THE EUROPA
WORLD
YEAR BOOK
2003

THE EUROPA WORLD YEAR BOOK 2003

VOLUME I

PART ONE: INTERNATIONAL ORGANIZATIONS
PART TWO: AFGHANISTAN–JORDAN

Europa Publications
Taylor & Francis Group

LONDON AND NEW YORK

First published 1926

© Europa Publications 2003
11 New Fetter Lane, London, EC4P 4EE, England
(A member of the Taylor & Francis Group)

ISBN 1-85743-227-4 (The Set)
1-85743-175-8 (Vol. I)
ISSN 0071-2302
Library of Congress Catalog Card Number 59-2942

Typeset by Ignition UK and printed by Unwin Brothers Limited
The Gresham Press
Old Woking, Surrey

FOREWORD

THE EUROPA WORLD YEAR BOOK (formerly THE EUROPA YEAR BOOK: A WORLD SURVEY) was first published in 1926. Since 1960 it has appeared in annual two-volume editions, and has become established as an authoritative reference work, providing a wealth of detailed information on the political, economic and commercial institutions of the world.

Volume I contains a comprehensive listing of more than 1,650 international organizations and the first part of the alphabetical survey of countries of the world, from Afghanistan to Jordan. Volume II contains countries from Kazakhstan to Zimbabwe.

The International Organizations section gives extensive coverage to the United Nations and its related agencies and bodies. There are also detailed articles concerning some 60 other major international and regional organizations; entries for many affiliated organizations appear within these articles. In addition, briefer details of more than 1,000 other international organizations appear in a separate section which starts on page 329. A comprehensive Index of International Organizations can be found at the end of Volume I.

Each country is covered by an individual chapter, containing: an introductory survey including recent history, economic affairs, government, defence, education, and public holidays; an economic and demographic survey using the latest available statistics on area and population, health and welfare, agriculture, forestry, fishing, industry, finance, trade, transport, tourism, the media, and education; and a directory section containing names, addresses and other useful facts about government, political parties, diplomatic representation, judiciary, religious groups, the media, telecommunications, banks, insurance, trade and industry, development organizations, chambers of commerce, industrial and trade associations, utilities, trade unions, transport and tourism.

Launched simultaneously with publication of the 2003 edition of THE EUROPA WORLD YEAR BOOK is EUROPA WORLD ONLINE, incorporating sophisticated search and browse functions that allow access to the entire content of the print edition, as well as specially commissioned visual and statistical content. An ongoing programme of updates of key areas of information will ensure the currency of content, and will enhance the richness of the information for which THE EUROPA WORLD YEAR BOOK is renowned. Details of this prestigious new resource are available at www.europaworldonline.com.

Readers are referred to our annual regional surveys, AFRICA SOUTH OF THE SAHARA, CENTRAL AND SOUTH-EASTERN EUROPE, EASTERN EUROPE, RUSSIA AND CENTRAL ASIA, THE FAR EAST AND AUSTRALASIA, THE MIDDLE EAST AND NORTH AFRICA, SOUTH AMERICA, CENTRAL AMERICA AND THE CARIBBEAN, THE USA AND CANADA and WESTERN EUROPE, for additional analysis of the geography, history and economy of these areas. More detailed coverage of international organizations may be found in THE EUROPA DIRECTORY OF INTERNATIONAL ORGANIZATIONS.

The information is extensively revised and updated by a variety of methods, including direct mailing to all the institutions listed. Many other sources are used, such as national statistical offices, government departments and diplomatic missions. The editors thank the innumerable individuals and organizations throughout the world whose generous co-operation in providing current information for this edition is invaluable in presenting the most accurate and up-to-date material available.

May 2003.

ACKNOWLEDGEMENTS

The editors gratefully acknowledge particular indebtedness for permission to reproduce material from the following publications: the United Nations' *Demographic Yearbook, Statistical Yearbook, Monthly Bulletin of Statistics, Industrial Commodity Statistics Yearbook* and *International Trade Statistics Yearbook*; the United Nations Educational, Scientific and Cultural Organization's *Statistical Yearbook*; the Food and Agriculture Organization of the United Nations' Statistical Database and *Yearbook of Fishery Statistics*; the International Labour Office's Statistical Database and *Yearbook of Labour Statistics*; the World Bank's *World Bank Atlas, Global Development Finance, World Development Report* and *World Development Indicators*; the International Monetary Fund's Statistical Database and *International Financial Statistics* and *Government Finance Statistics Yearbook*; the World Tourism Organization's *Yearbook of Tourism Statistics*; and *The Military Balance 2002–2003*, a publication of the International Institute for Strategic Studies, Arundel House, 13–15 Arundel Street, London WC2R 3DX.

HEALTH AND WELFARE STATISTICS: SOURCES AND DEFINITIONS

Total fertility rate Source: WHO, *The World Health Report* (2002). The number of children that would be born per woman, assuming no female mortality at child-bearing ages and the age-specific fertility rates of a specified country and reference period.

Under-5 mortality rate Source: UNICEF, *The State of the World's Children* (2003). The ratio of registered deaths of children under 5 years to the total number of registered live births over the same period.

HIV/AIDS Source: UNAIDS. Estimated percentage of adults aged 15 to 49 years living with HIV/AIDS. < indicates 'fewer than'.

Health expenditure Source: WHO, *The World Health Report* (2002).
US $ per head (PPP)
International dollar estimates, derived by dividing local currency units by an estimate of their purchasing-power parity (PPP) compared with the US dollar. PPPs are the rates of currency conversion that equalize the purchasing power of different currencies by eliminating the differences in price levels between countries.
% of GDP
GDP levels for OECD countries follow the most recent UN System of National Accounts. For non-OECD countries a value was estimated by utilizing existing UN, IMF and World Bank data.
Public expenditure
Government health-related outlays plus expenditure by social schemes compulsorily affiliated with a sizeable share of the population, and extrabudgetary funds allocated to health services. Figures include grants or loans provided by international agencies, other national authorities, and sometimes commercial banks.

Access to water and sanitation Source: WHO, *Global Water Supply and Sanitation Assessment* (2000 Report). Defined in terms of the type of technology and levels of service afforded. For water, this includes house connections, public standpipes, boreholes with handpumps, protected dug wells, protected spring and rainwater collection; allowance is also made for other locally defined technologies. 'Access' is broadly defined as the availability of at least 20 litres per person per day from a source within 1 km of the user's dwelling. Sanitation is defined to include connection to a sewer or septic tank system, pour-flush latrine, simple pit or ventilated improved pit latrine, again with allowance for acceptable local technologies. Access to water and sanitation does not imply that the level of service or quality of water is 'adequate' or 'safe'.

Human Development Index (HDI) Source: UNDP, *Human Development Report* (2002). A summary of human development measured by three basic dimensions: prospects for a long and healthy life, measured by life expectancy at birth; knowledge, measured by adult literacy rate (two-thirds' weight) and the combined gross enrolment ratio in primary, secondary and tertiary education (one-third weight); and standard of living, measured by GDP per head (PPP US $). The index value obtained lies between zero and one. A value above 0.8 indicates high human development, between 0.5 and 0.8 medium human development, and below 0.5 low human development. A centralized data source for all three dimensions was not available for all countries. In some such cases other data sources were used to calculate a substitute value; however, this was excluded from the ranking. Other countries, including non-UNDP members, were excluded from the HDI altogether. In total, 173 countries were ranked for 2000.

CONTENTS

* A complete Index of International Organizations is to be found
  on p. 2343.

PART TWO
Afghanistan–Jordan

Index of International Organizations   2343

An Index of Territories is to be found at the end of Volume II.

ABBREVIATIONS

AB	Aktiebolag (Joint-Stock Company); Alberta
Abog.	Abogado (Lawyer)
Acad.	Academician; Academy
ACP	African, Caribbean and Pacific (countries)
ACT	Australian Capital Territory
AD	anno Domini
ADB	African Development Bank; Asian Development Bank
ADC	aide-de-camp
Adm.	Admiral
admin.	administration
AfDB	African Development Bank
AG	Aktiengesellschaft (Joint-Stock Company)
AH	anno Hegirae
a.i.	ad interim
AID	(US) Agency for International Development
AIDS	acquired immunodeficiency syndrome
AK	Alaska
Al.	Aleja (Alley, Avenue)
AL	Alabama
ALADI	Asociación Latinoamericana de Integración
Alt.	Alternate
AM	Amplitude Modulation
a.m.	ante meridiem (before noon)
amalg.	amalgamated
Apdo	Apartado (Post Box)
APEC	Asia-Pacific Economic Co-operation
approx.	approximately
Apt	Apartment
AR	Arkansas
AŞ	Anonim Şrketi (Joint-Stock Company)
A/S	Aktieselskab (Joint-Stock Company)
ASEAN	Association of South East Asian Nations
asscn	association
assoc.	associate
ASSR	Autonomous Soviet Socialist Republic
asst	assistant
AU	African Union
Aug.	August
auth.	authorized
Ave	Avenue
Avda	Avenida (Avenue)
Avv.	Avvocato (Lawyer)
AZ	Arizona
BC	British Columbia
BC	before Christ
Bd	Board
Bd, Bld, Blv., Blvd	Boulevard
b/d	barrels per day
BFPO	British Forces' Post Office
Bhd	Berhad (Public Limited Company)
Bldg	Building
blk	block
Blvr	Bulevar
BP	Boîte postale (Post Box)
br.(s)	branch(es)
Brig.	Brigadier
BSE	Bovine spongiform encephalopathy
BSEC	(Organization of) Black Sea Economic Co-operation
bte	boîte (box)
BTN	Brussels Tariff Nomenclature
bul.	bulvar (boulevard)
bulv.	bulvarīs (boulevard)
C	Centigrade
c.	circa; cuadra(s) (block(s))
CA	California
CACM	Central American Common Market
Cad.	Caddesi (Street)
CAP	Common Agricultural Policy
cap.	capital
Capt.	Captain
CARICOM	Caribbean Community and Common Market
CBSS	Council of Baltic Sea States
CCL	Caribbean Congress of Labour
Cdre	Commodore
CEMAC	Communauté économique et monétaire de l'Afrique centrale
Cen.	Central
CEO	Chief Executive Officer
CFA	Communauté Financière Africaine; Coopération Financière en Afrique centrale
CFP	Common Fisheries Policy; Communauté française du Pacifique; Comptoirs français du Pacifique
Chair.	Chairman/person/woman
Chih.	Chihuahua
CI	Channel Islands
Cia	Companhia
Cía	Compañía
CICP	Centre for International Crime Prevention
Cie	Compagnie
c.i.f.	cost, insurance and freight
C-in-C	Commander-in-Chief
circ.	circulation
CIS	Commonwealth of Independent States
CJD	Creutzfeldt-Jakob disease
cm	centimetre(s)
cnr	corner
CO	Colorado
Co	Company; County
c/o	care of
Coah.	Coahuila
Col	Colonel
Col.	Colima; Colonia
COMESA	Common Market for Eastern and Southern Africa
Comm.	Commission; Commendatore
Commdr	Commander
Commdt	Commandant
Commr	Commissioner
Cond.	Condiminio
Confed.	Confederation
Cont.	Contador (Accountant)
Corp.	Corporate
Corpn	Corporation
CP	Case Postale, Caixa Postal, Casella Postale (Post Box); Communist Party
CPSU	Communist Party of the Soviet Union
Cres.	Crescent
CSCE	Conference on Security and Co-operation in Europe
CSTAL	Confederación Sindical de los Trabajadores de América Latina
CT	Connecticut
CTCA	Confederación de Trabajadores Centro-americanos
Cttee	Committee
cu	cubic
cwt	hundredweight
DC	District of Columbia; Distrito Capital; Distrito Central
DE	Departamento Estatal; Delaware
Dec.	December
Del.	Delegación
Dem.	Democratic; Democrat
Dep.	Deputy
dep.	deposits
Dept	Department
devt	development
DF	Distrito Federal
Dgo	Durango
Diag.	Diagonal
Dir	Director
Div.	Division(al)
DM	Deutsche Mark
DMZ	demilitarized zone
DN	Distrito Nacional
Doc.	Docent
Dott.	Dottore/essa
Dr	Doctor
Dr.	Drive
Dra	Doctora
Dr Hab	Doktor Habilitowany (Assistant Professor)
dr.(e)	drachma(e)
Drs	Doctorandus
DU	depleted uranium
dwt	dead weight tons
E	East; Eastern
EBRD	European Bank for Reconstruction and Development
EC	European Community
ECA	(United Nations) Economic Commission for Africa
ECE	(United Nations) Economic Commission for Europe
ECLAC	(United Nations) Economic Commission for Latin America and the Caribbean
ECO	Economic Co-operation Organization
Econ.	Economist; Economics
ECOSOC	(United Nations) Economic and Social Council
ECOWAS	Economic Community of West African States
ECU	European Currency Unit
Edif.	Edificio (Building)
edn	edition
EEA	European Economic Area
EFTA	European Free Trade Association
e.g.	exempli gratia (for example)
EIB	European Investment Bank
eKv	electron kilovolt
EMS	European Monetary System
EMU	economic and monetary union
eMv	electron megavolt
Eng.	Engineer; Engineering
EP	Empresa Pública
ERM	exchange rate mechanism
ESACA	Emisora de Capital Abierto Sociedad Anónima
Esc.	Escuela; Escudos; Escritorio
ESCAP	(United Nations) Economic and Social Commission for Asia and the Pacific
ESCWA	(United Nations) Economic and Social Commission for Western Asia
esq.	esquina (corner)
est.	established; estimate; estimated
etc.	et cetera
EU	European Union
eV	eingetragener Verein

excl.   excluding
exec.   executive
Ext.   Extension

F   Fahrenheit
f.   founded
FAO   Food and Agriculture
                 Organization
f.a.s.   free alongside ship
Feb.   February
Fed.   Federation; Federal
FL   Florida
FM   frequency modulation
fmr(ly)   former(ly)
f.o.b.   free on board
Fr   Father
Fr.   Franc
Fri.   Friday
FRY   Federal Republic of Yugoslavia
ft   foot (feet)
FYRM   former Yugoslav republic of
                 Macedonia

g   gram(s)
GA   Georgia
GATT   General Agreement on Tariffs
                 and Trade
GCC   Gulf Co-operation Council
Gdns   Gardens
GDP   gross domestic product
Gen.   General
GeV   giga electron volts
GM   genetically modified
GmbH   Gesellschaft mit beschränkter
                 Haftung (Limited Liability
                 Company)
GMT   Greenwich Mean Time
GNI   gross national income
GNP   gross national product
Gov.   Governor
Govt   Government
Gro   Guerrero
grt   gross registered tons
Gto   Guanajuato
GWh   gigawatt hours

ha   hectares
HE   His/Her Eminence; His/Her
                 Excellency
hf   hlutafelag (Limited Company)
HI   Hawaii
HIPC   heavily indebted poor country
HIV   human immunodeficiency virus
hl   hectolitre(s)
HM   His/Her Majesty
Hon.   Honorary, Honourable
hp   horsepower
HQ   Headquarters
HRH   His/Her Royal Highness
HSH   His/Her Serene Highness

IA   Iowa
IBRD   International Bank for
                 Reconstruction and
                 Development (World Bank)
ICC   International Chamber of
                 Commerce; International
                 Criminal Court
ICFTU   International Confederation of
                 Free Trade Unions
ICRC   International Committee of the
                 Red Cross
ICTR   International Criminal Tribunal
                 for Rwanda
ICTY   International Criminal Tribunal
                 for the former Yugoslavia
ID   Idaho
IDA   International Development
                 Association
IDB   Inter-American Development
                 Bank
i.e.   id est (that is to say)

IFC   International Finance
                 Corporation
IGAD   Intergovernmental Authority on
                 Development
IL   Illinois
ILO   International Labour
                 Organization/Office
IMF   International Monetary Fund
in (ins)   inch (inches)
IN   Indiana
Inc, Incorp.
Incd   Incorporated
incl.   including
Ind.   Independent
INF   Intermediate-Range Nuclear
                 Forces
Ing.   Engineer
Insp.   Inspector
Int.   International
Inzå.   Engineer
IPU   Inter-Parliamentary Union
Ir   Engineer
IRF   International Road Federation
irreg.   irregular
Is   Islands
ISIC   International Standard
                 Industrial Classification
IT   information technology
ITU   International
                 Telecommunication Union
Iur.   Lawyer

Jal.   Jalisco
Jan.   January
Jnr   Junior
Jr   Jonkheer (Esquire); Junior
Jt   Joint

kg   kilogram(s)
KG   Kommandit Gesellschaft
                 (Limited Partnership)
kHz   kilohertz
KK   Kaien Kaisha (Limited
                 Company)
km   kilometre(s)
Kom.   Komnata (Room)
kor.   korpus (block)
KS   Kansas
kv.   kvartal (apartment block); kvar-
                 tira (apartment)
kW   kilowatt(s)
kWh   kilowatt hours
KY   Kentucky

LA   Louisiana
lauk   laukums (square)
lb   pound(s)
Lic.   Licenciado
Licda   Licenciada
LNG   liquefied natural gas
LPG   liquefied petroleum gas
Lt, Lieut   Lieutenant
Ltd   Limited

m   metre(s)
m.   million
MA   Massachusetts
Maj.   Major
Man.   Manager; managing
MB   Manitoba
mbH   mit beschränkter Haftung (with
                 limited liability)
Mc/s   megacycles per second
MD   Maryland
ME   Maine
Me   Maître
mem.(s)   member(s)
MEP   Member of the European
                 Parliament
Mercosul   Mercado Comum do Sul
                 (Southern Common Market)
Mercosur   Mercado Común del Sur
                 (Southern Common Market)

MEV, MeV   mega electron volts
Méx.   México
MFN   most favoured nation
mfrs   manufacturers
Mgr   Monseigneur; Monsignor
MHz   megahertz
MI   Michigan
MIA   missing in action
Mich.   Michoacán
MIGA   Multilateral Investment
                 Guarantee Agency
Mil.   Military
Mlle   Mademoiselle
mm   millimetre(s)
Mme   Madame
MN   Minnesota
MO   Missouri
Mon.   Monday
Mor.   Morelos
MOU   memorandum of understanding
MP   Member of Parliament
MS   Mississippi
MSS   Manuscripts
MT   Montana
MW   megawatt(s); medium wave
MWh   megawatt hour(s)

N   North; Northern
n.a.   not available
nab.   naberezhnaya (embankment,
                 quai)
NAFTA   North American Free Trade
                 Agreement
nám.   náměstí (square)
Nat.   National
NATO   North Atlantic Treaty
                 Organization
Nay.   Nayarit
NB   New Brunswick
NC   North Carolina
NCO   non-commissioned officer
ND   North Dakota
NE   Nebraska; North-East
NEPAD   New Partnership for Africa's
                 Development
NF   Newfoundland
NGO   non-governmental organization
NH   New Hampshire
NJ   New Jersey
NL   Nuevo León
NM   New Mexico
NMP   net material product
no   numéro, número (number)
no.   number
Nov.   November
nr   near
nrt   net registered tons
NS   Nova Scotia
NSW   New South Wales
NV   Naamloze Vennootschap
                 (Limited Company); Nevada
NW   North-West
NY   New York
NZ   New Zealand

OAPEC   Organization of Arab Petroleum
                 Exporting Countries
OAS   Organization of American States
OAU   Organization of African Unity
Oax.   Oaxaca
Oct.   October
OECD   Organisation for Economic Co-
                 operation and Development
OECS   Organisation of Eastern
                 Caribbean States
Of.   Oficina (Office)
OH   Ohio
OIC   Organization of the Islamic
                 Conference
OK   Oklahoma
ON   Ontario
OPEC   Organization of the Petroleum
                 Exporting Countries

opp.	opposite	S	South; Southern; San	TV	television
OR	Oregon	SA	Société Anonyme, Sociedad Anónima (Limited Company); South Australia	TX	Texas
Org.	Organization			u.	utca (street)
ORIT	Organización Regional Interamericana de Trabajadores	SAARC	South Asian Association for Regional Co-operation	u/a	unit of account
				UAE	United Arab Emirates
OSCE	Organization for Security and Co-operation in Europe	SAECA	Sociedad Anónima Emisora de Capital Abierto	UEE	Unidade Económica Estatal
				UEMOA	Union économique et monétaire ouest-africaine
		SADC	Southern African Development Community	UK	United Kingdom
p.	page			ul.	ulica, ulitsa (street)
p.a.	per annum	SAR	Special Administrative Region	UM	ouguiya
PA	Palestinian Authority; Pennsylvania	SARL	Sociedade Anônima de Responsabilidade Limitada (Joint-Stock Company of Limited Liability)	UN	United Nations
				UNAIDS	United Nations Joint Programme on HIV/AIDS
Parl.	Parliament(ary)				
pas.	passazh (passage)			UNCTAD	United Nations Conference on Trade and Development
per.	pereulok (lane, alley)	SARS	Severe Acute Respiratory Syndrome		
PE	Prince Edward Island			UNDCP	United Nations International Drug Control Programme
Perm. Rep.	Permanent Representative	Sat.	Saturday		
PF	Postfach (Post Box)	SC	South Carolina	UNDP	United Nations Development Programme
PK	Post Box (Turkish)	SD	South Dakota		
Pl.	Plac, Plads (square)	Sdn Bhd	Sendirian Berhad (Private Limited Company)	UNEP	United Nations Environment Programme
pl.	platz; place; ploshchad (square)				
PLC	Public Limited Company	SDR(s)	Special Drawing Right(s)	UNESCO	United Nations Educational, Scientific and Cultural Organization
PLO	Palestine Liberation Organization	SE	South-East		
		Sec.	Secretary		
p.m.	post meridiem (after noon)	Secr.	Secretariat	UNHCHR	UN High Commissioner for Human Rights
PMB	Private Mail Bag	Sen.	Senior; Senator		
PNA	Palestinian National Authority	Sept.	September	UNHCR	United Nations High Commissioner for Refugees
POB	Post Office Box	SER	Sua Eccellenza Reverendissima (His Eminence)		
pp.	pages			UNICEF	United Nations Children's Fund
PPP	purchasing-power parity	SFRY	Socialist Federal Republic of Yugoslavia	Univ.	University
PQ	Québec			UNRWA	United Nations Relief and Works Agency for Palestine Refugees in the Near East
PR	Puerto Rico	Sin.	Sinaloa		
pr.	prospekt (avenue)	SITC	Standard International Trade Classification		
Pres.	President				
PRGF	Poverty Reduction and Growth Facility	SJ	Society of Jesus	USA	United States of America
		SK	Saskatchewan	USAID	United States Agency for International Development
Prin.	Principal	SLP	San Luis Potosí		
Prof.	Professor	SMEs	small and medium-sized enterprises	USSR	Union of Soviet Socialist Republics
Propr	Proprietor				
Prov.	Province; Provincial; Provinciale (Dutch)	s/n	sin número (without number)	UT	Utah
		Soc.	Society		
prov.	provulok (lane)	Sok.	Sokak (Street)	VA	Virginia
PT	Perseroan Terbatas (Limited Company)	Son.	Sonora	VAT	Value-added Tax
		Şos.	Şosea (Road)	VEB	Volkseigener Betrieb (Public Company)
Pte	Private; Puente (Bridge)	SP	São Paulo		
Pty	Proprietary	SpA	Società per Azioni (Joint-Stock Company)	v-CJD	variant Creutzfeldt-Jakob disease
p.u.	paid up				
publ.	publication; published	Sq.	Square	Ven.	Venerable
Publr	Publisher	sq	square (in measurements)	Ver.	Veracruz
Pue.	Puebla	Sr	Senior; Señor	VHF	Very High Frequency
Pvt.	Private	Sra	Señora	VI	(US) Virgin Islands
		Srl	Società a Responsabilità Limitata (Limited Company)	Vic	Victoria
QC	Québec			Vn	Veien (Street)
Qld	Queensland	SSR	Soviet Socialist Republic	vol.(s)	volume(s)
Qro	Querétaro	St	Saint, Sint; Street	VT	Vermont
Q. Roo	Quintana Roo	Sta	Santa	vul.	vulitsa (street)
q.v.	quod vide (to which refer)	Ste	Sainte		
		str.	strada, stradă (street)	W	West; Western
Rag.	Ragioniere (Accountant)	str-la	stradelă (street)	WA	Western Australia; Washington (State)
Rd	Road	subs.	subscriptions; subscribed		
R(s)	rand; rupee(s)	Sun.	Sunday	WCL	World Confederation of Labour
reg., regd	register; registered	Supt	Superintendent	Wed.	Wednesday
reorg.	reorganized	sv.	Saint	WEU	Western European Union
Rep.	Republic; Republican; Representative	SW	South-West	WFP	World Food Programme
				WFTU	World Federation of Trade Unions
Repub.	Republic	Tab.	Tabasco		
res	reserve(s)	Tamps	Tamaulipas	WHO	World Health Organization
retd	retired	TAŞ	Turkiye Anonim Şirketi (Turkish Joint-Stock Company)	WI	Wisconsin
Rev.	Reverend			WSSD	World Summit on Sustainable Development
RI	Rhode Island	Tas	Tasmania		
RJ	Rio de Janeiro	TD	Teachta Dàla (Member of Parliament)	WTO	World Trade Organization
Rm	Room			WV	West Virginia
RN	Royal Navy	tech., techn.	technical	WY	Wyoming
ro-ro	roll-on roll-off	tel.	telephone		
RP	Recette principale	TEU	20-ft equivalent unit	yr	year
Rp.(s)	rupiah(s)	Thur.	Thursday	YT	Yukon Territory
RSFSR	Russian Soviet Federative Socialist Republic	TN	Tennessee	Yuc.	Yucatán
		Treas.	Treasurer		
Rt	Right	Tue.	Tuesday		

INTERNATIONAL TELEPHONE CODES

To make international calls to telephone and fax numbers listed in *The Europa World Year Book*, dial the international code of the country from which you are calling, followed by the appropriate country code for the organization you wish to call (listed below), followed by the area code (if applicable) and telephone or fax number listed in the entry.

	Country code	+ or – GMT*		Country code	+ or – GMT*
Afghanistan	93	+4½	Dominica	1 767	–4
Albania	355	+1	Dominican Republic	1 809	–4
Algeria	213	+1	Ecuador	593	–5
Andorra	376	+1	Egypt	20	+2
Angola	244	+1	El Salvador	503	–6
Antigua and Barbuda	1 268	–4	Equatorial Guinea	240	+1
Argentina	54	–3	Eritrea	291	+3
Armenia	374	+4	Estonia	372	+2
Australia	61	+8 to +10	Ethiopia	251	+3
Australian External Territories:			Fiji	679	+12
Australian Antarctic Territory	672	+3 to +10	Finland	358	+2
Christmas Island	61	+7	Finnish External Territory:		
Cocos (Keeling) Islands	61	+6½	Åland Islands	358	+2
Norfolk Island	672	+11½	France	33	+1
Austria	43	+1	French Overseas Departments:		
Azerbaijan	994	+5	French Guiana	594	–3
The Bahamas	1 242	–5	Guadeloupe	590	–4
Bahrain	973	+3	Martinique	596	–4
Bangladesh	880	+6	Réunion	262	+4
Barbados	1 246	–4	French Overseas Collectivité Départementale:		
Belarus	375	+2	Mayotte	269	+3
Belgium	32	+1	French Overseas Collectivité Territoriale:		
Belize	501	–6	Saint Pierre and Miquelon	508	–3
Benin	229	+1	French Overseas Territories:		
Bhutan	975	+6	French Polynesia	689	–9 to –10
Bolivia	591	–4	Wallis and Futuna Islands	681	+12
Bosnia and Herzegovina	387	+1	French Overseas Country:		
Botswana	267	+2	New Caledonia	687	+11
Brazil	55	–3 to –4	Gabon	241	+1
Brunei	673	+8	Gambia	220	0
Bulgaria	359	+2	Georgia	995	+4
Burkina Faso	226	0	Germany	49	+1
Burundi	257	+2	Ghana	233	0
Cambodia	855	+7	Greece	30	+2
Cameroon	237	+1	Grenada	1 473	–4
Canada	1	–3 to –8	Guatemala	502	–6
Cape Verde	238	–1	Guinea	224	0
The Central African Republic	236	+1	Guinea-Bissau	245	0
Chad	235	+1	Guyana	592	–4
Chile	56	–4	Haiti	509	–5
China, People's Republic	86	+8	Honduras	504	–6
Special Administrative Regions:			Hungary	36	+1
Hong Kong	852	+8	Iceland	354	0
Macao	853	+8	India	91	+5½
China (Taiwan)	886	+8	Indonesia	62	+7 to +9
Colombia	57	–5	Iran	98	+3½
The Comoros	269	+3	Iraq	964	+3
Congo, Democratic Republic	243	+1	Ireland	353	0
Congo, Republic	242	+1	Israel	972	+2
Costa Rica	506	–6	Italy	39	+1
Côte d'Ivoire	225	0	Jamaica	1 876	–5
Croatia	385	+1	Japan	81	+9
Cuba	53	–5	Jordan	962	+2
Cyprus	357	+2	Kazakhstan	7	+6
'Turkish Republic of Northern Cyprus'	90 392	+2	Kenya	254	+3
Czech Republic	420	+1	Kiribati	686	+12 to +13
Denmark	45	+1	Korea, Democratic People's Republic (North Korea)	850	+9
Danish External Territories:			Korea, Republic (South Korea)	82	+9
Faroe Islands	298	0	Kuwait	965	+3
Greenland	299	–1 to –4	Kyrgyzstan	996	+5
Djibouti	253	+3			

	Country code	+ or − GMT*		Country code	+ or − GMT*
Laos	856	+7	Singapore	65	+8
Latvia	371	+2	Slovakia	421	+1
Lebanon	961	+2	Slovenia	386	+1
Lesotho	266	+2	Solomon Islands	677	+11
Liberia	231	0	Somalia	252	+3
Libya	218	+1	South Africa	27	+2
Liechtenstein	423	+1	Spain	34	+1
Lithuania	370	+2	Sri Lanka	94	+6
Luxembourg	352	+1	Sudan	249	+2
Macedonia, former Yugoslav republic	389	+1	Suriname	597	−3
Madagascar	261	+3	Swaziland	268	+2
Malawi	265	+2	Sweden	46	+1
Malaysia	60	+8	Switzerland	41	+1
Maldives	960	+5	Syria	963	+2
Mali	223	0	Tajikistan	992	+5
Malta	356	+1	Tanzania	255	+3
Marshall Islands	692	+12	Thailand	66	+7
Mauritania	222	0	Timor-Leste	670	+9
Mauritius	230	+4	Togo	228	0
Mexico	52	−6 to −7	Tonga	676	+13
Micronesia, Federated States	691	+10 to +11	Trinidad and Tobago	1 868	−4
Moldova	373	+2	Tunisia	216	+1
Monaco	377	+1	Turkey	90	+2
Mongolia	976	+7 to +9	Turkmenistan	993	+5
Morocco	212	0	Tuvalu	688	+12
Mozambique	258	+2	Uganda	256	+3
Myanmar	95	$+6\frac{1}{2}$	Ukraine	380	+2
Namibia	264	+2	United Arab Emirates	971	+4
Nauru	674	+12	United Kingdom	44	0
Nepal	977	$+5\frac{3}{4}$	United Kingdom Crown		
Netherlands	31	+1	Dependencies	44	0
Netherlands Dependencies:			United Kingdom Overseas		
Aruba	297	−4	Territories:		
Netherlands Antilles	599	−4	Anguilla	1 264	−4
New Zealand	64	+12	Ascension Island	247	0
New Zealand's Dependent and Associated			Bermuda	1 441	−4
Territories:			British Virgin Islands	1 284	−4
Tokelau	690	−10	Cayman Islands	1 345	−5
Cook Islands	682	−10	Diego Garcia (British Indian		
Niue	683	−11	Ocean Territory)	246	+5
Nicaragua	505	−6	Falkland Islands	500	−4
Niger	227	+1	Gibraltar	350	+1
Nigeria	234	+1	Montserrat	1 664	−4
Norway	47	+1	Pitcairn Islands	872	−8
Norwegian External Territory:			Saint Helena	290	0
Svalbard	47	+1	Tristan da Cunha	2 897	0
Oman	968	+4	Turks and Caicos Islands	1 649	−5
Pakistan	92	+5	United States of America	1	−5 to −10
Palau	680	+9	United States Commonwealth		
Palestinian Autonomous Areas	970	+2	Territories:		
Panama	507	−5	Northern Mariana Islands	1 670	+10
Papua New Guinea	675	+10	Puerto Rico	1 787	−4
Paraguay	595	−4	United States External Territories:		
Peru	51	−5	American Samoa	1 684	−11
The Philippines	63	+8	Guam	1 671	+10
Poland	48	+1	United States Virgin Islands	1 340	−4
Portugal	351	0	Uruguay	598	−3
Qatar	974	+3	Uzbekistan	998	+5
Romania	40	+2	Vanuatu	678	+11
Russian Federation	7	+2 to +12	Vatican City	39	+1
Rwanda	250	+2	Venezuela	58	−4
Saint Christopher and Nevis	1 869	−4	Viet Nam	84	+7
Saint Lucia	1 758	−4	Yemen	967	+3
Saint Vincent and the Grenadines	1 784	−4	Zambia	260	+2
Samoa	685	−11	Zimbabwe	263	+2
San Marino	378	+1			
São Tomé and Príncipe	239	0			
Saudi Arabia	966	+3			
Senegal	221	0			
Serbia and Montenegro	381	+1			
Seychelles	248	+4			
Sierra Leone	232	0			

* Time difference in hours + or − Greenwich Mean Time (GMT). The times listed compare the standard (winter) times. Some countries adopt Summer (Daylight Saving) Time — i.e. + 1 hour — for part of the year.

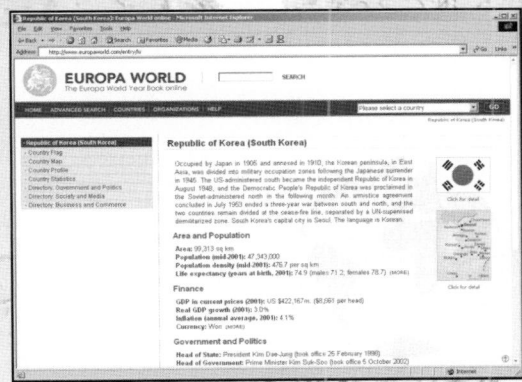

PART ONE
International Organizations

THE UNITED NATIONS

Address: United Nations, New York, NY 10017, USA.

Telephone: (212) 963-1234; **fax:** (212) 963-4879; **internet:** www.un.org.

The United Nations was founded in 1945 to maintain international peace and security and to develop international co-operation in addressing economic, social, cultural and humanitarian problems.

The United Nations was a name devised by President Franklin D. Roosevelt of the USA. It was first used in the Declaration by United Nations of 1 January 1942, when representatives of 26 nations pledged their governments to continue fighting together against the Axis powers.

The United Nations Charter (see p. 19) was drawn up by the representatives of 50 countries at the United Nations Conference on International Organization, which met at San Francisco from 25 April to 26 June 1945. The representatives deliberated on the basis of proposals put forward by representatives of China, the USSR, the United Kingdom and the USA at Dumbarton Oaks in August–October 1944. The Charter was signed on 26 June 1945. Poland, not represented at the Conference, signed it later but nevertheless became one of the original 51 members.

The United Nations officially came into existence on 24 October 1945, when the Charter had been ratified by China, France, the USSR, the United Kingdom and the USA, and by a majority of other signatories. United Nations Day is celebrated annually on 24 October.

The UN's chief administrative officer is the Secretary-General, elected for a five-year term by the General Assembly on the recommendation of the Security Council. He acts in that capacity at all meetings of the General Assembly, the Security Council, the Economic and Social Council, and the Trusteeship Council, and performs such other functions as are entrusted to him by those organs. He is required to submit an annual report to the General Assembly and may bring to the attention of the Security Council any matter which, in his opinion, may threaten international peace.

Secretary-General (1997–2006): Kofi Annan (Ghana).

Membership

MEMBERS OF THE UNITED NATIONS

(with assessments for percentage contributions to the UN budget for 2003, and year of admission)

Country	Assessment	Year
Afghanistan	0.00900	1946
Albania	0.00300	1955
Algeria	0.07000	1962
Andorra	0.00400	1993
Angola	0.00200	1976
Antigua and Barbuda	0.00200	1981
Argentina	1.45900	1945
Armenia	0.00200	1992
Australia	1.62700	1945
Austria	0.94700	1955
Azerbaijan	0.00400	1992
Bahamas	0.01200	1973
Bahrain	0.01800	1971
Bangladesh	0.01000	1974
Barbados	0.00900	1966
Belarus[1]	0.01900	1945
Belgium	1.12900	1945
Belize	0.00100	1981
Benin	0.00200	1960
Bhutan	0.00100	1971
Bolivia	0.00800	1945
Bosnia and Herzegovina	0.00400	1992
Botswana	0.01000	1966
Brazil	2.39000	1945
Brunei	0.03300	1984
Bulgaria	0.01300	1955
Burkina Faso	0.00200	1960
Burundi	0.00100	1962
Cambodia	0.00200	1955
Cameroon	0.00900	1960
Canada	2.55800	1945
Cape Verde	0.00100	1975
Central African Republic	0.00100	1960
Chad	0.00100	1960
Chile	0.21200	1945
China, People's Republic	1.53200	1945
Colombia	0.20100	1945
Comoros	0.00100	1975
Congo, Democratic Republic	0.00400	1960
Congo, Republic	0.00100	1960
Costa Rica	0.02000	1945
Côte d'Ivoire	0.00900	1960
Croatia	0.03900	1992
Cuba	0.03000	1945
Cyprus	0.03800	1960
Czech Republic[2]	0.20300	1993
Denmark	0.74900	1945
Djibouti	0.00100	1977
Dominica	0.00100	1978
Dominican Republic	0.02300	1945
Ecuador	0.02500	1945
Egypt	0.08100	1945
El Salvador	0.01800	1945
Equatorial Guinea	0.00100	1968
Eritrea	0.00100	1993
Estonia	0.01000	1991
Ethiopia	0.00400	1945
Fiji	0.00400	1970
Finland	0.52200	1955
France	6.46600	1945
Gabon	0.01400	1960
The Gambia	0.00100	1965
Georgia	0.00500	1992
Germany	9.76900	1973
Ghana	0.00500	1957
Greece	0.53900	1945
Grenada	0.00100	1974
Guatemala	0.02700	1945
Guinea	0.00300	1958
Guinea-Bissau	0.00100	1974
Guyana	0.00100	1966
Haiti	0.00200	1945
Honduras	0.00500	1945
Hungary	0.12000	1955
Iceland	0.03300	1946
India	0.34100	1945
Indonesia	0.20000	1950
Iran	0.27200	1945
Iraq	0.13600	1945
Ireland	0.29400	1955
Israel	0.41500	1949
Italy	5.06475	1955
Jamaica	0.00400	1962
Japan	19.51575	1956
Jordan	0.00800	1955
Kazakhstan	0.02800	1992
Kenya	0.00800	1963
Kiribati	0.00100	1999
Korea, Democratic People's Republic	0.00900	1991
Korea, Republic	1.85100	1991
Kuwait	0.14700	1963
Kyrgyzstan	0.00100	1992
Laos	0.00100	1955
Latvia	0.01000	1991
Lebanon	0.01200	1945
Lesotho	0.00100	1966
Liberia	0.00100	1945
Libya	0.06700	1955
Liechtenstein	0.00600	1990
Lithuania	0.01700	1991
Luxembourg	0.08000	1945
Macedonia, former Yugoslav republic	0.00600	1993
Madagascar	0.00300	1960
Malawi	0.00200	1964
Malaysia	0.23500	1957
Maldives	0.00100	1965
Mali	0.00200	1960
Malta	0.01500	1964
Marshall Islands	0.00100	1991
Mauritania	0.00100	1961
Mauritius	0.01100	1968
Mexico	1.08600	1945
Micronesia, Federated States	0.00100	1991
Moldova	0.00200	1992
Monaco	0.00400	1993
Mongolia	0.00100	1961

Morocco	0.04400	1956
Mozambique	0.00100	1975
Myanmar	0.01000	1948
Namibia	0.00700	1990
Nauru	0.00100	1999
Nepal	0.00400	1955
Netherlands	1.73800	1945
New Zealand	0.24100	1945
Nicaragua	0.00100	1945
Niger	0.00100	1960
Nigeria	0.06800	1960
Norway	0.64600	1945
Oman	0.06100	1971
Pakistan	0.06100	1947
Palau	0.00100	1994
Panama	0.01800	1945
Papua New Guinea	0.00600	1975
Paraguay	0.01600	1945
Peru	0.11800	1945
Philippines	0.1000	1945
Poland	0.37800	1945
Portugal	0.46200	1955
Qatar	0.03400	1971
Romania	0.05800	1955
Russia[3]	1.20000	1945
Rwanda	0.00100	1962
Saint Christopher and Nevis	0.00100	1983
Saint Lucia	0.00200	1979
Saint Vincent and the Grenadines	0.00100	1980
Samoa (formerly Western Samoa)	0.00100	1976
San Marino	0.00200	1992
São Tomé and Príncipe	0.00100	1975
Saudi Arabia	0.55400	1945
Senegal	0.00500	1960
Serbia and Montenegro[4]	0.02000	2000
Seychelles	0.00200	1976
Sierra Leone	0.00100	1961
Singapore	0.39300	1965
Slovakia[2]	0.04300	1993
Slovenia	0.08100	1992
Solomon Islands	0.00100	1978
Somalia	0.00100	1960
South Africa	0.40800	1945
Spain	2.51875	1955
Sri Lanka	0.01600	1955
Sudan	0.00600	1956
Suriname	0.00200	1975
Swaziland	0.00200	1968
Switzerland	—	2002
Sweden	1.02675	1946
Syria	0.08000	1945
Tajikistan	0.00100	1992
Tanzania	0.00400	1961
Thailand	0.29400	1946
Timor-Leste	—	2002
Togo	0.00100	1960
Tonga	0.00100	1999
Trinidad and Tobago	0.01600	1962
Tunisia	0.03000	1956
Turkey	0.44000	1945
Turkmenistan	0.00300	1992
Tuvalu	0.00100	2000
Uganda	0.00500	1962
Ukraine[1]	0.05300	1945
United Arab Emirates	0.20200	1971
United Kingdom	5.53600	1945
USA	22.00000	1945
Uruguay	0.08000	1945
Uzbekistan	0.01100	1992
Vanuatu	0.00100	1981
Venezuela	0.20800	1945
Viet Nam	0.01600	1977
Yemen[5]	0.00600	1947/67
Zambia	0.00200	1964
Zimbabwe	0.00800	1980

Total Membership: 191 (April 2003)

[1] Until December 1991 both Belarus and Ukraine were integral parts of the USSR and not independent countries, but had separate UN membership.

[2] Czechoslovakia, which had been a member of the UN since 1945, ceased to exist as a single state on 31 December 1992. In January 1993, as Czechoslovakia's legal successors, the Czech Republic and Slovakia were granted UN membership, and seats on subsidiary bodies that had previously been held by Czechoslovakia were divided between the two successor states.

[3] Russia assumed the USSR's seat in the General Assembly and its permanent seat on the Security Council (see p. 13) in December 1991, following the USSR's dissolution.

[4] Admitted as the Federal Republic of Yugoslavia. Present name was adopted in February 2003.

[5] The Yemen Arab Republic (admitted to the UN as Yemen in 1947) and the People's Democratic Republic of Yemen (admitted as Southern Yemen in 1967) merged to form the Republic of Yemen in May 1990.

SOVEREIGN STATES NOT IN THE UNITED NATIONS
(April 2003)

China (Taiwan)   Vatican City (Holy See)

Diplomatic Representation

MEMBER STATES' PERMANENT MISSIONS TO THE UNITED NATIONS
(with Permanent Representatives—April 2003)

Afghanistan: 360 Lexington Ave, 11th Floor, New York, NY 10017; tel. (212) 972-1212; fax (212) 972-1216; e-mail afgwatan@aol.com; Dr RAVAN A. G. FARHÂDI.

Albania: 320 East 79th St, New York, NY 10021; tel. (212) 249-2059; fax (212) 535-2917; e-mail albania@un.int; ZEF MAZI.

Algeria: 326 East 48th St, New York, NY 10017; tel. (212) 750-1960; fax (212) 759-5274; e-mail mission@algeria-un.org; internet www.algeria-un.org; ABDALLAH BAALI.

Andorra: 2 United Nations Plaza, 25th Floor, New York, NY 10017; tel. (212) 750-8064; fax (212) 750-6630; e-mail andorra@un.int; JULI MINOVES TRIQUELL.

Angola: 125 East 73rd St, New York, NY 10021; tel. (212) 861-5656; fax (212) 861-9295; e-mail ang-un@angolamissionun.org; internet www.angolamissionun.org; ISMAEL ABRAÃO GASPAR MARTINS.

Antigua and Barbuda: 610 Fifth Ave, Suite 311, New York, NY 10020; tel. (212) 541-4117; fax (212) 757-1607; e-mail antigua@un.int; internet www.un.int/antigua; Dr PATRICK ALBERT LEWIS.

Argentina: 1 United Nations Plaza, 25th Floor, New York, NY 10017; tel. (212) 688-6300; fax (212) 980-8395; e-mail argentina@un.int; internet www.un.int/argentina; ARNOLDO M. LISTRE.

Armenia: 119 East 36th St, New York, NY 10016; tel. (212) 686-9079; fax (212) 686-3934; e-mail armenia@un.int; internet www.un.int/armenia; Dr MOVSES ABELIAN.

Australia: 150 East 42nd St, 33rd Floor, New York, NY 10017; tel. (212) 351-6600; fax (212) 351-6610; e-mail australia@un.int; internet www.australiaun.org; JOHN DAUTH.

Austria: 823 United Nations Plaza, 8th Floor, New York, NY 10017; tel. (212) 949-1840; fax (212) 953-1302; e-mail austria@un.int; internet www.un.int/austria; GERHARD PFLANZELTER.

Azerbaijan: 866 United Nations Plaza, Suite 560, New York, NY 10017; tel. (212) 371-2559; fax (212) 371-2784; e-mail azerbaijan@un.int; YASHAR ALIYEV.

Bahamas: 231 East 46th St, New York, NY 10017; tel. (212) 421-6925; fax (212) 759-2135; e-mail bahamas@un.int; PAULETTE A. BETHEL.

Bahrain: 866 Second Ave, 14th/15th Floor, New York, NY 10017; tel. (212) 223-6200; fax (212) 319-0687; e-mail bahrain@un.int; www.un.int/bahrain; TAWFEEQ AHMED KHALIL ALMANSOOR.

Bangladesh: 821 United Nations Plaza, 8th Floor, New York, NY 10017; tel. (212) 867-3434; fax (212) 972-4038; e-mail bangladesh@un.int; internet www.un.int/bangladesh; Dr IFTEKHAR AHMED CHOWDHURY.

Barbados: 800 Second Ave, 2nd Floor, New York, NY 10017; tel. (212) 867-8431; fax (212) 986-1030; e-mail barbados@un.int; JUNE YVONNE CLARKE.

Belarus: 136 East 67th St, New York, NY 10021; tel. (212) 535-3420; fax (212) 734-4810; e-mail belarus@un.int; internet www.un.int/belarus; SERGEI LING.

Belgium: 823 United Nations Plaza, 4th Floor, New York, NY 10017; tel. (212) 378-6300; fax (212) 681-7618; e-mail belgium@un.int; internet www.un.int/belgium; JEAN DE RUYT.

Belize: 800 Second Ave, Suite 400G, New York, NY 10017; tel. (212) 593-0999; fax (212) 593-0932; e-mail blzun@undp.org; STUART LESLIE.

Benin: 4 East 73rd St, New York, NY 10021; tel. (212) 249-6014; fax (212) 988-3714; e-mail benin@un.int; internet www.un.int/benin; JOEL WASSI ADECHI.

Bhutan: 2 United Nations Plaza, 27th Floor, New York, NY 10017; tel. (212) 826-1919; fax (212) 826-2998; e-mail pmbnewyork@aol.com; LYONPO OM PRADHAN.

Bolivia: 211 East 43rd St, 8th Floor, Room 802, New York, NY 10017; tel. (212) 682-8132; fax (212) 682-8133; e-mail bolivia@un.int; JAVIER MURILLO DE LA ROCHA.

Bosnia and Herzegovina: 866 United Nations Plaza, Suite 580, New York, NY 10017; tel. (212) 751-9015; fax (212) 751-9019; e-mail bosnia@un.int; internet www.un.int/bosnia; MIRZA KUSLJUGIC.

Botswana: 103 East 37th St, New York, NY 10016; tel. (212) 889-2277; fax (212) 725-5061; e-mail botswana@un.int; LEGWAILA JOSEPH LEGWAILA.

Brazil: 747 Third Ave, 9th Floor, New York, NY 10017; tel. (212) 372-2600; fax (212) 371-5716; e-mail braun@delbrasonu.org; internet www.un.int/brazil; RONALDO MOTA SARDENBERG.

Brunei: 771 First Ave, New York, NY 10017; tel. (212) 697-3465; fax (212) 697-9889; e-mail info@bruneimission-ny.org; ABDUL GHAFOR SHOFRY.

Bulgaria: 11 East 84th St, New York, NY 10028; tel. (212) 737-4790; fax (212) 472-9865; e-mail bulgaria@un.int; internet www.un.int/bulgaria; STEFAN TAFROV.

Burkina Faso: 115 East 73rd St, New York, NY 10021; tel. (212) 288-7515; fax (212) 772-3562; e-mail burkinafaso@un.int; MICHEL KAFANDO.

Burundi: 336 East 45th St, 12th Floor, New York, NY 10017; tel. (212) 499-0001; fax (212) 499-0006; e-mail burundi@un.int; MARC NTETURUYE.

Cambodia: 866 United Nations Plaza, Suite 420, New York, NY 10017; tel. (212) 223-0676; fax (212) 223-0425; e-mail cambodia@un.int; internet www.un.int/cambodia; OUCH BORITH.

Cameroon: 22 East 73rd St, New York, NY 10021; tel. (212) 794-2296; fax (212) 249-0533; e-mail info@cameroonmission.org; internet www.cameroonmission.org; MARTIN BELINGA EBOUTOU.

Canada: 1 Dag Hammarskjöld Plaza, 885 Second Ave, 14th Floor, New York, NY 10017; tel. (212) 848-1100; fax (212) 848-1195; e-mail canada@un.int; internet www.un.int/canada; PAUL HEINBECKER.

Cape Verde: 27 East 69th St, New York, NY 10021; tel. (212) 472-0333; fax (212) 794-1398; e-mail capeverde@un.int; LUIS DE MATOS MONTEIRO DA FONSECA.

Central African Republic: 386 Park Ave South, Room 1114, New York, NY 10016; tel. (212) 679-8089; fax (212) 545-8326; e-mail caf@un.int; FERNAND POUKRE-KONO.

Chad: 211 East 43rd St, Suite 1703, New York, NY 10017; tel. (212) 986-0980; fax (212) 986-0152; e-mail chad@un.int; LAOTEGGUEL-NODJI KOUMTOG.

Chile: 3 Dag Hammarskjöld Plaza, 305 East 47th St, 10th/11th Floor, New York, NY 10017; tel. (212) 832-3323; fax (212) 832-0236; e-mail chile@un.int; internet www.un.int/chile; JUAN GABRIEL VALDES.

China, People's Republic: 350 East 35th St, New York, NY 10016; tel. (212) 655-6100; fax (212) 634-7626; e-mail chinamission_un@fmprc.gov.cn; internet www.china-un.org; WANG YING-FAN.

Colombia: 140 East 57th St, 5th Floor, New York, NY 10022; tel. (212) 355-7776; fax (212) 371-2813; e-mail colombia@colombiaun.org; internet www.colombiaun.org; LUIS GUILLERMO GIRALDO.

Comoros: 420 East 50th St, New York, NY 10022; tel. (212) 972-8010; fax (212) 983-4712; e-mail comoros@un.int; internet www.un.int/comoros; Chargé d'affaires a.i. MAHMOUD MOHAMED ABOUD.

Congo, Democratic Republic: 866 United Nations Plaza, Suite 511, New York, NY 10017; tel. (212) 319-8061; fax (212) 319-8232; e-mail drcongo@un.int; internet www.un.int/drcongo; CHRISTIAN ILEKA ATOKI.

Congo, Republic: 14 East 65th St, New York, NY 10021; tel. (212) 744-7840; fax (212) 744-7975; e-mail congo@un.int; BASILE IKOUEBE.

Costa Rica: 211 East 43rd St, Room 903, New York, NY 10017; tel. (212) 986-6373; fax (212) 986-6842; e-mail pmnu@rree.go.cr; internet www.un.int/costarica; BERND H. NIEHAUS.

Côte d'Ivoire: 46 East 74th St, New York, NY 10021; tel. (212) 717-5555; fax (212) 717-4492; e-mail ivorycoast@un.int; internet www.un.int/cotedivoire; Chargé d'affaires AHIPEAUD GUEBO NOËL EMMANUEL.

Croatia: 820 Second Ave, 19th Floor, New York, NY 10017; tel. (212) 986-1585; fax (212) 986-2011; e-mail croatia@un.int; internet www.un.int/croatia; Dr IVAN ŠIMONOVIĆ.

Cuba: 315 Lexington Ave and 38th St, New York, NY 10016; tel. (212) 689-7215; fax (212) 779-1697; e-mail cuba@un.int; internet www.un.int/cuba; BRUNO RODRíGUEZ PARRILLA.

Cyprus: 13 East 40th St, New York, NY 10016; tel. (212) 481-6023; fax (212) 685-7316; e-mail cyprus@un.int; internet www.un.int/cyprus; SOTIRIOS ZACKHEOS.

Czech Republic: 1109–1111 Madison Ave, New York, NY 10028; tel. (212) 535-8814; fax (212) 772-0586; e-mail un.newyork@embassy.mzv.cz; internet www.czechembassy.org; HYNEK KMONICEK.

Denmark: 1 Dag Hammarskjöld Plaza, 885 Second Ave, 18th Floor, New York, NY 10017; tel. (212) 308-7009; fax (212) 308-3384; e-mail nycmis@um.dk; internet www.un.int/denmark; ELLEN MARG-RETHE LØJ.

Djibouti: 866 United Nations Plaza, Suite 4011, New York, NY 10017; tel. (212) 753-3163; fax (212) 223-1276; e-mail djibouti@nyct.net; ROBLE OLHAYE.

Dominica: 800 Second Ave, Suite 400H, New York, NY 10017; tel. (212) 949-0853; fax (212) 808-4975; e-mail dominica@un.int; SIMON PAUL RICHARDS.

Dominican Republic: 144 East 44th St, 4th Floor, New York, NY 10017; tel. (212) 867-0833; fax (212) 986-4694; e-mail undomrep@aol.com; internet www.un.int/dr; MARINO DE JESÚS VILLANUEVA CALLOT.

Ecuador: 866 United Nations Plaza, Room 516, New York, NY 10017; tel. (212) 935-1680; fax (212) 935-1835; e-mail ecuador@un.int; internet www.un.int/ecuador; LUIS BENIGNO GALLEGOS CHIRIBOGA.

Egypt: 304 East 44th St, New York, NY 10017; tel. (212) 503-0300; fax (212) 949-5999; e-mail egypt@un.int; AHMED ABOUL GHEIT.

El Salvador: 46 Park Ave, New York, NY 10016; tel. (212) 679-1616; fax (212) 725-7831; e-mail elsalvador@un.int; VICTOR MANUEL LAGOS PIZZATI.

Equatorial Guinea: 57 Magnolia Ave, Mount Vernon, NY 10553; tel. (914) 667-8999; fax (914) 667-8778; e-mail eqguinea@un.int; TEODORO BIYOGO NSUE.

Eritrea: 800 Second Ave, 18th Floor, New York, NY 10017; tel. (212) 687-3390; fax (212) 687-3138; e-mail eritrea@un.int; internet www.un.int/eritrea; AHMED TAHIR BADURI.

Estonia: 600 Third Ave, 26th Floor, New York, NY 10016; tel. (212) 883-0640; fax (212) 883-0648; e-mail mission.newyork@mfa.ee; MERLE PAJULA.

Ethiopia: 866 Second Ave, 3rd Floor, New York, NY 10017; tel. (212) 421-1830; fax (212) 754-0360; e-mail ethiopia@un.int; internet www.un.int/ethiopia; Dr ABDULMEJID HUSSEIN.

Fiji: 630 Third Ave, 7th Floor, New York, NY 10017; tel. (212) 687-4130; fax (212) 687-3963; e-mail fiji@un.int; ISIKIA RABICI SAVUA.

Finland: 866 United Nations Plaza, Suite 222, New York, NY 10017; tel. (212) 355-2100; fax (212) 759-6156; e-mail sanomat.yke@formin.fi; internet www.un.int/finland; MARJATTA RASI.

France: 1 Dag Hammarskjöld Plaza, 245 East 47th St, 44th Floor, New York, NY 10017; tel. (212) 308-5700; fax (212) 421-6889; e-mail france@un.int; internet www.un.int/france; JEAN-MARC ROCHEREAU DE LA SABLIERE.

Gabon: 18 East 41st St, 9th Floor, New York, NY 10017; tel. (212) 686-9720; fax (212) 689-5769; e-mail gabon@un.int; DENIS DANGUE RÉWAKA.

The Gambia: 800 Second Ave, Suite 400F, New York, NY 10017; tel. (212) 949-6640; fax (212) 808-4975; e-mail gambia@un.int; CRISPIN GREY-JOHNSON.

Georgia: 1 United Nations Plaza, 26th Floor, New York, NY 10021; tel. (212) 759-1949; fax (212) 759-1832; e-mail georgia@un.int; internet www.un.int/georgia; REVAZ ADAMIA.

Germany: 871 United Nations Plaza, New York, NY 10017; tel. (212) 940-0400; fax (212) 940-0402; e-mail germany@un.int; internet www.germany-info.org/un; Dr GUNTER PLEUGER.

Ghana: 19 East 47th St, New York, NY 10017; tel. (212) 832-1300; fax (212) 751-6743; e-mail ghanaperm@aol.com; NANA EFFAH-APENTENG.

Greece: 866 Second Ave, 13th Floor, New York, NY 10017; tel. (212) 888-6900; fax (212) 888-4440; e-mail mission@greeceun.org; internet www.greeceun.org; ADAMANTIOS VASSILAKIS.

Grenada: 800 Second Ave, Suite 400K, New York, NY 10017; tel. (212) 599-0301; fax (212) 599-1540; e-mail grenada@un.int; Dr LAMUEL A. STANISLAUS.

Guatemala: 57 Park Ave, New York, NY 10016; tel. (212) 679-4760; fax (212) 685-8741; e-mail guatemala@un.int; internet www.un.int/guatemala; GERT ROSENTHAL.

Guinea: 140 East 39th St, New York, NY 10016; tel. (212) 687-8115; fax (212) 687-8248; e-mail guinea@un.int; MAMADY TRAORÉ.

Guinea-Bissau: 211 East 43rd St, Room 704, New York, NY 10017; tel. (212) 338-9394; fax (212) 293-0264; e-mail guinea-bissau@un.int; Chargé d'affaires a.i. JOÃO SOARES DA GAMA.

Guyana: 866 United Nations Plaza, Suite 555, New York, NY 10017; tel. (212) 527-3232; fax (212) 935-7548; e-mail guyana@un.int; SAMUEL R. INSANALLY.

Haiti: 801 Second Ave, Room 600, New York, NY 10017; tel. (212) 370-4840; fax (212) 661-8698; e-mail haiti@un.int; JEAN-CLAUDE ALEXANDRE.

Honduras: 866 United Nations Plaza, Suite 417, New York, NY 10017; tel. (212) 752-3370; fax (212) 223-0498; e-mail m.suazo@worldnet.att.net; internet www.un.int/honduras; MANUEL ACOSTA BONILLA.

Hungary: 227 East 52nd St, New York, NY 10022; tel. (212) 752-0209; fax (212) 755-5395; e-mail hungary@un.int; internet www.un.int/hungary; LÁSZLÓ MOLNÁR.

Iceland: 800 Third Ave, 36th Floor, New York, NY 10022; tel. (212) 593-2700; fax (212) 593-6269; e-mail icecon.ny@utn.stjr.is; internet brunnur.stjr.is/embassy/newyork.nsf/pages/index.html; THORSTEINN INGÓLFSSON.

India: 235 East 43rd St, New York, NY 10017; tel. (212) 490-9660; fax (212) 490-9656; e-mail india@un.int or indiaun@prodigy.net; internet www.un.int/india; VIJAY K. NAMBIAR.

Indonesia: 325 East 38th St, New York, NY 10016; tel. (212) 972-8333; fax (212) 972-9780; e-mail ptri@indonesiamission-ny.org; internet www.indonesiamission-ny.org.

Iran: 622 Third Ave, 34th Floor, New York, NY 10017; tel. (212) 687-2020; fax (212) 867-7086; e-mail iran@un.int; internet www.un.int/iranDr MOHAMMAD JAVAD ZARIF.

Iraq: 14 East 79th St, New York, NY 10021; tel. (212) 737-4433; fax (212) 772-1794; e-mail missionofiraq@nyc.rr.com; internet www.iraqi-mission.org; MOHAMMED AL-DOURY.

Ireland: 1 Dag Hammarskjöld Plaza, 885 Second Ave, 19th Floor, New York, NY 10017; tel. (212) 421-6934; fax (212) 752-4726; e-mail ireland@un.int; internet www.un.int/ireland; RICHARD RYAN.

Israel: 800 Second Ave, New York, NY 10017; tel. (212) 499-5510; fax (212) 499-5516; e-mail israel@un.int; internet www.israel-un.org; DAN GILLERMAN.

Italy: 2 United Nations Plaza, 24th Floor, New York, NY 10017; tel. (212) 486-9191; fax (212) 486-1036; e-mail italy@un.int; internet www.italyun.org; MARCELLO SPATAFORA.

Jamaica: 767 Third Ave, 9th Floor, New York, NY 10017; tel. (212) 935-7509; fax (212) 935-7607; e-mail jamaica@un.int; internet www.un.int/jamaica; STAFFORD OLIVER NEIL.

Japan: 866 United Nations Plaza, 2nd Floor, New York, NY 10017; tel. (212) 223-4300; fax (212) 751-1966; e-mail mission@un-japan.org; internet www.un.int/japan; KOICHI HARAGUCHI.

Jordan: 866 United Nations Plaza, Suite 552, New York, NY 10017; tel. (212) 832-9553; fax (212) 832-5346; e-mail jordan@un.int; Prince ZEID RA'AD ZEID AL-HUSSEIN.

Kazakhstan: 866 United Nations Plaza, Suite 586, New York, NY 10017; tel. (212) 230-1900; fax (212) 230-1172; e-mail kazakhstan@un.int; internet www.un.int/kazakhstan; Dr MADINA JARBUSSYNOVA.

Kenya: 866 United Nations Plaza, Room 486, New York, NY 10017; tel. (212) 421-4740; fax (212) 486-1985; e-mail kenya@un.int; internet www.un.int/kenya/; BOB F. JALANG'O.

Korea, Democratic People's Republic: 820 Second Ave, 13th Floor, New York, NY 10017; tel. (212) 972-3105; fax (212) 972-3154; dprk@un.int; PAK GIL YON.

Korea, Republic: 335 East 45th St, New York, NY 10017; tel. (212) 439-4000; fax (212) 986-1083; e-mail korea@un.int; internet www.un.int/korea; SUN JOUN-YUNG.

Kuwait: 321 East 44th St, New York, NY 10017; tel. (212) 973-4300; fax (212) 370-1733; e-mail kuwait@kuwaitmission.com; internet www.kuwaitmission.com; MOHAMMAD A. ABULHASAN.

Kyrgyzstan: 866 United Nations Plaza, Suite 477, New York, NY 10017; tel. (212) 486-4214; fax (212) 486-5259; e-mail kyrgyzstan@un.int; KAMIL BAIALINOV.

Laos: 317 East 51st St, New York, NY 10022; tel. (212) 832-2734; fax (212) 750-0039; e-mail lao@un.int; internet www.un.int/lao; ALOUNKÈO KITTIKHOUN.

Latvia: 333 East 50th St, New York, NY 10022; tel. (212) 838-8877; fax (212) 838-8920; e-mail irppanony@aol.com; GINTS JEGERMANIS.

Lebanon: 866 United Nations Plaza, Room 531–533, New York, NY 10017; tel. (212) 355-5460; fax (212) 838-2819; e-mail lebanon@un.int; Chargé d'affaires a.i. Houssam Asaad Diab.

Lesotho: 204 East 39th St, New York, NY 10016; tel. (212) 661-1690; fax (212) 682-4388; e-mail lesotho@un.int; internet www.un.int/lesotho; PERCY M. MANGOAELA.

Liberia: 820 Second Ave, 13th Floor, New York, NY 10017; tel. (212) 687-1033; fax (212) 687-1035; e-mail liberia@un.int; LAMI KAWAH.

Libya: 309-315 East 48th St, New York, NY 10017; tel. (212) 752-5775; fax (212) 593-4787; e-mail info@libya-un.org; internet www.libya-un.org; ABUZED OMAR DORDA.

Liechtenstein: 633 Third Ave, 27th Floor, New York, NY 10017; tel. (212) 599-0220; fax (212) 599-0064; e-mail liechtenstein@un.int; internet www.un.int/liechtenstein; CHRISTIAN WENAWESER.

Lithuania: 420 Fifth Ave, 3rd Floor, New York, NY 10018; tel. (212) 354-7820; fax (212) 354-7833; e-mail lithuania@un.int; internet www.un.int/lithuania; GEDIMINAS SERKSNYS.

Luxembourg: 17 Beekman Pl., New York, NY 10022; tel. (212) 935-3589; fax (212) 935-5896; e-mail luxun@undp.org; internet www.un.int/luxembourg; HUBERT WURTH.

Macedonia, former Yugoslav republic: 866 United Nations Plaza, Suite 517, New York, NY 10017; tel. (212) 308-8504; fax (212) 308-8724; e-mail macedonia@un.int; internet www.un.int/macedonia; Dr SRGJAN KERIM.

Madagascar: 820 Second Ave, Suite 800, New York, NY 10017; tel. (212) 986-9491; fax (212) 986-6271; e-mail repermad@ren.com; internet www.un.int/madagascar; ZINA ANDRIANARIVELO-RAZAFY.

Malawi: 600 Third Ave, 21st Floor, New York, NY 10016; tel. (212) 949-0180; fax (212) 599-5021; e-mail malawi@un.int; ISAAC CHIKWEKWERE LAMBA.

Malaysia: 313 East 43rd St, New York, NY 10017; tel. (212) 986-6310; fax (212) 490-8576; e-mail malaysia@un.int; internet www.un.int/malaysia; RASTAM MOHAMAD ISA.

Maldives: 820 Second Ave, Suite 800CE, New York, NY 10017; tel. (212) 599-6195; fax (212) 661-6405; e-mail mdv@undp.org; internet www.un.int/maldives; Dr MOHAMED LATHEEF.

Mali: 111 East 69th St, New York, NY 10021; tel. (212) 737-4150; fax (212) 472-6778; e-mail info@mali-un.org; MOCTAR OUANE.

Malta: 249 East 35th St, New York, NY 10016; tel. (212) 725-2345; fax (212) 779-7097; e-mail mltun@un.int; WALTER BALZAN.

Marshall Islands: 800 Second Ave, 18th Floor, New York, NY 10017; tel. (212) 983-3040; fax (212) 983-3202; e-mail marshallislands@un.int; ALFRED CAPELLE.

Mauritania: 211 East 43rd St, Suite 2000, New York, NY 10017; tel. (212) 986-7963; fax (212) 986-8419; e-mail mauritania@un.int; MAHFOUDH OULD DEDDACH.

Mauritius: 211 East 43rd St, 15th Floor, New York, NY 10017; tel. (212) 949-0190; fax (212) 697-3829; e-mail mauritius@un.int; JAGDISH KOONJUL.

Mexico: 2 United Nations Plaza, 28th Floor, New York, NY 10017; tel. (212) 752-0220; fax (212) 688-8862; e-mail mexico@un.int; internet www.un.int/mexico; ADOLFO MIGUEL AGUILAR ZINSER.

Micronesia, Federated States: 820 Second Ave, Suite 17A, New York, NY 10017; tel. (212) 697-8370; fax (212) 697-8295; e-mail fsmun@fsmgov.org; internet www.fsmgov.org/fsmun; MASAO NAKAYAMA.

Moldova: 573-577 Third Ave, New York, NY 10016; tel. (212) 682-3523; fax (212) 682-6274; e-mail moldova@un.int; internet www.un.int/modova; VSEVOLOD GRIGORE.

Monaco: 866 United Nations Plaza, Suite 520, New York, NY 10017; tel. (212) 832-0721; fax (212) 832-5358; e-mail monaco@un.int; www.un.int/monaco; JACQUES LOUIS BOISSON.

Mongolia: 6 East 77th St, New York, NY 10021; tel. (212) 737-3874; fax (212) 861-9460; e-mail mongolia@un.int; internet www.un.int/mongolia; BAATAR CHOISUREN.

Morocco: 866 Second Ave, 6th and 7th Floors, New York, NY 10017; tel. (212) 421-1580; fax (212) 980-1512; e-mail morocco@un.int; internet www.un.int/morocco; MOHAMED BENNOUNA.

Mozambique: 420 East 50th St, New York, NY 10022; tel. (212) 644-5965; fax (212) 644-5972; e-mail mozambique@un.int; internet www.un.int/mozambique; FILIPE CHIDUMO.

Myanmar: 10 East 77th St, New York, NY 10021; tel. (212) 535-1310; fax (212) 737-2421; e-mail myanmar@un.int; KYAW TINT SWE.

Namibia: 135 East 36th St, New York, NY 10016; tel. (212) 685-2003; fax (212) 685-1561; e-mail namibia@un.int; internet www.un.int/namibia; MARTIN ANDJABA.

Nauru: 800 Second Ave, Suite 400D, New York, NY 10017; tel. (212) 937-0074; fax (212) 937-0079; VINCI NEIL CLODUMAR.

Nepal: 820 Second Ave, Suite 17BB, New York, NY 10017; tel. (212) 370-3988; fax (212) 953-2038; e-mail nepal@un.int; internet www.un.int/nepal; MURARI RAJ SHARMA.

Netherlands: 235 East 45th St, 16th Floor, New York, NY 10017; tel. (212) 697-5547; fax (212) 370-1954; e-mail netherlands@un.int; internet www.pvnewyork.org; DIRK JAN VAN DEN BERG.

New Zealand: 1 United Nations Plaza, 25th Floor, New York, NY 10017; tel. (212) 826-1960; fax (212) 758-0827; e-mail nz@un.int; internet www.nzmissionny.org; DON MACKAY.

Nicaragua: 820 Second Ave, Suite 801, New York, NY 10017; tel. (212) 490-7997; fax (212) 286-0815; e-mail nicaragua@un.int; internet www.un.int/nicaragua; EDUARDO J. SEVILLA SOMOZA.

Niger: 417 East 50th St, New York, NY 10022; tel. (212) 421-3260; fax (212) 753-6931; e-mail nigerun@aol.com; internet www.un.int/niger; OUSMANE MOUTARI.

Nigeria: 828 Second Ave, New York, NY 10017; tel. (212) 953-9130; fax (212) 697-1970; e-mail nigeria@un.int; ARTHUR C. I. MBANEFO.

Norway: 825 Third Ave, 39th Floor, New York, NY 10017; tel. (212) 421-0280; fax (212) 688-0554; e-mail delun@mfa.no; internet www.un.norway-un.org; OLE PETER KOLBY.

Oman: 866 United Nations Plaza, Suite 540, New York, NY 10017; tel. (212) 355-3505; fax (212) 644-0070; e-mail oman@un.int; FUAD MUBARAK AL-HINAI.

Pakistan: 8 East 65th St, New York, NY 10021; tel. (212) 879-8600; fax (212) 744-7348; e-mail pakistan@un.int; internet www.un.int/pakistan; MUNIR AKRAM.

Palau: New York; e-mail palau@un.int.

Panama: 866 United Nations Plaza, Suite 4030, New York, NY 10017; tel. (212) 421-5420; fax (212) 421-2694; e-mail emb@panama_msun.org; RAMÓN A. MORALES.

Papua New Guinea: 201 East 42nd St, Suite 405, New York, NY 10017; tel. (212) 557-5001; fax (212) 557-5009; e-mail png@un.int; ROBERT GUBA AISI.

Paraguay: 211 East 43rd St, Suite 400, New York, NY 10017; tel. (212) 687-3490; fax (212) 818-1282; e-mail paraguay@un.int; ELADIO LOIZAGA.

Peru: 820 Second Ave, Suite 1600, New York, NY 10017; tel. (212) 687-3336; fax (212) 972-6975; e-mail peru@un.int; OSWALDO DE RIVERO.

Philippines: 556 Fifth Ave, 5th Floor, New York, NY 10036; tel. (212) 764-1300; fax (212) 840-8602; e-mail misunphil@idt.net; internet www.un.int/phillipines; Chargé d'affaires a.i. ENRIQUE A. MANALO.

Poland: 9 East 66th St, New York, NY 10021; tel. (212) 744-2506; fax (212) 517-6771; e-mail poland@un.int; internet www.un.int/poland; JANUSZ STANCZYK.

Portugal: 866 Second Ave, 9th Floor, New York, NY 10017; tel. (212) 759-9444; fax (212) 355-1124; e-mail portugal@un.int; internet www.un.int/portugal; Gonçalo de Santa Clara Gomes.

Qatar: 809 United Nations Plaza, 4th Floor, New York, NY 10017; tel. (212) 486-9335; fax (212) 758-4952; e-mail newyork@mofa.gov.qa; NASSIR BIN ABDULAZIZ AL-NASSER.

Romania: 573–577 Third Ave, New York, NY 10016; tel. (212) 682-3273; fax (212) 682-9746; e-mail romania@un.int; internet www.un.int/romania; ALEXANDRU A. NICULESCU.

Russia: 136 East 67th St, New York, NY 10021; tel. (212) 861-4900; fax (212) 628-0252; e-mail rusun@un.int; internet www.un.int/russia; SERGEI V. LAVROV.

Rwanda: 124 East 39th St, New York, NY 10016; tel. (212) 679-9010; fax (212) 679-9133; e-mail rwanda@un.int; STANISLAS KAMANZI.

Saint Christopher and Nevis: 414 East 75th St, 5th Floor, New York, NY 10021; tel. (212) 535-1235; fax (212) 535-6858; e-mail sknmission@aol.com; Dr JOSEPH R. CHRISTMAS.

Saint Lucia: 800 Second Ave, 9th Floor, New York, NY 10017; tel. (212) 697-9360; fax (212) 697-4993; e-mail stlucia@un.int; internet www.un.int/stlucia; EARL STEPHEN HUNTLEY.

Saint Vincent and the Grenadines: 801 Second Ave, 21st Floor, New York, NY 10017; tel. (212) 687-4490; fax (212) 949-5946; e-mail stvg@un.int; MARGARET HUGHES FERRARI.

Samoa: 800 Second Ave, Suite 400J, New York, NY 10017; tel. (212) 599-6196; fax (212) 599-0797; e-mail samoa@un.int; TUILOMA NERONI SLADE.

San Marino: 327 East 50th St, New York, NY 10022; tel. (212) 751-1234; fax (212) 751-1436; e-mail sanmarinoun@hotmail.com; GIAN NICOLA FILIPPI BALESTRA.

São Tomé and Príncipe: 400 Park Ave, 7th Floor, New York, NY 10022; tel. (212) 317-0533; fax (212) 317-0580; e-mail stp@un.int; Chargé d'affaires a.i. DOMINGOS AUGUSTO FERREIRA.

Saudi Arabia: 405 Lexington Ave, 56th Floor, New York, NY 10017; tel. (212) 697-4830; fax (212) 983-4895; e-mail saudi-mission@un.int; internet www.saudi-un-ny.org; FAWZI BIN ABDUL MAJEED SHOBOKSHI.

Senegal: 238 East 68th St, New York, NY 10021; tel. (212) 517-9030; fax (212) 517-3032; e-mail senegal@un.int; internet www.un.int/senegal; PAPA LOUIS FALL.

Serbia and Montenegro: 854 Fifth Ave, New York, NY 10021; tel. (212) 879-8700; fax (212) 879-8705; e-mail yugoslavia@un.int; internet www.un.int/serbia-montenegro; DEJAN ŠAHOVIĆ.

Seychelles: 800 Second Ave, Room 400C, New York, NY 10017; tel. (212) 972-1785; fax (212) 972-1786; e-mail seychelles@un.int; CLAUDE MOREL.

Sierra Leone: 245 East 49th St, New York, NY 10017; tel. (212) 688-1656; fax (212) 688-4924; e-mail sierraleone@un.int; JOE ROBERT PEMAGBI.

Singapore: 231 East 51st St, New York, NY 10022; tel. (212) 826-0840; fax (212) 826-2964; e-mail sgpun@prodigy.net; internet www.mfa.gov.sg/newyork; KISHORE MAHBUBANI.

Slovakia: 866 United Nations Plaza, Suite 494, New York, NY 10017; tel. (212) 980-1558; fax (212) 980-3295; e-mail slovakia@un.int; PETER TOMKA.

Slovenia: 600 Third Ave, 24th Floor, New York, NY 10016; tel. (212) 370-3007; fax (212) 370-1824; e-mail mny@mzz-dkp.gov.si; internet www.un.int/slovenia; ROMAN KIRN.

Solomon Islands: 800 Second Ave, Suite 8008, New York, NY 10017; tel. (212) 599-6193; fax (212) 661-8925; e-mail solomonislands@un.int; Chargé d'affaires a.i. JEREMIAH MANELE.

Somalia: 425 East 61st St, Suite 702, New York, NY 10021; tel. (212) 688-9410; fax (212) 759-0651; e-mail somalianet@hotmail.com; internet www.iaed.org/somalia; AHMED ABDI HASHI.

South Africa: 333 East 38th St, 9th Floor, New York, NY 10016; tel. (212) 213-5583; fax (212) 692-2498; e-mail soafun@worldnet.att.net; internet www.southafrica-newyork.net/pmun; DUMISANI SHADRACK KUMALO.

Spain: 823 United Nations Plaza, 9th Floor, New York, NY 10017; tel. (212) 661-1050; fax (212) 949-7247; e-mail spain@spainun.org; internet www.spainun.org; INOCENCIO F. ARIAS.

Sri Lanka: 630 Third Ave, 20th Floor, New York, NY 10017; tel. (212) 986-7040; fax (212) 986-1838; e-mail srilanka@un.int; CHITHAMBARANATHAN MAHENDRAN.

Sudan: 655 Third Ave, Suite 500-510, New York, NY 10017; tel. (212) 573-6033; fax (212) 573-6160; e-mail sudan@un.int; ELFATIH MOHAMED AHMED ERWA.

Suriname: 866 United Nations Plaza, Suite 320, New York, NY 10017; tel. (212) 826-0660; fax (212) 980-7029; e-mail suriname@un.int; internet www.un.int/suriname EWALD WENSLEY LIMON.

Swaziland: 408 East 50th St, New York, NY 10022; tel. (212) 371-8910; fax (212) 754-2755; e-mail swaziland@un.int; CLIFFORD SIBUSIO MAMBA.

Sweden: 1 Dag Hammarskjöld Plaza, 885 Second Ave, 46th Floor, New York, NY 10017; tel. (212) 583-2500; fax (212) 832-0389; e-mail sweden@un.int; internet www.un.int/sweden; PIERRE SCHORI.

Switzerland: 633 Third Ave, 29th floor, New York, NY 10017; tel. (212) 286 1540; fax (212) 286 1555 ; e-mail vertretung-un@nyc.rep.admin.ch; internet www.uno.admin.ch/sub_uno/e/uno.html; JENÖ C.A. STAEHELIN.

Syria: 820 Second Ave, 15th Floor, New York, NY 10017; tel. (212) 661-1313; fax (212) 867-3985; e-mail syria@un.int; internet www.syria-un.org; Dr MIKHAIL WEHBE.

Tajikistan: 136 East 67th St, New York, NY 10021; tel. (212) 744-2196; fax (212) 472-7645; e-mail tajikistan@un.int; RASHID ALIMOV.

Tanzania: 205 East 42nd St, 13th Floor, New York, NY 10017; tel. (212) 972-9160; fax (212) 682-5232; e-mail; DAUDI NGELAUTWA MWAKAWAGO.

Thailand: 351 East 52nd St, New York, NY 10022; tel. (212) 754-2230; fax (212) 754-2535; e-mail thailand@un.int; CHUCHAI KASEMSARN.

Timor-Leste: 866, Second Ave, 9th floor, New York, NY 10017; tel. (212) 759 3675; fax (212) 759 4196 ; e-mail timor-leste@un.int; internet www.un.int/timor-leste; JOSé LUíS GUTERRES.

Togo: 112 East 40th St, New York, NY 10016; tel. (212) 490-3455; fax (212) 983-6684; e-mail togo@un.int; e-mail onu@republicoftogo.com; ROLAND YAO KPOTSRA.

Tonga: 800 Second Ave, Suite 400B, New York, NY 10017; tel. (212) 5996190; fax (212) 8084975; e-mail tongaunmission@aol.com; S. TU'A TAUMOEPEAU-TUPOU.

Trinidad and Tobago: 820 Second Ave, 5th Floor, New York, NY 10017; tel. (212) 697-7620; fax (212) 682-3580; e-mail tto@un.int; PHILIP R.A.SEALY.

Tunisia: 31 Beekman Pl., New York, NY 10022; tel. (212) 751-7503; fax (212) 751-0569; e-mail tunisia@un.int; internet www.tunisiaonline.com/tunisia-un/index.html; ALI HACHANI.

Turkey: 821 United Nations Plaza, 10th Floor, New York, NY 10017; tel. (212) 949-0150; fax (212) 949-0086; e-mail turkey@un.int; internet www.un.int/turkey; MEHMET UMIT PAMIR.

Turkmenistan: 866 United Nations Plaza, Suite 424, New York, NY 10021; tel. (212) 486-8908; fax (212) 486-2521; e-mail turkmenistan@un.int; AKSOLTAN T. ATAEVA.

Tuvalu: 800 Second Ave, Suite 400B, New York, N.Y. 10017; tel. (212) 490-0534; fax (212) 808-4975; ENELE SOSENE SOPOAGA.

Uganda: 336 East 45th St, New York, NY 10017; tel. (212) 949-0110; fax (212) 687-4517; e-mail ugandaamb@aol.com; internet www.un.int/uganda; Prof. MATIA MULAMBA SEMAKULA KIWANUKA.

Ukraine: 220 East 51st St, New York, NY 10022; tel. (212) 759-7003; fax (212) 355-9455; e-mail mail@uamission.org; internet www.uamission.org; VALERIY P. KUCHINSKY.

United Arab Emirates: 747 Third Ave, 36th Floor, New York, NY 10017; tel. (212) 371-0480; fax (212) 371-4923; e-mail uae@un.int; ABDULAZIZ NASSER R. AL-SHAMSI.

United Kingdom: 1 Dag Hammarskjöld Plaza, 885 2nd Ave, New York, NY 10017; tel. (212) 745-9200; fax (212) 745-9316; e-mail uk@un.int; internet www.ukun.org; Sir JEREMY GREENSTOCK (until July 2003), Sir EMYR JONES PARRY (designate).

USA: 799 United Nations Plaza, New York, NY 10017; tel. (212) 415-4000; fax (212) 415-4443; e-mail usa@un.int; internet www.un.int/usa; JOHN DIMITRI NEGROPONTE.

Uruguay: 866 United Nations Plaza, Suite 322, New York, NY 10017; tel. (212) 752-8240; fax (212) 593-0935; e-mail uruguay@un.int; internet www.un.int/uruguay; FELIPE H. PAOLILLO.

Uzbekistan: 866 United Nations Plaza, Suite 326, New York, NY 10017; tel. (212) 486-4242; fax (212) 486-7998; e-mail uzbekistan@un.int; ALISHER VOHIDOV.

Vanuatu: 866 United Nations Plaza, 3rd Floor, New York, NY 10017; tel. (212) 425-9600; fax (212) 425-9653; e-mail vanuatu@un.int; Chargé d'affaires a.i. SELWYN ARUTANGAI.

Venezuela: 335 East 46th St, New York, NY 10017; tel. (212) 557-2055; fax (212) 557-3528; e-mail venezuela@un.int; internet www.un.int/venezuela; MILOS ALCALAY.

Viet Nam: 866 United Nations Plaza, Suite 435, New York, NY 10017; tel. (212) 644-0594; fax (212) 644-5732; e-mail vietnamun@aol.com; internet www.un.int/vietnam; NGUYEN THANH CHAU.

Yemen: 413 East 51st St, New York, NY 10022; tel. (212) 355-1730; fax (212) 750-9613; e-mail yemen@un.int; internet www.un.int/yemen; ABDULLAH M. AS-SAIDI.

Zambia: 237 East 52nd St, New York, NY 10022; tel. (212) 888-5770; fax (212) 888-5213; e-mail zambia@un.int; internet www.un.int/zambia; MWELWA CHAMBIKABALENSHI CHIBOTWE CHUSHI MUSAMBACHI.

Zimbabwe: 128 East 56th St, New York, NY 10022; tel. (212) 980-9511; fax (212) 308-6705; e-mail zimbabwe@un.int; T. J. B. BONIFACE GUWA CHIDYAUSIKU.

OBSERVERS

Non-member states, inter-governmental organizations, etc., which have received an invitation to participate in the sessions and the work of the General Assembly as Observers, maintaining permanent offices at the UN.

Non-member states

Holy See: 25 East 39th St, New York, NY 10016; tel. (212) 370-7885; fax (212) 370-9622; e-mail vatobservny@qwest.net; internet www.holyseemission.org; Most Rev. CELESTINO MIGLIORE, Titular Archbishop of Canosa.

Inter-governmental organizations*

African Union: 346 East 50th St, New York, NY 10022; tel. (212) 319-5490; fax (212) 319-7135; AMADOU KÉBÉ.

Asian-African Legal Consultative Organization: 404 East 66th St, Apt 12C, New York, NY 10021; tel. (212) 734-7608; e-mail aalco@un.int; K. BHAGWAT-SINGH (INDIA).

Caribbean Community: 97-40 62nd Drive, 15K, Rego Park, NY 11374-1336; tel. and fax (718) 896-1179; e-mail caribcomun@un.int; HAMID MOHAMMED.

Commonwealth Secretariat: 800 Second Ave, 4th Floor, New York, NY 10017; tel. (212) 599-6190; fax (212) 808-4975; e-mail comsec@thecommonwealth.org.

European Community: European Commission Delegation in New York, 305 East 47th St, New York, NY 10017; tel. (212) 371-3804; fax (212) 758-2718; e-mail euinfo@delusny.cec.eu.int; internet www.europa-eu-un.org; Head of delegation: John B. Richardson. Liaison Office of the General Secretariat of the Council of Ministers of the European Union, 345 East 46th St, 6th Floor, New York, NY 10017; tel. (212) 292-8600; fax (212) 681-6266; the Observer is the Permanent Representative to the UN of the country currently exercising the Presidency of the Council of Ministers of the European Union.

La Francophonie: 801 Second Ave, Suite 605, New York, NY 10017; tel. (212) 867-6771; fax (212) 867-3840; e-mail francophonie@un.int; RIDHA BOUABID.

International Organization for Migration: 122 East 42nd St, Suite 1610, New York, NY 10168; tel. (212) 681-7000; fax (212) 867-5887; e-mail unobserver@iom.int; ROBERT G. PAIVA.

International Seabed Authority: 1 United Nations Plaza, Room 1140, New York, NY 10017; tel. (212) 963-6470; fax (212) 963-0908.

International Tribunal for the Law of the Sea: 1 United Nations Plaza, Room 1142, New York, NY 10017, tel. (212) 963-6480; fax (212) 963-0908.

League of Arab States: 747 Third Ave, 35th Floor, New York, NY 10017; tel. (212) 838-8700; fax (212) 355-3909; e-mail las@un.int; YAHIA AL-MAHMASSANI.

Organization of the Islamic Conference: 130 East 40th St, 5th Floor, New York, NY 10016; tel. (212) 883-0140; fax (212) 883-0143; e-mail oic@un.int; internet www.un.int/oic; MOKHTAR LAMANI.

World Conservation Union—IUCN: 406 West 66th St, New York, NY 10021; tel. and fax (212) 734-7608.

* The following inter-governmental organizations have a standing invitation to participate as Observers, but do not maintain permanent offices at the United Nations:

    African, Caribbean and Pacific Group of States
    African Development Bank
    Agency for the Prohibition of Nuclear Weapons in Latin America and the Caribbean

    Andean Community
    Association of Caribbean States
    Central American Integration System
    Commonwealth of Independent States
    Council of Europe
    Economic Co-operation Organization
    International Criminal Police Organization (Interpol)
    Inter-Parliamentary Union
    Latin American Economic System
    Latin American Parliament
    Organisation for Economic Co-operation and Development
    Organization for Security and Co-operation in Europe
    Organization of American States
    Organization of the Black Sea Economic Co-operation
    Permanent Court of Arbitration
    Pacific Islands Forum

Other observers

International Committee of the Red Cross: 801 Second Ave, 18th Floor, New York, NY 10017; tel. (212) 599-6021; fax (212) 599-6009; e-mail mail@icrc.delnyc.org; SYLVIE JUNOD.

International Federation of Red Cross and Red Crescent Societies: 630 Third Ave, Suite 2104, New York, NY 10017; tel. (212) 338-0161; fax (212) 338-9832; e-mail redcross@un.int; ENCHO GOSPODINOV.

Palestine: 115 East 65th St, New York, NY 10021; tel. (212) 288-8500; fax (212) 517-2377; e-mail mission@palestine-un.org; internet www.palestine-un.org; Dr NASSER AL-KIDWA.

Sovereign Military Order of Malta: 216 East 47th St, 8th Floor, New York, NY 10017; tel. (212) 355-6213; fax (212) 355-4014; e-mail sm-malta@un.int; JOSÉ ANTONIO LINATI-BOSCH.

United Nations Information Centres/Services

Afghanistan: (temporarily inactive).

Algeria: 9A rue Emile Payen, Hydra, Algiers; tel. (2) 691212; fax (2) 692315; e-mail unic.dz@undp.org; internet www.unic.org.dz.

Argentina: Junín 1940, 1°, 1113 Buenos Aires; tel. (1) 803-7671; fax (1) 804-7545; e-mail buenosaires@unic.org.ar; internet www.unic.org.ar (also covers Uruguay).

Australia: POB 4045, 46-48 York St, 5th Floor, Sydney, NSW 2001; tel. (2) 9262-5111; fax (2) 9262-5886; e-mail unic@un.org.au; internet www.un.org.au (also covers Fiji, Kiribati, Nauru, New Zealand, Samoa, Tonga, Tuvalu and Vanuatu).

Austria: POB 500, Vienna International Centre, 1400 Vienna; tel. (1) 26060-4666; fax (1) 26060-5899; e-mail unis@unis.unvienna.org; internet www.unis.unvienna.org (also covers Hungary, Slovakia and Slovenia).

Bahrain: POB 26004, Bldg 69, Rd 1901, Manama 319; tel. (973) 311-676; fax (973) 311-692; e-mail unic.bahrain@undp.org (also covers Qatar and the United Arab Emirates).

Bangladesh: POB 3658, House 60, Rd 11A, Dhanmondi, Dhaka 1209; tel. (2) 8118600; fax (2) 8112343; e-mail unic.dhaka@undp.org; internet www.unicdhaka.org.

Belgium: Montoyerstraat 14, 1000 Brussels; tel. (2) 289-28-90; fax (2) 502-40-61; e-mail unic@unbenelux.org; internet www.unbenelux.org (also covers Luxembourg, the Netherlands and the European Union institutions).

Bolivia: Apdo 9072, Calle 14 esq. S. Bustamante, Ed. Metrobol II, Calacoto, La Paz; tel. (2) 2795544; fax (2) 2795963; e-mail unicbol@nu.org.bo; internet www.no.org.bo/cinu.

Brazil: Palacio Itamaraty, Avda Marechal Floriano 196, 20080-002 Rio de Janeiro; tel. (21) 253-2211; fax (21) 233-5753; e-mail info unic@unicrio.org.br; internet www.unicrio.org.br.

Burkina Faso: BP 135, ave Georges Konseiga, Secteur no 4, Ouagadougou; tel. 30-60-76; fax 31-13-22; e-mail cinu.oui@fasonet.bf; internet www.cinu-burkina.org (also covers Chad, Mali and Niger).

Burundi: BP 2160, ave de la Révolution 117, Bujumbura; tel. (2) 225018; fax (2) 241798; e-mail unicbuj@cbinf.com.

Cameroon: PB 836, Immeuble Kamdem, rue Joseph Clère, Yaoundé; tel. 22-50-43; fax 23-51-73; e-mail unic@un.cm; internet www.un.cm/cinu (also covers the Central African Republic and Gabon).

Chile: Edif. Naciones Unidas, Avda Dag Hammarskjöld, Casilla 179-D, Santiago; tel. (2) 210-2000; fax (2) 208-1946; e-mail dpisantiago@eclac.cl.

Colombia: Apdo Aéreo 058964; Calle 100, No. 8A–55, 10°, Santafé de Bogotá 2; tel. (1) 257-6044; fax (1) 257-6244; e-mail uniccol@mbox.unicc.org; internet www.onucolombia.org (also covers Ecuador and Venezuela).

Congo, Democratic Republic: PB 7248, blvd du 30 juin, Kinshasa; tel. 884-5537; fax 884-3675; e-mail unic.kinshasa@undp.org.

Congo, Republic: POB 13210, ave Foch, Case ORTF 15, Brazzaville; tel. 814447; fax 812744; e-mail prosper.mihindou@undp.org.

Czech Republic: nam. Kinských 6, 150 00 Prague 5; tel. (2) 57199831; fax (2) 47316761; e-mail unicprg@terminal.cz; internet www.unicprague.cz.

Denmark: Midtermolen 3, 2100 Copenhagen Ø; tel. 35-46-73-00; fax 35-46-73-01; e-mail unic@un.dk; internet www.un.dk (also covers Finland, Iceland, Norway and Sweden).

Egypt: POB 982, World Trade Centre, 1191 Corniche El Nil, Boulak, Cairo; tel. (2) 5315593; fax (2) 3553705; e-mail info@unic-eg.org; internet www.unic-eg.org (also covers Saudi Arabia).

El Salvador: (temporarily inactive).

Ethiopia: POB 3001, Africa Hall, Addis Ababa; tel. (1) 515826; fax (1) 510365; e-mail ecainfo@un.org.

France: 1 rue Miollis, 75732 Paris Cédex 15; tel. 1-45-68-10-00; fax 1-43-06-46-78; e-mail cinu@onu.fr; internet www.onu.fr.

Germany: 53175 Bonn, Haus Cartanjen, Martin-Luther-King-Str. 8; 53153 Bonn; tel. (228) 815-2770; fax (228) 815-2777; e-mail unic@uno.de; internet www.uno.de.

Ghana: POB 2339, Gamel Abdul Nassar/Liberia Roads, Accra; tel. (21) 665511; fax (21) 7010930; e-mail info@unicar.org.gh (also covers Sierra Leone).

Greece: 36 Amalia Ave, 105 58; Athens; tel. (1) 5230640; fax (1) 5233639; e-mail unicgre@unic.gr; internet www.unic.gr (also covers Cyprus and Israel).

India: 55 Lodi Estate, New Delhi 110 003; tel. (11) 462-8877; fax (11) 462-0293; internet www.unic.org.in (also covers Bhutan).

Indonesia: Gedung Surya, 14th Floor, 9 Jalan M. H. Thamrin Kavling, Jakarta 10350; tel. (21) 3983-1011; fax (21) 3983-1010; e-mail unicjak@cbn.net.id.

Iran: POB 15875-4557; 185 Ghaem Magham Farahani Ave, Tehran 15868; tel. (21) 873-1534; fax (21) 204-4523; e-mail unic@unic.un.or.ir; internet www.unic-ir.org.

Italy: Palazzetto Venezia, Piazza San Marco 50, 00186 Rome; tel. (06) 6789907; fax (06) 6793337; e-mail onuitalia@onuitalia.it; internet www.onuitalia.it (also covers the Holy See, Malta and San Marino).

Japan: UNU Bldg, 8th Floor, 53-70 Jingumae S-chome, Shibuya-ku, Tokyo 150 0001; tel. (3) 5467-4451; fax (3) 5467-4455; e-mail unic@untokyo.jp; internet www.unic.or.jp (also covers Palau).

Kenya: POB 30552, United Nations Office, Gigiri, Nairobi; tel. (20) 623292; fax (20) 624349; e-mail unic@unep.org; internet www.unicnairobi.org (also covers Seychelles and Uganda).

Lebanon: Riad es-Solh Sq., POB 11-8575-4956, Chouran, Beirut; tel. (1) 981301; fax (1) 981516; e-mail unic-beirut@un.org (also covers Jordan, Kuwait and Syria).

Lesotho: POB 301, Maseru 100; tel. (22) 312496; fax (22) 310042; e-mail unic.maseru@undp.org.

Liberia: Dubar Bldg, Virginia, Monrovia; tel. 2260195; fax 205407; e-mail registry.1r@undp.org.

Libya: POB 286, Shara Muzzafar al-Aftas, Hay al-Andalous, Tripoli; tel. (21) 4777885; fax (21) 4777343; e-mail fo.lby@undp.org.

Madagascar: PB 1348, 22 rue Rainitovo, Antsahavola, Antananarivo; tel. (20) 2224115; fax (20) 33315; e-mail unic.ant@dts.mg; internet www.onu.dts.mg.

Mexico: Presidente Masaryk 29, 6°, México 11 570, DF; tel. (52) 5263-9724; fax (52) 5203-8638; e-mail infounic@un.org.mx; internet www.cinu.org.mx (also covers Cuba and the Dominican Republic).

Morocco: BP 601, Angle Charia Ibnouzaid 6, Rabat; tel. (7) 7686-33; fax (7) 7683-77; e-mail unicmor@unicmor.ma; internet www.cinu.org.ma.

Myanmar: POB 230, 6 Natmauk Rd, Yangon; tel. (1) 292619; fax (1) 292911; e-mail unic.myanmar@undp.org.

Namibia: Private Bag 13351, Paratus Bldg, 372 Independence Ave, Windhoek; tel. (61) 233034; fax (61) 233036; e-mail unic@un.na; internet www.un.na/unic.htm.

Nepal: POB 107, UN House, Kathmandu; tel. (1) 524366; fax (1) 523991; e-mail registry.np@undp.org.

Nicaragua: Apdo 3260, Palacio de la Cultura, Managua; tel. (2) 664253; fax (2) 222362; e-mail cedoc@sdnnic.org.ni.

Nigeria: POB 1068, 17 Kingsway Rd, Ikoyi, Lagos; tel. 269-4886; fax (1) 269-1934; e-mail uniclag@unicnig.org.

Pakistan: POB 1107, House No. 26, 88th St, G-6/3, Islamabad; tel. (51) 270610; fax (51) 271856; e-mail unic@isb.paknet.com.pk; internet www.un.org.pk/unic.

Panama: POB 6-9083, El Dorado; Banco Central Hispano Edif., 1°, Calle Gerardo Ortega y Av. Samuel Lewis, Panama City; tel. (7) 233-0557; fax (7) 223-2198; e-mail cinup@cciglobal.net.pa; internet www.cinup.org.

Paraguay: Casilla de Correo 1107, Edif. City, 3°, Asunción; tel. (21) 614443; fax (21) 449611; e-mail unic.py@undp.org.

Peru: POB 14-0199, Lord Cochrane 130, San Isidro, Lima 27; tel. (1) 441-8745; fax (1) 441-8735; e-mail informes@uniclima.org.pe; internet www.uniclima.org.pe.

Philippines: NEDA Bldg, Ground Floor, 106 Amorsolo St, Legaspi Village, Makati City, Manila; tel. (2) 8920611; fax (2) 8163011; e-mail infocentre@unicmanila.org (also covers Papua New Guinea and Solomon Islands).

Poland: 00-608 Warsaw, Al. Niepodległości 186; 02-514 Warsaw, POB 1; tel. (22) 8259245; fax (22) 8255785; e-mail unic.pl@undp.org; internet www.unic.un.org.pl.

Portugal: Rua Latino Coelho No. 1, Edif. Aviz, Bloco A1, 10°, 1000 Lisbon; tel. (1) 319-0790; fax (1) 352-0559; e-mail uniclisbon@onuportugal.pt; internet www.onuportugal.pt.

Romania: POB 1-701, 16 Aurel Vlaicu St, Bucharest; tel. (1) 2113242; fax (1) 2113506; e-mail unic@undp.ro.

Russia: 4/16 Glazovsky Per., Moscow; tel. (095) 241-2894; fax (095) 230-2138; e-mail dpi-moscow@unic.ru; internet www.unic.ru.

Senegal: BP 154, Immeuble UNESCO, 12 ave Roume, Dakar; tel. 823-30-70; fax 822-26-79; e-mail cinu.dakar@sentoo.sn; internet www.cinu-dakar.org (also covers Cape Verde, Côte d'Ivoire, The Gambia, Guinea, Guinea-Bissau and Mauritania).

South Africa: Metro Park Bldg, 351 Schoeman St, POB 12677, Pretoria 0126; tel. (12) 338-5077; fax (12) 320-1122; e-mail unic@un.org.za.

Spain: Avda General Perón 32-1°, 28020 Madrid; tel. (91) 5558087; fax (91) 5971231; e-mail unicspa@mbox.unicc.org.

Sri Lanka: POB 1505, 202–204 Bauddhaloka Mawatha, Colombo 7; tel. (1) 580691; fax (1) 581116; e-mail anusha.atukorale@undp.org.

Sudan: POB 1992, UN Compound, Gamma'a Ave, Khartoum; tel. (11) 773121; fax (11) 773128; e-mail unic.sd@undp.org (also covers Somalia).

Switzerland: Palais des Nations, 1211 Geneva 10; tel. (22) 917-2300, fax (22) 917-0030; e-mail press_geneva@unog.ch; internet www.unog.ch/unis/unis1.htm (also covers Bulgaria).

Tanzania: POB 9224, Old Boma Bldg, Morogoro Rd/Sokoine Drive, Dar es Salaam; tel. (22) 2119510; fax (22) 2112923; e-mail fo.tza@undp.org.

Thailand: ESCAP, United Nations Bldg, Rajdamnern Ave, Bangkok 10200; tel. (2) 288-1234; fax (2) 288-1000; e-mail unisbkk.unescap@un.org; internet www.unescap.org/unic (also covers Cambodia, Hong Kong, Laos, Malaysia, Singapore and Viet Nam).

Togo: BP 911, 107 blvd du 13 janvier, Lomé; tel. and fax 2212306; e-mail cinutogo@laposte.tg (also covers Benin).

Trinidad and Tobago: POB 130, Bretton Hall, 16 Victoria Ave, Port of Spain; tel. 623-4813; fax 623-4332; e-mail unicpos@unicpos.org.tt (also covers Antigua and Barbuda, the Bahamas, Barbados, Belize, Dominica, Grenada, Guyana, Jamaica, the Netherlands Antilles, Saint Christopher and Nevis, Saint Lucia, Saint Vincent and the Grenadines and Suriname).

Tunisia: BP 863, 61 blvd Bab-Benat, Tunis; tel. (71) 560-203; fax (71) 568-811; e-mail onu.tunis@planet.tn; internet www.onu.org.tn.

Turkey: PK 407, Birlik Mahallesi, 2 Cad. No. 11, 06610 Cankaya, Ankara; tel. (312) 4541051; fax (312) 4961499; e-mail unic@un.org.tr; internet www.un.org.tr/unic.html.

United Kingdom: Millbank Tower, 21st Floor, 21-24 Millbank, London, SW1P 4QH; tel. (20) 7630-1981; fax (20) 7976-6478; e-mail info@uniclondon.org; internet www.unitednations.org.uk (also covers Ireland).

USA: 1775 K St, NW, Suite 400, Washington, DC 20006; tel. (202) 331-8670; fax (202) 331-9191; e-mail unicwash@unicwash.org; internet www.unicwash.org.

Yemen: POB 237, Handhal St, 4 Al-Boniya Arca, San'a; tel. (1) 274000; fax (1) 274043; e-mail unicyem@ynet.ye.

Zambia: POB 32905, Lusaka 10101; tel. (1) 228487; fax (1) 222958; unic@zamnet.zam (also covers Botswana, Malawi and Swaziland).

Zimbabwe: POB 4408, Sanders House, 2nd Floor, First St/Jason Moyo Ave, Harare; tel. (4) 777060; fax (4) 750476; e-mail unic@samara.co.uk; internet www.samara.co.zw/unic.

OTHER UNITED NATIONS OFFICES

Armenia: 375001 Yerevan, 14 Karl Libknekht St, 1st Floor; tel. (3741) 560-212; fax (3741) 561-406; e-mail dpi@undpi.am; internet www.undpi.am.

Azerbaijan: 370001 Baku, 3 Isteglialiyat St; tel. (12) 98-98-88; fax (12) 98-32-35; e-mail dpi@un.azeri.com; internet www.un-az.org/dpi.

Belarus: 220050 Minsk, 17 Kirov St, 6th Floor; tel. 2278149; fax 22260340; e-mail dpi_by@un.dp.org; internet www.un.minsk.by.

Eritrea: POB 5366, Andinet St, Zone 4 Admin. 07, Airport Rd, Asmara; tel. (1) 182166; fax (1) 1801081; e-mail fo.eri@undp.org.

Georgia: 380079 Tbilisi, Eristavi St 9; tel. (32) 998558; fax (32) 250271; e-mail registry.ge@undp.org; internet www.undp.org.ge.

Kazakhstan: 480100 Almaty, Tole bi 67; tel. (3272) 69-53-27; fax (3272) 58-26-54; e-mail registry.kz@undp.org.

Ukraine: 01021 Kiev-21, Klovsky Uzviz, 1; tel. (44) 253-55-59; fax (44) 253-26-07; e-mail registry@unkiev.ua; internet www.un.kiev.ua.

Uzbekistan: 700029 Tashkent, 4 Taras Shevchenko St; tel. (371) 139-09-77; fax (371) 133-69-65; e-mail registry.uz@undp.org; internet www.undp.uz.

Conferences

Global conferences are convened regularly by the United Nations. Special sessions of the General Assembly (see p. 12) assess progress achieved in the implementation of conference action plans. The following conferences and special sessions were scheduled for 2002–03:

International Conference on Financing for Development (March 2002: Monterrey, Mexico).

Second World Assembly on Ageing (April 2002: Madrid, Spain).

Special Session of the General Assembly on Children (May 2002).

World Food Summit: Five Years Later (June 2002: Rome, Italy).

World Summit on Sustainable Development (Aug./Sept. 2002: Johannesburg, South Africa).

International Conference on the Safety of Transport of Radioactive Material (July 2003: Vienna, Austria).

International Ministerial Conference of Landlocked and Transit Developing Countries and Donor Countries and International Financial and Development Institutions on Transit Transport Co-operation (Aug. 2003: Almaty, Kazakhstan).

World Summit on the Information Society (Dec. 2003: Geneva, Switzerland).

Global Biotechnology Forum (Dec. 2003: Santiago, Chile).

Co-ordinating Bodies

The 27-member United Nations System Chief Executives Board for Co-ordination—CEB, founded in 1946 as the Administrative Committee on Co-ordination and renamed in 2001, convenes at least twice a year under the chairmanship of the Secretary General to co-ordinate UN system-wide policies, activities and management issues. In 1997 the United Nations Development Group (UNDG) was established, under the chairmanship of the Administrator of UNDP (q.v.), uniting the heads of some 20 UN funds, programmes and departments concerned with sustainable development, in order to promote coherent policy at country level. Project management services are provided throughout the UN system of entities and organizations, as well as to certain bilateral donors, international financial institutions and governments, by the United Nations Office for Project Services—UNOPS. UNOPS, founded in 1995 and a member of the UNDG, is self-financing and in 2001 delivered services valued at US $505m. and authorized the disbursement of loans totalling $196m. The Inter-Agency Standing Committee—IASC, founded in 1992, comprises the executive heads of 17 leading UN and other agencies and NGO consortia, who convene at least twice a year under the leadership of the Emergency Relief Co-ordinator (see OCHA, p. 37). It co-ordinates and administers the international response to complex and major humanitarian disasters, and the development of relevant policies.

Finance

The majority of the UN's peace-keeping operations (q.v.) are financed separately from the UN's regular budget by assessed contributions from member states.

In recent years the UN has suffered financial difficulties, owing to an expansion of the organization's political and humanitarian activities and delay on the part of member states in paying their contributions. In 1993 the UN Secretary-General formulated a series of economy measures to be applied throughout the organization, in order to avert a financial crisis. However, the fragility of the UN's financial situation persisted, partly owing to delays in the process between approval of a peace-keeping operation and receipt of contributions for that budget. At 31 December 2001 members owed the UN some US $2,110m., compared with $2,260m. at the end of the previous year, of which $1,823m. was for peace-keeping operations and $44m. for international tribunals. Of the total amount of unpaid assessments the USA owed $1,456m. During 2001, however, 135 members paid their regular budget assessments in full and total receipts from member states amounted to the highest level of contributions in the organization's history.

In 1997 a US business executive announced a donation of US $1,000m., to be paid in regular instalments over a 10-year period, to finance humanitarian and environmental programmes. A UN International Partnership Trust Fund was established to administer the donation. In the same year the UN Secretary-General pledged to implement administrative reforms of the UN and proposed a reduction in the organization's budget. A Development Account was established in December under the Secretary-General's reform programme; administrative savings were to be channelled through this to finance development projects. In late 1999 the Secretary-General stated that a further reduction in the UN budget would compromise the organization's capacity to implement mandated activities. In December 2000 the General Assembly approved a restructuring of scale of assessment calculations, the methodology and accuracy of which had been contested in recent years, particularly by the USA. For the period 2001–03 the level of US contributions to the regular annual budget was reduced from 25% to 22%, while annual contributions were raised for several nations with rapidly developing economies. The budget for 2002–03 totalled $2,625.2m., representing a 3% reduction in real terms compared with in the budget for the previous biennium.

TWO-YEAR BUDGET OF THE UNITED NATIONS (US $'000)

	2002–03
Overall policy-making, direction and co-ordination	499,141.1
Political affairs	248,094.1
International justice and law	59,103.1
International co-operation for development	273,137.6
Regional co-operation for development	335,182.7
Human rights and humanitarian affairs	123,457.5
Public information	144,719.2
Common support services	428,530.5
Internal oversight	20,296.9
Jointly-financed activities and special expenses	77,777.1
Capital expenditures	45,423.6
Staff assessment	348,250.3
Development Account	13,065.0
Total	**2,625,178.7**

United Nations Publications

Africa Recovery (quarterly).

Annual Report of the Secretary-General on the Work of the Organization.

Basic Facts About the United Nations.

Demographic Yearbook.

Development Update (2 a month).

Index to Proceedings (of the General Assembly; the Security Council; the Economic and Social Council; the Trusteeship Council).

International Law Catalogue.

Monthly Bulletin of Statistics.

Population and Vital Statistics Report (quarterly).

Statistical Yearbook (also on CD-Rom).

The UN Chronicle (quarterly).

United Nations Disarmament Yearbook.

United Nations Juridical Yearbook.

World Economic and Social Survey.

World Situation and Prospects.

World Statistics Pocketbook.

Yearbook of the United Nations.

Other UN publications are listed in the chapters dealing with the agencies concerned.

Secretariat

According to the UN Charter the Secretary-General is the chief administrative officer of the organization, and he may appoint further Secretariat staff as required. The principal departments and officers of the Secretariat are listed below. The chief administrative staff of the UN Regional Commissions and of all the subsidiary organs of the UN are also members of the Secretariat staff and are listed in the appropriate chapters. The Secretariat staff also includes a number of special missions and special appointments, including some of senior rank.

In November 2001 the total number of staff of the Secretariat holding appointments continuing for a year or more was approximately 15,287, including those serving away from the headquarters, but excluding staff working for the UN specialized agencies and subsidiary organs.

In July 1997 the Secretary-General initiated a comprehensive reform of the administration of the UN and abolished some 1,000 Secretariat posts. A Senior Management Group was established as part of a new Secretariat leadership and management structure, to enhance day-to-day efficiency and accountability. The reforms aimed to restructure the Secretariat's substantive work programme around the UN's five core missions, i.e. peace and security, economic and social affairs, development co-operation, humanitarian affairs and human rights. During 1997 the Centre for Human Rights and the Office of the High Commissioner for Human Rights were consolidated into a single office under the reform process, while a new Office for Drug Control and Crime Prevention was established, within the framework of the UN Office in Vienna, to integrate efforts to combat crime, drug abuse and terrorism. A new Office of the Iraq Programme was established in October to undertake and co-ordinate activities relating to the oil-for-food programme (see Security Council, p. 13). In December the General Assembly endorsed a recommendation of the Secretary-General to create the position of Deputy Secretary-General, who was to assist in the management of Secretariat operations, in particular the ongoing reform process, and represent the Secretary-General as required.

In December 2001, on the recommendation of the Secretary-General, the General Assembly established the Office of the High Representative for the Least Developed Countries, Landlocked Developing Countries and Small Island Developing States. In May 2002 the Secretary-General appointed the first United Nations Security Co-ordinator.

SECRETARY-GENERAL
KOFI ANNAN (Ghana).

DEPUTY SECRETARY-GENERAL
LOUISE FRÉCHETTE (Canada).

EXECUTIVE OFFICE OF THE SECRETARY-GENERAL
Under-Secretary-General, Chief of Staff: S. IQBAL RIZA (Pakistan).
Assistant Secretary-General, Special Adviser: MICHAEL DOYLE (USA).
Assistant Secretary-General, External Relations: GILLIAN SORENSEN (USA).

DEPARTMENT FOR DISARMAMENT AFFAIRS
Under-Secretary-General: JAYANTHA DHANAPALA (Sri Lanka).

DEPARTMENT OF ECONOMIC AND SOCIAL AFFAIRS
Under-Secretary-General: NITIN DESAI (India).
Assistant Secretary-General, Special Adviser on Gender Issues and the Advancement of Women: ANGELA KING (Jamaica).
Assistant Secretary-General, Policy Co-ordination and Inter-Agency Affairs: PATRIZIO CIVILI (Italy).

DEPARTMENT OF GENERAL ASSEMBLY AFFAIRS AND CONFERENCE SERVICES
Under-Secretary-General: JIAN CHEN (China).
Assistant Secretary-General: MILES STOBY (Guyana).

DEPARTMENT OF MANAGEMENT
Under-Secretary-General: CATHERINE BERTINI (USA).
Assistant Secretary-General, Controller: JEAN-PIERRE HALBWACHS (Mauritius).

Assistant Secretary-General, Human Resources: RAFIAH SALIM (Malaysia).
Assistant Secretary-General, Central Support: TOSHIYUKI NIWA (Japan).

DEPARTMENT OF PEACE-KEEPING OPERATIONS
Under-Secretary-General: JEAN-MARIE GUÉHENNO (France).
Assistant Secretary-General: HÉDI ANNABI (Tunisia).
Assistant Secretary-General: MICHAEL SHEEHAN (USA).

DEPARTMENT OF POLITICAL AFFAIRS
Under-Secretary-General: Sir KIERAN PRENDERGAST (United Kingdom).
Assistant Secretary-General: DANILO TÜRK (Slovenia).
Assistant Secretary-General: TULIAMENI KALOMEH (Namibia).

DEPARTMENT OF PUBLIC INFORMATION
Under-Secretary-General: SHASHI THAROOR (India).

OFFICE FOR THE CO-ORDINATION OF HUMANITARIAN AFFAIRS
Under-Secretary-General for Humanitarian Affairs and Emergency Relief Co-ordinator: KENZO OSHIMA (Japan).

OFFICE FOR DRUG CONTROL AND CRIME PREVENTION
Under-Secretary-General: ANTONIO MARIA COSTA (Italy).

OFFICE OF INTERNAL OVERSIGHT SERVICES
Under-Secretary-General: DILEEP NAIR (Singapore).

OFFICE OF THE IRAQ PROGRAMME
Assistant Secretary-General: BENON V. SEVAN (Cyprus).

OFFICE OF THE HIGH REPRESENTATIVE FOR THE LEAST DEVELOPED COUNTRIES, LANDLOCKED DEVELOPING COUNTRIES AND SMALL ISLAND DEVELOPING STATES
Under-Secretary-General and High Representative: ANWARUL KARIM CHOWDHURY (Bangladesh).

OFFICE OF LEGAL AFFAIRS
Under-Secretary-General, The Legal Counsel: HANS CORELL (Sweden).
Assistant Secretary-General: RALPH ZACKLIN (United Kingdom).

OFFICE OF THE UNITED NATIONS SECURITY CO-ORDINATIOR
Assistant Secretary-General and UN Security Co-ordinator: TUN MYAT (Myanmar).

OFFICE OF THE SPECIAL REPRESENTATIVE OF THE SECRETARY-GENERAL FOR CHILDREN AND ARMED CONFLICT
Under-Secretary-General: OLARA OTUNNU (Uganda).

OFFICE OF THE UNITED NATIONS HIGH COMMISSIONER FOR HUMAN RIGHTS
Address: Palais des Nations, 1211 Geneva 10, Switzerland.
Telephone: (22) 9179000; **fax:** (22) 9179010; **internet:** www.unhchr.ch.
High Commissioner: SERGIO VIEIRA DE MELLO (Brazil).

GENEVA OFFICE
Address: Palais des Nations, 1211 Geneva 10, Switzerland.
Telephone: (22) 907-12-34; **fax:** (22) 917-90-10; **internet:** www.unog.ch.
Director-General: SERGEI ORDZONIKIDZE (Russia).

NAIROBI OFFICE

Address: POB 30552, Nairobi, Kenya.

Telephone and fax: (22) 62-4266.

Director-General: Dr KLAUS TÖPFER (Germany).

VIENNA OFFICE

Address: Vienna International Centre, POB 500, 1400 Vienna, Austria.

Telephone: (1) 26060-0; **fax:** (1) 26333-89; **internet:** www.un.or.at.

Director-General: ANTONIO MARIA COSTA (Italy).

General Assembly

The General Assembly was established as a principal organ of the United Nations under the UN Charter (see p. 19). It first met on 10 January 1946. It is the main deliberative organ of the United Nations, and the only one composed of representatives of all the UN member states. Each delegation consists of not more than five representatives and five alternates, with as many advisers as may be required. The Assembly meets regularly for three months each year, and special sessions may also be held. It has specific responsibility for electing the Secretary-General and members of other UN councils and organs, and for approving the UN budget and the assessments for financial contributions by member states. It is also empowered to make recommendations (but not binding decisions) on questions of international security and co-operation.

The regular session of the General Assembly commences in mid-September. After the election of its President and other officers, the Assembly opens its general debate, a two-week period during which the head of each delegation makes a formal statement of his or her government's views on major world issues. Since 1997 the Secretary-General has presented his report on the work of the UN at the start of the general debate. The Assembly then begins examination of the principal items on its agenda: it acts directly on a few agenda items, but most business is handled by the six Main Committees (listed below), which study and debate each item and present draft resolutions to the Assembly. After a review of the report of each Main Committee, the Assembly formally approves or rejects the Committee's recommendations. On designated 'important questions', such as recommendations on international peace and security, the admission of new members to the United Nations, or budgetary questions, a two-thirds majority is needed for adoption of a resolution. Other questions may be decided by a simple majority. In the Assembly, each member has one vote. Voting in the Assembly is sometimes replaced by an effort to find consensus among member states, in order to strengthen support for the Assembly's decisions: the President consults delegations in private to find out whether they are willing to agree to adoption of a resolution without a vote; if they are, the President can declare that a resolution has been so adopted.

Special sessions of the Assembly may be held to discuss issues which require particular attention (e.g. illicit drugs) and 'emergency special sessions' may also be convened to discuss situations on which the UN Security Council has been unable to reach a decision (for example, in 2000 on Israel's construction of new settlements in east Jerusalem). A special session of the Assembly entitled Gender Equality, Development and Peace for the 21st Century, reviewing the UN Fourth World Conference on Women, held at Beijing, People's Republic of China, in 1995, was held in June 2000. During that month a special session reviewing the World Summit for Social Development, held at Copenhagen in 1995, was also convened. Two special sessions took place in June 2001: the first assessed the outcome of the UN Conference on Human Settlements (Habitat II, held in Istanbul, Turkey, in 1996), and the second considered issues related to the global epidemic of HIV/AIDS. A special session on children, reviewing progress made since the World Summit for Children, held in 1990, and the adoption in 1989 of the Convention on the Rights of the Child, was convened in May 2002.

The Assembly's 55th session (from September 2000) was designated as the Millennium Assembly. In early September a Millennium Summit of UN heads of state or government was convened to debate 'The Role of the United Nations in the 21st Century'. The Millennium Summit issued a declaration identifying the values and principles that should guide the organization in key areas including peace, development, environment, human rights, protection of the vulnerable, and the special needs of the African continent; and specified six fundamental values underlying international relations: freedom; equality; solidarity; tolerance; respect for nature; and a sense of shared responsibility for the global economy and social development. The summit adopted the following so-called Millennium Development Goals (MDGs), each incorporating specific targets to be attained by 2015: the eradication of extreme poverty and hunger; attainment of universal primary education; promotion of gender equality and empowerment of women; reduction of child mortality rates; improvement in maternal health rates; combating

HIV/AIDS, malaria and other diseases; ensuring environmental sustainability; and the development of a global partnership for development. Reform of the Security Council and the need for increased UN co-operation with the private sector, non-governmental organizations and civil society in pursuing its goals were also addressed by the summit. Progress in attaining the MDGs was to be reviewed on a regular basis.

President of 57th Session (from September 2002): JAN KAVAN (Czech Republic).

MAIN COMMITTEES

There are six Main Committees, on which all members have a right to be represented. Each Committee includes an elected Chairperson and two Vice-Chairs.

First Committee: Disarmament and International Security.

Second Committee: Economic and Financial.

Third Committee: Social, Humanitarian and Cultural.

Fourth Committee: Special Political and Decolonization.

Fifth Committee: Administrative and Budgetary.

Sixth Committee: Legal.

OTHER SESSIONAL COMMITTEES

General Committee: f. 1946; composed of 28 members, including the Assembly President, the 21 Vice-Presidents of the Assembly and the Chairs of the six Main Committees.

Credentials Committee: f. 1946; composed of nine members appointed at each Assembly session.

POLITICAL AND SECURITY MATTERS

Special Committee on Peace-keeping Operations: f. 1965; 34 appointed members.

Disarmament Commission: f. 1978 (replacing body f. 1952); 61 members.

UN Scientific Committee on the Effects of Atomic Radiation: f. 1955; 21 members.

Committee on the Peaceful Uses of Outer Space: f. 1959; 61 members; has a Legal Sub-Committee and a Scientific and Technical Sub-Committee.

Ad Hoc Committee on the Indian Ocean: f. 1972; 44 members.

Committee on the Exercise of the Inalienable Rights of the Palestinian People: f. 1975; 25 members.

Special Committee on the Implementation of the Declaration on Decolonization: f. 1961; 24 members.

Ad Hoc Committee on Terrorism: f. 1996 .

DEVELOPMENT

Commission on Science and Technology for Development: f. 1992; 33 members.

Committee on Energy and Natural Resources Development: f. 1998; 24 members.

United Nations Environment Programme (UNEP) Governing Council: f. 1972; 58 members (see p. 49).

LEGAL QUESTIONS

International Law Commission: f. 1947; 34 members elected for a five-year term; originally established in 1946 as the Committee on the Progressive Development of International Law and its Codification.

Advisory Committee on the UN Programme of Assistance in Teaching, Study, Dissemination and Wider Appreciation of International Law: f. 1965; 25 members.

UN Commission on International Trade Law: f. 1966; 36 members.

Special Committee on the Charter of the United Nations and on the Strengthening of the Role of the Organization: f. 1975; composed of all UN members.

There is also a UN Administrative Tribunal and a Committee on Applications for Review of Administrative Tribunal Judgments.

ADMINISTRATIVE AND FINANCIAL QUESTIONS

Advisory Committee on Administrative and Budgetary Questions: f. 1946; 16 members appointed for three-year terms.

Committee on Contributions: f. 1946; 18 members appointed for three-year terms.
International Civil Service Commission: f. 1972; 15 members appointed for four-year terms.
Committee on Information: f. 1978, formerly the Committee to review UN Policies and Activities; 95 members.

There is also a Board of Auditors, Investments Committee, UN Joint Staff Pension Board, Joint Inspection Unit, UN Staff Pension Committee, Committee on Conferences, and Committee for Programme and Co-ordination.

Security Council

The Security Council was established as a principal organ under the United Nations Charter (see p. 19); its first meeting was held on 17 January 1946. Its task is to promote international peace and security in all parts of the world.

MEMBERS

Permanent members:

People's Republic of China, France, Russia, United Kingdom, USA.

The remaining 10 members are normally elected (five each year) by the General Assembly for two-year periods (five countries from Africa and Asia, two from Latin America, one from eastern Europe, and two from western Europe and others).

Non-permanent members as at 1 January 2003:

Bulgaria, Cameroon, Guinea, Mexico, Syria (term expires 31 December 2003).

Angola, Chile, Germany, Pakistan, Spain (term expires 31 December 2004).

Rotation of the Presidency in 2003:

France (January); Germany (February); Guinea (March); Mexico (April); Pakistan (May); Russia (June); Spain (July); Syria (August); United Kingdom (September); USA (October); Angola (November); Bulgaria (December).

ORGANIZATION

The Security Council has the right to investigate any dispute or situation which might lead to friction between two or more countries, and such disputes or situations may be brought to the Council's attention either by one of its members, by any member state, by the General Assembly, by the Secretary-General or even, under certain conditions, by a state which is not a member of the United Nations.

The Council has the right to recommend ways and means of peaceful settlement and, in certain circumstances, the actual terms of settlement. In the event of a threat to or breach of international peace or an act of aggression, the Council has powers to take 'enforcement' measures in order to restore international peace and security. These include severance of communications and of economic and diplomatic relations and, if required, action by air, land and sea forces.

All members of the United Nations are pledged by the Charter to make available to the Security Council, on its call and in accordance with special agreements, the armed forces, assistance and facilities necessary to maintain international peace and security. These agreements, however, have not yet been concluded.

The Council is organized to be able to function continuously. The Presidency of the Council is held monthly in turn by the member states in English alphabetical order. Each member of the Council has one vote. On procedural matters decisions are made by the affirmative vote of any nine members. For decisions on other matters the required nine affirmative votes must include the votes of the five permanent members. This is the rule of 'great power unanimity' popularly known as the 'veto' privilege. In practice, an abstention by one of the permanent members is not regarded as a veto. Any member, whether permanent or non-permanent, must abstain from voting in any decision concerning the pacific settlement of a dispute to which it is a party. Any member of the UN that is party to a dispute under consideration by the Council may participate in the Council's discussions without a vote.

Consideration of reform of the Security Council commenced in 1993 at the 48th Session of the General Assembly, which established a Working Group to assess the issue. In October 1994 a general debate of the General Assembly revealed widespread support for expanding the Security Council to 20 seats and awarding permanent membership to Japan and Germany. In March 1997 the President of the General Assembly formally introduced a proposal for reform, which envisaged a Council consisting of 24 members, including five new permanent members and four new non-permanent members. In September 2000 the UN Millennium Summit declared support for continued discussions on reform of the Council. A summit meeting of the Council convened during the Millennium Summit issued a declaration on ensuring an effective role for the Council in maintaining international peace and security, with particular reference to Africa.

ACTIVITIES

As the UN organ primarily responsible for maintaining peace and security, the Security Council is empowered to deploy UN forces in the event that a dispute leads to fighting. It may also authorize the use of military force by a coalition of member states or a regional organization. During 2002 the Security Council continued to monitor closely all existing peace-keeping missions and the situations in countries where missions were being undertaken, and to authorize extensions of their mandates accordingly. In March the Council authorized the establishment of a UN Assistance Mission in Afghanistan (UNAMA), to work alongside the International Security Assistance Force, and in May established the UN Mission of Support in East Timor (UNMISET) to assist the stability and security of the newly-independent state. In August the Council adjusted the mandate of the UN Mission in Ethiopia and Eritrea (UNMEE) to support the implementation of decisions adopted by the Boundary Commission, including demining activities, and in December the Council authorized the expansion of the mission in the Democratic Republic of the Congo (MONUC) to co-ordinate the process of disarmament, demobilization, repatriation and reintegration. The mandates of the UN Mission in Bosnia and Herzegovina (UNMIBH) and the UN Mission of Observers in Prevlaka (UNMOP) were terminated in December. (For details of UN observer missions and peace-keeping operations, see pp. 62–68.)

On 12 September 2001 the Security Council expressed its unequivocal condemnation of the terrorist attacks against targets in the USA, which had occurred on the previous day. It expressed its readiness to combat terrorism and reiterated the right to individual or collective self-defence in accordance with the UN Charter. At the end of September the Council adopted Resolution 1373 establishing a Counter-Terrorism Committee to monitor a range of measures to combat international terrorism, including greater international co-operation and information exchange and suppressing the financing of terrorist groups. A special session of the Council at ministerial level was convened on the issue of terrorism in mid-November. Throughout 2002 the Council reviewed the work of the Committee and urged all states to submit reports on efforts to implement Resolution 1373, as well as to ratify relevant international conventions and protocols. In January 2003 the Council met at ministerial level to discuss international terrorism, including the issue of particular states maintaining stocks of weapons of mass destruction. The meeting adopted a resolution urging intensified efforts to combat terrorism and full co-operation, within a deadline of the end of March, with the Counter-Terrorism Committee.

The imposition of sanctions by the Security Council as a means of targeting regimes and groupings that are deemed to threaten international peace and security has increased significantly in recent years and has been subjected to widespread scrutiny regarding enforceability and the potential adverse humanitarian consequences for general populations. In the latter respect the Council has, since 1999, incorporated clauses on humanitarian assessment in its resolutions; the sanctions that took effect against the Taliban regime in Afghanistan in January 2001 were the first to entail mandatory monitoring of the humanitarian impact. In 2000 a proposal was submitted to the Council regarding the establishment of a permanent body to monitor sanctions violations. The UN Secretary-General established a special committee in April 2000 to evaluate sanctions policy. A draft version of the committee's final report, issued in February 2001, recommended that future Security Council resolutions enforcing sanctions should clearly specify intended goals and targets, include incentives to reward partial compliance, and focus in particular on the finances of leaders. In April 2000 the Council authorized the establishment of a temporary monitoring mechanism to investigate alleged violations of the sanctions imposed against the UNITA rebels in Angola, owing to their failure to implement earlier Council resolutions demanding compliance with the obligations of the peace process in that country. The mandate of the mechanism was extended in 2001. In mid-2000 the Council's sanctions committee organized a public hearing to assess the role played in the conflict by the illicit diamond trade; the participants included representatives of interested states, regional and international organizations, the global diamond industry and of civil society, as well as individual experts. (It had become evident that the ongoing conflicts in Sierra Leone and Angola were fuelled by rebel groups' illegal exploitation of diamond resources and use of the proceeds derived therefrom to purchase armaments.) In July 2000 the Council voted to prohibit the exportation of all rough diamonds from Sierra Leone that had not been officially certified by that country's Government. In December a panel of experts appointed by the Council issued a report on the connections between the illicit exportation of diamonds from Sierra Leone and the international trade in armaments. In March 2001 the Council banned the purchase of diamonds exported from Liberia, and demanded that the Liberian authorities refrain from purchasing so-called 'conflict diamonds' from illegal sources and cease providing support to rebel organizations, with particular reference to the main rebel grouping active in Sierra Leone. (The Council also re-imposed an embargo on the sale or supply of armaments to Liberia and imposed diplomatic restrictions on high-level Liberian government officials, with effect from May.) In early February 2003 the Council endorsed a new certification scheme, known as the Kimberley Process, which had entered into effect on 1 January following an agreement reached by some 30 governments to regulate the trade in rough diamonds and eliminate the illegal sale of diamonds to fund conflicts. In May 2002 the Council suspended the travel restrictions on senior officials of the UNITA movement in Angola, following the signing of a cease-fire agreement ending hostilities in that country. All sanctions against UNITA were removed in December and the relevant Sanctions Committee, established pursuant to a resolution adopted in 1993, was dissolved.

In December 1996 the Security Council approved the implementation of Resolution 986, which was adopted in April 1995, to provide for the limited sale of Iraqi petroleum to enable the purchase of humanitarian supplies and the provision of contributions to the UN Compensation Committee (which had been established to settle claims against Iraq resulting from the Gulf War). Exports of petroleum up to a value of US $1,000m. every 90 days were to be permitted under the agreement; the Council was responsible for renewing the mandate of the agreement and for approving contracts for the sale of petroleum and the purchase of food and medical goods. In February 1998, despite ongoing tensions between the Iraqi Government and the UN Special Commission (UNSCOM), which had been established in 1991 to monitor the disposal of weapons, the Council approved a resolution expanding the so-called oil-for-food programme to allow for sales of petroleum up to a value of $5,256m. every 180 days (superseding a resolution to extend the programme at its existing level, which was authorized in December 1997). In October 1999 the Council agreed to permit Iraq to generate a further $3,040m. in the next 180-day period of the oil-for-food agreement, accounting for the shortfall of authorized revenue that had not yet been generated. In mid-December the Council approved a six-month extension of the programme. A few days later it adopted Resolution 1284, establishing a new policy towards Iraq. The resolution provided for an unlimited ceiling on petroleum exports under the agreed humanitarian programme, and for a suspension of sanctions dependent upon Iraq's co-operation with a new arms inspection body, the UN Monitoring, Verification and Inspection Commission (UNMOVIC) that was to replace UNSCOM, whose inspectors had withdrawn from Iraq in December 1998. At the end of March 2000 the Council doubled the maximum permitted revenue that Iraq might use to purchase petroleum industry spare parts and other equipment under the ongoing programme. In that month, during a Council meeting on Iraq, the Secretary-General stated that the oil-for-food programme represented a moral dilemma for the UN as it appeared insufficiently to meet the humanitarian requirements of the Iraqi population. In early December the Iraqi regime, while agreeing the terms of the next (ninth) 180-day phase of the programme, temporarily suspended exports of petroleum once again during a dispute with the sanctions committee over the pricing mechanism for its oil sales. It was reported in mid-December that the Iraqi administration had implemented the illicit surcharge. The Council urged buyers of Iraqi oil not to pay the premium. A new sanctions regime was discussed during 2001. This envisaged facilitating the transfer of civilian and humanitarian goods to Iraq, while tightening border checks for military or other illegal trading. Dis-

agreements among Council members concerned the extra responsibility placed on Iraq's neighbouring countries and the compilation of a list of 'controlled' items requiring special approval to be imported into Iraq. The existing oil-for-food scheme was extended in early July, after Russia confirmed that it would veto the new proposals, and again in November. At that time, however, the Council approved a draft Goods for Review List (GDL), which it intended to enter into effect in the following year, subject to further negotiations. In May 2002 the Council adopted Resolution 1409 to implement the new sanctions regime. The programme was extended for a further 180 days in December, although negotiations continued regarding adjustments to the GRL, advocated by the USA to tighten the restrictions on military-related items. Further goods to be subject to approval were agreed by the Council at the end of that month.

In September 2002 the US President, George W. Bush, expressed concern that Iraq was challenging international security owing to its non-compliance with previous UN resolutions relating to the elimination of weapons of mass destruction. Subsequently, diplomatic discussions intensified regarding the need for a new UN resolution on Iraq, amidst increasing pressure from the US administration to initiate military action. An open debate was held in the Security Council in October, at the request of the Non-aligned Movement. On 8 November the Council adopted Resolution 1441 providing for an enhanced inspection mission and a detailed timetable according to which Iraq would have a final opportunity to comply with its disarmament obligations. The Council determined to convene again upon receipt of any report of non-compliance. Following Iraq's acceptance of the resolution, inspectors from UNMOVIC and the IAEA arrived in Iraq in late November, with Council authorization to have unrestricted access to all areas and the right to interview Iraqi scientists and weapons experts. In early December Iraq submitted a declaration of all aspects of its weapons programmes, as required under Resolution 1441. In early January 2003 UNMOVIC's Executive Chairman, Dr Hans Blix, briefed the Council on Iraq's declaration and the inspection activities. A full update was presented to the Council on 27 January, as required by Resolution 1441 60 days after the resumption of inspections. The Director-General of the IAEA, Dr Mohammad el-Baradei, called for an ongoing mandate for his inspectors to clarify the situation regarding nuclear weapons. However, Blix declared that Iraq had potentially misled the UN on aspects of its chemical and biological weapons programmes and urged more active and substantive co-operation on the part of the Iraqi authorities to determine the existence or otherwise of proscribed items and activities. His report prompted further extensive international debate regarding Iraq's acceptance of its disarmament obligations and appropriate consequent measures, including the need for a new Council resolution to enforce Resolution 1441. On 14 February Blix reported to the Council that the Iraqi authorities had recently become more active in proposing and undertaking measures to co-operate with UNMOVIC, and on 7 March he noted that Iraq had started to destroy, under UNMOVIC supervision, its Al Samoud 2 missiles and associated items, having accepted the conclusion of an international panel that these exceeded the permissable range decreed by the Council. Blix declared that the destruction to date of 34 Al Samoud 2 missiles and other items represented a 'substantial measure of disarmament', and that a significant Iraqi effort was under way to clarify a major source of uncertainty regarding quantities of biological and chemical weapons that had been unilaterally destroyed in 1991. Blix stated that UNMOVIC inspectors would require a number of further months in which to verify sites and items, analyse documents, interview relevant persons and draw conclusions, with a view to verifying Iraq's compliance with Resolution 1441. Meanwhile, debate continued within the Council regarding the degree to which Iraq had co-operated 'immediately, unconditionally and actively' with UNMOVIC, as required by Resolution 1441, with the USA, United Kingdom and Spain declaring that Iraq had not made sufficient efforts to disarm and insisting upon immediate full co-operation, failing which military force should be used to remove the incumbent regime, and France, Germany and Russia demanding that UNMOVIC be given more time to fulfil its mandate. On 19 March, presenting to the Council UNMOVIC's draft work programme (required under Resolution 1284 to be formulated within a fixed period after the commencement of inspection activities), Blix stated that the Commission's experts had found that the Iraqi authorities had hitherto supplied only limited new information that would be of substantial assistance in resolving outstanding issues of concern. On the previous day UNMOVIC personnel had been withdrawn from Iraq in view of the abandonment by the USA, United Kingdom and Spain of an attempt to win the Council's support for the initiation of military action, and consequent ultimatum by the USA that the Iraqi leadership should leave the country immediately or face a military invasion. Unilateral military action by US, British and allied forces commenced on 20 March.

During 2002 the Council continued to provide a forum for discussion of the situation in the Middle East and the escalating violence in the West Bank and Gaza and in Israel. In March the Council adopted Resolution 1397 which envisaged two separate states of Israel and Palestine existing within secure and recognized borders. In April the Council called for Israel to withdraw its troops from Palestinian cities, following a massive military incursion, and expressed grave concern at the humanitarian situation in Jenin refugee camp, which had been a particular target of Israel's efforts to repress Palestinian extremists resulting in more than one hundred deaths and widespread destruction of the camp's infrastructure. The Council expressed support for an initiative of the UN Secretary-General to establish a fact-finding mission to investigate events surrounding the military assault on Jenin. In early May, however, many speakers in a Council open debate denounced Israel's refusal to co-operate with the inquiry. The Council remained actively concerned with the security situation in the region and efforts to achieve a peace plan. In September the Council demanded that Israel refrain from any further military action in the city of Ramallah and withdraw all forces to positions held prior to September 2000. The resolution also called upon the Palestinian Authority to bring to justice those responsible for acts of terrorism against Israel.

In 2002 the Council held several meetings to consider the situation in Africa, with particular concern to improve conflict prevention and co-operation with other regional and sub-regional organizations. A high-level debate was organized in January, and in May a debate was convened on conflict prevention and resolution in Africa. A separate session, concerned with the political, economic and security situation in Central Africa, was held in October. In December the Council discussed the severe food shortages being experienced by many countries in southern and western Africa and in the Horn of Africa. In November the Council considered the final report of an expert panel on the illegal exploitation of natural resources in the Democratic Republic of the Congo. In November 2001 the Council adopted as a resolution specific commitments and measures to protect children from the effects of armed conflict and to meet their humanitarian needs. The abuse of children in armed conflicts was the subject of a further presidential statement issued in May 2002. Other ongoing themes considered by the Council included women, peace and security, the illicit trade in small arms and light weapons, and civilians in armed conflict. A presidential statement issued in October proposed that countries formulate national registers of arms brokers to counter illicit brokering of small arms and impose stricter penalties for illicit trading activities. In March a Council presidential statement identified core objectives for the protection of civilians in conflict situations. An open debate on the subject was held in December.

COMMITTEES

In April 2003 there were two **Standing Committees**, each composed of representatives of all Council member states:

Committee of Experts on Rules of Procedure (studies and advises on rules of procedure and other technical matters);

Committee on the Admission of New Members.

Ad hoc Committees, which are established as needed, comprise all Council members and meet in closed session:

Governing Council of the UN Compensation Commission established by Security Council Resolution 692 (1991).

Security Council Committee on Council Meetings away from Headquarters.

Security Council Committee established pursuant to Resolution 1373 (2001) concerning Counter-Terrorism.

Within this category are the Sanctions Committees, which may be established to oversee economic or political enforcement measures, imposed by the Security Council to maintain or restore international peace and security. At April 2003 the following committees were operational:

Security Council Committee established pursuant to Resolution 1343 (2001) concerning Liberia;

Security Council Committee established pursuant to Resolution 1267 (1999) concerning Afghanistan;

Security Council Committee established pursuant to Resolution 1132 (1997) concerning Sierra Leone;

Security Council Committee established pursuant to Resolution 918 (1994) concerning Rwanda;

Security Council Committee established pursuant to Resolution 751 (1992) concerning Somalia;

Security Council Committee established pursuant to Resolution 748 (1992) concerning Libya;

Security Council Committee established pursuant to Resolution 661 (1990) concerning the situation between Iraq and Kuwait.

AD HOC INTERNATIONAL TRIBUNALS

In May 1993 the Security Council, acting under Article VII of the UN Charter, adopted Resolution 827, which established an ad hoc 'war crimes' tribunal. The so-called International Tribunal for the Prosecution of Persons Responsible for Serious Violations of International Humanitarian Law Committed in the Territory of the Former Yugoslavia (also referred to as the International Criminal Tribunal for the former Yugoslavia—ICTY) was inaugurated in The Hague, Netherlands, in November. The ICTY consists of a Chief Prosecutor's office, and 16 permanent judges, of whom 11 sit in three trial chambers and five sit in a seven-member appeals chamber (with the remaining two appeals chamber members representing the ICTR, see below). In addition, a maximum at any one time of 9 ad litem judges, drawn from a pool of 27, serve as required. Public hearings were initiated in November 1994. The first trial proceedings commenced in May 1996, and the first sentence was imposed by the Tribunal in November. In July and November 1995 the Tribunal formally charged the Bosnian Serb political and military leaders Radovan Karadžić and Gen. Ratko Mladić, on two separate indictments, with genocide, crimes against humanity, violation of the laws and customs of war and serious breaches of the Geneva Conventions. In July 1996 the Tribunal issued international warrants for their arrest. Amended indictments, confirmed in May 2000, and announced in October and November, respectively, included the withdrawal of the fourth charge against Mladić. Karadžić and Mladić remained at large in early 2003. In April 2000 Momčilo Krajišnik, a senior associate of Karadžić, was detained by the ICTY, charged with genocide, war crimes and crimes against humanity. Biljana Plavšić, a further former Bosnian Serb political leader, surrendered to the Tribunal in January 2001, also indicted on charges of genocide, war crimes and crimes against humanity. In the following month three Bosnian Serb former soldiers were convicted by the ICTY of utilizing mass rape and the sexual enslavement of women as instruments of terror in wartime. In February 2003 Plavšić was sentenced to eleven years' imprisonment, having pleaded guilty in October 2002 to one of the charges against her (persecutions: a crime against humanity). (Under a plea agreement reached with the Tribunal the remaining charges had been withdrawn.) In mid-1998 the ICTY began investigating reported acts of violence against civilians committed by both sides in the conflict in the southern Serbian province of Kosovo and Metohija. In early 1999 there were reports of large-scale organized killings, rape and expulsion of the local Albanian population by Serbian forces. In April ICTY personnel visited refugee camps in neighbouring countries in order to compile evidence of the atrocities, and obtained intelligence information from NATO members regarding those responsible for the incidents. In May the then President of the then Federal Republic of Yugoslavia (FRY, renamed Serbia and Montenegro in February 2003), Slobodan Milošević, was indicted, along with three senior government ministers and the chief-of-staff of the army, charged with crimes against humanity and violations of the customs of war committed in Kosovo since 1 January 1999; international warrants were issued for their arrests. In June, following the establishment of an international force to secure peace in Kosovo, the ICTY established teams of experts to investigate alleged atrocities at 529 identified grave sites. The new FRY administration, which had assumed power following legislative and presidential elections in late 2000, contested the impartiality of the ICTY, proposing that Milošević and other members of the former regime should be tried before a national court. In April 2001 Milošević was arrested by the local authorities in Belgrade. Under increasing international pressure, the Federal Government approved his extradition in June, and he was immediately transferred to the ICTY, where he was formally charged with crimes against humanity committed in Kosovo in 1999. A further indictment of crimes against humanity committed in Croatia during 1991–92 was confirmed in October 2001, and a third indictment, which included charges of genocide committed in Bosnia and Herzegovina in 1991–95, was confirmed in November 2001. In early February 2002 the Appeals Chamber ordered that the three indictments be considered in a single trial. The trial commenced later in that month. Milošević, however, continued to protest at the alleged illegality of his arrest and refused to recognize the jurisdiction of the Court. The case was expected to continue until the end of 2004. In August 2001 the ICTY passed its first sentence of genocide, convicting a former Bosnian Serb military commander, Gen. Radislav Kristić, for his role in the deaths of up to 8,000 Bosnian Muslim men and boys in Srebrenića in July 1995. In January 2003 Fatmir Limaj, an ethnic Albanian deputy in the Kosovo parliament and former commander of the Kosovo Liberation Army (KLA), was indicted by the ICTY on several counts of crimes against humanity and war crimes that were allegedly committed in mid-1998 against Serb and Albanian detainees at the KLA's Lapusnik prison camp. Limaj was arrested in Slovenia in February 2003 and transferred to ICTY custody in early March. At that time 23 arrest warrants remained outstanding. Of those who had appeared in proceedings before the Tribunal, 13 were awaiting appeal, nine were serving sentence and nine had been acquitted. Five people had completed their sentences. It was envisaged that the Tribunal's trial activities would be terminated by 2008.

President of the ICTY: THEODOR MERON (USA).

Registrar: HANS HOLTHUIS (Netherlands).

Address: Public Information Unit, POB 13888, 2501 EW The Hague, Netherlands.

Telephone: (70) 512-5233; **fax:** (70) 512-5355; **internet:** www.un.org/icty.

In November 1994 the Security Council adopted Resolution 955, establishing an International Criminal Tribunal for Rwanda (ICTR) to prosecute persons responsible for genocide and other serious violations of humanitarian law that had been committed in Rwanda and by Rwandans in neighbouring states. Its temporal jurisdiction was limited to the period 1 January to 31 December 1994. The Tribunal consists of 11 permanent judges, of whom nine sit in three trial chambers (based in Arusha, Tanzania) and two sit in the seven-member appeals chamber that is shared with the ICTY and based at The Hague. The Tribunal is served by the same Prosecutor as the ICTY. In August 2002 the UN Security Council endorsed a proposal by the ICTR President to elect a pool of 18 *ad litem* judges to the Tribunal with a view to accelerating its activities and bringing them to a conclusion by 2008. A high security detention facility had been built within the compound of the prison in Arusha. The first plenary session of the Tribunal was held in The Hague in June 1995; formal proceedings at its permanent headquarters in Arusha were initiated in November. The first trial of persons charged by the Tribunal commenced in January 1997, and sentences were imposed in July. In September 1998 the former Rwandan Prime Minister, Jean Kambanda, and a former mayor of Taba, Jean-Paul Akayesu, both Hutu extremists, were found guilty of genocide and crimes against humanity; Kambanda subsequently became the first person ever to be sentenced under the 1948 Convention on the Prevention and Punishment of the Crime of Genocide. In October 2000 the Tribunal rejected an appeal by Kambanda. In November 1999 the Rwandan Government temporarily suspended co-operation with the Tribunal in protest at a decision of the appeals chamber to release an indicted former government official owing to procedural delays. (The appeals chamber subsequently reversed this decision.) In 2001 two ICTR investigators employed on defence teams were arrested and charged with genocide, having been found to be working at the Tribunal under assumed identities. Relations between the Rwandan Government and the ICTR deteriorated again in 2002, with the Chief Prosecutor accusing the Rwandan authorities of failing to facilitate the travel of witnesses to the Tribunal and withholding access to documentary materials, and counter accusations by the Rwandan Government that the Tribunal's progess was too slow, that further suspected perpetrators of genocide had been inadvertantly employed by the Tribunal and that Rwandan witnesses attending the Tribunal had not received sufficient protection. Reporting to the UN Security Council in July, the Chief Prosecutor alleged that the Rwandan non-co-operation ensued from her recent decision to indict former members of the Tutsi-dominated Rwanda Patriotic Army for human rights violations committed against Hutus in 1994. In June 2002 proceedings commenced against Eliezer Niyitegeka, a former minister of information accused of genocide, conspiracy to commit genocide, direct public incitement to genocide through the state media, and crimes against humanity. In August Augustin Bizimungu, the former chief of the Rwandan armed forces, was arrested in Angola and transferred to the ICTR, indicted on charges of genocide, conspiracy to commit genocide and crimes against humanity. The trial of Theoneste Bagosora, a former military commander accused of masterminding the genocide, commenced, after considerable procedural delays, in September. At November 2001 some 74 people had been indicted by the ICTR. By February 2003 one person had been acquitted and ten people had been convicted by the Tribunal. Eight trials, involving 20 individuals, were under way at that time.

President of the ICTR: (vacant).

Registrar: Adama Dieng (Senegal).

Address: Arusha International Conference Centre, POB 6016, Arusha, Tanzania.

Telephone: (212) 963 2850; **fax:** (212) 963 2848; **e-mail:** ictr-press@un.org; **internet:** www.ictr.org.

Both Tribunals are supported by teams of investigators and human rights experts working in the field to collect forensic and other evidence in order to uphold indictments. Evidence of mass graves resulting from large-scale unlawful killings has been uncovered in both regions.

Chief Prosecutor: CARLA DEL PONTE (Switzerland).

Trusteeship Council

The Trusteeship Council (comprising the People's Republic of China—a non-active member until May 1989, France, Russia, the United Kingdom and the USA) was established to supervise United Nations Trust Territories through their administering authorities and to promote the political, economic, social and educational advancement of their inhabitants towards self-government or independence (see Charter, p. 19). On 1 October 1994 the last territory remaining under UN trusteeship, the Republic of Palau (part of the archipelago of the Caroline Islands), declared its independence under a compact of free association with the USA, its administering authority. The Security Council terminated the Trusteeship Agreement on 10 November, having determined that the objectives of the agreement had been fully attained. On 1 November the Trusteeship Council formally suspended its operations; thereafter it was to be convened on an extraordinary basis as required.

Economic and Social Council—ECOSOC

ECOSOC promotes world co-operation on economic, social, cultural and humanitarian problems. (See Charter, p. 19.)

MEMBERS

Fifty-four members are elected by the General Assembly for three-year terms: 18 are elected each year. Membership is allotted by regions as follows: Africa 14 members, western Europe and others 13, Asia 11, Latin America 10, eastern Europe 6.

President (2003): GERT ROSENTHAL (Guatemala).

ORGANIZATION

The Council, which meets annually for four to five weeks between May and July, alternately in New York and Geneva, is mainly a central policy-making and co-ordinating organ. It has a co-ordinating function between the UN and the specialized agencies, and also makes consultative arrangements with approved voluntary or non-governmental organizations which work within the sphere of its activities. The Council has functional and regional commissions to carry out much of its detailed work.

During 2002 ECOSOC pursued discussions with the IMF and World Bank regarding the outcome of the International Conference on Financing for Development and the meeting of the Development Committee and International and Monetary and Financial Committee.

SESSIONAL COMMITTEES

Each sessional committee comprises the 54 members of the Council: there is a First (Economic) Committee, a Second (Social) Committee and a Third (Programme and Co-ordination) Committee.

FUNCTIONAL COMMISSIONS

Commission on Crime Prevention and Criminal Justice: f. 1992; aims to formulate an international convention on crime prevention and criminal justice; 40 members.

Commission on Human Rights: f. 1946; seeks greater respect for the basic rights of man, the prevention of discrimination and the protection of minorities; reviews specific instances of human rights violation and dispatches rapporteurs to investigate allegations of abuses in particular countries; provides policy guidance; works on declarations, conventions and other instruments of international law; meets annually for six weeks; 53 members. There is a Sub-Commission on the Promotion and Protection of Human Rights, comprising working groups on issues such as slavery, indigenous populations, detention and communications.

Commission on Narcotic Drugs: f. 1946; mainly concerned in combating illicit traffic; 53 members. There is a Sub-Commission on Illicit Drug Traffic and Related Matters in the Near and Middle East.

Commission on Population and Development: f. 1946; advises the Council on population matters and their relation to socio-economic conditions; 47 members.

Commission on Science and Technology for Development: f. 1992; works on the restructuring of the UN in the economic, social and related fields; 33 members.

Commission for Social Development: f. 1946 as the Social Commission; advises ECOSOC on issues of social and community development; 46 members.

Commission on the Status of Women: f. 1946; aims at equality of political, economic and social rights for women, and supports the right of women to live free of violence; 45 members.

Commission on Sustainable Development: f. 1993 to oversee integration into the UN's work of the objectives set out in 'Agenda 21', the programme of action agreed by the UN Conference on Environment and Development in June 1992; 53 members.

Statistical Commission: Standardizes terminology and procedure in statistics and promotes the development of national statistics; 24 members.

COMMITTEES AND SUBSIDIARY BODIES

Commission on Human Settlements: f. 1977.
Committee for Development Policy: f. 1965.

Committee on Energy and Natural Resources for Development: f. 1998.
Committee on Negotiations with Intergovernmental Agencies: f. 1946.
Committee on Non-Governmental Organizations: f. 1946.
Committee for Programme and Co-ordination: f. 1962.
Permanent Forum on Indigenous Issues: f. 2000.
United Nations Forum on Forests: f. 2000.
There is also an *ad hoc* open-ended working group on informatics.

REGIONAL COMMISSIONS
(see pp. 27–36)

Economic Commission for Africa—ECA.
Economic Commission for Europe—ECE.
Economic Commission for Latin America and the Caribbean—ECLAC.
Economic and Social Commission for Asia and the Pacific—ESCAP.
Economic and Social Commission for Western Asia—ESCWA.

RELATED BODIES

Board of Trustees of the International Research and Training Institute for Women (INSTRAW): 11 members (see p. 72).
International Narcotics Control Board: f. 1964; 13 members.
Programme Co-ordination Board for the Joint UN Programme on HIV/AIDS (UNAIDS): f. 1995; 22 members.
UNDP/UNFPA Executive Board: 36 members, elected by ECOSOC (see p. 46).
UNHCR Executive Committee: 53 members, elected by ECOSOC (see p. 53).
UNICEF Executive Board: 36 members, elected by ECOSOC (see p. 41).
WFP Executive Board: one-half of the 36 members are elected by ECOSOC, one-half by the FAO; governing body of the World Food Programme (see p. 74).

International Court of Justice

Address: Peace Palace, Carnegieplein 2, 2517 KJ The Hague, Netherlands.
Telephone: (70) 302-23-23; **fax:** (70) 364-99-28; **e-mail:** information@icj-cij.org; **internet:** www.icj-cij.org.
Established in 1945, the Court is the principal judicial organ of the UN. All members of the UN are parties to the Statute of the Court. (See Charter, p. 19.)

THE JUDGES

(April 2003; in order of precedence)

	Term Ends*
President: SHI JIUYONG (People's Republic of China)	2012
Vice-President: RAYMOND RANJEVA (Madagascar)	2009
Judges:	
GILBERT GUILLAUME (France)	2009
ABDUL G. KOROMA (Sierra Leone)	2012
VLADLEN S. VERESHCHETIN (Russia)	2006
ROSALYN HIGGINS (United Kingdom)	2009
GONZALO PARRA-ARANGUREN (Venezuela)	2009
PIETER H. KOOIJMANS (Netherlands)	2006
JOSÉ FRANCISCO REZEK (Brazil)	2006
AWN SHAWKAT AL-KHASAWNEH (Jordan)	2009
THOMAS BUERGENTHAL (USA)	2009
NABIL ELARABY (Egypt)	2006
HISASHI OWADA (Japan)	2012
BRUNO SIMMER (Germany)	2012
PETER TOMKA (Slovakia)	2012

Registrar: PHILIPPE COUVREUR (Belgium)
* Each term ends on 5 February of the year indicated.

The Court is composed of 15 judges, each of a different nationality, elected with an absolute majority by both the General Assembly and the Security Council. Representation of the main forms of civilization and the different legal systems of the world are borne in mind in their election. Candidates are nominated by national panels of jurists.

The judges are elected for nine years and may be re-elected; elections for five seats are held every three years. The Court elects its President and Vice-President for each three-year period. Members may not have any political, administrative, or other professional occupation, and may not sit in any case with which they have been otherwise connected than as a judge of the Court. For the purposes of a case, each side—consisting of one or more States—may, unless the Bench already includes a judge with a corresponding nationality, choose a person from outside the Court to sit as a judge on terms of equality with the Members. Judicial decisions are taken by a majority of the judges present, subject to a quorum of nine Members. The President has a casting vote.

FUNCTIONS

The International Court of Justice operates in accordance with a Statute which is an integral part of the UN Charter. Only States may be parties in cases before the Court; those not parties to the Statute may have access in certain circumstances and under conditions laid down by the Security Council.

The Jurisdiction of the Court comprises:

1. All cases which the parties refer to it jointly by special agreement (indicated in the list below by a stroke between the names of the parties).

2. All matters concerning which a treaty or convention in force provides for reference to the Court. About 700 bilateral or multilateral agreements make such provision. Among the more noteworthy: Treaty of Peace with Japan (1951), European Convention for Peaceful Settlement of Disputes (1957), Single Convention on Narcotic Drugs (1961), Protocol relating to the Status of Refugees

(1967), Hague Convention on the Suppression of the Unlawful Seizure of Aircraft (1970).

3. Legal disputes between States which have recognized the jurisdiction of the Court as compulsory for specified classes of dispute. Declarations by the following 63 States accepting the compulsory jurisdiction of the Court are in force (although many with reservations): Australia, Austria, Barbados, Belgium, Botswana, Bulgaria, Cambodia, Cameroon, Canada, the Democratic Republic of the Congo, Costa Rica, Côte d'Ivoire, Cyprus, Denmark, the Dominican Republic, Egypt, Estonia, Finland, The Gambia, Georgia, Greece, Guinea, Guinea-Bissau, Haiti, Honduras, Hungary, India, Japan, Kenya, Lesotho, Liberia, Liechtenstein, Luxembourg, Madagascar, Malawi, Malta, Mauritius, Mexico, Nauru, the Netherlands, New Zealand, Nicaragua, Nigeria, Norway, Pakistan, Panama, Paraguay, the Philippines, Poland, Portugal, Senegal, Serbia and Montenegro, Somalia, Spain, Sudan, Suriname, Swaziland, Sweden, Switzerland, Togo, Uganda, the United Kingdom and Uruguay.

Disputes as to whether the Court has jurisdiction are settled by the Court.

Judgments are without appeal, but are binding only for the particular case and between the parties. States appearing before the Court undertake to comply with its Judgment. If a party to a case fails to do so, the other party may apply to the Security Council, which may make recommendations or decide upon measures to give effect to the Judgment.

Advisory opinions on legal questions may be requested by the General Assembly, the Security Council or, if so authorized by the Assembly, other United Nations organs or specialized agencies.

Rules of Court governing procedure are made by the Court under a power conferred by the Statute.

In July 1993 the Court established a seven-member Chamber for Environmental Matters, in view of the world-wide expansion of environmental law and protection.

CONSIDERED CASES

Judgments

Since 1946 more than 80 cases have been referred to the Court by States. Some were removed from the list as a result of settlement or discontinuance, or on the grounds of a lack of basis for jurisdiction. Cases which have been the subject of a Judgment by the Court include: Monetary Gold Removed from Rome in 1943 (Italy *v.* France, United Kingdom and USA); Sovereignty over Certain Frontier Land (Belgium/Netherlands); Arbitral Award made by the King of Spain on 23 December 1906 (Honduras *v.* Nicaragua); Temple of Preah Vihear (Cambodia *v.* Thailand); South West Africa (Ethiopia and Liberia *v.* South Africa); Northern Cameroons (Cameroon *v.* United Kingdom); North Sea Continental Shelf (Federal Republic of Germany/Denmark and Netherlands); Appeal relating to the Jurisdiction of the ICAO Council (India *v.* Pakistan); Fisheries Jurisdiction (United Kingdom *v.* Iceland; Federal Republic of Germany *v.* Iceland); Nuclear Tests (Australia *v.* France; New Zealand *v.* France); Aegean Sea Continental Shelf (Greece *v.* Turkey); United States of America Diplomatic and Consular Staff in Tehran (USA *v.* Iran); Continental Shelf (Tunisia/Libya); Delimitation of the Maritime Boundary in the Gulf of Maine Area (Canada/USA); Continental Shelf (Libya/Malta); Application for revision and interpretation of the Judgment of 24 February 1982 in the case concerning the Continental Shelf (Tunisia *v.* Libya); Military and Paramilitary Activities in and against Nicaragua (Nicaragua *v.* USA); Frontier Dispute (Burkina Faso/Mali); Delimitation of Maritime Boundary (Denmark *v.* Norway); Maritime Boundaries (Guinea-Bissau *v.* Senegal); Elettronica Sicula SpA (USA *v.* Italy); Land, Island and Maritime Frontier Dispute (El Salvador/Honduras) (in one aspect of which Nicaragua was permitted to intervene); Delimitation of Maritime Boundary in the area between Greenland and Jan Mayen island (Denmark *v.* Norway); Maritime Delimitation and Territorial Questions between Qatar and Bahrain (Qatar *v.* Bahrain); Territorial Dispute (Libya/Chad); East Timor (Portugal *v.* Australia); the Gabčíkovo-Nagymaros Hydroelectric Project (Hungary *v.* Slovakia), aspects of which were still under consideration in early 2003; Fisheries Jurisdiction (Spain *v.* Canada); Delimitation of the Boundary around Kasikili Sedudu Island (Botswana *v.* Namibia); La Grand case (Germany *v.* USA); Arrest Warrant of 11 April 2000 (Democratic Republic of the Congo *v.* Belgium); and Land and Maritime Boundary between Cameroon and Nigeria (Cameroon *v.* Nigeria, with Equatorial Guinea intervening).

Other cases under consideration, or pending before the Court, in early 2003 were: cases brought by Libya against the United Kingdom and the USA concerning questions of interpretation and application of the 1971 Montreal Convention arising from the aerial incident at Lockerbie, United Kingdom, in 1988; a case brought by Iran against the USA concerning the destruction of oil platforms; cases brought by Bosnia and Herzegovina and Croatia against the Federal Republic of Yugoslavia (FRY) concerning the application of the 1948 Convention on the Prevention and Punishment of the Crime of Genocide and an application, brought by the FRY, for revision of a judgment in 1996; a case concerning sovereignty over Pulau Ligatan and Pulau Sipadan brought by Indonesia and Malaysia; a case brought by Guinea against the Democratic Republic of the Congo (DRC) concerning the treatment of a Guinean business executive, Ahmadou Sadio Diallo; cases concerning the legality of the use of force brought by the FRY against Belgium, Canada, France, Germany, Italy, the Netherlands, Portugal and the United Kingdom; cases brought by the DRC against Uganda and against Rwanda, regarding armed activities on the territory of the DRC; dispute between Nicaragua and Honduras concerning maritime delimitation in the Caribbean Sea; a case brought by Liechtenstein against Germany regarding compensation for property of Liechtenstein nationals seized as a consequence of the Second World War; a case brought by Nicaragua against Colombia concerning territory and maritime delimitation in the western Caribbean; a case regarding a frontier dispute brought by Benin and Niger; an application, requested by El Salvador, for review of a 1992 judgment in the case concerning Land, Island and Maritime Frontier Dispute; and a request by Mexico for the indication of provisional measures in a case against the USA concerning the Vienna Convention on Consular Relations.

Advisory Opinions

Matters on which the Court has delivered an Advisory Opinion at the request of the United Nations General Assembly, or an organ thereof, include the following: Condition of Admission of a State to Membership in the United Nations; Competence of the General Assembly for the Admission of a State to the United Nations; Interpretation of the Peace Treaties with Bulgaria, Hungary and Romania; International Status of South West Africa; Reservations to the Convention on the Prevention and Punishment of the Crime of Genocide; Effect of Awards of Compensation Made by the United Nations Administrative Tribunal (UNAT); Western Sahara; Application for Review of UNAT Judgment No. 333; Applicability of the Obligation to Arbitrate under Section 21 of the United Nations Headquarters Agreement of 26 June 1947 (relating to the closure of the Observer Mission to the United Nations maintained by the Palestine Liberation Organization).

An Advisory Opinion has been given at the request of the Security Council: Legal Consequences for States of the continued presence of South Africa in Namibia (South West Africa) notwithstanding Security Council resolution 276 (1970).

In 1989 (at the request of the UN Economic and Social Council—ECOSOC) the Court gave an Advisory Opinion on the Applicability of Article 6, Section 22, of the Convention on the Privileges and Immunities of the United Nations. The Court has also, at the request of UNESCO, given an Advisory Opinion on Judgments of the Administrative Tribunal of the ILO upon Complaints made against UNESCO, and on the Constitution of the Maritime Safety Committee of the Inter-Governmental Maritime Consultative Organization, at the request of IMCO. In July 1996 the Court delivered Advisory Opinions on the Legality of the Use by a State of Nuclear Weapons in Armed Conflict, requested by WHO, and on the Legality of the Use or Threat of Nuclear Weapons, requested by the UN General Assembly. In April 1999 the Court delivered an Advisory Opinion, requested by ECOSOC, on the Difference Relating to Immunity from Legal Process of a Special Rapporteur of the Commission on Human Rights.

Finance

The UN budget appropriation for the Court for the two year period 2002–03 amounted to US $23,837m.

Publications

Acts and Documents, No. 5 (contains Statute and Rules of the Court, the Resolution concerning its internal judicial practice and other documents).

Bibliography (annually).

Pleadings (Written Pleadings and Statements, Oral Proceedings, Correspondence): series.

Reports (Judgments, Opinions and Orders): series.

Yearbook.

INTERNATIONAL CRIMINAL COURT

Address: Maanweg 174, 2516 AB The Hague, Netherlands.

Telephone: (70) 515-85-15; **fax:** (70) 515-85-15; **e-mail:** pio@icc-cpi.int; **internet:** www.icc-cpi.int.

The International Criminal Court (ICC) was established by the Rome Statute on the International Criminal Court, adopted by 120 states in July 1998. The Rome Statute (and therefore the temporal jurisdiction of the ICC) entered into force on 1 July 2002, 60 days after ratification by the requisite 60th signatory state in April. The ICC is a permanent, independent body, in relationship with the United Nations, that aims to promote the rule of law and punish the most serious international crimes. The Rome Statute reaffirms the principles of the UN Charter and states that the relationship between the Court and the United Nations system is to be determined by a relationship agreement to be concluded by the states parties to the Rome Statute and the UN General Assembly. Under the draft relationship agreement, approved by the Assembly of States Parties to the Rome Statute in September 2002, there was to be mutual exchange of information and documentation to the fullest extent and co-operation and consultation on practical matters, and the Court might, if deemed appropriate, submit reports on its activities to the UN Secretary-General and propose to the Secretary-General items for consideration by the United Nations. The Court comprises the Presidency (consisting of a President and first and second Vice-Presidents), Chambers (including a Pre-Trial Division, Trial Division and Appeals Division) with 18 permanent judges, Office of the Prosecutor, and Registry. In early February 2003 the first judges were elected to the Court. Judges must each have a different nationality and equitably represent the major legal systems of the world, a fair geographical distribution, and a fair proportion of men and women. They are elected by secret ballot at a meeting of the Assembly of States Parties to the Rome Statute convened for that purpose. The President and Vice-Presidents were to be elected by an absolute majority of the judges. The first Prosecutor was to be elected in April, by an absolute majority at a meeting of the Assembly of States Parties to the Rome Statute. By 26

February 2003 139 states had signed and 89 states had ratified the Rome Statute.

THE JUDGES
(April 2003)

	Term
RENÉ BLATTMANN (Bolivia)	6 years
MAUREEN HARDING CLARK (Ireland)	9 years
FATOUMATA DEMBELE DIARRA (Mali)	9 years
ADRIAN FULFORD (United Kingdom)	9 years
KARL HUDSON-PHILLIPS (Trinidad and Tobago)	9 years
CLAUDE JORDA (France)	6 years
HANS-PETER KAUL (Germany)	3 years
PHILIPPE KIRSCH (Canada)	6 years
ERKKI KOURULA (FINLAND)	3 years
AKUA KUENYEHIA (Ghana)	3 years
ELIZABETH ODIO BENITO (Costa Rica)	9 years
GHEORGHIOS PIKIS (Cyprus)	6 years
NAVANETHEM PILLAY (South Africa)	6 years
MAURO POLITI (Italy)	6 years
TUILOMA NERONI SLADE (Samoa)	3 years
SANG-HYUN SONG (Republic of Korea)	3 years
SYLVIA DE FIGUEIREDO STEINER (Brazil)	9 years
ANITA USACKA (Latvia)	6 years

Prosecutor: LUIS MORENO OCAMPO (Argentina).

Charter of the United Nations
(Signed 26 June 1945)

We the peoples of the United Nations determined
  to save succeeding generations from the scourge of war, which twice in our lifetime has brought untold sorrow to mankind, and
  to reaffirm faith in fundamental human rights, in the dignity and worth of the human person, in the equal rights of men and women and of nations large and small, and
  to establish conditions under which justice and respect for the obligations arising from treaties and other sources of international law can be maintained, and
  to promote social progress and better standards of life in larger freedom,

And for these ends
  to practise tolerance and live together in peace with one another as good neighbours, and
  to unite our strength to maintain international peace and security, and
  to ensure, by the acceptance of principles and the institution of methods, that armed force shall not be used, save in the common interest, and
  to employ international machinery for the promotion of the economic and social advancement of all peoples,

Have resolved to combine our efforts to accomplish these aims.
  Accordingly, our respective Governments, through representatives assembled in the city of San Francisco, who have exhibited their full powers found to be in good and due form, have agreed to the present Charter of the United Nations and do hereby establish an international organization to be known as the United Nations.

I. PURPOSES AND PRINCIPLES

Article 1
The Purposes of the United Nations are:
1. To maintain international peace and security, and to that end: to take effective collective measures for the prevention and removal of threats to the peace, and for the suppression of acts of aggression or other breaches of the peace, and to bring about by peaceful means, and in conformity with the principles of justice and international law, adjustment or settlement of international disputes or situations which might lead to a breach of the peace:
2. To develop friendly relations among nations based on respect for the principle of equal rights and self-determination of peoples, and to take other appropriate measures to strengthen universal peace;

3. To achieve international co-operation in solving international problems of an economic, social, cultural, or humanitarian character, and in promoting and encouraging respect for human rights and for fundamental freedoms for all without distinction as to race, sex, language, or religion; and
4. To be a centre for harmonizing the accusations of nations in the attainment of these common ends.

Article 2
The Organization and its Members, in pursuit of the Purposes stated in Article 1, shall act in accordance with the following Principles.
1. The Organization is based on the principle of the sovereign equality of all its Members.
2. All Members, in order to ensure to all of them the rights and benefits resulting from membership, shall fulfil in good faith the obligations assumed by them in accordance with the present Charter.
3. All Members shall settle their international disputes by peaceful means in such a manner that international peace and security, and justice, are not endangered.
4. All Members shall refrain in their international relations from the threat or use of force against the territorial integrity or political independence of any state, or in any manner inconsistent with the Purposes of the United Nations.
5. All Members shall give the United Nations every assistance in any action it takes in accordance with the present Charter, and shall refrain from giving assistance to any state against which the United Nations is taking preventive or enforcement action.
6. The Organization shall ensure that states which are not Members of the United Nations act in accordance with these Principles so far as may be necessary for the maintenance of international peace and security.
7. Nothing contained in the present Charter shall authorize the United Nations to intervene in matters which are essentially within the domestic jurisdiction of any state or shall require the Members to submit such matters to settlement under the present Charter; but this principle shall not prejudice the application of enforcement measures under Chapter VII.

II. MEMBERSHIP

Article 3
The original Members of the United Nations shall be the states which, having participated in the United Nations Conference on

International Organization at San Francisco, or having previously signed the Declaration by United Nations of January 1, 1942, sign the present Charter and ratify it in accordance with Article 110.

Article 4

1. Membership in the United Nations is open to all other peace-loving states which accept the obligations contained in the present Charter and, in the judgement of the Organization, are able and willing to carry out these obligations.

2. The admission of any such state to membership in the United Nations will be effected by a decision of the General Assembly upon the recommendation of the Security Council.

Article 5

A member of the United Nations against which preventive or enforcement action has been taken by the Security Council may be suspended from the exercise of the rights and privileges of membership by the General Assembly upon the recommendation of the Security Council. The exercise of these rights and privileges may be restored by the Security Council.

Article 6

A Member of the United Nations which has persistently violated the Principles contained in the present Charter may be expelled from the Organization by the General Assembly upon the recommendation of the Security Council.

III. ORGANS

Article 7

1. There are established as the principal organs of the United Nations: a General Assembly, a Security Council, an Economic and Social Council, a Trusteeship Council, an International Court of Justice, and a Secretariat.

2. Such subsidiary organs as may be found necessary may be established in accordance with the present Charter.

Article 8

The United Nations shall place no restrictions on the eligibility of men and women to participate in any capacity and under conditions of equality in its principal and subsidiary organs.

IV. THE GENERAL ASSEMBLY
Composition

Article 9

1. The General Assembly shall consist of all the Members of the United Nations.

2. Each Member shall have not more than five representatives in the General Assembly.

Functions and Powers

Article 10

The General Assembly may discuss any questions or any matters within the scope of the present Charter or relating to the powers and functions of any organs provided for in the present Charter, and, except as provided in Article 12, may make recommendations to the Members of the United Nations or to the Security Council or to both on any such questions or matters.

Article 11

1. The General Assembly may consider the general principles of co-operation in the maintenance of international peace and security, including the principles governing disarmament and the regulation of armaments, and may make recommendations with regard to such principles to the Members or to the Security Council or to both.

2. The General Assembly may discuss any questions relating to the maintenance of international peace and security brought before it by any Member of the United Nations, or by the Security Council, or by a state which is not a Member of the United Nations in accordance with Article 35, paragraph 2, and, except as provided in Article 12, may make recommendations with regard to any such question to the state or states concerned or to the Security Council or both. Any such question on which action is necessary shall be referred to the Security Council by the General Assembly either before or after discussion.

3. The General Assembly may call the attention of the Security Council to situations which are likely to endanger international peace and security.

4. The powers of the General Assembly set forth in this Article shall not limit the general scope of Article 10.

Article 12

1. While the Security Council is exercising in respect of any dispute or situation the functions assigned to it in the present Charter, the General Assembly shall not make any recommendations with regard to that dispute or situation unless the Security Council so requests.

2. The Secretary-General, with the consent of the Security Council, shall notify the General Assembly at each session of any matters relative to the maintenance of international peace and security which are being dealt with by the Security Council and shall similarly notify the General Assembly, or the Members of the United Nations if the General Assembly is not in session, immediately the Security Council ceases to deal with such matters.

Article 13

1. The General Assembly shall initiate studies and make recommendations for the purpose of:

(a) promoting international co-operation in the political field and encouraging the progressive development of international law and its codification;

(b) promoting international co-operation in the economic, social, cultural, educational, and health fields, and assisting in the realization of human rights and fundamental freedoms for all without distinction as to race, sex, language, or religion.

2. The further responsibilities, functions and powers of the General Assembly with respect to matters mentioned in paragraph 1(b) above are set forth in Chapters IX and X.

Article 14

Subject to the provision of Article 12, the General Assembly may recommend measures for the peaceful adjustment of any situation, regardless of origin, which it deems likely to impair the general welfare or friendly relations among nations, including situations resulting from a violation of the provisions of the present Charter setting forth the Purposes and Principles of the United Nations.

Article 15

1. The General Assembly shall receive and consider annual and special reports from the Security Council; these reports shall include an account of the measures that the Security Council has decided upon or taken to maintain international peace and security.

2. The General Assembly shall receive and consider reports from the other organs of the United Nations.

Article 16

The General Assembly shall perform such functions with respect to the international trusteeship system as are assigned to it under Chapters XII and XIII, including the approval of the trusteeship agreements for areas not designated as strategic.

Article 17

1. The General Assembly shall consider and approve the budget of the Organization.

2. The expenses of the Organization shall be borne by the Members as apportioned by the General Assembly.

3. The General Assembly shall consider and approve any financial and budgetary arrangements with specialized agencies referred to in Article 57 and shall examine the administrative budgets of such specialized agencies with a view to making recommendations to the agencies concerned.

Voting

Article 18

1. Each Member of the General Assembly shall have one vote.

2. Decisions of the General Assembly on important questions shall be made by a two-thirds majority of the members present and voting. These questions shall include: recommendations with respect to the maintenance of international peace and security, the election of the non-permanent Members of the Security Council, the election of the Members of the Economic and Social Council, the election of Members of the Trusteeship Council in accordance with paragraph 1(c) of Article 86, the admission of new Members to the United Nations, the suspension of the rights and privileges of membership, the expulsion of Members, questions relating to the operation of the trusteeship system, and budgetary questions.

3. Decisions on other questions, including the determination of additional categories of questions to be decided by a two-thirds majority, shall be made by a majority of the members present and voting.

Article 19

A Member of the United Nations which is in arrears in the payment of its financial contributions to the Organization shall have no vote in the General Assembly if the amount of its arrears equals or exceeds the amount of the contributions due from it for the preceding two full years. The General Assembly may, nevertheless, permit such a Member to vote if it is satisfied that the failure to pay is due to conditions beyond the control of the Member.

Procedure

Article 20

The General Assembly shall meet in regular annual sessions and in such special sessions as occasion may require. Special sessions shall be convoked by the Secretary-General at the request of the Security Council or of a majority of the members of the United Nations.

Article 21

The General Assembly shall adopt its own rules of procedure. It shall elect its President for each session.

Article 22

The General Assembly may establish such subsidiary organs as it deems necessary for the performance of its functions.

V. THE SECURITY COUNCIL

Composition

Article 23

1. The Security Council shall consist of 11 Members of the United Nations. The Republic of China*, France, the Union of Soviet Socialist Republics†, the United Kingdom of Great Britain and Northern Ireland, and the United States of America shall be permanent members of the Security Council. The General Assembly shall elect six other Members of the United Nations to be non-permanent members of the Security Council, due regard being specially paid, in the first instance to the contribution of Members of the United Nations to the maintenance of international peace and security and to the other purposes of the Organization, and also to equitable geographical distribution.

2. The non-permanent members of the Security Council shall be elected for a term of two years. In the first election of the non-permanent members, however, three shall be chosen for a term of one year. A retiring member shall not be eligible for immediate re-election.

3. Each member of the Security Council shall have one representative.

Functions and Powers

Article 24

1. In order to ensure prompt and effective action by the United Nations, its Members confer on the Security Council primary responsibility for the maintenance of international peace and security, and agree that in carrying out its duties under this responsibility the Security Council acts on their behalf.

2. In discharging these duties the Security Council shall act in accordance with the Purposes and Principles of the United Nations. The specific powers granted to the Security Council for the discharge of these duties are laid down in Chapters VI, VII, VIII and XII.

3. The Security Council shall submit annual and, when necessary, special reports to the General Assembly for its consideration.

Article 25

The Members of the United Nations agree to accept and carry out the decisions of the Security Council in accordance with the present Charter.

Article 26

In order to promote the establishment and maintenance of international peace and security with the least diversion for armaments of the world's human and economic resources, the Security Council shall be responsible for formulating, with the assistance of the Military Staff Committee referred to in Article 47, plans to be submitted to the Members of the United Nations for the establishment of a system for the regulation of armaments.

Voting

Article 27

1. Each member of the Security Council shall have one vote.

2. Decisions of the Security Council on procedural matters shall be made by an affirmative vote of seven members.

3. Decisions of the Security Council on all other matters shall be made by an affirmative vote of seven members including the concurring votes of the permanent members; provided that, in decisions under Chapter VI, and under paragraph 3 of Article 52, a party to a dispute shall abstain from voting.

---

* From 1971 the Chinese seat in the UN General Assembly and its permanent seat in the Security Council were occupied by the People's Republic of China.

† In December 1991 Russia assumed the former USSR's seat in the UN General Assembly and its permanent seat in the Security Council.

Procedure

Article 28

1. The Security Council shall be so organized as to be able to function continuously. Each member of the Security Council shall for this purpose be represented at all times at the seat of the Organization.

2. The Security Council shall hold periodic meetings at which each of its members may, if it so desires, be represented by a member of the government or by some other specially designated representative.

3. The Security Council may hold meetings at such places other than the seat of the Organization as in its judgment will best facilitate its work.

Article 29

The Security Council may establish such subsidiary organs as it deems necessary for the performance of its functions.

Article 30

The Security Council shall adopt its own rules of procedure, including the method of selecting its President.

Article 31

Any Member of the United Nations which is not a member of the Security Council may participate, without vote, in the discussion of any question brought before the Security Council whenever the latter considers that the interests of that Member are specially affected.

Article 32

Any Member of the United Nations which is not a member of the Security Council or any state which is not a Member of the United Nations, if it is a party to a dispute under consideration by the Security Council, shall be invited to participate, without vote, in the discussion relating to the dispute. The Security Council shall lay down such conditions as it deems just for the participation of a state which is not a Member of the United Nations.

VI. PACIFIC SETTLEMENT OF DISPUTES

Article 33

1. The parties to any dispute, the continuance of which is likely to endanger the maintenance of international peace and security, shall, first of all, seek a solution by negotiation, enquiry, mediation, conciliation, arbitration, judicial settlement, resort to regional agencies or arrangements, or other peaceful means of their own choice.

2. The Security Council shall, when it deems necessary, call upon the parties to settle their disputes by such means.

Article 34

The Security Council may investigate any dispute, or any situation which might lead to international friction or give rise to a dispute, in order to determine whether the continuance of the dispute or situation is likely to endanger the maintenance of international peace and security.

Article 35

1. Any Member of the United Nations may bring any dispute, or any situation of the nature referred to in Article 34, to the attention of the Security Council or of the General Assembly.

2. A state which is not a Member of the United Nations may bring to the attention of the Security Council or of the General Assembly any dispute to which it is a party if it accepts in advance, for the purposes of the dispute, the obligations of pacific settlement provided in the present Charter.

3. The proceedings of the General Assembly in respect of matters brought to its attention under this Article will be subject to the provisions of Articles 11 and 12.

Article 36

1. The Security Council may, at any stage of a dispute of the nature referred to in Article 33 or of a situation of like nature, recommend appropriate procedures or methods of adjustment.

2. The Security Council should take into consideration any procedures for the settlement of the dispute which have already been adopted by the parties.

3. In making recommendations under this Article the Security Council should also take into consideration that legal disputes should as a general rule be referred by the parties to the International Court of Justice in accordance with the provisions of the statute of the Court.

Article 37

1. Should the parties to a dispute of the nature referred to in Article 33, fail to settle it by the means indicated in that Article, they shall refer it to the Security Council.

2. If the Security Council deems that the continuance of the dispute is in fact likely to endanger the maintenance of international peace and security, it shall decide whether to take action under Article 36 or to recommend such terms of settlement as it may consider appropriate.

Article 38

Without prejudice to the provisions of Articles 33 to 37, the Security Council may, if all the parties to any dispute so request, make recommendations to the parties with a view to a pacific settlement of the dispute.

VII. ACTION WITH RESPECT TO THREATS TO THE PEACE, BREACHES OF THE PEACE, AND ACTS OF AGGRESSION

Article 39

The Security Council shall determine the existence of any threat to the peace, breach of the peace, or act of aggression and shall make recommendations, or decide what measures shall be taken in accordance with Articles 41 and 42, to maintain or restore international peace and security.

Article 40

In order to prevent an aggravation of the situation, the Security Council may, before making the recommendations or deciding upon the measures provided for in Article 39, call upon the parties concerned to comply with such provisional measures as it deems necessary or desirable. Such provisional measures shall be without prejudice to the rights, claims, or position of the parties concerned. The Security Council shall duly take account of failure to comply with such provisional measures.

Article 41

The Security Council may decide what measures not involving the use of armed force are to be employed to give effect to its decisions, and it may call upon the Members of the United Nations to apply such measures. These may include complete or partial interruption of economic relations and of rail, sea, air, postal, telegraphic, radio, and other means of communication, and the severance of diplomatic relations.

Article 42

Should the Security Council consider that measures provided for in Article 41 would be inadequate or have proved to be inadequate, it may take such action by air, sea, or land forces as may be necessary to maintain or restore international peace and security. Such action may include demonstrations, blockade, and other operations by air, sea, or land forces of Members of the United Nations.

Article 43

1. All Members of the United Nations, in order to contribute to the maintenance of international peace and security, undertake to make available to the Security Council, on its call and in accordance with a special agreement or agreements, armed forces, assistance, and facilities, including rights of passage, necessary for the purpose of maintaining international peace and security.

2. Such agreement or agreements shall govern the numbers and types of forces, their degree of readiness and general location, and the nature of the facilities and assistance to be provided.

3. The agreement or agreements shall be negotiated as soon as possible on the initiative of the Security Council. They shall be concluded between the Security Council and Members or between the Security Council and groups of Members and shall be subject to ratification by the signatory states in accordance with their respective constitutional processes.

Article 44

When the Security Council has decided to use force it shall, before calling upon a Member not represented on it to provide armed forces in fulfilment of the obligations assumed under Article 43, invite that Member, if the Member so desires, to participate in the decisions of the Security Council concerning the employment of contingents of that Member's armed forces.

Article 45

In order to enable the United Nations to take urgent military measures, Members shall hold immediately available national air-force contingents for combined international enforcement action. The strength and degree of readiness of these contingents and plans for their combined action shall be determined, within the limits laid down in the special agreement and agreements referred to in Article 43, by the Security Council with the assistance of the Military Staff Committee.

Article 46

Plans for the application of armed force shall be made by the Security Council with the assistance of the Military Staff Committee.

Article 47

1. There shall be established a Military Staff Committee to advise and assist the Security Council on all questions relating to the Security Council's military requirements for the maintenance of international peace and security, the employment and command of forces placed at its disposal, the regulation of armaments, and possible disarmament.

2. The Military Staff Committee shall consist of the Chiefs of Staff of the permanent members of the Security Council or their representatives. Any Member of the United Nations not permanently represented on the Committee shall be invited by the Committee to be associated with it when the efficient discharge of the Committee's responsibilities requires the participation of that Member in its work.

3. The Military Staff Committee shall be responsible under the Security Council for the strategic direction of any armed forces placed at the disposal of the Security Council. Questions relating to the command of such forces shall be worked out subsequently.

4. The Military Staff Committee, with the authorization of the Security Council and after consultation with appropriate regional agencies, may establish regional sub-committees.

Article 48

1. The action required to carry out the decisions of the Security Council for the maintenance of international peace and security shall be taken by all the Members of the United Nations or by some of them, as the Security Council may determine.

2. Such decisions shall be carried out by the Members of the United Nations directly and through their action in the appropriate international agencies of which they are members.

Article 49

The Members of the United Nations shall join in affording mutual assistance in carrying out the measures decided upon by the Security Council.

Article 50

If preventive or enforcement measures against any state are taken by the Security Council, any other state, whether a Member of the United Nations or not, which finds itself confronted with special economic problems arising from the carrying out of those measures shall have the right to consult the Security Council with regard to a solution of those problems.

Article 51

Nothing in the present Charter shall impair the inherent right of individual or collective self-defence if an armed attack occurs against a Member of the United Nations, until the Security Council has taken measures necessary to maintain international peace and security. Measures taken by Members in the exercise of this right of self-defence shall be immediately reported to the Security Council and shall not in any way affect the authority and responsibility of the Security Council under the present Charter to take at any time such action as it deems necessary in order to maintain or restore international peace and security.

VIII. REGIONAL ARRANGEMENTS

Article 52

1. Nothing in the present Charter precludes the existence of regional arrangements or agencies for dealing with such matters relating to the maintenance of international peace and security as are appropriate for regional action, provided that such arrangements or agencies and their activities are consistent with the Purposes and Principles of the United Nations.

2. The Members of the United Nations entering into such arrangements or constituting such agencies shall make every effort to achieve pacific settlement of local disputes through such regional agencies before referring them to the Security Council.

3. The Security Council shall encourage the development of pacific settlement of local disputes through such regional arrangements or by such regional agencies either on the initiative of the states concerned or by reference from the Security Council.

4. This Article in no way impairs the application of Articles 34 and 35.

Article 53

1. The Security Council shall, where appropriate, utilize such regional arrangements or agencies for enforcement action under its authority. But no enforcement action shall be taken under regional arrangements or by regional agencies without the authorization of the Security Council, with the exception of measures against any enemy state, as defined in paragraph 2 of this Article, provided for pursuant to Article 107 or in regional arrangements directed against renewal of aggressive policy on the part of any such state, until such time as the Organization may, on request of the Governments

concerned, be charged with the responsibility for preventing further aggression by such a state.

2. The term enemy state as used in paragraph 1 of this Article applies to any state which during the Second World War has been an enemy of any signatory of the present Charter.

Article 54

The Security Council shall at all times be kept fully informed of activities undertaken or in contemplation under regional arrangements or by regional agencies for the maintenance of international peace and security.

IX. INTERNATIONAL ECONOMIC AND SOCIAL CO-OPERATION

Article 55

With a view to the creation of conditions of stability and well-being which are necessary for peaceful and friendly relations among nations based on respect for the principle of equal rights and self-determination of peoples, the United Nations shall promote:

(a) higher standards of living, full employment, and conditions of economic and social progress and development;

(b) solutions of international economic, social, health, and related problems; and international cultural and educational co-operation; and

(c) universal respect for, and observance of, human rights and fundamental freedoms for all without distinction as to race, sex, language, or religion.

Article 56

All Members pledge themselves to take joint and separate action in co-operation with the Organization for the achievement of the purposes set forth in Article 55.

Article 57

1. The various specialized agencies, established by intergovernmental agreement and having wide international responsibilities, as defined in their basic instruments, in economic, social, cultural, educational, health, and related fields, shall be brought into relationship with the United Nations in accordance with the provisions of Article 63.

2. Such agencies thus brought into relationship with the United Nations are hereinafter referred to as specialized agencies.

Article 58

The Organization shall make recommendations for the co-ordination of the policies and activities of the specialized agencies.

Article 59

The Organization shall, where appropriate, initiate negotiations among the states concerned for the creation of any new specialized agencies required for the accomplishment of the purposes set forth in Article 55.

Article 60

Responsibility for the discharge of the functions of the Organization set forth in this Chapter shall be vested in the General Assembly and, under the authority of the General Assembly, in the Economic and Social Council, which shall have for this purpose the powers set forth in Chapter X.

X. THE ECONOMIC AND SOCIAL COUNCIL

Composition

Article 61

1. The Economic and Social Council shall consist of 18 Members of the United Nations elected by the General Assembly.

2. Subject to the provisions of paragraph 3, six members of the Economic and Social Council shall be elected each year for a term of three years. A retiring member shall be eligible for immediate re-election.

3. At the first election, 18 members of the Economic and Social Council shall be chosen. The term of office of six members so chosen shall expire at the end of one year, and of six other members at the end of two years, in accordance with arrangements made by the General Assembly.

4. Each member of the Economic and Social Council shall have one representative.

Functions and Powers

Article 62

1. The Economic and Social Council may make or initiate studies and reports with respect to international economic, social, cultural, educational, health, and related matters and may make recommendations with respect to any such matters to the General Assembly, to the Members of the United Nations, and to the specialized agencies concerned.

2. It may make recommendations for the purpose of promoting respect for, and observance of, human rights and fundamental freedoms for all.

3. It may prepare draft conventions for submission to the General Assembly, with respect to matters falling within its competence.

4. It may call, in accordance with the rules prescribed by the United Nations, international conferences on matters falling within its competence.

Article 63

1. The Economic and Social Council may enter into agreements with any of the agencies referred to in Article 57, defining the terms on which the agency concerned shall be brought into relationship with the United Nations. Such agreements shall be subject to approval by the General Assembly.

2. It may co-ordinate the activities of the specialized agencies through consultation with and recommendations to such agencies and through recommendations to the General Assembly and to the Members of the United Nations.

Article 64

1. The Economic and Social Council may take appropriate steps to obtain regular reports from the specialized agencies. It may make arrangements with the Members of the United Nations and with specialized agencies to obtain reports on the steps taken to give effect to its own recommendations and to recommendations on matters falling within its competence made by the General Assembly.

2. It may communicate its observations on these reports to the General Assembly.

Article 65

The Economic and Social Council may furnish information to the Security Council and shall assist the Security Council upon its request.

Article 66

1. The Economic and Social Council shall perform such functions as fall within its competence in connection with the carrying out of the recommendations of the General Assembly.

2. It may, with the approval of the General Assembly, perform services at the request of Members of the United Nations and at the request of specialized agencies.

3. It shall perform such other functions as are specified elsewhere in the present Charter or as may be assigned to it by the General Assembly.

Voting

Article 67

1. Each member of the Economic and Social Council shall have one vote.

2. Decisions of the Economic and Social Council shall be made by a majority of the members present and voting.

Procedure

Article 68

The Economic and Social Council shall set up commissions in economic and social fields and for the promotion of human rights, and such other commissions as may be required for the performance of its functions.

Article 69

The Economic and Social Council shall invite any Member of the United Nations to participate, without vote, in its deliberations on any matter of particular concern to that Member.

Article 70

The Economic and Social Council may make arrangements for representatives of the specialized agencies to participate, without vote, in its deliberations and in those of the commissions established by it, and for its representatives to participate in the deliberations of the specialized agencies.

Article 71

The Economic and Social Council may make suitable arrangements for consultation with non-governmental organizations which are concerned with matters within its competence. Such arrangements may be made with international organizations and, where appropriate, with national organizations after consultation with the Member of the United Nations concerned.

Article 72

1. The Economic and Social Council shall adopt its own rules of procedure, including the method of selecting its President.

2. The Economic and Social Council shall meet as required in accordance with its rules, which shall include provision for the convening of meetings on the request of a majority of its members.

XI. NON-SELF-GOVERNING TERRITORIES

Article 73

Members of the United Nations which have or assume responsibilities for the administration of territories whose peoples have not yet attained a full measure of self-government recognize the principle that the interests of the inhabitants of these territories are paramount, and accept as a sacred trust the obligation to promote to the utmost, within the system of international peace and security established by the present Charter, the well-being of the inhabitants of these territories, and, to this end:

(a) to ensure, with due respect for the culture of the peoples concerned, their political, economic, social, and educational advancement, their just treatment, and their protection against abuses;

(b) to develop self-government, to take due account of the political aspirations of the peoples, and to assist them in the progressive development of their free political institutions, according to the particular circumstances of each territory and its peoples and their varying stages of advancement;

(c) to further international peace and security;

(d) to promote constructive measures of development, to encourage research, and to co-operate with one another and, when and where appropriate, with specialized international bodies with a view to the practical achievement of the social, economic, and scientific purposes set forth in this Article; and

(e) to transmit regularly to the Secretary-General for information purposes, subject to such limitations as security and constitutional considerations may require, statistical and other information, of a technical nature relating to economic, social, and educational conditions in the territories for which they are respectively responsible other than those territories to which Chapters XII and XIII apply.

Article 74

Members of the United Nations also agree that their policy in respect of the territories to which this Chapter applies, no less than in respect of their metropolitan areas, must be based on the general principles of good-neighbourliness, due account being taken of the interests and well-being of the rest of the world, in social, economic, and commercial matters.

XII. INTERNATIONAL TRUSTEESHIP SYSTEM

Article 75

The United Nations shall establish under its authority an international trusteeship system for the administration and supervision of such territories as may be placed thereunder by subsequent individual agreements. These territories are hereinafter referred to as trust territories.

Article 76

The basic objectives of the trusteeship system, in accordance with the Purposes of the United Nations laid down in Article 1 of the present Charter, shall be:

(a) to further international peace and security;

(b) to promote the political, economic, social, and educational advancement of the inhabitants of the trust territories, and their progressive development towards self-government or independence as may be appropriate to the particular circumstances of each territory and its peoples and the freely expressed wishes of the peoples concerned, and as may be provided by the terms of each trusteeship agreement;

(c) to encourage respect for human rights and for fundamental freedoms for all without distinction as to race, sex, language, or religion, and to encourage recognition of the interdependence of the peoples of the world; and

(d) to ensure equal treatment in social, economic, and commercial matters for all Members of the United Nations and their nationals, and also equal treatment for the latter in the administration of justice, without prejudice to the attainment of the foregoing objectives and subject to the provisions of Article 80.

Article 77

1. The trusteeship system shall apply to such territories in the following categories as may be placed thereunder by means of trusteeship agreements:

(a) territories now held under mandate;

(b) territories which may be detached from enemy states as a result of the Second World War; and

(c) territories voluntarily placed under the system by states responsible for their administration.

2. It will be a matter for subsequent agreement as to which territories in the foregoing categories will be brought under the trusteeship system and upon what terms.

Article 78

The trusteeship system shall not apply to territories which have become Members of the United Nations, relationship among which shall be based on respect for the principle of sovereign equality.

Article 79

The terms of trusteeship for each territory to be placed under the trusteeship system, including any alteration or amendment, shall be agreed upon by the states directly concerned, including the mandatory power in the case of territories held under mandate by a Member of the United Nations, and shall be approved as provided for in Articles 83 and 85.

Article 80

1. Except as may be agreed upon in individual trusteeship agreements, made under Articles 77, 79, and 81, placing each territory under the trusteeship system, and until such agreements have been concluded, nothing in this Chapter shall be construed in or of itself to alter in any manner the rights whatsoever of any states or any peoples or the terms of existing international instruments to which Members of the United Nations may respectively be parties.

2. Paragraph 1 of this Article shall not be interpreted as giving grounds for delay or postponement of the negotiation and conclusion of agreements for placing mandated and other territories under the trusteeship system as provided for in Article 77.

Article 81

The trusteeship agreement shall in each case include the terms under which the trust territory will be administered and designate the authority which will exercise the administration of the trust territory. Such authority, hereinafter called the administering authority, may be one or more states or the Organization itself.

Article 82

There may be designated, in any trusteeship agreement, a strategic area or areas which may include part or all of the trust territory to which the agreement applies, without prejudice to any special agreement or agreements made under Article 43.

Article 83

1. All functions of the United Nations relating to strategic areas, including the approval of the terms of the trusteeship agreements and of their alteration or amendment, shall be exercised by the Security Council.

2. The basic objectives set forth in Article 76 shall be applicable to the people of each strategic area.

3. The Security Council shall, subject to the provisions of the trusteeship agreements and without prejudice to security considerations, avail itself of the assistance of the Trusteeship Council to perform those functions of the United Nations under the trusteeship system relating to political, economic, social, and educational matters in the strategic areas.

Article 84

It shall be the duty of the administering authority to ensure that the trust territory shall play its part in the maintenance of international peace and security. To this end the administering authority may make use of volunteer forces, facilities, and assistance from the trust territory in carrying out the obligations towards the Security Council undertaken in this regard by the administering authority, as well as for local defence and the maintenance of law and order within the trust territory.

Article 85

1. The functions of the United Nations with regard to trusteeship agreements for all areas not designated as strategic, including the approval of the terms of the trusteeship agreements and of their alteration or amendment, shall be exercised by the General Assembly.

2. The Trusteeship Council, operating under the authority of the General Assembly, shall assist the General Assembly in carrying out these functions.

XIII. THE TRUSTEESHIP COUNCIL*

Composition

Article 86

1. The Trusteeship Council shall consist of the following Members of the United Nations:

(a) those Members administering trust territories:

(b) such of those Members mentioned by name in Article 23 as are not administering trust territories; and

(c) as many other Members elected for three-year terms by the General Assembly as may be necessary to ensure that the total number of members of the Trusteeship Council is equally divided between those Members of the United Nations which administer trust territories and those which do not.

2. Each member of the Trusteeship Council shall designate one specially qualified person to represent it therein.

Functions and Powers

Article 87

The General Assembly and, under its authority, the Trusteeship Council, in carrying out their functions, may:

(a) consider reports submitted by the administering authority;

(b) accept petitions and examine them in consultation with the administering authority;

(c) provide for periodic visits to the respective trust territories at times agreed upon with the administering authority; and

(d) take these and other actions in conformity with the terms of the trusteeship agreements.

Article 88

The Trusteeship Council shall formulate a questionnaire on the political, economic, social, and educational advancement of the inhabitants of each trust territory, and the administering authority for each trust territory within the competence of the General Assembly shall make an annual report to the General Assembly upon the basis of such questionnaire.

Voting

Article 89

1. Each member of the Trusteeship Council shall have one vote.

2. Decisions of the Trusteeship Council shall be made by a majority of the members present and voting.

Procedure

Article 90

1. The Trusteeship Council shall adopt its own rules of procedure, including the method of selecting its President.

2. The Trusteeship Council shall meet as required in accordance with its rules, which shall include provision for the convening of meetings on the request of a majority of its members.

Article 91

The Trusteeship Council shall, when appropriate, avail itself of the assistance of the Economic and Social Council and of the specialized agencies in regard to matters with which they are respectively concerned.

XIV. THE INTERNATIONAL COURT OF JUSTICE

Article 92

The International Court of Justice shall be the principal judicial organ of the United Nations. It shall function in accordance with the annexed Statute, which is based upon the Statute of the Permanent Court of International Justice and forms an integral part of the present Charter.

Article 93

1. All Members of the United Nations are *ipso facto* parties to the Statute of the International Court of Justice.

2. A state which is not a Member of the United Nations may become a party to the Statute of the International Court of Justice on condition to be determined in each case by the General Assembly upon the recommendation of the Security Council.

Article 94

1. Each Member of the United Nations undertakes to comply with the decision of the International Court of Justice in any case to which it is a party.

2. If any party to a case fails to perform the obligations incumbent upon it under a judgment rendered by the Court, the other party may have recourse to the Security Council, which may, if it deems necessary, make recommendations or decide upon measures to be taken to give effect to the judgment.

Article 95

Nothing in the present Charter shall prevent Members of the United Nations from entrusting the solution of their differences to other tribunals by virtue of agreements already in existence or which may be concluded in the future.

Article 96

1. The General Assembly or the Security Council may request the International Court of Justice to give an advisory opinion on any legal question.

2. Other organs of the United Nations and specialized agencies, which may at any time be so authorized by the General Assembly, may also request advisory opinions of the Court on legal questions arising within the scope of their activities.

XV. THE SECRETARIAT

Article 97

The Secretariat shall comprise a Secretary-General and such staff as the Organization may require. The Secretary-General shall be appointed by the General Assembly upon the recommendation of the Security Council. He shall be the chief administrative officer of the Organization.

Article 98

The Secretary-General shall act in that capacity in all meetings of the General Assembly, of the Security Council, of the Economic and Social Council, and of the Trusteeship Council, and shall perform such other functions as are entrusted to him by these organs. The Secretary-General shall make an annual report to the General Assembly on the work of the Organization.

Article 99

The Secretary-General may bring to the attention of the Security Council any matter which in his opinion may threaten the maintenance of international peace and security.

Article 100

1. In the performance of their duties the Secretary-General and the staff shall not seek or receive instructions from any government or from any other authority external to the Organization. They shall refrain from any action which might reflect on their position as international officials responsible only to the Organization.

2. Each Member of the United Nations undertakes to respect the exclusively international character of the responsibilities of the Secretary-General and the staff and not to seek to influence them in the discharge of their responsibilities.

Article 101

1. The staff shall be appointed by the Secretary-General under regulations established by the General Assembly.

2. Appropriate staffs shall be permanently assigned to the Economic and Social Council, the Trusteeship Council, and, as required, to other organs of the United Nations. These staffs shall form a part of the Secretariat.

3. The paramount consideration in the employment of the staff and in the determination of the conditions of service shall be the necessity of securing the highest standards of efficiency, competence, and integrity. Due regard shall be paid to the importance of recruiting the staff on as wide a geographical basis as possible.

XVI. MISCELLANEOUS PROVISIONS

Article 102

1. Every treaty and every international agreement entered into by any Member of the United Nations after the present Charter comes into force shall as soon as possible be registered with the Secretariat and published by it.

2. No party to any such treaty or international agreement which has not been registered in accordance with the provisions of paragraph 1 of this Article may invoke that treaty or agreement before any organ of the United Nations.

Article 103

In the event of a conflict between the obligations of the Members of the United Nations under the present Charter and their obligations under any other international agreement, their obligations under the present Charter shall prevail.

---

* On 1 October 1994 the Republic of Palau, the last remaining territory under UN trusteeship, became independent. The Trusteeship Council formally suspended operations on 1 November; subsequently it was to be convened, as required, on an extraordinary basis.

Article 104

The Organization shall enjoy in the territory of each of its Members such legal capacity as may be necessary for the exercise of its functions and the fulfilment of its purposes.

Article 105

1. The Organization shall enjoy in the territory of each of its Members such privileges and immunities as are necessary for the fulfilment of its purposes.

2. Representatives of the Members of the United Nations and officials of the Organization shall similarly enjoy such privileges and immunities as are necessary for the independent exercise of their functions in connection with the Organization.

3. The General Assembly may make recommendations with a view to determining the details of the application of paragraphs 1 and 2 of this Article or may propose conventions to the Members of the United Nations for this purpose.

XVII. TRANSITIONAL SECURITY ARRANGEMENTS

Article 106

Pending the coming into force of such special agreements referred to in Article 43 as in the opinion of the Security Council enable it to begin the exercise of its responsibilities under Article 42, the parties to the Four-Nation Declaration signed at Moscow, October 30, 1943, and France, shall, in accordance with the provisions of paragraph 5 of that Declaration, consult with one another and as occasion requires with other Members of the United Nations with a view to such joint action on behalf of the Organization as may be necessary for the purpose of maintaining international peace and security.

Article 107

Nothing in the present Charter shall invalidate or preclude action, in relation to any state which during the Second World War has been an enemy of any signatory to the present Charter, taken or authorized as a result of that war by the Governments having responsibility for such action.

XVIII. AMENDMENTS

Article 108

Amendments to the present Charter shall come into force for all Members of the United Nations when they have been adopted by a vote of two-thirds of the members of the General Assembly and ratified in accordance with their respective constitutional processes by two-thirds of the Members of the United Nations, including all the permanent members of the Security Council.

Article 109

1. A General Conference of the Members of the United Nations for the purpose of reviewing the present Charter may be held at a date and place to be fixed by a two-thirds vote of the members of the General Assembly and by a vote of any seven members of the Security Council. Each Member of the United Nations shall have one vote in the conference.

2. Any alteration of the present Charter recommended by a two-thirds vote of the conference shall take effect when ratified in accordance with their respective constitutional processes by two-thirds of the Members of the United Nations including all the permanent members of the Security Council.

3. If such a conference has not been held before the tenth annual session of the General Assembly following the coming into force of the present Charter, the proposal to call such a conference shall be placed on the agenda of that session of the General Assembly, and the conference shall be held if so decided by a majority vote of the members of the General Assembly and by a vote of any seven members of the Security Council.

XIX. RATIFICATION AND SIGNATURE

Article 110

1. The present Charter shall be ratified by the signatory states in accordance with their respective constitutional processes.

2. The ratifications shall be deposited with the Government of the United States of America, which shall notify all the signatory states of each deposit as well as the Secretary-General of the Organization when he has been appointed.

3. The present Charter shall come into force upon the deposit of ratifications by the Republic of China, France, the Union of Soviet Socialist Republics, the United Kingdom of Great Britain and Northern Ireland, and the United States of America, and by a majority of the other signatory states. A protocol of the ratifications deposited shall thereupon be drawn up by the Government of the United States of America which shall communicate copies thereof to all the signatory states.

4. The states signatory to the present Charter which ratify it after it has come into force will become original Members of the United Nations on the date of the deposit of their respective ratifications.

Article 111

The present Charter, of which the Chinese, French, Russian, English, and Spanish texts are equally authentic, shall remain deposited in the archives of the Government of the United States of America. Duly certified copies thereof shall be transmitted by that Government to the Governments of the other signatory states.

IN FAITH WHEREOF the representatives of the Governments of the United Nations have signed the present Charter.

DONE at the city of San Francisco the twenty-sixth day of June, one thousand nine hundred and forty-five.

Amendments

The following amendments to Articles 23 and 27 of the Charter came into force in August 1965.

Article 23

1. The Security Council shall consist of 15 Members of the United Nations. The Republic of China, France, the Union of Soviet Socialist Republics, the United Kingdom of Great Britain and Northern Ireland, and the United States of America shall be permanent members of the Security Council. The General Assembly shall elect 10 other Members of the United Nations to be non-permanent members of the Security Council, due regard being specially paid, in the first instance to the contribution of Members of the United Nations to the maintenance of international peace and security and to the other purposes of the Organization, and also to equitable geographical distribution.

2. The non-permanent members of the Security Council shall be elected for a term of two years. In the first election of the non-permanent members after the increase of the membership of the Security Council from 11 to 15, two of the four additional members shall be chosen for a term of one year. A retiring member shall not be eligible for immediate re-election.

3. Each member of the Security Council shall have one representative.

Article 27

1. Each member of the Security Council shall have one vote.

2. Decisions of the Security Council on procedural matters shall be made by an affirmative vote of nine members.

3. Decisions of the Security Council on all other matters shall be made by an affirmative vote of nine members including the concurring votes of the permanent members; provided that, in decisions under Chapter VI and under paragraph 3 of Article 52, a party to a dispute shall abstain from voting.

The following amendments to Article 61 of the Charter came into force in September 1973.

Article 61

1. The Economic and Social Council shall consist of 54 Members of the United Nations elected by the General Assembly.

2. Subject to the provisions of paragraph 3, 18 members of the Economic and Social Council shall be elected each year for a term of three years. A retiring member shall be eligible for immediate re-election.

3. At the first election after the increase in the membership of the Economic and Social Council from 27 to 54 members, in addition to the members elected in place of the nine members whose term of office expires at the end of that year, 27 additional members shall be elected. Of these 27 additional members, the term of office of nine members so elected shall expire at the end of one year, and of nine other members at the end of two years, in accordance with arrangements made by the General Assembly.

4. Each member of the Economic and Social Council shall have one representative.

The following amendment to Paragraph 1 of Article 109 of the Charter came into force in June 1968.

Article 109

1. A General Conference of the Members of the United Nations for the purpose of reviewing the present Charter may be held at a date and place to be fixed by a two-thirds vote of the members of the General Assembly and by a vote of any nine members of the Security Council. Each Member of the United Nations shall have one vote in the conference.

Economic Commission for Europe—ECE

Address: Palais des Nations, 1211 Geneva 10, Switzerland.
Telephone: (22)-917-44-44; **fax:** (22)-917-05-05; **e-mail:** info
.ece@unece.org; **internet:** www.unece.org.

The UN Economic Commission for Europe was established in 1947. It provides a regional forum for governments from European countries, the USA, Canada, Israel and central Asian republics to study the economic, environmental and technological problems of the region and to recommend courses of action. ECE is also active in the formulation of international legal instruments and the setting of international norms and standards.

MEMBERS

Albania	Liechtenstein
Andorra	Lithuania
Armenia	Luxembourg
Austria	Macedonia, former Yugoslav
Azerbaijan	republic
Belarus	Malta
Belgium	Moldova
Bosnia and Herzegovina	Monaco
Bulgaria	Netherlands
Canada	Norway
Croatia	Poland
Cyprus	Portugal
Czech Republic	Romania
Denmark	Russia
Estonia	San Marino
Finland	Serbia and Montenegro
France	Slovakia
Georgia	Slovenia
Germany	Spain
Greece	Sweden
Hungary	Switzerland
Iceland	Tajikistan
Ireland	Turkey
Israel	Turkmenistan
Italy	Ukraine
Kazakhstan	United Kingdom
Kyrgyzstan	USA
Latvia	Uzbekistan

Organization

(April 2003)

COMMISSION

ECE, with ECAFE (now ESCAP), was the earliest of the five regional economic commissions set up by the UN Economic and Social Council. The Commission holds an annual plenary session and several informal sessions, and meetings of subsidiary bodies are convened throughout the year.

Chairman: CLYDE KULL (Estonia).

SECRETARIAT

The secretariat services the meetings of the Commission and its subsidiary bodies and publishes periodic surveys and reviews, including a number of specialized statistical bulletins on timber, housing, building, and transport (see list of publications below). It maintains close and regular liaison with the United Nations Secretariat in New York, with the secretariats of the other UN regional commissions and of other UN organizations, including the UN Specialized Agencies, and with other intergovernmental organizations. The Executive Secretary also carries out secretarial functions for the Executive Body of the 1979 Convention on Long-range Transboundary Air Pollution and its protocols. The ECE and UN Secretariats also service the ECOSOC Committee of Experts on the Transport of Dangerous Goods.

Executive Secretary: BRIGITA SCHMÖGNEROVÁ (Slovakia).

Activities

The guiding principle of ECE activities is the promotion of sustainable development. Within this framework, ECE's main objectives are to provide assistance to countries of central and eastern Europe in their transition from centrally-planned to market economies and to achieve the integration of all members into the European and global economies. Environmental protection, transport, statistics, trade facilitation and economic analysis are all principal topics in the ECE work programme, which also includes activities in the fields of timber, energy, trade, industry, and human settlements.

The 52nd plenary session of the ECE, held in April 1997, introduced a programme of reform, reducing the number of principal subsidiary bodies from 14 to seven, in order to concentrate resources on the core areas of work listed below, assisted by sub-committees and groups of experts. The Commission also determined to strengthen economic co-operation within Europe and to enhance co-operation and dialogue with other sub-regional organizations.

Committee on Environmental Policy: Provides policy direction for the ECE region and promotes co-operation among member governments in developing and implementing policies for environmental protection, rational use of natural resources, and sustainable development; supports the integration of environmental policy into sectoral policies; seeks solutions to environmental problems, particularly those of a transboundary nature; assists in strengthening environmental management capabilities, particularly in countries in transition; prepares ministerial conferences (normally held every four years—2003: Kiev, Ukraine); develops and promotes the implementation of international agreements on the environment; and assesses national policies and legislation.

Committee on Human Settlements: Reviews trends and policies in the field of human settlements; undertakes studies and organizes seminars; promotes international co-operation in the field of housing and urban and regional research; assists the countries of central and eastern Europe, which are currently in the process of economic transition, in reformulating their policies relating to housing, land management, sustainable human settlements, and planning and development.

Committee on Sustainable Energy: Exchanges information on general energy problems; work programme comprises activities including labelling classification systems and related legal and policy frameworks; liberalization of energy markets, pricing policies and supply security; harmonization of energy policies and practices; development of regional sustainable energy strategies for the 21st century; rational use of energy, efficiency and conservation; energy infrastructure including interconnection of electric power and gas networks; coal and thermal power generation in the context of sustainable energy development; Energy Efficiency Project; promotion and development of a market-based Gas Industry in Economies in Transition—Gas Centre programme; and technical assistance and operational activities in energy for the benefit of countries with economies in transition.

Committee for Trade, Industry and Enterprise Development: A forum for studying means of expanding and diversifying trade among European countries, as well as with countries in other regions, and for drawing up recommendations on how to achieve these ends. Analyses trends, problems and prospects in intra-European trade; explores means of encouraging the flow of international direct investment into the newly opening economies of central and eastern Europe; promotes new or improved methods of trading by means of marketing, industrial co-operation, contractual guides, and the facilitation of international trade procedures (notably through the Electronic Data Interchange for Administration, Commerce and Transport—UN/EDIFACT, a flexible single international standard).

Conference of European Statisticians: Promotes improvement of national statistics and their international comparability in economic, social, demographic and environmental fields; promotes co-ordination of statistical activities of international organizations active in Europe and North America; and responds to the increasing need for international statistical co-operation both within the ECE region and between the region and other regions. Works very closely with FAO, OECD and the EU.

Inland Transport Committee: Promotes a coherent, efficient, safe and sustainable transport system through the development of international agreements, conventions and other instruments covering a wide range of questions relating to road, rail, inland water and combined transport, including infrastructure, border-crossing facilitation, road traffic safety, limitation of air pollution and noise, requirements for the construction of road vehicles and other transport regulations, particularly in the fields of transport of dangerous goods and perishable foodstuffs. Also considers transport trends and economics and compiles transport statistics. Assists central and eastern European countries, as well as ECE member states from central Asia, in developing their transport systems and infrastructures.

Timber Committee: Regularly reviews markets for forest products; analyses long-term trends and prospects for forestry and timber;

keeps under review developments in the forest industries, including environmental and energy-related aspects. Subsidiary bodies run jointly with FAO deal with forest technology, management and training and with forest economics and statistics.

SUB-REGIONAL PROGRAMMES

Southeast European Co-operative Initiative—SECI: initiated in December 1996, in order to encourage co-operation among countries of the sub-region and to facilitate their access to the process of European integration. Nine *ad hoc* Project Groups have been established to undertake preparations for the following selected projects: trade facilitation; transport infrastructure, in particular road and rail networks; financial policies to promote small and medium-sized enterprises; co-operation to combat crime and corruption; energy efficiency demonstration zone networks; interconnection of natural gas networks; co-operation among securities markets; and the recovery programme for rivers, lakes and adjacent seas (with particular emphasis on the Danube River Basin). Activities are overseen by a SECI Agenda Committee and a SECI Business Advisory Council. Participating countries: Albania, Bosnia and Herzegovina, Bulgaria, Croatia, Greece, Hungary, the former Yugoslav republic of Macedonia, Moldova, Romania, Slovenia and Turkey.

Special Programme for the Economies of Central Asia—SPECA: initiated in March 1998 as a joint programme of the ECE and ESCAP. Aims to strengthen sub-regional co-operation, in particular in the following areas: the development of transport infrastructure and facilitation of cross-border activities; the rational use of energy and water; regional development and attraction of foreign investment; and development of multiple routes for pipeline transportation of hydrocarbons to global markets. In February 2002 SPECA's Regional Advisory Committee endorsed the terms of reference for the establishment of a Business Advisory Council of SPECA, which aimed to bring together business representatives from participating countries and from their major trading and economic partners. The inaugural session of the Council was held in June, in Almaty, Kazakhstan. Participating countries: Kazakhstan, Kyrgyzstan, Tajikistan, Turkmenistan and Uzbekistan.

Finance

ECE's budget for the two years 2002–03 was US $40.0m.

Publications

ECE Annual Report.
Annual Bulletin of Housing and Building Statistics for Europe and North America.
Annual Bulletin of Transport Statistics for Europe and North America.
ECE Highlights (3 a year).
The ECE in the Age of Change.
Economic Survey of Europe (2 a year).
Statistical Journal of the UNECE (quarterly).
Statistical Standards and Studies.
Statistics of Road Traffic Accidents in Europe and North America.
Timber Bulletin (6 a year).
Timber Committee Yearbook (annually).
Trends in Europe and North America: Statistical Yearbook of the ECE (annually).
The UN in your Daily Life – Economic Commission for Europe.
UN Manual of Tests and Criteria of Dangerous Goods.
UN Recommendations on the Transport of Dangerous Goods.
UNECE International Legal Instruments, Norms and Standards.
The UNECE Works for Quality and Safety: Norms and Standards.
Women and Men in Europe and North America.
World Robotics (annually).
Studies on air pollution, forestry and timber, water, gas, energy; environmental performance reviews; country profiles on the housing sector; transport agreements; customs conventions; maps; trade and investment briefings and guides; reports on fertility and family, gender, migration and population ageing; statistical bulletins; sectoral studies; discussion papers.

Reports, proceedings of meetings, technical documents, codes of conduct, codes of practice, guide-lines to governments, etc.

Economic and Social Commission for Asia and the Pacific—ESCAP

Address: United Nations Bldg, Rajdamnern Ave, Bangkok 10200, Thailand.

Telephone: (2) 288-1234; **fax:** (2) 288-1000; **e-mail:** unisbkk.unescap@un.org; **internet:** www.unescap.org.

The Commission was founded in 1947 to encourage the economic and social development of Asia and the Far East; it was originally known as the Economic Commission for Asia and the Far East (ECAFE). The title ESCAP, which replaced ECAFE, was adopted after a reorganization in 1974.

MEMBERS

Afghanistan	Korea, Democratic	Papua New Guinea
Armenia	People's Republic	Philippines
Australia	Korea, Republic	Russia
Azerbaijan	Kyrgyzstan	Samoa
Bangladesh	Laos	Singapore
Bhutan	Malaysia	Solomon Islands
Brunei	Maldives	Sri Lanka
Cambodia	Marshall Islands	Tajikistan
China, People's	Micronesia, Federated	Thailand
Republic	States	Tonga
Fiji	Mongolia	Turkey
France	Myanmar	Turkmenistan
Georgia	Nauru	Tuvalu
India	Nepal	United Kingdom
Indonesia	Netherlands	USA
Iran	New Zealand	Uzbekistan
Japan	Pakistan	Vanuatu
Kazakhstan	Palau	Viet Nam
Kiribati		

ASSOCIATE MEMBERS

American Samoa	Hong Kong	Northern Mariana
Cook Islands	Macao	Islands
French Polynesia	New Caledonia	
Guam	Niue	

Organization

(April 2003)

COMMISSION

The Commission meets annually at ministerial level to examine the region's problems, to review progress, to establish priorities and to decide upon the recommendations of the Executive Secretary or the subsidiary bodies of the Commission.

Ministerial and intergovernmental conferences on specific issues may be held on an *ad hoc* basis with the approval of the Commission, although, from 1998, no more than one ministerial conference and five intergovernmental conferences may be held during one year.

COMMITTEES AND SPECIAL BODIES

The following advise the Commission and help to oversee the work of the Secretariat:

Committee on the Environment and Natural Resources Development: meets annually.

Committee on Regional Economic-Co-operation: meets every two years, with a high-level Steering Group, which meets annually to discuss and develop policy options.

Committee on Socio-economic Measures to Alleviate Poverty in Rural and Urban Areas: meets annually.

Committee on Statistics: meets every two years.

Committee on Transport, Communications, Tourism and Infrastructure Development: meets annually.

Special Body on Least-Developed and Land-locked Developing Countries: meets every two years.

Special Body on Pacific Island Developing Countries: meets every two years.

In addition, an Advisory Committee of permanent representatives and other representatives designated by members of the Commission functions as an advisory body.

SECRETARIAT

The Secretariat operates under the guidance of the Commission and its subsidiary bodies. It consists of two servicing divisions, covering administration and programme management, in addition to the following substantive divisions: Poverty and Development; Statistics; Trade and Investment; Transport and Tourism; Environment and Sustainable Development; Information, Communication and Space Technology; and Emerging Social Issues.

The Secretariat also includes the ESCAP/UNCTAD Joint Unit on Transnational Corporations and the UN information services.

Executive Secretary: KIM HAK-SU (Republic of Korea).

SUB-REGIONAL OFFICE

ESCAP Pacific Operations Centre (EPOC): Private Mail Bag 9004, Port Vila, Vanuatu; tel. 23458; fax 23921; e-mail escap@ vanuatu.com.vu; f. 1984, to provide effective advisory and technical assistance at a sub-regional level and to identify the needs of island countries. Dir NIKENIKE VUROBARAVU.

Activities

ESCAP acts as a UN regional centre, providing the only intergovernmental forum for the whole of Asia and the Pacific, and executing a wide range of development programmes through technical assistance, advisory services to governments, research, training and information.

In 1992 ESCAP began to reorganize its programme activities and conference structures in order to reflect and serve the region's evolving development needs. The approach that was adopted focused on regional economic co-operation, poverty alleviation through economic growth and social development, and environmental and sustainable development.

Regional economic co-operation. Provides technical assistance and advisory services. Aims to enhance institutional capacity-building; gives special emphasis to the needs of least developed, land-locked and island developing countries, and to economies in transition in accelerating their industrial and technological advancement, promoting their exports, and furthering their integration into the region's economy; supports the development of electronic commerce and other information technologies in the region; and promotes the intra-regional and inter-subregional exchange of trade, investment and technology through the strengthening of institutional support services such as regional information networks.

Development research and policy analysis. Aims to increase the understanding of the economic and social development situation in the region, with particular attention given to sustainable economic growth, poverty alleviation, the integration of environmental concerns into macroeconomic decisions and policy-making processes, and enhancing the position of the region's disadvantaged economies. The sub-programme is responsible for the provision of technical assistance, and the production of relevant documents and publications.

Social development. The main objective is to assess and respond to regional trends and challenges in social policy and human resources development, with particular emphasis on the planning and delivery of social services and training programmes for disadvantaged groups, including the poor, youths, women, the disabled, and the elderly. The sub-programme aims to strengthen the capacity of public and non-government institutions to address the problems of such marginalized social groups and to foster partnerships between governments, the private sector, community organizations and all other involved bodies. Implements global and regional mandates, such as the Programme of Action of the World Summit for Social Development and the Jakarta Plan of Action on Human Resources Development. The Biwako Millennium Framework for Action towards an Inclusive, Barrier-free and Rights-based Society for Persons with Disabilities in Asia and the Pacific was adopted by ESCAP as a regional guide-line underpinning the Asian and Pacific Decade of Disabled Persons (2003–12). In 1998 ESCAP initiated a programme of assistance in establishing a regional network of Social Development Management Information Systems (SOMIS). ESCAP collaborated with other agencies towards the adoption, in November 2001, of a Regional Platform on Sustainable Development for Asia and the Pacific. The Commission undertook regional preparations for the World Summit on Sustainable Development, which was held in Johannesburg, South Africa, in August/September 2002.

Population and rural and urban development. Aims to assess and strengthen the capabilities of local institutions in rural and urban development, as well as increasing the capacity of governmental and non-governmental organizations to develop new approaches to poverty alleviation and to support food security for rural households. Promotes the correct use of agro-chemicals in order to increase food supply and to achieve sustainable agricultural development and administers the Fertilizer Advisory Development and Information Network for Asia and the Pacific (FADINAP). Rural employment opportunities and the access of the poor to land, credit and other productive assets are also considered by the sub-programme. Undertakes technical co-operation and research in the areas of ageing, female economic migration and reproductive health, and prepares specific publications relating to population. Implements global and regional mandates, such as the Programme of Action of the International Conference on Population and Development. The Secretariat co-ordinates the Asia-Pacific Population Information Network (POPIN). The fifth Asia and Pacific Population Conference, sponsored by ESCAP, was held in Bangkok, Thailand, in December 2002.

Environment and natural resources development. Concerned with strengthening national capabilities to achieve environmentally-sound and sustainable development by integrating economic concerns, such as the sustainable management of natural resources, into economic planning and policies. The sub-programme was responsible for implementation of the Regional Action Programme for Environmentally Sound and Sustainable Development for the period 1996–2000. Other activities have included the promotion of integrated water resources development and management, including water quality and a reduction in water-related natural disasters; strengthening the formulation of policies in the sustainable development of land and mineral resources; the consideration of energy resource options, such as rural energy supply, energy conservation and the planning of power networks; and promotion of the use of space technology applications for environmental management, natural disaster monitoring and sustainable development.

Transport, communications, tourism and infrastructure development. Aims to develop inter- and intra-regional transport links to enhance trade and tourism, mainly through implementation of an Asian Land Transport Infrastructure Development project. Other activities are aimed at improving the planning process in developing infrastructure facilities and services, in accordance with the regional action programme of the New Delhi Action Plan on Infrastructure Development in Asia and the Pacific, which was adopted at a ministerial conference held in October 1996, and at enhancing private sector involvement in national infrastructure development through financing, management, operations and risk-sharing. A Ministerial Conference on Infrastructure Development was organized by ESCAP in November 2001. The meeting concluded a memorandum of understanding, initially signed by ESCAP, Kazakhstan, the Republic of Korea, Mongolia and Russia, to facilitate the transport of container goods along the Trans-Asian Railway. The sub-programme aims to reduce the adverse environmental impact of the provision of infrastructure facilities and to promote more equitable and easier access to social amenities. Tourism concerns include the development of human resources, improved policy planning for tourism development, greater investment in the industry, and minimizing the environmental impact of tourism.

Statistics. Provides training and advice in priority areas, including national accounts statistics, gender statistics, population censuses and surveys, and the management of statistical systems. Supports co-ordination throughout the region of the development, implementation and revision of selected international statistical standards. Disseminates comparable socio-economic statistics, with increased use of the electronic media, promotes the use of modern information technology in the public sector and trains senior-level officials in the effective management of information technology.

Throughout all the sub-programmes, ESCAP aims to focus particular attention on the needs and concerns of least developed, land-locked and island developing nations, and economies in transition in the region.

CO-OPERATION WITH THE ASIAN DEVELOPMENT BANK

In July 1993 a memorandum of understanding was signed by ESCAP and the Asian Development Bank (ADB—q.v.), outlining priority areas of co-operation between the two organizations. These were: regional and sub-regional co-operation; issues concerning the least-developed, land-locked and island developing member countries; poverty alleviation; women in development; population; human resource development; the environment and natural resource management; statistics and data bases; economic analysis; transport and communications; and industrial restructuring and privatization. The two organizations were to co-operate in organizing workshops, seminars and conferences, in implementing joint projects, and in exchanging information and data on a regular basis.

ASSOCIATED BODIES

Asian and Pacific Centre for Transfer of Technology: APCTT Bldg, POB 4575, New Delhi 110 016, India; tel. (11) 26966509; fax (11) 26856274; e-mail infocentre@apctt.org; internet www.apctt.org; f. 1977 to assist countries of the ESCAP region by strengthening their capacity to develop, transfer and adopt technologies relevant to the region, and to identify and to promote regional technology development and transfer. Dir Dr JÜRGEN H. BISCHOFF. Publs *Asia Pacific Tech Monitor, VATIS Updates on Biotechnology, Food Processing, Ozone Layer Protection, Non-Conventional Energy,* and *Waste Technology* (each every 2 months), *International Technology and Business Opportunities: Catalogue*(quarterly).

Asian and Pacific Centre for Agricultural Engineering and Machinery: China International Science & Technology Convention Centre, 12 Yumin Rd, Madian, Deshengmenwai, Chaoyang District, Beijing 100029, People's Republic of China; f. 1977 as Regional Network for Agricultural Engineering and Machinery, elevated to regional centre May 2002; aims to reduce poverty by enhancing technical co-operation throughout the region, and promotes agricultural engineering and machinery and the region's agro-based biotechnologies. Mems: Bangladesh, People's Republic of China, India, Indonesia, Iran, Nepal, Pakistan, Philippines, Republic of Korea, Sri Lanka, Thailand, Viet Nam. Dir TAPIO JUOKSLAHTI.

ESCAP/WMO Typhoon Committee: c/o UNDP, POB 7285, ADC, Pasay City, Metro Manila, Philippines; tel. (632) 3733443; fax (2) 3733419; e-mail tcs@philonline.com; f. 1968; an intergovernmental body sponsored by ESCAP and WMO for mitigation of typhoon damage. It aims at establishing efficient typhoon and flood warning systems through improved meteorological and telecommunication facilities. Other activities include promotion of disaster preparedness, training of personnel and co-ordination of research. The committee's programme is supported from national resources and also by UNDP and other international and bilateral assistance. Mems: Cambodia, People's Republic of China, Hong Kong, Japan, Democratic People's Republic of Korea, Republic of Korea, Laos, Macao, Malaysia, Philippines, Singapore, Thailand, USA, Viet Nam. Co-ordinator of Secretariat: Dr ROMAN L. KINTANAR.

Regional Co-ordination Centre for Research and Development of Coarse Grains, Pulses, Roots and Tuber Crops in the Humid Tropics of Asia and the Pacific (CGPRT Centre): Jalan Merdeka 145, Bogor 16111, Indonesia; tel. (251) 343277; fax (251) 336290; e-mail cgprt@cbn.net.id; internet www.cgprt.org.sg; f. 1981; initiates and promotes research, training and publications on the production, marketing and use of these crops. Dir Dr NOBUYOSHI MAENO. Publs *Palawija News* (quarterly), working paper series, monograph series and statistical profiles.

Statistical Institute for Asia and the Pacific: JETRO-IDE Building, 2-2 Wakaba 3-chome, Mihama-ku, Chiba-shi, Chiba 261-8787, Japan; tel. (43) 2999782; fax (43) 2999780; e-mail staff@unsiap .or.jp; internet www.unsiap.or.jp; f. 1970; trains government statisticians; prepares teaching materials, provides facilities for special studies and research of a statistical nature, assists in the development of training on official statistics in national and sub-regional centres. Dir TOMAS P. AFRICA (Philippines).

WMO/ESCAP Panel on Tropical Cyclones: Technical Support Unit, c/o Pakistan Meteorological Dept, POB 1214, H-8, Islamabad, Pakistan; tel. (51) 9257314; fax (51) 432588; e-mail tsupmd@hot mail.com; f. 1973 to mitigate damage caused by tropical cyclones in the Bay of Bengal and the Arabian Sea; mems: Bangladesh, India, Maldives, Myanmar, Pakistan, Sri Lanka, Thailand. Co-ordinator of Secretariat Dr QAMAR-UZ-ZAMAN CHAUDHRY.

Finance

For the two-year period 2002–03 ESCAP's regular budget, an appropriation from the UN budget, was US $52.8m. The regular budget is supplemented annually by funds from various sources for technical assistance.

Publications

Annual Report.

Agro-chemicals News in Brief (quarterly).

Asia-Pacific Development Journal (2 a year).

Asia-Pacific in Figures (annually).

Asia-Pacific Population Journal (quarterly).

Asia-Pacific Remote Sensing and GIS Journal (2 a year).

Atlas of Mineral Resources of the ESCAP Region.

Confluence (water resources newsletter, 2 a year).

Economic and Social Survey of Asia and the Pacific (annually).

Environmental News Briefing (every 2 months).

ESCAP Energy News (2 a year).

ESCAP Human Resources Development Newsletter (2 a year).

ESCAP Population Data Sheet (annually).

ESCAP Tourism Newsletter (2 a year).

Fertilizer Trade Information Monthly Bulletin.

Foreign Trade Statistics of Asia and the Pacific (annually).

Government Computerization Newsletter (irregular).

Industry and Technology Development News for Asia and the Pacific (annually).

Poverty Alleviation Initiatives (quarterly).

Regional Network for Agricultural Machinery Newsletter (3 a year).

Small Industry Bulletin for Asia and the Pacific (annually).

Social Development Newsletter (2 a year).

Space Technology Applications Newsletter (quarterly).

Statistical Indicators for Asia and the Pacific (quarterly).

Statistical Newsletter (quarterly).

Statistical Yearbook for Asia and the Pacific.

Trade and Investment Information Bulletin (monthly).

Transport and Communications Bulletin for Asia and the Pacific (annually).

Water Resources Journal (quarterly).

Bibliographies; country and trade profiles; commodity prices; statistics.

Economic Commission for Latin America and the Caribbean—ECLAC

Address: Edif. Naciones Unidas, Avda Dag Hammarskjöld, Casilla 179D, Santiago, Chile.
Telephone: (2) 2102000; **fax:** (2) 2080252; **e-mail:** dpisantiago@eclac.cl; **internet:** www.eclac.org.

The UN Economic Commission for Latin America was founded in 1948 to co-ordinate policies for the promotion of economic development in the Latin American region. The current name of the Commission was adopted in 1984.

MEMBERS

Antigua and Barbuda	Costa Rica	Haiti
Argentina	Cuba	Honduras
Bahamas	Dominica	Italy
Barbados	Dominican Republic	Jamaica
Belize	Ecuador	Mexico
Bolivia	El Salvador	Netherlands
Brazil	France	Nicaragua
Canada	Grenada	Panama
Chile	Guatemala	Paraguay
Colombia	Guyana	Peru
Saint Christopher and Nevis	Spain	Portugal
Saint Lucia	Suriname	United Kingdom
Saint Vincent and the Grenadines	Trinidad and Tobago	USA
		Uruguay
		Venezuela

ASSOCIATE MEMBERS

Anguilla	Montserrat	Puerto Rico
Aruba	Netherlands Antilles	United States Virgin Islands
British Virgin Islands		

Organization

(April 2003)

COMMISSION

The Commission normally meets every two years in one of the Latin American capitals. The 29th session was held in Brasilia in May 2002, and the 30th session was to be held in Puerto Rico, in 2004. The Commission has established the following permanent bodies:

Caribbean Development and Co-operation Committee.

Central American Development and Co-operation Committee.

Committee of High-Level Government Experts.

Committee of the Whole.

Regional Conference on the Integration of Women into the Economic and Social Development of Latin America and the Caribbean.

Regional Council for Planning.

SECRETARIAT

The Secretariat employs more than 500 staff and is headed by the the Offices of the Executive Secretary and of the Secretary of the Commission. ECLAC's work programme is carried out by the following divisions: Economic Development; Social Development; International Trade and Integration; Production, Productivity and Management; Statistics and Economic Projections; Environment and Human Settlements; Natural Resources and Infrastructure; Documents and Publications; and Population. There are also units for information and conference services, women and development and special studies, an electronic information section, and a support division of administration.

Executive Secretary: JOSÉ ANTONIO OCAMPO (Colombia).
Secretary of the Commission: DANIEL BLANCHARD.

SUB-REGIONAL OFFICES

Caribbean: 63 Park St, Chic Bldg, 3rd Floor, POB 1113, Port of Spain, Trinidad and Tobago; tel. 623-5595; fax 623-8486; e-mail registry@eclacpos.org; internet www.eclacpos.org; f. 1956; covers non-Spanish-speaking Caribbean countries; Dir LEN ISHMAEL.

Central America and Spanish-speaking Caribbean: Avda Presidente Masaryk 29, 11570 México, DF; tel. (5) 250-1555; fax (5) 531-1151; e-mail cepal@un.org.mx; internet www.eclac.org.mx; f. 1951; covers Central America and Spanish-speaking Caribbean countries; Dir REBECA GRYNSPAN.

There are also national offices, in Santafé de Bogotá, Brasília, Buenos Aires and Montevideo and a liaison office in Washington, DC.

Activities

ECLAC collaborates with regional governments in the investigation and analysis of regional and national economic problems, and provides guidance in the formulation of development plans. Its activities include research; analysis; publication of information; provision of technical assistance; participation in seminars and conferences; training courses; and co-operation with national, regional and international organizations.

The 26th session of the Commission, which was held in San José, Costa Rica, in April 1996, considered means of strengthening the economic and social development of the region, within the framework of a document prepared by ECLAC's Secretariat, and adopted a resolution which defined ECLAC as a centre of excellence, charged with undertaking an analysis of specific aspects of the development process, in collaboration with member governments. The meeting also reviewed the impact on ECLAC of the ongoing process of reform throughout the UN system. In May 1998 the 27th session of the Commission, held in Oranjestad, Aruba, approved the ongoing reform programme, and in particular efforts to enhance the effectiveness and transparency of ECLAC's activities. The main topics of debate at the meeting were public finances, fiscal management and social and economic development. The Commission adopted a Fiscal Covenant, incorporating measures to consolidate fiscal adjustment and to strengthen public management, democracy and social equity, which was to be implemented throughout the region and provide the framework for further debate at national and regional level. ECLAC's 28th session, convened in Mexico City in April 2000, debated a document prepared by the Secretariat which proposed that the pursuit of social equity, sustainable development and 'active citizenship' (with emphasis on the roles of education and employment) should form the basis of future policy-making in the region.

ECLAC's 29th session, which was held in Brasilia, Brazil, in May 2002, focused on the process of globalization. The meeting adopted the Brasilia Resolution, which outlined a strategic agenda to meet the challenges of globalization. Proposed action included the consolidation of democracy, strengthening social protection, the formulation of policies to reduce macroeconomic and financial vulnerability, and the development of sustainable and systemic competitiveness. The objectives of the agenda were to achieve a guaranteed supply of general public goods, to overcome, steadily, the imbalances in the world order, and to build, gradually, an international social agenda based on rights. The Resolution requested that ECLAC strengthen its work in the relevant areas.

ECLAC works closely with other agencies within the UN system and with other regional and multinational organizations. ECLAC is co-operating with the OAS and the Inter-American Development Bank in the servicing of intergovernmental groups undertaking preparatory work for the establishment of a Free Trade Area of the Americas. In May 2001 ECLAC hosted the first meeting of the Americas Statistics Conference. In January 2002 ECLAC hosted an Interregional Conference on Financing for Development, held in Mexico City, which it had organized as part of the negotiating process prior to the World Summit on Financing for Development, held in March. In June senior representatives of ECLAC, UNDP, the World Bank and the Inter-American Development Bank signed a Protocol of Intentions with a commitment to co-ordinate activities in pursuit of the development goals proclaimed by the so-called Millennium Summit meeting of the General Assembly in September 2000. ECLAC was to adapt the objectives of the goals to the reality of countries in the region. ECLAC provides regional support to the UN Information and Communication Technologies Task Force, which was established in November 2001. A working meeting on the establishment of a regional network under the Task Force, in order to plan and monitor the development of digital technology in the region, was held in June 2002. In late January 2003 a regional conference was convened, in the Dominican Republic, in preparation for a World Summit on the Information Society, scheduled to be held later in that year.

Latin American and Caribbean Institute for Economic and Social Planning—ILPES: Edif. Naciones Unidas, Avda Dag

Hammarskjöld, Casilla 1567, Santiago, Chile; tel. (2) 2102506; fax (2) 2066104; e-mail pdekock@eclac.cl; internet www.eclac.org/ilpes; f. 1962; supports regional governments through the provision of training, advisory services and research in the field of public planning policy and co-ordination. Dir JOSÉ ANTONIO OCAMPO.

Latin American Demographic Centre—CELADE: Edif. Naciones Unidas, Avda Dag Hammarskjöld, Casilla 179D, Santiago, Chile; tel. (2) 2102002; fax (2) 2080252; e-mail djaspers@eclac.cl; internet www.eclac.org/celade; f. 1957, became an integral part of ECLAC in 1975; provides technical assistance to governments, universities and research centres in demographic analysis, population policies, integration of population factors in development planning, and data processing; conducts three-month courses on demographic analysis for development and various national and regional seminars; provides demographic estimates and projections, documentation, data processing, computer packages and training. Officer-in-Charge MIGUEL VILLA.

Finance

For the two-year period 2000–01 ECLAC's regular budget, an appropriation from the UN, amounted to US $78.9m. In addition, extra-budgetary activities are financed by governments, other organizations, and UN agencies, including UNDP, UNFPA and UNICEF.

Publications

Boletín del Banco de Datos del CELADE (annually).
Boletín demográfico (2 a year).
Boletín de Facilitación del Comercio y el Transporte (monthly).
CEPAL Review (Spanish and English, 3 a year).
CEPALINDEX (annually).
Co-operation and Development (Spanish and English, quarterly).
DOCPAL Resúmenes (population studies, 2 a year).
ECLAC Notes / Notas de la CEPAL (every 2 months).
Economic Survey of Latin America and the Caribbean (Spanish and English, annually).
Foreign Investment in Latin America and the Caribbean (annually).
Latin America and the Caribbean in the World Economy (annually).
Latin American Projections 2001–02.
Notas de Población (2 a year).
PLANINDEX (2 a year).
Preliminary Overview of the Economies of Latin America and the Caribbean (annually).
Social Panorama of Latin America (annually).
Statistical Yearbook for Latin America and the Caribbean (Spanish and English).
Studies, reports, bibliographical bulletins.

Economic Commission for Africa—ECA

Address: Africa Hall, POB 3001, Addis Ababa, Ethiopia.
Telephone: (1) 517200; **fax:** (1) 514416; **e-mail:** ecainfo@uneca.org; **internet:** www.uneca.org.

The UN Economic Commission for Africa was founded in 1958 by a resolution of the UN Economic and Social Council (ECOSOC) to initiate and take part in measures for facilitating Africa's economic development.

MEMBERS

Algeria	Eritrea	Niger
Angola	Ethiopia	Nigeria
Benin	Gabon	Rwanda
Botswana	The Gambia	São Tomé and
Burkina Faso	Ghana	Príncipe
Burundi	Guinea	Senegal
Cameroon	Guinea-Bissau	Seychelles
Cape Verde	Kenya	Sierra Leone
Central African	Lesotho	Somalia
Republic	Liberia	South Africa
Chad	Libya	Sudan
Comoros	Madagascar	Swaziland
Congo, Democratic	Malawi	Tanzania
Republic	Mali	Togo
Congo, Republic	Mauritania	Tunisia
Côte d'Ivoire	Mauritius	Uganda
Djibouti	Morocco	Zambia
Egypt	Mozambique	Zimbabwe
Equatorial Guinea	Namibia	

Organization

(April 2003)

COMMISSION

The Commission may only act with the agreement of the government of the country concerned. It is also empowered to make recommendations on any matter within its competence directly to the government of the member or associate member concerned, to governments admitted in a consultative capacity, and to the UN Specialized Agencies. The Commission is required to submit for prior consideration by ECOSOC any of its proposals for actions that would be likely to have important effects on the international economy.

CONFERENCE OF MINISTERS

The Conference, which meets every two years, is attended by ministers responsible for economic or financial affairs, planning and development of governments of member states, and is the main deliberative body of the Commission.

The Commission's responsibility to promote concerted action for the economic and social development of Africa is vested primarily in the Conference, which considers matters of general policy and the priorities to be assigned to the Commission's programmes, considers inter-African and international economic policy, and makes recommendations to member states in connection with such matters.

OTHER POLICY-MAKING BODIES

A Conference of Ministers of Finance and a Conference of Ministers responsible for economic and social development and planning meet in alternate years to formulate policy recommendations. Each is served by a committee of experts. Five intergovernmental committees of experts attached to the Sub-regional Development Centres (see below) meet annually and report to the Commission through a Technical Preparatory Committee of the Whole, which was established in 1979 to deal with matters submitted for the consideration of the Conference.

Seven other committees meet regularly to consider issues relating to the following policy areas: women and development; development information; sustainable development; human development and civil society; industry and private sector development; natural resources and science and technology; and regional co-operation and integration.

SECRETARIAT

The Secretariat provides the services necessary for the meeting of the Conference of Ministers and the meetings of the Commission's subsidiary bodies, carries out the resolutions and implements the programmes adopted there. It comprises an Office of the Executive Secretary, the African Centre for Gender and Development and the following eight divisions: Food Security and Sustainable Development; Development Management; Development Information Services; Regional Co-operation and Integration; Programme Planning, Finance and Evaluation; Economic and Social Policy; Human Resources and System Management; Conference and General Services.

Executive Secretary: KINGSLEY Y. AMOAKO (Ghana).

SUB-REGIONAL DEVELOPMENT CENTRES

Multinational Programming and Operational Centres (MULPOCs) were established, in 1977, to implement regional development programmes. In May 1997 the Commission decided to transform the MULPOCs into Sub-regional Development Centres (SRDCs) in order to enable member states to play a more effective role in the process of African integration and to facilitate the integration efforts of the other UN agencies active in the sub-regions. In addition, the SRDCs were to act as the operational arms of ECA at national and sub-regional levels: to ensure harmony between the objectives of sub-regional and regional programmes and those defined by the Commission; to provide advisory services; to facilitate sub-regional economic co-operation, integration and development; to collect and disseminate information; to stimulate policy dialogue; and to promote gender issues.

Central Africa: POB 836, Yaoundé, Cameroon; tel. 23-14-61; fax 23-31-85; e-mail casrdrc@un.cm; Dir ADDO IRO.

Eastern Africa: POB 4654, Kigali, Rwanda; tel. 86549; fax 86546; e-mail easrdc@rwandatel1.rwanda1.com; Dir MBAYE DIOUF.

Northern Africa: POB 316, Tangier, Morocco; tel. (39) 322345; fax (39) 340357; e-mail srdc-na@uneca.org; Dir ABDELOUAHAB REZIG.

Southern Africa: POB 30647, Lusaka, Zambia; tel. (1) 228503; fax (1) 236949; e-mail srdcsa-uneca@un-un.org; internet www.uneca-org.zm; Dir Dr ROBERT M. OKELLO.

West Africa: POB 744, Niamey, Niger; tel. 72-29-61; fax 72-28-94; e-mail srdcwest@eca.ne; Dir JEGGAN C. SENGHOR.

Activities

The Commission's activities are designed to encourage sustainable socio-economic development in Africa and to increase economic co-operation among African countries and between Africa and other parts of the world. The Secretariat has been guided in its efforts by major regional strategies including the Abuja Treaty establishing the African Economic Community signed under the aegis of the Organization of African Unity (OAU, now African Union—AU) in 1991, the UN System-wide Special Initiative on Africa (launched in 1996, see below), and the UN New Agenda for the Development of Africa covering the period 1991–2000. ECA was designated as the main body responsible for identifying and preparing programmes on economic and corporate governance under the New Partnership for Africa's Development (NEPAD), launched in October 2001 (q.v.). ECA's main programme areas for the period 1996–2001 were based on an Agenda for Action, which was announced by the OAU Council of Ministers in March 1995 and adopted by African heads of state in June, with the stated aim of 'relaunching Africa's economic and social development'. The five overall objectives were to facilitate economic and social policy analysis and implementation; to ensure food security and sustainable development; to strengthen development management; to harness information for development; and to promote regional co-operation and integration. In all its activities ECA aimed to promote the themes of capacity-building and of fostering leadership and the empowerment of women in Africa. ECA's African Centre for Gender and Development manages a Fund for African Women's Development to support capacity-building activities.

DEVELOPMENT INFORMATION SERVICES

The Development Information Services Division (DISD) has responsibility for co-ordinating the implementation of the Harnessing Information Technology for Africa project (in the context of the UN System-wide Special Initiative on Africa) and for implementing the African Information Society Initiative (AISI), a framework for creating an information and communications infrastructure; for overseeing quality enhancement and dissemination of statistical databases; for improving access to information by means of enhanced library and documentation services and output; and for strengthening geo-information systems for sustainable development. In addition, ECA encourages member governments to liberalize the telecommunications sector and stimulate imports of computers in order to enable the expansion of information technology throughout Africa. ECA manages the Information Technology Centre for Africa, based in Addis Ababa.

Regional statistical development activities are managed through the Co-ordinating Committee on African Statistical Development (CASD, established in 1992). The CASD facilitates the harmonization of statistical systems and methodologies at regional and national level; establishes mechanisms for the continuous exchange of information between governments, national agencies and regional and sub-regional bodies, and all bilateral and multilateral agencies; identifies and proposes new lines of action; and informs the Conference of African Planners, Statisticians and Population and Information Specialists on the progress of the Addis Ababa Plan of Action for Statistical Development in the 1990s (adopted in 1992). In May 1997 five task forces were established to undertake the CASD's activities; these covered the following areas: improving e-mail connectivity; monitoring the implementation of the Addis Ababa Plan of Action; strengthening statistical training programme for Africa (STPA) centres; assisting with the formation of census and household survey data service centres in up to five pilot countries, and with the establishment of a similar regional ECA service centre; and establishing live databases, comprising core macro and sectoral statistical indicators, initially as a pilot project, with eventual links to a regional database facility.

ECA assists its member states in (i) population data collection and data processing; (ii) analysis of demographic data obtained from censuses or surveys; (iii) training demographers at the Regional Institute for Population Studies (RIPS) in Accra, Ghana, and at the Institut de formation et de recherche démographiques (IFORD) in Yaoundé, Cameroon; (iv) formulation of population policies and integrating population variables in development planning, through advisory missions and through the organization of national seminars on population and development; and (v) dissemination of demographic information. The strengthening of national population policies was an important element of ECA's objective of ensuring food security in African countries.

In August 2000 ECA launched the Africa Knowledge Networks Forum (AKNF). The Forum, to be convened on an annual basis under ECA auspices, was to facilitate co-operation in information-sharing and research between professional research and development networks, and also between these and policy-makers, educators, civil society organizations and the private sector. It was to provide technical support to the ADF process (see below).

DEVELOPMENT MANAGEMENT

ECA aims to assist governments, public corporations, universities and the private sector in improving their financial management; strengthening policy-making and analytical capacities; adopting measures to redress skill shortages; enhancing human resources development and utilization; and promoting social development through programmes focusing on youth, people with disabilities and the elderly. The Secretariat organizes training workshops, seminars and conferences at national, subregional and regional levels for ministers, public administrators and senior policy-makers, as well as for private and non-governmental organizations. ECA aims to increase the participation of women in economic development and incorporates this objective into its administrative activities and work programmes.

Following the failure to implement many of the proposals under the UN Industrial Development Decade for Africa (IDDA, 1980–90) and the UN Programme of Action for African Economic Recovery and Development (1986–90), a second IDDA was adopted by the Conference of African Ministers of Industry in July 1991. The main objectives of IDDA II (1993–2003) included the consolidation and rehabilitation of existing industries, the expansion of new investments, and the promotion of small-scale industries and technological capabilities. In June 1996 a conference, organized by ECA, was held in Accra, Ghana, with the aim of reviving private investment in Africa in order to stimulate the private sector and promote future economic development. In October 1999 the first African Development Forum (ADF) was held in Addis Ababa, Ethiopia. The ADF process was initiated by ECA to formulate an agenda for effective, sustainable development in African countries through dialogue and partnership between governments, academics, the private sector, donor agencies etc. It was intended that the process would focus towards an annual meeting concerned with a specific development issue. The first Forum was convened on the theme 'The Challenge to Africa of Globalization and the Information Age'. It reviewed the AISI (see above) and formulated country action plans and work programmes. The four issues addressed were: strengthening Africa's information infrastructure; Africa and the information economy; information and communication technologies for improved governance; and democratizing access to the information society. The second ADF, convened in October 2000, in Addis Ababa, on the theme 'AIDS: the Greatest Leadership Challenge', addressed the impact on Africa of the HIV/AIDS epidemic and issued a Consensus and Plan of Action. The third ADF, held in March 2002, addressed the theme 'Defining Priorities for Regional Integration'.

In 1997 ECA hosted the first of a series of meetings on good governance, in the context of the UN System-wide Special Initiative on Africa. The second African Governance Forum (AGF II) was held in Accra, Ghana, in June 1998. The Forum focused on accountability and transparency, which participants agreed were essential elements in promoting development in Africa and should involve commitment from both governments and civil organizations. AGF III was convened in June 1999 in Bamako, Mali, to consider issues relating to conflict prevention, management and governance. The fourth AGF, which took place in Kampala, Uganda, in September 2000, focused on parliamentary processes and their role in consolidating good governance on the continent. AGF V, addressing the role of local government in reducing poverty in Africa, was held in Maputo, Mozambique, in May 2002.

ECONOMIC AND SOCIAL POLICY

The Economic and Social Policy division concentrates on the following areas: economic policy analysis, trade and debt, social policy and poverty analysis, and the co-ordination and monitoring of special issues and programmes. Monitoring economic and social trends in the African region and studying the development problems concerning it are among the fundamental tasks of the Commission, while the special issues programme updates legislative bodies regarding the progress made in the implementation of initiatives affecting the continent. Every year the Commission publishes the *Survey of Economic and Social Conditions in Africa* and the *Economic Report on Africa*.

The Commission gives assistance to governments in general economic analysis, fiscal, financial and monetary management, trade liberalization, regional integration and planning. ECA's work on economic planning has been broadened in recent years, in order to give more emphasis to macro-economic management in a mixed economy approach: a project is being undertaken to develop short-term forecasting and policy models to support economic management. The Commission has also undertaken a major study of the informal sector in African countries. Special assistance is given to least-developed, land-locked and island countries which have a much lower income level than other countries and which are faced with heavier constraints. Studies are also undertaken to assist longer-term planning.

In May 1994 ECA ministers of economic and social development and of planning, meeting in Addis Ababa, adopted a *Framework Agenda for Building and Utilizing Critical Capacities in Africa*. The agenda aimed to identify new priority areas to stimulate development by, for example, strengthening management structures, a more efficient use of a country's physical infrastructure and by expanding processing or manufacturing facilities.

ECA aims to strengthen African participation in international negotiations. To this end, assistance has been provided to member states in the ongoing multilateral trade negotiations under the World Trade Organization; in the annual conferences of the IMF and the World Bank; in negotiations with the EU; and in meetings related to economic co-operation among developing countries. Studies have been prepared on problems and prospects likely to arise for the African region from the implementation of the Common Fund for Commodities and the Generalized System of Trade Preferences (both supervised by UNCTAD); the impacts of exchange-rate fluctuations on the economies of African countries; and on the long-term implications of different debt arrangements for African economies. ECA assists individual member states by undertaking studies on domestic trade, expansion of intra-African trade, trans-national corporations, integration of women in trade and development, and strengthening the capacities of state-trading organizations. ECA encourages the diversification of production, the liberalization of cross-border trade and the expansion of domestic trade structures, within regional economic groupings, in order to promote intra-African trade. ECA also helps to organize regional and 'All-Africa' trade fairs.

In March/April 1997 the Conference of African Ministers of Finance, meeting in Addis Ababa, reviewed a new initiative of the World Bank and IMF to assist the world's most heavily indebted poor countries (numbering 42 at mid-2002, of which 33 were in sub-Saharan Africa). While the Conference recognized the importance of the involvement of multilateral institutions in assisting African economies to achieve a sustainable level of development, it criticized aspects of the structural adjustment programmes imposed by the institutions and advocated more flexible criteria to determine eligibility for the new scheme.

ECA aims to improve the socio-economic prospects of women through the promotion of equal access to resources and opportunities and equal participation in decision-making.

FOOD SECURITY AND SUSTAINABLE DEVELOPMENT

In the early 1990s reports were compiled on the development, implementation and sound management of environmental programmes at national, sub-regional and regional levels. ECA members adopted a common African position for the UN Conference on Environment and Development, held in June 1992. In 1995 ECA published its first comprehensive report and statistical survey of human development issues in African countries. The *Human Development in Africa Report*, which was to be published every two years, aimed to demonstrate levels of development attained, particularly in the education and child health sectors, to identify areas of concern and to encourage further action by policy-makers and development experts. ECA is actively involved in the promotion of food security in African countries through raising awareness of the relationship between population, food security, the environment and sustainable development; encouraging the advancement of science and technology in member states; and providing policy analysis support and technical advisory services.

PROGRAMME PLANNING, FINANCE AND EVALUATION

ECA provides guidance in the formulation of policies towards the achievement of Africa's development objectives to the policy-making organs of the UN and the AU. It contributes to the work of the General Assembly and other specialized agencies by providing an African perspective in the preparation of development strategies. In March 1996 the UN announced its System-wide Special Initiative on Africa to mobilize resources and to implement a series of political and economic development objectives over a 10-year period. ECA's Executive Secretary is the Co-Chairperson, with the Administrator of the UNDP, of the Steering Committee for the Initiative.

REGIONAL CO-OPERATION AND INTEGRATION

The Regional Co-operation and Integration Division administers the transport and communications and mineral and energy sectors, in addition to its activities concerning the Sub-regional Development Centres (SRDCs—see above), the integrated development of transboundary water resources, and facilitating and enhancing the process of regional economic integration. In June 2002 ECA issued its first *Annual Report on Regional Integration*.

ECA was appointed lead agency for the second United Nations Transport and Communications Decade in Africa (UNTACDA II), covering the period 1991–2000. The principal aim of UNTACDA II was the establishment of an efficient, integrated transport and communications system in Africa. The specific objectives of the programme included: (i) the removal of physical and non-physical barriers to intra-African trade and travel, and improvement in the road transport sector; (ii) improvement in the efficiency and financial viability of railways; (iii) development of Africa's shipping capacity and improvement in the performance of Africa's ports; (iv) development of integrated transport systems for each lake and river basin; (v) improvement of integration of all modes of transport in order to carry cargo in one chain of transport smoothly; (vi) integration of African airlines, and restructuring of civil aviation and airport management authorities; (vii) improvement in the quality and availability of transport in urban areas; (viii) development of integrated regional telecommunications networks; (ix) development of broadcasting services, with the aim of supporting socio-economic development; and (x) expansion of Africa's postal network. In April 2002 African ministers of transport and communications met to assess the outcome of UNTACDA II. ECA and the World Bank jointly co-ordinate the Sub-Saharan Africa Transport Policy Program (SSATP), established in 1987, which aims to facilitate policy development and related capacity-building in the continent's transport sector. The regional Road Management Initiative (RMI) under the SSATP seeks to encourage a partnership between the public and private sectors to manage and maintain road infrastructure more efficiently and thus to improve country-wide communications and transportation activities. In 2002 17 countries were particpating in the RMI. The Rural Travel and Transport Programme, another component of the SSATP, had 18 participating countries in 2002. The Urban Mobility component aims to improve sub-Saharan African urban transport services, while the Trade and Transport component aims to enhance the international competitiveness of regional economies through the establishment of more cost-effective services for shippers. The Railway Restructuring element focuses on the provision of financially sustainable railway enterprises. The third African road safety congress was held in April 1997, in Pretoria, South Africa. The congress, which was jointly organized by ECA and the OECD, aimed to increase awareness of the need to adopt an integrated approach to road safety problems. Other transport priorities have included consideration of a new African air transport policy, workshops on port restructuring, and regional and country analyses of transport trends and reforms.

The Fourth Regional Conference on the Development and Utilization of Mineral Resources in Africa, held in March 1991, adopted an action plan that included the formulation of national mineral exploitation policies; and the promotion of the gemstone industry, small-scale mining and the iron and steel industry. ECA supports the Southern African Mineral Resources Development Centre in Dar-es-Salaam, Tanzania, and the Central African Mineral Development Centre in Brazzaville, Republic of the Congo, which provide advisory and laboratory services to their respective member states.

ECA's Energy Programme provides assistance to member states in the development of indigenous energy resources and the formulation of energy policies to extricate member states from continued energy crises. In 1997 ECA strengthened co-operation with the World Energy Council and agreed to help implement the Council's African Energy Programme.

ECA assists member states in the assessment and use of water resources and the development of river and lake basins common to more than one country. ECA encourages co-operation between countries with regard to water issues and collaborates with other UN agencies and regional organizations to promote technical and economic co-operation in this area. ECA has been particularly active in efforts to promote the integrated development of the water resources of the Zambezi river basin and of Lake Victoria.

In all of its activities ECA aims to strengthen institutional capacities in order to support the process of regional integration, and aims to assist countries to implement existing co-operative agreements, for example by promoting the harmonization of macroeconomic and taxation policies and the removal of non-tariff barriers to trade.

ASSOCIATED BODY

Information Technology Centre for Africa—ITCA: POB 3001, Addis Ababa, Ethiopia; tel. (1) 314520; fax (1) 515829; e-mail mfaye@uneca.org; internet www.uneca.org/itca; aims to strengthen the continent's communications infrastructure and promote the use of information and communications technologies in planning and policy-making; stages exhibitions and provides training facilities.

Finance

For the two-year period 2000–01 ECA's regular budget, an appropriation from the UN budget, was an estimated US $78.5m.

Publications

Africa in Figures.
African Statistical Yearbook.
African Trade Bulletin (2 a year).

African Women's Report (annually).
Africa's Population and Development Bulletin.
Annual Report on Regional Integration.
Compendium of Intra-African and Related Foreign Trade Statistics.
Directory of African Statisticians (every 2 years).
ECA Development Policy Review.
ECA Environment Newsletter (3 a year).
ECANews (monthly).
Economic Report on Africa (annually).
Focus on African Industry (2 a year).
GenderNet (annually).
Human Development in Africa Report (every 2 years).
Human Rights Education.
Report of the Executive Secretary (every 2 years).
SSATP Progress Report (irregular).
Survey of Economic and Social Conditions in Africa (annually).
Country reports, policy and discussion papers, reports of conferences and meetings, training series, working paper series.

Economic and Social Commission for Western Asia—ESCWA

Address: Riad es-Solh Sq., POB 11-8575, Beirut, Lebanon.
Telephone: (1) 981301; **fax:** (1) 981510; **e-mail:** unescwa@escwa.org.lb; **internet:** www.escwa.org.lb.

The UN Economic Commission for Western Asia was established in 1974 by a resolution of the UN Economic and Social Council (ECOSOC), to provide facilities of a wider scope for those countries previously served by the UN Economic and Social Office in Beirut (UNESOB). The name 'Economic and Social Commission for Western Asia' (ESCWA) was adopted in 1985.

MEMBERS

Bahrain	Palestine
Egypt	Qatar
Iraq	Saudi Arabia
Jordan	Syria
Kuwait	United Arab Emirates
Lebanon	Yemen
Oman	

Organization

(April 2003)

COMMISSION

The sessions of the Commission (held every two years) are attended by delegates from member states. Representatives of UN bodies and specialized agencies, regional organizations, other UN member states, and non-governmental organizations having consultative status with ECOSOC may attend as observers.

PREPARATORY COMMITTEE

The Committee, formerly the Technical Committee, has the task of reviewing programming issues and presenting recommendations in that regard to the sessions of the Commission. It is the principal subsidiary body of the Commission and functions as its policy-making structure. Six specialized inter-governmental committees have been established to consider specific areas of activity, to report on these to the Preparatory Committee and to assist the Committee in formulating ESCWA's medium-term work programmes.

Statistics Committee: established in 1992; meets every two years.
Committee on Social Development: established in 1994; meets every two years.
Committee on Energy: established in 1995; meets every two years.
Committee on Water Resources: established in 1995; meets every two years.
Committee on Transport: established in 1997; meets annually.
Committee on Liberalization of Foreign Trade and Economic Globalization: established in 1997; meets every two years.

In addition, a Consultative Committee on Scientific Technological Development and Technological Innovation was established in 2001, and was to meet every two years, comprising experts from public institutions, the private sector, civil society and research centres.

SECRETARIAT

The Secretariat comprises an Executive Secretary, a Deputy Executive Secretary, a Senior Adviser and Secretary of the Commission, an Information Services Unit and divisions for administrative services and programme planning and technical co-operation. ESCWA's technical and substantive activities are undertaken by the following divisions: energy, natural resources and environment; social development issues and policies; economic development issues and policies; sectoral issues and policies; and statistics. The Secretariat administers the UN Regional Co-ordination Group for the ESCWA region, which was established in March 1999.
Executive Secretary: MERVAT M. TALLAWY (Egypt).

Activities

ESCWA is responsible for proposing policies and actions to support development and to further economic co-operation and integration in western Asia. ESCWA undertakes or sponsors studies of economic social and development issues of the region, collects and disseminates information, and provides advisory services to member states in various fields of economic and social development. It also organizes conferences and intergovernmental and export group meetings and sponsors training workshops and seminars.

Much of ESCWA's work is carried out in co-operation with other UN bodies, as well as with other international and regional organizations, for example the League of Arab States (q.v.) the Co-operation Council for the Arab States of the Gulf (GCC, q.v.) and the Organization of the Islamic Conference (OIC, q.v.). In April 2001 ESCWA convened an inaugural consultative meeting with representatives of more than 100 non-governmental organizations, in order to strengthen co-operation with civil society.

In late 2001 ESCWA initiated a pilot scheme to support the socio-economic development of local communities in southern Lebanon. A project to upgrade skills and the capacities of small businesses commenced in April 2002, within the framework of the so-called ESCWA Assistance for Southern Lebanon (EASL) programme, while two vocational training centres became operational in mid-2002.

ESCWA works within the framework of medium-term plans, which are divided into two-year programmes of action and priorities. The Commission restructured its work programme in the mid-1990s, which focused ESCWA activities from 15 to five sub-programmes. A further reorganization of the sub-programmes was implemented in 1997 to provide the framework for activities in the medium-term period 1998–2001. In May 2001 the Commission approved a work programme for 2002–03 on the basis of the existing sub-programme structure.

MANAGEMENT OF NATURAL RESOURCES AND ENVIRONMENT

The main objective of the sub-programme is to promote regional co-ordination and co-operation in the management of natural resources, in particular water resources and energy, and the protection of the environment. Work in this area aims to counter the problem of an increasing shortage of freshwater resources and deterioration in water quality resulting from population growth, agricultural land-use and socio-economic development, by supporting measures for more rational use and conservation of water resources, and by promoting public awareness and community participation in water and environmental protection projects. In addition, ESCWA assists governments in the formulation and implementation of capacity-building programmes and the development of surface and ground-water resources. In 2002–03 ESCWA aimed to promote greater co-operation among member and non-member countries in the management and use of shared water resources.

ESCWA supports co-operation in the establishment of electricity distribution and supply networks throughout the region and promotes the use of alternative sources of energy and the development of new and renewable energy technologies. Similarly, ESCWA promotes the application of environmentally sound technologies in order to achieve sustainable development, as well as measures to recycle resources, minimize waste and reduce the environmental impact of transport operations and energy use. Under the sub-programme ESCWA collaborates with national, regional and international organizations in monitoring and reporting on emerging environmental issues and to pursue implementation of Agenda 21, which was adopted at the June 1992 UN Conference on Environment and Development, with particular regard to land and water resource management and conservation.

IMPROVEMENT OF THE QUALITY OF LIFE

ESCWA's key areas of activity in this sub-programme are population, sustainable human development, the advancement of women and gender equality, and human settlements. The sub-programme was designed to pursue the implementation of recommendations relevant to the region of the four UN world conferences held on these themes during the mid-1990s.

ESCWA's objectives with regard to population are to increase awareness and understanding of links between population factors and poverty, human rights and the environment, and to strengthen the capacities of member states to analyse and assess demographic trends and migration. In the area of human development ESCWA aims to further the alleviation of poverty and to generate a sustainable approach to development through, for example, greater involvement of community groups in decision-making and projects to strengthen production and income-generating capabilities. The sub-programme incorporates activities to ensure all gender-related recommendations of the four world conferences could be pursued in the region, including support for the role of the family and assistance to organizations for monitoring and promoting the advancement of women. With regard to human settlements, the objectives of the sub-programme are to monitor and identify problems resulting from rapid urbanization and social change, to promote understanding and awareness of the problems and needs of human settlements, and to strengthen the capacity of governments in the region in formulating appropriate policies and strategies for sustainable human settlement development. In 2002–03 ESCWA's priorities were to develop and promote social policies and strategies with the emphasis on family cohesion, the advancement of women, poverty reduction, disabled and ageing populations, population dynamics, and the security of tenure. It also aimed to promote transparent and accountable governance, based on greater participation of civil society. In February 2002 ESCWA organized a ministerial preparatory meeting for the World Assembly on Ageing, which was convened, in Madrid, Spain, in April. The meeting adopted an Arab Plan on the Elderly up to the Year 2012.

ECONOMIC DEVELOPMENT AND GLOBAL CHANGES

During the period 2002–03 ESCWA aimed to assist member states to achieve sustainable economic development in the region and to integrate more fully into the world economy. Under the sub-programme ESCWA aimed to assist member countries to identify the challenges and opportunities created by the World Trade Organ-

ization (WTO) and other regional groupings, in particular with regard to free trade areas, the liberalization and management of financial markets, and the promotion of foreign direct investment. It also intended to improve the analysis of economic developments and the formulation of economic management policies, as well as to provide guidance on alternative development strategies to reduce the dominance of the petroleum sector. In June 2002 ESCWA organized a workshop for the business community and an expert group meeting to discuss the outcome of the WTO ministerial conference, which was held in Doha, Qatar, in November 2001, and future trade negotiations under the agreed Development Agenda.

CO-ORDINATION OF POLICIES AND HARMONIZATION OF NORMS AND REGULATIONS FOR SECTORAL DEVELOPMENT

This sub-programme is concerned with the harmonization of standards throughout the region in the areas of transport, industry, agriculture and technology. ESCWA aims to promote co-operation among member states in transport and infrastructure policies and greater uniformity of safety and legal standards, the latter with a view to facilitating border crossings between countries in the region. ESCWA, similarly, aims to assist local industries to meet regional and international standards and regulations, as well as to improve the competitiveness of industries through the development of skills and policies and greater co-operation with other national and regional support institutions. In May 2001 ESCWA member states adopted an Agreement on International Transport System in the Arab Mashreq, which had been formulated by the Secretariat with the aim of establishing a unified transportation network linking all countries in the region. In 2002–03 ESCWA envisaged pursuing activities to promote the harmonization of norms and standards for sustainable development within the region. ESCWA also aimed to provide support for the co-ordination of sectoral policies, in particular with regard to poverty-related issues, and to develop and disseminate related statistics, information and electronic data.

CO-ORDINATION AND HARMONIZATION OF STATISTICS AND INFORMATION DEVELOPMENT

In the medium-term ESCWA intended to develop the statistical systems of member states in order to improve the relevance and accuracy of economic and social data, and to implement measures to make the information more accessible to planners and researchers. Priorities for the biennium 2002–03 included activities to improve human and institutional capacities, in particular in the use of statistical tools for data analysis, to expand the adoption and implementation of international statistical methods, and to promote co-operation to further the regional harmonization of statistics.

Finance

ESCWA's share of the UN budget for the two years 2000–01 was US $50.3m., compared with $49.5m. for the previous biennium.

Publications

All publications are annual, unless otherwise indicated.
Agriculture and Development in Western Asia.
ESCWA Update (monthly).
External Trade Bulletin of the ESCWA Region.
National Accounts Studies of the ESCWA Region.
Population Bulletin of the ESCWA Region.
Prices and Financial Statistics in the ESCWA Region.
Socio-economic Data Sheet (every 2 years).
Statistical Abstract of the ESCWA Region.
Survey of Economic and Social Developments in the ESCWA Region.
Transport Bulletin.
Weekly News.

OTHER UNITED NATIONS BODIES

Office for the Co-ordination of Humanitarian Affairs— OCHA

Address: United Nations Plaza, New York, NY 10017, USA.
Telephone: (212) 963-1234; **fax:** (212) 963-1312; **e-mail:** ochany@ un.org; **internet:** www.reliefweb.int/ocha_ol/.

OCHA was established in January 1998 as part of the UN Secretariat, with a mandate to co-ordinate international humanitarian assistance and to provide policy and other advice on humanitarian issues. It replaced the Department of Humanitarian Affairs, established in 1992.

Organization

(April 2003)

OCHA has headquarters in New York, and in Geneva, Switzerland, and it maintains a field presence in 34 locations in Africa, Europe and Asia. In 2002 there were 964 staff posts, one-quarter of which were based at the headquarters.

Under Secretary-General for Humanitarian Affairs and Emergency Relief Co-ordinator: KENZO OSHIMA (Japan).

Activities

OCHA's mandate is to work with UN agencies, governments, intergovernmental humanitarian organizations and non-governmental organizations to ensure that a prompt, co-ordinated and effective response is provided to complex emergencies and natural disasters. OCHA monitors developments throughout the world and undertakes contingency planning. It liaises with UN Resident Co-ordinators, Humanitarian Co-ordinators and country teams, and reaches agreement with other UN bodies regarding the division of responsibilities, which may include field missions to assess requirements, organizing Consolidated Inter-agency Appeals for financial assistance (see below), and mobilizing other resources. The Emergency Relief Co-ordinator is the principal adviser to the UN Secretary-General on humanitarian issues. He chairs the Inter-Agency Standing Committee (IASC), which co-ordinates and administers the international response to humanitarian disasters and the development of relevant policies. The Co-ordinator also acts as Convener of the Executive Committee for Humanitarian Affairs, which provides a forum for humanitarian agencies, as well as the political and peace-keeping departments of the UN Secretariat, to exchange information on emergency situations and humanitarian issues. In 2001 OCHA started to implement the recommendations of an internal review process aimed at strengthening its three core functions of co-ordination, advocacy and policy development. During that year a new strategic planning process was also initiated.

OCHA maintains internet-based Integrated Regional Information Networks (IRINs). The first IRIN was created in 1995 in Nairobi, Kenya, to disseminate information on the humanitarian situation in central and east Africa. Additional IRINs have since been established in Abidjan, Côte d'Ivoire (covering west Africa), Johannesburg, South Africa (for southern Africa) and Islamabad, Pakistan (for central Asia). A complementary service, ReliefWeb, launched in 1996, monitors crises and publishes information on the internet.

OCHA's Humanitarian Emergency and Response Co-ordination branches (based, respectively, at the New York and Geneva headquarters) co-operate in mobilizing and co-ordinating international emergency assistance. The Response Co-ordination branch facilitates and participates in situation assessment missions; prepares briefings and issues Situation Reports to inform the international community on ongoing humanitarian crises, the type and level of assistance required and action being undertaken; and provides administrative support to OCHA field offices. The Emergency Services branch, based at the Geneva headquarters, undertakes disaster-preparedness activities and manages international rapid response missions in the field. UN Disaster Assessment and Co-ordination (UNDAC) teams, established by OCHA with the aid of donor governments, are available for immediate deployment to help to determine requirements and to co-ordinate assistance in those countries affected by disasters, for example by establishing reliable telecommunications and securing other logistical support. OCHA maintains a Central Register of Disaster Management Capacities, which may be available for international assistance. In addition, a stockpile of emergency equipment and supplies is maintained at the UN Humanitarian Response Depot in Brindisi, Italy, ready for immediate dispatch. A joint OCHA/UNEP Environment Unit mobilizes and co-ordinates international assistance in environmental emergency situations. In January 2002 a Unit on Internal Displacement was established within OCHA with the aim of strengthening international assistance for people displaced from their homes by civil conflict and natural disasters.

OCHA facilitates the Consolidated Inter-agency Appeal Process (CAP), which aims to organize a co-ordinated response to resource mobilization following humanitarian crises. Under guide-lines adopted by the IASC in 1994, the CAP was clearly defined as a programming mechanism rather than simply an appeal process. Technical guide-lines adopted in 1999 established a framework for developing a Common Humanitarian Action Plan (CHAP) to address a crisis, co-ordinating the relevant inter-agency appeal (on the basis of the CHAP), and preparing strategic monitoring reports. CAP appeals for 2003, seeking an estimated US $3,000m., were issued in November 2002; they concerned complex humanitarian crises affecting some 50m. people in 30 countries and regions. A Central Emergency Revolving Fund (CERF), under the authority of the Emergency Relief Co-ordinator, enables humanitarian agencies to provide an immediate response to emergencies, before donor contributions become available. Agencies borrowing from the fund are required to reimburse the amount loaned within a certain period of time, which is not to exceed one year.

Finance

OCHA's budgetary requirements for 2002 were an estimated US $70m., of which about $9m. was to be provided from the regular budget of the UN.

Publication

OCHA News (weekly).

Office for Drug Control and Crime Prevention—ODCCP

Address: Vienna International Centre, POB 500, A-1400 Vienna, Austria.
Telephone: (1) 26060-0; **fax:** (1) 26060-5866; **e-mail:** odccp@odccp.org; **internet:** www.odccp.org/odccp/index.html.

The Office was established in November 1997 to strengthen the UN's integrated approach to issues relating to drug control, crime prevention and international terrorism. It comprises two principal components: the United Nations International Drug Control Programme and the Centre for International Crime Prevention, both headed by the ODCCP Executive Director.

In March 1999 a new UN Global Programme against Money Laundering (GPML) was established within the framework of the ODCCP to assist governments with formulating legislation against money laundering and establishing and maintaining appropriate frameworks to counter the problem. GPML activities include the provision of technical assistance, training, and the collection, research and analysis of crime data. The Programme, in collaboration with other governmental organizations, law enforcement agencies and academic institutions, co-ordinates the International Money Laundering Information Network (IMoLIN), an internet-based information resource (accessible at www.imolin.org). IMoLIN incorporates the Anti-Money Laundering International Database (a comprehensive database on money-laundering legislation throughout the world that constituted a key element in ODCCP activities in support of the elaboration of the International Convention against Transnational Organized Crime—see below). At the first GPML Forum, held in the Cayman Islands in March 2000, the governments of 31 participating 'offshore' financial centres agreed in principle to adopt internationally-accepted standards of financial regulation and measures against money laundering.

The ODCCP's Terrorism Prevention Branch, established in 1999, researches trends in terrorist activity and assists countries with improving their capabilities to investigate and prevent acts of terrorism. The Branch promotes international co-operation in combating the problem, is compiling a database on global terrorism, and has initiated a study into the connections between terrorist activity and other forms of crime.

Executive Director: ANTONIO MARIA COSTA (Italy).

UNITED NATIONS INTERNATIONAL DRUG CONTROL PROGRAMME—UNDCP

UNDCP was established in 1991 to co-ordinate the activities of all UN specialized agencies and programmes in matters of international drug control. The structures of the former Division of Narcotic Drugs, the UN Fund for Drug Abuse Control and the secretariat of the International Narcotics Control Board (see below) were integrated into the new body. Accordingly, UNDCP became the focal point for promoting the UN Decade Against Drug Abuse (1991–2000) and for assisting member states to implement the Global Programme of Action that was adopted by the UN General Assembly in 1990 with the objective of achieving an international society free of illicit drugs and drug abuse. At a special summit meeting of the General Assembly, held in June 1998, heads of state and representatives of some 150 countries adopted a global strategy, formulated on the basis of UNDCP proposals, to reduce significantly the production of and demand for illicit substances by 2008. UNDCP subsequently launched the Global Assessment Programme on Drug Abuse (GAP), which aimed to establish one global and nine regional drug abuse data systems to collect and evaluate data on the extent of and patterns of illegal substance abuse. In the context of drug supply reduction UNDCP's Illicit Crop Monitoring Programme (ICMP) supports the development of comprehensive monitoring systems in the six countries believed to account for some 90% of illicit opium and coca production (Afghanistan, Bolivia, Colombia, Laos, Myanmar and Peru); a global monitoring component of the ICMP provides technical assistance to the national monitoring systems. The ICMP is facilitated by a combination of satellite sensing (with the assistance of the European Space Agency, q.v.), aerial surveillance and ground-level surveys, which provide a reliable collection and analysis mechanism for data on the production of illicit substances. UNDCP's Alternative Development Programme supports projects to create alternative sources of income for farmers economically dependent on the production of illicit narcotic crops. UNDCP aims to suppress trafficking in these substances and supports efforts to enhance regional and cross-border co-operation in implementing law enforcement initiatives. UNDCP serves as an international centre of expertise and information on drug abuse control, with the capacity to provide legal and technical assistance in relevant areas of concern. It supports governments in efforts to strengthen their institutional capacities for drug control (for example, drug identification and drug law enforcement training) and to prepare and implement national drug control 'action plans'.

UNDCP's approach to reducing demand for illicit drugs combines strategies in the areas of prevention, treatment and rehabilitation. It sponsors activities to generate public awareness of the harmful effects of drug abuse, for example through its Global Youth Network project, which was established in 1998 with the aim of involving young people in prevention activities, and through the system of goodwill ambassadors associated with its 'Sports Against Drugs' campaign. UNDCP works with governments, as well as non-governmental and private organizations and local community partners, in the detection, treatment, rehabilitation and social reintegration of drug addicts. It also undertakes research to monitor the drugs problem: for example, assessing the characteristics of drug-takers and the substances being used in order to help identify people at risk of becoming drug-takers and to enhance the effectiveness of national programmes to address the issue (see also the GAP, above).

UNDCP promotes implementation of the following major treaties which govern the international drug control system: the Single Convention on Narcotic Drugs (1961) and a Protocol amending the Convention (1972); the Convention on Psychotropic Substances (1971); and the UN Convention against Illicit Traffic in Narcotic Drugs and Psychotropic Substances (1988). Among other important

provisions, these treaties aim to restrict severely the production of narcotic drugs, while ensuring an adequate supply for medical and scientific purposes, to prevent profits obtained from the illegal sale of drugs being diverted into legal usage and to secure the extradition of drug-traffickers and the transfer of proceedings for criminal prosecution. UNDCP assists countries to adapt their national legislation and drug policies to facilitate their compliance with these conventions and to enhance co-ordinated inter-governmental efforts to control the movement of narcotic drugs. UNDCP services meetings of the International Narcotics Control Board, an independent body responsible for promoting and monitoring government compliance with the provisions of the drug control treaties, and of the Commission on Narcotic Drugs, which, as a functional committee of ECOSOC (q.v.), is the main policy-making organ within the UN system on issues relating to international drug abuse control.

UNDCP co-operates closely with other international, regional and non-governmental organizations and maintains dialogue with agencies advocating drug abuse control. It is a co-sponsor, with ILO, UNDP, UNESCO, UNFPA, UNICEF, WHO and the World Bank of the Joint UN Programme on HIV/AIDS (UNAIDS), which was established on 1 January 1996. UNDCP's participation is in recognition of the importance of international drug control efforts in preventing the spread of HIV/AIDS.

Finance

The UNDCP Fund receives an allocation from the regular budget of the UN, although voluntary contributions from member states and private organizations represent the majority (about 90%) of its resources. The proposed budget for the two-year period 2002–03 amounted to US $168.4m., including programme expenditure of $130.0m.

Publications

Bulletin on Narcotics (quarterly).

Global Illicit Drug Trends.

ODCCP Update (quarterly).

Technical Series.

World Drug Report.

CENTRE FOR INTERNATIONAL CRIME PREVENTION—CICP

The CICP, established in 1997, is the UN body responsible for crime prevention, criminal justice and criminal law reform. It oversees the application of international standards and norms relating to these areas, for example the Minimum Rules for the Treatment of Prisoners, Conventions against Torture, and Other Cruel, Inhuman or Degrading Treatment or Punishment, and Safeguards Guaranteeing the Protection of the Rights of Those Facing the Death Penalty. The Centre provides member states with technical assistance to strengthen national capacities to establish appropriate legal and criminal justice systems and to combat transnational organized crime (see below). The CICP supports the Commission on Crime Prevention and Criminal Justice, a functional committee of ECOSOC, which provides guidance in developing global anti-crime policies. In 1999 the CICP initiated three new programmes: a Global Programme against Corruption, a Global Programme against Trafficking in Human Beings (trafficking in human beings for sexual exploitation or forced labour is regarded as the fastest-growing area of international organized crime), and a Global Programme on Organized Crime, which aimed to analyse emerging transnational criminal organizations and assist countries to formulate strategies to combat the problem. The CICP supported member states in the preparation of the UN Convention against Transnational Organized Crime, which was adopted by the General Assembly in August 2000; the so-called Palermo Convention, with two additional Protocols on trafficking in human beings and the smuggling of migrants, was opened for signature in December at a UN conference on combating organized crime held in Sicily, Italy. By November 2002 the Convention had been signed by 143 states and ratified by 23. In January of that year the CICP participated in a preparatory meeting on the formulation of a UN Convention against Corruption.

The CICP promotes research and undertakes studies of new forms of crime prevention, in collaboration with the UN Interregional Crime and Justice Research Institute (UNICRI, q.v.). It also maintains a UN Crime and Justice Information Network database (UNCJIN), which provides information on national crime statistics, publications and links to other relevant intergovernmental agencies and research and academic institutes.

Following the major terrorist attacks perpetrated against targets in the USA in September 2001 several UN member states urged that the CICP and the ODCCP's Terrorism Prevention Branch be strengthened to combat potential future global terrorist threats.

Finance

The Centre has an annual administrative budget of US $3m., and approximately $3m. is budgeted annually for projects.

Publications

Forum on Crime and Society.
Global Report on Crime and Justice.

The United Nations and Juvenile Justice: A Guide to International Standards and Best Practices.

Office of the United Nations High Commissioner for Human Rights—OHCHR

Address: Palais Wilson, 52 rue de Paquis, 1201 Geneva, Switzerland.
Telephone: (22) 9179290; **fax:** (22) 9179022; **e-mail:** scrt.hchr@unog.ch; **internet:** www.unhchr.ch.

The Office is a body of the UN Secretariat and is the focal point for UN human rights activities. Since September 1997 it has incorporated the Centre for Human Rights.

Organization

(April 2003)

HIGH COMMISSIONER

In December 1993 the UN General Assembly decided to establish the position of a United Nations High Commissioner for Human Rights (UNHCHR) following a recommendation of the World Conference on Human Rights, held in Vienna, Austria, in June of that year. The High Commissioner, who is the UN official with principal responsibility for UN human rights activities, is appointed by the UN Secretary-General, with the approval of the General Assembly, for a four-year term in office, renewable for one term.

High Commissioner: SERGIO VIEIRA DE MELLO (Brazil).

Deputy to the High Commissioner: Dr BERTRAND GANGAPERSAND RAMCHARAN (Guyana).

ADMINISTRATION

The work of the Office is conducted by the following branches: Research and Right to Development, responsible for human rights policy development, undertaking research and providing information to the High Commissioner and other human rights experts, working groups, etc.; Support Services, which provides administrative support to UN human rights mechanisms, including the Commission on Human Rights and its working groups, and the Sub-commission on the Promotion and Protection of Human Rights and its working groups; and Activities and Programmes, which conducts field operations, provides advice and technical assistance to governments, and implements special procedures relating to human rights concerns. The Office also comprises a Staff Office, an Administrative Section and a branch office in New York, USA.

FIELD PRESENCES

As the Office's involvement in field work has expanded, a substantial structure of field presences has developed to strengthen this aspect of the Office's work. In 2002 there were field presences in 20 countries, covering the following areas: Abkhazia (Georgia), Afghanistan, Angola, Bosnia and Herzegovina, Burundi, Cambodia, Central African Republic, Chad, Colombia, Croatia, the Democratic Republic of the Congo, Gaza (Emerging Palestinian Autonomous Areas), Guatemala, Guinea-Bissau, Liberia, Madagascar, Sierra Leone, Somalia, South Africa and the provinces of Kosovo and Serbia (Federal Republic of Yugoslavia, now Serbia and Montenegro).

Activities

The mandate of the OHCHR incorporates the following functions and responsibilities: the promotion and protection of human rights throughout the world; the reinforcement of international co-operation in the field of human rights; the promotion of universal ratification and implementation of international standards; the establishment of a dialogue with governments to ensure respect for human rights; and co-ordination of efforts by other UN programmes and organs to promote respect for human rights. Upon request OHCHR undertakes assessments of national human rights needs, in consultation with governments. Through the provision of guidance and training it supports the establishment of independent national human rights institutions. The Office may also study and react to cases of serious violations of human rights, and may undertake diplomatic efforts to prevent violations. It also produces educational and other information material to enhance understanding of human rights. The High Commissioner was designated as the co-ordinator of the UN Decade for Human Rights Education (1995–2004). OHCHR co-operates with academic bodies and non-governmental organizations working the area of human rights.

OHCHR was the lead agency in undertaking preparations for the World Conference against Racism, Racial Discrimination, Xenophobia and Related Intolerance, convened in Durban, South Africa, in August/September 2001 and attended by representatives of 168 governments. The following five core themes were addressed at Durban: sources, causes, forms and contemporary manifestations of racism; victims; prevention, education and protection measures; provision of remedies and redress (i.e. compensation); and future strategies to achieve full and effective equality. The Conference adopted the 'Durban Declaration' and a Programme of Action, in accordance with which national plans of action were to be implemented by participating states: universal ratification of the International Convention on the Elimination of all Forms of Racism (ICERD) was to be aimed for by 2005, with the broadest possible ratification of other human rights instruments, and national legislation was to be improved in line with the ICERD. OHCHR was to play a leading role in following up the implementation of the Programme of Action; on the recommendation of the Conference an interim Anti-discrimination Unit was established within the Office for this purpose.

OHCHR field offices and operations ('field presences'—see above) undertake a variety of activities, such as training and other technical assistance, support for Special Rapporteurs (usually appointed by the Commission on Human Rights to investigate human rights emergencies), monitoring and fact-finding. Increasingly they provide support to conflict prevention, peace-making, peace-keeping and peace-building activities. OHCHR co-operates with the UN Department of Peace-keeping Operations and Department of Political Affairs in developing the human rights component of peace-keeping and peace-building missions.

The OHCHR quick response desk co-ordinates urgent appeals for assistance in addressing human rights emergencies. The High Commissioner issues reports on human rights emergencies to the Commission on Human Rights. During 2001 the High Commissioner presented reports on investigations into allegations of violations of human rights in Chechnya, Colombia, East Timor (now Timor-Leste), Sierra Leone, and the West Bank and Gaza.

TECHNICAL CO-OPERATION PROGRAMME

The UN Technical Co-operation Programme in the Field of Human Rights was established in 1955 to assist states, at their request, to strengthen their capacities in the observance of democracy, human rights, and the rule of law. Examples of work undertaken within the framework of the programme include training courses and workshops on good governance and the observance of human rights, expert advisory services on the incorporation of international human rights standards into national legislation and policies and on the formulation of national plans of action for the promotion and protection of human rights, fellowships, the provision of information and documentation, and consideration of promoting a human rights culture. In recent years the Programme, one of the key components of OHCHR's activities, has expanded to undertake UN system-wide human rights support activities, for example in the area of peace-keeping (see above).

Finance

The Office is financed from the regular budget of the UN, as well as by a number of voluntary and trust funds. OHCHR launched its first annual appeal to the international community for voluntary contributions in 2000. For 2002 some US $22.5m. was provisionally allocated under the regular budget, while OHCHR appealed for $55.8m. in voluntary contributions.

Publications

Annual Report.

Fact sheet series.

Human Rights Quarterly.

Human rights study series.

Professional training series.

Other reference material, reports, proceedings of conferences, workshops, etc.

United Nations Human Settlements Programme— UN-Habitat

Address: POB 30030, Nairobi, Kenya.

Telephone: (20) 623141; **fax:** (20) 624265; **e-mail:** infohabitat@ unhabitat.org; **internet:** www.unhabitat.org.

UN-Habitat (formerly the United Nations Centre for Human Settlements, UNCHS-Habitat, established in October 1978 to service the intergovernmental Commission on Human Settlements) became a full UN programme in January 2002, in accordance with a decision of the General Assembly in December 2001. UN-Habitat serves as a focus for human settlements activities in the UN system.

Organization

(April 2003)

GOVERNING COUNCIL

The Governing Council (formerly the Commission on Human Settlements) meets once every two years and has 58 members, serving for four years. Sixteen members are from Africa, 13 from Asia, six from eastern European countries, 10 from Latin America and 13 from western Europe and other countries. The Committee of Permanent Representatives to UN-Habitat, which meets at least four times a year, functions as an inter-sessional subsidiary body of the Governing Council. The Governing Council reports to the UN General Assembly through ECOSOC (q.v.).

SECRETARIAT

The Secretariat services the Governing Council, implements its resolutions and ensures the integration and co-ordination of technical co-operation, research and policy advice. Its Work Programme incorporates the following priority areas, as defined by the Governing Council: Shelter and social services; Urban management; Environment and infrastructure; and Assessment, information and monitoring. The Secretariat is responsible for monitoring the implementation of the objectives of the Second UN Conference on Human Settlements, Habitat II, which was held in Istanbul, Turkey, in June 1996.

Executive Director: ANNA KAJUMULO TIBAIJUKA (Tanzania).

Activities

Nearly one-half of the world's population lives in towns and cities. UN-Habitat supports the UN Millennium development target of improving significantly the lives of at least 100m. slum dwellers by 2020. It supports and conducts capacity-building and operational research, provides technical co-operation and policy advice, and disseminates information with the aim of strengthening the development and management of human settlements.

In June 1996 representatives of 171 national governments and of more than 500 municipal authorities attending Habitat II adopted a Global Plan of Action (the 'Habitat Agenda'), which incorporated detailed programmes of action to realize economic and social development and environmental sustainability, and endorsed the conference's objectives of ensuring 'adequate shelter for all' and 'sustainable human settlements development in an urbanizing world'. UN-Habitat provides the leadership and serves as a focal point for the implementation of the Agenda. In 1999 UNCHS (Habitat) approved a set of 23 resolutions to reduce poverty, improve shelter and environmental conditions, promote good governance, and improve the status of women. A special session of the UN General Assembly, entitled Istanbul + 5, was held in June 2001 to report on the implementation of the recommendations of the Habitat II conference. The special session adopted a Declaration on Cities and Other Human Settlements in the New Millennium that reaffirmed commitment to the objectives of the Habitat Agenda and

urged an intensification of efforts towards eradicating widespread poverty, which was identified as the main impediment to achieving these, and towards promoting good governance. The special session also resolved to increase international co-operation in several other areas, including addressing HIV/AIDS, urban crime and violence, environmental issues, and the problems posed by conflicts and refugees; and recommended the enhancement of the status and role of UNCHS (Habitat). Consequently, in December 2001 the General Assembly authorized the elevation of the body to a full UN programme with a strengthened mandate to address and implement the Habitat Agenda and, in January 2002, UN-Habitat was inaugurated.

UN-Habitat maintains a Global Urban Observatory to monitor implementation of the Habitat Agenda and to report on local and national plans of action, international and regional support programmes and ongoing research and development. The Observatory, which incorporates the Best Practices and Local Leadership Programme and the Urban Indicators Programme, operates through an international network of regional and national institutions, all of which provide local training in appropriate data collection methods and in the development, adoption and maintenance of reliable information systems.

Through its Women in Human Settlements Development Programme, which was established in 1990, the Programme—then UNCHS (Habitat)—ensured that the issue of human settlements was included in the agenda of the UN Fourth World Conference on Women, which was held in Beijing, People's Republic of China, in September 1995, and successfully incorporated the right of women to ownership of land and property into the Global Platform for Action which resulted from the conference. An advisory board, the Huairou Commission, comprising women from 'grass-roots' groups, non-governmental organizations, the UN and research and political institutions, has since been established to ensure a link between the Beijing and Habitat Agendas and the inclusion of gender issues in the follow-up to Habitat II.

UN-Habitat participates in implementing the human settlements component of Agenda 21, which was adopted at the UN Conference on Environment and Development in June 1992, and is also responsible for the chapter of Agenda 21 that refers to solid waste management and sewage-related issues. The Programme implements a programme entitled 'Localizing Agenda 21', to assist local authorities in developing countries to address local environmental and infrastructure-related problems. It also collaborates with national governments, private-sector and non-governmental institutions and UN bodies to achieve the objectives of Agenda 21. The Settlement Infrastructure and Environment Programme was initiated in 1992 to support developing countries in improving the environment of human settlements through policy advice and planning, infrastructure management and enhancing awareness of environmental and health concerns in areas such as water, sanitation, waste management and transport. In October 2002 UN-Habitat launched a Water and Sanitation Trust Fund aimed at supporting the goal of halving the proportion of the world's population lacking access to basic sanitation or clean water by 2015, that was set by the World Summit on Sustainable Development (WSSD), held in Johannesburg, South Africa, during August/September to assess strategies for strengthening the implementation of Agenda 21. An Urban Management Programme aims to strengthen the contribution of cities and towns in developing countries towards human development, including economic growth, social advancements, the reduction of poverty and the improvement of the environment. The Programme, which is active in 120 cities, is an international technical co-operation project, of which UN-Habitat is the executing agency, the World Bank is an associated agency, while UNDP provides core funding and monitoring. The Programme is operated through regional offices, in collaboration with bilateral and multilateral support agencies, and brings together national and local authorities, community leaders and representatives of the private sector to consider specific issues and solutions to urban problems. The related Safer Cities Programme was initiated in 1996. A Sustainable Cities Programme, operated jointly with UNEP, is concerned with incorporating environmental issues into urban planning and management, in order to ensure sustainable and equitable development. The Programme is active in some 20 cities world-wide, although a prepared series of policy guide-lines is used in many others. Some 95% of the Programme's resources are spent at city level to strengthen the capacities of municipal authorities and their public-, private- and community-sector partners in the field of environmental planning and management, with the objective that the concepts and approaches of the Programme are replicated throughout the region. UN-Habitat provided the secretariat of the inaugural World Urban Forum, held in April/May 2002 with participation by national governments and Habitat Agenda partners. The Forum, which represents a merger of the former Urban Environment Forum and International Forum on Urban Poverty, aims to promote international co-operation in shelter and urban development issues. In addition, UN-Habitat supports training and other activities designed to strengthen management development (in particular in the provision and maintenance of services and facilities) at local and community level. UN-Habitat's Global Campaign for Secure Tenure and Global Campaign on Urban Governance both emphasize urban poverty reduction. UN-Habitat focused on the theme of 'Sustainable Urbanization' as its main contribution to the WSSD held in August/September 2002 (see above).

Increasingly the Programme is being called upon to contribute to the relief, rehabilitation and development activities undertaken by the UN in areas affected by regional and civil conflict. It has been actively involved in the reconstruction of human settlements and other development activities in Afghanistan, as well as contributing to reconstruction programmes in Timor-Leste, Iraq, Myanmar, Rwanda and Somalia. From January 2000–November 2002 it administered a Housing and Property Directorate that was established in post-conflict Kosovo and Metohija, within the framework of the UN's interim administration in the province. UN-Habitat also provides assessment and technical support in the aftermath of natural disasters. Reconstruction and recovery activities are co-ordinated by the Risk and Disaster Management Unit.

Finance

UN-Habitat's work programme is financed from the UN regular budget, the Habitat and Human Settlements Foundation and from extra-budgetary resources. The approved budget for the two-year period 2002–03 amounted to US $24m.

Publications

Global Report on Human Settlements (annually).

Habitat Debate (quarterly).

Technical reports and studies, occasional papers, bibliographies, directories.

United Nations Children's Fund—UNICEF

Address: 3 United Nations Plaza, New York, NY 10017, USA.
Telephone: (212) 326-7000; **fax:** (212) 887-7465; **e-mail:** info@unicef.org; **internet:** www.unicef.org.
UNICEF was established in 1946 by the UN General Assembly as the UN International Children's Emergency Fund, to meet the emergency needs of children in post-war Europe and China. In 1950 its mandate was changed to respond to the needs of children in developing countries. In 1953 the General Assembly decided that UNICEF should continue its work, as a permanent arm of the UN system, with an emphasis on programmes giving long-term benefits to children everywhere, particularly those in developing countries. In 1965 UNICEF was awarded the Nobel Peace Prize.

Organization

(April 2003)

EXECUTIVE BOARD

The Executive Board, as the governing body of UNICEF, comprises 36 member governments from all regions, elected in rotation for a three-year term by ECOSOC. The Board establishes policy, reviews programmes and approves expenditure. It reports to the General Assembly through ECOSOC.

SECRETARIAT

The Executive Director of UNICEF is appointed by the UN Secretary-General in consultation with the Executive Board. The administration of UNICEF and the appointment and direction of staff are the responsibility of the Executive Director, under policy directives laid down by the Executive Board, and under a broad authority delegated to the Executive Director by the Secretary-General. In December 2001 there were some 5,600 UNICEF staff positions, of which about 85% were in the field.
Executive Director: CAROL BELLAMY (USA).

UNICEF REGIONAL OFFICES

UNICEF has a network of eight regional and 126 field offices serving 162 countries and territories. Its offices in Tokyo, Japan, and Brussels, Belgium, support fund-raising activities; UNICEF's supply division is administered from the office in Copenhagen, Demark. A research centre concerned with child development is based in Florence, Italy.
The Americas and the Caribbean: Apdo 3667, Balboa Ancon, Panamá, Panama; tel. (507) 315-7400; fax (507) 317-0258; e-mail tacro@unicef.org; internet www.uniceflac.org.
Central and Eastern Europe, Commonwealth of Independent States and Baltic States: Palais des Nations, 1211 Geneva 10,

Switzerland; tel. (22) 9095111; fax (22) 9095909; internet www.unicef.org/programme/highlights/cee.
East Asia and the Pacific: POB 2-154, Bangkok 10200, Thailand; tel. (2) 2805931; fax (2) 2803563; e-mail eapro@unicef.org.
Eastern and Southern Africa: POB 44145, Nairobi, Kenya; tel. (2) 621234; fax (2) 622678; e-mail nairobiro@unicef.org.
Europe: Palais des Nations, 1211 Geneva 10, Switzerland; tel. (22) 9095111; fax (22) 9095900.
Middle East and North Africa: POB 1551, UNICEF House, Tla'a al-Ali al Dahak Bin Soufian St, 11821 Amman, Jordan; tel. (6) 5539977; fax (6) 5538880; e-mail menaro@unicef.org.jo.
South Asia: POB 5815, Leknath Marg, Kathmandu, Nepal; tel. 417082; fax 419479; e-mail rosa@unicef.org.
West and Central Africa: BP 443, Abidjan 04, Côte d'Ivoire; tel. 213131; fax 227607; e-mail wcaro@unicef.org.

OTHER UNICEF OFFICES

UNICEF Innocenti Research Centre: Piazza SS. Annunziata 2, 50122 Florence, Italy; tel. (055) 20330; fax (055) 244817; e-mail florence@unicef.org; internet www.unicef-icdc.org; f. 1988 as International Child Development Centre; aims to strengthen UNICEF's research capability and to support the Fund's advocacy for children world-wide.
Belgium: ave des Arts 20, 1000 Brussels; tel. (2) 2305970; fax (2) 2303462; e-mail info@unicef.be; internet unicef.be.
UNICEF Supply Division: UNICEF Plads, Freeport 2100, Copenhagen; tel. (45) 35273527; fax (45) 35269421; e-mail supply@unicef.org; internet www.supply.unicef.dk.
Japan: UN Bldg, 8th Floor, 53-70, Jingumae 5-chome, Shibuya-ku, Tokyo 150, Japan; tel. (3) 5467-4431; fax (3) 5467-4437; e-mail unicefjp@sepia.ocn.ne.jp; internet unicef.or.jp.

NATIONAL COMMITTEES

UNICEF is supported by 37 National Committees, mostly in industrialized countries, whose volunteer members, numbering more than 100,000, raise money through various activities, including the sale of greetings cards. The Committees also undertake advocacy and awareness campaigns on a number of issues and provide an important link with the general public.

Activities

UNICEF is dedicated to the well-being of children, adolescents and women and works for the realization and protection of their rights within the frameworks of the Convention on the Rights of the Child, which was adopted by the UN General Assembly in 1989 and by 2003 was almost universally ratified, and of the Convention on the Elimination of All Forms of Discrimination Against Women, adopted by the UN General Assembly in 1979. Promoting the full implementation of the Conventions, UNICEF aims to ensure that children world-wide are given the best possible start in life and attain a good level of basic education, and that adolescents are given every opportunity to develop their capabilities and participate successfully in society. The Fund also continues to provide relief and rehabilitation assistance in emergencies. Through its extensive field network in some 162 developing countries and territories, UNICEF undertakes, in co-ordination with governments, local communities and other aid organizations, programmes in health, nutrition, education, water and sanitation, the environment, gender issues and development, and other fields of importance to children. Emphasis is placed on low-cost, community-based programmes. UNICEF programmes are increasingly focused on supporting children and women during critical periods of their life, when intervention can make a lasting difference, i.e. early childhood, the primary school years, adolescence and the reproductive years. Priorities include early years development, immunization strategies, girls' education, combating the spread and impact of HIV/AIDS, and strengthening the protection of children against violence, exploitation and abuse.

UNICEF was instrumental in organizing the World Summit for Children, held in September 1990 and attended by representatives from more than 150 countries, including 71 heads of state or government. The Summit produced a Plan of Action which recognized the rights of the young to 'first call' on their countries' resources and formulated objectives for the year 2000, including: (i) a reduction of the 1990 mortality rates for infants and children under five years by one-third, or to 50–70 per 1,000 live births, whichever is lower; (ii) a reduction of the 1990 maternal mortality rate by one-half; (iii) a reduction by one-half of the 1990 rate for severe malnutrition among children under the age of five; (iv) universal access to safe drinking water and to sanitary means of excreta disposal; and (v) universal access to basic education and completion of primary education by at least 80% of children. UNICEF supported the efforts of governments to achieve progress towards these objectives. The Fund played a leading role in helping governments and other partners prepare for the UN General Assembly special session on Children, which was held in May 2002 to assess the outcome of the 1990 summit and to determine a set of actions and objectives for the next 10 years. At the session the General Assembly adopted a document entitled 'A World Fit for Children', reaffirming its commitment to the agenda of the 1990 summit, and outlining a plan of action for the attainment of new goals and targets in the areas of education, health and the protection of children.

In 2000 UNICEF launched a new initiative, the Global Movement for Children—comprising governments, private- and public-sector bodies, and individuals—which aimed to rally world-wide support to improve the lives of all children and adolescents. In April 2001 a 'Say Yes for Children' campaign was adopted by the Global Movement, identifying 10 critical actions required to further its objectives. These were: eliminating all forms of discrimination and exclusion; putting children first; ensuring a caring environment for every child; fighting HIV/AIDS; eradicating violence against and abuse and exploitation of children; listening to children's views; universal eduation; protecting children from war; safeguarding the earth for children; and combating poverty. UNICEF was to co-ordinate the campaign.

UNICEF, in co-operation with other UN agencies, promotes universal access to and completion of basic and good quality education. The Fund, with UNESCO, UNDP, UNFPA and the World Bank, co-sponsored the World Conference on Education for All, held in Thailand in March 1990, and undertook efforts to achieve the objectives formulated by the conference, which included the elimination of disparities in education between boys and girls. UNICEF participated in and fully supports the objectives and framework for action adopted by the follow-up World Education Forum in Dakar, Senegal, in April 2000. The Fund supports education projects in sub-Saharan Africa, South Asia and countries in the Middle East and North Africa, and implements a Girls' Education Programme in more than 60 developing countries, which aims to increase the enrolment of girls in primary schools. More than 120m. children world-wide, of whom nearly 53% are girls, remain deprived of basic education. In December 2002 UNICEF initiated the '25 by 2005' initiative, which aimed to eliminate gender disparities in education in 25, mainly African and Asian, countries by 2005.

Through UNICEF's efforts the needs and interests of children were incorporated into Agenda 21, which was adopted as a plan of action for sustainable development at the UN Conference on Environment and Development, held in June 1992. In mid-1997, at the UN General Assembly's Special Session on Sustainable Development, UNICEF highlighted the need to improve safe water supply, sanitation and hygiene, and thereby reduce the risk of diarrhoea and other water-borne diseases, as fundamental to fulfilment of

child rights. The Fund has supported initiatives to provide the benefits of safe water, sanitation and hygiene education to communities in developing countries. UNICEF also works with UNEP to promote environment issues of common concern and with the World Wide Fund for Nature to support the conservation of local ecosystems.

UNICEF aims to break the cycle of poverty by advocating for the provision of increased development aid to developing countries, and aims to help poor countries obtain debt relief and to ensure access to basic social services. To this end it supports NetAid, an internet-based strategy to promote sustainable development and combat extreme poverty. UNICEF is the leading agency in promoting the 20/20 initiative, which was endorsed at the World Summit for Social Development, held in Copenhagen, Denmark, in March 1995. The initiative encourages the governments of developing and donor countries to allocate at least 20% of their domestic budgets and official development aid respectively, to health care, primary education and low-cost safe water and sanitation.

UNICEF estimates that the births of some 50m. children annually are not officially registered, and urges universal registration in order to prevent the abuse of children without proof of age and nationality, for example through trafficking, forced labour, early marriage and military recruitment. The Fund, which vigorously opposes the exploitation of children as a violation of their basic human rights, works with ILO and other partners to promote an end to exploitative and hazardous child labour, and supports special projects to provide education, counselling and care for the estimated 250m. children between the ages of five and 14 years working in developing countries. UNICEF played a major role at the World Congress against Commercial Sexual Exploitation of Children, held in Stockholm, Sweden, in 1996, which adopted a Declaration and Agenda for Action to end the sexual exploitation of children. UNICEF also actively participated in the International Conference on Child Labour held in Oslo, Norway, in November 1997. The Conference adopted an Agenda for Action to eliminate the worst forms of child labour, including slavery-like practices, forced labour, commercial sexual exploitation and the use of children in drugs-trafficking and other hazardous forms of work. UNICEF supports the 1999 ILO Worst Forms of Child Labour Convention, which aims at the prohibition and elimination of the worst forms of child labour. In 1999 UNICEF launched a global initiative, Education as a Preventive Strategy Against Child Labour, with the aim of providing education to children forced to miss school because of work. The Fund helped to draft and promotes full ratification and implementation of an Optional Protocol to the Convention of the Rights of the Child concerning the sale of children, child prostitution and pornography, which was adopted in May 2000 and entered into force in January 2002. UNICEF co-sponsored and actively participated in the Second Congress Against Commercial Sexual Exploitation of Children held in Yokohama, Japan, in December 2001.

Child health is UNICEF's largest programme sector, accounting for some 40% of programme expenditure in 2000. UNICEF estimates that around 10m. children under five years of age die each year, mainly in developing countries, and the majority from largely preventable causes. UNICEF has worked with WHO and other partners to increase global immunization coverage against the following six diseases: measles, poliomyelitis, tuberculosis, diphtheria, whooping cough and tetanus. In 2000 UNICEF, in partnership with WHO, governments and other partners, helped to immunize 550m. children under five years of age in 53 countries against polio. In 1999 UNICEF, WHO, the World Bank and a number of public- and private-sector partners launched the Global Alliance for Vaccines and Immunization (GAVI), which aimed to protect children of all nationalities and socio-economic groups against vaccine-preventable diseases. GAVI's strategy included improving access to sustainable immunization services, expanding the use of existing vaccines, accelerating the development and introduction of new vaccines and technologies and promoting immunization coverage as a focus of international development efforts. UNICEF and WHO also work in conjunction on the Integrated Management of Childhood Illness programme to control diarrhoeal dehydration, a major cause of death among children under five years of age in the developing world. UNICEF-assisted programmes for the control of diarrhoeal diseases promote the low-cost manufacture and distribution of pre-packaged salts or home-made solutions. The use of 'oral rehydration therapy' has risen significantly in recent years, and is believed to prevent more than 1m. child deaths annually. During 1990–2000 diarrhoea-related deaths were reduced by one-half. UNICEF also promotes the need to improve sanitation and access to safe water supplies in developing nations in order to reduce the risk of diarrhoea and other water-borne diseases (see 20/20 initiative, above). To control acute respiratory infections, another leading cause of death in children under five in developing countries, UNICEF works with WHO in training health workers to diagnose and treat the associated diseases. As a result, the level of child deaths from pneumonia and other respiratory infections has been reduced by one-half since 1990. Around 1m. children die from malaria every year, mainly in sub-

Saharan Africa. In October 1998 UNICEF, together with WHO, UNDP and the World Bank, inaugurated a new global campaign, Roll Back Malaria, to fight the disease. UNICEF supports control programmes in more than 30 countries.

According to UNICEF estimates, around 27% of children under five years of age are underweight, while each year malnutrition contributes to about one-half of the child deaths in that age group and leaves millions of others with physical and mental disabilities. More than 2,000m. people world-wide (mainly women and children in developing countries) are estimated to be deficient in one or more essential vitamins and minerals, such as vitamin A, iodine and iron. UNICEF supports national efforts to reduce malnutrition, for example, fortifying staple foods with micronutrients, widening women's access to education, improving household food security and basic health services, and promoting sound child-care and feeding practices. Since 1991 more than 15,000 hospitals in at least 136 countries have been designated 'baby-friendly', having implemented a set of UNICEF and WHO recommendations entitled '10 steps to successful breast-feeding'. In 1996 UNICEF expressed its concern at the impact of international economic embargoes on child health, citing as an example the extensive levels of child malnutrition recorded in Iraq. UNICEF remains actively concerned at the levels of child malnutrition and accompanying diseases in Iraq and in the Democratic People's Republic of Korea, which has also suffered severe food shortages centres.

UNICEF estimates that almost 515,000 women die every year during pregnancy or childbirth, largely because of inadequate maternal health care. For every maternal death, approximately 30 further women suffer permanent injuries or chronic disabilities as a result of complications during pregnancy or childbirth. With its partners in the Safe Motherhood Initiative—UNFPA, WHO, the World Bank, the International Planned Parenthood Federation, the Population Council, and Family Care International—UNICEF promotes measures to reduce maternal mortality and morbidity, including improving access to quality reproductive health services, educating communities about safe motherhood and the rights of women, training midwives, and expanding access to family planning services.

UNICEF is concerned at the danger posed by HIV/AIDS to the realization of children's rights. It is estimated that one-half of all new HIV infections occur in young people. At the end of 2002 3.2m. children under 15 were living with HIV/AIDS. Some 800,000 children under 15 were newly infected during that year, while 610,000 died as a result of AIDS. It was estimated that about one-half of all new HIV infections during 2002 occurred in young people, aged 15–24. It is estimated that more than 13m. children world-wide have lost one or both parents to AIDS since the start of the epidemic. UNICEF's priorities in this area include prevention of infection among young people, reduction in mother-to-child transmission, care and protection of orphans and other vulnerable children, and care and support for children, young people and parents living with HIV/AIDS. UNICEF works closely in this field with governments and co-operates with other UN agencies in the Joint UN Programme on HIV/AIDS (UNAIDS), which became operational on 1 January 1996. In July 2002 UNICEF, UNAIDS and WHO jointly produced a study entitled *Young People and HIV/AIDS: Opportunity in Crisis*, examining young people's sexual behaviour patterns and knowledge of HIV/AIDS.

UNICEF provides emergency relief assistance, supports education, health, mine-awareness and psychosocial activities and helps to demobilize and rehabilitate child soldiers in countries and territories affected by violence and social disintegration. It assists children orphaned or separated from their parents and made homeless

through armed conflict. In recent years several such emergency operations have been undertaken, including in Afghanistan, Angola, Burundi, Kosovo, Liberia, Sierra Leone and Sudan. In 1999 UNICEF adopted a Peace and Security Agenda to help guide international efforts in this field. Emergency education assistance includes the provision of 'Edukits' in refugee camps and the reconstruction of school buildings. In the area of health the Fund co-operates with WHO to arrange 'days of tranquility' in order to facilitate the immunization of children in conflict zones. Psychosocial assistance activities include special programmes to assist traumatized children and help unaccompanied children to be reunited with parents or extended families.

An estimated 300,000 children are involved in armed conflicts as soldiers, porters and forced labourers. UNICEF encourages ratification of the Optional Protocol to the Convention on the Rights of the Child on the involvement of children in armed conflict, which was adopted by the General Assembly in May 2000 and entered into force in February 2002, and bans the compulsory recruitment of combatants below 18 years. The Fund also urges states to make unequivocal statements endorsing 18 as the minimum age of voluntary recruitment to the armed forces. UNICEF was an active participant in the so-called 'Ottawa' process (supported by the Canadian Government) to negotiate an international ban on anti-personnel land-mines which, it was estimated, killed and maimed between 8,000 and 10,000 children every year. The Convention on the Prohibition of the Use, Stockpiling, Production and Transfer of Anti-Personnel Mines and on their Destruction was adopted in December 1997 and entered into force in March 1999. By January 2003 the Convention had been ratified by 131 countries. UNICEF is committed to campaigning for its universal ratification and full implementation, and also supports mine-awareness campaigns.

Finance

UNICEF is funded by voluntary contributions from governments and non-governmental and private-sector sources. Total income in 2000 amounted to US $1,139m., of which 64% was from governments and intergovernmental organizations. Total expenditure in 2000 amounted to $1,111m.

UNICEF's income is divided into contributions for 'regular resources' (used for country programmes of co-operation approved by the Executive Board, programme support, and management and administration costs) and contributions for 'other resources' (for special purposes, including expanding the outreach of country programmes of co-operation and ensuring capacity to deliver critical assistance to women and children for example during humanitarian crises). In 2000 contributions for 'regular resources' totalled US $563m. and those for 'other resources' amounted to $576m.

Publications

Facts and Figures (in English, French and Spanish).

The State of the World's Children (annually, in Arabic, English, French, Russian and Spanish and about 30 other national languages).

UNICEF Annual Report (in English, French and Spanish).

UNICEF at a Glance (annually, in English, French and Spanish).

Reports; series on children and women; nutrition; education; children's rights; children in wars and disasters; working children; water; sanitation and the environment; analyses of the situation of children and women in individual developing countries.

United Nations Conference on Trade and Development—UNCTAD

Address: Palais des Nations, 1211 Geneva 10, Switzerland.

Telephone: (22) 9071234; **fax:** (22) 9070057; **e-mail:** ers@unctad.org; **internet:** www.unctad.org.

UNCTAD was established in December 1964. It is the principal instrument of the UN General Assembly concerned with trade and development, and is the focal point within the UN system for integrated activities relating to trade, finance, technology, investment and sustainable development. It aims to maximize the trade and development opportunities of developing countries, in particular least-developed countries, and to assist them to adapt to the increasing globalization and liberalization of the world economy.

Organization

(April 2003)

CONFERENCE

The Conference is the organization's highest policy-making body and normally meets every four years at ministerial level in order to formulate major policy guide-lines and to decide on UNCTAD's forthcoming programme of work. The tenth session was held in Bangkok, Thailand, in February 2000; the 11th session was scheduled to be convened in Brazil in 2004. As well as its 191 members, many intergovernmental and non-governmental organizations (NGOs) participate in UNCTAD's work as observers.

TRADE AND DEVELOPMENT BOARD

The Trade and Development Board is the executive body of UNCTAD. It comprises elected representatives from 146 UNCTAD member states and is responsible for ensuring the overall consistency of UNCTAD's activities, as well as those of its subsidiary bodies. The Board meets for a regular annual session lasting about 10 days, at which it examines global economic issues. It may also meet a further three times a year in order to address management or institutional matters.

COMMISSIONS

The Trade and Development Board has three Commissions: the Commission on Trade in Goods and Services and Commodities; the Commission on Investment, Technology and Related Financial Issues; and the Commission on Enterprise, Business Facilitation and Development. The Commissions meet once a year in regular session and may convene up to 10 Expert Meetings a year on specific issues.

SECRETARIAT

The secretariat comprises the following Divisions: Globalization and Development Strategies; International Trade in Goods and Services and Commodities; Investment, Technology and Enterprise Development; Services Infrastructure for Development and Trade Efficiency. It also incorporates the Office of the Special Co-ordinator for Least Developed, Land-locked, and Small Island Developing States.

The UNCTAD secretariat, comprising some 400 staff, undertakes policy analysis; monitoring, implementation and follow-up of decisions of intergovernmental bodies; technical co-operation in support of UNCTAD's policy objectives; and information exchanges and consultations of various types.

Secretary-General: RUBENS RICÚPERO (Brazil).

Activities

In February 2000 the 10th session of the Conference, held in Bangkok, Thailand, adopted the Bangkok Declaration, which stated the importance of promoting equitable and sustainable development in view of increasing global interdependence, trade liberalization and advances in technology. The Declaration emphasized UNCTAD's commitment to a fair, non-discriminatory and fully-integrated multilateral trading system that would not tolerate the marginalization of the world's least developed economies, and urged that the next round of multilateral trade negotiations address development issues. The Declaration noted the need for increased policy coherence at national and international level, and for more effective co-operation and co-ordination among multilateral institutions. It recommended open debate on global development issues by all development partners, including the private sector, NGOs, academics and politicians. The Conference also adopted a Plan of Action which assessed the consequences of globalization for development, recommended measures to be implemented by the international community, and provided a strategic framework for UNCTAD's future work programme.

INTERNATIONAL TRADE

During the 1980s UNCTAD focused on its role of providing a forum for the negotiation of international agreements on commodities, including cocoa, jute, rubber and tropical timber. (Such agreements are designed to ensure the stabilization of conditions in the trade of the commodities concerned.) UNCTAD's monitoring and facilitation of international commodity agreements has subsequently continued. The establishment of the Common Fund for Commodities (q.v.) was agreed by UNCTAD in 1980, and the Fund came into operation in September 1989. More recently UNCTAD has been concerned to assist countries to adopt risk management and financial strategies against commodity dependence and price fluctuation, and to encourage diversification to reduce dependence on single commodities. Under the Bangkok agreements, UNCTAD was committed to improve market transparency and the availability of information, in particular through the improved use of technology.

Since the 1970s UNCTAD has been actively involved in work relating to restrictive business practices. In 1980 the UN General Assembly adopted a set of mutually agreed equitable principles and rules for the control of restrictive business practices, which had been negotiated under UNCTAD auspices. An Intergovernmental Group of Experts monitors and reviews its implementation. UNCTAD provides technical assistance to developing countries in the formulation and enforcement of competition legislation and consumer protection law and policies. It is also responsible for reviewing the developmental impact of international agreements on

competition law. Through its Programme on Dispute Settlements UNCTAD provides training on aspects of settlement in international trade, investment and intellectual property disputes. In 2003 UNCTAD was to organize a series of regional workshops on dispute settlement to meet the specific interests of regional developing countries. UNCTAD has established a Commercial Diplomacy Programme to provide training and capacity-building to strengthen the participation and effectiveness of developing member countries in international and regional trade negotiations.

During the 1990s UNCTAD undertook research into the design and implementation of a multilateral system to trade emissions of so-called greenhouse gases. UNCTAD's Carbon Market Programme analyses the impact of measures to address climate change through the reduction of greenhouse gas emissions and works to promote a fair and effective global carbon market. In June 1997, in co-operation with the Earth Council, UNCTAD established a Greenhouse Gas Emissions Trading Policy Forum to support the development of a plurilateral emissions market. In June 1999 the International Emissions Trading Association (IETA) was established, sponsored by UNCTAD and the Earth Council. The IETA, which was envisaged as a successor to the Forum, comprised commercial companies, business organizations and regional and national trading associations, as well as invited international organizations, research institutes and NGOs. It was to serve as a forum for the exchange of information and ideas relating to international emissions trading and as a means of developing the market in emission permit trading, which was scheduled to be launched in 2008. During the initial phase of the IETA's operations UNCTAD provided temporary secretariat support.

UNCTAD is responsible for the Generalized System of Preferences (GSP), initiated in 1971, whereby a proportion of both agricultural and manufactured goods that are exported by developing countries receive preferential tariff treatment by certain developed countries, Russia and several central European countries. UNCTAD monitors changes in and amendments to national GSP schemes and reviews the use of these schemes by beneficiary developing countries. In addition, the Commission on Trade in Goods and Services and Commodities (see above) is responsible for providing a forum to examine the operation of schemes, the benefits they offer and the future role of the GSP. In March 2001 the European Union introduced a new initiative, the so-called Everything but Arms scheme, to amend the GSP regime in member countries to provide free market access to all products from LDCs (see below), except arms and munitions, and with special provisions for rice, sugar and bananas. UNCTAD's database of trade control measures has been made available through a Trade Analysis and Information System (TRAINS). A Trade Analysis Branch was established in 1999 to improve the understanding of current and emerging issues in international trade of concern to developing countries.

In 1996 UNCTAD launched a BIOTRADE Initiative to stimulate trade and investment in biological resources, as a basis for equitable, sustainable development. Under the Initiative UNCTAD has established partnerhips with national and regional organizations, using their local knowledge and expertise to develop and implement biodiversity programmes. The Initiative also supports the development of appropriate policies and legislation to support the sustainable trade and investment in biodiversity, i.e. to address issues such as benefit sharing, intellectual property rights and poverty alleviation. In 2002 work was progressing, in collaboration with the International Trade Centre, to develop a BioTrade Facilitation Programme, which aimed to promote the trade in biodiversity products and services through arrangements that would enhance sustainable bio-resources management, product development, value-adding processing and marketing.

INVESTMENT, TECHNOLOGY AND ENTERPRISE DEVELOPMENT

UNCTAD has been mandated as the organ within the UN system responsible for negotiating a multilateral framework governing direct foreign investment that would protect the interests of the poorest countries, taking account of the work already undertaken by OECD in this area. In UNCTAD's revised approach, encouragement of foreign direct investment and of domestic private enterprise in developing countries and countries in transition have become central to the agency's work. UNCTAD is increasingly seeking the input and participation of non-governmental groups, such as academics, NGOs and business representatives, in its intergovernmental machinery, where appropriate. UNCTAD's Division of Investment, Technology and Enterprise Development organizes regional meetings, technical symposia and training courses in aspects of international investment agreements. It also conducts Investment Policy Reviews to assess and promote a country's investment potential. Within the Division the Advisory Service on Investment and Training (ASIT) executes the technical assistance programme for investment promotion strategies. UNCTAD'S Commission on Investment, Technology and Related Financial Issues undertakes the functions of the former ECOSOC Commission on

International Investment and Transnational Corporations, which aimed to provide an understanding of the nature of foreign direct investment and transnational corporations, to secure effective international agreements and to strengthen the capacity of developing countries in their dealings with transnational corporations through an integrated approach, including research, information and technical assistance. A subsidiary body—the Intergovernmental Group of Experts on International Standards of Accounting and Reporting—aimed to improve the availability of information disclosed by transnational corporations. In November 1997 the UN General Assembly endorsed a proposal of the UN Secretary-General that the Group report directly through the UNCTAD Commission on Investment, Technology and Related Financial Issues.

The Commission on Enterprise, Business Facilitation and Development advises countries on policy-related issues and training activities concerning the development of entrepreneurship. It facilitates the exchange of experiences on the formulation and implementation of enterprise development strategies, including privatization, public-sector co-operation and the special problems relating to enterprise development in countries in economic transition. Since 1996 UNCTAD has administered Empretec, initially started as a pilot programme in 1988, which undertakes capacity-building activities to develop institutional structures supportive of enterprise and small business ventures. The programme also aims to foster business links with other transnational corporations.

Since May 1993 UNCTAD has serviced the ECOSOC Commission on Science and Technology for Development, which provides a forum for discussion of the following issues relating to science and technology for development: technology for small-scale economic activities to address the basic needs of low-income countries; gender implications of science and technology for developing countries; science and technology and the environment; the contribution of technologies to industrialization in developing countries; and the role of information technologies, in particular in relation to developing countries. The Commission meets every two years.

SERVICES INFRASTRUCTURE

Activities to enhance transport and trade logistics constitute an important component of UNCTAD's efforts to improve the participation of developing countries in international trade. It convenes expert meetings, extends technical support and organizes specialized training activities. In March 1999, at a diplomatic conference held under the auspices of UNCTAD and the International Maritime Organization (IMO), an International Convention on the Arrest of Ships was adopted. Other initiatives have resulted in the adoption of the UN Convention on the Carriage of Goods by Sea (Hamburg Rules—1978), the UN Convention on International Multimodal Transport (1980), the UN Convention on a Code of Conduct for Liner Conferences (effective from 1983), the UN Convention on Conditions for Registration of Ships (1986), and the International Convention on Maritime Liens and Mortgages. UNCTAD administers a Port Training Programme, as part of its TrainforTrade initiative, which emphasizes the need for human resources and capacity-building activities to support trading efforts by developing countries. UNCTAD promotes the use of e-commerce as a means of development. It publishes an annual *E-Commerce and Development Report* which analyses issues that influence the expansion of e-commerce in developing countries and identifies means of promoting its use in order to support economic and social development. UNCTAD organized a meeting on e-finance at the UN International Conference on Financing for Development, which was held in Monterrey, Mexico, in March 2002. During the 1980s UNCTAD developed an Automated System for Customs Data (ASYCUDA), which by 2002 was operational in more than 80 countries. It serves as a customs management system, using international standards, covering essential trade procedures, such as customs declarations, accounting procedures and transit documentation. In March 2002 UNCTAD inaugurated a fully electronic version of ASYCUDA to enable transactions to be undertaken using the internet. A software package, Advance Cargo Information System (ACIS), enables shipping lines and railway companies to track the movement of cargo. Through the use of ACIS and ASYCUDA UNCTAD aims to enhance the effective exchange of information in order to counter customs fraud.

In November 2002 the Global Trade Point Network (GTPNet), which was launched by UNCTAD in 1994 as an electronic source of trade-related information for use by small and medium-sized enterprises, was transferred to the World Trade Point Federation, an organization established by UNCTAD in 2000 to represent the programme's beneficiaries and to maintain the network of trade points.

LEAST DEVELOPED COUNTRIES

UNCTAD aims to give particular attention to the needs of the world's 49 least developed countries (LDCs—as defined by the UN). The eighth session of the Conference requested that detailed analyses of the socio-economic situations and domestic policies of the LDCs, their resource needs, and external factors affecting their economies be undertaken as part of UNCTAD's work programme. The ninth session determined that particular attention be given to the problems of the LDCs in all areas of UNCTAD's work. The 10th session focused on the impact of globalization on developing economies and on means of improving trade opportunities for the LDCs. UNCTAD served as the secretariat for the Third UN Conference on the Least Developed Countries, which took place in Brussels, Belgium, in May 2001. The Conference, which was attended by more than 6,500 participants from governments, NGOs and other elements of civil society, considered issues including governance, peace and social stability, enhancing productive capacities, intellectual property and development, infrastructure development, and financing growth and development. A Programme of Action for 2001–10, which had been elaborated by LDCs and their development partners, was adopted by the Conference. UNCTAD was to support its implementation, with particular emphasis on the needs of land-locked and small island developing states.

GLOBALIZATION AND DEVELOPMENT

UNCTAD works to promote policies and strategies at national and international level in support of development, and analyses issues, such as financial crises, to support sustainable economic management. It contributed to the implementation and review of the UN New Agenda for the Development of Africa in the 1990s (UNNADF). UNCTAD provides assistance to developing countries in the area of debt-management, and in seeking debt relief from their creditors. UNCTAD is responsible for the software component of a joint programme with the World Bank to extend technical co-operation to developing countries in the field of debt management. The assistance is based on the development and distribution of software (the Debt Management and Financial Analysis System—DMFAS) designed to enable debtor countries to analyse data, make projections, and to plan strategies for debt repayment and reorganization. At the end of 2001 the programme was operational in 60 countries. UNCTAD provides training for operators in the use of the software, and for senior officials, to increase their awareness of institutional reforms which might be necessary for effective debt management. In 1995 UNCTAD initiated a programme of technical assistance to support the Palestinian people, within the context of involvement with Palestinian economy which had begun in 1979 with a study of the economic situation in the occupied territories.

The Secretariat provided technical assistance to developing countries in connection with the Uruguay Round of multilateral trade negotiations (see WTO). The International Trade Centre in Geneva is operated jointly by WTO and UNCTAD. In February 2002 UNCTAD initiated a new capacity-building and technical assistance programme to help developing countries in trade negotiations resulting from the WTO meeting held in Doha, Qatar, in November 2001.

Finance

The operational expenses of UNCTAD are borne by the regular budget of the UN, and amount to approximately US $50m. annually. Technical co-operation activities, financed from extra-budgetary resources, amount to some $25m. annually.

Publications

E-commerce and Development Report (annually).

Least Developed Countries Report (annually).

Monthly Commodity Price Bulletin.

Review of Maritime Transport (annually).

Trade and Development Report (annually).

Transnational Corporations (3 a year).

UNCTAD Commodity Yearbook.

UNCTAD Handbook of Statistics (annually, also available on CD-Rom).

UNCTAD News (3 a year).

World Commodity Survey.

World Investment Report (annually).

United Nations Development Programme—UNDP

Address: One United Nations Plaza, New York, NY 10017, USA.
Telephone: (212) 906-5295; **fax:** (212) 906-5364; **e-mail:** hq@undp.org; **internet:** www.undp.org.

The Programme was established in 1965 by the UN General Assembly. Its central mission is to help countries to eradicate poverty and achieve a sustainable level of human development, an approach to economic growth that encompasses individual well-being and choice, equitable distribution of the benefits of development, and conservation of the environment. UNDP advocates for a more inclusive global economy.

Organization

(April 2003)

UNDP is responsible to the UN General Assembly, to which it reports through ECOSOC.

EXECUTIVE BOARD

The Executive Board is responsible for providing intergovernmental support to, and supervision of, the activities of UNDP and the UN Population Fund (UNFPA). It comprises 36 members: eight from Africa, seven from Asia, four from eastern Europe, five from Latin America and the Caribbean and 12 from western Europe and other countries.

SECRETARIAT

In recent years UNDP has implemented a process aimed at restructuring and improving the efficiency of its administration. Offices and divisions at the Secretariat include: an Operations Support Group; Offices of the United Nations Development Group, the Human Development Report, Audit and Performance Review, and Communications; and Bureaux for Crisis Prevention and Recovery, Resources and Strategic Partnerships, Development Policy, and Management. Five regional bureaux, all headed by an assistant administrator, cover: Africa; Asia and the Pacific; the Arab states; Latin America and the Caribbean; and Europe and the Commonwealth of Independent States. There is also a Division for Global and Interregional Programmes.

Administrator: MARK MALLOCH BROWN (United Kingdom).
Associate Administrator: Dr ZÉPHIRIN DIABRÉ (Burkina Faso).

COUNTRY OFFICES

In almost every country receiving UNDP assistance there is an office, headed by the UNDP Resident Representative, who usually also serves as UN Resident Co-ordinator, responsible for the co-ordination of all UN technical assistance and operational development activities, advising the Government on formulating the country programme, ensuring that field activities are undertaken, and acting as the leader of the UN team of experts working in the country. The offices function as the primary presence of the UN in most developing countries.

Activities

As the world's largest source of grant-funded technical assistance for developing countries, UNDP provides advisory and support services to governments and UN teams. Assistance is mostly non-monetary, comprising the provision of experts' services, consultancies, equipment and training for local workers, including fellowships for advanced study abroad. UNDP supports programme countries in attracting aid and utilizing it efficiently. The Programme is committed to allocating some 88% of its regular resources to low-income developing countries. Developing countries themselves contribute significantly to the total project costs in terms of personnel, facilities, equipment and supplies.

Since the mid-1990s UNDP has strengthened its focus on results, streamlining its management practices and promoting clearly defined objectives for the advancement of sustainable human development. Under 'UNDP 2001', an extensive internal process of reform initiated during the late 1990s, UNDP placed increased emphasis on its activities in the field and on performance and accountability, focusing on the following priority areas: democratic governance; poverty reduction; crisis prevention and recovery; energy and environment; promotion of information and communications technology; and combating HIV/AIDS. In 2001 UNDP established six Thematic Trust Funds, covering each of these areas, to enable increased support of thematic programme activities. Gender equality and the provision of country-level aid co-ordination services are also

important focus areas. In accordance with the more results-oriented approach developed under the 'UNDP 2001' process the Programme introduced a new Multi-Year Funding Framework (MYFF), the first phase of which covered the period 2000–03. The MYFF outlines the country-driven goals around which funding is to be mobilized, integrating programme objectives, resources, budget and outcomes. It provides the basis for the Administrator's Business Plans for the same duration and enables policy coherence in the implementation of programmes at country, regional and global levels. A Results-Oriented Annual Report (ROAR) was produced for the first time in 2000 from data compiled by country offices and regional programmes. It was hoped that UNDP's greater focus on performance would generate increased voluntary contributions from donors, thereby strengthening the Programme's core resource base. In September 2000 the first ever Ministerial Meeting of ministers of development co-operation and foreign affairs and other senior officials from donor and programme countries, convened in New York, USA, endorsed UNDP's shift to a results-based orientation.

From the mid-1990s UNDP also determined to assume a more active and integrative role within the UN system-wide development framework. UNDP Resident Representatives—usually also serving as UN Resident Co-ordinators, with responsibility for managing inter-agency co-operation on sustainable human development initatives at country level—were to play a focal role in implementing this approach. In order to promote its co-ordinating function UNDP allocated increased resources to training and skill-sharing programmes. In late 1997 the UNDP Administrator was appointed to chair the UN Development Group (UNDG), which was established as part of a series of structural reform measures initiated by the UN Secretary-General, with the aim of strengthening collaboration between all UN funds, programmes and bodies concerned with development. The UNDG promotes coherent policy at country level through the system of UN Resident Co-ordinators (see above), the Common Country Assessment mechanism (CCA, a country-based process for evaluating national development situations), and the UN Development Assistance Framework (UNDAF, the foundation for planning and co-ordinating development operations at country level, based on the CCA). Within the framework of the Administrator's Business Plans for 2000–03 a new Bureau for Resources and Strategic Partnerships was established to build and strengthen working partnerships with other UN bodies, donor and programme countries, international financial institutions and development banks, civil society organizations and the private sector. The Bureau was also to serve UNDP's regional bureaux and country offices through the exchange of information and promotion of partnership strategies.

UNDP has a catalyst and co-ordinating function as the focus of UN system-wide efforts to achieve the so-called Millennium Development Goals (MDGs), pledged by governments attending a summit meeting of the UN General Assembly in September 2000. The objectives included a reduction by 50% in the number of people with income of less than US $1 a day and those suffering from hunger and lack of safe drinking water by 2015. Other commitments made concerned equal access to education for girls and boys, the provision of universal primary education, the reduction of maternal mortality by 75%, and the reversal of the spread of HIV/AIDS and other diseases. UNDP plays a leading role in efforts to integrate the MDGs into all aspects of the UN activities at country level. The Programme supports the formulation of MDG Reports for all developing countries.

UNDP aims to help governments to reassess their development priorities and to design initiatives for sustainable human development. UNDP country offices support the formulation of national human development reports (NHDRs), which aim to facilitate activities such as policy-making, the allocation of resources and monitoring progress towards poverty eradication and sustainable development. In addition, the preparation of Advisory Notes and Country Co-operation Frameworks by UNDP officials helps to highlight country-specific aspects of poverty eradiction and national strategic priorities. In January 1998 the Executive Board adopted eight guiding principles relating to sustainable human development that were to be implemented by all country offices, in order to ensure a focus to UNDP activities. A network of nine Sub-regional Resource Facilities (SURFs) has been established to strengthen and co-ordinate UNDP's technical assistance services. Since 1990 UNDP has published an annual *Human Development Report*, incorporating a Human Development Index, which ranks countries in terms of human development, using three key indicators: life expectancy, adult literacy and basic income required for a decent standard of living. In 1997 a Human Poverty Index and a Gender-related Development Index, which assesses gender equality on the basis of life expectancy, education and income, were introduced into the Report for the first time.

UNDP's activities to facilitate poverty eradication include support for capacity-building programmes and initiatives to generate sustainable livelihoods, for example by improving access to credit, land and technologies, and the promotion of strategies to improve education and health provision for the poorest elements of populations (with a focus on women and girls). In 1996 UNDP launched the Poverty Strategies Initiative (PSI) to strengthen national capacities to assess and monitor the extent of poverty and to combat the problem. All PSI projects were to involve representatives of governments, the private sector, social organizations and research institutions in policy debate and formulation. In early 1997 a UNDP scheme to support private-sector and community-based initiatives to generate employment opportunities, MicroStart, became operational. UNDP supports the Caribbean Project Development Facility and the Africa Project Development Facility, which are administered by the International Finance Corporation (q.v.) and which aim to develop the private sector in these regions in order to generate jobs and sustainable livelihoods. With the World Bank, UNDP helps governments of developing countries applying for international debt relief to draft Poverty Reduction Stategy Papers.

Approximately one-quarter of all UNDP programme resources support national efforts to ensure efficient and accountable governance and to build effective relations between the state, the private sector and civil society, which are essential to achieving sustainable development. UNDP undertakes assessment missions to help ensure free and fair elections and works to promote human rights, a transparent and competent public sector, a competent judicial system and decentralized government and decision-making. Within the context of the UN System-wide Special Initiative on Africa, UNDP supports the Africa Governance Forum which convenes annually to consider aspects of governance and development. In July 1997 UNDP organized an International Conference on Governance for Sustainable Growth and Equity, which was held in New York, USA. At the World Conference on Governance held in Manila, the Philippines, in May/June 1999, UNDP sponsored a series of meetings held on the subject of Building Capacities for Governance. In April of that year UNDP and the Office of the High Commissioner for Human Rights launched a joint programme to strengthen capacity-building in order to promote the integration of human rights issues into activities concerned with sustainable human development.

UNDP plays a role in developing the agenda for international co-operation on environmental and energy issues, focusing on the relationship between energy policies, environmental protection, poverty and development. UNDP supports the development of national programmes that emphasize the sustainable management of natural resources, for example through its Sustainable Energy Initiative, which promotes more efficient use of energy resources and the introduction of renewable alternatives to conventional fuels. UNDP is also concerned with forest management, the aquatic environment and sustainable agriculture and food security. Within UNDP's framework of urban development activities the Local Initiative Facility for Urban Environment (LIFE) undertakes small-scale environmental projects in low-income communities, in collaboration with local authorities and community-based groups. Other initiatives include the Urban Management Programme and the Public-Private Partnerships Programme for the Urban Environment, which aimed to generate funds, promote research and support new technologies to enhance sustainable environments in urban areas. In 1996 UNDP initiated a process of collaboration between city authorities world-wide to promote implementation of the commitments made at the 1995 Copenhagen summit for social development (see below) and to help to combat aspects of poverty and other urban problems, such as poor housing, transport, the management of waste disposal, water supply and sanitation. The first Forum of the so-called World Alliance of Cities Against Poverty was convened in October 1998, in Lyon, France. The second Forum took place in April 2000 in Geneva, Switzerland, and the third Forum was held in April 2002 in Huy, Belgium.

UNDP collaborates with other UN agencies in countries in crisis and with special circumstances to promote relief and development efforts, in order to secure the foundations for sustainable human development and thereby increase national capabilities to prevent or pre-empt future crises. In particular, UNDP is concerned to achieve reconciliation, reintegration and reconstruction in affected countries, as well as to support emergency interventions and management and delivery of programme aid. In 1995 the Executive Board decided that 5% of total UNDP regular resources be allocated to countries in 'special development situations', i.e. urgently requiring major, integrated external support. Special development initiatives include the demobilization of former combatants, rehabilitation of communities for the sustainable reintegration of returning populations, the restoration and strengthening of democratic institutions, and clearance of anti-personnel land-mines. UNDP has established a mine action unit within its Bureau for Crisis Prevention and Recovery (formerly the Emergency Response Division), in order to

strengthen national de-mining capabilities. In December 1996 UNDP launched the Civilian Reconstruction Teams programme, creating some 5,000 jobs for former combatants in Liberia to work on the rehabilitation of that country's infrastructure. In January 2002 UNDP, the World Bank and the Asian Development Bank announced the results of a jointly-prepared preliminary 'needs assessment' report for reconstruction efforts in Afghanistan: it was estimated that US $15,000m. in donor financing would be required over 10 years, of which $5,000m. would need to be provided in the first 2.5 years. UNDP is the focal point within the UN system for strengthening national capacities for natural disaster reduction (prevention, preparedness and mitigation relating to natural, environmental and technological hazards). UNDP's Disaster Management Programme oversees the system-wide Disaster Management Training Programme.

UNDP is a co-sponsor, jointly with WHO, the World Bank, UNICEF, UNESCO, UNDCP, ILO and UNFPA, of the Joint UN Programme on HIV and AIDS (UNAIDS), which became operational on 1 January 1996. UNAIDS co-ordinates UNDP's HIV and Development Programme. UNDP regards the HIV/AIDS pandemic as a major challenge to development, and advocates for making HIV/AIDS a focus of national planning; supports decentralized action against HIV/AIDS at community level; helps to strengthen national capacities at all levels to combat the disease; and aims to link support for prevention activities, education and treatment with broader development planning and responses. UNDP places a particular focus on combating the spread of HIV/AIDS through the promotion of women's rights. Within the UN system UNDP also has responsibility for co-ordinating activities following global UN conferences. In March 1995 government representatives attending the World Summit for Social Development, which was held in Copenhagen, Denmark, approved initiatives to promote the eradication of poverty, to increase and reallocate official development assistance to basic social programmes and to promote equal access to education. The Programme of Action adopted at the meeting advocated that UNDP support the implementation of social development programmes, co-ordinate these efforts through its field offices and organize efforts on the part of the UN system to stimulate capacity-building at local, national and regional levels. The PSI (see above) was introduced following the summit. A special session of the General Assembly to review the implementation of the summit's objectives was convened in June 2000. Following the UN Fourth World Conference on Women, held in Beijing, People's Republic of China, in September 1995, UNDP led inter-agency efforts to ensure the full participation of women in all economic, political and professional activities, and assisted with further situation analysis and training activities. (UNDP also created a Gender in Development Office to ensure that women participate more fully in UNDP-sponsored activities.) In June 2000 a special session of the General Assembly (Beijing + 5) was convened to review the conference. UNDP played an important role, at both national and international levels, in preparing for the second UN Conference on Human Settlements (Habitat II), which was held in Istanbul, Turkey, in June 1996 (see the UN Human Settlements Programme, p. 40). At the conference UNDP announced the establishment of a new facility, which was designed to promote private-sector investment in urban infrastructure. A special session of the UN General Assembly, entitled Istanbul + 5, was held in June 2001 to report on the implementation of the recommendations of the Habitat II conference.

UNDP aims to ensure that, rather than creating an ever-widening 'digital divide', ongoing rapid advancements in information technology are harnessed by poorer countries to accelerate progress in achieving sustainable human development. UNDP advises governments on technology policy, promotes digital entrepreneurship in programme countries and works with private-sector partners to provide reliable and affordable communications networks. The Bureau for Development Policy operates the Information and Communication Technologies for Development Programme, which aims to promote sustainable human development through increased utilization of information and communications technologies globally. The Programme aims to establish technology access centres in developing countries. A Sustainable Development Networking Programme focuses on expanding internet connectivity in poorer countries through building national capacities and supporting local internet sites. UNDP has used mobile internet units to train people even in isolated rural areas. In 1999 UNDP, in collaboration with an international communications company, Cisco Systems, and other partners, launched NetAid, an internet-based forum (accessible at www.netaid.org) for mobilizing and co-ordinating fundraising and other activities aimed at alleviating poverty and promoting sustainable human development in the developing world. With Cisco Systems and other partners, UNDP has worked to establish academies of information technology to support training and capacity-building in developing countries. By February 2002 70 academies had been established in 34 countries. UNDP and the World Bank jointly host the secretariat of the Digital Opportunity Task Force, a partnership between industrialized and developing countries, business and non-governmental organizations that was established in 2000. UNDP is a partner in the Global Digital Technology Initiative, launched in 2002 to strengthen the role of information and communications technologies in achieving the development goals of developing countries.

In 1996 UNDP implemented its first corporate communications and advocacy strategy, which aimed to generate public awareness of the activities of the UN system, to promote debate on development issues and to mobilize resources by increasing public and donor appreciation of UNDP. UNDP sponsors the International Day for the Eradication of Poverty, held annually on 17 October.

Finance

UNDP and its various funds and programmes are financed by the voluntary contributions of members of the United Nations and the Programme's participating agencies, as well as through cost-sharing by recipient governments and third-party donors. In 2001 total voluntary contributions amounted to an estimated US $2,580m, of which $652m. was for regular (core) resources. Donor co-finance, including trust funds and cost-sharing by third parties, amounted to $672m. in 2001, while cost-sharing by programme country governments amounted to more than $1,100m. In 2001 field programme expenditure under UNDP's regular programme totalled $1,526.2m.

Publications

Annual Report of the Administrator.
Choices (quarterly).
Global Public Goods: International Co-operation in the 21st Century.
Human Development Report (annually, also available on CD-ROM).
Poverty Report (annually).
Results-Oriented Annual Report.

Associated Funds and Programmes

UNDP is the central funding, planning and co-ordinating body for technical co-operation within the UN system. A number of associated funds and programmes, financed separately by means of voluntary contributions, provide specific services through the UNDP network. UNDP manages a trust fund to promote economic and technical co-operation among developing countries.

CAPACITY 2015

UNDP initiated Capacity 2015 at the World Summit for Sustainable Development, which was held in August/September 2002. Capacity 2015 aims to to support developing countries in expanding their capabilities to meet the Millennium Development Goals pledged by governments at a summit meeting of the UN General Assembly in September 2000.

GLOBAL ENVIRONMENT FACILITY—GEF

The GEF, which is managed jointly by UNDP, the World Bank and UNEP, began operations in 1991 and was restructured in 1994. Its aim is to support projects concerning climate change, the conservation of biological diversity, the protection of international waters, reducing the depletion of the ozone layer in the atmosphere, and (since October 2002) arresting land degradation and addressing the issue of persistent organic pollutants. The GEF acts as the financial mechanism for the Convention on Biological Diversity and the UN Framework Convention on Climate Change. UNDP is responsible for capacity-building, targeted research, pre-investment activities and technical assistance. UNDP also administers the Small Grants Programme of the GEF, which supports community-based activities by local non-governmental organizations, and the Country Dialogue Workshop Programme, which promotes dialogue on national priorities with regard to the GEF. In August 2002 32 donor countries pledged $2,920m. for the third periodic replenishment of GEF funds (GEF-3), covering the period 2002–06. During 1991–2002 the GEF allocated $4,000m. in grants and raised $12,000m. in co-financing from other sources in support of more than 1,000 projects in more than 140 developing nations.

Internet: www.gefweb.org.

Chair. and CEO: MOHAMMED T. EL-ASHRY.

MONTREAL PROTOCOL

UNDP assists countries to eliminate the use of ozone-depleting substances (ODS), in accordance with the Montreal Protocol to the Vienna Convention for the Protection of the Ozone Layer (see p. 51), through the design, monitoring and evaluation of ODS phase-out projects and programmes. In particular, UNDP provides technical assistance and training, national capacity-building and demonstration projects and technology transfer investment projects. By mid-2001, through the Executive Committee of the Montreal Protocol, UNDP had completed 822 projects and activities concerned with eliminating ozone-depleting substances.

UNDP DRYLANDS DEVELOPMENT CENTRE—DDC

The Centre, based in Nairobi, Kenya, was established in February 2002, superseding the former UN Office to Combat Desertification and Drought (UNSO). (UNSO had been established following the conclusion, in October 1994, of the UN Convention to Combat Desertification in Those Countries Experiencing Serious Drought and/or Desertification, Particularly in Africa; in turn, UNSO had replaced the former UN Sudano–Sahelian Office.) The DDC was to focus on the following areas: ensuring that national development planning takes account of the needs of dryland communities, particularly in poverty reduction strategies; helping countries to cope with the effects of climate variability, especially drought, and to prepare for future climate change; and addressing local issues affecting the utilization of resources.

Director: PHILIP DOBIE.

PROGRAMME OF ASSISTANCE TO THE PALESTINIAN PEOPLE—PAPP

PAPP, established in 1978, is committed to strengthening newly-created institutions in the Israeli-occupied Territories and emerging Palestinian autonomous areas, to creating employment opportunities and to stimulating private and public investment in the area to enhance trade and export potential. Examples of PAPP activities include the following: construction of sewage collection networks and systems in the northern Gaza Strip; provision of water to 500,000 people in rural and urban areas of the West Bank and Gaza; construction of schools, youth and health centres; support to vegetable and fish traders through the construction of cold storage and packing facilities; and provision of loans to strengthen industry and commerce.

Internet: www.papp.undp.org.

UNITED NATIONS CAPITAL DEVELOPMENT FUND—UNCDF

The Fund was established in 1966 and became fully operational in 1974. It invests in poor communities in least-developed countries through local governance projects and microfinance operations, with the aim of increasing such communities' access to essential local infrastructure and services and thereby improving their productive capacities and self-reliance. UNDCF encourages participation by local people and local governments in the planning, implementation and monitoring of projects. The Fund aims to promote the interests of women in community projects and to enhance their earning capacities. In 1998 the Fund nominated 15 less-developed countries in which to concentrate subsequent programmes. A Special Unit for Microfinance (SUM), established in 1997 as a joint UNDP/UNCDF operation, was fully integrated into UNCDF in 1999. UNCDF/SUM helps to develop financial services for poor communities and supports UNDP's MicroStart initiative. UNCDF's annual programming budget amounts to some US $40m.

Internet: www.uncdf.org.

Executive Secretary: NORMAND LAUZON.

UNITED NATIONS DEVELOPMENT FUND FOR WOMEN—UNIFEM

UNIFEM is the UN's lead agency in addressing the issues relating to women in development and promoting the rights of women worldwide. The Fund provides direct financial and technical support to enable low-income women in developing countries to increase earnings, gain access to labour-saving technologies and otherwise improve the quality of their lives. It also funds activities that include women in decision-making related to mainstream development projects. In 2001 UNIFEM approved 67 new projects and continued to support some 204 ongoing programmes world-wide. In that year UNIFEM's Trust Fund in Support of Actions to Eliminate Violence Against Women (established in 1996) provided grants to 21 national and regional programmes. During 1996–2001 the Trust Fund awarded grants totalling US $5.3m. in support of 127 initiatives in more than 70 countries. UNIFEM has supported the preparation of national reports in 30 countries and used the priorities identified in these reports and in other regional initiatives to formulate a Women's Development Agenda for the 21st century. Through these efforts, UNIFEM played an active role in the preparation for the UN Fourth World Conference on Women, which was held in Beijing, People's Republic of China, in September 1995. UNIFEM participated at a special session of the General Assembly convened in June 2000 to review the conference, entitled Women 2000: Gender Equality, Development and Peace for the 21st Century (Beijing + 5). In March 2001 UNIFEM, in collaboration with International Alert, launched a Millennium Peace Prize for Women. In January 2002 UNIFEM appealed for US $12m. to support women's leadership in the ongoing peace-building and reconstruction process in Afghanistan. UNIFEM maintains that the empowerment of women is a key to combating the HIV/AIDS pandemic, in view of the fact that women and adolescent girls are often culturally, biologically and economically more vulnerable to infection and more likely to bear responsibility for caring for the sick. In March 2002 UNIFEM launched a three-year programme aimed at making the gender and human rights dimensions of the pandemic central to policy-making in ten countries. A new online resource (www.genderandaids.org) on the gender dimensions of HIV/AIDS, was launched in February 2003. UNIFEM was a co-founder of WomenWatch (accessible online at www.un.org/womenwatch), a UN system-wide resource for the advancement of gender equality. Programme expenditure in 2001 totalled $25.4m.

Headquarters: 304 East 45th St, 15th Floor, New York, NY 10017, USA; tel. (212) 906-6400; fax (212) 906-6705; e-mail unifem@undp .org; internet www.unifem.undp.org.

Director: NOELEEN HEYZER (Singapore).

UNITED NATIONS VOLUNTEERS—UNV

The United Nations Volunteers is an important source of middle-level skills for the UN development system supplied at modest cost, particularly in the least-developed countries. Volunteers expand the scope of UNDP project activities by supplementing the work of international and host-country experts and by extending the influence of projects to local community levels. UNV also supports technical co-operation within and among the developing countries by encouraging volunteers from the countries themselves and by forming regional exchange teams comprising such volunteers. UNV is involved in areas such as peace-building, elections, human rights, humanitarian relief and community-based environmental programmes, in addition to development activities.

The UN International Short-term Advisory (UNISTAR) Programme, which is the private-sector development arm of UNV, has increasingly focused its attention on countries in the process of economic transition. Since 1994 UNV has administered UNDP's Transfer of Knowledge Through Expatriate Nationals (TOKTEN) programme, which was initiated in 1977 to enable specialists and professionals from developing countries to contribute to development efforts in their countries of origin through short-term technical assignments.

At 31 January 2003 3,201 UNVs were serving in 130 countries. At that time the total number of people who had served under the initiative amounted to more than 30,000 in some 140 countries.

Headquarters: POB 260111, 53153 Bonn, Germany; tel. (228) 8152000; fax (228) 8152001; e-mail information@unvolunteers.org; internet www.unvolunteers.org.

Executive Co-ordinator: SHARON CAPELING-ALAKIJA.

United Nations Environment Programme—UNEP

Address: POB 30552, Nairobi, Kenya.
Telephone: (20) 621234; **fax:** (20) 624489; **e-mail:** cpiinfo@unep .org; **internet:** www.unep.org.

The United Nations Environment Programme was established in 1972 by the UN General Assembly, following recommendations of the 1972 UN Conference on the Human Environment, in Stockholm, Sweden, to encourage international co-operation in matters relating to the human environment.

Organization
(April 2003)

GOVERNING COUNCIL

The main functions of the Governing Council, which meets every two years, are to promote international co-operation in the field of the environment and to provide general policy guidance for the direction and co-ordination of environmental programmes within the UN system. It comprises representatives of 58 states, elected by the UN General Assembly, for four-year terms, on a regional basis. The Council is assisted in its work by a Committee of Permanent Representatives.

HIGH-LEVEL COMMITTEE OF MINISTERS AND OFFICIALS IN CHARGE OF THE ENVIRONMENT

The Committee was established by the Governing Council in 1997, with a mandate to consider the international environmental agenda and to make recommendations to the Council on reform and policy issues. In addition, the Committee, comprising 36 elected members, was to provide guidance and advice to the Executive Director, to enhance UNEP's collaboration and co-operation with other multilateral bodies and to help to mobilize financial resources for UNEP.

SECRETARIAT

Offices and divisions at UNEP headquarters include the the the Office of the Executive Director; the Secretariat for Governing Bodies; Offices for Evaluation and Oversight, Programme Co-ordination and Management, and Resource Mobilization; and divisions of communications and public information, early warning and assessment, policy development and law, policy implementation, technology and industry and economics, regional co-operation and representation, environmental conventions, and GEF co-ordination.

Executive Director: Dr KLAUS TÖPFER (Germany).

REGIONAL OFFICES

Africa: POB 30552, Nairobi, Kenya; tel. (20) 624292; fax (20) 623928; internet www.unep.org/roa.

Asia and the Pacific: UN Bldg, 10th Floor, Rajdamnern Ave, Bangkok 10200, Thailand; tel. (2) 288-1870; fax (2) 280-3829; e-mail uneproap@un.org; internet www.roap.unep.org.

Europe: 11–13 chemin des Anémones, 1219 Châtelaine, Geneva, Switzerland; tel. (22) 9178279; fax (22) 9178024; e-mail roe@unep.ch; internet www.unep.ch/roe.

Latin America and the Caribbean: Blvd de los Virreyes 155, Lomas Virreyes, 11000 México, DF, Mexico; tel. (52) 52024841; fax (52) 52020950; e-mail registro@rolac.unep.mx; internet www.rolac .unep.mx.

North America: 1707 H St NW, Washington, DC 20006, USA; tel. (202) 785-0465; fax (202) 785-2096; e-mail uneprona@un.org; internet www.rona.unep.org.

West Asia: POB 10880, Manama, Bahrain; tel. 276072; fax 276075; e-mail uneprowa@unep.org.bh; internet www.unep.org.bh.

OTHER OFFICES

Convention on International Trade in Endangered Species of Wild Fauna and Flora (CITES): 15 chemin des Anémones, 1219 Châtelaine, Geneva, Switzerland; tel. (22) 9178139; fax (22) 7973417; e-mail cites@unep.ch; internet www.cites.org; Sec.-Gen. WILLEM WOUTER WIJNSTEKERS (Netherlands).

Global Programme of Action for the Protection of the Marine Environment from Land-based Activities: POB 16227, 2500 The Hague, Netherlands; tel. (70) 3114460; fax (70) 3456648; e-mail gpa@unep.nl; internet www.gpa.unep.org; Co-ordinator Dr VEERLE VANDEWEERD.

New York Office: DC-2 Bldg, Room 0803, 2 United Nations Plaza, New York, NY 10017, USA; tel. (212) 963-8210; fax (212) 963-7341; internet www.nyo.unep.org.

Regional Co-ordinating Unit for East Asian Seas: UN Bldg, 10th Floor, Rajdamnern Ave, Bangkok 10200, Thailand; tel. (2) 288-1234; fax (2) 267-0808; e-mail kirkman.unescap@un.org; internet www. unep.org/water/regseas/easian/htm; Co-ordinator HUGH KIRKMAN.

Regional Co-ordinating Unit for the Caribbean Environment Programme: 14-20 Port Royal St, Kingston, Jamaica; tel. 9229267; fax 9229292; e-mail uneprcuja@cwjamaica.com; internet www.cep .unep.org; Co-ordinator NELSON ANDRADE COLMENARES.

Secretariat of the Basel Convention: CP 356, 13–15 chemin des Anémones, 1219 Châtelaine, Geneva, Switzerland; tel. (22) 9178218; fax (22) 7973454; e-mail sbc@unep.ch; internet www.basel.int; Exec. Sec. SACHIKO KUWABARA-YAMAMOTO.

Secretariat of the Convention on Biological Diversity: World Trade Centre, 393 St Jacques St West, Suite 300, Montréal, QC, Canada H2Y 1N9; tel. (514) 288-2220; fax (514) 288-6588; e-mail secretariat@biodiv.org; internet www.biodiv.org; Exec. Sec. HAM-DALLAH ZEDAN.

Secretariat of the Multilateral Fund for the Implementation of the Montreal Protocol: 1800 McGill College Ave, 27th Floor, Montréal, QC, Canada H3A 3J6; tel. (514) 282-1122; fax (514) 282-0068; e-mail secretariat@unmfs.org; internet www.unmfs.org; Chief Dr OMAR EL-ARINI.

UNEP Arab League Liaison Office: POB 212, Cairo, Egypt; tel. (2) 3361349; fax (2) 3370658.

UNEP/CMS (Convention on the Conservation of Migratory Species of Wild Animals) **Secretariat:** Martin-Luther-King-Str. 8, 53175 Bonn, Germany; tel. (228) 8152401; fax (228) 8152449; e-mail cms@unep.de; internet www.wcmc.org.uk/cms; Exec. Sec. ARNULF MÜLLER-HELMBRECHT.

UNEP Chemicals: International Environment House, 11–13 chemin des Anémones, 1219 Châtelaine, Geneva, Switzerland; tel. (22) 9171234; fax (22) 7973460; e-mail chemicals@unep.ch; internet www.chem.unep.ch; Dir JAMES B. WILLIS.

UNEP Co-ordinating Unit for the Mediterranean Action Plan (MEDU): Leoforos Vassileos Konstantinou 48, POB 18019, 11610 Athens, Greece; tel. (210) 7273100; fax (210) 7253196; e-mail unepmedu@unepmap.gr; internet www.unepmap.org; Co-ordinator LUCIEN CHABASON.

UNEP Division of Technology, Industry and Economics: Tour Mirabeau, 39–43, Quai André Citroën, 75739 Paris Cédex 15, France; tel. 1-44-37-14-41; fax 1-44-37-14-74; e-mail unep.tie@unep.fr; internet www.uneptie.org/; Dir JACQUELINE ALOISI DE LARDEREL.

UNEP International Environmental Technology Centre (IETC): 2-110 Ryokuchi koen, Tsurumi-ku, Osaka 538-0036, Japan; tel. (6) 6915-4581; fax (6) 6915-0304; e-mail ietc@unep.or.jp; internet www.unep.or.jp; Dir STEVE HALLS.

UNEP Ozone Secretariat: POB 30552, Nairobi, Kenya; tel. (20) 623850; fax (20) 623913; e-mail ozoneinfo@unep.org; internet www.unep.org/ozone/; Officer-in-Charge MICHAEL GRABER.

UNEP Secretariat for the UN Scientific Committee on the Effects of Atomic Radiation: Vienna International Centre, Wagramerstrasse 5, POB 500, 1400 Vienna, Austria; tel. (1) 26060-4330; fax (1) 26060-5902; e-mail norman.gentner@unvienna.org; internet www.unscear.org; Sec. Dr NORMAN GENTNER.

Activities

UNEP serves as a focal point for environmental action within the UN system. It aims to maintain a constant watch on the changing state of the environment; to analyse the trends; to assess the problems using a wide range of data and techniques; and to promote projects leading to environmentally sound development. It plays a catalytic and co-ordinating role within and beyond the UN system. Many UNEP projects are implemented in co-operation with other UN agencies, particularly UNDP, the World Bank group, FAO, UNESCO and WHO. About 45 intergovernmental organizations outside the UN system and 60 international non-governmental organizations have official observer status on UNEP's Governing Council, and, through the Environment Liaison Centre in Nairobi, UNEP is linked to more than 6,000 non-governmental bodies concerned with the environment. UNEP also sponsors international conferences, programmes, plans and agreements regarding all aspects of the environment.

In February 1997 the Governing Council, at its 19th session, adopted a ministerial declaration (the Nairobi Declaration) on UNEP's future role and mandate, which recognized the organization as the principal UN body working in the field of the environment and as the leading global environmental authority, setting and overseeing the international environmental agenda. In June a special session of the UN General Assembly, referred to as the 'Rio + 5', was convened to review the state of the environment and progress achieved in implementing the objectives of the UN Conference on Environment and Development (UNCED), held in Rio de Janeiro, Brazil, in June 1992. The meeting adopted a Programme for Further Implementation of Agenda 21 (a programme of activities to promote sustainable development, adopted by UNCED) in order to intensify efforts in areas such as energy, freshwater resources and technology transfer. The meeting confirmed UNEP's essential role in advancing the Programme and as a global authority promoting a coherent legal and political approach to the environmental challenges of sustainable development. An extensive process of restructuring and realignment of functions was subsequently initiated by UNEP, and a new organizational structure reflecting the decisions of the Nairobi Declaration was implemented during 1999. UNEP played a leading role in preparing for the World Summit on Sustainable Development (WSSD), held in August/September 2002 in Johannesburg, South Africa, to assess strategies for strengthening the implementation of Agenda 21. Governments participating in the conference adopted the Johannesburg Declaration and WSSD Plan of Implementation, in which they strongly reaffirmed commitment to the principles underlying Agenda 21 and also pledged

support to all internationally-agreed development goals, including the UN Millennium Development Goals adopted by governments attending a summit meeting of the UN General Assembly in September 2000. Participating governments made concrete commitments to attaining several specific objectives in the areas of water, energy, health, agriculture and fisheries, and biodiversity. These included a reduction by one-half in the proportion of people worldwide lacking access to clean water or good sanitation by 2015, the restocking of depleted fisheries by 2015, a reduction in the ongoing loss in biodiversity by 2010, and the production and utilization of chemicals without causing harm to human beings and the environment by 2020. Participants determined to increase usage of renewable energy sources and to develop by 2005 integrated water resources management and water efficiency plans. A large number of partnerships between governments, private sector interests and civil society groups were announced at the conference.

In May 2000 UNEP sponsored the first annual Global Ministerial Environment Forum (GMEF), held in Malmö, Sweden, and attended by environment ministers and other government delegates from more than 130 countries. Participants reviewed policy issues in the field of the environment and addressed issues such as the impact on the environment of population growth, the depletion of earth's natural resources, climate change and the need for fresh water supplies. The Forum issued the Malmö Declaration, which identified the effective implementation of international agreements on environmental matters at national level as the most pressing challenge for policy-makers. The Declaration emphasized the importance of mobilizing domestic and international resources and urged increased co-operation from civil society and the private sector in achieving sustainable development. The second GMEF, held in Nairobi in February 2001, addressed means of strengthening international environmental governance, establishing an Open-Ended Intergovernmental Group of Ministers or Their Representatives (IGM) to prepare a report on possible reforms. GMEF-3, held in Cartagena, Colombia, in February 2002, considered UNEP's participation in the forthcoming WSSD, with a focus on environmental guidance issues.

ENVIRONMENTAL ASSESSMENT AND EARLY WARNING

The Nairobi Declaration resolved that the strengthening of UNEP's information, monitoring and assessment capabilities was a crucial element of the organization's restructuring, in order to help establish priorities for international, national and regional action, and to ensure the efficient and accurate dissemination of emerging environmental trends and emergencies.

In 1995 UNEP launched the Global Environment Outlook (GEO) process of environmental assessment. UNEP is assisted in its analysis of the state of the global environment by an extensive network of collaborating centres. Reports on the process are issued every two–three years. (The first *Global Environment Outlook*, GEO-I, was published in January 1997, and the second, *GEO 2000*, in September 1999, and *GEO-3* in May 2002.) UNEP is leading a major Global International Waters Assessment (GIWA) to consider all aspects of the world's water-related issues, in particular problems of shared transboundary waters, and of future sustainable management of water resources. UNEP is also a sponsoring agency of the Joint Group of Experts on the Scientific Aspects of Marine Environmental Pollution and contributes to the preparation of reports on the state of the marine environment and on the impact of land-based activities on that environment. In November 1995 UNEP published a Global Biodiversity Assessment, which was the first comprehensive study of biological resources throughout the world. The UNEP-World Conservation Monitoring Centre (UNEP-WCMC), established in June 2000, provides biodiversity-related assessment. UNEP is a partner in the International Coral Reef Action Network—ICRAN, which was established in 2000 to manage and protect coral reefs world-wide. In June 2001 UNEP launched the Millennium Ecosystems Assessment, which is expected to be completed in 2004. Other major assessments under way in 2002 included GIWA (see above); the Assessment of Impact and Adaptation to Climate Change; the Solar and Wind Energy Resource Assessment; the Regionally-Based Assessment of Persistent Toxic Substances; the Land Degradation Assessment in Drylands; and the Global Methodology for Mapping Human Impacts on the Biosphere (GLOBIO) project.

UNEP's environmental information network includes the Global Resource Information Database (GRID), which converts collected data into information usable by decision-makers. The INFOTERRA programme facilitates the exchange of environmental information through an extensive network of national 'focal points'. By early 2003 177 countries were participating in the network. Through INFOTERRA UNEP promotes public access to environmental information, as well as participation in environmental concerns. UNEP aims to establish in every developing region an Environment and Natural Resource Information Network (ENRIN) in order to make available technical advice and manage environmental information and data for improved decision-making and action-planning in countries most in need of assistance. UNEP aims to integrate its information resources in order to improve access to information and to promote its international exchange. This has been pursued through UNEPnet, an internet-based interactive environmental information- and data-sharing facility, and Mercure, a telecommunications service using satellite technology to link a network of 16 earth stations throughout the world.

UNEP's information, monitoring and assessment structures also serve to enhance early-warning capabilities and to provide accurate information during an environmental emergency.

POLICY DEVELOPMENT AND LAW

UNEP aims to promote the development of policy tools and guide-lines in order to achieve the sustainable management of the world environment. At a national level it assists governments to develop and implement appropriate environmental instruments and aims to co-ordinate policy initiatives. Training workshops in various aspects of environmental law and its applications are conducted. UNEP supports the development of new legal, economic and other policy instruments to improve the effectiveness of existing environmental agreements.

UNEP was instrumental in the drafting of a Convention on Biological Diversity (CBD) to preserve the immense variety of plant and animal species, in particular those threatened with extinction. The Convention entered into force at the end of 1993; by December 2002 187 countries and the European Community were parties to the CBD. The CBD's Cartagena Protocol on Biosafety (so-called as it had been addressed at an extraordinary session of parties to the CBD convened in Cartagena, Colombia, in February 1999) was adopted at a meeting of parties to the CBD held in Montreal, Canada, in January 2000. The Protocol regulates the transboundary movement and use of living modified organisms resulting from biotechnology (such as genetically modified—GM—seeds and crops), in order to reduce any potential adverse effects on biodiversity and human health. It establishes an Advanced Informed Agreement procedure to govern the import of such organisms. By December 2002 the Protocol had been ratified by 45 states. In January of that year UNEP launched a major project aimed at supporting developing countries with assessing the potential health and environmental risks and benefits of GM crops, in preparation for the Protocol's entry into force. In February the parties to the CBD and other partners convened a conference, in Montreal, to address ways in which the traditional knowledge and practices of local communities could be preserved and used to conserve highly-threatened species and ecosystems. The sixth conference of parties to the CBD, held in April 2002, adopted detailed voluntary guide-lines concerning access to genetic resources and sharing the benefits attained from such resources with the countries and local communities where they originate; a global work programme on forests; and a set of guiding principles for combating alien invasive species. UNEP supports co-operation for biodiversity assessment and management in selected developing regions and for the development of strategies for the conservation and sustainable exploitation of individual threatened species (e.g. the Global Tiger Action Plan). It also provides assistance for the preparation of individual country studies and strategies to strengthen national biodiversity management and research. UNEP administers the Convention on International Trade in Endangered Species of Wild Flora and Fauna (CITES), which entered into force in 1975.

In October 1994 87 countries, meeting under UN auspices, signed a Convention to Combat Desertification (see UNDP Drylands Development Centre, p. 48), which aimed to provide a legal framework to counter the degradation of drylands. An estimated 75% of all drylands have suffered some land degradation, affecting approximately 1,000m. people in 110 countries. UNEP continues to support the implementation of the Convention, as part of its efforts to protect land resources. UNEP also aims to improve the assessment of dryland degradation and desertification in co-operation with governments and other international bodies, as well as identifying the causes of degradation and measures to overcome these.

UNEP is the lead UN agency for promoting environmentally sustainable water management. It regards the unsustainable use of water as the most urgent environmental and sustainable development issue, and estimates that two-thirds of the world's population will suffer chronic water shortages by 2025, owing to rising demand for drinking water as a result of growing populations, decreasing quality of water because of pollution, and increasing requirements of industries and agriculture. In 2000 UNEP adopted a new water policy and strategy, comprising assessment, management and co-ordination components. The Global International Waters Assessment (see above) is the primary framework for the assessment component. The management component includes the Global Programme of Action (GPA) for the Protection of the Marine Environment from Land-based Activities (adopted in November 1995), and UNEP's freshwater programme and regional seas programme. The GPA for the Protection of the Marine Environment for Land-based Activities focuses on the effects of activities such as pollution on freshwater resources, marine biodiversity and the coastal ecosystems of small-island developing states. UNEP aims to develop a similar global instrument to ensure the integrated management of freshwater resources. It promotes

international co-operation in the management of river basins and coastal areas and for the development of tools and guide-lines to achieve the sustainable management of freshwater and coastal resources. UNEP provides scientific, technical and administrative support to facilitate the implementation and co-ordination of 14 regional seas conventions and 13 regional plans of action, and is developing a strategy to strengthen collaboration in their implementation. The new water policy and strategy emphasizes the need for improved co-ordination of existing activities. UNEP aims to play an enhanced role within relevant co-ordination mechanisms, such as the UN open-ended informal consultation process on oceans and the law of the sea.

In 1996 UNEP, in collaboration with FAO, began to work towards promoting and formulating a legally-binding international convention on prior informed consent (PIC) for hazardous chemicals and pesticides in international trade, extending a voluntary PIC procedure of information exchange undertaken by more than 100 governments since 1991. The Convention was adopted at a conference held in Rotterdam, Netherlands, in September 1998, and was to enter into force on being ratified by 50 signatory states. It aimed to reduce risks to human health and the environment by restricting the production, export and use of hazardous substances and enhancing information exchange procedures. By March 2003 the Convention had been ratified by 41 signatory states.

In conjunction with UN-Habitat, UNDP, the World Bank and other organizations and institutions, UNEP promotes environmental concerns in urban planning and management through the Sustainable Cities Programme, as well as regional workshops concerned with urban pollution and the impact of transportation systems. In 1994 UNEP inaugurated an International Environmental Technology Centre (IETC), with offices in Osaka and Shiga, Japan, in order to strengthen the capabilities of developing countries and countries with economies in transition to promote environmentally-sound management of cities and freshwater reservoirs through technology co-operation and partnerships.

UNEP has played a key role in global efforts to combat risks to the ozone layer, resultant climatic changes and atmospheric pollution. UNEP worked in collaboration with the World Meteorological Organization to formulate the UN Framework Convention on Climate Change (UNFCCC), with the aim of reducing the emission of gases that have a warming effect on the atmosphere, and has remained an active participant in the ongoing process to review and enforce its implementation (see WMO, p. 124, for further details, including on the Kyoto Protocol to the UNFCCC). UNEP was the lead agency in formulating the 1987 Montreal Protocol to the Vienna Convention for the Protection of the Ozone Layer (1985), which provided for a 50% reduction in the production of chlorofluorocarbons (CFCs) by 2000. An amendment to the Protocol was adopted in 1990, which required complete cessation of the production of CFCs by 2000 in industrialized countries and by 2010 in developing countries; these deadlines were advanced to 1996 and 2006, respectively, in November 1992. In 1997 the ninth Conference of the Parties (COP) to the Vienna Convention adopted a further amendment which aimed to introduce a licensing system for all controlled substances. The eleventh COP, meeting in Beijing, People's Republic of China, in November/December 1999, adopted the Beijing Amendment, which imposed tighter controls on the import and export of hydrochlorofluorocarbons, and on the production and consumption of bromochloromethane (Halon-1011, an industrial solvent and fire extinguisher). The Beijing Amendment entered into force in December 2001. A Multilateral Fund for the Implementation of the Montreal Protocol was established in June 1990 to promote the use of suitable technologies and the transfer of technologies to developing countries. UNEP, UNDP, the World Bank and UNIDO are the sponsors of the Fund, which by July 2001 had approved financing for some 3,850 projects in 124 developing countries at a cost of US $1,200m. Commitments of $440m. were made to the fourth replenishment of the Fund, covering the three-year period 2000–02.

POLICY IMPLEMENTATION

UNEP's Division of Environmental Policy Implementation incorporates two main functions: technical co-operation and response to environmental emergencies.

With the UN Office for the Co-ordination of Humanitarian Assistance (OCHA), UNEP has established a joint Environment Unit to mobilize and co-ordinate international assistance and expertise for countries facing environmental emergencies and natural disasters. In mid-1999 UNEP and UN-Habitat jointly established a Balkan Task Force (subsequently renamed UNEP Balkans Unit) to assess the environmental impact of NATO's aerial offensive against the Federal Republic of Yugoslavia (now Serbia and Montenegro). In November 2000 the Unit led a field assessment to evaluate reports of environmental contamination by debris from NATO ammunition containing depleted uranium. A final report, issued by UNEP in March 2001, concluded that there was no evidence of widespread contamination of the ground surface by depleted uranium and that the radiological and toxicological risk to the local population was negligible. It stated, however, that considerable scientific uncertainties remained, for example as to the safety of groundwater and the longer-term behaviour of depleted uranium in the environment, and recommended precautionary action. In December 2001 UNEP established a new Post-conflict Assessment Unit, which replaced, and extended the scope of, the Balkans Unit. In 2002 the Post-conflict Assessment Unit was undertaking activities in Afghanistan as well as the Balkans.

UNEP, together with UNDP and the World Bank, is an implementing agency of the Global Environment Facility (GEF, see p. 48), which was established in 1991 as a mechanism for international co-operation in projects concerned with biological diversity, climate change, international waters and depletion of the ozone layer. UNEP services the Scientific and Technical Advisory Panel, which provides expert advice on GEF programmes and operational strategies.

TECHNOLOGY, INDUSTRY AND ECONOMICS

The use of inappropriate industrial technologies and the widespread adoption of unsustainable production and consumption patterns have been identified as being inefficient in the use of renewable resources and wasteful, in particular in the use of energy and water. UNEP aims to encourage governments and the private sector to develop and adopt policies and practices that are cleaner and safer, make efficient use of natural resources, incorporate environmental costs, ensure the environmentally sound management of chemicals, and reduce pollution and risks to human health and the environment. In collaboration with other organizations and agencies UNEP works to define and formulate international guide-lines and agreements to address these issues. UNEP also promotes the transfer of appropriate technologies and organizes conferences and training workshops to provide sustainable production practices. Relevant information is disseminated through the International Cleaner Production Information Clearing House. UNEP, together with UNIDO, has established eight National Cleaner Production Centres to promote a preventive approach to industrial pollution control. In October 1998 UNEP adopted an International Declaration on Cleaner Production, with a commitment to implement cleaner and more sustainable production methods and to monitor results; the Declaration had 267 signatories at December 2001, including representatives of 45 governments. In 1997 UNEP and the Coalition for Environmentally Responsible Economies initiated the Global Reporting Initiative, which, with participation by corporations, business associations and other organizations and stakeholders, develops guide-lines for voluntary reporting by companies on their economic, environmental and social performance. In April 2002 UNEP launched the 'Life-Cycle Initiative', which aims to assist governments, businesses and other consumers with adopting environmentally-sound policies and practice, in view the upward trend in global consumption patterns.

UNEP provides institutional servicing to the Basel Convention on the Control of Transboundary Movements of Hazardous Wastes and their Disposal, which was adopted in 1989 with the aim of preventing the disposal of wastes from industrialized countries in countries that have no processing facilities. In March 1994 the second meeting of parties to the Convention determined to ban the exportation of hazardous wastes between industrialized and developing countries. The third meeting of parties to the Convention, held in 1995, proposed that the ban should be incorporated into the Convention as an amendment. The resulting so-called Ban Amendment (prohibiting exports of hazardous wastes for final disposal and recycling from states parties belonging to the OECD and, or, European Union, and from Liechtenstein, to any other state party to the Convention) required ratification by three-quarters of the 62 signatory states present at the time of adoption before it could enter into effect; by February 2003 the Ban Amendment had been ratified by 36 parties. In 1998 the technical working group of the Convention agreed a new procedure for clarifying the classification and characterization of specific hazardous wastes. The fifth full meeting of parties to the Convention, held in December 1999, adopted the Basel Declaration outlining an agenda for the period 2000–10, with a particular focus on minimizing the production of hazardous wastes. At February 2003 the number of parties to the Convention totalled 155. In December 1999 132 states adopted a Protocol to the Convention to address issues relating to liability and compensation for damages from waste exports. The governments also agreed to establish a multilateral fund to finance immediate clean-up operations following any environmental accident.

The UNEP Chemicals office was established to promote the sound management of hazardous substances, central to which was the International Register of Potentially Toxic Chemicals (IRPTC). UNEP aims to facilitate access to data on chemicals and hazardous wastes, in order to assess and control health and environmental risks, by using the IRPTC as a clearing house facility of relevant information and by publishing information and technical reports on the impact of the use of chemicals.

UNEP's OzonAction Programme works to promote information exchange, training and technological awareness. Its objective is to strengthen the capacity of governments and industry in developing countries to undertake measures towards the cost-effective phasing-out of ozone-depleting substances. UNEP also encourages the development of alternative and renewable sources of energy. To achieve this, UNEP is supporting the establishment of a network of centres to research and exchange information of environmentally-sound energy technology resources.

REGIONAL CO-OPERATION AND REPRESENTATION

UNEP maintains six regional offices. These work to initiate and promote UNEP objectives and to ensure that all programme formulation and delivery meets the specific needs of countries and regions. They also provide a focal point for building national, sub-regional and regional partnership and enhancing local participation in UNEP initiatives. Following UNEP's reorganization a co-ordination office was established at headquarters to promote regional policy integration, to co-ordinate programme planning, and to provide necessary services to the regional offices.

UNEP provides administrative support to several regional conventions, for example the Lusaka Agreement on Co-operative Enforcement Operations Directed at Illegal Trade in Wild Flora and Fauna, which entered into force in December 1996 having been concluded under UNEP auspices in order to strengthen the implementation of the CBD and CITES in Eastern and Central Africa. UNEP also organizes conferences, workshops and seminars at national and regional levels, and may extend advisory services or technical assistance to individual governments.

CONVENTIONS

UNEP aims to develop and promote international environmental legislation in order to pursue an integrated response to global environmental issues, to enhance collaboration among existing convention secretariats, and to co-ordinate support to implement the work programmes of international instruments.

UNEP has been an active participant in the formulation of several major conventions (see above). The Division of Environmental Conventions is mandated to assist the Division of Policy Development and Law in the formulation of new agreements or protocols to existing conventions. Following the successful adoption of the Rotterdam Convention in September 1998, UNEP played a leading role in formulating a multilateral agreement to reduce and ultimately eliminate the manufacture and use of Persistent Organic Pollutants (POPs), which are considered to be a major global environmental hazard. The agreement on POPs, concluded in December 2000 at a conference sponsored by UNEP in Johannesburg, South Africa, was adopted by 127 countries in May 2001.

UNEP has been designated to provide secretariat functions to a number of global and regional environmental conventions (see above for list of offices).

COMMUNICATIONS AND PUBLIC INFORMATION

UNEP's public education campaigns and outreach programmes promote community involvement in environmental issues. Further communication of environmental concerns is undertaken through the media, an information centre service and special promotional events, including World Environment Day, photograph competitions, and the awarding of the Sasakawa Prize (to recognize distinguished service to the environment by individuals and groups) and of the Global 500 Award for Environmental Achievement. In 1996 UNEP initiated a Global Environment Citizenship Programme to promote acknowledgment of the environmental responsibilities of all sectors of society.

Finance

UNEP derives its finances from the regular budget of the United Nations and from voluntary contributions to the Environment Fund. A budget of US $119.9m. was authorized for the two-year period 2002–03, of which $100m. was for programme activities (see below), $14.9m. for management and administration, and $5m. for fund programme reserves.

APPROVED BUDGET FOR FUND PROGRAMME ACTIVITIES, 2002–03

	(US $'000)
Environmental Assessment and Early Warning . .	23,000
Policy Development and Law	13,925
Policy Implementation	8,000
Technology, Industry and Economics . . .	21,350
Regional Co-operation and Representation . .	21,025
Environment Conventions	6,975
Communications and Public Information . . .	5,725
Total	100,000

Publications

Annual Report.

APELL Newsletter (2 a year).
Cleaner Production Newsletter (2 a year).
Climate Change Bulletin (quarterly).
Connect (UNESCO-UNEP newsletter on environmental degradation, quarterly).
EarthViews (quarterly).
Environment Forum (quarterly).
Environmental Law Bulletin (2 a year).
Financial Services Initiative (2 a year).
GEF News (quarterly).
Global Environment Outlook (every 2–3 years).
Global Water Review.
GPA Newsletter.
IETC Insight (3 a year).

Industry and Environment Review (quarterly).
Leave it to Us (children's magazine, 2 a year).
Managing Hazardous Waste (2 a year).
Our Planet (quarterly).
OzonAction Newsletter (quarterly).
Tierramerica (weekly).
Tourism Focus (2 a year).
UNEP Chemicals Newsletter (2 a year).
UNEP Update (monthly).
World Atlas of Coral Reefs.
World Atlas of Biodiversity.
World Atlas of Desertification.
Studies, reports, legal texts, technical guide-lines, etc.

United Nations High Commissioner for Refugees—UNHCR

Address: CP 2500, 1211 Geneva 2 dépôt, Switzerland.
Telephone: (22) 7398111; **fax:** (22) 7397312; **e-mail:** unhcr@unhcr.ch; **internet:** www.unhcr.ch.

The Office of the High Commissioner was established in 1951 to provide international protection for refugees and to seek durable solutions to their problems.

Organization

(April 2003)

HIGH COMMISSIONER

The High Commissioner is elected by the United Nations General Assembly on the nomination of the Secretary-General, and is responsible to the General Assembly and to the UN Economic and Social Council (ECOSOC).

High Commissioner: RUUD LUBBERS (Netherlands).
Deputy High Commissioner: MARY ANN WYRSCH (USA).

EXECUTIVE COMMITTEE

The Executive Committee of the High Commissioner's Programme (ExCom), established by ECOSOC, gives the High Commissioner policy directives in respect of material assistance programmes and advice in the field of international protection. In addition, it oversees UNHCR's general policies and use of funds. ExCom, which comprises representatives of 57 states, both members and non-members of the UN, meets once a year.

ADMINISTRATION

Headquarters include the Executive Office, comprising the offices of the High Commissioner, the Deputy High Commissioner and the Assistant High Commissioner. There are separate offices for the Inspector General, the Special Envoy in the former Yugoslavia, and the Director of the UNHCR liaison office in New York. The other principal administrative units are the Division of Communication and Information, the Department of International Protection, the Division of Resource Management, and the Department of Operations, which is responsible for the five regional bureaux covering Africa; Asia and the Pacific; Europe; the Americas and the Caribbean; and Central Asia, South-West Asia, North Africa and the Middle East. At July 2002 there were 268 UNHCR field offices in 114 countries. At that time UNHCR employed 5,523 people, including short-term staff, of whom 4,654 (or 84%) were working in the field.

Activities

The competence of the High Commissioner extends to any person who, owing to well-founded fear of being persecuted for reasons of race, religion, nationality or political opinion, is outside the country of his or her nationality and is unable or, owing to such fear or for reasons other than personal convenience, remains unwilling to accept the protection of that country; or who, not having a nationality and being outside the country of his or her former habitual residence, is unable or, owing to such fear or for reasons other than personal convenience, is unwilling to return to it. This competence may be extended, by resolutions of the UN General Assembly and decisions of ExCom, to cover certain other 'persons of concern', in addition to refugees meeting these criteria. Refugees who are assisted by other UN agencies, or who have the same rights or obligations as nationals of their country of residence, are outside the mandate of UNHCR.

In recent years there has been a significant shift in UNHCR's focus of activities. Increasingly UNHCR has been called upon to support people who have been displaced within their own country (i.e. with similar needs to those of refugees but who have not crossed an international border) or those threatened with displacement as a result of armed conflict. In addition, greater support has been given to refugees who have returned to their country of origin, to assist their reintegration, and UNHCR is working to enable local communities to support the returnees, frequently through the implementation of Quick Impact Projects (QIPs).

At December 2001 the refugee population world-wide provisionally totalled 12.1m. and UNHCR was concerned with an estimated further 940,791 asylum-seekers, 462,723 recently returned refugees and 6.3m. others (of whom an estimated 5.0m. were internally displaced persons—IDPs).

World Refugee Day, sponsored by UNHCR, is held annually on 20 June.

INTERNATIONAL PROTECTION

As laid down in the Statute of the Office, UNHCR's primary function is to extend international protection to refugees and its second function is to seek durable solutions to their problems. In the exercise of its mandate UNHCR seeks to ensure that refugees and asylum-seekers are protected against *refoulement* (forcible return), that they receive asylum, and that they are treated according to internationally recognized standards. UNHCR pursues these objectives by a variety of means that include promoting the conclusion and ratification by states of international conventions for the protection of refugees. UNHCR promotes the adoption of liberal practices of asylum by states, so that refugees and asylum-seekers are granted admission, at least on a temporary basis.

The most comprehensive instrument concerning refugees that has been elaborated at the international level is the 1951 United Nations Convention relating to the Status of Refugees. This Convention, the scope of which was extended by a Protocol adopted in 1967, defines the rights and duties of refugees and contains provisions dealing with a variety of matters which affect the day-to-day lives of refugees. The application of the Convention and its Protocol is supervised by UNHCR. Important provisions for the treatment of refugees are also contained in a number of instruments adopted at the regional level. These include the 1969 Convention Governing the Specific Aspects of Refugee Problems adopted by OAU (now AU) member states in 1969, the European Agreement on the Abolition of Visas for Refugees, and the 1969 American Convention on Human Rights.

UNHCR has actively encouraged states to accede to the 1951 United Nations Refugee Convention and the 1967 Protocol: 144 states had acceded to either or both of these basic refugee instruments by September 2002. An increasing number of states have also adopted domestic legislation and/or administrative measures to implement the international instruments, particularly in the field of procedures for the determination of refugee status. UNHCR has sought to address the specific needs of refugee women and children, and has also attempted to deal with the problem of military attacks on refugee camps, by adopting and encouraging the acceptance of a set of principles to ensure the safety of refugees. In recent years it has formulated a strategy designed to address the fundamental causes of refugee flows. In 2001, in response to widespread concern about perceived high numbers of asylum-seekers and large-scale international economic migration and human trafficking, UNHCR initiated a series of Global Consultations on International Protection with the signatories to the 1951 Convention and 1967 Protocol, and other interested parties, with a view to strengthening both the application and scope of international refugee legislation. A consultation of 156 Governments, convened in Geneva, in December, reaffirmed commitment to the central role played by the Convention and Protocol. The final consultation, held in May 2002, focused on durable solutions and the protection of refugee women and children. Subsequently, based on the findings of the Global Consultations process, UNHCR developed an Agenda on Protection with six main objectives: strengthening the implementation of the 1951 Convention and 1967 Protocol; the protection of refugees within broader migration movements; more equitable sharing of burdens and responsibilities and building of capacities to receive and protect refugees; addressing more effectively security-related concerns; increasing efforts to find durable solutions; and meeting the protection needs of refugee women and children. The Agenda was endorsed by the Executive Council in October.

ASSISTANCE ACTIVITIES

The first phase of an assistance operation uses UNHCR's capacity of emergency preparedness and response. This enables UNHCR to address the immediate needs of refugees at short notice, for example, by employing specially-trained emergency teams and maintaining stockpiles of basic equipment, medical aid and materials. A significant proportion of UNHCR expenditure is allocated to the next phase of an operation, providing 'care and maintenance' in stable refugee circumstances. This assistance can take various forms, including the provision of food, shelter, medical care and essential supplies. Also covered in many instances are basic services, including education and counselling.

As far as possible, assistance is geared towards the identification and implementation of durable solutions to refugee problems—this being the second statutory responsibility of UNHCR. Such solutions generally take one of three forms: voluntary repatriation, local integration or resettlement in another country. Voluntary repatriation is increasingly the preferred solution, given the easing of political tension in many regions from which refugees have fled. Where voluntary repatriation is feasible, the Office assists refugees to overcome obstacles preventing their return to their country of origin. This may be done through negotiations with governments involved, or by providing funds either for the physical movement of refugees or for the rehabilitation of returnees once back in their own country.

POPULATIONS OF CONCERN TO UNHCR BY REGION* ('000 persons, at 31 December 2001, provisional figures)

	Refugees†	Asylum-seekers	Returned refugees‡	Others of concern§	Total
Africa . . .	3,305	107	267	494	4,174
Asia . . .	5,770	33	49	2,968	8,820
Europe . .	2,228	335	146	2,146	4,855
Latin America	37	8	0	720	765
North America	645	442	—	—	1,087
Oceania . .	65	16	—	0	81
Total . . .	**12,051**	**941**	**463**	**6,328**	**19,783**

* In accordance with the regional classification of the UN's Department for Economic and Social Affairs, under which Africa includes countries of North Africa, and Asia incorporates Cyprus and Turkey and all countries of the Middle East not located on the African continent. Latin America covers Central and South America and the Caribbean.
† Includes persons recognized as refugees under international law, and also people receiving temporary protection and assistance outside their country but who have not been formally recognized as refugees.
‡ Refugees who returned to their place of origin during 2001.
§ Mainly internally displaced persons (IDPs) and former IDPs who returned to their place of origin during 2001.

POPULATIONS OF CONCERN TO UNHCR BY COUNTRY* ('000 persons, at 31 December 2001, provisional figures)

	Refugees	Asylum-seekers	Returned refugees†	Others of concern
Africa				
Algeria	169.4	0.1	0.0	—
Angola	12.3	0.9	13.2	202.0
Burundi	27.9	8.0	27.9	62.0
Congo, Democratic Republic . .	362.0	0.3	1.1	3.5
Congo, Republic . .	119.1	2.4	0.7	—
Côte d'Ivoire . . .	126.2	2.4	—	—
Ethiopia	152.6	0.0	9.4	—
Guinea	178.4	0.9	—	—
Kenya	239.2	12.6	—	—
Liberia	54.6	—	2.5	196.1
Sierra Leone . .	10.5	0.3	92.3	—
Sudan	349.2	0.0	5.2	—
Tanzania . . .	668.1	21.3	2.0	—
Uganda	199.7	0.6	0.2	—
Zambia	284.2	0.5	—	—
Asia				
Afghanistan . . .	0.0	—	26.1	1,200.0
Armenia . . .	264.3	0.0	0.0	—
Azerbaijan . . .	0.4	6.6	0.0	573
China, People's Republic‡ . .	295.3	0.0	—	—
Georgia . . .	7.9	—	0.0	264.2
India	169.5	0.2	—	—
Iran	1,868.0	—	0.0	—
Iraq	128.1	0.4	2.0	—
Kazakhstan . . .	19.5	0.0	0.0	100.0
Kuwait	1.3	0.1	—	138.0
Nepal	130.9	0.0	—	—
Pakistan	2,198.8	0.6	0.0	—
Sri Lanka . . .	0.0	0.0	0.0	683.3
Thailand . . .	110.7	0.4	—	0.0
Europe				
Bosnia and Herzegovina	32.7	0.4	18.7	518.4
France	131.6	34.6	—	—
Germany . . .	903.0	85.5	—	—
FYR Macedonia . .	4.4	0.1	90.0	74.5
Netherlands . . .	152.3§	78.6	—	—
Russia	18.0	0.7	0.3	1,120.8
Sweden	146.5§	17.6	—	—
United Kingdom . .	148.6§	39.4	—	—
Yugoslavia . . .	400.3	0.1	25.6	351.1
Latin America				
Colombia . . .	0.2	0.0	0.2	720.0
North America				
Canada	129.2§	45.8	—	—
USA	515.8§	395.9	—	—

* The list includes only those countries having 100,000 or more persons of concern to UNHCR.
† See table above for definitions.
‡ Excluding Hong Kong Special Administrative Region.
§ Figure estimated by UNHCR on the basis of previous average annual arrivals and/or recognition of asylum-seekers.

ORIGIN OF MAJOR REFUGEE POPULATIONS AND PERSONS IN REFUGEE-LIKE SITUATIONS*

('000 persons, 31 December 2001, provisional figures)

Origin	Refugees
Afghanistan	3,809.6
Burundi	554.0
Iraq	530.1
Sudan	489.5
Angola	470.6
Sierra Leone	440.0
Somalia	439.9
Bosnia and Herzegovina	426.0

* Information on the origin of refugees is not available for a number of, mainly industrialized, countries. Data exclude some 3.9m. Palestinian refugees who come under the mandate of UNRWA (q.v.). Palestinians who are outside the UNRWA area of operation, for example those in Iraq and Libya, are considered to be of concern to UNHCR.

When voluntary repatriation is not an option, efforts are made to assist refugees to integrate locally and to become self-supporting in their countries of asylum. This may be done either by granting loans to refugees, or by assisting them, through vocational training or in other ways, to learn a skill and to establish themselves in gainful occupations. One major form of assistance to help refugees re-establish themselves outside camps is the provision of housing. In cases where resettlement through emigration is the only viable solution to a refugee problem, UNHCR negotiates with governments in an endeavour to obtain suitable resettlement opportunities, to encourage liberalization of admission criteria and to draw up special immigration schemes. During 2000 an estimated 39,500 refugees were resettled under UNHCR auspices.

In the early 1990s UNHCR aimed to consolidate efforts to integrate certain priorities into its programme planning and implementation, as a standard discipline in all phases of assistance. The considerations include awareness of specific problems confronting refugee women, the needs of refugee children, the environmental impact of refugee programmes and long-term development objectives. In an effort to improve the effectiveness of its programmes, UNHCR has initiated a process of delegating authority, as well as responsibility for operational budgets, to its regional and field representatives, increasing flexibility and accountability. An Evaluation and Policy Analysis Unit reviews systematically UNHCR's operational effectiveness.

EAST ASIA, SOUTH ASIA AND THE PACIFIC

In June 1989 an international conference was convened by UNHCR in Geneva to discuss the ongoing problem of refugees and displaced persons in and from the Indo-Chinese peninsula. The participants adopted the Comprehensive Plan of Action for Indo-Chinese Refugees (CPA), which provided for the 'screening' of all Vietnamese arrivals in the region to determine their refugee status, the resettlement of 'genuine' refugees and the repatriation (described as voluntary 'in the first instance') of those deemed to be economic migrants. A steering committee of the international conference met regularly to supervise the plan. In March 1996 UNHCR confirmed that it was to terminate funding for the refugee camps (except those in Hong Kong) at the end of June to coincide with the formal conclusion of the CPA; however, it pledged to support transitional arrangements regarding the completion of the repatriation process and maintenance of the remaining Vietnamese 'non-refugees' during the post-CPA phase-out period, as well as to continue its support for the reintegration and monitoring of returning nationals in Viet Nam and Laos. The prospect of forcible repatriation provoked rioting and violent protests in many camps throughout the region. By mid-1996 more than 88,000 Vietnamese and 22,000 Laotians had returned to their countries of origin under the framework of the CPA, with Malaysia and Singapore having completed the repatriation process. In late July the Philippines Government agreed to permit the remaining camp residents to settle permanently in that country. In September the remaining Vietnamese refugees detained on the island of Galang, in Indonesia, were repatriated, and in February 1997 the last camp for Vietnamese refugees in Thailand was formally closed. In mid-June of that year the main Vietnamese detention camp in Hong Kong was closed. However, the scheduled repatriation of all remaining Vietnamese before the transfer of sovereignty of the territory to the People's Republic of China (PRC) at the end of June was not achieved. In early 1998 the Hong Kong authorities formally terminated the policy of granting a port of first asylum to Vietnamese 'boat people'. In February 2000 UNHCR, which had proposed the integration of the remaining Vietnamese as a final durable solution to the situation, welcomed a decision by the Hong Kong authorities to offer permanent residency status to the occupants of the last remaining Vietnamese detention camp (totalling 973 refugees and 435 'non-refugees'). By the end of May, when the camp was closed, more than 200 Vietnamese had failed to apply for residency. At 31 December 2001 UNHCR was providing assistance to an estimated further 295,276 Vietnamese refugees in mainland PRC. In 1995, in accordance with an agreement concluded with the Chinese Government, UNHCR initiated a programme to redirect its local assistance to promote long-term self-sufficiency in the poorest settlements, including support for revolving-fund rural credit schemes. UNHCR favours the local integration of the majority of the Vietnamese refugee population in the PRC as a durable solution to the situation.

The conclusion of a political settlement of the conflict in Cambodia in October 1991 made possible the eventual repatriation of some 370,000 Cambodian refugees and displaced persons by April 1993. Meanwhile, however, thousands of ethnic Vietnamese (of whom there were estimated to be 200,000 in Cambodia) fled to Viet Nam, as a result of violence perpetrated against them by Cambodian armed groups. In March 1994 25,000 supporters of the Khmers Rouges in Cambodia fled across the border into Thailand, following advances by government forces. The refugees were immediately repatriated by the Thai armed forces into Khmer Rouge territory,

which was inaccessible to aid agencies. In July 1997 armed conflict between opposing political forces in northern Cambodia resulted in large-scale population movement. A voluntary repatriation programme was initiated in October, and in late March 1999 UNHCR announced that the last Cambodian refugees had left camps in Thailand, the majority having been repatriated to north-western Cambodia. A UNHCR programme was initiated to monitor the welfare of returnees and assist in their reintegration; this was terminated at the end of 2000. At 31 December 2001 there were still some 15,945 Cambodian refugees in Viet Nam. In January 2002 UNHCR signed an agreement with the Governments of Viet Nam and Cambodia for the safe repatriation of an estimated 1,000 Montagnards who had fled from the Central Highland provinces of Viet Nam during 2001. UNHCR was to be permitted unlimited access to the region to assist and monitor the return process. In March 2002, however, UNCHR withdrew from the agreement owing to alleged intimidation of refugees and UN staff.

In 1991–92 thousands of people of Nepalese ethnic origin living in Bhutan sought refuge from alleged persecution by fleeing to Nepal. In December 2000 Bhutan and Nepal reached agreement on a joint verification mechanism for the repatriation of the refugees, which had been hitherto the principal issue precluding a resolution of the situation. The first verification of Bhutanese refugees was undertaken in March 2001, and it was envisaged that voluntary repatriations would commence during 2002. At the end of 2001 there were an estimated 110,780 Bhutanese refugees in Nepal, the majority of whom were receiving UNHCR assistance in the form of food, shelter, medical care and water.

A temporary cessation of hostilities between the Sri Lankan Government and Tamil separatists in early 1995 greatly facilitated UNHCR's ongoing efforts to repatriate Sri Lankan Tamils who had fled to India. However, later in that year an offensive by Sri Lankan government troops against the northern Jaffna peninsula caused a massive displacement of the local Tamil population and effectively ended the repatriation process. Increasing insecurity from late 1999 prompted further population displacements. However, fewer movements were recorded in 2001. In July UNHCR suspended its activities in Mallavi, northern Sri Lanka, owing to security concerns. By 31 December there were 683,286 Sri Lankan internally displaced persons of concern to UNHCR, as well as an estimated 64,061 Sri Lankan refugees in 116 camps in southern India. At that time India's total refugee population of some 169,549 also included 11,972 refugees from Afghanistan and 92,344 from the PRC (mainly Tibetans).

From April 1991 increasing numbers of Rohingya Muslims in Myanmar fled into Bangladesh to escape brutality and killings perpetrated by the Myanma armed forces. UNHCR launched an international appeal for financial aid for the refugees, at the request of Bangladesh, and collaborated with other UN agencies in providing humanitarian assistance. UNHCR refused to participate in a programme of repatriation of the Myanma refugees agreed by Myanmar and Bangladesh, on the grounds that no safe environment existed for them to return to. In May 1993 a memorandum of understanding between UNHCR and Bangladesh was signed, whereby UNHCR would be able to monitor the repatriation process and ensure that people were returning of their own free will. In November a memorandum of understanding, signed with the Myanma Government, secured UNHCR access to the returnees. The first refugees returned to Myanmar with UNHCR assistance at the end of April 1994. They and all subsequent returnees were provided with a small amount of cash, housing grants and two months' food rations, and were supported by several small-scale reintegration projects. Attempts by UNHCR to find a local solution for those unwilling to return to Myanmar have been met with resistance by the Bangladeshi Government. By the end of December 2001 an estimated 22,106 Myanma refugees still remained in camps in Bangladesh and were receiving basic care from UNHCR.

In the early 1990s members of ethnic minorities in Myanmar attempted to flee attacks by government troops into Thailand; however, the Thai Government refused to recognize them as refugees or to offer them humanitarian assistance. In December 1997 Thailand and Myanmar agreed to commence 'screening' the refugees to determine those who had fled persecution and those who were economic migrants. By the end of 2001 there were an estimated 110,313 people in camps along the Myanma–Thai border, the majority of whom were Karen (Kayin) refugees.

In April 1999, following the announcement by the Indonesian Government, in January, that it would consider a form of autonomy or independence for East Timor, some 26,000 Indonesian settlers left their homes as a result of clashes between opposing groups and uncertainty regarding the future of the territory. The popular referendum on the issue, conducted at the end of August, and the resulting victory for the independence movement, provoked a violent reaction by pro-integration militia. UNHCR, along with other international personnel, was forced to evacuate the territory in early September. At that time there were reports of forced mass deportations of East Timorese to West Timor, while a large number of others fled their homes into remote mountainous areas of East Timor. In mid-September UNHCR staff visited West Timor to review the state of refugee camps, allegedly under the control of militia, and to persuade the authorities to permit access for humanitarian personnel. It was estimated that 250,000–260,000 East Timorese had fled to West Timor, of whom some 230,000 were registered in 28 camps at the end of September. At that time there were also an estimated 190,000–300,000 people displaced within East Timor, although the International Committee of the Red Cross estimated that a total of 800,000 people, or some 94% of the population, had been displaced, or deported, during the crisis. The arrival of multinational troops, from 20 September, helped to stabilize the region and enable the safe receipt and distribution of food supplies, prompting several thousands to return from hiding. Most homes, however, along with almost all other buildings in the capital, Dili, had been destroyed. In early October UNHCR, together with the International Organization for Migration, initiated a repatriation programme for the refugees in West Timor. However, despite an undertaking by the Indonesian Government in mid-October that it would ensure the safety of all refugees and international personnel, persistent intimidation by anti-independence militia impeded the registration and repatriation processes. UNHCR initially aimed to complete the repatriation programme by mid-2001, prior to the staging of elections to a Constituent Assembly by the UN Transitional Administration in East Timor (UNTAET, which assumed full authority over the territory in February 2000). However, in September 2000 UNHCR suspended its activities in West Timor, following the murder by militiamen there of three of its personnel. A UN Security Council resolution, adopted soon afterwards, deplored this incident and strongly urged the Indonesian authorities to disable the militia and to guarantee the future security of all refugees and humanitarian personnel. In mid-September UNTAET and the Indonesian Government signed a Memorandum of Understanding on co-operation in resolving the refugee crisis. However, despite a subsequent operation by the Indonesian security forces to disarm the militia, intimidation of East Timorese refugees reportedly persisted, and UNHCR did not redeploy personnel to West Timor. The Office did, however, liaise with other humanitarian organizations to facilitate continuing voluntary repatriations, which have been encouraged by the Indonesian authorities. UNHCR's operation in East Timor aimed to promote the safe voluntary repatriation of refugees, monitor returnees, support their reintegration through the implementation of QIPs, pursue efforts towards sustainable development and the rehabilitation of communities, and to promote reconciliation and respect for human rights. At the beginning of January 2002 the Indonesian Government terminated the provision of food assistance to refugees remaining in camps in West Timor. In July, following a series of protests by refugees, the Government announced that it would resume the distribution of rice, although it reiterated that all repatriation assistance would terminate on 31 August. In mid-May East Timor (now Timor-Leste) achieved independence. At that time almost 205,000 East Timorese refugees were reported to have returned since October 1999, while more than 50,000 were believed to remain in West Timorese camps. UNHCR and the newly-elected administration were co-operating to encourage further repatriation, as well as to assist with Timor-Leste's accession to the international instruments of protection and with the development of new national refugee protection legislation.

CENTRAL ASIA, SOUTH-WEST ASIA, NORTH AFRICA AND THE MIDDLE EAST

From 1979, as a result of civil strife in Afghanistan, there was a massive movement of refugees from that country into Pakistan and Iran creating the world's largest refugee population, which reached a peak of almost 6.3m. people in 1990. In 1988 UNHCR agreed to provide assistance for the voluntary repatriation of refugees, both in ensuring the rights of the returning population and in providing material assistance such as transport, immunization, and supplies of food and other essentials. In April 1992, following the establishment of a new Government in Afghanistan, refugees began to repatriate in substantial numbers, although, meanwhile, large numbers of people continued to flee into Pakistan as a result of persisting insecurity. From October 1996 an escalation of hostilities in northern and western regions of Afghanistan resulted in further massive population displacement. By the end of 1998 the total number of returnees from Iran and Pakistan since 1988 amounted to more than 4.2m. In recent years UNHCR, with other UN agencies, attempted to meet the immediate needs of IDPs and recent returnees in Afghanistan through systematic monitoring and, for example, by initiating small-scale multi-sectoral QIPs to improve shelter, rural water supply and local infrastructure; organizing income-generating and capacity-building activities; and providing food and tools. However, the ongoing civil conflict, as well as successive severe droughts and harsh winter conditions, caused renewed population displacement, precluding a settlement of the refugee situation and entailing immense difficulties in undertaking comprehensive relief efforts.

Activities were disrupted by periodic withdrawals of UN international personnel owing to security concerns. The humanitarian crisis worsened considerably during 2000. At the end of that year, an estimated total of 1.3m. Afghan refugees were sheltering in Iran (the same as at the end of 1999), 2m. in Pakistan (compared with 1.2m. at end-1999), 15,350 in Tajikistan, and some 12,760 in India. In mid-2001 UNHCR warned that the food insecurity in the country was continuing to deteriorate and that population movements were ongoing. In September, prompted by the threat of impending military action directed by a US-led global coalition against targets in the Taliban-administered areas of Afghanistan, UNHCR launched a US $252m. appeal to finance an emergency relief operation to cope with a potentially large further movement of Afghan refugees and IDPs. Although all surrounding countries imposed 'closed border' policies (with Pakistan reportedly permitting limited entry to Afghans in possession of correct travel documentation), it was envisaged that, were the security situation to deteriorate significantly, large numbers of Afghans might attempt to cross into the surrounding countries (mainly Iran and Pakistan) at unsecured points of entry. UNHCR urged the adoption of more liberal border policies and began substantially to reinforce its presence in Iran and Pakistan. Activities being undertaken included the supply of basic relief items such as tents and health and hygiene kits and assistance with the provision of community services such as education for school-age children. The construction and maintenance of new camps near the Pakistan-Afghanistan border was initiated in co-operation with the Pakistan Government and other agencies, and it was also planned to construct new refugee shelters in Iran. Emergency contingency plans were also formulated for a relief initiative to assist a projected further 500,000 IDPs (in addition to the large numbers of people already displaced) inside Afghanistan. Large population movements out of cities were reported from the start of the international political crisis. An estimated 6m. Afghans (about one-quarter of the total population) were believed to be extremely vulnerable, requiring urgent food aid and other relief supplies. In mid-September all foreign UN field staff were withdrawn from Afghanistan for security reasons; meanwhile, in order to address the humanitarian situation, a Crisis Group was established by several UN agencies, including UNHCR, and a crisis management structure came into operation at UNHCR headquarters. In October (when air-strikes were initiated against Afghanistan) UNHCR opened a staging camp at a major crossing point on the Afghanistan-Pakistan border, and put in place a system for monitoring new refugee arrivals (implemented by local people rather than by UNHCR personnel). It was estimated that from October 2001–January 2002 about 50,000 Afghan refugees entered Pakistan officially, while about 150,000 crossed into the country at unofficial border points; many reportedly sought refuge with friends and relatives. Much smaller movements into Iran were reported. Spontaneous repatriations also occurred during that period (reportedly partly owing to the poor conditions at many camps in Pakistan), and UNHCR-assisted IDP returns were also undertaken. UNHCR resumed operations within Afghanistan in mid-November 2001, distributing supplies and implementing QIPs, for example the provision of warm winter clothing. From that month some 130,000 Afghan refugees in Pakistan were relocated from inadequate accommodation to new camps. At December 2001 there were an estimated 1.48m. Afghan refugees in Iran, 2.20m. in Pakistan and 15,300 in Tajikistan. On 1 March 2002 UNHCR initiated, jointly with the new interim Afghan administration, an assisted repatriation programme. Each returning family was to receive food and basic household items, as well as information about security and mine-awareness. UNHCR also concluded tripartite accords on repatriation with the Afghan authorities and with Iran and Pakistan. The pace of returns far exceeded expectations, and by early August more than 1.2m. Afghan refugees had registered to return under the programme, while some 200,000 had returned spontaneously. UNHCR had assisted a further 200,000 IDPs to return to their home areas. In early August UNHCR signed a new agreement with the Iranian Government to grant access to Afghans in detention centres throughout that country and to undertake a screening programme for asylum-seekers, in order to deal with the problem of undocumented refugees. However, at the same time UNHCR expressed its concern at reports that the Iranian authorities were applying pressure on long-term refugees to return to Afghanistan involuntarily.

In late 1992 people began to flee civil conflict in Tajikistan and to seek refuge in Afghanistan. During 1993 an emergency UNHCR operation established a reception camp to provide the 60,000 Tajik refugees with basic assistance, and began to move them away from the border area to safety. In December a tripartite agreement was concluded by UNHCR and the Tajik and Afghan Governments regarding the security of refugees returning to Tajikistan. UNHCR monitored the repatriation process and provided materials for the construction of almost 20,000 homes. The operation was concluded by the end of 1997. Nevertheless, at the end of 2000, there were still nearly 60,000 Tajik refugees remaining in other countries of the former USSR, of whom 14,120 were receiving assistance from

UNHCR. During 2000–02 an initiative was being implemented to integrate locally some 10,000 Tajik refugees of Kyrgyz ethnic origin in Kyrgyzstan and 12,500 Tajik refugees of Turkmen origin in Turkmenistan. Some 2,500 Tajik refugees were expected to return to Tajikistan in 2002. From late 2001 about 9,000 Afghan refugees repatriated from Tajikistan under the auspices of UNHCR and the International Organization for Migration. UNHCR expressed concern following the adoption by the Tajikistan authorities in May 2002 of refugee legislation that reportedly contravened the 1951 Convention relating to the Status of Refugees and its 1967 Protocol.

In March–May 1991, following the war against Iraq by a multi-national force, and the subsequent Iraqi suppression of resistance in Kurdish areas in the north of the country, there was massive movement of some 1.5m., mainly Kurdish, refugees into Iran and Turkey. UNHCR was designated the principal UN agency to attempt to alleviate the crisis. In May the refugees began to return to Iraq in huge numbers and UNHCR assisted in their repatriation, establishing relief stations along their routes from Iran and Turkey. Following the war to liberate Kuwait UNHCR gave protection and assistance to Iraqis, Bidoon (stateless people) and Palestinians who were forced to leave that country. In May 2000 the Kuwaiti authorities determined that all Bidoon still resident in the country should register officially with the national authorities by 27 June; while it was agreed that citizenship requirement restrictions would be eased for some 36,000 Bidoon who had been enumerated at a population census in 1965, the remaining stateless residents (numbering an estimated 75,000) were to be required to apply for short-term residency permits. At 31 December 2001 there were, provisionally, 1,255 registered refugees in Kuwait, however, it was estimated that an additional 138,000 people in Kuwait were of concern to UNHCR, mainly Bidoons, Iraqis and Palestinians. In March 2003, following the initiation of US-led military action against Iraq, UNHCR and the International Federation of Red Cross and Red Crescent Societies (q.v.) signed an agreement on co-operation in providing humanitarian relief in Iraq and neighbouring countries.

In April 1994 UNHCR initiated a programme to provide food and relief assistance to Turkish Kurds who had fled into northern Iraq. In September 1996 fighting escalated among the Kurdish factions in northern Iraq. By the time a cease-fire agreement was concluded in November some 65,000 Iraqi Kurds had fled across the border into Iran. UNHCR, together with the Iranian Government, provided these new refugees with basic humanitarian supplies. By the end of the year, however, the majority of refugees had returned to Iraq, owing to poor conditions in the temporary settlements, security concerns at being located in the border region and pressure from the Iranian authorities. In December, UNHCR announced its intention to withdraw from the Atroush camp in northern Iraq, which housed an estimated 15,000 Turkish Kurds, following several breaches of security in the camp. UNHCR proceeded to transfer 3,500 people to other local settlements, and continued to provide humanitarian assistance to those refugees who had settled closer to Iraqi-controlled territory but who had been refused asylum. During 1997–2000 some 2,200 Turkish Kurds repatriated from Iraq with assistance from UNHCR. At 31 December 2001 the refugee population in Iraq amounted to an estimated 128,142, of whom about 39,200 were being assisted by UNHCR. The total refugee population included some 90,000 Palestinians, 23,680 Iranian Kurds, and 13,136 Kurds from Turkey. In addition, there were an estimated 1,968 returned refugees in Iraq of concern to UNHCR. At that time there was still a substantial Iraqi refugee population in the region, mainly comprising the 386,000 people in Iran. In March 2001 the Governments of Iran and Iraq concluded a bilateral accord on the voluntary repatriation of some 5,000 Iranians and 5,000 Iraqis; UNHCR was to assist with the implementation of the agreement. During 2002 UNHCR was providing counseling to those refugee families to enable them to make a decision on repatriation.

In June 1992 people fleeing the civil war and famine in Somalia began arriving in Yemen in large numbers. UNHCR set up camps to accommodate some 50,000 refugees, providing them with shelter, food, water and sanitation. As a result of civil conflict in Yemen in mid-1994, a large camp in the south of the country was demolished and other refugees had to be relocated, while the Yemen authorities initiated a campaign of forcible repatriation. During 1998–mid-2000 the refugee population in Yemen expanded, owing to an influx of Somalis fleeing civil conflict and, to a lesser extent, people displaced by the 1998–2000 Eritrea–Ethiopia border conflict. The relocation of refugees to a newly-constructed camp at al-Kharaz, central Yemen, commenced in late 2000. At December 2001 Yemen was hosting an estimated 69,468 mostly Somali, refugees.

UNHCR co-ordinates humanitarian assistance for the estimated 165,000 Sahrawis registered as refugees in four camps in the Tindouf area of Algeria. In September 1997 an agreement was reached on implementing the 1991 Settlement Plan for the Western Sahara. Accordingly, UNHCR was to help organize the registration and safe return of some 120,000 Sahrawi refugees provisionally identified as eligible to vote in the planned referendum on the future of the territory. In addition, UNHCR was to facilitate the reintegration of the returnees and monitor their rehabilitation. By early 2003, however little progress had been achieved towards the implementation of the Settlement Plan and subsequent alternative settlement proposals.

AFRICA

UNHCR has provided assistance to refugee and internally displaced populations in many parts of the continent where civil conflict, violations of human rights, drought, famine or environmental degradation have forced people to flee their home regions. The majority of African refugees and returnees are located in countries that are themselves suffering major economic problems and are thus unable to provide the basic requirements of the uprooted people. Furthermore, UNHCR has often failed to receive adequate international financial support to implement effective relief programmes. At 31 December 2001 there were an estimated 4.2m. people of concern to UNHCR in sub-Saharan Africa (of a world-wide total of 19.8m.), of whom 3.3m. were refugees, 421,574 internally displaced, and 308,804 recent returnees.

The Horn of Africa, afflicted by famine, separatist violence and ethnic conflict, has experienced large-scale population movements in recent years. Following the overthrow of the regime of former Somali president Siad Barre in January 1991 hundreds of thousands of Somalis fled to neighbouring countries. In 1992 UNHCR initiated a repatriation programme for the massive Somali and Ethiopian refugee populations in Kenya, which included assistance with reconstruction projects and the provision of food to returnees and displaced persons. However, continuing instability in many areas of Somalia impeded the completion of the repatriation process to that country and resulted in further population displacement. The conclusion of the first Somali national reconciliation conference in August 2000 was expected to accelerate repatriations, although many areas of the country subsequently remained unstable, drought-affected and lacking in basic services. During 1992–2001 more than 420,000 Somali refugees returned to their country. In 2001 some 50,216 Somali refugees repatriated from Ethiopia. During that year UNHCR, with other partners, was implementing community-based QIPs, aimed at facilitating long-term self-reliance by improving local education and health provision, water supply and productive capacity. By the end of 2001 there remained an estimated total Somali refugee population of 309,264, of whom 143,180 were in Kenya and 67,129 were in Ethiopia. By November 1997 UNHCR estimated that some 600,000 Ethiopians had repatriated from neighbouring countries, either by spontaneous or organized movements. The voluntary repatriation operation of Ethiopian refugees from Sudan (which commenced in 1993) was concluded in mid-1998. With effect from 1 March 2000 UNHCR withdrew the automatic refugee status of Ethiopians who left their country before 1991. Transportation and rehabilitation assistance were provided for 9,321 of these, who wished to repatriate. At 31 December 2001 there remained an estimated total Ethiopian refugee population of 58,903, of whom 8,306 were being assisted by UNHCR; some 16,120 Ethiopians remained in Sudan (with 642 assisted by UNHCR) and 13,541 were in Kenya (4,533 assisted by UNHCR). At that time Ethiopia itself was hosting a total of 152,554 refugees (of whom the majority were Sudanese), while Kenya was sheltering 239,221 (mainly Somalis).

From 1992 some 500,000 Eritreans took refuge in Sudan as a result of separatist conflicts; however, by 1995 an estimated 125,000 had returned spontaneously, in particular following Eritrea's accession to independence in May 1993. A UNHCR repatriation programme to assist the remaining refugees, which had been delayed for various political, security and funding considerations, was initiated in November 1994. Its implementation, however, was hindered by a shortfall in donor funding and by differences between the Eritrean and Sudanese Governments, and Sudan continued to host substantial numbers of Eritrean refugees. Renewed conflict between Eritrea and Ethiopia, which commenced in 1998, had, by mid-1999, resulted in the displacement of some 350,000 Eritreans and 300,000 Ethiopians. In mid-2000, following an escalation of the conflict in May, UNHCR reported that some 95,000 Eritreans had sought refuge in Sudan, while smaller numbers had fled to Djibouti and Yemen. Following the conclusion of a cease-fire agreement between Eritrea and Ethiopia in June, UNHCR initiated an operation to repatriate the most recent wave of Eritrean refugees from Sudan, and also inaugurated a scheme (which had been scheduled to start in May) to repatriate 147,000 long-term refugees. During the latter part of 2000 25,000 Eritreans repatriated from Sudan with UNHCR assistance, and a further 5,000 returned in spontaneous movements. At 31 December 2001 the total number of Eritreans sheltering in Sudan was estimated at 324,546, of whom 129,880 were receiving UNHCR assistance. UNHCR assisted with the repatriation of 32,741 (of a planned 62,000) recent and long-term Eritrean refugees from Sudan from May–December 2001. UNHCR and other agencies were collaborating to rehabilitate areas of Eritrea that were receiving returnees. During 2001 UNHCR withdrew assistance to Eritrean

IDPs, whose numbers had declined from a peak of 300,000 to about 45,000 by May.

At 31 December 2001 an estimated 489,505 Sudanese remained exiled as refugees, mainly in Uganda, Ethiopia, the Democratic Republic of the Congo (DRC), Kenya and the Central African Republic, owing to continuing civil unrest in southern Sudan. Some 404,089 were receiving assistance from UNHCR. The Ugandan Government, hosting an estimated 176,766 Sudanese refugees at that time (156,766 UNHCR-assisted), has provided new resettlement sites and, jointly with UNHCR and other partners, has developed a Self-Reliance Strategy, which envisages achieving self-sufficiency for the long-term refugee population through integrating services for refugees into existing local structures. It was reported that about one-quarter of refugees in Uganda achieved self-sufficiency in food in 2001.

In West Africa the refugee population increased substantially during 1992 and the first half of 1993, with the addition of new refugees fleeing unrest in Togo, Liberia and Senegal. In accordance with a Liberian peace agreement, signed in July 1993, UNHCR was responsible for the repatriation of Liberian refugees who had fled to Guinea, Côte d'Ivoire and Sierra Leone. UNHCR also began to provide emergency relief to the displaced population within the country. Persisting political insecurity prevented any solution to the refugee problem, and in mid-1996 UNHCR suspended its preparatory activities for a large-scale repatriation and reintegration operation of Liberian refugees, owing to an escalation in hostilities. In early 1997 the prospect of a peaceful settlement in Liberia prompted a spontaneous movement of refugees returning home, and in April UNHCR initiated an organized repatriation of Liberian refugees from Ghana. The establishment of a democratically-elected Liberian government in August and the consolidation of the peace settlement were expected to accelerate the return of refugees and other displaced persons. However, the process was hindered by logistical difficulties, the persisting volatility particularly of some border regions, and alleged atrocities perpetrated by Liberian troops. During 1998 and 1999 an estimated 15,000 Liberians fled to Guinea from insecurity in the Lofa area of northern Liberia; meanwhile, UNHCR was forced to suspend its operations in Lofa. By the end of 2000 nearly 400,000 Liberians were reported to have repatriated, more than one-third with UNHCR assistance. UNHCR has organized QIPs to facilitate the reintegration of the returnees. Mounting insecurity in southern Guinea from September 2000 (see below) accelerated the return of Liberian refugees from camps there. However, during 2001 some 80,000 Liberians were displaced from their homes and refugee camps for Sierra Leoneans were disrupted, owing to an escalation of violence particularly in the Lofa and Gbarpolu areas. UNHCR's repatriation and reintegration activities were suspended throughout 2001. At 31 December there were still an estimated 244,574 Liberian refugees (166,614 UNHCR-assisted), of whom 122,846 were in Côte d'Ivoire and 82,792 in Guinea (only 21,871 of the latter UNHCR-assisted). At that time there were 196,116 Liberian IDPs of concern to UNHCR.

Further large-scale population displacement in West Africa followed an escalation of violence in Sierra Leone in early 1995. By December 1996 there were nearly 370,000 Sierra Leonean refugees in Liberia and Guinea, while a further 654,600 internally displaced Sierra Leoneans were of concern to UNHCR. The repatriation of Sierra Leonean refugees from Liberia was initiated in February 1997. However, the programme was suspended in May, owing to renewed political violence, which forced UNHCR staff to evacuate the country, and the seizure of power by military forces. Thousands of people fled to other parts of the country, as well as to neighbouring countries to escape the hostilities. Following the intervention of the ECOMOG multinational force (authorized by ECOWAS, q.v.) and the conclusion of a peace agreement in October, residents of the Sierra Leone capital, Freetown, who had been displaced by the conflict, began to return. In February 1998 ECOMOG troops took control of Freetown from the rebel military forces, and in the following month the elected President, Ahmed Tejan Kabbah, was reinstated as Head of State. None the less, large numbers of Sierra Leoneans continued to cross the borders into neighbouring countries, owing to ongoing violence in the northern and eastern regions of the country and severe food shortages. In early 1999 anti-government forces again advanced on Freetown, prompting heavy fighting with ECOMOG troops and the displacement of thousands more civilians. In February a reported 200,000 people fled the town of Kenema in south-eastern Sierra Leone following attacks by rebel militia. In May a cease-fire agreement was concluded between the Government and opposition forces, and a formal peace accord was signed in early July, under which the rebels were to be disarmed and demobilized; however, the agreement broke down in May 2000. The resumption of hostilities delayed a planned repatriation operation and displaced an estimated 50,000 people from their homes. A new cease-fire agreement was signed by the Sierra Leone Government and the principal rebel group in early November. Meanwhile, persistent insecurity in northeastern and some border areas of Sierra Leone prompted further movements of Sierra Leonean refu-

gees to Guinea during 2000. From September, however, unrest in southern Guinea (see below) caused some Sierra Leonean refugees who had been sheltering in camps there to repatriate. In 2001 UNHCR, while assisting, with the International Organization for Migration, returns by sea from the Guinean capital Conakry to Freetown, organized radio broadcasts to southern Guinea warning Sierra Leoneans against attempting to escape the unrest there by returning over the land border into volatile northeastern and other border areas of Sierra Leone. During that year UNHCR provided transportation to assist some 30,173 Sierra Leoneans wishing to repatriate from Guinea. A further 50,000 Sierra Leoneans were estimated to have repatriated spontaneously. However, owing to security considerations, the majority of returnees were unable to return to their home communities and were, therefore, accommodated in temporary settlements within host communities. It was hoped that during 2002 as many as 100,000 Sierra Leoneans would return to their places of origin, in view of the successful staging of legislative and presidential elections in May and the consolidation of the peace process. At 31 December 2001 there were an estimated 95,527 Sierra Leonean refugees in Guinea and 54,717 in Liberia. Some 55,291 of the Sierra Leonean refugees in Guinea and 38,757 of those in Liberia were being assisted by UNHCR. There were also 92,330 recently returned refugees in Sierra Leone of concern to UNHCR. UNHCR's activities in assisting Sierra Leonean refugees remaining in Liberia during 2001 included a focus on the prevention of sexual and gender-based violence in refugee camps.

In August 2000 the security sitiuation in southern border areas of Guinea deteriorated owing to increasing insurgencies by rebels from Liberia and Sierra Leone, which displaced a large number of Guineans from their homes and also endangered an estimated 460,000 mainly Liberian and Sierra Leonean refugees (see above) accommodated in Guinean camps. In mid-September UNHCR and other aid organizations withdrew their international personnel and suspended food distribution in these areas following the murder by armed rebels of a member of UNHCR staff. Insecurity, hunger and mounting hostility from elements of the local population subsequently led significant numbers of refugees to flee the unprotected camps. Many sought to reach northern Guinea, while some returned spontaneously to their countries of origin. Following an escalation in fighting between Guinean government forces and insurgent rebels in early December refugee movements intensified; however, it was reported that an estimated 180,000 refugees and 70,000 IDPs remained stranded without humanitarian assistance in the southwestern Bec de Perroquet area. Later in December UNHCR dispatched emergency teams to assist with the relocation of refugees who had escaped the conflict zone. In February 2001 the High Commissioner negotiated with the parties to the conflict for the establishment of a humanitarian 'lifeline' to enable the delivery of assistance to and possible evacuation of the refugees and IDPs trapped at Bec de Perroquet: conveys of food aid began to reach the area at the end of that month. Meanwhile, UNHCR opened five new refugee settlements in central Guinea and, supported by the Guinean authorities, dispatched search teams into Bec de Perroquet in an attempt to find and evacuate refugees still stranded there. UNHCR withdrew from Beq de Perroquet at the end of May. During 2001 a total of 63,662 mainly Sierra Leonean refugees were relocated.

UNHCR provided assistance to 120,000 people displaced by the extreme insecurity that developed in Côte d'Ivoire from September 2002. From November UNHCR assisted some 40,000 Liberian refugees who had been sheltering in western Côte d'Ivoire to return to Liberia; spontanoeus returns by Liberians were also reported. UNHCR planned to transfer some 5,000 extremely vulnerable Liberian refugees from Côte d'Ivoire to a third country.

Since 1993 the Great Lakes region of central Africa has experienced massive population displacement, causing immense operational challenges and demands on the resources of international humanitarian and relief agencies. In October of that year a military coup in Burundi prompted some 580,000 people to flee into Rwanda and Tanzania, although many had returned by early 1994. By May 1994, however, an estimated 860,000 people from Burundi and Rwanda had fled to neighbouring states (following a resurgence of ethnic violence in both countries), including 250,000 mainly Rwandan Tutsi refugees who entered Tanzania over a 24-hour period in late April in the most rapid mass exodus ever witnessed by UNHCR. In May UNHCR began an immediate operation to airlift emergency supplies to the refugees. For the first time in an emergency operation UNHCR organized support to be rendered in the form of eight defined 'service packages', for example, to provide domestic fuel, road servicing and security or sanitation facilities. Despite overcrowding in camps and a high incidence of cholera and dysentery (particularly in camps in eastern Zaire, where many thousands of Rwandan Hutus had sought refuge following the establishment of a new Government in July) large numbers of refugees refused to accept UNHCR-assisted repatriation, owing to fears of reprisal ethnic killings. In September reports of mass ethnic violence in Rwanda, which were disputed by some UN agencies, continued to disrupt UNHCR's policy of repatriation and to prompt returnees to cross the border back into Zaire. Security in the refugee camps, which was undermined by the presence of military and political elements of the former Rwandan regime, remained an outstanding concern for UNHCR. A resurgence of violence in Burundi, in February 1995, provoked further mass population movements. However, in March the Tanzanian authorities, reportedly frustrated at the lack of international assistance for the refugees and the environmental degradation resulting from the camps, closed Tanzania's border with Burundi, thus preventing the admission into the country of some 100,000 Rwandan Hutu refugees who were fleeing camps in Burundi. While persisting disturbances in Rwanda disrupted UNHCR's repatriation programme, in April Rwandan government troops employed intimidation tactics to force some 90,000 internally displaced Hutus to leave a heavily-populated camp in the south-west of the country; other small camps were closed. In August the Zairean Government initiated a short-lived programme of forcible repatriation of the estimated 1m. Rwandan and 70,000 Burundian Hutu refugees remaining in the country, which prompted as many as 100,000 refugees to flee the camps into the surrounding countryside. In September Rwanda agreed to strengthen its reception facilities and to provide greater security and protection for returnees, in collaboration with UNHCR, in order to prepare for any large-scale repatriation. UNHCR, meanwhile, expanded its information campaign, to promote the return of refugees, and enhanced its facilities at official border entry points. In December UNHCR negotiated an agreement between the Rwandan and Tanzanian authorities concerning the repatriation of the estimated 500,000 Rwandans remaining in camps in Tanzania. UNHCR agreed to establish a separate camp in north-west Tanzania in order to accommodate elements of the refugee population that might disrupt the repatriation programme. The repatriation of Rwandan refugees from all host countries was affected by reports of reprisals against Hutu returnees by the Tutsi-dominated Government in Rwanda. In February 1996 the Zairean Government renewed its efforts to accelerate the repatriation process, owing to concerns that the camps were becoming permanent settlements and that they were being used to train and rearm a Hutu militia. In July the Burundian Government forcibly repatriated 15,000 Rwandan refugees, having announced the closure of all remaining refugee camps. The repatriation programme was condemned by UNHCR and was suspended by the country's new military authorities, but only after many more thousands of refugees had been obliged to return to Rwanda and up to 30,000 had fled to Tanzania.

In October 1996 an escalation of hostilities between Zairean government forces, accused by Rwanda of arming the Hutu *Interahamwe* militia, and Zairean (Banyamulenge) Tutsis, who had been the focus of increasingly violent assaults, resulted in an extreme humanitarian crisis. Some 250,000 refugees fled 12 camps in the east of the country, including 90,000 Burundians who returned home. An estimated 500,000 refugees regrouped in Muganga camp, west of Goma, with insufficient relief assistance, following the temporary evacuation of international aid workers. UNHCR appealed to all Rwandan Hutu refugees to return home, and issued assurances of the presence of human rights observers in Rwanda to enhance their security. In November, with the apparent withdrawal of *Interahamwe* forces and the advance of the Tutsi-dominated Alliance des forces démocratiques pour la libération du Congo–Zaïre (AFDL), an estimated 600,000 refugees unexpectedly returned to Rwanda; however, concern remained on the part of the international community for the substantial number of Rwandan Hutu refugees at large in eastern Zaire. Further mass movement of Rwandan refugee populations occurred in December, owing to the threat of forcible repatriation by the Tanzanian Government, which had announced its intention of closing all camps by the end of the year. UNHCR initiated a repatriation programme; however, 200,000 refugees, unwilling to return to Rwanda, fled their camps. The majority of the refugees were later identified by the Tanzanian national army and escorted to the Rwandan border. By the end of December some 483,000 refugees had returned to Rwanda from Tanzania.

In February 1997 violence in Zaire intensified, which prompted some 56,000 Zaireans to flee into Tanzania and disrupted the distribution of essential humanitarian supplies to refugees remaining in Zaire. An estimated 170,000 refugees abandoned their temporary encampment at Tingi-Tingi, fearing attacks by the advancing AFDL forces. About 75,000 reassembled at Ubundu, south of Kisangani, while the fate of the other refugees remained uncertain. In March and April continued reports of attacks on refugee camps by AFDL forces and local Zaireans, resulted in large numbers of people fleeing into the surrounding countryside, with the consequent deaths of many of the most vulnerable members of the refugee population from disease and starvation. At the end of April the leader of the AFDL, Laurent-Désiré Kabila, ordered the repatriation of all Rwandan Hutu refugees by the UN within 60 days. Emergency air and land operations to evacuate some 185,000 refugees who had regrouped into temporary settlements were initiated a few days later. The repatriation process, however, was hindered by administrative and logistical difficulties and lack of co-operation on the part of the AFDL forces. By June an estimated 215,000 Rwandans were still missing or dispersed throughout the former Zaire (renamed the Democratic Republic of the Congo—DRC—by the AFDL in May). In the following months relations between the Kabila Government and UNHCR deteriorated as a result of several incidences of forcible repatriations of refugees to Rwanda and reports that the authorities were hindering a UN investigation into alleged abuses of human rights, committed against the Rwandan Hutu refugees by AFDL forces. In August an agreement was concluded to provide for the voluntary repatriation of some 75,000 refugees from the DRC remaining in Tanzania, under UNHCR supervision. However, the conflict that erupted in the DRC in August 1998 (see below) led to further large population movements. The repatriation of the estimated 260,000 Burundians remaining in Tanzania was also impeded, from early 1998, by an escalation of violence, which destabilized areas of return for both refugees and IDPs. In December 1997 a tripartite agreement was signed to provide for the organized repatriation of the remaining former Zairean refugees in Rwanda, with both Governments agreeing to observe strict conditions of security for the refugees on both sides of the border.

During the late 1990s UNHCR resolved to work, in co-operation with UNDP and WFP, to rehabilitate areas previously inhabitated by refugees in central African countries of asylum and undertook to repair roads, bridges and other essential transport infrastructure, improve water and sanitation facilities, and strengthen the education sector. However, the political stability of the region remained extremely uncertain, and, from August 1998, DRC government forces and rebels became involved in a civil war in which the militaries of several regional governments were also implicated. From late 1998 substantial numbers of DRC nationals fled to neighbouring countries (mainly Tanzania and Zambia) or were displaced within the DRC. Meanwhile, the DRC, in turn, was hosting a significant refugee population. Although a cease-fire agreement was signed by all parties to the conflict in July 1999, this did not begin to be implemented until early 2001, when Kabila was assassinated and succeeded as President by his son, Maj.-Gen. Joseph Kabila. The implementation of a plan for the phased disengagement of local and foreign forces, agreed in December 2000, was initiated in 2001, as a result of which UNHCR made preparatory plans for eventual mass refugee returns. Nevertheless, insecurity continued to prevail particularly in northeastern areas of the DRC, resulting in continuing population displacements. The major populations of concern to UNHCR in the Great Lakes region at 31 December 2001 were, provisionally, as follows: 362,012 refugees in the DRC; 89,885 IDPs, returned IDPs and returned refugees in Burundi; and a refugee population of 668,107 (498,082 UNHCR-assisted) remaining in Tanzania, which was coping with new influxes of refugees, mainly from Burundi and the DRC. In 2001 UNHCR was providing education, environmental protection and healthcare programmes at camps in Tanzania, and was focusing on the empowerment of women. Of an expected 60,000 refugee returns to Burundi in that year, only 27,866 were registered, owing to continuing insecurity. Nevertheless, in 2002, the Office aimed to facilitate a substantial number of repatriations to Burundi and some returns to Rwanda. The security of international aid personnel in the Great Lakes region has been of concern; UNHCR suspended all non-essential operations in Burundi from October 1999–April 2000, following the murder there of two UN personnel.

In mid-1997 an estimated 40,000 refugees from the Republic of the Congo fled to the DRC, following a short-lived outbreak of civil conflict. In December a memorandum of understanding was signed by representatives of the two Governments and of UNHCR, providing for their immediate repatriation. From late 1998 the resumption of conflict in the Republic of the Congo disrupted UNHCR humanitarian efforts in that country and caused significant numbers of Congolese to seek refuge in the DRC and Gabon, and the internal displacement of as many as 500,000 people. Following the agreement of a cease-fire in December the majority of IDPs returned home. More than 60,000 Congolese refugees had repatriated by the end of 2000. In 2001 2,000 Congolese refugees repatriated spontaneously from Gabon, leaving a Congolese refugee population of 15,000 in that country at the end of the year. A tripartite accord on their voluntary repatriation was concluded by UNHCR and the Congolese and Gabon Governments during 2001. UNHCR aimed to cease repatriation support by the end of 2002, by which time it was envisaged that most refugees would have returned. Some 2,900 Congolese refugees remained in the DRC at 31 December 2001. During 2000 more than 80,000 refugees from the DRC sought protection in the Republic of the Congo, which was hosting 92,678 refugees from the DRC at end-2001.

In 1994 continuing civil conflict in Angola caused some 370,000 people to leave their home areas. Prior to the signing of a peace settlement in November, UNHCR provided assistance to 112,000 internally displaced Angolans and returnees, although military activities, which hindered accessibility, undermined the effectiveness of the assistance programme. In mid-1995, following a consolidation of the peace process in Angola, UNHCR appealed for US \$44m. to support the voluntary repatriation of some 300,000 Angolan refugees over a two-and-a-half-year operation. By June 1996 implementation of the repatriation programme was delayed, reportedly owing to poor accommodation and other facilities for returnees, limited progress in confining and disarming opposition troops and the continued hazard of land-mines throughout the country. During 1997 an estimated 53,000 Angolans voluntarily returned from the DRC and Zambia, bringing the total returnees to some 130,000 since mid-1995. In November 1997 UNHCR resolved to implement an operation to provide for the repatriation and reintegration of the remaining Angolan refugees by June 1999. UNHCR allocated \$15.7m. to support the repatriation process and other activities in Angola, including strengthening the country's road infrastructure, monitoring areas of return, the implementation of reintegration projects and promoting links with other development programmes. In May 1998, however, the security situation in Angola deteriorated, and at the end of June UNHCR declared a temporary suspension of the repatriation operation. The renewed violence also resulted in further population displacement, with refugee movements into the DRC continuing during 1998–2001. In July 2000 UNHCR expanded its operations in Angola to support IDPs by providing emergency humanitarian assistance and helping IDP communities and local administrations with the provision of basic services, demining and the rehabilitation of local infrastructures. At the end of the year UNHCR was providing assistance to some 257,508 Angolan IDPs. By December 2001 an estimated 470,630 Angolans were sheltering in neighbouring countries, including 218,154 in Zambia and 186,879 in the DRC. It was estimated that in all some 3m.-4m. Angolans were displaced from their homes during the 1980s and 1990s. In 2002 the Office aimed to provide limited support to IDPs and returnees, and to provide basic assistance, including food and primary education, for the estimated 12,000 refugees and asylum-seekers (mainly from the DRC) sheltering in the country.

THE AMERICAS AND THE CARIBBEAN

In May 1989, when an International Conference on Central American Refugees (CIREFCA) was held in Guatemala, there were some 146,400 refugees receiving UNHCR assistance (both for emergency relief and for longer-term self-sufficiency programmes) in the region, as well as an estimated 1.8m. other refugees and displaced persons. UNHCR and UNDP were designated as the principal UN organizations to implement the CIREFCA plan of action for the repatriation or resettlement of refugees, alongside national co-ordinating committees. UNHCR QIPs were implemented in the transport, health, agricultural production and other sectors to support returnee reintegration (of both refugees and internally displaced persons) into local communities, and to promote the self-sufficiency of the returning populations. Implementation of UNHCR's programme for the repatriation of some 45,000 Guatemalan refugees in Mexico began in January 1993 with a convoy of 2,400 people. UNHCR initiated projects to support the reintegration of Guatemalan returnees, and in 1994–95 undertook a campaign to clear undetonated explosives in forest areas where they had resettled. The CIREFCA process was formally concluded in June 1994, by which time some 118,000 refugees had voluntarily returned to their countries of origin under the auspices of the programme, while thousands of others had integrated into their host countries. In December a meeting was held, in San José, Costa Rica, to commemorate the 10th anniversary of the Cartagena Declaration, which had provided a comprehensive framework for refugee protection in the region. The meeting adopted the San José Declaration on Refugees and Displaced Persons, which aimed to harmonize legal criteria and procedures to consolidate actions for durable solutions of voluntary repatriation and local integration in the region. UNHCR's efforts in the region have subsequently emphasized legal issues and refugee protection, while assisting governments to formulate national legislation on asylum and refugees. At the end of 2001 the outstanding population of concern to UNHCR in Central America was estimated at 25,500, including 11,654 Guatemalan refugees remaining in Mexico; it was estimated that more than 5,000 Guatemalan refugees had received Mexican citizenship since 1996 under a fast-track naturalization programme, and that a further 5,000 might benefit from the programme by the end of 2003. At December 2001 Costa Rica was hosting a refugee population estimated at 8,104, the majority of whom were Nicaraguans and newly-arrived refugees from Colombia. During 2001 some 5,018 Colombians applied for asylum in Costa Rica, compared with 1,456 in 2000.

In 1999 the Colombian Government approved an operational plan proposed by UNHCR to address a massive population displacement that has arisen in that country in recent years (escalating from 1997), as a consequence of ongoing internal conflict and alleged human rights abuses committed by armed groups. At the end of 2001 some 720,000 IDPs were of concern to UNHCR and believed to require urgent assistance; many of these had congregated near Colombia's borders with Ecuador, Panama and Venezuela. An increase in cross-border movements of Colombian refugees into neighbouring countries was reported throughout that year; UNHCR intensified its border-monitoring activities to enhance its capacity to forecast and react to new population movements. The Office has assisted with the implementation of an IDP registration plan, provided training in emergency response to displacements, and supported ongoing changes in the country's legislative framework for IDPs. UNHCR has also co-operated with UNICEF to improve the provision of education to displaced children. During 2001 UNHCR aimed to increase its emergency preparedness in relation to the ongoing conflict in Colombia by building up stockpiles of relief items in neighbouring countries and by developing contingency plans with other partners to enable the rapid deployment of personnel to border areas should the exodus of refugees from Colombia intensify further.

Canada and the USA are major countries of resettlement for refugees. UNHCR provides counselling and legal services for asylum-seekers in these countries. At 31 December 2001 the estimated refugee populations totalled 129,200 in Canada and 515,800 in the USA, while asylum-seekers numbered 45,800 and 395,900 respectively.

EUROPE

The political changes in Eastern and Central Europe during the early 1990s resulted in a dramatic increase in the number of asylum-seekers and displaced people in the region. UNHCR was the agency designated by the UN Secretary-General to lead the UN relief operation to assist those affected by the conflict in the former Yugoslavia. It was responsible for the supply of food and other humanitarian aid to the besieged capital of Bosnia and Herzegovina, Sarajevo, and to Muslim and Croatian enclaves in the country, under the armed escort of the UN Protection Force. Assistance was provided not only to Bosnian refugees in Croatia and displaced people within Bosnia and Herzegovina's borders, but also, in order to forestall further movements of people, to civilians whose survival was threatened. The operation was often seriously hampered by armed attacks (resulting, in some cases, in fatalities), distribution difficulties and underfunding from international donors. The Dayton peace agreement, which was signed in December 1995 bringing an end to the conflict, secured the right for all refugees and displaced persons freely to choose their place of residence within the new territorial arrangements of Bosnia and Herzegovina. Thus, the immediate effect of the peace accord was further population displacement, including a mass exodus of almost the entire Serb population of Sarajevo. Under the peace accord, UNHCR was responsible for planning and implementing the repatriation of all Bosnian refugees and displaced persons, then estimated at 2m.; however, there were still immense obstacles to freedom of movement, in particular for minorities wishing to return to an area dominated by a different politico-ethnic faction. By the end of 2001 there was still an estimated total Bosnian refugee population of some 425,979, of whom some 166,134 were receiving assistance from UNHCR. The majority of the Bosnian refugee population were in the Federal Republic of Yugoslavia (FRY, now Serbia and Montenegro). In addition, there were 18,665 recently returned refugees and 80,172 returned IDPs of concern to UNHCR in Bosnia and Herzegovina and 438,253 IDPs who had yet to return home. Returns by refugees and IDPs (including significant numbers of refugees returning to areas where they represented minority ethnic communities) accelerated during 2000 and 2001, owing to an improvement in security conditions. In 2001 so-called 'minority returns' totalled 92,061, bringing the total number of minority returns since 1998 to 287,000. In July 2002 the heads of state of Bosnia and Herzogovina, Croatia and the FRY met in Sarajevo with a view to resolving a number of outstanding issues including the return of remaining refugees.

From March 1998 attacks by Serbian forces against members of a separatist movement in the southern Serbian province of Kosovo and Metohija resulted in large-scale population displacement. Of particular concern were some 50,000 people who had fled to the surrounding mountains, close to the Albanian border, without shelter or adequate provisions. In October the withdrawal of Serbian troops and the involvement of the international community in the provision of aid and monitoring of the situation in Kosovo was thought to have prompted substantial numbers to have returned home. However, in December there were reports of renewed attacks by Serbian forces on the local Albanian population, which persisted into 1999. The failure of peace negotiations prompted further displacement, and in late March an estimated 95,000 people fled their homes following the withdrawal of international observers of the OSCE and the commencement of a NATO operation, which aimed to halt the Serbian attacks and compel the FRY to agree to a peace settlement. By mid-April UNHCR estimated that up to 1.3m. Kosovar Albanians had been displaced since the fighting began in 1998, with reports that thousands had been forcibly expelled by Serbian troops in recent weeks. UNHCR attempted to provide emergency relief to the thousands of refugees who fled to neighbouring countries, and expressed concern for those remaining in the province, of whom up to 400,000 were thought to be living without shelter. In early April 1999 UNHCR condemned the decision of the authorities in the former Yugoslav republic of Macedonia (FYRM) forcibly to evacuate some 30,000 refugees from camps in Blace, near the FRY border, and subsequently to close the border to further refugees. At that time UNHCR helped to co-ordinate an international effort to evacuate substantial numbers of the refugees to third countries, and issued essential identity and travel documents. In Albania UNHCR funded transport to relocate an estimated 250,000 people from the border town of Kukës, where resources and the local infrastructure were strained by the massive population influx, to other sites throughout the country. At the start of June the Kosovar refugee population totalled some 443,300 people in Albania, 247,800 in the FYRM, 69,300 in Montenegro, and 21,700 in Bosnia and Herzegovina, while under a joint Humanitarian Evacuation Programme with the International Organization for Migration, more than 90,000 refugees had been evacuated to 29 countries. UNHCR organized host families to receive a large proportion of the refugees, while additional shelter was provided in the form of tented camps and collective centres. In mid-June, following a cease-fire accord and an agreement by the FRY to withdraw all forces and paramilitary units, UNHCR initiated a large-scale registration operation of Kosovar refugees and began to deliver emergency provisions to assist the displaced population within Kosovo. Despite warnings of anti-personnel devices and lack of shelter, UNHCR estimated that some 477,000 refugees had returned in a spontaneous repatriation movement by the end of June. Meanwhile, it was reported that a total of 170,000 Serbs left Kosovo, fearing reprisal attacks by returning ethnic Albanians; in addition, some 50,000 members of the Roma minority moved out of the province. In September UNHCR estimated that one-third of all homes in Kosovo had been destroyed or seriously damaged during the conflict, prompting concerns regarding the welfare of returning refugees and IDPs in the coming winter months. UNHCR distributed 'shelter kits' to assist the process of reconstruction of homes, and proceeded to accelerate the distribution of blankets and winter clothing, as well as of fuel, food, water, and the provision of medical care throughout Serbia and Montenegro. By the end of 1999 the majority of refugees had returned to Kosovo. In mid-2000 UNHCR scaled down its emergency humanitarian activities in Kosovo and provided a UN Humanitarian Co-ordinator to oversee the transition to long-term reconstruction and development, in co-operation with the UN Interim Administration Mission in Kosovo (UNMIK). UNHCR and OSCE have periodically jointly assessed the situation of minority communities in Kosovo; in May 2002 the two organizations reported that discrimination against and intimidation of minorities in the province was prevalent, hindering minority returns and integration. From mid-2001 more than 5,000 ethnic Albanians returned to Serbia from Kosovo, where they had sought refuge.

In response to the mounting insecurity in the FYRM from early 2001, as conflict escalated between ethnic Albanian rebels and government troops, 81,000 Macedonian refugees fled to Kosovo (of whom several thousand repatriated promptly) and 12,000 to southern Serbia during February–August, while over that period more than 50,000 people became displaced within the FYRM. In June UNHCR appealed for funds to finance the provision of emergency humanitarian assistance to the Macedonian refugees, and opened a registration centre in Kosovo. Repatriations accelerated following the conclusion in August of a framework peace agreement between the opposing parties; by April 2002 some 4,000 Macedonian refugees remained in Kosovo, while 16,800 persons remained displaced withing the FYRM; in many cases the latter feared returning to communities in which they would belong to an ethnic minority.

In December 1992 UNHCR dispatched teams to establish offices in both Armenia and Azerbaijan to assist people displaced as a result of the war between the two countries and to provide immediate relief. A cease-fire agreement was signed between the two sides in May 1994, although violations of the accord were subsequently reported and relations between the two countries remained tense. At the end of 2001 the region was still supporting a massive displaced population, including 264,327 Azerbaijani refugees in Armenia and 572,955 IDPs of concern to UNHCR in Azerbaijan. UNHCR's humanitarian activities have focused on improving shelter, in particular for the most vulnerable among the refugee population, and promoting economic self-sufficiency and stability.

In Georgia, where almost 300,000 people left their homes as a result of civil conflict from 1991, UNHCR has attempted to encourage income-generating activities among the displaced population, to increase the Georgian Government's capacity to support those people and to assist the rehabilitation of people returning to their areas of origin. In late 1999 an estimated 7,000 refugees fleeing insecurity in Chechnya (see below) entered Georgia. By September 2002 there remained no return movements of Chechen refugees from Georgia, and about 265,000 IDPs in that country (affected by the ongoing conflicts in Abkhazia and South Ossetia). UNHCR has delivered food to the Chechen refugees and the host families with whom some 80% are staying, and has also assisted the refugees through shelter renovation, psycho-social support and the provision of child-care facilities and health and community development support, as well as monitoring refugee–host family relations.pa From 1994 UNHCR pursued a process to establish a comprehensive approach to the problems of refugees, returnees, IDPs and migrants in the Commonwealth of Independent States (CIS). A regional conference convened in Geneva, Switzerland, in May 1996, endorsed a framework of activities aimed at managing migratory flows and at developing institutional capacities to prevent mass population displacements. At that time it was estimated that more than 9m. former citizens of the USSR had relocated since its disintegration as a result of conflict, economic pressures and ecological disasters. By June 2002 (with the accession of Ukraine) all CIS member states excepting Uzbekistan had acceded to the 1951 Convention.

In March 1995 UNHCR initiated an assistance programme for people displaced as a result of conflict in the separatist republic of Chechnya (the Chechen Republic of Ichkeriya), the Russian Federation, as part of a UN inter-agency relief effort, in collaboration with the International Committee of the Red Cross (ICRC). UNHCR continued its activities in 1996, at the request of the Russian Government, at which time the displaced population within Chechnya and in the surrounding republics totalled 490,000. During 1997 UNHCR provided reintegration assistance to 25,000 people who returned to Chechnya, despite reports of sporadic violence. The security situation in the region deteriorated sharply in mid-1999, following a series of border clashes and incursions by Chechen separatist forces into the neighbouring republic of Dagestan. In September Russian military aircraft began an aerial offensive against suspected rebel targets in Chechnya, and at the end of the month ground troops moved into the republic. By November an estimated 225,000 Chechens had fled to neighbouring Ingushetiya. UNHCR dispatched food supplies to assist the IDPs and, from February 2000, periodically sent relief convoys into Chechnya, where there was still a substantial displaced population; the poor security situation, however, prevented other UNHCR deployment within Chechnya. In late 2000 UNHCR assisted with the construction of the first tented camp to provide adequate winter shelter for Chechens in Ingushetiya; many others were being sheltered in local homes. About 155,000 Chechens remained in Ingushetiya at the end of 2001.

CO-OPERATION WITH OTHER ORGANIZATIONS

UNHCR works closely with other UN agencies, intergovernmental organizations and non-governmental organizations (NGOs) to increase the scope and effectiveness of its operations. Within the UN system UNHCR co-operates, principally, with the World Food Programme in the distribution of food aid, UNICEF and the World Health Organization in the provision of family welfare and child immunization programmes, OCHA in the delivery of emergency humanitarian relief, UNDP in development-related activities and the preparation of guide-lines for the continuum of emergency assistance to development programmes, and the Office of the UN High Commissioner for Human Rights. UNHCR also has close working relationships with the International Committee of the Red Cross and the International Organization for Migration. In 2002 UNHCR worked with 510 NGOs as 'implementing partners', enabling UNHCR to broaden the use of its resources while maintaining a co-ordinating role in the provision of assistance.

TRAINING

UNHCR organizes training programmes and workshops to enhance the capabilities of field workers and non-UNHCR staff, in the following areas: the identification and registration of refugees; people-orientated planning; resettlement procedures and policies; emergency response and management; security awareness; stress management; and the dissemination of information through the electronic media.

Finance

The United Nations' regular budget finances a proportion of UNHCR's administrative expenditure. The majority of UNHCR's programme expenditure (about 98%) is funded by voluntary contributions, mainly from governments. The Private Sector and Public Affairs Service, established in 2001, aims to increase funding from non-governmental donor sources, for example by developing partnerships with foundations and corporations. Following approval of the Unified Annual Programme Budget any subsequently-identified requirements are managed in the form of Supplementary Programmes, financed by separate appeals. The total budget for 2002 amounted to US $925.4m.

Publications

Refugees (quarterly, in English, French, German, Italian, Japanese and Spanish).

Refugee Resettlement: An International Handbook to Guide Reception and Integration.

Refugee Survey Quarterly.

The State of the World's Refugees (every 2 years).

UNHCR Handbook for Emergencies.

Press releases, reports.

United Nations Peace-keeping Operations

Address: Department of Peace-keeping Operations, Room S-3727-B, United Nations, New York, NY 10017, USA.

Telephone: (212) 963-8077; **fax:** (212) 963-9222; **internet:** www.un.org/Depts/dpko/.

United Nations peace-keeping operations have been conceived as instruments of conflict control. The UN has used these operations in various conflicts, with the consent of the parties involved, to maintain international peace and security, without prejudice to the positions or claims of parties, in order to facilitate the search for political settlements through peaceful means such as mediation and the good offices of the Secretary-General. Each operation is established with a specific mandate, which requires periodic review by the Security Council. United Nations peace-keeping operations fall into two categories: peace-keeping forces and observer missions.

Peace-keeping forces are composed of contingents of military and civilian personnel, made available by member states. These forces assist in preventing the recurrence of fighting, restoring and maintaining peace, and promoting a return to normal conditions. To this end, peace-keeping forces are authorized as necessary to undertake negotiations, persuasion, observation and fact-finding. They conduct patrols and interpose physically between the opposing parties. Peace-keeping forces are permitted to use their weapons only in self-defence.

Military observer missions are composed of officers (usually unarmed), who are made available, on the Secretary-General's request, by member states. A mission's function is to observe and report to the Secretary-General (who, in turn, informs the UN Security Council) on the maintenance of a cease-fire, to investigate violations and to do what it can to improve the situation.

Peace-keeping forces and observer missions must at all times maintain complete impartiality and avoid any action that might affect the claims or positions of the parties. In January 1995 the UN Secretary-General presented a report to the Security Council, reassessing the UN's role in peace-keeping. The document stipulated that UN forces in conflict areas should not be responsible for peace-enforcement duties, and included a proposal for the establishment of a 'rapid reaction' force which would be ready for deployment within a month of being authorized by the Security Council. In September 1997 the UN Secretary-General established a staff to plan and organize the formation of the so-called UN Stand-by Forces High Readiness Brigade (SHIRBRIG). SHIRBRIG, based in Denmark, was declared available to the UN in January 2000. By March 2003 Argentina, Austria, Canada, Denmark, Italy, the Netherlands, Norway, Poland, Romania and Sweden had formally committed troops to the force. SHIRBRIG became fully operational in late 2000 with the deployment of troops to the newly-authorized UN Mission in Ethiopia and Eritrea (UNMEE, see below) for a duration of six months. A Stand-by Arrangements System (UNSAS) became operational in 1994; at February 2003 some 77 countries were participating in the system by making available specialized civilian and military personnel, as well as other services and equipment. In August 2000 a report on UN peace-keeping activities prepared by a team of experts appointed by the Secretary-General assessed the aims and requirements of peace-keeping operations and recommended several measures to improve the performance of the Department of Peace-Keeping Operations (DPKO), focusing on its planning and management capacity from the inception of an operation through to post-conflict peace-building activities, and on its rapid response capability. Proposed reforms included the establishment of a body to improve co-ordination of information and strategic analysis requirements; the promotion of partnership arrangements between member states (within the context of UNSAS, see above) enabling the formation of several coherent multinational brigades, and improved monitoring of the preparedness of potential troop contributor nations, with a view to facilitating the effective deployment of most operations within 30 days of their authorization in a Security Council resolution; the adoption of 'on-call' reserve lists to ensure the prompt deployment of civilian police and specialists; the preparation of a global logistics support strategy; and a restructuring of the DPKO to improve administrative efficiency.

The study also urged an increase in resources for funding peace-keeping operations and the adoption of a more flexible financing mechanism, and emphasized the importance of the UN's conflict prevention activities. In November the Security Council, having welcomed the report, adopted guide-lines aimed at improving its management of peace-keeping operations, including providing missions with clear and achievable mandates. In June 2001 the Council adopted a resolution incorporating a Statement of principles on co-operation with troop-contributing countries, which aimed to strengthen the relationship between those countries and the UN and to enhance the effectiveness of peace-keeping operations.

The UN's peace-keeping forces and observer missions are financed in most cases by assessed contributions from member states of the organization. In recent years a significant expansion in the UN's peace-keeping activities has been accompanied by a perpetual financial crisis within the organization, as a result of the increased financial burden and some member states' delaying payment. At 31 December 2002 outstanding assessed contributions to the peace-keeping budget amounted to some US $1,340m.

By March 2003 the UN had undertaken a total of 54 peace-keeping operations, of which 13 were authorized in the period 1948–88 and 41 since 1988, reaching a peak in 1993 with a total deployment of more than 80,000 troops from 77 countries. At December 2002 89 countries were contributing some 39,636 military personnel and civilian police to the 13 ongoing operations.

In 2002 the UN maintained 13 peace-building missions; of these, two were directly supported by the DPKO: the UN Assistance Mission in Afghanistan (UNAMA), established by a resolution of the Security Council in March, and the UN Mission in Angola (UNMA), established by the Council in August.

UNITED NATIONS DISENGAGEMENT OBSERVER FORCE—UNDOF

Headquarters: Camp Faouar, Syria.

Commander: Maj.-Gen. Bo Wranker (Sweden).

UNDOF was established for an initial period of six months by a UN Security Council resolution in May 1974, following the signature in Geneva of a disengagement agreement between Syrian and Israeli forces. The mandate has since been extended by successive resolutions. The initial task of the Force was to take over territory evacuated in stages by the Israeli troops, in accordance with the disengagement agreement, to hand over territory to Syrian troops, and to establish an area of separation on the Golan Heights.

UNDOF continues to monitor the area of separation; it carries out inspections of the areas of limited armaments and forces; uses its best efforts to maintain the cease-fire; and undertakes activities of a humanitarian nature, such as arranging the transfer of prisoners and war-dead between Syria and Israel. The Force operates exclusively on Syrian territory.

At 28 February 2003 the Force comprised 1,043 troops; it is assisted by approximately 80 military observers of UNTSO's Observer Group Golan, and supported by 125 international and local civilian personnel. Further UNTSO military observers help UNDOF in the performance of its tasks, as required. The General Assembly appropriated US $40.8m. to cover the cost of the operation for the period 1 July 2002–30 June 2003.

UNITED NATIONS INTERIM ADMINISTRATION MISSION IN KOSOVO— UNMIK

Headquarters: Priština, Kosovo.

Special Representative of the UN Secretary-General and Head of Mission: Michael Steiner (Germany).

Principal Deputy Special Representative of the UN Secretary-General: Charles H. Brayshaw (USA).

Deputy Special Representative for Police and Justice: JEAN-CHRISTIAN CADY (France).

Deputy Special Representative for Civil Administration: FRANCESCO BASTAGLI (Italy).

Deputy Special Representative for (OSCE) Institution Building in Kosovo: PASCAL FIESCHI (France).

Deputy Special Representative for (EU) Reconstruction in Kosovo: ANDY BEARPARK (United Kingdom).

In June 1999 NATO suspended a 10-week aerial offensive against the then Federal Republic of Yugoslavia (now Serbia and Montenegro), following an agreement by the Serbian authorities to withdraw all security and paramilitary forces from the southern province of Kosovo and Metohija, where Serbian repression of a separatist movement had prompted a humanitarian crisis and co-ordinated international action to resolve the conflict. On 10 June the UN Security Council adopted Resolution 1244, which outlined the terms of a political settlement for Kosovo and provided for the deployment of international civilian and security personnel. The security presence, termed the Kosovo Peace Implementation Force (KFOR), was to be led by NATO, while the UN was to oversee all civilian operations. UNMIK was established under the terms of Resolution 1244 as the supreme legal and executive authority in Kosovo, with responsibility for all civil administration and for facilitating the reconstruction and rehabilitation of the province as an autonomous region. For the first time in a UN operation other organizations were mandated to co-ordinate aspects of the mission in Kosovo, under the UN's overall jurisdiction. The four key elements, or Pillars, of UNMIK were (i) humanitarian affairs (led by UNHCR); (ii) civil administration; (iii) democratization and institution-building (OSCE); and (iv) economic reconstruction (EU). At the end of the first year of UNMIK's presence the element of humanitarian assistance was phased out. A new Pillar (i), concerned with police and justice, was established in May 2001, under the direct leadership of the UN. On arriving in the province at the end of June 1999 UNMIK and KFOR established a Joint Implementation Commission to co-ordinate and supervise the demilitarization of the Kosovo Liberation Army. UNMIK initiated a mass information campaign (and later administered new radio stations in Kosovo) to urge co-operation with the international personnel in the province and tolerance for all ethnic communities. A Mine Co-ordinating Centre supervised efforts to deactivate anti-personnel devices and to ensure the safety of the returning ethnic Albanian population. In mid-July the UN Secretary-General's permanent Special Representative took office, and chaired the first meeting of the Kosovo Transitional Council (KTC), which had been established by the UN as a multi-ethnic consultative organ, the highest political body under UNMIK, to help to restore law and order in the province and to reintegrate the local administrative infrastructure. In August a Joint Advisory Council on Legislative Matters was constituted, with representatives of UNMIK and the local judiciary, in order to consider measures to eliminate discrimination from the province's legal framework. At the end of July UNMIK personnel began to supervise customs controls at Kosovo's international borders. Other developments in the first few months of UNMIK's deployment included the establishment of joint commissions on energy and public utilities, education, and health, a Technical Advisory Commission on establishing a judiciary and prosecution service, and, in October, the establishment of a Fuel Supervisory Board to administer the import, sale and distribution of petroleum. Central financial institutions for the province were inaugurated in November. In the same month UNMIK established a Housing and Property Directorate and Claims Commission in order to resolve residential property disputes. In September the KTC agreed to establish a Joint Security Committee, in response to concerns at the escalation of violence in the province, in particular attacks on remaining Serbian civilians. In mid-December the leaders of the three main political groupings in Kosovo agreed on provisional power-sharing arrangements with UNMIK for the administration of Kosovo until the holding of elections, scheduled for 2000. The agreement on the so-called Kosovo-UNMIK Joint Interim Administrative Structure established an eight-member executive Interim Administrative Council and a framework of administrative departments. The KTC was to maintain its consultative role. In January 2000 UNMIK oversaw the inauguration of the Kosovo Protection Corps, a civilian agency comprising mainly former members of the newly-demilitarized Kosovo Liberation Army, which was to provide an emergency response service and a humanitarian assistance capacity, to assist in de-mining operations and contribute to rebuilding local infrastructure. In August UNMIK, in view of its mandate to assist with the regeneration of the local economy, concluded an agreement with a multinational consortium to rehabilitate the important Trepca non-ferrous mining complex. During mid-2000 UNMIK organized the voter registration process for the forthcoming territory-wide municipal elections. These were held in late October with a strong voter turnout, although participation by minority communities was low. In mid-December the Supreme Court of Kosovo was inaugurated,

comprising 16 judges appointed by the Special Representative. During 2000 UNMIK police and KFOR co-operated in conducting joint security operations; the establishment of a special security task force to combat ethnically-motivated political violence, comprising senior UNMIK police and KFOR members, was agreed in June. From January 2001 UNMIK international travel documents were distributed to Kosovars without Yugoslav passports. From early June, in response to ongoing concern at violence between ethnic Albanians and security forces in the former Yugoslav republic of Macedonia (FYRM), UNMIK designated 19 authorized crossing points at Kosovo's international borders with Albania and the FYRM, and its boundaries with Montenegro and Serbia. In mid-May the Special Representative of the Secretary-General signed the Constitutional Framework on Interim Self-Government, providing for the establishment of a Constitutional Assembly; elections to the proposed Assembly were scheduled to take place in mid-November. UNMIK undertook efforts to register voters, in particular those from minority ethnic groups, and to continue to facilitate the return of displaced persons to their home communities. The last session of the KTC was held in October, and a general election was conducted, as scheduled, on 17 November. In December the Special Representative of the Secretary-General inaugurated the new 120-member Assembly. However, disagreements ensued among the three main political parties represented in the Assembly concerning the appointment of the positions of President and Prime Minister. In February 2002 Michael Steiner, recently appointed as the new Special Representative of the Secretary-General, negotiated an agreement with the leaders of the main political parties that resolved the deadlock in establishing the Interim Government. Accordingly, in March the new President, Prime Minister and Interim Government were inaugurated, enabling the commencement of the process of developing self-governing institutions. In November the mission established the UNMIK Administration—Mitrovica, superseding parallel institutions that had operated hitherto in Serb-dominated northern Mitrovica, and thereby extending UNMIK's authority over all Kosovo. During that month a second series of municipal elections took place. Reporting to the UN Security Council in February 2003 Steiner detailed his priorities for that year as: intensifying efforts to facilitate a reduction in politically and ethnically motivated violence, organized crime and corruption; institution-building and developing the legal system to provide a solid basis for attracting investment to Kosovo, with a view to creating jobs and reducing unemployment; consolidating a multi-ethnic society; and transferring competencies from UNMIK to the provisional institutions of self-government. In March a Transfer Council was established with responsibility for the latter process.

At January 2003 UNMIK comprised 4,446 civilian police officers, 39 military personnel, and an additional 1,022 international civilian personnel and 3,243 local civilian personnel. The General Assembly apportioned US $345.0m. to finance the operation during the period 1 July 2002–30 June 2003.

UNITED NATIONS INTERIM FORCE IN LEBANON—UNIFIL

Headquarters: Naqoura, Lebanon.

Personal Representative of the UN Secretary-General for Southern Lebanon: STAFFAN DE MISTURA (Sweden).

Commander: Maj.-Gen. LALIT MOHAN TEWARI (India).

UNIFIL was established by UN Security Council Resolution 425 in March 1978, following an invasion of Lebanon by Israeli forces. The force was mandated to confirm the withdrawal of Israeli forces, to restore international peace and security, and to assist the Government of Lebanon in ensuring the return of its effective authority in southern Lebanon. UNIFIL also extended humanitarian assistance to the population of the area, particularly following the second Israeli invasion of Lebanon in 1982. UNIFIL has provided civilians with food, water, fuel; medical and dental services; and some veterinary assistance. In April 1992, in accordance with its mandate, UNIFIL completed the transfer of part of its zone of operations to the control of the Lebanese army.

In March 1998 the Israeli Government announced that it recognized Security Council Resolution 425, requiring the unconditional withdrawal of its forces from southern Lebanon. It stipulated, however, that any withdrawal of its troops must be conditional on receiving security guarantees from the Lebanese authorities. A formal decision to this effect, adopted on 1 April, was rejected by the Lebanese and Syrian Governments. In mid-April 2000 the Israeli Government formally notified the UN Secretary-General of its intention to comply forthwith and in full with Resolution 425. Later in that month the UN Secretary-General dispatched a team of experts to study the technical aspects of the impending implementation of Resolution 425, and sent a delegation, led by both his Special Co-ordinator for the Middle East Peace Process, Terje Roed-Larsen, and the Commander of UNIFIL, to consult with regional Governments and groupings. The withdrawal of Israeli troops commenced in mid-May, and the final contingent was reported to have left Lebanon on 24 May. Meanwhile, the Security Council endorsed an operational plan to enable UNIFIL to verify the withdrawal. All concerned parties were urged to co-operate with UNIFIL in order to ensure the full implementation of the resolution. In accordance with its mandate, UNIFIL was to be disbanded following the resumption by the Lebanese Government of effective authority and the normal responsibilities of a state throughout the area, including the re-establishment of law and order structures. In mid-June the UN Secretary-General confirmed that Israeli forces had been fully evacuated from southern Lebanon. Soon afterwards UNIFIL reported several Israeli violations of the line of withdrawal, the so-called Blue Line. The Israeli Government agreed to rectify these by the end of July, and on 24 July the UN Secretary-General confirmed that no serious violations remained. UNIFIL, reinforced with additional troops, patrolled the area vacated by the Israeli forces, monitored the line of withdrawal, undertook demining activities, and continued to provide humanitarian assistance. From August 2000 the Lebanese Government deployed a Joint Security Force to the area and began re-establishing local administrative structures and reintegrating basic services into the rest of the country. However, the authorities declined to deploy military personnel along the border zone, on the grounds that a comprehensive peace agreement with Israel would first need to be achieved. In November, following two serious violations of the Blue Line in the previous month by both Israeli troops and Hezbollah militia, the Security Council urged the Lebanese Government to take effective control of the whole area vacated by Israel and to assume international responsibilities. In January 2001 the UN Secretary-General reported that UNIFIL no longer exercised control over the area of operation, which remained relatively stable. The Security Council endorsed his proposals to reconfigure the Force in order to focus on its remaining mandate of maintaining and observing the cease-fire along the line of withdrawal; this was completed by the end of 2002. During 2001 several incidents involving Hezbollah attacks on Israeli military positions and frequent air violations of the area of withdrawal by Israeli military aircraft were reported. In response to an increase from early 2002 in incidents generating tension in the area of UNIFIL's operation, reportedly perpetrated by Hezbollah and other militants, and continuous Israeli air violations of the Blue Line, the Secretary-General's Personal Representative for Southern Lebanon and Terje Roed-Larsen undertook diplomatic efforts aimed at restoring stability, and, despite restrictions on its movements, UNIFIL increased its patrols. In January 2003 the UN Secretary-General reported that the number of ground violations of the Blue Line had decreased significantly although sporadic Israeli overflights, resulting in anti-aircraft fire by Hezbollah, continued. The Force's mandate was most recently extended until 31 July 2003.

At 28 February 2003 the Force comprised 2,023 troops, assisted by some 50 military observers of UNTSO's Observer Group Lebanon, and also by some 411 international and local civilian staff. The General Assembly appropriation for the operation for the period 1 July 2002–30 June 2003 amounted to US $117.1m.

UNITED NATIONS IRAQ-KUWAIT OBSERVATION MISSION—UNIKOM

Headquarters: normally Umm Qasr, Iraq. The mission was withdrawn in March 2003 (see below).

Commander: Maj.-Gen. FRANCISZEK GAGOR (Poland).

UNIKOM was established by a UN Security Council resolution in April 1991, to monitor a 200-km demilitarized zone along the border between Iraq and Kuwait. The task of the mission was to deter violations of the border, to monitor the Khor Abdullah waterway between Iraq and Kuwait, and to prevent military activity within the zone. In February 1993 the Security Council adopted a resolution to strengthen UNIKOM, following incursions into Kuwaiti territory by Iraqi personnel. The resolution enabled the use of physical action to prevent or redress violations of the demilitarized zone or the newly-defined boundary between Iraq and Kuwait. UNIKOM subsequently assisted with the relocation of Iraqi citizens from Kuwait, which was completed in February 1994; provided technical support to other UN operations in the area (especially the Iraq–Kuwait Boundary Demarcation Commission, which was terminated in 1993); and has facilitated the humanitarian activities of the International Committee of the Red Cross. A maritime operation to monitor the Khor Abdullah waterway was initiated in February 2000. In mid-March 2003 UNIKOM's mandate was suspended and the mission's personnel were withdrawn owing to the commencement of US-led military action against Iraq.

At 28 February 2003 UNIKOM comprised 917 troops and 194 military observers, assisted by some 230 international and local civilian support staff. The UN General Assembly appropriated US $52.9m. for the maintenance of the mission for the period 1 July 2002–30 June 2003; two-thirds of UNIKOM's total costs are funded by voluntary contributions from Kuwait.

UNITED NATIONS MILITARY OBSERVER GROUP IN INDIA AND PAKISTAN—UNMOGIP

Headquarters: Rawalpindi, Pakistan (November–April), Srinagar, India (May–October).

Chief Military Observer: Maj.-Gen. PERTTI JUHANI PUONTI (Finland).

The Group was established in 1948 by UN Security Council resolutions aiming to restore peace in the region of Jammu and Kashmir, the status of which had become a matter of dispute between the Governments of India and Pakistan. Following a cease-fire which came into effect in January 1949, the military observers of UNMOGIP were deployed to assist in its observance. There is no periodic review of UNMOGIP's mandate. In 1971, following the signature of a new cease-fire agreement, India claimed that UNMOGIP's mandate had lapsed, since it was originally intended to monitor the agreement reached in 1949. Pakistan, however, regarded UNMOGIP's mission as unchanged, and the Group's activities have continued, although they have been somewhat restricted on the Indian side of the 'line of control', which was agreed by India and Pakistan in 1972.

At 28 February 2003 there were 45 military observers deployed on both sides of the 'line of control', supported by 71 international and local civilian personnel. The operation was allocated US $9.2m. from the regular budget of the UN for 2003.

UNITED NATIONS MISSION FOR THE REFERENDUM IN WESTERN SAHARA—MINURSO

Headquarters: el-Aaiún, Western Sahara.

Special Representative of the UN Secretary-General and Chief of Mission: WILLIAM LACY SWING (USA).

Personal Envoy of the UN Secretary-General: JAMES A. BAKER, III (USA).

Commander: Maj.-Gen. GYORGY SZARAZ (HUNGARY).

In April 1991 the UN Security Council endorsed the establishment of MINURSO to verify a cease-fire in the disputed territory of Western Sahara, which came into effect in September 1991, and to implement a settlement plan, involving the repatriation of Western Saharan refugees (in co-ordination with UNHCR), the release of all Sahrawi political prisoners, and the organization of a referendum on the future of the territory. Western Sahara is claimed by Morocco, the administering power since 1975, and by the Algerian-supported Frente Popular para la Liberación de Saguia el Hamra y Río de Oro—Frente Polisario. Although originally envisaged for January 1992, the referendum was postponed indefinitely. In 1992 and 1993 the UN Secretary-General's Special Representative organized negotiations between the Frente Polisario and the Moroccan Government, who were in serious disagreement regarding criteria for eligibility to vote in the plebiscite (in particular, the Moroccan Government insisted that more than 100,000 members of ethnic groups who had been forced to leave the territory under Spanish rule prior to the last official census in 1974, the results of which were to be used as a basis for voter registration, should be allowed to participate in the referendum). In March 1993 the Security Council advocated that further efforts should be made to compile a satisfactory electoral list and to resolve the outstanding differences on procedural issues. An Identification Commission was consequently established to begin the process of voter registration, although this was obstructed by the failure of the Moroccan Government and the Frente Polisario to pursue political dialogue. The identification and registration operation was formally initiated in August 1994; however, the process was complicated by the dispersed nature of the Western Saharan population. In December 1995 the UN Secretary-General reported that the identification of voters had stalled, owing to persistent obstruction of the process on the part of the Moroccan and Frente Polisario authorities; at the end of May 1996 the Security Council endorsed a recommendation of the Secretary-General to suspend the identification process until all sides demonstrate their willingness to co-operate with the mission. The Security Council decided that MINURSO's operational capacity should be reduced by 20%, with sufficient troops retained to monitor and verify the cease-fire.

In early 1997 the new Secretary-General of the UN, Kofi Annan, attempted to revive the possibility of an imminent resolution of the dispute, amid increasing concerns that the opposing authorities were preparing for a resumption of hostilities in the event of a collapse of the existing cease-fire, and appointed James Baker, a former US Secretary of State, as his Personal Envoy to the region. In June Baker obtained the support of Morocco and the Frente Polisario, as well as Algeria and Mauritania (which border the disputed territory), to conduct further negotiations in order to advance the referendum process. Direct talks between senior representatives of the Moroccan Government and the Frente Polisario authorities were initiated later in that month, in Lisbon, Portugal, under the auspices of the UN, and attended by Algeria and Mauritania in an observer capacity. In September the two sides concluded an agreement which aimed to resolve the outstanding issues of contention and enable the referendum to be conducted in late 1998. The agreement included a commitment by both parties to identify eligible Sahrawi voters on an individual basis, in accordance with the results of the 1974 census, and a code of conduct to ensure the impartiality of the poll. In October 1997 the Security Council endorsed a recommendation of the Secretary-General to increase the strength of the mission, to enable it to supervise nine identification centres. The process of voter identification resumed in December 1997. The agenda for the settlement plan envisaged that the identification process would be followed by a process of appeal, the publication of a final list of voters, and then by a transitional period, under UN authority, during which all Sahrawi refugees would be repatriated. The referendum was scheduled to be conducted in December 1998.

In January 1998 the Security Council approved the deployment of an engineering unit to support MINURSO in its demining activities. By early September of that year the initial identification process had been completed, with a total of 147,350 voters identified, including 87,238 since December 1997. However, the controversial issue of the eligibility of 65,000 members of three Saharan tribal groups remained unresolved. In October the Security Council endorsed a series of measures proposed by the Secretary-General to advance the referendum, including a strengthened Identification Commission to consider requests from any applicant from the three disputed tribal groups on an individual basis. The proposals also incorporated the need for an agreement by both sides with UNHCR with regard to arrangements for the repatriation of refugees. In November, following a visit to the region by the Secretary-General, the Frente Polisario accepted the proposals, and in March 1999 the Moroccan Government signed an agreement with the UN to secure the legal basis of the MINURSO operation. In May the Moroccan Government and the Frente Polisario agreed in principle to a draft plan of action for cross-border confidence measures. A new timetable envisaged the referendum being held in July 2000. In July 1999 the UN published the first part of a provisional list of 84,251 qualified voters. The appeals process then commenced. In late November almost 200 Moroccan prisoners of war were released by the Frente Polisario, following a series of negotiations led by the Special Representative of the UN Secretary-General. The identification of applicants from the three disputed Saharan tribal groups was completed at the end of December. In January 2000 the second, final part of the provisional list of qualified voters was issued, and a six-week appeals process ensued. In December 1999 the Security Council acknowledged that persisting disagreements obstructing the implementation of the settlement plan (mainly concerning the processing and analysis of appeals, the release of remaining prisoners and the repatriation of refugees) precluded any possibility of conducting the planned referendum before 2002.

In June 2001 the Personal Envoy of the Secretary-General elaborated a draft Framework Agreement on the Status of Western Sahara as an alternative to the settlement plan. The draft Agreement envisaged the disputed area remaining part of Morocco, but with substantial devolution of authority. Any referendum would be postponed. The Security Council, when granting an extension of MINURSO's mandate until November, authorized Baker to discuss the proposals with all concerned parties. However, the Frente Polisario and Algeria rejected the draft Agreement. In November the Security Council, at the insistence of the Frente Polisario, requested the opinion of the UN Legal Counsel regarding the legality of two short-term reconnaissance licences granted by Morocco to international petroleum companies for operation in Western Sahara. In that month the Council extended MINURSO's mandate until the end of February 2002. In January the new Special Representative of the UN Secretary-General, William Lacy Swing, visited the region and met with leaders of both sides. He welcomed the release by the Frente Polisario of a further 115 Moroccan prisoners, but urged both sides to release all long-term detainees. In July 2002 the Frente Polisario released a further 101 Moroccan prisoners, leaving a total of 1,260 long-term detainees, of whom 816 had been held for more than 20 years. Further visits to the region were undertaken by Lacy Swing during the year, and also in early 2003, when he presented to both sides and to the Governments of neighbouring states a new proposal for a political settlement, providing for self-determination, that had been requested by Resolution 1429 of the Security Council. MINURSO's mandate was extended for two and three month intervals, respectively, in February and April 2002, and in July was

extended to 31 January 2003, in support of the Special Representative's ongoing diplomatic efforts. A further extension, to 31 March, was granted so that all parties could consider the latest settlement proposal.

The mission has headquarters in the north and south of the disputed territory, and there is a liaison office in Tindouf, Algeria, which was established in order to maintain contact with the Frente Polisario (which is based in Algeria) and the Algerian Government.

At 31 December 2002 MINURSO comprised 217 military observers, 27 troops and 25 civilian police observers, supported by 290 international and local civilian personnel. The General Assembly appropriation to cover the cost of the mission for the period 1 July 2002–30 June 2003 amounted to US \$43.4m.

UNITED NATIONS MISSION IN ETHIOPIA AND ERITREA—UNMEE

Headquarters: Asmara, Eritrea; Addis Ababa, Ethiopia.

Special Representative of the Secretary-General and Head of Mission: LEGWAILA JOSEPH LEGWAILA (Botswana).

Commander: Maj.-Gen. ROBERT GORDON (United Kingdom).

At the end of July 2000 the Security Council authorized the establishment of UNMEE to facilitate compliance with and verify a cease-fire agreement that had been signed by the Governments of Eritrea and Ethiopia in mid-June (having been mediated by the Organization of African Unity—OAU, now African Union—AU, q.v.), with a view to settling a two-year border conflict between the two countries. In mid-September the Security Council authorized the deployment of up to 4,200 military personnel (including 220 military observers) to the operation, which was given an initial six-month mandate. The Security Council emphasized that UNMEE's mandate would be terminated on completion of the process to delimit and demarcate the Eritrea-Ethiopia border. In December the Eritrean and Ethiopian authorities concluded a full peace accord, providing for the establishment of an Eritrea-Ethiopia Boundary Commission mandated to delimit the border on the basis of relevant colonial treaties and international law. The eventual decision of the Commission was to be accepted by both parties as 'final and binding'. In February 2001 the Military Co-ordination Commission (which had been established jointly by the UN and the OAU in accordance with the cease-fire accord to address military and technical aspects of the peace process, and had met for the first time in December 2000) agreed a timetable to enable Eritrean and Ethiopian forces, monitored by UNMEE, to redeploy in order to establish a 25-km temporary security zone in the border area; the security zone was declared operational in mid-April 2001. UNMEE was subsequently to continue to monitor both forces, to co-ordinate and provide technical assistance for demining activities in the vacated and adjacent areas, and to co-ordinate local humanitarian and human rights activities by UN and other agencies. From mid-2001 UNMEE repeatedly protested against alleged restrictions placed on its freedom of movement by the Eritrean authorities in areas adjoining the security zone, as these impeded the mission's capability to monitor the redeployment of that country's forces. In January 2002 the Security Council, noting that Eritrea had started to permit UNMEE delegates to visit certain parts of the adjacent areas on submission of 24 hours' notice, urged that the mission be allowed full freedom of movement. The Council also requested that the Eritrean Government disclose details of an alleged continuing military and police presence within the temporary security zone, and that it conclude a status of forces agreement with the Secretary-General. In mid-April the Eritrea-Ethiopia Boundary Commission published its decision on the delimitation of the two countries' common border. The Secretary-General urged Eritrea and Ethiopia to implement the decision without delay. UNMEE was to monitor the next phase of the peace process, involving the border's physical demarcation. In addition, the mission was to undertake demining activities in the area, in order to facilitate the demarcation; to determine with both sides technical modalities for the transfer of territory; and to provide logistical and administrative support for the Boundary Commission's field office. In August the Security Council adjusted the mission's mandate to support the implementation of decisions adopted by the Boundary Commission. During late April and early May the Ethiopian Government temporarily closed the Ethiopian border to UNMEE personnel, claiming that UNMEE had not consulted sufficiently with it regarding the mission's logistical support for, and the transfer of personnel to, the Boundary Commission's field office; that the Commission had not established its field presence on the Ethiopian side of the border; and that UNMEE had inappropriately permitted journalists to visit a border village. In March 2003 the Secretary-General noted that the movements of UNMEE personnel were still being restricted by the Eritrean authorities. In that month UNMEE's mandate was extended for a further six months, until 15 September.

At 28 February 2003 UNMEE comprised 3,852 troops, 207 military observers, and 490 international and local civilian personnel. The proposed budget for the mission amounted to US $200.9m. for the period 1 July 2002–30 June 2003.

UNITED NATIONS MISSION IN SIERRA LEONE—UNAMSIL

Headquarters: Freetown, Sierra Leone.

Special Representative of the Secretary-General and Chief of Mission: OLUYEMI ADENIJI (Nigeria).

Commander: Lt-Gen. DANIEL ISHMAEL OPANDE (Kenya).

Chief Military Observer: Maj.-Gen. SYED ATHAR ALI (Pakistan).

In July 1998 the Security Council established a UN observer mission in Sierra Leone (UNOMSIL) to monitor the military and security situation in that country following the restoration of a democratically-elected government. UNOMSIL was authorized to oversee the disarmament and demobilization of former combatants, as well as the voluntary disarmament of members of the civilian defence force, and to assist in monitoring respect for international humanitarian law. The Special Representative, with the civilian component of the mission, was authorized to advise the Sierra Leonea authorities on police practice, training and reform, and to help to address the country's human rights needs. UNOMSIL was to work closely with forces of the Economic Community for West African States (ECOWAS) in promoting peace and national reconciliation. In January 1999, following a sudden escalation of hostilities, the UN Security Council extended the mandate of UNOMSIL for a further two months, although it acknowledged that several UNOMSIL military observers, together with civilian support staff, would withdraw to Conakry, Guinea, until the security situation improved. In March the Security Council condemned the ongoing violation of human rights in Sierra Leone and urged all neighbouring countries to prevent the cross-border supply of armaments to anti-government forces. None the less, the Council extended the mission's mandate until mid-June and, subsequently, until mid-December. In August the Security Council authorized a provisional expansion of UNOMSIL of up to 210 military observers, in order to support the implementation of a peace agreement that had been signed by the parties to the Sierra Leone conflict in July, in Lomé, Togo. In October the Council authorized the establishment of the UN Mission in Sierra Leone (UNAMSIL), comprising up to 6,000 military personnel, to help to consolidate peace in that country. UNAMSIL was mandated to co-operate with the Sierra Leone Government and all other parties to enforce the cease-fire accord and Lomé peace agreement, to implement a plan for the disarmament, demobilization and reintegration of all former combatants, and to facilitate the delivery of humanitarian assistance. The mission was to assume responsibility for all civilian, political and military components of UNOMSIL, the mandate of which was terminated with immediate effect. In February 2000 the Council expanded UNAMSIL's mandate to include the provision of security at key locations and government installations, assistance to the Sierra Leone law enforcement authorities, and the safe keeping and subsequent disposal of military equipment collected from former combatants. The Council also enlarged the mission's authorized strength from 6,000 to 11,100 military personnel.

During early 2000, in contravention of the Lomé accord, Sierra Leone rebels repeatedly obstructed the implementation of the disarmament and demobilization programme. In May, following an attack on a contingent of UNAMSIL troops in the previous month, rebels killed several mission personnel and captured and detained around 500 others; these were all released later in the month. In response to the breakdown in security the United Kingdom deployed a force in Sierra Leone in early May, with a mandate to evacuate British nationals; the presence of the British troops was also regarded, however, as a deterrent to any escalation in rebel activities pending the arrival of UNAMSIL reinforcements. In mid-May the Security Council approved a further increase in the mission's authorized strength, providing for a total of 13,000 military personnel. The United Kingdom withdrew most of its force in the following month, leaving a small contingent to train Sierra Leone government troops and undertake security duties. In mid-July UNAMSIL mounted a successful operation to release 233 of its personnel, who had been surrounded by rebels in eastern Sierra Leone since the end of May. The Security Council adopted a resolution in July banning the direct and indirect importation of rough diamonds from rebel-controlled areas of Sierra Leone, following mounting concern at the role played by illicit diamond exploitation in motivating and funding anti-government activities. In August the Security Council recommended that UNAMSIL should be strengthened to enable it to secure approach routes to the Lungi and Freetown peninsulas and to counter continuing attacks by armed rebels. The Security Council asked the Secretary-General to assess the number of additional troops that would be required to achieve this. A new cease-fire

agreement, entailing the recommencement of the disarmament, demobilization and reintegration plan, was signed by the Sierra Leone Government and the principal rebel group in early November. In March 2001 the Council expanded the mission's authorized maximum strength to 17,500 military personnel and also approved a revised concept of operations that envisaged the deployment of UNAMSIL troops, government representatives, and international humanitarian personnel into rebel-controlled areas, with a view to re-establishing basic services and the authority of the state. In December the Security Council noted that the Sierra Leone Government, assisted by UNAMSIL, had yet to establish full authority over the rebel-dominated diamond-producing areas of the country.

In January 2002 the Security Council welcomed the significant progress that had been achieved in the implementation of the disarmament, demobilization and reintegration plan, including the official completion of the disarmament element during that month. In March the mission's mandate was extended until 30 September. In support of legislative and presidential elections that were staged in Sierra Leone in mid-May, UNAMSIL temporarily redeployed some 11,000 troops to high-risk areas of the country, and provided practical assistance to the Sierra Leone police, to the country's National Electoral Commisssion, and to electoral observer teams. At this time UNAMSIL intensified patrols of border areas with Liberia in response to increasing incursions by Liberian rebels into Sierra Leone. Following the elections, UNAMSIL was to continue to support the Sierra Leone Government in restoring the nation-wide authority of the state; in consolidating peace, security and national reconciliation; in promoting the rehabilitation of the judicial system and respect for human rights; and by addressing outstanding issues such as the reintegration of former combatants. In September, in view of the prevailing generally stable security situation in much of Sierra Leone, the UN Secretary-General presented proposals to the Security Council for the downsizing of UNAMSIL to a force strength of about 5,000 by the end of 2004, dependent upon the achievement of certain benchmarks in areas such as security.

At 28 February 2003 UNAMSIL comprised 15,255 troops and 256 military observers, assisted by 52 civilian police and 864 international and local civilian personnel. The proposed budget for the mission amounted to US $699.8m. for the period 1 July 2002–31 July 2003.

UNITED NATIONS MISSION IN THE DEMOCRATIC REPUBLIC OF THE CONGO—MONUC

Headquarters: Kinshasa, Democratic Republic of the Congo.

Liaison offices are situated in Bujumbura (Burundi); Addis Ababa (Ethiopia); Windhoek (Namibia); Kigali (Rwanda); Kampala (Uganda); Lusaka (Zambia); and Harare (Zimbabwe).

Special Representative of the UN Secretary-General and Chief of Mission: AMOS NAMANGA NGONGI (Cameroon).

Commander: Maj.-Gen. MOUNTAGA DIALLO (Senegal).

In August 1999 the UN Security Council authorized the deployment of up to 90 military liaison personnel to support implementation of a cease-fire agreement for the Democratic Republic of the Congo (DRC) which had been signed in Lusaka, Zambia, in July, by the heads of state of the DRC, Angola, Namibia, Rwanda, Uganda and Zimbabwe. The Council approved the establishment of MONUC in late November. With an initial mandate until 1 March 2000, the mission was, in co-operation with a Joint Military Commission comprising representatives of the parties to the conflict, to oversee the implementation of the agreement, including monitoring the cease-fire and the disengagement of forces. The mission was also mandated to facilitate the delivery of humanitarian assistance and to develop a mine action plan and undertake emergency demining activities. The first phase of MONUC's operations entailed the deployment of unarmed liaison and technical assessment officers, as well as other multi-disciplinary personnel, previously authorized by the Council, to the capitals of the states party to the Lusaka accord and, where possible, to rebel group headquarters. In February 2000 the Security Council authorized the expansion of the mission to comprise up to 5,537 military personnel, including up to 500 observers, thereby enabling the commencement of the second phase of the operation, under which military observers were to be dispatched to the DRC to monitor and verify the cease-fire and disengagement of forces. In April a sub-plan on military disengagement and redeployment was agreed in Kampala, Uganda, by the parties to the conflict and, in December, a revised sub-plan was adopted in Harare, Zimbabwe. However, by early 2001 the Lusaka cease-fire accord and Kampala and Harare sub-plans remained to be implemented and only a small contingent of MONUC observers had been deployed in the DRC. In mid-February the Security Council adopted a resolution demanding that the parties to the conflict commence the phased disengagement and redeployment of their forces by mid-March and stipulating that plans for the full withdrawal of foreign troops and the disarmament, demobilization and resettlement of militia must be prepared and adopted by mid-May. The resolution raised the maximum number of military observers to 550, to be stationed around four regional headquarters; the deployment of up to 1,900 armed security personnel to protect these bases was also authorized. River boat units were to be deployed to assist with the transportation of observers and supplies and to reinforce the mission's presence; it was hoped that commercial activity along river routes would thus also be supported. In mid-March the initial phase of military disengagement was reported to have commenced. Small contingents of MONUC troops were deployed in the DRC from March, including, in the following month, to the strategic rebel-occupied northeastern town of Kisangani. In June the Security Council approved a revised concept of operations for MONUC, entailing the establishment of a civilian police element, enhancing the mission's presence in Kisangani and strengthening its logistic support capabilities. In October 2002 the UN Secretary-General reported that 90 teams of military observers were stationed at 50 sites in the DRC. Preparations were under way for the implementation of the mission's third phase of operations (authorized at the end of 2001), which was to entail the deployment of a full peace-keeping force to oversee the complete withdrawal of foreign troops from DRC territory and the disarmament, demobilization and reintegration of rebel forces. In December 2002 the UN Security Council authorized the expansion of the mission to co-ordinate this process.

Some progress towards the implementation of the Lusaka cease-fire accord was achieved at the Inter-Congolese Dialogue held in Sun City, South Africa, from mid-February–mid-April 2002, when a bilateral power-sharing agreement was concluded between the DRC Government and Mouvement de libération du Congo—MLC rebels supported by the Ugandan Government. In mid-May a failed mutiny attempt by dissident rebels in Kisangani led to an outbreak of violence that resulted in at least 50 civilian fatalities. MONUC conducted patrols of the city and provided protection to a number of individuals who considered their lives to be at risk. Subsequently the Rwandan-backed Rassemblement congolais pour la démocratie (RCD)-Goma rebels controlling Kisangani accused the Special Representative of the Secretary-General of displaying a pro-Government bias and announced that he and several mission personnel were 'banned' from the area occupied by the grouping. A resolution of the Security Council in early June demanded that the RCD-Goma rebels cease their obstruction of the mission's activities in Kisangani immediately. MONUC continued to maintain an increased level of patrols.

Following the adoption in July and August 2002, respectively, of the so-called Pretoria agreement between the DRC and Rwandan Governments, and Luanda agreement between the DRC and Ugandan Governments, nearly all Rwandan and Ugandan forces were withdrawn before the end of that year. Meanwhile, troop withdrawals were also initiated by Angola, Burundi, Namibia and Zimbabwe. MONUC observed the departure of the foreign forces. In December the All-Inclusive Agreement on the Transition in the DRC, providing for the staging of elections in the DRC after a transition period of 24 months, was signed by the participants in the Inter-Congolese Dialogue, in Pretoria, South Africa. MONUC's mandate has been successively extended, most recently to 30 June 2003.

At 28 February 2003 MONUC comprised 3,889 troops, 476 military observers and 49 civilian police, assisted by 1,263 international and local civilian personnel. The proposed budget for the mission amounted to US $608.3m. for the period 1 July 2002–30 June 2003, funded from a Special Account comprising assessed contributions from UN member states.

UNITED NATIONS MISSION OF SUPPORT IN EAST TIMOR—UNMISET

Headquarters: Dili, Timor-Leste.

Special Representative of the UN Secretary-General and Transitional Administrator: KAMALESH SHARMA (India).

Commander: Maj.-Gen. TAN HUCK GIM (Singapore).

Chief Military Observer: Brig.-Gen. PEDRO ROCHA PENA MADEIRA (PORTUGAL).

Chief of Civilian Police: Chief Superintendent PETER MILLER (Canada).

UNMISET was established on 20 May 2002, initially with a mandate for one year, when Timor-Leste (East Timor) attained its independence. It succeeded the UN Transitional Administration in East Timor (UNTAET), which had been established in October 1999 to govern the territory on an interim basis following the outcome of a popular referendum in favour of independence from Indonesia. UNMISET was to provide assistance to core administrative structures, to extend interim law enforcement and public security services, to assist the development of a national police force, and to contribute to the maintenance of external and internal security. The civilian component of UNMISET was to include a Serious Crimes Unit and a Human Rights Unit, as well as focal points for gender and HIV/AIDS. The Mission was mandated to devolve all operational responsibilities to the Timor-Leste authorities within two years. In March 2003 the UN Secretary-General reported that, owing to an escalation in insecurity (including riots and attacks by armed groups) in Timor-Leste from November 2002, and the current early stage in the development of the national police force, original plans swiftly to downsize the mission should be revised. He proposed adjustments to the configuration and military strategy of UNMISET, aimed at facilitating the restoration of stability.

At 28 February 2003 UNMISET comprised 3,761 troops, 672 civilian police officers and 108 military observers, supported by 1,427 international and local civilian personnel. The cost of the operation for the period 1 July 2002–30 June 2003 was estimated at US $305m; this was to be financed by a Special Account.

UNITED NATIONS OBSERVER MISSION IN GEORGIA—UNOMIG

Headquarters: Sukhumi, Georgia.

Special Representative of the UN Secretary-General and Head of Mission: HEIDI TAGLIAVINI (Switzerland).

Chief Military Observer: Maj.-Gen. KAZI ASHFAQ AHMED (Bangladesh).

UNOMIG was established in August 1993 to verify compliance with a cease-fire agreement, signed in July between the Government of Georgia and the Abkhazian separatist movement. The mission was the UN's first undertaking in the former USSR. In October the UN Secretary-General stated that a breakdown in the cease-fire agreement had invalidated UNOMIG's mandate. He proposed, however, to maintain, for information purposes, the eight-strong UNOMIG team in the city of Sukhumi, which had been seized by Abkhazian forces in late September. In late December the Security Council authorized the deployment of additional military observers in response to the signing of a memorandum of understanding by the conflicting parties earlier that month. Further peace negotiations, which were conducted in January–March 1994 under the authority of the UN Secretary-General's Special Envoy, achieved no political consensus. In July the Security Council endorsed the establishment of a Commonwealth of Independent States (CIS, q.v.) peace-keeping force to verify a cease-fire agreement that had been signed in May. At the same time the Security Council increased UNOMIG's authorized strength and expanded the mission's mandate to incorporate the following tasks: to monitor and verify the implementation of the agreement and to investigate reported violations; to observe the operation of the CIS peace-keeping force; to verify that troops and heavy military equipment remain outside the security zone and the restricted weapons zone; to monitor the storage of the military equipment withdrawn from the restricted zones; to monitor the withdrawal of Georgian troops from the Kodori Gorge region to locations beyond the Abkhazian frontiers; and to patrol regularly the Kodori Gorge. Peace negotiations were pursued in 1995, despite periodic outbreaks of violence in Abkhazia. In July 1996 the Security Council urged the Abkhazian side to accelerate significantly the process of voluntary return of Georgian refugees and displaced persons to Abkhazia. In October the Council decided to establish a human rights office as part of UNOMIG. In May 1997 the Security Council issued a Presidential Statement urging greater efforts towards achieving a peaceful solution to the dispute. The Statement endorsed a proposal of the UN Secretary-General to strengthen the political element of UNOMIG to enable the mission to assume a more active role in furthering a negotiated settlement. In July direct discussions between representatives of the Georgian and Abkhazian authorities, the first in more than two years, were held under UN auspices. In early 1998 the security situation in Abkhazia deteriorated. Following an outbreak of violence in May the conflicting parties signed a cease-fire accord, which incorporated an agreement that UNOMIG and CIS forces would continue to work to create a secure environment to allow for the return of displaced persons to the Gali region of Abkhazia. In addition, the UN Security Council urged both parties to establish a protection unit to ensure the safety of UN military observers. In December 2000, following a series of detentions and hostage-takings of Mission personnel in the Kodori Gorge during late 1999 and 2000, UNOMIG suspended patrols of that area. Reviewing the operation in January 2001 the UN Secretary-General expressed concern at the recent recurrent abductions and urged the Abkhazian side to cease imposing restrictions on the mission's freedom of movement. Although contacts between the Georgian and Abkhazian authorities continued in 2001, progress towards the conclusion of a durable political settlement remained stalled by an *impasse* between the two sides regarding the future political status of Abkhazia. A Programme of Action on confidence-building measures was concluded in March; however, the negotiation process was interrupted from April, owing to increasing insecurity in the conflict zone and the ongoing activities of illegal armed groups. In October a UNOMIG helicopter was shot down in the Kodori Gorge, resulting in the deaths of nine people. UNOMIG suspended its patrols of the area. In January 2002 a protocol was signed between the conflicting parties providing for the withdrawal of Georgian troops from the upper Kodori valley and the resumption of UN ground patrols. Further discussion on implementation of the protocol resulted in the first joint patrol being conducted in late March. On 2 April a protocol was concluded by both sides for a final withdrawal of Georgian troops and the resumption of regular UNOMIG/CIS patrols. Renewed diplomatic efforts to secure a political agreement initially focused on a paper of Basic Principles for the Distribution of Competences between Tbilisi and Sukhumi, which had been prepared by the Special Representative of the UN Secretary-General. The document was rejected as a basis for negotiations by the Abkhazian leadership; however, discussions were held between the leadership of the two sides to consider measures to stabilize further the situation in the Kodori Gorge. Both sides agreed to resolve all outstanding issues by peaceful means. By early 2003 no further progress towards the commencement of negotiations had been achieved. UNOMIG co-operates closely with the CIS peace-keeping force, and a joint UNOMIG–CIS fact-finding team undertakes investigations of violent incidents. UNOMIG's mandate was most recently extended until 31 July 2003.

At 28 February 2003 UNOMIG comprised 117 military observers, supported by 269 international and local civilian personnel. The General Assembly budget appropriation for the mission for the period 1 July 2002–30 June 2003 amounted to US $33.1m.

UNITED NATIONS PEACE-KEEPING FORCE IN CYPRUS—UNFICYP

Headquarters: Nicosia, Cyprus.

Special Adviser to the UN Secretary-General: ALVARO DE SOTO (Peru).

Acting Special Representative of the UN Secretary-General and Chief of Mission: ZBIGNIEW WLOSOWICZ (Poland).

Commander: Lt.-Gen. JIN HA HWANG (Republic of Korea).

UNFICYP was established in March 1964 by a UN Security Council resolution (initially for a three-month duration, subsequently periodically extended) to prevent a recurrence of fighting between the Greek and Turkish Cypriot communities, and to contribute to the maintenance of law and order and a return to normal conditions. The Force controls a 180-km buffer zone, established (following the Turkish intervention in 1974) between the cease-fire lines of the Turkish forces and the Cyprus National Guard. It is mandated to investigate and act upon all violations of the cease-fire and buffer zone. The Force also performs humanitarian functions, such as facilitating the supply of electricity and water across the cease-fire lines, and offering emergency medical services. In August 1996 serious hostilities between elements of the two communities in the UN-controlled buffer zone resulted in the deaths of two people and injuries to many others, including 12 UN personnel. Following further intercommunal violence, UNFICYP advocated the prohibition of all weapons and military posts along the length of the buffer zone. The Force also proposed additional humanitarian measures to improve the conditions of minority groups living in the two parts of the island. In reports to the Security Council, the UN Secretary-General has consistently recognized UNFICYP as being indispensable to maintaining calm on the island and to creating the best conditions for his good offices. In July 1997 a new series of direct negotiations between the leaders of the two communities was initiated, under the auspices of the UN Secretary-General's Special Adviser; however, the talks were suspended at the end of that year. In November 1999 the leaders of the two communities agreed to participate in proximity negotiations, to be mediated by the UN. The first round of these took place in New York, in December. A second and third round were convened in Geneva, Switzerland, in February and July 2000, respectively. A fourth round of proximity talks was held in New York in September and a fifth round in Geneva, in November. In December 2001 the leaders of the two communities met together, in the presence of the Special Adviser, and agreed to begin a series of direct talks in the following month. In May the Secretary-General visited Cyprus. Further meetings between the Secretary-General and the two leaders took place in September (in Paris) and October (New York). In November he submitted to them for consideration a document providing the basis for a comprehensive settlement agreement; a revised version of the document was released in the following month. In a report issued in November the Secretary-General noted that the two leaders were jointly addressing the outstanding issue of missing persons, and also that a number of restrictions placed on UNFICYP's activities during 2000 by the Turkish Cypriot authorities and Turkish forces remained in place. A further revised version of the draft settlement document was presented to the leaders of the two communities during a visit by the Secretary-General to Cyprus in late February 2003. He urged that both sides put this to separate simultaneous referenda at the end of March, in the hope that, were the agreement approved, Cyprus would be able subsequently to accede to the European Union in a re-united state.

At 28 February 2003 UNFICYP had an operational strength of 1,253 military personnel and 35 civilian police officers, supported by 149 international and local civilian staff. Over the period 1 July 2002–30 June 2003 the proposed cost of maintaining the force amounted to US $45.6m., including voluntary contributions from the Governments of Cyprus and of Greece amounting to $15.2m. and $6.5m., respectively.

UNITED NATIONS TRUCE SUPERVISION ORGANIZATION—UNTSO

Headquarters: Government House, Jerusalem.

Chief-of-Staff: Maj.-Gen. CARL A. DODD (Ireland).

UNTSO was established initially to supervise the truce called by the UN Security Council in Palestine in May 1948 and has assisted in the application of the 1949 Armistice Agreements. Its activities have evolved over the years, in response to developments in the Middle East and in accordance with the relevant resolutions of the Security Council. There is no periodic renewal procedure for UNTSO's mandate.

UNTSO observers assist UN peace-keeping forces in the Middle East, at present UNIFIL and UNDOF (see above). The mission maintains offices in Beirut, Lebanon and Damascus, Syria. In addition, UNTSO operates a number of outposts in the Sinai region of Egypt to maintain a UN presence there. UNTSO observers have been available at short notice to form the nucleus of new peace-keeping operations.

The operational strength of UNTSO at 28 February 2003 was 155 military observers, supported by 217 international and local civilian staff. UNTSO expenditures are covered by the regular budget of the United Nations. The cost of the operation in 2003 was estimated to be US $25.9m.

United Nations Population Fund—UNFPA

Address: 220 East 42nd St, New York, NY 10017, USA.

Telephone: (212) 297-5020; **fax:** (212) 297-4911; **internet:** www.unfpa.org.

Created in 1967 as the Trust Fund for Population Activities, the UN Fund for Population Activities (UNFPA) was established as a Fund of the UN General Assembly in 1972 and was made a subsidiary organ of the UN General Assembly in 1979, with the UNDP Governing Council (now the Executive Board) designated as its governing body. In 1987 UNFPA's name was changed to the United Nations Population Fund (retaining the same acronym).

Organization

(April 2003)

EXECUTIVE DIRECTOR

The Executive Director, who has the rank of Under-Secretary-General of the UN, is responsible for the overall direction of the Fund, working closely with governments, other United Nations bodies and agencies, and non-governmental and international organizations to ensure the most effective programming and use of resources in population activities.

Executive Director: THORAYA A. OBAID (Saudi Arabia).

EXECUTING AGENCIES

UNFPA provides financial and technical assistance to developing countries at their request. In many projects assistance is extended through member organizations of the UN system (in particular, FAO, ILO, UNESCO, WHO), although projects are executed increasingly by national governments themselves. The Fund may also call on the services of international, regional and national non-governmental and training organizations, as well as research institutions. In addition, eight UNFPA regional technical support teams, composed of experts from the UN, its specialized agencies and non-governmental organizations, assist countries at all stages of project/programme development and implementation.

FIELD ORGANIZATION

UNFPA operates field offices, each headed by an UNFPA Representative, in more than 100 countries. In other countries UNFPA uses UNDP's field structure of Resident Representatives as the main mechanism for performing its work. The field offices assist governments in formulating requests for aid and co-ordinate the work of the executing agencies in any given country or area. UNFPA has eight regional technical support teams (see above).

Activities

The major functions of UNFPA, according to its mandate, are: to advance the knowledge and capacity to respond to needs in population and family planning; to promote awareness of population problems in developed and developing countries and possible strategies to deal with them; to assist countries, at their request, in dealing with their population problems, in the forms and means best suited to the individual countries' requirements; and to play a leading role in the UN system in promoting population programmes and support and co-ordinate projects.

In co-operation with the UN Population Division, UNFPA played an important role in preparing for and conducting the International Conference on Population and Development (ICPD), held in Cairo, Egypt, in September 1994. UNFPA's then Executive Director, Dr Nafis Sadik, acted as Secretary-General of the Conference, which was attended by representatives of 182 countries. The Fund was appointed as the lead body within the UN system responsible for following up and implementing the Programme of Action adopted by the ICPD. This outlined the objectives to be pursued for the next 20 years (despite reservations recorded by the representatives of some predominantly Roman Catholic and Islamic countries, concerning sections which they regarded as endorsing abortion and sexual promiscuity). The Programme's objectives envisaged universal access to reproductive health and family planning services, a reduction in infant, child and maternal mortality, a life expectancy at birth of 75 years or more, and universal access to primary education for all children by 2015. The Programme emphasized the necessity of empowering and educating women, in order to achieve successful sustainable human development. Annual expenditure required for the implementation of the objectives was estimated to amount to US $17,000m. in 2000, increasing to $21,700m. in 2015: of these amounts, the international community or donor countries would need to contribute about one-third. During 1995 UNFPA undertook to redefine its programme directions, resource allocations and policy guide-lines in order to implement effectively the recommendations of the ICPD Programme of Action. The Executive Board subsequently endorsed the following as core programme areas: Reproductive Health, including family planning and sexual health; Population and Development Strategies; and Advocacy (for example, human rights, education, basic health services and the empowerment of women) (see below). A special session of the UN General Assembly (entitled ICPD + 5, and attended by delegates from 177 countries) was held in June/July 1999 to assess progress in achieving the objectives of the Cairo Conference and to identify priorities for future action. ICPD + 5 adopted several key actions for further implementation of the Programme of Action. These included advancing understanding of the connections between poverty, gender inequalities, health, education, the environment, financial and human resources, and development; focusing on the economic and social implications of demographic change; greater incorporation of gender issues into social and development policies and greater involvement of women in decision-making processes; greater support for HIV/AIDS prevention activities; and strengthened political commitment to the reproductive health of adolescents. Several new objectives were adopted by the special session, including the achievement of 60% availability of contraceptives and reproductive health care services by 2005, 80% by 2010, with universal availability by 2015.

UNFPA is participating in the UN System-wide Special Initiative on Africa that was initiated by the UN Secretary-General in March 1996. UNFPA's principal involvement is to assist countries to implement efforts for reproductive health and to promote the integration of population considerations into development planning. UNFPA collaborates with other UN agencies and international experts to develop a reliable, multidisciplinary set of indicators to measure progress towards achieving the objectives of different global conferences and to help formulate reproductive health programmes and monitor their success. UNFPA co-operates with other UN agencies in the Joint UN Programme on HIV/AIDS (UNAIDS), which became operational on 1 January 1996. The Fund organized a high-level panel discussion on the theme 'Gender and HIV/AIDS' at the UN General Assembly special session on HIV/AIDS held in June 2001.

REPRODUCTIVE HEALTH

UNFPA recognizes that improving reproductive health is an essential requirement for improving the general welfare of the population and the basis for empowering women and achieving sustainable social and economic development. The ICPD succeeded in raising the political prominence of reproductive health issues and stimulating consideration by governments of measures to strengthen and restructure their health services and policies. UNFPA encourages the integration of family planning into all maternal, child and other reproductive health care. Its efforts to improve the quality of these services include support for the training of health-care personnel and promoting greater accessibility. Many reproductive health projects focus on the reduction of maternal mortality (i.e. those related to pregnancy), which was included as a central objective of the ICPD Programme, and recognized as a legitimate element of international human rights instruments concerning the right to life/survival. Through its Global Initiative on Safe Motherhood, UNFPA supports projects to reduce maternal death, which amount to about 500,000 each year, in 89 countries. Efforts have focused on improving accessibility to essential obstetric care and ensuring the provision of skilled attendance to women in labour. The ICPD reported that a major cause of maternal deaths was unsafe abortions, and urged governments to confront the issue as a major public health concern. UNFPA is also concerned with reducing the use of abortion (i.e. its use as a means of family planning), and with preventing infertility, reproductive tract infections and sexually-transmitted diseases, including HIV/AIDS. Special attention is given to the specific needs of adolescents, for example through education and counselling initiatives, and to women in emergency situations. UNFPA distributes emergency reproductive health supplies (including home delivery kits), with a focus on HIV-prevention, to regions affected by conflict or natural disaster and supports training and the construction of clinics and other health facilities following humanitarian crises. UNFPA also supports research into contraceptives and training in contraceptive technology. The Fund's Global Initiative on Reproductive Health Commodity Security organizes in-depth studies on national contraceptive requirements and aims to ensure an adequate supply of contraceptives and reproductive health supplies to developing countries. UNFPA encourages partnerships between private-sector interests and the governments of developing nations, with a view to making affordable commercial contraceptive products more easily available to consumers and thereby enabling governments to direct subsidies at the poorest sectors of society. In 2001 the Fund met 44 urgent requests for supplies through its Global Contraceptive Commodities Programme.

POPULATION AND DEVELOPMENT STRATEGIES

UNFPA helps countries to formulate and implement comprehensive population policies as a central part of any strategies to achieve sustainable development. The Fund aims to ensure that the needs and concerns of women are incorporated into development and population policies. Under this programme area UNFPA provides assistance and training for national statistical offices in undertaking basic data collection, for example censuses and demographic surveys. UNFPA also provides assistance for analysis of demographic and socio-economic data, for research on population trends and for the formulation of government policies. It supports a programme of fellowships in demographic analysis, data processing and cartography. In October 2001 UNFPA organized a meeting of experts on population ageing in preparation for the Second World Assembly on Ageing, which was held in April 2002.

ADVOCACY

UNFPA's advocacy role is incorporated into all its programming activities in support of the objectives of the ICPD. Consequently, the Fund aims to encourage the participation of women at all levels of decision- and policy-making and supports programmes that improve the access of all girls and women to education and grant women equal access to land, credit and employment opportunities. UNFPA's annual *State of World Population Report* has consistently focused on the improved welfare of women as an issue of basic human rights; this includes the eradication of all forms of gender discrimination, entitlement to reproductive choice and a zero-tolerance approach to the protection of women from sexual and domestic violence and coercion. UNFPA helps to promote awareness of these objectives and to incorporate them into national programmes. In 1997 UNFPA appointed a special ambassador to generate international awareness of the dangers of female genital mutilation. UNFPA emphasizes the role of knowledge and prevention in combating the spread of HIV/AIDS. There are special programmes on youth, on ageing and on migration, and the Fund is currently increasing educational and research activities in the area of population and the environment. UNFPA attempts to increase awareness of the issue of population through regional and national seminars, publications (see below) and audio-visual aids, participation in conferences, and through a pro-active relationship with the mass media. In 1999 UNFPA promoted observance of 12 October as the symbolic day on which the world's population was estimated to reach 6,000m.

Finance

UNFPA is supported entirely by voluntary contributions from donor countries. In 2001 UNFPA's income totalled US $396.5m. of which $268.7m. was for regular resources and $127.8m. for trust funds and other cost-sharing arrangements. Income in 2002 was projected to be $ 305.2m. Country programme expenditure in 2001 totalled some $144m., and a further $27.7m. was spent on regional and interregional projects. Of total programme expenditure in 2001 about 70% was allocated to reproductive health care.

Publications

Annual Report.
AIDS Update (annually).
Dispatches (10 a year, in English, French and Spanish).
Inventory of Population Projects in Developing Countries around the World (annually in English and French).
Populi (quarterly, in English, French and Spanish).
State of World Population Report (annually).
Reports and reference works; videotapes and radio programmes.

United Nations Relief and Works Agency for Palestine Refugees in the Near East—UNRWA

Addresses: Gamal Abd an-Nasser St, Gaza City; Bayader Wadi Seer, POB 140157, Amman 11814, Jordan.
Telephone (Gaza City): (7) 6777333; **fax:** (7) 6777555.
Telephone (Amman): (6) 5826171; **fax:** (6) 5826177.
E-mail: unrwapio@unrwa.org; **internet:** www.un.org/unrwa/.

UNRWA was established by the UN General Assembly to provide relief, health, education and welfare services for Palestine refugees in the Near East, initially on a short-term basis. UNRWA began operations in May 1950 and, in the absence of a solution to the refugee problem, its mandate has subsequently been extended by the General Assembly.

Organization

(April 2003)

UNRWA employs an international staff of about 120 and more than 22,500 local staff, mainly Palestine refugees. In mid-1996 the agency's headquarters were relocated, from Vienna, Austria, to Gaza and Jordan. The Commissioner-General is the head of all UNRWA operations and reports directly to the UN General Assembly. UNRWA has no governing body, but its activities are reviewed annually by a 10-member Advisory Commission comprising representatives of the governments of:

Belgium	Jordan	Turkey
Egypt	Lebanon	United Kingdom
France	Syria	USA
Japan		

Commissioner-General: PETER HANSEN (Denmark).

FIELD OFFICES

Each field office is headed by a director and has departments responsible for education, health and relief and social services programmes, finance, administration, supply and transport, legal affairs and public information.

Gaza: POB 61; Al Azhar Rd, Rimal Quarter, Gaza City; tel. (7) 2824508; fax (7) 6777444.

Jordan: POB 484; Al Zubeidi Bldg, Mustafa Bin Abdullah St, Tla'a Al-Ali, Amman; tel. (6) 5607194; fax (6) 5685476.

Lebanon: POB 11-0947, Beirut 1107 2060; Bir Hassan, Ghobeiri, Beirut; tel. (1) 822415; fax (1) 840469.

Syria: POB 4313; UN Compound, Mezzah Highway/Beirut Rd, Damascus; tel. (11) 6133035; fax (11) 6133047.

West Bank: POB 19149; Sheik Jarrah Qtr, East Jerusalem; tel. (2) 5890400; fax (2) 5322714.

LIAISON OFFICES

Egypt: 2 Dar-el-Shifa St, Garden City, POB 227, Cairo; tel. (2) 354-8502; fax (2) 354-8504.

Switzerland: Rm 92-93 Annexe Le Bocage, Palais des Nations, 1211 Geneva; tel. (22) 9171166; fax (22) 9170956.

USA: 2 United Nations Plaza, Room DC 2-1755, New York, NY 10017; tel. (212) 963-2255; fax (212) 935-7899.

Activities

ASSISTANCE ACTIVITIES

Since 1950 UNRWA has been the main provider of relief, health, education and social services for Palestine refugees in Lebanon, Syria, Jordan, the West Bank and the Gaza Strip. For UNRWA's purposes, a Palestine refugee is one whose normal residence was in Palestine for a minimum of two years before the 1948 conflict and who, as a result of the Arab–Israeli hostilities, lost his or her home and means of livelihood. To be eligible for assistance, a refugee must reside in one of the five areas in which UNRWA operates and be in need. A refugee's descendants who fulfil certain criteria are also eligible for UNRWA assistance. At 30 June 2002 UNRWA was providing essential services to 3,973,360 registered refugees (see table). Of these, an estimated 1,262,867 (32%) were living in 59 camps serviced by the Agency, while the remaining refugees had settled in the towns and villages already existing.

UNRWA's three principal areas of activity are education, health, and relief and social services. Some 89% of the Agency's 2002 general fund budget was devoted to these three operational programmes.

Education accounted for 52% of UNRWA's 2002 budget. In the 2001/02 school year there were 486,020 pupils enrolled in 644 UNRWA schools, and 16,933 educational staff. UNRWA also operated eight vocational and teacher-training centres, which provided a total of 4,884 training places. UNRWA awarded 197 scholarships for study at Arab universities in 2001/02. Technical co-operation for the Agency's education programme is provided by UNESCO.

Health services accounted for 18% of UNRWA's 2002 general fund budget. At mid-2002 there were 122 primary health care units providing outpatient medical care, disease prevention and control, maternal and child health care and family planning services, of which 88 also offered dental care. At that time the number of health staff totalled 3,607. During 2001 patient visits to UNRWA medical units numbered 8.8m. UNRWA also operates a small hospital in the West Bank and offers assistance towards emergency and other secondary treatment, mainly through contractual agreements with non-governmental and private hospitals. Technical assistance for the health programme is provided by WHO.

Relief and social services accounted for 10% of UNRWA's general fund budget for 2002. These services comprise the distribution of food rations, the provision of emergency shelter and the organization of welfare programmes for the poorest refugees (at 30 June 2002 229,404 refugees, or 5.8% of the total registered refugee population, were eligible to receive special hardship assistance). In 2002 UNRWA provided technical and financial support to 71 women's programme centres, 27 youth activity centres and 36 community-based rehabilitation centres.

In order to encourage Palestinian self-reliance the Agency issues grants to ailing businesses and loans to families who qualify as special hardship cases. In 1991 UNRWA launched an income generation programme, which provides capital loans to small businesses and micro-enterprises with the objective of creating sustainable employment and eliminating poverty, particularly in the Occupied Territories. By 30 June 2002 53,036 loans, with a total estimated value of US $68.7m., had been issued to new and existing Palestinian-owned enterprises.

SPECIAL PROGRAMMES

Following the signing of the Declaration of Principles by the Palestine Liberation Organization and the Israeli Government in September 1993, UNRWA initiated a Peace Implementation Programme (PIP) to improve services and infrastructure for Palestinian refugees. In September 1994 the first phase of the programme (PIP I) was concluded after the receipt of US $93.2m. in pledged donations. PIP I projects included the construction of 33 schools and 24 classrooms and specialized education rooms, the rehabilitation of 4,700 shelters, the upgrading of solid waste disposal facilities throughout the Gaza Strip and feasibility studies for two sewerage systems. It was estimated that these projects created more than 5,500 jobs in the Gaza Strip for an average period of four months each. By the end of 2000 the total number of PIP projects, including those under the second phase of the programme (PIP II), amounted to 496, while funds received or pledged to the Programme totalled $255.6m.

Since 1993 UNRWA has been engaged in the construction, equipping and commissioning of a 232-bed hospital in the Gaza Strip, with funds from the European Union and its member states. The outpatient facilities opened in July 2000. The hospital and an affiliated nursing college were to be integrated into the health care system of the Palestinian (National) Authority (PA), once the process of commissioning had been completed.

AID TO DISPLACED PERSONS

After the renewal of Arab–Israeli hostilities in the Middle East in June 1967, hundreds of thousands of people fled from the fighting and from Israeli-occupied areas to east Jordan, Syria and Egypt. UNRWA provided emergency relief for displaced refugees and was additionally empowered by a UN General Assembly resolution to provide 'humanitarian assistance, as far as practicable, on an emergency basis and as a temporary measure' for those persons other than Palestine refugees who were newly displaced and in urgent need. In practice, UNRWA lacked the funds to aid the other displaced persons and the main burden of supporting them devolved on the Arab governments concerned. The Agency, as requested by the Government of Jordan in 1967 and on that Government's behalf, distributes rations to displaced persons in Jordan who are not registered refugees of 1948.

RECENT EMERGENCIES

In November 2000 UNRWA launched an emergency humanitarian appeal for US $39.1m. in additional funds to assist Palestinian refugees affected by the most recent escalation of violence in the region and the Israeli-imposed blockade on PA-controlled territory. UNRWA became the lead agency with responsibility for the co-ordination and delivery of emergency assistance, as well as for monitoring the immediate needs of the local populations. A second appeal was made by the Agency in April 2001, for some $37.2m., and a third emergency appeal, for $77m., was issued in June to provide basic food and medical supplies until the end of the year. The additional resources were also required to fund a programme of emergency workdays, which aimed to provide employment and income for labourers with dependents, while improving the local infrastructure. In addition, UNRWA intended to provide extra schooling days to make up for those missed because of the fighting, trauma counselling for children, and post-injury rehabilitation. In mid-January 2002 UNRWA reacted immediately to assess the needs of refugees following the demolition of 54 shelters by Israeli forces, and provided emergency supplies, including tents, blankets, mats and food. A fourth emergency appeal, for some $117.1m., was launched at the end of January to provide food aid, medical care, shelter reconstruction and emergency work programmes for refugees in the affected areas. In February the Commissioner-General protested at the Israeli bombing of Gaza City and at the damage caused by Israeli security forces in the Palestinian towns of Jenin and Nablus. In March the Commissioner-General expressed deep concern at the worsening humanitarian situation in the Palestinian territories, as well as his outrage at the death of an UNRWA staff member during an Israeli incursion into Tulkarem camp. Later in that month UNRWA assessed the damage inflicted against UNRWA infrastructure during March amounted to $3.8m. In early April UNRWA efforts to deliver emergency food and medical supplies to Ramallah hospital and other areas in the West Bank were hindered by attacks and threats by Israeli troops. The Commissioner-General expressed concern at the deteriorating security and humanitarian situation and for the welfare of detained and besieged UN workers. In mid-April UNRWA was permitted limited access to Jenin refugee camp, which had experienced extensive fighting during a two-week period of occupation by Israeli forces. UNRWA delivered food and water and attempted to co-ordinate international efforts to send search and rescue teams into the camp. It also undertook to reintroduce essential services and to initiate the reconstruction of refugee homes. At the same time UNRWA noted with concern the entry restrictions imposed by Israel against the Gaza Strip, which were causing extreme food shortages. In May UNRWA organized a conference of 28 countries to highlight the need for an additional $70m. to meet the humanitarian requirements resulting from the Israeli incursions. In July UNRWA requested $55.7m. in additional aid, at meetings held in Jerusalem and Amman. Of the total amount, $26m. was allocated for emergency shelter repair and reconstruction. In December UNRWA launched an appeal for $93.7m. to fund emergency relief efforts in the first six months of 2003. Some $32.4m. was to be allocated to a large-scale emergency food aid programme, which aimed to reach 1.3m. people suffering malnutrition.

STATISTICS

Refugees Registered with UNRWA (30 June 2002)

Country	Number	% of total
Jordan	1,679,623	42.3
Gaza Strip	878,977	22.1
West Bank	626,532	15.8
Syria	401,185	10.1
Lebanon	387,043	9.7
Total	**3,973,360**	**100.0**

Finance

UNRWA is financed almost entirely by voluntary contributions from governments and the European Union, the remainder being provided by UN bodies, non-governmental organizations, business corporations and private sources, which also contribute to extra-budgetary activities. UNRWA's general fund budget for 2002 amounted to US $330.7m., with an additional $55.5m. in project financing. The total proposed budget for 2003 budget amounted to $405.5m.

Publication

Annual Report of the Commissioner-General of UNRWA.

United Nations Training and Research Institutes

UNITED NATIONS INSTITUTE FOR DISARMAMENT RESEARCH—UNIDIR

Address: Palais des Nations, 1211 Geneva 10, Switzerland.

Telephone: (22) 9173186; **fax:** (22) 9170176; **e-mail:** unidir@unog.ch; **internet:** www.undir.org.

UNIDIR is an autonomous institution within the United Nations. It was established by the General Assembly in 1980 for the purpose of undertaking independent research on disarmament and related problems, particularly international security issues. UNIDIR's statute became effective on 1 January 1985.

The work of the Institute is based on the following objectives: to provide the international community with more diversified and complete data on problems relating to international security, the armaments race and disarmament in all fields, so as to facilitate progress towards greater global security and towards economic and social development for all peoples; to promote informed participation by all states in disarmament efforts; to assist ongoing negotiations on disarmament, and continuing efforts to ensure greater international security at a progressively lower level of armaments, in particular nuclear weapons, by means of objective studies and analyses; and to conduct long-term research on disarmament in order to provide a general insight into the problems involved and to stimulate new initiatives for negotiations. UNIDIR's activities are divided into the following three areas: global security and disarmament, regional security and disarmament, and human security and disarmament.

The work programme of UNIDIR is reviewed annually and is subject to approval by its Board of Trustees. During 2002 UNIDIR conducted research and organized seminars on a range of issues, including: peace-building and practical disarmament in West Africa; the costs of disarmament; contemporary issues in arms control and disarmament (the so-called Geneva Forum); development of a *Handbook on Verification and Compliance*; strengthening the role of regional organizations in treaty implementation; prevention of the proliferation of biological weapons; the impact of missile proliferation and the potential deployment of theatre and national missile defences; and weapons stockpile destruction and management in South Africa. Research projects are conducted within the Institute, or commissioned to individual experts or research organizations. For some major studies, multinational groups of experts are established. The Institute offers internships, in connection with its research programme. UNIDIR maintains a database on research institutes (DATARIs) in the field of international security (accessible at dataris.sipri.org).

The Institute is financed mainly by voluntary contributions from governments and public or private organizations. A contribution to the costs of the Director and staff may be provided from the UN regular budget.

The Director of UNIDIR reports annually to the General Assembly on the activities of the Institute. The UN Secretary-General's Advisory Board on Disarmament Studies functions as UNIDIR's Board of Trustees.

Director: PATRICIA LEWIS (United Kingdom).

Publications: *Disarmament Forum* (quarterly), *UNIDIR Newsletter* (quarterly); research reports (6 a year); research papers (irregular).

UNITED NATIONS INSTITUTE FOR TRAINING AND RESEARCH—UNITAR

Address: Palais des Nations, 1211 Geneva 10, Switzerland.

Telephone: (22) 9171234; **fax:** (22) 9178047; **e-mail:** info@unitar.org; **internet:** www.unitar.org.

UNITAR was established in 1963, as an autonomous body within the United Nations, in order to enhance the effectiveness of the latter body in achieving its major objectives. In recent years the main focus of the Institute has shifted to training and capacity-building, with basic research being conducted only if extra-budgetary funds are made available. Training is provided at various levels for personnel on assignments under the United Nations and its specialized agencies or under organizations operating in related fields. In 2002 UNITAR programmes included courses on the management of international affairs; peace-keeping; the application of environmental law; debt, financial management and negotiation; foreign economic relations; chemicals and waste management; climate change; information and communication technologies; and the special needs of women and children affected by conflict. Most training programmes are designed and conducted in Geneva. The

New York office, established in 1996, organizes the training of delegates at United Nations headquarters. In October 2001 UNITAR, in collaboration with the authorities in Hiroshima, Japan, initiated the Hiroshima Programmes, which aimed to organize training activities in the Asia and Pacific region to promote peace and security and economic and social development. Also in 2001, in partnership with UNOPS, the International Training Center for Local Actors (CIFAL) was inaugurated in Divonne-les-Bains, France, to assist with UN crisis situation management activities and focus on the role of local communities in emergency humanitarian responses.

UNITAR offers a fellowship programme in peace-making and preventive diplomacy to provide advanced training for international and national civil servants in conflict analysis and mediation. It also organizes, jointly with the UN Office for Legal Affairs, an annual fellowship programme in international law.

UNITAR is financed by voluntary contributions from UN member states, by donations from foundations and other non-governmental sources, and by income generated by its Reserve Fund.

Executive Director: MARCEL A. BOISARD (Switzerland).

UNITED NATIONS INTERNATIONAL RESEARCH AND TRAINING INSTITUTE FOR THE ADVANCEMENT OF WOMEN— INSTRAW

Address: Calle César Nicolás Pensón 102-A, POB 21747, Santo Domingo, Dominican Republic.

Telephone: (809) 685-2111; **fax:** (809) 685-2117; **e-mail:** comments@un-instraw.org; **internet:** www.un-instraw.org.

The Institute was established by ECOSOC, and endorsed by the General Assembly, in 1976, following a recommendation of the World Conference on the International Women's Year (1975). INSTRAW provides training, conducts research and collects and disseminates relevant information in order to stimulate and to assist the advancement of women and their integration in the development process, both as participants and beneficiaries. In 1999 INSTRAW initiated a process of restructuring to implement a strategic mandate to use new information and communication technologies. In June 2000 INSTRAW inaugurated the Gender Awareness Information and Networking System (GAINS), an internet-based database on research and training materials. During 2001–02 INSTRAW's work programme focused on: building partnerships for gender equality; women and men in the information society; and the impact of globalization.

INSTRAW is an autonomous body of the UN, funded by voluntary contributions from UN member states, inter- and non-governmental organizations, foundations and other private sources. An 11-member Board of Trustees meets annually to formulate the principles and guide-lines for the activities of INSTRAW and to consider the current work progamme and budget proposals, and reports to ECOSOC. The Institute maintains a liaison office at the UN Secretariat in New York.

Director: SAVITRI BUTCHEY (Malaysia) (acting).

Publications: *INSTRAW News* (2 a month); training materials, research studies.

UNITED NATIONS INTERREGIONAL CRIME AND JUSTICE RESEARCH INSTITUTE— UNICRI

Address: Viale Maestri del Lavoro 10, 10127 Turin, Italy.

Telephone: (011) 6537111; **fax:** (011) 6313368; **e-mail:** unicri@unicri.it; **internet:** www.unicri.it.

The Institute was established in 1968 as the United Nations Social Defence Research Institute. Its present name was adopted by a resolution of ECOSOC in 1989. The Institute undertakes research, training and information activities in the fields of crime prevention and criminal justice, at international, regional and national levels.

In collaboration with national governments, UNICRI aims to establish a reliable base of knowledge and information on organized crime; to identify strategies for the prevention and control of crime, within the framework of contributing to socio-economic development and protecting human rights; and to design systems to support policy formulation, implementation and evaluation. UNICRI organizes workshops and conferences, and promotes the exchange of information through its international documentation centre on criminology. Main areas of activity during 2003 included global programmes against trafficking in human beings, corruption and organized crime.

UNICRI is funded by the United Nations Crime Prevention and Criminal Justice Fund, which is financed by voluntary contributions from UN member states, non-governmental organizations, academic institutions and other concerned bodies.

Director: ALBERTO BRADANINI (Italy).

Publications: *UNICRI Journal* (2 a year); training materials, research studies.

UNITED NATIONS RESEARCH INSTITUTE FOR SOCIAL DEVELOPMENT—UNRISD

Address: Palais des Nations, 1211 Geneva 10, Switzerland.

Telephone: (22) 9173020; **fax:** (22) 9170650; **e-mail:** info@unrisd .org; **internet:** www.unrisd.org.

UNRISD was established in 1963 as an autonomous body within the United Nations, to conduct multi-disciplinary research into the social dimensions of contemporary problems affecting development.

The Institute aims to provide governments, development agencies, grass-roots organizations and scholars with a better understanding of how development policies and processes of economic, social and environmental change affect different social groups.

UNRISD research is undertaken in collaboration with a network of national research teams drawn from local universities and research institutions. UNRISD aims to promote and strengthen research capacities in developing countries. Its main focus areas are the eradication of poverty; the promotion of democracy and human rights; environmental sustainability; gender equality; and the effects of globalization. During the period 2000–05 UNRISD's main programme areas and areas of research were: civil society and social movements; democracy, governance and human rights; identities, conflict and cohesion; social policy development; and technology, business and society.

The Institute is supported by voluntary grants from governments, and also receives financing from other UN organizations, and from various other national and international agencies.

Director: THANDIKA MKANDAWIRE (Sweden).

Publications: *UNRISD Social Development News* (1–2 a year), discussion papers and monographs, special reports, programme and occasional papers.

UNITED NATIONS SYSTEM STAFF COLLEGE

Address: Viale Maestri del Lavoro 10, 10127 Turin, Italy.

Telephone: (011) 6535906; **fax:** (011) 6535901; **e-mail:** unscp@ itcilo.it; **internet:** www.unssc.org/unscp.

In July 2001 the UN General Assembly approved a statute for the UN System Staff College (UNSSC), which, it envisaged, would provide knowledge management, training and continuous learning opportunities for all UN personnel, with a view to developing UN system-wide co-operation and operational effectiveness. The inaugural meeting of the Board of Governors was held in November, and the College formally began operations on 1 January 2002. It aims to promote the exchange of knowledge and shared learning, to administer learning and training workshops, as well as distance learning opportunities, to provide support and expert advice, and to act as a clearing house for learning activities. The College administers a Systems Programme, including the Resident Co-Ordinator System Project and Early Warning and Preventive Measures: Building UN Capacity Project; and a Learning Programme, including the Strategic Communication Project, Knowledge Management Project and Global Learning Network on Partnerships Project.

The UNSSC is financed by a combination of course fees, voluntary grants from governments and contributions in kind from various UN organizations in the form of staff secondments.

Director: JOHN MACHIN (United Kingdom).

UNITED NATIONS UNIVERSITY—UNU

Address: 53–70, Jingumae 5-chome, Shibuya-ku, Tokyo 150-8925, Japan.

Telephone: (3) 3499-2811; **fax:** (3) 3499-2828; **e-mail:** mbox@hq .unu.edu; **internet:** www.unu.edu.

The University is sponsored jointly by the United Nations and UNESCO. It is an autonomous institution within the United Nations, guaranteed academic freedom by a charter approved by the General Assembly in 1973. It is governed by a 28-member University Council of scholars and scientists, of whom 24 are appointed by the Secretary-General of the UN and the Director-General of UNESCO (who, together with the Executive Director of UNITAR, are *ex-officio* members of the Council; the Rector is also on the Council). The University is not traditional in the sense of having students or awarding degrees, but works through networks of collaborating institutions and individuals. These include Associated Institutions (universities and research institutes linked with the UNU under general agreements of co-operation). The UNU undertakes multi-disciplinary research on problems that are the concern of the United Nations and its agencies, and works to strengthen research and training capabilities in developing countries. It provides post-graduate fellowships for scientists and scholars from developing countries, and conducts various training activities in association with its programme. Its main thematic programme areas are peace; governance; development; science, technology and society; and environment.

The UNU's research and training centres and programmes include the World Institute of Development Economics Research (UNU/WIDER) in Helsinki, Finland; the Institute for New Technologies (UNU/INTECH) in Maastricht, Netherlands; the International Institute for Software Technology (UNU/IIST) in Macao; the UNU Institute for Natural Resources in Africa (UNU/INRA) in Accra, Ghana (with a mineral resources unit in Lusaka, Zambia); the UNU Programme for Biotechnology in Latin America and the Caribbean (UNU/BIOLAC), based in Caracas, Venezuela; the UNU Leadership Academy (UNU/LA) in Amman, Jordan; the Institute of Advanced Studies (UNU/IAS), based in Tokyo, Japan; the UNU International Network on Water, Environment and Health (UNU/INWEH) in Ontario, Canada, the UNU International Network on Water, Environment and Health (UNU/INWEH) in Hamilton, Canada; the UNU Programme on Comparative Regional Integration Studies (UNU/CRIS), in Bruges, Belgium; the UNU Food and Nutrition Programme for Human and Social Development, based at Cornell University, USA; the UNU Geothermal Training Programme (UNU/GTP) and UNU Fisheries Training Programme (UNU/FTP), both based in Iceland; and the Initiative on Conflict Resolution and Ethnicity (INCORE), jointly managed by UNU and the University of Ulster.

The UNU is financed by voluntary contributions from UN member states. The budget for 2002–03 amounted to US $73.5m.

Rector: Prof. HANS J. A. VAN GINKEL (Netherlands).

Publications: *UNU Nexions* (2 a year), *Work In Progress* (1–2 a year), *WIDERAngle* (2 a year), *Africa Research* (irregular), regular journals, abstracts, research papers.

UNIVERSITY FOR PEACE

Address: POB 138-6100, San José, Costa Rica.

Telephone: 205-9000; **fax:** 249-1929; **e-mail:** info@upeace.org; **internet** www.upeace.org.

The University for Peace was established by the United Nations in 1980 to conduct research on, *inter alia*, disarmament, mediation, the resolution of conflicts, the preservation of the environment, international relations, peace education and human rights. The Council of the University (the governing body, comprising 15 members) was reconstituted in March 1999, meeting for the first time since 1994. In May 1999 the Council initiated a programme of extensive reforms and expansion. A programme of short courses for advanced international training was reintroduced in 2001. In September 2002 Masters degrees became available in International Law and the Settlement of Disputes, Human Rights Studies, Natural Resources and Sustainable Development, Gender and Peace-Building, and International Peace Studies. In 2000 a University for Peace Centre and Policy Institute was established in Geneva, Switzerland, and an Institute for Media, Peace and Security was inaugurated, with administrative headquarters in Paris, France. In 2001 the World Centre for Research and Training in Conflict Resolution was established in Bogotá, Colombia. The University has a global network of partner institutions. In January 2002 the University launched its Africa Programme, which aims to build African capacity for education, training and research on matters related to peace and security.

Rector and Chief Executive Officer: MARTIN LEES (United Kingdom).

World Food Programme—WFP

Address: Via Cesare Giulio Viola 68, Parco dei Medici, 00148 Rome, Italy.

Telephone: (06) 6513-1; **fax:** (06) 6513-2840; **e-mail:** wfpinfo@wfp.org; **internet:** www.wfp.org.

WFP, the principal food aid organization of the United Nations, became operational in 1963. It aims to alleviate acute hunger by providing emergency relief following natural or man-made humanitarian disasters, and supplies food aid to people in developing countries to eradicate chronic undernourishment, to support social development and to promote self-reliant communities.

Organization

(April 2003)

EXECUTIVE BOARD

The governing body of WFP is the Executive Board, comprising 36 members, 18 of whom are elected by the UN Economic and Social Council (ECOSOC) and 18 by the Council of the Food and Agriculture Organization (FAO). The Board meets four times each year at WFP headquarters.

SECRETARIAT

WFP's Executive Director is appointed jointly by the UN Secretary-General and the Director-General of FAO and is responsible for the management and administration of the Programme. In 2001 there were 2,567 permanent staff members, of whom about 70% were working in the field. WFP administers some 87 country offices, in order to provide operational, financial and management support at a more local level, and has established seven regional bureaux, located in Bangkok, Thailand (for Asia), Cairo, Egypt (for the Middle East, Central Asia and the Mediterranean), Rome, Italy (for Eastern Europe), Managua, Nicaragua (for Latin America and the Caribbean), Yaoundé, Cameroon (for Central Africa), Kampala, Uganda (for Eastern and Southern Africa), and Dakar, Senegal (for West Africa).

Executive Director: JAMES T. MORRIS (USA).

Activities

WFP is the only multilateral organization with a mandate to use food aid as a resource. It is the second largest source of assistance in the UN, after the World Bank group, in terms of actual transfers of resources, and the largest source of grant aid in the UN system. WFP handles more than one-third of the world's food aid. WFP is also the largest contributor to South–South trade within the UN system, through the purchase of food and services from developing countries. WFP's mission is to provide food aid to save lives in refugee and other emergency situations, to improve the nutrition and quality of life of vulnerable groups and to help to develop assets and promote the self-reliance of poor families and communities. WFP aims to focus its efforts on the world's poorest countries and to provide at least 90% of its total assistance to those designated as 'low-income food-deficit'. At the World Food Summit, held in November 1996, WFP endorsed the commitment to reduce by 50% the number of undernourished people, no later than 2015. During 2001 WFP food assistance benefited some 77m. people world-wide, of whom 20m. received aid through development projects, 43m. through emergency operations, and 14m. through rehabilitation programmes. Total food deliveries amounted to 4.2m. metric tons in 82 countries.

WFP aims to address the causes of chronic malnourishment, which it identifies as poverty and lack of opportunity. It emphasizes the role played by women in combating hunger, and endeavours to address the specific nutritional needs of women, to increase their access to food and development resources, and to promote girls' education. It also focuses resources on supporting the food security of households and communities affected by HIV/AIDS and on promoting food security as a means of mitigating extreme poverty and vulnerability and thereby combating the spread of HIV/AIDS. In February 2003 WFP and the Joint UN Programme on HIV/AIDS (UNAIDS) concluded an agreement to jointly address the relationship between HIV/AIDS, regional food shortages and chronic hunger, with a particular focus on Africa, South-East Asia and the Caribbean.

In the early 1990s there was a substantial shift in the balance between emergency relief and development assistance provided by WFP, owing to the growing needs of victims of drought and other natural disasters, refugees and displaced persons. By 1994 two-thirds of all food aid was for relief assistance and one-third for development, representing a direct reversal of the allocations five years previously. In addition, there was a noticeable increase in aid given to those in need as a result of civil war, compared with commitments for victims of natural disasters. Accordingly, WFP has developed a range of mechanisms to enhance its preparedness for emergency situations and to improve its capacity for responding effectively to situations as they arise. A new programme of emergency response training was inaugurated in 2000, while security concerns for personnel was incorporated as a new element into all general planning and training activities. Through its Vulnerability Analysis and Mapping (VAM) project, WFP aims to identify potentially vulnerable groups by providing information on food security and the capacity of different groups for coping with shortages, and to enhance emergency contingency-planning and long-term assistance objectives. In early 2003 VAM field units were operational in more than 50 countries. WFP also co-operates with other UN agencies including FAO (undertaking joint activities in 24 countries in 2001), IFAD (conducting joint activities in 14 countries in that year) and UNHCR. The key elements of WFP's emergency response capacity are its strategic stores of food and logistics equipment, stand-by arrangements to enable the rapid deployment of personnel, communications and other essential equipment, and the Augmented Logistics Intervention Team for Emergencies (ALITE), which undertakes capacity assessments and contingency-planning. During 2000 WFP led efforts, undertaken with other UN humanitarian agencies, for the design and application of local UN Joint Logistics Centre facilities, which aimed to co-ordinate resources in an emergency situation. In 2001 a new UN Humanitarian Response Depot was opened in Brindisi, Italy, under the direction of WFP experts, for the storage of essential rapid response equipment. In that year the Programme published a set of guide-lines on contingency planning.

In 2001 the main regional focus of WFP relief activities was sub-Saharan Africa, which accounted for 53% of total emergency operational expenditure. Food aid was supplied to more than 9m. people from countries in the Horn of Africa owing to severe drought in the previous year and continuing poor rainfall; to 130,000 people displaced from their homes by flooding in Malawi; and to war-affected populations in Angola, the Democratic Republic of the Congo and southern Sudan. Other major emergency operations undertaken in 2001 included the provision of aid to communities affected by earthquakes in El Salvador, India and Peru; to drought-affected communities in Central America; to ethnic Albanian former refugees returning to Kosovo; and to Palestinians affected by the ongoing insecurity in the West Bank and Gaza Strip. In recent years WFP has been actively concerned with the food situation in the Democratic People's Republic of Korea (DPRK), which has required substantial levels of emergency food supplies, owing to natural disasters and consistently poor harvests. By mid-1999 an estimated 1.5m.–3.5m. people had died of starvation in the DPRK since 1995. During 2000 an estimated 9.4m. people in the DPRK received WFP assistance. WFP's eighth emergency operation in the DPRK, covering the period January–December 2003, aimed to provide food aid to 6.4m. people, at a cost of US $201m. In February 2003 WFP and other UN agencies urged continuing international support for humanitarian activities in the DPRK in order to maintain progress achieved since 1999 in reducing the rate of malnutrition. WFP has also been active in Afghanistan, where civil conflict and severe drought have caused massive food insecurity and population displacement. In March 2001 WFP launched an appeal for $76m. to fund a new one-year emergency operation to assist 3.8m. Afghans. In August WFP reported a substantial cereal deficit in the country and identified widespread pre-famine conditions. Accordingly, the operation was expanded to provide assistance to 5.5m. people, with new funding requirements amounting to $151m., in order to meet its objectives, which included delivering food to those threatened with starvation, providing subsidized bread to urban communities, and encouraging farmers to engage in productive activities. In mid-September, however, the delivery of food aid to Afghanistan was suspended and all international personnel were withdrawn owing to a deterioration in the security situation and expectation of imminent military action by a US-led coalition against the then Taliban regime. Food shipments to northern areas of the country were resumed later in that month. Meanwhile, in readiness for a predicted mass influx of refugees from Afghanistan, WFP staff were mobilized in neighbouring countries and emergency supplies stockpiled in border regions. The first delivery of humanitarian supplies by air was undertaken in late October. By mid-December, despite the withdrawal of the Taliban authorities, the distribution of aid was still seriously hampered by poor rural infrastructure, adverse weather conditions and ongoing security concerns. In April 2002 WFP launched a new nine-month US $285m. operation for Afghanistan with a focus on recovery and rehabiliation rather than relief. In addition to the provision of 1.2m. metric tons of emergency food aid, activities aimed at assisting 9m. Afghans included food for workers engaged in reconstructing the country's infrastructure and for farmers concerned with rehabilitating irrigation systems, an expansion of bakery projects staffed by women, and support for school feeding projects targeting 1m. children. In July 2002 WFP appealed for US $507m. in order to provide food assistance for some 10.2m. people suffering severe food insecurity in Lesotho, Malawi, Mozambique, Swaziland, Zambia and Zimbabwe. During that month the UN Secretary-General appointed the WFP Executive Director as his Special Envoy on the ongoing humanitarian crisis in the region, which was attributed to the combined effects of drought, flooding and, in some cases, alleged economic mismanagement, aggravated by the effects of the regional epidemic of HIV/AIDS. In December WFP initiated Africa Hunger Alert, a campaign aimed at assisting an estimated total of 38m. people affected by severe food insecurity in sub-Saharan Africa; by that time some 13m. people were reported to be suffering famine conditions in southern Africa.

Through its development activities, WFP aims to alleviate poverty in developing countries by promoting self-reliant families and communities. Food is supplied, for example, as an incentive in development self-help schemes and as part-wages in labour-intensive projects of many kinds. In all its projects WFP aims to assist the most vulnerable groups and to ensure that beneficiaries have an adequate and balanced diet. Activities supported by the Programme include the settlement and resettlement of groups and communities; land reclamation and improvement; irrigation; the development of forestry and dairy farming; road construction; training of hospital staff; community development; and human resources development such as feeding expectant or nursing mothers and schoolchildren, and support for education, training and health programmes. In 2001 WFP supported development projects in 55 countries, which benefited some 20m. people. School feeding projects benefited 15m. children during that year. During 2001 WFP initiated a new Global School Feeding Campaign to strengthen international co-operation to expand educational opportunities for poor children and to improve the quality of the teaching environment.

Following a comprehensive evaluation of its activities, WFP is increasingly focused on linking its relief and development activities to provide a continuum between short-term relief and longer-term rehabilitation and development. In order to achieve this objective, WFP aims to integrate elements that strengthen disaster mitigation into development projects, including soil conservation, reafforestation, irrigation infrastructure, and transport construction and rehabilitation; and to promote capacity-building elements within relief operations, e.g. training, income-generating activities and environmental protection measures. In 1999 WFP adopted a new Food Aid

and Development policy, which aims to use food assistance both to cover immediate requirements and to create conditions conducive to enhancing the long-term food security of vulnerable populations. During that year WFP began implementing Protracted Relief and Recovery Operations (PRROs), where the emphasis is on fostering stability, rehabilitation and long-term development for victims of natural disasters, displaced persons and refugees. PRROs were to be introduced no later than 18 months after the initial emergency operation, and to last no more than three years. When undertaken in collaboration with UNHCR and other international agencies, WFP was to be responsible for mobilizing basic food commodities and for related transport, handling and storage costs. In 2001 PRROs, involving the provision of 818,700 metric tons of food, were being undertaken in 41 countries.

OPERATIONAL EXPENDITURE IN 2001, BY REGION AND TYPE* (US $ '000, provisional figures)

Region	Development	Relief	Special operations	Total (incl. others†)
Sub-Saharan Africa .	95,235	744,209	18,304	863,728
Asia	79,158	463,886	10,347	555,395
Latin America and the Caribbean .	38,547	18,910	—	57,456
North Africa and the Middle East . .	12,179	17,325	—	53,036
Europe and the CIS .	—	152,903	493	165,267
Total	**225,118**	**1,397,233**	**29,160**	**1,744,074**

* Excludes programme support and administrative costs.
† Includes trust fund expenditures and operational expenditures that cannot be apportioned by project/operation.

Finance

The Programme is funded by voluntary contributions from donor countries and intergovernmental bodies such as the European Union. Contributions are made in the form of commodities, finance and services (particularly shipping). Commitments to the International Emergency Food Reserve (IEFR), from which WFP provides the majority of its food supplies, and to the Immediate Response Account of the IEFR (IRA), are also made on a voluntary basis by donors. In 2001 contributions by donors provided 83% of WFP's food requirements. WFP's operational expenditure in that year amounted to some US $1,744m., while administrative costs totalled $244.7m. for the two-year period 2000–01.

Publications

Annual Report.
Food and Nutrition Handbook.
School Feeding Handbook.

SPECIALIZED AGENCIES WITHIN THE UN SYSTEM

Food and Agriculture Organization of the United Nations—FAO

Address: Viale delle Terme di Caracalla, 00100 Rome, Italy.
Telephone: (06) 5705-1; **fax:** (06) 5705-3152; **e-mail:** fao.hq@fao.org; **internet:** www.fao.org.

FAO, the first specialized agency of the UN to be founded after the Second World War, aims to alleviate malnutrition and hunger, and serves as a co-ordinating agency for development programmes in the whole range of food and agriculture, including forestry and fisheries. It helps developing countries to promote educational and training facilities and the creation of appropriate institutions.

MEMBERS

184 members (including the European Union as a member organization): see Table on pp. 125–127.

Organization

(April 2003)

CONFERENCE

The governing body is the FAO Conference of member nations. It meets every two years, formulates policy, determines the Organization's programme and budget on a biennial basis, and elects new members. It also elects the Director-General of the Secretariat and the Independent Chairman of the Council. Every other year, FAO also holds conferences in each of its five regions (see below).

COUNCIL

The FAO Council is composed of representatives of 49 member nations, elected by the Conference for staggered three-year terms. It is the interim governing body of FAO between sessions of the Conference. The most important standing Committees of the Council are: the Finance and Programme Committees, the Committee on Commodity Problems, the Committee on Fisheries, the Committee on Agriculture and the Committee on Forestry.

SECRETARIAT

The total number of FAO staff in May 2002 was 3,700, of whom 1,500 were professional staff and 2,200 general service staff. About one-half of the Organization's staff were based at headquarters. Work is supervised by the following Departments: Administration and Finance; General Affairs and Information; Economic and Social Policy; Agriculture; Forestry; Fisheries; Sustainable Development; and Technical Co-operation.
Director-General: JACQUES DIOUF (Senegal).

REGIONAL OFFICES

Africa: POB 1628, Accra, Ghana; tel. (21) 665343; fax (21) 234003; e-mail fao-raf@fao.org; Regional Rep. M. J. OMAR.

Asia and the Pacific: Maliwan Mansion, Phra Atit Rd, Bangkok 10200, Thailand; tel. (662) 697-4000; fax (662) 697-4445; e-mail fao-rap@fao.org; internet www.fao.or.th; Regional Rep. HE CHANGCHUI.

Europe: Viale delle Terme di Caracalla, Room A-304, 00100 Rome, Italy; tel. (06) 57051; fax (06) 5705 3152; internet www.fao.org/regional/europe; Regional Rep. CLAUDE FORTHOMME.

Latin America and the Caribbean: Avda Dag Hammarskjöld 3241, Casilla 10095, Vitacura, Santiago, Chile; tel. (2) 337-2102; fax (2) 337-2101; e-mail fao-rlc@field.fao.org; internet www.fao.org/regional/lamerica/default.htm; Regional Rep. GUSTAVO GORDILLO DE ANDA.

Near East: 11 El-Eslah el-Zerai St, Dokki, POB 2223, Cairo, Egypt; tel. (2) 3372229; fax (2) 3495981; e-mail fao-rne@fao.org; Regional Rep. M. ZEHNI.

In addition, the following Sub-regional Offices are operational: in Harare, Zimbabwe (for Southern and Eastern Africa); in Bridgetown, Barbados (for the Caribbean); in Tunis, Tunisia (for North Africa); in Budapest, Hungary (for Central and Eastern Europe); and in Apia, Samoa (for the Pacific Islands).

JOINT DIVISION AND LIAISON OFFICES

Joint FAO/IAEA Division of Nuclear Techniques in Food and Agriculture: Wagramerstrasse 5, 1400 Vienna, Austria; tel. (1) 20600; fax (1) 20607.

European Union: blvd Simon Bolivar, 1000 Brussels, Belgium; tel. (2) 203-8587; fax (2) 203-8589; e-mail fao-lobr@fao.org; Dir MANFRED LINDAU.

Japan: 6F Yokohama International Organizations Centre, Pacifico-Yokohama, 1-1-1, Minato Mirai, Nishi-ku, Yokohama 220-0012; tel. (45) 222-1101; fax (45) 222-1103.

North America: Suite 300, 2175 K St, NW, Washington, DC 20437, USA; tel. (202) 653-2400; fax (202) 653-5760; e-mail fao-lowa@fao.org; Dir C. H. RIEMENSCHNEIDER.

United Nations: Suite DC1-1125, 1 United Nations Plaza, New York, NY 10017, USA; tel. (212) 963-6036; fax (212) 963-5425; e-mail fao-lony@field.fao.org; Dir HOWARD W. HJORT.

Activities

FAO aims to raise levels of nutrition and standards of living by improving the production and distribution of food and other commodities derived from farms, fisheries and forests. FAO's ultimate objective is the achievement of world food security, 'Food for All'. The organization provides technical information, advice and assistance by disseminating information; acting as a neutral forum for discussion of food and agricultural issues; advising governments on policy and planning; and developing capacity directly in the field.

In November 1996 FAO hosted the World Food Summit, which was held in Rome and was attended by heads of state and senior government representatives of 186 countries. Participants approved the Rome Declaration on World Food Security and the World Food Summit Plan of Action, with the aim of halving the number of people afflicted by undernutrition, at that time estimated to total 828m. world-wide, by no later than 2015. A review conference to assess progress in achieving the goals of the summit, entitled World Food Summit: Five Years Later, held in June 2002, reaffirmed commitment to this objective. During that month FAO announced the formulation of a global 'Anti-Hunger Programme', which aimed to promote investment in the agricultural sector and rural development, with a particular focus on small farmers, and to enhance food access for those most in need, for example through the provision of school meals, schemes to feed pregnant and nursing mothers and food-for-work programmes. In late 2002 FAO reported that an estimated 840m. people were undernourished during the period 1998–2000; of these 799m. resided in developing countries, 30m. in states with economies in transition and 11m. in industrialized countries.

In November 1999 the FAO Conference approved a long-term Strategic Framework for the period 2000–15, which emphasized national and international co-operation in pursuing the goals of the 1996 World Food Summit. The Framework promoted interdisciplinarity and partnership, and defined three main global objectives: constant access by all people to sufficient nutritionally adequate and safe food to ensure that levels of undernourishment were reduced by 50% by 2015 (see above); the continued contribution of sustainable agriculture and rural development to economic and social progress and well-being; and the conservation, improvement and sustainable use of natural resources. It identified five corporate strategies (each supported by several strategic objectives), covering the following areas: reducing food insecurity and rural poverty; ensuring enabling policy and regulatory frameworks for food, agriculture, fisheries and forestry; creating sustainable increases in the supply and availability of agricultural, fisheries and forestry products; conserving and enhancing sustainable use of the natural resource base; and generating knowledge. The November 2001 FAO Conference adopted a medium-term plan covering 2002–07 and a work programme for 2000–03, both on the basis of the Strategic Framework.

FAO organizes an annual series of fund-raising events, 'TeleFood', some of which are broadcast on television and the internet, in order to raise public awareness of the problems of hunger and malnutrition. Since its inception in 1997 public donations to Tele-Food have exceeded US $10m., financing more than 1,000 'grass-roots' projects in more than 100 countries. The projects have provided tools, seeds and other essential supplies directly to small-scale farmers, and have been especially aimed at helping women.

In 1999 FAO signed a memorandum of understanding with UNAIDS on strengthening co-operation. In December 2001 FAO,

IFAD and WFP determined to strengthen inter-agency collaboration in developing strategies to combat the threat posed by the HIV/AIDS epidemic to food security, nutrition and rural livelihoods. During that month experts from those organizations and UNAIDS held a technical consultation on means of mitigating the impact of HIV/AIDS on agriculture and rural communities in affected areas.

The Technical Cooperation Department has responsibility for FAO's operational activities, including policy development assistance to member countries; investment support; and the management of activities associated with the development and implementation of country, sub-regional and regional programmes. The Department manages the technical co-operation programme (TCP, which funds 13% of FAO's field programme expenditures), and mobilizes resources.

AGRICULTURE

FAO's most important area of activity is crop production, accounting annually for about one-quarter of total field programme expenditure. FAO assists developing countries in increasing agricultural production, by means of a number of methods, including improved seeds and fertilizer use, soil conservation and reforestation, better water resource management techniques, upgrading storage facilities, and improvements in processing and marketing. FAO places special emphasis on the cultivation of under-exploited traditional food crops, such as cassava, sweet potato and plantains.

In 1985 the FAO Conference approved an International Code of Conduct on the Distribution and Use of Pesticides, and in 1989 the Conference adopted an additional clause concerning 'Prior Informed Consent' (PIC), whereby international shipments of newly banned or restricted pesticides should not proceed without the agreement of importing countries. Under the clause, FAO aims to inform governments about the hazards of toxic chemicals and to urge them to take proper measures to curb trade in highly toxic agrochemicals while keeping the pesticides industry informed of control actions. In 1996 FAO, in collaboration with UNEP, publicized a new initiative which aimed to increase awareness of, and to promote international action on, obsolete and hazardous stocks of pesticides remaining throughout the world (estimated in 2001 to total some 500,000 metric tons). In September 1998 a new legally-binding treaty on trade in hazardous chemicals and pesticides was adopted at an international conference held in Rotterdam, Netherlands. The so-called Rotterdam Convention required that hazardous chemicals and pesticides banned or severely restricted in at least two countries should not be exported unless explicitly agreed by the importing country. It also identified certain pesticide formulations as too dangerous to be used by farmers in developing countries, and incorporated an obligation that countries halt national production of those hazardous compounds. The treaty was to enter into force on being ratified by 50 signatory states. FAO was co-operating with UNEP to provide an interim secretariat for the Convention. In July 1999 a conference on the Rotterdam Convention, held in Rome, established an Interim Chemical Review Committee with responsibility for recommending the inclusion of chemicals or pesticide formulations in the PIC procedure. As part of its continued efforts to reduce the environmental risks posed by over-reliance on pesticides, FAO has extended to other regions its Integrated Pest Management (IPM) programme in Asia and the Pacific on the use of safer and more effective methods of pest control, such as biological control methods and natural predators (including spiders and wasps), to avert pests. In February 2001 FAO warned that some 30% of pesticides sold in developing countries did not meet internationally accepted quality standards. A revised International Code of Conduct on the Distribution and Use of Pesticides, adopted in November 2002, aimed to reduce the inappropriate distribution and use of pesticides and other toxic compounds, particularly in developing countries.

FAO's Joint Division with the International Atomic Energy Agency (IAEA) tests controlled-release formulas of pesticides and herbicides that gradually free their substances and can limit the amount of agrochemicals needed to protect crops. The Joint FAO-IAEA Division is engaged in exploring biotechnologies and in developing non-toxic fertilizers (especially those that are locally available) and improved strains of food crops (especially from indigenous varieties). In the area of animal production and health, the Joint Division has developed progesterone-measuring and disease diagnostic kits, of which thousands have been delivered to developing countries. FAO's plant nutrition activities aim to promote nutrient management, such as the Integrated Plant Nutritions Systems (IPNS), which are based on the recycling of nutrients through crop production and the efficient use of mineral fertilizers.

The conservation and sustainable use of plant and animal genetic resources are promoted by FAO's Global System for Plant Genetic Resources, which includes five databases, and the Global Strategy on the Management of Farm Animal Genetic Resources. An FAO programme supports the establishment of gene banks, designed to maintain the world's biological diversity by preserving animal and plant species threatened with extinction. FAO, jointly with UNEP, has published a document listing the current state of global livestock genetic diversity. In June 1996 representatives of more than 150 governments convened in Leipzig, Germany, at a meeting organized by FAO (and hosted by the German Government) to consider the use and conservation of plant genetic resources as an essential means of enhancing food security. The meeting adopted a Global Plan of Action, which included measures to strengthen the development of plant varieties and to promote the use and availability of local varieties and locally-adapted crops to farmers, in particular following a natural disaster, war or civil conflict. In November 2001 the FAO Conference adopted the International Treaty on Plant Genetic Resources for Food and Agriculture, which was to provide a framework to ensure access to plant genetic resources and to related knowledge, technologies and funding. The Treaty was to enter into force once it had been ratified by 40 signatory states; at February 2003 it had been ratified by 15 states.

An Emergency Prevention System for Transboundary Animal and Plant Pests and Diseases (EMPRES) was established in 1994 to strengthen FAO's activities in the prevention, early warning of, control and, where possible, eradication of pests and highly contagious livestock diseases (which the system categorizes as epidemic diseases of strategic importance, such as rinderpest or foot-and-mouth; diseases requiring tactical attention at international or regional level, e.g. Rift Valley fever; and emerging diseases, e.g. bovine spongiform encephalopathy—BSE). EMPRES has a desert locust component, and has published guide-lines on all aspects of desert locust monitoring. FAO has assumed responsibility for technical leadership and co-ordination of the Global Rinderpest Eradication Programme (GREP), which has the objective of eliminating the disease by 2010. Following technical consulations in late 1998, an Intensified GREP was launched. In November 1997 FAO initiated a Programme Against African Trypanosomiasis, which aimed to counter the disease affecting cattle in almost one-third of Africa. EMPRES promotes Good Emergency Management Practices (GEMP) in animal health. The system is guided by the annual meeting of the EMPRES Expert Consultation.

FAO's organic agriculture programme provides technical assistance and policy advice on the production, certification and trade of organic produce. In July 2001 the FAO/WHO Codex Alimentarius Commission adopted guide-lines on organic livestock production, covering organic breeding methods, the elimination of growth hormones and certain chemicals in veterinary medicines, and the use of good quality organic feed with no meat or bone meal content.

ENVIRONMENT

At the UN Conference on Environment and Development (UNCED), held in Rio de Janeiro, Brazil, in June 1992, FAO participated in several working parties and supported the adoption of Agenda 21, a programme of activities to promote sustainable development. FAO is responsible for the chapters of Agenda 21 concerning water resources, forests, fragile mountain ecosystems and sustainable agriculture and rural development. FAO was designated by the UN General Assembly as the lead agency for co-ordinating the International Year of Mountains (2002), which aimed to raise awareness of mountain ecosystems and to promote the conservation and sustainable development of mountainous regions.

FISHERIES

FAO's Fisheries Department consists of a multi-disciplinary body of experts who are involved in every aspect of fisheries development from coastal surveys, conservation management and use of aquatic genetic resources, improvement of production, processing and storage, to the compilation and analysis of statistics, development of computer databases, improvement of fishing gear, institution-building and training. In November 1993 the FAO Conference adopted an agreement to improve the monitoring and control of fishing vessels operating on the high seas that are registered under 'flags of convenience', in order to ensure their compliance with internationally accepted marine conservation and management measures. In March 1995 a ministerial meeting of fisheries adopted the Rome Consensus on World Fisheries, which identified a need for immediate action to eliminate overfishing and to rebuild and enhance depleting fish stocks. In November the FAO Conference adopted a Code of Conduct for Responsible Fishing, which incorporated many global fisheries and aquaculture issues (including fisheries resource conservation and development, fish catches, seafood and fish processing, commercialization, trade and research) to promote the sustainable development of the sector. In February 1999 the FAO Committee on Fisheries adopted new international measures, within the framework of the Code of Conduct, in order to reduce over-exploitation of the world's fish resources, as well as plans of action for the conservation and management of sharks and the reduction in the incidental catch of seabirds in longline fisheries. The voluntary measures were endorsed at a ministerial meeting, held in March and attended by representatives of some 126 countries, which issued a declaration to promote the implementation of the Code of Conduct and to achieve sustainable management of fisheries and aquaculture. In March 2001 FAO adopted an international plan of action to address the continuing problem of so-called illegal, unreported and unregulated fishing (IUU). In that year FAO estimated that about one-half of major marine fish stocks were fully exploited, one-quarter under-exploited, at least 15% over-exploited, and 10% depleted or recovering from depletion. IUU was estimated to account for up to 30% of total catches in certain fisheries. In October FAO and the Icelandic Government jointly organized the Reykjavik Conference on Responsible Fisheries in the Marine Ecosystem, which adopted a declaration on pursuing responsible and sustainable fishing activities in the context of ecosystem-based fisheries management (EBFM). EBFM involves determining the boundaries of individual marine ecosystems, and maintaining or rebuilding the habitats and biodiversity of each of these so that all species will be supported at levels of maximum production. FAO promotes aquaculture (which contributes almost one-third of annual global fish landings) as a valuable source of animal protein and income-generating activity for rural communities. In February 2000 FAO and the Network of Aquaculture Centres in Asia and the Pacific (NACA, q.v.) jointly convened a Conference on Aquaculture in the Third Millennium, which was held in Bangkok, Thailand, and attended by participants representing more than 200 governmental and non-governmental organizations. The Conference debated global trends in aquaculture and future policy measures to ensure the sustainable development of the sector. It adopted the Bangkok Declaration and Strategy for Aquaculture Beyond 2000. In December 2001 FAO issued a report based on the technical proceedings of the conference.

FORESTRY

FAO focuses on the contribution of forestry to food security, on effective and responsible forest management and on maintaining a balance between the economic, ecological and social benefits of forest resources. The Organization has helped to develop national forestry programmes and to promote the sustainable development of all types of forest. FAO administers the global Forests, Trees and People Programme, which promotes the sustainable management of tree and forest resources, based on local knowledge and management practices, in order to improve the livelihoods of rural people in developing countries. FAO's Strategic Plan for Forestry was approved in March 1999; its main objectives were to maintain the environmental diversity of forests, to realise the economic potential of forests and trees within a sustainable framework, and to expand access to information on forestry.

NUTRITION

The International Conference on Nutrition, sponsored by FAO and WHO, took place in Rome in December 1992. It approved a World Declaration on Nutrition and a Plan of Action, aimed at promoting efforts to combat malnutrition as a development priority. Since the conference, more than 100 countries have formulated national plans of action for nutrition, many of which were based on existing development plans such as comprehensive food security initiatives, national poverty alleviation programmes and action plans to attain the targets set by the World Summit for Children in September 1990. In October 1996 FAO, WHO and other partners jointly organized the first World Congress on Calcium and Vitamin D in Human Life, held in Rome. In January 2001 a joint team of FAO and WHO experts issued a report concerning the allergenicity of foods derived from biotechnology (i.e. genetically modified—GM foods). In July the Codex Alimentarius Commission agreed the first global principles for assessing the safety of GM foods, and approved a series of maximum levels of environmental contaminants in food. FAO and WHO jointly convened a Global Forum of Food Safety Regulators in Marrakech, Morocco, in January 2002. In April the two organizations announce a joint review of their food standards operations, including the activities of the Codex Alimentarius Commission.

PROCESSING AND MARKETING

An estimated 20% of all food harvested is lost before it can be consumed, and in some developing countries the proportion is much higher. FAO helps reduce immediate post-harvest losses, with the introduction of improved processing methods and storage systems. It also advises on the distribution and marketing of agricultural produce and on the selection and preparation of foods for optimum nutrition. Many of these activities form part of wider rural development projects. Many developing countries rely on agricultural products as their main source of foreign earnings, but the terms under which they are traded are usually more favourable to the industrialized countries. FAO continues to favour the elimination of export subsidies and related discriminatory practices, such as protectionist measures that hamper international trade in agricultural commodities. FAO has organized regional workshops and national projects in order to help member states to implement World Trade Organization regulations, in particular with regard to agricultural policy, intellectual property rights, sanitary and phytosanitary measures, technical

barriers to trade and the international standards of the Codex Alimentarius. FAO evaluates new market trends and helps to develop improved plant and animal quarantine procedures. In November 1997 the FAO Conference adopted new guide-lines on surveillance and on export certification systems in order to harmonize plant quarantine standards. FAO participates in PhAction, a forum of 12 agencies that was established in 1999 to promote post-harvest research and the development of effective post-harvest services and infrastructure.

FOOD SECURITY

FAO's policy on food security aims to encourage the production of adequate food supplies, to maximize stability in the flow of supplies, and to ensure access on the part of those who need them. In 1994 FAO initiated the Special Programme for Food Security (SPFS), designed to assist low-income countries with a food deficit to increase food production and productivity as rapidly as possible, primarily through the widespread adoption by farmers of improved production technologies, with emphasis on areas of high potential. FAO was actively involved in the formulation of the Plan of Action on food security that was adopted at the World Food Summit in November 1996, and was to be responsible for monitoring and promoting its implementation. In March 1999 FAO signed agreements with IFAD and WFP that aimed to increase co-operation within the framework of the SPFS. A budget of US $10.5m. was allocated to the SPFS for the two-year period 2002–03. In early 2003 the SPFS was operational in 74 countries categorized as 'low-income food-deficit', of which 42 were in Africa. The Programme promotes South-South co-operation to improve food security and the exchange of knowledge and experience. By March 2002 26 bilateral co-operation agreements were in force, for example, between Pakistan and Swaziland and Viet Nam and Benin.

FAO's Global Information and Early Warning System (GIEWS), which become operational in 1975, maintains a database on and monitors the crop and food outlook at global, regional, national and sub-national levels in order to detect emerging food supply difficulties and disasters and to ensure rapid intervention in countries experiencing food supply shortages. It publishes regular reports on the weather conditions and crop prospects in sub-Saharan Africa and in the Sahel region, issues special alerts which describe the situation in countries or sub-regions experiencing food difficulties, and recommends an appropriate international response. FAO's annual publication *State of Food Insecurity in the World* is based on data compiled by the Organization's Food Insecurity and Vulnerability Information and Mapping Systems programme.

An Inter-Agency Task Force on the UN Response to Long-Term Food Security, Agricultural Development and Related Aspects in the Horn of Africa, appointed by the UN Secretary-General in April 2000, is chaired by the Director-General of FAO.

FAO INVESTMENT CENTRE

The Investment Centre was established in 1964 to help countries to prepare viable investment projects that will attract external financing. The Centre focuses its evaluation of projects on two fundamental concerns: the promotion of sustainable activities for land management, forestry development and environmental protection, and the alleviation of rural poverty. In 2000–01 90 projects were approved, representing a total investment of some US $4,670m.

EMERGENCY RELIEF

FAO works to rehabilitate agricultural production following natural and man-made disasters by providing emergency seed, tools, and technical and other assistance. Jointly with the United Nations, FAO is responsible for WFP (q.v.), which provides emergency food supplies and food aid in support of development projects. FAO's Division for Emergency Operations and Rehabilitation was responsible for preparing the emergency agricultural relief component of the 2002 UN inter-agency appeals for 17 countries and regions.

INFORMATION

FAO collects, analyses, interprets and disseminates information through various media, including an extensive internet site. It issues regular statistical reports, commodity studies, and technical manuals in local languages (see list of publications below). Other materials produced by the FAO include information booklets, reference papers, reports of meetings, training manuals and audiovisuals.

FAO's internet-based interactive World Agricultural Information Centre (WAICENT) offers access to agricultural publications, technical documentation, codes of conduct, data, statistics and multimedia resources. FAO compiles and co-ordinates an extensive range of international databases on agriculture, fisheries, forestry, food and statistics, the most important of these being AGRIS (the International Information System for the Agricultural Sciences and Technology) and CARIS (the Current Agricultural Research Information System). Statistical databases include the GLOBEFISH databank and electronic library, FISHDAB (the Fisheries Statistical Data-base), FORIS (Forest Resources Information System), and GIS (the Geographic Information System). In addition, FAOSTAT provides access to updated figures in 10 agriculture-related topics.

In June 2000 FAO organized a high-level Consultation on Agricultural Information Management (COAIM), which aimed to increase access to and use of agricultural information by policy-makers and others. The second COAIM was held in September 2002.

World Food Day, commemorating the foundation of FAO, is held annually on 16 October.

FAO Councils and Commissions

(Based at the Rome headquarters unless otherwise indicated.)

African Commission on Agricultural Statistics: c/o FAO Regional Office for Africa, POB 1628, Accra, Ghana: f. 1961 to advise member countries on the development and standardization of food and agricultural statistics; 37 member states.

African Forestry and Wildlife Commission: f. 1959 to advise on the formulation of forest policy and to review and co-ordinate its implementation on a regional level; to exchange information and advise on technical problems; 42 member states.

Asia and Pacific Commission on Agricultural Statistics: c/o FAO Regional Office, Maliwan Mansion, Phra Atit Rd, Bangkok 10200, Thailand; f. 1962 to review the state of food and agricultural statistics in the region and to advise member countries on the development and standardization of agricultural statistics; 25 member states.

Asia and Pacific Plant Protection Commission: c/o FAO Regional Office, Maliwan Mansion, Phra Atit Rd, Bangkok 10200, Thailand; f. 1956 (new title 1983) to strengthen international co-operation in plant protection to prevent the introduction and spread of destructive plant diseases and pests; 25 member states.

Asia-Pacific Fishery Commission: c/o FAO Regional Office, Maliwan Mansion, Phra Atit Rd, Bangkok 10200, Thailand; f. 1948 to develop fisheries, encourage and co-ordinate research, disseminate information, recommend projects to governments, propose standards in technique and management measures; 20 member states.

Asia-Pacific Forestry Commission: internet www.apfcweb.org; f. 1949 to advise on the formulation of forest policy, and review and co-ordinate its implementation throughout the region; to exchange information and advise on technical problems; 29 member states.

Caribbean Plant Protection Commission: f. 1967 to preserve the existing plant resources of the area.

Commission for Controlling the Desert Locust in the Eastern Region of its Distribution Area in South West Asia: f. 1964 to carry out all possible measures to control plagues of the desert locust in Afghanistan, India, Iran and Pakistan.

Commission for Controlling the Desert Locust in the Near East: c/o FAO Regional Office for the Near East, POB 2223, Cairo, Egypt; f. 1967 to promote national and international research and action with respect to the control of the desert locust in the Near East.

Commission for Controlling the Desert Locust in North-West Africa: f. 1971 to promote research on control of the desert locust in NW Africa.

Commission for Inland Fisheries of Latin America: f. 1976 to promote, co-ordinate and assist national and regional fishery and limnological surveys and programmes of research and development leading to the rational utilization of inland fishery resources.

Commission on Genetic Resources for Food and Agriculture: internet www.fao.org/ag/cgrfa/default.htm; f. 1983 as the Commission on Plant Genetic Resources, renamed in 1995; provides a forum for negotiation on the conservation and sustainable utilization of genetic resources for food and agriculture, and the equitable sharing of benefits derived from their use; 164 mems.

European Commission on Agriculture: f. 1949 to encourage and facilitate action and co-operation in technological agricultural problems among member states and between international organizations concerned with agricultural technology in Europe.

European Commission for the Control of Foot-and-Mouth Disease: www.fao.org/ag/AGA/AGAH/EUFMD/default.htm; f. 1953 to promote national and international action for the control of the disease in Europe and its final eradication.

European Forestry Commission: f. 1947 to advise on the formulation of forest policy and to review and co-ordinate its implementation on a regional level; to exchange information and to make recommendations; 27 member states.

European Inland Fisheries Advisory Commission: internet www.fao.org/fi/body/eifac/eifac.asp; f. 1957 to promote improvements in inland fisheries and to advise member governments and FAO on inland fishery matters; 34 mems.

FAO/WHO Codex Alimentarius Commission: internet www.codexalimentarius.net; f. 1962 to make proposals for the co-ordination of all international food standards work and to publish a code of international food standards; established Intergovernmental Task Force on Foods Derived from Biotechnology in 1999; 165 member states.

General Fisheries Council for the Mediterranean—GFCM: internet www.fao.org/fi/body/rfb/index.htm; f. 1952 to develop aquatic resources, to encourage and co-ordinate research in the fishing and allied industries, to assemble and publish information, and to recommend the standardization of equipment, techniques and nomenclature.

Indian Ocean Fishery Commission: f. 1967 to promote national programmes, research and development activities, and to examine management problems; 41 member states.

International Poplar Commission: f. 1947 to study scientific, technical, social and economic aspects of poplar and willow cultivation; to promote the exchange of ideas and material between research workers, producers and users; to arrange joint research programmes, congresses, study tours; to make recommendations to the FAO Conference and to National Poplar Commissions.

International Rice Commission: internet www.fao.org/ag/AGP/AGPC/doc/field/commrice/welcome.htm; f. 1949 to promote national and international action on production, conservation, distribution and consumption of rice, except matters relating to international trade; 60 member states.

Latin American and Caribbean Forestry Commission: f. 1948 to advise on formulation of forest policy and review and co-ordinate its implementation throughout the region; to exchange information and advise on technical problems; 31 member states.

Near East Forestry Commission: f. 1953 to advise on formulation of forest policy and review and co-ordinate its implementation throughout the region; to exchange information and advise on technical problems; 20 member states.

Near East Regional Commission on Agriculture: c/o FAO Regional Office, POB 2223, Cairo, Egypt; f. 1983 to conduct periodic reviews of agricultural problems in the region; to promote the formulation and implementation of regional and national policies and programmes for improving production of crops and livestock; to strengthen the management of crops, livestock and supporting services and research; to promote the transfer of technology and regional technical co-operation; and to provide guidance on training and human resources development.

North American Forestry Commission: f. 1959 to advise on the formulation and co-ordination of national forest policies in Canada, Mexico and the USA; to exchange information and to advise on technical problems; three member states.

Regional Animal Production and Health Commission for Asia and the Pacific: c/o FAO Regional Office, Maliwan Mansion, Phra Atit Rd, Bangkok 10200, Thailand; internet www.aphca.org; f. 1973 to promote livestock development in general, and national and international research and action with respect to animal health and husbandry problems in the region; 15 member states.

Regional Commission on Land and Water Use in the Near East: f. 1967 to review the current situation with regard to land and water use in the region; to identify the main problems concerning the development of land and water resources which require research and study and to consider other related matters.

Western Central Atlantic Fishery Commission: f. 1973 to assist international co-operation for the conservation, development and utilization of the living resources, especially shrimps, of the Western Central Atlantic.

Finance

FAO's Regular Programme, which is financed by contributions from member governments, covers the cost of FAO's Secretariat, its Technical Co-operation Programme (TCP) and part of the cost of several special action programmes. The proposed budget for the two years 2002–03 totalled US $651.8m. Much of FAO's technical assistance programme is funded from extra-budgetary sources, predominantly by trust funds that come mainly from donor countries and international financing institutions. The single largest contributor is the United Nations Development Programme (UNDP, q.v.). In 2001 total field programme expenditure amounted to $367m.

Publications

Animal Health Yearbook.
Commodity Review and Outlook (annually).

Environment and Energy Bulletin.
Ethical Issues in Food and Agriculture.
Fertilizer Yearbook.
Food Crops and Shortages (6 a year).
Food Outlook (5 a year).
Food Safety and Quality Update (monthly; electronic bulletin)*Forest Resources Assessment.*
Plant Protection Bulletin (quarterly).
Production Yearbook.
Quarterly Bulletin of Statistics.
The State of Food and Agriculture (annually).

The State of Food Insecurity in the World (annually).
The State of World Fisheries and Aquaculture (every two years).
The State of the World's Forests (every 2 years).
Trade Yearbook.
Unasylva (quarterly).
Yearbook of Fishery Statistics.
Yearbook of Forest Products.
World Animal Review (quarterly).
World Watch List for Domestic Animal Diversity.
Commodity reviews; studies; manuals.

International Atomic Energy Agency—IAEA

Address: POB 100, Wagramerstrasse 5, 1400 Vienna, Austria.

Telephone: (1) 26000; **fax:** (1) 26007; **e-mail:** official.mail@iaea.org; **internet:** www.iaea.org/worldatom.

The International Atomic Energy Agency (IAEA) is an intergovernmental organization, established in 1957 in accordance with a decision of the General Assembly of the United Nations. Although it is autonomous, the IAEA is administratively a member of the United Nations, and reports on its activities once a year to the UN General Assembly. Its main objectives are to enlarge the contribution of atomic energy to peace, health and prosperity throughout the world and to ensure, so far as it is able, that assistance provided by it or at its request or under its supervision or control is not used in such a way as to further any military purpose.

MEMBERS

135 members: see Table on pp. 125–127.

Organization

(April 2003)

GENERAL CONFERENCE

The Conference, comprising representatives of all member states, convenes each year for general debate on the Agency's policy, budget and programme. It elects members to the Board of Governors, and approves the appointment of the Director-General; it admits new member states.

BOARD OF GOVERNORS

The Board of Governors consists of 35 member states: 22 elected by the General Conference for two-year periods and 13 designated by the Board from among member states which are advanced in nuclear technology. It is the principal policy-making body of the Agency and is responsible to the General Conference. Under its own authority, the Board approves all safeguards agreements, important projects and safety standards. In 1999 the General Conference adopted a resolution on expanding the Board's membership to 43, to include 18 states designated as the most advanced in nuclear technology. The resolution required ratification by two-thirds of member states to come into effect.

SECRETARIAT

The Secretariat, comprising about 2,200 staff, is headed by the Director-General, who is assisted by six Deputy Directors-General. The Secretariat is divided into six departments: Technical Co-operation; Nuclear Energy; Nuclear Safety; Nuclear Sciences and Applications; Safeguards; Management. A Standing Advisory Group on Safeguards Implementation advises the Director-General on technical aspects of safeguards.

Director-General: Dr MOHAMMAD EL-BARADEI (Egypt).

Activities

In recent years the IAEA has implemented several reforms of its management structure and operations. The Agency's functions can be divided into the following categories: technology (assisting research on and practical application of atomic energy for peaceful uses), and safety and verification (ensuring that special fissionable and other materials, services, equipment and information made available by the Agency or at its request or under its supervision are not used for any non-peaceful purpose).

TECHNICAL CO-OPERATION AND TRAINING

The IAEA provides assistance in the form of experts, training and equipment to technical co-operation projects and applications worldwide, with an emphasis on radiation protection and safety-related activities. Training is provided to scientists, and experts and lecturers are assigned to provide specialized help on specific nuclear applications.

FOOD AND AGRICULTURE

In co-operation with FAO (q.v.), the Agency conducts programmes of applied research on the use of radiation and isotopes in fields including: efficiency in the use of water and fertilizers; improvement of food crops by induced mutations; eradication or control of destructive insects by the introduction of sterilized insects (radiation-based Sterile Insect Technique); improvement of livestock nutrition and health; studies on improving efficacy and reducing residues of pesticides, and increasing utilization of agricultural wastes; and food preservation by irradiation. The programmes are implemented by the Joint FAO/IAEA Division of Nuclear Techniques in Food and Agriculture and by the FAO/IAEA Agriculture and Biotechnology Laboratory, based at IAEA's laboratory complex in Seibersdorf, Austria. A new Training and Reference Centre for Food and Pesticide Control opened at Seibersdorf in mid-1999. The Centre was to support the implementation of national legislation and trade agreements ensuring the quality and safety of food products in international trade.

LIFE SCIENCES

In co-operation with the World Health Organization (WHO, q.v.), the IAEA promotes the use of nuclear techniques in medicine, biology and health-related environmental research, provides training, and conducts research on techniques for improving the accuracy of radiation dosimetry.

In 2001 the IAEA/WHO Network of Secondary Standard Dosimetry Laboratories (SSDLs) comprised 80 laboratories in 62 member states. The Agency's Dosimetry Laboratory in Seibersdorf performs dose inter-comparisons for both SSDLs and radiotherapy centres. The IAEA undertakes maintenance plans for nuclear laboratories; national programmes of quality control for nuclear medicine instruments; quality control of radioimmunoassay techniques; radiation sterilization of medical supplies; and improvement of cancer therapy.

PHYSICAL AND CHEMICAL SCIENCES

The Agency's programme in physical sciences includes industrial applications of isotopes and radiation technology; application of nuclear techniques to mineral exploration and exploitation; radiopharmaceuticals; and hydrology, involving the use of isotope techniques for assessment of water resources. Nuclear data services are provided, and training is given for nuclear scientists from developing countries. The Physics, Chemistry and Instrumentation Laboratory at Seibersdorf supports the Agency's research in human health, industry, water resources and environment.

NUCLEAR POWER

At the end of 2001 there were 438 nuclear power plants in operation throughout the world, providing about 16% of total electrical energy generated during the year. There were also 32 reactors under construction. The Agency helps developing member states to introduce nuclear-powered electricity-generating plants through assistance with planning, feasibility studies, surveys of manpower and infrastructure, and safety measures. It publishes books on numerous aspects of nuclear power, and provides training courses on safety in nuclear power plants and other topics. An energy data bank collects and disseminates information on nuclear technology, and a power-reactor information system monitors the technical performance of nuclear power plants. There is increasing interest in the use of nuclear reactors for seawater desalination and radiation hydrology techniques to provide potable water. In July 1992 the EC, Japan, Russia and the USA signed an agreement to co-operate in the engineering design of an International Thermonuclear Experimental Reactor (ITER). The project aimed to demonstrate the scientific and technological feasibility of fusion energy, with the aim of providing a source of clean, abundant energy in the 21st century. An Extension Agreement, signed in 1998, provided for the continuation of the project. In November 2000 the International Project on Innovative Nuclear Reactors and Fuel Cycles (INPRO) was inaugurated. INPRO aimed to promote nuclear energy as a means of meeting future sustainable energy requirements and to facilitate the exchange of information by member states to advance innovations in nuclear technology.

RADIOACTIVE WASTE MANAGEMENT

The Agency provides practical help to member states in the management of radioactive waste. The Waste Management Advisory Programme (WAMAP) was established in 1987, and undertakes advisory missions in member states. A code of practice to prevent the illegal dumping of radioactive waste was drafted in 1989, and another on the international trans-boundary movement of waste was drafted in 1990. A ban on the dumping of radioactive waste at sea came into effect in February 1994, under the Convention on the Prevention of Marine Pollution by Dumping of Wastes and Other Matters (see IMO, p. 97). The IAEA was to determine radioactive levels, for purposes of the Convention, and provide assistance to countries for the safe disposal of radioactive wastes. The Agency has issued modal regulations for the air, sea and land transportation of all radioactive materials.

In September 1997 IAEA adopted a Joint Convention on the Safety of Spent Fuel Management and on the Safety of Radioactive Waste Management. The first internationally-binding legal device to address such issues, the Convention was to ensure the safe storage and disposal of nuclear and radioactive waste, during both the construction and operation of a nuclear power plant, as well as following its closure. The Convention entered into force in June 2001, and had been ratified by 30 parties at November 2002.

NUCLEAR SAFETY

The IAEA's nuclear safety programme encourages international co-operation in the exchange of information, promoting implementation of its safety standards and providing advisory safety services. It includes the IAEA International Nuclear Event Scale; the Incident Reporting System; an emergency preparedness programme (which maintains an Emergency Response Centre); operational safety review teams; the 15-member International Nuclear Safety Advisory Group (INSAG); the Radiation Protection Advisory Team; and a safety research co-ordination programme. The safety review teams provide member states with advice on achieving and maintaining a high level of safety in the operation of nuclear power plants, while research programmes establish risk criteria for the nuclear fuel cycle and identify cost-effective means to reduce risks in energy systems. By the end of 1998 53 member states had agreed to report all nuclear events, incidents and accidents according to the International Nuclear Event Scale. In May the Director-General initiated a review of the Agency's nuclear strategy, proposing the development of national safety profiles, more active promotion of safety services and improved co-operation at governmental and non-governmental levels.

The revised edition of the Basic Safety Standards for Radiation Protection (IAEA Safety Series No. 9) was approved in 1994. The Nuclear Safety Standards programme, initiated in 1974 with five codes of practice and more than 60 safety guides, was revised in 1987 and again in 1995.

Following a serious accident at the Chornobyl (Chernobyl) nuclear power plant in Ukraine (then part of the USSR) in April 1986, two conventions were formulated by the IAEA and entered into force in October. The first, the Convention on Early Notification of a Nuclear Accident, commits parties to provide information about nuclear accidents with possible trans-boundary effects at the earliest opportunity (it had 87 parties by March 2003); and the second commits parties to endeavour to provide assistance in the event of a nuclear accident or radiological emergency (this had 84 parties by March 2003). During 1990 the IAEA organized an assessment of the consequences of the Chernobyl accident, undertaken by an international team of experts, who reported to an international conference on the effects of the accident, convened at the IAEA headquarters in Vienna in May 1991. In February 1993 INSAG published an updated report on the Chernobyl incident, which emphasized the role of design factors in the accident, and the need to implement safety measures in the RBMK-type reactor. In March 1994 an IAEA expert mission visited Chernobyl and reported continuing serious deficiencies in

safety at the defunct reactor and the units remaining in operation. An international conference reviewing the radiological consequences of the accident, 10 years after the event, was held in April 1996, co-sponsored by the IAEA, WHO and the European Commission. The last of the Chernobyl plant's three operating units was officially closed in December 2000. The IAEA was to offer a wide range of assistance during Chernobyl's decommissioning period, the first stage of which was expected to have a duration of five years.

In September 1999 the IAEA activated its Emergency Response Centre, following a serious incident at a fuel conversion facility in Tokaimura, Japan. The Centre was used to process information from the Japanese authorities and to ensure accurate reporting of the event. In October a three-member IAEA team of experts visited the site to undertake a preliminary investigation into the causes and consequences of the accident.

An International Convention on Nuclear Safety was adopted at an IAEA conference in June 1994. The Convention applies to land-based civil nuclear power plants: adherents commit themselves to fundamental principles of safety, and maintain legislative frameworks governing nuclear safety. The Convention entered into force in October 1996. The first Review Meeting of Contracting Parties to the Convention was held in April 1999. By October 2002 54 states had ratified the Convention.

In September 1997 more than 80 member states adopted a protocol to revise the 1963 Vienna Convention on Civil Liability for Nuclear Damage, fixing the minimum limit of liability for the operator of a nuclear reactor at 300m. Special Drawing Rights (SDRs, the accounting units of the IMF) in the event of an accident. The amended protocol also extended the length of time during which claims may be brought for loss of life or injury. The amended protocol had been signed by 15 countries and ratified by four at February 2003. A Convention on Supplementary Compensation for Nuclear Damage established a further compensatory fund to provide for the payment of damages following an accident; contributions to the Fund were to be calculated on the basis of the nuclear capacity of each member state. The Convention had 13 signatories and three contracting states by February 2003.

In July 1996 the IAEA co-ordinated a study on the radiological situation at the Mururoa and Fangatauta atolls, following the French nuclear test programmes in the South Pacific. Results published in May 1998 concluded there was no radiological health risk and that neither remedial action nor continued environmental monitoring was necessary.

The IAEA is developing a training course on measurement methods and risk analysis relating to the presence of depleted uranium (which can be used in ammunition) in post-conflict areas. In November 2000 IAEA specialists participated in a fact-finding mission organized by UNEP in Kosovo and Metohija, which aimed to assess the environmental and health consequences of the use of depleted uranium in ammunition by NATO during its aerial offensive against the Federal Republic of Yugoslavia (now Serbia and Montenegro) in 1999. (A report on the situation was published by UNEP in March 2001.)

In May 2001 the IAEA convened an international conference to address the protection of nuclear material and radioactive sources from illegal trafficking. In September, in view of the perpetration of major terrorist attacks against targets in the USA during that month, the IAEA General Conference addressed the potential for nuclear-related terrorism. It adopted a resolution that emphasized the importance of the physical protection of nuclear material in preventing its illicit use or the sabotage of nuclear facilities and nuclear materials. Three main potential threats were identified: the acquisition by a terrorist group of a nuclear weapon; acquisition of nuclear material to construct a nuclear weapon or cause a radiological hazard; and violent acts against nuclear facilities to cause a radiological hazard. In March 2002 the Board of Governors approved in principle an action plan to improve global protection against acts of terrorism involving nuclear and other radioactive materials. The plan addressed the physical protection of nuclear materials and facilities; the detection of malicious activities involving radioactive materials; strengthening national control systems; the security of radioactive sources; evaluation of security and safety at nuclear facilities; emergency response to malicious acts or threats involving radioactive materials; ensuring adherence to international guidelines and agreements; and improvement of programme co-ordination and information management. It was estimated that the Agency's upgraded nuclear security activities would require significant additional annual funding. In March 2003 the IAEA organized an International Conference on Security of Radioactive Sources, held in Vienna.

DISSEMINATION OF INFORMATION

The International Nuclear Information System (INIS), which was established in 1970, provides a computerized indexing and abstracting service. Information on the peaceful uses of atomic energy is collected by member states and international organizations and sent to the IAEA for processing and dissemination (see list of publications below). The IAEA also co-operates with FAO in an information system for agriculture (AGRIS) and with the World Federation of Nuclear Medicine and Biology, and the non-profit Cochrane Collaboration, in maintaining an electronic database of best practice in nuclear medicine. The IAEA Nuclear Data Section provides cost-free data centre services and co-operates with other national and regional nuclear and atomic data centres in the systematic world-wide collection, compilation, dissemination and exchange of nuclear reaction data, nuclear structure and decay data, and atomic and molecular data for fusion.

SAFEGUARDS

The Treaty on the Non-Proliferation of Nuclear Weapons (known also as the Non-Proliferation Treaty or NPT), which entered into force in 1970, requires each 'non-nuclear-weapon state' (one which had not manufactured and exploded a nuclear weapon or other nuclear explosive device prior to 1 January 1967) which is a party to the Treaty to conclude a safeguards agreement with the IAEA. Under such an agreement, the state undertakes to accept IAEA safeguards on all nuclear material in all its peaceful nuclear activities for the purpose of verifying that such material is not diverted to nuclear weapons or other nuclear explosive devices. In May 1995 the Review and Extension Conference of parties to the NPT agreed to extend the NPT indefinitely, and reaffirmed support for the IAEA's role in verification and the transfer of peaceful nuclear technologies. At the next review conference, held in April/May 2000, the five 'nuclear-weapon states'— the People's Republic of China, France, Russia, the United Kingdom and the USA—issued a joint statement pledging their commitment to the ultimate goal of complete nuclear disarmament under effective international controls. By March 2003 181 non-nuclear-weapon states and the five nuclear-weapon states were parties to the Treaty, but a number of non-nuclear-weapon states had not complied, within the prescribed time-limit, with their obligations under the Treaty regarding the conclusion of the relevant safeguards agreement with the Agency. The Democratic Republic of Korea (DPRK), which had acceded to the NPT in December 1985, announced its immediate withdrawal from the Treaty in January 2003 (see below).

The five nuclear-weapon states have concluded safeguards agreements with the Agency that permit the application of IAEA safeguards to all their nuclear activities, excluding those with 'direct national significance'. A Comprehensive Nuclear Test Ban Treaty (CTBT) was opened for signature in September 1996, having been adopted by the UN General Assembly. The Treaty was to enter into international law upon ratification by all 44 nations with known nuclear capabilities. A separate verification organization was to be established, based in Vienna. A Preparatory Commission for the treaty organization became operational in 1997. By March 2003 166 countries had signed the CTBT and 98 had ratified it, including 31 of the 44 states with nuclear capabilities. However, the US Senate rejected ratification of the CTBT in October 1999.

Several regional nuclear weapons treaties require their member states to conclude comprehensive safeguards agreements with the IAEA. By December 2001 31 of the 32 states party to the Treaty for the prohibition of Nuclear Weapons in Latin America (Tlatelolco Treaty) had concluded safeguards agreements with the Agency, as had all 11 signatories of the South Pacific Nuclear-Free Zone Treaty (Rarotonga Treaty). The IAEA also aims to administer full applications of safeguards with the ten states party to the Treaty in the South-East Asia Nuclear-Weapon Free Zone (Treaty of Bangkok, adopted in 1995) and the states party to the African Nuclear-Weapon Free Zone Treaty (Pelindaba Treaty, adopted in 1996). In September 2002 experts from Kazakhstan, Kyrgyzstan, Tajikistan, Turkmenistan and Uzbekistan, meeting in Samarkand, Uzbekistan, approved the draft text of a treaty on establishing a Central Asian Nuclear Weapon Free Zone. At the end of 2001 a total of 225 IAEA safeguards agreements were in force with 142 states. Of these, 71 states had declared significant nuclear activities and were under inspection. At the end of the same year there were 908 nuclear installations and locations containing nuclear material subject to IAEA safeguards. A total of 2,487 inspections were conducted in that year. Expenditure on the Safeguards Regular Budget for 2001 was US $70.0m; extra-budgetary programme expenditure amounted to $15.2m. During 2000 the IAEA established an imagery database of nuclear sites; digital image surveillance systems had been installed in 24 countries by the end of the year.

In April 1992 the DPRK ratified a safeguards agreement with the IAEA. In late 1992 and early 1993, however, the IAEA unsuccessfully requested access to two non-declared sites in the DPRK, where it was suspected that material capable of being used for the manufacture of nuclear weapons was stored. In March 1993 the DPRK announced its intention of withdrawing from the NPT: it suspended its withdrawal in June, but continued to refuse full access to its nuclear facilities for IAEA inspectors. In May 1994 the DPRK began to refuel an experimental nuclear power reactor at Yongbyon, but refused to allow the IAEA to analyse the spent fuel rods in order to ascertain whether plutonium had been obtained

from the reactor for possible military use. In June the IAEA Board of Governors halted IAEA technical assistance to the DPRK (except medical assistance) because of continuous violation of the NPT safeguards agreements. In the same month the DPRK withdrew from the IAEA (though not from the NPT); however, it allowed IAEA inspectors to remain at the Yongbyon site to conduct safeguards activites. In October the Governments of the DPRK and the USA concluded an agreement whereby the former agreed to halt construction of two new nuclear reactors, on condition that it received international aid for the construction of two 'light water' reactors (which could not produce materials for the manufacture of nuclear weapons). The DPRK also agreed to allow IAEA inspections of all its nuclear sites, but only after the installation of one of the 'light water' reactors had been completed (entailing a significant time lapse). In November IAEA inspectors visited the DPRK to initiate verification of the suspension of the country's nuclear programme, in accordance with the agreement concluded in the previous month. From 1995 the IAEA pursued technical discussions with the DPRK authorities as part of the Agency's efforts to achieve the full compliance of the DPRK with the IAEA safeguards agreement. By the end of 1999 the canning of spent fuel rods from the Yongbyon nuclear power reactor was completed. However, little overall progress had been achieved, owing to the obstruction of inspectors by the authorities in that country, including their refusal to provide samples for analysis. The IAEA was unable to verify the suspension of the nuclear programme and declared that the DPRK continued to be in non-compliance with its NPT safeguards agreement. In accordance with a decision of the General Conference in September 2001, IAEA inspectors subsequently resumed a continuous presence in the DPRK. The DPRK authorities permitted low-level inspections of the Yongbyon site by an IAEA technical team in January and May 2002. It was envisaged at that time that the new 'light water' reactors would become operational by 2008. However, in December 2002 the DPRK authorities disabled IAEA safeguards surveillance equipment placed at three facilities in Yongbyon and took measures to restart reprocessing capabilities at the site, requesting the immediate withdrawal of the Agency's inspectors. (The inspectors were withdrawn at the end of the month.) In early January 2003 the IAEA Board of Governors adopted a resolution deploring the DPRK's non-co-operation and urging its immediate and full compliance with the Agency. Shortly afterwards, however, the DPRK announced its withdrawal from the NPT, stating that it would limit its nuclear activities to peaceful purposes. In late February the IAEA condemned the reported successful reactivation of the Yongbyon reactor.

In April 1991 the UN Security Council requested the IAEA to conduct investigations into Iraq's capacity to produce nuclear weapons, following the end of the war between Iraq and the UN-authorized, US-led multinational force. The IAEA was to work closely with a UN Special Commission of experts (UNSCOM), established by the Security Council, whose task was to inspect and dismantle Iraq's weapons of mass destruction (including chemical and biological weapons). In July the IAEA declared that Iraq had violated its safeguards agreement with the IAEA by not submitting nuclear material and relevant facilities in its uranium-enrichment programme to the Agency's inspection. This was the first time that a state party to the NPT had been condemned for concealing a programme of this nature. In October the sixth inspection team, composed of UNSCOM and representatives of the IAEA, was reported to have obtained conclusive documentary evidence that Iraq had a programme for developing nuclear weapons. By February 1994 all declared stocks of nuclear-weapons-grade material had been removed from Iraq. Subsequently, the IAEA pursued a programme of long-term surveillance of nuclear activity in Iraq, under a mandate issued by the UN Security Council. In September 1996 Iraq submitted to the IAEA a 'full, final and complete' declaration of its nuclear activities. However, in September–October 1997 the IAEA recommended that Iraq disclose further equipment, materials and information relating to its nuclear programme. In April 1998 IAEA technical experts were part of a special group that entered eight presidential sites in Iraq to collect baseline data, in accordance with a Memorandum of Understanding concluded between the UN Secretary-General and the Iraqi authorities in February. The accord aimed to ensure full Iraqi co-operation with UNSCOM and IAEA personnel. In August, however, Iraq suspended co-operation with UN inspectors, which prevented IAEA from implementing its programme of ongoing monitoring and verification (OMV) activities. Iraq's action was condemned by the IAEA General Conference in September. In October IAEA reported that while there was no evidence of Iraq having produced nuclear weapons or having retained or obtained a capability for the production of nuclear weapons, the Agency was unable to guarantee that all items had been found. All IAEA inspectors were temporarily relocated from Iraq to Bahrain in November, in accordance with a decision to withdraw UNSCOM personnel owing to Iraq's failure to agree to resume co-operation. In March 2000 UNSCOM was replaced by a new arms inspection body, the UN Monitoring, Verification and

Inspection Commission (UNMOVIC, q.v.). Although the IAEA carried out inventory verifications of nuclear material in Iraq in January 2000, January 2001 and January 2002, pursuant to Iraq's NPT safeguards agreement, full inspection activities in conjunction with UNMOVIC remained suspended. In September 2002 the US President expressed concern that Iraq was challenging international security owing to its non-compliance with successive UN resolutions relating to the elimination of weapons of mass destruction. In November the UN Security Council adopted Resolution 1441 providing for an enhanced inspection mission and a detailed timetable according to which Iraq would have a final opportunity to comply with its disarmament obligations. Following Iraq's acceptance of the resolution, experts from the IAEA's so-called Iraq Nuclear Verification Office and UNMOVIC resumed inspections on 27 November, with Council authorization to have unrestricted access to all areas and the right to interview Iraqi scientists and weapons experts. In early December Iraq submitted a declaration of all aspects of its weapons programmes, as required under Resolution 1441. In January 2003 Dr Mohammad el-Baradei, the IAEA Director-General, requested an ongoing mandate for his inspectors to clarify the situation regarding nuclear weapons. In mid-March el-Baradei reported that no evidence had been found of nuclear weapons programme activities in Iraq. At that time, however, IAEA and UNMOVIC personnel were withdrawn from Iraq owing to the unilateral initiation of military action against the Iraqi regime by US and allied forces.

In late 1997 the IAEA began inspections in the USA to verify the conversion for peaceful uses of nuclear material released from the military sector. In 1998 the United Kingdom announced that substantial quantities of nuclear material previously in its military programme would become available for verification under its voluntary offer safeguards agreement.

In June 1995 the Board of Governors approved measures to strengthen the safeguards system, including allowing inspection teams greater access to suspected nuclear sites and to information on nuclear activities in member states, reducing the notice time for inspections by removing visa requirements for inspectors and using environmental monitoring (i.e. soil, water and air samples) to test for signs of radioactivity. In April 1996 the IAEA initiated a programme to prevent and combat illicit trafficking of nuclear weapons, and in May 1998 the IAEA and the World Customs Organization (q.v.) signed a Memorandum of Understanding to enhance co-operation in the prevention of illicit nuclear trafficking. In May 1997 the Board of Governors adopted a model additional protocol approving measures to strengthen safeguards further, in order to ensure the compliance of non-nuclear-weapon states with IAEA commitments. The new protocol compelled member states to provide inspection teams with improved access to information concerning existing and planned nuclear activities, and to allow access to locations other than known nuclear sites within that country's territory. By March 2003 29 states had ratified additional protocols to their safeguards agreements.

IAEA's Safeguards Analytical Laboratory analyses nuclear fuel-cycle samples collected by IAEA safeguards inspectors. The Agency's Marine Environment Laboratory, in Monaco, studies radionuclides and other ocean pollutants.

NUCLEAR FUEL CYCLE

The Agency promotes the exchange of information between member states on technical, safety, environmental, and economic aspects of nuclear fuel cycle technology, including uranium prospecting and the treatment and disposal of radioactive waste; it provides assistance to member states in the planning, implementation and operation of nuclear fuel cycle facilities and assists in the development of advanced nuclear fuel cycle technology. Every two years, in collaboration with the OECD, the Agency prepares estimates of world uranium resources, demand and production.

Finance

The Agency is financed by regular and voluntary contributions from member states. Expenditure approved under the regular budget for 2003 amounted to some US $249m., and the target for voluntary contributions to finance the IAEA technical assistance and co-operation programme in that (and the following) year was $75m.

Publications

Annual Report.
IAEA Bulletin (quarterly).
IAEA Newsbriefs (every 2 months).
IAEA Yearbook.
INIS Atomindex (bibliography, 2 a month).
INIS Reference Series.
INSAG Series.
Legal Series.
Meetings on Atomic Energy (quarterly).
The Nuclear Fuel Cycle Information System: A Directory of Nuclear Fuel Cycle Facilities.
Nuclear Fusion (monthly).
Nuclear Safety Review (annually).
Panel Proceedings Series.
Publications Catalogue (annually).
Safety Series.
Technical Directories.
Technical Reports Series.

International Bank for Reconstruction and Development—IBRD (World Bank)

Address: 1818 H St, NW, Washington, DC 20433, USA.
Telephone: (202) 477-1234; **fax:** (202) 477-6391; **e-mail:** pic@worldbank.org; **internet:** www.worldbank.org.

The IBRD was established in December 1945. Initially it was concerned with post-war reconstruction in Europe; since then its aim has been to assist the economic development of member nations by making loans where private capital is not available on reasonable terms to finance productive investments. Loans are made either directly to governments, or to private enterprises with the guarantee of their governments. The World Bank, as it is commonly known, comprises the IBRD and the International Development Association (IDA, q.v.). The affiliated group of institutions, comprising the IBRD, the IDA, the International Finance Corporation (IFC, q.v.), the Multilateral Investment Guarantee Agency (MIGA, q.v.) and the International Centre for Settlement of Investment Disputes (ICSID, see below), is now referred to as the World Bank Group.

MEMBERS

There are 184 members: see Table on pp. 125–127. Only members of the International Monetary Fund (IMF, q.v.) may be considered for membership in the World Bank. Subscriptions to the capital stock of the Bank are based on each member's quota in the IMF, which is designed to reflect the country's relative economic strength. Voting rights are related to shareholdings.

Organization

(April 2003)

Officers and staff of the IBRD serve concurrently as officers and staff in the IDA. The World Bank has offices in New York, Brussels, Paris (for Europe), Frankfurt, London, Geneva and Tokyo, as well as in more than 100 countries of operation. Country Directors are located in some 28 country offices.

BOARD OF GOVERNORS

The Board of Governors consists of one Governor appointed by each member nation. Typically, a Governor is the country's finance minister, central bank governor, or a minister or an official of comparable rank. The Board normally meets once a year.

EXECUTIVE DIRECTORS

With the exception of certain powers specifically reserved to them by the Articles of Agreement, the Governors of the Bank have delegated their powers for the conduct of the general operations of the World Bank to a Board of Executive Directors which performs its duties on a full-time basis at the Bank's headquarters. There are 24 Executive Directors (see table below); each Director selects an Alternate. Five Directors are appointed by the five members having the largest number of shares of capital stock, and the rest are elected by the Governors representing the other members. The President of the Bank is Chairman of the Board.

The Executive Directors fulfill dual responsibilities. First, they represent the interests of their country or groups of countries. Second, they exercise their authority as delegated by the Governors in overseeing the policies of the Bank and evaluating completed projects. Since the Bank operates on the basis of consensus (formal votes are rare), this dual role involves frequent communication and consultations with governments so as to reflect accurately their views in Board discussions.

The Directors consider and decide on Bank policy and on all loan and credit proposals. They are also responsible for presentation to the Board of Governors at its Annual Meetings of an audit of accounts, an administrative budget, the *Annual Report* on the operations and policies of the World Bank, and any other matter that, in their judgement, requires submission to the Board of Governors. Matters may be submitted to the Governors at the Annual Meetings or at any time between Annual Meetings.

PRINCIPAL OFFICERS

The principal officers of the Bank are the President of the Bank, four Managing Directors, two Senior Vice-Presidents and 23 Vice-Presidents.

President and Chairman of Executive Directors: JAMES D. WOLFENSOHN (USA).

Managing Directors: SHENGMAN ZHANG (People's Republic of China), PETER L. WOICKE (Germany), JEFFREY GOLDSTEIN (USA), Dr MAMPHELA RAMPHELE (South Africa).

Vice-President and Corporate Secretary: CHEIKH IBRAHIMA FALL (Senegal).

Activities

FINANCIAL OPERATIONS

IBRD capital is derived from members' subscriptions to capital shares, the calculation of which is based on their quotas in the International Monetary Fund (q.v.). At 30 June 2002 the total subscribed capital of the IBRD was US $189,505m., of which the paid-in portion was $11,476m. (6.1%); the remainder is subject to call if required. Most of the IBRD's lendable funds come from its borrowing, on commercial terms, in world capital markets, and also from its retained earnings and the flow of repayments on its loans. IBRD loans carry a variable interest rate, rather than a rate fixed at the time of borrowing.

IBRD loans usually have a 'grace period' of five years and are repayable over 15 years or fewer. Loans are made to governments, or must be guaranteed by the government concerned, and are normally made for projects likely to offer a commercially viable rate of return. In 1980 the World Bank introduced structural adjustment lending, which (instead of financing specific projects) supports programmes and changes necessary to modify the structure of an economy so that it can restore or maintain its growth and viability in its balance of payments over the medium term.

The IBRD and IDA together made 229 new lending and investment commitments totalling US $19,519.4m. during the year ending 30 June 2002, compared with 225 (amounting to $17,250.6m.) in the previous year. During 2001/02 the IBRD alone approved commitments totalling $11,451.8m. (compared with $10,487.1m. in the previous year), of which $4,894.7m. (43%) was allocated to Europe and Central Asia and $4,188.1m. (37%) to Latin America and the Caribbean (see table). Disbursements by the IBRD in the year ending 30 June 2002 amounted to $11,256m. (For details of IDA operations, see separate chapter on IDA.)

IBRD operations are supported by medium- and long-term borrowings in international capital markets. During the year ending 30 June 2002 the IBRD's net income amounted to US $2,778m.

The World Bank's primary objectives are the achievement of sustainable economic growth and the reduction of poverty in developing countries. In the context of stimulating economic growth the Bank promotes both private-sector development and human resource development and has attempted to respond to the growing demands by developing countries for assistance in these areas. In March 1997 the Board of Executive Directors endorsed a 'Strategic Compact', providing for a programme of reforms, to be implemented over a period of 30 months, to increase the effectiveness of the Bank in achieving its central objective of poverty reduction. The reforms included greater decentralization of decision-making, and investment in front-line operations, enhancing the administration of loans, and improving access to information and co-ordination of Bank activities through a knowledge management system comprising four thematic networks: the Human Development Network; the Environmentally and Socially Sustainable Development Network;

the Finance, Private Sector and Infrastructure Development Network; and the Poverty Reduction and Economic Management Network. In 2000/01 the Bank adopted a new two-year Strategic Framework which emphasized two essential approaches for Bank support: strengthening the investment climate and prospects for sustainable development in a country, and supporting investment in the poor. In September 2001 the Bank announced that it was to join the UN as a full partner in implementing the so-called Millennium Development Goals, and was to make them central to its development agenda. The objectives, which were approved by governments attending a special session of the UN General Assembly in September 2000, included a reduction by 50% in the number of people with an income of less than US $1 a day and those suffering from hunger and lack of safe drinking water by 2015. The Bank was closely involved in preparations for the International Conference on Financing for Development, which was held in Monterrey, Mexico, in March 2002. The meeting adopted the Monterrey Consensus, which outlined measures to support national development efforts and to achieve the Millennium Development Goals.

The Bank's efforts to reduce poverty include the compilation of country-specific assessments and the formulation of country assistance strategies (CASs) to review and guide the Bank's country programmes. Since August 1998 the Bank has published CASs, with the approval of the government concerned. In 1998/99 the Bank's Executive Directors endorsed a Comprehensive Development Framework (CDF) to effect a new approach to development assistance based on partnerships and country responsibility, with an emphasis on the interdependence of the social, structural, human, governmental, economic and environmental elements of development. The Framework, which aimed to enhance the overall effectiveness of development assistance, was formulated after a series of consultative meetings organized by the Bank and attended by representatives of governments, donor agencies, financial institutions, non-governmental organizations, the private sector and academics.

In December 1999 the Bank introduced a new approach to implement the principles of the CDF, as part of its strategy to enhance the debt relief scheme for heavily indebted poor countries (see below). Applicant countries were requested to formulate a national strategy to reduce poverty, to be presented in the form of a Poverty Reduction Strategy Papers (PRSP). In cases where there might be some delay in issuing a full PRSP, it was permissible for a country to submit a less detailed 'interim' PRSP (I-PRSP) in order to secure the preliminary qualification for debt relief. During 2001/02 seven countries completed PRSPs and nine countries issued interim papers. In 2000/01 the Bank introduced a new Poverty Reduction Support Credit to help low-income countries to implement the policy and institutional reforms outlined in their PRSP. The first credits were approved for Uganda and Viet Nam in May and June respectively. In January 2002 a PRSP public review conference, attended by more than 200 representatives of donor agencies, civil society groups, and developing country organizations was held as part of an ongoing review of the scheme by the Bank and the IMF.

In September 1996 the World Bank/IMF Development Committee endorsed a joint initiative to assist heavily indebted poor countries (HIPCs) to reduce their debt burden to a sustainable level, in order to make more resources available for poverty reduction and economic growth. A new Trust Fund was established by the World Bank in November to finance the initiative. The Fund, consisting of an initial allocation of US $500m. from the IBRD surplus and other contributions from multilateral creditors, was to be administered by IDA. Of the 41 HIPCs identified by the Bank, 33 were in sub-Saharan Africa. In April 1997 the World Bank and the IMF announced that Uganda was to be the first beneficiary of the initiative, enabling the Ugandan Government to reduce its external debt by some 20%, or an estimated $338m. In early 1999 the World Bank and IMF initiated a comprehensive review of the HIPC initiative. By April meetings of the Group of Seven industrialized nations (G-7) and of the governing bodies of the Bank and IMF indicated a consensus that the scheme needed to be amended and strengthened, in order to allow more countries to benefit from the initiative, to accelerate the process by which a country may qualify for assistance, and to enhance the effectiveness of debt relief. In June the G-7 and Russia, meeting in Cologne, Germany, agreed to increase contributions to the HIPC Trust Fund and to cancel substantial amounts of outstanding debt, and proposed more flexible terms for eligibility. In September the Bank and IMF reached an agreement on an enhanced HIPC scheme, with further revenue to be generated through the revaluation of a percentage of IMF gold reserves. Under the enhanced initiative it was agreed that, during the initial phase of the process to ensure suitability for debt relief, each applicant country should formulate a PRSP, and should demonstrate prudent financial management in the implementation of the strategy for at least one year, with support from the IDA and IMF. At the pivotal 'decision point' of the process, having thus developed and successfully applied the poverty reduction strategy, applicant countries still deemed to have an unsustainable level of debt were to qualify for interim debt relief from the IMF and IDA, as well as relief on

EXECUTIVE DIRECTORS AND THEIR VOTING POWER (30 June 2002)

Executive Director	Casting Votes of	IBRD Total votes	IBRD % of total	IDA Total votes	IDA % of total
Appointed:					
CAROLE BROOKINS	USA	265,219	16.45	1,913,640	14.52
YUZO HARADA	Japan	127,250	7.89	1,461,212	11.09
ECKHARD DEUTSCHER . . .	Germany	72,649	4.51	940,076	7.13
TOM SCHOLAR	United Kingdom	69,647	4.32	658,718	5.00
PIERRE DUQUESNE	France	69,647	4.32	579,342	4.40
Elected:					
PHILIPPE M. PEETERS (Belgium)	Austria, Belarus*, Belgium, Czech Republic, Hungary, Kazakhstan, Luxembourg, Slovakia, Slovenia, Turkey	77,669	4.82	592,203	4.49
MOISES PINEDA (Mexico) . .	Costa Rica, El Salvador, Guatemala, Honduras, Mexico, Nicaragua, Spain, Venezuela*	72,786	4.51	291,969	2.22
PIETER STEK (Netherlands) . .	Armenia, Bosnia and Herzegovina, Bulgaria*, Croatia, Cyprus, Georgia, Israel, the former Yugoslav republic of Macedonia, Moldova, Netherlands, Romania*, Ukraine*	72,208	4.48	478,024	3.63
TERRIE O'LEARY (Canada) . .	Antigua and Barbuda*, The Bahamas*, Barbados, Belize, Canada, Dominica, Grenada, Guyana, Ireland, Jamaica*, Saint Christopher and Nevis, Saint Lucia, Saint Vincent and the Grenadines	62,217	3.86	560,547	4.25
JAIME RUIZ (Colombia) . .	Brazil, Colombia, Dominican Republic, Ecuador, Haiti, Panama, Philippines, Suriname*, Trinidad and Tobago	58,124	3.61	392,696	2.98
FRANCO PASSACANTANDO (Italy). .	Albania, Greece, Italy, Malta*, Portugal, San Marino*	55,938	3.47	517,721	3.93
NEIL F. HYDEN (Australia) .	Australia, Cambodia, Kiribati, Republic of Korea, Marshall Islands, Federated States of Micronesia, Mongolia, New Zealand, Palau, Papua New Guinea, Samoa, Solomon Islands, Vanuatu	55,800	3.46	396,886	3.01
C. M. VASUDEV† (India) . .	Bangladesh, Bhutan, India, Sri Lanka	54,945	3.41	546,804	4.15
AHMED SADOUDI (Algeria). .	Algeria, Ghana, Iran, Iraq, Morocco, Pakistan, Tunisia	54,052	3.35	253,710	1.93
FINN JØNCK (Denmark) . .	Denmark, Estonia*, Finland, Iceland, Latvia, Lithuania*, Norway, Sweden	54,039	3.35	652,246	4.95
GIRMAI ABRAHAM (Eritrea) . .	Angola, Botswana, Burundi, Eritrea, The Gambia, Kenya, Lesotho, Liberia, Malawi, Mozambique, Namibia*, Nigeria, Seychelles*, Sierra Leone, South Africa, Sudan, Swaziland, Tanzania, Uganda, Zambia, Zimbabwe	53,962	3.35	476,109	3.61
PIETRO VEGLIO (Switzerland) .	Azerbaijan, Kyrgyzstan, Poland, Switzerland, Tajikistan, Turkmenistan*, Uzbekistan	46,096	2.86	467,821	3.55
ZU GUANGYAO	People's Republic of China	45,049	2.79	247,345	1.88
YAHYA ABDULLAH M. ALYAHYA .	Saudi Arabia	45,045	2.79	471,464	3.58
ALEXY G. KVASOV‡	Russia	45,045	2.79	35,991	0.27
MAHDY ISMAIL ALJAZZAF (Kuwait)	Bahrain*, Egypt, Jordan, Kuwait, Lebanon, Libya, Maldives, Oman, Qatar*, Syria, United Arab Emirates, Yemen	43,984	2.73	283,980	2.16
ABDUL AZIZ M. YAACOB (Malaysia).	Brunei*, Fiji, Indonesia, Laos, Malaysia, Myanmar, Nepal, Singapore*, Thailand, Tonga, Viet Nam	41,096	2.55	345,372	2.62
MARIO SOTO-PLATERO (Uruguay) .	Argentina, Bolivia, Chile, Paraguay, Peru, Uruguay*	37,499	2.33	237,131	1.80
BASSARY TOURÉ (Mali). . . .	Benin, Burkina Faso, Cameroon, Cape Verde, Central African Republic, Chad, Comoros, Democratic Republic of the Congo, Republic of the Congo, Côte d'Ivoire, Djibouti, Equatorial Guinea, Gabon, Guinea, Guinea-Bissau, Madagascar, Mali, Mauritania, Mauritius, Niger, Rwanda, São Tomé and Príncipe, Senegal, Togo	32,252	2.00	374,898	2.85

Note: Afghanistan (550 votes in IBRD and 13,557 in IDA), Ethiopia (1,228 votes in IBRD and 23,053 in IDA) and Somalia (802 votes in IBRD and 10,506 in IDA) did not participate in the 2000 regular election of Executive Directors. Serbia and Montenegro (1,847 votes in IBRD and 25,109 in IDA) and Timor-Leste (767 votes in IBRD and 558 in IDA) became members after that election.

* Member of IBRD only (not IDA).
† Took office 1 August 2002.
‡ Took office 1 July 2002.

highly concessional terms from other official bilateral creditors and multilateral institutions. During the ensuing 'interim period' countries were required successfully to implement further economic and social development reforms, as a final demonstration of suitability for securing full debt relief at the 'completion point' of the scheme. Data produced at the decision point was to form the base for calculating the final debt relief (in contrast to the original initiative, which based its calculations on projections of a country's debt stock at the completion point). In the majority of cases a sustainable level of debt was targeted at 150% of the net present value (NPV) of the debt in relation to total annual exports (compared with 200%–250% under the original initiative). Other countries with a lower debt-to-export ratio were to be eligible for assistance under the scheme, providing that their export earnings were at least 30% of GDP (lowered from 40% under the original initiative) and government revenue at least 15% of GDP (reduced from 20%). At November 2002 six countries (Bolivia, Burkina Faso, Mauritania, Mozambique, Tanzania and Uganda) had reached completion point under the enhanced HIPC initiative, while 21 countries had reached their decision point (including Côte d'Ivoire, reached under the original scheme). At that time total assistance committed under the HIPC initiative amounted to $25,102m., or $41,520m. in total estimated nominal debt service relief, of which the Bank's share was $6,394m.

During 2000/01 the World Bank strengthened its efforts to counter the problem of HIV and AIDS in developing countries. In September 2000 a new Multi-Country HIV/AIDS Programme for Africa (MAP) was launched, in collaboration with UNAIDS and other major donor agencies and non-governmental organizations. Some US $500m. was allocated to the initiative and was used to support efforts in seven countries. In February 2002 the Bank approved an additional $500m. for a second phase of MAP, which was envisaged to assist HIV/AIDS schemes in a further 12 countries, as well as regional activities. During 2000/01 the Bank also approved two operations under an HIV/AIDS initiative for the Caribbean. In November 2001 the Bank appointed its first Global HIV/AIDS Adviser.

In addition to providing financial services, the Bank also undertakes analytical and advisory services, and supports learning and capacity-building, in particular through the World Bank Institute (see below), the Staff Exchange Programme and knowledge-sharing initiatives. The Bank has supported efforts, such as the Global Development Gateway, to disseminate information on development issues and programmes

TECHNICAL ASSISTANCE

The provision of technical assistance to member countries has become a major component of World Bank activities. The economic and sector work (ESW) undertaken by the Bank is the vehicle for considerable technical assistance. In addition, project loans and credits may include funds earmarked specifically for feasibility studies, resource surveys, management or planning advice, and training. The Economic Development Institute has become one of the most important of the Bank's activities in technical assistance. It provides training in national economic management and project analysis for government officials at the middle and upper levels of responsibility. It also runs overseas courses aiming to build up local training capability, and administers a graduate scholarship programme.

The Bank serves as an executing agency for projects financed by the UN Development Programme. It also administers projects financed by various trust funds.

Technical assistance (usually reimbursable) is also extended to countries that do not need Bank financial support, e.g. for training and transfer of technology. The Bank encourages the use of local consultants to assist with projects and stimulate institutional capability.

The Project Preparation Facility (PPF) was established in 1975 to provide cash advances to prepare projects that may be financed by the Bank. In December 1994 the PPF's commitment authority was increased from US $220m. to $250m. In 1992 the Bank established an Institutional Development Fund (IDF), which became operational on 1 July; the purpose of the Fund was to provide rapid, small-scale financial assistance, to a maximum value of $500,000, for capacity-building proposals.

In March 1996 a new programme to co-ordinate development efforts in Africa was announced by the UN Secretary-General. The World Bank was to facilitate the mobilization of the estimated US $25,000m. required to achieve the objectives of the Special Initiative over a 10-year period. In addition, the Bank was to provide technical assistance to enable countries to devise economic plans (in particular following a period of civil conflict), agricultural development programmes and a common strategy for African countries to strengthen the management capacities of the public sector.

ECONOMIC RESEARCH AND STUDIES

In the 1990s the World Bank's research, conducted by its own research staff, was increasingly concerned with providing information to reinforce the Bank's expanding advisory role to developing countries and to improve policy in the Bank's borrowing countries. The principal areas of current research focus on issues such as maintaining sustainable growth while protecting the environment and the poorest sectors of society, encouraging the development of the private sector, and reducing and decentralizing government activities.

Consultative Group on International Agricultural Research—CGIAR: founded in 1971 under the sponsorship of the World Bank, FAO and UNDP. (In 1995 UNEP was invited to become the fourth sponsoring member, and in 2001/02 IFAD became a co-sponsor.) The Bank is chairman of the Group (which includes governments, private foundations and multilateral development agencies) and provides its secretariat. The Group was formed to raise financial support for international agricultural research work for improving crops and animal production in the developing countries; it supports 16 research centres. Its work is focused on the following five research areas: increasing productivity; protecting the environment; saving biodiversity; improving policies; and strengthening national research. In 2001 member contributions amounted to US $336m. Dir FRANCISCO REIFSCHNEIDER (Brazil).

CO-OPERATION WITH OTHER ORGANIZATIONS

The World Bank co-operates closely with other UN bodies, at the project level, particularly in the design of social funds and social action programmes. It collaborates with the IMF in implementing economic adjustment programmes in developing countries. The Bank holds regular consultations with the European Union and OECD on development issues, and the Bank-NGO Committee provides an annual forum for discussion with non-governmental organizations (NGOs). In September 1995 the Bank initiated the Information for Development Programme (InfoDev) with the aim of fostering partnerships between governments, multilateral institutions and private-sector experts in order to promote reform and investment in developing countries through improved access to information technology. Strengthening co-operation with external partners was a fundamental element of the Comprehensive Development Framework, which was adopted in 1998/99 (see above). In

2001/02 a Partnership Approval and Tracking System was implemented to provide information on the Bank's regional and global partnerships.

In June 1995 the World Bank joined other international donors (including regional development banks, other UN bodies, Canada, France, the Netherlands and the USA) in establishing a Consultative Group to Assist the Poorest (CGAP), which was to channel funds to the most needy through grass-roots agencies. An initial credit of approximately US $200m. was committed by the donors. The Bank manages the CGAP Secretariat, which is responsible for the administration of external funding and for the evaluation and approval of project financing. The CGAP provides technical assistance, training and strategic advice to microfinance institutions and other relevant bodies. As an implementing agency of the Global Environment Facility (GEF, see p. 48) the Bank assists countries to prepare and supervise GEF projects relating to biological diversity, climate change and other environmental protection measures.

In 1997 a Partnerships Group was established to strengthen the Bank's work with development institutions, representatives of civil society and the private sector. The Group established a new Development Grant Facility, which became operational in October, to support partnership initiatives and to co-ordinate all of the Bank's grant-making activities. Also in 1997 the Bank, in partnership with the IMF, UNCTAD, UNDP, the World Trade Organization (WTO) and International Trade Commission, established an Integrated Framework for Trade-related Assistance to Least Developed Countries, at the request of the WTO, to assist those countries to integrate into the global trading system and improve basic trading capabilities.

The Bank is a lead organization in providing reconstruction assistance following natural disasters or conflicts, usually in collaboration with other UN agencies or international organizations, and through special trust funds. In April 1999 the World Bank and the IMF convened an international meeting of governments and agencies to review the immediate response of the international community to meet the humanitarian, economic and financial needs of the six Balkan countries most affected by the conflict in Kosovo and Metohija, a southern province of Serbia (then Federal Republic of Yugoslavia—FRY, now Serbia and Montenegro). The meeting also aimed to consider areas for future co-operation and measures to promote economic recovery and growth in those countries. In July the World Bank and European Commission organized an international conference to mobilize funds for post-conflict rehabilitation in Kosovo. A new trust fund for the FRY became operational in 2000/01. The Bank is a trustee, with the Asian Development Bank, of the Trust Fund for East Timor, which was established in December 1999, with donations of some US $147m., to channel support during the transition towards independence. In November 2001 the Bank worked with UNDP and the Asian Development Bank to assess the needs of Afghanistan following the removal of the Taliban authorities in that country. At an International Conference on Reconstruction Assistance to Afghanistan, held in Tokyo, Japan, in January 2002, the Bank's President proposed extending US $500m. in assistance over a 30-month period, and providing an immediate amount of $50m.–$70m. in grants. In May an Afghanistan Reconstruction Trust Fund was established to provide a co-ordinated financing mechanism to support the interim administration in that country. The Bank is the Administrator of the Trust, which is managed jointly by the Bank, Asian Development Bank, Islamic Development Bank and the UNDP.

The Bank conducts co-financing and aid co-ordination projects with official aid agencies, export credit institutions, and commercial banks. During the year ending 30 June 2002 a total of 109 IBRD and IDA projects involved co-financers' contributions amounting to US $4,700m., or 26% of total bank lending.

EVALUATION

The Operations Evaluation Department is an independent unit within the World Bank, which studies and publishes the results of projects after a loan has been fully disbursed, so as to identify problems and possible improvements in future activities. In 1996 a Quality Assurance Group was established to monitor the effectiveness of the Bank's operations and performance.

In September 1993 the Bank's Board of Executive Directors agreed to establish an independent Inspection Panel, consistent with the Bank's objective of improving project implementation and accountability. The panel, which became operational in September 1994, was to conduct independent investigations and report on complaints concerning the design, appraisal and implementation of development projects supported by the Bank. By mid-2002 the panel had received 26 formal requests for inspection. In 2001/02 the Panel received three new requests for inspection, relating to power projects in Uganda, a loan scheme in Papua New Guinea, and infrastructure projects in Paraguay and Argentina.

IBRD INSTITUTIONS

World Bank Institute—WBI: founded in March 1999 by merger of the Bank's Learning and Leadership Centre, previously responsible for internal staff training, and the Economic Development Institute (EDI), which had been established in 1955 to train government officials concerned with development programmes and policies. The new Institute aimed to emphasize the Bank's priority areas through the provision of training courses and seminars relating to poverty, crisis response, good governance and anti-corruption strategies. The Institute co-ordinated a process of consultation and dialogue with researchers and other representatives of civil society to examine poverty for the 2000/01 *World Development Report*. During 1999/2000 the WBI expanded its programmes through distance learning, global knowledge networks, and use of new technologies. Under the EDI a World Links for Development programme was initiated to connect schools in developing countries with partner establishments in industrialized nations via the internet. A new initiative, Global Development Learning Network (GDLN), aimed to expand access to information and learning opportunities through the internet, videoconferences and organized exchanges. At mid-2002 37 GDLN distance learning centers were operational and 42 sites were under development. Vice-Pres. FRANNIE LÉAUTIER (Tanzania/France).

International Centre for Settlement of Investment Disputes—ICSID: founded in 1966 under the Convention of the Settlement of Investment Disputes between States and Nationals of Other States. The Convention was designed to encourage the growth of private foreign investment for economic development, by creating the possibility, always subject to the consent of both parties, for a Contracting State and a foreign investor who is a national of another Contracting State to settle any legal dispute that might arise out of such an investment by conciliation and/or arbitration before an impartial, international forum. The governing body of the Centre is its Administrative Council, composed of one representative of each Contracting State, all of whom have equal voting power. The President of the World Bank is (*ex officio*) the non-voting Chairman of the Administrative Council.

At December 2002 136 countries had signed and ratified the Convention to become ICSID Contracting States. At that time the Centre had considered 68 cases, while 46 were pending. Sec.-Gen. KO-YUNG TUNG (Japan).

Publications

Abstracts of Current Studies: The World Bank Research Program (annually).

Annual Report on Operations Evaluation.

Annual Report on Portfolio Performance.

Annual Review of Development Effectiveness.

EDI Annual Report.

Global Commodity Markets (quarterly).

Global Development Finance (annually, also on CD-Rom and online).

Global Economic Prospects (annually).

ICSID Annual Report.

ICSID Review—Foreign Investment Law Journal (2 a year).

Joint BIS-IMF-OECD-World Bank Statistics on External Debt (quarterly, also available on the internet at www.worldbank.org/data/jointdebt.html).

New Products and Outreach (EDI, annually).

News from ICSID (2 a year).

Poverty Reduction Strategies Newsletter (quarterly).

Research News (quarterly).

Staff Working Papers.

Transition (every 2 months).

World Bank Annual Report.

World Bank Atlas (annually).

World Bank Economic Review (3 a year).

The World Bank and the Environment (annually).

World Bank Research Observer.

World Development Indicators (annually, also on CD-Rom and online).

World Development Report (annually, also on CD-Rom).

World Bank Statistics

LENDING OPERATIONS, BY SECTOR
(projects approved, year ending 30 June; US $ million)

	2001	2002
Agriculture, fishing and forestry	695.5	1,247.9
Education	1,094.7	1,384.6
Energy and mining	1,530.7	1,974.6
Finance	2,253.4	2,862.4
Health and other social services	2,521.2	2,366.1
Industry and trade	718.3	1,394.5
Information and communication	216.9	153.2
Law, justice and public administration	3,843.0	5,199.6
Transportation	3,105.2	2,390.1
Water, sanitation and flood protection	1,271.1	546.0
Total	17,250.6	19,519.4

IBRD INCOME AND EXPENDITURE
(US $ million, year ending 30 June)

Revenue	2001	2002
Income from loans:		
Interest	8,052	6,779
Commitment charges	91	82
Income from investments and securities	1,701	831
Other income	171	184
Total income	10,015	7,876

Expenditure	2001	2002
Interest on borrowings	7,021	4,793
Amortization of issuance and prepayment costs	131	110
Interest on securities sold under repurchase agreements and payable-for-cash collateral received	6	4
Administrative expenses	881	876
Contributions to special programmes	147	176
Provision for loan losses	676	-15
Other financial expenses	9	8
Total	8,871	5,952
Operating income	1,144	1,924
Effects of adjustment and accounting charge	345	854
Net income	1,489	2,778

IBRD LOANS AND IDA CREDITS APPROVED, BY SECTOR AND REGION (1 July 2001–30 June 2002; US $ million)

Sector	Africa	East Asia and Pacific	South Asia	Europe and Central Asia	Latin America and the Caribbean	Middle East and North Africa	Total
Agriculture, fishing and forestry.	210.4	151.2	328.1	470.4	85.0	75.2	1,247.9
Education	472.6	134.6	95.9	83.2	560.4	2.9	1,384.6
Energy and mining	490.3	314.5	504.8	218.0	445.6	1.3	1,974.6
Finance	192.8	219.2	310.0	1,295.9	734.1	110.5	2,862.4
Health and other social services	616.6	243.8	278.7	524.7	660.5	41.7	2,366.1
Industry and trade	266.7	9.4	443.1	552.1	51.4	71.7	1,394.5
Information and communication	33.8	11.1	12.4	9.6	16.5	69.9	153.2
Law, justice and public administration . . .	906.9	115.2	632.5	2,170.9	1,299.5	74.7	5,199.6
Transportation	491.1	540.2	758.1	67.1	463.1	70.9	2,390.1
Water, sanitation and flood protection . .	112.2	34.4	144.9	131.7	49.8	73.1	546.0
Total	**3,793.5**	**1,773.6**	**3,508.4**	**5,523.6**	**4,365.8**	**554.5**	**19,519.4**
of which: IBRD	41.8	982.4	893.0	4,894.7	4,188.1	451.8	11,451.8
IDA	3,751.6	791.2	2,615.4	628.9	177.8	102.7	8,067.6
Number of operations	65	27	22	48	53	14	229

IBRD OPERATIONS AND RESOURCES, 1998–2002 (US $ million, years ending 30 June)

	1997/98	1998/99	1999/2000	2000/01	2001/02
Loans approved	21,086	22,182	10,919	10,487	11,452
Gross disbursements	19,232	18,205	10,918	11,784	11,256
New medium- to long-term borrowings . .	27,748	21,846	15,206	17,223	22,803
Net income	1,243	1,518	1,991	1,489	2,778
Subscribed capital	186,436	188,220	188,606	189,505	189,505
Net loans and callable guarantees outstanding . .	106,947	117,694	117,181	115,390	117,984

Source: *World Bank Annual Report 2002.*

International Development Association—IDA

Address: 1818 H Street, NW, Washington, DC 20433, USA.
Telephone: (202) 477-1234; **fax:** (202) 477-6391; **internet:** www.worldbank.org/ida.
The International Development Association began operations in November 1960. Affiliated to the IBRD (see above), IDA advances capital to the poorer developing member countries on more flexible terms than those offered by the IBRD.

MEMBERS

164 members: see Table on pp. 125–127.

Organization

(April 2003)

Officers and staff of the IBRD serve concurrently as officers and staff of IDA.
President and Chairman of Executive Directors: JAMES D. WOLFENSOHN (*ex officio*).

Activities

IDA assistance is aimed at the poorer developing countries (i.e. those with an annual GNP per capita of less than US $885 in 2001 dollars qualified for assistance in 2002/03). Under IDA lending conditions, credits can be extended to countries whose balance of payments could not sustain the burden of repayment required for IBRD loans. Terms are more favourable than those provided by the IBRD; credits are for a period of 35 or 40 years, with a 'grace period' of 10 years, and carry no interest charges. At mid-2002 81 countries were eligible for IDA assistance, including several small-island economies with a GNP per head greater than $885, but which would

otherwise have little or no access to Bank funds, and 14 so-called 'blend borrowers' (such as India), which are entitled to borrow from both the IDA and IBRD. IDA administers a Trust Fund, which was established in November 1996 as part of a World Bank/IMF initiative to assist heavily indebted poor countries (HIPCs, see IBRD).

IDA's total development resources, consisting of members' subscriptions and supplementary resources (additional subscriptions and contributions), are replenished periodically by contributions from the more affluent member countries. In November 1998 representatives of 39 donor countries agreed to provide US $11,600m. for the 12th replenishment of IDA funds, enabling total lending to amount to an estimated $20,500m. in the period July 1999–June 2002. The new IDA-12 resources were to be directed towards the following objectives: investing in people; promoting good governance; promoting broad-based growth; and protecting the environment. Discussions on the 13th replenishment of IDA funds commenced in February 2001, and for the first time involved representatives of borrowing countries, civil society and other public groups. A final commitment, providing for some US $23,000m. in resources in the period 1 July 2002–30 June 2005, was concluded in early July 2002.

During the year ending 30 June 2001 IDA credits totalling US $8,067.6m. were approved. Of total IDA assistance during that year, $3,751.6m. (46.5%) was for Africa and $2,615.4m. (32.4%) was for South Asia (see table above). The largest borrowers of IDA credits were India ($1,296.5m. for six projects), Pakistan ($800.0m. for two projects) and Viet Nam ($593.0m. for five projects). Some 70% of new lending was for investment projects, in particular for the provision of basic social services and public administration, some 25% was in the form of adjustment credits.

Publication

Annual Report.

IDA OPERATIONS AND RESOURCES, 1998–2002 (US $ million, years ending 30 June)

	1997/98	1998/99	1999/2000	2000/01	2001/02
Commitments*	7,508	6,812	4,358	6,764	8,068
Disbursements	5,630	6,023	5,177	5,492	6,612

* Excluding HIPC development grants.
Source: *World Bank Annual Report 2002*.

International Finance Corporation—IFC

Address: 2121 Pennsylvania Ave, NW, Washington, DC 20433, USA.

Telephone: (202) 473-9331; **fax:** (202) 974-4384; **e-mail:** information@ifc.org; **internet:** www.ifc.org.

IFC was founded in 1956 as a member of the World Bank Group to stimulate economic growth in developing countries by financing private-sector investments, mobilizing capital in international financial markets, and providing technical assistance and advice to governments and businesses.

MEMBERS

175 members: see Table on pp. 125–127.

Organization

(April 2003)

IFC is a separate legal entity in the World Bank Group. Executive Directors of the World Bank also serve as Directors of IFC. The President of the World Bank is *ex officio* Chairman of the IFC Board of Directors, which has appointed him President of IFC. Subject to his overall supervision, the day-to-day operations of IFC are conducted by its staff under the direction of the Executive Vice-President.

PRINCIPAL OFFICERS

President: JAMES D. WOLFENSOHN (USA).
Executive Vice-President: PETER L. WOICKE (Germany).

REGIONAL AND INDUSTRY DEPARTMENTS

Seven Regional Departments cover: sub-Saharan Africa; East Asia and the Pacific; South Asia; Central and Eastern Europe; Southern Europe and Central Asia; Latin America and the Caribbean; and the Middle East and North Africa. These aim to develop strategies for member countries, promote businesses, and strengthen relations with governments and the private sector. The Industry Departments include Agribusiness; Global Financial Markets; Global Information and Communications Technologies (jointly managed with the World Bank); Global Manufacturing and Services; Health and Education; Infrastructure; Oil, Gas, Mining and Chemicals (jointly managed with the World Bank); Power; Private Equity and Investment Funds; Small and Medium Enterprises (jointly managed with the World Bank); Syndications and International Securities; and Trust Funds.

REGIONAL AND RESIDENT MISSIONS

There are Regional and Resident Missions in Argentina, Australia, Bolivia, Brazil, Cambodia, Cameroon, People's Republic of China, Colombia, Côte d'Ivoire, Egypt, Ghana, Guatemala, India, Japan, Kazakhstan, Kenya, Laos, Mauritius, Mexico, Nepal, Paraguay, Poland, Russia, South Africa, Turkey, Uruguay, Viet Nam and Zimbabwe. There are also Special Representatives in France, Germany and the United Kingdom (for Europe), and other programme co-ordinators, managers and investment officers in more than 30 additional countries.

Activities

IFC aims to promote economic development in developing member countries by assisting the growth of private enterprise and effective capital markets. It finances private sector projects, through loans, the purchase of equity, quasi-equity products, and risk management services, and assists governments to create conditions that stimulate the flow of domestic and foreign private savings and investment. IFC may provide finance for a project that is partly state-owned, provided that there is participation by the private sector and that the project is operated on a commercial basis. IFC also mobilizes additional resources from other financial institutions, in particular through syndicated loans, thus providing access to international capital markets. IFC provides a range of advisory services to help to improve the investment climate in developing countries and offers technical assistance to private enterprises and governments.

To be eligible for financing, projects must be profitable for investors, as well as financially and economically viable, must benefit the economy of the country concerned, and must comply with IFC's environmental and social guide-lines. IFC aims to promote best corporate governance and management methods and sustainable business practices, and encourages partnerships between governments, non-governmental organizations and community groups. In mid-2002 IFC published its first Sustainability Review, reflecting its emphasis on sustainability as a key strategic and corporate priority.

IFC's authorized capital is US $2,450m. At 30 June 2002 paid-in capital was $2,360m. The World Bank was originally the principal source of borrowed funds, but IFC also borrows from private capital markets. IFC's net income amounted to $215m. in 2001/02, compared with $345m. in the previous year.

In the year ending 30 June 2002 project financing approved by IFC amounted to US $5,835m. for 223 projects in 63 countries and regions (compared with $5,357m. for 240 projects in 77 countries in the previous year). Of the total approved, $4,006m. was for IFC's own account, while $1,829m. was in the form of loan syndications and underwriting of securities issues and investment funds by more than 100 participant banks and institutional investors. Generally, the IFC limits its financing to less than 25% of the total cost of a project, but may take up to a 35% stake in a venture (although never as a majority shareholder). Disbursements for IFC's account amounted to $1,498m. in 2001/02 (compared with $1,535m. in the previous year).

During 2001/02 total financing commitments for 204 new projects amounted to US $3,610m.. The largest proportion of commitments was allocated to Latin America and the Caribbean (41%); East Asia and the Pacific and Europe and Central Asia both received 21%, South Asia and sub-Saharan Africa 7%, and the Middle East and North Africa received 4%. The Corporation invests in a wide variety of business and financial institutions in a broad range of sectors. In 2001/02 more than one-third of total financing committed (34%) was for financial services. Other financing included transportation, warehousing and utilities (17%), information technologies (9%), construction and real estate (8%), and non-metallic mineral product manufacturing (6%).

IFC offers risk-management services, assisting institutions to avoid financial risks that arise from changes in interest rates, in exchange rates or in commodity prices. In 2001/02 IFC approved 11 risk-management projects for companies and banks, bringing the total number of projects approved since the introduction of the service in 1990 to 104 in 39 countries.

In 1999/2000 the IFC and World Bank advisory services were integrated into the Private Sector Advisory Services (PSAS). PSAS advises governments and private enterprises on policy, transaction implementation and foreign direct investment. The Foreign Investment Advisory Service (FIAS), established in 1986, provides advice on promoting foreign investment and strengthening the country's investment framework at the request of governments. During 2001/02 FIAS completed 50 advisory projects. Under the Technical Assistance Trust Funds Program (TATF), established in 1988, IFC manages resources contributed by various governments and agencies to provide finance for feasibility studies, project identification studies and other types of technical assistance relating to project preparation.

IFC has helped to establish several regional facilities which aim to assist small-scale entrepreneurs to develop business proposals and generate funding for their projects. For each of the facilities listed below IFC is the executing agency, and their activities are co-ordinated by the Small and Medium Enterprise (SME) Department.

The Africa Project Development Facility (APDF) was established in 1986 by IFC, UNDP and the African Development Bank, and has headquarters in Johannesburg, South Africa, with other offices in Cape Town (South Africa), Cameroon, Ghana, Kenya, and Nigeria. The Facility also promotes capacity-building for SMEs, local business associations and financial institutions. It works closely with the African Management Services Company (AMSCo, established in 1989, with headquarters in Amsterdam, the Netherlands) which helps to find qualified senior executives and technical personnel to work with African companies, assist in the training of local managers, and provide management support The South Pacific Project Facility, based in Sydney, Australia, was established in 1991, mainly to assist local businesses in the IFC Pacific Island member countries. A separate office in Port Moresby, Papua New Guinea, was opened in 1997. The Mekong Project Development Facility was inaugurated in 1995, and became operational in 1997, specifically to support the development of SMEs in Cambodia, Laos and Viet Nam.

IFC's SME Department also works with external donors to establish development facilities. In September 2000 the Southeast Europe Enterprise Development (SEED) initiative was formally launched at its headquarters in Sarajevo, Bosnia and Herzegovina, as a five-year scheme to support the development of the private-sector in Albania, Bosnia and Herzegovina, Kosovo, the former Yugoslav republic of Macedonia, and the Federal Republic of Yugoslavia (now Serbia and Montenegro). In June of that year the IFC approved the establishment of a China Project Development Facility to support the development of SMEs within the People's Republic of China. The Facility's headquarters in Chengdu, Sichuan Province, became operational in 2001/02. Both these initiatives highlighted the following three strategic targets: to provide support services at enterprise level; to assist the development of local private sector support institutions; and to advocate ways to improve the business-enabling environment. Also in 2000 a Private Enterprise Partnership, jointly funded by IFC and donor governments, was initiated to implement programmes to develop financial markets in the former Soviet Union, as well as to improve corporate governance practices and business support services in order to enhance the investment and business environment. An SME Capacity Building Facility provides financial support for local projects and development facilities which aim to stimulate small business growth.

Publications

Annual Report.
Emerging Stock Markets Factbook (annually).
Impact (quarterly).
Lessons of Experience (series).
Results on the Ground (series).
Review of Small Businesses (annually).
Discussion papers and technical documents.

IFC OPERATIONS AND RESOURCES, 1993–2002 (fiscal years ending 30 June)

	1993	1994	1995	1996	1997	1998	1999	2000	2001	2002
Approved investments										
Number of new projects	185	231	213	264	276	304	255	259	239	223
Total financing (US $ million)	3,936	4,287	5,467	8,118	6,722	5,905	5,280	5,846	5,357	5,835
Total project costs* (US $ million)	17,422	15,839	19,352	19,633	17,945	15,726	15,578	21,136	16,747	15,514
Disbursements (IFC's own account, US $ million)	1,106	1,537	1,808	2,053	2,003	2,054	2,102	2,210	1,535	1,498
Resources and income (US $ million)										
Borrowings	5,565	6,531	7,993	8,956	10,123	11,162	12,429	14,919	15,457	16,581
Paid-in capital	1,423	1,658	1,875	2,076	2,229	2,337	2,350	2,358	2,360	2,360
Retained earnings	1,280	1,538	1,726	2,071	2,503	2,749	2,998	3,378	3,723	3,938
Net income	142	258	188	346	432	246	249	380	345	215

* Including investment mobilized from other sources.
Source: *IFC Annual Report 2002.*

Multilateral Investment Guarantee Agency—MIGA

Address: 1818 H Street, NW, Washington, DC 20433, USA.
Telephone: (202) 473-6163; **fax:** (202) 522-2630; **internet:** www.miga.org.
MIGA was founded in 1988 as an affiliate of the World Bank. Its mandate is to encourage the flow of foreign direct investment to, and among, developing member countries, through the provision of political risk insurance and investment marketing services to foreign investors and host governments, respectively.

MEMBERS

MIGA has 161 member countries. Membership is open to all countries that are members of the World Bank.

Organization
(April 2003)

MIGA is legally and financially separate from the World Bank. It is supervised by a Council of Governors (comprising one Governor and one Alternate of each member country) and an elected Board of Directors (of no less than 12 members).
President: JAMES D. WOLFENSOHN (USA).
Executive Vice-President: MOTOMICHI IKAWA (Japan).

Activities

The convention establishing MIGA took effect in April 1988. Authorized capital was US $1,082m. In April 1998 the Board of Directors approved an increase in MIGA's capital base. A grant of $150m. was transferred from the IBRD as part of the package, while the capital increase (totalling $700m. callable capital and $150m. paid-in capital) was approved by MIGA's Council of Governors in April 1999. A three-year subscription period then commenced, covering the period April 1999–March 2002. At 30 June 2002 total subscriptions to the capital stock amounted to $1,713m., of which $328m. was paid-in.

MIGA guarantees eligible investments against losses resulting from non-commercial risks, under four main categories:

(i) transfer risk resulting from host government restrictions on currency conversion and transfer;

(ii) risk of loss resulting from legislative or administrative actions of the host government;

(iii) repudiation by the host government of contracts with investors in cases in which the investor has no access to a competent forum;

(iv) the risk of armed conflict and civil unrest.

Before guaranteeing any investment, MIGA must ensure that it is commercially viable, contributes to the development process and is not harmful to the environment. During the fiscal year 1998/99 MIGA and IFC appointed the first Compliance Advisor and Ombudsman to consider the concerns of local communities directly affected by MIGA or IFC sponsored projects. In February 1999 the Board of Directors approved an increase in the amount of political risk insurance available for each project, from US $75m. to $200m.

During the year ending 30 June 2002 MIGA issued 58 investment insurance contracts for 33 projects in 24 countries with a value of US $1,357m., compared with 66 contracts valued at $2,000m. in the previous financial year. The amount of direct investment associated with the contracts in 2001/02 totalled approximately $4,700m. (compared with $5,200m. in 2000/01), bringing the total estimate investment facilitated since 1988 to $45,800m. through 597 contracts.

MIGA administers two investment guarantee trust funds, for Bosnia and Herzegovina and for the West Bank and Gaza Strip, to underwrite investment in post-conflict reconstruction activities.

MIGA also provides policy and advisory services to promote foreign investment in developing countries and in transitional economies, and disseminates information on investment opportunities. In October 1995 MIGA established a new network on investment opportunities, which connected investment promotion agencies (IPAs) throughout the world on an electronic information network. The so-called IPA*net* aimed to encourage further investments among developing countries, to provide access to comprehensive information on investment laws and conditions and to strengthen links between governmental, business and financial associations and investors. A new version of IPA*net* was launched in 1997 (and can be accessed at www.ipanet.net). In June 1998 MIGA initiated a new internet-based facility, 'PrivatizationLink', to provide information on investment opportunities resulting from the privatization of industries in developing economies. In October 2000 a specialized facility within the service was established to facilitate investment in Russia (russia.privatizationlink.com). During 2000/01 an office was established in Paris, France, to promote and co-ordinate European investment in developing countries, in particular in Africa and Eastern Europe. In September 2002 a new regional office was inaugurated in Singapore, in order to facilitate foreign investment in Asia. In April MIGA launched a new service, 'FDIXchange', to provide potential investors, advisors and financial institutions with up-to-date market analysis and information on foreign direct investment opportunities in emerging economies (accessible at www.fdixchange.com).

Publications

Annual Report.
Investment Promotion Quarterly (electronic news update).
MIGA News (quarterly).

International Civil Aviation Organization—ICAO

Address: 999 University St, Montreal, QC H3C 5H7, Canada.
Telephone: (514) 954-8219; **fax:** (514) 954-6077; **e-mail:** icaohq@icao.int; **internet:** www.icao.int.

The Convention on International Civil Aviation was signed in Chicago in 1944. As a result, ICAO was founded in 1947 to develop the techniques of international air navigation and to help in the planning and improvement of international air transport.

MEMBERS

188 members: see Table on pp. 125–127.

Organization

(April 2003)

ASSEMBLY

Composed of representatives of all member states, the Assembly is the organization's legislative body and meets at least once every three years. It reviews the work of the organization, sets out the work programme for the next three years, approves the budget and determines members' contributions. The 33rd Assembly was held in September/October 2001.

COUNCIL

Composed of representatives of 33 member states, elected by the Assembly. It is the executive body, and establishes and supervises subsidiary technical committees and makes recommendations to member governments; meets in virtually continuous session; elects the President, appoints the Secretary-General, and administers the finances of the organization. The Council is assisted by the Air Navigation Commission (on technical matters), the Air Transport Committee (on economic matters), the Committee on Joint Support of Air Navigation Services and the Finance Committee. The functions of the Council are:

 (i) to adopt international standards and recommended practices and incorporate them as annexes to the Convention on International Civil Aviation;

 (ii) to arbitrate between member states on matters concerning aviation and implementation of the Convention;

 (iii) to investigate any situation which presents avoidable obstacles to development of international air navigation;

 (iv) to take whatever steps are necessary to maintain safety and regularity of operation of international air transport;

 (v) to provide technical assistance to the developing countries under the UN Development Programme and other assistance programmes.

President of the Council: Dr ASSAD KOTAITE (Lebanon).

SECRETARIAT

The Secretariat, headed by a Secretary-General, is divided into five main divisions: the Air Navigation Bureau, the Air Transport Bureau, The Technical Co-operation Bureau, the Legal Bureau, and the Bureau of Administration and Services.

Secretary-General: RENATO CLÁUDIO COSTA PEREIRA (Brazil).

REGIONAL OFFICES

Asia and Pacific: 252/1 Vipavadee Rangsit Rd, Ladyao, Chatuchak, POB 11, Bangkok 10900, Thailand; tel. (2) 537-8189; fax (2) 537-8199; e-mail icao-apac@bangkok.icao.int; internet www.icao.int/apac; Regional Dir L. B. SHAH.

Eastern and Southern Africa: Limuru Rd, Gigiri, POB 46294, Nairobi, Kenya; tel. (20) 622395; fax (20) 623028; e-mail icao@icao.unon.org;internet www.icao.int/esaf; Regional Dir L. MOLLEL.

Europe and North Atlantic: 3 bis, Villa Emile-Bergerat, 92522 Neuilly-sur-Seine Cédex, France; tel. 1- 46-41-85-85; fax 1-46-41-85-00; e-mail icaoeurnat@paris.icao.int; internet www.icao.int/eurnat; Regional Dir C. EIGL.

Middle East: Egyptian Civil Aviation Complex, Cairo Airport Rd, Cairo, Egypt; tel. (2) 267-4840; fax (2) 2674843; e-mail icao@idsc.net.eg; internet www.icao.int/mid; Regional Dir A. ZERHOUNI.

North America, Central America and the Caribbean: Apdo Postal 5-377, CP 06500, México 5, DF, Mexico; tel. (52) 5552503211; fax (52)5552032757; e-mail icaonacc@mexico.icao.int; internet www.icao.int/nacc; Regional Dir R. YBARRA.

South America: Apdo 4127, Lima 100, Peru; tel. (1) 575-1646; fax (1) 575-0974; e-mail mail@lima.icao.int; internet www.lima.icao.int; Regional Dir JOSé MIGUEL CAPPI.

Western and Central Africa: 15 blvd de la République, BP 2356, Dakar, Senegal; tel. 839-9393; fax 823-6926; e-mail icaodkr@icao.sn; internet www.icao.int/wacaf; Regional Dir AMADOU CHEIFFOU.

Activities

ICAO aims to ensure the safe and orderly growth of civil aviation; to encourage skills in aircraft design and operation; to improve airways, airports and air navigation; to prevent the waste of resources in unreasonable competition; to safeguard the rights of each contracting party to operate international air transport; and to prevent discriminatory practices. ICAO collects and publishes statistics relating to civil aviation.

SAFETY AND SECURITY

ICAO aims to enhance all aspects of air safety and security. A Global Aviation Safety Plan (GASP) was initiated in 1998 to promote new safety measures. ICAO assists member countries to develop appropriate educational and training activities. It also supports programmes to assist the victims of aircraft accidents. The 32nd Assembly, held in September/October 1998, endorsed the establishment of a Universal Safety Oversight Audit Programme, to provide for mandatory, systematic and harmonized safety audits regularly to be undertaken in member states in fields including the airworthiness of aircraft, flight operations and personnel licensing. The Programme became operational on 1 January 1999 with the aim of auditing all member states and compiling an Audit Findings and Differences Database over an initial three-year period. In October 1998 a protocol to the Chicago Convention, prohibiting the use of weapons against civil aircraft in flight, entered into effect, having been adopted in 1984 following an attack on a Korean Airlines passenger flight. During the late 1990s ICAO implemented a programme to address potential malfunctions, resulting from the date change at the start of the new century, of systems affecting the safety, regularity and efficiency of international civil aviation operations; this entailed the harmonization of regional contingency plans and the development of an extensive inventory of air traffic systems and aviation facilities. In 2000 ICAO developed model legislation to cover offences committed on board aircraft by unruly passengers (other than hijacking, sabotage etc., which are already governed by international legislation). Following the major terrorist attacks perpetrated against targets in the USA in September 2001, involving the use of hijacked aircraft as weapons, the 33rd Assembly—held in September/October—adopted a Declaration on the Misuse of Civil Aircraft as Weapons of Destruction and Other Terrorist Acts involving Civil Aviation. The Declaration urged a review of the Organization's aviation security programme and consideration of the initiation of a programme to audit airport security arrangements and member states' civil aviation security programmes. The Assembly also approved the concept of an International Financial Facility for Aviation Safety. In October the Council established a Special Group on Aviation War Risk Insurance to make recommendations on the development of a co-ordinated and long-term approach in this area. A high-level ministerial conference, convened under ICAO auspices in February 2002 to discuss preventing, combating and eradicating acts of terrorism involving civil aviation, and strengthening the Organization's role in overseeing the adoption and national implementation of security-related standards and procedures, endorsed a global Aviation Security Plan of Action and reaffirmed the responsibility of states to ensure aviation security on their territories. The Plan provided for continued implementation of the Universal Safety Oversight Audit Programme until the end of 2004; development of an effective global response to emerging threats; strengthened security-related provisions of the Convention on International Civil Aviation; and enhanced co-ordination of regional and sub-regional audit programmes.

NAVIGATION

ICAO projects relating to navigation have included automated data interchange systems, all-weather navigation, obstacle clearances and the use of space technology in air navigation. In March 1998 the ICAO Council adopted a Global Air Navigation Plan for Communications, Navigation, Surveillance, and Air Traffic Management (CNS/ATM) Systems. In May an international conference was held in Rio de Janeiro, Brazil, to consider implementation of the CNS/ATM systems. The conference urged greater financing and co-operation between states to ensure that the CNS/ATM becomes the basis of a global ATM system. An Air Traffic Management Operational Concept Panel, which was to develop standards and recommend procedures for the development of an integrated ATM system, was convened for the first time in March/April 1999. In October 1998 the Assembly adopted a Charter on the Rights and Obligations of States relating to Global Navigation Satellite Systems (GNSS) to serve as an interim framework on the GNSS. A long-term legal framework on principles governing the GNSS, including a new international convention, remained under consideration in 2002.

ENVIRONMENT

International standards and guide-lines for noise certification of aircraft and international provisions for the regulation of aircraft engine emissions have been adopted and published in Annex 16 to the Chicago Convention. However, these remain under consideration. ICAO was recognized in the Kyoto Protocol to the Framework Convention on Climate Change as the global body through which industrialized nations were to pursue the limitation or reduction of so-called greenhouse gas emissions from international aviation. In 1998 ICAO's Committee on Aviation Environmental Protection recommended a reduction of 16% in the permissible levels of nitrogen oxides emitted by aircraft engines. The new limits, to be applicable to new engine designs from 2003, were adopted by the ICAO Council in early 1999. In June 2001 the Council adopted a stricter noise standard (applicable from 1 January 2006) for jet and large propeller-driven aircraft, as well as new noise limits for helicopters and new provisions concerning re-certification. In October the Assembly approved a series of measures developed by the Committee concerning a balanced approach to aircraft noise and based on the following elements: quieter aircraft; land-use planning and management in the vicinity of airports; operational procedures for noise abatement; and operating restrictions.

ICAO SPECIFICATIONS

These are contained in annexes to the Chicago Convention, and in three sets of Procedures for Air Navigation Services (PANS Documents). The specifications are periodically revised in keeping with developments in technology and changing requirements. The 18 annexes to the Convention include personnel licensing, rules relating to the conduct of flights, meteorological services, aeronautical charts, airiground communications, safety specifications, identification, air-traffic control, rescue services, environmental protection, security and the transporting of dangerous goods. Technical Manuals and Circulars are issued to facilitate implementation.

ICAO REGIONAL PLANS

These set out the technical requirements for air navigation facilities in the nine ICAO regions; Regional Offices offer assistance (see addresses above). Because of growth in air traffic and changes in the pattern of air routes, the Plans are periodically amended. ICAO maintains a structure of Planning and Implementation Regional Groups.

TECHNICAL CO-OPERATION

ICAO's Technical Co-operation Bureau promotes the implementation of ICAO Standards and Recommended Practices, including the CNS/ATM and safety oversight measures, and assists developing countries in the execution of various projects, financed by UNDP and other sources.

ICAO works in close co-operation with other UN bodies, such as the World Meteorological Organization, the International Telecommunication Union, the Universal Postal Union, the World Health Organization and the International Maritime Organization. Non-governmental organizations which also participate in ICAO's work include the International Air Transport Association (q.v.), the Airports Council International (q.v.), the International Federation of Air Line Pilots' Associations (q.v.), and the International Council of Aircraft Owner and Pilot Associations.

Finance

ICAO is financed mainly by contributions from member states. The 33nd Session of the Assembly, held in September/October 2001, approved budget allocations of US $56.7m. for 2002, $57.6m. for 2003 and $60.5m. for 2004.

Publications

Aircraft Accident Digest.

Air Navigation Plans.

Annual Civil Aviation Report.

Civil Aviation Statistics of the World (annually).

ICAO Journal (10 a year, in English, French and Spanish; quarterly digest in Russian).

Lexicon of Terms.

Transition (CNS/ATM newsletter, quarterly).

Conventions, agreements, rules of procedures, regulations, technical publications and manuals.

International Fund for Agricultural Development—IFAD

Address: Via del Serafico 107, 00142 Rome, Italy.

Telephone: (06) 54591; **fax:** (06) 5043463; **e-mail:** ifad@ifad.org; **internet:** www.ifad.org.

IFAD was established in 1977, following a decision by the 1974 UN World Food Conference, with a mandate to combat hunger and eradicate poverty on a sustainable basis in the low-income, food-deficit regions of the world. Funding operations began in January 1978.

MEMBERS

162 members: see Table on pp. 125–127.

Organization

(April 2003)

GOVERNING COUNCIL

Each member state is represented in the Governing Council (the Fund's highest authority) by a Governor and an Alternate. Sessions are held annually with special sessions as required. The Governing Council elects the President of the Fund (who also chairs the Executive Board) by a two-thirds majority for a four-year term. The President is eligible for re-election.

EXECUTIVE BOARD

Consists of 18 members and 18 alternates, elected by the Governing Council, who serve for three years. The Executive Board is responsible for the conduct and general operation of IFAD and approves loans and grants for projects; it holds three regular sessions each year.

Following agreement on the fourth replenishment of the Fund's resources in February 1997, the governance structure of the Fund was amended. Former Category I countries (i.e. industrialized donor countries) were reclassified as List A countries and were awarded a greater share of the 1,800 votes in the Governing Council and Executive Board, in order to reflect their financial contributions to the Fund. Former Category II countries (petroleum-exporting developing donor countries) were reclassified as List B countries, while recipient developing countries, formally Category III countries, were termed as List C countries, and divided into three regional Sub-Lists. Where previously each category was ensured equal representation on the Executive Board, the new allocation of seats was as follows: eight List A countries, four List B, and two of each Sub-List C group of countries.

President and Chairman of Executive Board: LENNART BÅGE (Sweden).

Vice-President: JOHN WESTLEY (USA).

DEPARTMENTS

IFAD has three main administrative departments: the Economic Policy and Resource Strategy Department; the Programme Management Department (with five regional Divisions and a Technical Advisory Division); and the Management and Personnel Services Department (including Office of the Secretary, Management Information Systems, Personnel Division, and Administrative and Protocol Services). At December 2001 IFAD had 313 staff positions.

Activities

IFAD provides financing primarily for projects designed to improve food production systems in developing member states and to strengthen related policies, services and institutions. In allocating resources IFAD is guided by: the need to increase food production in the poorest food-deficit countries; the potential for increasing food production in other developing countries; and the importance of improving the nutrition, health and education of the poorest people in developing countries, i.e. small-scale farmers, artisanal fishermen, nomadic pastoralists, indigenous populations, rural women, and the rural landless. All projects emphasize the participation of beneficiaries in development initiatives, both at the local and national level. Issues relating to gender and household food security are incorporated into all aspects of its activities. IFAD is committed to achieving the so-called Millennium Development Goals, pledged by governments attending a special session of the UN General Assembly in September 2000, and, in particular, the objective to reduce by 50% the proportion of people living in extreme poverty by 2015. In 2001 the Fund introduced new measures to improve monitoring and impact evaluation, in particular to assess its contribution to achieving the Millennium Goals. IFAD's Strategic Framework for 2002–06 reiterates its commitment to enabling the rural poor to overcome their poverty. Accordingly, the Fund's efforts were to focus on the following objectives: strengthening the capacity of the rural poor and their organizations; improving equitable access to productive natural resources and technology; and increasing access to financial services and markets. Within this Framework the Fund has also formulated regional strategies for rural poverty reduction, based on a series of regional poverty assessments.

IFAD is a leading repository in the world of knowledge, resources and expertise in the field of rural hunger and poverty alleviation. In 2001 it renewed its commitment to becoming a global knowledge institution for rural poverty-related issues. Through its technical assistance grants, IFAD aims to promote research and capacity-building in the agricultural sector, as well as the development of technologies to increase production and alleviate rural poverty. In recent years IFAD has been increasingly involved in promoting the use of communication technology to facilitate the exchange of information and experience among rural communities, specialized institutions and organizations, and IFAD-sponsored projects. Within the strategic context of knowledge management, IFAD has supported initiatives to support regional electronic networks, such as ENRAP in Asia and the Pacific and FIDAMERICA in Latin America and the Caribbean, as well as to develop other lines of communication between organizations, local agents and the rural poor.

IFAD is empowered to make both grants and loans. Grants are limited to 7.5% of the resources committed in any one financial year. Loans are available on highly concessionary, intermediate and ordinary terms. Highly concessionary loans carry no interest but have an annual service charge of 0.75% and a repayment period of 40 years, including a 10-year grace period. Intermediate term loans are subject to a variable interest charge, equivalent to 50% of the interest rate charged on World Bank loans, and are repaid over 20 years. Ordinary loans carry a variable interest charge equal to that charged by the World Bank, and are repaid over 15–18 years. In 2001 highly concessionary loans represented almost 83% of total lending in that year. In order to increase the impact of its lending resources on food production, the Fund seeks as much as possible to attract other external donors and beneficiary governments as cofinanciers of its projects. In 2001 external cofinancing accounted for some 27% of all project funding, while domestic contributions, i.e. from recipient governments and other local sources, accounted for 32%.

At the end of 2001 total IFAD loans approved since 1978 amounted to US $7,303.3m. for 603 projects. During the same period the Fund approved 1,563 research and technical assistance grants, at a cost of $418.7m. In 2001 IFAD approved $403.1m. for 25 projects, as follows: $174.0m. for 11 projects in sub-Saharan Africa, (or 43.1% of the total committed in that year), $107.1m. for six operations in Asia and the Pacific (26.6%), $69.2m. for four projects in Latin America and the Caribbean (17.2%) and $52.9m. for four projects in the Near East and North Africa (13.1%). Technical assistance grants amounting to $30.8m. (for research, training and project preparation and development), were awarded, bringing the total financial assistance approved in 2001 to $433.9m., compared with $441.8m. in 2000.

IFAD's development projects usually include a number of components, such as infrastructure (e.g. improvement of water supplies, small-scale irrigation and road construction); input supply (e.g. improved seeds, fertilizers and pesticides); institutional support (e.g. research, training and extension services); and producer incentives (e.g. pricing and marketing improvements). IFAD also attempts to enable the landless to acquire income-generating assets: by increasing the provision of credit for the rural poor, it seeks to free them from dependence on the capital market and to generate productive activities.

In addition to its regular efforts to identify projects and programmes, IFAD organizes special programming missions to certain selected countries to undertake a comprehensive review of the constraints affecting the rural poor, and to help countries to design strategies for the removal of these constraints. In general, projects based on the recommendations of these missions tend to focus on institutional improvements at the national and local level to direct inputs and services to small farmers and the landless rural poor. Monitoring and evaluation missions are also sent to check the progress of projects. During 2001 IFAD conducted 24 programme and project evaluations, as part of its commitment to improving the impact of poverty reduction efforts.

The Fund supports projects that are concerned with environmental conservation, in an effort to alleviate poverty that results from the deterioration of natural resources. In addition, it extends environmental assessment grants to review the environmental consequences of projects under preparation. In October 1997 IFAD was appointed to administer the Global Mechanism of the Convention to Combat Desertification in those Countries Experiencing Drought and Desertification, particularly in Africa, which entered into force in December 1996. The Mechanism was envisaged as a means of mobilizing and channelling resources for implementation of the Convention. A series of collaborative institutional arrangements were to be concluded between IFAD, UNDP and the World Bank in order to facilitate the effective functioning of the Mechanism. In May 2001 the Global Environmental Facility approved IFAD as an executing agency.

In February 1998 IFAD inaugurated a new Trust Fund to complement the multilateral debt initiative for Heavily Indebted Poor Countries (HIPCs—see World Bank p. 84). The Fund was intended to assist IFAD's poorest members deemed to be eligible under the initiative to channel resources from debt repayments to communities in need. In February 2000 the Governing Council approved full participation by IFAD in the enhanced HIPC debt initiative agreed by the World Bank and IMF in September 1999.

During 1998 the Executive Board endorsed a policy framework for the Fund's provision of assistance in post-conflict situations, with the aim of achieving a continuum from emergency relief to a secure basis from which to pursue sustainable development. In July 2001 IFAD and UNAIDS signed a memorandum of understanding on developing a co-operation agreement. A meeting of technical experts from IFAD, FAO, WFP and UNAIDS, held in December, addressed means of mitigating the impact of HIV/AIDS on food security and rural livelihoods in affected regions.

During the late 1990s IFAD established several partnerships within the agribusiness sector, with a view to improving performance at project level, broadening access to capital markets, and encouraging the advancement of new technologies. Since 1996 it has chaired the Support Group of the Global Forum on Agricultural Research, which facilitates dialogue between research centers and institutions, farmers' organizations, non-governmental bodies, the private sector and donors. In October 2001 IFAD became a co-sponsor of the Consultative Group on International Agricultural Research (CGIAR, see p. 86).

Finance

In accordance with the Articles of Agreement establishing IFAD, the Governing Council periodically undertakes a review of the adequacy of resources available to the Fund and may request members to make additional contributions. The fifth replenishment of IFAD funds, covering the period 2000–02, amounted to US $460m. and became effective in September 2001. The provisional budget for administrative expenses for 2001 amounted to $53.6m.

Publications

Annual Report.
IFAD Update (2 a year).
Rural Poverty Report (annually).
Staff Working Papers (series).

International Labour Organization—ILO

Address: 4 route des Morillons, 1211 Geneva 22, Switzerland.
Telephone: (22) 799-6111; **fax:** (22) 798-8685; **e-mail:** ilo@ilo.org; **internet:** www.ilo.org.

ILO was founded in 1919 to work for social justice as a basis for lasting peace. It carries out this mandate by promoting decent living standards, satisfactory conditions of work and pay and adequate employment opportunities. Methods of action include the creation of international labour standards; the provision of technical co-operation services; and research and publications on social and labour matters. In 1946 ILO became a specialized agency associated with the UN. It was awarded the Nobel Peace Prize in 1969. ILO's tripartite structure gives representation to employers' and workers' organizations alongside governments.

MEMBERS

175 members: see Table on pp. 125–127.

Organization

(April 2003)

INTERNATIONAL LABOUR CONFERENCE

The supreme deliberative body of ILO, the Conference meets annually in Geneva, with a session devoted to maritime questions when necessary; it is attended by about 2,000 delegates, advisers and observers. National delegations are composed of two government delegates, one employers' delegate and one workers' delegate. Non-governmental delegates can speak and vote independently of the views of their national government. The conference elects the Governing Body and adopts International Labour Conventions and Recommendations. Every two years the Conference adopts the ILO Budget.

The President and Vice-Presidents hold office for the term of the Conference only.

GOVERNING BODY

ILO's executive council meets three times a year in Geneva to decide policy and programmes. It is composed of 28 government members, 14 employers' members and 14 workers' members. Ten seats are reserved for 'states of chief industrial importance': Brazil, the People's Republic of China, France, Germany, India, Italy, Japan, Russia, the United Kingdom and the USA. The remaining 18 are elected from other countries every three years. Employers' and workers' members are elected as individuals, not as national candidates.

Among the Committees formed by the Governing Body are: the Committee on Freedom of Association; the Programme, Financial and Administrative Committee; the Building Sub-Committee; the Committee on Legal Issues and International Labour Standards; the Sub-Committee on Multinational Enterprises; the Working Party on Policy regarding the Revision of Standards; the Committee on Employment and Social Policy; the Committee on Sectoral and Technical Meetings and Related Issues; the Committee on Technical Co-operation; and the Working Party on the Social Dimensions of the Liberalization of International Trade.

Chairperson (2002–03): LORD BRETT (United Kingdom).
Employers' Vice-Chairman: DANIEL FUNES DE RIOJA (Argentina).
Workers' Vice-Chairman: EUI-YOUG CHUNG (Republic of Korea).

INTERNATIONAL LABOUR OFFICE

The International Labour Office is ILO's secretariat, operational headquarters and publishing house. It is staffed in Geneva and in the field by about 2,250 people of some 120 nationalities. Operations are decentralized to regional, area and branch offices in nearly 40 countries.

Director-General: JUAN O. SOMAVÍA (Chile).

REGIONAL OFFICES

Regional Office for Africa: BP 3960, Abidjan 01, Côte d'Ivoire.
Regional Office for the Americas: Apdo Postal 3638, Lima 1, Peru.
Regional Office for Arab States: POB 11-4088, Beirut, Lebanon.
Regional Office for Asia and the Pacific: POB 2-349, Bangkok 10200, Thailand.
Regional Office for Europe and Central Asia: 4 route des Morillons, 1211 Geneva 22, Switzerland.

Activities

ILO identified the following four principal themes as strategic objectives for its 2002–03 work programme: to promote and realize standards and fundamental principles and rights at work; to create greater opportunities for women and men to secure decent employment and income; to enhance the coverage and effectiveness of social protection for all; and to strengthen tripartism and social dialogue.

STANDARDS AND FUNDAMENTAL PRINCIPLES AND RIGHTS AT WORK

One of ILO's primary functions is the adoption by the International Labour Conference of conventions and recommendations setting minimum labour standards. Through ratification by member states, conventions create binding obligations to put their provisions into effect. Recommendations provide guidance as to policy and practice. At June 2001 a total of 184 conventions and 192 recommendations had been adopted, ranging over a wide field of social and labour matters, based on the following principles: freedom of association, the abolition of forced and child labour, and the elimination of discrimination in employment promotion, training and the protection of workers. Together they form the International Labour Code. By January 2002 more than 7,000 ratifications of the conventions had been registered by member states. The Committee of Experts on the Application of Conventions and Recommendations and the Conference Committee on the Application of Standards monitor the adoption of international labour standards. In June 1998 a Declaration on Fundamental Principles and Rights at Work, establishing seven fundamental labour standards, was adopted by the Conference. All member states were obliged to observe the four principles upon which these standards were based (see above), whether or not they had ratified the corresponding international conventions.

From 1996 ILO resolved to strengthen its efforts, working closely with UNICEF, to encourage member states to ratify and to implement relevant international standards on child labour. In June 1999 the International Labour Conference adopted the Worst Forms of Child Labour Convention (No. 182); the convention entered into force in November 2000. By January 2003 it had been ratified by 132 states. The Organization helped to organize an International Conference on Child Labour, convened in The Hague, Netherlands, in February 2002. In May ILO issued a global study entitled *A Future without Child Labour'*, in which it estimated that one-eighth of the world's children were exposed to the worst forms of child labour. The first annual World Day against Child Labour, sponsored by ILO, was held on 12 June. By early 2003 more than 90 countries were taking part in ILO's International Programme for the Elimination of Child Labour (IPEC, established in 1992), with emphasis placed on the elimination of the most severe forms of labour such as hazardous working conditions and occupations, child prostitution and trafficking of children. In addition, IPEC gives special attention to children who are particularly vulnerable, for example those under 12 years of age.

In 2000 the Global Compact, an initiative of the UN Secretary-General, was inaugurated; this comprised leaders in the fields of business, labour and civil society who undertook to promote human rights, the fundamental principles of ILO, and protection of the environment.

DECENT EMPLOYMENT AND INCOME

ILO aims to monitor, examine and report on the situation and trends in employment throughout the world, and considers the effects on employment and social justice of economic trade, investment and related phenomena. A programme on crisis response and reconstruction addresses the effect on employment of armed conflicts, natural disasters, social movements or political transitions, and financial and economic disruptions. In 2002 ILO estimated that some 180m. workers world-wide were unemployed and that 550m. were earning less than US $1 a day. Some 6.9% of the labour force in the world's industrialized countries and 13.5% of the labour force in countries with economies in transition were estimated to be unemployed.

ILO's programme sector on skills, knowledge and employability supports governments in structuring policies for improved investment in learning and training for enhanced employability, productivity and social inclusion. The programme focuses on promoting access to training and decent work for specific groups, such as youths, the disabled, and workers in the informal economy, and on protecting the rights of the elderly. The job creation and enterprise development programme aims to assist governments, employers, workers and other related groups with fostering a successful business environment, for example through the identification and implementation of appropriate policies, legal frameworks and management strategies, the promotion of access to business development and training services, and the promotion of local economic development programmes. The Tripartite Declaration of Principles concerning Multinational Enterprises and Social Policy, adopted in 1977 and amended in 2000, provides international guide-lines—agreed by governments and employers' and workers' organizations—on investment policy and practice. ILO's gender promotion programme aims to promote effective gender mainstreaming and the creation of more and better jobs for women and men. The impact of current global financial and economic trends on employment creation, poverty alleviation and social exclusion are addressed by ILO's social finance programme. In February 2002 ILO established a World Commission on the Social Dimension of Globalization to consider means of utilizing economic globalization to stimulate economic growth and reduce poverty. ILO is formulating a Global Employment Agenda, a comprehensive framework for managing changes to employment derived from the developing global economy, through investment in knowledge and skills, maintaining a healthy labour market and ensuring adequate social safety nets.

ILO maintains technical relations with the IMF, the World Bank, OECD, the WTO and other international organizations on global economic issues, international and national strategies for employment, structural adjustment, and labour market and training policies. A number of employment policy reviews have been carried out by ILO within the framework of the UN Administrative Committee on Co-ordination Task Force on Full Employment and Sustainable Livelihoods.

SOCIAL PROTECTION FOR ALL

Access to an adequate level of social protection is recognized in ILO's 1944 Declaration of Philadelphia, as well as in a number of international labour standards, as a basic right of all individuals. ILO aims to enable countries to extend social protection to all groups in society and to improve working conditions and safety at work. The fundamental premise of ILO's programme sector on socio-economic security is that basic security for all is essential for productive work and human dignity in the future global economy. The achievement of basic security is deemed to entail the attainment of basic humanitarian needs, including universal access to health services and a decent level of education. The programme aims to address the following concerns: what constitutes socio-economic security and insecurity in member countries; identifying the sources of such insecurity; and identifying economic, labour and social policies that could improve socio-economic security while promoting sustainable economic growth. The programme focuses on the following dimensions of work-based security: security in the labour market (the provision of adequate employment opportunities); employment security (for example, protection against dismissal); occupational security (the opportunity to develop a career); work security (protection against accidents, illness and stress at work); skill reproduction security; income security; and representation security (the right to collective representation in the labour market, through independent trade unions and employers associations, etc.). ILO's Social Security Policy and Development Branch assists member states and constituents in the design, reform and implementation of social security policies based on the principles embodied in international labour standards, with a special focus on developing strategies to extend social security coverage. The Branch provides general research and analysis of social security issues; extends technical assistance to member states for designing, reforming and expanding social security schemes; provides services to enable community-based organizations to develop their own social security systems; promotes and oversees the implementation of ILO standards on social security; develops training programmes and materials; and disseminates information. The Financial, Actuarial and Statistical Branch assists with the long-term financial planning of social protection systems.

ILO's Global Programme on Safety, Health and the Environment aims to protect workers in hazardous occupations (e.g. agriculture, mining and construction); to provide protection to vulnerable groups of workers outside the scope of normal protection measures; to improve the capacity of governments and employers' and workers' organizations to address workers' well-being, extend the scope of occupational health care, etc.; and to ensure that policy-makers recognize and document the social and economic impact of implementing measures that enhance workers' protection. ILO's Conditions of Work Branch conducts research and provides advocacy, training and technical co-operation to governments and employers' and workers' organizations. The International Labour Migration Branch focuses on protecting the rights, and promoting the integration, of migrant workers, forging international consensus on the management of migration, and furthering knowledge of international migration. ILO's Global Programme on HIV/AIDS and the World of Work, formally established in November 2000, issued a code of practice in May 2001, focusing on prevention; management and mitigation of the impact of HIV/AIDS on the world of work; support for HIV/AIDS-affected workers; and eliminating discrimination on the basis of perceived HIV status. In October ILO became the eighth co-sponsor (with UNICEF, UNDP, UNFPA, UNESCO, WHO, the World Bank and UNDCP) of the Joint UN Programme on HIV/AIDS (UNAIDS), which was established on 1 January 1996 to co-ordinate and strengthen world-wide action against HIV/AIDS.

In November 2002 the Governing Body approved a pilot project to consider the development of a proposed 'Global Social Trust'. It was envisaged that such a Trust, to be funded by international donors, might eventually assist with the provision of basic social security benefits and access to health and education services for workers in least developed and low-income countries.

TRIPARTISM AND SOCIAL DIALOGUE

This area was identified as one of the four strategic objectives in order to concentrate and reinforce ILO's support for strengthening the process of tripartism, the role and activities of its tripartite constituents (i.e. governments, employers and workers' organizations), and, in particular, their capacity to engage in and to promote the use of social dialogue. ILO recognizes that the enactment of labour laws, and ensuring their effective enforcement, collective bargaining and other forms of co-operation are important means of promoting social justice. It aims to assist governments and employers' and workers' organizations to establish sound labour relations, to adapt labour laws to meet changing economic and social needs, and to improve labour administration.

INTERNATIONAL LABOUR CONFERENCE

89th Session: June 2001. Adopted a Convention and Recommendation on Agricultural Safety and Health. (It is estimated that about one-half of occupational fatalities annually occur in the agricultural sector, primarily as a result of exposure to pesticides and other toxins or accidents with machinery.) The Director-General presented a report entitled 'Reducing the Decent Work Deficit', emphasizing the need to implement the Organization's agenda on decent work at policy level. Determined to send a high level team to evaluate the situation in Myanmar, welcoming the Myanmar Government's decision to co-operate with ILO by promising freedom of movement, access to and protection of witnesses. Considered a global report on forced labour and examined a report by the Director-General on the condition of workers in the Occupied Territories.

90th Session: June 2002. Adopted a new Recommendation on the Promotion of Co-operatives, a new Protocol to the Occupational Safety and Health Convention, 1981 (No. 155), and a recommendation on drafting an updated list of occupational diseases to supplement Schedule 1 of ILO's Employment Injury Benefits Convention, 1964. Also approved proposals for a new ILO programme of work to focus on employment generation, social protection and poverty reduction for informal economy workers. It was envisaged that the proposed programme would provide a roadmap for extending the application of basic rights and access to the benefits of labour standards and the global economy. Determined to continue pursuing dialogue with the Myanmar Government on ending the use of forced labour in that country. Focused special attention on reports of abduction, trafficking and forced labour in Sudan, in contravention of the Forced Labour Convention, 1930 (No. 29), and on alleged breaches of the Freedom of Association and Protection of the Right to Organize Convention 1948 (No. 87) by Venezuela, while welcoming a request by the Ethiopian Government for technical assistance to facilitate compliance with the latter convention.

MEETINGS

Meetings scheduled for 2003, in addition to the regular Governing Body sessions, included: the Tripartite Meeting on the Future of Employment in the Tobacco Sector; Tripartite Meeting on the Employment Effects of Mergers and Acquisitions in Commerce; Tripartite Meeting on Challenges and Opportunities Facing Public Utilities; High-Level Tripartite Working Group on Maritime Labour Standards; Meeting of Experts on Labour Standards in the Fishing Sector; International Workers' Symposium on Decent Work in Agriculture; Joint ILO/UNESCO Committee of Experts on the Application of the Recommendations concerning Teaching Personnel; Meeting of Experts to Develop a Code of Practice on Violence and Stress at Work in Services; Tripartite Meeting on Best Practices in Work Flexibility Schemes and their Impact on the Quality of Working Life in the Chemical Industries; and the Meeting of Experts on Security, Safety and Health in Ports.

INTERNATIONAL INSTITUTE FOR LABOUR STUDIES

Established in 1960 and based at ILO's Geneva headquarters, the Institute promotes the study and discussion of policy issues of concern to ILO and its constituents, i.e. government, employers and workers. The core theme of the Institute's activities is the interaction between labour institutions, development and civil society in a global economy. It identifies emerging social and labour issues by developing new areas for research and action, and encourages dialogue on social policy between the tripartite constituency of ILO and the international academic community and other experts. The Institute maintains research networks, conducts courses, seminars and social policy forums, and supports internships and visiting scholar and internship programmes.

INTERNATIONAL TRAINING CENTRE OF ILO

Address: Corso Unità d'Italia 125, 10127 Turin, Italy.

The Centre became operational in 1965. The ILO Director-General is Chairman of the Board of the Centre. It provides programmes for directors in charge of technical and vocational institutions, training officers, senior and middle-level managers in private and public enterprises, trade union leaders, and technicians, primarily from the developing regions of the world. Since 1991 the Centre has been increasingly used by UN agencies to provide training for improving the management of development and for building national capacities to sustain development programmes.

Finance

The proposed regular budget for the two years 2004–05 was US $434.0m.

Publications

(in English, French and Spanish unless otherwise indicated)

Bulletin of Labour Statistics (quarterly).

Global Employment Trends.

International Labour Review (quarterly).

International studies, surveys, works of practical guidance or reference (on questions of social policy, manpower, industrial relations, working conditions, social security, training, management development, etc.).

Key Indicators of the Labour Market.

Labour Law Documents (selected labour and social security laws and regulations; 3 a year).

Official Bulletin (3 a year).

Reports for the annual sessions of the International Labour Conference, etc. (also in Arabic, Chinese and Russian).

World Employment Report (every 2 years).

World Labour Report (every 2 years).

World of Work (magazine issued in several languages; 5 a year).

Yearbook of Labour Statistics.

Also maintains a database on international labour standards, ILOLEX, and a database on national labour law, NATLEX, in electronic form.

International Maritime Organization—IMO

Address: 4 Albert Embankment, London, SE1 7SR, United Kingdom.

Telephone: (20) 7735-7611; **fax:** (20) 7587-3210; **e-mail:** info@imo.org; **internet:** www.imo.org.

The Inter-Governmental Maritime Consultative Organization (IMCO) began operations in 1959, as a specialized agency of the UN to facilitate co-operation among governments on technical matters affecting international shipping. Its main functions are the achievement of safe and efficient navigation, and the control of pollution caused by ships and craft operating in the marine environment. IMCO became IMO in 1982.

MEMBERS

162 members and three associate members: see Table on pp. 125–127.

Organization

(April 2003)

ASSEMBLY

The Assembly consists of delegates from all member countries, who each have one vote. Associate members and observers from other governments and the international agencies are also present. Regular sessions are held every two years. The Assembly is responsible for the election of members to the Council and approves the appointment of the Secretary-General of the Secretariat. It considers reports from all subsidiary bodies and decides the action to be taken on them; it votes the agency's budget and determines the work programme and financial policy. The 22nd regular session of the Assembly was held in London in November 2001.

The Assembly also recommends to members measures to promote maritime safety and to prevent and control maritime pollution from ships.

COUNCIL

The Council is the governing body of the Organization between the biennial sessions of the Assembly. Its members, representatives of 40 states, are elected by the Assembly for a term of two years. The Council appoints the Secretary-General; transmits reports by the subsidiary bodies, including the Maritime Safety Committee, to the Assembly, and reports on the work of the Organization generally; submits budget estimates and financial statements with comments and recommendations to the Assembly. The Council normally meets twice a year. In June 2002 the Council established an *ad hoc* working group to draft a five-year strategic plan for the Organization, to incorporate a new mission statement: 'secure and efficient shipping on clean oceans'. The Council also approved in principle the concept of an IMO Model Audit Scheme, which was to advise and assess member states on the implementation of relevant IMO Convention standards.

Facilitation Committee: Constituted by the Council in May 1972 as a subsidiary body, this Committee deals with measures to facilitate maritime travel and transport and matters arising from the 1965 Facilitation Convention. Membership is open to all IMO member states.

MARITIME SAFETY COMMITTEE

The Maritime Safety Committee is open to all IMO members. The Committee meets at least once a year and submits proposals to the Assembly on technical matters affecting the safety of shipping. In December 2002 a conference of contracting states to the 1974 International Convention on Safety of Life at Sea (see below) adopted a series of security measures relating to the international maritime and port industries that had been formulated by the Safety Committee in view of the major terrorist attacks perpetrated against targets in the USA in September 2001.

Sub-Committees:

Bulk Liquids and Gases*.
Carriage of Dangerous Goods, Solid Cargoes and Containers.
Fire Protection.
Flag State Implementation*.
Radiocommunications and Search and Rescue.
Safety of Navigation.
Ship Design and Equipment.
Stability and Load Lines and Fishing Vessel Safety.
Standards of Training and Watchkeeping.

* Also sub-committees of the Marine Environment Protection Committee.

LEGAL COMMITTEE

Established by the Council in June 1967 to deal initially with problems connected with the loss of the tanker *Torrey Canyon*, and subsequently with any legal problems laid before IMO. Membership open to all IMO member states.

MARINE ENVIRONMENT PROTECTION COMMITTEE

Established by the eighth Assembly (1973) to co-ordinate IMO's work on the prevention and control of marine pollution from ships, and to assist IMO in its consultations with other UN bodies, and with international organizations and expert bodies in the field of marine pollution. Membership is open to all IMO members.

TECHNICAL CO-OPERATION COMMITTEE

Constituted by the Council in May 1972, this Committee evaluates the implementation of UN Development Programme projects for which IMO is the executing agency, and generally reviews IMO's technical assistance programmes. Its membership is open to all IMO member states.

SECRETARIAT

The Secretariat consists of the Secretary-General and a staff appointed by the Secretary-General and recruited on as wide a geographical basis as possible.

Secretary-General: WILLIAM A. O'NEIL (Canada).

Divisions of the Secretariat:

Administrative
Conference
Legal Affairs and External Relations
Marine Environment
Maritime Safety
Technical Co-operation

Activities

In addition to the work of its committees and sub-committees, the organization works in connection with the following Conventions, of which it is the depository:

Convention on Facilitation of International Maritime Traffic, 1965. Came into force in March 1967.

International Convention on Load Lines, 1966. Came into force in July 1968.

International Convention on Tonnage Measurement of Ships, 1969. Convention embodies a universal system for measuring ships' tonnage. Came into force in 1982.

International Convention relating to Intervention on the High Seas in Cases of Oil Pollution Casualties, 1969. Came into force in May 1975. A Protocol adopted in 1973 came into force in 1983.

International Convention on Civil Liability for Oil Pollution Damage, 1969. Came into force in June 1975.

Intenational Convention on the Establishment of an International Fund for Compensation for Oil Pollution Damage, 1971. Came into force in October 1978.

Convention relating to Civil Liability in the Field of Maritime Carriage of Nuclear Material, 1971. Came into force in 1975.

Special Trade Passenger Ships Agreement, 1971. Came into force in 1974.

Convention on the International Regulations for Preventing Collisions at Sea, 1972. Came into force in July 1977.

Convention on the Prevention of Marine Pollution by Dumping of Wastes and Other Matter, 1972. Came into force in August 1975. Extended to include a ban on low-level nuclear waste in November 1993; came into force in February 1994.

International Convention for Safe Containers, 1972. Came into force in September 1977.

International Convention for the Prevention of Pollution from Ships, 1973 (as modified by the Protocol of 1978). Came into force in October 1983. Extended to include regulations to prevent air pollution in September 1997; amendments will come into force 12 months after 15 countries whose combined fishing fleets constitute 50% of the world's merchant fleet have become parties thereto.

International Convention on Safety of Life at Sea, 1974. Came into force in May 1980. A Protocol drawn up in 1978 came into force in May 1981. Numerous extensions and amendments.

Athens Convention relating to the Carriage of Passengers and their Luggage by Sea, 1974. Came into force in April 1987.

Convention on the International Maritime Satellite Organization, 1976. Came into force in July 1979.

Convention on Limitation of Liability for Maritime Claims, 1976. Came into force in December 1986.

International Convention for the Safety of Fishing Vessels, Torremolinos, 1977. Will come into force 12 months after 15 countries whose combined fishing fleets constitute 50% of world fishing fleets of 24 metres in length and over have become parties thereto.

International Convention on Standards of Training, Certification and Watchkeeping for Seafarers, 1978. Came into force in April 1984; restructured by amendments that entered into force in February 1997.

International Convention on Maritime Search and Rescue, 1979. Came into force in June 1985.

Paris Memorandum of Understanding on Port State Control, 1982.

International Convention for the Suppression of Unlawful Acts against the Safety of International Shipping, 1988. Came into force in March 1992.

Protocol for the Suppression of Unlawful Acts against the Safety of Fixed Platform located on the Continental Shelf, 1988. Came into force in March 1992.

International Convention on Salvage, 1989. Came into force in July 1996.

International Convention on Oil Pollution, Preparedness, Response and Co-operation, 1990. Came into force on 13 May 1995.

International Convention on Liability and Compensation for Damage in Connection with the Carriage of Hazardous and Noxious Substances by Sea, 1996. Will come into force 18 months after 12 states of which four have not less than 2m. units of gross tonnage have become parties thereto.

International Convention on Civil Liability for Bunker Oil Pollution Damage, 2001.

Convention on Control of Harmful Anti-fouling Systems on Ships, 2001. Will enter into force 12 months after 25 states representing 25% of the world's merchant shipping tonnage have become parties thereto.

ASSOCIATED INSTITUTES

IMO Maritime Law Institute—IMLI: POB 31, Msida, MSD 01, Malta; tel. 319343; fax 343092; e-mail imli@maltanet.net; internet www.imli.org; provides training for maritime lawyers. Dir Prof. DAVID ATTARD.

International Maritime Academy—IMA: via E. Weiss 15, 34127 Trieste, Italy; tel. (40) 350829; fax (40) 350322; e-mail imoima@imoima.org; internet www.imoima.org; provides postgraduate training for seafarers and onshore staff employed in maritime-related fields; Dir PIETRO MARIN.

Regional Marine Pollution Emergency Response Centre for the Mediterranean Sea—REMPEC: Manoel Island, GZR 03, Malta; tel. 337296; fax 339951; e-mail rempec@waldonet.mt; internet www.rempec.org; f. 1976 as the Regional Oil Combating

Centre for the Mediterranean Sea. Administered by IMO in conjunction with the Regional Seas Programme of the UN Environment Programme. Aims to develop measures to combat pollution in the Mediterranean. Dir ROBERTO PATRUNO.

World Maritime University—WMU: POB 500, Citadellsvägen 29, 201 24 Malmö, Sweden; tel. (40) 356300; fax (40) 128442; e-mail info@wmu.se; internet www.wmu.se; f. by IMO in 1983. Offers postgraduate courses in various maritime disciplines, mainly for students from developing countries. Rector K. LAUBSTEIN. Publs *WMU Newsletter, WMU Handbook, WMU Journal of Maritime Affairs*, several books on maritime issues.

Finance

Contributions are received from the member states. The budget appropriation for the two years 2002–03 amounted to £39.5m.

Publications

IMO News (quarterly).

Numerous specialized publications, including international conventions of which IMO is depositary.

International Monetary Fund—IMF

Address: 700 19th St, NW, Washington, DC 20431, USA.
Telephone: (202) 623-7300; **fax:** (202) 623-6220; **e-mail:** publicaffairs@imf.org; **internet:** www.imf.org.

The IMF was established at the same time as the World Bank in December 1945, to promote international monetary co-operation, to facilitate the expansion and balanced growth of international trade and to promote stability in foreign exchange.

MEMBERS

184 members: see Table on pp. 125–127.

Organization

(April 2003)

Managing Director: HORST KÖHLER (Germany).
First Deputy Managing Director: ANNE KRUEGER (USA).
Deputy Managing Directors: SHIGEMITSU SUGISAKI (Japan); EDUARDO ANINAT (Chile).

BOARD OF GOVERNORS

The highest authority of the Fund is exercised by the Board of Governors, on which each member country is represented by a Governor and an Alternate Governor. The Board normally meets once a year. The Board of Governors has delegated many of its powers to the Executive Directors. However, the conditions governing the admission of new members, adjustment of quotas and the election of Executive Directors, as well as certain other important powers, remain the sole responsibility of the Board of Governors. The voting power of each member on the Board of Governors is related to its quota in the Fund (see p. 102).

In September 1999 the Board of Governors adopted a resolution to transform the Interim Committee of the Board of Governors (established 1974) into the International Monetary and Financial Committee (IMFC). The IMFC, which held its inaugural meeting in April 2000, comprises 24 members, representing the same countries or groups of countries as those on the Board of Executive Directors (see below). It advises and reports to the Board on matters relating to the management and adaptation of the international monetary and financial system, sudden disturbances that might threaten the system and proposals to amend the Articles of Agreement, but has no decision-making authority.

The Development Committee (the Joint Ministerial Committee of the Boards of Governors of the World Bank and the IMF on the Transfer of Real Resources to Developing Countries, created in 1974, with a structure similar to that of the IMFC) reviews development policy issues and financing requirements.

BOARD OF EXECUTIVE DIRECTORS

The 24-member Board of Executive Directors, responsible for the day-to-day operations of the Fund, is in continuous session in Washington, under the chairmanship of the Fund's Managing Director or Deputy Managing Directors. The USA, the United Kingdom, Germany, France and Japan each appoint one Executive Director. There is also one Executive Director each from the People's Republic of China, Russia and Saudi Arabia, while the remainder are elected by groups of the remaining countries. As in the Board of Governors, the voting power of each member is related to its quota in the Fund, but in practice the Executive Directors normally operate by consensus.

The Managing Director of the Fund serves as head of its staff, which is organized into departments by function and area. At 31 December 2001 the Fund staff employed 2,633 staff members (with a further 343 additional authorized staff positions) from 133 countries.

Activities

The purposes of the IMF, as defined in the Articles of Agreement, are:

(i) To promote international monetary co-operation through a permanent institution which provides the machinery for consultation and collaboration on monetary problems.

(ii) To facilitate the expansion and balanced growth of international trade, and to contribute thereby to the promotion and maintenance of high levels of employment and real income and to the development of members' productive resources.

(iii) To promote exchange stability, to maintain orderly exchange arrangements among members, and to avoid competitive exchange depreciation.

(iv) To assist in the establishment of a multilateral system of payments in respect of current transactions between members and in the elimination of foreign exchange restrictions which hamper the growth of trade.

(v) To give confidence to members by making the general resources of the Fund temporarily available to them, under adequate safeguards, thus providing them with the opportunity to correct maladjustments in their balance of payments, without resorting to measures destructive of national or international prosperity.

(vi) In accordance with the above, to shorten the duration of and lessen the degree of disequilibrium in the international balances of payments of members.

In joining the Fund, each country agrees to co-operate with the above objectives. In accordance with its objective of facilitating the expansion of international trade, the IMF encourages its members to accept the obligations of Article VIII, Sections two, three and four, of the Articles of Agreement. Members that accept Article VIII undertake to refrain from imposing restrictions on the making of payments and transfers for current international transactions and from engaging in discriminatory currency arrangements or multiple currency practices without IMF approval. By mid-2002 152 members had accepted Article VIII status.

The financial crises of the late 1990s, notably in several Asian countries, Brazil and Russia, contributed to widespread discussions concerning the strengthening of the international monetary system. In April 1998 the Executive Board identified the following fundamental aspects of the debate: reinforcing international and domestic financial systems; strengthening IMF surveillance; promoting greater availability and transparency of information regarding member countries' economic data and policies; emphasizing the central role of the IMF in crisis management; and establishing effective procedures to involve the private sector in forestalling or resolving financial crises. During 1999/2000 the Fund implemented several measures in connection with its ongoing efforts to appraise and reinforce the global financial architecture, including, in March 2000, the adoption by the Executive Board of a strengthened framework to safeguard the use of IMF resources. During 2000 the Fund established the IMF Center, in Washington, DC, which aimed to promote awareness and understanding of its activities. In September the Fund's new Managing Director announced his intention to focus and streamline the principals of conditionality (which links Fund financing with the implementation of specific economic policies by the recipient countries) as part of the wider reform of the international financial system. A comprehensive review was undertaken, during which the issue was considered by public forums and representatives of civil society. New guide-lines on conditionality, which *inter alia* aimed to promote national ownership of policy reforms and to introduce specific criteria for the implementation of conditions given different states' circumstances, were approved by the Executive Board in September 2002. In 2000/01 the Fund established an International Capital Markets Department to improve its understanding of financial markets and a separate Consultative Group on capital markets to serve as a forum for regular dialogue between the Fund and representatives of the private sector.

In early 2002 a position of Director for Special Operations was created to enhance the Fund's ability to respond to critical situations affecting member countries. In February the newly-appointed Director immediately assumed leadership of the staff team working with the authorities in Argentina to help that country to overcome its extreme economic and social difficulties. In September the IMFC approved further detailed consideration of a sovereign debt restructuring mechanism (SDRM), which aimed to establish a procedure to enable countries with an unsustainable level of debt to renegotiate loans more effectively. In January 2003 the IMF hosted a conference for representatives from the financial sector and civil society and other public officials and academics to discuss aspects of the SDRM.

SURVEILLANCE

Under its Articles of Agreement, the Fund is mandated to oversee the effective functioning of the international monetary system. Accordingly, the Fund aims to exercise firm surveillance over the exchange rate policies of member states and to assess whether a country's economic situation and policies are consistent with the objectives of sustainable development and domestic and external stability. The Fund's main tools of surveillance are regular, bilateral consultations with member countries conducted in accordance with Article IV of the Articles of Agreement, which cover fiscal and monetary policies, balance of payments and external debt developments, as well as policies that affect the economic performance of a country, such as the labour market, social and environmental issues and good governance, and aspects of the country's capital accounts, and finance and banking sectors. In April 1997, in an effort to improve the value of surveillance by means of increased transparency, the Executive Board agreed to the voluntary issue of Press Information Notices (PINs) (on the internet and in *IMF Economic Reviews*), following each member's Article IV consultation with the Board, to those member countries wishing to make public the Fund's views. Other background papers providing information on and analysis of economic developments in individual countries continued to be made available. In addition, World Economic Outlook discussions are held, normally twice a year, by the Executive Board to assess policy implications from a multilateral perspective and to monitor global developments.

The rapid decline in the value of the Mexican peso in late 1994 and the financial crisis in Asia, which became apparent in mid-1997, focused attention on the importance of IMF surveillance of the economies and financial policies of member states and prompted the Fund to enhance the effectiveness of its surveillance and to encourage the full and timely provision of data by member countries in order to maintain fiscal transparency. In April 1996 the IMF established the Special Data Dissemination Standard (SDDS), which was intended to improve access to reliable economic statistical information for member countries that have, or are seeking, access to international capital markets. In March 1999 the IMF undertook to strengthen the Standard by the introduction of a new reserves data template. By late 2002 52 countries had subscribed to the Standard. In December 1997 the Executive Board approved a new General Data Dissemination System (GDDS), to encourage all member countries to improve the production and dissemination of core economic data. The operational phase of the GDDS commenced in May 2000. The Fund maintains a Dissemination Standards Bulletin Board (accessible at dsbb.imf.org), which aims to ensure that information on SDDS subscribing countries is widely available.

In April 1998 the then Interim Committee adopted a voluntary Code of Good Practices on Fiscal Transparency: Declaration of Principles, which aimed to increase the quality and promptness of official reports on economic indicators, and in September 1999 it adopted a Code of Good Practices on Transparency in Monetary and Financial Policies: Declaration of Principles. The IMF and World Bank jointly established a Financial Sector Assessment Programme (FSAP) in May 1999, initially as a pilot project, which aimed to promote greater global financial security through the preparation of confidential detailed evaluations of the financial sectors of individual countries. Assessments were undertaken of 12 industrialized countries, emerging market economies and developing countries. During 2000 the FSAP was extended to cover a further 24 countries. It remained under regular review by the Boards of Governors of the Fund and World Bank. As part of the FSAP, Fund staff may conclude a Financial System Stability Assessment (FSSA), addressing issues relating to macroeconomic stability and the strength of a country's financial system. A separate component of the FSAP are Reports on the Observance of Standards and Codes (ROSCs), which are compiled after an assessment of a country's implementation and observance of internationally recognized financial standards. In March

2000 the IMF Executive Board adopted a strengthened framework to safeguard the use of IMF resources. All member countries making use of Fund resources were to be required to publish annual central bank statements audited in accordance with internationally accepted standards. It was also agreed that any instance of intentional misreporting of information by a member country should be publicized. In the following month the Executive Board approved the establishment of an Independent Evaluation Office to conduct objective evaluations of IMF policy and operations. In August the Executive Board adopted a Code of Conduct to guide its activities.

In April 2001 the Executive Board agreed on measures to enhance international efforts to counter money-laundering, in particular through the Fund's ongoing financial supervision activities and its programme of assessment of offshore financial centres. In November the IMFC, in response to the terrorist attacks against targets in the USA, which had occurred in September, resolved, *inter alia*, to strengthen the Fund's focus on surveillance, and, in particular, to extend measures to counter money-laundering to include the funds of terrorist organizations. It determined to accelerate efforts to assess offshore centres and to provide technical support to enable poorer countries to meet international financial standards.

SPECIAL DRAWING RIGHTS

The special drawing right (SDR) was introduced in 1970 as a substitute for gold in international payments, and was intended eventually to become the principal reserve asset in the international monetary system. SDRs are allocated to members in proportion to their quotas. In October 1996 the Executive Board agreed to a new allocation of SDRs in order to achieve their equitable distribution among member states (i.e. all members would have an equal number of SDRs relative to the size of their quotas). In particular, this was deemed necessary since 38 countries that had joined the Fund since the last allocation of SDRs in 1981 had not yet received any of the units of account. In September 1997 at the annual meeting of the Executive Board, a resolution approving a special allocation of SDR 21,400m. was passed, in order to ensure an SDR to quota ratio of 29.32%, for all member countries. The resolution was to come into effect following its acceptance by 60% of member countries, having 85% of the total voting power. (At 30 April 2002 118 members, holding 73% of the voting power, had agreed to the proposal.)

From 1974 to 1980 the SDR was valued on the basis of the market exchange rate for a basket of 16 currencies, belonging to the members with the largest exports of goods and services; since 1981 it has been based on the currencies of the five largest exporters (France, Germany, Japan, the United Kingdom and the USA), although the list of currencies and the weight of each in the SDR valuation basket is revised every five years. In January 1999 the IMF incorporated the new currency of the European Economic and Monetary Union, the euro, into the valuation basket; it replaced the French and German currencies, on the basis of their conversion rates with the euro as agreed by the EU. From 1 January 2001 the relative weights assigned to the currencies in the valuation basket were redistributed. The value of the SDR averaged US $1.29484 during 2002, and at 31 December 2002 stood at $1.35952.

The Second Amendment to the Articles of Agreement (1978) altered and expanded the possible uses of the SDR in transactions with other participants. These 'prescribed holders' of the SDRs have the same degree of freedom as Fund members to buy and sell SDRs and to receive or use them in loans, pledges, swaps, donations or settlement of financial obligations. In 2001/02 there were 16 'prescribed holders': the African Development Bank and the African Development Fund, the Arab Monetary Fund, the Asian Development Bank, the Bank of Central African States, the Bank for International Settlements, the Central Bank of West African States, the East African Development Bank, the Eastern Caribbean Central Bank, the European Central Bank, the International Bank for Reconstruction and Development, the International Development Association, the International Fund for Agricultural Development, the Islamic Development Bank, the Latin American Reserve Fund and the Nordic Investment Bank.

QUOTAS

Each member is assigned a quota related to its national income, monetary reserves, trade balance and other economic indicators. A member's subscription is equal to its quota and is payable partly in SDRs and partly in its own currency. The quota determines a member's voting power, which is based on one vote for each SDR 100,000 of its quota *plus* the 250 votes to which each member is entitled. A member's quota also determines its access to the financial resources of the IMF, and its allocation of SDRs.

Quotas are reviewed at intervals of not more than five years, to take into account the state of the world economy and members' different rates of development. Special increases, separate to the general review, may be made in exceptional circumstances. These have been approved by the Fund for the People's Republic of China in 1980 and 2001, for Saudi Arabia in 1981, and for Cambodia in

BOARD OF EXECUTIVE DIRECTORS (January 2003)

Director	Casting Votes of	Total Votes	%
Appointed:			
NANCY P. JACKLIN	USA	371,743	17.10
KEN YAGI	Japan	133,378	6.14
KARLHEINZ BISCHOFBERGER	Germany	130,332	6.00
PIERRE DUQUESNE	France	107,635	4.95
TOM SCHOLAR	United Kingdom	107,635	4.95
Elected:			
WILLY KIEKENS (Belgium)	Austria, Belarus, Belgium, Czech Republic, Hungary, Kazakhstan, Luxembourg, Slovakia, Slovenia, Turkey	111,696	5.14
J. DE BEAUFORT WIJNHOLDS (Netherlands)	Armenia, Bosnia and Herzegovina, Bulgaria, Croatia, Cyprus, Georgia, Israel, the former Yugoslav republic of Macedonia, Moldova, Netherlands, Romania, Ukraine	105,412	4.85
HERNÁN OYARZÁBAL (Venezuela)	Costa Rica, El Salvador, Guatemala, Honduras, Mexico, Nicaragua, Spain, Venezuela	92,989	4.28
PIER CARLO PADOAN (Italy)	Albania, Greece, Italy, Malta, Portugal, San Marino, Timor-Leste	90,968	4.19
IAN E. BENNETT (Canada)	Antigua and Barbuda, Bahamas, Barbados, Belize, Canada, Dominica, Grenada, Ireland, Jamaica, Saint Christopher and Nevis, Saint Lucia, Saint Vincent and the Grenadines	80,636	3.71
ÓLAFUR ÍSLEIFSSON (Iceland)	Denmark, Estonia, Finland, Iceland, Latvia, Lithuania, Norway, Sweden	76,276	3.51
MICHAEL J. CALLAGHAN (Australia)	Australia, Kiribati, Republic of Korea, Marshall Islands, Federated States of Micronesia, Mongolia, New Zealand, Palau, Papua New Guinea, Philippines, Samoa, Seychelles, Solomon Islands, Vanuatu	72,423	3.33
SULAIMAN M. AL-TURKI	Saudi Arabia	70,105	3.23
ISMAILA USMAN (Nigeria)	Angola, Botswana, Burundi, Eritrea, Ethiopia, The Gambia, Kenya, Lesotho, Liberia, Malawi, Mozambique, Namibia, Nigeria, Sierra Leone, South Africa, Sudan, Swaziland, Tanzania, Uganda, Zambia, Zimbabwe	69,968	3.22
Sri MULYANI INDRAWATI (Indonesia)	Brunei, Cambodia, Fiji, Indonesia, Laos, Malaysia, Myanmar, Nepal, Singapore, Thailand, Tonga, Viet Nam	69,019	3.18
A. SHAKOUR SHAALAN (Egypt)	Bahrain, Egypt, Iraq, Jordan, Kuwait, Lebanon, Libya, Maldives, Oman, Qatar, Syria, United Arab Emirates, Yemen	64,008	2.95
WEI BENHUA	People's Republic of China	63,942	2.94
FRITZ ZURBRÜGG (Switzerland)	Azerbaijan, Kyrgyzstan, Poland, Serbia and Montenegro, Switzerland, Tajikistan, Turkmenistan, Uzbekistan	61,827	2.84
ALEKSEI V. MOZHIN	Russia	59,704	2.75
MURILO PORTUGAL (Brazil)	Brazil, Colombia, Dominican Republic, Ecuador, Guyana, Haiti, Panama, Suriname, Trinidad and Tobago	53,422	2.46
ABBAS MIRAKHOR (Iran)	Afghanistan, Algeria, Ghana, Iran, Morocco, Pakistan, Tunisia	53,247	2.45
YAGA V. REDDY (India)	Bangladesh, Bhutan, India, Sri Lanka	52,112	2.40
GUILLERMO LE FORT (Chile)	Argentina, Bolivia, Chile, Paraguay, Peru, Uruguay	43,395	2.00
DAMIAN ONDO MAÑE (Equatorial Guinea)	Benin, Burkina Faso, Cameroon, Cape Verde, Central African Republic, Chad, Comoros, Democratic Republic of the Congo, Republic of the Congo, Côte d'Ivoire, Djibouti, Equatorial Guinea, Gabon, Guinea, Guinea-Bissau, Madagascar, Mali, Mauritania, Mauritius, Niger, Rwanda, São Tomé and Príncipe, Senegal, Togo	30,749	1.41

Note: At January 2003 member countries' votes totalled 2,173,313, while votes in the Board of Executive Directors totalled 2,172,621. The latter total does not include the votes of Somalia, which did not participate in the 2002 election of Executive Directors.

1984. In June 1990 the Board of Governors authorized proposals for a Ninth General Review of quotas. Total quotas were to be increased by roughly 50% (depending on various factors). At the same time the Board of Governors stipulated that the quota increase could occur only after the Third Amendment of the IMF's Articles of Agreement had come into effect. The amendment provides for the suspension of voting and other related rights of members that do not fulfil their obligations under the Articles. By September 1992 the necessary proportion of IMF members had accepted the amendment, and it entered into force in November. The Tenth General Review of quotas was concluded in December 1994, with the Board recommending no further increase in quotas. However, the Board resolved to monitor closely the Fund's liquidity. In October 1996 the Fund's Managing Director advocated an increase in quotas under the latest review of at least two-thirds in the light of the IMF's reduced liquidity position. (The IMF had extended unprecedentedly large amounts in stand-by arrangements during the period 1995–96, notably to Mexico and Russia.) In January 1998 the Board of Governors adopted a resolution in support of an increase in quotas of 45%, subject to approval by member states constituting 85% of total quotas (as at December 1997). Sufficient consent had been granted by January 1999 to enable the Eleventh General Review of Quotas to enter into effect. The Twelfth General Review was initiated in December 2001, and was concluded at the end of January 2003 without an increase in quotas. At that time total quotas in the Fund amounted to SDR 212,731.3m.

RESOURCES

Members' subscriptions form the basic resource of the IMF. They are supplemented by borrowing. Under the General Arrangements to Borrow (GAB), established in 1962, the 'Group of Ten' industrialized nations (G-10—Belgium, Canada, France, Germany, Italy, Japan, the Netherlands, Sweden, the United Kingdom and the USA) and Switzerland (which became a member of the IMF in May 1992 but which had been a full participant in the GAB from April 1984) undertake to lend the Fund as much as SDR 17,000m. in their own currencies, to assist in fulfilling the balance-of-payments requirements of any member of the group, or in response to requests to the Fund from countries with balance-of-payments problems that could threaten the stability of the international monetary system. In 1983 the Fund entered into an agreement with Saudi Arabia, in association with the GAB, making available SDR 1,500m., and other borrowing arrangements were completed in 1984 with the Bank for International Settlements, the Saudi Arabian Monetary Agency, Belgium and Japan, making available a further SDR 6,000m. In 1986 another borrowing arrangement with Japan made available SDR 3,000m. In May 1996 GAB participants concluded an agreement in principle to expand the resources available for borrowing to SDR 34,000m., by securing the support of 25 countries with the financial capacity to support the international monetary system. The so-called New Arrangements to Borrow (NAB) was approved by the Executive Board in January 1997. It was to enter into force, for an initial five-year period, as soon as the five largest potential creditors participating in NAB had approved the initiative and the total credit arrangement of participants endorsing the scheme had reached at least SDR 28,900m. While the GAB credit arrangement was to remain in effect, the NAB was expected to be the first facility to be activated in the event of the Fund's requiring supplementary resources. In July 1998 the GAB was activated for the first time in more than 20 years in order to provide funds of up to US $6,300m. in support of an IMF emergency assistance package for Russia (the first time the GAB had been used for a non-participant). The NAB became effective in November, and was used for the first time as part of an extensive programme of support for Brazil, which was adopted by the IMF in early December.

DRAWING ARRANGEMENTS

Exchange transactions within the Fund take the form of members' purchases (i.e. drawings) from the Fund of the currencies of other members for the equivalent amounts of their own currencies. Fund resources are available to eligible members on an essentially short-term and revolving basis to provide members with temporary assistance to contribute to the solution of their payments problems. Before making a purchase, a member must show that its balance of payments or reserve position makes the purchase necessary. Apart from this requirement, reserve tranche purchases (i.e. purchases that do not bring the Fund's holdings of the member's currency to a level above its quota) are permitted unconditionally.

With further purchases, however, the Fund's policy of 'conditionality' means that a member requesting assistance must agree to adjust its economic policies, as stipulated by the IMF. All requests other than for use of the reserve tranche are examined by the Executive Board to determine whether the proposed use would be consistent with the Fund's policies, and a member must discuss its proposed adjustment programme (including fiscal, monetary, exchange and trade policies) with IMF staff. Purchases outside the reserve tranche are made in four credit tranches, each equivalent to 25% of the member's quota; a member must reverse the transaction by repurchasing its own currency (with SDRs or currencies specified by the Fund) within a specified time. A credit tranche purchase is usually made under a 'Stand-by Arrangement' with the Fund, or under the Extended Fund Facility. A Stand-by Arrangement is normally of one or two years' duration, and the amount is made available in instalments, subject to the member's observance of 'performance criteria'; repurchases must be made within three-and-a-quarter to five years. An Extended Arrangement is normally of three years' duration, and the member must submit detailed economic programmes and progress reports for each year; repurchases must be made within four-and-a-half to 10 years. A member whose payments imbalance is large in relation to its quota may make use of temporary facilities established by the Fund using borrowed resources, namely the 'enlarged access policy' established in 1981, which helps to finance Stand-by and Extended Arrangements for such a member, up to a limit of between 90% and 110% of the member's quota annually. Repurchases are made within three-and-a-half to seven years. In October 1994 the Executive Board approved a temporary increase in members' access to IMF resources, on the basis of a recommendation by the then Interim Committee. The annual access limit under IMF regular tranche drawings, Stand-by Arrangements and Extended Fund Facility credits was increased from 68% to 100% of a member's quota, with the cumulative access limit remaining at 300% of quota. The arrangements were extended, on a temporary basis, in November 1997.

In addition, special-purpose arrangements have been introduced, all of which are subject to the member's co-operation with the Fund to find an appropriate solution to its difficulties. During late 1999 the Fund undertook a review of its non-concessional lending facilities. The Buffer Stock Financing Facility (BSFF), established in 1969 in order to enable members to pay their contributions to the buffer stocks which were intended to stabilize markets for primary commodities, was abolished in January 2000, having last been used in 1984. In January 2000 the Executive Board also resolved to eliminate the contingency component of the former Compensatory and Contingency Financing Facility, established in 1988, reforming it as the Compensatory Financing Facility (CCF). The CCF provides compensation to members whose export earnings are reduced as a result of circumstances beyond their control, or which are affected by excess costs of cereal imports. In December 1997 the Executive Board established a new Supplemental Reserve Facility (SRF) to provide short-term assistance to members experiencing exceptional balance-of-payments difficulties resulting from a sudden loss of market confidence. Repayments were to be made within one to one-and-a-half years of the purchase, unless otherwise extended by the Board. The SRF was activated immediately to provide SDR 9,950m. to the Republic of Korea, as part of a Stand-by Arrangement amounting to SDR 15,550m., the largest amount ever committed by the Fund. (With additional financing from governments and international institutions, the total assistance 'package' for the Republic of Korea reached an estimated US $57,000m.) In July 1998

SDR 4,000m. was made available to Russia under the SRF and, in December, some SDR 9,100m. was extended to Brazil under the SRF as part of a new Stand-by Arrangement. In January 2001 some SDR 2,100m. in SRF resources were approved for Argentina as part of an SDR 5,187m. Stand-by Arrangement augmentation. (In January 2002 the Executive Board approved an extension of one year for Argentina's SRF repayments.) In April 1999 an additional facility, the Contingent Credit Lines (CCL), was established to provide short-term financing on similar terms to the SRF in order to prevent more stable economies being affected by adverse international financial developments and to maintain investor confidence. Under the CCL member countries were to have short-term access to up to 500% of their quota, subject to meeting various economic criteria stipulated by the Fund. No funds under the CCL were committed in 2001/02.

In October 1995 the Interim Committee of the Board of Governors endorsed recent decisions of the Executive Board to strengthen IMF financial support to members requiring exceptional assistance. An Emergency Financing Mechanism was established to enable the IMF to respond swiftly to potential or actual financial crises, while additional funds were made available for short-term currency stabilization. (The Mechanism was activated for the first time in July 1997, in response to a request by the Philippines Government to reinforce the country's international reserves, and was subsequently used during that year to assist Thailand, Indonesia and the Republic of Korea, and, in July 1998, Russia.) Emergency assistance was also to be available to countries in a post-conflict situation, in addition to existing arrangements for countries having been affected by natural disasters, to facilitate the rehabilitation of their economies and to improve their eligibility for further IMF concessionary arrangements.

In November 1999 the Fund's existing facility to provide balance-of-payments assistance on concessional terms to low-income member countries, the Enhanced Structural Adjustment Facility, was reformulated as the Poverty Reduction and Growth Facility (PRGF), with greater emphasis on poverty reduction and sustainable development as key elements of growth-orientated economic strategies. Assistance under the PRGF (for which 77 countries were deemed eligible) was to be carefully matched to specific national requirements. Prior to drawing on the facility each recipient country was, in collaboration with representatives of civil society, non-governmental organizations and bilateral and multilateral institutions, to develop a national poverty reduction strategy, which was to be presented in a Poverty Reduction Strategy Paper (PRSP). PRGF loans carry an interest rate of 0.5% per year and are repayable over 10 years, with a five-and-a-half-year grace period; each eligible country is normally permitted to borrow up to 140% of its quota (in exceptional circumstances the maximum access can be raised to 185%). A PGRF Trust replaced the former ESAF Trust.

The PRGF supports, through long-maturity loans and grants, IMF participation in a joint initiative, with the World Bank, to provide exceptional assistance to heavily indebted poor countries (HIPCs), in order to help them to achieve a sustainable level of debt management. The initiative was formally approved at the September 1996 meeting of the Interim Committee, having received the support of the 'Paris Club' of official creditors, which agreed to increase the relief on official debt from 67% to 80%. In all, 41 HIPCs were identified, of which 33 were in sub-Saharan Africa. In April 1997 Uganda was approved as the first beneficiary of the initiative (see World Bank, p. 84). Resources for the HIPC initiative are channelled through the PRGF Trust. In early 1999 the IMF and World Bank initiated a comprehensive review of the HIPC scheme, in order to consider modifications of the initiative and to strengthen the link between debt relief and poverty reduction. A consensus emerged among the financial institutions and leading industrialized nations to enhance the scheme, in order to make it available to more countries, and to accelerate the process of providing debt relief. In September the IMF Board of Governors expressed its commitment to undertaking an off-market transaction of a percentage of the Fund's gold reserves (i.e. a sale, at market prices, to central banks of member countries with repayment obligations to the Fund, which were then to be made in gold), as part of the funding arrangements of the enhanced HIPC scheme; this was undertaken during the period December 1999–April 2000. Under the enhanced initiative it was agreed that countries seeking debt relief should first formulate, and successfully implement for at least one year, a national poverty reduction strategy (see above). In May 2000 Uganda became the first country to qualify for full debt relief under the enhanced scheme. By November 2002 six countries had reached completion point under the enhanced HIPC initiative, while 21 eligible countries had reached their decision point (including Côte d'Ivoire, reached under the original scheme). At that time a total of $25,102m. in NPV terms had been committed, of which the Fund's share was $2,043m.

During 2001/02 the IMF approved funding commitments for new arrangements amounting to SDR 41,219m., compared with SDR 14,333m. in the previous year. Of the total amount, SDR 39,438m.

was committed under nine new Stand-by Arrangements and the augmentation of two already in place (for Argentina and Turkey). Nine new PRGF arrangements were approved in 2001/02, amounting to SDR 1,781m., while augmentations of four existing commitments were also approved. During 2001/02 members' purchases from the general resources account amounted to SDR 29,194m., compared with SDR 9,599m. in the previous year, with the main users of IMF resources being Turkey (SDR 16,200m.), Argentina (SDR 5,922m.) and Brazil (SDR 5,277m.). Outstanding IMF credit at 30 April 2002 totalled SDR 58,698m., compared with SDR 48,662m. as at the previous year. In August the Fund approved its largest ever Stand-by credit amounting to SDR 22,800m. in support of the Brazilian Government's efforts to secure economic and financial stability.

TECHNICAL ASSISTANCE

Technical assistance is provided by special missions or resident representatives who advise members on every aspect of economic management, while more specialized assistance is provided by the IMF's various departments. In 2000/01 the IMFC determined that technical assistance should be central to IMF's work in crisis prevention and management, in capacity-building for low-income countries, and in restoring macroeconomic stability in countries following a financial crisis. Technical assistance activities subsequently underwent a process of review and reorganization to align them more closely with IMF policy priorities and other initiatives, for example the Financial Stability Assessment Programme. The majority of technical assistance is provided by the Departments of Monetary and Exchange Affairs, of Fiscal Affairs and of Statistics, and by the IMF Institute. The Institute, founded in 1964, trains officials from member countries in financial analysis and policy, balance-of-payments methodology and public finance; it also gives assistance to national and regional training centres. In May 1998 an IMF—Singapore Regional Training Institute (an affiliate of the IMF Institute) was inaugurated, in collaboration with the Singaporean Government, in order to provide training for officials from the Asia-Pacific region. The IMF is a co-sponsor, with UNDP and the Japan administered account, of the Joint Vienna Institute, which was opened in the Austrian capital in October 1992 and which trains officials from former centrally-planned economies in various aspects of economic management and public administration. In January 1999 the IMF, in co-operation with the African Development Bank and the World Bank, announced the establishment of a Joint Africa Institute, in Abidjan, Côte d'Ivoire, which was to offer training to officials from African countries from the second half of the year. The IMF Institute also co-operates with other established regional training centres and institutes in order to refine its delivery of technical assistance and training services. During 2000/01 the Institute established a new training programme with government officials in the People's Republic of China and agreed to establish a regional training centre for Latin America in Brazil. A Caribbean Regional Technical Assistance Centre (CARTAC), located in Barbados, began operations in November 2001. In October 2002 an East African Regional Technical Assistance Centre (East AFRITAC), based in Dar es Salaam, Tanzania, was inaugurated as the first of a planned series of sub-regional centres in Africa with the objective of developing local capacity in economic and financial management. In the previous month the IMF signed a memorandum of understanding with the African Capacity Building Foundation (q.v.) to strengthen collaboration, in particular within the context of a new IMF Africa Capacity-Building Initiative.

Publications

Annual Report.

Balance of Payments Statistics Yearbook.

Direction of Trade Statistics (quarterly and annually).

Finance and Development (quarterly, published jointly with the World Bank).

Global Financial Stability Report (quarterly).

Government Finance Statistics Yearbook.

IMF Economic Reviews (3 a year).

IMF Research Bulletin (quarterly).

IMF Survey (2 a month).

International Financial Statistics (monthly and annually, also on CD-ROM).

Joint BIS-IMF-OECD-World Bank Statistics on External Debt (quarterly).

Staff Papers (quarterly).

World Economic Outlook (2 a year).

Occasional papers, economic and financial surveys, pamphlets, booklets.

Statistics

QUOTAS (SDR million)

	31 January 2003
Afghanistan*	(161.9) 120.4
Albania	48.7
Algeria	1,254.7
Angola	286.3
Antigua and Barbuda	13.5
Argentina	2,117.1
Armenia	92.0
Australia	3,236.4
Austria	1,872.3
Azerbaijan	160.9
Bahamas	130.3
Bahrain	135.0
Bangladesh	533.3
Barbados	67.5
Belarus	386.4
Belgium	4,605.2
Belize	18.8
Benin	61.9
Bhutan	6.3
Bolivia	171.5
Bosnia and Herzegovina	169.1
Botswana	63.0
Brazil	3,036.1
Brunei	215.2
Bulgaria	640.2
Burkina Faso	60.2
Burundi	77.0
Cambodia	87.5
Cameroon	185.7
Canada	6,369.2
Cape Verde	9.6
Central African Republic	55.7
Chad	56.0
Chile	856.1
China, People's Republic	6,369.2
Colombia	774.0
Comoros	8.9
Congo, Democratic Republic	533.0
Congo, Republic	84.6
Costa Rica	164.1
Côte d'Ivoire	325.2
Croatia	365.1
Cyprus	139.6
Czech Republic	819.3
Denmark	1,642.8
Djibouti	15.9
Dominica	8.2
Dominican Republic	218.9
Ecuador	302.3
Egypt	943.7
El Salvador	171.3
Equatorial Guinea	32.6
Eritrea	15.9
Estonia	65.2
Ethiopia	133.7
Fiji	70.3
Finland	1,263.8
France	10,738.5
Gabon	154.3
The Gambia	31.1
Georgia	150.3
Germany	13,008.2
Ghana	369.0
Greece	823.0
Grenada	11.7
Guatemala	210.2
Guinea	107.1
Guinea-Bissau	14.2
Guyana	90.9
Haiti†	(81.9) 60.7
Honduras	129.5
Hungary	1,038.4
Iceland	117.6
India	4,158.2
Indonesia	2,079.3
Iran	1,497.2
Iraq*	(1,188.4) 504.0
Ireland	838.4
Israel	928.2
Italy	7,055.5

— continued	31 January 2003
Jamaica	273.5
Japan	13,312.8
Jordan	170.5
Kazakhstan	365.7
Kenya	271.4
Kiribati	5.6
Korea, Republic	1,633.6
Kuwait	1,381.1
Kyrgyzstan	88.8
Laos†	52.9
Latvia	126.8
Lebanon	203.0
Lesotho	34.9
Liberia†	(129.2) 71.3
Libya	1,123.7
Lithuania	144.2
Luxembourg	279.1
Macedonia, former Yugoslav republic	68.9
Madagascar	122.2
Malawi	69.4
Malaysia	1,486.6
Maldives	8.2
Mali	93.3
Malta	102.0
Marshall Islands	3.5
Mauritania	64.4
Mauritius	101.6
Mexico	2,585.8
Micronesia, Federated States	5.1
Moldova	123.2
Mongolia	51.1
Morocco	588.2
Mozambique	113.6
Myanmar	258.4
Namibia	136.5
Nepal	71.3
Netherlands	5,162.4
New Zealand	894.6
Nicaragua	130.0
Niger	65.8
Nigeria	1,753.2
Norway	1,671.7
Oman	194.0
Pakistan	1,033.7
Palau	3.1
Panama	206.6
Papua New Guinea	131.6
Paraguay	99.9
Peru	638.4
Philippines	879.9
Poland	1,369.0
Portugal	867.4
Qatar	263.8
Romania	1,030.2
Russia	5,945.4
Rwanda	80.1
Saint Christopher and Nevis	8.9

— continued	31 January 2003
Saint Lucia	15.3
Saint Vincent and the Grenadines	8.3
Samoa	11.6
San Marino	17.0
São Tomé and Príncipe	7.4
Saudi Arabia	6,985.5
Senegal	161.8
Serbia and Montenegro	467.7
Seychelles	8.8
Sierra Leone	103.7
Singapore	862.5
Slovakia	357.5
Slovenia	231.7
Solomon Islands	10.4
Somalia†	(81.7) 44.2
South Africa	1,868.5
Spain	3,048.9
Sri Lanka	413.4
Sudan†	(315.1) 169.7
Suriname	92.1
Swaziland	50.7
Sweden	2,395.5
Switzerland	3,458.5
Syria	293.6
Tajikistan	87.0
Tanzania	198.9
Thailand	1,081.9
Timor-Leste	8.2
Togo	73.4
Tonga	6.9
Trinidad and Tobago	335.6
Tunisia	286.5
Turkey	964.0
Turkmenistan	75.2
Uganda	180.5
Ukraine	1,372.0
United Arab Emirates	611.7
United Kingdom	10,738.5
USA	37,149.3
Uruguay	306.5
Uzbekistan	275.6
Vanuatu	17.0
Venezuela	2,659.1
Viet Nam	329.1
Yemen	243.5
Zambia	489.1
Zimbabwe	353.4

* At 31 January 2003 these members had not yet consented to their increased quotas under the Eleventh General Review. The proposed quotas are those in parentheses.
† At 31 January 2003 these members had overdue obligations and were therefore ineligible to consent to the increase in quotas under the Eleventh General Review (which came into effect in January 1999). The figures listed are those determined under previous reviews, while the figures in parentheses are the proposed Eleventh General Review quotas.

FINANCIAL ACTIVITIES (SDR million, year ending 30 April)

Type of Transaction	1997	1998	1999	2000	2001	2002
Total disbursements	5,644	20,973	24,897	6,890	10,229	30,146
Purchases by facility (General Resources Account)*	4,939	20,000	24,071	6,377	9,599	29,194†
Loans under SAF/PRGF arrangements	705	973	826	513	630	952
Repurchases and repayments	7,196	4,385	11,092	23,627	11,831	19,984
Repurchases	6,668	3,789	10,465	22,993	11,243	19,207
Trust Fund and SAF/PRGF loan repayments	529	596	627	634	588	777
Total outstanding credit provided by Fund (end of year)	40,488	56,026	67,175	50,370	48,662	58,698
Of which:						
General Resources Account	34,539	49,701	60,651	43,968	42,219	52,081
SAF Arrangements	954	730	565	456	432	341
PRGF Arrangements‡	4,904	5,505	5,870	5,857	5,951	6,188
Trust Fund	90	90	89	89	89	89

* Including reserve tranche purchases.
† Comprising (in SDR million): 126 in reserve tranche purchases, 17,219 in Stand-by Arrangements and credit tranche purchases, 958 under the Extended Fund Facility, and 10,891 under the Supplemental Reserve Facility.
‡ Including Saudi Fund for Development associated loans.
Source: *International Monetary Fund Annual Report 2002.*

International Telecommunication Union—ITU

Address: Place des Nations, 1211 Geneva 20, Switzerland.
Telephone: (22) 7305111; **fax:** (22) 7337256; **e-mail:** itumail@itu.int;
internet: www.itu.int.

Founded in 1865, ITU became a specialized agency of the UN in 1947. It acts *inter alia* to encourage world co-operation for the improvement and national use of telecommunications to promote technical development, to harmonize national policies in the field, and to promote the extension of telecommunications throughout the world.

MEMBERS

189 member states: see Table on pp. 125-127. More than 650 scientific and technical companies, public and private operators, broadcasters and other organizations are also ITU members.

Organization

(April 2003)

PLENIPOTENTIARY CONFERENCE

The supreme organ of ITU; normally meets every four years. The main tasks of the Conference are to elect ITU's leadership, establish policies, revise the Constitution and Convention (see below) and approve limits on budgetary spending. The 2002 Conference was held in Marrakesh, Morocco, in September/October.

WORLD CONFERENCES ON INTERNATIONAL TELECOMMUNICATIONS

The World Conferences on International Telecommunications are held at the request of members and after approval by the Plenipotentiary Conference. The World Conferences are authorized to review and revise the regulations applying to the provision and operation of international telecommunications services. As part of the 1993 restructuring of ITU, separate Conferences were to be held by three sectors (see below): Radiocommunication Conferences (to be held every two or three years); Telecommunication Standardization Assemblies (to be held every four years or at the request of one-quarter of ITU members); and Telecommunication Development Conferences (to be held every four years).

ITU COUNCIL

The Council meets annually in Geneva and is composed of 46 members elected by the Plenipotentiary Conference.

The Council ensures the efficient co-ordination and implementation of the work of the Union in all matters of policy, administration and finance, in the interval between Plenipotentiary Conferences, and approves the annual budget.

GENERAL SECRETARIAT

The Secretary-General is elected by the Plenipotentiary Conference, and is responsible to it for the Secretariat's work, and for the Union's administrative and financial services. The Secretariat's staff totals about 790, representing 83 nationalities; the official and working languages are Arabic, Chinese, English, French, Russian and Spanish.

Secretary-General: YOSHIO UTSUMI (Japan).

Deputy Secretary-General: ROBERTO BLOIS MONTES DE SOUZA (Brazil).

Constitution and Convention

Between 1865 and 1992 each Plenipotentiary Conference adopted a new Convention of ITU. At the Additional Plenipotentiary Conference held in December 1992, in Geneva, Switzerland, a new Constitution and Convention were signed. They were partially amended by the following two Plenipotentiary Conferences held in Kyoto, Japan, in 1994, and Minneapolis, USA, in 1998. The Constitution contains the fundamental provisions of ITU, whereas the Convention contains other provisions which complement those of the Constitution and which, by their nature, require periodic revision.

The Constitution establishes the purposes and structure of the Union, contains the general provisions relating to telecommunications and special provisions for radio, and deals with relations with the UN and other organizations. The Convention establishes the functioning of the Union and the three sectors, and contains the general provisions regarding conferences and assemblies. Both instruments are further complemented by the administrative regulations listed below.

INTERNATIONAL TELECOMMUNICATIONS REGULATIONS

The International Telecommunications Regulations were adopted in 1988 and entered into force in 1990. They establish the general principles relating to the provision and operation of international telecommunication services offered to the public. They also establish rules applicable to administrations and recognized private operating agencies. Their provisions are applied to both wire and wireless telegraph and telephone communications in so far as the Radio Regulations do not provide otherwise. The 2002 Plenipotentiary Conference determined to initiate a review process of the International Telecommunications Regulations and agreed to convene a World Conference on International Telecommunications within four to five years, on the basis of recommendations arising from the review.

RADIO REGULATIONS

The Radio Regulations, which first appeared in 1906, include general rules for the assignment and use of frequencies and the associated orbital positions for space stations. They include a Table of Frequency Allocations (governing the use of radio frequency bands between 9 kHz and 400 GHz) for the various radio services (*inter alia* radio broadcasting, television, radio astronomy, navigation aids, point-to-point service, maritime mobile, amateur).

The 1979 World Administrative Radio Conference undertook a complete revision of the radio spectrum allocation. Partial revisions were also made by subsequent world and regional administrative radio conferences, particularly with reference to space radiocommunications, using satellites. The last revision of the Radio Regulations was signed in Istanbul, Turkey, in 2000.

Activities

In December 1992 an Additional Plenipotentiary Conference was held in Geneva, Switzerland, which agreed on reforms to the structure and functioning of ITU. As a result, ITU comprised three sectors corresponding to its main functions: standardization; radiocommunication; and development. Separate sector conferences were to be held. In October 1994 the ordinary Plenipotentiary Conference, held in Kyoto, Japan, adopted ITU's first strategic plan. A second strategic plan, for the period 1999–2003, was adopted by the conference, convened in Minneapolis, USA, in October/November 1998. The plan recognized new trends and developments in the world telecommunication environment, such as globalization, liberalization, and greater competition, assessed their implications for ITU, and proposed new strategies and priorities to enable ITU to function effectively. The conference approved the active involvement of ITU in governance issues relating to the internet, and recommended that a World Summit on the Information Society be convened, given the rapid developments in that field. Accordingly, the Union is undertaking a lead role in organizing the summit, under the auspices of the UN Secretary-General, which was scheduled to be held in two phases: the first to take place in Geneva in December 2003, and the second in Tunisia in 2005. In October 2002 the Plenipotentiary Conference, convened in Marrakesh, Morocco, adopted a strategic plan for the period 2004–07 which emphasized ITU's role in facilitating universal access to the global information economy and society. ITU was to take a lead role in UN initiatives concerning information and communication technologies and support all efforts to bridge the international digital divide.

RADIOCOMMUNICATION SECTOR

The role of the sector is to ensure an equitable and efficient use of the radio-frequency spectrum by all radiocommunication services, to conduct studies, and to adopt recommendations on sector issues. The Radio Regulations are reviewed and revised by the World Radiocommunication Conferences. The technical work on issues to be considered by the conferences is conducted by Radiocommunication Assemblies, on the basis of recommendations made by Study Groups. These groups of experts study technical questions relating to radiocommunications, according to a study programme formulated by the Assemblies. The Assemblies may approve, modify or reject any recommendations of the Study Groups, and are authorized to establish new groups or to abolish others. The procedural rules used in the application of the Radio Regulations were to be considered by a Radio Regulations Board, which may also perform duties relating to the allocation and use of frequencies and consider cases of interference. The sector administers ITU's 'International Mobile Telecommunication-2000' initiative relating to third generation (3G) mobile communication systems, which aims to provide wireless access to the global telecommunication infrastructure through satellite and terrestrial systems.

The administrative work of the sector is the responsibility of the Radiocommunication Bureau, which is headed by an elected Director. The Bureau co-ordinates the work of Study Groups, provides administrative support for the Radio Regulations Board, and works alongside the General Secretariat to prepare conferences and to provide relevant assistance to developing countries. The Director is assisted by an Advisory Group.

Director: Valery Timofeev (Russia).

TELECOMMUNICATION STANDARDIZATION SECTOR

The sector was established to study technical, operational and tariff issues in order to standardize telecommunications throughout the world. The sector's conferences consider draft standards, referred to as Recommendations, which, if approved, establish ITU guidelines to guarantee the effective provision of telecommunication services. According to the priority given to different issues concerning draft standards, the conferences may maintain, establish or abolish Study Groups. Recommendations may be approved outside of the four-year interval between conferences if a Study Group concludes such action to be urgent. According to the 1999–2003 strategic plan, one of the priorities for the sector was to be the formulation of recommendations relating to Internet Protocol-based networks, as well as more general recommendations to keep pace with the rapid technological developments and expansion of market demand. A World Telecommunication Standardization Assembly was held in Montréal, Canada, in September/October 2000, to approve settlement rates for international connections. The meeting also approved the establishment of a management board to oversee the implementation of 3G mobile services. The 2004–07 strategic plan determined that the sector take a greater and more effective role in standards relating to the information society, and co-ordinate work undertaken by other relevant bodies.

Preparations for conferences and other meetings of the sector are made by the Telecommunication Standardization Bureau (ITU-T). It administers the application of conference decisions, as well as relevant provisions of the International Telecommunications Regulations. ITU-T is headed by an elected Director, who is assisted by an Advisory Group. The Director reports to conferences and to the ITU Council on the activities of the sector.

Director: Houlin Zhao (People's Republic of China).

TELECOMMUNICATION DEVELOPMENT SECTOR

The sector's objectives are to facilitate and enhance telecommunications development by offering, organizing and co-ordinating technical co-operation and assistance activities, to promote the development of telecommunication networks and services in developing countries, to facilitate the transfer of appropriate technologies and the use of resources, and to provide advice on issues specific to telecommunications. The sector implements projects under the UN development system or other funding arrangements. The 2004–07 strategic plan emphasized the need for the sector to assist developing countries gain access to and realize the benefits of information and communication technologies.

The sector holds conferences regularly to encourage international co-operation in the development of telecommunications, and to determine strategies for development. Conferences consider the result of work undertaken by Study Groups on issues of benefit to developing countries, including development policy, finance, network planning and operation of services.

The administrative work of the sector is conducted by the Telecommunication Development Bureau, which may also study specific problems presented by a member state. The Director of the Bureau reports to conferences and the ITU Council, and is assisted by an Advisory Board.

Director: Hamedoun I. Touré (Mali).

INFORMATION

ITU issues numerous technical and statistical publications (see below) and maintains a library and archives. It also offers the use of an on-line computer-based telecom information exchange service (TIES), which provides access to ITU databases, document exchange, and other telecommunication information.

Finance

The 1998 Plenipotentiary Conference approved a maximum budget of 333.6m. Swiss francs for the two-year period 2002–03.

Publications

ITU Internet Reports.

ITU News (10 a year, in English, French and Spanish).

World Telecommunication Development Report.

Conventions, statistics, regulations, technical documents and manuals, conference documents.

United Nations Educational, Scientific and Cultural Organization—UNESCO

Address: 7 place de Fontenoy, 75352 Paris 07 SP, France.
Telephone: 1-45-68-10-00; **fax:** 1-45-67-16-90; **e-mail:** scg@unesco.org; **internet:** www.unesco.org.
UNESCO was established in 1946 'for the purpose of advancing, through the educational, scientific and cultural relations of the peoples of the world, the objectives of international peace and the common welfare of mankind'.

MEMBERS

188 members, and six associate members: see Table on pp. 125–127.

Organization

(April 2003)

GENERAL CONFERENCE

The supreme governing body of the Organization, the Conference meets in ordinary session once in two years and is composed of representatives of the member states.

EXECUTIVE BOARD

The Board, comprising 58 members, prepares the programme to be submitted to the Conference and supervises its execution; it meets twice or sometimes three times a year.

SECRETARIAT

Director-General: Koichiro Matsuura (Japan).

CO-OPERATING BODIES

In accordance with UNESCO's constitution, national Commissions have been set up in most member states. These help to integrate work within the member states and the work of UNESCO.

PRINCIPAL REGIONAL OFFICES

Africa

Regional Bureau for Education: BP 3311, Dakar, Senegal; tel. 823-83-93; fax 849-23-23; e-mail dakar@unesco.org; Dir A. Parsuramen.

Regional Bureau for Science: POB 30592, Nairobi, Kenya; tel. (20) 21-59-91; fax (20) 62-12-34; e-mail nairobi@unesco.org; f. 1965 to execute UNESCO's regional science programme, and to assist in the planning and execution of national programmes; Dir Paul B. Vitta.

UNESCO International Institute for Capacity Building in Africa—UNESCO-IICBA: POB 2305, Addis Ababa, Ethiopia; tel. (1) 55-75-86; fax (1) 55-75-85; e-mail webmaster@unesco-iicba.org; internet www.unesco-iicba.org; f. 1999 to promote capacity building in the following areas: teacher education, curriculum development; educational policy, planning and management, and distance education; Dir Dr Fay King Chung.

Arab States

Regional Office for Education in the Arab States: POB 5244, ave Cité Sportive, Beirut, Lebanon; tel. (1) 850075; fax (1) 824854; e-mail beirut@unesco.org; internet www.unesco.org; Dir V. Billeh.

Regional Office for Science and Technology in the Arab States—ROSTAS: 8 Abdel Rahman Fahmy St, Garden City, Cairo 11511, Egypt; tel. (2) 7945599; fax (2) 78945296; e-mail cairo@unesco.org; internet www.unesco-cairo.org; also covers informatics; Dir Dr MOHAMED EL-DEEK.

Regional Office for Social and Human Sciences in the Arab Region: POB 363, 12 rue de Rhodes-Notre Dame, 1002 Tunis, Tunisia; tel. (1) 790947; fax (1) 791588; e-mail tunis@unesco.org; liaison office with the Arab League Educational, Cultural and Scientific Organization; Dir FRANCISCO CARRILLO-MONTESINOS.

Asia and the Pacific

Regional Office for Science and Technology for South-East Asia: UN Building (2nd Floor), Jalan M. H. Thamrin 14, Tromol Pos 1273/JKT, Jakarta 10002, Indonesia; tel. (21) 3141308; fax (21) 3150382; e-mail uhjak@unesco.org; internet www.unesco.or.id; Dir Prof. STEPHEN HILL.

UNESCO Asia and Pacific Regional Bureau for Education: 920 Sukhumvit Rd, POB 967, Bangkok 10110, Thailand; tel. (2) 391-0577; fax (2) 391-0866; e-mail bangkok@unescobkk.org; internet www.unescobkk.org; Dir SHELDON SCHAEFFER.

Europe and North America

European Centre for Higher Education (CEPES): Str. Stirbei Vodă 39, 70732 Bucharest, Romania; tel. (1) 3159956; fax (1) 3123567; e-mail cepes@cepes.ro; internet www.cepes.ro; Dir JAN SADLAK.

Regional Office for Science and Technology for Europe: Palazzo Loredan degli Ambasciatori, 1262/A Dorsoduro, 30123 Venice, Italy; tel. (041) 522-5535; fax (041) 528-9995; e-mail roste@unesco.org; internet www.unesco.org/venice; Dir Prof. PIERRE LASSERRE.

Latin America and the Caribbean

Caribbean Network of Educational Innovation for Development: POB 423, Bridgetown, St Michael, Barbados; tel. 427-4771; fax 436-0094; e-mail unesco@ribsurf.com; internet www.unesco.org/ext/field/carneid; Head of Office R. COLLEEN WINTER-BRAITHWAITE.

International Institute for Higher Education in Latin America and the Caribbean (IESALC): Ave Los Chorros, c/c Calle Acueducto, Edif. Asovincar, Altos de Sebucan, Apdo 68394, Caracas 1062 A, Venezuela; tel. (2) 283-1411; fax (2) 283-1454; e-mail caracas@unesco.org; internet www.iesalc.unesco.org.ve; Dir CLAUDIO RAMA VITALE.

Regional Office for Culture in Latin America and the Caribbean (ORCALC): Apdo 4158, Havana 4, Cuba; tel. (7) 832-7741; fax (7) 833-3144; e-mail havana@unesco.org.cu; internet www.unesco.org.cu; f. 1950; activities include research and programmes of cultural development and cultural tourism; maintains a documentation centre and a library of 14,500 vols; Dir FRANCISCO JOSÉ LACAYO PARAJÓN. Publs *Oralidad* (annually), *Boletín Electrónico* (quarterly).

Regional Office for Education in Latin America and the Caribbean (OREALC): Calle Enrique Delpiano 2058, Plaza Pedro de Valdivia, Casilla 3187, Santiago, Chile; tel. (2) 2049032; fax (2) 2091875; e-mail unesco@unesco.org.cl; internet www.unesco.cl; Dir ANA LUIZA MACHADO PINHEIRO.

Regional Office for Science for Latin America and the Caribbean: Calle Dr Luis Piera 1992, 2°, Casilla 859, 11000 Montevideo, Uruguay; tel. (2)413-2075; fax (2) 413-2094; e-mail orcyt@unesco.org.uy; internet www.unesco.org.uy; Dir MIGUEL ANGEL ENRÍQUES BERCIANO.

Activities

In November 2001 the General Conference approved a medium-term strategy to guide UNESCO during the period 2002–07. The Conference adopted a new unifying theme for the organization: 'UNESCO contributing to peace and human development in an era of globalization through education, the sciences, culture and communication'. UNESCO's central mission as defined under the strategy was to contribute to peace and human development in the globalized world through its four programme domains (Education, Natural and Social and Human Sciences, Culture, and Communication and Information), incorporating the following three principal dimensions: developing universal principles and norms to meet emerging challenges and protect the 'common public good'; promoting pluralism and diversity; and promoting empowerment and participation in the emerging knowledge society through equitable access, capacity-building and knowledge-sharing. Programme activities were to be focused particularly on supporting disadvantaged and excluded groups or geographic regions. The organization aimed to decentralize its operations in order to ensure more country-driven programming. UNESCO's overall work programme for 2002–03 comprised the following major programmes: education; natural sciences; social and human sciences; culture; and communication and information. Basic education; fresh water resources and ecosystems; the ethics of science and technology; diversity, intercultural pluralism and dialogue; and universal access to information, especially in the public domain, were designated as the priority themes. The work programme incorporated two transdisciplinary projects—eradication of poverty, especially extreme poverty; and the contribution of information and communication technologies to the development of education, science and culture and the construction of a knowledge society. UNESCO aims to promote a culture of peace. The UN General Assembly designated UNESCO as the lead agency for co-ordinating the International Decade for a Culture of Peace and Non-Violence for the Children of the World (2001–10), with a focus on education, and the UN Literacy Decade (2003–12). In the implementation of all its activities UNESCO aims to contribute to achieving the UN Millennium Goal of halving levels of extreme poverty by 2015.

Since the 1990s Africa has been a priority focus of UNESCO's activities. In November 2001 UNESCO organized an international seminar entitled *Forward-looking approaches and innovative strategies to promote the development of Africa in the 21st century*, which aimed to review UNESCO's strategy on Africa in the light of the recently-launched New Partnership on Africa's Development (q.v.).

EDUCATION

Since its establishment UNESCO has devoted itself to promoting education in accordance with principles based on democracy and respect for human rights.

In March 1990 UNESCO, with other UN agencies, sponsored the World Conference on Education for All. 'Education for All' was subsequently adopted as a guiding principle of UNESCO's contribution to development. UNESCO advocates 'Literacy for All' as a key component of 'Education for All', regarding literacy as essential to basic education and to social and human development. In April 2000 several UN agencies, including UNESCO and UNICEF, and other partners sponsored the World Education Forum, held in Dakar, Senegal, to assess international progress in achieving the goal of 'Education for All' and to adopt a strategy for further action (the 'Dakar Framework'), with the aim of ensuring universal basic education by 2015. The Forum launched the Global Initiative for Education for All. The Dakar Framework emphasized the role of improved access to education in the reduction of poverty and in diminishing inequalities within and between societies. UNESCO was appointed as the lead agency in the implementation of the Framework. UNESCO's role in pursuing the goals of the Dakar Forum was to focus on co-ordination, advocacy, mobilization of resources, and information-sharing at international, regional and national levels. It was to oversee national policy reforms, with a particular focus on the integration of 'Education for All' objectives into national education plans, which were to be produced by all member countries by 2002. UNESCO's work programme on Education for 2002–03 aimed to promote an effective follow-up to the Forum and comprised the following two main components: Basic Education for All: Meeting the Commitments of the Dakar World Education Forum; and Building Knowledge Societies through Quality Education and a Renewal of Education Systems. 'Basic Education for All', signifying the promotion of access to learning opportunities throughout the lives of all individuals, including the most disadvantaged, was designated as the principal theme of the programme and was deemed to require urgent action. The second part of the strategy was to improve the quality of educational provision and renew and diversify education systems, with a view to ensuring that educational needs at all levels were met. This component included updating curricular programmes in secondary education, strengthening science and technology activities and ensuring equal access to education for girls and women. (UNESCO supports the UN Girls' Education Initiative, established following the Dakar Forum.) The work programme focused on the importance of knowledge, information and communication in the increasingly globalized world, and the significance of education as a means of empowerment for the poor and of enhancing basic quality of life.

In December 1993 the heads of government of nine highly-populated developing countries (Bangladesh, Brazil, the People's Republic of China, Egypt, India, Indonesia, Mexico, Nigeria and Pakistan), meeting in Delhi, India, agreed to co-operate, with the objective of achieving comprehensive primary education for all children and of expanding further learning opportunities for children and adults. By September 1999 all of the so-called 'E-9' (or Education-9) countries had officially signed the 'Delhi Declaration' issued by the meeting. An evaluation of the 'E-9' initiative was to be conducted during the period of UNESCO's 2002–03 work programme.

Within the UN system, UNESCO is responsible for providing technical assistance and educational services in the context of emergency situations. This includes providing education to refugees and displaced persons, as well as assistance for the rehabilitation of national education systems. In Palestine, UNESCO collaborates with UNRWA (q.v.) to assist with the training of teachers, educational planning and rehabilitation of schools.

UNESCO is concerned with improving the quality, relevance and efficiency of higher education. It assists member states in reforming their national systems, organizes high-level conferences for Ministers of Education and other decision-makers, and disseminates research papers. A World Conference on Higher Education was convened in October 1998 in Paris, France. The Conference adopted a World Declaration on Higher Education for the 21st Century, incorporating proposals to reform higher education, with emphasis on access to education, and educating for individual development and active participation in society. The Conference also approved a framework for Priority Action for Change and Development of Higher Education, which comprised guide-lines for governments and institutions to meet the objectives of greater accessibility, as well as improved standards and relevancy of higher education.

The International Institute for Educational Planning and the International Bureau of Education (see below) undertake training, research and the exchange of information on aspects of education. A UNESCO Institute for Education, based in Hamburg, Germany, researches literacy activities and the evolution of adult learning systems. UNESCO aims to promote the use of new information and communication technologies in the expansion of learning opportunities. A joint UNESCO/ILO committee of experts has been established to consider strategies for enhancing the status of the teaching profession. The UNESCO International Institute for Capacity Building in Africa, based in Addis Ababa, Ethiopia, promotes capacity building in teacher education, curriculum development, educational policy, planning and management, and distance education.

The April 2000 World Education Forum recognized the global HIV/AIDS pandemic to be a significant challenge to the attainment of 'Education for All'. UNESCO, as a co-sponsor of UNAIDS, takes an active role in promoting formal and non-formal preventive health education.

NATURAL SCIENCES

In November 1999 the General Conference endorsed a Declaration on Science and the Use of Scientific Knowledge and an agenda for action, which had been adopted at the World Conference on Science, held in June/July 1999, in Budapest, Hungary. UNESCO was to co-ordinate the follow-up to the conference and, in conjunction with the International Council for Science (q.v.), to promote initiatives in international scientific partnership. The following were identified as priority areas of UNESCO's work programme on Natural Sciences for 2002–03: Science and Technology: Capacity-building and Management; and Sciences, Environment and Sustainable Development. Water Security in the 21st Century was designated as the principal theme, involving addressing threats to water resources and their associated ecosystems. UNESCO was the lead UN agency involved in the preparation of the first *World Water Development Report*, issued in March 2003. UNESCO was a joint co-ordinator of the International Year of Freshwater (2003), which aimed to raise global awareness of the importance of improving the protection and management of fresh water resources. The Science and Technology component of the programme focused on the follow-up of the World Conference on Science, involving the elaboration of national policies on science and technology; strengthening science education; improving university teaching and enhancing national research capacities; and reinforcing international co-operation in mathematics, physics, chemistry, biology, biotechnology and the engineering sciences. UNESCO aims to contribute to bridging the divide between community-held traditional knowledge and scientific knowledge.

UNESCO aims to improve the level of university teaching of the basic sciences through training courses, establishing national and regional networks and centres of excellence, and fostering co-operative research. In carrying out its mission, UNESCO relies on partnerships with non-governmental organizations and the world scientific communities. With the International Council of Scientific Unions and the Third World Academy of Sciences, UNESCO operates a short-term fellowship programme in the basic sciences and an exchange programme of visiting lecturers. In September 1996 UNESCO initiated a 10-year World Solar Programme, which aimed to promote the application of solar energy and to increase research, development and public awareness of all forms of ecologically-sustainable energy use.

UNESCO has over the years established various forms of intergovernmental co-operation concerned with the environmental sciences and research on natural resources, in order to support the recommendations of the June 1992 UN Conference on Environment and Development and, in particular, the implementation of 'Agenda 21' to promote sustainable development. The International Geological Correlation Programme, undertaken jointly with the International Union of Geological Sciences, aims to improve and facilitate global research of geological processes. In the context of the International Decade for Natural Disaster Reduction (declared in 1990), UNESCO conducted scientific studies of natural hazards and means of mitigating their effects and organized several disaster-related workshops. The International Hydrological Programme considers scientific aspects of water resources assessment and management; and the Intergovernmental Oceanographic Commission (IOC, q.v.) focuses on issues relating to oceans, shorelines and marine resources, in particular the role of the ocean in climate and global systems. The IOC has

been actively involved in the establishment of a Global Coral Reef Monitoring Network and is developing a Global Ocean Observing System. An initiative on Environment and Development in Coastal Regions and in Small Islands is concerned with ensuring environmentally-sound and sustainable development by strengthening management of the following key areas: freshwater resources; the mitigation of coastline instability; biological diversity; and coastal ecosystem productivity. UNESCO hosts the secretariat of the World Water Assessment Programme on freshwater resources.

UNESCO's Man and the Biosphere Programme supports a world-wide network of biosphere reserves (comprising 425 sites in 95 countries in February 2003), which aim to promote environmental conservation and research, education and training in biodiversity and problems of land use (including the fertility of tropical soils and the cultivation of sacred sites). In October 2002 UNESCO announced that the 138 biospheres in mountainous areas would play a leading role in a new Global Change Monitoring Programme aimed at assessing the impact of global climate changes. Following the signing of the Convention to Combat Desertification in October 1994, UNESCO initiated an International Programme for Arid Land Crops, based on a network of existing institutions, to assist implementation of the Convention.

Abdus Salam International Centre for Theoretical Physics: based in Trieste, Italy, the Centre brings together scientists from the developed and developing countries. With support from the Italian Government, the Centre has been operated jointly by the IAEA and UNESCO since 1970. At the end of 1995 administrative responsibility for the Centre was transferred to UNESCO, although IAEA remained a partner in the operations of the Centre. Each year it offers seminars followed by a research workshop, as well as short topical seminars, training courses, symposia and panels. Independent research is also carried out. The programme concentrates on condensed matter physics, high-energy physics, mathematics, physics of weather and climate, structure and nonlinear dynamics of the earth, and microprocessors; Dir KATEPALLI R. SREENIVASEN.

SOCIAL AND HUMAN SCIENCES

UNESCO is mandated to contribute to the world-wide development of the social and human sciences and philosophy, which it regards as of great importance in policy-making and maintaining ethical vigilance. The structure of UNESCO's Social and Human Sciences programme takes into account both an ethical and standard-setting dimension, and research, policy-making, action in the field and future-oriented activities. UNESCO's work programme for 2002–03 on Social and Human Sciences comprised three main components: The Ethics of Science and Technology; Promotion of Human Rights, Peace and Democratic Principles; and Improvement of Policies Relating to Social Transformations and Promotion of Anticipation and Prospective Studies. The priority Ethics of Science and Technology element aimed to reinforce UNESCO's role as an intellectual forum for ethical reflection on challenges related to the advance of science and technology; oversee the follow-up of the Universal Declaration on the Human Genome and Human Rights (see below); promote education in science and technology; ensure UNESCO's role in promoting good practices through encouraging the inclusion of ethical guiding principles in policy formulation and reinforcing international networks; and to promote international co-operation in human sciences and philosophy. The Social and Human Sciences programme had the main intellectual and conceptual responsibility for the transdisciplinary theme 'eradication of poverty, especially extreme poverty'.

UNESCO aims to promote and protect human rights and acts as an interdisciplinary, multicultural and pluralistic forum for reflection on issues relating to the ethical dimension of scientific advances, for example in biogenetics, new technology, and medicine. In May 1997 the International Bioethics Committee, a group of 36 specialists who meet under UNESCO auspices, approved a draft version of a Universal Declaration on the Human Genome and Human Rights, in an attempt to provide ethical guide-lines for developments in human genetics. The Declaration, which identified some 100,000 hereditary genes as 'common heritage', was adopted by the UNESCO General Conference in November and committed states to promoting the dissemination of relevant scientific knowledge and co-operating in genome research. The November Conference also resolved to establish an 18-member World Commission on the Ethics of Scientific Knowledge and Technology (COMEST) to serve as a forum for the exchange of information and ideas and to promote dialogue between scientific communities, decision-makers and the public. UNESCO hosts the secretariat of COMEST. COMEST met for the first time in April 1999 in Oslo, Norway. Its second meeting, which took place in December 2001 in Berlin, Germany, focused on the ethics of energy, fresh water and outer space.

In 1994 UNESCO initiated an international social science research programme, the Management of Social Transformations (MOST), to promote capacity-building in social planning at all levels of decision-making. UNESCO sponsors several research fellowships in the social sciences. In other activities UNESCO promotes the rehabilitation of underprivileged urban areas, the research of socio-cultural factors affecting demographic change, and the study of family issues.

UNESCO aims to assist the building and consolidation of peaceful and democratic societies. An international network of institutions and centres involved in research on conflict resolution is being established to support the promotion of peace. Other training, workshop and research activities have been undertaken in countries that have suffered conflict. The Associated Schools Project (ASPnet—comprising 6,483 institutions in 166 countries in early 2003) has, for 50 years, promoted the principles of peace, human rights, democracy and international co-operation through education. An International Youth Clearing House and Information Service (INFOYOUTH) aims to increase and consolidate the information available on the situation of young people in society, and to heighten awareness of their needs, aspirations and potential among public and private decision-makers. UNESCO also focuses on the educational and cultural dimensions of physical education and sport and their capacity to preserve and improve health. Fundamental to UNESCO's mission is the rejection of all forms of discrimination. It disseminates scientific information aimed at combating racial prejudice, works to improve the status of women and their access to education, and promotes equality between men and women.

CULTURE

In undertaking efforts to preserve the world's cultural and natural heritage UNESCO has attempted to emphasize the link between culture and development. In November 2001 the General Conference adopted the UNESCO Universal Declaration on Cultural Diversity, which affirmed the importance of intercultural dialogue in establishing a climate of peace. The work programme on Culture for 2002–03 included the following interrelated components: Reinforcing Normative Action in the Field of Culture; Protecting Cultural Diversity and Promoting Cultural Pluralism and Intercultural Dialogue; and Strengthening Links between Culture and Development. The focus was to be on all aspects of cultural heritage, and on the encouragement of cultural diversity and dialogue between cultures and civilizations. Under the 2002–03 programme UNESCO aimed to launch the Global Alliance on Cultural Diversity, a six-year initiative to promote partnerships between governments, non-governmental bodies and the private sector, with a view to supporting cultural diversity through the strengthening of cultural industries and the prevention of cultural piracy. UNESCO was designated as the lead agency for co-ordinating the UN Year for Cultural Heritage, celebrated in 2002.

UNESCO's World Heritage Programme, inaugurated in 1978, aims to protect historic sites and natural landmarks of outstanding universal significance, in accordance with the 1972 UNESCO Convention Concerning the Protection of the World Cultural and Natural Heritage, by providing financial aid for restoration, technical assistance, training and management planning. By June 2002 the 'World Heritage List' comprised 730 sites in 125 countries, of which 563 had cultural significance, 144 were natural landmarks, and 23 were of 'mixed' importance. Examples include: the Great Barrier Reef in Australia, the Galapagos Islands (Ecuador), Chartres Cathedral (France), the Taj Mahal at Agra (India), Auschwitz concentration camp (Poland), the historic sanctuary of Machu Picchu (Peru), Robben Island (South Africa), the Serengeti National Park (Tanzania), and the archaeological site of Troy (Turkey). UNESCO also maintains a 'List of World Heritage in Danger', comprising 33 sites at June 2002, in order to attract international attention to sites particularly at risk from the environment or human activities. In early 2001 UNESCO condemned an edict by the fundamentalist Islamist Taliban regime in Afghanistan ordering the destruction of all statues in that country which, owing to their representation of human likenesses, were regarded as non-Islamic. In March UNESCO protested strongly against the reported destruction by order of the Taliban of two ancient monuments of Buddha at Bamiyan. In October 2002 UNESCO's Executive Board approved the establishment of an International Co-ordination Committee for the Safeguarding of Afghanistan's Cultural Heritage, to be administered by UNESCO with participation by other agencies and organizations, donor nations and experts. The formulation of a Declaration against the Intentional Destruction of Cultural Heritage was authorized by the General Conference in November 2001. In addition, the November General Conference adopted the Convention on the Protection of the Underwater Cultural Heritage, covering the protection from commercial exploitation of shipwrecks, submerged historical sites, etc., situated in the territorial waters of signatory states. UNESCO also administers the 1954 Hague Convention on the Protection of Cultural Property in the Event of Armed Conflict and the 1970 Convention on the Means of Prohibiting and Preventing the Illicit Import, Export and Transfer of Ownership of Cultural Property. In 1992 a World Heritage Centre was established to enable rapid mobilization of international technical assistance for the preservation of cultural sites. Through the World Heritage Information Network (WHIN), a world-wide network of more than 800 information providers, UNESCO promotes global awareness and information exchange.

UNESCO supports efforts for the collection and safeguarding of humanity's non-material 'intangible' heritage, including oral traditions, music, dance and medicine. In May 2001 UNESCO awarded the title of 'Masterpieces of the Oral and Intangible Heritage of Humanity' to 19 cultural spaces (i.e. physical or temporal spaces hosting recurrent cultural events) and popular forms of expression deemed to be of outstanding value. UNESCO produces an *Atlas of the World's Languages in Danger of Disappearing*. The most recent edition, issued in February 2002, reported that, of some 6,000 languages spoken world-wide, about one-half were endangered.

UNESCO encourages the translation and publication of literary works, publishes albums of art, and produces records, audiovisual programmes and travelling art exhibitions. It supports the development of book publishing and distribution, including the free flow of books and educational material across borders, and the training of editors and managers in publishing. UNESCO is active in preparing and encouraging the enforcement of international legislation on copyright.

In December 1992 UNESCO established the World Commission on Culture and Development, to strengthen links between culture and development and to prepare a report on the issue. The first World Conference on Culture and Development was held in June 1999, in Havana, Cuba. Within the context of the UN's World Decade for Cultural Development (1988–97) UNESCO launched the Silk Roads Project, as a multi-disciplinary study of the interactions among cultures and civilizations along the routes linking Asia and Europe, and established an International Fund for the Promotion of Culture, awarding two annual prizes for music and the promotion of arts. In April 1999 UNESCO celebrated the completion of a major international project, the *General History of Africa*.

COMMUNICATION AND INFORMATION

In 2001 UNESCO introduced a major programme, 'Information for All', as the principal policy-guiding framework for the Communication and Information sector. The organization works towards establishing an open, non-exclusive knowledge society based on information-sharing and incorporating the socio-cultural and ethical dimensions of sustainable development. It promotes the free flow of, and universal access to information, knowledge, data and best practices, through the development of communications infrastructures, the elimination of impediments to freedom of expression, and the promotion of the right to information; through encouraging international co-operation in maintaining libraries and archives; and through efforts to harness informatics for development purposes and strengthen member states' capacities in this field. Activities include assistance with the development of legislation and training programmes in countries where independent and pluralistic media are emerging; assistance in the monitoring of media independence, pluralism and diversity; promotion of exchange programmes and study tours; and improving access and opportunities for women in the media. UNESCO recognizes that the so-called global 'digital divide', in addition to other developmental differences between countries, generates exclusion and marginalization, and that increased participation in the democratic process can be attained through strengthening national communication and information capacities. UNESCO promotes the upholding of human rights in the use of cyberspace. The organization was to participate in the World Summit on the Information Society, scheduled to take place in Geneva, Switzerland, in December 2003. The work programme on Communication and Information for 2002–03 comprised the following components: Promoting Equitable Access to Information and Knowledge Especially in the Public Domain; and Promoting Freedom of Expression and Strengthening Communication Capacities. During 2002–03 UNESCO was to evaluate its interactive internet-based WebWorld Portal, which aims to provide global communication and information services at all levels of society. UNESCO's Memory of the World project aims to preserve in digital form, and thereby to promote wide access to, the world's documentary heritage.

In regions affected by conflict UNESCO supports efforts to establish and maintain an independent media service. This strategy is largely implemented through an International Programme for the Development of Communication (IPDC—see below). In Cambodia, Haiti and Mozambique UNESCO participated in the restructuring of the media in the context of national reconciliation and in Bosnia and Herzegovina it assisted in the development of independent media. In December 1998 the Israeli–Palestinian Media Forum was established, to foster professional co-operation between Israeli and Palestinian journalists. IPDC provides support to communication and media development projects in the developing world, including the establishment of news agencies and newspapers and training editorial and technical staff. Since its establishment in 1982 IPDC has financed some 1,000 projects in more than 130 countries.

In March 1997 the first International Congress on Ethical, Legal and Societal Aspects of Digital Information ('InfoEthics') was held in Monte Carlo, Monaco. At the second 'InfoEthics' Congress, held in October 1998, experts discussed issues concerning privacy, confidentiality and security in the electronic transfer of information. UNESCO maintains an Observatory on the Information Society, which provides up-to-date information on the development of new information and communications technologies, analyses major trends, and aims to raise awareness of related ethical, legal and societal issues. A UNESCO Institute for Information Technologies in Education was established in Moscow, Russia in 1998. In 2001 the UNESCO Institute for Statistics was established in Montréal, Canada.

Finance

UNESCO's activities are funded through a regular budget provided by contributions from member states and extrabudgetary funds from other sources, particularly UNDP, the World Bank, regional banks and other bilateral Funds-in-Trust arrangements. UNESCO co-operates with many other UN agencies and international non-governmental organizations.

UNESCO's Regular Programme budget for the two years 2002–03 was US $544.4m., the same as for the previous biennium. Extrabudgetary funds for 2002–03 were estimated at $320m.

Publications

(mostly in English, French and Spanish editions; Arabic, Chinese and Russian versions are also available in many cases)

Atlas of the World's Languages in Danger of Disappearing.
Copyright Bulletin (quarterly).
Encyclopedia of Life Support Systems (internet-based).
International Review of Education (quarterly).
International Social Science Journal (quarterly).
Museum International (quarterly).
Nature and Resources (quarterly).
Prospects (quarterly review on education).
UNESCO Courier (monthly, in 27 languages).
UNESCO Sources (monthly).
UNESCO Statistical Yearbook.
World Communication Report.
World Educational Report (every 2 years).
World Heritage Review (quarterly).
World Information Report.
World Science Report (every 2 years).
Books, databases, video and radio documentaries, statistics, scientific maps and atlases.

INTERGOVERNMENTAL COMMITTEE FOR PHYSICAL EDUCATION AND SPORT

Address: 7 place de Fontenoy, 75352 Paris, France.

Established by UNESCO in 1978 to serve as a permanent intergovernmental body in the field of physical education and sport.

The Committee is composed of 30 representatives of member states of UNESCO, elected by the General Conference.

Among its many activities aimed at further development of physical education and sport throughout the world, the Committee is responsible for supervising the planning and implementation of UNESCO's programme of activities in physical education and sport, promoting international co-operation in this area and facilitating the adoption and implementation of an International Charter of physical education and sport.

INTERNATIONAL BUREAU OF EDUCATION—IBE

Address: POB 199, 1211 Geneva 20, Switzerland.
Telephone: (22) 9177800; **fax:** (22) 9177801; **e-mail:** doc.centre@ibe.unesco.org; **internet:** www.ibe.unesco.org.

Founded in 1925, the IBE became an intergovernmental organization in 1929 and was incorporated into UNESCO in 1969. The Bureau's fundamental mission is to deal with matters concerning educational content, methods, and teaching/learning strategies. In addition, the IBE, as an observatory of educational trends and innovations, has assumed responsibilities in the field of educational information. It

publishes a quarterly review of education and a newsletter, in addition to various monographs and reference works. The Council of the IBE is composed of representatives of 28 member states of UNESCO, designated by the General Conference. The International Conference on Education is held periodically.

Director: Cecilia Braslavsky (Argentina).

INTERNATIONAL CENTRE FOR TECHNICAL AND VOCATIONAL EDUCATION AND TRAINING

Address: Gorrestr. 15, 53113 Bonn, Germany.
Telephone: (228) 243370; **fax:** (228) 2433777; **e-mail:** bonn@unesco.org.

The Institute, inaugurated in April 2002, promotes high-quality lifelong technical and vocational education in UNESCO's member states, with a particular focus on young people, girls and women, and the disadvantaged.

Director: Rupert Maclean.

INTERNATIONAL INSTITUTE FOR EDUCATIONAL PLANNING—IIEP

Address: 7–9 rue Eugène Delacroix, 75116 Paris, France.
Telephone: 1-45-03-77-00; **fax:** 1-40-72-83-66; **e-mail:** information@iiep.unesco.org; **internet:** www.unesco.org/iiep.

The Institute was established by UNESCO in 1963 to serve as a world centre for advanced training and research in educational planning. Its purpose is to help all member states of UNESCO in their social and economic development efforts, by enlarging the fund of knowledge about educational planning and the supply of competent experts in this field.

Legally and administratively a part of UNESCO, the Institute is autonomous, and its policies and programme are controlled by its own Governing Board, under special statutes voted by the General Conference of UNESCO.

A satellite office of the IIEP was opened in Buenos Aires, Argentina, in June 1998.

Director: Gudmund Hernes (Norway).

UNESCO INSTITUTE FOR EDUCATION

Address: Feldbrunnenstr. 58, 20148 Hamburg, Germany.
Telephone: (40) 448-0410; **e-mail:** uie@unesco.org; **internet:** www.unesco.org/education/uie/institute/about.shtml.

UNESCO established the Institute in 1951 as a research, training, information, documentation and publishing centre, with a particular focus on adult basic and further education and adult literacy.

Director: Adama Ouane (Mali).

UNESCO INSTITUTE FOR INFORMATION TECHNOLOGIES IN EDUCATION

Address: 8 Kedrova St, 117292 Moscow, Russia.
Telephone: (95) 1292990; **fax:** (95) 1291225; **e-mail:** info@iite.ru; **internet:** www.iite.ru/iite.

The Institute aims to formulate policies regarding the development of, and to support and monitor the use of, information and communication technologies in education. The Institute also conducts research and organizes training programmes.

Director: Vladimir Kinelev.

UNESCO INSTITUTE FOR STATISTICS

Address: CP 6128, Succursale Centre-Ville, Montréal, QC, H3C 3J7, Canada.
Telephone: (514) 343-6880; **fax:** (514) 343-6882; **e-mail:** uis@unesco.org; **internet:** www.uis.unesco.org.

The Institute for Statistics, established in 2001, collects and analyzes national statistics on education, science, technology, culture and communications.

Director: Denise Lievesley.

United Nations Industrial Development Organization—UNIDO

Address: Vienna International Centre, POB 300, 1400 Vienna, Austria.

Telephone: (1) 26026; **fax:** (1) 2692669; **e-mail:** unido@unido.org; **internet:** www.unido.org.

UNIDO began operations in 1967, as an autonomous organization within the UN Secretariat, and became a specialized agency of the UN in 1985. UNIDO's objective is to promote sustainable industrial development in developing nations and states with economies in transition. It aims to assist such countries to integrate fully into the global economic system by mobilizing knowledge, skills, information and technology to promote productive employment, competitive economies and sound environment.

MEMBERS

169 members: see Table on pp. 125–127.

Organization

(April 2003)

GENERAL CONFERENCE

The General Conference, which consists of representatives of all member states, meets once every two years. It is the chief policy-making organ of the Organization, and reviews UNIDO's policy concepts, strategies on industrial development and budget. The ninth General Conference was held in Vienna, Austria, in December 2001.

INDUSTRIAL DEVELOPMENT BOARD

The Board consists of 53 members elected by the General Conference for a four-year period. It reviews the implementation of the approved work programme, the regular and operational budgets and other General Conference decisions, and, every four years, recommends a candidate for the post of Director-General to the General Conference for appointment.

PROGRAMME AND BUDGET COMMITTEE

The Committee, consisting of 27 members elected by the General Conference for a two-year term, assists the Industrial Development Board in preparing work programmes and budgets.

SECRETARIAT

The Secretariat comprises the office of the Director-General and three divisions, each headed by a Managing Director: Programme Development and Technical Co-operation; Programme Co-ordination and Field Operations; and Administration. In 2002 the Secretariat comprised 553 staff members.

Director-General: CARLOS ALFREDO MAGARIÑOS (Argentina).

FIELD REPRESENTATION

In December 2001 UNIDO had 18 country and nine functioning regional offices. There were 108 permanent field staff.

Activities

In its efforts to promote the advancement and integration of industry, UNIDO fulfils two core functions. Firstly, as a global forum, it generates and disseminates knowledge relating to industrial matters and provides a platform for policy- and decision-makers to enhance co-operation, establish dialogue and develop partnerships to address effectively challenges to sustainable industrialization. Secondly, as a technical co-operation agency, UNIDO designs and implements programmes to support national industrial development efforts. It also offers specialized support for programme development. The two core functions are complementary and mutually supportive: policy-makers benefit from experience gained in technical co-operation projects, while, by helping to define priorities, the Organization's analytical work identifies where technical co-operation will have greatest impact.

UNIDO's services are designed to be easily integrated into country-specific packages, and local ownership ensures a custom-made approach. The comprehensive services provided by UNIDO cover:

  (i) Industrial governance;
  (ii) Promotion of investment and technology;
  (iii) Quality infrastructure and productivity;
  (iv) Private-sector development;

  (v) The Montreal Protocol;
  (vi) Industrial development and the Kyoto Protocol;
  (vii) Environmental management.
  (viii) Support for agro-industry production.

Between 1993 and 1998 UNIDO implemented a major restructuring programme in order to respond to changes in the global economy and industrial development. The seventh session of the General Conference, held in December 1997, endorsed a Business Plan on the Future Role and Functions of UNIDO, which regrouped the Organization's activities into two main areas—Strengthening of industrial capacities, and Cleaner and sustainable industrial development. According to the Plan, activities were to be concentrated in support of the development and mainstreaming of small and medium-sized enterprises—SMEs (identified as the principal means for achieving equitable and sustainable industrial development), in support of agro-based industries and their integration into national industrial structures, and in least-developed countries (LDCs), in particular in Africa, with emphasis on service provision at regional and sub-regional level. In December 1999, at its eighth session, the General Conference approved funding arrangements for a new strategy of developing integrated industrial service packages designed specifically for individual countries. (Some 44 of these were being implemented at December 2001, with a total value of US $257.1m. The first regional integrated programme was initiated in 2001, covering six West African countries—see below.)

In 2001 UNIDO's investment promotion and institutional capacity-building activities delivered US $84.9m. in technical co-operation to developing countries and economies in transition in seven priority areas: industrial policy forumulation and implementation; statistics and information networks; metrology, standardization, certification and accreditation; continuous improvement and quality management; investment and technology promotion; policy framework for SMEs; policy for women's entrepreneurship and entrepreneurship development. UNIDO has extended its networking with the private sector while assisting developing countries and economies in transition with capacity-building for sustained industrial growth. Promotion of business partnerships, for example, has been strengthened through the Organization's world-wide network of investment and technology promotion offices, investment promotion units, and subcontracting and partnership exchanges, as well as through the Asia-Africa Investment and Technology Promotion Centre. UNIDO has pursued efforts to overcome the so-called 'digital divide' between and within countries. The Organization has helped to develop electronic and mobile business for SMEs in developing countries and economies in transition. It has also launched an internet-based electronic platform, UNIDO Exchange (accessible at (www.unido.org/exchange), for sharing intelligence and fostering business partnerships. UNIDO's Technology Foresight initiative, launched in 1999, involves the systematic visualization of long-term developments in the areas of science, technology, industry, economy and society, with the aim of identifying technologies capable of providing future economic and social benefits. The initiative is being implemented in Latin America and the Caribbean and in Central and Eastern Europe and the CIS.

Through strategic alliances with international certification and standards organizations UNIDO is assisting enterprises in developing countries to overcome technical barriers while improving product quality and access to international markets. UNIDO's industrial business development services—such as business incubators, rural entrepreneurship development and SME cluster development—for SME support institutions are aimed at enabling SMEs to play a key role in economic growth.

UNIDO provides advice to governmental agencies and industrial institutions to improve the management of human resources. The Organization also undertakes training projects to develop human resources in specific industries, and aims to encourage the full participation of women in economic progress through gender awareness programmes and practical training to improve women's access to employment and business opportunities.

UNIDO participated in the Third United Nations Conference on the Least-Developed Countries (UN-LDCs III), held in Brussels, Belgium, in May 2001. The Organization launched a package of 'deliverables' (special initiatives) in support of the Programme of Action adopted by the Conference, which emphasized the importance of productive capacity in the international development agenda. These related to energy, market access (the enablement of LDCs to participate in international trade), and SME networking and cluster development (with a particular focus on agro-processing and metalworking). A new post of UNIDO Co-ordinator for LDCs was created in 2001.

As a result of the reforms introduced in the 1990s, UNIDO shifted its programming modality from a project-based framework to one with a national scope. Emphasis was given to industrialization in Africa, owing to the prevalence of LDCs there and the necessity to reduce regional inequalities in view of increasing globalization. The national integrated industrial service packages (see above) emphasize capacity-building for the enhancement of industrial competitiveness and private-sector development, which is regarded as a major priority for the transformation of African economies. The basic philosophy has been to identify, jointly with key stakeholders in major industrial sub-sectors, the basic tools required to determine their national industrial development needs and priorities. This process has facilitated the definition and establishment of comprehensive national medium-term and long-term industrial development agenda. By 2001 national programmes, valued at an estimated US $151.3m., had been developed for 18 African countries. In 2001 a West African regional integrated programme was launched, with a special focus on agro-industries in Benin, Burkino Faso, Guinea, Niger, Senegal and Togo. In 1996 UNIDO formally inaugurated the Alliance for Africa's Industrialization, which constituted the industrial sector element of the UN System-wide Special Initiative on Africa. This aimed to promote development of the continent's natural resources, strengthen labour resources and build government capacities in order to exploit new global markets, in particular in the agro-industrial sector. The Organization supported the Conference on Industrial Partnership and Investment in Africa, held in October 1999 in Dakar, Senegal, which aimed to provide a forum for developing industrial partnerships and promote industrial development. UNIDO was to be responsible for the technical implementation of a regional programme on quality management and standardization, covering the member countries of the Union économique et monétaire ouest-africaine—UEMOA, q.v.), to be undertaken in collaboration with the European Union, that was approved in 2000. In addition, a technical support programme to improve the level of fish exports has been approved.

UNIDO is increasingly involved in general environmental projects. As one of the four implementing agencies of the Multilateral Fund for the Implementation of the Montreal Protocol, UNIDO assists developing countries in efforts gradually to reduce the use of ozone-depleting substances. It is also involved in implementing the Kyoto Protocol of the Framework Convention on Climate Change (relating to greenhouse gas emissions) in old factories world-wide. In 1994 UNIDO and UNEP launched the National Cleaner Production Centres Programme; by 2001 19 Centres had been established world-wide.

UNIDO also supports collaborative efforts between countries with complementary experience or resources in specific sectors. The investment and technology promotion network publicizes investment opportunities, provides information to investors and promotes business contacts between industrialized and developing countries and economies in transition. UNIDO is increasingly working to achieve investment promotion and transfer of technology and knowledge among developing countries. The Organization has developed several databases, including the Biosafety Information Network Advisory Service (BINAS), the Business Environment Strategic Toolkit (BEST), Industrial Development Abstracts (IDA, providing information on technical co-operation), and the International Referral System on Sources of Information (IRS).

UNIDO established and operates the International Centre for Science and High Technology, based in Trieste (Italy); the International Centre for Advancement of Manufacturing Technology in Bangalore (India); the Centre for the Application of Solar Energy in Perth (Australia); the International Centre of Medicine Biotechnology in Obolensk (Russia); and the International Materials Assessment and Application Centre in Rio de Janeiro (Brazil).

Finance

The regular budget for the two years 2002–03 amounted to €133.7m., financed by assessed contributionss payable by member states. There was an operational budget of some €22.0m. for the same period, financed from the reinbursement of support costs pertaining to technical co-operation and other services for the same period. UNIDO's technical co-operation expenditure was budgeted at €193.5m. In 2001 allocations were received from UNDP, the Multilateral Fund for the Implementation of the Montreal Protocol on Substances that Deplete the Ozone Layer, the Global Environment Facility, and the Common Fund for Commodities. In addition, voluntary contributions were received from member states. The Industrial Development Fund is used by UNIDO to finance development projects that fall outside the usual systems of multilateral funding.

Publications

African Industry 2000: The Challenge of Going Global.
Annual Report.
Development of Clusters and Networks of SMEs.
Gearing up for a New Development Agenda.
Industry for Growth into the New Millennium.
International Yearbook of Industrial Statistics (annually).
Manual for the Evaluation of Industrial Projects.
Manual for Small Industrial Businesses.
Reforming the UN System—UNIDO's Need-Driven Model.
UNIDOScope (monthly, electronic newsletter).
Using Statistics for Process Control and Improvement: An Introduction to Basic Concepts and Techniques.
World Industrial Development Report.
World Information Directory of Industrial Technology and Investment Support Services.
Several other manuals; guide-lines; numerous working papers and reports.

Universal Postal Union—UPU

Address: Case Postale, 3000 Berne 15, Switzerland.
Telephone: (31) 3503111; **fax:** (31) 3503110; **e-mail:** info@upu.int; **internet:** www.upu.int.

The General Postal Union was founded by the Treaty of Berne (1874), beginning operations in July 1875. Three years later its name was changed to the Universal Postal Union. In 1948 the UPU became a specialized agency of the UN. The UPU promotes the sustainable development of high-quality, universal, efficient and accessible postal services.

MEMBERS

189 members: see Table on pp. 125–127.

Organization

(April 2003)

CONGRESS

The supreme body of the Union is the Universal Postal Congress, which meets, in principle, every five years. Congress focuses on general principles and broad policy issues. It is responsible for the Constitution (the basic act of the Union), the General Regulations (which contain provisions relating to the application of the Constitution and the operation of the Union), changes in the provision of the Universal Postal Convention, approval of the strategic plan and budget parameters, formulation of overall policy on technical co-operation, and for elections and appointments. Amendments to the Constitution are recorded in Additional Protocols, of which there are currently six. The 22nd Congress was held in Beijing, People's Republic of China, in August/September 1999; the 23rd Congress was to be held in Bucharest, Romania, in September/October 2004.

COUNCIL OF ADMINISTRATION

The Council, created by the Seoul Congress, 1994, to replace the former Executive Council, meets annually at Berne. It is composed of a Chairman and representatives of 41 member countries of the Union elected by the Universal Postal Congress on the basis of an equitable geographical distribution. It is responsible for supervising the affairs of the Union between Congresses. The Council also considers policies that may affect other sectors, such as standardization and quality of service, provides a forum for considering the implications of governmental policies with respect to competition, deregulation, and trade-in-service issues for international postal services, and considers intergovernmental aspects of technical co-operation. The Council approves the Union's budget, supervises the activities of the International Bureau and takes decisions regarding UPU contacts with other international agencies and bodies. It is also responsible for promoting and co-ordinating all aspects of technical assistance among member countries.

POSTAL OPERATIONS COUNCIL (POC)

As the technical organ of the UPU, the Council, which holds annual sessions and comprises 40 elected member countries, is responsible for the operational, economic and commercial aspects of international postal services. The POC has the authority to amend and enact the Detailed Regulations of the Universal Postal Convention, on the basis of decisions made at Congress. It promotes the studies undertaken by some postal services and the introduction of new postal products. It also prepares and issues recommendations for member countries concerning uniform standards of practice. On the recommendation of the 1999 Beijing Congress the POC established a Standards Board with responsibility for approving standards relating to telematics, postal technology and Electronic Data Interchange (EDI). The POC aims to assist national postal services to modernize postal products, including letter and parcel post, financial services and expedited mail services.

INTERNATIONAL BUREAU

The day-to-day administrative work of UPU is executed through the International Bureau, which provides secretariat and support facilities for the UPU's bodies. It serves as an instrument of liaison, information and consultation for the postal administration of the member countries and promotes technical co-operation among Union members. It also acts as a clearing house for the settlement of accounts between postal administrations for inter-administration charges related to the exchange of postal items and international reply coupons. The Bureau supports the technical assistance programmes of the UPU and serves as an intermediary between the UPU, the UN, its agencies and other international organizations, customer organizations and private delivery services. Increasingly the Bureau has assumed a greater role in certain areas of postal administration, for example, the application of telematics, postal technology and EDI through its Postal Technology Centre, the development of postal markets, and the monitoring of quality of postal services world-wide.

Director-General of the International Bureau: THOMAS E. LEAVEY (USA).

Activities

The essential principles of the Union are the following:

   (i) to develop social, cultural and commercial communication between people through the efficient operation of the postal services;

   (ii) to guarantee freedom of transit and free circulation of postal items;

   (iii) to ensure the organization, development and modernization of the postal services;

   (iv) to promote and participate in postal technical assistance between member countries;

   (v) to ensure the interoperability of postal networks by implementing a suitable policy of standardization;

   (vi) to meet the changing needs of customers; and

   (vii) to improve the quality of service.

In addition to the Constitution and the General Regulations, the Universal Postal Convention is also a compulsory Act of the UPU (binding on all member countries), in view of its importance in the postal field and historical value. The Convention and its Detailed Regulations contain the common rules applicable to the international postal service and provisions concerning letter- and parcel-post. The Detailed Regulations are agreements concluded by the national postal administrations elected by Congress to the POC. The POC is empowered to revise and enact these, taking into account decisions made at Congress.

The Postal Payment Services Agreement and its Regulations, adopted by the 1999 Beijing Congress to replace the former Money Orders, Giro and Cash-on-Delivery Agreements, is an optional arrangement. Not all member countries have acceded to this Agreement.

In recent years the UPU has reviewed its activities and has focused on the following factors underlying the modern postal environment: the growing role played by technology, with electronic communications expected to develop at more than twice the rate of physical mail during 2000–05; the expanding reach of the effects of globalization; and the need to make the customer the focus of new competitive strategies. The 1999 Universal Congress adopted the Beijing Postal Strategy, detailing a number of objectives to be pursued by governments, postal administrations and restricted unions, and the UPU permanent bodies, over the period 2000–04. The strategy incorporated the following themes: ensuring the provision of a universal post service; strengthening quality of service in the international postal network; increasing the economic viability of the international postal network; responding effectively to postal market requirements through improved market knowledge and product development; enabling, through postal reform and development, the attainment of maximum benefit from technological, economic and regulatory changes in the postal environment; and strengthening co-operation among stakeholders. The Beijing Congress authorized the establishment of a high-level group to consider the future development of the UPU. Issues under consideration in this respect have included defining the future scope of the Union's activities, participation by non-governmental organizations, and reforms to the Union's structure, processes and finances. In October 2001, on the recommendation of the high-level group, the Administrative Council approved the establishment of a consultative committee representing external stakeholders in postal systems. This was to be inaugurated following the 2004 Congress. The group also recommended that the founding Acts of the UPU should be amended to distinguish clearly the separate roles of governments and postal operators in UPU bodies. The Beijing Congress also approved the creation of an Advisory Group (comprising members of UPU bodies and of other organizations), and of a Quality of Service Fund. The Fund, to be financed by industrialized member countries, was to support service improvement projects in developing member states. In October 2002 the UPU organized a strategy conference entitled 'Future Post', at which delegates representing governments and postal services addressed challenges confronting the postal industry.

Finance

The 1999 Beijing Congress agreed to replace the Union's annual budget with a biennial budget from 2001. The approved budget for 2001–02 amounted to 71.4m. Swiss francs. All of the UPU's regular budget expenses are financed by member countries, based on a contribution class system. Members are listed in 11 classes, establishing the proportion that they should pay.

Publications

POST 2005: Follow-up and Trends.
Postal Statistics.
Union Postale (quarterly, in French, German, English, Arabic, Chinese, Spanish and Russian).
*UPU Technical Standards.*Other guides and industry reports.

World Health Organization—WHO

Address: Ave Appia 20, 1211 Geneva 27, Switzerland.
Telephone: (22) 7912111; **fax:** (22) 7913111; **e-mail:** info@who.int; **internet:** www.who.int.

WHO, established in 1948, is the lead agency within the UN system concerned with the protection and improvement of public health.

MEMBERS

192 members and two associate members: see Table on pp. 125–127.

Organization

(April 2003)

WORLD HEALTH ASSEMBLY

The Assembly meets in Geneva, once a year; it is responsible for policy making and the biennial programme and budget; appoints the Director-General, admits new members and reviews budget contributions.

EXECUTIVE BOARD

The Board is composed of 32 health experts designated by, but not representing, their governments; they serve for three years, and the World Health Assembly elects 10–12 member states each year to the Board. It meets at least twice a year to review the Director-General's programme, which it forwards to the Assembly with any recommendations that seem necessary. It advises on questions referred to it by the Assembly and is responsible for putting into effect the decisions and policies of the Assembly. It is also empowered to take emergency measures in case of epidemics or disasters.

Chairman: KYAW MYINT (Myanmar).

SECRETARIAT

Director-General: Dr GRO HARLEM BRUNDTLAND (Norway) (until 20 July 2003); Dr JONG-WOOK LEE (Republic of Korea) (designate).

Executive Directors: Dr ANARFI ASAMOA-BAAH (Ghana) (Health Technology and Pharmaceuticals), MARYAN BAQUEROT (General Management), Dr DAVID L. HEYMANN (USA) (Communicable Diseases), Dr CHRISTOPHER MURRAY (Evidence and Information for Policy), Dr DAVID NABARRO (United Kingdom) (Sustainable Development and Healthy Environments), Dr TOMRIS TÜRMEN (Turkey) (Family and Community Health), Dr DEREK YACH (South Africa) (Non-communicable Diseases and Mental Health); NADIA YOUNES (Egypt) (External Relations and Governing Bodies).

Chef de Cabinet (Office of the Director-General): DENIS AITKIN (United Kingdom).

REGIONAL OFFICES

Each of WHO's six geographical regions has its own organization consisting of a regional committee representing the member states and associate members in the region concerned, and a regional office staffed by experts in various fields of health.

Africa: Cité du Djoue BP 06, Brazzaville, Republic of the Congo; tel. and fax 83-91-00; e-mail regafro@whoafr.org; internet www.afro.who.int/; Dir Dr EBRAHIM MALICK SAMBA (The Gambia).

Americas: Pan-American Health Organization, 525 23rd St, NW, Washington, DC 20037, USA; tel. (202) 974-3000; fax (202) 974-3663; e-mail director@paho.org; internet www.paho.org; Dir Dr MIRTA ROSES PERIAGO (Argentina).

Eastern Mediterranean: WHO Post Office, Abdul Razzak al Sanhouri St, Cairo (Nasr City) 11371, Egypt; tel. (2) 6702535; fax (2) 6702492; e-mail emro@emro.who.int; internet www.emro.who.int; Dir Dr HUSSEIN ABDUL-RAZZAQ GEZAIRY.

Europe: 8 Scherfigsvej, 2100 Copenhagen Ø, Denmark; tel. (1) 39-17-17-17; fax (1) 39-17-18-18; e-mail webmaster@who.dk; internet www.who.dk; Dir Dr MARC DANZON (France).

South-East Asia: World Health House, Indraprastha Estate, Mahatma Gandhi Rd, New Delhi 110002, India; tel. (11) 3370804; fax (11) 3379507; e-mail pandeyh@whosea.org; internet www.whosea.org; Dir Dr UTON MUCHTAR RAFEI (Indonesia).

Western Pacific: POB 2932, Manila 1000, Philippines; tel. (2) 5288001; fax (2) 5211036; e-mail postmaster@who.org.ph; internet www.wpro.who.int; Dir Dr SHIGERU OMI (Japan).

Activities

WHO's objective is stated in the constitution as 'the attainment by all peoples of the highest possible level of health'. 'Health' is defined as 'a state of complete physical, mental and social well-being and not merely the absence of disease and infirmity'. In November 2001 WHO issued the International Classification of Functioning, Disability and Health (ICF) to act as an international standard and guide-lines for determining health and disability.

WHO acts as the central authority directing international health work, and establishes relations with professional groups and government health authorities on that basis.

It provides, on request from member states, technical and policy assistance in support of programmes to promote health, prevent and control health problems, control or eradicate disease, train health workers best suited to local needs and strengthen national health systems. Aid is provided in emergencies and natural disasters.

A global programme of collaborative research and exchange of scientific information is carried out in co-operation with about 1,200 national institutions. Particular stress is laid on the widespread communicable diseases of the tropics, and the countries directly concerned are assisted in developing their research capabilities.

It keeps diseases and other health problems under constant surveillance, promotes the exchange of prompt and accurate information and of notification of outbreaks of diseases, and administers the International Health Regulations. It sets standards for the quality control of drugs, vaccines and other substances affecting health. It formulates health regulations for international travel.

It collects and disseminates health data and carries out statistical analyses and comparative studies in such diseases as cancer, heart disease and mental illness.

It receives reports on drugs observed to have shown adverse reactions in any country, and transmits the information to other member states.

It promotes improved environmental conditions, including housing, sanitation and working conditions. All available information on effects on human health of the pollutants in the environment is critically reviewed and published.

Co-operation among scientists and professional groups is encouraged. The organization negotiates and sustains national and global partnerships. It may propose international conventions and agreements, and develops and promotes international norms and standards. The organization promotes the development and testing of new technologies, tools and guide-lines. It assists in developing an informed public opinion on matters of health.

HEALTH FOR ALL

WHO's first global strategy for pursing 'Health for all' was adopted in May 1981 by the 34th World Health Assembly. The objective of 'Health for all' was identified as the attainment by all citizens of the world of a level of health that would permit them to lead a socially and economically productive life, requiring fair distribution of available resources, universal access to essential health care, and the promotion of preventive health care. In May 1998 the 51st World Health Assembly renewed the initiative, adopting a global strategy in support of 'Health for all in the 21st century', to be effected through regional and national health policies. The new approach was to build on the primary health care approach of the initial strategy, but was to strengthen the emphasis on quality of life, equity in health and access to health services. The following have been identified as minimum requirements of 'Health for All':

Safe water in the home or within 15 minutes' walking distance, and adequate sanitary facilities in the home or immediate vicinity;

Immunization against diphtheria, pertussis (whooping cough), tetanus, poliomyelitis, measles and tuberculosis;

Local health care, including availability of essential drugs, within one hour's travel;

Trained personnel to attend childbirth, and to care for pregnant mothers and children up to at least one year old.

In July 1998 Dr Gro Harlem Brundtland officially took office as the new Director-General of WHO. She immediately announced an extensive reform of the organization, including restructuring the WHO technical programmes into nine groups, or 'clusters', each headed by an Executive Director. The groups are as follows: Communicable Diseases; Non-communicable Diseases and Mental Health; Family and Community Health; Sustainable Development and Healthy Environments; Health Technology and Pharmaceuticals; Evidence and Information for Policy; External affairs and Governing Bodies; General Management; and Office of the Director-General (including audit, oversight and legal activities). In 2000 WHO adopted a new corporate strategy, entailing a stronger focus on performance and programme delivery through standardized plans of action, and increased consistency and efficiency throughout the organization.

The Tenth General Programme of Work, for the period 2002–05, defined a policy framework for pursuing the principal objectives of building healthy populations and combating ill health. The Programme took into account: increasing understanding of the social, economic, political and cultural factors involved in achieving better health and the role played by better health in poverty reduction; the increasing complexity of health systems; the importance of safeguarding health as a component of humanitarian action; and the need for greater co-ordination among development organizations. It incorporated four interrelated strategic directions: lessening excess mortality, morbidity and disability, especially in poor and marginalized populations; promoting healthy lifestyles and reducing risk factors to human health arising from environmental, economic, social and behavioural causes; developing equitable and financially fair health systems; and establishing an enabling policy and an institutional environment for the health sector and promoting an effective health dimension to social, economic, environmental and development policy.

COMMUNICABLE DISEASES

WHO identifies infectious and parasitic communicable diseases as a major obstacle to social and economic progress, particularly in developing countries, where, in addition to disabilities and loss of productivity and household earnings, they cause nearly one-half of all deaths. Emerging and re-emerging diseases, those likely to cause epidemics, increasing incidence of zoonoses (diseases passed from animals to humans either directly or by insects) attributable to environmental changes, outbreaks of unknown etiology, and the undermining of some drug therapies by the spread of antimicrobial resistance are main areas of concern. In recent years WHO has noted the global spread of communicable diseases through international travel, voluntary human migration and involuntary population displacement.

WHO's Communicable Diseases group works to reduce the impact of infectious diseases world-wide through surveillance and response; prevention, control and eradication strategies; and research and product development. Combating malaria and tuberculosis (TB) are organization-wide priorities and, as such, are supported not only by their own areas of work but also by activities undertaken in other areas. The group seeks to identify new technologies and tools, and to foster national development through strengthening health services and the better use of existing tools. It aims to strengthen global monitoring of important communicable disease problems. The group advocates a functional approach to disease control. It aims to create consensus and consolidate partnerships around targeted diseases and collaborates with other groups at all stages to provide an integrated response. In April 2000 WHO and several partner institutions in epidemic surveillance established a Global Outbreak Alert and Response Network. Through the Network WHO aims to maintain constant vigilance regarding outbreaks of disease and to link world-wide expertise to provide an immediate response capability. From March 2003 WHO, through the Network, was co-ordinating the international investigation into the global spread of Severe Acute Respiratory Syndrome (SARS), a previously unknown atypical pneumonia. A Global Fund to Fight AIDS, TB and Malaria was established, with WHO participation, in 2001 (see below).

A Ministerial Conference on Malaria, organized by WHO, was held in October 1992, attended by representatives from 102 member countries. The Conference adopted a plan of action for the 1990s for the control of the disease, which kills an estimated 1m. people every year and affects a further 300m.–500m. Some 90% of all cases are in sub-Saharan Africa. WHO assists countries where malaria is endemic to prepare national plans of action for malaria control in accordance with its Global Malaria Control Strategy, which emphasizes strengthening local capabilities, for example through training, for effective health control. In July 1998 WHO declared the control of malaria a priority concern, and in October the organization formally launched the 'Roll Back Malaria' programme, in conjunction with UNICEF, the World Bank and UNDP, which aimed to halve the prevalence of malaria by 2010. Emphasis was to be placed on strengthening local health systems and on the promotion of inexpensive preventive measures, including the use of bednets treated with insecticides. The global Roll Back Malaria partnership, linking governments, development agencies, and other parties, aims to mobilize resources and support for controlling the disease. WHO, with several private- and public-sector partners, supports the development of more effective anti-malaria drugs and vaccines through the 'Medicines for Malaria' venture.

In 1995 WHO established a Global Tuberculosis Programme to address the challenges of the TB epidemic, which had been declared a global emergency by the Organization in 1993. According to WHO estimates, one-third of the world's population carries the TB bacillus, and 2m.–3m. people die from the disease each year. WHO provides technical support to all member countries, with special attention given to those with high TB prevalence, to establish effective national tuberculosis control programmes. WHO's strategy for TB control includes the use of DOTS (direct observation treatment, short-course), standardized treatment guide-lines, and result accountability through routine evaluation of treatment outcomes. Simultaneously, WHO is encouraging research with the aim of further disseminating DOTS, adapting DOTS for wider use, developing new tools for prevention, diagnosis and treatment, and containing new threats such as the HIV/TB co-epidemic. In March 1999 WHO announced the launch of a new initiative, 'Stop TB', in partnership with the World Bank, the US Government and a coalition of non-governmental organizations, which aimed to promote DOTS to ensure its use in 85% of detected cases by 2005 (compared with around one-quarter in 1999). The global target for case detection by 2005 was 70%. However, inadequate control of DOTS in some areas, leading to partial and inconsistent treatments, has resulted in the development of drug-resistant and, often, incurable strains of the disease. The incidence of so-called multidrug-resistant TB (MDR-TB) strains, that are unresponsive to the two main anti-TB drugs, has risen in recent years. During 2001 WHO was developing and testing DOTS-Plus, a strategy for controlling the spread of MDR-TB in areas of high prevalence. In 2001 WHO estimated that more than 8m. new cases of TB were occurring world-wide each year, of which the largest concentration was in south-east Asia. It envisaged a substantial increase in new cases by 2005, mainly owing to the severity of the HIV/TB co-epidemic. TB is the principal cause of death for people infected with the HIV virus. In March 2001 the Global TB Drug Facility was launched under the 'Stop TB' initiative; this aimed to increase access to high-quality anti-TB drugs for sufferers in developing countries. In October the 'Stop TB' partnership announced a Global Plan to Stop TB, which envisaged the expansion of access to DOTS; the advancement of MDR-TB preven-

tion measures; the development of anti-TB drugs entailing a shorter treatment period; and the implementation of new strategies for treating people with HIV and TB.

One of WHO's major achievements was the eradication of smallpox. Following a massive international campaign of vaccination and surveillance (begun in 1958 and intensified in 1967), the last case was detected in 1977 and the eradication of the disease was declared in 1980. In May 1996 the World Health Assembly resolved that, pending a final endorsement, all remaining stocks of the smallpox virus were to be destroyed on 30 June 1999, although 500,000 doses of smallpox vaccine were to remain, along with a supply of the smallpox vaccine seed virus, in order to ensure that a further supply of the vaccine could be made available if required. In May 1999, however, the Assembly authorized a temporary retention of stocks of the virus until 2002. In late 2001, in response to fears that illegally-held virus stocks could be used in acts of biological terrorism (see below), WHO reassembled a team of technical experts on smallpox. In January 2002 the Executive Board determined that stocks of the virus should continue to be retained, to enable research into more effective treatments and vaccines.

In 1988 the World Health Assembly declared its commitment to the eradication of poliomyelitis by the end of 2000 and launched the Global Polio Eradication Initiative. In August 1996 WHO, UNICEF and Rotary International, together with other national and international partners, initiated a campaign to 'Kick Polio out of Africa', with the aim of immunizing more than 100m. children in 46 countries against the disease over a three-year period. In 2000 WHO adopted a strategic plan for the eradication of polio covering the period 2001–05, which envisaged the effective use of National Immunization Days (NIDs) to secure global interruption of polio transmission by the end of 2002, with a view to achieving certification of the global eradication of polio by the end of 2005. (In conflict zones so-called 'days of tranquility' have been negotiated to facilitate the implementation of NIDs.) Meanwhile, routine immunization services were to be strengthened. A post-certification immunization policy for polio was to be formulated. By the end of 2001 the number of confirmed polio cases world-wide had declined to 483 in 10 countries, from 35,000 in 125 countries in 1988 (the actual number of cases in 1988 was estimated at around 350,000). In 2001 575m. children in 94 countries world-wide were immunized through the use of NIDS. In that year Vitamin A was also administered during NIDS in some 60 countries in order to combat nutritional deficiencies in children. By December 2002, however, the number of confirmed cases of polio stood at 1,924, 1,599 of which were in India. Six other countries were still known to be or suspected of being polio endemic at that time: Afghanistan, Egypt, Niger, Nigeria, Pakistan and Somalia. WHO has declared the following regions 'polio-free': the Americas (1994); Western Pacific (2000); and Europe (2002).

The Onchocerciasis Control Programme in West Africa (OCP) was initiated in 1974 to eliminate onchocerciasis, which can cause blindness, as a major public health problem and an impediment to socio-economic development in 11 countries of the region. In January 1996 a new initiative, the African Programme for Onchocerciasis Control (APOC), covering 19 countries outside West Africa, became operational, with funding co-ordinated by the World Bank and with WHO as the executing agency. In December 1994 WHO announced that the OCP was to be terminated by the end of 2002, by which time it was estimated that 40m. people would have been protected from the disease and 600,000 people prevented from blindness. In May 1999 WHO reported that the OCP, based in Ouagadougou, Burkina Faso, was to be transformed into a Multi-disease Surveillance Centre. The Onchocerciasis Elimination Programme in the Americas (OEPA), launched in 1992, co-ordinates work to control the disease in six endemic countries of Latin America. In January 1998 a new 20-year programme to eliminate lymphatic filariasis was initiated, with substantial funding and support from two major pharmaceutical companies, and in collaboration with the World Bank, the Arab Fund for Economic and Social Development and the governments of Japan, the United Kingdom and the USA. A regional intergovernmental commission is implementing a programme to eliminate South American trypanosomiasis ('Chagas disease', which causes the deaths of some 45,000 people each year and infects a further 16m.–18m.) from the Southern Cone region of Latin America; it is hoped that this goal will be achieved by 2010. The countries of the Andean region of Latin America initiated a plan for the elimination of transmission of Chagas disease in February 1997; a similar plan was launched by Central American governments in October.

WHO is committed to the elimination of leprosy (the reductionn of the prevalence of leprosy to less than one case per 10,000 population). The use of a highly effective combination of three drugs (known as multi-drug therapy—MDT) resulted in a reduction in the number of leprosy cases world-wide from 10m.–12m. in 1988 to 597,000 in 2000. The number of countries having more than one case of leprosy per 10,000 had declined to from to 15 by 2000, compared with 122 in 1985. In 2000 the world-wide leprosy prevalence rate stood at 1.4 cases per 10,000 people, although the rate in the 11 most endemic countries was 4.5 cases per 10,000. India has more than one-half of all active leprosy cases. The Global Alliance for the Elimination of Leprosy, launched in November 1999 by WHO, in collaboration with governments of affected countries and several private partners, including a major pharmaceutical company, aims to bring about the eradication of the disease by the end of 2005, through the continued use of MDT treatment. In July 1998 the Director-General of WHO and representatives of more than 20 countries, meeting in Yamoussoukro, Côte d'Ivoire, signed a declaration on the control of another mycobacterial disease, Buruli ulcer.

The Special Programme for Research and Training in Tropical Diseases, established in 1975 and sponsored jointly by WHO, UNDP and the World Bank, as well as by contributions from donor countries, involves a world-wide network of some 5,000 scientists working on the development and application of vaccines, new drugs, diagnostic kits and preventive measures, and an applied field research on practical community issues affecting the target diseases.

The objective of providing immunization for all children by 1990 was adopted by the World Health Assembly in 1977. Six diseases (measles, whooping cough, tetanus, poliomyelitis, tuberculosis and diphtheria) became the target of the Expanded Programme on Immunization (EPI), in which WHO, UNICEF and many other organizations collaborated. As a result of massive international and national efforts, the global immunization coverage increased from 20% in the early 1980s to the targeted rate of 80% by the end of 1990. This coverage signified that more than 100m. children in the developing world under the age of one had been successfully vaccinated against the targeted diseases, the lives of about 3m. children had been saved every year, and 500,000 annual cases of paralysis as a result of polio had been prevented. In 1992 the Assembly resolved to reach a new target of 90% immunization coverage with the six EPI vaccines; to introduce hepatitis B as a seventh vaccine (with the aim of an 80% reduction in the incidence of the disease in children by 2001); and to introduce the yellow fever vaccine in areas where it occurs endemically.

In June 2000 WHO released a report entitled 'Overcoming Antimicrobial Resistance', in which it warned that the misuse of antibiotics could render some common infectious illnesses unresponsive to treatment. At that time WHO issued guide-lines which aimed to mitigate the risks associated with the use of antimicrobials in livestock reared for human consumption.

NON-COMMUNICABLE DISEASES AND MENTAL HEALTH

The Non-communicable Diseases and Mental Health group comprises departments for the surveillance, prevention and management of uninfectious diseases, such as those arising from an unhealthy diet, and departments for health promotion, disability, injury prevention and rehabilitation, mental health and substance abuse. Surveillance, prevention and management of non-communicable diseases, tobacco, and mental health are organization-wide priorities.

Tobacco use, unhealthy diet and physical inactivity are regarded as common, preventable risk factors for the four most prominent non-communicable diseases: cardiovascular diseases, cancer, chronic respiratory disease and diabetes. WHO aims to monitor the global epidemiological situation of non-communicable diseases, to co-ordinate multinational research activities concerned with prevention and care, and to analyse determining factors such as gender and poverty. In mid-1998 the organization adopted a resolution on measures to be taken to combat non-communicable diseases; their prevalence was anticipated to increase, particularly in developing countries, owing to rising life expectancy and changes in lifestyles. For example, between 1995 and 2025 the number of adults affected by diabetes was projected to increase from 135m. to 300m. In 2001 chronic diseases reportedly accounted for about 59% of the estimated 56.5m. total deaths globally and for 46% of the global burden of disease. In February 1999 WHO initiated a new programme, 'Vision 2020: the Right to Sight', which aimed to eliminate avoidable blindness (estimated to be as much as 80% of all cases) by 2020. Blindness was otherwise predicted to increase by as much as twofold, owing to the increased longevity of the global population. In co-operation with the International Association for the Study of Obesity WHO has studied obesity-related issues. The International Task Force on Obesity, affiliated to the IASO, aims to encourage the development of new policies for managing obesity. WHO and FAO jointly commissioned an expert report on the relationship of diet, nutrition and physical activity to chronic diseases, which was published in March 2003.

WHO's programmes for diabetes mellitus, chronic rheumatic diseases and asthma assist with the development of national initiatives, based upon goals and targets for the improvement of early detection, care and reduction of long-term complications. WHO's cardiovascular diseases programme aims to prevent and control the major cardiovascular diseases, which are responsible for more than 14m. deaths each year. It is estimated that one-third of these deaths could have been prevented with existing scientific knowledge The programme on cancer control is concerned with the prevention of

cancer, improving its detection and cure and ensuring care of all cancer patients in need. In 1998 a five-year programme to improve cancer care in developing countries was established, sponsored by private enterprises.

The WHO Human Genetics Programme manages genetic approaches for the prevention and control of common hereditary diseases and of those with a genetic predisposition representing a major health importance. The Programme also concentrates on the further development of genetic approaches suitable for incorporation into health care systems, as well as developing a network of international collaborating programmes.

WHO works to assess the impact of injuries, violence and sensory impairments on health, and formulates guide-lines and protocols for the prevention and management of mental problems. The health promotion division promotes decentralized and community-based health programmes and is concerned with developing new approaches to population ageing and encouraging healthy life-styles and self-care. It also seeks to relieve the negative impact of social changes such as urbanization, migration and changes in family structure upon health. WHO advocates a multi-sectoral approach—involving public health, legal and educational systems—to the prevention of injuries, which represent 16% of the global burden of disease. It aims to support governments in developing suitable strategies to prevent and mitigate the consequences of violence, unintentional injury and disability. Several health promotion projects have been undertaken, in collaboration between WHO regional and country offices and other relevant organizations, including: the Global School Health Initiative, to bridge the sectors of health and education and to promote the health of school-age children; the Global Strategy for Occupational Health, to promote the health of the working population and the control of occupational health risks; Community-based Rehabilitation, aimed at providing a more enabling environment for people with disabilities; and a communication strategy to provide training and support for health communications personnel and initiatives. In 2000 WHO, UNESCO, the World Bank and UNICEF adopted the joint Focusing Resources for Effective School Health (FRESH Start) approach to promoting life skills among adolescents.

In July 1997 the fourth International Conference on Health Promotion (ICHP) was held in Jakarta, Indonesia, where a declaration on 'Health Promotion into the 21st Century' was agreed. The fifth ICHP was convened in June 2000, in Mexico City, Mexico.

Mental health problems, which include unipolar and bipolar affective disorders, psychosis, epilepsy, dementia, Parkinson's disease, multiple sclerosis, drug and alcohol dependency, and neuropsychiatric disorders such as post-traumatic stress disorder, obsessive compulsive disorder and panic disorder, have been identified by WHO as significant global health problems. Although, overall, physical health has improved, mental, behavioural and social health problems are increasing, owing to extended life expectancy and improved child mortality rates, and factors such as war and poverty. WHO aims to address mental problems by increasing awareness of mental health issues and promoting improved mental health services and primary care.

The Substance Abuse department is concerned with problems of alcohol, drugs and other substance abuse. Within its Programme on Substance Abuse (PSA), which was established in 1990 in response to the global increase in substance abuse, WHO provides technical support to assist countries in formulating policies with regard to the prevention and reduction of the health and social effects of psychoactive substance abuse. PSA's sphere of activity includes epidemiological surveillance and risk assessment, advocacy and the dissemination of information, strengthening national and regional prevention and health promotion techniques and strategies, the development of cost-effective treatment and rehabilitation approaches, and also encompasses regulatory activities as required under the international drugs-control treaties in force.

The Tobacco or Health Programme aims to reduce the use of tobacco, by educating tobacco-users and preventing young people from adopting the habit. In 1996 WHO published its first report on the tobacco situation world-wide. According to WHO, about one-third of the world's population aged over 15 years smoke tobacco, which causes approximately 3.5m. deaths each year (through lung cancer, heart disease, chronic bronchitis and other effects). In 1998 the 'Tobacco Free Initiative', a major global anti-smoking campaign, was established. In May 1999 the World Health Assembly endorsed the formulation of a Framework Convention on Tobacco Control (FCTC) to help to combat the increase in tobacco use (although a number of tobacco growers expressed concerns about the effect of the convention on their livelihoods). The draft Framework Convention was finalized in March 2003; it was envisaged that the Convention would be adopted by the World Health Assembly in May. The greatest increase in tobacco use is forecast to occur in developing countries.

FAMILY AND COMMUNITY HEALTH

WHO's Family and Community Health group addresses the following areas of work: child and adolescent health, research and programme development in reproductive health, making pregnancy safer, women's health, and HIV/AIDS. Making pregnancy safer and HIV/AIDS are organization-wide priorities. The group's aim is to improve access to sustainable health care for all by strengthening health systems and fostering individual, family and community development. Activities include newborn care; child health, including promoting and protecting the health and development of the child through such approaches as promotion of breast-feeding and use of the mother-baby package, as well as care of the sick child, including diarrhoeal and acute respiratory disease control, and support to women and children in difficult circumstances; the promotion of safe motherhood and maternal health; adolescent health, including the promotion and development of young people and the prevention of specific health problems; women, health and development, including addressing issues of gender, sexual violence, and harmful traditional practices; and human reproduction, including research related to contraceptive technologies and effective methods. In addition, WHO aims to provide technical leadership and co-ordination on reproductive health and to support countries in their efforts to ensure that people: experience healthy sexual development and maturation; have the capacity for healthy, equitable and responsible relationships; can achieve their reproductive intentions safely and healthily; avoid illnesses, diseases and injury related to sexuality and reproduction; and receive appropriate counselling, care and rehabilitation for diseases and conditions related to sexuality and reproduction.

In September 1997 WHO, in collaboration with UNICEF, formally launched a programme advocating the Integrated Management of Childhood Illness (IMCI), following successful regional trials in more than 20 developing countries during 1996–97. IMCI recognizes that pneumonia, diarrhoea, measles, malaria and malnutrition cause some 70% of the approximately 11m. childhood deaths each year, and recommends screening sick children for all five conditions, to obtain a more accurate diagnosis than may be achieved from the results of a single assessment. WHO's Division of Diarrhoeal and Acute Respiratory Disease Control encourages national programmes aimed at reducing childhood deaths as a result of diarrhoea, particularly through the use of oral rehydration therapy and preventive measures. The Division is also seeking to reduce deaths from pneumonia in infants through the use of a simple case-management strategy involving the recognition of danger signs and treatment with an appropriate antibiotic.

The HIV/AIDS epidemic represents a major threat to human well-being and socio-economic progress. Some 95% of those known to be infected with HIV/AIDS live in developing countries, and AIDS-related illnesses are the leading cause of death in sub-Saharan Africa. At December 2002 an estimated 42m. adults and children world-wide were living with HIV/AIDS, of whom 5m. were newly infected during that year. WHO's Global Programme on AIDS, initiated in 1987, was concluded in December 1995. A Joint UN Programme on HIV/AIDS (UNAIDS) became operational on 1 January 1996, sponsored by WHO, the World Bank, UNICEF, UNDP, UNESCO and UNFPA. (The UN International Drug Control Programme became the seventh sponsoring agency of UNAIDS in 1999, and in 2001 ILO became the eighth sponsor.) The UNAIDS secretariat is based at WHO headquarters. WHO established an Office of HIV/AIDS and Sexually-Transmitted Diseases in order to ensure the continuity of its global response to the problem, which included support for national control and education plans, improving the safety of blood supplies and improving the care and support of AIDS patients. In addition, the Office was to liaise with UNAIDS and to make available WHO's research and technical expertise. Sufferers of HIV/AIDS in developing countries have often failed to receive advanced antiretroviral (ARV) treatments that are widely available in industrialized countries, owing to their high cost. In May 2000 the World Health Assembly adopted a resolution urging WHO member states to improve access to the prevention and treatment of HIV-related illnesses and to increase the availability and affordability of drugs. WHO, with UNAIDS, UNICEF, UNFPA, the World Bank, and major pharmaceutical companies, participates in the 'Accelerating Access' initiative, which aims to expand access to care, support and ARVs for people with HIV/AIDS. In March 2002, under its 'Access to Quality HIV/AIDS Drugs and Diagnostics' programme, WHO published a comprehensive list of HIV-related medicines deemed to meet standards recommended by the Organization. In April WHO issued the first treatment guide-lines for HIV/AIDS cases in poor communities, and endorsed the inclusion of HIV/AIDS drugs in its *Model List of Essential Drugs* (see below) in order to encourage their wider availability. The secretariat of the International HIV Treatment Access Coalition, founded in December 2002 by governments, non-governmental organizations, donors and others to facilitate access to ARVs for people in low and middle income countries, is based at WHO headquarters. In June 2001

governments participating in a special session of the UN General Assembly on HIV/AIDS adopted a Declaration of Commitment on HIV/AIDS. A WHO-UNAIDS HIV Vaccine Initiative was launched in 2000. In July a meeting of the Group of Seven industrialized nations and Russia (G-8), convened in Genoa, Italy, announced the formation of a new Global Fund to Fight AIDS, TB and Malaria (as previously proposed by the UN Secretary-General and recommended by the World Health Assembly). The Fund, a partnership between governments, UN bodies (including WHO) and other agencies, and private-sector interests, aimed to disburse US $700m.–$800m. in grants during 2002, thereby increasing annual global expenditure on combating those diseases by about 50%. WHO supports governments in developing effective health-sector responses to the HIV/AIDS epidemic through enhancing the planning and managerial capabilities, implementation capacity, and resources of health systems. In February 2003 WHO and FAO jointly published a manual on nutritional care for people living with HIV/AIDS.

By the late 1990s many countries had failed significantly to reduce inequalities in healthcare, to improve the health of poor and disadvantaged people or to improve the sustainability of health systems, owing to weak national health systems and the insufficient use of evidence-based, cost-effective treatment methods. In addition, there was a lack of systems to monitor improvements in health services and to determine overall changes in health. The Family and Community Health group, therefore, aims to address these problems and works to ensure that treatment concerning children, adolescents and women, and reproductive health, HIV/AIDS and other sexually transmitted infections, is effectively provided. WHO assists countries to expand and improve the functioning of their health infrastructure in order to ensure wider access to care, hospital services and health education. It works with countries to ensure continuity and quality of care at all levels, by well-trained health personnel.

In March 1996 WHO's Centre for Health Development opened at Kobe, Japan. The Centre researches health developments and other determinants to strengthen policy decision-making within the health sector.

Joint UN Programme on HIV/AIDS—UNAIDS: 20 ave Appia, 1211 Geneva 27, Switzerland; tel. (22) 7913666; fax (22) 7914187; e-mail unaids@unaids.org; internet www.unaids.org. Established in 1996 to lead, strengthen and support an expanded response to the global HIV/AIDS pandemic; activities focus on prevention, care and support, reducing vulnerability to infection, and alleviating the socioeconomic and human effects of HIV/AIDS; co-sponsors: WHO, UNICEF, UNDP, UNFPA, UNDCP, ILO, UNESCO, the World Bank; Exec. Dir PETER PIOT (Belgium).

SUSTAINABLE DEVELOPMENT AND HEALTHY ENVIRONMENTS

The Sustainable Development and Healthy Environments group focuses on the following areas of work: health in sustainable development; nutrition; health and environment; food safety; and emergency preparedness and response. Food safety is an organization-wide priority.

WHO promotes recognition of good health status as one of the most important assets of the poor. The Sustainable Development and Healthy Environment group seeks to monitor the advantages and disadvantages for health, nutrition, environment and development arising from the process of globalization (i.e. increased global flows of capital, goods and services, people, and knowledge); to integrate the issue of health into poverty reduction programmes; and to promote human rights and equality. Adequate and safe food and nutrition is a priority programme area. WHO collaborates with FAO, the World Food Programme, UNICEF and other UN agencies in pursuing its objectives relating to nutrition and food safety. An estimated 780m. people world-wide cannot meet basic needs for energy and protein, more than 2,000m. people lack essential vitamins and minerals, and 170m. children are estimated to be malnourished. In December 1992 WHO and FAO hosted an international conference on nutrition, at which a World Declaration and Plan of Action on Nutrition was adopted to make the fight against malnutrition a development priority. Following the conference, WHO promoted the elaboration and implementation of national plans of action on nutrition. WHO aims to support the enhancement of member states' capabilities in dealing with their nutrition situations, and addressing scientific issues related to preventing, managing and monitoring protein-energy malnutrition; micronutrient malnutrition, including iodine deficiency disorders, vitamin A deficiency, and nutritional anaemia; and diet-related conditions and non-communicable diseases such as obesity (increasingly affecting children, adolescents and adults, mainly in industrialized countries), cancer and heart disease. In 1990 the World Health Assembly resolved to eliminate iodine deficiency (causing mental retardation); a strategy of universal salt iodization was launched in 1993. In collaboration with other international agencies, WHO is implementing a comprehensive strategy for promoting appropriate infant, young child and maternal nutrition, and for dealing effectively with nutritional emergencies in large populations. Areas of emphasis include promoting health-care practices that enhance successful breast-feeding; appropriate complementary feeding; refining the use and interpretation of body measurements for assessing nutritional status; relevant information, education and training; and action to give effect to the International Code of Marketing of Breast-milk Substitutes. The food safety programme aims to protect human health against risks associated with biological and chemical contaminants and additives in food. With FAO, WHO establishes food standards (through the work of the Codex Alimentarius Commission and its subsidiary committees) and evaluates food additives, pesticide residues and other contaminants and their implications for health. The programme provides expert advice on such issues as food-borne pathogens (e.g. listeria), production methods (e.g. aquaculture) and food biotechnology (e.g. genetic modification). In July 2001 the Codex Alimentarius Commission adopted the first global principles for assessing the safety of GM foods. In March 2002 an intergovernmental task force established by the Commission finalized 'principles for the risk analysis of foods derived from biotechnology', which were to provide a framework for assessing the safety of genetically-modified—GM foods and plants. In the following month WHO and FAO announced a joint review of their food standards operations. In February 2003 the The FAO/WHO Project and Fund for Enhanced Participation in Codex was launched to support the participation of poorer countries in the Commission's activities.

WHO's programme area on environment and health undertakes a wide range of initiatives to tackle the increasing threats to health and well-being from a changing environment, especially in relation to air pollution, water quality, sanitation, protection against radiation, management of hazardous waste, chemical safety and housing hygiene. Some 1,100m. people world-wide have no access to clean drinking water, while a further 2,400m. people are denied suitable sanitation systems. WHO helped launch the Water Supply and Sanitation Council in 1990 and regularly updates its *Guidelines for Drinking Water Quality*. In rural areas, the emphasis continues to be on the provision and maintenance of safe and sufficient water supplies and adequate sanitation, the health aspects of rural housing, vector control in water resource management, and the safe use of agrochemicals. In urban areas, assistance is provided to identify local environmental health priorities and to improve municipal governments' ability to deal with environmental conditions and health problems in an integrated manner; promotion of the 'Healthy City' approach is a major component of the Programme. Other Programme activities include environmental health information development and management, human resources development, environmental health planning methods, research and work on problems relating to global environment change, such as UV-radiation. A report considering the implications of climate change on human health, prepared jointly by WHO, WMO and UNEP, was published in July 1996. The WHO Global Strategy for Health and Environment, developed in response to the WHO Commission on Health and Environment which reported to the UN Conference on Environment and Development in June 1992, provides the framework for programme activities. In December 2001 WHO published a report on the relationship between macroeconomics and health.

WHO's work in the promotion of chemical safety is undertaken in collaboration with ILO and UNEP through the International Programme on Chemical Safety (IPCS), the Central Unit for which is located in WHO. The Programme provides internationally-evaluated scientific information on chemicals, promotes the use of such information in national programmes, assists member states in establishment of their own chemical safety measures and programmes, and helps them strengthen their capabilities in chemical emergency preparedness and response and in chemical risk reduction. In 1995 an Inter-organization Programme for the Social Management of Chemicals was established by UNEP, ILO, FAO, WHO, UNIDO and OECD, in order to strengthen international co-operation in the field of chemical safety. In 1998 WHO led an international assessment of the health risk from bendocine disruptors (chemicals which disrupt hormonal activities). In January 2001 WHO sent a team of experts to Kosovo and Metohija (Federal Republic of Yugoslavia—FRY, now Serbia and Montenegro) to assess the potential impact on the health of the local population of exposure to depleted uranium, which had been used by NATO in ammunition during its aerial offensive against the FRY in 1999.

Following the major terrorist attacks perpetrated against targets in the USA in September 2001, WHO focused renewed attention on the potential deliberate use of infectious diseases, such as anthrax and smallpox, or of chemical agents, in acts of biological or chemical terrorism. In September 2001 WHO issued draft guide-lines entitled 'Health Aspects of Biological and Chemical Weapons'.

Within the UN system, WHO's Department of Emergency and Humanitarian Action co-ordinates the international response to emergencies and natural disasters in the health field, in close co-operation with other agencies and within the framework set out by

the UN's Office for the Co-ordination of Humanitarian Affairs. In this context, WHO provides expert advice on epidemiological surveillance, control of communicable diseases, public health information and health emergency training. Its emergency preparedness activities include co-ordination, policy-making and planning, awareness-building, technical advice, training, publication of standards and guide-lines, and research. Its emergency relief activities include organizational support, the provision of emergency drugs and supplies and conducting technical emergency assessment missions. The Division's objective is to strengthen the national capacity of member states to reduce the adverse health consequences of disasters. In responding to emergency situations, WHO always tries to develop projects and activities that will assist the national authorities concerned in rebuilding or strengthening their own capacity to handle the impact of such situations In May 2001 WHO participated with governments and other international agencies in a joint exercise to evaluate national and international procedures for responding to a nuclear emergency.

HEALTH TECHNOLOGY AND PHARMACEUTICALS

WHO's Health Technology and Pharmaceuticals group, made up of the departments of essential drugs and other medicines, vaccines and other biologicals, and blood safety and clinical technology, covers the following areas of work: essential medicines—access, quality and rational use; immunization and vaccine development; and world-wide co-operation on blood safety and clinical technology. Blood safety and clinical technology are an organization-wide priority.

The Department of Essential Drugs and Other Medicines promotes public health through the development of national drugs policies and global guide-lines and through collaboration with member countries to promote access to essential drugs, the rational use of medicines and compliance with international drug-control requirements. The department comprises four teams: Policy Access and Rational Use; the Drug Action Programme; Quality, Safety and the Regulation of Medicines; and Traditional Medicine.

The Department of Vaccines and Other Biologicals undertakes activities related to quality assurance and safety of biologicals; vaccine development; vaccine assessment and monitoring; access to technologies; and the development of policies and strategies aimed at maximizing the use of vaccines.

The Policy Access and Rational Use team and the Drug Action Programme assist in the development and implementation by member states of pharmaceutical policies, in ensuring a supply of essential drugs of good quality at low cost, and in the rational use of drugs. Other activities include global and national operational research in the pharmaceutical sector, and the development of technical tools for problem solving, management and evaluation. The Policy Access and Rational Use team also has a strong advocacy and information role, promulgated through a periodical, the *Essential Drugs Monitor*, an extensive range of technical publications, and an information dissemination programme targeting developing countries.

The Quality, Safety and Regulation of Medicines team supports national drug-regulatory authorities and drug-procurement agencies and facilitates international pharmaceutical trade through the exchange of technical information and the harmonization of internationally respected norms and standards. In particular, it publishes the *International Pharmacopoeia*, the *Consultative List of International Nonproprietary Names for Pharmaceutical Substances*, and annual and biennial reports of Expert Committees responsible for determining relevant international standards for the manufacture and specification of pharmaceutical and biological products in international commerce. It provides information on the safety and efficacy of drugs, with particular regard to counterfeit and substandard projects, to health agencies and providers of health care, and it maintains the pharmaceuticals section of the UN *Consolidated List of Products whose Consumption and/or Sale have been Banned, Withdrawn, Severely Restricted or Not Approved by Governments*. The *WHO Model List of Essential Drugs* is updated about every two years and is complemented by corresponding model prescribing information; the 12th *Model List* was published in 2002 and identified 325 essential drugs, including 12 ARVs and 60 further essential medicines for HIV/AIDS. In September 2002 WHO issued the first *WHO Model Formulary*, which gives detailed information on the safe and effective use of all essential drugs.

The Traditional Medicine team encourages and supports member states in the integration of traditional medicine into national health-care systems and in the appropriate use of traditional medicine, in particular through the provision of technical guide-lines, standards and methodologies. In May 2002 WHO adopted a strategy on the regulation of traditional medicine and complementary or alternative medicines (TM/CAM).

In January 1999 the Executive Board adopted a resolution on WHO's Revised Drug Strategy which placed emphasis on the inequalities of access to pharmaceuticals, and also covered specific aspects of drugs policy, quality assurance, drug promotion, drug donation, independent drug information and rational drug use. Plans of action involving co-operation with member states and other international organizations were to be developed to monitor and analyse the pharmaceutical and public health implications of international agreements, including trade agreements. In April 2001 experts from WHO and the World Trade Organization participated in a workshop to address ways of lowering the cost of medicines in less developed countries. In the following month the World Health Assembly adopted a resolution urging member states to promote equitable access to essential drugs, noting that this was denied to about one-third of the world's population. WHO participates with other partners in the 'Accelerating Access' initiative, which aims to expand access to antiretroviral drugs for people with HIV/AIDS (see above).

WHO reports that 2m. children die each year of diseases for which common vaccines exist. In September 1991 the Children's Vaccine Initiative (CVI) was launched, jointly sponsored by the Rockefeller Foundation, UNDP, UNICEF, the World Bank and WHO, to facilitate the development and provision of children's vaccines. The CVI has as its ultimate goal the development of a single oral immunization shortly after birth that will protect against all major childhood diseases. An International Vaccine Institute was established in Seoul, Republic of Korea, as part of the CVI, to provide scientific and technical services for the production of vaccines for developing countries. In September 1996 WHO, jointly with UNICEF, published a comprehensive survey, entitled *State of the World's Vaccines and Immunization*. In 1999 WHO, UNICEF, the World Bank and a number of public- and private-sector partners formed the Global Alliance for Vaccines and Immunization (GAVI), which aimed to expand the provision of existing vaccines and to accelerate the development and introduction of new vaccines and technologies, with the ultimate goal of protecting children of all nations and from all socio-economic backgrounds against vaccine-preventable diseases.

WHO supports states in ensuring access to safe blood, blood products, transfusions, injections, and health-care technologies.

EVIDENCE AND INFORMATION FOR HEALTH POLICY

The Evidence and Information for Health Policy group addresses the following areas of work: evidence for health policy; health information management and dissemination; and research policy and promotion and organization of health systems. Through the generation and dissemination of evidence the Evidence and Information for Health Policy group aims to assist policy-makers assess health needs, choose intervention strategies, design policy and monitor performance, and thereby improve the performance of national health systems. The group also supports international and national dialogue on health policy.

WHO co-ordinates the Health InterNetwork Access to Research Initiative (HINARI), which was launched in July 2001 to enable relevant authorities in developing countries to access more than 2,000 biomedical journals through the internet at no or greatly reduced cost, in order to improve the world-wide circulation of scientific information; some 28 medical publishers participate in the initiative.

HEALTH DAYS

World Health Day is observed on 7 April every year, and is used to promote awareness of a particular health topic ('Shape the Future of Life, Healthy Environments for Children', in 2003). World Leprosy Day is held every year on 30 January, World TB Day on 24 March, World No Tobacco Day on 31 May, World Heart Day on 24 September, World Mental Health Day on 10 October, World Diabetes Day, in association with the International Diabetes Federation, on 14 November, World AIDS Day on 1 December, and World Asthma Day on 11 December.

ASSOCIATED AGENCY

International Agency for Research on Cancer: 150 Cours Albert Thomas, 69372 Lyon Cédex 08, France; tel. 4-72-73-84-85; fax 4-72-73-85-75; e-mail postmaster@iarc.fr; internet www.iarc.fr. Established in 1965 as a self-governing body within the framework of WHO, the Agency organizes international research on cancer. It has its own laboratories and runs a programme of research on the environmental factors causing cancer. Members: Argentina, Australia, Belgium, Brazil, Canada, Denmark, Finland, France, Germany, Italy, Japan, Netherlands, Norway, Sweden, Switzerland, United Kingdom, USA. Dir Dr PAUL KLEIHUES (Germany).

Finance

WHO's regular budget is provided by assessment of member states and associate members. An additional fund for specific projects is provided by voluntary contributions from members and other sources, including UNDP and UNFPA.

A regular budget of US $842.7m. was proposed for the two years 2002–03, the same as for the previous biennium.

WHO budget appropriations by region, 2002–03

Region	Amount ('000 US dollars)	% of total budget
Africa	186,472	22.13
Americas	74,682	8.86
South-East Asia	93,022	11.04
Europe	52,771	6.26
Eastern Mediterranean	83,390	9.90
Western Pacific	73,262	8.69
Headquarters	279,055	33.12
Total	842,654	100.00

Publications

Action against Infection (newsletter).

Bulletin of WHO (monthly).

Environmental Health Criteria.

International Digest of Health Legislation (quarterly).

International Classification of Functioning, Disability and Health—ICF.

International Statistical Classification of Diseases and Related Health Problems, Tenth Revision, 1992–1994 (versions in 37 languages).

Model List of Essential Drugs (biennially).

Weekly Epidemiological Record.

WHO Drug Information (quarterly).

WHO Model Formulary.

World Health Report (annually).

World Health Statistics Annual.

Technical report series; catalogues of specific scientific, technical and medical fields available.

World Intellectual Property Organization—WIPO

Address: 34 chemin des Colombettes, BP 18, 1211 Geneva 20, Switzerland.
Telephone: (22) 3389111; **fax:** (22) 7335428; **e-mail:** wipo.mail@wipo.int; **internet:** www.wipo.int.

WIPO was established by a Convention signed in Stockholm in 1967, which came into force in 1970. It became a specialized agency of the UN in December 1974.

MEMBERS

179 members: see Table on pp. 125–127.

Organization

(April 2003)

GENERAL ASSEMBLY

The General Assembly is one of the three WIPO governing bodies, and is composed of all states that are party to the WIPO Convention and that are also members of any of the WIPO-administered Unions (see below). In November 2002 the Assembly comprised 168 members. The Assembly meets in ordinary session once every two years to agree on programmes and budgets. It elects the Director-General, who is the executive head of WIPO.

CONFERENCE

All member states are represented in the Conference, which meets in ordinary session once every two years to adopt budgets and programmes.

CO-ORDINATION COMMITTEE

Countries belonging to the Committee are elected from among the member states of WIPO, the Paris and Berne Unions, and, *ex officio*, Switzerland. At November 2002 there were 79 members of the Committee, including three *ad hoc* members and Switzerland. It meets in ordinary session once a year.

INTERNATIONAL BUREAU

The International Bureau, as WIPO's secretariat, prepares the meetings of the various bodies of WIPO and the Unions, mainly through the provision of reports and working documents. It organizes the meetings, and sees that the decisions are communicated to all concerned, and, as far as possible, that they are carried out.

The International Bureau implements projects and initiates new ones to promote international co-operation in the field of intellectual property. It acts as an information service and publishes reviews. It is also the depositary of most of the treaties administered by WIPO.

Director-General: Dr KAMIL IDRIS (Sudan).

More than 170 non-governmental organizations have observer status at WIPO. There are two advisory bodies: the Policy Advisory Commission (comprising eminent politicians, diplomats, lawyers and public officials) and the Industry Advisory Commission (comprising senior business representatives).

Activities

WIPO works to ensure that the rights of creators and owners of intellectual property are protected throughout the world, with a view to facilitating the advancement of science, technology and the arts and promoting international trade. Intellectual property comprises two principal branches: industrial property (patents and other rights in technological inventions, rights in trademarks, industrial designs, appellations of origin, etc.) and copyright and neighbouring rights (in literary, musical, artistic, photographic and audiovisual works).

WIPO administers and encourages member states to sign and enforce international treaties relating to the protection of intellectual property, of which the most fundamental are the Paris Convention for the Protection of Industrial Property (1883), the Berne Convention for the Protection of Literary and Artistic Works (1886), and the Patent Co-operation Treaty (PCT). WIPO's main areas of activity are progressive development of international intellectual property law, global protection systems and services, and co-operation for development. The Organization seeks to simplify and harmonize national intellectual property legislation and procedures (for example through implementation of the Trademark Law Treaty, 1994, and development of the Patent Law Treaty, 2000), provide services for international applications for industrial property rights, exchange information on intellectual property, provide training and

legal and technical assistance to developing countries, facilitate the resolution of private intellectual property disputes, and develop the use of information technology for storing, accessing and using valuable intellectual property information.

The rapid advancement of digital communications networks has posed challenges regarding the protection and enforcement of intellectual property rights. WIPO has undertaken a range of initiatives to address the implications for copyright and industrial property law, and for electronic commerce transcending national jurisdictions. WIPO's Electronic Commerce Section co-ordinates programmes and activities relating to the intellectual property aspects of electronic commerce. In September 1999 WIPO organized the first International Conference on Electronic Commerce and Intellectual Property; a 'Digital Agenda' was launched by the Organization at the Conference. The second International Conference on Electronic Commerce and Intellectual Property was held in September 2001. A WIPO Summit on Intellectual Property and the Knowledge Economy was scheduled to be held in Beijing, People's Republic of China, in April 2003.

In view of the advances in technology and economic globalization in recent years WIPO has focused increasingly on the relationship between intellectual property and issues such as traditional knowledge, biological diversity, environmental protection and human rights. In 1998–99 WIPO prepared the first ever report on the intellectual property concerns of holders of traditional knowledge. In April 2000 the organization convened its first Meeting on Intellectual Property and Genetic Resources. A WIPO Intergovernmental Committee on Intellectual Property and Genetic Resources, Traditional Knowledge and Folklore was established in September.

In September 2001 member states approved the WIPO Patent Agenda, a process of global consultations aimed at creating a blueprint for the development of the international patent system.

PROGRESSIVE DEVELOPMENT OF INTERNATIONAL PROPERTY LAW

One of WIPO's major activities is the progressive development and application of international norms and standards. The Organization prepares new treaties and undertakes the revision of the existing treaties that it administers. WIPO administers international classifications established by treaties and relating to inventions, marks and industrial designs: periodically it reviews these to ensure their improvement in terms of coverage and precision. WIPO also carries out studies on issues in the field of intellectual property that could be the subject of model laws or guide-lines for implementation at national or international levels. The organization is increasingly active in harmonizing and simplifying procedures in order to make the registration of intellectual property more easily accessible. WIPO aims to keep pace with rapid developments in the intellectual property domain. Standing committees have been formed by member states to examine questions of substantive law or harmonization in the organization's main fields of activity and to ensure that the interests of member states are addressed promptly.

CO-OPERATION FOR DEVELOPMENT

WIPO aims to modernize national intellectual property systems. It offers assistance to increase the capabilities of developing countries to benefit from the international intellectual property framework, with a view to promoting the optimal use of human and other resources and thereby contributing to national prosperity. WIPO supports governments with intellectual property-related institution-building, human resources development, and preparation and implementation of legislation. The WIPO Worldwide Academy, created in 1998, undertakes training, teaching and research on intellectual property matters, focusing particularly on developing countries. The Academy maintains a Distance Learning Centre using on-line facilities, digital multimedia technology and video conferencing. WIPO's Information and Documentation Centre holds extensive reference materials. Under its Digital Agenda WIPO aims to assist the integration of developing countries into the internet environment, particularly through the use of WIPONET, a global digital network of intellectual property information capable of transmitting confidential data that was launched in January 2001. The organization is also implementing the Intellectual Property Digital Libraries database project and maintains the WIPO Collection of Laws for Electronic Access (CLEA) multi-lingual database.

WIPO advises countries on obligations under the World Trade Organization's agreement on Trade-Related Aspects of Intellectual Property Rights (TRIPS). The two organizations are undertaking a joint technical co-operation initiative to assist least-developed countries to harmonize their national legislative and administrative structures in compliance with the TRIPS accord by 1 January 2006.

WIPO presented a programme of action to the Third UN Conference on the Least-Developed Countries (UN-LDCs III, held in Brussels, Belgium in May 2001), which was aimed at strengthening LDC's intellectual property systems.

A new programme focusing on the intellectual property concerns of small and medium-sized enterprises was approved by the WIPO General Assembly in September 2000. An International Forum on Intellectual Property and SMEs, organized jointly by WIPO and the Italian Government in Milan, Italy in February 2001, adopted the Milan Plan of Action for helping SMEs to benefit fully from the intellectual property system.

GLOBAL PROTECTION SYSTEMS AND SERVICES

WIPO administers a small number of treaties, covering inventions (patents), trademarks and industrial designs, under which one international registration or filing has effect in any of the relevant signatory states. The services provided by WIPO under such treaties simplify the registration process and reduce the cost of making individual applications or filings in each country in which protection for a given intellectual property right is sought. The most widely used of these treaties is the PCT, under which a single international patent application is valid in all signatory countries selected by the applicant. The PCT system has expanded rapidly in recent years. Through its Information Management for the PCT (IMPACT) project WIPO aims to automate fully the operations of the PCT. The corresponding treaties concerning the international registration of trademarks and industrial designs are, respectively, the Madrid Agreement (and its Protocol), and the Hague Agreement. WIPO's Advisory Committee on Enforcement of Industrial Property Rights assesses best practices and procedures for the effective enforcement of intellectual property rights.

WIPO maintains the following international registration services:

International registration of trademarks: operating since 1893; during 2001 there were approximately 24,000 registrations and renewals of trademarks; publ. *WIPO Gazette of International Marks* (every two weeks).

International deposit of industrial designs: operating since 1928; during 2001 approximately 4,200 deposits, renewals and prolongations of industrial designs were made; publ. *International Designs Bulletin* (monthly).

International applications for patents: operating since 1978; during 2001 103,947 record copies of international applications for patents under the PCT were received; publ. *PCT Gazette* (weekly).

WIPO also maintains the WIPO Arbitration and Mediation Centre, which became operational on 1 October 1994, to facilitate the settlement of intellectual property disputes between private parties. The Centre also organizes arbitrator and mediator workshops and assists in the development of WIPO model contract clauses and industry-specific resolution schemes. The Centre operates a Domain Name Dispute Resolution Service, which plays a leading role in reviewing cases of conflict between trademarks and internet domain names, in accordance with the Uniform Domain Name Dispute Resolution Policy that was, on WIPO's recommendation, adopted by the Internet Corporation for Assigned Names and Numbers (ICANN, q.v.) in October 1999. In 2001 1,506 cases concerning disputes over generic top-level domains were filed with the Centre. WIPO's first Internet Domain Name Process, a series of international consultations, undertaken in 1999, issued several recommendations for controlling the abuse of trademarks on the internet. A second Internet Domain Name Process, completed in 2001, addressed the improper registration of other identifiers ('cybersquatting'), including standard non-proprietary names for pharmaceutical substances, names and acronyms of intergovernmental organizations, geographical indications and terms, and trade names. WIPO maintains an online database of cybersquatting cases (accessible at arbiter.wipo.int/domains/search).

PARIS AND BERNE CONVENTIONS

International Union for the Protection of Industrial Property (Paris Convention): the treaty was signed in Paris in 1883, and last revised in 1967; there were 162 members of the Union's Assembly at November 2002 and two parties to the Convention that were not Assembly members. Member states must accord to nationals and residents of other member states the same advantages under their laws relating to the protection of inventions, trademarks and other subjects of industrial property as they accord to their own nationals.

International Union for the Protection of Literary and Artistic Works (Berne Union): the treaty was signed in Berne in 1886 and last revised in 1971; there were 146 members of the Union's Assembly at November 2002 and three parties to the Convention that were not Assembly members. Members of the Union's Assembly must accord the same protection to the copyright of nationals of other member states as to their own. The treaty also prescribes minimum standards of protection, for example, that copyright protection generally continues throughout the author's

life and for 50 years after. It includes special provision for the developing countries.

OTHER AGREEMENTS

(Status at October 2002, unless otherwise indicated)

International Protection of Industrial Property:

Madrid Agreement of 14 April 1891, for the Repression of False or Deceptive Indications of Source on Goods; 33 states party to the Agreement.

Madrid Agreement of 14 April 1891, Concerning the International Registration of Marks; 52 states party to the Agreement.

The Hague Agreement of 6 November 1925, Concerning the International Deposit of Industrial Designs; 30 states party to the Agreement.

Nice Agreement of 15 June 1957, Concerning the International Classification of Goods and Services for the Purposes of the Registration of Marks; 69 states party to the Agreement.

Lisbon Agreement of 31 October 1958, for the Protection of Appellations of Origin and their International Registration; 20 states party to the Agreement.

Locarno Agreement of 8 October 1968, Establishing an International Classification for Industrial Designs; 41 states party to the Agreement.

Patent Co-operation Treaty of 19 June 1970 (PCT); 117 states party to the Treaty.

Strasbourg Agreement of 24 March 1971, Concerning the International Patent Classification (IPC); 53 states party to the Agreement.

Vienna Agreement of 12 June 1973, Establishing an International Classification of the Figurative Elements of Marks; 19 states party to the Agreement.

Budapest Treaty of 28 April 1977, on the International Recognition of the Deposit of Micro-organisms for the Purposes of Patent Procedure; 55 states party to the Treaty.

Nairobi Treaty of 26 September 1981, on the Protection of the Olympic Symbol; 41 states party to the Treaty.

Trademark Law Treaty of 27 October 1994; 31 states party to the Treaty (at 25 November 2002).

Protocol Relating to the Madrid Agreement Concerning the International Registration of Marks, signed on 28 June 1989; 56 contracting states.

Geneva Act of the Hague Agreement Concerning the International Registration of Industrial Designs, 1999; not yet entered into force.

Patent Law Treaty, 2000; not yet entered into force.

Copyright and Special International Protection of the Rights of Performers, Producers of Phonograms and Broadcasting Organizations ('Neighbouring Rights'):

Rome Convention, 26 October 1961, for the Protection of Performers, Producers of Phonograms and Broadcasting Organizations; 70 states party to the Convention.

Geneva Convention, 29 October 1971, for the Protection of Producers of Phonograms against Unauthorized Duplication of their Phonograms; 69 states party to the Convention.

Brussels Convention, 21 May 1974, Relating to the Distribution of Programme-carrying Signals Transmitted by Satellite; 24 states party to the Convention.

Treaty on the International Registration of Audiovisual Works, 1989; 13 states party to the Treaty.

Performances and Phonograms Treaty, 1996; 38 states party to the Treaty (at 15 November 2002).

Copyright Treaty, 1996; 38 states party to the Treaty (at 4 November 2002).

Finance

The proposed budget for the two years 2002–03 amounted to 678.4m. Swiss francs. Some 85% of WIPO's revenue derives from the international registration systems maintained by the Organization; the remainder derives mainly from contributions by member states.

Publications

Annual Report.

Les appellations d'origine (annually, in French).

Essential Elements of Intellectual Property (CD-Rom).

Industrial Property and Copyright (monthly in English and French; bimonthly in Spanish).

Industrial Property Statistics (CD-Rom).

Intellectual Property in Asia and the Pacific (quarterly in English).

Intellectual Property Profile of the Least-Developed Countries.

International Designs Bulletin (monthly in English and French, also on CD-Rom).

PCT Gazette (weekly in English and French).

PCT Newsletter (monthly in English).

WIPO Academy Review .

WIPO Gazette of International Marks (every two weeks, in English and French, also on CD-Rom).

WIPO Magazine (monthly in English, French and Spanish).

A collection of industrial property and copyright laws and treaties; a selection of publications related to intellectual property.

World Meteorological Organization—WMO

Address: 7 bis, ave de la Paix, CP 2300, 1211 Geneva 2, Switzerland.

Telephone: (22) 7308111; **fax:** (22) 7308181; **e-mail:** ipa@www.wmo.ch; **internet:** www.wmo.ch.

The WMO was established in 1950 and was recognized as a Specialized Agency of the UN in 1951, operating in the fields of meteorology, climatology, operational hydrology and related fields, as well as their applications.

MEMBERS

185 members: see Table on pp. 125–127.

Organization

(April 2003)

WORLD METEOROLOGICAL CONGRESS

The supreme body of the Organization, the Congress, is convened every four years and represents all members; it adopts regulations, and determines policy, programme and budget. Fourteenth Congress: May 2003.

EXECUTIVE COUNCIL

The Council has 36 members and meets at least yearly to prepare studies and recommendations for the Congress; it supervises the implementation of Congress resolutions and regulations, informs members on technical matters and offers advice.

SECRETARIAT

The secretariat acts as an administrative, documentary and information centre; undertakes special technical studies; produces publications; organizes meetings of WMO constituent bodies; acts as a link between the meteorological and hydrometeorological services of the world, and provides information for the general public.

Secretary-General: Prof. G. O. P. Obasi (Nigeria).

REGIONAL ASSOCIATIONS

Members are grouped in six Regional Associations (Africa, Asia, Europe, North and Central America, South America and South-West Pacific), whose task is to co-ordinate meteorological activity within their regions and to examine questions referred to them by the Executive Council. Sessions are held at least once every four years.

TECHNICAL COMMISSIONS

The Technical Commissions are composed of experts nominated by the members of the Organization. Sessions are held at least once every four years. The Commissions cover the following areas: Basic Systems; Climatology; Instruments and Methods of Observation; Atmospheric Sciences; Aeronautical Meteorology; Agricultural Meteorology; Hydrology; Marine Meteorology.

Activities

WORLD WEATHER WATCH PROGRAMME

Combining facilities and services provided by the members, the Programme's primary purpose is to make available meteorological and related geophysical and environmental information enabling them to maintain efficient meteorological services. Facilities in regions outside any national territory (outer space, ocean areas and Antarctica) are maintained by members on a voluntary basis.

Antarctic Activities: co-ordinate WMO activities related to the Antarctic, in particular the surface and upper-air observing programme, plan the regular exchange of observational data and products needed for operational and research purposes, study problems related to instruments and methods of observation peculiar to the Antarctic, and develop appropriate regional coding practices. Contacts are maintained with scientific bodies dealing with Antarctic research and with other international organizations on aspects of Antarctic meteorology.

Data Management: This aspect of the Programme monitors the integration of the different components of the World Weather Watch (WWW) Programme, with the intention of increasing the efficiency of, in particular, the Global Observing System, the Global Data Processing System and the Global Telecommunication System. The Data Management component of the WWW Programme develops data handling procedures and standards for enhanced forms of data representation, in order to aid member countries in processing large volumes of meteorological data. It also supports the co-ordinated transfer of expertise and technology to developing countries.

Emergency Response Activities: assist national meteorological services to respond effectively to man-made environmental emergencies, particularly nuclear accidents, through the development, co-ordination and implementation of WMO/IAEA established procedures and response mechanisms for the provision and exchange of observational data and specialized transport model products.

Global Data Processing System: consists of World Meteorological Centres (WMCs) in Melbourne (Australia), Moscow (Russia) and Washington, DC (USA), 40 Regional/Specialized Meteorological Centres (RSMCs) and 187 National Meteorological Centres. The WMCs and RSMCs provide analyses, forecasts and warnings for exchange on the Global Telecommunications System. Some centres concentrate on the monitoring and forecasting of environmental quality and special weather phenomena, such as tropical cyclones, monsoons, droughts, etc., which have a major impact on human safety and national economies. These analyses and forecasts are designed to assist the members in making local and specialized forecasts.

Global Observing System: Simultaneous observations are made at more than 10,000 land stations. Meteorological information is also received from 3,000 aircraft, 7,000 ships, 600 drifting buoys, and nine polar orbiting and six geostationary meteorological satellites. About 160 members operate some 1,300 ground stations equipped to receive picture transmissions from geostationary and polar-orbiting satellites.

Global Telecommunication System: provides telecommunication services for the rapid collection and exchange of meteorological information and related data; consists of (a) the Main Telecommunication Network (MTN), (b) six Regional Meteorological Telecommunication networks, and (c) the national telecommunication networks. The system operates through 183 National Meteorological Centres, 29 Regional Telecommunications Hubs and the three WMCs.

Instruments and Methods of Observation Programme: promotes the world-wide standardization of meteorological and geophysical instruments and methods of observation and measurement to meet agreed accuracy requirements. It provides related guidance material and training assistance in the use and maintenance of the instruments.

System Support Activity: provides guidance and support to members in the planning, establishment and operation of the WWW. It includes training, technical co-operation support, system and methodology support, operational WWW evaluations, advanced technology support, an operations information service, and the WWW referral catalogue.

Tropical Cyclone Programme: established in response to UN General Assembly Resolution 2733 (XXV), aims at the development of national and regionally co-ordinated systems to ensure that the loss of life and damage caused by tropical cyclones and associated floods, landslides and storm surges are reduced to a minimum. The programme supports the transfer of technology, and includes five regional tropical cyclone bodies covering more than 60 countries, to improve warning systems and for collaboration with other international organizations in activities related to disaster mitigation.

WORLD CLIMATE PROGRAMME

Adopted by the Eighth World Meteorological Congress (1979), the World Climate Programme (WCP) comprises the following components: World Climate Data and Monitoring Programme (WCDMP), World Climate Applications and Services Programme (WCASP), World Climate Impact Assessment and Response Strategies Programme (WCIRP), World Climate Research Programme (WCRP). The WCP is supported by the Global Climate Observing System (GCOS), which provides comprehensive observation of the global climate system, involving a multi-disciplinary range of atmospheric, oceanic, hydrologic, cyrospheric and biotic properties and processes. In 1997/98 the GCOS was particularly active in monitoring the impact of the El Niño weather phenomenon on the climate system. The objectives of the WCP are: to use existing climate information to improve economic and social planning; to improve the understanding of climate processes through research, so as to determine the predictability of climate and the extent of man's influence on it; and to detect and warn governments of impending climate variations or changes, either natural or man-made, which may significantly affect critical human activities.

Co-ordination of the overall Programme is the responsibility of the WMO, along with direct management of the WCDMP and WCASP. The UN Environment Programme (UNEP, q.v.) has accepted responsibility for the WCIRP, while the WCRP is jointly administered by WMO, the International Council of Scientific Unions (ICSU, q.v.) and UNESCO's Intergovernmental Oceanographic Commission. Other organizations involved in the Programme include FAO, WHO, and the Consultative Group on International Agricultural Research (CGIAR). The WCP Co-ordinating Committee co-ordinates the activities of the four components of the Programme and liaises with other international bodies concerned with climate. In addition, the WCP supports the WMO/UNEP Intergovernmental Panel on Climate Change and the implementation of international agreements, such as the UN Framework Convention on Climate Change (see below).

World Climate Applications and Services Programme (WCASP): promotes applications of climate knowledge in the areas of food production, water, energy (especially solar and wind energy), urban planning and building, human health, transport, tourism and recreation.

World Climate Data and Monitoring Programme (WCDMP): aims to make available reliable climate data for detecting and monitoring climate change for both practical applications and research purposes. The major projects are: the Climate Change Detection Project (CCDP); development of climate data bases; computer systems for climate data management (CLICOM); the World Data and Information Referral Service (INFOCLIMA); the Climate Monitoring System; and the Data Rescue (DARE) project.

World Climate Impact Assessment and Response Strategies Programme (WCIRP): aims to make reliable estimates of the socio-economic impact of climate changes, and to assist in forming national policies accordingly. It concentrates on: study of the impact of climate variations on national food systems; assessment of the impact of man's activities on the climate, especially through increasing the amount of carbon dioxide and other radiatively active gases in the atmosphere; and developing the methodology of climate impact assessments.

World Climate Research Programme (WCRP): organized jointly with the Intergovernmental Oceanographic Commission of UNESCO and the ICSU, to determine to what extent climate can be predicted, and the extent of man's influence on climate. Its three specific objectives are: establishing the physical basis for weather predictions over time ranges of one to two months; understanding and predicting the variability of the global climate over periods of several years; and studying the long-term variations and the response of climate to natural or man-made influence over periods of several decades. Studies include: changes in the atmosphere caused by emissions of carbon dioxide, aerosols and other gases; the effect of cloudiness on the radiation balance; the effect of ground water storage and vegetation on evaporation; the Arctic and Antarctic climate process; and the effects of oceanic circulation changes on the global atmosphere. The 10-year Tropical Ocean and Global Atmosphere Project, which ended in 1994, developed forecasting techniques used to monitor the climate phenomenon, El Niño, in 1997–98.

ATMOSPHERIC RESEARCH AND ENVIRONMENT PROGRAMME

This major programme aims to help members to implement research projects; to disseminate relevant scientific information; to draw the attention of members to outstanding research problems of major importance, such as atmospheric composition and environment changes; and to encourage and help members to incorporate the results of research into operational forecasting or other appropriate techniques, particularly when such changes of procedure require international co-ordination and agreement.

Global Atmosphere Watch (GAW): This is a world-wide system that integrates most monitoring and research activities involving the measurement of atmospheric composition, and is intended to serve as an early warning system to detect further changes in atmospheric concentrations of 'greenhouse' gases, changes in the ozone layer and in long-range transport of pollutants, including acidity and toxicity of rain, as well as the atmospheric burden of aerosols. The instruments of these globally standardized observations and related research are a set of 22 global stations in remote areas and, in order to address regional effects, some 200 regional stations measuring specific atmospheric chemistry parameters, such as ozone and acid deposition. GAW is the main contributor of data on chemical composition and physical characteristics of the atmosphere to the GCOS. Through GAW, WMO has collaborated with the UN Economic Commission for Europe (ECE) and has been responsible for the meteorological part of the Monitoring and Evaluation of the Long-range Transmission of Air Pollutants in Europe. In this respect, WMO has arranged for the establishment of two Meteorological Synthesizing Centres (Oslo, Norway, and Moscow, Russia) which provide daily analysis of the transport of pollution over Europe. GAW also gives attention to atmospheric chemistry studies, prepares scientific assessments and encourages integrated environmental monitoring. Quality Assurance Science Activities Centres have been established to ensure an overall level of quality in GAW. Atmospheric composition information is maintained by and available through a series of six GAW World Data Centres. GAW operates the GAW Urban Environment Meteorological Research Programme (GURME), which assists National Meteorological and Hydrological Services (NMHSs) in dealing with regional and urban pollution monitoring forecasting, through the provision of guide-lines and information on the requisite measuring and modelling infrastructures, and by bringing together NMHSs, regional and city administrations and health authorities. GURME is being developed in co-operation with the World Health Organization.

Physics and Chemistry of Clouds and Weather Modification Research Programme: encourages scientific research on cloud physics and chemistry, with special emphasis on interaction between clouds and atmospheric chemistry, as well as weather modification such as precipitation enhancement ('rain-making') and hail suppression. It provides information on world-wide weather modification projects, and guidance in the design and evaluation of experiments. It also studies the chemistry of clouds and their role in the transport, transformation and dispersion of pollution.

Tropical Meteorology Research Programme: aims at the promotion and co-ordination of members' research efforts into such important problems as monsoons, tropical cyclones, meteorological aspects of droughts in the arid zones of the tropics, rain-producing tropical weather systems, and the interaction between tropical and mid-latitude weather systems. This should lead to a better understanding of tropical systems and forecasting, and thus be of economic benefit to tropical countries.

Weather Prediction Research Programmes: The programmes assist members in exchanging the results of research on weather prediction and long-range forecasting by means of international conferences and technical reports and progress reports on numerical weather prediction, in order to improve members' weather services. The Programme on Very Short- and Short-range Weather Prediction Research is designed to promote and co-ordinate research activities by members, with a view to improving forecast accuracy over a period extending to three or four days. The Programme on Medium- and Long-range Weather Prediction Research is aimed at the improvement and better co-ordination of members' research activities in weather prediction beyond day four, including monthly and seasonal forecasting.

World Weather Research Programme: Promotes the development and application of improved weather forecasting techniques. The Programme is primarily concerned with forecasting weather events that have the potential to cause considerable socio-economic dislocation. Advances in forecasting capability are pursued through a combination of improved scientific understanding (gained through field experiments and research), forecast technique development, the demonstration of new forecasting capabilities, and the transfer of these advances to all NMHSs in conjunction with related training.

APPLICATIONS OF METEOROLOGY PROGRAMME

Public Weather Services Programme: assists members in providing reliable and effective weather and related services for the benefit of the public. The main objectives of the programme are: to strengthen members' capabilities to meet the needs of the community through the provision of comprehensive weather and related services, with particular emphasis on public safety and welfare; and to foster a better understanding by the public of the capabilities of national meteorological services and how best to use their services.

Agricultural Meteorology Programme: the study of weather and climate as they affect agriculture and forestry, the selection of crops and their protection from disease and deterioration in storage, soil conservation, phenology and physiology of crops and productivity and health of farm animals; the Commission for Agricultural Meteorology supervises the applications projects and also advises the Secretary-General in his efforts to co-ordinate activities in support of food production. There are also special activities in agrometeorology to monitor and combat drought and desertification, to apply climate and real-time weather information in agricultural planning and operations, and to help improve the efficiency of the use of human labour, land, water and energy in agriculture; close co-operation is maintained with FAO, centres of CGIAR and UNEP.

Aeronautical Meteorology Programme: to provide operational meteorological information required for safe, regular and efficient air navigation, as well as meteorological assistance to non-real-time activities of the aviation industry. The objective is to ensure the world-wide provision of cost-effective and responsive meteorological services, in support of safe, regular and efficient aviation operations. The programme is implemented at global, regional and national levels by the Commission for Aeronautical Meteorology (CAeM) playing a major role, taking into account relevant meteorological developments in science and technology, studying aeronautical requirements for meteorological services, promoting international standardization of methods, procedures and techniques, and considering requirements for basic and climatological data as well as aeronautical requirements for meteorological observations and specialized instruments and enhanced understanding and awareness of the impact of aviation on the environment. Activities under this programme are carried out, where relevant, with the International Civil Aviation Organization (ICAO, q.v.) and in collaboration with users of services provided to aviation.

Marine Meteorology and Associated Oceanographic Activities Programme: operational monitoring of the oceans and the maritime atmosphere; collection, exchange, archival recording and management of marine data; processing of marine data, and the provision of marine meteorological and oceanographic services in support of the safety of life and property at sea and of the efficient and economic operation of all sea-based activities. The joint WMO/Intergovernmental Oceanographic Commission (IOC) Technical Commission for Oceanography and Marine Meteorology (JCOMM) has broad responsibilities in the overall management of the programme. Many programme elements are undertaken jointly with the IOC, within the context of JCOMM, and also of the Global Ocean Observing System (GOOS). Close co-operation also occurs with the International Maritime Organization (IMO, q.v.), as well as with other bodies both within and outside the UN system.

HYDROLOGY AND WATER RESOURCES PROGRAMME

The overall objective of this major programme is to apply hydrology to meet the needs of sustainable development and use of water and related resources; for the mitigation of water-related disasters; and to ensure effective environment management at national and international levels. The Programme consists of the following mutually supporting component programmes:

Programme on Basic Systems in Hydrology (BSH): provides the basis and framework for the majority of the scientific and technical aspects of WMO activities in hydrology and water resources. The BSH covers the collection, transmission and storage of data, the implementation of the Hydrological Operational Multipurpose System (HOMS), and the development of the World Hydrological Cycle Observing System (WHYCOS).

Programme on Forecasting and Applications in Hydrology (FAH): covers aspects of the Hydrology and Water Resources Programme relating to hydrological modelling and forecasting, and to the application of hydrology in studies of global change. The FAH organizes activities in support of water resources development and management, and hazard mitigation, and conducts studies on climate change and environmental protection. The Programme is linked to the World Climate and Tropical Cyclone programmes.

Programme on Sustainable Development of Water Resources (SDW): encourages the full participation of hydrological services in national planning and in the implementation of actions consequent to the relevant recommendations of the United Nations Conference on Environment and Development (UNCED, held in Rio de Janeiro, Brazil, in 1992), and of its review conference in 1997.

Programme on Capacity Building in Hydrology and Water Resources (CBH): provides a framework under which National Hydrological Services (NHSs) can request advice and assistance. Supports NHSs' capacity-building efforts.

Programme on Water-related Issues (WRI): maintains WMO's important role in international activities relating to water resource assessment and hydrological forecasting. A major aspect of this component programme is the Organization's collaboration with other UN agencies. In addition, the WRI involves joint activities with international river basin commissions and with scientific and technical non-governmental organizations.

Specific support for the transfer of operational technology is provided through the Hydrological Operational Multipurpose System (HOMS).

Other WMO programmes contain hydrological elements, which are closely co-ordinated with the Hydrology and Water Resources Programme. These include the Tropical Cyclone Programme, the World Climate Programme, and the Global Energy and Water Budget Experiment of the World Climate Research Programme.

EDUCATION AND TRAINING PROGRAMME

The overall objective of this programme is to assist members in developing adequately trained staff to meet their responsibilities for providing meteorological and hydrological information services.

Activities include surveys of the training requirements of member states, the development of appropriate training programmes, the monitoring and improvement of the network of WMO Regional Meteorological Training Centres, the organization of training courses, seminars and conferences and the preparation of training materials. The Programme also arranges individual training programmes and the provision of fellowships. There are about 500 trainees in any one year. About 300 fellowships are awarded annually. Advice is given on training materials, resources and expertise between members. A Panel of Experts on Education and Training was set up by the Executive Council to serve as an advisory body on all aspects of technical and scientific education and of training in meteorology and operational hydrology.

TECHNICAL CO-OPERATION PROGRAMME

The objective of the WMO Technical Co-operation Programme is to assist developing countries in improving their meteorological and hydrological services so that they can serve the needs of their people more effectively. This is through improving, *inter alia*, their early warning systems for severe weather; their agricultural-meteorological services, to assist in more reliable and fruitful food production; and the assessment of climatological factors for economic planning. At a regional level the Programme concentrates on disaster prevention and mitigation. In 2000 the cost of the assistance to developing countries, administered or arranged by the Technical Co-operation Programme, was US $16.6m.

United Nations Development Programme (UNDP): WMO provides assistance in the development of national meteorological and hydrological services, in the application of meteorological and hydrological data to national economic development, and in the training of personnel. Assistance in the form of expert missions, fellowships and equipment was provided to 18 countries in 2000 at a cost of US $2.6m., financed by UNDP.

Voluntary Co-operation Programme (VCP): WMO assists members in implementing the World Weather Watch Programme to develop an integrated observing and forecasting system. Member governments contribute equipment, services and fellowships for training, in addition to cash donations. During 2000 167 projects in 778 countries received support under the VCP, while 124 short-term and 78 long-term fellowships were being implemented in the framework of the programme. Contributions to the VCP totalled US $8.4m. in 2000.

WMO also carries out assistance projects under Trust Fund arrangements, financed by national authorities, either for activities in their own country or in a beneficiary country and managed by UNDP, the World Bank and UNEP. Such arrangements provided one-third of total Programme funds in 2000.

Financial support from WMO's regular budget for fellowships, group training, technical conferences and study tours amounted to US $800,000 in 2000.

CO-OPERATION WITH OTHER BODIES

As a Specialized Agency of the UN, WMO is actively involved in the activities of the UN system. In addition, WMO has concluded a number of formal agreements and working arrangements with international organizations both within and outside the UN system, at the intergovernmental and non-governmental level. As a result, WMO participates in major international conferences convened under the auspices of the UN or other organizations.

Intergovernmental Panel on Climate Change (IPCC): established in 1988 by WMO and UNEP; comprises some 3,000 scientists as well as other experts and representatives of all UN member governments. Approximately every five years the IPCC assesses all available scientific, technical and socio-economic information on anthropogenic climate change. IPCC provides, on request, scientific, technical and socio-economic advice to the parties to the Conference of the Parties to the UN Framework Convention on Climate Change (UNFCCC) and to its subsidiary bodies, and compiles reports on specialized topics, such as *Aviation and the Global Atmosphere* and *Regional Impacts of Climate Change*. The IPCC informs and guides, but does not prescribe, policy. In December 1995 the IPCC presented evidence to 120 governments, demonstrating 'a discernible human influence on global climate'. In 2001 the Panel issued its *Third Assessment Report*, in which it confirmed this finding and presented new and strengthened evidence attributing most global climate warming over the past 50 years to human activities. IPCC's fourth report was scheduled to be issued in 2007.

Secretariat of the UN Framework Convention on Climate Change: Haus Carstanjen, Martin-Luther-King-Strasse 8, 53175 Bonn, Germany; tel. (228) 815-1000; fax (228) 815-1999; e-mail secretariat@unfccc.int; internet unfccc.int. WMO and UNEP worked together to formulate the Convention, in response to the first report of the IPCC, issued in August 1990, which predicted an increase in the concentration of 'greenhouse' gases (i.e. carbon dioxide and other gases that have a warming effect on the atmosphere) owing to human activity. The UNFCCC was signed in May 1992 and formally adopted at the UN Conference on Environment and Development, held in June. It entered into force in March 1994. It commited countries to submitting reports on measures being taken to reduce the emission of greenhouse gases and recommended stabilizing these emissions at 1990 levels by 2000; however, this was not legally-binding. In July 1996, at the second session of the Conference of the Parties (COP) of the Convention, representatives of developed countries declared their willingness to commit to legally-binding objectives for emission limitations in a specified timetable. Multilateral negotiations ensued to formulate a mandatory treaty on greenhouse gas emissions. At the third COP, held in Kyoto, Japan, in December 1997, 38 industrial nations endorsed mandatory reductions of emissions of the six most harmful gases by an average of 5.2% from 1990 levels, between 2008 and 2012. The so-called Kyoto Protocol was to enter into force on being ratified by countries representing 55% of the world's carbon dioxide emissions in 1990. Many of the Protocol's operational details, however, remained to be determined. The fourth COP, convened in Buenos Aires, Argentina, in November 1998, adopted a plan of action to promote implementation of the UNFCCC and to finalize the operational details of the Kyoto Protocol. These included the Clean Development Mechanism, by which industrialized countries may obtain credits towards achieving their reduction targets by assisting developing countries to implement emission-reducing measures, and a system of trading emission quotas. The fifth COP, held in Bonn, Germany, in October/November 1999, and the first session of the sixth COP, convened in The Hague, Netherlands, in November 2000, failed to reach agreement on the implementation of the Buenos Aires plan of action, owing to a lack of consensus on several technical matters, including the formulation of an effective mechanism for ascertaining compli-

ance under the Kyoto Protocol, and adequately defining a provision of the Protocol under which industrialized countries may obtain credits towards achieving their reduction targets in respect of the absorption of emissions resulting from activities in the so-called land-use, land-use change and forestry (LULUCF) sector. Further, informal, talks were held in Ottawa, Canada, in early December. Agreement on implementing the Buenos Aires action plan was finally achieved at the second session of the sixth COP, held in Bonn in July 2001. The seventh COP, convened in Marrakech, Morocco, in October/November, formally adopted the decisions reached in July, and elected 15 members to the Executive Board of the Clean Development Mechanism. The eighth COP, convened in New Dehli, India, in October/November 2002, issued the Dehli Declaration, urging states parties that had not done so already to ratify the Kyoto Protocol, and urging the integration of climate change objectives in key areas into national sustainable development strategies. In March the USA (the most prolific national producer of harmful gas emissions) announced that it would not ratify the Kyoto Protocol. By December 2002 the Protocol had been ratified by 100 signatory states, requiring only ratification by Russia to enable it to enter into force.

INTERNATIONAL DAY

World Meteorological Day is observed every year on 23 March. The theme in 2003 was 'Our Future Climate'.

Finance

WMO is financed by contributions from members on a proportional scale of assessment. The assessed regular budget for the four years 2000–03 was 248.8m. Swiss francs; additional expenditure of 3.5m. Swiss francs was also authorized to be used for high priority activities. Outside this budget, WMO implements a number of projects as executing agency for UNDP or else under trust-fund arrangements.

Publications

Annual Report.
Statements on the Status of the Global Climate.
WMO Bulletin (quarterly in English, French, Russian and Spanish).
Reports, technical regulations, manuals and notes and training publications.

Membership of the United Nations and its Specialized Agencies

(at April 2003)

	UN	IAEA	IBRD	IDA	IFC	IMF	FAO[1]	IFAD[2]	IMO[3]	ICAO[4]	ILO	ITU[5]	UNESCO[6]	UNIDO	UPU[7]	WHO[8]	WMO[9]	WIPO
Afghanistan	x	x	x	x	x	x	x	x		x	x	x	x	x	x	x	x	
Albania	x	x	x	x	x	x	x	x	x	x	x	x	x	x	x	x	x	x
Algeria	x	x	x	x	x	x	x	x	x	x	x	x	x	x	x	x	x	x
Andorra	x									x		x	x		x		x	x
Angola	x		x	x	x	x	x	x	x	x	x	x	x	x	x	x	x	x
Antigua and Barbuda	x		x		x	x	x	x	x	x		x	x		x	x	x	x
Argentina	x	x	x	x	x	x	x	x	x	x	x	x	x	x	x	x	x	x
Armenia	x	x	x	x	x	x	x		x	x	x	x	x	x	x	x	x	x
Australia	x	x	x	x	x	x	x	x	x	x	x	x	x	x	x	x	x	x
Austria	x	x	x	x	x	x	x	x	x	x	x	x	x	x	x	x	x	x
Azerbaijan	x	x	x	x	x	x	x		x	x	x	x	x	x	x	x	x	x
Bahamas	x		x		x	x	x		x	x	x	x	x	x	x	x	x	x
Bahrain	x		x		x	x	x	x	x	x	x	x	x	x	x	x	x	x
Bangladesh	x	x	x	x	x	x	x	x	x	x	x	x	x	x	x	x	x	x
Barbados	x		x	x	x	x	x	x		x	x	x	x	x	x	x	x	x
Belarus	x	x	x		x	x				x	x	x	x	x	x	x	x	x
Belgium	x	x	x	x	x	x	x	x	x	x	x	x	x	x	x	x	x	x
Belize	x		x	x	x	x	x	x	x	x	x	x	x	x	x	x	x	x
Benin	x		x	x	x	x	x	x		x	x	x	x	x	x	x	x	x
Bhutan	x		x	x			x			x		x		x		x	x	
Bolivia	x	x	x	x	x	x	x	x	x	x	x	x	x	x	x	x	x	x
Bosnia and Herzegovina	x	x	x	x	x	x	x	x	x	x	x	x	x	x	x	x	x	x
Botswana	x	x	x	x	x	x	x	x		x	x	x	x	x	x	x	x	x
Brazil	x	x	x	x	x	x	x	x	x	x	x	x	x	x	x	x	x	x
Brunei	x		x			x			x	x		x				x	x	x
Bulgaria	x	x	x		x	x		x	x	x	x	x	x	x	x	x	x	x
Burkina Faso	x	x	x	x	x	x	x	x		x	x	x	x	x	x	x	x	x
Burundi	x		x	x	x	x	x	x		x	x	x	x	x	x	x	x	x
Cambodia	x		x	x	x	x	x	x	x	x	x	x	x	x	x	x	x	x
Cameroon	x	x	x	x	x	x	x	x	x	x	x	x	x	x	x	x	x	x
Canada	x	x	x	x	x	x	x	x	x	x	x	x	x	x	x	x	x	x
Cape Verde	x		x	x		x	x	x	x	x	x	x	x	x	x	x	x	x
Central African Republic	x		x	x	x	x	x	x		x	x	x	x	x	x	x	x	x
Chad	x		x	x	x	x	x	x		x	x	x	x	x	x	x	x	x
Chile	x	x	x	x	x	x	x	x	x	x	x	x	x	x	x	x	x	x
China, People's Republic	x	x	x	x	x	x	x	x	x	x	x	x	x	x	x	x	x	x
Colombia	x	x	x	x	x	x	x	x	x	x	x	x	x	x	x	x	x	x
Comoros	x		x	x		x	x	x	x		x	x	x	x	x	x	x	
Congo, Democratic Republic	x	x	x	x	x	x	x	x	x	x	x	x	x	x	x	x	x	x
Congo, Republic	x		x	x	x	x	x	x	x	x	x	x	x	x	x	x	x	x
Costa Rica	x	x	x	x	x	x	x	x	x	x	x	x	x	x	x	x	x	x
Côte d'Ivoire	x	x	x	x	x	x	x	x	x	x	x	x	x	x	x	x	x	x
Croatia	x	x	x		x	x	x	x	x	x	x	x	x	x	x	x	x	x
Cuba	x	x					x		x	x	x	x	x	x	x	x	x	x
Cyprus	x	x	x		x	x	x	x	x	x	x	x	x	x	x	x	x	x
Czech Republic	x	x	x	x	x	x	x	x	x	x	x	x	x	x	x	x	x	x
Denmark	x	x	x	x	x	x	x	x	x	x	x	x	x	x	x	x	x	x
Djibouti	x		x	x	x	x	x	x	x	x	x	x	x	x	x	x	x	x
Dominica	x		x	x	x	x	x		x		x	x	x	x	x	x	x	x
Dominican Republic	x	x	x	x	x	x	x	x		x	x	x	x	x	x	x	x	x
Ecuador	x	x	x	x	x	x	x	x	x	x	x	x	x	x	x	x	x	x
Egypt	x	x	x	x	x	x	x	x	x	x	x	x	x	x	x	x	x	x
El Salvador	x	x	x	x	x	x	x	x	x	x	x	x	x	x	x	x	x	x
Equatorial Guinea	x		x	x		x	x	x	x	x	x	x	x	x	x	x	x	x
Eritrea	x	x	x	x	x	x	x	x	x	x	x	x	x	x		x		x
Estonia	x	x	x		x	x		x	x	x	x	x	x		x	x	x	x
Ethiopia	x		x	x	x	x	x	x	x	x	x	x	x	x	x	x	x	x
Fiji	x		x	x	x	x	x	x	x	x	x	x	x	x	x	x	x	x
Finland	x	x	x	x	x	x	x	x	x	x	x	x	x	x	x	x	x	x
France	x	x	x	x	x	x	x	x	x	x	x	x	x	x	x	x	x	x
Gabon	x	x	x	x	x	x	x	x	x	x	x	x	x	x	x	x	x	x
The Gambia	x		x	x	x	x	x	x	x	x	x	x	x	x	x	x	x	x
Georgia	x	x	x	x	x	x	x	x	x	x	x	x	x	x	x	x	x	x
Germany	x	x	x	x	x	x	x	x	x	x	x	x	x	x	x	x	x	x
Ghana	x	x	x	x	x	x	x	x	x	x	x	x	x	x	x	x	x	x
Greece	x	x	x		x	x	x	x	x	x	x	x	x	x	x	x	x	x
Grenada	x		x	x	x	x	x	x	x	x	x	x	x	x	x	x	x	x
Guatemala	x	x	x	x	x	x	x	x	x	x	x	x	x	x	x	x	x	x

continued

	UN	IAEA	IBRD	IDA	IFC	IMF	FAO[1]	IFAD[2]	IMO[3]	ICAO[4]	ILO	ITU[5]	UNESCO[6]	UNIDO	UPU[7]	WHO[8]	WMO[9]	WIPO
Guinea	x		x	x	x	x	x	x	x	x	x	x	x	x	x	x	x	x
Guinea-Bissau	x		x	x	x	x	x	x	x	x	x	x	x	x	x	x	x	x
Guyana	x		x	x	x	x	x	x	x	x	x	x	x	x	x	x	x	x
Haiti	x	x	x	x	x	x	x	x	x	x	x	x	x	x	x	x	x	x
Honduras	x	x	x	x	x	x	x	x	x	x	x	x	x	x	x	x	x	x
Hungary	x	x	x	x	x	x	x	x	x	x	x	x	x	x	x	x	x	x
Iceland	x	x	x	x	x	x	x		x	x	x	x	x	x	x	x	x	x
India	x	x	x	x	x	x	x	x	x	x	x	x	x	x	x	x	x	x
Indonesia	x	x	x	x	x	x	x	x	x	x	x	x	x	x	x	x	x	x
Iran	x	x	x	x	x	x	x	x	x	x	x	x	x	x	x	x	x	x
Iraq	x	x	x	x	x	x	x	x	x	x	x	x	x	x	x	x	x	x
Ireland	x	x	x	x	x	x	x	x	x	x	x	x	x	x	x	x	x	x
Israel	x	x	x	x	x	x	x	x	x	x	x	x	x	x	x	x	x	x
Italy	x	x	x	x	x	x	x	x	x	x	x	x	x	x	x	x	x	x
Jamaica	x	x	x		x	x	x	x	x	x	x	x	x	x	x	x	x	x
Japan	x	x	x	x	x	x	x	x	x	x	x	x	x	x	x	x	x	x
Jordan	x	x	x	x	x	x	x	x	x	x	x	x	x	x	x	x	x	x
Kazakhstan	x	x	x	x	x	x	x		x	x	x	x	x	x	x	x	x	x
Kenya	x	x	x	x	x	x	x	x	x	x	x	x	x	x	x	x	x	x
Kiribati	x		x	x	x	x	x		x	x		x		x	x	x	x	x
Korea, Democratic People's Republic	x						x		x	x		x	x	x	x	x	x	x
Korea, Republic	x	x	x	x	x	x	x	x	x	x	x	x	x	x	x	x	x	x
Kuwait	x	x	x	x	x	x	x	x	x	x	x	x	x	x	x	x	x	x
Kyrgyzstan	x	x	x	x	x	x	x			x	x	x	x	x	x	x	x	x
Laos	x		x	x	x	x	x	x		x	x	x	x	x	x	x	x	x
Latvia	x	x	x	x	x	x	x		x	x	x	x	x	x	x	x	x	x
Lebanon	x	x	x	x	x	x	x	x	x	x	x	x	x	x	x	x	x	x
Lesotho	x		x	x	x	x	x	x	x	x	x	x	x	x	x	x	x	x
Liberia	x	x	x	x	x	x	x	x	x	x	x	x	x	x	x	x	x	x
Libya	x	x	x	x	x	x	x	x	x	x	x	x	x	x	x	x	x	x
Liechtenstein	x	x										x			x	x		x
Lithuania	x	x	x	x	x	x	x		x	x	x	x	x	x	x	x	x	x
Luxembourg	x	x	x	x	x	x	x	x	x	x	x	x	x	x	x	x	x	x
Macedonia, former Yugoslav republic	x		x	x	x	x	x	x	x	x	x	x	x	x	x	x	x	x
Madagascar	x	x	x	x	x	x	x	x	x	x	x	x	x	x	x	x	x	x
Malawi	x		x	x	x	x	x	x	x	x	x	x	x	x	x	x	x	x
Malaysia	x	x	x	x	x	x	x	x	x	x	x	x	x	x	x	x	x	x
Maldives	x		x	x	x	x	x		x	x	x	x	x	x	x	x	x	x
Mali	x		x	x	x	x	x	x		x	x	x	x	x	x	x	x	x
Malta	x	x	x			x	x		x	x	x	x	x	x	x	x	x	x
Marshall Islands	x		x	x	x	x	x		x	x		x	x		x	x	x	
Mauritania	x		x	x	x	x	x	x	x	x	x	x	x	x	x	x	x	x
Mauritius	x	x	x	x	x	x	x	x	x	x	x	x	x	x	x	x	x	x
Mexico	x	x	x	x	x	x	x	x	x	x	x	x	x	x	x	x	x	x
Micronesia, Federated States of	x		x	x	x	x				x		x			x	x	x	
Moldova	x	x	x	x	x	x	x		x	x	x	x	x	x	x	x	x	x
Monaco	x	x					x			x		x	x		x	x	x	x
Mongolia	x	x	x	x	x	x	x	x	x	x	x	x	x	x	x	x	x	x
Morocco	x	x	x	x	x	x	x	x	x	x	x	x	x	x	x	x	x	x
Mozambique	x		x	x	x	x	x	x	x	x	x	x	x	x	x	x	x	x
Myanmar	x	x	x	x	x	x	x		x	x	x	x	x	x	x	x	x	x
Namibia	x		x	x	x	x	x	x	x	x	x	x	x	x	x	x	x	x
Nauru	x						x			x		x				x		
Nepal	x		x	x	x	x	x	x		x	x	x	x	x	x	x	x	x
Netherlands	x	x	x	x	x	x	x	x	x	x	x	x	x	x	x	x	x	x
New Zealand	x	x	x	x	x	x	x	x	x	x	x	x	x	x	x	x	x	x
Nicaragua	x	x	x	x	x	x	x	x	x	x	x	x	x	x	x	x	x	x
Niger	x	x	x	x	x	x	x	x	x	x	x	x	x	x	x	x	x	x
Nigeria	x	x	x	x	x	x	x	x	x	x	x	x	x	x	x	x	x	x
Norway	x	x	x	x	x	x	x	x	x	x	x	x	x	x	x	x	x	x
Oman	x		x	x	x	x	x	x	x	x	x	x	x	x	x	x	x	x
Pakistan	x	x	x	x	x	x	x	x	x	x	x	x	x	x	x	x	x	x
Palau	x		x	x	x	x			x	x			x			x		
Panama	x	x	x		x	x	x	x	x	x	x	x	x	x	x	x	x	x
Papua New Guinea	x		x	x	x	x	x	x	x	x	x	x	x	x	x	x	x	x
Paraguay	x	x	x	x	x	x	x	x	x	x	x	x	x	x	x	x	x	x
Peru	x	x	x	x	x	x	x	x	x	x	x	x	x	x	x	x	x	x
Philippines	x	x	x	x	x	x	x	x	x	x	x	x	x	x	x	x	x	x
Poland	x	x	x	x	x	x	x	x	x	x	x	x	x	x	x	x	x	x
Portugal	x	x	x	x	x	x	x		x	x	x	x	x	x	x	x	x	x
Qatar	x	x	x			x	x		x	x	x	x	x	x	x	x	x	x
Romania	x	x	x		x	x	x		x	x	x	x	x	x	x	x	x	x
Russia	x	x	x		x	x			x	x	x	x	x	x	x	x	x	x
Rwanda	x		x	x	x	x	x	x		x	x	x	x	x	x	x	x	x
Saint Christopher and Nevis	x		x	x	x	x	x	x			x		x	x	x	x		x

continued

	UN	IAEA	IBRD	IDA	IFC	IMF	FAO[1]	IFAD[2]	IMO[3]	ICAO[4]	ILO	ITU[5]	UNESCO[6]	UNIDO	UPU[7]	WHO[8]	WMO[9]	WIPO
Saint Lucia	x		x	x	x	x	x	x	x	x	x	x	x	x	x	x	x	x
Saint Vincent and the Grenadines	x		x	x		x	x	x	x	x	x	x	x	x	x	x		x
Samoa	x		x	x	x	x	x	x	x	x		x	x	x	x	x	x	x
San Marino	x		x			x	x		x	x	x	x	x	x	x	x		x
São Tomé and Príncipe	x		x	x		x	x	x	x	x	x	x	x	x	x	x	x	x
Saudi Arabia	x	x	x	x	x	x	x	x	x	x	x	x	x	x	x	x	x	x
Senegal	x	x	x	x	x	x	x	x	x	x	x	x	x	x	x	x	x	x
Serbia and Montenegro	x	x	x	x	x	x	x	x	x	x	x	x	x	x	x	x	x	x
Seychelles	x	x	x			x	x	x	x	x	x	x	x	x	x	x	x	x
Sierra Leone	x	x	x	x	x	x	x	x	x	x	x	x	x	x	x	x	x	x
Singapore	x	x	x	x	x	x			x	x	x	x	x	x	x	x	x	x
Slovakia	x	x	x	x	x	x	x		x	x	x	x	x	x	x	x	x	x
Slovenia	x	x	x	x	x	x	x		x	x	x	x	x	x	x	x	x	x
Solomon Islands	x		x	x	x	x	x	x	x	x	x	x	x	x	x	x	x	x
Somalia	x		x	x	x	x	x	x	x	x	x	x	x	x	x	x	x	x
South Africa	x	x	x	x	x	x	x	x	x	x	x	x	x	x	x	x	x	x
Spain	x	x	x	x	x	x	x	x	x	x	x	x	x	x	x	x	x	x
Sri Lanka	x	x	x	x	x	x	x	x	x	x	x	x	x	x	x	x	x	x
Sudan	x	x	x	x	x	x	x	x	x	x	x	x	x	x	x	x	x	x
Suriname	x		x			x	x	x	x	x	x	x	x	x	x	x	x	x
Swaziland	x		x	x	x	x	x	x	x	x	x	x	x	x	x	x	x	x
Sweden	x	x	x	x	x	x	x	x	x	x	x	x	x	x	x	x	x	x
Switzerland	x	x	x	x	x	x	x	x	x	x	x	x	x	x	x	x	x	x
Syria	x	x	x	x	x	x	x	x	x	x	x	x	x	x	x	x	x	x
Tajikistan	x	x	x	x	x	x	x	x	x	x	x	x	x	x	x	x	x	x
Tanzania	x	x	x	x	x	x	x	x	x	x	x	x	x	x	x	x	x	x
Thailand	x	x	x	x	x	x	x	x	x	x	x	x	x	x	x	x	x	x
Timor-Leste	x		x	x		x												
Togo	x		x	x	x	x	x	x	x	x	x	x	x	x	x	x	x	x
Tonga	x		x	x	x	x	x		x	x		x	x	x	x	x	x	x
Trinidad and Tobago	x		x	x	x	x	x	x	x	x	x	x	x	x	x	x	x	x
Tunisia	x	x	x	x	x	x	x	x	x	x	x	x	x	x	x	x	x	x
Turkey	x	x	x	x	x	x	x	x	x	x	x	x	x	x	x	x	x	x
Turkmenistan	x	x	x		x	x			x	x	x	x	x	x	x	x	x	x
Tuvalu	x														x	x	x	
Uganda	x	x	x	x	x	x	x	x		x	x	x	x	x	x	x	x	x
Ukraine	x	x	x	x	x	x	x		x	x	x	x	x	x	x	x	x	x
United Arab Emirates	x	x	x	x	x	x	x	x	x	x	x	x	x	x	x	x	x	x
United Kingdom	x	x	x	x	x	x	x	x	x	x	x	x	x	x	x	x	x	x
USA	x	x	x	x	x	x	x	x	x	x	x	x	x	x	x	x	x	x
Uruguay	x	x	x		x	x	x	x	x	x	x	x	x	x	x	x	x	x
Uzbekistan	x	x	x	x	x	x			x	x	x	x	x	x	x	x	x	x
Vanuatu	x		x	x	x	x			x	x		x	x	x	x	x	x	x
Vatican City		x										x			x			x
Venezuela	x	x	x		x	x	x	x	x	x	x	x	x	x	x	x	x	x
Viet Nam	x	x	x	x	x	x	x	x	x	x	x	x	x	x	x	x	x	x
Yemen	x	x	x	x	x	x	x	x	x	x	x	x	x	x	x	x	x	x
Zambia	x	x	x	x	x	x	x	x	x	x	x	x	x	x	x	x	x	x
Zimbabwe	x	x	x	x	x	x	x	x	x	x	x	x	x	x	x	x	x	x

[1] The Cook Islands, Niue and the European Union are members of FAO.
[2] The Cook Islands is a member of IFAD.
[3] Hong Kong, Macau and are associate members of IMO.
[4] The Cook Islands is a member of ICAO.
[5] Members also include British Overseas Territories, French Overseas Territories and United States Territories.
[6] The Cook Islands and Niue are members of UNESCO; Aruba, the British Virgin Islands, the Cayman Islands, Macau, the Netherlands Antilles and Tokelau are associate members.
[7] Members also include British Overseas Territories and the Netherlands Antilles and Aruba.
[8] The Cook Islands and Niue are members of WHO; Puerto Rico and Tokelau are associate members.
[9] Members also include British Caribbean Territories, the Cook Islands, French Polynesia, Hong Kong, Macau, the Netherlands Antilles and Aruba, New Caledonia and Niue.

AFRICAN DEVELOPMENT BANK—ADB

Address: angle des trois rues, rue du Ghana, rue Pierre de Coubertin et rue Hedi Nouira, BP 323, 1002 Tunis Belvedere, Tunisia (temporary address).

Telephone: (71) 333-511; **fax:** (71) 251-933; **e-mail:** afdb@afdb.org; **internet:** www.afdb.org.

Established in 1964, the Bank began operations in July 1966, with the aim of financing economic and social development in African countries. The Bank's headquarters are normally based in Abidjan, Côte d'Ivoire. In February 2003, however, in view of ongoing insecurity in Côte d'Ivoire, the Bank's operations were relocated on a temporary basis to Tunis, Tunisia (see above).

AFRICAN MEMBERS

Algeria	Equatorial Guinea	Namibia
Angola	Eritrea	Niger
Benin	Ethiopia	Nigeria
Botswana	Gabon	Rwanda
Burkina Faso	The Gambia	São Tomé and
Burundi	Ghana	Príncipe
Cameroon	Guinea	Senegal
Cape Verde	Guinea-Bissau	Seychelles
Central African	Kenya	Sierra Leone
Republic	Lesotho	Somalia
Chad	Liberia	South Africa
Comoros	Libya	Sudan
Congo,	Madagascar	Swaziland
Democratic	Malawi	Tanzania
Republic	Mali	Togo
Congo, Republic	Mauritania	Tunisia
Côte d'Ivoire	Mauritius	Uganda
Djibouti	Morocco	Zambia
Egypt	Mozambique	Zimbabwe

There are also 24 non-African members.

Organization

(April 2003)

BOARD OF GOVERNORS

The highest policy-making body of the Bank. Each member country nominates one Governor, usually its Minister of Finance and Economic Affairs, and an alternate Governor or the Governor of its Central Bank. The Board meets once a year. It elects the Board of Directors and the President.

BOARD OF DIRECTORS

The Board consists of 18 members (of whom six are non-African), elected by the Board of Governors for a term of three years, renewable once; it is responsible for the general operations of the Bank. The Board meets on a weekly basis.

OFFICERS

The President is responsible for the organization and the day-to-day operations of the Bank under guidance of the Board of Directors. The President is elected for a five-year term and serves as the Chairman of the Board of Directors. In 2000 the Bank initiated a process of organizational restructuring as part of a new Bank Vision, approved by the Board of Governors in the previous year. The objectives of the reorganization were to give greater priority to client needs, strategically oriented planning, and human resources management. A new structure was introduced on 1 January 2002. Accordingly, the number of Vice-Presidents was increased from three to five, responsible for Planning, Policy and Research; Corporate Management; Operations, Central and West Regions; Operations, North, East and South Regions; and Finance.

Executive President and Chairman of Board of Directors: OMAR KABBAJ (Morocco).

Secretary-General: PHILIBERT AFRIKA (Rwanda).

FINANCIAL STRUCTURE

The ADB Group of development financing institutions comprises the African Development Fund (ADF) and the Nigeria Trust Fund (NTF), which provide concessional loans, and the African Development Bank itself. The group uses a unit of account (UA), which, at April 2001, was valued at US \$1.2063.

The capital stock of the Bank was at first exclusively open for subscription by African countries, with each member's subscription consisting of an equal number of paid-up and callable shares. In 1978, however, the Governors agreed to open the capital stock of the Bank to subscription by non-regional states on the basis of nine principles aimed at maintaining the African character of the institution. The decision was finally ratified in May 1982, and the participation of non-regional countries became effective on 30 December. It was agreed that African members should still hold two-thirds of the share capital, that all loan operations should be restricted to African members, and that the Bank's President should always be an African national. In May 1998 the Board of Governors approved an increase in capital of 35%, and resolved that the non-African members' share of the capital be increased from 33.3% to 40%. In 2000 the ADB's authorized capital was US \$28,495m. At the end of 2000 subscribed capital was \$26,772m. (of which the paid-up portion was \$2,628m.).

Activities

At the end of 2000 total loan and grant approvals by the ADB Group since the beginning of its operations amounted to US \$39,116m. Of that amount agriculture received the largest proportion of assistance (19.3%), while transport received 16.3%, multi-sector activities 14.4%, and finance 12.8%. In 2000 the group approved 143 loans and grants amounting to \$2,585m., compared with \$1,764m. for 92 loans and grants in the previous year.

A new credit policy, adopted in May 1995, effectively disqualified 39 low-income regional members, deemed to be non-creditworthy, from receiving non-concessional ADB financing, in an attempt to reduce the accumulation of arrears. The ADB Group estimated that its capital requirements for the period 1997–2001 would amount to US \$46,500m. to allow for greater flexibility in its lending. In September 1997 the Bank established a Supplementary Financing Mechanism, to provide countries eligible for ADF funds with quick-disbursing resources to meet interest payments on outstanding Bank debt. The Bank allocated UA 222m. for the mechanism, which became operational in March 1998.

The ADB contributed funds for the establishment in 1986 of the Africa Project Development Facility, which assists the private sector in Africa by providing advisory services and finance for entrepreneurs: it is managed by the International Finance Corporation (IFC). In 1989 the ADB, in co-ordination with IFC and UNDP, created the African Management Services Company (AMSCo) which provides management support and training to private companies in Africa. The Bank is one of three multilateral donors, with the World Bank and UNDP, supporting the African Capacity Building Foundation (q.v.), which was established in 1991 to strengthen and develop institutional and human capacity in support of sustainable development activities.

The Bank also provides technical assistance to regional member countries in the form of experts' services, pre-investment feasibility studies, and staff training; much of this assistance is financed through bilateral aid funds contributed by non-African member states. The Bank's African Development Institute provides training for officials of regional member countries in order to enhance the management of Bank-financed projects and, more broadly, to strengthen national capacities for promoting sustainable development. In 1990 the ADB established the African Business Round Table (ABR), which is composed of the chief executives of Africa's leading corporations. The ABR aims to strengthen Africa's private sector, promote intra-African trade and investment, and attract foreign investment to Africa. The ABR is chaired by the ADB's Executive President. At its fourth annual meeting, held in Arusha, Tanzania, in March 1994, the ABR resolved to establish an African Investment Bank, in co-operation with the ADB, which was to provide financial services to African companies. In November 1999 a Joint Africa Institute, which had been established by the Bank, the World Bank and the IMF, was formally inaugurated in Abidjan, Côte d'Ivoire. The Institute aimed to enhance training opportunities in economic policy and management and to strengthen capacity-building in the region.

In 1990 a Memorandum of Understanding (MOU) for the Reinforcement of Co-operation between the Organization of African Unity, now African Union, the UN's Economic Commission for Africa and the ADB was signed by the three organizations. A joint secretariat supports co-operation activities between the organizations. In 1999 a Co-operation Agreement was formally concluded between the Bank and theCommon Market for Eastern and Southern Africa (COMESA). In March 2000 the Bank signed an MOU on its strategic partnership with the World Bank. Other MOUs were signed during that year with the United Nations Industrial Development Organization, the World Food Programme, and the Arab Maghreb Union. Since 1996 the Bank has collaborated closely with international partners, in particular the World Bank, in efforts to address the problems of heavily indebted poor countries (HIPCs) (see World Bank, see p. 83). Following the introduction of an enhanced framework for the initiative, extending the number of eligible African countries from 25 to 31, the Bank has been actively involved in the preparation of Poverty Reduction Strategy Papers, that provide national frameworks for poverty reduction programmes. At 31 December 2000 the Bank had approved US $635.8m. (in 1999 net present value terms) to 10 countries under the enhanced HIPC initiative.

AFRICAN DEVELOPMENT BANK (ADB)

The Bank makes loans at a variable rate of interest, which is adjusted twice a year, plus a commitment fee of 0.75%. Loan approvals amounted to US $1,099.0m. for 38 loans in 2000. Since October 1997 new fixed and floating rate loans have also been made available.

Group Loan and Grant Approvals by Country
(millions of UA)

Country	1999	2000	Cumulative total*
Algeria	157.46	89.25	1,739.92
Angola	—	—	294.14
Benin	12.27	27.34	304.86
Botswana	—	2.78	327.71
Burkina Faso	10.00	10.96	315.85
Burundi	—	0.37	276.33
Cameroon	21.95	26.46	603.82
Cape Verde	0.13	5.74	153.96
Central African Republic	—	—	139.39
Chad	21.10	12.00	305.63
Comoros	—	—	64.74
Congo, Democratic Republic	—	—	936.20
Congo, Republic	—	—	278.18
Côte d'Ivoire	32.67	28.66	1,060.21
Djibouti	—	0.81	91.76
Egypt	53.55	—	1,488.23
Equatorial Guinea	—	—	67.19
Eritrea	—	2.30	39.90
Ethiopia	—	4.08	1,048.35
Gabon	—	—	596.81
Gambia	5.65	12.91	188.31
Ghana	16.16	40.75	628.22
Guinea	—	22.86	480.04
Guinea Bissau	—	0.38	157.64
Kenya	15.50	28.62	554.91
Lesotho	6.05	11.74	277.59
Liberia	0.37	—	153.62
Madagascar	26.10	22.89	424.90
Malawi	24.24	11.73	521.85
Mali	21.94	20.75	432.16
Mauritania	23.02	1.80	265.06
Mauritius	—	14.87	166.82
Morocco	19.60	79.87	2,789.95
Mozambique	37.25	118.56	754.77
Namibia	7.10	—	62.13
Niger	—	—	210.50
Nigeria	36.51	43.40	1,982.78
Rwanda	—	19.87	298.69
São Tomé and Príncipe	4.20	—	93.78
Senegal	24.75	30.00	463.89
Seychelles	7.09	—	89.49
Sierra Leone	9.21	0.39	168.35
Somalia	—	—	150.40
South Africa	82.59	75.76	272.55
Sudan	0.35	0.37	350.52
Swaziland	11.11	—	200.04
Tanzania	28.15	7.71	642.93
Togo	12.18	—	170.68
Tunisia	262.97	115.28	2,534.84
Uganda	32.54	82.77	640.89
Zambia	33.77	31.65	604.20
Zimbabwe	118.23	0.37	726.53
Total	1,175.76	1,006.47	27,592.59

*Since the initial operation of the three institutions (1967 for ADB, 1974 for ADF and 1976 for NTF).

Source: *Annual Report 2000*.

AFRICAN DEVELOPMENT FUND (ADF)

The Fund commenced operations in 1974. It grants interest-free loans to low-income African countries for projects with repayment over 50 years (including a 10-year grace period) and with a service charge of 0.75% per annum. Grants for project feasibility studies are made to the poorest countries.

In 1991 a sixth replenishment of the Fund's resources amounting to US $3,340m. was approved for 1991–93. Negotiations for the seventh replenishment of the Fund's resources commenced in May 1993. However, in May 1994, donor countries withheld any new funds owing to dissatisfaction with the Bank's governance. In May 1996, following the implementation of various institutional reforms to strengthen the Bank's financial management and decision-making capabilities and to reduce its administrative costs, an agreement was concluded on the seventh replenishment of the ADF. Donor countries pledged some $2,690m. for the period 1996–98. An additional allocation of $420m. was endorsed at a special donors' meeting held in Osaka, Japan, in June. The ADF aimed to offer concessional assistance to 42 African countries over the period 1996–98. The seventh replenishment provided for the establishment of an ADF Microfinance Initiative (AMINA), initially for a two-year period, to support small-scale capacity-building projects. In January 1999 negotiations on the eighth replenishment of the Fund were concluded with an agreement to provide additional resources amounting to $3,437m. The replenishment was approved by the Board of Governors in May, and came into effect in December.

In 2000 102 ADF loans and grants were approved amounting to US $1,472.2m.

NIGERIA TRUST FUND (NTF)

The Agreement establishing the Nigeria Trust Fund was signed in February 1976 by the Bank and the Government of Nigeria. The Fund is administered by the Bank and its loans are granted for up to 25 years, including grace periods of up to five years, and carry 0.75% commission charges and 4% interest charges. The loans are intended to provide financing for projects in co-operation with other lending institutions. The Fund also aims to promote the private sector and trade between African countries by providing information on African and international financial institutions able to finance African trade.

During 1999 negotiations on a revised Agreement and replenishment of the Fund's resources were undertaken. Three loans were approved during 2000 amounting to US $13.9m.

Summary of Bank Group Activities
(US $ million)

	1999	2000	Cumulative total*
ADB loans			
Number	22.00	38.00	832.00
Amount approved	1,082.56	1,098.99	24,054.71
Disbursements	700.62	535.42	16,098.25
ADF loans and grants			
Number	70.00	102.00	1,577.00
Amount approved	681.93	1,472.17	114,726.70
Disbursements	504.94	352.99	9,093.46
NTF loans			
Number	—	3.00	61.00
Amount approved	—	13.92	334.19
Disbursements	10.27	8.28	235.79
Group total			
Number	92.00	143.00	2,470.00
Amount approved	1,764.49	2,585.08	39,115.59
Disbursements	1,215.83	896.68	25,427.49

*Since the initial operations of the three institutions (1967 for ADB, 1974 for ADF and 1976 for NTF).

Source: *Annual Report 2000*.

ASSOCIATED INSTITUTIONS

The ADB actively participated in the establishment of five associated institutions:

Africa Reinsurance Corporation—Africa-Re: Reinsurance House, 46 Marina, PMB 12765, Lagos, Nigeria; tel. (1) 2663323; fax (1) 2668802; e-mail info@africa-re.com; internet www.africa-re.com; f. 1977; started operations in 1978; its purpose is to foster the development of the insurance and reinsurance industry in Africa and to promote the growth of national and regional underwriting capacities; auth. cap. US $50m., of which the ADB holds 10%; there are 12 directors, one appointed by the Bank; mems: 41 countries, the ADB, and some 90 insurance and reinsurance cos; Man. Dir BAKARY KAMARA; publ. *The African Reinsurer* (annually).

129

African Export-Import Bank—Afreximbank: POB 404 Gezira, Cairo 11568; World Trade Centre Bldg, 1191 Corniche el-Nil, Cairo 11221, Egypt; tel. (2) 5780282; fax (2) 5780277; e-mail mail@afreximbank.com; internet www.afreximbank.com; f. 1993; aims to increase the volume of African exports and to expand intra-African trade by financing exporters and importers directly and indirectly through trade finance institutions, such as commercial banks; in Nov. 2001, under the auspices of Afreximbank, a Memorandum of General Principles was signed by African bankers for the establishment of an African Bankers Forum; auth. cap. US $750m. paid-up cap. $146.2m. (Dec. 2001); Pres. CHRISTOPHER C. EDORDU; Exec. Vice-Pres. JEAN-LOUIS EKRA; publ. *Annual Report.*

Association of African Development Finance Institutions—AADFI: Immeuble AIAFD, blvd Latrille, rue J61, Cocody Deux Plateaux, Abidjan 04, Côte d'Ivoire; tel. 22-52-33-89; fax 22-52-25-84; e-mail adfi@aviso.ci; f. 1975; aims to promote co-operation among financial institutions in the region in matters relating to economic and social development, research, project design, financing and the exchange of information; mems: 92 in 43 African and non-African countries; Pres. GERSHOM MUMBA; Sec.-Gen. J. A. AMIHERE (acting); publs *Annual Report, AADFI Information Bulletin* (quarterly), *Finance and Development in Africa* (2 a year).

Shelter-Afrique (Société pour l'habitat et le logement territorial en Afrique): Longonot Rd, POB 41479, Nairobi, Kenya; tel. (20) 2722305; fax (20) 2722024; e-mail info@shelterafrique.co.ke; internet www.shelterafrique.org; f. 1982 to finance housing in ADB mem. countries; share cap. is US $300m., held by 40 African countries, the ADB, Africa-Re and the Commonwealth Development Corpn; Man. Dir P. M'BAYE.

Société Internationale Financière pour les Investissements et le Développement en Afrique—SIFIDA: 22 rue François-Perréard, BP 310, 1225 Chêne-Bourg/Geneva, Switzerland; tel. (22) 8692000; fax (22) 8692001; e-mail headoffice@sifida.com; internet www.sifida.com; f. 1970 by 120 financial and industrial institutions, including the ADB and the IFC following a restructuring in 1996, the main shareholders are BNP/Paribas and its six banking affiliates in West and Central Africa. SIFIDA is active in the fields of trade and equity participation finance in Africa and also provides financial advisory services, notably in the context of project finance, privatizations and debt conversion; auth. cap. US $75m., subscribed cap. $12.5m; Chair. PIERRE MARIANI; Man. Dir PHILIPPE SÉCHAUD; publ. *African Banking Directory* (annually).

Publications

Annual Report.
ADB Business Bulletin (10 a year).
ADB Statistical Pocketbook.
ADB Today (every 2 months).
African Development Report (annually).
African Development Review.
Annual Procurement Report.
Basic Information (annually).
Economic Research Papers.
Quarterly Operational Summary.
Summaries of operations in each member country and various background documents.

AFRICAN UNION—AU

Address: POB 3243, Addis Ababa, Ethiopia.
Telephone: (1) 51-7700; **fax:** (1) 51-2622; **e-mail:** tpst@africa-union.org; **internet:** www.africa-union.org.
In May 2001 the Constitutive Act of the African Union entered into force. In July 2002 the African Union (AU) became fully operational, replacing the Organization of African Unity (OAU), which had been founded in 1963. The AU aims to support unity, solidarity and peace among African states; to promote and defend African common positions on issues of shared interest; to encourage human rights, democratic principles and good governance; to advance the development of member states by encouraging research and by working to eradicate preventable diseases; and to promote sustainable development and political and socio-economic integration, including co-ordinating and harmonizing policy between the continent's various 'regional economic communities' (see below).

FORMATION

There were various attempts at establishing an inter-African organization from the 1950s. In November 1958 Ghana and Guinea (later joined by Mali) drafted a Charter that was to form the basis of a Union of African States. In January 1961 a conference was held at Casablanca, attended by the heads of state of Ghana, Guinea, Mali, Morocco, and representatives of Libya and of the provisional government of the Algerian Republic (GPRA). Tunisia, Nigeria, Liberia and Togo declined the invitation to attend. An African Charter was adopted and it was decided to set up an African Military Command and an African Common Market.

Between October 1960 and March 1961 three conferences were held by French-speaking African countries, at Abidjan, Brazzaville and Yaoundé, Cameroon. None of the 12 countries that attended these meetings had been present at the Casablanca Conference. These conferences led eventually to the signing in September 1961, at Tananarive, of a charter establishing the Union africaine et malgache, later the Organisation commune africaine et mauricienne (OCAM).

In May 1961 a conference was held at Monrovia, Liberia, attended by the heads of state or representatives of 19 countries: Cameroon, Central African Republic, Chad, Congo Republic (ex-French), Côte d'Ivoire, Dahomey, Ethiopia, Gabon, Liberia, Madagascar, Mauritania, Niger, Nigeria, Senegal, Sierra Leone, Somalia, Togo, Tunisia and Upper Volta. Meeting again (with the exception of Tunisia and with the addition of the ex-Belgian Congo Republic) in January 1962 at Lagos, Nigeria, they established a permanent secretariat and a standing committee of finance ministers, and accepted a draft charter for an Organization of Inter-African and Malagasy States.

It was the Conference of Addis Ababa, convened in 1963, which finally brought together African states despite the regional, political and linguistic differences that divided them. The foreign ministers of 32 African states attended the Preparatory Meeting held in mid-May: Algeria, Burundi, Cameroon, Central African Republic, Chad, Congo (Brazzaville) (now Republic of the Congo), Congo (Léopoldville) (now Democratic Republic of the Congo), Côte d'Ivoire, Dahomey (now Benin), Ethiopia, Gabon, Ghana, Guinea, Liberia, Libya, Madagascar, Mali, Mauritania, Morocco, Niger, Nigeria, Rwanda, Senegal, Sierra Leone, Somalia, Sudan, Tanganyika (now Tanzania), Togo, Tunisia, Uganda, the United Arab Republic (Egypt) and Upper Volta (now Burkina Faso).

The topics discussed by the meeting were: (i) creation of an Organization of African States; (ii) co-operation among African states in the following fields: economic and social; education, culture and science; collective defence; (iii) decolonization; (iv) apartheid and racial discrimination; (v) effects of economic grouping on the economic development of Africa; (vi) disarmament; (vii) creation of a Permanent Conciliation Commission; and (viii) Africa and the United Nations.

The Heads of State Conference that opened on 23 May 1963 drew up the Charter of the Organization of African Unity, which was then signed by the heads of 30 states on 25 May. The Charter was essentially functional and reflected a compromise between the concept of a loose association of states favoured by the Monrovia Group and the federal idea supported by the Casablanca Group, and in particular by Ghana.

In May 1994 the Abuja Treaty Establishing the African Economic Community (AEC, signed in June 1991) entered into force. The formation of the Community was expected to be a gradual process, to be completed by 2028.

An extraordinary summit meeting, convened in September 1999, in Sirte, Libya, at the request of the Libyan leader Col al-Qaddafi, determined to establish an African Union, based on the principles and objectives of the OAU and AEC, but furthering African co-operation, development and integration. Heads of state declared their commitment to accelerating the establishment of regional institutions, including a pan-African parliament, court of justice and central bank, as well as the implementation of economic and monetary union, as provided for by the Abuja Treaty Establishing the AEC. In July 2000 at the annual OAU summit meeting, held at Lomé, Togo, 27 heads of state and government signed the draft Constitutive Act of the African Union, which was to enter into force one month after ratification by two-thirds of member states' legislatures; this was achieved on 26 May 2001. The Union was inaugurated, replacing the OAU, on 9 July 2002, at a summit meeting of heads of state and government held in Durban, South Africa, following a transitional period of one year after the endorsement of the Act in July 2001. (During the transitional year, pending the transfer of all assets and liabilities to the Union, the OAU Charter remained in effect. A review of all OAU treaties was implemented, with those deemed relevant retained by the AU.) During an initial interim period, from July 2002–July 2003, the establishment of the AU's main policy organs and other institutions was to be finalized; the four key organs were launched in July 2002. Morocco is the only African country that is not a member of the AU (see below).

The AU aims to strengthen and advance the process of African political and socio-economic integration initiated by the OAU. The Union operates on the basis of both the Constitutive Act and the Abuja Treaty. It is envisaged that the process of implementing the Abuja Treaty will be accelerated. A protocol to the Treaty, establishing a Pan-African Parliament was opened for signature under the OAU in March 2001, and a protocol relating to the establishment of a Peace and Security Council was adopted at the July 2002 inaugural summit meeting of the AU.

MEMBERS*

Algeria	Eritrea	Nigeria
Angola	Ethiopia	Rwanda
Benin	Gabon	São Tomé and
Botswana	The Gambia	Príncipe
Burkina Faso	Ghana	Senegal
Burundi	Guinea	Seychelles
Cameroon	Guinea-Bissau	Sierra Leone
Cape Verde	Kenya	Somalia
Central African	Lesotho	South Africa
Republic	Liberia	Sudan
Chad	Libya	Swaziland
The Comoros	Madagascar†	Tanazania
Congo, Democratic	Malawi	Togo
Republic	Mali	Tunisia
Congo, Republic	Mauritania	Uganda
Côte d'Ivoire	Mauritius	Zambia
Djibouti	Mozambique	Zimbabwe
Egypt	Namibia	
Equatorial Guinea	Niger	

* The Sahrawi Arab Democratic Republic (SADR–Western Sahara) was admitted to the OAU in February 1982, following recognition by more than one-half of the member states, but its membership was disputed by Morocco and other states which claimed that a two-thirds majority was needed to admit a state whose existence was in question. Morocco withdrew from the OAU with effect from November 1985, and has not applied to join the AU. The SADR ratified the Constitutive Act in December 2000 and is a full member of the AU.

† Madagascar was suspended from meetings of the AU in July 2002, having been suspended from the OAU in the previous month.

Note: The Constitutive Act stipulates that member states in which Governments accede to power by unconstitutional means are liable to suspension from participating in the Union's activities and to the imposition of sanctions by the Union.

Organization

(April 2003)

ASSEMBLY

The Assembly, comprising member countries' Heads of State and Government, is the supreme organ of the Union and meets at least once a year to determine and monitor the Union's priorities and common policies and to adopt its annual work programme. Resolutions are passed by a two-thirds majority, procedural matters by a simple majority. Extraordinary sessions may be convened at the request of a member state and on approval by a two-thirds majority. A chairperson is elected at each meeting from among the members, to hold office for one year. The Assembly ensures compliance by member states with decisions of the Union, adopts the biennial budget, will appoint judges of the planned Court of Justice, and hears and settles disputes between member states. The first regular Assembly meeting was held in Durban, South Africa, in July 2002. (July 2003: Maputo, Mozambique. Subsequently the Assembly was to meet in Addis Ababa, Ethiopia, in alternate years.) The first extraordinary summit meeting was convened in Addis Ababa in February 2003.

Chairperson: (2002/03) THABO MBEKI (Pres. of South Africa).

EXECUTIVE COUNCIL

Consists of ministers of foreign affairs and others and meets at least twice a year (in February and July), with provision for extraordinary sessions. The Council's Chairperson is the Minister of Foreign Affairs (or another competent authority) of the country that has provided the Chairperson of the Assembly. Prepares meetings of, and is responsible to, the Assembly. Determines the issues to be submitted to the Assembly for decision, co-ordinates and harmonizes the policies, activities and initiatives of the Union in areas of common interest to member states, monitors the implementation of policies and decisions of the Assembly.

PERMANENT REPRESENTATIVES COMMITTEE

The Committee, which comprises Ambassadors accredited to the AU and meets at least once a month, is responsible to, advises and prepares meetings of the Executive Council, including its agenda and draft decisions.

COMMISSION

(An Interim Commission was to be operational from July 2002–July 2003.) The Commission is permanent secretariat of the organization. It comprises a Chairperson (elected for a four-year term of office by the Assembly), Deputy Chairperson and eight Commissioners (responsible for: peace and security; political affairs; infrastructure and energy; social affairs; human resources, science and technology; trade and industry; rural economy and agriculture; and economic affairs) who are elected on the basis of equal geographical distribution. Members of the Commission serve a term of four years and may stand for re-election for one further term of office. Further support staff assist the smooth functioning of the Commission. The Commission represents the Union under the guidance of and as mandated by the Assembly and the Executive Council, and reports to the Executive Council. It deals with administrative issues, implements the decisions of of the Union, and acts as the custodian of the Constitutive Act and Protocols, and other agreements. Its work covers the following domains: control of pandemics; disaster management; international crime and terrorism; environmental management; negotiations relating to external trade; negotiations relating to external debt; population, migration, refugees and displaced persons; food security; socio-economic integration; and all other areas where a common position has been established by Union member states. It has responsibility for the co-ordination of AU activities and meetings.

Interim Chairperson: AMARA ESSY (Côte d'Ivoire).

SPECIALIZED TECHNICAL COMMITTEES

There are specialized committees for monetary and financial affairs; rural economy and agricultural matters; trade, customs and immigration; industry, science and technology, energy, natural resources and environment; transport, communications and tourism; health, labour and social affairs; and education, culture and human resources. These have responsibility for implementing the Union's programmes and projects.

Note: In May 2002 a 15-member High Level Advisory Panel of Eminent Persons was formed to make recommendations on key aspects of the finalization of the OAU–AU transition process and on possible action by the AU during the 2002–03 interim period. The Panel was to be disbanded in late 2003. At early 2003 several organs of the AU remained to be established, including a Pan-African Parliament comprising elected representatives from the Union's five principal regions (northern, eastern, southern, western and central); a Court of Justice, which was to pass judgment on alleged human rights abuses; an Economic, Social and Cultural Council, which was to have an advisory function and was to comprise representatives of civic and professional bodies; and a 15-country Peace and Security Council. In addition three financial instititions were to be inaugurated to manage the financing of programmes and projects: an African Central Bank, an African Monetary Fund, and an African Investment Bank.

Finance

The AU inherited substantial debts owed by member states to the OAU (totalling some US $52m. at May 2002). The annual budget is $32m.

Activities

The AU has the following areas of interest: peace and security; political affairs; infrastructure and energy; social affairs; human resources, science and technology; trade and industry; rural economy and agriculture; and economic affairs. In July 2001 the

OAU adopted a New African Initiative, which was subsequently renamed the New Partnership for Africa's Development (see below). NEPAD, which was officially launched in October, represents a long-term strategy for socio-economic recovery in Africa and aims to promote the strengthening of democracy and economic management in the region. The heads of state of Algeria, Egypt, Nigeria, Senegal and South Africa have played leading roles in its preparation and management. In June 2002 NEPAD heads of state and government adopted a Declaration on Democracy, Political, Economic and Corporate Governance and announced the development of an African Peer Review Mechanism (whose secretariat was to be hosted by the UN Economic Commission for Africa). Meeting during that month the Group of Seven industrialized nations and Russia (the G-8) welcomed the formation of NEPAD and adopted an Africa Action Plan in support of the initiative. NEPAD is ultimately answerable to the AU Assembly. The inaugural summit of the Assembly, held in Durban, South Africa, in July 2002, issued a Declaration on the Implementation of NEPAD, which urged all member states to adopt the Declaration on Democracy, Political, Economic and Corporate Governance and to participate in the peer-review process.

PEACE AND SECURITY

Pending the ratification and entry into force of the Protocol on the Peace and Security Council, adopted by the first AU summit of heads of state and government in July 2002, the 1993 Cairo Declaration on the OAU Mechanism for Conflict Prevention, Management and Resolution was to remain in effect. The Protocol provides for the inauguration of an AU collective security and early warning mechanism, comprising a 15-country Peace and Security Council, operational at the levels of heads of state and government, ministers of foreign affairs, and permanent representatives, to be supported by a five-member advisory Panel of the Wise, a Continental Early Warning System, an African Standby Force and a Peace Fund (superseding the OAU Peace Fund, which was established in June 1993 and had received contributions of US $42m. by March 2002). The activities of the Peace and Security Council were to include the promotion of peace, security and stability; early warning and preventive diplomacy; peace-making mediation; peace support operations and intervention; peace-building activities and post-conflict reconstruction; and humanitarian action and disaster management. The Council was to implement the common defence policy of the Union, and to ensure the implementation of the 1999 OAU Convention on the Prevention and Combating of Terrorism (which provided for the exchange of information to help counter terrorism and for signatory states to refrain from granting asylum to terrorists). Member states were to set aside standby troop contingents for the planned African Standby Force, which was mandated to undertake observation, monitoring and other peace-support missions; to deploy in member states as required to prevent the resurgence or escalation of violence; to intervene in member states as required to restore stability; to conduct post-conflict disarmament and demobilization and other peace-building activities; and to provide emergency humanitarian assistance. The Council was to harmonize and co-ordinate the activities of other regional security mechanisms.

The extraordinary OAU summit meeting convened in Sirte, Libya in September 1999 determined to hold a regular ministerial Conference on Security, Stability, Development and Cooperation in Africa (CSSDCA): the first CSSDCA took place in Abuja, Nigeria, in May 2000. The CSSDCA process provides a forum for the development of policies aimed at advancing the common values of the AU and AEC in the areas of peace, security and co-operation. In December 2000 OAU heads of state and government adopted the Bamako Declaration, concerning arresting the circulation of small arms on the continent.

In recent years the OAU was involved in peace-making and peace-building activities in several African countries and regions. Military observer missions were deployed in Rwanda (1991–93), Burundi (1993–96), the Comoros (1998–2002), the Democratic Republic of the Congo (from 1999) and Eritrea and Ethiopia (from 2000). In February 2002 the OAU mediated talks between President Didier Ratsiraka of Madagascar and the official opposition leader Marc Ravalomanana, who established a rival Madagascan government during that month, having also claimed victory at the presidential election held in that country in December 2001. In March 2002 the OAU held talks with each of the disputing sides in the Madagascan political crisis, facilitating the conclusion in mid-April of the so-called Dakar Agreement, providing for the formation of an interim government of national unity, pending the staging of a new presidential election. However, in the following month Ravalomanana was declared President by a Madagascan constitutional court. In view of significant opposition to this decision, the OAU determined not to recognize the Ravalomanana administration and, in June, suspended Madagascar from its meetings. In July the newly inaugurated AU upheld this decision, suspending the country from AU meetings pending the staging of free and fair elections leading to the establishment of a legitimate and democratic government. In February 2003, in view of new parliamentary elections that were held in December 2002 (resulting in a majority of seats for supporters of Ravalomanana), the Mechanism for Conflict Prevention, Management and Resolution recommended that Madagascar's suspension should be revoked by the next regular summit meeting of the AU Assembly, scheduled to convene in July. An extraordinary summit meeting of the Assembly, held in February 2003, urged support for a peace accord concluded in January by parties to the conflict that had erupted in Côte d'Ivoire in September 2002. In April 2003 the AU authorized the establishment of the 3,500-member African Mission in Burundi to oversee the implementation of cease-fire accords in that country, support the disarmament and demobilization of former combatants, and ensure favourable conditions for the deployment of a future UN peace-keeping presence.

INFRASTRUCTURE, ENERGY AND THE ENVIRONMENT

Meeting in Lomé, Togo, in July 2001, OAU heads of state and government authorized the establishment of an African Energy Commission—AFREC, which was to increase co-operation in energy matters between Africa and other regions. The convention establishing AFREC had six signatories at January 2002.

In 1964 the OAU adopted a Declaration on the Denuclearization of Africa, and in April 1996 it adopted the African Nuclear Weapons Free Zone Treaty (also known as the 'Pelindaba Treaty'), which identifies Africa as a nuclear weapon-free zone and promotes co-operation in the peaceful uses of nuclear energy.

In 1968 OAU member states adopted the African Convention on the Conservation of Nature and Natural Resources. The Bamako Convention on the Ban of the Import into Africa and the Control of Transboundary Movement and Management of Hazardous Wastes within Africa was adopted by OAU member states in 1991 and entered into force in April 1998.

POLITICAL AND SOCIAL AFFAIRS

The African Charter on Human and People's Rights, which was adopted by the OAU in 1981 and entered into force in October 1986, provided for the establishment of an 11-member African Commission on Human and People's Rights, based in Banjul, The Gambia. The African Charter on the Rights and Welfare of the Child was opened for signature in July 1990, but has not yet entered into force. In March 2001 the OAU adopted a Protocol to the Abuja Treaty Establishing the AEC relating to the Pan-African Parliament. Once established the Parliament was to have an advisory and consultative function.

The July 2002 inaugural summit meeting of AU heads of state and government adopted a Declaration Governing Democratic Elections in Africa, providing guide-lines for the conduct of national elections in member states and outlining the AU's electoral observation and monitoring role. In March an OAU observer team found the Zimbabwean presidential election, held in controversial circumstances during that month, to have been conducted freely and fairly. In recent years several large population displacements have occurred in Africa, mainly as a result of violent conflict. In 1969 OAU member states adopted the Convention Governing the Specific Aspects of Refugee Problems in Africa, which entered into force in June 1974. The Convention promotes close co-operation with UNHCR. The AU maintains a Special Refugee Contingency Fund to provide relief assistance and to support repatriation activities, education projects, etc. for displaced people in Africa. The AU aims to address pressing health issues affecting member states, including the eradication of endemic parasitic and infectious diseases and improving access to medicines. An African Summit on HIV/AIDS, Tuberculosis and other related Infectious Diseases was convened, under OAU auspices, in March 2001. An AU Scientific, Technical and Research Commission is based in Lagos, Nigeria, and a Centre for Linguistic and Historical Studies by Oral Tradition is based in Niamey, Niger.

TRADE, INDUSTRY AND ECONOMIC CO-OPERATION

In October 1999 a conference on Industrial Partnerships and Investment in Africa was held in Dakar, Senegal, jointly organized by the OAU with UNIDO, the ECA, the African Development Bank and the Alliance for Africa's Industrialization. In June 1997 the first meeting between ministers of the OAU and the European Union (EU) was convened in New York, USA. In April 2000 the first EU–Africa summit of heads of state and government was held in Cairo, Egypt, under the auspices of the EU and OAU. The summit adopted the Cairo Plan of Action, which addressed areas including economic integration, trade and investment, private-sector development in Africa, human rights and good governance, peace and security, and development issues such as education, health and food security. A second EU–Africa summit meeting, scheduled to be held in April 2003, in Lisbon, Portugal, was postponed, owing to disagreements concerning participation by President Mugabe of Zimbabwe, against whom the EU had imposed sanctions. More than 200 business representatives participated in an AU Business Summit, convened in July 2002, in Durban, South Africa, alongside the inaugural AU summit of heads of state and government.

The AU aims to reduce obstacles to intra-African trade and to reverse the continuing disproportionate level of trade conducted by many African countries with their former colonial powers.

In June 1991 the OAU Assembly of Heads of State signed the Abuja Treaty Establishing the African Economic Community (AEC). The Treaty was to enter into force after ratification by two-thirds of member states. The Community was to be established by 2028, following a gradual six-phase process involving the co-ordination, harmonization and progressive integration of the activities of all existing and future sub-regional economic unions. (There are 14 so-called 'regional economic communities'—RECs in Africa, including the following major RECs that are regarded as the five pillars, or building blocks, of the AEC: the Common Market for Eastern and Southern Africa—COMESA, the Communauté économique des états de l'Afrique centrale—CEEAC, the Economic Community of West African States—ECOWAS, the Southern African Development Community—SADC, and the Union of the Arab Maghreb. The subsidiary RECs are: the Communauté économique et monétaire de l'Afrique centrale—CEMAC, the Community of Sahel-Saharan States—CEN-SAD, the East African Community—EAC, the Economic Community of the Great Lakes Countries, the Intergovernmental Authority on Development—IGAD, the Indian Ocean Commission—IOC, the Mano River Union, the Southern African Customs Union, and the Union économique et monétaire ouest-africaine—UEMOA.) The main policy-making organ of the AEC was to be an Economic and Social Council. The Abuja Treaty entered into force on 12 May 1994, having been ratified by the requisite number of OAU member states. The inaugural meeting of the AEC took place in June 1997.

Specialized Agencies

African Accounting Council: POB 11223, Kinshasa, Democratic Republic of the Congo; tel. (12) 33567; f. 1979; provides assistance to institutions in member countries on standardization of accounting; promotes education, further training and research in accountancy and related areas of study; publ. *Information and Liaison Bulletin* (every two months).

African Civil Aviation Commission—AFCAC: 15 blvd de la République, BP 2356, Dakar, Senegal; tel. 839-93-73; fax 823-26-61; e-mail secretariat@afcac-cafac.org; internet www.afcac-cafac.sn; f. 1969 to encourage co-operation in all civil aviation activities; promotes co-ordination and better utilization and development of African air transport systems and the standardization of aircraft, flight equipment and training programmes for pilots and mechanics; organizes working groups and seminars, and compiles statistics; Pres. MAMDOUH HESHMAT (Egypt); Sec. CHARLES M. DIOP.

Pan-African Institution of Education for Development—PIED: 29 ave de la Justice, BP 1764, Kinshasa I, Democratic Republic of the Congo; tel. (12) 34527; e-mail baseeduc@hotmail.com; f. 1973, became specialized agency in 1986, present name adopted 2001; undertakes educational research and training, focuses on co-operation and problem-solving, acts as an observatory for education; Publs *Bulletin d'Information* (quarterly), *Revue africaine des sciences de l'éducation* (2 a year), *Répertoire africain des institutions de recherche* (annually).

Pan-African News Agency—PANAPRESS: BP 4650, Dakar, Senegal; tel. 824-14-10; fax 824-13-90; internet www.panapress.com; regional headquarters in Khartoum, Sudan; Lusaka, Zambia; Kinshasa, Democratic Republic of the Congo; Lagos, Nigeria; Tripoli, Libya; began operations in May 1983, restructured in late 1990s; receives information from national news agencies and circulates news in English and French; Dir-Gen. BABACAR FALL; publ. *PANA Review*.

Pan-African Postal Union—PAPU: POB 6026, Arusha, Tanzania; tel. (27) 2508606; fax (27) 2508603; e-mail papu@habari.co.tz; f. 1980 to extend members' co-operation in the improvement of postal services; Sec.-Gen. JILANI BEN HADDADA; publ. *PAPU Bulletin*.

Pan-African Railways Union: BP 687, Kinshasa, Democratic Republic of the Congo; tel. (12) 23861; f. 1972 to standardize, expand, co-ordinate and improve members' railway services; the ultimate aim is to link all systems; main organs: Gen. Assembly, Exec. Bd, Gen. Secr., five tech. cttees. mems in 30 African countries.

Pan-African Telecommunications Union: POB 7248, Kinshasa, Democratic Republic of the Congo; f. 1977; co-ordinates devt of telecommunications networks and services in Africa.

Supreme Council for Sports in Africa: BP 1363, Yaoundé, Cameroon; tel. and fax 23-95-80; Sec.-Gen. Dr AWOTURE ELEYAE (Nigeria); publs *SCSA News* (6 a year), *African Sports Movement Directory* (annually).

ASSOCIATED PARTNERSHIP

New Partnership for Africa's Development (NEPAD): POB 1234, Midrand, Halfway House, 1685 South Africa (secretariat); tel. (11) 313-3716; fax (11) 313-3583; e-mail africam@nepad.org; internet www.nepad.org; f. 2001 as a long-term strategy to promote socio-economic development in Africa; adopted Declaration on Democracy, Political, Economic and Corporate Governance and the African Peer Review Mechanism in June 2002; heads of state implementation cttee comprises representatives of 20 countries (four from each of the AU's five regions: northern, eastern, southern, western and central); steering cttee, comprising Algeria, Egypt, Nigeria, Senegal and South Africa, meets once a month; Implementation Cttee Chair. Gen. (retd) OLUSEGUN OBASANJO (Pres. of Nigeria); Steering Cttee Chair. Prof. WISEMAN NKUHLU (South Africa).

ANDEAN COMMUNITY OF NATIONS

(COMUNIDAD ANDINA DE NACIONES—CAN)

Address: Avda Paseo de la República 3895, San Isidro, Lima 27; Apdo 18-1177, Lima 18, Peru.

Telephone: (1) 4111400; **fax:** (1) 2213329; **e-mail:** contacto@comunidadandina.org; **internet:** www.comunidadandina.org.

The organization was established in 1969 as the Acuerdo de Cartagena (the Cartagena Agreement), also referred to as the Grupo Andino (Andean Group) or the Pacto Andino (Andean Pact). In March 1996 member countries signed a Reform Protocol of the Cartagena Agreement, in accordance with which the Andean Group was superseded in August 1997 by the Andean Community of Nations (CAN, generally referred to as the Andean Community). The Andean Community was to promote greater economic, commercial and political integration under a new Andean Integration System (Sistema Andino de Integración), comprising the organization's bodies and institutions. The Community covers an area of 4,710,000 sq km, with some 113m. inhabitants.

MEMBERS

| Bolivia | Colombia | Ecuador | Peru | Venezuela |

Note: Chile withdrew from the Andean Group in 1976. Panama has observer status with the Community.

Organization

(April 2003)

ANDEAN PRESIDENTIAL COUNCIL

The presidential summits, which had been held annually since 1989, were formalized under the 1996 Reform Protocol of the Cartagena Agreement as the Andean Presidential Council. The Council is the highest-level body of the Andean Integration System, and provides the political leadership of the Community.

COMMISSION

The Commission consists of a plenipotentiary representative from each member country, with each country holding the presidency in turn. The Commission is the main policy-making organ of the Andean Community, and is responsible for co-ordinating Andean trade policy.

COUNCIL OF FOREIGN MINISTERS

The Council of Foreign Ministers meets annually or whenever it is considered necessary, to formulate common external policy and to co-ordinate the process of integration.

GENERAL SECRETARIAT

The General Secretariat (formerly the Junta) is the body charged with implementation of all guide-lines and decisions issued by the bodies listed above. It submits proposals to the Commission for facilitating the fulfilment of the Community's objectives. Members are appointed for a three-year term. They supervise technical officials assigned to the following Departments: External Relations, Agricultural Development, Press Office, Economic Policy, Physical Integration, Programme of Assistance to Bolivia, Industrial Development, Programme Planning, Legal Affairs, Technology. Under the reforms agreed in March 1996 the Secretary-General is elected by the Council of Foreign Ministers for a five-year term, and has enhanced powers to adjudicate in disputes arising between member states. In August 1997 the General Secretariat assumed the functions of the Board of the Cartagena Agreement.

Secretary-General: GUILLERMO FERNÁNDEZ DE SOTO (Colombia).

PARLIAMENT

Parlamento Andino: Carrera 7A, No. 13–58, Of. 401, Santafé de Bogotá, Colombia; tel. (1) 284-4191; fax (1) 284-3270; e-mail pandino@cable.net.co; internet www.parlamentoandino.org; f. 1979; comprises five members from each country, and meets in each capital city in turn; makes recommendations on regional policy; in April 1997 a new protocol was adopted which provided for the election of members by direct and universal voting; in November 1998 Venezuela put the new voting mechanism into practice; the remaining Community countries were expected to complete the process by 2007; Pres. JHANNETT MADRIZ SOTILLO; Sec.-Gen. Dr RUBÉN VÉLEZ NÚÑEZ.

COURT OF JUSTICE

Tribunal de Justicia de la Comunidad Andina: Calle Roca 450 y Seis de Diciembre, Quito, Ecuador; tel. (2) 529998; fax (2) 565007; e-mail tjca@impsat.net.ec; internet www.altesa.net/tribunal; f. 1979, began operating in 1984; a protocol approved in May 1996 (which came into force in August 1999) modified the Court's functions; its main responsibilities are to resolve disputes among member countries and interpret community legislation; comprises five judges, one from each member country, appointed for a renewable period of six years; the Presidency is assumed annually by each judge in turn.

Activities

In May 1979, at Cartagena, Colombia, the Presidents of the five member countries signed the 'Mandate of Cartagena', which envisaged greater economic and political co-operation, including the establishment of more sub-regional development programmes (especially in industry). In May 1989 the Group undertook to revitalize the process of Andean integration, by withdrawing measures that obstructed the programme of trade liberalization, and by complying with tariff reductions that had already been agreed upon. In May 1991, in Caracas, Venezuela, a summit meeting of the Andean Group agreed the framework for the establishment of a free-trade area on 1 January 1992 (achieved in February 1993) and for an eventual Andean common market (see below, under Trade).

In March 1996 heads of state, meeting in Trujillo, Peru, agreed to a substantial restructuring of the Andean Group. The heads of state signed the Reform Protocol of the Cartagena Agreement, providing for the establishment of the Andean Community of Nations, which was to have more ambitious economic and political objectives than the Group. Consequently, in August 1997 the Andean Community was inaugurated, and the Group's Junta was replaced by a new General Secretariat, headed by a Secretary-General with enhanced executive and decision-making powers. The initiation of these reforms was designed to accelerate harmonization in economic matters, particularly the achievement of a common external tariff. In September 1996 the Group agreed to negotiate a free-trade agreement with the Mercado Común del Sur (Mercosur). (Disunity among the Andean nations had been evident in June, when Bolivia had agreed to enter into free-trade negotiations with Mercosur on a unilateral basis, thus becoming an associate member of that grouping.) In April 1997 the Peruvian Government announced its intention to withdraw from the Cartagena Agreement, owing to disagreements about the terms of Peru's full integration into the Community's trading system. Later in that month the heads of state of the four other members attended a summit meeting, in Sucre, Bolivia, and reiterated their commitment to strengthening regional integration. A high-level group of representatives was established to pursue negotiations with Peru regarding its future relationship with the Community (agreement was reached in June—see below). In April 2001 Venezuela announced that it intended to apply for membership of Mercosur (while retaining its membership of the Community).

At the 13th presidential summit, held in Valencia, Venezuela, in June 2001, heads of state adopted an Andean Co-operation Plan for the Control of Illegal Drugs and Related Offences, which was to promote a united approach to combating these problems. An executive committee was to be established under the accord to oversee implementation of an action plan. It was also agreed that an Andean passport system should enter into effect no later than December 2005. In January 2002 a special Andean presidential summit, held in Santa Cruz, Bolivia, reiterated the objective of creating a common market and renewing efforts to strengthen sub-regional integration, including the adoption of a common agricultural policy and the standardization of macroeconomic policies.

In June 2002 ministers of defence and of foreign affairs of the Andean Community approved an Andean Charter for Peace and Security, establishing principles and commitments for the formulation of a policy on sub-regional security, the establishment of a zone of peace, joint action in efforts to counter terrorism, and the limitation of external defence spending. Other provisions of the Charter included commitments to eradicate illegal trafficking in firearms, ammunition and explosives, to expand and reinforce confidence-building measures, and to establish verification mechanisms to strengthen dialogue and efforts in those areas. In January 2003 the Community and Interpol concluded a co-operation agreement providing for collaboration in combating national and transnational crime.

TRADE

Trade within the group increased by about 37% annually between 1978 and 1980. A council for customs affairs met for the first time in January 1982, aiming to harmonize national legislation within the group. In December 1984 the member states launched a common currency, the Andean peso, aiming to reduce dependence on the US dollar and to increase regional trade. The new currency was to be backed by special contributions to the Fondo Andino de Reservas (now the Fondo Latinoamericano de Reservas) amounting to US $80m., and was to be 'pegged' to the US dollar, taking the form of financial drafts rather than notes and coins. In May 1986 a formula for trade among member countries was agreed, in order to restrict the number of products exempted from trade liberalization measures to 40 'sensitive' products.

The 'Caracas Declaration' of May 1991 provided for the establishment of an Andean free-trade area, which entered into effect (excluding Peru—see below) in February 1993. Heads of state also agreed in May 1991 to create a common external tariff (CET), to standardize member countries' trade barriers in their dealings with the rest of the world, and envisaged the eventual creation of an Andean common market. In December heads of state defined four main levels of external tariffs (between 5% and 20%). The conclusion of negotiations, however, was subsequently delayed, notably by Ecuador's request for numerous exceptions and by a deterioration in relations between Peru and Venezuela during 1992 (following the suspension of the Peruvian Constitution in April), which halted progress completely. In August the Group approved a request by Peru for the suspension of its rights and obligations under the Pact, thereby enabling the other members to proceed with negotiations on the CET. Peru was readmitted as a full member of the Group in 1994, but participated only as an observer in the ongoing negotiations.

In November 1994 ministers of trade and integration, meeting in Quito, Ecuador, concluded a final agreement on a four-tier structure of external tariffs (although Bolivia was to retain a two-level system). The CET agreement, which came into effect in February 1995, covered 90% of the region's imports which were to be subject to the following tariff bands: 5% for raw materials; 10%–15% for semi-manufactured goods; and 20% for finished products. In order to reach an agreement, special treatment and exemptions were granted, while Peru, initially, was to remain a 'non-active' member of the accord: Bolivia was to maintain external tariffs of 5% and 10%, Ecuador was permitted to apply the lowest rate of 5% to 990 items and was granted an initial exemption from tariffs on 400 items, while Colombia and Venezuela were granted 230 items to be subject to special treatment for four years. In June 1997 an agreement was concluded to ensure Peru's continued membership of the Community, which provided for that country's integration into the free-trade area. The Peruvian Government determined to eliminate customs duties on some 2,500 products with immediate effect, and it was agreed that the process be completed by 2005. However, negotiations were to continue with regard to the replacement of Peru's single tariff on products from outside the region with the Community's scale of external duties.

In May 1999 the Community adopted a policy on border integration and development to prepare the border regions of member countries for the envisaged free circulation of people, goods, capital and services, while consolidating sub-regional security. Community heads of state, meeting in January 2002 at a special Andean presidential summit, agreed to consolidate and improve the free-trade zone by mid-2002 and apply a new common external tariff (CET, with four levels, i.e. 0%, 5%, 10% and 20%) by December 2003. To facilitate this process a common agricultural policy was to be adopted, and macroeconomic policies were to be harmonized. In June 2002 ministers of foreign affairs approved a schedule of activities relating to the new CET. In October member governments determined the new tariff levels applicable to 62% of products and agreed the criteria for negotiating levels for the remaining 38%.

EXTERNAL RELATIONS

In September 1995 heads of state of member countries identified the formulation of common positions on foreign relations as an important part of the process of relaunching the integration initiative. A Protocol Amending the Cartagena Agreement was signed in June 1997 to confirm the formulation of a common foreign policy. During 1998 the General Secretariat held consultations with government experts, academics, representatives of the private sector and other interested parties to help formulate a document on guide-lines for a common foreign policy. The guide-lines, establishing the principles, objectives and mechanisms of a common foreign policy, were approved by the Council of Foreign Ministers in 1999. Councils on Trade and Investment between the Andean Community and the USA, and between the Community and Canada, have been established to strengthen bilateral trading relations. At the special Andean presidential summit in January 2002, members reiterated their intention to appeal to the US Congress to renew and extend the Andean Trade Preferences Act, which expired in December 2001. The Group has also sought to strengthen relations with the European Union, and a co-operation agreement was signed between the two blocs in April 1993. A Euro-Andean Forum is held periodically to promote mutual co-operation, trade and investment. In February 1998 the Community signed a co-operation and technical assistance agreement with the EU in order to combat drugs trafficking. At the first summit meeting of Latin American, Caribbean and EU leaders held in Rio de Janeiro, Brazil, in June 1999, Community–EU discussions were held on strengthening economic, trade and political co-operation and on the possibility of eventually concluding an Association Agreement. In May 2002 the European Union adopted a Regional Strategy for the Andean Community covering the period 2002–06. The second Latin America, Caribbean and EU summit meeting, held in that month in Madrid, Spain, welcomed a new initiative to negotiate an agreement on political dialogue and co-operation, envisaging that this would strengthen the basis for subsequent negotiations on the proposed Association Agreement. In October the European Commission adopted a recommendation on the initiation of negotiations on the new political dialogue and co-operation agreement. In March 2003 the Commisson committed €2m. to financing a three-year project to improve and harmonize Andean Community legislation on competition.

In March 2000 the Andean Community concluded an agreement to establish a political consultation and co-operation mechanism with the People's Republic of China. At the first ministerial meeting within this framework, which took place in October 2002, it was agreed that consultations would be held thereafter on a biennial basis. A high-level meeting between senior officials from Community member states and Japan was organized in December 2002; further consultations were to be convened, aimed at cultivating closer relations.

In April 1998, at the 10th Andean presidential summit, an agreement was signed with Panama establishing a framework for negotiations providing for the conclusion of a free-trade accord by the end of 1998 and for Panama's eventual associate membership of the Community. Also in April 1998 the Community signed a framework agreement with Mercosur on the establishment of a free-trade accord. Although negotiations between the Community and Mercosur were subsequently delayed, bilateral agreements between the countries of the two groupings were extended. A preferential tariff agreement was concluded between Brazil and the Community in July 1999; the accord entered into effect, for a period of two years, in August. In August 2000 a preferential tariff agreement concluded with Argentina entered into force. The Community commenced negotiations on drafting a preferential tariff agreement with (jointly) El Salvador, Guatemala and Honduras in March of that year. In September leaders of the Community and Mercosur, meeting at a summit of Latin American heads of state, determined to relaunch negotiations, with a view to establishing a free-trade area. In July 2001 ministers of foreign affairs of the two groupings approved the establishment of a formal mechanism for political dialogue and co-ordination in order to facilitate negotiations and to enhance economic and social integration. In December 2002 Andean Community and Mercosur heads of state signed an economic complementation agreement, providing for the merger of their respective free-trade areas by 2004.

In March 1998 ministers of trade from 34 countries, meeting in San José, Costa Rica, concluded an agreement on the structure of negotiations for the establishment of a Free Trade Area of the Americas (FTAA). The process was formally initiated by heads of state, meeting in Santiago, Chile, in the following month. The Community negotiated as a bloc to obtain chairmanship of three of the nine negotiating groups: on market access (Colombia), on competition policy (Peru), and on intellectual property (Venezuela). The Community insisted that the final declaration issued by the meeting include recognition that the varying levels of development of the participating countries should be taken into consideration throughout the negotiating process. In April 2001, convened in Quebec City, Canada, leaders of the participating countries determined to conclude negotiations on the FTAA by January 2005, with the Agreement to enter into force by December at the latest.

In August 1999 the Secretary-General of the Community visited Guyana in order to promote bilateral trading opportunities and to strengthen relations with the Caribbean Community. The Community held a meeting on trade relations with the Caribbean Community during 2000.

INDUSTRY

Negotiations began in 1970 for the formulation of joint industrial programmes, particularly in the petrochemicals, metal-working and motor vehicle sectors, but disagreements over the allocation of different plants, and the choice of foreign manufacturers for co-operation, prevented progress and by 1984 the more ambitious schemes had been abandoned. Instead, emphasis was to be placed on assisting small and medium-sized industries, particularly in the agro-industrial and electronics sectors, in co-operation with national industrial organizations.

An Andean Agricultural Development Programme was formulated in 1976 within which 22 resolutions aimed at integrating the Andean agricultural sector were approved. In 1984 the Andean Food Security System was created to develop the agrarian sector, replace imports progressively with local produce, and improve rural living conditions. In April 1998 the Presidential Council instructed the Commission, together with ministers of agriculture, to formulate an Andean Common Agricultural Policy, including measures to harmonize trade policy instruments and legislation on animal and plant health. The 12th Andean presidential summit, held in June 2000, authorized the adoption of the concluded Policy and the enforcement of a plan of action for its implementation. In January 2002, at the special Andean presidential summit, it was agreed that all countries in the bloc would adopt price stabilization mechanisms for agricultural products.

In May 1987 member countries signed the Quito Protocol, modifying the Cartagena Agreement, to amend the strict rules that had formerly been imposed on foreign investors in the region. The Protocol entered into force in May 1988. Accordingly, each government was to decide which sectors were to be closed to foreign participation, and the period within which foreign investors must transfer a majority shareholding to local investors was extended to 30 years (37 years in Bolivia and Ecuador). In March 1991 the Protocol was amended, with the aim of further liberalizing foreign investment and stimulating an inflow of foreign capital and technology. External and regional investors were to be permitted to repatriate their profits (in accordance with the laws of the country concerned) and there was no stipulation that a majority shareholding must eventually be transferred to local investors. A further directive, adopted in March, covered the formation of 'Empresas Multinacionales Andinas' (multinational enterprises) in order to ensure that at least two member countries have a shareholding of 15% or more of the capital, including the country where the enterprise was to be based. These enterprises were entitled to participate in sectors otherwise reserved for national enterprises, subject to the same conditions as national enterprises in terms of taxation and export regulations, and to gain access to the markets of all member countries.

In November 1988 member states established a bank, the Banco Intermunicipal Andino, which was to finance public works.

In May 1995 the Group initiated a programme to promote the use of cheap and efficient energy sources and greater co-operation in the energy sector. The programme planned to develop a regional electricity grid.

In September 1999 Colombia, Ecuador and Venezuela signed an accord to facilitate the production and sale of vehicles within the region. The agreement became effective in January 2000, with a duration of 10 years.

TRANSPORT AND COMMUNICATIONS

The Andean Community has pursued efforts to improve infrastructure throughout the region. In 1983 the Commission formulated a plan to assist land-locked Bolivia, particularly through improving roads connecting it with neighbouring countries and the Pacific Ocean. An 'open skies' agreement, giving airlines of member states equal rights to airspace and airport facilities within the grouping, was signed in May 1991. In June 1998 the Commission approved the establishment of an Andean Commission of Land Transportation Authorities, which was to oversee the operation and development of land transportation services. Similarly, an Andean Committee of Water Transportation Authorities has been established to ensure compliance with Community regulations regarding ocean transportation activities. The Community aims to facilitate the movement of goods throughout the region by the use of different modes of transport ('multimodal transport') and to guarantee operational standards. It also intends to harmonize Community transport regulations and standards with those of Mercosur countries.

In August 1996 a regulatory framework was approved for the development of a commercial Andean satellite system. In December 1997 the General Secretariat approved regulations for granting authorization for the use of the system; the Commission subsequently granted the first Community authorization to an Andean multinational enterprise (Andesat), comprising 48 companies from all five member states. The system was expected to be fully operational from mid-2002. In 1994 the Community initiated efforts to establish digital technology infrastructure throughout the Community: the resulting Andean Digital Corridor comprises ground, underwater and satellite routes providing a series of cross-border interconnections between the member countries. The Andean Internet System, which aims to provide internet protocol-based services throughout the Community, was operational in Colombia, Ecuador and Venezuela in 2000, and was due to be extended to all five member countries. In May 1999 the Andean Committee of Telecommunications Authorities agreed to remove all restrictions to free trade in telecommunications services (excluding sound broadcasting and television) by 1 January 2002. The Committee also determined to formulate provisions on interconnection and the safeguarding of free competition and principles of transparency within the sector.

Asociación de Empresas de Telecomunicaciones de la Comunidad Andina—ASETA: Calle La Pradera 510 y San Salvador, Casilla 17-1106042, Quito, Ecuador; tel. (2) 563-812; fax (2) 562-499; e-mail info@aseta.org; internet www.aseta.org; f. 1974; co-ordinates improvements in national telecommunications services, in order to contribute to the further integration of the countries of the Andean Community; Sec.-Gen. MARCELO LÓPEZ ARJONA.

SOCIAL INTEGRATION

Several formal agreements and institutions have been established within the framework of the grouping to enhance social development and welfare (see below). The Community aims to incorporate these bodies into the process of enhanced integration and to promote greater involvement of representatives of civil society. In May 1999 the 11th Andean presidential summit adopted a 'multidimensional social agenda' focusing on job creation and on improvements in the fields of education, health and housing throughout the Community. In June 2000 the 12th presidential summit instructed the Andean institutions to prepare individual programmes aimed at consolidating implementation of the Community's integration programme and advancing the development of the social agenda. At a special presidential summit in January 2002, corresponding ministers were directed to meet during the first half of the year to develop a Community strategy to complement national efforts in this area. The heads of state also accepted an invitation by Peruvian President Alejandro Toledo to convene a conference of Community ministers of defence and of foreign affairs in Peru, in April, to consider a proposal to reduce defence expenditures, in order to assign more resources to poverty-reduction initiatives.

INSTITUTIONS

Consejo Consultivo Empresarial Andino (Andean Business Advisory Council): Paseo de la República 3895, Lima, Peru; tel. (1) 4111400; fax (1) 2213329; e-mail rsuarez@comunidadandina.org; first meeting held in November 1998; an advisory institution within the framework of the Sistema Andino de Integración; comprises elected representatives of business organizations; advises Community ministers and officials on integration activities affecting the business sector; Pres. PEDRO CARMONA ESTANGA.

Consejo Consultivo Laboral Andino (Andean Labour Advisory Council): Central Obrera Boliviana, Calle Pisagua 618, La Paz, Bolivia; tel. and fax (2) 28-0420; internet www.ccla.org.pe; an advis-

ory institution within the framework of the Sistema Andino de Integración; comprises elected representatives of labour organizations; advises Community ministers and officers on related labour issues; Pres. JULIO CARRASCAL PUENTES (Colombia).

Convenio Andrés Bello (Andrés Bello Agreement): Paralela Autopista Norte, Avda 13 85–60, Bogotá DC 53465, Colombia; tel. (1) 6449292; fax (1) 6100139; e-mail ecobello@col1.telecom.com.co; internet www.cab.int.co; f. 1970, modified in 1990; aims to promote integration in the educational, technical and cultural sectors; mems: Bolivia, Chile, Colombia, Cuba, Ecuador, Panama, Paraguay, Peru, Spain, Venezuela.

Convenio Hipólito Unanue (Hipólito Unanue Agreement): Edif. Cartagena, Paseo de la República 3832, 3°, Lima, Peru; tel. (1) 4226862; fax (1) 4409285; e-mail postmaster@conhu.org.pe; internet www.conhu.org.pe; f. 1971 on the occasion of the first meeting of Andean ministers of health; aims to enhance the development of health services, and to promote regional co-ordination in areas such as environmental health, disaster preparedness and the prevention and control of drug abuse.

Convenio Simón Rodríguez (Simón Rodríguez Agreement): Paseo de la República 3895, esq. Aramburú, San Isidro, Lima 27, Peru; tel. (1) 4111400; fax (1) 2213329; promotes a convergence of social and labour conditions throughout the Community, for example, working hours and conditions, employment and social security policies, and to promote the participation of workers and employers in the sub-regional integration process.

Corporación Andina de Fomento—CAF (Andean Development Corporation): Torre CAF, Avda Luis Roche, Altamira, Apdo 5086, Caracas, Venezuela; tel. (2) 2092111; fax (2) 28457544; e-mail infocaf@caf.com; internet www.caf.com; f. 1968, began operations in 1970; aims to encourage the integration of the Andean countries by specialization and an equitable distribution of investments; conducts research to identify investment opportunities, and prepares the resulting investment projects; gives technical and financial assistance; and attracts internal and external credit; auth. cap. US $3,000m. subscribed or underwritten by the governments of member countries, or by public, semi-public and private-sector institutions authorized by those governments; the Board of Directors comprises representatives of each country at ministerial level; mems: the Andean Community, Argentina, Brazil, Chile, Jamaica, Mexico, Panama, Paraguay, Spain, Trinidad and Tobago, and 18 private banks in the Andean region; Exec. Pres. ENRIQUE GARCÍA RODRÍGUEZ (Bolivia).

Fondo Latinoamericano de Reservas—FLAR (Latin American Reserve Fund): Edif. Banco de Occidente, Carrera 13, No. 27–47, 10°, Santafé de Bogotá, Colombia; tel. (1) 2858511; fax (1) 2881117; e-mail flar@flar.net; internet www.flar.net; f. 1978 as the Fondo Andino de Reservas to support the balance of payments of member countries, provide credit, guarantee loans, and contribute to the harmonization of monetary and financial policies; adopted present name in 1991, in order to allow the admission of other Latin American countries; in 1992 the Fund began extending credit lines to commercial for export financing; ii is administered by an Assembly of the ministers of finance and economy of the member countries, and a Board of Directors comprising the Presidents of the central banks of the member states; in October 1995 it was agreed to expand the Fund's capital from US $800m. to $1,000m. the increase became effective on 30 June 1997; Exec. Pres. ROBERTO GUARNIERI (Venezuela); Sec.-Gen. BORIS HERNÁNDEZ (Colombia).

Universidad Andina Simón Bolívar (Simón Bolívar Andean University): Calle Real Audiencia 73, Casilla 608-33, Sucre, Bolivia; tel. (64) 60265; fax (64) 60833; e-mail uasb@uasb.edu.bo; internet www.uasb.edu.bo; f. 1985; institution for postgraduate study and research; promotes co-operation between other universities in the Andean region; branches in Quito (Ecuador), La Paz (Bolivia), Caracas (Venezuela) and Cali (Colombia); Pres. Dr JULIO GARRET AILLÓN.

Publications

Gaceta Oficial del Acuerdo de Cartagena.
Trade and Investment Guide.
Reports, working papers.

ARAB FUND FOR ECONOMIC AND SOCIAL DEVELOPMENT—AFESD

Address: POB 21923, Safat, 13080 Kuwait.
Telephone: 4844500; **fax:** 4815760; **e-mail:** hq@arabfund.org; **internet:** www.arabfund.org.
Established in 1968 by the Economic Council of the Arab League, the Fund began its operations in 1974. It participates in the financing of economic and social development projects in the Arab states.

MEMBERSHIP

Twenty-one members (see table of subscriptions below)

Organization

(April 2003)

BOARD OF GOVERNORS

The Board of Governors consists of a Governor and an Alternate Governor appointed by each member of the Fund. The Board of Governors is considered as the General Assembly of the Fund, and has all powers.

BOARD OF DIRECTORS

The Board of Directors is composed of eight Directors elected by the Board of Governors from among Arab citizens of recognized experience and competence. They are elected for a renewable term of two years.
The Board of Directors is charged with all the activities of the Fund and exercises the powers delegated to it by the Board of Governors.
Director-General and Chairman of the Board of Directors: ABDLATIF YOUSUF AL-HAMAD.

FINANCIAL STRUCTURE

In 1982 the authorized capital was increased from 400m. Kuwaiti dinars (KD) to KD 800m., divided into 80,000 shares having a value of KD 10,000 each. At the end of 2001 paid-up capital was KD 663.04m.

SUBSCRIPTIONS (KD million, December 2001)*

Algeria	64.78	Oman		17.28
Bahrain	2.16	Palestine		1.10
Djibouti	0.02	Qatar		6.75
Egypt	40.50	Saudi Arabia		159.07
Iraq	31.76	Somalia		0.21
Jordan	17.30	Sudan		11.06
Kuwait	169.70	Syria		24.00
Lebanon	2.00	Tunisia		6.16
Libya	59.85	United Arab Emirates		28.00
Mauritania	0.82	Yemen		4.52
Morocco	16.00			
		Total		**663.04**

* 100 Kuwaiti dinars = US $325.6 (December 2001).

Activities

Pursuant to the Agreement Establishing the Fund (as amended in 1997 by the Board of Governors), the purpose of the Fund is to contribute to the financing of economic and social development projects in the Arab states and countries by:
  1. Financing economic development projects of an investment character by means of loans granted on concessionary terms to governments and public enterprises and corporations, giving preference to projects which are vital to the Arab entity, as well as to joint Arab projects;
  2. Financing private sector projects in member states by providing all forms of loans and guarantees to corporations and enterprises (possessing juridical personality), participating in their equity capital, and providing other forms of financing and the requisite financial, technical and advisory services, in accordance with such regulations and subject to such conditions as may be prescribed by the Board of Directors;
  3. Forming or participating in the equity capital of corporations possessing juridical personality, for the implementation and financing of private sector projects in member states, including the provision and financing of technical, advisory and financial services;
  4. Establishing and administering special funds with aims compatible with those of the Fund and with resources provided by the Fund or other sources;
  5. Encouraging, directly or indirectly, the investment of public and private capital in a manner conducive to the development and growth of the Arab economy;
  6. Providing expertise and technical assistance in the various fields of economic development.

LOANS BY MEMBER, 2001

Member	Project	Amount (KD million)
Algeria	Pumping and conveyance of water from Bani Haroun	31.0
Djibouti	Development of the education sector	4.0
Egypt	Cairo North power generation station	27.0
Lebanon	Conveyance of water from Litani to Southern Lebanon	31.0
Mauritania	Connecting Boghe to Manantali electrical grid	4.0
	Debt reduction	14.0
	Nouakchott–Nouadhibou road	16.0
Morocco	Casablanca–el-Jadida motorway	15.0
Sudan	Atbara–Haiya–Port Sudan road	25.0
Syria	Expansion of Nasrieh power plant and conversion to combined cycle	25.0
Tunisia	Tunis–Mjaz el-Bab motorway	25.0
	Developmental credit lines	11.0
Yemen	Sayhat–Nishtun road	26.0
	San'a International Airport development	28.0
Total		**282.0**

LOANS BY SECTOR, 2001

Sector	Amount (KD million)	%
Agriculture and rural development	31.0	11.0
Energy and electricity	56.0	19.8
Industry and mining	11.0	3.9
Transport and telecommunications	135.0	47.9
Water and sewerage	31.0	11.0
Other	18.0	6.4
Total	**282.0**	**100.0**

The Fund co-operates with other Arab organizations such as the Arab Monetary Fund, the League of Arab States and OAPEC in preparing regional studies and conferences, for example in the areas of human resource development, demographic research and private sector financing of infrastructure projects. It also acts as the secretariat of the Co-ordination Group of Arab National and Regional Development Financing Institutions. These organizations also work together to produce a *Joint Arab Economic Report*, which considers economic and social developments in the Arab states.
During 2001 the Fund approved 14 new loans, totalling KD 282m., for projects in 10 member countries. At the end of that year total lending since 1974 amounted to KD 3,855.7m., which helped to finance 417 projects in 17 Arab countries.
The total number of technical assistance grants provided by the end of 2001 was 678, with a value of KD 89.1m. During 2001 the Fund extended 28 new grants, totalling KD 5.0m., of which 63% was to enhance institution building and to support training in specialized Arab scientific and research centres, while 24% was for general studies and other research activities.
In December 1997 AFESD initiated an Arab Fund Fellowships Programme, which aimed to provide grants to Arab academics to conduct university teaching or advanced research.

ARAB MONETARY FUND

Address: Arab Monetary Fund Bldg, Corniche Rd, POB 2818, Abu Dhabi, United Arab Emirates.
Telephone: (2) 6215000; **fax:** (2) 6326454; **e-mail:** centralmail@amfad.org.ae; **internet:** www.amf.org.ae.

The Agreement establishing the Arab Monetary Fund was approved by the Economic Council of Arab States in Rabat, Morocco, in April 1976 and entered into force on 2 February 1977.

MEMBERS

Algeria	Oman
Bahrain	Palestine
Djibouti	Qatar
Egypt	Saudi Arabia
Iraq*	Somalia*
Jordan	Sudan*
Kuwait	Syria
Lebanon	Tunisia
Libya	United Arab Emirates
Mauritania	Yemen
Morocco	

* From July 1993 loans to Iraq, Somalia and Sudan were suspended as a result of non-repayment of debts to the Fund. Sudan was readmitted in April 2000, following a settlement of its arrears, but subsequently defaulted on further loan repayments. At 31 December 2001 the three countries' arrears to the Fund totalled AAD 158.2m.

Organization

(April 2003)

BOARD OF GOVERNORS

The Board of Governors is the highest authority of the Arab Monetary Fund. It formulates policies on Arab economic integration and liberalization of trade among member states. With certain exceptions, it may delegate to the Board of Executive Directors some of its powers. The Board of Governors is composed of a governor and a deputy governor appointed by each member state for a term of five years. It meets at least once a year; meetings may also be convened at the request of half the members, or of members holding half of the total voting power.

BOARD OF EXECUTIVE DIRECTORS

The Board of Executive Directors exercises all powers vested in it by the Board of Governors and may delegate to the Director-General such powers as it deems fit. It is composed of the Director-General and eight non-resident directors elected by the Board of Governors. Each director holds office for three years and may be re-elected.

DIRECTOR-GENERAL

The Director-General of the Fund is appointed by the Board of Governors for a renewable five-year term, and serves as Chairman of the Board of Executive Directors.

The Director-General supervises a Committee on Loans and a Committee on Investments to make recommendations on loan and investment policies to the Board of Executive Directors, and is required to submit an Annual Report to the Board of Governors.

Director-General and Chairman of the Board of Executive Directors: Dr JASSIM ABDULLAH AL-MANNAI.

FINANCE

The Arab Accounting Dinar (AAD) is a unit of account equivalent to three IMF Special Drawing Rights. (The average value of the SDR in 2002 was US $1.29484.)

Each member paid, in convertible currencies, 5% of the value of its shares at the time of its ratification of the Agreement and another 20% when the Agreement entered into force. In addition, each member paid 2% of the value of its shares in its national currency regardless of whether it is convertible. The second 25% of the capital was to be subscribed by the end of September 1979, bringing the total paid-up capital in convertible currencies to AAD 131.5m. An increase in requests for loans led to a resolution by the Board of Governors in April 1981, giving members the option of paying the balance of their subscribed capital. This payment became obligatory in July 1981, when total approved loans exceeded 50% of the already paid-up capital in convertible currencies. In April 1983 the authorized capital of the Fund was increased from AAD 288m. to AAD

600m. The new capital stock comprised 12,000 shares, each having the value of AAD 50,000. At the end of 2000 total paid-up capital was AAD 324.1m.

CAPITAL SUBSCRIPTIONS (million Arab Accounting Dinars, 31 December 2001)

Member	Paid-up capital
Algeria	42.40
Bahrain	5.00
Djibouti	0.25
Egypt	32.00
Iraq	42.40
Jordan	5.40
Kuwait	32.00
Lebanon	5.00
Libya	13.44
Mauritania	5.00
Morocco	15.00
Oman	5.00
Palestine	2.16
Qatar	10.00
Saudi Arabia	48.40
Somalia	4.00
Sudan	10.00
Syria	7.20
Tunisia	7.00
United Arab Emirates	19.20
Yemen	15.40
Total*	**324.09**

* Excluding Palestine's share, which was deferred by a Board of Governors' resolution in 1978.

Activities

The creation of the Arab Monetary Fund was seen as a step towards the goal of Arab economic integration. It assists member states in balance of payments difficulties, and also has a broad range of aims. The Articles of Agreement define the Fund's aims as follows:

(a) to correct disequilibria in the balance of payments of member states;

(b) to promote the stability of exchange rates among Arab currencies, to render them mutually convertible, and to eliminate restrictions on current payments between member states;

(c) to establish policies and modes of monetary co-operation to accelerate Arab economic integration and economic development in the member states;

(d) to tender advice on the investment of member states' financial resources in foreign markets, whenever called upon to do so;

(e) to promote the development of Arab financial markets;

(f) to promote the use of the Arab dinar as a unit of account and to pave the way for the creation of a unified Arab currency;

(g) to co-ordinate the positions of member states in dealing with international monetary and economic problems; and

(h) to provide a mechanism for the settlement of current payments between member states in order to promote trade among them.

The Arab Monetary Fund functions both as a fund and a bank. It is empowered:

(a) to provide short- and medium-term loans to finance balance of payments deficits of member states;

(b) to issue guarantees to member states to strengthen their borrowing capabilities;

(c) to act as intermediary in the issuance of loans in Arab and international markets for the account of member states and under their guarantees;

(d) to co-ordinate the monetary policies of member states;

(e) to manage any funds placed under its charge by member states;

(f) to hold periodic consultations with member states on their economic conditions; and

(g) to provide technical assistance to banking and monetary institutions in member states.

Loans are intended to finance an overall balance of payments deficit and a member may draw up to 75% of its paid-up subscription, in convertible currencies, for this purpose unconditionally (automatic loans). A member may, however, obtain loans in excess of this limit, subject to agreement with the Fund on a programme aimed at reducing its balance of payments deficit (ordinary and extended loans, equivalent to 175% and 250% of its quota respectively). From 1981 a country receiving no extended loans was entitled to a loan under the Inter-Arab Trade Facility (discontinued in 1989) of up to 100% of its quota. In addition, a member has the right to borrow up to 50% of its paid-up capital in order to cope with an unexpected deficit in its balance of payments resulting from a decrease in its exports of goods and services or a large increase in its imports of agricultural products following a poor harvest (compensatory loans).

Automatic and compensatory loans are repayable within three years, while ordinary and extended loans are repayable within five and seven years respectively. Loans are granted at concessional and uniform rates of interest which increase with the length of the period of the loan. In 1988 the Fund's executive directors agreed to modify their policy on lending, placing an emphasis on the correction of economic imbalances in recipient countries. In 1996 the Fund established the Structural Adjustment Facility, providing up to 75% of a member's paid-up subscription. This may include a technical assistance component comprising a grant of up to 2% of the total loan.

Over the period 1978–2001 the Fund extended 121 loans amounting to AAD 896,894m. During 2001 the Fund approved six loans, amounting to AAD 69,305m., while loan disbursements amounted to AAD 73,629m.

The Fund's technical assistance activities are extended through either the provision of experts to the country concerned or in the form of specialized training of officials of member countries. In view of the increased importance of this type of assistance, the Fund established, in 1988, the Economic Policy Institute (EPI) which offers regular training courses and specialized seminars for middle-level and senior staff, respectively, of financial and monetary institutions of the Arab countries. On 1 April 1999 the Fund signed a memorandum of understanding with the International Monetary Fund to establish a joint regional training programme. During 2001 five training courses were organized by the EPI under this joint programme.

LOANS APPROVED, 1978–2001

Type of loan	Number of loans	Amount (AAD '000)
Automatic	56	290,250
Ordinary	11	104,566
Compensatory	14	99,085
Extended	19	223,451
Structural Adjustment Facility	10	114,812
Inter-Arab Trade Facility (cancelled in 1989)	11	64,730
Total	**121**	**896,894**

LOANS APPROVED, 2001

Borrower	Type of loan	Amount (AAD million)
Egypt	Compensatory	15,750
	Automatic	23,625
Jordan	Structural Adjustment Facility	5,214
Morocco	Structural Adjustment Facility	14,504
Tunisia	Compensatory	3,450
	Structural Adjustment Facility	6,762
Total		**69,305**

TRADE PROMOTION

Arab Trade Financing Program (ATFP): POB 26799, Arab Monetary Fund Bldg, 7th Floor, Corniche Rd, Abu Dhabi, United Arab Emirates; tel. (2) 6316999; fax (2) 6316793; e-mail atfphq@atfp .org.ae; internet www.atfp.org.ae; f. 1989 to develop and promote trade between Arab countries and to enhance the competitive ability of Arab exporters; operates by extending lines of credit to Arab exporters and importers through national agencies (some 132 agencies designated by the monetary authorities of 18 Arab countries in Dec. 2002); the Arab Monetary Fund provided 50% of ATFP's authorized capital of US $500m. participation was also invited from private and official Arab financial institutions and joint Arab/foreign institutions; ATFP administers the Inter-Arab Trade Information Network (IATIN), and organizes Buyers-Sellers meetings to promote Arab goods; Chair. and Chief Exec. Dr JASSIM ABDULLAH AL-MANNAI; publs *Annual Report*(Arabic and English), *IATIN Quarterly Bulletin*(Arabic).

Publications

Annual Report.

AMDB Bulletin (quarterly).

Arab Countries: Economic Indicators (annually).

Balance of Payments and External Public Debt of Arab the Countries (annually).

Foreign Trade of the Arab Countries (annually).

Joint Arab Economic Report (annually).

Money and Credit in the Arab Countries.

National Accounts of the Arab Countries (annually).

Reports on commodity structure (by value and quantity) of member countries' imports from and exports to other Arab countries; other studies on economic, social, management and fiscal issues.

ASIA-PACIFIC ECONOMIC CO-OPERATION—APEC

Address: 438 Alexandra Rd, 14th Floor, Alexandra Point, Singapore 119958.

Telephone: 62761880; **fax:** 62761775; **e-mail:** info@mail.apecsec .org.sg; **internet:** www.apecsec.org.sg.

Asia-Pacific Economic Co-operation (APEC) was initiated in November 1989, in Canberra, Australia, as an informal consultative forum. Its aim is to promote multilateral economic co-operation on issues of trade and investment.

MEMBERS

Australia	Japan	Philippines
Brunei	Korea, Republic	Russia
Canada	Malaysia	Singapore
Chile	Mexico	Taiwan*
China, People's Republic	New Zealand	Thailand
Hong Kong	Papua New Guinea	USA
Indonesia	Peru	Viet Nam

*Admitted as Chinese Taipei.

Organization

(April 2003)

ECONOMIC LEADERS' MEETINGS

The first meeting of APEC heads of government was convened in November 1993, in Seattle, USA. Subsequently, each annual meeting of APEC ministers of foreign affairs and of economic affairs has been followed by an informal gathering of the leaders of the APEC economies, at which the policy objectives of the grouping are discussed and defined. The 10th Leaders' Meeting was held in Mexico, in October 2002; the 2003 meeting was scheduled to be held in October, in Bangkok, Thailand.

MINISTERIAL MEETINGS

APEC ministers of foreign affairs and ministers of economic affairs meet annually. These meetings are hosted by the APEC Chair, which rotates each year, although it was agreed, in 1989, that alternate Ministerial Meetings were to be convened in an ASEAN member country. A Senior Officials' Meeting (SOM) convenes regularly between Ministerial Meetings to co-ordinate and administer the budgets and work programmes of APEC's committees and working groups. Other meetings of ministers are held on a regular basis to enhance co-operation in specific areas.

SECRETARIAT

In 1992 the Ministerial Meeting, held in Bangkok, Thailand, agreed to establish a permanent secretariat to support APEC activities, and approved an annual budget of US $2m. The Secretariat became operational in February 1993. The Executive Director is appointed from the member economy chairing the group and serves a one-year term. A Deputy Executive Director is appointed by the member economy designated to chair APEC in the following year.

Executive Director: PIAMSAK MILINTACHINDA (Thailand).

Deputy Executive Director: MARIO ARTAZA (Chile).

COMMITTEES AND GROUPS

Budget and Management Committee—BMC: f. 1993 as Budget and Administrative Committee, present name adopted 1998; advises APEC senior officials on budgetary, administrative and managerial issues. The Committee reviews the operational budgets of APEC committees and groups, evaluates their effectiveness and conducts assessments of group projects.

Committee on Trade and Investment—CTI: f. 1993 on the basis of a Declaration signed by ministers meeting in Seattle, USA, in order to facilitate the expansion of trade and the development of a liberalized environment for investment among member countries; undertakes initiatives to improve the flow of goods, services and technology in the region. In May 1997 an APEC Tariff Database was inaugurated, with sponsorship from the private sector. A new Market Access Group was established in 1998 to administer CTI activities concerned with non-tariff measures. In 2001 the CTI finalized a set of non-binding Principles on Trade Facilitation. The development of the nine principles was intended to help eliminate procedural and administrative impediments to trade and to increase trading opportunities.

Economic Committee—EC: f. 1994 following an agreement, in November, to transform the existing *ad hoc* group on economic trends and issues into a formal committee; aims to enhance APEC's capacity to analyse economic trends and to research and report on issues affecting economic and technical co-operation in the region. In addition, the Committee is considering the environmental and development implications of expanding population and economic growth.

Sub-Committee on Economic and Technical Co-operation—ESC: f. 1998 to assist the SOM with the co-ordination of APEC's economic and technical co-operation programme (ECOTECH); monitors and evaluates project implementation and also supervises the work of the Group on Economic Infrastructure (GEI), which carries out projects designed to strengthen economic and technical co-operation in infrastructure. The ESC co-ordinated the development of APEC's Human-Capacity Building Strategy in 2001.

In addition, the following Working Groups promote and co-ordinate practical co-operation between member countries in different activities: Agricultural technical co-operation; Energy; Fisheries; Human resources development; Industrial science and technology; Marine resource conservation; Small and medium enterprises (SMEs); Telecommunications and Information; Tourism; Trade promotion; and Transportation. (See below for more detailed information.)

ADVISORY COUNCIL

APEC Business Advisory Council (ABAC): Equitable Card Center Bldg, 8th Floor, 203 Salcedo St, Legaspi Village, Makati City 1229, Philippines; tel. (2) 8436001; fax (2) 8454832; e-mail abacsec@pfgc.ph; internet www.abaconline.org; an agreement to establish ABAC, comprising up to three senior representatives of the private sector from each APEC member economy, was concluded at the Ministerial Meeting held in November 1995. ABAC was mandated to advise member states on the implementation of APEC's Action Agenda and on other business matters, and to provide business-related information to APEC fora. ABAC meets three or four times each year and holds a dialogue with APEC economic leaders prior to their annual informal meeting. ABAC's first meeting, convened in June 1996 in Manila, the Philippines, resolved to accelerate the liberalization of regional trade. In 1998 ABAC focused on measures to alleviate the effects of the financial crisis in Asia, in particular, by enhancing confidence in the private sector, as well as efforts to support SMEs, to develop electronic commerce in the region and to advise on APEC Individual Action Plans (IAPs, see below). In 2000 ABAC addressed the relevance of APEC to the challenges of globalization and, in its annual report to APEC leaders, issued several recommendations, including support for a new round of multilateral trade negotiations; enhancement of the IAP process, with increased implementation of electronic IAPs (e-IAPS); implementation of a proposed food system for member states; the establishment of an APEC Institute of Directors Forum; and the adoption of a regulatory framework conducive to the development of e-commerce. In 2001 ABAC concentrated on the challenges posed by globalization; the

impact on APEC members of the global economic slowdown; and capacity-building in financial systems. ABAC's declared theme for 2002 was Sharing Development to Reinforce Global Security. At a meeting in February the Council considered the relationship between global security and its work to facilitate trade and investment flows. In April ABAC organized a Business on Alert Workshop, which addressed security issues in the business sector. Chair. TIMOTHY ONG TEK MONG (Brunei).

Activities

APEC was initiated in 1989 as a forum for informal discussion between the then six ASEAN members and their six dialogue partners in the Pacific, and, in particular, to promote trade liberalization in the Uruguay Round of negotiations, which were being conducted under the General Agreement on Tariffs and Trade (GATT). The Seoul Declaration, adopted by ministers meeting in the Republic of Korea in November 1991, defined the objectives of APEC.

ASEAN countries were initially reluctant to support any more formal structure of the forum, or to admit new members, owing to concerns that it would undermine ASEAN's standing as a regional grouping and be dominated by powerful non-ASEAN economies. In August 1991 it was agreed to extend membership to the People's Republic of China, Hong Kong and Taiwan (subject to conditions imposed by the People's Republic of China, including that a Taiwanese official of no higher than vice-ministerial level should attend the annual meeting of ministers of foreign affairs). Mexico and Papua New Guinea acceded to the organization in November 1993, and Chile joined in November 1994. The summit meeting held in November 1997 agreed that Peru, Russia and Viet Nam should be admitted to APEC at the 1998 meeting, but imposed a 10-year moratorium on further expansion of the grouping.

In September 1992 APEC ministers agreed to establish a permanent secretariat. In addition, the meeting created an 11-member non-governmental Eminent Persons Group (EPG), which was to assess trade patterns within the region and propose measures to promote co-operation. At the Ministerial Meeting in Seattle, USA, in November 1993, members agreed on a framework for expanding trade and investment among member countries, and to establish a permanent committee (the CTI, see above) to pursue these objectives.

In August 1994 the EPG proposed the following timetable for the liberalization of all trade across the Asia-Pacific region: negotiations for the elimination of trade barriers were to commence in 2000 and be completed within 10 years in developed countries, 15 years in newly-industrialized economies and by 2020 in developing countries. Trade concessions could then be extended on a reciprocal basis to non-members in order to encourage world-wide trade liberalization, rather than isolate APEC as a unique trading bloc. In November 1994 the meeting of APEC heads of government adopted the Bogor Declaration of Common Resolve, which endorsed the EPG's timetable for free and open trade and investment in the region by the year 2020. Other issues incorporated into the Declaration included the implementation of GATT commitments in full and strengthening the multilateral trading system through the forthcoming establishment of the World Trade Organization (WTO), intensifying development co-operation in the Asia-Pacific region and expanding and accelerating trade and investment programmes.

During 1995 meetings of APEC officials and other efforts to substantiate the trade liberalization agreement revealed certain differences among members regarding the timetable and means of implementing the measures, which were to be agreed upon at the 1995 Economic Leaders' Meeting. The principal concern, expressed notably by the USA, focused on whether tariff reductions were to be achieved by individual trade liberalization plans or based on some reciprocal or common approach. In August the EPG issued a report, to be considered at the November Leaders' Meeting, which advocated acceleration of tariff reductions and other trade liberalization measures agreed under GATT; the establishment of a dispute mediation service to reduce and settle regional trade conflicts; and a review of new trade groupings within the APEC region. Further proposals for the implementation of the Bogor Declaration objectives were presented, in September, by the Pacific Business Forum, comprising APEC business representatives. The recommendations included harmonization of product quality, the establishment of one-stop investment agencies in each APEC country, training and technology transfers and the implementation of visa-free business travel by 1999. In November 1995 the Ministerial Meeting decided to dismantle the EPG, and to establish an APEC Business Advisory Council (ABAC), consisting of private-sector representatives.

In November 1995 APEC heads of government, meeting in Osaka, Japan, adopted an Action Agenda as a framework to achieve the commitments of the Bogor Declaration. Part One of the Agenda identified action areas for the liberalization of trade and investment and the facilitation of business, for example, customs procedures, rules of origin and non-tariff barriers. It incorporated agreements that the process was to be comprehensive, consistent with WTO commitments, comparable among all APEC economies and non-discriminatory. Each member economy was to ensure the transparency of its laws, regulations and procedures affecting the flow of goods, services and capital among APEC economies and to refrain from implementing any trade protection measures. A second part of the Agenda was to provide a framework for further economic and technical co-operation between APEC members in areas such as energy, transport, infrastructure, SMEs and agricultural technology. In order to resolve a disagreement concerning the inclusion of agricultural products in the trade liberalization process, a provision for flexibility was incorporated into the Agenda, taking into account diverse circumstances and different levels of development in APEC member economies. Liberalization measures were to be implemented from January 1997 (i.e. three years earlier than previously agreed) and were to be subject to annual reviews. A Trade and Investment Liberalization and Facilitation Special Account was established to finance projects in support of the implementation of the Osaka Action Agenda. In May 1996 APEC senior officials met in Cebu, the Philippines, to review Individual Action Plans—IAPs, annual reports submitted by each member state on progress in the implementation of trade liberalization measures—and to achieve some coherent approach to tariff liberalization prior to the Leaders' Meeting in November.

In November 1996 the Economic Leaders' Meeting, held in Subic Bay, the Philippines, approved the Manila Action Plan for APEC (MAPA), which had been formulated at the preceding Ministerial Meeting, held in Manila. MAPA incorporated the IAPs and other collective measures aimed at achieving the trade liberalization and co-operation objectives of the Bogor Declaration, as well as the joint activities specified in the second part of the Osaka Agenda. Heads of government also endorsed a US proposal to eliminate tariffs and other barriers to trade in information technology products by 2000 and determined to support efforts to conclude an agreement to this effect at the forthcoming WTO conference; however, they insisted on the provision of an element of flexibility in achieving trade liberalization in this sector.

The 1997 Economic Leaders' Meeting, held in Vancouver, Canada, in November, was dominated by concern at the financial instability that had affected several Asian economies during 1997. The final declaration of the summit meeting endorsed a framework of measures that had been agreed by APEC deputy ministers of finance and central bank governors at an emergency meeting convened in the previous week in Manila, the Philippines (the so-called Manila Framework for Enhanced Asian Regional Co-operation to Promote Financial Stability). The meeting, attended by representatives of the IMF, the World Bank and the Asian Development Bank, committed all member economies receiving IMF assistance to undertake specified economic and financial reforms, and supported the establishment of a separate Asian funding facility to supplement international financial assistance (although this was later rejected by the IMF). APEC ministers of finance and governors of central banks were urged to accelerate efforts for the development of the region's financial and capital markets and to liberalize capital flows in the region. Measures were to include strengthening financial market supervision and clearing and settlement infrastructure, the reform of pension systems, and promoting co-operation among export credit agencies and financing institutions. The principal item on the Vancouver summit agenda was an initiative to enhance trade liberalization, which, the grouping insisted, should not be undermined by the financial instability in Asia. The following 15 economic sectors were identified for 'early voluntary sectoral liberalization' ('EVSL'): environmental goods and services; fish and fish products; forest products; medical equipment and instruments; toys; energy; chemicals; gems and jewellery; telecommunications; oilseeds and oilseed products; food; natural and synthetic rubber; fertilizers; automobiles; and civil aircraft. The implementation of EVSL was to encompass market opening, trade facilitation, and economic and technical co-operation activities. The heads of government subsequently requested the authorities in each member state to formulate details of tariff reductions in these sectors by mid-1998, with a view to implementing the measures in 1999. (In June 1998, however, ministers of trade, meeting in Malaysia, failed to conclude an agreement on early tariff reductions, in part owing to Japan's reluctance to liberalize trade in fish and forest products.) In Vancouver APEC Economic Leaders also declared their support for an agreement to liberalize financial services (which was successfully negotiated under the auspices of the WTO in December 1997) and for the objective of reducing the emission of 'greenhouse gases', which was under consideration at a global conference, held in Kyoto, Japan, in December (resulting in the adoption of the Kyoto Protocol to the UN Framework Convention on Climate Change).

In May 1998 APEC finance ministers met in Canada to consider the ongoing financial and economic crisis in Asia and to review progress in implementing efforts to alleviate the difficulties experienced by several member economies. The ministers agreed to pursue

activities in the following three priority areas: capital market development, capital account liberalization and strengthening financial systems (including corporate governance). The region's economic difficulties remained the principal topic of discussion at the Economic Leaders' Meeting held in Kuala Lumpur, Malaysia, in November. A final declaration reiterated their commitment to co-operation in pursuit of sustainable economic recovery and growth, in particular through the restructuring of financial and corporate sectors, promoting and facilitating private-sector capital flows, and efforts to strengthen the global financial system. The meeting endorsed a proposal of ABAC to establish a partnership for equitable growth, with the aim of enhancing business involvement in APEC's programme of economic and technical co-operation. Other initiatives approved included an Agenda of APEC Science and Technology Industry Co-operation into the 21st Century (for which the People's Republic of China announced it was to establish a special fund), and an Action Programme on Skills and Development in APEC. Japan's persisting opposition to a reduction of tariffs in the fish and forestry sectors again prevented the conclusion of tariff negotiations under the EVSL scheme, and it was therefore agreed that responsibility for managing the tariff reduction element of the initiative should be transferred to the WTO. The meeting was divided by political differences regarding human rights and, in particular, the treatment by the Malaysian authorities of the imprisoned former Deputy Prime Minister, Anwar Ibrahim. A declaration of support for the democratic reform movement in Malaysia by the US representative dominated discussions at the start of the summit meeting and provoked a formal complaint from the Malaysian Government.

In September 1999 political dialogue regarding the civil conflict in East Timor (now Timor-Leste) dominated the start of the annual meetings of the grouping, held in Auckland, New Zealand, although the issue remained separate from the official agenda. Ministers of foreign affairs, convened in emergency session, declared their support for the establishment of a multinational force, under UN auspices, to restore peace in the territory and determined to provide humanitarian and technical assistance to facilitate the process of reconstruction and rehabilitation. The Economic Leaders' Meeting considered measures to sustain the economic recovery in Asia and endorsed the APEC Principles to Enhance Competition and Regulatory Reform (for example, transparency, accountability, non-discrimination) as a framework to strengthen APEC markets and to enable further integration and implementation of the IAPs. The meeting endorsed a report prepared during the year by an *ad hoc* task force concerning an ABAC proposal for the development of an APEC food system. Also under discussion was the forthcoming round of multilateral trade negotiations, to be initiated by the WTO. The heads of government proposed the objective of completing a single package of trade agreements within three years and endorsed the abolition of export subsidies for agricultural products. The meeting determined to support the efforts of the People's Republic of China, Russia, Taiwan and Viet Nam to accede to WTO membership.

The Economic Leaders' Meeting for 2000, held in Brunei in November, noted the generally strong recovery from the Asian economic crisis of 1997–98 and reiterated support for APEC's goals. The heads of government urged that an agenda for the now-stalled round of multilateral trade negotiations should be formulated without further delay. The meeting endorsed a plan of action to promote the utilization of advances in information and communications technologies in member economies, for the benefit of all citizens. It adopted the aim of tripling the number of people in the region with access to the internet by 2005, and determined to co-operate with business and education sector interests to attract investment and expertise in the pursuit of this goal. A proposal that the Democratic People's Republic of Korea be permitted to participate in APEC working groups was approved at the meeting.

The 2001 Economic Leaders' Meeting, held in October, in Shanghai, People's Republic of China, condemned the terrorist attacks against targets in the USA of the previous month and resolved to take action to combat the threat of international terrorism. The heads of state declared terrorism to be a direct challenge to APEC's vision of free, open and prosperous economies, and concluded that the threat made the continuing move to free trade, with its aim of bolstering economies, increasing prosperity and encouraging integration, even more of a priority. The meeting stressed the importance of sharing the benefits of globalization. The leaders also expressed their determination to address the effects on APEC countries of the prevailing global economic downturn. They noted that the reforms carried out after the 1997–98 financial crisis had strengthened APEC economies, and advocated timely policy actions in the coming year to rebuild confidence and boost growth. Human capacity-building was a central theme. The heads of state committed support to the launch of the next round of WTO multilateral trade negotiations and applauded the recent successful conclusion of negotiations on WTO membership for the People's Republic of China. The meeting adopted the Shanghai Accord, which identified development goals for APEC during its second decade and clarified measures for achieving the Bogor goals within the agreed timetable.

Among other initiatives, the Accord suggested broadening and updating the Osaka Action Agenda to reflect developments in the new economy. The meeting also outlined the e-APEC Strategy developed by the e-APEC Task Force established after the Brunei Economic Leaders' meeting. Considering issues of entrepreneurship, structural and regulatory reform, competition, intellectual property rights and information security, the strategy aimed to facilitate technological development in the region.

In September 2002 a meeting of APEC ministers of finance was held in Los Cabos, Mexico. Ministers discussed the importance of efforts to combat money-laundering and the financing of terrorism. The meeting also focused on ways to strengthen global and regional economic growth, to advance fiscal and financial reforms and to improve the allocation of domestic savings for economic development. The theme of the 2002 Economic Leaders' Meeting, held in the following month in Los Cabos, Mexico, was 'Expanding the Benefits of Co-operation for Economic Growth and Development— Implementing the Vision'. The Meeting issued a statement on the implementation of APEC standards of transparency in trade and investment liberalization and facilitation.

WORKING GROUPS

APEC's structure of working groups aims to promote practical and technical co-operation in specific areas, and to help implement individual and collective action plans in response to the directives of the Economic Leaders and meetings of relevant ministers. APEC recognizes sustainable development as a key issue cross-cutting all forum activities. In 1997 APEC leaders declared their commitment to the integration of women into the mainstream of APEC activities.

Agricultural Technical Co-operation: Formally established as an APEC Expert's Group in 1996, and incorporated into the system of working groups in 2000. The group aims to enhance the role of agriculture in the economic growth of the region and to promote co-operation in the following areas: conservation and utilization of plant and animal genetic resources; research, development and extension of agricultural biotechnology; processing, marketing, distribution and consumption of agricultural products; plant and animal quarantine and pest management; development of an agricultural finance system; sustainable agriculture; and agricultural technology transfer and training. The group has primary responsibility for undertaking recommendations connected with the implementation of the proposed APEC food system. In 2001 the group conducted projects on human resource development in post-harvest technology and on capacity-building, safety assessment and communication in biotechnology.

Energy: Responsible for the development of the energy component of the 1995 Action Agenda. APEC ministers responsible for energy convened for the first time in 1996 to discuss major energy challenges confronting the region and to provide guidance for the working group. The group's main objectives were determined as: the enhancement of regional energy security and improvement of the fuel supply market for the power sector; the development and implementation of programmes of work promoting the adoption of environmentally sound energy technologies and promoting private-sector investment in regional power infrastructure; the development of energy efficiency guide-lines; and the standardization of testing facilities and results. In March 1999 the group resolved to establish a business network to improve relations and communications with the private sector. The first meeting of the network took place in April. In October 1998 APEC energy ministers, meeting in Okinawa, Japan, emphasized the role of the energy sector in stimulating economic activity and stressed the need to develop infrastructure, improve energy efficiency and accelerate the development of natural gas reserves. In May 2000 ministers meeting in San Diego, USA, launched the APEC 21st Century Renewable Energy Initiative, which aims to encourage co-operation in and advance the utilization of renewable energy technologies, envisaging the establishment of a Private Sector Renewable Energy Forum.

Fisheries: Aims to maximize the economic benefits and sustainability of fisheries resources for all APEC members. Recent concerns include food safety, the quality of fish products and resource management. In 1996 the group initiated a four-year study on trade and investment liberalization in the sector, in the areas of tariffs, non-tariff barriers and investment measures and subsidies. In 1997 the group organized two technical workshops on seafood inspection systems, and conducted a workshop addressing destructive fishing techniques. The first APEC Aquaculture Forum, which considered the sustainable development of aquaculture in the region and the development of new markets for APEC fish products, was held in Taipei, Taiwan, in June 1998. In May 1999 new guide-lines were adopted to encourage the participation of the private sector in the activities of the working group. The group's first business forum was convened in July 2000.

Human Resources Development: Comprises three networks promoting co-operation in different areas of human resources, training

and education: the Capacity Building Network, with a focus on human capacity building, including management and technical skills development and corporate governance; the Education Network, promoting effective learning systems and supporting the role of education in advancing individual, social and economic development; and the Labour and Social Protection Network, concerned with promoting social integration through the strengthening of labour markets, the development of labour market information and policy, and improvements in working conditions and social safety net frameworks. The working group undertakes activities through these networks to implement ministerial and leaders' directives, as well as the 'Medium Term Strategic Priorities', which were formulated in January 1997. A voluntary network of APEC Study Centers links higher education and research institutions in member economies. In January 1998 the working group established a Task Force on the Human Resource and Social Impacts of the Financial Crisis. Private-sector participation in the working group has been strengthened by the establishment of a network of APEC senior executives responsible for human resources management. Recent activities have included programmes on information technology in the learning society; the implementation of standards and accreditation in supply chain management; and child labour.

Industrial Science and Technology: Aims to contribute to sustainable development in the region, improve the availability of information, enhance human resources development in the sector, improve the business climate, promote policy dialogue and review and facilitate networks and partnerships. Accordingly, the group has helped to establish an APEC Virtual Centre for Environmental Technology Exchange in Japan; a Science and Technology Industrial Parks Network; an International Molecular Biology Network for the APEC Region; an APEC Centre for Technology Foresight, based in Thailand; and the APEC Science and Technology Web, an online database. In 2001 the group worked on developing a Strategy to Combat HIV/AIDS and Other Infectious Diseases, as requested by the Economic Leaders' meeting in 2000. A dialogue on the subject was initiated with the World Health Organization.

Marine Resource Conservation: Promotes initiatives within APEC to protect the marine environment and its resources. In 1996 a five-year project was initiated for the management of red tide and harmful algal blooms in the APEC region. An APEC Action Plan for Sustainability of the Marine Environment was adopted by ministers responsible for the environment, meeting in June 1997. The Plan aimed to promote regional co-operation, an integrated approach to coastal management, the prevention, reduction and control of marine pollution, and sustainable development. Efforts were also being undertaken to establish an Ocean Research Network of centres of excellence in the Pacific. In December 1997 the group organized a workshop, in Hong Kong, on the impact of destructive fishing practices on the marine environment. A workshop was held in Australia, in April 1998, on preventing maritime accidents and pollution in the Pacific region. In April 1999 the group organized a training course, held in Hong Kong, on the satellite remote sensing of algal blooms. Strategies to encourage private-sector participation in promoting the sustainable management of marine resources were endorsed by the group in June 2000. Four main themes were identified for the Action Plan in the 21st century: balancing coastal development and resource protection; ensuring sustainable fisheries and aquaculture; understanding and observing the oceans and seas; and promoting economic and technical co-operation in oceans management.

Small and Medium Enterprises: The group was established in 1995, as the Ad Hoc Policy Level Group on Small and Medium Enterprises, with a temporary mandate to oversee all APEC activities relating to SMEs. It supported the establishment of an APEC Centre for Technical Exchange and Training for Small and Medium Enterprises, which was inaugurated at Los Baños, near Manila, the Philippines, in September 1996. A five-year action plan for SMEs was endorsed in 1998. The group was resdesignated as a working group, with permanent status, in 2000. In 2000 and 2001 the group considered issues relating to globalization, innovation, human resource development, information technology and e-commerce, financing, and the forming of strategic alliances with other SMEs and larger firms.

Telecommunications and Information: Incorporates four steering groups concerned with different aspects of the development and liberalization of the sector—Liberalization; Business facilitation; Development co-operation; and Human resource development. Activities are guided by directives of ministers responsible for telecommunications, who first met in 1995, in the Republic of Korea, and adopted a Seoul Declaration on Asia Pacific Information Infrastructure (APII). The second ministerial meeting, held in Gold Coast, Australia, in September 1996, adopted more detailed proposals for liberalization of the sector in member economies. In June 1998 ministers, meeting in Singapore, agreed to remove technical barriers to trade in telecommunications equipment (although Chile and New Zealand declined to sign up to the arrangement). At their fourth meeting, convened in May 2000 in Cancún, Mexico, telecommunications ministers approved a programme of action that included measures to bridge the 'digital divide' between developed and developing member economies, and adopted the APEC Principles on International Charging Arrangements for Internet Services and the APEC Principles of Interconnection.

Tourism: Established in 1991, with the aim of promoting the long-term sustainability of the tourism industry, in both environmental and social terms. The group administers a Tourism Information Network and an APEC Centre for Sustainable Tourism. In 1998 the group initiated a project to assess the impact of the Asian financial crisis on regional tourism and to identify strategies to counter any negative effects. The first meeting of APEC ministers of tourism, held in the Republic of Korea in July 2000, adopted the Seoul Declaration on the APEC Tourism Charter. The group's work plan is based on four policy goals inherent in the Seoul Declaration, namely, the removal of impediments to tourism business and investment; increased mobility of visitors and increased demand for tourism goods and services; sustainable management of tourism; and enhanced recognition of tourism as a vehicle for economic and social development. At a meeting of the working group in April 2001, APEC and the Pacific Asia Travel Association (PATA) adopted a Code for Sustainable Tourism. The Code is designed for adoption and implementation by a variety of tourism companies and government agencies. It urges members to conserve the natural environment, ecosystems and biodiversity; respect local traditions and cultures; conserve energy; reduce pollution and waste; and ensure that regular environmental audits are carried out. In November 2001 the working group considered the impact on tourism of the September terrorist attacks on the USA. The group noted that while the short-term negative effects could be substantial, a return to long-term growth could be expected in the following year. The group advocated work to improve the quality and timeliness of tourism data, to enable accurate assessment of the situation. In July 2002 APEC ministers of tourism met for the second time, in Manzanillo, Mexico, and adopted a declaration that reiterated the importance of tourism to regional economies.

Trade Promotion: Aims to promote trade, as a key aspect of regional economic co-operation, through activities to enhance trade financing, skills and training, information and networking (for example, through the establishment of APEC Net, providing information to the business community via the internet, accessible at www.apecnet.org.sg), and co-operation with the private sector and public agencies, including trade promotion organizations. Organizes an APEC International Trade Fair, the fourth of which was held in Jakarta, Indonesia, in October 2000.

Transportation: Undertakes initiatives to enhance the efficiency and safety of the regional transportation system, in order to facilitate the development of trade. The working group focuses on three main areas: improving the competitiveness of the transportation industry; promoting a safe and environmentally-sound regional transportation system; and human resources development, including training, research and education. The group has published surveys, directories and manuals on all types of transportation systems, and has compiled an inventory on regional co-operation on oil spills preparedness and response arrangements. A Road Transportation Harmonization Project aims to provide the basis for common standards in the automotive industry in the Asia-Pacific region. The group has established an internet database on ports and the internet-based Virtual Centre for Transportation Research, Development and Education. It plans to develop a regional action plan on the implementation of Global Navigation Satellite Systems, in consultation with the relevant international bodies.

Publications

ABAC Report to APEC Leaders (annually).

APEC Economic Outlook (annually).

APEC Economies Beyond the Asian Crisis.

APEC Energy Handbook (annually).

APEC Energy Statistics (annually).

Foreign Direct Investment and APEC Economic Integration (irregular).

Guide to the Investment Regimes of the APEC Member Economies.

Key APEC Documents (annually).

The State of Economic and Technical Co-operation in APEC.

Towards Knowledge-based Economies in APEC.

Trade and Investment Liberalization in APEC.

Working group reports, regional directories, other irregular surveys.

ASIAN DEVELOPMENT BANK—ADB

Address: 6 ADB Ave, Mandaluyong City, 0401 Metro Manila, Philippines; POB 789, 0980 Manila, Philippines.

Telephone: (2) 6324444; **fax:** (2) 6362444; **e-mail:** information@adb.org; **internet:** www.adb.org.

The ADB commenced operations in December 1966. The Bank's principal functions are to provide loans and equity investments for the economic and social advancement of its developing member countries, to give technical assistance for the preparation and implementation of development projects and programmes and advisory services, to promote investment of public and private capital for development purposes, and to respond to requests from developing member countries for assistance in the co-ordination of their development policies and plans.

MEMBERS

There are 44 member countries and territories within the ESCAP region and 17 others (see list of subscriptions below).

Organization

(April 2003)

BOARD OF GOVERNORS

All powers of the Bank are vested in the Board, which may delegate its powers to the Board of Directors except in such matters as admission of new members, changes in the Bank's authorized capital stock, election of Directors and President, and amendment of the Charter. One Governor and one Alternate Governor are appointed by each member country. The Board meets at least once a year.

BOARD OF DIRECTORS

The Board of Directors is responsible for general direction of operations and exercises all powers delegated by the Board of Governors, which elects it. Of the 12 Directors, eight represent constituency groups of member countries within the ESCAP region (with about 65% of the voting power) and four represent the rest of the member countries. Each Director serves for two years and may be re-elected.

Three specialized committees (the Audit Committee, the Budget Review Committee and the Inspection Committee), each comprising six members, assist the Board of Directors in exercising its authority with regard to supervising the Bank's financial statements, approving the administrative budget, and reviewing and approving policy documents and assistance operations.

The President of the Bank, though not a Director, is Chairman of the Board.

Chairman of Board of Directors and President: TADAO CHINO (Japan).

Vice-Presidents: JOSEPH B. EICHENBERGER (USA), JOHN LINTJER (Netherlands), MYOUNG-HO SHIN (Republic of Korea).

ADMINISTRATION

The Bank had 2,163 staff at 31 December 2001.

On 1 January 2002 the Bank implemented a new organizational structure, which had been under review in 2001. The reorganization aimed to strengthen the Bank's country and sub-regional focus, as well as its capacity for poverty reduction and implementing its long-term strategic framework. Five regional departments cover East and Central Asia, the Mekong, the Pacific, South Asia, and South East Asia. Other departments and offices include Private Sector Operations, Central Operations Services, Regional and Sustainable Development, Strategy and Policy, Cofinancing Operations, and Economics and Research, as well as other administrative units.

There are Bank Resident Missions in Bangladesh, Cambodia, the People's Republic of China, India, Indonesia, Kazakhstan, Kyrgyzstan, Laos, Mongolia, Nepal, Pakistan, Sri Lanka, Uzbekistan and Viet Nam, all of which report to the head of the regional department. In addition, there is a country office in the Philippines and there are Extended Missions in Gujarat, India and in Papua New Guinea, Special Liaison Offices in Timor-Leste and Afghanistan, and a South Pacific Regional Mission, based in Vanuatu. Representative Offices are located in Tokyo, Japan, Frankfurt am Main, Germany (for Europe), and Washington, DC, USA (for North America).

Secretary: BINDU N. LOHANI.

General Counsel: ARTHUR M. MITCHELL.

INSTITUTE

ADB Institute—ADBI: Kasumigaseki Bldg, 8th Floor, 2–5 Kasumigaseki 3-chome, Chiyoda-ku, Tokyo 100-6008, Japan; tel. (3) 3593-5500; fax (3) 3593-5571; e-mail info@adbi.org; internet www .adbi.org; f. 1997 as a subsidiary body of the ADB to research and analyse long-term development issues and to disseminate development practices through training and other capacity-building activities; Dean Dr PETER McCAWLEY (Australia).

FINANCIAL STRUCTURE

The Bank's ordinary capital resources (which are used for loans to the more advanced developing member countries) are held and used entirely separately from its Special Funds resources (see below). A fourth General Capital Increase (GCI IV), amounting to US $26,318m. (or some 100%), was authorized in May 1994. At the final deadline for subscription to GCI IV, on 30 September 1996, 55 member countries had subscribed shares amounting to $24,675.4m.

At 31 December 2001 the position of subscriptions to the capital stock was as follows: authorized US $43,834m.; subscribed $43,628m.

The Bank also borrows funds from the world capital markets. Total borrowings during 2001 amounted to US $1,607m. (compared with $1,693m. in 2000). At 31 December 2001 total outstanding borrowings amounted to $24,880.8m.

In July 1986 the Bank abolished the system of fixed lending rates, under which ordinary operations loans had carried interest rates fixed at the time of loan commitment for the entire life of the loan. Under the new system the lending rate is adjusted every six months, to take into account changing conditions in international financial markets.

SPECIAL FUNDS

The Asian Development Fund (ADF) was established in 1974 in order to provide a systematic mechanism for mobilizing and administering resources for the Bank to lend on concessionary terms to the least-developed member countries. In 1998 the Bank revised the terms of ADF. Since 1 January 1999 all new project loans are repayable within 32 years, including an eight-year grace period, while quick-disbursing programme loans have a 24-year maturity, also including an eight-year grace period. The previous annual service charge was redesignated as an interest charge, including a portion to cover administrative expenses. The new interest charges on all loans are 1%–1.5% per annum. At 31 December 2001 total ADF loans approved amounted to US $25,714m. for 917 loans, while cumulative disbursements from ADF resources totalled $17,552m.

Successive replenishments of the Fund's resources amounted to US $809m. for the period 1976–78, $2,150m. for 1979–82, $3,214m. for 1983–86, $3,600m. for 1987–90, $4,200m. for 1992–95, and $6,300m. for 1997–2000. In September 2000 25 donor countries pledged $2,910m. towards the ADF's seventh replenishment (ADF VIII), which totalled $5,650m. to provide resources for the period 2001–04; repayments of earlier ADF loans were to provide the remaining $2,740m. ADF VIII became effective in June 2001.

The Bank provides technical assistance grants from its Technical Assistance Special Fund (TASF). By the end of 2001, the Fund's total resources amounted to US $911.0m., of which $829.7m. had been utilized or committed. The Japan Special Fund (JSF) was established in 1988 to provide finance for technical assistance by means of grants, in both the public and private sectors. The JSF aims to help developing member countries restructure their economies, enhance the opportunities for attracting new investment, and recycle funds. The Japanese Government had committed a total of 94,300m. yen (equivalent to some $813.5m.) to the JSF by the end of 2001 (of which $774.2m. had been utilized). In March 1999 an Asian Currency Crisis Support Facility (ACCSF) was established, for a three-year period, as an independent component of the JSF to provide additional technical assistance, interest payment assistance and guarantees to countries most affected by financial instability, i.e. Indonesia, Republic of Korea, Malaysia, Philippines and Thailand. At the end of 2001 the Japanese Government, as the sole financier of the fund, had contributed 27,500m. yen (some $241.0m.) to the new Facility. The Japanese Government also funds the Japan Scholarship Program, under which 1,334 scholarships had been awarded to recipients from 34 member countries between 1988 and 2001, and the

ADB Institute Special Fund, which was established to finance the initial operations of the new Institute (see above). By 31 December 2001 cumulative commitments to the Special Fund amounted to 7,500m. yen (or $61.5m.). In May 2000 the Japan Fund for Poverty Reduction was established, with an initial contribution of 10,000m. yen (approximately $92.6m.), supplemented in 2001 by an additional 7,900m. yen, of $65.0m.) from the Japanese Government, to support ADB-financed poverty reduction and social development activities. A Japan Fund for Information and Community Technology (ICT) was established in July 2001, for a three-year period, to promote the development and use of ICT in developing member countries. The Fund was established with an initial contribution of 1,273m. yen (or $10.7m.) from the Japanese Government.

The majority of grant funds in support of the Bank's technical assistance activities are provided by bilateral donors under channel financing arrangements (CFAs). Since 1980, when the first CFA was negotiated, 151 technical assistance grants had been financed under CFAs at the end of 2001, with a total value of $73.7m. CFAs may also be processed as a thematic financing tool, for example concerned with renewable energy, water or poverty reduction, enabling more than one donor to contribute.

Activities

Loans by the ADB are usually aimed at specific projects. In responding to requests from member governments for loans, the Bank's staff assesses the financial and economic viability of projects and the way in which they fit into the economic framework and priorities of development of the country concerned. In 1987 the Bank adopted a policy of lending in support of programmes of sectoral adjustment, not limited to specific projects; such loans were not to exceed 15% of total Bank public sector lending. In 1999 the Board of Directors increased the ceiling on programme lending to 20% of the annual total. In 1985 the Bank decided to expand its assistance to the private sector, hitherto comprising loans to development finance institutions, under government guarantee, for lending to small and medium-sized enterprises; a programme was formulated for direct financial assistance, in the form of equity and loans without government guarantee, to private enterprises. In 1992 a Social Dimensions Unit was established as part of the central administrative structure of the Bank, which contributed to the Bank's increasing awareness of the importance of social aspects of development as essential components of sustainable economic growth. During the early 1990s the Bank also aimed to expand its role as project financier by providing assistance for policy formulation and review and promoting regional co-operation, while placing greater emphasis on individual country requirements. In accordance with its medium-term strategy for 1995–98 the Bank resolved to promote sound development management, by integrating into its operations and projects the promotion of governance issues, such as capacity-building, legal frameworks and openness of information. During that period the Bank also introduced a commitment to assess development projects for their impact on the local population and to avoid all involuntary resettlement where possible and established a formal procedure for grievances, under which the Board may authorize an inspection of a project, by an independent panel of experts, at the request of the affected community or group. In 1998 the Bank approved a new anticorruption strategy.

The currency instability and ensuing financial crises affecting many Asian economies in the second half of 1997 and in 1998 prompted the Bank to reflect on its role in the region. The Bank resolved to strengthen its activities as a broad-based development institution, rather than solely as a project financier, through lending policies, dialogue, co-financing and technical assistance. A Task Force on Financial Sector Reform was established to review the causes and effects of the regional financial crisis. The Task Force identified the Bank's initial priorities as being to accelerate banking and capital market reforms in member countries, to promote market efficiency in the financial, trade and industrial sectors, to promote good governance and sound corporate management, and to alleviate the social impact of structural adjustments. In mid-1999 the Bank approved a technical assistance grant to establish an internet-based Asian Recovery Information Centre, within a new Regional Monitoring Unit, which aimed to facilitate access to information regarding the economic and social impact of the Asian financial crisis, analyses of economic needs of countries, reform programmes and monitoring of the economic recovery process. In November the Board of Directors approved a new overall strategy objective of poverty reduction, which was to be the principal consideration for all future Bank lending, project financing and technical assistance. The strategy incorporated key aims of supporting sustainable, grass-roots based economic growth, social development and good governance. The Board also approved a health sector policy, to concentrate resources on basic primary healthcare, and initiated reviews of the Bank's private sector strategy and the efficiency of resident missions. During 2000 the Bank began to refocus its country strategies, projects and lending targets to complement the poverty reduction strategy. In addition, it initiated a process of wide-ranging discussions to formulate a long-term strategic framework for the next 15 years, based on the target of reducing by 50% the incidence of extreme poverty by 2015. The framework, establishing the operational priorities and principles for reducing poverty, was approved in March 2001. At the same time a medium-term strategy, for the period 2001–05, was approved, which aimed to enhance the development impact of the Bank's assistance and to define the operational priorities within the context of the strategic agenda.

SUBSCRIPTIONS AND VOTING POWER*
(31 December 2001)

Country	Subscribed capital (% of total)	Voting power (% of total)
Regional:		
Afghanistan	0.034	0.366
Australia	5.892	5.053
Azerbaijan	0.453	0.701
Bangladesh	1.040	1.171
Bhutan	0.006	0.344
Cambodia	10.050	0.379
China, People's Republic	6.562	5.588
Cook Islands	0.003	0.341
Fiji	0.069	0.394
Hong Kong	0.555	0.783
India	6.447	5.497
Indonesia	5.546	4.776
Japan	15.893	13.053
Kazakhstan	0.821	0.996
Kiribati	0.004	0.342
Korea, Republic	5.130	4.443
Kyrgyzstan	0.305	0.583
Laos	0.014	0.350
Malaysia	2.773	2.557
Maldives	0.004	0.342
Marshall Islands	0.003	0.341
Micronesia, Federated States	0.004	0.342
Mongolia	0.015	0.351
Myanmar	0.555	0.783
Nauru	0.004	0.342
Nepal	0.150	0.459
New Zealand	1.564	1.590
Pakistan	2.218	2.114
Papua New Guinea	0.096	0.415
Philippines	2.426	2.280
Samoa	0.003	0.342
Singapore	0.347	0.616
Solomon Islands	0.007	0.344
Sri Lanka	0.591	0.811
Taiwan	1.109	1.226
Tajikistan	0.292	0.572
Thailand	1.386	1.448
Tonga	0.004	0.342
Turkmenistan	0.258	0.545
Tuvalu	0.001	0.340
Uzbekistan	0.686	0.888
Vanuatu	0.007	0.344
Viet Nam	0.348	0.617
Sub-total	63.674	65.515
Non-regional:		
Austria	0.347	0.616
Belgium	0.347	0.616
Canada	5.327	4.600
Denmark	0.347	0.616
Finland	0.347	0.616
France	2.370	2.235
Germany	4.405	3.863
Italy	1.840	1.811
Netherlands	1.045	1.175
Norway	0.347	0.616
Spain	0.347	0.616
Sweden	0.347	0.616
Switzerland	0.594	0.814
Turkey	0.347	0.616
United Kingdom	2.080	2.003
USA	15.893	13.053
Sub-total	36.326	34.485
Total	100.000	100.000

*Portugal was admitted as a non-regional member of the Bank in April 2002; Timor-Leste became the Bank's 61st member in July.

In 2001 the Bank approved 76 loans in 60 projects amounting to US $5,339.0m. (compared with $5,653m. for 74 projects in 2000). Loans from ordinary capital resources in 2001 totalled $3,977.4m., while loans from the ADF amounted to $1,361.6m. Private-sector operations approved amounted to $67.9m., which included direct loans without government guarantee of $37.5m. and equity investments of $30.4m. The largest proportion of assistance, amounting to some 27% of total lending, was allocated to transport and communications projects. Disbursements of loans during 2001 amounted to $3,873.9m., bringing cumulative disbursements to $62,168.0m.

In 2001 grants approved for technical assistance (e.g. project preparation, consultant services and training) amounted to US $146.4m. for 257 projects, with $59.8m. deriving from the Bank's ordinary resources and the TASF, $53.8m. from the JSF, $16.1m. from the ACCSF, and $16.7m. from bilateral and multilateral sources. The Bank's Operations Evaluation Office prepares reports on completed projects, in order to assess achievements and problems. In April 2000 the Bank announced that, from 2001, some new loans would be denominated in local currencies, in order to ease the repayment burden on recipient economies.

The Bank co-operates with other international organizations active in the region, particularly the World Bank group, the IMF, UNDP and APEC, and participates in meetings of aid donors for developing member countries. In May 2001 the Bank and UNDP signed a memorandum of understanding (MOU) on strategic partnership, in order to strengthen co-operation in the reduction of poverty, for example the preparation of common country assessments and a common database on poverty and other social indicators. Also in 2001 the Bank signed an MOU with the World Bank on administrative arrangements for co-operation, providing a framework for closer co-operation and more efficient use of resources. In early 2002 the Bank worked with the World Bank and UNDP to assess the preliminary needs of the interim administration in Afghanistan, in preparation for an International Conference on Reconstruction Assistance to Afghanistan, held in late January, in Tokyo. The Bank pledged to work with its member governments to provide highly concessional grants and loans of some US $500m., with a particular focus on road reconstruction, basic education, and agricultural irrigation rehabilitation. A new policy concerning co-operation with non-governmental organizations (NGOs) was approved by the Bank in 1998. During 2001 57% of the public sector projects were prepared with NGO involvement.

Finance

Internal administrative expenses amounted to US $220.7m. in 2001, and were projected to total $240.0m. in 2002.

Publications

ADB Business Opportunities (monthly).

ADB Institute Newsletter.

ADB Review (6 a year).

Annual Report.

Asian Development Outlook (annually).

Asian Development Review (2 a year).

Basic Statistics (annually).

Key Indicators of Developing Asian and Pacific Countries (annually).

Law and Policy Reform Bulletin (annually).

Loan Disbursement Handbook.

Studies and technical assistance reports, information brochures, guide-lines, sample bidding documents, staff papers.

Statistics

BANK ACTIVITIES BY SECTOR

	Loan Approvals (US $ million)		
	2001		1968–2001
Sector	Amount	%	%
Agriculture and natural resources	603.48	11.30	18.34
Energy	662.90	12.42	20.87
Finance	565.02	10.58	14.53
Industry and non-fuel minerals	86.00	1.61	3.47
Social infrastructure	492.10	9.22	16.10
Transport and communications	1,425.50	26.70	20.17
Multi-sector and others	1,504.00	28.17	6.51
Total	5,339.00	100.00	100.00

LENDING ACTIVITIES BY COUNTRY (US $ million)

Country	Loans approved in 2001		
	Ordinary Capital	ADF	Total
Bangladesh	138.70	159.20	297.90
Bhutan	—	7.00	7.00
Cambodia	—	75.20	75.20
China, People's Republic. . .	997.00	—	997.00
India	1,500.00	—	1,500.00
Indonesia	400.00	100.00	500.00
Kyrgyzstan	—	75.00	75.00
Laos	—	65.00	65.00
Maldives	—	17.50	17.50
Marshall Islands	4.00	8.00	12.00
Micronesia, Federated States .	—	13.02	13.02
Mongolia.	—	35.69	35.69
Nepal	—	95.60	95.60
Pakistan	593.20	363.60	956.80
Papua New Guinea	70.00	5.90	75.90
Philippines	105.00	—	105.00
Samoa	—	6.00	6.00
Sri Lanka	60.00	86.00	146.00
Tajikistan	—	3.60	3.60
Uzbekistan	72.00	—	72.00
Viet Nam	17.50	243.09	260.59
Regional	20.00	—	20.00
Total	3,977.40	1,361.60	5,339.00

LENDING ACTIVITIES
(in %)

Country	1993–97		1998–2001	
	Ordinary Capital	ADF	Ordinary Capital	ADF
Bangladesh	0.2	21.2	1.8	15.9
Bhutan	—	0.3	—	0.8
Cambodia	—	2.5	—	5.4
China, People's Republic .	23.4	—	25.5	—
Cook Islands	—	0.2	—	0.0
Fiji	0.2	—	—	—
India	13.0	—	20.8	—
Indonesia	22.2	3.7	22.9	5.3
Kazakhstan	1.6	0.8	0.3	—
Kiribati	—	—	—	0.2
Korea, Republic	18.4	—	—	—
Kyrgyzstan	—	3.5	—	5.5
Laos	—	5.8	—	3.4
Malaysia	0.9	—	—	—
Maldives	—	0.2	—	0.6
Marshall Islands	—	0.5	0.0	0.5
Micronesia, Federated States	—	0.5	—	0.4
Mongolia	—	4.8	—	2.6
Nauru	—	—	0.0	—
Nepal	0.2	5.2	—	8.5
Pakistan	4.1	20.5	8.0	14.3
Papua New Guinea . . .	0.2	0.6	1.1	1.0
Philippines	6.7	3.1	9.2	0.2
Samoa	—	0.0	—	0.5
Solomon Islands	—	0.0	—	0.7
Sri Lanka	0.0	7.8	0.8	12.2
Tajikistan	—	—	—	2.1
Thailand	8.5	—	5.9	—
Tonga	—	0.2	—	—
Tuvalu	—	—	—	0.1
Uzbekistan	0.3	0.3	2.2	—
Vanuatu	—	0.1	—	0.4
Viet Nam	0.1	18.2	0.6	15.4
Regional	—	—	0.9	4.0
Total	100.0	100.0	100.0	100.0
Value (US $ million) . .	21,828.8	7,139.5	16,941.0	5,011.7

Source: *ADB Annual Report 2001.*

ASSOCIATION OF SOUTH EAST ASIAN NATIONS— ASEAN

Address: 70A Jalan Sisingamangaraja, POB 2072, Jakarta 12110, Indonesia.

Telephone: (21) 7262991; **fax:** (21) 7398234; **e-mail:** public@asean .or.id; **internet:** www.aseansec.org.

ASEAN was established in August 1967 in Bangkok, Thailand, to accelerate economic progress and to increase the stability of the South-East Asian region.

MEMBERS

Brunei	Malaysia	Singapore
Cambodia	Myanmar	Thailand
Indonesia	Philippines	Viet Nam
Laos		

Organization

(April 2003)

SUMMIT MEETING

The highest authority of ASEAN, bringing together the heads of government of member countries. The first meeting was held in Bali, Indonesia, in February 1976. The 30th anniversary of the founding of ASEAN was commemorated at an informal gathering of heads of government in Kuala Lumpur, Malaysia, in December 1997. The sixth summit meeting was convened in Hanoi, Viet Nam, in December 1998 and informal summit meetings were held in Manila, Philippines, in November 1999 and in Singapore, in November 2000. The seventh summit meeting took place in Bandar Seri Begawan, Brunei, in November 2001. The eighth meeting was held in Phnom-Penh, Cambodia, in November 2002.

MINISTERIAL MEETINGS

The ASEAN Ministerial Meeting (AMM), comprising ministers of foreign affairs of member states, meets annually, in each member country in turn, to formulate policy guide-lines and to co-ordinate ASEAN activities. These meetings are followed by 'post-ministerial conferences' (PMCs), where ASEAN ministers of foreign affairs meet with their counterparts from countries that are 'dialogue partners' as well as with ministers from other countries. Ministers of economic affairs also meet once a year, to direct ASEAN economic co-operation. Joint Ministerial Meetings, consisting of ministers of foreign affairs and of economic affairs are convened prior to a summit meeting, and may be held at the request of either group of ministers. Other ministers meet regularly to promote co-operation in different sectors.

STANDING COMMITTEE

The Standing Committee normally meets every two months. It consists of the minister of foreign affairs of the host country and ambassadors of the other members accredited to the host country.

SECRETARIATS

A permanent secretariat was established in Jakarta, Indonesia, in 1976 to form a central co-ordinating body. The Secretariat comprises four bureaux relating to: Programme Co-ordination and External Relations; Trade, Industry and Services; Investment, Finance and Surveillance; and Economic and Functional Co-operation. The Secretary-General holds office for a five-year term, and is assisted by two Deputy Secretaries-General. In each member country day-to-day work is co-ordinated by an ASEAN National Secretariat.

Secretary-General: Ong Keng Yong (Singapore).

Deputy Secretaries-General: Tran Duc Minh (Viet Nam), Ahmad Mokhtar Selat (Malaysia).

COMMITTEES AND SENIOR OFFICIALS' MEETINGS

Ministerial meetings are serviced by 29 committees of senior officials, supported by 122 technical working groups. There is a network of subsidiary technical bodies comprising sub-committees, expert groups, *ad hoc* working groups and working parties.

To support the conduct of relations with other countries and international organizations, ASEAN committees (composed of heads of diplomatic missions) have been established in 14 foreign capitals: those of Australia, Belgium, Canada, the People's Republic of China, France, India, Japan, the Republic of Korea, New Zealand, Pakistan, Russia, Switzerland, the United Kingdom and the USA. There is also an ASEAN committee in New York (USA).

Activities

ASEAN was established in 1967 with the signing of the ASEAN Declaration, otherwise known as the Bangkok Declaration, by the ministers of foreign affairs of Indonesia, Malaysia, the Philippines, Singapore and Thailand. Brunei joined the organization in January 1984, shortly after attaining independence. Viet Nam was admitted as the seventh member of ASEAN in July 1995. Laos and Myanmar joined in July 1997 and Cambodia was formally admitted in April 1999, fulfilling the organization's ambition to incorporate all 10 countries in the sub-region.

TRADE AND ECONOMIC CO-OPERATION

A Basic Agreement on the Establishment of ASEAN Preferential Trade Arrangements was concluded in 1977, but by mid-1987 the system covered only about 5% of trade between member states, since individual countries were permitted to exclude any 'sensitive' products from preferential import tariffs. In December 1987 the meeting of ASEAN heads of government resolved to reduce such exclusions to a maximum of 10% of the number of items traded and to a maximum of 50% of the value of trade, over the next five years (seven years for Indonesia and the Philippines).

In January 1992 heads of government, meeting in Singapore, signed an agreement to create an 'ASEAN Free Trade Area' (AFTA) by 2008. In accordance with the agreement, a common effective preferential tariff (CEPT) scheme came into effect in January 1993. The CEPT covered all manufactured products, including capital goods, and processed agricultural products (which together accounted for two-thirds of intra-ASEAN trade), but was to exclude unprocessed agricultural products. Tariffs were to be reduced to a maximum of 20% within a period of five to eight years and to 0%–5% during the subsequent seven to 10 years. Fifteen categories were designated for accelerated tariff reduction, including vegetable oils, rubber products, textiles, cement and pharmaceuticals. Member states were, however, still to be permitted exclusion for certain 'sensitive' products. In October 1993 ASEAN trade ministers agreed to modify the CEPT, with only Malaysia and Singapore having adhered to the original tariff reduction schedule. The new AFTA programme, under which all member countries except Brunei were scheduled to begin tariff reductions from 1 January 1994, substantially enlarged the number of products to be included in the tariff-reduction process (i.e. on the so-called 'inclusion list') and reduced the list of products eligible for protection. In September 1994 ASEAN ministers of economic affairs agreed to accelerate the implementation of AFTA, advancing the deadline for its entry into operation from 2008 to 1 January 2003. Tariffs were to be reduced to 0%–5% within seven to 10 years, or within five to eight years for products designated for accelerated tariff cuts. In July 1995 Viet Nam was admitted as a member of ASEAN and was granted until 2006 to implement the AFTA trade agreements. In December 1995 heads of government, at a meeting convened in Bangkok, agreed to extend liberalization to certain service industries, including banking, telecommunications and tourism. In July 1997 Laos and Myanmar became members of ASEAN and were granted a 10-year period, from 1 January 1998, to comply with the AFTA schedule.

In December 1998, meeting in Hanoi, Viet Nam, heads of government approved a Statement on Bold Measures, detailing ASEAN's strategies to deal with the economic crisis that had prevailed in the region since late 1997. These included incentives to attract investors, for example a three-year exemption on corporate taxation, accelerated implementation of the ASEAN Investment Area (AIA, see below), and advancing the AFTA deadline, for the original six members, to 2002, with some 85% of products to be covered by the arrangements by 2000, and 90% by 2001. It was envisaged that the original six members and the new members would achieve the elimination of all tariffs by 2015 and 2018, respectively. The Hanoi Plan of Action, which was also adopted at the meeting as a framework for the development of the organization over the period 1999–2004, incorporated a series of measures aimed at strengthening macroeconomic and financial co-operation and enhancing economic integration. In April 1999 Cambodia, on being admitted as a full member of ASEAN, signed an agreement to implement the tariff reduction programme over a 10-year period, commencing 1 January 2000. Cambodia also signed a declaration endorsing the commitments of the 1998 Statement on Bold Measures. In May 2000 Malaysia was granted a special exemption to postpone implementing tariff reductions on motor vehicles for two years from 1 January 2003. In November 2000 a protocol was approved permitting further temporary exclusion of products from the CEPT scheme for countries experiencing economic difficulties. On 1 January 2002 AFTA was formally realized among the original six signatories (Brunei, Indonesia, Malaysia, the Philippines, Singapore and Thailand), which had achieved the objective of reducing to less than 5% trade restrictions on 96.24% of products on the inclusion list. Some 98.36% of tariff lines for the core six AFTA members were on the inclusion list at that time. Tariffs on trade in products on the inclusion list for these countries averaged less than 2.9% in 2002.

To complement AFTA in facilitating intra-ASEAN trade, member countries are committed to the removal of non-tariff barriers (such as quotas), the harmonization of standards and conformance measures, and the simplification and harmonization of customs procedures. In June 1996 the Working Group on Customs Procedures completed a draft legal framework for regional co-operation, designed to simplify and harmonize customs procedures, legislation and product classification. The agreement was signed in March 1997 at the inaugural meeting of ASEAN finance ministers. (Laos and Myanmar signed the customs agreement in July and Cambodia assented to it in April 1999.) In 2001 ASEAN finalized its system of harmonized tariff nomenclature. Implementation began in 2002, with training on the new system to be given to public- and private-sector officials over the course of the year.

At the seventh summit meeting, held in Brunei, in November 2001 heads of government noted the challenges posed by the severe global economic slowdown, at a time when ASEAN countries were beginning to emerge from the 1997–98 crisis. Members discussed moving beyond the group's existing free-trade and investment commitments by deepening market liberalization. Specifically, it was proposed that negotiations on the liberalization of intra-ASEAN trade in services be accelerated. The third round of negotiations on liberalizing trade in services began at the end of 2001; it was scheduled to be completed by 2004. Members also agreed to start negotiations on mutual recognition arrangements for professional services. The summit meeting stated that tariff preferences would be extended to ASEAN's newer members from January 2002, under the ASEAN Integration System of Preferences (AISP), thus allowing Cambodia, Laos, Myanmar and Viet Nam tariff-free access to the more developed ASEAN markets earlier than the previously agreed target date of 2010.

In November 2000 heads of government endorsed an Initiative for ASEAN Integration (IAI), which aimed to reduce economic disparities within the region through effective co-operation, in particular, in training and other educational opportunities. In July 2002 the AMM endorsed an IAI Work Plan, which focused on the following priority areas: human resources development; infrastructure; information communications technology; and regional economic integration. An IAI Development Co-operation Forum was held in August.

At the eighth summit meeting, held in November 2002, in Phnom-Penh, Cambodia, ASEAN heads of state considered the Phnom-Penh Agenda, comprising the following four elements: collaboration with an ongoing initiative to promote economic co-operation in the Greater Mekong subregion, with a view to accelerating the pace of ASEAN integration; promoting ASEAN as a single tourist destination; solidarity for peace and security, especially in combating terrorism; and progress in sustainable natural resources management, including the ratification of the Kyoto Protocol to the UN Framework Convention on Climate Change.

In 1991 ASEAN ministers discussed a proposal of the Malaysian Government for the formation of an economic grouping, to be composed of ASEAN members, the People's Republic of China, Hong Kong, Japan, the Republic of Korea and Taiwan. In July 1993 ASEAN ministers of foreign affairs agreed a compromise, whereby the grouping was to be a caucus within APEC, although it was to be co-ordinated by ASEAN's meeting of economy ministers. In July 1994 ministers of foreign affairs of nine prospective members of the group held their first informal collective meeting; however, no progress was made towards forming the proposed East Asia Economic Caucus. There was renewed speculation on the formation of an East Asian grouping following the onset of the Asian financial crisis of the late 1990s. At an informal meeting of leaders of ASEAN countries, China, Japan and the Republic of Korea, held in November 1999, all parties (designating themselves 'ASEAN + 3') issued a Joint Statement on East Asian Co-operation, in which they agreed to strengthen regional unity, and addressed the long-term possibility of establishing an East Asian common market and currency. Meeting in May 2000, in Chiang Mai, Thailand, ASEAN + 3 ministers of economic affairs proposed the establishment of an enhanced currency-swap mechanism, enabling countries to draw on liquidity support to defend their economies during balance-of-payments difficulties or speculative currency attacks and to prevent future financial crises. In July ASEAN + 3 ministers of foreign affairs convened an inaugural formal summit in Bangkok, Thailand, and in October ASEAN + 3 economic affairs ministers agreed to hold their hitherto twice-yearly informal meetings on an institutionalized basis. In November an informal meeting of ASEAN + 3 leaders approved further co-operation in various sectors and initiated a feasibility study into a proposal to establish a regional free trade area. In May 2001 ASEAN + 3 ministers of economic affairs endorsed a series of projects for co-operation in information technology, environment, small and medium-sized enterprises, Mekong Basin development, and harmonization of standards. In the same month the so-called Chiang Mai initiative on currency-swap arrangements was formally approved by ASEAN + 3 finance ministers. A meeting of the ASEAN + 3 leaders was held alongside the seventh ASEAN summit in November 2001. Malaysia offered to host an ASEAN + 3 secretariat; however the establishment of a formal secretariat for the grouping remained under discussion in 2002. In October 2001 ASEAN + 3 agriculture and forestry ministers met for the first time, and discussed issues of poverty alleviation, food security, agricultural research and human resource development. The first meeting of ASEAN + 3 tourism ministers was held in January 2002. In July ASEAN + 3 ministers of foreign affairs declared their support for other regional initiatives, namely an Asia Co-operation Dialogue, which was initiated by the Thai Government in June, and an Initiative for Development in East Asia (IDEA), which had been announced by the Japanese Government in January. An IDEA ministerial meeting was convened in Tokyo, in August.

INDUSTRY

The ASEAN-Chambers of Commerce and Industry (CCI) aims to enhance ASEAN economic and industrial co-operation and the participation in these activities of the private sector. In March 1996 a permanent ASEAN-CCI secretariat became operational at the ASEAN Secretariat. The first AIA Council-Business Sector Forum was convened in September 2001, with the aim of developing alliances between the public and private sectors. The seventh ASEAN summit in November resolved to encourage the private sector to convene a regular ASEAN Business Summit. It was also agreed to set up an ASEAN Business Advisory Council.

The ASEAN Industrial Co-operation (AICO) scheme, initiated in 1996, encourages companies in the ASEAN region to undertake joint manufacturing activities. Products derived from an AICO arrangement benefit immediately from a preferential tariff rate of 0%–5%. The AICO scheme superseded the ASEAN industrial joint venture scheme, established in 1983. The attractiveness of the scheme is expected slowly to diminish as ASEAN moves towards the full implementation of the CEPT scheme. ASEAN has initiated studies of new methods of industrial co-operation within the grouping, with the aim of achieving further integration.

The ASEAN Consultative Committee on Standards and Quality (ACCSQ) aims to promote the understanding and implementation of quality concepts, considered to be important in strengthening the economic development of a member state and in helping to eliminate trade barriers. ACCSQ comprises three working groups: standards and information; conformance and assessment; and testing and calibration. In September 1994 an *ad hoc* Working Group on Intellectual Property Co-operation was established, with a mandate to formulate a framework agreement on intellectual property co-operation and to strengthen ASEAN activities in intellectual property protection. ASEAN aims to establish, by 2004, a regional electronic database, to strengthen the administration of intellectual property. ASEAN is also developing a Regulatory Trademark Filing System, as a first step towards the creation of an ASEAN Trademark System.

In 1988 the ASEAN Fund was established, with capital of US $150m., to provide finance for portfolio investments in ASEAN countries, in particular for small and medium-sized enterprises (SMEs). The Hanoi Plan of Action, which was adopted by ASEAN heads of state in December 1998, incorporated a series of initiatives to enhance the development of SMEs, including training and technical assistance, co-operation activities and greater access to information.

FINANCE, BANKING AND INVESTMENT

In 1987 heads of government agreed to accelerate regional financial co-operation, to support intra-ASEAN trade and investment. They adopted measures to increase the role of ASEAN currencies in regional trade, to assist negotiations on the avoidance of double taxation, and to improve the efficiency of tax and customs administrators. An ASEAN Reinsurance Corporation was established in 1988, with initial authorized capital of US $10m. In December 1995 the summit meeting proposed the establishment of an ASEAN Investment Area (AIA). Other measures to attract greater financial resource flows in the region, including an ASEAN Plan of Action for the Promotion of Foreign Direct Investment and Intra-ASEAN Investment, were implemented during 1996.

In February 1997 ASEAN central bank governors agreed to strengthen efforts to combat currency speculation through the established network of foreign-exchange repurchase agreements. However, from mid-1997 several Asian currencies were undermined by speculative activities. Subsequent unsuccessful attempts to support the foreign-exchange rates contributed to a collapse in the value of financial markets in some countries and to a reversal of the region's economic growth, at least in the short term, while governments undertook macro-economic structural reforms. In early December ASEAN ministers of finance, meeting in Malaysia, agreed to liberalize markets for financial services and to strengthen surveillance of member country economies, to help prevent further deterioration of the regional economy. The ministers also endorsed a proposal for the establishment of an Asian funding facility to provide emergency assistance in support of international credit and structural reform programmes. At the informal summit meeting held later in December, ASEAN leaders issued a joint statement in which they expressed the need for mutual support to counter the region's financial crisis and urged greater international assistance to help overcome the situation and address the underlying problems. The heads of government also resolved to accelerate the implementation of the AIA.

In July 1998 the ASEAN Ministerial Meeting endorsed the decisions of finance ministers, taken in February, to promote greater use of regional currencies for trade payments and to establish an economic surveillance mechanism. In October ministers of economic affairs, meeting in Manila, the Philippines, signed a framework agreement on the AIA, which was expected to provide for equal treatment of domestic and other ASEAN direct investment proposals within the grouping by 2010, and of all foreign investors by 2020. The meeting also confirmed that the proposed ASEAN Surveillance Process (ASP), to monitor the economic stability and financial systems of member states, would be implemented with immediate effect, and would require the voluntary submission of economic information by all members to a monitoring committee, to be based in Jakarta, Indonesia. The ASP and the framework agreement on the AIA were incorporated into the Hanoi Plan of Action, adopted by heads of state in December 1998. The December summit meeting also resolved to accelerate reforms, particularly in the banking and financial sectors, in order to strengthen the region's economies, and to promote the liberalization of the financial services sector.

In March 1999 ASEAN ministers of trade and industry, meeting in Phuket, Thailand, as the AIA Council, agreed to open their manufacturing, agriculture, fisheries, forestry and mining industries to foreign investment. Investment restrictions affecting those industries were to be eliminated by 2003 in most cases, although Laos and Viet Nam were granted until 2010. In addition, ministers adopted a number of measures to encourage investment in the region, including access to three-year corporate income-tax exemptions, and tax allowances of 30% for investors. The AIA agreement formally entered into force in June 1999, having been ratified by all member countries. Under the agreement, member countries submitted individual action plans for 2000–04, noting specific action to be taken in the areas of investment promotion, facilitation and liberalization. In September 2001 ministers agreed to accelerate the full realization of the AIA for non-ASEAN investors in manufacturing, agriculture, forestry, fishing and mining sectors. The date for full implementation was advanced to 2010 for the original six ASEAN members and to 2015 for the newer members.

In November 2001 ASEAN heads of state considered the difficulties facing member countries as a result of the global economic and political uncertainties following the terrorist attacks on the USA in September. The summit meeting noted the recent decline in foreign direct investment and the erosion of the region's competitiveness. Short-term priorities were stated to be the stimulation of economies to lessen the impact of reduced external demand, and the adoption of appropriate fiscal and monetary policies, together with a renewed commitment to structural reform.

In April 2002 ASEAN economy ministers signed an agreement to facilitate intra-regional trade in electrical and electronic equipment by providing for the mutual recognition of standards (for example, testing and certification). The agreement was also intended to lower the costs of trade in those goods, thereby helping to maintain competitiveness.

SECURITY

In 1971 ASEAN members endorsed a declaration envisaging the establishment of a Zone of Peace, Freedom and Neutrality (ZOPFAN) in the South-East Asian region. This objective was incorporated in the Declaration of ASEAN Concord, which was adopted at the first summit meeting of the organization, held in Bali, Indonesia, in February 1976. (The Declaration also issued guide-lines for co-operation in economic development and the promotion of social justice and welfare.) Also in February 1976 a Treaty of Amity and Co-operation was signed by heads of state, establishing principles of mutual respect for the independence and sovereignty of all nations, non-interference in the internal affairs of one another and settlement of disputes by peaceful means. The Treaty was amended in December 1987 by a protocol providing for the accession of Papua New Guinea and other non-member countries in the region; it was reinforced by a second protocol, signed in July 1998.

In December 1995 ASEAN heads of government, meeting in Bangkok, signed a treaty establishing a South-East Asia Nuclear-Weapon Free Zone (SEANWFZ). The treaty was also signed by Cambodia, Myanmar and Laos. It was extended to cover the offshore economic exclusion zones of each country. On ratification by all parties, the Treaty was to prohibit the manufacture or storage of nuclear weapons within the region. Individual signatories were to decide whether to allow port visits or transportation of nuclear weapons by foreign powers through territorial waters. The Treaty entered into force on 27 March 1997. ASEAN senior officials were mandated to oversee implementation of the Treaty, pending the establishment of a permanent monitoring committee. In July 1999 the People's Republic of China and India agreed to observe the terms of the SEANWFZ.

In January 1992 ASEAN leaders agreed that there should be greater co-operation on security matters within the grouping, and that ASEAN's post-ministerial conferences (PMCs) should be used as a forum for discussion of questions relating to security with dialogue partners and other countries. In July 1992 the ASEAN Ministerial Meeting issued a statement calling for a peaceful resolution of the dispute concerning the strategically significant Spratly Islands in the South China Sea, which are claimed, wholly or partly, by the People's Republic of China, Viet Nam, Taiwan, Brunei, Malaysia and the Philippines. (In February China had introduced legislation that defined the Spratly Islands as belonging to its territorial waters.) Viet Nam's accession to ASEAN in July 1995, bringing all the Spratly Islands claimants except China and Taiwan into the grouping, was expected to strengthen ASEAN's position of negotiating a multilateral settlement on the islands. In 1999 ASEAN established a special committee to formulate a code of conduct for the South China Sea to be observed by all claimants to the Spratly Islands. A draft code of conduct was approved in November 1999. China, insisting that it would adopt the proposed code only as a set of guide-lines and not as a legally-binding document, resolved not to strengthen its presence on the islands. In 2000 and 2001 it participated in discussions with ASEAN officials concerning the document. In November 2002 ASEAN and China's foreign ministers adopted a Declaration on the Conduct of Parties in the South China Sea, agreeing to promote a peaceful environment and durable solutions for the area, to resolve territorial disputes by peaceful means, to refrain from undertaking activities that would aggravate existing tensions (such as settling unpopulated islands and reefs), and to initiate a regular dialogue of defence officials.

In July 1997 ASEAN ministers of foreign affairs reiterated their commitment to the principle of non-interference in the internal affairs of other countries. However, the group's efforts in Cambodia (see below) marked a significant shift in diplomatic policy towards one of 'constructive intervention', which had been proposed by Malaysia's Deputy Prime Minister in recognition of the increasing interdependence of the region. At the Ministerial Meeting in July 1998 Thailand's Minister of Foreign Affairs, supported by his Philippine counterpart, proposed that the grouping formally adopt a policy of 'flexible engagement'. The proposal, based partly on concerns that the continued restrictions imposed by the Myanma authorities on dissident political activists was damaging ASEAN relations with its dialogue partners, was to provide for the discussion of the affairs of other member states when they have an impact on neighbouring countries. While rejecting the proposal, other ASEAN ministers agreed to pursue a more limited version, referred to as 'enhanced interaction', and to maintain open dialogue within the grouping. In September 1999 the unrest prompted by the popular referendum on the future of East Timor (now Timor-Leste) and the resulting humanitarian crisis highlighted the unwillingness of some ASEAN member states to intervene in other member countries and undermined the political unity of the grouping. A compromise agreement, enabling countries to act on an individual basis rather than as representatives of ASEAN, was formulated

prior to an emergency meeting of ministers of foreign affairs, held during the APEC meetings in Auckland, New Zealand. Malaysia, the Philippines, Singapore and Thailand declared their support for the establishment of a multinational force to restore peace in East Timor and committed troops to participate in the Australian-led operation. At their informal summit in November 1999 heads of state approved the establishment of an ASEAN Troika, which was to be constituted as an *ad hoc* body comprising the foreign ministers of the Association's current, previous and future chairmanship with a view to providing a rapid response mechanism in the event of a regional crisis.

On 12 September 2001 ASEAN issued a ministerial statement on international terrorism, condemning the attacks of the previous day in the USA and urging greater international co-operation to counter terrorism. The seventh summit meeting in November issued a Declaration on a Joint Action to Combat Terrorism. This condemned the September attacks, stated that terrorism was a direct challenge to ASEAN's aims, and affirmed the grouping's commitment to strong measures to counter terrorism. The summit encouraged member countries to sign (or ratify) the International Convention for the Suppression of Financing of Terrorism, to strengthen national mechanisms against terrorism, and to work to deepen co-operation, particularly in the area of intelligence exchange; international conventions to combat terrorism would be studied to see if they could be integrated into the ASEAN structure, while the possibility of developing a regional anti-terrorism convention was discussed. The summit noted the need to strengthen security co-operation to restore investor confidence. In its Declaration and other notes, the summit explicitly rejected any attempt to link terrorism with religion or race, and expressed concern for the sufferings of innocent Afghanis during the US military action against the Taliban authorities in Afghanistan. The summit's final Declaration was worded so as to avoid any mention of the US action, to which Muslim ASEAN states such as Malaysia and Indonesia were strongly opposed. Several ASEAN countries offered to assist in peace-keeping and reconstruction in Afghanistan, following the removal of the Taliban and establishment of an interim authority.

In June 1999 the first ministerial meeting to consider issues relating to transnational crime was convened. Regular meetings of senior officials and ministers were subsequently held. The third ministerial meeting, in October 2001, considered initiatives to combat transnational crime, which was defined as including terrorism, trafficking in drugs, arms and people, money-laundering, cyber-crime, piracy and economic crime. In May 2002 ministers responsible for transnational crime issues convened a Special Ministerial Meeting on Terrorism, held in Kuala Lumpur, Malaysia. The meeting approved a work programme to implement a plan of action to combat transitional crime, including information exchange, the development of legal arrangements for extradition, prosecution and seizure, the enhancement of co-operation in law enforcement, and the development of regional security training programmes. In a separate initiative Indonesia, Malaysia and the Philippines signed an agreement on information exchange and the establishment of communication procedures. Cambodia acceded to the agreement in July.

ASEAN Regional Forum—ARF: In July 1993 the meeting of ASEAN ministers of foreign affairs sanctioned the establishment of a forum to discuss and promote co-operation on security issues within the region, and, in particular, to ensure the involvement of the People's Republic of China in regional dialogue. The ARF was informally initiated during that year's PMC, comprising the ASEAN countries, its dialogue partners (at that time—Australia, Canada, the EC, Japan, the Republic of Korea, New Zealand and the USA), and the People's Republic of China, Laos, Papua New Guinea, Russia and Viet Nam. The first formal meeting of the ARF was conducted in July 1994, following the Ministerial Meeting held in Bangkok, Thailand, and it was agreed that the ARF would be convened on an annual basis. The 1995 meeting, held in Brunei, in August, attempted to define a framework for the future of the Forum. It was perceived as evolving through three stages: the promotion of confidence-building (including disaster relief and peace-keeping activities); the development of preventive diplomacy); and the elaboration of approaches to conflict. The 19 ministers of foreign affairs attending the meeting (Cambodia participated for the first time) recognized that the ARF was still in the initial stage of implementing confidence-building measures. The ministers, having conceded to a request by China not to discuss explicitly the Spratly Islands, expressed concern at overlapping sovereignty claims in the region. In a further statement, the ministers urged an 'immediate end' to the testing of nuclear weapons, then being undertaken by the French Government in the South Pacific region. The third ARF, convened in July 1996, which was attended for the first time by India and Myanmar, agreed a set of criteria and guiding principles for the future expansion of the grouping. In particular, it was decided that the ARF would only admit as participants countries that had a direct influence on the peace and security of the East Asia and Pacific region. The ARF held in July 1997 reviewed progress made in developing the first two 'tracks' of the ARF process, through the structure of inter-sessional working groups and meetings. The Forum's consideration of security issues in the region was dominated by concern at the political situation in Cambodia; support was expressed for ASEAN mediation to restore stability within that country. Myanmar and Laos attended the ARF for the first time. Mongolia was admitted into the ARF at its meeting in July 1998. India rejected a proposal that Pakistan attend the meeting to discuss issues relating to both countries' testing of nuclear weapons. The meeting ultimately condemned the testing of nuclear weapons in the region, but declined to criticize specifically India and Pakistan. In July 1999 the ARF warned the Democratic People's Republic of Korea (DPRK) not to conduct any further testing of missiles over the Pacific. At the seventh meeting of the ARF, convened in Bangkok, Thailand, in July 2000, the DPRK was admitted to the Forum. The meeting considered the positive effects and challenges of globalization, including the possibilities for greater economic interdependence and for a growth in transnational crime. The eighth ARF meeting in July 2001 in Hanoi, Viet Nam, pursued these themes, and also discussed the widening development gap between nations. The meeting agreed to enhance the role of the ARF Chairman, enabling him to issue statements on behalf of ARF participants and to organize events during the year. In March and April 2002 ARF workshops were held on financial measures against terrorism and on the prevention of terrorism, respectively. The ninth ARF meeting, held in Bandar Seri Begawan, Brunei, in July, assessed regional and international security developments, and issued a statement of individual and collective intent to prevent any financing of terrorism. The statement included commitments by participants to freeze the assets of suspected individuals or groups, to implement international financial standards and to enhance co-operation and the exchange of information. In October the Chairman, on behalf of all ARF participants, condemned the terrorist bomb attacks committed against tourist targets in Bali, Indonesia.

Since 2000 the ARF has published the *Annual Security Outlook*, to which participating countries submit assessments of the security prospects in the region.

EXTERNAL RELATIONS

ASEAN's external relations have been pursued through a dialogue system, initially with the objective of promoting co-operation in economic areas with key trading partners. The system has been expanded in recent years to encompass regional security concerns and co-operation in other areas, such as the environment. The ARF (see above) emerged from the dialogue system, and more recently the formalized discussions of ASEAN with Japan, China and the Republic of Korea (ASEAN + 3) has evolved as a separate process with its own strategic agenda.

European Union: In March 1980 a co-operation agreement was signed between ASEAN and the European Community (EC, as the EU was known prior to its restructuring on 1 November 1993), which provided for the strengthening of existing trade links and increased co-operation in the scientific and agricultural spheres. A Joint Co-operation Committee met in November (and annually thereafter). An ASEAN-EC Business Council was launched in December 1983, and three European Business Information Councils have since been established, in Malaysia, the Philippines and Thailand, to promote private-sector co-operation. The first meeting of ministers of economic affairs from ASEAN and EC member countries took place in October 1985. In December 1990 the Community adopted new guidelines on development co-operation, with an increase in assistance to Asia, and a change in the type of aid given to ASEAN members, emphasizing training, science and technology and venture capital, rather than assistance for rural development. In October 1992 the EC and ASEAN agreed to promote further trade between the regions, as well as bilateral investment, and made a joint declaration in support of human rights. An EU-ASEAN Junior Managers Exchange Programme was initiated in November 1996, as part of efforts to promote co-operation and understanding between the industrial and business sectors in both regions. An ASEAN-EU Business Network was established in Brussels in 2001, to develop political and commercial contacts between the two sides.

In May 1995 ASEAN and EU senior officials endorsed an initiative to strengthen relations between the two economic regions within the framework of an Asia-Europe Meeting of heads of government (ASEM). The first ASEM was convened in Bangkok, Thailand, in March 1996, at which leaders approved a new Asia-Europe Partnership for Greater Growth. The second ASEM summit meeting, held in April 1998, focused heavily on economic concerns. In February 1997 ministers of foreign affairs of countries participating in ASEM met in Singapore. Despite ongoing differences regarding human rights issues, in particular concerning ASEAN's granting of full membership status to Myanmar and the situation in East Timor (which precluded the conclusion of a new co-operation agreement), the

Ministerial Meeting issued a final joint declaration, committing both sides to strengthening co-operation and dialogue on economic, international and bilateral trade, security and social issues. A protocol to the 1980 co-operation agreement was signed, enabling the participation of Viet Nam in the dialogue process. In November 1997 a session of the Joint Co-operation Committee was postponed and later cancelled, owing to a dispute concerning objections by the EU to the participation of Myanmar. A compromise agreement, allowing Myanma officials to attend meetings as 'silent' observers, was concluded in November 1998. However, a meeting of the Joint Co-operation Committee, scheduled to take place in January 1999, was again cancelled, owing to controversy over perceived discrimination by the EU against Myanmar's status. The meeting was finally convened in Bangkok, Thailand, in late May. The third ASEM summit meeting was convened in Seoul, Korea in October 2000. In December an ASEAN-EU Ministerial Meeting was held in Vientiane, Laos. Both sides agreed to pursue dialogue and co-operation and issued a joint declaration that accorded support for the efforts of the UN Secretary-General's special envoy towards restoring political dialogue in Myanmar. Myanmar agreed to permit an EU delegation to visit the country, and opposition leaders, in early 2001. In September 2001 the Joint Co-operation Committee met for the first time since 1999 and resolved to strengthen policy dialogue, in particular in areas fostering regional integration. Four new EC delegations were to be established—in Cambodia, Laos, Myanmar and Singapore. The fourth ASEM summit meeting was held in September 2002, in Copenhagen, Denmark.

People's Republic of China: Efforts to develop consultative relations between ASEAN and China were initiated in 1993. Joint Committees on economic and trade co-operation and on scientific and technological co-operation were subsequently established. The first formal consultations between senior officials of the two sides were held in April 1995. In July 1996, in spite of ASEAN's continued concern at China's territorial claims to the Spratly Islands in the South China Sea, China was admitted to the PMC as a full dialogue partner. In February 1997 a Joint Co-operation Committee was established to co-ordinate the China-ASEAN dialogue and all aspects of relations between the two sides. Relations were further strengthened by the decision to form a joint business council to promote bilateral trade and investment. China participated in the informal summit meeting held in December, at the end of which both sides issued a joint statement affirming their commitment to resolving regional disputes through peaceful means. A second meeting of the Joint Co-operation Committee was held in March 1999. China was a participant in the first official ASEAN + 3 meeting of foreign ministers, which was convened in July 2000. An ASEAN-China Experts Group was established in November, to consider future economic co-operation and free trade opportunities. The Group held its first meeting in April 2001 and proposed a Framework on Economic Co-operation and the establishment of an ASEAN-China free-trade area within 10 years (with differential treatment and flexibility for newer ASEAN members). Both proposals were endorsed at the seventh ASEAN summit meeting in November 2001. China also agreed to grant preferential tariff treatment for some goods from Cambodia, Laos and Myanmar. In November 2002 an agreement on economic co-operation was concluded by the ASEAN member states and China.

Japan: The ASEAN-Japan Forum was established in 1977 to discuss matters of mutual concern in trade, investment, technology transfer and development assistance. The first meeting between the two sides at ministerial level was held in October 1992. At this meeting, and subsequently, ASEAN requested Japan to increase its investment in member countries and to make Japanese markets more accessible to ASEAN products, in order to reduce the trade deficit with Japan. Since 1993 ASEAN-Japanese development and cultural co-operation has expanded under schemes including the Inter-ASEAN Technical Exchange Programme, the Japan-ASEAN Co-operation Promotion Programme and the ASEAN-Japan Friendship Programme. In December 1997 Japan, attending the informal summit meeting in Malaysia, agreed to improve market access for ASEAN products and to provide training opportunities for more than 20,000 young people in order to help develop local economies. In December 1998 ASEAN heads of government welcomed a Japanese initiative, announced in October, to allocate US $30,000m. to promote economic recovery in the region. At the same time the Japanese Prime Minister announced a further package of $5,000m. to be made available as concessionary loans for infrastructure projects. In mid-2000 a new Japan-ASEAN General Exchange Fund (JAGEF) was established to promote and facilitate the transfer of technology, investment and personnel. In November 1999 Japan, along with the People's Republic of China and the Republic of Korea, attending an informal summit meeting of ASEAN, agreed to strengthen economic and political co-operation with the ASEAN countries, to enhance political and security dialogue, and to implement joint infrastructure and social projects. Japan participated in the first official ASEAN + 3 meeting of foreign ministers, which was convened in

July 2000. An ASEAN-Japan Experts Group, similar to that for China, was to be established to consider how economic relations between the two sides can be strengthened. In recent years Japan has provided information technology (IT) support to ASEAN countries, and has offered assistance in environmental and health matters and for educational training and human resource development (particularly in engineering).

Australia and New Zealand: In 1999 ASEAN and Australia undertook to development the ASEAN-Australia Development Co-operation Programme (AADCP), to replace an economic co-operation programme which had begun in 1974. In August 2002 the two sides signed a formal memorandum of understanding on the AADCP. It was to comprise three core elements, with assistance amounting to $A45m.: a Program Stream, to address medium-term issues of economic integration and competitiveness; a Regional Partnerships Scheme for smaller collaborative activities; and the establishment of a Regional Economic Policy Support Facility within the ASEAN Secretariat. All components were to be fully operational by 2003. Co-operation relations with New Zealand are based on the Inter-Institutional Linkages Programme and the Trade and Investment Promotion Programme, which mainly provide assistance in forestry development, dairy technology, veterinary management and legal aid training. An ASEAN-New Zealand Joint Management Committee was established in November 1993, to oversee the implementation of co-operation projects. New Zealand's English Language Training for Officials Programme is among the most important of these projects. In September 2001 ASEAN ministers of economic affairs signed a Framework for Closer Economic Partnership (CEP) with their counterparts from Australia and New Zealand (the Closer Economic Relations—CER—countries), and agreed to establish a Business Council to involve the business communities of all countries in the CEP. The CEP was perceived as a first step towards the creation of a free-trade area between ASEAN and CER countries. The establishment of such an area would strengthen the grouping's bargaining position regionally and multilaterally, and bring benefits such as increased foreign direct investment and the possible relocation of industry.

Other countries: The USA gives assistance for the development of small and medium-sized businesses and other projects, and supports a Center for Technology Exchange. In 1990 ASEAN and the USA established an ASEAN-US Joint Working Group, whose purpose is to review ASEAN's economic relations with the USA and to identify measures by which economic links could be strengthened. In recent years, dialogue has increasingly focused on political and security issues. In early August 2002 ASEAN ministers of foreign affairs met with their US counterpart, and signed a Joint Declaration for Co-operation to Combat International Terrorism. ASEAN-Canadian co-operation projects include fisheries technology, the telecommunications industry, use of solar energy, and a forest seed centre. A Working Group on the Revitalization of ASEAN-Canada relations met in February 1999. At a meeting in Bangkok in July 2000, the two sides agreed to explore less formal avenues for project implementation.

In July 1991 the Republic of Korea was accepted as a 'dialogue partner' in ASEAN, and in December a joint ASEAN-Korea Chamber of Commerce was established. In 1995 co-operation projects on human resources development, science and technology, agricultural development and trade and investment policies were implemented. The Republic of Korea participated in ASEAN's informal summit meetings in December 1997 and November 1999 (see above), and took part in the first official ASEAN + 3 meeting of foreign ministers, convened in July 2000. The Republic's assistance in the field of information technology (IT) has become particularly valuable in recent years. In March 2001, in a sign of developing co-operation, ASEAN and the Republic of Korea exchanged views on political and security issues in the region for the first time. The ASEAN-Korea Work Programme for 2001–03 covers, among other areas, the environment, transport, science and technology and cultural sectors.

In July 1993 both India and Pakistan were accepted as sectoral partners, providing for their participation in ASEAN meetings in sectors such as trade, transport and communications and tourism. An ASEAN-India Business Council was established, and met for the first time, in New Delhi, in February 1995. In December 1995 the ASEAN summit meeting agreed to enhance India's status to that of a full dialogue partner; India was formally admitted to the PMC in July 1996. At a meeting of the ASEAN-India Working Group in March 2001 the two sides agreed to pursue co-operation in new areas, such as health and pharmaceuticals, social security and rural development. The fourth meeting of the ASEAN-India Joint Co-operation Committee in January 2002 agreed to strengthen co-operation in these areas and others, including technology. The first ASEAN-India meeting at the level of heads of state was scheduled to be held in November. An ASEAN-Pakistan Joint Business Council met for the first time in February 2000. In early 2001 both sides agreed to co-operate in projects relating to new and renewable energy resources, IT, agricultural research and transport and communications.

In March 2000 the first ASEAN-Russia business forum opened in Kuala Lumpur, Malaysia.

Indo-China: In July 1992 Viet Nam and Laos signed ASEAN's Treaty on Amity and Co-operation and subsequently participated in ASEAN meetings and committees as observers. Viet Nam was admitted as a full member of ASEAN in July 1995. In that month Myanmar signed ASEAN's Treaty on Amity and Co-operation. In July 1996 ASEAN granted Myanmar observer status and admitted it to the ARF, despite the expression of strong reservations by (among others) the Governments of Australia, Canada and the USA owing to the human rights situation in Myanmar. In November ASEAN heads of government, attending an informal summit meeting in Jakarta, Indonesia, agreed to admit Myanmar as a full member of the grouping at the same time as Cambodia and Laos. While Cambodia's membership was postponed, Laos and Myanmar were admitted to ASEAN in July 1997.

Cambodia was accorded observer status in July 1995. In May 1997 ASEAN ministers of foreign affairs confirmed that Cambodia, together with Laos and Myanmar, was to be admitted to the grouping in July of that year. In mid-July, however, Cambodia's membership was postponed owing to the deposition of Prince Ranariddh, and the resulting civil unrest. Later in that month Cambodia's *de facto* leader, Second Prime Minister Hun Sen, agreed to ASEAN's pursuit of a mediation role in restoring stability in the country and in preparing for democratic elections. In early August the ministers of foreign affairs of Indonesia, the Philippines and Thailand, representing ASEAN, met Hun Sen to confirm these objectives. A team of ASEAN observers joined an international monitoring mission to supervise the election held in Cambodia in July 1998. International approval of the conduct of the election, and consequently of Hun Sen's victory, prompted ASEAN to agree to reconsider Cambodia's admission into the Association. In December, following the establishment of a coalition administration in Cambodia, the country was welcomed, by the Vietnamese Government, as the 10th member of ASEAN, despite an earlier meeting of ministers of foreign affairs failing to reach a consensus decision. Its formal admission took place on 30 April 1999.

In June 1996 ministers of ASEAN countries, and of the People's Republic of China, Cambodia, Laos and Myanmar adopted a framework for ASEAN-Mekong Basin Development Co-operation. The initiative aimed to strengthen the region's cohesiveness, with greater co-operation on issues such as drugs-trafficking, labour migration and terrorism, and to facilitate the process of future expansion of ASEAN. Groups of experts and senior officials were to be convened to consider funding issues and proposals to link the two regions, including a gas pipeline network, rail links and the establishment of a common time zone. In December 1996 the working group on rail links appointed a team of consultants to conduct a feasibility study of the proposals. The completed study was presented at the second ministerial conference on ASEAN-Mekong Basin Development Co-operation, convened in Hanoi, Viet Nam, in July 2000. At the November 2001 summit China pledged US $5m. to assist with navigation along the upper stretches of the Mekong River, while other means by which China could increase its investment in the Mekong Basin area were considered. At the meeting the Republic of Korea was invited to become a core member of the grouping. Other growth regions sponsored by ASEAN include the Brunei, Indonesia, Malaysia, Philippines, East ASEAN Growth Area (BIMP-EAGA), the Indonesia, Malaysia, Singapore Growth Triangle (IMS-GT), the Indonesia, Malaysia, Thailand Growth Triangle (IMT-GT), and the West-East Corridor within the Mekong Basin Development initiative.

AGRICULTURE, FISHERIES AND FORESTRY

In October 1983 a ministerial agreement on fisheries co-operation was concluded, providing for the joint management of fish resources, the sharing of technology, and co-operation in marketing. In July 1994 a Conference on Fisheries Management and Development Strategies in the ASEAN region resolved to enhance fish production through the introduction of new technologies, aquaculture development, improvements of product quality and greater involvement by the private sector.

Co-operation in forestry is focused on joint projects, funded by ASEAN's dialogue partners, which include a Forest Tree Seed Centre, an Institute of Forest Management and the ASEAN Timber Technology Centre. In April 1995 representatives of the ASEAN Secretariat and private-sector groups met to co-ordinate the implementation of a scheme to promote the export of ASEAN agricultural and forestry products. In recent years ASEAN has urged member countries to take action to prevent illegal logging in order to prevent the further degradation of forest resources.

ASEAN holds an emergency rice reserve, amounting to 87,000 metric tons, as part of its efforts to ensure food security in the region. There is an established ASEAN programme of training and study exchanges for farm workers, agricultural experts and members of agricultural co-operatives. During 1998 ASEAN was particularly concerned with the impact of the region's economic crisis on the agricultural sector, and the possible effects of climatic change. In September ministers of agriculture and forestry, meeting in Hanoi, Viet Nam, endorsed a Strategic Plan of Action on ASEAN Co-operation in Food, Agriculture and Forestry for 1999–2004. The Plan focused on programmes and activities aimed at enhancing food security, the international competitiveness of ASEAN food, agri-culture and forestry products, promoting the sustainable use and conservation of natural resources, encouraging greater involvement by the private sector in the food and agricultural industry, and strengthening joint approaches on international and regional issues. An ASEAN Task Force has been formed to harmonize regulations on agricultural products derived from biotechnology. In December 1998 heads of state resolved to establish an ASEAN Food Security Infor-mation Service to enhance the capacity of member states to forecast and manage food supplies. In 1999 agriculture ministers endorsed guide-lines on assessing risk from genetically modified organisms (GMOs) in agriculture, to ensure a common approach. In 2001 work was undertaken to increase public and professional awareness of GMO issues, through workshops and studies.

MINERALS AND ENERGY

The ASEAN Centre for Energy (ACE), based in Jakarta, Indonesia, provides an energy information network, promotes the establish-ment of interconnecting energy structures among ASEAN member countries, supports the development of renewable energy resources and encourages co-operation in energy efficiency and conservation. An ASEAN energy business forum is held annually and attended by representatives of the energy industry in the private and public sectors. Efforts to establish an ASEAN electricity grid were initiated in 1990. An ASEAN Interconnection Masterplan Study Working Group was established in April 2000 to formulate a study on the power grid. In November 1999 a Trans-ASEAN Gas Pipeline Task Force was established. In July 2002 ASEAN ministers of energy signed a Memorandum of Understanding to implement the pipeline project, involving seven interconnections. The meeting also approved initial plans for the implementation of the regional power grid initiative. ASEAN has forged partnerships with the EU and Japan in the field of energy, under the ASEAN Plan of Action for Energy Co-operation, running from 1999–2004.

A Framework of Co-operation in Minerals was adopted by an ASEAN working group of experts in August 1993. The group has also developed a programme of action for ASEAN co-operation in the development and utilization of industrial minerals, to promote the exploration and development of mineral resources, the transfer of mining technology and expertise, and the participation of the private sector in industrial mineral production. The programme of action is implemented by an ASEAN Regional Development Centre for Min-eral Resources, which also conducts workshops and training pro-grammes relating to the sector.

TRANSPORT AND COMMUNICATIONS

ASEAN aims to promote greater co-operation in the transport and communications sector, and in particular, to develop multi-modal transport; to harmonize road transport laws and regulations; to improve air space management; to develop ASEAN legislation for the carriage of dangerous goods and waste by land and sea; and to achieve interoperability and interconnectivity in telecommunica-tions. The summit meeting of December 1998 agreed to work to develop a trans-ASEAN transportation network by 2000, comprising principal routes for the movement of goods and people. (The deadline for the full implementation of the agreement was subsequently moved to the end of 2000.) In September 1999 ASEAN ministers of transport and communications resolved to establish working groups to strengthen co-operation within the sector and adopted a pro-gramme of action for development of the sector in 1999–2004. By September 2001, under the action programme, a harmonized road route numbering system had been completed, a road safety imple-mentation work plan agreed, and two pilot courses, on port manage-ment and traffic engineering and safety, had been adopted. A Framework Agreement on Facilitation of Goods in Transport entered into force in October 2000.

ASEAN is seeking to develop a Competitive Air Services Policy, possibly as a first step towards the creation of an ASEAN Open Skies Policy. In September 2000 a meeting of transport ministers agreed to embark on a study to formulate maritime shipping policy, to cover, *inter alia*, issues of transshipment, the competitiveness of ports, liberalization, and the integration of maritime shipping into the overall transport system. In October 2001 ministers approved the third package of commitments for the air and transport sectors under the ASEAN framework agreement on services (according to which member countries were to liberalize the selling and marketing of air and maritime transport services. The summit meeting held in November reaffirmed the large-scale Singapore–Kunming rail link

as a priority transport project. Emphasis was also put on smaller-scale (and cheaper) projects in 2001.

In October 1999 an e-ASEAN initiative was launched, aiming to promote and co-ordinate electronic commerce and internet utiliza-tion. In November 2000 the informal meeting of ASEAN heads of government approved an e-ASEAN Framework Agreement to fur-ther the aims of the initiative. The Agreement incorporated commit-ments to develop and strengthen ASEAN's information infrastruc-ture, in order to provide for universal and affordable access to communications services. Tariff reduction on IT products was to be accelerated, with the aim of eliminating all tariffs in the sector by 2010. In July 2001 ministers of foreign affairs discussed measures for the economic liberalization of IT products and for developing IT capabilities in poorer member countries. In the same month the first meeting of ASEAN ministers responsible for telecommunications was held, in Kuala Lumpur, Malaysia, during which a Ministerial Understanding on ASEAN co-operation in telecommunications and IT was signed. In September ASEAN ministers of economic affairs approved a list of information and communications technology (ICT) products eligible for the elimination of duties under the e-ASEAN Framework Agreement. This was to take place in three annual tranches, commencing in 2003 for the six original members of ASEAN and in 2008 for the newer member countries. During 2001 ASEAN continued to develop a reference framework for e-commerce legislation; it aimed to have e-commerce legislation in place in all member states by 2003. The second ASEAN telecommunications ministerial meeting was held in Manila, Philippines, in August 2002. The meeting issued a declaration incorporating commitments to exploit ASEAN's competitive position in the field of ICT and to fulfil the obligations of the e-ASEAN Framework Agreement. The ministers also resolved to enhance co-operation with China, Japan and Korea with regard to ICT.

SCIENCE AND TECHNOLOGY

ASEAN's Committee on Science and Technology (COST) supports co-operation in food science and technology, meteorology and geo-physics, microelectronics and IT, biotechnology, non-conventional energy research, materials science and technology, space technology applications, science and technology infrastructure and resources development, and marine science. There is an ASEAN Science Fund, used to finance policy studies in science and technology and to support information exchange and dissemination.

The Hanoi Plan of Action, adopted in December 1998, envisaged a series of measures aimed at promoting development in the fields of science and technology, including the establishment of networks of science and technology centres of excellence and academic institu-tions, the creation of a technology scan mechanism, the promotion of public- and private-sector co-operation in scientific and techno-logical (particularly IT) activities, and an increase in research on strategic technologies. In September 2001 the ASEAN Ministerial Meeting on Science and Technology, convened for its first meeting since 1998, approved a new framework for implementation of ASEAN's Plan of Action on Science and Technology during the period 2001–04. The Plan aimed to help less developed member countries become competitive in the sector and integrate into regional co-operation activities.

ENVIRONMENT

A ministerial meeting on the environment in April 1994 approved long-term objectives on environmental quality and standards for the ASEAN region, aiming to enhance joint action in addressing envi-ronmental concerns. At the same time, ministers adopted standards for air quality and river water to be achieved by all ASEAN member countries by 2010. In June 1995 ministers agreed to co-operate to counter the problems of transboundary pollution.

In December 1997 ASEAN heads of state endorsed a Regional Haze Action Plan to address the environmental problems resulting from forest fires, which had afflicted several countries in the region throughout that year. A Haze Technical Task Force undertook to implement the plan in 1998, with assistance from the UN Environ-ment Programme. In March ministers of the environment requested international financial assistance to help mitigate the dangers of forest fires in Indonesia, which had suffered an estimated US $1,000m. in damage in 1997. Sub-regional fire-fighting arrangement working groups for Sumatra and Borneo were established in April 1998 and in May the Task Force organized a regional workshop to strengthen ASEAN capacity to prevent and alleviate the haze caused by the extensive fires. A pilot project of aerial surveillance of the areas in the region most at risk of forest fires was initiated in July. In December heads of government resolved to establish an ASEAN Regional Research and Training Centre for Land and Forest Fire Management by 2004. In March 2002 members of the workings groups on sub-regional fire-fighting arrangements for Sumatra and Borneo agreed to intensify early warning efforts and surveillance activities in order to reduce the risks of forest fires. In June ASEAN ministers of the environment signed an Agreement on Transboundary Haze Pollution, which was intended to provide a legal basis for the Regional Haze Action Plan. The Agreement required member countries to co-operate in the prevention and mitigation of haze pollution, for example, by responding to requests for information by other states and facilitating the transit of personnel and equipment in case of disaster. The Agreement also provided for the establishment of an ASEAN Co-ordination Centre for Transboundary Haze Pollution Control. An ASEAN Specialized Meteorological Centre (ASMC) based in Singapore, plays a primary role in long-range climatological forecasting, early detection and monitoring of fires and haze.

In April 2000 ministers adopted a Strategic Plan of Action on the Environment for 1999–2004. Activities under the Plan focus on issues of coastal and marine erosion, nature conservation and biodiversity, the implementation of multilateral environmental agreements, and forest fires and haze. Other ASEAN environmental objectives include the implementation of a water conservation programme and the formation and adoption of an ASEAN protocol on access to genetic resources. An ASEAN Regional Centre for Biodiversity Conservation (ARCBC) was established in February 1999. It held several workshops in 2000 and 2001, on issues including genetically modified organisms, access to genetic resources and data sharing. In May 2001 environment ministers launched the ASEAN Environment Education Action Plan (AEEAP), with the aim of making citizens 'environmentally literate', and willing and able to participate in sustainable regional development.

SOCIAL DEVELOPMENT

ASEAN concerns in social development include youth development, the role of women, health and nutrition, education, labour affairs and disaster management. In December 1993 ASEAN ministers responsible for social affairs adopted a Plan of Action for Children, which provided a framework for regional co-operation for the survival, protection and development of children in member countries. ASEAN supports efforts to combat drug abuse and illegal drugs-trafficking. It aims to promote education and drug-awareness campaigns throughout the region, and administers a project to strengthen the training of personnel involved in combating drug abuse. In October 1994 a meeting of ASEAN Senior Officials on Drug Matters approved a three-year plan of action on drug abuse, providing a framework for co-operation in four priority areas: preventive drug education; treatment and rehabilitation; law enforcement; and research. In July 1998 ASEAN ministers of foreign affairs signed a Joint Declaration for a Drug-Free ASEAN, which envisaged greater co-operation among member states, in particular in information exchange, educational resources and legal procedures, in order to eliminate the illicit production, processing and trafficking of narcotic substances by 2020. (This deadline was subsequently advanced to 2015.)

The seventh ASEAN summit meeting, held in November 2001, declared work on combating HIV and AIDS to be a priority. The second phase of a work programme to combat AIDS and provide help for sufferers was endorsed at the meeting. Heads of government expressed their readiness to commit the necessary resources for prevention and care, and to attempt to obtain access to cheaper drugs. More than 1.5m. people in South-East Asia were known to be infected with the HIV virus. An ASEAN task force on AIDS has been operational since March 1993.

In December 1998 ASEAN leaders approved a series of measures aimed at mitigating the social impact of the financial and economic crises that had affected many countries in the region. Plans of Action were formulated on issues of rural development and poverty eradication, while Social Safety Nets, which aimed to protect the most vulnerable members of society, were approved. The summit meeting emphasized the need to promote job generation as a key element of strategies for economic recovery and growth. The fourth meeting of ministers of social welfare in August 2001 noted the need for a holistic approach to social problems, integrating social and economic development. The summit meeting in November considered the widening development gap between ASEAN members and concluded that bridging this gap was a priority, particularly with respect to developing human resources and infrastructure and providing access to IT.

In January 1992 the ASEAN summit meeting resolved to establish an ASEAN University Network (AUN) to hasten the development of a regional identity. A draft AUN Charter and Agreement were adopted in 1995. The Network aims to strengthen co-operation

within the grouping, develop academic and professional human resources and transmit information and knowledge. The 17 universities linked in the network carry out collaborative studies and research programmes. At the seventh ASEAN summit in November 2001 heads of government agreed to establish the first ASEAN University, in Malaysia.

TOURISM

National Tourist Organizations from ASEAN countries meet regularly to assist in co-ordinating the region's tourist industry, and a Tourism Forum is held annually to promote the sector. The first formal meeting of ASEAN ministers of tourism was held in January 1998, in Cebu, the Philippines. The meeting adopted a Plan of Action on ASEAN Co-operation in Tourism, which aimed to promote intra-ASEAN travel, greater investment in the sector, joint marketing of the region as a single tourist destination and environmentally sustainable tourism. In January 1999 the second meeting of ASEAN ministers of tourism agreed to appoint country co-ordinators to implement various initiatives, including the designation of 2002 as 'Visit ASEAN Millennium Year'; research to promote the region as a tourist destination in the 21st century, and to develop a cruise-ship industry; and the establishment of a network of ASEAN Tourism Training Centres to develop new skills and technologies in the tourism industry by 2001. The third meeting of tourism ministers, held in Bangkok, Thailand, in January 2000, agreed to reformulate the Visit ASEAN Millennium Year initiative as a long-term Visit ASEAN programme. This was formally launched in January 2001 at the fourth ministerial meeting. The first phase of the programme, implemented in 2001, promoted brand awareness through an intense marketing effort; the second phase, initiated at the fifth meeting of tourism ministers, held in Yogyakarta, Indonesia, in January 2002, was to direct campaigns towards end-consumers. Ministers urged member states to abolish all fiscal and non-fiscal travel barriers, to encourage tourism, including intra-ASEAN travel. A seminar on sustainable tourism was held in Malaysia in October 2001. In November 2002 the eighth summit of heads of state adopted a framework agreement on ASEAN co-operation in tourism, aimed at facilitating domestic and intra-regional travel.

CULTURE AND INFORMATION

Regular workshops and festivals are held in visual and performing arts, youth music, radio, television and films, and print and interpersonal media. In addition, ASEAN administers a News Exchange and provides support for the training of editors, journalists and information officers. In 2000 ASEAN adopted new cultural strategies, with the aims of raising awareness of the grouping's objectives and achievements, both regionally and internationally. The strategies included: producing ASEAN cultural and historical educational materials; promoting cultural exchanges (especially for young people); and achieving greater exposure of ASEAN cultural activities and issues in the mass media. It was agreed to work towards the creation of an ASEAN Cultural Heritage Network, for use by professionals and the public, by 2002.

In July 1997 ASEAN ministers of foreign affairs endorsed the establishment of an ASEAN Foundation to promote awareness of the organization and greater participation in its activities; this was inaugurated in July 1998 and is based at the ASEAN secretariat building (www.aseanfoundation.org). The Foundation's work programme for 2000–03 has four major goals: promotion of awareness of ASEAN activities; reinforcement of ASEAN solidarity; promotion of development co-operation in poverty alleviation and related issues; and organizational development.

Publications

Annual Report.

AFTA Brochure.

ASEAN Investment Report (annually).

ASEAN State of the Environment Report (1st report: 1997; 2nd report: 2000).

ASEAN Update (6 a year).

Business ASEAN (6 a year).

Public Information Series, Briefing Papers, Documents Series, educational materials.

BANK FOR INTERNATIONAL SETTLEMENTS—BIS

Address: Centralbahnplatz 2, 4052 Basel, Switzerland.
Telephone: (61) 2808080; **fax:** (61) 2809100; **e-mail:** emailmaster@bis.org; **internet:** www.bis.org.

The Bank for International Settlements was founded pursuant to the Hague Agreements of 1930 to promote co-operation among national central banks and to provide additional facilities for international financial operations.

Organization

(April 2003)

GENERAL MEETING

The General Meeting is held annually in June and is attended by representatives of the central banks of countries in which shares have been subscribed. At March 2002 the central banks of the following authorities were entitled to attend and vote at General Meetings of the BIS: Argentina, Australia, Austria, Belgium, Bosnia and Herzegovina, Brazil, Bulgaria, Canada, the People's Republic of China, Croatia, the Czech Republic, Denmark, Estonia, Finland, France, Germany, Greece, Hong Kong, Hungary, Iceland, India, Ireland, Italy, Japan, the Republic of Korea, Latvia, Lithuania, the former Yugoslav republic of Macedonia, Malaysia, Mexico, the Netherlands, Norway, Poland, Portugal, Romania, Russia, Saudi Arabia, Singapore, Slovakia, Slovenia, South Africa, Spain, Sweden, Switzerland, Thailand, Turkey, the United Kingdom and the USA. The European Central Bank became a shareholder in December 1999.

BOARD OF DIRECTORS

The Board of Directors is responsible for the conduct of the Bank's operations at the highest level, and comprises the Governors in office of the central banks of Belgium, France, Germany, Italy, the United Kingdom and the USA, each of whom appoints another member of the same nationality. The statutes also provide for the election to the Board of not more than nine Governors of other member central banks: those of Canada, Japan, the Netherlands, Sweden and Switzerland are elected members of the Board.

Chairman of the Board and President of the Bank: NOUT WELLINK (Netherlands).

MANAGEMENT

The Bank has a staff of about 500 employees, from 35 countries. In July 1998 the BIS inaugurated its first overseas administrative unit, the Representative Office for Asia and the Pacific, which was based in Hong Kong. In November 2001 an agreement was concluded to open a Representative Office for the Americas in Mexico City, Mexico.

General Manager: MALCOLM D. KNIGHT (Canada).

Activities

The BIS is an international financial institution whose role is to promote international monetary and financial co-operation, and to fulfil the function of a 'central banks' bank'. Although it has the legal form of a company limited by shares, it is an international organization governed by international law, and enjoys special privileges and immunities in keeping with its role (a Headquarters Agreement was concluded with Switzerland in 1987). The participating central banks were originally given the option of subscribing the shares themselves or arranging for their subscription in their own countries: thus the BIS also has some private shareholders, but they have no right of participation in the General Meeting. Some 86% of the total share capital is in the hands of central banks and 14% is held by private shareholders. In January 2001 an extraordinary general meeting amended the Bank's statutes to restrict ownership to central banks. Accordingly, all shares held by private shareholders were to be repurchased at a specified rate of compensation.

FINANCE

The authorized capital of the Bank is 1,500m. gold francs, divided into 600,000 shares of 2,500 gold francs each.

Statement of Account*

(In millions of gold francs; units of 0.29032258 . . . gram of fine gold —Art. 4 of the Statutes; 31 March 2002)

Assets		%
Gold (bars).	3,209.9	3.66
Cash on hand and on sight a/c with banks	3,292.3	3.75
Treasury bills.	9,588.1	10.93
Time deposits and advances . .	45,538.0	51.92
Securities at term	25,271.6	28.81
Miscellaneous.	814.5	0.93
Total	87,714.4	100.00

Liabilities		%
Authorized cap.: 1,500,000,000		
Issued cap.: 1,292,912,500		
viz. 529,165 shares of which 25% paid up	330.7	0.38
Reserves	3,307.8	3.77
Deposits (gold)	2,531.4	2.89
Deposits (currencies) . . .	79,486.4	90.62
Miscellaneous.	2,005.5	2.29
Dividend payable on 1 July . .	52.6	0.06
Total	87,714.4	100.00

* Assets and liabilities in US dollars are converted at a fixed rate of US \$208 per fine ounce of gold (equivalent to 1 gold franc = \$1.94149 . . .) and all other items in currencies on the basis of market rates against the US dollar.

BANKING OPERATIONS

The BIS assists central banks in managing and investing their monetary reserves: in 2001 some 120 international financial institutions and central banks from all over the world had deposits with the BIS, representing around 7% of world foreign exchange reserves.

The BIS uses the funds deposited with it partly for lending to central banks. Its credit transactions may take the form of swaps against gold; covered credits secured by means of a pledge of gold or marketable short-term securities; credits against gold or currency deposits of the same amount and for the same duration held with the BIS; unsecured credits in the form of advances or deposits; or standby credits, which in individual instances are backed by guarantees given by member central banks. In addition, the Bank undertakes operations in foreign exchange and in gold, both with central banks and with the markets.

In 1982, faced with the increasingly critical debt situation of some Latin American countries and the resultant threat to the viability of the international financial system, the BIS granted comparatively large-scale loans to central banks that did not number among its shareholders: the central banks of Argentina, Brazil and Mexico were granted bridging loans pending the disbursement of balance-of-payments credits extended by the IMF. These facilities amounted to almost US \$3,000m., all of which had been repaid by the end of 1983. The Bank subsequently made similar loans, but with decreasing frequency. Since 1990 the BIS has contributed funds to bridging facilities arranged for the central banks of Venezuela, Guyana, Hungary, Romania, the former Yugoslav republic of Macedonia, Mexico (in 1995) and Thailand (in August 1997). Within the framework of an international financial programme, approved in support of the Brazilian economy in late 1998, the Bank was to co-ordinate a credit facility of up to \$13,280m. in favour of the Banco Central do Brasil. Funds were provided with the backing or guarantee of 19 central banks; the load was repaid in full in April 2000.

The BIS also engages in traditional types of investment: funds not required for lending to central banks are placed in the market as deposits with commercial banks and purchases of short-term negotiable paper, including Treasury bills. Such operations constitute a major part of the Bank's business.

Because the central banks' monetary reserves must be available at short notice, they can only be placed with the BIS at short term, for fixed periods and with clearly defined repayment terms. The BIS has to match its assets to the maturity structure and nature of its commitments, and must therefore conduct its business with special regard to maintaining a high degree of liquidity.

The Bank's operations must be in conformity with the monetary policy of the central banks of the countries concerned. It is not permitted to make advances to governments or to open current accounts in their name. Real estate transactions are also excluded.

INTERNATIONAL MONETARY CO-OPERATION

Governors of central banks meet for regular discussions at the BIS to co-ordinate international monetary policy and ensure orderly conditions on the international financial markets. There is close co-operation with the IMF and the World Bank. The BIS participates in meetings of the so-called Group of 10 (G-10) industrialized nations (see IMF, see p. 98), which has been a major forum for discussion of international monetary issues since its establishment in 1962. Governors of central banks of the G-10 countries convene for regular Basle Monthly Meetings. In 1971 a Standing Committee of the G-10 central banks was established at the BIS to consider aspects of the development of Euro-currency markets. In February 1999 the G-10 renamed the body the Committee on the Global Financial System, and approved a revised mandate to undertake systematic short-term monitoring of global financial system conditions; longer-term analysis of the functioning of financial markets; and the articulation of policy recommendations aimed at improving market functioning and promoting stability. The Committee was to meet four times a year.

In 1974 the Governors of central banks of the G-10 set up the Basle Committee on Banking Supervision (whose secretariat is provided by the BIS) to co-ordinate banking supervision at the international level. The Committee pools information on banking supervisory regulations and surveillance systems, including the supervision of banks' foreign currency business, identifies possible danger areas and proposes measures to safeguard the banks' solvency and liquidity. An International Conference of Banking Supervisors is held every two years. In 1997 the Committee published new guidelines, entitled Core Principles for Effective Banking Supervision, that were intended to provide a comprehensive set of standards to ensure sound banking. In 1998 the Committee was concerned with the development and implementation of the Core Principles, particularly given the ongoing financial and economic crisis affecting several Asian countries and instability of other major economies. In January 2001 the Committee issued preliminary proposals on capital adequacy rules; a new regime was scheduled to come into effect in 2004. A Financial Stability Institute was established in 1998, jointly by the BIS and Basle Committee, to enhance the capacity of central banks and supervisory bodies to implement aspects of the Core Principles, through the provision of training programmes and other policy workshops.

In February 1999 ministers of finance and governors of the central banks of the Group of Seven (G-7) industrialized nations approved the establishment of a Financial Stability Forum to strengthen co-operation among the world's largest economies and economic bodies, to improve the monitoring of international finance and to prevent a recurrence of the economic crises of 1997 and 1998. The General Manager of the BIS was appointed to chair the Forum for an initial three-year term. The first meeting of the Forum, comprising representatives of G-7 ministries of finance and central banks, and of international financial institutions and regulatory bodies, took place at the headquarters of the IMF in Washington, DC, USA, in April 1999. Three working groups were established to study aspects of highly leveraged, or unregulated, institutions, offshore financial centres, and short-term capital flows. In November the Forum constituted additional groups to review deposit insurance schemes and to consider measures to promote implementation of international standards. In March 2001 the Forum convened for its seventh meeting and considered, *inter alia*, measures to combat the financing of terrorism and the progress of offshore financial centres in strengthening their supervisory, regulatory and other practices.

The Bank organizes and provides the secretariat for periodic meetings of experts, such as the Group of Computer Experts, the Committee on Payment and Settlement Systems, the Group of Experts on Monetary and Economic Data Bank Questions, which aims to develop a data bank service for the G-10 central banks and the BIS, and the Committee of Experts on Gold and Foreign Exchange, which monitors financial market developments.

Since January 1998 the BIS has hosted the secretariat of the International Association of Insurance Supervisors, which aims to promote co-operation within the insurance industry with regard to effective supervision and the development of domestic insurance markets. It also hosts the secretariat of the International Association of Deposit Insurers, founded in May 2002.

RESEARCH

The Bank's Monetary and Economic Department conducts research, particularly into monetary and financial questions; collects and publishes data on securities markets and international banking developments; and organizes a data bank for central banks. The BIS Annual Report provides an independent analysis of monetary and economic developments. Statistics on international banking and on external indebtedness are also published regularly.

AGENCY AND TRUSTEE FUNCTIONS

Throughout its history the BIS has undertaken various duties as Trustee Fiscal Agent or Depository with regard to international loan agreements. From October 1986 the BIS performed the functions of Agent for the private European Currency Unit (ECU) clearing and settlement system, in accordance with the provisions of successive agreements concluded between the then ECU Banking Association (now Euro Banking Association—EBA), based in Paris, and the BIS. This arrangement was terminated following the introduction of the euro on 1 January 1999, when the ECU clearing system was replaced by a new euro clearing system of the EBA. At that time 62 banks had been granted the status of clearing bank by the EBA.

In April 1994 the BIS assumed new functions in connection with the rescheduling of Brazil's external debt, which had been agreed by the Brazilian Government in November 1993. In accordance with two collateral pledge agreements, the BIS acts in the capacity of Collateral Agent to hold and invest collateral for the benefit of the holders of certain US dollar-denominated bonds, maturing in 15 or 30 years, which have been issued by Brazil under the rescheduling arrangements. The Bank acts in a similar capacity for Peru, in accordance with external debt agreements concluded in November 1996 and a collateral agreement signed with the BIS in March 1997, and for Côte d'Ivoire, under a restructuring agreement signed in May 1997 and collateral agreement signed in March 1998.

Publications

Annual Report (in English, French, German and Italian).

The BIS Consolidated International Banking Statistics (every 6 months).

BIS Papers (series).

Central Bank Survey of Foreign Exchange and Derivatives Market Activity (3 a year).

Joint BIS-IMF-OECD-World Bank Statistics on External Debt (quarterly).

Quarterly Review: International Banking and Financial Market Developments (English, French, German and Italian).

Regular OTC Derivatives Market Statistics (every 6 months).

CARIBBEAN COMMUNITY AND COMMON MARKET— CARICOM

Address: Bank of Guyana Building, POB 10827, Georgetown, Guyana.
Telephone: (2) 226-9289; **fax:** (2) 226-7816; **e-mail:** carisec1@caricom.org; **internet:** www.caricom.org.

CARICOM was formed in 1973 by the Treaty of Chaguaramas, signed in Trinidad, as a movement towards unity in the Caribbean; it replaced the Caribbean Free Trade Association (CARIFTA), founded in 1965. A revision of the Treaty of Chaguaramas (by means of nine separate Protocols), in order to institute greater regional integration and to establish a CARICOM single market and economy (CSME), was instigated in the 1990s and completed in July 2001.

MEMBERS

Antigua and Barbuda	Jamaica
Bahamas*	Montserrat
Barbados	Saint Christopher and Nevis
Belize	Saint Lucia
Dominica	Saint Vincent and the Grenadines
Grenada	Suriname
Guyana	Trinidad and Tobago
Haiti	

* The Bahamas is a member of the Community but not the Common Market.

Anguilla   Cayman Islands
British Virgin Islands   Turks and Caicos Islands

Note: Aruba, Bermuda, the Cayman Islands, Colombia, the Dominican Republic, Mexico, the Netherlands Antilles, Puerto Rico and Venezuela have observer status with the Community.

Organization

(April 2003)

HEADS OF GOVERNMENT CONFERENCE AND BUREAU

The Conference is the final authority of the Community and determines policy. It is responsible for the conclusion of treaties on behalf of the Community and for entering into relationships between the Community and international organizations and states. Decisions of the Conference are generally taken unanimously. Heads of government meet annually, although inter-sessional meetings may be convened.

At a special meeting of the Conference, held in Trinidad and Tobago in October 1992, participants decided to establish a Heads of Government Bureau, with the capacity to initiate proposals, to update consensus and to secure the implementation of CARICOM decisions. The Bureau became operational in December, comprising the Chairman of the Conference, as Chairman, as well as the incoming and outgoing Chairmen of the Conference, and the Secretary-General of the Conference, in the capacity of Chief Executive Officer.

COMMUNITY COUNCIL OF MINISTERS

In October 1992 CARICOM heads of government agreed that a Caribbean Community Council of Ministers should be established to replace the existing Common Market Council of Ministers as the second highest organ of the Community. Protocol I amending the Treaty of Chaguaramas, to restructure the organs and institutions of the Community, was formally adopted at a meeting of CARICOM heads of government in February 1997 and was signed by all member states in July. The inaugural meeting of the Community Council of Ministers was held in Nassau, the Bahamas, in February 1998. The Council consists of ministers responsible for community affairs, as well as other government ministers designated by member states, and is responsible for the development of the Community's strategic planning and co-ordination in the areas of economic integration, functional co-operation and external relations.

MINISTERIAL COUNCILS

The principal organs of the Community are assisted in their functions by the following bodies, established under Protocol I amending the Treaty of Chaguaramas: the Council for Trade and Economic Development (COTED); the Council for Foreign and Community Relations (COFCOR); the Council for Human and Social Development (COHSOD); and the Council for Finance and Planning (COFAP). The Councils are responsible for formulating policies, promoting their implementation and supervising co-operation in the relevant areas.

SECRETARIAT

The Secretariat is the main administrative body of the Caribbean Community. The functions of the Secretariat are: to service meetings of the Community and of its Committees; to take appropriate follow-up action on decisions made at such meetings; to carry out studies on questions of economic and functional co-operation relating to the region as a whole; to provide services to member states at their request in respect of matters relating to the achievement of the objectives of the Community.

Secretary-General: EDWIN W. CARRINGTON (Trinidad and Tobago).

Deputy Secretary-General: (vacant).

Activities

REGIONAL INTEGRATION

In 1989 CARICOM heads of government established the 15-member West Indian Commission to study regional political and economic integration. The Commission's final report, submitted in July 1992, recommended that CARICOM should remain a community of sovereign states (rather than a federation), but should strengthen the integration process and expand to include the wider Caribbean region. It recommended the formation of an Association of Caribbean States (ACS, see p. 338), to include all the countries within and surrounding the Caribbean Basin. In November 1997 the Sec-

retaries-General of CARICOM and the ACS signed a Co-operation Agreement to formalize the reciprocal procedures through which the organizations work to enhance and facilitate regional integration. The Heads of Government Conference that was held in October 1992 established an Inter-Governmental Task Force, which was to undertake preparations for a reorientation of CARICOM. In February 1993 it presented a draft Charter of Civil Society for the Community, which set out principles in the areas of democracy, government, parliament, freedom of the press and human rights. The Charter was signed by Community heads of government in February 1997. Suriname was admitted to the organization in July 1995. In July 1997 the Heads of Government Conference agreed to admit Haiti as a member, although the terms and conditions of its accession to the organization had yet to be negotiated. These were finalized in July 1999. In July 2001 the CARICOM Secretary-General formally inaugurated a CARICOM Office in Haiti, which aimed to provide technical assistance in preparation of Haiti's accession to the Community. In January 2002 a CARICOM special mission visited Haiti, following an escalation of the political violence which had started in the previous month. Ministers of foreign affairs emphasized the need for international aid for Haiti when they met their US counterpart in February. Haiti was admitted as the 15th member of CARICOM at the Heads of Government Conference, held in July.

In August 1998 CARICOM and the Dominican Republic signed a free-trade accord, covering trade in goods and services, technical barriers to trade, government procurement, and sanitary and phytosanitary measures and standards. A protocol to the agreement was signed in April 2000, following the resolution of differences concerning exempted items. The accord was ratified by the Dominican Republic in February 2001 and entered partially into force on 1 December (except in Guyana, Suriname and the Bahamas).

In July 1999 CARICOM heads of government endorsed proposals to establish a Caribbean Court of Justice (CCJ), which, it was provisionally agreed, would be located in Port of Spain, Trinidad and Tobago. The Court was intended to replace the Judicial Committee of the Privy Council as the Court of Final Appeal for those countries recognizing its jurisdiction, and was also to adjudicate on trade disputes and on the interpretation of the CARICOM Treaty. An agreement establishing the Court was formally signed by 10 member countries in February 2001. Meeting in July 2002, heads of government mandated the Caribbean Development Bank to establish a trust fund, amounting to US \$100m., to finance the Court, and urged member states to implement the necessary measures to enable the Court's inauguration in late 2003.

In November 2001 the CARICOM Secretary-General formally inaugurated a Caribbean Regional Technical Assistance Centre (CARTAC), in Barbados. The Centre was intended to provide technical advice and training to officials from member countries and the Dominican Republic in support of the region's development, with particular focus on fiscal management, financial sector supervision and regulation, and the compilation of statistics. The IMF was to manage the Centre's operations, while UNDP was to provide administrative and logistical support.

In early July 2002 a conference was held, in Liliendaal, Guyana, attended by representatives of civil society and the CARICOM heads of government. The meeting issued a statement of principles on 'Forward Together', recognizing the role of civil society in meeting the challenges to the region. It was agreed to hold regular meetings and to establish a task force to develop a regional strategic framework for pursuing the main recommendations of the conference.

CO-ORDINATION OF FOREIGN POLICY

The co-ordination of foreign policies of member states is listed as one of the main objectives of the Community in its founding treaty. Activities include: strengthening of member states' position in international organizations; joint diplomatic action on issues of particular interest to the Caribbean; joint co-operation arrangements with third countries and organizations; and the negotiation of free-trade agreements with third countries and other regional groupings. This last area of activity has assumed increasing importance since the agreement in 1994 by almost all the governments of countries in the Americas to establish a 'Free Trade Area of the Americas' (FTAA) by 2005. In April 1997 CARICOM inaugurated a Regional Negotiating Machinery body to co-ordinate and strengthen the region's presence at external economic negotiations. The main focus of activities has been the establishment of the FTAA, ACP relations with the EU, and multilateral trade negotiations under the WTO.

In July 1991 Venezuela applied for membership of CARICOM, and offered a non-reciprocal free-trade agreement for CARICOM exports to Venezuela, over an initial five-year period. In October 1993 the newly-established Group of Three (Colombia, Mexico and Venezuela) signed joint agreements with CARICOM and Suriname on combating drugs-trafficking and environmental protection. In June 1994 CARICOM and Colombia concluded an agreement on trade, economic and technical co-operation, which, *inter alia*, gives special treatment to the least-developed CARICOM countries. CARICOM has observer status in the Latin American Rio Group (see p. 351).

In 1992 Cuba applied for observer status within CARICOM, and in July 1993 a joint commission was inaugurated to establish closer ties between CARICOM and Cuba and to provide a mechanism for regular dialogue. In July 1997 the heads of government agreed to pursue consideration of a free-trade accord between the Community and Cuba. A Trade and Economic Agreement was signed by the two sides in July 2000, and a CARICOM office was established in Cuba, in February 2001. In February 1992 ministers of foreign affairs from CARICOM and Central American states met to discuss future co-operation, in view of the imminent conclusion of the North American Free Trade Agreement (see p. 270) (NAFTA) between the USA, Canada and Mexico. It was agreed that a consultative forum would be established to discuss the possible formation of a Caribbean and Central American free-trade zone. In October 1993 CARICOM declared its support for NAFTA, but requested a 'grace period', during which the region's exports would have parity with Mexican products, and in March 1994 requested that it should be considered for early entry into NAFTA. In July 1996 the heads of government expressed strong concern over the complaint lodged with the World Trade Organization (WTO) by the USA, Ecuador, Guatemala and Honduras regarding the European Union's import regime on bananas, which gives preferential access to bananas from the ACP countries (see the EU, see p. 234). CARICOM requested the US Government to withdraw its complaint and to negotiate a settlement. Nevertheless, WTO panel hearings on the complaint were initiated in September. Banana producers from the ACP countries were granted third-party status, at the insistence of the Eastern Caribbean ambassador to the EU, Edwin Laurent. In December a special meeting of the Heads of Government Conference was convened, in Barbados, in order to formulate a common position on relations with the USA, in particular with respect to measures to combat illegal drugs-trafficking, following reports that the US Government was planning to impose punitive measures against certain regional authorities, owing to their perceived failure to implement effective controls on illicit drugs.

In May 1997 CARICOM heads of government met the then US President, Bill Clinton, to discuss issues of mutual concern. A partnership for prosperity and security was established at the meeting, and arrangements were instituted for annual consultations between the ministers of foreign affairs of CARICOM countries and the US Secretary of State. However, the Community failed to secure a commitment by the USA to grant the region's exports 'NAFTA-parity' status, or to guarantee concessions to the region's banana industry, following a temporary ruling of the WTO, issued in March, upholding the US trade complaint. The WTO ruling was confirmed in May and endorsed by the WTO dispute settlement body in September. The USA's opposition to a new EU banana policy (which was to terminate the import licensing system, extending import quotas to 'dollar' producers, while maintaining a limited duty-free quota for Caribbean producers) was strongly criticized by CARICOM leaders, meeting in July 1998. In March 1999 the Inter-Sessional meeting of the Conference of Heads of Government issued a statement condemning the imposition by the USA of sanctions against a number of EU imports, in protest at the revised EU banana regime, and the consequences of this action on Caribbean economies, and agreed to review its co-operation with the USA under the partnership for prosperity and security.

During 1998 CARICOM was particularly concerned by the movement within Nevis to secede from its federation with Saint Christopher. In July heads of government agreed to dispatch a mediation team to the country (postponed until September). The Heads of Government Conference held in March 1999 welcomed the establishment of a Constitutional Task Force by the local authorities to prepare a draft constitution, on the basis of recommendations of a previous constitutional commission and the outcome of a series of public meetings. In July 1998 heads of government expressed concern at the hostility between the Government and opposition groupings in Guyana. The two sides signed an agreement, under CARICOM auspices, and in September a CARICOM mediation mission visited Guyana to promote further dialogue. CARICOM has declared its support for Guyana in its territorial disputes with Venezuela and Suriname. In June 2000 CARICOM initiated negotiations following Suriname's removal of petroleum drilling equipment from Guyanan territorial waters. In March 2000 heads of government issued a statement supporting the territorial integrity and security of Belize in that country's ongoing border dispute with Guatemala. CARICOM subsequently urged both countries to implement the provisions of an agreement signed in November. In December 2001 a CARICOM mission observed a general election in Trinidad and Tobago. Following an inconclusive outcome to the election, a delegation from CARICOM visited that country in late January 2002.

In July 2000 the Heads of Government meeting issued a statement strongly opposing the OECD Harmful Tax Initiative, under which punitive measures had been threatened against 35 countries, including CARICOM member states, if they failed to tighten tax-

ation legislation. The meeting also condemned a separate list, issued by the OECD's Financial Task Force on Money Laundering (FATF, see p. 343), which identified 15 countries, including five Caribbean states, of failing to counter effectively international money-laundering. The statement reaffirmed CARICOM's commitment to fighting financial crimes and support for any necessary reform of supervisory practices or legislation, but insisted that national taxation jurisdictions, and specifically competitive regimes designed to attract offshore business, was not a matter for OECD concern. CARICOM remained actively involved in efforts to counter the scheme, and in April 2001 presented its case to the US President. In September the FATF issued a revised list of 19 'unco-operative jurisdictions', including Dominica, Grenada, St Christopher and Nevis and St Vincent and the Grenadines. In early 2002 most Caribbean states concluded a provisional agreement with the OECD to work to improve the transparency and supervision of offshore sectors.

In February 2002 the first meeting of heads of state and of government of CARICOM and the Central American Integration System convened in Belize City. The meeting aimed to strengthen co-operation between the groupings, in particular in international negotiations, efforts to counter transnational organized crime, and support for the regions' economies.

ECONOMIC CO-OPERATION

The Caribbean Community's main field of activity is economic integration, by means of a Caribbean Common Market which replaced the former Caribbean Free Trade Association. The Secretariat and the Caribbean Development Bank undertake research on the best means of facing economic difficulties, and meetings of the Chief Executives of commercial banks and of central bank officials are also held with the aim of strengthening regional co-operation.

In July 1984 heads of government agreed to establish a common external tariff (CET) on certain products, in order to protect domestic industries, although implementation of the CET was considerably delayed (see below). They also urged the necessity of structural adjustment in the economies of the region, including measures to expand production and reduce imports. In 1989 the Conference of Heads of Government agreed to implement, by July 1993, a series of measures to encourage the creation of a single Caribbean market. These included the establishment of a CARICOM Industrial Programming Scheme; the inauguration of the CARICOM Enterprise Regime; abolition of passport requirements for CARICOM nationals travelling within the region; full implementation of the rules of origin and the revised scheme for the harmonization of fiscal incentives; free movement of skilled workers; removal of all remaining regional barriers to trade; establishment of a regional system of air and sea transport; and the introduction of a scheme for regional capital movement. A CARICOM Export Development Council, established in November 1989, undertook a three-year export development project to stimulate trade within CARICOM and to promote exports outside the region.

In August 1990 CARICOM heads of government mandated the governors of CARICOM members' central banks to begin a study of the means to achieve a monetary union within CARICOM; they also institutionalized meetings of CARICOM ministers of finance and senior finance officials, to take place twice a year.

The initial deadline of 1 January 1991 for the establishment of a CET was not achieved, and in July a new deadline of 1 October was set for those members which had not complied—Antigua and Barbuda, Belize, Montserrat, Saint Christopher and Nevis and Saint Lucia, whose governments feared that the tariff would cause an increase in the rate of inflation and damage domestic industries. This deadline was later (again unsuccessfully) extended to February 1992. The tariff, which imposed a maximum level of duty of 45% on imports, was also criticized by the World Bank, the IMF and the US Government as being likely to reduce the region's competitiveness. At a special meeting, held in October 1992, CARICOM heads of government agreed to reduce the maximum level of tariffs to between 30% and 35%, to be in effect by 30 June 1993 (the level was to be further lowered, to 25%–30% by 1995). The Bahamas, however, was not party to these trading arrangements (since it is a member of the Community but not of the Common Market), and Belize was granted an extension for the implementation of the new tariff levels. At the Heads of Government Conference, held in July 1995 in Guyana, Suriname was admitted as a full member of CARICOM and acceded to the treaty establishing the Common Market. It was granted until 1 January 1996 for implementation of the tariff reductions.

The 1995 Heads of Government Conference approved additional measures to promote the single market. The free movement of skilled workers (mainly graduates from recognized regional institutions) was to be permitted from 1 January 1996. At the same time an agreement on the mutual protection and provision of social security benefits was to enter into force. In July 1996 the heads of government decided that CARICOM ministers of finance, central bank governors and planning agencies should meet more frequently to address single market issues and agreed to extend the provisions of free movement to sports people, musicians and others working in the arts and media.

In July 1997 the heads of government, meeting in Montego Bay, Jamaica, agreed to accelerate economic integration, with the aim of completing a single market by 1999. At the meeting 11 member states signed Protocol II amending the Treaty of Chaguaramas, which constituted a central element of a CARICOM Single Market and Economy (CSME), providing for the right to establish enterprises, the provision of services and the free movement of capital and labour throughout participating countries. A regional collaborative network was established to promote the CSME. In July 1998, at the meeting of heads of government, held in Saint Lucia, an agreement was signed with the Insurance Company of the West Indies to accelerate the establishment of a Caribbean Investment Fund, which was to mobilize foreign currency from extra-regional capital markets for investment in new or existing enterprises in the region. Some 60% of all funds generated were to be used by CARICOM countries and the remainder by non-CARICOM members of the ACS.

In November 2000 a special consultation on the single market and economy was held in Barbados, involving CARICOM and government officials, academics, and representatives of the private sector, labour organizations, the media, and other regional groupings. In February 2001 heads of government agreed to establish a new high-level sub-committee to accelerate the establishment of the CSME and to promote its objectives. The sub-committee was to be supported by a Technical Advisory Council, comprising representatives of the public and private sectors. By June all member states had signed and declared the provisional application of Protocol II, which had received two ratifications. By mid-2002 nine countries had completed the fourth phase of the CET.

In October 2001 CARICOM heads of government, meeting in a special emergency meeting, considered the impact on the region's economy of the terrorist attacks perpetrated against targets in the USA in the previous month. The meeting resolved to enhance aviation security, to implement promotion and marketing campaigns in support of the tourist industry, and to approach international institutions to assist with emergency financing. The economic situation, which had been further adversely affected by the reduced access to the EU banana market, the economic downturn in the USA, and the effects on the investment climate of the OECD Harmful Taxation Initiative, was considered at the Heads of Government Conference, held in Guyana, in July 2002. Heads of government agreed to meeting in August in special session to elaborate a programme to revive the economy, on the basis of the work of a newly-appointed technical team. A technical committee was also established in July to develop proposals for a regional stabilization programme, and a Stabilization Fund. An inter-sessional Heads of Government Conference that was held in in February 2003, in Port-of-Spain, Trinidad and Tobago, considered a proposal that the Fund should be established with initial capital of US $60m., rising to $180m. within five years.

CRIME AND SECURITY

In December 1996 CARICOM heads of government determined to strengthen comprehensive co-operation and technical assistance to combat illegal drugs-trafficking. The Conference decided to establish a Caribbean Security Task Force to help formulate a single regional agreement on maritime interdiction, incorporating agreements already concluded by individual members. A Regional Drugs Control Programme at the CARICOM Secretariat aims to co-ordinate regional initiatives with the overall objective of reducing the demand and supply of illegal substances. In July 2001 the Prime Minister of Antigua and Barbuda, Lester Bird, proposed the establishment of a rapid response unit to deal with drugs-related and other serious crimes. Heads of government agreed, instead, to establish a task force to be responsible for producing recommendations for a forthcoming meeting of national security advisers. In October, heads of government convened an emergency meeting in Nassau, the Bahamas, to consider the impact of the terrorist attacks against the USA which had occurred in September. The meeting determined to convene immediately the so-called Task Force on Crime and Security in order to implement new policy directives. It was agreed to enhance co-ordination and collaboration of security services throughout the region, in particular in intelligence gathering, analysis and sharing in relation to crime, illicit drugs and terrorism, and to strengthen security at airports, seaports and borders. In July 2002 heads of government agreed on a series of initiatives recommended by the Task Force to counter the escalation in crime and violence. These included strengthening border controls, preparing national anti-crime master plans, establishing broad-based National Commissions on law and order and strengthening the exchange of information and intelligence.

INDUSTRY AND ENERGY

A protocol relating to the CARICOM Industrial Programming Scheme (CIPS), approved in 1988, is the Community's instrument for promoting the co-operative development of industry in the region. Protocol III amending the Treaty of Chaguaramas, with respect to industrial policy, was opened for signature in July 1998. At June 2001 it had been signed by 13 member states, provisionally applied by 12, and ratified by one.

The Secretariat has established a national standards bureau in each member country to harmonize technical standards, and supervises the metrication of weights and measures. In 1999 members agreed to establish a new CARICOM Regional Organization of Standards and Quality (CROSQ) to develop common regional standards and resolve disputes. CROSQ, located in Barbados, became operational in 2002.

The CARICOM Alternative Energy Systems Project provides training, assesses energy needs and conducts energy audits. Efforts in regional energy development are directed at the collection and analysis of data for national energy policy documents.

TRANSPORT, COMMUNICATIONS AND TOURISM

A Caribbean Confederation of Shippers' Councils represents the interests of regional exporters and importers. In July 1990 the Caribbean Telecommunications Union was established to oversee developments in regional telecommunications.

In 1988 a Consultative Committee on Caribbean Regional Information Systems (CCCRIS) was established to evaluate and monitor the functioning of existing information systems and to seek to co-ordinate and advise on the establishment of new systems.

A Summit of Heads of Government on Tourism, Trade and Transportation was held in Trinidad and Tobago, in August 1995, to which all members of the ACS and regional tourism organizations were invited. In 1997 CARICOM heads of government considered a number of proposals relating to air transportation, tourism, human resource development and capital investment, which had been identified by Community ministers of tourism as critical issues in the sustainable development of the tourist industry. The heads of government requested ministers to meet regularly to develop tourism policies, and in particular to undertake an in-depth study of human resource development issues in early 1998. A new fund to help train young people from the region in aspects of the tourist industry was inaugurated in July 1997, in memory of the former Prime Minister of Jamaica, Michael Manley. A regional summit on tourism, in recognition of the importance of the industry to the economic development of the region, was held in the Bahamas, in December 2001.

A Multilateral Agreement Concerning the Operations of Air Services within the Caribbean Community entered into force in November 1998, providing a formal framework for the regulation of the air transport industry and enabling CARICOM-owned and -controlled airlines to operate freely within the region. In July 1999 heads of government signed Protocol VI amending the Treaty of Chaguaramas providing for a common transportation policy, with harmonized standards and practices, which was to be an integral component of the development of a single market and economy. In November 2001 representatives of national civil aviation authorities signed a memorandum of understanding, providing for the establishment of a regional body, with the aim of promoting the development of a Regional Aviation Oversight Safety System.

AGRICULTURE AND FISHERIES

In July 1996 the CARICOM summit meeting agreed to undertake wide-ranging measures in order to modernize the agricultural sector and to increase the international competitiveness of Caribbean agricultural produce. The CARICOM Secretariat was to support national programmes with assistance in policy formulation, human resource development and the promotion of research and technology development in the areas of productivity, marketing, agri-business and water resources management. During 1997 CARICOM Governments continued to lobby against a complaint lodged at the WTO with regard to the EU's banana import regime (offering favourable conditions to ACP producers—see above) and to generate awareness of the economic and social importance of the banana industry to the region. Protocol V amending the Treaty of Chaguaramas, which was concerned with agricultural policy, was opened for signature by heads of government in July 1998. At June 2001 it had been signed and provisionally applied by 13 member states, and ratified by one (Guyana). In July 2002 heads of government approved an initiative to develop a CARIFORUM Special Programme for Food Security.

In February 2003 the CARICOM Secretariat was mandated to draft a proposal for a common fisheries policy that was to be presented to the next Conference of Heads of State, scheduled to be convened in July in Jamaica.

HEALTH AND EDUCATION

In 1986 CARICOM and the Pan-American Health Organization launched 'Caribbean Co-operation in Health' with projects to be undertaken in six main areas: environmental protection, including the control of disease-bearing pests; development of human resources; chronic non-communicable diseases and accidents; strengthening health systems; food and nutrition; maternal and child health care; and population activities. In 2001 CARICOM co-ordinated a new regional partnership to reduce the spread and impact of HIV and AIDS in member countries. All countries were to prepare national strategic plans to facilitate access to funding to combat the problem. A meeting of the so-called Pan-Caribbean Partnership against HIV/AIDS (PANCAP) was convened in November. In February 2002 PANCAP initiated regional negotiations with pharmaceutical companies to secure reductions in the cost of anti-retroviral drugs. A Caribbean Environmental Health Institute (see below) aims to promote collaboration among member states in all areas of environmental management and human health. In July 2001 heads of government, meeting in the Bahamas, issued the Nassau Declaration on Health, advocating greater regional strategic co-ordination and planning in the health sector, institutional reform, and increased resources.

CARICOM educational programmes have included the improvement of reading in schools through assistance for teacher-training; and ensuring the availability of low-cost educational material throughout the region. In July 1997 CARICOM heads of government adopted the recommendations of a ministerial committee, which identified priority measures for implementation in the education sector. These included the objective of achieving universal, quality secondary education and the enrolment of 15% of post-secondary students in tertiary education by 2005, as well as improved training in foreign languages and science and technology. From the late 1990s youth activities have been increasingly emphasized by the Community. These have included new programmes for disadvantaged youths, a mechanism for youth exchange and the convening of a Caribbean Youth Parliament.

EMERGENCY ASSISTANCE

A Caribbean Disaster Emergency Response Agency (CDERA) was established in 1991 to co-ordinate immediate disaster relief, primarily in the event of hurricanes. During 1997 CARICOM Governments remained actively concerned with the situation in Montserrat, which had suffered a series of massive volcanic eruptions. At the Heads of Government Conference in July, the Community pledged humanitarian, economic and technical assistance and resolved to help mobilize external assistance from regional and international donor countries and institutions. In March 1998 CARICOM heads of government agreed to establish a team, comprising representatives of the CARICOM Secretariat, CDERA and the Caribbean Development Bank, to assist the Montserrat Government in formulating programmes to provide a secure future for the island. In November the Community determined to support the countries of Central America in their reconstruction and rehabilitation efforts following the devastation caused by 'Hurricane Mitch', and to co-ordinate the provision of immediate humanitarian assistance by CARICOM member countries.

INSTITUTIONS

The following are among the institutions formally established within the framework of CARICOM.

Assembly of Caribbean Community Parliamentarians: c/o CARICOM Secretariat; an intergovernmental agreement on the establishment of a regional parliament entered into force in August 1994; inaugural meeting held in Barbados, in May 1996. Comprises up to four representatives of the parliaments of each member country, and up to two of each associate member. It aims to provide a forum for wider community involvement in the process of integration and for enhanced deliberation on CARICOM affairs; authorized to issue recommendations for the Conference of Heads of Government and to adopt resolutions on any matter arising under the Treaty of Chaguaramas.

Caribbean Agricultural Research and Development Institute —CARDI: UWI Campus, St Augustine, Trinidad and Tobago; tel. 645-1205; fax 645-1208; e-mail infocentre@cardi.org; internet www.cardi.org; f. 1975; aims to contribute to the competitiveness and sustainability of Caribbean agriculture by generating and transferring new and appropriate technologies and by developing effective partnerships with regional and international entities; Exec. Dir Bruce Laukner; publs *CARDI Weekly*, *Procicaribe News*, *CARDI Annual Report*, Technical bulletin series.

Caribbean Centre for Development Administration— CARICAD: 1st Floor, Weymouth Corporate Centre, Roebuck St, St Michael, Barbados; tel. 4278535; fax 4361709; e-mail caricad@caribsurf.com; internet www.caricad.org; f. 1980; aims to assist governments in the reform of the public sector and to strengthen their managerial capacities for public administration; promotes the involvement of the private sector, non-governmental organizations and other bodies in all decision-making processes; Exec. Dir Dr P. I. Gomes.

Caribbean Disaster Emergency Response Agency—CDERA: The Garrison, St Michael, Barbados; tel. 436-9651; fax 437-7649; e-mail cdera@caribsurf.com; internet www.cdera.org; f. 1991 for activities, see Emergency Assistance above; Regional Co-ordinator Jeremy Collymore.

Caribbean Environmental Health Institute—CEHI: POB 1111, The Morne, Castries, St Lucia; tel. 4522501; fax 4532721; e-mail cehi@candw.lc; internet www.cehi.org.lc; f. 1980 (began operations in 1982); provides technical and advisory services to member states in formulating environmental health policy legislation and in all areas of environmental management (for example, solid waste management, water supplies, beach and air pollution, and pesticides control); promotes, collates and disseminates relevant research; conducts courses, seminars and workshops throughout the region; Exec. Dir Vincent Sweeney.

Caribbean Food and Nutrition Institute—CFNI: UWI Campus, POB 140, St Augustine, Trinidad and Tobago; tel. 663-1544; e-mail cfni@cablenett.net; internet www.cfni.paho.org; f. 1967 to serve the governments and people of the region and to act as a catalyst among persons and organizations concerned with food and nutrition through research and field investigations, training in nutrition, dissemination of information, advisory services and production of educational material; mems: all English-speaking Caribbean territories, including the mainland countries of Belize and Guyana; Dir Dr Fitzroy Henry; publs *Cajanus* (quarterly), *Nyam News* (monthly), *Nutrient-Cost Tables* (quarterly), educational material.

Caribbean Meteorological Organization—CMO: POB 461, Port of Spain, Trinidad and Tobago; tel. 624-4481; fax 623-3634; e-mail hqcmo@tstt.net.tt; f. 1951 to co-ordinate regional activities in meteorology, operational hydrology and allied sciences; became an associate institution of CARICOM in 1973; comprises a headquarters unit, a Council of Government Ministers, the Caribbean Meteorological Foundation and the Caribbean Meteorological Institute, located in Barbados; mems: govts of 16 countries and territories represented by the National Meteorological and Hydro-meteorological Services; Co-ordinating Dir Tyrone W. Sutherland.

ASSOCIATE INSTITUTIONS

Caribbean Development Bank: POB 408, Wildey, St Michael, Barbados; tel. 431-1600; fax 426-7269; e-mail info@caribank.org; internet www.caribank.org; f. 1969 to stimulate regional economic growth through support for agriculture, industry, transport and other infrastructure, tourism, housing and education; subscribed cap. US \$687.2m. (Dec. 1999); in 1999 net approvals totalled \$146.6m. for 16 projects; at the end of 1999 cumulative grant and loan disbursements totalled \$1,275.0m.; the Special Development Fund was replenished in 1996; mems: CARICOM states, and Canada, the People's Republic of China, Colombia, Germany, Italy, Mexico, United Kingdom, Venezuela; Pres. Dr. Compton Bourne.

Caribbean Law Institute: University of the West Indies, Cave Hill Campus, POB 64, Bridgetown, Barbados; tel. 417-4560; fax 417-4138.

Other Associate Institutions of CARICOM, in accordance with its constitution, are the University of Guyana, the University of the West Indies and the Secretariat of the Organisation of Eastern Caribbean States (see p. 341).

Publications

Annual Report.
Caribbean Trade and Investment Report.
CARICOM View (quarterly).
Statistics — News and Views (2 a year).

CENTRAL AMERICAN INTEGRATION SYSTEM

(SISTEMA DE LA INTEGRACIÓN CENTROAMERICANA—SICA)

Address: Blv. Orden de Malta 470, Urb. Santa Elena, Antiguo Cuscatlán, San Salvador, El Salvador.

Telephone: 289-6131; **fax:** 289-6124; **e-mail:** sgsic@sicanet.org.sv; **internet:** www.sgsica.org.

Founded in December 1991, when the heads of state of six Central American countries signed the Protocol of Tegucigalpa to the agreement establishing the Organization of Central American States (f. 1951), creating a new framework for regional integration. A General Secretariat of the Sistema de la Integración Centroamericana (SICA) was inaugurated in February 1993 to co-ordinate the process of political, economic, social cultural and environmental integration and to promote democracy and respect for human rights throughout the region.

MEMBERS

Belize	Guatemala	Nicaragua
Costa Rica	Honduras	Panama
El Salvador		

OBSERVERS

Dominican Republic	Taiwan

Organization

(April 2003)

SUMMIT MEETINGS

The meetings of heads of state of member countries serve as the supreme decision-making organ of SICA.

COUNCIL OF MINISTERS

Ministers of Foreign Affairs of member states meet regularly to provide policy direction for the process of integration.

CONSULTATIVE COMMITTEE

The Committee comprises representatives of business organizations, trade unions, academic institutions and other federations concerned with the process of integration in the region. It is an integral element of the integration system and assists the Secretary-General in determining the policies of the organization.

President: RICARDO SOL.

GENERAL SECRETARIAT

The General Secretariat of SICA was established in February 1993 to co-ordinate the process of enhanced regional integration. It comprises the following divisions: inter-institutional relations; research and co-operation; legal and political affairs; economic affairs; and communications and information.

In September 1997 Central American Common Market (CACM) heads of state, meeting in the Nicaraguan capital, signed the Managua Declaration in support of further regional integration and the establishment of a political union. A commission was to be established to consider all aspects of the policy and to formulate a timetable for the integration process. In February 1998 SICA heads of state resolved to establish a Unified General Secretariat to integrate the institutional aspects of SICA (see below) in a single office, to be located in San Salvador. The process was ongoing in early 2003.

Secretary-General: Dr OSCAR ALFREDO SANTAMARÍA.

SPECIALIZED TECHNICAL SECRETARIATS

Secretaría Ejecutiva de la Comisión Centroamericana de Ambiente y Desarrollo—SE-CCAD: Blv. Orden de Malta 470, Santa Elena, Antiguo Cuscatlán, San Salvador, El Salvador; tel. 289-6131; fax 289-6124; e-mail mcastro@sgsica.org; internet ccad .sgsica.org; f. 1989 to enhance collaboration in the promotion of sustainable development and environmental protection; Exec. Sec. MAURICIO CASTRO SALAZAR.

Secretaría General de la Coordinación Educativa y Cultural Centroamericana—SG-CECC: 175m norte de la esquina oeste del ICE, Sabana Norte, San José, Costa Rica; tel. 232-3783; fax 231-2366; e-mail sgcecc@sol.racsa.co.cr; f. 1982; promotes development of regional programmes in the fields of education and culture; Sec.-Gen. MARVIN HERRERA ARAYA.

Secretaría Permanente del Tratado General de Integración Económica Centroamericana (SIECA): 4A Avda 10–25, Zona 14, Apdo 1237, 01901 Guatemala City, Guatemala; tel. (2) 368-2151; fax (2) 368-1071; e-mail sieca@pronet.net.gt; internet www.sieca.org.gt; f. 1960 to assist the process of economic integration and the creation of a Central American Common Market (CACM—established by the organization of Central American States under the General Treaty of Central American Economic Integration, signed in December 1960 and ratified by Costa Rica, Guatemala, El Salvador, Honduras and Nicaragua in September 1963); supervises the correct implementation of the legal instruments of economic integration, carries out relevant studies at the request of the CACM, and arranges meetings; comprises departments covering the working of the CACM: negotiations and external trade policy; external co-operation; systems and statistics; finance and administration; also includes a unit for co-operation with the private sector and finance institutions, and a legal consultative committee; Sec.-Gen. HAROLDO RODAS MELARA; publs *Anuario Estadístico Centroamericano de Comercio Exterior*, *Carta Informativa* (monthly), *Cuadernos de la SIECA* (2 a year), *Estadísticas Macroeconómicas de Centroamérica* (annually), *Series Estadísticas Seleccionadas de Centroamérica* (annually), *Boletín Informativo* (fortnightly).

Secretaría Técnica del Consejo de la Integración Social—ST-CIS: Blv. Orden de Malta 470, Santa Elena, Antiguo Cuscatlán, San Salvador, El Salvador; tel. 289-6131; fax 289-6124; e-mail hmorgado@sgsica.org.sv; f. 1995; Dir-Gen. Dr HUGO MORGADO.

OTHER SPECIALIZED SECRETARIATS

Direccíon de Turismo de la Secretaría General del SICA—SITCA: Blv. Orden de Malta 470, Santa Elena, Antiguo Cuscatlán, San Salvador, El Salvador; tel. 289-6131; fax 289-6124; e-mail econtreras@sgsica.org.sv; f. 1965 to develop regional tourism activities; Sec.-Gen. EDGARDO CONTRERAS SCHNEIDER.

Secretaría del Consejo Agropecuario Centroamericano—SCAC: Sede del IICA, Apdo Postal 55-2200 Coronado, San José, Costa Rica; tel. 216-0303; fax 216-0285; e-mail rguillen@iica.ac.cr; f. 1991 to determine and co-ordinate regional policies and programmes relating to agriculture and agroindustry; Sec-Gen. RÓGER GUILLÉN BUSTOS.

Secretaría Ejecutiva del Consejo Monetario Centroamericano—SECMCA (Central American Monetary Council): Ofiplaza del Este, Edif. C, 75m. oeste de la Rotonda la Bandera, San Pedro Montes de Oca, Apdo Postal 5438-1000, San José, Costa Rica; tel. 280-9522; fax 281-0169; e-mail secma@sol.racsa.co.cr; internet www .secmca.org; f. 1964 by the presidents of Central American central banks, to co-ordinate monetary policies; Exec. Sec. MIGUEL CHORRO; publs *Boletín Estadístico* (annually), *Informe Económico* (annually).

Secretaría Ejecutiva de la Comisión Centroamericana de Transporte Marítimo—COCATRAM: Contiguo a Mansión Teolinda, Barrio Bolonia, Apdo Postal 2423, Managua, Nicaragua; tel. (2) 222-3560; fax (2) 222-2759; e-mail cocatram@ibw.com.ni; internet www.cocatram.org.ni; f. 1981; Exec. Sec. ALFONSO BREUILLET GALINDO; publs *Boletín Informativo*.

PARLIAMENT

12A Avda 33-04, Zona 5, Guatemala City, Guatemala 01005; tel. (2) 339-0466; fax (2) 334-6670; e-mail guatemala@parlacen.org.gt; internet www.parlacen.org.gt.

Officially inaugurated in 1991. Comprises representatives of El Salvador, Guatemala, Honduras, Nicaragua and Panama. In February 1998 heads of state of member countries resolved to limit the number of deputies to 10–15 from each country.

President: (2002/03) AUGUSTO VELA MENA (Guatemala).

COURT OF JUSTICE

Apdo Postal 907 Managua, Nicaragua; tel. 266-6273; fax 266-8486; e-mail cortecen@tmx.com.ni; internet www.ccj.org.ni.

Officially inaugurated in 1994. Tribunal authorized to consider disputes relating to treaties agreed within the regional integration system. In February 1998 Central American heads of state agreed to limit the number of magistrates in the Court to one per country.

President: (2002/03) Dr RAFAEL CHAMORRO MORA.

AD HOC INTERGOVERNMENTAL SECRETARIATS

Comisión para el Desarollo Científico y Tecnológico para Centroamérica y Panamá—CTCAP (Committee for the Scientific and Technological Development of Central America and Panama): Antigua base de Clayton, Édif. 213, Panamá, Panama; tel. 317-0014; fax 317-0026; e-mail espinoza@ns.hondunet.net; internet www.senacyt.gob.pa/ctcap; f. 1975; Pres. Dr Gonzalo Córdova (Panama).

Consejo Centroamericano de Instituciones de Seguridad Social—COCISS (Central American Council of Social Security Institutions): Apdo 10105, San José, Costa Rica; tel. 257-0122; fax 233-1850; e-mail cociss@ccss.sa.cr; internet www.ccss.sa.cr/cociss/idcociss.htm; f. 1992; Pres. Dr Rodolfo Piza Rocafort.

Consejo del Istmo Centroamericano de Deportes y Recreación—CODICADER (Committee of the Central American Isthmus for Sport and Recreation): Palacio Nacional de los Deportes, Edif. Administrativo, 3°, San Salvador, El Salvador; tel. 271-3080; fax 271-5681; f. 1992; Dir. Roberto Hernández.

Unidad Técnica del Consejo Centroamericano de Vivienda y Asentamientos Humanos—CCVAH (Central American Council on Housing and Human Settlements): Avda la Paz 244, Tegucigalpa, Honduras; tel. 236-5804; fax 236-6560; f. 1992; Co-ordinator a.i. Armando Enrique Sánchez.

Secretaría Ejecutiva del Consejo de Electrificación de América Central—CEAC (Central American Electrification Council): 9A Calle Pte 950, Edif. CEL, Centro de Gobierno, San Salvador, El Salvador; tel. 211-6175; fax 211-6239; e-mail jmontesi@cel.gob.sv; internet www.ceac-ca.org.sv; f. 1985; Exec. Sec Jorge Salomón Montesinos.

OTHER REGIONAL INSTITUTIONS

Finance

Banco Centroamericano de Integración Económica—BCIE (Central American Bank for Economic Integration): Blv. Suyapa, Contigua a Banco de Honduras, Apdo 772, Tegucigalpa, Honduras; tel. 228-2182; fax 228-2183; e-mail webmail-hn@bcie.org; internet www.bcie.hn; f. 1961 to promote the economic integration and balanced economic development of member countries; finances public and private development projects, particularly those related to industrialization and infrastructure; by March 1999 cumulative lending amounted to US \$5,238m. for 1,763 loans; auth. cap. \$2,000m; regional mems: Costa Rica, El Salvador, Guatemala, Honduras, Nicaragua; non-regional mems: Argentina, the People's Republic of China, Colombia, Mexico; Pres. Pablo Schneider; publs *Annual Report, Revista de la Integración y el Desarrollo de Centroamérica.*

Public Administration

Centro de Coordinación para la Prevención de Desastres Naturales en América Central—CEPREDENAC: Antigua Base de Howard, Ave. Rencher, Edif. 707, Panamá, Panama; tel. 316-0065; fax 316-0074; e-mail secretaria@cepredenac.org; internet www.cepredenac.org; Exec. Sec. Gerónimo Giusto Robelo.

Comisión Centroamericana Permanente para la Erradicación de la Producción, Tráfico, Consumo y Uso Ilícitos de Estupefacientes y Sustancias Psicotrópicas y Delitos Conexos—CCP (Permanent Central American Committee for the Eradication of Illicit Production, Traffic, Consumption and Use of Narcotics and Psychotropic Substances and Associated Crimes): Edif. de Comisiones, 1°, Tegucigalpa, Honduras; tel. 237-0568; fax 238-3960; f. 1993; Pres. Dr Carlos Sosa Coello.

Instituto Centroamericano de Administración Pública—ICAP (Central American Institute of Public Administration): Apdo Postal 10025-1000 San José, Costa Rica; tel. 234-1011; fax 225-2049; e-mail icapcr@sol.racsa.co.cr; internet www.icap.ac.cr; f. 1954 by the five Central American Republics and the United Nations, with later participation by Panama, the Institute aims to train the region's public servants, provide technical assistance and carry out research leading to reforms in public administration; Dir Dr Hugo Zelaya Cálix.

Secretaría Ejecutiva de la Comisión Regional de Recursos Hidráulicos—SE-CRRH: Apdo Postal 1527-1200, Pavas, San José, Costa Rica; tel. 296-4641 ; fax 296-0047; e-mail crrhcr@sol.racsa.co.cr; internet www.crrh.imn.ac.cr; f. 1966; mems: Belize, Costa Rica, El Salvador, Guatemala, Honduras, Nicaragua, Panama; Exec. Dir Max Campos Ortiz.

Education and Health

Comité Coordinador Regional de Instituciones de Agua Potable y Saneamiento de Centroamérica, Panamá y República Dominicana—CAPRE: De la casa Italia, 100m. al sur y 100 al este, diagonal a farmacia Umaña, Barrio Francisco Peralta, San Pedro de Montes de OCA, San José, Costa Rica; tel. 280-4460; fax 280-4414; e-mail capregtz@sol.racsa.co.cr; f. 1979; Dir Liliana Arce Umaña.

Consejo Superior Universitario Centroamericano—CSUCA (Central American University Council): Ciudad Universitaria Rodrigo Facio, San Pedro de Montes de Oca, Apdo Postal 37-2060 San José, Costa Rica; tel. 225-2744; fax 234-0071; e-mail rsol@cariari.ucr.ac.cr; internet www.csuca.ac.cr; f. 1948 to guarantee academic, administrative and economic autonomy for universities and to encourage regional integration of higher education; maintains libraries and documentation centres; Council of 32 mems; mems: 16 universities, in Belize, Costa Rica (four), El Salvador, Guatemala, Honduras (two), Nicaragua (four) and Panama (three); Sec.-Gen. Dr Ricardo Sol Sol Arriaza (El Salvador); publs *Estudios Sociales Centroamericanos* (quarterly), *Cuadernos de Investigación* (monthly), *Carta Informativa de la Secretaría General* (monthly).

Instituto de Nutrición de Centroamérica y Panamá (Institute of Nutrition of Central America and Panama—INCAP): Calzada Roosevelt, Zona 11, Apdo Postal 1188, Guatemala City, Guatemala; tel. (2) 473-6518 ; fax (2) 473–6529; e-mail hdelgado@incap.ops-oms.org; internet www.incap.org.gt; f. 1949 to promote the development of nutritional sciences and their application and to strengthen the technical capacity of member countries to reach food and nutrition security; provides training and technical assistance for nutrition education and planning; conducts applied research; disseminates information; maintains library (including about 600 periodicals); administered by the Pan American Health Organization (PAHO) and the World Health Organization; mems: CACM mems and Belize and Panama; Dir Dr Hernán L. Delgado; publ. *Annual Report.*

Organismo Internacional Regional de Sanidad Agropecuaria—OIRSA (International Regional Organization of Plant Protection and Animal Health): Avda República Federal de Alemania, Calle Ramón Belloso y final pasaje Isolde, Edif. OIRSA, Col. Escalon, San Salvador, El Salvador; tel. 263-1123; fax 263-1128; e-mail orgoirsa@gbm.net; internet ns1.oirsa.org.sv; f. 1953 for the prevention of the introduction of animal and plant pests and diseases unknown in the region; research, control and eradication programmes of the principal pests present in agriculture; technical assistance and advice to the ministries of agriculture and livestock of member countries; education and qualification of personnel; mems: Belize, Costa Rica, Dominican Republic, El Salvador, Guatemala, Honduras, Mexico, Nicaragua, Panama; Exec. Dir Dr Celio Humberto Barreto Ortega.

Transport and Communications

Comisión Técnica de Telecomunicaciones—COMTELCA (Technical Commission for Telecommunications): Col. Palmira, Edif. Alfa, 608 Avda Brasil, Apdo 1793, Tegucigalpa, Honduras; tel. 220-6666; fax 220-1197; e-mail alexm@comtelca.hn; internet www.comtelca.org; f. 1966 to co-ordinate and improve the regional telecommunications network; Dir-Gen. Héctor Leonel Rodríguez Milla.

Corporación Centroamericana de Servicios de Navegación Aérea—COCESNA (Central American Air Navigation Service Corporation): Apdo 660, Aeropuerto de Toncontín, Tegucigalpa, Honduras; tel. 234-3360; fax 234-2550; e-mail sec-interna@cocesna.org; internet www.cocesna.hn; f. 1960 ; offers radar air traffic control services, aeronautical telecommunications services, flight inspections and radio assistance services for air navigation; administers the Central American Aeronautical School; Exec. Pres. Eduardo José Marín.

Activities

In June 1990 the presidents of the Central American Common Market (CACM) countries (Costa Rica, El Salvador, Guatemala, Honduras and Nicaragua) signed a declaration welcoming peace initiatives in El Salvador, Guatemala and Nicaragua, and appealing for a revitalization of CACM, as a means of promoting lasting peace in the region. In December the presidents committed themselves to the creation of an effective common market, proposing the opening of negotiations on a comprehensive regional customs and tariffs policy by March 1991, and the introduction of a regional 'anti-dumping' code by December 1991. They requested the support of multilateral lending institutions through investment in regional development, and the cancellation or rescheduling of member countries' debts. In December 1991 the heads of state of the five CACM countries and Panama signed the Protocol of Tegucigalpa, and in February 1993 the General Secretariat of SICA was inaugurated to co-ordinate the integration process in the region.

In February 1993 the European Community (EC) signed a new framework co-operation agreement with the CACM member states extending the programme of economic assistance and political dialogue initiated in 1984; a further co-operation agreement with the European Union (as the EC had become) was signed in early 1996.

In October 1993 the presidents of the CACM countries and Panama signed a protocol to the 1960 General Treaty, committing themselves to full economic integration in the region (with a common external tariff of 20% for finished products and 5% for raw materials and capital goods) and creating conditions for increased free trade. The countries agreed to accelerate the removal of internal non-tariff barriers, but no deadline was set. Full implementation of the protocol was to be 'voluntary and gradual', owing to objections on the part of Costa Rica and Panama. In May 1994, however, Costa Rica committed itself to full participation in the protocol. In March 1995 a meeting of the Central American Monetary Council discussed and endorsed a reduction in the tariff levels from 20% to 15% and from 5% to 1%. However, efforts to adopt this as a common policy were hindered by the implementation of these tariff levels by El Salvador on a unilateral basis, from 1 April, and the subsequent modifications by Guatemala and Costa Rica of their external tariffs. In March 2002 Central American leaders adopted the San Salvador Plan of Action for Central American Economic Integration, establishing several objectives as the basis for the creation, by 1 January 2004, of a regional customs union, with a single tariff.

In December 1994 the SICA member states and the USA signed the Central American-United States of America Joint Declaration (CONCAUSA), covering co-operation in the following areas: conservation of biodiversity, sound management of energy, environmental legislation, and sustainable economic development. In June 2001 the SICA states and the USA signed a renewed and expanded CONCAUSA, now also covering co-operation in addressing climate change, and in disaster preparedness. In May 1997 the heads of state of CACM member countries, together with the Prime Minister of Belize, conferred with the then US President, Bill Clinton, in San José, Costa Rica. The leaders resolved to establish a Trade and Investment Council to promote trade relations; however, Clinton failed to endorse a request from CACM members that their products receive preferential access to US markets, on similar terms to those from Mexico agreed under the NAFTA accord. During the 1990s the Central American Governments pursued negotiations to conclude free-trade agreements with Mexico, Panama and the members of the Caribbean Community and Common Market (CARICOM). Nicaragua signed a bilateral accord with Mexico in December (Costa Rica already having done so in 1994). El Salvador, Guatemala and Honduras jointly concluded a free-trade arrangement with Mexico in May 2000. In November 1997, at a special summit meeting of CACM heads of state, an agreement was reached with the President of the Dominican Republic to initiate a gradual process of incorporating that country into the process of Central American integration, with the aim of promoting sustainable development throughout the region. The first sectors for increased co-operation between the two sides were to be tourism, health, investment promotion and air transport. A free-trade accord with the Dominican Republic was concluded in April 1998, and formally signed in November.

In November 1998 Central American heads of state held an emergency summit meeting to consider the devastation in the region caused by 'Hurricane Mitch'. The Presidents urged international creditors to write off the region's estimated debts of US $16,000m. to assist in the economic recovery of the countries worst-affected. They also reiterated requests for preferential treatment for the region's exports within the NAFTA framework. In October 1999 the heads of state adopted a strategic framework for the period 2000–04 to strengthen the capacity for the physical, social, economic and environmental infrastructure of Central American countries to withstand the impact of natural disasters. In particular, pro-

grammes for the integrated management and conservation of water resources, and for the prevention of forest fires were to be implemented.

In June 2001 the heads of state and representatives of Belize, Costa, Rica, El Salvador, Guatemala, Honduras, Mexico, Nicaragua and Panama agreed to activate the Puebla-Panama Plan (PPP) to promote sustainable social and economic development in the region and to reinforce integration efforts among Central America and the southern states of Mexico (referred to as Mesoamerica). The heads of state identified the principal areas for PPP initiatives, including tourism, road integration, telecommunications, energy interconnection, and the prevention and mitigation of disasters. In June 2002 the heads of state of seven countries, and the Vice-President of Panama, convened in Mérida, Mexico during an investment fair to promote the Plan and reiterated their support for the regional initiatives. The meeting was also held within the framework of the Tuxtla dialogue mechanism, so-called after an agreement signed in 1991 between Mexico and Central American countries, to discuss co-ordination between the parties, in particular in social matters, health, education and the environment.

In April 2001 Costa Rica concluded a free-trade accord with Canada; the other four CACM countries commenced negotiations with Canada in November with the aim of reaching a similar agreement. In February 2002 heads of state of SICA countries convened an extraordinary summit meeting in Managua, Nicaragua, at which they resolved to implement measures to further the political and economic integration of the region. The leaders determined to pursue initial proposals for a free-trade pact with the USA during the visit to the region of US President George W. Bush in the following month, and, more generally, to strengthen trading relations with the European Union (EU). They also pledged to resolve all regional conflicts by peaceful means. Earlier in February the first meeting of heads of state or government of SICA and CARICOM countries took place in Belize, with the aim of strengthening political and economic relations between the two groupings. The meeting agreed to work towards concluding common negotiating positions, for example in respect of the FTAA and World Trade Organization.

In May 2002 ministers of foreign affairs of Central America and the EU agreed upon a new agenda for a formalized dialogue and on priority areas of action, including environmental protection, democracy and governance, and poverty reduction. The meeting determined to aim to commence negotiations on an Association Agreement by the end of 2004. It was agreed that meetings between the two sides, at ministerial level, were to be held each year. The EU has allocated €74.5m. to finance co-operation programmes under its Regional Strategy for Central America covering the period 2002–06; these were to focus on strengthening the role of civil society in the process of regional integration, reducing vulnerability to natural disasters, and environmental improvement.

The summit meeting of heads of state, convened in December 2002, in San José, Costa Rica, adopted the 'Declaration of San José', supporting the planned establishment of the Central American customs union (see above), and endorsing the initiation of negotiations with the USA on the creation by the end of that year of a new Central American Free Trade Area (CAFTA). Negotiations on the CAFTA between the CACM countries and the USA commenced in January 2003. The establishment of a new Central American Tourism Agency was also announced at the summit.

COMMON MARKET FOR EASTERN AND SOUTHERN AFRICA—COMESA

Address: COMESA Centre, Ben Bella Rd, POB 30051, 101101 Lusaka, Zambia.

Telephone: (1) 229726; **fax:** (1) 225107; **e-mail:** comesa@comesa.int; **internet:** www.comesa.int.

The COMESA treaty was signed by member states of the Preferential Trade Area for Eastern and Southern Africa (PTA) in November 1993. COMESA formally succeeded the PTA in December 1994. COMESA aims to promote regional economic and social development.

MEMBERS

Angola	Malawi
Burundi	Mauritius
Comoros	Namibia
Congo, Democratic Republic	Rwanda
Djibouti	Seychelles
Egypt	Sudan
Eritrea	Swaziland
Ethiopia	Uganda
Kenya	Zambia
Madagascar	Zimbabwe

Organization

(April 2003)

AUTHORITY

The Authority of the Common Market is the supreme policy organ of COMESA, comprising heads of state or of government of member countries. The inaugural meeting of the Authority took place in Lilongwe, Malawi, in December 1994. The eighth summit meeting was held in Khartoum, Sudan, in March 2003.

COUNCIL OF MINISTERS

Each member government appoints a minister to participate in the Council. The Council monitors COMESA activities, including supervision of the Secretariat, recommends policy direction and development, and reports to the Authority.

A Committee of Governors of Central Banks advises the Authority and the Council of Ministers on monetary and financial matters.

COURT OF JUSTICE

The inaugural session of the COMESA Court of Justice was held in March 2001. The sub-regional Court is vested with the authority to settle disputes between member states and to adjudicate on matters concerning the interpretation of the COMESA treaty. The Court is composed of seven judges, who serve terms of five years' duration.

President: AKILANO MOLADE AKIWUMI (Kenya).

SECRETARIAT

COMESA's Secretariat comprises the following divisions: Trade, customs and monetary harmonization; Investment promotion and private sector development; Infrastructure development; and Information and networking. The COMESA/SADC task force operates from the secretariats of both organizations.

Secretary-General: J. E. O. (ERASTUS) MWENCHA (Kenya).

Activities

COMESA aims to promote economic and social progress in member states. Since its establishment in 1994 COMESA has pursued efforts to strengthen the process of regional economic integration that was initiated under the PTA, in order to help member states achieve sustainable economic growth. In May 1999 COMESA established a Free-Trade Area (FTA) Committee to facilitate and co-ordinate preparations for the establishment of the common market envisaged under the COMESA treaty. An extraordinary summit of COMESA heads of state or government, held in October 2000, established the FTA, with nine initial members: Djibouti, Egypt, Kenya, Madagascar, Malawi, Mauritius, Sudan, Zambia and Zimbabwe. The final deadline for all states to join was initially 30 April 2002. This was, however, subsequently extended to December 2004. Trading practices within the FTA were fully liberalized, including the elimination of non-tariff barriers, thereby enabling the free internal movement of goods, services and capital. It was envisaged that a regional customs union would be established by December 2004, with a common external tariff set at 0%, 5%, 15% and 30% for, respectively, capital goods, raw materials, intermediate goods and final goods. In 2002 a COMESA Fund was under development, in order to assist member states address structural imbalances in their economies. COMESA also plans to form an economic community (entailing monetary union and the free movement of people between member states) by 2014. COMESA aims to formulate a common investment procedure to promote domestic, cross-border and direct foreign investment by ensuring the free movement of capital, services and labour. Heads of regional investment agencies, meeting in August 2000, developed a plan of action for the creation of a common investment agency to facilitate the establishment of a common investment area, in accordance with recommendations by the Authority. The development of a protocol to the COMESA treaty on the Free Movement of Persons, Labour, Services, the Right of Establishment and Residence is under way. In October 2001 COMESA concluded a Trade and Investment Framework Agreement with the USA.

A clearing house (based in Harare, Zimbabwe) dealing with credit arrangements and balance of payments issues became operational under the PTA in 1984 in order to facilitate intra-regional trade. The clearing house remained an integral part of the COMESA infrastructure, although its role was diminished by the liberalization of foreign exchange markets in the majority of member countries. The fourth COMESA business forum (held in Cairo, Egypt, in May 2001) proposed that the Clearing House should be reformed to facilitate money transfers without the use of foreign currency. In April 1997 the Authority approved the introduction of the COMESA dollar (CMD), with a value equivalent to that of the US currency, to replace the UAPTA (introduced by the PTA). An Automated System of Customs Data (ASYCUDA) has been established to facilitate customs administration in all COMESA member states. Through support for capacity-building activities and the establishment of other specialized institutions (see below) COMESA aims to reinforce its objectives of regional integration. In August 2001 COMESA officially inaugurated the African Trade Insurance Agency (ATI), based in Nairobi, Kenya, with Burundi, Kenya, Malawi, Rwanda, Tanzania, Uganda and Zambia as initial members. The ATI manages COMESA's Regional Trade Faciliation Project, promoting trade and investment activities throughout the region.

Co-operation programmes have been implemented by COMESA in the industrial, agricultural, energy and transport and communications sectors. A regional food security programme aimes to ensure continuous adequate food supplies. In 1997 COMESA Heads of State advocated that the food sector be supported by the immediate implementation of an irrigation action plan for the region. The organization also supports the establishment of common agricultural standards and phytosanitary regulations throughout the region in order to stimulate trade in food crops. Meeting in November 2002, COMESA ministers of agriculture determined to formulate a regional policy on genetically-modified organisms. Other organization-wide initiatives include a road customs declaration document, a regional customs bond guarantee scheme, and schemes for third party motor vehicle insurance and regional travellers cheques. A Trade Information Network co-ordinates information on the production and marketing of goods manufactured and traded in the region. COMESA is implementing the new COMESA Information Network, which aims to develop the utilization by member states of advanced information and communication technologies. A COMESA Telecommunications Company (COMTEL) was registered in May 2000. In January 2003 the Association of Regulators of Information and Communication for Eastern and Southern Africa was launched, under the auspices of COMESA. The first COMESA trade fair was held in Nairobi, Kenya, in May 1999. The first COMESA economic forum was held in Cairo, Egypt, in February 2000.

In May 1999 the COMESA Authority resolved to establish a Committee on Peace and Security comprising ministers of foreign affairs from member states. It was envisaged that the Committee would convene at least once a year to address matters concerning regional stability. (Instability in certain member states was regarded as a potential threat to the successful implementation of the FTA.) The Committee met for the first time in 2000. It was announced in September 2002 that the COMESA Treaty was to be amended to provide for the establishment of a formal conflict prevention and resolution structure to be governed by member countries' heads of state.

Since COMESA's establishment there have been concerns on the part of member states, as well as other regional non-member countries, in particular South Africa, of adverse rivalry between COMESA and the Southern African Development Community (SADC) and of a duplication of roles. In 1997 Lesotho and Mozambique terminated their membership of COMESA owing to concerns that their continued participation in the organization was incompatible with their SADC membership. Tanzania withdrew from COMESA in September 2000, reportedly also in view of its dual commitment to that organization and to the SADC. The summit meeting of COMESA heads of state or government held in May of that year expressed support for an ongoing programme of co-operation by the secretariats of COMESA and the SADC aimed at reducing the duplication of roles between the two organizations, and urged further mutual collaboration. A co-ordinating COMESA/SADC task force was established in 2001. COMESA has co-operated with other sub-regional organizations to finalize a common position on co-operation between African ACP countries and the EU under the Cotonou Agreement (concluded in June 2000, see European Union).

COMESA INSTITUTIONS

African Trade Insurance Agency—ATI: based in Nairobi, Kenya; f. 2001; Man. Dir BERNARD DE HALDERANG.

COMESA Bankers Association: Private Bag 271, Blantyre, Malawi; tel. (1) 621503; fax (1) 621204; e-mail info@comesabankers.org; internet www.comesabankers.org; aims to strengthen co-operation between banks in the region; organizes training activities; conducts studies to harmonize banking laws and operations; initiated a project to combat bank fraud and money laundering in December 2000; mems: commercial banking orgs in Burundi, Egypt, Eritrea, Ethiopia, Malawi, Rwanda, Swaziland, Sudan, Uganda; Exec. Sec. MARY NKOSI (acting).

COMESA Leather and Leather Products Institute—LLPI: POB 5538, Addis Ababa, Ethiopia; tel. (1) 510361; fax (1) 512799; e-mail comesa.llpi@telecom.net.et; f. 1990 as the PTA Leather Institute; mems: Govts of 16 COMESA mem. states; Dir Dr GEREMEW DEBELE.

COMESA Metallurgical Industries Association—COMESAMIA: Kampala, Uganda; f. 1999; aims to advance capabilities in the production, processing and marketing of metals and allied engineering products, and to develop co-operation and networking in the sector.

Compagnie de réassurance de la Zone d'échanges préférentiels—ZEP-RE (PTA Reinsurance Co): Anniversary Towers, University Way, POB 42769, Nairobi, Kenya; tel. (2) 212792; fax (2) 224102; e-mail mail@zep-re.com; internet www.zep-re.com; f. 1992 (began operations on 1 January 1993); provides local reinsurance services and training to personnel in the insurance industry; auth. cap. CMD 27.3m; Man. Dir S. M. LUBASI.

Eastern and Southern African Trade and Development Bank: NSSF Bldg, 23rd Floor, Bishop's Rd, POB 48596, Nairobi, Kenya; tel. (2) 712260; fax (2) 711510; e-mail infoserv@ptabank.co.ke; internet www.ptabank.co.ke; f. 1983 as PTA Development Bank; aims to mobilize resources and finance COMESA activities to foster regional integration; promotes investment and co-financing within the region; shareholders 16 COMESA mem. states and the African Development Bank; cumulative project approvals totalled CMD 181.9m. at Dec. 2000; cap. p.u. CMD 67.4m. (Dec. 2000); Pres. Dr MICHAEL GONDWE; Dir Dr BWALYA K. E. NG'ANDU.

Federation of National Associations of Women in Business—FEMCOM: c/o COMESA Secretariat; f. 1993 to provide links between female business executives throughout the region and to promote greater awareness of relevant issues at policy level.

Finance

COMESA is financed by member states. The organization's activities have been undermined by delays by some countries in paying membership dues.

Publications

Annual Report of the Council of Ministers.

Asycuda Newsletter.

COMESA Journal.

COMESA Trade Directory (annually).

COMESA Trade Information Newsletter (monthly).

Demand/supply surveys, catalogues and reports.

THE COMMONWEALTH

Address: Commonwealth Secretariat, Marlborough House, Pall Mall, London, SW1Y 5HX, United Kingdom.

Telephone: (20) 7839-3411; **fax:** (20) 7930-0827; **e-mail:** info@commonwealth.int; **internet:** www.thecommonwealth.org.

The Commonwealth is a voluntary association of 54 independent states, comprising about one-quarter of the world's population. It includes the United Kingdom and most of its former dependencies, and former dependencies of Australia and New Zealand (themselves Commonwealth countries).

The evolution of the Commonwealth began with the introduction of self-government in Canada in the 1840s; Australia, New Zealand and South Africa became independent before the First World War. At the Imperial Conference of 1926 the United Kingdom and the Dominions, as they were then called, were described as 'autonomous communities within the British Empire, equal in status', and this change was enacted into law by the Statute of Westminster, in 1931.

The modern Commonwealth began with the entry of India and Pakistan in 1947, and of Sri Lanka (then Ceylon) in 1948. In 1949, when India decided to become a republic, the Commonwealth Heads of Government agreed to replace allegiance to the British Crown with recognition of the British monarch as Head of the Commonwealth, as a condition of membership. This was a precedent for a number of other members (see Heads of State and Heads of Government, below).

MEMBERS*

Antigua and	Kenya	Samoa
Barbuda	Kiribati	Seychelles
Australia	Lesotho	Sierra Leone
Bahamas	Malawi	Singapore
Bangladesh	Malaysia	Solomon Islands
Barbados	Maldives	South Africa
Belize	Malta	Sri Lanka
Botswana	Mauritius	Swaziland
Brunei	Mozambique	Tanzania
Cameroon	Namibia	Tonga
Canada	Nauru	Trinidad and Tobago
Cyprus	New Zealand	Tuvalu
Dominica	Nigeria	Uganda
Fiji	Pakistan	United Kingdom
The Gambia	Papua New Guinea	Vanuatu
Ghana	Saint Christopher	Zambia
Grenada	and Nevis	Zimbabwe
Guyana	Saint Lucia	
India	Saint Vincent and	
Jamaica	the Grenadines	

* Ireland, South Africa and Pakistan withdrew from the Commonwealth in 1949, 1961 and 1972 respectively. In October 1987 Fiji's membership was declared to have lapsed (following the proclamation of a republic there). It was readmitted in October 1997, but

was suspended from participation in meetings of the Commonwealth in June 2000. Fiji was formally readmitted to Commonwealth meetings in December 2001 following the staging of free and fair legislative elections in August/September. Pakistan rejoined the Commonwealth in October 1989; however, it was suspended from participation in meetings in October 1999. South Africa rejoined in June 1994. Nigeria's membership was suspended in November 1995; it formally resumed membership in May 1999, when a new civilian government was inaugurated. Tuvalu, previously a special member of the Commonwealth with the right to participate in all activities except full Meetings of Heads of Government, became a full member in September 2000. In March 2002 Zimbabwe was suspended from participation in meetings of the Commonwealth.

Dependencies and Associated States

Australia:	British Antarctic Territory
Ashmore and Cartier Islands	British Indian Ocean
Australian Antarctic	Territory
Territory	British Virgin Islands
Christmas Island	Cayman Islands
Cocos (Keeling) Islands	Channel Islands
Coral Sea Islands Territory	Falkland Islands
Heard Island and the	Gibralter
McDonald Islands	Isle of Man
Norfolk Island	Montserrat
New Zealand:	Pitcairn Islands
Cook Islands	St Helena
Niue	Ascension
Ross Dependency	Tristan da Cunha
Tokelau	South Georgia and the South
United Kingdom:	Sandwich Islands
Anguilla	Turks and Caicos Islands
Bermuda	

HEADS OF STATE AND HEADS OF GOVERNMENT

At April 2003 21 member countries were monarchies and 33 were republics. All Commonwealth countries accept Queen Elizabeth II as the symbol of the free association of the independent member nations and as such the Head of the Commonwealth. Of the 33 republics, the offices of Head of State and Head of Government were combined in 22: Botswana, Cameroon, Cyprus, The Gambia, Ghana, Guyana, Kenya, Kiribati, Malawi, Maldives, Mozambique, Namibia, Nauru, Nigeria, Seychelles, Sierra Leone, South Africa, Sri Lanka, Tanzania, Uganda, Zambia and Zimbabwe. The two offices were separated in the remaining 11: Bangladesh, Dominica, Fiji, India, Malta, Mauritius, Pakistan, Samoa, Singapore, Trinidad and Tobago and Vanuatu.

Of the monarchies, the Queen is Head of State of the United Kingdom and of 15 others, in each of which she is represented by a Governor-General: Antigua and Barbuda, Australia, the Bahamas,

Barbados, Belize, Canada, Grenada, Jamaica, New Zealand, Papua New Guinea, Saint Christopher and Nevis, Saint Lucia, Saint Vincent and the Grenadines, Solomon Islands and Tuvalu. Brunei, Lesotho, Malaysia, Swaziland and Tonga are also monarchies, where the traditional monarch is Head of State.

The Governors-General are appointed by the Queen on the advice of the Prime Ministers of the country concerned. They are wholly independent of the Government of the United Kingdom.

HIGH COMMISSIONERS

Governments of member countries are represented in other Commonwealth countries by High Commissioners, who have a status equivalent to that of Ambassadors.

Organization

(April 2003)

The Commonwealth is not a federation: there is no central government nor are there any rigid contractual obligations such as bind members of the United Nations.

The Commonwealth has no written constitution but its members subscribe to the ideals of the Declaration of Commonwealth Principles unanimously approved by a meeting of heads of government in Singapore in 1971. Members also approved the 1977 statement on apartheid in sport (the Gleneagles Agreement); the 1979 Lusaka Declaration on Racism and Racial Prejudice; the 1981 Melbourne Declaration on relations between developed and developing countries; the 1983 New Delhi Statement on Economic Action; the 1983 Goa Declaration on International Security; the 1985 Nassau Declaration on World Order; the Commonwealth Accord on Southern Africa (1985); the 1987 Vancouver Declaration on World Trade; the Okanagan Statement and Programme of Action on Southern Africa (1987); the Langkawi Declaration on the Environment (1989); the Kuala Lumpur Statement on Southern Africa (1989); the Harare Commonwealth Declaration (1991); the Ottawa Declaration on Women and Structural Adjustment (1991); the Limassol Statement on the Uruguay Round of multilateral trade negotiations (1993); the Millbrook Commonwealth Action Programme on the Harare Declaration (1995); the Edinburgh Commonwealth Economic Declaration (1997); the Fancourt Commonwealth Declaration on Globalization and People-centred Development (1999); and the Coolum Declaration on the Commonwealth in the 21st Century: Continuity and Renewal (2002).

MEETINGS OF HEADS OF GOVERNMENT

Meetings are private and informal and operate not by voting but by consensus. The emphasis is on consultation and exchange of views for co-operation. A communiqué is issued at the end of every meeting. Meetings are normally held every two years in different capitals in the Commonwealth. The last meeting was held in Coolum, near Brisbane, Australia, in March 2002.

OTHER CONSULTATIONS

Meetings at ministerial and official level are also held regularly. Since 1959 finance ministers have met in a Commonwealth country in the week prior to the annual meetings of the IMF and the World Bank. Meetings on education, legal, women's and youth affairs are held at ministerial level every three years. Ministers of health hold annual meetings, with major meetings every three years, and ministers of agriculture meet every two years. Ministers of trade, labour and employment, industry, science and the environment also hold periodic meetings.

Senior officials—cabinet secretaries, permanent secretaries to heads of government and others—meet regularly in the year between meetings of heads of government to provide continuity and to exchange views on various developments.

COMMONWEALTH SECRETARIAT

The Secretariat, established by Commonwealth heads of government in 1965, operates as an international organization at the service of all Commonwealth countries. It organizes consultations between governments and runs programmes of co-operation. Meetings of heads of government, ministers and senior officials decide these programmes and provide overall direction.

The Secretariat is headed by a secretary-general (elected by heads of government), assisted by three deputy secretaries-general. One deputy is responsible for political affairs, one for economic and social affairs, and one for development co-operation (including the Commonwealth Fund for Technical Co-operation—see below). The Secretariat comprises 12 Divisions in the fields of political affairs; legal and constitutional affairs; information and public affairs; administration; economic affairs; human resource development; gender and youth affairs; science and technology; economic and legal advisory services; export and industrial development; management and training services; and general technical assistance services. It also includes a non-governmental organizations desk, a unit for strategic planning and evaluation, and a human rights unit.

In 2000 the Secretariat adopted the following as its guiding mission: working for all people of the Commonwealth as a force for democracy and good governance, as a platform for global consensus-building, and as a source of practical assistance for sustainable development.

Secretary-General: Rt Hon. DONALD (DON) C. McKINNON (New Zealand).

Deputy Secretary-General (Political): FLORENCE MUGASHA (Uganda).

Deputy Secretary-General (Economic and Social): (vacant).

Deputy Secretary-General (Development Co-operation): WINSTON A. COX (Barbados).

Activities

INTERNATIONAL AFFAIRS

In October 1991 heads of government, meeting in Harare, Zimbabwe, issued the Harare Commonwealth Declaration, in which they reaffirmed their commitment to the Commonwealth Principles declared in 1971, and stressed the need to promote sustainable development and the alleviation of poverty. The Declaration placed emphasis on the promotion of democracy and respect for human rights and resolved to strengthen the Commonwealth's capacity to assist countries in entrenching democratic practices. The meeting also welcomed the political reforms introduced by the South African Government to end the system of apartheid and urged all South African political parties to commence negotiations on a new constitution as soon as possible. The meeting endorsed measures on the phased removal of punitive measures against South Africa. In December a group of six eminent Commonwealth citizens was dispatched to observe multi-party negotiations on the future of South Africa and to assist the process where possible. In October 1992, in a fresh attempt to assist the South African peace process, a Commonwealth team of 18 observers was sent to monitor political violence in the country. A second phase of the Commonwealth Mission to South Africa (COMSA) began in February 1993. COMSA issued a report in May in which it urged a concerted effort to build a culture of political tolerance in South Africa. In a report on its third phase, issued in December, COMSA appealed strongly to all political parties to participate in the transitional arrangements leading to democratic elections. In October the Commonwealth heads of government, meeting in Limassol, Cyprus, agreed that a democratic and non-racial South Africa would be invited to join the organization. They endorsed the removal of all economic sanctions against South Africa, but agreed to retain the arms embargo until a post-apartheid, democratic government had been established.

In November 1995 Commonwealth heads of government, convened in New Zealand, formulated and adopted the Millbrook Commonwealth Action Programme on the Harare Declaration, to promote adherence by member countries to the fundamental principles of democracy and human rights (as proclaimed in the 1991 Declaration). The Programme incorporated a framework of measures to be pursued in support of democratic processes and institutions, and actions to be taken in response to violations of the Harare Declaration principles, in particular the unlawful removal of a democratically-elected government. A Commonwealth Ministerial Action Group on the Harare Declaration (CMAG) was to be established to implement this process and to assist the member country involved to comply with the Harare principles. On the basis of this Programme, the leaders suspended Nigeria from the Commonwealth with immediate effect, following the execution by that country's military Government of nine environmental and human rights protesters and a series of other violations of human rights. The meeting determined to expel Nigeria from the Commonwealth if no 'demonstrable progress' had been made towards the establishment of a democratic authority by the time of the next summit meeting. In addition, the Programme formulated measures to promote sustainable development in member countries, which was considered to be an important element in sustaining democracy, and to facilitate consensus-building within the international community. Earlier in the meeting a statement was issued declaring the 'overwhelming majority' of Commonwealth governments to be opposed to nuclear-testing programmes being undertaken in the South Pacific region. However, in view of events in Nigeria, the issue of nuclear testing and disagreement among member countries did not assume the significance anticipated.

In December 1995 CMAG convened for its inaugural meeting in London. The Group, comprising the ministers of foreign affairs of Canada, Ghana, Jamaica, Malaysia, New Zealand, South Africa, the United Kingdom and Zimbabwe (with membership to be reconstituted periodically), commenced by considering efforts to restore democratic government in the three Commonwealth countries then under military regimes, i.e. The Gambia, Nigeria and Sierra Leone. At the second meeting of the Group, in April 1996, ministers commended the conduct of presidential and parliamentary elections in Sierra Leone and the announcement by The Gambia's military leaders to proceed with a transition to civilian rule. In June a three-member CMAG delegation visited The Gambia to reaffirm Commonwealth support of the transition process in that country and to identify possible areas of further Commonwealth assistance. In August the Gambian authorities issued a decree removing the ban on political activities and parties, although shortly afterwards they prohibited certain parties and candidates involved in political life prior to the military take-over from contesting the elections. CMAG recommended that in such circumstances no Commonwealth observers should be sent to either the presidential or parliamentary elections, which were held in September 1996 and January 1997 respectively. Following the restoration of a civilian Government in early 1997, CMAG requested the Commonwealth Secretary-General to extend technical assistance to The Gambia in order to consolidate the democratic transition process. In April 1996 it was noted that the human rights situation in Nigeria had continued to deteriorate. CMAG, having pursued unsuccessful efforts to initiate dialogue with the Nigerian authorities, outlined a series of punitive and restrictive measures (including visa restrictions on members of the administration, a cessation of sporting contacts and an embargo on the export of armaments) that it would recommend for collective Commonwealth action in order to exert further pressure for reform in Nigeria. Following a meeting of a high-level delegation of the Nigerian Government and CMAG in June, the Group agreed to postpone the implementation of the sanctions, pending progress on the dialogue. (Canada, however, determined, unilaterally, to impose the measures with immediate effect; the United Kingdom did so in accordance with a decision of the European Union to implement limited sanctions against Nigeria.) A proposed CMAG mission to Nigeria was postponed in August, owing to restrictions imposed by the military authorities on access to political detainees and other civilian activists in that country. In September the Group agreed to proceed with the visit and to delay further a decision on the implementation of sanction measures. CMAG, without the participation of the representative of the Canadian Government, undertook its ministerial mission in November. In July 1997 the Group reiterated the Commonwealth Secretary-General's condemnation of a military coup in Sierra Leone in May, and decided that the country's participation in meetings of the Commonwealth should be suspended pending the restoration of a democratic government.

In October 1997 Commonwealth heads of government, meeting in Edinburgh, the United Kingdom, endorsed CMAG's recommendation that the imposition of sanctions against Nigeria be held in abeyance pending the scheduled completion of a transition programme towards democracy by October 1998. It was also agreed that CMAG be formally constituted as a permanent organ to investigate abuses of human rights throughout the Commonwealth. Jamaica and South Africa were to be replaced as members of CMAG by Barbados and Botswana, respectively.

In March 1998 CMAG, at its ninth meeting, commended the efforts of ECOWAS in restoring the democratically-elected Government of President Ahmed Tejan Kabbah in Sierra Leone, and agreed to remove all restrictions on Sierra Leone's participation in Commonwealth activities. Later in that month, a representative mission of CMAG visited Sierra Leone to express its support for Kabbah's administration and to consider the country's needs in its process of reconstruction. At the CMAG meeting held in October members agreed that Sierra Leone should no longer be considered under the Group's mandate; however, they urged the Secretary-General to continue to assist that country in the process of national reconciliation and to facilitate negotiations with opposition forces to ensure a lasting cease-fire. A Special Envoy of the Secretary-General was appointed to co-operate with the UN, ECOWAS and the OAU (now African Union—AU) in monitoring the implementation of the Sierra Leone peace process, and the Commonwealth has supported the rebuilding of the Sierra Leone police force. In September 2001 CMAG recommended that Sierra Leone be removed from its remit, but that the Secretary-General should continue to monitor developments there.

In April 1998 the Nigerian military leader, Gen. Sani Abacha, confirmed his intention to conduct a presidential election in August, but indicated that, following an agreement with other political organizations, he was to be the sole candidate. In June, however, Abacha died suddenly. His successor, Gen. Abdulsalam Abubakar, immediately released several prominent political prisoners, and in early July agreed to meet with the Secretaries-General of the UN and the Commonwealth to discuss the release of the imprisoned opposition leader, Chief Moshood Abiola. Abubakar also confirmed his intention to abide by the programme for transition to civilian rule by October. In mid-July, however, shortly before he was to have been liberated, Abiola died. The Commonwealth Secretary-General

subsequently endorsed a new transition programme, which provided for the election of a civilian leader in May 1999. In October 1998 CMAG, convened for its 10th formal meeting, acknowledged Abubakar's efforts towards restoring a democratic government and recommended that member states begin to remove sanctions against Nigeria and that it resume participation in certain Commonwealth activities. The Commonwealth Secretary-General subsequently announced a programme of technical assistance to support Nigeria in the planning and conduct of democratic elections. Staff teams from the Commonwealth Secretariat observed local government, and state and governorship elections, held in December and in January 1999, respectively. A Commonwealth Observer Group was also dispatched to Nigeria to monitor preparations and conduct of legislative and presidential elections, held in February. While the Group reported several irregularities in the conduct of the polling, it confirmed that, in general, the conditions had existed for free and fair elections and that the elections were a legitimate basis for the transition of power to a democratic, civilian government. In April CMAG voted to readmit Nigeria to full membership on 29 May, upon the installation of the new civilian administration.

In 1999 the Commonwealth Secretary-General appointed a Special Envoy to broker an agreement in order to end a civil dispute in Honiara, Solomon Islands. An accord was signed in late June, and it was envisaged that the Commonwealth would monitor its implementation. In October a Commonwealth Multinational Police Peace Monitoring Group was stationed in Solomon Islands; this was renamed the Commonwealth Multinational Police Assistance Group in February 2000. Following further internal unrest, however, the Group was disbanded. In June CMAG determined to send a new mission to Solomon Islands in order to facilitate negotiations between the opposing parties, to convey the Commonwealth's concern and to offer assistance. The Commonwealth welcomed the peace accord concluded in Solomon Islands in October, and extended its support to the International Peace Monitoring Team which was established to oversee implementation of the peace accords. CMAG welcomed the conduct of parliamentary elections held in Solomon Islands in December 2001.

In June 1999 an agreement was concluded between opposing political groups in Zanzibar, having been facilitated by the good offices of the Secretary-General; however, this was only partially implemented. In mid-October a special meeting of CMAG was convened to consider the overthrow of the democratically-elected Government in Pakistan in a military coup. The meeting condemned the action as a violation of Commonwealth principles and urged the new authorities to declare a timetable for the return to democratic rule. CMAG also resolved to send a four-member delegation, comprising the ministers of foreign affairs of Barbados, Canada, Ghana and Malaysia, to discuss this future course of action with the military regime. Pakistan was suspended from participation in meetings of the Commonwealth with immediate effect. The suspension, pending the restoration of a democratic government, was endorsed by heads of government, meeting in November, who requested that CMAG keep the situation in Pakistan under review. At the meeting, held in Durban, South Africa, CMAG was reconstituted to comprise the ministers of foreign affairs of Australia, Bangladesh, Barbados, Botswana, Canada, Malaysia, Nigeria and the United Kingdom. It was agreed that no country would serve for more than two consecutive two-year terms. CMAG was requested to remain actively involved in the post-conflict development and rehabilitation of Sierra Leone and the process of consolidating peace. In addition, it was urged to monitor persistent violations of the Harare Declaration principles in all countries. Heads of government also agreed to establish a new ministerial group on Guyana and to reconvene a ministerial committee on Belize, in order to facilitate dialogue in ongoing territorial disputes with neighbouring countries. The meeting established a 10-member Commonwealth High Level Review Group to evaluate the role and activities of the Commonwealth. In 2000 the Group initiated a programme of consultations to proceed with its mandate and established a working group of experts to consider the Commonwealth's role in supporting information technology capabilities in member countries.

In June 2000, following the overthrow in May of the Fijian Government by a group of armed civilians, and the subsequent illegal detention of members of the elected administration, CMAG suspended Fiji's participation in meetings of the Commonwealth pending the restoration of democratic rule. In September, upon the request of CMAG, the Secretary-General appointed a Special Envoy to support efforts towards political dialogue and a return to democratic rule in Fiji. The Special Envoy undertook his first visit in December. In December 2001, following the staging of democratic legislative elections in August/September, Fiji was readmitted to Commonwealth meetings on the recommendation of CMAG.

In March 2001 CMAG resolved to send a ministerial mission to Zimbabwe, in order to relay to the government the Commonwealth's concerns at the ongoing violence and abuses of human rights in that country, as well as to discuss the conduct of parliamentary elections and extend technical assistance. The mission was rejected by the

Zimbabwe Government, which queried the basis for CMAG's intervention in the affairs of an elected administration. In September, under the auspices of a group of Commonwealth foreign ministers partly derived from CMAG, the Zimbabwe Government signed the Abuja Agreement, which provided for the cessation of illegal occupations of white-owned farms and the resumption of the rule of law, in return for financial assistance to support the ongoing process of land reform in that country. In January 2002 CMAG expressed strong concern at the continuing violence and political intimidation in Zimbabwe. The summit of Commonwealth heads of government convened in early March (see below) also expressed concern at the situation in Zimbabwe, and, having decided on the principle that CMAG should be permitted to engage with any member Government deemed to be in breach of the organization's core values, mandated a Commonwealth Chairperson's Committee on Zimbabwe to determine appropriate action should an impending presidential election (scheduled to be held during that month) be found not to have been conducted freely and fairly. Following the publication by a Commonwealth observer team of an unfavourable report on the conduct of the election, the Committee decided to suspend Zimbabwe from meetings of the Commonwealth for one year. In March 2003, the Committee concluded that the suspension should remain in force pending consideration by the next summit of heads of government, scheduled to be held in December, in Abuja, Nigeria.

In March 2002, meeting in Coolum, near Brisbane, Australia, Commonwealth heads of government adopted the Coolum Declaration on the Commonwealth in the 21st Century: Continuity and Renewal, which reiterated commitment to the organization's principles and values. Leaders at the meeting condemned all forms of terrorism; welcomed the Millennium Development Goals of the UN General Assembly; called on the Secretary-General to constitute a high-level expert group on implementing the objectives of the Fancourt Declaration; pledged continued support for small states; and urged renewed efforts to combat the spread of HIV/AIDS. The meeting adopted a report on the future of the Commonwealth drafted by the High Level Review Group. The document recommended strengthening the Commonwealth's role in conflict prevention and resolution and support of democratic practices; enhancing the good offices role of the Secretary-General; better promoting member states' economic and development needs; strengthening the organization's role in facilitating member states' access to international assistance; and promoting increased access to modern information and communications technologies. The meeting expanded CMAG's mandate to enable the Group to consider action against serious violations of the Commonwealth's core values perpetrated by elected administrations (such as that in Zimbabwe, see above) as well as by military regimes. A the summit CMAG was reconstituted to comprise the ministers of foreign affairs of Australia, the Bahamas, Bangladesh, Botswana, India, Malta, Nigeria and Samoa.

A Commonwealth team of observers dispatched to monitor legislative and provincial elections that were held in Pakistan in October 2002 found them to have been well-organized and conducted in a largely transparent manner. The team made several recommendations on institutional and procedural issues. CMAG subsequently expressed concern over the promulgation of new legislation in Pakistan following the imposition earlier in the year of a number of extra-constitutional measures. CMAG determined that Pakistan should continue to be suspended from meetings of the Commonwealth, pending a review of the role and functioning of its democratic institutions. In November a Commonwealth Expert Group on Papua New Guinea, established in the previous month to review the electoral process in that country (in view of unsatisfactory legislative elections that were conducted there in July), made several recommendations aimed at enhancing the future management of the electoral process. A Commonwealth observer team dispatched to monitor legislative elections held in Kenya in December found, despite some areas of concern, the electoral process to have been credible and the results to have expressed the wishes of the people.

Political Affairs Division: assists consultation among member governments on international and Commonwealth matters of common interest. In association with host governments, it organizes the meetings of heads of government and senior officials. The Division services committees and special groups set up by heads of government dealing with political matters. The Secretariat has observer status at the United Nations, and the Division manages a joint office in New York to enable small states, which would otherwise be unable to afford facilities there, to maintain a presence at the United Nations. The Division monitors political developments in the Commonwealth and international progress in such matters as disarmament, the concerns of small states, dismantling of apartheid and the Law of the Sea. It also undertakes research on matters of common interest to member governments, and reports back to them. The Division is involved in diplomatic training and consular co-operation.

In 1990 Commonwealth heads of government mandated the Division to support the promotion of democracy by monitoring the preparations for and conduct of parliamentary, presidential or other elections in member countries at the request of national governments. By the end of 2000 the Commonwealth had dispatched more than 30 electoral missions in accordance with this mandate.

A new expert group on good governance and the elimination of corruption in economic management convened for its first meeting in May 1998. In November 1999 Commonwealth heads of government endorsed a Framework for Principles for Promoting Good Governance and Combating Corruption, which had been drafted by the group. The conference of heads of government that met in Coolum in March 2002, endorsed a Commonwealth Local Government Good Practice Scheme, to be managed by the Commonwealth Local Government Forum (established in 1995).

LAW

Legal and Constitutional Affairs Division: promotes and facilitates co-operation and the exchange of information among member governments on legal matters. It administers, jointly with the Commonwealth of Learning, a distance training programme for legislative draftsmen and assists governments to reform national laws to meet the obligations of international conventions. The Division organizes the triennial meeting of ministers, Attorneys General and senior ministry officials concerned with the legal systems in Commonwealth countries. It has also initiated four Commonwealth schemes for co-operation on extradition, the protection of material cultural heritage, mutual assistance in criminal matters and the transfer of convicted offenders within the Commonwealth. It liaises with the Commonwealth Magistrates' and Judges' Association, the Commonwealth Legal Education Association, the Commonwealth Lawyers' Association (with which it helps to prepare the triennial Commonwealth Law Conference for the practising profession), the Commonwealth Association of Legislative Counsel, and with other international non-governmental organizations. The Division provides in-house legal advice for the Secretariat. The quarterly *Commonwealth Law Bulletin* reports on legal developments in and beyond the Commonwealth.

The Division's Commercial Crime Unit assists member countries to combat financial and organized crime, in particular transborder criminal activities, and promotes the exchange of information regarding national and international efforts to combat serious commercial crime through a quarterly publication, *Commonwealth Legal Assistance News* and the *Crimewatch* bulletin.

ECONOMIC CO-OPERATION

In October 1997 Commonwealth heads of government, meeting in Edinburgh, the United Kingdom, signed an Economic Declaration that focused on issues relating to global trade, investment and development and committed all member countries to free-market economic principles. The Declaration also incorporated a provision for the establishment of a Trade and Investment Access Facility within the Secretariat in order to assist developing member states in the process of international trade liberalization and promote intra-Commonwealth trade.

In May 1998 the Commonwealth Secretary-General appealed to the Group of Eight industrialized nations to accelerate and expand the initiative to ease the debt burden of the most heavily indebted poor countries (HIPCs) (see World Bank andIMF). In October Commonwealth finance ministers, convened in Ottawa, Canada, reiterated their appeal to international financial institutions to accelerate the HIPC initiative. The meeting also issued a Commonwealth Statement on the global economic crisis and endorsed several proposals to help to counter the difficulties experienced by several countries. These measures included a mechanism to enable countries to suspend payments on all short-term financial obligations at a time of emergency without defaulting, assistance to governments to attract private capital and to manage capital market volatility, and the development of international codes of conduct regarding financial and monetary policies and corporate governance. In March 1999 the Commonwealth Secretariat hosted a joint IMF-World Bank conference to review the HIPC scheme and initiate a process of reform. In November Commonwealth heads of government, meeting in South Africa, declared their support for measures undertaken by the World Bank and IMF to enhance the HIPC initiative. At the end of an informal retreat the leaders adopted the Fancourt Commonwealth Declaration on Globalization and People-Centred Development, which emphasized the need for a more equitable spread of wealth generated by the process of globalization, and expressed a renewed commitment to the elimination of all forms of discrimination, the promotion of people-centred development and capacity-building, and efforts to ensure developing countries benefit from future multilateral trade liberalization measures. In June 2002 the Commonwealth Secretary-General urged more generous funding of the HIPC initiative. Meetings of ministers of finance from Commonwealth African member countries participating in the HIPC initiative have been convened in Lilongwe, Malawi in February 2002, in London in September, and in Dar es Salaam, Tanzania, in March 2003.

In February 1998 the Commonwealth Secretariat hosted the first Inter-Governmental Organizations Meeting to promote co-operation between small island states and the formulation of a unified policy approach to international fora. A second meeting was convened in March 2001, where discussions focused on the forthcoming WTO ministerial meeting and the OECD's harmful tax competition initiative. In September 2000 Commonwealth finance ministers, meeting in Malta, reviewed the OECD initiative and agreed that the measures, affecting many member countries with offshore financial centres, should not be imposed on governments. The ministers mandated the involvement of the Commonwealth Secretariat in efforts to resolve the dispute; a joint working group was subsequently established by the Secretariat with the OECD. In April 2002 a meeting on international co-operation in the financial services sector, attended by representatives of international and regional organizations, donors and senior officials from Commonwealth countries, was held under Commonwealth auspices in Saint Lucia.

The first meeting of governors of central banks from Commonwealth countries was held in June 2001 in London.

Economic Affairs Division: organizes and services the annual meetings of Commonwealth ministers of finance and the ministerial group on small states and assists in servicing the biennial meetings of heads of government and periodic meetings of environment ministers. It engages in research and analysis on economic issues of interest to member governments and organizes seminars and conferences of government officials and experts. The Division undertook a major programme of technical assistance to enable developing Commonwealth countries to participate in the Uruguay Round of multilateral trade negotiations and has assisted the African, Caribbean and Pacific (ACP) group of countries in their trade negotiations with the European Union. It continues to help developing countries to strengthen their links with international capital markets and foreign investors. The Division also services groups of experts on economic affairs that have been commissioned by governments to report on, among other things, protectionism; obstacles to the North-South negotiating process; reform of the international financial and trading system; the debt crisis; management of technological change; the special needs of small states; the impact of change on the development process; environmental issues; women and structural adjustment; and youth unemployment. A Commonwealth Secretariat Debt Recording and Management System has been developed by the Economic and Legal Advisory Services Division, which operates the system for the benefit of member countries and concerned organizations. The Economic Affairs Division co-ordinates the Secretariat's environmental work and manages the Iwokrama International Centre for Rainforest Conservation and Development.

The Division played a catalytic role in the establishment of a Commonwealth Equity Fund, initiated in September 1990, to allow developing member countries to improve their access to private institutional investment, and promoted a Caribbean Investment Fund. The Division supported the establishment of a Commonwealth Private Investment Initiative (CPII) to mobilize capital, on a regional basis, for investment in newly-privatized companies and in small and medium-sized businesses in the private sector. The first regional fund under the CPII was launched in July 1996. The Commonwealth Africa Investment Fund (Comafin), was to be managed by the United Kingdom's official development institution, the Commonwealth Development Corporation, to assist businesses in 19 countries in sub-Saharan Africa, with initial resources of US $63.5m. In August 1997 a fund for the Pacific Islands was launched, with an initial capital of $15.0m. A $200m. South Asia Regional Fund was established at the Heads of Government Meeting in October. In October 1998 a fund for the Caribbean states was inaugurated, at a meeting of Commonwealth finance ministers. The 2001 summit of Commonwealth heads of government authorized the establishment of a new fund for Africa (Comafin II): this was inaugurated in March 2002, and attracted initial capital in excess of $200m.

HUMAN RESOURCES

Human Resource Development Division: consists of two departments concerned with education and health. The Division co-operates with member countries in devising strategies for human resource development.

The **Education Department** arranges specialist seminars, workshops and co-operative projects, and commissions studies in areas identified by ministers of education, whose three-yearly meetings it also services. Its present areas of emphasis include improving the quality of and access to basic education; strengthening the culture of science, technology and mathematics education in formal and non-formal areas of education; improving the

quality of management in institutions of higher learning and basic education; improving the performance of teachers; strengthening examination assessment systems; and promoting the movement of students between Commonwealth countries. The Department also promotes multi-sectoral strategies to be incorporated in the development of human resources. Emphasis is placed on ensuring a gender balance, the appropriate use of technology, promoting good governance, addressing the problems of scale particular to smaller member countries, and encouraging collaboration between governments, the private sector and other non-governmental organizations.

The **Health Department** organizes ministerial, technical and expert group meetings and workshops, to promote co-operation on health matters, and the exchange of health information and expertise. The Department commissions relevant studies and provides professional and technical advice to member countries and to the Secretariat. It also supports the work of regional health organizations and promotes health for all people in Commonwealth countries.

Gender and Youth Affairs Division: consists of the Gender Affairs Department and the Commonwealth Youth Affairs Department.

The **Gender Affairs Department** is responsible for the implementation of the 1995 Commonwealth Plan of Action on Gender and Development, which was endorsed by the Heads of Government in order to achieve gender equality in the Commonwealth. The main objective of the Plan is to ensure that gender is incorporated into all policies, programmes, structures and procedures of member states and of the Commonwealth Secretariat. A further gender equality plan, 'Advancing the Commonwealth Agenda in the New Millennium', covers the period 2000–05. The Department is also addressing specific concerns such as the integration of gender issues into national budgetary processes, increasing the participation of women in politics and conflict prevention and resolution (with the objective of raising the level of female participation to 30%), and the promotion of human rights, including the elimination of violence against women and girls.

The **Youth Affairs Department** administers the Commonwealth Youth Programme (CYP), funded through separate voluntary contributions from governments, which seeks to promote the involvement of young people in the economic and social development of their countries. The CYP was awarded a budget of £2.3m. for 2002–03. It provides policy advice for governments and operates regional training programmes for youth workers and policymakers through its centres in Africa, Asia, the Caribbean and the Pacific. It conducts a Youth Study Fellowship scheme, a Youth Project Fund, a Youth Exchange Programme (in the Caribbean), and a Youth Service Awards Scheme, holds conferences and seminars, carries out research and disseminates information. In 1995 a Commonwealth Youth Credit Initiative was launched, in order to provide funds, training and advice to young entrepreneurs. In May 1998 a Commonwealth ministerial meeting, held in Kuala Lumpur, Malaysia, approved a new Plan of Action on Youth Empowerment to the Year 2005. In March 2002 Commonwealth heads of government approved the Youth for the Future initiative involving technology and skills development and promoting youth enterprise.

SCIENCE

Science and Technology Division: is partially funded and governed by the Commonwealth Science Council, consisting of 35 member governments, which aims to enhance the scientific and technological capabilities of member countries, through co-operative research, training and the exchange of information. Current priority areas of work are concerned with the promotion of sustainable development and cover biological diversity and genetic resources, water resources, and renewable energy. The Science Council was allocated a budget of £900,000 for 2002–03.

TECHNICAL CO-OPERATION

Commonwealth Fund for Technical Co-operation—CFTC: f. 1971 to facilitate the exchange of skills between member countries and to promote economic and social development. It is administered by the Commonwealth Secretariat and financed by voluntary subscriptions from member governments. The CFTC responds to requests from member governments for technical assistance, such as the provision of experts for short- or medium-term projects, advice on economic or legal matters, in particular in the areas of natural resources management and public-sector reform, and training programmes. Since 1995 the CFTC has operated a volunteer scheme, the Commonwealth Service Abroad Programme, for senior professionals willing to undertake short-term assignments. The CFTC also administers the Langkawi awards for the study of environmental issues, which is funded by the Canadian Government. The CFTC budget for 2002–03 amounted to £22.2m.

CFTC activities are implemented by the following divisions:

Economic and Legal Advisory Services Division: serves as an in-house consultancy, offering advice to governments on macro-economic and financial management, capital market and private-sector development, debt management, the development of natural resources, and the negotiation of maritime boundaries and fisheries access agreements;

Export and Industrial Development Division: advises on all aspects of export marketing and the development of tourism, industry, small businesses and enterprises. Includes an Agricultural Development Unit, which provides technical assistance in agriculture and renewable resources;

General Technical Assistance Services Division: provides short- and long-term experts in all fields of development;

Management and Training Services Division: provides integrated packages of consultancy and training to enhance skills in areas such as public sector reform and the restructuring of enterprises, and arranges specific country and overseas training programmes.

The Secretariat also includes an Administration Division, a Strategic Planning and Evaluation Unit, and an Information and Public Affairs Division, which produces information publications, and radio and television programmes, about Commonwealth co-operation and consultation activities.

Finance

The Secretariat's budget for 2002–03 was £11.4m. Member governments meet the cost of the Secretariat through subscriptions on a scale related to income and population.

Publications

Commonwealth Currents (quarterly).

Commonwealth Law Bulletin (2 a year).

Commonwealth Organisations (directory).

In Common (quarterly newsletter of the Youth Programme).

International Development Policies (quarterly).

Link In to Gender and Development (annually).

Report of the Commonwealth Secretary-General (every 2 years).

The Commonwealth Yearbook.

Numerous reports, studies and papers (catalogue available).

Commonwealth Organizations

(In the United Kingdom, unless otherwise stated)

PRINCIPAL BODIES

Commonwealth Foundation: Marlborough House, Pall Mall, London, SW1Y 5HY; tel. (20) 7930-3783; fax (20) 7839 8157; e-mail geninfo@commonwealth.int; internet www .commonwealthfoundation.com; f. 1966; intergovernmental body promoting people-to-people interaction, and collaboration within the non-governmental sector of the Commonwealth; supports non-governmental organizations, professional associations and Commonwealth arts and culture; awards an annual Commonwealth Writers' Prize; funds are provided by Commonwealth govts; Chair GRACA MACHEL (Mozambique); Dir COLIN BALL (United Kingdom); publ. *Commonwealth People* (quarterly).

The Commonwealth of Learning—COL: 1285 West Broadway, Suite 600, Vancouver, BC V6H 3X8, Canada; tel. (604) 775-8200; fax (604) 775-8210; e-mail info@col.org; internet www.col.org; f. 1987 by Commonwealth Heads of Government to promote the devt and sharing of distance education and open learning resources, including materials, expertise and technologies, throughout the Commonwealth and in other countries; implements and assists with national and regional educational programmes; acts as consultant to international agencies and national governments; conducts seminars and studies on specific educational needs; COL is financed by Commonwealth governments on a voluntary basis; in 1999 heads of government endorsed an annual core budget for COL of US $9m; Pres. and CEO Dato' Prof. GAJARAJ DHANARAJAN (Malaysia); publs *Connections, EdTech News.*

The following represents a selection of other Commonwealth organizations:

AGRICULTURE AND FORESTRY

Commonwealth Forestry Association: POB 142, Bicester, OX1 6ZJ; tel. (1865) 820935; fax (871) 2209682; e-mail cfa@ cfa-international.org; internet www.cfa-international.org; f. 1921; produces, collects and circulates information relating to world forestry and promotes good management, use and conservation of forests and forest lands throughout the world; mems: 1,000; Chair. Prof. J. BURLEY; publs *International Forestry Review* (quarterly), *Commonwealth Forestry News* (quarterly), *Commonwealth Forestry Handbook* (irregular).

Standing Committee on Commonwealth Forestry: Forestry Commission, 231 Corstorphine Rd, Edinburgh, EH12 7AT; tel. (131) 314-6137; fax (131) 334-0442; e-mail libby.jones@forestry.gsi.gov.uk; f. 1923 to provide continuity between Confs, and to provide a forum for discussion on any forestry matters of common interest to mem. govts which may be brought to the Cttee's notice by any mem. country or organization; 54 mems; 2001 Conference: Freemantle, Australia; 2005 Conference: Sri Lanka; Sec. LIBBY JONES; publ. *Newsletter* (quarterly).

COMMONWEALTH STUDIES

Institute of Commonwealth Studies: 28 Russell Sq., London, WC1B 5DS; tel. (20) 7862-8844; fax (20) 7862-8820; e-mail ics@sas .ac.uk; internet www.sas.ac.uk/commonwealthstudies; f. 1949 to promote advanced study of the Commonwealth; provides a library and meeting place for postgraduate students and academic staff engaged in research in this field; offers postgraduate teaching; Dir Prof. TIMOTHY SHAW; publs *Annual Report, Collected Seminar Papers, Newsletter, Theses in Progress in Commonwealth Studies.*

COMMUNICATIONS

Commonwealth Telecommunications Organization: Clareville House, 26–27 Oxendon St, London, SW1Y 4EL; tel. (20) 7930-5516; fax (20) 7930-4248; e-mail info@cto.int; internet www.cto.int; f. 1967; aims to enhance the development of telecommunications in Commonwealth countries and contribute to the communications infrastructure required for economic and social devt, through a devt and training programme; Exec. Dir Dr DAVID SOUTER; publ. *CTO Briefing* (3 a year).

EDUCATION AND CULTURE

Association of Commonwealth Universities—ACU: John Foster House, 36 Gordon Sq., London, WC1H 0PF; tel. (20) 7380-6700; fax (20) 7387-2655; e-mail info@acu.ac.uk; internet www.acu .ac.uk; f. 1913; ; promotes international co-operation and understanding; provides assistance with staff and student mobility and development programmes; researches and disseminates information about universities and relevant policy issues; organizes major meetings of Commonwealth universities and their representatives; acts as a liaison office and information centre; administers scholarship and fellowship schemes; operates a policy research unit; mems: 480 universities in 36 Commonwealth countries or regions; Sec.-Gen. Prof. MICHAEL GIBBONS; publs include: *Yearly Review* (annually) *Commonwealth Universities Yearbook,* (annually) *ACU Bulletin* (4 a year) *Report of the Council of the ACU* (annually) *Who's Who of Executive Heads: Vice-Chancellors, Presidents, Principals and Rectors, International Awards,* Student Information Papers (study abroad series).

Commonwealth Association for Education in Journalism and Communication—CAEJC: c/o Faculty of Law, University of Western Ontario, London, ON N6A 3K7, Canada; tel. (519) 6613348; fax (519) 6613790; e-mail caejc@julian.uwo.ca; f. 1985; aims to foster high standards of journalism and communication education and research in Commonwealth countries and to promote co-operation among institutions and professions; c. 700 mems in 32 Commonwealth countries; Pres. Prof. SYED ARABI IDID (Malaysia); Sec. Prof. ROBERT MARTIN (Canada); publ. *CAEJAC Journal* (annually).

Commonwealth Association of Science, Technology and Mathematics Educators—CASTME: c/o Education Dept, Human Resource Development Division, Commonwealth Secretariat, Marlborough House, Pall Mall, London, SW1Y 5HX; tel. (20) 7747-6282; fax (20) 7747-6287; e-mail v.goel@commonwealth.int; f. 1974; special emphasis is given to the social significance of education in these subjects; organizes an Awards Scheme to promote effective teaching and learning in these subjects, and biennial regional seminars; Pres. Sir HERMANN BONDI; Hon. Sec. Dr VED GOEL; publ. *CASTME Journal* (quarterly).

Commonwealth Council for Educational Administration and Management: c/o Assistant to the Deputy Vice Chancellor, Research and Development, Auckland University of Technology, POB 12 397, Penrose, Auckland 1135, New Zealand ; tel. (9) 917 9566 ; fax (9) 917 9501 ; e-mail jo.howse@aut.ac.nz; f. 1970; aims to foster quality in professional development and links among educational administrators; holds nat. and regional confs, as well as visits and seminars; mems: 24 affiliated groups representing 3,000 persons; Pres. Jo Howse; (New Zealand); publs *Managing Education Matters* (2 a year), *International Studies in Educational Administration* (2 a year).

Commonwealth Institute: 230 Kensington High St, London, W8 6NQ; tel. (20) 7603-4535; fax (20) 7603-4525; e-mail info@commonwealth.org.uk; internet www.commonwealth.org.uk; f. 1893 as the Imperial Institute; restructured as an independent pan-Commonwealth agency Jan. 2000; governed by a Bd of Trustees elected by the Bd of Governors; Commonwealth High Commissioners to the United Kingdom act as ex-officio Governors; the Inst. houses a Commonwealth Resource and Literature Library and a Conference and Events Centre; supplies educational resource mater ials and training throughout the United Kingdom; provides internet services to the Commonwealth; operates as an arts and conference centre, running a Commonwealth-based cultural programme; a five-year strategic plan, entitled 'Commonwealth 21', was inaugurated in 1998; Chair. JUDITH HANRATTY; Chief Exec. DAVID FRENCH; publ. *Annual Review*.

League for the Exchange of Commonwealth Teachers: 7 Lion Yard, Tremadoc Rd, London, SW4 7NQ; tel. (20) 7498-1101; fax (20) 7720-5403; e-mail info@lect.org.uk; internet www.lect.org.uk; f. 1901; promotes educational exchanges between teachers in Australia, the Bahamas, Barbados, Bermuda, Canada, Guyana, India, Jamaica, Kenya, Malawi, New Zealand, Pakistan, South Africa and Trinidad and Tobago; Dir ANNA TOMLINSON; publs *Annual Report, Exchange Teacher* (annually).

HEALTH

Commonwealth Medical Association: BMA House, Tavistock Sq., London, WC1H 9JP; tel. (20) 7272-8492; fax (20) 7272-1663; e-mail office@commat.org; internet www.commedast.org; f. 1962 for the exchange of information; provision of tech. co-operation and advice ; formulation and maintenance of a code of ethics; liaion with WHO and other UN agencies on health issues; meetings of its Council are held every three years; mems: medical asscns in Commonwealth countries; Sec. Dr JANE RICHARDS.

Commonwealth Pharmaceutical Association: 1 Lambeth High St, London, SE1 7JN; tel. (20) 7572-2364; fax (20) 7572-2508; e-mail bfalconbridge@rpsgb.org.uk; f. 1970 to promote the interests of pharmaceutical sciences and the profession of pharmacy in the Commonwealth to maintain high professional standards, encourage links between members and the creation of nat. asscns; and to facilitate the dissemination of information; holds confs (every four years) and regional meetings; mems: 39 pharmaceutical asscns; Sec. TONY MOFFAT; publ. *Quarterly Newsletter*.

Commonwealth Society for the Deaf: 34 Buckingham Palace Rd, London, SW1W 0RE; tel. (20) 7233-5700; fax (20) 7233-5800; e-mail sound.seekers@btinternet.com;   internet   www.sound-seekers.org .uk; promotes the health, education and general welfare of the deaf in developing Commonwealth countries; encourages and assists the development of educational facilities, the training of teachers of the deaf, and the provision of support for parents of deaf children; organizes visits by volunteer specialists to developing countries; provides audiological equipment and organizes the training of audiological maintenance technicians; conducts research into the causes and prevention of deafness; CEO Brig. J. A. DAVIS; publ. *Annual Report*.

Sight Savers International: Grosvenor Hall, Bolnore Rd, Haywards Heath,West Sussex, RH16 4BX; tel. (1444) 446600; fax (1444) 446688; e-mail generalinformation@sightsavers.org; internet www .sightsavers.org; f. 1950 to prevent blindness and restore sight in developing countries, and to provide education and community-based training for incurably blind people; operates in collaboration with local partners, with high priority given to training local staff; Chair. Sir JOHN COLES; Dir RICHARD PORTER; publ. *Sight Savers News*.

INFORMATION AND THE MEDIA

Commonwealth Broadcasting Association: 17 Fleet St, London, EC4Y 1AA; tel. (20) 7583-5550; fax (20) 7583-5549; e-mail cba@cba .org.uk; internet www.cba.org.uk; f. 1945; gen. confs are held every two years (2002: Manchester, United Kingdom); mems: 97 in 57 countries; Pres. GEORGE VALARINO; Sec.-Gen. ELIZABETH SMITH; publs *Commonwealth Broadcaster* (quarterly), *Commonwealth Broadcaster Directory* (annually).

Commonwealth Institute: see under Education.

Commonwealth Journalists Association: 17 Nottingham St, London, W1M 3RD; tel. (20) 7486-3844; fax (20) 7486-3822; e-mail ian.cjalon@virgin.net;   internet   www.ozemail.com.au/&ub .nft;pwessels/cja.html; f. 1978 to promote co-operation between journalists in Commonwealth countries, organize training facilities and

confs, and foster understanding among Commonwealth peoples; Pres. MURRAY BURT; Exec. Dir IAN GILLHAM.

Commonwealth Press Union (Asscn of Commonwealth Newspapers, News Agencies and Periodicals): 17 Fleet St, London, EC4Y 1AA; tel. (20) 7583-7733; fax (20) 7583-6868; e-mail 106156.3331@ compuserve.com; internet www.cpu.org.uk; f. 1950; promotes the welfare of the Commonwealth press; provides training for journalists and organizes biennial confs; mems: c. 1,000 newspapers, news agencies, periodicals in 42 Commonwealth countries; Dir LINDSAY ROSS; publs *CPU News, Annual Report*.

LAW

Commonwealth Lawyers' Association: c/o The Law Society, 114 Chancery Lane, London, WC2A 1PL; tel. (20) 7320-5911; fax (20) 7831-0057;   e-mail   cla@lawsociety.org.uk;   internet   www .commonwealthlawyers.com; f. 1983 (fmrly the Commonwealth Legal Bureau); seeks to maintain and promote the rule of law throughout the Commonwealth, by ensuring that the people of the Commonwealth are served by an independent and efficient legal profession; upholds professional standards and promotes the availability of legal services; assists in organizing the triennial Commonwealth law confs; Pres. CYRUS DAS (1999–2003); Exec. Sec. CHRISTINE AMOH; publs *The Commonwealth Lawyer, Clarion*.

Commonwealth Legal Advisory Service: c/o British Institute of International and Comparative Law, Charles Clore House, 17 Russell Sq., London, WC1B 5JP; tel. (20) 7862-5151; fax (20) 7862-5152; e-mail info@biicl.org; financed by the British Institute and by contributions from Commonwealth govts; provides research facilities for Commonwealth govts and law reform commissions.

Commonwealth Legal Education Association: c/o Legal and Constitutional Affairs Division, Commonwealth Secretariat, Marlborough House, Pall Mall, London, SW1Y 5HX; tel. (20) 7747-6415; fax (20) 7747-6406; e-mail clea@commonwealth.int; internet www .clea.org.uk; f. 1971 to promote contacts and exchanges and to provide information regarding legal education; Gen. Sec. JOHN HATCHARD; publs *Commonwealth Legal Education Association Newsletter* (3 a year), *Directory of Commonwealth Law Schools* (every 2 years).

Commonwealth Magistrates' and Judges' Association: Uganda House, 58/59 Trafalgar Sq., London, WC2N 5DX; tel. (20) 7976-1007; fax (20) 7976-2395; e-mail info@cmja.org; internet www .cmja.org; f. 1970 to advance the administration of the law by promoting the independence of the judiciary, to further education in law and crime prevention and to disseminate information; confs and study tours; corporate membership for asscns of the judiciary or courts of limited jurisdiction; assoc. membership for individuals; Pres. Hon. Chief Justice RICHARD BANDA; Sec.-Gen. Dr KAREN BREWER; publ. *Commonwealth Judicial Journal* (2 a year).

PARLIAMENTARY AFFAIRS

Commonwealth Parliamentary Association: Westminster House, Suite 700, 7 Millbank, London, SW1P 3JA; tel. (20) 7799-1460; fax (20) 7222-6073; e-mail hq.sec@cpahq.org; internet www .cpahq.org; f. 1911 to promote understanding and co-operation between Commonwealth parliamentarians; organization: Exec. Cttee of 32 MPs responsible to annual Gen. Assembly; 170 brs throughout the Commonwealth; holds annual Commonwealth Parliamentary Confs and seminars; also regional confs and seminars; Sec.-Gen. Hon. DENIS MARSHALL; publ. *The Parliamentarian* (quarterly).

PROFESSIONAL AND INDUSTRIAL RELATIONS

Commonwealth Association of Architects: 66 Portland Pl., London, W1N 4AD; tel. (20) 7490-3024; fax (20) 72532592; e-mail caa@gharchitects.demon.co.uk; internet www.archexchange.org; f. 1964; an asscn of 38 socs of architects in various Commonwealth countries; objectives: to facilitate the reciprocal recognition of professional qualifications; to provide a clearing house for information on architectural practice, and to encourage collaboration. Plenary confs every three years; regional confs are also held; Exec. Dir TONY GODWIN; publs *Handbook, Objectives and Procedures: CAA Schools Visiting Boards, Architectural Education in the Commonwealth* (annotated bibliography of research), *CAA Newsnet* (2 a year), a survey and list of schools of architecture.

Commonwealth Association for Public Administration and Management—CAPAM: 1075 Bay St, Suite 402, Toronto, ON M5S 2B1, Canada; tel. (416) 920-3337; fax (416) 920-6574; e-mail capam@ capam.ca; internet www.capam.comnet.mt/; f. 1994; aims to promote sound management of the public sector in Commonwealth countries and to assist those countries undergoing political or financial reforms; an international awards programme to reward innovation within the public sector was introduced in 1997, and is awarded every 2 years; Pres. Hon. JOCELYNE BOURGON (Canada); Exec. Dir ART STEVENSON (Canada).

Commonwealth Trade Union Council: Congress House, 23–28 Great Russell St, London, WC1B 3LS; tel. (20) 7467-1301; fax (20) 7436-0301; e-mail info@commonwealthtuc.org; internet www .commonwealthtuc.org; f. 1979; links trade union national centres (representing more than 30m. trade union mems) throughout the Commonwealth; promotes the application of democratic principles and core labour standards, works closely with other international trade union orgs; Dir ANNIE WATSON; publ. *Annual Report.*

SCIENCE AND TECHNOLOGY

Commonwealth Engineers' Council: c/o Institution of Civil Engineers, One Great George St, London, SW1P 3AA; tel. (20) 7222-7722; fax (20) 7233-1806; e-mail international@ice.org.uk; f. 1946; the Council meets every two years to provide an opportunity for engineering institutions of Commonwealth countries to exchange views on collaboration; there is a standing cttee on engineering education and training; organizes seminars on related topics; Sec.Gen. TOM FOULKES.

Commonwealth Geological Surveys Forum: c/o Commonwealth Science Council, CSC Earth Sciences Programme, Marlborough House, Pall Mall, London, SW1Y 5HX; tel. (20) 7839-3411; fax (20) 7839-6174; e-mail comsci@gn.apc.org; f. 1948 to promote collaboration in geological, geochemical, geophysical and remote sensing techniques and the exchange of information; Geological Programme Officer Dr SIYAN MALOMO.

SPORT

Cmmonwealth Games Federation: 4th Floor, 26 Upper Brooke Street,, London; tel. (20) 7491-8801; fax (20) 7409-7803; e-mail info@ thecgf.com; internet www.thecgf.com; the Games were first held in 1930 and are now held every four years; participation is limited to competitors representing the mem. countries of the Commonwealth; held in Manchester, United Kingdom, in 2002; mems: 72 affiliated bodies; Pres. HRH THE EARL OF WESSEX; CEO. MICHAEL HOOPER.

YOUTH

Commonwealth Youth Exchange Council: 7 Lion Yard, Tremadoc Rd, London, SW4 7NQ; tel. (20) 7498-6151; fax (20) 7720-5403; e-mail mail@cyec.demon.co.uk; f. 1970; promotes contact between groups of young people of the United Kingdom and other Commonwealth countries by means of educational exchange visits, provides information for organizers and allocates grants; 224 mem. orgs; Dir V. S. G. CRAGGS; publs *Contact* (handbook), *Exchange* (newsletter), *Safety and Welfare* (guide-lines for Commonwealth Youth Exchange groups).

Duke of Edinburgh's Award International Association: Award House, 7-11 St Matthew St, London, SW1P 2JT; tel. (20) 7222-4242; fax (20) 7222-4141; e-mail sect@intaward.org; internet www .intaward.org; f. 1956; offers a programme of leisure activities for young people, comprising Service, Expeditions, Physical Recreation, and Skills; operates in more than 60 countries (not confined to the Commonwealth); International Sec.-Gen. PAUL ARENGO-JONES; publs *Award World* (2 a year), *Annual Report*, handbooks and guides.

MISCELLANEOUS

British Commonwealth Ex-Services League: 48 Pall Mall, London, SW1Y 5JG; tel. (20) 7973-7263; fax (20) 7973-7308; links the ex-service orgs in the Commonwealth, assists ex-servicemen of the Crown and their dependants who are resident abroad; holds triennial confs; Grand Pres. HRH THE DUKE OF EDINBURGH; Sec.-Gen. COL BRIAN NICHOLSON; publ. *Annual Report.*

Commonwealth Countries League: 96 High Street, Hampton Wick, Kingston-upon-Thames KT1 4DQ; tel. (20) 8943 3001; fax (20) 8458 0763; f. 1925 to secure equal opportunities and status between men and women in the Commonwealth, to act as a link between Commonwealth women's orgs, and to promote and finance secondary education of disadvantaged girls of high ability in their own countries, through the CCL Educational Fund; holds meetings with speakers and an annual Conf., organizes the annual Commonwealth Fair for fund-raising; individual mems and affiliated socs in the Commonwealth; Sec.-Gen. FLOI STEWART-MURRAY; publ. *CCL Newsletter* (3 a year).

Commonwealth War Graves Commission: 2 Marlow Rd, Maidenhead, Berks, SL6 7DX; tel. (1628) 634221; fax (1628) 771208; e-mail general.enq@cwgc.org; internet www.cwgc.org; casualty and cemetery enquiries e-mail casualty.enq@cwgc.org; f. 1917 (as Imperial War Graves Commission); responsible for the commemoration in perpetuity of the 1.7m. members of the Commonwealth Forces who died during the wars of 1914–18 and 1939–45; provides for the marking and maintenance of war graves and memorials at some 23,000 locations in 150 countries; mems: Australia, Canada, India, New Zealand, South Africa, United Kingdom; Pres. HRH THE DUKE OF KENT; Dir-Gen. RICHARD KELLAWAY.

Joint Commonwealth Societies' Council: c/o Royal Commonwealth Society, 18 Northumberland Ave, London, WC2N 5BJ; tel. (20) 7930-6733; fax (20) 7930-9705; e-mail jcsc@rcsint.org; internet www.commonwealthday.com; f. 1947; provides a forum for the exchange of information regarding activities of mem. orgs which promote understanding among countries of the Commonwealth; co-ordinates the distribution of the Commonwealth Day message by Queen Elizabeth, organizes the observance of the Commonwealth Day and produces educational materials relating to the occasion; mems: 16 unofficial Commonwealth orgs and four official bodies; Chair. Sir PETER MARSHALL; Sec. NICHOLAS. J. HERCULES.

Royal Commonwealth Society: 18 Northumberland Ave, London, WC2N 5BJ; tel. (20) 7930-6733; fax (20) 7930-9705; e-mail info@ rcsint.org; internet www.rcsint.org; f. 1868 to promote international understanding of the Commonwealth and its people; organizes meetings and seminars on topical issues, and cultural and social events; library housed by Cambridge University Library; Chair. Baroness PRASHAR; Dir STUART MOLE; publs *Annual Report, Newsletter* (3 a year), conference reports.

Royal Over-Seas League: Over-Seas House, Park Place, St James's St, London, SW1A 1LR; tel. (20) 7408-0214; fax (20) 7499-6738; e-mail info@rosl.org.uk; internet www.rosl.org.uk; f. 1910 to promote friendship and understanding in the Commonwealth; club houses in London and Edinburgh; membership is open to all British subjects and Commonwealth citizens; Chair. Sir COLIN IMRAY; Dir-Gen. ROBERT F. NEWELL; publ. *Overseas* (quarterly).

The Victoria League for Commonwealth Friendship: 55 Leinster Sq., London, W2 4PW; tel. (20) 7243-2633; fax (20) 7229-2994; f. 1901; aims to further personal friendship among Commonwealth peoples and to provide hospitality for visitors; maintains Student House, providing accommodation for students from Commonwealth countries; has brs elsewhere in the UK and abroad; Chair. JOHN KELLY; Gen. Sec. JOHN M. W. ALLAN; publ. *Annual Report.*

THE COMMONWEALTH OF INDEPENDENT STATES— CIS

Address: 220000 Minsk, Kirava 17, Belarus.

Telephone: (172) 22-35-17; **fax:** (172) 27-23-39; **e-mail:** postmaster@www.cis.minsk.by; **internet:** www.cis.minsk.by.

The Commonwealth of Independent States is a voluntary association of 12 (originally 11) states, established at the time of the collapse of the USSR in December 1991.

MEMBERS

Armenia	Moldova
Azerbaijan	Russia
Belarus	Tajikistan
Georgia	Turkmenistan
Kazakhstan	Ukraine
Kyrgyzstan	Uzbekistan

Note: Azerbaijan signed the Alma-Ata Declaration (see below), but in October 1992 the Azerbaijan legislature voted against ratification of the foundation documents by which the Commonwealth of Independent States had been established in December 1991. Azerbaijan formally became a member of the CIS in September 1993, after the legislature voted in favour of membership. Georgia was admitted to the CIS in December 1993.

Organization

(April 2003)

COUNCIL OF HEADS OF STATE

This is the supreme body of the CIS, on which all the member states of the Commonwealth are represented at the level of head of state, for discussion of issues relating to the co-ordination of Commonwealth activities and the development of the Minsk Agreement. Decisions of the Council are taken by common consent, with each state having equal voting rights. The Council meets at least twice a year. An extraordinary meeting may be convened on the initiative of the majority of Commonwealth heads of state. From January 2003 the chairmanship of the Council was to be rotated among member states.

COUNCIL OF HEADS OF GOVERNMENT

This Council convenes for meetings at least once every three months; an extraordinary sitting may be convened on the initiative of a majority of Commonwealth heads of government. The two Councils may discuss and take necessary decisions on important domestic and external issues, and may held joint sittings.

Working and auxiliary bodies, composed of authorized representatives of the participating states, may be set up on a permanent or interim basis on the decision of the Council of Heads of State and the Council of Heads of Government.

CIS EXECUTIVE COMMITTEE

The Executive Committee was established by the Council of Heads of State in April 1999 to supersede the existing Secretariat, the Inter-state Economic Committee and other working bodies and committees, in order to improve the efficient functioning of the organization. The Executive Committee co-operates closely with other CIS bodies including the councils of foreign ministers and defence ministers; the Economic Council; Council of Border Troops Commanders; the Collective Security Council; the Secretariat of the Council of the Inter-parliamentary Assembly; and the Inter-state Committee for Statistics.

Executive Secretary and Chairman of the Executive Committee: YURII YAROV.

Activities

On 8 December 1991 the heads of state of Belarus, Russia and Ukraine signed the Minsk Agreement, providing for the establishment of a Commonwealth of Independent States. Formal recognition of the dissolution of the USSR was incorporated in a second treaty (the Alma-Ata Declaration), signed by 11 heads of state in the then Kazakh capital, Alma-Ata (Almaty), later in that month.

In March 1992 a meeting of the CIS Council of Heads of Government decided to establish a commission to examine the resolution that 'all CIS member states are the legal successors of the rights and obligations of the former Soviet Union'. Documents relating to the legal succession of the Soviet Union were signed at a meeting of Heads of State in July. In April an agreement establishing an Inter-parliamentary Assembly (IPA), signed by Armenia, Belarus, Kazakhstan, Kyrgyzstan, Russia, Tajikistan and Uzbekistan, was published. The first Assembly was held in Bishkek, Kyrgyzstan, in September, attended by delegates from all these countries, with the exception of Uzbekistan.

A CIS Charter was formulated at the meeting of the heads of state in Minsk, Belarus, in January 1993. The Charter, providing for a defence alliance, an inter-state court and an economic co-ordination committee, was to serve as a framework for closer co-operation and was signed by all of the members except Moldova, Turkmenistan and Ukraine.

In May 1994 the CIS and UNCTAD signed a co-operation accord. A similar agreement was concluded with the UN Economic Commission for Europe in June 1996. Working contacts have also been established with ILO, UNHCR, WHO and the European Union. In June 1998 the IPA approved a decision to sign the European Social Charter (see Council of Europe); a declaration of co-operation between the Assembly and the OSCE Parliamentary Assembly was also signed.

In November 1995, at the Council of Heads of Government meeting, Russia expressed concern at the level of non-payment of debts by CIS members, which, it said, was hindering further integration. At the meeting of the Council in April 1996 a long-term plan for the integrated development of the CIS, incorporating measures for further socio-economic, military and political co-operation, was approved.

In March 1997 the then Russian President, Boris Yeltsin, admitted that the CIS institutional structure had failed to ameliorate the severe economic situation of certain member states. Nevertheless, support for the CIS as an institution was reaffirmed by the participants during the meeting. At the heads of state meeting held in Chişinău, Moldova, in October, Russia was reportedly criticized by the other country delegations for failing to implement CIS agreements, for hindering development of the organization and for failing to resolve regional conflicts. Russia, for its part, urged all member states to participate more actively in defining, adopting and implementing CIS policies. Meeting in April 1998 heads of state emphasized the necessity of improving the activities of the CIS and of reforming its bureaucratic structure. Reform of the CIS was also the main item on the agenda of the eleventh IPA, held in June. It was agreed that an essentially new institution needed to be created, taking into account the relations between the states in a new way. In the same month the first plenary meeting of a special forum, convened to address issues of restructuring the CIS, was held. Working groups were to be established to co-ordinate proposals and draft documents. However, in October reform proposals drawn up by 'experienced specialists' and presented by the Executive Secretary were unanimously rejected as inadequate by the 12 member states. In March 1999 Boris Yeltsin, acting as Chairman of the Council of Heads of State, dismissed the then Executive Secretary, Boris Berezovskii, owing to alleged misconduct and neglect of duties. The decision was endorsed by the Council of Heads of Government meeting in April. The Council also adopted guide-lines for restructuring the CIS and for the future development of the organization. Economic co-operation was to be a priority area of activity, and in particular, the establishment of a free-trade zone. Vladimir Putin, then acting President of the Russian Federation, was elected as the new Chairman of the Council of Heads of State at a CIS summit held in Moscow in January 2000. Meeting in June, a summit of the Councils of Heads of State and Government issued a declaration concerning the maintenance of strategic stability, approved a plan and schedule for pursuing economic integration, and adopted a programme for combating international terrorism (perceived to be a significant threat in central Asia) during 2000–03. The Council of Heads of Government also approved a programme of action to guide the organization's activities until 2005. An informal CIS 10-year 'jubilee' summit, convened in November 2001, adopted a statement identifying the collective pursuit of stable socio-economic development and integration on a global level as the organization's principal objective. A summit of heads of state convened in January 2003 agreed that the position of Chairman of the Council of Heads of State (hitherto held by consecutive Russian presidents) should be rotated henceforth among member states. Leonid Kuchma, the President of Ukraine, was elected as the new Chairman.

Member states of the CIS have formed alliances of various kinds among themselves, thereby potentially undermining the unity of the Commonwealth. In March 1996 Belarus, Kazakhstan, Kyrgyzstan and the Russian Federation signed the Quadripartite Treaty for greater integration. This envisaged the establishment of a 'New Union', based, initially on a common market and customs union, and was to be open to all CIS members and the Baltic states. Consequently these countries (with Tajikistan) became founding members of the Eurasian Economic Community, inaugurated in October 2001. In April 1996 Belarus and Russia signed the Treaty on the Formation of a Community of Sovereign Republics (CSR), which provided for extensive economic, political and military co-operation. In April 1997 the two countries signed a further Treaty of Union and, in addition, initialled the Charter of the Union, which detailed the procedures and institutions designed to develop a common infrastructure, a single currency and a joint defence policy within the CSR, with the eventual aim of 'voluntary unification of the member states'. The Charter was signed in May and ratified by the respective legislatures the following month. The Union's Parliamentary Assembly, comprising 36 members from the legislature of each country, convened in official session for the first time shortly afterwards. Azerbaijan, Georgia, Moldova and Ukraine co-operated increasingly during the late 1990s as the so-called GUAM Group, which envisaged implementing joint economic and transportation initiatives and establishing a sub-regional free-trade zone. In October 1997 the GUAM countries agreed collectively to establish a Eurasian Trans-Caucasus transportation corridor. Uzbekistan joined in April 1999, creating GUAAM. The group agreed in September 2000 to convene regular annual summits of member countries' heads of state and to organize meetings of ministers of foreign affairs at least twice a year. Russia, Armenia, Azerbaijan and Georgia convene regular meetings as the 'Caucasian Group of Four'.

ECONOMIC AFFAIRS

At a meeting of the Council of Heads of Government in March 1992 agreement was reached on repayment of the foreign debt of the former USSR. Agreements were also signed on pensions, joint tax policy and the servicing of internal debt. In May an accord on repayment of inter-state debt and the issue of balance-of-payments statements was adopted by the heads of government, meeting in Tashkent, Uzbekistan. In July it was decided to establish an economic court in Minsk.

The CIS Charter, formulated in January 1993 and signed by seven of the 10 member countries, provided for the establishment of an economic co-ordination committee. In February, at a meeting of the heads of foreign economic departments, a foreign economic council was formed. In May all member states, with the exception of Turkmenistan, adopted a declaration of support for increased economic union and, in September, agreement was reached by all states except Ukraine and Turkmenistan on a framework for economic union, including the gradual removal of tariffs and creation of a currency union. Turkmenistan was subsequently admitted as a full member of the economic union in December 1993 and Ukraine as an associate member in April 1994.

At the Council of Heads of Government meeting in September 1994 all member states, except Turkmenistan, agreed to establish an Inter-state Economic Committee to implement economic treaties adopted within the context of an economic union. The establishment of a payments union to improve the settlement of accounts was also agreed. In April 1998 CIS heads of state resolved to incorporate the functions of the Inter-state Economic Committee, along with those of other working bodies and sectional committees, into a new CIS Executive Committee.

In October 1997 seven heads of government signed a document on implementing the 'concept for the integrated economic development of the CIS'. The development of economic co-operation between the member states was a priority task of the special forum on reform held in June 1998. In the same month an economic forum, held in St Petersburg, Russia, acknowledged the severe economic conditions prevailing in certain CIS states.

Guide-lines adopted by the Council of Heads of State in April 1999 concerning the future development of the CIS identified economic co-operation and the establishment of a free-trade zone (see Trade) as priority areas for action. The plan of action for the development of the CIS until 2005, adopted by the Council of Heads of Government in June 2000, outlined medium-term economic co-operation measures, including the formulation of intergovernmental accords to provide the legal basis for the free movement of services, capital, people, etc.; the development of private business and markets; and joint participation in the implementation of major economic projects.

TRADE

Agreement was reached on the free movement of goods between republics at a meeting of the Council of Heads of State in February 1992, and in April 1994 an agreement on the creation of a CIS free-trade zone (envisaged as the first stage of economic union) was concluded. In July a council of the heads of customs committees, meeting in Moscow, approved a draft framework for customs legislation in CIS countries, to facilitate the establishment of a free-trade zone. The framework was approved by all the participants, with the exception of Turkmenistan. In April 1999 CIS heads of state signed a protocol to the 1994 free-trade area accord, which aimed to accelerate co-operation. In June 2000 the Council of Heads of State adopted a plan and schedule for the implementation of priority measures related to the creation of the free-trade zone, and in early 2003 it was announced that an accord formally establishing the zone could be adopted by CIS heads of state in September.

At the first session of the Inter-state Economic Committee in November 1994 draft legislation regarding a customs union was approved. In March 1998 Russia, Belarus, Kazakhstan and Kyrgyzstan signed an agreement establishing a customs union, which was to be implemented in two stages: firstly, the removal of trade restrictions and the unification of trade and customs regulations; followed by the integration of economic, monetary and trade policies (see above). The development of a customs union and the strengthening of intra-CIS trade were objectives endorsed by all participants, with the exception of Georgia, at the Council of Heads of Government meeting held in March 1997. In February 1999 Tajikistan signed the 1998 agreement to become the fifth member of the customs union. In October 1999 the heads of state of the five member states of the customs union reiterated their political determination to implement the customs union and approved a programme to harmonize national legislation to create a single economic space. In May 2000 the heads of state announced their intention to raise the status of the customs union to that of an inter-state economic organization, and, in October, the leaders signed a treaty establishing the Eurasian Economic Community. Under the new structure member states aimed to formulate a unified foreign economic policy, and collectively to pursue the creation of the planned single economic space. In the following month the five member governments signed an agreement enabling visa-free travel within the new Community. (Earlier in 2000 Russia had withdrawn from a CIS-wide visa-free travel arrangement agreed in 1992.) In December 2000 member states of the Community adopted several documents aimed at facilitating economic co-operation. The Eurasian Economic Community, governed by an inter-state council based in Astana, Kazakhstan, was formally inaugurated in October 2001.

The CIS maintains a 'loose co-ordination' on issues related to applications by member states to join the WTO.

BANKING AND FINANCE

In February 1992 CIS heads of state agreed to retain the rouble as the common currency for trade between the republics. However, in July 1993, in an attempt to control inflation, notes printed before 1993 were withdrawn from circulation and no new ones were issued until January 1994. Despite various agreements to recreate the 'rouble zone', including a protocol agreement signed in September 1993 by six states, it effectively remained confined to Tajikistan, which joined in January 1994, and Belarus, which joined in April. Both those countries proceeded to introduce national currencies in May 1995. In January 1993, at the signing of the CIS Charter, all 10 member countries endorsed the establishment of an inter-state bank to facilitate payments between the republics and to co-ordinate monetary-credit policy. Russia was to hold 50% of shares in the bank, but decisions were to be made only with a two-thirds majority approval. In December 2000, in accordance with the CSR and Treaty of Union (see above), the Presidents of Belarus and Russia signed an agreement providing for the adoption by Belarus of the Russian currency from 1 January 2005, and for the introduction of a new joint Union currency by 1 January 2008.

DEFENCE

An Agreement on Armed Forces and Border Troops was concluded on 30 December 1991, at the same time as the Agreement on Strategic Forces. This confirmed the right of member states to set up their own armed forces and appointed Commanders-in-Chief of the Armed Forces and of the Border Troops, who were to elaborate joint security procedures. In February 1992 an agreement was signed stipulating that the commander of the strategic forces was subordinate to the Council of Heads of States. Eight states agreed on a unified command for general-purpose (i.e. non-strategic) armed forces for a transitional period of two years. Azerbaijan, Moldova and Ukraine resolved to establish independent armed forces.

In January 1992 Commissions on the Black Sea Fleet (control of which was disputed by Russia and Ukraine) and the Caspian Flotilla (the former Soviet naval forces on the Caspian Sea) were established. The defence and stability of CIS external borders and the status of strategic and nuclear forces were among topics discussed at the meeting of heads of state and of government, in Bishkek, in October. The formation of a defence alliance was provided for in the CIS Charter formulated in January 1993 and signed by seven of the

10 member countries; a proposal by Russia to assume control of all nuclear weapons in the former USSR was rejected at the same time.

In June 1993 CIS defence ministers agreed to abolish CIS joint military command and to abandon efforts to maintain a unified defence structure. The existing CIS command was to be replaced, on a provisional basis, by a 'joint staff for co-ordinating military co-operation between the states of the Commonwealth'. It was widely reported that Russia had encouraged the decision to abolish the joint command, owing to concerns at the projected cost of a CIS joint military structure and support within Russia's military leadership of bilateral military agreements with the country's neighbours. In December the Council of Defence Ministers agreed to establish a secretariat to co-ordinate military co-operation as a replacement to the joint military command. In November 1995 the Council of Defence Ministers authorized the establishment of a Joint Air Defence System, to be co-ordinated largely by Russia. A CIS combat duty system was to be created in 1999–2005. Russia and Belarus are also developing a joint air-defence unit in the context of the CSR (see above).

In September 1996 the first meeting of the inter-state commission for military economic co-operation was held; a draft agreement on the export of military projects and services to third countries was approved. The basic principles of a programme for greater military and technical co-operation were approved by the Council of Defence Ministers in March 1997. In April 1998 the Council proposed drawing up a draft programme for military and technical co-operation between member countries and also discussed procedures advising on the use and maintenance of armaments and military hardware. Draft proposals relating to information security for the military were approved by the Council in December. It was remarked that the inadequate funding of the Council was impeding co-operation. In May 2001 a draft plan for military co-operation until 2005 was agreed.

In August 1996 the Council of Defence Ministers condemned what it described as the political, economic and military threat implied in any expansion of NATO. The statement was not signed by Ukraine. The eighth plenary session of the IPA, held in November, urged NATO countries to abandon plans for the organization's expansion. Strategic co-operation between NATO and CIS member states increased from the mid-1990s, particularly with Russia and Ukraine. In the late 1990s the USA established bilateral military assistance programmes for Azerbaijan, Georgia, and Uzbekistan. Uzbekistan and other central Asian CIS states played a support role in the US-led action initiated in late 2001 against the then Taliban-held areas of Afghanistan (see below).

REGIONAL SECURITY

At a meeting of heads of government in March 1992 agreements on settling inter-state conflicts were signed by all participating states (except Turkmenistan). At the same meeting an agreement on the status of border troops was signed by five states. In May a five-year Collective Security Agreement was signed. In July further documents were signed on collective security and it was agreed to establish joint peacemaking forces to intervene in CIS disputes. In April 1999 Armenia, Belarus, Kazakhstan, Kyrgyzstan, Russia and Tajikistan signed a protocol to extend the Collective Security Agreement for a further five-year period.

In September 1993 the Council of Heads of State agreed to establish a Bureau of Organized Crime, to be based in Moscow. A meeting of the Council of Border Troop Commanders in January 1994 prepared a report on the issue of illegal migration and drug trade across the external borders of the CIS; Moldova, Georgia and Tajikistan did not attend. A programme to counter organized crime within the CIS was approved by heads of government, meeting in Moscow, in April 1996. In March 2001 CIS interior ministers agreed to strengthen co-operation in combating transnational organized crime, in view of reportedly mounting levels of illicit drugs-trafficking in the region.

In February 1995 a non-binding memorandum on maintaining peace and stability was adopted by heads of state, meeting in Almaty. Signatories were to refrain from applying military, political, economic or other pressure on another member country, to seek the peaceful resolution of border or territorial disputes and not to support or assist separatist movements active in other member countries. In April 1998 the Council of Defence Ministers approved a draft document proposing that coalition forces be provided with technical equipment to enhance collective security.

In June 1998, at a session of the Council of Border Troop Commanders, some 33 documents were signed relating to border co-operation. A framework protocol on the formation and expedient use of a border troops reserve in critical situations was discussed and signed by several participants. A register of work in scientific and engineering research carried out in CIS countries in the interests of border troops was also adopted.

In June 1998 CIS interior ministers, meeting in Tashkent, Uzbekistan, adopted a number of co-operation agreements, including a framework for the exchange of information between CIS law-enforcement agencies; it was also decided to maintain contact with Interpol.

An emergency meeting of heads of state in October 1996 discussed the ongoing conflict in nearby Afghanistan and the consequent threat to regional security. The participants requested the UN Security Council to adopt measures to resolve the situation. The IPA subsequently reiterated the call for a cessation of hostilities in that country. In May 2000 the six signatory states to the Collective Security Agreement pledged to strengthen military co-operation in view of the perceived threat to their security from the Taliban regime in Afghanistan. It was reported that a mechanism had been approved that would enable parties to the Agreement to purchase arms from Russia at special rates. In October the parties to the Collective Security Agreement signed an agreement on the Status of Forces and Means of Collective Security Systems, establishing a joint rapid deployment function. The so-called CIS Collective Rapid Reaction Force was to be assembled to combat insurgencies, with particular reference to trans-border terrorism from Afghanistan, and also to deter trans-border illegal drugs trafficking (see above). In June 2001 a CIS anti-terrorism centre was established in Moscow. The centre was to co-ordinate counter-terrorism activities and to compile a database of international terrorist organizations operating in member states. In October, in response to the major terrorist attacks perpetrated in September against targets in the USA—allegedly co-ordinated by Afghanistan-based militant fundamentalist Islamist leader Osama bin Laden—the parties to the Collective Security Treaty adopted a new anti-terrorism plan. In November the head of the co-ordinating Collective Security Council identified combating international terrorism as the main focus of the Collective Security Agreement at that time. The signatory countries to the Collective Security Agreement participate in regular so-called 'CIS Southern Shield' joint military exercises. In October 2002 a central Asian subdivision of the CIS anti-terrorism centre was established in Bishkek, Kyrgyzstan. The formation of a new regional security organization, the Central Asian Co-operation Pact, was announced in February of that year by Kazakhstan, Kyrgyzstan, Tajikistan and Uzbekistan.

The fourth plenary session of the IPA in March 1994 established a commission for the resolution of the conflicts in the secessionist regions of Nagornyi Karabakh (Azerbaijan) and Abkhazia (Georgia) and endorsed the use of CIS peace-keeping forces. In the following month Russia agreed to send peace-keeping forces to Georgia, and the dispatch of peace-keeping forces was approved by the Council of Defence Ministers in October. The subsequent session of the IPA in October adopted a resolution to send groups of military observers to Abkhazia and to Moldova. The inter-parliamentary commission on the conflict between Abkhazia and Georgia proposed initiating direct negotiations with the two sides in order to reach a peaceful settlement.

In December 1994 the Council of Defence Ministers enlarged the mandate of the commander of the CIS collective peace-keeping forces in Tajikistan: when necessary CIS military contingents were permitted to engage in combat operations without the prior consent of individual governments. At the Heads of State meeting in Moscow in January 1996 Georgia's proposal to impose sanctions against Abkhazia was approved, in an attempt to achieve a resolution of the conflict. Provisions on arrangements relating to collective peace-keeping operations were approved at the meeting; the training of military and civilian personnel for these operations was to commence in October. In March 1997 the Council of Defence Ministers agreed to extend the peace-keeping mandates for CIS forces in Tajikistan and Abkhazia (following much disagreement, the peace-keepers' mandate in Abkhazia was further renewed in October). At a meeting of the Council in January 1998 a request from Georgia that the CIS carry out its decisions to settle the conflict with Abkhazia was added to the agenda. The Council discussed the promotion of military co-operation and the improvement of peace-making activities, and declared that there was progress in the formation of the collective security system, although the situation in the North Caucasus remained tense. In April President Yeltsin requested that the Armenian and Azerbaijani presidents sign a document to end the conflict in Nagornyi Karabakh; the two subsequently issued a statement expressing their support for a political settlement of the conflict. A document proposing a settlement of the conflict in Abkhazia was also drawn up, but the resolutions adopted were not accepted by Abkhazia. Against the wishes of the Abkhazian authorities, the mandate for the CIS troops in the region was extended to cover the whole of the Gali district. The mandate expired in July 1998, but the forces remained in the region while its renewal was debated. In April 1999 the Council of Heads of State agreed to a retrospective extension of the operation's mandate; the mandate has subsequently continued to be renewed at six-monthly intervals. The mandate of the CIS peace-keeping operation in Tajikistan was terminated in June 2000. In February 2001 it was reported that regulations had been drafted for the inistitution of a CIS Special Envoy for the Settlement of Conflicts.

LEGISLATIVE CO-OPERATION

An agreement on legislative co-operation was signed at an Inter-Parliamentary Conference in January 1992; joint commissions were established to co-ordinate action on economy, law, pensions, housing, energy and ecology. The CIS Charter, formulated in January 1993, provided for the establishment of an inter-state court. In October 1994 a Convention on the rights of minorities was adopted at the meeting of the Heads of State. In May 1995, at the sixth plenary session of the IPA, several acts to improve co-ordination of legislation were approved, relating to migration of labour, consumer rights, and the rights of prisoners of war.

The creation of a Council of Ministers of Internal Affairs was approved at the Heads of State meeting in January 1996; the Council was to promote co-operation between the law-enforcement bodies of member states. At the 10th plenary session of the IPA in December 1997 14 laws, relating to banking and financial services, education, ecology and charity were adopted. At the IPA session held in June 1998 10 model laws relating to social issues were approved,

including a law on obligatory social insurance against production accidents and occupational diseases, and on the general principles of regulating refugee problems.

OTHER ACTIVITIES

The CIS has held a number of discussions relating to the environment. In July 1992 agreements were concluded to establish an Inter-state Ecological Council. It was also agreed in that month to establish an Inter-state Television and Radio Company (ITRC). In February 1995 the IPA established a Council of Heads of News Agencies, in order to promote the concept of a single information area.

A Petroleum and Gas Council was created at a Heads of Government meeting in March 1993, to guarantee energy supplies and to invest in the Siberian petroleum industry. The Council was to have a secretariat based in Tyumen, Siberia. In the field of civil aviation, the inter-state economic committee agreed in February 1997 to establish an Aviation Alliance to promote co-operation between the countries' civil aviation industries.

CO-OPERATION COUNCIL FOR THE ARAB STATES OF THE GULF

Address: POB 7153, Riyadh 11462, Saudi Arabia.

Telephone: (1) 482-7777; **fax:** (1) 482-9089; **internet:** www.gcc-sg.org.

More generally known as the Gulf Co-operation Council (GCC), the organization was established on 25 May 1981 by six Arab states.

MEMBERS

Bahrain	Oman	Saudi Arabia
Kuwait	Qatar	United Arab Emirates

Organization

(April 2003)

SUPREME COUNCIL

The Supreme Council is the highest authority of the GCC. It comprises the heads of member states and meets annually in ordinary session, and in emergency session if demanded by two or more members. The Council also convenes an annual consultative meeting. The Presidency of the Council is undertaken by each state in turn, in alphabetical order. The Supreme Council draws up the overall policy of the organization; it discusses recommendations and laws presented to it by the Ministerial Council and the Secretariat General in preparation for endorsement. The GCC's charter provided for the creation of a commission for the settlement of disputes between member states, to be attached to and appointed by the Supreme Council. The Supreme Council convenes the commission for the settlement of disputes on an *ad hoc* basis to address altercations between member states as they arise.

MINISTERIAL COUNCIL

The Ministerial Council consists of the foreign ministers of member states (or other ministers acting on their behalf), meeting every three months, and in emergency session if demanded by two or more members. It prepares for the meetings of the Supreme Council, and draws up policies, recommendations, studies and projects aimed at developing co-operation and co-ordination among member states in various spheres. GCC ministerial committees have been established in a number of areas of co-operation; sectoral ministerial meetings are held periodically.

CONSULTATIVE COMMISSION

The Consultative Commission comprising 30 members (five from each member state) nominated for a three-year period, acts as an advisory body, considering matters referred to it by the Supreme Council.

SECRETARIAT GENERAL

The Secretariat assists member states in implementing recommendations by the Supreme and Ministerial Councils, and prepares reports and studies, budgets and accounts. The Secretary-General is appointed by the Supreme Council for a three-year term renewable

once. The position is rotated among member states in order to ensure equal representation. Assistant Secretary-Generals are appointed by the Ministerial Council upon the recommendation of the Secretary-General. The Secretariat comprises the following divisions and departments: political affairs; economic affairs; military affairs; human and environmental affairs; the Office of the Secretary-General, Finance and Administrative Affairs; a patent bureau; an administrative development unit; an internal auditing unit; an information centre; and a telecommunications bureau (based in Bahrain). All member states contribute in equal proportions towards the budget of the Secretariat.

Secretary-General: ABDUL RAHMAN BIN HAMAD AL-ATTIYA (Qatar).

Assistant Secretary-General for Political Affairs: Dr HAMAD ALI AS-SULAYTI (Bahrain).

Assistant Secretary-General for Economic Affairs: AJLAN BEN ALI AL-KUWARI (Qatar).

Assistant Secretary-General for Military Affairs: Maj.-Gen. ALI IBN SALEM AL MUAMARI (Oman).

Note: In December 2001 the Supreme Council admitted Yemen (which applied to join the organization as a full member in 1996) as a member of the GCC's Arab Bureau of Education for the Gulf States), as a participant in meetings of GCC ministers of health and of labour and social affairs, and, alongside the GCC member states, as a participant in the biennial Gulf Cup football tournament. The Council also authorized the establishment of a Supreme Defence Council. This was to be composed of defence ministers meeting on an annual basis to consider security matters and supervise the implementation of the organization's joint defence pact.

Activities

The GCC was established following a series of meetings of foreign ministers of the states concerned, culminating in an agreement on the basic details of its charter on 10 March 1981. The Charter was signed by the six heads of state on 25 May. It describes the organization as providing 'the means for realizing co-ordination, integration and co-operation' in all economic, social and cultural affairs.

ECONOMIC CO-OPERATION

In November 1981 GCC ministers drew up a 'unified economic agreement' covering freedom of movement of people and capital, the abolition of customs duties, technical co-operation, harmonization of banking regulations and financial and monetary co-ordination. At the same time GCC heads of state approved the formation of a Gulf Investment Corporation, to be based in Kuwait (see below). In March 1983 customs duties on domestic products of the Gulf states were abolished, and new regulations allowing free movement of workers and vehicles between member states were also introduced. A common minimum customs levy (of between 4% and 20%) on foreign imports was imposed in 1986. In February 1987 the governors of the member states' central banks agreed in principle to co-ordinate their rates of exchange, and this was approved by the Supreme Council in November. It was subsequently agreed to link the Gulf currencies to a 'basket' of other currencies. In April 1993 the Gulf central bank governors decided to allow Kuwait's currency to become part of the GCC monetary system that was established following Iraq's invasion of Kuwait in order to defend the Gulf currencies. In May 1992 GCC trade ministers announced the objective of establishing a GCC common market. Meeting in September GCC ministers reached agreement on the application of a unified system of tariffs by March 1993. A meeting of the Supreme Council, held in December 1992, however, decided to mandate GCC officials to formulate a plan for the introduction of common external tariffs, to be presented to the Council in December 1993. Only the tax on tobacco products was to be standardized from March 1993, at a rate of 50% (later increased to 70%). In April 1994 ministers of finance agreed to pursue a gradual approach to the unification of tariffs. A technical committee, which had been constituted to consider aspects of establishing a customs union, met for the first time in June 1998. In November 1999 the Supreme Council concluded an agreement to establish the customs union by 1 March 2005. However, in December 2001 the Supreme Council, meeting in Muscat, Oman, adopted a new agreement on regional economic union ('Economic Agreement Between the Arab GCC States'), which superseded the 1981 'unified economic agreement'. The new accord brought forward the deadline for the establishment of the proposed customs union to 1 January 2003 and provided for a standard tariff level of 5% for foreign imports (with the exception of 53 essential commodities previously exempted by the Supreme Council). The agreement also provided for the introduction, by 1 January 2010, of a GCC single currency, linked to the US dollar. The necessary economic performance measures for monetary union were to be established by the end of 2005. The Supreme Council also authorized the creation of a new independent authority for overseeing the unification of specifications and standards throughout member states. The GCC customs union was launched, as planned, on 1 January 2003.

In April 1993 GCC central bank governors agreed to establish a joint banking supervisory committee, in order to devise rules for GCC banks to operate in other member states. In December 1997 GCC heads of state authorized guide-lines to this effect. These were to apply only to banks established at least 10 years previously with a share capital of more than US $100m.

The first annual GCC Economic Forum was be held in Muscat, Oman, in November 2002.

TRADE AND INDUSTRY

In 1982 a ministerial committee was formed to co-ordinate trade policies and development in the region. Technical subcommittees were established to oversee a strategic food reserve for the member states, and joint trade exhibitions (which were generally held every year until responsibility was transferred to the private sector in 1996). In 1986 the Supreme Council approved a measure whereby citizens of GCC member states were enabled to undertake certain retail trade activities in any other member state, with effect from 1 March 1987. In September 2000 GCC ministers of commerce agreed to establish a technical committee to promote the development of electronic commerce and trade among member states.

In 1976 the GCC member states formed the Gulf Organization for Industrial Consulting, based in Doha, Qatar, which promotes regional industrial development. In 1985 the Supreme Council endorsed a common industrial strategy for the Gulf states. It approved regulations stipulating that priority should be given to imports of GCC industrial products, and permitting GCC investors to obtain loans from GCC industrial development banks. In November 1986 resolutions were adopted on the protection of industrial products, and on the co-ordination of industrial projects, in order to avoid duplication. In 1989 the Ministerial Council approved the Unified GCC Foreign Capital Investment Regulations, which aimed to attract foreign investment and to co-ordinate investments amongst GCC countries. Further guide-lines to promote foreign investment in the region were formulated during 1997. In December 1999 the Supreme Council amended the conditions determining rules of origin on industrial products in order to promote direct investment and intra-Community trade. In December 1992 the Supreme Council endorsed Patent Regulations for GCC member states to facilitate regional scientific and technological research. A GCC Patent Office for the protection of intellectual property in the region, was established in 1998.

In December 1998 the Supreme Council approved a long-term strategy for regional development, covering the period 2000–25, which had been formulated by GCC ministers of planning. The strategy aimed to achieve integrated, sustainable development in all member states and the co-ordination of national development plans. The Supreme Council also approved a framework Gulf population strategy formulated by the ministers of planning. In December 2000 the Supreme Council agreed gradually to limit, by means of the imposition of quotas and deterrent taxation measures, the numbers of foreign workers admitted to member states, in order to redress the current demographic imbalance resulting from the large foreign

population resident in the region (believed to comprise more than one-third of the overall population). Unified procedures and measures for facilitating the intra-regional movement of people and commercial traffic were adopted by the Supreme Council in December 2001, as well as unified standards in the areas of education and healthcare.

AGRICULTURE

A unified agricultural policy for GCC countries was endorsed by the Supreme Council in November 1985. Co-operation in the agricultural sector extends to consideration of the water resources in the region. Between 1983 and 1990 ministers also approved proposals for harmonizing legislation relating to water conservation, veterinary vaccines, insecticides, fertilizers, fisheries and seeds. A permanent committee on fisheries aims to co-ordinate national fisheries policies, to establish designated fishing periods and to undertake surveys of the fishing potential in the Arabian (Persian) Gulf. In February 2001 GCC ministers responsible for water and electricity determined to formulate a common water policy for the region, which experiences annual shortfalls of water. Unified agricultural quarantine laws were adopted by the Supreme Council in December 2001.

TRANSPORT, COMMUNICATIONS AND INFORMATION

During 1985 feasibility studies were undertaken on new rail and road links between member states, and on the establishment of a joint coastal transport company. A scheme to build a 1,700-km railway to link all the member states and Iraq (and thereby the European railway network) was postponed, owing to its high estimated cost. In November 1993 ministers agreed to request assistance from the International Telecommunication Union on the establishment of a joint telecommunications network, which had been approved by ministers in 1986. The region's telecommunications systems were to be integrated through underwater fibre-optic cables and a satellite-based mobile telephone network. In the mid-1990s GCC ministers of information began convening on a regular basis with a view to formulating a joint external information policy. In November 1997 GCC interior ministers approved a simplified passport system to facilitate travel between member countries.

ENERGY

In 1982 a ministerial committee was established to co-ordinate hydrocarbons policies and prices. Ministers adopted a petroleum security plan to safeguard individual members against a halt in their production, to form a stockpile of petroleum products, and to organize a boycott of any non-member country when appropriate. In December 1987 the Supreme Council adopted a plan whereby a member state whose petroleum production was disrupted could 'borrow' petroleum from other members, in order to fulfil its export obligations. GCC petroleum ministers hold occasional co-ordination meetings to discuss the agenda and policies of OPEC, to which all six member states belong.

During the early 1990s proposals were formulated to integrate the electricity networks of the six member countries. In the first stage of the plan the networks of Saudi Arabia, Bahrain, Kuwait and Qatar would be integrated; those of the United Arab Emirates (UAE) and Oman would be interconnected and finally linked to the others in the second stage. In December 1997 GCC heads of state declared that work should commence on the first stage of the plan, under the management of an independent authority. The estimated cost of the project was more than US $6,000m. However, it was agreed not to invite private developers to participate in construction of the grid, but that the first phase of the project be financed by member states (to contribute 35% of the estimated $2,000m. required), and by loans from commercial banking and international monetary institutions. The Gulf Council Interconnection Authority was established in 1999, with its headquarters in Dammam, Saudi Arabia.

CULTURAL CO-OPERATION

The GCC Folklore Centre, based in Doha, Qatar, was established in 1983 to collect, document and classify the regional cultural heritage, publish research, sponsor and protect regional folklore, provide a database on Gulf folklore, and to promote traditional culture through education.

REGIONAL SECURITY

Although no mention of defence or security was made in the original charter, the summit meeting which ratified the charter also issued a statement rejecting any foreign military presence in the region. The Supreme Council meeting in November 1981 agreed to include defence co-operation in the activities of the organization: as a result, defence ministers met in January 1982 to discuss a common security policy, including a joint air defence system and standardization of weapons. In November 1984 member states agreed to form the

Peninsula Shield Force for rapid deployment against external aggression, comprising units from the armed forces of each country under a central command to be based in north-eastern Saudi Arabia.

In October 1987 (following an Iranian missile attack on Kuwait, which supported Iraq in its war against Iran) GCC ministers of foreign affairs issued a statement declaring that aggression against one member state was regarded as aggression against them all. In December the Supreme Council approved a joint pact on regional co-operation in matters of security. In August 1990 the Ministerial Council condemned Iraq's invasion of Kuwait as a violation of sovereignty, and demanded the withdrawal of all Iraqi troops from Kuwait. The Peninsula Shield Force was not sufficiently developed to be deployed in defence of Kuwait. During the crisis and the ensuing war between Iraq and a multinational force which took place in January and February 1991, the GCC developed closer links with Egypt and Syria, which, together with Saudi Arabia, played the most active role among the Arab countries in the anti-Iraqi alliance. In March the six GCC nations, Egypt and Syria formulated the 'Declaration of Damascus', which announced plans to establish a regional peace-keeping force. The Declaration also urged the abolition of all weapons of mass destruction in the area, and recommended the resolution of the Palestinian question by an international conference. In June Egypt and Syria, whose troops were to have formed the largest proportion of the proposed peace-keeping force, announced their withdrawal from the project, reportedly as a result of disagreements with the GCC concerning the composition of the force and the remuneration involved. A meeting of ministers of foreign affairs of the eight countries took place in July, but agreed only to provide mutual military assistance when necessary. In September 1992 the signatories of the Damascus Declaration adopted a joint statement on regional questions, including the Middle East peace process and the dispute between the UAE and Iran (see below), but rejected an Egyptian proposal to establish a series of rapid deployment forces which could be called upon to defend the interests of any of the eight countries. A meeting of GCC ministers of defence in November agreed to maintain the Peninsula Shield Force. In November 1993 GCC ministers of defence approved a proposal for the significant expansion of the Force and for the incorporation of air and naval units. Ministers also agreed to strengthen the defence of the region by developing joint surveillance and early warning systems. A GCC military committee was established, and convened for the first time in April 1994, to discuss the implementation of the proposals. However, the expansion of the Peninsula Shield Force was not implemented. Joint military training exercises were conducted by troops from five GCC states (excluding Qatar) in northern Kuwait in March 1996. In December 1997 the Supreme Council approved plans for linking the region's military telecommunications networks and establishing a common early warning system. In December 2000 GCC leaders adopted a joint defence pact aimed at enhancing the grouping's defence capability. The pact formally committed member states to defending any other member state from external attack, envisaging the expansion of the Peninsula Shield Force from 5,000 to 22,000 troops and the creation of a new rapid deployment function within the Force. In March 2001 the GCC member states inaugurated the first phase of the long-envisaged joint air defence system. In December GCC heads of state authorized the establishment of a supreme defence council, comprising member states' ministers of defence, to address security-related matters and supervise the implementation of the joint defence pact. The council was to convene on an annual basis. Meeting in emergency session in early February 2003 GCC ministers of defence and foreign affairs agreed to deploy the Peninsuala Field Force in Kuwait, in view of the then impending US military action against neighbouring Iraq. The full deployment of 3,000 Peninsula Shield troops to Kuwait was completed in early March.

In 1992 Iran extended its authority over the island of Abu Musa, which it had administered under a joint arrangement with the UAE since 1971. In September 1992 the GCC Ministerial Council condemned Iran's continued occupation of the island and efforts to consolidate its presence, and reiterated support of UAE sovereignty over Abu Musa, as well as the largely uninhabited Greater and Lesser Tunb islands (also claimed by Iran). All three islands are situated the approach to the Strait of Hormuz, through which petroleum exports are transported. In December 1994 the GCC supported the UAE's request that the dispute be referred to the International Court of Justice (ICJ).

In September 1992 a rift within the GCC was caused by an incident on the disputed border between Saudi Arabia and Qatar. Qatar's threat to boycott a meeting of the Supreme Council in December was allayed at the last minute as a result of mediation efforts by the Egyptian President. At the meeting, which was held in UAE, Qatar and Saudi Arabia agreed to establish a joint technical committee to demarcate the disputed border. In November 1994 a security agreement, to counter regional crime and terrorism, was concluded by GCC states. The pact, however, was not signed by Kuwait, which claimed that a clause concerning the extradition of offenders was in contravention of its constitution; Qatar did not

attend the meeting, held in Riyadh, owing to its ongoing dispute with Saudi Arabia. During 1995 the deterioration of relations between Qatar and other GCC states threatened to undermine the Council's solidarity. In December Qatar publicly displayed its dissatisfaction at the appointment, without a consensus agreement, of Saudi Arabia's nominee as the new Secretary-General by failing to attend the final session of the Supreme Council, held in Muscat, Oman. However, at a meeting of ministers of foreign affairs in March 1996, Qatar endorsed the new Secretary-General, following an agreement on future appointment procedures, and reasserted its commitment to the organization. In June Saudi Arabia and Qatar agreed to reactivate the joint technical committee in order to finalize the demarcation of their mutual border: border maps drafted by the committee were approved by both sides in December 1999. In December 1996 Qatar hosted the annual GCC summit meeting; however, Bahrain refused to attend, owing to Qatar's 'unfriendly attitude' and a long-standing dispute between the two countries (referred by Qatar to the ICJ in 1991) concerning the sovereignty of the Hawar islands, and of other islands, maritime and border areas. The issue dominated the meeting, which agreed to establish a four-member committee to resolve the conflicting sovereignty claims. In January 1997 the ministers of foreign affairs of Kuwait, Oman, Saudi Arabia and the UAE, meeting in Riyadh, formulated a seven-point memorandum of understanding to ease tensions between Bahrain and Qatar. The two countries refused to sign the agreement; however, in March both sides announced their intention to establish diplomatic relations at ambassadorial level. In March 2001 the ICJ ruled on the dispute between Bahrain and Qatar concerning the sovereignty of the Hawar Islands and other territorial boundaries, awarding Bahrain sovereignty of the Hawar islands, while supporting Qatar's sovereignty over other disputed territories. The GCC welcomed the judgement, which was accepted by the Governments of both countries.

In May 1997 the Ministerial Council, meeting in Riyadh, expressed concern at Turkey's cross-border military operation in northern Iraq and urged the withdrawal of Turkish troops from Iraqi territory. In December the Supreme Council reaffirmed the need to ensure the sovereignty and territorial integrity of Iraq. At the same time, however, the Council expressed concern at the escalation of tensions in the region, owing to Iraq's failure to co-operate with the UN Special Commission (UNSCOM). The Council also noted the opportunity to strengthen relations with Iran, in view of political developments in that country. In February 1998 the US Defense Secretary visited each of the GCC countries in order to generate regional support for any punitive military action against Iraq, given that country's obstruction of UN weapons inspectors. Kuwait was the only country to declare its support for the use of force (and to permit the use of its bases in military operations against Iraq), while other member states urged a diplomatic solution to the crisis. Qatar pursued a diplomatic initiative to negotiate directly with the Iraqi authorities, and during February, the Qatari Minister of Foreign Affairs became the most senior GCC government official to visit Iraq since 1990. The GCC supported an agreement concluded between the UN Secretary-General and the Iraqi authorities at the end of February 1998, and urged Iraq to co-operate with UNSCOM in order to secure an end to the problem and a removal of the international embargo against the country. This position was subsequently reiterated by the Supreme Council. (In December 1999 UNSCOM was replaced by a new arms inspection body, the UN Monitoring, Verification and Inspection Commission—UNMOVIC.) In December 2000 Kuwait and Saudi Arabia rejected a proposal by the Qatari Government, supported by the UAE, that the GCC should soften its policy on Iraq and demand the immediate removal of the international embargo against that country. During that month the Supreme Council determined to establish a committee with the function of touring Arab states to explain the GCC's Iraq policy. In September 2002 the US Secretary of State met representatives of the GCC to discuss ongoing US pressure on the UN Security Council to draft a new resolution insisting that Iraq comply with previous UN demands, setting a time frame for such compliance and authorizing the use of force against Iraq in response to non-compliance. In March 2003, in response to the initiation of US-led miiltary action against Iraq for perceived non-compliance with the resulting Security Council resolution (1441, adopted in November 2002), the GCC Secretary-General urged the resumption of negotiations in place of military conflict. He also expressed regret that the Saddam Hussein regime had failed to co-operate sufficiently with the UN, in disregard of the GCC's recommendations.

The GCC has condemned repeated military exercises conducted by Iran in the waters around the disputed islands of Abu Musa and Greater and Lesser Tunb as a threat to regional security and a violation of the UAE's sovereignty. Nevertheless, member countries have pursued efforts to strengthen relations with Iran. In May 1999 President Khatami undertook a state visit to Qatar, Saudi Arabia and Syria, prompting concern on the part of the UAE that its support within the GCC and the solidarity of the grouping were being undermined. In June a meeting of GCC ministers of foreign affairs was adjourned, owing to reported disagreements between Saudi Arabia and the UAE. Diplomatic efforts secured commitments, issued by both countries later in that month, to co-operate fully within the GCC. In early July the Ministerial Council reasserted GCC support of the UAE's sovereignty claim over the three disputed islands and determined to establish a committee, comprising the ministers of foreign affairs of Oman, Qatar and Saudi Arabia and the GCC Secretary-General, to resolve the dispute. In December the Supreme Council extended the mandate of the committee to establish a mechanism for direct negotiations between UAE and Iran. Iran, however, refused to co-operate with the committee; consequently, the committee's mandate was terminated in January 2001. In March the Ministerial Council demanded that Iran cease the construction of buildings for settlement on the disputed islands, and reiterated its support for the UAE's sovereignty claim.

EXTERNAL RELATIONS

In June 1988 an agreement was signed by GCC and European Community (EC) ministers on economic co-operation; this took effect from January 1990. Under the accord a joint ministerial council (meeting on an annual basis) was established, and working groups were subsequently created to promote co-operation in several specific areas, including business, energy, the environment and industry. In October 1990 GCC and EC ministers of foreign affairs commenced negotiations on formulating a free-trade agreement. In October 1995 a conference was held in Muscat, Oman, which aimed to strengthen economic co-operation between European Union (EU, as the restructured EC was now known) and GCC member states, and to promote investment in both regions. GCC heads of state, meeting in December 1997, condemned statements issued by the European Parliament, as well as by other organizations, regarding human rights issues in member states and insisted they amounted to interference in GCC judicial systems. In January 2003 the GCC established a customs union (see above), which was a precondition of the proposed GCC-EU free-trade agreement. Free-trade negotiations were continuing in early 2003.

In September 1994 GCC ministers of foreign affairs decided to end the secondary and tertiary embargo on trade with Israel. In February 1995 a ministerial meeting of signatories of the Damascus Declaration adopted a common stand, criticizing Israel for its refusal to renew the nuclear non-proliferation treaty. In December 1996 the foreign ministers of the Damascus Declaration states, convened in Cairo, requested the USA to exert financial pressure on Israel to halt the construction of settlements on occupied Arab territory. In December 2001 GCC heads of state issued a statement holding Israeli government policy responsible for the escalating crisis in the Palestinian territories. The consultative meeting of heads of state held in May 2002 declared its support for a Saudi-proposed initiative aimed at achieving a peaceful resolution of the crisis.

In June 1997 ministers of foreign affairs of the Damascus Declaration states agreed to pursue efforts to establish a free-trade zone throughout the region, which they envisaged as the nucleus of a future Arab common market. (Meanwhile, the League of Arab States has also initiated efforts to create a Greater Arab Free Trade Area.)

The GCC-USA Economic Dialogue, which commenced in 1985, convenes periodically as a government forum to promote co-operation between the GCC economies and the USA. Since the late 1990s private-sector interests have been increasingly represented at sessions of the Dialogue. It was announced in March 2001 that a business forum was to be established under the auspices of the Dialogue, to act as a permanent means of facilitating trade and investment between the GCC countries and the USA.

The GCC Secretary-General denounced the major terrorist attacks that were perpetrated in September 2001 against targets in the USA. Meeting in an emergency session in mid-September, in Riyadh, Saudi Arabia, GCC foreign ministers agreed to support the aims of the developing international coalition against terrorism. Meanwhile, however, member states urged parallel international resolve to halt action by the Israeli security forces against Palestinians. In December the Supreme Council declared the organization's full co-operation with the anti-terrorism coalition.

INVESTMENT CORPORATION

Gulf Investment Corporation (GIC): Joint Banking Center, Kuwait Real Estate Bldg, POB 3402, Safat 13035, Kuwait; tel. 2431911; fax 2448894; e-mail gic@gic.com.kw; f. 1983 by the six member states of the GCC, each contributing US $350m. of the total capital of $2,100m. total assets $19,500m. (1999); investment chiefly in the Gulf region, financing industrial projects (including pharmaceuticals, chemicals, steel wire, aircraft engineering, aluminium, dairy produce and chicken-breeding); GIC provides merchant banking and financial advisory services, and in 1992 was appointed to advise the Kuwaiti Government on a programme of privatization; Chair. IBRAHIM ABDUL-KARIM; Gen. Man. HISHAM A. RAZZUQI; Publ. *The GIC Gazetteer*(annually).

Gulf International Bank: POB 1017, Al-Dowali Bldg, 3 Palace Ave, Manama 317, Bahrain; tel. 534000; fax 522633; e-mail info@gib.com.bh; internet www.gibonline.com; f. 1976 by the six GCC states and Iraq; became a wholly-owned subsidiary of the GIC (without Iraqi shareholdings) in 1991; in April 1999 a merger with Saudi Investment Bank was concluded; cap. US $1,000m., dep. $10,949.7m., total assets $15,232.0m. (Dec. 2001); Chair. EBRAHIM BIN KHALIFA AL-KHALIFA; CEO Dr KHALED M. AL-FAYEZ.

Publications

GCC News (monthly).
At-Ta'awun (periodical).

COUNCIL OF ARAB ECONOMIC UNITY

Address: 1191 Corniche en-Nil, 12th Floor, POB 1, Mohammed Fareed, Cairo, Egypt.
Telephone: (2) 5755321; **fax:** (2) 5754090.
Established in 1957 by the Economic Council of the League of Arab States. The first meeting of the Council of Arab Economic Unity was held in 1964.

MEMBERS

Egypt	Palestine
Iraq	Somalia
Jordan	Sudan
Libya	Syria
Mauritania	Yemen

Organization

(April 2003)

COUNCIL

The Council consists of representatives of member states, usually ministers of economy, finance and trade. It meets twice a year; meetings are chaired by the representative of each country for one year.

GENERAL SECRETARIAT

Entrusted with the implementation of the Council's decisions and with proposing work plans, including efforts to encourage participation by member states in the Arab Economic Unity Agreement. The Secretariat also compiles statistics, conducts research and publishes studies on Arab economic problems and on the effects of major world economic trends.

General Secretary: Dr AHMED GOWEILI (Egypt).

COMMITTEES

There are seven standing committees: preparatory, follow-up and Arab Common Market development; Permanent Delegates; budget; economic planning; fiscal and monetary matters; customs and trade planning and co-ordination; statistics. There are also seven *ad hoc* committees, including meetings of experts on tariffs, trade promotion and trade legislation.

Activities

The Council undertakes to co-ordinate measures leading to a customs union subject to a unified administration; conduct market and commodity studies; assist with the unification of statistical terminology and methods of data collection; conduct studies for the formation of new joint Arab companies and federations; and to formulate specific programmes for agricultural and industrial co-ordination and for improving road and railway networks.

ARAB COMMON MARKET

Based on a resolution passed by the Council in August 1964; its implementation was to be supervised by the Council. Customs duties and other taxes on trade between the member countries were to be eliminated in stages prior to the adoption of a full customs union, and ultimately all restrictions on trade between the member countries, including quotas, and restrictions on residence, employment and transport, were to be abolished. In practice little progress was achieved in the development of an Arab common market during 1964–2000. However, efforts towards liberalizing intra-Arab trade were intensified in 2001. A meeting of Council ministers of economy and trade convened in Baghdad, Iraq, in June, issued the 'Baghdad Declaration' on establishing an, initially, quadripartite free-trade area comprising Egypt, Iraq, Libya and Syria; future participation by other member states was urged by the Council's General Secretary. The initiative was envisaged as a cornerstone of the Greater Arab Free Trade Area—GAFTA, which was being implemented by the Arab League. The meeting also approved an executive programme for developing the common market and a 10-year strategy for joint Arab economic action, determined to establish a compensation fund to support the integration of the least developed Arab states into the regional economy, and agreed to provide technical assistance for Arab states aiming to join the WTO. It was reported in late 2001 that Palestine had also applied to join the free-trade area, and that consideration of its application would delay the zone's entry into force. In May Egypt, Jordan, Morocco and Tunisia (all participants in the Euro-Mediterranean Partnership—see European Union), meeting in Agadir, Morocco, had agreed to establish the Mediterranean Arab Free Trade Area (MAFTA) as a cornerstone of a planned larger Arab-Mediterranean free trade area. In 2002 the Council was considering a draft general framework for Arab economic action in the areas of investment, technology, trade and joint ventures (see below) covering the next 20 years. In December the Secretary-General of the Council announced the finalization of an Arab investment plan detailing some 4,000 investment opportunities.

JOINT VENTURES

A number of multilateral organizations in industry and agriculture have been formed on the principle that faster development and economies of scale may be achieved by combining the efforts of member states. In industries that are new to the member countries Arab Joint Companies are formed, while existing industries are co-ordinated by the setting up of Arab Specialized Unions. The unions are for closer co-operation on problems of production and marketing, and to help companies deal as a group in international markets. The companies are intended to be self-supporting on a purely commercial basis; they may issue shares to citizens of the participating countries. The joint ventures are:

Arab Joint Companies::

Arab Company for Drug Industries and Medical Appliances —ACDIMA: POB 925161, Amman 11190, Jordan; tel. (6) 5821618; fax (6) 5821649; e-mail acdima@go.com.jo; internet www.acdima .com; f. 1976.

Arab Company for Electronic Commerce: f. 2001.

Arab Company for Industrial Investment: POB 3385, Alwiyah, Baghdad, Iraq; tel. 718-9215; fax 718-0710.

Arab Company for Livestock Development: POB 5305, Damascus, Syria; tel. 666037.

Arab Mining Company: POB 20198, Amman, Jordan; tel. (6) 5663148; fax (6) 5684114; e-mail armico@go.com.jo; f. 1974.

Specialized Arab Unions and Federations::

Arab Co-operative Federation: POB 57640, Baghdad, Iraq; tel. (1) 888-8121; f. 1985.

Arab Federation for Paper, Printing and Packaging Industries: POB 5456, Baghdad, Iraq; tel. (1) 887-2384; fax (1) 886-9639; f. 1977; 250 mems.

Arab Federation of Chemical Fertilizers Producers: Cairo, Egypt; f. 1976.

Arab Federation of Engineering Industries: POB 509, Baghdad, Iraq; tel. (1) 776-1101; f. 1975.

Arab Federation of Leather Industries: POB 2188, Damascus, Syria; f. 1978; activities currently suspended.

Arab Federation of Shipping: POB 1161, Baghdad, Iraq; tel. (1) 717-4540; fax (1) 717-7243; f. 1979; 22 mems.

Arab Federation of Textile Industries: POB 620, Damascus, Syria; f. 1976; activities currently suspended.

Arab Federation of Travel Agents: POB 7090, Amman, Jordan.

Arab Seaports Federation: Alexandria, Egypt; f. 1977.

Arab Steel Union: Algiers, Algeria; f. 1972.

Arab Sugar Federation: POB 195, Khartoum, Sudan; f. 1977; activities currently suspended.

Arab Union for Cement and Building Materials: POB 9015, Damascus, Syria; tel. (11) 6118598; fax (11) 6111318; e-mail aucbm@ net.sy; internet www.aucbm.org; f. 1977; 22 mem. countries, 100 mem. cos.

Arab Union for Information Technology.

Arab Union of Fish Producers: POB 15064, Baghdad, Iraq; tel. (1) 551-1261; f. 1976.

Arab Union of Food Industries: POB 13025, Baghdad, Iraq; f. 1976.

Arab Union of Hotels and Tourism: Beirut, Lebanon; f. 1994.

Arab Union of Land Transport: POB 926324, Amman 11110, Jordan; tel. (6) 5663153; fax (6) 5664232; f. 1978.

Arab Union of the Manufacturers of Pharmaceuticals and Medical Appliances: POB 81150, Amman 11181, Jordan; tel. (6) 4654306; fax (6) 4648141; f. 1986.

Arab Union of the Manufacturers of Tyres and Rubber Products: Alexandria, Egypt; f. 1993.

Arab Union of Railways: POB 6599, Aleppo, Syria; tel. (21)2667270; fax (21) 2686000; f. 1979.

General Arab Insurance Federation: POB 611, 11511 Cairo, Egypt; tel. (2) 5743177; fax (2) 5762310; f. 1964.

General Union of Arab Agricultural Workers and Co-operatives: Tripoli, Libya; f. 1993.

Union of Arab Contractors: Cairo, Egypt; f. 1995.

Union of Arab Investors: Cairo, Egypt; f. 1995.

Publications

Annual Bulletin for Arab Countries' Foreign Trade Statistics.
Annual Bulletin for Official Exchange Rates of Arab Currencies.
Arab Economic Unity Bulletin (2 a year).
Demographic Yearbook for Arab Countries.
Economic Report of the General Secretary (2 a year).
Guide to Studies prepared by Secretariat.
Progress Report (2 a year).
Statistical Yearbook for Arab Countries.
Yearbook for Intra-Arab Trade Statistics.
Yearbook of National Accounts for Arab Countries.

COUNCIL OF BALTIC SEA STATES—CBSS

Address: Strömsberg, POB 2010, 103 11 Stockhölm, Sweden.

Telephone: (8) 440-19-20; **fax:** (8) 440-19-44; **e-mail:** cbss@cbss.st; **internet:** www.cbss.st.

The Council of Baltic Sea States (CBSS) was established in 1992 to develop co-operation between member states.

MEMBERS

Denmark	Iceland	Poland
Estonia	Latvia	Russia
Finland	Lithuania	Sweden
Germany	Norway	

The European Commission also has full membership status.

Organization

(April 2003)

PRESIDENCY

The presidency is occupied by member states for one year, on a rotating basis. Summit meetings of heads of government are convened every two years. The last summit meeting was held in St Petersburg, Russia, in June 2002.

COUNCIL

The Council comprises the ministers of foreign affairs of each member state and a representative of the European Commission. The Council meets annually and aims to serve as a forum for guidance, direction of work and overall co-ordination among participating states. The minister of foreign affairs of the presiding country acts as Chairman of the Council and is responsible for co-ordinating the Council's activities between ministerial sessions, with assistance from the Committee of Senior Officials. (Other ministers also convene periodically, on an *ad hoc* basis by their own decision.)

COMMITTEE OF SENIOR OFFICIALS—CSO

The Committee consists of senior officials of the ministries of foreign affairs of the member states and of the European Commission. It serves as a discussion forum for matters relating to the work of the Council and undertakes inter-sessional activities. The Chairman of the Committee, from the same country serving as President of the CBSS, meets regularly with the previous and future Chairmen. The so-called Troika aims to maintain information co-operation, promote better exchange of information, and ensure more effective decision-making.

SECRETARIAT

In October 1998 the presidency inaugurated a permanent secretariat in Stockholm. The tasks of the secretariat include the preparation of summit meetings, annual sessions of ministers of foreign affairs, and other meetings of high-level officials and experts, the provision of technical support to the presidency regarding the implementation of plans, maintaining contacts with other sub-regional organizations, and strengthening awareness of the Council and its activities. The Secretariat includes an Energy Unit (established in April 2000), Baltic 21 Unit (January 2001) and a Children's Unit (June 2002).

Director: HANNU HALINEN (Finland).

COMMISSIONER ON DEMOCRATIC DEVELOPMENT

Amagertorv 142, POB 1165, 1010 Copenhagen K, Denmark; tel. 33-91-22-88; fax 33-91-22-96; e-mail mail@cbsscommissioner.org; internet www.cbss-commissioner.org.

The ministerial session held in May 1994 agreed to appoint an independent Commissioner on democratic institutions and human rights to serve a three-year term of office, from October of that year. In July 1997, at the sixth ministerial session held in Riga, Latvia, the Commissioner's term of office was extended by a further three years. The ninth ministerial session, held in Bergen, Norway, in June 2000, revised and renewed the Commissioner's mandate, until September 2003.

Commissioner on Democratic Development: HELLE DEGN (Denmark).

Activities

The CBSS was established in March 1992 as a forum to enhance and strengthen co-operation between countries in the Baltic Sea region. At a meeting of the Council in Kalmar, Sweden, in July 1996, ministers adopted an Action Programme as a guide-line for CBSS activities. The main programme areas covered stable and participatory political development; economic integration and prosperity; and protection of the environment. The third summit meeting of

CBSS heads of government, held at Kolding, Denmark, in April 2000, recommended a restructuring of the organization to consolidate regional intergovernmental, multilateral co-operation in all sectors. In June the ninth meeting of the CBSS Council approved the summit's recommendations. The 10th ministerial session, held in Hamburg, Germany, in June 2001, adopted a set of guide-lines regarding the strengthening of the CBSS.

At the first Baltic Sea States summit, held in Visby, Sweden, in May 1996, heads of government agreed to establish a Task Force on organized crime to counter drugs-trafficking, strengthen judicial co-operation, increase the dissemination of information, impose regional crime-prevention measures, improve border controls and provide training. In January 1998 the second summit meeting, convened in Riga, Latvia, agreed to extend the mandate of the Task Force until the end of 2000 and to enhance co-operation in the areas of civic security and border control. In April 2000 the third Baltic Sea States summit prolonged the Task Force's mandate further, until the end of 2004. The 2000 summit also authorized the establishment of a Task Force on Communicable Disease Control (TFCDC).

The Council has founded a number of working groups, comprising experts in specific fields, which aim to report on and recommend action on issues of concern to the Council. In early 2003 there were five groups working under the auspices of the CSO: the working group on assistance to democratic institutions, based in Riga, Latvia; the working group on economic co-operation, based in Bonn, Germany; the working group on nuclear and radiation safety, based in Helsinki, Finland; the working group on youth co-operation, based in Kiel, Germany; and the working group for co-operation on children at risk, based in Reykjavik, Iceland. The Swedish Special Group originated as a working group with a mandate to support the elimination of the sexual exploitation of children for commercial purposes in the Baltic Sea region. The Group helped to organize a conference on the subject held in Tallinn, Estonia, in September 1998.

A Baltic Business Advisory Council was established in 1996. In July 1998 ministers of trade of member states met in Vilnius, Lithuania, to discuss the development of small and medium-sized enterprises. Ministers agreed to strengthen links between member states, to implement measures to increase access to information in the region and to improve procedures for commercial border crossings.

In January 2001 the CBSS Council agreed to establish a unit in the CBSS secretariat to implement Baltic 21, the regional variant (adopted by the CBSS in 1998) of 'Agenda 21', the programme of action agreed by the UN Conference on Environment and Development, held in Rio de Janeiro, Brazil, in June 1992. Baltic 21 comprised a programme of 30 projects throughout the region, which aim to promote sustainable development in the agriculture, forestry and fisheries, energy, industry, tourism, transport, and spatial planning sectors. The Baltic Sea Region Energy Co-operation (BASREC) has its own secretariat function and council of senior energy officials, administered by the CBSS secretariat. BASREC also has *ad hoc* groups on electricity markets, gas markets, energy efficiency and climate change.

The CBSS contributed to the implementation of the European Union's Northern Dimension Action Plan (NDAP) for 2000–03 through the formulation, in collaboration with other regional groupings, of a 'List of Priorities and Projects'. In March 2003 the Committee of Senior Officials met to consider the organization's contribution to the NDAP for 2004–06.

Finance

Contributions of the governments of the Council's 11 member states finance the Secretariat and the Commissioner on Democratic Development. Ongoing activities and co-operation projects are funded through voluntary contributions from member states on the basis of special contribution schemes.

Publication

Newsletter (monthly).

THE COUNCIL OF EUROPE

Address: 67075 Strasbourg Cédex, France.

Telephone: 3-88-41-20-00; **fax:** 3-88-41-27-81; **e-mail:** pointi@coe
.int; **internet:** www.coe.int.

The Council was founded in May 1949 to achieve a greater unity
between its members, to facilitate their social progress and to uphold
the principles of parliamentary democracy, respect for human rights
and the rule of law. Membership has risen from the original 10 to 44.

MEMBERS*

Albania	Liechtenstein
Andorra	Lithuania
Armenia	Luxembourg
Austria	Macedonia, former Yugoslav
Azerbaijan	republic
Belgium	Malta
Bulgaria	Moldova
Bosnia and Herzegovina	Netherlands
Croatia	Norway
Cyprus	Poland
Czech Republic	Portugal
Denmark	Romania
Estonia	Russia
Finland	San Marino
France	Slovakia
Georgia	Slovenia
Germany	Spain
Greece	Sweden
Hungary	Switzerland
Iceland	Turkey
Ireland	Ukraine
Italy	United Kingdom
Latvia	

* The Holy See, Canada, Japan, Mexico and the USA have observer
status with the organization. The Serbia and Montenegro parliament has special 'guest status' at the Parliamentary Assembly,
while the parliaments of Canada, Israel and Mexico have observer
status with the Assembly.

Organization

(April 2003)

COMMITTEE OF MINISTERS

The Committee consists of the ministers of foreign affairs of all
member states (or their deputies); it decides with binding effect all
matters of internal organization, makes recommendations to governments and draws up conventions and agreements; it also discusses matters of political concern, such as European co-operation,
compliance with member states' commitments, in particular concerning the protection of human rights, and considers possible co-
ordination with other institutions, such as the European Union (EU)
and the Organization for Security and Co-operation in Europe
(OSCE). The Committee meets weekly at deputies level and twice a
year (usually in May and November) at ministerial level..

CONFERENCES OF SPECIALIZED MINISTERS

There are 19 Conferences of specialized ministers, meeting regularly
for intergovernmental co-operation in various fields.

PARLIAMENTARY ASSEMBLY

President: PETER SCHIEDER (Austria).

Chairman of the Socialist Group: TERRY DAVIS (United Kingdom).

Chairman of the Group of the European People's Party: RENÉ
VAN DER LINDEN (Netherlands).

**Chairman of the European Democratic (Conservative)
Group:** DAVID ATKINSON (United Kingdom).

Chairman of the Liberal Democratic and Reformers' Group:
MÁTYÁS EÖRSI (Hungary).

Chairman of the Unified European Left Group: JAAKKO LAAKSO
(Finland).

Members are elected or appointed by their national parliaments
from among the members thereof; political parties in each delegation
follow the proportion of their strength in the national parliament.
Members do not represent their governments, speaking on their own
behalf. At January 2003 the Assembly had 306 members (and 301

substitutes): 18 each for France, Germany, Italy, Russia and the
United Kingdom; 12 each for Poland, Spain, Turkey and Ukraine; 10
for Romania; seven each for Belgium, the Czech Republic, Greece,
Hungary, the Netherlands and Portugal; six each for Austria, Azer-
baijan, Bulgaria, Sweden and Switzerland; five each for Bosnia and
Herzegovina, Croatia, Denmark, Finland, Georgia, Moldova,
Norway and Slovakia; four each for Albania, Armenia, Ireland and
Lithuania; three each for Cyprus, Estonia, Iceland, Latvia, Lux-
embourg, the former Yugoslav republic of Macedonia, Malta and
Slovenia; and two each for Andorra, Liechtenstein and San Marino.
The parliaments of Israel, Canada and Mexico have permanent
observer status, while that of Serbia and Montenegro has special
'guest status'. (Belarus's special status was suspended in January
1997.)

The Assembly meets in ordinary session once a year. The session
is divided into four parts, generally held in the last full week of
January, April, June and September. The Assembly submits Recommendations to the Committee of Ministers, passes Resolutions, and
discusses reports on any matters of common European interest. It is
also a consultative body to the Committee of Ministers, and elects
the Secretary-General, the Deputy Secretary-General, the Secretary-General of the Assembly, the Council's Commissioner for
Human Rights, and the members of the European Court of Human
Rights.

Standing Committee: represents the Assembly when it is not in
session, and may adopt Recommendations to the Committee of
Ministers and Resolutions on behalf of the Assembly. Consists of the
President, Vice-Presidents, Chairmen of the Political Groups,
Chairmen of the Ordinary Committees and Chairmen of national
delegations. Meets usually three times a year.

Ordinary Committees: political; legal and human rights; economic
and development; social, health and family affairs; culture, science
and education; environment, agriculture, and local and regional
authorities; migration, refugees and demography; rules of procedure
and immunities; equal opportunities; honouring of obligations and
commitments by member states of the Council of Europe.

CONGRESS OF LOCAL AND REGIONAL AUTHORITIES OF EUROPE—CLRAE

The Congress was established in 1994, incorporating the former
Standing Conference of Local and Regional Authorities, in order to
protect and promote the political, administrative and financial
autonomy of local and regional European authorities by encouraging
central governments to develop effective local democracy. The Congress comprises two chambers—a Chamber of Local Authorities and
a Chamber of Regions—with a total membership of 306 elected
representatives (and 306 elected substitutes). Annual sessions are
mainly concerned with local government matters, regional planning,
protection of the environment, town and country planning, and
social and cultural affairs. A Standing Committee, drawn from all
national delegations, meets between plenary sessions of the Congress. Four Statutory Committees (Institutional; Sustainable Development; Social Cohesion; Culture and Education) meet twice a year
in order to prepare texts for adoption by the Congress.

The Congress advises the Council's Committee of Ministers and
the Parliamentary Assembly on all aspects of local and regional
policy and co-operates with other national and international organizations representing local government. The Congress monitors
implementation of the European Charter of Local Self-Government,
which was opened for signature in 1985 and provides common
standards for effective local democracy. Other legislative guide-lines
for the activities of local authorities and the promotion of democracy
at local level include the 1980 European Outline Convention on
Transfrontier Co-operation, and its Additional Protocol which was
opened for signature in 1995, a Convention on the Participation of
Foreigners in Public Life at Local Level (1992), and the European
Charter for Regional or Minority Languages (1992). In addition, the
European Urban Charter defines citizens' rights in European towns
and cities, for example in the areas of transport, urban architecture,
pollution and security.

President: HERWIG VAN STAA (Austria).

SECRETARIAT

Secretary-General: Dr WALTER SCHWIMMER (Austria).

Deputy Secretary-General: MAUD DE BOER-BUQUICCHIO (Netherlands).

Secretary-General of the Parliamentary Assembly: BRUNO
HALLER (France).

Activities

In an effort to harmonize national laws, to put the citizens of member countries on an equal footing and to pool certain resources and facilities, the Council of Europe has concluded a number of conventions and agreements covering particular aspects of European co-operation. Since 1989 the Council has undertaken to increase co-operation with all countries of the former Eastern bloc and to facilitate their accession to the organization. In October 1997 heads of state or government of member countries convened for only the second time (the first meeting took place in Vienna, in October 1993—see below) with the aim of formulating a new social model to consolidate democracy throughout Europe. The meeting endorsed a Final Declaration and an Action Plan, which established priority areas for future Council activities, including fostering social cohesion; protecting civilian security; promoting human rights; enhancing joint measures to counter cross-border illegal trafficking; and strengthening democracy through education and other cultural activities. In addition, the meeting generated renewed political commitment to the Programme of Action against Corruption, which has become a key element of Council activities.

A Multidisciplinary Group on International Action against Terrorism, established in 2001, has updated the 1977 European Convention on the Suppression of Terrorism. In 2001 the Council's Committee of Ministers adopted a set of 'Guide-lines on Human Rights and the Fight against Terrorism'.

HUMAN RIGHTS

The promotion and development of human rights is one of the major tasks of the Council of Europe. The European Convention for the Protection of Human Rights and Fundamental Freedoms (European Convention on Human Rights) was opened for signature in 1950. The Steering Committee for Human Rights is responsible for intergovernmental co-operation in the field of human rights and fundamental freedoms; it works to strengthen the effectiveness of systems for protecting human rights, to identify potential threats and challenges to human rights, and to encourage education and provide information on the subject. The Committee has been responsible for the elaboration of several conventions and other legal instruments including Protocol No. 12 of the European Convention on Human Rights, adopted in June 2000, which enforces a general prohibition of discrimination; and Protocol No. 13, adopted in May 2002, which guarantees the abolition of the death penalty in all circumstances (including in time of war).

The Committee was responsible for the preparation of the European Ministerial Conference on Human Rights, held in Rome in November 2000, which commemorated the 50th anniversary of the adoption of the European Convention on Human Rights. The Conference highlighted, in particular, 'the need to reinforce the effective protection of human rights in domestic legal systems as well as at the European level'.

The 1993 Vienna summit meeting also agreed to restructure the control mechanism for the protection of human rights, mainly the procedure for the consideration of cases, in order to reduce the length of time before a case is concluded. As a result, Protocol (No. 11) to the European Convention on Human Rights was opened for signature by member states in May 1994. The then existing institutions (i.e. the European Commission of Human Rights and the European Court of Human Rights) were consequently replaced in November 1998 (when Protocol No. 11 entered into force) by a single Court, working on a full-time basis.

The second summit meeting of the Council's heads of state and government, held in Strasbourg, France, in October 1997, welcomed a proposal to institute a Council of Europe Commissioner for Human Rights to promote respect for human rights in member states; this office was established by a resolution of the Council's Committee of Ministers in May 1999.

The November 2000 European Ministerial Conference on Human Rights commemorated the 50th anniversary of the European Convention on Human Rights and agreed an agenda for the Council's future human rights activities. This included work on a future reform of the control system of the Convention, in order to preserve its effectiveness despite the rising number of individual applications. In November 2002, in this regard, the Committee of Ministers adopted a Declaration on The Court of Human Rights for Europe.

Commissioner for Human Rights: ALVARO GIL-ROBLES (Spain).

European Court of Human Rights

The Court has compulsory jurisdiction and is competent to consider complaints lodged by states party to the European Convention and by individuals, groups of individuals or non-governmental organizations claiming to be victims of breaches of the Convention's guarantees. The Court comprises one judge for each contracting state. The Court sits in three-member Committees, empowered to declare applications inadmissible in the event of unanimity and where no further examination is necessary, seven-member Chambers, and a 17-member Grand Chamber. Chamber judgments become final three months after delivery, during which period parties may request a rehearing before the Grand Chamber, subject to acceptance by a panel of five judges. Grand Chamber judgments are final. The Court's final judgments are binding on respondent states and their execution is supervised at regular intervals by the Committee of Ministers. Execution of judgments includes payment of pecuniary just satisfaction awarded by the Court, adoption of specific individual measures to erase the consequences of the violations found (such as striking out of impugned convictions from criminal records, reopening of judicial proceedings, etc.), and general measures to prevent new similar violations (e.g. constitutional and legislative reforms, changes of domestic case-law and administrative practice, etc.) At January 2002 18,383 applications were pending before the Court.

President: LUZIUS WILDHABER (Switzerland).

Registrar: PAUL MAHONEY (United Kingdom).

European Committee for the Prevention of Torture and Inhuman or Degrading Treatment or Punishment—CPT

The Committee was established under the 1987 Convention for the Prevention of Torture as an integral part of the Council of Europe's system for the protection of human rights. The Committee, comprising independent experts, aims to examine the treatment of persons deprived of their liberty with a view to strengthening, if necessary, the protection of such persons from torture and from inhuman or degrading treatment or punishment. It conducts periodic visits to police stations, prisons, detention centres, and all other sites where persons are deprived of their liberty by a public authority, in all states parties to the Convention, and may also undertake *ad hoc* visits when the Committee considers them necessary. By January 2003 the Committee had undertaken 98 periodic visits and 48 *ad hoc* visits. After each visit the Committee drafts a report of its findings and any further advice or recommendations, based on dialogue and co-operation.

President: SILVIA CASALE (United Kingdom).

European Social Charter

The European Social Charter, in force since 1965, is the counterpart of the European Convention on Human Rights, in the field of protection of economic and social rights. A revised Charter, which amended existing guarantees and incorporated new rights, was opened for signature in May 1996, and entered into force on 1 July 1999. By January 2003 43 of the 44 member states had signed the Charter, some 32 of which had ratified it. Rights guaranteed by the Charter concern all individuals in their daily lives in matters of housing, health, education, employment, social protection, movement of persons and non-discrimination. The European Committee of Social Rights considers reports submitted to it annually by member states. It also considers collective complaints submitted in the framework of an Additional Protocol (1995), providing for a system which entered into force in July 1998, permitting trade unions, employers' organizations and NGOs to lodge complaints on alleged violations of the Charter. The Committee, composed of 13 members (to be expanded to 15 from January 2005), decides on the conformity of national situations with the Charter. When a country does not bring a situation into conformity, the Committee of Ministers may, on the basis of decisions prepared by a Governmental Committee (composed of representatives of each Contracting Party), issue recommendations to the state concerned, inviting it to change its legislation or practice in accordance with the Charter's requirements.

President of the European Committee of Social Rights: JEAN-MICHEL BELORGEY (France).

FRAMEWORK CONVENTION FOR THE PROTECTION OF NATIONAL MINORITIES

In 1993 the first summit meeting of Council of Europe heads of state and government, held in Vienna, mandated the Committee of Ministers to draft 'a framework convention specifying the principle that States commit themselves to respect in order to assure the protection of national minorities'. A special committee was established to draft the so-called Framework Convention for the Protection of National Minorities, which was then adopted by the Committee in November 1994. The Convention was opened for signature in February 1995, entering into force in February 1998. Contracting parties (35 States at January 2003) are required to submit reports on the implementation of the treaty at regular intervals to an Advisory Committee composed of 18 independent experts. The Advisory Committee adopts an opinion on the implementation of the Framework Convention by the contracting party, on the basis of which the Committee of Ministers adopts a resolution. At January 2003 23 opinions and 14 resolutions had been adopted.

President of the Advisory Committee: RAINER HOFMANN.

RACISM AND INTOLERANCE

In October 1993 heads of state and of government, meeting in Vienna, resolved to reinforce a policy to combat all forms of intolerance, in response to the increasing incidence of racial hostility and intolerance towards minorities in European societies. A European Commission against Racism and Intolerance (ECRI) was established by the summit meeting to analyse and assess the effectiveness of legal, policy and other measures taken by member states to combat these problems. It became operational in March 1996. Members of ECRI are designated by governments on the basis of their recognized expertise in the field, although participate in the Commission in an independent capacity. ECRI undertakes activities in three programme areas: country-by-country approach; work on general themes; and ECRI and civil society. In the first area of activity, ECRI analyses the situation regarding racism and intolerance in each of the member states, in order to advise governments on measures to combat these problems. In December 1998 ECRI completed a first round of reports for all Council members. A follow-up series of reports were prepared during the four-year period 1999–2002. ECRI's work on general themes includes the preparation of policy recommendations and guide-lines on issues of importance to combating racism and intolerance. ECRI also collects and disseminates examples of good practices relating to these issues. Under the third programme area ECRI aims to disseminate information and raise awareness of the problems of racism and intolerance among the general public.

A Committee on the Rehabilitation and Integration of People with Disabilities supports co-operation between member states in this field and undertakes studies in order to promote legislative and administrative action.

MEDIA AND COMMUNICATIONS

Article 10 of the European Convention on Human Rights (freedom of expression and information) forms the basis for the Council of Europe's mass media activities. Implementation of the Council of Europe's work programme concerning the media is undertaken by the Steering Committee on the Mass Media (CDMM), which comprises senior government officials and representatives of professional organizations, meeting in plenary session twice a year. The CDMM is mandated to devise concerted European policy measures and appropriate legal instruments. Its underlying aims are to further freedom of expression and information in a pluralistic democracy, and to promote the free flow of information and ideas. The CDMM is assisted by various specialist groups and committees. Policy and legal instruments have been developed on subjects including: exclusivity rights; media concentrations and transparency of media ownership; protection of journalists in situations of conflict and tension; independence of public-service broadcasting, protection of rights holders; legal protection of encrypted television services; media and elections; protection of journalists' sources of information; and the independence and functions of broadcasting regulatory authorities. These policy and legal instruments (mainly in the form on non-binding recommendations addressed to member governments) are complemented by the publication of studies, analyses and seminar proceedings on topics of media law and policy. The CDMM has also prepared a number of international binding legal instruments, including the European Convention on Transfrontier Television (adopted in 1989 and ratified by 25 countries by 31 December 2002), the European Convention on the legal protection of services based on or consisting of conditional access (signed by eight countries and ratified by two at the end of 2002), and the European Convention relating to questions on copyright law and other rights in the context of transfrontier broadcasting by satellite (ratified by two countries and signed by seven other member states and the European Community at the end of 2002). CDMM areas of activity in 2002 included: self-regulation of internet services; credibility of information disseminated online; media and privacy; the regulation of digital broadcasting services; and media and terrorism.

SOCIAL COHESION

In June 1998, the Committee of Ministers established the European Committee for Social Cohesion (CDCS). The CDCS has the following responsibilities: to co-ordinate, guide and stimulate co-operation between member States with a view to promoting social cohesion in Europe, to develop and promote integrated, multidisciplinary responses to social issues, and to promote the social standards embodied in the European Social Charter and other Council of Europe instruments, including the European Code of Social Security. The CDCS is also responsible for executing the terms of reference of the European Code of Social Security, the European Convention on Social Security and the European Agreement on 'au pair' Placement. The CDCS has agreed on policy guide-lines on access to employment, housing and social protection. In November 2002 it adopted a report on *Access to Social Rights in Europe*, and in early 2003 it was drafting a Recommendation on the subject. It also supervises a programme of work on families and children.

The European Code of Social Security and its Protocol entered into force in 1968; by March 2003 the Code and Protocol had been ratified by Belgium, Germany, Luxembourg, the Netherlands, Norway, Portugal and Sweden, while the Code alone had, additionally, been ratified by Cyprus, the Czech Republic, Denmark, France, Greece, Ireland, Italy, Spain, Switzerland, Turkey and the United Kingdom. These instruments set minimum standards for medical care and the following benefits: sickness, old-age, unemployment, employment injury, family, maternity, invalidity and survivor's benefit. A revision of these instruments, aiming to provide higher standards and greater flexibility, was completed for signature in 1990 and had been signed by 14 states at March 2003.

The European Convention on Social Security, in force since 1977, now applies in Austria, Belgium, Italy, Luxembourg, the Netherlands, Portugal, Spain and Turkey; most of the provisions apply automatically, while others are subject to the conclusion of additional multilateral or bilateral agreements. The Convention is concerned with establishing the following four fundamental principles of international law on social security: equality of treatment, unity of applicable legislation, conservation of rights accrued or in course of acquisition, and payment of benefits abroad. In 1994 a Protocol to the Convention, providing for the enlargement of the personal scope of the Convention, was opened for signature. By March 2003 it had been signed by Austria, the Czech Republic, Greece and Luxembourg, and had been ratified by Portugal.

HEALTH

Through a series of expert committees, the Council aims to ensure constant co-operation in Europe in a variety of health-related fields, with particular emphasis on patients' rights, for example: equity in access to health care, quality assurance, health services for institutionalized populations (prisoners, elderly in homes), discrimination resulting from health status and education for health. These efforts are supplemented by the training of health personnel.

Improvement of blood transfusion safety and availability of blood and blood derivatives has been ensured through European Agreements and guide-lines. Advances in this field and in organ transplantation are continuously assessed by expert committees.

Eighteen states co-operate in a Partial Agreement to protect the consumer from potential health risks connected with commonplace or domestic activities. The committees of experts of the Public Health Committee provide the scientific base for national and international regulations regarding products which have a direct or indirect impact on the human food chain, pesticides, pharmaceuticals and cosmetics.

The 1992 Recommendation on A Coherent Policy for People with Disabilities contains the policy principles for the rehabilitation and integration of people with disabilities. This model programme recommends that governments of all member states develop comprehensive and co-ordinated national disability policies taking account of prevention, diagnosis, treatment education, vocational guidance and training, employment, social integration, social protection, information and research. It has set benchmarks, both nationally and internationally. The 1995 Charter on the Vocational Assessment of People with Disabilities states that a person's vocational abilities and not disabilities should be assessed and related to specific job requirements. The 2001 Resolution on Universal Design aims to improve the accessibility, recommending the inclusion of Universal Design principles in the training for vocations working on the built environment. The 2001 Resolution on New Technologies recommends formulating national strategies to ensure that people with disabilities benefit from new technologies. Current activities include: air travel, community living, disability prevention, and women with disabilities. Tailor-made programmes for Central and Eastern European countries take account of their specific requirements. The Council of Europe designated 2003 as the European Year of People with Disabilities.

In the co-operation group to combat drug abuse and illicit drugs trafficking (Pompidou Group), 34 states work together, through meetings of ministers, officials and experts, to counteract drug abuse. The Group follows a multidisciplinary approach embracing in particular legislation, law enforcement, prevention, treatment, rehabilitation and data collection.

The Convention on the Elaboration of a European Pharmacopoeia (establishing legally binding standards for medicinal substances, auxiliary substances, pharmaceutical preparations, vaccines for human and veterinary use and other articles) entered into force in eight signatory states in May 1974: in January 2003 30 states and the European Union were parties to the Convention. WHO and 16 European and non-European states participate as observers in the sessions of the European Pharmacopoeia Commission. In 1994 a procedure on certification of suitability to the European Pharmacopoeia monographs for manufacturers of substances for pharmaceutical use was established. In 2002 almost 1,100 certificates were granted. A network of official control laboratories for human and veterinary medicines was established in 1995, open to all signatory countries to the Convention and observers at the Pharmacopoeia Commission. The fourth edition of the European Pharmacopoeia, in force since 1 January 2002, is updated three times a year in its electronic version, and includes some 1,800 harmonized European standards, or 'monographs', 300 general methods of analysis and 2,002 reagents.

In April 1997 the first international convention on biomedicine was opened for signature at a meeting of health ministers of member states, in Oviedo, Spain. The so-called Convention for the Protection of Human Rights and the Dignity of Human Beings with Respect to the Applications of Biology and Medicine incorporated provisions on scientific research, the principle of informed patient consent, organ and tissue transplants and the prohibition of financial gain and disposal of a part of the human body. It entered into force on 1 November 1999 (see below).

POPULATION AND MIGRATION

The European Convention on the Legal Status of Migrant Workers, in force since 1983, has been ratified by France, Italy, the Netherlands, Norway, Portugal, Spain, Sweden and Turkey, and was signed by Moldova in July 2002. The Convention is based on the principle of equality of treatment for migrant workers and the nationals of the host country as to housing, working conditions, and social security. The Convention also upholds the principle of the right to family reunion. An international consultative committee, representing the parties to the Convention, monitors the application of the Convention.

In 1996 the European Committee on Migration concluded work on a project entitled 'The Integration of Immigrants: Towards Equal Opportunities' was concluded and the results were presented at the sixth conference of European ministers responsible for migration affairs, held in Warsaw, Poland. At the conference a new project, entitled 'Tensions and Tolerance: Building better integrated communities across Europe' was initiated; it was concluded in 1999. The Committee was responsible for activities concerning Roma/Gypsies in Europe, in co-ordination with other relevant Council of Europe bodies. The Committee is also jointly responsible, with the *ad hoc* Committee of Experts on the legal aspects of territorial asylum, refugees and stateless persons, for the examination of migration issues arising at the pan-European level.

The European Population Committee, an intergovernmental committee of scientists and government officials responsible for population matters, monitors and analyses population trends throughout Europe and informs governments, research centres and the public of demographic developments and their impact on policy decisions. It compiles an annual statistical review of demographic developments (covering 46 European states) and publishes the results of studies on population issues, such as *Fertility and new types of households and family formation in Europe* (2001), and *Trends in mortality and differential mortality in Europe* (2001). Future publications were to include studies on the demographic characteristics of immigrant populations, the demographic consequences of economic transition in the countries of central and eastern Europe, and social exclusion.

COUNCIL OF EUROPE DEVELOPMENT BANK

The Council of Europe Development Bank was established in April 1956 by the Committee of Ministers, initially as the Resettlement Fund, and later as the Council of Europe Social Development Fund, and then renamed again in November 1999. It is a multilateral development bank with a social mandate, promoting social development by granting loans for projects with a social purpose. Projects aimed at solving social problems related to the presence of refugees, displaced persons or forced migrants are a priority. In addition, the Bank finances projects in other fields that contribute directly to strengthening social cohesion in Europe: job creation and preservation in small and medium-sized enterprises; social housing; improving urban living conditions; health and education infrastructure, protection of the environment, and rural modernisation; protection and rehabilitation of the historic heritage. At November 2002 the Bank had a subscribed capital of €3,160m. It is currently funding 167 projects in 28 countries. Its lending activities have been increasingly targeted at central and eastern European countries. Since 1995 the Bank has approved 66 projects in 14 transition countries, supported by a cumulative total of €1,800m. worth of loans.

EQUALITY BETWEEN WOMEN AND MEN

The Steering Committee for Equality between Women and Men (CDEG—an intergovernmental committee of experts) is responsible for encouraging action at both national and Council of Europe level to promote equality of rights and opportunities between the two sexes. Assisted by various specialist groups and committees, the CDEG is mandated to establish analyses, studies and evaluations, to examine national policies and experiences, to work out concerted policy strategies and measures for implementing equality and, as necessary, to prepare appropriate legal and other instruments. It is

also responsible for preparing the European Ministerial Conferences on Equality between Women and Men. The main areas of CDEG activities are the comprehensive inclusion of the rights of women (for example, combating violence against women and trafficking in human beings) within the context of human rights; the issue of equality and democracy, including the promotion of the participation of women in political and public life; projects aimed at studying the specific equality problems related to cultural diversity, migration and minorities; positive action in the field of equality between men and women and the mainstreaming of equality into all policies and programmes at all levels of society. In October 1998 the Committee of Ministers adopted a Recommendation to member states on gender mainstreaming; in May 2000 it approved a Recommendation on action against trafficking in human beings for the purpose of sexual exploitation; and in April 2002 it adopted a Recommendation on the protection of women against violence.

LEGAL MATTERS

The European Committee on Legal Co-operation develops co-operation between member states in the field of law, with the objective of harmonizing and modernizing public and private law, including administrative law and the law relating to the judiciary. The Committee is responsible for expert groups which consider issues relating to administrative law, efficiency of justice, family law, nationality, information technology and data protection.

Numerous conventions and Recommendations have been adopted, and followed up by appropriate committees or groups of experts, on matters which include: efficiency of justice, nationality, legal aid, rights of children, data protection, information technology, children born out of wedlock, animal protection, adoption, information on foreign law, and the legal status of non-governmental organizations. In addition, a new draft Convention on contact concerning children was adopted in May 2002.

In December 1999 the Convention for the Protection of Human Rights and the Dignity of Human Beings with Respect to the Applications of Biology and Medicine: Convention on Human Rights and Biomedicine entered into force, as the first internationally-binding legal text to protect people against the misuse of biological and medical advances. It aims to preserve human dignity and identify, rights and freedoms, through a series of principles and rules. Additional protocols develop the Convention's general provisions by means of specialized texts. A Protocol prohibiting the medical cloning of human beings was approved by Council heads of state and government in October 1997 and entered into force on 1 March 2001. A Protocol on the transplantation of human organs and tissue was opened for signature in January 2002. Work on draft protocols relating to biomedical research, protection of the human embryo and foetus, and genetics is ongoing. A draft Recommendation on xenotransplantation is currently being considered by the Committee of Ministers.

In 2001 an Additional Protocol to the Convention for the protection of individuals with regard to automatic processing of personal data was adopted. The Protocol, which opened for signature in November, concerned supervisory authorities and transborder data flows. By April 2003 it had been signed by 21 states, and ratified by three (Germany, Slovakia and Sweden).

In 2001 the the European Committee for Social Cohesion (CDCS) approved three new conventions on contact concerning children, legal aid, and 'Information Society Services'. In 2002 the CDCS approved a Recommendation on mediation on civil matters and a resolution establishing the European Commission for the Efficiency of Justice (CEPEJ). The aims of the CEPEJ are: to improve the efficiency and functioning of the justice system of memeber states, with a view to ensuring that everyone within their jurisdiction can enforce their legal rights effectively, increasing citizen confidence in the system; and enabling better implementation of the international legal instruments of the Council of Europe concerning efficiency and fairness of justice.

The Consultative Council of European Judges has prepared a framework global action plan for judges in Europe. In addition, it has contributed to the implementation of this programme by the adoption of opinions on standards concerning the independence of the judiciary and the irremovability of judges, and on the funding and management of courts.

A Committee of Legal Advisors on Public and International Law (CAHDI), comprising the legal advisors of ministers of foreign affairs of member states and of several observer states, is authorized by the Committee of Ministers to examine questions of public international law, and to exchange and, if appropriate, to co-ordinate the views of member states. The CAHDI functions as a European observatory of reservations to international treaties. Recent activities of the CAHDI include the preparation of a Recommendation on reactions to inadmissible reservations to international treaties, the publication of a report on state practice with regard to state succession and recognition, and another on expression of consent of states to be bound by a treaty. In 2002 the CAHDI was conducting research into the practice of states with regard to immunities of states and their property.

An *ad hoc* Committee of Experts on the Legal Aspects of Territorial Asylum, Refugees and Stateless Persons (CAHAR) proposes solutions to practical and legal problems relating to its area of expertise and works towards harmonizing rules and practices to be followed in Europe in matters of asylum and refugees. It reviews national and international developments and formulates appropriate legal instruments (mainly Recommendations) for discussion and adoption by the Committee of Ministers. Over the years the Committee has drafted a number of pan-European standards, and in 2002 it prepared a draft recommendation relating to the detention of asylum seekers. The CAHAR has also adopted a series of opinions for the Committee of Ministers on issues relating to refugees and displaced persons in member states. It works closely with other international bodies, in particular UNHCR and the Council's Parliamentary Assembly.

With regard to crime, expert committees and groups operating under the authority of the European Committee on Crime Problems have prepared conventions on such matters as extradition, mutual assistance, recognition and enforcement of foreign judgments, transfer of proceedings, suppression of terrorism, transfer of prisoners, compensation payable to victims of violent crime, money-laundering, confiscation of proceeds from crime, cybercrime and corruption. In 2002 member states concluded an additional Protocol to the 2001 Convention on cybercrime relating to the criminalization of acts of a racist and xenophobic nature committed through computer systems.

The Group of States Against Corruption (GRECO) became operational in 1999 and became a permanent body of the Council in 2002. By the end of that year it had 34 members (33 member states of the Council of Europe and the USA). A monitoring mechanism, based on mutual evaluation and peer pressure, GRECO assesses members' compliance with Council instruments for combating corruption. Its First Round Evaluations were completed by the end of 2002. A Second Round Evaluation commenced in 2003, reviewing Proceeds of Corruption, Public Administration and Corruption, and Legal Persons and Corruption. It was then to cover member states' compliance with, *inter alia*, requirements of the Criminal Law Convention on Corruption, which entered into force in July 2002. The evaluation procedure of GRECO is confidential but it has become practice to make reports public after their adoption.

The select committee of Experts on the Evaluation of Anti-Money laundering Measures (MONEYVAL) became operational in 1998. It is responsible for mutual evaluation of the anti-money laundering measures in place in 25 Council of Europe states that are not members of the Financial Action Task Force (FATF), . The MONEYVAL mechanism is based on FATF practices and procedures. States are evaluated against the relevant international standards in the legal, financial and law enforcement sectors. In the legal sector this includes evaluation of states' obligations under the Council of Europe Convention on Laundering, Search Seizure and Confiscation of the Proceeds from Crime. After the terrorist attacks against targets in the USA on 11 September 2001, the Comittee of Ministers adopted revised terms of reference, which specifically include the evaluation of measures to combat the financing of terrorism. MONEYVAL completed its first round of onsite visits in 2000 and subsequently adopted all first round reports. Its second round, focusing even more closely on the effectiveness of national systems, began in 2001 and was expected to be completed during 2003. The evaluations of MONEYVAL are confidential, but summaries of adopted reports are made public.

A Criminological Scientific Council, composed of specialists in law, psychology, sociology and related sciences, advises the Committee and organizes criminological research conferences and colloquia. A Council for Penological Co-operation organizes regular high-level conferences of directors of prison administration and is responsible for collating statistical information on detention and community sanctions in Europe. The Council prepared the European Prison Rules in 1987 and the European Rules on Community Sanctions (alternatives to imprisonment) in 1992. A council for police matters was established in 2002.

In May 1990 the Committee of Ministers adopted a Partial Agreement to establish the European Commission for Democracy through Law, to be based in Venice, Italy. The so-called Venice Commission was enlarged in February 2002 and at early 2003 comprised all Council of Europe member states. The Commission is composed of independent legal and political experts, mainly senior academics, supreme or consitutional court judges, members of national parliaments, and senior public officers. Its main activity is constitutional assistance and may supply opinions upon request, made through the Committee of Ministers, by the Parliamentary Assembly, the Secretary-General or any member states of the Commission . Other states and international organizations may request opinions with the consent of the Committee of Ministers. The Commission is active throughout the constitutional domain, and has worked on issues including legislation on constitutional courts and national minor-

ities, electoral law and other legislation with implications for national democratic institutions. The creation of the Council for Democratic elections institutionalized co-operation in the areaof elections between the Venice Commission, the Parliamentary Assembly of the Council of Europe, and the Congress of Regional and Local Authorities of Europe.The Commission disseminates its work through the UniDem (University for Democracy) programme of seminars, the CODICES database, and the *Bulletin of Constitutional Case-Law*.

The promotion of local and regional democracy and of transfrontier co-operation constitutes a major aim of the Council's intergovernmental programme of activities. The Steering Committee on Local and Regional Democracy (CDLR) serves as a forum for representatives of member states to exchange information and pursue co-operation in order to promote the decentralization of powers, in accordance with the European Charter on Local Self-Government. The CDLR's principal objective is to improve the legal, institutional and financial framework of local democracy and to encourage citizen participation in local and regional communities. In December 2001 the Committee of Ministers adopted a Recommendation on citizens' participation in public life at local level, drafted on the basis of the work conducted by the CDLR. The CDLR publishes comparative studies and national reports, and aims to identify guide-lines for the effective implementation of the principles of subsidiarity and solidarity. Its work also constitutes a basis for the provision of aid to central and eastern European countries in the field of local democracy. The CDLR is responsible for the preparation and follow-up of Conferences of Ministers responsible for local and regional government.

Intergovernmental co-operation with the CDLR is supplemented by specific activities aimed at providing legislative advice, supporting reform and enhancing management capabilities and democratic participation in European member and non-member countries. These activities are specifically focused on the democratic stability of central and eastern European countries. The programmes for democratic stability in the field of local democracy draw inspiration from the European Charter of Local Self-Government, operating at three levels of government: at intergovernmental level, providing assistance in implementing reforms to reinforce local or regional government, in compliance with the Charter; at local or regional level, co-operating with local and regional authorities to build local government capacity; and at community level, co-operating directly with individual authorities to promote pilot initiatives. Working methods include: awareness-raising conferences; legislative opinion involving written opinions, expert round-tables and working groups; and seminars, workshops and training at home and abroad.

The policy of the Council of Europe on transfrontier co-operation between territorial communities or authorities is implemented through two committees. The Committee of Experts on Transfrontier Co-operation (LR -CT), working under the supervision of the CDLR, aims to monitor the implementation of the European Outline Convention on Transfrontier Co-operation between Territorial Communities or Authorities; to make proposals for the elimination of obstacles, in particular of a legal nature, to transfrontier and interterritorial co-operation; and to compile 'best practice' examples of transfrontier co-operation in various fields of activity. In 2002 the Committee of Ministers adopted a draft recommendation on the mutual aid and assistance between central and local authorities in the event of disasters affecting frontier areas. A Committee of Advisers for the development of transfrontier co-operation in central and eastern Europe is composed of six members appointed or elected by the Secretary-General, the Committee of Ministers and the Congress of Local and Regional Authorities of Europe. Its task is to guide the promotion of transfrontier co-operation in central and eastern European countries, with a view to fostering good neighbourly relations between the frontier populations, especially in particularly sensitive regions. Its programme comprises: conferences and colloques designed to raise awareness on the Outline Convention; meetings in border regions between representatives of local communities with a view to strengthening mutual trust; and legal assistance to, and restricted meetings with, national and local representatives responsible for preparing the legal texts for ratification and/or implementation of the Outline Convention. The priority areas which had been outlined by the Committee of Advisers include South-East Europe, northern Europe around the Baltic Sea, the external frontiers of an enlarged European Union, and the Caucasus.

EDUCATION, CULTURE AND HERITAGE

The European Cultural Convention covers education, culture, heritage, sport and youth. Programmes on education, higher education, culture and cultural heritage are managed by four steering committees.

The education programme consists of projects on education for democratic citizenship and human rights, history teaching, the

European dimension of education and interreligious dialogue, instruments and policies for plurilingualism, equitable education policies responding to new social, economic and technological realities, and bilateral co-operation for education renewal. Other activities include the partial agreement for the European Centre for Modern Languages located in Graz, Austria, the In Service Educational Staff Training Programme, the Network for School Links and Exchanges, and the European Schools Day competition, organized in co-operation with the European Union. The Council of Europe's main focus in the field of higher education is on the Bologna Proccess aiming to establish a European Higher Education Area by 2010.

In December 2000 the Committee of Ministers adopted a Declaration on Cultural Diversity, formulated in consultation with other organizations (including the European Union and UNESCO), which created a framework for developing a European approach to valuing cultural diversity. A European Charter for Regional or Minority languages entered into force in 1998, with the aim of protecting regional or minority languages, which are considered to be a threatened aspect of Europe's cultural heritage. It was intended to promote the use in private and public life of languages traditionally used within a state's territory. The Charter provides for a monitoring system enabling states, the Council of Europe and individuals to observe and follow up its implementation.

The Council of Europe's activities related to cultural policy focus on the following prioriy areas: standard-setting; cultural policy reviews; conflict prevention; comparative studies on cultural diversity, and partnership programmes; archives; the MOSAIC and STAGE projects (co-operation with South-East Europe and the South Caucasus, respectively); and the Action Plan for Russia.

The European Convention for the Protection of Audiovisual Heritage and its Protocol were opened for signature in November 2001. The Eurimages support fund helps to finance co-production of films. The Convention for the Protection of the Architectural Heritage and the Protection of the Archaeological Heritage provide a legal framework for European co-operation in these areas. The European Heritage Network is a being developed to facilitate the work of professionals and state institutions and the dissemination of good practices in more than 30 countries of the states party to the European Cultural Convention.

YOUTH

In 1972 the Council of Europe established the European Youth Centre (EYC) in Strasbourg. A second residential centre was created in Budapest in 1995. The centres, run with and by international non-governmental youth organizations representing a wide range of interests, provide about 50 residential courses a year (study sessions, training courses, symposia). A notable feature of the EYC is its decision-making structure, by which decisions on its programme and general policy matters are taken by a Programming Committee composed of an equal number of youth organizations and government representatives.

The European Youth Foundation (EYF) aims to provide financial assistance to European activities of non-governmental youth organizations and began operations in 1973. Since that time more than 380 organizations have received financial aid for carrying out international activities, while more than 210,000 young people have participated in meetings supported by the Foundation. The European Steering Committee for Intergovernmental Co-operation in the Youth Field conducts research in youth-related matters and prepares for ministerial conferences.

SPORT

The Committee for the Development of Sport, founded in November 1977, oversees sports co-operation and development on a pan-European basis, bringing together all the 48 states party to the European Cultural Convention. Its activities focus on the implementation of the European Sport Charter and Code of Sports Ethics (adopted in 1992 and revised in 2002), the role of sport in society, the provision of assistance in sports reform to new member states in central and eastern Europe, and the practice of both recreational and high level sport. A Charter on Sport for Disabled Persons was adopted in 1986. The Committee also prepares the Conferences of European Ministers responsible for Sport and has been responsible for drafting two important conventions to combat negative influences on sport. The European Convention on Spectator Violence and Misbehaviour at Sport Events (1985) provides governments with practical measures to ensure crowd security and safety, particularly at football matches. The Anti-Doping Convention (1989) has been ratified by nearly 40 European countries, and is also open to non-European states.

ENVIRONMENT AND SUSTAINABLE DEVELOPMENT

In 1995 a pan-European biological and landscape diversity strategy, formulated by the Committee of Ministers, was endorsed at a ministerial conference of the UN Economic Commission for Europe, which was held in Sofia, Bulgaria. The strategy was to be implemented jointly by the Council of Europe and UNEP, in close co-operation with the European Community. In particular, it provided for implementation of the Convention on Biological Diversity.

At March 2002 45 states and the European Community had ratified a Convention on the Conservation of European Wildlife and Natural Habitats, which entered into force in June 1982 and gives total protection to 693 species of plants, 89 mammals, 294 birds, 43 reptiles, 21 amphibians, 115 freshwater fishes, 113 invertebrates and their habitats. The Convention established a network of protected areas known as the 'Emerald Network'. The Council's NATUROPA Centre provides information and documentation on the environment, through periodicals and campaigns. The Council awards the European Diploma for protection of sites of European significance, supervises a network of biogenetic reserves, and co-ordinates conservation action for threatened animals and plants.

Regional disparities constitute a major obstacle to the process of European integration. Conferences of ministers of regional planning are held to discuss these issues. In 2000 they adopted guiding principles for sustainable development of the European continent and, in 2001, a resolution detailing a ten-point programme for greater cohesion among the Regions of Europe.

EXTERNAL RELATIONS

Agreements providing for co-operation and exchange of documents and observers have been concluded with the United Nations and its agencies, and with most of the European inter-governmental organizations and the Organization of American States. Particularly close relations exist with the EU, OECD, and the OSCE. Relations with non-member states, other organizations and non-governmental organizations are co-ordinated by the Directorate General of Political Affairs.

Israel, Canada and Mexico are represented in the Parliamentary Assembly by observer delegations, and certain European and other non-member countries participate in or send observers to certain meetings of technical committees and specialized conferences at intergovernmental level. Full observer status with the Council was granted to the USA in 1995, to Canada and Japan in 1996 and to Mexico in 1999. The Holy See has had a similar status since 1970.

The European Centre for Global Interdependence and Solidarity (the 'North–South Centre') was established in Lisbon, Portugal, in 1990, in order to provide a framework for European co-operation in this area and to promote pluralist democracy and respect for human rights. The Centre is co-managed by parliamentarians, governments, non-governmental organizations and local and regional authorities. Its activities are divided into three programmes: public information and media relations; education and training for global interdependence; and dialogue for global partnership. The Centre organizes workshops, seminars and training courses on global interdependence and convenes international colloquies on human rights.

During the early 1990s the Council of Europe established a structure of programmes to assist the process of democratic reform in central and eastern European countries that had formerly been under communist rule. In October 1997 the meeting of heads of state or of government of Council members agreed to extend the programmes as the means by which all states are assisted to meet their undertakings as members of the Council. These specific co-operation programmes were mainly concerned with the development of the rule of law; the protection and promotion of human rights; and strengthening local democracy. A scheme of Democratic Leadership Programmes has also been established for the training of political leaders. Within the framework of the co-operation programme 22 information and documentation centres/offices have been established in 17 countries of central and eastern Europe. A secretariat representation to co-ordinate the Council's contribution to the UN operation in Kosovo was established in Priština (the capital of Kosovo and Metohija), in mid-1999.

Finance

The budget is financed by contributions from members on a proportional scale of assessment (using population and gross domestic product as common indicators). The 2003 budget totalled €175.5m.

Publications

The Council of Europe: 800 million Europeans (introductory booklet).

Activities Report (in English and French).

The Bulletin (newsletter of the CLRAE, 3 a year).

The Europeans (electronic bulletin of the Parliamentary Assembly).

Naturopa (3 a year, in 15 languages).

Bulletin On Constitutional Case-Law (3–4 times a year, in English and French).

The Pompidou Group Newsletter (3 a year).

Penological Information Bulletin (annually, in English and French).

Human Rights Information Bulletin (monthly, in English and French.).

ECONOMIC COMMUNITY OF WEST AFRICAN STATES —ECOWAS

Address: ECOWAS Secretariat and Conference Centre, 60 Yakubu Gowon Crescent, Asokoro, Abuja, Nigeria.

Telephone: (9) 3147647; **fax:** (9) 3147646; **e-mail:** info@ecowasmail .net; **internet:** www.ecowas.int.

The Treaty of Lagos, establishing ECOWAS, was signed in May 1975 by 15 states, with the object of promoting trade, co-operation and self-reliance in West Africa. Outstanding protocols bringing certain key features of the Treaty into effect were ratified in November 1976. Cape Verde joined in 1977. A revised ECOWAS treaty, designed to accelerate economic integration and to increase political co-operation, was signed in July 1993.

MEMBERS

Benin	Ghana	Niger
Burkina Faso	Guinea	Nigeria
Cape Verde	Guinea-Bissau	Senegal
Côte d'Ivoire	Liberia	Sierra Leone
The Gambia	Mali	Togo

Organization

(April 2003)

AUTHORITY OF HEADS OF STATE AND GOVERNMENT

The Authority is the supreme decision-making organ of the Community, with responsibility for its general development and realization of its objectives. The Chairman is drawn from the member states in turn. In August 1997 ECOWAS heads of state decided that the Authority (previously convened on an annual basis) should meet twice each year to enhance monitoring and co-ordination of the Community's activities.

COUNCIL OF MINISTERS

The Council consists of two representatives from each member country; a chairman is drawn from each country in turn. It meets at least twice a year, and is responsible for the running of the Community.

EXECUTIVE SECRETARIAT

The Executive Secretary is elected for a four-year term, which may be renewed once only.

Executive Secretary: MOHAMED IBN CHAMBAS (Ghana).

SPECIALIZED TECHNICAL COMMISSIONS

There are eight commissions, comprising representatives of each member state, which prepare Community projects and programmes in the following areas:

(i) Food and Agriculture;

(ii) Industry, Science and Technology, and Energy;

(iii) Environment and Natural Resources;

(iv) Transport, Communications, and Tourism;

(v) Trade, Customs, Taxation, Statistics, and Money and Payments;

(vi) Political, Judicial and Legal Affairs, Regional Security, and Integration;

(vii) Human Resources, Information, and Social and Cultural Affairs; and

(viii) Administration and Finance.

ECOWAS PARLIAMENT

The inaugural session of the 120-member ECOWAS Parliament, based in Abuja, Nigeria, was held in November 2000. Members of the Parliament are elected for five-year terms. Each ECOWAS member state is allocated a minimum of five seats; the distribution of the remaining 45 seats is proportionate to the relative sizes of member states' populations. There is a co-ordinating administrative bureau, comprising a speaker, elected for a five-year term of office, and other elected officials. There are 13 technical committees covering the Parliament's areas of activity, including defence and security, economics and finance, energy, environment and natural resources, foreign affairs, human rights, laws and regulations, rural develop-

ment, transport and communications, and women's and children's affairs.

Speaker: Prof. ALI NOUHOUM DIALLO (Mali).

ECOWAS COURT OF JUSTICE

The Court of Justice, established in January 2001, is based in Abuja, Nigeria, and comprises seven judges who serve a five-year renewable term of office.

Chief Justice: HASSINE DONLI (Nigeria).

ECOWAS FUND FOR CO-OPERATION, COMPENSATION AND DEVELOPMENT

BP 2704, blvd du 13 Janvier, Lomé, Togo; tel. 216864; fax 218684; e-mail info-fund@ecowasmail.net; internet www.ecowas-fund.org.

The Fund is administered by a Board of Directors. The chief executive of the Fund is the Managing Director, who holds office for a renewable term of four years. There is a staff of 100. The authorized cap. of the Fund is US $500m.; paid-up cap. totalled $84m. in 2000. In 1988 agreements were reached with the African Development Bank and the Islamic Development Bank on the co-financing of projects and joint training of staff. Efforts have been initiated to enhance the Fund's financial resources, by opening its capital to non-regional participants. At a summit of ECOWAS heads of state and government in December 1999 it was announced that the Fund was to be converted into the ECOWAS Investment and Development Bank, which was to have two divisions, a Regional Investment Bank and a Regional Development Fund.

Managing Director: DRABO D. BARTHELAMY.

Activities

ECOWAS aims to promote co-operation and development in economic, social and cultural activity, particularly in the fields for which specialized technical commissions (see above) are appointed, to raise the standard of living of the people of the member countries, increase and maintain economic stability, improve relations among member countries and contribute to the progress and development of Africa. ECOWAS is committed to abolishing all obstacles to the free movement of people, services and capital, and to promoting: harmonization of agricultural policies; common projects in marketing, research and the agriculturally-based industries; joint development of economic and industrial policies and elimination of disparities in levels of development; and common monetary policies. The ECOWAS treaty provides for compensation for states whose import duties are reduced through trade liberalization and contains a clause permitting safeguard measures in favour of any country affected by economic disturbances through the application of the treaty.

Initial slow progress in achieving many of ECOWAS' aims was attributed to the reluctance of some governments to implement policies at the national level, their failure to provide the agreed financial resources, and the absence of national links with the Secretariat; to the high cost of compensating loss of customs revenue; and to the existence of numerous other intergovernmental organizations in the region (in particular the Union économique et monétaire ouest-africaine—UEMOA, which replaced the francophone Communauté économique de l'Afrique de l'ouest in 1994). In respect of the latter obstacle to progress, however, ECOWAS and UEMOA resolved in February 2000 to create a single monetary zone (see below). In October ECOWAS and the European Union (EU) held their first joint high-level meeting, at which the EU pledged financial support for ECOWAS' economic integration programme, and, in April 2001 it was announced that the IMFhad agreed to provide technical assistance for the programme.

A revised treaty for the Community was drawn up by an ECOWAS Committee of Eminent Persons in 1991–92, and was signed at the ECOWAS summit conference that took place in Cotonou, Benin, in July 1993. The treaty, which was to extend economic and political co-operation among member states, designated the achievement of a common market and a single currency as economic objectives, while in the political sphere it envisaged the establishment of an ECOWAS parliament, an economic and social council, and an ECOWAS court of justice to enforce Community decisions. The treaty also formally assigned the Community with the responsibility of preventing and settling regional conflicts. At a summit meeting held in Abuja, Nigeria, in August 1994, ECOWAS heads of state and government signed a protocol agreement for the establishment of a regional parliament. The meeting also adopted a Convention on Extradition of non-political offenders. The new ECOWAS treaty entered into effect in August 1995, having received the required number of ratifications. A draft protocol providing for the creation of a mechanism for the prevention, management and settlement of conflicts, and for the maintenance of peace in the region, was approved by ECOWAS heads of state and government in December 1999. The protocol establishing the ECOWAS Parliament came into effect in March 2000. The inaugural session of the Parliament was held in Abuja, Nigeria, in November, and in January 2001 the seven judges of the ECOWAS Court of Justice were sworn in. At December 2000 the revised ECOWAS treaty had been ratified by 13 member states (all but Cape Verde, Guinea Bissau and Mauritania; Mauritania left the grouping at the end of that month).

In May 2002 the ECOWAS Authority met in Yamoussoukro, Côte d'Ivoire, to develop a regional plan of action for the implementation of the New Partnership for Africa's Development (NEPAD).

TRADE AND MONETARY UNION

Under the founding ECOWAS treaty elimination of tariffs and other obstructions to trade among member states, and the establishment of a common external tariff, were planned over a transitional period of 15 years, from 1975. At the 1978 Conference of Heads of State and Government it was decided that from May 1979 no member state might increase its customs tariff on goods from another member. This was regarded as the first step towards the abolition of customs duties within the Community. During the first two years import duties on intra-community trade were to be maintained, and then eliminated in phases over the next eight years. Quotas and other restrictions of equivalent effect were to be abolished in the first 10 years. It was envisaged that in the remaining five years all differences between external customs tariffs would be abolished.

In 1980 ECOWAS heads of state and government decided to establish a free-trade area for unprocessed agricultural products and handicrafts from May 1981. Tariffs on industrial products made by specified community enterprises were also to be abolished from that date, but implementation was delayed by difficulties in defining the enterprises. From 1 January 1990 tariffs were eliminated on 25 listed items manufactured in ECOWAS member states. Over the ensuing decade, tariffs on other industrial products were to be eliminated as follows: the 'most-developed' countries of ECOWAS (Côte d'Ivoire, Ghana, Nigeria and Senegal) were to abolish tariffs on 'priority' products within four years and on 'non-priority' products within six years; the second group (Benin, Guinea, Liberia, Sierra Leone and Togo) were to abolish tariffs on 'priority' products within six years, and on 'non-priority' products within eight years; and the 'least-developed' members (Burkina Faso, Cape Verde, The Gambia, Guinea-Bissau, Mali and Niger) were to abolish tariffs on 'priority' products within eight years and on 'non-priority' products within 10 years. By December 2000 only Benin had removed tariffs on all industrial products. By mid-2002 an estimated 1,500 products had been approved under the trade liberalization scheme.

In 1990 ECOWAS heads of state and government agreed to adopt measures that would create a single monetary zone and remove barriers to trade in goods that originated in the Community. ECOWAS regards monetary union as necessary to encourage investment in the region, since it would greatly facilitate capital transactions with foreign countries. In September 1992 it was announced that, as part of efforts to enhance monetary co-operation and financial harmonization in the region, the West African Clearing House was to be restructured as the West African Monetary Agency (WAMA, see , see p. 192). As a specialized agency of ECOWAS, WAMA was to be responsible for administering an ECOWAS exchange rate system (EERS) and for establishing the single monetary zone. A credit guarantee scheme and travellers' cheque system were to be established in association with the EERS. The agreement founding WAMA was signed by the Governors of the central banks of ECOWAS member states, meeting in Banjul, The Gambia, in March 1996. In July the Authority agreed to impose a common value-added tax (VAT) on consumer goods, in order to rationalize indirect taxation and to stimulate greater intra-Community trade. In August 1997 ECOWAS heads of state and government appointed an *ad hoc* monitoring committee to promote and oversee the implementation of trade liberalization measures and the establishment of a single monetary zone. The meeting also authorized the introduction of the regional travellers' cheque scheme. In October 1998 the travellers' cheque scheme was formally inaugurated at a meeting of ECOWAS heads of state. The cheques were to be issued by WAMA in denominations of a West African Unit of Account and convertible into each local currency at the rate of one Special Drawing Right (SDR—see IMF, see p. 98). The cheques entered into circulation on 1 July 1999. In March 1998 senior customs officials of ECOWAS countries agreed to harmonize customs policies and administrations, in order to facilitate intra-Community trade, and to pursue the objective of establishing a common external tariff

by 2000. However, this deadline was not met. In December 1999 the ECOWAS Authority determined to pursue a 'Fast Track Approach' to economic integration, involving a two-track implementation of related measures. In April 2000 seven, predominantly anglophone, ECOWAS member states—Cape Verde, The Gambia, Ghana, Guinea, Liberia, Nigeria and Sierra Leone—issued the 'Accra Declaration', in which they agreed to establish by 1 January 2003 a second West African monetary union (the West African Monetary Zone—WAMZ) to co-exist initially alongside UEMOA, which unites eight, mainly francophone, ECOWAS member states. As preconditions for adopting a single currency and common monetary and exchange rate policy, the member states of the second West African monetary union were to attain a number of convergence criteria, including: a satisfactory level of price stability; sustainable budget deficits; a reduction in inflation; and the maintenance of an adequate level of foreign exchange reserves. The two complementary monetary unions were expected to harmonize their economic programmes, with a view to effecting an eventual merger, as outlined in an action plan adopted by ECOWAS and UEMOA in February 2000. The ECOWAS Authority summit held in December in Bamako, Mali, adopted an Agreement Establishing the WAMZ, approved the establishment of a West African Monetary Institute to prepare for the formation of a West African Central Bank, and determined that the harmonization of member countries' tariff structures should be accelerated to facilitate the implementation of the planned customs union. In December 2001 the Authority determined that the currency of the WAMZ (and eventually the ECOWAS-wide currency) would be known as the 'eco' and authorized the establishment during 2002 of an exchange rate mechanism. (This was achieved in April.) In November 2002 the heads of state and government of the planned WAMZ determined to postpone its inauguration and the launch of the eco until 1 July 2005, owing to slower than anticipated progress in achieving the convergence criteria required for monetary union. The establishment of the proposed West African Central Bank was to be effected during January 2003–June 2005. The heads of state and government also agreed that a forum of ministers of finance from the planned second monetary union should be convened on a regular basis to ensure the effective implementation of fiscal policies.

In December 1992 ECOWAS ministers agreed on the institutionalization of an ECOWAS trade fair, in order to promote trade liberalization and intra-Community trade. The first trade fair, which was held in Dakar, Senegal, in May/June 1995, was attended by some 400 private businesses from member states. A second trade fair was staged in Accra, Ghana, in March 1999, and a third fair was held in Lomé, Togo, in March 2003.

TRAVEL, TRANSPORT AND COMMUNICATIONS

In 1979 ECOWAS heads of state signed a Protocol relating to free circulation of the region's citizens and to rights of residence and establishment of commercial enterprises. The first provision (the right of entry without a visa) came into force in 1980. An optional ECOWAS travel certificate, valid for travel within the Community in place of a national passport, was established in July 1985. The second provision of the 1979 Protocol, allowing unlimited rights of residence, was signed in 1986 (although Nigeria indicated that unskilled workers and certain categories of professionals would not be allowed to stay for an indefinite period) and came into force in 1989. The third provision, concerning the right to establish a commercial enterprise in another member state was signed in 1990. In July 1992 the ECOWAS Authority formulated a Minimum Agenda for Action for the implementation of Community agreements regarding the free movement of goods and people, for example the removal of non-tariff barriers, the simplification of customs and transit procedures and a reduction in the number of control posts on international roads. By mid-1996 the ECOWAS summit meeting observed that few measures had been adopted by member states to implement the Minimum Agenda, and emphasized that it remained a central element of the Community's integration process. In April 1997 Gambian and Senegalese finance and trade officials concluded an agreement on measures to facilitate the export of goods via Senegal to neighbouring countries, in accordance with ECOWAS protocols relating to inter-state road transit arrangements. An Inter-state Road Transit Authority has been established. A Brown Card scheme provides recognized third-party liability insurance throughout the region. In October 2001 an ECOWAS passport was reported to be ready for issuance; the ECOWAS travel certificate was to remain in operation, while national passports were to be gradually eliminated over a period of five years.

In February 1996 ECOWAS and several private-sector partners established ECOAir Ltd, based in Abuja, Nigeria, which was to develop a regional airline. It was envisaged that ECOAir would become operative in 2002. The establishment of a regional shipping company, ECOMARINE, is also planned.

In August 1996 the initial phase of a programme to improve regional telecommunications was reported to have been completed.

Some US \$35m. had been granted for project financing in eight ECOWAS countries. A second phase of the programme (INTELCOM II), which aimed to modernize and expand the region's telecommunications services, was initiated by ECOWAS heads of state in August 1997. A West African Telecommunications Regulators' Association was established, under the auspices of ECOWAS, in September 2000.

A programme for the development of an integrated regional road network was adopted in 1980. Under the programme, two major trans-regional roads were to be completed: the Trans-Coastal Highway, linking Lagos, Nigeria, with Nouackchott, Mauritania (4,767 km); and the Trans-Sahelian Highway, linking Dakar, Senegal, with N'Djamena, Chad (4,633 km). By the end of 2000 about 83% of the trans-coastal route was reportedly complete, and about 87% of the trans-Sahelian route.

ECONOMIC AND INDUSTRIAL DEVELOPMENT

In November 1984 ECOWAS heads of state and government approved the establishment of a private regional investment bank, to be known as Ecobank Transnational Inc. The bank, which was based in Lomé, Togo, opened in March 1988. ECOWAS has a 10% share in the bank. By the end of 2000 Ecobank affiliates were operating in 11 member countries.

The West African Industrial Forum, sponsored by ECOWAS, is held every two years to promote regional industrial investment. Community ministers of industry are implementing an action plan on the formulation of a West African Industrial Master Plan identifying strategies for stimulating regional economic development and attracting external investment.

In September 1995 Nigeria, Ghana, Togo and Benin resolved to develop a gas pipeline to connect Nigerian gas supplies to the other countries. In August 1999 the participating countries, together with two petroleum companies operating in Nigeria, signed an agreement on the financing and construction of the pipeline, which was expected to become operational in 2002. During 2000 a Community initiative to connect the electricity supply networks throughout the region was under consideration. The implementation of a planned energy exchange scheme, known as the West African Power Pool Project, is envisaged as a means of efficiently utilizing the region's hydro-electricity and thermal power capabilities by transferring power from surplus producers to countries unable to meet their energy requirements. ECOWAS is developing an initiative aimed at promoting the use of renewable energy resources.

REGIONAL SECURITY

In 1990 a Standing Mediation Committee was formed to mediate disputes between member states. Member states reaffirmed their commitment to refrain from aggression against one another at a summit conference in 1991. The revised ECOWAS treaty, signed in July 1993, incorporates a separate provision for regional security, requiring member states to work towards the maintenance of peace, stability and security.

In December 1997 an extraordinary meeting of ECOWAS heads of state and government was convened in Lomé, Togo, to consider the future stability and security of the region. It was agreed that a permanent mechanism be established for conflict prevention and the maintenance of peace. ECOWAS leaders also reaffirmed their commitment to pursuing dialogue to prevent conflicts, co-operating in the early deployment of peace-keeping forces and implementing measures to counter trans-border crime and the illegal trafficking of armaments and drugs. At the meeting ECOWAS leaders acknowledged ECOMOG's role in restoring constitutional order in Liberia and expressed their appreciation of the force's current efforts in Sierra Leone (see below). In March 1998 ECOWAS ministers of foreign affairs, meeting in Yamoussoukro, Côte d'Ivoire, resolved that ECOMOG should become the region's permanent peace-keeping force, and upheld the decision of heads of state regarding the establishment of a new body, which should be used to observe, analyse and monitor the security situation in the West African region. Ministers agreed to undertake a redefinition of the command structure within the organization in order to strengthen decision-making and the legal status of the ECOMOG force.

In July 1998 ECOWAS ministers of defence and of security adopted a draft mechanism for conflict management, peace-keeping and security, which provided for ECOWAS intervention in the internal affairs of member states, where a conflict or military uprising threatened the region's security. In October the ECOWAS Authority determined to implement a renewable three-year ban on the import, export or manufacture of small armaments in order to enhance the security of the sub-region. (The ban was renewed for a further three years in July 2001.) The Authority also issued a declaration on the control and prevention of drug abuse, agreeing to allocate US \$150,000 to establish an Eco-Drug Fund to finance regional activities in countering substance abuse.

The summit meeting of ECOWAS heads of state and government held in December 1999 in Lomé, Togo, approved a draft protocol to the organization's treaty, providing for the establishment of a Permanent Mechanism for the Prevention, Management and Settlement of Conflicts and the Maintenance of Peace in the Region, as envisaged at their conference in December 1997, and for the creation in connection with the Mechanism of a Mediation and Security Council, to comprise representatives of 10 member states, elected for two-year terms. The Mediation and Security Council was to be supported by an advisory Council of Elders, comprising 32 eminent statesmen from the region. ECOMOG was to be transformed from an *ad hoc* cease-fire monitoring group into a permanent standby force available for immediate deployment to avert emerging conflicts in the region.

In 2002 ECOWAS, with assistance from the USA, was developing an early warning system for monitoring threats to regional security.

Peace-keeping operations

In August 1990 an ECOWAS Cease-fire Monitoring Group (ECOMOG—initially comprising about 4,000 troops from The Gambia, Ghana, Guinea, Nigeria and Sierra Leone) was dispatched to Liberia in an attempt to enforce a cease-fire between conflicting factions there, to restore public order, and to establish an interim government, until elections could be held. In November a temporary cease-fire was agreed by the protagonists in Liberia, and an interim president was installed by ECOMOG. Following the signature of a new cease-fire agreement a national conference, organized by ECOWAS in March 1991, established a temporary government, pending elections to be held in early 1992. In June 1991 ECOWAS established a committee (initially comprising representatives of five member states, later expanded to nine) to co-ordinate the peace negotiations. In September, at a meeting in Yamoussoukro, Côte d'Ivoire, held under the aegis of the ECOWAS committee, two of the rival factions in Liberia agreed to encamp their troops in designated areas and to disarm under ECOMOG supervision. During the period preceding the proposed elections, ECOMOG was to occupy Liberian air and sea ports, and create a 'buffer zone' along the country's border with Sierra Leone. By September 1992, however, ECOMOG had been unable either to effect the disarmament of two of the principal military factions, the National Patriotic Front of Liberia (NPFL) and the United Liberation Movement of Liberia for Democracy (ULIMO), or to occupy positions in substantial areas of the country, as a result of resistance on the part of the NPFL. The proposed elections were consequently postponed indefinitely.

In October 1992 ECOMOG began offensive action against NPFL positions, with a campaign of aerial bombardment. In November ECOWAS imposed a land, sea and air blockade on the NPFL's territory, in response to the Front's refusal to comply with the Yamoussoukro accord of October 1991. In April 1993 ECOMOG announced that the disarmament of ULIMO had been completed, amid widespread accusations that ECOMOG had supported ULIMO against the NPFL, and was no longer a neutral force. An ECOWAS-brokered cease-fire agreement was signed in Cotonou, Benin, in July, and took effect on 1 August. In September a UN observer mission (UNOMIL) was established in Liberia to work alongside ECOMOG in monitoring the process of disarming troops, as well as to verify the impartiality of ECOMOG.

In September 1994 leaders of Liberia's main military factions, having negotiated with representatives of ECOWAS, the Organization of African Unity (OAU, now the African Union—AU) and the UN, signed an amendment to the Cotonou accord in Akosombo, Ghana. This provided for a new five-member Council of State, in the context of a cease-fire, as a replacement to the expired interim executive authority, and established a new timetable for democratic elections. In early 1995 negotiations to secure a peace settlement, conducted under ECOWAS auspices, collapsed, owing to disagreement on the composition of the new Council of State. In May, in an attempt to ease the political deadlock, ECOWAS heads of state and of government met leaders of the six main warring factions. Under continuing pressure from the international community, the leaders of the Liberian factions signed a new peace accord, in Abuja, Nigeria, in August. This political development led to renewed efforts on the part of ECOWAS countries to strengthen ECOMOG, and by October Burkina Faso, Nigeria, Ghana and Guinea had pledged troop contributions to increase the force strength from 7,268 to 12,000. In accordance with the peace agreement, ECOMOG forces, with UNOMIL, were to be deployed throughout Liberia and along its borders to prevent the flow of arms into the country and to monitor the disarmament of the warring parties. In December an attack on ECOMOG troops, by a dissident ULIMO faction (ULIMO–J), disrupted the deployment of the multinational forces and the disarmament process, which was scheduled to commence in mid-January 1996. At least 16 members of the peace-keeping force were killed in the fighting that ensued. Clashes between ECOMOG and the ULIMO–J forces continued in the west of the country in late December 1995 and early January 1996, during which time 130 Nigerian members of ECOMOG were held hostage. In April, following a series of violations of the cease-fire, serious hostilities erupted in the Liberian capital, Monrovia, between government forces and dissident troops. An initial agreement to end the fighting, negotiated under ECOWAS auspices, was unsuccessful; however, it secured the release of several civilians and soldiers who had been taken hostage during the civil disruption. Later in April a further cease-fire agreement was concluded, under the aegis of the US Government, the UN and ECOWAS. In May ministers of foreign affairs of the countries constituting the ECOWAS Committee of Nine advocated that all armed factions be withdrawn from Monrovia and that ECOMOG troops be deployed throughout the capital in order to re-establish the city's 'safe-haven' status. According to the Committee's demands, all property, armaments and equipment seized unlawfully from civilians, ECOMOG and other international organizations during the fighting were to be returned, while efforts to disarm the warring factions and to pursue the restoration of democracy in the country were to be resumed. At the end of May the deployment of ECOMOG troops was initiated. In August a new cease-fire accord was signed by the leaders of the principal factions in Liberia, which envisaged the completion of the disarmament process by the end of January 1997, with elections to be held in May. The disarmament process began in November 1996, and by the end of January 1997 ECOMOG confirmed that 23,000 of the targeted 30,000–35,000 soldiers had been disarmed. The deadline for disarmament was extended by seven days, during which time a further 1,500 soldiers were reported to have been disarmed. However, vigilant attacks by remaining armed faction fighters persisted. The Committee of Nine announced in February that presidential and legislative elections would be held in May, later revising the election schedule to mid-July. ECOMOG was to withdraw from Liberia six months after the election date, until which time it had proposed to offer security for the incoming government and to provide training for a new unified Liberian army. The Committee also agreed, in consultation with the Council of State, to replace the existing Electoral Commission with a new Commission comprising seven members, to reflect all aspects of Liberian society. The Chairman would be selected from among the seven, in consultation with ECOWAS, which along with the UN and the OAU, would act as a 'technical adviser' to the Commission. ECOMOG deployed additional troops, who were joined by other international observers in ensuring that the elections were conducted in the necessary conditions of security. In August, following the inauguration of Charles Taylor (formerly leader of the NPFL) as Liberia's democratically-elected President, ECOWAS heads of state agreed that the ECOMOG force in Liberia was to be reconstituted and would henceforth assist in the process of national reconstruction, including the restructuring of the armed and security forces, and the maintenance of security; it was further envisaged that ECOMOG's mandate (officially due to expire in February 1998) would be extended in agreement with the Liberian Government. A Status of Forces Agreement, which defined ECOMOG's post-conflict responsibilities (i.e. capacity-building and maintenance of security) and imposed conditions on the peace-keeping forces remaining in the country, was signed by the Liberian Government and ECOWAS in June 1998. Relations with the Taylor administration, however, deteriorated, owing to accusations that ECOMOG was providing assistance to opposition groupings. The tense political situation, therefore, and the need for greater resources in Sierra Leone, resulted in ECOMOG transferring its headquarters from Monrovia to Freetown in Sierra Leone. The transfer was reported to have been completed by October, with just two ECOMOG battalions remaining in Liberia. The ECOMOG mission in Liberia was effectively terminated in October 1999 when the final declared stocks of rebel armaments were destroyed. In April 2001 the ECOWAS Authority determined to send a Mediation and Security Council mission to Liberia to monitor compliance with a resolution of the UN Security Council imposing sanctions on the Liberian regime. An ECOWAS military team was sent to Liberia in June 2002 to assess continuing unrest in the country. ECOWAS welcomed a Liberian Leadership Forum that was staged in the following month, in Ouagadougou, Burkina Faso, to address means of achieving peace and reconciliation.

In August 1999 a regional meeting was convened, under ECOWAS auspices, to attempt to defuse escalating tensions between Liberia and Guinea following an incursion into northern Liberia by Guinean rebel forces earlier in that month. In September representatives of eight member countries determined to establish a monitoring body to supervise the border region between Guinea, Liberia and Sierra Leone. Insecurity in the area escalated in the latter part of 2000, particularly in southern Guinea, which was increasingly subjected to insurgencies by Sierra Leonean RUF rebels, combated forcefully by Guinean troops, and prompting massive displacement of and severe hardship for the local population, which included significant numbers of refugees who had fled unrest in Liberia and Sierra Leone. Relations between the three countries deteriorated swiftly, amidst mutual accusations and counter-accusations concerning the provision of external support for dissidents in their respective territories. Allegations that the RUF rebels were supported by the Liberian authorities were the subject of a report issued by an independent UN panel of experts in December. During that month

the ECOWAS Authority approved the deployment of a 1,700-strong ECOMOG interposition force to act as a buffer in the Guinea-Liberia-Sierra Leone border region, in order to deter the rebel activity and thereby alleviate the ongoing humanitarian crisis. (In early October the grouping's newly-formed Mediation and Security Council had authorized the deployment of a military observer mission to the area.) Meanwhile, the governments of the three (Mano River Union) countries agreed to disarm rebel groups and to prevent these from entering neighbouring countries from their territories. However, the political crisis subsequently intensified, amid mutual expulsions of diplomatic personnel. In April 2001, by which time the presidents of Guinea and Liberia had still not signed the Status of Force Agreement necessary to enable the deployment of the proposed ECOMOG interposition force, the ECOWAS Authority agreed to postpone the deployment indefinitely. In that month an ECOWAS committee, comprising the presidents of Mali, Nigeria and Togo, was established to mediate a resolution to the crisis. From August ministers of foreign affairs and defence from the three Mano River Union countries held a series of meetings to address the situation. The deployment of the ECOMOG interposition force remained suspended.

In May 1997 the democratically-elected Sierra Leonean leader, President Ahmed Tejan Kabbah, was overthrown by a military coup involving officers of the national army and RUF rebels. Nigerian forces based in Sierra Leone as part of a bilateral defence pact attempted to restore constitutional order. Their numbers were strengthened by the arrival of more than 700 Nigerian soldiers and two naval vessels which had been serving under the ECOMOG mandate in neighbouring Liberia. At the end of June ECOWAS ministers of foreign affairs, convened in Conakry, Guinea, agreed to pursue the objective of restoring a democratic government in Sierra Leone through dialogue and the imposition of economic sanctions. In July a five-member ECOWAS committee, comprising the foreign ministers of Côte d'Ivoire, Ghana, Guinea, Liberia and Nigeria, together with representatives of the OAU, negotiated an agreement with the so-called Armed Forces Revolutionary Council (AFRC) in Sierra Leone to establish an immediate cease-fire and to pursue efforts towards the restoration of constitutional order. In August ECOWAS heads of state reaffirmed the Community's condemnation of the removal of President Kabbah and officially endorsed a series of punitive measures against the AFRC authorities in order to accelerate the restoration of democratic government. The meeting mandated ECOMOG to maintain and monitor the cease-fire and to prevent all goods, excepting essential humanitarian supplies, from entering that country. It was also agreed that the committee on Sierra Leone include Liberia and be convened at the level of heads of state. In October the UN Security Council imposed an embargo on the sale or supply of armaments to Sierra Leone and authorized ECOWAS to ensure implementation of these measures. ECOMOG conducted a number of attacks against commercial and military targets, with the aim of upholding the international sanctions, and clashes occurred between ECOMOG troops and AFRC/RUF soldiers, in particular around the area of Freetown's Lungi international airport which had been seized by ECOMOG. Despite the escalation in hostilities, the ECOWAS Committee of Five pursued negotiations with the military authorities, and at the end of October both sides signed a peace agreement, in Conakry, Guinea, providing for an immediate end to all fighting and the reinstatement of Kabbah's Government by April 1998; all combatants were to be disarmed and demobilized under the supervision of a disarmament committee comprising representatives of ECOMOG, the military authorities and local forces loyal to President Kabbah. In November 1997, however, the peace process was undermined by reports that ECOMOG forces had violated the cease-fire agreement following a series of air raids on Freetown, which ECOMOG claimed to have been in retaliation for attacks by AFRC/RUF-operated anti-aircraft equipment, and a demand by the AFRC authorities that the Nigerian contingent of ECOMOG leave the country. In mid-February 1998, following a series of offensive attacks against forces loyal to the military authorities, ECOMOG assumed control of Freetown and arrested several members of the AFRC/RUC regime. Some 50 AFRC officials were arrested by troops serving under ECOMOG on arrival at James Spriggs Payne Airport in Liberia, prompting protests from the Liberian Government at the Nigerian military intervention. An 11-member supervisory task force, which included the ECOMOG Commander, was established in Sierra Leone to maintain order, pending Kabbah's return from exile. ECOMOG troops subsequently also monitored the removal of the embargo against the use of the airport and port facilities in Freetown. Kabbah returned to Sierra Leone in March and installed a new administration. It was agreed that ECOMOG forces were to remain in the country in order to ensure the full restoration of peace and security, to assist in the restructuring of the armed forces and to help to resolve the problems of the substantial numbers of refugees and internally displaced persons. In early May ECOWAS Chiefs of Staff, meeting in Accra, Ghana, urged member states to provide more troops and logistical support to strengthen the ECOMOG force in

Sierra Leone (at that time numbering some 10,000 troops), which was still involved in ongoing clashes with remaining rebel soldiers in eastern regions of the country. The UN established an Observer Mission in Sierra Leone (UNOMSIL) in July, which was to monitor the cease-fire, mainly in areas secured by ECOMOG troops. In October ECOMOG transferred its headquarters to Freetown, in order, partly, to reinforce its presence in the country. In January 1999 rebel soldiers attacked the capital and engaged in heavy fighting with ECOMOG forces, amid reports that the Liberian Government was supporting the rebels. Nigeria dispatched several thousand additional troops to counter the rebel advance and to secure the border with Liberia. In February, however, once ECOMOG had regained control of Freetown, the Nigerian Government expressed its desire to withdraw all its troops from the peace-keeping force by May, owing to financial restraints. Efforts to negotiate a peace settlement were initiated, with the Chairman of ECOWAS at that time, President Gnassingbé Eyadéma of Togo, actively involved in mediation between the opposing groups, despite persisting reports of fighting between ECOMOG and rebel soldiers in areas east of the capital. A cease-fire agreement was concluded in May, and a political settlement was signed, by Kabbah and the RUF leader, in Lomé, Togo, in July. ECOMOG's mandate in Sierra Leone was adapted to support the consolidation of peace in that country and national reconstruction. In October UNOMSIL was replaced by the UN Mission in Sierra Leone (UNAMSIL), which was to assist with the implementation of the Lomé accord and to assume many of the functions then being performed by ECOMOG, including the provision of security at Lungi international airport and at other key installations, buildings and government institutions in the Freetown area. In consequence the ECOMOG contingent was withdrawn in April 2000. However, following a resurgence of RUF violence in April and May, when as many as 500 members of UNAMSIL (which had not been deployed to full strength) were captured by the rebels, ECOWAS heads of government agreed to reinforce the UN peacekeeping operation with some 3,000 regional troops. A UN Security Council mission to Sierra Leone in September recommended the establishment of a mechanism to co-ordinate the formulation and implementation by the UN, ECOWAS, the Sierra Leone Government and other parties of a unified strategy to resolve the insecurity in Sierra Leone. A new cease-fire accord was agreed by the Sierra Leone Government and the RUF in November, in Abuja, Nigeria, and in January 2002 the process (monitored by UNAMSIL) of disarming, demobilizing and reintegrating former combatants was completed. An ECOWAS observer team was dispatched to monitor legislative and presidential elections that were held in Sierra Leone in May. In April 2001 representatives of the Mediation and Security Council were dispatched to Liberia to monitor, jointly with a UN delegation, the Liberian Government's compliance with a UN Security Council Resolution aimed at ending support for and eradicating RUF activity in that country, and at terminating illicit trading there in Sierra Leonean diamonds.

In July 1998 ECOWAS ministers of defence and of foreign affairs met to consider the political unrest in Guinea-Bissau, following an unsuccessful attempt by rebel soldiers, in June, to overthrow the Government of President João Vieira, and urged both sides to co-operate in negotiating a settlement. An ECOWAS Committee of Seven on Guinea-Bissau (comprising the ministers of foreign affairs of Burkina Faso, Côte d'Ivoire, The Gambia, Ghana, Guinea, Nigeria and Senegal) was established and met for the first time in August. In late August, following mediation by ECOWAS representatives and a contact group of the Comunidade dos Países de Língua Portuguesa (CPLP), which had secured an initial cease-fire, an agreement was signed by the conflicting parties providing for an end to hostilities, the reopening of the international airport to facilitate the provision of humanitarian supplies, and for independent supervision of the cease-fire agreement. ECOWAS subsequently held discussions with the CPLP in order to co-ordinate efforts to secure peace in Guinea-Bissau. In late October ECOWAS heads of state endorsed the deployment of ECOMOG forces in Guinea-Bissau. On 1 November the two sides in the dispute, meeting in Abuja, Nigeria, signed a peace accord under ECOWAS auspices, which reinforced the August cease-fire and incorporated an agreement to establish a government of national unity. ECOMOG forces were to replace all foreign troops, mainly Senegalese, currently in Guinea-Bissau, supervise the security of the border region between those two countries, and enable humanitarian organizations to have free access to those needing assistance. In addition ECOMOG was to be responsible for monitoring the conduct of presidential and legislative elections, scheduled to be held in 1999. In early February President Vieira and the rebel leader Gen. Manè signed a cease-fire accord, under ECOWAS auspices. A new Government of National Unity was established later in that month and an ECOMOG Interposition Force began to be dispatched to Guinea-Bissau. In early May, however, President Vieira was ousted by the rebel forces. Meeting later in that month, in Lomé, Togo, ECOWAS ministers of foreign affairs condemned the overthrow of Vieira. They resolved to withdraw the ECOMOG contingent, at that time numbering 600 troops

from Benin, Gabon, Niger and Togo, owing to the political developments and lack of finances. By early June all ECOMOG troops had left Guinea-Bissau.

At the end of September 2002 an extraordinary summit meeting of ECOWAS heads of state and government was convened in Accra, Ghana, to address the violent unrest that had erupted in Côte d'Ivoire during that month, commencing with an attempted *coup d'état* by disloyal elements of the country's armed forces. The summit meeting condemned the attempt to overthrow democratic rule and constitutional order and established a high-level contact group, comprising the heads of state of Ghana, Guinea-Bissau, Mali, Niger, Nigeria and Togo, to prevail upon the rebels to end hostilities, and to negotiate a general framework for the resolution of the crisis. The contact group helped to mediate a cease-fire in the following month; this was to be monitored by an ECOWAS military mission in Côte d'Ivoire (ECOMICI), which was also to be responsible for ensuring safe passage for deliveries of humanitarian assistance. In March 2003, following the conclusion in January by the parties to the conflict of a peace agreement, signed at Marcoussis, France, ECOWAS chiefs of staff endorsed the expansion of ECOMICI from 1,264 to a maximum of 3,411 men.

In May 2000 the ECOWAS Authority authorized the initiation of an inquiry into the link between illicit trading in diamonds and ongoing rebel activity in the region, with a particular focus on Liberia and Sierra Leone.

ENVIRONMENTAL PROTECTION

ECOWAS promotes implementation of the UN Convention on Desertification Control and supports programmes initiated at national and sub-regional level within the framework of the treaty. Together with the Permanent Inter-State Committee on Drought Control in the Sahel (CILSS). ECOWAS has been designated as a project leader for implementing the Convention in West Africa. Other environmental initiatives include a regional meteorological project to enhance meteorological activities and applications, and in particular to contribute to food security and natural resource management in the sub-region. ECOWAS pilot schemes have formed the basis of integrated control projects for the control of floating weeds in five water basins in West Africa, which had hindered the development of the local fishery sectors. A rural water supply programme aims to ensure adequate water for rural dwellers in order to improve their living standards. The first phase of the project focused on schemes to develop village and pastoral water points in Burkina Faso, Guinea, Mali, Niger and Senegal, with funds from various multilateral donors.

AGRICULTURE AND FISHING

In November 1995 an agro-industrial forum, jointly organized by ECOWAS and the EU, was held in Dakar, Senegal. The forum aimed to facilitate co-operation between companies in the two regions, to develop the agro-industrial sector in West Africa and to promote business opportunities.

In February 2001 ECOWAS ministers of agriculture adopted an action plan for the formulation of a common agricultural policy, as envisaged under the ECOWAS treaty. The Community enforces a transhumance certification scheme for facilitating the monitoring of animal movement and animal health surveillance and protection in the sub-region.

SOCIAL PROGRAMME

Four organizations have been established within ECOWAS by the Executive Secretariat: the Organization of Trade Unions of West Africa, which held its first meeting in 1984; the West African Youth Association; the West African Universities' Association; and the West Africa Women's Association (whose statutes were approved by a meeting of ministers of social affairs in May 1987). Regional sports competitions are held annually. The West African Health Organization (WAHO) was established in 2000 by merger of the West African Health Community and the Organization for Co-ordination and Co-operation in the Struggle against Endemic Diseases. In December 2001 the ECOWAS summit of heads of state and government adopted a plan of action aimed at combating trafficking in human beings and authorized the establishment of an ECOWAS Criminal Intelligence Bureau.

INFORMATION AND MEDIA

In March 1990 ECOWAS ministers of information formulated a policy on the dissemination of information about ECOWAS throughout the region and the appraisal of attitudes of its population towards the Community. The ministers established a new information commission. In November 1991 a conference on press communication and African integration, organized by ECOWAS, recommended the creation of an ECOWAS press card, judicial safeguards to protect journalists, training programmes for journalists and the establishment of a regional documentation centre and data bank. In November 1994 the commission of social and cultural affairs, meeting in Lagos, Nigeria, endorsed a series of measures to promote west African integration. These included special radio, television and newspaper features, sporting events and other competitions or rallies. In December 2000 the Council of Ministers approved a new policy on the dissemination of information about the Community's activities.

SPECIALIZED AGENCIES

West African Monetary Agency: 11–13 ECOWAS St, PMB 218, Freetown, Sierra Leone; tel. 224485; fax 223943; e-mail wama@sierratel.sl; f. 1975 as West African Clearing House; administers transactions between its 10 member central banks in order to promote sub-regional trade and monetary co-operation; administers ECOWAS travellers' cheques scheme. Mems: Banque Centrale des Etats de l'Afrique de l'Ouest (serving Benin, Burkina Faso, Côte d'Ivoire, Guinea-Bissau, Mali, Niger, Senegal, Togo) and the central banks of Cape Verde, The Gambia, Ghana, Guinea, Liberia, Mauritania, Nigeria and Sierra Leone; Dir-Gen. ANTOINE M. F. NDIAYE (Senegal); publ. *Annual Report*.

West African Monetary Institute: Premier Towers, 8th/9th Floors, Cantonments 75, Accra, Ghana; tel. (21) 676-901; fax (21) 676-903; e-mail info@wami-imao.org; internet www.ecowas.int/wami-imao/; f. by the ECOWAS Authority summit in December 2000 to prepare for the establishment of a West African Central Bank; Dir-Gen. Dr MICHAEL OLUFEMI OJO.

West African Health Organization—WAHO: BP 153 Bobo-Dioulasso 01, Burkina Faso; tel. (226) 975772; fax (226) 975772; e-mail wahooas@fasonet.bf; f. 2000 by merger of the West African Health Community (f. 1978) and the Organization for Co-ordination and Co-operation in the Struggle against Endemic Diseases (f. 1960); aims to harmonize member states' health policies and to promote research, training, the sharing of resources and diffusion of information; Dir-Gen. Dr KABBA T. JOINER; publ. *Bulletin Bibliographique* (quarterly).

Finance

ECOWAS is financed by contributions from member states, although there is a poor record of punctual payment of dues, which has hampered the work of the Secretariat. Arrears in contributions to the Secretariat were reported to total US $27m. at 31 December 2001. Under the revised treaty, ECOWAS was to receive revenue from a community tax, based on the total value of imports from member countries. In July 1996 the summit meeting approved a protocol on a community levy, providing for the imposition of a 0.5% tax on the value of imports from a third country. In August 1997 the Authority of Heads of State and Government determined that the community levy should replace budgetary contributions as the organization's principal source of finance. The protocol came into force in January 2000, having been ratified by nine member states, with the substantive regime entering into effect on 1 January 2003.

The provisional budget for 2002 amounted to approximately US $9.6m.

Publications

Annual Report.
Contact.
ECOWAS National Accounts.
ECOWAS News.
West African Bulletin.

ECONOMIC CO-OPERATION ORGANIZATION—ECO

Address: 1 Golbou Alley, Kamranieh St, POB 14155-6176, Tehran, Iran.
Telephone: (21) 2831733; **fax:** (21) 2831732; **e-mail:** registry@ecosecretariat.org; **internet:** www.ecosecretariat.org.

The Economic Co-operation Organization (ECO) was established in 1985 as the successor to the Regional Co-operation for Development, founded in 1964.

MEMBERS

Afghanistan	Kyrgyzstan	Turkey
Azerbaijan	Pakistan	Turkmenistan
Iran	Tajikistan	Uzbekistan
Kazakhstan		

The 'Turkish Republic of Northern Cyprus' has been granted special guest status.

Organization

(April 2003)

SUMMIT MEETING

The first summit meeting of heads of state and of government of member countries was held in Tehran in February 1992. Summit meetings are generally held at least once every two years. The seventh summit meeting was convened in Istanbul, Turkey, in October 2002.

COUNCIL OF MINISTERS

The Council of Ministers, comprising ministers of foreign affairs of member states, is the principal policy- and decision-making body of ECO. It meets at least once a year.

REGIONAL PLANNING COUNCIL

The Council, comprising senior planning officials or other representatives of member states, meets at least once a year. It is responsible for reviewing programmes of activity and evaluating resultsachieved, and for proposing future plans of action to the Council of Ministers.

COUNCIL OF PERMANENT REPRESENTATIVES

Permanent representatives or Ambassadors of member countries accredited to Iran meet regularly to formulate policy for consideration by the Council of Ministers and to promote implementation of decisions reached at ministerial or summit level.

SECRETARIAT

The Secretariat is headed by a Secretary-General, who is supported by two Deputy Secretaries-General. The following Directorates administer and co-ordinate the main areas of ECO activities: Trade and investment; Transport and communications; Energy, minerals and environment; Industry and agriculture (to be renamed Human development); Project research; Economic research and statistics; and Co-ordination and international relations.

Secretary-General: SAYED MOJTABA ARASTOU (Iran).

Activities

The Regional Co-operation for Development (RCD) was established in 1964 as a tripartite arrangement between Iran, Pakistan and Turkey, which aimed to promote economic co-operation between member states. ECO replaced the RCD in 1985, and seven additional members were admitted to the Organization in November 1992. The main areas of co-operation are transport (including the building of road and rail links, of particular importance as seven member states are landlocked), telecommunications and post, trade and investment, energy (including the interconnection of power grids in the region), minerals, environmental issues, industry, and agriculture. ECO priorities and objectives for each sector are defined in the Quetta Plan of Action and the İstanbul Declaration; an Almaty Outline Plan, which was adopted in 1993, is specifically concerned with the development of regional transport and communication infrastructure. The period 1998–2007 has been designated as the ECO Decade of Transport and Communications.

In 1990 an ECO College of Insurance was inaugurated. A joint Chamber of Commerce and Industry was established in 1993. The third ECO summit meeting, held in Islamabad, Pakistan, in March 1995, concluded formal agreements on the establishment of several other regional institutes and agencies: an ECO Trade and Development Bank, in İstanbul, Turkey (with main branches in Tehran, Iran, and Islamabad, Pakistan), a joint shipping company, airline, and an ECO Cultural Institute, all to be based in Iran, and an ECO Reinsurance Company and an ECO Science Foundation, with head-quarters in Pakistan. In addition, heads of state and of government endorsed the creation of an ECO eminent persons group and signed the following two agreements in order to enhance and facilitate trade throughout the region: the Transit Trade Agreement (which entered into force in December 1997) and the Agreement on the Simplification of Visa Procedures for Businessmen of ECO Countries (which came into effect in March 1998). The sixth ECO summit meeting, held in June 2000 in Tehran, urged the completion of the necessary formalities for the creation of the planned ECO Trade and Development Bank and ECO Reinsurance Company. In May 2001 the Council of Ministers agreed to terminate the ECO airline project, owing to its unsustainable cost, and to replace it with a framework agreement on co-operation in the field of air transport.

In September 1996, at an extraordinary meeting of the ECO Council of Ministers, held in Izmir, Turkey, member countries signed a revised Treaty of Izmir, the Organization's fundamental charter. An extraordinary summit meeting, held in Ashgabat, Turkmenistan, in May 1997, adopted the Ashgabat Declaration, emphasizing the importance of the development of the transport and communications infrastructure and the network of transnational petroleum and gas pipelines through bilateral and regional arrangements in the ECO area. In May 1998, at the fifth summit meeting, held in Almaty, Kazakhstan, ECO heads of state and of government signed a Transit Transport Framework Agreement and a memorandum of understanding to help combat the cross-border trafficking of illegal goods. The meeting also agreed to establish an ECO Educational Institute in Ankara, Turkey. In June 2000 the sixth ECO summit encouraged member states to participate in the development of information and communication technologies through the establishment of a database of regional educational and training institutions specializing in that field. The ECO heads of state and government also reconfirmed their commitment to the Ashgabat Declaration. In December 2001 ECO organized its first workshop on energy conservation and efficiency in Ankara. The seventh ECO summit, held in Istanbul, Turkey, in October 2002, adopted the Istanbul Declaration, which outlined a strengthened and more pro-active economic orientation for the Organization

Convening in conference for the first time in early March 2000, ECO ministers of trade signed a Framework Agreement on ECO Trade Co-operation (ECOFAT), which established a basis for the expansion of intra-regional trade. The Framework Agreement envisaged the eventual adoption of an ECO Trade Agreement (ECOTA), providing for the gradual elimination of regional tariff and non-tariff

barriers between member states. ECO and the International Trade Centre are jointly implementing a project on expanding intra-ECO trade. In November the first meeting of ECO ministers responsible for energy and petroleum, convened in Islamabad, adopted a plan of action for regional co-operation on energy and petroleum matters over the period 2001–05. The first meeting of ECO ministers of agriculture, convened in July 2002, in Islamabad, Pakistan, adopted a declaration on co-operation in the agricultural sector, which specified that member states would contribute to agricultural rehabilitation in Afghanistan and considered instigating a mechanism for the regional exchange of agricultural and cattle products. In December the first meeting of ECO ministers of the environment, held in Tehran, adopted an action plan for co-operation in environmental issues covering the period 2003–07.

ECO staged its third trade fair in Bandar Anzali, Iran, in July 1998. The fourth fair, scheduled to be held in Karachi, Pakistan, in May 2002, was postponed. The Organization maintains ECO TradeNet, an internet-based repository of regional trade information. ECO has co-operation agreements with several UN agencies and other international organizations in development-related activities. An ECO-UN International Drug Control Programme (UNDCP) Project on Drug Control and Co-ordination Unit commenced operations in Tehran in July 1999. ECO has been granted observer status at the UN, OIC and WTO.

In November 2001 the UN Secretary-General requested ECO to take an active role in efforts to restore stability in Afghanistan and to co-operate closely with his special representative in that country. In June 2002 the ECO Secretary-General participated in a tripartite ministerial conference on co-operation for development in Afghanistan that was convened under the auspices of the UN Development Programme and attended by representatives from Afghanistan, Iran and Pakistan. The ECO summit meeting in October authorized the establishment of a fund to provide financial assistance for reconstruction activities in Afghanistan.

Finance
Member states contribute to a centralized administrative budget.

Publications
ECO Annual Economic Report.
ECO Bulletin (quarterly).

EUROPEAN BANK FOR RECONSTRUCTION AND DEVELOPMENT—EBRD

Address: One Exchange Square, 175 Bishopsgate, London, EC2A 2EH, United Kingdom.
Telephone: (20) 7338-6000; **fax:** (20) 7338-6100; **e-mail:** generalenquiries@ebrd.com; **internet:** www.ebrd.com.
The EBRD was founded in May 1990 and inaugurated in April 1991. Its object is to contribute to the progress and the economic reconstruction of the countries of central and eastern Europe which undertake to respect and put into practice the principles of multi-party democracy, pluralism, the rule of law, respect for human rights and a market economy.

MEMBERS
Countries of Operations:

Albania	Lithuania
Armenia	Macedonia, former Yugoslav
Azerbaijan	republic
Belarus	Moldova
Bosnia and Herzegovina	Poland
Bulgaria	Romania
Croatia	Russia
Czech Republic	Serbia and Montenegro
Estonia	Slovakia
Georgia	Slovenia
Hungary	Tajikistan
Kazakhstan	Turkmenistan
Kyrgyzstan	Ukraine
Latvia	Uzbekistan

EU members*:

Austria	Italy
Belgium	Luxembourg
Denmark	Netherlands
Finland	Portugal
France	Spain
Germany	Sweden
Greece	United Kingdom
Ireland	

EFTA members:

Iceland	Norway
Liechtenstein	Switzerland

Other countries:

Australia	Malta
Canada	Mexico
Cyprus	Mongolia
Egypt	Morocco
Israel	New Zealand
Japan	Turkey
Republic of Korea	USA

* The European Community and the European Investment Bank are also shareholder members in their own right.

Organization

(April 2003)

BOARD OF GOVERNORS

The Board of Governors, to which each member appoints a Governor and an alternate, is the highest authority of the EBRD.

BOARD OF DIRECTORS

The Board is responsible for the organization and operations of the EBRD. The Governors elect 23 directors for a three-year term and a President for a term of four years. Vice-Presidents are appointed by the Board on the recommendation of the President.

ADMINISTRATION

The EBRD's operations are conducted by its Banking Department, headed by the First Vice-President. The other departments are: Finance; Human Resources and Administration; Evaluation, Operational and Environmental Support; Internal Audit; Communications; and Offices of the Secretary-General, the General Counsel and the Chief Economist. A structure of country teams, industry teams and operations support units oversee the implementation of projects. The EBRD has 32 local offices in all 27 of its countries of operations. There were some 913 regular staff at the end of 2001.

President: JEAN LEMIERRE (France).

First Vice-President: NOREEN DOYLE (USA).

Activities

In April 1996 EBRD shareholders, meeting in Sofia, Bulgaria, agreed to increase the Bank's capital from ECU 10,000m. to ECU 20,000m., to enable the Bank to continue, and to enhance, its lending programme (the ECU was replaced by the euro, with an equivalent value, from 1 January 1999). It was agreed that 22.5% of the new resources, was to be paid-up, with the remainder as 'callable' shares. Contributions were to be paid over a 13-year period from April 1998. By 31 December 2001 paid-up capital amounted to €5,197m.

PROJECT FINANCING COMMITTED BY COUNTRY

	2001		Cumulative to 31 Dec. 2001	
	Number	Amount € million	Number	Amount € million
Albania	1	19	14	126
Armenia	0	0	6	140
Azerbaijan . . .	0	17	11	393
Belarus	0	7	6	190
Bosnia and Herzegovina	4	52	15	201
Bulgaria	3	60	34	536
Croatia	9	281	36	937
Czech Republic . .	3	88	35	869
Estonia	1	15	37	367
Georgia	1	12	15	249
Hungary	3	129	59	1,357
Kazakhstan . . .	5	177	19	797
Kyrgyzstan . . .	1	5	13	190
Latvia	3	43	24	353
Lithuania	3	83	24	437
Macedonia, former Yugoslav republic	1	33	14	270
Moldova	1	10	17	211
Poland	14	588	110	2,560
Romania	4	282	56	2,017
Russia	18	822	128	4,276
Slovakia	7	345	32	899
Slovenia	1	52	23	414
Tajikistan	2	21	6	38
Turkmenistan . .	0	1	4	177
Ukraine	6	176	44	1,294
Uzbekistan . . .	2	107	17	690
Yugoslavia* . . .	7	233	7	233
Total	**102**	**3,656**	**807**	**20,219**

Note: Operations may be counted as fractional numbers if multiple sub-loans are grouped under one framework agreement.

* Renamed as Serbia and Montenegro in February 2003.

Source: EBRD, *Annual Report 2001*.

PROJECT FINANCING COMMITTED BY SECTOR

	2001		Cumulative to 31 Dec. 2001	
	Number	Amount € million	Number	Amount € million
Financial institutions				
Bank equity	6	184	80	1,023
Bank lending. . . .	8	591	112	3,031
Equity funds	6	175	63	1,220
Non-bank financial institutions	7	93	24	236
Micro and small business programmes . .	6	64	19	403
Industry and commerce				
Agribusiness	12	299	86	1,466
Natural resources . .	5	196	38	1,633
Property, tourism and shipping	4	148	43	831
Telecommunications, informatics and media	8	297	53	1,730
Infrastructure				
Energy efficiency . .	3	53	12	233
Municipal and environmental infrastructure . . .	9	188	39	1,095
Power and energy . .	4	364	41	1,873
Transport	8	401	68	2,611
General industry				
General industry . .	16	604	128	2,835
Total	**102**	**3,656**	**807**	**20,219**

The Bank aims to assist the transition of the economies of central Europe, southern and eastern Europe and the Caucasus, and central Asia and Russia towards a market economy system, and to encourage private enterprise. The Agreement establishing the EBRD specifies that 60% of its lending should be for the private sector, and that its operations do not displace commercial sources of finance. The Bank helps the beneficiaries to undertake structural and sectoral reforms, including the dismantling of monopolies, decentralization, and privatization of state enterprises, to enable these countries to become fully integrated in the international economy. To this end, the Bank promotes the establishment and improvement of activities of a productive, competitive and private nature, particularly small and medium-sized enterprises (SMEs), and works to strengthen financial institutions. It mobilizes national and foreign capital, together with experienced management teams, and helps to develop an appropriate legal framework to support a market-orientated economy. The Bank provides extensive financial services, including loans, equity and guarantees, and aims to develop new forms of financing and investment in accordance with the requirements of the transition process. The EBRD's founding Agreement specifies that all operations are to be undertaken in the context of promoting environmentally sound and sustainable development. It undertakes environmental audits and impact assessments in areas of particular concern, which enable the Bank to incorporate environmental action plans into any project approved for funding. An Environment Advisory Council assists with the development of policy and strategy in this area.

The economic crisis in Russia, in August 1998, undermined the viability of many proposed projects and adversely affected the Bank's large portfolio of Russian investments. In March 1999, partly in response to the region's economic difficulties, the Board of Directors approved a new medium-term strategy for 2000–03, which focused on advancing the process of transition. Key aspects of the strategy were to develop a sound financial sector and investment climate in its countries of operations; to provide leadership for the development of SMEs; to promote infrastructure development; and to ensure a balanced and focused project portfolio. In April 1999 the Bank and the European Commission launched a new SME Finance Facility, with committed funds of €125m., to provide equity and loan financing for SMEs in countries seeking accession to the EU. During 2001 the Bank directed substantial investment to the so-called accession countries, and supported the development of institutions in areas including financial regulation, competition policy and telecommunications. During 2001 the Bank also further strengthened measures to improve institutional governance, in particular to combat money-laundering. A Trade Facilitation Programme, which extends bank guarantees in order to promote trading capabilities in the region, was expanded during 1999. By the end of 2001 63 issuing banks in 21 countries of operations, together with 144 confirming banks in 50 countries world-wide, were participating in the Programme. During 1999 the Bank participated in international efforts to secure economic and political stability in the Balkans, following the conflict in Kosovo. Subsequently the Bank has promoted the objectives of the Stability Pact for South-Eastern Europe by expanding its commitments in the region and by taking a lead role among international financial institutions in promoting private sector development. During 2001 the Bank committed €678m. to 46 new projects in the six Stability Pact countries. In October the Bank development an Action Plan for Central Asia in order to accelerate development and economic stability in the countries neighbouring Afghanistan, as part of a wider objective of securing peace in the region.

In the year ending 31 December 2001 the EBRD approved 102 operations, involving funds of €3,656m., compared with €2,673m. for 95 operations in the previous year. During 2001 30% of all project financing committed was allocated to the financial sector, in order to support the development and restructuring of sound financial institutions and to make more funds available, through banks and local intermediaries, for small-scale private enterprises.

A high priority is given to attracting external finance for Bank-sponsored projects, in particular in countries at advanced stages of transition, from government agencies, international financial institutions, commercial banks and export credit agencies. The EBRD's Technical Co-operation Funds Programme (TCFP) aims to facilitate access to the Bank's capital resources for countries of operations by providing support for project preparation, project implementation and institutional development. In 2001 the EBRD committed €128.4m. to finance 367 consultancy assignments under the TCFP, bringing the total amount committed since 1991 to €763.4m. for 2,989 assignments. Resources for technical co-operation originate from regular TCFP contributions, specific agreements and contributions to Special Funds. The Baltic Investment Programme, which is administered by Nordic countries, consists of two special funds to co-finance investment and technical assistance projects in the private sectors of Baltic states. The Funds are open to contributions from all EBRD member states. The Russia Small Business Special Funds, established in October 1993, support local SMEs through similar investment and technical co-operation activities. Other financing mechanisms that the EBRD uses to address the needs of the region include Regional Venture Funds, which invest equity in privatized companies, in particular in Russia, and provide relevant management assistance, and the Central European Agency Lines, which disburse lines of credit to small-scale projects through local intermediaries. A TurnAround Management Programme (TAM) provides practical assistance to senior managers of industrial enterprises to facilitate the expansion of businesses in a market economy. A Business Advisory Services programme complements TAM by undertaking projects to improve competitiveness, strategic planning, marketing and financial management in SMEs. In 2001 the Bank collaborated with other donor institutions and partners to initiate a Northern Dimension Environmental Partnership to strengthen and co-ordinate environmental projects in northern Europe.

The Bank administers a Nuclear Safety Account (NSA), which was established in 1993 to fund a multilateral programme of action for the improvement of safety in nuclear power plants of the former eastern bloc. At the end of 2001 14 countries and the European Community had pledged funds amounting to some €260.6m. to the NSA. At that time short-term projects to improve safety at plants in Bulgaria, Lithuania, Russia and Ukraine had been completed.

In 1997 the G-7, together with the European Community and Ukraine, endorsed the creation of a supplemental multilateral funding mechanism to assist Ukraine in repairing the protective sarcophagus covering the faulty Chornobyl (Chernobyl) reactor, under the Chornobyl Unit 4 Shelter Implementation Plan (SIP). The EBRD's Board of Directors approved the participation of the Bank in September 1997. The rules of the so-called Chornobyl Shelter Fund, which the EBRD was to administer, were approved in November and the Fund became operational in the following month. In 1995 the G-7 requested that the Bank fund the completion of two new nuclear reactors in Ukraine, to provide alternative energy sources to the Chornobyl power-station, which, it was agreed, was to be shut down in December 2000. A study questioning the financial viability of the proposed reactors threatened funding in early 1997; a second survey, carried out by the EBRD, pronounced the plan viable, although environmental groups continued to dispute the proposals. In July 2000 donor countries committed additional funds to the SIP, raising the total pledged to €766m. In December the Chornobyl power station was closed. The NSA is financing the construction of two major pre-decommissioning facilities in Ukraine, which were scheduled to be completed in 2003. In June 2000 the Bank approved the establishment of three International Decommissioning Support Funds, to assist the governments of Bulgaria, Lithuania and Slovakia in their commitments to close certain reactors. By the end of 2001 all three funds had become operational, with contributions totaling €358m. by 15 countries and the European Commission.

Publications

Annual Report.

Environments in Transition (2 a year).

Law in Transition (2 a year).

Transition Report (annually).

EUROPEAN FREE TRADE ASSOCIATION—EFTA

Address: (secretariat headquarters): 9–11 rue de Varembé, 1211 Geneva 20, Switzerland.

Telephone: (22) 332-26-26; **fax:** (22) 332-26-99; **e-mail:** mail.gva@efta.int; **internet:** www.efta.int.

Established in 1960, EFTA aimed to bring about free trade in industrial goods and to contribute to the liberalization and expansion of world trade. EFTA now serves as the structure through which three of its members participate in the European Economic Area (EEA), together with the 15 member states of the European Union. In June 2002 a revised EFTA Convention entered into force, replacing the original Convention that had been in effect since 1960.

MEMBERS

Iceland	Norway
Liechtenstein	Switzerland

Three founder members subsequently left EFTA and joined the European Community (EC): Denmark (1973), the United Kingdom (1973) and Portugal (1986). Finland, formerly an associate member of EFTA, became a full member on 1 January 1986. Liechtenstein joined EFTA as a full member in September 1991, having hitherto had associate status through its customs union with Switzerland. Austria, Sweden (both founder members) and Finland left the Association on 31 December 1994 to become members of the European Union (as the EC had been restyled).

Organization

(April 2003)

EFTA COUNCIL

The Council is EFTA's governing body. The Chair is held for six months by each country in turn. The Council's decisions are binding on member states and must be unanimous. The Council is assisted by a substructure of committees and working groups.

EFTA STANDING COMMITTEES

Board of Auditors.

Budget Committee.

Committee of Members of Parliament of the EFTA Countries.

Committee of Origin and Customs Experts.

Committee on Technical Barriers to Trade.

Committee on Third Country Relations.

Committee of Trade Experts.

Consultative Committee.

Steering Committee of the Portuguese Fund.

MATTERS RELATED TO THE EEA

The treaty establishing the EEA, which entered into force in 1994, provided for an institutional structure to enhance its operations. An EEA Council, comprising ministers of all signatory countries, provides policy direction, while a Joint Committee, comprising representatives of the EFTA states in the EEA, the European Commission and EU member states, is responsible for the day-to-day management of EEA matters. A Standing Committee serves as the forum of consultation within EFTA, consisting of representatives from Iceland, Liechtenstein and Norway and observers from Switzerland. It is assisted by five Subcommittees (for free movement of goods; free movement of capital and services; free movement of persons; flanking and horizontal policies; and legal and institutional matters) and a number of Working Groups. An independent EFTA Surveillance Authority and an EFTA Court have also been established to provide judicial control.

SECRETARIAT

The secretariat headquarters, in Geneva, Switzerland, provides support to the EFTA Council and on third country relations, as well as servicing the operation of certain conventions and schemes. About one-third of secretariat staff are deployed at headquarters. The secretariat division, based in Brussels, Belgium, and employing most of the remaining staff, and assists member states on EEA matters. The Office of the Statistical Adviser is based in Luxembourg, and a Customs Officer is based in Paris, France. (Brussels division): 74 rue de Trèves, 1040 Brussels, Belgium; tel. (2) 286-17-11; fax (2) 286-17-50; e-mail mail.bxl@efta.int

Secretary-General: WILLIAM ROSSIER (Switzerland).

Activities

The creation of a single market including all the countries in Western Europe was the ultimate objective of EFTA when it was created in 1960. Member states were, however, not ready or able to accept the far-reaching political and economic implications of joining the EC, which was established in 1958. EFTA's first target, the creation of free trade in industrial goods between its members, was achieved by the end of 1966. By 1991 tariffs or import duties had been removed on all imports except agricultural products. The revised EFTA Convention that was adopted by member states in Vaduz, Liechtenstein, in June 2001, and entered into force in June 2002, provided for strengthened economic integration between the four countries.

EEA

In 1972 EFTA member states signed bilateral agreements with the EC, which established free trade in most industrial goods between them from 1 July 1977. The last restrictions on free industrial trade were abolished from 1 January 1984. In April of that year ministers from all EFTA and EC member countries agreed on general guidelines for developing the EFTA-EC relationship. Their Declaration (known as the Luxembourg Declaration) recommended intensified efforts to improve the free circulation of industrial products between their countries, and closer co-operation beyond the framework of the free-trade agreements, in fields such as education, the environment, social policy, and research and development. In March 1989 the EFTA heads of government issued a declaration reaffirming their commitment to establish a European Economic Area (EEA), consisting of all the member states of EFTA and the EC. Formal negotiations on the establishment of the EEA commenced in June 1990, and the Agreement was signed in Oporto, Portugal, in May 1992. In December a Swiss referendum voted to oppose ratification of the EEA treaty. The ministers of trade of the remaining 18 member countries, however, signed an adjustment protocol in March 1993, allowing the EEA to be established without Switzerland. The EEA entered into force on 1 January 1994. Liechtenstein joined the EEA on 1 May 1995, having amended its customs union agreement and secured the support of the majority of its population in a national referendum. The EEA Agreement provided for the removal of all restrictions on the movement of goods, persons, services and capital within the area, effectively extending the internal market of the EU to the three EFTA countries within the EEA. In addition, the Agreement provided for co-operation in areas such as the environment, social policy, education and training, tourism, culture, consumer protection and small and medium-sized enterprises. To main-

tain homogeneity within the EEA, the Agreement is amended on a continuous basis to ensure that relevant EU legislation is extended to the EFTA EEA grouping. Bilateral agreements on strengthening Switzerland–EU trade entered into force in June 2002. The revised EFTA Convention that entered into force in that month extended to Iceland, Liechtenstein and Norway the main provisions of these bilateral trade agreements. In January 2003 the EEA members states and the EU's ten candidate countries commenced negotiations on the enlargement of the EEA following the accession of the candidate countries to the EU (scheduled to take place on 1 May 2004 with the entry into force of the EU Accession Treaty, adopted in mid-April 2003). The legal text of the EEA Enlargement Instrument, including EEA-relevant technical adaptations and transitional arrangements, has been prepared on the basis of the EU Accession Treaty.

THIRD COUNTRY RELATIONS

In recent years EFTA developed an extensive network of contractual relations in central and eastern Europe and in the Mediterranean region. EFTA is currently in the process of extending the geographical scope of its third country relations, and has engaged in negotiations with other countries, and regional and sub-regional groupings, from beyond Europe and the Mediterranean. In a declaration adopted in Geneva in December 1999, to commemorate the 40th anniversary of EFTA's foundation, ministers reaffirmed their commitment to the further development of the Association's network of free-trade agreements, and indicated the potential for broadening the scope of the agreements to include fields such as services and investment, these being of growing importance in the increasingly interdependent global economy. The network was extended across the Atlantic by the declaration on trade and investment co-operation concluded with Mercosur in 2000 and the free-trade agreement concluded with Mexico in 2001 (see below); the latter was the most comprehensive agreement developed to date, covering areas including services and investment and public procurement.

EFTA has concluded free-trade agreements with: Turkey (in December 1991); with Czechoslovakia (March 1992) (with protocols on succession with the Czech Republic and Slovakia in April 1993); with Israel (September 1992); with Poland and Romania (December 1992); with Bulgaria and Hungary (March 1993); with Slovenia (July 1995); with Estonia, Latvia and Lithuania (December 1995); with Morocco (which was granted a 12-year transitional period to phase out customs duties) (June 1997); with the Palestinian National Authority (November 1998); with the former Yugoslav Republic of Macedonia (June 2000); with Mexico (July 2001); with Singapore (January 2003); and with Chile (March 2003). In addition, declarations on co-operation (with a view to securing a free-trade agreement) are in force with: Albania (signed in December 1992); with Egypt and Tunisia (December 1995); with Jordan and Lebanon (June 1997); with Croatia, Ukraine and the Co-operation Council for the Arab States of the Gulf (June 2000); with Serbia and Montenegro (then the Federal Republic of Yugoslavia) and Mercosur (the latter a declaration on trade and investment co-operation) (December 2000); and with Algeria (December 2002). In 2003 EFTA was to continue pursuing negotiations on free-trade agreements with Canada (initiated in 1998), Egypt, Lebanon, South Africa and Tunisia.

Although Portugal withdrew from EFTA in 1985, EFTA decided to maintain an industrial development fund (established in 1976) for that country, for the 25-year period originally foreseen.

Finance

Net budget for 2003: 21.0m. Swiss francs.

Publications

EFTA Annual Report.

EFTA Bulletin.

EFTA Traders' ABC (CD-Rom).

Factsheets, legal documents.

EUROPEAN SPACE AGENCY—ESA

Address: 8–10 rue Mario Nikis, 75738 Paris Cédex 15, France.
Telephone: 1-53-69-76-54; **fax:** 1-53-69-75-60; **e-mail:** contactesa@esa.int; **internet:** www.esa.int.

ESA was established in 1975 to provide for, and to promote, European co-operation in space research and technology, and their applications, for exclusively peaceful purposes. It replaced the European Space Research Organisation (ESRO) and the European Launcher Development Organisation (both founded in 1962)

MEMBERS*

Austria	Netherlands
Belgium	Norway
Denmark	Portugal
Finland	Spain
France	Sweden
Germany	Switzerland
Ireland	United Kingdom
Italy	

*Canada has signed an agreement for close co-operation with ESA, including representation on the ESA Council.

Organization

(April 2003)

Director-General: (until 30 June 2003) Antonio Rodotà (Italy), Jean-Jacques Dordain (from 1 July 2003).

COUNCIL

The Council is composed of representatives of all member states. It is responsible for formulating policy and meets at ministerial or delegate level.

PROGRAMME BOARDS AND COMMITTEES

The Council is assisted in its work by five specialized Programme Boards, which oversee the management of the following ESA activities: Communication Satellite Programmes; Satellite Navigation; Earth Observation; Human Spaceflight, Research and Applications; and Ariane Launcher. The other principal bodies of the ESA administrative structure are the Committees for Administration and Finance, Industrial Policy, Science Programme, International Relations, and Security.

ESA CENTRES

European Space Research and Technology Centre (ESTEC): Noordwijk, Netherlands. ESA's principal technical establishment, at which the majority of project teams are based, together with the space science department and the technological research and support engineers; provides the appropriate testing and laboratory facilities.

European Space Operations Centre (ESOC): Darmstadt, Germany. Responsible for all satellite operations and the corresponding ground facilities and communications networks.

European Space Research Institute (ESRIN): Frascati, Italy. Responsible for the corporate exploitation of Earth observation data from space.

European Astronaut Centre (EAC): Köln, Germany. As a subsidiary of the Directorate of Human Spaceflight, manages all European astronaut activities and trains European and international partner astronauts on the European elements of the International Space Station. The Centre employs 16 European astronauts.

ESA also helps to maintain the Space Centre at Kourou, French Guyana, which is used for the Ariane launchers.

ESA had some 1,870 permanent staff at March 2003.

Activities

ESA's tasks are to define and put into effect a long-term European space policy of scientific research and technological development and to encourage all members to co-ordinate their national programmes with those of ESA to ensure that Europe maintains a competitive position in the field of space technology. ESA's basic activities cover studies on future projects, technological research, shared technical investments, information systems and training programmes. These, and the science programme, are mandatory activities to which all members must contribute; other programmes are optional and members may determine their own level of participation. In November 2000 the ESA Council and the Council of the European Union adopted parallel resolutions endorsing a European strategy for space. The strategy, which had been jointly prepared in 1999 and was entitled *Europe and Space: A New Chapter*, aimed to strengthen the foundation for European space activities; advance scientific knowledge; and to use the technical capabilities developed in connection with space activities to secure wider economic and social benefits. ESA collaborated with the European Commision in the preparation of a Green Paper on EU Space Policy, which assessed Europe's strengths and weaknesses in the sector. Following a period of consultation and debate, a White Paper and action plan detailingconcrete proposals were to be drafted later in the year.

ESA is committed to pursuing international co-operation to achieve its objective of developing the peaceful applications of space technology. ESA works closely with both the US National Aeronautics and Space Administration (NASA) and the Russian Aviation and Space Agency (Rosaviakosmos). In February 2003 ESA and the Russian Government signed an Agreement on Co-operation and Partnership in the Exploration and Use of Outer Space for Peaceful Purposes (to be implemented by Rosaviakosmos), succeeding a similar agreement concluded with the USSR in 1990. In recent years ESA has developed a co-operative relationship with Japan, in particular in data relay satellites and the exchange of materials for the International Space Station. ESA has also concluded co-operation agreements with the Czech Republic, Greece, Hungary, Poland and Romania, providing for technical training and joint projects in the fields of space science, Earth observation and telecommunications. ESA assists other transitional and developing countries to expand their space activities. It works closely with other international organizations, in particular the European Union and EUMETSAT (q.v.). ESA has observer status with the UN Committee on the Peaceful Uses of Outer Space and co-operates closely with the UN's Office of Outer Space Affairs, in particular through the organization of a training and fellowship programme.

SCIENCE

The first European scientific space programmes were undertaken under the aegis of ESRO, which launched seven satellites during 1968–72. The Science Programme is a mandatory activity of the Agency and forms the basis of co-operation between member states. The first astronomical satellite (COS–B) was launched by ESA in August 1975. By March 2002 ESA had launched 17 scientific satellites and probes, among the most successful being the Giotto probe, launched in 1985 to study the composition of Halley's comet and reactivated in 1990 to observe the Grigg-Skjellerup comet in July 1992, and Hipparcos, which, between 1989 and 1993, determined the precise astronomic positions and distances of more than 1m. stars. In November 1995 ESA launched the Infrared Space Observatory, which has successfully conducted pre-planned scientific studies providing data on galaxy and star formation and on interstellar matter. ESA is collaborating with NASA in the Ulysses space project (a solar polar mission), the Solar and Helispheric Observatory (SOHO), launched in 1995 to study the internal structure of the sun, and the Hubble Space Telescope. In October 1997 the Huygens space probe was launched under the framework of a joint NASA–ESA project (the Cassini/Huygens mission) to study the planet Saturn and its largest moon, Titan, where it aims to land in 2004. In December 1999 the X-Ray Multimirror Mission (XMM–Newton) was launched from Kourou, French Guyana. It was envisaged that XMM–Newton, the most powerful x-ray telescope ever placed in orbit, would investigate the origin of galaxies, the formation of black holes, etc. Four cluster satellites, launched from Baikonur, Russia, in July/August 2000, were, in association with SOHO, to explore the interaction between the Earth's magnetic field and electrically-charged particles transported on the solar wind. In October 2002 INTEGRAL (International Gamma-Ray Astrophysical Laboratory) was successfully launched by a Russian Proton vehicle, to study the most violent events perceptible in the Universe.

ESA's space missions are an integral part of its long-term science programme, Horizon 2000, which was initiated in 1984. In 1994 a new set of missions was defined, to enable the inclusion of projects using new technologies and participation in future international space activities, which formed the Horizon 2000 Plus extension covering the period 2005–16. Together they were called Horizons 2000.

In May 2002 the Science Programme Committee initiated a new programme, COSMIC VISION, covering the period 2002–12. Under the programme three main projects—Astrophysics, Solar System Science, and Fundamental Physics—were to be developed in production groups, missions within each to be built synergistically, where possible using common technologies and engineering teams:

Astrophysics: Production Group 2: Herschel, exploring the infrared and microwave Universe; Planck, studying the cosmic microwave background; Eddington, searching for extra-solar planets and studying the stellar seismology. (These missions were to be launched during 2007–08.) Group 3: GAIA, the ultimate galaxy mapper (to be launched no later than 2012).

Solar System Science: Group 1: Rosetta, to 'rendez-vous' and land on a comet (launch date as yet undecided); Mars Express, a Mars orbiter carrying the Beagle2 lander (to be launched in 2003); Venus Express, a Venus orbiter (2005). Group 2: SMART-1, which was to demonstrate solar propulsion technology while on on course to the Moon (2003); BepiColombo, a mission to Mercury; Solar Orbiter to take a closer look at the Sun. (These missions were to be launched in 2011–12).

Fundamental Physics: SMART 2, a technology demonstration mission (to be launched in 2006); a joint mission with NASA, searching for gravitational waves (2011).

In addition, the Agency is committed to co-operation with NASA on JWST (James Webb Space Telescope), the successor of the Hubble Space telescope, scheduled to be launched in 2010. The Herschel Space Observatory, designed to investigate the formation of stars and galaxies, was scheduled to be launched in 2007.

EARTH OBSERVATION

ESA has contributed to the understanding and monitoring of the Earth's environment through its satellite projects. Since 1977 ESA has launched seven Meteosat spacecraft into geosynchronous orbit, which have provided continuous meteorological data, mainly for the purposes of weather forecasting. The Meteosat systems are financed and owned by EUMETSAT, but were operated by ESA until December 1995. ESA and EUMETSAT have collaborated on the development of a successor to the Meteosat weather satellites (Meteosat Second Generation—MSG) to provide enhanced geostationary data coverage. The first satellite, MSG-1, was launched in August 2002. ESA and EUMETSAT have also begun development of the METOP/EPS (EUMETSAT Polar System) programme, to provide observations from polar orbit. The first METOP satellite was scheduled for launch in 2005.

In 1991 ESA launched the ERS–1 satellite, which carried sophisticated instruments to measure the Earth's surface and its atmosphere. A second ERS satellite was launched in April 1995 with the specific purpose of measuring the stratospheric and tropospheric ozone. ENVISAT, the largest and most advanced European-built observation satellite, was launched in February 2002 from Kourou, French Guyana. ENVISAT aims to provide a detailed assessment of the impact of human activities on the Earth's atmosphere, and land and coastal processes, and to monitor exceptional natural events, such as volcanic eruptions.

In June 1998 the ESA Council approved the initiation of activities related to the Living Planet Programme, designed to increase understanding of environmental issues. In May 1999 the Council committed funds for a research mission, Cryosat, to be undertaken, in order to study the impact of global warming on polar ice caps. Cryosat was due to be launched in 2004. Future missions also include the Gravity Field and Steady-State Ocean Circulation Explorer (GOCE), scheduled to be launched in 2006; the GOCE mission was to use a unique measurement technique to recover geodetic precision data on the Earth's gravity field.

As part of the Treaty Enforcement Services using Earth Observation (TESEO) initiative, agreed in 2001, ESA satellites provide data for a wide range of environmental activities including monitoring wetlands, ensuring compliance with Kyoto Protocol emission targets and combatting desertification. Similarly, ESA has agreements with UNESCO to protect wildlife and sites of historic interest, in support of the Convention Concerning the Protection of the World Cultural and Natural Heritage.

TELECOMMUNICATIONS

ESA commenced the development of communications satellites in 1968. These have since become the largest markets for space use and have transformed global communications, with more than 100 satellites circling the Earth for the purposes of telecommunications. The main series of operational satellites developed by ESA are the European Communications Satellites (ECS), based on the original orbital test satellite and used by EUTELSAT, and the Maritime Communications Satellites (MARECS), which have been leased for operations to INMARSAT

In 1989 ESA launched an experimental civilian telecommunications satellite, Olympus, to develop and demonstrate new broadcasting services. An Advanced Relay and Technology Mission Satellite (ARTEMIS) has been developed by ESA to test and operate new telecommunications techniques, and in particular to enable the relay of information directly between satellites. ARTEMIS was launched in July 2001. In 1998 ESA, together with the EU and

EUROCONTROLcontinued to implement a satellite-based navigation system to be used for civilian aircraft and maritime services, similar to the two existing systems operational for military use. ESA was also working with the EU and representatives of the private sector to enhance the region's role in the development of electronic media infrastructure to meet the expanding global demand. In May 1999 the Council approved funding for a satellite multimedia programme, Artes 3, which aimed to support the development of satellite systems and services for delivering information through high-speed internet access.

NAVIGATION

ESA, in co-operation with the European Commission and Eurocontrol, is implementing the EGNOS System.. EGNOS is the European contribution to the Global Navigation Satellite System phase 1 (GNSS-1) and will provide an improved navigation and positioning service for all users of the (American) GPS and (Russian) GLONASS systems. EGNOS was to become operational in 2004, and was to serve as a major regional component of a seamless, world-wide augmentation system for navigation, aimed at meeting the demanding requirements for aircraft navigation, and comprising (in addition to EGNOS in Europe): WAAS in the USA, MSAS in Japan and GAGAN in India. ESA and the European Commission are also collaborating to design and develop a European satellite and navigation system, *Galileo.* The project will consist of about 30 satellites, a global network of tracking stations, and central control facilities in Europe. The satellites are due to be launched between 2005 and 2008, with an initial *Galileo* service to be available from 2006. The GNSS aims to use the *Galileo,* GPS and GLONASS systems to provide an integrated satellite navigation service of unprecedented accuracy and global coverage under civilian control.

LAUNCHERS

The European requirement for independent access to space first manifested itself in the early 1970s against the background of strategic and commercial interests in telecommunications and Earth observation. As a consequence, and based on knowledge gained through national programmes, ESA began development of a space launcher. The resulting Ariane rocket was first launched in December 1979. The project, which incorporated four different launchers; Ariane-1 to Ariane-4, subsequently became an essential element of ESA's programme activities and, furthermore, developed a successful commercial role in placing satellites into orbit. The last flight of Ariane-4 took place in February 2003. From 1985 ESA worked to develop the more powerful Ariane-5 launcher, which has been in commercial operation since 1999, launched from the ESA facility at the Guyana Space Centre. In December 2000 the ESA Council approved the Vega Small Launcher Development and the P80 Advanced Solid Propulsion Stage programmes. The first Vega launch is due to take place in mid-2006. A Future Launcher Preparatory Programme is being defined.

HUMAN SPACEFLIGHT

Europe has gained access to human space technology and operations through Spacelab, which ESA developed as the European contribution to the US Space Shuttle Programme, and through the two joint Euromir missions on the Russian space station, Mir. Spacelab has flown into space 25 times and, with the Euromir projects, has enabled ESA to conduct, using its own astronauts, research into life and physical sciences under microgravity conditions. Since the mid-1980s ESA has supported space research in the life and physicial sciences through its microgravity programmes. A considerable scientific output has been achieved in key areas such as crystal growth, solidification physics, fluid sciences, thermophysical properties, molecular and cell biology, developmental biology, exobiology and human physiology. The latest microgravity programme, approved in November 2001, is the ESA Programme in Life and Physical Sciences and Applications (ELIPS). ESA is a partner in the International Space Station (ISS), which was initiated by the US Government in 1984, and subsequently developed as a joint project between five partners-Canada, Europe, Japan, Russia and the USA. ESA's main contributions to the ISS are the Columbus Laboratory (due to be launched in 2004); and the Automated Transfer Vehicle—ATV (due to be launched by Ariane-5, with the first flight scheduled for 2004), which is to provide logistical support to the Space Station. The Columbus laboratory will accommodate European multi-user research facilities: Biolab; Fluid Science Laboratory, European Physiology Modules, Material Science Laboratory (all being developed within the Microgravity Facilities for the Columbus Programme); and European Drawer Rack and European Stowage Rack (both within the ISS Utilisation Programme). Once in orbit, Columbus will accommodate 10 active racks. In the framework of the ISS agreements with the USA, ESA is allocated 51% usage of Columbus, the other five racks being allocated to NASA. In addition to the experiment accommodation capabilities on Columbus, the European Zero-G Airbus, operated under ESA contract by Nove-space, provides European researchers short-duration access to microgravity conditions for a wide variety of experiments, ranging from precursor experiments for the ISS to student experiments. Droptowers and sounding rockets provide additional short-duration opportunities. The ESA Directorate of Human Spaceflight also provides European researchers with flight opportunities on unmanned Russian Foton and Bion capsules.

Finance

All member states contribute to ESA's mandatory programme activities, on a scale based on their national income, and are free to decide on their level of commitment in optional programmes, such as telecommunications, the Ariane project and future space station and platform projects. The 2003 budget amounted to about €2,700m., including 23.5% for launchers, 22.2% for human spaceflight, 13.5% for space science, 13.4 % for earth observation, 5.5% for telecommunications, and 2% for navigation.

Publications

ESA Annual Report.
ESA Bulletin (quarterly).
EDUnews.
Earth Observation Quarterly.
On Station.
Reaching for the Skies (quarterly).
PFF—Preparing for the Future.
CONNECT.
Spacelink (newsletter).
Eurocomp (newsletter).
ECSL News.
Monographs and conference proceedings.

THE EUROPEAN UNION—EU

The European Coal and Steel Community (ECSC) was created by a treaty signed in Paris on 18 April 1951 (effective from 25 July 1952) to pool the coal and steel production of the six original members (see below). It was seen as a first step towards a united Europe. The European Economic Community (EEC) and European Atomic Energy Community (Euratom) were established by separate treaties signed in Rome on 25 March 1957 (effective from 1 January 1958), the former to create a common market and to approximate economic policies, the latter to promote growth in nuclear industries. The common institutions of the three Communities were established by a treaty signed in Brussels on 8 April 1965 (effective from 1 July 1967).

The EEC was formally changed to the European Community (EC) under the Treaty on European Union (effective from 1 November 1993), although in practice the term EC had been used for several years to describe the three Communities together. The new Treaty established a European Union (EU), which introduced citizenship thereof and aimed to increase intergovernmental co-operation in economic and monetary affairs; to establish a common foreign and security policy; and to introduce co-operation in justice and home affairs. The EU was placed under the supervision of the European Council (comprising Heads of State or Government of member countries), while the EC continued to exist, having competence in matters relating to the Treaty of Rome and its amendments.

The Treaty of Paris establishing the ECSC expired on 23 July 2002. A series of events and ceremonies were held to mark the occasion, including a symposium on the history and future of the EU. Upon expiry of the Treaty, which resulted in the termination of the ECSC legal regime and procedures and the dissolution of the ECSC Consultative Committee, the ECSC's assets and liabilities were transferred to the overall EU budget, while rights and obligations arising from international agreements drawn up between the ECSC and third countries were to be devolved to the EC.

No final decision has been made on a headquarters for the Union. Meetings of the principal organs take place in Brussels, Luxembourg and Strasbourg.

MEMBERS

Austria	Germany*	Netherlands*
Belgium*	Greece	Portugal
Denmark	Ireland	Spain
Finland	Italy*	Sweden
France*	Luxembourg*	United Kingdom

*Original members. Denmark, Ireland and the United Kingdom joined on 1 January 1973, and Greece on 1 January 1981. In a referendum held in February 1982, the inhabitants of Greenland voted to end their membership of the Community, entered into when under full Danish rule. Greenland's withdrawal took effect from 1 February 1985. Portugal and Spain became members on 1 January 1986. Following the reunification of Germany in October 1990, the former German Democratic Republic immediately became part of the Community, although a transitional period was to be allowed before certain Community legislation took effect there. Austria, Finland and Sweden became members on 1 January

1995. In October 2002 the European Council confirmed that 10 candidate countries (Cyprus, Czech Republic, Estonia, Hungary, Latvia, Lithuania, Malta, Poland, Slovakia and Slovenia) fulfilled the political criteria and would be able to fulfil the economic criteria for membership from the beginning of 2004. The accession negotiations were concluded at the Copenhagen summit in December 2003, and the Accession Treaty was signed in Athens in April 2003.

PERMANENT REPRESENTATIVES OF MEMBER STATES

Austria: GREGOR WOSCHNAGG, 30 ave de Cortenbergh, 1040 Brussels; tel. (2) 234-53-00; fax (2) 235-63-00; e-mail austria.press@pophost.eunet.be.

Belgium: JAN DE BOCK, Rond-point Schuman 6, 1040 Brussels; tel. (2) 233-21-11; fax (2) 231-10-75; e-mail belgoeurop@skynet.be.

Denmark: POUL SKYTTE CHRISTOFFERSEN, 73 rue d'Arlon, 1040 Brussels; tel. (2) 233-08-11; fax (2) 230-93-84; e-mail brurep@um.dk.

Finland: EIKKA KOSONEN, 100 rue de Trèves, 1040 Brussels; tel. (2) 287-84-11; fax (2) 287-84-00; e-mail press.eue@formin.fi; internet www.uunet.be/finland/.

France: PIERRE SELLAL, 14 place de Louvain, 1000 Brussels; tel. (2) 229-82-11; fax (2) 229-82-82; e-mail firstname.lastname@diplomatie.fr; internet www.rpfrance.org.

Germany: Dr WILHELM SCHÖNFELDER, 19-21 rue J. de Lalaing, 1040 Brussels; tel. (2) 238-18-11; fax (2) 238-19-78.

Greece: ARISTIDE AGATHOCLES, 25 rue Montoyer, 1000 Brussels; tel. (2) 551-56-11; fax (2) 551-56-51; e-mail mea.bruxelles@rp-grece.be.

Ireland: ANNE ANDERSON, 89-93 rue Froissart, 1040 Brussels; tel. (2) 230-85-80; fax (2) 230-32-03; e-mail reppermirl@online.be.

Italy: UMBERTO VATTANI, 9–11 rue du Marteau, 1000 Brussels; tel. (2) 220-04-11; fax (2) 219-34-49; e-mail rpue@rpue.it; internet www.rpue.it.

Luxembourg: NICOLAS SCHMIT, 75 ave de Cortenbergh, 1000 Brussels; tel. (2) 737-56-00; fax (2) 737-56-10; e-mail secretariat@rpue.etat.lu.

Netherlands: T. J. A. M. DE BRUIJN, 48 ave Herrmann Debroux, 1160 Brussels; tel. (2) 679-15-11; fax (2) 679-17-75.

Portugal: ALVARO MENDONÇA E MOURA, 12 ave de Cortenbergh, 1040 Brussels; tel. (2) 286-42-00; fax (2) 231-00-26; e-mail reper@reper.portugal.be.

Spain: CARLOS BASTARRECHE SAGÜES, 52 blvd du Régent, 1000 Brussels; tel. (2) 509-86-11; fax (2) 511-19-40.

Sweden: SVEN-OLOF PETERSSON, 30 square de Meeûs, 1000 Brussels; tel. (2) 289-56-00; fax (2) 289-56-00; e-mail representationen.bryssel@foreign.ministry.se.

United Kingdom: Sir NIGEL SHEINWALD (until Aug. 2003), JOHN GRANT (designate), 10 ave d'Auderghem, 1040 Brussels; tel. (2) 287-82-11; fax (2) 287-83-98; internet ukrep.fco.gov.uk.

PERMANENT MISSIONS TO THE EUROPEAN UNION
(April 2003)

Afghanistan: 32 ave Raphaël, 75016 Paris, France; tel. 1-45-25-05-29; fax 1-45-24-46-87; Chargé d'affaires a.i. MEHRABODIN MASSTAN.

Albania: 42 rue Alphonse Hottat, 1050 Brussels; tel. (2) 640-35-44; fax (2) 640-31-77; e-mail amba.brux@skynet.be; Ambassador FERIT HOXHA.

Algeria: 209 ave Molière, 1050 Brussels; tel. (2) 343-50-78; fax (2) 343-51-68; e-mail info@algerian-embassy.be; internet www.algerian-embassy.be.htm; Ambassador HALIM BENATTALLAH.

Andorra: 10 rue de la Montagne, 1000 Brussels; tel. (2) 513-28-06; fax (2) 513-07-41; e-mail ambassade@andorra.be; Ambassador MERITXELL MATEU I PI.

Angola: 182 rue Franz Merjay, 1180 Brussels; tel. (2) 346-18-80; fax (2) 344-08-94; Ambassador ARMANDO MATEUS CADETE.

Argentina: 225 ave Louise (7e étage), Boîte 2, 1050 Brussels; tel. (2) 648-93-71; fax (2) 648-08-04; Ambassador JUAN JOSÉ URANGA.

Armenia: 157 rue Franz Merjay, 1060 Brussels; tel. and fax (2) 346-56-67; Ambassador V. CHITECHIAN.

Australia: 6-8 rue Guimard, 1040 Brussels; tel. (2) 286-05-00; fax (2) 230-68-02; e-mail pub.affs.brussels@dfat.gov.au; internet www.austemb.be; Ambassador JOANNA HEWITT.

Bahamas: 10 Chesterfield St, London, W1J 5JL, United Kingdom; tel. (20) 7408-4488; fax (20) 7499-9937; e-mail information@bahamashclondon.net; Ambassador BASIL G. O'BRIEN.

Bangladesh: 29-31 rue Jacques Jordaens, 1000 Brussels; tel. (2) 640-55-00; fax (2) 646-59-98; Ambassador MUHAMMAD ZAMIR.

Barbados: 100 ave F. D. Roosevelt, 1050 Brussels; tel. (2) 732-17-37; fax (2) 732-32-66; e-mail brussels@foreign.gov.bb; internet www.foreign.barbadosgov.org; Ambassador ERROL L. HUMPHREY.

Belize: 100 rue des Aduatiques, 1040 Brussels; tel. (2) 732-62-04; fax (2) 732-62-46; e-mail ecs.embassies@skynet.be; Ambassador YVONNE HYDE.

Benin: 5 ave de l'Observatoire, 1180 Brussels; tel. (2) 375-06-74; fax (2) 375-83-26; Ambassador EULOGE HINVI.

Bhutan: 17-19 chemin du Champ d'Anier, 1209 Geneva, Switzerland; tel. (22) 7990890; fax (22) 7990899; e-mail mission.bhutan.ties.itu.int; Ambassador BAP KESANG.

Bolivia: 176 ave Louise, Boîte 6, 1050 Brussels; tel. (2) 627-00-10; fax (2) 647-47-82; e-mail embajada.bolivia@embolbrus.be; Ambassador ARTURO SUÁREZ VARGAS.

Bosnia and Herzegovina: 9 rue Paul Lauters, 1000 Brussels; tel. (2) 644-00-47; fax (2) 644-16-98; e-mail mission.bih.brussels@euronet.be; Ambassador VITOMIR MILES RAGUZ.

Botswana: 169 ave de Tervuren, 1150 Brussels; tel. (2) 735-20-70; fax (2) 735-63-18; Ambassador SASALA CHASALA GEORGE.

Brazil: 30 ave F.D. Roosevelt, 1050 Brussels; tel. (2) 640-20-40; fax (2) 648-80-40; e-mail missao@braseuropa.be; Ambassador JOSÉ ALFREDO GRAÇA LIMA.

Brunei: 238 ave F. D. Roosevelt, 1050 Brussels; tel. (2) 675-08-78; fax (2) 672-93-58; e-mail kedutaan-brunei.brussels@skynet.be; Ambassador PENGIRAN MASHOR AHMAD.

Bulgaria: 7 ave Moscicki, 1180 Brussels; tel. (2) 374-84-68; fax (2) 374-91-88; e-mail missionlog@village.eunet.be; Ambassador ANTOINETTE PRIMATAROVA.

Burkina Faso: 16 place Guy d'Arezzo, 1180 Brussels; tel. (2) 345-99-12; fax (2) 345-06-12; e-mail ambassade.burkina@skynet.be; Ambassador KADRÉ DÉSIRÉ OUÉDRAOGO.

Burundi: 46 square Marie-Louise, 1040 Brussels; tel. (2) 230-45-35; fax (2) 230-78-83; e-mail ambassade.burundi@skynet.be; internet www.burundi.gov.bi; Ambassador JONATHAS NIYUNGEKO.

Cameroon: 131-133 ave Brugmann, 1190 Brussels; tel. (2) 345-18-70; fax (2) 344-57-35; Ambassador ISABELLE BASSONG.

Canada: 2 ave de Tervuren, 1040 Brussels; tel. (2) 741-06-60; fax (2) 741-06-29; e-mail breec@dfait-maeci.gc.ca; internet www.dfait-maeci.gc.ca/eu-mission; Ambassador JEREMY KINSMAN.

Cape Verde: 29 ave Jeanne, 1050 Brussels; tel. (2) 643-62-70; fax (2) 646-33-85; e-mail emb.caboverde@skynet.be; Ambassador FERNANDO WAHNON FERREIRA.

Central African Republic: 416 blvd Lambermont, 1030 Brussels; tel. (2) 242-28-80; fax (2) 215-13-11; Ambassador ARMAND GUY ZOUNGUERE-SOKAMBI.

Chad: 52 blvd Lambermont, 1030 Brussels; tel. (2) 215-19-75; fax (2) 216-35-26; Ambassador ABDERAHIM YACOUB N'DIAYE.

Chile: 13 blvd St Michel, 1040 Brussels; tel. (2) 743-36-60; fax (2) 736-49-94; e-mail misue@misionchile-ue.org; Ambassador ALBERTO VAN KLAVEREN.

China, People's Republic: 443-445 ave de Tervueren, 1150 Brussels; tel. (2) 771-33-09; fax (2) 779-28-95; Ambassador SONG MINGJIANG.

Colombia: 96A ave F.D. Roosevelt, 1050 Brussels; tel. (2) 649-56-79; fax (2) 646-54-91; e-mail colombia@emcolbru.org; Ambassador ROBERT ARENAS BONILLA.

Comoros: 128 ave Paul Hymans, 1200 Brussels; tel. (2) 779-58-38; fax (2) 779-58-38; e-mail ambacom.bxl@skynet.be; Ambassador SULTAN CHOUZOUR.

Congo, Democratic Republic: 30 rue Marie de Bourgogne, 1040 Brussels; tel. (2) 513-66-10; fax (2) 514-04-03; Ambassador MAHAMOUD SOILIH.

Congo, Republic: 16-18 ave F. D. Roosevelt, 1050 Brussels; tel. (2) 648-38-56; fax (2) 648-42-13; Ambassador JACQUES OBIA.

Costa Rica: 489 ave Louise (4e étage), 1050 Brussels; tel. (2) 640-55-41; fax (2) 648-31-92; e-mail embcrbel@infonie.be; Ambassador MARIO FERNÁNDEZ-SILVA.

Côte d'Ivoire: 234 ave F. D. Roosevelt, 1050 Brussels; tel. (2) 672-95-77; fax (2) 672-04-91; Ambassador MARIE GOSSET.

Croatia: 50 ave des Arts, Boîte 14, 1000 Brussels; tel. (2) 500-09-20; fax (2) 512-03-38; Ambassador ŽELJKO MATIĆ.

Cuba: 77 rue Robert Jones, 1180 Brussels; tel. (2) 343-00-20; fax (2) 344-96-91; Ambassador RENÉ MUJICA CANTELAR.

Cyprus: 2 square Ambiorix, 1000 Brussels; tel. (2) 735-35-10; fax (2) 735-45-52; e-mail cyprus.embassy@skynet.be; Ambassador K. KORNELIOU.

Czech Republic: 15 rue Caroly, 1050 Brussels; tel. (2) 213-01-11; fax (2) 213-01-85; e-mail eu.brussels@embassy.mzv.cz; Ambassador PAVEL TELIČKA.

Djibouti: 26 rue Emile-Menier, 75116 Paris, France; tel. 1-47-27-49-22; fax 1-45-53-52-53; Ambassador MOHAMED MOUSSA CHEHEM.

Dominica: 42 rue de Livourne, 1000 Brussels; tel. (2) 534-26-11; fax (2) 539-40-09; e-mail ecs.embassies@skynet.be; Ambassador EDWIN P. J. LAURENT.

Dominican Republic: 12 ave Bel Air, 1180 Brussels; tel. (2) 346-49-35; fax (2) 346-51-52; Ambassador CLARA JOSELYN QUIÑONES RODRÍGUEZ.

Ecuador: 363 ave Louise, 1050 Brussels; tel. (2) 644-30-50; fax (2) 644-28-13; Ambassador ALFREDO PINOARGOTE CEVALLOS.

Egypt: 44 ave Léo Errera, 1180 Brussels; tel. (2) 345-52-53; fax (2) 343-65-33; Ambassador MUHAMMAD CHABANE.

El Salvador: 171 ave de Tervueren, 1150 Brussels; tel. (2) 733-04-85; fax (2) 735-02-11; Ambassador JOAQUÍN RODEZNA MUNGUIA.

Equatorial Guinea: 17 ave Jupiter, 1190 Brussels; tel. (2) 346-25-09; fax (2) 346-33-09; e-mail guineaecuatorial.brux@skynet.be; Ambassador AURÉLIO MBA OLO ANDEME.

Eritrea: 15-17 ave de Wolvendael, 1180 Brussels; tel. (2) 374-44-34; fax (2) 372-07-30; e-mail eebb@pophost.eunet.be; Ambassador ANDEBRHAN WELDEGIORGIS.

Estonia: 1-3 rue Marie-Thérèse, 1000 Brussels; tel. (2) 227-39-10; fax (2) 227-39-25; e-mail eu.all@eu.estemb.be; Ambassador VÄINO REINART.

Ethiopia: 231 ave de Tervueren, Brussels; tel. (2) 771-32-94; fax (2) 771-49-14; Ambassador PETER GABRIEL ROBLEH.

Fiji: 66 ave de Cortenbergh (7e étage), Boîte 7, 1000 Brussels; tel. (2) 736-90-50; fax (2) 736-14-58; e-mail info@fijiembassy.be; internet www.fijiembassy.be; Ambassador ISIKELI ULUINAIRAI MATAITOGA.

Gabon: 112 ave Winston Churchill, 1180 Brussels; tel. (2) 340-62-10; fax (2) 346-46-69; e-mail bs.175335@skynet.be; Ambassador RENÉ MAKONGO.

The Gambia: 126 ave F. D. Roosevelt, 1050 Brussels; tel. (2) 640-10-49; fax (2) 646-32-77; e-mail gambianmission@hotmail.com; Ambassador ALIEU M. NGUM.

Georgia: 15 rue Vergote, 1030 Brussels; tel. (2) 732-85-50; fax (2) 732-85-47; e-mail geoemb.bru@skynet.be; Ambassador KONSTANTIN ZALDASTANISHVILI.

Ghana: 7 blvd Gén. Wahis, 1030 Brussels; tel. (2) 705-82-20; fax (2) 705-66-53; e-mail head@ghembassy.arc.be; internet www.ghanabru.net; Ambassador NANA OYE-MANSA YEBOOAA I DOMPIAHENE.

Grenada: 123 rue de Laeken, 1000 Brussels; tel. (2) 223-73-03; fax (2) 223-73-07; Ambassador FABIAN A. REDHEAD.

Guatemala: 185 ave Winston Churchill, 1180 Brussels; tel. (2) 345-90-58; fax (2) 344-64-99; e-mail obguab@infoboard.be; Ambassador EDMOND MULET LESIEUR.

Guinea: 75 ave Roger Vandendriessche, 1150 Brussels; tel. (2) 771-01-26; fax (2) 762-60-36; Ambassador KAZALIOU BALDE.

Guinea-Bissau: 70 ave F. D. Roosevelt, 1050 Brussels; tel. (2) 647-08-90; fax (2) 640-43-12; Chargé d'affaires a.i. JOSÉ FONSECA.

Guyana: 12 ave du Brésil, 1000 Brussels; tel. (2) 675-62-16; fax (2) 675-55-98; e-mail embassy.guyana@skynet.be; Ambassador KENNETH F. S. KING.

Haiti: 139 Chaussée de Charleroi, 1060 Brussels; tel. (2) 649-73-81; fax (2) 640-60-80; e-mail amb.haiti.bel@skynet.be; Ambassador YOLETTE AZOR-CHARLES.

Holy See: 5-9 ave des Franciscains, 1150 Brussels; tel. (2) 762-20-05; fax (2) 762-20-32; Apostolic Nuncio Most Rev. PIER LUIGI CELATA (Titular Archbishop of Doclea).

Honduras: 3 ave des Gaulois (5e étage), 1040 Brussels; tel. (2) 734-00-00; fax (2) 735-26-26; e-mail ambassade.honduras@chello.com; Ambassador TEODOLINDA BANEGAS DE MAKRIS.

Hungary: 44 ave du Vert Chasseur, 1180 Brussels; tel. (2) 379-09-00; fax (2) 372-07-84; e-mail titkarsag@humisbeu.be; internet www.humiseu.be; Ambassador ENDRE JUHÁSZ.

Iceland: 74 rue de Trèves, 1040 Brussels; tel. (2) 286-17-00; fax (2) 286-17-70; e-mail icemb.brussel@utn.stjr.is; internet www.iceland.org/be; Ambassador KJARTAN JÓHANNSSON.

India: 217 chaussée de Vleurgat, 1050 Brussels; tel. (2) 640-91-40; fax (2) 648-96-38; e-mail info@indembassy.be; internet www.indembassy.be; Ambassador C. DASGUPTA.

Indonesia: 38 blvd de la Woluwe, 1200 Brussels; tel. (2) 779-09-15; fax (2) 772-82-10; Ambassador POEDJI KOENTARSO.

Iran: 415 ave de Tervueren, 1150 Brussels; tel. (2) 762-37-45; fax (2) 762-39-15; e-mail eiri.bxl@skynet.be; Ambassador ABOLGHASEM DELFI.

Iraq: 23 ave des Aubépines, 1180 Brussels; tel. (2) 374-59-92; fax (2) 374-76-15; e-mail ambassade.irak@skynet.be; Chargé d'affaires a.i. Dr RIADH AL-WEYESAHDI S. HAMOUDI.

Israel: 40 ave de l'Observatoire, 1180 Brussels; tel. (2) 373-55-00; fax (2) 373-56-17; e-mail parl-eu@brussels.mfa.gov.il; Ambassador HARRY KNEY-TAL.

Jamaica: 2 ave Palmerston, 1000 Brussels; tel. (2) 230-11-70; fax (2) 230-37-09; e-mail emb.jam.brussels@skynet.be; Ambassador EVADNE COYE.

Japan: 5-6 Sq. de Meeûs, 1000 Brussels; tel. (2) 500-77-11; fax (2) 513-32-41; e-mail inf@jmission-eu-be; internet www.jmission-eu.be; Ambassador TAKAYUKI KIMURA.

Jordan: 104 ave F. D. Roosevelt, 1050 Brussels; tel. (2) 640-77-55; fax (2) 640-27-96; Ambassador Dr UMAYYA TOUKAN.

Kazakhstan: 30 ave Van Bever, 1180 Brussels; tel. (2) 374-95-62; fax (2) 374-50-91; Ambassador AKHMETZHAN S. YESIMOV.

Kenya: 208 ave Winston Churchill, 1180 Brussels; tel. (2) 340-10-40; fax (2) 340-10-50; e-mail kenbrussels@hotmail.com; Ambassador PETER OLE NKURAIYIA.

Kiribati: c/o Ministry of Foreign Affairs, POB 68, Bairiki, Tarawa; tel. 21342; fax 21466.

Korea, Republic: 173-175 chaussée de la Hulpe, 1170 Brussels; tel. (2) 675-57-77; fax (2) 675-52-21; Ambassador LEE JAI-CHUN.

Kuwait: 43 ave F. D. Roosevelt, 1050 Brussels; tel. (2) 647-79-50; fax (2) 646-12-98; e-mail embassy.kwt@euronet.be; Ambassador ABDULAZEEZ A. AL-SHARIKH.

Kyrgyzstan: 133 rue Tenbosch, 1050 Brussels; tel. (2) 534-63-99; fax (2) 534-23-25; Ambassador CHINGIZ TOREKULOVICH AITMATOV.

Laos: 74 ave Raymond Poincaré, 75116 Paris, France; tel. 1-45-53-02-98; fax 1-47-57-27-89; Ambassador KHAMPHAN SIMMALAVONG.

Latvia: 39-41 rue d'Arlon, Boîte 6, 1000 Brussels; tel. (2) 282-03-60; fax (2) 282-03-69; e-mail missioneu@mfa.gov.lv; Ambassador ANDRIS PIEBALGS.

Lebanon: 2 rue Guillaume Stocq, 1050 Brussels; tel. (2) 645-77-60; fax (2) 645-77-69; Ambassador FAWZI FAWAZ.

Lesotho: 45 blvd Général Wahis, 1030 Brussels; tel. (2) 705-39-76; fax (2) 705-67-79; e-mail lesothobruemb@skynet.be; Ambassador MOLIEHI MATHATO ADEL MATLANYANE.

Liberia: 50 ave du Château, 1081 Brussels; tel. (2) 414-73-17; fax (2) 411-09-12; Ambassador Dr CECIL T. O. BRANDY.

Libya: 28 ave Victoria, 1050 Brussels; tel. (2) 649-21-12; Ambassador HAMED AHMED ELHOUDERI.

Liechtenstein: 1 Place du Congrès, 1000 Brussels; tel. (2) 229-39-00; fax (2) 219-35-45; e-mail ambassade.liechtenstein@bbru.llv.li; Ambassador Prince NIKOLAUS VON LIECHTENSTEIN.

Lithuania: 5 rue Belliard, 1040 Brussels; tel. (2) 771-01-40; fax (2) 771-45-97; e-mail office@lt-mission-eu.be; internet http://users.skynet.be/lt-mission-eu; Ambassador OSKARAS JUSYS.

Macedonia, former Yugoslav republic: 128 ave de Tervueren, 1150 Brussels; tel. (2) 732-91-08; fax (2) 732-91-11; Ambassador SASKO STEFKOV.

Madagascar: 276 ave de Tervueren, 1150 Brussels; tel. (2) 770-17-26; fax (2) 772-37-31; e-mail pierre.rabarivola@ambassademadagascar.be; internet www.ambassademadagascar.be; Ambassador Dr PIERRE RABARIVOLA.

Malawi: 15 rue de la Loi, 1040 Brussels; tel. (2) 231-09-80; fax (2) 231-10-66; Ambassador JERRY ALEXANDER ALIKOPAGA JANA.

Malaysia: 414A ave de Tervueren, 1150 Brussels; tel. (2) 776-03-40; fax (2) 762-67-67; e-mail embassy.malaysia@euronet.be; Ambassador Dato' M. M. SATHIAH.

Maldives: 212 East 47th St, Apt 15B, New York, NY 10017, USA; tel. (212) 688-0776.

Mali: 487 ave Molière, 1050 Brussels; tel. (2) 345-74-32; fax (2) 344-57-00; Ambassador AHMED MOHAMED AG HAMANI.

Malta: 44 rue Jules Lejeune, 1050 Brussels; tel. (2) 343-01-95; fax (2) 343-01-06; Ambassador VICTOR CAMILLERI.

Mauritania: 6 ave de la Colombie, 1050 Brussels; tel. (2) 672-47-47; fax (2) 672-20-51; Ambassador MOHAMED SALEM OULD LEKHAL.

Mauritius: 68 rue des Bollandistes, 1040 Brussels; tel. (2) 733-99-88; fax (2) 734-40-21; e-mail ambmaur@skynet.be; Ambassador S. GUNESSEE.

Mexico: 94 ave F.D. Roosevelt, 1050 Brussels; tel. (2) 629-07-11; fax (2) 644-08-19; e-mail mex-ue@pophost.eunet.be; Ambassador PORFIRIO MUÑOZ-LEDO Y LAZO DE LA VEGA.

Mongolia: 18 ave Besme, 1190 Brussels; tel. (2) 344-69-74; fax (2) 344-32-15; e-mail brussels.mn.embassy@chello.be; Ambassador SODOV ONON.

Morocco: 275 ave Louise, 1050 Brussels; tel. (2) 736-11-00; fax (2) 734-64-68; e-mail sifamabruxe@infoboard.be; Chargé d'affaires a.i. AICHA BELARBI SAUBRY.

Mozambique: 97 blvd Saint-Michel, 1040 Brussels; tel. (2) 736-25-64; fax (2) 735-62-07; e-mail embamoc.bru@skynet.be; Ambassador ALVARO MANUEL TRINIDADE DA SILVA.

Myanmar: Schumannstrasse 112, 53113 Bonn, Germany; tel. (228) 210091; fax (228) 219316; Ambassador U TUN NGWE.

Namibia: 454 ave de Tervueren, 1150 Brussels; tel. (2) 771-14-10; fax (2) 771-96-89; e-mail nam.emb@brutele.be; Ambassador Dr ZEDEKIA JOSEF NGAVIRUE.

Nepal: 68 ave Winston Churchill, 1180 Brussels; tel. (2) 346-26-58; fax (2) 344-13-61; e-mail rne.bru@skynet.be; Ambassador NARAYAN S. THAPA.

New Zealand: 1 square de Meeûs, 1000 Brussels; tel. (2) 512-10-40; fax (2) 513-48-56; e-mail nzemb.brussels@skynet.be; Ambassador DELL HIGGIE.

Nicaragua: 55 ave de Wolvendael, 1180 Brussels; tel. (2) 375-64-34; fax (2) 375-71-88; Ambassador ALVARO PORTA BERMÚDEZ.

Niger: 78 ave F. D. Roosevelt, 1050 Brussels; tel. (2) 648-61-40; fax (2) 648-27-84; Ambassador HOUSSEINI ABDOU-SALEYE.

Nigeria: 288 ave de Tervueren, 1150 Brussels; tel. (2) 762-52-00; fax (2) 762-37-63; Ambassador GABRIEL SAM AKUNWAFOR.

Norway: 17 rue Archimède, 1000 Brussels; tel. (2) 234-11-11; fax (2) 234-11-50; Ambassador EINAR M. BULL.

Oman: 50 ave d'Iéna, 75116 Paris, France; tel. 1-47-23-01-63; fax 1-47-23-77-10; Ambassador MUHAMMAD BIN SULTAN AL-BUSAIDI.

Pakistan: 57 ave Delleur, 1170 Brussels; tel. (2) 673-80-07; fax (2) 675-83-94; e-mail parepbru_econ@infoboard.be; Ambassador SAIDULLA KHAN DEHLAVI.

Panama: 390-392 ave Louise, 1050 Brussels; tel. (2) 649-07-29; fax (2) 648-92-16; e-mail panama@antrasite.be; Chargé d'affaires a.i. ELENA BARLETTA DE NOTTEBOHM.

Papua New Guinea: 430 ave de Tervueren, 1150 Brussels; tel. (2) 779-08-26; fax (2) 772-70-88; Ambassador GABRIEL KOIBA PEPSON.

Paraguay: 475 ave Louise (12e étage), 1050 Brussels; tel. (2) 649-90-55; fax (2) 647-42-48; Ambassador MANUEL MARÍA CÁCERES.

Peru: 179 ave de Tervueren, 1150 Brussels; tel. (2) 733-33-19; fax (2) 733-48-19; e-mail comunicaciones@embassy-of-peru.be; Ambassador JOSÉ URRUTIA.

Philippines: 297 ave Molière, 1050 Brussels; tel. (2) 340-33-77; fax (2) 345-64-25; e-mail pleu.pe@skynet.be; internet www.philembassy.be; Ambassador CLEMENCIO F. MONTESA.

Poland: 282-284 ave de Tervueren, 1150 Brussels; tel. (2) 777-72-00; fax (2) 777-72-97; e-mail mail@pol-mission-eu.be; internet www.pol-mission.eu.be; Ambassador MAREK GRELA.

Qatar: 71 ave F. D. Roosevelt, 1050 Brussels; tel. (2) 640-29-00; fax (2) 648-40-78; e-mail qatar@infonie.be; Chargé d'affaires a.i. MOHAMED AL-HAIYKI.

Romania: 107 rue Gabrielle, 1180 Brussels; tel. (2) 344-41-45; fax 344-24-79; e-mail rommis@pophost.eunet.be; internet www.roumisue.org; Ambassador LAZAR COMANESCU.

Russia: 56 ave Louis Lepoutre, 1060 Brussels; tel. (2) 343-03-39; fax (2) 346-24-53; e-mail misrusce@interpac.be; Ambassador VASILII LIKHACHEN.

Rwanda: 1 ave des Fleurs, 1150 Brussels; tel. (2) 763-07-02; fax (2) 763-07-53; e-mail ambarwanda.@skynet.be; internet www.ambarwanda.be; Ambassador JACQUES BIHOZAGARA.

Saint Christopher and Nevis: 42 rue de Livourne, 1000 Brussels; tel. (2) 534-26-11; fax (2) 539-40-09; e-mail ecs.embassies@skynet.be; Ambassador EDWIN P. J. LAURENT.

Saint Lucia: 42 rue de Livourne, 1000 Brussels; tel. (2) 534-26-11; fax (2) 539-40-09; e-mail ecs.embassies@skynet.be; Ambassador EDWIN P. J. LAURENT.

Saint Vincent and the Grenadines: 42 rue de Livourne, 1000 Brussels; tel. (2) 534-26-11; fax (2) 539-40-09; e-mail ecs.embassies@skynet.be; Ambassador EDWIN P. J. LAURENT.

Samoa: 123 ave F. D. Roosevelt, Boîte 14, 1050 Brussels; tel. (2) 660-84-54; fax (2) 675-03-36; e-mail samoa.emb.bxl@skynet.be; Ambassador TAUILIILI UILI MEREDITH.

San Marino: 62 ave F.D. Roosevelt, 1050 Brussels; tel. (2) 644-22-24; fax (2) 644-20-57; Ambassador SAVINA ZAFFERANI.

São Tomé and Príncipe: 175 ave de Tervueren, 1150 Brussels; tel. and fax (2) 734-88-15; e-mail ambassade.sao.tome@skynet.be; Chargé d'affaires a.i. ARMINDO DE BRITO FERNANDES.

Saudi Arabia: 45 ave F. D. Roosevelt, 1050 Brussels; tel. (2) 649-20-44; fax (2) 647-24-92; Ambassador NASSIR AL-ALASSAF.

Senegal: 196 ave F. D. Roosevelt, 1050 Brussels; tel. (2) 673-00-97; fax (2) 675-04-60; Ambassador SALIOU CISSE.

Serbia and Montenegro: 11 ave Emile Demot, 1000 Brussels; tel. (2) 649-83-65; fax (2) 649-08-78; Ambassador DRAGOSLAV JOVANOVIĆ.

Seychelles: 51 ave Mozart, 75016 Paris, France; tel. 1-42-30-57-47; fax 1-42-30-57-40; e-mail ambsey@aol.com; Ambassador CALLIXTE FRANÇOIS-XAVIER D'OFFAY.

Sierra Leone: 410 ave de Tervueren, 1150 Brussels; tel. (2) 771-00-53; fax (2) 771-82-30; Ambassador FODE M. DABOR.

Singapore: 198 ave F. D. Roosevelt, 1050 Brussels; tel. (2) 660-29-79; fax (2) 660-86-85; e-mail amb.eu@singembbru.be; Ambassador A. SELVERAJAH.

Slovakia: 79 ave Cortenbergh, 1000 Brussels; tel. (2) 743-68-11; fax (2) 743-68-88; e-mail slovakmission@pmsreu.be; Ambassador JURAJ MIGAS.

Slovenia: 30 ave Marnix, 1000 Brussels; tel. (2) 512-44-66; fax (2) 512-09-97; e-mail mission.bruxelles@mzz-dkp.sigor.si; Ambassador MARKO KRANJEC.

Solomon Islands: 13 ave de L'Yser, Boîte 3, 1040 Brussels; tel. (2) 732-70-85; fax (2) 732-68-85; Ambassador ROBERT SISILO.

Somalia: 26 rue Dumont d'Urville, 75116 Paris, France; tel. 1-45-00-76-51; Ambassador (vacant).

South Africa: 26 rue de la Loi, Boîtes 7–8, 1040 Brussels; tel. (2) 285-44-00; fax (2) 285-44-87; e-mail embassy.southafrica@belgium.online.be; Ambassador JERRY M. MATJILA.

Sri Lanka: 27 rue Jules Lejeune, 1050 Brussels; tel. (2) 344-53-94; fax (2) 344-67-37; e-mail sri.lanka@euronet.be; Ambassador C. R. JAYASINGHE.

Sudan: 124 ave F. D. Roosevelt, 1050 Brussels; tel. (2) 647-51-59; fax (2) 648-34-99; Ambassador ALI YOUSEF AHMED.

Suriname: 379 ave Louise, 1050 Brussels; tel. (2) 640-11-72; fax (2) 646-39-62; e-mail sur.amb.bru@online.be; Ambassador GERARD OTMAR HIWAT.

Swaziland: 188 ave Winston Churchill, 1180 Brussels; tel. (2) 347-47-71; fax (2) 347-46-23; Ambassador Dr THEMBAYENA ANNASTASIA DLAMINI.

Switzerland: 1 place du Luxembourg, 1050 Brussels; tel. (2) 286-13-11; fax (2) 230-45-09; e-mail vertretung@brm.rep.admin.ch; Ambassador DANTE MARTINELLI.

Syria: 3 ave F. D. Roosevelt, 1050 Brussels; tel. (2) 648-01-35; fax (2) 646-40-18; Ambassador (vacant).

Tanzania: 363 ave Louise (7e étage), 1050 Brussels; tel. (2) 640-65-00; fax (2) 646-80-26; Ambassador ALI ABEID AMAN KARUME.

Thailand: 2 square du Val de la Cambre, 1050 Brussels; tel. (2) 640-68-10; fax (2) 648-30-66; e-mail thaibxl@pophost.eunet.be; internet www.waw.be/rte-be; Ambassador SURAPONG POSAYANOND.

Togo: 264 ave de Tervueren, 1150 Brussels; tel. (2) 770-17-91; fax (2) 771-50-75; Ambassador OHARA KATI KORGA.

Tonga: 36 Molyneux St, London, W1H 6AB, United Kingdom; tel. (20) 7724-5828; fax (20) 7723-9074; e-mail tongahicommission@btinternet.com; Ambassador FETU'UTOLU TUPOU.

Trinidad and Tobago: 14 ave de la Faisanderie, 1150 Brussels; tel. (2) 762-94-15; fax (2) 772-27-83; e-mail information@ttm.eunet.be; Chargé d'affaires a. i. S. N. GORDON.

Tunisia: 278 ave de Tervueren, 1150 Brussels; tel. (2) 771-73-95; fax (2) 771-94-33; Ambassador TAHAR SIOUD.

Turkey: 4 rue Montoyer, 1000 Brussels; tel. (2) 513-28-36; fax (2) 511-0450; e-mail turkdelegeu@euronet.be; Ambassador NIHAT AKYOL.

Tuvalu: c/o Prime Minister's Office, Vaiaku, Funafuti, Tuvalu.

Uganda: 317 ave de Tervueren, 1150 Brussels; tel. (2) 762-58-25; fax (2) 763-04-38; e-mail ugembrus@brutele.be; Ambassador KAMIMA NTAMBI.

Ukraine: 7 rue Guimard, 1040 Brussels; tel. (2) 511-46-09; fax (2) 512-40-45; Ambassador ROMAN SHPEK.

United Arab Emirates: 73 ave F. D. Roosevelt, 1050 Brussels; tel. (2) 640-60-00; fax (2) 646-24-73; e-mail uae-embassy@skynet.be; Ambassador ABDEL HADI ABDEL WAHID AL-KHAJA.

USA: 40 blvd du Régent, Boîte 3, 1000 Brussels; tel. (2) 500-27-74; fax (2) 512-57-20; e-mail useu@usinfo.be; internet www.useu.be; Ambassador ROCKWELL A. SCHNABEL.

Uruguay: 22 ave F. D. Roosevelt, 1050 Brussels; tel. (2) 640-11-69; fax (2) 648-29-09; e-mail uruemb@euronet.be; Ambassador GUILLERMO VALLES.

Vanuatu: c/o Prime Minister's Office, POB 110, Port Vila, Vanuatu.

Venezuela: 10 ave F. D. Roosevelt, 1050 Brussels; tel. (2) 639-03-40; fax (2) 647-88-20; e-mail embajada@venezuela-eu.org; Ambassador LUISA ROMERO BERMÙDEZ.

Viet Nam: 130 ave de la Floride, 1180 Brussels; tel. (2) 374-91-33; fax (2) 374-93-76; Ambassador HUYNH ANH DZUNG.

Yemen: 114 ave F. D. Roosevelt, 1050 Brussels; tel. (2) 646-52-90; fax (2) 646-29-11; Ambassador GAZEM A. K. AL-AGHBARI.

Zambia: 469 ave Molière, 1060 Brussels; tel. (2) 343-56-49; fax (2) 347-43-33; Ambassador GRIFFIN KAFWIMBI NYIRONGO.

Zimbabwe: 11 square Joséphine Charlotte, 1200 Brussels; tel. (2) 762-58-08; fax (2) 762-96-05; Ambassador KELEBERT NKOMANI.

Union Institutions

Originally each of the Communities had its own Commission (High Authority in the case of the ECSC) and Council, but a treaty transferring the powers of these bodies to a single Commission and a single Council came into effect in 1967.

EUROPEAN COMMISSION

Address: 200 rue de la Loi, 1049 Brussels, Belgium.

Telephone: (2) 299-11-11; **fax:** (2) 295-01-38; **internet:** www.europa.eu.int/comm/index.htm.

MEMBERS OF THE COMMISSION
(with their responsibilities: April 2003)

President, responsible for the Secretariat General, the Forward Studies Unit, the Legal Service and the Media and Communication: ROMANO PRODI (Italy).

Vice-President, responsible for Administrative Reform, Personnel and Administration, Linguistic Services, Protocol and Security and the Internal Audit Service: NEIL KINNOCK (United Kingdom).

Vice-President, responsible for Relations with the European Parliament, Relations with the Committee of the Regions, the Economic and Social Commitee, and the Ombudsman, Transport (including Trans-European Networks) and Energy: LOYOLA DE PALACIO (Spain).

Commissioner, responsible for Competition: MARIO MONTI (Italy).

Commissioner, responsible for Agriculture, Rural Development and Fisheries: FRANZ FISCHLER (Austria).

Commissioner, responsible for Enterprise, Competitiveness, Innovation and the Information Society: ERKKI LIIKANEN (Finland).

Commissioner, responsible for the Internal Market, Financial Services, Customs and Taxation: FRITS BOLKESTEIN (Netherlands).

Commissioner, responsible for Science, Research and Development and the Joint Research Centre: PHILIPPE BUSQUIN (Belgium).

Commissioner, responsible for Economic and Financial Affairs, Monetary Matters and the Statistical Office: PEDRO SOLBES MIRA (Spain).

Commissioner, responsible for Development Aid and Co-operation and the Humanitarian Aid Office: POUL NIELSON (Denmark).

Commissioner, responsible for the Enlargement Process, including the Pre-accession Strategy: GÜNTER VERHEUGEN (Germany).

Commissioner, responsible for External Relations, the Common Foreign and Security Policy, Delegations to Non-member Countries and the Common Service for External Relations: CHRISTOPHER PATTEN (United Kingdom).

Commissioner, responsible for Trade Policy and the Instruments of Trade Policy: PASCAL LAMY (France).

Commissioner, responsible for Public Health; and Consumer Protection: DAVID BYRNE (Ireland).

Commissioner, responsible for Regional Policy, the Cohesion Fund and the Intergovernmental Conference: MICHEL BARNIER (France).

Commissioner, responsible for Citizens' Europe, Transparency, Education and Culture and the Publications Office: VIVIANE REDING (Luxembourg).

Commissioner, responsible for the Budget, Financial Control and the Prevention of Fraud: MICHAELE SCHREYER (Germany).

Commissioner, responsible for the Environment and Nuclear Safety: MARGOT WALLSTRÖM (Sweden).

Commissioner, responsible for Freedom, Security and Justice: ANTÓNIO VITORINO (Portugal).

Commissioner, responsible for Employment and Social Affairs and Equal Opportunities: ANNA DIAMANTOPOULOU (Greece).

The functions of the Commission are fourfold: to ensure the application of the provisions of the Treaties and of the provisions enacted by the institutions of the Communities in pursuance thereof; to formulate recommendations or opinions in matters which are the subject of the Treaties, where the latter expressly so provides or where the Commission considers it necessary; to dispose, under the conditions laid down in the Treaties, of a power of decision of its own and to participate in the preparation of acts of the Council of the European Union and of the European Parliament; and to exercise the competence conferred on it by the Council of the European Union for the implementation of the rules laid down by the latter.

The Commission may not include more than two members having the nationality of the same state; the number of members of the Commission may be amended by a unanimous vote of the Council of the European Union. In the performance of their duties, the members of the Commission are forbidden to seek or accept instructions from any Government or other body, or to engage in any other paid or unpaid professional activity.

The members of the Commission are nominated by the Governments of the member states acting in common agreement normally for a renewable term of five years. From January 1995, under the terms of the Treaty on European Union, the nominated President and other members of the Commission must be approved as a body by the European Parliament before they can take office. Once approved, the Commission may nominate one or two of its members as Vice-President. Any member of the Commission, if he or she no longer fulfils the conditions required for the performance of his or her duties, or commits a serious offence, may be declared removed from office by the Court of Justice. The Court may furthermore, on the petition of the Council of the European Union or of the Commission itself, provisionally suspend any member of the Commission from his or her duties. The European Parliament has the authority to dismiss the entire Commission.

In January 1999 Commissioners accused of mismanagement and corruption retained their positions following a vote of censure by Parliament. However, Parliament proceeded to appoint a five-member Committee of Independent Experts to investigate allegations of fraud, mismanagement and nepotism within the Commission. In early March two new codes of conduct for Commissioners were announced. On 15 March the Committee published a report that criticized the Commission's failure to control the administration and to take responsibility for the budget and other measures implemented by each department. The report also identified individual Commissioners as guilty of nepotism and mismanagement and proposed the establishment of a new independent unit to investigate fraud. As a consequence of the report the Commission agreed, collectively, to resign, although Commissioners were to retain their positions, and exercise limited duties, until their successors were appointed. In late March EU heads of state and of government nominated Romano Prodi, the former Italian Prime Minister, as the next President of the Commission. His appointment, and the team of Commissioners that he had appointed in the interim, were duly ratified by Parliament in September. However, Parliament made ratification subject to conditions, forming the foundation of a future inter-institutional agreement between itself and the Commission: while it did not lose any of its powers, the Commission undertook to be more open in its future dealings with the Parliament.

In February 2002 a Convention on the Future of Europe was opened in Brussels, chaired by the French former President Valéry Giscard d'Estaing. The convention, which had been agreed upon at the Laeken summit in 2001, included in its rebate 60 or more topics aimed at reforming EU institutions to ensure the smooth functioning of the Union after enlargement. Topics discussed included the future of EU policymaking, and the division of powers; reform to the current rotating system of presidency; Europe's role on the world stage and its legal identity; and the possibility of a future name change for the Union.

In October 2002 the convention published a draft new constitution for Europe, which paved the way for future reform. Its terms included the possible creation of a powerful new president of the EU who would report to national leaders, as well as the creation of an EU minister of foreign affairs. The draft constitution also included plans to give the EU the legal power to sign treaties and sit on international bodies as a legal body in its own right, and also proposed to end the system of national vetoes on all issues except that of admitting new member states. It outlined plans to give all Europeans the right to dual citizenship — ie. of the EU as well as of a member state. The terms of the draft plan were due to be submitted to national leaders in June 2003. In separate proposals published in January 2003, France and Germany proposed a dual presidency for the Union, with a powerful new head of the European Council, with the power to lead foreign policy, working alongside a separate president of the Commission. The proposals gained the support of the United Kingdom, Spain and Denmark in January 2003.

ADMINISTRATION

Offices are at the address of the European Commission unless otherwise stated.

GENERAL SERVICES

Secretariat-General of the Commission: Sec.-Gen. DAVID O'SULLIVAN.

Statistical Office (EUROSTAT): Bâtiment Jean Monnet, rue Alcide de Gasperi, 2920 Luxembourg; tel. 4301-33-107; fax 4301-33-015; e-mail media.support@eurostat.cec.be; internet europa.eu.int/eurostat.html; Dir-Gen. YVES FRANCHET.

Press and Communication: Dir JONATHAN FAULL.

Office for Official Publications of the European Union (EUROP): 2 rue Mercier, 2985 Luxembourg; tel. 2929-1; fax 2929-44619; e-mail europ@opoce.cec.be; internet eur-op.eu.int; Dir-Gen. THOMAS L. CRANFIELD.

European Anti-fraud Office: Dir-Gen. FRANZ-HERMANN BRÜNER.

POLICIES

Agriculture: Dir-Gen. JOSÉ MANUEL SILVA RODRÍGUEZ.

Competition: Dir-Gen. PHILIP LOWE.

Economic and Financial Affairs: Dir-Gen. KLAUS REGLING.

Education and Culture: Dir-Gen. NIKOLAUS VAN DER PAS.

Employment and Social Affairs: Dir-Gen. ODILE QUINTIN.

Energy and Transport: Dir-Gen. FRANÇOIS LAMOUREUX.

Enterprise: Dir-Gen. JEAN-PAUL MINGASSON.

Environment: Dir-Gen. CATHERINE DAY.

Fisheries: Dir-Gen. JÖRGEN HOLMQUIST.

Health and Consumer Protection: Dir-Gen. ROBERT COLEMAN.

Information Society: Dir-Gen. FABIO COLASANTI.

Internal Market: Dir-Gen. ALEXANDER SCHAUB.

Joint Research Centre: Dir-Gen. FINBARR MCSWEENEY.

Justice and Home Affairs: Dir-Gen. ADRIAN FORTESCUE.

Regional Policy: Dir-Gen. GRAHAM MEADOWS.

Research: Dir-Gen. ACHILLEAS MITSOS.

Taxation and Customs Union: Dir-Gen. ROBERT VERRUE.

EXTERNAL RELATIONS

Development: Dir-Gen. KOOS RICHELLE.

Enlargement: Dir-Gen. ENEKO LANDÁBURU ILLARRAMENDI.

EuropeAid—Co-operation Office: Dir-Gen. GIORGIO BONACCI.

External Relations: Dir-Gen. GUY LEGRAS.

Humanitarian Aid Office (ECHO): Dir COSTANZA ADINOLFI.

Trade: Dir-Gen. MOGENS PETER CARL.

INTERNAL SERVICES

Budget: Dir-Gen. LUIS ROMERO REQUENA.

Financial Control: Dir-Gen. EDITH KITZMANTEL.

Group of Policy Advisers Internal Audit Service: Dir-Gen. JULES MUIS.

Joint Interpreting and Conference Service: Head of Service MARCO BENEDETTI.

Legal Service: Dir-Gen. MICHEL PETITE.

Personnel and Administration: Dir-Gen. HORST REICHENBACH.

Translation Service: Dir-Gen. MICHEL VANDEN ABEELE.

THE EUROPEAN COUNCIL

The heads of state or of government of the member countries meet at least twice a year, in the member state which currently exercises the presidency of the Council of the European Union, or in Brussels.

Until 1975 summit meetings were held less frequently, on an *ad hoc* basis, usually to adopt major policy decisions regarding the future development of the Community. In answer to the evident need for more frequent consultation at the highest level, it was decided at the summit meeting in Paris, in December 1974, to hold the meetings on a regular basis, under the rubric of the European Council. There was no provision made for the existence of the European Council in the Treaty of Rome, but its position was acknowledged and regularized in the Single European Act (1987). Its role was further strengthened in the Treaty on European Union, which entered into force on 1 November 1993. As a result of the Treaty, the European Council became directly responsible for common policies within the fields of Common Foreign and Security Policy and Justice and Home Affairs.

COUNCIL OF THE EUROPEAN UNION

The Council of the European Union (until 1994 known formally as the Council of Ministers of the European Community and still frequently referred to as the Council of Ministers) is the only institution that directly represents the member states. It is the Community's principal decision-making body, acting on proposals made by the Commission, and is responsible for ensuring the co-ordination of the general economic policies of the member states and for taking the decisions necessary to implement the Treaties. The Council is composed of representatives of the member states, each Government delegating to it one of its members, according to the subject to be discussed. These meetings are generally referred to as the Agriculture Council, Telecommunications Council, etc. The Foreign Affairs, Economics and Finance ('ECOFIN') and Agriculture Councils normally meet once a month. The office of President is exercised for a term of six months by each member of the Council in rotation (January–June 2003: Greece; July–December 2003: Italy). Meetings of the Council are convened and chaired by the President, acting on his or her own initiative or at the request of a member or of the Commission.

The Treaty of Rome prescribed three types of voting: simple majority, qualified majority and unanimity. The votes of its members are weighted as follows: France, Germany, Italy and the United Kingdom 10; Spain 8; Belgium, Greece, the Netherlands and Portugal 5; Austria and Sweden 4; Denmark, Finland and Ireland 3; Luxembourg 2. Out of a total number of votes of 87, 62 are required for a qualified majority decision, making 26 votes sufficient for a blocking minority. During negotiations for enlargement of the EU, an agreement was reached, in March 1994, on new rules regulating voting procedures in the expanded Council, in response to concerns on the part of Spain and the United Kingdom that their individual influence would be diminished. Under the 'Ioannina compromise' (named after the Greek town where the agreement was concluded) 23–25 opposing votes were to be sufficient to continue debate of legislation for a 'reasonable period' until a consensus decision is reached. Amendments to the Treaty of Rome (the Single European Act), effective from July 1987, restricted the right of 'veto', and were expected to accelerate the development of a genuine common market: they allowed proposals relating to the dismantling of barriers to the free movement of goods, persons, services and capital to be approved by a majority vote in the Council, rather than by a unanimous vote. Unanimity would still be required, however, for certain areas, including harmonization of indirect taxes, legislation on health and safety, veterinary controls, and environmental protection; individual states would also retain control over immigration rules, prevention of terrorism and drugs-trafficking. The Treaty of Amsterdam, which came into force on 1 May 1999, extended the use of qualified majority voting to limited policy areas.

The Single European Act introduced a 'co-operation procedure' whereby a proposal adopted by a qualified majority in the Council must be submitted to the European Parliament for approval: if the Parliament rejects the Council's common position, unanimity shall be required for the Council to act on a second reading, and if the Parliament suggests amendments, the Commission must re-examine the proposal and forward it to the Council again. A 'co-decision procedure' was introduced in 1993 by the Treaty on European Union. The procedure allows a proposal to be submitted for a third reading by a so-called 'Conciliation Committee', composed equally of Council representatives and members of the European Parliament. The Treaty of Amsterdam simplified the co-decision procedure, and extended it to matters previously resolved under the co-operation procedure, although the latter remained in place for matters concerning economic and monetary union.

Under the Treaty of Amsterdam, the Secretary-General of the Council also took the role of 'High Representative', responsible for the co-ordination of common foreign and security policy. The Secretary-General is supported by a policy planning and early warning unit. In June 1999 Javier Solana Madariaga, at that time Secretary-General of NATO, was designated as the first Secretary-General of the Council.

The Treaty of Nice, initialled in February 2001, addresses institutional issues that remained outstanding under the Treaty of Amsterdam and which had to be settled before the enlargement of the EU from 2003, and various other issues not directly connected with enlargement. The main focus of the Treaty is the establishment of principles governing the new distribution of seats in the European Parliament, the new composition of the Commission and a new definition of qualified majority voting within the European Council. It stipulates that, with effect from the appointment of the next European Commission, in January 2005, the five largest member states (France, Germany, Italy, Spain and the United Kingdom) will lose their present right each to nominate two Commissioners. Instead, all member states will be entitled to nominate one member of the Commission, which may be enlarged to an upper limit of 26 Commissioners. Were the number of EU member states to expand beyond 26, the Council would set a limit on Commission membership, at 26 Commissioners or fewer, to be appointed on a rotational basis. The powers of the President of the Commission are enhanced. The new weighting system for existing members' votes within the European Council, effective from 1 January 2005, is as follows: France, Germany, Italy and the United Kingdom 29; Spain 27; Netherlands 13; Greece, Belgium and Portugal 12; Sweden and Austria 10; Denmark, Finland and Ireland 7; Luxembourg 4. Of the total number of 237 votes (based on the current 15 member states), a majority of 169 (71.3%) would be required for the adoption of a decision by the Council. The number of weighted votes needed for the adoption of a decision (referred to as the 'qualified majority threshold') was to be reassessed on the accession of each new member state. Qualified majority voting was to be applied to 30 additional policy areas that were presently subject to national vetos. The Treaty also provides for a major reform of the EU's legal system, and for changes to the rules on decision-making within the European Central Bank and the European Investment Bank. Under the terms of the Treaty some alterations are made to the EU's common foreign and security policy, mainly entailing an increased role for the EU in crisis prevention and conflict management activities, with the development of a regional military rapid response capability (the so-called Rapid Reaction Force—RRF, see Security and Defence). The Treaty of Nice entered into force on 1 February 2002, having been formally ratified by all the member states.

PERMANENT REPRESENTATIVES

Preparation and co-ordination of the Council's work is entrusted to a Committee of Permanent Representatives (COREPER), meeting in Brussels, consisting of the ambassadors of the member countries to the Union. A staff of national civil servants assists each ambassador.

GENERAL SECRETARIAT

Justus Lipsius Bldg, 175 rue de la Loi, 1048 Brussels, Belgium; tel. (2) 285-61-11; fax (2) 285-73-97; e-mail public.relations@consilium.eu.int; internet ue.eu.int.

Secretary-General and High Representative: JAVIER SOLANA MADARIAGA.

Deputy Secretary-General: PIERRE DE BOISSEAU.

Secretary-General's Private Office: Dir and Head of Cabinet ALBERTO NAVARRO GONZÁLEZ.

Legal Service: Dir-Gen. (Juriconsult of the Council) JEAN-CLAUDE PIRIS.

Directorates-General:

A (Administration and Protocol): Dir-Gen. VITTORIO GIFFO.

B (Agriculture and Fisheries): Dir-Gen. ÁNGEL BOIXAREU CARRERA.

C (Internal Market, Customs Union, Industrial Policy, Telecommunications, Information Society, Research, Energy and Transport): Dir-Gen. KLAUS GRETSCHMANN.

E (External Economic Relations and Common Foreign and Security Policy) (*): Dir-Gen. ROBERT COOPER.

F (Press and Communications): Dir-Gen. HANS BRUNMAYR.

G (Economic and Financial Affairs and European Monetary Union) (EMU): Dir-Gen. SIXTEN KORKMAN.

H (Justice and Home Affairs): Dir-Gen. CHARLES ELSEN.

I (Environmental and Consumer Protection, Civil Protection, Health, Foodstuffs Legislation, Drug Addiction, AIDS Education and Youth, Culture and Audio-visual Media): Dir-Gen. KERSTIN NIBLAEUS.
* Directorate-General D no longer exists.

EUROPEAN PARLIAMENT

Address: Centre Européen, Plateau du Kirchberg, BP 1601, 2929 Luxembourg.

Telephone: 4300-1; **fax:** 4300-29494; **internet:** www.europarl.eu.int.

PRESIDENT AND MEMBERS
(April 2003)

President: PAT COX (Ireland).

Members: 626 members, apportioned as follows: Germany 99 members; France, Italy and the United Kingdom 87 members each; Spain 64; the Netherlands 31; Belgium, Greece and Portugal 25 each; Sweden 22; Austria 21; Denmark and Finland 16 each; Ireland 15; Luxembourg 6. Members are elected for a five-year term by direct universal suffrage by the citizens of the member states. Members sit in the Chamber in political, not national, groups.

The tasks of the European Parliament are: amending legislation, scrutinizing the Union budget and exercising a measure of democratic control over the executive organs of the European Communities, the Commission and the Council. It has the power to dismiss the European Commission by a vote of censure. Increases in parliamentary powers have been brought about through amendments to the Treaty of Rome. The Single European Act, which entered into force on 1 July 1987, introduced, in certain circumstances where the Council normally adopts legislation through majority voting, a co-operation procedure involving a second parliamentary reading, enabling Parliament to amend legislation. Community agreements with third countries require parliamentary approval. The Treaty on European Union, which came into force in November 1993, introduced the co-decision procedure, permitting a third parliamentary reading (see Council of the European Union, above). The Treaty also gives Parliament the right to veto legislation, and allows Parliament a vote of approval for a new Commission. Parliament appoints the European Ombudsman, who investigates reports of maladministration in Community institutions. The Treaty of Amsterdam, which entered into force in May 1999, expanded and simplified Parliament's legislative role.

Political Groupings

	Distribution of seats (April 2003)
Group of the European People's Party	232
Party of European Socialists	175
Group of the European Liberal, Democrat and Reform Party	53
Confederal Group of the European United Left/Nordic Green Left	49
Green/European Free Alliance	45
Union for a Europe of the Nations	23
Group for a Europe of Democracies and Diversities	18
Non-attached	31
Total	**626**

Parliament has an annual session, divided into about 12 one-week meetings, normally held in Strasbourg, France. The session opens with the March meeting. Committees and political group meetings and additional sittings of Parliament are held in Brussels.

The budgetary powers of Parliament (which, with the Council, forms the Budgetary Authority of the Communities) were increased to their present status by a treaty of 22 July 1975. Under this treaty, it can amend non-agricultural spending and reject the draft budget, acting by a majority of its members and two-thirds of the votes cast.

Parliament is run by a Bureau comprising the President, 14 Vice-Presidents elected from its members by secret ballot to serve for two-and-a-half years, and the five members of the College of Quaestors. The Conference of Presidents is the political governing body of Parliament, with responsibility for formulating the agenda for plenary sessions and the timetable for the work of parliamentary bodies, and for establishing the terms of reference and the size of committees and delegations. It comprises the President of Parliament and Chairmen of the political groupings.

There are Standing Parliamentary Committees on Foreign Affairs, Human Rights, Common Security, and Defence Policy; Agriculture and Rural Development; Budgets; Budgetary Control; Economic and Monetary Affairs; Legal Affairs and the Internal Market; Industry, External Trade, Research and Energy; Employment and Social Affairs; Public Health and Consumer Policy; Culture, Youth, Education, the Media and Sport; Development and Co-operation; Fisheries; Constitutional Affairs; Petitions; and Women's Rights and Equal Opportunities.

The first direct elections to the European Parliament took place in June 1979, and Parliament met for the first time in July. The second elections were held in June 1984 (with separate elections held in Portugal and Spain in 1987, following the accession of these two countries to the Community), the third in June 1989, the fourth in June 1994. Direct elections to the European Parliament were held in Sweden in September 1995, and in Austria and Finland in October 1996. The fifth European Parliament was elected in June 1999.

EUROPEAN OMBUDSMAN

Address: ave du President Robert Schuman 1, BP 403, 67001 Strasbourg Cédex, France.

Telephone: 3-88-17-40-01; **fax:** 3-88-17-90-62; **e-mail:** euro-ombudsman@europarl.eu.int; **internet:** www.euro-ombudsman.eu.int.

The position was created by the Treaty on European Union, and the first Ombudsman took office in July 1995. The Ombudsman is appointed by the European Parliament for a renewable five-year term. He is authorized to receive complaints regarding maladministration in Community institutions and bodies (except in the Court of Justice and Court of First Instance), to make recommendations, and to refer any matters to the Parliament.

European Ombudsman: NIKIFOROS DIAMANDOUROS.

COURT OF JUSTICE OF THE EUROPEAN COMMUNITIES

Address: Palais de la Cour de Justice, blvd Konrad Adenauer, Kirchberg, 2925 Luxembourg.

Telephone: 4303-1; **fax:** 4303-2600; **internet:** www.curia.eu.int.

The task of the Court of Justice is to ensure the observance of law in the interpretation and application of the Treaties setting up the three Communities. The 15 Judges and the eight Advocates General are appointed for renewable six-year terms by the Governments of the member states. The President of the Court is elected by the Judges from among their number for a renewable term of three years. The majority of cases are dealt with by one of the six chambers, each of which consists of a President of Chamber and two or four Judges. The Court may sit in plenary session in cases of particular importance or when a member state or Community institution that is a party to the proceedings so requests. The Court has jurisdiction to award damages. It may review the legality of acts (other than recommendations or opinions) of the Council, the Commission or the European Central Bank, of acts adopted jointly by the European Parliament and the Council and of Acts adopted by Parliament and intended to produce legal effects *vis-à-vis* third parties. It is also competent to give judgment on actions by a member state, the Council or the Commission on grounds of lack of competence, of infringement of an essential procedural requirement, of infringement of a Treaty or of any legal rule relating to its application, or of misuse of power. The Court of Justice may hear appeals, on a point of law only, from the Court of First Instance.

The Court is also empowered to hear certain other cases concerning the contractual and non-contractual liability of the Communities and disputes between member states in connection with the objects of the Treaties. It also gives preliminary rulings at the request of national courts on the interpretation of the Treaties, of Union legislation, and of the Brussels Convention on Jurisdiction and the Enforcement of Judgments in Civil and Commercial Matters. During 2001 398 new cases were completed, while 839 cases were pending.

Composition of the Court
(in order of precedence, as at March 2003)

President of the Court of Justice: GIL CARLOS RODRÍGUEZ IGLESIAS (Spain).

Judge: JEAN-PIERRE PUISSOCHET (France).

Judge: MELCHIOR WATHELET (Belgium).

Judge: ROMAIN SCHINTGEN (Luxembourg).

Advocate General: JEAN MISCHO (Luxembourg).

Judge: CHRISTIAAN WILLEM ANTON TIMMERMANS (Netherlands).

Advocate General: FRANCIS JACOBS (United Kingdom).

Judge: CLAUS CHRISTIAN GULMANN (Denmark).

Judge: DAVID ALEXANDER OGILVY EDWARD (United Kingdom).

Judge: ANTONIO MARIO LA PERGOLA (Italy).

Advocate General: PHILIPPE LÉGER (France).

President of the First and Fifth Chambers: PETER JANN (Austria).

Advocate General: DÁMASO RUIZ-JARABO COLOMER (Spain).

First Advocate General: SIEGBERT ALBER (Germany).

Judge: VASSILIOS SKOURIS (Greece).

President of the Third and Sixth Chambers: FIDELMA O'KELLY MACKEN (Ireland).

President of the Second Chamber: NINON COLNERIC (Germany).

President of the Fourth Chamber: STIG VON BAHR (Sweden).

Advocate General: ANTONIO TIZZANO (Italy).

Judge: JOSÉ NARCISO DA CUNHA RODRIGUES (Portugal).

Advocate General: LEENDERT A. GEELHOED (Netherlands).

Advocate General: CHRISTINE STIX-HACKL (Austria).

Judge: ALLAN ROSAS (Finland).

Registrar: ROGER GRASS (France).

COURT OF FIRST INSTANCE OF THE EUROPEAN COMMUNITIES

Address: blvd Konrad Adenauer, 2925 Luxembourg.

Telephone: 4303-1; **fax:** 4303-2100; **internet:** www.curia.eu.int.

The Court of First Instance was established by the European Council by a decision of October 1988, and began operations in 1989. The Court has jurisdiction to hear and determine cases brought by natural or legal persons and which had hitherto been dealt with by the Court of Justice. During 2001 the Court considered 327 cases, while 786 were pending.

Composition of the Court of First Instance
(in order of precedence, as at March 2003)

President of Chamber: BO VESTERDORF (Denmark).

Judge: RAFAEL GARCÍA -VALDECASAS Y FERNÁNDEZ (Spain).

Judge: KOENRAAD LENAERTS (Belgium).

Judge: VIRPI E. TIILI (Finland).

Judge: NICHOLAS JAMES FORWOOD (United Kingdom).

Judge: PERNILLA LINDH (Sweden).

Judge: JOSEF AZIZI (Austria).

President of the Court of First Instance: RUI MANUEL GENS DE MOURA RAMOS (Portugal).

President of Chamber: JOHN D. COOKE (Ireland).

President of Chamber: MARC JAEGER (Luxembourg).

Judge: JÖRG PIRRUNG (Germany).

Judge: ARJEN W. H. MEIJ (Netherlands).

President of Chamber: MIHALIS VILARAS (Greece).

Judge: PAOLO MENGOZZI (Italy).

Judge: HUBERT LEGAL (France).

Registrar: HANS JUNG (Germany).

COURT OF AUDITORS OF THE EUROPEAN COMMUNITIES

Address: 12 rue Alcide de Gasperi, 1615 Luxembourg.

Telephone: 4398-45410; **fax:** 4398-46430; **e-mail:** euraud@eca.eu.int; **internet:** www.eca.eu.int.

The Court of Auditors was created by the Treaty of Brussels, which was signed on 22 July 1975, and commenced its duties in late 1977. It was given the status of an institution on a par with the Commission, the Council, the Court of Justice and the Parliament by the Treaty on European Union. It is the institution responsible for the external audit of the resources managed by the three Communities and the European Union. It consists of 15 members who are appointed for six-year terms by unanimous decision of the Council of the European Union, after consultation with the European Parliament. The members elect the President from among their number for a term of three years.

The Court is organized and acts as a collegiate body. It adopts its decisions by a majority of its members. Each member, however, has a direct responsibility for the audit of certain sectors of Union activities.

The Court examines the accounts of all expenditure and revenue of the European Communities and of any body created by them in so far as the relevant constituent instrument does not preclude such examination. It examines whether all revenue has been received and all expenditure incurred in a lawful and regular manner and whether the financial management has been sound. The audit is based on records, and if necessary is performed directly in the institutions of the Communities, in the member states and in other countries. In the member states the audit is carried out in co-operation with the national audit bodies. The Court of Auditors draws up an annual report after the close of each financial year. The Court provides the Parliament and the Council with a statement of assurance as to the reliability of the accounts, and the legality and regularity of the underlying transactions. It may also, at any time, submit observations on specific questions (usually in the form of special reports) and deliver opinions at the request of one of the institutions of the Communities. It assists the European Parliament and the Council in exercising their powers of control over the implementation of the budget, in particular in the framework of the annual discharge procedure, and gives its prior opinion on the financial regulations, on the methods and procedure whereby the budgetary revenue is made available to the Commission, and on the formulation of rules concerning the responsibility of authorizing officers and accounting officers and concerning appropriate arrangements for inspection.

President: JUAN MANUEL FABRA VALLÉS (Spain).

Audit Group I: JEAN-FRANÇOIS BERNICOT, HEDDA VON WEDEL, DAVID BOSTOCK.

Audit Group II: GIORGIO CLEMENTE, JØRGEN MOHR, FRANÇOIS COLLING, LARS TOBISSON.

Audit Group III: HUBERT WEBER, MAARTEN ENGWIRDA, ROBERT REYNDERS.

Audit Group IV: AUNUS SALMI, MORTEN LOUIS LEVYSOHN, IOANNIS SARMAS.

Secretary-General: MICHEL HERVÉ.

EUROPEAN CENTRAL BANK

Address: 60066 Frankfurt am Main, Kaiserstr. 29, Postfach 160319, Germany.

Telephone: (69) 13440; **fax:** (69) 13446000; **internet:** www.ecb.int.

The European Central Bank (ECB) was formally established on 1 June 1998, replacing the European Monetary Institute, which had been operational since January 1994. The Bank has the authority to issue the single currency, the euro, which replaced the European Currency Unit (ECU) on 1 January 1999, at the beginning of Stage III of Economic and Monetary Union (EMU), in accordance with the provisions of the Treaty on European Union ('the Maastricht

Treaty'). The Bank's leadership is provided by a six-member executive board, appointed for a non-renewable term of eight years (it should be noted that the Statute of the European System of Central Banks—ESCB—provides for a system of staggered appointments to the first executive board for members other than the President in order to ensure continuity), which is responsible for the preparation of meetings of the governing council, the implementation of monetary policy in accordance with the guide-lines and decisions laid down by the governing council and for the current business of the ECB. The ECB and the national central banks of EU member states together comprise the ESCB. The governing council of the ESCB, which consists of ECB executive board members and the governors of central banks of countries participating in EMU, meets twice a month. The general council comprises the President, the Vice-President and the governors of the central banks of all EU member states.

President: WILLEM (WIM) F. DUISENBERG (Netherlands), JEAN-CLAUDE TRICHET (France)(from July 2003).

Vice-President: LUCAS PAPADEMOS (Greece).

Executive Board: SIRKKA HÄMÄLÄINEN (Finland), OTMAR ISSING (Germany), TOMMASO PADOA-SCHIOPPA (Italy), EUGENIO DOMINGO SOLANS (Spain).

EUROPEAN INVESTMENT BANK

Address: 100 blvd Konrad Adenauer, 2950 Luxembourg.

Telephone: 4379-1; **fax:** 4377-04; **e-mail:** info@eib.org; **internet:** www.eib.org.

The European Investment Bank (EIB) is the EU's international financing institution, and was created in 1958 by the six founder member states of the European Economic Community. The shareholders are the 15 member states of the EU. In 2002 subscribed capital stood at €150,000m. The bulk of the EIB's resources comes from borrowings, principally public bond issues or private placements on capital markets inside and outside the Union. In 2002 the Bank raised €38,016m. in resources, of which 779% was in Community currencies.

The EIB's principal task, defined by the Treaty of Rome, is to work on a non-profit basis, making or guaranteeing loans for investment projects which contribute to the balanced and steady development of EU member states. Throughout the Bank's history, priority has been given to financing investment projects which further regional development within the Community. The EIB also finances projects that improve communications, protect and improve the environment, promote urban development, strengthen the competitive position of industry and encourage industrial integration within the Union, support the activities of small and medium-sized enterprises (SMEs), and help ensure the security of energy supplies. The EIB also provides finance for developing countries in Africa, the Caribbean and the Pacific, under the terms of the Lomé Convention (q.v.); for countries in the Mediterranean region, under a new Euro-Mediterranean investment facility established in 2002, and for Accession countries in central and eastern Europe.

In 2002 total financing contracts signed by the EIB, both inside and outside the European Union, amounted to €39,618m., compared with €36,776m. in 2001, bringing cumulative operations to €172,8561m. since 1998.

The Board of Governors of the EIB, which usually meets only once a year, lays down general directives on credit policy, approves the annual report and accounts and decides on capital increases. The Board of Directors meets once a month, and has sole power to take decisions in respect of loans, guarantees and borrowings. Its members are appointed by the Governors for a renewable five-year term following nomination by the member states. The Bank's President presides over meetings of the Board of Directors. The day-to-day management of operations is the responsibility of the Management Committee, which is the EIB's collegiate executive body and recommends decisions to the Board of Directors. It comprises the President and seven Vice-Presidents, nominated for six-year terms by the Board of Directors and approved by the Board of Governors. The Audit Committee, which reports to the Board of Governors regarding the management of operations and the maintenance of the Bank's accounts, is an independent body comprising three members who are appointed by the Board of Governors for a renewable three-year term.

Board of Governors: One minister (usually the minister of finance) from each member state.

Board of Directors: Twenty-five directors and 13 alternates (senior officials from finance or economic ministries, public-sector banks or credit institutions), appointed for a renewable five-year term, of whom 24 and 12 respectively are nominated by the member states; one director and one alternate are nominated by the Commission of the European Communities.

Management Committee

President: PHILIPPE MAYSTADT.

Vice-Presidents: WOLFGANG ROTH, EWALD NOWOTNY, PETER SEDGWICK, ISABEL MARTÍN CASTELLÁ, MICHAEL G. TUTTY, GERLANDO GENUARDI, PHILIPPE DE FONTAINE VIVE.

FINANCE CONTRACTS SIGNED

Recipient	2002 Amount (€ million)	2002 %	1998–2002 Amount (€ million)	1998–2002 %
Austria	998	2.5	3,489	2.0
Belgium	479	1.2	2,430	1.4
Denmark	1,027	2.6	4,826	2.8
Finland	744	1.9	3,011	1.7
France	4,023	10.2	18,209	10.5
Germany	6,504	16.4	29,103	16.9
Greece	1,072	2.7	6,607	3.8
Ireland	400	1.0	1,647	1.0
Italy	6,041	15.2	25,451	14.8
Luxembourg	74	0.2	489	0.3
Netherlands	538	1.4	2,295	1.3
Portugal	1,770	4.5	8,515	4.9
Spain	5,426	13.7	21,302	12.3
Sweden	720	1.8	3,490	2.0
United Kingdom	3,328	8.4	15,175	8.8
Other*	300	0.8	1,174	0.7
EU total	**33,442**	**84.4**	**147,213**	**85.2**
Central and east European candidate countries	3,421	8.6	13,435	7.8
Cyprus and Malta	220	0.6	575	0.3
Candidate countries total	3,641	9.2	14,010	8.1
Mediterranean countries (except Cyprus and Malta)	1,588	4.0	5,890	3.4
ACP-Overseas countries and territories and South Africa	348	0.9	2,772	1.6
Latin America and Asia	174	0.4	1,921	1.1
Balkans	425	1.1	1,050	0.6
Partner countries total	**2,534**	**6.4**	**11,633**	**6.7**
Total	**39,618**	**100.0**	**172,856**	**100.0**

* Projects with a European dimension located outside the member states.

ECONOMIC AND SOCIAL COMMITTEE

Address: 2 rue Ravenstein, 1000 Brussels.

Telephone: (2) 546-90-11; **fax:** (2) 513-48-93; **internet:** www.esc.eu.int.

The Committee was set up by the 1957 Rome Treaties. It is advisory and is consulted by the Council of the European Union or by the European Commission, particularly with regard to agriculture, free movement of workers, harmonization of laws and transport, as well as legislation adopted under the Euratom Treaty. In certain cases consultation of the Committee by the Commission or the Council is mandatory. In addition, the Committee has the power to deliver opinions on its own initiative.

The Committee has 222 members: 24 each from France, Germany, Italy and the United Kingdom, 21 from Spain, 12 each from Austria, Belgium, Greece, the Netherlands, Portugal and Sweden, nine from Denmark, Finland and Ireland, and six from Luxembourg. One-third represents employers, one-third employees, and one-third various interest groups (e.g. agriculture, small enterprises, consumers). The Committee is appointed for a renewable term of four years by the unanimous vote of the Council of the European Union. Members are nominated by their governments, but are appointed in their personal capacity and are not bound by any mandatory instructions. The Committee is served by a permanent and independent General Secretariat, headed by the Secretary-General.

President: ROGER BRIESCH (France).

Vice-Presidents: GÖKE DANIE FRERICHS (Germany), LEIF E. NIELSEN (Denmark).

Secretary-General: PATRICK VENTURINI.

COMMITTEE OF THE REGIONS

Address: rue Montoyer 92-102, 1000 Brussels.

Telephone: (2) 282-22-11; **fax:** (2) 282-23-25; **internet:** www.cor.eu
.int.

The Treaty on European Union provided for a committee to be
established, with advisory status, comprising representatives of
regional and local bodies throughout the EU. The first meeting of the
Committee was held in March 1994. It may be consulted on EU
proposals concerning economic and social cohesion, trans-European
networks, public health, education and culture, and may issue an
opinion on any issue with regional implications. The Committee
meets in plenary session five times a year.

The number of members of the Committee is equal to that of the
Economic and Social Committee. Members are appointed for a
renewable term of four years by the Council, acting unanimously on
the proposals from the respective member states. The Committee
elects its principal officers from among its members for a two-year
term.

President: Sir ALBERT BORE (United Kingdom).

First Vice-President: REINHOLD BOCKLET.

OTHER BODIES

EUROPEAN INVESTMENT FUND—EIF

Address: 43 ave J. F. Kennedy, 2968 Luxembourg.

Telephone: 4266-881; **fax:** 4266-88200; **e-mail:** info@eif.org;
internet: www.eif.org.

The European Investment Fund was founded in 1994 as a specialized financial institution to support the growth of small and
medium-sized enterprises (SMEs). Its operations are focused on the
provision of venture capital, through investment in funds that
support SMEs, and on guarantee activities to facilitate access to
finance for SMEs. In all its activities the Fund aims to maintain a
commercial approach to investment, and to apply risk-sharing principles. Since 1998 the Fund has managed the European Technology
Faculty (ETF)—Start-Up, and the SME Guarantee Facility. A new
legal framework for these operations, under the Multiannual Programme (MAP) for enterprise and entrepreneurship was approved
in December 2001, with a budget of €317m. During 2002 the Fund
signed €1,250m. for guarantee operations and €471.5m. for 36
investments in venture capital funds. Authorized capital totals
€2,000m., held by the European Investment Bank (60.75%), the
European Commission (30.00%), and other European banks and
financial institutions (9.25%).

Chief Executive: WALTER CERNOIA.

ADVISORY COMMITTEES

There are advisory committees dealing with all aspects of EU policy.
Consultation with some committees is compulsory in the procedure
for drafting EC legislation.

In addition to the consultative bodies listed above there are
several hundred special interest groups representing every type of
interest within the Union. All these hold unofficial talks with the
Commission.

AGENCIES

Community Plant Variety Office
Address: POB 2141, 49021 Angers Cedex 2.

Address: 3 blvd Foch, 49100 Angers, France.

Telephone: 2-41-25-64-00; **fax:** 2-41-25-64-10; **e-mail:** cpvo@cpvo
.eu.int; **internet:** www.cpvo.eu.int.

Began operations in April 1995, with responsibility for granting
intellectual property rights for plant varieties. Supervised by an
Administrative Council, and managed by a President, appointed by
the Council of the European Union. A Board of Appeal has been
established to consider appeals against certain technical decisions
taken by the Office.

President: BARTELD P. KIEWIET.

European Agency for Reconstruction
POB 10177, 54626 Thessaloniki; Egnatia 4, 54626 Thessaloniki,
Greece; tel. (2310) 505100; fax (2310) 505172; e-mail info@ear.eu.int;
internet www.ear.eu.int.

Established in February 2000 (upon a Council regulation of
November 1999) to assume responsibilities of the European Commission's Task Force for the Reconstruction of Kosovo (which had
become operational in July 1999 following the end of hostilities in
the southern Serbian province of Kosovo and Metohija). The Agency's mandate is to prepare and implement reconstruction and refugee return programmes for Kosovo, as well as for other parts of
Serbia and Montenegro. In December 2001 the Agency assumed
responsibility for the EU's main assistance programmes in the
former Yugoslav republic of Macedonia.

Director: RICHARD ZINK.

European Agency for Safety and Health at Work
Gran Vía 33, 48009 Bilbao, Spain; tel. (94) 479-43-60; fax (94) 479-
43-83; e-mail information@osha.eu.int; internet www.osha.eu.int.

Began operations in 1996. Aims to encourage improvements in the
working environment, and to make available all necessary technical,
scientific and economic information for use in the field of health and
safety at work. A 48-member Administrative Board comprising
representatives from each member state's government, employers'
and workers' organizations, and three representatives from the
European Commission, adopts the Agency's work programme and
other strategic decisions of the Agency, and appoints the Director.
The Agency supports a network of Focal Points in each member
state.

Director: HANS-HORST KONKOLEWSKY.

European Agency for the Evaluation of Medicinal Products (EMEA)
7 Westferry Circus, Canary Wharf, London, E14 4HB, United
Kingdom; tel. (20) 7418-8400; fax (20) 7418-8416; e-mail mail@emea
.eudra.org; internet www.emea.eu.int.

Established in 1993 for the authorization and supervision of medicinal products for human and veterinary use. In 2003 the Agency's
proposed budget was €94.113m.

Chairman of the Management Board: KEITH JONES (United
Kingdom).

**Chairman of the Committee for Proprietary Medicinal Prod-
ucts (CPMP):** Dr DANIEL BRASSEUR.

**Chairman of the Committee for Veterinary Medicinal Prod-
ucts (CVMP):** Dr STEVE DEAN.

**Chairman of the Committee for Orphan Medicinal Products
(COMP) :** JOSEP TORRENT FARNELL.

Executive Director: THOMAS LÖNNGREN.

European Aviation Safety Agency (EASA)
internet http://europa.eu.int/agencies/easa/index-en.htm.

Established by regulation of the European Parliament in July 2002;
the mission of the agency is to establish and maintain a high,
uniform level of civil aviation safety and environmental protection in
Europe. The agency was expected to start operating fully in September 2003.

European Centre for the Development of Vocational Training (CEDEFOP)
POB 22427, Thessaloniki; Europe 123, 57001 Thessaloniki, Greece;
tel. (31) 490111; fax (31) 490102; e-mail info@cedefop.eu.int.

Assists policy-makers and other officials in member states and
partner organizations in issues relating to vocational training policies, and assists the European Commission in the development of
these policies. Manages a European Training Village internet site.

Director: JOHAN VAN RENS (Netherlands).

European Environment Agency (EEA)
6 Kongens Nytorv, 1050 Copenhagen K, Denmark; tel. 33-36-71-00;
fax 33-36-71-99; e-mail eea@eea.eu.int; internet www.eea.eu.int.

Became operational in 1994, having been approved in 1990, to
gather and supply information to assist the implementation of
Community policy on environmental protection and improvement.
In 2003 the Agency's budget amounted to around €23m. The Agency
publishes a report on the state of the environment every three years.

Chairman of the Management Board: KEES ZOETMAN (Netherlands).

Chairman of the Scientific Committee: Prof. BEDRICH MOLDAN.

Executive Director: JACQUELINE MCGLADE (Spain).

European Food Safety Authority (EFSA)
1 rue Genève, 1140 Brussels; fax (2) 299-56-01; internet www.efsa
.eu.int/.

Established by a regulation of the European Parliament in 2002; the
primary responsibility of the authority is to provide independent

scientific advice on all matters with a direct or indirect impact on food safety.

Executive Director: GEOFFREY PODGER.

European Foundation for the Improvement of Living and Working Conditions

Wyattville Rd, Loughlinstown, Dublin 18, Ireland; tel. (1) 204-3100; fax (1) 282-6456; e-mail postmaster@eurofound.eu.int; internet www.eurofound.eu.int.

Established in 1975 to develop strategies for the medium- and long-term improvement of industrial relations, living conditions and working conditions. The Foundation publishes a bi-monthly newsletter.

Chairman of the Administrative Board: MARC BOISNEL.

Director: RAYMOND-PIERRE BODIN.

European Maritime Safety Agency (EMSA)

internet http://europa.eu.int/agencies/emsa/index-en.htm.

Established by a regulation of the European Parliament in June 2002; the primary responsibility of the authority is to provide technical and scientific advice to the Commission in the field of maritime safety and prevention of pollution by ships.

Executive Director: WILLEM DE RUITER.

European Monitoring Centre for Drugs and Drug Addiction (EMCDDA)

Palacete Mascarenhas, Rua da Cruz de Sta. Apolónia 23–25, 1149 Lisbon, Portugal; tel. (1) 21811-30-00; fax (1) 21811-17-11; e-mail info@emcdda.eu.int; internet www.emcdda.eu.int.

Founded in 1993, and became fully operational at the end of 1995, with the aim of providing member states with objective, reliable and comparable information on drugs and drug addiction in order to assist in combating the problem. The Centre co-operates with other European and international organizations and non-Community countries. The Centre publishes an *Annual Report on the State of the Drugs Problem in Europe*. A newsletter, *Drugnet Europe*, is published every two months.

Chairman of the Management Board: MIKE TRACE (Germany).

Executive Director: GEORGES ESTIEVENART (France).

European Monitoring Centre on Racism and Xenophobia

Rahlgasse 3. 1060 Vienna, Austria; tel. (1) 580300; fax (1) 5803099; e-mail office@eumc.eu.int; internet www.eumc.eu.int.

Established by a decision of the European Council in June 1997, and began operations in July 1998. Aims to review issues relating to racism, xenophobia and anti-semitism and to promote best practices to combat the problem. Working to establish a European Information Network on Racism and Xenophobia (RAXEN).

Chairman of Executive Board: ROBERT PURKISS (United Kingdom).

Director: Dr BEATE WINKLER.

European Training Foundation (ETF)

Villa Gualino, Viale Settimio Severo 65, 10133 Turin, Italy; tel. (011) 630-22-22; fax (011) 630-22-00; e-mail info@etf.eu.int; internet www .etf.eu.int.

Established in 1995 with the aim of contributing to the development of the vocational training systems of designated central and eastern European countries. In 1998 the Foundation's responsibilities were extended to include certain non-member Mediterranean countries and Mongolia.

Chairman of the Governing Board: KLAUS VAN DER PAS.

Director: PETER G. M. DE ROOIJ.

Office for Harmonization in the Internal Market (Trade Marks and Designs) (OHIM)

Avda de Europa 4, 03080 Alicante, Spain; tel. (96) 513-91-00; fax (96) 513-91-73; e-mail information@oami.eu.int; internet www.oami.eu .int.

Established in 1993 to promote and control trade marks and designs throughout the European Union.

Chairman of the Administrative Board: CARL-ANDERS IFVARSSON.

Chairman of the Budget Committee: PETER LAWRENCE.

President: WUBBO DE BOER.

Translation Centre for the Bodies of the European Union

Bâtiment Nouvel Hémicycle, 1 rue de Fort Thungen, 1499 Luxembourg; tel. 4217-11200; fax 4217-11220; e-mail cdt@eu.int; internet www.cdt.eu.int.

Established in 1994 to meet the translation needs of other decentralized Community agencies.

Director: FRANCISCO DE VICENTE.

Activities of the Community

AGRICULTURE

Co-operation in the Community has traditionally been at its most highly organized in the area of agriculture. The objectives of the Common Agricultural Policy (CAP) are described in the Treaty of Rome. The markets for agricultural products have been progressively organized following three basic principles: (i) unity of the market (products must be able to circulate freely within the Community and markets must be organized according to common rules); (ii) Community preference (products must be protected from low-cost imports and from fluctuations on the world market); (iii) common financial responsibility: the European Agricultural Guidance and Guarantee Fund (EAGGF) finances, through its Guarantee Section, all public expenditure intervention, storage costs, marketing subsidies and export rebates.

Agricultural prices are, in theory, fixed each year at a common level for the Community as a whole, taking into account the rate of inflation and the need to discourage surplus production of certain commodities. Export subsidies are paid to enable farmers to sell produce at the lower world market prices without loss. These subsidies account for some 50% of agricultural spending. When market prices of certain cereals, sugar, some fruits and vegetables, dairy produce and meat fall below a designated level the Community intervenes, and buys a certain quantity which is then stored until prices recover. During the 1980s expanding production led to food surpluses, costly to maintain, particularly in dairy produce, beef, cereals and wine, and to the destruction of large quantities of fruit and vegetables.

Agriculture is by far the largest item on the Community budget, accounting for about two-thirds of annual expenditure, mainly for supporting prices through the EAGGF Guarantee Section (appropriations for which amounted to €44,505m., or 45% of total commitment appropriations, in 2002). A system of 'stabilizers' was introduced in February 1988, imposing an upper limit on the production of certain products. Any over-production would result in a decrease in the guaranteed intervention price for the following year. Similar 'stabilizers' were later imposed on production of oilseeds, protein feed crops, wine, sugar, fruit and vegetables, tobacco, olive oil, cotton and mutton.

In 1990 the CAP was criticized during the 'Uruguay Round' of negotiations on the General Agreement on Tariffs and Trade (GATT, see World Trade Organization—WTO, see p. 323). The US Government demanded massive reductions in the EC's agricultural and export subsidies, on the grounds that they disrupted world markets. In November Community ministers of agriculture agreed to accept proposals by the Commission for a reduction of 30% in agricultural subsidies over a 10-year period. In May 1992, on the basis of proposals made by the Commission in 1991, ministers adopted a number of reforms, which aimed to transfer the Community's agricultural support from upholding prices to maintaining farmers' incomes, thereby removing the incentive to over-produce. Intervention prices were reduced by 29% for cereals, 15% for beef and poultry and 5% for dairy products. Farmers were to be compensated for the price reductions by receiving additional grants, which, in the case of crops, took the form of a subsidy per hectare of land planted. To qualify for these subsidies, arable farmers (except for those with the smallest farms) were to be obliged to remove 15% of their land from cultivation (the 'set-aside' scheme). Incentives were to be given for alternative uses of the withdrawn land (e.g. forestry). The reform reduced prices payable for cereals to the level of those prevailing in the international market.

In May 1992 the US Government threatened to impose a large increase in import tariffs on European products, in retaliation against subsidies paid by the EC to oilseed producers, which, the US Government claimed, led to unfair competition for US exports of soya beans. In November, however, agreement was reached between the USA and the European Commission: the USA agreed that limits should be imposed on the area of EC land on which cultivation of oilseed was permitted. The USA also agreed to accept a reduction of 21% in the volume and 36% in the value of the EC's subsidized exports of farm produce, over a six-year period (the amounts being based on average production during 1986–90). These agreements formed the basis of the GATT agricultural accord, which was concluded as part of the Uruguay Round trade agreement in mid-December 1993.

The Commission estimated that between September 1992 and the end of July 1993, as a result of the turmoil in the exchange-rate mechanism (see Economic Co-operation), an extra ECU 1,500m. was spent in price-support payments to farmers. In February 1995 ministers adopted a new agrimonetary regime, which limited the amount of compensation paid to farmers as a result of currency fluctuations. Further amendments, introduced in June, abandoned the existing common exchange rate, used to calculate compensation payments, and introduced two rates: one for currencies linked to the Deutsche Mark and one for all other EU currencies. Attempts by some member states to reform the system further were unsuccessful, and in October ministers agreed that national governments would be permitted to compensate farmers who had suffered loss of income as a result of currency fluctuations. The Commission is allowed to recover from member states sums that they have paid out under the CAP without sufficient guarantees of legitimacy or without adequate regard to control and verification.

In June 1995 the guaranteed intervention price for beef was decreased by 5% and that for cereals by 7.5%. In September ministers agreed to reduce the level of compulsory 'set-aside' for 1996/97 to 10%, in response to much lower food surpluses in the EU and high world prices for cereal crops. In July 1996 agriculture ministers agreed on a further reduction in the 'set-aside' rate for cereals to 5%. Fruit and vegetable production subsidies were fixed at no more than 4% of the value of total marketed production, rising to 4.5% in 1999. The aim was to improve competitiveness in the European market and avoid the widespread destruction of surplus fruit and vegetables that had taken place in previous years.

In March 1998 the Commission outlined firm proposals for reform of the CAP as part of its 'Agenda 2000', concerning the enlargement of the EU and the Community's budget for 2000–06, published in July 1997. The plans envisaged imposing limits on subsidies and reductions of up to 30% in guaranteed prices, to allow compliance with WTO rules. In June 1998 the Commission adopted proposals to introduce new agrimonetary arrangements for a period of three years from January 1999, owing to the launch of the euro. The arrangements were to compensate farmers in those EU member states not participating in the process of economic and monetary union (EMU) for currency fluctuations until 2002. Farmers in countries taking part in EMU were also to be compensated for reductions in prices and aid payments resulting from the abolition of currency differentials. In 2000, as a result of the appreciation of the currencies in Denmark, Sweden and the United Kingdom, agrimonetary measures were fixed to compensate these countries for the reduction in certain direct payments converted into national currencies.

In March 1999 EU ministers of agriculture reached a compromise agreement on reform of the CAP, which proposed reductions of up to 20% in guaranteed prices and increases in milk quotas from 2003/04. The plans were approved by heads of state and of government later that month, although they were modified to include less dramatic reductions in the guaranteed prices for cereals and to delay reforms to the dairy sector until 2005/06. According to the final agreement on the reforms, guaranteed prices for cereals were to be reduced by 7.5% in both 2000 and 2001 and the 'set-aside' rate was to be fixed at 10% until 2006. Guaranteed prices for beef were to be abolished and the 'basic price' offered for the meat was to decrease by a total of 20% over a three-year period from 2000 (more far-reaching reform for the beef sector was later proposed, as a result of the BSE crisis. Direct annual payments to farmers were to be increased, thereby compensating farmers for the reductions in guaranteed prices and removing incentives for over-production. A proposed limit on payments made to farmers, which aimed at preventing large-scale producers from receiving excessive compensation, failed to win approval. The CAP budget was expected to stabilize at some €4,500m. until 2006, although some officials expressed concern that the reforms were not sufficiently far-reaching to achieve this aim.

In 2000 the CAP reforms under Agenda 2000 relating to arable crops, beef and veal, milk and milk products, financing and rural development, were adopted. As a result of the reforms, the annual price-setting exercise in 2000 involved just six sectors: pig meat, sugar, silkworms, sheep meat, goat meat, and monthly increases for cereal and rice, on a multi-annual basis. For sugar, prices and amounts were set only until the end of the 2000/01 marketing year, when the production quota regime was due to expire. In April 2000, in the wake of sharper cyclical price movements on the market for pig meat, the Commission proposed introducing a regulatory fund into the market organization. This would aim to stabilize incomes, by collecting revenue when the situation was favourable and making payments in more difficult times.

Throughout 2000 the process of simplifying agricultural legislation continued, notably through the streamlining of the import and export licensing procedures. In December the varying procedures on the promotion of agricultural products in the internal market were replaced by one harmonized system. In January 2000 the Commission adopted a communication on the integration of environmental concerns into the CAP, whereby additional payments to farmers who adopt extra environmental protection measures were under consideration.

A further element of reform is the enlargement of the CAP to encompass the wider rural population. The policy of rural development under the CAP (described as the 'second pillar' of the CAP in Agenda 2000) aims to restore and increase the competitiveness of rural areas, through supporting employment, diversification and population growth. In addition, producers are to be rewarded for the preservation of rural heritage. Specifically, the policy will provide funds for the modernization of agricultural holdings, for establishing young farmers, for training and for early retirement. Forestry is recognized as an integral part of rural development (previous treaties on the EU made no provision for a comprehensive common forestry policy). During 1999 and 2000 member states developed rural development programmes for 2000–06. In June 2000 the Commission began the process of approval of these schemes, to which annual expenditure of €4,300m. had been committed. In late 2000 rural development programmes for a number of applicant countries were also adopted. These are drawn up under the EU's Special Accession Programme for Agriculture and Rural Development (SAPARD), which aims to help candidate countries manage structural adjustment in their agricultural sectors. Pre-accession aid of €520m per year is provided under SAPARD for 2000-06.

In January 2003 the Commission endorsed a radical reform package for the Common Agricultural Policy (CAP). Its recommendations included a number of measures relating to aid mechanisms and the promotion of rural development. The proposal aimed to stabilize markets and improve the common market organizations (the first pillar of the CAP), by introducing simpler and more sustainable direct support, and channeling a share of subsidies into rural development funds (the second pillar). Measures include the proposal that direct aid should be separated from production, with payments made conditional on compliance with environmental, food safety, animal welfare and occupational safety standards. Payments to large and medium-sized farms were to be reduced, to achieve a fairer distribution of the annual €42,000m. budget. The Commission also proposed to improve the competitiveness of Community agriculture by continuing to reduce guaranteed fixed prices for a number of products such as cereals, milk and rice, continuing a reform that had been in progress since 1992. The issue of CAP reform remains controversial, with several member states, led by France, bitterly opposed to the plans.

A further issue during 2002 related to the implications for the CAP of enlargement of the EU in 2004, when 10 new members join the Union: measures discussed included the adoption of agricultural trade concessions for candidate countries, in the form of tariff quotas for agricultural products. In October 2002 it was agreed that the enlargement process would be part-funded by a deal to cap farm subsidies at 2006 levels until 2013, and that candidate countries would be offered direct farm payments at 25% of the level paid to existing member states, rising in stages to 100% in 10 years.

The EU has adopted a number of measures on the safety of agricultural produce. In 1986 the first case of bovine spongiform encephalopathy (BSE) in UK cattle was noted. The use of meat and bone meal (MBM) in animal feed was identified as being responsible for the disease, which causes the brain tissue of cattle to degenerate, and was banned for use in cattle feed in 1988. The use of certain cuts of offal in human foodstuffs was prohibited in the United Kingdom in the following year. In July 1994 strict controls on carcass beef trade were imposed, with the time-scale for the prohibition of exports from diseased herds extended from two to six years. The agreement temporarily resolved a dispute between the United Kingdom and Germany, which had attempted to impose a unilateral ban on UK beef exports, provoking that country to seek a judicial ruling on the action by the European Court of Justice. New fears about possible links between BSE and Creutzfeldt-Jakob disease (CJD), which affects humans, led to a collapse in consumer confidence in the European beef market in early 1996. In March the Commission accepted that member countries could unilaterally stop imports of UK beef on health grounds, pending a decision by a committee of scientific and veterinary experts from all member states. At the end of the month the Commission agreed a full ban on exports from the United Kingdom of live cattle, beef and beef products. In 1996 the UK Government proposed a programme of selective slaughter and the implementation of new national legislation to ensure that MBM products were excluded from the manufacture of animal feeds. However, the planned cull was later abandoned, with the country proposing instead a much smaller slaughter scheme. In July the European Court of Justice rejected the UK Government's application for the beef export ban to be suspended. At the end of 1996 the Commission was estimated to have spent some ECU 1,500m., including ECU 850m. as compensation paid to beef farmers, on dealing with the consequences of the BSE crisis.

In December 1996 the UK Government yielded to the European Commission's demand for a more substantial cull. The Commission also stated that the United Kingdom was to submit plans for a certified BSE-free herd scheme, to provide computerized evidence that cattle herds had had no contact with other animals infected with BSE, before a phased removal of the export embargo could begin. In June 1997 the United Kingdom's plans for monitoring and preventing BSE were judged by the Commission to be inadequate. In July the United Kingdom was reported by the Commission to have engaged in the illegal export of beef, while in late June the Commission commenced infringement proceedings against 10 EU countries accused of evading the full implementation of hygiene procedures for the eradication of BSE. In July agriculture ministers voted to introduce a complete ban on the use for any purpose of 'specified risk materials' (SRMs—i.e. those most likely to carry BSE) from cattle, sheep and goats. The introduction of the ban was postponed until January 1999, as a result of opposition from a number of EU member states, particularly Germany, as well as the USA. The scope of legislation on undesirable substances in animal feed was extended in May 2002, to cover additives, with the aim of enhancing the safety of animal feed.

In May 1998 the Commission agreed to ease the export ban on UK beef, to allow the export of deboned beef from Northern Irish herds certified as BSE-free for eight years, from June. In November the Agriculture Council fully endorsed the United Kingdom's Date-based Export Scheme, which permitted the export of deboned beef produced from animals born after August 1996 and tracked by an official monitoring system. In October 1998 Portugal was banned from exporting beef and live cattle, following a two-fold increase in reported cases of BSE in the country. The ban on Portuguese beef exports was originally supposed to expire after nine months, but restrictions only began to be removed in March 2001.

In July 1999 the United Kingdom was deemed to have met all of the conditions pertaining to the lifting of the ban on its beef exports; the European Commission announced that exports would be permitted to resume from 1 August. In January 2000 the Commission commenced legal action against the French Government over its continued unilateral ban on imports of UK beef. In December 2001 the European Court of Justice ordered France to lift its ban. The Commission also started legal action against Germany in February 2000, but abandoned this the following month when Germany agreed to revoke the ban. France finally lifted its ban on British beef in October 2002.

In June 2000 a new surveillance system to improve the detection of BSE was introduced. In the following month the EU established a system for identifying and registering bovine animals and for labelling beef and beef products. The aim was to introduce, from September, a compulsory beef-labelling system making beef traceable 'from stable to table'. (The rules were further tightened in January 2002, to oblige producers to indicate precisely where animals had been born and reared.)

In December 2000, as an emergency measure to boost confidence in European beef, agriculture ministers determined to ban from the regional food chain (with effect from 1 January 2001) all cattle aged more than 30 months, unless these had been tested and proven not to be infected with the disease. The age limit was lowered to 24 months in June 2001. Also in June the EU set out further rules on the use of animal materials excluded from the human food chain. The ban on the use of MBM in feed for pigs and poultry, first adopted in January, was extended.

By January 2001 incidences of BSE infection had been reported in 11 of the 15 member countries (with the number of confirmed cases in France and Ireland increasing significantly in 2000). The BSE epidemic in the United Kingdom had eased progressively since its peak in 1993, but in early 2001 around 30 suspected cases were still being reported every week. In December EU vets and scientists reported that they believed the incidence of BSE in UK cattle to be far higher than official figures indicated. By September 2001 the total official number of cases of BSE in the EU stood at 181,946, of which 180,019 had occurred in the United Kingdom.

Following an outbreak of foot-and-mouth disease on farms in the United Kingdom in February 2001, the EU imposed a temporary ban on imports of UK livestock products. Three days after the first cases were reported, all movement of susceptible livestock in the United Kingdom was stopped. The culling of sheep imported from the United Kingdom to other member states began in February. An EU-wide ban on assembly points and markets for all potentially affected species was imposed (with exceptions for direct transport to slaughter-houses and other farms) and measures were adopted requiring the disinfection of vehicles travelling from the United Kingdom to other member states. Cases of foot-and-mouth disease were also noted in the Netherlands, France and Ireland. These three countries were declared free of the disease in September. During the outbreak, the USA and other third countries imposed import restrictions on fresh meat and livestock from the EU. As the outbreak waned, the EU announced that its policy on vaccination (currently used only as a temporary emergency measure on animals awaiting slaughter and destruction, rather than pre-emptively, to prevent infection) would be reviewed. In January 2002 the United Kingdom regained 'clear' status, without recourse to vaccination. In December 2002 the European Parliament adopted a resolution on measures to control foot-and-mouth disease in the EU; its proposals included the use of vaccination as a preventative option in the event of any future outbreak.

In April 1999 a dispute arose between the EU and the USA after the EU announced plans to ban all imports of US beef, as a result of traces of growth hormones found in imported meat that was supposed to be hormone-free. In May the EU informed the WTO that it would not be able to lift its ban on US hormone-treated beef by 13 May 1999, as the WTO had ordered that it should. The USA subsequently imposed sanctions, and the dispute persisted throughout 2000 and 2001.

In June 1999 the USA impounded all imports of European pork and poultry, because of the possibility that these might have been contaminated by a carcinogen, dioxin, extremely high levels of which had been discovered in some Belgian supplies of animal feedstuffs. The European Commission had already prohibited the sale of some Belgian food products. In 2000, following the successful completion in Belgium of a programme to detect dioxins on farms and in produce, the Commission lifted the restrictions on Belgium. As part of ongoing efforts to tighten controls relating to animal health, the Commission adopted a proposal for a directive on measures to control classical swine fever in 2000. In June 2001 random testing for transmissible spongiform encephalopathies (TSEs, including scrapie) was introduced for sheep and goats.

The EU has also adopted a number of protective measures to prevent the introduction of organisms harmful to plants and plant products. In 2000 the Commission adopted four directives determining the maximum levels of pesticide residues permitted in products of plant origin. In mid-2001, noting consumer interest in organic products, the Council invited discussion towards a future action plan to promote organic food and farming. By the end of 2000 there were 541 registered names (protected geographical indications —PGI—and protected designations of origin—PDO) of agricultural products and foodstuffs in the EU.

The EU's Food and Veterinary Office was established in April 1997 to ensure that the laws on food safety, animal health and welfare and plant health are applied in all member states. The office carries out audits and checks on food safety in member states and in third countries exporting agricultural produce to the EU. Legislation establishing the European Food Safety Authority (EFSA) was signed in January 2002; the new body will provide independent scientific advice and support and to give the public information on food risks. It will have no regulatory or judicial power, but will co-operate closely with similar bodies in the member states. The first meeting of the EFSA management board took place in September 2002, while its Advisory Forum was convened for the first time in March 2003.

In April 2000 a team of EU experts was set up to provide advice on issues concerning genetically-modified (GM) crops and food products. A draft directive regulating the planting, testing and sale of GM products was approved by the European Parliament in February 2001. Among other provisions, this requires a risk assessment to be carried out for each GM organism (GMO), and the creation of a public register of all GMOs released for trial and for commercial purposes. Additional rules on the labelling and tracing of GM foods took effect in October 2002. The EU envisaged that these would be sufficiently stringent to allow the issue of marketing permits for new GM products. The planned European Food Safety Authority was to carry out risk assessments and participate in the authorization process.

In June 1995 the Agriculture Council agreed to new rules on the welfare of livestock during transport. The agreement, which came into effect in 1996, limited transport of livestock to a maximum of eight hours in any 24-hour period, and stipulated higher standards for their accommodation and care while in transit. In January 1996 the Commission proposed a ban on veal crates, which was to come into effect from January 1998. In April 2001 the Commission adopted new rules for long-distance animal transport, setting out the required standards of ventilation, temperature and humidity control. In June 1999 EU agriculture ministers agreed to end battery egg production within the EU by 2012; in December 2000 a regulation was adopted requiring EU producers to indicate the rearing method on eggs and egg-packaging. In December 2002 the European Council suggested the establishment of a system of exchange of information between member states on aspects of animal welfare.

FISHERIES

The Common Fisheries Policy (CFP) came into effect in January 1983 after seven years of negotiations, particularly concerning the problem of access to fishing-grounds. In 1973 a 10-year agreement had been reached, whereby member states could have exclusive access to waters up to six nautical miles (11.1 km) or, in some cases, 12 miles from their shores; 'historic rights' were reserved in certain cases for foreign fishermen who had traditionally fished within a country's waters. In 1977 the Community set up a 200-mile (370-km) fishing zone around its coastline (excluding the Mediterranean) within which all members would have access to fishing. The 1983 agreement confirmed the 200-mile zone and allowed exclusive national zones of six miles with access between six and 12 miles from the shore for other countries according to specified historic rights. Rules furthering conservation (e.g. standards for fishing tackle) were imposed under the policy, with checks by a Community fisheries inspectorate. Total allowable catches (TACs) are fixed annually by species, divided into national quotas under the renewable Multiannual Guidance Programme (MAGP). The Commission monitors compliance with the quotas and TACs and with technical measures in Community and some international waters.

In 1990 it was reported that stocks of certain species of fish in EC waters had seriously diminished. Consequently a reduction in quotas was agreed, together with the imposition of a compulsory eight-day period in each month during which fishermen in certain areas (chiefly the North Sea) would stay in port, with exemptions for fishermen using nets with larger meshes that would allow immature fish to escape. In 1992 the compulsory non-fishing period was increased to 135 days between February and December (with similar exemptions).

In December 1992 EC ministers agreed to extend the CFP for a further 10-year period. Two years later ministers concluded a final agreement on the revised CFP, allowing Spain and Portugal to be integrated into the policy by 1 January 1996. A compromise accord was reached regarding access to waters around Ireland and off south-west Great Britain (referred to as the 'Irish box'), by means of which up to 40 Spanish vessels were granted access to 80,000 sq miles of the 90,000 sq mile area. However, the accord was strongly opposed by Irish and UK fishermen. In April 1995 seven Spanish vessels were seized by the Irish navy, allegedly for fishing illegally in the Irish Sea. In October fisheries ministers agreed to a regime to control fishing in the 'Irish box', introducing stricter controls and instituting new surveillance measures.

The organization of fish marketing involves common rules on quality and packing and a system of guide prices established annually by the Council. Fish are withdrawn from the market if prices fall too far below the guide price, and compensation may then be paid to the fishermen. Export subsidies are paid to enable the export of fish onto the lower-priced world market and import levies are imposed to prevent competition from low-priced imports. A new import regime took effect from May 1993. This enables regional fishermens' associations to increase prices to a maximum of 10% over the Community's reference price, although this applies to both EU and imported fish.

Initially, structural assistance actions for fisheries were financed by the EAGGF. Following the reform of the structural funds in 1993, a separate fund, the Financial Instrument for Fisheries Guidance (FIFG), was set up. The instrument's principal responsibilities include the decommissioning of vessels and the creation, with foreign investors, of joint ventures designed to reduce the fishing effort in EU waters. The fund also supports the building and modernizing of vessels, developments in the aquaculture sector and the creation of protected coastal areas. In addition, it finances contributions to redundancy payments.

The proposals put forward in May 1996 by the European Commission for the fourth MAGP, covering 1997–2002, envisaged catch reductions of up to 40% for species most at risk, and set targets and detailed rules for restructuring fishing fleets in the EU. The draft MAGP IV failed to gain approval at the meeting of fisheries ministers held in November 1996. The UK Government, in October, insisted that it would not accept additional limits on catches without action to stop quota-hopping, in which UK-registered boats are bought by operators in other EU countries (mainly Spain and the Netherlands), which are thus able to gain part of the UK fishing quotas. (In mid-1998 the UK Government received approval from the Commission to introduce new licensing conditions from 1 January 1999 that would compel the owners of boats involved in 'quota-hopping' to establish economic links with the United Kingdom.) In April 1997, following a number of concessions by the Commission, ministers approved MAGP IV. The programme fixed catch reductions at 30% for species most at risk and at 20% for other over-fished species.

In June 1998 the Council overcame long-standing objections from a number of member states and adopted a ban on the use of drift nets in the Atlantic Ocean and the Mediterranean Sea, in an attempt to prevent the unnecessary deaths of marine life such as dolphins and sharks. The ban, introduced in January 2002, partially implemented a 1992 UN resolution demanding a complete cessation of drift-net fishing. A series of compensatory measures aims to rectify any short-term detrimental impact on EU fishing fleets.

A meeting of the European Council in Helsinki, in December 1999, requested the Fisheries Council to formulate a strategy for the integration of environmental issues into the CFP. It was agreed that the CFP should adopt the principles of the EU's environmental policy, including recognizing the precedence of preventative action, the need to rectify environmental damage at source and the economic responsibility of the 'authors' of environmental damage. In March 2001 the Commission adopted a series of action plans designed to integrate the protection of biodiversity into fisheries policies, building on the Community biodiversity strategy presented in 1998.

With concern over stocks continuing to mount, an emergency 11-week ban on deep-sea cod fishing over 40,000 sq miles of the North Sea was introduced in February 2001. In March similar emergency measures for the west of Scotland entered into effect, while emergency measures for the northern hake catch were adopted in June. Measures for the Irish Sea had been instituted in 2000. In December 2001 the Fisheries Council fixed TACs for 2002, incorporating further substantial reductions, with the aim of achieving 'biologically acceptable' levels of stocks. It was agreed to extend MAGP IV until June 2002. In the same month the Commission presented its long-term recovery plans for cod and hake. Under the plans, the Commission proposed establishing a procedure for setting TACs so as to achieve a significant increase in mature fish stocks, with limits on the fishing effort fixed in accordance with the TACs. The plans also provided for the temporary closure of areas where endangered species have congregated, and allowed for more generous EU aid for the decommissioning of vessels (aid for the modernization of vessels, which tends to increase the fishing catch, was to be reduced). The Commission proposed catch limits for deep-water fish stocks (including blue ling, red seabream and black scabbardfish) for the first time in December.

In April 2001 a Green Paper on the future of the CFP was presented. The paper stated that a balance between fishing effort and resources must be reached, to achieve a sustainable future for the industry. It concluded that a 'thorough and urgent reform' was needed. Proposals included the imposition of a multi-annual strategy for TAC and quota management; the development of a new fleet policy; measures to enhance the EU's profile in regional fisheries organizations; and the creation of an EU-wide joint inspection structure.

Radical reform of the CFP, aimed at ensuring the sustainable development of the industry, was announced during 2002; the Commission proposed a new multiannual framework for the conservation of resources and the management of fisheries, incorporating environmental concerns. Under its terms, quotas for cod catches in the North Sea were to be reduced by 45% in 2003, while catches of whiting and haddock were to be cut by 50%. Fishermen were to be guaranteed only nine days a month at sea (with some leeway to extend this to 15 days in some circumstances) and public funding for new fishing boats was to be abolished after 2004. As a further part of the reform, in April 2002 the Commission proposed to abandon the MAGP system and replace it with a more effective system for monitoring fishing capacity.

Agreements have been signed with other countries (Norway, Sweden, Canada and the USA) allowing reciprocal fishing rights and other advantages, and with some African countries that receive assistance in strengthening their fishing industries in return for allowing EU boats to fish in their waters. Following the withdrawal of Greenland from the Community in February 1985, Community vessels retained fishing rights in Greenland waters, in exchange for financial compensation. Under a four-year agreement signed with Morocco in November 1995, the size of catches by EU vessels fishing in Moroccan waters was reduced by 20%–40% for various species, and the EU provided financial compensation to Morocco amounting to ECU 355m. Morocco decided that it would not renew the fishing agreement with the EU in 1999, and the accord became void at the end of November. In November 2001 the Commission agreed an aid package of €197m. to convert the Spanish and Portuguese fleets that fished Moroccan waters, including €63m. for social measures to aid the crews of the boats. In January 2003 Morocco lifted its ban on fishing by EU vessels for a three-month period as a goodwill gesture following an oil spill which polluted much of the Spanish coast; officials were optimistic that this would lead to a further agreement about fishing in Moroccan waters.

During 2002 fisheries agreements were concluded or renewed with several countries, including Angola, Cape Verde, Gabon, Guinea, Guinea-Bissau, Kiribati, Mozambique, Senegal, Seychelles, and South Africa.

RESEARCH AND TECHNOLOGY

In the amendments to the Treaty of Rome, effective from July 1987, a section on research and technology was included for the first time, defining the extent of Community co-operation in this area. Most of the funds allocated to research and technology are granted to companies or institutions that apply to participate in EU research programmes. In March 1996 task forces established by the Commission presented a report identifying priority topics for European research: the car of tomorrow; educational software and multimedia; new generation aircraft; vaccines and viral diseases; trains and railway systems of the future; intermodal transport; maritime systems; and the environment, with a particular focus on water resources.

In January 2000 the Commission launched an initiative to establish a European Research Area (ERA). The aim was to promote the more effective use of scientific resources within a single area, in order to enhance the EU's competitiveness and create jobs. ERA will provide venture capital and tax breaks for research and high-technology start-up companies.

The creation of ERA will be supported through the sixth framework programme for research and technological development, which was launched in 2002. Covering the period 2002-06, the programme, which had a budget of €16,270m., aimed to integrate research capacities in Europe (for example by establishing networks of excellence and jointly-implemented national programmes), and to concentrate on priority areas such as genomics, information technology and food safety. The candidate countries that were to join the enlarged EU were to be integrated into the programme's framework, while international co-operation was also to be stressed.

The European Strategic Programme for Research and Development in Information Technology (ESPRIT) was inaugurated in 1984 and concentrated on five key areas: advanced micro-electronics; software technology; advanced information processing; office automation; and computer integrated manufacturing. The programme was financed half by the EU and half by the participating research institutes, universities and industrial companies. ESPRIT was integrated into the EU's Information Society Technologies (IST) initiative under the fifth framework programme. The IST initiative is designed to accelerate the emergence of an information society in Europe by promoting the development of high-quality, affordable services.

In July 1997 the European Parliament approved the Life Patent Directive, a proposal aiming to harmonize European rules on gene patenting in order to promote research into genetic diseases, despite objections over the ethical implications. In December 2000 the EU agreed to establish a parliamentary committee to examine new developments in human genetics. In late 2001 the Commission set up a website to encourage debate on stem cell research, aiming to create a dialogue between experts and the public. The EU is also participating actively in the international human genome project, which seeks to characterize the genomes of humans and other organisms, through mapping and sequencing of their DNA.

The EU is making efforts to integrate space science into its research activities, and is increasingly collaborating with the European Space Agency (ESA). In November 2000 the EU and ESA adopted a joint European strategy for space. In March 2002 the EU approved the development of the 'Galileo' civil satellite navigation and positioning system. Start-up costs are projected at €3,250m.; the system will require €220m. a year for maintenance from 2008.

In February 2000 the European Parliament called for action to be taken to combat the under-representation of women in science. In June the Commission began an assessment of the gender balance in the specific projects carried out under the fifth framework programme. The Commission is working towards a target of 40% participation by women at all levels in the implementation and management of research programmes.

Following a further reorganization in September 2001, the Community's own Joint Research Centre (JRC) comprises six institutes, based at Ispra (Italy), Geel (Belgium), Karlsruhe (Germany), Seville (Spain) and Petten (Netherlands). In 2000 the JRC restructured its work around four areas: safety of food and chemicals; the environment; the dependability of information systems and services; and nuclear safety and safeguards. In particular, it prioritized work on genetically-modified organisms. Nuclear work accounted for about 27% of total JRC activities in 2000, with the share accounted for by non-nuclear work increasing. The JRC also provides technical assistance to applicant countries. During 2002 the JRC's work centred on sustainable development and exposure to health hazards in the context of food, chemicals, pollution, water supply and noise. The new Science Strategy Directorate, based in Brussels, serves as a link between the JRC institutes and European policymakers.

In March 2002 the European Council agreed that investment in research and development (R & D) in the EU should be increased, with the aim of approaching 3% of GDP by 2010, compared with 1.9% in 2000. The Commission subsequently adopted a communication on the means to promote such an increase, such as highly qualified human resources, a strong public research base, an appropriate competitive environment and favourable fiscal conditions.

The EU also co-operates with non-member countries (particularly EFTA states) in bilateral research projects. The Commission and 19 European countries (including the members of the EU as individuals) participate in the 'Eureka' programme of research in advanced technology, which was relaunched in 1999. The programme, focusing on robotics, engineering, IT and environmental science, allows resources to be pooled and promotes collaboration. In 2000 Croatia, Israel and Latvia joined Eureka. In addition, the Community research and development information service ('Cordis') disseminates findings in this field, with eight databases, while the 'Value' programme funds the publication and dissemination of technical reports from specific research projects. In 1994 a European Technology Assessment Network (ETAN) was developed to improve the dissemination of technological research findings; under the fifth framework programme this was replaced by the Strategic Analysis

of Specific Political Issues (Strata) programme, which sets up groups of experts and works to develop networks.

ENERGY

The treaty establishing the European Atomic Energy Community ('Euratom') came into force on 1 January 1958. This was designed to encourage the growth of the nuclear energy industry in the Community by conducting research, providing access to information, supplying nuclear fuels, building reactors and establishing common laws and procedures. A common market for nuclear materials was introduced in 1959 and there is a common insurance scheme against nuclear risks. In 1977 the Commission began granting loans on behalf of Euratom to finance investment in nuclear power stations and the enrichment of fissile materials. An agreement with the International Atomic Energy Authority entered into force in 1977, to facilitate co-operation in research on nuclear safeguards and controls. The EU's Joint Research Centre (JRC, see under Research and Technology) conducts research on nuclear safety and the management of radioactive waste.

The Joint European Torus (JET) is an experimental thermonuclear machine designed to pioneer new processes of nuclear fusion, using the 'Tokamak' system of magnetic confinement to heat gases to very high temperatures and bring about the fusion of tritium and deuterium nuclei. Switzerland is also a member of the JET project. Since 1974 work has been proceeding at Culham in the United Kingdom, and the project was formally inaugurated in April 1984. In 1991 JET became the first fusion facility in the world to achieve significant production of controlled fusion power. In 1988 work began with representatives of Japan, the former USSR and the USA on the joint design of an International Thermonuclear Experimental Reactor (ITER), based on JET. The aim of ITER was to demonstrate the scientific and technical capacities of fusion energy for peaceful purposes. The European Fusion Development Agreement (EFDA), which entered into force in January 1999, and a new JET implementing agreement, which came into force in January 2000, provides the framework for the collective use of the JET facilities.

Legislation on the completion of the 'internal energy market', adopted in 1990, aimed to encourage the sale of electricity and gas across national borders in the Community by opening national networks to foreign supplies, obliging suppliers to publish their prices and co-ordinating investment in energy. Energy ministers reached agreement in June 1996 on rules for the progressive liberalization of the electricity market. Twenty-five per cent of the market was to be opened up from mid-February 1999, rising to 33% by 2003. Belgium and Ireland were to implement the agreement in 2000, while Greece would be exempt until 2001. In November 1999 the Commission commenced legal action against France and Luxembourg for failure to meet the February deadline for opening their electricity markets. In December 1997 the Council agreed rules to allow the gas market to be opened up in three stages, over a 10-year period. The staged scheme allowed the largest gas suppliers to receive temporary exemptions from trade liberalization if the presence of competitors caused demand for supplies to drop below the amount that the distributor was contracted to purchase in the long term.

In 2001 the Commission amended the timetable for liberalizing the electricity and gas markets: by 2003 all non-domestic consumers were to have the freedom to choose their electricity supplier; by 2004 non-domestic consumers were to have the freedom to choose their gas supplier; and by 2005 all consumers, domestic and non-domestic, would be able to choose both suppliers. The Commission further proposed that the management of transmission and distribution grids should be legally separated from production and sales activities (except for small-scale distribution companies). It was suggested that network access tariffs should be published and approved by national regulators before entering into force, and that a regulator should be established for each member state. To create a genuine single market, the Commission proposed adopting rules on tariff-setting across borders, developing a European infrastructure plan for electricity and gas, and negotiating reciprocal agreements on the opening of electricity markets with the EU's neighbours. In June 2002 the European Council confirmed amended target dates for the complete two-stage liberalization of the markets: opening up by July 2004 for non-domestic users and by July 2007 for domestic users (the latter target had been extended in the face of opposition among member countries, with France in particular reluctant to liberalize fully its electricity market for domestic customers).

The Commission has consistently urged the formation of an effective overall energy policy. The five-year 'SAVE' programme, introduced in 1991, emphasized the improvement of energy efficiency, reduction of the energy consumption of vehicles and the use of renewable energy. A second five-year programme, SAVE II, was initiated in 1995, covering 1996–2000. This aimed to continue the work of the first programme and to establish energy efficiency as a criterion for all EU projects. In February 2002 SAVE was integrated into the 'Energy, Environment and Sustainable Development—EESD' thematic programme initiated under the fifth framework programme for 1998–2002. The 'Carnot' programme, which promotes the use of clean technologies for solid fuels, and the ETAP multi-annual programme of studies and forecasts in the energy sector, were also integrated into the fifth framework programme. As the fifth framework programme came to an end in 2002, the Commission put forward a proposal for a new multi-annual programme for action in the field of energy for the period 2003-06. The programme aimed to focus on security of energy supply, rational and effective use of energy, and promotion of renewable energy. In November 2002 a budget of €190m. was agreed for the programme.

In 1990 the Council established the ALTENER programme, which aimed to increase the contribution of renewable energy sources (RES), such as wind, solar, biomass and small-scale hydropower, within the Community. The programme finished at the end of 1997, having supported 278 projects since 1993, at a cost of ECU 26.9m. A replacement programme for 1998–2002, ALTENER II, was allocated a budget of €77m. A Green Paper on ways of promoting RES in the EU was issued in November 1996. These sources provided less than 6% of the total energy produced in the EU at that time. In May 1998, following the publication of a report by the Commission in late 1997, the Council committed the EU to increasing the use of RES to 12% by 2010. The Campaign for Take-Off, initiated after the 1997 report, set out a framework for action, with four main objectives: developing 1m. photovoltaic systems; establishing wind-farm-generating capacity of 10,000 MW; reaching 10,000 MW (thermal) of biomass installation; and integrating RES to meet the total electricity requirements of 100 communities. The Renewable Energy Partnership scheme works to involve public and private partners in the campaign. In May 2000 the EU set out a fourfold strategy on the promotion of electricity from RES in the internal energy market, based on the 1997 report: member states were to set and comply with national targets for the future consumption of energy from RES, consistent with the commitments entered into under the Kyoto protocol (see under Environment Policy), and to introduce a system for certifying the origin of electricity from RES; operators of transmission and district networks were to be encouraged to give priority to RES electricity; and measures were to be taken to establish a harmonized support system for RES producers. In December an action plan on energy efficiency was adopted, setting out measures to integrate energy efficiency into other EU policies and programmes. In January 2000 the Commission submitted a proposal for an EU energy-efficiency labelling programme

Energy ministers from the EU member states and 12 Mediterranean countries agreed at a meeting held in June 1996 in Trieste, Italy, to develop a Euro-Mediterranean gas and electricity network. The first Euro-Med Energy Forum was held in May 1997, and an action plan to develop the network was adopted at a Euro-Med conference of energy ministers in May 1998. In May 2002 a Euro-Med conference of energy ministers discussed the issue of security of energy supply in the Mediterranean region. In 1997 a programme for the Optimal Use of Energy Resources in Latin America (ALURE) began the implementation of projects in that region. In 1997 the Community agreed to help a number of eastern European countries to overcome energy problems by means of the Interstate Oil and Gas to Europe programme (INOGATE). This programme, which was to receive €50m. over a five-year period, aimed to improve energy flows in eastern Europe and to increase the access of newly independent countries to European markets. INOGATE forms part of the TACIS programme (see under External Relations). In July 2002 the Commission adopted a communication on energy co-operation with developing countries, and proposed a framework for EU external action in this field.

The EU also promotes trans-European energy networks (TENs, see under Transport Policy), with the aim of improving the operation of the internal energy market and reinforcing the security of supplies. In 2001 90 projects of common interest for electricity and gas TENS had been identified. These included linking isolated networks; developing interconnections between member states and with third countries; introducing natural gas to new regions; and increasing the capacity for the transmission, reception and storage of natural gas.

In a communication in September 2000 the Commission set out the broad lines of a new EU strategy on nuclear safety in central and eastern Europe and the former Soviet states. The strategy entailed supporting those countries in their efforts to improve operating safety, strengthening their regulatory frameworks, and closing reactors that could not be upgraded to an acceptable standard. The SURE programme of action under the fifth framework programme aimed to improve safety and co-operation in the nuclear sector with countries participating in the TACIS programme. In December 2000, in accordance with its commitments, the Commission approved a grant of €25m. from the TACIS budget for 2000 for the closure of the Chernobyl (Chornobyl) nuclear power station in Ukraine, to cover part of the cost of the resulting temporary power shortfall. A Euratom loan of €558m. was granted for completion of the replacement reactors. In November 1999 the Commission indicated the need to strengthen the EU's 'Northern Dimension' energy policy (covering Scandinavia, the Baltic states and northwest Russia.)

In November 2000 the Commission adopted a Green Paper on the security of energy supply, which was aimed at launching a broad debate on the role of each energy source, with regard to the security of supply, sustainable development, questions of enlargement, and action needed to combat climate change. Security of supply is of vital importance as the EU currently meets 50% of its energy requirements through imports. In October 2000, in response to a sharp rise in petroleum prices, the Commission issued a communication emphasizing the importance of dialogue between the major producer and consumer countries and the need to adjust priorities with a view to maintaining prices at a stable level.

The issue of enlargement of the EU has brought implications for nuclear safety, since five of the 10 candidate countries have nuclear reactors, mostly of the old Soviet design. In November 2002 the Commission proposed the establishment of a new Community reference framework for nuclear safety standards, with plans for a directive setting out basic obligations and general principles relating to the safety of nuclear installations.

INDUSTRY, ENTERPRISE AND BUSINESS POLICY

Industrial co-operation was the earliest activity of the Community. The treaty establishing the European Coal and Steel Community (ECSC) came into force in July 1952, and by the end of 1954 nearly all barriers to trade in coal, coke, steel, pig-iron and scrap iron had been removed. The ECSC treaty expired in July 2002, and the provisions of the ECSC treaty were incorporated in the EEC treaty, on the grounds that it was no longer appropriate to treat the coal and steel sectors separately.

In the late 1970s and 1980s measures were adopted to restructure the steel industry in response to a dramatic reduction in world demand for steel. These included production capacity quotas and a reduction of state subsidies. In November 1992 the Commission announced a three-year emergency programme to further restructure the industry, following a reduction of 30% in steel prices over the previous two years. In December 1993 ministers approved aid totalling ECU 7,000m. to achieve a further reduction in annual capacity at a number of state-owned steel plants. The industry failed to achieve the required reduction in capacity of 19m. metric tons, and in October 1994 the Commission decided to abandon the restructuring plan, although the social measures, which allocated ECU 240m. to compensate for job losses, were to be maintained. Output of crude steel totalled 156m. tons in 1995, reversing the downward trend of previous years. In December 1996 the Commission adopted a new code on steel aid, for the period 1997–2002. The new code stipulated the conditions under which member states could grant aid to steel companies, namely for research and development, environmental protection, and for full or partial closures of capacity. In October 1997 the Commission announced plans to finance, using ECSC reserves, research of benefit to the coal and steel industries amounting to some ECU 40m. each year, after the expiry of the ECSC Treaty in 2002. In 2000 total EU steel production was estimated at 163m. tons. In January 2002 the Commission adopted a draft forward programme for steel for 2002, aimed at strengthening the EU's competitive position in this sector. In 2002 the Commission adopted a report on state aid to the coal industry, and in particular the results of restructuring, rationalization and modernization in the member states that still produce coal.

The European textile and clothing industry has been seriously affected by overseas competition over an extended period. The Community participates in the Multi-fibre Arrangement (MFA, see WTO, see p. 323), to limit imports from low-cost suppliers overseas. A proposal by the Commission in October 1996 to accelerate liberalization of the textiles and clothing market in the EU provoked anger among industry leaders in member states, because no reciprocal concessions, in the form of removal of trade barriers, were being obtained from the major textile-exporting countries in other parts of the world. A proposal by the Commission to impose duties of between 3% and 36% on imports of unfinished cotton fabrics, to counter alleged 'dumping' by several developing countries, was opposed by a majority of EU member states. The proposal aimed to help weaving industries (mainly in France and Italy), which had been adversely affected by the developing countries' practice of sharply undercutting their prices. Duties were provisionally introduced, for a period of six months, in late 1996. In March 1998 provisional duties of between 14% and 32.5% were imposed on imports of unbleached cotton from six countries, despite opposition by nine EU member states. Ministers of foreign affairs voted to remove duties in October. An action plan for the industry was drawn up in 1997. This was designed to improve competitiveness, facilitate structural adjustment in the industry and improve conditions of employment and training. In December 2000 the Commission published a report on the implementation of the plan, noting that there was still insufficient investment in research and innovation. The 2000 report established future priorities for the sector, focusing on preparations for the enlargement of the EU and systems for co-operation in the 'new economy'. During 2002 the European Council approved bilateral agreements on textiles between the EC and Brazil, Nepal and Cambodia, while India, Thailand and the Philippines were reported to be considering reciprocal market-opening deals with the EU for trade in textiles.

Production in EU member states' shipyards has fallen drastically since the 1970s, mainly as a result of competition from shipbuilders in the Far East. In the first half of the 1980s a Council directive allowed for subsidies to help reorganize the shipbuilding industry and to increase efficiency, but subsequently, rigorous curbs on state aid to the industry were introduced. The permitted maximum percentage of state aid for shipbuilding was reduced from 28% of the value of each vessel in 1987 to 9% in 1992. In July 1994 the EU signed an accord with Japan, the USA, the Republic of Korea and the Nordic countries to end subsidies to the shipbuilding industry from 1996, subject to ratification by member states. However, subsidies available in several EU countries in 1996 were higher than the official ceiling, and state aid was also given for industrial restructuring (for example, for modernization of east German shipyards) and for rescuing state-owned yards in difficulties (as in Spain). In October 1997 the Commission proposed to maintain state aid until the end of 2000; it was eventually phased out in early 2001. In April 2002 the Commission adopted its fifth report on the state of world shipbuilding. It confirmed previous observations that, in the absence of an international agreement, the market was facing a serious crisis, owing to the extremely low prices offered by South Korean shipyards. In May 2002 the EU agreed to launch WTO procedures against South Korea, and to establish a 'temporary defensive mechanism' of state subsidies to protect European shipbuilding against unfair South Korean practices.

The Commission has made a number of proposals for the development of the information technology (IT) industry in Europe, particularly in view of the superiority of Japan and the USA in the market for advanced electronic circuits. Under the fifth framework programme for 1998–2002, several of the EU's IT programmes were integrated into an overall Information Society Technologies (IST) programme (see under Research and Technology), designed to facilitate the development of IT in Europe. Various other initiatives to promote e-commerce and IT to businesses are under way (see under Telecommunications and Information Technology).

Harmonization of national company law to form a common legal structure within the Community has led to the adoption of directives on disclosure of information, company capital, internal mergers, the accounts of companies and of financial institutions, the division of companies, the qualification of auditors, single-member private limited companies, mergers, take-over bids and the formation of joint ventures. In September 2002 the European Council prepared an action plan on 'corporate governance', aimed at improving and modernizing the regulatory framework of company law, by looking at issues such as executives' pay and audit practices. Ministers also agreed to discuss the creation of a regulatory body to oversee corporate governance across the EU. The Community Patent Convention was signed in 1975. In June 1997 the Commission published a consultative document containing proposals to simplify the European patent system through the introduction of a unitary Community patent, which would remove the need to file patent applications with individual member states. The Commission hoped to have the patent in place by the end of 2001, but disagreements between member states resulted in this deadline being missed. Once established, the patent was to be issued by the European Patent Office (EPO), based in Munich. An Office for Harmonization in the Internal Market (OHIM), based in Alicante, Spain, was established in December 1993, and is responsible for the registration of Community trade-marks and for ensuring that these receive uniform protection throughout the EU. Numerous directives have been adopted on the technical harmonization and standardization of products (e.g. on safety devices in motor vehicles, labelling of foodstuffs and of dangerous substances, and classification of medicines).

The liberalization of Community public procurement has played an important role in the establishment of the internal market. A directive on public supplies contracts (effective from January 1989, or from March 1992 in Greece, Portugal and Spain) stipulated that major purchases of supplies by public authorities should be offered for tender throughout the Community. Public contracts for construction or civil engineering works in excess of ECU 5m. were to be offered for tender throughout the EC from July 1990 (March 1992 for Greece, Portugal and Spain). From January 1993 the liberalization of procurement was extended to include public utilities in the previously excluded sectors of energy, transport, drinking-water and telecommunications. In mid-1998 business leaders proposed introducing independent ombudsmen to monitor the operation of public procurement throughout the EU and to verify its compliance with competition rules. An action plan was adopted in 1998 for revitalizing public procurement policy. In particular, it aimed to make

contract award procedures clearer and more flexible. During 2002 the European Parliament adopted a regulation aimed at simplifying the rules on procurement of contract notices, by introducing a single system for classifying public procurement, to be used by all public authorities. The Commission has launched the Système d'information pour les marchés publics (SIMAP) programme, which gives information on rules, procedures and opportunities in the public procurement market. SIMAP aims to encourage the optimum use of IT in public procurement; the March 2000 Lisbon summit set the goal of bringing EU and government procurement fully online by 2003.

In October 2001 the Commission presented a strategy for company taxation in the EU, suggesting the introduction of a single consolidated tax base, to eliminate the large variations in effective company tax rates across the EU. The Commission noted that a new approach was needed, in view of increasing globalization and economic integration in the internal market as well as developments such as economic and monetary union (EMU, see under Economic Co-operation). In that month the European Council also adopted two legislative instruments enabling companies to form a European Company (known as a Societas Europaea—SE). A vital element of the internal market, the legislation gave companies operating in more than one member state the option of establishing themselves as single companies, thereby able to function throughout the EU under one set of rules and through a unified management system; companies might be merged to establish an SE. The legislation was aimed at making cross-border enterprise management more flexible and less bureaucratic, and at helping to improve competitiveness.

The Business Co-operation Centre, established in 1973, supplies information to businesses and introduces firms from 70 different countries wishing to co-operate or form links. The Business Co-operation Network (BC-Net) links enterprises, both public and private, which wish to form alliances with others (e.g. licensing agreements), on a confidential basis. The Business Environment Simplification Task Force was established in September 1997 to consider ways of improving legislation and of removing hindrances to the development of businesses, especially small and medium-sized enterprises (SMEs). It presented its report in 1998; the subsequent action plan, designed to improve the overall environment for business, was endorsed in April 1999.

In September 1995 a Commission report outlined proposals to improve the business environment for SMEs in particular, by improving fiscal policies and access to finance, and introducing measures aimed at reducing delays in payments and lowering the costs of international transactions. In March 1996 the Commission agreed new guide-lines for state aid to SMEs. Aid for the acquisition of patent rights, licences, expertise, etc., was to be allowed at the same level as that for tangible investment. In July 1997 the I-TEC scheme was inaugurated, with a budget of ECU 7.5m., to encourage SMEs to invest in new technology. By mid-1998 I-TEC had facilitated investments amounting to over ECU 250m. A Charter for Small Enterprises, approved in June 2000, aimed to support SMEs in areas such as education and training, the development of regulations, and taxation and financial matters, and to increase representation of the interests of small businesses at national and EU level. In October 2001 SMEs comprised 98% of all EU enterprises and employed almost 75m. people. The EU has repeatedly stated that it views small businesses as a vital source of economic growth and employment creation; in December 2001 the Commission appointed an 'SME Envoy' to act as a representative for, and a contact with, SMEs.

The European Investment Bank (see p. 207) provides finance for small businesses by means of 'global loans' to financial intermediaries. A mechanism providing small businesses with subsidized loans was approved by ministers in April 1992. In 2001, noting that SMEs were gradually switching from loan finance to other instruments, including equity, the EU began an initiative to develop European venture capital markets.

A network of 39 Euro Info Centres (EICs), aimed particularly at small businesses, began work in 1987. A total of 270 EICs and 11 Euro Info Correspondence Centres were in operation in 2000. The EU's other information services for business include the Community Research and Development Information Service (Cordis, see under Research and Technology) and the internet-based Dialogue with Business, which brings together advice and data from various sources.

Meeting in Lisbon, in March 2000, the European Council set the EU the new strategic goal of transforming itself into the most competitive and dynamic economy in the world over the following decade. In January 2000 the EU's Directorate-Generals for Industry and SMEs and for Innovation were transformed into one Directorate-General for Enterprise Policy. The Commission subsequently adopted a multiannual programme on enterprise and entrepreneurship covering the period 2001–05, aimed particularly at SMEs. It was noted that business start-ups should be made easier and the cost of doing business in Europe lowered. Stronger measures were proposed for the protection of intellectual property rights (IPRs), and the harmonization of legislation on IPRs was advocated (differences between national laws in this respect could constitute protectionist barriers to the EU's principle of free movement of goods and services). The programme's overall objective was to create a dynamic, sustainable, innovation-based environment for EU businesses and to develop a climate of confidence among investors.

In order to analyse the EU's performance, the Commission has established innovation and enterprise policy scoreboards; these involve a set of performance indicators that serve as a benchmark for evaluating progress, looking at indicators such as home internet access, high technology patents, public Research and Development, ICT expenditure as a proportion of GDP, employment in high-technology manufacturing, etc. The European Innovation Scoreboard (EIS) for 2002 concluded, among other things, that trends in the EU have been improving faster than in the USA for five of the eight comparable indicators (and for all seven comparable indicators for Japan). The EIS also considered candidate countries, and found that while there were many negative trends in human resources indicators and for Research and Development, almost all individual candidate countries did have strengths in particular areas. A network of 68 Innovation Relay Centres (IRCs) has been established to facilitate the transfer of technologies in Europe; having completed their first phase of activity during 2002, their contracts were extended until 2004.

Through its joint European venture programme, the EU backs the establishment of joint ventures between enterprises from at least two member states. The European Business Angels Network (EBAN) provides a means of introduction between SMEs and investors and encourages the exchange of expertise. The Commission also promotes inter-industry co-operation between enterprises in the EU and in third countries through the Euro-Med Industrial Co-operation working party, the Transatlantic Business Dialogue (TABD), the EU-Japan Centre for Industrial Co-operation, and the Mercosur-Europe Business Forum (MEBF).

COMPETITION POLICY

The Treaty of Rome establishing the European Economic Community provided for the creation of a common market based on the free movement of goods, persons, services and capital. The EU's competition policy aims to guarantee the unity of this internal market, by providing access to a range of high-quality goods and services, at competitive prices. It seeks to prevent anti-competitive practices by companies or national authorities, and to outlaw monopolization, protective agreements and abuses of dominant positions. Overall, it aims to create a climate favourable to innovation, while protecting the interests of consumers.

The Commission has wide investigative powers in the area of competition policy. It may act on its own initiative, or after a complaint from a member state, firm or individual, or after being notified of agreements or planned state aid. Before taking a decision, the Commission organizes hearings; its decisions can be challenged before the Court of First Instance and the Court of Justice, or in national courts. In 2000 the Commission recommended measures to strengthen its investigative powers. In April 2002 the Commission adopted the XXXIst Report on Competition Policy, which assessed activity in the field in 2001.

State aid—which ranges from discrimination in favour of public enterprises to the granting of aid to private-sector companies—is contrary to the principles of competition policy. The EU does not attempt to ban state aid completely, but encourages a reduction in its overall level and works to ensure that all aid granted is compatible with the principles of the common market. The procedural rules on state aid were consolidated and clarified in a regulation in 1999. There are several exemptions, notably regarding the provision of aid to small and medium-sized enterprises (SMEs) and for training. The EU has drawn up 'regional aid maps' designed to concentrate aid in those regions with the most severe development problems.

The Treaty of Rome prohibits agreements and concerted practices between firms resulting in the prevention, restriction or distortion of competition within the common market. This ban applies both to horizontal agreements (between firms at the same stage of the production process) and vertical agreements (between firms at different stages). The type of agreements and practices that are prohibited include: price-fixing; imposing conditions on sale; seeking to isolate market segments; imposing production or delivery quotas; agreements on investments; establishing joint sales offices; market-sharing agreements; creating exclusive collective markets; agreements leading to discrimination against other trading parties; collective boycotting; and voluntary restraints on competitive behaviour. Certain types of co-operation considered as positive, such as agreements promoting technical and economic progress, may be exempt.

In addition, mergers that would significantly impede competition in the common market are banned. The Commission examines prospective mergers in order to decide whether they are compatible with competition principles. In December 2001 the Commission launched a review of its handling of mergers and acquisitions, focusing on the speed of decisions and on bringing European competition standards in line with those in the USA and elsewhere.

In 2000 the EU received 345 notifications under the merger regulation. All mergers are subject to various conditions. In July 2001 the EU blocked a merger between two US companies for the first time on the grounds that EU companies would be adversely affected.

The Commission is attempting to abolish monopolies in the networks supplying basic services to member states. In June 2002 the Council adopted a directive on the opening up of postal services. Liberalization is also being pursued in the gas and electricity, telecommunications and transport sectors . In addition, efforts are being made to integrate aspects of environment policy and issues of sustainable development into competition policy. In return, competition law must be respected when environmental initiatives are put into place. In July 2002 the Commission approved a plan to open the car industry to greater competition, by applying new Europe-wide rules for car sales, giving car dealers the freedom to operate anywhere in the EU. The reforms, which were strongly opposed by car manufacturers and by the French and German Governments, were due to come into effect in 2005.

In April 1999 reforms to competition policy were proposed in a White Paper presented by the Commission. The reforms aim to transfer responsibility for much of the routine enforcement of EU competition rules to national authorities and courts. Under the proposals companies would have to notify the EU's competition watchdog only of mergers and acquisitions, but not of other agreements, thereby freeing the Commission from the need to process every deal. The European Parliament began to debate the reforms in January 2000.

The international affairs unit of the Directorate-General for Competition co-operates with foreign competition authorities (particularly in the USA) and promotes competition instruments in applicant countries, where it also provides technical assistance. The unit works within the framework of international organizations such as the WTO, the Organisation for Economic Co-operation and Development (OECD) and the United Nations Conference on Trade and Development (UNCTAD).

TELECOMMUNICATIONS AND INFORMATION TECHNOLOGY

In 1990 proposals were adopted by the Council on the co-ordinated introduction of a European public paging system and of cellular digital land-based mobile communications. In 1991 the Council adopted a directive requiring member states to liberalize their rules on the supply of telecommunications terminal equipment, thus ending the monopolies of national telecommunications authorities. In the same year the Council adopted a plan for the gradual introduction of a competitive market in satellite communications. In October 1995 the Commission adopted a directive liberalizing the use of cable telecommunications, requiring member states to permit a wide range of services, in addition to television broadcasts, on such networks. The EU market for mobile telephone networks was opened to full competition as a result of a directive adopted by the Commission in January 1996, according to which member states were to abolish all exclusive and special rights in this area, and establish open and fair licensing procedures for digital services. The telecommunications market was to be fully deregulated by 1998, although extensions to the deregulation schedule were agreed for a number of member states. In October 1997 the Commission announced plans to commence legal proceedings against those member states that had not yet adopted the legislation necessary to permit the liberalization of the telecommunications market. Spain agreed to bring forward the full deregulation of its telecommunications market from January 2003 to 1998, which meant that all the major EU telecommunications markets were open to competition from 1998. In March 2000 the EU resolved that telecommunications markets throughout the Community should be fully liberalized and integrated by 2002. In September 2002 the Commission adopted a directive on competition in the telecommunications market, which replaced six existing liberalization directives. Under its provisions, member states may no longer permit exclusive rights for the operation of electronic communications networks or services.

In July 1998 the Commission identified 14 cases of unfair pricing after commencing an investigation into the charges imposed by telecommunications companies for interconnection between fixed and mobile telephone networks. In December the Commission suspended some of its investigations, after a number of companies introduced price reductions. In February 2000 the Commission requested that national competition authorities, telecommunications regulators, mobile network operators and service providers give information on conditions and price structures for national and international mobile services. The EU has registered concern at the lack of competition in the mobile market.

In July 2000 a comprehensive reform of the regulatory framework for telecommunications—the so-called 'telecoms package'—was launched. The reform aimed to update EU regulations to take account of changes in the telecommunications, media and information technology (IT) sectors. Noting the continuing convergence of these sectors, the Commission aimed to develop a single regulatory framework for all transmission networks and associated services, in order to exploit the full potential for growth, competition and job creation. The Commission recommended, as a priority, introducing a regulation on unbundled access to the local loop (the final connection of telephone wires into the home). The lack of competition in this part of the network was considered a significant obstacle to the widespread provision of low-cost internet access. The regulation obliged incumbent operators to permit shared and full access to the local loop by the end of 2000. (In December 2001 the Commission initiated infringement procedures against Greece, Portugal and Germany for failure to ensure this.) The EU has also made efforts to increase broadband use, which provides faster access to the internet. The Commission is working to develop a policy framework for so-called third-generation (3G) mobile communications within the EU, including an agreement on a regulatory framework for broadband networks. In December 2001 Parliament voted to adopt a compromise telecoms package. This gives the Commission powers to oversee national regulatory regimes and, in some cases, to overrule national regulatory authorities. It is designed to reduce the dominant market position of monopolies and to open the market to competition. The package includes a framework directive and three specific directives (covering issues of authorization, access and interconnection, universal service and users' rights) and measures to ensure harmonized conditions in radio spectrum policy.

The EU is undertaking efforts to make the internet more user-friendly, with targeted online services, technical support and information technology training for those at risk of 'digital exclusion'. A high-level group on Employment and the Social Dimension of the Information Society (ESDIS) was established in 1998 to focus on promoting digital inclusion. At the European Council meeting held in January 2000, referred to as the 'dot.com summit', the Commission agreed to put all remaining e-commerce legislation in place by the end of the year. The Lisbon European Council meeting in March 2000 set the EU a new strategic goal of transforming itself into the most competitive and dynamic knowledge-based economy in the world. The Commission presented the Council with a draft action plan entitled 'eEurope 2002: an information society for all'. Priority actions under the plan include developing cheaper internet access; establishing online healthcare and government services; updating schools' networks; training all teachers in internet use; developing a faster internet for use by researchers and students; promoting the use of smart cards for secure electronic access; providing internet access to basic public services by 2003; and encouraging participation by the disabled. Internet access for all schoolchildren in the Community was to be achieved by 2001. During 2002 the European Council approved a new eEurope 2005 action plan, following on from the earlier eEurope 2002 plan. The new plan aims to create an environment favourable to private investment and job creation, to modernize public services and to give everyone the opportunity to participate in the global information society. The EU aims to ensure that the movement into the digital age is socially inclusive and serves to build consumer trust. In December 2000 the Commission's programme on European digital content was adopted. Recognizing that a large proportion of the material on the internet originated in the USA, this sought to develop the regional potential in this area. In June 2001 a communication on the security of electronic networks and information systems was adopted, considering problems and possible solutions. The '.eu' domain name was formally adopted by the European Parliament in April 2002, giving a European identity for providers of services and information.

The EU maintains several information society programmes. The Community's overall Information Society Technologies (IST) programme (see under Research and Technology) is designed to accelerate the emergence of an information society and promotes the development of high-quality, efficient, affordable services. The Interchange of Data between Administrations (IDA) initiative supports the rapid electronic exchange of information between EU administrations. An action plan promoting safer use of the internet, extended in March 2002 until December 2004, aims to combat illegal and harmful content on global networks.

In 1992 a White Paper proposed the establishment of trans-European networks (TENs) in telecommunications, energy and transport (see under those sections), in order to improve infrastructure and assist in the development of the common market. Following the liberalization of the telecommunications market in 1998, efforts in this area were concentrated on support for the development of broadband networks and multimedia applications.

TRANSPORT POLICY

The establishment of a common transport policy is stipulated in the Treaty of Rome, with the aim of gradually standardizing the national regulations that hinder the free movement of traffic within the Community, such as the varying safety and licensing rules, diverse restrictions on the size of lorries, and frontier-crossing formalities. A White Paper in 1992 set out a common transport policy for the EU. The paper proposed the establishment of trans-European networks (TENs) to improve transport, telecommunications and energy infrastructure throughout the Community, as well as the integration of transport systems and measures to protect the environment and improve safety. An action programme for 1995–2000 set out initiatives in three basic areas: developing integrated transport systems based on advanced technologies; improving the functioning of the single market through transport policy; and improving transport links between the EU and third countries. A new action plan based on this was adopted for 1998–2004. Significant progress has been made, through harmonization and liberalization, towards the achievement of a single transport market.

The overall aim of the EU's TENs policy, which included so-called intelligent transport systems, was to unite the 15 national networks into a single European network, by eliminating bottlenecks and adding missing links. The 2000–06 budget for the 14 TENs projects totalled €4,600m., funded in part by the European Regional Development Fund, the European Investment Bank and the European Investment Fund. In addition, efforts are being made to increase the private-sector involvement in financing TENs, through the development of public-private partnerships (PPPs). The majority of the financial backing, however, is provided by individual member states. In April 1997 plans were announced to extend the TENs scheme into central and eastern Europe.

In recent years the EU has focused on integrating environmental issues and questions of sustainable development into transport policy. In September 2001 the Commission adopted a White Paper on Transport Policy for 2010. This set out a framework designed to accommodate the forecast strong growth in demand for transport, on a sustainable basis. The new policy aimed to shift the balance between modes of transport by 2010, by revitalizing railways, promoting maritime and inland waterway transport systems, and by linking up different kinds of transport. The paper proposed an action plan and a strategy designed gradually to break the link between economic and transport growth, with the aim of reducing pressure on the environment and relieving congestion.

In 1986 transport ministers agreed on a system of Community-wide permits for commercial vehicles, to facilitate the crossing of frontiers, and in 1993 they agreed on measures concerning road haulage. A common tax system for trucks using EC roads was to lead to the full liberalization of road 'cabotage' (whereby road hauliers may provide services in the domestic market of another member state) by 1998. In May 1998 transport ministers approved legislation compelling member governments to clear serious obstructions, such as truck blockades, that hinder the free movement of goods. The White Paper on Transport Policy adopted in September 2001 proposed the harmonization of petrol taxes across the EU.

In 1991 directives were adopted by the Council on the compulsory use of safety belts in vehicles weighing less than 3.5 metric tons. Further regulations applying to minibuses and coaches were to be introduced, following approval by the Commission in mid-1996. In June 2000 the Commission issued a communication setting out measures to improve the safety and efficiency of road transport and to ensure fair competition. These included road traffic monitoring, the regulation of employed drivers' working time, and regularity of employment conditions. In November 2002 the European Parliament adopted a directive on speed limitation devices for certain categories of motor vehicles, including haulage vehicles and passenger vehicles carrying more than eight passengers.

In the late 1980s ministers of transport approved measures to contribute to the liberalization of air transport within the Community. In 1990 ministers agreed to make further reductions in guaranteed quotas for a country's airlines on routes to another country, and to liberalize air cargo services. In 1992 they approved an 'open skies' arrangement that would allow any EC airline to operate domestic flights within another member state (with effect from 1 April 1997). In June 1996 the ministers of transport approved a limited mandate for the Commission to negotiate an 'open skies' agreement with the USA, under which a common EU–US aviation area would be created. However, the USA wished to negotiate on the basis of a full mandate. In October 1998 ministers failed to award a full mandate to the Commission. In November 2002 the European Court of Justice ruled that bilateral 'open-skies' treaties between countries were illegal if they discriminated against airlines from other member states; the ruling was in response to a case brought by the Commission against eight member states that had concluded such agreements with the USA.

In July 1994, despite the recommendations of a 'Committee of Wise Men' for tighter controls on subsidies awarded to airlines, as part of efforts to increase competitiveness within the industry, the Commission approved substantial subsidies that had been granted by the French and Greek governments to their respective national airlines. Subsequently, the Commission specified that state assistance could be granted to airlines 'in exceptional, unforeseen circumstances, outside the control of the company'. In June 1998 the European Court of Justice declared the subsidies awarded by the French Government illegal. However, in the following month the Commission stated that the subsidies were valid, as they had been accompanied by restructuring measures and certain competition guarantees. Following the major terrorist attacks perpetrated against targets in the USA in September 2001, and the consequent difficulties suffered by the air transport sector, the EU ruled that a degree of aid or compensation was permissible, but stressed that this must not lead to distortion of competition. The Commission approved a one-month loan to the Belgian national airline, Sabena (which subsequently collapsed), and agreed to compensate airlines for revenues lost in the immediate aftermath of the attacks. However, further subsidies were refused.

In early 1999 a dispute arose between the EU and the USA over the introduction of new EU legislation to curb aircraft noise. Initially, the EU proposed to prevent aircraft fitted with hush kits from flying in the EU after 1 April 2002 unless they were already operating there before 1 April 1999 (aircraft fitted with hush kits create more noise than newer aircraft, use more fuel and cause more pollution). The legislation was subsequently amended to avert the threat of a temporary boycott of some European flights by the US authorities, but the dispute persisted. The USA lodged an official complaint with the International Civil Aviation Organisation in March 2000.

In July 2002 the European Parliament adopted a regulation creating a European Aviation Safety Agency (EASA). The EASA was to cover all aircraft registered in member states, unless agreed otherwise. The Commission has also formulated ground rules for enquiries into civil air incidents and has issued proposals for assessing the safety of aircraft registered outside the EU. In October 2001 the Commission proposed establishing common rules in the field of civil aviation safety, to strengthen public confidence in air transport following the terrorist attacks on the USA. Issues addressed included securing cockpits, improving air-ground communications and using video cameras in aircraft. Member states also agreed to incorporate into Community law co-operation arrangements on security measures. These measures covered control of access to sensitive areas of airports and aircraft, control of passengers and hand luggage, control and monitoring of hold luggage, and training of ground staff.

In December 1999 the Commission presented a communication on streamlining air-traffic control to create a Single European Sky. Based on several lines of action, proposals include the joint management of airspace; the establishment of a strong EU regulator; and the gradual integration of civilian and military air traffic management. The overall aim was to restructure the EU's airspace on the basis of traffic, rather than national frontiers. The plans have proved controversial (in June 2002 a strike by European air-traffic controllers, protesting against the plan, caused major disruption to air travel), but in December 2002 EU transport ministers agreed on a package of measures under which the separate European air traffic control providers would be regulated as a single entity, and EU airspace over 28,500 feet (approximately 8,690 m) would be under unified control.

In 1986 progress was made towards the establishment of a common maritime transport policy, with the adoption of regulations on unfair pricing practices, safeguard of access to cargoes, application of competition rules and the eventual elimination of unilateral cargo reservation and discriminatory cargo-sharing arrangements. In December 1990 the Council approved, in principle, the freedom for shipping companies to provide maritime transport anywhere within the Community. Cabotage by sea began to be phased in from January 1993. The introduction of cabotage, and the need to improve conditions, resulted in the adoption of measures relating to competition policy, the prevention of unfair pricing practices, standards for ships engaged in transport of dangerous goods, and working conditions. The conditions governing admission to the occupation were also defined. Cabotage was introduced in the inland waterway transport sector in 1993. The inland waterways market was liberalized by January 2000, although obstacles to the functioning of the single market subsequently persisted, including differing technical regulations among member states and numerous bilateral agreements.

In March 2000 the Commission adopted a communication on the safety of the seaborne oil trade. It proposed the introduction of a first package of short-term measures to strengthen controls, including the right to refuse access to substandard ships, more stringent inspections and a generalization of the ban on single-hull oil tankers. In May the Commission adopted a proposal to harmonize procedures between bulk carriers and terminals, in order to reduce the risk of accidents caused by incorrect loading and unloading. In

the same month the Commission signed a memorandum of understanding with several countries on the establishment of the Equasis database, intended to provide information on the safety and quality of ships. In December the Commission set out a second package of safety measures, together with legislative proposals relating to the establishment of these bodies. Broad agreement was reached on the first package, and the EU agreed to accelerate the phasing in of double-hull tankers. In June 2002 the European Parliament established by regulation the European Maritime Safety Agency; its tasks were to include preparing legislation in the field of maritime safety, co-ordination of investigations following accidents at sea, assisting member states in implementing maritime safety measures, and providing assistance to the candidate countries.

In April 1998 the Commission published a report on railway policy, with the aim of achieving greater harmonization, the regulation of state subsidies and the progressive liberalization of the rail freight market. The Commission proposed the immediate liberalization of 5% of the market, increasing to 15% after five years and to 25% after 10 years. In October 1999 EU transport ministers concluded an agreement that was regarded as a precursor to the full liberalization of the rail-freight market. The agreement provided for the extension of access to a planned Trans-European Rail Freight Network (TERFN, covering some 50,000 km), with a charging system designed to ensure optimum competitiveness.

In December 2000 the EU adopted the first 'Railway Package'. This aimed to open up the TERFN to international goods services by 2003, and to open the rest of the network by 2008. Following the presentation of the White Paper on Transport Policy for 2010, the Commission made more radical proposals to revitalize the railways in its second Railway Package, adopted in January 2002. Under the framework of the second package, the EU aimed to open up the entire network, including national networks, by 2006. Other measures included developing a common approach to rail safety; bolstering principles of interoperability; and setting up a European Railway Agency. Rail transport's share of the total freight market declined from 21% in 1970 to 8% by the end of 2001. The EU aims also to liberalize progressively passenger rail services.

In February 2002 a proposal for the Marco Polo programme, successor to the earlier PACT (pilot action for combined transport) scheme, was adopted; the programme aims to promote the shift of road freight to shipping, rail and inland waterway during the period 2003–07, with a proposed budget of €115m. The programme was expected to be fully operational by 2003.

JUSTICE AND HOME AFFAIRS

Under the Treaty on European Union, EU member states undertook to co-operate in the areas of justice and home affairs, particularly in relation to the free movement of people between member states. Issues of common interest were defined as asylum policy; border controls; immigration; drug addiction; fraud; judicial co-operation in civil and criminal matters; customs co-operation; and police co-operation for the purposes of combating terrorism, drugs-trafficking and other serious forms of international crime. The EU's current action plan for justice and home affairs covers the period 2000–04. In view of the sensitivity of many of the issues involved in this sphere, the EU affords great weight to the positions and opinions of individual states. There tends to be a greater degree of flexibility than in other areas, and requirements are frequently less stringent.

A European Police Office (Europol), facilitating the exchange of information between police forces, operates from The Hague, Netherlands. A special Europol unit dealing with the trafficking of illicit drugs and nuclear and radioactive materials began work in 1994. Europol's mandate has been extended to cover illegal immigrants, stolen vehicles, paedophilia and terrorist activities, and, since November 2000, money-laundering. Europol had a budget of €48.5m. for 2002.

The EU convention on extradition, signed by ministers of justice in September 1996 prior to ratification by national governments, simplified and accelerated procedures in this area, reduced the number of cases where extradition could be refused, and made it easier to extradite members of criminal organizations. In November 1997 the Commission proposed an extension to European law to allow civil and commercial judgments made in the courts of member states to be enforced throughout the whole of the EU. A regulation on the mutual recognition and enforcement of such judgments came into force in March 2001 across the EU, with the exception of Denmark. The EU recognizes that some harmonization of legal standards may be required for mutual recognition to be effective. In 2000 a convention on mutual assistance in criminal matters was adopted. This contained provisions on a number of specific forms of mutual assistance (such as criminal hearings by video and telephone conference and cross-border investigations).

The Grotius-Civil programme of incentives and exchanges for legal practitioners was established in 1996. It was designed to aid judicial co-operation between member states by improving reciprocal knowledge of legal and judicial systems. The successor programme, Grotius II, focused on general and criminal law. The establishment of a European legal training network for judges has also been proposed. In addition, in February 2002 the EU established a 'Eurojust' unit, composed of prosecutors, magistrates and police officers from member states, to help co-ordinate prosecutions and support investigations into incidences of serious organized crime. A European Police College (CEPOL) has also been created to train senior members of Community police departments, as well as officers from the central and eastern European states. CEPOL consists of a network of existing national training institutes; a permanent institution may eventually be created.

In March 2000 an action programme entitled 'The prevention and control of organized crime: a European strategy' was adopted. A European crime prevention network was formally established in May 2001. There are also agreements within the EU on co-operation between financial intelligence units and between police forces for the purposes of combating child pornography. In addition, the EU has a common strategy designed to help Russia combat organized crime. The EU runs the FALCONE programme—a series of incentives, training opportunities and exchanges for those responsible for the fight against organized crime in individual member states. The STOP (sexual treatment of persons) programme operates a similar system for those responsible for combating trade in humans and the sexual exploitation of children. The EU has focused recent efforts on preventing child pornography on the internet. In September 2001 member states harmonized their definitions of human trafficking and set common minimum jail sentences. In June 2000 an action plan was approved on combating usage of and trafficking illicit drugs. The plan, covering the period 2000–04, identified a range of measures to be implemented. The European Monitoring Centre for Drugs and Drug Addiction (EMCDDA) is based in Lisbon, Portugal. In September 2000 Norway became the first non-EU state to be admitted to EMCDDA. The EU is working with other third countries to tackle issues of drugs demand and supply.

The EU's draft Charter of Fundamental Rights, signed in December 2000, outlines the rights and freedoms recognized by the EU. It includes civil, political, economic and social rights, with each based on a previous charter, convention, treaty or jurisprudence. The charter may be used to challenge decisions taken by the Community institutions and by member states when implementing EU law.

The Justice and Home Affairs Council held an emergency meeting in September 2001 following the terrorist attacks on the USA. It determined a number of measures to be taken to improve security in the Community. First, the Council sought to reach a common definition of acts of terrorism, and to establish higher penalties for such acts. The new definition included cyber and environmental attacks. The Council decided that, for the perpetrators of terrorist attacks, as well as those involved in other serious crimes (including trafficking in arms, people and drugs and money-laundering), the process of extradition would ultimately be replaced by a procedure for hand-over based on a European arrest warrant. In the meantime, member states were urged to take the necessary steps to allow the existing conventions on extradition to enter into force. The member states reached agreement on the arrest warrant in December; under the agreement, covering 32 serious offences, EU countries may no longer refuse to extradite their own nationals. The warrant was scheduled to come into force in January 2004. The Council also determined to accelerate the implementation of the convention on mutual assistance in criminal matters and to establish a joint investigation team. Member states were encouraged to ratify the convention on combating the financing of terrorism and to exercise greater rigour in the issuing of travel documents. The heads of the security and intelligence services of member states met in October, in the first EU-wide meeting of this kind, to discuss the co-ordinated action to be taken to curb terrorism. They were to meet in regular sessions thereafter. A team of counter-terrorist specialists, established within Europol, was to produce an assessment of terrorist threats to EU states, indicating the likely nature and location of any such attacks. Rapid links were being forged with US counterparts—in December Europol signed a co-operation agreement on the exchange of strategic information (excluding personal data) with the USA; in December 2002 the agreement was extended also to include the exchange of personal data. The heads of the EU's anti-terrorist units also held a meeting following the September 2001 attacks, to discuss issues such as joint training exercises, equipment sharing, the joint procurement of equipment and possible joint operations. Prior to these emergency meetings, intelligence and security information had been shared bilaterally and on a small scale, impeding Europol's effectiveness.

Measures related to the abolition of customs formalities at intra-community frontiers were completed by mid-1991, and entered into force in January 1993. However, disagreements remained among member governments concerning the free movement of persons: discussions continued in 1992 on the abuse of open frontiers by organized crime, particularly for drugs-trafficking; on extradition procedures; and on rules of asylum and immigration. In June 1990

Belgium, France, Germany, Luxembourg and the Netherlands, meeting in Schengen, Luxembourg, signed a convention to implement an earlier agreement (concluded in 1985 at the same location), abolishing frontier controls on the free movement of persons from 1993. Delay in the establishment of the Schengen Information System (SIS), providing a computer network on criminals and illegal immigrants for use by the police forces of signatory states, resulted in the postponement of the implementation of the new agreement. Seven countries (Belgium, France, Germany, Luxembourg, the Netherlands, Portugal and Spain) agreed to implement the agreement with effect from March 1995. Frontier controls at airports on those travelling between the seven countries were dismantled during a three-month transition period, which ended on 1 July 1995. However, after that date the French government announced that it would retain land-border controls for a further six months, claiming that drugs-trafficking and illegal immigration had increased as a result of the agreement. In March 1996 France decided to lift its border controls with Spain and Germany while maintaining controls on borders with the Benelux countries, mainly owing to fears concerning the transportation of illicit drugs from the Netherlands via Belgium and Luxembourg. Italy joined the 'Schengen Group' in October 1997, and Austria in December. Border controls for both countries were removed in 1998. Denmark, Finland and Sweden (and non-EU members Norway and Iceland) were admitted as observers of the accord from 1 May 1996. The latter agreement was framed in such a way as to enable the first three countries to accede to the Schengen agreement in the future without adversely affecting the border-free zone provided by the Nordic Passport Union. In April 1998 Sweden voted to join the 'Schengen Group'. Denmark and Finland were also reported to be making preparations for membership. In March 1999 signatories of the Schengen accords on visa-free border crossings began to waive visa requirements with Estonia, Latvia and Lithuania. The Treaty of Amsterdam, which came into effect on 1 May 1999, incorporated the so-called Schengen *'acquis'* (comprising the 1985 agreement, 1990 convention and additional accession protocols and executive decisions), in order to integrate it into the framework of the EU. The Treaty permitted the United Kingdom and Ireland to maintain permanent jurisdiction over their borders and rules of asylum and immigration. Countries acceding to the EU after 2000 were automatically to adhere to the Schengen arrangements. The Schengen agreement came into force in the Nordic states in March 2001, while in February 2002 the Council approved Ireland's participation in some of the provisions of the Schengen acquis.

The EC defined objectives on the subject of asylum that were to be met within five years of the Amsterdam Treaty entering into force. These included: establishing criteria and mechanisms for determining which member state was responsible for considering an asylum application; setting minimum standards for the reception of asylum seekers (covering issues of residence and freedom of movement, financial and material assistance, work, healthcare, family unity and schooling of minors, among others); establishing rules for the temporary protection of refugees; setting minimum standards for conditions to obtain refugee status and for having this withdrawn; determining measures to be taken against illegal immigration, including the use of repatriation; and formulating rulings relating to other third country nationals. The need to develop a common policy on immigration was expressed more strongly in the late 1990s, with the number of immigrants forecast to increase in coming years. In February 2002 the European Council adopted a comprehensive plan to combat illegal immigration. Priority areas included visa policy, readmission and repatriation policies, the monitoring of borders, the role of Europol and penalties.

In November 2000 the Commission adopted a communication outlining a common asylum procedure and providing for a uniform status, valid throughout the EU, for persons granted asylum. Efforts towards a full harmonization of the rules on immigration continued. In March 2001 a common list of countries whose citizens required visas to enter the EU was finally adopted. The EU has also developed the so-called 'Eurodac' database for co-ordinating information on the movements of asylum-seekers; Eurodac allows for the comparison of fingerprints of refugees. In September 2001 the Commission launched a directive establishing a common European definition of a refugee, aimed at curtailing so-called 'asylum shopping' (in which a person moves from one state to another until reaching one prepared to give protection). The EU was also seeking to develop common repatriation procedures for unsuccessful claimants. (Under current arrangements refugees may simply be repatriated to the EU state from which they arrived.) In June 2002 a summit of the European Council in Seville, Spain, discussed the issues of asylum and immigration. The meeting's priority was to continue the progress towards a common asylum policy, by establishing minimum standards and procedures for member states. At the summit the United Kingdom and Spain were forced to mitigate contentious proposals to reduce aid to countries that refuse to co-operate with the EU on immigration. The number of people seeking asylum in the EU fell to 384,530 in 2001, compared with 675,460 in 1992.

The European Refugee Fund, with funds of €216m. for 2000–04, was established in September 2000. It aims to support the efforts of member states to receive refugees and, with a reserve of €10m., allows emergency measures to be taken in the event of a sudden, mass influx. The Odysseus programme of training, exchange and co-operation assists officials working in the field of asylum and immigration. A high-level working group on asylum and migration was set up in December 1998. It implements action plans in the main source countries for immigration to western Europe (Afghanistan and the surrounding region; Iraq; Morocco; Somalia; Sri Lanka; and Albania and Kosovo). In 2000 and 2001 there was particular concern at the level of illegal immigration from the West Balkans; the establishment of a network of national immigration liaison offices was planned in that region to help control illegal immigration flows.

In July 2001, noting the problems likely to arise in the future from labour shortages and ageing populations in EU countries, the Commission proposed the introduction of a 'green card' system. If adopted, this would consider age, profession and language skills, in order to help regulate legal immigration and fill gaps in the labour market.

EDUCATION, CULTURE AND BROADCASTING

The Treaty of Rome, although not covering education directly, gave the Community the role of establishing general principles for implementing a common vocational training policy. The Treaty on European Union urged greater co-operation on education policy, including encouraging exchanges and mobility for students and teachers, distance learning and the development of European studies. In July 2000 the EU's Economic and Social Committee adopted a report on education in Europe. The Committee considered the development of a more integrated education strategy for Europe and advocated the study of new approaches to schooling, including differing structures and wider objectives, more diverse fields of learning and greater use of modern technologies.

The postgraduate European University Institute was founded in Florence in 1972, with departments of history, economics, law, and political and social sciences, together with a European Policy Unit and a European Culture Research Centre. In 2000 there were some 450 research students. In April 1998 202 research and teaching projects were approved for EU universities, including the establishment of 25 Jean Monnet European Centres of Excellence. The Jean Monnet project also finances the establishment of Jean Monnet chairs at universities worldwide; there were 601 such chairs by 2002.

In September 1980 an educational information network, 'Eurydice', began operations, with a central unit in Brussels and national units providing data on the widely varying systems of education within member states. In 1987 the Council adopted a European Action Scheme for the Mobility of University Students ('Erasmus'). The scheme was expanded to include EFTA member states from 1992. The 'Lingua' programme promoted the teaching of foreign languages in the Community. From 1 January 1995 the Erasmus and Lingua schemes were incorporated into a new Community programme, 'Socrates', with a budget of ECU 850m for 1995–99. In 2002/03, under Erasmus, financial assistance was given to 1,845 higher education establishments and to 107 projects to develop joint syllabuses. Some 111,084 students and 14,356 teachers participated in educational exchanges. In addition to Erasmus, Socrates incorporates the Comenius strand (which financed 10,200 school partnerships in 2002); the Gruntvig strand (which deals with adult education and gave aid to more than 50 projects in 2002); and the Minerva strand (for open and distance learning, which supported 70 projects). The second phase of Socrates runs from 2000–06, with a budget of €1,850m. It is prioritizing the learning of EU languages (2001 was nominated the European Year of Languages); the promotion of mobility in education; innovation in educational practices; and life-long learning.

The Trans-European Mobility Programme for University Studies (TEMPUS) was launched in 1990 to foster co-operation between institutions of higher education and their counterparts in central and eastern Europe, as part of the wider aid programme to those countries. Under the second phase of the scheme (TEMPUS II) for 1994–98, the former Soviet republics were eligible to participate. TEMPUS III covers 2000–06. Under this third phase, the programme has widened its remit to cover certain non-academic institutions, as well as extending geographical coverage to include Mediterranean non-member countries; a budget of €106m. was agreed for this in 2002. The European Training Foundation, based in Turin, supports TEMPUS projects as part of its general assistance for the development of vocational training in EU partner countries. The Foundation deals with those countries eligible to participate in the EU's Phare, CARDS, TACIS and MEDA programmes (see under External Relations).

In 1975 a European Centre for the Development of Vocational Training (CEDEFOP) was established in Berlin, Germany. The centre relocated to Thessaloniki, Greece, in 1995. The priority areas for the centre in 2000–03 included promoting key skills and lifelong learning; developing new ways of learning; and supporting employment and competitiveness. Between 1995 and 1999 the Leonardo da Vinci programme for vocational training supported more than 3,000 projects. The second phase of the programme (2000–06) had a budget of €1,150m. In January 2000 a programme for the promotion of European pathways for work-linked training, including apprenticeship, came into force. This involved the introduction of the new EU 'Europass Training' document, which attests to periods of training completed in another member state.

In April 2000 the EU's 'Youth' community action programme for 2000–06 was adopted, with a budget of €520m. This incorporated all the previous youth programmes and related activities, including Youth for Europe, which covered the period 1995–99, and the European Voluntary Service (EVS) programmes. The overall objective of the new programme was to help young people contribute to the building of Europe and to foster a spirit of initiative. Around 11,500 projects were financed under the programme in 2002. From the outset Youth included applicant countries. The new Socrates, Leonardo da Vinci and Youth programmes were officially launched in March 2000. Together, they aimed to halve, by 2010, the number of people aged 18–24 who had completed only the first part of secondary education; promote life-long learning; encourage electronic learning; develop a European certificate of competence in information technology (IT); and promote mobility.

In May 2000 the Commission adopted an initiative entitled 'e-Learning: designing tomorrow's education' as part of its overall 'e-Europe' action plan (see under Telecommunications and Information Technology). One of the main objectives of the e-Europe programme was to encourage the use of the internet in schools and universities. A Commission report in January 2000 considered the use of IT in schools and the possibilities for development. The report noted problems such as the rapid obsolescence of technical equipment, the need for lower costs and greater reliability in internet use, and the need for training, particularly at secondary level.

The Commission organizes the annual so-called 'Netd@ys' Europe, aimed at exchanging and disseminating experience in the use of new media, especially the internet, as a teaching, learning and cultural resource. Non-member countries are involved in the initiative, which is held over the course of one week. The 2000 Netd@ys concentrated on the changing role of teachers and trainers, and the capacity of new technologies to improve quality of life, especially for people in isolated areas. During 2002 more than 400 projects on the theme of 'image' from around 30 countries received the Netd@ys label.

The EU's Culture 2000 framework programme, with a budget of €167m., replaced the Raphael, Kaleidoscope and Ariane programmes. The new framework programme, ending in 2004, was to focus on the following themes: legislation of benefit to cultural projects; the cultural aspects of existing support policies; and the incorporation of culture into the field of external relations. Culture 2000 supported more than 230 projects in 2002.

The European City of Culture initiative was launched in 1985 (it was renamed the Cultural Capital of Europe initiative in 1999). Member states designate cities, which receive a subsidy from the Commission. As part of the so-called Cardiff process of integration of environmental and sustainable development issues (see under Environment Policy), the Commission is bound to make efforts to preserve cultural heritage in the formulation of other policies.

In 1989 ministers of foreign affairs adopted a directive ('television without frontiers') establishing minimum standards for television programmes to be broadcast freely throughout the Community: limits were placed on the amount of time devoted to advertisements, a majority of programmes broadcast were to be from the Community, where practicable, and governments were allowed to forbid the transmission of programmes considered morally harmful. The 'Media' programme was introduced in 1991 to provide financial support to the television and film industry. 'Media II', covering 1996–2000, was followed by Media Plus, covering 2001–05, with a budget of €400m. Media Plus was to take account of the new regulatory environment (see under Telecommunications and Information Technology), and aimed to encourage the development, distribution and marketing of European audiovisual material.

During 2002 the scope of the Media programme was extended to include nine candidate countries. In November the Commission adopted a 'television without frontiers' communication on the promotion and distribution of television programmes, and proposed a revision of the broadcasting directive in the light of technological developments in the field of television broadcasting.

SOCIAL POLICY

The Single European Act, which entered into force in 1987, added to the original Treaty of Rome articles that emphasized the need for 'economic and social cohesion' in the Community, i.e. the reduction of disparities between the various regions. This was to be achieved principally through the existing 'structural funds'—the European

Regional Development Fund, the European Social Fund, and the Guidance Section of the European Agricultural Guidance and Guarantee Fund (EAGGF, see p. 236). In 1988 the Council declared that Community operations through the structural funds, the European Investment Bank (EIB) and other financial instruments should have five priority objectives: (i) promoting the development and structural adjustment of the less-developed regions (where gross domestic product per head is less than 75% of the Community average); (ii) converting the regions, frontier regions or parts of regions seriously affected by industrial decline; (iii) combating long-term unemployment among people above the age of 25; (iv) providing employment for young people (aged under 25); and (v) with a view to the reform of the common agricultural policy (CAP), speeding up the adjustment of agricultural structures and promoting the development of rural areas.

In 1989 the Commission proposed a Charter on the Fundamental Social Rights of Workers (Social Charter), covering freedom of movement, fair remuneration, improvement of working conditions, the right to social security, freedom of association and collective wage agreements, the development of participation by workers in management, and sexual equality. The Charter was approved by the heads of government of all Community member states, except the United Kingdom, in December. On the insistence of the United Kingdom, the chapter on social affairs of the Treaty on European Union, negotiated in December 1991, was omitted from the Treaty to form a separate protocol.

In September 1994 ministers adopted the first directive to be approved under the Social Charter, concerning the establishment of mandatory works councils in multinational companies. After lengthy negotiations, it was agreed that the legislation was to apply to companies employing more than 1,000 people, of whom 150 worked in at least two EU member states. The United Kingdom was excluded from the directive; however, UK companies operating in other European countries were to participate in the scheme (although without counting UK-based employees towards the applicability thresholds). The directive came into force in September 1996. In April 1996 the Commission proposed that part-time, fixed-term and temporary employees should receive comparable treatment to permanent, full-time employees. A directive ensuring equal treatment for part-time employees was adopted by the Council in December 1997. A directive on parental leave, the second directive to be adopted under the Social Charter, provided for a statutory minimum of three months' unpaid leave to allow parents to care for young children, and was adopted in June 1996.

In May 1997 the new United Kingdom Government approved the Social Charter, which was to be incorporated into the Treaty of Amsterdam. The Treaty, which entered into force in May 1999, included a new chapter on employment. In December 1999 the Council adopted amendments extending the two directives adopted under the Charter to include the United Kingdom. In November 1998 the Commission proposed a directive compelling companies employing more than 50 staff to consult workers about decisions likely to cause significant organizational or contractual changes. In June 2001, after significant opposition from the United Kingdom, agreement was reached on an amended proposal, under which the directive would be implemented gradually and the United Kingdom granted an exemption from the legislation for seven years. In October the European Parliament rejected this transitional arrangement, and negotiations resumed.

The Treaty of Amsterdam authorized the European Council to take action against all types of discrimination. Several directives and programmes on gender equality and equal opportunities have been approved and the Commission has initiated legal proceedings against a number of member states before the European Court of Justice for infringements. In June 2000 the Commission presented a framework strategy on gender equality for 2001–05, aimed at altering roles and eliminating stereotypes. A directive agreed in June 2001 brought together case law and other directives on non-discrimination in employment and vocational training. The directive increased protection for women returning to work after maternity leave and for men on paternity leave (where this exists) and tightened the rules on sexual harassment. In June 2000 the Council adopted a directive implementing the principle of equal treatment regardless of racial or ethnic origin in employment, education, social security, healthcare and access to goods and services. This was followed in November by a directive establishing a framework for equal treatment regardless of religion or belief, disability, age or sexual orientation. The European Monitoring Centre on Racism and Xenophobia, created in 1997, was inaugurated in April 2000. It is based in Vienna and maintains an information network and database.

Numerous directives on health and safety in the workplace have been adopted by the Community. The creation of a Major Accident Hazards Bureau (MAHB) was announced by the Commission in February 1996. Based at the Joint Research Centre at Ispra in Italy, its purpose is to help prevent industrial accidents in the EU. There is also a European Agency for Health and Safety at Work, located in Bilbao, Spain. In June 2000 the Commission drafted a list of exposure limits for chemicals at work. In September a directive on protection from exposure to biological agents was adopted, incorporating guidelines for pregnant women and new mothers. In June 1993 the Working Time directive was approved, restricting the working week to 48 hours, except where overtime arrangements are agreed with trade unions. In October ministers adopted further legislation limiting the number of hours worked by young people. The United Kingdom secured a dispensation to delay implementation of these measures for four years. The Working Time directive, which also prescribed minimum rest periods and a minimum of four weeks' paid holiday a year, had to be implemented by late November 1996. Certain categories of employee were exempt from the maximum 48-hour week rule, including those in the transport sector, fishermen and junior hospital doctors. In April 2000 a Conciliation Committee comprising MEPs and the Council of Ministers reached agreement on extending the directive to cover most excluded workers (further talks were held on extending the directive to workers in the road transport sector). The extension was to be phased in under transitional arrangements and could, for example, take 12 years to apply to junior doctors.

The European Foundation for the Improvement of Living and Working Conditions (Dublin), established in 1975, undertakes four-year research programmes in the field of employment, sustainable development, equal opportunities, social cohesion, health and well-being, and participation. The European Work Organisation Network also considers questions relating to the quality of working life. It has stressed the importance of organizational innovation to allow businesses to adapt to change.

The European Confidence Pact for Employment was launched by the Commission in January 1996 as a comprehensive strategy to combat unemployment, involving a common approach by public authorities, employers and employees. An employment body, EURES, launched in November 1994, operates as a network of 450 advisers with access to two European databases listing job vacancies in the EU and in Norway and Iceland. During 1996–97 EURES assisted more than 1m. people. (Its website can be accessed at europa.eu.int/jobs/eures.)

An employment summit was held in Luxembourg in November 1997. The conference focused on four themes: employability, entrepreneurship, equal opportunities and adaptability, and committed member governments to providing training or work placements for unemployed young people within six months, and for the long-term unemployed within 12 months. Member states also agreed to reduce taxation on labour-intensive service industries from 1 July 1998 and to produce national action plans for employment. Under the European employment strategy, initiated in 1997, an employment package is presented each year. The package contains reports on member states' performances, individual recommendations and policy guidelines for the future. In 2000 some 3m. jobs were created under the employment strategy. The overall EU employment rate averaged 63.3% in 2000. In March 2001 a meeting of the European Council in Stockholm established a target employment rate of 67% by 2005 (57% for women) and of 50% for older workers (aged 55–64) by 2010, when the target for full employment was 70%.

In March 2000 the Commission adopted a communication entitled 'Building an inclusive Europe', which discussed methods of combating poverty and social exclusion. In June the Commission adopted a new Agenda for Social Policy for 2000–05. This aimed to modernize the overall European social model, in order to address the challenges resulting from changes in employment, the development of the knowledge-based economy, the forthcoming enlargement of the EU, and issues related to globalization. The new strategy is geared towards integrating economic, social and employment policies. A European Social Protection Committee was also established in June. In addition, the EU runs MISSOC—the Mutual Information System on Social Protection in EU member states and the European Economic Area.

During 2002 the Commission presented a series of proposals on social policy, including the Community strategy for health and safety at work, a directive on the status of temporary workers and a communication on corporate social responsibility. In November 2002 the Commission adopted a draft joint employment report for 2002, in which it noted that the EU's employment performance had continued to improve during 2001, but member states were asked to continue their efforts to reform labour markets. The EU has also launched a Community action programme to encourage action between member states to combat social exclusion, by drawing up comparable indicators in areas such as poverty, aiming to increase living standards and quality of life, and to promote economic and social cohesion.

EU activities relating to disability include the HELIOS programme for disabled people, which focuses on mobility, integration and independence, and the Technology Initiative for Disabled and Elderly people (TIDE), which aims to develop technologies to improve the living conditions of these groups.

CONSUMER PROTECTION AND HEALTH

Consumer protection is one of the stated priorities of EU policy, and has been implemented via a series of action programmes covering areas such as safety of products and services (e.g. food additives, safety of toys and childcare articles, packaging and labelling of goods), protecting consumers' economic and legal interests, and promoting consumer representation. A number of measures have been taken to strengthen consumer power, by promoting consumer associations and drawing up a requirement for fair commercial practices.

In February 1997 the Commission extended the function of its directorate-general on consumer policy to incorporate consumer health protection. This decision (which followed widespread consumer concerns regarding the BSE crisis), was designed to ensure that sufficient importance was given to food safety. In November a Scientific Steering Committee was established to provide advice on consumer health issues. Eight sectoral steering committees were formed at the same time, covering a range of public health and consumer protection issues. Five of the committees were devoted to food safety, one to cosmetic and non-food products, one to medicinal products and medical devices, and one to issues of toxicity and the environment. In July 1998 an Institute for Health and Consumer Protection, attached to the Commission's Joint Research Centre, was established to improve research in this field.

In January 2000 the Commission adopted a White Paper on food safety, proposing a comprehensive, integrated approach covering foodstuffs from 'farm to table'. The paper envisaged a programme of measures, including legislation on the responsibilities of food and feedstuff manufacturers and the traceability of products. Stringent rules and appropriate checks at all stages of the production chain were to be introduced and the importance of clear labelling was emphasized.

The European Council's 2000 directive on the labelling, presentation and advertizing of foodstuffs aimed to ensure that essential, objective information was given to consumers. The White Paper on food safety proposed that certain substances recognized scientifically as being sources of allergies should be included in lists of ingredients on labels. From October 1999 food products labelled as 'GM-free' in the EU were permitted to contain up to 1% of GM material. In July 2001 the Commission developed its rules on the labelling and tracing of GM organisms (GMOs, see Agriculture).

In May 2002 the Commission presented its new strategy for consumer policy for 2002–06. The priorities are: to ensure a high common level of consumer protection; to guarantee effective enforcement of consumer protection rules; and to involve consumer organizations in EU policies. Specific measures agreed in 2002 included a proposal for a harmonization on rules for consumer credit, as well as a resolution on labelling of video and computer games, aimed at ensuring their suitability for young people. The same year saw an extension of the monitoring of certain foodstuffs, to include labelling of irradiated foods, authorization of two new sweeteners, and labelling and marketing of food supplements. In 2002 the European Food Safety Authority was formally established (see Agriculture), with a wide brief to cover all stages of food production and supply right through to consumers.

In May 2000 the Commission adopted a communication on the EU's overall health strategy, together with a proposal for a plan of action in the field of public health. The plan had three priorities: the introduction of a comprehensive information system; the development of a mechanism to respond rapidly to health threats; and promotion and prevention measures. In September 2002 the European Parliament adopted a programme of Community action in the field of public health for the period 2003–08, with a budget of €312m. The three basic objectives of the programme were: to improve health-related information; to boost swift and co-ordinated response to threats to health; and to promote health and prevent diseases.

Various epidemiological surveillance systems are in operation, covering major communicable diseases. An early warning and response system to help member states deal with outbreaks of diseases was in place by the end of 2000. The EU implements a number of individual action plans, including one to combat cancer: 41 new projects were adopted under this in 2000. In 2000 funding was also granted to the prevention and treatment of drug dependence (€5.3m.), pollution-related diseases (€1.8m.), rare diseases (€1.2m), HIV/AIDS and other communicable diseases (€10.9m.), and to health promotion, information, education and training (€3.8m.), health monitoring (€3.6m.) and injury prevention (€2.6m.). Under the Treaty on European Union, the EU assumed responsibility for the problem of drug addiction; a European Monitoring Centre for Drugs and Drug Addiction (EMCDDA, see under Justice and Home Affairs) was established in Lisbon, Portugal, in 1995. In April 2003 plans were announced for a new European Centre for Disease Prevention and Control, with the aim of improving the surveillance of infectious diseases and co-ordinating response to epidemics across member states. It was hoped that the Centre would become operational by 2005.

ENVIRONMENT POLICY

Environmental action by the EU was initiated in 1972. Four successive action programmes were complemented by a variety of legislation, including regulations on air and water pollution (e.g. 'acid rain', pollution by fertilizers and pesticides, and emissions from vehicles), directives on the transport of hazardous waste across national boundaries, measures on waste treatment, noise abatement and the protection of natural resources, and legislation to guarantee freedom of access to information on the environment held by public authorities. The Maastricht Treaty on European Union, which entered into force in November 1993, gave environmental action policy status, and the Treaty of Amsterdam identified sustainable development as one of the Community's overall aims.

The Community's fifth environmental action programme (1993–2000), entitled 'Towards Sustainability', aimed to address the root causes of environmental degradation, by raising public awareness and working to change the behaviour of authorities, enterprises and the general public. The programme focused on anticipating, as well as addressing, environmental problems. A 1998 communication on the so-called 'Cardiff Process' of integrating environmental considerations into all EU policies confirmed this programme's broad approach. The Commission recognized that full integration was a long-term aim. For the short term, it identified two priority objectives: the fulfilment of the environmental measures contained in the Agenda 2000 action programme (relating for example to the reform of the Common Agricultural Policy and to EU enlargement), and the implementation of the Kyoto Protocol (see below).

The EU's sixth environmental action programme was adopted by the European Parliament in July 2002, and emphasized the continuing importance of the integration of environmental considerations into other EU policies, focusing on four priority areas: climate change, nature and biodiversity, environment and health, and natural resources and waste.

The Community's programme of research and technological development on the environment, carried out on a shared-cost basis by various scientific institutions, covers the economic and social aspects of environmental issues and the EU's participation in global change programmes. The programme is open to all European countries. A separate programme covers research in marine science and technology. In 1990 the EC established the European Environment Agency (EEA, see p. 208) to monitor environmental issues and provide advice. The agency, which became operational in November 1994, also provides targeted information to policymakers and the public and disseminates comparable environmental data.

In 1996 the LIFE programme was established as a financial instrument to promote the development and implementation of environmental policy. LIFE funds priority activities in EU member states and provides technical assistance to countries in central and eastern Europe and the Mediterranean. The LIFE programme entered its third phase, covering 2000–04, in July 2000. The programme (with a total budget of €640m.) is subdivided into LIFE-Environment (addressing the further development of environmental policy and receiving 47% of funds); LIFE-Nature (managing conservation of wild birds and natural habitats and also receiving 47% of funds); and LIFE-Third countries (contributing to the development of environmental policy and action programmes in third countries, with 6% of funds). In view of the impending enlargement of the EU the poor state of the environment in some central and eastern European countries has become a pressing issue.

In 1985 the Community (and a number of individual member states) ratified the Vienna Convention for the Protection of the Ozone Layer, and in 1987 the Community signed a protocol to the treaty, controlling the production of chlorofluorocarbons. In 1990 ministers of the environment undertook to ban the production of chlorofluorocarbons by mid-1997; the introduction of the ban was later brought forward to 1996. In July 1998 the Commission proposed committing EU countries to the progressive elimination of remaining ozone-depleting substances, by introducing a ban on the sale and use of CFCs and imposing production limits on HCFCs, which were originally introduced to replace CFCs. In 1990 ministers agreed to stabilize emissions of carbon dioxide, believed to be responsible for 'global warming', at 1990 levels by 2000 (2005 for the United Kingdom). In December 1997, at the third conference of parties to the UN Framework Convention on Climate Change (UNFCCC), agreement was reached on the Kyoto Protocol, under which emissions of six greenhouse gases were to be reduced by 8% between 2008 and 2012, in comparison with 1990 levels. In June 1998 ministers of the environment agreed upon individual emission targets for each EU member state. The Kyoto Protocol was formally approved by the European Council in April 2002.

In March 2000 the Commission noted that emissions were actually rising in relation to 1990 levels. In that month the Commission adopted a Green Paper on the trading of greenhouse gas emissions within the EU, exploring the role that such a scheme could play in the fulfilment of the Kyoto commitments. At the same time, the European Climate Change Programme (ECCP) was adopted.

This outlined the strategy needed to meet commitments under the Kyoto Protocol and aimed to incorporate climate-change concerns into various EU policies. Six working groups were established under the programme, covering energy supply; energy consumption; transport; industry; research; and the mechanisms of the Kyoto Protocol. In January 2000 the EU's Theseo 2000-Solve experiment was launched; this was the largest experiment ever undertaken to study the ozone layer above northern Europe.

In June 1996 the Commission agreed a strategy, drawn up in collaboration with the European petroleum and car industries, for reducing harmful emissions from road vehicles by between 60% and 70% by 2010. In late June 1998 EU member states reached an 'auto-oil' agreement to reduce air pollution. The agreement committed member states to the progressive elimination of leaded petrol by 2000 (with limited exemptions until 2005). From 2000 petrol-powered road vehicles were to be fitted with 'on-board diagnostic' (OBD) systems to monitor emissions. Diesel vehicles were to be installed with OBD systems by 2005. In July the Commission announced plans to decrease pollution from nuclear power stations by reducing emissions of sulphur dioxides, nitrogen oxides and dust by one-half. The auto-oil agreement entered a second phase—auto-oil II—in 1997, terminating in 2000. It forecast and assessed likely trends in emissions and air quality and established a framework to determine options for reducing emissions. The Clean Air for Europe (CAFE) programme was endorsed by the European Parliament in March 2002. Continuing the auto-oil principles, this aimed to develop an air-quality policy covering all emissions sources by 2004.

In September 2000 the EU adopted a directive on end-of-life vehicles (ELVs), containing measures for the collection, treatment, recovery and disposal of such waste. The ruling forces manufacturers to pay for the disposal of new cars from July 2002 and of old cars from January 2007. The directive set recycling and recovery targets, restricted the use of heavy metals in new cars from 2003, and specified that ELVs might only be dismantled by authorized agencies. In June 2000 the Commission adopted two proposals on the management of waste from electronic and electrical equipment. The EU aimed to implement a directive in this field by 2004, making manufacturers of such equipment similarly responsible for the disposal of used goods.

A regulation revising EU laws on trade in wild animals and plants was adopted by ministers of the environment in December 1996. This aimed to tighten controls and improve the enforcement of restrictions on trade in endangered species. A series of directives adopted in 2002 formulated new EU policy on the conservation of wild birds, fishing and protection for certain species of whales. Every three years the Commission publishes an official report on the conservation of wild birds; the latest report, in March 2002, identified a decline of almost 25% in wild bird species in Europe, despite efforts made over the last 20 years.

The voluntary Eco-Management and Audit Scheme (EMAS) was launched in April 1995. Under the scheme, participating industrial companies undergo an independent audit of their environmental performance. In addition, the EU awards 'eco-labels' for products that limit harmful effects on the environment (excluding foodstuffs, drinks and pharmaceutical products, among others). The criteria to be met are set by the EU Eco-Labelling Board (EUEB).

SECURITY AND DEFENCE

Under the Single European Act, which came into force on 1 July 1987 (amending the Treaty of Rome), it was formally stipulated for the first time that member states should inform and consult each other on foreign policy matters (as was already, in practice, often the case).

The Maastricht Treaty on European Union, which came into force on 1 November 1993, provided for joint action by member governments in matters of common foreign and security policy (CFSP), and envisaged the eventual formation of a European security and defence policy (ESDP), with the possibility of a common defence force. The Western European Union (WEU, see p. 318), to which all EU members except Denmark, Greece and Ireland belong, was to be developed as the 'defence component' of the Union, but member states' existing commitments to NATO were to be honoured. The CFSP is the province of the EU (as opposed to the EC), and decisions in this field are made by the European Council and the Council of the European Union.

The Treaty of Amsterdam, which entered into force in May 1999, aimed to strengthen the concept of a CFSP within the Union and incorporated a process of common strategies to co-ordinate external relations with a third party. Under the Amsterdam Treaty, WEU was to provide the EU with access to operational capability for undertaking the so-called 'Petersberg tasks' relating to crisis management, including humanitarian, peace-keeping and peace-making operations. Accordingly, a High Representative, responsible for the co-ordination of the CFSP, was to be appointed to represent the EU at international meetings. In late March representatives of the Commission and NATO held a joint meeting, for the first time,

to discuss the conflict in the southern Serbian province of Kosovo. In April a meeting of NATO heads of state and government determined that NATO's equipment, personnel and infrastructure would be available to any future EU military operation. In June the European Council, meeting in Cologne, determined to strengthen the ESDP, and initiated a process of assuming direct responsibility for the Petersberg tasks, which were placed at the core of the ESDP process. In October 1999 Javier Solana, hitherto Secretary-General of NATO, was appointed as Secretary-General of the Council of the European Union and as the EU's High Representative. In the following month he also became the Secretary-General of WEU, providing for a very high degree of co-operation between the two organizations. The process of transferring the crisis-management responsibilities of WEU to the EU was finalized by July 2001.

The June 1999 Cologne meeting of the European Council stated that the EU must have a capacity for autonomous action, without prejudice to actions by NATO and acknowledging the supreme prerogatives of the UN Security Council. In December 1999, following consultation with NATO, the European Council, meeting in Helsinki, adopted the European Defence Initiative, comprising the following goals: by 2003 the EU should be able to deploy within 60 days and for a period of up to one year a rapid reaction force, comprising up to 60,000 national troops from member states capable of implementing the full range of Petersberg tasks. The force was to be militarily self-sustaining, with all services and support provided, and was to include smaller, rapid response elements. In November EU member states took part in a Capabilities Commitment Conference to assess the need to upgrade assets. The Council stressed the need to work on measures in the field of command and control, intelligence and strategic transport. In late 2001 defence ministers acknowledged that certain military capabilities, including strategic airlift, would not be available until 2006. Nevertheless, in December 2001 the EU announced that the force was, theoretically, ready, although only as yet capable of undertaking small-scale crisis management tasks. Further negotiations on the organization and funding of the force took place in 2002, but were hampered by disputes between Greece and Turkey on the role of the new body; a deal was finally agreed at the Copenhagen summit in December about sharing planning resources with NATO, in theory clearing the way for the beginning of EU military operations. In January 2003 EU forces were deployed for the first time in an international peace-keeping role, when, in a small-scale operation, 500 officers were dispatched to Bosnia and Herzegovina to take over from the existing UN force.

In December 1999 the Helsinki meeting of the European Council proposed the establishment of three permanent military institutions: a Political and Security Committee (PSC), a Military Body and a Military Staff. In February 2000 the EU set up an interim PSC and an interim Military Body. When fully established, the PSC was to monitor the international situation, help define policies and assess their implementation, encourage dialogue and, under the auspices of the Council, take responsibility for the political direction of capability development. In the event of a crisis situation, it was to oversee the strategic direction of any military response, propose political objectives and supervise their enactment. The Military Body was to give military advice to the PSC, and was to comprise the chiefs of defence of member states, represented by military delegates. It was to serve as a forum for military consultation and co-operation and was to deal with risk assessment, the development of crisis management and military relations with non-EU European NATO members, accession countries, and NATO itself. Meanwhile, the Military Staff, comprising experts seconded by the member states, was to provide the EU with an early-warning capability, and would conduct assessments of situations, take responsibility for strategic planning for the Petersberg tasks and implement the Military Body's policies. Permanent arrangements have been agreed for EU–NATO consultation and co-operation in this area.

In June 2000 the EU established a civilian crisis management committee. The Feira meeting of the European Council in that month defined four priority areas for civilian crisis management: developing the role of the police; strengthening the rule of law; strengthening civilian administrations; and improving civil protection. As part of the general rapid reaction force (see above), the EU aimed to be able to deploy up to 5,000 police officers for international missions by 2003. In February 2001 the Council adopted a regulation creating a rapid reaction mechanism (RRM) to improve the EU's civilian capacity to respond to crises. The mechanism bypasses cumbersome decision-making processes, to enable civilian experts in fields such as mine clearance, customs, police training, election-monitoring, institution-building, media support, rehabilitation and mediation to be mobilized speedily. The RRM was granted funds of €25m. for 2002. During that year it was used to intervene in various crisis situations, including emergency reconstruction work in Afghanistan, peace initiatives in Somalia, Ethiopia, Eritrea, Sudan, Nepal and Sri Lanka, and emergency aid for Palestinians.

In October 2002 an extraordinary session of the Brussels European Council adopted a European action plan to combat terrorism, which aimed to contribute to a global anti-terrorism strategy. Its priority objectives included deepening political dialogue with third countries, strengthening arrangements for shared intelligence and using military or civilian capabilities to protect civilian populations in the event of terrorist attack. In December 2002 EU ministers of justice agreed to allow the exchange of information on crime and terrorist suspects between European and US agencies.

Under the European code of conduct on arms exports the EU publishes an annual report on defence exports based on confidential information provided by each member state. EU member states must withhold export licences to countries where it is deemed that arms sales might lead to political repression or external aggression. The Community funds projects aimed at the collection and destruction of weapons in countries emerging from conflict. The EU is strongly committed to nuclear non-proliferation. Under its programme of co-operation with Russia, it works to dismantle or destroy nuclear, chemical and biological weapons and weapons of mass destruction.

FINANCIAL SERVICES AND CAPITAL MOVEMENTS

Freedom of capital movement and the creation of a uniform financial area were regarded as vital for the completion of the EU's internal market by 1992. In 1987, as part of the liberalization of the flow of capital, a Council directive came into force whereby member states were obliged to remove restrictions on three categories of transactions: long-term credits related to commercial transactions; acquisition of securities; and the admission of securities to capital markets. In June 1988 the Council of Ministers approved a directive whereby all restrictions on capital movements (financial loans and credits, current and deposit account operations, transactions in securities and other instruments normally dealt in on the money market) were to be removed by 1 July 1990. A number of countries were permitted to exercise certain restrictions until the end of 1992, and further extensions were then granted to Portugal and Greece. With the entry into force of the Maastricht Treaty in November 1993, the principle of full freedom of capital movements was incorporated into the structure of the EU.

The EU worked to develop a single market in financial services throughout the 1990s. In October 1998 the Commission drew up a framework for action in the financial services sector. This noted that investors should be free to invest their assets without legal, administrative or information barriers, and proposed that this could be achieved through the further harmonization of accounting rules; by eliminating restrictions on investments by supplementary pension and life-assurance funds; by developing a level playing field for similar financial products; and by harmonizing the prudential and tax aspects of the EU's regulatory framework. The communication was followed by a Financial Services Action Plan (FSAP) in May 1999, with three strategic objectives: to establish a single market in wholesale financial services; to make retail markets open and secure; and to strengthen the rules on prudential supervision, to keep pace with new sources of financial risk. The prudential supervision of financial conglomerates (entities offering a range of financial services in areas such as banking, insurance and securities), which are developing rapidly, has been identified as an area of particular importance. Individual targets included removing the outstanding barriers to raising capital within the EU; creating a coherent legal framework for supplementary pension funds; and providing greater legal certainty in cross-border securities trading. During 2002 a directive was drawn up on the supplementary supervision of such businesses, in recognition of the increasing consolidation in the financial sector and the emergence of cross-sector financial groups.

The deadline for meeting the targets of the FSAP was set as 2005. During 2002 the Commission reported on progress made towards the implementation of the plan, recognizing that tangible progress had been made but stressing the need to maintain the pace in order to meet the original 2005 deadline.

In July 2001 progress towards the creation of a single financial market was impeded by the European Parliament's rejection of a proposed takeover directive that had been under negotiation for 12 years. The directive had aimed to ensure that shareholders were treated in the same way throughout the EU after takeover bids, and had sought to create a single Community framework governing takeovers.

A directive on Community banking, adopted in 1977, laid down common prudential criteria for the establishment and operation of banks in member states. A second banking directive, adopted in 1989, aimed to create a single community licence for banking, thereby permitting a bank established in one member country to open branches in any other. The directive entered into force on 1 January 1993. Related measures were subsequently adopted, with the aim of ensuring the capital adequacy of credit institutions and the prevention of 'money-laundering' by criminals. In September

1993 ministers approved a directive on a bank deposit scheme to protect account-holders: banks were to be obliged to raise protection to 90% on the first ECU 20,000 in an account from 1 January 1995. These directives were consolidated into one overall banking directive in March 2000. Non-bank institutions may be granted a 'European passport' once they have complied with the principles laid down in the EU's first banking directive on the mutual recognition of licences, prudential supervision and supervision by the home member state. Non-bank institutions must also comply with the directive on money-laundering.

In September 2000 a directive was issued governing the actions of non-bank institutions with regard to the issuance of 'electronic money' (money stored on an electronic device, for example, a chip card or in a computer memory). The directive authorized non-bank institutions to issue electronic money on a non-professional basis, with the aim of promoting a level playing field with other credit institutions. Other regulations oblige the institutions to redeem electronic money at par value in coins and bank notes, or by transfer without charge.

In May 2001 a directive on the reorganization and winding up of failed credit institutions with branches in more than one member state was agreed; it was to enter into force in May 2004. The directive recognizes the principle of home country control and requires certain information to be given to creditors. It also enforces co-operation between supervisory authorities.

In July 1994 the third insurance co-ordination directives came into effect, relating to life assurance and non-life insurance, were adopted, creating a framework for an integrated Community insurance market. The directives provide greater access for insurance companies and customers to the European market, guarantee greater protection for purchasers of life assurance policies and prohibit substantive control of rates. A new directive on life assurance was adopted in November 2002, superseding all previous directives in this field. Community legislation also covers motor-vehicle liability insurance and legal protection insurance. The EU's insurance committee works to improve co-operation with national supervisory authorities.

In May 1993 ministers adopted a directive on investment services, which (with effect from 1 January 1996) allowed credit institutions to offer investment services in any member state, on the basis of a licence held in one state. The 1999 FSAP aimed to achieve the further convergence of national approaches to investment, in order to increase the effectiveness of the 1993 directive.

In late 1999 the Commission put forward proposals to remove tax barriers and investment restrictions affecting cross-border pension schemes. At present, variations among member states in the tax liability of contributions to supplementary pension schemes obstruct the transfer of pension rights from one state to another, contradicting the Treaty of Rome's principles of free movement. In October 2000 a specific legal framework for institutions for occupational retirement provision (IORPs) was proposed. This seeks to abolish barriers to investment by pension funds and would permit the cross-border management of IORP pension schemes, with mutual recognition of the supervisory methods in force. In February 2003 the European Parliament's economic and monetary affairs committee agreed a number of amendments to the draft occupational pensions directive (IORP directive), which is designed to allow workers of multi-national companies to have access to cross-border employer pension schemes.

In November 1997 the Commission adopted proposals to co-ordinate tax policy among member states. The measures, including a code of conduct on corporate taxation, aimed to simplify the transfer of royalty and interest payments between member states and to prevent the withholding of taxes. In February 1999 Parliament endorsed a proposal by the Commission to harmonize taxation further, through the co-ordination of savings taxes. In November 2000 finance ministers agreed on a proposed 'tax savings' directive. This set out rules on the exchange of information on savings accounts of individuals resident in one EU country and receiving interest in another. Ministers agreed that for a seven-year transitional period member states must either exchange information on the savings income of non-residents or apply a withholding tax. Standards would be in place for the full exchange of information when the transitional period expired. Agreement on the issue was reached in July 2001. However, in December Austria, Luxembourg and Belgium abandoned the agreement, insisting that they would only comply if other 'tax havens' in Europe, such as Monaco, Liechtenstein and Switzerland, were compelled to amend their banking secrecy laws. During 2002 the Commission reported on the progress of negotiations with these and other countries regarding the adoption by such countries of equivalent taxation measures to ensure effective taxation within the Community.

Two other proposed directives were issued in November 2000, the first relating to interest and royalties and the second concerning the code of conduct for business taxation. Together with the tax savings directive, these are known as the 'EU tax package'.

The EU's action plan on combating fraud in financial services covers the period 2001–03. The May 2000 convention on mutual assistance in criminal matters (see under Justice and Home Affairs) commits member states to co-operation in combating economic and financial crime. In May 2001 the Council adopted a framework decision on preventing fraud and counterfeiting in non-cash means of payment, recognizing this as a criminal offence. A conference in Paris, France, in February 2002 agreed to tackle money laundering by setting minimum secrecy levels and compelling internet service providers to identify operators of suspect financial deals. The conference was attended by members of the European Parliament, as well as by representatives of seven candidate countries and Russia. Following the terrorist attacks on the USA in September 2001, the EU attempted to accelerate the adoption of the convention combating the financing of terrorism, and began work on a new directive on 'freezing' assets or evidence related to terrorist crimes.

In January 2001 the Commission launched a complaints network for out-of-court settlements in the financial sector (FIN-NET), to help consumers find amicable solutions in cases where the supplier is in another member state. In September the EU agreed harmonized rules on the cross-border distance-selling of financial services.

ECONOMIC CO-OPERATION

A review of the economic situation is presented annually by the Commission, analysing recent developments and short- and medium-term prospects. Economic policy guide-lines for the following year are adopted annually by the Council.

The following objectives for the end of 1973 were agreed by the Council in 1971, as the first of three stages towards European economic and monetary union:

the narrowing of exchange-rate margins to 2.25%; creation of a medium-term pool of reserves; co-ordination of short- and medium-term economic and budgetary policies; a joint position on international monetary issues; harmonization of taxes; creation of the European Monetary Co-operation Fund (EMCF); and creation of the European Regional Development Fund.

The narrowing of exchange margins (the 'snake') came into effect in 1972; however, Denmark, France, Ireland, Italy and the United Kingdom later floated their currencies, with only Denmark permanently returning to the arrangement. Sweden and Norway also linked their currencies to the 'snake', but Sweden withdrew from the arrangement in August 1977, and Norway withdrew in December 1978.

The European Monetary System (EMS) came into force in March 1979, with the aim of creating closer monetary co-operation, leading to a zone of monetary stability in Europe, principally through an exchange-rate mechanism (ERM), supervised by the ministries of finance and the central banks of member states. Not all Community members participated in the ERM: Greece did not join, Spain joined only in June 1989, the United Kingdom in October 1990 and Portugal in April 1992. To prevent wide fluctuations in the value of members' currencies against each other, the ERM fixed for each currency a central rate in European Currency Units (ECUs, see below), based on a 'basket' of national currencies; a reference rate in relation to other currencies was fixed for each currency, with established fluctuation margins (until July 1993, 6% for the Portuguese escudo and the Spanish peseta, 2.25% for others). Central banks of the participating states intervened by buying or selling currencies when the agreed margin was likely to be exceeded. Each member placed 20% of its gold reserves and dollar reserves, respectively, into the EMCF, and received a supply of ECUs to regulate central bank interventions. Short- and medium-term credit facilities were given to support the balance of payments of member countries. The EMS was initially put under strain by the wide fluctuations in the exchange rates of non-Community currencies and by the differences in economic development among members, which led to nine realignments of currencies in 1979–83. Subsequently, greater stability was achieved, with only two realignments of currencies between 1984 and 1988. In September 1992, however, with great pressure on currency markets, the Italian and Spanish currencies were devalued by 7% and 5% respectively within the ERM and Italian and British membership was suspended; in November the Portuguese and Spanish currencies were both devalued by 6% within the ERM. In May 1993 the Spanish and Portuguese currencies were further devalued (by 8% and 6.5%, respectively). In late July, as a result of intensive currency speculation on European financial markets (forcing the weaker currencies to the very edge of their permitted margins), the ERM almost collapsed. In response to the crisis, EC finance ministers decided to widen the fluctuation margins allowed for each currency to 15%, except in the cases of Germany and the Netherlands, which agreed to maintain their currencies within the original 2.25% limits. The 15% margins were regarded as allowing for so much fluctuation in exchange rates as to represent a virtual suspension of the ERM; however, some countries, notably France and Belgium, expressed determination to adhere as far as possible to the original 'bands' in order to fulfil the conditions for eventual monetary union. In practice, during 1994, most currencies remained within the former 2.25% and 6% bands. Austria became a member of the EMS in January 1995, and its currency was subject to ERM conditions. While Sweden decided to remain outside the EMS, Finland joined in October 1996. In November the Italian lira was readmitted to the ERM.

In September 1988 a committee (chaired by Jacques Delors, then President of the European Commission, and comprising the governors of member countries' central banks, representatives of the European Commission and outside experts) was established to discuss European monetary union. The resulting 'Delors plan' was presented to heads of government in June 1989, who agreed to begin the first stage of the process of monetary union—the drafting of a treaty on the subject—in 1990. The Intergovernmental Conference on Economic and Monetary Union was initiated in December 1990, and continued to work (in parallel with the Intergovernmental Conference on Political Union) throughout 1991. The Intergovernmental Conference was responsible for the drafting of the economic and monetary provisions of the Treaty on European Union, which was agreed by the European Council in December 1991 and which came into force on 1 November 1993. The principal feature of the Treaty's provisions on economic and monetary union (EMU) was the gradual introduction of a single currency, to be administered by a single central bank. During the remainder of Stage I, member states were to adopt programmes for the 'convergence' of their economies and ensure the complete liberalization of capital movements. Stage II began on 1 January 1994, and included the establishment of a European Monetary Institute (EMI), replacing the EMCF and comprising governors of central banks and a president appointed by heads of government. Heads of government were to decide, not later than 31 December 1996, whether a majority of member states fulfilled the necessary conditions for the adoption of a single currency: if so, they were to establish a date for the beginning of Stage III. If no date had been set by the end of 1997, Stage III was to begin on 1 January 1999, and was to be confined to those members that did fulfil the necessary conditions. After the establishment of a starting date for Stage III, the European Central Bank (ECB) and a European System of Central Banks were to be set up to replace the EMI. During Stage III, exchange rates were to be irrevocably fixed, and a single currency introduced. Member states that had not fulfilled the necessary conditions for the adoption of a single currency would be exempt from participating. The United Kingdom was to be allowed to make a later, separate decision on whether to proceed to Stage III, while Denmark reserved the right to submit its participation in Stage III to a referendum. The near-collapse of the ERM in July 1993 cast serious doubts on the agreed timetable for monetary union, although in October the EC heads of government reaffirmed their commitment to the objective.

In December 1995 the European Council, meeting in Madrid, confirmed that Stage III of Economic and Monetary Union was to begin on 1 January 1999. The economic conditions for member states wishing to enter Stage III (including an annual budget deficit of no more than 3% of annual gross domestic product—GDP—and total public debt of no more than 60% of annual GDP) were also confirmed. The meeting decided that the proposed single currency would be officially known as the 'euro'. Participants in EMU were to be selected in early 1998, on the basis of economic performance during 1997. In October 1996 the Commission issued a draft regulation on a proposed 'Stability and Growth Pact', intended to ensure that member countries maintained strict budgetary discipline during Stage III of monetary union. Another draft regulation formed the legal framework for the euro, confirming that it would be the single currency of participating countries from 1 January 1999. During a transitional period of up to three years, national currencies would remain in circulation, having equivalent legal status to the euro. The communication outlined the main features of a new ERM, which would act as a 'waiting room' for countries preparing to join the single currency. Member countries remaining outside the monetary system, whether or not by choice, would still be part of the single market.

Although all 15 members of the EU endorsed the principle of monetary union, with France and Germany the most ardent supporters, certain countries were known to have political doubts about joining. In October 1997 both the United Kingdom and Sweden confirmed that they would not participate in EMU from 1999. Denmark was also to remain outside the single currency.

Technical preparations for the euro were confirmed during a meeting of the European Council in Dublin in December 1996. The heads of government endorsed the new ERM and the legal framework for the euro and agreed to the proposed 'Stability and Growth Pact'. In March 1998 the Commission and the European Investment Bank (EIB) published reports on the progress made by member states towards the fulfilment of convergence criteria. The Commission concluded that Greece alone failed to satisfy the necessary conditions. However, the EIB warned that Italy and Belgium, with public-debt ratios of over 100% of GDP, had made insufficient progress towards the reduction of debt levels. In March Greece was admitted to the ERM, causing a 14% devaluation of its national currency. In early May 1998 heads of state and of government confirmed that Greece failed to fulfil the conditions required for the adoption of a single currency from 1999, and that 11 countries would take part in Stage III of EMU. After substantial debate, the European Council agreed to appoint Willem (Wim) Duisenberg, governor of the central bank of the Netherlands, as the President of the new ECB. The Vice-President and the remaining four members of the ECB's executive board were also appointed. The meeting agreed that existing ERM central rates were to be used to determine the final rates of exchange between national currencies and the euro, which would be adopted on 1 January 1999. The ECB, which was established on 1 June 1998 and ceremonially launched on 30 June, was to be accountable to a European Forum, comprising members of the European Parliament (MEPs) and chairmen of the finance committees of the national parliaments of EU member countries.

In September 1998 Sweden and the United Kingdom came under pressure to join the successor to the ERM, ERM2, launched on 1 January 1999, as a precondition of future participation in EMU. In October 1998 ministers discussed Greece's convergence programme for 1998–2001; this sought to allow Greece to join the single currency from 1 January 2001. On 31 December 1998 the ECOFIN Council adopted the conversion rates for the national currencies of the countries participating in the single currency. The euro was formally launched on 1 January 1999. Both Greece and Denmark joined ERM2. In September 2000 some 53% of Danish voters participating in a national referendum rejected the adoption of the euro. On 1 January 2001 Greece became the twelfth EU member state to adopt the euro, in the first enlargement of the euro area since its inception. Sweden announced in November 2002 that it would hold a referendum on adoption of the euro in September 2003.

The Stability and Growth Pact, which was designed to sustain confidence in the euro, is seen as the cornerstone of monetary union. Under its original terms member states were obliged to keep budget deficits within 3% of GDP, or face fines, and to bring their budgets close to balance by 2004. However, during 2002 the Pact was heavily criticized for being inflexible (including some criticism from Romano Prodi, President of the Commission), when a number of countries (including Portugal and Germany) could not meet its requirements, and in September the 2004 deadline was extended by two years for certain countries (France, Germany, Italy and Portugal), while some concessionary provision was introduced to allow countries with low levels of long-term debt, such as the United Kingdom and Ireland, to increase investment spending by running larger short-term budget deficits. The Pact faces additional pressure with the pending enlargement of the EU, as its framework will have to apply to the 10 candidate countries, even though their economies are very diverse. A summit was scheduled to take place in Brussels in the first half of 2003 to discuss reforming the terms of the Pact.

The euro

With the creation of the European Monetary System (EMS), a new monetary unit, the European Currency Unit (ECU), was adopted. Its value and composition were identical to those of the European Unit of Account (EUA) already used in the administrative fields of the Community. The ECU was a composite monetary unit, in which the relative value of each currency was determined by the gross national product and the volume of trade of each country.

The ECU, which was assigned the function of the unit of account used by the European Monetary Co-operation Fund (EMCF), was also used as the denominator for the exchange-rate mechanism (ERM); as the denominator for operations in both the intervention and the credit mechanisms; and as a means of settlement between monetary authorities of the European Community. From April 1979 the ECU was also used as the unit of account for the purposes of the Common Agricultural Policy (CAP). From 1981 it replaced the EUA in the general budget of the Community; the activities of the European Development Fund (EDF) under the Lomé Convention; the balance sheets and loan operations of the European Investment Bank (EIB); and the activities of the European Coal and Steel Community (ECSC). In June 1985 measures were adopted by the governors of the Community's central banks, aiming to strengthen the EMS by expanding the use of the ECU, for example, by allowing international monetary institutions and the central banks of non-member countries to become 'other holders' of ECUs.

In June 1989 it was announced that, with effect from 20 September, the Portuguese and Spanish currencies were to be included in the composition of the ECU. From that date the amounts of the national currencies included in the composition of the ECU were 'weighted' as follows (in percentages): Belgian franc 7.6; Danish krone 2.5; French franc 19.0; Deutsche Mark 30.1; Greek drachma 0.8; Irish pound 1.1; Italian lira 10.2; Luxembourg franc 0.3; Netherlands guilder 9.4; Portuguese escudo 0.8; Spanish peseta 5.3; and the United Kingdom pound sterling 13.0. The composition of the ECU

'basket' of currencies was 'frozen' with the entry into force of the Treaty on European Union on 1 November 1993. This was not affected by the accession to the EU of Austria, Finland and Sweden; consequently those countries' currencies were not represented in the ECU 'basket'.

As part of Stage III of the process of economic and monetary union (EMU), the ECU was replaced by a single currency, the euro (€), on 1 January 1999, at a conversion rate of 1:1.

In April 1998 ministers agreed that banks should make no charge for the conversion of accounts or payments of national currency into euros, during a transitional period. In July agreement was reached with trade and consumer groups to establish a voluntary scheme allowing retailers to display prices in euros and to accept payments made in euros without imposing any additional charges.

A payments settlement system, known as Target (Trans-European Automated Real-time Gross Settlement Express Transfer), was introduced for countries participating in EMU on 4 January 1999. By 2002 Target had become one of the world's largest payment systems, and was considered to be making a considerable contribution to the integration of the euro money market and the smooth implementation of the single monetary policy.

On 1 January 2002 the euro entered into circulation in the 12 participating countries. By the end of February the former national currencies of all the participating countries had been withdrawn. The introduction of the new currency took place without major problems, and even ahead of the official phasing out of national currencies the changeover was functioning smoothly; by the beginning of February the euro was used in over 95% of cash transactions.

The euro's value in national currencies is calculated and published daily. By mid-1999 the value of the euro had declined by some 12% against the US dollar compared with its value on introduction. Its decline was attributed to the relatively high degree of economic growth taking place in the USA compared with rates in the euro zone. Signs of economic recovery, especially in Germany, led to the strengthening of the euro against the US dollar in the second half of 1999. However, this renewal of confidence was not sustained and the euro dropped below parity level with the dollar in December. The ECB raised interest rates four times during the six months to May 2000, in an attempt to combat the failure in confidence. In September 2000 the monetary authorities of the USA and Japan, concerned about the impact of the weakness of the euro on the world economy, intervened jointly with the ECB in exchange markets. In November 2000 the currency reached its lowest recorded level. The euro rallied briefly in early 2001, but by June its value was declining once again. The ECB lowered interest rates four times during 2001 (including in September, as part of a joint effort by central banks to counteract the economic effects of the terrorist attacks on the USA). By November the currency had lost about one-fifth of its value against the US dollar since its launch in 1999.

Immediately following the introduction of the euro in the 12 participating countries in January 2002, its value rose significantly; during 2002 it continued to appreciate against other currencies, reaching parity with the US dollar in June, a stage which marked its highest level since February 2000. By April 2003 the euro stood at €1 = US$1.08.

In March 2000 Belgium, France and the Netherlands announced the pending merger of their stock exchanges, to form a joint exchange, EURONEXT, with a view to facilitating cross-border euro commerce. This was achieved in September. Once fully operative, EURONEXT was to be the first fully integrated cross-border European market for equities, bonds, derivatives and commodities.

External Relations

The EU has diplomatic relations in its own right with many countries, and with international organizations, and participates as a body in international conferences on trade and development, such as the 'Uruguay Round' of trade negotiations, under the General Agreement on Tariffs and Trade (GATT—see WTO, see p. 323), and the 'Doha Round' launched by WTO in November 2001. It has observer status at the United Nations. Agreements have been signed with numerous countries and groups of countries, allowing for co-operation in trade and other matters. Association agreements were initially signed between the EC and other European countries for the purpose of customs union or possible accession. After the decline of Communism in eastern Europe in 1989, it was decided that the new states, many of which expressed a desire to become full members of the EC, should be offered association status in the first instance. The resulting agreements are known as 'Europe Agreements'. Co-operation agreements are less comprehensive, and seek to facilitate economic co-operation with both European and non-European countries. Prior to 1989 they represented the preferred form of relationship with eastern European countries. Within the framework of the Stabilization and Association Process the EU is negotiating Stabilization and Association Agreements with Balkans countries, with the long-term goal of admitting them as members. In addition several Euro-Mediterranean association agreements have been concluded. The Union is a party to various international conventions (in some of these to the exclusion of the individual member states).

CENTRAL AND EASTERN EUROPE

During the late 1980s the extensive political changes and reforms in eastern European countries led to a strengthening of links with the EC. Agreements on trade and economic co-operation were concluded with Hungary (1988), Poland (1989), the USSR (1989), Czechoslovakia (1988—on trade only—and 1990), Bulgaria (1990), the German Democratic Republic (GDR—1990) and Romania (1990). In July 1989 the EC was entrusted with the co-ordination of aid from member states of the Organisation for Economic Co-operation and Development (OECD, see p. 277) to Hungary and Poland ('Operation PHARE'—Poland/Hungary Aid for Restructuring of Economies): this programme was subsequently extended to include Albania, Bulgaria, the Czech Republic, Slovakia, Romania and the Baltic states (Estonia, Latvia and Lithuania). Community heads of government agreed in December 1989 to establish a European Bank for Reconstruction and Development (EBRD, see p. 193), with participation by member states of the OECD and the Council for Mutual Economic Assistance, to promote investment in eastern Europe; the EBRD began operations in April 1991. In June 1995 the European Council agreed to provide total funding under the PHARE programme of ECU 6,693m. to central and eastern European countries for the period 1995–99.

'Europe Agreements' between the EC and Czechoslovakia, Hungary and Poland were signed in December 1991, with the aim of establishing a free-trade area within 10 years and developing political co-operation. In April 1994 Hungary and Poland submitted formal applications for EU membership. The Czech Republic applied formally in January 1996. In June 1991 the EC established diplomatic relations with Albania, and in May 1992 an agreement on trade and co-operation was signed. Europe Agreements were initialled with Romania in October, and with Bulgaria in March 1993. In June 1995 Romania formally applied for EU membership, followed by Bulgaria in December. In June 1993 the European Council approved measures to accelerate the opening of EC markets to goods from central and eastern European countries, with customs duties on many industrial items to be removed by the end of 1994. In September 1993 a co-operation agreement with Slovenia came into force; a Europe Agreement was signed in 1996, and Slovenia then formally applied for EU membership. An interim agreement, implementing the measures approved in June 1993, entered into force on 1 January 1997, providing for the gradual establishment of a free-trade area during a transitional period of six years. In December 2000 a preferential trade regime between Slovenia and the EU entered into effect.

Trade and co-operation agreements with the three Baltic states were signed in May 1992. In July 1994 free-trade agreements with these countries were finalized by the EU, coming into effect on 1 January 1995. The EU concluded Europe Agreements with the Baltic states in June 1995. In October 1995 Latvia submitted a formal application for EU membership. Formal applications by Estonia and Lithuania were submitted in December.

In 1991 the EC established the Technical Assistance to the Commonwealth of Independent States (TACIS) programme, to promote the development of successful market economies and foster democracy in the countries of the former USSR through the provision of expertise and training. (TACIS initially extended assistance to the Baltic states. In 1992, however, these became eligible for assistance under PHARE and withdrew from TACIS.) The TACIS/EBRD Bangkok Facility provides EU financing to assist in the preparation for, and implementation of, EBRD investment in the CIS region. In 1994 Mongolia also became eligible for TACIS assistance. The TACIS programme's budget for 2000–06 was €3,138m.

In 1992 EU heads of government decided to replace the agreement on trade and economic co-operation that had been concluded with the USSR in 1989 with new Partnership and Co-operation Agreements (PCAs), providing a framework for closer political, cultural and economic relations between the EU and the former republics of the USSR. The PCAs are preceded by preliminary Interim Agreements. An Interim Agreement with Russia on trade concessions came into effect in February 1996, giving EU exporters improved access to the Russian market for specific products, and at the same time abolishing quantitative restrictions on some Russian exports to the EU. In December 1997 a PCA with Russia entered into force. The first meeting of the Co-operation Council for the EU-Russia PCA took place in January 1998, and, in July, an EU-Russia Space Dialogue was established. In June 1999 the EU adopted a Common Strategy on Russia. This aimed to promote the consolidation of democracy and rule of law in the country; the integration of Russia into the common European economic and social space; and regional stability and security. At the sixth EU-Russia summit in October 2000 the two sides agreed to initiate a regular energy dialogue, with the aim of establishing an EU-Russia Energy Partnership. During 2002 two EU-Russia summits were held, at which each party reconfirmed its commitment to democratic principles and human rights, and its determination to continue the fight against international terrorism, drugs trafficking and illegal immigration. Discussion also centred on the issue of Kaliningrad, a Russian enclave between Poland and Lithuania, and its future status following the accession of these two countries. In the face of opposition from Russia, the EU insisted that residents of Kaliningrad would need a visa to cross EU territory; the matter was eventually resolved by a compromise agreement on a special multiple re-entry transit pass for residents of the enclave.

In February 1994 the EU Council of Ministers agreed to pursue closer economic and political relations with Ukraine, following an agreement by that country to renounce control of nuclear weapons on its territory. A PCA was signed by the two sides in June. In December EU ministers of finance approved a loan totalling ECU 85m., conditional on Ukraine's implementation of a strategy to close the Chernobyl (Chornobyl) nuclear power plant. An Interim Trade Agreement with Ukraine came into force in February 1996; this was replaced by a PCA in March 1998. In December 1999 the EU adopted a Common Strategy on Ukraine, aimed at developing a strategic partnership on the basis of the PCA. The Chernobyl plant closed in December 2000. The EU has provided funding to cover the interim period prior to the completion of two new reactors (supported by the EBRD and the European Atomic Energy Community—Euratom) to replace the plant's generating capacity. The EU has also been involved in social regeneration projects in the Chernobyl area.

An Interim Agreement with Belarus was signed in March 1996. However, in February 1997 the EU suspended negotiations for the conclusion of the Interim Agreement and for a PCA in view of serious reverses to the development of democracy in that country. EU technical assistance programmes were suspended, with the exception of aid programmes and those considered directly beneficial to the democratic process. In 1999 the EU announced that the punitive measures would be withdrawn gradually upon the attainment of certain benchmarks. In 2000 the EU criticized the Belarus Government for failing to accept its recommendations on the conduct of legislative elections held in October. By July 1999 PCAs had entered into force with all the CIS states except for Belarus, Tajikistan and Turkmenistan. In November 2002 the EU member states imposed a travel ban on President Alyaksandr Lukashenka of Belarus, as a protest against his authoritarian rule and the declining human rights situation in the country.

In May 1994 a Conference on Stability in Europe was convened in Paris to discuss the prevention of ethnic and territorial conflicts in central and eastern Europe. In particular, the conference sought to secure bilateral 'good-neighbour' accords between nine European countries that were regarded as potential future members of the EU (Bulgaria, the Czech Republic, Estonia, Hungary, Latvia, Lithuania, Poland, Romania and Slovakia). These countries, together with EU member states and other European countries (including Belarus, Moldova, Russia and Ukraine), signed a 'Stability Pact' in Paris in March 1995.

In July 1997 the European Commission published a report entitled 'Agenda 2000', which presented the Commission's new 'reinforced pre-accession strategy', uniting all the existing forms of support, including PHARE, into a single 'Accession Partnership' (AP) programme for each country. The APs, approved by the Commission in March 1998, were designed to support each country's preparations for accession by identifying priority areas and providing financial assistance. Each AP was complemented by a 'National Programme for the Adoption of the Acquis' (NPAA). (The acquis communautaire is the entire body of legislation of the European Community.) In 2000 the EU's PHARE and other schemes for the then five countries with SAAs (see below) were streamlined into the CARDS (Community Assistance for Reconstruction, Democratization and Stabilization) programme, now the EU's main channel for financial and technical assistance to the countries of southeastern Europe. A total of €4,650m. was allocated under CARDS for 2000–06.

Concurrently with Agenda 2000 the Commission published 'Opinions' on the application for membership of each of the candidate countries. It proposed that accession negotiations should commence with the Czech Republic, Estonia, Hungary, Poland and Slovenia. It was recommended that discussions with Bulgaria, Latvia, Lithuania, Romania and Slovakia be deferred, owing to the need for further economic or democratic reform in those countries. Accession negotiations at ministerial level commenced on 10 November 1998 with the first group of applicant countries. In December 1999 it was agreed to initiate accession negotiations with Bulgaria, Latvia, Lithuania, Romania and Slovakia; these commenced in February 2000. Two Eastern European programmes designed to aid candidate countries in their efforts towards accession began in 2000. The Special Accession Programme for Agriculture and Rural Development (SAPARD) aims to help candidate countries manage the problems of structural adjustment in their agricultural sectors. It has an annual budget of €250m. The Instrument for Structural Policies for Preaccession (ISPA) has a budget for 2000–06 of €1,040m. Funds are available for infrastructure projects in the environment and transport sectors of candidate countries.

At the Copenhagen summit in December 2002, an historic agreement was reached when the European Council agreed that 10 candidate countries, including eight in central and eastern Europe (the Czech Republic, Estonia, Hungary, Latvia, Lithuania, Poland, Slovakia and Slovenia) should join the EU in May 2004. By the summit accession negotiations covering more than 30 issues, including free movement of goods, capital, persons and services; agriculture; fisheries; company law; energy; the environment; external relations; and so on had been completed with all of the candidate countries, thus allowing them to be formally accepted as members. Financing agreements were signed with each of the 10 countries concerned during 2002, with financial assistance earmarked for projects such as cross-border co-operation, phasing out nuclear plants, agricultural development schemes, etc., in readiness for accession. At the Copenhagen summit the EU agreed to increase aid to the 10 states to €40,800m. for 2004–06. The largest share of the money was allocated to Poland; the Polish Government had been negotiating for extra assistance to compensate for the reduction in subsidies to its farmers, in the form of higher production quotas and extended tariff protection, but accepted a package of immediate direct budgetary assistance in place of longer-term regional aid. A referendum on EU membership was to take place in Poland in 2003; in Estonia an earlier referendum had resulted in a 39% vote in favour. The leaders of the new member states signed the accession treaty in Athens in April 2003.

Following the introduction on 1 July 1990 of monetary, economic and social union between the Federal Republic of Germany and the GDR, and the formal integration of the two countries on 3 October, Community legislation was introduced within the former GDR over a transitional period.

A co-operation agreement was signed with Yugoslavia in 1980 (but not ratified until April 1983), allowing tariff-free imports and Community loans. New financial protocols were signed in 1987 and 1991. However, EC aid was suspended in July 1991, following the declarations of independence by the Yugoslav republics of Croatia and Slovenia, and the subsequent outbreak of civil conflict. Efforts were made in the ensuing months by EC ministers of foreign affairs to negotiate a peaceful settlement between the Croatian and Serbian factions, and a team of EC observers was maintained in Yugoslavia from July onwards, to monitor successive cease-fire agreements. In October the EC proposed a plan for an association of independent states, to replace the Yugoslav federation: this was accepted by all the Yugoslav republics except Serbia, which demanded a redefining of boundaries to accommodate within Serbia all predominantly Serbian areas. In November the application of the Community's co-operation agreements with Yugoslavia was suspended (with exemptions for the republics which co-operated in the peace negotiations). In January 1992 the Community granted diplomatic recognition to the former Yugoslav republics of Croatia and Slovenia, and in April it recognized Bosnia and Herzegovina, while withholding recognition from Macedonia (owing to pressure from the Greek Government, which feared that the existence of an independent Macedonia would imply a claim on the Greek province of the same name). In May EC ambassadors were withdrawn from Belgrade, in protest at Serbia's support for aggression by Bosnian Serbs against other ethnic groups in Bosnia and Herzegovina, and in the same month the Community imposed a trade embargo on Serbia and Montenegro.

New proposals for a settlement of the Bosnian conflict, submitted by EC and UN mediators in 1993, were accepted by the Bosnian Croats and by the Bosnian Government in March, but rejected by the Bosnian Serbs. In June the European Council pledged more rigorous enforcement of sanctions against Serbia. In July, at UN/EC talks in Geneva, all three parties to the Bosnian war agreed on a plan to divide Bosnia and Herzegovina into three separate republics; however, the Bosnian Government rejected the proposals for the share of territory to be allotted to the Muslim community.

In April 1994, following a request from EU ministers of foreign affairs, a Contact Group, consisting of France, Germany, the United Kingdom, the USA and Russia, was initiated to undertake peace negotiations. The following month ministers of foreign affairs of the

USA, Russia and the EU (represented by five member states) jointly endorsed a proposal to divide Bosnia and Herzegovina in proportions of 49% to the Bosnian Serbs and 51% to the newly-established Federation of Muslims and Croats. The proposal was rejected by the Bosnian Serb assembly in July and had to be abandoned after the Muslim-Croat Federation withdrew its support subsequent to the Bosnian Serb vote. In July the EU formally assumed political control of Mostar, in southern Bosnia and Herzegovina, in order to restore the city's administrative infrastructure and secure peace.

Despite some criticism of US policy towards the former Yugoslavia, in September 1995 the EU supported US-led negotiations in Geneva to devise a plan to end the conflict in Bosnia and Herzegovina. The plan closely resembled the previous proposals of the Contact Group: two self-governing entities were to be created within Bosnia and Herzegovina, with 51% of territory being allocated to the Muslim-Croat Federation, and 49% to Bosnian Serbs. The proposals were finally agreed after negotiations in Dayton, USA, in November 1995, and an accord was signed in Paris in December. During 1991–2000 Bosnia and Herzegovina received a total of €1,032m. in assistance from the EU. In 2000 the EU published a 'road map' for Bosnia and Herzegovina, outlining measures that must be undertaken by the Government prior to the initiation of a feasibility study on the formulation of a Stabilization and Association Agreement (SAA). In September 2002 the Commission reported that Bosnia and Herzegovina had essentially adhered to the terms of the road map. In January 2003 a new European Union Police Mission (EUPM) took over from the UN peace-keeping force in Bosnia and Herzegovina, with a budget of €38m. for 2003.

Negotiations towards a trade and co-operation agreement with Croatia began in June 1995, but talks were suspended in early August, following Croatia's military offensive in the Krajina region, which was strongly criticized by the EU. A CTF was established in Croatia in February 2000. An SAA with Croatia entered into force in October 2001.

In January 1996 the EU announced its intention to recognize Yugoslavia (Serbia and Montenegro), despite the opposition of the USA. During 1996–99 the EU allocated ECU 1,000m. for the repatriation of refugees, restructuring the economy and technical assistance, in addition to ECU 1,000m. in humanitarian aid provided since the beginning of the conflict in the former Yugoslavia.

In December 1993 six member states of the EU formally recognized the former Yugoslav republic of Macedonia (FYRM) as an independent state, but in February 1994 Greece imposed a commercial embargo against the FYRM, on the grounds that the use of the name and symbols (e.g. on the state flag) of 'Macedonia' was a threat to Greek national security. In March, however, ministers of foreign affairs of the EU decided that the embargo was in contravention of EU law, and in April the Commission commenced legal proceedings in the European Court of Justice against Greece. In September 1995 Greece and the FYRM began a process of normalizing relations, after the FYRM agreed to change the design of its state flag. In October Greece ended its economic blockade of the FYRM. A trade and co-operation agreement with the FYRM entered into force in January 1998. In April 2001 an SAA was signed with the FYRM. At the same time, an interim agreement was adopted, allowing for trade-related matters of the SAA to enter into effect in June, without the need for formal ratification by the national parliaments of the EU member states. (The SAA provided for the EU to open its markets to 95% of exports from the FYRM.) However, the Macedonian Government was informed that it would be required to deliver concessions to the ethnic Albanian minority population prior to entering into the agreement. In 2002 the remit of the European Agency for Reconstruction, which had been originally established to administer aid programmes in Kosovo, was extended to include the FYRM. The EU made humanitarian payments of €3m. to the FYRM in 2002.

In March 1997 the EU sent two advisory delegations to Albania to help to restore order after violent unrest and political instability erupted in that country. A request by the Albanian Government for the deployment of EU peace-keeping troops was refused, but it was announced in early April that the EU was to provide humanitarian aid of some ECU 2m., to be used for emergency relief. In September 2002 the European Parliament voted in support of opening negotiations for an SAA with Albania, following satisfactory progress in that country, with regard to presidential elections and electoral reform.

In 1998 the escalation of violence in Kosovo and Metohija (Federal Republic of Yugoslavia), between Serbs and the ethnic Albanian majority, prompted the imposition of sanctions by EU ministers of foreign affairs. In March ministers agreed to impose an arms embargo, to halt export credit guarantees to Yugoslavia and to restrict visas for Serbian officials. A ban on new investment in the region was imposed in June. In the same month military observers from the EU, Russia and the USA were deployed to Kosovo. In September the EU agreed to deny JAT, the Yugoslav airline, landing rights in EU countries. During the following month the Yugoslav Government allowed a team of international experts to investigate atrocities in the region, under an EU mandate. Several EU countries participated in the NATO military offensive against Yugoslavia, which was initiated in March 1999 owing to the continued repression of ethnic Albanians in Kosovo by Serbian forces. Ministers approved a new series of punitive measures in April, including an embargo on the sale or supply of petroleum to the Yugoslav authorities and an extension of a travel ban on Serbian official and business executives. Humanitarian assistance was extended to provide relief for the substantial numbers of refugees who fled Kosovo amid the escalating violence, in particular to assist the Governments of Albania and the FYRM.

In September 1999 EU foreign ministers agreed to ease sanctions in force against Kosovo and Montenegro. In October the EU began to implement an 'Energy for Democracy' initiative, with the objective of supplying some €5m.-worth of heating oil to Serbian towns controlled by groups in opposition to the then Yugoslav President Slobodan Milošević. In February 2000 the EU suspended its ban on the Yugoslav national airline. However, the restrictions on visas for Serbian officials were reinforced. Kosovo received a total of €474.7m. under EU programmes in 2000 and the EU remained the largest financial contributor to the province in 2001.

In May 2000 the EU agreed an emergency aid package to support Montenegro against destabilization by Serbia. Following the election of a new FRY administration in late 2000 the EU immediately withdrew all remaining sanctions, with the exception of those directed against Milošević and his associates, and pledged financial support of €200m. The FRY was welcomed as a full participant in the stabilization and association process (see below). It was announced that a CTF would be set up when conditions permitted. The EU insisted that the FRY must co-operate fully with the International Criminal Tribunal for the Former Yugoslavia (ICTY). Following the arrest of Milošević by the FRY authorities in April 2001, the first part of the EU's aid package for that year (amounting to €240m.) was released. During 2002 EU humanitarian aid to Serbia totalled €37.5m., to assist the large numbers of refugees and displaced persons.

At a Balkan summit convened in Zagreb, Croatia, in November 2000, the EU pledged €4,650m. for reconstruction aid to the region over the period 2000–06. The allocation of aid in 2002 for the Balkans was half that of 2001, owing to the return to relative normality in the region and the decline in humanitarian needs.

In June 1999 the EU, in conjunction with the Group of Seven industrialized nations and Russia (the G-8), regional governments and other organizations concerned with the stability of the region, launched the Stability Pact for South-Eastern Europe, which was placed under the auspices of the OSCE. For its part, the EU proposed to offer customized SAAs (see above) to Albania, Bosnia, Croatia, Macedonia and, eventually, the FRY, provided that they fulfilled certain conditions. (The FRY was excluded from the Pact until October 2000, following the staging there of democratic presidential elections.) Since the establishment of the Pact, heads of state and government of the South-East European countries have met regularly in the framework of the South East Europe Co-operation Process (SEECP). At the Stability Pact's first regional funding conference, held in March 2000, a 'quick start package', comprising 244 projects, was announced; by June 2001 some 201 projects were under way.

OTHER EUROPEAN COUNTRIES

The members of the European Free Trade Association (EFTA) concluded bilateral free trade agreements with the EEC and the ECSC during the 1970s. On 1 January 1984 the last tariff barriers were eliminated, thus establishing full free trade for industrial products between the Community and EFTA members. Some EFTA members subsequently applied for membership of the EC: Austria in 1989, Sweden in 1991, and Finland, Switzerland and Norway in 1992. Formal negotiations on the creation of a 'European Economic Area' (EEA), a single market for goods, services, capital and labour among EC and EFTA members, began in June 1990, and were concluded in October 1991. The agreement was signed in May 1992 (after a delay caused by a ruling of the Court of Justice of the EC that a proposed joint EC-EFTA court, for adjudication in disputes, was incompatible with the Treaty of Rome; EFTA members then agreed to concede jurisdiction to the Court of Justice on cases of competition involving both EC and EFTA members, and to establish a special joint committee for other disputes). In a referendum in December Swiss voters rejected ratification of the agreement, and the remaining 18 countries signed an adjustment protocol in March 1993, allowing the EEA to be established without Switzerland (which was to have observer status). The EEA entered into force on 1 January 1994. Formal negotiations on the accession to the EU of Austria, Finland and Sweden began on 1 February, and those on Norway's membership started on 1 April. Negotiations were concluded with Austria, Finland and Sweden on 1 March 1994, and with Norway on 16 March, having been delayed by issues concerning the fisheries sector. Heads of government of the four countries signed treaties of accession to the EU in June, which were to come into

effect from 1995, subject to approval by a national referendum in each country. Accession to the EU was endorsed by the electorates of Austria, Finland and Sweden in June, October and November respectively. Norway's accession was rejected by a referendum conducted at the end of November. Austria, Finland and Sweden became members of the EU on 1 January 1995. Liechtenstein, which became a full member of EFTA in September 1991, joined the EEA on 1 May 1995. Negotiations conducted with Switzerland since 1992 on the formulation of a new bilateral economic arrangement proceeded slowly. The main obstacles to an agreement concerned Switzerland's work permit quotas for EU citizens, and the weight limit on trucks passing through its territory. In December 1996 it was reported that Switzerland had agreed to phase out the use of work permit quotas within six years of a treaty being signed. In early December 1998 political agreement was reached with Switzerland to abolish the weight limit and instead impose road-haulage charges on trucks weighing 40 metric tons or more. Later in that month an interim trade agreement was concluded. In December 2002 talks aimed at fighting fraud and tax evasion took place between EU and Swiss officials; the EU was keen to gain further concessions from Switzerland regarding improved access to information for EU tax authorities.

A trade agreement with Andorra entered into force on 1 January 1991, establishing a customs union for industrial products, and allowing duty-free access to the EC for certain Andorran agricultural products. In January 1998 negotiations on a co-operation agreement with Andorra were finalized. However, the agreement remains to be adopted. Negotiations on a trade agreement with San Marino were concluded in December 1991.

THE MIDDLE EAST AND THE MEDITERRANEAN

A scheme to negotiate a series of parallel trade and co-operation agreements encompassing almost all of the non-member states on the coast of the Mediterranean was formulated by the EC in 1972. Association agreements, intended to lead to customs union or the eventual full accession of the country concerned, had been signed with Greece (which eventually became a member of the Community in 1981) in 1962, Turkey in 1964 and Malta in 1971; a fourth agreement was signed with Cyprus in 1972. These established free access to the Community market for most industrial products and tariff reductions for most agricultural products. Annexed were financial protocols under which the Community was to provide concessional finance. During the 1970s a series of agreements covering trade and economic co-operation were concluded with the Arab Mediterranean countries and Israel, all establishing free access to EC markets for most industrial products. Access for agricultural products was facilitated, although some tariffs remained. In 1982 the Commission formulated an integrated plan for the development of its own Mediterranean regions and recommended the adoption of a new policy towards the non-Community countries of the Mediterranean. This was to include greater efforts towards diversifying agriculture, in order to avoid surpluses of items such as citrus fruits, olive oil and wine (which the Mediterranean countries all wished to export to the Community) and to reduce these countries' dependence on imported food. From 1 January 1993 the majority of agricultural exports from Mediterranean non-Community countries were granted exemption from customs duties.

In June 1995 the European Council endorsed a proposal by the Commission to reform and strengthen the Mediterranean policy of the EU. The initiative envisaged the eventual establishment of a Euro-Mediterranean Economic Area (EMEA), to be preceded by a gradual liberalization of trade within the region through bilateral and regional free-trade arrangements, and the adoption of financial and technical measures to support the implementation of structural reforms in Mediterranean partner countries. In November 1995 a conference of foreign affairs ministers of the EU member states, 11 Mediterranean non-member countries (excluding Libya) and the Palestinian authorities was convened in Barcelona, Spain. The conference endorsed the agreement on the EMEA and resolved to establish a permanent Euro-Mediterranean ministerial dialogue. It issued the 'Barcelona Declaration', endorsing commitments to uphold democratic principles and to pursue greater co-operation in the control of international crime, drugs-trafficking and illegal migration. The Declaration set the objective of establishing a Euro-Mediterranean free-trade area by 2010. The process of co-operation and dialogue under this agreement became known as the Euro-Mediterranean Partnership (or 'Barcelona Process'). In September 1998 the Commission proposed measures to extend the single market to the Mediterranean countries and sought to formulate common rules on customs and taxation, free movement of goods, public procurement, intellectual property, financial services, data protection and accounting.

In April 1997 the second Euro-Mediterranean Conference of ministers of foreign affairs was held, in Malta, to review implementation of the partnership strategy. Euro-Mediterranean foreign ministers convened for a third conference in April 1999, in Stuttgart, Germany. The Stuttgart conference agreed that Libya could eventually become a partner in the process, following the removal of UN sanctions on that country and acceptance of the full terms of the Barcelona Declaration. Libya subsequently attended some meetings as an observer. A fourth conference, convened in November 2000, in Marseilles, France, focused on the adoption of a new common strategy for the Mediterranean, aimed at strengthening the Barcelona Process. With economic, financial, social and cultural components, the new approach involved increased political dialogue with partnership countries as well as further efforts to improve security, democracy and human rights. The sixth Euro-Mediterranean Conference, in Valencia, in April 2002, reaffirmed the principles of the Barcelona Declaration and adopted an action plan covering different fields of the partnership, and in particular speeding up progress towards the creation of the Euro-Mediterranean free-trade area.

The EU's primary financial instrument for the implementation of the Euro-Mediterranean Partnership has been the MEDA programme, providing support for the reform of economic and social structures within partnership countries. The legal basis of the MEDA programme was the MEDA Regulation, adopted in July 1996. Financial aid commitments under MEDA I (covering 1995–99) amounted to ECU 3,400m. In 1999 the MEDA Regulation was reviewed and revised. The amended programme was named MEDA II. Covering the period 2000–06, MEDA II was granted a budget of €5,350m.

The first Euro-Mediterranean Energy Forum was convened in May 1997 and a second Energy Forum was held in May 1998; a number of other sectoral conferences have been organized. The inaugural meeting of a Euro-Mediterranean Parliamentary Forum was convened in Brussels in October 1998. The second meeting of the Forum took place in Brussels in February 2001. (The meeting will now be held annually.) The first Euro-Mediterranean ministerial meeting on trade was convened in May 2001; ministers have agreed to hold regular meetings within this framework, and the second such meeting took place in Toledo, Spain, in March 2002.

In 1987 Turkey applied for membership of the EC. In 1989 the European Commission stated that, for formal negotiations on Turkish membership to take place, it would be necessary for Turkey to restructure its economy, improve its observance of human rights, and harmonize its relations with Greece. Negotiations in early 1995 to conclude a customs union agreement with Turkey were obstructed by the opposition of Greece. In early March, however, Greece removed its veto on the customs union, having received assurance on the accession of Cyprus to the EU. Ratification of the agreement by the European Parliament was delayed until mid-December, owing to concern over issues of human rights, in particular the policies of the Turkish Government towards the country's Kurdish population. In July 1990 Cyprus and Malta made formal applications to join the Community. In June 1993 the European Commission approved the eligibility of both countries to join the Community, and membership negotiations commenced in February 2000. In December 2002 the European Council agreed to admit Cyprus and Malta (along with eight other candidate countries) to the Union from May 2004. However the northern (Turkish) part of Cyprus was to be excluded unless a reunification plan was agreed, and the latest round of peace talks between the Greek and Turkish Cypriot areas ended in failure in March 2003, with no further negotiations scheduled. In contrast, progress in Malta was boosted in March 2003 by a referendum on EU membership (at which 53.6% voted in favour of membership) and an election victory the following month for the pro-EU Nationalist Party. In April 2003 the Maltese Prime Minister joined the leaders of other candidate countries (including Cyprus) in Athens to sign the accession treaty in preparation for the 2004 enlargement of the EU. From August 1999, when a devastating earthquake struck northwestern Turkey, a *rapprochement* began to take place between Greece and Turkey. Greece lifted its long-standing veto on disbursements of aid to Turkey and the EU made a loan of €600m. to the Turkish Government to assist reconstruction. This improvement in relations culminated, at the Helsinki summit meeting of EU leaders in December, in a formal invitation to Turkey to present its candidacy for EU membership. In December 2002 the Commission agreed on a programme of pre-accession financial assistance for Turkey, which had received financial assistance during the year of €142m., but at the same time refused to give the Turkish Government a firm date for accession talks as a candidate country, deciding instead to review Turkey's progress towards meeting membership terms in December 2004.

Co-operation agreements concluded in the 1970s with the Maghreb countries (Algeria, Morocco and Tunisia), the Mashreq countries (Egypt, Jordan, Lebanon and Syria) and Israel covered free access to the Community market for industrial products, customs preferences for certain agricultural products, and financial aid in the form of grants and loans from the European Investment Bank. A co-operation agreement negotiated with the Republic of Yemen was non-preferential. In June 1992 the EC approved a proposal to conclude new bilateral agreements with the Maghreb countries, incorporating the following components: political dialogue; financial,

economic, technical and cultural co-operation; and the eventual establishment of a free-trade area. A Euro-Mediterranean Association Agreement with Tunisia was signed in July 1995 and entered into force in March 1998. A similar agreement with Morocco entered into force in March 2000. (In July 1987 Morocco applied to join the Community, but its application was rejected on the grounds that it is not a European country.) The EU's relations with Algeria have been affected by political and civil instability in that country and by concerns regarding the Government's respect for human rights and democratic principles. In March 1997 negotiations were initiated between the European Commission and representatives of the Algerian government on a Euro-Mediterranean Association Agreement that would incorporate political commitments relating to democracy and human rights; this was signed in April 2002. A Euro-Mediterranean Association Agreement with Egypt was signed in June 2001. In May of that year, Egypt, together with Jordan, Tunisia and Morocco, issued the Agadir Declaration, providing for the establishment of a free-trade area, as a cornerstone of the planned Euro-Mediterranean free-trade area. Negotiations for the conclusion of an Association Agreement with Syria were initiated in July 1996, and continued during 2002. An Association Agreement with Jordan entered into force in May 2002. A similar agreement with Lebanon was signed in June 2002.

In January 1989 the EC and Israel eliminated the last tariff barriers to full free trade for industrial products. A Euro-Mediterranean Association Agreement with Israel was signed in 1995, providing further trade concessions and establishing an institutional political dialogue between the two parties. The agreement entered into force in June 2000. Following the signing of the September 1993 Israeli-Palestine Liberation Organization (PLO) peace agreement, the EC committed substantial funds in humanitarian assistance for the Palestinians. A Euro-Mediterranean Interim Association Agreement on Trade and Co-operation was signed with the PLO in January 1997 and entered into force in July. The agreement confirmed existing trade concessions offered to the Palestinians since 1986 and provided for free trade to be introduced during an initial five-year period. In April 1998 the EU and the Palestinian (National) Authority (PA) signed a security co-operation agreement, which provided for regular meetings to promote joint efforts on security issues, in particular in combating terrorism. The EU approved an assistance programme for the Palestinians in November totalling ECU 500m.; this was to cover the period 1999–2003. In April 1999 the European Parliament demanded an investigation into the handling of Commission funds to Palestinian-controlled areas of the West Bank and Gaza. At that time the EU was reported to be the largest donor to the PA. The escalation of violence between Israel and the Palestinians from September 2000 resulted in a significant deterioration of EU–Israel relations. During 2002 the EU criticized Israel for its policy of restricting the movements of Yasser Arafat, the Palestinian President, and in May of that year Israel alleged that EU funding to the Palestinian Authority was being diverted for terrorist activities, although the EU insisted that its aid was closely monitored by the IMF. EU aid to the Palestinians was increased during 2002, to a total of US $17.7m. for the year. The EU formed part of the quartet (alongside the UN, the USA and Russia) which in September 2002 put forward a three-stage peace plan, including provision for free elections for the Palestinian people, the creation of a Palestinian state and negotiations between Israel and Palestine, aiming at a final settlement by 2005.

A new co-operation agreement with Yemen, incorporating a political element (i.e. commitments to democratic principles and respect for human rights), and providing for 'most favoured nation' treatment, entered into force in July 1998.

Talks were held with Iran in April 1992 on the establishment of a co-operation accord. In December the Council of Ministers recommended that a 'critical dialogue' be undertaken with Iran, owing to the country's significance to regional security. In April 1997 the 'critical dialogue' was suspended and ambassadors were recalled from Iran, following a German court ruling that found the Iranian authorities responsible for ordering the murder of four Kurdish dissidents in Berlin in 1992. Later that month ministers of foreign affairs resolved to restore diplomatic relations with Iran, in order to protect the strong trading partnership. During 2002 attempts were made to improve relations with Iran, as negotiations began in preparation for a Trade and Co-operation Agreement. An eventual trade deal was to be linked to progress in political issues including human rights, weapons proliferation and counter-terrorism.

An co-operation agreement between the EC and the countries of the Gulf Co-operation Council (GCC), which entered into force in January 1990, provided for co-operation in industry, energy, technology and other fields. Negotiations on a full free-trade pact began in October 1990, but it was expected that any agreement would involve transition periods of some 12 years for the reduction of European tariffs on 'sensitive products' (i.e. petrochemicals). In November 1999 the GCC Supreme Council agreed to establish a customs union (a precondition of the proposed EU-GCC free-trade agreement) by March 2005. Free-trade negotiations continued throughout 2002.

Contacts with the Arab world in general take place within the framework of the 'Euro-Arab Dialogue', established in 1973 to provide a forum for discussion of economic issues through working groups on specific topics. Following a decision in 1989 to reactivate the Dialogue, meetings were suspended in 1990 as a result of Iraq's invasion of Kuwait. In April 1992 senior EC and Arab officials agreed to resume the process.

The increased tension in the Middle East in the run-up to the US-led military action in Iraq in March 2003 placed considerable strain on relations between member states of the EU, and exposed the lack of a common EU policy on Iraq. A summit of EU foreign ministers in Denmark in August 2002 emphasized the EU's support for the UN weapons inspectors in Iraq, and in January 2003 the EU warned the USA that only the UN Security Council could determine whether military action was justified. In the same month (which saw the beginning of the six-month Greek presidency in the EU) an EU diplomatic mission led by the Greek foreign minister visited seven Arab states in an effort to avert war. Divisions remained between member states, with the United Kingdom, Spain, Italy, Portugal and Denmark supporting the US policy, while France and Germany led the other members in opposing the impending conflict, or, at the least, in insisting on a second UN resolution. In February 2003 the European Council held an extraordinary meeting to discuss the crisis in Iraq, and issued a statement reconfirming its commitment to the UN. The EU set aside €15m. for humanitarian aid for Iraq, with further funds available for emergency aid, but also made it clear that the Union would not willingly pay for the reconstruction of Iraq after the conflict, which it had not fully supported in the first case without a UN resolution.

LATIN AMERICA

A non-preferential trade agreement was signed with Uruguay in 1974, and economic and commercial co-operation agreements with Mexico in 1975 and Brazil in 1980. A five-year co-operation agreement with the members of the Central American Common Market and with Panama entered into force in 1987, as did a similar agreement with the member countries (see below) of the Andean Group (now the Andean Community). Co-operation agreements were signed with Argentina and Chile in 1990, and in that year tariff preferences were approved for Bolivia, Colombia, Ecuador and Peru, in support of those countries' efforts to combat drugs-trafficking. In May 1992 an interinstitutional co-operation agreement was signed with the Southern Common Market (Mercosur); in the following month the EC and the member states of the Andean Group (Bolivia, Colombia, Ecuador, Peru and Venezuela) initialled a new co-operation agreement, which was to broaden the scope of economic and development co-operation and enhance trade relations, and a new co-operation agreement was signed with Brazil. In July 1993 the EC introduced a tariff regime to limit the import of bananas from Latin America, in order to protect the banana-producing countries of the ACP group, then linked to the EC by the Lomé Convention (see below). In June 1995 a Commission communication advocated greater economic co-operation with Cuba. This policy was strongly supported by a resolution of the European Parliament in January 1996, but was criticized by the US Government, which continued to maintain an economic embargo against Cuba. In April 2000 Cuba rejected the Cotonou Agreement (see below), following criticism by some European governments of its human rights record.

During 1996–2000 the EU forged closer links with Latin America, by means of strengthened political ties, an increase in economic integration and free trade, and co-operation in other areas. In April 1997 the EU extended further trade benefits to the countries of the Andean Community. In July the EU and Mexico concluded an Economic Partnership, Political Co-operation and Co-operation Agreement and an interim agreement on trade. The accords were signed in December. The main part of the interim agreement entered into effect in July 2000 and the co-operation agreement entered into force in October. In November 1999 the EU and Mexico concluded a free-trade agreement which, on implementation, was to lead to the removal of all tariffs on bilateral trade in industrial products by 2007. The first summit meeting of all EU and Latin American heads of state or government was held in Rio de Janeiro, Brazil, in June 1999.

In June 1996 the EU and Chile signed a framework agreement on political and economic co-operation, which provided for a process of bilateral trade liberalization, as well as co-operation in other industrial and financial areas. An EU-Chile Joint Council was established. In November 1999 the EU and Chile commenced practical negotiations on developing closer political and economic co-operation, within the framework of the proposed EU-Mercosur/Chile association agreement (see below). In November 2002 EU and Chile signed an association and free-trade agreement in Brussels; it provided for the liberalization of trade within seven years for industrial products and 10 years for agricultural products.

The first ministerial conference between the EC and the then 11 Latin American states of the Rio Group took place in April 1991; thereafter high-level joint ministerial meetings have been held on a regular basis. In late December 1994 the EU and Mercosur signed a joint declaration that aimed to promote trade liberalization and greater political co-operation. In September 1995, at a meeting in Montevideo, Uruguay, a framework agreement on the establishment of a free-trade regime between the two organizations was initialled. The agreement was formally signed in December. In July 1998 the Commission voted to commence negotiations towards an interregional association agreement with Mercosur and Chile, which would strengthen existing co-operation agreements. Negotiations were initiated in April 2000.

A second EU-Latin America/Caribbean summit took place in Madrid, Spain, in May 2002, and covered co-operation in political, economic, social and cultural fields, while in November of the same year the eighth EU-Mercosur negotiating meeting took place in Brasilia. Officials hoped that the agreement would be ready by 2004. During 2002 the Argentine economy was severely affected by recession, and the EU responded by temporarily increasing import quotas for Argentine meat in response to a request from the Argentine Government. In November 2002 the EU signed a memorandum of agreement on co-operation with Brazil for the period 2001–06.

During 2002 €123m. was committed to financial and technical co-operation with Latin America, covering projects in the field of the environment and rural development, regional integration, economic development and the strengthening of intra-regional trade.

ASIA AND AUSTRALASIA

Relations between the EU and ASEAN are based on the Co-operation Agreement of 1980. Under this agreement, joint committee meetings are held approximately every 18 months. There are also regular ministerial meetings and post-ministerial conferences. In addition, the EU is a member of the ASEAN Regional Forum (ARF), a security grouping designed to promote peace and stability, established in 1994. In December of that year the European Council endorsed a new strategy for Asia, which recognized the region's increasing economic and political importance and pledged to strengthen bilateral and regional dialogue. The strategy aimed to enhance the development of trade and investment, promote peace and security, and assist the less-developed countries in Asia. In May 1995 ASEAN and EU senior officials endorsed an initiative to convene an Asia-Europe Meeting of heads of government (ASEM). The first Asia-Europe meeting (ASEM) was held in March 1996 in Bangkok, Thailand. It was agreed to launch an Asia-Europe Partnership for Greater Growth, in order to expand trade, investment and technology transfer. An Asia-Business Forum was to be formed, as well as an Asia-Europe Foundation in Singapore to promote educational and cultural exchanges. The second ASEM summit, convened in the United Kingdom in April 1998, was dominated by economic and financial concerns, and both sides' declared intention to prevent a return to protectionist trading policies. The meeting established an ASEM Trust Fund, under the auspices of the World Bank, to alleviate the social impact of the financial crisis. Other initiatives adopted by ASEM were an Asia-Europe Co-operation Framework to co-ordinate political, economic and financial co-operation, a Trade Facilitation Action Plan, and an Investment Promotion Action Plan, which incorporated a new Investment Experts Group. The meeting resolved to promote efforts to strengthen relations in all areas, and to establish a series of working bodies to promote specific areas of co-operation. ASEM heads of government convened for the third time in Seoul, Republic of Korea, in October 2000. ASEM III welcomed the ongoing *rapprochement* between the two Korean nations, declared a commitment to the promotion of human rights, and endorsed several initiatives related to globalization and information technology. The meeting established a new Asia-Europe Co-operation Framework (AECF), identifying ASEM's principles and priorities for the next 10 years. ASEM IV took place in Copenhagen, Denmark, in September 2002. Statements were subsequently adopted on co-operation in the fight against international terrorism, and on the situation in the Korean peninsula. Economic issues were also discussed, and in particular the need to continue the WTO 'Doha' negotiating round. At the same time the first EU-Korea summit was held; discussion centred on the reduction in customs barriers and aid to shipbuilding.

In September 2001 the EU adopted a new Communication on relations with Asia for the coming decade. Representing an updating of the 1994 strategy, this focused on strengthened partnership, particularly in the areas of politics, security, trade and investment. It aimed to reduce poverty and to promote democracy, good governance and the rule of law throughout the region. Partnerships and alliances on global issues were to be forged. A fundamental aim was to strengthen the EU's presence in Asia, promoting mutual awareness and knowledge on both sides.

Bilateral non-preferential co-operation agreements were signed with Bangladesh, India, Pakistan and Sri Lanka between 1973 and

1976. A further agreement with India, extended to include co-operation in trade, industry, energy, science and finance, came into force in December 1981. A third agreement, which entered into effect in August 1994, included commitments to develop co-operation between the two sides and improve market access, as well as for the observance of human rights and democratic principles. The first EU–India summit meeting was held in Lisbon in June 2000. A new and extended agreement with Pakistan on commercial and economic co-operation entered into force in May 1986; in May 1992 an agreement was signed on measures to stimulate private investment in Pakistan. A new accord with Sri Lanka, designed to promote co-operation in areas such as trade, investment and protection of the environment, entered into force in April 1995. A similar agreement with Nepal entered into force in June 1996. In July 1996 EU Governments authorized the European Commission to conclude similar agreements with Bangladesh and Pakistan. A draft co-operation agreement was initialled with Pakistan in April 1998. However, following the October 1999 military coup in Pakistan, the agreement was suspended. Political dialogue with Pakistan recommenced on an *ad hoc* basis in November 2000, and the co-operation agreement was signed in November 2001. The new co-operation accord with Bangladesh was signed in May 2000.

A trade agreement was signed with the People's Republic of China (PRC) in 1978, and renewed in May 1985. In June 1989, following the violent repression of the Chinese pro-democracy movement by the PRC Government, the EC imposed economic sanctions on that country. In October 1990 it was decided that relations with the PRC should be 'progressively normalized'. The EU has supported the PRC's increased involvement in the international community and, in particular, supported its application for membership of the WTO (eventually approved in 2001). The first EU-PRC meeting of heads of government was convened in April 1998. In November the President of the Commission made an official visit to the PRC and urged that country to remove trade restrictions imposed on European products. In the same month the EU and Hong Kong signed a co-operation agreement to combat drugs-trafficking and copyright piracy. A bilateral trade agreement between the EU and the PRC was concluded in May 2000, removing a major barrier to the PRC's accession to the WTO; this was approved in November 2001. A third EU-PRC summit meeting was held in Beijing in October 2000. At the fourth summit, convened in September 2001, the two sides agreed to strengthen and widen political dialogue and to continue discussions on human rights issues. In March 2002 the European Commission approved a strategy document setting out a framework for co-operation between the EU and China over the period 2002–06, and in September the fifth EU-China summit discussed trade relations and future co-operation on illegal immigrants and tourism.

In October 1997 the EU and the Republic of Korea signed an agreement regarding a reciprocal opening of markets for telecommunications equipment, following a protracted dispute, which had led the EU to lodge a complaint with the WTO. In September 1997, however, the Commission submitted a further complaint to the WTO, accusing the Republic of Korea of tax discrimination against European spirits exporters. In the same month the EU joined the Korean Peninsular Energy Development Organization, an initiative to increase nuclear safety and reduce the risk of nuclear proliferation from the energy programme of the Democratic People's Republic of Korea (DPRK). In September 1999, for the first time ever, ministerial-level discussions took place between the EU and the DPRK at the United Nations General Assembly. In May 2001 the EU announced that it was to establish diplomatic relations with the DPRK.

In June 1992 the EC signed trade and co-operation agreements with Mongolia and Macao, with respect for democracy and human rights forming the basis of envisaged co-operation. The sixth EU-Mongolia co-operation council met in Brussels in November 2002. A co-operation accord was formally signed with Viet Nam in July 1995, under which the EU agreed to increase quotas for Vietnamese textile products, to support the country's efforts to join the WTO and to provide aid for environmental and public management projects. The agreement entered into force in June 1996. A permanent EU mission to Viet Nam was established in February 1996. In October the EU imposed strict limits on entry visas for Myanmar officials, because of Myanmar's refusal to allow the Commission to send a mission to investigate allegations of forced labour. In March 1997 EU ministers of foreign affairs agreed to revoke Myanmar's special trade privileges under the Generalized System of Preferences (GSP). In November a meeting of EU and ASEAN officials was postponed, owing to Myanmar's insistence (then as a full member of the ASEAN grouping) that it should attend with full observer status. After several further delays, the meeting was finally convened, with Myanmar as a 'silent' observer, in late May 1999. The EU has successively extended its ban on arms exports to Myanmar and its prohibition on the issuing of visas, and in October 2002 the European Council confirmed its common position that progress on human rights and democratization in Myanmar was insufficient. Non-preferential co-operation agreements were signed with Laos and

Cambodia in April 1997. The agreement with Laos entered into force on 1 December; the agreement with Cambodia was postponed owing to adverse political developments in that country. In 1998 the EU provided financial assistance to support preparations for a general election in Cambodia, and dispatched observers to monitor the election, which was held in July. In September 1999 the EU briefly imposed an arms embargo against Indonesia, which was at that time refusing to permit the deployment of an international peace-keeping force in East Timor.

Textiles exports by Asian countries have caused concern in the EU, owing to the depressed state of its textiles industry. In 1982 bilateral negotiations were held under the Multi-fibre Arrangement (MFA, see WTO) with Asian producers, notably Hong Kong, the Republic of Korea and Macao. Agreements were eventually reached involving reductions in clothing quotas and 'anti-surge' clauses to prevent flooding of European markets. In 1986 new bilateral negotiations were held and agreements were reached with the principal Asian textile exporters, for the period 1987–91 (later extended to December 1993, when the 'Uruguay Round' of GATT negotiations was finally concluded): in most cases a slight increase in quotas was permitted. Under the conclusions of the Uruguay Round, the MFA was to be progressively eliminated over a 10-year period. In January 1995 bilateral textiles agreements, signed by the EU with India, Pakistan and the PRC, specified certain trade liberalization measures to be undertaken, including an increase of the PRC's silk export quota and a removal of trade barriers on small-business and hand-loom textile products from India, while including commitments from the Asian countries for greater efforts to combat textile and design fraud.

Numerous discussions have been held since 1981 on the Community's increasing trade deficit with Japan, and on the failure of the Japanese market to accept more European exports. In July 1991 the heads of government of Japan and of the EC signed a joint declaration on closer co-operation in both economic and political matters. In the same month an agreement was reached on limiting exports of Japanese cars to the EC until the end of 1999. The agreement did not include vehicles produced in Europe by Japanese companies. The European office of the EU-Japan Industrial Co-operation Centre was opened in Brussels in June 1996; the Centre, which was established in 1987 as a joint venture between the Japanese Government and the European Commission, sought to boost industrial co-operation between the EU and Japan. In October 1996 the WTO upheld a long-standing complaint brought by the EU that Japanese taxes on alcoholic spirits discriminated against certain European products. In January 1998 an EU-Japan summit meeting was held, followed by a meeting at ministerial level in October. Subsequent summits (the 11th was held in July 2002) have aimed to strengthen dialogue.

The EU has pledged assistance for the reconstruction of Afghanistan following the removal of the Taliban regime, and in 2002 announced development aid of €1,000m. for the period 2002–06, in addition to humanitarian aid.

In 2000 the EU contributed €19m. to a Trust Fund established by the World Bank to finance reconstruction activities in East Timor. In December the EU hosted the third multilateral conference of donors to the territory. During 2002 the EU provided €650,000 in development aid for East Timor.

Regular consultations are held with Australia at ministerial level. In January 1996 the Commission proposed a framework agreement to formalize the EU's trade and political relationship with that country. However, in September negotiations were suspended, following the Australian Government's objections to the human rights clause contained in all EU international agreements. In June 1997 a joint declaration was signed, committing both sides to greater political, cultural and economic co-operation. Despite intensive negotiations between the EU and the New Zealand Government in 1996, no conclusion was reached regarding import duties. In March 1997 New Zealand took the case to the WTO, which later ruled against the EU. A joint declaration detailing areas of co-operation and establishing a consultative framework to facilitate the development of these was signed in May 1999. Mutual recognition agreements were also signed with Australia and New Zealand in 1999, with the aim of facilitating bilateral trade in industrial products.

CANADA AND THE USA

A framework agreement for commercial and economic co-operation between the Community and Canada was signed in Ottawa in 1976. It was superseded in 1990 by a Declaration on EC-Canada Relations. In 1995 relations with Canada were strained as a result of a dispute regarding fishing rights in the north-west Atlantic Ocean. An agreement on a new division of quotas between EU and Canadian fishermen was concluded in April. In February 1996 the Commission proposed closer ties with Canada, and an action plan including early warning to avoid trade disputes, elimination of trade barriers, and promotion of business contacts. An action plan and joint political declaration were signed in December. Two EU-Canada summits took place in 2002; numerous issues were discussed including improved co-operation to combat terrorism, heightened co-operation in research, science and technology, the strengthening of trade relations, and collaboration on environmental issues.

A number of specific agreements have been concluded between the Community and the USA: a co-operation agreement on the peaceful use of atomic energy entered into force in 1959, and agreements on environmental matters and on fisheries came into force in 1974 and 1984 respectively. Additional agreements provide for co-operation in other fields of scientific research and development, while bilateral contacts take place in many areas not covered by a formal agreement.

The USA has frequently criticized the Common Agricultural Policy, which it sees as creating unfair competition for American exports by its system of export refunds and preferential agreements. A similar criticism has been levelled at Community subsidies to the steel industry. In October 1985 and September 1986 agreements were reached on Community exports of steel to the USA until September 1989 (subsequently extended until March 1992). In January 1993 the USA announced the imposition of substantial duties on imports of steel from 19 countries, including seven EC member states, as an 'anti-dumping' measure. Meanwhile, a further trade dispute emerged between the EC and the USA regarding the liberalization of public procurement of services (e.g. telecommunications, transport and power). In early December the EC and the USA undertook intensive trade negotiations, which facilitated the conclusion of GATT's Uruguay Round of talks by the deadline of 15 December.

A 'Transatlantic Declaration' on EC-US relations was agreed in November 1990: the two parties agreed to consult each other on important matters of common interest, and to increase formal contacts. A new Trans-Atlantic Agenda for EU-US relations was signed by the US President and the Presidents of the European Commission and European Council at a meeting in Madrid, Spain, in December 1995. In October 1996 EU ministers of foreign affairs agreed to pursue in the WTO a complaint regarding the effects on European businesses of the USA's trade embargo against Cuba, formulated in the Helms-Burton Act. In April 1997 the EU and the USA approved a temporary resolution of the Helms-Burton dispute, whereby the US Administration was to limit the application of sanctions in return for a formal suspension of the WTO case. In mid-1996 the US Congress had adopted legislation imposing an additional trade embargo (threatening sanctions against any foreign company investing more than US \$40m. in energy projects in a number of prescribed states, including Iran and Libya), the presence of which further complicated the EU-US debate in September 1997, when a French petroleum company, Total, provoked US anger, owing to its proposed investment in an Iranian natural gas project. In May 1998 an EU-USA summit meeting reached agreement on a 'Trans-Atlantic Economic Partnership' (TEP), to remove technical trade barriers, eliminate industrial tariffs, establish a free-trade area in services, and further liberalize measures relating to government procurement, intellectual property and investment. The agricultural and audio-visual sectors were to be excluded from the agreement. Initial objections from France were overcome when the EU and the USA reached a resolution to the dispute on sanctions legislation. The USA agreed to exempt European companies from the trade embargo on Iran and Libya, and to seek congressional approval for an indefinite waiver for the Helms-Burton Act, thereby removing the threat of sanctions from Total. The EU had allowed the WTO case to lapse in April, but it warned that a new WTO panel would be established if the USA took action against European companies trading with Cuba. In return, the EU agreed to increase co-operation in combating terrorism and the proliferation of weapons of mass destruction and to discourage investment in expropriated property. Following approval by the Council in November, it was agreed that implementation of the TEP would begin in advance of an EU-USA summit meeting in December. The EU-USA summit meeting held in June 1999 issued the 'Bonn Declaration', pledging a 'full and equal partnership' in economic, political and security matters.

In July 1997 the EU became involved in intensive negotiations with the US aircraft company, Boeing, over fears that its planned merger with McDonnell Douglas would harm European interests. In late July the EU approved the merger, after Boeing accepted concessions including an agreement to dispense with exclusivity clauses for 20-year supply contracts and to maintain McDonnell Douglas as a separate company for a period of 10 years. In June the EU and the USA agreed to introduce a mutual recognition agreement, which was to enable goods (including medicines, pharmaceutical products, telecommunications equipment and electrical apparatus) undergoing tests in Europe to be marketed in the USA or Canada without the need for further testing. In May 1997 the WTO upheld a US complaint against the EU's ban on imports of hormone-treated beef,

which had led to a retaliatory US ban on meat imports from the EU. Negotiations took place in 1998 regarding the enforcement of European meat hygiene regulations (see under Agriculture), the reform of the EU's banana import regime (see Lomé Convention, below) and the application of a data protection law, which empowers national regulators to stop the transfer of personal information to countries judged to have inadequate data protection arrangements (including the USA). In July the Commission submitted a complaint to the WTO regarding tax exemptions granted to US companies exporting goods via subsidiaries established in tax-free countries (foreign sales corporations). Agreement on the banana dispute was eventually reached in May 2001.

Relations between the EU and the USA were strained by a number of issues during 2002. In May Romano Prodi, the President of the Commission, accused the USA of consistently breaching world trade laws, following the decision by US President George Bush to impose tariffs of up to 30% on steel imports, while long-standing concerns about US unilateralism (for example on environmental matters), and criticism from the USA of the EU's Galileo satellite network system (which the USA claimed could compromise NATO operations) further added to the strain. During the dispute over steel, in March 2002 the EU drew up a list of US products that would face sanctions (in the form of 100% tariffs) if the USA refused to grant the EU's request for compensation for lost steel trade. However, in September the EU voted to shelve retaliatory measures against the USA and wait instead for a ruling from the WTO, due in 2003.

In political matters, some member states also criticized the USA's objections to the establishment of the International Criminal Court (which eventually came into effect in the Hague in 2003), while the EU also criticized the USA for its strategy on Iraq (see The Middle East and the Mediterranean), adopting the line that only the UN Security Council could determine whether military action was justified.

GENERALIZED PREFERENCES

In July 1971 the Community introduced a generalized system of preferences (GSP) for tariffs in favour of developing countries, ensuring duty-free entry to the EC of all otherwise dutiable manufactured and semi-manufactured industrial products, including textiles—but subject in certain circumstances to preferential limits. Preferences, usually in the form of a tariff reduction, are also offered on some agricultural products. In 1980 the Council agreed to the extension of the scheme for a second decade (1981–90): at the same time it adopted an operational framework for industrial products, which gives individual preferential limits based on the degree of competitiveness of the developing country concerned. From the end of 1990 an interim scheme was in operation, pending the introduction of a revised scheme based on the outcome of the 'Uruguay Round' of GATT negotiations on international trade (which were finally concluded in December 1993). Since 1977 the Community has progressively liberalized GSP access for the least-developed countries by according them duty-free entry on all products and by exempting them from virtually all preferential limits. In 1992–93 the GSP was extended to Albania, the Baltic states, the CIS and Georgia; in September 1994 it was extended to South Africa.

In December 1994 the European Council adopted a revised GSP to operate during 1995–98. It provided additional trade benefits to encourage the introduction by governments of environmentally sound policies and of internationally-recognized labour standards. Conversely, a country's preferential entitlement could be withdrawn, for example, if it permitted forced labour. Under the new scheme preferential tariffs amounted to 85% of the common customs duty for very sensitive products (for example, most textile products), and 70% or 35% for products classified as sensitive (for example, chemicals, electrical goods). The common customs duty was suspended for non-sensitive products (for example, paper, books, cosmetics). In accordance with the EU's foreign policy objective of focusing on the development of the world's poorest countries, duties were eliminated in their entirety for 49 least-developed countries. Duties were also suspended for a further five Latin American countries, conditional on the implementation of campaigns against the production and trade of illegal drugs.

A new GSP for 1999–2001 largely extended the existing scheme unchanged. The next GSP regulation, for 2002–04, was revised to expand product coverage and improve preferential margins.

AID TO DEVELOPING AND NON-EU COUNTRIES

The main channels for Community aid to developing countries are the Cotonou Agreement (see below) and the Mediterranean Financial Protocols, but technical and financial aid, and assistance for refugees, training, trade promotion and co-operation in industry, energy, science and technology is also provided to about 30 countries in Asia and Latin America. The EC International Investment Partners facility, established in 1988, promotes private-sector investment in Asian, Latin American and Mediterranean countries, especially in the form of joint ventures. The European Community Humanitarian Office (ECHO) was established in 1991 with a mandate to co-ordinate emergency aid provided by the Community and became fully operational in early 1993. ECHO finances operations conducted by non-governmental organizations and international agencies, with which it works in partnership. During 2002 the main recipient areas for humanitarian aid were Afghanistan, Chechnya, the Middle East, Sudan, Congo, North Korea and Colombia; in that year the EU provided humanitarian aid worth a total of €537.8m., of which 37% was allocated to ACP countries, and 8% each to the Balkans and the independent states of the former Soviet Union. In April 1999 ECHO signed a framework partnership agreement with the International Federation of Red Cross and Red Crescent Societies to promote effective co-operation in the provision of humanitarian assistance.

EU-ACP PARTNERSHIP

From 1976 to February 2000 the principal means of co-operation between the Community and developing countries were the Lomé Conventions, concluded by the EU and African, Caribbean and Pacific (ACP) countries. The First Lomé Convention (Lomé I), which was concluded at Lomé, Togo, in February 1975 and came into force on 1 April 1976, replaced the Yaoundé Conventions and the Arusha Agreement. Lomé I was designed to provide a new framework of co-operation, taking into account the varying needs of developing ACP countries. The Second Lomé Convention entered into force on 1 January 1981. The Third Lomé Convention came into force on 1 March 1985 (trade provisions) and 1 May 1986 (aid). The Fourth Lomé Convention, which had a 10-year commitment period, was signed in December 1989: its trade provisions entered into force on 1 March 1990, and the remainder entered into force in September 1991. In June 2000, meeting in Cotonou, Benin, EU and ACP heads of state and government concluded a new 20-year partnership accord with 77 ACP states. The so-called Cotonou Agreement was to enter into effect once it had been ratified by the European Parliament and by the ACP national legislatures. By April 2003 all 15 of the EU member states and 64 ACP countries had ratified the Agreement.

ACP-EU Institutions

Council of Ministers: one minister from each signatory state; one co-chairman from each of the two groups; meets annually.

Committee of Ambassadors: one ambassador from each signatory state; chairmanship alternates between the two groups; meets at least every six months.

Joint Assembly: EU and ACP are equally represented; attended by parliamentary delegates from each of the ACP countries and an equal number of members of the European Parliament; one co-chairman from each of the two groups; meets twice a year.

Secretariat of the ACP-EU Council of Ministers: 175 rue de la Loi, 1048 Brussels; tel. (2) 285-61-11; fax (2) 285-74-58.

Centre for the Development of Enterprise (CDE): 52 ave Herrmann Debroux, 1160 Brussels, Belgium; tel. (2) 679-18-11; fax (2) 679-26-03; e-mail director@cdi.be; internet www.cdi.be; f. 1977 to encourage and support the creation, expansion and restructuring of industrial companies (mainly in the fields of manufacturing and agro-industry) in the ACP states by promoting co-operation between ACP and European companies, in the form of financial, technical or commercial partnership, management contracts, licensing or franchise agreements, sub-contracts, etc. manages the Pro€Invest programme; Dir FERNANDO MATOS ROSA.

Technical Centre for Agricultural and Rural Co-operation: Postbus 380, 6700 AJ Wageningen, Netherlands; tel. (317) 467100; fax (317) 460067; e-mail cta@cta.nl; internet www.agricta.org; f. 1983 to provide ACP states with better access to information, research, training and innovations in agricultural development and extension; Dir CARL B. GREENIDGE.

ACP Institutions

ACP Council of Ministers.

ACP Committee of Ambassadors.

ACP Secretariat: ACP House, 451 ave Georges Henri, Brussels, Belgium; tel. (2) 743-06-00; fax (2) 735-55-73; e-mail info@acpsec .org; internet www.acpsec.org; Sec.-Gen. JEAN-ROBERT GOULONGANA (Gabon).

The ACP States

Angola	Mali
Antigua and Barbuda	Marshall Islands
Bahamas	Mauritania
Barbados	Mauritius
Belize	Federated States of
Benin	Micronesia
Botswana	Mozambique
Burkina Faso	Namibia
Burundi	Nauru
Cameroon	Niger
Cape Verde	Niger
Central African Republic	Niue
Chad	Palau
Comoros	Papua New Guinea
Congo, Democratic Republic	Rwanda
Congo, Republic	Saint Christopher and Nevis
Cook Islands	Saint Lucia
Côte d'Ivoire	Saint Vincent and the
Djibouti	Grenadines
Dominica	Samoa
Dominican Republic	São Tomé and Príncipe
Equatorial Guinea	Senegal
Eritrea	Seychelles
Ethiopia	Sierra Leone
Fiji	Solomon Islands
Gabon	Somalia
The Gambia	South Africa
Ghana	Sudan
Grenada	Suriname
Guinea	Swaziland
Guinea-Bissau	Tanzania
Guyana	Togo
Haiti	Tonga
Jamaica	Trinidad and Tobago
Kenya	Tuvalu
Kiribati	Uganda
Lesotho	Vanuatu
Liberia	Zambia
Madagascar	Zimbabwe
Malawi	

Under Lomé I, the Community committed ECU 3,052.4m. for aid and investment in developing countries, through the European Development Fund (EDF) and the European Investment Bank (EIB). Provision was made for over 99% of ACP (mainly agricultural) exports to enter the EC market duty free, while certain products which compete directly with Community agriculture, such as sugar, were given preferential treatment but not free access. The Stabex (Stabilization of Export Earnings) scheme was designed to help developing countries to withstand fluctuations in the price of their agricultural products, by paying compensation for reduced export earnings.

The Second Lomé Convention (1981–85) envisaged Community expenditure of ECU 5,530m.: it extended some of the provisions of Lomé I, and introduced new fields of co-operation, including a scheme (Sysmin) to safeguard exports of mineral products.

Lomé III made commitments of ECU 8,500m., including loans of ECU 1,100m. from the EIB. Innovations included an emphasis on agriculture and fisheries, and measures to combat desertification; assistance for rehabilitating existing industries or sectoral improvements; improvements in the efficiency of the Stabex system (now covering a list of 48 agricultural products) and of Sysmin; simplification of the rules of origin of products; the promotion of private investment; co-operation in transport and communications; cultural and social co-operation; restructuring of emergency aid, and more efficient procedures for technical and financial assistance.

The Fourth Lomé Convention was to cover the period 1990–99 (subsequently extended to February 2000). The budget for financial and technical co-operation for 1990–95 amounted to ECU 12,000m., of which ECU 10,800m. was from the EDF (including ECU 1,500m. for Stabex and ECU 480m. for Sysmin) and ECU 1,200m. from the EIB. The budget for the second five years was ECU 14,625m., of which ECU 12,967m. was from the EDF, and ECU 1,658m. from the EIB. Under Lomé IV, the obligation of most of the ACP states to contribute to the replenishment of Stabex resources, including the repayment of transfers made under the first three Conventions, was removed. In addition, special loans made to ACP member countries were to be cancelled, except in the case of profit-orientated businesses. Other innovations included the provision of assistance for structural adjustment programmes (amounting to ECU 1,150m.); increased support for the private sector, environmental protection, and control of growth in population; and measures to avoid increasing the recipient countries' indebtedness (e.g. by providing Stabex and Sysmin assistance in the form of grants, rather than loans).

On 1 July 1993 the EC introduced a regime covering the import of bananas into the Community. This was designed to protect the banana industries of ACP countries (mostly in the Caribbean), which were threatened by the availability of cheaper bananas, produced by countries in Latin America. The new regime guaranteed 30% of the European market to ACP producers, and established an annual quota of 2m. metric tons for bananas imported from Latin America, which would incur a uniform duty of 20%, while imports above this level were to be subject to a tariff of ECU 850 per ton. In February 1994 a dispute panel of GATT upheld a complaint, brought by five Latin American countries, that the EU banana import regime was in contravention of free-trade principles. An agreement was reached in March, under which the EU increased the annual quota for Latin American banana imports. However, in 1995 the USA, supported by Guatemala, Honduras and Mexico (and subsequently by Ecuador), filed a complaint with the WTO against the EU's banana regime. In May 1997 the WTO concluded that the EU banana import regime violated 19 free-trade regulations. The EU appealed against the ruling in July, but in September the WTO's dispute settlement body endorsed the original verdict. However, the allocation of preferential tariffs to ACP producers, covered by a waiver since late 1994, was upheld. In October 1997 the EU agreed to amend its banana import regime to comply with the WTO ruling. An arbitration report, published in January 1998, compelled the EU to implement changes by 1 January 1999. In June 1998 EU ministers of agriculture approved a reform of the import regime, providing for two separate quota systems, granting Latin American producers greater access to the European market, with a quota of 2.53m. tons (at a tariff of ECU 75 per ton), while ACP countries would have a quota of 857,000 tons (tariff-free). The quota systems, which were to apply from 1 January 1999, were approved by the Commission in October. However, in November the USA proposed the imposition of duties of 100% on a number of European imports, in protest at the reform, which it continued to regard as discriminatory and incompatible with WTO provisions. In March 1999, the USA imposed provisional measures against a diverse range of EU products, prompting the EU to issue a complaint with the WTO. In April an arbitration panel of the WTO confirmed that the EU had failed to conform its banana regime with WTO rules and formally authorized the USA to impose trade sanctions, valued at US \$191.4m. A satisfactory accord, involving the adoption by the EU of a new system of licences and quotas to cover the period 2001–06 and the introduction of a new tariff-only system from 2006, was eventually reached by the EU and USA in April 2001, subject to approval by EU member states; the USA consequently agreed to suspend its punitive trade sanctions.

In September 1993 the Community announced plans to revise and strengthen its relations with the ACP countries under the Lomé Convention. In May 1994 representatives of EU member states and ACP countries initiated the mid-term review of Lomé IV. The Community reiterated its intention to maintain the Convention as an aid instrument but emphasized that stricter conditions relating to the awarding of aid would be imposed, based on standards of human rights, human resource development and environmental protection. In June 1995 the European Council agreed to provide ECU 14,625m. for the second phase of Lomé IV, of which ECU 12,967m. was to be allocated from the EDF and ECU 1,658m. in loans from the EIB. Agreement was also reached on revision of the 'country-of-origin' rules for manufactured goods, a new protocol on the sustainable management of forest resources and a joint declaration on support for the banana industry. The agreement was subsequently endorsed by an EU-ACP ministerial group, and the revised Convention was signed in November, in Mauritius. In March 1997 the Commission proposed granting debt relief assistance of ECU 25m. each year for the period 1997–2000 to the 11 heavily-indebted poor countries (as identified by the World Bank and the IMF) forming part of the ACP group. Funding was to be used to support international efforts to reduce debt and encourage the economic prospects of such countries. In May 2001 the EU announced that it would cancel all outstanding debts arising from its trade accords with former colonies of member states.

In June 1995 negotiations opened with a view to concluding a wide-ranging trade and co-operation agreement with South Africa, including the eventual creation of a free-trade area (FTA). The accord was approved by heads of state and of government in March 1999, after agreement was reached to eliminate progressively, over a 12-year period, the use of the terms 'port' and 'sherry' to describe South African fortified wines. The accord provided for the removal of duties from about 99% of South Africa's industrial exports and some 75% of its agricultural products within 10 years, while South Africa was to liberalize its market for some 86% of EU industrial goods (with protection for the motor vehicle and textiles industries), within a 12-year period. The accord also introduced increased development assistance for South Africa after 1999. The long-delayed agreement was finally signed in January 2002, allowing South African wines freer access to the European market. Under the terms of the agreement South Africa was allowed to export 42m. litres of wine a year

duty-free to the EU, in exchange for abandoning the use of names such as 'sherry', 'port', 'ouzo' or 'grappa'. In March 1997 the Commission approved a Special Protocol for South Africa's accession to the Lomé Convention, and in April South Africa attained partial membership. Full membership was withheld, as South Africa was not regarded as, in all respects, a developing country, and was therefore not entitled to aid provisions. A special provision was introduced into the revised Lomé Convention to allow Somalia to accede, should constitutional government be established in that country prior to the expiry of the Convention.

Intensive debate took place from 1995 on the future of relations between the ACP states and the EU, in view of the increasingly global nature of the EU's foreign policies, and particular the growing emphasis it was placing on relations with central and eastern Europe and countries of the Mediterranean rim. In November 1996 the Commission published a consultative document to consider the options for future ACP-EU relations. The document focused on the areas of trade, aid and politics, and included proposals to encourage competitiveness, to support private-sector investment and to enhance democracy. The report suggested abolishing or restructuring Stabex and Sysmin, and considered altering the grouping of the ACP states for the purpose of implementing economic agreements. The ultimate aim of the document was to foster conditions in which the EU and the ACP countries could co-exist as equal partners. In November 1997 the first summit of heads of state of ACP countries was held in Libreville, Gabon. The ACP council of ministers prepared a mandate for negotiations towards a renewed Lomé Convention, which was approved by the Commission in January 1998. The Joint Assembly of ACP ministers, meeting in Mauritius in April, and the ACP-EU Council of Ministers, meeting in Barbados in May, discussed proposals for future ACP-EU relations after the expiry of Lomé IV. The ACP states emphasized that they should be regarded as a single entity, with recognition for the individual requirements of each region, and that any renewed partnership should continue to support the elimination of poverty as its main objective. In late June EU ministers of foreign affairs approved preliminary directives for the negotiation of a new partnership agreement. The ministers agreed to allow Cuba to participate in the negotiations, with observer status, but emphasized that their decision would have no influence on any future accession discussions should Cuba wish to join the Lomé Convention. In November Cuba formally applied for full membership. Formal negotiations on the conclusion of a successor agreement to the Lomé Convention were initiated at the end of September and were concluded in February 2000: the new partnership accord was signed by ACP and EU heads of state and government in June of that year in Cotonou, Benin. The so-called Cotonou Agreement was to enter into effect following ratification by the European Parliament and the ACP national legislatures, and was to cover the period 2000–20. It comprised the following main elements: increased political co-operation; the enhanced participation of civil society in ACP–EC partnership affairs; a strong focus on the reduction of poverty; reform of the existing structures for financial co-operation; and a new framework for economic and trade co-operation. Under the provisions of the new accord, the EU was to negotiate free-trade arrangements (replacing the previous non-reciprocal trade preferences) with the most developed ACP countries during 2000–08; these would be structured around a system of regional free-trade zones, and would be designed to ensure full compatibility with WTO provisions. Once in force, the agreements would be subject to revision every five years. An assessment to be conducted in 2004 would identify those mid-ranking ACP nations also capable of entering into such free-trade deals. Meanwhile, the least-developed ACP nations were to benefit from an EU initiative to allow free access for most of their products by 2005. The preferential agreements currently in force would be retained initially (phase I), in view of a waiver granted by the WTO; thereafter ACP–EU trade was to be gradually liberalized over a period of 12–15 years (phase II). It was envisaged that Stabex and Sysmin would be eliminated gradually.

The first meeting of the ACP–EU Joint Parliamentary Assembly following the signing of the Cotonou Agreement was held in Brussels in October 2000. In total, the EU provided €3,612m. in financing for ACP countries in 2000. The EDF had funds of €13,500m. to cover the first five years of operation of the Cotonou Agreement. In February 2001 the EU agreed to phase out trade barriers on imports of everything but military weapons from the world's 48 least developed countries, 39 of which were in the ACP group. Duties on sugar, rice, bananas and some other products were to remain until 2009.

The fourth plenary session of the joint ACP-EU Joint Parliamentary Assembly was held in Cape Town, South Africa, in March 2002, at which the ninth EDF was discussed. The plan was to be organized along sub-regional lines, with countries grouped into west Africa, central Africa, the Caribbean, the Pacific Region, eastern and southern Africa (partly via the Southern Africa Development Community, SADC). One major programme set up on behalf of the ACP countries and financed by the EDF was the new Pro€Invest programme, which was launched in 2002, with funding of €110m. over a seven-year period.

In September 2002 the European Council adopted a mandate on the new system of European Partnership Agreements (EPAs), as outlined in the Cotonou Agreement, which were to replace all non-reciprocal trade preferences with the most developed ACP countries. Priority was to be given to the furthering of sustainable development and the eradication of poverty, as well as the protection of ACP economies against certain effects of globalization.

Although the Cotonou Agreement had not been fully ratified in 2002, parts of it were able to be put into practice owing to measures giving effect to some of its provisions in advance. This proved particularly relevant during 2002 with Article 96 of the Agreement, which provides for suspension of the Agreement in specific countries in the event of violation of one of its essential elements (respect for human rights, democratic principles and the rule of law). In January 2002 action was taken against Zimbabwe, when financing of most projects was suspended. In contrast, co-operation was resumed with Côte d'Ivoire and the Comoros in February, but Fiji and Liberia still remained subject to Article 96. During 2002 the European Council condemned the worsening human rights situation in Zimbabwe, describing the elections held there in 2002 as deeply flawed, and imposed a range of targeted sanctions including a travel ban and freezing of assets of certain members of the leadership, an arms embargo, and the suspension of development aid. In February 2003 it was announced that the second Europe-Africa summit, scheduled to take place in Lisbon, Portugal, in April, had had to be postponed indefinitely when EU leaders decided that they could not find a way to exclude the Zimbabwean leader, Robert Mugabe. At the same time the EU sanctions against Zimbabwe were renewed.

Finance

THE COMMUNITY BUDGET

The general budget of the European Union covers all EEC and Euratom expenditure. The Commission is responsible for implementing the budget. Under the Council decision of 24 June 1988 all revenue (except that expressly designated for supplementary research and technological development programmes) is used without distinction to finance all expenditure, and all budget expenditure must be covered in full by the revenue entered in the budget. Any amendment of this decision requires the unanimous approval of the Council and must be ratified by the member states. The Treaty of Rome requires member states to release funds to cover the appropriations entered in the budget.

Each Community institution draws up estimates of its expenditure, and sends them to the Commission before 1 July of the year preceding the financial year (1 January–31 December) in question. The Commission consolidates these estimates in a preliminary draft budget, which it sends to the Council by 1 September. Expenditure is divided into two categories: that necessarily resulting from the Treaties (compulsory expenditure) and other (non-compulsory) expenditure. The draft budget must be approved by a qualified majority in the Council, and presented to Parliament by 5 October. Parliament may propose modifications to compulsory expenditure, and may (within the limits of the 'maximum rate of increase', dependent on growth of member states' gross national product—GNP—and budgets) amend non-compulsory expenditure. The budget must normally be declared finally adopted 75 days after the draft is presented to Parliament. If the budget has not been adopted by the beginning of the financial year, monthly expenditure may amount to one-twelfth of the appropriations adopted for the previous year's budget. The Commission may (even late in the year during which the budget is being executed) revise estimates of revenue and expenditure, by presenting supplementary and/or amending budgets.

Expenditure under the general budget is financed by 'own resources', comprising agricultural duties (on imports of agricultural produce from non-member states), customs duties, application of value-added tax (VAT) on goods and services, and (since 1988) a levy based on the GNP of member states. Member states are obliged to collect 'own resources' on the Community's behalf. From May 1985 arrangements were introduced for the correction of budgetary imbalances, as a result of which the United Kingdom received compensation in the form of reductions in VAT payments. In 1988 it was decided by the Community's heads of government to set a maximum amount for 'own resources' that might be called up in any one year.

The general budget contains the expenditures of the six main Community institutions—the Commission, the Council, Parliament, the Court of Justice, the Court of Auditors, and the Economic and Social Committee and the Committee of the Regions—of which

Commission expenditure (covering administrative costs and expenditure on operations) forms the largest proportion. The Common Agricultural Policy accounts for about 50% of total expenditure, principally in agricultural guarantees. In 1988 it was decided (as part of a system of budgetary discipline agreed by the Council) that the rate of increase in spending on agricultural guarantees between 1988 and a given year was not to exceed 74% of the growth rate of Community GNP during the same period. In December 1992 it was agreed to increase the upper limit on Community expenditure from 1.2% of the EC's combined GNP to 1.27% in 1999. 'Agenda 2000', concerning financial arrangements for the period 2000–2006, proposed maintaining the limit at 1.27% from 2000. In December 1994, taking into account the enlargement of the EU to 15 countries (from 1 January 1995) it was agreed to set a level of maximum expenditure at ECU 75,500m. in 1995, increasing to ECU 87,000m. in 1999, at constant 1992 prices. Agenda 2000 proposed that maximum annual expenditure would increase to €104,600m. at 1999 prices, by 2006.

The general budget for 2003, adopted in December 2002, allocated €98,6865m. in total commitment appropriations, virtually the same as the previous year. Of the total, €5.2m. were for administration, €47.4m. for agriculture, € 34.0m. for structural operations, €6.8m. for internal policies, €5.0m. for external action, and €3.4m. for pre-accession assistance.

STRUCTURAL FUNDS

The Community's 'structural funds' comprise the Guidance Section of the European Agricultural Guidance and Guarantee Fund, the European Regional Development Fund, the European Social Fund and the Cohesion Fund. There is also a financial instrument for fisheries guidance. In accordance with the Single European Act (1987), reforms of the Community's structural funds were adopted by the Council with effect from 1 January 1989, with the aim of more accurate identification of priority targets, and greater selectivity to enable action to be concentrated in the least-favoured regions (see Social Policy, see p. 220). 'Agenda 2000', which was approved by the Council in March 1999, provided for the reform of the structural funds to make available some €213,000m. for 2000–2006, at 1999 prices. During 2002 the European Council established a new European Union Solidarity Fund, designed as a disaster relief fund in response to the flooding that affected Germany, Austria and several candidate countries during the summer of that year. A budget of €1,000m. per year was agreed for the Fund in November 2002.

Cohesion Fund

The Treaty on European Union and its protocol on economic and social cohesion provided for the establishment of a 'Cohesion Fund', which began operating on 1 April 1993, with a budget of ECU 1,500m. for the first year. This was to subsidize projects in the fields of the environment and trans-European energy and communications networks in member states with a per caput GNP of less than 90% of the Community average (in practice, this was to mean Greece, Ireland, Portugal and Spain). Commitments under the fund in the budget appropriations for 2002 amounted to €2,791m. The fund's total budget for the period 2000–06 was €18,000m.

European Agricultural Guidance and Guarantee Fund (EAGGF)—Guidance Section

Created in 1962, the European Agricultural Guidance and Guarantee Fund is administered by the Commission. The Guidance section covers expenditure on Community aid for projects to improve farming conditions in the member states. It includes aid for poor rural areas and the structural adjustment of rural areas, particularly in the context of the reform of the common agricultural policy (CAP). This aid is usually granted in the form of financial contributions to programmes also supported by the member governments themselves. Commitments to the EAGGF in 2002 amounted to €2,630m.

European Regional Development Fund—ERDF

Payments began in 1975. The Fund is intended to compensate for the unequal rate of development in different regions of the Community, by encouraging investment and improving infrastructure in 'problem regions'. In 2002 commitments to the Fund totalled €13,429m.

European Social Fund

internet: europa.eu.int/comm/dgo5/esf/en/index.htm.

The Fund (established in 1960) provides resources with the aim of combating long-term unemployment and facilitating the integration into the labour market of young people and the socially disadvantaged. It also supports schemes to help workers to adapt to industrial changes. Commitments to the Fund in 2002 amounted to €4,780m.

BUDGET EXPENDITURE APPROPRIATIONS FOR THE ACTIVITIES OF THE EUROPEAN COMMISSION
(€ million)

	2002	2003
Section III 'Commission' (part B)		
EAGGF Guarantee Section	44,480.2	44,762.5
Structural operations, other agricultural and regional operations, transport and fisheries	32,287.1	33,330.5
Training, youth, culture, audiovisual media, information and other social operations	888.2	879.6
Energy, Euratom nuclear safeguards and environment	189.3	250.8
Consumer protection, internal market, industry and trans-European networks	1,124.2	1,165.7
Research and technological development	3,751.7	3,650.0
External actions	7,387.0	7,687.6
Common foreign and security policy	35.0	50.0
Guarantees, reserves and compensation	335.2	366.2
Subtotal	90,477.9	92,142.9
Section III 'Commission' (part A)	3,424.8	3,489.5
Other institutions	1,753.7	1,870.6
Total expenditure	95,656.4	97,502.9

Note: The funds allocated to the other Community institutions were to be supplemented by the institutions' own resources.

REVENUE (€ million)

Source of revenue	2002	2003
Agricultural duties	1.180.2	1,173.1
Sugar and isoglucose levies	864.8	728.8
Customs duties	12,918.9	14,285.2
Own resources collection costs	−3,725.7	−4,046.8
Regularization of collection costs for 2001	−2,023.0	—
VAT own resources	22,687.4	24,121.2
GNP-based own resources	45,850.6	59,404.0
Balance of VAT and GNP own resources from previous years	−53.5	n.a.
Surplus available from previous year	15,375.0	1,000.0
Other revenue	1,257.0	837.4
Total	94,331.7	97,502.9

Source: European Commission, *General Report* (2002).

MEMBER STATES' PAYMENTS

Country (€ million)	Contribution for 2003	% of total
Austria	2,177.8	2.3
Belgium	3,667.0	3.8
Denmark	2,016.9	2.1
Finland	1,448.6	1.5
France	16,576.5	17.3
Germany	22,010.2	23.0
Greece	1,639.4	1.7
Ireland	1,252.5	1.3
Italy	13,606.5	14.2
Luxembourg	231.7	0.2
Netherlands	5,741.9	6.0
Portugal	1,427.9	1.5
Spain	7,800.2	8.2
Sweden	2,550.9	2.7
United Kingdom	13,517.6	14.1
Total	95,665.6	100.0

Publications*

Bulletin of the European Union (10 a year).
The Courier (every 2 months, on ACP-EU affairs).
European Economy (every 6 months, with supplements).
European Voice (weekly).
General Report on the Activities of the European Union (annually).
Official Journal of the European Communities.
Publications of the European Communities (quarterly).
EUR-Lex Website (treaties, legislation and judgments, internet europa.eu.int/eur-lex/en/index.html).

Information sheets, background reports and statistical documents.

* Most publications are available in all the official languages of the Union. They are obtainable from the ; Office for Official Publications of the European Communities, 2 rue Mercier, 2985 Luxembourg ; tel. 29291 ; fax 495719 ; e-mail europ@opoce.cec.be ; internet eur-op.eu.int.

THE FRANC ZONE

Address: Direction des Relations Internationales et Européennes (Service de la Zone Franc), Banque de France, 39 rue Croix-des-Petits-Champs, 75049, Paris Cédex 01, France.
Telephone: 1-42-92-31-46; **fax:** 1-42-92-39-88; **e-mail:** comozof@banque-france.fr; **internet:** www.banque-france.fr/fr/zonefr/main.htm.

MEMBERS*

Benin	French Overseas
Burkina Faso	Territories
Cameroon	Gabon
Central African Republic	Guinea-Bissau
Chad	Mali
The Comoros	Niger
Republic of the Congo	Senegal
Côte d'Ivoire	Togo
Equatorial Guinea	

* The following states withdrew from the Franc Zone during the period 1958–73: Guinea, Tunisia, Morocco, Algeria, Mauritania and Madagascar. Equatorial Guinea, formerly a Spanish territory, joined the Franc Zone in January 1985, and Guinea-Bissau, a former Portuguese territory, joined in May 1997. Prior to 1 January 2002, when the transition to a single European currency (euro) was finalized (see below), the Franc Zone also included Metropolitan France; the French Overseas Collectivités Territoriales (Mayotte and St Pierre and Miquelon); and the French Overseas Departments. The French Overseas Territories— New Caledonia, French Polynesia and the Wallis and Futuna Islands—continued to use the franc CFP (franc des Comptoirs français du Pacifique, 'French Pacific franc') following the transition to the euro.

Apart from Guinea and Mauritania, all of the countries that formerly comprised French West and Equatorial Africa are members of the Franc Zone. The former West and Equatorial African territories are still grouped within the two currency areas that existed before independence, each group having its own variant on the CFA, issued by a central bank: the franc de la Communauté Financière d'Afrique ('franc CFA de l'Ouest'), issued by the Banque centrale des états de l'Afrique de l'ouest—BCEAO, and the franc Coopération financière en Afrique centrale ('franc CFA central'), issued by the Banque des états de l'Afrique centrale—BEAC.

The Comoros, formerly a French Overseas Territory, did not join the Franc Zone following its unilateral declaration of independence in 1975. However, the franc CFA was used as the currency of the new state and the Institut d'émission des Comores continued to function as a Franc Zone organization. In 1976 the Comoros formally assumed membership. In July 1981 the Banque centrale des Comores replaced the Institut d'émission des Comores, establishing its own currency, the Comoros franc.

The Franc Zone operates on the basis of agreements concluded between France and each group of member countries, and the Comoros. The currencies in the Franc Zone were formerly linked with the French franc at a fixed rate of exchange. However, following the introduction of the euro (European single currency) in January 1999, within the framework of European economic and monetary union, in which France was a participant, the Franc Zone currencies were effectively linked at fixed parity to the euro (i.e. parity was based on the fixed conversion rate for the French franc and the euro). From 1 January 2002, when European economic and monetary union was finalized and the French franc withdrawn from circulation, the franc CFA, Comoros franc and franc CFP became officially pegged to the euro, at a fixed rate of exchange. (In accordance with Protocol 13 on France, appended to the 1993 Maastricht Treaty on European Union, France was permitted to continue issuing currencies in its Overseas Territories—i.e. the franc CFP—following the completion of European economic and monetary union.) All the convertibility arrangements previously concluded between France and the Franc Zone remained in force. Therefore Franc Zone currencies are freely convertible into euros, at the fixed exchange rate, guaranteed by the French Treasury. Each group of member countries, and the Comoros, has its own central issuing bank, with overdraft facilities provided by the French Treasury. (The issuing authority for the French Overseas Territories is the Institut d'émission d'outre-mer, based in Paris.) Monetary reserves are held mainly in the form of euros. The BCEAO and the BEAC are authorized to hold up to 35% of their foreign exchange holdings in currencies other than the euro. Franc Zone ministers of finance normally meet twice a year to review economic and monetary co-operation. The meeting is normally attended by the French Minister of Co-operation and Francophony.

During the late 1980s and early 1990s the economies of the African Franc Zone countries were adversely affected by increasing foreign debt and by a decline in the prices paid for their principal export commodities. The French Government, however, refused to devalue the franc CFA, as recommended by the IMF. In 1990 the Franc Zone governments agreed to develop economic union, with integrated public finances and common commercial legislation. In April 1992, at a meeting of Franc Zone ministers, a treaty on the insurance industry was adopted, providing for the establishment of a regulatory body for the industry, the Conférence Intrafricaine des Marchés d'Assurances (CIMA), and for the creation of a council of Franc Zone ministers responsible for the insurance industry, with its secretariat in Libreville, Gabon. (A code of conduct for members of CIMA entered into force in February 1995.) At the meeting held in April 1992 ministers also agreed that a further council of ministers was to be created with the task of monitoring the social security systems in Franc Zone countries. A programme drawn up by Franc Zone finance ministers concerning the harmonization of commercial legislation in member states through the establishment of l'Organisation pour l'Harmonisation du Droit des Affaires en Afrique (OHADA) was approved by the Franco-African summit in October. A treaty to align corporate and investment regulations was signed by 11 member countries in October 1993.

In August 1993, in view of financial turmoil related to the continuing weakness of the French franc and the abandonment of the European exchange rate mechanism, the BCEAO and the BEAC determined to suspend repurchasing of francs CFA outside the Franc Zone. Effectively this signified the temporary withdrawal of guaranteed convertibility of the franc CFA with the French franc. Devaluations of the franc CFA and the Comoros franc (by 50% and 33.3%, respectively) were implemented in January 1994. Following the devaluation the CFA countries embarked on programmes of economic adjustment, including restrictive fiscal and wage policies and other monetary, structural and social measures, designed to stimulate growth and to ensure eligibility for development assistance from international financial institutions. France established a special development fund of FFr 300m. to alleviate the immediate social consequences of the devaluation, and announced substantial debt cancellations. In April the French Government announced assistance amounting to FFr 10,000m. over three years to Franc Zone countries undertaking structural adjustment programmes. The IMF, which had strongly advocated a devaluation of the franc CFA, and the World Bank approved immediate soft-credit loans, technical assistance and cancellations or rescheduling of debts. In June 1994 heads of state (or representatives) of African Franc Zone countries convened in Libreville, Gabon, to review the effects of the currency realignment. The final communiqué of the meeting urged further international support for the countries' economic development efforts. In April 1995 Franc Zone finance ministers, meeting in Paris, recognized the positive impact of the devaluation on agricultural export sectors, in particular in west African countries. In January 1996 Afristat, a research and training institution based in Bamako, Mali, commenced activities, having been established in accordance with a decision by the Franc Zone member countries and the French Government made in September 1993. Afristat aims to support national statistical organizations in participating states in order to strengthen their economic management capabilities. The IMF and the World Bank have continued to support economic development efforts in the Franc Zone. France provides debt relief to Franc Zone member states eligible under the World Bank's HIPC (see p. 84). In April 2001 the African Franc Zone member states determined jointly to develop anti-money laundering legislation.

In February 2000 UEMOA and ECOWAS adopted an action plan for the creation of a single West African Monetary Zone and consequent replacement of the franc Communauté financière africaine by a single West African currency (see below).

CURRENCIES OF THE FRANC ZONE

1 franc CFA = €0.00152. CFA stands for Communauté financière africaine in the West African area and for Coopération financière en Afrique centrale in the Central African area. Used in the monetary areas of West and Central Africa respectively.

1 Comoros franc = €0.00201. Used in the Comoros, where it replaced the franc CFA in 1981.

1 franc CFP = €0.00839. CFP stands for Comptoirs français du Pacifique. Used in New Caledonia, French Polynesia and the Wallis and Futuna Islands.

WEST AFRICA

Union économique et monétaire ouest-africaine (UEMOA): BP 543, Ouagadougou, Burkina Faso; tel. 31-88-73; fax 31-88-72; e-mail commission@uemoa.bf; internet www.uemoa.int; f. 1994; replaced the Communauté économique de l'Afrique de l'ouest–CEAO; promotes regional monetary and economic convergence, and envisages the eventual creation of a sub-regional common market. A preferential tariff scheme, eliminating duties on most local products and reducing by 30% import duties on many Union-produced industrial goods, became operational on 1 July 1996; in addition, from 1 July, a community solidarity tax of 0.5% was imposed on all goods from third countries sold within the Union, in order to strengthen UEMOA's capacity to promote economic integration. (This was increased to 1% in December 1999.) In June 1997 UEMOA heads of state and government agreed to reduce import duties on industrial products originating in the Union by a further 30%. An inter-parliamentary committee, recognized as the predecessor of a UEMOA legislature, was inaugurated in Mali in March 1998. In September Côte d'Ivoire's stock exchange was transformed into the Bourse regionale des valeurs mobilières, a regional stock exchange serving the Union, in order to further economic integration. In August 1999 an inter-parliamentary committee, recognized as the predecessor of a UEMOA legislature, adopted a draft treaty on the establishment of a UEMOA parliament. On 1 January 2000 internal tariffs were eliminated on all local products (including industrial goods) and a joint external tariff system, reportedly in five bands of between 0% and 20%, was imposed on goods deriving from outside the new customs union. Guinea-Bissau was excluded from the arrangement owing to its unstable political situation. The UEMOA member countries also belong to ECOWAS and, in accordance with an action plan adopted by the two organizations in February 2000, aim to harmonize UEMOA's economic programme with that of a planned second West African monetary union (the West African Monetary Zone), scheduled to be established in July 2005 by the remaining—mainly anglophone—ECOWAS member states. A merger of the two complementary monetary unions, and the replacement of the franc Communauté financière africaine by a new single West African currency, is then envisaged. Mems: Benin, Burkina Faso, Côte d'Ivoire, Guinea-Bissau, Mali, Niger, Senegal and Togo; Pres. MOUSSA TOURÉ (Senegal).

Union monétaire ouest-africaine (UMOA) (West African Monetary Union): established by Treaty of November 1973, entered into force 1974; in 1990 the UMOA Banking Commission was established, which is responsible for supervising the activities of banks and financial institutions in the region, with the authority to prohibit the operation of a banking institution. UMOA constitutes an integral part of UEMOA.

Banque centrale des états de l'Afrique de l'ouest (BCEAO): ave Abdoulaye Fadiga, BP 3108, Dakar, Senegal; tel. 839-05-00; fax 823-93-35; e-mail akangni@bceao.int; internet www.bceao.int; f. 1962; central bank of issue for the mems of UEMOA; cap. and res 844,377m. francs CFA (Dec. 1999); mems: Benin, Burkina Faso, Côte d'Ivoire, Guinea-Bissau, Mali, Niger, Senegal and Togo; Gov. CHARLES KONAN BANNY (Côte d'Ivoire); Sec.-Gen. MICHEL K. KLOUSSEH (Togo); publs *Annual Report, Notes d'Information et Statistiques* (monthly), *Annuaire des banques, Bilan des banques et établissements financiers* (annually).

Banque ouest-africaine de développement (BOAD): 68 ave de la Libération, BP 1172, Lomé, Togo; tel. 221-42-44; fax 221-52-67; e-mail boadsiege@boad.org; internet www.boad.org; f. 1973 to promote the balanced development of mem. states and the economic integration of West Africa; auth. cap. 35,000m. francs CFA, subscribed cap. 33,680m. francs CFA (Dec. 2000); a Guarantee Fund for Private Investment in West Africa, established jtly by BOAD and the European Investment Bank in Dec. 1994, aims to guarantee medium- and long-term credits to private sector businesses in the region; mems: Benin, Burkina Faso, Côte d'Ivoire, Guinea-Bissau,

Mali, Niger, Senegal, Togo; Pres. Dr YAYI BONI (Benin); Vice-Pres. ALPHA TOURÉ; publs *Rapport Annuel*, *BOAD en Bref* (quarterly).

Bourse Régionale des Valeurs Mobilières—BVRM: 18 ave Joseph Anoma, BP 3802, Abidjan 01, Côte d'Ivoire; tel. 20-32-66-85; fax 20-32-66-84; e-mail brvm@brvm.org; internet www.brvm.org; f. 1998; Pres. COULIBALY TIEMKOKO YADE; Man. JEAN-PAUL GILLET.

CENTRAL AFRICA

Communauté économique et monétaire de l'Afrique centrale (CEMAC): BP 969, Bangui, Central African Republic; tel. and fax 61-21-35; e-mail sgudeac@intnet.cf; f. 1998; formally inaugurated as the successor to the Union douanière et économique de l'Afrique centrale (UDEAC, f. 1966) at a meeting of heads of state held in Malabo, Equatorial Guinea, in June 1999; aims to promote the process of sub-regional integration within the framework of an economic union and a monetary union; CEMAC was also to comprise a parliament and sub-regional tribunal; UDEAC established a common external tariff for imports from other countries and administered a common code for investment policy and a Solidarity Fund to counteract regional disparities of wealth and economic development; mems: Cameroon, Central African Republic, Chad, Republic of the Congo, Equatorial Guinea, Gabon; Sec.-Gen. JEAN NKUETE.

At a summit meeting in December 1981, UDEAC leaders agreed in principle to form an economic community of Central African states (Communauté économique des états de l'Afrique centrale—CEEAC), to include UDEAC members and Burundi, Rwanda, São Tomé and Príncipe and Zaire (now Democratic Republic of the Congo). CEEAC began operations in 1985.

Banque de développement des états de l'Afrique centrale (BDEAC): place du Gouvernement, BP 1177, Brazzaville, Republic of the Congo; tel. 81-18-85; fax 81-18-80; f. 1975; cap. 20,716m. francs CFA (Dec. 2000); shareholders: Cameroon, Central African Republic, Chad, Republic of the Congo, Gabon, Equatorial Guinea, ADB, BEAC, France, Germany and Kuwait; Chair. ERIC SORONGOPE; Gen. Man. ANICET G. DOLOGUELE.

Banque des états de l'Afrique centrale (BEAC): ave Mgr François Xavier Vogt, BP 1917, Yaoundé, Cameroon; tel. 23-40-30; fax 23-33-29; f. 1973 as the central bank of issue of Cameroon, the Central African Republic, Chad, Republic of the Congo, Equatorial Guinea and Gabon; a monetary market, incorporating all national financial institutions of the BEAC countries, came into effect on 1 July 1994; cap. 45,000m. francs CFA (Dec. 1998); Gov. JEAN-FÉLIX MAMALEPOT; publs *Rapport annuel*, *Etudes et statistiques* (monthly).

CENTRAL ISSUING BANKS

Banque centrale des Comores: place de France, BP 405, Moroni, Comoros; tel. (73) 1002; fax (73) 0349; e-mail bcc@snpt.km; f. 1981; cap. 1,100m. Comoros francs (Dec. 1997); Gov. SAÏD AHMED SAÏD ALI.

Banque centrale des états de l'Afrique de l'ouest: see above.

Banque des états de l'Afrique centrale: see above.

Institut d'émission d'outre-mer—IEOM: 5 rue Roland Barthes, 75598 Paris Cédex 12, France; tel. 1-53-44-41-41; fax 1-43-47-51-34; internet www.ieom.fr; f. 1966; issuing authority for the French Overseas Territories; Pres. JEAN-PAUL REDOUIN; Dir-Gen. JEAN-MICHEL SEVERINO; Dir THIERRY CORNAILLE.

FRENCH ECONOMIC AID

France's connection with the African Franc Zone countries involves not only monetary arrangements, but also includes comprehensive French assistance in the forms of budget support, foreign aid, technical assistance and subsidies on commodity exports.

Official French financial aid and technical assistance to developing countries is administered by the following agencies:

Agence française de développement—AFD: 5 rue Roland Barthes, 75598 Paris Cédex 12, France; tel. 1-53-44-31-31; fax 1-44-87-99-39; e-mail com@afd.fr; internet www.afd.fr/; f. 1941; fmrly the Caisse française de développement—CFD; French development bank which lends money to member states and former member states of the Franc Zone and several other states, and executes the financial operations of the FAC (see below). Following the devaluation of the franc CFA in January 1994, the French Government cancelled some 25,000m. French francs in debt arrears owed by member states to the CFD. The CFD established a Special Fund for Development and the Exceptional Facility for Short-term Financing to help alleviate the immediate difficulties resulting from the devaluation. A total of FFr 4,600m. of financial assistance was awarded to Franc Zone countries in 1994. In early 1994 the CFD made available funds totalling 2,420m. francs CFA to assist the establishment of CEMAC (see above). Serves as the secretariat for the Fonds français pour l'environnement mondial (f. 1994). Since 2000 the AFD has been implementing France's support of the World Bank's HIPC initiative; Dir-Gen. JEAN-MICHEL SEVERINO.

Fonds de Solidarité Prioritaire—FSP: 20 rue Monsieur, 75007 Paris, France; tel. 1-53-69-37-29; fax 1-53-69-37-55; f. 2000, taking over from the Fonds d'aide et de coopération (f. 1959) the administration of subsidies from the French Government to 54 countries of the Zone de Solidarité prioritaire; FSP is administered by the Ministry of Co-operation and Francophony, which allocates budgetary funds to it.

INTER-AMERICAN DEVELOPMENT BANK—IDB

Address: 1300 New York Ave, NW, Washington, DC 20577, USA.

Telephone: (202) 623-1000; **fax:** (202) 623-3096; **e-mail:** pic@iadb .org;; **internet:** www.iadb.org.

The Bank was founded in 1959 to promote the individual and collective development of Latin American and Caribbean countries through the financing of economic and social development projects and the provision of technical assistance. Membership was increased in 1976 and 1977 to include countries outside the region.

MEMBERS

Argentina	Ecuador	Norway
Austria	El Salvador	Panama
Bahamas	Finland	Paraguay
Barbados	France	Peru
Belgium	Germany	Portugal
Belize	Guatemala	Slovenia
Bolivia	Guyana	Spain
Brazil	Haiti	Suriname
Canada	Honduras	Sweden
Chile	Israel	Switzerland
Colombia	Italy	Trinidad and
Costa Rica	Jamaica	Tobago
Croatia	Japan	United Kingdom
Denmark	Mexico	USA
Dominican	Netherlands	Uruguay
Republic	Nicaragua	Venezuela

Organization

(April 2003)

BOARD OF GOVERNORS

All the powers of the Bank are vested in a Board of Governors, consisting of one Governor and one alternate appointed by each member country (usually ministers of finance or presidents of central banks). The Board meets annually, with special meetings when necessary. The 44th annual meeting of the Board of Governors took place in Milan, Italy, in March 2003.

BOARD OF EXECUTIVE DIRECTORS

The Board of Executive Directors is responsible for the operations of the Bank. It establishes the Bank's policies, approves loan and technical co-operation proposals that are submitted by the President of the Bank, and authorizes the Bank's borrowings on capital markets.

There are 12 executive directors and 12 alternates. Each Director is elected by a group of two or more countries, except the Directors representing Canada and the USA. The USA holds 30% of votes on the Board, in respect of its contribution to the Bank's capital. The Board has four standing committees, relating to: Policy and evaluation; Organization, human resources and board matters; Budget, financial policies and audit; and Programming. A steering committee was established in 1997.

ADMINISTRATION

The Bank comprises three Regional Operations Departments, as well as the following principal departments: Finance; Legal; Research; Integration and Regional Programmes; Private Sector; External Relations; Sustainable Development; Information Technology and General Services; Strategic Planning and Budget; and Human Resources. There are also Offices of the Auditor-General, the Multilateral Investment Fund, and the External Relations Advisor. An Office of Evaluation and Oversight, reporting directly to the Board of Executive Directors, was established in 2000 as part of a reorganization of the Bank's evaluation system. The Bank has country offices in each of its borrowing member states, and special offices in Paris, France and in Tokyo, Japan. At the end of 2001 there were 1,730 Bank staff (excluding the Board of Executive Directors and the Evaluation Office). The administrative budget for 2002 amounted to US $347m.

President: ENRIQUE V. IGLESIAS (Uruguay).

Executive Vice-President: DENNIS E. FLANNERY (USA).

Activities

Loans are made to governments, and to public and private entities, for specific economic and social development projects and for sectoral reforms. These loans are repayable in the currencies lent and their terms range from 12 to 40 years. Total lending authorized by the Bank by the end of 2001 amounted to US $110,565m. During 2001 the Bank approved loans totalling $7,854m., compared with $5,266m. in 2000. Disbursements on authorized loans amounted to $6,459m. in 2001, compared with $7,069m. in the previous year.

The subscribed ordinary capital stock, including inter-regional capital, which was merged into it in 1987, totalled US $100,959.4m. at the end of 2001, of which $4,340.7m. was paid-in and $96,618.7m. was callable. The callable capital constitutes, in effect, a guarantee of the securities which the Bank issues in the capital markets in order to increase its resources available for lending. Replenishments are usually made every four years. In July 1995 the eighth general increase of the Bank's authorized capital was ratified by member countries: the Bank's resources were to be increased by $41,000m. to $102,000m.

In 2001 the Bank borrowed the equivalent of US $7,097m. on the international capital markets, bringing total borrowings outstanding to more than $42,186m. at the end of the year. During 2001 net earnings amounted to $1,009m. in ordinary capital resources and $129m. from the Fund for Special Operations (see below), and at the end of that year the Bank's total reserves were $8,922m.

The Fund for Special Operations enables the Bank to make concessional loans for economic and social projects where circumstances call for special treatment, such as lower interest rates and longer repayment terms than those applied to loans from the ordinary resources. The Board of Governors approved US $200m. in new contributions to the Fund in 1990, and in 1995 authorized $1,000m. in extra resources for the Fund. During 2001 the Fund made 24 loans totalling $443m., compared with loans amounting to $297m. in the previous year.

In January 1993 a Multilateral Investment Fund was established, as an autonomous fund administered by the Bank, to promote private sector development in the region. The 21 Bank members who signed the initial draft agreement in 1992 to establish the Fund pledged to contribute US $1,200m. The Fund's activities are undertaken through three separate facilities concerned with technical co-operation, human resources development and small enterprise development. In 2000 a specialist working group, established to consider MIF operations, recommended that it target its resources on the following core areas of activity: small business development; microenterprise; market functioning; and financial and capital markets. During 2001 the Fund approved $94m. for 66 projects. In June 2002 the Fund approved $1.2m. to assist the financial intelligence units in eight South American countries in their efforts to counter money laundering.

In 1998 the Bank agreed to participate in a joint initiative by the International Monetary Fund and the World Bank to assist heavily indebted poor countries (HIPCs) to maintain a sustainable level of debt. Four member countries were eligible for assistance under the initiative (Bolivia, Guyana, Honduras and Nicaragua). Also in 1998, following projections of reduced resources for the Fund for Special Operations, borrowing member countries agreed to convert about US $2,400m. in local currencies held by the Bank, in order to maintain a convertible concessional Fund for poorer countries, and to help to reduce the debt-servicing payments under the HIPC initiative. In mid-2000 a committee of the Board of Governors endorsed a financial framework for the Bank's participation in an enhanced HIPC initiative (see p. 84), which aimed to broaden the eligibility criteria and accelerate the process of debt reduction. The Bank's total contribution to the initiative was estimated to be

$1,100m. By December 2001 the Bank had approved interim debt relief for all four eligible member countries under the enhanced HIPC initiative, and had assisted the preparation of national Poverty Reduction Strategy Papers, a condition of reaching the 'completion point' of the process.

The Bank supports a range of consultative groups, in order to strengthen donor co-operation with countries in the Latin America and Caribbean region. In December 1998 the Bank established an emergency Consultative Group for the Reconstruction and Transformation of Central America to co-ordinate assistance to countries that had suffered extensive damage as a result of Hurricane Mitch. The Bank hosted the first meeting of the group in the same month, which was attended by government officials, representatives of donor agencies and non-governmental organizations and academics. A total of US $6,200m. was pledged in the form of emergency aid, longer-term financing and debt relief. A second meeting of the group was held in May 1999, in Stockholm, Sweden, at which the assistance package was increased to some $9,000m., of which the Bank and World Bank committed $5,300m. In March 2001 the group convened, in Madrid, Spain, to promote integration and foreign investment in Central America. The meeting, organized by the Bank, was also used to generate $1,300m. in commitments from international donors to assist emergency relief and reconstruction efforts in El Salvador following an earthquake earlier in the year. In October the Bank organized a consultative group meeting in support of a Social Welfare and Alternative Preventive Development Programme for Ecuador, to which donor countries committed $266m. Other consultative groups co-ordinated by the Bank include ones to support the peace process in Colombia, and in Guatemala. In November the Bank hosted the first meeting of a Network for the Prevention and Mitigation of Natural Disasters in Latin America and the Caribbean, which was part of a regional policy dialogue, sponsored by the Bank to promote broad debate on strategic issues.

Distribution of loans (US $ million)

Sector	2001	%	1961–2001	%
Productive Sectors				
Agriculture and fisheries .	683.2	8.7	12,278.1	11.1
Industry, mining and tourism . . .	1,060.2	13.5	11,367.7	10.3
Science and technology .	6.8	0.1	1,616.7	1.5
Physical Infrastructure				
Energy	303.7	3.9	16,022.2	14.5
Transportation and communications . .	391.7	5.0	12,870.1	11.6
Social Sectors				
Sanitation	123.0	1.6	8,803.5	8.0
Urban development . .	168.8	2.1	6,622.3	6.0
Education	711.5	9.1	4,911.7	4.4
Social investment . .	1,784.8	22.7	8,910.7	8.1
Health	110.3	1.4	2,107.7	1.9
Environment . . .	79.5	1.0	1,541.8	1.4
Microenterprise . . .	0.0	0.0	381.2	0.3
Other				
Public-sector reform and modernization . .	2,419.1	30.8	19,309.0	17.4
Export financing . .	11.0	0.1	1,536.7	1.4
Other	0.0	0.0	2,285.4	2.1
Total	**7,853.5**	**100.0**	**110,564.8**	**100.0**

Source: *Annual Report, 2001.*

An increasing number of donor countries have placed funds under the Bank's administration for assistance to Latin America, outside the framework of the Ordinary Resources and the Bank's Special Operations. These trust funds, totalling some 58 in 2000, include the Social Progress Trust Fund (set up by the USA in 1961); the Venezuelan Trust Fund (set up in 1975); the Japan Special Fund (1988); and other funds administered on behalf of Austria, Belgium, Canada, Denmark, Finland, France, Israel, Italy, Japan, the Netherlands, Norway, Portugal, Spain, Sweden, Switzerland, the United Kingdom and the EU. A Program for the Development of Technical Co-operation was established in 1991, which is financed by European countries and the EU. Total cumulative lending from all these trust funds was $1,719.3m. for loans approved by the end of 2001, of which $1,646.6m. had been disbursed. During 2001 cofinancing by bilateral and multilateral sources amounted to $628.8m., which helped to finance 22 national and two regional projects.

The Bank provides technical co-operation to help member countries to identify and prepare new projects, to improve loan execution, to strengthen the institutional capacity of public and private agencies, to address extreme conditions of poverty and to promote small- and micro-enterprise development. The Bank has established a special co-operation programme to facilitate the transfer of experience and technology among regional programmes. In 2001 the Bank approved 376 technical co-operation operations, totalling US $71m., mainly financed by income from the Fund for Special Operations and donor trust funds. The Bank supports the efforts of the countries of the region to achieve economic integration and has provided extensive technical support for the formulation of integration strategies in the Andean, Central American and Southern Cone regions. The Bank is also supporting the initiative to establish a Free Trade Area of the Americas (FTAA) by 2005 and has provided technical assistance, developed programming strategies and produced a number of studies on relevant integration and trade issues. During the period 1998–2000 the Bank contributed an estimated $15,000m. to projects in support of the goals of the summit meetings of the Americas, for example, strengthening democratic systems, alleviating poverty, and promoting economic integration. In 2001 the Bank took a lead role in a Central American regional initiative, the Puebla-Panama Plan, which aimed to consolidate integration and support for social and economic development.

INSTITUTIONS

Instituto para la Integración de América Latina y el Caribe (Institute for the Integration of Latin America and the Caribbean): Esmeralda 130, 17°, 1035 Buenos Aires, Argentina; tel. (11) 4320-1850; fax (11) 4320-1865; e-mail int/inl@iadb.org; internet www.iadb.org/intal; f. 1965 under the auspices of the Inter-American Development Bank; forms part of the Bank's Integration and Regional Programmes Department; undertakes research on all aspects of regional integration and co-operation and issues related to international trade, hemispheric integration and relations with other regions and countries of the world; activities come under four main headings: regional and national technical co-operation projects on integration; policy fora; integration fora; and journals and information; maintains an extensive Documentation Center and various statistical databases; Dir JUAN JOSÉ TACCONE; publs *Integración y Comercio/Integration and Trade* (2 a year), *Intal Monthly Newsletter*, *Informe Andino/Andean Report*, *CARICOM Report*, *Informe Centroamericano/Central American Report*, *Informe Mercosur/Mercosur Report* (2 a year).

Inter-American Institute for Social Development—INDES: 1350 New York Ave, NW, Washington, DC, 20057, USA; e-mail indes@iadb.org; internet www.iadb.org/indes; commenced operations in 1995; aims to support the training of senior officials from public sector institutions and organizations involved with social policies and social services; organizes specialized sub-regional courses and seminars and national training programmes; produces teaching materials and also serves as a forum for the exchange of ideas on social reform; during 2001 four courses were conducted, and other national training programmes were organized in six countries; Dir NOHRA REY DE MARULANDA.

Inter-American Investment Corporation—IIC: 1300 New York Ave, NW, Washington, DC 20057, USA; tel. (202) 623-3900; fax (202) 623-2360; e-mail iicmail@iadb.org; internet www.iadb.org/iic; f. 1986 as a legally autonomous affiliate of the Inter-American Development Bank, to promote the economic development of the region; commenced operations in 1989; initial capital stock was US $200m., of which 55% was contributed by developing member nations, 25.3% by the USA, and the remainder by non-regional members; in total, the IIC has 42 shareholders (26 Latin American and Caribbean countries, 13 European countries, Israel, Japan and the USA); places emphasis on investment in small and medium-sized enterprises without access to other suitable sources of equity or long-term loans; in 2001 the IIC approved equity investments and loans totalling $128m. for 19 transactions; duringn that year the Board of Governors of the IADB agreed to increase the IIC's capital by $500m. Gen. Man. JACQUES ROGOZINSKI; publ. *Annual Report* (in English, French, Portuguese and Spanish).

Publications

Annual Report (in English, French, Portuguese and Spanish).

Annual Report on Oversight and Evaluation.

Annual Report on the Environment and Natural Resources (in English and Spanish).

Economic and Social Progress in Latin America (annually, in English and Spanish).

Equidad (2 a year).

IDB América (monthly, English and Spanish).

IDB Projects (10 a year, in English).

IFM (Infrastructure and Financial Markets) Review (quarterly).

Latin American Economic Markets (quarterly).

Proceedings of the Annual Meeting of the Boards of Governors of the IDB and IIC (in English, French, Portuguese and Spanish).

Social Development Newsletter (2 a year).

Brochure series, occasional papers, working papers, reports.

Yearly and cumulative loans and guarantees, 1961–2001 (US $ million; after cancellations and exchange adjustments)

Country	Total Amount		Ordinary Capital*		Fund for Special Operations		Funds in Administration	
	2001	1961–2001	2001	1961–2001	2001	1961–2001	2001	1961–2001
Argentina	1,655.9	16,757.2	1,655.9	16,063.3	—	644.9	—	49.0
Bahamas	46.2	334.6	46.2	332.6	—	—	—	2.0
Barbados	8.8	377.5	8.8	315.7	—	42.8	—	19.0
Belize	7.0	92.2	7.0	92.2	—	—	—	—
Bolivia	113.2	2,832.8	—	970.5	113.2	1,791.1	—	71.2
Brazil	2,055.5	23,651.5	2,055.5	21,963.8	—	1,558.5	—	129.2
Chile	60.4	4,602.3	60.4	4,357.2	—	203.3	—	41.8
Colombia	800.0	8,471.0	800.0	7,651.5	—	759.3	—	60.2
Costa Rica	22.4	2,088.6	22.4	1,598.8	—	351.8	—	138.0
Dominican Republic	275.0	2,234.7	275.0	1,450.5	—	699.0	—	85.2
Ecuador	65.1	3,615.0	65.1	2,596.6	—	931.1	—	87.3
El Salvador	277.0	2,792.6	277.0	1,902.7	—	745.8	—	144.1
Guatemala	32.2	2,212.0	32.2	1,514.4	—	627.5	—	70.1
Guyana	53.3	747.6	—	102.3	53.3	638.4	—	6.9
Haiti	—	752.8	—	—	—	746.5	—	6.3
Honduras	96.4	2,175.5	—	484.3	96.4	1,625.8	—	65.4
Jamaica	112.0	1,618.6	112.0	1,255.8	—	163.8	—	199.0
Mexico	1,102.0	14,401.5	1,102.0	13,791.2	—	559.0	—	51.3
Nicaragua	180.0	1,841.4	—	243.0	180.0	1,533.5	—	64.9
Panama	35.7	1,866.0	35.7	1,543.4	—	280.0	—	42.6
Paraguay	22.2	1,699.7	22.2	1,116.2	—	571.7	—	11.8
Peru	343.3	5,408.0	343.3	4,768.9	—	418.1	—	221.0
Suriname	14.7	72.6	14.7	70.3	—	2.3	—	—
Trinidad and Tobago	—	951.1	—	895.3	—	30.6	—	25.2
Uruguay	303.9	2,576.8	303.9	2,430.9	—	104.1	—	41.8
Venezuela	97.5	3,730.3	97.5	3,556.0	—	101.4	—	72.9
Regional	74.0	2,660.6	74.0	2,450.3	—	197.2	—	13.1
Total	**7,853.5**	**110,564.8**	**7,410.8**	**93,518.0**	**442.7**	**15,327.5**	**—**	**1,719.3**

* Includes private sector loans, net of participations.

INTERGOVERNMENTAL AUTHORITY ON DEVELOPMENT—IGAD

Address: BP 2653, Djibouti.

Telephone: 354050; **fax:** 356994; **e-mail:** igad@igadregion.org; **internet:** www.igadregion.org.

The Intergovernmental Authority on Development (IGAD), established in 1996 to supersede the Intergovernmental Authority on Drought and Development (IGADD, founded in 1986), aims to co-ordinate the sustainable socio-economic development of member countries, to combat the effects of drought and desertification, and to promote regional food security.

MEMBERS

Djibouti	Kenya	Sudan
Eritrea	Somalia	Uganda
Ethiopia		

Organization

(April 2003)

ASSEMBLY

The Assembly, consisting of heads of state and of government of member states, is the supreme policy-making organ of the Authority. It holds a summit meeting at least once a year. The ninth Assembly meeting of heads of state and of government was held in Khartoum, Sudan in January 2002. The chairmanship of the Assembly rotates among the member countries on an annual basis.

Chairman: (2002/03) Lt-Gen. OMAR HASSAN AHMAD AL-BASHIR (Sudan).

COUNCIL OF MINISTERS

The Council of Ministers is composed of the minister of foreign affairs and one other minister from each member state. It meets at least twice a year and approves the work programme and the annual budget of the Secretariat.

COMMITTEE OF AMBASSADORS

The Committee of Ambassadors comprises the ambassadors or plenipotentiaries of member states to Djibouti. It convenes as regularly as required to advise and assist the Executive Secretary concerning the interpretation of policies and guide-lines and the realization of the annual work programme.

SECRETARIAT

The Secretariat, the executive body of IGAD, is headed by the Executive Secretary, who is appointed by the Assembly for a term of four years, renewable once. In addition to the Office of the Executive Secretary, the Secretariat comprises the following three divisions: Agriculture and Environment; Economic Co-operation; and Political and Humanitarian Affairs.

Executive Secretary: Dr ATTALLA HAMAD BASHIR (Sudan).

Activities

IGADD was established in 1986 by Djibouti, Ethiopia, Kenya, Somalia, Sudan and Uganda, to combat the effects of aridity and desertification arising from the severe drought and famine that has periodically affected the Horn of Africa. Eritrea became a member of IGADD in September 1993, following its proclamation as an independent state. In April 1995, at an extraordinary summit meeting held in Addis Ababa, Ethiopia, heads of state and of government resolved to reorganize and expand the Authority. In March 1996 IGAD was endorsed to supersede IGADD, at a second extraordinary summit meeting of heads of state and of government, held in Nairobi, Kenya. The meeting led to the adoption of an agreement for a new organizational structure and the approval of an extended mandate to co-ordinate and harmonize policy in the areas of economic co-operation and political and humanitarian affairs, in addition to its existing responsibilities for food security and environmental protection.

IGAD aims to achieve regional co-operation and economic integration. To facilitate this IGAD assists the governments of member states to maximize resources and co-ordinates efforts to initiate and implement regional development programmes and projects. In this context, IGAD promotes the harmonization of policies relating to agriculture and natural resources, communications, customs, trade and transport; the implementation of pro-grammes in the fields of social sciences, research, science and technology; and effective participation in the global economy. Meetings between IGAD foreign affairs ministers and the IGAD Joint Partners' Forum, comprising the grouping's donors, are convened periodically to discuss issues such as food security and humanitarian affairs.

FOOD SECURITY AND ENVIRONMENTAL PROTECTION

IGAD seeks to achieve regional food security, the sustainable development of natural resources and environmental protection, and to encourage and assist member states in their efforts to combat the consequences of drought and other natural and man-made disasters. The region suffers from recurrent droughts, which severely impede crop and livestock production. Natural and man-made disasters increase the strain on resources, resulting in annual food deficits. About 80% of the IGAD sub-region is classified as arid or semi-arid, and some 40% of the region is unproductive, owing to severe environmental degradation. Activities to improve food security and preserve natural resources have included: the introduction of remote-sensing services; the development of a Marketing Information System and of a Regional Integrated Information System (RIIS); the establishment of training and credit schemes for fishermen; research into the sustainable production of drought-resistant, high-yielding crop varieties; transboundary livestock disease control and vaccine production; the control of environmental pollution; the promotion of alternative sources of energy in the home; the management of integrated water resources; the promotion of community-based land husbandry; training programmes in grain marketing; and the implementation of the International Convention to Combat Desertification.

ECONOMIC CO-OPERATION

The Economic Co-operation division concentrates on the development of a co-ordinated infrastructure for the region, in particular in the areas of transport and communications, to promote foreign, cross-border and domestic trade and investment opportunities. IGAD seeks to harmonize national transport and trade policy and thereby facilitate the free movement of people, goods and services. The improvements to infrastructure also aim to facilitate more timely interventions to conflicts, disasters and emergencies in the sub-region. Projects to be undertaken by the end of 2001 included: the construction of missing segments of the Trans-African Highway and the Pan African Telecommunications Network; the removal of barriers to trade and communications; improvements to ports and inland container terminals; and the modernization of railway and telecommunications services. In November 2000 the IGAD Assembly determined to establish an integrated rail network connecting all member countries. In addition, the heads of state and government considered the possibility of drafting legislation to facilitate the expansion of intra-IGAD trade. The development of economic co-operation has been impeded by persisting conflicts in the sub-region (see below).

POLITICAL AND HUMANITARIAN AFFAIRS

The field of political and humanitarian affairs focuses on conflict prevention, management and resolution through dialogue. The division's primary aim is to restore peace and stability to member countries affected by conflict, in order that resources may be diverted for development purposes. Efforts have been pursued to strengthen capacity for conflict prevention and to relieve humanitarian crises. In September 1995 negotiations between the Sudanese Government and opposition leaders were initiated, under the auspices of IGAD, with the aim of resolving the conflict in southern Sudan; these were subsequently reconvened periodically. In March 2001 IGAD's mediation committee on southern Sudan, chaired by President Daniel arap Moi of Kenya, publicized a seven-point plan for a peaceful settlement of the conflict. In early June, at a regional summit on the situation in Sudan convened by IGAD, it was agreed that a permanent negotiating forum comprising representatives of the parties to the conflict would be established at the Authority's secretariat. In May–August 2000 a conference aimed at securing peace in Somalia was convened in Arta, Djibouti, under the auspices of IGAD. The conference appointed a transitional Somali legislature, which then elected an interim national president. The eighth summit of IGAD heads of state and government, held in Khartoum, Sudan, in November, welcomed the conclusion in September of an agreement of reconciliation between the new Somali interim administration and a prominent opposition alliance, and determined that those member countries that neighboured Somalia (the 'frontline states' of Djibouti, Ethiopia and Kenya) should co-operate in assisting the process of reconstruction and reconciliation in that country. The summit appointed a special envoy to implement IGAD's directives concerning the Somali situation. Following the violent escalation of a border dispute between Eritrea and Ethiopia in mid-1998 IGAD supported efforts by the Organization of African Unity (now African Union) to mediate a cease-fire between the two sides. This was achieved in mid-2000.

The ninth IGAD summit meeting, held in Khartoum in January 2002, adopted a protocol to IGAD's founding agreement establishing a conflict early warning and response mechanism (CEWARN). CEWARN, which was to be based in Addis Ababa, Ethiopia, was to collect and analyse information for the preparation of periodic early warning reports concerning the potential outbreak of violent conflicts in the region. The summit meeting determined that a new conference for promoting reconciliation in Somalia (where insecurity continued to prevail) should be convened, under IGAD's auspices. The leaders also issued a statement condemning international terrorism and urged Somalia, in particular, to make a firm commitment to eradicating terrorism. The inaugural meeting of CEWARN was held in June. In mid-July the Sudanese Government and the main rebel grouping in that country signed a framework peace agreement, under IGAD auspices, in Machakos, Kenya. A cease-fire agreement was concluded by the parties to the conflict in October 2002, and in early 2003 IGAD was finalizing arrangements for the deployment of a 24-member verification and monitoring team to oversee compliance with the accord. Meanwhile, peace negotiations were continuing under IGAD auspices. The second Somalia reconciliation conference held, under IGAD auspices, in October 2002, in Eldoret, Kenya, issued a Declaration on Cessation of Hostilities, Structures and Principles of the Somalia National Reconciliation Process, as a basis for the pursuit of a peace settlement. In February 2003, in view of reported violations of the cease-fire, the three frontline states established a committee to monitor the implementation of the Declaration.

Publications

Annual Report.

IGAD News (2 a year).

Proceedings of the Summit of Heads of State and Government; Reports of the Council of Ministers' Meetings.

INTERNATIONAL CHAMBER OF COMMERCE—ICC

Address: 38 cours Albert 1er, 75008 Paris, France.

Telephone: 1-49-53-28-28; **fax:** 1-49-53-28-59; **e-mail:** icc@iccwbo.org; **internet:** www.iccwbo.org.

The ICC was founded in 1919 to promote free trade and private enterprise, provide practical services and represent business interests at governmental and intergovernmental levels.

MEMBERS

ICC membership comprises corporations, national professional and sectoral associations, business and employer federations, chambers of commerce, and individuals involved in international business from more than 130 countries. National Committees or Groups have been formed in some 70 countries and territories to co-ordinate ICC objectives and functions at the national level.

Organization

(April 2003)

COUNCIL

The Council is the governing body of the organization. It meets twice a year and is composed of members nominated by the National Committees. Ten direct members, from countries where no National Committee exists, may also be invited to participate. The Council elects the President and Vice-President for terms of two years.

President: JEAN RENÉ FOURTOU (France).

EXECUTIVE BOARD

The Executive Board consists of 15–30 members appointed by the Council on the recommendation of the President and nine *ex-officio*-members. Members serve for a three-year term, one-third of the members retiring at the end of each year. It ensures close direction of ICC activities and meets at least three times each year.

INTERNATIONAL SECRETARIAT

The ICC secretariat is based at International Headquarters in Paris, with additional offices maintained in Geneva and New York principally for liaison with the United Nations and its agencies. The Secretary-General is appointed by the Council on the recommendation of the Executive Board.

Secretary-General: MARIA LIVANOS CATTAUI (Switzerland).

NATIONAL COMMITTEES AND GROUPS

Each affiliate is composed of leading business organizations and individual companies. It has its own secretariat, monitors issues of concern to its national constituents, and draws public and government attention to ICC policies.

CONGRESS

The ICC's supreme assembly, to which all member companies and organizations are invited to send senior representatives. Congresses are held regularly, in a different place on each occasion, with up to 2,000 participants. The 34th Congress was held in Denver, USA, in May 2002, on the theme of 'Trade, Technology and Partnership—The Business of Building a Better World'.

CONFERENCES

ICC Conferences was created in 1996 to disseminate ICC expertise in the fields of international arbitration, trade, banking and commercial practice, by means of a world-wide programme of conferences and seminars.

Activities

The various Commissions of the ICC (listed below) are composed of at least 500 practising business executives and experts from all sectors of economic life, nominated by National Committees. ICC recommendations must be adopted by a Commission following consultation with National Committees, and then approved by the Council or Executive Board, before they can be regarded as official ICC policies. Meetings of Commissions are generally held twice a year. Working Parties are frequently constituted by Commissions to undertake specific projects and report back to their parent body. Officers of Commissions, and specialized Working Parties, often meet in the intervals between Commission sessions. The Commissions produce a wide array of specific codes and guide-lines of direct use to the world business community; formulate statements and initiatives for presentation to governments and international bodies; and comment constructively and in detail on proposed actions by intergovernmental organizations and governments that are likely to affect business. In January 1997 the ICC opened its first regional office, in the Hong Kong Special Administrative Region.

ICC works closely with other international organizations. ICC members, the heads of UN economic organizations and the OECD convene for annual discussions on the world economy. The Commission on International Trade and Investment Policy campaigns against protectionism in world trade and in support of the World Trade Organization (WTO). The ICC also works closely with the European Union, commenting on EU directives and making recommendations on, for example, tax harmonization and laws relating to competition.

ICC plays a part in combating international crime connected with commerce through its Commercial Crime Services, based in London, United Kingdom, and Kuala Lumpur, Malaysia. These comprise: the Commercial Crime Bureau; the International Maritime Bureau, which combats maritime fraud, including insurance fraud and the theft of cargoes; and the Counterfeiting Intelligence Bureau, established in 1985 to investigate counterfeiting in trade-marked goods, copyrights and industrial designs.

The ICC provides a framework for international commercial disputes, mainly through the ICC International Court of Arbitration, which was established in 1923. The Court received more than 590 requests for arbitration in 2002. Other ICC services for dispute resolution include its Rules of Arbitration, its Alternative Dispute Resolution, and the International Centre for Expertise, which administers ICC Rules of Expertise and Rules for Documentary Credit and Dispute Resolution Expertise (DOCDEX).

The ICC has developed rules and guide-lines relating to electronic transactions, including guide-lines for ethical advertising on the internet and for data protection. In September 1999 it presented model clauses for company contracts involving the electronic transfer of personal information. The Geneva Business Dialogue was held in Switzerland in September. The primary subjects discussed were the importance of globalization in business and the need to avoid protectionist reactions to recent economic upheaval. The ICC has also devised a system of standard trade definitions most commonly used in international sales contracts. A fully revised and updated version of these, Incoterms 2000, entered into effect on 1 January 2000.

Policy and Technical Commissions:
Commission on Air Cargo
Commission on Air Transport
Commission on Arbitration
Commission on Banking Technique and Practice
Commission on Business in Society
Commission on Competition
Commission on Customs and Trade Regulations
Commission on Energy
Commission on Environment
Commission on Extortion and Bribery
Commission on Financial Services and Insurance
Commission on Intellectual and Industrial Property
Commission on International Commercial Practice
Commission on Maritime Transport
Commission on Marketing, Advertising and Distribution
Commission on Surface Transport

Commission on Taxation
Commission on Telecommunications and Information Technologies
Commission on Trade and Investment Policy
Special Groups:
Corporate Economist Advisory Group
Electronic Commerce Project
Standing Committee on Extortion and Bribery
Bodies for the Settlement of Disputes:
International Centre for Technical Expertise
International Court of Arbitration
International Maritime Arbitration Organization
Other Bodies:
ICC Centre for Maritime Co-operation
ICC Commercial Crime Bureau
ICC Corporate Security Services
ICC Counterfeiting Intelligence Bureau
ICC Cybercrime Unit
ICC Institute of International Business Law and Practice
ICC International Maritime Bureau
ICC-WTO Economic Consultative Committee
Institute of World Business Law
World Chambers Federation

Finance

The International Chamber of Commerce is a private organization financed partly by contributions from National Committees and other members, according to the economic importance of the country which each represents, and partly by revenue from fees for various services and from sales of publications.

Publications

Annual Report.
Business World (electronic magazine).
Documentary Credits Insight (quarterly).
Handbook.
ICC Contact (newsletter).
ICC International Court of Arbitration Bulletin.
IGO Report.
Numerous publications on general and technical business and trade-related subjects.

INTERNATIONAL CONFEDERATION OF FREE TRADE UNIONS—ICFTU

Address: 5 blvd du Roi Albert II, bte 1, 1210 Brussels, Belgium.

Telephone: (2) 224-0211; **fax:** (2) 201-5815; **e-mail:** internetpo@ icftu.org; **internet:** www.icftu.org.

ICFTU was founded in 1949 by trade union federations which had withdrawn from the World Federation of Trade Unions (see p. 322). It aims to promote the interests of working people and to secure recognition of workers' organizations as free bargaining agents; to reduce the gap between rich and poor; and to defend fundamental human and trade union rights. It campaigns for the adoption by the World Trade Organization of a social clause, with legally-binding minimum labour standards, and regularly provides economic analysis and proposals at international meetings. In March 2001 ICFTU launched a two-year campaign to promote the eradication of child labour. In March 2002 it presented a report on the social dimensions of globalization, at the first meeting of the ILO World Commission on Globalization. See also the World Confederation of Labour, see p. 320).

MEMBERS
231 organizations in 150 countries with 158m. members (April 2003).

Organization
(April 2003)

WORLD CONGRESS
The Congress, the highest authority of ICFTU, normally meets every four years. The 17th Congress was held in Durban, South Africa, in April 2000.

Delegations from national federations vary in size according to membership. The Congress examines past activities, maps out future plans, elects the Executive Board and the General Secretary, considers the functioning of the regional machinery, examines financial reports and social, economic and political situations. It works through plenary sessions and through technical committees which report to the plenary sessions.

EXECUTIVE BOARD
The Board meets not less than once a year, for about three days, usually at Brussels, or at the Congress venue; it comprises 53 members elected by Congress and nominated by areas of the world. The General Secretary is an *ex-officio* member. After each Congress the Board elects a President and at least seven Vice-Presidents.

The Board considers administrative questions; hears reports from field representatives, missions, regional organizations and affiliates, and makes resultant decisions; and discusses finances, applications for affiliation, and problems affecting world labour. It elects a steering committee of 19 to deal with urgent matters between Board meetings.

President: FACKSON SHAMENDA (Zambia).

PERMANENT COMMITTEES

Steering Committee: Administers the General Fund, comprising affiliation fees, and the International Solidarity Fund, constituting additional voluntary contributions.

Economic and Social Committee.

Human and Trade Union Rights Committee.

***ICFTU/ITS Working Party on Trade Union Education.**

***ICFTU/ITS Occupational Health, Safety, and the Environment Working Party.**

***ICFTU/ITS Working Party on Multinational Companies.**

Peace, Security and Disarmament Committee.

Youth Committee.

Women's Committee.

* A joint body of the ICFTU and International Trade Secretariats.

SECRETARIAT

Departments at headquarters include: Economic and Social Policy; Trade Union Rights; Projects, Co-ordination and Education (comprising units for Projects and Trade Union Education); Equality (including Youth); Finance and Administration; Press and Publications. There are also the Co-ordination Unit for Central and Eastern Europe, the Electronic Data Processing Unit, Personnel, Co-ordination and Regional Liaison Desks for the Americas, Africa and Asia.

General Secretary: GUY RYDER (United Kingdom).

BRANCH OFFICES

ICFTU Geneva Office: 46 ave Blanc, 1202 Geneva, Switzerland; tel. (22) 738-4202; fax (22) 738-1082; e-mail icftu.ge@geneva.icftu.org; Dir DAN CUNNIAH.

ICFTU Moscow Office: 2142, Leninsky Prospekt 42, 117119 Moscow, Russia; tel. (95) 938-7356; fax (95) 938-7304; e-mail icftumos@cq.ru.

ICFTU United Nations Office: 211 East 43rd St, Suite 710, New York, NY 10017, USA; tel. (212) 370-0180; fax (212) 370-0188; e-mail icftuny@igc.org; Perm. Rep. GEMMA ADABA.

There are also Permanent Representatives accredited to FAO (Rome), UNIDO and IAEA (Vienna), and to UNEP and UN-Habitat (Nairobi).

REGIONAL ORGANIZATIONS

ICFTU African Regional Organization—AFRO: POB 67273, Kenya Re Towers, 4th Floor, Upper Hill, Off Ragati Rd, POB 67273, Nairobi, Kenya; tel. (22) 244336; fax (22) 215072; e-mail info@ictfuafro.org; internet www.icftu-afro.org; f. 1957; mems: 5m. workers in 36 African countries; Gen. Sec. ANDREW KAILEMBO (Tanzania).

ICFTU Asian and Pacific Regional Organization—APRO: 73 Bras Basah Rd, NTUC Trade Union House, Singapore 189556; tel. (65) 6222-6294; fax (65) 6221-7380; e-mail gs@icftu-apro.org; internet www.icftu-apro.org; f. 1951; mems: 33m. in 38 orgs in 29 countries; Gen. Sec. NORIYUKI SUZUKI.

Inter-American Regional Organization of Workers—ORIT: Avda Andrés Eloy Blanco, Edif. José Vargas, 15 Los Caobos, Caracas, Venezuela; tel. (2) 578-3538; fax (2) 578-1702; e-mail sedeorit@cioslorit.org; internet www.cioslorit.org; f. 1951; mems: national unions in 28 countries and territories; Gen. Sec. LUIS A. ANDERSON.

There are Field Representatives in various parts of Africa. In addition, a number of Project Planners for development co-operation travel in different countries.

Finance

Affiliated federations pay a standard fee of €165.1 (2002), or its equivalent in other currencies, per 1,000 members per annum, which covers the establishment and routine activities of the ICFTU headquarters in Brussels, and partly subsidizes the regional organizations.

An International Solidarity Fund was set up in 1956 to assist unions in developing countries, and workers and trade unionists victimized by repressive political measures. It provides legal assistance and supports educational activities. In cases of major natural disasters affecting workers token relief aid is granted.

Publications

Survey of Trade Union Rights (annually).

Trade Union World (official journal, monthly).

These periodicals are issued in English, French and Spanish. In addition the Congress report is issued in English. Numerous other publications on labour, social protection and trade union training have been published in various languages.

Associated International Trade Secretariats

Education International—EI: 5 blvd du Roi Albert II (8ème étage), 1210 Brussels, Belgium; tel. (2) 224-0680; fax (2) 224-0606; e-mail headoffice@ei-ie.org; internet www.ei-ie.org; f. 1993 by merger of the World Confederation of Organizations of the Teaching Profession (f. 1952) and the International Federation of Free Teachers' Unions (f. 1951); mems: 311 national orgs of teachers' trade unions representing 25m. members in 159 countries and territories; holds Congress every three years (July 2001: Kathmandu, Nepal); Pres. MARY HATWOOD FUTRELL (USA); Sec.-Gen. FRED VAN LEEUWEN (Netherlands); publs *Worlds of Education Education International* (quarterly) (both in English, French and Spanish).

International Federation of Building and Woodworkers—IFBWW: 54 route des Acacias, 1227 Carouge, Switzerland; tel. (22) 8273777; fax (22) 8273770; e-mail info@ifbww.org; internet www.ifbww.org; f. 1934; mems: 287 national unions with a membership of more than 10m. workers in 124 countries; organization: Congress, Executive Committee; Pres. ROEL DE VRIES (Netherlands); Sec.-Gen. ANITA NORMARK (Sweden); publ. *IFBWW News* (2 a month).

International Federation of Chemical, Energy, Mine and General Workers' Unions—ICEM: 109 ave Emile de Béco, B-1050 Brussels, Belgium; tel. (2) 626-2020; fax (2) 648-4316; e-mail info@icem.org; internet www.icem.org; f. 1995 by merger of the International Federation of Chemical, Energy and General Workers' Unions (f. 1907) and the Miners' International Federation (f. 1890); mems: 403 trade unions covering approximately 20m. workers in 115 countries; main sectors cover energy industries; chemicals; pharmaceuticals and biotechnology; mining and extraction; pulp and paper; rubber; ceramics; glass; building materials; and environmental services; Pres. JOHN MAITLAND; Gen. Sec. FRED HIGGS; publs *ICEM Info* (quarterly), *ICEM Focus on Health, Safety and Environment* (2 a year), *ICEM Update* Irregular.

International Federation of Journalists—IFJ: International Press Centre, 155 rue de la Loi, 1040 Brussels, Belgium; tel. (2) 235-2200; fax (2) 235-2219; e-mail ifj@ifj.org; internet www.ifj.org; f. 1952 to link national unions of professional journalists dedicated to the freedom of the press, to defend the rights of journalists, and to raise professional standards; it conducts surveys, assists in trade union training programmes, organizes seminars and provides information; it arranges fact-finding missions in countries where press freedom is under pressure, and issues protests against the persecution and detention of journalists and the censorship of the mass media; holds Congress every three years: (June 2001: Seoul, Republic of Korea); mems: 147 unions in 106 countries, comprising 450,000 individuals; Pres. CHRIS WARREN (Australia); Gen. Sec. AIDAN WHITE (UK); publ. *IFJ Direct Line* every two months.

International Metalworkers' Federation—IMF: 54 bis, route des Acacias, CP 1516, 1227 Geneva, Switzerland; tel. (22) 308-5050; fax (22) 308-5055; e-mail info@imfmetal.org; internet www.imfmetal.org; f. 1893; Mems: national orgs covering 24.8m. workers in 207 unions in 101 countries; holds Congress every four years; has six regional offices; seven industrial departments; World Company Councils for unions in multinational corporations; Pres. KLAUS ZWICKEL (Germany); Gen. Sec. MARCELLO MALENTACCHI; pPubls *IMF News Briefs* (weekly), *Metal World* (quarterly).

International Textile, Garment and Leather Workers' Federation—ITGLWF: rue Joseph Stevens 8 (boîte 4), 1000 Brussels, Belgium; tel. (2) 512-2606; fax (2) 511-0904; e-mail office@itglwf.org; internet www.itglwf.org; f. 1970; mems: 217 unions covering 10m. workers in 110 countries; holds Congress every four years: (June 2000: Norrköping, Sweden); Pres. PETER BOOTH (UK); Gen. Sec. NEIL KEARNEY (Ireland); publ. *ITGLWF Newsletter* (quarterly).

International Transport Workers' Federation—ITF: 49–60 Borough Rd, London, SE1 1DR, United Kingdom; tel. (20) 7403-2733; fax (20) 7357-7871; e-mail mail@itf.org.uk; internet www.itf .org.uk; f. 1896; mems: national trade unions covering 5m. workers in 604 unions in 137 countries; holds Congress every four years; has eight Industrial Sections; Pres. UMRAOMAL PUROHIT (India); Gen. Sec. DAVID COCKROFT (UK); publ. *Transport International* (quarterly).

International Union of Food, Agricultural, Hotel, Restaurant, Catering, Tobacco and Allied Workers' Associations—IUF: 8 rampe du Pont-Rouge, 1213 Petit-Lancy, Switzerland; tel. (22) 793-2233; fax (22) 793-2238; e-mail iuf@iuf.org; internet www .iuf.org; f. 1920; mems: 336 affiliated organizations covering about 12m. workers in 120 countries; holds Congress every five years; Pres. GARY NEBEKER (USA); Gen. Sec. TOMOJI MISATO; publs bi-monthly bulletins.

Public Services International—PSI: 45 ave Voltaire, BP9, 01211 Ferney-Voltaire Cédex, France; tel. 4-50-40-64-64; fax 4-50-40-73-20; e-mail psi@world-psi.org; internet www.world-psi.org; f. 1907; mems: 620 unions and professional associations covering 20m.

workers in 149 countries (at Oct. 2002); holds Congress every five years; Pres. YLVA THÖRN (Sweden); Gen. Sec. HANS ENGELBERTS (Netherlands); publ. *Focus* (quarterly).

Union Network International—UNI: ave Reverdil 8–10, 1260 Nyon, Switzerland; tel. (22) 365-2100; fax (22) 365-2121; e-mail contact@union-network.org; internet www.union-network.org; f. 2000 by merger of Communications International (CI), the International Federation of Commercial, Clerical, Professional and Technical Employees (FIET), the International Graphical Federation (IGF), and Media and Entertainment International (MEI); mems: 900 unions in more than 140 countries, representing 15.5m. people; activities cover the following 12 sectors: commerce; electricity; finance; graphical; hair and beauty; professional and information technology staff; media, entertainment and the arts; postal; property services; social insurance and private health care; telecommunications; and tourism; first World Congress convened in Berlin, Germany, in September 2001; Pres. MAJ-LEN REMAHL (Finland); Gen. Sec. PHILIP J. JENNINGS (United Kingdom); publs *UNIinfo* (quarterly), *UNInet News* (monthly).

INTERNATIONAL OLYMPIC COMMITTEE

Address: Château de Vidy, 1007 Lausanne, Switzerland.

Telephone: (21) 6216111; **fax:** (21) 6216216; **internet:** www .olympic.org.

The International Olympic Committee was founded in 1894 to ensure the regular celebration of the Olympic Games.

Organization

(April 2003)

INTERNATIONAL OLYMPIC COMMITTEE

The International Olympic Committee (IOC) is a non-governmental international organization comprising 128 members, who are representatives of the IOC in their countries and not their countries' delegates to the IOC. In addition there are 25 Honorary members and five Honor members. The members meet in session at least once a year. In accordance with reforms adopted in December 1999, the Committee was to comprise a maximum of 115 members (130 until 31 December 2003), including 15 active Olympic athletes, 15 National Olympic Committee presidents, 15 International Sports Federation presidents, and 70 other individuals. A nominations committee has been established under the reform programme to select qualified candidates to stand for election to the IOC.

The IOC is the final authority on all questions concerning the Olympic Games and the Olympic movement. There are 199 recognized National Olympic Committees, which are the sole authorities responsible for the representation of their respective countries at the Olympic Games. The IOC may give recognition to International Federations which undertake to adhere to the Olympic Charter, and which govern sports that comply with the IOC's criteria.

An International Council for Arbitration for Sport (ICAS) has been established. ICAS administers the Court of Arbitration for Sport which hears cases brought by competitors.

EXECUTIVE BOARD

The session of the IOC delegates to the Executive Board the authority to manage the IOC's affairs. The President of the Board is elected for an eight-year term, and is eligible for re-election once for an additional term of four years. The Vice-Presidents are elected for four-year terms, and may be re-elected after a minimum interval of four years. Members of the Board are elected to hold office for four years. The Executive Board generally meets four to five times per year.

President: Dr JACQUES ROGGE (Belgium).

Vice-Presidents: RICHARD KEVAN GOSPER (Australia), THOMAS BACH (Germany), JAMES L. EASTON (USA), VITALY SMIRNOV (Russia).

Members of the Board: SERGEI BUBKA (Ukraine), FRANCO CARRARO (Italy), OTTAVIO CINQUANTA (Italy), ZHENLIANG HE (People's Republic of China), TONI KHOURY (Lebanon), GUNILLA LINDBERG (Sweden), LAMBIS W. NIKOLAOU (Greece), DENIS OSWALD (Switzerland), MARIO VÁZQUEZ RAÑA (Mexico).

IOC COMMISSIONS

Athletes' Commission: f. 1981; comprising active and retired athletes, represents their interests; may issue recommendations to the Executive Board.

Commission for Culture and Olympic Education: f. 2000 by merger of the Culture Commission (f. 1968) and the IOC Commission for the International Olympic Academy and Olympic Education (f. 1961).

Co-ordination Commission for the Olympic Games: f. after the election of a host city to oversee and assist the organizing committee in the planning and management of the games.

Ethics Commission: f. 1999 to develop and monitor rules and principles to guide the selection of hosts for the Olympic Games, and the organization and execution of the Games.

Medical Commission: f. 1967; concerned with the protection of the health of athletes, respect for medical and sport ethics, and equality for all competing athletes.

Olympic Collectors' Commission: f. 1993; aims to increase awareness of Olympic philately, numismatics, and other memorabilia.

Olympic Games Study Commission: f. 2002; makes recommendations on means of controlling the cost, complexity and size of the Summer and Winter Games.

Olympic Programme Commission: reviews, and analyses the Olympic programme of sports, disciplines and events; develops recommendations on the principles and structure of the programme.

Olympic Solidarity Commission: f. 1961; assists National Olympic Committees (NOCs); responsible for managing and administering the share of television rights allocated to NOCs.

Sport and Environment Commission: f. 1995 to promote environmental protection and sustainable development.

Sport for All Commission: f. 1983 to encourage and support the principles of Sport for All.

Women and Sport Working Group: f. 1995 to advise the Executive Board on policies to promote women in sport.

ADMINISTRATION

The administration of the IOC is under the authority of the Director-General and the Secretary-General, who are appointed by the Executive Board, on the proposal of the President.

Director-General: FRANÇOIS CARRARD.

Secretary-General: FRANÇOISE ZWEIFEL.

Activities

The fundamental principles of the Olympic movement are:

Olympism is a philosophy of life, exalting and combining, in a balanced whole, the qualities of body, will and mind. Blending sport with culture, education and respect for the environment, Olympism seeks to create a way of life based on the joy found in effort, the educational value of good example and respect for universal fundamental ethical principles.

Under the supreme authority of the IOC, the Olympic movement encompasses organizations, athletes and other persons who agree to be guided by the Olympic Charter. The criterion for belonging to the Olympic movement is recognition by the IOC.

The goal of the Olympic movement is to contribute to building a peaceful and better world by educating youth through sport practised without discrimination of any kind and in the Olympic spirit, which requires mutual understanding with a spirit of friendship, solidarity and fair-play.

The activity of the Olympic movement is permanent and universal. It reaches its peak with the bringing together of the athletes of the world at the great sport festival, the Olympic Games.

The Olympic Charter is the codification of the fundamental principles, rules and bye-laws adopted by the IOC. It governs the organization and operation of the Olympic movement and stipulates the conditions for the celebration of the Olympic Games.

In March 1998, at a meeting organized with other international sports governing bodies, it was agreed to form a working group to defend the principle of self-regulation in international sports organizations, against possible interference by the EU. At a meeting in August methods of containing the increase in drugs abuse in sport were discussed. In January 1999, following publication of the results of an investigation into allegations of corruption and bribery, six members of the Committee were recommended for expulsion while investigations into the conduct of other officials were to be pursued. In March an extraordinary session of the IOC was convened, at which the six Committee members were expelled for violating rules relating to Salt Lake City's bid to host the Olympic Winter Games in 2002 (four other members had already resigned, while Executive Board member Un Yong Kim had received disciplinary action). The President of the IOC retained his position after receiving a vote of confidence. The session approved far-reaching reforms, including the introduction of an interim procedure to select the host city for the Winter Games in 2006, by means of which an election college was to choose two finalists from the six cities submitting bids. Visits by IOC members to any of the bid cities were prohibited. In addition, the meeting approved the establishment of an independent Ethics Commission to oversee cities' bids to host the Olympic Games (see above) and an IOC 2000 Commission to review the bidding process after 2006 and the internal structure of the organization. A declaration on drugs and sport was also adopted by the meeting. In November 1999, an independent World Anti-Doping Agency (WADA, see below) was established by the IOC, and an Anti-Doping Code entered into effect on 1 January 2000. In December 1999 the IOC adopted 50 reforms proposed by the IOC 2000 Commission during the Extraordinary 110th Session. The changes aimed to create a more open, responsive and accountable organization, and included the elimination of member visits to bid cities, the application of terms of office, limiting the expansion of the Summer Games, and the election of 15 active athletes to the IOC membership. In 2000, prior to the Sydney 'Summer' Olympic Games, held in September of that year, WADA conducted about 2,200 out-of-competition drugs tests, involving competitors from more than 80 nations and supplementing significantly the IOC's ongoing out-of-competition drugs testing programme. The Agency established a 15-member team of independent observers to oversee doping control operations at the Sydney Games. Participants attending the World Conference on Doping in Sport, held in Copenhagen, Denmark, in March 2003, adopted the Copenhagen Declaration on Doping in Sport and promoted the World Anti-Doping Code, formulated by WADA, as the basis for combating doping in sport.

In July 2000 the International Olympic Committee established a subsidiary International Olympic Truce Foundation, and an International Olympic Truce Centre, based in Athens, Greece, with the aim of promoting a culture of peace through the pursuit of sport and the Olympic ideals. A new president of the IOC's Executive Board was elected at the 112th Session, held in Moscow, Russia, in July 2001. In early 2002 the Olympic Games Study Commission was established to address means of reducing the cost and complexity of the Games. The Commission was to present a full report of its findings to the 115th Session of the IOC, scheduled to be convened in Prague, Czech Republic, in July 2003. In November 2002 the Olympic Programme Commission made a full review of the sports programme for the first time since 1936. It decided to cap the

number of sports at 28, the number of events at 300, and the number of participating athletes at 10,500.

ASSOCIATED AGENCY

World Anti-Doping Agency—WADA: f. 1999 to promote and co-ordinate efforts to achieve drug-free sport; has five committees: Ethics and Education; Finance and Administration; Health, Medical and Research; Legal; Standards and Harmonization; Chair. RICHARD W. POUND; Dir Gen. HARRI SYVÄSALMI.

THE GAMES OF THE OLYMPIAD

The Olympic Summer Games take place during the first year of the Olympiad (period of four years) which they are to celebrate. They are the exclusive property of the IOC, which entrusts their organization to a host city seven years in advance.

1896	Athens	1960	Rome
1900	Paris	1964	Tokyo
1904	St Louis	1968	Mexico City
1908	London	1972	Munich
1912	Stockholm	1976	Montreal
1920	Antwerp	1980	Moscow
1924	Paris	1984	Los Angeles
1928	Amsterdam	1988	Seoul
1932	Los Angeles	1992	Barcelona
1936	Berlin	1996	Atlanta
1948	London	2000	Sydney
1952	Helsinki	2004	Athens
1956	Melbourne	2008	Beijing

The programme of the Games must include at least 15 of the total number of Olympic sports (sports governed by recognized International Federations and admitted to the Olympic programme by decision of the IOC at least seven years before the Games). The Olympic summer sports are: aquatics (including swimming, diving and water polo), archery, athletics, badminton, baseball, basketball, boxing, canoeing, cycling, equestrian sports, fencing, football, gymnastics, handball, field hockey, judo, modern pentathlon, rowing, sailing, shooting, softball, table tennis, tae kwondo, tennis, triathlon, volleyball, weight-lifting, wrestling.

OLYMPIC WINTER GAMES

The Olympic Winter Games comprise competitions in sports practised on snow and ice. From 1994 onwards, they were to be held in the second calendar year following that in which the Games of the Olympiad take place.

1924	Chamonix	1972	Sapporo
1928	St Moritz	1976	Innsbruck
1932	Lake Placid	1980	Lake Placid
1936	Garmisch-Partenkirchen	1984	Sarajevo
1948	St Moritz	1988	Calgary
1952	Oslo	1992	Albertville
1956	Cortina d'Ampezzo	1994	Lillehammer
1960	Squaw Valley	1998	Nagano
1964	Innsbruck	2002	Salt Lake City
1968	Grenoble	2006	Turin

The Winter Games may include biathlon, bobsleigh, curling, ice hockey, luge, skating and skiing.

Finance

The International Olympic Committee derives marketing revenue from the sale of broadcast rights, the Olympic Partners sponsorship Programme, local sponsorship, ticketing, and licensing. Some 8% of this is retained for the Committee's operational budget, with the remainder allocated to Olympic organizing committees, National Olympic Committees and teams, and international sports federations.

Publication

Olympic Review (6 a year).

INTERNATIONAL ORGANIZATION FOR MIGRATION—IOM

Address: 17 route des Morillons, CP 71, 1211 Geneva 19, Switzerland.

Telephone: (22) 7179111; **fax:** (22) 7986150; **e-mail:** info@iom.int; **internet:** www.iom.int.

The Intergovernmental Committee for Migration (ICM) was founded in 1951 as a non-political and humanitarian organization with a predominantly operational mandate, including the handling of orderly and planned migration to meet specific needs of emigration and immigration countries; and the processing and movement of refugees, displaced persons and other individuals in need of international migration services to countries offering them resettlement opportunities. In 1989 ICM's name was changed to the International Organization for Migration (IOM). IOM was admitted as an observer to the UN General Assembly in October 1992.

MEMBERS

Albania	Finland	Panama
Algeria	France	Paraguay
Angola	Georgia	Peru
Argentina	Germany	Philippines
Armenia	Greece	Poland
Australia	Guatemala	Portugal
Austria	Guinea	Romania
Azerbaijan	Guinea-Bissau	Rwanda
Bangladesh	Haiti	Senegal
Belgium	Honduras	Serbia and
Belize	Hungary	Montenegro
Benin	Iran	Sierra Leone
Bolivia	Ireland	Slovakia
Bulgaria	Israel	Slovenia
Burkina Faso	Italy	Sri Lanka
Cambodia	Japan	Sudan
Canada	Jordan	Sweden
Cape Verde	Kazakhstan	Switzerland
Chile	Kenya	Tajikistan
Colombia	Korea, Republic	Tanzania
Congo, Democratic	Kyrgyzstan	Thailand
Republic	Latvia	Tunisia
Congo, Republic	Liberia	Uganda
Costa Rica	Lithuania	Ukraine
Côte d'Ivoire	Luxembourg	United Kingdom
Croatia	Madagascar	USA
Cyprus	Mali	Uruguay
Czech Republic	Mexico	Venezuela
Denmark	Morocco	Yemen
Dominican	Netherlands	Zambia
Republic	Nicaragua	Zimbabwe
Ecuador	Nigeria	
Egypt	Norway	
El Salvador	Pakistan	

Observers: Afghanistan, Belarus, Bhutan, Bosnia and Herzegovina, Brazil, People's Republic of China, Cuba, Estonia, Ethiopia, Ghana, Holy See, India, Indonesia, Jamaica, , Libya, former Yugoslav republic of Macedonia, Malta, Mauritania, Moldova, Mozambique, Namibia, Nepal, New Zealand, Papua New Guinea, Russia, San Marino, São Tomé and Príncipe, Somalia, Sovereign Military Order of Malta, Spain, Turkey, Turkmenistan and Viet Nam. In addition, some 50 international governmental and non-governmental organizations hold observer status with IOM.

Organization

(April 2003)

IOM is governed by a Council which is composed of representatives of all member governments, and has the responsibility for making final decisions on policy, programmes and financing. An Executive Committee of nine member governments elected by the Council prepares the work of the Council and makes recommendations on the basis of reports from the Sub-Committee on Budget and Finance and the Sub-Committee on the Co-ordination of Transport.

Director General: BRUNSON MCKINLEY (USA).

Deputy Director General: NDIORO NDIAYE (Senegal).

Activities

IOM aims to provide assistance to member governments in meeting the operational challenges of migration, to advance understanding of migration issues, to encourage social and economic development through migration and to work towards effective respect of the human dignity and well-being of migrants. It provides a full range of migration assistance to, and sometimes *de facto* protection of, migrants, refugees, displaced persons and other individuals in need of international migration services. This includes recruitment, selection, processing, medical examinations, and language and cultural orientation courses, placement, activities to facilitate reception and integration and other advisory services. IOM co-ordinates its refugee activities with the UN High Commissioner for Refugees (UNHCR) and with governmental and non-governmental partners. In May 1997 IOM and UNHCR signed a memorandum of understanding which aimed to facilitate co-operation between the two organizations. Since it commenced operations in February 1952 IOM has provided assistance to an estimated 11m. migrants.

IOM operates within the framework of the main service areas outlined below. It also administers special programmes. In June 2001 IOM established a Migration Policy and Research Programme to strengthen the capacity of governments to manage migration effectively, and to contribute to a better understanding of migration issues. IOM was designated as one of the implementing organizations of the settlement agreement concluded between survivors of the Nazi holocaust and Swiss banks. IOM established the Holocaust Victim Assets Programme (HVAP) to process claims made by certain target groups. A German Forced Labour Compensation Programme (GFLCP) was founded to process applications for claims of forced labour and personal injury and for property loss. The deadline for filing claims under both programmes was 31 December 2001.

MOVEMENTS

IOM's constitution mandates the organization to provide for the organized transfer of migrants, refugee displaced persons, and others to countries offering to receive them. Accordingly, IOM provides assistance to persons fleeing conflict situations, to refugees being resettled in third countries or repatriated, to stranded individuals, to internally and externally displaced persons, to other persons compelled to leave their homelands, to individuals seeking to reunite with other members of their families and to migrants involved in regular migration, including qualified migrants travelling under the Facilitated Passage Programme. IOM provides these individuals with secure, reliable, cost-effective services, including counselling, document processing, medical examination, transportation, language training, and cultural orientation and integration assistance. IOM offers discounted transport services and assistance during departure, transit and arrival.

IOM movements are undertaken by the Movement Management Department, which is also responsible for statistical recording of IOM activities and for the development of effective procedures and operational guide-lines. In a humanitarian emergency situation, the department assumes the focal point of IOM operations until field missions are prepared to co-ordinate activities. From April–June 1999 IOM co-operated with UNHCR and the OSCE to facilitate the evacuation of refugees from Kosovo and Metohija (Federal Republic of Yugoslavia, now Serbia and Montenegro), following an escalation of violence against the local Albanian population by Serbian forces and the initiation of a NATO military offensive. The joint Humanitarian Evacuation Programme included land transportation to move substantial numbers of refugees away from overcrowded camps in the border region of the former Yugoslav republic of Macedonia (FYRM), and the provision of charter flights to evacuate those refugees most at need to third countries. IOM was also involved in implementing a programme to register the refugees in Albania, the FYRM and Montenegro, and to reissue identification documents where necessary.

ASSISTED RETURNS SERVICE

IOM assists migrants to return home, on a voluntary basis. These people may include unsuccessful asylum seekers, stranded students, labour migrants, and qualified nationals. IOM provides return services directly to the migrant, as well as in co-operation with other organizations to assist wider groups of people. As with its movements service, IOM provides assistance at each stage of the process, i.e. pre-departure, transportation, and post-arrival. It aims to act in a mediating role between the countries and governments of origin, transit and destination and often extends assistance through a period of rehabilitation, to longer-term reconstruction and development efforts.

Since its establishment IOM has been involved in the voluntary repatriation of refugees, displaced persons, and other vulnerable groups. Between 1996 and 1998 more than 160,000 Bosnians were assisted to return voluntarily under IOM auspices. In June 1999, following the end of the conflict in Kosovo and Metohija, IOM co-ordinated the return movement of refugees and worked with the UN mission and UNHCR to assist returnees to move to their final destination in Kosovo. From July 1999–December 2000 IOM assisted some 170,000 Kosovars to return to the province.

In the period October 1999–December 2000 IOM assisted 115,000 East Timorese, who had fled violence between Indonesian forces and separitist groups in September 1999, to return to the territory (now independent Timor-Leste) from camps in West Timor, and participated in reconstruction activities. A joint IOM/UNHCR programme to facilitate the return of Afghan refuees from Iran commenced in April 2000. In late 2001 the IOM was actively involved in assisting Afghans who had left their homes during renewed fighting between Taliban and oposition forces and the US bombing raids against Taliban and other military targets in Afghanistan. IOM was the co-ordinating agency for the largest camp, located in Maslakh, which had an estimated population of 120,000. A registration process was conducted in February 2002. IOM aimed to provide transport assistance, in co-operation with UNHCR, to 400,000 Afghan refugees from Iran by the end of 2002; however, transport assistance activities were suspended indefinitely in May, owing to insufficient funding. In 2001 IOM assisted with the repatriation of Sierra Leonean refugees from Guinea, following an escalation of violence in the south of that country which had rendered refugee camps vulnerable to attack and largely inaccessible to humanitarian aid agencies. In April 2003, following the US-led military action initiated in March against the Saddam Hussain regime in Iraq, IOM launched the Iraq Transition Initiative, aimed at addressing the priority community requirements of post-conflict Iraq. The programme was to facilitate the reintegration of internally displaced people, refugees and former combatants, to stabilize populations, and to establish links between local communities and regional and national authorities. During that month IOM announced that it would launch a programme to repatriate some 21,500 third-country nationals (mainly from Burkina Faso, Guinea and Mali) who had been displaced by the ongoing violent unrest in Côte d'Ivoire and had become stranded in that country, Liberia and Mali.

IOM aims to contribute towards alleviating economic and social problems through the recruitment and selection of high-level workers and professionals to fill positions in priority sectors of the economy in developing countries for which qualified persons are not available locally, taking into account national development priorities as well as the needs and concerns of receiving communities. IOM screens possible returnees, identifies employment opportunities and provides reintegration assistance. Selection Migration programmes help qualified professionals to migrate to countries in need of specific expertise when the country cannot find the required skills from within or through the return of nationals. Integrated Experts programmes provide temporary expatriate expertise to states for up to six years: these experts transfer their skills to their working partners and contribute directly to productive output. Programmes of Intraregional Co-operation in the field of qualified human resources encourage collective self-reliance among developing countries by fostering the exchange of governmental experts and the transfer of professionals and technicians within a given region. IOM maintains recruitment offices throughout the world. In November 1996 IOM established a Return of Qualified Nationals (RQN) programme to facilitate the employment of refugees returning to Bosnia and Herzegovina. By December 1999, when the programme was terminated, more than 750 professionals had been placed in jobs in that country. In 2001 IOM initiated a Programme for the Return of Judiciary and Prosecutors to Minority Areas in Bosnia and Herzegovina.

An RQN programme has been established for Timor-Leste, and a programme to encourage the Return and Reintegration of Qualified Afghan Nationals is under way. In addition, IOM operates a Return of Qualified African Nationals scheme. IOM and the EU jointly fund a scheme to support Rwandan students abroad and encourage their return to Rwanda.

In recent years IOM has increasingly assisted in the return home and reintegration of demobilized soldiers, police officials, and their dependents. During 1997–99 IOM undertook a programme of assistance for demobilized soldiers and their families in Angola. IOM was also involved in the resettlement of demobilized forces in Guatemala in 1998. In mid-1999 IOM established an Information Counselling and Referral Service (ICRS) to undertake the registration of former combatants in Kosovo and assist their rehabilitation. From July–November 1999 the ICRS registered 25,723 demobilized soldiers from the Kosovo Liberation Army; during that period IOM helped 4,122 of the former combatants to start their own businesses or to find other permanent employment.

COUNTER TRAFFICKING

IOM aims to counter the growing problem of smuggling and trafficking in migrants, which has resulted in several million people being exploited by criminal agents and employers. IOM aims to provide shelter and assistance for victims of trafficking; to provide legal and medical assistance to migrants uncovered in transit or in the receiving country; and to offer voluntary return and reintegration assistance. IOM organizes mass information campaigns in countries of origin, in order to highlight the risks of smuggling and trafficking, and aims to raise general awareness of the problem. It also provides training to increase the capacity of governments and other organizations to counter irregular migration. Since 1996 IOM has worked in Cambodia and Thailand to help victims of trafficking to return home. A transit centre has been established on the border between the two countries, where assessments are carried out, advice is given, and the process of tracing families is undertaken. During 2001 IOM operated a pilot project for the return of trafficked migrants to Bosnia and Herzogovina.

TECHNICAL CO-OPERATION ON MIGRATION

Through its technical co-operation programmes IOM offers advisory services on migration to governments, intergovernmental agencies and non-governmental organizations. They aim to assist in the formation and implementation of effective and coherent migration policy, legislation and administration. IOM technical co-operation also focuses on capacity building projects such as training courses for government migration officials, and analysis of and suggestions for solving emerging migration problems. Throughout these activities IOM aims to maintain an emphasis on the rights and well-being of migrants, and in particular to ensure that the specific needs of migrant women are incorporated into programmes and policies.

MASS INFORMATION

IOM furthers the understanding of migration through mass information campaigns, in particular to provide migrants with enough knowledge to make informed decisions. In recent years information campaigns have addressed migrant rights, trafficking in women and children, migration and health, promoting the image of migrants, and amnesty programmes. Information campaigns may also inform refugees and displaced persons on the nature and extent of humanitarian aid during an emergency. Information programmes may be implemented to address a specific need, or as part of a wider strategy for migration management. Through its research IOM has developed mechanisms to gather information on potential migrants' attitudes and motivations, as well as on situations which could lead to irregular migration flows. Trends in international migration point to information as an essential resource for individuals making life-changing decisions about migrating; for governments setting migration policies; for international, regional or non-governmental organizations designing migration programmes; and for researchers, the media and individuals analyzing and reporting on migration.

MIGRATION HEALTH

IOM's migration health services aim to ensure that migrants are fit to travel, do not pose a danger to those travelling with them, and that they receive medical attention and care when necessary. IOM also undertakes research and other technical support and policy development activities in the field of health care. Medical screening of prospective migrants is routinely conducted, along with immunizations and specific counselling, e.g. for HIV/AIDS. IOM administers programmes for disabled refugees and undertakes medical evacuation of people affected by conflict. Under its programmes for health assistance and advice, IOM conducts health education programmes, training for health professionals in post-conflict regions, and assessments of availability and access to health care for migrant populations. IOM provides assistance for post-emergency returning populations, through the rehabilitation of health infrastructures, provision of medical supplies, mental health programmes, and training of personnel. In September 1999 IOM established a one-year Psychosocial and Trauma Response in Kosovo project, to enhance the local capacity to respond to problems arising from the conflict and mass displacement. Following the end of the project, during which 37 people graduated as counsellors, IOM developed a new programme to establish community psychosocial centres, to train a further 40 counsellors and to enhance access to psychosocial support for ethnic minorities.

IOM collaborates with government health authorities and relevant intergovernmental and non-governmental organizations. In September 1999 IOM and UNAIDS signed a co-operation framework to promote awareness on HIV/AIDS issues relating to displaced populations, and to ensure the needs of migrants are incorporated into national and regional AIDS strategies. In October IOM and WHO signed an agreement to strengthen collaborative efforts to improve the health care of migrants. IOM maintains a database of its tuberculosis diagnostic and treatment programmes, which facilitates the management of the disease. An information system on immigration medical screening data was being developed to help to analyse disease trends among migrants.

INTERNATIONAL CENTRE FOR MIGRATION AND HEALTH:
11 route du Nant-d'Avril, 1214 Geneva, Vernier, Switzerland; tel. (22) 7831080; fax (22) 7831087; e-mail icmh@worldcom.ch; internet www.icmh.ch.

Established in March 1995, by IOM and the University of Geneva, with the support of WHO, to respond to the growing needs for information, documentation, research, training and policy development in migration health; designated a WHO collaborating centre, in August 1996, for health-related issues among people displaced by disasters.
Co-ordinator: Dr MANUEL CARBALLO.

Finance

The approved IOM budget for 2000 amounted to US \$208.4m. for operations and 34.1m. Swiss francs for administration.

Publications

International Migration (quarterly).
IOM News (quarterly, in English, French and Spanish).
Migration and Health (quarterly).
Report by the Director General (in English, French and Spanish).
Trafficking in Migrants (quarterly).
World Migration Report (annually).
Research reports, *IOM Info Sheets* surveys and studies.

INTERNATIONAL RED CROSS AND RED CRESCENT MOVEMENT

The International Red Cross and Red Crescent Movement is a worldwide independent humanitarian organization, comprising three components: the International Committee of the Red Cross (ICRC), founded in 1863; the International Federation of Red Cross and Red Crescent Societies (the Federation), founded in 1919; and National Red Cross and Red Crescent Societies in 178 countries.

Organization

INTERNATIONAL CONFERENCE
The supreme deliberative body of the Movement, the Conference comprises delegations from the ICRC, the Federation and the National Societies, and of representatives of States Parties to the Geneva Conventions (see below). The Conference's function is to determine the general policy of the Movement and to ensure unity in the work of the various bodies. It usually meets every four to five years, and is hosted by the National Society of the country in which it is held. The 27th International Conference was held in Geneva, Switzerland, in October/November 1999.

STANDING COMMISSION
The Commission meets at least twice a year in ordinary session. It promotes harmony in the work of the Movement, and examines matters which concern the Movement as a whole. It is formed of two representatives of the ICRC, two of the Federation, and five members of National Societies elected by the Conference.

COUNCIL OF DELEGATES
The Council comprises delegations from the National Societies, from the ICRC and from the Federation. The Council is the body where the representatives of all the components of the Movement meet to discuss matters that concern the Movement as a whole.
In November 1997 the Council adopted an Agreement on the organization of the activities of the Movement's components. The Agreement aimed to promote increased co-operation and partnership between the Movement's bodies, clearly defining the distribution of tasks between agencies. In particular, the Agreement aimed to ensure continuity between international operations carried out in a crisis situation and those developed in its aftermath.

Fundamental Principles of the Movement

Humanity: The International Red Cross and Red Crescent Movement, born of a desire to bring assistance without discrimination to the wounded on the battlefield, endeavours, in its international and national capacity, to prevent and alleviate human suffering wherever it may be found. Its purpose is to protect life and health and to ensure respect for the human being. It promotes mutual understanding, friendship, co-operation and lasting peace amongst all peoples.

Impartiality: It makes no discrimination as to nationality, race, religious beliefs, class or political opinions. It endeavours to relieve the suffering of individuals, being guided solely by their needs, and to give priority to the most urgent cases of distress.

Neutrality: In order to continue to enjoy the confidence of all, the Movement may not take sides in hostilities or engage in controversies of a political, racial, religious or ideological nature.

Independence: The Movement is independent. The National Societies, while auxiliaries in the humanitarian services of their governments and subject to national laws, must retain their autonomy so that they may always be able to act in accordance with the principles of the Movement.

Voluntary Service: It is a voluntary relief movement not prompted by desire for gain.

Unity: There can be only one Red Cross or Red Crescent Society in any one country. It must be open to all. It must carry on its humanitarian work throughout the territory.

Universality: The International Red Cross and Red Crescent Movement, in which all National Societies have equal status and share equal responsibilities and duties in helping each other, is worldwide.

In 1997 all constituent parts of the Movement (National Societies, the ICRC and the International Federation of Red Cross and Red Crescent Societies) adopted the Seville Agreement on co-operation in the undertaking of international relief activities. The Agreement excludes activities that are entrusted to individual components by the statutes of the Movement or the Geneva Conventions.

International Committee of the Red Cross—ICRC

Address: 19 ave de la Paix, 1202 Geneva, Switzerland.
Telephone: (22) 7346001; **fax:** (22) 7332057; **e-mail:** press.gva@icrc
.org; **internet:** www.icrc.org.
Founded in 1863, the ICRC is at the origin of the Red Cross and Red
Crescent Movement, and co-ordinates all international humani-
tarian activities conducted by the Movement in situations of conflict.
New statutes of the ICRC, incorporating a revised institutional
structure, were adopted in June 1998 and came into effect in July.

Organization

(April 2003)

INTERNATIONAL COMMITTEE

The ICRC is an independent institution of a private character
composed exclusively of Swiss nationals. Members are co-opted, and
their total number may not exceed 25. The international character of
the ICRC is based on its mission and not on its composition.

President: JAKOB KELLENBERGER.

Vice-Presidents: Prof. JACQUES FORSTER, ANNE PETITPIERRE.

ASSEMBLY

Under the new decision-making structures, approved in 1998, the
Assembly was defined as the supreme governing body of the ICRC.
It formulates policy, defines the Committee's general objectives and
strategies, oversees its activities, and approves its budget and
accounts. The Assembly is composed of the members of the ICRC,
and is collegial in character. The President and Vice-Presidents of
the ICRC hold the same offices in the Assembly.

ASSEMBLY COUNCIL

The Council (formerly the Executive Board) is a subsidiary body of
the Assembly, to which the latter delegates certain of its responsibilities. It prepares the Assembly's activities and takes decisions on
matters within its competence. The Council is composed of five
members elected by the Assembly and is chaired by the President of
the ICRC.

Members: JAKOB KELLENBERGER, ERNST A. BRUGGER, Prof. JACQUES
FORSTER, JAKOB NÜESCH, JEAN ABT, JEAN DE COURTEN.

DIRECTORATE

The Directorate is the executive body of the ICRC, overseeing the
efficient running of the organization and responsible for the application of the general objectives and institutional strategies decided by
the Assembly. Members are appointed by the Assembly to serve a
four-year term. The Director of Operations is responsible for running
the following divisions at headquarters: the Central Tracing Agency
and Protection Division; Health and Relief Division; Logistics Division; International Organizations Division; and the External
Resources Division.

Director-General: ANGELO GNAEDINGER.

Members: PIERRE KRAEHENBUEL (Director of Operations), FRANÇOIS
BUGNION (Director for International Law and Co-operation), JACQUES
STROUN (Director of Human Resources and Finance), DORIS PFISTER
(Director of Resources and Operational Support), YVES DACCORD
(Director of Communication).

Activities

The International Committee of the Red Cross was founded in 1863
in Geneva, by Henry Dunant and four of his friends. The original
purpose of the Committee was to promote the foundation, in every
country, of a voluntary relief society to assist wounded soldiers on
the battlefield (the origin of the National Societies of the Red Cross
or Red Crescent), as well as the adoption of a treaty protecting
wounded soldiers and all those who come to their rescue. The
mission of the ICRC was progressively extended through the Geneva
Conventions (see below). The present activities of the ICRC consist
in giving legal protection and material assistance to military and
civilian victims of wars (international wars, internal strife and
disturbances) and in promoting and monitoring the application of
international humanitarian law. The ICRC takes into account the
legal standards and the specific cultural, ethical and religious features of the environment in which it operates. It aims to influence
the conduct of all actual and potential perpetrators of violence by
seeking direct dialogue with combatants. In 1990 the ICRC was

granted observer status at the United Nations General Assembly.
The ICRC overall programme of activities covers the following areas:

The protection of vulnerable individuals and groups under international humanitarian law, including activities related to
ensuring respect for detainees (monitoring prison conditions),
respect for civilians, reuniting relatives separated in conflict situations and restoring family links, and tracing missing persons.

The implementation of assistance activities, aimed at restoring a
sufficient standard of living to victims of armed conflict, including
the provision of medical aid and emergency food supplies, initiatives to improve water supply, basic infrastructure and access
to health care, and physical rehabilitation assistance (for example
to assist civilians injured by land-mines).

Preventive action, including the development and implementation
of international humanitarian law and dissemination of humanitarian principles, with a view to protecting non-combatants from
violence.

Co-operation with National Societies.

In January 1996 an ICRC Advisory Service became operational; this
was intended to assist national authorities in their implementation
of humanitarian law and to provide a basis for consultation, analysis
and harmonization of legislative texts. A Documentation Centre has
also been established for exchanging information on national measures and activities aimed at promoting humanitarian law in countries. The Centre is open to all states and National Societies, as well
as to interested institutions and the general public.
In 1996 the ICRC launched the 'Avenir' project to define the
organization's future role, in recognition of significant changes in
the world situation and the consequent need for changes in humanitarian action. Four main priorities were identified: improving the
status of international humanitarian action and knowledge of and
respect for humanitarian law; carrying out humanitarian action in
closer proximity to victims, with long-term plans and identified
priorities; strengthening dialogue with all parties (including
launching joint appeals with other organizations if necessary, and
the establishment of a combined communication and information
dissemination unit); and increasing the ICRC's efficiency. In April
1998 the Assembly endorsed a plan of action, based on these priorities. In November 1999 the 27th International Conference of the
Red Cross and Red Crescent adopted a further plan of action for the
movement, covering the four-year period 2000–03. The plan incorporated the following three main objectives: to strengthen respect for
international humanitarian law, including the conformity of
weapons with legal guide-lines, in order to protect victims of armed
conflict; to improve national and international preparedness to
respond effectively to disaster situations, as well as to improve
mechanisms of co-operation and protection of humanitarian personnel working in the field; and strategic partnerships to improve
the lives of vulnerable people through health initiatives, measures to
reduce discrimination and violence, and strengthening National
Societies' capacities and their co-operation with other humanitarian
organizations.
The ICRC consistently reviews the 1980 UN Convention on prohibitions or restrictions on the use of certain conventional weapons
which may be deemed to be excessively injurious or to have indiscriminate effects (ratified by 90 states at April 2003) and its protocols. In September 1997 the ICRC participated in an international
conference, held in Oslo, Norway, at which a Convention was
adopted, prohibiting 'the use, stockpiling, production and transfer of
anti-personnel mines' and ensuring their destruction. The treaty
was opened for signature in December and became legally-binding
on 1 March 1999 for the 66 states that had then ratified it. By April
2003 the treaty had been ratified by 132 states. In April 1998 the
Swiss Government established a Geneva International Centre for
Humanitarian Demining, in co-operation with the United Nations
and the ICRC, to co-ordinate the destruction of landmines world-
wide.
In 1995 the ICRC adopted a 'Plan of Action concerning Children in
Armed Conflicts', to promote the principle of non-recruitment and
non-participation in armed conflict of children under the age of 18
years. A co-ordinating group was established, with representatives
of the individual National Societies and the International Federation of Red Cross and Red Crescent Societies. The ICRC participated in drafting the Optional Protocol to the Convention on the
Rights of the Child, which was adopted by the UN General Assembly
in May 2000 and entered into force in February 2002, raising from 15
to 18 years the minimum age for recruitment in armed conflict.
The ICRC's presence in the field is organized under the following
three categories: responsive action, aimed at addressing the immediate effects of crises; remedial action, with an emphasis on rehabilitation; and environment-building activities, aimed at creating

political, institutional, humanitarian and economic situations that are suitable for generating respect for human rights. ICRC operational delegations focus on responsive action and remedial action, while environment-building is undertaken by ICRC regional delegations. The regional delegations undertake humanitarian diplomacy efforts (e.g. networking, promoting international humanitarian law and distributing information), logistical support to operational delegations, and their own operations; they also have an early warning function, alerting the ICRC to developing conflict situations. The ICRC targets its activities at the following groups: 'victims', comprising civilians affected by violent crises, people deprived of their freedom, and the wounded and sick; and institutions and individuals with influence, i.e. national and local authorities, security forces, representatives of civil society, and Red Cross or Red Crescent National Societies. Children, women and girls, internally displaced people and missing persons are of particular concern to the ICRC.

During 2001 the ICRC distributed around 130,000 metric tons of relief supplies, including food, clothing, blankets and tents, in 60 countries. In that year ICRC representatives visited some 346,807 prisoners held in more than 70 countries. Contacts were mediated between around 865,465 family members separated by conflict, and more than 1,897 persons reported as missing were traced. Assistance including medicines and equipment was provided for 134 hospitals in 22 countries world-wide, and permanent surgical teams were maintained in medical centres in Afghanistan, East Timor (now Timor-Leste), Kenya, Sierra Leone and Sudan, and short-term surgical presences were funded in five other African countries and the Solomon Islands. During the year the ICRC participated in orthopaedic projects in 22 countries, including the manufacturing and fitting of artificial limbs. In early 2003 the ICRC was actively concerned with around 80 conflicts and was undertaking major operations in Afghanistan, Angola, the Caucasus, Colombia, the Democratic Republic of the Congo, Ethiopia, Iraq, Israel and the Palestinian territories, Rwanda, Somalia and Sudan. In March, following the initiation of US-led military action against the Saddam Hussain regime in Iraq, the ICRC signed an agreement with UNHCR on co-operation in providing humanitarian relief in Iraq and neighbouring countries. In April, following the fall of the Iraqi regime, the ICRC urged the US-led coalition to protect Iraq's essential infrastructure, such as hospitals and water supply facilities, from damage by looters and rioters. In 2002 operations in Africa were allocated some 39.7% of the total field budget; Europe and North America 19.2%; Asia and the Pacific 17.4%; the Middle East and North Africa 9.3%; and Latin America and the Caribbean 6.3%. (Some 8.1% of field expenditure was held as an operational reserve.)

THE GENEVA CONVENTIONS

In 1864, one year after its foundation, the ICRC submitted to the states called to a Diplomatic Conference in Geneva a draft international treaty for 'the Amelioration of the Condition of the Wounded in Armies in the Field'. This treaty was adopted and signed by 12 states, which thereby bound themselves to respect as neutral wounded soldiers and those assisting them. This was the first Geneva Convention.

With the development of technology and weapons, the introduction of new means of waging war, and the manifestation of certain phenomena (the great number of prisoners of war during World War I; the enormous number of displaced persons and refugees during World War II; the internationalization of internal conflicts in recent years), the necessity was felt of having other international treaties to protect new categories of war victims. The ICRC, for more than 134 years, has been the leader of a movement to improve and complement international humanitarian law.

There are now four Geneva Conventions, adopted on 12 August 1949: I—to protect wounded and sick in armed forces on land, as well as medical personnel; II—to protect the same categories of people at sea, as well as the shipwrecked; III—concerning the treatment of prisoners of war; IV—for the protection of civilians in time of war; and there are two Additional Protocols of 8 June 1977, for the protection of victims in international armed conflicts (Protocol I) and in non-international armed conflicts (Protocol II).

By January 2003 189 states were parties to the Geneva Conventions; 161 were parties to Protocol I and 156 to Protocol II.

In April 2000 a joint working group on the emblems of the National Red Cross and Red Crescent Societies recommended the formulation of a Third Additional Protocol to the Geneva Conventions, designating a new official emblem so that National Societies could be recognized in countries that did not wish to be represented by either current symbol or did not wish to choose between the two.

Finance

The ICRC's work is financed by a voluntary annual grant from governments parties to the Geneva Conventions, voluntary contributions from National Red Cross and Red Crescent Societies and by gifts and legacies from private donors. The ICRC's total budget for 2002 amounted to some 915.6m. Swiss francs, of which 765.8m. Swiss francs were allocated to field operations.

Publications

Annual Report (editions in English, French and Spanish).

The Geneva Conventions (texts and commentaries).

ICRC News (weekly, English, French, German and Spanish editions).

International Review of the Red Cross (quarterly in English and French; annually in Arabic, Russian and Spanish).

The Protocols Additional.

Yearbook of International Humanitarian Law (annually).

Various publications on subjects of Red Cross interest (medical studies, international humanitarian law, etc.), some in electronic form.

International Federation of Red Cross and Red Crescent Societies

Address: 17 chemin des Crêts, Petit-Saconnex, CP 372, 1211 Geneva 19, Switzerland.

Telephone: (22) 7304222; **fax:** (22) 7330395; **e-mail:** secretariat@ifrc.org; **internet:** www.ifrc.org.

The Federation was founded in 1919 (as the League of Red Cross Societies). It works on the basis of the Principles of the Red Cross and Red Crescent Movement to inspire, facilitate and promote all forms of humanitarian activities by the National Societies, with a view to the prevention and alleviation of human suffering, and thereby contribute to the maintenance and promotion of peace in the world. The Federation acts as the official representative of its member societies in the field. The Federation maintains close relations with many inter-governmental organizations, the United Nations and its Specialized Agencies, and with non-governmental organizations. It has permanent observer status with the United Nations.

MEMBERS

National Red Cross and Red Crescent Societies in 178 countries in April 2003, with a total of 97m. members and volunteers.

Organization

(April 2003)

GENERAL ASSEMBLY

The General Assembly is the highest authority of the Federation and meets every two years in commission sessions (for development, disaster relief, health and community services, and youth) and plenary sessions. It is composed of representatives from all National Societies that are members of the Federation.

GOVERNING BOARD

The Board (formerly the Executive Council) meets every six months and is composed of the President of the Federation, nine Vice-Presidents, representatives of 16 National Societies elected by the Assembly, and the Chairman of the Finance Commission. Its functions include the implementation of decisions of the General Assembly; it also has powers to act between meetings of the Assembly.

COMMISSIONS

Development Commission.

Disaster Relief Commission.

Finance Commission.

Health and Community Services Commission.

Youth Commision.

The Commissions meet, in principle, twice a year, just before the Governing Board. Members are elected by the Assembly under a system that ensures each Society a seat on one Commission.

SECRETARIAT

The Secretariat assumes the statutory responsibilities of the Federation in the field of relief to victims of natural disasters, refugees and civilian populations who may be displaced or exposed to abnormal hardship. In addition, the Secretariat promotes and co-ordinates assistance to National Societies in developing their basic structure and their services to the community. From 2000 the Secretariat underwent a process of restructuring. In 2003 there were some 230 staff at the Secretariat, employed in the following divisions (created in 2000): programme and co-ordination, disaster management and co-ordination, knowledge-sharing, monitoring and evaluation, advocacy and communication, and corporate services.

Secretary-General: DIDIER J. CHERPITEL (France).

Activities

In October 1999 the Assembly adopted Strategy 2010, outlining the Federation's objectives and strategies for the next 10 years, in order to address new demands placed on it, for example by the proliferation of other humanitarian groups, restricted finance, and pressure from donors for efficiency, transparency and results. The Strategy involved a significant restructuring of the organization.

DISASTER RESPONSE

The Federation supports the establishment of emergency response units, which aim to act effectively and independently to meet the needs of victims of natural or man-made disasters. The units cover basic health care provision, referral hospitals, water sanitation, logistics, telecommunications and information units. The Federation advises National Societies in relief health. In the event of a disaster the following areas are covered: communicable disease alleviation and vaccination; psychological support and stress management; health education; the provision of medicines; and the organization of mobile clinics and nursing care. The Societies also distribute food and clothing to those in need and assist in the provision of shelter and adequate sanitation facilities and in the management of refugee camps.

DEVELOPMENT

The Federation undertakes capacity-building activities with the National Societies to train and develop staff and volunteers and to improve management structures and processes, in particular in the area of disaster-preparedness. Blood donor programmes are often undertaken by National Societies, sometimes in conjunction with WHO. The Federation supports the promotion of these programmes and the implementation of quality standards. Other activities in the health sector aim to strengthen existing health services and promote community-based health care and first aid; the prevention of HIV/AIDS and substance abuse; and health education and family planning initiatives. The Federation also promotes the establishment and development of education and service programmes for children and for other more vulnerable members of society, including the elderly and disabled. Education projects support the promotion of humanitarian values.

Finance

The permanent Secretariat of the Federation is financed by the contributions of member Societies on a pro-rata basis. Each relief action is financed by separate, voluntary contributions, and development programme projects are also financed on a voluntary basis.

Publications

Annual Report.

Handbook of the International Red Cross and Red Crescent Movement (with the ICRC).

Red Cross, Red Crescent (quarterly, English, French and Spanish).

Weekly News.

World Disasters Report (annually).

Newsletters on several topics; various guides and manuals for Red Cross and Red Crescent activities.

INTERNATIONAL SEABED AUTHORITY

Address: 14–20 Port Royal St, Kingston, Jamaica.

Telephone: 922-9105; **fax:** 922-0195; **e-mail:** postmaster@isa.org.jm; **internet:** www.isa.org.jm.

The Authority is an autonomous international organization established in accordance with the 1982 United Nations Convention on the Law of the Sea and 1994 Agreement Relating to the Implementation of Part XI of the Convention. The Authority was founded in November 1994 and became fully operational in June 1996.

Organization

(April 2003)

ASSEMBLY

The Assembly is the supreme organ of the Authority, consisting of representatives of all member states. It formulates policies, approves the budget and elects Council members. The first session of the Assembly was initiated in November 1994 and was continued at a meeting in February/March 1995. The session was concluded in August 1995, having failed to reach agreement on the composition of the Council (see below) and to elect a Secretary-General of the Authority. In March 1996 the Assembly concluded the first part of its second session, having constituted the 36-member Council and elected, by consensus, the first Secretary-General of the Authority. The seventh session of the Assembly was held in August 2002.

COUNCIL

The Council, elected by the Assembly, acts as the executive organ of the Authority. It consists of 36 members, comprising the four states that are the largest importers or consumers of seabed minerals, the four largest investors in seabed minerals, the four major exporters of seabed minerals, six developing countries representing special interests, and 18 members covering all the geographical regions.

LEGAL AND TECHNICAL COMMISSION

The Legal and Technical Commission, comprising 24 experts, assists the Council by making recommendations concerning sea-bed activities, assessing the environmental implications of activities in the area and proposing measures to protect the marine environment.

FINANCE COMMITTEE

The Committee, comprising 15 experts, was established to make recommendations to the Assembly and the Council on all financial and budgetary issues.

SECRETARIAT

The Secretariat provides administrative services to all the bodies of the Authority and implements the relevant work programmes. It comprises the Office of the Secretary-General, Offices of Resources and Environmental Monitoring, Legal Affairs, and Administration and Management. Under the terms of the 1994 Agreement Relating to the Implementation of Part XI of the Convention, the Secretariat is performing the functions of the Enterprise, the organ through which the Authority carries out deep sea-bed mining operations (directly or through joint ventures). It is envisaged that the Enterprise will eventually operate independently of the Secretariat.

Secretary-General: SATYA N. NANDAN (Fiji).

Activities

The Authority, functioning as an autonomous international organization in relationship with the UN, implements the Convention on the Law of the Sea (which was adopted in April 1982 and entered into force in November 1994). All states party to the Convention (142 at March 2003) are members. The Convention covers the uses of ocean space: navigation and overflight, resource exploration and exploitation, conservation and pollution, and fishing and shipping; as well as governing conduct on the oceans; defining maritime zones; establishing rules for delineating sea boundaries; assigning legal rights, duties and responsibilities to states; and providing machinery for the settlement of disputes. Its main provisions are as follows:

Coastal states are allowed sovereignty over their territorial waters of up to 12 nautical miles in breadth; foreign vessels are to be allowed 'innocent passage' through these waters.

Ships and aircraft of all states are allowed 'transit passage' through straits used for international navigation.

Archipelagic states (composed of islands) have sovereignty over a sea area enclosed by straight lines drawn between the outermost points of the islands.

Coastal states and inhabited islands are entitled to proclaim a 200-mile exclusive economic zone with respect to natural resources and jurisdiction over certain activities (such as protection and preservation of the environment), and rights over the adjacent continental shelf, up to 350 miles from the shore under specified circumstances.

All states have freedom of navigation, overflight, scientific research and fishing on the high seas, but must co-operate in measures to conserve living resources.

A 'parallel system' is to be established for exploiting the international seabed, where all activities are to be supervised by the International Seabed Authority.

States are bound to control pollution and co-operate in forming preventive rules, and incur penalties for failing to combat pollution.

Marine scientific research in the zones under national jurisdiction is subject to the prior consent of the coastal state, but consent may be denied only under specific circumstances.

States must submit disputes on the application and interpretation of the Convention to a compulsory procedure entailing decisions binding on all parties. An International Tribunal for the Law of the Sea is to be established.

In July 1994 the UN General Assembly adopted the Agreement Relating to the Implementation of Part XI of the Convention. The original Part XI, concerning the exploitation of the international ocean bed, and particularly the minerals to be found there (chiefly manganese, cobalt, copper and nickel), envisaged as the 'common heritage of mankind', had not been supported by the USA and other industrialized nations on the grounds that countries possessing adequate technology for deep-sea mining would be insufficiently represented in the Authority; that the operations of private mining consortia would be unacceptably limited by the stipulations that their technology should be shared with the Authority's 'Enterprise' and that production should be limited in order to protect land-based mineral producers. Under the 1994 Agreement there was to be no mandatory transfer of technology, the Enterprise was to operate according to commercial principles and there were to be no production limits, although a compensation fund was to assist land-

based producers adversely affected by seabed mining. Several industrial nations then ratified the Convention and Agreement (which entered into force in July 1996), although the USA had not yet ratified either by early 2003. An agreement on the implementation of the provisions of the Convention relating to the conservation and management of straddling and highly migratory fish stocks was opened for signature in December 1995 and entered into force in December 2001.

In July 2000 the Authority adopted the Regulations for Prospecting and Exploration for Polymetallic Nodules in the Area. In 2001 and 2002, pursuant to the Regulations, exploration contracts were signed with six out of seven registered pioneer investors who had submitted plans of work for deep seabed exploration. During 1998–2002 the Authority organized five workshops on (i) development of guide-lines for the assessment of the possible environmental impacts arising from exploration for polymetallic nodules; (ii) proposed technologies for deep seabed mining of polymetallic nodules; (iii) the available knowledge on mineral resources other than polymetallic nodules in the deep seabed; (iv) a standardized system of data interpretation; and (v) international co-operation and collaboration in marine scientific research on the deep oceans. A sixth workshop was scheduled to be held in May 2003 on the establishment of a geologic model for the assessment of polymetallic nodule resources in the Clarion-Clipperton Fracture Zone (CCFZ) of the equatorial north Pacific Ocean. The Authority is developing a database on polymetallic nodules (POLYDAT), and has also made significant progress towards the establishment of a central data repository for all marine minerals in the seabed.

Finance

The Authority's budget is the responsibility of the Finance Committee. The budget for the Authority for the biennium 2003–04 was US $10.5m. The administrative expenses of the Authority are met by assessed contributions of its members.

Publications

Handbook (annually).

The Law of the Sea: Compendium of Basic Documents.

Selected decisions of sessions of the Authority, consultations, documents, rules of procedure, etc.

Associated Institutions

The following were also established under the terms of the Convention:

Commission on the Limits of the Continental Shelf: Division for Ocean Affairs and the Law of the Sea, Room DC2-0450, United Nations, New York, NY 10017, USA; tel. (212) 963-3966; fax (212) 963-5847; e-mail doalos@un.org; internet www.un.org/Depts/los/clcs_new/clcs_home.htm; 21 members, serving a five-year term (the first election of members took place in March 1997 and the second was held in April 2002); responsible for making recommendations regarding the establishment of the outer limits of the continental shelf of a coastal state, where the limit extends beyond 200 nautical miles (370 km).

International Tribunal for the Law of the Sea: Am internationalen Seegerichtshof 1, Hamburg, Germany; tel. (40) 356070; fax (40) 35607275; e-mail itlos@itlos.org; internet www.itlos.org; inaugurated in Oct. 1996; 21 judges; responsible for interpreting the Convention and ruling on disputes brought by states party to the Convention on matters within its jurisdiction; Registrar PHILIPPE GAUTIER (Belgium).

INTER-PARLIAMENTARY UNION—IPU

Address: 5 chemin du Pommier, CP 330, 1218 Le Grand Saconnex/Geneva, Switzerland.
Telephone: (22) 9194150; **fax:** (22) 9194160; **e-mail:** postbox@mail.ipu.org; **internet:** www.ipu.org.

Founded in 1889, the IPU aims to promote peace, co-operation and representative democracy by providing a forum for multilateral political debate between representatives of national parliaments.

MEMBERS

National parliaments of 144 sovereign states; five international parliamentary associations (associate members).

Organization

(April 2003)

INTER-PARLIAMENTARY CONFERENCE

The Conference is the main statutory body of the IPU, comprising eight to 10 representatives from each member parliament. It meets twice a year to discuss current issues in world affairs and to make political recommendations. Other specialized conferences may also be held. The Conference is assisted by the following four plenary Study Committees: on Political Questions, International Security and Disarmament; Parliamentary, Juridical and Human Rights Questions; Economic and Social Questions; and Education, Science, Culture and the Environment.

INTER-PARLIAMENTARY COUNCIL

The Council comprises two representatives of each member parliament, usually from different political groups. It is responsible for approving membership and the annual programme and budget of the IPU, and for electing the Secretary-General. The Council may consider substantive issues and adopt resolutions and policy statements, in particular on the basis of recommendations from its subsidiary bodies.

President: Sergio Páez Verdugo (Chile).

MEETING OF WOMEN PARLIAMENTARIANS

The Meeting is a mechanism for co-ordination between women parliamentarians. Since 1975 the Meeting has been convened twice a year, on the occasion of IPU statutory meetings, to discuss subjects of common interest, to formulate strategies to develop the IPU's women's programme, to strengthen their influence within the organization and to ensure that women are elected to key positions. The Meeting is assisted by a Co-ordinating Committee.

SUBSIDIARY BODIES

In addition to the thematic Study Committees of the IPU Conference, various other committees and groups undertake and co-ordinate IPU activities in specific areas. All these bodies are subsidiary to the IPU Council:

Committee on the Human Rights of Parliamentarians;

Committee for Sustainable Development;

Committee on Middle East Questions;

Group of Facilitators for Cyprus;

Ad hoc Committee to Promote Respect for International and Humanitarian Law;

CSCM Process and CSCM Co-ordinating Committee (concerned with security and co-operation in the Mediterranean);

Co-ordinating Committee of the Meeting of Women MPs;

Gender Partnership Group;

Management Board of the Staff Pension Fund.

EXECUTIVE COMMITTEE

The Committee, comprising 12 members and presided over by the President of the Council, oversees the administration of the IPU and advises the Council on membership, policy and programme, and any other matters referred to it.

SECRETARIAT

Secretary-General: Anders B. Johnsson (Sweden).

Activities

PROMOTION OF REPRESENTATIVE DEMOCRACY

This is one of the IPU's core areas of activity, and covers a wide range of concerns, such as democracy, gender issues, human rights and ethnic diversity, parliamentary action to combat corruption, and links between democracy and economic growth. In September 1997 the Council adopted a Universal Declaration on Democracy. The IPU subsequently published a study entitled *Democracy: Its Principles and Achievements*.

The IPU administers a Programme for the Study and Promotion of Representative Institutions, which aims to improve knowledge of the functioning of national parliaments by gathering and disseminating information on their constitutional powers and responsibilities, structure, and membership, and on the electoral systems used. The IPU also organizes international seminars and gatherings for parliamentarians, officials, academics and other experts to study the functioning of parliamentary institutions. A Technical Co-operation Programme aims to mobilize international support in order to improve the capabilities, infrastructure and technical facilities of national parliaments and enhance their effectiveness. Under the Programme, the IPU may provide expert advice on the structure of legislative bodies, staff training, and parliamentary working procedures, and provide technical equipment and other resources. The IPU provided technical assistance for the drafting of Timor-Leste's Constitution, which was adopted by the then East Timor Constituent Assembly in March 2002. In that year the IPU was implementing 11 projects aimed at strengthening the capacity of 10 national parliaments. Plans were under way to establish a Parliamentary Resource Centre at the Union's headquarters.

IPU teams of observers have overseen elections in Namibia, in 1989, in Cambodia (1993), and in El Salvador (1994). Their duties included observing the process of voter registration, the election campaign and voting, and verifying the results. In 1993 the Council resolved that the IPU be present at all national elections organized, supervised or verified by the United Nations. The IPU has reported on the rights and responsibilities of election observers and issued guide-lines on the holding of free and fair elections. These include a *Declaration on Criteria for Free and Fair Elections*, together with a study on the subject, and Codes of Conduct for Elections.

The IPU maintains a special database (PARLINE) on parliaments of the world, giving access to information on the structure and functioning of all existing parliaments, and on national elections. It conducts regular world studies on matters regarding the structure and functioning of parliaments. It also maintains a separate database (PARLIT) comprising literature from around the world on constitutional, electoral and parliamentary matters.

In August/September 2000 the IPU organized the first international conference of speakers of national parliaments.

INTERNATIONAL PEACE AND SECURITY

The IPU aims to promote conflict resolution and international security through political discussion. Certain areas of conflict are monitored by the Union on an ongoing basis (for example, Cyprus and the Middle East), while others are considered as they arise. In the 1990s the IPU was particularly concerned with the situation in the former Yugoslavia, and condemned incidents of violations of humanitarian law and supported efforts to improve the lives of those affected by the conflict. In March 2002 the 107th Inter-Parliamentary Conference urged both sides in the escalating conflict in the Middle East to observe a cease-fire, to resume political negotiations, and to ensure the safety of all Israeli and Palestinian people. An extensive programme of activities is undertaken by the IPU with regard to the Mediterranean region. In June 1992 the first Conference on Security and Co-operation in the Mediterranean (CSCM) took place; the objectives outlined at the Conference have been integrated as a structured process of the IPU. A second CSCM was held in Valletta, Malta, in November 1995, and a third was convened at Marseilles, France, in March/April 2000. Intermediary thematic meetings are held between plenary conferences, while consultations among parties to the CSCM process take place every six months.

The IPU has worked constantly to promote international and regional efforts towards disarmament, as part of the process of enhancing peace and security. Issues that have been discussed by the Conference include nuclear non-proliferation, a ban on testing of nuclear weapons, and a global register of arms transfers.

SUSTAINABLE DEVELOPMENT

The Committee for Sustainable Development guides the IPU's work in this area, with a broad approach of linking economic growth with social, democratic, human welfare and environmental considerations. Issues of world economic and social development on which the IPU has approved recommendations include employment in a globalizing world, the globalization of economy and liberalization of trade, Third World debt and its impact on the integration of those countries affected into the process of globalization, international mass migration and other demographic problems, and the right to food. The IPU co-operates with programmes and agencies of the UN, in particular in the preparation of major socio-economic conferences, including the World Summit for Social Development, which was held in Copenhagen, Denmark, in March 1995, the Fourth World Conference on Women, held in Beijing, People's Republic of China, in September 1995, and the World Food Summit, held in Rome, Italy, in November 1996. In September 1996 a tripartite meeting of parliamentary, governmental and inter-governmental representatives, convened at the UN headquarters in New York, considered legislative measures to pursue the objectives of the World Summit for Social Development; a follow-up meeting was held in March 1999. In November/December 1998 the IPU, in co-operation with FAO, organized an Inter-Parliamentary Conference concerned with 'Attaining the World Food Summit's Objectives through a Sustainable Development Strategy'. The IPU assisted with preparations for the World Food Summit: Five Years Later, held in Rome, Italy, in June 2002.

Activities to protect the environment are undertaken within the framework of sustainable development. In 1984 the first Inter-Parliamentary Conference on the Environment, convened in Nairobi, Kenya, advocated the inclusion of environmental considerations into the development process. The IPU was actively involved in the preparation of the UN Conference on Environment and Development (UNCED), which was held in Rio de Janeiro, Brazil, in June 1992. Subsequently the IPU's environment programme has focused on implementing the recommendations of UNCED, and identifying measures to be taken at parliamentary level to facilitate that process. The IPU also monitors the actual measures taken by national parliaments to pursue the objective of sustainable development, as well as emerging environmental problems. In 1997 the IPU published the *World Directory of Parliamentary Bodies for Environment*.

HUMAN RIGHTS AND HUMANITARIAN LAW

The IPU frequently considers human rights issues and makes relevant recommendations at its statutory Conferences and during specialized meetings, and aims to incorporate human rights concerns, including employment, the rights of minorities, and gender issues, in all areas of activity. A five-member Committee on the Human Rights of Parliamentarians is responsible for the consideration of complaints relating to alleged violations of the human rights of members of parliament, for example state harassment, arbitrary arrest and detention, unfair trail and violation of parliamentary immunity, based on a procedure adopted by the IPU in 1976. The Committee conducts hearings and site missions to investigate a complaint and communicates with the authorities of the country concerned. If no settlement is reached at that stage, the Committee may then publish a report for the Inter-Parliamentary Council and submit recommendations on specific measures to be adopted. During 2002 the Committee addressed 72 cases of human rights violations against current or former members of parliament; of these, some 27 were closed, the majority with a satisfactory settlement.

The IPU works closely with the International Committee of the Red Cross to uphold respect for international humanitarian law. It supports the implementation of the Geneva Conventions and their Additional Protocols, and the adoption of appropriate national legislation. In 1995 the Council adopted a special resolution to establish a reporting mechanism at the parliamentary level to ensure respect for international humanitarian law. Consequently IPU initiated a world survey on legislative action regarding the application of international humanitarian law, as well as efforts to ban anti-personnel land-mines. In April and September 1998 the Council adopted special resolutions on parliamentary action to secure the entry into force and implementation of the Convention on the Prohibition of the Use, Stockpiling, Production and Transfer of Anti-personnel Mines and on their Destruction, which was signed by representatives of some 120 countries meeting in Ottawa, Canada, in December 1997. Further resolutions to that effect were adopted by the Inter-Parliamentary Conference in October 1999 and in April 2001.

In 1998 the IPU published a *World Directory of Parliamentary Human Rights Bodies*

WOMEN IN POLITICS

The IPU aims to promote the participation of women in the political and parliamentary decision-making processes, and, more generally, in all aspects of society. It organizes debates and events on these issues and compiles a statistical database on women in politics, compiled by regular world surveys. The IPU also actively addresses wider issues of concern to women, such as literacy and education, women in armed conflicts, women's contribution to development, and women in the electoral process. The eradication of violence against women was the subject of a special resolution adopted by the Conference in 1991. The Meeting of Women MPs has monitored efforts by national authorities to implement the recommendations outlined in the resolution. In 1996 the IPU promoted the Framework for Model Legislation on Domestic Violence, formulated by the UN Special Rapporteur on the issue, which aimed to assist national parliaments in preparing legislation to safeguard women. At the Fourth World Conference on Women, held in Beijing, in September 1995, the IPU organized several events to bring together parliamentarians and other leading experts, diplomats and officials to promote the rights of women and of children. In February 1997 the IPU organized a Specialized Inter-Parliamentary Conference, in New Delhi, India, entitled 'Towards partnership between men and women in politics'. Following the Conference the IPU decided to establish a Gender Partnership Group, comprising two men and two women, within the Executive Committee, to ensure that IPU activities and decisions serve the interests and needs of all members of the population. The Group was authorized to report to the IPU Council.

The IPU aims to promote the importance of women's role in economic and social development and their participation in politics as a democratic necessity, and recognizes the crucial role of the media in presenting the image of women. Within the context of the 1997 New Delhi Conference, the IPU organized a second Round Table on the Image of Women Politicians in the Media (the first having been convened in November 1989). The debate urged fair and equal representation of women politicians by the media and for governments to revise their communications policies to advance the image of female parliamentarians.

EDUCATION, SCIENCE AND CULTURE

Activities in these sectors are often subject to consideration by statutory Conferences. Resolutions of the Conference have focused on the implementation of educational and cultural policies designed to foster greater respect for demographic values, adopted in April 1993; on bioethics and its implications world-wide for human rights protection, adopted in April 1995; and on the importance of education and culture as prerequisites for securing sustainable development (with particular emphasis on the education of women and the application of new information technologies), necessitating their high priority status in national budgets, adopted in April 2001. Specialized meetings organized by the IPU have included the Asia and Pacific Inter-Parliamentary Conference on 'Science and technology for regional sustainable development', held in Tokyo, Japan, in June 1994, and the Inter-Parliamentary Conference on 'Education, science, culture and communication on the threshold of the 21st century', organized jointly with UNESCO, and held in Paris, France, in June 1996.

Finance

The IPU is financed by its members from public funds. The 2003 annual budget totalled 9.5m. Swiss francs. In addition external financial support, primarily from UNDP, is received for some special activities.

Publications

Activities of the Inter-Parliamentary Union (annually).

IPU Information Brochure (annually).

World Directory of Parliaments (annually).

The World of Parliaments (quarterly).

Other handbooks, reports and surveys, documents, conference proceedings.

ISLAMIC DEVELOPMENT BANK

Address: POB 5925, Jeddah 21432, Saudi Arabia.

Telephone: (2) 6361400; **fax:** (2) 6366871; **e-mail:** idbarchives@isdb.org.sa; **internet:** www.isdb.org.

The Bank is an international financial institution that was established following a conference of Ministers of Finance of member countries of the Organization of the Islamic Conference (OIC), held in Jeddah in December 1973. Its aim is to encourage the economic development and social progress of member countries and of Muslim communities in non-member countries, in accordance with the principles of the Islamic *Shari'a* (sacred law). The Bank formally opened in October 1975.

MEMBERS

There are 54 members.

Organization

(April 2003)

BOARD OF GOVERNORS

Each member country is represented by a governor, usually its Minister of Finance, and an alternate. The Board of Governors is the supreme authority of the Bank, and meets annually. The 27th Annual Meeting was held in Ouagadougou, Burkina Faso, in October 2002.

BOARD OF EXECUTIVE DIRECTORS

The Board consists of 14 members, seven of whom are appointed by the seven largest subscribers to the capital stock of the Bank; the remaining seven are elected by Governors representing the other subscribers. Members of the Board of Executive Directors are elected for three-year terms. The Board is responsible for the direction of the general operations of the Bank.

ADMINISTRATION

In addition to the President of the Bank, there are three Vice-Presidents, responsible for Operations, Trade and Policy, and Finance and Administration.

President of the Bank and Chairman of the Board of Executive Directors: Dr AHMED MOHAMED ALI.

Vice-President Operations: Dr AMADOU BOUBACAR CISSE.

Vice-President Trade and Policy: Dr SYED JAAFAR AZNAN.

Vice-President Finance and Administration: MUZAFAR AL HAJ MUZAFAR.

REGIONAL OFFICES

Kazakhstan: c/o Director, External Aid Co-ordination Dept, 93–95 Ablay-Khan Ave, 480091 Almaty; tel. (3272) 62-18-68; fax (3272) 69-61-52; Dir ZEINAL ABIDIN.

Malaysia: Level 11, Front Wing, Bank Industri, Jalan Sultan Ismail, POB 13671, 50818 Kuala Lumpur; tel. (3) 2946627; fax (3) 2946626; Dir SALEH AMRAN BIN JAMAN (acting).

Morocco: 177 Ave John Kennedy, Souissi 10105, POB 5003, Rabat; tel. (7) 757191; fax (7) 775726; Dir HANI SALIM SUNBUL.

FINANCIAL STRUCTURE

The authorized capital of the Bank is 6,000m. Islamic Dinars (divided into 600,000 shares, having a value of 10,000 Islamic Dinars each). The Islamic Dinar (ID) is the Bank's unit of account and is equivalent to the value of one Special Drawing Right of the IMF (SDR 1 = US \$1.35930 at 26 March 2003).

Subscribed capital amounts to ID 4,000m.

SUBSCRIPTIONS

(million Islamic Dinars, as at 5 April 2000)

Afghanistan	5.00	Maldives	2.50
Albania	2.50	Mali	4.92
Algeria	124.26	Mauritania	4.92
Azerbaijan	4.92	Morocco	24.81
Bahrain	7.00	Mozambique	2.50
Bangladesh	49.29	Niger	12.41
Benin	4.92	Oman	13.78
Brunei	12.41	Pakistan	124.26
Burkina Faso	12.41	Palestine	9.85
Cameroon	12.41	Qatar	49.23
Chad	4.92	Saudi Arabia	997.17
Comoros	2.50	Senegal	12.42
Djibouti	2.50	Sierra Leone	2.50
Egypt	346.00	Somalia	2.50
Gabon	14.77	Sudan	19.69
The Gambia	2.50	Suriname	2.50
Guinea	12.41	Syria	5.00
Guinea-Bissau	2.50	Tajikistan	2.50
Indonesia	124.26	Togo	2.50
Iran	349.97	Tunisia	9.85
Iraq	13.05	Turkey	315.47
Jordan	19.89	Turkmenistan	2.50
Kazakhstan	2.50	Uganda	12.41
Kuwait	496.64	United Arab	
Kyrgyzstan	2.50	Emirates	283.03
Lebanon	4.92	Yemen	24.81
Libya	400.00		
Malaysia	79.56	**Total**	**4,060.54**

* Côte d'Ivoire became a member of the Bank after this date.

Activities

The Bank adheres to the Islamic principle forbidding usury, and does not grant loans or credits for interest. Instead, its methods of project financing are: provision of interest-free loans (with a service fee), mainly for infrastructural projects which are expected to have a marked impact on long-term socio-economic development; provision of technical assistance (e.g. for feasibility studies); equity participation in industrial and agricultural projects; leasing operations, involving the leasing of equipment such as ships, and instalment sale financing; and profit-sharing operations. Funds not immediately needed for projects are used for foreign trade financing. Under the Import Trade Financing Operations (ITFO) scheme, funds are used for importing commodities for development purposes (i.e. raw materials and intermediate industrial goods, rather than consumer goods), with priority given to the import of goods from other member countries (see table). The Longer-term Trade Financing Scheme (LTTFS) was introduced in 1987/88 to provide financing for the export of non-traditional and capital goods. During AH 1419 the LTTFS was renamed the Export Financing Scheme (EFS). A special programme under the EFS became operational in AH 1419, on the basis of a memorandum of understanding signed between the Bank and the Arab Bank for Economic Development in Africa (BADEA), to finance Arab exports to non-Arab League members of the OAU (now African Union).

The Bank's Special Assistance programme was initiated in AH 1400 to support the economic and social development of Muslim communities in non-member countries, in particular in the education and health sectors. It also aimed to provide emergency aid in times of natural disasters, and to assist Muslim refugees throughout the world. Operations undertaken by the Bank are financed by the Waqf Fund (formerly the Special Assistance Account). Other assistance activities include scholarship programmes, technical co-operation projects and the sacrificial meat utilization project.

By 5 April 2000 the Bank had approved a total of ID 4,947.98m. for project financing and technical assistance, a total of ID 11,125.24m. for foreign trade financing, and ID 402.59m. for special assistance operations, excluding amounts for cancelled operations. During the Islamic year 1420 (17 April 1999 to 5 April 2000) the Bank approved a total of ID 1,522.80m., for 230 operations.

The Bank approved 39 loans in the year ending 5 April 2000, amounting to ID 179.70m. (compared with 38 loans, totalling ID 159.79m., in the previous year). These loans supported projects concerned with the construction and modernization of schools and health centres, infrastructural improvements, and agricultural developments. During the year ending 5 April 2000 the Bank's disbursements totalled ID 871m., bringing the total cumulative disbursements since the Bank began operations to ID 11,010m.

Operations approved, Islamic year 1420
(17 April 1999–5 April 2000)

Type of operation	Number of operations	Total amount (million Islamic Dinars)
Ordinary operations	112	725.49
Project financing . . .	77	718.31
Technical assistance . .	35	7.19
Trade financing operations*. .	64	805.85
Waqf Fund operations . .	54	21.46
Total †	230	1,522.80

* Including ITFO, the EFS, the Islamic Bank's Portfolio and the UIF.
† Excluding cancelled operations.

Project financing and technical assistance by sector, Islamic year 1420
(17 April 1999–5 April 2000)

Sector	Number of operations	Amount (million Islamic Dinars)	%
Agriculture and agro-industry	18	87.51	12.1
Industry and mining . .	4	71.40	9.8
Transport and communications . . .	17	99.25	13.7
Public utilities	18	222.18	30.6
Social sectors	39	183.74	25.3
Financial services/Other* .	16	61.41	8.5
Total †	112	725.49	100.0

* Mainly approved amounts for Islamic banks.
† Excluding cancelled operations.

During AH 1420 the Bank approved 35 technical assistance operations for 19 countries (as well as six regional projects) in the form of grants and loans, amounting to ID 7.19m.

Import trade financing approved during the Islamic year 1420 amounted to ID 651.34m. for 39 operations in 12 member countries. By the end of that year cumulative import trade financing amounted to ID 9,480.37m., of which 37.4% was for imports of crude petroleum, 26.4% for intermediate industrial goods, 7.5% for vegetable oil and 6.4% for refined petroleum products. Export financing approved under the EFS amounted to ID 61.32m. for 15 operations in nine countries in AHh 1420. In the same year the Bank's Portfolio for Investment and Development, established in AH 1407 (1986–87), approved eight operations amounting to US $106.6m. (or approximately ID 79.1m.). Since its introduction, the Portfolio has approved net financing operations amounting to $1,490.1m. (or ID 1,106.0m.).

The Bank's Unit Investment Fund (UIF) became operational in 1990, with the aim of mobilizing additional resources and providing a profitable channel for investments conforming to *Shari'a*. The initial issue of the UIF was US $100m., which has subsequently been increased to $325m. The Fund finances mainly private-sector industrial projects in middle-income countries. The UIF also finances short-term trade financing operations: two were approved in AH 1420, amounting to $19.0m. In October 1998 the Bank announced the establishment of a new fund to invest in infrastructure projects in member states. The Bank committed $250m. to the fund, which was to comprise $1,000m. equity capital and a

$500m. Islamic financing facility. In September 1999 the Bank's Board of Executive Directors approved the establishment of an Islamic Corporation for the Development of the Private Sector, which aimed to identify opportunities in the private sector, provide financial products and services compatible with Islamic law, and expand access to Islamic capital markets for private companies in member countries. The Bank was to retain 50% of the authorized capital of $1,000m., with the remainder owned by member countries (30%) and public financial institutions (20%). In November 2001 the Bank signed an agreement with Malaysia, Bahrain, Indonesia and Sudan for the establishment of an Islamic financial market. In April 2002 the Bank, jointly with governors of central banks and the Accounting and Auditing Organization for Islamic Financial Institutions, concluded an agreement, under the auspices of the IMF, for the establishment of an Islamic Financial Services Board. The Board, which was to be located in Kuala Lumpur, Malaysia, was intended to elaborate and harmonize standards for best practices in the regulation and supervision of the Islamic financial services industry.

During AH 1420 the Bank approved 54 Waqf Fund operations, amounting to ID 21.5m. Of the total financing, 28 operations provided assistance for Muslim communities in 18 non-member countries.

By the end of AH 1420 the Bank's scholarships programme for Muslim communities in non-member countries had benefited some 5,343 students, at a cost of ID 27m., since it began in 1983. The Merit Scholarship Programme, initiated in AH 1412 (1991–92), aims to develop scientific, technological and research capacities in member countries through advanced studies and/or research. During the second five-year phase of the initiative, which commenced in January 1997, 20 scholars each year were expected to be placed in academic centres of excellence in Australia, Europe and the USA under the programme. In December 1997 the Board of Executive Directors approved a new scholarship programme designed specifically to assist scholars from 18 least-developed member countries to study for a masters degree in science and technology. A total of 190 scholarships were expected to have been awarded by AH 1423. The Bank's Programme for Technical Co-operation aims to mobilize technical capabilities among member countries and to promote the exchange of expertise, experience and skills through expert missions, training, seminars and workshops. During AH 1420 74 projects were implemented under the programme. The Bank also undertakes the distribution of meat sacrificed by Muslim pilgrims: in AH 1420 meat from approximately 416,699 animals was distributed to the needy in 26 countries.

SUBSIDIARY ORGANS

Islamic Corporation for the Insurance of Investment and Export Credit (ICIEC): POB 15722, Jeddah 21454, Saudi Arabia; tel. (2) 6445666; fax (2) 6379504; e-mail idb.iciec@isdb.org.sa; internet www.iciec.org; f. 1994; aims to promote trade and the flow of investments among member countries of the OIC through the provision of export credit and investment insurance services; auth. cap. ID 100m., subscribed cap. ID 95.0m. (March 2001); Man. Dr ABDEL RAHMAN A. TAHA; Mems: 29 OIC member states.

Islamic Research and Training Institute: POB 9201, Jeddah 21413, Saudi Arabia; tel. (2) 6361400; fax (2) 6378927; e-mail maljarhi@isdb.org.sa; internet www.irti.org; f. 1982 to undertake research enabling economic, financial and banking activities to conform to Islamic law, and to provide training for staff involved in development activities in the Bank's member countries; The Institute also organizes seminars and workshops, and holds training courses aimed at furthering the expertise of government and financial officials in Islamic developing countries; Dir Dr MABID ALI AL-JARHI; Publs *Annual Report, Journal of Islamic Economic Studies*, various research studies, monographs, reports.

Publication

Annual Report.

LATIN AMERICAN INTEGRATION ASSOCIATION—LAIA

(ASOCIACIÓN LATINOAMERICANA DE INTEGRACIÓN—ALADI)

Address: Cebollatí 1461, Casilla 577, 11200 Montevideo, Uruguay.
Telephone: (2) 410-1121; **fax:** (2) 419-0649; **e-mail:** sgaladi@aladi .org; **internet:** www.aladi.org.

The Latin American Integration Association was established in August 1980 to replace the Latin American Free Trade Association, founded in February 1960.

MEMBERS

Argentina	Colombia	Paraguay
Bolivia	Cuba	Peru
Brazil	Ecuador	Uruguay
Chile	Mexico	Venezuela

Observers: People's Republic of China, Costa Rica, Dominican Republic, El Salvador, Guatemala, Honduras, Italy, Nicaragua, Panama, Portugal, Romania, Russia, Spain and Switzerland; also the UN Economic Commission for Latin America and the Caribbean (ECLAC), the UN Development Programme (UNDP), the European Union, the Inter-American Development Bank, the Organization of American States, the Andean Development Corporation, the Inter-American Institute for Co-operation on Agriculture, the Latin American Economic System, and the Pan American Health Organization.

Organization

(April 2003)

COUNCIL OF MINISTERS

The Council of Ministers of Foreign Affairs is responsible for the adoption of the Association's policies. It meets when convened by the Committee of Representatives.

EVALUATION AND CONVERGENCE CONFERENCE

The Conference, comprising plenipotentiaries of the member governments, assesses the Association's progress and encourages negotiations between members. It meets when convened by the Committee of Representatives.

COMMITTEE OF REPRESENTATIVES

The Committee, the permanent political body of the Association, comprises a permanent and a deputy representative from each member country. Permanent observers have been accredited by 15 countries and eight international organizations (see above). The Committee is the main forum for the negotiation of ALADI's initiatives and is responsible for the correct implementation of the Treaty and its supplementary regulations. There are the following auxiliary bodies:

Advisory Commission on Customs Valuation.

Advisory Commission on Financial and Monetary Affairs.

Advisory Council for Export Financing.

Advisory Council for Customs Matters.

Budget Commission.

Commission for Technical Support and Co-operation.

Council for Financial and Monetary Affairs: comprises the Presidents of member states' central banks, who examine all aspects of financial, monetary and exchange co-operation.

Council on Transport for Trade Facilitation.

Entrepreneurial Advisory Council.

Labour Advisory Council.

Meeting of Directors of National Customs Administrations.

Nomenclature Advisory Commission.

Sectoral Councils.

Tourism Council.

GENERAL SECRETARIAT

The General Secretariat is the technical body of the Association; it submits proposals for action, carries out research and evaluates activities. The Secretary-General is elected for a three-year term, which is renewable. There are two Assistant Secretaries-General.

Secretary-General: (2002–05) JUAN FRANCISCO ROJAS PENSO (Venezuela).

Activities

The Latin American Free Trade Association (LAFTA) was an intergovernmental organization, created by the Treaty of Montevideo in February 1960 with the object of increasing trade between the Contracting Parties and of promoting regional integration, thus contributing to the economic and social development of the member countries. The Treaty provided for the gradual establishment of a free-trade area, which would form the basis for a Latin American Common Market. Reduction of tariff and other trade barriers was to be carried out gradually until 1980.

By 1980, however, only 14% of annual trade among members could be attributed to LAFTA agreements, and it was the richest states which were receiving most benefit. In June it was decided that LAFTA should be replaced by a less ambitious and more flexible organization, the Latin American Integration Association (Asociación Latinoamericana de Integración—ALADI), established by the 1980 Montevideo Treaty, which came into force in March 1981, and was fully ratified in March 1982. Instead of across-the-board tariff cuts, the Treaty envisaged an area of economic preferences, comprising a regional tariff preference for goods originating in member states (in effect from 1 July 1984) and regional and partial scope agreements (on economic complementation, trade promotion, trade in agricultural goods, scientific and technical co-operation, the environment, tourism, and other matters), taking into account the different stages of development of the members, and with no definite timetable for the establishment of a full common market.

The members of ALADI are divided into three categories: most developed (Argentina, Brazil and Mexico); intermediate (Chile, Colombia, Peru, Uruguay and Venezuela); and least developed (Bolivia, Cuba—which joined the Association in August 1999, Ecuador and Paraguay), enjoying a special preferential system. In 2000 the value of exports within ALADI amounted to US $42,860m., compared with $34,776m. in 1999. The countries of the Southern Common Market (Mercosur) accounted for more than one-half of this total. The value of exports within ALADI was estimated at $43,210m. in 2001, an increase of only 0.8% compared with the previous year. In 2002 intra-subregional exports declined by 14.9%. By 2004 75% of all intra-ALADI trade was expected to be free of trade restrictions.

Certain LAFTA institutions were retained and adapted by ALADI, e.g. the Reciprocal Payments and Credits Agreement (1965, modified in 1982) and the Multilateral Credit Agreement to Alleviate Temporary Shortages of Liquidity, known as the Santo Domingo Agreement (1969, extended in 1981 to include mechanisms for counteracting global balance-of-payments difficulties and for assisting in times of natural disaster).

By August 1998 98 agreements had entered into force. Seven were 'regional agreements' (in which all member countries participate). These agreements included a regional tariff preference agreement, whereby members allow imports from other member states to enter with tariffs 20% lower than those imposed on imports from other countries, and a Market Opening Lists agreement in favour of the three least developed member states, which provides for the total elimination of duties and other restrictions on imports of certain products. The remaining 91 agreements were 'partial scope agreements' (in which two or more member states participate), including: renegotiation agreements (pertaining to tariff cuts under LAFTA); trade agreements covering particular industrial sectors; the agreements establishing (Mercosur) and the Group of Three (G3); and agreements covering agriculture, gas supply, tourism, environmental protection, books, transport, sanitation and trade facilitation. A new system of tariff nomenclature, based on the 'harmonized system', was adopted from 1 January 1990 as a basis for common trade negotiations and statistics. General regimes on safeguards and rules of origin entered into force in 1987.

The Secretariat convenes meetings of entrepreneurs in various private industrial sectors, to encourage regional trade and co-operation. In early 2001 ALADI conducted a survey on small and medium-sized enterprises in order to advise the Secretary-General in formulating a programme to assist those businesses and enhance their competitiveness.

A feature of ALADI is its 'outward' projection, allowing for multilateral links or agreements with Latin American non-member countries or integration organizations, and with other developing countries or economic groups outside the continent. In February 1994 the Council of Ministers of Foreign Affairs urged that ALADI should become the co-ordinating body for the various bilateral, multilateral and regional accords (with the Andean Community, Mercosur and G3, etc.), with the aim of eventually forming a region-wide common market. The General Secretariat initiated studies in preparation for a programme to undertake this co-ordinating work. At the same meeting in February there was a serious disagreement regarding the proposed adoption of a protocol to the Montevideo Treaty to enable Mexico to participate in the North American Free Trade Agreement (NAFTA), while remaining a member of ALADI. Brazil, in particular, opposed such a solution. However, in June the first Interpretative Protocol to the Montevideo Treaty was signed by the Ministers of Foreign Affairs: the Protocol allows member states to establish preferential trade agreements with developed nations, with a temporary waiver of the most-favoured nation clause (article 44 of the Treaty), subject to the negotiation of unilateral compensation.

Mercosur (which comprises Argentina, Brazil, Paraguay and Uruguay, with Chile and Bolivia as associate members) aims to conclude free-trade agreements with the other members of ALADI. In March 2001 ALADI signed a co-operation agreement with the Andean Community to facilitate the exchange of information and consolidate regional and subregional integration. In December 2002 Mercosur and the Andean Commmunity determined to merge their respective free trade areas by 2004. Those ALADI member states remaining outside Mercosur and the Andean Community—Cuba, Chile and Mexico—would be permitted to apply to join the larger free trade zone.

Publications

Empresarios en la Integración (monthly, in Spanish).
Noticias ALADI (monthly, in Spanish).
Estadísticas y Comercio (quarterly, in Spanish).
Reports, studies, brochures, texts of agreements.

LEAGUE OF ARAB STATES

Address: POB 11642, Arab League Bldg, Tahrir Square, Cairo, Egypt.
Telephone: (2) 575-0511; **fax:** (2) 574-0331; **internet:** www.arableagueonline.org/arableague/index_en.jsp.

The League of Arab States (more generally known as the Arab League) is a voluntary association of sovereign Arab states, designed to strengthen the close ties linking them and to co-ordinate their policies and activities and direct them towards the common good of all the Arab countries. It was founded in March 1945.

MEMBERS

Algeria	Lebanon	Somalia
Bahrain	Libya*	Sudan
Comoros	Mauritania	Syria
Djibouti	Morocco	Tunisia
Egypt	Oman	United Arab
Iraq	Palestine†	Emirates
Jordan	Qatar	Yemen
Kuwait	Saudi Arabia	

* In October 2002 Libya announced that it was to withdraw from the League.
† Palestine is considered an independent state, and therefore a full member of the League.

Organization

(April 2003)

COUNCIL

The supreme organ of the Arab League, the Council consists of representatives of the member states, each of which has one vote, and a representative for Palestine. The Council meets ordinarily every March, normally at the League headquarters, at the level of heads of state ('kings, heads of state and emirs'), and in March and September at the level of foreign ministers. The summit-level meeting reviews all issues related to Arab national security strategies, co-ordinates supreme policies of the Arab states towards regional and international issues, reviews recommendations and reports submitted to it by meetings at foreign minister level, appoints the Secretary-General of the League, and is mandated to amend the League's Charter. Decisions of the summit-level Council are passed on a consensus basis. Foreign ministers' meetings assess the implementation of summit resolutions, prepare relevant reports, and make arrangements for subsequent summits. Committees comprising a smaller group of foreign ministers may be appointed to follow up closely summit resolutions. Extraordinary summit-level meetings may be held at the request of one member state or the Secretary-General, if approved by a two-thirds majority of member states. Extraordinary sessions of ministers of foreign affairs may be held at the request of two member states or of the Secretary-General. The presidency of ordinary meetings is rotated in accordance with the alphabetical order of the League's member states. Unanimous decisions of the Council are binding upon all member states of the League; majority decisions are binding only on those states which have accepted them.

The Council is supported by technical and specialized committees advising on financial and administrative affairs, information affairs and legal affairs. In addition, specialized ministerial councils have been established to formulate common policies for the regulation and the advancement of co-operation in the following sectors: communications; electricity; environment; health; housing and construction; information; interior; justice; social affairs; tourism; transportation; and youth and sports.

GENERAL SECRETARIAT

The administrative and financial offices of the League. The Secretariat carries out the decisions of the Council, and provides financial and administrative services for the personnel of the League. General departments comprise: the Bureau of the Secretary-General, Arab Affairs, Economic Affairs, Information Affairs, Legal Affairs, Palestine Affairs, Political International Affairs, Military Affairs, Social Affairs, Administrative and Financial Affairs, and Internal Audit. In addition, there is a Documentation and Information Centre, an Arab League Centre in Tunis, an Arab Fund for Technical Assistance in African States, a Higher Arab Institute for Translation in Algiers, a Music Academy in Baghdad, and a Special Bureau for Boycotting Israel, based in Damascus, Syria (see below). The following bodies have also been established: an administrative court, an investment arbitration board and a higher auditing board.

The Secretary-General is appointed at summit meetings of the Council by a two-thirds' majority of the member states, for a five-year, renewable term. He appoints the Assistant Secretaries-General and principal officials, with the approval of the Council. He has the rank of ambassador, and the Assistant Secretaries-General have the rank of ministers plenipotentiary.

Secretary-General: AMR MUHAMMAD MOUSSA (Egypt).

DEFENCE AND ECONOMIC CO-OPERATION

Groups established under the Treaty of Joint Defence and Economic Co-operation, concluded in 1950 to complement the Charter of the League.

Arab Unified Military Command: f. 1964 to co-ordinate military policies for the liberation of Palestine.

Economic and Social Council: compares and co-ordinates the economic policies of the member states; supervises the activities of the Arab League's specialized agencies. The Council is composed of ministers of economic affairs or their deputies; decisions are taken by majority vote. The first meeting was held in 1953. In February 1997 the Economic and Social Council adopted the Executive Programme of the League's (1981) Agreement to Facilitate and Develop Trade Among Arab Countries, with a view to establishing a Greater Arab Free Trade Area (see below).

Joint Defence Council: supervises implementation of those aspects of the treaty concerned with common defence. Composed of foreign and defence ministers; decisions by a two-thirds' majority vote of members are binding on all.

Permanent Military Commission: established 1950; composed of representatives of army general staffs; main purpose: to draw up plans of joint defence for submission to the Joint Defence Council.

ARAB DETERRENT FORCE

Created in June 1976 by the Arab League Council to supervise successive attempts to cease hostilities in Lebanon, and afterwards to maintain the peace. The mandate of the Force has been successively renewed. The Arab League summit conference in October 1976 agreed that costs were to be paid in the following percentage contributions: Saudi Arabia and Kuwait 20% each, the United Arab Emirates 15%, Qatar 10% and other Arab states 35%.

OTHER INSTITUTIONS OF THE LEAGUE

Other bodies established by resolutions adopted by the Council of the League:

Administrative Tribunal of the Arab League: f. 1964; began operations 1966.

Arab Fund for Technical Assistance to African Countries: f. 1975 to provide technical assistance for development projects by providing African and Arab experts, grants for scholarships and training, and finance for technical studies.

Higher Auditing Board: comprises representatives of seven member states, elected every three years; undertakes financial and administrative auditing duties.

Investment Arbitration Board: examines disputes between member states relating to capital investments.

Special Bureau for Boycotting Israel: POB 437, Damascus, Syria; f. 1951 to prevent trade between Arab countries and Israel, and to enforce a boycott by Arab countries of companies outside the region that conduct trade with Israel.

SPECIALIZED AGENCIES

All member states of the Arab League are also members of the Specialized Agencies, which constitute an integral part of the Arab League. (See also entries on Arab Fund for Economic and Social Development, the Arab Monetary Fund, Council of Arab Economic Unity and the Organization of Arab Petroleum Exporting Countries)

Arab Academy for Science, Technology and Maritime Transport—AASTMT: POB 1029, Alexandria, Egypt; tel. (3) 5602388; fax (3) 5622525; internet www.aast.edu/web/main.jsp; f. 1975 as Arab Maritime Transport Academy; provides specialized training in marine transport, engineering, technology and management; Dir-Gen. Dr GAMAL ED-DIN MOUKHTAR; publs *Maritime Research Bulletin* (monthly), *Journal of the Arab Academy for Science Technology and Maritime Transport* (2 a year).

Arab Administrative Development Organization—ARADO: POB 2692 Al-Horreia, Heliopolis, Cairo, Egypt; tel. (2) 4175401; fax (2) 4175407; e-mail arado@arado.org; internet www.arado.org; f. 1961 (as Arab Organization of Administrative Sciences), became operational in 1969; administration development, training, consultancy, research and studies, information, documentation; promotes Arab and international co-operation in administrative sciences; includes Arab Network of Administrative Information; 20 Arab state members; library of 26,000 volumes, 400 periodicals; Dir-Gen. Dr MOHAMED IBRAHIM AL-TWEGRI; publs *Arab Journal of Administration* (biannual), *Management Newsletter* (quarterly), research series, training manuals.

Arab Atomic Energy Agency—AAEA: POB 402, al-Manzah 1004, 1004 Tunis, Tunisia; tel. (71) 709464; fax (71) 711330; e-mail aaea@aaea.org.tn; f. 1988 to co-ordinate research into the peaceful uses of atomic energy; Dir-Gen. Prof. Dr MAHMOUD NASREDDINE (Lebanon); publs *The Atom and Development* (quarterly), other publs in the field of nuclear sciences and their applications in industry, biology, medicine, agriculture, food irradiation and seawater desalination.

Arab Bank for Economic Development in Africa (Banque arabe pour le développement économique en Afrique—BADEA): Sayed Abd ar-Rahman el-Mahdi St, POB 2640, Khartoum 11111, Sudan; tel. (11) 773646; fax (11) 770600; e-mail badea@badea.org; internet www.badea.org; f. 1973 by Arab League; provides loans and grants to African countries to finance development projects; paid-up cap. US $1,500m. (Dec. 2001); ; in 2001 the Bank approved loans and grants totalling $124m.; by the end of 2001 total loans and grants approved since funding activities began in 1975 amounted to $2,211.3m.; subscribing countries: all countries of Arab League, except the Comoros, Djibouti, Somalia and Yemen; recipient countries: all countries of the African Union, except those belonging to the Arab League; Chair. AHMAD ABDALLAH AL-AKEIL (Saudi Arabia); Dir-Gen. MEDHAT SAMI LOTFY (Egypt); publs *Annual Report Co-operation for Development* (quarterly), Studies on Afro-Arab co-operation, periodic brochures.

Arab Centre for the Study of Arid Zones and Dry Lands—ACSAD: POB 2440, Damascus, Syria; tel. (11) 5743039; fax (11) 5743037; e-mail acsad@net.sy; internet www.acsad.org; f. 1971 to conduct regional research and development programmes related to water and soil resources, plant and animal production, agro-meteorology, and socio-economic studies of arid zones; the Centre holds conferences and training courses and encourages the exchange of information by Arab scientists; Dir-Gen. Dr ADEL SAFER.

Arab Industrial Development and Mining Organization: rue France, Zanagat Al Khatawat, POB 8019, Rabat, Morocco; tel. (7) 772600; fax (7) 772188; e-mail aidmo@arifonet.org.ma; internet www.arifonet.org.ma; f. 1990 by merger of Arab Industrial Development Organization, Arab Organization for Mineral Resources and Arab Organization for Standardization and Metrology; comprises a 13-member Executive Council, a High Consultative Committee of Standardization, a High Committee of Mineral Resources and a Co-ordination Committee for Arab Industrial Research Centres; a Ministerial Council, of ministers of member states responsible for industry, meets every two years; Dir-Gen. TALA'AT BEN DAFER; publs *Arab Industrial Development* (monthly and quarterly newsletters).

Arab Labour Organization: POB 814, Cairo, Egypt; f. 1965 for co-operation between member states in labour problems; unification of labour legislation and general conditions of work wherever possible; research; technical assistance; social insurance; training, etc. the organization has a tripartite structure: governments, employers and workers; Dir-Gen. IBRAHIM GUDIR; publs *ALO Bulletin* (monthly), *Arab Labour Review* (quarterly), *Legislative Bulletin* (annually), series of research reports and studies concerned with economic and social development issues in the Arab world.

Arab League Educational, Cultural and Scientific Organization—ALECSO: POB 1120, Tunis, Tunisia; tel. (71) 784-466; fax (71) 784-965; e-mail alecso@email.ati.tn; internet www.slis.uwm.edu/ALECSO/; f. 1970 to promote and co-ordinate educational, cultural and scientific activities in the Arab region; Regional units: Arab Centre for Arabization, Translation, Authorship, and Publication—Damascus, Syria; Institute of Arab Manuscript—Cairo, Egypt; Institute of Arab Research and Studies—Cairo, Egypt; Khartoum Institute for Arabic Language—Khartoum, Sudan; and the Arabization Co-ordination Bureau—Rabat, Morocco; Dir-Gen. Dr MONGI BOUSNINA; publs *Arab Journal of Culture Arab Journal of Science Arab Bulletin of Publications Statistical Yearbook Journal of the Institute of Arab Manuscripts Arab Magazine for Information Science.*

Arab Organization for Agricultural Development—AOAD: St no. 7, Al-Amarat, POB 474, Khartoum, Sudan; tel. (11) 472176; fax (11) 471402; e-mail aoad@sudanmail.net; internet www.aoad.org; f. 1970; began operations in 1972 to contribute to co-operation in agricultural activities, and in the development of natural and human resources for agriculture; compiles data, conducts studies, training and food security programmes; includes Arab Institute of Forestry and Range, Arab Centre for Information and Early Warning, and Arab Centre for Agricultural Documentation; Dir-Gen. Dr SALEM AL-LOZI; publs *Agricultural Statistics Yearbook Annual Report on Agricultural Development the State of Arab Food Security* (annually), *Agriculture and Development in the Arab World* (quarterly), *Accession Bulletin* (every 2 months), *AOAD Newsletter* (monthly), *Arab Agricultural Research Journal Arab Journal for Irrigation Water Management* (2 a year).

Arab Satellite Communications Organization—ARABSAT: King Fahd Express Rd (Ollaya St), POB 1038, Riyadh, 11431 Saudi Arabia; tel. (1) 4820000; fax (1) 4887999; e-mail albidnah@arabsat.com; internet www.arabsat.com; f. 1976; regional satellite telecommunications organization providing television, telephone and data exchange services to members and private users; operates three satellites, which cover all Arab and Mediterranean countries, controlled by a Primary Control Station in Dirab, Saudi Arabia, and a Secondary Control Facility, based in Dkhila, Tunisia; Dir-Gen. SAAD IBN ABD AL-AZIZ AL-BIDNAH (Saudi Arabia).

Arab States Broadcasting Union—ASBU: POB 250, 1080 Tunis Cedex; 6 rue des Entrepreneurs, zone industrielle Charguia 2, Ariana Aéroport, Tunisia; tel. (71) 703854; fax (71) 703855; e-mail asbu@asbu.intl.tn; internet www.asbu.org.tn; f. 1969 to promote Arab fraternity, co-ordinate and study broadcasting subjects, to exchange expertise and technical co-operation in broadcasting; conducts training and audience research; mems: 21 Arab radio and TV stations and six foreign associates; Exec. Chair. Dr FAYEZ AL SAYEGH (Syria); publ. *ASBU Review* (quarterly).

Inter-Arab Investment Guarantee Corporation: POB 23568, Safat 13096, Kuwait; tel. 4844500; fax 4815741; internet www.iaigc.org; f. 1975; insures Arab investors for non-commercial risks, and export credits for commercial and non-commercial risks; undertakes research and other activities to promote inter-Arab trade and investment; cap. p.u. US $81m., res $168m. (Dec. 2000); mems: 22 Arab governments; Dir-Gen. MAMOUN IBRAHIM HASSAN; publs *News Bulletin* (monthly), *Arab Investment Climate Report* (annually).

External Relations

ARAB LEAGUE OFFICES AND INFORMATION CENTRES ABROAD

Established by the Arab League to co-ordinate work at all levels among Arab embassies abroad.

Austria: Kärntner Ring 17, 1010 Vienna; e-mail arab.league .vienna@aon.at.

Belgium: 28 ave de l'Uruguay, 1000 Brussels; e-mail ligue.etats .arabes@skynet.be.

China, People's Republic: 1-14-2 Lian Ma He, Tayuan Diplomatic Building, Beijing 100600; e-mail lasj@a-a.net.cn.

Ethiopia: POB 5768, Addis Ababa; e-mail arague.et@telecom.net .et.

France: 36 rue Fortuny, 75017 Paris; e-mail leap@pelnet.com.

Germany: Markgrafenstr. 25, 10117 Berlin.

India: F-63 Poorvo MargVasant Vihar, New Delhi; e-mail las@ mantraonline.com.

Italy: Piazzale delle Belle Arti 6, 001961 Rome; e-mail legaarab@ shareware.it.

Russia: 28 Koniouch Kovskaya, 123242 Moscow; e-mail ligarab@ granit.ru.

Spain: Paseo de la Castellana 180, 60°, 28046 Madrid; e-mail liga .arabe@terra.es.

Switzerland: 9 rue du Valais, 1202 Geneva; e-mail saad.alfarargi@ ties.itu.int.

United Kingdom: 52 Green St, London, W1Y 3RH; e-mail las@ jamia-uk.dmon.co.uk.

USA: 1100 17th St, NW, Suite 602, Washington, DC 20036; 747 Third Ave, 35th Floor, New York, NY 10017 (UN Office); e-mail arableague@aol.com.

Record of Events

1945 Pact of the Arab League signed, March.

1946 Cultural Treaty signed.

1950 Joint Defence and Economic Co-operation Treaty.

1952 Agreements on extradition, writs and letters of request, nationality of Arabs outside their country of origin.

1953 Formation of Economic and Social Council.
Convention on the privileges and immunities of the League.

1954 Nationality Agreement.

1956 Agreement on the adoption of a Common Tariff Nomenclature.

1962 Arab Economic Unity Agreement.

1964 First summit conference of Arab heads of state, Cairo, January.
First meeting of Council of Arab Economic Unity, June. Arab Common Market Agreement endorsed by the Council, August. Second summit conference welcomed establishment of Palestine Liberation Organization (PLO), September.

1969 Fifth summit conference, Rabat. Call for mobilization of all Arab nations against Israel.

1977 Tripoli Declaration, December. Decision of Algeria, Iraq, Libya and Yemen PDR to boycott League meetings in Egypt in response to President Sadat's visit to Israel.

1979 Council meeting resolved to withdraw Arab ambassadors from Egypt; to recommend severance of political and diplomatic relations with Egypt; to suspend Egypt's membership of the League on the date of the signing of its formal peace treaty with Israel (26 March); to transfer the headquarters of the League to Tunis; to condemn US policy regarding its role in concluding the Camp David agreements (in September 1978) and the peace treaty; to halt all bank loans, deposits, guarantees or facilities, as well as all financial or technical contributions and aid to Egypt; to prohibit trade exchanges with the Egyptian state and with private establishments dealing with Israel.

1981 In November the 12th summit conference, held in Fez, Morocco, was suspended owing to disagreement over a Saudi Arabian proposal known as the Fahd Plan, which included not only the Arab demands on behalf of the Palestinians, as

approved by the UN General Assembly, but also an implied *de facto* recognition of Israel.

1982 The 12th summit conference was reconvened in September. It adopted a peace plan, which demanded Israel's withdrawal from territories occupied in 1967, and removal of Israeli settlements in these areas; freedom of worship for all religions in the sacred places; the right of the Palestinian people to self-determination, under the leadership of the PLO; temporary supervision for the West Bank and the Gaza Strip; the creation of an independent Palestinian state, with Jerusalem as its capital; and a guarantee of peace for all the states of the region by the UN Security Council.

1983 The summit meeting due to be held in November was postponed owing to members' differences of opinion concerning Syria's opposition to Yasser Arafat's chairmanship of the PLO, and Syrian support of Iran in the war against Iraq.

1984 In March an emergency meeting established an Arab League committee to encourage international efforts to bring about a negotiated settlement of the Iran–Iraq war. In May ministers of foreign affairs adopted a resolution urging Iran to stop attacking non-belligerent ships and installations in the Gulf region: similar attacks by Iraq were not mentioned.

1985 In August an emergency summit conference was boycotted by Algeria, Lebanon, Libya, Syria and Yemen PDR, while of the other 16 members only nine were represented by their heads of state. Two commissions were set up to mediate in disagreements between Arab states (between Jordan and Syria, Iraq and Syria, Iraq and Libya, and Libya and the PLO).

1986 In July King Hassan of Morocco announced that he was resigning as chairman of the next League summit conference, after criticism by several Arab leaders of his meeting with the Israeli Prime Minister earlier that month. A ministerial meeting, held in October, condemned any attempt at direct negotiation with Israel.

1987 An extraordinary summit conference was held in November, mainly to discuss the war between Iran and Iraq. Contrary to expectations, the participants unanimously agreed on a statement expressing support for Iraq in its defence of its legitimate rights, and criticizing Iran for its procrastination in accepting the UN Security Council Resolution 598 of July, which had recommended a cease-fire and negotiations on a settlement of the conflict. The meeting also stated that the resumption of diplomatic relations with Egypt was a matter to be decided by individual states.

1988 In June a summit conference agreed to provide finance for the PLO to continue the Palestinian uprising in Israeli-occupied territories. It reiterated a demand for the convening of an international conference, attended by the PLO, to seek to bring about a peaceful settlement in the Middle East (thereby implicitly rejecting recent proposals by the US Government for a conference that would exclude the PLO).

1989 In January an Arab League group, comprising six ministers of foreign affairs, began discussions with the two rival Lebanese governments on the possibility of a political settlement in Lebanon. At a summit conference, held in May, Egypt was readmitted to the League. The Conference expressed support for the chairman of the PLO, Yasser Arafat, in his recent peace proposals made before the UN General Assembly, and reiterated the League's support for proposals that an international conference should be convened to discuss the rights of Palestinians: in so doing, it accepted UN Security Council Resolutions 242 and 338 on a peaceful settlement in the Middle East and thus gave tacit recognition to the State of Israel. The meeting also supported Arafat in rejecting Israeli proposals for elections in the Israeli-occupied territories of the West Bank and the Gaza Strip. A new mediation committee was established, with a six-month mandate to negotiate a cease-fire in Lebanon, and to reconvene the Lebanese legislature with the aim of holding a presidential election and restoring constitutional government in Lebanon. In September the principal factions in Lebanon agreed to observe a cease-fire, and the surviving members of the Lebanese legislature (originally elected in 1972) met at Ta'if, in Saudi Arabia, in October, and approved the League's proposed 'charter of national reconciliation'.

1990 In May a summit conference, held in Baghdad, Iraq (which was boycotted by Syria and Lebanon), criticized recent efforts by Western governments to prevent the development of advanced weapons technology in Iraq. In August an emergency summit conference was held to discuss the invasion and annexation of Kuwait by Iraq. Twelve members (Bahrain, Djibouti, Egypt, Kuwait, Lebanon, Morocco, Oman, Qatar, Saudi Arabia, Somalia, Syria and the United Arab Emirates) approved a resolution condemning Iraq's action, and demanding the withdrawal of Iraqi forces from Kuwait and the reinstatement of the Government. The 12 states expressed support for the Saudi Arabian Government's invitation to the USA to send forces to defend Saudi Arabia; they also agreed to impose economic sanctions on Iraq, and to provide troops for an Arab defensive force in Saudi Arabia. The remaining member states, however, condemned the presence of foreign troops in Saudi Arabia, and their ministers of foreign affairs refused to attend a meeting, held at the end of August, to discuss possible solutions to the crisis. The dissenting countries also rejected the decision, taken earlier in the year, to return the League's headquarters from Tunis to Cairo. None the less, the official transfer of the League's headquarters to Cairo took place at the end of October. In November King Hassan of Morocco urged the convening of an Arab summit conference, in an attempt to find an 'Arab solution' to Iraq's annexation of Kuwait. However, the divisions in the Arab world over the issue meant that conditions for such a meeting could not be agreed.

1991 The first meeting of the Arab League since August 1990 took place in March, attended by representatives of all 21 member nations, including Iraq. Discussion of the recently-ended war against Iraq was avoided, in an attempt to re-establish the unity of the League. In September, despite deep divisions between member states, it was agreed that a committee should be formed to co-ordinate Arab positions in preparation for the US-sponsored peace talks between Arab countries and Israel. (In the event, an *ad hoc* meeting, attended by Egypt, Jordan, Syria, the PLO, Saudi Arabia—representing the Gulf Co-operation Council (GCC), and Morocco—representing the Union of the Arab Maghreb, was held in October, prior to the start of the talks.) In December the League expressed solidarity with Libya, which was under international pressure to extradite two government agents who were suspected of involvement in the explosion which destroyed a US passenger aircraft over Lockerbie, United Kingdom, in December 1988.

1992 The League attempted to mediate between the warring factions in Somalia. In March the League appointed a committee to seek to resolve the disputes between Libya and the USA, the United Kingdom and France over the Lockerbie bomb and the explosion which destroyed a French passenger aircraft over Niger in September 1989. The League condemned the UN's decision, at the end of March, to impose sanctions against Libya, and appealed for a negotiated solution. In September the League's Council issued a condemnation of Iran's alleged occupation of three islands in the Persian (Arabian) Gulf that were claimed by the United Arab Emirates, and decided to refer the issue to the UN.

1993 In April the Council approved the creation of a committee to consider the political and security aspects of water supply in Arab countries. In the same month the League pledged its commitment to the Middle East peace talks, but warned that Israel's continued refusal to repatriate the Palestinians based in Lebanon remained a major obstacle to the process. In September the Council admitted the Comoros as the 22nd member of the League. Following the signing of the Israeli-PLO peace accord in September the Council convened in emergency session, at which it approved the agreement, despite opposition from some members, notably Syria. In November it was announced that the League's boycott of commercial activity with Israel was to be maintained.

1994 The League condemned a decision of the GCC, announced in late September, to end the secondary and tertiary trade embargo against Israel, by which member states refuse to trade with international companies which have investments in Israel. A statement issued by the League insisted that the embargo could be removed only on the decision of the Council. Earlier in September the Council endorsed a recommendation that the UN conduct a census of Palestinian refugees, in the absence of any such action taken by the League.

1995 In March Arab ministers of foreign affairs approved a resolution urging Israel to renew the Nuclear Non-Proliferation Treaty (NPT). The resolution stipulated that failure by Israel to do so would cause Arab states to seek to protect legitimate Arab interests by alternative means. In May an extraordinary session of the Council condemned a decision by Israel to confiscate Arab-owned land in East Jerusalem for resettlement. The Israeli Government announced the suspension of its expropriation plans. In September the Council discussed plans for a regional court of justice and for an Arab Code of Honour to prevent the use of force in disputes between Arab states.

1996 In March, following protests by Syria and Iraq that extensive construction work in southern Turkey was restricting water supply in the region, the Council determined that the waters of the Euphrates and Tigris rivers be shared equitably between the three countries. In April an emergency meeting of the Council issued a further endorsement of Syria's position in the dispute with Turkey. The main objective of the meeting, which was convened at the request of Palestine, was to attract international attention to the problem of radiation from an Israeli nuclear reactor. The Council requested an immediate technical inspection of the site by the UN, and further demanded that Israel be obliged to sign the NPT to ensure the eradication of its nuclear weaponry. In June an extraordinary summit conference of League heads of state was convened, the first since 1990, in order to formulate a united Arab response to the election, in May, of a new government in Israel and to the prospects for peace in the Middle East. At the conference, which was attended by heads of state of 13 countries and senior representatives of seven others (Iraq was excluded from the meeting in order to ensure the attendance of the Gulf member states), Israel was urged to honour its undertaking to withdraw from the Occupied Territories, including Jerusalem, and to respect the establishment of an independent Palestinian state, in order to ensure the success of the peace process. A final communiqué of the meeting warned that Israeli co-operation was essential to prevent Arab states' reconsidering their participation in the peace process and the re-emergence of regional tensions. Meanwhile, there were concerns over increasing inter-Arab hostility, in particular between Syria and Jordan, owing to the latter's relations with Israel and allegations of Syrian involvement in recent terrorist attacks against Jordanian targets. In early September the League condemned US missile attacks against Iraq as an infringement of that country's sovereignty. In addition, it expressed concern at the impact on Iraqi territorial integrity of Turkish intervention in the north of Iraq. Later in September the League met in emergency session, following an escalation of civil unrest in Jerusalem and the Occupied Territories. The League urged the UN Security Council to prevent further alleged Israeli aggression against the Palestinians. In November the League criticized Israel's settlement policy, and at the beginning of December convened in emergency session to consider measures to end any expansion of the Jewish population in the West Bank and Gaza.

1997 In March the Council met in emergency session, in response to the Israeli Government's decision to proceed with construction of a new settlement at Har Homa (Jabal Abu-Ghunaim) in East Jerusalem. The Council pledged its commitment to seeking a reversal of the decision and urged the international community to support this aim. At the end of March ministers of foreign affairs of Arab League states agreed to end all efforts to secure normal diplomatic relations with Israel (although binding agreements already in force with Egypt, Jordan and Palestine were exempt) and to close diplomatic offices and missions while construction work continued in East Jerusalem. In addition, ministers recommended reactivating the economic boycott against Israel until comprehensive peace was achieved in the region and suspending Arab participation in the multilateral talks that were initiated in 1991 to further the peace process. Earlier in the year, in February, the Economic and Social Council adopted the Executive Programme of the (1981) Agreement to Facilitate and Develop Trade Among Arab Countries, with a view to creating a Greater Arab Free Trade Area (GAFTA), which aimed to facilitate and develop inter-Arab trade through the reduction and eventual elimination of customs duties over a 10-year period (at a rate of 10% per year), with effect from 1 January 1998. (According to schedule the fifth 10% reduction was achieved in January 2002.) The Council agreed to supervise the implementation of the free trade agenda and formally to review its progress twice a year. In June the League condemned Turkey's military incursion into northern Iraq and demanded a withdrawal of Turkish troops from Iraqi territory. Meeting in September, ministers of foreign affairs of member states advocated a gradual removal of international sanctions against Libya, and agreed that member countries should permit international flights to leave Libya for specific humanitarian and religious purposes and when used for the purposes of transporting foreign nationals. Ministers also voted to pursue the decision, adopted in March, not to strengthen relations with Israel. Several countries urged a formal boycott of the forthcoming Middle East and North Africa economic conference, in protest at the lack of progress in the peace process (for which the League blamed Israel, which was due to participate in the conference). However, the meeting upheld a request by the Qatari Government, the host of the conference, that each member should decide individually whether to attend. In the event, only seven Arab League countries participated in the conference, which was held in Doha in mid-November, while the Secretary-General of the League decided not to attend as the organization's official representative. In November the League criticized the decision of the US Government to impose economic sanctions against Sudan. The League also expressed concern at the tensions arising from Iraq's decision not to co-operate fully with UN weapons inspectors, and held several meetings with representatives of the Iraqi administration in an effort to secure a peaceful conclusion to the impasse.

1998   In early 1998 the Secretary-General of the League condemned the use or threat of force against Iraq and continued to undertake diplomatic efforts to secure Iraq's compliance with UN Security Council resolutions. The League endorsed the agreement concluded between the UN Secretary-General and the Iraqi authorities in late February, and reaffirmed its commitment to facilitating the eventual removal of the international embargo against Iraq. A meeting of the Council in March, attended by ministers of foreign affairs of 16 member states, rejected Israel's proposal to withdraw from southern Lebanon, which was conditional on the deployment by the Lebanese Government of extra troops to secure Israeli territory from attack, and, additionally, urged international support to secure Israel's withdrawal from the Golan Heights. In April Arab League ministers of the interior and of justice adopted the Arab Convention for the Suppression of Terrorism, which incorporated security and judicial measures, such as extradition arrangements and the exchange of evidence. The agreement was to enter into effect 30 days after being ratified by at least seven member countries. (This was achieved in May 2000.) In August the League denounced terrorist bomb attacks against the US embassies in Kenya and Tanzania. Nevertheless, it condemned US retaliatory military action, a few days later, against suspected terrorist targets in Afghanistan and Sudan, and endorsed a request by the Sudanese Government that the Security Council investigate the incident. In the same month the USA and United Kingdom accepted a proposal of the Libyan Government, supported by the Arab League, that the suspects in the Lockerbie case be tried in The Hague, Netherlands, under Scottish law. Among items concluded by the Council at its meeting in September were condemnation of Turkey's military co-operation with Israel and a request that the UN dispatch a fact-finding mission to examine conditions in the Israeli-occupied territories and alleged violations of Palestinian property rights. In November, following an escalation of tensions between the Iraqi authorities and UN weapons inspectors, the Secretary-General reiterated the League's opposition to the use of force against Iraq, but urged Iraq to maintain a flexible approach in its relations with the UN. The League condemned the subsequent bombing of strategic targets in Iraq, conducted by US and British military aircraft from mid-December, and offered immediate medical assistance to victims of the attacks.

1999   An emergency meeting of ministers of foreign affairs, held in late January to formulate a unified Arab response to the aerial attacks on targets in Iraq and attended by representatives of 18 member states, expressed concern at the military response to the stand-off between Iraq and the UN, and agreed to establish a seven-member *ad hoc* committee to consider the removal of punitive measures against Iraq within the framework of UN resolutions. However the Iraqi delegation withdrew from the meeting in protest at the final statement, which included a request that Iraq recognize Kuwait's territorial integrity. In March the League's Council determined that member states would suspend sanctions imposed against Libya, once arrangements for the trial of the suspects in the Lockerbie case had been finalized. (The suspects were transferred to a detention centre in the Netherlands in early April, whereupon the UN Security Council suspended its sanctions against Libya.) The meeting also expressed support for a UN resolution convening an international conference to facilitate the implementation of agreements applying to Israel and the Occupied Territories, condemned Israel's refusal to withdraw from the Occupied Territories without a majority vote in favour from its legislature, as well as its refusal to resume the peace negotiations with Lebanon and Syria that had ended in 1996, and advocated the publication of evidence of Israeli violence against Palestinians. The Council considered other issues, including the need to prevent further Israeli expansion in Jerusalem and the problem of Palestinian refugees, and reiterated demands for international support to secure Israel's withdrawal from the Golan Heights. In May the League expressed its concern at the political situation in the Comoros, following the

removal of the government and establishment of a new military regime in that country at the end of April. In June the League condemned an Israeli aerial attack on Beirut and southern Lebanon. In September Iraq chaired a meeting of the Council for the first time since 1990. The meeting considered a range of issues, including the Middle East peace process, US military aid to Israel, and a dispute with the Walt Disney corporation regarding a forthcoming exhibition which appeared to depict Jerusalem as the capital of Israel. Later in September an extraordinary meeting of League senior media and information officials was convened to discuss the latter issue. Negotiations with representatives of Disney were pursued and the implied threat of an Arab boycott of the corporation was averted following assurances that the exhibition would be apolitical. In October the Secretary-General of the League condemned the Mauritanian authorities for concluding an agreement with Israel to establish diplomatic relations. In November the League, in conjunction with the Arab Monetary Fund and the Palestinian Monetary Authority, convened a symposium on the planned issuance of a Palestinian currency. The League demanded that Israel compensate Palestinians for alleged losses incurred by their enforced use of the Israeli currency. In late December, prior to a short-lived resumption of Israeli-Syrian peace negotiations, the League reaffirmed its full support for Syria's position.

2000   In February the League strongly condemned an Israeli aerial attack on southern Lebanon; the League's Council changed the venue of its next meeting, in March, from its Cairo headquarters to Beirut as a gesture of solidarity with Lebanon. During March the Secretary-General of the League expressed regret over Iraq's failure to join the *ad hoc* committee established in early 1999 (see above) and also over Iraq's refusal to co-operate with the recently established UN Monitoring, Verification and Inspection Commission (UNMOVIC). The League welcomed the withdrawal of Israeli forces from southern Lebanon in May, although it subsequently condemned continuing territorial violations by the Israeli military. In June the League concluded a co-operation accord with UNHCR; the two bodies agreed to exchange documents and data. At a meeting of the Council in early September, foreign ministers adopted an Appendix to the League's Charter, providing for the Council to meet ordinarily every March at the level of a summit conference of heads of state ('kings, heads of state and emirs'). The Council was to continue to meet at the level of foreign ministers every March and September. In addition, resolutions were passed urging international bodies to avoid participating in conferences in Jerusalem, reiterating a threatened boycott of a US chain of restaurants which was accused of operating a franchise in an Israeli settlement in the West Bank, and opposing an Israeli initiative for a Jewish emblem to be included as a symbol of the International Red Cross and Red Crescent Movement. At an emergency summit conference convened in late October in response to mounting insecurity in Jerusalem and the Occupied Territories, 15 Arab heads of state, senior officials from six countries and Yasser Arafat, the Palestinian National Authority leader, strongly rebuked Israel, which was accused of inciting the ongoing violent disturbances by stalling the progress of the peace process. The summit determined to 'freeze' co-operation with Israel, requested the formation of an international committee to conduct an impartial assessment of the situation, urged the UN Security Council to establish a mechanism to bring alleged Israeli 'war' criminals to trial, and requested the UN to approve the creation of an international force to protect Palestinians residing in the Occupied Territories. The summit also endorsed the establishment of an 'Al-Aqsa Fund', with a value of US $800m., which was to finance initiatives aimed at promoting the Arab and Islamic identity of Jerusalem, and a smaller 'Jerusalem Intifada Fund' to support the families of Palestinians killed in the unrest. A follow-up committee was subsequently established to implement the resolutions adopted by the emergency summit.

2001   In early January a meeting of League foreign ministers reviewed a proposed framework agreement, presented by outgoing President Clinton of the USA, which aimed to resolve the continuing extreme tension between the Israeli and Palestinian authorities. The meeting agreed that the issues dominating the stalled Middle East peace process should not be redefined, strongly objecting to a proposal that, in exchange for Palestinian assumption of control over Muslim holy sites in Jerusalem, Palestinians exiled at the time of the foundation of the Israeli state in 1948 should forgo their claimed right to return to their former homes. At the end of January, following the completion of the trial in The Hague, Netherlands, of the two Libyans accused of complicity in the

Lockerbie case (one of whom was found guilty and one of whom was acquitted), the Secretary-General of the League urged the UN Security Council fully to terminate the sanctions against Libya that had been suspended in 1999. Meeting in mid-March the League's Council pledged that member states would not consider themselves bound by the (inactive) UN sanctions. The Council also reiterated the League's opposition to the economic sanctions maintained by the USA against Sudan, welcomed the political *rapprochement* achieved in the Comoros in February, and accused Iran of threatening regional security by conducting military manoeuvres on the three disputed islands in the Persian (Arabian) Gulf that were also claimed by the United Arab Emirates. In late March the League's first ordinary annual summit-level Council was convened, in Amman, Jordan. The summit issued the Amman Declaration, which emphasized the promotion of Arab unity, and demanded the reversal of Israel's 1967 occupation of Arab territories and the removal of the UN sanctions against Iraq. The Declaration also urged all member states to accelerate implementation of the GAFTA initiative. (It was reported prior to the summit that 15 of the League's 22 member states were making sufficient progress in realizing the requisite trade liberalization measures.) Heads of state attending the summit meeting requested that the League consider means of reactivating the now relaxed Arab economic boycott of Israel, and agreed that the Jordanian King should mediate contacts between Iraq and Kuwait. At the summit Amr Moussa, hitherto Egypt's minister of foreign affairs, was appointed as the League's new Secretary-General. In May a meeting of League ministers of foreign affairs determined that all political contacts with Israel should be suspended in protest at aerial attacks by Israel on Palestinian targets in the West Bank. In July representatives of 13 member countries met in Damascus, Syria, under the auspices of the Special Bureau for Boycotting Israel. The meeting declared unanimous support for reactivated trade measures against Israeli companies and foreign businesses dealing with Israel. In August an emergency meeting of ministers of foreign affairs of Arab League states was convened at the request of the Palestinian authorities to address the recent escalation of hostilities and Israel's seizure of institutions in East Jerusalem. The meeting, which was attended by the League's Secretary-General and the leader of the Palestinian (National) Authority (PA), Yasser Arafat, aimed to formulate a unified Arab response to the situation. The meeting followed an emergency gathering of information ministers of member countries, at which it was agreed to provide political and media support to the Palestinian position. An emergency meeting of the League's Council convened in mid-September in response to recent major terrorist attacks on the USA allegedly perpetrated by militant Islamist fundamentalists, condemned the atrocities, while urging respect for the rights of Arab and Muslim US citizens. The Secretary-General subsequently emphasized the need for co-ordinated global anti-terrorist action to have clearly defined goals and to be based on sufficient consultations and secure evidence. He also deplored anti-Islamic prejudice, stated that US-led military action against any Arab state would not be supported and that Israeli participation in an international anti-terrorism alliance would be unacceptable, and urged a review of the UN sanctions regime against Iraq and an accelerated settlement to the Palestinian-Israeli crisis. A meeting of League foreign ministers in Doha, in early October, condemned international terrorism but did not express support for retaliatory military action by the USA and its allies. In December a further emergency meeting of League foreign affairs ministers was held to discuss the deepening Middle East crisis.

2002 In January the League appointed a commissioner responsible for promoting dialogue between civilizations. The commissioner was mandated to encourage understanding in Western countries of Arab and Muslim civilization and viewpoints, with the aim of redressing perceived negative stereotypes (especially in view of the Islamist fundamentalist connection to the September 2001 terrorist atrocities). In early March a meeting of League foreign ministers agreed to support an initiative proposed by Crown Prince Abdullah of Saudi Arabia aimed at brokering a peaceful settlement to the by then critical Palestinian-Israeli crisis. The Saudi-backed plan—entailing the restoration of 'normal' Arab relations with Israel and acceptance of its right to exist in peace and security, in exchange for a full Israeli withdrawal from the Occupied Territories, the establishment of an independent Palestinian state with East Jerusalem as its capital, and the return of refugees—was unanimously endorsed, as the first ever pan-Arab Palestinian–Israeli peace initiative, by the

summit-level Council held in Beirut in late March. The plan urged compliance with Security Council Resolution 194 concerning the return of Palestinian refugees to Israel, or appropriate compensation for their property; however, precise details of eligibility criteria for the proposed return, a contentious issue owing to the potentially huge numbers of refugees and descendants of refugees involved, were not elaborated. Conditions imposed by Israel on Yasser Arafat's freedom of movement deterred him from attending the summit. The Egyptian and Jordanian leaders failed to attend. The Arab leaders also agreed that external threats to the security of any Arab country (with particular reference to Iraq) would be regarded as an attack on the security of all Arab states, demanded respect for Iraq's sovereignty, and reiterated demands for the withdrawal of international sanctions against Iraq. A *rapprochement* between Iraq and Kuwait occurred at the summit meeting when the Iraqi envoy representing Saddam Hussain declared Iraq's respect for Kuwait's sovereignty and security. A committee of nine foreign ministers (representing Bahrain, Egypt, Jordan, Lebanon, Morocco, Palestine, Saudi Arabia, Syria and Yemen) was appointed to co-ordinate activities related to following up the summit's decisions (issued in its 'Beirut Declaration'). At the end of March the League's Secretary-General condemned the Israeli military's siege of Yasser Arafat's presidential compound in Ramallah (initiated in retaliation against a succession of Palestinian bomb attacks on Israeli civilians). An extraordinary Council meeting held in April at the request of Palestine to consider the 'unprecedented deterioration' of the situation in the Palestinian territories accused certain states (notably the USA) of implementing a pro-Israeli bias that enabled Israel to act outside the scope of international law and to ignore relevant UN resolutions, and accused Israel of undermining international co-operation in combating terrorism by attempting to equate its actions towards the Palestinian people with recent anti-terrorism activities conducted by the USA. A meeting organized by the Special Bureau for Boycotting Israel at the end of April in Damascus, Syria, was attended by representatives of all League member states except for Egypt, Jordan and Mauritania (which have relations with Israel). The meeting agreed to expand boycott measures and assessed the status of 17 companies believed to have interests in Israel. Israel's termination of its siege of Arafat's Ramallah compound in early May was welcomed by the Secretary-General. In early June the League appointed a special representative to Somalia to assist with the ongoing reconciliation efforts in that country. A meeting of Arab information ministers in mid-June launched a US $22.5m. campaign to combat Israel's Palestine policy through the international media. Following an aerial raid by the Israeli military on targets in Gaza in late July, the League urged a halt in the export of weaponry, particularly F-16 military aircraft, to Israel. In early August the Secretary-General expressed strong concern at US threats to attack Iraq in view of its failure to implement UN resolutions, stating that such action would seriously undermine regional stability. A Council meeting held in early September reiterated its complete opposition to the threat of aggression against any Arab country, including Iraq, and demanded the withdrawal of the sanctions against that country. The meeting agreed to intensify Arab efforts to expose Israeli atrocities against the Palestinians and urged the international community to provide protection and reparations for Palestinians. The Council authorized the establishment of a committee to address the welfare of imprisoned Palestinians and urged the USA and UK to reconsider their policies on exporting weaponry to Israel, while issuing a resolution concerning the danger posed by Israel's possession of weapons of mass destruction. The Council deplored the USA's continuing active imposition of sanctions against Libya and endorsed Libya's right to claim compensation in respect of these. In addition, a committee was established to encourage peace efforts in Sudan. In mid-September, following an ultimatum by the USA that military action against Iraq would ensue were the UN to fail within a short time limit to ensure the elimination of any Iraqi-held weapons of mass destruction, the League urged Iraq to negotiate the return of UN weapons inspectors with a view to avoiding confrontation. Soon afterwards, following tripartite consultations between the Secretary-General of the League, the UN Secretary-General and the Iraqi foreign minister concerning the implementation of UN resolutions and eventual withdrawal of UN sanctions, Iraq agreed to admit UNMOVIC personnel. In early October the Secretary-General expressed concern at new US legislation aimed at securing the relocation of the USA's embassy in Israel from Tel Aviv to Jerusalem, stating that this represented a symbolic acceptance of Jerusalem as the Israeli capital, in contravention of relevant UN resolutions. Later in that month Libya announced plans to withdraw from the League. An emergency meeting of the Council convened in early November reviewed the recent adoption by the UN Security Council of Resolution 1441, establishing a stict time frame for Iraqi compliance with UN demands and authorizing the use of force against Iraq in response to non-compliance. The Council urged Iraq to co-operate with UNMOVIC and IAEA inspection teams, requested the inclusion of Arab weapons inspectors on the teams, and urged that the resolution should not be used as a pretext to launch a war against Iraq, emphasizing the importance of a peaceful resolution of the situation.

2003 A summit-level meeting of the Council, held in Sharm el-Sheik, Egypt, at the beginning of March, issued a final communiqué rejecting threatened aggression against Iraq, reiterating that the Saddam Hussain regime should co-operate with UN weapons inspectors, urging that the inspectors be given enough time to complete their work, and declaring that the League would form a committee of diplomats to explain its position to concerned international parties. In late March, following the initiation of US-led military action against the Saddam Hussain regime, the Council adopted a resolution condemning the invasion. In early April the Secretary-General expressed his regret that the Arab states had failed to prevent the ongoing war, and urged the development of a new regional security order. Later in that month, following the overthrow of the Saddam Hussain regime, the League participated in a joint meeting of Arab organizations convened to consider means of assisting the Iraqi people.

FINANCE

In September 2002 the Council approved a budget of US $35m. for the Secretariat in 2003.

Publications

Arab Perspectives—Sh'oun Arabiyya (monthly).
Journal of Arab Affairs (monthly).
Bulletins of treaties and agreements concluded among the member states, essays, regular publications circulated by regional offices.

NORDIC COUNCIL

Address: Store Strandstræde 18, 1021 Copenhagen K, Denmark.
Telephone: 3396-0400; **fax:** 3311-1870; **e-mail:** nordisk-rad@ nordisk-rad.dk; **internet:** www.norden.org.

The Nordic Council was founded in 1952 for co-operation between the Nordic parliaments and governments. The four original members were Denmark, Iceland, Norway and Sweden; Finland joined in 1955, and the Faroe Islands and Åland Islands were granted representation in 1970 within the Danish and Finnish delegations respectively. Greenland had separate representation within the Danish delegation from 1984. Co-operation was first regulated by a Statute, and subsequently by the Helsinki Treaty of 1962. The Nordic region has a population of about 24m.

MEMBERS

Denmark (with the autonomous territories of the Faroe Islands and Greenland)	Finland (with the autonomous territory of the Åland Islands) Iceland	Norway Sweden

Organization

(April 2003)

COUNCIL

The Nordic Council is not a supranational parliament, but a forum for co-operation between the parliaments and governments of the Nordic countries. The Nordic Council of Ministers (see below)co-ordinates the activities of the governments of the Nordic countries when decisions are to be implemented.

The Council comprises 87 members, elected annually by and from the parliaments of the respective countries (Denmark 16 members; Faroes 2; Greenland 2; Finland 18; Åland 2; Iceland 7; Norway 20; Sweden 20). The various parties are proportionately represented in accordance with their representation in the national parliaments. Sessions of the Council consider proposals submitted by Council members, by the Council of Ministers or national governments. The sessions also follow up the outcome of past decisions and the work of the various Nordic institutions. The Plenary Assembly, which convenes once a year, is the highest body of the Nordic Council. Government representatives participate in the Assembly, but do not have the right to vote.

The Council has initiated and overseen extensive efforts to strengthen Nordic co-operation at the political, economic and social level. In 1995 the following were adopted as the priority focus areas ('pillars') of Nordic co-operation: intra-Nordic co-operation, with the emphasis on cultural, education and research co-operation; co-operation with the EU and the European Economic Area, focusing on promoting Nordic values and interests in a broader European context; and co-operation with the Adjacent Areas, i.e. the Baltic States, north-west Russia and the Arctic Area/Barents Sea, where Nordic governments are committed to furthering democracy, security and sustainable development. In September 2000 a Nordic Advisory Panel, appointed in 1999, recommended that the three-pillar basis of Nordic co-operation should be replaced by a theme-based, 'circular' structure. Meeting in Copenhagen, Denmark, in November 2000, the Council endorsed new guide-lines for policy and administrative reforms, in order to develop a better correspondence between the work of the Council and national parliaments. The reform process was also intended to facilitate co-operation with the Nordic Council of Ministers and the implementation of recommendations. Co-operation with non-member states remained a priority focus of the Council's activities.

STANDING COMMITTEES

Council members are assigned to the following Standing Committees: the Culture and Education Committee, Citizens and Consumer Rights Committee, Environment and Natural Resource Committee, Welfare Committee, and the Business and Industry Committee.

PRESIDIUM

The day-to-day work of the Nordic Council is directed by a Presidium, consisting of 13 members of national legislatures. The Presidium is the Council's highest decision-making body between sessions. The Presidium secretariat is headed by a Council Director. Each delegation to the Nordic Council has a secretariat at its national legislature.

Director: FRIDA NOKKEN.

Publications

Note: the titles listed below are joint publications of the Nordic Council and Nordic Council of Ministers.

Norden this Week (electronic newsletter in the languages of the region and English).
Norden the Top of Europe (monthly newsletter in English, German and French).
Politik i Norden (magazine in the languages of the region).
Yearbook of Nordic Statistics (in English, Finnish and Swedish).
Books and pamphlets on Nordic co-operation; summaries of Council sessions.

NORDIC COUNCIL OF MINISTERS

Address: Store Strandstræde 18, 1255 Copenhagen K, Denmark.
Telephone: 3396-0200; **fax:** 3396-0202; **internet:** www.norden.org.
The Governments of Denmark, Finland, Iceland, Norway and Sweden co-operate through the Nordic Council of Ministers. This co-operation is regulated by the Treaty of Co-operation between Denmark, Finland, Iceland, Norway and Sweden of 1962 (amended in 1971, 1974, 1983, 1985, 1993 and 1995) and the Treaty between Denmark, Finland, Iceland, Norway and Sweden concerning cultural co-operation of 1971 (amended in 1983 and 1985). Although the Prime Ministers do not meet formally within the Nordic Council of Ministers, they have decided to take a leading role in overall Nordic co-operation. The Ministers of Defence and Foreign Affairs do not meet within the Council of Ministers. These ministers, however, meet on an informal basis.

MEMBERS

Denmark   Finland   Iceland   Norway   Sweden
Greenland, the Faroe Islands and the Åland Islands also participate as autonomous regions.

Organization

(April 2003)

COUNCIL OF MINISTERS

The Nordic Council of Ministers holds formal and informal meetings and is attended by ministers with responsibility for the subject under discussion. Each member state also appoints a minister in its own cabinet as Minister for Nordic Co-operation.

Decisions of the Council of Ministers must be unanimous, except for procedural questions, which may be decided by a simple majority of those voting. Abstention constitutes no obstacle to a decision. Decisions are binding on the individual countries, provided that no parliamentary approval is necessary under the constitution of any of the countries. If such approval is necessary, the Council of Ministers must be so informed before its decision.

Meetings are concerned with: agreements and treaties, guidelines for national legislation, recommendations from the Nordic Council, financing joint studies, setting up Nordic institutions.

The Council of Ministers reports each year to the Nordic Council on progress in all co-operation between member states, as well as on future plans.

SECRETARIAT

The Office of the Secretary-General is responsible for co-ordination and legal matters (including co-ordination of work related to the European integration process and to the development of eastern Europe).

The work of the Secretariat is divided into the following departments:

Cultural and educational co-operation, research, advanced education, computer technology.

Budget and administration.

Environmental protection, finance and monetary policy, fisheries, industry and energy, regional policy, agriculture and forestry.

Information.

Labour market issues, social policy and health care, occupational environment, consumer affairs, equal opportunities.

Secretary-General: SØREN CHRISTENSEN (Denmark).

COMMITTEES

Nordic Co-operation Committee: for final preparation of material for the meetings of Ministers of Nordic Co-operation.

Senior Executives' Committees: prepare the meetings of the Council of Ministers and conduct research at its request. There are a number of sub-committees. The Committees cover the subjects listed under the Secretariat (above).

Activities

The Nordic Council of Ministers has designated the following as priority areas of activity: technological development; welfare; the internal market in the Nordic countries; the environment and sustainable development; and co-operation with neighbouring countries and regions, and has adopted the following strategic objectives for the period 2003–05: active support for the implementation of the European Union's Action Plan for the Northern Dimension (see below); increased co-operation with Northwest Russia and Kaliningrad; the identification of new projects in the Arctic; restructuring co-operation with the Baltic states; and improved co-operation and division of activities among actors in the Adjacent Areas. A long-term cross-sectoral Strategy for a Sustainable Nordic Region and the Adjacent Areas covering the period 2001–20 was adopted in 2001. The strategy established targets for regional sustainable development, focusing on climate change, biodiversity, genetics, cultural environment, the oceans, chemicals and food safety. The new Nordic strategy for sustainable development was a priority area of activity for the Nordic Council of Ministers in 2002, alongside children and young people, and food safety.

ECONOMIC AND FINANCIAL CO-OPERATION

Nordic economic and financial co-operation aims to promote regional economic, ecological and socially sustainable growth, without inflation, with high employment, and supporting the Nordic social welfare model. It also aims to continue preparing the way for economic integration within the Nordic area and with Europe, and to promote issues of common Nordic concern internationally. Co-operation is undertaken in the following areas: freer markets for goods and services; measures on training and employment; elimination of trade barriers; liberalization of capital movements; research and development; export promotion; taxes and other levies; and regional policy. The Environment and Economics Group commissions environmental and economic analyses of areas of joint Nordic interest, e.g. ecological taxes and duties, cost-effective solutions to international environmental problems, and financing; and disseminates internationally analyses of and other information on Nordic environmental/economic issues.

Nordic Development Fund: f. 1989; supports activities by national administrations for overseas development with resources amounting to €330m.

Nordic Environmental Finance Corporation—NEFCO: f. 1990 to finance environmental projects in Central and Eastern Europe; cap. €80m. administers the Nordic Environmental Development Fund (NEDF, authorized in 1999 to finance environmental projects in the Barents Sea and Baltic Sea areas during 1999–2003).

Nordic Industrial Fund: f. 1973 to provide grants, subsidies and loans for industrial research and development projects of interest to more than one member country.

Nordic Investment Bank—NIB: f. under an agreement of December 1975 to provide finance and guarantees for the implementation of investment projects and exports; total assets €15,900m. (Dec. 2002); the main sectors of the Bank's activities are energy, metal and wood-processing industries (including petroleum extraction) and manufacturing; in 1982 a separate scheme for financing investments in developing countries was established; in 1997 an Environmental Loan Facility was established to facilitate environmental investments in the Nordic Adjacent Areas.

Nordic Project Fund—NoPEF: f. 1982 to strengthen the international competitiveness of Nordic exporting companies, and to promote industrial co-operation in international projects (e.g. in environmental protection); grants loans to Nordic companies for feasibility expenses relating to projects.

NORDTEST: f. 1973 as an inter-Nordic agency for technical testing and standardization of methods and of laboratory accreditation.

RELATIONS WITH THE EU, EASTERN EUROPE AND THE ARCTIC

In 1991 the theme 'Norden in Europe' was identified as an area of high priority for the coming years by the Council. Nordic co-operation was to be used to co-ordinate member countries' participation in the western European integration process, based on EC and EC/EFTA co-operation. Since 1995, when Finland and Sweden acceded to the European Union (joining Denmark, already a member of that organization), Europe and the EU have been an integrated part of the work of Nordic co-operation. Under the Finnish presidency of the EU in the second half of 1999 the 'Northern Dimension', a strategy covering the Nordic region and Adjacent Areas, was adopted by the EU. The Nordic Council of Ministers actively supports the Action Plan on the Northern Dimension, which was adopted by the EU in June 2000.

Since 1991 the Nordic Council of Ministers has developed its co-operation relating to the Baltic countries and north-west Russia, in order to contribute to peace, security and stability in Europe. Co-operation measures aim to promote democracy, the establishment of market economies, respect for civil rights and the responsible use of resources in these areas. The Nordic Council of Ministers has co-operated with the Arctic Council since that body's establishment in 1996. The Nordic 'Working Programme of the Adjacent Areas' comprises the following major components: Nordic Information Offices in Tallinn, Riga, Vilnius and St Petersburg, which co-ordinate Nordic projects and activities, promote regional contact at all levels and provide information about the Nordic countries in general and Nordic co-operation specifically; the Nordic Grants Scheme for the Baltic States and Northwest Russia, which supports networks linking universities and research institutions, and also awards grants to facilitate network-building in the NGO sector; a grants scheme for public servants and an exchange programme for parliamentarians; and the Nordic Council of Ministers Project Activities. In 1998 the Council of Ministers adopted a Framework Action Plan for Children and Young Adults in the Adjacent Areas. In 2000 the Council of Ministers implemented a review of the strategic goals for co-operation with the Adjacent Areas in view of the administrative, democratic and economic reforms implemented by the Baltic States and their planned accession to the EU; progress achieved towards strengthening regional and EU co-operation with Russia; and an increase in Nordic and international bilateral co-operation measures in the Adjacent Areas. In March of that year the Nordic Investment Bank and the Nordic Environmental Finance Corporation signed a framework agreement with the EU and other partners on providing funding to assist the planned accession to the EU of the Baltic states and other central and east European countries.

A new strategy for activities in the Adjacent Areas and a separate Arctic Programme of Co-operation were approved by the Council of Ministers in 2001. It was agreed that co-operation should focus primarily on the following themes: the Nordic welfare model (including healthcare and gender equality); sustainable utilization of resources (including environmental and energy issues); children and youth issues; culture mediation; and consumer policy and food safety. It was envisaged that cross-border co-operation along the boundaries with Russia and Belarus would assume a growing significance. The programme for co-operation with the Arctic (introduced in 2003) was to take into account subsequent developments since the formation of the Arctic Council.

The 2003 budget for co-operation with the Adjacent Areas and the Arctic totalled 86m. Danish kroner in 2003, jointly funded by NEFCO, NOPEF, NIB and bilateral financing.

COMMUNICATIONS AND TRANSPORT

The main areas of co-operation have been concerned with international transport, the environment, infrastructure, road research, transport for the disabled and road safety.

EMPLOYMENT

In 1954 an agreement entered into force on a free labour market between Denmark, Finland, Norway and Sweden. Iceland became a party to the agreement in 1982 and the Faroe Islands in 1992. In 1982 an agreement on worker training and job-oriented rehabilitation came into effect. There is a joint centre for labour market training at Övertorneå in Sweden. A convention on the working environment was signed in 1989. The Nordic Institute for Advanced Training in Occupational Health is based in Helsinki, Finland.

GENDER EQUALITY

A Nordic co-operation programme on equality between women and men began in 1974. The main areas of co-operation have been the integration of equality aspects into all activities covered by the organization (i.e. 'mainstreaming'), working conditions, education, social welfare and family policy, housing and social planning, and women's participation in politics. In June 2000 the Council of Ministers determined that each ministerial group should take responsibility for gender equality in its own sphere of activities. In 2001–05 the main areas of concern were: incorporating the equality dimension into national budgetary policy; men and equality; and the prevention of violence against women.

ENVIRONMENT

A Nordic Environmental Action Plan constituted the overall guidelines for Nordic co-operation in this field over the period 2001–04. The long-term cross-sectoral Strategy for a Sustainable Nordic Region and the Adjacent Areas covering the period 2001–20, adopted in 2001, had a strong focus on climate change, biodiversity, and the oceans. Under the Strategy environmental considerations were applied across a wide spectrum of issues, such as globalization, communications technology, natural resources, consumption patterns, renewable resources, air and sea pollutants and poverty reduction. During 2002 priority areas in the environment sector

included work on a proposal to establish a testing ground for the mechanisms of the Kyoto Protocol to the UN Framework Convention on Climate Change; Nordic co-operation on chemicals; and Nordic co-operation on products and waste. The preparation of a Nordic Millennium Ecosystem Assessment was to commence in that year. The Nordic countries promote a high level of ambition as the basis for the environmental work conducted in the EU and at an international level.

ENERGY AND INDUSTRY

Co-operation in the energy sector focuses on energy-saving, energy and the environment, climate policy, the energy market, and the introduction of new and renewable sources of energy. A Nordic Co-operation Programme on Business Policy for 2002–05 represented the first joint Nordic initiative concerning the trade and industry sector.

CONSUMER AFFAIRS

The main areas of co-operation are in safety legislation, consumer education and information and consumers' economic and legal interests. In 2002 the Nordic Council of Ministers was promoting changes in consumption habits and production that would benefit sustainable development.

AGRICULTURE, FORESTRY, FISHERIES AND FOOD

Efforts to develop co-operation in both the fisheries and agriculture and forestry sectors have been undertaken with the aim of integrating environmental aspects into the relevant policies and strategies. In 2002 work was under way to promote sustainable development in agricultural production within the framework of the Strategy for a Sustainable Nordic Region and the Adjacent Areas for 2001–20. Priorities included ensuring food security through ecologically and economically sustainable production methods and an emphasis on quality, with reference to related areas such as food safety, biological diversity and genetic resources. A conference of Nordic ministers with responsibility for food was to be convened during 2002 to discuss the development of a regional action plan for food safety. Nordic co-operation on forestry issues includes joint participation in international processes concerned with forestry management. Co-operation on fisheries aims to promote the sustainable development of the fishing industry as an important economic asset and to ensure a balanced approach to the exploitation of regional marine resources.

LAW

The five countries have similar legal systems and tend towards uniformity in legislation and interpretation of law. Much of the preparatory committee work within the national administrations on new legislation involves consultation with the neighbour countries.

Citizens of one Nordic country working in another are in many respects given the status of nationals. In all the Nordic countries they already have the right to vote in local elections in the country of residence. The changing of citizenship from one Nordic country to another has been simplified, and legislation on marriage and on children's rights amended to achieve the greatest possible parity.

There are special extradition facilities between the countries and further stages towards co-operation between the police and the courts have been adopted. In October 1996 justice ministers of the Nordic countries agreed to strengthen police co-operation in order to counter an increase in violent crime perpetrated by gangs. Emphasis is also placed on strengthening co-operation to combat the sexual abuse of children.

There is a permanent Council for Criminology and a Nordic Institute for Maritime Law in Oslo.

In 2002 the following were priority areas of co-operation: addressing criminal activity motivated by Nazi or racist ideologies; family law; and debt collection issues.

REGIONAL POLICY

The Council of Ministers has aimed to develop cross-border co-operation between the Nordic countries and co-operation with the EU and the Baltic countries, and to give greater priority to exchanging knowledge and information.

SOCIAL WELFARE AND HEALTH

Existing conventions and other co-operation directives ensure that Nordic citizens have the same rights, benefits and obligations in each Nordic country, with regard to sickness, parenthood, occupational injury, unemployment, disablement and old-age pension. Uniform provisions exist concerning basic pension and supplementary pension benefits when moving from one Nordic country to another. In 1993 Nordic representatives signed an agreement providing for a common Nordic labour market for health professionals. Numerous joint initiatives have been undertaken in the social welfare and health sectors within the framework of the co-operating institutions.

A programme on Nordic co-operation on illicit drugs for 2001–05 aimed to include the Adjacent Areas in the Council of Ministers' activities in this field.

Institutions:
Nordic Committee on Disability
Nordic Committee on Social Security Statistics
Nordic Council for Alcohol and Drug Research, Helsinki, Finland
Nordic Council on Medicines, Uppsala, Sweden
Nordic Education Programme for Social Service Development, Gothenburg, Sweden
Nordic Medico-statistical Committee, Copenhagen, Denmark
Nordic School of Public Health, Gothenburg, Sweden
Nordic Staff Training Centre for Deaf-blind Services, Dronninglund, Denmark
Scandinavian Institute of Dental Materials, Haslum, Norway

EDUCATIONAL AND SCIENTIFIC CO-OPERATION

Education: Nordic co-operation in the educational field includes the objective content and means of education, the structure of the educational system and pedagogical development work. Strategic, long-term investment in human resources, particularly education and research, form part of the basis of the Nordic welfare model. Nordic co-operation on information and communication technology aims to promote universal access to information, with a view to strengthening democracy, Nordic culture, electronic commerce and business networking.

The Nordic Council of Ministers finances the following co-operating bodies, permanent institutions and joint programmes:
Nordic-Baltic Scholarship Scheme.
Nordic Folk Academy.
Nordic Institute in Finland.
Nordic Language and Literature Courses.
NORDPLUS (Nordic Programme for Mobility of University Students and Teachers).
Nordic programmes for mobility of pupils, students, and teachers at primary and secondary school level (NORDPLUS-Junior and others).
Nordic School Data Network (ODIN).
Nordic Summer University.
Programme of Action for Nordic Language Co-operation.
Steering Committee for Nordic Co-operation on General and Adult Education.
Steering Committee for Nordic Co-operation in Higher Education.
Steering Committee for Nordic Educational Co-operation (primary and secondary school).

Research: Nordic co-operation in research comprises information on research activities and research findings, joint research projects, joint research institutions, the methods and means in research policy, the organizational structure of research and co-ordination of the national research programmes.

Much of the research co-operation activities at the more permanent joint research institutions consists of establishing science contacts in the Nordic areas by means of grants, visiting lecturers, courses and symposia.

The research institutions and research bodies listed below receive continuous financial support via the Nordic cultural budget. In many cases, these joint Nordic institutions ensure a high international standard that would otherwise have been difficult to maintain at a purely national level.
Nordic Academy for Advanced Study.
Nordic Committee for Bioethics.
Nordic Council for Scientific Information and Research Libraries.
Nordic Institute of Asian Studies.
Nordic Institute of Maritime Law.
Nordic Institute for Theoretical Physics.
Nordic Programme for Arctic Research.
Nordic Sámi Institute.
Nordic Science Policy Council.
Nordic Vulcanological Institute.
Research Programme on the Nordic Countries and Europe.

Cultural activities: Cultural co-operation is based on the Nordic Agreement on Cultural Affairs Co-operation, adopted in 1971, and aims to promote the linguistic and cultural heritage of the Nordic nations. Co-operation includes artistic and other cultural exchange between the Nordic countries; activities relating to libraries, museums, radio, television, film and digitalized culture; promotion of activities within organizations with general cultural aims, including youth and sports organizations; the improvement of conditions for the creative and performing arts; and encouragement for artists and cultural workers. Exhibitions and performances of Nordic culture are organized abroad. A Nordic Multimedia Fund is planned. In 2000 Nordic ministers responsible for Sámi affairs and the leaders of Sámi parliaments (the Sámi being the indigenous population of the northern areas of Norway, Sweden, Finland and north-western Russia) established a permanent co-operation, with the aim of strengthening Sámi languages, culture, business and community life. The Sámi co-operation was to be informally linked to the Nordic Council of Ministers. In October 2001 the ministers for Sámi affairs agreed to appoint a committee of experts to present (by 2003) the draft text of a Nordic Sámi Convention.

Joint projects include:

Fund for Mobility of Young Nordic Artists—SLEIPNIR.
Nordic Amateur Theatre Council.
Nordic Art Centre.
Nordic Co-operation in Athletics.
Nordic Council Literature Prize.
Nordic Council Music Prize.
Nordic Documentation Centre for Mass Communication Research.
Nordic Film and Television Fund.
Nordic House in the Faroe Islands.
Nordic House in Reykjavík.
Nordic Institute in Åland.
Nordic Institute of Contemporary Art.
Nordic Institute in Greenland.
Nordic Literature and Libraries Committee.
Nordic Music Committee.
Nordic Theatre and Dance Committee.
Nordic Visual Art Committee.
Steering Committee on Culture and Mass Media.
Steering Committee on Nordic Cultural Projects Abroad.
Valhalla (a network for children's and youth culture).

NORDIC CULTURAL FUND

The Nordic Cultural Fund was established through a separate agreement between the governments of the Nordic countries in 1966, and began operating in 1967, with the aim of supporting the needs of cultural life in the Nordic countries. A Board of 11 members administers and distributes the resources of the Fund and supervises its activities. Five of the members are appointed by the Nordic Council and five by the Nordic Council of Ministers (of culture and education), for a period of two years. The autonomous territories (the Åland islands, the Faroe Islands and Greenland) are represented by one member on the Board, appointed alternately by the Nordic Council and the Nordic Council of Ministers. The Fund is located within and administered by the Secretariat of the Nordic Council of Ministers. It considers applications for assistance for research, education and general cultural activities; grants may also be awarded for the dissemination of information concerning Nordic culture within and outside the region.

Finance

Joint expenses are divided according to an agreed scale in proportion to the relative national product of the member countries. The 2002 budget of the Nordic Council of Ministers amounted to 774m. Danish kroner. Various forms of co-operation are also financed directly from the national budgets.

NORTH AMERICAN FREE TRADE AGREEMENT—NAFTA

Address: Canadian section: Royal Bank Centre, 90 Sparks St, Suite 705, Ottawa, ON K1P 5B4.

Telephone: (613) 992-9388; **fax:** (613) 992-9392.

Address: Mexican section: Blvd Adolfo López Mateos 3025, 2°, Col Héroes de Padierna, 10700 Mexico, DF.

Telephone: (5) 629-9630; **fax:** (5) 629-9637.

Address: US section: 14th St and Constitution Ave, NW, Room 2061, Washington, DC 20230.

Telephone: (202) 482-5438; **fax:** (202) 482-0148; **e-mail:** info@nafta-sec-alena.org; **internet:** www.nafta-sec-alena.org.

The North American Free Trade Agreement (NAFTA) grew out of the free-trade agreement between the USA and Canada that was signed in January 1988 and came into effect on 1 January 1989. Negotiations on the terms of NAFTA, which includes Mexico in the free-trade area, were concluded in October 1992 and the Agreement was signed in December. The accord was ratified in November 1993 and entered into force on 1 January 1994. The NAFTA Secretariat is composed of national sections in each member country.

MEMBERS

Canada	Mexico	USA

MAIN PROVISIONS OF THE AGREEMENT

Under NAFTA almost all restrictions on trade and investment between Canada, Mexico and the USA were to be gradually removed over a 15-year period. Most tariffs were eliminated immediately on agricultural trade between the USA and Mexico, with tariffs on 6% of agricultural products (including corn, sugar, and some fruits and vegetables) to be abolished over the 15 years. Tariffs on automobiles and textiles were to be phased out over 10 years in all three countries. Mexico was to open its financial sector to US and Canadian investment, with all restrictions to be removed by 2007. Barriers to investment were removed in most sectors, with exemptions for petroleum in Mexico, culture in Canada and airlines and radio communications in the USA. Mexico was to liberalize government procurement, removing preferential treatment for domestic companies over a 10-year period. In transport, heavy goods vehicles were to have complete freedom of movement between the three countries by 2000. An interim measure, whereby transport companies could apply for special licences to travel further within the borders of each country than the existing limit of 20 miles (32 km), was postponed in December 1995, shortly before it was scheduled to come into effect. The postponement was due to concerns, on the part of the US Government, relating to the implementation of adequate safety standards by Mexican truck-drivers. The 2000 deadline for the free circulation of heavy goods vehicles was not met, owing to the persistence of these concerns. In February 2001, however, a five-member NAFTA panel of experts appointed to adjudicate on the dispute ruled that the USA was violating the Agreement. The panel demanded that the US authorities consider entry applications from Mexican-based truck companies on an individual basis. In April 1998 the fifth meeting of the three-member ministerial Free Trade Commission (see below), held in Paris, France, agreed to remove tariffs on some 600 goods, including certain chemicals, pharmaceuticals, steel and wire products, textiles, toys, and watches, from 1 August. As a result of the agreement, a number of tariffs were eliminated as much as 10 years earlier than had been originally planned.

In the case of a sudden influx of goods from one country to another that adversely affects a domestic industry, the Agreement makes provision for the imposition of short-term 'snap-back' tariffs.

Disputes are to be settled in the first instance by intergovernmental consultation. If a dispute is not resolved within 30 to 40 days, a government may call a meeting of the Free Trade Commission. In October 1994 the Commission established an Advisory Committee on Private Commercial Disputes to recommend procedures for the resolution of such disputes. If the Commission is unable to settle the issue a panel of experts in the relevant field is appointed to adjudicate. In June 1996 Canada and Mexico announced their decision to refer the newly-enacted US 'Helms-Burton' legislation on trade with Cuba to the Commission. They claimed that the legislation, which provides for punitive measures against foreign companies that engage in trade with Cuba, imposed undue restrictions on Canadian and Mexican companies and was, therefore, in contravention of NAFTA. However, at the beginning of 1997 certain controversial provisions of the Helms-Burton legislation were suspended for a period of six months by the US administration. In April these were again suspended, as part of a compromise agreement with the European Union. The relevant provisions continued to be suspended at six-monthly intervals, and remained suspended in early 2002. An Advisory Committee on Private Commercial Disputes Regarding Agricultural Goods was formed in 1998.

In December 1994 NAFTA members issued a formal invitation to Chile to seek membership of the Agreement. Formal discussions on Chile's entry began in June 1995, but were stalled in December when the US Congress failed to approve 'fast-track' negotiating authority for the US Government, which was to have allowed the latter to negotiate a trade agreement with Chile, without risk of incurring a line-by-line veto from the US Congress. In February 1996 Chile began high-level negotiations with Canada on a wide-ranging bilateral free-trade agreement. Chile, which already had extensive bilateral trade agreements with Mexico, was regarded as advancing its position with regard to NAFTA membership by means of the proposed accord with Canada. The bilateral agreement, which provided for the extensive elimination of customs duties by 2002, was signed in November 1996 and ratified by Chile in July 1997. However, in November 1997 the US Government was obliged to request the removal of the 'fast-track' proposal from the legislative agenda, owing to insufficient support within Congress.

In April 1998 heads of state of 34 countries, meeting in Santiago, Chile, agreed formally to initiate the negotiating process to establish a Free Trade Area of the Americas (FTAA). The US Government had originally proposed creating the FTAA through the gradual extension of NAFTA trading privileges on a bilateral basis. However, the framework agreed upon by ministers of trade of the 34 countries, meeting in March, provided for countries to negotiate and accept FTAA provisions on an individual basis and as part of a sub-regional economic bloc. It was envisaged that the FTAA would exist alongside the sub-regional associations, including NAFTA. In April 2001, meeting in Quebec City, Canada, leaders of the participating countries agreed to conclude the negotiations on the FTAA by January 2005 to enable it to enter into force by the end of that year.

ADDITIONAL AGREEMENTS

During 1993, as a result of domestic pressure, the new US Government negotiated two 'side agreements' with its NAFTA partners, which were to provide safeguards for workers' rights and the environment. A Commission for Labour Co-operation was established under the North American Agreement on Labour Co-operation (NAALC) to monitor implementation of labour accords and to foster co-operation in that area. The North American Commission for Environmental Co-operation (NACEC) was initiated to combat pollution, to ensure that economic development was not environmentally damaging and to monitor compliance with national and NAFTA environmental regulations. Panels of experts, with representatives from each country, were established to adjudicate in cases of alleged infringement of workers' rights or environmental damage. The panels were given the power to impose fines and trade sanctions, but only with regard to the USA and Mexico; Canada, which was opposed to such measures, was to enforce compliance with NAFTA by means of its own legal system. In 1995 the North American Fund for Environmental Co-operation (NAFEC) was established. NAFEC, which is financed by the NACEC, supports community environmental projects.

In February 1996 the NACEC consented for the first time to investigate a complaint brought by environmentalists regarding non-compliance with domestic legislation on the environment. Mexican environmentalists claimed that a company that was planning to build a pier for tourist ships (a project that was to involve damage to a coral reef) had not been required to supply adequate environmental impact studies. The NACEC was limited to presenting its findings in such a case, as it could only make a ruling in the case of complaints brought by one NAFTA government against another. The NACEC allocates the bulk of its resources to research undertaken to support compliance with legislation and agreements on the environment. However, in October 1997 the council of NAFTA ministers of the environment, meeting in Montréal, Canada, approved a new structure for the NACEC's activities. The NACEC's main objective was to be the provision of advice concerning the environmental impact of trade issues. It was also agreed that the Commission was further to promote trade in environmentally-sound products and to encourage private-sector investment in environmental trade issues.

With regard to the NAALC, National Administration Offices have been established in each of the three NAFTA countries in order to monitor labour issues and to address complaints about non-compliance with domestic labour legislation. However, punitive measures in the form of trade sanctions or fines (up to US $20m.) may only be imposed in the specific instances of contravention of national legislation regarding child labour, a minimum wage or health and safety standards. A Commission for Labour Co-operation has been established (see below) and incorporates a council of ministers of labour of the three countries.

In August 1993 the USA and Mexico agreed to establish a Border Environmental Co-operation Commission (BECC) to assist with the co-ordination of projects for the improvement of infrastructure and to monitor the environmental impact of the Agreement on the US–Mexican border area, where industrial activity was expected to intensify. The Commission is located in Ciudad Juárez, Mexico. By early 2003 the BECC had certified 70 projects, at a cost of US \$1,339.1m. In October 1993 the USA and Mexico concluded an agreement to establish a North American Development Bank (NADB or NADBank), which was mandated to finance environmental and infrastructure projects along the US–Mexican border.

Commission for Labour Co-operation: 1211 Connecticut Ave, NW Suite 200, Washington, DC 20036, USA; tel. (202) 464-1100; fax (202) 464-9487; e-mail info@naalc.org; internet www.naalc.org; f. 1994; Exec. Dir Dr Alfonso Oñate Laborde (Mexico); publ. *Annual Report.*

North American Commission for Environmental Co-operation—NACEC: 393 rue St Jacques West, Bureau 200, Montréal, QC H2Y IN9, Canada; tel. (514) 350-4300; fax (514) 350-4314; e-mail info@ccemtl.org; internet www.cec.org; f. 1994; Exec. Dir Victor Shantora (acting); publs *Annual Report, Taking Stock* (annually), industry reports, policy studies.

North American Development Bank—NADB/NADBank: 203 St Mary's, Suite 300, San Antonio, TX 78205, USA; tel. (210) 231-8000; fax (210) 231-6232; internet www.nadbank.org; at March 2002 the NADB had authorized capital of US \$3,000m., subscribed equally by Mexico and the USA, of which \$450m. was paid-up; Man. Dir Raul Rodriguez (Mexico); publs *Annual Report, NADBank News.*

NORTH ATLANTIC TREATY ORGANIZATION—NATO

Address: blvd Léopold III, 1110 Brussels, Belgium.
Telephone: (2) 707-41-11; **fax:** (2) 707-45-79; **e-mail:** natodoc@hq.nato.int; **internet:** www.nato.int.

The Atlantic Alliance was established on the basis of the 1949 North Atlantic Treaty as a defensive political and military alliance of a group of European states (then numbering 10) and the USA and Canada. The Alliance aims to provide common security for its members through co-operation and consultation in political, military and economic fields, as well as scientific, environmental, and other non-military aspects. The objectives of the Alliance are implemented by NATO. Following the collapse of the communist governments in central and eastern Europe, from 1989 onwards, and the dissolution of the Warsaw Pact (which had hitherto been regarded as the Alliance's principal adversary) in 1991, NATO has undertaken a fundamental transformation of its structures and policies to meet the new security challenges in Europe.

MEMBERS*

Belgium	Hungary	Poland
Canada	Iceland	Portugal
Czech Republic	Italy	Spain
Denmark	Luxembourg	Turkey
France	Netherlands	United Kingdom
Germany	Norway	USA
Greece		

* Greece and Turkey acceded to the Treaty in 1952, and the Federal Republic of Germany in 1955. France withdrew from the integrated military structure of NATO in 1966, although remaining a member of the Atlantic Alliance; in 1996 France resumed participation in some, but not all, of the military organs of NATO. Spain acceded to the Treaty in 1982, but remained outside the Alliance's integrated military structure until 1999. The Czech Republic, Hungary and Poland were formally admitted as members of NATO in March 1999. In March 2003 membership accords were adopted by Bulgaria, Estonia, Latvia, Lithuania, Romania, Slovakia and Slovenia; these states were scheduled to join NATO in May 2004.

Organization

(April 2003)

NORTH ATLANTIC COUNCIL

The Council, the highest authority of the Alliance, is composed of representatives of the 16 member states. It meets at the level of Permanent Representatives, ministers of foreign affairs, or heads of state and government, and, at all levels, has effective political and decision-making authority. Ministerial meetings are held at least twice a year. Occasional meetings of defence ministers are also held. At the level of Permanent Representatives the Council meets at least once a week.

The Secretary-General of NATO is Chairman of the Council, and each year a minister of foreign affairs of a member state is nominated honorary President, following the English alphabetical order of countries.

Decisions are taken by common consent and not by majority vote. The Council is a forum for wide consultation between member governments on major issues, including political, military, economic and other subjects, and is supported by the Senior or regular Political Committee, the Military Committee and other subordinate bodies.

PERMANENT REPRESENTATIVES

Belgium: Dominique Struye de Swielande.
Canada: David Wright.
Czech Republic: Karel Kovanda.
Denmark: Niels Egelund.
France: Benoît d'Aboville.
Germany: Gebhardt von Moltke.
Greece: Vassilis Kaskarelis.
Hungary: János Herman.
Iceland: Gunnar Gunnarsson.
Italy: Maurizio Moreno.
Luxembourg: Patrick Heck.
Netherlands: Michiel Patijn.
Norway: Kai Eide.
Poland: Jerzy Nowak.
Portugal: Fernando Andresen-Guimarães.
Spain: Juan Prat y Coll.
Turkey: Ahmet Uzumcu.
United Kingdom: Dr Emyr Jones Parry.
USA: R. Nicholas Burns.

Note: NATO partner countries are represented by heads of diplomatic missions or liaison officers located at NATO headquarters.

DEFENCE PLANNING COMMITTEE

Most defence matters are dealt with in the Defence Planning Committee, composed of representatives of all member countries except France. The Committee provides guidance to NATO's military authorities and, within the field of its responsibilities, has the same functions and authority as the Council. Like the Council, it meets regularly at ambassadorial level and assembles twice a year in ministerial sessions, when member countries are represented by their ministers of defence.

NUCLEAR PLANNING GROUP

Defence ministers of countries participating in the Defence Planning Committee meet regularly in the Nuclear Planning Group (NPG) to discuss specific policy issues relating to nuclear forces, such as safety, deployment issues, nuclear arms control and proliferation. The NPG is supported by a Staff Group, composed of representatives of all members participating in the NPG, which meets at least once a week.

OTHER COMMITTEES

There are also committees for political affairs, economics, military medical services, armaments, defence review, science, the environment, infrastructure, logistics, communications, civil emergency planning, information and cultural relations, and civil and military budgets. In addition, other committees consider specialized subjects such as NATO pipelines, air traffic management, etc. Since 1992 most of these committees consult on a regular basis with representatives from central and eastern European countries.

INTERNATIONAL SECRETARIAT

The Secretary-General is Chairman of the North Atlantic Council, the Defence Planning Committee and the Nuclear Planning Group. He is the head of the International Secretariat, with staff drawn from the member countries. He proposes items for NATO consultation and is generally responsible for promoting consultation and co-operation in accordance with the provisions of the North Atlantic Treaty. He is empowered to offer his help informally in cases of disputes between member countries, to facilitate procedures for settlement.

Secretary-General: Lord ROBERTSON OF PORT ELLEN (United Kingdom).

Deputy Secretary-General: ALESSANDRO MINUTO RIZZO (Italy).

There is an Assistant Secretary-General for each of the operational divisions listed below.

PRINCIPAL DIVISIONS

Division of Political Affairs: maintains political liaison with national delegations and international organizations; prepares reports on political subjects for the Secretary-General and the Council, and provides the administrative structure for the management of the Alliance's political responsibilities, including disarmament and arms control; Asst Sec.-Gen. GÜNTHER ALTENBURG (Germany).

Division of Defence Planning and Operations: studies all matters concerning the defence of the Alliance, and co-ordinates the defence review and other force planning procedures of the Alliance; Asst Sec.-Gen. Dr EDGAR BUCKLEY (United Kingdom).

Division of Defence Support: promotes the most efficient use of the Allies' resources in the production of military equipment and its standardization; Asst Sec.-Gen. ROBERT BELL (USA).

Division of Security Investment, Logistics and Civil Emergency Planning: supervises the technical and financial aspects of the security investment programme; provides guidance, co-ordination and support to the activities of NATO committees or bodies active in the field of consumer logistics and civil emergency planning; Asst Sec.-Gen. JUAN MARTINEZ-ESPARZA (Spain).

Division of Scientific and Environmental Affairs: advises the Secretary-General on scientific matters of interest to NATO; responsible for promoting and administering scientific exchange programmes between member countries, research fellowships, advanced study institutes and special programmes of support for the scientific and technological development of less-advanced member countries; Asst Sec.-Gen. JEAN FOURNET (France).

Military Organization

MILITARY COMMITTEE

Composed of the allied Chiefs-of-Staff, or their representatives, of all member countries: the highest military body in NATO under the authority of the Council. Meets at least twice a year at Chiefs-of-Staff level and remains in permanent session with Permanent Military Representatives. It is responsible for making recommendations to the Council and Defence Planning Committee and Nuclear Planning Group on military matters and for supplying guidance on military questions to Supreme Allied Commanders and subordinate military authorities. The Committee is supported by an International Military Staff.

In December 1995 France agreed to rejoin the Military Committee, which it formally left in 1966.

Chairman: Gen. HARALD KUJAT (Germany).

COMMANDS

Allied Command Europe—ACE: Casteau, Belgium—Supreme Headquarters Allied Powers Europe—SHAPE; Supreme Allied Commander Europe—SACEUR Gen. JAMES L. JONES (USA).

Allied Command Atlantic—ACLANT: Norfolk, Virginia, USA; Supreme Allied Commander Atlantic—SACLANT Adm. IAN FORBES (USA).

Activities

The common security policy of the members of the North Atlantic Alliance is to safeguard peace through the maintenance of political solidarity and adequate defence at the lowest level of military forces needed to deter all possible forms of aggression. Each year, member countries take part in a Defence Review, designed to assess their contribution to the common defence in relation to their respective capabilities and constraints. Allied defence policy is reviewed periodically by ministers of defence.

Since the 1980s the Alliance has been actively involved in co-ordinating policies with regard to arms control and disarmament issues designed to bring about negotiated reductions in conventional forces, intermediate and short-range nuclear forces and strategic nuclear forces. A Verification Co-ordinating Committee was established in 1990. In April 1999 the summit meeting determined to improve co-ordination on issues relating to weapons of mass destruction through the establishment of a separate centre at NATO headquarters.

Political consultations within the Alliance take place on a permanent basis, under the auspices of the North Atlantic Council (NAC), on all matters affecting the common security interests of the member countries, as well as events outside the North Atlantic Treaty area.

Co-operation in scientific and technological fields as well as co-operation on environmental challenges takes place in the NATO Science Committee and in its Committee on the Challenges of Modern Society. Both these bodies operate an expanding international programme of science fellowships, advance study institutes and research grants. NATO has also pursued co-operation in relation to civil emergency planning. These activities represent NATO's 'Third Dimension'.

At a summit meeting of the Conference on Security and Co-operation in Europe (CSCE, now renamed as the Organization for Security and Co-operation in Europe, OSCE, see p. 283) in November 1990, the member countries of NATO and the Warsaw Pact signed an agreement limiting Conventional Armed Forces in Europe (CFE), whereby conventional arms would be reduced to within a common upper limit in each zone. The two groups also issued a Joint Declaration, stating that they were no longer adversaries and that none of their weapons would ever be used 'except in self-defence'. Following the dissolution of the USSR the eight former Soviet republics with territory in the area of application of the CFE Treaty committed themselves to honouring its obligations in June 1992. In March 1992, under the auspices of the CSCE, the ministers of foreign affairs of the NATO and of the former Warsaw Pact countries (with Russia, Belarus, Ukraine and Georgia taking the place of the USSR) signed the 'Open Skies' treaty. Under this treaty, aerial reconnaissance missions by one country over another were to be permitted, subject to regulation. At the summit meeting of the OSCE in December 1996 the signatories of the CFE Treaty agreed to begin negotiations on a revised treaty governing conventional weapons in Europe. In July 1997 the CFE signatories concluded an agreement on Certain Basic Elements for Treaty Adaptation, which provided for substantial reductions in the maximum levels of conventional military equipment at national and territorial level, replacing the previous bloc-to-bloc structure of the Treaty.

An extensive review of NATO's structures was initiated in June 1990, in response to the fundamental changes taking place in central and eastern Europe. In November 1991 NATO heads of government, convened in Rome, recommended a radical restructuring of the organization in order to meet the demands of the new security environment, which was to involve further reductions in military forces in Europe, active involvement in international peace-keeping operations, increased co-operation with other international institutions and close co-operation with its former adversaries, the USSR and the countries of eastern Europe. The basis for NATO's new force structure was incorporated into a new Strategic Concept, which was adopted in the Rome Declaration issuing from the summit meeting. The concept provided for the maintenance of a collective defence capability, with a reduced dependence on nuclear weapons. Substantial reductions in the size and levels of readiness of NATO forces were undertaken, in order to reflect the Alliance's strictly defensive nature, and forces were reorganized within a streamlined integrated command structure. Forces were categorized into immediate and rapid reaction forces (including the ACE Rapid Reaction Corps—ARRC, which was inaugurated in October 1992), main defence forces and augmentation forces, which may be used to reinforce any NATO region or maritime areas for deterrence, crisis management or defence. In December the NAC, meeting at ministerial level, endorsed a new military structure, which envisaged a reduction in the number of NATO command headquarters from 65 to 20, and instructed the military authorities of the Alliance to formulate a plan for the transitional process. During 1998 work was undertaken on the formulation of a new Strategic Concept, reflecting the changing security environment and defining NATO's future role and objectives, which recognized a broader sphere of influence of NATO in the 21st century and confirmed NATO to be the principal generator of security in the Euro-Atlantic area. It emphasized NATO's role in crisis management and a renewed commitment to partnership and dialogue. The document was approved at a special summit meeting, convened in Washington, USA, in April 1999, to commemorate the 50th anniversary of the Alliance. A separate initiative was approved to assist member states to adapt their defence capabilities to meet changing security requirements, for example improving the means of troop deployment and equipping and protecting forces. A High-Level Steering Group was established to oversee implementation of the Defence Capabilities Initiative. The Washington meeting, which had been envisaged as a celebration of NATO's achievements since its foundation, was, however, dominated by consideration of the situation in the southern Serbian province of Kosovo and Metohija and the conduct of its military offensive against the Federal Republic of Yugoslavia, initiated in late March (see below).

In January 1994 NATO heads of state and government welcomed the entry into force of the Maastricht Treaty, establishing the European Union (EU, superseding the EC). The Treaty included an agreement on the development of a common foreign and security policy, which was intended to be a mechanism to strengthen the European pillar of the Alliance. NATO subsequently co-operated with the Western European Union (WEU) in support of the development of a European Security and Defence Identity. In June 1996 NATO ministers of foreign affairs reached agreement on the implementation of the 'Combined Joint Task Force (CJTF) concept', which had been adopted in January 1994. Measures were to be taken to establish the 'nuclei' of these task forces at certain NATO headquarters, which would provide the basis for missions that could be activated at short notice for specific purposes such as crisis management and peace-keeping. It was also agreed to make CJTFs available for operations undertaken by WEU. In conjunction with this, WEU was to be permitted to make use of Alliance hardware and capabilities (in practice, mostly belonging to the USA) subject to the endorsement of the NAC. The summit meeting, held in April 1999, confirmed NATO's willingness to establish a direct NATO-EU relationship. In February 2000 the first joint NATO-WEU crisis management exercise was conducted. However, in accordance with decisions taken by the EU in late 1999 and 2000 to implement a common security and defence policy, it was agreed that routine NATO-WEU consultation mechanisms were to be suspended. The first formal meeting of the Military Committees of the EU and NATO took place in June 2001 to exchange information relating to the development of EU-NATO security co-operation. In order to support an integrated security structure in Europe, NATO also co-operates with the OSCE and has provided assistance for the development of the latter's conflict prevention and crisis management activities.

In January 2001 NATO established an *ad hoc* working committee in response to concerns expressed by several member governments regarding the health implications of the use of depleted uranium munitions during the Alliance's military intervention in the Balkans. The committee was to co-ordinate the compilation of information regarding the use of depleted uranium and to co-operate with the Yugoslav authorities in the rehabilitation of the local environment. An extraordinary meeting of chiefs of military medical services, including surgeons-general and medical experts, was also convened to consider the issue.

On 12 September 2001 the NAC agreed to invoke, for the first time, Article 5 of the North Atlantic Treaty, providing for collective self-defence, in response to the terrorist attacks against targets in the USA of the previous day. The measure was formally implemented in early October after the US authorities presented evidence substantiating claims that the attacks had been directed from abroad. The NAC endorsed eight specific US requests for logistical and military support in its efforts to counter terrorism, including enhanced sharing of intelligence and full access to airfields and ports in member states. It also agreed to dispatch five surveillance aircraft to help to patrol US airspace and directed the standing naval force to the Eastern Mediterranean. In December NATO ministers of defence initiated a review of military capabilities and defences with a view to strengthening its ability to counter international terrorism.

In February–April 2003 NATO deployed surveillance aircraft and missile defences in Turkey, and provided assistance with civil emergency planning, to defend that country from possible repercussions of the US-led military action against neighbouring Iraq that was initiated in March.

PARTNERSHIPS

In May 1997 a Euro-Atlantic Partnership Council (EAPC) was inaugurated as a successor to the North Atlantic Co-operation Council (NACC), that had been established in December 1991 to provide a forum for consultation on political and security matters with the countries of central and eastern Europe, including the

former Soviet republics. An EAPC Council was to meet monthly at ambassadorial level and twice a year at ministerial level. It was to be supported in its work by a steering committee and a political committee. The EAPC was to pursue the NACC Work Plan for Dialogue, Partnership and Co-operation and incorporate it into a new Work Plan, which was to include an expanded political dimension of consultation and co-operation among participating states. The Partnership for Peace (PfP) programme, which was established in January 1994 within the framework of the NACC, was to remain an integral element of the new co-operative mechanism. The PfP incorporated practical military and defence-related co-operation activities that had originally been part of the NACC Work Plan. Participation in the PfP requires an initial signature of a framework agreement, establishing the common principles and objectives of the partnership, the submission of a presentation document, indicating the political and military aspects of the partnership and the nature of future co-operation activities, and thirdly, the development of individual partnership programmes establishing country-specific objectives. In June 1994 Russia, which had previously opposed the strategy as being the basis for future enlargement of NATO, signed the PfP framework document, which included a declaration envisaging an 'enhanced dialogue' between the two sides. Despite its continuing opposition to any enlargement of NATO, in May 1995 Russia agreed to sign a PfP Individual Partnership Programme, as well as a framework document for NATO-Russian dialogue and co-operation beyond the PfP. During 1994 a Partnership Co-ordination Cell (PCC), incorporating representatives of all partnership countries, became operational in Mons, Belgium. The PCC, under the authority of the NAC, aims to co-ordinate joint military activities and planning in order to implement PfP programmes. The first joint military exercises with countries of the former Warsaw Pact were conducted in September. NATO began formulating a PfP Status of Forces Agreement (SOFA) to define the legal status of Allies' and partners' forces when they are present on each other's territory; the PfP SOFA was opened for signature in June 1995. The new EAPC was to provide a framework for the development of an enhanced PfP programme, which NATO envisaged would become an essential element of the overall European security structure. Accordingly, the military activities of the PfP were to be expanded to include all Alliance missions and incorporate all NATO committees into the PfP process, thus providing for greater co-operation in crisis management, civil emergency planning and training activities. In addition, all PfP member countries were to participate in the CJTF concept through a structure of Partners Staff Elements, working at all levels of the Alliance military structure. Defence ministers of NATO and the 27 partner countries were to meet regularly to provide the political guidance for the enhanced Planning and Review Process of the PfP. In December 1997 NATO ministers of foreign affairs approved the establishment of a Euro-Atlantic Disaster Response Co-ordination Centre (EDRCC), and a non-permanent Euro-Atlantic Disaster Response Unit. The EDRCC was inaugurated in June 1998 and immediately commenced operations to provide relief to ethnic Albanian refugees fleeing the conflict in the Serbian province of Kosovo. In November the NAC approved the establishment of a network of PfP training centres, the first of which was inaugurated in Ankara, Turkey. The centres were a key element of a Training and Education Programme, which was endorsed at the summit meeting in April 1999. During 2000 *ad hoc* working groups were convened to consider EAPC involvement in global humanitarian action against mines, the challenge of small arms and light weapons, and prospects for regional co-operation in South-Eastern Europe and in the Caucasus. The EAPC Action Plan for 2002–04 aimed to promote new approaches to co-operation in the combating of international terrorism.

The enlargement of NATO, through the admission of new members from the former USSR and eastern and central European countries, was considered to be a progressive means of contributing to the enhanced stability and security of the Euro-Atlantic area. In December 1996 NATO ministers of foreign affairs announced that invitations to join the Alliance would be issued to some former eastern bloc countries during 1997. The NATO Secretary-General and member governments subsequently began intensive diplomatic efforts to secure Russia's tolerance of these developments. It was agreed that no nuclear weapons or large numbers of troops would be deployed on the territory of any new member country in the former Eastern bloc. In May 1997 NATO and Russia signed the Founding Act on Mutual Relations, Co-operation and Security, which provided for enhanced Russian participation in all NATO decision-making activities, equal status in peace-keeping operations and representation at the Alliance headquarters at ambassadorial level, as part of a recognized shared political commitment to maintaining stability and security throughout the Euro-Atlantic region. A NATO-Russian Permanent Joint Council (PJC) was established under the Founding Act, and met for the first time in July; the Council provided each side the opportunity for consultation and participation in the other's security decisions, but without a right of veto. In March 1999 Russia condemned NATO's military action against the Federal Republic of

Yugoslavia and announced the suspension of all relations within the framework of the Founding Act, as well as negotiations on the establishment of a NATO mission in Moscow. The PJC convened once more in May 2000, and subsequent meetings were held in June and December. In February 2001 the NATO Secretary-General agreed with the then acting Russian President a joint statement of commitment to pursuing dialogue and co-operation. A NATO information office was opened in Moscow in that month. The PJC condemned major terrorist attacks perpetrated against the USA in September and pledged to strengthen Russia-NATO co-operation with a view to combating international terrorism. In December an agreement was concluded by NATO ministers of foreign affairs and their Russian counterpart to establish an eventual successor body to the PJC. The new NATO-Russia Council, in which NATO member states and Russia were to have equal status in decision-making, was inaugurated in May 2002. The Council aimed to strengthen co-operation in issues including counter-terrorism, crisis management, nuclear non-proliferation, and arms control. In March 2003 NATO membership accords were adopted by Bulgaria, Estonia, Latvia, Lithuania, Romania, Slovakia and Slovenia; these states were scheduled to join NATO in May 2004.

In May 1997 NATO ministers of foreign affairs, meeting in Sintra, Portugal, concluded an agreement with Ukraine providing for enhanced co-operation between the two sides; the so-called Charter on a Distinctive Relationship was signed at the NATO summit meeting held in Madrid, Spain, in July. In May 1998 NATO agreed to appoint a permanent liaison officer in Ukraine to enhance co-operation between the two sides and assist Ukraine to formulate a programme of joint military exercises. The first NATO-Ukraine meeting at the level of heads of state took place in April 1999. A NATO-Ukraine Commission met for the first time in March 2000.

The Madrid summit meeting in July 1997 endorsed the establishment of a Mediterranean Co-operation Group to enhance NATO relations with Egypt, Israel, Jordan, Mauritania, Morocco and Tunisia. The Group was to provide a forum for regular political dialogue between the two groupings and to promote co-operation in training, scientific research and information exchange. In April 1999 NATO heads of state endorsed measures to strengthen the so-called Mediterranean Dialogue. Algeria joined the Mediterranean Dialogue in February 2000.

In July 1997 heads of state and government formally invited the Czech Republic, Hungary and Poland to begin accession negotiations, with the aim of extending membership to those countries in April 1999. During 1997 concern was expressed on the part of some member governments with regard to the cost of expanding the Alliance; however, in November the initial cost of incorporating the Czech Republic, Hungary and Poland into NATO was officially estimated at US $1,300m. over a 10-year period, which was widely deemed to be an acceptable figure. Accession Protocols for the admission of those countries were signed in December and required ratification by all member states. The three countries formally became members of NATO in March 1999. In April the NATO summit meeting, held in Washington, DC, USA, initiated a new Membership Action Plan to extend practical support to aspirant member countries and to formalize a process of reviewing applications. Albania, Bulgaria, Estonia, Latvia, Lithuania, Romania, Slovakia, Slovenia and the former Yugoslav republic of Macedonia were participating in the Membership Action Plan in 2001.

PEACE-KEEPING ACTIVITIES

During the 1990s NATO increasingly developed its role as a mechanism for peace-keeping and crisis management. In June 1992 NATO ministers of foreign affairs, meeting in Oslo, Norway, announced the Alliance's readiness to support peace-keeping operations under the aegis of the CSCE on a case-by-case basis: NATO would make both military resources and expertise available to such operations. In July NATO, in co-operation with WEU, undertook a maritime operation in the Adriatic Sea to monitor compliance with the UN Security Council's resolutions imposing sanctions against the Yugoslav republics of Serbia and Montenegro. In October NATO was requested to provide, staff and finance the military headquarters of the United Nations peace-keeping force in Bosnia and Herzegovina, the UN Protection Force in Yugoslavia (UNPROFOR). In December NATO ministers of foreign affairs expressed the Alliance's readiness to support peace-keeping operations under the authority of the UN Security Council. From April 1993 NATO fighter and reconnaissance aircraft began patrolling airspace over Bosnia and Herzegovina in order to enforce the UN prohibition on military aerial activity over the country. In addition, from July NATO aircraft provided protective cover for UNPROFOR troops operating in the 'safe areas' established by the UN Security Council. In February 1994 NATO conducted the first of several aerial strikes against artillery positions that were violating heavy-weapons exclusion zones imposed around 'safe areas' and threatening the civilian populations. Throughout the conflict the Alliance also provided

transport, communications and logistics to support UN humanitarian assistance in the region.

The peace accord for the former Yugoslavia, which was initialled in Dayton, USA, in November 1995, and signed in Paris in December, provided for the establishment of a NATO-led Implementation Force (IFOR) to ensure compliance with the treaty, in accordance with a strictly defined timetable and under the authority of a UN Security Council mandate. In early December a joint meeting of allied foreign and defence ministers endorsed the military structure for the peace mission, entitled Operation Joint Endeavour, which was to involve approximately 60,000 troops from 31 NATO and non-NATO countries. The mission was to be under the overall authority of the Supreme Allied Commander Europe (ACE), with the Commander of the ACE Rapid Reaction Corps providing command on the ground. IFOR, which constituted NATO's largest military operation ever, formally assumed responsIbility for peace-keeping in Bosnia and Herzegovina from the UN on 20 December.

By mid-1996 the military aspects of the Dayton peace agreement had largely been implemented under IFOR supervision, including the withdrawal of former warring parties to behind agreed lines of separation and the release of prisoners of war. Substantial progress was achieved in the demobilization of soldiers and militia and in the cantonment of heavy weaponry. However, in August and September the Bosnian Serbs obstructed IFOR weapons inspections and the force was obliged to threaten the Serbs with strong military retaliation to secure access to the arms sites. During 1996 IFOR personnel undertook many activities relating to the civilian reconstruction of Bosnia and Herzegovina, including the repair of roads, railways and bridges; reconstruction of schools and hospitals; delivery of emergency food and water supplies; and emergency medical transportation. IFOR also co-operated with, and provided logistical support for, the Office of the High Representative of the International Community in Bosnia and Herzegovina, which was charged with overseeing implementation of the civilian aspects of the Bosnian peace accord. IFOR assisted the OSCE in preparing for and overseeing the all-Bosnia legislative elections that were held in September, and provided security for displaced Bosnians who crossed the interentity boundary in order to vote in their towns of origin. In December NATO ministers of foreign affairs approved a follow-on operation, with an 18-month mandate, to be known as the Stabilization Force (SFOR). SFOR was to be about one-half the size of IFOR, but was to retain 'the same unity of command and robust rules of engagement' as the previous force. SFOR became operational on 20 December. Its principal objective was to maintain a safe environment at a military level to ensure that the civil aspects of the Dayton peace accord could be fully implemented, including the completion of the de-mining process, the repatriation of refugees and preparations for municipal elections. In July 1997 NATO heads of government expressed their support for a more determined implementation of SFOR's mandate permitting the arrest of people sought by the International Criminal Tribunal for the Former Yugoslavia (ICTY, see p. 15) if they were discovered within the normal course of duties. A few days later troops serving under SFOR seized two former Serb officials who had been indicted on charges of genocide. SFOR has subsequently undertaken this objective as part of its operational activities. From mid-1997 SFOR assisted efforts to maintain the security and territorial integrity of the Republika Srpska in the face of violent opposition from nationalist supporters of the former President, Radovan Karadžić, based in Pale. In August NATO authorized SFOR to use force to prevent the use of the local media to incite violence, following attacks on multinational forces by Serb nationalists during attempts to regain control of police buildings. In November SFOR provided the general security framework, as well as logistical and communications assistance, in support of the OSCE's supervision of legislative elections that were conducted in the Republika Srpska. In December NATO ministers of defence confirmed that SFOR would be maintained at its current strength of some 31,000 troops, subject to the periodic six-monthly reviews. In February 1998 NATO resolved to establish within SFOR a specialized unit to respond to civil unrest and uphold public security. At the same time the NAC initiated a series of security co-operation activities to promote the development of democratic practices and defence mechanisms in Bosnia and Herzegovina. In October 1999 the NAC formally agreed to implement a reduction in SFOR's strength to some 20,000 troops, as well as a revision of its command structure, in response to the improved security situation in Bosnia and Herzegovina. In 2001 some 35 countries contributed troops to SFOR. Its main activities continued to be in support of the peace process, assisting the collection and disposal of illegal weapons, distributing humanitarian aid, and rebuilding the country's infrastructure. In May 2002, in view of the improved security environment in Bosnia and Herzegovina, NATO determined to reduce SFOR to 12,000 troops by the end of the year.

In March 1998 an emergency session of the NAC was convened at the request of the Albanian Government, which was concerned at the deteriorating security of its border region with the Serbian province of Kosovo and Metohija, following intensified action by the

Kosovo Liberation Army (KLA) and retaliatory attacks by Serbian security forces. In mid-June NATO defence ministers authorized the formulation of plans for airstrikes against Serbian targets. A few days later some 80 aircraft dispatched from 15 NATO bases flew close to Albania's border with Kosovo, in an attempt to demonstrate the Alliance's determination to prevent further reprisals against the ethnic Albanian population. In September NATO defence ministers urged a diplomatic solution to the conflict, but insisted that, with an estimated 50,000 refugees living without shelter in the mountainous region bordering Albania, their main objective was to avert a humanitarian disaster. In late September the UN Security Council issued a resolution (1199) demanding an immediate cease-fire in Kosovo, the withdrawal of the majority of Serbian military and police forces, co-operation by all sides with humanitarian agencies, and the initiation of political negotiations on some form of autonomy for the province. Plans for NATO airstrikes were finalized in early October. However, the Russian Government remained strongly opposed to the use of force and there was concern among some member states whether there was sufficient legal basis for NATO action without further UN authorization. Nevertheless, in mid-October, following Security Council condemnation of the humanitarian situation in Kosovo, the NAC agreed on limited airstrikes against Serbian targets, with a 96-hour delay on the 'activation order'. At the same time the US envoy to the region, Richard Holbrooke, concluded an agreement with President Milošević to implement the conditions of UN Resolution 1199. A 2,000-member international observer force, under the auspices of the OSCE, was to be established to monitor compliance with the agreement, supported by a NATO Co-ordination Unit, based in the former Yugoslav republic of Macedonia (FYRM), to assist with aerial surveillance. In mid-November NATO ambassadors approved the establishment of a 1,200–1,800 strong multinational force, under French command, to assist in any necessary evacuation of OSCE monitors. A NATO Kosovo Verification Command Centre was established in Kumanovo, north-east FYRM, in November; however, President Milošević warned that the dispatch of foreign troops into Kosovo would be treated as an act of aggression.

In January 1999 NATO ambassadors convened in an emergency session following the discovery of the bodies of 45 ethnic Albanians in the Kosovan village of Racak. The meeting demanded that Serbia co-operate with an inquiry into the incident by the Prosecutor of the ICTY, guarantee the security and safety of all international personnel, withdraw security forces (which had continued to undertake offensives within Kosovo), and uphold the cease-fire. Intensive diplomatic efforts, co-ordinated by the six-country 'Contact Group' on the former Yugoslavia, succeeded in bringing both sides in the dispute to talks on the future of Kosovo. During the first stage of negotiations, held in Rambouillet, France, a provisional framework for a political settlement was formulated, based on a form of autonomy for Kosovo (to be reviewed after a three-year period), and incorporating a mandate for a NATO force of some 28,000 troops to monitor its implementation. The talks were suspended in late February with neither side having agreed to the accord. On the resumption of negotiations in mid-March representatives of the KLA confirmed that they would sign the peace settlement. President Milošević, however, continued to oppose the establishment of a NATO force in Kosovo and, despite further diplomatic efforts by Holbrooke, declined to endorse the agreement in accordance with a deadline imposed by the Contact Group. Amid reports of renewed Serbian violence against Albanian civilians in Kosovo, the NAC subsequently reconfirmed its support for NATO military intervention.

On 24 March 1999 an aerial offensive against the Federal Republic of Yugoslavia (now Serbia and Montenegro) was initiated by NATO, with the declared aim of reducing that country's capacity to commit attacks on the Albanian population. The first phase of the allied operation was directed against defence facilities, followed, a few days later, by the second phase which permitted direct attacks on artillery positions, command centres and other military targets in a declared exclusion zone south of the 44th parallel. The escalation of the conflict prompted thousands of Albanians to flee Kosovo, while others were reportedly forced from their homes by Serbian security personnel, creating massive refugee populations in neighbouring countries. In early April NATO ambassadors agreed to dispatch some 8,000 troops, as an ACE Mobile Force Land operation (entitled 'Operation Allied Harbour'), to provide humanitarian assistance to the estimated 300,000 refugees in Albania at that time and to provide transportation to relieve overcrowded camps, in particular in border areas. Refugees in the FYRM were to be assisted by the existing NATO contingent (numbering some 12,000 troops by early April), which was permitted by the authorities in that country to construct new camps for some 100,000 displaced Kosovans. An additional 1,000 troops were transferred from the FYRM to Albania in mid-May in order to construct a camp to provide for a further 65,000 refugees. In mid-April NATO ministers of foreign affairs, meeting in special session, expressed extreme concern at the refugee situation throughout the region. The ministers also clarified the conditions necessary to halt the offensive, which included Serbia's

agreement to an international military presence in Kosovo, provision for the safe return of all refugees and an undertaking to work on the basis of the Rambouillet accord. Russia continued to pursue diplomatic efforts to secure a peaceful settlement to the conflict, however, Milošević's reported agreement to allow an unarmed international force in Kosovo, conditional on the immediate end to the NATO campaign, was dismissed by NATO governments. From early April there was increasing evidence of civilian casualties resulting from NATO's aerial bombing of transport, power and media infrastructure and suspected military targets. In mid-April NATO initiated an inquiry following the bombing of a convoy of lorries which resulted in the deaths of some 69 refugees. In the following month NATO was obliged to apologise to the authorities of the People's Republic of China after the accidental bombing of its embassy in Belgrade. At the same time there was widespread concern among governments at increasing evidence of systematic killings and ethnic violence being committed by Serbian forces within Kosovo, and at the estimated 100,000 Albanian men unaccounted for among the massive displaced population. NATO's 50th anniversary summit meeting, held in Washington, USA, in late April, was dominated by consideration of the conflict and of the future stability of the region. A joint statement declared the determination of all Alliance members to increase economic and military pressure on President Milošević to withdraw forces from Kosovo. In particular, the meeting agreed to prevent shipments of petroleum reaching Serbia through Montenegro, to complement the embargo imposed by the EU and a new focus of the bombing campaign which aimed to destroy the fuel supply within Serbia. However, there was concern on the part of several NATO governments on the legal and political aspects of implementing the embargo. The meeting failed to adopt a unified position on the use of ground forces, which many expert commentators insisted, throughout the campaign, were necessary to secure NATO's objectives. In May ministers of foreign affairs of the Group of Seven industrialized nations and Russia (the G-8) agreed on general principles for a political solution, which was to form the basis of UN Security Council resolution. Later in that month NATO estimated that a future Kosovo Peace Implementation Force (KFOR), installed to guarantee a settlement, would require at least 48,000 troops. Following further intensive diplomatic efforts to secure a cease-fire in Kosovo, on 9 June a Military Technical Agreement was signed between NATO and the Federal Republic of Yugoslavia, incorporating a timetable for the withdrawal of all Serbian security personnel. On the following day the UN Security Council adopted Resolution 1244, which authorized an international security presence in Kosovo, under NATO, and an international civilian presence, the UN Interim Administration Mission in Kosovo (UNMIK). The NAC subsequently suspended the airstrike campaign, which, by that time, had involved some 38,000 sorties. KFOR was organized into six brigades, under the leadership of France, Germany, Italy, USA and the United Kingdom (with responsibility for two brigades). An initial force of 20,000 troops entered Kosovo on 12 June. A few days later an agreement was concluded with Russia, whose troops had also entered Kosovo and taken control of Pristina airport, which provided for the joint responsibility of the airstrip with a NATO contingent and for the participation of some 3,600 Russian troops in KFOR, reporting to the country command in each sector. On 20 June the withdrawal of Yugoslav troops from Kosovo was completed, providing for the formal ending of NATO's air campaign. The KLA undertook to demilitarize and transform the force, as required under Resolution 1244, which was reported to have been achieved in September. KFOR's immediate responsibility was to provide a secure environment to facilitate the safe return of refugees, and, pending the full deployment of UNMIK, to assist the reconstruction of infrastructure and civil and political institutions. In addition, NATO troops were to assist personnel of the international tribunal to investigate sites of alleged violations of human rights and mass graves. From August an escalation of ethnic violence and deterioration of law and order in some parts of the province was an outstanding concern. In January 2000 NATO agreed that the Eurocorps defence force (see under WEU) would assume command of KFOR headquarters in April. At that time KFOR's main concerns were to protect the minority populations, maintain security and reintegrate members of the KLA into civilian life. KFOR was also to continue to work closely with UNMIK in the provision of humanitarian aid, the rehabilitation of infrastructure and the development of civil administration. In February an emergency meeting of the NAC was convened to review the situation in the divided town of Titova Mitrovica, northern Kosovo, where violent clashes had occurred between the ethnic populations and five people had died during attempts by KFOR to impose order. The NAC expressed its determination to reinforce KFOR's troop levels. In September KFOR undertook to protect ethnic Serbians who were eligible to vote in a general election in the Federal Republic of Yugoslavia, and in the following month KFOR worked with OSCE and UN personnel to maintain a secure environment and provide logistical assistance for the holding of municipal elections in Kosovo. During the year KFOR attempted to prevent the movement and stockpiling of illegal armaments in the region. In November there was a marked deterioration in the security situation in Kosovo, and KFOR attempted to halt several outbreaks of cross-border violence. In February 2001 NATO conducted negotiations with the Yugoslav Government regarding new security arrangements to prevent further attacks on the local population in southern Serbia and to counter illegal arms-trafficking. A Weapons Destruction Programme was successfully conducted by KFOR between April 2000–December 2001; a second programme was initiated in March 2002, while an Ammunition Destruction Programme commenced in January.

In March 2001 Albanian separatists in the FYRM escalated their campaign in the north of that country. KFOR troops attempted to prevent Kosovo Albanians from supporting the rebels, fighting as the National Liberation Army (NLA), in order to avert further violence and instability. NATO dispatched military and political missions to meet with the Macedonian authorities, and agreed that Serbian troops were to be permitted to enter the ground safety zone in the Presevo valley (bordering on Kosovo and the FYRM) to strengthen security and prevent it becoming a safe haven for the rebel fighters. The Secretary-General also requested an additional 1,400 troops from member countries to reinforce border security. In mid-March the NLA seized strategic positions around Tetovo, in north-west FYRM. After several days of conflict Macedonian troops initiated an offensive against the rebel strongholds, prompting thousands of Albanians to flee into Kosovo. Nevertheless, hostilities intensified again from late April, resulting in further population displacements. In June NATO troops supervised the withdrawal of some 300 armed Albanian rebels who had been besieged in a town neighbouring Skopje, the Macedonian capital. A cease-fire agreement, mediated by NATO, was concluded by the Macedonian authorities and Albanian militants in early July, as a prelude to negotiations on a political settlement. Meanwhile, NATO, at the request of the Macedonian Government, was drafting contingency plans to deploy troops in the FYRM with a mandate to supervise the voluntary disarmament of the Albanian militants and to collect and destroy their weapons, on condition that both sides showed commitment to maintaining the cease-fire and pursuing peace talks. In mid-July, however, ethnic Albanian insurgents in the Tetovo area were reportedly violating the cease-fire accord. An agreement regarding disarmament and conditions for ethnic minorities, as well as for the immediate withdrawal of troops, was concluded in August. Some 3,800 NATO troops were deployed at the end of that month, under so-called Operation Essential Harvest. At the end of the operation's 30-day mandate almost 4,300 guns had been surrendered, together with 400,000 mines, grenades and ammunition rounds. The NLA formally disbanded, in accordance with the peace agreement. The NAC approved a successor mission, comprising 700 troops, initially with a three-month mandate (subsequently suspended), to protect the civilian observers of the accord (to be deployed by the EU and OSCE). In June 2002 a team from NATO headquarters met with the Macedonian authorities to discuss measures to enhance the country's co-operation with the Alliance.

In April 2003 NATO determined to enhance its support to the International Security Assistance Force in Afghanistan, mandated by the United Nations Security Council in December 2001 to assist the Afghan Interim Authority in maintaining security; NATO was to assume responsibility for command, co-ordination and planning of the operation later in 2003.

Nato Agencies

1. Civilian production and logistics organizations responsible to the NAC:

Central Europe Pipeline Management Agency—CEPMA: BP 552, 78005 Versailles, France; tel. 1-39-24-49-00; fax 1-39-55-65-39; f. 1957; responsible for the 24-hour operation of the Central Europe Pipeline System and its storage and distribution facilities.

NATO Air Command Control System Management Agency— NACMA: 8 rue de Genève, 1140 Brussels, Belgium; tel. (2) 707-41-11; fax (2) 707-87-77; internet www.nacma.nato.int; conducts planning, system engineering, implementation and configuration management for NATO's ACCS programme.

NATO Airborne Early Warning and Control Programme Management Organisation—NAPMO: Akerstraat 7, 6445 CL Brunssum, Netherlands; fax (45) 5254373; f. 1978; responsible for the management and implementation of the NATO Airborne Early Warning and Control Programme.

NATO Consultation, Command and Control Agency—NC3A: 1110 Brussels, Belgium; tel. (2) 707-43-58; fax (2) 708-87-70; internet www.nc3a.nato.int; works within the framework of the NATO C3 Organization (f. 1996 by restructuring of the NATO Communications and Information Systems Organization and the Tri-Service Group on Communications and Electronics, incorpor-

ating the former Allied Data Systems Interoperability Agency, the Allied Naval Communications Agency and the Allied Tactical Communications Agency); provides scientific advice and assistance to NATO military and political authorities; helps to develop, procure and implement cost-effective system capabilities to support political consultations and military command and control functions; also maintains offices in The Hague.

NATO CIS Operating and Support Agency—NACOSA: maintains NATO's communications and information system (CIS); supervised by the NC3 Board.

> **NATO CIS School:** 04010 Borgo Riave, Latina, Italy; tel. (0773) 6771; fax (0773) 662467; f. 1959; provides advanced training to civilian and military personnel in the operation and maintenance of NATO's communications and information system; conducts orientation courses for partner countries.

NATO EF 2000 and Tornado Development, Production and Logistics Management Agency—NETMA: Insel Kammerstrasse 12–14, Postfach 1302, 82008 Unterhaching, Germany; tel. (89) 666800; fax (89) 6668055; replaced the NATO Multirole Combat Aircraft (MRCA) Development and Production Management Agency (f. 1969) and the NATO European Fighter (EF) Aircraft Development, Production and Logistics Management Agency (f. 1987); responsible for the joint development and production of the European Fighter Aircraft and the MRCA (Tornado).

NATO HAWK Management Office: 26 rue Galliéni, 92500 Rueil-Malmaison, France; tel. 1-47-08-75-00; fax 1-47-52-10-99; e-mail bgohnhmo@csi.com; f. 1959 to supervise the multinational production and upgrading programmes of the HAWK surface-to-air missile system in Europe; Gen. Man. A. BOCCHI.

NATO Helicopter Design and Development Production and Logistics Management Agency—NAHEMA: Le Quatuor, Bâtiment A, 42 route de Galice, 13082 Aix-en-Provence Cédex 2, France; tel. 4-42-95-92-00; fax 4-42-64-30-50.

NATO Maintenance and Supply Agency—NAMSA: 8302 Capellen, Luxembourg; tel. 30-631; fax 30-87-21; internet www.namsa.nato.int; f. 1958; supplies spare parts and logistic support for a number of jointly-used weapon systems, missiles and electronic systems; all member nations except Iceland participate.

2. Responsible to the Military Committee:

NATO Defense College—NADEFCOL: Via Giorgio Pelosi 1, 00143 Rome-Cecchiguola, Italy; tel. (06) 505259; f. 1951 to train officials for posts in NATO organizations or in national ministries.

NATO Frequency Management Sub-Committee—FMSC: 1100 Brussels, Belgium; tel. (2) 707-55-28; replaced the Allied Radio Frequency Agency (f. 1951); the FMSC is the frequency authority of the Alliance and establishes and co-ordinates all policy concerned with the military use of the radio frequency spectrum.

NATO Standardization Agency—NSA: 1110 Brussels, Belgium; tel. (2) 707-55-76; fax (2) 707-57-18; e-mail nsa@hq.nato.int; lead agent for the development, co-ordination and assessment of operational standardization, in order to enhance interoperability; initiates, co-ordinates, supports and administers standardization activities conducted under the authority of the NATO Committee for Standardization.

Research and Technology Organization—RTO: BP 25, 7 rue Ancelle, 92201 Neuilly-sur-Seine Cédex, France; tel. 1-55-61-22-00; fax 1-55-61-22-99; e-mail mailbox@rta.nato.int; internet www.rta.nato.int; f. 1998 by merger of the Advisory Group for Aerospace Research and Development and the Defence Research Group; brings together scientists and engineers from member countries for exchange of information and research co-operation (formally established 1998); provides scientific and technical advice for the Military Committee, for other NATO bodies and for member nations; comprises a Research and Technology Board and a Research and Technology Agency, responsible for implementing RTO's work programme.

3. Responsible to Supreme Allied Commander Atlantic (SACLANT):

NATO SACLANT Undersea Research Centre— SACLANTCEN: Viale San Bartolomeo 400, 19138 La Spezia, Italy; tel. (0187) 5271; fax (0187) 527420; e-mail library@saclantc.nato.int; internet www.saclantc.nato.int; f. 1959 to conduct research in support of NATO operational requirements in antisubmarine warfare and mine counter-measures.

4. Responsible to Supreme Allied Commander Europe (SACEUR):

NATO (SHAPE) School: Am Rainenbichl 54, 82487 Oberammergau, Germany; tel. (88) 224477; fax (88) 221035; e-mail postmaster@natoschool-shape.de; internet www.natoschool-shape.de; f. 1975; acts as a centre for training military and civilian personnel of NATO countries, and, since 1991, for officials from partner countries, in support of NATO policies, operations and objectives.

Finance

As NATO is an international, not a supra-national, organization, its member countries themselves decide the amount to be devoted to their defence effort and the form which the latter will assume. Thus, the aim of NATO's defence planning is to develop realistic military plans for the defence of the alliance at reasonable cost. Under the annual defence planning process, political, military and economic factors are considered in relation to strategy, force requirements and available resources. The procedure for the co-ordination of military plans and defence expenditures rests on the detailed and comparative analysis of the capabilities of member countries. All installations for the use of international forces are financed under a common-funded infrastructure programme. In accordance with the terms of the Partnership for Peace strategy, partner countries undertake to make available the necessary personnel, assets, facilities and capabilities to participate in the programme. The coun-

tries also share the financial cost of military exercises in which they participate. The administrative (or 'civil') budget, which includes the NATO Science Programme, amounted to US \$133m. in 2000. The total military budget approved for 2001 amounted to \$716m. (including the operating costs of NATO command structures in the former Yugoslavia, but excluding the costs of assignment of military personnel, met by the contributing countries).

Publications

NATO publications (in English and French, with some editions in other languages) include:
NATO Basic Fact Sheets.
NATO Final Communiqués.
NATO Handbook.
NATO in the 21st Century.
NATO Review (quarterly in 11 languages; annually in Icelandic).
NATO Update (weekly, electronic version only).
Economic and scientific publications

ORGANISATION FOR ECONOMIC CO-OPERATION AND DEVELOPMENT—OECD

Address: 2 rue André-Pascal, 75775 Paris Cédex 16, France.

Telephone: 1-45-24-82-00; **fax:** 1-45-24-85-00; **e-mail:** webmaster@ oecd.org; **internet:** www.oecd.org.

OECD was founded in 1961, replacing the Organisation for European Economic Co-operation (OEEC) which had been established in 1948 in connection with the Marshall Plan. It constitutes a forum for governments to discuss, develop and attempt to co-ordinate their economic and social policies. The Organisation aims to promote policies designed to achieve the highest level of sustainable economic growth, employment and increase in the standard of living, while maintaining financial stability and democratic government, and to contribute to economic expansion in member and non-member states and to the expansion of world trade.

MEMBERS

Australia	Hungary	Norway
Austria	Iceland	Poland
Belgium	Ireland	Portugal
Canada	Italy	Slovakia
Czech Republic	Japan	Spain
Denmark	Republic of Korea	Sweden
Finland	Luxembourg	Switzerland
France	Mexico	Turkey
Germany	Netherlands	United Kingdom
Greece	New Zealand	USA

The European Commission also takes part in OECD's work.

Organization

(April 2003)

COUNCIL

The governing body of OECD is the Council, at which each member country is represented. The Council meets from time to time (usually once a year) at the level of government ministers, with the chairmanship rotated among member states. It also meets regularly at official level, when it comprises the Secretary-General and the Permanent Representatives of member states to OECD. It is responsible for all questions of general policy and may establish subsidiary bodies as required, to achieve the aims of the Organisation. Decisions and recommendations of the Council are adopted by mutual agreement of all its members.

Heads of Permanent Delegations
(with ambassadorial rank)

Australia: IAN K. FORSYTH.
Austria: ULRICH STACHER.
Belgium: RÉGINE DE CLERCQ.
Canada: SUZANNE HURTUBISE.
Czech Republic: JIRI MACESKA.
Denmark: PETER BRÜCKNER.
Finland: JORMA JULIN.
France: DOMINIQUE PERREAU.
Germany: HANS STEFAN KRUSE.
Greece: GEORGE E. KRIMPAS.
Hungary: KAROLY LOTZ.
Iceland: SIGRIDUR ASDIS SNAEVARR.
Ireland: JOHN ROWAN.
Italy: FRANCESCO OLIVIERI.
Japan: SEIICHIRO NOBORU.
Republic of Korea: KYUNG-TAE LEE.
Luxembourg: JEAN-MARC HOSCHEIT.
Mexico: CLAUDE HELLER.
Netherlands: FRANZ ENGERING.
New Zealand: ADRIAN H. MACEY.
Norway: TANYA H. STORM.
Poland: JAN BIELAWSKI.
Portugal: BASILIO HORTA.
Slovakia: DUSAN BELLA.
Spain: ELENA PISONERO RUIZ.
Sweden: ANDERS FERM.
Switzerland: WILHELM B. JAGGI.
Turkey: SENCAR OZSOY.
United Kingdom: CHRISTOPHER CRABBIE.
USA: JEANNE L. PHILLIPS.

Participant with Special Status

European Commission: JOHN MADDISON (United Kingdom).

EXECUTIVE COMMITTEE

The Executive Committee prepares the work of the Council. It is also called upon to carry out specific tasks where necessary. In addition to its regular meetings, the Committee meets occasionally in special sessions attended by senior government officials.

SECRETARIAT

The Council, the committees and other bodies in OECD are assisted by an independent international secretariat headed by the Secretary-General. An Executive Director is responsible for the management of administrative support services.

Secretary-General: DONALD J. JOHNSTON (Canada).

Deputy Secretaries-General: RICHARD E. HECKLINGER (USA), HERWIG SCHLÖGL (Germany), SEIICHI KONDO (Japan), BERGLIND ASGEIRSDOTTIR (Iceland).

Executive Director: PIERRE-DOMINIQUE SCHMIDT (Belgium).

AUTONOMOUS AND SEMI-AUTONOMOUS BODIES

Centre for Educational Research and Innovation—CERI: f. 1968; includes all member countries; Dir JOHN MARTIN.

Development Centre.

European Conference of Ministers of Transport.

Financial Action Task Force on Money Laundering.

International Energy Agency (see p. 281).

Nuclear Energy Agency (see p. 282).

Activities

The greater part of the work of OECD, which covers all aspects of economic and social policy, is prepared and carried out in about 200 specialized bodies (committees, working parties, etc.); all members are normally represented on these bodies, except on those of a restricted nature.

ECONOMIC POLICY

Through its work on economic policy, OECD aims to promote stable macroeconomic environments in member and non-member countries and the equitable distribution of income. The main organ for the consideration and direction of economic policy is the Economic Policy Committee, which comprises governments' chief economic advisers and central bankers, and meets two or three times a year. It has several working parties and groups, the most important of which are Working Party No. 1 on Macro-Economic and Structural Policy Analysis, Working Party No. 3 on Policies for the Promotion of Better International Payments Equilibrium, and the Working Group on Short-Term Economic Prospects. In 2001 the Committee's priority work areas included the interaction between labour and product markets, tax reform, issues related to the ageing of OECD populations, and the development of human capital.

The Economic and Development Review Committee, comprising all member countries, is responsible for the annual examination of the economic situation and macro economic and structural policies of each member country. A report, including specific policy recommendations, is issued every 12 to 18 months on each country, after an examination carried out by the Committee. This process of peer review has been extended to other branches of the Organisation's work (agriculture, environment, manpower and social affairs, scientific policy and development aid efforts).

STATISTICS

Statistical data and related methodological information are collected from member governments and, where possible, consolidated, or converted into an internationally comparable form. The Statistics Directorate maintains data required for macroeconomic forecasting, i.e. national accounts, the labour force, foreign trade, prices, output, and monetary, financial, industrial and other short-term statistics. Work is also undertaken to develop new statistics and new statistical standards and systems in areas of emerging policy interest (such as sustainable development). In addition, the Directorate passes on to non-member countries member states' experience in compiling statistics. In 2000 a project to reform OECD's statistical system was launched, and in 2001 a new strategy began to be defined. The overall aim was to improve the efficiency and quality of the statistics produced and to counter some of the problems inherent in the decentralized system. (Other specialist directorates also collect statistics and maintain databases.) A co-ordinated framework for collecting, processing, storing, retrieving, analysing and disseminating data was to be developed, with precise guide-lines issued to all directorates and integrated programmes across the Organisation. The Directorate aims to expand contacts with other international and national statistical authorities.

DEVELOPMENT CO-OPERATION

The Development Assistance Committee (DAC) is the principal body through which the Organisation deals with issues relating to co-operation with developing countries and is one of the key forums in which the major bilateral donors work together to increase their effectiveness in support of sustainable development. The DAC holds an annual high-level meeting of ministers or heads of aid agencies. Work is supported by the Development Co-operation Directorate, which monitors aid programmes and resource flows, compiles statistics and seeks to establish codes of practice in aid. There is also a working party on aid evaluation, a working party on gender equality, a network on good governance and capacity development, a network on conflict, peace and development co-operation, and a working party on the financial aspects of development assistance.

Guided by the Development Partnerships Strategy formulated in 1996, the DAC's mission is to foster co-ordinated, integrated, effective and adequately financed international efforts in support of sustainable economic and social development. Recognizing that developing countries themselves are ultimately responsible for their own development, the DAC concentrates on how international co-operation can contribute to the population's ability to overcome poverty and participate fully in society. Principal activities include: adopting authoritative policy guide-lines; conducting periodic critical reviews of members' programmes of development co-operation; providing a forum for dialogue, exchange of experience and the building of international consensus on policy and management issues; and publishing statistics and reports on aid and other resource flows to developing countries and countries in transition. A working set of indicators of development progress has been established by the DAC, in collaboration with experts from UN agencies (including the World Bank) and from developing countries.

The Development Partnerships Strategy was followed up by a report entitled *Shaping the 21st Century—The Contribution Of Development Co-operation* , which outlined a series of poverty reduction and development objectives. In 2000 the Partnership for Poverty Reduction was launched, with the aim of establishing a partnership approach for bilateral co-operation with developing countries. In late 2000 the DAC established a Task Force on Donor Practices, which aimed to strengthen partner countries' ownership of development programmes by improving and co-ordinating donor practices. In April 2001 OECD adopted a Recommendation on Untying Official Development Assistance to the Least Developed Countries, in accordance with which recipient countries may use aid to purchase goods and services from any state, not just the donor country.

In May 1999 the Executive Committee in Special Session considered OECD's role in South-East Europe once a peace settlement had been agreed on the future of Kosovo and Metohija, in southern Serbia. The Committee determined that OECD should collaborate with the World Bank, IMF and other agencies to promote economic and social development in countries bordering the Federal Republic of Yugoslavia, in order to strengthen political stability throughout the region.

PUBLIC MANAGEMENT

The Public Management Committee, and its secretariat, the Public Management Service (PUMA) are concerned with issues of governance, including: the formulation of policies and their implementation; the allocation of resources; building and strengthening effective government structures; human resource management; and questions of accountability, ethics and corruption, consultation and transparency. PUMA serves as a forum for senior officials responsible for the central management systems of government, providing information, analysis and recommendations on public management and governing capacity. In view of recent changes in the environment for government management, PUMA has addressed the greater role afforded to sub-national governments by decentralization and the use of new information and communication technologies. A joint initiative of OECD and the EU, operating within PUMA, supports good governance in countries of Central and Eastern Europe. The so-called Support for Improvement in Governance and Management (SIGMA) programme advises countries on improving their administrative efficiency and promotes the adherence of public-sector staff to democratic values and ethics and respect for the rule of law. SIGMA also helps to strengthen capacities at the level of central government to address the challenges of EU integration, and greater global interdependence.

CO-OPERATION WITH NON-MEMBER ECONOMIES

The Centre for Co-operation with Non-Members (CCNM) was established in January 1998, by merger of the Centre for Co-operation with Economies in Transition (founded in 1990) and the Liaison and Co-ordination Unit. It serves as the focal point for the development of policy dialogue with non-member economies, managing multi-country, thematic, regional and country programmes. An Emerging Market Economy Forum brings together non-member economies engaged in market-orientated policy reform of interest to members.

Recent topics discussed included tax evasion, the regulation of securities markets and foreign direct investment policy. There is also a General Programme for the Transition Economies of Europe and Central Asia (covering a broad range of economic and social policy issues, as well as structural adjustment), a Baltic Regional Programme, and a General Programme for South Eastern Europe.

The Centre manages OECD's various Global Forums, which discuss a wide range of specific issues. An Emerging Market Economy Forum brings together non-member economies engaged in market-orientated policy reform of interest to members. Recent topics discussed have included tax evasion, the regulation of securities markets and foreign direct investment policy.

Non-member economies are invited, on a selective basis by the CCNM, to participate in or observe the work of certain OECD committees and working parties. The Centre also provides a limited range of training activities in support of policy implementation and institution building. Five multilateral tax centres provide workshops and seminars for senior officials in tax administration and policy. OECD, through the CCNM, co-sponsors the Centre for Private Sector Development in İstanbul, Turkey, with the Turkish and German Governments. This assists various countries to develop the necessary framework and policies for a market economy and integration into the world economy. The CCNM also sponsors the Joint Vienna Institute, which offers a variety of administrative, economic and financial management courses to participants from transition economies. The Centre co-ordinates and maintains OECD's relations with other international organizations.

INTERNATIONAL TRADE

OECD's Trade Committee supports the continued liberalization and efficient operation of the multilateral trading system, with the aim of contributing to the expansion of world trade on a non-discriminatory basis. Its activities include examination of issues concerning trade relations among member countries as well as relations with non-member countries, and consideration and discussion of trade measures taken by a member country which adversely affect another's interests. Through its working parties, the Committee analyses trade issues relating to, for example, the environment and agriculture. It holds regular consultations with civil society organizations.

Through its export credit agreement, OECD maintains an export credit system, stipulating generous financial terms and conditions, and serves as a forum for the discussion and co-ordination of export credit policies. The Working Party on Export Credits and Credit Guarantees works to achieve a level playing field in this area.

The Trade Committee considers the challenges that are presented to the existing international trading system by financial or economic instability, the process of globalization of production and markets and the ensuing deeper integration of national economies. OECD provided support to the multilateral trade negotiations conducted under the General Agreement on Tariffs and Trade (GATT), assisting member countries to analyse the effects of the trade accords and promoting its global benefits. Following the entry into force of the World Trade Organization (WTO) agreements in 1995, OECD continued to study and assess aspects of the international trade agenda. In November 1999 OECD published a report on the impact of further trade liberalization on developing countries, in preparation for the next round of multilateral trade negotiations (which were launched by WTO in November 2001). In 2000 all OECD governments adopted a set of revised guide-lines for multinational enterprises.

FINANCIAL, FISCAL AND ENTERPRISE AFFAIRS

Promoting the efficient functioning of markets and enterprises and strengthening the multilateral framework for trade and investment is the responsibility of a number of OECD committees under the Directorate for Financial, Fiscal and Enterprise Affairs. The Directorate works to encourage policy convergence, provides policy guidelines, gives examples of best practice and maintains benchmarks to measure progress.

The Committee on Capital Movements and Invisible Transactions monitors the implementation of the Codes of Liberalization of Invisible Transactions and of Current Invisible Operations as legally binding norms for all member countries. The Committee on International Investment and Multinational Enterprises monitors the OECD Guide-lines for Multinational Enterprises, a corporate Code of Conduct recommended by OECD member governments, business and labour units. A Declaration on International Investment and Multinational Enterprises, while non-binding, contains commitments on the conduct and treatment of foreign-owned enterprises established in member countries. Negotiations on a Multilateral Agreement on Investment (MAI), initiated by OECD ministers in 1995 to provide a legal framework for international investment, broke down in October 1998, although 'informal consultation' on the issue was subsequently continued.

The Committee on Competition Law and Policy promotes the harmonization of national competition policies, co-operation in competition law enforcement, common merger reporting rules and pro-competitive regulatory reform, the development of competition laws and institutions, and efforts to change policies that restrain competition. The Committee on Financial Markets exercises surveillance over recent developments, reform measures and structural and regulatory conditions in financial markets. It aims to promote international trade in financial services, to encourage the integration of non-member countries into the global financial system, and to improve financial statistics. The Insurance Committee monitors structural changes and reform measures in insurance markets. Its programme of work for 2001–02 focused on the liberalization of insurance markets, financial insolvency, co-operation on insurance and reinsurance policy, the monitoring and analysis of regulatory and structural developments, and private pensions and health insurance. A working party on private pensions meets twice a year.

The Committee on Fiscal Affairs has recently focused its efforts on the tax implications of the globalization of national economies. Its activities include promoting the removal of tax barriers and monitoring the implementation and impact of major tax reforms, as well as developing a neutral tax framework for electronic commerce. Since 1998 OECD has promoted co-ordinated action for the elimination of so-called 'harmful' tax practices, designed to reduce the incidence of international money-laundering, and the level of potential tax revenue lost by OECD members. In mid-2000 it launched an initiative to abolish 'harmful tax systems', identifying a number of offshore jurisdictions as 'tax havens' lacking financial transparency, and inviting these to co-operate with the Organisation by amending national financial legislation. Several of the countries and territories named agreed to follow a timetable for reform, with the aim of eliminating such practices by the end of 2005. Others, however, were reluctant to participate. (The USA also strongly opposed the initiative.) In April 2002 OECD announced that co-ordinated defensive measures would be implemented against non-complying jurisdictions ('un-co-operative tax havens') from early 2003. The Organisation has also highlighted examples of preferential tax regimes in member countries. OECD provides the secretariat for the Financial Action Task Force on Money Laundering (FATF, q.v.).

In May 1997 the OECD Council endorsed plans to introduce a global ban on the corporate bribery of public officials; the OECD Convention on Bribery of Foreign Public Officials in International Business Transactions entered into force in February 1999. By February 2002 the Convention had been ratified by 34 countries. In May 1999 ministers endorsed a set of OECD Principles for Corporate Governance, covering ownership and control of corporate entities, the rights of shareholders, the role of stakeholders, transparency, disclosure and the responsibilities of boards. In 2000 these became one of the 12 core standards of global financial stability, and they are used as a benchmark by other international financial institutions. OECD also collaborates with the World Bank and other organizations to promote good governance world-wide, for example through regional round tables and the Global Corporate Governance Forum.

FOOD, AGRICULTURE AND FISHERIES

The Committee for Agriculture reviews major developments in agricultural policies, deals with the adaptation of agriculture to changing economic conditions, elaborates forecasts of production and market prospects for the major commodities, manages a programme to develop product standards in agriculture, identifies best practices for limiting the impact of agricultural production on the environment, promotes the use of sustainable practices in the sector, considers questions of agricultural development in emerging and transition economies, and evaluates progress towards the integration of the agro-food sector into the multilateral trading system. OECD agriculture ministers have agreed on the long-term objective of seeking a substantial reduction in agricultural support. A separate Fisheries Committee carries out similar tasks in its sector, and, in particular, analyses the consequences of policy measures with a view to promoting responsible and sustainable fisheries. OECD is currently seeking to develop indicators measuring economic and social sustainability in the fisheries sector.

TERRITORIAL DEVELOPMENT

The Territorial Development Service assists central governments with the design and implementation of more effective, area-based strategies, encourages the emergence of locally driven initiatives for economic development, and promotes better integration of local and national approaches. Territorial policies have recently emphasized the need to mobilize local resources to enhance regional competitiveness and to create employment. The Service comprises two intergovernmental bodies—the Local Economic and Employment Development Committee and the Territorial Development Policy Committee—which share an overall work programme emphasizing the need for innovative policy initiatives and exchange of knowledge in a wide range of policies, such as entrepreneurship and technology diffusion and issues of social exclusion and urban deprivation. The two Committees select and analyse territorial data in order to produce reviews of economic performance and prospects. In 2000 the areas of focus of the Territorial Development Policy Committee included metropolitan governance.

ENVIRONMENT

The OECD Environment Directorate works in support of the Environment Policy Committee (EPOC) on environmental issues. EPOC assesses performance; encourages co-operation on environmental policy; promotes the integration of environmental and economic policies; works to develop principles, guide-lines and strategies for effective environmental management; provides a forum for member states to address common problems and share data and experience; and promotes the sharing of information with non-member states. Working parties consider a range of issues, in some cases collaborating with other Directorates (for example, the Working Parties on Trade and Environment and on Agriculture and Environment). An Experts Group on Climate Change, based in the Environment Directorate, undertakes studies related to international agreements on climate change.

In April 1998 environment ministers of member countries agreed upon a set of 'Shared Goals for Action', with four principal aims: to promote strong national policies and effective regulatory structures for the protection of the natural environment and human health; to promote an integrated policy approach, encouraging coherence among economic, environmental and social policies; to strengthen international co-operation in meeting global and regional environmental commitments; and to support participation, transparency, the provision of information and accountability in environmental policy-making at all levels. In May 2001 ministers adopted an Environmental Strategy for the 21st Century, containing recommendations for future work. The Strategy, which was to be implemented by 2010, focused on fostering sustainable development, and strengthening co-operation with non-member countries and partnerships with the private sector and civil society. Fundamental objectives included the efficient use of renewable and non-renewable resources; the avoidance of irreversible damage; the maintenance of ecosystems; and separating environmental pressures from economic growth. The Strategy identified several issues requiring urgent action, such as the generation of municipal waste, increased car and air travel, greenhouse gas emissions, groundwater pollution, and the exploitation of marine fisheries. It aimed to ensure the implementation of agreed policies and the formulation of new ones.

The Environment Directorate also provides the secretariat for the Task Force for the Implementation of the Environmental Action Programme in Central and Eastern Europe, which encourages countries in Eastern Europe and the CIS to take environmental issues into consideration in the process of economic restructuring. The first cycle of 32 Environmental Performance Reviews of member and selected non-member countries was completed in 2000. The second cycle commenced in 2001. The Directorate aims to improve understanding of past and future trends through the collection and dissemination of environmental data.

In a report to the Secretary-General in late 1997 an advisory group on the environment, comprising non-governmental experts, recommended that OECD should evolve into the principal intergovernmental organization providing the analytical and comparative framework of policy necessary for industrialized countries to make the transition to sustainable development. At a meeting in April 1998 ministers from member countries reiterated that the achievement of sustainable development was a priority, and recommended wide-ranging projects over the forthcoming three years in areas relating to technology, the effects of climate change, the environmental impact of subsidies, and the creation of indicators of sustainability, in order comprehensively to address the economic, social and environmental dimensions of sustainable development. In May 2001 OECD ministers of the environment, convened in Paris, France, adopted the OECD Environmental Strategy for the First Decade of the 21st Century, as well as the use of a set of key environmental indicators and guide-lines for the provision of environmentally sustainable transport.

SCIENCE, TECHNOLOGY AND INDUSTRY

The principal objective of the Directorate for Science, Technology and Industry is to assist member countries in formulating and implementing policies that optimize the contribution of science, technology, industrial development and structural change to economic growth, employment and social development. The Committee for Scientific and Technological Policy reviews national and international policy issues relating to science and technology. It provides indicators and analysis on emerging trends in these fields, identifies and promotes best practices, and offers a forum for dialogue. Important themes include: the management and reform of science systems; the development of policies to promote the innovative capacity of

members' economies; and policy responses to the globalization of science and technology.

A working party on biotechnology was established in 1993 and its mandate was renewed in 1998. Among the priority topics in its most recent work programme were scientific and technological infrastructure, and the relation of biotechnology to sustainable industrial development. In 1992 a megascience forum was established to bring together senior science policy-makers for consultations regarding large scientific projects and programmes. It was succeeded, in 1999, by the Global Science Forum. The Forum's research programme for 2002 included elementary particle physics, neuroinformatics, radio astronomy and the radio spectrum. In 2000 multilateral negotiations on establishing a Global Biodiversity Information Facility (GBIF) were concluded. The GBIF was to connect global biodiversity databases in order to make available a wide range of online data.

The Committee for Information, Computer and Communications Policy monitors developments in telecommunications and information technology and their impact on competitiveness and productivity, with a new emphasis on technological and regulatory convergence. It also promotes the development of new rules (e.g. guide-lines on information security) and analyses trade and liberalization issues. The Committee maintains a database of communications indicators and telecommunications tariffs. In December 1999 the OECD Council adopted a set of Guide-lines for Consumer Protection in the Context of Electronic Commerce. OECD supports the Digital Opportunities Task Force (Dot.force) which was established in June 2000 by the Group of Seven industrialized nations and Russia (the G-8) to recommend action with a view to eliminating the so-called 'digital divide' between developed and less developed countries and between different population sectors within nations. OECD's Global Conference on Telecommunications Policy for the Digital Environment, held in January 2002, stressed the importance of competition in the sector and the need for regulatory reform.

The Committee on Industry and the Business Environment focuses on industrial production; business performance; innovation and competitiveness in industrial and services sectors; and policies for private sector development in member and selected non-member economies. In recent years the Committee has addressed issues connected with globalization, regulatory reform, small and medium-sized enterprises (SMEs), and the role of industry in sustainable development. Business and industry policy fora explore a variety of issues with the private sector and develop recommendations. Issues addressed recently include environmental strategies for industry and new technologies. A working party on SMEs conducts an ongoing review of the contribution of SMEs to growth and employment and carries out a comparative assessment of best practice policies. OECD, in conjunction with the Italian Government, organized its first conference on SMEs in Bologna, Italy, in June 2000. Databases enabling internationally comparable monitoring of structural change in areas of science and technology, investment, production, employment and trade have been prepared by a working party on statistics.

The Transport Division of the Directorate for Science, Technology and Industry considers aviation, maritime, shipbuilding, road and intermodal transport issues. A road transport research programme covers all aspects of road transport, including its integration into overall transport systems and multimodal transport strategies. Two databases on road transport research and road safety are maintained. The Maritime Transport and Steel Committees aim to promote multilateral solutions to sectoral friction and instability based on the definition and monitoring of rules. The Working Party on Shipbuilding seeks to establish normal competitive conditions in that sector, especially through dialogue with non-OECD countries. In June 1994 negotiations between leading shipbuilding nations, conducted under OECD auspices, concluded a multilateral agreement to end state subsidies to the industry. However, continued failure by the US Congress to ratify the agreement disrupted its entry into force. The Tourism Committee promotes sustained growth in the tourism sector and encourages the integration of tourism issues into other policy areas.

EDUCATION, EMPLOYMENT, LABOUR AND SOCIAL AFFAIRS

The Employment, Labour and Social Affairs Committee is concerned with the development of the labour market and selective employment policies to ensure the utilization of human capital at the highest possible level and to improve the quality and flexibility of working life, as well as the effectiveness of social policies; it plays a central role in addressing OECD's concern to reduce high and persistent unemployment through the creation of high-quality jobs. The Committee's work covers such issues as the role of women in the economy, industrial relations, international migration, measurements of unemployment, and the development of an extensive social database. The Committee also carries out single-country and thematic reviews of labour-market policies and social assistance systems. It has assigned a high priority to work on the policy implications of an ageing population and on indicators of human capital investment.

The Health Policy Unit of the Employment, Labour and Social Affairs Committee provides analysis to policymakers on health care and health expenditure issues, and analyses the organization and performance of health systems. A new OECD Health Project was launched in 2001. The Non-Member Economies and International Migration Division works on social policy issues in emerging economies and economies in transition, especially relating to education and labour market reforms and to the economic and social aspects of migration. The Education Committee analyses policies for education and training at all levels, carries out education and training policy reviews and produces education data and indicators. An adult literacy survey conducted by the Committee was concluded in June 2000. During 2001 'lifelong learning' was a priority focus area. Together, the Employment, Labour and Social Affairs and Education Committees seek to provide for the greater integration of labour market and educational policies and the prevention of social exclusion.

OECD's Centre for Educational Research and Innovation (CERI) promotes the development of research activities in education together with experiments of an advanced nature designed to test innovations in educational systems and to stimulate research and development.

RELATIONS WITH OTHER INTERNATIONAL ORGANIZATIONS

Under a Protocol signed at the same time as the OECD Convention, the European Commission generally takes part in the work of OECD. EFTA may also send representatives to OECD meetings. Formal relations exist with a number of other international organizations, including the ILO, FAO, IMF, IBRD, UNCTAD, UNIDO, WHO, IAEA, APEC and the Council of Europe. A few non-governmental organizations have been granted consultative status, notably the Business and Industry Advisory Committee to OECD (BIAC) and the Trade Union Advisory Committee to OECD (TUAC).

Finance

In 2000 OECD's total budget amounted to 1,200m. French francs.

Publications

Activities of OECD (Secretary-General's Annual Report).

Agricultural Outlook (annually).

Energy Balances (quarterly).

Energy Prices and Taxes (quarterly).

Financial Market Trends (3 a year).

Financial Statistics (Part 1 (domestic markets): monthly; Part 2 (international markets): monthly; Part 3 (OECD member countries): 25 a year).

Foreign Trade Statistics (monthly).

Higher Education Management and Policy (3 a year).

Indicators of Industry and Services Activity (quarterly).

International Trade by Commodities Statistics (5 a year).

Joint BIS-IMF-OECD-World Bank Statistics on External Debt (quarterly).

Main Developments in Trade (annually).

Main Economic Indicators (monthly).

Monthly Statistics of International Trade.

National Accounts Quarterly.

OECD Economic Outlook (2 a year).

OECD Economic Studies (2 a year).

OECD Economic Surveys (every 12 to 18 months for each country).

OECD Employment Outlook (annually).

OECD Journal of Competition Law and Policy (quarterly).

The OECD Observer (every 2 months).

Oil and Gas Statistics (quarterly).

PEB Exchange (newsletter of the Programme on Educational Building, 3 a year).

Quarterly Labour Force Statistics.

Short-term Economic Indicators: Transition Economies (quarterly).

Numerous specialized reports, working papers, books and statistics on economic and social subjects (about 130 titles a year, both in English and French) are also published.

International Energy Agency—IEA

Address: 9 rue de la Fédération, 75739 Paris Cédex 15, France.

Telephone: 1-40-57-65-00; **fax:** 1-40-57-65-59; **e-mail:** info@iea .org; **internet:** www.iea.org.

The Agency was established by the OECD Council in 1974 to develop co-operation on energy questions among participating countries.

MEMBERS

Australia	Greece	Norway
Austria	Hungary	Portugal
Belgium	Ireland	Spain
Canada	Italy	Sweden
Czech Republic	Japan	Switzerland
Denmark	Republic of Korea	Turkey
Finland	Luxembourg	United Kingdom
France	Netherlands	USA
Germany	New Zealand	

The European Commission is also represented.

Organization

(April 2003)

GOVERNING BOARD

Composed of ministers or senior officials of the member governments. Meetings are held every two years at ministerial level and five times a year at senior official level. Decisions may be taken by a weighted majority on a number of specified subjects, particularly concerning emergency measures and the emergency reserve commitment; a simple weighted majority is required for procedural decisions and decisions implementing specific obligations in the agreement. Unanimity is required only if new obligations, not already specified in the agreement, are to be undertaken.

SECRETARIAT

The Secretariat comprises the following four divisions: Standing Group on Long-Term Co-operation; Standing Group on the Oil Market; Standing Group on Emergency Questions; Committee on Energy Research and Technology (with working parties); Committee on Non-Member Countries; Coal Industry Advisory Board; and Industry Advisory Board.

Executive Director: CLAUDE MANDIL (France).

Activities

The Agreement on an International Energy Programme was signed in November 1974 and formally entered into force in January 1976. The Programme commits the participating countries of the International Energy Agency to share petroleum in emergencies, to strengthen their long-term co-operation in order to reduce dependence on petroleum imports, to increase the availability of information on the petroleum market, to co-operate in the development and co-ordination of energy policies, and to develop relations with the petroleum-producing and other petroleum-consuming countries. The IEA issues energy statistics and publications and provides information and analysis on the energy sector. It sponsors conferences, symposia and workshops to enhance international co-operation among member and non-member states.

An emergency petroleum-sharing plan has been established, and the IEA ensures that the necessary technical information and facilities are in place so that it can be readily used in the event of a reduction in petroleum supplies. The IEA undertakes emergency response reviews and workshops, and publishes an Emergency Management Manual to facilitate a co-ordinated response to a severe disruption in petroleum supplies. A separate division monitors and reports on short-term developments in the petroleum market. It also considers other related issues, including international crude petroleum pricing, petroleum trade and stock developments and investments by major petroleum-producing countries.

The IEA Long-Term Co-operation Programme is designed to strengthen the security of energy supplies and promote stability in world energy markets. It provides for co-operative efforts to conserve energy, to accelerate the development of alternative energy sources by means of both specific and general measures, to strengthen research and development of new energy technologies and to remove legislative and administrative obstacles to increased energy supplies. Regular reviews of member countries' efforts in the fields of energy conservation and accelerated development of alternative energy sources assess the effectiveness of national programmes in relation to the objectives of the Agency.

The IEA also reviews the energy situation in non-member countries, in particular the petroleum-producing countries of the Middle East and Central and Eastern European countries. In the latter states the IEA has provided technical assistance for the development of national energy legislation, regulatory reform and energy efficiency projects.

The IEA aims to contribute to the energy security of member countries through energy technology and research and development projects, in particular those concerned with energy efficiency, conservation and protection of the environment. The IEA promotes international collaboration in this field and the participation of energy industries to facilitate the application of new technologies, through effective transfer of knowledge, technology innovation and training. Member states adopt Implementing Agreements, which provide mechanisms for collaboration and information exchange in specific areas, for example, electric vehicle technologies, electric demand-side management and photovoltaic power systems. Non-member states are encouraged to participate in these Agreements. The Agency sponsors conferences, symposia and workshops to further enhance international co-operation among member and non-member countries.

In recent years the IEA has increased its focus on issues related to the environment and sustainable development. In 2000 and 2001 it supported analysis of actions to mitigate climate change, studies of the implications of the Kyoto Protocol to the UN Framework Convention on Climate Change, and analysis of policies designed to reduce greenhouse gas emissions, including emissions trading. (In June/July 2000 it organized an emissions-trading simulation involving 17 countries.) The Agency also analyses the regulation and reform of energy markets, especially for electricity and gas. The IEA Regulatory Forum held in February 2002 considered the implications for security of supply and public service of competition in energy markets.

Publications

Coal Information (annually).

Electricity Information (annually).

Natural Gas Information (annually).

Oil Information (annually).

Oil Market Report (monthly).

World Energy Outlook (annually).

Reports, studies, statistics, country reviews.

OECD Nuclear Energy Agency—NEA

Address: Le Seine Saint-Germain, 12 blvd des Îles, 92130 Issy-les-Moulineaux, France.

Telephone: 1-45-24-10-10; **fax:** 1-45-24-11-10; **e-mail:** nea@nea.fr; **internet:** www.nea.fr.

The NEA was established in 1958 to further the peaceful uses of nuclear energy. Originally a European agency, it has since admitted OECD members outside Europe.

MEMBERS

All members of OECD (except New Zealand and Poland).

Organization

(April 2003)

STEERING COMMITTEE FOR NUCLEAR ENERGY

Meets twice a year. Comprises senior representatives of member governments, presided over by a chairman.

SECRETARIAT

Director-General: LUIS ENRIQUE ECHÁVARRI (Spain).

Deputy Director-General: CAROL KESSLER (USA).

MAIN COMMITTEES

Committee on Nuclear Regulatory Activities.

Committee on Radiation Protection and Public Health.

Committee on the Safety of Nuclear Installations.

Committee for Technical and Economic Studies on Nuclear Energy Development and the Fuel Cycle.

Nuclear Law Committee.

Nuclear Science Committee.

Radioactive Waste Management Committee.

NEA DATA BANK

The Data Bank was established in 1978, as a successor to the Computer Programme Library and the Neutron Data Compilation Centre. The Data Bank develops and supplies data and computer programmes for nuclear technology applications to users in laboratories, industry, universities and other areas of interest. Under the supervision of the Nuclear Science Committee, the Data Bank collates integral experimental data, and functions as part of a network of data centres to provide direct data services. It was responsible for co-ordinating the development of the Joint Evaluation Fission and Fusion (JEFF) data reference library, and works with the Radioactive Waste Management Division of the NEA on the Thermonuclear Database project (see below).

Activities

The mission of the Agency is to assist its member countries in maintaining and further developing—through international co-operation—the scientific, technological and legal bases required for the safe, environmentally-friendly and economical use of nuclear energy for peaceful purposes. The Agency maintains a continual survey with the co-operation of other organizations, notably the International Atomic Energy Agency (IAEA), of world uranium resources, production and demand, and of economic and technical aspects of the nuclear fuel cycle.

A major part of the Agency's work is devoted to the safety and regulation of nuclear power, including co-operative studies and projects related to the prevention of nuclear accidents and the long-term safety of radioactive waste disposal systems. It is also concerned with the harmonization of nuclear legislation and the dissemination of information on nuclear law issues. A Nuclear Development Committee provides members with statistics and analysis on nuclear resources, economics, technology and prospects. The NEA also co-operates with non-member countries of Central and Eastern Europe and the CIS in areas such as nuclear safety, radiation protection and nuclear law.

JOINT PROJECTS

Nuclear Safety

OECD Halden Reactor Project: Halden, Norway; experimental boiling heavy water reactor, which became an OECD project in 1958. From 1964, under successive agreements with participating countries, the reactor has been used for long-term testing of water reactor fuels and for research into automatic computer-based control of nuclear power stations. The main focus is on nuclear fuel safety and man-machine interface. Some 100 nuclear energy research institutions and authorities in 20 countries support the project.

OECD International Common Cause Data Exchange—ICDE Project: initiated in 1994 and formally operated by the NEA since April 1998; encourages multilateral co-operation in the collection and analysis of data on common cause failure (CCF) events occurring at nuclear power plants, with the aim of enabling greater understanding and prevention of such events; nine participating countries.

OECD-IPSN CABRI Water Loop Project: revised programme initiated in 2000; conducted at the Institute for Protection and Nuclear Safety (IPSN), based in France; investigates the capacity of high burn-up fuel to withstand sharp power peaks that may occur in power reactors owing to rapid reactivity insertion in the reactor core (i.e. reactivity-initiated accidents); 11 participating countries.

OECD MASCA Project: initiated in 2000 as a follow-up to the NEA-sponsored RASPLAV Project, which studied the behaviour of molten core material in a reactor pressure vessel during a severe accident; MASCA is undertaking additional tests in order to resolve remaining uncertainties related to the heat load that the reactor vessel can support during an accident involving core melt; scheduled for completion in 2003; 17 participating countries.

OECD Melt Coolability and Concrete Interaction—MCCI Project: initiated 2002; conducted at the Argonne National Laboratory, USA; aims to provide experimental data on severe accident molten core coolability and interaction with containment concrete, contributing to improved accident management; eight participating countries.

OECD SETH Project: covering the period 2001–05; conducted at the Paul Scherrer Institute PANDA facility, based in Switzerland, and the Siemens Primär Kreislauf, Germany; researches important thermal-hydraulic phenomena in support of accident management; 14 participating countries.

Bubbler Condenser Project: initiated 2002; conducted at the Electrogorsk Research and Engineering Centre, Russia; performs thermal-hydraulic and structural experiments to resolve outstanding issues surrounding the bubbler condenser function for VVER-213 reactors; six participating countries

Sandia Lower Head Failure Project: initiated in 1999; conducted at the Sandia National Laboratory, USA; researches the rupture behaviour of the reactor pressure vessel lower head and, consequently, provides information for the development of severe accident management strategies; eight participating countries

Radioactive Waste Management

Co-operative Programme for the Exchange of Scientific and Technical Information Concerning Nuclear Installation Decommissioning Projects Programme: initiated in 1985; promotes exchange of technical information and experience for ensuring that safe, economic and optimum environmental options for decommissioning are used; 12 participating countries

Sorption Project: phase II commenced in 2000; comprises benchmark exercises co-ordinated by the NEA; aims to evaluate various approaches used to model sorption phenomena in the context of performance assessments of geologic disposal concepts for the disposal of radioactive waste in deep geological formations; 10 participating countries and 16 participating organizations

Thermonuclear Database—TDB Project: phase II commenced in 1998; aims to develop a quality-assured, comprehensive thermodynamic database of selected chemical elements for use in the safety assessment of radioactive waste repositories; data are selected by review teams; 13 participating countries and 17 participating organizations

Radiation Protection

Information System on Occupational Exposure—ISOE: initiated in 1992 and co-sponsored by the IAEA; maintains largest database world-wide on occupational exposure to ionizing radiation at nuclear power plants; participants: 452 reactors in 28 countries; the system also contains information from 39 nuclear reactors which are either defunct or actively decommissioning

Finance

The Agency's annual budget amounts to €11m.

Publications

Annual Report.

NEA News (2 a year).

Nuclear Energy Data (annually).

Nuclear Law Bulletin (2 a year).

Publications on a range of issues relating to nuclear energy, reports and proceedings.

ORGANIZATION FOR SECURITY AND CO-OPERATION IN EUROPE—OSCE

Address: 1010 Vienna, Kärntner Ring 5–7, Austria.

Telephone: (1) 514-36-0; **fax:** (1) 514-36-105; **e-mail:** info@osce.org; **internet:** www.osce.org.

The OSCE was established in 1972 as the Conference on Security and Co-operation in Europe (CSCE), providing a multilateral forum for dialogue and negotiation. It produced the Helsinki Final Act of 1975 on East–West relations (see below). The areas of competence of the CSCE were expanded by the Charter of Paris for a New Europe (1990), which transformed the CSCE from an *ad hoc* forum to an organization with permanent institutions, and the Helsinki Document 1992 (see 'Activities'). In December 1994 the summit conference adopted the new name of OSCE, in order to reflect the Organization's changing political role and strengthened secretariat.

PARTICIPATING STATES

Albania	Greece	Portugal
Andorra	Hungary	Romania
Armenia	Iceland	Russia
Austria	Ireland	Serbia and
Azerbaijan	Italy	Montenegro
Belarus	Kazakhstan	Slovakia
Belgium	Kyrgyzstan	Slovenia
Bosnia and	Latvia	Spain
Herzegovina	Liechtenstein	Sweden
Bulgaria	Lithuania	Switzerland
Canada	Luxembourg	Tajikistan
Croatia	Macedonia, former	Turkey
Cyprus	Yugoslav republic	Turkmenistan
Czech Republic	Malta	Ukraine
Denmark	Moldova	United Kingdom
Estonia	Monaco	USA
Finland	Netherlands	Uzbekistan
France	Norway	Vatican City (Holy
Georgia	Poland	See)
Germany		

Organization

(April 2003)

SUMMIT CONFERENCES

Heads of state or government of OSCE participating states normally meet every two or three years to set priorities and political orientation of the Organization. The most recent conference was held in İstanbul, Turkey, in November 1999.

MINISTERIAL COUNCIL

The Ministerial Council (formerly the Council of Foreign Ministers) comprises ministers of foreign affairs of member states. It is the central decision-making and governing body of the OSCE and meets every year in which no summit conference is held.

SENIOR COUNCIL

The Senior Council (formerly the Council of Senior Officials—CSO) is responsible for the supervision, management and co-ordination of OSCE activities. Member states are represented by senior political officers, who convene at least twice a year in Prague, Czech Republic, and once a year as the Economic Forum.

PERMANENT COUNCIL

The Council, which is based in Vienna, is responsible for day-to-day operational tasks. Members of the Council, comprising the permanent representatives of member states to the OSCE, convene weekly. The Council is the regular body for political consultation and decision-making, and may be convened for emergency purposes.

FORUM FOR SECURITY CO-OPERATION—FSC

The FSC, comprising representatives of delegations of member states, meets weekly in Vienna to negotiate and consult on measures aimed at strengthening security and stability throughout Europe. Its main objectives are negotiations on arms control, disarmament, and confidence- and security-building; regular consultations and intensive co-operation on matters related to security; and the further reduction of the risks of conflict. The FSC is also responsible for the implementation of confidence- and security-building measures (CSBMs); the preparation of seminars on military doctrine; the holding of annual implementation assessment meetings; and the provision of a forum for the discussion and clarification of information exchanged under agreed CSBMs.

CHAIRMAN-IN-OFFICE—CIO

The CIO is vested with overall responsibility for executive action. The position is held by a minister of foreign affairs of a member state for a one-year term. The CIO may be assisted by a troika, consisting of the preceding, current and succeeding chairpersons; *ad hoc* steering groups; or personal representatives, who are appointed by the CIO with a clear and precise mandate to assist the CIO in dealing with a crisis or conflict.

Chairman-in-Office: JAAP DE HOOP SCHEFFER (Netherlands).

SECRETARIAT

The Secretariat comprises two principal departments: the Conflict Prevention Centre (including an Operations Centre), which focuses on the support of the CIO in the implementation of OSCE policies, in particular the monitoring of field activities and co-operation with other international bodies; and the Department for Support Services and Budget, responsible for technical and administrative support activities. The OSCE maintains an office in Prague, Czech Republic, which assists with documentation and information activities, and a liaison office in Central Asia, based in Tashkent, Uzbekistan.

The position of Secretary-General was established in December 1992 and the first appointment to the position was made in June 1993. The Secretary-General is the representative of the CIO and is responsible for the management of OSCE structures and operations.

Secretary-General: JÁN KUBIŠ (Slovakia).

Co-ordinator of OSCE Economic and Environmental Activities: MARCIN SWIECICKI (Poland).

HIGH COMMISSIONER ON NATIONAL MINORITIES

POB 20062, 2500 EB The Hague, Netherlands; tel. (70) 3125500; fax (70) 3635910; e-mail hcnm@hcnm.org; internet www.osce.org/hcnm.

The establishment of the office of High Commissioner on National Minorities was proposed in the 1992 Helsinki Document, and endorsed by the Council of Foreign Ministers in Stockholm, Sweden in December 1992. The role of the High Commissioner is to identify ethnic tensions that might endanger peace, stability or relations between OSCE participating states, and to promote their early resolution. The High Commissioner may issue an 'early warning' for the attention of the Senior Council of an area of tension likely to degenerate into conflict. The High Commissioner is appointed by the Ministerial Council, on the recommendation of the Senior Council, for a three-year term.

High Commissioner: ROLF EKÉUS (Sweden).

OFFICE FOR DEMOCRATIC INSTITUTIONS AND HUMAN RIGHTS—ODIHR

Aleje Ujazdowskie 19, 00-517 Warsaw, Poland; tel. (22) 520-06-00; fax (22) 520-06-05; e-mail office@odihr.osce.waw.pl; internet www.osce.org.odihr.

Established in July 1999, the ODIHR has responsibility for promoting human rights, democracy and the rule of law. The Office provides a framework for the exchange of information on and the promotion of democracy-building, respect for human rights and elections within OSCE states. In addition, it co-ordinates the monitoring of elections and provides expertise and training on constitutional and legal matters.

Director: CHRISTIAN STROHAL (Switzerland).

OFFICE OF THE REPRESENTATIVE ON FREEDOM OF THE MEDIA

Kärntner Ring 5–7, 1010 Vienna, Austria; tel. (1) 512-21-450; fax (1) 512-21-459; e-mail pm-fom@osce.org; internet www.osce.org/fom.

The office was founded in 1998 to strengthen the implementation of OSCE commitments regarding free, independent and pluralistic media.

Representative: FREIMUT DUVE (Germany).

PARLIAMENTARY ASSEMBLY

Rädhusstraede 1, 1466 Copenhagen K, Denmark; tel. 33-37-80-40; fax 33-37-80-30; e-mail osce@oscepa.dk; internet www.osce.org/pa.

The OSCE Parliamentary Assembly, which is composed of 317 parliamentarians from 55 participating countries, was inaugurated in July 1992, and meets annually. The Assembly comprises a Standing Committee, a Bureau and three General Committees and is supported by a Secretariat in Copenhagen, Denmark.

President: ADRIAN SEVERIN (Romania).

Secretary-General: R. SPENCER OLIVER.

OSCE Related Bodies

COURT OF CONCILIATION AND ARBITRATION

266 route de Lausanne, 1292 Chambésy, Geneva, Switzerland; tel. (22) 7580025; fax (22) 7582510; e-mail cca.osce@bluewin.ch.

The establishment of the Court of Conciliation and Arbitration was agreed in 1992 and effected in 1994. OSCE states that have ratified the OSCE Convention on Conciliation and Arbitration may submit a dispute to the Court for settlement by the Arbitral Tribunal or the Conciliation Commission.

President: ROBERT BADINTER.

JOINT CONSULTATIVE GROUP—JCG

The states that are party to the Treaty on Conventional Armed Forces in Europe (CFE), which was concluded within the CSCE framework in 1990, established the Joint Consultative Group (JCG). The JCG, which meets in Vienna, addresses questions relating to compliance with the Treaty; enhancement of the effectiveness of the Treaty; technical aspects of the Treaty's implementation; and disputes arising out of its implementation. There are currently 30 states participating in the JCG.

OPEN SKIES CONSULTATIVE COMMISSION

The Commission represents all states parties to the 1992 Treaty on Open Skies, and promotes its implementation. Its regular meetings are serviced by the OSCE secretariat.

Activities

In July 1990 heads of government of the member countries of the North Atlantic Treaty Organization (NATO) proposed to increase the role of the CSCE 'to provide a forum for wider political dialogue in a more united Europe'. The Charter of Paris for a New Europe, which undertook to strengthen pluralist democracy and observance of human rights, and to settle disputes between participating states by peaceful means, was signed in November. At the summit meeting the Treaty on Conventional Armed Forces in Europe (CFE), which had been negotiated within the framework of the CSCE, was signed by the member states of NATO and of the Warsaw Pact. The Treaty limits non-nuclear air and ground armaments in the signatory countries. In April 1991 parliamentarians from the CSCE countries agreed on the creation of a pan-European parliamentary assembly. Its first session was held in Budapest, Hungary, in July 1992.

The Council of Foreign Ministers met for the first time in Berlin, Germany, in June 1991. The meeting adopted a mechanism for consultation and co-operation in the case of emergency situations, to be implemented by the Council of Senior Officials (CSO, which was subsequently renamed the Senior Council). A separate mechanism regarding the prevention of the outbreak of conflict was also adopted, whereby a country can demand an explanation of 'unusual military activity' in a neighbouring country. These mechanisms were utilized in July in relation to the armed conflict in Yugoslavia between the Republic of Croatia and the Yugoslav Government. In mid-August a meeting of the CSO resolved to reinforce considerably the CSCE's mission in Yugoslavia and in September the CSO agreed to impose an embargo on the export of armaments to Yugoslavia. In October the CSO resolved to establish an observer mission to monitor the observance of human rights in Yugoslavia.

In January 1992 the Council of Foreign Ministers agreed that the Conference's rule of decision-making by consensus was to be altered to allow the CSO to take appropriate action against a participating state 'in cases of clear and gross violation of CSCE commitments'. This development was precipitated by the conflict in Yugoslavia, where the Yugoslav Government was held responsible by the majority of CSCE states for the continuation of hostilities. It was also agreed at the meeting that the CSCE should undertake fact-finding and conciliation missions to areas of tension, with the first such mission to be sent to Nagornyi Karabakh, the largely Armenian-populated enclave in Azerbaijan.

In March 1992 CSCE participating states reached agreement on a number of confidence-building measures, including commitments to exchange technical data on new weapons systems; to report activation of military units; and to prohibit military activity involving very large numbers of troops or tanks. Later in that month at a meeting of the Council of Foreign Ministers, which opened the Helsinki Follow-up Conference, the members of NATO and the former members of the Warsaw Pact (with Russia, Belarus, Ukraine and Georgia taking the place of the USSR) signed the Open Skies Treaty. Under the treaty, aerial reconnaissance missions by one country over another were permitted, subject to regulation. An Open Skies Consultative Commission was subsequently established (see above).

The summit meeting of heads of state and government that took place in Helsinki, Finland, in July 1992 adopted the Helsinki Document 1992, in which participating states defined the terms of future CSCE peace-keeping activities. Conforming broadly to UN practice, peace-keeping operations would be undertaken only with the full consent of the parties involved in any conflict and only if an effective cease-fire were in place. The CSCE may request the use of the military resources of NATO, the CIS, the EU, Western European Union (WEU) or other international bodies. (NATO and WEU had recently changed their Constitutions to permit the use of their forces for CSCE purposes.) The Helsinki Document declared the CSCE a 'regional arrangement' in the sense of Chapter VIII of the UN's Charter, which states that such a regional grouping should attempt to resolve a conflict in the region before referring it to the Security Council. In 1993 the First Implementation Meeting on Human Dimension Issues (the CSCE term used with regard to issues concerning human rights and welfare) took place. The Meeting, for which the ODIHR serves as a secretariat, provides a now annual forum for the exchange of news regarding OSCE commitments in the fields of human rights and democracy.

In December 1993 a Permanent Committee (now renamed the Permanent Council) was established in Vienna, providing for greater political consultation and dialogue through its weekly meetings. In December 1994 the summit conference redesignated the CSCE as the Organization for Security and Co-operation in Europe —OSCE and endorsed the role of the Organization as the primary instrument for early warning, conflict prevention and crisis management in the region. The conference adopted a 'Code of Conduct on Politico-Military Aspects of Security', which set out principles to guide the role of the armed forces in democratic societies. The summit conference that was held in Lisbon, Portugal, in December 1996 agreed to adapt the CFE Treaty, in order to further arms-reduction negotiations on a national and territorial basis. The conference also adopted the 'Lisbon Declaration on a Common and Comprehensive Security Model for Europe for the 21st Century', committing all parties to pursuing measures to ensure regional security. A Security Model Committee was established and began to meet regularly during 1997 to consider aspects of the Declaration, including the identification of risks and challenges to future European security; enhancing means of joint co-operative action within the OSCE framework in the event of non-compliance with OSCE commitments by participating states; considering other new arrangements within the OSCE framework that could reinforce security and stability in Europe; and defining a basis of co-operation between the OSCE and other relevant organizations to co-ordinate security enforcement. In November 1997 the Office of the Representative on Freedom of the Media was established in Vienna, to support the OSCE's activities in this field. In the same month a new position of Co-ordinator of OSCE Economic and Environmental Activities was created.

In November 1999 OSCE heads of state and of government, convened in İstanbul, Turkey, signed a new Charter for European Security, which aimed to formalize existing norms regarding the observance of human rights and to strengthen co-operation with other organizations and institutions concerned with international security. The Charter focused on measures to improve the operational capabilities of the OSCE in early warning, conflict prevention, crisis management and post-conflict rehabilitation. Accordingly, Rapid Expert Assistance and Co-operation (REACT) teams were to be established to enable the Organization to respond rapidly to requests from participating states for assistance in crisis situations. The REACT programme became operational in April 2001. At the İstanbul meeting a revised CFE Treaty was also signed, providing for a stricter system of limitations and increased transparency, which was to be open to other OSCE states not currently signatories. The US and EU governments determined to delay ratification of the Agreement of the Adaptation of the Treaty until Russian troop levels in the Caucasus had been reduced.

In April 2000 the OSCE High Commissioner on National Minorities issued a report reviewing the problems confronting Roma and Sinti populations in OSCE member states. In April 2001 the ODIHR launched a programme of assistance for the Roma communities of south-eastern Europe. The OSCE and UN Office for Drug Control and Crime Prevention (ODCCP) jointly organized a conference in October 2000, supported by the Governments of Kazakhstan, Kyrgyzstan, Tajikistan, Turkmenistan and Uzbekistan and attended by representatives of 67 states and 44 international organizations, which aimed to promote co-operation, democratization, security and stability in Central Asia and to address the threat of drugs-trafficking, organized crime and terrorism in the sub-region. In November an OSCE Document on Small Arms and Light Weapons was adopted, aimed at curtailing the spread of armaments in member states. A workshop on implementation of the Document was held in February 2002. In mid-November 2000 the Office of the Representative on Freedom of the Media organized a conference, staged in Dushanbe, Tajikistan, of journalists from Kazakhstan, Kyrgyzstan, Tajikistan and Uzbekistan. In February 2001 the ODIHR established an Anti-Trafficking Project Fund to help to finance its efforts to combat trafficking in human beings. In July the OSCE Parliamentary Assembly adopted a resolution concerned with strengthening transparency and accountability within the Organization.

In September 2001 the Secretary-General condemned the major terrorist attacks perpetrated against targets in the USA, allegedly by militant Islamist fundamentalists. In early October OSCE member states unanimously adopted a statement in support of the developing US-led global coalition against international terrorism. Meanwhile, the Organization determined to establish a working group on terrorism to draft an action plan on counter-terrorism measures. In December the Ministerial Council, meeting in Romania, approved the 'Bucharest Action Plan' outlining the Organization's contribution to countering terrorism. A Personal Representative for Terrorism was appointed by the CIO in January 2002 to co-ordinate the implementation of the initiatives. Later in December 2001 the OSCE sponsored, with the ODCCP, an International Conference on Security and Stability in Central Asia, held in Bishek, Kyrgyzstan. The meeting, which was attended by representatives of more than 60 countries and organizations, was concerned with strengthening efforts to counter terrorism and providing effective support to the Central Asian states. In October 2002 the ODIHR and the Government of Azerbaijan organized an international conference on religious freedom and combating terrorism.

OSCE MISSIONS AND FIELD ACTIVITIES

In 2002 there were long-term OSCE missions in Bosnia and Herzegovina, Croatia, Georgia, the former Yugoslav republic of Macedonia, Moldova, Tajikistan, the Federal Republic of Yugoslavia (now Serbia and Montenegro), and Kosovo. (OSCE Missions to Latvia and Estonia were terminated at the end of 2001.) The OSCE was also undertaking field activities in Albania, Armenia, Azerbaijan, Belarus, Chechnya, Kazakhstan, Kyrgyzstan, Turkmenistan, and Uzbekistan. The OSCE has institutionalized structures to assist in the implementation of certain bilateral agreements. At April 2002 there were OSCE representatives to the Russian-Latvian Joint Commission on Military Pensioners and to the Estonian Government Commission on Military Pensioners.

In August 1995 the CIO appointed a Personal Representative concerned with the conflict between Armenia and Azerbaijan in the Nagornyi Karabakh region. The OSCE provided a framework for discussions between the two countries through its 11-nation Minsk Group, which from early 1997 was co-chaired by France, Russia and the USA. In October 1997 Armenia and Azerbaijan reached agreement on OSCE proposals for a political settlement; however, the concessions granted by the Armenian President, Levon Ter-Petrossian, which included the withdrawal of troops from certain strategic areas of Nagornyi Karabakh precipitated his resignation in February 1998. The proposals were rejected by his successor, Robert Kocharian. Nevertheless, meetings of the Minsk Group continued in 1998 and both countries expressed their willingness to recommence negotiations. The then CIO, Bronisław Geremek, met with the leaders of both countries in November and persuaded them to exchange prisoners of war. In July 1999 the OSCE Permanent Council approved the establishment of an Office in Yerevan (Armenia), which began operations in February 2000. The Office works independently of the Minsk Group, to promote OSCE principles within the country in order to support political and economic stability. It aims to contribute to the development of democratic institutions and to the strengthening of civil society. An Office in Baku (Azerbaijan) opened in July 2000. In November 2001 the Office in Yerevan presented a report on trafficking in human beings in Armenia, which had been compiled as a joint effort by the OSCE, IOM and UNICEF. In March 2002 the CIO visited the region to discuss prospects for peace, and the OSCE's role in the process.

In January 1995 Russia agreed to an OSCE proposal to send a fact-finding mission to assist in the conflict between the Russian authorities and an independence movement in Chechnya. The mission criticized the Russian army for using excessive force against Chechen rebels and civilians; reported that violations of human rights had been perpetrated by both sides in the conflict; and urged Russia to enforce a cease-fire to allow the delivery of humanitarian supplies by international aid agencies to the population of the city. An OSCE Assistance Group to Chechnya mediated between the two sides, and, in July, brokered a cease-fire agreement between the Russian military authorities in Chechnya and the Chechen rebels. A further peace accord was signed, under the auspices of the OSCE, in May 1996, but the truce was broken in July. A more conclusive cease-fire agreement was signed by the two parties to the conflict in August. In January 1997 the OSCE assisted in the preparation and monitoring of general elections conducted in Chechnya. The Assistance Group remained in the territory to help with post-conflict rehabilitation, including the promotion of democratic institutions and respect for human rights. In December 1998, however, the Assistance Group relocated from its headquarters in Groznyi (also known as Dzokhar from March of that year) to Moscow, owing to the deteriorating security situation. It continued to co-ordinate the delivery of humanitarian aid and implementation of other assistance projects. In September 1999, in response to resurgent separatist activity, Russian launched a military offensive against Chechnya. In early November an OSCE mission arrived in the neighbouring republic of Ingushetia to assess the condition and needs of the estimated 200,000 refugees who had fled the hostilities; however, the officials were prevented by the Russian authorites from travelling into Chechnya. The issue dominated the OSCE summit meeting, held in İstanbul, Turkey, later in that month. The meeting insisted upon a political solution to the conflict and called for an immediate cease-fire. An agreement was reached with the Russian President to allow the CIO to visit the region, and to an OSCE role in initiating political dialogue. In February 2000 the CIO welcomed the Russian Government's appointment of a Presidential Representative for Human Rights in Chechnya. In June 2001 the Assistance Group to Chechnya resumed operations inside the territory from a new office in Znamenskoye. An OSCE/ODIHR delegation visited Chechnya during that month to evaluate the prevailing humanitarian and human rights situation.

In December 1999 the Permanent Council, at the request of the Government of Georgia expanded the mandate of the existing OSCE Mission to Georgia to include monitoring that country's border with Chechnya. The first permanent observation post opened in February 2000 and the monitoring team was fully deployed by July. In December 2001 the Permanent Council approved an expansion in the border monitoring mission to cover the border between Georgia and Ingushetia. The OSCE Mission to Georgia was established in 1992 to work towards a political settlement between disputing factions within the country. Since 1994 the Mission has contributed to efforts to define the political status of South Ossetia and has supported UN peace-keeping and human rights activities in Abkhazia.

In late 1996 the OSCE declared the constitutional referendum held in Belarus in November to be illegal and urged that country's Government to ensure political freedoms and respect for human rights. In September 1997 the Permanent Council determined to establish an OSCE Advisory and Monitoring Group to assist with the process of democratization; the Group commenced operations in February 1998. It has subsequently been active in strengthening civil society, organizing training seminars and workshops in electoral practices, monitoring the human rights situation, including the registration of political parties and the development of an independent media, and in mediating between the President and opposition parties. In October the OSCE Parliamentary Assembly formed an *ad hoc* Committee on Belarus, to act as a working group to support and intensify the organization's work in the country. The OSCE/ODIHR declared legislative elections held in Belarus in October 2000 not to have been conducted freely and fairly, and pronounced that presidential elections held in September 2001 had not met the standards required by the Organization.

An OSCE Mission to Moldova was established in February 1993, in order to assist the conflicting parties to pursue negotiations on a political settlement, as well as to observe the military situation in the region and to provide advice on issues of human and minority rights, democratization and the repatriation of refugees. In December 1999 the Permanent Council, with the approval of the Russian Government, authorized an expansion of the Mission's mandate to ensure the full removal and destruction of Russian ammunition and armaments and to co-ordinate financial and technical assistance for the withdrawal of foreign troops and the destruction of weapons. In June 2001 the Mission established a tripartite working group, with representatives of the Russian Ministry of Defence and the local authorities in Transdniestrian to assist and support the process of disposal of munitions.

In 1999 an OSCE Project Co-ordinator in Ukraine was established, following the successful conclusion of the OSCE Mission to Ukraine (which had been established in November 1994). The Project Co-ordinator is responsible for pursuing co-operation between Ukraine and the OSCE and providing technical assistance in areas including legal reform, freedom of the media, trafficking in human rights, and the work of the human rights Ombudsman. In April 2002 an ODIHR Election Observation Mission monitored parliamentary elections held in Ukraine.

In March 1997 the OSCE dispatched a fact-finding mission to Albania to help restore political and civil stability, which had been undermined by the collapse of national pyramid saving schemes at the start of the year. At the end of that month the Permanent Council agreed to establish an OSCE Presence in Albania. OSCE efforts focused on reaching a political consensus on new legislation for the conduct of forthcoming elections to establish a government of national reconciliation. Voting took place in June/July, with 500 OSCE observers providing technical electoral assistance and helping to monitor the voting. In December the Permanent Council confirmed that the Presence should provide the framework for co-ordinating other international efforts in the country. In March 1998 the OSCE Presence was mandated to monitor the country's borders with the Kosovan region of southern Serbia and to prevent any spillover effects from the escalating crisis. This role was reduced following the political settlement for Kosovo and Metohija concluded in mid-1999. In June 1998 the OSCE observed local elections in Albania. It became the Co-Chair, with the EU, of the Friends of Albania group, which then brought together countries and international bodies concerned with the situation in Albania for the first time in September. (The sixth annual meeting of the group was held in April 2002.) In October 1998 the Permanent Council determined to enhance the Presence's role in border-monitoring activities. With other organizations, the OSCE was involved in the preparation of the country's draft constitution, finalized in October, and an ODIHR Election Observation Mission was established to observe the referendum on the constitution held in November. The OSCE Presence in Albania has subsequently provided advice and support to the Albanian Government regarding democratization, the rule of law, the media, human rights, election preparation and monitoring, and the development of civil society. It supports an Economics and Environment Office. The Presence also monitors the Government's weapons collection programme.

The OSCE Mission to Bosnia and Herzegovina was established in December 1995 to achieve the objectives of the peace accords for the former Yugoslavia, in particular to oversee the process of democratization. The OSCE's efforts to organize and oversee the Bosnian national elections, which were held on 14 September 1996, was the largest-ever electoral operation undertaken by the organization, with some 1,200 electoral observers deployed. The OSCE subsequently monitored Bosnian municipal elections, twice rescheduled by the organization and eventually held in September 1997, and the elections to the National Assembly of the Serb Republic and to the Bosnian Serb presidency in November. In 1998 the mission was charged with organizing the second post-war general elections in Bosnia and Herzegovina (comprising elections to the legislature of Bosnia and Herzegovina, the Federation and the Serb Republic, and to the presidencies of Bosnia and Herzegovina and the Serb Republic). The mission assisted with the registration of voters and, in September, was responsible for the supervision of the elections at polling stations within and outside the country. The final results of the election to the Bosnian Serb presidency were delayed, owing to the unexpected victory of an extreme nationalist which, it was feared, could jeopardize the peace process. The OSCE immediately emphasized the necessity of maintaining the process. It also insisted on the need to transfer responsibility for the electoral process to the national authorities for future elections. In March 1999 the OSCE initiated an educational campaign relating to new election laws. However a permanent electoral legal framework had not been approved by the time of legislative elections held in November 2000; the OSCE was therefore active in both preparing and monitoring these. The Mission's responsibility for elections in the country ended in November 2001 when a new permanent Election Commission was inaugurated. However, it was to continue to provide support for the Commission's secretariat. Other key areas of Mission activity continued to be the promotion of democratic values, monitoring and promoting respect for human rights, and implementation of arms control and security-building measures. An Agreement on Regional Arms Control was signed in 1995, providing for confidence- and security-building measures and a reduction in excess armaments. The Mission has established consultative commissions to promote dialogue among military personnel from different entities within the country. An audit of the entities' defence budgets was conducted in 2001.

The OSCE Mission to Croatia was established in April 1996 to provide assistance and expertise in the field of human and minority rights, and to assist in the implementation of legislation and the development of democratic institutions. The Mission's mandate was extended in June 1997 in order to enhance its capacity to protect human rights, in particular the rights of minorities, to monitor the return and treatment of refugees and displaced persons, and to make specific recommendations to the Croatian authorities. In March 1998, following the integration of the disputed region into Croatia, the OSCE criticized the conditions imposed by the Croatian Government for the return of Serb refugees, stating that the right to return to one's own country is inalienable and must not depend on the fulfilment of conditions. The Mission conducts extensive field monitoring to facilitate the return of refugees and displaced persons. In October 1998 the Mission assumed the responsibilities of the United Nations Police Support Group (UNPSG). The OSCE Police Monitoring Group, comprising a maximum of 120 unarmed OSCE civilian police monitors, was deployed in the region, representing the Organization's first police-monitoring role. The Group was terminated in October 2000, although the OSCE was to continue to advise on and monitor police activities in Croatia. The OSCE was also to be responsible for monitoring the border regions, with particular concern for customs activities. The OSCE/ODIHR monitored legislative and presidential elections held in Croatia in January 2000. Local government elections were held in May 2001.

In mid-1998 the OSCE was involved in the mediation effort to resolve the conflict between the Serbian authorities and ethnic Albanian separatists in the formerly autonomous province of Kosovo and Metohija. In October, following months of diplomatic effort and the threat of NATO air strikes, Yugoslav President Slobodan Milošević agreed to comply with UN Security Council Resolution 1199, which required an immediate cease-fire, Serbian troop withdrawals, the commencement of meaningful peace negotiations, and unrestricted access for humanitarian aid. Under a peace plan proposed by the US special envoy, Richard Holbrooke, President Milošević agreed to the formation of a 2,000-member OSCE Kosovo Verification Mission (KVM) to monitor compliance, in addition to surveillance flights by unarmed NATO aircraft. The KVM was to patrol the region to ensure the withdrawal of Serbian military and police units, and to oversee the safe return of refugees and the non-harassment of ethnic Albanian inhabitants. It was also to monitor border control activities and accompany police units in Kosovo, when necessary, to assist them to perform their normal policing roles. The mission's mandate was formally established on 25 October 1998 for a period of one year. Upon achievement of a political settlement defining the area's self-government, and its subsequent implementation, the KVM was to be responsible for supervising elections in Kosovo, assisting in the establishment of democratic institutions and developing a Kosovo police force. The long-term mission was accepted in return for the eventual removal of Yugoslavia's suspension from the OSCE. However, sporadic fighting continued in the province, and the monitoring force began unofficially to assume a peace-keeping role. In January 1999 the KVM successfully negotiated for the release of eight Yugoslav soldiers held hostage by the separatist forces. Later in that month following the KVM's denunciation of the killing of some 45 ethnic Albanians by Serbian security forces in the village of Racak, President Milošević ordered the head of the mission, William Walker, to leave the region. This was later revoked. Meanwhile, OSCE monitors were forced to withdraw from Racak under fire from Serbian troops. An emergency meeting of the OSCE in Vienna agreed to maintain the mission. However, on 19 March, following the failure of negotiations to resolve the crisis, the CIO decided to evacuate the 1,380 unarmed monitors, owing to the deteriorating security situation in Kosovo. NATO commenced an aerial offensive against Yugoslavia in late March. In early April the CIO condemned the mass expulsion of ethnic Albanians from Kosovo and other violations of human rights committed by Serbian forces. Later in the same month the CIO, at a meeting of a ministerial troika attended by the Secretary-General, announced that the OSCE was willing to assist in the implementation of a political settlement in Kosovo. The OSCE was also concerned with measures to prevent the crisis affecting the other Balkan states. Within the framework of

a political settlement for Kosovo, which was formally concluded in June, the OSCE (whose Mission in Kosovo, mandated to comprise 1,400 personnel, was established on 1 July) was responsible for democracy- and institution-building under the auspices of the UN Interim Administration Mission for Kosovo (UNMIK). OSCE monitors were deployed to assess the human rights situation throughout the region, and in August a new OSCE-administered police training school was inaugurated. (By the end of 2001 5,700 police officers had trained under the OSCE police education programme.) In December 1999 the OSCE published a report on the situation in Kosovo, which confirmed that Serbian forces had conducted systematic abuses of human rights but also raised suspicion against the KLA for organizing retribution attacks against Serbian civilians later in the year. In February 2000 the OSCE Mission established an Institute for Civil Administration to train public officials in principles of democratic governance. A Kosovo Law Centre was established in June to provide technical assistance to the legal community, with a view to promoting democratic principles and human rights. In the following month the Department for Democratic Governance and Civil Society was established by UNMIK, and was to be administered by the OSCE Mission. In August an Ombudsperson, nominated by the OSCE, was appointed to a new Office of the Ombudsperson, which became operational in November: the role of the Ombudsperson was to investigate and mediate claims of human rights violations arising within Kosovo. The OSCE was responsible for registering about 1m. voters prior to municipal elections that were held in Kosovo in October. During 2001 the Mission assisted the registration process for voting in a general election, and supervised the polling which took place in November. In early 2002 the Mission initiated training sessions for members of the new Kosovo Assembly. At that time the Mission was restructured, consolidating the number of field offices from 21 to nine.

In November 2000 the Federal Republic of Yugoslavia (FRY) was admitted into the OSCE. An OSCE Mission to the FRY, to assist in the areas of democracy and protection of human rights and in the restructing and training of law enforcement agencies and the judiciary, was approved by the Permanent Council in January 2001 and inaugurated in March. In March 2002 members of the Mission were facilitating the census process in southern Serbia.

The OSCE Spillover Monitor Mission to Skopje was established in 1992 to help to prevent the conflict in the former Yugoslavia from destabilizing the former Yugoslav republic of Macedonia (FYRM). Its principal mandate is to monitor the border region, as well as monitoring human rights and promoting the development of democratic institutions, including an independent media. The Mission is also concerned with mediating between inter-ethnic groups in the country, and has provided support for implementation of a framework political agreement signed in August 2001 through the deployment of international confidence-building monitors and police advisers. In December OSCE monitors accompanied multi-ethnic police officers to areas of early conflict, as part of the August agreement. In March 2002 OSCE signed its first memorandum of understanding with the European Commission, in respect to policing operations in FYRM.

In March 2000 the OSCE adopted a Regional Strategy for South-Eastern Europe, aimed at enhancing co-operation amongst its presences in the region. The OSCE was actively involved in co-ordinating the Stability Pact for South-Eastern Europe, which was initiated, in June 1999, as a collaborative plan of action by the EU, Group of Seven industrialized nations and Russia (the G-8), regional governments and other organizations concerned with the stability of the region. (This can be accessed at www.stabilitypact.org.) A meeting of participants in the Pact was convened to coincide with the OSCE summit meeting, held in November. In October 2001 the OSCE organized a Stability Pact regional conference, held in Bucharest, Romania. A memorandum of understanding between the OSCE Mission to the FRY and the Stability Pact was signed in December.

The OSCE Mission to Tajikistan was established in December 1993, and began operations in February 1994. The Mission worked with the UN Mission of Observers to Tajikistan (UNMOT) to promote a peace process in that country, and was a guarantor of the peace agreement concluded in June 1997. The Mission remained actively concerned with promoting respect for human rights, assisting the development of the local media, locating missing persons, and the fair distribution of humanitarian aid. Following multi-party parliamentary elections, held in February 2000, the Mission's focus was to be on post-conflict rehabilitation. In April 2002 the Mission initiated a one-year project to promote access to environmental information and network-building among young people concerned with ecology.

In December 2000 the Permanent Council renamed the OSCE Liaison Office in Central Asia the OSCE Centre in Tashkent. The Centre aims to promote OSCE principles within Uzbekistan; it also functions as an information exchange between OSCE bodies and participating Central Asian states and as a means of liaising with OSCE presences in the region. In July 1998 the Permanent Council determined to open OSCE Centres in Bishkent (Kyrgyzstan), Almaty (Kazakhstan), and Ashgabad (Turkmenistan), all of which opened in January 1999. In general the Centres were to encourage each country's integration into the OSCE, and implementation of its principles, and to focus on the economic, environmental, human and political aspects of security. In January 2000, for the first time, the OSCE refused to dispatch official observers to monitor presidential elections in a member state, owing to concerns about the legitimacy of elections held in Kazakhstan. Subsequently the Centre in Almaty, with the ODIHR and the OSCE Parliamentary Assembly, initiated a round table on elections project to improve electoral legislation, thus strengthening the political system. The project concluded in January 2002, when participants presented a list of recommendations to the national parliament.

Japan, the Republic of Korea and Thailand have the status of 'partners for co-operation' with the OSCE, while Algeria, Egypt, Israel, Jordan, Morocco and Tunisia are 'Mediterranean partners for co-operation'. Regular consultations are held with these countries in order to discuss security issues of common concern.

Finance

All activities of the institutions, negotiations, *ad hoc* meetings and missions are financed by contributions from member states. The budget for 2003 amounted to €185.7m., of which some 84% was allocated to OSCE missions and field activities.

Publications

Annual Report of the Secretary-General.

The Caucasus: In Defence of the Future.paDecision Manual (annually).

OSCE Handbook (annually).

OSCE Newsletter (monthly).

ORGANIZATION OF AMERICAN STATES—OAS

(ORGANIZACIÓN DE LOS ESTADOS AMERICANOS—OEA)

Address: 17th St and Constitution Ave, NW, Washington, DC 20006, USA.

Telephone: (202) 458-3000; **fax:** (202) 458-6319; **e-mail:** pi@oas.org; **internet:** www.oas.org.

The ninth International Conference of American States (held in Bogotá, Colombia, in 1948) established the Organization of American States by adopting the Charter (succeeding the International Union of American Republics, founded in 1890). The Charter was subsequently amended by the Protocol of Buenos Aires (creating the annual General Assembly), signed in 1967, enacted in 1970, and by the Protocol of Cartagena de Indias, which was signed in 1985 and enacted in 1988. The purpose of the Organization is to strengthen the peace and security of the continent; to promote and consolidate representative democracy, with due respect for the principle of non-intervention; to prevent possible causes of difficulties and to ensure the peaceful settlement of disputes that may arise among the member states; to provide for common action in the event of aggression; to seek the solution of political, juridical and economic problems that may arise among them; to promote, by co-operative action, their economic, social and cultural development; to achieve an effective limitation of conventional weapons; and to devote the largest amount of resources to the economic and social development of the member states.

MEMBERS

Antigua and Barbuda	Guyana
Argentina	Haiti
Bahamas	Honduras
Barbados	Jamaica
Belize	Mexico
Bolivia	Nicaragua
Brazil	Panama
Canada	Paraguay
Chile	Peru
Colombia	Saint Christopher and Nevis
Costa Rica	Saint Lucia
Cuba*	Saint Vincent and the Grenadines
Dominica	Suriname
Dominican Republic	Trinidad and Tobago
Ecuador	USA
El Salvador	Uruguay
Grenada	Venezuela
Guatemala	

* The Cuban Government was suspended from OAS activities in 1962.

Permanent Observers: Algeria, Angola, Armenia, Austria, Azerbaijan, Belgium, Bosnia and Herzegovina, Bulgaria, Croatia, Cyprus, Czech Republic, Denmark, Egypt, Equatorial Guinea, Estonia, Finland, France, Georgia, Germany, Ghana, Greece, the Holy See, Hungary, India, Ireland, Israel, Italy, Japan, Kazakhstan, the Republic of Korea, Latvia, Lebanon, Morocco, the Netherlands, Norway, Pakistan, Philippines, Poland, Portugal, Qatar, Romania, Russia, Saudi Arabia, Serbia and Montenegro, Slovakia, Spain, Sri Lanka, Sweden, Switzerland, Thailand, Tunisia, Turkey, Ukraine, the United Kingdom, Yemen and the European Union.

Organization

(April 2003)

GENERAL ASSEMBLY

The Assembly meets annually and may also hold special sessions when convoked by the Permanent Council. As the supreme organ of the OAS, it decides general action and policy.

MEETINGS OF CONSULTATION OF MINISTERS OF FOREIGN AFFAIRS

Meetings are convened, at the request of any member state, to consider problems of an urgent nature and of common interest to member states, or to serve as an organ of consultation in cases of armed attack or other threats to international peace and security. The Permanent Council determines whether a meeting should be convened and acts as a provisional organ of consultation until ministers are able to assemble.

PERMANENT COUNCIL

The Council meets regularly throughout the year at OAS headquarters. It is composed of one representative of each member state with the rank of ambassador; each government may accredit alternate representatives and advisers and when necessary appoint an interim representative. The office of Chairman is held in turn by each of the representatives, following alphabetical order according to the names of the countries in Spanish. The Vice-Chairman is determined in the same way, following reverse alphabetical order. Their terms of office are three months.

The Council acts as an organ of consultation and oversees the maintenance of friendly relations between members. It supervises the work of the OAS and promotes co-operation with a variety of other international bodies including the United Nations. The official languages are English, French, Portuguese and Spanish.

INTER-AMERICAN COUNCIL FOR INTEGRAL DEVELOPMENT—CIDI

The Council was established in 1996, replacing the Inter-American Economic and Social Council and the Inter-American Council for Education, Science and Culture. Its aim is to promote co-operation among the countries of the region, in order to accelerate economic and social development. CIDI's work focuses on eight areas: social development and education; cultural development; the generation of productive employment; economic diversification, integration and trade liberalization; strengthening democratic institutions; the exchange of scientific and technological information; the development of tourism; and sustainable environmental development. An Executive Secretary for Integral Development provides CIDI with technical and secretarial services.

Executive Secretary: RONALD SCHEMAN (USA).

Inter-American Agency for Co-operation and Development: f. November 1999 as a subsidiary body of CIDI to accelerate the development of Latin America and the Caribbean through technical co-operation and training programmes. In particular, the Agency aimed to formulate strategies for mobilizing external funds for OAS co-operation initiatives; establish criteria for the promotion and exchange of co-operation activities; prepare co-operation accords and evaluate project requests and results; and review mechanisms for promoting scholarships and professional exchange programmes. Approximately 1,500 students are trained each year under Agency programmes. The Executive Secretary for Integral Development serves as the Agency's Director-General.

GENERAL SECRETARIAT

The Secretariat, the central and permanent organ of the Organization, performs the duties entrusted to it by the General Assembly, Meetings of Consultation of Ministers of Foreign Affairs and the Councils.

Secretary-General: CÉSAR GAVIRIA TRUJILLO (Colombia).

Assistant Secretary-General: LUIGI R. EINAUDI (USA).

INTER-AMERICAN COMMITTEES AND COMMISSIONS

Inter-American Juridical Committee—IAJC (Comité Jurídico Interamericano): Rua Senador Vergueiro 81, Rio de Janeiro, RJ 22230-000, Brazil; tel. (21) 558-3204; fax (21) 558-4600; e-mail sdsouza@oas.org; composed of 11 jurists, nationals of different member states, elected for a period of four years, with the possibility of re-election. The Committee's purposes are: to serve as an advisory body to the Organization on juridical matters; to promote the progressive development and codification of international law; and to study juridical problems relating to the integration of the developing countries in the hemisphere, and, in so far as may appear desirable, the possibility of attaining uniformity in legislation; Chair. JOÃO GRANDINO RODAS.

Inter-American Commission on Human Rights (Comisión Interamericana de Derechos Humanos): 1889 F St, NW, Washington, DC 20006, USA; tel. (202) 458-6002; fax (202) 458-3992; e-mail cidhoea@oas.org; internet www.cidh.oas.org; f. 1960; comprises seven members; promotes the observance and protection of human rights in the member states of the OAS; examines and reports on the human rights situation in member countries, and provides consultative services; during 2000 it received 681 written complaints, and opened 110 new cases related to 25 member states; Exec. Sec. SANTIAGO CANTON.

Inter-American Court of Human Rights—IACHR (Corte Interamericana de Derechos Humanos): Apdo Postal 6906-1000, San José, Costa Rica; tel. 234-0581; fax 234-0584; e-mail corteidh@corteidh.or.cr; internet www.corteidh.or.cr; f. 1978, as an autonomous judicial institution whose purpose is to apply and interpret the American Convention on Human Rights (which entered into force in 1978: at December 2002 the Convention had been ratified by 24 OAS member states, of which 21 had accepted the competence of the Court); comprises seven jurists from OAS member states; Pres. ANTÔNIO A. CANÇADO TRINDADE; Sec. MANUEL E. VENTURA-ROBLES.

Inter-American Drug Abuse Control Commission (Comisión Interamericana para el Control del Abuso de Drogas—CICAD): c/o OAS General Secretariat, 1889 F St, NW, Washington, 8th Floor, DC 20006-4499, USA; tel. (202) 458-3178; fax (202) 458-3658; e-mail oidcicad@oas.org; internet www.cicad.oas.org; f. 1986 by the OAS to promote and facilitate multilateral co-operation in the control and prevention of the trafficking, production and use of illegal drugs, and related crimes; mems 34 countries; Exec. Sec. DAVID R. BEALL; publs *Statistical Survey* (annually), *Directory of Governmental Institutions Charges with the Fight Against the Illicit Production, Trafficking, Use and Abuse of Narcotic Drugs and Psychotropic Substances Evaluation of Progress in Drug Control Progress Report in Drug Control—Implementation in Recommendations* (twice a year).

Inter-American Telecommunication Commission (Comisión Interamericana de Telecomunicaciones—CITEL): 1889 F St, NW, Washington, DC 20006, USA; tel. (202) 458-3004; fax (202) 458-6854; e-mail citel@oas.org; internet www.citel.oas.org; f. 1993 to promote the development of telecommunications in the region; mems 35 countries; Exec. Sec. CLOVIS JOSÉ BAPTISTA NETO.

Inter-American Committee on Ports (Comisión Interamericana de Puertos—CIP): 1889 F St, NW, Washington, DC 20006, USA; tel. (202) 458-3871; fax (202) 458-3517; e-mail cgallegos@oas.org; f. 1998 to further OAS activities in the sector (previously undertaken by Inter-American port conferences); aims to develop and co-ordinate member state policies in port administration and management; the first meeting of the Committee took place in October 1999; three technical advisory groups were established to advise on port oper-

ations, port security, and navigation safety and environmental protection; an Executive Board meets annually; Sec. CARLOS GALLEGOS.

Activities

In December 1994 the first Summit of the Americas was convened in Miami, USA. The meeting endorsed the concept of a Free Trade Area of the Americas (FTAA), and also approved a Plan of Action to strengthen democracy, eradicate poverty and promote sustainable development throughout the region. The OAS subsequently embarked on an extensive process of reform and modernization to strengthen its capacity to undertake a lead role in implementing the Plan. The Organization realigned its priorities in order to respond to the mandates emerging from the Summit and developed a new institutional framework for technical assistance and co-operation, although many activities continued to be undertaken by the specialized or associated organizations of the OAS (see below). In 1998, following the second Summit of the Americas, held in April, in Santiago, Chile, the OAS established an Office of Summit Follow-Up, in order to strengthen its servicing of the meetings, and to co-ordinate tasks assigned to the Organization. The third Summit, convened in Quebec City, Canada, in April 2001, reaffirmed the central role of the OAS in implementing decisions of the summit meetings and instructed the Organization to pursue the process of reform in order to enhance its operational capabilities, in particular in the areas of human rights, combating trade in illegal drugs, and enforcement of democratic values. The Summit declaration stated that commitment to democracy was a requirement for a country's participation in the summit process. The meeting also determined that the OAS was to be the technical secretariat for the process, assuming many of the responsibilities previously taken by the host country.

TRADE AND ECONOMIC INTEGRATION

A trade unit was established in 1995 in order to strengthen the Organization's involvement in trade issues and the process of economic integration, which became a priority area following the first Summit of the Americas. The unit was to provide technical assistance in support of the establishment of the FTAA, and to co-ordinate activities between regional and sub-regional integration organizations. In 2002 the unit was providing technical support to the nine FTAA negotiating groups: market access; investment; services; government procurement; dispute settlement; agriculture; intellectual property rights; subsidies, anti-dumping and countervailing duties; and competition policy. In April 2001 the third Summit of the Americas requested the OAS to initiate an analysis of corporate social responsibility. At the Summit it was agreed that negotiations to establish the FTAA should be concluded by January 2005, to allow the trade pact to enter into force no later than December of that year.

The unit operates in consultation with a Special Committee on Trade, which was established in 1993, comprising high-level officials representing each member state. The Committee studies trade issues, provides technical analyses of the economic situation in member countries and the region, and prepares reports for ministerial meetings of the FTAA. The OAS also administers an Inter-American Foreign Trade Information System which facilitates the exchange of information.

DEMOCRACY AND CIVIL SOCIETY

Two principal organs of the OAS, the Inter-American Commission on Human Rights and the Inter-American Court of Human Rights, work to secure respect for human rights in all member countries. The OAS aims to encourage more member governments to accept jurisdiction of the Court. The OAS also collaborates with member states in the strengthening of representative institutions within government and as part of a democratic civil society. The third Summit of the Americas, convened in April 2001, mandated the OAS to formulate an Inter-American Democratic Charter. The Charter was adopted in September at a special session of the Assembly. Central to the Charter's five chapters was democracy and its relationship to human rights, integral development and combating poverty.

Through its Unit for the Promotion of Democracy, established in 1990, the OAS provides electoral technical assistance to member states and undertakes missions to observe the conduct of elections. By the end of 2001 the OAS had conducted more than 60 electoral missions in 18 countries. The OAS also supports societies in post-conflict situations and recently-installed governments to promote democratic practices.

In June 1991 the OAS General Assembly approved a resolution on representative democracy, which authorized the Secretary-General to summon a session of the Permanent Council in cases where a democratically-elected government had been overthrown or democratic procedures abandoned in member states. The Council could then convene an *ad hoc* meeting of ministers of foreign affairs to consider the situation. The procedure was invoked following political developments in Haiti, in September 1991, and Peru, in April 1992. Ministers determined to impose trade and diplomatic sanctions against Haiti and sent missions to both countries. The resolution was incorporated into the Protocol of Washington, amending the OAS charter, which was adopted in December 1992 and entered into force in September 1997. A high-level OAS mission was dispatched to Peru in June 2000 to assist with the process of 'strengthening its institutional democratic system', following allegations that the Peruvian authorities had manipulated the re-election of that country's President in May. The mission subsequently co-ordinated negotiations between the Peruvian Government and opposition organizations. In August the OAS Secretary-General undertook the first of several high-level missions to negotiate with the authorities in Haiti in order to resolve the political crisis resulting from a disputed general election in May. (An OAS electoral monitoring team was withdrawn from Haiti in July prior to the second round of voting owing to concern at procedural irregularities.) In January 2001, following a meeting with the Haitian Prime Minister, the Assistant Secretary-General recommended that the OAS renew its efforts to establish a dialogue between the government, opposition parties and representatives of civil society in that country. In May the OAS and CARICOM undertook a joint mission to Haiti in order to assess prospects for a democratic resolution to the political uncertainties, and in June the OAS General Assembly issued a resolution urging all parties in Haiti to respect democratic order. At the end of that month the OAS Secretary-General led a visit of the joint mission to Haiti, during which further progress was achieved on the establishment of a new electoral council. Following political and social unrest in Haiti in December 2001, the OAS and CARICOM pledged to conduct an independent investigation into the violence, and in March 2002 an agreement to establish a special OAS mission to Haiti was signed in the capital, Port-au-Prince. The independent commission of inquiry reported to the OAS at the beginning of July, and listed a set of recommendations relating to law reform, security and other confidence-building measures to help to secure democracy in Haiti.

In April 2002 a special session of the General Assembly was convened to discuss the ongoing political instability in Venezuela. In January 2003 the OAS announced the establishment of the so-called Group of Friends, composed of representatives from Brazil, Chile, Mexico, Spain, Portugal and the USA, to support its efforts to resolve the ongoing crisis in Venezuela. In March the OAS Secretary-General was invited by Venezuelan opposition groupings to mediate negotiations with the Government.

The OAS Assistance Programme for Demining in Central America (PADCA) was established in 1992, as part of efforts to facilitate the social and economic rehabilitation of the region. By 2002 the programme had provided training for more than 1,100 de-mining experts and assisted six countries in the clearance of some 75,000 anti-personnel devices, as well as in the destruction of more than 500,000 landmines from military stock-piles. Technical support was provided by the Inter-American Defense Board (see below)

The OAS formulated an Inter-American Programme of Co-operation to Combat Corruption in order to address the problem at national level and, in 1996, adopted a Convention against Corruption. The first conference of the parties to the Convention was held in Buenos Aires, Argentina, in May 2001. In June the General Assembly approved the proposed establishment of a verification mechanism, including a policy-making annual conference and an intergovernmental committee of experts. At July 2002 the Convention had been ratified by 27 member states. A working group on transparency aims to promote accountability throughout the public sector and supports national institutions responsible for combating corruption. In 1997 the OAS organized a meeting of experts to consider measures for the prevention of crime. The meeting adopted a work programme which included commitments to undertake police training in criminology and crime investigation, to exchange legal and practical knowledge, and to measure crime and violence in member countries.

REGIONAL SECURITY

In 1991 the General Assembly established a working group to consider issues relating to the promotion of co-operation in regional security. A Special Commission on Hemispheric Security was subsequently established, while two regional conferences have been held on security and confidence-building measures. Voluntary practices agreed by member states include the holding of border meetings to co-ordinate activities, co-operation in natural disaster management, and the exchange of information on military exercises and expenditure. From 1995 meetings of ministers of defence have been convened regularly, which provide a forum for discussion of security matters. The OAS aims to address the specific security concerns of small-island states, in particular those in the Caribbean, by adopting a multidimensional approach to counter their vulnerability, for example through efforts to strengthen democracy, to combat organized crime, to mitigate the effects of natural disasters and other environmental hazards, and to address the problem of HIV/AIDS.

In June 2000 the OAS General Assembly, convened in Windsor, Canada, established a Fund for Peace in support of the peaceful settlement of territorial disputes. In 2001 the Fund was supporting efforts to resolve disputes between Belize and Guatemala and between Honduras and Nicaragua. In June an agreement was concluded to enable an OAS Civilian Verification Mission to visit Honduras and Nicaragua in order to monitor compliance with previously agreed confidence-building measures. The Mission was to be financed by the Fund for Peace.

The OAS is actively involved in efforts to combat the abuse and trafficking of illegal drugs, and in 1996 members approved a Hemispheric Anti-drug Strategy, reiterating their commitment to addressing the problem. In 1998 the Inter-American Drug Abuse Control Commission (CICAD) established a Multilateral Evaluation Mechanism (MEM) to measure aspects of the drug problem and to co-ordinate an evaluation process under which national plans of action to combat drugs trafficking were to be formulated. The first hemispheric drugs report was published by MEM in January 2001 and in February 34 national reports produced under MEM were issued together with a series of recommendations for action. A meeting to review and strengthen MEM was convened in April. In January 2002 MEM published a progress report on the implementation of the recommendations, in which it stated that the countries of the Americas had made a 'significant effort' to adopt the recommendations, although in some instances they had encountered difficulties owing to a lack of technical or financial resources. It was reported that advances had been made in developing national anti-drugs plans, measuring land under illicit cultivation, and adopting procedures against money-laundering. Since 1996 an OAS group of experts has undertaken efforts to assist countries in reducing the demand for illegal substances. Activities include the implementation of prevention programmes for street children; the development of communication strategies; and education and community projects relating to the prevention of drug dependence. In January 2003 CICAD issued reports covering the period 2001–02, including recommendations on measures that individual countries could take to strengthen national anti-drug efforts.

The first Specialized Inter-American Conference on Terrorism was held in Lima, Peru, in April 1996. A Declaration and Plan of Action were adopted, according to which member states agreed to co-operate and implement measures to combat terrorism and organized crime. A second conference was held in Mar del Plata, Argentina, in 1998, which culminated in the adoption of the Commitment of Mar del Plata. Member states recommended the establishment of an Inter-American Committee against Terrorism (CICTE) to implement decisions relating to judicial, police and intelligence co-operation. The Committee held its first session in Miami, USA, in October 1999; a second meeting was convened in January 2002. Two special sessions of the CICTE were held in October and November 2001, following the terrorist attacks on targets in the USA in September. In June 2002, at the OAS General Assembly, held in Bridgetown, Barbados, 30 heads of state and of government signed an Inter-American Convention against Terrorism. The Assembly also adopted a Declaration of Bridgetown on the multidimensional approach to hemispheric security. In 2002 the CICTE On-Line Anti-terrorism Database came into operation.

SOCIAL DEVELOPMENT AND EDUCATION

In June 1996 the OAS established a specialized unit for social development and education to assist governments and social institutions of member states to formulate public policies and implement initiatives relating to employment and labour issues, education development, social integration and poverty elimination. It was also to provide technical and operational support for the implementation of inter-American programmes in those sectors, and to promote the exchange of information among experts and professionals working in those fields. In June 1997 the OAS approved an Inter-American Programme to Combat Poverty. The unit serves as the technical secretariat for annual meetings on social development that were to be convened within the framework of the Programme. The unit also administers the Social Networks of Latin America and the Caribbean project, and its co-ordinating committee, which promotes sub-regional co-operation to combat poverty and discrimination. From 1999 the unit implemented a project funded by the Inter-American Development Bank to place interns and trainees within the Social Network institutions and to promote exchanges between the institutions.

The first meeting of ministers of education of the Americas was held in Bras‡lia, Brazil, in July 1998, based on the mandate of the second Summit of the Americas. The meeting approved an Inter-American Education Programme, formulated by the unit for social development and education, which incorporated the following six priority initiatives: education for priority social sectors; strengthening educational management and institutional development; education for work and youth development; education for citizenship and sustainability in multicultural societies; training in the use of new technologies in teaching the official languages of the OAS; and training of teachers and education administrators. Other programmes in the education sector are undertaken with international agencies and non-governmental organizations.

The OAS supports member states to formulate and implement programmes to promote productive employment and vocational training, to develop small businesses and other employment generation initiatives, and to regulate labour migration. In 1998 the OAS initiated the Labour Market Information System project, which aimed to provide reliable and up-to-date indicators of the labour situation in member countries, to determine the impact of economic policy on the labour situation, and to promote the exchange of information among relevant national and regional institutions. Labour issues were addressed by the second Summit of the Americas, and, following an Inter-American Conference of Labour Ministers, held in Viña del Mar, Chile, in October 1998, two working groups were established to consider the globalization of the economy and its social and labour dimension and the modernization of the state and labour administration. In June 2002 the Pan-American Health Organization (PAHO) and Inter-American Institute for Co-operation on Agriculture (IICA) signed an agreement to increase co-operation in matters relating to health and agriculture, in order to combat poverty in rural communities.

SUSTAINABLE DEVELOPMENT AND THE ENVIRONMENT

In 1996 a summit meeting on social development adopted a plan of action, based on the objectives of the UN Conference on the Environment and Development, which was held in Rio de Janeiro, Brazil, in June 1992. The OAS was to participate in an inter-agency group to monitor implementation of the action plan. The OAS has subsequently established new financing mechanisms and networks of experts relating to aspects of sustainable development. Technical co-operation activities include multinational basin management; a strategic plan for the Amazon; natural disaster management; and the sustainable development of border areas in Central America and South America. In December 1999 the Inter-American Council for Integral Development approved a policy framework and recommendations for action of a new Inter-American Strategy for Public Participation in Decision-making for Sustainable Development.

The following initiatives have also been undertaken: a Caribbean Disaster Mitigation Project, to help those countries to counter and manage the effects of natural disasters; a Post-Georges Disaster Mitigation initiative specifically to assist countries affected by Hurricane Georges; a Natural Hazards Project to provide a general programme of support to assess member states' vulnerability, to provide technical assistance and training to mitigate the effects of a disaster, and to assist in the planning and formulation of development and preparedness policies; the Renewable Energy in the Americas initiative to promote co-operation and strengthen renewable energy and energy efficiency; an Inter-American Water Resources Network, which aims to promote collaboration, training and the exchange of information within the sector; and a Water Level Observation Network for Central America to provide support for coastal resources management, navigation and disaster mitigation in the countries affected by Hurricane Mitch.

SCIENCE AND TECHNOLOGY

The OAS supports and develops activities to contribute to the advancement of science and technology throughout the Americas, and to promote its contribution to social and sustainable development. In particular, it promotes collaboration, dissemination of information and improved communication between experts and institutions working in the sector. Specialized bodies and projects have been established to promote activities in different fields, for example metrology; co-operation between institutions of accreditation, certification and inspection; the development of instruments of measurements and analysis of science and technology; chemistry; the development of technical standardization and related activities; and collaboration between experts and institutions involved in biotechnology and food technology. The OAS also maintains an information system to facilitate access to databases on science and technology throughout the region.

TOURISM AND CULTURE

A specialized unit for tourism was established in 1996 in order to strengthen and co-ordinate activities for the sustainable development of the tourism industry in the Americas. The unit supports regional and sub-regional conferences and workshops, as well as the Inter-American Travel Congress, which was convened for the first time in 1993 to serve as a forum to formulate region-wide tourism

policies. The unit also undertakes research and analysis of the industry.

In 1998 the OAS approved an Inter-American Programme of Culture to support efforts being undertaken by member states and to promote co-operation in areas such as cultural diversity; protection of cultural heritage; training and dissemination of information; and the promotion of cultural tourism. The OAS also assists with the preparation of national and multilateral cultural projects, and co-operates with the private sector to protect and promote cultural assets and events in the region.

COMMUNICATIONS

In June 1993 the OAS General Assembly approved the establishment of an Inter-American Telecommunication Commission. The body has technical autonomy, within the statute and mandate agreed by the Assembly. It aims to facilitate and promote the development of communications in all member countries, in collaboration with the private sector and other organizations, and serves as the principal advisory body of the OAS on matters related to telecommunications.

Finance

The OAS budget for 2003, approved by the General Assembly in mid-2002, amounted to US $84.4m., of which $76.0m. was to come from the regular fund, and $4.4m. from voluntary fund contributions.

Publications

(in English and Spanish)

Américas (6 a year).
Annual Report.
Catalog of Publications (annually).
Ciencia Interamericana (quarterly).
La Educación (quarterly).
Statistical Bulletin (quarterly).
Numerous cultural, legal and scientific reports and studies.

Specialized Organizations and Associated Agencies

Inter-American Children's Institute (Instituto Americano del Niño—IIN): Avda 8 de Octubre 2904, POB 16212, Montevideo 11600, Uruguay; tel. (2) 487-2150; fax (2) 487-3242; e-mail iin@redfacil.com.uy; internet www.iin.oea.org; f. 1927; promotes the regional implementation of the Convention on the Rights of the Child, assists in the development of child-oriented public policies; promotes co-operation between states; and aims to develop awareness of problems affecting children and young people in the region. The Institute organizes workshops, seminars, courses, training programmes and conferences on issues relating to children, including, for example, the rights of children, children with disabilities, and the child welfare system. It also provides advisory services, statistical data and other relevant information to authorities and experts throughout the region; Dir-Gen. ALEJANDRO BONASSO; publs *Boletín* (quarterly), *IINfancia* (2 a year).

Inter-American Commission of Women (Comisión Interamericana de Mujeres—CIM): 1889 F St, NW, Suite 880 Washington, DC 20006, USA; tel. (202) 458-6084; fax (202) 458-6094; e-mail spcim@oas.org; f. 1928 for the extension of civil, political, economic, social and cultural rights for women; in 1991 a Seed Fund was established to provide financing for grass-roots projects consistent with the Commission's objectives; Pres. YADIRA HENRÍQUEZ (Dominican Republic); Exec. Sec. CARMEN LOMELLIN (USA).

Inter-American Committee Against Terrorism (Comité Interamericano Contra el Terrorismo—CICTE): 17th St and Constitution Ave, NW, Washington, DC 20006, USA; tel. (202) 458-3000; fax (202) 458-3967; internet www.cicte.oas.org; f. 1999 to enhance the exchange of information via national authorities (including the establishment of an Inter-American database on terrorism issues), formulate proposals to assist member states in drafting counter-terrorism legislation in all states, compile bilateral, sub-regional, regional and multilateral treaties and agreements signed by member states and promote universal adherence to international counter-terrorism conventions, strengthen border co-operation and travel documentation security measures, and develop activities for training and crisis management; Exec. Sec. STEVEN MONBLATT (USA).

Inter-American Defense Board (Junta Interamericana de Defensa—JID): 2600 16th St, NW, Washington, DC 20441, USA; tel. (202) 939-7490; internet www.jid.org; works in liaison with member governments to plan and train for the common security interests of the western hemisphere; operates the Inter-American Defense College; Chair. Maj.-Gen. CARL H. FREEMAN (USA).

Inter-American Indigenous Institute (Instituto Indigenista Interamericano—III): Avda de las Fuentes 106, Col. Jardines del Pedregal, Delegación Álvaro Obregón, 01900 México, DF, Mexico; tel. (5) 595-8410; fax (5) 595-4324; e-mail ininin@data.net.mx; internet www.indigenista.org; f. 1940; conducts research on the situation of the indigenous peoples of America; assists the exchange of information; promotes indigenous policies in member states aimed at the elimination of poverty and development within Indian communities, and to secure their position as ethnic groups within a democratic society; Hon. Dir Dr GUILLERMO ESPINOSA VELASCO (Mexico); Publs *América Indígena* (quarterly), *Anuario Indigenista*.

Inter-American Institute for Co-operation on Agriculture—IICA (Instituto Interamericano de Cooperación para la Agricultura): Apdo Postal 55–2200 San Isidro de Coronado, San José, Costa Rica; tel. 216-0222; fax 216-0233; e-mail iicahq@iica.ac.cr; internet www .iica.int; f. 1942 (as the Inter-American Institute of Agricultural Sciences: new name 1980); supports the efforts of member states to improve agricultural development and rural well-being; encourages co-operation between regional organizations, and provides a forum for the exchange of experience; Dir-Gen. Dr CHELSTON W. D. BRATHWAITE (Barbados); publs *Annual Report, Comuniica* (quarterly).

Pan American Development Foundation—PADF (Fundación Panamericana para el Desarrollo): 2600 16th St, NW, Washington, DC 20009-4202, USA; tel. (202) 458-3969; fax (202) 458-6316; e-mail padf-dc@padf.org; internet www.padf.org; f. 1962 to improve economic and social conditions in Latin America and the Caribbean through providing low-interest credit for small-scale entrepreneurs, vocational training, improved health care, agricultural development and reafforestation, and strengthening local non-governmental organizations; provides emergency disaster relief and reconstruction assistance; Pres. ALEXANDER WATSON; Exec. Dir. FRANK D. GÓMEZ.

Pan American Health Organization—PAHO (Organización Panamericana de la Salud): 525 23rd St, NW, Washington, DC 20037, USA; tel. (202) 974-3000; fax (202) 974-3663; e-mail webmaster@paho.org; internet www.paho.org; f. 1902; co-ordinates regional efforts to improve health; maintains close relations with national health organizations and serves as the Regional Office for the Americas of the World Health Organization; Dir Dr MIRTA ROSES PERIAGO (Argentina).

Pan-American Institute of Geography and History—PAIGH (Instituto Panamericano de Geografía e Historia–IPGH): Ex-Arzobispado 29, 11860 México, DF, Mexico; tel. (5) 277-5888; fax (5) 271-6172; e-mail ipgh@laneta.apc.org; internet www.ipgh.org.mx; f. 1928; co-ordinates and promotes the study of cartography, geophysics, geography and history; provides technical assistance, conducts training at research centres, distributes publications, and organizes technical meetings; Sec.Gen. CARLOS A.ZELAYA CARVALLO YÁNEZ (Chile); Publs *Boletín Aéreo* (quarterly), *Revista Cartográfica* (2 a year), *Revista Geográfica* (2 a year), *Revista Historia de América* (2 a year), *Revista de Arqueología Americana* (2 a year), *Revista Geofísica* (2 a year), *Folklore Americano* (2 a year), *Boletín de Antropología Americana* (2 a year).

ORGANIZATION OF ARAB PETROLEUM EXPORTING COUNTRIES—OAPEC

Address: POB 20501, Safat 13066, Kuwait.

Telephone: 4844500; **fax:** 4815747; **e-mail:** oapec@qualitynet.net; **internet:** www.oapecorg.org.

OAPEC was established in 1968 to safeguard the interests of members and to determine ways and means for their co-operation in various forms of economic activity in the petroleum industry. OAPEC member states contributed 28.2% of total world petroleum production in 2001 and 12.3% of total global natural gas output in 2000. At the end of 2001 OAPEC member states accounted for an estimated 60.1% of total global oil reserves and 24.6% of total global reserves of natural gas.

MEMBERS

Algeria	Kuwait	Saudi Arabia
Bahrain	Libya	Syria
Egypt	Qatar	United Arab Emirates
Iraq		

Organization

(April 2003)

MINISTERIAL COUNCIL

The Council consists normally of the ministers of petroleum of the member states, and forms the supreme authority of the Organization, responsible for drawing up its general policy, directing its activities and laying down its governing rules. It meets twice yearly, and may hold extraordinary sessions. Chairmanship is on an annual rotation basis.

EXECUTIVE BUREAU

Assists the Council to direct the management of the Organization, approves staff regulations, reviews the budget, and refers it to the Council, considers matters relating to the Organization's agreements and activities and draws up the agenda for the Council. The Bureau comprises one senior official from each member state. Chairmanship is by rotation on an annual basis, following the same order as the Ministerial Council chairmanship. The Bureau convenes at least three times a year.

GENERAL SECRETARIAT

Secretary-General: ABDULAZIZ A. AL-TURKI (Saudi Arabia).

Besides the Office of the Secretary-General, there are four departments: Finance and Administrative Affairs, Information and Library, Technical Affairs, and Economics. The last two form the Arab Centre for Energy Studies (which was established in 1983). At the end of 2001 there were 21 professional staff members and 31 general personnel at the General Secretariat.

JUDICIAL TRIBUNAL

The Tribunal comprises seven judges from Arab countries. Its task is to settle differences in interpretation and application of the OAPEC Agreement, arising between members and also between OAPEC and its affiliates; disputes among member countries on petroleum activities falling within OAPEC's jurisdiction and not under the sovereignty of member countries; and disputes that the Ministerial Council decides to submit to the Tribunal.

President: FARIS ABDUL RAHMAN AL-WAGAYAN.

Registrar: Dr RIAD RASHAD AL-DAOUDI.

Activities

OAPEC co-ordinates different aspects of the Arab petroleum industry through the joint undertakings described below. It co-operates with the League of Arab States and other Arab organizations, and attempts to link petroleum research institutes in the Arab states. It organizes or participates in conferences and seminars, many of which are held jointly with non-Arab organizations in order to enhance Arab and international co-operation. OAPEC collaborates with the AFESD, the Arab Monetary Fund and the League of Arab States in compiling the annual *Joint Arab Economic Report*, which is issued by the Arab Monetary Fund.

OAPEC provides training in technical matters and in documentation and information. The General Secretariat also conducts technical and feasibility studies and carries out market reviews. It provides information through a library, 'databank' and the publications listed below.

The invasion of Kuwait by Iraq in August 1990, and the subsequent international embargo on petroleum exports from Iraq and Kuwait, severely disrupted OAPEC's activities. In December the OAPEC Council decided to establish temporary headquarters in

Cairo while Kuwait was under occupation. The Council resolved to reschedule overdue payments by Iraq and Syria over a 15-year period, and to postpone the Fifth Arab Energy Conference from mid-1992 to mid-1994. The Conference was held in Cairo, Egypt, in May 1994. In June OAPEC returned to its permanent headquarters in Kuwait. The Sixth Arab Energy Conference was held in Damascus, Syria, in May 1998, with the theme of 'Energy and Arab Co-operation'. The seventh conference, focusing on the same theme, was convened in May 2002, in Cairo, Egypt. It was attended by OAPEC ministers of petroleum and energy, senior officials from other Arab states, and representatives of invited institutions and organizations concerned with energy issues.

Finance

The General Secretariat's budget for 2002 amounted to 1,606,300 Kuwaiti dinars (KD). A budget of 82,500 KD was approved for the Judicial Tribunal.

Publications

Annual Statistical Report.

Energy Resources Monitor (quarterly, Arabic).

OAPEC Monthly Bulletin (Arabic and English editions).

Oil and Arab Co-operation (quarterly, Arabic).

Secretary-General's Annual Report (Arabic and English editions).

Papers, studies, conference proceedings.

OAPEC-Sponsored Ventures

Arab Maritime Petroleum Transport Company—AMPTC: POB 22525, Safat 13086, Kuwait; tel. 4844500; fax 4842996; f. 1973 to undertake transport of crude petroleum, gas, refined products and petro-chemicals, and thus to increase Arab participation in the tanker transport industry; auth. cap. US $200m. Gen. Man. SULAYMAN AL-BASSAM.

Arab Petroleum Investments Corporation—APICORP: POB 9599, Dammam 31423, Saudi Arabia; tel. (3) 847-0444; fax (3) 847-0022; e-mail apicorp@apicorp-arabia.com; internet www.apicorp-arabia.com; f. 1975 to finance investments in petroleum and petrochemicals projects and related industries in the Arab world and in developing countries, with priority being given to Arab joint ventures; projects financed include gas liquefaction plants, petrochemicals, tankers, oil refineries, pipelines, exploration, detergents, fertilizers and process control instrumentation; auth. cap. US $1,200m. subs. cap. $460m. shareholders: Kuwait, Saudi Arabia and United Arab Emirates (17% each), Libya (15%), Iraq and Qatar (10% each), Algeria (5%), Bahrain, Egypt and Syria (3% each). Chair. ABDULLAH A. AZ-ZAID (Saudi Arabia); Gen. Man. and CEO RASHEED AL-MARAJ.

Arab Detergent Chemicals Company—ARADET: POB 27864, el-Monsour, Baghdad, Iraq; tel. (1) 541-9893; f. 1981; produces and markets linear alkyl benzene; an additional project to construct a sodium tripolyphosphate plant has been suspended temporarily owing to the trade embargo against Iraq; APICORP and the Iraqi Government each hold 32% of shares in the co; auth. cap. 72m. Iraqi dinars; subs. cap. 60m. Iraqi dinars.

Arab Petroleum Services Company—APSCO: POB 12925, Tripoli, Libya; tel. (21) 45861; fax (21) 3331930; f. 1977 to provide petroleum services through the establishment of companies specializing in various activities, and to train specialized personnel; auth. cap. 100m. Libyan dinars; subs. cap. 15m. Libyan dinars; Chair. AYAD HUSSEIN AD-DALI; Gen. Man. ISMAIL AL-KORAITLI.

Arab Drilling and Workover Company: POB 680, Suani Rd, km 3.5, Tripoli, Libya; tel. (21) 800064; fax (21) 805945; f. 1980; 40%-owned by APSCO; auth. cap. 12m. Libyan dinars; Gen. Man. MUHAMMAD AHMAD ATTIGA.

Arab Geophysical Exploration Services Company—AGESCO: POB 84224, Airport Rd, Tripoli, Libya; tel. (21) 4804863; fax (21) 4803199; f. 1985; 40%-owned by APSCO; auth. cap. 12m. Libyan dinars; subs. cap. 4m. Libyan dinars; Gen. Man. AYAD HUSSEIN AD-DALI.

Arab Well Logging Company (AWLCO): POB 6225, Baghdad, Iraq; tel. (1) 541-8259; f. 1983; wholly-owned subsidiary of APSCO; provides well-logging services and data interpretation; auth. cap. 7m. Iraqi dinars.

Arab Petroleum Training Institute—APTI: POB 6037, Al-Tajeyat, Baghdad, Iraq; tel. (1) 523-4100; fax (1) 521-0526; f. 1978 to provide instruction in many technical and managerial aspects of the oil industry; from Dec. 1994 the Institute was placed under the trusteeship of the Iraqi Govt; the arrangement was scheduled to come to an end in Dec. 1998; Dir HAZIM A. AS-SULTAN.

Arab Shipbuilding and Repair Yard Company—ASRY: POB 50110, Hidd, Bahrain; tel. 671111; fax 670236; e-mail asryco@batelco.com.bh; internet www.asry.net; f. 1974 to undertake repairs and servicing of vessels; operates a 500,000 dwt dry dock in Bahrain; two floating docks operational since 1992; has recently diversified it activities, e.g. into upgrading oil rigs; cap. (auth. and subs.) US $340m. Chair. EID ABDULLA YOUSIF (Bahrain); Chief Exec. MOHAMED M. AL-KHATEEB.

ORGANIZATION OF THE BLACK SEA ECONOMIC CO-OPERATION—BSEC

Address: İstinye Cad. Müşir Fuad Paşa Yalısı, Eski Tersane 80860 İstinye-İstanbul, Turkey.

Telephone: (212) 229-63-30; **fax:** (212) 229-63-36; **e-mail:** bsec@turk.net; **internet:** www.bsec.gov.tr.

The Black Sea Economic Co-operation (BSEC) was established in 1992 to strengthen regional co-operation, particularly in the field of economic development. In June 1998, at a summit meeting held in Yalta, Ukraine, participating countries signed the BSEC Charter, thereby officially elevating BSEC to regional organization status. The Charter entered into force on 1 May 1999, at which time BSEC formally became the Organization of the Black Sea Economic Co-operation, retaining the same acronym.

MEMBERS

Albania	Georgia	Russia
Armenia	Greece	Turkey
Azerbaijan	Moldova	Ukraine
Bulgaria	Romania	

Note: Observer status has been granted to Egypt, France, Germany, Israel, Italy, Poland, Slovakia and Tunisia. The BSEC Business Council, International Black Sea Club, and the Energy Charter Conference also have observer status. Iran, the former Yugoslav republic of Macedonia, Serbia and Montenegro and Uzbekistan have applied for full membership.

Organization

(April 2003)

PRESIDENTIAL SUMMIT

The Presidential Summit, comprising heads of state or government of member states, represents the highest authority of the body.

COUNCIL

The Council of Ministers of Foreign Affairs is BSEC's principal decision-making organ. Ministers meet twice a year to review progress and to define new objectives. Chairmanship of the Council rotates among members; the Chairman-in-Office co-ordinates the activities undertaken by BSEC. The Council is supported by a Committee of Senior Officials.

PARLIAMENTARY ASSEMBLY

1 Hareket Kösku, Dolmabahçe Sarayi, Besiktas, 80680 İstanbul, Turkey; tel. (212) 227-6070; fax (212) 227-6080; e-mail vdeiv@pabsec .org; internet www.pabsec.org.

The Parliamentary Assembly, consisting of the representatives of the national parliaments of member states, was created in February 1993 to provide a legal basis for the implementation of decisions within the BSEC framework. It comprises three committees concerning economic, commercial, technological and environmental affairs; legal and political affairs; and cultural, educational and social affairs.

PERMANENT INTERNATIONAL SECRETARIAT

The Secretariat commenced operations in March 1994. Its tasks are, primarily, of an administrative and technical nature, and include the maintenance of archives, and the preparation and distribution of documentation. Much of the organization's activities are undertaken by 15 working groups, each headed by an Executive Manager, and by various *ad hoc* groups and meetings of experts.

Secretary-General: Valeri Chechelashvili (Georgia).

Activities

In June 1992, at a summit meeting held in İstanbul, heads of state and of government signed the summit declaration on BSEC, and adopted the Bosphorus statement, which established a regional structure for economic co-operation. The grouping attained regional organization status in May 1999 (see above). The Organization's main areas of co-operation include transport; communications; trade and economic development; banking and finance; energy; tourism; agriculture and agro-industry; health care and pharmaceuticals; environmental protection; science and technology; the exchange of statistical data and economic information; collaboration between customs authorities; and combating organized crime, drugs-trafficking, trade in illegal weapons and radioactive materials, and terrorism. In order to promote regional co-operation, the organization also aims to strengthen the business environment by providing support for small and medium-sized enterprises; facilitating closer contacts between businesses in member countries; progres-

sively eliminating obstacles to the expansion of trade; creating appropriate conditions for investment and industrial co-operation, in particular through the avoidance of double taxation and the promotion and protection of investments; encouraging the dissemination of information concerning international tenders organized by member states; and promoting economic co-operation in free-trade zones.

In recent years BSEC has undergone a process of reform aimed at developing a more project-based orientation. In April 2001 the Council adopted the so-called BSEC Economic Agenda for the Future Towards a More Consolidated, Effective and Viable BSEC Partnership, which provided a roadmap for charting the implementation of the Organization's goals. In 2002 a project development fund was established and a regional programme of governance and institutional renewal was launched. Under the new orientation the roles of BSEC's Committee of Senior Officials and network of country-co-ordinators were to be enhanced.

BSEC aims to foster relations with other international and regional organizations, and has been granted observer status at the UN General Assembly. In 1999 BSEC agreed upon a Platform of Co-operation for future structured relations with the European Union. The main areas in which BSEC determined to develop co-operation with the EU were transport, energy and telecommunications infrastructure; trade and the promotion of foreign direct investment; sustainable development and environmental protection, including nuclear safety; science and technology; and combating terrorism and organized crime. BSEC supports the Stability Pact for South-Eastern Europe, initiated in June 1999 as a collaborative plan of action by the EU, the Group of Seven industrialized nations and Russia (the G-8), regional governments and other organizations concerned with the stability of the region. The Declaration issued by BSEC's decennial anniversary summit, held in Istanbul in June 2002, urged that collaboration with the EU should be enhanced.

A BSEC Business Council was established in İstanbul in December 1992 by the business communities of member states. It has observer status at the BSEC, and aims to identify private and public investment projects, maintain business contacts and develop programmes in various sectors. A Black Sea Trade and Development Bank has been established, in Thessaloníki, Greece, as the organization's main funding institution, to finance and implement joint regional projects. It began operations on 1 July 1999. The European Bank for Reconstruction and Development (EBRD) was entrusted as the depository for all capital payments made prior to its establishment. A BSEC Co-ordination Centre, located in Ankara, Turkey, aims to promote the exchange of statistical and economic information. In September 1998 a Black Sea International Studies Centre was inaugurated in Athens, Greece, in order to undertake research concerning the BSEC, in the fields of economics, industry and technology. The transport ministers of BSEC member states adopted a Transport Action Plan in March 2001, which envisaged reducing the disparities in regional transport systems and integrating the BSEC regional transport infrastructure with wider international networks and projects.

BSEC has supported implementation of the Bucharest Convention on the Protection of the Black Sea Against Pollution, adopted by Bulgaria, Georgia, Romania, Russia, Turkey and Ukraine in April 1992. In October 1996 those countries adopted the Strategic Action Plan for the Rehabilitation and Protection of the Black Sea (BSSAP), to be implemented by the Commission of the Bucharest Convention.

ORGANIZATION OF THE ISLAMIC CONFERENCE—OIC

Address: Kilo 6, Mecca Rd, POB 178, Jeddah 21411, Saudi Arabia.
Telephone: (2) 680-0800; **fax:** (2) 687-3568; **e-mail:** info@oic-oci
.org; **internet:** www.oic-oci.org.

The Organization was formally established in May 1971, when its
Secretariat became operational, following a summit meeting of
Muslim heads of state at Rabat, Morocco, in September 1969, and
the Islamic Foreign Ministers' Conference in Jeddah in March 1970,
and in Karachi, Pakistan, in December 1970.

MEMBERS

Afghanistan	Indonesia	Palestine
Albania	Iran	Qatar
Algeria	Iraq	Saudi Arabia
Azerbaijan	Jordan	Senegal
Bahrain	Kazakhstan	Sierra Leone
Bangladesh	Kuwait	Somalia
Benin	Kyrgyzstan	Sudan
Brunei	Lebanon	Suriname
Burkina Faso	Libya	Syria
Cameroon	Malaysia	Tajikistan
Chad	Maldives	Togo
The Comoros	Mali	Tunisia
Côte d'Ivoire	Mauritania	Turkey
Djibouti	Morocco	Turkmenistan
Egypt	Mozambique	Uganda
Gabon	Niger	United Arab
The Gambia	Nigeria	Emirates
Guinea	Oman	Uzbekistan
Guinea-Bissau	Pakistan	Yemen
Guyana		

Note: Observer status has been granted to Bosnia and Herzegovina,
the Central African Republic, Thailand, the Muslim community of
the 'Turkish Republic of Northern Cyprus', the Moro National
Liberation Front (MNLF) of the southern Philippines, the United
Nations, the African Union, the Non-Aligned Movement, the League
of Arab States, the Economic Co-operation Organization, the Union
of the Arab Maghreb and the Co-operation Council for the Arab
States of the Gulf.

Organization

(April 2003)

SUMMIT CONFERENCES

The supreme body of the Organization is the Conference of Heads of
State, which met in 1969 at Rabat, Morocco, in 1974 at Lahore,
Pakistan, and in January 1981 at Mecca, Saudi Arabia, when it was
decided that summit conferences would be held every three years in
future. Ninth Conference: Doha, Qatar, November 2000. An extraordinary summit conference was convened in Doha, Qatar, in March
2003, to consider the ongoing situation in Iraq.

CONFERENCE OF MINISTERS OF FOREIGN AFFAIRS

Conferences take place annually, to consider the means for implementing the general policy of the Organization, although they may
also be convened for extraordinary sessions.

SECRETARIAT

The executive organ of the Organization, headed by a Secretary-
General (who is elected by the Conference of Ministers of Foreign
Affairs for a four-year term, renewable only once) and four Assistant
Secretaries-General (similarly appointed).

Secretary-General: Dr ABDELOUAHED BELKEZIZ (Morocco).

At the summit conference in January 1981 it was decided that an
International Islamic Court of Justice should be established to
adjudicate in disputes between Muslim countries. Experts met in
January 1983 to draw up a constitution for the court; however, by
2002 it was not yet in operation.

STANDING COMMITTEES

Al-Quds Committee: f. 1975 to implement the resolutions of the
Islamic Conference on the status of Jerusalem (Al-Quds); it meets at
the level of foreign ministers; maintains the Al-Quds Fund; Chair.
King MOHAMMAD VI OF MOROCCO.

**Standing Committee for Economic and Commercial Co-oper-
ation—COMCEC:** f. 1981; Chair. AHMET NECDET SEZER (Pres. of
Turkey).

**Standing Committee for Information and Cultural Affairs—
COMIAC:** f. 1981; Chair. ABDOULAYE WADE (Pres. of Senegal).

**Standing Committee for Scientific and Technological Co-
operation—COMSTECH:** f. 1981; Chair. Gen. PERVEZ MUSHARRAF
(Pres. of Pakistan).

Other committees comprise the Islamic Peace Committee, the Permanent Finance Committee, the Committee of Islamic Solidarity
with the Peoples of the Sahel, the Eight-Member Committee on the
Situation of Muslims in the Philippines, the Six-Member Committee
on Palestine, and the *ad hoc* Committee on Afghanistan. In addition,
there is an Islamic Commission for Economic, Cultural and Social
Affairs and OIC contact groups on Bosnia and Herzegovina, Kosovo,
Jammu and Kashmir, and Sierra Leone.

Activities

The Organization's aims, as proclaimed in the Charter that was
adopted in 1972, are:

(i) To promote Islamic solidarity among member states;

(ii) To consolidate co-operation among member states in the economic, social, cultural, scientific and other vital fields, and to
arrange consultations among member states belonging to international organizations;

(iii) To endeavour to eliminate racial segregation and discrimination and to eradicate colonialism in all its forms;

(iv) To take necessary measures to support international peace
and security founded on justice;

(v) To co-ordinate all efforts for the safeguard of the Holy Places
and support of the struggle of the people of Palestine, and help
them to regain their rights and liberate their land;

(vi) To strengthen the struggle of all Muslim people with a view to
safeguarding their dignity, independence and national rights; and

(vii) To create a suitable atmosphere for the promotion of co-
operation and understanding among member states and other
countries.

The first summit conference of Islamic leaders (representing 24
states) took place in 1969 following the burning of the Al Aqsa
Mosque in Jerusalem. At this conference it was decided that Islamic
governments should 'consult together with a view to promoting close
co-operation and mutual assistance in the economic, scientific, cultural and spiritual fields, inspired by the immortal teachings of
Islam'. Thereafter the foreign ministers of the countries concerned
met annually, and adopted the Charter of the Organization of the
Islamic Conference in 1972.

At the second Islamic summit conference (Lahore, Pakistan,
1974), the Islamic Solidarity Fund was established, together with a
committee of representatives which later evolved into the Islamic
Commission for Economic, Cultural and Social Affairs. Subsequently, numerous other subsidiary bodies have been set up (see
below).

ECONOMIC CO-OPERATION

A general agreement for economic, technical and commercial co-
operation came into force in 1981, providing for the establishment of
joint investment projects and trade co-ordination. This was followed
by an agreement on promotion, protection and guarantee of investments among member states. A plan of action to strengthen economic co-operation was adopted at the third Islamic summit conference in 1981, aiming to promote collective self-reliance and the
development of joint ventures in all sectors. In 1994 the 1981 plan of
action was revised; the reformulated plan placed greater emphasis
on private-sector participation in its implementation. Although several meetings of experts were subsequently held to discuss some of
the 10 priority focus areas of the plan, little progress was achieved
in implementing it during the 1990s.

The fifth summit conference, held in 1987, approved proposals for
joint development of modern technology, and for improving scientific
and technical skills in the less developed Islamic countries. The first
international Islamic trade fair was held in Jeddah, Saudi Arabia, in
March 2001.

In 1991 22 OIC member states signed a framework agreement
concerning the introduction of a system of trade preferences among
member states. It was envisaged that, if implemented, this would
represent the first step towards the eventual establishment of an

Islamic common market. In May 2001 the OIC Secretary-General urged increased progress in the ratification of the framework agreement. An OIC group of experts was considering the implications of the proposed creation of such a common market.

CULTURAL CO-OPERATION

The Organization supports education in Muslim communities throughout the world, and was instrumental in the establishment of Islamic universities in Niger and Uganda (see below). It organizes seminars on various aspects of Islam, and encourages dialogue with the other monotheistic religions. Support is given to publications on Islam both in Muslim and Western countries. The OIC organizes meetings at ministerial level to consider aspects of information policy and new technologies.

HUMANITARIAN ASSISTANCE

Assistance is given to Muslim communities affected by wars and natural disasters, in co-operation with UN organizations, particularly UNHCR. The countries of the Sahel region (Burkina Faso, Cape Verde, Chad, The Gambia, Guinea, Guinea-Bissau, Mali, Mauritania, Niger and Senegal) receive particular attention as victims of drought. In April 1999 the OIC resolved to send humanitarian aid to assist the displaced ethnic Albanian population of Kosovo and Metohija, in southern Serbia. Several member states have provided humanitarian assistance to the Muslim population affected by the conflict in Chechnya. During 2001 the OIC was providing emergency assistance to Afghanistan, and in October established an Afghan People Assistance Fund. The OIC also administers a Trust Fund for the urgent return of refugees and the displaced to Bosnia and Herzegovina.

POLITICAL CO-OPERATION

Since its inception the OIC has called for vacation of Arab territories by Israel, recognition of the rights of Palestinians and of the Palestine Liberation Organization (PLO) as their sole legitimate representative, and the restoration of Jerusalem to Arab rule. The 1981 summit conference called for a *jihad* (holy war—though not necessarily in a military sense) 'for the liberation of Jerusalem and the occupied territories'; this was to include an Islamic economic boycott of Israel. In 1982 Islamic ministers of foreign affairs decided to establish Islamic offices for boycotting Israel and for military co-operation with the PLO. The 1984 summit conference agreed to reinstate Egypt (suspended following the peace treaty signed with Israel in 1979) as a member of the OIC, although the resolution was opposed by seven states.

In August 1990 a majority of ministers of foreign affairs condemned Iraq's recent invasion of Kuwait, and demanded the withdrawal of Iraqi forces. In August 1991 the Conference of Ministers of Foreign Affairs obstructed Iraq's attempt to propose a resolution demanding the repeal of economic sanctions against the country. The sixth summit conference, held in Senegal in December, reflected the divisions in the Arab world that resulted from Iraq's invasion of Kuwait and the ensuing war. Twelve heads of state did not attend, reportedly to register protest at the presence of Jordan and the PLO at the conference, both of which had given support to Iraq. Disagreement also arose between the PLO and the majority of other OIC members when a proposal was adopted to cease the OIC's support for the PLO's *jihad* in the Arab territories occupied by Israel, in an attempt to further the Middle East peace negotiations.

In August 1992 the UN General Assembly approved a non-binding resolution, introduced by the OIC, that requested the UN Security Council to take increased action, including the use of force, in order to defend the non-Serbian population of Bosnia and Herzegovina (some 43% of Bosnians being Muslims) from Serbian aggression, and to restore its 'territorial integrity'. The OIC Conference of Ministers of Foreign Affairs, which was held in December, demanded anew that the UN Security Council take all necessary measures against Serbia and Montenegro, including military intervention, in order to protect the Bosnian Muslims.

A report by an OIC fact-finding mission, which in February 1993 visited Azad Kashmir while investigating allegations of repression of the largely Muslim population of the Indian state of Jammu and Kashmir by the Indian armed forces, was presented to the 1993 Conference. The meeting urged member states to take the necessary measures to persuade India to cease the 'massive human rights violations' in Jammu and Kashmir and to allow the Indian Kashmiris to 'exercise their inalienable right to self-determination'. In September 1994 ministers of foreign affairs, meeting in Islamabad, Pakistan, agreed to establish a contact group on Jammu and Kashmir, which was to provide a mechanism for promoting international awareness of the situation in that region and for seeking a peaceful solution to the dispute. In December OIC heads of state approved a resolution condemning reported human rights abuses by Indian security forces in Kashmir.

In July 1994 the OIC Secretary-General visited Afghanistan and proposed the establishment of a preparatory mechanism to promote national reconciliation in that country. In mid-1995 Saudi Arabia, acting as a representative of the OIC, pursued a peace initiative for Afghanistan and issued an invitation for leaders of the different factions to hold negotiations in Jeddah.

A special ministerial meeting on Bosnia and Herzegovina was held in July 1993, at which seven OIC countries committed themselves to making available up to 17,000 troops to serve in the UN Protection Force in the former Yugoslavia (UNPROFOR). The meeting also decided to dispatch immediately a ministerial mission to persuade influential governments to support the OIC's demands for the removal of the arms embargo on Bosnian Muslims and the convening of a restructured international conference to bring about a political solution to the conflict. In December 1994 OIC heads of state, convened in Morocco, proclaimed that the UN arms embargo on Bosnia and Herzegovina could not be applied to the Muslim authorities of that Republic. The Conference also resolved to review economic relations between OIC member states and any country that supported Serbian activities. An aid fund was established, to which member states were requested to contribute between US $500,000 and $5m., in order to provide further humanitarian and economic assistance to Bosnian Muslims. In relation to wider concerns the conference adopted a Code of Conduct for Combating International Terrorism, in an attempt to control Muslim extremist groups. The code commits states to ensuring that militant groups do not use their territory for planning or executing terrorist activity against other states, in addition to states refraining from direct support or participation in acts of terrorism. In a further resolution the OIC supported the decision by Iraq to recognize Kuwait, but advocated that Iraq comply with all UN Security Council decisions.

In July 1995 the OIC contact group on Bosnia and Herzegovina (at that time comprising Egypt, Iran, Malaysia, Morocco, Pakistan, Saudi Arabia, Senegal and Turkey), meeting in Geneva, declared the UN arms embargo against Bosnia and Herzegovina to be 'invalid'. Several Governments subsequently announced their willingness officially to supply weapons and other military assistance to the Bosnian Muslim forces. In September a meeting of all OIC ministers of defence and foreign affairs endorsed the establishment of an 'assistance mobilization group' which was to supply military, economic, legal and other assistance to Bosnia and Herzegovina. In a joint declaration the ministers also demanded the return of all territory seized by Bosnian Serb forces, the continued NATO bombing of Serb military targets, and that the city of Sarajevo be preserved under a Muslim-led Bosnian Government. In November the OIC Secretary-General endorsed the peace accord for the former Yugoslavia, which was concluded, in Dayton, USA, by leaders of all the conflicting factions, and reaffirmed the commitment of Islamic states to participate in efforts to implement the accord. In the following month the OIC Conference of Ministers of Foreign Affairs, convened in Conakry, Guinea, requested the full support of the international community to reconstruct Bosnia and Herzegovina through humanitarian aid as well as economic and technical co-operation. Ministers declared that Palestine and the establishment of fully-autonomous Palestinian control of Jerusalem were issues of central importance for the Muslim world. The Conference urged the removal of all aspects of occupation and the cessation of the construction of Israeli settlements in the occupied territories. In addition, the final statement of the meeting condemned Armenian aggression against Azerbaijan, registered concern at the persisting civil conflict in Afghanistan, demanded the elimination of all weapons of mass destruction and pledged support for Libya (affected by the US trade embargo). Ministers determined that an intergovernmental group of experts should be established in 1996 to address the situation of minority Muslim communities residing in non-OIC states.

In December 1996 OIC ministers of foreign affairs, meeting in Jakarta, Indonesia, urged the international community to apply pressure on Israel in order to ensure its implementation of the terms of the Middle East peace process. The ministers reaffirmed the importance of ensuring that the provisions of the Dayton Peace Agreement for the former Yugoslavia were fully implemented, called for a peaceful settlement of the Kashmir issue, demanded that Iraq fulfil its obligations for the establishment of security, peace and stability in the region and proposed that an international conference on peace and national reconciliation in Somalia be convened. The ministers elected a new Secretary-General who confirmed that the organization would continue to develop its role as an international mediator. In March 1997, at an extraordinary summit held in Pakistan, OIC heads of state and of government reiterated the organization's objective of increasing international pressure on Israel to ensure the full implementation of the terms of the Middle East peace process. An 'Islamabad Declaration' was also adopted, which pledged to increase co-operation between members of the OIC. In June the OIC condemned the decision by the US House of Representatives to recognize Jerusalem as the Israeli capital. The Secretary-General of the OIC issued a statement rejecting the US decision as counter to the role of the USA as sponsor of the Middle East peace plan.

In early 1998 the OIC appealed for an end to the threat of US-led military action against Iraq arising from a dispute regarding access granted to international weapons inspectors. The crisis was averted by an agreement concluded between the Iraqi authorities and the UN Secretary-General in February. In March OIC ministers of foreign affairs, meeting in Doha, Qatar, requested an end to the international sanctions against Iraq. Additionally, the ministers urged all states to end the process of restoring normal trading and diplomatic relations with Israel pending that country's withdrawal from the occupied territories and acceptance of an independent Palestinian state. In April the OIC, jointly with the UN, sponsored new peace negotiations between the main disputing factions in Afghanistan, which were conducted in Islamabad, Pakistan. In early May, however, the talks collapsed and were postponed indefinitely. In September the Secretaries-General of the OIC and UN agreed to establish a joint mission to counter the deteriorating security situation along the Afghan–Iranian border, following the large-scale deployment of Taliban troops in the region and consequent military manoeuvres by the Iranian authorities. They also reiterated the need to proceed with negotiations to conclude a peaceful settlement in Afghanistan. In December the OIC appealed for a diplomatic solution to the tensions arising from Iraq's withdrawal of co-operation with UN weapons inspectors, and criticized subsequent military air-strikes, led by the USA, as having been conducted without renewed UN authority. An OIC Convention on Combating International Terrorism was adopted in 1998. An OIC committee of experts responsible for formulating a plan of action for safeguarding the rights of Muslim communities and minorities met for the first time in 1998.

In early April 1999 ministers of foreign affairs of the countries comprising OIC's contact group met to consider the crisis in Kosovo. The meeting condemned Serbian atrocities being committed against the local Albanian population and urged the provision of international assistance for the thousands of people displaced by the conflict. The group resolved to establish a committee to co-ordinate relief aid provided by member states. The ministers also expressed their willingness to help to formulate a peaceful settlement and to participate in any subsequent implementation force. In June an OIC Parliamentary Union was inaugurated; its founding conference was convened in Tehran, Iran.

In early March 2000 the OIC mediated contacts between the parties to the conflict in Afghanistan, with a view to reviving peace negotiations. Talks, held under OIC auspices, ensued in May. In November OIC heads of state attended the ninth summit conference, held in Doha, Qatar. In view of the significant deterioration in relations between Israel and the Palestinian (National) Authority during late 2000, the summit issued a Declaration pledging solidarity with the Palestinian cause and accusing the Israeli authorities of implementing large-scale systematic violations of human rights against Palestinians. The summit also issued the Doha Declaration, which reaffirmed commitment to the OIC Charter and undertook to modernize the organization's organs and mechanisms. Both the elected Government of Afghanistan and the Taliban sent delegations to the Doha conference. The summit determined that Afghanistan's official participation in the OIC, suspended in 1996, should not yet be reinstated. In early 2001 a high-level delegation from the OIC visited Afghanistan in an attempt to prevent further destruction of ancient statues by Taliban supporters.

In May 2001 the OIC convened an emergency meeting, following an escalation of Israeli-Palestinian violence. The meeting resolved to halt all diplomatic and political contacts with the Israeli government, while restrictions remained in force against Palestinian-controlled territories. In June the OIC condemned attacks and ongoing discrimination against the Muslim Community in Myanmar. In the same month the OIC Secretary-General undertook a tour of six African countries—Burkina Faso, The Gambia, Guinea, Mali, Niger and Senegal, to promote co-operation and to consider further OIC support for those states. In August the Secretary-General condemned Israel's seizure of several Palestinian institutions in East Jerusalem and aerial attacks against Palestinian settlements. The OIC initiated high-level diplomatic efforts to convene a meeting of the UN Security Council in order to discuss the situation.

In September 2001 the OIC Secretary-General strongly condemned major terrorist attacks perpetrated against targets in the USA. Soon afterwards the US authorities rejected a proposal by the Taliban regime that an OIC observer mission be deployed to monitor the activities of the Saudi Arabian-born exiled militant Islamist fundamentalist leader Osama bin Laden, who was accused by the US Government of having co-ordinated the attacks from alleged terrorist bases in the Taliban-administered area of Afghanistan. An extraordinary meeting of OIC ministers of foreign affairs, convened in early October, in Doha, Qatar, to consider the implications of the terrorist atrocities, condemned the attacks and declared its support for combating all manifestations of terrorism within the framework of a proposed collective initiative co-ordinated under the auspices of the UN. The meeting, which did not pronounce directly on the

recently-initiated US-led military retaliation against targets in Afghanistan, urged that no Arab or Muslim state should be targeted under the pretext of eliminating terrorism. It determined to establish a fund to assist Afghan civilians. In February 2002 the Secretary-General expressed concern at statements of the US administration describing Iran and Iraq (as well as the Democratic People's Republic of Korea) as belonging to an 'axis of evil' involved in international terrorism and the development of weapons of mass destruction. In early April OIC foreign ministers convened an extraordinary session on terrorism, in Kuala Lumpur, Malaysia. The meeting issued the 'Kuala Lumpur Declaration', which reiterated member states' collective resolve to combat terrorism, recalling the organization's 1994 code of conduct and 1998 convention to this effect; condemned attempts to associate terrorist activities with Islamists or any other particular creed, civilization or nationality, and rejected attempts to associate Islamic states or the Palestinian struggle with terrorism; rejected the implementation of international action against any Muslim state on the pretext of combating terrorism; urged the organization of a global conference on international terrorism; and urged an examination of the root causes of international terrorism. In addition, the meeting strongly condemned Israel's ongoing military intervention in areas controlled by the Palestinian (National) Authority. The meeting adopted a plan of action on addressing the issues raised in the declaration. Its implementation was to be co-ordinated by a 13-member committee on international terrorism. Member states were encouraged to sign and ratify the Convention on Combating International Terrorism in order to accelerate its implementation. In June ministers of foreign affairs, meeting in Khartoum, Sudan, issued a declaration reiterating the OIC call for an international conference to be convened, under UN auspices, in order clearly to define terrorism and to agree on the international procedures and mechanisms for combating terrorism through the UN. The conference also repeated demands for the international community to exert pressure on Israel to withdraw from all Palestinian-controlled territories and for the establishment of an independent Palestinian state. It endorsed the peace plan for the region that had been adopted by the summit meeting of the League of Arab States in March.

In June 2002 the OIC Secretary-General expressed his concern at the escalation of tensions between Pakistan and India regarding Kashmir. He urged both sides to withdraw their troops and to refrain from the use of force. In the following month the OIC pledged its support for Morocco in a territorial dispute with Spain over the small island of Perejil, but called for a negotiated settlement to resolve the issue.

An extraordinary summit conference of Islamic leaders convened in Doha, Qatar, in early March 2003 to consider the ongoing Iraq crisis, welcomed the Saddam Hussain regime's acceptance of UN Security Council Resolution 1441 and consequent co-operation with UN weapons inspectors, and emphatically rejected any military strike against Iraq or threat to the security of any other Islamic state. The conference also urged progress towards the elimination of all weapons of mass destruction in the Middle East, including those held by Israel.

Finance

The OIC's activities are financed by mandatory contributions from member states. The budget for 2002/03 totalled US $11.4m.

SUBSIDIARY ORGANS

Islamic Centre for the Development of Trade: Complexe Commercial des Habous, ave des FAR, BP 13545, Casablanca, Morocco; tel. (2) 314974; fax (2) 310110; e-mail icdt@icdt.org; internet www.icdt.org; f. 1983 to encourage regular commercial contacts, harmonize policies and promote investments among OIC mems; Dir-Gen. ALLAL RACHDI; publs *Tijaris: International and Inter-Islamic Trade Magazine* (bi-monthly), *Inter-Islamic Trade Report* (annually).

Islamic Jurisprudence (Fiqh) Academy: POB 13917, Jeddah, Saudi Arabia; tel. (2) 667-1664; fax (2) 667-0873; internet www.fiqhacademy.org.sa; f. 1982; Sec.-Gen. SHEIKH MOHAMED HABIB IBN AL-KHODHA.

Islamic Solidarity Fund: c/o OIC Secretariat, POB 178, Jeddah 21411, Saudi Arabia; tel. (2) 680-0800; fax (2) 687-3568; f. 1974 to meet the needs of Islamic communities by providing emergency aid and the finance to build mosques, Islamic centres, hospitals, schools and universities; Chair. Sheikh NASIR ABDULLAH BIN HAMDAN; Exec. Dir ABDULLAH HERSI.

Islamic University in Uganda: POB 2555, Mbale, Uganda; Kampala Liaison Office: POB 7689, Kampala; tel. (45) 33502; fax (45) 34452; e-mail iuiu@info.com.co.ug; tel. (41) 236874; fax (41) 254576; f. 1988 to meet the educational needs of Muslim populations in

English-speaking African countries; mainly financed by OIC; Principal Officer Prof. MAHDI ADAMU.

Islamic University of Niger: BP 11507, Niamey, Niger; tel. 723903; fax 733796; f. 1984; provides courses of study in *Shari'a* (Islamic law) and Arabic language and literature; also offers courses in pedagogy and teacher training; receives grants from Islamic Solidarity Fund and contributions from OIC member states; Rector Prof. ABDELALI OUDHRIRI.

Islamic University of Technology—IUT: GPO Box 3003, Board Bazar, Gazipur 1704, Dhaka, Bangladesh; tel. (2) 980-0960; fax (2) 980-0970; e-mail vc@int-dhaka.edu; internet www.iutoic-dhaka.edu; f. 1981 as the Islamic Centre for Technical and Vocational Training and Resources, named changed to Islamic Institute of Technology in 1994, current name adopted in June 2001; aims to develop human resources in OIC mem. states, with special reference to engineering, technology, tech. and vocational education and research; 224 staff and 1,000 students; library of 23,000 vols. Vice-Chancellor Prof. Dr M. ANWAR HOSSAIN; publs *News Bulletin* (annually), annual calendar and announcement for admission, reports, human resources development series.

Research Centre for Islamic History, Art and Culture—IRCICA: POB 24, Beşiktaş 80692, İstanbul, Turkey; tel. (212) 2591742; fax (212) 2584365; e-mail ircica@superonline.com; internet www.ircica.org; f. 1980; library of 50,000 vols; Dir-Gen. Prof. Dr EKMELEDDİN IHSANOĞLU; publs *Newsletter* (3 a year), monographical studies.

Statistical, Economic and Social Research and Training Centre for the Islamic Countries: Attar Sok 4, GOP 06700, Ankara, Turkey; tel. (312) 4686172; fax (312) 4673458; e-mail oicankara@sesrtcic.org; internet www.sesrtcic.org; f. 1978; Dir-Gen. ERDİNÇ ERDÜN; publs *Journal of Economic Co-operation among Islamic Countries* (quarterly), *InfoReport* (quarterly), *Statistical Yearbook* (annually).

SPECIALIZED INSTITUTIONS

International Islamic News Agency—IINA (IINA): King Khalid Palace, Madinah Rd, POB 5054, Jeddah, Saudi Arabia; tel. (2) 665-8561; fax (2) 665-9358; e-mail iina@ogertel.com; internet www .islamicnews.org; f. 1972; distributes news and reports daily on events in the Islamic world, in Arabic, English and French; Dir-Gen. ABDULWAHAB KASHIF.

Islamic Development Bank: POB 5925, Jeddah 21432, Saudi Arabia; tel. (2) 636-1400; fax (1) 636-6871; e-mail archives@isdb.org .sa; internet www.isdb.org; f. 1975; promotes the economic and social development of OIC member countries and Muslim communities in non-member countries; provides assistance in the form of loans and grants for technical aid, in accordance with the principles of the Islamic *Shari'a* (sacred law); Pres. and Chair. Dr AHMED MOHAMED ALI; Sec.-Gen. Dr ABDERRAHIM OMRANA.

Islamic Educational, Scientific and Cultural Organization—ISESCO: BP 755, Rabat 10104, Morocco; tel. (7) 772433; fax (7) 772058; e-mail cid@isesco.org.ma; internet www.isesco.org.ma; f. 1982; Dir-Gen. Dr ABDULAZIZ BIN OTHMAN AL-TWAIJRI; publs *ISESCO Newsletter* (quarterly), *Islam Today* (2 a year), *ISESCO Triennial*.

Islamic States Broadcasting Organization—ISBO: POB 6351, Jeddah 21442, Saudi Arabia; tel. (2) 672-1121; fax (2) 672-2600; e-mail isbo@isbo.org; internet www.isbo.org; f. 1975; Sec.-Gen. HUSSEIN AL-ASKARY.

The Islamic Development Bank (see p. 257) is also a Specialized Institution of the OIC.

AFFILIATED INSTITUTIONS

International Association of Islamic Banks—IAIB: King Abdulaziz St, Queen's Bldg, 23rd Floor, Al-Balad Dist, POB 9707, Jeddah 21423, Saudi Arabia; tel. (2) 651-6900; fax (2) 651-6552; f. 1977 to link financial institutions operating on Islamic banking principles; activities include training and research; mems: 192 banks and other financial institutions in 34 countries; Sec.-Gen. SAMIR A. SHAIKH.

Islamic Chamber of Commerce and Industry: POB 3831, Clifton, Karachi 75600, Pakistan; tel. (21) 5874756; fax (21) 5870765; e-mail icci@icci-oic.org; internet icci-oic.org; f. 1979 to promote trade and industry among member states; comprises nat. chambers or feds of chambers of commerce and industry; Sec.-Gen. AQEEL AHMAD AL-JASSEM.

Islamic Committee for the International Crescent: POB 17434, Benghazi, Libya; tel. (61) 95823; fax (61) 95829; f. 1979 to attempt to alleviate the suffering caused by natural disasters and war; Sec.-Gen. Dr AHMAD ABDALLAH CHERIF.

Islamic Solidarity Sports Federation: POB 5844, Riyadh 11442, Saudi Arabia; tel. and fax (1) 482-2145; f. 1981; Sec.-Gen. Dr MOHAMMAD SALEH GAZDAR.

Organization of Islamic Capitals and Cities—OICC: POB 13621, Jeddah 21414, Saudi Arabia; tel. (2) 698-1953; fax (2) 698-1053; e-mail secrtriat@oicc.org; internet www.oicc.org; f. 1980 to promote and develop co-operation among OICC mems, to preserve their character and heritage, to implement planning guide-lines for the growth of Islamic cities and to upgrade standards of public services and utilities in those cities; Sec.-Gen. OMAR ABDULLAH KADI.

Organization of the Islamic Shipowners' Association: POB 14900, Jeddah 21434, Saudi Arabia; tel. (2) 663-7882; fax (2) 660-4920; e-mail oisa@sbm.net.sa; f. 1981 to promote co-operation among maritime cos in Islamic countries; In 1998 mems approved the establishment of a new commercial venture, the Bakkah Shipping Company, to enhance sea transport in the region; Sec.-Gen. Dr ABDULLATIF A. SULTAN.

World Federation of Arab-Islamic Schools: POB 3446, Jeddah, Saudi Arabia; tel. (2) 670-0019; fax (2) 671-0823; f. 1976; supports Arab-Islamic schools world-wide and encourages co-operation between the institutions; promotes the dissemination of the Arabic language and Islamic culture; supports the training of personnel.

ORGANIZATION OF THE PETROLEUM EXPORTING COUNTRIES—OPEC

Address: Obere Donaustrasse 93, 1020 Vienna, Austria.

Telephone: (1) 211-12-279; **fax:** (1) 214-98-27; **e-mail:** info@opec .org; **internet:** www.opec.org.

OPEC was established in 1960 to link countries whose main source of export earnings is petroleum; it aims to unify and co-ordinate members' petroleum policies and to safeguard their interests generally. In 1976 OPEC member states established the OPEC Fund for International Development.

OPEC's share of world petroleum production was 40.7% in 2001 (compared with 44.7% in 1980 and 54.7% in 1974). OPEC members were estimated to possess 79.8% of the world's known reserves of crude petroleum in 2001; about two-thirds of these were in the Middle East. In 2000 OPEC members possessed about 44.4% of known reserves of natural gas and accounted for 20.1% of total global output of natural gas.

MEMBERS

Algeria	Kuwait	Saudi Arabia
Indonesia	Libya	United Arab Emirates
Iran	Nigeria	Venezuela
Iraq	Qatar	

Organization

(April 2003)

CONFERENCE

The Conference is the supreme authority of the Organization, responsible for the formulation of its general policy. It consists of representatives of member countries, who examine reports and recommendations submitted by the Board of Governors. It approves the appointment of Governors from each country and elects the Chairman of the Board of Governors. It works on the unanimity principle, and meets at least twice a year.

BOARD OF GOVERNORS

The Board directs the management of the Organization; it implements resolutions of the Conference and draws up an annual budget. It consists of one governor for each member country, and meets at least twice a year.

MINISTERIAL MONITORING COMMITTEE

The Committee (f. 1982) is responsible for monitoring price evolution and ensuring the stability of the world petroleum market. As such, it is charged with the preparation of long-term strategies, including the allocation of quotas to be presented to the Conference. The Committee consists of all national representatives, and is normally convened four times a year. A Ministerial Monitoring Sub-committee, reporting to the Committee on production and supply figures, was established in 1993.

ECONOMIC COMMISSION

A specialized body operating within the framework of the Secretariat, with a view to assisting the Organization in promoting stability in international prices for petroleum at equitable levels; consists of a Board, national representatives and a commission staff; meets at least twice a year.

SECRETARIAT

Secretary-General: Dr ALVARO SILVA CALDERON (Venezuela).

Research Division: comprises three departments:

Data Services Department: Maintains and expands information services to support the research activities of the Secretariat and those of member countries; collects, collates and analyses statistical information and provides essential data for forecasts and estimates necessary for OPEC medium- and long-term strategies.

Energy Studies Department: Energy Section monitors, forecasts and analyses developments in the energy and petrochemical industries and their implications for OPEC, and prepares forecasts of demands for OPEC petroleum and gas. Petroleum Section assists the Board of the Economic Commission in determining the relative values of OPEC crude petroleum and gases and in developing alternative methodologies for this purpose.

Petroleum Market Analysis Department: Monitors and analyses short-term oil market indicators and world economic developments, factors affecting the supply and demand balance, policy developments affecting prices and petroleum demand, crude oil and product market performance, stocks, spot price movements and refinery utilization.

Division Director: Dr ADNAN SHIHAB-ELDIN (Kuwait).

Administration and Human Resources Department: Responsible for all organization methods, provision of administrative services for all meetings, personnel matters, budgets, accounting and internal control; reviews general administrative policies and industrial relations practised throughout the oil industry; Head S. J. SENUSSI.

Public Relations and Information Department: Concerned with communicating OPEC objectives, decisions and actions; produces and distributes a number of publications, films, slides and tapes; and disseminates news of general interest regarding the Organization and member countries on energy and other related issues. Operates a daily on-line news service, the OPEC News Agency (OPECNA). An OPEC Library contains an extensive collection of energy-related publications; Head (vacant).

Legal Office: Provides legal advice, supervises the Secretariat's legal commitments, evaluates legal issues of concern to the Organization and member countries, and recommends appropriate action; Legal Officer DOLORES DOBARRO DE TORRES (Venezuela).

Office of the Secretary-General: Provides the Secretary-General with executive assistance in maintaining contacts with governments, organizations and delegations, in matters of protocol and in the preparation for and co-ordination of meetings; Officer-in-Charge KARIN CHACIN.

Note: In September 2000 the Conference agreed that regular meetings of heads of state or government should be convened every five years.

Record of Events

1960   The first OPEC Conference was held in Baghdad in September, attended by representatives from Iran, Iraq, Kuwait, Saudi Arabia and Venezuela.

1961   Second Conference, Caracas, January. Qatar was admitted to membership; a Board of Governors was formed and statutes agreed.

1962   Fourth Conference, Geneva, April and June. Protests were addressed to petroleum companies against price cuts introduced in August 1960. Indonesia and Libya were admitted to membership.

1965   In July the Conference reached agreement on a two-year joint production programme, implemented from 1965 to 1967, to limit annual growth in output to secure adequate prices.

1967   Abu Dhabi was admitted to membership.

1969   Algeria was admitted to membership.

1970   Twenty-first Conference, Caracas, December. Tax on income of petroleum companies was raised to 55%.

1971   A five-year agreement was concluded in February between the six producing countries in the Gulf and 23 international petroleum companies (Tehran Agreement). Nigeria was admitted to membership.

1972   In January petroleum companies agreed to adjust petroleum revenues of the largest producers after changes in currency exchange rates (Geneva Agreement).

1973   OPEC and petroleum companies concluded an agreement whereby posted prices of crude petroleum were raised by 11.9% and a mechanism was installed to make monthly adjustments to prices in future (Second Geneva Agreement). Negotiations with petroleum companies on revision of the Tehran Agreement collapsed in October, and the Gulf states unilaterally declared 70% increases in posted prices, from US $3.01 to $5.11 per barrel. In December the Conference resolved to increase the posted price by nearly 130%, to $11.65 per barrel, from 1 January 1974. Ecuador was admitted to full membership and Gabon became an associate member.

1974   As a result of Saudi opposition to the December price increase, prices were held at current level for first quarter (and subsequently for the remainder of 1974). Abu Dhabi's membership was transferred to the United Arab Emirates (UAE). A meeting in June increased royalties charged to petroleum companies from 12.5% to 14.5% in all member states except Saudi Arabia. A meeting in September increased governmental take by about 3.5% through further increases in royalties on equity crude to 16.67% and in taxes to 65.65%, except in Saudi Arabia.

1975   OPEC's first summit meeting of heads of state or government was held in Algiers in March. Gabon was admitted to full membership. A ministerial meeting in September agreed to raise prices by 10% for the period until June 1976.

1976   The OPEC Fund for International Development was created in May. In December 11 member states endorsed a rise in basic prices of 10% as of 1 January 1977, and a further 5% rise as of 1 July 1977. However, Saudi Arabia and the UAE decided to raise their prices by 5% only.

1977   Following an earlier waiver by nine members of the 5% second stage of the price increase, Saudi Arabia and the UAE announced in July that they would both raise their prices by 5%. As a result, a single level of prices throughout the organization was restored. Because of continued disagreements between the 'moderates', led by Saudi Arabia and Iran, and the 'radicals', led by Algeria, Libya and Iraq, the Conference, held in December, was unable to settle on an increase in prices.

1978   The June Conference agreed that price levels should remain stable until the end of the year. In December it was decided to raise prices in four instalments, in order to compensate for the effects of the depreciation of the US dollar. These would bring a rise of 14.5% over nine months, but an average increase of 10% for 1979.

1979   At an extraordinary meeting in March members decided to raise prices by 9%. In June the Conference agreed minimum and maximum prices that seemed likely to add between 15% and 20% to import bills of consumer countries. The December Conference agreed in principle to convert the OPEC Fund into a development agency with its own legal personality.

1980   In June the Conference decided to set the price for a marker crude at US $32 per barrel, and that the value differentials which could be added above this ceiling (on account of quality and geographical location) should not exceed $5 per barrel. The planned OPEC summit meeting in Baghdad in November was postponed indefinitely because of the Iran–Iraq war, but the scheduled ministerial meeting went ahead in Bali in December, with both Iranians and Iraqis present. A ceiling price of $41 per barrel was fixed for premium crudes.

1981 In May attempts to achieve price reunification were made, but Saudi Arabia refused to increase its US $32 per barrel price unless the higher prices charged by other countries were lowered. Most of the other OPEC countries agreed to cut production by 10% so as to reduce the surplus. An emergency meeting in Geneva in August again failed to unify prices, although Saudi Arabia agreed to reduce production by 1m. barrels per day (b/d). In October OPEC countries agreed to increase the Saudi marker price to $34 per barrel, with a ceiling price of $38 per barrel.

1982 In March an emergency meeting of petroleum ministers was held in Vienna and agreed (for the first time in OPEC's history) to defend the Organization's price structure by imposing an overall production ceiling of 18m. b/d. In December the Conference agreed to limit OPEC production to 18.5m. b/d in 1983 but postponed the allocation of national quotas pending consultations among the respective governments.

1983 In January an emergency meeting of petroleum ministers, fearing a collapse in world petroleum prices, decided to reduce the production ceiling to 17.5m. b/d, but failed to agree on individual production quotas or on adjustments to the differentials in prices charged for the high-quality crude petroleum produced by Algeria, Libya and Nigeria compared with that produced by the Gulf States. In February Nigeria cut its prices to US $30 per barrel, following a collapse in its production. To avoid a 'price war' OPEC set the official price of marker crude at $29 per barrel, and agreed to maintain existing price differentials at the level agreed on in March 1982, with the temporary exception that the differentials for Nigerian crudes should be $1 more than the price of the marker crude. It also agreed to maintain the production ceiling of 17.5m. b/d and allocated quotas for each member country except Saudi Arabia, which was to act as a 'swing producer' to supply the balancing quantities to meet market requirements.

1984 In October the production ceiling was lowered to 16m. b/d. In December price differentials for light (more expensive) and heavy (cheaper) crudes were slightly altered in an attempt to counteract price-cutting by non-OPEC producers, particularly Norway and the United Kingdom.

1985 In January members (except Algeria, Iran and Libya) effectively abandoned the marker price system. During the year production in excess of quotas by OPEC members, unofficial discounts and barter deals by members, and price cuts by non-members (such as Mexico, which had hitherto kept its prices in line with those of OPEC) contributed to a weakening of the market.

1986 During the first half of the year petroleum prices dropped to below US $10 per barrel. In April ministers agreed to set OPEC production at 16.7m. b/d for the third quarter of 1986 and at 17.3m. b/d for the fourth quarter. Algeria, Iran and Libya dissented. Discussions were also held with non-member countries (Angola, Egypt, Malaysia, Mexico and Oman), which agreed to co-operate in limiting production, although the United Kingdom declined. In August all members, with the exception of Iraq (which demanded to be allowed the same quota as Iran and, when this was denied it, refused to be a party to the agreement), agreed upon a return to production quotas, with the aim of cutting production to 14.8m. b/d (about 16.8m. b/d including Iraq's production) for the ensuing two months. This measure resulted in an increase in prices to about $15 per barrel, and was extended until the end of the year. In December members (with the exception of Iraq) agreed to return to a fixed pricing system at a level of $18 per barrel as the OPEC reference price, with effect from 1 February 1987. OPEC's total production for the first half of 1987 was not to exceed 15.8m. b/d.

1987 In June, with prices having stabilized, the Conference decided that production during the third and fourth quarters of the year should be limited to 16.6m. b/d (including Iraq's production). However, total production continued to exceed the agreed levels. In December ministers decided to extend the existing agreement for the first half of 1988, although Iraq, once more, refused to participate.

1988 By March prices had fallen below US $15 per barrel. In April non-OPEC producers offered to reduce the volume of their petroleum exports by 5% if OPEC members would do the same. Saudi Arabia, however, refused to accept further reductions in production, insisting that existing quotas should first be more strictly enforced. In June the previous production limit (15.06m. b/d, excluding Iraq's production) was again renewed for six months, in the hope that increasing demand would be sufficient to raise prices. By October, however, petroleum prices were below $12 per barrel. In November a new agreement was reached, limiting total production (including that of Iraq) to 18.5m. b/d, with effect from 1 January 1989. Identical quotas were agreed for Iran and Iraq.

1989 In June (when prices had returned to about US $18 per barrel) ministers agreed to increase the production limit to 19.5m. b/d for the second half of 1989. However, Kuwait and the UAE indicated that they would not feel bound to observe this limit. In September the production limit was again increased, to 20.5m. b/d, and in November the limit for the first half of 1990 was increased to 22m. b/d.

1990 In May members resolved to adhere more strictly to the agreed production quotas, in response to a sharp decline in prices. By late June, however, it was reported that total production had decreased by only 400,000 b/d, and prices remained at about US $14 per barrel. In July Iraq threatened to take military action against Kuwait unless it reduced its petroleum production. In the same month OPEC members agreed to limit output to 22.5m. b/d. In August Iraq invaded Kuwait, and petroleum exports by the two countries were halted by an international embargo. Petroleum prices immediately increased to exceed $25 per barrel. Later in the month an informal consultative meeting of OPEC ministers placed the July agreement in abeyance, and permitted a temporary increase in production of petroleum, of between 3m. and 3.5m. b/d (mostly by Saudi Arabia, the UAE and Venezuela). In September and October prices fluctuated in response to political developments in the Gulf region, reaching a point in excess of $40 per barrel in early October, but falling to about $25 per barrel by the end of the month. In December a meeting of OPEC members voted to maintain the high levels of production and to reinstate the quotas that had been agreed in July, once the Gulf crisis was over. During the period August 1990–February 1991 Saudi Arabia increased its petroleum output from 5.4m. to 8.5m. b/d. Seven of the other OPEC states also produced in excess of their agreed quotas.

1991 In March, in an attempt to reach the target of a minimum reference price of US $21 per barrel, ministers agreed to reduce production from 23m. b/d to 22.3m. b/d, although Saudi Arabia refused to return to its pre-August 1990 quota. In June ministers decided to maintain the ceiling of 22.3m. b/d into the third quarter of the year, since Iraq and Kuwait were still unable to export their petroleum. In September it was agreed that OPEC members' production for the last quarter of 1991 should be raised to 23.65m. b/d, and in November the OPEC Conference decided to maintain the increased production ceiling during the first quarter of 1992. From early November, however, the price of petroleum declined sharply, owing to lower than anticipated demand.

1992 The Ministerial Monitoring Committee, meeting in February, decided to impose a production ceiling of 22.98m. b/d with immediate effect. In May ministers agreed to maintain the production restriction during the third quarter of 1992. Kuwait, which was resuming production in the wake of the extensive damage inflicted on its oil-wells by Iraq during the Gulf War, was granted a special dispensation to produce without a fixed quota. During the first half of 1992 member states' petroleum output consistently exceeded agreed levels, with Saudi Arabia and Iran the principal over-producers. In June, at the UN Conference on Environment and Development, OPEC's Secretary-General expressed its member countries' strong objections to the tax on fossil fuels (designed to reduce pollution) proposed by the EC. In September agreement was reached on a production ceiling of 24.2m. b/d for the final quarter of 1992, in an attempt to raise the price of crude petroleum to the OPEC target of US $21 per barrel. At the Conference, held in November, Ecuador formally resigned from OPEC, the first country ever to do so, citing as reasons the high membership fee and OPEC's refusal to increase Ecuador's quota. The meeting agreed to restrict production to 24.58m. b/d for the first quarter of 1993 (24.46m. b/d, excluding Ecuador).

1993 In February a quota was set for Kuwait for the first time since the onset of the Gulf crisis. Kuwait agreed to produce 1.6m. b/d (400,000 less than current output) from 1 March, on the understanding that this would be substantially increased in the third quarter of the year. The quota for overall production from 1 March was set at 23.58m. b/d. A Ministerial Monitoring Sub-committee was established to supervise compliance with quotas. In June OPEC ministers decided to 'roll over' the overall quota of 23.58m. b/d into the third quarter of the year. However, Kuwait rejected its new allocation of 1.76m. b/d, demanding a quota of at least 2m. In July discussions between Iraq and the UN on the possible supervised sale of Iraqi petroleum depressed petroleum prices to below

US $16 per barrel. The Monitoring Sub-committee urged member states to adhere to their production quotas (which were exceeded by a total of 1m. b/d in July). At the end of September an extraordinary meeting of the Conference agreed on a raised production ceiling of 24.52m. b/d, to be effective for six months from 1 October. Kuwait accepted a quota of 2m. b/d, which brought the country back into the production ceiling mechanism. Iran agreed on an allocation of 3.6m. b/d, while Saudi Arabia consented to freeze production at current levels, in order to support petroleum prices which remained persistently low. In November the Conference rejected any further reduction in production. Prices subsequently fell below $14.

1994   In March OPEC ministers opted to maintain the output quotas agreed in September 1993 until the end of the year, and urged non-OPEC producers to freeze their production levels. (Iraq failed to endorse the agreement, recognizing only the production agreement adopted in July 1990.) At the meeting Saudi Arabia resisted a proposal from Iran and Nigeria, both severely affected by declines in petroleum revenue, to reduce its production by 1m. b/d in order to boost prices. In November ministers endorsed a proposal by Saudi Arabia to maintain the existing production quota (of 24.52m. b/d) until the end of 1995.

1995   In January it was reported that Gabon was reconsidering its membership of OPEC, owing to difficulties in meeting its budget contribution. During the first half of the year Gabon consistently exceeded its quota of 287,000 b/d, by 48,000 b/d, and the country failed to send a delegate to the ministerial Conference in June. At the Conference ministers expressed concern at OPEC's falling share of the world petroleum market. The Conference criticized the high level of North Sea production, by Norway and the United Kingdom, and urged collective production restraint in order to stimulate prices. In November the Conference agreed to extend the existing production quota (24.52m. b/d) for a further six months, in order to stabilize prices. During the year, however, output remained in excess of the production quotas, at some 25.58m. b/d.

1996   The possibility of a UN-Iraqi agreement permitting limited petroleum sales dominated OPEC concerns in the first half of the year and contributed to price fluctuations in the world markets. By early 1996 output by OPEC countries was estimated to be substantially in excess of quota levels; however, the price per barrel remained relatively buoyant (the average basket price reaching US $21 in March), owing largely to unseasonal cold weather in the northern hemisphere. In May a memorandum of understanding was signed between Iraq and the UN to allow the export of petroleum, up to a value of $2,000m. over a six-month period, in order to fund humanitarian relief efforts within that country. In June the Conference agreed to increase the overall output ceiling by 800,000 b/d, i.e. the anticipated level of exports from Iraq in the first six months of the agreement. Gabon's withdrawal from the Organization was confirmed at the meeting. As a result of these developments, the new production ceiling was set at 25.03m. b/d. Independent market observers expressed concern that, without any formal agreement to reduce overall production and given the actual widespread violation of the quota system, the renewed export of Iraqi petroleum would substantially depress petroleum prices. In September the Monitoring Sub-committee acknowledged that members were exceeding their production quotas, but declined to impose any punitive measures (owing to the steady increase in petroleum prices). In November the Conference agreed to maintain the existing production quota for a further six months. Also in that month, Iraq accepted certain disputed technical terms of the UN agreement, enabling the export of petroleum to commence in December.

1997   During the first half of the year petroleum prices declined, reaching a low of US $16.7 per barrel in early April, owing to the Iraqi exports, depressed world demand and persistent over-production. In June the Conference agreed to extend the existing production ceiling, of 25.03m. b/d, for a further six-month period. Member states resolved to adhere to their individual quotas in order to reduce the cumulative excess production of an estimated 2m. b/d; however, Venezuela, which (some sources claimed) was producing almost 800,000 b/d over its quota of 2.4m. b/d, declined to co-operate. An escalation in political tensions in the Gulf region in October, in particular Iraq's reluctance to co-operate with UN inspectors, prompted an increase in the price of crude petroleum to some $21.2 per barrel. Price fluctuations ensued, although there was a general downward trend. In November the OPEC Conference, meeting in Jakarta, approved a proposal by Saudi Arabia, to increase the overall production ceiling by

some 10%, with effect from 1 January 1998, in order to meet the perceived stable world demand and to reflect more accurately current output levels. At the same time the Iranian Government announced its intention to increase its production capacity and maintain its share of the quota by permitting foreign companies to conduct petroleum exploration in its territory.

1998   A decline in petroleum prices at the start of the year caused widespread concern, and speculation that this had resulted from the decision to increase production to 27.5m. b/d, coinciding with the prospect of a decline in demand from Asian economies that had been undermined by extreme financial difficulties and of a new Iraqi agreement with the UN with provision for increased petroleum exports. A meeting of the Monitoring Sub-committee, in late January, urged members to implement production restraint and resolved to send a monitoring team to member states to encourage compliance with the agreed quotas. (Venezuela remained OPEC's principal over-producer.) In February the UN Security Council approved a new agreement permitting Iraq to export petroleum valued at up to US $5,256m. every 180 days, although the Iraqi Government insisted that its production and export capacity was limited to $4,000m. In March Saudi Arabia, Venezuela and Mexico announced a joint agreement to reduce domestic production by 300,000 b/d, 200,000 b/d and 100,000 b/d respectively, with effect from 1 April, and agreed to co-operate in persuading other petroleum producing countries to commit to similar reductions. At the end of March an emergency ministerial meeting ratified the reduction proposals (the so-called 'Riyadh Pact'), which amounted to 1.245m. b/d pledged by OPEC members and 270,000 b/d by non-member states. Nevertheless, prices remained low, with over-production, together with lack of market confidence in member states' willingness to comply with the restricted quotas, an outstanding concern. In June Saudi Arabia, Venezuela and Mexico reached agreement on further reductions in output of some 450,000 b/d. Later in that month the Conference, having reviewed the market situation, agreed to implement a new reduction in total output of some 1.36m b/d, with effect from 1 July, reducing the total production target for OPEC members to 24.387m. b/d. Iran, which had been criticized for not adhering to the reductions agreed in March, confirmed that it would reduce output by 305,000 b/d. In early August petroleum prices fell below $12 per barrel. In September Iraq's petroleum production reached an estimated 2.4m. b/d, contributing to concerns of over-supply in the world market. In early November OPEC members attending a conference of the parties to the UN Framework Convention on Climate Change, held in Buenos Aires, Argentina, warned that they would claim compensation for any lost revenue resulting from initiatives to limit the emission of 'greenhouse gases' and reduce the consumption of petroleum. Later in November OPEC ministers, meeting in Vienna, resolved to maintain the existing production levels, but improve compliance. Subsequently, despite an escalation of tensions between the UN and Iraqi authorities, prices remained consistently around the level of $11 per barrel. Air-strikes initiated in December by the USA and United Kingdom against strategic targets in Iraq were not considered to have interrupted petroleum supplies and therefore had little impact on prices.

1999   In March ministers from Algeria, Iran, Mexico, Saudi Arabia and Venezuela, meeting in The Hague, Netherlands, agreed further to reduce petroleum production, owing to the continued weakness of the global market. Subsequently, petroleum prices rose by nearly 40%, after reaching the lowest price of US $9.9 per barrel in mid-February. Later in March OPEC confirmed a new reduction in output of 2.104m. b/d from 1 April, including commitments from non-OPEC members Mexico, Norway, Oman and Russia to decrease production by a total of 388,000 b/d. The agreement envisaged a total production target for OPEC member countries of 22.976m. b/d. By June total production by OPEC member states (excluding Iraq) had declined to a reported 23.25m. b/d (compared with 27.72m. in March). The evidence of almost 90% compliance with the new production quotas contributed to market confidence that stockpiles of petroleum would be reduced, and resulted in sustained price increases. In September OPEC ministers confirmed that the existing quotas would be maintained for a further six-month period. At the end of September the reference price for petroleum rose above $24, its highest level since January 1997. Prices remained buoyant during the rest of the year; however, there was increasing speculation at whether the situation was sustainable. At the end of November Iraq temporarily suspended its petroleum exports, totalling some 2.2m. b/d, pending agreement on a new phase of the 'oil-for-food' arrangement and

concern at the lack of progress on the removal of international sanctions.

2000   In March petroleum prices attained their highest level since the 1990 Gulf crisis, with the the reference price briefly exceeding US $34. At the end of that month OPEC ministers, meeting in Vienna, agreed to raise output by 1.45m. b/d, in order to ease supply shortages and thereby contain the surge in prices, with a view to restoring these to a more moderate level. A further increase in production, of 500,000 b/d, was approved by member states in June, to take effect from July (contingent on the reference price continuing to exceed $28 for 20 consecutive days). Prices remained high, reaching $34.6 in early September and leading to intense international pressure on OPEC to resolve the situation. OPEC ministers immediately announced that an increase in production of 800,000 b/d would take effect from 1 October and indicated that, were the reference price still to exceed $28 at the end of that month, an additional increase in output would be implemented. It was noted that a target band of $22–$28 per barrel was envisaged as an acceptable price level. The production agreement was supported by five non-OPEC member countries: Angola, Mexico, Norway, Oman and Russia. In late September both the Group of Seven industrialized nations (G-7) and the IMF issued warnings about the potential economic and social consequences of sustained high petroleum prices. Meanwhile the US administration agreed to release part of its strategic petroleum reserve. Towards the end of the month OPEC heads of state or government, convened at their first summit since 1975, issued the so-called 'Caracas Declaration' in which they resolved to promote market stability by developing 'remunerative, stable and competitive' pricing policies in conjunction with implementing a production policy that would secure OPEC member states an equitable share of world supply; by strengthening co-operation between the organization and other oil-exporting nations; and by developing communication between petroleum producers and consumers. The declaration also affirmed the organization's commitment to environmentally sound practice and to promoting sustainable global economic growth, social development and the eradication of poverty; supported research in technical and scientific fields; expressed concern that government taxation policies significantly inflate the end cost of petroleum; and agreed to convene future heads of state summits at regular five-yearly intervals. By the end of September petroleum prices had declined to just above $30 per barrel; this was attributed in part to an announcement by the Saudi Arabian Government that it would consider unilaterally raising output if prices were to remain at a high level. However, the decline in prices was short-lived, as the political crisis in the Middle East prompted a further series of increases: by 12 October the London Brent crude price exceeded $35 per barrel. From 31 October an additional increase in production, of 500,000 b/d was implemented, as planned for in early September. Meeting in mid-November the Conference appointed Dr Alí Rodríguez Araque as the new OPEC Secretary-General, with effect from January 2001. Addressing the Conference, Rodríguez identified the following contributory factors to the high level of petroleum prices other than the relationship between production and price levels: a decline in recent years in the refining capacity of the USA (the world's largest market), the high national taxes on consumption (particularly within the European Union), and price distortions deriving from speculation on futures markets. Attending the sixth conference of parties to the UN Framework Convention on Climate Change later in November OPEC reiterated its concern over the lost revenue that limits on 'greenhouse gas' emissions and reduced petroleum consumption would represent for member states, estimating this at $63,000m. per year.

2001   In mid-January, with a view to stabilizing petroleum prices that by now had fallen back to around US $25 per barrel, the Conference agreed to implement a reduction in production of 1.5m. b/d, to take effect on 1 February. A further reduction, of 1m. b/d, effective from 1 April, was approved by the Conference in mid-March, limiting overall production to 24.2m. b/d. In early June an extraordinary meeting of the Conference determined to maintain the production level, given that prices had stabilized within the agreed price range of $22–$28 per barrel, in spite of market reports forecasting reduced demand. A further extraordinary meeting was convened in early July, following Iraq's decision temporarily to suspend its petroleum exports under the UN programme, which again resolved to make no adjustment to the output ceiling. Later in that month, however, OPEC responded to a gradual decline in petroleum prices, which reached $22.78 in mid-July, by

announcing a ministerial agreement to reduce production by 1m. b/d, with effect from 1 September. Meeting in late September the Conference addressed the repercussions of recent major terrorist attacks on targets in the USA, which had caused significant market uncertainty. OPEC's spot basket reference price had fallen back to around $20 per barrel. The Conference declared its commitment to stabilizing the market and determined to leave production levels unchanged (at 23.2m. b/d) in order to ensure sufficient supplies. It agreed to establish an expert working group, comprising representatives of OPEC and non-OPEC producer countries, to evaluate future market developments and advance dialogue and co-operation. At a further meeting in December the Conference decided, in view of the prevailing global economic uncertainty and a decline in the average basket price level to $17–$18 in November and December, to prevent a further deterioration in petroleum prices by reducing output by a further 1.5m. b/d for six months from 1 January 2002, contingent upon the non-OPEC producers concurrently implementing a reduction in production amounting to 500,000 b/d. The Conference resolved to continue to develop contacts with the non-OPEC producer states. By the end of December 2001 the non-OPEC producers had committed themselves to a reduction in output totalling 462,500 b/d, which was considered by OPEC an adequate basis for lowering its own production ceiling to 21.70m. b/d from the start of 2002, as planned.

2002   Meeting in March the OPEC Conference welcomed a gradual improvement in the reference price (the spot basket price had averaged nearly US $19 in February), attributing this to a high level of compliance by member countries with their agreed production quotas and to ongoing support from non-OPEC producers. The latter were urged to maintain their voluntarily-imposed reductions in output. Six non-OPEC producers—Angola, Egypt, Mexico, Oman, Russia and Syria—attended the meeting as observers. Concern was expressed over the potentially destabilizing effects of the ongoing Middle East crisis. Prices rose significantly in early April following the imposition by Iraq of a one-month suspension of its oil exports in protest at the ongoing Israeli military intervention in areas controlled by the Palestinian (National) Authority. The ensuing reduction in global supply was compounded by constraints on Venezuelan production caused by a strike in the oil sector. It was reported at this time that the Iranian Government advocated the implementation of a general embargo by the Arab states on oil exports to Western countries perceived to be supporting Israeli actions. During April–early August the reference price stabilized at around $25. Meeting in June the Conference determined to maintain the existing production quota (21.70 b/d) and appointed a new Secretary-General, Dr Alvaro Silva Calderon, hitherto the Venezuelan the minister of energy and mines. In September the Conference agreed to maintain existing production levels until the end of 2002. In view of the threat to prices posed by persistent overproduction by some member states, the Conference, convened in December, determined to effect an increase in production quotas to 23 b/d from 1 January 2003 while simultaneously reducing market supply; strict compliance by member states with the new quotas was urged.

2003   Petroleum prices rose above OPEC's target range of US $22–$28 from mid-December 2002, exceeding $30 by early January 2003, owing to the reduction in actual output agreed in December 2002, compounded by the continuing industrial action in Venezuela (which was reducing overall levels of supply by about 2m. b/d), and the ongoing threat of US military action against Iraq (and consequent medium-term threat to Iraq's production of about 2.2m. b/d under the UN 'oil-for-food' arrangement). Meeting early in January the Conference agreed to raise the production ceiling to 24.5 b/d from 1 February with the aim of stabilizing the market. Prices subsequently continued to rise, with the spot basket reference price reaching $32 in February, but fell back to within the desired $22–$28 price range in March, mainly owing to a recovery in Venezuelan production by that time. Meeting in early March the Conference welcomed the resolution of Venezuela's previous supply difficulties, and decided to maintain the production ceiling at the level approved in January. The meeting resolved that, to ensure continuing stable supply, member states would make up from their available excess capacities the shortfall in production that would result in the event of war against Iraq. Later in that month, following the initiation of US-led military action against Iraq and the consequent temporary interruption in that country's production, the Secretary-General reiterated the cartel's resolve to implement this decision.

Finance

The budget for 2003 amounted to €17.6m., of which €1.1m. was to be financed by transfer from the Reserve Fund and the balance was to be contributed by member states.

Publications

Annual Report.

Annual Statistical Bulletin.

Monthly Oil Market Report.

OPEC Bulletin (monthly).

OPEC Review (quarterly).

Reports, information papers, press releases.

OPEC FUND FOR INTERNATIONAL DEVELOPMENT

Address: POB 995, 1011 Vienna, Austria.

Telephone: (1) 515-64-0; **fax:** (1) 513-92-38; **e-mail:** info@opecfund.org; **internet:** www.opecfund.org.

The Fund was established by OPEC member countries in 1976.

MEMBERS

Member countries of OPEC.

Organization

(April 2003)

ADMINISTRATION

The Fund is administered by a Ministerial Council and a Governing Board. Each member country is represented on the Council by its minister of finance. The Board consists of one representative and one alternate for each member country.

Chairman, Ministerial Council: Dr YOUSEF H. AL-EBRAHEEM (Kuwait).

Chairman, Governing Board: Dr SALEH A. AL-OMAIR (Saudi Arabia).

Director-General of the Fund: Dr YESUFU SEYYID ABDULAI (Nigeria).

FINANCIAL STRUCTURE

The resources of the Fund, whose unit of account is the US dollar, consist of contributions by OPEC member countries, and income received from operations or otherwise accruing to the Fund.

The initial endowment of the Fund amounted to US $800m. Its resources have been replenished three times, and have been further increased by the profits accruing to seven OPEC member countries through the sales of gold held by the International Monetary Fund. The pledged contributions to the OPEC Fund amounted to $3,435m. at the end of 2001, and paid-in contributions totalled some $2,990m.

Activities

The OPEC Fund for International Development is a multilateral agency for financial co-operation and assistance. Its objective is to reinforce financial co-operation between OPEC member countries and other developing countries through the provision of financial support to the latter on appropriate terms, to assist them in their economic and social development. The Fund was conceived as a collective financial facility which would consolidate the assistance extended by its member countries; its resources are additional to those already made available through other bilateral and multilateral aid agencies of OPEC members. It is empowered to:

(i) Provide concessional loans for balance-of-payments support;

(ii) Provide concessional loans for the implementation of development projects and programmes;

(iii) Make contributions and/or provide loans to eligible international agencies; and

(iv) Finance technical assistance and research through grants.

The eligible beneficiaries of the Fund's assistance are the governments of developing countries other than OPEC member countries, and international development agencies whose beneficiaries are developing countries. The Fund gives priority to the countries with the lowest income.

The Fund may undertake technical, economic and financial appraisal of a project submitted to it, or entrust such an appraisal to an appropriate international development agency, the executing national agency of a member country, or any other qualified agency. Most projects financed by the Fund have been co-financed by other development finance agencies. In each such case, one of the co-financing agencies may be appointed to administer the Fund's loan in association with its own. This practice has enabled the Fund to extend its lending activities to 109 countries over a short period of time and in a simple way, with the aim of avoiding duplication and complications. As its experience grew, the Fund increasingly resorted to parallel, rather than joint financing, taking up separate project components to be financed according to its rules and policies. In addition, it started to finance some projects completely on its own. These trends necessitated the issuance in 1982 of guide-lines for the procurement of goods and services under the Fund's loans, allowing for a margin of preference for goods and services of local origin or originating in other developing countries: the general principle of competitive bidding is, however, followed by the Fund. The loans are not tied to procurement from Fund member countries or from any other countries. The margin of preference for goods and services obtainable in developing countries is allowed on the request of the borrower and within defined limits. Fund assistance in the form of programme loans has a broader coverage than project lending. Programme loans are used to stimulate an economic sector or sub-sector, and assist recipient countries in obtaining inputs, equipment and spare parts. Besides extending loans for project and programme financing and balance of payments support, the Fund also undertakes other operations, including grants in support of technical assistance and other activities (mainly research), and financial contributions to other international institutions. In 1998 the Fund began to extend lines of credit to support private-sector activities in beneficiary countries. The so-called Private-Sector Facility aims to encourage the growth of private enterprises, in particular small and medium-sized enterprises, and to support the development of local capital markets.

OPEC FUND COMMITMENTS AND DISBURSEMENTS IN 2001

((US $ million))

	Commit-ments	Disburse-ments
Public-sector lending operations:	332.33	175.42
Project financing	273.83	159.82
Programme financing	—	6.00
HIPC initiative financing*	58.50	9.60
Private-sector lending operations	58.60	7.80
Grant Programme:	5.21	3.94
Technical assistance	3.04	2.93
Research and other activities	0.67	0.48
Emergency aid	1.50	0.54
Total	396.14	187.16

* Heavily Indebted Poor Countries initiative, jointly implemented by the International Monetary Fund and World Bank.

Project loans approved in 2001
((US $ million))

	Loans approved
Sector:	
Transportation	102.76
Agriculture and agro-industry	20.00
Education	60.89
Energy	16.90
Health	21.20
Telecommunications	2.50
Water supply and sewerage	26.30
Multisectoral	23.28
Total	273.83
Region*:	
Africa	162.29
Asia	92.24
Europe	2.70
Latin America and the Caribbean	16.60

*A total of 38 loans was approved for projects in 33 countries, benefiting 20 countries in Africa, nine in Asia, three in Latin America and the Caribbean, and one in Europe.

By the end of December 2001 the Fund had approved 913 loans since operations began in 1976, totalling US $4,873.7m., of which $3,698.3m. (or 75.9%) was for project financing, $724.2m. (14.9%) was for balance-of-payments support, $305.3m. (6.3%) was for programme financing and $145.8m. (3.0%) was allocated as financing for the Heavily Indebted Poor Countries (HIPC) initiative (see World Bank, see p. 84). Private sector operations totalled $111.7m. at that time. The Fund's 15th lending programme, approved for a three-year period, became effective on 1 January 2002.

Direct loans are supplemented by grants to support technical assistance, food aid and research. By the end of December 2001 568 grants, amounting to US $251.8m., had been extended, including $83.6m. to the Common Fund for Commodities (established by the UN Conference on Trade and Development—UNCTAD), $44.1m. in support of emergency relief operations, $99.1m. in technical assistance often in co-operation with UN agencies or other development organizations, and a special contribution of $20m. to the International Fund for Agricultural Development (IFAD). In addition, the OPEC Fund had committed $971.8m. to other international institutions by the end of 2001, comprising OPEC members' contributions to the resources of IFAD, and irrevocable transfers in the name of its members to the IMF Trust Fund. By the end of 2001 66.2% of total commitments had been disbursed.

During the year ending 31 December 2001 the Fund's total commitments amounted to US $332.3m. (compared with $284.4m. in 2000). These commitments included 38 public sector project loans, amounting to $273.8m., and nine loans, totalling $58.5m., to finance debt-relief under the HIPC initiative. The largest proportion of project loans (37.5%) was to support improvements in the transportation sector in 12 countries and included road connections to remote rural areas in Benin, Cameroon, Chad, Malawi, Senegal and Tanzania, rehabilitation of major highways in Ethiopia, the Republic of Korea and Lebanon, the expansion of the international airport in Ethiopia and modernization of railways in Pakistan. The education sector received 22.2% of loans, which supported the construction and improvement of primary level facilities in Angola, Côte d'Ivoire, Equatorial Guinea and Kenya, secondary education improvements in Mozambique and the expansion of a specialized technology institute in India. Four loans (9.6% of the total) were allocated to improve water supply and sewerage in Albania, Haiti, Honduras and Yemen. Five health sector loans accounted for 7.7% of the total and were allocated to fund hospital improvements in Lesotho and Zambia, HIV/AIDS activities in Chad and Djibouti, and laboratory facilities in Burkina Faso.

During 2001 the Fund approved US $5.21m. for 37 grants, of which $3.04m. was for technical assistance activities, $671,000 for research, and $1.50m. to support emergency humanitarian operations in El Salvador, India, Algeria, Cuba and Honduras, as well as other humanitarian activities in Mongolia, for Afghan refugees in Pakistan and for Palestinians receiving medical care in Austria.

Publications

Annual Report (in Arabic, English, French and Spanish).
OPEC Fund Newsletter (3 a year).
Occasional papers and documents.

PACIFIC COMMUNITY

Address: BP D5, 98848 Nouméa Cédex, New Caledonia.

Telephone: 26-20-00; **fax:** 26-38-18; **e-mail:** spc@spc.int; **internet:** www.spc.org.nc/.

In February 1947 the Governments of Australia, France, the Netherlands, New Zealand, the United Kingdom, and the USA signed the Canberra Agreement establishing the South Pacific Commission, which came into effect in July 1948. (The Netherlands withdrew from the Commission in 1962, when it ceased to administer the former colony of Dutch New Guinea, now Papua, formerly known as Irian Jaya, part of Indonesia.) In October 1997 the 37th South Pacific Conference, convened in Canberra, Australia, agreed to rename the organization the Pacific Community, with effect from 6 February 1998. The Secretariat of the Pacific Community (SPC) services the Community, and provides research, technical advice, training and assistance in economic, social and cultural development to 22 countries and territories of the Pacific region. It serves a population of about 6.8m., scattered over some 30m. sq km, more than 98% of which is sea.

MEMBERS

American Samoa	Niue
Australia	Northern Mariana Islands
Cook Islands	Palau
Fiji	Papua New Guinea
France	Pitcairn Islands
French Polynesia	Samoa
Guam	Solomon Islands
Kiribati	Tokelau
Marshall Islands	Tonga
Federated States of	Tuvalu
Micronesia	United Kingdom
Nauru	USA
New Caledonia	Vanuatu
New Zealand	Wallis and Futuna Islands

Organization

(April 2003)

CONFERENCE OF THE PACIFIC COMMUNITY

The Conference is the governing body of the Community (replacing the former South Pacific Conference) and is composed of representatives of all member countries and territories. The main responsibilities of the Conference, which meets annually, are to appoint the Director-General, to determine major national or regional policy issues in the areas of competence of the organization and to note changes to the Financial and Staff Regulations approved by the Committee of Representatives of Governments and Administrations (CRGA).

COMMITTEE OF REPRESENTATIVES OF GOVERNMENTS AND ADMINISTRATIONS (CRGA)

This Committee comprises representatives of all member states and territories, having equal voting rights. It meets annually to consider the work programme evaluation conducted by the Secretariat and to discuss any changes proposed by the Secretariat in the context of regional priorities; to consider and approve any policy issues for the organization presented by the Secretariat or by member countries and territories; to consider applicants and make recommendations for the post of Director-General; to approve the administrative and work programme budgets; to approve amendments to the Financial and Staff Regulations; and to conduct annual performance evaluations of the Director-General.

SECRETARIAT

The Secretariat of the Pacific Community—SPC—is headed by a Director-General and two Deputy Directors-General, based in Suva, Fiji, and Nouméa, New Caledonia. Three administrative Divisions cover Land Resources, Marine Resources and Social Resources. The

Secretariat also provides information services, including library facilities, publications, translation and computer services. The organization has about 250 staff members.

Director-General: LOURDES PANGELINAN (Guam).

Senior Deputy Director-General: Dr JIMMIE RODGERS (Solomon Islands).

Deputy Director-General: YVES CORBEL (France).

Regional Office: Private Mail Bag, Suva, Fiji; tel. 3370733; fax 3370021; e-mail spcsuva@spc.org.fj.

Activities

The SPC provides, on request of its member countries, technical assistance, advisory services, information and clearing-house services aimed at developing the technical, professional, scientific, research, planning and management capabilities of the regional population. The SPC also conducts regional conferences and technical meetings, as well as training courses, workshops and seminars at the regional or country level. It provides small grants-in-aid and awards to meet specific requests and needs of members. In November 1996 the Conference agreed to establish a specific Small Islands States fund to provide technical services, training and other relevant activities. The organization's three programme divisions are: land resources, marine resources and social resources. The Pacific Community oversees the maritime programme and telecommunications policy activities of the Pacific Islands Forum Secretariat.

In 1998 the SPC adopted a Corporate Plan for 1999–2003, the main objectives of which included developing national capabilities in 'value-adding' technology; enhancing the integration of cross-sectoral issues (such as economics, gender, culture and community education) into national planning and policy-making processes; and developing a co-ordinated human resources programme as a focal point for providing information, advice and support to the regional population. The 1999 Conference, held in Tahiti in December, adopted the 'Déclaration de Tahiti Nui', a mandate that detailed the operational policies and mechanisms of the Pacific Community, taking into account operational changes not covered by the founding Canberra Agreement. The Déclaration was regarded as a 'living document' that would be periodically revised to record subsequent modifications of operational policy. The SPC has signed memoranda of understanding with WHO, the Forum Fisheries Agency, the South Pacific Regional Environment Programme (SPREP), and several other partners. The organization participates in meetings of the Council of Regional Organizations in the Pacific (CROP, see under Pacific Islands Forum Secretariat). Representatives of the SPC, SPREP and the South Pacific Applied Geoscience Commission hold periodic 'troika' meetings to develop regional technical co-operation and harmonization of work programmes.

LAND RESOURCES

The land resources division comprises two major programmes: agriculture (incorporating advice and specific activities in crop improvement and plant protection; animal health and production services; and agricultural resource economics and information); and forestry (providing training, technical assistance and information in forestry management and agroforestry). Objectives of the agriculture programme, based in Suva, Fiji, include the promotion of land and agricultural management practices that are both economically and environmentally sustainable; strengthening national capabilities to reduce losses owing to crop pests (insects, pathogens and weeds) and animal diseases already present, and to prevent the introduction of new pests and diseases; and facilitating trade through improved quarantine procedures. Forestry activities include the implementation, jointly with other partners, of the Pacific Islands Forests and Trees Support Project, which is concerned with natural forest management and conservation, agroforestry and development and the use of tree and plant resources; and of the Pacific-German Regional Forestry Project. A Pacific Regional Agricultural Programme (PRAP), funded by the European Union, was introduced by eight member states in 1990. The SPC assumed responsibility for administering PRAP in 1998.

MARINE RESOURCES

The SPC aims to support and co-ordinate the sustainable development and management of inshore fisheries resources in the region, to undertake scientific research in order to provide member governments with relevant information for the sustainable development and management of tuna and billfish resources in and adjacent to the South Pacific region, and to provide data and analytical services to national fisheries departments. The main components of the Community's fisheries activities are the Coastal Fisheries Programme (CFP), the Oceanic Fisheries Programme (OFP), and the

Regional Maritime Programme (RMP). The CFP is divided into the following sections: community fisheries (research and assessment of and development support for people occupied in subsistence and artisanal fisheries); fisheries training; sustainable fisheries development; reef fisheries assessment and management; fisheries information; and post-harvest development (offering advice and training in order to improve handling practices, storage, seafood product development, quality control and marketing). The OFP consists of the following three sections: statistics and monitoring; tuna ecology and biology; and stock assessment and modelling. The statistics and monitoring section maintains a database of industrial tuna fisheries in the region. The OFP contributed research and statistical information for the formulation of the Convention for the Conservation and Management of Highly Migratory Fish Stocks in the Western and Central Pacific, which aimed to establish a regime for the sustainable management of tuna reserves, and was opened for signature in Honolulu in September 2000. (The convention had been ratified by four states at February 2002.) The SPC and European Commission were jointly to launch the Pacific Regional Oceanic and Coastal Fisheries Project (PROCFISH) in 2002. The oceanic component of the project aimed to assist the OFP with advancing knowledge of tuna fisheries ecosystems, while the coastal element was to produce the first comparative regional baseline assessment of reef fisheries. The RMP advises member governments in the fields of policy, law and training. In early 2002 the RMP launched the model Pacific Islands Maritime Legislation and Regulations as a framework for the development of national maritime legislation. The SPC administers the Pacific Island Aquaculture Network, a forum for promoting regional aquaculture development.

The SPC hosts the Pacific Office of the World Fish Center (the International Centre for Living Aquatic Resources Management—ICLARM); the SPC and the World Fish Center have jointly implemented a number of projects.

SOCIAL RESOURCES

The Social Resources Division comprises the Community Health Programme and the Socio-economic Programme (including sub-programmes and sections on statistics; population and demography; rural energy development; youth issues; culture; women's and gender equality; community education training; and media training).

The Community Health Programme aims to implement health promotion programmes; to assist regional authorities to strengthen health information systems and to promote the use of new technology for health information development and disease control (for example, through the Public Health Surveillance and Disease Control Programme); to promote efficient health services management; and to help all Pacific Islanders to attain a level of health and quality of life that will enable them to contribute to the development of their communities. The Community Health Services also work in the areas of non-communicable diseases and nutrition (with particular focus on the high levels of diabetes and heart disease in parts of the region); environmental health, through the improvement of water and sanitation facilities; and reducing the incidence of HIV/AIDS and other sexually-transmitted diseases (STDs), tuberculosis, and vector-borne diseases such as malaria and dengue fever. The SPC operates a project (mainly funded by Australia and New Zealand), to prevent AIDS and STDs among young people through peer education and awareness. It is also responsible for implementing the Pacific Regional Vector-Borne Diseases Project, established in 1996, which focuses particularly on Fiji, Vanuatu and the Solomon Islands.

The Statistics Programme assists governments and administrations in the region to provide effective and efficient national statistical services through the provision of training activities, a statistical information service and other advisory services. A Regional Conference of Statisticians facilitates the integration and co-ordination of statistical services throughout the region.

The Population and Demography Programme provides technical support in population, demographic and development issues to member governments, other SPC programmes, and organizations active in the region. The Programme aims to assist governments effectively to analyse data and utilize it into the formulation of national development policies and programmes. The Programme organizes national workshops in population and development planning, provides short-term professional attachments, undertakes demographic research and analysis, and disseminates information.

The Rural Energy Development Programme provides technical assistance and advice to member states on the utilization of sustainable energy resources, and incorporates a regional rural renewable energy project, sponsored by Australia and France.

The Pacific Youth Resource Bureau (PWRB) co-ordinates the implementation of the Pacific Youth Strategy 2005, which aims to develop opportunities for young people to play an active role in society. The PYRB provides non-formal education and support for youth, community workers and young adults in community development subjects and provides grants to help young people find employ-ment. It also advises and assists the Pacific Youth Council in promoting a regional youth identity. The Pacific Women's Resource Bureau (PWRB) aims to promote the social, economic and cultural advancement of women in the region by assisting governments and regional organizations to include women in the development plan-ning process. The PWRB also provides technical and advisory serv-ices, advocacy and management support training to groups con-cerned with women in development and gender and development, and supports the production and exchange of information regarding women.

The Cultural Programme aims to preserve and promote the cul-tural heritage of the Pacific Islands. The Programme assists with the training of librarians, archivists and researchers and promotes instruction in local languages, history and art at schools in member states and territories. The SPC acts as the secretariat of the Council of Pacific Arts, which organizes the Festival of Pacific Arts on a four-yearly basis.

The SPC regional office in Suva, Fiji, administers a Community Education Training Centre (CETC), which conducts a seven-month training course for up to 36 women community workers annually, with the objective of training women in methods of community development so that they can help others to achieve better living conditions for island families and communities. The Regional Media Centre provides training, technical assistance and production mate-rials in all areas of the media for member countries and territories, community work programmes, donor projects and regional non-governmental organizations. The Centre comprises a radio broad-cast unit, a graphic design and publication unit and a TV and video unit.

In 2000 the SPC's Information Technology and Communication Unit launched ComET, a satellite communications project aimed at linking more closely the organization's headquarters in New Cale-donia and regional office in Fiji. The Information and Communica-tions Programme is developing the use of modern communication technology as an invaluable resource for problem-solving, regional

networking, and uniting the Community's scattered, often physi-cally isolated, island member states. In conjunction with the Secre-tariat of the Pacific Islands Forum the SPC convened the first regional meeting of Information and Communication Technology workers, researchers and policy-makers in August 2001. The meeting addressed strategies for the advancement of new informa-tion technologies in member countries.

Finance

The organization's core budget, funded by assessed contributions from member states, finances executive and administrative expendi-tures, the Information and Communications Programme, and sev-eral professional and support positions that contribute to the work of the three programme divisions (i.e. Land Resources, Marine Resources and Social Resources). The non-core budget, funded mainly by aid donors and in part by Community member states, mostly on a contractual basis, finances the SPC's technical services. Administrative expenditure for 2000 amounted to US $2.5m.

Publications

Annual Report.

Fisheries Newsletter (quarterly).

Pacific Aids Alert Bulletin (quarterly).

Pacific Island Nutrition (quarterly).

Regional Tuna Bulletin (quarterly).

Report of the Conference of the Pacific Community.

Women's Newsletter (quarterly).

Technical publications, statistical bulletins, advisory leaflets and reports.

PACIFIC ISLANDS FORUM

MEMBERS

Australia	Niue
Cook Islands	Palau
Fiji	Papua New Guinea
Kiribati	Samoa
Marshall Islands	Solomon Islands
Federated States of	Tonga
Micronesia	Tuvalu
Nauru	Vanuatu
New Zealand	

Note: New Caledonia was admitted as an observer at the Forum in 1999. Timor-Leste was granted 'special observer' status in 2002.

The Pacific Islands Forum (which changed its name from South Pacific Forum in October 2000) was founded as the gathering of Heads of Government of the independent and self-governing states of the South Pacific. Its first meeting was held on 5 August 1971, in Wellington, New Zealand. It provides an opportunity for informal discussions to be held on a wide range of common issues and problems and meets annually or when issues require urgent atten-tion. The Forum has no written constitution or international agree-ment governing its activities nor any formal rules relating to its purpose, membership or conduct of meeting. Decisions are always reached by consensus, it never having been found necessary or desirable to vote formally on issues. In October 1994 the Forum was granted observer status by the General Assembly of the United Nations.

Since 1989 each Forum has been followed by 'dialogues' with representatives of other countries with a long-term interest in and commitment to the region. In October 1995 the Forum Governments suspended France's 'dialogue' status, following that country's re-sumption of the testing of nuclear weapons in French Polynesia. France was reinstated as a 'dialogue partner' in September 1996. In 2002 'dialogue partners' comprised Canada, the People's Republic of China, France, Indonesia, Japan, the Republic of Korea, Malaysia, Philippines, the United Kingdom, the USA, and the European Union. India was to be admitted as a dialogue partner in 2003.

The South Pacific Nuclear-Free Zone Treaty (Treaty of Raro-tonga), prohibiting the acquisition, stationing or testing of nuclear weapons in the region, came into effect in December 1986, following ratification by eight states. The USSR signed the protocols to the

treaty (whereby states possessing nuclear weapons agree not to use or threaten to use nuclear explosive devices against any non-nuclear party to the Treaty) in December 1987 and ratified them in April 1988; the People's Republic of China did likewise in December 1987 and October 1988 respectively. The other three major nuclear powers, however, intimated that they did not intend to adhere to the Treaty. In July 1993 the Forum petitioned the USA, the United Kingdom and France, asking them to reconsider their past refusal to sign the Treaty in the light of the end of the 'Cold War'. In July 1995, following the decision of the French Government to resume testing of nuclear weapons in French Polynesia, members of the Forum resolved to increase diplomatic pressure on the three Governments to sign the Treaty. In October the United Kingdom, the USA and France announced their intention to accede to the Treaty, by mid-1996. While the decision was approved by the Forum, it urged the Governments to sign with immediate effect, thus accelerating the termination of France's testing programme. Following France's deci-sion, announced in January 1996, to end the programme four months earlier than scheduled, representatives of the Governments of the three countries signed the Treaty in March.

In 1990 five of the Forum's smallest island member states formed an economic sub-group to address their specific concerns, in particu-lar economic disadvantages resulting from a poor resource base, absence of a skilled work-force and lack of involvement in world markets. In September 1997 the 28th Forum, convened in Rar-otonga, the Cook Islands, endorsed the inclusion of the Marshall Islands as the sixth member of the Smaller Island States sub-group. Representatives of the grouping, which also includes Kiribati, the Cook Islands, Nauru, Niue and Tuvalu, meet regularly. In February 1998 senior Forum officials, for the first time, met with representa-tives of the Caribbean Community and the Indian Ocean Commis-sion, as well as other major international organizations, to discuss means to enhance consideration and promotion of the interests of small island states. Small island member states have been partic-ularly concerned about the phenomenon of global warming and its potentially damaging effects on the region (see below).

The 23rd Forum, held in Honiara, Solomon Islands, in July 1992, welcomed France's suspension of its nuclear-testing programme until the end of the year, but urged the French Government to make the moratorium permanent. Forum members discussed the deci-sions made at the UN Conference on Environment and Development held in June, and approved the Cook Islands' proposal to host a 'global conference for small islands'. The Niue Fisheries Surveillance and Law Enforcement Co-operation Treaty was signed by members, with the exception of Fiji, Kiribati and Tokelau, which were awaiting endorsement from their legislatures. The treaty provided for co-operation in the surveillance of fisheries resources and in defeating drugs-trafficking and other organized crime. Forum leaders also adopted a separate declaration on future priorities in law enforcement co-operation.

At the 24th Forum, held in Yaren, Nauru, in August 1993 it was agreed that effective links needed to be established with the broader Asia-Pacific region, with participation in Asia-Pacific Economic Co-operation (APEC), where the Forum has observer status, to be utilized to the full. The Forum urged an increase in intra-regional trade and asked for improved opportunities for Pacific island countries exporting to Australia and New Zealand. New Caledonia's right to self-determination was supported. Environmental protection measures and the rapid growth in population in the region, which was posing a threat to economic and social development, were also discussed by the Forum delegates.

The 25th Forum was convened in Brisbane, Australia, in August 1994 under the theme of 'Managing Our Resources'. In response to the loss of natural resources as well as of income-earning potential resulting from unlawful logging of timber by foreign companies, Forum members agreed to impose stricter controls on the exploitation of forestry resources and to begin negotiations to standardize monitoring of the region's resources. The Forum also agreed to strengthen its promotion of sustainable exploitation of fishing stocks, reviewed preparations of a convention to control the movement and management of radioactive waste within the South Pacific and discussed the rationalization of national airlines, on a regional or sub-regional basis, to reduce operational losses.

The 26th Forum, held in Madang, Papua New Guinea, in September 1995, was dominated by extreme hostility on the part of Forum Governments to the resumption of testing of nuclear weapons by France in the South Pacific region. The decision to recommence testing, announced by the French Government in June, had been instantly criticized by Forum Governments. The 26th Forum reiterated their demand that France stop any further testing, and also condemned the People's Republic of China for conducting nuclear tests in the region. The meeting endorsed a draft Code of Conduct on the management and monitoring of indigenous forest resources in selected South Pacific countries, which had been initiated at the 25th Forum; however, while the six countries concerned committed themselves to implementing the Code through national legislation, its signing was deferred, owing to an initial unwillingness on the part of Papua New Guinea and Solomon Islands. The Forum did adopt a treaty to ban the import into the region of all radioactive and other hazardous wastes, and to control the transboundary movement and management of these wastes (the so-called Waigani Convention). The Forum agreed to reactivate the ministerial committee on New Caledonia, comprising Fiji, Nauru and Solomon Islands, which was to monitor political developments in that territory prior to its referendum on independence, scheduled to be held in 1998. In addition, the Forum resolved to implement and pursue means of promoting economic co-operation and long-term development in the region. In December 1995 Forum finance ministers, meeting in Port Moresby, Papua New Guinea, discussed the issues involved in the concept of 'Securing Development Beyond 2000' and initiated an assessment project to further trade liberalization efforts in the region.

The 27th Forum, held in Majuro, the Marshall Islands, in September 1996, supported the efforts of the French Government to improve relations with countries in the South Pacific and agreed to readmit France to the post-Forum dialogue. The Forum meeting recognized the importance of responding to the liberalization of the global trading system by reviewing the region's economic tariff policies, and of assisting members in attracting investment for the development of the private sector. The Forum advocated that a meeting of economy ministers of member countries be held each year. The Forum was also concerned with environmental issues: in particular, it urged the ratification and implementation of the Waigani Convention by all member states, the promotion of regional efforts to conserve marine resources and to protect the coastal environment, and the formulation of an international, legally-binding agreement to reduce emissions by industrialized countries of so-called 'greenhouse gases'. Such gases contribute to the warming of the earth's atmosphere (the 'greenhouse effect') and to related increases in global sea-levels, and have therefore been regarded as a threat to low-lying islands in the region. The Forum requested the ministerial committee on New Caledonia (established by the 1990 Forum to monitor, in co-operation with the French authorities, political developments in the territory) to pursue contacts with all parties there and to continue to monitor preparations for the 1998 referendum.

In July 1997 the inaugural meeting of Forum economy ministers was convened in Cairns, Australia. It formulated an Action Plan to encourage the flow of foreign investment into the region by committing members to economic reforms, good governance and the implementation of multilateral trade and tariff policies. The meeting also commissioned a formal study of the establishment of a free-trade agreement between Forum island states. The 28th Forum, held in Rarotonga, the Cook Islands, in September, considered the economic challenges confronting the region. However, it was marked by a failure to conclude a common policy position on mandatory targets for reductions in 'greenhouse gas' emissions, owing to an ongoing dispute between Australia and other Forum Governments.

The 29th Forum, held in Pohnpei, Federated States of Micronesia, in August 1998, considered the need to pursue economic reforms and to stimulate the private sector and foreign investment in order to ensure economic growth. Leaders reiterated their support for efforts to implement the economic Action Plan and to develop a framework for a free-trade agreement, and endorsed specific recommendations of the second Forum Economic Ministers Meeting, which was held in Fiji, in July, including the promotion of competitive telecommunications markets, the development of information infrastructures and support for a new economic vulnerability index at the UN to help determine least developed country status. The Forum was also concerned with environmental issues, notably the shipment of radioactive wastes, the impact of a multinational venture to launch satellites from the Pacific, the need for ongoing radiological monitoring of the Mururoa and Fangataufa atolls, and the development of a South Pacific Whale Sanctuary. The Forum adopted a Statement on Climate Change, which urged all countries to ratify and implement the gas emission reductions agreed upon by UN member states in December 1997 (the so-called Kyoto Protocol of the UN Framework Convention on Climate Change), and emphasized the Forum's commitment to further measures for verifying and enforcing emission limitation.

In October 1999 the 30th Forum, held in Koror, Palau, endorsed in principle the establishment of a regional free-trade area (FTA), which had been approved at a special ministerial meeting held in June. The FTA was to be implemented from 2002 over a period of eight years for developing member countries and 10 years for smaller island states and least developed countries. The Forum requested officials from member countries to negotiate the details of a draft agreement on the FTA (the so-called Pacific Island Countries Trade Agreement—PICTA), including possible extensions of the arrangements to Australia and New Zealand. The heads of government adopted a Forum Vision for the Pacific Information Economy, which recognized the importance of information technology infrastructure for the region's economic and social development and the possibilities for enhanced co-operation in investment, job creation, education, training and cultural exchange. Forum Governments also expressed concern at the shipment of radioactive waste through the Pacific and determined to pursue negotiations with France, Japan and the United Kingdom regarding liability and compensation arrangements; confirmed their continued support for the multinational force and UN operations in East Timor (now Timor-Leste); and urged more countries to adopt and implement the Kyoto Protocol to limit the emission of 'greenhouse gases'. In addition, the Forum agreed to rename the grouping (hitherto known as the South Pacific Forum) the Pacific Islands Forum, to reflect the expansion of its membership since its establishment; the new designation took effect at the 31st Forum, which was convened in Tarawa, Kiribati, at the end of October 2000.

At the 31st Forum the heads of government discussed the escalation in regional insecurity that had occurred since the previous Forum. Concern was expressed over the unrest that prevailed during mid-2000 in Fiji and Solomon Islands, and also over ongoing political violence in the Indonesian province of Irian Jaya (now Papua). The Forum adopted the Biketawa Declaration, which outlined a mechanism for responding to any future such crises in the region while urging members to undertake efforts to address the fundamental causes of instability. The detrimental economic impact of the disturbances in Fiji and Solomon Islands was noted. The Forum endorsed a proposal to establish a Regional Financial Information Sharing Facility and national financial intelligence units, and welcomed the conclusion in June by the European Union and ACP states (which include several Forum members) of the Cotonou Agreement. The Forum also reiterated support for the prompt implementation of the Kyoto Protocol.

In August 2001, convened at the 32nd Forum, in Nauru, nine regional leaders adopted PICTA, providing for the establishment of the FTA (as envisaged at the 30th Forum). A related Pacific Agreement on Closer Economic Relations (PACER), envisaging the phased establishment of a regional single market including the signatories to PICTA and Australia and New Zealand, was also adopted. The Forum expressed concern at the refusal of the USA (responsible for about one-quarter of world-wide 'greenhouse gas' emissions) to ratify the Kyoto Protocol. In response to an ongoing initiative by the Organisation of Economic Co-operation and Development (OECD) to eliminate the operation of 'harmful tax systems', the Forum reaffirmed the sovereign right of nations to establish individual tax regimes and urged the development of a new co-operative framework to address issues relating to financial transparency. (OECD had identified the Cook Islands, the Marshall Islands, Nauru and Niue as so-called 'tax havens' lacking financial transparency and had demanded that they impose stricter legislation to address the incidence of international money-laundering on their territories.) Forum leaders also reiterated protests against the shipment of radioactive materials through the region.

The 33rd Forum, held in Suva, Fiji, in August 2002, adopted the the Nasonini Declaration on Regional Security, which recognized the need for immediate and sustained regional action to combat international terrorism and transnational crime, in view of the perceived increased threat to global and regional security following

the major terrorist attacks perpetrated against targets in the USA in September 2001. Regional leaders also approved a Pacific Island Regional Ocean Policy, which aimed to ensure the future sustainable use of the ocean and its resources by Pacific Island communities and external partners. In addition the Forum urged OECD to adopt a more flexible approach in the implementation of its ongoing harmful tax initiative; welcomed the third assessment report on climate change issued in 2001 by the WMO/UNEP Intergovernmental Panel on Climate Change and reiterated demands for a world-wide reduction in greenhouse gas emissions; invited member island states to declare their coastal waters as whale sanctuaries; and urged the development of a Pacific Regional Plan of Action against HIV/AIDS.

Pacific Islands Forum Secretariat

Address: Private Mail Bag, Suva, Fiji.
Telephone: 3312600; **fax:** 3305573; **e-mail:** info@forumsec.org.fj; **internet:** www.forumsec.org.fj.

The South Pacific Bureau for Economic Co-operation (SPEC) was established by an agreement signed on 17 April 1973, at the third meeting of the South Pacific Forum (now Pacific Islands Forum) in Apia, Western Samoa (now Samoa). SPEC was renamed the South Pacific Forum Secretariat in 1988; this, in turn, was redesignated as the Pacific Islands Forum Secretariat in October 2000.

Organization
(April 2003)

FORUM OFFICIALS COMMITTEE
The Forum Officials Committee is the Secretariat's executive board. It comprises representatives and senior officials from all member countries. It meets twice a year, immediately before the meetings of the Pacific Islands Forum and at the end of the year, to discuss in detail the Secretariat's work programme and annual budget.

SECRETARIAT
The Secretariat undertakes the day-to-day activities of the Forum. It is headed by a Secretary-General, with a staff of some 70 people drawn from the member countries. The Secretariat comprises the following four Divisions: Corporate Services; Development and Economic Policy; Trade and Investment; and Political, International and Legal Affairs.

Secretary-General: NOEL LEVI (Papua New Guinea).
Deputy Secretary-General: IOSEFA MAIAVA (Samoa).

Activities

The Secretariat's aim is to enhance the economic and social well-being of the people of the South Pacific, in support of the efforts of national governments.

The Secretariat's trade and investment services extend advice and technical assistance to member countries in policy, development, export marketing, and information dissemination. Trade policy activities are mainly concerned with improving private sector policies, for example investment promotion, assisting integration into the world economy (including the provision of information and technical assistance to member states on WTO-related matters and supporting Pacific Island ACP states with preparations for negotiations on trade partnership with the EU under the Cotonou Agreement), and the development of businesses. The Secretariat aims to assist both island governments and private sector companies to enhance their capacity in the development and exploitation of export markets, product identification and product development. A trade exhibition was held in French Polynesia in 1997, and support was granted to provide for visits to overseas trade fairs and the development of promotional materials. A regional trade and investment database is being developed. The Trade and Investment Division of the Secretariat co-ordinates the activities of the regional trade offices located in Australia, New Zealand and Japan (see below). A representative trade office in Beijing, People's Republic of China, opened in January 2002.

In 2002 the Trade and Investment Division was preparing for the implementation of two major regional trade accords signed by Forum heads of state in August 2001: the Pacific Island Countries

Trade Agreement (PICTA), providing for the establishment of a Pacific Island free-trade area (FTA); and the related Pacific Agreement on Closer Economic Relations (PACER), incorporating trade and economic co-operation measures and envisaging an eventual single regional market comprising the PICTA FTA and Australia and New Zealand. It was envisaged that negotiations on free-trade agreements between Pacific Island states and Australia and New Zealand, with a view to establishing the larger regional single market envisaged by PACER, would commence within eight years of PICTA's entry into force. SPARTECA (see below) would remain operative pending the establishment of the larger single market, into which it would be subsumed. Under the provisions of PACER, Australia and New Zealand were to provide technical and financial assistance to PICTA signatory states in pursuing the objectives of PACER.

In 1981 the South Pacific Regional Trade and Economic Co-operation Agreement (SPARTECA) came into force. SPARTECA aimed to redress the trade deficit of the Pacific Island countries with Australia and New Zealand. It is a non-reciprocal trade agreement under which Australia and New Zealand offer duty-free and unrestricted access or concessional access for specified products originating from the developing island member countries of the Forum. In 1985 Australia agreed to further liberalization of trade by abolishing (from the beginning of 1987) duties and quotas on all Pacific products except steel, cars, sugar, footwear and garments. In August 1994 New Zealand expanded its import criteria under the agreement by reducing the rule of origin requirement for garment products from 50% to 45% of local content. In response to requests from Fiji, Australia agreed to widen its interpretation of the agreement by accepting as being of local content manufactured products that consist of goods and components of 50% Australian content. A new Fiji/Australia Trade and Economic Relations Agreement (AFTERA) was concluded in March 1999 to complement SPARTECA and compensate for certain trade benefits that were in the process of being withdrawn.

In April 2001 the Secretariat convened a meeting of seven member island states—Cook Islands, the Marshall Islands, Nauru, Niue, Samoa, Tonga and Vanuatu—as well as representatives from Australia and New Zealand, to address the regional implications of the OECD's Harmful Tax Competition Initiative. Under the initiative, designed to reduce the level of potential tax revenue lost by OECD member states to offshore 'tax havens', 35 jurisdictions, including these seven Pacific Island states, were required to amend national financial legislation by the end of July. States that did not comply would be designated as 'non-co-operative' and might be targeted by 'defensive measures'. The meeting requested the OECD to engage in conciliatory negotiations with the listed Pacific Island states. At the August 2001 Forum (by which time Cook Islands, the Marshall Islands, Nauru and Niue had been identified as non-co-operative) leaders reiterated this stance, proclaiming the sovereign right of nations to establish individual tax regimes, and supporting the development of a new co-operative framework to address financial transparency concerns. In December the Secretariat hosted a workshop for officials from nine member states concerned with combating financial crime. The workshop was attended and sponsored by several partner organizations and bodies, including the IMF.

The Political, International and Legal Affairs Division of the Secretariat organizes and services the meetings of the Forum, disseminates its views, administers the Forum's observer office at the United Nations, and aims to strengthen relations with other regional and international organizations, in particular APEC and ASEAN. The Division's other main concern is to promote regional co-operation in law enforcement and legal affairs, and it provides technical support for the drafting of legal documents and for law enforcement capacity-building. In 1997 the Secretariat undertook an assessment to survey the need for specialist training in dealing with money laundering in member countries. In recent years the Forum Secretariat has been concerned with assessing the legislative reforms and other commitments needed to ensure implementation of the 1992 Honiara Declaration on Law Enforcement Co-operation. The Division assists member countries to ratify and implement the 1988 UN Convention against Illicit Trafficking in Narcotic Drugs and Psychotropic Substances. In December 1998 the Secretariat initiated a five-year programme to strengthen regional law enforcement capabilities, in particular to counter cross-border crimes such as money-laundering and drugs-trafficking. All member states, apart from Australia and New Zealand, were to participate in the initiative. In December 2001 the first ever Forum Election Observer Group was dispatched to monitor legislative elections held in Solomon Islands. A conference of Forum immigration ministers convened in that month expressed concern at rising levels of human-trafficking and illegal immigration in the region, and recommended that member states become parties to the 2000 UN Convention Against Transnational Organized Crime.

The Secretariat helps to co-ordinate environmental policy. With support from the Australian Government, it administers a network of stations to monitor sea-levels and climate change throughout the Pacific region. In recent years the Secretariat has played an active role in supporting regional participation at meetings of the Conference of the Parties to the UN Framework Convention on Climate Change.

The Development and Economic Policy Division of the Secretariat aims to co-ordinate and promote co-operation in development activities and programmes throughout the region. The Division administers a Short Term Advisory Service, which provides consultancy services to help member countries meet economic development priorities, and a Fellowship Scheme to provide practical training in a range of technical and income-generating activities. A Small Island Development Fund aims to assist the economic development of this sub-group of member countries (i.e. the Cook Islands, Kiribati, the Marshall Islands, Nauru, Niue and Tuvalu) through project financing. A separate fellowship has also been established to provide training to the Kanak population of New Caledonia, to assist in their social, economic and political development. The Division aims to assist regional organizations to identify development priorities and to provide advice to national governments on economic analysis, planning and structural reforms. The Secretariat chairs the Council of Regional Organizations in the Pacific (CROP), an *ad hoc* committee comprising the heads of eight regional organizations, which aims to discuss and co-ordinate the policies and work programmes of the various agencies in order to avoid duplication of or omissions in their services to member countries.

The Secretariat services the Pacific Group Council of ACP states receiving assistance from the EU, and in early 1993 a joint unit was established within the Secretariat headquarters to assist Pacific ACP countries and regional organizations in submitting projects to the EU for funding.

The Forum established the Pacific Forum Line and the Association of South Pacific Airlines (see below), as part of its efforts to promote co-operation in regional transport. On 1 January 1997 the work of the Forum Maritime Programme, which included assistance for regional maritime training and for the development of regional maritime administrations and legislation, was transferred to the regional office of the South Pacific Commission (renamed the Pacific Community from February 1998) at Suva. At the same time responsibility for the Secretariat's civil aviation activities was transferred to individual countries, to be managed at a bilateral level. Telecommunications policy activities were also transferred to the then South Pacific Commission at the start of 1997. In May 1998 ministers responsible for aviation in member states approved a new regional civil aviation policy, which envisaged liberalization of air services, common safety and security standards and provisions for shared revenue.

Finance

The Governments of Australia and New Zealand each contribute some 37% of the annual budget and the remaining amount is shared by the other member Governments. Extra-budgetary funding is contributed mainly by Australia, New Zealand, Japan, the EU and France. Forum officials approved a budget of $F 15.4m. for the Secretariat's 2002 work programme.

Publications

Annual Report.

Forum News (quarterly).

Forum Trends.

Forum Secretariat Directory of Aid Agencies.

South Pacific Trade Directory.

SPARTECA (guide for Pacific island exporters).

Reports of meetings; profiles of Forum member countries.

Associated and Affiliated Organizations

Association of South Pacific Airlines—ASPA: POB 9817, Nadi Airport, Nadi, Fiji; tel. 6723526; fax 6720196; f. 1979 at a meeting of airlines in the South Pacific, convened to promote co-operation among the member airlines for the development of regular, safe and economical commercial aviation within, to and from the South Pacific. mems: 16 regional airlines, two associates; Chair. SEMISI TAUMOEPEAU; Sec.-Gen. GEORGE E. FAKTAUFON.

Forum Fisheries Agency—FFA: POB 629, Honiara, Solomon Islands; tel. (677) 21124; fax (677) 23995; e-mail info@ffa.int; f. 1979 to promote co-operation in fisheries among coastal states in the region; collects and disseminates information and advice on the living marine resources of the region, including the management, exploitation and development of these resources; provides assistance in the areas of law (treaty negotiations, drafting legislation, and co-ordinating surveillance and enforcement), fisheries development, research, economics, computers, and information management; a Vessel Monitoring System, to provide automated data collection and analysis of fishing vessel activities throughout the region, was inaugurated by the FFA in 1998; on behalf of its 16 member countries, the FFA administers a multilateral fisheries treaty, under which vessels from the USA operate in the region, in exchange for an annual payment; Dir VICTORIO UHERBELAU; publs *FFA News Digest* (every two months), *FFA Reports.*

Pacific Forum Line: POB 796, Auckland, New Zealand; tel. (9) 356-2333; fax (9) 356-2330; e-mail info@pflnz.co.nz; internet www.pflnz.co.nz; f. 1977 as a joint venture by South Pacific countries, to provide shipping services to meet the special requirements of the region; operates three container vessels; conducts shipping agency services in Australia, Fiji, New Zealand and Samoa, and stevedoring in Samoa; Chair. T. TUFUI; CEO W. J. MACLENNAN.

Pacific Islands Centre—PIC: Sotobori Sky Bldg, 5th Floor, 2-11 Ichigayahonmura-cho, Shinjuku-ku,, Tokyo 162-0845, Japan; tel. (3) 3268-8419; fax (3) 3268-6311; e-mail info@pic.or.jp;; internet www.pic.or.jp; f. 1996 to promote and to facilitate trade, investment and tourism among Forum members and Japan. Dir AKIRA OUCHI.

South Pacific Trade Commission (Australia Office): Level 30, Piccadilly Tower, 133 Castlereagh St, Sydney, NSW 2000, Australia; tel. (2) 9283-5933; fax (2) 9283-5948; e-mail info@sptc.gov.au; internet www.sptc.gov.au; f. 1979; assists Pacific Island Governments and business communities to identify market opportunities in Australia and promotes investment in the Pacific Island countries; Senior Trade Commr AIVU TAUVASA (Papua New Guinea).

South Pacific Trade Commission (New Zealand Office): Flight Centre, 48 Emily Pl., Auckland, New Zealand; tel. (9) 3020465; fax (9) 3776642; e-mail parmeshc@sptc.org.nz; internet www.sptc.org.nz; Senior Trade Commr PARMESH CHAND.

SOUTH ASIAN ASSOCIATION FOR REGIONAL CO-OPERATION—SAARC

Address: POB 4222, Kathmandu, Nepal.
Telephone: (1) 221785; **fax:** (1) 227033; **e-mail:** saarc@saarc-sec
.org; **internet:** www.saarc-sec.org.

The South Asian Association for Regional Co-operation (SAARC) was formally established in 1985 in order to strengthen and accelerate regional co-operation, particularly in economic development.

MEMBERS

Bangladesh	Nepal
Bhutan	Pakistan
India	Sri Lanka
Maldives	

Organization

(April 2003)

SUMMIT MEETING

Heads of state and of government of member states represent the body's highest authority, and a summit meeting is normally held annually. The 11th SAARC summit meeting was convened in Kathmandu, Nepal, in January 2002. (It had been postponed from November 1999 owing to a deterioration in relations at that time between India and Pakistan.)

COUNCIL OF MINISTERS

The Council of Ministers comprises the ministers of foreign affairs of member countries, who meet twice a year. The Council may also meet in extraordinary session at the request of member states. The responsibilities of the Council include formulation of policies, assessing progress and confirming new areas of co-operation.

STANDING COMMITTEE

The Committee consists of the secretaries of foreign affairs of member states. It has overall responsibility for the monitoring and co-ordination of programmes and financing, and determines priorities, mobilizes resources and identifies areas of co-operation. It usually meets twice a year, and submits its reports to the Council of Ministers. The Committee is supported by an *ad hoc* Programming Committee made up of senior officials, who meet to examine the budget of the Secretariat, confirm the Calendar of Activities and resolve matters assigned to it by the Standing Committee.

TECHNICAL COMMITTEES

SAARC's Integrated Programme of Action is implemented by seven Technical Committees (reduced from 11 since 2000) covering: Agriculture and rural development; Energy; Environment, meteorology and forestry; Human resource development; Science and technology; Social development; and Transport and communications. Each committee is headed by a representative of a member state and meets annually.

SECRETARIAT

The Secretariat was established in 1987 to co-ordinate and oversee SAARC activities. It comprises the Secretary-General and a Director from each member country. The Secretary-General is appointed by the Council of Ministers, after being nominated by a member state. The ninth summit meeting of heads of state and of government, held in Malé, Maldives, in 1997, extended the Secretary-General's term of office from two to three years. The Director is nominated by member states and appointed by the Secretary-General for a term of three years, although this may be increased in special circumstances.
Secretary-General: Q. A. M. A. Rahim (Bangladesh).

Activities

The first summit meeting of SAARC heads of state and government, held in Dhaka, Bangladesh, in December 1985, resulted in the signing of the Charter of the South Asian Association for Regional Co-operation (SAARC). In August 1993 ministers of foreign affairs of seven countries, meeting in New Delhi, India, adopted a Declaration on South Asian Regional Co-operation and launched an Integrated Programme of Action (IPA), which identified the main areas for regional co-operation. The ninth summit meeting, held in May 1997, authorized the establishment of a Group of Eminent Persons to review the functioning of the IPA. On the basis of the group's recommendations a reconstituted IPA, to be administered by a more efficient arrangement of Technical Committees, was initiated in June 2000.

SAARC is committed to improving quality of life in the region by accelerating economic growth, social progress and cultural development; promoting self-reliance; encouraging mutual assistance; increasing co-operation with other developing countries; and co-operating with other regional and international organizations. The SAARC Charter stipulates that decisions should be made unanimously, and that 'bilateral and contentious issues' should not be discussed. Regular meetings, at all levels, are held to further co-operation in areas covered by the Technical Committees (see above). A priority objective is the eradication of poverty in the region, and in 1993 SAARC endorsed an Agenda of Action to help achieve this. A framework for exchanging information on poverty eradication has also, since, been established. In 1998 the 10th summit meeting resolved to formulate a SAARC Social Charter, which was to incorporate agreed objectives in areas such as poverty eradication, promotion of health and nutrition, and the protection of children. Representatives of civil society, academia, non-governmental organizations and government were to be involved in the process of drafting the Charter, under the auspices of an inter-governmental expert group, which met for the first time in April 2001. The 11th SAARC summit meeting, held in Kathmandu, Nepal, in January 2002, adopted a convention on regional arrangements for the promotion of child welfare in South Asia. The 11th summit also determined to reinvigorate regional poverty reduction activities in the context of the UN General Assembly's Millennium Goal of halving extreme poverty by 2015, and of other internationally-agreed commitments. The summit also urged the development of a regional strategy for preventing and combating HIV/AIDS and other communicable diseases; the SAARC Tuberculosis Centre (see below) was to play a co-ordinating role in this area.

A Committee on Economic Co-operation (CEC), comprising senior trade officials of member states, was established in July 1991 to monitor progress concerning trade and economic co-operation issues. In the same year the summit meeting approved the creation of an inter-governmental group to establish a framework for the promotion of specific trade liberalization measures. A SAARC Chamber of Commerce (SCCI) became operational in 1992, with headquarters in Karachi, Pakistan. (The SCCI headquarters were subsequently transferred to Islamabad, Pakistan.) In April 1993 ministers signed a SAARC Preferential Trading Arrangement (SAPTA), which came into effect in December 1995. The 10th summit meeting proposed a series of measures to accelerate progress in the next round of SAPTA trade negotiations, including a reduction in the domestic content requirements of SAPTA's rules of origin, greater tariff concessions on products being actively traded and the removal of certain discriminatory and non-tariff barriers. By the third, and most recent, round of trade negotiations under SAPTA, held in November 1998, 3,456 products had been identified as eligible for preferential trade tariffs. In December 1995 the Council resolved that the ultimate objective for member states should be the establishment of a South Asian Free Trade Area (SAFTA), superseding SAPTA. An *ad hoc* inter-governmental expert group was constituted to formulate a framework treaty to realize SAFTA. The 11th summit urged that the draft treaty on a regulatory framework for SAFTA be finalized by the end of 2002.

In January 1996 the first SAARC Trade Fair was held, in New Delhi, India, to promote intra-SAARC commerce. At the same time SAARC ministers of commerce convened for their first meeting to discuss regional economic co-operation. A group on customs co-operation was established in 1996 to harmonize trading rules and regulations within the grouping, to simplify trade procedures and to upgrade facilities. In 1999 a regional action plan to harmonize national standards, quality control and measurements came into effect. A second SAARC trade fair was held at Colombo, Sri Lanka, in 1998, and the third was held in Islamabad, Pakistan, in early September 2001. In August 2001 SAARC commerce ministers met, in New Delhi, to discuss a co-ordinated approach to the World Trade Organization negotiations that were held in November.

An Agricultural Information Centre was founded in 1988, in Dhaka, Bangladesh, to serve as a central institution for the dissemination of knowledge and information in the agricultural sector. It maintains a network of centres in each member state, which provide for the efficient exchange of technical information and for strengthening agricultural research. An agreement establishing a Food Security Reserve to meet emergency food requirements was signed in November 1987, and entered into force in August 1988. The Board of the Reserve meets annually to assess the food security of the region. At March 2001 the Reserve contained some 241,580 metric tons of grain. Other regional institutions include the SAARC Tuberculosis Centre in Thimi, Nepal, which opened in July 1992 with the aim of preventing and reducing the prevalence of the disease in the region through the co-ordination of tuberculosis control programmes, research and training; a SAARC Documentation Centre, established in New Delhi in May 1994; and a SAARC Meteorological Research Centre which opened in Dhaka in January 1995. A Human Resources Development Centre was established in Islamabad, Pakistan in 1999. Regional funds include a SAARC-Japan Special Fund established in September 1993. One-half of the fund's resources, which were provided by the Japanese Government, was to be used to finance projects identified by Japan, including workshops and cultural events, and one-half was to be used to finance projects identified by SAARC member states. The eighth SAARC summit meeting, held in New Delhi in May 1996, established a South Asian Development Fund, comprising a Fund for Regional Projects, a Regional Fund and a fund for social development and infrastructure building.

A SAARC Youth Volunteers Programme (SYVOP) enables young people to work in other member countries in the agriculture and forestry sectors. The Programme is part of a series of initiatives designed to promote intra-regional exchanges and contact. A Youth Awards Scheme to reward outstanding achievements by young people was inaugurated in 1996. Founded in 1987, the SAARC Audio-visual Exchange Programme (SAVE) broadcasts radio and television programmes on social and cultural affairs to all member countries, twice a month, in order to disseminate information about SAARC and its members. From 2001 SAVE was to organize an annual SAARC Telefilm festival. The SAARC Consortium of Open and Distance Learning was established in 2000. A Visa Exemption Scheme, exempting 21 specified categories of person from visa requirements, with the aim of promoting closer regional contact, became operational in March 1992. A SAARC citizens forum promotes interaction among the people of South Asia. In addition, SAARC operates a fellowships, scholarships and chairs scheme and a scheme for the promotion of organized tourism.

At the third SAARC summit, held in Kathmandu in November 1987, member states signed a regional convention on measures to counteract terrorism. The convention, which entered into force in August 1988, commits signatory countries to the extradition or prosecution of alleged terrorists and to the implementation of preventative measures to combat terrorism. Monitoring desks for terrorist and drugs offences have been established to process information relating to those activities. The first SAARC conference on co-operation in police affairs, attended by the heads of the police forces of member states, was held in Colombo in July 1996. The conference discussed the issues of terrorism, organized crime, the extradition of criminals, drugs-trafficking and drug abuse. A convention on narcotic drugs and psychotropic substances was signed during the fifth SAARC summit meeting, held in Malé in 1990. The convention entered into force in September 1993, following its ratification by member states. It is implemented by a co-ordination group of drug law enforcement agencies. At the 11th SAARC summit member states adopted a convention on the prevention of trafficking in women and children for prostitution.

SAARC co-operates with other regional and international organizations. In February 1993 SAARC signed a memorandum of understanding with UNCTAD, whereby both parties agreed to exchange information on trade control measures regionally and in 50 developed and developing countries, respectively, in order to increase transparency and thereby facilitate trade. In February 1994 SAARC signed a framework co-operation agreement with ESCAP to enhance co-operation on development issues through a framework of joint studies, workshops and information exchange. A memorandum of understanding with the European Commission was signed in July 1996. SAARC has also signed co-operation agreements with UNICEF (in 1993), the Asia Pacific Telecommunity (1994), UNDP (1995), UNDCP (1995), the International Telecommunication Union (1997), the Canadian International Development Agency (1997), WHO (2000), and UNIFEM (2001). An informal dialogue at ministerial level has been conducted with ASEAN and the European Union since 1998. SAARC and WIPO hold regular consultations concerning regional co-operation on intellectual property rights, and regular consultations are convened with the WTO.

Finance

The national budgets of member countries provide the resources to finance SAARC activities. The Secretariat's annual budget is shared among member states according to a specified formula.

Publications

SAARC News (7/8 a year).
SPECTRUM (irregular).

Regional Apex Bodies

Association of Persons of the Legal Communities of the SAARC Countries—SAARCLAW: Pioneer House, Shahayog Marg, Anamnagar, Kathmandu, Nepal; tel. (1) 221340; fax (1) 226770; e-mail saarclaw@wlink.com.np; internet www.saarclaw.org; f. 1991; recognized as a SAARC regional apex body in July 1994; aims to enhance exchanges and co-operation amongst the legal communities of the sub-region and to promote the development of law; Pres. Laxman Aryal (Nepal); Sec.-Gen. Bharat Raj Upreti (Nepal).

SAARC Chamber of Commerce and Industry—SCCI: House 5, St 59, F-8/4, Islamabad, Pakistan; tel. (51) 2281395; fax (51) 2281390; e-mail saarc@isb.comsats.net.pk; internet www.saarcnet .org; f. 1992; promotes economic and trade co-operation throughout the sub-region and greater interaction between the business communities of member countries; organizes SAARC Economic Co-operation Conferences and Trade Fairs; Pres. Padma Jyoti (Nepal); Sec.-Gen. Abul Hasan.

South Asian Federation of Accountants—SAFA: f. 1984; recognized as a SAARC regional apex body in Jan. 2002; aims to develop regional co-ordination for the accountancy profession.

Other recognized regional bodies include the South Asian Association for Regional Co-operation of Architects, the Association of Management Development Institutions, the SAARC Federation of University Women, the SAARC Association of Town Planners, the SAARC Cardiac Society, the Association of SAARC Speakers and Parliamentarians, the Federation of State Insurance Organizations of SAARC Countries, the Federation of State Insurance Organizations of SAARC Countries, the SAARC Diploma Engineers Forum, the Radiological Society of SAARC Countries, the SAARC Teachers' Federation, the SAARC Surgical Care Society and the Foundation of SAARC Writers and Literature.

SOUTHERN AFRICAN DEVELOPMENT COMMUNITY— SADC

Address: SADC House, Government Enclave, Private Bag 0095, Gaborone, Botswana.

Telephone: 351863; **fax:** 372848; **e-mail:** registry@sadc.int; **internet:** www.sadc.int.

The first Southern African Development Co-ordination Conference (SADCC) was held at Arusha, Tanzania, in July 1979, to harmonize development plans and to reduce the region's economic dependence on South Africa. On 17 August 1992 the 10 member countries of the SADCC signed a treaty establishing the Southern African Development Community (SADC), which replaced the SADCC. The treaty places binding obligations on member countries, with the aim of promoting economic integration towards a fully developed common market. A tribunal was to be established to arbitrate in the case of disputes between member states arising from the treaty. By September 1993 all of the member states had ratified the treaty; it came into effect on 5 October. A protocol on the establishment of the long-envisaged SADC tribunal was adopted in 2000. The Protocol on

Politics, Defence and Security Co-operation, regulating the structure, operations and functions of the Organ on Politics, Defence and Security, established in June 1996 (see under Regional Security), was adopted and opened for signature in August 2001. A troika system, comprising the current, incoming and outgoing SADC chairmanship, operates at the level of the Summit, Council of Ministers and Standing Committee of Officials, and co-ordinates the Organ on Politics, Defence and Security. Other member states may be co-opted into the troika as required. A system of SADC national committees, comprising representatives of government, civil society and the private sector, oversees the implementation of regional programmes at country level and helps to formulate new regional strategies. In recent years SADC institutions have been undergoing a process of intensive restructuring.

MEMBERS

Angola	Malawi	South Africa
Botswana	Mauritius	Swaziland
Congo, Democratic	Mozambique	Tanzania
Republic	Namibia	Zambia
Lesotho	Seychelles	Zimbabwe

Organization

(April 2003)

SUMMIT MEETING

The meeting is held at least once a year and is attended by heads of state and government or their representatives. It is the supreme policy-making organ of the SADC and is responsible for the appointment of the Executive Secretary. A report on the restructuring of the SADC, adopted by an extraordinary summit held in Windhoek, Namibia, in March 2001, recommended that biannual summit meetings should be convened.

COUNCIL OF MINISTERS

Representatives of SADC member countries at ministerial level meet at least once a year.

STANDING COMMITTEE OF OFFICIALS

The Committee, comprising senior officials, usually from the ministry responsible for economic planning or finance, acts as the technical advisory body to the Council. It meets at least once a year. Members of the Committee also act as a national contact point for matters relating to SADC.

SECRETARIAT

Executive Secretary: Dr PAKEREESAMY ('PREGA') RAMSAMY (Mauritius).

The extraordinary summit held in March 2001 determined that the mandate and resources of the Secretariat should be strengthened. A Department of Strategic Planning, Gender and Development and Policy Harmonization was established, comprising permanently-staffed Directorates covering the four priority areas of integration, as follows: trade, industry, finance and investment; infrastructure and services; food, agriculture and natural resources; and social and human development and special programmes. The Community's 21 sectors were to be divided among the new Directorates. An Integrated Committee of Ministers (ICM) was to oversee the four priority areas of integration, monitor the Directorates, facilitate the co-ordination and harmonization of cross-sectoral activities, and provide policy guidance to the Secretariat. The ICM would be responsible to the Council of Ministers.

Activities

In July 1979 the first Southern African Development Co-ordination Conference was attended by delegations from Angola, Botswana, Mozambique, Tanzania and Zambia, with representatives from donor governments and international agencies. In April 1980 a regional economic summit conference was held in Lusaka, Zambia, and the Lusaka Declaration, a statement of strategy entitled 'Southern Africa: Towards Economic Liberation', was approved. The members aimed to reduce their dependence on South Africa for rail and air links and port facilities, imports of raw materials and manufactured goods, and the supply of electric power. In 1985, however, an SADCC report noted that since 1980 the region had become still more dependent on South Africa for its trade outlets, and the 1986 summit meeting, although it recommended the adoption of economic sanctions against South Africa, failed to establish a timetable for doing so.

In January 1992 a meeting of the SADCC Council of Ministers approved proposals to transform the organization (by then expanded to include Lesotho, Malawi, Namibia and Swaziland) into a fully integrated economic community, and in August the treaty establishing the SADC (see above)was signed. An SADC Programme of Action—SPA was to combine the strategies and objectives of the organization's sectoral programmes. (By the end of 2001 nearly 500 projects had been initiated under the SPA.) South Africa became a member of the SADC in August 1994, thus strengthening the objective of regional co-operation and economic integration. Mauritius became a member in August 1995. In September 1997 SADC heads of state agreed to admit the Democratic Republic of the Congo (DRC) and Seychelles as members of the Community.

A possible merger between the SADC and the Preferential Trade Area for Eastern and Southern African States (PTA), which consisted of all the members of the SADC apart from Botswana and had similar aims of enhancing economic co-operation, was rejected by the SADC's Executive Secretary in January 1993. He denied that the two organizations were duplicating each other's work, as had been suggested. However, concerns of regional rivalry with the PTA's successor, the Common Market for Eastern and Southern Africa (COMESA), persisted. In August 1996 an SADC–COMESA ministerial meeting advocated the continued separate functioning of the two organizations. A programme of co-operation between the secretariats of the SADC and COMESA, aimed at reducing all duplication of roles between the two organizations, was ongoing in 2003. A co-ordinating SADC/COMESA task force was established in 2001.

In September 1994 the first meeting of ministers of foreign affairs of the SADC and the European Union (EU) was held in Berlin, Germany. The two sides agreed to establish working groups to promote closer trade, political, regional and economic co-operation. In particular, a declaration issued from the meeting specified joint objectives, including a reduction of exports of weapons to southern Africa and of the arms trade within the region, promotion of investment in the region's manufacturing sector and support for democracy at all levels. A consultative meeting between representatives of the SADC and EU was held in February 1995, in Lilongwe, Malawi, at which both groupings resolved to strengthen security in the southern African region. A second SADC–EU ministerial meeting, held in Namibia in October 1996, endorsed a Regional Indicative Programme to enhance co-operation between the two organizations over the next five years. The third ministerial meeting took place in Vienna, Austria, in November 1998. In September 1999 the SADC signed a co-operation agreement with the US Government, which incorporated measures to promote US investment in the region, and commitments to support HIV/AIDS assessment and prevention programmes and to assist member states to develop environmental protection capabilities. The fourth SADC–EU ministerial meeting, convened in Gaborone, Botswana, in November 2000, adopted a joint declaration on the control of small arms and light weapons in the SADC region. The meeting also emphasized that the termination of illicit trading in diamonds would be a major contributory factor in resolving the ongoing conflicts in Angola and the DRC (see below). The fifth SADC-EU ministerial meeting was held in Maputo, Mozambique, in November 2002.

In April 1997 the SADC announced the establishment of a Parliamentary Forum to promote democracy, human rights and good governance throughout the region. Membership was to be open to national parliaments of all SADC countries, and was to offer fair representation for women. Representatives were to serve for a period of five years. The Parliamentary Forum, with its headquarters in Windhoek, Namibia, was to receive funds from member parliaments, governments and charitable and international organizations. In September SADC heads of state endorsed the establishment of the Forum as an autonomous institution. A regional women's parliamentary caucus was inaugurated in April 2002.

In 2001 the recommendations of the report on the restructuring of the SADC's institutions, adopted by an extraordinary summit meeting convened in March, were being implemented, in order to facilitate the effective application of the objectives of the organization's treaty and of the SPA. The Community's sectoral system was being reorganized under four new directorates: trade, industry, finance and investment; infrastructure and services; food, agriculture and natural resources; and social and human development and special programmes. These were to be administered from the secretariat in Gaborone to ensure greater efficiency (the previous system of directorates had been decentralized). The report outlined a common agenda for the organization, which covered the promotion of poverty reduction measures and of sustainable and equitable socio-economic development, promotion of democratic political values and systems, and the consolidation of peace and security. The extraordinary summit meeting held in March 2001 authorized the establishment of an integrated ministerial committee mandated to formulate a five-year Regional Indicative Strategic Development Plan.

In August 2001 the SADC established a task force, comprising representatives of five member countries, to address the ongoing political crisis in Zimbabwe. The Community sent two separate observer teams to monitor the controversial presidential election held in Zimbabwe in March 2002; the SADC Council of Ministers team found the election to have been conducted freely and fairly, while the Parliamentary Forum group was reluctant to endorse the poll. Having evaluated both reports, the Community approved the election.

REGIONAL SECURITY

In November 1994 SADC ministers of defence, meeting in Arusha, Tanzania, approved the establishment of a regional rapid-deployment peace-keeping force, which could be used to contain regional conflicts or civil unrest in member states. In April 1997 a training programme was held, which aimed to inform troops from nine SADC countries of UN peace-keeping doctrines, procedures and strategies. The exercise took place in Zimbabwe at a cost of US $900,000, provided by the British Government and the Zimbabwe National Army. A peace-keeping exercise involving 4,000 troops was held in South Africa, in April 1999. An SADC Mine Action Committee has been established to monitor and co-ordinate the process of removing anti-personnel land devices from countries in the region.

In June 1996 SADC heads of state and government, meeting in Gaborone, Botswana, inaugurated a new Organ on Politics, Defence and Security, which was expected to enhance co-ordination of national policies and activities in these areas. The objectives of the body were, *inter alia* to safeguard the people and development of the region against instability arising from civil disorder, inter-state conflict and external aggression; to undertake conflict prevention, management and resolution activities, by mediating in inter-state and intra-state disputes and conflicts, pre-empting conflicts through an early-warning system and using diplomacy and peace-keeping to achieve sustainable peace; to promote the development of a common foreign policy, in areas of mutual interest, and the evolution of common political institutions; to develop close co-operation between the police and security services of the region; and to encourage the observance of universal human rights, as provided for in the charters of the UN and OAU (now African Union—AU). In October the Organ convened, at summit level, to consider measures to promote the peace process in Angola; however, there were disagreements within SADC regarding its future status, either as an integrated part of the Community (favoured by South Africa) or as a more autonomous body (supported by Zimbabwe).

In August 1998 the Zimbabwean Government convened a meeting of the heads of state of seven SADC member states to discuss the escalation of civil conflict in the DRC and the threat to regional security, with Rwanda and Uganda reportedly having sent troops to assist anti-government forces. Later in that month ministers of defence and defence officials of several SADC countries declared their support for an initiative of the Zimbabwean Government to send military assistance to the forces loyal to President Kabila in the DRC. South Africa, which did not attend the meeting, rejected any military intervention under SADC auspices and insisted that the organization would pursue a diplomatic initiative. Zimbabwe, Angola and Namibia proceeded to send troops and logistical support to counter rebel Congolese forces. The Presidents of those countries failed to attend an emergency meeting of heads of state, convened by President Mandela of South Africa, which called for an immediate cease-fire and presented a 10-point-peace plan. A further emergency meeting, held in early September and attended by all SADC leaders, agreed to pursue negotiations for a peaceful settlement of the conflict. Some unity within the grouping was restored by Mandela's endorsement of the objective of supporting Kabila as the legitimate leader in the DRC. Furthermore, at the annual SADC summit meeting, held in Mauritius, it was agreed that discussion of the report on the security Organ, scheduled to have been presented to the conference, would be deferred to a specially convened summit meeting (although no date was agreed). Talks attended by Angola, the DRC, Namibia, Rwanda, Uganda, Zambia and Zimbabwe, conducted in mid-September, in Victoria Falls, agreed in principle on a cease-fire in the DRC but failed to conclude a detailed peace accord. Fighting continued to escalate, and in October Zimbabwe, Angola and Namibia resolved to send reinforcements to counter the advancing rebel forces. Meanwhile, in September representatives of the SADC attempted to mediate between government and opposition parties in Lesotho amidst a deteriorating security situation in that country. At the end of the month, following an attempt by the Lesotho military to seize power, South Africa, together with Botswana, sent troops into Lesotho to restore civil order. The operation, which was declared to have been conducted under SADC auspices, prompted widespread criticism owing to the troops' involvement in heavy fighting with opposition forces. A committee was established by SADC to secure a cease-fire in Lesotho. Also at the end of September SADC chiefs of staff agreed that the Community would assist the Angolan Government to eliminate the UNITA movement, owing to its adverse impact on the region's security. In October an SADC ministerial team, comprising representatives of South Africa,

Botswana, Mozambique and Zimbabwe, negotiated an accord between the opposing sides in Lesotho providing for the conduct of democratic elections. The withdrawal of foreign troops from Lesotho was initiated at the end of April 1999, and was reported to have been completed by mid-May.

During the first half of 1999 Zambia's President Chiluba pursued efforts, under SADC auspices, to negotiate a political solution to the conflict in the DRC. Troops from the region, in particular from Angola and Zimbabwe, remained actively involved in the struggle to uphold Kabila's administration. SADC ministers of defence and of foreign affairs convened in Lusaka, in June, in order to secure a cease-fire agreement. An accord was finally signed in July between Kabila, leaders of the rebel forces and foreign allies of both sides. All foreign troops were to be withdrawn within nine months according to a schedule to be drawn up by the UN, OAU and a Joint Military Commission. However, the disengagement and redeployment of troops from front-line positions did not commence until February 2001. The SADC welcomed peace accords signed by the DRC Government with Ugandan-backed rebels and with the Rwandan Government, respectively in April and July 2002. In August 2001 SADC heads of state resolved to support the continuing imposition of sanctions by the UN Security Council against the UNITA rebels in Angola; it was agreed to promote the international certification system for illicit trade in rough diamonds (believed to finance UNITA's activities), to install mobile radar systems that would detect illegal cross-border flights in the region, and to establish a body to compile information and to devise a strategy for terminating the supply of petroleum products to UNITA. The SADC welcomed the cease-fire that was signed by the Angolan Government and UNITA in April 2002.

In August 2000 proposals were announced (strongly supported by South Africa, see above) to develop the Organ for Politics, Defence and Security as a substructure of the SADC, with subdivisions for defence and international diplomacy, to be chaired by a member country's head of state, working within a troika system; these were approved at the extraordinary summit held in March 2001. A Protocol on Politics, Defence and Security Co-operation, regulating the structure, operations and functions of the Organ, was adopted and opened for signature in August. The protocol was to be implemented by an Inter-state Politics and Diplomacy Committee.

The March 2001 extraordinary SADC summit adopted a Declaration on Small Arms, promoting the curtailment of the proliferation of and illicit trafficking in light weapons in the region. A Protocol on Firearms, Ammunition and Other Related Materials has also been adopted. In July SADC ministers of defence approved a draft regional defence pact, providing for a mechanism to prevent conflict involving member countries and for member countries to unite against outside aggression. In January 2002 an extraordinary summit of SADC heads of state, held in Blantyre, Malawi, adopted a Declaration against Terrorism. An SADC peace-keeping exercise was conducted in February 2002 in Tanzania, jointly with Tanzanian and Ugandan forces.

INFRASTRUCTURE AND SERVICES

At the SADC's inception transport was seen as the most important area to be developed, on the grounds that, as the Lusaka Declaration noted, without the establishment of an adequate regional transport and communications system, other areas of co-operation become impractical. Priority was to be given to the improvement of road and railway services into Mozambique, so that the landlocked countries of the region could transport their goods through Mozambican ports instead of South African ones. The Southern African Transport and Communications Commission (SATCC) was established, in Maputo, Mozambique, in order to undertake the SADC's activities in this sector. During 1995 the SATCC undertook a study of regional transport and communications to provide a comprehensive framework and strategy for future courses of action. A task force was also established to identify measures to simplify procedures at border crossings throughout southern Africa. In 1996 the SATCC Road Network Management and Financing Task Force was established. An SADC Transport Investment Forum was convened in Windhoek, Namibia, in April 2001. In March the Association of Southern African National Road Agencies (ASANRA) was established to foster the development of an integrated regional transportation system. Eleven railways in the region form the Interconnected Regional Rail Network (IRRN), comprising nearly 34,000km of route track.

The SADC's development projects in the transport and communications sector have aimed to address missing links and over-stretched sections of the regional network, as well as to improve efficiency, operational co-ordination and human resource development, such as management training projects. Other sectoral objectives have been to ensure the compatibility of technical systems within the region and to promote the harmonization of regulations relating to intra-regional traffic and trade. In 1997 Namibia announced plans, supported by the SADC, to establish a rail link with Angola in order to form a trade route similar to that created in

Mozambique, on the western side of southern Africa. In March 1998 the final stage of the trans-Kalahari highway, linking ports on the east and west coasts of southern Africa, was officially opened. In July 1999 a 317-km rail link between Bulawayo, Zimbabwe, and the border town of Beitbridge, administered by the SADC as its first build-operate-transfer project, was opened.

The SADC promotes greater co-operation in the civil aviation sector, in order to improve efficiency and to reverse a steady decline in the region's airline industries. Within the telecommunications sector efforts have been made to increase the capacity of direct exchange lines and international subscriber dialling (ISD) services. In January 1997 the Southern African Telecommunications Regional Authority (SATRA), a regulatory authority, was established. SADC policy guide-lines on 'making information and communications technology a priority in turning the SADC into an information-based economy' were adopted in November 2001. Policy guide-lines and model regulations on tariffs for telecommunications services have also been adopted. An SADC Expedited Mail Service operates in the postal services sector. The SATCC's Technical Unit oversees the region's meteorological services and issues a regular *Drought-Watch for Southern Africa* bulletin, a monthly *Drought Overview* bulletin and forewarnings of impending natural disasters. The SADC is developing a regional strategy aimed at improving the early warning capabilities of national meteorological services

The tourism sector operates within the context of national and regional socio-economic development objectives. It comprises four components: tourism product development; tourism marketing and research; tourism services; and human resources development and training. The SADC has promoted tourism for the region at trade fairs in Europe, and has initiated a project to provide a range of promotional material and a regional tourism directory. In 1993 the Council approved the implementation of a project to design a standard grading classification system for tourist accommodation in the region, which had been completed with the assistance of the World Tourism Organization. In September 1997 the legal charter for the establishment of a new Regional Tourism Organization for Southern Africa (RETOSA), to be administered jointly by SADC officials and private-sector operators, was signed by ministers of tourism. RETOSA assists member states to formulate tourism promotion policies and strategies. During 1999 a feasibility study on the development of the Upper Zambezi basin as a site for eco-tourism was initiated. Consultations are under way on the development of a common visa (UNIVISA) system to promote tourism in the region.

Areas of activity in the energy sector include: joint petroleum exploration, training programmes for the petroleum sector and studies for strategic fuel storage facilities; promotion of the use of coal; development of hydroelectric power and the co-ordination of SADC generation and transmission capacities; new and renewable sources of energy, including pilot projects in solar energy; assessment of the environmental and socio-economic impact of wood-fuel scarcity and relevant education programmes; and energy conservation. In July 1995 SADC energy ministers approved the establishment of the Southern African Power Pool, whereby all member states were to be linked into a single electricity grid. (Several grids are already integrated and others are being rehabilitated.) At the same time, ministers endorsed a protocol to promote greater co-operation in energy development within the SADC, providing for the establishment of an Energy Commission, responsible for 'demand-side' management, pricing, ensuring private-sector involvement and competition, training and research, collecting information, etc. The energy sector administers a joint SADC Petroleum Exploration Programme. In September 1997 heads of state endorsed an Energy Action Plan to proceed with the implementation of co-operative policies and strategies in four key areas of energy: trade, information exchange, training and organizational capacity-building, and investment and financing. A technical unit of the Energy Commission was to be responsible for implementation of the Action Plan.

FOOD, AGRICULTURE AND NATURAL RESOURCES

The food, agriculture and natural resources directorate combines the following sectors: agricultural research and training; inland fisheries; forestry; wildlife; marine fisheries and resources; food security; livestock production and animal disease control; environment and land management; and water. According to SADC figures, agriculture contributes one-third of the region's GNP, accounts for about one-quarter of total earnings of foreign exchange and employs some 80% of the labour force. The principal objectives in this field are regional food security, agricultural development and natural resource development.

The Southern African Centre for Co-operation in Agricultural Research (SACCAR), was established in Gaborone, Botswana, in 1985. It aims to strengthen national agricultural research systems, in order to improve management, increase productivity, promote the development and transfer of technology to assist local farmers, and improve training. Examples of activity include: a sorghum and millet improvement programme; a land and water management research programme; a root crop research network; agroforestry research, implemented in Malawi, Tanzania, Zambia and Zimbabwe; and a grain legume improvement programme, comprising separate research units for groundnuts, beans and cowpeas. The SADC's Plant Genetic Resources Centre was established in 1988, near Lusaka, Zambia, to collect, conserve and utilize indigenous and exotic plant genetic resources and to develop appropriate management practices.

The sector for livestock production and animal disease control has aimed to improve breeding methods in the region through the Management of Farm Animal Genetic Research Programme. It also seeks to control diseases such as contagious bovine pleuro-pneumonia, foot and mouth disease and heartwater through diagnosis, monitoring and vaccination programmes. An *Animal Health Mortality Bulletin* is published, as is a monthly *Animal Disease Situation Bulletin*, which alerts member states to outbreaks of disease in the region.

The SADC aims to promote inland and marine fisheries as an important, sustainable source of animal protein. Marine fisheries are also considered to be a potential source of income of foreign exchange. In May 1993 the first formal meeting of SADC ministers of marine fisheries convened in Namibia, and it was agreed to hold annual meetings. In April 1997 it was agreed that Namibia would co-ordinate the establishment of inspectorates to monitor and control marine fisheries in the region for a period of five years. The development of fresh water fisheries is focused on aquaculture projects, and their integration into rural community activities. The environment and land management sector is concerned with sustainability as an essential quality of development. It aims to protect and improve the health, environment and livelihoods of people living in the southern African region; to preserve the natural heritage and biodiversity of the region; and to support regional economic development on a sustainable basis. The sector also focuses on capacity-building, training, regional co-operation and the exchange of information in all areas related to the environment and land management. It administers an SADC Environmental Exchange Network and the Community's Land Degradation and Desertification Control Programme. The sector also undertakes projects for the conservation and sustainable development of forestry and wildlife. In 1999 the Protocol on Wildlife Conservation and Law Enforcement was adopted by SADC heads of state.

Under the food security programme, the Regional Early Warning Unit aims to anticipate and prevent food shortages through the provision of information relating to the food security situation in member states. As a result of the drought crisis experience, SADC member states have agreed to inform the food security sector of their food and non-food requirements on a regular basis, in order to assess the needs of the region as a whole. A regional food reserve project was also to be developed. In June 2002 the SADC predicted a regional cereals deficit of 5.3m. metric tons for 2002/03, owing to both severe drought and flooding, and estimated that 12.8m. people throughout the region would require food assistance by March 2003, mainly in Lesotho, Malawi, Mozambique, Swaziland, Zambia and Zimbabwe. The SADC Regional Disaster Response Task Force recommended a number of strategies for managing the situation.

Following the severe drought in the region in 1991/92, the need for water resource development became a priority. The water sector was established as a separate administrative unit in August 1996, although the terms of reference of the sector were only formally approved by the Council, meeting in Windhoek, Namibia, in February 1997. The sector aims to promote the equitable distribution and effective management of water resources. In April a workshop was held in Swaziland concerning the implementation of a new SADC Protocol on Shared Watercourse Systems. A regional strategic action plan for integrated water resources development and management in the SADC region was being implemented during 1999–2004.

TRADE, INDUSTRY, FINANCE AND INVESTMENT

Under the treaty establishing the SADC, efforts were to be undertaken to achieve regional economic integration. The trade and industry sector aims to facilitate this by the creation of an enabling investment and trade environment in SADC countries, the establishment of a single regional market, by progressively removing barriers to the movement of goods, services and people, and the promotion of cross-border investment. The sector supports programmes for industrial research and development and standardization and quality assurance. The sector of finance and investment was established to mobilize industrial investment resources and to co-ordinate economic policies and the development of the financial sector. During 1995 work continued on the preparation of two protocols on trade co-operation and finance and investment, which were to provide the legal framework for integration. In August 1996 SADC member states signed the Protocol on Trade, providing for the establishment of a regional free-trade area, through the gradual elimination of tariff barriers over an eight-year period, at a summit meeting held in Lesotho. (Angola, the DRC and Seychelles are not signatories to the Protocol.) In September 1999 representatives of the private sector in SADC member states, meeting in Mauritius, agreed to establish an Association of SADC Chambers of Commerce. The Protocol on Trade entered into force in January 2000, and an Amendment Protocol on Trade was adopted in August, incorporating renegotiated technical details on the gradual elimination of tariffs, rules of origin, customs co-operation, special industry arrangements and dispute settlement procedures. The implementation phase of the Protocol on Trade commenced in September. In accordance with a revised schedule, all intra-SADC trade tariffs were to be removed by 2012, with about 85% to be withdrawn by 2008. Annual meetings are convened to review the work of expert teams in the areas of standards, quality, assurance, accreditation and metrology.

The mining sector contributes about 10% of the SADC region's annual GDP. The principal objective of the SADC's programme of action on mining is to stimulate increased local and foreign investment in the sector, through the assimilation and dissemination of data, prospecting activities, and participation in promotional fora. In December 1994 the SADC held a mining forum, jointly with the EU, in Lusaka, Zambia, with the aim of demonstrating to potential investors and promoters the possibilities of mining exploration in the region. A second mining investment forum was held in Lusaka in December 1998. A further SADC-EU mining investment forum ('Mines 2000') was held in Lusaka, Zambia, in October 2000. Subsequently a Mines 2000 follow-up programme has been implemented. Other objectives of the mining sector are the improvement of industry training, increasing the contribution of small-scale mining, reducing the illicit trade in gemstones and gold, increasing co-operation in mineral exploration and processing, and minimizing the adverse impact of mining operations on the environment. At the summit meeting, held in September 1997, SADC heads of state signed a protocol providing for the harmonization of policies and programmes relating to the development and exploitation of mineral resources in the region. Experts from SADC countries have participated in technical meetings convened to consider recommendations on the international certification of rough diamonds, as proposed by the UN General Assembly. (The illicit trade in so-called 'conflict diamonds' and other minerals is believed to have motivated and financed many incidences of rebel activity in the continent, for example in Angola and the DRC.) In August 2001 SADC heads of state determined to promote the international certification system.

In July 1998 a Banking Association was officially constituted by representatives of SADC member states. The Association was to establish international banking standards and regional payments systems, organize training and harmonize banking legislation in the region. In April 1999 governors of SADC central banks determined to strengthen and harmonize banking procedures and technology in order to facilitate the financial integration of the region. Efforts to harmonize stock exchanges in the region were also initiated in 1999.

SOCIAL AND HUMAN DEVELOPMENT AND SPECIAL PROGRAMMES

The SADC helps to supply the region's requirements in skilled manpower by providing training in the following categories: high-level managerial personnel; agricultural managers; high- and medium-level technicians; artisans; and instructors. The Technical Committee on Accreditation and Certification aims to harmonize and strengthen the education and training systems in the SADC through initiatives such as the standardization of curricula and examinations. The human resources development sector aims to determine active labour market information systems and institutions in the region, improve education policy analysis and formulation, and address issues of teaching and learning materials in the region. It administers an Intra-regional Skills Development Programme. The sector has initiated a programme of distance education to enable greater access to education, and operates the SADC's scholarship and training awards programme. In September 1997 heads of state, meeting in Blantyre, Malawi, endorsed the establishment of a Gender Department within the Secretariat to promote the advancement and education of women. A Declaration on Gender and Development was adopted. At the same time representatives of all member countries (except Angola) signed a Protocol on Education and Training, which was to provide a legal framework

for co-operation in this sector; this entered into force in July 2000. In 2001 a gender audit study of aspects of the SADC SPA was finalized. An SADC regional human development report for 2000 was published in 2001 by UNDP and the Southern African Regional Institute for Policy Studies. SADC has adopted a Protocol on Combating Illicit Drugs, and operates a regional drugs control programme, funded by the EU. In October 2000 an SADC Epidemiological Network on Drug Use was established to enable the systematic collection of narcotics-related data.

In August 1999 an SADC protocol on health was adopted. The SADC has adopted a strategic framework (2000-04) and programme of action for tackling HIV/AIDS, which are endemic in the region. In December 1999 a multisectoral sub-committee on HIV/AIDS was established. In August 2000 the SADC adopted a set of guide-lines to underpin any future negotiations with major pharmaceutical companies on improving access to and reducing the cost of drugs to combat HIV/AIDS. The SADC is implementing a Southern African Tuberculosis Control Initiative (SATCI); the SATCI TB/HIV Co-ordinator took office in February 2001. In May 2000 an SADC Malaria Task Force was established.

The employment and labour sector was founded in 1996. It seeks to promote employment and harmonize legislation concerning labour and social protection. Its activities include: the implementation of International Labour Standards, the improvement of health and safety standards in the workplace, combating child labour and the establishment of a statistical database for employment and labour issues.

A culture and information sector was established in 1990. Following the ratification of the treaty establishing the Community, the sector was expected to emphasize regional socio-cultural development as part of the process of greater integration. The SADC Press Trust was established, in Harare, Zimbabwe, to disseminate information about the SADC and to articulate the concerns and priorities of the region. Public education initiatives have commenced to encourage the involvement of people in the process of regional integration and development, as well as to promote democratic and human rights' values. A new project, 'Information 21', is to be implemented under the sector, in collaboration with the SADC secretariat and the Southern African Research and Documentation Centre, with the aim of promoting community-building and greater participation in decision-making at all levels of government. In 1994 the SADC Festival on Arts and Culture project was initiated. In connection with this, South Africa was to organize an interdisciplinary festival of arts and culture in 2002. In May 2000 ministers of arts and culture meeting in Lilongwe, Malawi, proposed that inter-disciplinary and monodisciplinary festivals should be alternated on a two-yearly basis. Thus it was decided that the following mono-disciplinary festivals should be held: music (2004); theatre (2008) and visual arts (2012). An SADC Cultural Fund was established in 1996. A draft SADC protocol on piracy and protection of copyright and neighbouring rights has been prepared.

Finance

The SADC's administrative budget for 2002–03, approved by the Council in February 2002, amounted to US $12.8m., to be financed mainly by contributions from member states. At June 2001 members reportedly owed some $10.2m. in unpaid arrears.

Publications

Quarterly Food Security Bulletin.
SACCAR Newsletter (quarterly).
SADC Annual Report.
SADC Energy Bulletin.
SADC Today (six a year).
SATCC Bulletin (quarterly).
SKILLS.
SPLASH.

SOUTHERN COMMON MARKET— MERCOSUR/MERCOSUL

(MERCADO COMÚN DEL SUR/MERCADO COMUM DO SUL)

Address: Edif. Mercosur, Luis Piera 1992, 1°, 11200 Montevideo, Uruguay.

Telephone: (2) 412-9024; **fax:** (2) 418-0557; **e-mail:** sam@mercosur .org.uy; **internet:** www.mercosur.org.uy.

Mercosur (known as Mercosul in Portuguese) was established in March 1991 by the heads of state of Argentina, Brazil, Paraguay and Uruguay with the signature of the Treaty of Asunción. The primary objective of the Treaty is to achieve the economic integration of member states by means of a free flow of goods and services between member states, the establishment of a common external tariff, the adoption of common commercial policy, and the co-ordination of macroeconomic and sectoral policies. The Ouro Preto Protocol, which was signed in December 1994, conferred on Mercosur the status of an international legal entity with the authority to sign agreements with third countries, group of countries and international organizations.

MEMBERS

Argentina	Brazil	Paraguay	Uruguay

Chile and Bolivia are associate members.

Organization

(April 2003)

COMMON MARKET COUNCIL

The Common Market Council (Consejo del Mercado Común) is the highest organ of Mercosur and is responsible for leading the integration process and for taking decisions in order to achieve the objectives of the Asunción Treaty.

COMMON MARKET GROUP

The Common Market Group (Grupo Mercado Común) is the executive body of Mercosur and is responsible for implementing concrete measures to further the integration process.

TRADE COMMISSION

The Trade Commission (Comisión de Comercio del Mercosur) has competence for the area of joint commercial policy and, in particular, is responsible for monitoring the operation of the common external tariff (see below). The Brasília Protocol may be referred to for the resolution of trade disputes between member states.

JOINT PARLIAMENTARY COMMISSION

The Joint Parliamentary Commission (Comisión Parlamentaria Conjunta) is made up of parliamentarians from the member states and is charged with accelerating internal national procedures to implement Mercosur decisions, including the harmonization of country legislation.

CONSULTATIVE ECONOMIC AND SOCIAL FORUM

The Consultative Economic and Social Forum (Foro Consultivo Económico-Social) comprises representatives from the business community and trade unions in the member countries and has a consultative role in relation to Mercosur.

ADMINISTRATIVE SECRETARIAT

Director: REGINALDO BRAGA ARCURI (Brazil).

Activities

Mercosur's free-trade zone entered into effect on 1 January 1995, with tariffs removed from 85% of intra-regional trade. A regime of gradual removal of duties on a list of special products was agreed, with Argentina and Brazil given four years to complete this process while Paraguay and Uruguay were allowed five years. Regimes governing intra-zonal trade in the automobile and sugar sectors remained to be negotiated. Mercosur's customs union also came into force at the start of 1995, comprising a common external tariff of 0%–20%. A list of exceptions from the common external tariff was also agreed; these products were to lose their special status and be subject to the general tariff system concerning foreign goods by 2006. The value of intra-Mercosur trade was estimated to have tripled during the period 1991–95 and was reported to have amounted to US \$20,400m. in 1998. However, intra-subregional trade was reported to have declined to \$15,200m. in 1999, stabilizing at about 15,000m. in 2000. The financial crisis that escalated in Argentina during late 2001 had a detrimental effect on intra-Mercosur trade.

In December 1995 Mercosur presidents affirmed the consolidation of free trade as Mercosur's 'permanent and most urgent goal'. To this end they agreed to prepare norms of application for Mercosur's customs code, accelerate paper procedures and increase the connections between national computerized systems. It was also agreed to increase co-operation in the areas of agriculture, industry, mining, energy, communications, transport and tourism, and finance. At this meeting Argentina and Brazil reached an accord aimed at overcoming their dispute regarding the trade in automobiles between the two countries. They agreed that cars should have a minimum of 60% domestic components and that Argentina should be allowed to complete its balance of exports of cars to Brazil, which had earlier imposed a unilateral quota on the import of Argentine cars. In June 1995 Mercosur ministers responsible for the environment agreed to harmonize environmental legislation and to form a permanent sub-group of Mercosur

In May 1996 Mercosur parliamentarians met with the aim of harmonizing legislation on patents in member countries. In December Mercosur heads of state, meeting in Fortaleza, Brazil, approved agreements on harmonizing competition practices (by 2001), integrating educational opportunities for post-graduates and human resources training, standardizing trading safeguards applied against third-country products (by 2001) and providing for intra-regional cultural exchanges. An Accord on Subregional Air Services was signed at the meeting (including by the heads of state of Bolivia and Chile) to liberalize civil transport throughout the region. In addition, the heads of state endorsed texts on consumer rights that were to be incorporated into a Mercosur Consumers' Defence Code, and agreed to consider the establishment of a bank to finance the integration and development of the region.

In June 1996 the Joint Parliamentary Commission agreed that Mercosur should endorse a 'Democratic Guarantee Clause', whereby a country would be prevented from participation in Mercosur unless democratic, accountable institutions were in place. The clause was adopted by Mercosur heads of state at the summit meeting held in San Luis de Mendoza, Argentina, later in the month. The presidents approved the entry into Mercosur of Bolivia and Chile as associate members. An Economic Complementation Accord with Bolivia, which includes Bolivia in Mercosur's free-trade zone, but not in the customs union, was signed in December 1995 and was to come into force on 1 January 1997. In December 1996 the Accord was extended until 30 April 1997, when a free-trade zone between Bolivia and Mercosur was to become operational. Measures of the free-trade agreement, which was signed in October 1996, were to be implemented over a transitional period commencing on 28 February 1997 (revised from 1 January). Chile's Economic Complementation Accord with Mercosur entered into effect on 1 October 1996, with duties on most products to be removed over a 10-year period (Chile's most sensitive products were given 18 years for complete tariff elimination). Chile was also to remain outside the customs union, but was to be involved in other integration projects, in particular infrastructure projects designed to give Mercosur countries access to both the Atlantic and Pacific Oceans (Chile's Pacific coast was regarded as Mercosur's potential link to the economies of the Far East).

In June 1997 the first meeting of tax administrators and customs officials of Mercosur member countries was held, with the aim of enhancing information exchange and promoting joint customs inspections. During 1997 Mercosur's efforts towards regional economic integration were threatened by Brazil's adverse external trade balance and its Government's measures to counter the deficit, which included the imposition of import duties on certain products. In November the Brazilian Government announced that it was to increase its import tariff by 3%, in a further effort to improve its external balance. The measure was endorsed by Argentina as a means of maintaining regional fiscal stability. The new external tariff, which was to remain in effect until 31 December 2000, was formally adopted by Mercosur heads of state at a meeting held in Montevideo, Uruguay, in December 1997. At the summit meeting a separate Protocol was signed providing for the liberalization of trade in services and government purchases over a 10-year period. In order to strengthen economic integration throughout the region, Mercosur leaders agreed that Chile, while still not a full member of the organization, be integrated into the Mercosur political structure, with equal voting rights. In December 1998 Mercosur heads of state agreed on the establishment of an arbitration mechanism for disputes between members, and on measures to standardize human, animal and plant health and safety regulations throughout the grouping. In March 1998 the ministers of the interior of Mercosur countries, together with representatives of the Governments of Chile and Bolivia, agreed to implement a joint security arrangement for the border region linking Argentina, Paraguay and Brazil. In particular, the initiative aimed to counter drugs-trafficking, money-laundering and other illegal activities in the area.

Tensions within Mercosur were compounded in January 1999 owing to economic instability in Brazil and its Government's decision effectively to devalue the national currency, the real. In March the grouping's efforts at integration were further undermined by political instability in Paraguay. As a consequence of the devaluation of its currency, Brazil's important automotive industry became increasingly competitive, to the detriment of that of Argentina. In April Argentina imposed tariffs on imports of Brazilian steel and, in July, the Argentine authorities approved a decree permitting restrictions on all imports from neighbouring countries, in order to protect local industries, prompting Brazil to suspend negotiations to resolve the trading differences between the two countries. Argentina withdrew the decree a few days later, but reiterated its demand for some form of temporary safeguards on certain products as compensation for their perceived loss of competitiveness resulting from the devalued real. An extraordinary meeting of the Common Market Council was convened, at Brazil's request, in August, in order to discuss the dispute, as well as measures to mitigate the effects of economic recession throughout the sub-region. However, little progress was made and the bilateral trade dispute continued to undermine Mercosur. Argentina imposed new restrictions on textiles and footwear, while, in September, Brazil withdrew all automatic import licences for Argentine products, which were consequently to be subject to the same quality control, sanitary measures and accounting checks applied to imports from non-Mercosur countries. The volume of intra-Mercosur trade shrank during 1999 as a consequence of the continuing dispute. In January 2000, however, the Argentine and Brazilian Governments agreed to refrain from adopting potentially divisive unilateral measures and resolved to accelerate negotiations on the resolution of ongoing differences. In March Mercosur determined to promote and monitor private accords to cover the various areas of contention, and also established a timetable for executing a convergence of regional macroeconomic policies. In June Argentina and Brazil signed a bilateral automobile agreement; however, a new sectoral trade regime failed to be approved by the summit meeting held later in that month. The Motor Vehicle Agreement, incorporating new tariffs and a nationalization index, was endorsed by all Mercosur leaders at a meeting convened in Florianopolis, Brazil, in December. The significant outcome of that meeting was the approval of criteria, formulated by Mercosur finance ministers and central bank governors, determining monetary and fiscal targets to achieve economic convergence. Annual inflation rates were to be no higher than 5% in 2002–05, and reduced to 4% in 2006 and 3% from 2007 (with an exception for Paraguay). Public debt was to be reduced to 40% of GDP by 2010, and fiscal deficits were to be reduced to no more than 3% of GDP by 2002. The targets aimed to promote economic stability throughout the region, as well as to reduce competitive disparities affecting the unity of the grouping. The Florianopolis summit meeting also recommended the formulation of social indicators to facilitate achieving targets in the reduction of poverty and the elimination of child labour. However, political debate surrounding the meeting was dominated by the Chilean Government's announcement that it had initiated bilateral free-trade discussions with the USA, which was considered, in particular by the Brazilian authorities, to undermine Mercosur's unified position at multilateral free-trade negotiations. Procedures to incorporate Chile as a full member of Mercosur were suspended.

In early 2001 Argentina imposed several emergency measures to strengthen its domestic economy, in contradiction of Mercosur's external tariffs. In March Brazil was reported to have accepted the measures, which included an elimination of tariffs on capital goods and an increase in import duties on consumer goods, as an exceptional temporary trade regime; this position was reversed by mid-2001 following Argentina's decision to exempt certain countries from import tariffs. In February 2002, at a third extraordinary meeting of the Common Market Council, held in Buenos Aires, Argentina, Mercosur heads of state expressed their support for Argentina's

application to receive international financial assistance, in the wake of that country's economic crisis. Although there were fears that the crisis might curb trade and stall economic growth across the region, Argentina's adoption of a floating currency made the prospect of currency harmonization between Mercosur member countries appear more viable. During the meeting it was also agreed that a permanent panel to consider trade disputes would be established in Asunción, Paraguay, comprising one legal representative from each of Mercosur's four member countries, plus one 'consensus' member. In December 2002 Mercosur ministers of justice signed an agreement permitting citizens of Mercosur member and associate member states to reside in any other Mercosur state, initially for a two-year period.

EXTERNAL RELATIONS

In December 1995 Mercosur and the EU signed a framework agreement for commercial and economic co-operation, which provided for co-operation in the economic, trade, industrial, scientific, institutional and cultural fields and the promotion of wider political dialogue on issues of mutual interest. In June 1997 Mercosur heads of state, convened in Asunción, reaffirmed the group's intention to pursue trade negotiations with the EU, Mexico and the Andean Community, as well as to negotiate as a single economic bloc in discussions with regard to the establishment of a Free Trade Area of the Americas (FTAA). Chile and Bolivia were to be incorporated into these negotiations. During 1997 negotiations to establish a free-trade accord with the Andean Community were hindered by differences regarding schedules for tariff elimination and Mercosur's insistence on a local content of 60% to qualify for rules of origin preferences. However, in April 1998 the two groupings signed an accord that committed them to the establishment of a free-trade area by January 2000. Negotiations in early 1999 failed to conclude an agreement on preferential tariffs between the two blocs, and the existing arrangements were extended on a bilateral basis. In March the Andean Community agreed to initiate free-trade negotiations with Brazil; a preferential tariff agreement was concluded in July. In August 2000 a similar agreement between the Community and Argentina entered into force. In September leaders of Mercosur and the Andean Community, meeting at a summit of Latin American heads of state, determined to relaunch negotiations. The establishment of a mechanism to support political dialogue and co-ordination between the two groupings, which aimed to enhance the integration process, was approved at the first joint meeting of ministers of foreign affairs in July 2001. In December 2002 Andean Community and Mercosur heads of state signed an economic complementation agreement, providing for the merger of their respective free-trade areas by 2004. Bilateral negotiations on a free-trade agreement between Mexico and Mercosur, initiated in 2001, were expected to be concluded during 2003. Negotiations between Mercosur and the EU on the conclusion of an Association Agreement commenced in 1999 and were ongoing in early 2003. In March 2003 Argentina and Brazil, with the backing of other Mercosur member states, formed the Southern Agricultural Council (CAS), which was to represent the interests of the grouping as a whole in negotiations with third countries.

In March 1998 ministers of trade of 34 countries agreed a detailed framework for negotiations to establish the FTAA by 2005. Mercosur secured support for its request that a separate negotiating group be established to consider issues relating to agriculture, as one of nine key sectors to be discussed. The FTAA negotiating process was formally initiated by heads of state of the 34 countries meeting in Santiago, Chile, in April 1998. In June Mercosur and Canada signed a Trade and Investment Co-operation Arrangement, which aimed to remove obstacles to trade and to increase economic co-operation between the two signatories. In July the European Commission proposed obtaining a mandate to commence negotiations with Mercosur and Chile towards a free-trade agreement, which, it was envisaged, would provide for the elimination of tariffs over a period of 10 years. However, Mercosur requested that the EU abolish agricultural subsidies as part of any accord. Negotiations between Mercosur, Chile and the EU were initiated in April 2000. Specific discussion of tariff reductions and market access commenced at the fifth round of negotiations, held in July 2001, at which the EU proposed a gradual elimination of tariffs on industrial imports over a 10-year period and an extension of access quotas for agricultural products. The summit meeting held in December 2000 was attended by the President of South Africa, and it was agreed that Mercosur would initiate free-trade negotiations with that country. In June 2001 Mercosur leaders agreed to pursue efforts to conclude a bilateral trade agreement with the USA, an objective previously opposed by the Brazilian authorities, while reaffirming their commitment to the FTAA process. Negotiations to conclude a bilateral trade accord with the USA were ongoing in 2002.

Finance

The annual budget for the secretariat, set at US $980,887 in 1999, is contributed by the four full member states.

Publication

Boletín Oficial del Mercosur (quarterly).

WESTERN EUROPEAN UNION—WEU

Address: 15 rue de l'Association, 1000 Brussels, Belgium.
Telephone: (2) 500-44-50; **fax:** (2) 500-44-70; **e-mail:** ueo .secretarygeneral@skynet.be; **internet:** www.weu.int.

Based on the Brussels Treaty of 1948, the Western European Union (WEU) was set up in 1955 as an intergovernmental organization for European co-operation in the field of security and defence. In the 1990s WEU was developed as the defence component of the European Union (EU), and as the means of strengthening the European pillar of the Atlantic Alliance under NATO. However, in June 1999 the European Council resolved to formulate a common European security and defence policy, incorporating the main crisis management responsibilities of WEU. Consequently, WEU relinquished these functions to the EU by July 2001.

MEMBERS*

Belgium	Luxembourg
France	Netherlands
Germany	Portugal
Greece	Spain
Italy	United Kingdom

* WEU has invited the other members of the EU to join the organization and has invited other European members of NATO to become Associate Members to enable them to participate fully in WEU activities. In November 1992 Denmark and Ireland took up observer status and on 1 January 1995 Austria, Finland and Sweden became Observers following their accession to the EU. Associate member status was granted to Iceland, Norway and Turkey in November 1992. Associate Partner status was granted to Bulgaria, the Czech Republic, Estonia, Hungary, Latvia, Lithuania, Poland, Romania and Slovakia in May 1994 and to Slovenia in June 1996. The Czech Republic, Hungary and Poland became Associate Partners in March 1999.

Organization

(April 2003)

COUNCIL

The Council is the WEU's main body, responsible for addressing all security and defence matters within WEU's remit. It is organized so as to be able to function on a permanent basis and may be convened at any time at the request of a member state. The Permanent Council, chaired by the WEU Secretary-General, is the central body responsible for day-to-day management of the organization and for assigning tasks to and co-ordinating the activities of the various working groups. It is composed of permanent representatives, supported by military delegates, and meets as often as required. The presidency of the Council is rotated between member states on a six-monthly basis.

SECRETARIAT-GENERAL

Secretary-General: Dr Javier Solana Madariaga (Spain).

WEU's Secretariat also headquarters the secretariats of the Western European Armaments Group (WEAG), a forum for armaments co-operation, and the Western European Armaments Organization (WEAO), which operates as a research cell.

ASSEMBLY

Address: 43 ave du Président Wilson, 75775 Paris Cédex 16, France; tel. 1-53-67-22-00; fax 1-53-67-22-01; e-mail assembly@weu .int; internet www.weu.int/assembly.

The Assembly of Western European Union is composed of the representatives of the Brussels Treaty powers to the Parliamentary Assembly of the Council of Europe. It meets at least twice a year, usually in Paris. The Assembly may proceed on any matter regarding the application of the Brussels Treaty and on any matter submitted to the Assembly for an opinion by the Council. Resolutions may be adopted in cases where this form is considered appropriate. When so directed by the Assembly, the President transmits such resolutions to international organizations, governments and national parliaments. An annual report is presented to the Assembly by the Council. In March 2000 an extraordinary meeting of the Assembly determined to initiate a process of transforming the body into the European Security and Defence Assembly (ESDA).

President: Jan Dirk Blaauw (Netherlands).

PERMANENT COMMITTEES OF THE ASSEMBLY

There are permanent committees on: Political Defence Questions; Technological and Aerospace Questions; Budgetary Affairs and Administration; Rules of Procedure and Privileges; and Parliamentary and Public Relations.

Activities

The Brussels Treaty was signed in 1948 by Belgium, France, Luxembourg, the Netherlands and the United Kingdom. It foresaw the potential for international co-operation in Western Europe and provided for collective defence and collaboration in economic, social and cultural activities. Within this framework, NATO and the Council of Europe (see chapters) were formed in 1949.

On the collapse in 1954 of plans for a European Defence Community, a nine-power conference was convened in London to try to reach a new agreement. This conference's decisions were embodied in a series of formal agreements drawn up by a ministerial conference held in Paris in October. The agreements entailed: arrangements for the Brussels Treaty to be strengthened and modified to include the Federal Republic of Germany and Italy, the ending of the occupation regime in the Federal Republic of Germany, and the invitation to the latter to join NATO. These agreements were ratified on 6 May 1955, on which date the seven-power Western European Union came into being. WEU was reactivated in October 1984 by restructuring its organization and by holding more frequent ministerial meetings, in order to harmonize members' views on defence questions, arms control and disarmament, developments in East-West relations, Europe's contribution to the Atlantic alliance, and European armaments co-operation.

In April 1990 ministers of foreign affairs and defence discussed the implications of recent political changes in central and eastern Europe, and mandated WEU to develop contacts with democratically elected governments there. In June 1992 an extraordinary meeting of WEU's Ministerial Council with the ministers of defence and foreign affairs of Hungary, Czechoslovakia, Poland, Romania, Bulgaria, Estonia, Latvia and Lithuania agreed on measures to enhance co-operation. The ministers were to meet annually, while a forum of consultation was to be established between the WEU Council and the ambassadors of the countries concerned, which was to meet at least twice a year. The focus of consultations was to be the security structure and political stability of Europe; the future development of the CSCE (now the OSCE); and arms control and disarmament, in particular the implementation of the Treaty on Conventional Armed Forces in Europe (the CFE Treaty) and the 'Open Skies' Treaty (see NATO for both). In May 1994 the Council of Ministers, meeting in Luxembourg, issued the Kirchberg Declaration, according the nine countries concerned (including the Czech Republic and Slovakia, which were the legal successors to Czechoslovakia) the status of Associate Partners of WEU, thereby suspending the forum of consultation.

The EC Treaty on European Union, which was agreed at Maastricht, in the Netherlands, in December 1991, and entered into force on 1 November 1993, referred to WEU as an 'integral part of the development of European Union' and requested WEU 'to elaborate and implement decisions and actions of the Union which have defence implications'. The Treaty also committed EU member countries to the 'eventual framing of a common defence policy which might in time lead to a common defence'. A separate declaration, adopted by WEU member states in Maastricht, defined WEU's role as being the defence component of the European Union but also as the instrument for strengthening the European pillar of the Atlantic Alliance, thus maintaining a role for NATO in Europe's defence and retaining WEU's identity as distinct from that of the EU. In January 1993 WEU's Council and Secretariat-General moved to Brussels (from Paris and London, respectively), in order to promote closer co-operation with both the EU and NATO, which have their head-quarters there.

In June 1992 WEU ministers of defence and foreign affairs convened in Petersberg, Germany, to consider the implementation of the Maastricht decisions. In the resulting 'Petersberg Declaration' member states declared that they were prepared to make available military units from the whole spectrum of their conventional armed forces for military tasks conducted under the authority of WEU. In addition to contributing to the common defence in accordance with Article V of the modified Brussels Treaty, three categories of missions were identified for the possible employment of military units under the aegis of WEU: humanitarian and rescue tasks; peace-keeping tasks; and crisis management, including peace-making. (Missions of this kind are often described as 'Petersberg tasks'.) The Petersberg Declaration stated that the WEU was prepared to support peace-keeping activities of the CSCE and UN Security Council on a case-by-case basis. A WEU planning cell was established in Brussels in October, which was to be responsible for preparing contingency plans for the employment of forces under WEU auspices for humanitarian operations, peace-keeping and crisis-management activities. It was expected that the same military units identified by member states for deployment under NATO would be used for military operations under WEU: this arrangement was referred to as 'double-hatting'. In May 1995 WEU ministers, convened in Lisbon, Portugal, agreed to strengthen WEU's operational capabilities through new structures and mechanisms, including the establishment of a politico-military group to advise on crises and crisis management, a Situation Centre able to monitor WEU operations and support decisions taken by the Council, and an Intelligence Section within the planning cell. WEU rules of engagement, with a view to implementing the missions identified in the Petersberg Declaration, were to be formulated.

In January 1994 NATO heads of state gave their full support to the development of a European Security and Defence Identity (ESDI) and to the strengthening of WEU. They declared their readiness to make collective assets of the Alliance available for WEU operations, and endorsed the concept of Combined Joint Task Forces (CJTFs), which was to provide separable, but not separate, military capabilities that could be employed by either organization. In May 1996 NATO and WEU signed a security agreement, which provided for the protection and shared use of classified information. In June NATO ministers, meeting in Berlin, Germany, agreed on a framework of measures to enable the implementation of the CJTF concept and the development of an ESDI within the Alliance. WEU was to be permitted to request the use of a CJTF headquarters for an operation under its command and to use Alliance planning capabilities and military infrastructure. In May 1998 the Council of both organizations approved a set of consultation arrangements as a guide to co-operation in a crisis situation. A framework document on principles and guide-lines for detailed practicalities of cases where NATO assets and/or capabilities were loaned to WEU was subsequently prepared.

In November 1994 a WEU ministerial meeting in Noordwijk, the Netherlands, adopted a set of preliminary conclusions on the formulation of a common European defence policy. The role and place of WEU in further European institutional arrangements were addressed by the EU's Intergovernmental Conference, which commenced in March 1996. The process was concluded in June 1997 with agreement having been reached on the Treaty of Amsterdam (see EU chapter). The Treaty, which was signed in October and entered into force on 1 May 1999, confirmed WEU as providing the EU with access to operational capability for undertaking the Petersberg tasks, which were incorporated into the revised Treaty. It advocated enhanced EU-WEU co-operation and referred to the possible integration of the WEU into the EU, should the European Council so decide (the United Kingdom being the main opponent). Following the entry into force of the Treaty of Amsterdam WEU and the EU approved a set of arrangements for enhanced co-operation. In June the EU determined to strengthen its common security and defence policy, and initiated a process of assuming direct responsibility for the Petersberg tasks. Javier Solana was appointed as the EU's first High Representative for foreign and security policy, and subsequently named as the new WEU Secretary-General, providing for the highest level of co-operation between the two organizations. In November WEU ministers adopted a series of recommendations,

based on the results of an audit of assets, to enable European countries to respond rapidly to conduct crisis management operations, to enhance collective capabilities in strategic intelligence and planning, and to strengthen military air, sea and transport equipment and capabilities for use in humanitarian and peace-keeping operations. By July 2001 the transfer of WEU's crisis management functions to the EU had been finalized, leaving commitments relating to collective defence as WEU's key focus area. The EU assumed responsibility for two former subsidiary bodies of the WEU (a Satellite Centre and the Paris-based Institute for Strategic Studies) in January 2002. The remaining functions of the restructured WEU related to the provision of military and other aid and assistance should a member state become the object of an armed attack in Europe, as provided for under the Brussels Treaty; institutional dialogue within the Assembly, support to the Western European Armaments Group and the Western European Armaments Organization, and other administrative tasks.

In the early 1990s WEU's operational capabilities were substantially developed. From mid-July 1992 warships and aircraft of WEU members undertook a monitoring operation in the Adriatic Sea, in co-ordination with NATO, to ensure compliance with the UN Security Council's resolutions imposing a trade and armaments embargo on Serbia and Montenegro. In mid-November the UN Security Council gave the NATO/WEU operation the power to search vessels suspected of attempting to flout the embargo. In June 1993 the Councils of WEU and NATO agreed to establish a unified command for the operation, which was to implement a Security Council resolution to strengthen the embargo against Serbia and Montenegro. Under the agreement, the Councils were to exert joint political control, and military instructions were to be co-ordinated within a joint *ad hoc* headquarters. In April WEU ministers offered civil assistance to Bulgaria, Hungary and Romania in enforcing the UN embargo on the Danube, and a monitoring mission began operations in June. In June 1996 the NATO/WEU naval monitoring mission in the Adriatic Sea was suspended, following the decision of the UN Security Council to remove the embargo on the delivery of armaments to the former Yugoslavia. WEU provided assistance for the administration of Mostar, Bosnia and Herzegovina, for which the EU assumed responsibility in July 1994.

In May 1997 WEU dispatched a Multinational Advisory Police Element (MAPE) to Albania to provide training and advice on restructuring the police force in that country. By the end of 1999 a new State Police Law, formulated with MAPE's support, had been ratified by the Albanian legislature, while some 3,000 police officers had been trained at centres in Tirana and Dürres and through field programmes. In February the WEU Council approved plans for an enhanced MAPE, with greater geographical coverage and operational mobility, with an initial mandate until April 2000. MAPE was being conducted by WEU at the request of the EU, enabling a large part of the costs to be met from the EU budget. In response to the escalation of conflict in the Serbian province of Kosovo and Metohija in 1999, MAPE assisted the Albanian authorities to establish an Emergency Crisis Group to help to administer and to assist the massive refugee population which entered Albania in March and April. MAPE terminated its operational activities in Albania on 31 May 2001.

In April 1999 WEU and Croatia signed an agreement to establish a WEU De-mining Assistance Mission (WEUDAM) in that country, upon a request by the Council of the EU. WEUDAM, which commenced activities in May, provided advice, technical expertise and training to the Croatian Mine Action Centre. WEUDAM was terminated on 31 November 2001.

In May 1992 France and Germany announced their intention to establish a joint defence force, the 'Eurocorps', which was to be based in Strasbourg, France, and which was intended to provide a basis for a European army under the aegis of WEU. This development caused concern among some NATO member countries, particularly the USA and United Kingdom, which feared that it represented a fresh attempt (notably on the part of France, which is outside NATO's military structure) to undermine the Alliance's role in Europe. In November, however, France and Germany stated that troops from the joint force could serve under NATO military command. This principle was recognized in an agreement signed in January 1993, which established links between the proposed joint force and NATO's military structure. In June Belgium opted to participate in the Eurocorps. In December Spain agreed to provide troops for the force. Luxembourg agreed to participate in May 1994. Eurocorps formally became operational on 30 November 1995. In June 1999 EU ministers decided that Eurocorps was to be transformed into a rapid reaction force, under EU authority. In May 1995 France, Italy, Spain and Portugal announced the establishment of two new forces, which were to be at the disposal of WEU as well as NATO and the UN: EUROFOR, consisting of up to 14,000 ground troops, to be based in Florence, Italy; and EUROMARFOR, a maritime force serving the Mediterranean. A number of other multinational forces are also designated as forces answerable to WEU (FAWEU) or that were to be available to WEU: the Multinational Division (Central), comprising Belgium, Germany, the Netherlands and the United Kingdom; the Headquarters of the First German-Netherlands Corps; the United Kingdom-Netherlands Amphibious Force; the Spanish-Italian Amphibious Force; and the European Air Group (EAG), comprising Belgium, France, Germany, Italy, Netherlands, Spain and the United Kingdom.

Publications

Account of the Session (WEU Assembly, 2 a year).
Annual Report of the Council.
Assembly of Western European Union: Texts adopted and Brief Account of the Session (2 a year).
Assembly documents and reports.

WORLD CONFEDERATION OF LABOUR—WCL

Address: 33 rue de Trèves, 1040 Brussels, Belgium.
Telephone: (2) 285-47-00; **fax:** (2) 230-87-22; **e-mail:** info@cmt-wcl.org; **internet:** www.cmt-wcl.org.

Founded in 1920 as the International Federation of Christian Trade Unions (IFCTU); reconstituted under present title in 1968. (See also the International Confederation of Free Trade Unions and the World Federation of Trade Unions.)

MEMBERS

Affiliated national federations and trade union internationals; about 26m. members in 116 countries.

Organization

(April 2003)

CONGRESS

The supreme and legislative authority, which convenes every four years (October 2001: Bucharest, Romania). Congress consists of delegates from national confederations and trade internationals. Delegates have votes according to the size of their organization. Congress receives official reports, elects the Executive Board, considers the future programme and any proposals.

CONFEDERAL BOARD

The Board meets annually, and consists of 47 members (including 23 representatives of national confederations and eight representatives of trade internationals) elected by Congress from among its members for four-year terms. It issues executive directions and instructions to the Secretariat.

SECRETARIAT-GENERAL

Secretary-General: WILLY THYS (Belgium).
Deputy Secretaries-General: EDUARDO ESTÉVEZ (Argentina), JAAP WIENEN (Netherlands).

REGIONAL AND OTHER OFFICES

Africa: Democratic Organization of African Workers' Trade Unions (ODSTA), BP 4401, Route International d'Atakpamé, Lomé, Togo; tel. 250710; fax 256113; e-mail odsta@café.tg; Pres. F. KIKONGI.

Asia: Brotherhood of Asian Trade Unionists (BATU), 1943 Taft Avenue, 1004 Malate, Manila, Philippines; tel. (2) 500709; fax (2) 5218335; e-mail batuasean@batunorm.org.ph; Pres. J. TAN.

Latin America: Latin-American Confederation of Workers (CLAT), Apdo 6681, Caracas 1010, Venezuela; tel. (32) 720794; fax (32) 720463; e-mail clat@telcel.net.ve; internet www.clat.org; Sec.-Gen. EDUARDO GARCÍA.

North America: c/o National Alliance of Postal and Federal Employees, 1628 11th St, NW, Washington, DC 20001, USA; tel. (202) 939-6325; fax (202) 939-6389; e-mail ptennas@patriot.net; Pres. JAMES McGEE.

Eastern Europe Liaison Office: Bucharest, Splaiul Independentei, nr 202, cam. 324, Sector 6, Romania; tel. and fax (1) 3101586; e-mail cmtest@alfa.rtel.ro.

Geneva Liaison Office: CP 122, 1 rue de Varembé, 1211 Geneva 20, Switzerland; tel. (22) 7482080; fax (22) 7482088; e-mail Beatrice.fauchere@suisse.cmt-wcl.org.

INTERNATIONAL INSTITUTES OF TRADE UNION STUDIES

Africa: Fondation panafricaine pour le développement économique, social et culturel (Fopadesc), Lomé, Togo.

Asia: BATU Social Institute, Manila, Philippines.
Latin America:
Instituto Andino de Estudios Sociales, Lima, Peru
Instituto Centro-Americano de Estudios Sociales (ICAES), San José, Costa Rica
Instituto del Cono Sur (INCASUR), Buenos Aires, Argentina
Instituto de Formación del Caribe, Willemstad, Curaçao, Netherlands Antilles
Universidad de Trabajadores de América Latina (UTAL)

Finance

Income is derived from affiliation dues, contributions, donations and capital interest.

Publications

Tele-flash (every 2 weeks).
Labor magazine (quarterly).
Reports of Congresses; Study Documents.

International Trade Union Federations

Federation of Professional Sportsmen: rue des Chantaeux 70, 1000 Brussels, Belgium; tel. (2) 500–28–30; fax (2) 500–28–32; e-mail sporta@acv-csc.be; Sec. DIRK DE VOS.

International Federation of Textile and Clothing Workers—IFTC: 27 Koning Albertlaan, 9000 Ghent, Belgium; tel. (9) 222-57-01; fax (9) 220-45-59; e-mail info@cnv.net; f. 1901; mems: unions covering 800,000 workers in 39 countries; Organization: Congress (every three years), Board, Exec. Committee; Pres. JACQUES JOURET (Belgium); Gen. Sec. BART BRUGGEMAN (Netherlands).

International Federation of Trade Unions of Employees in Public Service—INFEDOP: 39 rue Monteyer, 100 Brussels, Belgium; tel. (2) 230-38-65; fax (2) 231-14-72; e-mail info@infedop-eurofedop.com; f. 1922; mems: national federations of workers in public service, covering 4m. workers; Organization: World Congress (at least every five years), World Confederal Board (meets every year), 10 Trade Groups, Secretariat; Pres. GUY RASNEUR (Belgium); Sec.-Gen. FRITZ NEUGEBAUER (Austria); publ. *Servus* (monthly).

> **European Federation of Employees in Public Services—EUROFEDOP:** 39 rue Montoyer, 1000 Brussels, Belgium; tel. (2) 230-38-65; fax (2) 231-14-72; e-mail info@infedop-eurofedop.com; internet www.eurofedop.org; Chair. GUY RASNEUR (Belgium); Sec.-Gen. FRITZ NEUGEBAUER (Austria).

International Federation of Trade Unions of Transport Workers—FIOST: 33 rue de Trèves, 1040 Brussels, Belgium; tel. (2) 285-47-35; fax (2) 230-87-22; e-mail freddy.pools@cmt-wcl.org; f. 1921; mems: national federations in 28 countries covering 600,000 workers; Organization: Congress (every four years), Committee (meets twice a year), Executive Board; Pres. MICHEL BOVY (Belgium); Exec. Sec. FREDDY POOLS (Belgium); publ. *Labor* (6 a year).

World Confederation of Teachers—WCT: 33 rue de Trèves, 1040 Brussels, Belgium; tel. (2) 285-47-29; fax (2) 230-87-22; e-mail wct@cmt-wcl.org; internet www.wctcsme.org; f. 1963; mems: national federations of unions concerned with teaching; Organization: Congress (every four years), Council (at least once a year), Steering Committee; Pres. LOUIS VAN BENEDEN; Sec.-Gen. GASTON DE LA HAYE.

World Federation of Agriculture, Food, Hotel and Allied Workers—WFAFW: 33 rue de Trèves, 1040 Brussels, Belgium; tel. (2) 230-60-90; fax (2) 230-87-22; e-mail fmtaa@cmt-wcl.org; f. 1982; merger of former World Federation of Agricultural Workers and World Federation of Workers in the Food, Drink, Tobacco and Hotel Industries; mems: national federations covering 2,800,000 workers in 38 countries; Organization: Congress (every five years), World Board, Daily Management Board; Pres. ADRIAN COJOCARUN (Romania); Exec. Sec. JOSÉ GÓMEZ CERDA (Dominican Republic).

World Federation of Building and Woodworkers Unions—WFBW: 33 rue de Trèves, 1040 Brussels, Belgium; tel. (2) 285-02-11; fax (2) 230-74-43; e-mail piet.nelissen@cmt-wcl.org;; internet internet www.wflw-fmcb.org; f. 1936; mems: national federations covering 2,438,000 workers in several countries; Organization: Congress, Bureau, Permanent Secretariat; Pres. JACKY JACKERS; Sec.-Gen. DICK VAN DE KAMP (Netherlands); publ. *Bulletin*.

World Federation of Clerical Workers—WFCW: 33 rue de Trèves, 1040 Brussels, Belgium; tel. (2) 285-47-35; fax (2) 230-87-22; e-mail olga.nicolae@cmt-wcl.org; internet www.cmt-wcl.org; f. 1921; mems: national federations of unions and professional associations covering 700,000 workers in 57 countries; Organization: Congress (every four years), Council, Executive Board, Secretariat; Pres. ROEL ROTSHUIZEN (Netherlands); Sec. OLGA NICOLAI; publ. *Labor*.

World Federation of Industry Workers—WFIW: 33 rue de Trèves, 1040 Brussels, Belgium; e-mail piet.nelissen@cmt-wcl.org; f. 1985; mems: regional and national federations covering about 600,000 workers in 45 countries; Organization: Congress (every five years), World Board (every year), Executive Committee, six World Trade Councils; Pres. BART BRUGGEMAN; Gen. Sec. ITALO RODOMONTI; publ. *Labor*.

WORLD COUNCIL OF CHURCHES—WCC

Address: 150 route de Ferney, POB 2100, 1211 Geneva 2, Switzerland.
Telephone: (22) 7916111; **fax:** (22) 7910361; **e-mail:** info@wcc-coe.org; **internet:** www.wcc-coe.org.
The Council was founded in 1948 to promote co-operation between Christian Churches and to prepare for a clearer manifestation of the unity of the Church.

MEMBERS
There are 342 member Churches in more than 120 countries. Chief denominations: Anglican, Baptist, Congregational, Lutheran, Methodist, Moravian, Old Catholic, Orthodox, Presbyterian, Reformed and Society of Friends. The Roman Catholic Church is not a member but sends official observers to meetings.

Organization
(April 2003)

ASSEMBLY
The governing body of the World Council, consisting of delegates of the member Churches, it meets every seven or eight years to frame policy and consider some main themes. It elects the Presidents of the Council, who serve as members of the Central Committee. The eighth Assembly was held at Harare, Zimbabwe, in December 1998. The ninth Assembly was scheduled to be convened at Porto Alegre, Brazil, in 2006.
Presidium: Dr AGNES ABOUM (Kenya), Rev. KATHRYN K. BANNISTER (USA), Bishop JABEZ L. BRYCE (Fiji), His Eminence CHRYSOSTOMOS OF EPHESUS (Greece), Dr MOON-KYU KANG (Republic of Korea), Bishop FEDERICO J. PAGURA (Argentina), Bishop EBERHARDT RENZ (Germany), His Holiness IGNATIUS ZAKKA I (Syria).

CENTRAL COMMITTEE
Appointed by the Assembly to carry out its policies and decisions, the Committee consists of 158 members chosen from Assembly delegates. It meets every 12 to 18 months.
The Central Committee comprises the Programme Committee and the Finance Committee. Within the Programme Committee there are advisory groups on issues relating to communication, women, justice, peace and creation, youth, ecumenical relations, and inter-religious relations. There are also five commissions and boards.
Moderator: His Holiness ARAM I (CATHOLICOS OF CILICIA) (Armenian Apostolic Church, Lebanon).
Vice-Moderators: Justice SOPHIA O. A. ADINYIRA (Ghana), Dr MARION S. BEST (Canada).

EXECUTIVE COMMITTEE
Consists of the Presidents, the Officers and 20 members chosen by the Central Committee from its membership to prepare its agenda, expedite its decisions and supervise the work of the Council between meetings of the Central Committee. Meets every six months.

GENERAL SECRETARIAT
The General Secretariat implements the policies laid down by the WCC, and co-ordinates the work of the programme units described below. The General Secretariat is also responsible for the Ecumenical Centre Library and an Ecumenical Institute, at Bossey, which provides training in ecumenical leadership.
General Secretary: Rev. Dr KONRAD RAISER (Germany).

Activities
Following the Assembly in Harare in December 1998 the work of the WCC was restructured. Activities were grouped into four 'clusters':

RELATIONSHIPS
The cluster group on relationships carries out the Council's work in promoting unity and community. There are teams on Church and Ecumenical Relations; Relations and Ecumenical Sharing; Inter-religious Relations and Dialogue; and International Relations. Two programmes—Action by Churches Together (ACT) and the Ecumenical Church Loan Fund (ECLOF)—are included in this grouping.

ISSUES AND THEMES
This grouping, dealing with issues and themes encompassed by the aims of the Council, comprises four teams: Faith and Order; Mission and Evangelism; Justice, Peace, Creation; and Education and Ecumenical Formation.

COMMUNICATION
The Communication cluster unites those parts of the Council involved in the provision of public information, documentation, and the production of publications.

FINANCE, SERVICES AND ADMINISTRATION
This grouping comprises the following teams: Finance, Human Resources, Income Monitoring and Development, Computer Information Services, and Building Services.
In February 2001 the WCC launched its Decade to Overcome Violence (2001–10) during which various events were to be held on the themes of reconciliation, peace and justice.

Finance
The main contributors to the WCC's budget are the churches and their agencies, with funds for certain projects contributed by other organizations. The 2002 budget amounted to 52.5m. Swiss francs.

Publications
Catalogue of periodicals, books and audio-visuals.
Current Dialogue (2 a year).
Echoes (2 a year).
Ecumenical News International (weekly).
Ecumenical Review (quarterly).
International Review of Mission (quarterly).
Ministerial Formation (quarterly).
Overcoming Violence (quarterly).
WCC News (quarterly).
WCC Yearbook.

WORLD FEDERATION OF TRADE UNIONS—WFTU

Address: Branická 112, 14701 Prague 4, Czech Republic.
Telephone: (2) 4446-2140; **fax:** (2) 4446-1378; **e-mail:** wftu@login
.cz; **internet:** www.wftu.cz.

The Federation was founded in 1945, on a world-wide basis. A number of members withdrew from the Federation in 1949 to establish the International Confederation of Free Trade Unions (see p. 244). (See also the World Confederation of Labour (see p. 320).)

MEMBERS

Affiliated or associated national federations (including the six Trade Unions Internationals) in 126 countries representing some 135m. individuals.

Organization

(April 2003)

WORLD TRADE UNION CONGRESS

The Congress meets every five years. It reviews WFTU's work, endorses reports from the executives, and elects the General Council. The size of the delegations is based on the total membership of national federations. The Congress is also open to participation by non-affiliated organizations. The 14th Congress was held in New Delhi, India, in March 2000.

GENERAL COUNCIL

The General Council meets three times between Congresses, and comprises members and deputies elected by Congress from nominees of national federations. Every affiliated or associated organization and Trade Unions International has one member and one deputy member.

The Council receives reports from the Presidential Council, approves the plan and budget and elects officers.

PRESIDENTIAL COUNCIL

The Presidential Council meets twice a year and conducts most of the executive work of WFTU. It comprises a President, elected each year from among its members, the General Secretary and 18 Vice-Presidents.

SECRETARIAT

The Secretariat consists of the General Secretary, and six Deputy General Secretaries. It is appointed by the General Council and is responsible for general co-ordination, regional activities, national trade union liaison, press and information, administration and finance.

WFTU has regional offices in New Delhi, India (for the Asia-Pacific region), Havana, Cuba (covering the Americas), Dakar, Senegal (for Africa), Damascus, Syria (for the Middle East) and in Moscow, Russia (covering the CIS countries).

General Secretary: ALEKSANDR ZHARIKOV (Russia).

Finance

Income is derived from affiliation dues, which are based on the number of members in each trade union federation.

Publication

Flashes from the Trade Unions (fortnightly, in English, French and Spanish; monthly in Arabic and Russian).

Trade Unions Internationals

The following autonomous Trade Unions Internationals (TUIs) are associated with WFTU:

Trade Unions International of Agriculture, Food, Commerce, Textile and Allied Workers: f. 1997 by merger of the TUI of Agricultural, Forestry and Plantation Workers (f. 1949), the TUI of Food, Tobacco, Hotel and Allied Industries Workers (f. 1949), the TUI of Workers in Commerce (f. 1959) and the TUI of Textile, Clothing, Leather and Fur Workers (f. 1949); Pres. FREDDY HUCK (France); Gen. Sec. DMITRII DOZORIN (Russia).

Trade Unions International of Public and Allied Employees: 4 Windsor Pl., New Delhi 110 001, India; tel. (11) 331-1829; fax (11) 331-1849; e-mail aisgef@ca12.vsnl.net.in; internet www .tradeunionindia.org; f. 1949; mems: 34m. in 152 unions in 54 countries; Branch Commissions: State, Municipal, Postal and Telecommunications, Health, Banks and Insurance; Pres. CHRISTOS ALEKKOU CHRISTOU (Cyprus); Gen. Sec. SUKOMAL SEN (India); publ. *Information Bulletin* (in three languages).

Trade Unions International of Transport Workers: Tengerszem U. 21/B , 1142 Budapest, Hungary; tel. and fax (1) 2851593; f. 1949; holds International Trade Conference (every 4 years) and General Council (annually); mems: 95 unions from 37 countries; Pres. NASR ZARIF MOUHREZ (Syria); Gen. Sec. JÓZSEF TÓTH (Hungary); publ. *TUI Reporter* (every 2 months, in English and Spanish).

Trade Unions International of Workers of the Building, Wood and Building Materials Industries (Union Internationale des Syndicats des Travailleurs du Bâtiment, du Bois et des Matériaux de Construction—UITBB): Box 281, 00101 Helsinki, Finland; tel. (9) 693-1130; fax (9) 693-1020; e-mail rguitbb@kaapeli.fi; internet ww .uitbb.org; f. 1949; mems: unions in 50 countries, grouping 2m. workers; Sec.-Gen. JOSÉ DINIS (Portugal); publ. *Bulletin*.

Trade Unions International of Workers in the Energy, Metal, Chemical, Oil and Related Industries: c/o 3a Calle Maestro Antonio Caso 45, Col. Tabacalera, 06470 Mexico City, Mexico; tel. and fax (55) 5546-3200; e-mail uis@uis-tui.org; internet www.uis-tui .org; f. 1998 by merger of the TUI of Chemical, Oil and Allied Workers (f. 1950), the TUI of Energy Workers (f. 1949) and the TUI of Workers in the Metal Industry (f. 1949); Gen. Sec. ROSENDO FLORES FLORES (Mexico); publ. *Bulletin*.

World Federation of Teachers' Unions: 6/6 Kalicharan Ghosh Rd, Kolkata 700 050, India; tel. (33) 2528-4786; fax (33) 2557-1293; f. 1946; mems: 132 national unions of teachers and educational and scientific workers in 78 countries, representing over 24m. individuals; Pres. LESTURUGE ARIYAWANSA (Sri Lanka); Gen. Sec. MRINMOY BHATTACHARYYA (India); publ *Teachers of the World* (quarterly, in English).

WORLD TRADE ORGANIZATION—WTO

Address: Centre William Rappard, rue de Lausanne 154, 1211 Geneva, Switzerland.

Telephone: (22) 7395111; **fax:** (22) 7314206; **e-mail:** enquiries@wto .org; **internet:** www.wto.org.

The WTO is the legal and institutional foundation of the multilateral trading system. It was established on 1 January 1995, as the successor to the General Agreement on Tariffs and Trade (GATT).

MEMBERS*

Albania	Georgia	Niger
Angola	Germany	Nigeria
Antigua and	Ghana	Norway
Barbuda	Greece	Oman
Argentina	Grenada	Pakistan
Australia	Guatemala	Panama
Austria	Guinea	Papua New Guinea
Bahrain	Guinea-Bissau	Paraguay
Bangladesh	Guyana	Peru
Barbados	Haiti	Philippines
Belgium	Honduras	Poland
Belize	Hong Kong	Portugal
Benin	Hungary	Qatar
Bolivia	Iceland	Romania
Botswana	India	Rwanda
Brazil	Indonesia	Saint Christopher
Brunei	Ireland	and Nevis
Bulgaria	Israel	Saint Lucia
Burkina Faso	Italy	Saint Vincent and the
Burundi	Jamaica	Grenadines
Cameroon	Japan	Senegal
Canada	Jordan	Sierra Leone
Central African	Kenya	Singapore
Republic	Korea, Republic	Slovakia
Chad	Kuwait	Slovenia
Chile	Kyrgyzstan	Solomon Islands
China, People's	Latvia	South Africa
Republic	Lesotho	Spain
China, Republic†	Liechtenstein	Sri Lanka
Colombia	Lithuania	Suriname
Congo, Democratic	Luxembourg	Swaziland
Republic	Macau	Sweden
Congo, Republic	Macedonia, former	Switzerland
Costa Rica	Yugoslav republic	Tanzania
Côte d'Ivoire	Madagascar	Thailand
Croatia	Malawi	Togo
Cuba	Malaysia	Trinidad and
Cyprus	Maldives	Tobago
Czech Republic	Mali	Tunisia
Denmark	Malta	Turkey
Djibouti	Mauritania	Uganda
Dominica	Mauritius	United Arab
Dominican Republic	Mexico	Emirates
Ecuador	Moldova	United Kingdom
Egypt	Mongolia	USA
El Salvador	Morocco	Uruguay
Estonia	Mozambique	Vanuatu
Fiji	Myanmar	Venezuela
Finland	Namibia	Zambia
France	Netherlands	Zimbabwe
Gabon	New Zealand	
The Gambia	Nicaragua	

* The European Community also has membership status.

† Admitted as the Separate Customs Territory of Taiwan, Penghu, Kinmen and Matsu (referred to as Chinese Taipei).

Note: In early 2003 a further 30 governments had requested to join the WTO, and their applications were under consideration by accession working parties. Accession requests had also been received from Syria and Libya in late 2001, for which working parties had not yet been established.

Organization

(April 2003)

MINISTERIAL CONFERENCE

The Ministerial Conference is the highest authority of the WTO. It is composed of representatives of all WTO members at ministerial level, and may take decisions on all matters under any of the multilateral trade agreements. The Conference is required to meet at least every two years. The fourth Conference was held in Doha, Qatar, in November 2001; the fifth Conference was scheduled to be convened in Mexico in September 2003.

GENERAL COUNCIL

The General Council, which is also composed of representatives of all WTO members, is required to report to the Ministerial Conference and conducts much of the day-to-day work of the WTO. The Council convenes as the Dispute Settlement Body, to oversee the trade dispute settlement procedures, and as the Trade Policy Review Body, to conduct regular reviews of the trade policies of WTO members. The Council delegates responsibility to three other major Councils: for trade-related aspects of intellectual property rights, for trade in goods and for trade in services.

TRADE NEGOTIATIONS COMMITTEE

The Committee was established in November 2001 by the Declaration of the fourth Ministerial Conference, held in Doha, Qatar, to supervise the agreed agenda of trade negotiations. It was to operate under the authority of the General Council and was mandated to establish negotiating mechanisms and subsidiary bodies for each subject under consideration. A structure of negotiating groups and a declaration of principles and practices for the negotiations were formulated by the Committee in February 2002

SECRETARIAT

The WTO Secretariat comprises some 550 staff. Its responsibilities include the servicing of WTO delegate bodies, with respect to negotiations and the implementation of agreements, undertaking accession negotiations for new members and providing technical support and expertise to developing countries. In July 1999 member states reached a compromise agreement on the appointment of a new Director-General, having postponed the decision several times after failing to achieve the required consensus. Two candidates were appointed to serve consecutive three-year terms-in-office. In December 2001 the Director-General announced that the Secretariat was to be reorganized, in order to provide greater support to developing countries.

In June 2001 a WTO Training Institute was established, at the Secretariat, to extend the provision of training activities previously undertaken. Courses were to be held on trade policy, WTO dispute settlement rules and procedures, and other specialized topics; other programmes included training-of-trainers programmes and distance-learning services.

Director-General: SUPACHAI PANITCHPAKDI (Thailand).

Deputy Directors-General: RODERICK ABBOT (United Kingdom), KIPKORIR ALY AZAD RANA (Kenya), FRANCISCO THOMPSON-FLORES (Brazil), RUFUS YERXA (USA).

Activities

The Final Act of the Uruguay Round of GATT multilateral trade negotiations, which were concluded in December 1993, provided for extensive trade liberalization measures and for the establishment of a permanent structure to oversee international trading procedures. The Final Act was signed in April 1994, in Marrakesh, Morocco. At the same time a separate accord, the Marrakesh Declaration, was signed by the majority of GATT contracting states, endorsing the establishment of the WTO. The essential functions of the WTO are: to administer and facilitate the implementation of the results of the Uruguay Round; to provide a forum for multilateral trade negotiations; to administer the trade dispute settlement procedures; to review national trade policies; and to co-operate with other international institutions, in particular the IMF and World Bank, in order to achieve greater coherence in global economic policy-making.

The WTO Agreement contains some 29 individual legal texts and more than 25 additional Ministerial declarations, decisions and understandings, which cover obligations and commitments for member states. All these instruments are based on a few fundamental principles, which form the basis of the WTO Agreement. An integral part of the Agreement is 'GATT 1994', an amended and updated version of the original GATT Agreement of 1947, which was formally concluded at the end of 1995. Under the 'most-favoured nation' (MFN) clause, members are bound to grant to each other's products treatment no less favourable than that accorded to the products of any third parties. A number of exceptions apply, principally for customs unions and free-trade areas and for measures in favour of and among developing countries. The principle of 'national treatment' requires goods, having entered a market, to be treated no less favourably than the equivalent domestically-produced goods. Secure and predictable market access, to encourage trade, investment and job creation, may be determined by 'binding' tariffs, or customs duties. This process means that a tariff level for a particular product becomes a commitment by a member state, and cannot be increased without compensation negotiations with its main trading partners. Other WTO agreements also contribute to predictable trading conditions by demanding commitments from member countries and greater transparency of domestic laws and national trade policies. By permitting tariffs, whilst adhering to the guide-lines of being non-discriminatory, the WTO aims to promote open, fair and undistorted competition.

The WTO aims to encourage development and economic reform among the increasing number of developing countries and countries with economies in transition participating in the international trading system. These countries, particularly the least-developed states, have been granted transition periods and greater flexibility to implement certain WTO provisions. Industrial member countries are encouraged to assist developing nations by their trading conditions and by not expecting reciprocity in trade concession negotiations. In addition, the WTO operates a limited number of technical assistance programmes, mostly relating to training and the provision of information technology.

Finally, the WTO Agreement recognizes the need to protect the environment and to promote sustainable development. A new Committee on Trade and Environment was established to identify the relationship between trade policies, environmental measures and sustainable development and to recommend any appropriate modifications of the multilateral trading provisions. There was much contention over the compatibility of environmental and free-trade concerns in 1998, which was highlighted by a dispute settlement relating to shrimp-fishing in Asia.

At the 1996 Conference representatives of some 28 countries signed a draft Information Technology Agreement (ITA), which aimed to eliminate tariffs on the significant global trade in IT products by 2000. By late February 1997 some 39 countries, representing the required 90% share of the world's IT trade, had consented to implement the ITA. It was signed in March, and was to cover the following main product categories: computers; telecommunications products; semiconductors or manufacturing equipment; software; and scientific instruments. Tariff reductions in these sectors were to be undertaken in four stages, commencing in July, and subsequently on 1 January each year, providing for the elimination of all tariffs by the start of 2000. (By February 2001 there were 56 participants in the ITA.) In February 1999 the WTO announced plans to investigate methods of removing non-tariff barriers to trade in IT products, such as those resulting from non-standardization of technical regulations. A one-year work programme on non-tariff measures was approved by the Committee of Participants on the Expansion of Trade in IT Products in November 2000.

At the end of the Uruguay Round a 'built-in' programme of work for the WTO was developed. In addition, the Ministerial Conferences in December 1996 and May 1998 addressed a range of issues. The final declaration issued from the Ministerial Conference in December 1996 incorporated a text on the contentious issue of core labour standards, although it was emphasized that the relationship between trade and labour standards was not part of the WTO agenda. The text recognized the International Labour Organization's competence in establishing and dealing with core labour standards and endorsed future WTO/ILO co-operation. The declaration also included a plan of action on measures in favour of the world's least-developed countries, to assist these countries in enhancing their trading opportunities. The second Conference, convened in May 1998, decided against imposing customs duties on international electronic transactions, and agreed to establish a comprehensive work programme to address the issues of electronic commerce. The Conference also supported the creation of a framework of international rules to protect intellectual property rights and provide security and privacy in transactions. Developing countries were assured that their needs in this area would be taken into account. Members agreed to begin preparations for the launch of comprehensive talks on global trade liberalization. In addition, following repeated mass public demonstrations against free trade, it was agreed to try to increase the transparency of the WTO and improve public understanding of the benefits of open global markets.

Formal negotiations on the agenda of a new multilateral trade 'round', which was scheduled to be launched at the third Ministerial Conference, to be held in Seattle, USA, in late November/December 1999, commenced in September 1998. While it was confirmed that further liberalization of agriculture and services was to be considered, no consensus was reached (in particular between the Cairns Group of countries and the USA, and the EU, supported by Japan) on the terms of reference or procedures for these negotiations prior to the start of the Conference. In addition, developing countries criticized renewed efforts, mainly by the USA, to link trade and labour standards and to incorporate environmental considerations into the discussions. Efforts by the EU to broaden the talks to include investment and competition policy were also resisted by the USA. The conduct of the Ministerial Conference was severely disrupted by public demonstrations by a diverse range of interest groups concerned with the impact of WTO accords on the environment, workers' rights and developing countries. The differences between member states with regard to a formal agenda failed to be resolved during extensive negotiations, and the Conference was suspended. At a meeting of the General Council, convened later in December, member countries reached an informal understanding that any agreements concluding on 31 December would be extended. Meanwhile, the Director-General attempted to maintain a momentum for proceeding with a new round of trade negotiations, although it was considered unlikely to be initiated before 2001. In February 2000 the General Council agreed to resume talks with regard to agriculture and services, and to consider difficulties in implementing the Uruguay Accord, which was a main concern of developing member states. The Council also urged industrialized nations to pursue an earlier initiative to grant duty-free access to the exports of least developed countries. In May the Council resolved to initiate a series of Special Sessions to consider implementation of existing trade agreements, and approved more flexible provisions for implementation of TRIPS (see below), as part of ongoing efforts to address the needs of developing member states and strengthen their confidence in the multilateral trading system.

During 2001 negotiations were undertaken to reach agreement on further trade liberalization. A draft accord was approved by the General Council in October. The fourth Ministerial Conference, held in Doha, Qatar, in November, adopted a final declaration providing a mandate for a three-year agenda for negotiations on a range of subjects, commencing 1 January 2002. Most of the negotiations were to be concluded, on 1 January 2005, as a single undertaking, i.e. requiring universal agreement on all matters under consideration. A new Trade Negotiations Committee was established to supervise the process, referred to as the Doha Development Round. Several aspects of existing agreements were to be negotiated, while new issues included WTO rules, such as subsidies, regional trade agreements and anti-dumping measures, and market access. The Declaration incorporated a commitment to negotiate issues relating to trade and the environment, including fisheries subsidies, environmental labeling requirements, and the relationship between trade obligations of multilateral environment agreements and WTO rules. The Conference approved a separate decision on implementation-related issues, to address the concerns of developing countries in meeting their WTO commitments. Several implementation issues were agreed at the meeting, while others were incorporated into the Development Agenda. Specific reference was made in the Declaration to providing greater technical co-operation and capacity-building assistance to WTO developing country members. A Doha Development Agenda Global Trust Fund was established in late 2001, with a core budget of CHF 15m., to help finance technical support for trade liberalization in less developed member states. On assuming office in September 2002 the new WTO Director-General, Supachai Panitchpakdi, announced that the ongoing trade negotiations should be brought to a swift conclusion, and that this goal would be supported by the strengthening of the following four pillars of the Organization: beneficial use of the legal framework binding together the multilateral system; technical and capacity-building assistance to least-developed and developing countries; greater coherence in international economic policy-making; and the WTO's functioning as an institution.

AGRICULTURE

The Final Act of the Uruguay Round extended previous GATT arrangements for trade in agricultural products through new rules and commitments to ensure more predictable and fair competition in the sector. All quantitive measures limiting market access for agricultural products were to be replaced by tariffs (i.e. a process of 'tariffication'), enabling more equal protection and access opportunities. All tariffs on agricultural items were to be reduced by 36% by developed countries, over a period of six years, and by 24% by developing countries (excluding least-developed member states) over 10 years. A special treatment clause applied to 'sensitive' products (mainly rice) in four countries, for which limited import restrictions could be maintained. Efforts to reduce domestic support measures for agricultural products were to be based on calculations of total aggregate measurements of support (Total AMS) by each member state. A 20% reduction in Total AMS was required by developed countries over six years, and 13% over 10 years by developing countries. No reduction was required of least-developed countries. Developed member countries were required to reduce the value and quantity of direct export subsidies by 36% and 21% respectively (on 1986–90 levels) over six years. For developing countries these reductions were to be two-thirds those of developed nations, over 10 years. A specific concern of least-developed and net-food importing developing countries, which had previously relied on subsidized food products, was to be addressed through other food aid mechanisms and assistance for agricultural development. The situation was to be monitored by WTO's Committee on Agriculture. Negotiations on the further liberalization of agricultural markets were part of the WTO 'built-in' programme for 2000 or earlier, but remained a major area of contention. In March 2000 negotiations on market access in the agricultural sector commenced, under an interim chairman owing to a disagreement among participating states. By November 2001 121 countries had submitted proposals for the next stage of negotiations. The Doha Declaration, approved in that month, established a timetable for further negotiations on agriculture, which were to be concluded as part of the single undertaking on 1 January 2005. A compromise agreement was reached with the EU to commit to a reduction in export subsidies, with a view to phasing them out (without a firm deadline for their elimination). Member states agreed to aim for further reductions in market access restrictions and domestic support mechanisms, and to incorporate non-trade concerns, including environmental protection, food security and rural development, into the negotiations.

The Agreement on the Application of Sanitary and Phytosanitary Measures aims to regulate world-wide standards of food safety and animal and plant health in order to encourage the mutual recognition of standards and conformity, so as to facilitate trade in these products. The Agreement includes provisions on control inspection and approval procedures. In September 1997, in the first case to be brought under the Agreement, a dispute panel of the WTO ruled that the EU's ban on imports of hormone-treated beef and beef products from the USA and Canada was in breach of international trading rules. In January 1998 the Appellate Body upheld the panel's ruling, but expressed its support for restrictions to ensure food standards if there was adequate scientific evidence of risks to human health. The EU maintained the ban, against resistance from the USA, while it carried out scientific risk assessments.

TEXTILES AND CLOTHING

From 1974 the Multi-fibre Arrangement (MFA) provided the basis of international trade concerning textiles and clothing, enabling the major importers to establish quotas and protect their domestic industries, through bilateral agreements, against more competitive low-cost goods from developing countries. MFA restrictions that were in place on 31 December 1994 were carried over into the new agreement and were to be phased out through integration into GATT 1994, under which they would be subject to the same rules applying to other industrial products. This was to be achieved in four stages: products accounting for 16% of the total volume of textiles and clothing imports (at 1990 levels) were to be integrated from 1 January 1995; a further 17% on 1 January 1998; and not less than a further 18% on 1 January 2002, with all remaining products to be integrated by 1 January 2005.

TRADE IN SERVICES

The General Agreement on Trade in Services (GATS), which was negotiated during the GATT Uruguay Round, is the first set of multilaterally-agreed and legally-enforceable rules and disciplines ever negotiated to cover international trade in services. The GATS comprises a framework of general rules and disciplines, annexes addressing special conditions relating to individual sectors and national schedules of market access commitments. A Council for Trade in Services oversees the operation of the agreement.

The GATS framework consists of 29 articles, including the following set of basic obligations: total coverage of all internationally-traded services; national treatment, i.e. according services and service suppliers of other members no less favourable treatment than that accorded to domestic services and suppliers; MFN treatment (see above), with any specific exemptions to be recorded prior to the implementation of the GATS, with a limit of 10 years duration; transparency, requiring publication of all relevant national laws and legislations; bilateral agreements on recognition of standards and qualifications to be open to other members who wish to negotiate accession; no restrictions on international payments and transfers; progressive liberalization to be pursued; and market access and national treatment commitments to be bound and recorded in national schedules. These schedules, which include exemptions to the MFN principles, contain the negotiated and guaranteed conditions under which trade in services is conducted and are an integral part of the GATS.

Annexes to the GATS cover the movement of natural persons, permitting governments to negotiate specific commitments regarding the temporary stay of people for the purpose of providing a service; the right of governments to take measures in order to ensure the integrity and stability of the financial system; the role of telecommunications as a distinct sector of economic activity and as a means of supplying other economic activities; and air transport services, excluding certain activities relating to traffic rights.

At the end of the Uruguay Round governments agreed to continue negotiations in the following areas: basic telecommunications, maritime transport, movement of natural persons and financial services. The Protocol to the GATS relating to movement of natural persons was concluded in July 1995. In May 1996 the USA withdrew from negotiations to conclude an agreement on maritime transport services. At the end of June the participating countries agreed to suspend the discussions and to recommence negotiations in 2000.

In July 1995 some 29 members signed an interim agreement to grant greater access to the banking, insurance, investment and securities sectors from August 1996. Negotiations to strengthen the agreement and to extend it to new signatories (including the USA, which had declined to sign the agreement, claiming lack of reciprocity by some Asian countries) commenced in April 1997. A final agreement was successfully concluded in mid-December: 102 countries endorsed the elimination of restrictions on access to the financial services sectors from 1 March 1999, and agreed to subject those services to legally-binding rules and disciplines. In late January 1999 some 35 signatory states had yet to ratify the financial services agreement, and its entry into force was postponed. Negotiations on trade in basic telecommunications began in May 1994 and were scheduled to conclude in April 1996. Before the final deadline, however, the negotiations were suspended, owing to US concerns, which included greater access to satellite telecommunications markets in Asia and greater control over foreign companies operating from the domestic markets. An agreement was finally concluded by the new deadline of 15 February 1997. Accordingly the largest telecommunications markets, i.e. the USA, the EU and Japan, were to eliminate all remaining restrictions on domestic and foreign competition in the industry by 1 January 1998 (although delays were granted to Spain, until December 1998, Ireland, until 2000, and Greece and Portugal, until 2003). The majority of the 69 signatories to the accord also agreed on common rules to ensure that fair competition could be enforced by the WTO disputes settlement mechanism, and pledged their commitment to establishing a regulatory system for the telecommunications sector and guaranteeing transparency in government licensing. The agreement entered into force on 5 February 1998, having been rescheduled, owing to the delay on the part of some signatory countries (then totalling 72 states) in ratifying the accord and incorporating the principles of industry regulation into national legislation. The negotiations to liberalize trade in services were formally reopened in 2000, while new guide-lines and procedures for the negotiations were approved in March 2001. The negotiations were incorporated into the Doha Agenda and were to be concluded as part of a single undertaking by 1 January 2005.

INTELLECTUAL PROPERTY RIGHTS

The WTO Agreement on Trade-Related Aspects of Intellectual Property Rights (TRIPS) recognizes that widely varying standards in the protection and enforcement of intellectual property rights and the lack of multilateral disciplines dealing with international trade in counterfeit goods have been a growing source of tension in international economic relations. The TRIPS agreement aims to ensure that nationals of member states receive equally favourable treatment with regard to the protection of intellectual property and that adequate standards of intellectual property protection exist in all WTO member countries. These standards are largely based on the obligations of the Paris and Berne Conventions of WIPO (see p. 119), however, the agreement aims to expand and enhance these where necessary, for example: computer programmes, to be protected as literary works for copyright purposes; definition of trade marks eligible for protection; stricter rules of geographical indications of consumer products; a 10-year protection period for industrial designs; a 20-year patent protection available for all inventions; tighter protection of layout design of integrated circuits; and protection for trade secrets and 'know-how' with a commercial value.

Under the agreement member governments are obliged to provide procedures and remedies to ensure the effective enforcement of intellectual property rights. Civil and administrative procedures outlined in the TRIPS include provisions on evidence, injunctions, judicial authority to order the disposal of infringing goods, and criminal procedures and penalties, in particular for trade-mark counterfeiting and copyright piracy. A one-year period was envisaged for developed countries to bring their legislation and practices into conformity with the agreement. Developing countries were to do so in five years (or 10 years if an area of technology did not already have patent protection) and least-developed countries in 11 years. A Council for Trade-Related Property Rights monitors the compliance of governments with the agreement and its operation. During 2000 the implementation of TRIPS was one of the key areas of contention among WTO members. In November WTO initiated a review of TRIPS, although this was expected to consider alteration of the regime rather than of its implementation. At that time some 70 developing countries were failing to apply TRIPS rules. In November 2001 the WTO Ministerial Conference sought to resolve the ongoing dispute regarding the implementation of TRIPS in respect of pharmaceutical patents in developing countries. A separate declaration aimed to clarify a flexible interpretation of TRIPS in order for governments to meet urgent public health priorities. The deadline for some of the poorest countries to apply provisions on pharmaceutical patents was extended to 1 January 2016. The TRIPS Council was mandated to undertake further consideration of problems concerning compulsory licensing. The Doha Declaration also committed the Council to concluding, by the next Ministerial Conference, scheduled to be held in 2003, negotiations on a multilateral registration system for geographical indications for wines and spirits.

LEGAL FRAMEWORK

In addition to the binding agreements mentioned above, WTO aims to provide a comprehensive legal framework for the international trading system. Under GATT 1994 'anti-dumping' measures were permitted against imports of a product with an export price below its normal value, if these imports were are likely to cause damage to a domestic industry. The WTO agreement provides for greater clarity and more-detailed rules determining the application of these measures and determines settlement procedures in disputes relating to anti-dumping actions taken by WTO members. In general, anti-dumping measures were to be limited to five years. WTO's Agreement on Subsidies and Countervailing Measures is intended to expand on existing GATT agreements. It classifies subsidies into three categories: prohibited, which may be determined by the Dispute Settlement Body and must be immediately withdrawn; actionable, which must be withdrawn or altered if the subsidy is found to cause adverse effects on the interests of other members; and non-actionable, for example subsidies involving assistance to industrial research, assistance to disadvantaged regions or adaptation of facilities to meet new environmental requirements. The Agreement also contains provisions on the use of duties to offset the effect of a subsidy (so-called countervailing measures) and establishes procedures for the initiation and conduct of investigations into this action. Countervailing measures must generally be terminated within five years of their imposition. Least-developed countries, and developing countries with gross national product per capita of less than US $1,000, are exempt from disciplines on prohibited export subsidies; however, these were to be eliminated by 2003 in all other developing countries and by 2002 in countries with economies in transition.

WTO members may take safeguard actions to protect a specific domestic industry from a damaging increase of imported products. However, the WTO agreement aims to clarify criteria for imposing safeguards, their duration (normally to be no longer than four years, which may be extended to eight years) and consultations on trade compensation for the exporting countries. At 1 December 1995 50 member states had notified the Committee on Safeguards of the WTO Secretariat of their existing domestic safeguard legislations, as required under the agreement. Any measures to protect domestic industries through voluntary export restraints or other market-sharing devices were to be phased out by the end of 1998, or a year later for one specific safeguard measure, subject to mutual agreement of the members directly concerned. Safeguard measures are not applicable to products from developing countries as long as their share of imports of the product concerned does not exceed 3%.

Further legal arrangements act to ensure the following: that technical regulations and standards (including testing and certification procedures) do not create unnecessary obstacles to trade; that import licensing procedures are transparent and predictable; that the valuation of goods for customs purposes are fair and uniform; that GATT principles and obligations apply to import preshipment inspection activities; the fair and transparent administration of rules of origin; and that no investment measures which may restrict or distort trade may be applied. A Working Group on Notification Obligations and Procedures aims to ensure that members fulfil their notification requirements, which facilitate the transparency and surveillance of the trading rules.

PLURILATERAL AGREEMENTS

The majority of GATT agreements became multilateral obligations when the WTO became operational in 1995; however, four agreements, which have a selective group of signatories, remained in effect. These so-called plurilateral agreements, the Agreement on Trade in Civil Aircraft, the Agreement on Government Procurement, the International Dairy Agreement and the International Bovine Meat Agreement, aim to increase international co-operation and fair and open trade and competition in these areas. Each of the agreements establish their own management bodies, which are required to report to the General Council.

TRADE POLICY REVIEW MECHANISM

The mechanism, which was established provisionally in 1989, was given a permanent role in the WTO. Through regular monitoring and surveillance of national trade policies the mechanism aims to increase the transparency and understanding of trade policies and practices and to enable assessment of the effects of policies on the world trading system. In addition, it records efforts made by governments to bring domestic trade legislation into conformity with WTO provisions and to implement WTO commitments. Reviews are conducted in the Trade Policy Review Body on the basis of a policy statement of the government under review and an independent report prepared by the WTO Secretariat. Under the mechanism the world's four largest traders, the European Union, the USA, Japan and Canada, were to be reviewed every two years. Special groups were established to examine new regional free-trade arrangements and the trade policies of acceding countries. In February 1996 a single Committee on Regional Trade Agreements was established, superseding these separate working parties. The Committee aimed to ensure that these groupings contributed to the process of global trade liberalization and to study the implications of these arrangements on the multilateral system. At the Ministerial Conference held in December 1996 it was agreed to establish a new working group to conduct a study of transparency in government procurement practices.

SETTLEMENT OF DISPUTES

A separate annex to the WTO agreement determines a unified set of rules and procedures to govern the settlement of all WTO disputes, substantially reinforcing the GATT procedures. WTO members are committed not to undertake unilateral action against perceived violations of the trade rules, but to seek recourse in the dispute settlement mechanism and abide by its findings.

The first stage of the process requires bilateral consultations between the members concerned in an attempt to conclude a mutually-acceptable solution to the issue. These may be undertaken through the good offices and mediation efforts of the Director-General. Only after a consultation period of 60 days may the complainant ask the General Council, convened as the Dispute Settlement Body (DSB), to establish an independent panel to examine the case, which then does so within the terms of reference of the agreement cited. Each party to the dispute submits its arguments and then presents its case before the panel. Third parties which notify their interest in the dispute may also present views at the first substantive meeting of the panel. At this stage an expert review group may be appointed to provide specific scientific or technical advice. The panel submits sections and then a full interim report of its findings to the parties, who may then request a further review involving additional meetings. A final report should be submitted to the parties by the panel within six months of its establishment, or within three months in cases of urgency, including those related to perishable goods. Final reports are normally adopted by the DSB within 60 days of issuance. In the case of a measure being found to be inconsistent with the relevant WTO agreement, the panel recommends ways in which the member may bring the measure into conformity with the agreement. However, under the WTO mechanism either party has the right to appeal against the decision and must notify the DSB of its intentions before adoption of the final report. Appeal proceedings, which are limited to issues of law and the legal interpretation covered by the panel report, are undertaken by three members of the Appellate Body within a maximum period of 90 days. The report of the Appellate Body must be unconditionally accepted by the parties to the dispute (unless there is a consensus within the DSB against its adoption). If the recommendations of the panel or appeal report are not implemented immediately, or within a 'reasonable period' as determined by the DSB, the parties are obliged to negotiate mutually-acceptable compensation pending full implementation. Failure to agree compensation may result in the DSB authorizing the complainant to suspend concessions or obligations against the other party. In any case the DSB monitors the implementation of adopted recommendations or rulings, while any outstanding cases remain on its agenda until the issue is resolved. By April 2002 254 trade complaints had been notified to the WTO since 1995, on some 180 different issues.

In late 1997 the DSB initiated a review of the WTO's understanding on dispute settlement, as required by the Marrakesh Agreement. The Doha Declaration, which was adopted in November 2001, mandated further negotiations to be conducted on the review and on additional proposals to amend the dispute procedure as a separate undertaking from the rest of the work programme. Negotiations were to be concluded by May 2003.

CO-OPERATION WITH OTHER ORGANIZATIONS

WTO is mandated to pursue co-operation with the IMF and the World Bank, as well as with other multilateral organizations, in order to achieve greater coherence in global economic policy-making. In November 1994 the preparatory committee of the WTO resolved not to incorporate the new organization into the UN structure as a specialized agency. Instead, co-operation arrangements with the IMF and World Bank were to be developed. In addition, efforts were pursued to enhance co-operation with UNCTAD in research, trade and technical issues. The Directors-General of the two organizations agreed to meet at least twice a year in order to develop the working relationship. In particular, co-operation was to be undertaken in WTO's special programme of activities for Africa, which aimed to help African countries expand and diversify their trade and benefit from the global trading system. Since 1997 WTO has co-operated with the IMF, ITC, UNCTAD, UNDP and World Bank in an Integrated Framework for trade-related technical assistance to least developed countries. In 2000 WTO led efforts to enhance activities under this grouping.

International Trade Centre (UNCTAD/WTO): Palais des Nations, 1211 Geneva 10, Switzerland; tel. (22) 7300111; fax (22) 7334439; e-mail itcreg@intracen.org; internet www.intracen.org; f. 1964 by GATT; jointly operated with the UN (through UNCTAD) since 1968; ITC works with developing countries in product and market development, the development of trade support services, trade information, human resource development, international purchasing and supply management, and needs assessment and pro-gramme design for trade promotion; publs *International Trade Forum* (quarterly), market studies, handbooks, etc.

Executive Director: J. DENIS BÉLISLE.

Finance

The WTO's 2002 budget amounted to 143m. Swiss francs, financed mainly by contributions from members in proportion to their share of total trading conducted by WTO members.

Publications

Annual Report (2 volumes).

International Trade Statistics (annually).

World Trade Review (3 a year).

WTO Focus (monthly).

OTHER INTERNATIONAL ORGANIZATIONS

OTHER INTERNATIONAL ORGANIZATIONS

Agriculture, Food, Forestry and Fisheries

(For organizations concerned with agricultural commodities, see Commodities (see p. 335))

African Timber Organization—ATO: BP 1077, Libreville, Gabon; tel. 732928; fax 734030; e-mail oab-gabon@internetgabon .com; f. 1976 to enable members to study and co-ordinate ways of ensuring the optimum utilization and conservation of their forests; mems: 13 African countries; Sec.-Gen. (vacant); publs *ATO Information Bulletin* (quarterly), *International Magazine of African Timber* (2 a year).

Asian Vegetable Research and Development Center—AVRDC: POB 42, Shanhua, Tainan 741, Taiwan; tel. (6) 5837801; fax (6) 5830009; e-mail avrdcbox@netra.avrdc.org.tw; internet www .avrdc.org.tw; f. 1971; aims to enhance the nutritional well-being and raise the incomes of the poor in rural and urban areas of developing countries, through improved varieties and methods of vegetable production, marketing and distribution; runs an experimental farm, laboratories, gene-bank, greenhouses, quarantine house, insectarium, library and weather station; provides training for research and production specialists in tropical vegetables; exchanges and disseminates vegetable germplasm through regional centres in the developing world; serves as a clearing-house for vegetable research information; and undertakes scientific publishing; mems: Australia, France, Germany, Japan, Republic of Korea, Philippines, Taiwan, Thailand, USA; Dir-Gen. Dr THOMAS A. LUMPKIN; publs *Annual Report, Technical Bulletin, Proceedings, Centerpoint* (4 a year).

CAB International—CABI: Wallingford, Oxon, OX10 8DE, United Kingdom; tel. (1491) 832111; fax (1491) 833508; e-mail cabi@cabi .org; internet www.cabi.org; f. 1929 as the Imperial Agricultural Bureaux (later Commonwealth Agricultural Bureaux), current name adopted in 1985; aims to improve human welfare world-wide through the generation, dissemination and application of scientific knowledge in support of sustainable development; places particular emphasis on sustainable agriculture, forestry, human health and the management of natural resources, with priority given to the needs of developing countries; compiles and publishes extensive information (in a variety of print and electronic forms) on aspects of agriculture, forestry, veterinary medicine, the environment and natural resources, Third World rural development and others; maintains regional centres in Kenya, Malaysia, Pakistan, Switzerland, Trinidad and Tobago, and the United Kingdom; mems: 40 countries; Dir-Gen. Dr DENIS BLIGHT.

CABI Bioscience: Bakeham Lane, Egham, Surrey, TW20 9TY, United Kingdom; tel. (1491) 829000; fax (1491) 829100; e-mail bioscience@cabi.org; internet www.cabi-bioscience.org; f. 1998 by integration of the following four CABI scientific institutions: International Institute of Biological Control; International Institute of Entomology; International Institute of Parasitology; International Mycological Institute; undertakes research, consultancy, training, capacity-building and institutional development measures in sustainable pest management, biosystematics and molecular biology, ecological applications and environmental and industrial microbiology; maintains centres in Kenya, Malaysia, Pakistan, Switzerland, Trinidad and the United Kingdom; Dir DAVID DENT.

Collaborative International Pesticides Analytical Council Ltd—CIPAC: c/o Dr M. D. Müller, Swiss Federal Res. Station, 8820 Waedenswil, Switzerland; tel. (1) 7836412; fax (1) 7836439; e-mail markus.mueller@faw.admin.ca; internet www.cipac.org; f. 1957 to organize international collaborative work on methods of analysis for pesticides used in crop protection; mems: in 46 countries; Chair. Dr MARKUS D. MÜLLER (Switzerland); Sec. Dr LÁZLÓ BURA (Hungary).

Desert Locust Control Organization for Eastern Africa—DLCOEA: POB 30023, Nairobi, Kenya; tel. (20) 501704; fax (20) 505137; e-mail delco@insightkenya.com; f. 1962 to promote effective control of desert locust in the region and to conduct research into the locust's environment and behaviour; also assists member states in the monitoring, forecasting and extermination of other migratory pests; mems: Djibouti, Eritrea, Ethiopia, Kenya, Somalia, Sudan, Tanzania, Uganda; Dir PETER O. ODIYO; Co-ordinator J. M. GATIMU;

publs *Desert Locust Situation Reports*(monthly), *Annual Report*, technical reports.

European and Mediterranean Plant Protection Organization —EPPO: 1 rue Le Nôtre, 75016 Paris, France; tel. 1-45-20-77-94; fax 1-42-24-89-43; e-mail hq@eppo.fr; internet www.eppo.org; f. 1951, present name adopted in 1955; aims to promote international co-operation between government plant protection services to prevent the introduction and spread of pests and diseases of plants and plant products; mems: governments of 44 countries and territories; Chair. OLIVER FÉLIX; Dir-Gen. Dr IAN M. SMITH; publs *EPPO Bulletin, Data Sheets on Quarantine Organisms, Guidelines for the Efficacy Evaluation of Pesticides, Crop Growth Stage Keys, Summary of the Phytosanitary Regulations of EPPO Member Countries, Reporting Service.*

European Association for Animal Production—EAAP (Fédération européenne de zootechnie): Via Nomentana 134A, 00162 Rome, Italy; tel. (06) 86329141; fax (06) 86329263; e-mail eaap@eaap.org; internet www.eaap.org; f. 1949 to help improve the conditions of animal production and meet consumer demand; holds annual meetings; mems: asscns in 37 countries; Pres. A. AUMAITRE (France); publ. *Livestock Production Science* (16 a year).

European Association for Research on Plant Breeding—EUCARPIA: c/o Plant Breeding Department, University of Agricultural Sciences, Gregor Mendel Str. 33, 1180 Vienna, Austria; tel. (1) 47654-3309; fax (1) 47654-3342; e-mail vollmann@eucarpia.org; internet www.eucarpia.org; f. 1956 to promote scientific and technical co-operation in the plant breeding field; mems: 1,000 individuals, 64 corporate mems. Pres. Prof. PETER RUCKENBAUER (Austria); Sec. Dr JOHANN VOLLMANN (Austria); publ. *Bulletin.*

European Confederation of Agriculture—CEA: 23 rue de la Science, bte 23, 1040 Brussels, Belgium; tel. (2) 230-43-80; fax (2) 230-46-77; e-mail cea@pophost.eunet.be; f. 1889 as International Confederation, re-formed in 1948 as European Confederation; represents the interests of European agriculture in the international field; provides social security for independent farmers and foresters in the member countries; mems: 300 mems. in 30 countries; Pres. BEN GILL (UK); Gen. Sec. CHRISTOPHE HÉMARD (France); publs *CEA Dialog, Annual Report.*

European Grassland Federation: c/o Dr Willy Kessler, Swiss Federal Research Station for Agroecology and Agriculture, FAL Reckenholzstr. 191, Postfach 8046 Zürich, Switzerland; tel. and fax (317) 416386; e-mail egf-secr@pckassa.com; internet www .europeangrassland.org; f. 1963 to facilitate and maintain liaison between European grassland organizations and to promote the interchange of scientific and practical knowledge and experience; holds General Meeting every two years and symposia at other times; mems: 29 full and eight corresponding mem. countries in Europe; Pres. Dr PAUL STEFFEN; Sec. Dr WILLY KESSLER; publ. *Proceedings (Grassland Science in Europe).*

European Livestock and Meat Trading Union—UECBV: 81A rue de la Loi, 1040 Brussels, Belgium; tel. (2) 230-46-03; fax (2) 230-94-00; e-mail uecbv@pophost.eunet.be; internet uecbv.eunet.be; f. 1952 to study problems of the European livestock and meat trade and inform members of all relevant legislation; acts as an international arbitration commission; conducts research on agricultural markets, quality of livestock, and veterinary regulations; mems: national organizations in 23 countries, and the European Association of Livestock Markets; Pres. LAURENT SPANGHERO; Sec.-Gen. JEAN-LUC MERIAUX.

Inter-American Association of Agricultural Librarians, Documentalists and Information Specialists (Asociación Interamericana de Bibliotecarios, Documentalistas y Especialistas en Información Agrícolas—AIBDA): c/o IICA-CIDIA, Apdo 55-2200 Coronado, Costa Rica; tel. 216-0290; fax 216-0291; e-mail aibda@iica .ac.cr; internet www.iica.int/servicios/aibda; f. 1953 to promote professional improvement through technical publications and meetings, and to promote improvement of library services in agricultural sciences; mems: c. 400 in 29 countries and territories; Pres. GERARDO SÁNCHEZ AMBRIZ (Mexico); Exec. Sec. AURA MATA (Costa Rica); publs *Boletín Informativo* (3 a year), *Boletín Especial* (irregular), *Revista AIBDA* (2 a year), *AIBDA Actualidades* (4 or 5 a year).

Inter-American Tropical Tuna Commission—IATTC: S8604 La Jolla Shores Drive, La Jolla, CA 92037-1508, USA; tel. (858) 546-7100; fax (858) 546-7133; e-mail rallen@iattc.org; internet www.iattc

.org; f. 1950; administers two programmes, the Tuna-Billfish Programme and the Tuna-Dolphin Programme. The principal responsibilities of the Tuna-Billfish Programme are to study the biology of the tunas and related species of the eastern Pacific Ocean and to determine the effects of fishing and natural factors on their abundance, to recommend appropriate conservation measures in order to maintain stocks at levels which will afford maximum sustainable catches, and to collect information on compliance with Commission resolutions. The functions of the Tuna-Dolphin Programme are to monitor the abundance of dolphins and their mortality incidental to purse-seine fishing in the eastern Pacific Ocean, to study the causes of mortality of dolphins during fishing operations and promote the use of techniques and equipment that minimize these mortalities, to study the effects of different fishing methods on the various fish and other animals of the pelagic ecosystem, and to provide a secretariat for the International Dolphin Conservation Programme. mems: Costa Rica, Ecuador, El Salvador, France, Guatemala, Japan, Mexico, Nicaragua, Panama, Peru, USA, Vanuatu, Venezuela; Dir ROBIN L. ALLEN; publs *Bulletin* (irregular), *Annual Report, Stock Assessment Report* (annually), *Special Report* (irregular).

International Association for Cereal Science and Technology—ICC: Marxergasse 2, Postfach 47, 1033 Vienna, Austria; tel. (1) 707-72-02; fax (1) 707-72-04; e-mail gen.sec@icc.or.at; internet www.icc.or.at; f. 1955 (as the International Association for Cereal Chemistry; name changed 1986); aims to promote international co-operation in the field of cereal science and technology through the dissemination of information and the development of standard methods of testing and analysing products; mems: 49 mem. and six observer mem. states; Pres. JAN WILLEM VAN DER KAMP (Netherlands); Sec.-Gen. Dr HELMUT GLATTES (Austria).

International Association for Vegetation Science—IAVS: Alterra, Green World Research, POB 47, 6700 AA Wageningen, Netherlands; tel. (317) 477914; fax (317) 424988; e-mail j.h.j .schaminee@alterra.wag-ur.nl; internet www.iavs.org; f. 1938; mems: 1,500 in 70 countries; Chair. Prof. Dr E. O. BOX; Gen Sec. Dr J. H. J. SCHAMINÉE (Netherlands); publs *Phytocoenologia, Journal of Vegetation Science, Applied Vegetation Science.*

International Association of Agricultural Economists—IAAE: c/o Farm Foundation, 1211 West 22nd St, Suite 216, Oak Brook, IL 60523-2197, USA; tel. (630) 571-9393; fax (630) 571-9580; e-mail iaae@farmfoundation.org; internet www.iaae-agecon.org; f. 1929 to foster development of agricultural economic sciences; aims to further the application of research into agricultural processes; works to improve economic and social conditions for agricultural and rural life; mems: in 96 countries; Pres. JOACHIM VON BRAUN (Germany); Sec. and Treas. WALTER J. ARMBRUSTER (USA); publs *Agricultural Economics* (8 a year), *IAAE Newsletter* (2 a year).

International Association of Agricultural Information Specialists: c/o Margot Bellamy, 14 Queen St, Dorchester-on-Thames, Wallingford, Oxon OX10 7HR, United Kingdom; tel. (1865) 340054; e-mail margot.bellamy@fritillary.demon.co.uk; f. 1955 to promote agricultural library science and documentation and the professional interests of agricultural librarians and documentalists; affiliated to the International Federation of Library Assns and Institutions; mems: 600 in 84 countries; Pres. a.i. PAMELA ANDRÉ (USA); Sec.-Treas. MARGOT BELLAMY (UK); publs *Quarterly Bulletin, World Directory of Agricultural Information Resource Centres.*

International Association of Horticultural Producers—IAHP: Louis Pasteurlaan 6, POB 280,2700 AG Zoetermeen, Netherlands; tel. (79) 3470707; fax (79) 3470405; e-mail pt@tuinbouw.nl; internet www.aiph.org; f. 1948; represents the common interests of commercial horticultural producers in the international field; authorizes international horticultural exhibitions; mems: national asscns in 25 countries; Pres. BERND WERNER; Gen. Sec. TON BLOM (Netherlands); publ. *Yearbook of International Horticultural Statistics.*

International Bee Research Association—IBRA: 18 North Rd, Cardiff, CF10 3DT, United Kingdom; tel. (29) 2037-2409; fax (29) 2066-5522; e-mail info@ibra.org.uk; internet www.ibra.org.uk; f. 1949 to further bee research and provide an information service for bee scientists and bee-keepers world-wide; mems: 1,200 in 130 countries; Dir RICHARD JONES; Asst Dir Dr PAMELA MUNN; publs *Bee World* (quarterly), *Apicultural Abstracts* (quarterly), *Journal of Apicultural Research* (quarterly).

International Centre for Integrated Mountain Development—ICIMOD: POB 3226, Jawalakhel, Kathmandu, Nepal; tel. (1) 525313; fax (1) 524509; e-mail dits@icimod.org.np; internet www .icimod.org; f. 1983 to promote the well-being of mountain communities through effective socioeconomic development policies and programmes; advocates the sound management of fragile mountain habitats, especially in the Hindu Kush-Himalayan region; Dir-Gen. Dr GABRIEL CAMPBELL.

International Centre for Tropical Agriculture (Centro Internacional de Agricultura Tropical—CIAT): Apdo Aéreo 6713, Cali,

Colombia; tel. (2) 445-0000; fax (2) 445-0073; e-mail ciat@cgiar.org; internet www.ciat.cgiar.org; f. 1967 to contribute to the alleviation of hunger and poverty in tropical developing countries by using new techniques in agriculture research and training; focuses on production problems in field beans, cassava, rice and tropical pastures in the tropics; Dir-Gen. Dr JOACHIM VOSS; publs *Annual Report, Growing Affinities* (2 a year), *Pasturas Tropicales* (3 a year), catalogue of publications.

International Commission for the Conservation of Atlantic Tunas—ICCAT: Calle Corazón de Maria 8, 28020 Madrid, Spain; tel. (91) 4165600; fax (91) 4152612; e-mail info@iccat.es; internet www.iccat.es; f. 1969 under the provisions of the International Convention for the Conservation of Atlantic Tunas (1966) to maintain the populations of tuna and tuna-like species in the Atlantic Ocean and adjacent seas at levels that permit the maximum sustainable catch; collects statistics; conducts studies; mems: 34 contracting parties; Chair. M. MIYAHARA (Japan); Exec. Sec. Dr A. RIBEIRO LIMA (Portugal); publs *ICCAT Biennial Report, ICCAT Collective Vol. of Scientific PapersStatistical Bulletin* (annually), *Data Record* (annually).

International Commission of Sugar Technology (Commission Internationale Technique de Sucrerie—CITS): Marktbreiter Str. 74, 97199 Ochsenfurt, Germany; tel. (9331) 91450; fax (9331) 91462; f. 1949 to discuss investigations and promote scientific and technical research work; Pres. LÉON SUÉ (Belgium); Hon. Sec.-Gen. ROBERT PIECK.

International Committee for Animal Recording—ICAR: Villa del Ragno, Via Nomentana 134, 00161 Rome, Italy; tel. (06) 86329141; fax (06) 86329263; e-mail icar@eap.org; internet www .icar.org; f. 1951 to extend and improve the work of recording and to standardize methods; mems: in 58 countries; Pres. MARK JEFFRIES (New Zealand).

International Crops Research Institute for the Semi-Arid Tropics—ICRISAT: Patancheru 502 324, Andhra Pradesh, India; tel. (40) 23296161; fax (40) 23241239; e-mail icrisat@cgiar.org; internet www.icrisat.org; f. 1972 to promote the genetic improvement of crops and for research on the management of resources in the world's semi-arid tropics, with the aim of reducing poverty and protecting the environment; research covers all physical and socioeconomic aspects of improving farming systems on unirrigated land; Dir Dr WILLIAM D. DAR (Philippines); publs *ICRISAT Report* (annually), *SAT News* (2 a year), *International Chickpea and Pigeonpea Newsletter, International Arachis Newsletter, International Sorghum and Millet Newsletter* (annually), information and research bulletins.

International Dairy Federation—IDF: Diamant Bldg, 80 blvd Auguste Reyers, 1030 Brussels, Belgium; tel. (2) 733-98-88; fax (2) 733-04-13; e-mail info@fil-idf.org; internet www.fil-idf.org; f. 1903 to link all dairy asscns, in order to encourage the solution of scientific, technical and economic problems affecting the dairy industry; mems: national cttees in 41 countries; Dir-Gen. EDWARD HOPKIN (UK); publs *Bulletin of IDF, IDF Standards.*

International Federation of Agricultural Producers—IFAP: 60 rue St-Lazare, 75009 Paris, France; tel. 1-45-26-05-53; fax 1-48-74-72-12; e-mail ifap@ifap.org; internet www.ifap.org; f. 1946 to represent, in the international field, the interests of agricultural producers; encourages the exchange of information and ideas; works to develop understanding of world problems and their effects upon agricultural producers; encourages sustainable patterns of agricultural development; holds conference every two years; mems: national farmers' organizations and agricultural co-operatives of 71 countries; Pres. JACK WILKINSON (Canada); Sec.-Gen. DAVID KING; publs *The World Farmer* (monthly), *Proceedings of General Conferences.*

International Federation of Beekeepers' Associations—APIMONDIA: Corso Vittorio Emanuele II 101, 00186 Rome, Italy; tel. and fax (06) 6852286; fax (06) 6852287; e-mail apimondia@ mclink.it; internet www.apimondia.org; f. 1949; collects and brings up to date documentation on international beekeeping; carries out studies into the particular problems of beekeeping; organizes international congresses, seminars, symposia and meetings; co-operates with other international organizations interested in beekeeping, in particular, with the FAO; mems: 56 asscns from 52 countries; Pres. ASGER SØGAARD JØRGENSEN (Denmark); Sec.-Gen. RICCARDO JANNONI-SEBASTIANINI (Italy); publs *Apiacta* (quarterly, in English, French, German and Spanish), *Dictionary of Beekeeping Terms,* AGROVOC (thesaurus of agricultural terms), studies.

International Hop Growers' Convention: c/o Inštitut za hmeljarstvo in pivovarstvo, POB 51, 3310 Žalec, Slovenia; tel. (63) 712-16-18; fax (63) 712-16-20; e-mail martin.pavlovic@uni-lj.si; internet www.hmelj-giz.si/ihgc; f. 1950; acts as a centre for the collection of data and reports on hop production, beer exports and imports and sales, estimates the world crop and promotes scientific research;

mems: national asscns in 19 countries; Pres. MARTIN JOLLY (UK); Gen. Sec. Dr MARTIN PAVLOVIĆ.

International Institute for Beet Research—IIRB: ave de Tervuren 195, 1150 Brussels, Belgium; tel. (2) 737-70-90; fax (2) 737-70-99; e-mail mail@iirb.org; internet www.iirb.org; f. 1932 to promote research and the exchange of information; organizes meetings and study groups; mems: 600 in 33 countries; Pres. HANS-JÖRG GEBHARD (German); Sec.-Gen. RALPH BECKERS (Belgium).

International Institute of Tropical Agriculture—IITA: Oyo Rd, PMB 5320, Ibadan, Nigeria;; c/o Lambourn (UK) Ltd, Carolyn House, 26 Dingwall Rd., Croydon CR9 3EE, United Kindom (mailing addess); tel. (2) 241-2626; fax (2) 241-2221; e-mail ciat@cgiar.org; internet www.iita.org; f. 1967; principal financing arranged by the Consultative Group on International Agricultural Research—CGIAR (see p. 86), co-sponsored by the FAO, the IBRD and the UNDP; research programmes comprise crop management, improvement of crops and plant protection and health; conducts a training programme for researchers in tropical agriculture; maintains a library of 75,000 vols and data base; administers six agro-ecological research stations; Dir-Gen. Dr PETER HARTMAN (USA); publs *Annual Report, IITA Research* (quarterly), technical bulletins, research reports.

International Livestock Research Institute—ILRI: POB 30709, Nairobi, Kenya; tel. (20) 632311; fax (20) 631499; e-mail ilri-kenya@cgiar.org; internet www.cgiar.org/ilri; f. 1995 to supersede the International Laboratory for Research on Animal Diseases and the International Livestock Centre for Africa; conducts laboratory and field research on animal health and other livestock issues; carries out training programmes for scientists and technicians; maintains a specialized science library; Dir Dr CARLOS SERÉ; publs *Annual Report, Livestock Research for Development* (newsletter, 2 a year).

International Maize and Wheat Improvement Centre—CIMMYT: Apdo Postal 6-641, 06600 México, DF, Mexico; tel. (5) 804-2004; fax (5) 804-7558; e-mail cimmyt@cgiar.org; internet www.cimmyt.org; conducts world-wide research programme for sustainable maize and wheat cropping systems to help the poor in developing countries; Dir-Gen. Dr MASA IWANAGA.

International Organization for Biological Control of Noxious Animals and Plants: IOBC Permanent Secretariat, AGROPOLIS, ave Agropolis, 34394 Montpellier Cédex 5, France; e-mail iobc@agropolis.fr; internet www.oilb.agropolis.fr; f. 1955 to promote and co-ordinate research on the more effective biological control of harmful organisms; re-organized in 1971 as a central council with world-wide affiliations and six largely autonomous regional sections; Pres. Dr L.E. EHLER (USA); Sec.-Gen. Dr A. GASSMANN (Switzerland); publs *BioControl, Newsletter.*

International Organization of Citrus Virologists—IOCV: c/o C. N. Roistacher, Dept of Plant Pathology, Univ. of California, Riverside, CA 92521-0122, USA; tel. (909) 684-0934; fax (909) 684-4324; e-mail chester.r@worldnet.att.net; f. 1957 to promote research on citrus virus diseases at international level by standardizing diagnostic techniques and exchanging information; mems: 250; Chair. PEDRO MORENO; Sec. CHESTER N. ROISTACHER.

International Red Locust Control Organization for Central and Southern Africa—IRLCO-CSA: POB 240252, Ndola, Zambia; tel. (2) 612057; fax (2) 614285; e-mail locust@zamnet.zm; f. 1971 to control locusts in eastern, central and southern Africa; also assists in the control of African army-worm and quelea-quelea; mems: seven countries; Dir Dr AFETE DIVELIAS. GADABU; publs *Annual Report, Quarterly Report, Monthly Report,* scientific reports.

International Rice Research Institute—IRRI: Los Baños, Laguna, DAPO Box 7777, Metro Manila, Philippines; tel. (2) 845-0563; fax (2) 891-1292; e-mail irri@cgiar.org; internet www.irri.orgi; f. 1960; conducts research on rice, with the aim of developing technologies of environmental, social and economic benefit; works to enhance national rice research systems and offers training; operates Riceworld, a museum and learning centre about rice; maintains a library of technical rice literature; organizes international conferences and workshops; Dir-Gen. Dr RONALD P. CANTRELL; publs *Rice Literature Update, Hotline, Facts about IRRI, News about Rice and People, International Rice Research Notes.*

International Seed Testing Association—ISTA: Zürichstrasse 50, Postfach 308, 8303 Bassersdorf, Switzerland; tel. (1) 8386000; fax (1) 8386001; e-mail ista.office@ista.ch; internet www.seedtest .org; f. 1924 to promote uniformity and accurate methods of seed testing and evaluation in order to facilitate efficiency in production, processing, distribution and utilization of seeds; organizes meetings, workshops, symposia, training courses and triennial congresses; mems: 72 countries; Sec.-Gen. Dr M. MUSCHICK; Pres. Prof. Dr N. LEIST (Germany); publs *Seed Science and Technology* (3 a year), *Seed Testing International (ISTA News Bulletin)* (2 a year).

International Sericultural Commission—ISC: 25 quai Jean-Jacques Rousseau, 69350 La Mulatière, France; tel. 4-78-50-41-98; fax 4-78-86-09-57; f. 1948 to encourage the development of silk production; mems: governments of Brazil, Egypt, France, India, Indonesia, Iran, Japan, Lebanon, Madagascar, Romania, Thailand, Tunisia, Turkey; Sec.-Gen. Dr GÉRARD CHAVANCY (France); publ. *Sericologia* (quarterly).

International Service for National Agricultural Research—ISNAR: Laan van Nieuw Oost Indie 133, 2593 BM The Hague; POB 93375, 2509 AJ The Hague, Netherlands; tel. (70) 349-61-00; fax (70) 381-96-77; e-mail isnar@cgiar.org; internet www.isnar.cgiar.org; f. 1980 by the Consultative Group on International Agricultural Research—CGIAR (see p. 86) to strengthen national agricultural research systems in developing countries; promotes appropriate research policies, the creation of sustainable research institutions and improved research management; provides advisory, training and research services and information; Chair. MOÏSE MENSAH; Dir-Gen. STEIN W. BIE.

International Society for Horticultural Science—ISHS: Decroylaan 42 (01.21), POB 500, 3001 Leuven 1, Belgium; tel. (16) 22-94-27; fax (16) 22-94-50; e-mail info@ishs.org; internet www.ishs .org; f. 1959 to promote co-operation in horticultural science research; mems: 54 mem. countries, 300 organizations, 5,000 individuals; Pres. Dr NORMAN E. LOONEY (Canada); Exec. Dir Ir JOZEF VAN ASSCHE (Belgium); publs *Chronica Horticulturae* (quarterly), *Acta Horticulturae, Scientia Horticulturae* (monthly), *Horticultural Research International.*

International Union of Forest Research Organizations—IUFRO: 1140 Vienna-Hadersdorf, Austria; tel. (1) 877-01-51-0; fax (1) 877-01-51-50–0; internet iufro.boku.ac.at; e-mail iufro@forvie.ac .at; f. 1892; mems: 700 organizations in 115 countries, involving more than 15,000 scientists; Pres. Prof. RISTO SEPPÄLÄ (Finland); Sec. HEINRICH SCHMUTZENHOFER (Austria); publs *Annual Report, IUFRO News* (quarterly), *IUFRO World Series, IUFRO Occasional Paper Series, IUFRO Research Series.*

International Union for the Protection of New Plant Varieties (Union internationale pour la protection des obtentions végétales—UPOV): c/o 34 chemin des Colombettes, 1211 Geneva 20, Switzerland; tel. (22) 338-91-1153; fax (22) 733-03-36; e-mail upov .mail@wipo.intrg; internet www.upov.int; f. 1961 by the International Convention for the Protection of New Varieties of Plants (entered into force 1968, revised in 1972, 1978 and 1991); aims to encourage the development of new plant varieties and provide an effective system of protection. Admin. support provided by WIPO; mems: 52 signatory states; Pres. KARL OLOV ÖSTER; Dir.-Gen. Dr KAMIL IDRIS.

International Union of Soil Sciences: c/o Institute of Soil Science, University of Reading, POB 233, Reading RG6 6DW, United Kingdom; tel. (118) 378-6559; fax (118) 378-6666; e-mail iusss@rdg .ac.uk; internet www.iuss.org; f. 1924; mems: national academies or national soil science societies from 143 countries; Pres. Prof. DONALD SPARKS (UK); Sec.-Gen. Dr STEPHEN NORTCLIFF (UK); publ. *Bulletin* (2 a year).

International Whaling Commission—IWC: The Red House, 135 Station Rd, Impington, Cambridge, CB4 9NP, United Kingdom; tel. (1223) 233971; fax (1223) 232876; e-mail secretariat@iwcoffice.com; internet www.iwcoffice.org; f. 1946 under the International Convention for the Regulation of Whaling, for the conservation of world whale stocks; reviews the regulations covering whaling operations; encourages research; collects, analyses and disseminates statistical and other information on whaling. A ban on commercial whaling was passed by the Commission in July 1982, to take effect three years subsequently (in some cases, a phased reduction of commercial operations was not completed until 1988). A revised whale-management procedure was adopted in 1992, to be implemented after the development of a complete whale management scheme. mems: governments of 49 countries; Chair. Prof. BO FERNHOLM (Sweden); Sec. Dr NICOLA GRANDY; publ. *Annual Report.*

North Pacific Anadromous Fish Commission: 889 W. Pender St, Suite 502, Vancouver, BC V6C 3B2, Canada; tel. (604) 775-5550; fax (604) 775-5577; e-mail secretariat@npafc.org; f. 1993; mems: Canada, Japan, Russia, USA; Exec. Dir VLADIMIR FEDORENKO; publs *Annual Report, Newsletter* (2 a year), *Statistical Yearbook, Scientific Bulletin, Technical Report.*

Northwest Atlantic Fisheries Organization—NAFO: 2 Morris Drive, POB 638, Dartmouth, NS B2Y 3Y9, Canada; tel. (902) 468-5590; fax (902) 468-5538; e-mail info@nafo.ca; internet www.nafo.ca; f. 1979 (formerly International Commission for the Northwest Atlantic Fisheries); aims at optimum use, management and conservation of resources; promotes research and compiles statistics; Pres. E. OLTUSKI (Cuba); Exec. Sec. Dr J. FISHER; publs *Annual Report, Statistical Bulletin, Journal of Northwest Atlantic Fishery Science, Scientific Council Reports, Scientific Council Studies, Sampling Yearbook, Proceedings.*

World Association for Animal Production—WAAP: Villa del Ragno, Via Nomentana 134, 00162 Rome, Italy; tel. (06) 86329141; fax (06) 86329263; e-mail waap@waap.it; internet www.waap.it; f. 1965; holds world conference on animal production every five years; encourages, sponsors and participates in regional meetings, seminars and symposia; mems: 17 mem. organizations; Pres. AKKE J. VAN DER ZIJPP (Netherlands); Sec.-Gen. JEAN GEORGES BOYAZOGLU (Greece); publ. *WAAP Newsletter.*

World Association of Veterinary Food-Hygienists—WAVFH: Federal Institute for Health Protection of Consumers and Veterinary Medicine (BgVV), Diedersdorfer Weg 1, 12277 Berlin, Germany; tel. (30) 8412-2101; fax (30) 8412-2951; e-mail p.teufel@bgvv .de; f. 1955 to promote hygienic food control and discuss research; mems: national asscns in 40 countries; Pres. Prof. PAUL TEUFEL; Sec. Treas. Dr L. ELLERBROEK.

World Association of Veterinary Microbiologists, Immunologists and Specialists in Infectious Diseases: Ecole Nationale Vétérinaire d'Alfort, 7 ave du Général de Gaulle, 94704 Maisons-Alfort Cédex, France; tel. 1-43-96-70-21; fax 1-43-96-70-22; f. 1967 to facilitate international contacts in the fields of microbiology, immunology and animal infectious diseases; Pres. Prof. C. PILET (France); publs *Comparative Immunology, Microbiology and Infectious Diseases.*

WorldFish Center (International Centre for Living Aquatic Resources Management—ICLARM): Jalan Batu Maung, Batu Maung, 11960 Bayan Lepas, Penang; POB 500, 10670 Penang, Malaysia; tel. (4) 626-1606; fax (4) 626-5530; e-mail worldfishcenter@cgiar.org; internet www.worldfishcenter.org; f. 1973; became a mem. of the Consultative Group on International Agricultural Research—CGIAR (see p. 86) in 1992; aims to contribute to food security and poverty eradication in developing countries through the sustainable development and use of living aquatic resources; carries out research and promotes partnerships; Dir-Gen. MERYL J. WILLIAMS; publs *NAGA* (quarterly newsletter).

World Ploughing Organization—WPO: Søkildevej 17, 5270 Odense N, Denmark; tel. 65-97-80-06; fax 65-93-24-40; internet www.worldploughing.org; f. 1952 to promote the World Ploughing Contest in a different country each year, to improve techniques and promote better understanding of soil cultivation practices through research and practical demonstrations; arranges tillage clinics world-wide; mems: affiliates in 29 countries; Gen. Sec. CARL ALLESO; publ. *WPO Handbook* (annually).

World's Poultry Science Association—WPSA: c/o Dr P. C. M. Simons, Centre for Applied Poultry Research, 'Het Spelderholt', POB 31, 7360 AA Beekbergen, Netherlands; tel. (55) 506-6534; fax (55) 506-4858; e-mail p.c.m.simons@pp.agro.nl; internet www.wpsa .com; f. 1912 to exchange knowledge in the industry, to encourage research and teaching, to publish information relating to production and marketing problems, to promote World Poultry Congresses and co-operate with governments; mems: individuals in 95 countries, branches in 55 countries; Pres. Dr PETER HUNTON (Canada); Sec. Dr PIET C. M. SIMONS (Netherlands); publ. *The World Poultry Science Journal* (quarterly).

World Veterinary Association: Rosenlunds Allé 8, 2720 Vanlose, Denmark; tel. 38-71-01-56; fax 38-71-03-22; e-mail wva@ddd.dk; internet www.worldvet.org; f. 1959 as a continuation of the International Veterinary Congresses; organizes quadrennial congress; mems: organizations in 76 countries, 19 organizations of veterinary specialists as associate members; Pres. Dr HERBERT SCHNEIDER (Namibia); Exec. Sec. Dr LARS HOLSAAE.

Arts and Culture

Europa Nostra—Pan-European Federation for Heritage: Lange Voorhout 35, 2514 EC The Hague, Netherlands; tel. (70) 302-4050; fax (70) 361-7865; e-mail office@europanostra.org; internet www.europanostra.org; f. 1963; groups organizations and individuals concerned with the protection and enhancement of the European architectural and natural heritage and of the European environment; has consultative status with the Council of Europe; mems: 225 mem. organizations, more than 150 associate mems, more than 40 supporting bodies, more than 1,200 individual mems; Pres. HRH The Prince Consort of Denmark; Exec. Pres. OTTO VON DER GABLENTZ (Germany); Sec.-Gen. SNESKA QUAEDVLIEG-MIHAILOVIĆ.

European Association of Conservatoires, Music Academies and Music High Schools: POB 805, 3500 AV Utrecht, Netherlands; tel. (30) 236-12-42; fax (30) 236-12-90; e-mail aecinfo@aecinfo .org; internet www.aecinfo.org; f. 1953; aims to establish and foster contacts and exchanges between and represent the interests of members; initiates and supports international collaboration through research projects, congresses and seminars; mems: 187 mems, 22 associate mems. Pres. Dr IAN HORSBRUGH; Gen. Sec. JOHANNES JOHANSSON; publs *The European Cultural Heritage Review* (annually), *Europa Nostra Scientific Bulletin,* conference proceedings.

European Society of Culture: Guidecca 54P (Calle Michelangelo, Villa Hériot), 30133 Venice, Italy; tel. (041) 5230210; fax (041) 5231033; e-mail soceurcultur@flashnet.it; f. 1950 to unite artists, poets, scientists, philosophers and others through mutual interests and friendship in order to safeguard and improve the conditions required for creative activity; maintains a library of 10,000 volumes; mems: national and local centres, and 2,000 individuals, in 60 countries; Pres. Prof. VINCENZO CAPPELLETTI (Italy); Gen. Sec. Dott. MICHELLE CAMPAGNOLO-BOUVIER.

Inter-American Music Council (Consejo Interamericano de MúsicaCIDEM): 2511 P St NW, Washington, DC 20007, USA; f. 1956 to promote the exchange of works, performances and information in all fields of music, to study problems relative to music education, to encourage activity in the field of musicology, to promote folklore research and music creation, and to establish distribution centres for music material of the composers of the Americas; mems: national music societies of 33 American countries; Sec.-Gen. EFRAÍN PAESKY.

International Association of Art—IAA: Maison de l'UNESCO, 1 rue Miollis, 75732 Paris Cédex 15, France; tel. 1-45-68-26-55; fax 1-45-67-22-87; f. 1954; mems: 104 national committees; Pres. UNA WALKER; Sec.-Gen. J. C. DE SALINS; publ *IAA Newsletter* (quarterly).

International Association of Art Critics: 15 rue Martel, 75010 Paris, France; tel. 1-47-70-17-42; fax 1-47-70-17-81; e-mail paris .office@aica-int.org; internet www.aica-int.org; f. 1949 to increase co-operation in plastic arts, promote international cultural exchanges and protect the interests of mems; mems: 4,062 in 77 countries; Pres. HENRY MEYRIC HUGHES (UK); Sec.-Gen. RAMON TIO BELLIDO (France); publs *Annuaire, Newsletter* (quarterly).

International Association of Bibliophiles: Réserve des livres rares, Quai François Mauriac, 75706 Cédex 13, France; fax 1-53-79-54-60; f. 1963 to create contacts between bibliophiles and encourage book-collecting in different countries; organizes and encourages congresses, meetings, exhibitions and the award of scholarships; mems: 450; Pres. Conde DE ORGAZ (Spain); Sec.-Gen. JEAN-MARC CHATELAIN (France); publs *Le Bulletin du Bibliophile* (2 a year), yearbooks.

International Association of Literary Critics: 38 rue du Faubourg St-Jacques, 75014 Paris, France; tel. 1-53-10-12-13; fax 1-53-10-12-12; internet www.aicl.org; f. 1969; national centres in 34 countries; organizes congresses; Pres. ROBERT ANDRÉ; publ *Revue* (2 a year).

International Association of Museums of Arms and Military History—IAMAM: c/o Senior Curator, Koninklijk Nederlands Leger en Wapenmuseum, Delft, Netherlands; tel. (4) 221-94-16; fax (4) 221-94-01; e-mail claude.gaier@museedarmes.be; internet www .klm-mra.be/ICOMAM/index.htm; f. 1957; links museums and other scientific institutions with public collections of arms and armour and military equipment, uniforms, etc. holds triennial conferences and occasional specialist symposia; mems: 260 institutions in 60 countries. name change to International Cttee of Museums of Arms and Military History pending in 2003. Pres. GUY M. WILSON (UK); Sec.-Gen. JAN PIET PUYPE (Netherlands); publ *The Mohonk Courier.*

International Board on Books for Young People—IBBY: Nonnenweg 12, Postfach, 4003 Basel, Switzerland; tel. (61) 272-2917; fax (61) 272-2757; e-mail ibby@eye.ch; internet www.ibby.org; f. 1953 to support and link bodies in all countries connected with children's book work; encourages the distribution of good children's books; promotes scientific investigation into problems of juvenile books; presents the Hans Christian Andersen Award every two years to a living author and a living illustrator whose work is an outstanding contribution to juvenile literature; presents the IBBY-Asahi Reading Promotion Award annually to an organization that has made a significant contribution towards the encouragement of reading; sponsors International Children's Book Day (2 April); mems: national sections and individuals in more than 60 countries; Pres. PETER SCHNECK (Austria); Exec. Dir LEENA MAISSEN; publs *Bookbird* (quarterly, in English), *Congress Papers, IBBY Honour List* (every 2 years), special bibliographies.

International Centre for the Study of the Preservation and Restoration of Cultural Property—ICCROM: Via di San Michele 13, 00153 Rome, Italy; tel. (06) 585-531; fax (06) 5855-3349; e-mail iccrom@iccrom.org; internet www.iccrom.org; f. 1959; assembles documents on the preservation and restoration of cultural property; stimulates research and proffers advice; organizes missions of experts; undertakes training of specialists; mems: 104 countries; Dir-Gen. Dr NICHOLAS STANLEY-PRICE (UK); publ *Newsletter* (annually, in English and French).

International Centre of Films for Children and Young People (Centre international du film pour l'enfance et la jeunesse—CIFEJ): 3774 rue Saint-Denis, Bureau 200, Montréal, QC H2W 2M1,

Canada; tel. (514) 284-9388; fax (514) 284-0168; e-mail info@cifej .com; internet www.cifej.com; f. 1955; serves as a clearing house for information about: entertainment films (cinema and television) for children and young people, the influence of films on the young, and the regulations in force for the protection and education of young people; promotes production and distribution of suitable films and their appreciation; awards the CIFEJ prize at selected film festivals; mems: 163 mems in 53 countries; Exec. Dir JO-ANNE BLOUIN; publ *CIFEJ Info* (monthly).

International Committee for the Diffusion of Arts and Literature through the Cinema (Comité international pour la diffusion des arts et des lettres par le cinéma—CIDALC): 24 blvd Poissonnière, 75009 Paris, France; tel. 1-42-46-13-60; f. 1930 to promote the creation and release of educational, cultural and documentary films and other films of educational value, in order to contribute to closer understanding between peoples; awards medals and prizes for films of exceptional merit; mems: national committees in 19 countries; Pres. JEAN-PIERRE FOUCAULT (France); Sec.-Gen. MARIO VERDONE (Italy); publs *Annuaire CIDALC, Cinéma éducatif et culturel*.

International Comparative Literature Association—ICLA (Association Internationale de Littérature Comparée): c/o Paola Mildonian, Letterature Comparate, Dipartim. di Studi Anglo-Americani e Ibero-Americani, Università Ca' Foscari-Venezia, Ca' Garzoni, S. Marco 3417, 30124 Venice, Italy; tel. (041) 257-8427; fax (041) 257-8476; e-mail iclaweb@byu.edu; internet www.byu.edu/icla; f. 1954 to work for the development of the comparative study of literature in modern languages; mems: societies and individuals in 78 countries; Pres. KOJI KAWAMOTO; publs *ICLA Bulletin* (annually), *Literary Research* (2 a year).

International Confederation of Societies of Authors and Composers—World Congress of Authors and Composers: 20–26 blvd du Parc, 92200 Neuilly-sur-Seine, France; tel. 1-55-62-08-50; fax 1-55-62-08-60; e-mail cisac@cisac.org; internet www.cisac.org; f. 1926 to protect the rights of authors and composers; organizes biennial congress; mems: 204 mem. societies from 105 countries; Sec.-Gen. ERIC BAPTISTE.

International Council of Graphic Design Associations—ICOGRADA: POB 5, Forest 2, 1190 Brussels, Belgium; tel. (2) 344-58-43; fax (2) 344-71-38; e-mail secretariat@icograda.org; internet www.icograda.org; f. 1963; aims to raise standards of graphic design; promotes the exchange of information; organizes exhibitions and congresses; maintains library, slide collection and archive; mems: 68 asscns in 43 countries; Pres. ROBERT L. PETERS (Canada); Sec.-Gen. TIFFANY TURKINGTON (South Africa); publs *Newsletter* (quarterly), *Regulations and Guidelines governing International Design Competitions, Model Code of Professional Conduct*, other professional documents.

International Council of Museums—ICOM: Maison de l'UNESCO, 1 rue Miollis, 75732 Paris Cédex 15, France; tel. 1-47-34-05-00; fax 1-43-06-78-62; e-mail secretariat@icom.museum; internet www.icom.museum; f. 1946 to further international co-operation among museums and to advance museum interests; maintains with UNESCO the organization's documentation centre; mems: 17,000 individuals and institutions in 1409 countries; Pres. JACQUES PEROT (France); Sec.-Gen. MANUS BRINKMAN (Netherlands); publ *ICOM News—Nouvelles de l'ICOM—Noticias del ICOM* (quarterly).

International Council on Monuments and Sites—ICOMOS: 49–51 rue de la Fédération, 75015 Paris, France; tel. 1-45-67-67-70; fax 1-45-66-06-22; e-mail secretariat@icomos.org; internet www .icomos.org; f. 1965 to promote the study and preservation of monuments and sites and to arouse and cultivate the interest of public authorities and people of every country in their cultural heritage; disseminates the results of research into the technical, social and administrative problems connected with the conservation of the architectural heritage; holds triennial General Assembly and Symposium; mems: c. 7,000, 21 international committees, 105 national committees; Pres. Dr MICHAEL PETZET (Germany); Sec.-Gen. JEAN-LOUIS LUXEN (Belgium); publs *ICOMOS Newsletter* (quarterly), *Scientific Journal* (quarterly).

International Federation for Theatre Research—IFTR (Fédération Internationale pour la Recherche Théâtrale): c/o Dean of Arts & Humanities, Lancaster University, Lancaster, LA1 4YN, United Kingdom; e-mail d.whitton@lancaster.ac.uk; internet www .firt-iftr.org; f. 1955 by 21 countries at the International Conference on Theatre History, London; Pres. Prof. JOSETTE FÉRAL; Canada; Joint Secs-Gen. Prof. DAVID WHITTON; UK, Prof. CHRISTIANE PAGE; France; publs *Theatre Research International* (in association with Oxford University Press; 3 a year), *Bulletin* (2 a year).

International Federation of Film Archives (FédérationiInternationale des Archives du Film—FIAF): rue Defacqz 1, B-1000 Brussels, Belgium; tel. (2) 538-30-65; fax (2) 534-47-74; e-mail info@ fiafnet.org; internet www.fiafnet.org; f. 1938 to encourage the creation of audio-visual archives for the collection and conservation of the moving image heritage of every country; facilitates co-operation

and exchanges between film archives; promotes public interest in the art of the cinema; aids and conducts research; compiles new documentation; holds annual congress; mems: in 65 countries; Pres. IVAN TRUJILLO BOLIO (Mexico); Sec.-Gen. Dr STEVEN RICCI (USA); publs *Journal of Film Preservation* (2 a year), *FIAF International Film Archive Database* (2 a year).

International Federation of Film Producers' Associations (Fédération Internationale des associations de Producteurs de Films —FIAPF): 9 rue de l'Echelle, 75002 Paris, France; tel. 1-44-77-97-50; fax 1-42-56-16-52; e-mail infos@fiapf.org; internet fiapf.org; f. 1933 to represent film production internationally, to defend its general interests and promote its development; studies all cultural, legal, economic, technical and social problems related to film production; mems: national asscns in 23 countries; Pres. AURELIO DE LAURENTIIS (Italy); Dir-Gen. ANDRÉ CHAUBEAU (France).

International Institute for Children's Literature and Reading Research (Internationales Institut für Jugendliteratur und Leseforschung): 1040 Vienna, Mayerhofgasse 6, Austria; tel. (1) 50503-59; fax (1) 50503-5917; e-mail office@jugendliteratur.net; internet www.jugendliteratur.net; f. 1965 as an international documentation, research and advisory centre of juvenile literature and reading; maintains specialized library; arranges conferences and exhibitions; compiles recommendation lists; mems: individual and group members in 28 countries; Pres. Dr HILDE HAWLICEK; Dir KARIN HALLER; publ *1000 & 1 Buch* (quarterly).

International Institute for Conservation of Historic and Artistic Works: 6 Buckingham St, London, WC2N 6BA, United Kingdom; tel. (20) 7839-5975; fax (20) 7976-1564; e-mail iicon@ compuserve.com; internet www.iiconservation.org; f. 1950; mems: 3,350 individual, 450 institutional mems. Pres. ANDREW ODDY; Exec. Sec. PERRY SMITH; publs *Studies in Conservation* (quarterly), *Reviews in Conservation* (annually).

International Liaison Centre for Cinema and Television Schools (Centre international de liaison des écoles de cinéma et de télévision—CILECT): 8 rue Thérésienne, 1000 Brussels, Belgium; tel. (2) 511-98-39; fax (2) 511-98-39; e-mail hverh.cilect@skynet.be; internet www.cilect.org; f. 1955 to link higher teaching and research institutes and improve education of makers of films and television programmes; organizes conferences and student film festivals; runs a training programme for developing countries; mems: 107 institutions in 52 countries; Pres. CATERINA D'AMICO (Italy); Exec. Sec. HENRY VERHASSELT (Belgium); publ *Newsletter*.

International Music Council—IM: Maison de l'UNESCO, 1 rue Miollis, 75732 Paris Cédex 15, France; tel. 1-45-68-48-50; fax 1-43-06-87-98; e-mail imc@unesco.org; internet www.unesco.org/imc; f. 1949 to foster the exchange of musicians, music (written and recorded), and information between countries and cultures; mems: 34 international non-governmental organizations, national committees in 74 countries; Pres. KIFAH FAKHOURI (Jordan); Exec. Dir SILJA FISCHER (Germany).

Members of IMC include:

European Festivals Association: Château de Coppet, BP 26, 1296 Coppet, Switzerland; tel. (22) 776-8673; fax (22) 776-4275; e-mail geneva@eurofestival.net; internet www.euro-festival.net; f. 1952 to maintain high artistic standards and the representative character of art festivals; holds annual General Assembly; mems: 92 regular international performing arts festivals in 30 European countries, Israel, Japan, Lebanan and Mexico; Pres. FRANS DE RUITER; publ *Festivals* (annually).

International Association of Music Libraries, Archives and Documentation Centres—IAML: c/o Cataloguing Dept, Carleton Univ. Library, 1125 Colonel By Drive, Ottawa, ON K1S 5B6, Canada; tel. (613) 520-2600; fax (613) 520-3583; e-mail alison hall@carleton.ca; internet www.cilea.it/music/iame/ iamchome.htm; f. 1951; mems: 2,003 institutions and individuals in 58 countries; Pres. JOHN H. ROBERTS (USA); Sec.-Gen. ALISON HALL (Canada); publ *Fontes artis musicae* (quarterly).

International Council for Traditional Music—ICTM: Dept of Ethnomusicology, UCLA, 2539 Schoenberg, Box 957178, Los Angeles, California, CA 90095-7178, USA; tel. (310) 794-1858; fax (310) 206-4738; e-mail ictm@arts.ucla.edu; internet www .ethnomusic.ucla.edu/ictm; f. 1947 (as International Folk Music Council) to further the study, practice, documentation, preservation and dissemination of traditional music of all countries; holds conference every two years; mems: 1,650; Pres. Dr KRISTER MALM (Sweden); Sec.-Gen. Prof. ANTHONY SEEGER (USA); publs *Yearbook for Traditional Music, ICTM Bulletin* (2 a year), *Directory of Traditional Music* (every 2 years).

International Federation of Musicians: 21 bis rue Victor Massé, 75009 Paris, France; tel. 1-45-26-31-23; fax 1-45-26-31-57; e-mail fimparis@compuserve.com; internet www.fim-musicians .com/; f. 1948 to promote and protect the interests of musicians in affiliated unions; promotes international exchange of musicians; mems: 69 unions totalling 250,000 individuals in 57 countries; Pres. JOHN MORTON (UK); Gen. Sec. BENOÎT MACHUEL (France).

International Music Centre (Internationales Musikzentrum—IMZ): 1230 Vienna, Speisinger Str. 121–127, Austria; tel. (1) 889 03-15; fax (1) 889 03-1577; e-mail office@imz.at; internet www.imz .at; f. 1961 for the study and dissemination of music through technical media (film, television, radio, gramophone); organizes congresses, seminars and screenings on music in audio-visual media; holds courses and competitions designed to strengthen the relationship between performing artists and audio-visual media; mems: 110 ordinary mems and 30 associate mems in 33 countries, including 50 broadcasting organizations; Pres. HENK VAN DER MEULEN (Netherlands); Sec.-Gen. FRANZ A. PATAY (Austria); publ *IMZ-Magazine* (5 a year, in English).

International Society for Contemporary Music—ISCM: c/o Gaudeamus, Swammerdamstraat 38, 1091 RV Amsterdam, Netherlands; tel. (20) 6947349; fax (20) 6947258; e-mail info@iscm.nl; internet www.iscm.nl; f. 1922 to promote the development of contemporary music; organizes annual World Music Day; mems: organizations in 48 countries; Pres. RICHARD TSANG; Sec.-Gen. HENK HEUVELMANS.

Jeunesses Musicales International—JMI: Palais des Beaux-Arts, 10 rue Royale, 1000 Brussels, Belgium; tel. (2) 513-97-74; fax (2) 514-47-55; e-mail mail@jmi.net; internet www.jmi.net; f. 1945 to enable young people to develop, through music, and to stimulate contacts between member countries; mems: organizations in 40 countries; Sec.-Gen. DAG FRANZÉN; *JMI News*(6 a year).

World Federation of International Music Competitions—WFIMC: 104 rue de Carouge, 1205 Geneva, Switzerland; tel. (22) 3213620; fax (22) 7811418; e-mail fmcim@iprolink.ch; internet www.wfimc.org; f. 1957 to co-ordinate the arrangements for affiliated competitions and to exchange experience; holds General Assembly annually; mems: 112; Pres. MARIANNE GRANVIG; Sec.-Gen. RENATE RONNEFELD.

International PEN (A World Association of Writers): 9–10 Charterhouse Bldgs, Goswell Rd, London, EC1M 7AT, United Kingdom; tel. (20) 7253-4308; fax (20) 7253-5711; e-mail intpen@dircon.co.uk; internet www.internatpen.org; f. 1921 to promote co-operation between writers; mems: c. 14,000, 134 centres worldwide. International; Pres. HOMERO ARIDJIS; International Sec. TERRY CARLBOM; publ *PEN International* (2 a year, in English, French and Spanish, with the assistance of UNESCO).

International Theatre Institute—ITI: Maison de l'UNESCO, 1 rue Miollis, 75732 Paris Cédex 15, France; tel. 1-45-68-48-80; fax 1-45-66-50-40; e-mail iti@unesco.org; internet iti-worldwide.org; f. 1948 to facilitate cultural exchanges and international understanding in the domain of the theatre; holds conferences; mems: 87 member nations, each with an ITI national centre; Pres. MANFRED BEILHARZ (Germany); Sec.-Gen. a.i. ANDRÉ-LOUIS PERINETTI (France); publs *ITI News* (3 times a year in English and French); *World Theatre Directory* (biennially); *The World of Theatre* (biennially).

Organization of World Heritage Cities: 56 Saint-Pierre St, Suite 401, Quebec City, QC, G1K 4AI, Canada; tel. (418) 692-0000; fax (418) 692-5558; e-mail secretariat@ovpm.org; internet www.ovpm .org; f. 1993 to assist cities inscribed on the UNESCO World Heritage List to implement the Convention concerning the Protection of the World Cultural and Natural Heritage (1972); promotes co-operation between city authorities, in particular in the management and sustainable development of historic sites; holds a General Assembly, comprising the mayors of member cities, at least every two years; mems: 187 cities world-wide; Sec.-Gen. D. S. MYRVOLL (acting).

Pan-African Writers' Association—PAWA: PAWA House, Roman Ridge, POB C456, Cantonments, Accra, Ghana; tel. (21) 773-062; fax (21) 773-042; e-mail pawa@ghana.com; f. 1989 to link African creative writers, defend the rights of authors and promote awareness of literature; Sec.-Gen. ATUKWEI OKAI (Ghana).

Royal Asiatic Society of Great Britain and Ireland: 60 Queen's Gardens, London, W2 3AF, United Kingdom; tel. (20) 7724-4742; fax (20) 7706-4008; e-mail info@royalasiaticsociety.org; internet www .royalasiaticsociety.org; f. 1823 for the study of history and cultures of the East; mems: c. 700, branch societies in Asia; Pres. Prof. A. J. STOCKWELL; Sec. ADRIAN P. THOMAS; publ *Journal* (3 a year).

Society of African Culture (Société Africaine de Culture): 25 bis rue des Ecoles, 75005 Paris, France; tel. 1-43-54-15-88; fax 1-43-25-96-67; f. 1956 to create unity and friendship among scholars in Africa, for the encouragement of their own cultures; mems: national asscns and individuals in 44 countries and territories; Pres. AIMÉ CÉSAIRE; Gen. Sec. CHRISTIANE YANDÉ DIOP; publ *La Revue Présence Africaine* (2 a year).

United World Federation of United Cities: 41 rue de la République, 93200 Saint Denis, France; tel. 1-55-84-23-50; fax 1-55-84-23-51; e-mail contact@fmcu-uto.org; internet www.fmcu-uto.org; f. 1957, as the United Towns Organization, by Le Monde Bilingue (f. 1951); aims to set up permanent links between towns throughout the world, leading to social, cultural, economic and other exchanges favouring world peace, understanding and development; involved in sustainable development and environmental activities at municipal level; mem. of the Habitat II follow-up group; mems: 4,000 local and regional authorities throughout the world; World Pres. MERCEDES BRESSO; Sec.-Gen. PAOLO MORELLO; publs *Cités Unies* (quarterly, in French, English and Spanish), *Newsletter* (3 a year in English, French, Italian and Spanish).

World Crafts Council International: Anthrakitou 5 and Tsechouli Street, Kastro Ioanninon, 452 21 Ioannina, Greece; tel. (30) 26510-72315; fax (30) 26510-36695; e-mail wis@epcon.gr; internet www.wccwis.gr; f. 1964; aims to strengthen the status of crafts as a vital part of cultural life, to link crafts people around the world, and to foster wider recognition of their work; mems: national organizations in more than 87 countries; Pres. ELENA AVEROFF (Greece); publs *Annual Report*, *Newsletter* (2 a year) *WCC News* (in English and French).

Commodities

African Groundnut Council—AGC: Trade Fair Complex, Badagry Expressway Km 15, POB 3025, Lagos, Nigeria; tel. (1) 880982; fax (1) 887811; f. 1964 to advise producing countries on marketing policies; mems: Gambia, Mali, Niger, Nigeria, Senegal, Sudan; Chair. MUSTAFA BELLO (Nigeria); Exec. Sec. ELHADJ MOUR MAMADOU SAMB (Senegal); publ. *Groundnut Review*.

African Oil Palm Development Association—AFOPDA: 15 BP 341, Abidjan 15, Côte d'Ivoire; tel. 25-15-18; fax 21-97-06; f. 1985; seeks to increase production of, and investment in, palm oil; mems: Benin, Cameroon, Democratic Republic of the Congo, Côte d'Ivoire, Ghana, Guinea, Nigeria, Togo; Exec. Sec. BAUDELAIRE HOUNSINOU SOUROU.

African Petroleum Producers' Association—APPA: POB 1097, Brazzaville, Republic of the Congo; tel. 83-64-38; fax 83-67-99; f. 1987 by African petroleum-producing countries to reinforce co-operation among regional producers and to stabilize prices; council of ministers responsible for the hydrocarbons sector meets twice a year; first APPA Congress and Exhibition: Tripoli, Libya (March 2003); mems: Algeria, Angola, Benin, Cameroon, Democratic Republic of the Congo, Republic of the Congo, Côte d'Ivoire, Egypt, Equatorial Guinea, Gabon, Libya, Nigeria; Exec. Sec. MAXIME OBIANG-NZE; publ. *APPA Bulletin* (2 a year).

Asian and Pacific Coconut Community—APCC: 3rd Floor, Lina Bldg, Jalan H. R. Rasuna Said Kav. B7, Kuningan, Jakarta 10002, Indonesia; POB 1343, Jakarta 10013; tel. (21) 5221712; fax (21) 5221714; e-mail apcc@indo.net.id; internet www.apcc.org.sg; f. 1969 to promote and co-ordinate all activities of the coconut industry, to achieve higher production and better processing, marketing and research; organizes annual Coconut Technical Meeting (COCO-TECH); mems: Fiji, India, Indonesia, Kiribati, Malaysia, Federated States of Micronesia, Papua New Guinea, Philippines, Samoa, Solomon Islands, Sri Lanka, Thailand, Vanuatu, Viet Nam; assoc. mem.: Palau; Exec. Dir Dr P. RETHINAM; Sec. Gen. Dr ABDULLAH MOHD. TAHIR; publs *Cocomunity* (fortnightly), *CORD* (2 a year), *Statistical Yearbook*, *Cocoinfo International* (2 a year).

Association of Natural Rubber Producing Countries—ANRPC: Bangunan Getah Asli, 148 Jalan Ampang, 7th Floor, 50450 Kuala Lumpur, Malaysia; tel. (3) 2611900; fax (3) 2613014; e-mail anrpc@capo.jaring.my; f. 1970 to co-ordinate the production and marketing of natural rubber, to promote technical co-operation amongst members and to bring about fair and stable prices for natural rubber; holds seminars, meetings and training courses on technical and statistical subjects. A joint regional marketing system has been agreed in principle; mems: India, Indonesia, Malaysia, Papua New Guinea, Singapore, Sri Lanka, Thailand, Viet Nam; Sec.-Gen. G. W. S. K. DE SILVA; publs *ANRPC Statistical Bulletin* (quarterly), *ANRPC NewsletterANRPC Quarterly Natural Rubber Statistical Bulletin*.

Cocoa Producers' Alliance—CPA: National Assembly Complex, Tafawa Balewa Sq., POB 1718, Lagos, Nigeria; tel. (1) 2635506; fax (1) 2635684; e-mail info@copal-cpa.org; internet www.copal-cpa.org; f. 1962 to exchange technical and scientific information, to discuss problems of mutual concern to producers, to ensure adequate supplies at remunerative prices and to promote consumption; mems: Brazil, Cameroon, Côte d'Ivoire, Dominican Republic, Gabon, Ghana, Malaysia, Nigeria, São Tomé and Príncipe, Togo; Sec.-Gen. HOPE SONA EBAI.

Common Fund for Commodities: Postbus 74656, 1070 BR, Amsterdam, Netherlands; tel. (20) 575-4949; fax (20) 676-0231; e-mail managing.director@common-fund.org; internet www .common-fund.org; f. 1989 as the result of an UNCTAD negotiation conference; finances commodity development measures including research, marketing, productivity improvements and vertical diversification, with the aim of increasing the long-term competitiveness of particular commodities; paid-in capital US $165m; mems: 105 countries and the AU, EC and COMESA; Man. Dir (also Chief Exec. and Chair.) ROLF BOEHNKE.

European Aluminium Association—EEA: 12 ave de Broqueville, 1150 Brussels, Belgium; tel. (2) 775-63-63; fax (2) 779-05-31; e-mail eaa@eaa.be; internet www.eaa.net; f. 1981 to encourage studies, research and technical co-operation, to make representations to international bodies and to assist national asscns in dealing with national authorities; mems: individual producers of primary aluminium, 17 national groups for wrought producers, the Organization of European Aluminium Smelters, representing producers of recycled aluminium, and the European Aluminium Foil Association, representing foil rollers and converters; Chair. R. BELDA; Sec.-Gen. P. DE SCHRYNMAKERS; publs *Annual Report*, *EAA Quarterly Report*.

European Association for the Trade in Jute and Related Products: Adriaan Goekooplaan 5, POB 29822, 2502 LV, The Hague, Netherlands; tel. (70) 330-4659; fax (70) 351-2777; e-mail eurojute@verbondgroothandel.nl; f. 1970 to maintain contacts between national asscns, permit the exchange of information and represent the interests of the trade; carries out scientific research; mems: enterprises in eight European countries; Sec.-Gen. H. J. J. KRUIPER.

European Committee of Sugar Manufacturers: 182 ave de Tervueren, 1150 Brussels, Belgium; tel. (2) 762-07-60; fax (2) 771-00-26; e-mail cefs@cefs.org; internet www.cefs.org; f. 1954 to collect statistics and information, conduct research and promote co-operation between national organizations; mems: national asscns in 15 European countries; Pres. JOHANN MARIHART; Dir-Gen. J. L. BARJOL.

Group of Latin American and Caribbean Sugar Exporting Countries (Grupo de Países Latinoamericanos y del Caribe Exportadores de Azúcar—GEPLACEA): Paseo de la Reforma 1030, Lomas de Chapultepec, DF 11000 México, Mexico; tel. (55) 5520-9711; fax (55) 5520-5089; e-mail geplacea@dns.telecom.ipn.mx; internet www .geplacea.ipn.mx; f. 1974 to serve as a forum for consultation on the production and sale of sugar to contribute to the adoption of agreed positions at international meetings on sugar; to provide training and the transfer of technology; to exchange scientific and technical knowledge on agriculture and the sugar industry; to co-ordinate the various branches of sugar processing; and to co-ordinate policies of action, in order to achieve fair and remunerative prices; mems: 23 Latin American and Caribbean countries (accounting for about 45% of world sugar exports and 66% of world cane sugar production); Exec. Sec. LUIS EDUARDO ZEDILLO PONCE DE LEÓN.

Inter-African Coffee Organization—IACO (Organisation internationale du caf—OIAC): BP V210, Abidjan, Côte d'Ivoire; tel. 20-21-61-31; fax 20-21-62-12; e-mail oiac-iaco@aviso.ci; f. 1960 to adopt a common policy on the marketing and consumption of coffee; aims to foster greater collaboration in research technology transfer through the African Coffee Research Network (ACRN); seeks to improve the quality of coffee exports, and implement poverty reduction programmes; mems: 25 coffee-producing countries in Africa; Chair. BONAYA ADHI GODANA (Côte d'Ivoire); Sec.-Gen. JOSEFA LEONEL CORREIA SACKO (Angola).

International Cadmium Association: 12110 Sunset Hills Rd, Suite 110, Reston, VA 22090, USA; tel. (703) 709-1400; fax (703) 709-1402; f. 1976; covers all aspects of the production and use of cadmium and its compounds; includes almost all producers and users of cadmium; Chair. DAVID SINCLAIR (USA).

International Cocoa Organization—ICCO: 22 Berners St, London, W1P 3DB, United Kingdom; tel. (20) 7637-3211; fax (20) 7631-0114; e-mail exec.dir@icco.org; internet www.icco.org; f. 1973 under the first International Cocoa Agreement, 1972; The ICCO supervises the implementation of the agreements, and provides member governments with conference facilities and up-to-date information on the world cocoa economy and the operation of the agreements. The sixth International Cocoa Agreement was signed in March 2001; it will enter into force in October 2003; mems: 19 exporting countries and 23 importing countries; and the European Union; Officer in Charge Dr JAN VINGERHOETS (Netherlands); Council Chair. 2002–03 Dr J. A. MARTÍNEZ (Dominican Republic); publs *Quarterly Bulletin of Cocoa Statistics*, *Annual Report*, *World Cocoa Directory*, *Cocoa Newsletter*, studies on the world cocoa economy.

International Coffee Organization—ICO: 22 Berners St, London, W1T 4DD, United Kingdom; tel. (20) 7580-8591; fax (20) 7580-6129; e-mail info@ico.org; internet www.ico.org; f. 1963 under the International Coffee Agreement, 1962, which was renegotiated in 1968, 1976, 1983, 1994 (extended in 1999) and 2001; aims to improve international co-operation and provide a forum for inter-governmental consultations on coffee matters; to facilitate international trade in coffee by the collection, analysis and dissemination of statistics; to act as a centre for the collection, exchange and publication of coffee information; to promote studies in the field of coffee; and to encourage an increase in coffee consumption; mems: 45 exporting and 20 importing countries; Chair. of Council JACQUES THINSY (Belgium); Exec. Dir NÉSTOR OSORIO (Colombia).

International Confederation of European Sugar Beet Growers (Confédération internationale des betteraviers européens —CIBE): 29 rue du Général Foy, 75008 Paris, France; tel. 1-44-69-39–00; fax 1-42-93-28-93; f. 1925 to act as a centre for the co-ordination and dissemination of information about beet sugar production and the industry to represent the interests of sugar beet growers at an international level; mems: asscns in Austria, Belgium, Czech Republic, Denmark, Finland, France, Germany, Greece, Hungary, Ireland, Italy, Lithuania, Netherlands, Poland, Portugal, Romania, Slovakia, Spain, Sweden, Switzerland, United Kingdom; Pres. J. KIRSCH (Germany); Sec.-Gen. H. CHAVANES (France).

International Cotton Advisory Committee—ICAC: 1629 K St, NW, Suite 702, Washington, DC 20006-1636, USA; tel. (202) 463-6660; fax (202) 463-6950; e-mail secretariat@icac.org; internet www .icac.org; f. 1939 to observe developments in world cotton to collect and disseminate statistics; to suggest measures for the furtherance of international collaboration in maintaining and developing a sound world cotton economy; and to provide a forum for international discussions on cotton prices; mems: 43 countries; Exec. Dir Dr TERRY TOWNSEND (USA); publs *Cotton This Month*, *Cotton: Review of the World Situation*, *Cotton: World Statistics*, *The ICAC Recorder*.

International Grains Council—IGC: 1 Canada Sq., Canary Wharf, London, E14 5AE, United Kingdom; tel. (20) 7513-1122; fax (20) 7513-0630; e-mail igc@igc.org.uk; internet www.igc.org.uk; f. 1949 as International Wheat Council, present name adopted in 1995; responsible for the administration of the Grains Trade Convention of the International Grains Agreement, 1995; aims to further international co-operation in all aspects of trade in grains and to promote the freest possible flow of this trade, in particular, to support developing countries; seeks to contribute to the stability of the international grain market; acts as a forum for consultations between members; provides comprehensive information on the international grain market; mems: 28 countries and the EU; Exec. Dir. G. DENIS; publs *World Grain Statistics* (annually), *Wheat and Coarse Grain Shipments* (annually), *Report for the Fiscal Year* (annually), *Grain Market Report* (monthly), *Grain Market Indicators* (weekly) *Food Aid Shipments*.

International Jute Study Group—IJSG: 145 Monipuriparu, Near Farmgate, Tejgaon, Dhaka 1215, Bangladesh; tel. (2) 9125581; fax (2) 9125248; e-mail ijoinf@bdmail.net; f. 2002 as successor to International Jute Organization (f. 1984 in accordance with an agreement made by 48 producing and consuming countries in 1982, under the auspices of UNCTAD); aims to improve the jute economy and the quality of jute and jute products through research and development projects and market promotion; Sec.-Gen T. NANADAKUMAR.

International Lead and Zinc Study Group—ILZSG: 2 King St, London, SW1Y 6QP, United Kingdom; tel. (20) 7484-3300; fax (20) 7930-4635; e-mail root@ilzsg.org; internet www.ilzsg.org; f. 1959 for intergovernmental consultation on world trade in lead and zinc; conducts studies and provides information on trends in supply and demand; mems: 28 countries; Chair. A. IGNATOW (Canada); Sec.-Gen. DON SMALE; publ. *Lead and Zinc Statistics* (monthly).

International Molybdenum Association—IMOA: 2 Baron's Gate, 33 Rothschild Rd, London, W4 5HT, United Kingdom; tel. (20) 8742-2274; fax (20) 8742-7345; e-mail info@imoa.info; internet www .imoa.org.uk/; f. 1989; collates statistics; promotes the use of molybdenum; monitors health and environmental issues in the molybdenum industry; mems: 49; Pres. J. GRAELL; Sec.-Gen. MICHAEL MABY.

International Olive Oil Council: Príncipe de Vergara 154, 28002 Madrid, Spain; tel. (91) 59033638; fax (91) 5631263; e-mail iooc@ internationaloliveoil.org; internet www.internationaloliveoil.org; f. 1959 to administer the International Agreement on Olive Oil and Table Olives, which aims to promote international co-operation in connection with problems of the world economy for olive products; works to prevent unfair competition, to encourage the production and consumption of, and international trade in, olive products, and to reduce the disadvantages caused by fluctuations of supplies on the market; mems: of the 1986 Agreement (Fourth Agreement, amended and extended in 1993; last prolonged in 2002): nine mainly producing countries, five mainly importing country, and the European Commission; Dir a.i. AHMED TOUZANI; publs *Information Sheet of the IOOC* (fortnightly, in French and Spanish), *OLIVAE* (5 a year, in English, French, Italian and Spanish).

International Pepper Community—IPC: 4th Floor, Lina Bldg, Jalan H. R. Rasuna Said, Kav. B7, Kuningan, Jakarta 12920,

Indonesia; tel. (21) 5224902; fax (21) 5224905; e-mail ipc@indo.net .id; internet www.ipcnet.org; f. 1972 for promoting, co-ordinating and harmonizing all activities relating to the pepper economy; mems: Brazil, India, Indonesia, Malaysia, Federated States of Micronesia, Papua New Guinea, Sri Lanka, Thailand; Exec. Dir Dr K. P. G. MENON; publs *Pepper Statistical Yearbook, International Pepper News Bulletin* (quarterly), *Directory of Pepper Exporters, Directory of Pepper Importers, Weekly Prices Bulletin, Pepper Market Review*.

International Platinum Association: Kroegerstr. 5, Frankfurt-am-Main, 60313, Germany; tel. (69) 287941; fax (69) 283601; e-mail info@platinuminfo.net; internet www.platinuminfo.net; links principal producers and fabricators of platinum; Pres. DEREK G. ENGELBRECHT; Man. Dir MARCUS NURDIN.

International Rubber Study Group: Heron House, 109–115 Wembley Hill Rd, Wembley, HA9 8DA, United Kingdom; tel. (20) 8900-5400; fax (20) 8903-2848; e-mail irsg@compuserve.com; internet www.rubberstudy.org; f. 1944 to provide a forum for the discussion of problems affecting synthetic and natural rubber and to provide statistical and other general information on rubber; mems: 17 governments; Sec.-Gen. Dr A. F. S. BUDIMAN (Indonesia); publs *Rubber Statistical Bulletin* (monthly), *International Rubber Digest* (monthly), *Proceedings of International Rubber Forums* (annually), *World Rubber Statistics Handbook, Key Rubber Indicators, Rubber Statistics Yearbook* (annually), *Rubber Economics Yearbook* (annually), *Outlook for Elastomers* (annually).

International Silk Association: 34 rue de la Charité, 69002 Lyon, France; tel. 4-78-42-10-79; fax 4-78-37-56-72; e-mail isa-silk .ais-sole@wanadoo.fr; f. 1949 to promote closer collaboration between all branches of the silk industry and trade, develop the consumption of silk, and foster scientific research; collects and disseminates information and statistics relating to the trade and industry; organizes biennial Congresses; mems: employers' and technical organizations in 40 countries; Gen. Sec. X. LAVERGNE; publs *ISA Newsletter* (monthly), congress reports, standards, trade rules, etc.

International Spice Group: c/o International Trade Centre (UNCTAD/WTO), 54–56 rue de Montbrillant, 1202 Geneva, Switzerland; tel. (22) 730-01-01; fax (22) 730-02-54; e-mail itcreg@intracen .org; f. 1983 to provide a forum for producers and consumers of spices; works to increase the consumption of spices; mems: 33 producer countries, 15 importing countries; Chair. HERNAL HAMILTON (Jamaica).

International Sugar Organization: 1 Canada Sq., Canary Wharf, London, E14 5AA, United Kingdom; tel. (20) 7513-1144; fax (20) 7513-1146; e-mail exdir@isosugar.org; internet www.isosugar.org; administers the International Sugar Agreement (1992), with the objectives of stimulating co-operation, facilitating trade and encouraging demand; aims to improve conditions in the sugar market through debate, analysis and studies; serves as a forum for discussion; holds annual seminars and workshops; sponsors projects from developing countries; mems: 63 countries producing some 80% of total world sugar; Exec. Dir Dr P. BARON; publs *Sugar Year Book, Monthly Statistical Bulletin, Market Report and Press Summary, Quarterly Market Review*, seminar proceedings.

International Tea Committee Ltd—ITC: Sir John Lyon House, 5 High Timber St, London, EC4V 3NH, United Kingdom; tel. (20) 7248-4672; fax (20) 7329-6955; e-mail info@intteacomm.co.uk; internet www.intteacomm.co.uk; f. 1933 to administer the International Tea Agreement; now serves as a statistical and information centre; in 1979 membership was extended to include consuming countries; Producer mems: national tea boards or asscns in eight countries; consumer mems: United Kingdom Tea Assn, Tea Assn of the USA Inc., Comité européen du thé and the Tea Council of Canada; assoc. mems: Netherlands and UK ministries of agriculture, Cameroon Development Corpn; Chair. M. J. BUNSTON; publs *Annual Bulletin of Statistics, Monthly Statistical Summary*.

International Tea Promotion Association—ITPA: c/o Tea Board of Kenya, POB 20064, Nairobi, Kenya; tel. (20) 220241; fax (20) 331650; e-mail teaboardk@kenyaweb.com; internet www .teaboard.or.ke; f. 1979; mems: eight countries; Chair. GEORGE M. KIMANI; publ. *International Tea Journal* (2 a year).

International Tobacco Growers' Association—ITGA: Apdo 5, 6001-081 Castelo Branco, Portugal; tel. (72) 325901; fax (72) 325906; e-mail itga@mail.telepac.pt; internet www.tobaccoleaf.org; f. 1984 to provide a forum for the exchange of views and information of interest to tobacco producers; mems: 22 countries producing over 80% of the world's internationally traded tobacco; Pres. MARCELO QUEVEDO (Argentina); Exec. Dir ALBERT KAMULAGA (Malawi); publs *Tobacco Courier* (quarterly), *Tobacco Briefing*.

International Tropical Timber Organization—ITTO: International Organizations Center, 5th Floor, Pacifico-Yokohama, 1-1-1, Minato-Mirai, Nishi-ku, Yokohama 220-0012, Japan; tel. (45) 223-

1110; fax (45) 223-1111; e-mail itto@itto.or.jp; internet www.itto.or .jp; f. 1985 under the International Tropical Timber Agreement (1983); a new treaty, ITTA 1994, came into force in 1997; provides a forum for consultation and co-operation between countries that produce and consume tropical timber, and is dedicated to the sustainable development and conservation of tropical forests; facilitates progress towards 'Objective 2000', which aims to move as rapidly as possible towards achieving exports of tropical timber and timber products from sustainably managed resources; encourages, through policy and project work, forest management, conservation and restoration, the further processing of tropical timber in producing countries, and the gathering and analysis of market intelligence and economic information; mems: 31 producing and 25 consuming countries and the EU; Exec. Dir Dr MANOEL SOBRAL FILHO; publs *Annual Review and Assessment of the World Timber Situation, Tropical Timber Market Information Service* (every 2 weeks), *Tropical Forest Update* (quarterly).

International Tungsten Industry Association—ITIA: 2 Baron's Gate, 33 Rothschild Rd, London, W4 5HT, United Kingdom; tel. (20) 8742-2274; fax (20) 8742-7345; e-mail info@itia.info; internet www .itia.org.uk/; f. 1988 (fmrly Primary Tungsten Asscn, f. 1975); promotes use of tungsten; collates statistics; prepares market reports; monitors health and environmental issues in the tungsten industry; mems: 51; Pres. D. LANDSBERGER; Sec.-Gen. MICHAEL MABY.

International Vine and Wine Office (Office International de la Vigne et du Vin—OIV): 18 rue d'Aguesseau, 75008 Paris, France; tel. 1-44-94-80-80; fax 1-42-66-90-63; e-mail oiv@oiv.int; internet www .oiv.int; f. 1924 to study all the scientific, technical, economic and human problems concerning the vine and its products to spread knowledge and facilitate contacts between researchers; mems: 46 countries; Dir-Gen. GEORGES DUTRUC-ROSSET; France; publs *Bulletin de l'OIV* (every 2 months), *Lettre de l'OIV* (monthly), *Lexique de la Vigne et du Vin, Recueil des méthodes internationales d'analyse des vins, Code international des Pratiques oenologiques, Codex oenologique international*, numerous scientific publications.

International Zinc Association: 168 ave de Tervueren, Box 4, 1150 Brussels, Belgium; tel. (2) 776-00-70; fax (2) 776-00-89; e-mail email@iza.com; internet www.iza.com; f. 1990 to represent the world zinc industry; provide a forum for senior executives to address global issues requiring industry-wide action; consider new applications for zinc and zinc products; foster understanding of zinc's role in the environment; build a sustainable development policy; mems: 28 zinc-producing countries; Exec. Dir EDOUARD GERVAIS; publ. *Zinc Protects* (4 a year).

Lead Development Association International: 42 Weymouth St, London, W1G 6NP, United Kingdom; tel. (20) 7499-8422; fax (20) 7493-1555; e-mail enq@ldaint.org; internet www.ldaint.org; f. 1956; provides authoritative information on the use of lead and its compounds; Financed by lead producers and users in the United Kingdom, Europe and elsewhere; Dir Dr D. N. WILSON (UK).

Regional Association of Oil and Natural Gas Companies in Latin America and the Caribbean (Asociación Regional de Empresas de Petróleo y Gas Natural en Latinoamérica y el Caribe—ARPEL): Javier de Viana 2345, Casilla de correo 1006, 11200 Montevideo, Uruguay; tel. (2) 4106993; fax (2) 4109207; e-mail bsettembri@arpel.org.uy; internet www.arpel.org; f. 1965 as the Mutual Assistance of the Latin American Oil Companies; aims to initiate and implement activities for the development of the oil and natural gas industry in Latin America and the Caribbean; promotes the expansion of business opportunities and the improvement of the competitive advantages of its members; promotes guide-lines in support of competition in the sector; and supports the efficient and sustainable exploitation of hydrocarbon resources and the supply of products and services. Works in co-operation with international organizations, governments, regulatory agencies, technical institutions, universities and non-governmental organizations; mems: state enterprises, representing more than 90% of regional operations, in Argentina, Bolivia, Brazil, Canada, Chile, Colombia, Costa Rica, Cuba, Ecuador, Jamaica, Mexico, Nicaragua, Paraguay, Peru, Suriname, Trinidad and Tobago, Uruguay, Venezuela; Exec. Sec. JOSÉ FÉLIX GARCÍA GARCÍA; publ. *Boletín Técnico*.

Sugar Association of the Caribbean (Inc.)—SAC: c/o Caroni (1975) Ltd, Brechin Castle, Conva, Trinidad and Tobago; tel. 636-2449; fax 636-2847; f. 1942; mems: national sugar cos of Barbados, Belize, Guyana, Jamaica and Trinidad and Tobago, and Sugar Asscn of St Kitts–Nevis–Anguilla; Chair. RODERICK KARL JAMES; Sec. AZIZ MOHAMMED; publs *SAC Handbook, SAC Annual Report, Proceedings of Meetings of WI Sugar Technologists*.

Union of Banana-Exporting Countries (Unión de Países Exportadores de Banano—UPEB): Apdo 4273, Bank of America, piso 7, Panamá 5, Panama; tel. 263-6266; fax 264-8355; e-mail iicapan@pan .gbm.net; f. 1974 as an intergovernmental agency to assist in the cultivation and marketing of bananas and to secure prices; collects statistics; mems: Colombia, Costa Rica, Guatemala, Honduras,

Nicaragua, Panama, Venezuela; Exec. Dir a.i. ROLANDO GABRIELLI; publs *Informe UPEB*, *Fax UPEB*, *Anuario de Estadísticas*, bibliographies.

West Africa Rice Development Association—WARDA: 01 BP 2551 Bouaké 01, Côte d'Ivoire; tel. 31-65-93-00; fax 31-65-93-11; e-mail warda@cgiar.org; internet www.cgiar.org/warda; f. 1971 as a mem. of the network of agricultural research centres supported by the Consultative Group on International Agricultural Research (CGIAR, q.v.); aims to contribute to food security and poverty eradication in poor rural and urban populations, particularly in West and Central Africa, through research, partnerships, capacity strengthening and policy support on rice-based systems; promotes sustainable agricultural development based on environmentally-sound management of natural resources; maintains research stations in Côte d'Ivoire, Nigeria and Senegal; provides training and consulting services. WARDA; mems: 17 west African countries; Dir-Gen. Dr KANAYO F. NWANZE (Nigeria); publs *Program Report* (annually), *Participatory Varietal Selection* (annually), *Rice Interspecific Hybridization Project Research Highlights* (annually), *Biennial WARDA/National Experts Committee Meeting Reports*, *Inland Valley Newsletter*, *ROCARIZ Newsletter*, training series, proceedings, leaflets.

West Indian Sea Island Cotton Association (Inc.)—WISICA: c/o Barbados Agricultural Development Corporation, Fairy Valley, Christ Church, Barbados; mems: organizations in Antigua-Barbuda, Barbados, Jamaica, Montserrat and St Christopher and Nevis; Pres. LEROY ROACH; Sec. MICHAEL I. EDGHILL.

World Association of Beet and Cane Growers—WABCG: c/o IFAP, 60 rue St Lazare, 75009 Paris, France; tel. 1-45-26-05-53; fax 1-48-74-72-12; e-mail wabcg@ifap.org; internet www.ifap.org/wabcg; f. 1983 (formal adoption of Constitution, 1984); groups national organizations of independent sugar beet and cane growers; aims to boost the economic, technical and social development of the beet- and cane-growing sector; works to strengthen professional representation in international and national fora; serves as a forum for discussion and exchange of information; mems: 21 beet-growing organizations, 14 cane-growing organizations, from 30 countries; Pres. ROGER STEWART (South Africa); Sec. MICHEL HARDY; publs *World Sugar Farmer News* (quarterly), *World Sugar Farmer Fax Sheet*, *WABCG InfoFlash*, study reports.

World Federation of Diamond Bourses: 62 Pelikaanstraat, 2018 Antwerp, Belgium; tel. (3) 234-07-78; fax (3) 226-40-73; e-mail info@worldfed.com; internet www.worldfed.com; f. 1947 to protect the interests of affiliated organizations and their individual members and to settle or arbitrate in disputes; mems: 24 bourses in 15 countries; Pres. SHMUEL. SCHNITZER (Israel); Sec.-Gen. MICHAEL H. VAUGHAN (Belgium).

World Gold Council: 45 Pall Mall, London, SW1Y 5JG, United Kingdom; tel. (20) 7930-5171; fax (20) 7839-6561; e-mail info@gold.org; internet www.gold.org; f. 1987 as world-wide international asscn of gold producers, to promote the demand for gold; Chair. CHRIS THOMPSON; Chief Exec. JAMES E. BURTON (Japan).

World Sugar Research Organisation—WSRO: Science and Technology Centre, University of Reading, Earley Gate, Whiteknights Rd, Reading, RG6 6BZ, United Kingdom; tel. (118) 935-7000; fax (118) 935-7301; e-mail wsro@wsro.org; internet www.wsro.org; an alliance of sugar producers, processors, marketers and users; monitors and communicates research on role of sugar and other carbohydrates in nutrition and health; organizes conferences and symposia; operates a database of information; serves as a forum for exchange of views; mems: 73 orgs in 30 countries; Dir-Gen. Dr RIAZ KHAN; publs *WSRO Research Bulletin* (on-line, monthly), *WSRO Newsletter*, papers and conference proceedings.

Development and Economic Co-operation

African Capacity Building Foundation—ACBF: Intermarket Life Towers, 7th Floor, cnr Jason Moyo Ave/Sam Nujoma St, POB 1562, Harare, Zimbabwe; tel. (4) 790398; fax (4) 702915; e-mail root@acbf-pact.org; internet www.acbf-pact.org; f. 1991 by the World Bank, UNDP, the African Development Bank, African and non-African governments; assists African countries to strengthen and build local capacity in economic policy analysis and development management. Implementing agency for the Partnership for Capacity Building in Africa (PACT, established in 1999); Exec. Sec. Dr SOUMANA SAKO.

African Training and Research Centre in Administration for Development (Centre africain de formation et de recherche administratives pour le développement—CAFRAD): blvd Pavillon International, BP 310, Tangier, 90001 Morocco; tel. (212) 3942652; fax (212) 3932578; e-mail cafrad@cafrad.org; internet www.cafrad.org; f. 1964

by agreement between Morocco and UNESCO; undertakes research into administrative problems in Africa and documents results; provides a consultation service for governments and organizations; holds workshops to train senior civil servants; prepares the Biennial Pan-African Conference of Ministers of the Civil Service; mems: 37 African countries; Chair. M'HAMED EL KHALIFA; Dir-Gen. Prof. TIJJANI MUHAMMAD BANDE; publs *African Administrative Studies* (2 a year), *Research Studies*, *CAFRAD News* (2 a year, in Arabic, English and French), *Collection: Etudes et Documents, Répertoire des Consultants*.

Afro-Asian Rural Development Organization—AARDO: No. 2, State Guest Houses Complex, Chanakyapuri, New Delhi 110 021, India; tel. (11) 4100475; fax (11) 4672045; e-mail aardo@nde.vsnl.net.in; internet www.aardo.org; f. 1962 to act as a catalyst for the co-operative restructuring of rural life in Africa and Asia and to explore opportunities for the co-ordination of efforts to promote rural welfare and to eradicate hunger, thirst, disease, illiteracy and poverty; carries out collaborative research on development issues; organizes training; encourages the exchange of information; holds international conferences and seminars; awards 100 individual training fellowships at nine institutes in Egypt, India, Japan, the Republic of Korea and Taiwan; mems: 12 African countries, 14 Asian countries, one African associate; Sec.-Gen. Dr BAHAR MUNIP; publs *Afro-Asian Journal of Rural Development*, *Annual Report*, *AARDO Newsletter* (2 a year).

Agence Intergouvernementale de la Francophonie: 13 quai André Citroën, 75015 Paris, France; tel. 1-44-37-33-00; fax 1-45-79-14-98; internet agence.francophonie.org; f. 1970 as l'Agence de coopération culturelle et technique; promotes co-operation among French-speaking countries in the areas of education, culture, science and technology; implements decisions of the Sommet francophone (q.v.); technical and financial assistance has been given to projects in every member country, mainly to aid rural people; mems: 50 countries and territories; Gen. Dir SALIOU AKADIRI; publ. *Journal de l'Agence de la Francophonie* (6 a year).

Arab Authority for Agricultural Investment and Development—AAAID: POB 2102, Khartoum, Sudan; tel. (11) 780777; fax (11) 772600; e-mail info@aaaid.org; internet www.aaaid.org; f. 1976 to accelerate agricultural development in the Arab world and to ensure food security; acts principally by equity participation in agricultural projects in Iraq, Sudan and Tunisia; signed a co-operation agreement with IFAD in Nov. 2000; mems: 16 countries; Pres. and Chair. ABDUL KAREEM MOHAMMAD AL-AMRI; publ. *Journal of Agricultural Investment* (English and Arabic), *Extension and Investment Bulletins*, *Annual Report* (Arabic and English), *AAAID Newsletter* (quarterly).

Arab Co-operation Council: POB 2640, Khartoum, Sudan; tel. (11) 73646; f. 1989 to promote economic co-operation between member states, including free movement of workers, joint projects in transport, communications and agriculture, and eventual integration of trade and monetary policies; mems: Egypt, Iraq, Jordan, Yemen.

Arab Gulf Programme for the United Nations Development Organizations (AGFUND): POB 18371, Riyadh 11415, Saudi Arabia; tel. (1) 4418888; fax (1) 4412962; e-mail info@agfund.org; internet www.agfund.org; f. 1981 to provide grants for projects in mother and child care carried out by United Nations organizations, Arab non-governmental organizations and other international bodies, and to co-ordinate assistance by the nations of the Gulf; financing comes mainly from member states, all of which are members of OPEC; mems: Bahrain, Kuwait, Oman, Qatar, Saudi Arabia, UAE; Pres. HRH Prince TALAL BIN ABDUL AZIZ.

Arctic Council: c/o Ministry of Foreign Affairs, Raudararstigur 25,150 Reykjavik, Iceland; tel. 545 9900; fax 562 2373; e-mail arctic.council@utn.stjr.is; internet www.arctic-council.org; f. 1996 to promote co-ordination of activities in the Arctic region, in particular in the areas of education, development and environmental protection; mems: Canada, Denmark, Finland, Iceland, Norway, Russia, Sweden, USA; Chair. GUNNAR PÁLSSON;; Exec. Sec. BRYNDIS KJARTANSDÓTTIR.

Association of Caribbean States—ACS: 5–7 Sweet Briar Rd, St Clair, POB 660, Port of Spain, Trinidad and Tobago; tel. 622-9575; fax 622-1653; e-mail mail@acs-aec.org; internet www.acs-aec.org; f. 1994 by the Governments of the 13 CARICOM countries and Colombia, Costa Rica, Cuba, Dominican Republic, El Salvador, Guatemala, Haiti, Honduras, Mexico, Nicaragua, Suriname and Venezuela; Aims to promote economic integration, sustainable development and co-operation in the region; to co-ordinate participation in multilateral forums; to undertake concerted action to protect the environment, particularly the Caribbean Sea; and to co-operate in the areas of science and technology, health, trade, transport, tourism, education and culture. Policy is determined by a Ministerial Council and implemented by a Secretariat based in Port of Spain. In December 2001 a third Summit of Heads of State and

Government was convened in Venezuela; a Plan of Action focusing on issues of sustainable tourism, trade, transport and natural disasters was agreed; mems: 25 signatory states, five associate members, 14 observer countries; Sec.-Gen. Prof. Dr NORMAN GIRVAN (Jamaica).

Association of Development Financing Institutions in Asia and the Pacific—ADFIAP: Skyland Plaza, 2nd Floor, Sen. Gil J. Puyat Ave, Makati City, Metro Manila, 1200 Philippines; tel. (2) 816-1672; fax (2) 817-6498; e-mail inquire@adfiap.org; internet www .adfiap.org; f. 1976 to promote the interests and economic development of the respective countries of its member institutions, through development financing; mems: 65 institutions in 30 countries; Chair. ISOA KALOUMAIRA (Fiji); Sec.-Gen. ORLANDO P. PEÑA (Philippines); publs *Asian Banking Digest, Journal of Development Finance* (2 a year), *ADFIAP Newsletter, ADFIAP Accompli, DevTrade Finance*.

Benelux Economic Union: 39 rue de la Régence, 1000 Brussels, Belgium; tel. (2) 519-38-11; fax (2) 513-42-06; e-mail r.vanimpe@ benelux.be; internet www.benelux.be; f. 1960 to bring about the economic union of Belgium, Luxembourg and the Netherlands; aims to introduce common policies in the field of cross-border co-operation and harmonize standards and intellectual property legislation; structure comprises: Committee of Ministers; Council; Court of Justice; Consultative Inter-Parliamentary Council; the Economic and Social Advisory Council; and the General Secretariat; Sec.-Gen. Dr B. M. J. HENNEKAM (Netherlands); publs *Benelux Newsletter, Bulletin Benelux*.

Caribbean Council for Europe: Westminster Palace Gardens, Suite 18, 1–7 Artillery Row, London, SW1P 1RR, United Kingdom; tel. (20) 7799-1521; e-mail admin@caribbean-council.com; f. 1992 by the Caribbean Association of Industry and Commerce and other regional organizations, to represent the interests of the Caribbean private sector in the European Union; organizes regular Europe/Caribbean Conference; Chair. YESU PERSAUD; Exec. Dir DAVID JESSOP.

Caritas Internationalis (International Confederation of Catholic Organizations for charitable and social action): Palazzo San Calisto, 00120 Città del Vaticano; tel. (06) 6987-9799; fax (06) 6988-7237; e-mail caritas.internationalis@caritas.va; internet www.caritas.org; f. 1950 to study problems arising from poverty, their causes and possible solutions; national mem. organizations undertake assistance and development activities. The Confederation co-ordinates emergency relief and development projects, and represents mems at international level; mems: 154 national orgs; Pres. Mgr YOUHANNA-FOUAD EL-HAGE (Bishop of Imperatriz (Brazil)); Sec.-Gen. DUNCAN MACLAREN; publs *Caritas Matters* (quarterly), *Emergency Calling* (2 a year).

Colombo Plan: Bank of Ceylon Merchant Tower, 28 St Michael's Rd, Colombo 03, Sri Lanka; tel. (1) 564448; fax (1) 564531; e-mail cplan@slt.lk; internet www.colombo-plan.org; f. 1950 by seven Commonwealth countries, to encourage economic and social development in Asia and the Pacific; the Plan comprises the Programme for Public Administration, to provide training for officials in the context of a market-orientated economy; the Programme for Private Sector Development, which organizes training programmes to stimulate the economic benefits of development of the private sector; a Drug Advisory Programme, to encourage regional co-operation in efforts to control drug-related problems, in particular through human resources development; a programme to establish a South-South Technical Co-operation Data Bank, to collate, analyse and publish information in order to facilitate south-south co-operation; and a Staff College for Technician Education (see below). All programmes are voluntarily funded; developing countries are encouraged to become donors and to participate in economic and technical co-operation activities among developing mems; mems: 24 countries; Sec.-Gen. U. SARAT CHANDRAN (India); publs *Annual Report, Colombo Plan Focus* (quarterly), Consultative Committee proceedings (every 2 years).

Colombo Plan Staff College for Technician Education: POB 7500, Domestic Airport Post Office, NAIA, Pasay City 1300, Philippines; tel. (2) 631-0991; fax (2) 631-0996; e-mail cpsc@skyinet .net; internet www.cpsc.org.ph; f. 1973 with the support of member Governments of the Colombo Plan; aims to enhance the development of technician education systems in developing mem. countries; Dir MAN-GON PARK; publ. *CPSC Quarterly*.

Communauté économique des états de l'Afrique centrale (CEEAC) (Economic Community of Central African States): BP 2112, Libreville, Gabon; tel. 73-35-48; internet www.ceeac.org; f. 1983, operational 1 January 1985; aims to promote co-operation between member states by abolishing trade restrictions, establishing a common external customs tariff, linking commercial banks, and setting up a development fund, over a period of 12 years; works to combat drug abuse and to promote regional security; mems: 10 African countries; Sec.-Gen. LOUIS-SYLVAIN GOMA.

Community of Sahel-Saharan States (Communauté des états Sahelo–Sahariens—CEN-SAD): POB 4041, Aljazaer Sq., Tripoli, Libya; tel. and fax (21) 361-4832; fax (21) 333-2116; e-mail info@ cen-sad.org; internet www.cen-sad.org; f. 1998; frmrly known as COMESSA; aims to strengthen co-operation between signatory states in order to promote their economic, social and cultural integration and to facilitate conflict resolution and poverty alleviation; partnership agreements concluded with many orgs, including the AU, the UN and ECOWAS; mems: Benin, Burkina Faso, Central African Republic, Chad, Djibouti, Egypt, Eritrea, The Gambia, Libya, Mali, Morocco, Niger, Nigeria, Senegal, Somalia, Sudan, Togo, Tunisia; Sec.-Gen. Dr MOHAMMED AL-MADANI AL-AZHARI (Libya).

Conseil de l'Entente (Entente Council): 01 BP 3734, angle ave Verdier/rue de TessiÈres, Abidjan 01, Côte d'Ivoire; tel. 33-28-35; fax 33-11-49; f. 1959 to promote economic development in the region; the Council's Mutual Aid and Loan Guarantee Fund (Fonds d' entraide et de garantie des emprunts) finances development projects, including agricultural projects, support for small and medium-sized enterprises, vocational training centres, research into new sources of energy and building of hotels to encourage tourism. A Convention of Assistance and Co-operation was signed in Feb. 1996. Holds annual summit (2000: Kara, Togo); mems: Benin, Burkina Faso, Côte d'Ivoire, Niger, Togo; Sec.-Gen. PAUL KOUAMÉ; publ. *Rapport d'activité* (annually).

Communauté économique du bétail et de la viande (CEBV) du Conseil de l'Entente (Livestock and Meat Economic Community of the Entente Council): 01 BP 638 Ouagadougou, Burkina Faso; tel. 21-30-62-67; fax 21-30-62-68; e-mail cebv@cenatrin.bf; internet www.cenatrin.bf/cebv; f. 1970 to promote the production, processing and marketing of livestock and meat; negotiates between members and with third countries on technical and financial co-operation and co-ordinated legislation; attempts to co-ordinate measures to combat drought and cattle diseases; mems: states belonging to the Conseil de l'Entente; Exec. Sec. Dr ELIE LADIKPO (Togo).

Council of American Development Foundations (Consejo de Fundaciones Americanas de Desarrollo—SOLIDARIOS): Calle 6 No. 10 Paraíso, Apdo Postal 620, Santo Domingo, Dominican Republic; tel. (809) 549-5111; fax (809) 544-0550; e-mail solidarios@codetel.net .do; f. 1972; exchanges information and experience, arranges technical assistance, raises funds to organize training programmes and scholarships; administers development fund to finance programmes carried out by members through a loan guarantee programme; provides consultancy services. Mem. foundations provide technical and financial assistance to low-income groups for rural, housing and microenterprise development projects; mems: 18 institutional mems in 14 Latin American and Caribbean countries; Pres. MERCEDES P. DE CANALDA; Sec.-Gen. ISABEL C. ARANGO; publs *Solidarios* (quarterly), *Annual Report*.

Developing Eight (D-8): Müsir Fuad Pasa Yalisi, Eski Tersane, Emirgan, Cad. 90, 80860 İstanbul, Turkey; tel. (212) 2775513; fax (212) 2775519; internet www.mfa.gov.tr/d-8; inaugurated at a meeting of heads of state in June 1997; aims to foster economic co-operation between member states and to strengthen the role of developing countries in the global economy; project areas include trade and industry, agriculture, human resources, telecommunications, rural development, finance (including banking and privatization), energy, environment, and health. Third Summit meeting, convened in Cairo, Egypt, in Feb. 2001, discussed reducing trade barriers amongst member states and considered the impact of external debt on member economies; mems: Bangladesh, Egypt, Indonesia, Iran, Malaysia, Nigeria, Pakistan, Turkey; Exec. Dir AYHAN KAMEL.

Earth Council: POB 319-6100, San José, Costa Rica; tel. 205-1600; fax 249-3500; e-mail eci@ecouncil.ac.cr; internet www.ecouncil.ac.cr; f. 1992, following the UN Conference on Environment and Development; aims to promote and support sustainable development; supported the establishment of National Councils for Sustainable Development (NCSDs) and administers a programme to promote co-operation and dialogue and to facilitate capacity-building and training, with NCSDs; works, with other partner organizations, to generate support for an Earth Charter. The Earth Council Institute, comprising 18 members, functions as an advisory board to the Council; Chair. MAURICE STRONG (Canada); Pres. And CEO of Earth Council Institute FRANS van HAREN (Netherlands).

East African Community (EAC): AICC Bldg, Kilimanjaro Wing, 5th Floor, POB 1096, Arusha, Tanzania; tel. (27) 2504253; fax (27) 2504255; e-mail eac@eachq.org; internet www.eachq.org; f. Jan. 2001, following the adoption of a treaty on political and economic integration (signed in November 1999) by the heads of state of Kenya, Tanzania and Uganda, replacing the Permanent Tripartite Commission for East African Co-operation (f. 1993) and reviving the former East African Community (f. 1967; dissolved 1977); initial areas for co-operation were to be trade and industry, security, immigration, transport and communications, and promotion of investment; further objectives were the elimination of trade barriers and ensuring the free movement of people and capital within the grouping; Sec.-Gen. NUWE AMANYA-MUSHEGA.

Economic Community of the Great Lakes Countries (Communauté économique des pays des Grands Lacs—CEPGL): POB 58, Gisenyi, Rwanda; tel. 61309; fax 61319; f. 1976 main organs: annual Conference of Heads of State, Council of Ministers of Foreign Affairs, Permanent Executive Secretariat, Consultative Commission, Security Commission, three Specialized Technical Commissions; there are four specialized agencies: a development bank, the Banque de Développement des Etats des Grands Lacs (BDEGL) at Goma, Democratic Republic of the Congo; an energy centre at Bujumbura, Burundi; the Institute of Agronomic and Zootechnical Research, Gitega, Burundi; and a regional electricity company (SINELAC) at Bukavu, Democratic Republic of the Congo; mems: Burundi, the Democratic Republic of the Congo, Rwanda; publs *Grands Lacs* (quarterly review), *Journal* (annually).

Food Aid Committee: c/o International Grains Council, 1 Canada Sq., Canary Wharf, London, E14 5AE, United Kingdom; tel. (20) 7513-1122; fax (20) 7513-0630; e-mail igc-fac@igc.org.uk; internet www.igc.org.uk; f. 1967; responsible for administration of the Food Aid Convention—FAC (1999), a constituent element of the International Grains Agreement (1995); aims to make appropriate levels of food aid available on a consistent basis to maximize the impact and effectiveness of such assistance; provides a framework for co-operation, co-ordination and information-sharing among members on matters related to food aid. The 23 donor members pledge to supply a minimum of 5m. metric tons of food annually to developing countries and territories, mostly as gifts: in practice aid has usually exceeded 8m. tons annually. Secretariat support is provided by the International Grains Council; Exec. Dir G. DENIS; publ. *Report on shipments* (annually).

Gambia River Basin Development Organization (Organisation de mise en valeur du fleuve Gambie—OMVG): BP 2353, 13 passage Leblanc, Dakar, Senegal; tel. 822-31-59; fax 822-59-26; e-mail omvg@sentoo.sn; f. 1978 by Senegal and The Gambia; Guinea joined in 1981 and Guinea-Bissau in 1983. A masterplan for the integrated development of the Kayanga/Geba and Koliba/Corubal river basins has been developed, encompassing a projected natural resources management project; work on a hydraulic development plan for the Gambia river commenced in late 1996 and was completed in mid-1998; a pre-feasibility study on connecting the national electric grids of the four member states has been completed, and a feasibility study for the construction of the proposed Sambangalou hydroelectric dam, providing for energy transmission to all member states, commenced in Feb. 2002, with completion envisaged by Aug. 2003; maintains documentation centre; Exec. Sec. MAMADOU NASSIROU DIALLO.

Group of Three—G3: c/o Secretaría de Relaciones Exteriores, 1 Tlatelolco, Delegación Cuauhtémoc 06995, México, DF; e-mail gtres@sre.gob.mx; internet g3.sre.gob.mx; f. 1990 by Colombia, Mexico and Venezuela to remove restrictions on trade between the three countries; the trade agreement covers market access, rules of origin, intellectual property, trade in services, and government purchases, and entered into force in early 1994. Tariffs on trade between member states were to be removed on a phased basis. Co-operation was also envisaged in employment creation, the energy sector and the fight against cholera. The secretariat function rotates between the three countries on a two-yearly basis.

Indian Ocean Commission (IOC) (Commission de l'Océan Indien—COI): Q4, Ave Sir Guy Forget, BP 7, Quatre Bornes, Mauritius; tel. 425-9564; fax 425-2709; e-mail coi7@intnet.mu; internet coi.intnet.mu; f. 1982 to promote regional co-operation, particularly in economic development; projects include tuna-fishing development, protection and management of environmental resources and strengthening of meteorological services; tariff reduction is also envisaged; organizes an annual regional trade fair; mems: Comoros, France (representing the French Overseas Department of Réunion), Madagascar, Mauritius, Seychelles; Sec.-Gen. WILFRID BERTILE; publ. *La Gazette de la Commission de l'Océan Indien.*

Indian Ocean Rim Association for Regional Co-operation (IOR–ARC): Sorèze House, 14 Angus Rd, Vacoas, Mauritius; tel. 698-3979; fax 697-5390; e-mail iorarchq@intnet.mu; internet www.iornet.org; the first intergovernmental meeting of countries in the region to promote an Indian Ocean Rim initiative was convened in March 1995; charter to establish the Asscn was signed at a ministerial meeting in March 1997; aims to promote regional economic co-operation in fields of trade, investment, the environment, tourism, and science and technology. Third meeting of Council of Ministers held in Muscat, Oman, April 2001; mems: Australia, Bangladesh, India, Indonesia, Iran, Kenya, Madagascar, Malaysia, Mauritius, Mozambique, Oman, Seychelles, Singapore, South Africa, Sri Lanka, Tanzania, Thailand, United Arab Emirates and Yemen.

Dialogue Partner countries: People's Republic of China, Egypt, France, Japan, United Kingdom; Chair. MUSHTAQ AL-SALEH; Dir DEVDASLALL DUSORUTH (Mauritius).

Inter-American Planning Society (Sociedad Interamericana de Planificación—SIAP): c/o Revista Interamericana de Planificación, Casilla 01-05-1978, Cuenca, Ecuador; tel. (7) 823-860; fax (7) 823-949; e-mail siap1@siap.org.ec; f. 1956 to promote development of comprehensive planning; mems: institutions and individuals in 46 countries; Pres. Prof. PATRICIA A. WILSON (USA); Exec. Sec. LUIS E. CAMACHO (Colombia); publs *Correo Informativo* (quarterly), *Inter-American Journal of Planning* (quarterly).

International Bank for Economic Co-operation—IBEC: 107815 GSP Moscow B-78, 11 Masha Poryvaeva St, Russia; tel. (95) 975-38-61; fax (95) 975-22-02; f. 1963 by members of the Council for Mutual Economic Assistance (dissolved in 1991), as a central institution for credit and settlements following the decision in 1989–91 of most member states to adopt a market economy, the IBEC abandoned its system of multilateral settlements in transferable roubles, and (from 1 January 1991) began to conduct all transactions in convertible currencies. The Bank provides credit and settlement facilities for member states, and also acts as an international commercial bank, offering services to commercial banks and enterprises; mems: Bulgaria, Cuba, Czech Republic, Hungary, Mongolia, Poland, Romania, Russia, Slovakia, Viet Nam; Chair. VITALI S. KHOKHLOV; Man. Dirs V. SYTNIKOV, S. CONSTANTINESCU.

International Co-operation for Development and Solidarity (Co-opération internationale pour le développement et la solidarité—CIDSE): 16 rue Stévin, 1000 Brussels, Belgium; tel. (2) 230-77-22; fax (2) 230-70-82; e-mail postmaster@cidse.org; internet www.cidse.org; f. 1967 to link Catholic development organizations and assist in the co-ordination of projects; co-ordinates advocacy and lobbying; provides information; mems: 15 Catholic agencies in 14 countries and territories; Pres. JEAN-MARIE FARDEAU; Sec.-Gen. CHRISTIANE OVERKAMP.

International Investment Bank: 107078 Moscow, 7 Masha Poryvaeva St, Russia; tel. (95) 975-40-08; fax (95) 975-20-70; f. 1970 by members of the CMEA to grant credits for joint investment projects and the development of enterprises following the decision in 1989–91 of most member states to adopt a market economy, the Bank conducted its transactions (from 1 January 1991) in convertible currencies, rather than in transferable roubles. The Bank focuses on production and scientific and technical progress; mems: Bulgaria, Cuba, Czech Republic, Hungary, Mongolia, Poland, Romania, Russia, Slovakia, Viet Nam.

Inuit Circumpolar Conference: 170 Laurier Ave West, Suite 504, Ottawa, ON K1P 5V5, Canada; tel. (613) 563-2642; fax (613) 565-3089; e-mail icc@magma.ca; internet www.inuit.org; f. 1977 to protect the indigenous culture, environment and rights of the Inuit people (Eskimoes), and to encourage co-operation among the Inuit; conferences held every four years; mems: Inuit communities in Canada, Greenland, Alaska and Russia; Pres. AQQALUK LYNGE; Exec. Di HJALMAR DAHL; publ. *Silarjualiriniq.*

Lake Chad Basin Commission—LCBC: BP 727, N'Djamena, Chad; tel. 52-41-45; fax 52-41-37; e-mail lcbc@intnet.td; f. 1964 to encourage co-operation in developing the Lake Chad region and to promote the settlement of regional disputes; Work programmes emphasize the regulation of the utilization of water and other natural resources in the basin; the co-ordination of natural resources development projects and research; holds annual summit of heads of state; mems: Cameroon, Central African Republic, Chad, Niger, Nigeria; Exec. Sec. MUHAMMAD SANI ADAMU; publ. *Bibliographie générale de la cblt* (2 a year).

Latin American Association of Development Financing Institutions (Asociación Latinoamericana de Instituciones Financieras para el Desarrollo—ALIDE): Apdo Postal 3988, Paseo de la República 3211, Lima 100, Peru; tel. (1) 442-2400; fax (1) 442-8105; e-mail sg@alide.org.pe; internet www.alide.org.pe; f. 1968 to promote co-operation among regional development financing bodies; programmes: technical assistance; training; studies and research; technical meetings; information; projects and investment promotion; mems: 62 active, 8 assoc. and 8 collaborating (banks and financing institutions and development organizations in 22 Latin American countries, Slovenia and Spain); Sec.-Gen. ROMMEL ACEVEDO; publs *ALIDE Bulletin* (6 a year), *ALIDENOTICIAS Newsletter* (monthly), *Annual Report, Latin American Directory of Development Financing Institutions.*

Latin American Economic System (Sistema Económico Latinoamericano—SELA): Apdo 17035 1010–A; Torre Europa, 4°, Urb. Campo Alegre, Avda Francisco de Miranda, Caracas 1061, Venezuela;; Apdo 17035, Caracas 1010-A, Venezuela; tel. (212) 955-7111; fax (212) 951-5292; e-mail difusion@sela.org; internet www.sela.org; f. 1975 in accordance with the Panama Convention; aims to foster co-operation and integration among the countries of Latin America and the Caribbean, and to provide a permanent system of consultation and co-ordination in economic and social matters; conducts studies and other analysis and research; extends technical assistance to sub-regional and regional co-ordination bodies; provides library, information service and data bases on regional co-operation. The Latin American Council, the principal decision-making body of the System, meets annually at ministerial level and high-level regional consultation and co-ordination meetings are held; there is also a Permanent Secretariat; mems: 28 countries; Perm. Sec. (1999–2003) OTTO BOYE SOTO (Chile); publs *Capítulos del SELA* (3 a year), *Bulletin on Latin America and Caribbean Integration* (monthly), *SELA Antenna in the United States* (quarterly).

Liptako-Gourma Integrated Development Authority—LGA: POB 619, ave M. Thevenond, Ouagadougou, Burkina Faso; tel. (3) 30-61-48; f. 1972; scope of activities includes water infrastructure, telecommunications and construction of roads and railways; in 1986 undertook study on development of water resources in the basin of the Niger river (for hydroelectricity and irrigation); mems: Burkina Faso, Mali, Niger; Dir-Gen. GISANGA DEMBÉLÉ (Mali).

Mano River Union: Private Mail Bag 133, Delco House, Lightfoot Boston St, Freetown, Sierra Leone; tel. (22) 226883; f. 1973 to establish a customs and economic union between member states to accelerate development via integration; a common external tariff was instituted in 1977. Intra-union free trade was officially introduced in May 1981, as the first stage in progress towards a customs union. A non-aggression treaty was signed by heads of state in 1986. The Union was inactive for three years until mid-1994, owing to regional conflict and disagreements regarding funding. In January 1995 a Mano River Centre for Peace and Development was established, which was to be temporarily based in London. The Centre aims to provide a permanent mechanism for conflict prevention and resolution, and monitoring of human rights violations, and to promote sustainable peace and development. A new security structure was approved in 2000. In Aug. 2001 ministers of foreign affairs, security, internal affairs, and justice, meeting as the Joint Security Committee, resolved to deploy joint border security and confidence-building units, and to work to reestablish the free movement of people and goods; mems: Guinea, Liberia, Sierra Leone; Dir Dr ABDOULAYE DIALLO.

Mekong River Commission—MRC: 364 M. V. Preah Monivong, Sangkat Phsar Doerm Thkouv, Khan Chamkar Mon, POB 1112, Phnom Penh, Cambodia; tel. (23) 720979; fax (23) 720972; e-mail mrcs@mrcmekong.org; internet www.mrcmekong.org; f. 1995 as successor to the Committee for Co-ordination of Investigations of the Lower Mekong Basin (f. 1957); aims to promote and co-ordinate the sustainable development and use of the resources of the Mekong River Basin for navigational and non-navigational purposes, in order to assist the social and economic development of member states and preserve the ecological balance of the basin. Provides scientific information and policy advice; supports the implementation of strategic programmes and activities; organizes an annual donor consultative group meeting; maintains regular dialogue with Myanmar and the People's Republic of China; mems: Cambodia, Laos, Thailand, Viet Nam; Chief Exec. JOERN KRISTENSEN; publ. *Mekong News* (quarterly).

Niger Basin Authority (Autorité du bassin du Niger): BP 729, Niamey, Niger; tel. 723102; fax 735310; e-mail abasec@intnet.ne; internet www.abn-nba.org; f. 1964 (as River Niger Commission; name changed 1980) to harmonize national programmes concerned with the River Niger Basin and to execute an integrated development plan; compiles statistics; regulates navigation; runs projects on hydrological forecasting, environmental control; infrastructure and agro-pastoral development; mems: Benin, Burkina Faso, Cameroon, Chad, Côte d'Ivoire, Guinea, Mali, Niger, Nigeria; Exec. Sec. MOHAMMED BELLO TUGA (Nigeria); publ. *Bulletin.*

Niger Basin Initiative: POB 192, Entebbe, Uganda; tel. (41) 321329; fax (41) 320971; e-mail nbisec@nilesec.org; internet www.nilebasin.org; f. 1999; aims to achieve sustainable socio-economic development through the equitable use and benefits of the Nile Basin water resources and to create an enabling environment for the implementation of programmes with a shared vision. Highest authority is the Nile Basin Council of Ministers (Nile-COM); other activities undertaken by a Nile Basin Technical Advisory Committee (Nile-TAC); mems: Burundi, Democratic Republic of the Congo, Egypt, Eritrea, Ethiopia, Kenya, Rwanda, Sudan, Tanzania, Uganda; Exec. Dir Meraji O. Y. MSUYA (Tanzania).

Organisation of Eastern Caribbean States (OECS): POB 179, Morne Fortune, Castries, Saint Lucia; tel. 452-2537; fax 453-1628; e-mail oesec@oecs.org; internet www.oecs.org; f. 1981 by the seven states that formerly belonged to the West Indies Associated States (f. 1966); Aims to promote the harmonized development of trade and industry in member states; single market created on 1 January 1988. Principal institutions are: the Authority of Heads of Government (the supreme policy-making body), the Foreign Affairs Committee, the Defence and Security Committees, and the Economic

Affairs Committee. There is also an Export Development and Agricultural Diversification Unit—EDADU (based in Dominica); mems: Antigua and Barbuda, Dominica, Grenada, Montserrat, Saint Christopher and Nevis, Saint Lucia, Saint Vincent and the Grenadines; assoc. mems: Anguilla, British Virgin Islands; Dir-Gen. GEORGE GOODWIN.

Organization for the Development of the Senegal River (Organisation pour la mise en valeur du fleuve Sénégal—OMVS): c/o Haut-Commissariat, 46 rue Carnot, BP 3152, Dakar, Senegal; tel. 823-45-30; fax 823-47-62; e-mail omvssphc@sentoo.sn; internet www.omvs-hc.org; f. 1972 to promote the use of the Senegal river for hydroelectricity, irrigation and navigation; the Djama dam in Senegal provides a barrage to prevent salt water from moving upstream, and the Manantali dam in Mali is intended to provide a reservoir for irrigation of about 375,000 ha of land and for production of hydro-electricity and provision of year-round navigation for ocean-going vessels. In 1997 two companies were formed to manage the dams: Société de gestion de l'énergie de Manantali (SOGEM) and Société de gestion et d'exploitation du barrage de Djama (SOGED). Work began in 1997 on a hydro-electric power station on the Senegal River; mems: Mali, Mauritania, Senegal; Guinea has observer status; Pres. ABOUBACARY COULIBALY (Mali).

Organization for the Management and Development of the Kagera River Basin (Organisation pour l'aménagement et le développement du bassin de la rivière Kagera—OBK): BP 297, Kigali, Rwanda; tel. (7) 84665; fax (7) 82172; f. 1978; envisages joint development and management of resources, including the construction of an 80-MW hydroelectric dam at Rusumo Falls, on the Rwanda-Tanzania border, a 2,000-km railway network between the four member countries, road construction (914 km), and a telecommunications network between member states; mems: Burundi, Rwanda, Tanzania, Uganda; Exec. Sec. JEAN-BOSCO BALINDA.

Pacific Basin Economic Council—PBEC: 900 Fort St, Suite 1080, Honolulu, HI 96813, USA; tel. (808) 521-9044; fax (808) 521-8530; e-mail info@pbec.org; internet www.pbec.org; f. 1967; an asscn of business representatives aiming to promote business opportunities in the region, in order to enhance overall economic development; advises governments and serves as a liaison between business leaders and government officials; encourages business relationships and co-operation among members; holds business symposia; mems: 20 economies (Australia, Canada, Chile, People's Republic of China, Colombia, Ecuador, Hong Kong, Indonesia, Japan, Republic of Korea, Malaysia, Mexico, New Zealand, Peru, Philippines, Russia, Singapore, Taiwan, Thailand, USA); Chair. SUCK-RAI CHO; Pres. DALTON TANONAKA; publs *Pacific Journal* (quarterly), *Executive Summary* (annual conference report).

Pacific Economic Co-operation Council—PECC: 4 Nassim Rd, Singapore 258372; tel. 67379823; fax 67379824; e-mail peccsec@pecc.net; internet www.pecc.net; f. 1980; an independent, policy-orientated organization of senior research, government and business representatives from 25 economies in the Asia-Pacific region; aims to foster economic development in the region by providing a forum for discussion and co-operation in a wide range of economic areas; holds a General Meeting every 2 years; mems: Australia, Brunei, Canada, Chile, the People's Republic of China, Colombia, Ecuador, Hong Kong, Indonesia, Japan, the Republic of Korea, Malaysia, Mexico, Mongolia (assoc. mem.), New Zealand, Peru, Philippines, Russia, Singapore, Taiwan, Thailand, USA, Viet Nam and the Pacific Island Forum; French Pacific Territories (assoc. mem.); Dir-Gen. DAVID PARSONS; publs *Issues PECC* (quarterly), *Pacific Economic Outlook* (annually), *Pacific Food Outlook* (annually).

Pan-African Institute for Development—PAID: BP 4056, Douala, Cameroon; tel. and fax 342-80-30; e-mail ipd.sg@camnet.cm; internet www.paid-wa.org; f. 1964; gives training to people from African countries involved with development at grassroots, intermediate and senior levels (48 countries in 1998); emphasis is given to: development management and financing; agriculture and rural development; issues of gender and development; promotion of small and medium-sized enterprises; training policies and systems; environment, health and community development; research, support and consultancy services; and specialized training. There are four regional institutes: Central Africa (Douala), Sahel (Ouagadougou, Burkina Faso), West Africa (Buéa, Cameroon), Eastern and Southern Africa (Kabwe, Zambia) and a European office in Geneva; Pres. of the Governing Council Dr MBUKI V. MWAMUFIYA; publs *Newsletter* (2 a year), *Annual Progress Report*, *PAID Report* (quarterly).

Permanent Inter-State Committee on Drought Control in the Sahel (Comité permanent inter états de lutte contre la sécheresse au Sahel—CILSS): POB 7049, Ouagadougou 03, Burkina Faso; tel. 37-41-25; fax 37-41-32; e-mail cilss@fasonet.bf; internet www.cilssnet.org; f. 1973; works in co-operation with UNDP Drylands Development Centre; aims to combat the effects of chronic drought in the Sahel region, by improving irrigation and food production, halting deforestation and creating food reserves; initiated a series of projects to improve food security and to counter poverty, entitled Sahel 21; by Jan. 2002 heads of state of all members had signed a convention for the establishment of a Fondation pour le Développement Durable du Sahel; maintains Institut du Sahel at Bamako (Mali) and centre at Niamey (Niger); mems: Burkina Faso, Cape Verde, Chad, The Gambia, Guinea-Bissau, Mali, Mauritania, Niger, Senegal; Pres. AMADOU TOUMANI TOURÉ (Mali); Exec. Sec. MOUSSA S. MBENGA (The Gambia); publ. *Reflets Sahéliens* (quarterly).

Population Council: 1 Dag Hammarskjöld Plaza, New York, NY 10017, USA; tel. (212) 339-0500; fax (212) 755-6052; e-mail pubinfo@ popcouncil.org; internet www.popcouncil.org; f. 1952; aims to improve reproductive health and achieve a balance between people and resources; analyses demographic trends; conducts biomedical research to develop new contraceptives; works with private and public agencies to improve the quality and scope of family planning and reproductive health services; helps governments to design and implement population policies; communicates results of research. Four regional offices, in India, Mexico, Egypt and Ghana, and 15 country offices. Additional office in Washington, DC, USA, carries out world-wide operational research and activities for reproductive health and the prevention of HIV and AIDS; Chair. RODNEY B. WAGNER; Pres. LINDA MARTIN; publs *Studies in Family Planning* (quarterly), *Population and Development Review* (quarterly), *Population Briefs* (quarterly).

Society for International Development: Via Panisperna 207, 00184 Rome, Italy; tel. (06) 4872172; fax (06) 4872170; e-mail info@ sidint.org; internet www.sidint.org; f. 1957; a global network of individuals and institutions wishing to promote participative, pluralistic and sustainable development; builds partnerships with civil society groups and other sectors; fosters local initiatives and new forms of social experimentation; mems: over 3,000 in 115 countries, 60 local chapters; Pres. ENRIQUE IGLESIAS; Sec.-Gen. ROBERTO SAVIO; publs *Development* (quarterly), *Bridges* (bimonthly newsletter).

South Centre: Chemin du Champ-d'Anier 17–19, BP 228, 1211 Geneva 19, Switzerland; tel. (22) 7918050; fax (22) 7988531; e-mail south@southcentre.org; internet www.southcentre.org; f. 1990 as a follow-up mechanism of the South Commission (f. 1987); in 1995 established as an intergovernmental body to promote South–South solidarity and co-operation by generating ideas and action-oriented proposals on major policy issues; Chair. GAMANI COREA (Sri Lanka); publ. *South Letter* (weekly).

Union of the Arab Maghreb (Union du Maghreb arabe—UMA): 14 rue Zalagh, Agdal, Rabat, Morocco; tel. (37) 671-274; fax (37) 671-253; e-mail sg.uma@maghrebarabe.org; internet www .maghrebarabe.org; f. 1989; aims to encourage joint ventures and to create a single market; structure comprises a council of heads of state (meeting annually), a council of ministers of foreign affairs, a follow-up committee, fa consultative council of 30 delegates from each country, a UMA judicial court, and four specialized ministerial commissions. Chairmanship rotates annually between heads of state. A Maghreb Investment and Foreign Trade Bank, funding joint agricultural and industrial projects, has been established and a customs union created. In May 1999 the follow-up committee convened to formulate a programme to reactivate the Union; mems: Algeria, Libya, Mauritania, Morocco, Tunisia; Sec.-Gen. HABIB BOULARES AMAMOU (Tunisia).

Vienna Institute for Development and Co-operation (Wiener Institut für Entwicklungsfragen und Zusammenarbeit): Möllwaldplatz 5/3, 1040 Vienna, Austria; tel. (1) 713-35-94; fax (1) 713-35-94-73; e-mail office@vidc.org; internet www.vidc.org; f. 1987 (fmrly Vienna Institute for Development, f. 1964); disseminates information on the problems and achievements of developing countries; encourages increased aid-giving and international co-operation; conducts research; Pres. FRANZ VRANITZKY; Dir ERICH ANDLIK; publs *Report Series, Echo*.

Economics and Finance

African Centre for Monetary Studies—ACMS: 15 blvd Franklin Roosevelt, BP 4128, Dakar, Senegal; tel. 821-93-80; fax 822-73-43; e-mail caem@syfed.refer.sn; began operations 1978; aims to promote better understanding of banking and monetary matters; studies monetary problems of African countries and the effect on them of international monetary developments; seeks to enable African countries to co-ordinate strategies in international monetary affairs; established as an organ of the Association of African Central Banks (AACB) following a decision by the OAU Heads of State and Government; mems: all mems of the AACB; Chair. Dr PAUL A. OGWUMA (Nigeria); Dir MAMADOU SIDIBE.

African Insurance Organization—AIO: SNAC Building, 3rd Floor Flatters St, BP 5860, Douala, Cameroon; tel. 342-4758; fax 343-2008; e-mail aio@sprynet.com; internet www.africaninsurance .org; f. 1972 to promote the expansion of the insurance and reinsur-

ance industry in Africa, and to increase regional co-operation; holds annual conference, periodic seminars and workshops, and arranges meetings for reinsurers, brokers, consultant and regulators in Africa; has established African insurance 'pools' for aviation, petroleum and fire risks, and created asscns of African insurance educators, supervisory authorities and insurance brokers and consultants; Pres. TEWODROS TILAHUN (Ethiopia); Sec.-Gen. YOSEPH ASEFFA (Cameroon); publ. *African Insurance Annual Review*.

Asian Clearing Union—ACU: c/o Central Bank of the Islamic Republic of Iran, POB 11365/8531, Tehran, Iran; tel. (21) 2842076; fax (21) 2847677; e-mail acusecret@mail.iranet.net; f. 1974 to provide clearing arrangements, whereby members settle payments for intra-regional transactions among the participating central banks, on a multilateral basis, in order to economize on the use of foreign exchange and promote the use of domestic currencies in trade transactions among developing countries; part of ESCAP's Asian trade expansion programme; the Central Bank of Iran is the Union's agent; in September 1995 the ACU unit of account was changed from SDR to US dollars, with effect from 1 January 1996; mems: central banks of Bangladesh, Bhutan, India, Iran, Myanmar, Nepal, Pakistan, Sri Lanka; Sec.-Gen. MOHAMMAD FIROUZDOR; publs *Annual Report, Newsletter* (monthly).

Asian Reinsurance Corporation: 17th Floor, Tower B, Chamnan Phenjati Business Center, 65 Rama 9 Rd, Huaykwang, Bangkok 10320, Thailand; tel. (2) 245-2169; fax (2) 248-1377; e-mail asianre@ asianrecorp.com; internet www.asianrecorp.com; f. 1979 by ESCAP with UNCTAD, to operate as a professional reinsurer, giving priority in retrocessions to national insurance and reinsurance markets of member countries, and as a development organization providing technical assistance to countries in the Asia-Pacific region; cap. (auth.) US $15m., (p.u.) $8m. mems: Afghanistan, Bangladesh, Bhutan, People's Republic of China, India, Iran, Republic of Korea, Philippines, Sri Lanka, Thailand; Gen. Man. A. S. MALABANAN.

Association of African Central Banks—AACB: 15 blvd Franklin Roosevelt, BP 4128, Dakar, Senegal; tel. 821-93-80; fax 822-73-43; f. 1968 to promote contacts in the monetary and financial sphere, in order to increase co-operation and trade among member states; aims to strengthen monetary and financial stability on the African continent; mems: 36 African central banks representing 47 states; Chair. Dr PAUL A. OGWUMA (Nigeria).

Association of African Tax Administrators—AATA: POB 13255, Yaoundé, Cameroon; tel. 22-41-57; fax 23-18-55; f. 1980 to promote co-operation in the field of taxation policy, legislation and administration among African countries; mems: 20 states; Exec. Sec. OWONA PASCAL-BAYLON.

Association of Asian Confederation of Credit Unions—AACCU: 36/2 Moo 3, Soi Malee Suanson Ramkanheang Rd, Bangkapi, Bangkok 10240, Thailand; ; tel. (2) 374-3170; fax (2) 374-5321; e-mail ceo@aaccu.net; internet www.aaccu.net; links and promotes credit unions in Asia, provides research facilities and training programmes; mems: in 12 Asian countries; Pres. CHARLES YIP WAI KWONG (Hong Kong); CEO RANJITH HETTIARACHICHI (Thailand); publs *ACCU News* (every 2 months), *Annual Report and Directory*.

Association of European Institutes of Economic Research—AIECE (Association d'instituts européens de conjoncture économique): 3 place Montesquieu, 1348 Louvain-la-Neuve, Belgium; tel. (10) 47-34-26; fax (10) 47-39-45; e-mail olbrechts@ires.ucl.ac.be; internet www.aiece.org; f. 1957; provides a means of contact between member institutes; organizes two meetings annually, at which discussions are held on the economic situation and on a special theoretical subject; mems: 40 institutes in 20 European countries; Admin. Sec. PAUL OLBRECHTS.

Central Asian Bank for Co-operation and Development—CABCD: 115A Abay, Almaty, Kazakhstan; tel. (2) 422737; fax (2) 428627; f. 1994 to support trade and development in the sub-region; mems: Kazakhstan, Kyrgyzstan, Tajikistan, Uzbekistan.

Centre for Latin American Monetary Studies (Centro de Estudios Monetarios Latinoamericanos—CEMLA): Durango 54, Col. Roma, Del. Cuauhtémoc, 06700 México, DF, Mexico; tel. (55) 5533-0300; fax (55) 5525-4432; e-mail estudios@cemla.org; internet www .cemla.org; f. 1952; organizes technical training programmes on monetary policy, development finance, etc; runs applied research programmes on monetary and central banking policies and procedures; holds regional meetings of banking officials; mems: 31 associated members (Central Banks of Latin America and the Caribbean), 28 co-operating members (supervisory institutions of the region and non-Latin American Central Banks); Dir-Gen. KENNETH GILMORE COATES SPRY; publs *Bulletin* (every 2 months), *Monetaria* (quarterly), *Money Affairs* (2 a year).

Comité Européen des Assurances—CEA: 3 bis rue de la Chaussée d'Antin, F-75009 Paris, France; tel. 1-44-83-11-83; fax 1-47-70-03-75; internet www.cea.assur.org; f. 1953 to represent the interests of European insurers, to encourage co-operation between members, to allow the exchange of information and to conduct studies; mems: national insurance asscns of 30 countries; Pres. GIJSBERT J. SWALEF (Netherlands); Dir -Gen. DANIEL G. SCHANTÉ (France); publs *CEA INFO—Euro Brief* (every 2 months), *CEA Executive Update* (monthly newsletter), *European Insurance in Figures* (annually), *The European Life Insurance Market* (annually).

East African Development Bank: 4 Nile Ave, POB 7128, Kampala, Uganda; tel. (41) 230021; fax (41) 259763; e-mail admin@eadb.com; internet www.transafrica.org/eadb; f. 1967 by the former East African Community to promote development within Kenya, Tanzania and Uganda, which each hold 25.78% of the equity capital; the remaining equity is held by the African Development Bank and other institutional investors; total assets SDR 145m. (31 Dec. 2002); Chair. MWAGHAZI MWACHOFI; Dir-Gen. F. R. TIBEITA.

Eastern Caribbean Central Bank—ECCB: POB 89, Basseterre, St Christopher and Nevis; tel. 465-2537; fax 465-9562; e-mail eccbinfo@caribsurf.com; internet www.eccb-centralbank.org; f. 1983 by OECS governments; maintains regional currency (Eastern Caribbean dollar) and advises on the economic development of member states; mems: Anguilla, Antigua and Barbuda, Dominica, Grenada, Montserrat, Saint Christopher and Nevis, Saint Lucia, Saint Vincent and the Grenadines; Gov. Sir K. DWIGHT VENNER.

Econometric Society: Dept of Economics, Northwestern University, Evanston, IL 60208, USA; tel. (847) 491-3615; internet www.econometricsociety.org; f. 1930 to promote studies aiming at a unification of the theoretical-quantitative and the empirical-quantitative approaches to economic problems; mems: c. 7,000; Exec. Dir and Sec. JULIE P. GORDON; publ. *Econometrica* (6 a year).

European Federation of Finance House Associations—Eurofinas: Ave de Tervueren 267, 1150 Brussels, Belgium; tel. (2) 778-05-60; fax (2) 778-05-79; internet www.eurofinas.org; f. 1959 to study the development of instalment credit financing in Europe, to collate and publish instalment credit statistics, and to promote research into instalment credit practice; mems: finance houses and professional asscns in 16 European countries; Chair. GREGORIO D'OTTAVIANO CHIARAMONTI (Italy); Sec.-Gen. MARC BAERT; publs *Eurofinas Newsletter* (monthly), *Annual Report*, *Study Reports*.

European Federation of Financial Analysts Societies—EFFAS: Palais de la Bourse, Place de la Bourse, 75002 Paris, France; tel. 1-03-58-33-48; fax 1-03-58-33-35; e-mail claudia.stinnes@effas.com; internet www.effas.com; f. 1962 to co-ordinate the activities of European asscns of financial analysts; aims to raise the standard of financial analysis and improve the quality of information given to investors; encourages unification of national rules and draws up rules of profession; holds biennial congress; mems: 14,000 in 18 European countries; Pres. FRITZ H. RAU.

European Financial Management and Marketing Association—EFMA: 16 rue d'Aguesseau, 75008 Paris, France; tel. 1-47-42-52-72; fax 1-47-42-56-76; e-mail info@efma.com; internet www.efma.com; f. 1971 to link financial institutions by organizing seminars, conferences and training sessions and an annual Congress and World Convention, and by providing information services; mems: over 200 European financial institutions; Chair. ALFREDO SÁENZ ABAD (Spain); publ. *Newsletter*.

European Private Equity and Venture Capital Association—EVCA: 4 Minervastraat, 1930 Zaventem, Belgium; tel. (2) 715-00-20; fax (2) 725-07-04; e-mail evca@evca.com; internet www.evca.com; f. 1983 to link private equity and venture capital companies within Europe; provides information services; supports networking; organizes lobbies and campaigns; works to promote the asset class in Europe and worldwide; holds three conferences each year as well as seminars, organizes EVCA Institute training courses; mems: over 950; Chair.. MAX BURGER; Sec.-Gen. JAVIER ECHARRI; publs *Yearbook* (annually), *research and special papers; legal documents, industry guide-lines*.

Financial Action Task Force on Money Laundering—FATF (Groupe d'action financière sur le blanchiment de capitaux—GAFI): 2 rue André-Pascal, 75775 Paris Cédex 16, France; tel. 1-45-24-82-00; fax 1-45-24-85-00; e-mail contact@fatf.gafi.org; internet www1.oecd.org/fatf; f. 1989, on the recommendation of the Group of Seven industrialized nations (G-7), to develop and promote policies to combat money laundering and the financing of terrorism; formulated a set of Recommendations for member countries to implement; established regional task forces in the Caribbean, Asia-Pacific, Europe, Africa and South America; mems: 31 countries, the European Commission, and the Co-operation Council for the Arab States of the Gulf; Pres. JOCHEN SANIO; Exec. Sec. PATRICK MOULETTE; publ. *Annual Report*.

Fonds Africain de Garantie et de Co-opération Economique —FAGACE (African Guarantee and Economic Co-operation Fund): 01 BP 2045 RP, Cotonou, Benin; tel. 30-03-76; fax 30-02-84; e-mail fagace@intnet.bj; internet www.fagace.org; commenced operations in 1981; guarantees loans for development projects, provides loans

and grants for specific operations and supports national and regional enterprises. mems: nine African countries; Dir-Gen. LIBASSE SAMB.

International Accounting Standards Board—IASB: 30 Cannon St, London, EC4M 6XH, United Kingdom; tel. (20) 7246-6410; fax (20) 7246-6411; e-mail iasb@iasb.org.uk; internet www.iasb.org.uk; f. 1973 as International Accounting Standards Committee, reorganized and present name adopted 2001; aims to develop, in the public interest, a single set of high-quality, uniform, clear and enforceable global accounting standards requiring the submission of high-quality, transparent and comparable information in financial statements and other financial reporting, in order to assist participants in world-wide capital markets and other end-users to make informed decisions on economic matters; aims also to promote the use and rigorous application of these global accounting standards, and to bring about the convergence of these with national accounting standards; Chair. and CEO Sir DAVID TWEEDIE; publs *IASB Insight* (quarterly), *Bound Volume of International Accounting Standards* (annually), *Interpretations of International Accounting Standards*.

International Association for Research in Income and Wealth: Dept of Economics, New York University, 269 Mercer St, Room 700, New York, NY 10003, USA; tel. (212) 924-4386; fax (212) 366-5067; e-mail iariw@nyu.edu; internet www.econ.nyu.edu/iariw; f. 1947 to further research in the general field of national income and wealth and related topics by the organization of biennial conferences and other means; mems: approx. 375; Chair.. TIM SMEEDING; Exec. Sec. JANE FORMAN (USA); publ. *Review of Income and Wealth* (quarterly).

International Bureau of Fiscal Documentation—IBFD: H. J. E. Wenckebachweg 210, POB 20237, 1096 AS Amsterdam, Netherlands; tel. (20) 55-40-100; fax (20) 62-28-658; e-mail info@ibfd.org; internet www.ibfd.org; f. 1938 to supply information on fiscal law and its application; maintains library on international taxation; Pres. Prof. G. MAISTO; Chair. Prof. HUBERT M. A. L. HAMAEKERS; publs *Bulletin for International Fiscal Documentation, Asia Pacific Tax Bulletin, Derivatives and Financial Instruments, European Taxation, International VAT Monitor, International Transfer Pricing Journal, Supplementary Service to European Taxation* (all monthly), *Tax News Service* (weekly); studies, data bases, regional tax guides.

International Centre for Local Credit: Koninginnegracht 2, 2514 AA The Hague, Netherlands; tel. (70) 3750850; fax (70) 3454743; e-mail centre@bng.nl; f. 1958 to promote local authority credit by gathering, exchanging and distributing information and advice on member institutions and on local authority credit and related subjects; studies important subjects in the field of local authority credit; mems: 22 financial institutions in 16 countries; Sec.-Gen. P. P. VAN BESOUW (Netherlands); publs *Bulletin, Newsletter* (quarterly).

International Economic Association: 23 rue Campagne Première, 75014 Paris, France; tel. 1-43-27-91-44; fax 1-42-79-92-16; e-mail iea@iea-world.org; internet www.iea-world.com; f. 1949 to promote international collaboration for the advancement of economic knowledge and develop personal contacts between economists, and to encourage the provision of means for the dissemination of economic knowledge; mems: asscns in 59 countries; Pres. Prof. JANOS KORNAI (Hungary); Sec.-Gen. Prof. JEAN-PAUL FITOUSSI (France).

International Federation of Accountants: 535 5th Ave, 26th Floor, New York, NY 10017, USA; tel. (212) 286-9344; fax (212) 286-9570; e-mail mariahermann@ifac.org; internet www.ifac.org; f. 1977 to develop a co-ordinated world-wide accounting profession with harmonized standards; mems: 155 accountancy bodies in 113 countries; Pres. RENÉ RICOL; Chief Exec. IAN BALL; publ. *International Standards on Auditing*.

International Fiscal Association—IFA: World Trade Center, POB 30215, 3001 DE Rotterdam, Netherlands; tel. (10) 4052990; fax (10) 4055031; e-mail n.gensecr@ifa.nl; internet www.ifa.nl; f. 1938 to study international and comparative public finance and fiscal law, especially taxation; holds annual congresses; mems in 90 countries and branches in 46 countries; Pres. JEROME B. LIBIN (USA); Sec.-Gen. M. J. ELLIS (Netherlands); publs *Cahiers de Droit Fiscal International, Yearbook of the International Fiscal Association, IFA Congress Seminar Series*.

International Institute of Public Finance: University of the Saar, PO Box 151150, 66041 Saarbrücken, Germany; fax (681) 302-4369; e-mail sec@iipf.net; internet www.iipf.net; f. 1937; a private scientific organization aiming to establish contacts between people of every nationality, whose main or supplementary activity consists in the study of public finance; holds one meeting a year devoted to a certain scientific subject; Pres. HIROFUMI SHIBATA (Japan).

International Organization of Securities Commissions— IOSCO: Plaza de Carlos Trías Bertrán 7, Planta 3a, 28020 Madrid, Spain; tel. (91) 417-55-49; fax (91) 555-93-68; e-mail mail@oicv.iosco

.org; internet www.iosco.org; f. 1983 to facilitate co-operation between securities and futures regulatory bodies at the international level; mems: 168 agencies; Chair. FERNANDO TEIXEIRA DOS SANTOS; Sec.-Gen. PHILIPPE RICHARD; publ. *IOSCO News* (3 a year).

International Securities Market Association—ISMA: Rigistr. 60, POB, 8033 Zürich, Switzerland; tel. (1) 363-4222; fax (1) 363-7772; e-mail info@isma.org; internet www.isma.org; f. 1969 for discussion of questions relating to the international securities market, to issue rules governing their functions, and to maintain a close liaison between the primary and secondary markets in international securities; mems: 568 banks and major financial institutions in 48 countries; Chair. RIJNHARD W. F. VAN TETS (Netherlands); Chief Exec. and Sec.-Gen. JOHN L. LANGTON (Switzerland); publs *International Bond Manual*, daily Eurobond listing, electronic price information, weekly Eurobond guide, ISMA formulae for yield, members' register, ISMA quarterly comment, reports, etc.

International Union for Housing Finance: 3 Savile Row, London, W1S 3PB, United Kindom; tel. (20) 7494-2995; fax (20) 7734-6826; e-mail iuhf@housingfinance.org; internet www .housingfinance.org; f. 1914 to foster world-wide interest in savings and home-ownership and co-operation among members; encourages comparative study of methods and practice in housing finance; promotes development of appropriate legislation on housing finance; mems: 350 in 51 countries, 8 regional affiliates; Sec.-Gen. ADRIAN COLES; publs *Housing Finance International* (quarterly), *Directory*, *International Housing Finance Factbook* (every 2 years), *IUHF Newsletter* (3 a year).

Latin American Banking Federation (Federación Latino-americana de Bancos—FELABAN): Santafé de Bogotá, D.C., Colombia Cra 11A No. 93-67 Of. 202 A.A 091959,; tel. (1) 621-8617; fax (1) 621-7659; internet www.latinbanking.com; f. 1965 to co-ordinate efforts towards wide and accelerated economic development in Latin American countries; mems: 19 Latin American national banking asscns; Pres. of Board IGNACIO SALVATIERRA (Venezuela); Sec.-Gen. MARICIELO GLEN DE TOBÓN (Colombia).

World Council of Credit Unions—WOCCU: POB 2982, 5710 Mineral Point Rd, Madison, WI 53705, USA; tel. (608) 231-7130; fax (608) 238-8020; e-mail mail@woccu.org; internet www.woccu.org; f. 1970 to link credit unions and similar co-operative financial institutions and assist them in expanding and improving their services; provides technical and financial assistance to credit union asscns in developing countries; mems: 35,000 credit unions in 86 countries; CEO ARTHUR ARNOLD; publs *WOCCU Annual Report*, *Credit Union World* (3 a year), *Spotlights On Development*; technical monographs and brochures.

World Federation of Exchanges (International Federation of Stock Exchanges): 22 boulevard de Courcelles, 75017 Paris, France; tel. 1-44-01-05-45; fax 1-47-54-94-22; e-mail secretariat@ world-exchanges.org; internet www.world-exchanges.org; f. 1961; formerly Fédération Internationale des Bourses de Valeurs—FIBV; central reference point for the securities industry; offers member exchanges guidance in business strategies, and improvement and harmonization of management practices; works with public financial authorities to promote increased use of regulated securities and derivatives exchanges; mems: 59, and 23 corresponding exchanges; Pres. RICHARD A. GRASSO; Sec-Gen. THOMAS KRANTZ.

World Savings Banks Institute: 11 rue Marie Thérèse, 1000 Brussels, Belgium; tel. (2) 211-11-11; fax (2) 211-11-99; internet www.savings-banks.com; f. 1924 as International Savings Banks Institute, present name and structure adopted in 1994; promotes co-operation among members and the development of savings banks world-wide; mems: 109 banks and asscns in 92 countries; Pres. Dr HOLGEN BERNDT (Germany); publs *Annual Report*, *International Savings Banks Directory*, *Perspectives* (4–5 a year).

Education

Agence Universitaire de la Francophonie—AUF: BP 400, succ. Côte-des-Neiges, Montréal, QC H3S 2S7, Canada; tel. (514) 343-6630; fax (514) 343-5783; e-mail recteur@auf.org; internet www.auf .org; f. 1961; aims to develop a francophone university community, through building partnerships with students, teachers, institutions and governments; mems: 452 institutions; Pres. JEAN DU BOIS DE GAUDUSSON (Canada); Dir-Gen. and Rector MICHÈLE GENDREAU-MASSA-LOUX (France); publs *Universités* (quarterly), *UREF Actualités* (every 2 months), directories (Francophone universities, Professors from francophone universities, Departments of French studies world-wide).

Asian Confederation of Teachers: c/o FIT, 55 Abhinav Apt, Mahturas Rd Extn, Kandivli, Mumbai 400 067, India; tel. (22) 8085437; fax (22) 6240578; e-mail vsir@hotmail.com; f. 1990; mems in 10 countries and territories; Pres. MUHAMMAD MUSTAPHA; Sec.-Gen. VINAYAK SIRDESAI.

Asian and South Pacific Bureau of Adult Education—ASPBAE: c/o H. Bhargava, 1st Floor, Shroff Chambers, 259-261 Perin Nariman St, Fort, Mumbai 400 001, India; tel. (22) 22665942; fax (22) 22679154; e-mail aspbae@vsnl.com; internet www.aspbae .org; f. 1964 to assist non-formal education and adult literacy; organizes training courses and seminars; provides material and advice relating to adult education; mems in 36 countries and territories; Sec.-Gen. MARIA-LOURDES ALMAZAN-KHAN; publs *ASPBAE News* (3 a year), *ASPBAE Courier* (2 a year).

Association for Childhood Education International: 17904 Georgia Ave, Suite 215, Olney, MD 20832, USA; tel. (301) 570-2111; fax (301) 570-2212; e-mail aceihq@aol.com; internet www.udel.edu/ bateman/acei; f. 1892 to work for the education of children (from infancy through early adolescence) by promoting desirable conditions in schools, raising the standard of teaching, co-operating with all groups concerned with children, informing the public of the needs of children; mems: 12,000; Pres. NANCY L. QUISENBERRY; Exec. Dir GERALD C. ODLAND; publs *Childhood Education* (6 a year), *Professional Focus Newsletters*, *Journal of Research in Childhood Education* (2 a year), books on current educational subjects.

Association Montessori Internationale: Koninginneweg 161, 1075 CN Amsterdam, Netherlands; tel. (20) 6798932; fax (20) 6767341; e-mail info@montessori-ami.org; internet www .montessori-ami.org; f. 1929 to propagate the ideals and educational methods of Dr Maria Montessori on child development, without racial, religious or political prejudice; organizes training courses for teachers in 15 countries; Pres. RENILDE MONTESSORI; publ *Communications* (quarterly).

Association of African Universities—AAU: POB 5744, Accra North, Ghana; tel. (21) 774495; fax (21) 774821; e-mail info@aau.org; internet www.aau.org; f. 1967 to promote exchanges, contact and co-operation among African university institutions and to collect and disseminate information on research and higher education in Africa; mems: 132 university institutions; Sec.-Gen. Prof. FRANÇOIS RAJAOSON (Madagascar); publs *AAU Newsletter* (3 a year), *Directory of African Universities* (every 2 years).

Association of Arab Universities: POB 401, Jubeyha, Amman, Jordan; tel. (6) 5345131; fax (6) 5332994; e-mail secgen@aaru.edu.jo; internet www.aaru.edu.jo; f. 1964; a scientific conference is held every 3 years; council meetings held annually; mems: 149 universities; Sec.-Gen. Dr MARWAN RASIM KAMAL; publ *AARU Bulletin* (annually and quarterly, in Arabic).

Association of Caribbean University and Research Institutional Libraries—ACURIL: Apdo postal 23317, San Juan 00931-3317, Puerto Rico; tel. 790-8054; fax 764-2311; e-mail acuril@rrpac .upr.clu.edu; internet acuril.rrp.upr.edu; f. 1968 to foster contact and collaboration between mem. universities and institutes; ; holds conferences, meetings and seminars; circulates information through newsletters and bulletins; facilitates co-operation and the pooling of resources in research; encourages exchange of staff and students; mems: 250; Pres LUISA VIGO-CEPEDA (Puerto Rico); Exec.-Sec. ONEIDA R. ORTIZ (Puerto Rico); publ *Newsletter* (2 a year).

Association of South-East Asian Institutions of Higher Learning—ASAIHL: Secretariat, Ratasastra Bldg 2, Chulalong-korn University, Henri Dunant Rd, Bangkok 10330, Thailand; tel. (2) 251-6966; fax (2) 253-7909; e-mail oninnat@chula.ac.th; internet www.seameo.org/asaihl; f. 1956 to promote the economic, cultural and social welfare of the people of South-East Asia by means of educational co-operation and research programmes; and to cultivate a sense of regional identity and interdependence; collects and disseminates information, organizes discussions; mems: 160 university institutions in 14 countries; Pres. Prof. Tan Sri Dr SYED JALALUDIN SYED SALIM; Sec.-Gen. Dr NINNAT OLANVORAVUTH; publs *Newsletter*, *Handbook* (every 3 years).

Caribbean Examinations Council: The Garrison, St Michael 20, Barbados; tel. 436-6261; fax 429-5421; internet www.cxc.org; f. 1972; develops syllabuses and conducts examinations; mems: govts of 16 English-speaking countries and territories.

Catholic International Education Office: 60 rue des Eburons, 1000 Brussels, Belgium; tel. (2) 230-72-52; fax (2) 230-97-45; e-mail oiec@pophost.eunet.be; internet www3.planalfa.es/oiec; f. 1952 for the study of the problems of Catholic education throughout the world; co-ordinates the activities of members; represents Catholic education at international bodies; mems: 102 countries, 18 assoc. mems, 13 collaborating mems, 6 corresponding mems; Pres. Mgr CESARE NOSIGLIA; Sec.-Gen. ANDRÉS DELGADO HERNÁNDEZ; publs *OIEC Bulletin* (every 3 months, in English, French and Spanish), *OIEC Tracts on Education*.

Comparative Education Society in Europe—CESE: Institut für Augemeine Pädagogik, Humboldt-Universität zu Berlin, Unter den Linden 6, 10099 Berlin, Germany; tel. (30) 20934094; fax (30) 20931006; e-mail juergen.schriewer@educat.hu-berlin.de; internet www.ceseurope.org; f. 1961 to promote teaching and research in comparative and international education; organizes conferences and promotes literature; mems: in 49 countries; Pres. Prof. DONATELLA PALOMBA (Italy); Sec. and Treas. Prof. MIGUEL A. PEREYRA (Spain); publ *Newsletter* (quarterly).

Council of Legal Education—CLE: c/o Registrar, POB 323, Tunapuna, Trinidad and Tobago; tel. 662-5860; fax 662-0927; f. 1971; responsible for the training of members of the legal profession; mems: govts of 12 countries and territories.

European Association for the Education of Adults: rue Liedts 27, 1030 Brussels, Belgium; tel. (2) 513-5205; fax (2) 513-5734; e-mail eaea@eaea.org; internet www.eaea.org; f. 1953; aims to create a 'learning society' by encouraging demand for learning, particularly from women and excluded sectors of society; seeks to improve response of providers of learning opportunities and authorities and agencies; mems: 90 in 30 countries; Pres. JÁNOS TÓTH; Gen. Sec. ELLINOR HAASE; publs *EAEA Monograph Series*, newsletter.

European Cultural Foundation: Jan van Goyenkade 5, 1075 HN Amsterdam, Netherlands; tel. (20) 6760222; fax (20) 6752231; e-mail eurocult@eurocult.org; internet www.eurocult.org; f. 1954 as a non-governmental organization, supported by private sources, to promote activities of mutual interest to European countries on aspects of culture; maintains national committees in 23 countries and a transnational network of institutes and centres: European Institute of Education and Social Policy, Paris; Institute for European Environmental Policy, London, Madrid and Berlin; Association for Innovative Co-operation in Europe (AICE), Brussels; EURYDICE Central Unit (the Education Information Network of the European Community), Brussels; European Institute for the Media, Düsseldorf; European Foundation Centre, Brussels; Fund for Central and East European Book Projects, Amsterdam; Institute for Human Sciences, Vienna; East West Parliamentary Practice Project, Amsterdam; and Centre Européen de la Culture, Geneva. A grants programme, for European co-operation projects is also conducted; Pres. HRH Princess, Margriet of the Netherlands ; Sec.-Gen. GOTT-FRIED WAGNER; publs *Annual Report*, *Newsletter* (3 a year).

European Federation for Catholic Adult Education (Federation Européene pour l'Éducation Catholique des Adultes—FEECA): ave de Tervueren 221, 1150, Brussels, Belgium; tel. (2) 738-07-90; e-mail feeca@brutele.be; fax (2) 738-07-95; f. 1963 to strengthen international contact between mems and to assist with international research and practical projects in adult education; holds conference every two years; Pres. ERICA SCHUSTER (Austria); Sec. GEORG DÜCHS.

European Foundation for Management Development—EFMD: 88 rue Gachard, 1050 Brussels, Belgium; tel. (2) 629-08-10; fax (2) 629-08-11; e-mail info@efmd.be; internet www.efmd.be; f. 1971 through merger of European Association of Management Training Centres and International University Contact for Management Education; aims to help improve the quality of management development, disseminate information within the economic, social and cultural context of Europe and promote international co-operation; mems: over 390 institutions in 41 countries world-wide (26 in Europe); Pres. GERARD VAN SCHAIK; Dir-Gen. ERIC CORNUEL; publs *Forum* (3 a year), *The Bulletin*(3 a year), *Guide to European Business Schools and Management Centres* (annually).

European Union of Arabic and Islamic Scholars (Union Européenne des Arabisants et Islamisants—UEAI): c/o Prof. S. Naef, Univ. de Genève, Faculté des Lettres, 3 place de l'Université, 1211 Geneva 4, Switzerland; tel. (081) 5517840; fax (081) 5515386; e-mail silvia.naef@lettres.unige.ch; f. 1964 to organize congresses of Arabic and Islamic Studies; holds congresses every two years; mems: 300 in 28 countries; Pres. Prof. URBAIN VERMEULEN (Belgium); Sec. Prof. SILVIA NAEF (Italy).

European University Association—EUA: 42 rue de la Loi, 1040 Brussels, Belgium; tel. (2) 230-55-44; fax (2) 230-57-51; e-mail info@eua.unige.ch; internet www.unige.ch/eua/; f. 2001 by merger of the Association of European Universities and the Confederation of EU Rectors' Conferences; represents European universities and national rectors' conferences; promotes the development of a coherent system of European higher education and research; provides support and guidance to its mems; focuses policies and services on the creation of a European area for higher education and research. mems: 37 collective and 8 assoc. universities and rectors' conferences in 45 countries; Sec.-Gen. LESLEY WILSON; publs *Thema*, *Directory*, *Annual Report*.

Graduate Institute of International Studies (Institut universitaire de hautes études internationales—HEI): POB 36, 132 rue de Lausanne, 1211 Geneva 21, Switzerland; tel. (22) 908-57-00; fax (22) 908-57-10; e-mail info@hei.unige.ch; internet heiwww.unige.ch; f. 1927 to establish a centre for advanced studies in international relations of the present day; maintains a library of 147,000 vols; Pres. Prof. JEAN-MICHEL JACQUET; Sec.-Gen. SIMON WERMELINGER.

Inter-American Centre for Research and Documentation on Vocational Training (Centro Interamericano de Investigación y Documentación sobre Formación Profesional—CINTER-FOR): Avda Uruguay 1238, Casilla de correo 1761, Montevideo, Uruguay; tel. (2) 9020557; fax (2) 9021305; e-mail dirmvd@cinterfor.org.uy; internet www.ilo.org/public/english/region/ampro/cinterfor/; f. 1964 by the International Labour Organization for mutual help among the Latin American and Caribbean countries in planning vocational training; services are provided in documentation, research, exchange of experience; holds seminars and courses; Dir PEDRO DANIEL WEINBERG; publs *Bulletin* (3 a year), *Documentation* (2 a year), *Herramientas para la transformación*, *Trazos de la formación*, studies, monographs and technical office papers.

Inter-American Confederation for Catholic Education (Confederación Interamericana de Educación Católica—CIEC): Calle 78 No 12–16 (ofna 101), Apdo Aéreo 90036, Santafé de Bogotá 8 DE, Colombia; tel. (1) 255-3676; fax (1) 255-0513; e-mail ciec@cable.net.co; internet www.ciec.to; f. 1945 to defend and extend the principles and rules of Catholic education, freedom of education, and human rights; organizes congress every three years; Pres. RAMÓN E. RIVAS TOMASI (Venezuela); Sec. Gen. MARIA CONSTANZA ARANGO; publ *Educación Hoy*.

International Association for Educational and Vocational Guidance—IAEVG: c/o Linda Taylor, Essex Careers and Business Partnership, Westergaard House, The Matchyns, London Rd, Rivenhall, Essex, CM8 3HA, United Kingdom; tel. (1376) 391303; fax (1376) 391498; e-mail linda.taylor@careersbp.co.uk; internet www.iaevg.org; f. 1951 to contribute to the development of vocational guidance and promote contact between persons associated with it; mems: 40,000 from 60 countries; Pres. Dr BERNHARD JENSCHKE (Germany); Sec.-Gen. LINDA TAYLOR (UK); publs *Bulletin* (2 a year), *Newsletter* (3 a year).

International Association for the Development of Documentation, Libraries and Archives in Africa: Villa 2547 Dieuppeul II, BP 375, Dakar, Senegal; tel. 824-09-54; f. 1957 to organize and develop documentation and archives in all African countries; mems: national asscns, institutions and individuals in 48 countries; Sec.-Gen. ZACHEUS SUNDAY ALI (Nigeria).

International Association of Educators for World Peace: POB 3282, Mastin Lake Station, Huntsville, AL 35810-0282, USA; tel. (256) 534-5501; fax (256) 536-1018; e-mail mercieca@hiwaay.net; internet www.earthportals.com/portal_messenger/executivelistiaewp1.html; f. 1969 to develop education designed to contribute to the promotion of peaceful relations at personal, community and international levels; aims to communicate and clarify controversial views in order to achieve maximum understanding; helps put into practice the Universal Declaration of Human Rights; mems: 35,000 in 102 countries; Pres. Dr CHARLES MERCIECA (USA); Sec.-Gen. Dr SURYA NATH PRASAD (India); publs *Peace Progress* (annually), *IAEWP Newsletter* (6 a year), *Peace Education* (2 a year), *UN News* (monthly).

International Association of Papyrologists (Association Internationale de Papyrologues): Fondation Egyptologique Reine Elisabeth, Parc du Cinquantenaire 10, 1000 Brussels, Belgium; tel. (2) 741-73-64; e-mail amartin@ulb.ac.be; internet www.ulb.ac.be/assoc/aip/; f. 1947; links all those interested in Graeco-Roman Egypt, especially Greek texts; mem. of the International Federation of the Societies of Classical Studies; mems: about 400; Pres. Prof. DOROTHY J. THOMPSON (UK); Sec. Prof. ALAIN MARTIN (Belgium).

International Association of Physical Education in Higher Education (Association Internationale des Écoles Supérieures d'Éducation Physique—AIESEP): Faculdade de Motricidade Humana, Universidade Técnica de Lisboa, 1495-688 Cruz Quebrada, Lisbon, Portugal; tel. (21) 419-66-08; fax (21) 415-12-48; e-mail fcosta@fmh.utl.pt; f. 1962; organizes congresses, exchanges, and research in physical education; mems: institutions in 51 countries; Sec.-Gen. Dr FRANCISCO CARREIRO DA COSTA.

International Association of Universities—IAU International Universities Bureau—IUB: 1 rue Miollis, 75732 Paris cédex 15, France; tel. 1-45-68-48-00; fax 1-47-34-76-05; e-mail iau@unesco.org; internet www.unesco.org/iau; f. 1950 to allow co-operation at the international level among universities and other institutions of higher education; provides clearing-house services and operates the joint IAU/UNESCO Information Centre on Higher Education; conducts meetings and research on issues concerning higher education; mems: about 700 universities and institutions of higher education in some 150 countries, 31 international and national university organizations; Pres. HANS VAN GINKEL; Sec.-Gen. EVA EGRON-POLAK; publs *Higher Education Policy* (quarterly), *IAU Newsletter* (every 2 months), *International Handbook of Universities* (every 2 years), *Issues in Higher Education* (monographs), *World Academic Database* (CD-ROM, annually), *World List of Universities* (every 2 years).

International Association of University Professors and Lecturers—IAUPL (Association Internationale des Professeurs et

Maîtres de Conférence Universitaires): 87 rue de Rome, 75017 Paris, France; tel. 1-44-90-01-01; fax 1-44 90 08 87; e-mail autonomesup@aol.com; f. 1945 for the development of academic fraternity amongst university teachers and research workers; the protection of independence and freedom of teaching and research; the furtherance of the interests of all university teachers; and the consideration of academic problems; mems: federations in 13 countries.

International Baccalaureate Organization—IBO: Route des Morillons 15, Grand-Saconnex 1218, Geneva, Switzerland; tel. (22) 791-7740; fax (22) 791-0277; e-mail ibhq@ibo.org; internet www.ibo.org; f. 1967 to plan curricula and an international university entrance examination, the International Baccalaureate, recognized by major universities world-wide; offers the Primary Years Programme for children aged between 3 and 12, the Middle Years Programme for students in the 11–16 age range, and the Diploma Programme for 17–18 year olds; mems: 1,425 participating schools in 115 countries; Pres. of Council GREG CRAFTER (Australia); Dir-Gen. Prof. GEORGE WALKER.

International Catholic Federation for Physical and Sports Education (Fédération Internationale Catholique d'Education Physique et Sportive—FICEP): 22 rue Oberkampf, 75011 Paris, France; tel. 1-43-38-50-57; fax 43-14-06-65; f. 1911 to group Catholic asscns for physical education and sport of different countries and to develop the principles and precepts of Christian morality by fostering meetings, study and international co-operation; mems: 14 affiliated national federations representing about 3.5m. members; Pres. DICK WIJTE (Netherlands); Sec.-Gen. CLÉMENT SCHERTZINGER (France).

International Council for Adult Education—ICAE: 720 Bathurst St, Suite 500, Toronto, ON M5S 2R4, Canada; tel. (416) 588-1211; fax (416) 588-5725; e-mail icae@icae.ca; internet www.web.net/icae; f. 1973 as a partnership of adult learners, teachers and organizations; General Assembly meets every four years; mems: seven regional organizations and 85 national asscns in more than 80 countries; Pres. PAUL BÉLANGER; publs *Convergence, ICAE News*.

International Council for Open and Distance Education—ICDE: Lilleakerveien 23, 0283 Oslo, Norway; tel. 22-06-26-30; fax 22-06-26-31; e-mail icde@icde.no; internet www.icde.org; f. 1938 (name changed 1982); furthers distance (correspondence) education by promoting research, encouraging regional links, providing information and organizing conferences; mems: institutions, corporations and individuals in 120 countries; Pres. Elect JIM TAYLOR (Australia); Sec.-Gen. REIDAR ROLL (Norway); publ *Open Praxis* (2 a year).

International Federation for Parent Education—IFPE (Fédération internationale pour l'éducation des parents–FIEP): 1 ave Léon Journault, 92311 Sèvres Cédex, France; tel. 1-45-07-21-64; fax 1-46-26-69-27; e-mail fiep@sympatico.ca; f. 1964 to gather in congresses and colloquia experts from different scientific fields and those responsible for family education in their own countries and to encourage the establishment of family education where it does not exist; mems: 120; Pres. MONEEF GUITOUNI (Canada); publ *Lettre de la FIEP* (2 a year).

International Federation of Catholic Universities (Fédération internationale d'universités catholiques—FIUC): 21 rue d'Assas, 75270 Paris Cédex 06, France; tel. 1-44-39-52-26; fax 1-44-39-52-28; e-mail sgfiuc@bureau.fiuc.org; internet www.fiuc.org/; f. 1948; aims to ensure a strong bond of mutual assistance among all Catholic universities in the search for truth; to help to solve problems of growth and development, and to co-operate with other international organizations; mems: 191 in 41 countries; Pres. Rev. JAN PETERS (Netherlands); Sec.-Gen. GUY-RÉAL THIVIERGE (Canada); publ *Monthly Newsletter*.

International Federation of Library Associations and Institutions—IFLA: POB 95312, 2509 CH The Hague, Netherlands; tel. (70) 3140884; fax (70) 3834827; e-mail ifla@ifla.org; internet www.ifla.org; f. 1927 to promote international co-operation in librarianship and bibliography; mems: 1700 members in 150 countries; Pres. Elect KAY RASEROKA; Sec.-Gen. ROSS SHIMMON; publs *IFLA Annual Report, IFLA Directory, IFLA Journal, International Cataloguing and Bibliographic Control* (quarterly), *IFLA Professional Reports*.

International Federation of Organizations for School Correspondence and Exchange: Via Torino 256, 10015 Ivrea, Italy; tel. (0125) 234433; fax (0125) 234761; e-mail fioces@ipfs.org; internet ipfs.org/fioces.htm; f. 1929; aims to contribute to the knowledge of foreign languages and civilizations and to bring together young people of all nations by furthering international scholastic correspondence; mems: 78 national bureaux of scholastic correspondence and exchange in 21 countries; Pres. ALBERT V. RUTTER (Malta); Gen. Sec. LIVIO TONSO (Italy).

International Federation of Physical Education (Fédération internationale d'éducation physique—FIEP): c/o Prof. Robert Decker, 7–9 rue du X Octobre, 7243 Bereldange, Luxembourg; tel. and fax 33-94-81; e-mail robert.decker@ni.educ.lu; f. 1923; studies

physical education on scientific, pedagogic and aesthetic bases, with the aim of stimulating health, harmonious development or preservation, healthy recreation, and the best adaptation of the individual to the general needs of social life; organizes international congresses and courses; awards research prize; mems: from 112 countries; Vice-Pres. (Europe) Prof. ROBERT DECKER; publ *FIEP Bulletin* (trilingual edition in English, French, and Spanish, 3 a year).

International Federation of Teachers of Modern Languages: POB 216, Belgrave 3160, Australia; tel. 6139-754-4714; fax 6139-416-9899; e-mail djc@netspace.net.au; internet www.fiplv.org; f. 1931; holds meetings on every aspect of foreign-language teaching; has consultative status with UNESCO; mems: 28 national and regional language asscns and ten international unilingual asscns (teachers of English, Esperanto, French, German, Hungarian, Portuguese, Russian, and Spanish); Sec.-Gen. EYNAR LEUPOLD; publ *FIPLV World News* (quarterly, in English, French, German and Spanish).

International Federation of University Women—IFUW: 8 rue de l'Ancien Port, 1201 Geneva, Switzerland; tel. (22) 7312380; fax (22) 7380440; e-mail ifuw@ifuw.org; internet www.ifuw.org; f. 1919 to promote understanding and friendship among university women of the world to encourage international co-operation; to further the development of education; to represent university women in international organizations; to encourage the full application of members' skills to the problems which arise at all levels of public life; Affiliates: 72 national asscns with over 180,000 mems; Pres. Prof. REIKO AOKI (Japan); publs *IFUW News* (6 a year), triennial report.

International Federation of Workers' Education Associations: c/o POB 8703, Youngstorget, 0028 Oslo 1, Norway; tel. 23-06-12-88; fax 23-06-12-70; e-mail jmehlum@online.no; internet www.ifwea.org; f. 1947 to promote co-operation between non-governmental bodies concerned with workers' education; organizes clearing-house services; promotes exchange of information; holds international seminars, conferences and summer schools; Pres. DAN GALLIN (Switzerland); Gen. Sec. ASLAK LEESLAND (Norway); publ. *Worker's Education* (quarterly).

International Institute for Adult Education Methods: POB 19395/6194, 5th Floor, Golfam St, 19156 Tehran, Iran; tel. (21) 2220313; f. 1968 by UNESCO and the Government of Iran, to collect, analyse and distribute information on activities concerning methods of literacy training and adult education; sponsors seminars; maintains documentation service and library on literacy and adult education; Dir Dr MOHAMMAD REZA HAMIDIZADE; publs *Selection of Adult Education Issues* (monthly), *Adult Education and Development* (quarterly), *New Library Holdings* (quarterly).

International Institute of Iberoamerican Literature (Instituto Internacional de Literatura Iberoamericana): 1312 CL, University of Pittsburgh, PA 15260, USA; tel. (412) 624-0829; e-mail iilit@apvtt-edn; f. 1938 to advance the study of Iberoamerican literature, and intensify cultural relations among the peoples of the Americas;; mems: scholars and artists in 37 countries;; publs *Revista IberoamericanaMemorias*.

International Institute of Philosophy—IIP (Institut international de philosophie): 8 rue Jean-Calvin, 75005 Paris, France; tel. 1-43-36-39-11; e-mail inst.intern.philo@wanadoo.fr; f. 1937 to clarify fundamental issues of contemporary philosophy and to promote mutual understanding among thinkers of different backgrounds and traditions; mems: 101 in 36 countries; Pres. A. FAGOT-LARGEAULT (Finland); Sec.-Gen. P. AUBENQUE (France); publs *Bibliography of Philosophy* (quarterly), *Proceedings* of annual meetings, *Chroniques, Philosophy and World Community* (series), *Philosophical Problems Today, Controverses philosophiques*.

International Reading Association: 800 Barksdale Rd, POB 8139, Newark, DE 19714-8139, USA; tel. (302) 731-1600; fax (302) 731-1057; internet www.reading.org; f. 1956 to improve the quality of reading instruction at all levels, to promote the habit of lifelong reading, and to develop every reader's proficiency; mems: 90,000 in 99 countries; Pres. JERRY L. JOHNS; publs *The Reading Teacher* (8 a year), *Journal of Adolescent and Adult Literacy* (8 a year), *Reading Research Quarterly, Lectura y Vida* (quarterly in Spanish), *Reading Today* (6 a year).

International Schools Association—ISA: 10333 Diego Drive South, Boca Raton, FL 33428, USA; tel. (561) 883-3854; fax (561) 483-2004; e-mail info@isaschools.org; internet www.intschools.org; f. 1951 to co-ordinate work in international schools and promote their development; supports the maintenance of high standards and equal opportunities in international schools; carries out curriculum research; convenes annual conferences on problems of curriculum and educational reform; organizes occasional teachers' training workshops and specialist seminars; mems: 85 schools throughout the world; Pres. M. M. MANZITTI; Exec. Dir BERT TIMMERMANS; publs *Education Bulletin* (2 a year), *ISA Magazine* (annually), *Conference Report* (annually), curriculum studies (occasional).

International Society for Business Education: POB 20457, Carson City, NV 89721, USA; tel. (775) 882-1445; fax (775) 882-1449; e-mail lkantin@prodigy.net; internet www.siec-isbe.org; f. 1901; encourages international exchange of information; organizes international courses and congresses on business education; mems: 2,200 national organizations and individuals in 23 countries; Pres. MICHAELA FEVERSTEIN (Germany); Gen. Sec. G. LEE KANTIN (USA); publ *International Review for Business Education.*

International Society for Education through Art—INSEA: c/o Peter Hermans, Citogroep, POB 1109, 6801 BC Arnhem, Netherlands; fax (26) 3521202; e-mail insea@citogroep.nl; internet insea .unb.ca; f. 1951 to unite art teachers throughout the world, to exchange information and to co-ordinate research into art education; organizes international congresses and exhibitions of children's art; Pres. DOUG BOUGHTON (USA); Sec. Gen. DEBORAH SMITH-SHANK; publ *INSEA News* (3 a year).

International Society for Music Education—ISME: POB 909, Nedlands, WA 6909, Australia; tel. (8) 9389-5862; fax (8) 9386-2658; e-mail isme@isme.org; internet www.isme.org; f. 1953 to organize international conferences, seminars and publications on matters pertaining to music education; acts as advisory body to UNESCO in matters of music education; mems: national committees and individuals in 60 countries; Pres.Elect GARY MCPHERSON (USA); Sec.-Gen. JUDY THÖNELL (Australia); publs *Music Education International,ISME Newsletter, International Journal of Music Education.*

International Society for the Study of Medieval Philosophy: Collège Mercier, place du Cardinal Mercier 14, 1348 Louvain-la-Neuve, Belgium; tel. (10) 47-48-07; fax (10) 47-82-85; e-mail siepm@ isp.vcp.ac.be; internet www.isp.ucl.ac.be/isp/siepm/siepm.html; f. 1958 to promote the study of medieval thought and the collaboration between individuals and institutions in this field; organizes international congresses; mems: 576; Pres. Prof. DAVID LUSCOMBE (UK); Sec. Prof. JACQUELINE HAMESSE (Belgium); publ *Bulletin de Philosophie Médiévale* (annually).

International Youth Library (Internationale Jugendbibliothek): Schloss Blutenburg, 81247 Munich, Germany; tel. (89) 8912110; fax (89) 8117553; e-mail bib@ijb.de; internet www.ijb.de; f. 1949, since 1953 an associated project of UNESCO; promotes the international exchange of children's literature; provides study opportunities for specialists in childrens' books; maintains a library of 510,000 volumes in about 130 languages; Dir Dr BARBARA SCHARIOTH; publs *The White Ravens, IJB Report,* catalogues.

League of European Research Libraries (Ligue des bibliothèques européennes de recherche—LIBER): c/o Secretariat, Susan Vejlsgaard, Det Kongelige Bibliotek, POB 2149, 1016 Copenhagen K, Denmark; tel. 33-93-62-22; fax 33-91-95-96; e-mail sv@kb.dk; internet www.kb.dk/liber; f. 1971 to encourage collaboration between the general research libraries of Europe, and national and university libraries in particular; gives assistance in finding practical ways of improving the quality of the services provided; mems: 310 libraries and individuals in 33 countries; Dir-Gen. ERLAND KOLDING NIELSEN; Sec. PETER K. FOX (UK); publ *LIBER Quarterly.*

Organization of Ibero-American States for Education, Science and Culture (Organización de Estados Iberoamericanos para la Educación, la Ciencia y la Cultura—OEI): Centro de Recursos Documentales e Informáticos, Calle Bravo Murillo 38, 28015 Madrid, Spain; tel. (91) 594-43-82; fax (91) 594-32-86; e-mail oeimad@oei.es; internet www.oei.es; f. 1949 (as the Ibero-American Bureau of Education); promotes peace and solidarity between member countries, through education, science, technology and culture; provides information, encourages exchanges and organizes training courses; the General Assembly (at ministerial level) meets every four years; mems: govts of 20 countries; Sec.-Gen. FRANCISCO JOSÉ PIÑÓN; publ *Revista Iberoamericana de Educación* (quarterly).

Organization of the Catholic Universities of Latin America (Organización de Universidades Católicas de América Latina—ODUCAL): c/o Dr J. A. Tobías, Universidad del Salvador, Viamonte 1856, CP 1056, Buenos Aires, Argentina; tel. (11) 4813-1408; fax (11) 4812-4625; e-mail udes-rect@salvador.edu.ar; f. 1953 to assist the social, economic and cultural development of Latin America through the promotion of Catholic higher education in the continent; mems: 43 Catholic universities in 15 Latin American countries; Pres. Dr JUAN ALEJANDRO TOBÍAS (Argentina); publs *Anuario, Sapientia, Universitas.*

Pan-African Association for Literacy and Adult Education: c/o ANAFA, BP 10358, Dakar, Senegal; tel. 825-48-50; fax 824-43-30; e-mail anafa@metissacana.sn; f. 2000 to succeed African Asscn for Literacy and Adult Education (f. 1984); Co-ordinator Dr LAMINE KANE.

Southeast Asian Ministers of Education Organization—SEAMEO: Darakarn Bldg, 920 Sukhumvit Rd, Bangkok 10110, Thailand; tel. (2) 391-0144; fax (2) 381-2587; e-mail secretariat@ seameo.org; internet www.seameo.org; f. 1965 to promote co-operation among the Southeast Asian nations through projects in education, science and culture; SEAMEO has 14 regional centres including: BIOTROP for tropical biology, in Bogor, Indonesia; INNOTECH for educational innovation and technology; an Open-Learning Centre in Indonesia; RECSAM for education in science and mathematics, in Penang, Malaysia; RELC for languages, in Singapore; RIHED for higher education development in Bangkok, Thailand; SEARCA for graduate study and research in agriculture, in Los Baños, Philippines; SPAFA for archaeology and fine arts in Bangkok, Thailand; TROPMED for tropical medicine and public health with regional centres in Indonesia, Malaysia, Philippines and Thailand and a central office in Bangkok; VOCTECH for vocational and technical education; and the SEAMO Training Centre in Ho Chi Minh City, Viet Nam; mems: Brunei, Cambodia, Indonesia, Laos, Malaysia, Philippines, Singapore, Thailand, Viet Nam; assoc. mems: Australia, Canada, France, Germany, Netherlands, New Zealand; Pres. Dr EDILBERTO DE JESUS (Philippines); Dir Dr ARIEF S. SADIMAN (Indonesia); publs *Annual Report, Journal of Southeast Asian Education, SEAMEO Horizon ,SEAMEO Forum.*

Union of Latin American Universities (Unión de Universidades de América Latina—UDUAL): Edificio UDUAL, Apdo postal 70-232, Ciudad Universitaria, Del. Coyoacán, 04510 México, DF, Mexico; tel. (55) 5622-0991; fax (55) 5616-1414; f. 1949 to organize the interchange of professors, students, research fellows and graduates and generally encourage good relations between the Latin American universities; arranges conferences; conducts statistical research; maintains centre for university documentation; mems: 165 universities; Pres. Dr SALOMÓN LERNER FEBRES (Peru); Sec.-Gen. Dr JUAN JOSÉ SÁNCHEZ SOSA (Mexico); publs *Universidades* (2 a year), *Gaceta UDUAL* (quarterly), *Censo* (every 2 years).

Universal Esperanto Association (Universala Esperanto-Asocio): Nieuwe Binnenweg 176, 3015 BJ Rotterdam, Netherlands; tel. (10) 4361044; fax (10) 4361751; e-mail uea@inter.nl.net; internet www.uea.org; f. 1908 to assist the spread of the international language, Esperanto, and to facilitate the practical use of the language; mems: 62 affiliated national asscns and 19,750 individuals in 120 countries; Pres. RENATO CORSETTI (Italy); Gen. Sec. IVO OSIBOV (Croatia); publs *Esperanto* (monthly), *Kontakto* (every 2 months), *Jarlibro* (yearbook), *Esperanto Documents.*

World Association for Educational Research—WAER (Association mondiale des sciences de l'éducation—AMSE): c/o Madame Denise Lauzon, Faculty of Education, Sherbrooke Univ., 2500 blvd de l'Université Sherbrooke, QC J1K 2R1, Canada; e-mail denise .lauzon@courrier.usherb.ca; f. 1953, present title adopted 1977; aims to encourage research in educational sciences by organizing congresses, issuing publications and supporting the exchange of information; mems: societies and individual members in 50 countries; Pres. Prof. Dr YVES LENOIR; Gen. Sec and Treas. CÉLINE GARANT.

World Education Fellowship: 54 Fox Lane, London N13 4AL, United Kingdom; f. 1921 to promote education for international understanding, and the exchange and practice of ideas, together with research into progressive educational theories and methods; mems: sections and groups in 20 countries; Pres. Prof. SHINJO OKUDA (Japan); Chair. CHRISTINE WYKES (UK); Gen. Sec. GUADALUPE G. DE TURNER; UK; publ *The New Era in Education* (3 a year).

World Union of Catholic Teachers (Union mondiale des enseignants catholiques—UMEC): Piazza San Calisto 16, 00120 Città del Vaticano; tel. (06) 69887286; f. 1951; encourages the grouping of Catholic teachers for the greater effectiveness of Catholic schools, distributes documentation on Catholic doctrine with regard to education, and facilitates personal contacts through congresses, and seminars, etc; nationally and internationally; mems: 32 organizations in 29 countries; Pres. ARNOLD BACKX (Netherlands); Sec.-Gen. MICHAEL EMM (UK); publ *Nouvelles de l'UMEC.*

World University Service—WUS: International Co-ordination Office, c/o WUSC, 1404 Scott St, Ottawa, ON K1Y 2N2, Canada; tel. (613) 798-7477; fax (613) 798-0990; internet www.wusc.ca; f. 1920; links students, faculty and administrators in post-secondary institutions concerned with economic and social development, and seeks to protect their academic freedom and autonomy; seeks to extend technical, personal and financial resources of post-secondary institutions to under-developed areas and communities; provides scholarships at university level for refugees, displaced people, and returnees, and supports informal education projects for women; governed by an assembly of national committees; Chair. LEONARD W. CONOLLY (Canada); publs *WUS News, WUS and Human Rights* (quarterly).

Environmental Conservation

BirdLife International: Wellbrook Ct, Girton Rd, Cambridge, CB3 0NA, United Kingdom; tel. (1223) 277318; fax (1223) 277200; e-mail birdlife@birdlife.org.uk; internet www.birdlife.net; f. 1922 as the International Council for Bird Preservation; a global partnership of organizations that determines status of bird species throughout the world and compiles data on all endangered species; identifies conservation problems and priorities; initiates and co-ordinates conservation projects and international conventions; mems: partners in 60 countries, representatives in 31 countries; Chair. GERARD A. BERTRAND; Dir Dr MICHAEL RANDS (UK); publs *Bird Red Data Book*, *World Birdwatch* (quarterly), *Bird Conservation Series*, study reports.

Friends of the Earth International: Prins Hendrikkade 48, POB 19199, 1000 GD Amsterdam, Netherlands; tel. (20) 6221369; fax (20) 6392181; e-mail foei@foei.org; internet www.foei.org; f. 1971 to promote the conservation, restoration and rational use of the environment and natural resources through public education and campaigning; mems: 68 national groups; Publs *Link* (quarterly), .

Greenpeace International: Keizersgracht 176, 1016 DW Amsterdam, Netherlands; tel. (20) 5236222; fax (20) 5236200; e-mail supporter.services@ams.greenpeace.org; internet www.greenpeace .org; f. 1971 to campaign for the protection of the environment; aims to bear witness to environmental destruction, and to demonstrate solutions for positive change; mems: offices in 41 countries; Chair. ANNE SUMMERS (Australia); Exec. Dir GERD LEIPOLD (Germany).

Independent World Commission on the Oceans—IWCO: c/o Palácio de Belém, 1300 Lisbon, Portugal; tel. (1) 3637141; fax (1) 3636603; e-mail secretariat@world-oceans.org; internet www .world-oceans.org; f. 1995 to study ways of protecting maritime resources and coastal areas; Chair. MÁRIO SOARES.

International Commission for the Protection of the Rhine: Postfach 200253 56002 Koblenz; Hohenzollernstrasse 18, 56068 Koblenz, Germany; tel. (261) 12495; fax (261) 36572; e-mail sekretariat@iksr.de; internet www.iksr.org; f. 1950; prepares and commissions research on the nature of the pollution of the Rhine; proposes protection, ecological rehabilitation and flood prevention measures; mems: 23 delegates from France, Germany, Luxembourg, Netherlands, Switzerland and the EU; Pres. Prof. M. KRAFFT; Sec. J. H. OTERDOOM; Publ. *Annual Report*.

International Council on Mining and Metals—ICMM: 19 Stratford Place, London W1C 1BQ, United Kingdom; tel. (20) 7290-4920; e-mail info@icmm.com; internet www.icme.com/icme; f. 1991 (as the International Council on Metals and the Environment, present name adopted 2002) by metal-producing and mining companies to promote responsible environmental practices and policies in the mining, use, recycling and disposal of metals; mems: companies from six continents; Chair. Sir ROBERT WILSON (UK); Dep. Sec.-Gen. ANITA ROPER (Canada); publ. *ICME Newsletter* (quarterly).

South Pacific Regional Environment Programme—SPREP: POB 240, Apia, Samoa; tel. 21929; fax 20231; e-mail sprep@sprep .org.ws; internet www.sprep.org.ws; f. 1978 by the South Pacific Commission (where it was based), the South Pacific (now Pacific Islands) Forum, ESCAP and UNEP; formally established as an independent institution in June 1993 when members signed the *Agreement Establishing SPREP*; aims to promote regional co-operation in environmental matters, to assist members to protect and improve their shared environment, and to help members work towards sustainable development; mems: 22 Pacific islands, Australia, France, New Zealand, USA; Dir ASTERIO TAKESY (Federated States of Micronesia); publs *SPREP Newsletter* (quarterly), *CASO-Link* (quarterly), *La lettre de l'environnement* (quarterly), *South Pacific Sea Level and Climate Change Newsletter* (quarterly).

Wetlands International Africa, Europe, Middle East—AEME: POB 471, 6700 AL Wageningen, Netherlands; tel. (317) 478854; fax (317) 478850; e-mail post@wetlands.agro.nl; internet www.wetlands .org; f. 1995 by merger of several regional wetlands organizations; aims to sustain and restore wetlands, their resources and biodiversity through research, information exchange and conservation activities; promotes implementation of the 1971 Ramsar Convention on Wetlands; Chair. STEW MORRISON; CEO SIMON NASH; publs *Wetlands* (2 a year), other studies, technical publications, manuals, proceedings of meetings.

World Conservation Union—IUCN: 28 rue Mauverney, 1196 Gland, Switzerland; tel. (22) 9990000; fax (22) 9990002; e-mail mail@hq.iucn.org; internet www.iucn.org; f. 1948, as the International Union for Conservation of Nature and Natural Resources; supports partnerships and practical field activities to promote the conservation of natural resources, to secure the conservation of nature, and especially of biological diversity, as an essential foundation for the future; to ensure wise use of the earth's natural resources in an equitable and sustainable way; and to guide the development of human communities towards ways of life in enduring harmony with other components of the biosphere, developing programmes to protect and sustain the most important and threatened species and eco-systems and assisting governments to devise and carry out national conservation strategies; maintains a conservation library and documentation centre and units for monitoring traffic in wildlife; mems: government agencies in 98 countries and national and

international non-governmental organizations in 128 countries; 37 non-voting affiliate mems; Pres. YOLANDA KAKABADSE NAVARRO (Ecuador); Dir-Gen. ACHIM STEINER; publs *World Conservation Strategy*, *Caring for the Earth*, *Red List of Threatened Plants*, *Red List of Threatened Species*, *United Nations List of National Parks and Protected Areas*, *World Conservation* (quarterly) *IUCN Today*.

World Society for the Protection of Animals—WSPA: 89 Albert Embankment, London, SE1 7TP, United Kingdom; tel. (20) 7587-5000; fax (20) 7793-0208; e-mail wspa@wspa.org.uk; internet www .wspa.org.uk; f. 1981, incorporating the World Federation for the Protection of Animals (f. 1950) and the International Society for the Protection of Animals (f. 1959); promotes animal welfare and conservation by humane education, practical field projects, international lobbying and legislative work; Mems: more than 400 member societies in more than 100 countries; Chair. PETER DAVIES; Chief Exec. ANDREW DICKSON.

World Wide Fund for Nature—WWF: ave de Mont-Blanc, 1196 Gland, Switzerland; tel. (22) 3649111; fax (22) 3643239; e-mail kevans@wwfnet.org; internet www.panda.org; f. 1961 (as World Wildlife Fund); aims to stop the degradation of the natural environment, conserve bio-diversity, ensure the sustainable use of renewable resources, promote the reduction of pollution and wasteful consumption; mems: 27 national organizations, five associates, c. 5m. individual mems world-wide; Pres. Chief EMEKA ANYAOKU (Nigeria); Dir-Gen. Dr CLAUDE MARTIN.

Government and Politics

African Association for Public Administration and Management—AAPAM: POB 48677, Nairobi, Kenya; tel. (20) 52-19-44; fax (20) 52-18-45; e-mail aapam@africaonline.co.ke; f. 1971 to provide senior officials with a forum for the exchange of ideas and experience, to promote the study of professional techniques and to encourage research into African administrative problems; mems: 500 individual, 50 corporate; Pres. Dr JONATHAN CHILESHE (Zambia); Sec.-Gen. HUDSON MOSES BIGOGO (Kenya); publs *Newsletter* (quarterly), *Annual Seminar Report*, *African Journal of Public Administration and Management*, studies.

Afro-Asian Peoples' Solidarity Organization—AAPSO: 89 Abdel Aziz Al-Saoud St, POB 11559-61 Manial El-Roda, Cairo, Egypt; tel. (2) 3636081; fax (2) 3637361; e-mail aapso@idsc.gov.eg; f. 1958; acts among and for the peoples of Africa and Asia in their struggle for genuine independence, sovereignty, socio-economic development, peace and disarmament; mems: national committees and affiliated organizations in 66 countries and territories, assoc. mems in 15 European countries; Pres. Dr MOURAD GHALEB; Sec.-Gen. NOURI ABDUL RAZZAK HUSSEIN (Iraq); publs *Solidarity Bulletin* (monthly), *Development and Socio-Economic Progress* (quarterly), *Human Rights Newsletter* (6 a year).

Agency for the Prohibition of Nuclear Weapons in Latin America and the Caribbean (Organismo para la Proscripción de las Armas Nucleares en la América Latina y el Caribe—OPANAL): Schiller 326, 5°, Col Chapultepec Morales, 11570, México, DF, Mexico; tel. (55) 5255-2914; fax (55) 5255-3748; internet www .opanal.org; f. 1969 to ensure compliance with the Treaty for the Prohibition of Nuclear Weapons in Latin America (Treaty of Tlatelolco), 1967 to ensure the absence of all nuclear weapons in the application zone of the Treaty; to contribute to the movement against proliferation of nuclear weapons; to promote general and complete disarmament; to prohibit all testing, use, manufacture, acquisition, storage, installation and any form of possession, by any means, of nuclear weapons; the organs of the Agency comprise the General Conference, meeting every two years, the Council, meeting every two months, and the secretariat; a General Conference is held every two years; mems: 33 states that have fully ratified the Treaty; the Treaty has two additional Protocols: the first signed and ratified by France, the Netherlands, the United Kingdom and the USA, the second signed and ratified by China, the USA, France, the United Kingdom and Russia; Sec.-Gen. EDMUNDO VARGAS CARREÑO (Chile).

Alliance of Small Island States—AOSIS: c/o 800 Second Ave, Suite 400D New York, NY 10017, USA; tel. (212) 599-6196; fax (212) 599-0797; e-mail samoa@un.int; internet www.sidsne.org/aosis; f. 1990 as an *ad hoc* intergovernmental grouping to focus on the special problems of small islands and low-lying coastal developing states; mems: 43 island nations; Chair. TUILOMA NERONI SLADE (Samoa); publ. *Small Islands, Big Issues*.

ANZUS: c/o Dept of Foreign Affairs and Trade, Locked Bag 40, Queen Victoria Terrace, Canberra, ACT 2600, Australia; tel. (2) 6261-9111; fax (2) 6273-3577; internet www.dfat.gov.au; the ANZUS Security Treaty was signed in 1951 by Australia, New Zealand and the USA, and ratified in 1952 to co-ordinate partners' efforts for collective defence for the preservation of peace and security in the Pacific area, through the exchange of technical information and strategic intelligence, and a programme of exercises, exchanges and visits. In 1984 New Zealand refused to allow visits by US naval vessels that were either nuclear-propelled or potentially nuclear-armed, and this led to the cancellation of joint ANZUS military exercises: in 1986 the USA formally announced the suspension of its security commitment to New Zealand under ANZUS. Instead of the annual ANZUS Council meetings, bilateral talks were subsequently held every year between Australia and the USA. ANZUS continued to govern security relations between Australia and the USA, and between Australia and New Zealand; security relations between New Zealand and the USA were the only aspect of the treaty to be suspended. Senior-level contacts between New Zealand and the USA resumed in 1994. The Australian Govt invoked the Anzus Security Treaty for the first time following the international terrorist attacks against targets in the USA that were perpetrated in September 2001.

Association of Secretaries General of Parliaments: c/o Committee Office, House of Commons, London, SW1, United Kingdom; tel. (20) 7219-3754; e-mail phillipsris@parliament.uk; internet www.ipu.org/english/asgp.htm; f. 1938; studies the law, practice and working methods of different Parliaments; proposes measures for improving those methods and for securing co-operation between the services of different Parliaments; operates as a consultative body to the Inter-Parliamentary Union, and assists the Union on subjects within the scope of the Association; mems: c. 200 representing 145 countries; five assoc. institutions; Pres. (vacant); Jt Secs FRANK BOULIN (France), ROGER PHILLIPS (UK); publ. *Constitutional and Parliamentary Information* (2 a year).

Atlantic Treaty Association: 10 rue Crevaux, 75116 Paris, France; tel. 1-45-53-28-80; fax 1-47-55-49-63; e-mail ata sg@noos.fr; internet www.atasec.org; f. 1954 to inform public opinion on the North Atlantic Alliance and to promote the solidarity of the peoples of the North Atlantic; holds annual assemblies, seminars, study conferences for teachers and young politicians; mems: national asscns in the 19 member countries of NATO; 19 assoc. mems from central and eastern Europe, two observer mems; Chair. ALAN LEE WILLIAMS (UK); Sec.-Gen. ANTÓNIO BORGES DE CARVALHO (Portugal).

Baltic Council: f. 1993 by the Baltic Assembly, comprising 60 parliamentarians from Estonia, Latvia and Lithuania; the Council of Ministers of the three Baltic countries co-ordinates policy in the areas of foreign policy, justice, the environment, education and science.

Celtic League: 11 Cleiy Rhennee, Kirk Michael, Isle of Man, IM6 1HT, United Kingdom; tel. (1624) 877918; e-mail b.moffatt@advsys.co.im; internet www.manxman.co.im/cleague; f. 1961 to foster co-operation between the six Celtic nations (Ireland, Scotland, Man, Wales, Cornwall and Brittany), especially those actively working for political autonomy by non-violent means; campaigns politically on issues affecting the Celtic countries; monitors military activity in the Celtic countries; co-operates with national cultural organizations to promote the languages and culture of the Celts; mems: approx. 1,400 individuals in the Celtic communities and elsewhere; Chair. CATHAL Ó LUAIN; Gen. Sec. BERNARD MOFFAT; publ. *Carn* (quarterly).

Central European Initiative (CEI): CEI Executive Secretariat, Via Genova 9, 34121 Trieste, Italy; tel. (040) 7786777; fax (040) 360640; e-mail cei-es@cei-es.org; internet www.ceinet.org; f. 1989 as 'Quadrilateral' co-operation between Austria, Italy, Hungary and Yugoslavia, became 'Pentagonal' in 1990 with the admission of Czechoslovakia, and 'Hexagonal' with the admission of Poland in 1991, present name adopted in 1992, when Bosnia and Herzegovina, Croatia and Slovenia were admitted; the Czech Republic and Slovakia became separate mems in January 1993, and Macedonia also joined in that year; Albania, Belarus, Bulgaria, Romania and Ukraine joined the CEI in 1995 and Moldova in 1996; Serbia and Montenegro (then the Federal Republic of Yugoslavia) was admitted in 2000; aims to encourage regional and bilateral political and economic co-operation, working within the OSCE; Dir-Gen. Dr HARALD KREID.

Christian Democrat and Peoples' Parties International: 67 rue d'Arlon, 1040 Brussels, Belgium; tel. (2) 285–41–60; fax (2) 285-41-66; e-mail idc@idc-cdi.org; internet www.idc-cdi.org; f. 1961 to serve as a platform for the co-operation of political parties of Christian Social inspiration; mems: parties in 64 countries (of which 47 in Europe); Pres. JOSÉ MARÍA AZNAR (Spain); Exec. Sec. ANTONIO LÓPEZ ISTURIZ; publ *DC-Info* (quarterly), *Human Rights* (5 a year), *Documents* (quarterly).

Comunidade dos Países de Língua Portuguesa—CPLP (Community of Portuguese-Speaking Countries): rua S. Caetano 32, 1200-829 Lisbon, Portugal; tel. (1) 392-8560; fax (1) 392-8588; e-mail comunicacao@cplp.org; internet www.cplp.org; f. 1996; aims to produce close political, economic, diplomatic and cultural links between Portuguese-speaking countries and to strengthen the influence of the Lusophone commonwealth within the international community; mems: Angola, Brazil, Cape Verde, Guinea-Bissau, Mozambique, Portugal, São Tomé e Príncipe; Timor-Leste has observer status; Exec. Sec. Dr JOÃO AUGUSTO DE MÉDICIS.

Eastern Regional Organization for Public Administration—EROPA: One Burgundy Plaza, Suite 12M, 307 Katipunan Ave, Loyola Heights, Quezon City 1105, Metro Manila, Philippines; tel. (2) 433-8175; fax (2) 434-9223; e-mail eropa@eropa.org.ph; internet www.eropa.org.ph; f. 1960 to promote regional co-operation in improving knowledge, systems and practices of governmental administration, to help accelerate economic and social development; organizes regional conferences, seminars, special studies, surveys and training programmes. There are three regional centres: Training Centre (New Delhi), Local Government Centre (Tokyo), Development Management Centre (Seoul); mems: 12 countries, 111 organizations/groups, 483 individuals; Chair. KARINA C. DAVID; Sec.-Gen. PATRICIA A. STO TOMAS (Philippines); publs *EROPA Bulletin* (quarterly), *Asian Review of Public Administration* (2 a year).

European Movement: 25 Square de Meeus, 1000 Brussels, Belgium; tel. (2) 508-30-88; fax (2) 508-30-89; e-mail secretariat@europeanmovement.org; internet www.europeanmovement.org; f. 1947 by a liaison committee of representatives from European organizations, to study the political, economic and technical problems of a European Union and suggest how they could be solved and to inform and lead public opinion in the promotion of integration; Conferences have led to the creation of the Council of Europe, College of Europe, etc; mems: national councils and committees in 39 European countries, and several international social and economic organizations; Pres. JOSÉ MARIA GIL-ROBLES (Spain); Sec.-Gen. HENRIK H. KRÖNER.

European Union of Women—EUW: 2 Pittakou St, 105 58 Athens, Greece; tel. (1) 3314847; fax (1454) 3314817; e-mail fpetralia@parliament.gr; f. 1955 to increase the influence of women in the political and civic life of their country and of Europe; mems: national organizations in 21 countries; Chair. FANNY PALLI PETRALIA; Sec.-Gen. VASSO KOLLIA.

La Francophonie: 28 rue de Bourgogne, 75007 Paris, France; tel. 1-44-11-12-50; fax 1-44-11-12-76; e-mail oif@francophonie.org; internet www.francophonie.org; political grouping of French-speaking countries; conference of heads of state convened every two years to promote co-operation throughout the French-speaking world (2002: Beirut, Lebanon); mems: govts of 51 countries; Sec.-Gen. BOUTROS BOUTROS-GHALI (Egypt).

Gulf of Guinea Commission (Commission du Golfe de Guinée—CGG): f. 2001 to promote co-operation among mem; countries and the peaceful and sustainable development of natural resources in the sub-region; mems: Angola, Cameroon, the Repub. of the Congo, Equatorial Guinea, Gabon, Nigeria, Sao Tomé and Príncipe.

Hansard Society: 9 Kingsway, London, WC2B 6FX, United Kingdom; tel. (20) 7955-7459; fax (20) 7955-7492; e-mail hansard@hansard.lse.ac.uk; internet www.hansardsociety.org.uk; f. 1944 as Hansard Society for Parliamentary Government; aims to promote political education and research and the informed discussion of all aspects of modern parliamentary government; Dir CLARE ETTINGHAUSEN; publ. *Parliamentary Affairs* (quarterly).

International Alliance of Women: c/o Lenaustr. 5/2/12, 4053 Haid bei Ansfelden, Austria; tel. (7229) 876-34; e-mail mab@liwest.at; internet www.womenalliance.com; f. 1904 to obtain equality for women in all fields and to encourage women to assume decision-making responsibilities at all levels of society; lobbies at international organizations; mems: 78 national affiliates in 67 countries; Pres. PATRICIA GILES; publ. *International Women's News* (3 a year).

International Association for Community Development—IACD: 179 rue du Débarcadère, 6001 Marcinelle, Belgium; tel. (71) 44-72-78; fax (71) 47-11-04; internet www.iacdglobal.org; organizes annual international colloquium for community-based organizations; Sec.-Gen. PIERRE ROZEN; publ. *IACD Newsletter* (2 a year).

International Commission for the History of Representative and Parliamentary Institutions—CHRPI: c/o Dr David Dean, Dept of History, Carleton Univ., 400 Peterson Hall, 1125 Colonel By Drive, Ottawa, ON KIS 511, Canada; tel. (613) 520-2828; fax (613) 520-2819; internet www.univie.ac.at/ichrpi; f. 1936; promotes research into the origin and development of representative and parliamentary institutions worldwide; encourages wide and comparative study of such institutions, both current and historical; facilitates the exchange of information; mems: 300 individuals in 31 countries; Pres. WILHELM BRAUNEDER (Austria); Sec.-Gen. Dr DAVID DEAN (Canada); publs *Parliaments, Estates and Representation* (annually), studies.

International Democrat Union: c/o Queen Anne's Gate, London, SW1H 9AA, United Kingdom; tel. (20) 7222-0847; fax (20) 7222-5999; e-mail rnormington@idu.org; internet www.idu.org; f. 1983 as a group of centre and centre-right political parties; facilitates the exchange of information and views; promotes networking; organizes campaigning seminars for politicians and party workers; holds Party

Leaders' meetings every three or four years, also executive meetings and a Young Leaders' Forum; mems: political parties in 41 countries, 46 assoc. mems in regions; Exec. Sec. RICHARD NORMINGTON.

International Federation of Resistance Movements—FIR: c/o R. Maria, 5 rue Rollin, 75005 Paris, France; tel. 1-43-26-84-29; f. 1951; supports the medical and social welfare of former victims of fascism; works for peace, disarmament and human rights, and against fascism and neo-fascism; mems: 82 national organizations in 29 countries; Pres. ALIX LHOTE (France); Sec.-Gen. OSKAR WIES-FLECKER (Austria); publs *Feuille d'information* (in French and German), *Cahier d'informations médicales, sociales et juridiques* (in French and German).

International Institute for Peace: Möllwaldplatz 5, 1040 Vienna, Austria; tel. (1) 504-43-76; fax (1) 505-32-36; e-mail iip@aon.at; internet www.iip.at; f. 1957; non-governmental organization with consultative status at ECOSOC and UNESCO; studies conflict prevention; new structures in international law; security issues in Europe and world-wide; mems: individuals and corporate bodies invited by the executive board; Pres. ERWIN LANC (Austria); Dir PETER STANIA (Russia); publs *Peace and Security* (quarterly, in English), occasional papers (2 or 3 a year, in English and German).

International Institute for Strategic Studies—IISS: Arundel House, 13–15 Arundel St, London, WC2R 3DX, United Kingdom; tel. (20) 7379-7676; fax (20) 7836-3108; e-mail iiss@iiss.org; internet www.iiss.org; f. 1958; concerned with the study of the role of force in international relations, including problems of international strategy, the ethnic, political and social sources of conflict, disarmament and arms control, peace-keeping and intervention, defence economics, etc. independent of any government; mems: c. 3,000; Dir Dr JOHN M. W. CHIPMAN; publs *Survival* (quarterly), *The Military Balance* (annually), *Strategic Survey* (annually), *Adelphi Papers* (10 a year), *Strategic Comments* (10 a year).

International Lesbian and Gay Association—ILGA: 81 rue Marché-au-charbon, 1000 Brussels 1, Belgium; tel. and fax (2) 502-24-71; e-mail ilga@ilga.org; internet www.ilga.org; f. 1978; works to abolish legal, social and economic discrimination against homosexual and bisexual women and men, and transexuals, throughout the world; co-ordinates political action at an international level; co-operates with other supportive movements; 2001 world conference: Oakland, CA, USA; mems: 350 national and regional asscns in 80 countries; Secs-Gen. PHUMI MTETWA; publs *ILGA Bulletin* (quarterly), *GBLT Human Rights Annual Report*.

International Peace Bureau (IPB): 41 rue de Zürich, 1201 Geneva, Switzerland; tel. (22) 7316429; fax (22) 7389419; e-mail mailbox@ipb.org; internet www.ipb.org; f. 1892; promotes international co-operation for general and complete disarmament and the non-violent solution of international conflicts; co-ordinates and represents peace movements at the UN; conducts projects on the abolition of nuclear weapons and the role of non-governmental organizations in conflict prevention and resolution; mems: 220 peace organizations in 53 countries; Pres. CORA WEISS; Sec.-Gen. COLIN ARCHER; publs *IPB News* (quarterly), *IPB Geneva News*.

International Political Science Association—IPSA (Association Internationale de Science Politique—AISP): c/o Concordia Univ., 331 ave Docteur Penfield, Montréal, QC H3G 1C5, Canada; tel. (514) 848-8717; e-mail ipsa@alcor.concordia.ca; internet www.ipsa.ca; f. 1949; aims to promote the development of political science; mems: 41 national asscns, 100 institutions, 1,350 individual mems; Pres. DALCHOONG KIM (Republic of Korea); Sec.-Gen. GUY LACHAPELLE (Canada); publs *Participation* (3 a year), *International Political Science Abstracts* (6 a year), *International Political Science Review* (quarterly).

International Union of Local Authorities—IULA: POB 90646, 2509 LP, The Hague, Netherlands; tel. (70) 3066066; fax (70) 3500496; e-mail iula@iula.org; internet www.iula.org; f. 1913 to promote local government, improve local administration and encourage popular participation in public affairs; activities include organization of a biennial international congress; operation of specific 'task forces' (Association Capacity-Building, Women in Local Government, Information Technology); development of intermunicipal relations to provide a link between local authorities of countries; maintenance of a permanent office for the collection and distribution of information on municipal affairs; mems: in over 110 countries, seven regional sections; Pres. ALAN LLOYD; Sec.-Gen. JEREMY SMITH; publs various, on a range of local government issues.

International Union of Young Christian Democrats—IUYCD: 16 rue de la Victoire, 1060 Brussels, Belgium; tel. (2) 537-77-51; fax (2) 534-50-28; f. 1962; mems: national organizations in 59 countries and territories; Sec.-Gen. MARCOS VILLASMIL (Venezuela); publs *IUYCD Newsletter* (fortnightly), *Debate* (quarterly).

Jewish Agency for Israel—JAFI: POB 92, 48 King George St, Jerusalem, Israel; tel. (2) 6202297; fax (2) 6202412; e-mail elibir@jazo.org.il; internet www.jafi.org.il; f. 1929; reconstituted 1971 as an instrument through which world Jewry can work to develop a national home; constituents are: World Zionist Organization, United Israel Appeal, Inc. (USA), and Keren Hayesod; Chair. Exec. SALLAI MERIDOR; Chair. Bd. ALEX GRASS; Dir-Gen. Maj.-Gen. (retd) GIORA ROMM.

Latin American Parliament (Parlamento Latinoamericano): Avda Auro Soares de Moura Andrade 564, São Paulo, Brazil; tel. (11) 3824-6325; fax (11) 3824-0621; internet www.parlatino.org.br; f. 1965; permanent democratic institution, representative of all existing political trends within the national legislative bodies of Latin America; aims to promote the movement towards economic, political and cultural integration of the Latin American republics, and to uphold human rights, peace and security; Sec.-Gen. RAFAEL CORREA FLORES; publs *Acuerdos*, *Resoluciones de las Asambleas Ordinarias* (annually), *Parlamento Latinoamericano–Actividades de los Órganos*, *Revista Patria Grande* (annually), statements and agreements.

Liberal International: 1 Whitehall Place, London, SW1A 2HD, United Kingdom; tel. (20) 7839-5905; fax (20) 7925-2685; e-mail all@liberal-international.org; internet www.liberal-international.org; f. 1947; world union of 83 liberal parties in 58 countries; co-ordinates foreign policy work of member parties, and promotes freedom, tolerance, democracy, international understanding, protection of human rights and market-based economics; has consultative status at ECOSOC of United Nations and the Council of Europe; Pres. ANNEMIE NEYTS-UYTTEBROECK; Sec.-Gen. FREDERICA SABBATI; publ. *London Aerogramme* (quarterly).

Nato Parliamentary Assembly: 3 place du Petit Sablon, 1000 Brussels, Belgium; tel. (2) 513-28-65; fax (2) 514-18-47; e-mail secretariat@naa.be; internet www.nato-pa.int; f. 1955 as the NATO Parliamentarians' Conference; name changed 1966 to North Atlantic Assembly; renamed as above 1999; the inter-parliamentary assembly of the North Atlantic Alliance; holds two plenary sessions a year and meetings of committees (Political, Defence and Security, Economics and Security, Civil Dimension of Security, Science and Technology), where parliamentarians from North America, western Europe and eastern Europe (associate delegates) examine the problems confronting the Alliance and European security issues in general; Pres. DOUGLAS BEREUTER (USA); Sec.-Gen. SIMON LUNN (United Kingdom).

Non-aligned Movement—NAM: c/o Permanent Representative of South Africa to the UN, 333 East 38th St, 9th Floor, New York, NY 10016, USA (no permanent secretariat); tel. (212) 213-5583; fax (212) 692-2498; e-mail soafun@worldnet.att.net; internet www.nam.gov.za; f. 1961 by a meeting of 25 Heads of State, with the aim of linking countries that had refused to adhere to the main East-West military and political blocs; co-ordination bureau established in 1973; works for the establishment of a new international economic order, and especially for better terms for countries producing raw materials; maintains special funds for agricultural development, improvement of food production and the financing of buffer stocks; South Commission promotes co-operation between developing countries; seeks changes in the United Nations to give developing countries greater decision-making power; holds summit conference every three years; 13th conference (2003): Kuala Lumpur, Malaysia; mems: 113 countries.

Open Door International (for the Economic Emancipation of the Woman Worker): 16 rue Américaine, 1060 Brussels, Belgium; tel. (2) 537-67-61; f. 1929 to obtain equal rights and opportunities for women in the whole field of work; mems: in 10 countries; Hon. Sec. ADÈLE HAUWEL (Belgium).

Organization for the Prohibition of Chemical Weapons (OPCW): Johan de Wittlaan 32, 2517JR The Hague, Netherlands; tel. (70) 4163300; fax (70) 3063535; e-mail inquiries@opcw.org; internet www.opcw.org; f. 1997 to oversee implementation of the Chemical Weapons Convention, which aims to ban the development, production, stockpiling and use of chemical weapons; the Convention was negotiated under the auspices of the UN Conference on Disarmament and entered into force in April 1997, at which time the OPCW was inaugurated; governed by an Executive Council, comprising representatives of 41 States Parties, elected on a regional basis; undertakes mandatory inspections of member states party to the Convention (151 at March 2003); provisional 2003 budget: €68.6m; Dir-Gen. ROGELIO PFIRTER.

Organization of Solidarity of the Peoples of Africa, Asia and Latin America—OSPAAAL (Organización de Solidaridad de los Pueblos de Africa, Asia y América Latina): Apdo 4224, Calle C No 670 esq. 29, Vedado, Havana 10400, Cuba; tel. (7) 830-5136; fax (7) 833-3985; e-mail ospaal1966@enet.cu; internet www.tricontinental.cubaweb.cu; f. 1966 at the first Conference of Solidarity of the Peoples of Africa, Asia and Latin America, to unite, co-ordinate and encourage national liberation movements in the three continents, to oppose foreign intervention in the affairs of sovereign states, colonial and neo-colonial practices, and to fight against racialism and all forms of racial discrimination; favours the establishment of a new international economic order; mems: 56 organizations in 46 countries; Sec.-Gen. Juan Carretero Ibañez; publ. *Tricontinental* (quarterly).

Organization of the Cooperatives of America (Organización de las Cooperativas de América—OCA): Apdo Aéreo 241263, Carrera 11, No. 86-32 Of. 101, Santafé de Bogotá, DC, Colombia; tel. (1) 610-3296; fax (1) 610-1912; f. 1963 for improving socio-economic, cultural and moral conditions through the use of the co-operative system; works in every country of the continent; regional offices sponsor plans of activities based on the most pressing needs and special conditions of individual countries; mems: organizations in 23 countries and territories; Pres. Dr Armando Tovar Parada; Exec. Sec. Dr Carlos Julio Pineda; publs *OCA News* (monthly), *América Cooperativa* (3 a year).

Parliamentary Association for Euro-Arab Co-operation—PAEAC: 10 ave de la Renaiisance, 1040 Brussels, Belgium; tel. (2) 231-13-00; fax (2) 231-06-46; e-mail paeac@medea.be; internet www.medea.be; f. 1974 as an asscn of 650 parliamentarians of all parties from the national parliaments of the Council of Europe countries and from the European Parliament, to promote friendship and co-operation between Europe and the Arab world; Executive Committee holds annual joint meetings with Arab Inter-Parliamentary Union; represented in Council of Europe, Western European Union and European Parliament; works for the progress of the Euro-Arab Dialogue and a settlement in the Middle East that takes into account the national rights of the Palestinian people; Jt Chair. Michael Lanigan (Ireland), Roy Perry (UK); Sec.-Gen. Pol Marck (Belgium); publs *Information Bulletin* (quarterly), *Euro-Arab and Mediterranean Political Fact Sheets* (2 a year), conference notes.

Party of European Socialists (PES): 60 rue Wiertz, 1047 Brussels, Belgium; tel. (2) 284-29-76; fax (2) 230-17-66; e-mail pes@pes.org; internet www.pes.org; f. 1992 to replace the Confederation of the Socialist Parties of the EC (f. 1974); affiliated to Socialist International; mems: 20 member parties, 15 associate parties and 6 observer parties; Chair. Robin Cook (UK); Sec.-Gen. Antony Beumer; publs various, including statutes, manifestos and Congress documents.

Rio Group: f. 1987 at a meeting in Acapulco, Mexico, of eight Latin American government leaders, who agreed to establish a 'permanent mechanism for joint political action'; additional countries subsequently joined the Group (see below); holds annual summit meetings at presidential level. At the ninth presidential summit (Quito, Ecuador, September 1995) a 'Declaration of Quito' was adopted, which set out joint political objectives, including the strengthening of democracy; combating corruption, drugs-production and -trafficking and 'money laundering'; and the creation of a Latin American and Caribbean free trade area by 2005 (supporting the efforts of the various regional groupings). Opposes US legislation (the 'Helms-Burton' Act), which provides for sanctions against foreign companies that trade with Cuba; also concerned with promoting sustainable development in the region, the elimination of poverty, and economic and financial stability. The Rio Group holds annual ministerial conferences with the European Union (11th meeting held in Greece in March 2003; third summit of heads of state and govt scheduled to be held in Mexico in 2004; mems: Argentina, Bolivia, Brazil, Chile, Colombia, Costa Rica, Dominican Republic, Ecuador, El Salvador, Guatemala, Guyana, Honduras, Mexico, Nicaragua, Panama, Paraguay, Peru, Uruguay, Venezuela.

Shanghai Co-operation Organization—SCO: f. 2001, replacing the Shanghai Five (f. 1996 to address border disputes); comprises People's Republic of China, Kazakhstan, Kyrgyzstan, Russia, Tajikistan and Uzbekistan; aims to achieve security through mutual co-operation: promotes economic co-operation and measures to eliminate terrorism and drugs-trafficking; agreement on combating terrorism signed June 2001; an SCO anti-terrorism centre was to be established in Bishkek, Kyrgyzstan; holds annual summit meeting (2002: St Petersburg, Russia).

Socialist International: Maritime House, Clapham, London, SW4 0JW, United Kingdom; tel. (20) 7627-4449; fax (20) 7720-4448; e-mail secretariat@socialistinternational.org; internet www.socialistinternational.org; f. 1864; re-established in 1951; the world's oldest and largest asscn of political parties, grouping democratic socialist, labour and social democratic parties from every continent; provides a forum for political action, policy discussion and the exchange of ideas; works with many international organizations and trades unions (particularly members of ICFTU; holds Congress every three years. The Council meets twice a year, and regular conferences and meetings of party leaders are also held; committees and councils on a variety of subjects and in different regions meet frequently; mems: 89 full member, 25 consultative and 15 observer parties in 110 countries; There are three fraternal organizations and nine associated organizations, including: the Party of European Socialists (PES), the Group of the PES at the European Parliament

and the International Federation of the Socialist and Democratic Press; Pres. Antonio Guterres (Portugal); Gen. Sec. Luis Ayala (Chile); publ. *Socialist Affairs* (quarterly).

International Falcon Movement—Socialist Educational International: 3 rue Quinaux, 1030 Brussels, Belgium; tel. (2) 215-79-27; fax (2) 245-00-83; e-mail contact@ifm.sei.org; internet www.ifm.sei.org; f. 1924 to help children and adolescents develop international understanding and a sense of social responsibility and to prepare them for democratic life; co-operates with several institutions concerned with children, youth and education; mems: about 1m., 62 co-operating organizations in all countries; Pres. Östen Löugren (Sweden); Sec.-Gen. Uwe Ostendorff (Germany); publs *IFM-SEI Bulletin* (quarterly), *IFM-SEI World News*, *EFN Newsletter* (6 a year), *Asian Regional Bulletin*, *Latin American Regional Bulletin*.

International Union of Socialist Youth—IUSY: Amtshausgasse 4, 1050 Vienna, Austria; tel. (1) 523-12-67; fax (1) 523-12-679; e-mail iusy@iusy.org; internet www.iusy.org; f. 1907 as Socialist Youth International (present name adopted 1946), to educate young people in the principles of free and democratic socialism and further the co-operation of democratic socialist youth organizations; conducts international meetings, symposia, etc; mems: 134 youth and student organizations in 100 countries; Pres. Alvaro Elizalde Soto; Gen. Sec. Enzo Amendola (Italy); publs *IUSY Newsletter*, *FWG News*, *IUSY—You see us in Action*.

Socialist International Women: Maritime House, Old Town, Clapham, London, SW4 0JW, United Kingdom; tel. (20) 7627-4449; fax (20) 7720-4448; e-mail socintwomen@gn.apc.org; internet socintwomen.org; f. 1907 to promote the understanding among women of the aims of democratic socialism to facilitate the exchange of experience and views; to promote programmes opposing discrimination in society; and to work for human rights in general and for development and peace; mems: 131 organizations; Pres. Dolors Renau; Gen. Sec. Marlène Haas; publ. *Women and Politics* (quarterly).

Stockholm International Peace Research Institute—SIPRI: Signalistgatan 9, 169 70 Solna, Sweden; tel. (8) 655-97-00; fax (8) 655-97-33; e-mail sipri@sipri.se; internet www.sipri.se; f. 1966; carries out studies on international security and arms control issues, including on conflict and crisis management, peace-keeping and regional security, and chemical and biological warfare; mems: about 50 staff mems, half of whom are researchers; Dir Alyson J. K. Bailes (UK); Chair. Rolf Ekéus (Sweden); publs *SIPRI Yearbook: Armaments, Disarmament and International Security*, monographs and research reports.

Transparency International: Otto-Suhr-Allee 97-99, 10585 Berlin, Germany; tel. (30) 3438200; fax (30) 34703912; e-mail ti@transparency.de; internet www.transparency.de; f. 1993; aims to promote governmental adoption of anti-corruption practices and accountability at all levels of the public sector; works to ensure that international business transactions are conducted with integrity and without resort to corrupt practices; formulates an annual Corruption Perceptions Index, and a Bribe Payers Index, and an annual Global Corruption Report; holds International Anti-Corruption Conference every two years; Chair. Dr Peter Eigen.

Trilateral Commission: 1156 15th St, NW, Washington, DC 20005, USA; tel. (202) 467-5410; fax (202) 467-5415; e-mail admin@trilateral.org; internet www.trilateral.org; also offices in Paris and Tokyo; f. 1973 by private citizens of western Europe, Japan and North America, to encourage closer co-operation among these regions on matters of common concern by analysis of major issues the Commission seeks to improve public understanding of problems, to develop and support proposals for handling them jointly, and to nurture the habit of working together in the 'trilateral' area. The Commission issues 'task force' reports on such subjects as monetary affairs, political co-operation, trade issues, the energy crisis and reform of international institutions; mems: about 335 individuals eminent in academic life, industry, finance, labour, etc. those currently engaged as senior government officials are excluded; Chair. Thomas S. Foley, Yotaro Kobyashi, Peter Sutherland; Dirs Michael J. O'Neil, Tadashi Yamamto, Paul Revay; publs *Task Force Reports*, *Triangle Papers*.

Unrepresented Nations' and Peoples' Organization—UNPO: Eisenhowelaan 136, 2517 KN The Hague, Netherlands; tel. (70) 360-3318; fax (70) 360-3346; e-mail unpo@unpo.nl; internet www.unpo.org; f. 1991 to provide an international forum for indigenous and other unrepresented peoples and minorities; provides training in human rights, law, diplomacy and public relations to UNPO members; provides conflict resolution services; mems: 52 organisations representing occupied nations, indigenous peoples and minorities; Gen. Sec. Michael van Walt; publs *UNPO News*, *UNPO Yearbook*.

War Resisters' International: 5 Caledonian Rd, London, N1 9DX, United Kingdom; tel. (20) 7278-4040; fax (20) 7278-0444; e-mail office@wri-irg.org; internet www.wri-irg.org; f. 1921; encourages refusal to participate in or support wars or military service, collaborates with movements that work for peace and non-violent social change; mems: approx. 150,000; Chair. JOANNE SHEEHAN; Sec. ROBERTA BACIC; publ. *Peace News* (quarterly).

Women's International Democratic Federation—WIDF (Fédération Démocratique Internationale des Femmes—FDIF): c/o 'Femmes solidaires', 25 rue du Charolais, 75012 Paris, France; tel. 1-40-01-90-90; fax 1-40-01-90-81; e-mail fdif@fdif.eu.org; internet www.fdif.eu.org; f. 1945 to unite women regardless of nationality, race, religion or political opinion to enable them to work together to win and defend their rights as citizens, mothers and workers; to protect children; and to ensure peace and progress, democracy and national independence; structure: Congress, Secretariat and Executive Committee; mems: 629 organizations in 104 countries; Pres. SYLVIE JAN (France); Vice-Pres. MAYADA ABBASSI (Palestine); publs *Women of the Whole World* (6 a year), *Newsletter*.

World Council of Indigenous Peoples: 100 Argyle Ave, 2nd Floor, Ottawa, ON K2P 1B6, Canada; tel. (613) 230-9030; fax (613) 230-9340; e-mail wcip@net.web; f. 1975 to promote the rights of indigenous peoples and to support their cultural, social and economic development; comprises representatives of indigenous organizations from five regions: North, South and Central America, Pacific-Asia and Scandinavia; holds General Assembly every three years; Pres. CONRADO JORGE VALIENTE QUILPILDOR; publ. *WCIP Newsletter* (4–6 a year).

World Disarmament Campaign: 45–47 Blythe St, London, E2 6LN, United Kingdom; tel. (20) 7729-2523; f. 1980 to encourage governments to take positive and decisive action to end the arms race, acting on the four main commitments called for in the Final Document of the UN's First Special Session on Disarmament; aims to mobilize people of every country in a demand for multilateral disarmament, to encourage consideration of alternatives to the nuclear deterrent for ensuring world security, and to campaign for a strengthened role for the UN in these matters; Chair. Dr FRANK BARNABY, Dr TONY HART; publ. *World Disarm!* (6 a year).

World Federalist Movement: 777 UN Plaza, New York, NY 10017, USA; tel. (212) 599-1320; fax (212) 599-1332; e-mail wfm@igc .org; internet www.worldfederalist.org; f. 1947 to achieve a just world order through a strengthened United Nations to acquire for the UN the authority to make and enforce laws for the peaceful settlement of disputes, and to raise revenue under limited taxing powers; to establish better international co-operation in the areas of environment, development and disarmament; and to promote federalism throughout the world; mems: 23 member organizations and 16 assoc. organizations; Pres. Sir PETER USTINOV; Exec. Dir WILLIAM R. PACE; publ. *World Federalist News* (quarterly).

World Federation of United Nations Associations—WFUNA (Fédération Mondiale des Associations Pour les Nations Unies—FMANU): United Nations Room, DC1-1177, New York, NY 10017, USA; e-mail wfunany@wfuna.org; internet www.wfuna.org; f. 1946 to encourage popular interest and participation in United Nations programmes, discussion of the role and future of the UN, and education for international understanding; Plenary Assembly meets every two years; WFUNA has founded International Youth and Student Movement for the United Nations; mems: national asscns in 80 countries; Pres. HASHIM ABDUL HALIM (India); Sec.-Gen. DONALD BLINKEN; publ. *WFUNA News*.

World Peace Council: Othonos 10, Athens, Greece; tel. (1) 331-6326; fax (1) 322-4302; e-mail info@wpc-in.org; internet www.wpc-in .org; f. 1950 at the Second World Peace Congress, Warsaw; principles: the prevention of nuclear war; the peaceful co-existence of the various socio-economic systems in the world; settlement of differences between nations by negotiation and agreement; complete disarmament; elimination of colonialism and racial discrimination; and respect for the right of peoples to sovereignty and independence; mems: representatives of national organizations, groups and individuals from 140 countries, and of 30 international organizations; Executive Committee of 40 mems elected by world assembly held every three years; Exec. Sec. ATHANASSIOS PAFILIS; publ. *Peace Courier* (monthly).

Youth of the European People's Party—YEPP: 67 rue d'Arlon, 1047 Brussels, Belgium; tel. (2) 285-41-65; fax (2) 281-41-65; e-mail yepp@evppe.be; internet www.yepp.org; f. 1997 to unite national youth organizations of member parties of European Young Christian Democrats and Democrat Youth Community of Europe; aims to develop contacts between youth movements and advance general political debate; mems: 388 national organizations in 29 European countries; Exec. Sec. MARKUS PÖSENTRUP (Germany); publ. *YEPP News* (monthly).

Industrial and Professional Relations

(See also the chapters on ICFTU, WCL and WFTU)

Arab Federation of Petroleum, Mining and Chemicals Workers: POB 5339, Tripoli, Libya; tel. (21) 444-7597; fax (21) 444-9139; f. 1961 to establish industrial relations policies and procedures for the guidance of affiliated unions; promotes establishment of trade unions in the relevant industries in countries where they do not exist; publs *Arab Petroleum* (monthly), specialzed publications and statistics.

European Association for Personnel Management—EAPM: c/o CIPD, CIPD House, Camp Rd, Wimbledon, London, SW19 4OX; tel. (20) 8263-3273; fax (20) 8263-3806; e-mail f.wilson@ipd.co.uk; internet www.eapm.org; f. 1962 to disseminate knowledge and information concerning the personnel function of management, to establish and maintain professional standards, to define the specific nature of personnel management within industry, commerce and the public services, and to assist in the development of national asscns; mems: 26 national asscns; Pres. CHRISTOPH SCHAUB (Switzerland); Sec.-Gen. GEOFFREY ARMSTRONG (UK).

European Civil Service Federation—ECSF (Fédération de la Fonction Publique Européenne—FFPE): 200 rue de la Loi, L 102 6/14,1049 Brussels, Belgium; e-mail secretariat.politique@ffpe.org; internet www.ffpe.org; f. 1962 to foster the idea of a European civil service of staff of international organizations operating in western Europe or pursuing regional objectives; upholds the interests of civil service members; mems: local cttees in 12 European countries and individuals in 66 countries; Sec.-Gen. L. RIJNOUDT; publ. *Eurechos*.

European Construction Industry Federation (Fédération de l'Industrie Européenne de la Construction—FIEC): 66 ave Louise, 1050 Brussels, Belgium; tel. (2) 514-55-35; fax (2) 511-02-76; e-mail info@fiec.org; internet www.fiec.org; f. 1905 as International European Construction Federation, present name adopted 1999; mems: 32 national employers' organizations in 25 countries; Pres. WILHELM KÜCHLER (Germany); Dir-Gen. ULRICH PAETZOLD; publs *FIEC News*(2 a year), *Annual Report, Construction Activity in Europe*.

European Federation of Conference Towns: POB 182, 1040 Brussels, Belgium; tel. (2) 732-69-54; fax (2) 735-48-40; e-mail secretariat@efct.com; internet www.efct.com; lays down standards for conference towns; provides advice and assistance to its members and other organizations holding conferences in Europe; undertakes publicity and propaganda for promotional purposes; helps conference towns to set up national centres; Pres. HENRI CÉRAN (France); Exec. Dir ALINE LEGRAND.

European Federation of Lobbying and Public Affairs (Fédération européenne du lobbying et public afairs—FELPA): rue du Trône 61, 1050 Brussels, Belgium; tel. (2) 511-74-30; fax (2) 511-12-84; aims to enhance the development and reputation of the industry; encourages professionals active in the industry to sign a code of conduct outlining the ethics and responsibilities of people involved in lobbying or public relations work with the institutions of the EU; Pres. Y. DE LESPINAY.

European Industrial Research Management Association—EIRMA: 34 rue de Bassano, 75008 Paris, France; tel. 1-53-23-83-10; fax 1-47-20-05-30; e-mail info@eirma.asso.fr; internet www.eirma .asso.fr; f. 1966 under auspices of the OECD; a permanent body in which European science and technology firms meet to consider approaches to industrial innovation, support research and development, and take joint action to improve performance in their various fields; mems: 160 in 21 countries; Pres. LARS-GÖRAN ROSENGREN; Gen. Sec. ANDREW DEARING; publs *Annual Report, Conference Reports, Working Group Reports, Workshop Reports*.

European Trade Union Confederation—ETUC (Confédération européenne des syndicats): 5 blvd du Roi Albert II, 1210 Brussels, Belgium; tel. (2) 224-04-11; fax (2) 224-04-54; e-mail etuc@etuc.org; internet www.etuc.org; f. 1973; comprises 78 national trade union confederations and 11 European industrial federations in 34 European countries, representing 60m. workers; holds congress every four years; Pres. FRITZ VERZETNITSCH (Austria); Gen. Sec. EMILIO GABAGLIO (Italy).

Federation of International Civil Servants' Associations—FICSA: Palais des Nations, 1211 Geneva 10, Switzerland; tel. (22) 917-3150; fax (22) 917-0660; e-mail ficsa@ficsa.org; internet www .ficsa.org; f. 1952 to co-ordinate policies and activities of member asscns and unions, to represent staff interests before inter-agency and legislative organs of the UN and to promote the development of an international civil service; mems: 26 asscns and unions consisting of staff of UN organizations, 2 associate mems from non-UN organizations, 25 consultative asscns and 17 inter-organizational federations with observer status; Pres. ALI K. BASARAN; Gen. Sec. JANICE

ALBERT; publs *Annual Report, FICSA Newsletter, FICSA Update, FICSA circulars*.

International Association of Conference Interpreters: 10 ave de Sécheron, 1202 Geneva, Switzerland; tel. (22) 9081540; fax (22) 7324151; e-mail info@aiic.net; internet www.aiic.net; f. 1953 to represent professional conference interpreters, ensure the highest possible standards and protect the legitimate interests of mems; establishes criteria designed to improve the standards of training; recognizes schools meeting the required standards; has consultative status with the UN and several of its agencies; mems: 2,300 in 53 countries; Pres. JENNIFER MACKINTOSH (Switzerland); Exec. Sec. JOSYANE CRISTINA; publs *Code of Professional Conduct, Yearbook* (listing interpreters), etc.

International Association of Conference Translators: 15 route des Morillons, 1218 Le Grand-Saconnex, Geneva, Switzerland; tel. (22) 7910666; fax (22) 7885644; e-mail secretariat@aitc.ch; internet www.aitc.ch; f. 1962; represents revisers, translators, précis writers and editors working for international conferences and organizations; aims to protect the interests of those in the profession and help maintain high standards; establishes links with international organizations and conference organizers; mems: c. 450 in 33 countries; Pres. LUIS TURIANSKY; Exec. Sec. MARIE EL-ACHKAR; publs *Directory, Bulletin*.

International Association of Crafts and Small and Medium-Sized Enterprises—IACME: c/o Centre patronal, CP 1215, 1001 Lausanne, Switzerland; tel. (21) 796-33-54; fax (21) 796-33-11; e-mail iacme@centrepatronal.ch; f. 1947 to defend undertakings and the freedom of enterprise within private economy, to develop training, to encourage the creation of national organizations of independent enterprises and promote international collaboration, to represent the common interests of members and to institute exchange of ideas and information; mems: organizations in 26 countries; Chair. FRANCO MUSCARA; Gen. Sec. JACQUES DESGRAZ.

International Association of Mutual Insurance Companies—AISAM (Association internationale des sociétés d'assurance mutuelle): 29 Square de Meeus, 1000, Brussels, Belgium; tel. (2) 503-38-78; fax (2) 503-30-55; e-mail aisam@aisam.org; internet www .aisam.org; f. 1963 for the establishment of good relations between members and the protection of the general interests of private insurance based on the principle of mutuality; mems: over 200 in 25 countries; Pres. FILOMENO MIRA (Spain); Sec.-Gen. GÉRARD OUTTERS; publs *Mutuality* (2 a year), *AISAM Directory, Newsletter*.

International Federation of Actors (Fédération internationale des acteurs—FIA): Guild House, Upper St Martin's Lane, London, WC2H 9EG, United Kingdom; tel. (20) 7379-0900; fax (20) 7379-8260; e-mail info@fia-actors.com; internet www.fia-actors.com; f. 1952; Exec. Cttee meets annually, Congress convened every four years; mems: 100 performers' unions in 71 countries; Pres. TOMAS BOLME (Sweden); Gen. Sec. KATHERINE SAND.

International Federation of Air Line Pilots' Associations—IFALPA: Interpilot House, Gogmore Lane, Chertsey, Surrey, KT16 9AP, United Kingdom; tel. (1932) 571711; fax (1932) 570920; e-mail admin@ifalpa.org; internet www.ifalpa.org; f. 1948 to represent pilots at the ICAO and other industry fora and organizations, especially in technical and safety matters; establishes standards for air safety world-wide; seeks to ensure fair conditions of employment for pilots; mems: 95 asscns, over 100,000 pilots; Pres. Capt. TED MURPHY; publs *Interpilot* (2 a year), safety bulletins and news-sheets.

International Federation of Biomedical Laboratory Science—IFBLS: Office POB 2830,Hamilton, Ontario, ON L8N 3N8, Canada; tel. 905-528-8642; fax 905-528-4968; e-mail office@ifbls.org; internet www.iamlt.org; f. 1954 to allow discussion of matters of common professional interest; fmrly the International Association of Medical Laboratory Technologists (f. 1954); aims to promote globally the highest standards in the delivery of care, of professional training, and ethical and professional practices; develops and promotes active professional partnerships in health care at the international level; promotes and encourages participation of members in international activities; holds international congress every second year; mems: 180,000 in 40 countries; Pres. NOEL WHITE (Ireland); Pres. (designate) LENA MORGAN (Sweden); publs *MedTecInternational* (2 a year), *Newsletter* (6 a year).

International Federation of Business and Professional Women: POB 568, Horsham RH13 9ZP, United Kingdom; tel. (1403) 739343; fax (1403) 734432; e-mail bpwi@horsham.co.uk; internet www.bpwintl.com; f. 1930 to promote interests of business and professional women and secure combined action by such women; mems: national federations, associate clubs and individual associates, totalling more than 200,000 mems in over 100 countries; Pres. ANTOINETTE RUEGG (Switzerland); Exec. Sec. ANN R. TODD-LAMBIE (New Zealand); publ. *BPW News International*(monthly).

International Federation of Insolvency Professionals—INSOL: 2–3 Philpot Lane, London, EC3M 8AQ, United Kingdom;

tel. (20) 7929-6679; fax (20) 7929-6678; e-mail pennyr@insol.ision.co .uk; internet www.insol.org; f. 1982; comprises national asscns of accountants and lawyers specializing in corporate turnaround and insolvency; holds annual conference; mems: 36 asscns, with more than 7,700 individual members; Pres. JOHN LEES (Hong Kong); Exec. Dir CLAIRE BROUGHTON; publ. *INSOL World* (quarterly newsletter), *International Insolvency Review* (2 a year).

International Graphical Federation (Fédération graphique internationale): 17 rue des Fripiers, Galerie du Centre, bloc 2, 1000 Brussels, Belgium; tel. (2) 223-02-20; fax (2) 223-18-14; e-mail igf-fgi@enter.org; f. 1925; mems: national federations in 15 countries, covering 100,000 workers; Pres. L. VAN HAUDT (Belgium); Sec.-Gen. R. E. VAN KESTEREN (Netherlands).

International Industrial Relations Association—IIRA: c/o International Labour Office, 1211 Geneva 22, Switzerland; tel. (22) 7996841; fax (22) 7998541; e-mail iira@ilo.org; internet www.ilo.org/ iira; f. 1966 to encourage development of national asscns of specialists, facilitate the spread of information, organize conferences, and promote internationally planned research, through study groups and regional meetings; a World Congress is held every three years; mems: 39 asscns, 47 institutions and 1,100 individuals; Pres. Prof. MANFRED WEISS; Sec. Prof. TAYO FASHOYIN; publs *IIRA Bulletin* (3 a year), *IIRA Membership Directory, IIRA Congress proceedings*.

International Organisation of Employers—IOE: 26 chemin de Joinville, BP 68, 1216 Cointrin/Geneva, Switzerland; tel. (22) 929-00-00; fax (22) 929-00-01; internet www.ioe-emp.org; f. 1920, ; aims to establish and maintain contacts between mems and to represent their interests at the international level; works to promote free enterprise; and to assist the development of employers' organizations; General Council meets annually; there is a Management Board and a General Secretariat; mems: 136 federations in 132 countries; Chair. FRANÇOIS PERIGOT (France); Sec.-Gen. ANTONIO PEÑALOSA (Spain); publ. *IOE.net*.

International Organization of Experts—ORDINEX: 19 blvd Sébastopol, 75001 Paris, France; tel. 1-40-28-06-06; fax 1-40-28-03-13; e-mail contact@ordinex.org; internet www.ordinex.org; f. 1961 to establish co-operation between experts on an international level; mems: 600; Pres. FRANZ SCHREINER (Austria); Sec.-Gen. PIERRE ROYER (France); publ. *General Yearbook*.

International Public Relations Association—IPRA: Cheltonian House, Portsmouth Rd, Esher, Surrey KT10 9AA, United Kingdom; tel. (1372) 461188; fax (1372) 461159; e-mail iprasec@ btconnect.com; internet www.ipra.org; f. 1955 to provide for an exchange of ideas, technical knowledge and professional experience among those engaged in international public relations, and to foster the highest standards of professional competence; mems: 1000 in 95 countries; CEO JAMES HOLT; publs*Frontline* (quarterly), *Members' Manual* (annually).

International Society of City and Regional Planners—ISoCaRP: Willem Witsenplein 6, 2596 BK, The Hague, Netherlands; tel. (70) 3462654; fax (70) 3617909; e-mail secretariat@isocarp .org; internet www.isocarp.org; f. 1965 to promote better planning practice through the exchange of knowledge; holds annual international congress (2003: Cairo, Egypt); mems: 480 in 70 countries; Pres. ALFONSO VEGARA GOMEZ (Netherlands); Sec.-Gen. Prof. Dr MILICA BAJÍC BRKOVIC (Serbia and Montenegro); publs *News Bulletin* (quarterly), ; seminar and congress reports.

International Union of Architects (Union internationale des architectes—UIA): 51 rue Raynouard, 75016 Paris, France; tel. 1-45-24-36-88; fax 1-45-24-02-78; e-mail uia@uia-architectes.org; internet www.uia-architectes.org; f. 1948; holds triennial congress; mems: 106 countries; Pres. JAIME LERNER (Brazil); Sec.-Gen JEAN-CLAUDE RIGUET (France); publ. *Lettre d'informations* (monthly).

Latin American Federation of Agricultural and Food Industry Workers (Federación Latinoamericana de Trabajadores Campesinos y de la Alimentación—FELTAC): Avda Baralt esq. Conde a Padre Cierra, Edificio Bapgel, 4°, Oficina 42, Apdo 1422, Caracas 1010A, Venezuela; tel. (2) 863-2447; fax (2) 720463; e-mail lassofeltaca@cantv.net; f. 1961 to represent the interests of agricultural workers and workers in the food and hotel industries in Latin America; mems: national unions in 28 countries and territories; Sec.-Gen. JOSÉ LASSO; publ. *Boletín Luchemos* (quarterly).

Nordic Industry Workers' Federation (Nordiska Industriarbetarefederationen—NIF): Olof Palmes gata 11, 5th Floor, Box 1114, 111 81 Stockholm, Sweden; tel. (8) 7868500; fax (8) 105968; e-mail kent.karrlander.nif@industrifacket.se; f. 1901; promotes collaboration between affiliates representing workers in the chemicals, energy, garment, manufacturing, mining, paper and textile sectors in Denmark, Finland, Iceland, Norway and Sweden; supports sister unions economically and in other ways in labour market conflicts; mems: 400,000 in 17 unions; Pres. LEIF OHLSSON; Sec. KENT KÄRR-LANDER.

Organisation of African Trade Union Unity—OATUU: POB M386, Accra, Ghana; tel. (21) 508855; fax (21) 508851; e-mail oatuu@lghmail.com; internet www.ecouncil.ac.cr/ngoexch/oatuu2 .htm; f. 1973 as a single continental trade union org., independent of international trade union organizations; has affiliates from all African trade unions. Congress, the supreme policy-making body, is composed of four delegates per country from affiliated national trade union centres, and meets at least every four years; the General Council, composed of one representative from each affiliated trade union, meets annually to implement Congress decisions and to approve the annual budget; mems: trade union movements in 53 independent African countries; Sec.-Gen. Gen. HASSAN A. SUNMONU (Nigeria); publ. *The African Worker*.

Pan-African Employers' Confederation—PEC: c/o Mauritius Employers' Federation, Cerné House, 13 La Chaussée, Port Louis, Mauritius; tel. 212-1599; fax 212-6725; e-mail mef@intnet.mu; f. 1986 to link African employers' organizations and represent them at the AU, UN and ILO; representation in 39 countries on the continent; Sec.-Gen. AZAD JEETUN (Mauritius).

World Federation of Scientific Workers—WFSW (Fédération mondiale des travailleurs scientifiques—FMTS): Case 404, 263 rue de Paris, 93516 Montreuil, Cédex, France; tel. (1) 48-18-81-75; fax (1) 48-18-80-03; e-mail fmts@wanadoo.fr; internet assoc.wanadoo.fr/ fmts.wfsw; f. 1946 to improve the position of science and scientists, to assist in promoting international scientific co-operation and to promote the use of science for beneficial ends; studies and publicizes problems of general, nuclear, biological and chemical disarmament; surveys the position and activities of scientists; mems: organizations in 37 countries, totalling over 500,000 mems; Pres. ANDRÉ JAEGLÉ; Sec.-Gen. CHARLES DEMONS (UK); publ. *Scientific World* (quarterly, in English, Esperanto, German and Russian).

World Movement of Christian Workers—WMCW: 124 blvd du Jubilé, 1080 Brussels, Belgium; tel. (2) 421-58-40; fax (2) 421-58-49; e-mail mmtc@skynet.be; internet www.mmtc-wmcw-wbca.be; f. 1961 to unite national movements that advance the spiritual and collective well-being of workers; holds General Assembly every four years; mems: 47 affiliated movements in 39 countries; Sec.-Gen. NORBERT KLEIN; publ. *Infor-WMCW*.

World Union of Professions (Union mondiale des professions libérales): 38 rue Boissière, 75116 Paris, France; tel. 1-44-05-90-15; fax 1-44-05-90-17; e-mail info@umpl.com; internet www.umpl.com; f. 1987 to represent and link members of the liberal professions; mems: 27 national inter-professional organizations, two regional groups and 12 international federations; Pres. Dr CHRISTIAN RONDEAU.

Law

African Bar Association: 29/31 Obafemi Awolowo Way, Ikeja, Lagos, Nigeria (temporary address); tel. (1) 4936907; fax (1) 7752202; f. 1972; aims to uphold the rule of law, maintain the independence of the judiciary, and improve legal services; Pres. PETER ALA ADJETY (Ghana); Sec.-Gen. FEMI FELANA (Nigeria).

African Society of International and Comparative Law—ASICL: 402 Holloway Rd, London, M7 6PZ United Kingdom; tel. (20) 7609 3800; fax (20) 7609 5400; e-mail asicl@compuserve.com; f. 1986; promotes public education on law and civil liberties; aims to provide a legal aid and advice system in each African country, and to facilitate the exchange of information on civil liberties in Africa; Pres. MOHAMED BEDJAOUI; Sec. EMILE YAKPO (Ghana); publs *Newsletter* (every 2 months), *African Journal of International and Comparative Law* (quarterly).

Asian-African Legal Consultative Organization—AALCO: E-66, Vasant Marg, Vasant Vihar, New Delhi 110057, India; tel. (11) 6152251; fax (11) 6152041; e-mail aalco@ysnl.com; internet www .aalco.org; f. 1956 to consider legal problems referred to it by member countries and to serve as a forum for Afro-Asian co-operation in international law, including international trade law, and economic relations; provides background material for conferences, prepares standard/model contract forms suited to the needs of the region; promotes arbitration as a means of settling international commercial disputes; trains officers of member states; has permanent UN observer status; mems: 45 countries; Pres. Senator KANU G. AGABI SAN (Nigeria); Sec.-Gen. Dr WAFIK ZAHER KAMIL (Egypt).

Centre for International Environmental Law—CIEL: 1367 Connecticut Ave, NW, Suite 300, Washington, DC 20036, USA; tel. (202) 785-8700; fax (202) 785-8701; e-mail info@ciel.org; internet www.ciel.org; f. 1989; aims to solve environmental problems and promote sustainable societies through use of law; works to strengthen international and comparative environmental law and policy and to incorporate fundamental ecological principles into international law; provides a range of environmental legal services;

educates and trains environmental lawyers; Exec. Dir DANIEL B. MAGRAW.

Council of the Bars and Law Societies of the European Union —CCBE: 45 rue de Trèves, 1040 Brussels, Belgium; tel. (2) 234-65-10; fax (2) 234-65-11; e-mail ccbe@ccbe.org; internet www.ccbe.org; f. 1960; the officially recognized representative organization for the legal profession in the European Union and European Economic Area; liaises between the bars and law societies of member states and represents them before the European institutions; also maintains contact with other international organizations of lawyers; principal objective is to study all questions affecting the legal profession in member states and to harmonize professional practice; mems: 18 delegations (representing some 500,000 European lawyers), and observers from Bulgaria, Croatia, Cyprus, Czech Republic, Estonia, Hungary, Poland, Romania, Slovakia, Slovenia, Switzerland and Turkey; Pres. HELGE JAKOB KOLRUD; Sec.-Gen. JONATHAN GOLDSMITH.

Hague Conference on Private International Law: Scheveningseweg 6, 2517 KT, The Hague, Netherlands; tel. (70) 3633303; fax (70) 3604867; e-mail secretariat@hcch.net; internet www.hcch.net; f. 1893 to work for the unification of the rules of private international law; Permanent Bureau f. 1955; mems: 38 European and 24 other countries; Sec.-Gen. J. H. A. VAN LOON; publs *Proceedings of Diplomatic Sessions* (every 4 years), *Collection of Conventions*.

Institute of International Law (Institut de droit international): IUHEI, 132 rue de Lausanne, CP 36, 1211 Geneva 21, Switzerland; tel. (22) 9085720; fax (22) 9085710; e-mail gerardi@hei.unige.ch; f. 1873 to promote the development of international law through the formulation of general principles, in accordance with civilized ethical standards; provides assistance for the gradual and progressive codification of international law; mems: limited to 132 members and associates world-wide; Sec.-Gen. CHRISTIAN DOMINICÉ (Switzerland); publ. *Annuaire de l'Institut de Droit international*.

Inter-African Union of Lawyers—IAUL (Union interafricaine des avocats): BP14409, Libreville, Gabon; tel. 76-41-44; fax 74-54-01; f. 1980; holds congress every three years; Pres. ABDELAZIZ BENZAKOUR (Morocco); Sec.-Gen. FRANÇOIS XAVIER AGONDJO-OKAWE (Gabon); publ. *L'avocat africain* (2 a year).

Inter-American Bar Association—IABA: 1211 Connecticut Ave, NW, Suite 202, Washington, DC 20036, USA; tel. (202) 466-5944; fax (202) 466-9546; e-mail iaba@iaba.org; internet www.iaba.org; f. 1940 to promote the rule of law and to establish and maintain relations between asscns and organizations of lawyers in the Americas; mems: 90 asscns and 3,500 individuals in 27 countries; Pres. RAÚL LOZANO MERINO (Peru); Sec.-Gen. Dr LOUIS G. FERRAND (USA); publs *Newsletter* (quarterly), *Conference Proceedings*.

Intergovernmental Committee of the Universal Copyright Convention: Division of Arts and Cultural Enterprise, UNESCO, 7 place de Fontenoy, 75700 Paris, France; tel. 1-45-68-47-05; fax 1-45-68-55-89; e-mail rsy@unesco.org; established to study the application and operation of the Universal Copyright Convention and to make preparations for periodic revisions of this Convention; studies other problems concerning the international protection of copyright, in co-operation with various international organizations; mems: 18 states; publ. *Copyright Bulletin* (quarterly: digital format in English, French and Spanish; print format in Chinese and Russian).

International Association for the Protection of Industrial Property—AIPPI: Tödistrasse 16, 8027 Zürich 27, Switzerland; tel. (1) 280-58-80; fax (1) 280-58-85; e-mail mail@aippi.org; internet www.aippi.org; f. 1897 to encourage the development of legislation on the international protection of industrial property and the development and extension of international conventions, and to make comparative studies of existing legislation with a view to its improvement and unification; holds triennial congress; mems: 8,200 (national and regional groups and individual mems) in 108 countries; Pres. Dr GERD F. KUNZE (Australia); Sec.-Gen. VINCENZO M. PEDRAZZINI (Switzerland); publs *Yearbook*, reports.

International Association of Democratic Lawyers: 21 rue Brialmont, 1210 Brussels, Belgium; tel. and fax (2) 223-33-10; e-mail iadl@ist.cerist.dz; internet www.iadllaw.org; f. 1946 to facilitate contacts and exchange between lawyers, encourage study of legal science and international law and support the democratic principles favourable to the maintenance of peace and co-operation between nations; promotes the preservation of the environment; conducts research on labour law, private international law, agrarian law, etc. has consultative status with UN; mems: in 96 countries; Pres. JITENDRA SHARMA (India); Sec.-Gen. BEINUSZ SZMUKLER (Argentina); publ. *International Review of Contemporary Law*, (2 a year, in French, English and Spanish).

International Association of Juvenile and Family Court Magistrates—IAYFJM: 175 Andersonstown Rd, Belfast, BT11 9EA, Northern Ireland; tel. (28) 9061-5164; fax (28) 9061-8374; e-mail w .mccarney@btconnect.com; f. 1928 to support the protection of youth and family, and criminal behaviour and juvenile maladjustment; members exercise functions as juvenile and family court judges or within professional services linked to youth and family justice and welfare; organizes study groups, meetings and an international congress; mems: 23 national asscns; Pres. WILLY McCARNEY (Canada).

International Association of Law Libraries—IALL: POB 5709, Washington, DC 20016-1309, USA; e-mail ann.morrison@dal.ca; internet www.iall.org; f. 1959 to encourage and facilitate the work of librarians and others concerned with the bibliographic processing and administration of legal materials; mems: 600 from more than 50 countries (personal and institutional); Pres. HOLGER KNUDSEN (Germany); Sec. ANN MORRISON (Canada); publ. *International Journal of Legal Information* (3 a year).

International Association of Legal Sciences—IALS (Association internationale des sciences juridiques): c/o CISS, 1 rue Miollis, 75015 Paris, France; tel. 1-45-68-25-59; fax 1-45-66-76-03; f. 1950 to promote the mutual knowledge and understanding of nations and the increase of learning by encouraging throughout the world the study of foreign legal systems and the use of the comparative method in legal science; governed by a president and an executive committee of 11 members known as the International Committee of Comparative Law; sponsored by UNESCO; mems: national committees in 47 countries; Pres. Prof. WLADIMIR TOUMANOV (Russia); Sec.-Gen. M. LEKER (Israel).

International Association of Penal Law: 41 rue Bonado, 640000 Pau, France; tel. 5-59-98-08-24; fax 5-59-27-24-56; e-mail aidp-pau@infonie.fr; internet www.penal.org; f. 1924 to promote collaboration between those from different countries working in penal law, studying criminology, or promoting the theoretical and practical development of international penal law; mems: 1,800; Pres. Prof. M. C. BASSIOUNI; Sec.-Gen. Dr H. EPP; publs *Revue Internationale de Droit Pénal* (2 a year), *Nouvelles Etudes Penales.*

International Bar Association—IBA: 271 Regent St, London W1B 2AQ, United Kingdom; tel. (20) 7629-1206; fax (20) 7409-0456; e-mail iba@int-bar.org; internet www.ibanet.org; f. 1947; a non-political federation of national bar asscns and law societies; aims to discuss problems of professional organization and status; to advance the science of jurisprudence; to promote uniformity and definition in appropriate fields of law; to promote administration of justice under law among peoples of the world; to promote in their legal aspects the principles and aims of the United Nations; mems: 154 member organizations in 164 countries, 17,500 individual members in 173 countries; Pres. EMILIO CÁRDENAS (Argentina); Sec. Gen. FERNANDO POMBO (Spain); publs *International Business Lawyer* (11 a year), *International Bar News* (3 a year), *International Legal Practitioner* (quarterly), *Journal of Energy and Natural Resources Law* (quarterly).

International Commission of Jurists—ICJ: POB 216, 81A ave de Châtelaine, 1219 Châtelaine/Geneva, Switzerland; tel. (22) 9793800; fax (22) 9793801; e-mail info@icj.org; internet www.icj.org; f. 1952 to promote the implementation of international law and principles that advance human rights; provides legal expertise to ensure that developments in international law adhere to human rights principles and that international standards are implemented at the national level; maintains Centre for the Independence of Judges and Lawyers (f. 1978); mems: 81 sections and affiliates; Pres. Chief Justice ARTHUR CHASKALSON (Canada); Sec.-Gen. LOUISE DOS-WALD-BECK; publs *CIJL Yearbook, The Review, ICJ Newsletter*, special reports.

International Commission on Civil Status: 3 place Arnold, 67000 Strasbourg, France; e-mail ciec-sg@ciec1.org; internet www .ciec1.org; f. 1950 for the establishment and presentation of legislative documentation relating to the rights of individuals; carries out research on means of simplifying the judicial and technical administration with respect to civil status; mems: governments of Austria, Belgium, Croatia, France, Germany, Greece, Hungary, Italy, Luxembourg, Netherlands, Poland, Portugal, Spain, Switzerland, Turkey, United Kingdom; Pres. H. G. KOUMANTOS (Greece); Sec.-Gen. P. LAGARDE (France); publs *Guide Pratique international de l'état civil* (available on-line), various studies on civil status.

International Copyright Society (Internationale Gesellschaft für Urheberrecht—INTERGU): Rosenheimer Strasse 11, 81667 Munich, Germany; tel. (89) 480-03-00; fax (89) 480-03-969; f. 1954 to enquire scientifically into the natural rights of the author and to put the knowledge obtained to practical application world-wide, in particular in the field of legislation; mems: 393 individuals and corresponding organizations in 52 countries; Pres. Prof. REINHOLD KREILE; Gen. Sec. Dr MARTIN VOGEL; publs *Schriftenreihe* (61 vols), *Yearbook.*

International Council for Commercial Arbitration—ICCA: c/o Ulf Franke, POB 16050, 103 21 Stockholm, Sweden; tel. (8) 555-100-00; fax (8) 5663-16-50; e-mail info@arbitration-icca.org; internet www.arbitration-icca.org; promotes international arbitration and other forms of dispute resolution; convenes Congresses and Confer-ences for discussion and the presentation of papers; mems: 33 mems, 12 advisory mems; Pres. FALI S. NARIMAN (India); Sec.-Gen. ULF FRANKE (Sweden); publs *Yearbook on Commercial Arbitration, International Handbook on Commercial Arbitration, ICCA Congress Series.*

International Council of Environmental Law: Adenauerallee 214, 53113 Bonn, Germany; tel. (228) 2692-240; fax (228) 2692-250; e-mail 100651.317@compuserve.com; internet www.law.pace.edu/env/icelsite/icelhome.html; f. 1969 to exchange information and expertise on legal, administrative and policy aspects of environmental questions; Exec. Governors Dr WOLFGANG E. BURHENNE (Germany), Dr ABDULBAR AL-GAIN (Saudi Arabia); publs *Directory, References, Environmental Policy and Law, International Environmental Law—Multilateral Treaties*, etc.

International Criminal Police Organization—INTERPOL: 200 quai Charles de Gaulle, 69006 Lyon, France; tel. 4-72-44-70-00; fax 4-72-44-71-63; e-mail cp@interpol.int; internet www.interpol.int; f. 1923, reconstituted 1946; aims to promote and ensure mutual assistance between police forces in different countries; co-ordinates activities of police authorities of member states in international affairs; works to establish and develop institutions with the aim of preventing transnational crimes; centralizes records and information on international criminals; operates a telecommunications network of 179 stations; holds General Assembly annually; mems: official bodies of 179 countries; Sec.-Gen. RONALD K. NOBLE (USA); publs *International Criminal Police Review, International Crime Statistics, Stolen Works of Art* (CD Rom), *Interpol Guide to Vehicle Registration Documents* (annually).

International Customs Tariffs Bureau: 38 rue de l'Association, 1000 Brussels, Belgium; tel. (2) 501-87-74; fax (2) 218-30-25; e-mail bitd@euronet.be; internet www.bitd.org; f. 1890; serves as the executive instrument of the International Union for the Publication of Customs Tariffs; translates and publishes all customs tariffs in five languages—English, French, German, Italian, Spanish; mems: 71; Pres. MARC VAN CRAEN (Belgium); Dir DAVID DAVIES (UK); publs *International Customs Journal, Annual Report.*

International Development Law Institute—IDLI: Via di San Sebastianello 16, 00187 Rome, Italy; tel. (06) 6979261; fax (06) 6781946; e-mail idlo@idlo.int; internet www.idli.org; f. 1983; designs and conducts courses and seminars for lawyers, legal advisors and judges from developing countries, central and eastern Europe and the former USSR; also provides in-country training workshops; training programme addresses legal skills, international commercial law, economic law reform, governance and the role of the judiciary; Chair. JAMES HURLOCK; Dir-Gen. WILLIAM T. LORIS.

International Federation for European Law (Fédération Internationale pour le Droit Européen—FIDE): 113 ave Louise, 1050 Brussels, Belgium; tel. (2) 534-71-63; fax (2) 534-28-58; e-mail pia .conseil@euronet.be; internet www.fidelaw.org; f. 1961 to advance studies on European law among members of the European Community by co-ordinating activities of member societies; organizes conferences every two years; mems: 12 national asscns; Pres. ZACHA-RIAS SÜNDSTRÖM; Sec.-Gen. Prof. PETER-CHRISTIAN MÜLLER-GRAFF.

International Federation of Senior Police Officers (Fédération Internationale des Fonctionnaires Superieures de Police—FIFSP): FIFSP, Ministère de l'Intérieur, 127 rue Faubourg Saint Honoré, 75008 Paris, France; tel. 1-49-27-40-67; fax 1-45-62-48-52; f. 1950 to unite policemen of different nationalities, adopting the general principle that prevention should prevail over repression, and that the citizen should be convinced of the protective role of the police; established International Centre of Crime and Accident Prevention, 1976 and International Association against Counterfeiting, 1994; mems: 34 national organizations; Pres. JUAN GARCÍA LLOVERA; Sec.-Gen. JEAN-PIERRE HAVRIN (France); publ. *International Police Information* (quarterly, in English, French and German).

International Institute for the Unification of Private Law—UNIDROIT: Via Panisperna 28, 00184 Rome, Italy; tel. (06) 696211; fax (06) 69941394; e-mail unidroit.rome@unidroit.org; internet www .unidroit.org; f. 1926 to undertake studies of comparative law, to prepare for the establishment of uniform legislation, to prepare drafts of international agreements on private law and to organize conferences and publish works on such subjects; holds international congresses on private law and meetings of organizations concerned with the unification of law; maintains a library of 215,000 vols; mems: govts of 58 countries; Pres. Prof. BERARDINO LIBONATI (Italy); Sec.-Gen. Prof. HERBERT KRONKE (Germany); publs *Uniform Law Review* (quarterly), *Digest of Legal Activities of International Organizations*, etc.

International Institute of Space Law—IISL: c/o IAF, 3–5 rue Mario Nikis, 75015 Paris, France; tel. 1-45-67-42-60; fax 1-42-73-21-20; e-mail iaf@wanadoo.fr; internet www.iafastro.com; f. 1959 at the XI Congress of the International Astronautical Federation; organizes annual Space Law colloquium; studies juridical and sociological aspects of astronautics; makes awards; Pres. NANDASIRI JASEN-

TULIYANAARBOSA (USA); publs *Proceedings of Annual Colloquium on Space Law*, *Survey of Teaching of Space Law in the World*.

International Juridical Institute—IJI: Permanent Office for the Supply of International Legal Information, Spui 186, 2511 BW, The Hague, Netherlands; tel. (70) 3460974; fax (70) 3625235; e-mail iji@worldonline.nl; internet www.iji.nl; f. 1918 to supply information on any non-secret matter of international interest, respecting international, municipal and foreign law and the application thereof; Pres. A. V. M. STRUYCKEN; Dir A. L. G. A. STILLE.

International Law Association—ILA: Charles Clore House, 17 Russell Sq., London, WC1B 5DR, United Kingdom; tel. (20) 7323-2978; fax (20) 7323-3580; e-mail secretariat@ila-hq.org; internet www.ila-hq.org; f. 1873 for the study and advancement of international law, both public and private and the promotion of international understanding and goodwill; mems: 4,000 in 51 regional branches; 25 international cttees; Pres. Hon. Justice. S. P. BHARUCHA (Taiwan); Chair. Exec. Council Lord SLYNN OF HADLEY (UK); Sec.-Gen. DAVID J. C. WYLD (UK).

International Maritime Committee (Comité maritime international—CMI): Mechelsesteensweg 196, 2018 Antwerp, Belgium; tel. (3) 227-35-26; fax (3) 227-35-28; e-mail admin@cmi-imc.org; internet www.comitemaritime.org; f. 1897 to contribute to the unification of maritime law and to encourage the creation of national asscns; work includes drafting of conventions on collisions at sea, salvage and assistance at sea, limitation of shipowners' liability, maritime mortgages, etc. mems: national asscns in more than 50 countries; Pres. PATRICK J. S. GRIGGS (UK); Sec. Gen. ALEXANDER VON ZIEGLER (Switzerland); publs *CMI Newsletter*, *Year Book*.

International Nuclear Law Association—INLA: 29 sq. de Meeûs, 1000 Brussels, Belgium; tel. (2) 547-58-41; fax (2) 503-04-40; e-mail aidn.inla@skynet.be; internet www.aidn-inla.be; f. 1972 to promote international studies of legal problems related to the peaceful use of nuclear energy; holds conference every two years; mems: 500 in 30 countries; Sec.-Gen. V. VERBRAEKEN; publs *Congress reports*, *Une Histoire de 25 ans*.

International Penal and Penitentiary Foundation—IPPF (Fondation internationale pénale et pénitentiaire—FIPP): c/o Dr K. Hobe, Bundesministerium der Justiz, 10104 Berlin, Germany; tel. (30) 20259226; fax (30) 20259525; f. 1951 to encourage studies in the field of prevention of crime and treatment of delinquents; mems in 23 countries (membership limited to three people from each country) and corresponding mems; Pres. JORGE DE FIGUEIREDO DIAS (Portugal); Sec.-Gen. KONRAD HOBE (Germany).

International Police Association—IPA: 1 Fox Rd, West Bridgford, Nottingham, NG2 6AJ, United Kingdom; tel. (115) 945-5985; fax (115) 982-2578; e-mail isg@ipa-iac.org; internet www.ipa-iac.org; f. 1950 to permit the exchange of professional information, create ties of friendship between all sections of the police service and organize group travel and studies; mems: 3,500 in more than 59 countries; International Pres. MICHAEL ODYSSEOS; International Sec.-Gen. A. F. CARTER.

International Society for Labour Law and Social Security—ISLLSS: CP 500, CH-1211 Geneva 22, Switzerland; tel. (22) 7996961; fax (22) 7998749; e-mail bronstein@ilo.org; internet www.ilo.org/isllss; f. 1958 to encourage collaboration between labour law and social security specialists; holds World Congress every three years, as well as irregular regional congresses (Europe, Africa, Asia and Americas); mems: 66 national asscns of labour law officers; Pres. Prof. ROGER BLANPAIN (Belgium); Sec.-Gen. ARTURO BRONSTEIN.

International Union of Latin Notaries (Union Internationale du Notariat Latin—UINL): Via Locatelli 5, 20124 Milan, Italy; f. 1948 to study and standardize notarial legislation and promote the progress, stability and advancement of the Latin notarial system; mems: organizations and individuals in 70 countries; Sec. EMANUELE FERRARI; publs *Revista Internacional del Notariado* (quarterly), *Notarius International*.

Law Association for Asia and the Pacific—LAWASIA: GPO Box 3275, NT House, 11th Floor, 22 Mitchell St, Darwin, Northern Territory 0800, Australia; tel. (8) 8946-9500; fax (8) 8946-9505; e-mail lawasia@lawasia.asn.au; internet www.lawasia.asn.au; f. 1966; provides an international, professional network for lawyers to update, reform and develop law within the region; comprises five Sections and 21 Standing Committees in Business Law and General Practice areas, which organize speciality conferences; also holds a biennial conference (2001: Christchurch, New Zealand); mems: national orgs in 23 countries; 2,500 mems in 55 countries; publs *Directory* (annually), *LAWASIA Update* (quarterly), *Directory* (annually), *Journal* (annually).

Permanent Court of Arbitration: Peace Palace, Carnegieplein 2, 2517 KJ, The Hague, Netherlands; tel. (70) 3024165; fax (70) 3024167; e-mail bureau@pca-cpa.org; internet www.pca-cpa.org; f. by the Convention for the Pacific Settlement of International Disputes (1899, 1907); provides for the resolution of disputes involving combinations of states, private parties and intergovernmental organizations, under its own rules of procedure, by means of arbitration, conciliation and fact-finding; operates a secretariat, the International Bureau, which provides registry services and legal support to ad hoc tribunals and commissions; draws up lists of adjudicators with specific expertise; and maintains documentation on mass claims settlement processes; mems: governments of 97 countries; Sec.-Gen. TJACO VAN DEN HOUT (Netherlands); publs *Kluwer Law International Database* (ed), *Journal of International Arbitration* (ed), *World Trade and Arbitration Materials* (ed), *Peace Palace Papers* (ed), *International Law Seminars* (annually).

Society of Comparative Legislation: 28 rue Saint-Guillaume, 75007 Paris, France; tel. 1-44-39-86-23; fax 1-44-39-86-28; e-mail slc@legiscompare.com; internet www.legiscompare.com; f. 1869 to study and compare laws of different countries, and to investigate practical means of improving the various branches of legislation; mems: 600 in 48 countries; Pres. GUY CANIVET (France); Sec.-Gen. DAVID CAPITANT (France); publ. *Revue Internationale de Droit Comparé* (quarterly).

Union Internationale des Avocats (International Association of Lawyers): 25 rue du Jour, 75001 Paris, France; tel. 1-44-88-55-66; fax 1-44-88-55-77; e-mail uiacentre@wanadoo.fr; internet www.uianet.org; f. 1927 to promote the independence and freedom of lawyers, and defend their ethical and material interests on an international level; aims to contribute to the development of international order based on law; mems: 250 asscns and 3,000 lawyers in over 120 countries; Pres. ANTOINE AKL (Lebanon); Exec. Dir MARIE-PIERRE RICHARD.

Union of Arab Jurists—UAJ: POB 6026, Al-Mansour, Baghdad, Iraq; tel. (1) 5372371; fax (1) 53723693; f. 1975 to facilitate contacts between Arab lawyers, to safeguard the Arab legislative and judicial heritage, to encourage the study of Islamic jurisprudence; and to defend human rights; mems: national jurists asscns in 15 countries; Sec.-Gen. SHIBIB LAZIM AL-MALIKI; publ. *Al-Hukuki al-Arabi* (Arab Jurist).

Union of International Associations—UIA: 40 rue Washington, 1050 Brussels, Belgium; tel. (2) 640-41-09; fax (2) 643-61-99; e-mail uia@uia.be; internet www.uia.org; f. 1907, present title adopted 1910; aims to facilitate the evolution of the activities of the worldwide network of non-profit organizations, especially non-governmental and voluntary asscns; collects and disseminates information on such organizations; promotes research on the legal, administrative and other problems common to these asscns; mems: 200 in 54 countries; Sec.-Gen. ANDRÉ ONKELINX (Belgium); publs *Transnational Associations* (quarterly), *International Congress Calendar* (quarterly), *Yearbook of International Organizations*, *International Organization Participation* (annually), *Global Action Network* (annually), *Encyclopedia of World Problems and Human Potential*, *Documents for the Study of International Non-Governmental Relations*, *International Congress Science* series, *International Association Statutes* series, *Who's Who in International Organizations*.

World Jurist Association—WJA: 1000 Connecticut Ave, NW, Suite 202, Washington, DC 20036, USA; tel. (202) 466-5428; fax (202) 452-8540; e-mail wja@worldjurist.org; internet www.worldjurist.org; f. 1963; promotes the continued development of international law and the legal maintenance of world order; holds biennial world conferences, World Law Day and demonstration trials; organizes research programmes; mems: lawyers, jurists and legal scholars in 155 countries; Pres. HANS THÜMMEL (Germany); Exec. Vice-Pres. MARGARETHA M. HENNEBERRY (USA); publs *The World Jurist* (6 a year), Research Reports, *Law and Judicial Systems of Nations*, 4th revised edn (directory), *World Legal Directory*, *Law/Technology* (quarterly), *World Law Review* Vols I–V (World Conference Proceedings), *The Chief Justices and Judges of the Supreme Courts of Nations* (directory), work papers, newsletters and journals.

World Association of Judges—WJA: 1000 Connecticut Ave, NW, Suite 202, Washington, DC 20036, USA; tel. (202) 466-5428; fax (202) 452-8540; e-mail wja@worldjurist.org; f. 1966 to advance the administration of judicial justice through co-operation and communication among ranking jurists of all countries; Pres. Prince BOLA AJIBOLA (Nigeria).

World Association of Law Professors—WALP: 1000 Connecticut Ave, NW, Suite 202, Washington, DC 20036, USA; tel. (202) 466-5428; fax (202) 452-8540; e-mail wja@worldjurist.org; internet www.worldjurist.org; f. 1975 to improve scholarship and education in matters related to international law; Pres. SERAFIN V. C. GUINGONA (Philippines).

World Association of Lawyers—WAL: 1000 Connecticut Ave, NW, Suite 202, Washington, DC 20036, USA; tel. (202) 466-5428; fax (202) 452-8540; e-mail wja@worldjurist.org; internet www.worldjurist.org; f. 1975 to develop international law and improve lawyers' effectiveness in this field; Pres. JACK STREETER (USA).

Medicine and Health

Council for International Organizations of Medical Sciences —CIOMS: c/o WHO, ave Appia, 1211 Geneva 27, Switzerland; tel. (22) 7913467; fax (22) 7913111; e-mail cioms@who.int; internet www.cioms.ch; f. 1949 to serve the scientific interests of the international biomedical community; aims to facilitate and promote activities in biomedical sciences; runs long-term programmes on bioethics, health policy, ethics and values, drug development and use, and the international nomenclature of diseases; maintains collaborative relations with the UN; holds a general assembly every three years; mems: 67 organizations; Pres. Prof. JOHN H. BRYANT; Sec.-Gen. Prof. J. E. IDÁNPÁAN-HEIKKILÁ; publs *Reports on Drug Development and Use, Proceedings of CIOMS Conferences, International Nomenclature of DiseasesInternational Ethical Guide-lines for Biomedical Research Involving Human Subjects.*

MEMBERS OF CIOMS

Members of CIOMS include the following:

FDI World Dental Federation: L'Avant Centre, 13 chemin du Levant, 01210 Ferney Voltaire, France; tel. and fax 4-50-40-55-55; e-mail info@fdiworldental.org; internet www.fdiworldental.org; f. 1900; mems: 152 national dental asscns and 31 affiliates; Pres. Dr A. RATNANESAN (Malaysia); Exec. Dir Dr J. T. BARNARD (South Africa); publ. *International Dental Journal* (every 2 months).

International Association for the Study of the Liver: c/o Elise Hunchuck, 399 Bathurst St, 6B Fell Pavillion, Room 166, Toronto, ON M5T 2S8, Canada; tel. (416) 681-9135; fax (416) 703-0300; e-mail elise.hunchuck@utoronto.ca; f. 1962; Sec. ELISE HUNCHUCK.

International College of Surgeons—ICS: 1516 N. Lake Shore Drive, Chicago, IL 60610, USA; tel. (312) 642-3555; fax (312) 787-1624; e-mail info@icsglobal.org; internet www.icsglobal.org; f. 1935, as a world-wide federation of surgeons and surgical specialists for the advancement of the art and science of surgery; aims to create a common bond among the surgeons of all nations and promote the highest standards of surgery, without regard to nationality, creed, or colour; sends teams of surgeons to developing countries to teach local surgeons; provides research and scholarship grants, organizes surgical congresses around the world; manages the International Museum of Surgical Science in Chicago; mems: c. 8,000 in 112 countries; Pres. RAY A. DIETER (USA); Exec. Dir MAX C. DOWNHAM (USA); publ. *International Surgery* (quarterly).

International Diabetes Federation—IDF: 19 ave Emile de Mot, 1000 Brussels, Belgium; tel. (2) 538-55-11; fax (2) 538-51-14; e-mail luc.hendrickx@idf.org; internet www.idf.org; f. 1949 to help in the collection and dissemination of information on diabetes and to improve the welfare of people suffering from diabetes; mems: 175 asscns in 138 countries; Exec. Dir LUC HENDRICKX; publs *Diabetes Voice, Bulletin of the IDF* (quarterly).

International Federation of Clinical Neurophysiology: c/o Concorde Administration Ltd, 42 Canham Rd London, W3 7SR, United Kingdom; tel. (20) 8743-3106; fax (20) 8743-1010; e-mail ifcn@ifcn.info; internet www.elsevier.nl/homepage/sah/ifcn; f. 1949 to attain the highest level of knowledge in the field of electro-encephalography and clinical neurophysiology in all the countries of the world; mems: 48 organizations; Pres. Prof. FRANÇOIS MAUGUIÈRE (France); Sec. Prof. G. F. A. HARDING (UK); publs *Clinical Neurophysiology* (monthly), *Evoked Potentials* (every 2 months), *EMG and Motor Control* (every 2 months).

International Federation of Oto-Rhino-Laryngological Societies—IFOS: Oosterveldlaan 24, 2610 Wilrijk-Antwerp, Belgium; tel. and fax (3) 443-36-11; e-mail ifos@uia.ua.ac.be; internet www.ifosworld.org; f. 1965 to initiate and support programmes to protect hearing and prevent hearing impairment; holds Congresses every four years; Pres. NASSER KOTBY (Egypt); Sec.-Gen. JAN J. GROTE (Netherlands); publ. *IFOS Newsletter* (quarterly).

International Federation of Surgical Colleges: c/o Prof. S. W. A. Gunn, La Panetiere, 1279 Bogis-Bossey, Switzerland; tel. (22) 7762161; fax (22) 7766417; e-mail muldoon@mail.med.upenn.edu; f. 1958 to encourage high standards in surgical training; accepts volunteers to serve as surgical teachers in developing countries and co-operates with WHO in these countries; provides journals and text books for needy medical schools; conducts international symposia; offers travel grants; mems: colleges or asscns in 77 countries, 420 individual associates; Pres. Prof. JONATHAN L. MEAKINS (Canada); Hon. Sec. Prof. S. WILLIAM. A. GUNN (Switzerland); ; publ. *World Journal of Surgery.*

International League of Associations for Rheumatology—ILAR: c/o Prof. of Rheumatology and Rehabilitation, Univ. of Cairo, 19 Ismail Mohammed St, Jeddah Tower, Zamalek, Egypt; tel. (615) 343-9324; fax (615) 343-6478; internet www.ilar.org; f. 1927 to promote international co-operation for the study and control of rheumatic diseases to encourage the foundation of national leagues against rheumatism; to organize regular international congresses and to act as a connecting link between national leagues and international organizations; mems: 13,000; Pres. Prof. TAHSIN HADIDI (Chile); Sec.-Gen. Prof. SAMIR EL-BADAWY (USA); ; publs *Annals of the Rheumatic Diseases* (in the UK), *Revue du Rhumatisme* (in France), *Reumatismo* (in Italy), *Arthritis and Rheumatism* (in the USA), etc.

International Leprosy Association—ILA: c/o Univ. of Oxford, International Leprosy Association Global Project on the History of Leprosy, Wellcome Unit for The History of Medicine, 45–47 Banbury Rd, Oxford, OX2 6PE, United Kingdom; tel. (1865) 284627; fax (1865) 274605; f. 1931 to promote international co-operation in work on leprosy; holds congress every five years (2002: Brazil); Pres. Dr S. K. NOORDEEN; publ. *International Journal of Leprosy and Other Mycobacterial Diseases* (quarterly).

International Pediatric Association—IPA: c/o Hôpital Necker-Enfants Malades, 149 rue de Sèvres, 75743 Paris Cédex 15, France; tel. (1- 42-19-26-45; fax (716) 273-1038 1-42-19-26-44; internet www.ipa-france.net; f. 1912;; holds triennial congresses and regional and national workshops; mems: 135 national paediatric societies in 131 countries, 9 regional affiliate societies, 9 paediatric specialty societies; Pres. Dr. JANE SCHALLER (USA); Exec. Dir JACQUES SCMITZ (France); publ. *International Child Health* (quarterly).

International Rhinologic Society: c/o Prof. Clement, ENT-Dept, AZ-VUB, Laarbeeklaan 101, 1090 Brussels, Belgium; tel. (2) 477-60-02; fax (2) 477-64-23; e-mail knoctp@az.vub.ac.be; f. 1965; holds congress every four years; Pres. IN-YONG PARK (Republic of Korea); Sec. Prof. P. A. R. CLEMENT (Belgium); publ. *Rhinology.*

International Society of Audiology: University Hospital Rotterdam, Audiological Centre, Molewaterplein 40, 3015 GD Rotterdam, Netherlands; tel. (10) 463-4586; fax (10) 463-4240; e-mail info@isa-audiology.org; internet www.isa-audiology.org; f. 1952 to facilitate the knowledge, protection and rehabilitation of human hearing and to represent the interests of audiology professionals and of the hearing-impaired; organizes biannual Congress and workshops and seminars; mems: 300 individuals; Pres. Prof. A. QUARANTA; Gen. Sec. Dr J. VERSCHUURE; publ. *International Journal of Audiology* (every 2 months).

International Society of Dermatopathology—ISVD: c/o Mill House Veterinary Surgery, Kings Lynn, Norfolk, United Kingdom; tel. (1553) 771457; e-mail vets@vetcutis.freeserve.co.uk; internet www.vetcutis.freeserve.co.uk/vetcutis.freeserve.co.uk; f. 1958; groups professionals interested in the microscopic interpretation of skin diseases; aims to advance veterinary and comparative dermatopathology; encourages the development of technologies for the diagnosis of skin diseases in animals; promotes professional training; Pres. Dr THELMA LEE GROSS (USA); Sec. Dr DAVID H. SHEARER (UK).

International Society of Internal Medicine: Dept. of Medicine, Regional Hospital, 4900 Langenthal, Switzerland; tel. (62) 9163102; fax (62) 9164155; e-mail r.streuli@sro.ch; internet www.acponline.org/isim; f. 1948 to encourage research and education in internal medicine; mems: 58 national societies, 1,500 individuals in 65 countries; congress: Granada, Spain (2004); Pres. Prof. CHARLES R. K. HIND (USA); Sec. Prof. ROLF A. STREULI (Switzerland).

International Society of Physical and Rehabilitation Medicine—ISPRM: ISPRM Central Office,Werner van Cleemputte, Medicongress, 28–34 Waalpoel, 9960 Assenede, Belgium; tel. (9) 344-3959; fax (9) 344-4010; e-mail isprm@medicongress.com; internet www.isprm.org; f. 1999 by merger of International Federation of Physical Medicine and Rehabilitation (f. 1952) and International Rehabilitation Medicine Association (f. 1968); mems: in 68 countries; second international congress: Prague, Czech Republic (May 2003); Pres. Dr HAIM RING (Israel); Sec. Dr NAOICHI CHINO (Japan).

International Union against Cancer (Union internationale contre le cancer—UICC): 3 rue du Conseil Général, 1205 Geneva, Switzerland; tel. (22) 8091811; fax (22) 8091810; e-mail info@uicc.org; internet www.uicc.org; f. 1933 to promote the campaign against cancer on an international level; organizes International Cancer Congress every four years; administers the American Cancer Society UICC International Fellowships for Beginning Investigators (ACSBI), the Astrazeneca and Novartis UICC Transnational Cancer Research Fellowships (TCRF), the UICC International Cancer Technology Transfer Fellowships (ICRETT), the Yamagiwa-Yoshida Memorial UICC International Cancer Study Grants (YY), the Trish Greene UICC International Oncology Nursing Fellowships (IONF), the UICC Asia-Pacific Cancer Society Training Grants (APCASOT), and the Latin America UICC COPES Training and Education Fellowship (LACTEF); conducts worldwide programmes of campaign organization; public and professional education; and patient support, detection and diagnosis; and programmes on epidemiology and prevention; tobacco and cancer; the treatment of cancer; and tumour biology; mems: voluntary national organizations, cancer research and treatment organizations, institutes and governmental agencies in more than 80 countries; Pres. Dr JOHN SEFFRIN (USA); Exec. Dir ISABEL MORTARA (Switzerland); ; publs *UICC International Directory of Cancer Institutes and Organizations* (electronic version), *International Journal of Cancer* (36 a year), *UICC News* (quarterly), *International Calendar of Meetings on Cancer* (2 a year).

Latin American Association of National Academies of Medicine: Carrera 7, Santafé de Bogotá, Colombia; tel. and fax (571) 249-3122; e-mail alanam_colombia@hotmail.com; f. 1967; mems: 11 national Academies; Pres. Dr ROLANDO CALDERÓN VELASCO (Peru); Sec. Dr ZOÍLO CUÉLLAR-MONTOYA (Colombia).

Medical Women's International Association—MWIA: Wilhelm-Brand-Str.3, 44141 Dortmund, Germany; tel. (231) 94-32-771; fax (231) 94-32-773; e-mail mwia@aol.com; internet www.mwia.net; f. 1919 to facilitate contacts between women in medicine and to encourage co-operation in matters connected with international health problems; mems: national asscns in 43 countries, and individuals; Pres. Dr SHELLEY ROSS (Canada); Sec.-Gen. Dr WALTRAUD DIEKHAUS (Germany); publ. *MWIA UPDATE* (3 a year).

Organisation panafricaine de lutte contre le SIDA—OPALS: 15/21 rue de L'Ecole de Médecine, 75006 Paris, France; tel. 1-43-26-72-28; fax 1-43-29-70-93; e-mail opals@croix-rouge.fr; f. 1988;; disseminates information relating to the treatment and prevention of AIDS; provides training of medical personnel; promotes co-operation between African medical centres and specialized centres in the USA and Europe; Pres. Prof. MARC GENTILINI; publ. *OPALS Liaison*.

World Allergy Organization—IAACI: 611 East Wells St, Milwaukee, WI 53202, USA; tel. (414) 276-1791; fax (414) 276-3349; e-mail info@worldallergy.org; internet www.worldallergy.org; f. 1945, as International Association of Allergology and Clinical Immunology, to further work in the educational, research and practical medical aspects of allergic and immunological diseases; 2003 Congress: Vancouver, Canada; mems: 56 national societies and three regional orgs; Pres. Dr ALLEN P. KAPLAN (USA); until 2003; Sec.-Gen. Prof. G. WALTER CANONICA (Italy); publ. *Allergy and Clinical Immunology International* (6 a year).

World Federation for Medical Education—WFME (Fédération mondiale pour l'enseignement de la medicine): Univ. of Copenhagen Faculty of Health Sciences, Blegdamsvej 3, 2200 Copenhagen N, Denmark; tel. (353) 27103; fax (353) 27070; e-mail wfme@wfme.org; internet www.sund.ku.dk/wfme; f. 1972; aims to promote and integrate medical education world-wide; links regional and international asscns; has official relations with WHO, UNICEF, UNESCO, UNDP and the World Bank; Pres. Dr HANS KARLE; Exec. Dir BENTE HAGELUND.

World Federation of Associations of Paediatric Surgeons—WOFAPS: c/o Prof. J. Boix-Ochoa, Clinica Infantil 'Vall d'Hebron', Departamento de Cirugía Pediátrica, Valle de Hebron 119–129, Barcelona 08035, Spain; f. 1974; mems: 80 asscns; Pres. Prof. J. L. GROSFELD; Sec. Prof. J. BOIX-OCHOA.

World Federation of Neurology—WFN: 12 Chandos St, London, W1G 9DR, United Kingdom; tel. (20) 7323-4011; fax (20) 7323-4012; e-mail wfnlondon@aol.com; internet www.wfneurology.org; f. 1955 as International Neurological Congress, present title adopted 1957; aims to assemble members of various congresses associated with neurology and promote co-operation among neurological researchers. Organizes Congress every four years; mems: 23,000 in 89 countries; Pres. JUN KIMURA (Japan); Sec.-Treas. Dr RICHARD GODWIN-AUSTEN (UK); publs *Journal of the Neurological Sciences*, *World Neurology* (quarterly).

World Heart Federation: 5 ave du Mail, 1205 Geneva 12, Switzerland; tel. (22) 807-03-20; fax (22) 807-03-39; e-mail admin@worldheart.org; internet www.worldheart.org; f. 1978 as International Society and Federation of Cardiology, through merger of the International Society of Cardiology and the International Cardiology Federation, name changed as above 1998; aims to promote the study, prevention and relief of cardiovascular diseases through scientific and public education programmes and the exchange of materials; organizes world congresses every four years; mems: national cardiac societies and heart foundations in 84 countries; Pres. Dr PHILIP POOLE-WILSON (UK); Sec. Dr AYRTON BRANDÃO (Hungary); publs *CVD Prevention*, *Heartbeat* (quarterly).

World Medical Association—WMA: 13 chemin du Levant, POB 63, 01210 Ferney-Voltaire, France; tel. 4-50-40-75-75; fax 4-50-40-59-37; e-mail wma@wma.net; internet www.wma.net; f. 1947 to achieve the highest international standards in all aspects of medical education and practice, to promote closer ties among doctors and national medical asscns by personal contact and all other means, to study problems confronting the medical profession, and to present its views to appropriate bodies; holds an annual General Assembly; mems: 78 national medical asscns; Pres. Dr KATI MYLLYMAKI (Finland); Sec.-Gen. Dr DELON HUMAN (South Africa); publ. *The World Medical Journal* (6 a year).

World Organization of Gastroenterology (Organisation mondiale de gastro-entérologie—OMGE): c/o Bridget Fischer, Medconnect GmbH, Brünnsteinstr. 10, 81541 München, Germany; tel. (89) 41419240; fax (89) 41419245; e-mail omge@omge.org; internet www .omge.org; f. 1958 to promote clinical and academic gastroenterological practice throughout the world, and to ensure high ethical standards; mems: in 80 countries; Pres. Prof. GUIDO N. J. TYTGAT; Sec.-Gen. Dr HENRY COHEN.

World Psychiatric Association—WPA: Elmhurst Hospital/Mt Sinai School of Medicine, 79 Broadway, Room D-10-20, Elmhurst, NY 11373, USA; tel. (718) 334-5094; fax (718) 334-5096; e-mail wpasecretariat@wpanet.org; internet www.wpanet.org; f. 1961 for the exchange of information on problems of mental illness and to strengthen relations between psychiatrists in all countries; organizes World Psychiatric Congresses and regional and inter-regional scientific meetings; mems: 150,000 psychiatrists in 100 countries; Pres. AHMED OKASHA (Egypt); Sec.-Gen. JOHN COX (UK).

ASSOCIATE MEMBERS OF CIOMS

Associate members of CIOMS include the following:

Asia Pacific Academy of Ophthalmology—APAO: c/o Prof. Arthur S. M. Lim, Eye Clinic Singapura, 6A Napier Rd, 02-38 Gleneagles Annexe Block, Gleneagles Hospital, Singapore 258500; tel. 64666666; fax 67333360; f. 1956; holds Congress every two years; Pres. IAN CONSTABLE (Australia); Sec.-Gen. Prof. ARTHUR S. M. LIM (Singapore).

International Association of Medicine and Biology of the Environment—IAMBE: c/o 115 rue de la Pompe, 75116 Paris, France; tel. 1-45-53-45-04; fax 1-45-53-41-75; e-mail celine.abbou@ free.fr; f. 1971 with assistance from the UN Environment Programme; aims to contribute to the solution of problems caused by human influence on the environment; structure includes 13 technical commissions; mems: individuals and organizations in 79 countries; Hon. Pres. Prof. R. DUBOS; Pres. Dr C. ABBOU.

International Committee of Military Medicine—ICMM (Comité international de médecine militaire—CIMM): Hôpital Militaire Reine Astrid, rue Bruyn, 1120 Brussels, Belgium; tel. (2) 264-43-48; fax (2) 264-43-67; e-mail cimm.icmm@smd.be; internet www .cimm-icmm.org; f. 1921 as Permanent Committee of the International Congresses of Military Medicine and Pharmacy; name changed 1990; aims to increase co-operation and promote activities in the field of military medicine; considers issues relating to mass medicine, dentistry, military pharmacy, veterinary sciences and the administration and organization of medical care missions, among others; mems: official delegates from 94 countries; Chair. Lt-Gen. J. L. JANSEN VAN RENSBURG (South Africa); Sec.-Gen. Col Dr J. SANABRIA (Belgium); publ. *Revue Internationale des Services de Santé des Forces Armées* (quarterly).

International Council for Laboratory Animal Science—ICLAS: Canadian Council on Animal Care, 315–350 Albert St, Ottawa, ON K1R 1B1, Canada; tel. (450) 467-4221; fax (450) 467-6308; e-mail gdemers@ccac.ca; internet www.iclas.org; f. 1956; promotes the ethical care and use of laboratory animals in research, with the aim of advancing human and animal health; establishes standards and provides support resources; encourages international collaboration to develop knowledge; Pres. Prof. STEVEN PAKES (USA); Sec.-Gen. Dr GILLES DEMERS (Canada).

International Federation of Clinical Chemistry and Laboratory Medicine—IFCC: via Carlo Farini 81, 20159 Milan, Italy; tel. (2) 6680-9912; fax (2) 6078-1846; e-mail ifcc@ifcc.org; internet www.ifcc.org; f. 1952; mems: 78 national societies (about 33,000 individuals) and 33 corporate mems; Pres. Prof. MATHIAS M. MÜLLER (Austria); Sec. Dr RENZE BAIS (Australia); publs *Journal* (electronic version), *Annual Report*.

International Society of Blood Transfusion—ISBT: c/o Eurocongres Conference Management, Jan van Goyenkade 11, 1075 HP Amsterdam, Netherlands; tel. (20) 6794311; fax (20) 6737306; e-mail isbt@eurocongres.org; internet www.isbt-web.org; f. 1937; mems: c. 1,000 in 100 countries; Pres. H. E. HEIER; Sec.-Gen. Dr P. T. W. STRENGERS; publ. *Transfusion Today* (quarterly).

International Spinal Cord Society—ISCoS: National Spinal Injuries Centre, Stoke Mandeville Hospital, Aylesbury, Bucks, HP21 8AL, United Kingdom; tel. (1296) 315866; fax (1296) 315870; e-mail admin@iscos.org.uk; internet www.imsop.org.uk; f. 2001; formerly the International Medical Society of Paraplegia (f.1961); studies all problems relating to traumatic and non-traumatic lesions of the spinal cord, including causes, prevention, research and rehabilitation; promotes the exchange of information; assists in efforts to guide and co-ordinate research; Pres. Prof. T. IKATA; Hon. Sec. Prof. J. J. WYNDALE; publ. *Spinal Cord*.

Rehabilitation International: 25 East 21st St, New York, NY 10010, USA; tel. (212) 420-1500; fax (212) 505-0871; e-mail rehabintl@rehab-international.org;   internet   www

.rehab-international.org; f. 1922 to improve the lives of disabled people through the exchange of information and research on equipment and methods of assistance; organizes international conferences and co-operates with UN agencies and other international organizations; mems: organizations in 80 countries; Pres. LEX FRIEDEN; Sec.-Gen. TOMAS LAGERWALL; publs *International Rehabilitation Review*(annually), *Rehabilitación* (2 or 3 a year).

Transplantation Society (Société de Transplantation): Central Business Office, 205 Viger Ave West, Suite 201, Montreal, QC H2Z 1G2, Canada; tel. (514) 874-1998; fax (514) 874-1580; e-mail info@ transplantation-soc.org; internet www.transplantation-soc.org; f. 1966; over 3,000 members in 65 countries; Pres. Dr DAVID E. R. SUTHERLAND; Exec. Sec. (vacant).

World Federation of Associations of Poison Centres and Clinical Toxicology Centres: c/o Prof. Louis Roche, CIRC, 150 cours Albert-Thomas, 69372 Lyon, Cédex 2, France; tel. 7-874-1674; f. 1975 as World Federation of Associations of Clinical Toxicology Centres and Poison Control Centres; mems: 37; Pres. Dr HANS PERSSON (Sweden); Sec.-Gen. Prof. LOUIS ROCHE; ; publ. *Bulletin of the World Federation* (quarterly).

OTHER ORGANIZATIONS

Aerospace Medical Association—AsMA: 320 S. Henry St, Alexandria, VA 22314-3579, USA; tel. (703) 739-2240; fax (703) 739-9652; e-mail rrayman@asma.org; internet www.asma.org; f. 1929 as Aero Medical Association; aims to advance the science and art of aviation and space medicine; establishes and maintains co-operation between medical and allied sciences concerned with aerospace medicine; works to promote, protect, and maintain safety in aviation and astronautics; mems: individual, constituent and corporate in 75 countries; Pres. Dr CLAUDE THIBEAULT (Canada); Exec. Dir RUSSELL B. RAYMAN (USA); publ. *Aviation Space and Environmental Medicine* (monthly).

Asian-Pacific Dental Federation—APDF: c/o Dr J. Annan, 16 The Terrace, Wellington, New Zealand; tel. 4472-5516; fax 4472-5448; e-mail jannan@apdf.info; internet www.apdf.info; f. 1955 to establish closer relationships among dental asscns in Asian and Pacific countries and to encourage research on dental health in the region; holds Congress every year; mems: 23 national asscns; Pres. Dr KEE-TAEK LEE; Sec.-Gen. Dr JEFF ANNAN; ; publ. *Asian Dentist* (every 2 months).

Association for Paediatric Education in Europe—APEE (Association pour l'Enseignement de la Pédatrie en Europe—AEPE): c/o Dr Claude Billeaud, Dept. Néonatal Médicine, Maternité-CHU Pellegrin, 33076 Bordeaux Cédex, France; tel. 5-56-79-55-39; fax 5-56-79-61-56; e-mail claude.billeaud@neonata.u-bordeaux2.fr; internet www.atinternet.com/apee; f. 1970 to promote research and practice in educational methodology in paediatrics; mems: 120 in 20 European countries; Pres. Dr JUAN BRINES (Spain); Sec.-Gen. Dr CLAUDE BILLEAUD (France).

Association of National European and Mediterranean Societies of Gastroenterology—ASNEMGE: c/o Andrea Bauer, Vereinsmanagement Lassingleithnerplatz 2/3, 1020 Vienna, Austria; tel. 1-533-35-42; fax 1-535-10-45; e-mail info@asnemge.org; internet www.asnemge.org; f. 1947 to facilitate the exchange of ideas between gastroenterologists and to disseminate knowledge; organizes International Congress of Gastroenterology every four years; mems: in 37 countries, national societies and sections of national medical societies; Pres. Prof. PETER FERENCI (Austria); Sec. Prof. JØRGEN RASK-MADSEN (Denmark).

Balkan Medical Union (Uniunii Medicale Balcanice—UMB): POB 149, 1 rue G. Clémenceau, 70148 Bucharest, Romania; tel. (1) 3137857; fax (1) 3121570; f. 1932; studies medical problems, particularly ailments specific to the Balkan region; promotes a regional programme of public health; facilitates the exchange of information between doctors in the region; organizes research programmes and congresses; mems: doctors and specialists from Albania, Bulgaria, Cyprus, Greece, Moldova, Romania, Turkey and the former Yugoslav republics; Pres. Prof. H. CIOBANU (Moldova); publs *Archives de l'union médicale Balkanique* (quarterly), *Bulletin de l'union médicale Balkanique* (6 a year), *Annuaire*.

Cystic Fibrosis Worldwide: Bosbes 12, 5708 DA Helmond, Netherlands; tel. (492) 520-241; fax (492) 599-068; e-mail info@cfww.org; internet www.cfww.org; f. 2003 by merger of the International Association of Cystic Fibrosis Adults and International Cystic Fibrosis (Muscoviscidosis) Association (f. 1964); promotes the development of lay organizations and the advancement of knowledge among medical, scientific and health professionals in underdeveloped areas; convenes annual conference, 2003: Belfast, UK; 2004: Birmingham, UK; Pres. HERMAN WEGGEN (Netherlands); Sec. GINA STEEKAMER (Netherlands); publs: *Annual Report*, *CFW Newsletter* (quarterly), *Joseph Levy Lecture*, Physiotherapy booklet.

European Association for Cancer Research—EACR: c/o P. Saunders, The Pharmacy School, Univ. of Nottingham, University Park, Nottingham, NG7 2RD, United Kingdom; tel. and fax (115) 9515114; e-mail paul.saunders@nottingham.ac.uk; internet www .eacr.org; f. 1968 to facilitate contact between cancer research workers and to organize scientific meetings in Europe; mems: over 5,000 in more than 40 European and other countries; Pres. E. OLAH; Sec. Prof. HELGA ÖGMUNDSDÓTTIR (Iceland).

European Association for the Study of Diabetes—EASD: Rheindorfer Weg 3 40591 Düsseldorf, Germany Germany; tel. (211) 75-84-69; fax (211) 75-84-69; e-mail secretariat@easd.org; internet www.easd.org; f. 1965 to support research in the field of diabetes, to promote the rapid diffusion of acquired knowledge and its application; holds annual scientific meetings within Europe; mems: 6,000 in 101 European and other countries; Pres. Prof. P. A. HALBAN (Switzerland); Exec. Dir Dr VIKTOR JÖRGENS (Germany); publ. *Diabetologia* (13 a year).

European Association of Radiology: c/o Prof. Dr P. Vock, Institut für Diagnostische Radiologie der Universität Bern, Inselspital, 3010 Bern, Switzerland; tel. (31) 632-24-35; fax (31) 632-48-74; e-mail peter.vock@insel.ch; internet www.ear-online.org; f. 1962 to develop and co-ordinate the efforts of radiologists in Europe by promoting radiology in both biology and medicine, studying its problems, developing professional training and establishing contact between radiologists and professional, scientific and industrial organizations; mems: national asscns in 40 countries; Sec.-Gen. Prof. Dr PETER VOCK; publs *EAR Newsletter, European Radiology* (monthly).

European Association of Social Medicine: Corso Bramante 83, 10126 Turin, Italy; f. 1953 to provide co-operation between national asscns of preventive medicine and public health; mems: asscns in 14 countries; Pres. Dr JEAN-PAUL FOURNIER (France); Sec.-Gen. Prof. Dr ENRICO BELLI (Italy).

European Brain and Behaviour Society—EBSS: c/o Dr M. Ammassari-Teule, Istituto di Psicobiologia e Psicofarmacologia, CNR, IRCCS S. Lucia Foundation, Via Ardeatina 306, I-00179 Rome, Italy; tel. (06) 51501511; fax (06) 5034038; e-mail ebbs@ hsantalucia.it; internet www.ebbs-science.org; f. 1969; holds one conference a year and organizes workshops; Pres. SUSAN J. SARA (France); Sec.-Gen. Dr MARTINE AMMASSARI-TEULE (Italy); publ. *Newsletter*.

European Federation of Internal Medicine—EFIM: c/o Dr Davidson, Royal Sussex County Hospital, Eastern Rd, Brighton, BN2 5BE, United Kingdom; tel. (1273) 696955; fax (1273) 684554; e-mail chris.davidson@bsuh.nhs.uk; internet www.efim.org; f. 1969 as European Asscn of Internal Medicine (present name adopted 1996); aims to bring together European specialists, and establish communication between them, to promote internal medicine; organizes congresses and meetings; provides information; mems: 29 European societies of internal medicine; Pres. Prof. JAIME MERIO; Sec. Dr CHRISTOPHER DAVIDSON; publ. *European Journal of Internal Medicine* (8 a year).

European Health Management Association—EHMA: Vergemount Hall, Clonskeagh, Dublin 6, Ireland; tel. (1) 2839299; fax (1) 2838653; e-mail pcberman@ehma.org; internet www.ehma.org; f. 1966; aims to improve health care in Europe by raising standards of managerial performance in the health sector; fosters co-operation between health service organizations and institutions in the field of health-care management education and training; mems: 225 in 30 countries; Pres. Prof. JOAN HIGGINS; Dir PHILIP C. BERMAN; publs *Newsletter, Eurobriefing* (quarterly).

European League against Rheumatism—EULAR: Witikonerstr. 15, 8032 Zürich, Switzerland; tel. (1) 3839690; fax (1) 3839810; e-mail secretariat@eular.org; internet www.eular.org; f. 1947 to co-ordinate research and treatment of rheumatic complaints; holds an annual Congress; mems: in 41 countries; Exec. Sec. F. WYSS; publ. *Annals of the Rheumatic Diseases*.

European Organization for Caries Research—ORCA: c/o Lutz Stösser, Dept of Preventive Dentistry, Dental School of Erfurt, Univ. of Jena, Nordhauser Str. 78, 99089 Erfurt, Germany; tel. (361) 7411205; e-mail stoesser@zmkh.ef.uni-jena.de; internet www .orca-caries-research.org; f. 1953 to promote and undertake research on dental health, encourage international contacts, and make the public aware of the importance of care of the teeth; mems: research workers in 23 countries; Pres. Prof. BIRGIT ANGMAR-MANSSON (Sweden); Sec.-Gen. Prof. L. STÖSSER (Germany); publ. *Caries Research*.

European Orthodontic Society—EOS: Flat 20, 49 Hallam St, London, W1W 6JN, United Kingdom; tel. (20) 7935-2795; fax (20) 7323-0410; e-mail eoslondon@compuserve.com; internet www .eoseurope.org; f. 1907 (name changed in 1935), to advance the science of orthodontics and its relations with the collateral arts and sciences; mems: 2,784 in 80 countries; Sec. Prof. L. DERMANT; publ. *European Journal of Orthodontics* (6 a year).

European Union of Medical Specialists (Union Européenne des Médecins Spécialistes—UEMS): 20 ave de la Couronne, Brussels 1050, Belgium; tel. (2) 649-51-64; fax (2) 640-37-30; e-mail uems@skynet.be; internet www.uems.be; f. 1958 to harmonize and improve the quality of medical specialist practices in the EU and safeguard the interests of medical specialists; seeks formulation of common training policy; mems: two representatives each from Austria, Belgium, Denmark, Finland, France, Germany, Greece, Iceland, Ireland, Italy, Luxembourg, Netherlands, Norway, Portugal, Spain, Sweden, Switzerland, United Kingdom; Pres. Dr H. HALILA (Finland); Sec.-Gen. Dr B. MAILLET (Belgium).

Eurotransplant International Foundation: POB 2304, 2301 CH Leiden, Netherlands; tel. (71) 5795795; fax (71) 5790057; internet www.eurotransplant.nl; f. 1967; co-ordinates the exchange of organs for transplants in Austria, Belgium, Germany, Luxembourg, Netherlands and Slovenia; keeps register of c. 15,000 patients with all necessary information for matching with suitable donors in the shortest possible time; organizes transport of the organ and transplantation; collaborates with similar organizations in western and eastern Europe; Dirs Dr B. COHEN, Dr G. G. PERSIJN.

Federation of French-Language Obstetricians and Gynaecologists (Fedération des gynécologues et obstetriciens de langue française—FGOLF): Clinique Baudelocque, 123 blvd de Port-Royal, 75674 Paris Cédex 14, France; tel. 1-42-34-11-43; fax 1-42-34-12-31; f. 1920 for the scientific study of phenomena having reference to obstetrics, gynaecology and reproduction in general; mems: 1,500 in 50 countries; Pres. Prof. H. RUF (France); Gen. Sec. Prof. J. R. ZORN (France); publ. *Journal de Gynécologie Obstétrique et Biologie de la Reproduction* (8 a year).

Federation of the European Dental Industry (Fédération de l'Industrie Dentaire en Europe—FIDE): Kirchweg 2, 50858 Cologne, Germany; ; tel. (221) 948628; fax (221) 483428; e-mail shelton@fide-online.org; internet www.fide-online.org; f. 1957 to promote the interests of the dental industry; mems: national asscns in 10 European countries; Pres. and Chair. Dr ALESSANDRO GAMBERINI (Germany); Sec. HARALD RUSSEGGER (Germany).

General Association of Municipal Health and Technical Experts: 83 ave Foch, BP 3916, 75761 Paris Cédex 16, France; tel. 1-53-70-13-53; fax 1-53-70-13-40; e-mail aghtm@aghtm.org; internet www.aghtm.org; f. 1905 to study all questions related to urban and rural health; mems: in 35 countries; Dir-Gen. ALAIN LASALMONIE (France); publ. *TSM-Techniques, Sciences, Méthodes* (monthly).

Inter-American Association of Sanitary and Environmental Engineering (Asociación Interamericana de Ingeniería Sanitaria y Ambiental—AIDIS): Rua Nicolau Gagliardi 354, 05429-010 São Paulo, SP, Brazil; tel. (11) 3812-4080; fax (11) 3814-2441; e-mail aidis@aidis.org.br; internet www.aidis.org.br; f. 1948 to assist in the development of water supply and sanitation; mems: 32 countries; Pres. HORST OTTERSTETTER (Brazil); Exec. Dir LUIZ AUGUSTO DE LIMA PONTES (Brazil); publs *Revista Ingeniería Sanitaria* (quarterly), *Desafío* (quarterly).

International Academy of Aviation and Space Medicine—IAASM: c/o Dr G. Takahashi, 21 Antares Dr., Suite 112, Ottawa, ON K2E 7T8, Canada; tel. (613) 228-9345; fax (613) 228-0242; e-mail g.takahashi@sympatico.ca; internet www.iaasm.org; f. 1955 to facilitate international co-operation in research and teaching in the fields of aviation and space medicine; mems: in 42 countries; Pres. Dr ULF BALLDIN (USA); Sec.-Gen. Dr GEORGE TAKAHASHI (Canada).

International Academy of Cytology: Burgunderstr. 1, 79104 Freiburg, Germany; tel. (761) 292-3801; fax (761) 292-3802; e-mail centraloffice@cytology-iac.org; internet www.cytology-iac.org; f. 1957 to facilitate the international exchange of information on specialized problems of clinical cytology, to stimulate research and to standardize terminology; mems: 2,400; Pres. G. PETER VOOIJS; Sec. VOLKER SCHNEIDER; publs *Acta Cytologica, Analytical and Quantitative Cytology and Histology* (both every 2 months).

International Agency for the Prevention of Blindness—IAPB: L. V. Prasad Eye Institute, L. V. Prasad Marg, Banjara Hills, Hyderabad 500 034, India; tel. (40) 2354-5389; fax (40) 2354-8271; e-mail iapb@lvpeye.stph.net; internet www.iapb.org; f. 1975; promotes advocacy and information sharing on the prevention of blindness; aims to encourage the formation of national prevention of blindness committees and programmes; has an official relationship with WHO; Pres. Dr HANNAH B. FAAL (The Gambia); Sec.-Gen. Dr GULLAPALLI N. RAO (India); publ. *IAPB News*.

International Anatomical Congress: c/o Prof. Dr Wolfgang Kühnel, Institut für Anatomie, Medizinische Universität zu Lübeck, Ratzeburger Allee 160, 23538 Lübeck, Germany; tel. (451) 500-4030; fax (451) 500-4034; e-mail buchuel@anet.mu-luebeck.de; internet www.anet.mu-luebeck.de/anetpes.html; f. 1903; runs international congresses for anatomists to discuss research, teaching methods and terminology in the fields of gross and microscopical anatomy, histology, cytology, etc; Pres. J. ESPERENCA-PINE (Portugal); Sec.-Gen. Prof. Dr WOLFGANG KÜHNEL (Germany); publ. *Annals of Anatomy*.

International Association for Child and Adolescent Psychiatry and Allied Professions—IACAPAP: c/o Dr I. M. Goodyer, Univ. of Cambridge, Douglas House, 18b Trumpington Rd, Cambridge CB2 2AH, United Kingdom; tel. (1223) 336-098; fax (1223) 746-1225; e-mail ig104@cus.cam.ac.uk; internet www.iacapap.org; f. 1937 to promote scientific research in the field of child psychiatry by collaboration with allied professions; mems: national asscns and individuals in 42 countries; Pres. Prof. HELMUT REMSCHMIDT; Sec.-Gen. Dr IAN M. GOODYER; publs *The Child in the Family* (Yearbook of the IACAPP), *Newsletter*.

International Association for Dental Research—IADR: 1619 Duke St, Alexandria, VA 22314, USA; tel. (703) 548-0066; fax (703) 548-1883; e-mail research@iadr.com; internet www.dentalresearch.org; f. 1920 to encourage research in dentistry and related fields; holds annual meetings, triennial conferences and divisional meetings; Pres. Dr JOHN CLARKSON; Exec. Dir Dr ROBERT COLLINS.

International Association for the Study of Obesity—IASO:: 231 North Gower St, London, NW1 2NS, United Kingdom; e-mail inquiries@iaso.org; internet www.iaso.org; f. 1986; supports research into the prevention and management of obesity throughout the world and disseminates inormation regarding disease and accompanying health and social issues; incorporates the International Obesity Task Force; international congress every four years (2002: Sao Paulo, Brazil); Exec. Dir KATE BAILLIE.

International Association of Agricultural Medicine and Rural Health—IAAMRH: ul.Marszalkowska 82, 00517 Warsaw, Poland; tel. and fax (22) 623-6551; e-mail kris@krus.gov.pl; internet www.iaamrh.org; f. 1961 to study the problems of medicine in agriculture in all countries and to prevent the diseases caused by the conditions of work in agriculture; mems: 405; Pres. Dr ASHOK PATIL (India); Gen. Sec. Dr ANDRZEJ WOJTYLA (Poland).

International Association of Applied Psychology—IAAP: c/o Prof. José M. Prieto, Universidad Complutense, Facultad de Psicología, Despacho 2218, Somosaguas, 28223 Madrid, Spain; fax (91) 351-0091; e-mail iaap@psi.ucm.es; internet www.iaapsy.org; f. 1920, present title adopted in 1955; aims to establish contacts between those carrying out scientific work on applied psychology, to promote research and to encourage the adoption of measures contributing to this work; organizes International Congress of Applied Psychology every four years (2006: Athens, Greece) and co-sponsors International Congress of Psychology every two years (2004: Beijing, People's Republic of China); mems: 2,200 in 94 countries; Pres. Prof. MICHAEL FRESE (Germany); Sec.-Gen. Prof. JOSÉ. M. PRIETO (Spain); publ. *Applied Psychology: An International Review* (quarterly).

International Association of Asthmology—INTERASMA: c/o Prof. Hugo Neffen, Irigoyen Freyre 2670, 3000 Santa Fé, Argentina; tel. (42) 453-7638; fax (42) 456-9773; e-mail interasm@neffen.satlink.net; internet www.asmanet.com; f. 1954 to advance medical knowledge of bronchial asthma and allied disorders; mems: 1,100 in 54 countries; Pres. Prof. GAETANO MELILLO (Italy); Sec./Treas. Prof. H. NEFFEN; publs *Interasma News, Journal of Investigative Allergology and Clinical Immunology* (every 2 months), *Allergy and Clinical Immunology International* (every 2 months).

International Association of Gerontology—IAG: IAG Secretariat, Gerontology Research Centre, Simon Fraser Univ. at Harbour Centre 2800, 515 West Hastings St, Vancouver, BC V3C 5K3, Canada; tel. (604) 268-7972; fax (604) 291-5066; e-mail iag@sfu.ca; internet www.sfu.ca/iag; f. 1950 to promote research and training in all fields of gerontology and to protect the interests of gerontologic societies and institutions; holds World Congress every four years; mems: 63 national societies in 60 countries; Pres. Prof. GLORIA M. GUTMAN (Canada); Sec.-Gen. JOHN E. GRAY (Canada); publ. *IAG Newsletter* (2 a year).

International Association of Group Psychotherapy: c/o Dr D. Mattke, Rhein-Klinik, Bad Honnef, Leitender Arzt der Abteilung I, Luisenstr. 3, 53604 Bad Honnef, Germany; e-mail info@iagp.com; internet www.iagp.com; f. 1954; holds congresses every three years; mems: in 35 countries; Pres. SABAR RUSTOMJEE (Australia); Sec. Dr DANKWART MATTKE (Germany); publs *Newsletter, Forum* (2 a year),*Yearbook of Group Psychotherapies*.

International Association of Hydatidology: Florida 460, 3°, 1005 Buenos Aires, Argentina; tel. (11) 4322-2030; fax (11) 4325-8231; f. 1941; mems: 1,200 in 41 countries; Pres. Dr RAÚL MARTÍN MENDY; Sec.-Gen. Dr JORGE ALFREDO IRIARTE (Argentina); publs *Archivos Internacionales de la Hidatidosis* (every 2 years), *Boletín de Hidatidosis* (quarterly).

International Association of Logopedics and Phoniatrics—IALP: 43 Louis de Savoie, 1110 Morges, Switzerland; fax (21) 3209300; e-mail h.k.schutte@med.rug.nl; internet www1.ldc.lu.se/logopedi/IALP; f. 1924 to promote standards of training and research in human communication disorders, to establish information centres and communicate with kindred organizations; mems: 125,000 in 60 societies from 54 countries; Pres. Prof. HARM SCHUTTE (Netherlands); publ. *Folia Phoniatrica et Logopedica* (6 a year).

International Association of Oral and Maxillofacial Surgeons —IAOMS: 9700 W. Bryn Mawr, Suite 210, Rosemont, ILL 60018-5701, USA; tel. (847) 678-9370; fax (847) 678-9380; e-mail lsavler@iaoms.org; internet www.iaoms.org; f. 1963 to advance the science and art of oral and maxillofacial surgery; organizes biennial international conference; mems: over 3,000; Pres. PAUL J. STOELINGA (Netherlands); Exec. Dir VICTOR MONCARZ (Canada); publs *International Journal of Oral and Maxillofacial Surgery* (every 2 months), *Newsletter*.

International Brain Research Organization—IBRO: 51 blvd de Montmorency, 75016 Paris, France; tel. 1-46-47-92-92; fax 1-45-20-60-06; e-mail ibro@wanadoo.fr; internet www.ibro.org; f. 1958 to further all aspects of brain research; mems: 45 corporate, 16 academic and 51,000 individual; Pres. Prof. T. N. WIESEL (USA); Sec.-Gen. Prof. A. J. AGUAYO (Canada); publs *IBRO News, Neuroscience* (bi-monthly).

International Bronchoesophagological Society: Mayo Clinic, 13400 E. Shea Blvd, Scottsdale, AZ 85259, USA; e-mail helmers.richard@mayo.edu; f. 1951 to promote the progress of bronchoesophagology and to provide a forum for discussion among bronchoesophagologists with various medical and surgical specialities; holds Congress every two years; mems: 500 in 37 countries; Exec. Sec. Dr RICHARD A. HELMERS.

International Bureau for Epilepsy—IBE: POB 21, 2100 AA Heemstede, Netherlands; tel. (23) 5237411; fax (23) 5470119; e-mail ibe@sein.nl; internet www.ibe-epilepsy.org; f. 1961; collects and disseminates information about social and medical care for people with epilepsy; organizes international and regional meetings; advises and answers questions on social aspects of epilepsy; mems: 59 national epilepsy organizations; Sec.-Gen. ESPER CAVALHEIRO; publ. *International Epilepsy News* (quarterly).

International Catholic Committee of Nurses and Medico-Social Assistants (Comité International Catholique des Infirmières et Assistantes Médico-Sociales—CICIAMS): 43 Square Vergote, 1040 Brussels, Belgium; tel. (2) 732-10-50; fax (2) 734-84-60; e-mail an.verlinde@adamco.be; f. 1933 to group professional Catholic nursing asscns to represent Christian thought in the general professional field at international level; to co-operate in the general development of the profession and to promote social welfare; mems: 49 full, 20 corresponding mems; Pres. RICHARD LAI; Gen. Sec. AN VERLINDE; publ. *Nouvelles/News/Nachrichten* (3 a year).

International Cell Research Organization—ICRO (Organisation Internationale de Recherche sur la Cellule): c/o UNESCO, SC/BES/LSC, 1 rue Miollis, 75015 Paris, France; fax 1-45-68-58-16; e-mail icro@unesco.org; internet www.unesco.org/icro; f. 1962 to create, encourage and promote co-operation between scientists of different disciplines throughout the world for the advancement of fundamental knowledge of the cell, normal and abnormal; organizes international laboratory courses on modern topics of cell and molecular biology and biotechnology for young research scientists; mems: 400; Pres. Prof. JORGE E. ALLENDE (Chile); Exec. Sec. Prof. GEORGES N. COHEN (France).

International Centre for Diarrhoeal Disease Research, Bangladesh—ICDDR, B: GPO Box 128, Dhaka 1000Bangladesh; tel. (2) 8811751; fax (2) 8823116; e-mail info@icddrb.org; internet www.icddrb.org; f. 1960; undertakes research, training and information dissemination on diarrhoeal diseases, child health and child survival, reproductive health, women's health, nutrition, emerging infectious diseases, environmental health, vaccine evaluation and case management, with particular reference to developing countries; supported by 55 governments and international organizations; Dir Prof. DAVID A. SACK; Sec Dr SHAH ALAM; publs *Annual Report, Journal of Health, Population and Nutrition* (quarterly), *Glimpse* (quarterly), *Shasthya Sanglap* (3 a year), *DISC Bulletin* (weekly), scientific reports, working papers, monographs.

International Chiropractors' Association: 1110 North Glebe Rd, Suite 1000, Arlington, VA 22201, USA; tel. (703) 528-5000; fax (703) 528-5023; e-mail chiro@chiropractic.org; internet www.chiropractic.org; f. 1926 to promote advancement of the art and science of chiropractors; mems: 7,000 individuals, and affiliated asscns; Pres. Dr D. D. HUMBER; Exec. Dir RONALD M. HENDRICKSON; publs *International Review of Chiropractic* (every 2 months), *ICA Today* (every 2 months).

International Commission on Occupational Health—ICOH: Dept of Community, Occupational and Family Medicine, MD3, National University of Singapore, 16 Medical Drive, Singapore 117597; tel. 6874-49595; fax 6779-1489; e-mail icohsg@singnet.com.sg; internet www.icoh.org.sg; f. 1906, present name adopted 1985; aims to study and prevent pathological conditions arising from industrial work; arranges congresses on occupational medicine and the protection of workers' health; provides information for public authorities and learned societies; mems: 1,944 in 89 countries; Pres. Prof. BENGT KNAVE (Sweden); Sec.-Gen. Prof. CHIA KEE SENG (Singapore); publ. *Newsletter* (electronic version).

International Commission on Radiological Protection—ICRP: 17116 Stockholm, Sweden; tel. (8) 729-72-75; fax (8) 729-72-98; e-mail jack.valentin@ssi.se; internet www.icrp.org; f. 1928 to provide technical guidance and promote international co-operation in the field of radiation protection; committees on Radiation Effects, Doses from Radiation Exposure, Protection in Medicine, and the Application of Recommendations; mems: c. 70; Chair. Prof. R. H. CLARKE (UK); Scientific Sec. Dr J. VALENTIN (Sweden); publ. *Annals of the ICRP*.

International Council for Physical Activity and Fitness Research—ICPAFR: Prof. A. L. Claessens, Faculty of Physical Education and Physiotherapy, Catholic Univ. of Leuven, Tervuurse Vest 101, 3001 Heverlee (Leuven), Belgium; tel. (16) 32-90-83; fax (16) 32-91-97; e-mail albrecht.claessens@flok.kuleuven.ac.be; internet www.unipid.it/esterni/wwwmedic/servizi.htm; f. 1964 to construct international standardized physical fitness tests, to encourage research based upon the standardized tests and to enhance participation in physical activity; mems: some 35 countries; Pres. Prof. ALBRECHT L. CLAESSENS (Belgium); Sec. Treas. Prof. ANDREW HILLS; publs *International Guide to Fitness and Health*, proceedings of seminars and symposia, other fitness and health publs.

International Council of Nurses—ICN: 3 place Jean-Marteau, 1201 Geneva, Switzerland; tel. (22) 9080100; fax (22) 9080101; e-mail icn@icn.ch; internet www.icn.ch; f. 1899 to allow national asscns of nurses to work together to develop the contribution of nursing to the promotion of health; holds quadrennial Congresses; mems: 124 national nurses' asscns; Pres. CHRISTINE HANCOCK (UK); Exec. Dir JUDITH OULTON; publ. *The International Nursing Review* (4 a year, in English).

International Epidemiological Association—IEA: Suite 840, 111 Market Place, Baltimore, MD 21202-6709, USA; tel. (410) 223-1600; fax (410) 223-1620; e-mail harmenia@jhsph.edu; internet www.dundee.ac.uk/iea; f. 1954; mems: 2,237; Pres. and Chair. Dr RODOLFO SARACCI; Sec. Prof. HAROUTUNE ARMENIAN; publ. *International Journal of Epidemiology* (6 a year).

International Federation for Medical and Biological Engineering—IFMBE: c/o Heikki Terio, Dept of Biomedical Engineering, Huddinge Univ. Hospital, SE 14186, Stockholm, Sweden; tel. (8) 5858-0852; fax (8) 5858-0852; e-mail heikki.terio@mta.hs.sll.se; internet www.ifmbe.org; f. 1959; mems: organizations in 40 countries; Sec.-Gen. HEIKKI TERIO (Netherlands).

International Federation for Medical Psychotherapy—IFMP: c/o Prof. E. Heim, Tannackstr. 3, 3653 Oberhofen, Switzerland; tel. and fax (33) 2431141; e-mail senf-blum@t-online.de; f. 1946 to further research and teaching of psychotherapy; organizes international congresses; mems: c. 6,000 psychotherapists from around 40 countries, 36 societies; Pres. Dr EDGAR HEIM (Switzerland); Sec.-Gen. Prof. Dr WOLFGANG SENE (Germany).

International Federation of Fertility Societies—IFFS: c/o CSI, 337 rue de la Combe Caude, 34090 Montpellier, France; tel. 4-67-63-53-40; fax 4-67-41-94-27; e-mail algcsi@mnet.fr; f. 1951 to study problems of fertility and sterility; Pres. ROBERT F. HARRISON; Sec.-Gen. Prof. BERNARD HEDON; publ. *Newsletter* (2 a year).

International Federation of Gynecology and Obstetrics—FIGO: 70 Wimpole St, London, W1X 8AG, United Kingdom; tel. (20) 7224-3270; fax (20) 7935-0736; e-mail figo@figo.org; internet www.figo.org; f. 1954; aims to improve standards in gynaecology and obstetrics, promote better health care for women, facilitate the exchange of information, and perfect methods of teaching; mems: national societies in 102 countries; Pres. Dr SHIRISH S. SHETH (India); Sec.-Gen. Prof. G. BENAGIANO (Italy); publ. *International Journal of Obstetrics and Gynecology*.

International Federation of Ophthalmological Societies: c/o Dr Bruce E. Spivey, 945 Green St, San Francisco, CA 94133, USA; tel. (415) 409-8410; fax (415) 409-8403; e-mail icoph@icoph.org; internet www.icoph.org; f. 1927; works to support and develop ophthalmology, especially in developing countries; carries out education and assessment projects; promotes clinical standards; holds International Congress every four years; Pres. Prof. G. O. H. NAUMANN (Germany); Sec. Dr BRUCE E. SPIVEY.

International Hospital Federation—IHF (Fédération Internationale des Hôpitaux—FIH): 13 chemin du Levant,01210 Ferney Voltaire, France; tel. 4 -50-42-60-00; fax 4-50-42-60-01; e-mail info@ihf-fih.org; internet www.hospitalmanagement.net; f. 1947 for information exchange and education in hospital and health service matters; represents institutional health care in discussions with WHO; conducts conferences and courses on management and policy issues; mems in five categories: national hospital and health service organizations; professional asscns, regional organizations and individual hospitals; individual mems; professional and industrial mems; honorary mems; Dir-Gen. Prof. PER-GUNNAR SVENSSON; publs *World Hospitals and Health Services* (quarterly), *Hospitals International* (quarterly), *Hospital Management International (Yearbook1)*, *New World Health (Yearbook 2)*.

International League against Epilepsy—ILAE: 204 ave Marcel Thiry, 1200 Brussels, Belgium;; tel. (2) 774-9547; fax (2) 774-9690; e-mail dsartiaux@ilae-epilepsy.org; internet www.ilae-epilepsy.org; f. 1909 to link national professional asscns and to encourage research, including classification and the development of anti-epileptic drugs; collaborates with the International Bureau for Epilepsy and with WHO; mems: 72 asscns; Pres. GIULIANO AVANZINI; Sec.-Gen. NATALIO FEJERMAN.

International Narcotics Control Board—INCB: 1400 Vienna, POB 500, Austria; tel. (1) 260-60-42-77; fax (1) 260-60-58-67; e-mail secretariat@incb.org; internet www.incb.org; f. 1961 by the Single Convention on Narcotic Drugs, to supervise implementation of drug control treaties by governments; mems: 13 individuals; Pres. PHILIP EMATO (Iran); Sec. HERBERT SCHAEPE (Germany); publ. *Annual Report* (with three technical supplements).

International Opticians' Association: Godmersham Park Mansion, Godmersham, Canterbury, Kent, CT4 7DT, United Kingdom; tel. (1227) 733901; fax (1227) 733900; e-mail general@abdo.org.uk; internet www.abdo.org.uk; f. 1951 to promote the science of opthalmology, and to maintain and advance standards and effect co-operation in optical dispensing; Gen. Sec. Sir ANTHONY GARRETT; Pres. C. J. PACKFORD; publs *ABDO Frame Rule, Dispensing Optics* (monthly).

International Organization for Medical Physics—IOMP: c/o Prof. Gary D. Fullerton, UTHSCSA, Dept of Radiology, MSC 7800, 7703 Floyd Curl Drive, San Antonio, TX 78229-3900, USA; tel. (210) 567-5551; fax (210) 567-5549; e-mail iomp@uthscsa.edu; internet www.iomp.org; f. 1963 to organize international co-operation in medical physics, to promote communication between the various branches of medical physics and allied subjects, to contribute to the advancement of medical physics in all its aspects and to advise on the formation of national organizations; mems: national organizations of medical physics in over 70 countries; Pres. Prof. OSKAR CHOMICKI (Poland); Sec.-Gen. Prof. GARY FULLERTON; publ. *Medical Physics World*.

International Pharmaceutical Federation (Fédération Internationale Pharmaceutique—FIP): POB 84200, 2508 AE, The Hague, Netherlands; tel. (70) 302-1970; fax (70) 302-1999; e-mail secretariat@fip.org; internet www.fip.org; f. 1912;; aims to represent and serve pharmacy and pharmaceutical sciences world-wide and to improve access to medecines; holds World Congress of Pharmacy and Pharmaceutical Sciences annually; mems: 86 national pharmaceutical organizations in 62 countries, 55 associate, supportive and collective mems, 4,000 individuals; Dir A. J. M (TON) HOEK (Netherlands); publ. *International Pharmacy Journal* (2 a year).

International Psycho-Analytical Association—IPA: Broomhills, Woodside Lane, London, N12 8UD, United Kingdom; tel. (20) 8446-8324; fax (20) 8445-4729; e-mail ipa@ipa.org.uk; internet www.ipa.org.uk; f. 1908; holds meetings to define and promulgate the theory and teaching of psychoanalysis; acts as a forum for scientific discussions; controls and regulates training; contributes to the interdisciplinary area common to the behavioural sciences; mems: 11,000 in 34 countries; Pres. Prof. DANIEL WIDLÖCHER; Sec.-Gen. ALAIN GIBEAULT; publs *Bulletin, Newsletter*.

International Society for Cardiovascular Surgery—ISCVS: Cummings Center, Beverly, MA 01915, USA; tel. (978) 927-8330; fax (978) 524-8890; e-mail iscvs@prri.com; internet iscvs.vascularweb .org; f. 1950 to stimulate research on the diagnosis and therapy of cardiovascular diseases and to exchange ideas on an international basis; Pres. JAMES MAY (USA); Sec.-Gen. Dr LAZAR J. GREENFIELD (USA); publ. *Cardiovascular Surgery*.

International Society for Oneiric Mental Imagery Techniques: c/o Odile Dorkel, 56 rue Sedaine, 75011 Paris, France; tel. 1-47-00-16-63; e-mail odile.orkel@wanadoo.fr; links a group of research workers, technicians and psychotherapists using oneirism techniques under waking conditions, with the belief that a healing action cannot be dissociated from the restoration of creativity; mems: in 17 countries; Pres. ODILE DORKEL (France); Sec.-Gen. JEAN-FRANÇOIS CESARO (France).

International Society of Developmental Biologists: c/o Dr Paul T. van der Saag, Hubrecht Laboratorium/Netherlands Institute for Developmental Biology, Uppsalalaan 8, 3584 CT, Utrecht, Netherlands; tel. (30) 2510-211; e-mail directie@niob.knaw.nl; internet www.elsevier.com/inca/homepage/sah/isdb; f. 1911 as International Institute of Embryology; aims to promote the study of developmental biology and to encourage international co-operation among investigators in the field; mems: 850 in 33 countries; Pres. Prof. EDWARD M. DE ROBERTIS (USA); International Sec. Prof. BEN SCHERES (Netherlands); publ. *Mechanisms of Development*.

International Society of Lymphology: Room 4406, University of Arizona, 1501 North Campbell Ave, POB 245063, Tucson, AZ 85724-5063, USA; tel. (520) 626-6118; fax (520) 626-0822; e-mail lymph@u .arizona.edu; internet www.u.arizona.edu/~witte/ISL.htm; f. 1966 to further progress in lymphology through personal contacts and the exchange of ideas; mems: 375 in 42 countries; Pres. A. PISSAS (France); Sec.-Gen. M. H. WITTE (USA); publ. *Lymphology* (quarterly).

International Society of Neuropathology: c/o Prof. Hannu Kalimo, Dept of Pathology, Turku University Hospital, 20520 Turku, Finland; tel. (2) 2611685; fax (2) 3337456; e-mail hkalimo@ mailhost.utu.fi; internet brainpath.medsch.ucla.edu/isn/isnhome .htm; Pres. Prof. SAMUEL K. LUDWIN (Canada); Sec.-Gen. Prof. HANNU KALIMO (Finland).

International Society of Orthopaedic Surgery and Traumatology (Société Internationale de Chirurgie Orthopédique): 40 rue Washington, bte 9, 1050 Brussels, Belgium; tel. (2) 648-68-23; fax (2) 649-86-01; e-mail edsecr@sicot.org; internet www.sicot.org; f. 1929; convenes world congresses every three years; mems: 102 countries, 3,000 individuals; Pres. Prof. JOHN C. Y. LEONG; Sec.-Gen. MAURICE HINSENKAMP; publ. *Newsletter* (every 2 months).

International Society for the Psychopathology of Expression and Art Therapy—SIPE: c/o Dr G. Roux, 27 rue du mal Joffre, 64000 Pau, France; tel. and fax 5-59-27-69-74; e-mail sipearther@aol .com; internet perso.wanadoo.fr/art.therapy; f. 1959 to bring together specialists interested in the problems of expression and artistic activities in connection with psychiatric, sociological and psychological research; mems: 625; Pres. Dr G. ROUX (France); Sec.-Gen. J. L. SUDRES (France); publ. *Newsletter* (quarterly).

International Society of Radiology—ISR: 7910 Woodmont Ave, Suite 800, Bethesda, Maryland 20814-3095, USA; tel. (301) 657-2652; fax (301) 907-8768; e-mail isr@isradiology.org; internet www .isradiology.org; f. 1953 to promote radiology world-wide; International Commissions on Radiation Units and Measurements (ICRUM), on Radiation Protection (ICRP), and on Radiological Education (ICRE); organizes biannual International Congress of Radiology; collaborates with WHO; mems: more than 50 national radiological societies; Pres. G. KLEMPFNER; Sec.-Gen. CLAUDE MANELFE; Exec. Dir OTHA W. LINTON; publ *Newsletter*.

International Society of Surgery—ISS: Netzibodenstr. 34, POB 1527, 4133 Pratteln, Switzerland; tel. (61) 8159666; fax (61) 8114775; e-mail surgery@iss-sic.ch; internet www.iss-sic.ch; f. 1902 to promote understanding between surgical disciplines; groups surgeons to address issues of interest to all surgical specialists; supports general surgery as a training base for abdominal surgery, surgery with integuments and endocrine surgery; organizes congresses, 40th World Congress of Surgery: Bangkok, Thailand (August 2003); mems: 4,000; Admin. Dir. VICTOR BERTSCHI; Sec.-Gen. Prof. FELIX HARDER; publ. *World Journal of Surgery* (monthly).

International Union against Tuberculosis and Lung Disease —IUATLD: 68 blvd St Michel, 75006 Paris, France; tel. 1-44-32-03-60; fax 1-43-29-90-87; e-mail union@iuatld.org; internet www.iuatld .org; f. 1920 to co-ordinate the efforts of anti-tuberculosis and respiratory disease asscns, to mobilize public interest, to assist control programmes and research around the world, to collaborate with governments and WHO and to promote conferences; mems: asscns in 165 countries, 3,000 individual mems; Pres. Prof. ANNE FANNING; Exec. Dir Dr NILS BILLO; publs *The International Journal of Tuberculosis and Lung Disease* (in English, with summaries in French and Spanish; incl. conference proceedings), *Newsletter*.

International Union for Health Promotion and Education— IUHPE: Immeuble le Berry, 2 rue Auguste Comte, 92170 Vanves, France; tel. 1-46-45-00-59; fax 1-46-45-00-45; e-mail mclamarre@ iuhpe.org; internet www.iuhpe.org; f. 1951; provides an international network for the exchange of practical information on developments in health promotion and education; promotes research; encourages professional training for health workers, teachers, social workers and others; holds a World Conference on Health Promotion and Health Education every three years; organizes regional conferences and seminars; mems: in more than 90 countries; Pres. Prof. MAURICE MITTELMARK (Norway); Exec. Dir MARIE-CLAUDE LAMARRE (France); publs. *Health Promotion InternationalPromotion and Education* (quarterly, in English, French and Spanish).

International Union of Therapeutics: c/o Prof. A. Pradalier, Hôpital Louis Mourier, 178 rue des Renouillers, 92701 Colombes, France; tel. 1-47-60-67-05; e-mail secretariat.medecine4@emr .ap-hop-paris.fr; f. 1934; international congress held every other year; mems: 500 from 22 countries; Pres. Prof. A. PRADALIER.

Middle East Neurosurgical Society: c/o Dr Fuad S. Haddad, Neurosurgical Department, American University Medical Centre,

POB 113-6044, Beirut, Lebanon; tel. (1) 347348; fax (1) 342517; e-mail gfhaddad@aub.edu.lb; f. 1958 to promote clinical advances and scientific research among its members and to spread knowledge of neurosurgery and related fields among all members of the medical profession in the Middle East; mems: 684 in nine countries; Pres. Dr FUAD S. HADDAD; Hon. Sec. Dr GEDEON MOHASSEB.

Multiple Sclerosis International Federation—MSIF: 3rd Floor, Skyline House, 200 Union St, London, SE1 0LX, United Kingdom; tel. (20) 7620-1911; fax (20) 7620-1922; e-mail info@msif .org; internet www.msif.org; f. 1965; co-ordinates the work of national multiple sclerosis organizations throughout the world; encourages scientific research into multiple sclerosis and related neurological diseases; helps to develop new and existing multiple sclerosis organizations; collects and disseminates information; Pres. PETER W. SCHNUDT; Chief Exec. CHRISTINE PURDY; publs *MSIF Annual Review* (annually), *MS: The Guide to Treatment and Management* (every 2 years), *MS in Focus* (2 a year), *MSIF Directory* (annually), *How To* series (annually).

Organization for Co-ordination in the Struggle against Endemic Diseases in Central Africa (Organisation de coordination pour la lutte contre les endémies en Afrique Centrale—OCEAC): BP 288, Yaoundé, Cameroon; tel. 23-22-32; fax 23-00-61; e-mail oceac@camnet.cm; internet www.cm.refer.org/site_oceac; f. 1965 to standardize methods of controlling endemic diseases, to co-ordinate national action, and to negotiate programmes of assistance and training on a regional scale; mems: Cameroon, Central African Republic, Chad, Republic of the Congo, Equatorial Guinea, Gabon; Sec.-Gen. Dr AUGUSTE BILONGO-MANÉNÉ; publ. *Bulletin de Liaison et de Documentation* (quarterly).

Pan-American Association of Ophthalmology—PAAO: 1301 South Bowen Rd, Suite 365, Arlington, TX 76013, USA; tel. (817) 265-2831; fax (817) 275-3961; e-mail info@paao.org; internet www .paao.org; f. 1939 to promote friendship within the profession and the dissemination of scientific information; holds biennial Congress (2003: Puerto Rico); mems: national ophthalmological societies and other bodies in 39 countries; Pres. Dr RUBENS BELFORT, Jr (USA); Exec. Dir Dr CRISTIÁN LUCO (Chile); publs *The Pan American* (2 a year), *El Noticiero* (quarterly).

Pan-Pacific Surgical Association: POB 61479 Honolulu, HI 96839, Hawaii,, USA; tel. (808) 941-1010; fax (808) 536-4141; e-mail ppsa.info@panpacificsurgical.org; internet www.panpacificsurgical .org; f. 1929 to bring together surgeons to exchange scientific knowledge relating to surgery and medicine, and to promote the improvement and standardization of hospitals and their services and facilities; congresses are held every two years; mems: 2,716 regular, associate and senior mems from 44 countries; Pres. JOHN WONG; Chair. THOMAS KOSASA.

Society of French-speaking Neuro-Surgeons (Société de neurochirurgie de langue française—SNLF): c/o Prof. C .Raftopoulos, ave Hippocrate 10, 1200, Brussels, Belgium; tel. (2) 764-10-88; fax (2) 764-89-61; e-mail Raftopoulos@chir.ucl.ac.be; internet www.snclf .com; f. 1949; holds annual convention and congress; mems: 700; Pres. Prof. YVES KERAVEL (France); Sec. Prof. CHRISTIAN RAFTOPOULOS (Belgium); publ. *Neurochirurgie* (6 a year).

World Association for Disaster and Emergency Medicine—WADEM: 3330 University Ave, Room 352, Madison, WI 53705, USA; tel. (608) 263-2069; fax (608) 265-3037; e-mail mlb@medicine .wisc.edu; internet wadem.medicine.wisc.edu; f. 1976 to improve the world-wide delivery of emergency and humanitarian care in mass casualty and disaster situations, through training, symposia, and publications; mems: 600 in 62 countries; Pres. KNUT OLE SUNDNES (Norway); Sec. DEMETRIOS PYRROS (Greece); publ. *Prehospital and Disaster Medicine*.

World Association of Societies of Pathology and Laboratory Medecine—WASPaLM: c/o Japan Clinical Pathology Foundation for International Exchange, Sakura-Sugamo Bldg 7F, Sugamo 2-11-1, Toshima-ku, Tokyo 170, Japan; tel. (3) 3918-8161; fax (3) 3949-6168; internet www.waspalm.org; f. 1947 to link national societies and co-ordinate their scientific and technical means of action; promotes the development of anatomic and clinical pathology, especially by convening conferences, congresses and meetings, and through the interchange of publications and personnel; mems: 54 national asscns; Pres. Dr MIKIO MORI (Japan); Sec. KENNETH D. MCCLATCHEY (USA); publ. *Newsletter* (quarterly).

World Confederation for Physical Therapy—WCPT: 46–48 Grosvenor Gdns, London, SW1W 0EB, United Kingdom; tel. (20) 7881-9234; fax (20) 7881-9239; e-mail wcpt@dial.pipex.com; internet www.wcpt.org; f. 1951; represents physical therapy internationally; encourages high standards of physical therapy education and practice; promotes exchange of information among members, and the development of a scientific professional base through research; aims to contribute to the development of informed public opinion regarding physical therapy; holds seminars and workshops and quadrennial General Assembly; mems: 82 organizations; Pres.

SANDRA MERCER MOORE; Sec.-Gen. B. J. MYERS; publ. *Newsletter* (2 a year).

World Council of Optometry—WCO: 8360 Old York West, 4th Floor, Elkins Park, PA 19027, USA; e-mail wco@pco.edu; internet www.worldoptometry.org; f. 1927 to co-ordinate efforts to provide a good standard of ophthalmic optical (optometric) care throughout the world; enables exchange of ideas between different countries; focuses on optometric education; gives advice on standards of qualification; considers optometry legislation throughout the world; mems: 70 optometric organizations in 50 countries and four regional groups; Pres. Dr SCOTT D. BRISBIN (Canada); Exec. Dir Dr ANTONY DI STEFANO (USA); publ. *Interoptics* (quarterly).

World Federation for Mental Health—WFMH: POB 16810, Alexandria, VA 22302-0810, USA; tel. (703) 838-7543; fax (703) 519-7648; e-mail wfmh@erols.com; internet www.wfmh.org; f. 1948 to promote the highest standards of mental health; works with agencies of the United Nations in promoting mental health; assists other voluntary asscns in improving mental health services; mems: 250 national and international asscns in 115 countries; Pres.and Chief Exec. PRESTON J. GARRISON; publs *Newsletter* (quarterly), *Annual Report*.

World Federation of Hydrotherapy and Climatotherapy: Cattedra di Terapia Med. E Medic. Termal, Università degli Studi, via Cicognara 7, 20129 Milan, Italy; tel. (02) 50318456; fax (02) 50318461; e-mail umberto.solimene@unimi.it; internet www .femteconline.com; f. 1947 as International Federation of Thermalism and Climatism; present name adopted 1999; mems: in 36 countries; Pres. M. NIKOLAI A. STOROJENKO; Gen. Sec. Prof. UMBERTO SOLIMENE.

World Federation of Neurosurgical Societies—WFNS: c/o Prof. Edward R. Laws, Dept. of Neurological Surgery, Univ. of Virginia, Box 212, Health Science Center, Charlottesville, VA 22908, USA; tel. (804) 924-2650; fax (804) 924-5894; internet www.wfns.org; f. 1957 to assist in the development of neurosurgery and to help the formation of asscns; facilitates the exchange of information and encourages research; mems: 57 societies in 56 countries; Pres. Prof. ARMANDO BASSO; Sec. Prof. EDWARD R. LAWS, Jr.

World Federation of Occupational Therapists—WFOT: POB 30, Forrestfield, 6058 Western Australia, Australia; fax (8) 9453-9746; e-mail wfot@multiline.com.au; internet wfot.org.au; f. 1952 to further the rehabilitation of the physically and mentally disabled by promoting the development of occupational therapy in all countries; facilitates the exchange of information and publications; promotes research in occupational therapy; holds international congresses every four years; mems: national professional asscns in 50 countries, with total membership of c. 100,000; Pres. KIT SINCLAIR (Hong Kong); Hon. Sec. MARILYN PATTISON (Australia); publ. *Bulletin* (2 a year).

World Federation of Public Health Associations: c/o Allen Jones, APHA, 800 I St, NW, Washington, DC 20001-3710, USA; tel. (202) 777-2487; fax (202) 777-2534; e-mail allen.jones@apha.org; internet www.wfpha.org; f. 1967; brings together researchers, teachers, health service providers and workers in a multidisciplinary environment of professional exchange, studies and action; endeavours to influence policies and to set priorities to prevent disease and promote health; holds a triennial Congress: United Kingdom (2004); mems: 64 national public health asscns; Sec.-Gen. ALLEN JONES (USA); publs *WFPHA Report* (in English), and occasional technical papers.

World Federation of Societies of Anaesthesiologists—WFSA: Imperial House, 7th Floor, 15–19 Kingsway, London, WC2B 6TH, United Kingdom; tel. (20) 7836-5652; fax (20) 7836-5616; e-mail info@wfsa-office.org; internet www.anaesthesiologists.org; f. 1955; aims to make available the highest standards of anaesthesia to all peoples of the world; mems: 106 national societies; Pres. Dr K. BROWN (Australia); Sec. Prof. A. E. E. MEURSING; publs *World Anaesthesia Newsletter* (2 a year), *Annual Report*.

World Self-Medication Industry—WSMI: Centre International de Bureaux, 13 chemin du Levant, 01210 Ferney-Voltaire, France; tel. 450-28-47-28; fax 450-28-40-24; e-mail dwebber@wsmi.org; internet www.wsmi.org; Dir-Gen. Dr DAVID E. WEBBER.

Posts and Telecommunications

African Telecommunications Union: Posta Sacco Plaza, 11th Floor, Uhuru Highway, POB 35282 Nairobi, Kenya; tel. (20) 216678; fax (20) 219478; e-mail sg@atu-uat.org; internet www.atu-uat.org; f. 1999 as successor to Pan-African Telecommunications Union (f. 1977); promotes the rapid development of information communications in Africa, with the aim of making Africa an equal participant in the global information society; works towards universal service and access and full inter-country connectivity; promotes development and adoption of appropriate policies and regulatory frameworks; promotes financing of development; encourages co-operation between members and the exchange of information; advocates the harmonization of telecommunications policies; mems: in 46 countries; Sec.-Gen. M. JAN MUTAI.

Arab Permanent Postal Commission: c/o Arab League Bldg, Tahrir Sq., Cairo, Egypt; tel. (2) 5750511; fax (2) 5775626; f. 1952; aims to establish stricter postal relations between the Arab countries than those laid down by the Universal Postal Union, and to pursue the development and modernization of postal services in member countries; publs *APU Bulletin* (monthly), *APU Review* (quarterly), *APU News* (annually).

Arab Telecommunications Union: POB 2397, Baghdad, Iraq; tel. (1) 555-0642; f. 1953 to co-ordinate and develop telecommunications between member countries to exchange technical aid and encourage research; promotes establishment of new cable telecommunications networks in the region; Sec.-Gen. ABDUL JAFFAR HASSAN KHALAF IBRAHIM AL-ANI; publs *Arab Telecommunications Union Journal* (2 a year), *Economic and Technical Studies*.

Asia-Pacific Telecommunity: No. 12/49, Soi 5, Chaengwattana Rd, Thungsonghong, Bangkok 10210, Thailand; tel. (2) 573-0044; fax (2) 573-7479; e-mail aptmail@aptsec.org; internet www.aptsec.org; f. 1979 to cover all matters relating to telecommunications in the region; mems: Afghanistan, Australia, Bangladesh, Brunei, the People's Republic of China, India, Indonesia, Iran, Japan, the Republic of Korea, Laos, Malaysia, Maldives, Myanmar, Nauru, Nepal, Pakistan, the Philippines, Singapore, Sri Lanka, Thailand, Viet Nam; assoc. mems: Cook Islands, Hong Kong; two affiliated mems each in Indonesia, Japan and Thailand, three in the Republic of Korea, four in Hong Kong, one in Maldives and six in the Philippines; Exec. Sec. JONG-SOON LEE.

Asian-Pacific Postal Union: Post Office Bldg, 1000 Manila, Philippines; tel. (2) 470760; fax (2) 407448; f. 1962 to extend, facilitate and improve the postal relations between the member countries and to promote co-operation in the field of postal services; mems: 23 countries; Dir JORGE SARMIENTO; publs *Annual Report, Exchange Program of Postal Officials, APPU Newsletter*.

European Conference of Postal and Telecommunications Administrations: Ministry of Transport and Communications, Odos Xenofontos 13, 10191 Athens, Greece; tel. (1) 9236494; fax (1) 9237133; internet www.cept.org; f. 1959 to strengthen relations between member administrations and to harmonize and improve their technical services; set up Eurodata Foundation, for research and publishing; mems: 26 countries; Sec. Z. PROTOPSALTI; publ. *Bulletin*.

European Telecommunications Satellite Organization—EUTELSAT: 70 rue Balard, 75015, Paris Cédex 15, France; tel. 1-53-98-47-47; fax 1-53-98-37-00; internet www.eutelsat.com/; f. 1977 to operate satellites for fixed and mobile communications in Europe; EUTELSAT's in-orbit resource comprises 18 satellites; commercialises capacity in three satellites operated by other companies; mems: public and private telecommunications operations in 47 countries; Dir-Gen. GIULIANO BERRETTA.

INMARSAT (International Mobile Satellite Organization): 99 City Rd, London, EC1Y 1AX, United Kingdom; tel. (20) 7728-1000; fax (20) 7728-1044; internet www.inmarsat.org; f. 1979, as International Maritime Satellite Organization, to provide (from February 1982) global communications for shipping via satellites on a commercial basis; satellites in geo-stationary orbit over the Atlantic, Indian and Pacific Oceans provide telephone, telex, facsimile, telegram, low to high speed data services and distress and safety communications for ships of all nations and structures such as oil rigs; in 1985 the operating agreement was amended to include aeronautical communications, and in 1988 amendments were approved which allow provision of global land-mobile communications; in April 1999 INMARSAT was transferred to the private sector and became a limited company; an intergovernmental secretariat was to be maintained to monitor INMARSAT's public service obligations; mems: 86 countries; Chair. RICHARD VOS; Dir of Secretariat JERZY VONAU (Poland).

International Telecommunications Satellite Organization—INTELSAT: 3400 International Drive, NW, Washington, DC 20008-3098, USA; tel. (202) 944-6800; fax (202) 944-7860; internet www.intelsat.com; f. 1964 to establish a global commercial satellite communications system; Assembly of Parties attended by representatives of member governments, meets every two years to consider policy and long-term aims and matters of interest to members as sovereign states; meeting of Signatories to the Operating Agreement held annually; 24 INTELSAT satellites in geosynchronous orbit provide a global communications service; provides most of the world's overseas traffic; in 1998 INTELSAT agreed to establish a private enterprise, incorporated in the Netherlands, to administer six satellite services; mems: 143 governments; Dir-Gen. and Chief Exec. CONNY KULLMAN (Sweden).

Internet Corporation for Assigned Names and Numbers—ICANN: 4676 Admiralty Way, Suite 330, Marina del Rey, CA 90292-6601, USA; tel. (310) 823-9358; fax (310) 823-8649; e-mail icann@icann.org; internet www.icann.org; f. 1998; non-profit, private-sector body; aims to co-ordinate the technical management and policy development of the internet; comprises three Supporting Organizations to assist, review and develop recommendations on internet policy and structure relating to addresses, domain names, and protocol; Pres. and CEO STUART LYNN.

Pacific Telecommunications Council—PTC: 2454 S. Beretania St, 302 Honolulu, HI 96826, USA; tel. (808) 941-3789; fax (808) 944-4874; e-mail info@ptc.org; internet www.ptc.org; f. 1980 to promote the development, understanding and beneficial use of telecommunications and information systems/services throughout the Pacific region; provides forum for users and providers of communications services; sponsors annual conference and seminars; mems: 650 (corporate, government, academic and individual); Pres. JANE HURD; Exec. Dir HOYT ZIA; publ. *Pacific Telecommunications Review* (quarterly).

Postal Union of the Americas, Spain and Portugal (Unión Postal de las Américas, España y Portugal): Cebollatí 1468/70, 1°, Casilla de Correos 20.042, Montevideo, Uruguay; tel. (2) 4100070; fax (2) 4105046; e-mail secretariat@upaep.com.uy; internet www.upaep.com.uy; f. 1911 to extend, facilitate and study the postal relationships of member countries; mems: 27 countries; Sec.-Gen. MARIO FELMER KLENNER (Chile).

Press, Radio and Television

Asia-Pacific Broadcasting Union—ABU: POB 1164, 59700 Kuala Lumpur, Malaysia; tel. (3) 22823592; fax (3) 22825292; e-mail sg@abu.org.my; internet www.abu.org.my; f. 1964 to foster and co-ordinate the development of broadcasting in the Asia-Pacific area, to develop means of establishing closer collaboration and co-operation among broadcasting orgs, and to serve the professional needs of broadcasters in Asia and the Pacific; holds annual General Assembly; mems: 102 in 50 countries and territories; Pres. KATSUJI EBISAWA (Japan); Sec.-Gen. HUGH LEONARD; publs *ABU News* (every 2 months), *ABU Technical Review* (every 2 months).

Association for the Promotion of the International Circulation of the Press—DISTRIPRESS: 8002 Zürich, Beethovenstrasse 20, Switzerland; tel. (1) 2024121; fax (1) 2021025; e-mail info@distripress.ch; internet www.distripress.ch; f. 1955 to assist in the promotion of the freedom of the press throughout the world, supporting and aiding UNESCO in promoting the free flow of ideas; organizes meetings of publishers and distributors of newspapers, periodicals and paperback books, to promote the exchange of information and experience among members; mems: 458; Pres. ALFRED HEINTZE (Germany); Man. HEINZ E. GRAF (Switzerland); publs *Distripress Gazette, Who's Who*.

Association of European Journalists—AEJ: Balistraat 46, Den Haag, 2585 Netherlands; tel. (70) 3635875; fax (70) 3107217; e-mail hhetzel@atglobal.net; internet www.aej.org; f. 1963 to participate actively in the development of a European consciousness to promote deeper knowledge of European problems and secure appreciation by the general public of the work of European institutions; and to facilitate members' access to sources of European information; mems: 2,100 individuals and national asscns in 23 countries; Pres. HELMUT HETZEL (Netherlands); Sec.-Gen. JURAJ ALNER (Slovakia); publ. *Newsletter*.

Association of Private European Cable Operators: 1 blvd Anspach, boîte 25, 1000 Brussels, Belgium; tel. (2) 223-25-91; fax (2) 223-06-96; f. 1995 to promote the interests of independent cable operators and to ensure exchange of information on cable and telecommunications; carries out research on relevant technical and legal questions; mems: 27 organizations in 19 countries; Pres. M. DE SUTTER.

Broadcasting Organization of Non-aligned Countries—BONAC: c/o Cyprus Broadcasting Corpn, POB 4824, 1397 Nicosia, Cyprus; tel. (2) 422231; fax (2) 314050; e-mail rik@cybc.com.cy; f. 1977 to ensure an equitable, objective and comprehensive flow of information through broadcasting; Secretariat moves to the broadcasting organization of host country; mems: in 102 countries.

European Alliance of Press Agencies: Norrbackagatan 23, 11341 Stockholm; tel. (8) 301-324; e-mail erik-n@telia.com; internet www.pressalliance.com; f. 1957 to assist co-operation among members and to study and protect their common interests; annual assembly; mems: in 30 countries; Sec.-Gen. ERIK NYLÉN.

European Broadcasting Union—EBU: CP 45, Ancienne-Route 17A, 1218 Grand-Saconnex, Geneva, Switzerland; tel. (22) 7172111; fax (22) 74740003; e-mail ebu@ebu.ch; internet www.eurovision.net; f. 1950 in succession to the International Broadcasting Union; a professional asscn of broadcasting organizations, supporting the interests of members and assisting the development of broadcasting in all its forms; activities include the Eurovision news and programme exchanges and the Euroradio music exchanges; mems: 71 active (European) in 52 countries, and 45 associate in 28 countries; Pres. ARNE WESSBERG (Finland); Sec.-Gen. JEAN STOCK (France); publs *EBU Technical Review* (annually), *Diffusion* (2 a year).

IFRA: Washingtonplatz 1, 64287 Darmstadt, Germany; tel. (6151) 7336; fax (6151) 733800; e-mail info@ifra.com; internet www.ifra .com; f. 1961 as Inca-Fiej Research Assen to develop methods and techniques for the newspaper industry to evaluate standard specifications for raw materials for use in newspaper production; and to investigate economy and quality improvements for newspaper printing and publishing; mems: more than 1,300 newspapers, 400 suppliers; Pres. MURDOCH MACLENNAN; Man. Dir REINER MITTELBACH; publ. *Newspaper Techniques* (monthly, in English, French and German).

Inter-American Press Association—IAPA (Sociedad Interamericana de Prensa): Jules Dubois Bldg, 1801 SW 3rd Ave, Miami, FL 33129, USA; tel. (305) 634-2465; fax (305) 635-2272; e-mail info@ sipiapa.org; internet www.sipiapa.org; f. 1942 to guard the freedom of the press in the Americas to promote and maintain the dignity, rights and responsibilities of the profession of journalism; to foster a wider knowledge and greater interchange among the peoples of the Americas; mems: 1,400; Exec. Dir JULIO E. MUÑOZ; publ. *IAPA News*.

International Association of Broadcasting (Asociación Internacional de Radiodifusión—AIR): Cnel Brandzen 1961, Office 402, 11200 Montevideo, Uruguay; tel. (2) 4088129; fax (2) 4088121; e-mail airiab@distrinet.com.uy; internet www.airiab.com; f. 1946 to preserve free and private broadcasting to promote co-operation between the corporations and public authorities; to defend freedom of expression; mems: national asscns of broadcasters; Pres. Dr LUIS H. TARSITANO; Dir-Gen. Dr HÉCTOR OSCAR AMENGUAL; publ. *La Gaceta de AIR* (every 2 months).

International Association of Sound and Audiovisual Archives: c/o Eva Fønss-Jørgensen, Statsbiblioteket, 8000 Aarhus C, Denmark; tel. 89-46-20-51; fax 89-46-20-51; e-mail efj@ statsbiblioteket.dk; internet www.iasa-web.org; f. 1969; supports the professional exchange of sound and audiovisual documents, and fosters international co-operation between audiovisual archives in all fields, in particular in the areas of acquisition, documentation, access, exploitation copyright, and preservation; holds annual conference; mems: 410 individuals and institutions in 48 countries; Sec.-Gen. EVA FØNSS-JØRGENSEN; publs *IASA Journal* (2 a year), *IASA Information Bulletin* (quarterly).

International Catholic Union of the Press (Union catholique internationale de la presse—UCIP): 37–39 rue de Vermont, Case Postale 197, 1211 Geneva 20, Switzerland; tel. (22) 7340017; fax (22) 7340053; e-mail helo@ucip.ch; internet www.ucip.ch; f. 1927 to link all Catholics who influence public opinion through the press, to inspire a high standard of professional conscience and to represent the interest of the Catholic press at international organizations; mems: Federation of Catholic Press Agencies, Federation of Catholic Journalists, Federation of Catholic Dailies, Federation of Catholic Periodicals, Federation of Teachers in the Science and Technics of Information, Federation of Church Press Associations, Federation of Book Publishers, eight regional asscns; Pres. RERESA EE-CHOOI; Sec.-Gen. JOSEPH CHITTILAPPILLY (India); publ. *UCIP-Information*.

International Council for Film, Television and Audiovisual Communication (Conseil international du cinema de la television et de la communication audiovisuelle): 1 rue Miollis, 75732 Paris Cédex 15, France; tel. 1-45-68-48-55; fax 1-45-67-28-40; e-mail r .kalman@unesco.org; internet www.unesco.org/iftc; f. 1958 to support collaboration between UNESCO and professionals engaged in cinema, television and audiovisual communications; mems: 36 international film and television organizations; Pres. HISANORI ISOMURA; Sec.-Gen. Dr ROBERT E. KALMAN; publ. *Letter of Information* (monthly).

International Council of French-speaking Radio and Television Organizations (Conseil international des radios-télévisions d'expression française): 52 blvd Auguste-Reyers, 1044 Brussels, Belgium; tel. (2) 732-45-85; fax (2) 732-62-40; f. 1978 to establish links between French-speaking radio and television organizations; mems: 46 organizations; Sec.-Gen. ABDELKADER MARZOUKI (Tunisia).

International Federation of Press Cutting Agencies: Streulistr. 19, POB 8030 Zürich, Switzerland; tel. (1) 3888200; fax (1) 3888201; e-mail fibep@bluewin.ch; f. 1953 to improve the standing of the profession, prevent infringements, illegal practices and unfair competition; and to develop business and friendly relations among press cuttings agencies throughout the world. Annual meeting, 2003: Cape Town, South Africa; mems: 81 agencies; Pres. CARLOS BEGAS (Israel); Gen. Sec. THOMAS HENNE (Switzerland).

International Federation of the Cinematographic Press (Fédération Internationale de la Presse Cinématographique—

FIPRESCI): Schleissheimerstr. 83, 80797 Munich, Germany; tel. (89) 182303; fax (89) 184766; e-mail keder@fipresci.org; internet www.fipresci.org; f. 1930 to develop the cinematographic press and promote cinema as an art; organizes international meetings and juries in film festivals; mems: national organizations or corresponding members in 68 countries; Pres. DEREK MALCOLM (UK); Sec.-Gen. KLAUS EDER (Germany).

International Federation of the Periodical Press—FIPP: Queen's House, 55/56 Lincoln's Inn Fields, London, WC2A 3LJ, United Kingdom; tel. (20) 7404-4169; fax (20) 7404-4170; e-mail info@fipp.com; internet www.fipp.com; f. 1925; works through national asscns to promote optimum conditions for the development of periodical publishing; fosters formal and informal alliances between magazine publishers; mems: 35 national asscns representing 2,500 publishing cos and 75 international publishing cos and assoc. mems; Pres. and CEO PER R. MORTENSEN; Chair. AXEL GANZ (Germany); publ. *Magazine World* (6 a year).

International Federation of the Socialist and Democratic Press: CP 737, 1-2021 Milan, Italy; tel. (02) 8050105; f. 1953 to promote co-operation between editors and publishers of socialist newspapers; affiliated to the Socialist International (see p. 351); mems: about 100; Sec. UMBERTO GIOVINE.

International Institute of Communications: 3rd Floor, Westcott House, 35 Portland Place, London, W1B 1AE, United Kingdom; tel. (20) 7323-9672; fax (20) 7323-9625; e-mail enquiries@iicom.org; internet www.iicom.org; f. 1969 (as the International Broadcast Institute) to link all working in the field of communications, including policy makers, broadcasters, industrialists and engineers; holds local, regional and international meetings; undertakes research; mems: over 1,000 corporate, institutional and individual; Pres. BERNARD COURTOIS (Canada); Chair. BÄASHIR SHARIFF (Malaysia); publs *Intermedia* (quarterly), *Communications Technology Decisions* (2 a year).

International Maritime Radio Association: South Bank House, Black Prince Rd, London, SE1 7SJ, United Kingdom; tel. (20) 7587-1245; fax (20) 7587-1436; e-mail secgen@cirm.org; internet www .cirm.org; f. 1928 to study and develop means of improving marine radio communications and radio aids to marine navigation; mems: over 70 organizations and companies from the major maritime nations involved in marine electronics in the areas of radio communications and navigation; Pres. G. SEUTIN (Belgium); Sec.-Gen. and Chair. of Technical Cttee Capt. C. K. D. COBLEY.

International Press Institute—IPI: Spiegelgasse 2/29, 1010 Vienna, Austria; tel. (1) 5129011; fax (1) 5129014; e-mail ipi@ freemedia.at; internet www.freemedia.at; f. 1951 as a non-governmental organization of editors, publishers and news broadcasters supporting the principles of a free and responsible press; aims to defend press freedom; conducts training programmes and research; maintains a library; holds regional meetings and an annual World Congress; mems: about 2,000 from 110 countries; Pres. HUGO BUETLER (Switzerland); Dir JOHANN FRITZ (Austria); publs *IPI Global Journalist* (quarterly), *World Press Freedom Review* (annually).

International Press Telecommunications Council—IPTC: Royal Albert House, Sheet St, Windsor, Berks, SL4 1BE, United Kingdom; tel. (1753) 705051; fax (1753) 831541; e-mail m_director_iptc@iptc.org; internet www.iptc.org; f. 1965 to safeguard and promote the interests of the Press on all matters relating to telecommunications; keeps its members informed of current and future telecommunications developments; acts as the news information formal standards body; meets three times a year and maintains four committees and 10 working parties; mems: 44 press asscns, newspapers, news agencies and industry vendors; Chair. JOHN IOBST; Man. Dir MICHAEL STEIDL; publs *IPTC Spectrum* (annually), *IPTC Mirror* (monthly).

Latin-American Catholic Press Union: Apdo Postal 17-21-178, Quito, Ecuador; tel. (2) 548046; fax (2) 501658; f. 1959 to co-ordinate, promote and improve the Catholic press in Latin America; mems: national asscns and local groups in most Latin American countries; Pres. ISMAR DE OLIVEIRA SOARES (Brazil); Sec. CARLOS EDUARDO CORTÉS (Colombia).

Organization of Asia-Pacific News Agencies—OANA: c/o Xinhua News Agency, 57 Xuanwumen Xidajie, Beijing 100803, People's Republic of China; tel. (10) 3074762; fax (10) 3072707; internet www.oananews.com; f. 1961 to promote co-operation in professional matters and mutual exchange of news, features, etc. among the news agencies of Asia and the Pacific via the Asia-Pacific News Network (ANN); mems: Anadolu Ajansi (Turkey), Antara (Indonesia), APP (Pakistan), Bakhtar (Afghanistan), BERNAMA (Malaysia), BSS (Bangladesh), ENA (Bangladesh), Hindustan Samachar (India), IRNA (Iran), ITAR-TASS (Russia), Kaz-TAG (Kazakhstan), KABAR (Kyrgyzstan), KCNA (Korea, Democratic People's Republic), KPL (Laos), Kyodo (Japan), Lankapuvath (Sri Lanka), Montsame (Mongolia), PNA (Philippines), PPI (Pakistan), PTI (India), RSS (Nepal), Samachar Bharati (India), TNA (Thailand), UNB (Bangladesh), UNI (India), Viet Nam News Agency, Xinhua (People's Republic of China), Yonhap (Republic of Korea); Pres. GUO CHAOREN; Sec.-Gen. MIKHAIL GUSMANN.

Press Foundation of Asia: POB 1843, S & L Bldg, 3rd Floor, 1500 Roxas Blvd, Manila, Philippines; tel. (2) 5233223; fax (2) 5224365; e-mail pfa@pressasia.org; internet www.pressasia.org; f. 1967; an independent, non-profit making organization governed by its newspaper members; acts as a professional forum for about 200 newspapers in Asia; aims to reduce cost of newspapers to potential readers, to improve editorial and management techniques through research and training programmes and to encourage the growth of the Asian press; operates *Depthnews* feature service; mems: 200 newspapers; Exec. Chair. MAZLAN NORDIN (Malaysia); Chief Exec. MOCHTAR LUBIS (Indonesia); publs *Pressasia* (quarterly), *Asian Women* (quarterly).

Reporters sans Frontières: 5 rue Geoffroy Marie, 75009 Paris, France; tel. 1-44-83-84-84; fax 1-45-23-11-51; e-mail rsf@rsf.org; internet www.rsf.org; f. 1985 to defend press freedoms throughout the world; generates awareness of violations of press freedoms and supports journalists under threat or imprisoned as a result of their work; mems in 77 countries; Dir ROBERT MÉNARD; publs *Annual Report*, *La Lettre de Reporters sans Frontières* (monthly).

Union of National Radio and Television Organizations of Africa—URTNA: 101 rue Carnot, BP 3237, Dakar, Senegal; tel. 821-16-25; fax 822-51-13; e-mail urtnadkr@telecomplus.sn; f. 1962; co-ordinates radio and television services, including monitoring and frequency allocation, the exchange of information and coverage of national and international events among African countries; maintains programme exchange centre (Nairobi, Kenya), technical centre (Bamako, Mali), a centre for rural radio studies (Ouagadougou, Burkina Faso) and a centre for the exchange of television news (Algiers, Algeria); mems: 48 organizations and six associate members; Sec.-Gen. ABDELHAMID BOUKSANI; publ. *URTNA Review* (2 a year, in English and French).

World Association for Christian Communication—WACC: 357 Kennington Lane, London, SE11 5QY, United Kingdom; tel. (20) 7582-9139; fax (20) 7735-0340; e-mail wacc@wacc.org.uk; internet www.wacc.org.uk; f. 1975 to promote human dignity, justice and peace through freedom of expression and the democratization of communication; offers professional guidance on communication policies; interprets developments in and the consequences of global communication methods; works towards the empowerment of women; assists the training of Christian communicators; mems: more than 800 corporate and personal mems in 115 countries, organized in eight regional assocs; Pres. ALBERT VAN DEN HEUVEL; Gen.-Sec. R. L. NAYLOR; publs *Action*, newsletter (10 a year), *Media Development* (quarterly), *Communication Resource*, *Media and Gender Monitor* (both occasional).

World Association of Newspapers—WAN: 25 rue d'Astorg, 75008 Paris, France; tel. 1-47-42-85-00; fax 1-47-42-49-48; e-mail tbalding@wan.asso.fr; internet www.wan-press.org; f. 1948 to defend the freedom of the press, to safeguard the ethical and economic interests of newspapers and to study all questions of interest to newspapers at international level; mems: 71 national newspaper asscns, individual newspaper executives in 100 countries, 13 news agencies and nine regional and world-wide press groups; Pres. SEOK HYUN HONG (Republic of Korea); Dir-Gen. TIMOTHY BALDING; publ. *Newsletter*.

Religion

Agudath Israel World Organisation: Hacherut Sq., POB 326, Jerusalem 91002, Israel; tel. (2) 5384357; fax (2) 5383634; f. 1912 to help solve the problems facing Jewish people all over the world in the spirit of the Jewish tradition; holds World Congress (every five years) and an annual Central Council; mems: over 500,000 in 25 countries; Chair. J. M. ABRAMOWITZ (Jerusalem); Secs Rabbi MOSHE GEWIRTZ, Rabbi CHAIM WEINSTOCK; publs *Hamodia* (Jerusalem daily newspaper, in Hebrew; weekly in English), *Jewish Tribune* (London, weekly), *Jewish Observer* (New York, monthly), *Dos Yiddishe Vort* (New York, monthly), *Coalition* (New York), *Perspectives* (Toronto, monthly), *La Voz Judia* (Buenos Aires, monthly), *Jüdische Stimme* (Zürich, monthly).

All Africa Conference of Churches—AACC: POB 14205, Waiyaki Way, Nairobi, Kenya; tel. (20) 441483; fax (20) 443241; e-mail aacc-secretariat@maf.org; f. 1958; an organ of co-operation and continuing fellowship among Protestant, Orthodox and independent churches and Christian Councils in Africa; 2003 Assembly: Yaoundé, Cameroon; mems: 147 churches and affiliated Christian councils in 39 African countries; Pres. The Very Rev. Prof. KWESI DICKSON (Ghana); Gen. Sec. Canon CLEMENT JANDA (Uganda); publs *ACIS/APS Bulletin*, *ACLCA News*, *Tam Tam*.

Alliance Israélite Universelle—AIU: 45 rue La Bruyère, 75425 Paris Cédex 09, France; tel. 1-53-32-88-55; fax 1-48-74-51-33; e-mail info@aiu.org; internet www.aiu.org; f. 1860 to work for the emancipation and moral progress of the Jews; maintains 40 schools in eight countries; library of 120,000 vols; mems: 8,000 in 16 countries; Pres. ADY STEG; Dir JEAN-JACQUES WAHL (France); publs *Les Cahiers de l'Alliance Israélite Universelle* (3 a year, in French), *Les Cahiers du Judaïsme*, *The Alliance Review* (in English).

Bahá'í International Community: Bahá'í World Centre, POB 155, 31 001 Haifa, Israel; tel. (4) 8358394; fax (4) 8313312; e-mail opi@bwc.org; internet www.bahai.org; f. 1844 in Persia to promote the unity of mankind and world peace through the teachings of the Bahá'í religion, including the equality of men and women and the elimination of all forms of prejudice; maintains schools for children and adults world-wide, operates educational and cultural radio stations in the USA, Asia and Latin America; has 32 publishing trusts throughout the world; governing body: Universal House of Justice (nine mems elected by 182 National Spiritual Assemblies); mems: in 127,555 local communities (in 190 countries and 45 dependent territories or overseas departments); Sec.-Gen. ALBERT LINCOLN (USA); publs *Bahá'í World* (annually), *One Country* (quarterly, in 6 languages).

Baptist World Alliance: 6733 Curran St, McLean, VA 22101-6005, USA; tel. (703) 790-8980; fax (703) 893-5160; e-mail bwa@bwanet.org; internet www.bwanet.org; f. 1905; aims to unite Baptists, lead in evangelism, respond to people in need and defend human rights; mems: 191 Baptist unions and conventions comprising 42m. people in 200 countries and territories; Pres. Dr NILSON DO AMARAL FANINI (Brazil); Gen. Sec. Dr DENTON LOTZ; publ. *The Baptist World* (quarterly).

Caribbean Conference of Churches: POB 876, Port of Spain, Trinidad and Tobago; tel. 628-202; fax 628-2031; e-mail caconftt@trinidad.net; internet www.cariblife.com/pub/ccc; f. 1973; holds Assembly every five years; conducts study and research programmes; supports education and community projects; mems: 34 churches; Gen. Sec. GERARD GRANADO; publ. *Christian Action Newsletter* (quarterly).

Christian Conference of Asia—CCA: 96, 2nd District, Pak Tin Village, Mei Tin Rd, Shatin, NT, Hong Kong; tel. 26911068; fax 26924378; e-mail cca@cca.org.hkt; internet www.cca.org.hk; f. 1957 (present name adopted 1973) to promote co-operation and joint study in matters of common concern among the Churches of the region and to encourage interaction with other regional Conferences and the World Council of Churches; mems: more than 100 churches and councils of churches from 18 Asian countries; Gen. Sec. Dr AHN JAE WOONG; publ. *CCA News* (quarterly).

Christian Peace Conference: Prokopova 4, 130 00 Prague 3, Czech Republic; tel. (2) 22781800; fax (2) 22781801; e-mail christianpeace@volny.cz; internet www.volny.cz/christianpeace; f. 1958 as an international movement of theologians, clergy and laypeople, aiming to bring Christendom to recognize its share of guilt in both world wars and to dedicate itself to the service of friendship, reconciliation and peaceful co-operation of nations, to concentrate on united action for peace and justice, and to co-ordinate peace groups in individual churches and facilitate their effective participation in the peaceful development of society; works through five continental asscns, regional groups and member churches in many countries; Moderator Dr SERGIO ARCE MARTÍNEZ; Co-ordinator Rev. BRIAN G. COOPER; publs *CPC Information* (8 a year in English and German), occasional *Study Volume*.

Conference of European Churches—CEC: POB 2100, 150 route de Ferney, 1211 Geneva 2, Switzerland; tel. (22) 7916111; fax (22) 7916227; e-mail cec@cec-kek.org; internet www.cec-kek.org; f. 1959 as a regional ecumenical organization for Europe and a meeting-place for European churches, including members and non-members of the World Council of Churches; holds assemblies every six years; mems: 128 Protestant, Anglican, Orthodox and Old Catholic churches in all European countries; Gen. Sec. Rev. Dr KEITH CLEMENTS; publs *Monitor* (quarterly), CEC communiqués, reports.

Conference of International Catholic Organizations: 37–39 rue de Vermont, 1202 Geneva, Switzerland; tel. (22) 7338392; f. 1927 to encourage collaboration and agreement between the different Catholic international organizations in their common interests, and to contribute to international understanding; organizes international assemblies and meetings to study specific problems; permanent commissions deal with human rights, the new international economic order, social problems, the family health, education, etc. mems: 36 Catholic international organizations; Administrator FERNAUD VINCENT (Switzerland).

Consultative Council of Jewish Organizations—CCJO: 420 Lexington Ave, New York, NY 10170, USA; tel. (212) 808-5437; f. 1946 to co-operate and consult with the UN and other international bodies directly concerned with human rights and to defend the cultural, political and religious rights of Jews throughout the world; Sec.-Gen. WARREN GREEN (USA).

European Baptist Federation (EBF): Postfach 610340, 22423 Hamburg, Germany; tel. (40) 5509723; fax (40) 5509725; e-mail office@ebf.org; internet www.ebf.org; f. 1949 to promote fellowship and co-operation among Baptists in Europe to further the aims and objects of the Baptist World Alliance; to stimulate and co-ordinate evangelism in Europe; to provide for consultation and planning of missionary work in Europe and elsewhere in the world; mems: 49 Baptist Unions in European countries and the Middle East; Pres. DAVID COFFEY; Sec.-Treas. Rev. KARL-HEINZ WALTER (Germany).

European Evangelical Alliance: Wilhelmshoeher Allee 258, 34131 Kassel, Germany; tel. (561) 3149711; fax (561) 9387520; e-mail 100341.550@compuserve.com; internet www.hfe.org; f. 1953 to promote understanding and co-operation among evangelical Christians in Europe and to stimulate evangelism; mems: 25 national alliances from 24 countries, 6 pan-European asscns; Pres. DEREK COPLEY (UK); Sec. GORDON SHOWELL-ROGERS.

Friends World Committee for Consultation: 4 Byng Pl., London, WC1E 7LE, United Kingdom; tel. (20) 7388-0497; fax (20) 7383-4644; e-mail world@fwcc.quaker.org; internet www.quaker .org/fwcc/; f. 1937 to encourage and strengthen the spiritual life within the Religious Society of Friends (Quakers) to help Friends to a better understanding of their vocation in the world; and to promote consultation among Friends of all countries; representation at the United Nations as a non-governmental organization; mems: appointed representatives and individuals from 70 countries; Gen. Sec. ELIZABETH DUKE; publs *Friends World News* (2 a year), *Calendar of Yearly Meetings* (annually), *Quakers around the World* (handbook).

Initiatives of Change: POB 3, 1211 Geneva 20, Switzerland; tel. (22) 7330920; fax (22) 7330267; e-mail media@caux.ch; internet www.caux.ch; other international centres at Panchgani, India, Petropolis, Brazil, London, UK, and Gweru, Zimbabwe; f. 1921; aims to develop a new social order for better human relations and the elimination of political, industrial and racial antagonism; legally incorporated bodies in 20 countries; Pres. of Swiss foundation CORNELIO SOMMARUGA; publs *Changer* (French, 6 a year), *For a Change* (English, 6 a year), *Caux Information* (German, monthly).

International Association for Religious Freedom—IARF: 2 Market St, Oxford OX1 3EF, United Kingdom; tel. (1865) 202-744; fax (1865) 202-746; e-mail hq@iarf.net; internet iarf-religiousfreedom.net; f. 1900 as a world community of religions, subscribing to the principle of openness and upholding the United Nation's Universal Declaration on freedom of religion or belief; conducts religious freedom programmes, focusing on inter-religious harmony; holds regional conferences and triennial congress; mems: 100 groups in 27 countries; Pres. EIMERT VAN HERWIJNEN (Netherlands); Gen. Sec. ANDREW C. CLARK (UK); publ. *IARF World* (2 a year).

International Association of Buddhist Studies—IABS: c/o Prof. T. J. F. Tillemans, Section des langues et civilisations orientales, Université de Lausanne, 1015 Lausanne, Switzerland; tel. (761) 203-3158; fax (761) 203-3152; e-mail iabs.treasurer@orient .unil.ch; f. 1976; supports studies of Buddhist religion, philosophy and literature; holds international conference every three or four years; Gen. Sec. TOM J. F. TILLEMANS; publ. *Journal* (2 a year).

International Council of Christians and Jews—ICCJ: Martin Buber House, Werléstrasse 2, 64646 Heppenheim, Germany; tel. (6252) 93120; fax (6252) 68331; e-mail iccj_buberhouse@t-online.de; internet www.iccj.org; f. 1947 to promote mutual respect and co-operation; holds annual international colloquium, seminars, meetings for young people and for women; maintains a forum for Jewish–Christian–Muslim relations; mems: 36 national councils in 32 countries; Pres. Rev. Prof. JOHN T. PAWLIKOWSKI; Sec.-Gen. Rev. FRIEDHELM PIEPER; publs *ICCJ History*, *ICCJ Brochure*, conference documents.

International Council of Jewish Women: POB 12130, Local 4, Montevideo, Uruguay; tel. and fax (2) 628–5874; e-mail icjw@ montevideo.org.uy; internet www.icjw.org; f. 1912 to promote friendly relations and understanding among Jewish women throughout the world; campaigns for human and women's rights, exchanges information on community welfare activities, promotes volunteer leadership, sponsors field work in social welfare, co-sponsors the International Jewish Women's Human Rights Watch and fosters Jewish education; mems: affiliates totalling over 1.5m. members in 46 countries; Pres. SARA WINKOWSKI; publs *Newsletter*, *Links around the World* (2 a year, English and Spanish), *International Jewish Women's Human Rights Watch* (2 a year).

International Fellowship of Reconciliation—IFOR: Spoorstraat 38, 1815 BK Alkmaar, Netherlands; tel. (72) 512-30-14; fax (72) 515-11-02; e-mail office@ifor.org; internet www.ifor.org; f. 1919; international, spiritually-based movement committed to active non-violence as a way of life and as a means of building a culture of peace and non-violence; maintains branches, affiliates and groups in more than 50 countries; Int. Pres. JOHN SISSON (Switzerland); publs *IFOR*

in Action (quarterly), *Patterns in Reconciliation*, *Cross the Lines* (3 a year, in Arabic, English, French, Russian and Spanish), occasional paper series.

International Humanist and Ethical Union—IHEU: 47 Theobald's Rd, London, WC1X 8SP, United Kingdom; tel. (20) 7831-4817; fax (20) 7404-8641; internet www.iheu.org; f. 1952 to bring into asscn all those interested in promoting ethical and scientific humanism and human rights; mems: national organizations and individuals in 37 countries; Exec. Dir BABU R. R. GOGINENI; publ. *International Humanist News* (quarterly).

International Organization for the Study of the Old Testament: c/o Prof. Gordon, St Catharine's College, Cambridge CB2 1RL, United Kingdom; tel. (1223) 335118; fax (1223) 335110; f. 1950; holds triennial congresses; Pres. Prof. A. VAN DER KOOIJ (Netherlands); Sec. Prof. R. P. GORDON (UK); publ. *Vetus Testamentum* (quarterly).

Latin American Council of Churches (Consejo Latinoamericano de Iglesias—CLAI): Casilla 17-08-8522, Calle Inglaterra 32–113 y Mariana de Jesús, Quito, Ecuador; tel. and fax (2) 553996; fax (2) 529933; e-mail israel@clai.org.ec; internet www.clai.org.ec; f. 1982; mems: 147 churches in 19 countries; Gen. Sec. Rev. ISRAEL BATISTA.

Latin American Episcopal Council: Apartado Aéreo 51086, Santafé de Bogotá, Colombia; tel. (1) 612-1379; fax (1) 612-1929; e-mail celam@celam.org; internet www.celam.org; f. 1955 to study the problems of the Roman Catholic Church in Latin America and to co-ordinate Church activities; mems: the Episcopal Conferences of Central and South America and the Caribbean; Pres. Mgr JORGE E. JIMÉNEZ CARVAJAL (Colombia); publ. *CELAM* (6 a year).

Lutheran World Federation: 150 route de Ferney, POB 2100, 1211 Geneva 2, Switzerland; tel. (22) 7916111; fax (22) 7916111; e-mail info@lutheranworld.org; internet www.lutheranworld.org; f. 1947; groups 128 Lutheran Churches in 70 countries; provides inter-church aid and relief work in various areas of the globe; gives service to refugees, including resettlement; carries out theological research, conferences and exchanges; grants scholarship aid in various fields of church life; conducts inter-confessional dialogue with Roman Catholic, Seventh-day Adventist, Anglican and Orthodox churches; Pres. Rt Rev. Dr CHRISTIAN KRAUSE (Germany); Gen. Sec. Rev. Dr ISHMAEL NOKO (Zimbabwe); publs *Lutheran World Information* (English and German, daily e-mail news service and monthly print edition), *LWF Today* and *LWF Documentation* (both irregular).

Middle East Council of Churches: Makhoul St, Deep Bldg, POB 5376, Beirut, Lebanon; tel. and fax (1) 344894; internet www .mecchurches.org; f. 1974; mems: 28 churches; Pres Pope SHENOUDAH, III; Patriarch PETROS VII PAPAPETRO; Rev. Dr SELIM SAHYOUNI; Archbishop KYRILLOS BUSTROS; Gen. Sec. Rev. Dr RIAD JARJOUR; publs *MECC News Report* (monthly), *Al Montada News Bulletin* (quarterly, in Arabic), *Courrier oecuménique du Moyen-Orient* (quarterly), *MECC Perspectives* (3 a year).

Muslim World League—MWL (Rabitat al-Alam al-Islami): POB 537–538, Makkah, Saudi Arabia; tel. (2) 5422733; fax (2) 5436619; e-mail mwlhq@aol.com; internet www.arab.net/mwl; f. 1962; aims to advance Islamic unity and solidarity, and to promote world peace and respect for human rights; provides financial assistance for education, medical care and relief work; has 30 offices throughout the world; Sec.-Gen. Dr ABDULLAH BIN ABDULMOSHIN AL-TURKI; publs *Majalla al-Rabita* (monthly, Arabic), *Akhbar al-Alam al Islami* (weekly, Arabic), *Journal* (monthly, English).

Opus Dei (Prelature of the Holy Cross and Opus Dei): Viale Bruno Buozzi 73, 00197 Rome, Italy; tel. (06) 808961; e-mail newyork@ opusdei.org; internet www.opusdei.org; f. 1928 by St Josemaría Escrivá de Balaguer to spread, at every level of society, an increased awareness of the universal call to sanctity and apostolate in the exercise of one's work; mems: 82,715 Catholic laypeople and 1,788 priests; Prelate Most Rev. JAVIER ECHEVARRÍA; publ. *Romana, Bulletin of the Prelature* (every six months).

Pacific Conference of Churches: POB 208, 4 Thurston St, Suva, Fiji; tel. 3311277; fax 3303205; e-mail pacific@is.com.fj; f. 1961; organizes assembly every five years, as well as regular workshops, meetings and training seminars throughout the region; mems: 36 churches and councils; Moderator Pastor REUBEN MAGEKON; Gen. Sec. Rev. VALAMOTU PALU.

Pax Romana International Catholic Movement for Intellectual and Cultural Affairs—ICMICA; and International Movement of Catholic Students—IMCS: 15 rue du Grand-Bureau, POB 315, 1211 Geneva 24, Switzerland; tel. (22) 8230707; fax (22) 8230708; e-mail miicmica@paxromana.int.ch; internet www .pax-romana.org; f. 1921 (IMCS), 1947 (ICMICA), to encourage in members an awareness of their responsibilities as people and Christians in the student and intellectual milieux to promote contacts between students and graduates throughout the world and co-ordinate the contribution of Catholic intellectual circles to international life; mems: 80 student and 60 intellectual organizations in 80 countries; ICMICA—Pres. MARY J. MWINGIRA (Tanzania); Gen. Sec. ANSELMO LEE SEONG-HOON (Republic of Korea); IMCS—Gen. Secs WALTER PRYSTHON (Brazil), ROLAND RANAIVOARISON (Madagascar); publ. *Convergence* (3 a year).

Salvation Army: International HQ, 101 Queen Victoria St, London, EC4P 4EP, United Kingdom; tel. (20) 7332-0101; fax (20) 7236-4981; e-mail websa@salvationarmy.org; internet www.salvationarmy.org; f. 1865 to spread the Christian gospel and relieve poverty; emphasis is placed on the need for personal discipleship, and to make its evangelism effective it adopts a quasi-military form of organization. Social, medical and educational work is also performed in the 109 countries where the Army operates; Pres. Gen. JOHN LARSSON; Chief of Staff Commissioner ISRAEL L. GAITHER; publs The War Cry; (weekly).

Theosophical Society: Adyar, Chennai 600 020, India; tel. (44) 4915552; fax (44) 4902706; e-mail theossoc@satyam.net.in; internet www.ts-adyar.org; f. 1875; aims at universal brotherhood, without distinction of race, creed, sex, caste or colour; study of comparative religion, philosophy and science; investigation of unexplained laws of nature and powers latent in man; mems: 35,000 in 70 countries; Pres. RADHA S. BURNIER; Int. Sec. MARY ANDERSON; publs *The Theosophist* (monthly), *Adyar News Letter* (quarterly), *Brahmavidya* (annually).

United Bible Societies: 7th Floor, Reading Bridge House, Reading, RG1 8PJ, United Kingdom; tel. (118) 950-0200; fax (118) 950-0857; e-mail jphillips@ubs-wsc.org; internet www.biblesociety .org; f. 1946; co-ordinates the translation, production and distribution of the Bible by Bible Societies world-wide; works with national Bible Societies to develop religious programmes; mems: 136 Bible Societies in more than 200 countries; Pres. Dr SAMUEL ESCOBAR (Peru/USA); Gen. Sec. NEIL CROSBIE (UK); publs *Bulletin (1 or 2 a year)*, *The Bible Translator* (quarterly), *Publishing World* (3 a year), *Prayer Booklet* (annually), *Special Report* (3 or 4 a year), *World Report* (monthly).

Watch Tower Bible and Tract Society: (British section) The Ridgeway, London, NW7 1RN, United Kingdom; tel. (20) 8906-2211; fax (20) 8371-0051; e-mail pr@wtbts.org.uk; internet www .watchtower.org; f. 1881; 110 branches; serves as legal agency for Jehovah's Witnesses; Pres. RON DRAGE; Sec. and Treas. TOM CRUSE; publs *The Watchtower* (2 a month, in 146 languages), *Awake!* (2 a month, in 87 languages).

World Alliance of Reformed Churches (Presbyterian and Congregational): Box 2100, 150 route de Ferney, 1211 Geneva 2, Switzerland; tel. (22) 7916240; fax (22) 7916505; e-mail sn@warc.ch; internet www.warc.ch; f. 1970 by merger of WARC (Presbyterian) (f.1875) with International Congregational Council (f. 1891) to promote fellowship among Reformed, Presbyterian and Congregational churches; mems: 214 churches in 106 countries; Pres. Prof. CHOAN-SENG SONG; Gen. Sec. Dr SETRI NYOMI (Ghana); publs *Reformed World* (quarterly), *Up-Date*.

World Christian Life Community: Borgo S. Spirito 8, Casella Postale 6139, 00195 Rome, Italy; tel. (06) 6868079; fax (06) 6813–2497; e-mail mcvx.wclc@agora.it; f. 1953 as World Federation of the Sodalities of our Lady (first group f.1563) as a lay organization based on the teachings of Ignatius Loyola, to integrate Christian faith and daily living; mems: groups in 55 countries representing about 100,000 individuals; Pres. JOSÉ MARÍA RIERA; Exec. Sec. GILLES MICHAUD; publ. *Progressio* (in English, French and Spanish).

World Conference on Religion and Peace: 777 United Nations Plaza, New York, NY 10017, USA; tel. (212) 687-2163; fax (212) 983-0566; internet www.wcrp.org; f. 1970 to co-ordinate education and action of various world religions for world peace and justice; mems: religious organizations and individuals in 100 countries; Sec.-Gen. Dr WILLIAM VENDLEY; publ. *Religion for Peace*.

World Congress of Faiths: 2 Market St, Oxford, OX1 3EF, United Kingdom; tel. (1865) 202751; fax (1865) 202746; e-mail worldconfaiths@aol.com; internet www.worldfaiths.org; f. 1936 to promote a spirit of fellowship among mankind through an understanding of one another's religions, to bring together people of all nationalities, backgrounds and creeds in mutual respect and tolerance, to encourage the study and understanding of issues arising out of multi-faith societies, and to promote welfare and peace; mems: about 400; Pres Prof. KEITH WARD; Rev. MARCUS BRAYBROOKE; Chair. Rabbi JACQUELINE TABICK; publ. *Interreligious Insight* (quarterly).

World Evangelical Alliance: 141 Middle Rd 05-05, GSM Bldg, Singapore 188976, Singapore; tel. 3397900; fax 3383756; e-mail 100012.345@compuserve.com; internet www.worldevangelical.org; f. 1951 as World Evangelical Fellowship, on reorganization of World Evangelical Alliance (f. 1846), reverted to original name Jan. 2002; an int. grouping of national and regional bodies of evangelical Christians; encourages the organization of national fellowships and assists national mems in planning their activities; mems: national evangelical asscns in 110 countries; International Dir AUGUSTIN B.

VENCER, Jr; publs *Evangelical World* (monthly), *Evangelical Review of Theology* (quarterly).

World Fellowship of Buddhists: 616 Benjasiri Pk, Soi Medhinivet off Soi Sukhumvit 24, Bangkok 10110, Thailand; tel. (2) 661-1284; fax (2) 661-0555; e-mail wfb-hq@asianet.co.th; internet www .wfb-hq.org; f. 1950 to promote strict observance and practice of the teachings of the Buddha; holds General Conference every 2 years; 146 regional centres in 37 countries; Pres. PHAN WANNAMETHEE; Hon. Sec.-Gen. PHALLOP THAIARRY; publs *WFB Journal* (6 a year), *WFB Review* (quarterly), *WFB Newsletter* (monthly), documents, booklets.

World Hindu Federation: c/o Dr Jogendra Jha, Pashupati Kshetra, Kathmandu, Nepal; tel. (1) 470182; fax (1) 470131; e-mail hem@karki.com.np; f. 1981 to promote and preserve Hindu philosophy and culture to protect the rights of Hindus, particularly the right to worship. Executive Board meets annually; mems: in 45 countries and territories; Sec.-Gen. Dr JOGENDRA JHA (Nepal); publ. *Vishwa Hindu* (monthly).

World Jewish Congress: 501 Madison Ave, New York, NY 10022, USA; tel. (212) 755-5770; fax (212) 755-5883; internet www.wcj.org .il; f. 1936 as a voluntary asscn of representative Jewish communities and organizations throughout the world; aims to foster the unity of the Jewish people and ensure the continuity and development of their heritage; mems: Jewish communities in 84 countries; Pres. EDGAR M. BRONFMAN; Sec.-Gen. ISRAEL SINGER; publs *Gesher* (Hebrew quarterly, Israel), *Boletín Informativo OJI* (fortnightly, Buenos Aires).

World Methodist Council: International Headquarters, POB 518, Lake Junaluska, NC 28745, USA; tel. (704) 456-9432; fax (704) 456-9433; e-mail georgefreeman@mindspring.com; internet www .worldmethodistcouncil.org; f. 1881 to deepen the fellowship of the Methodist peoples, encourage evangelism, foster Methodist participation in the ecumenical movement and promote the unity of Methodist witness and service; mems: 77 churches in 132 countries, comprising 36m. individuals; Gen. Sec. GEORGE H. FREEMAN (USA); publ. *World Parish* (6 a year).

World Sephardi Federation: 13 rue Marignac, 1206 Geneva, Switzerland; tel. (22) 3473313; fax (22) 3472839; f. 1951 to strengthen the unity of Jewry and Judaism among Sephardi and Oriental Jews, to defend and foster religious and cultural activities of all Sephardi and Oriental Jewish communities and preserve their spiritual heritage, to provide moral and material assistance where necessary and to co-operate with other similar organizations; mems: 50 communities and organizations in 33 countries; Pres. NESSIM D. GAON; Sec.-Gen. SHIMON DERY.

World Student Christian Federation—WSCF: 5 route des Morillons, Grand-Saconnex, 1218 Geneva, Switzerland; tel. (22) 7988953; fax (22) 7982370; e-mail wscf@wscf.ch; internet www.wscf .org; f. 1895 to proclaim Jesus Christ as Lord and Saviour in the academic community, and to present students with the claims of the Christian faith over their whole life; holds General Assembly every four years; mems: 67 national Student Christian Movements, and 34 national correspondents; Chair. Rev. EJIKE OKORD (Nigeria); Secs-Gen. BEATE FAGERLI (Norway), LAWRENCE BREW (Ghana).

World Union for Progressive Judaism: 633 Third Ave, New York, NY 10017, USA; tel. (212) 249-0100; fax (212) 650-4099; internet wupj.org; f. 1926; promotes and co-ordinates efforts of Reform, Liberal, Progressive and Reconstructionist congregations throughout the world; supports new congregations; assigns and employs rabbis; sponsors seminaries and schools; organizes international conferences; maintains a youth section; mems: organizations and individuals in 30 countries; Pres. AUSTIN BEUTEL; Exec. Dir Rabbi RICHARD G. HIRSCH (Israel); publs *News Updates*, *International Conference Reports*, *European Judaism* (bi-annual).

World Union of Catholic Women's Organisations: 18 rue Notre-Dame-des-Champs, 75006 Paris, France; tel. 1-45-44-27-65; fax 1-42-84-04-80; e-mail wucwoparis@wanadoo.fr; internet www.wucwo .org; f. 1910 to promote and co-ordinate the contribution of Catholic women in international life, in social, civic, cultural and religious matters; mems: 20m. Pres. MARÍA EUGENIA DÍAZ DE PFENNICH (Mexico); Sec.-Gen. GILLIAN BADCOCK (UK); publ. *Women's Voice* (quarterly, in four languages).

Science

International Council for Science—ICSU: 51 blvd de Montmorency, 75016 Paris, France; tel. 1-45-25-03-29; fax 1-42-88-94-31; e-mail secretariat@icsu.org; internet www.icsu.org; f. 1919 as International Research Council; present name adopted 1931; new statutes adopted 1996; to co-ordinate international co-operation in theoretical and applied sciences and to promote national scientific research through the intermediary of affiliated national organizations; General Assembly of representatives of national and scientific members meets every three years to formulate policy. The following committees have been established: Cttee on Science for Food Security, Scientific Cttee on Antarctic Research, Scientific Cttee on Oceanic Research, Cttee on Space Research, Scientific Cttee on Water Research, Scientific Cttee on Solar-Terrestrial Physics, Cttee on Science and Technology in Developing Countries, Cttee on Data for Science and Technology, Programme on Capacity Building in Science, Scientific Cttee on Problems of the Environment, Steering Cttee on Genetics and Biotechnology and Scientific Cttee on International Geosphere-Biosphere Programme. The following services and Inter-Union Committees and Commissions have been established: Federation of Astronomical and Geophysical Data Analysis Services, Inter-Union Commission on Frequency Allocations for Radio Astronomy and Space Science, Inter-Union Commission on Radio Meteorology, Inter-Union Commission on Spectroscopy, Inter-Union Commission on Lithosphere; National mems: academies or research councils in 98 countries; Scientific mems and assocs: 26 international unions (see below) and 28 scientific associates; Pres. W. ARBER; Sec.-Gen. H. A. MOONEY; publs *ICSU Yearbook*, *Science International* (quarterly), *Annual Report*.

UNIONS FEDERATED TO THE ICSU

International Astronomical Union—IAU: 98 bis blvd d'Arago, 75014 Paris, France; tel. 1-43-25-83-58; fax 1-43-25-26-16; e-mail iau@iap.fr; internet www.iau.org; f. 1919 to facilitate co-operation between the astronomers of various countries and to further the study of astronomy in all its branches; organizes colloquia every two months; mems: organizations in 65 countries, and 9,000 individual mems; Pres. FRANCO PACINI (Italy); Gen. Sec. HANS RICKMAN (Sweden); publs *IAU Information Bulletin* (2 a year), *Symposia Series* (6 a year), *Highlights* (every 3 years).

International Geographical Union—IGU: Dept of Geography, University of Bonn, 53115 Bonn, Meckenheimer Allee 166, Germany; tel. (228) 739287; fax (228) 739272; e-mail secretariat@igu.bn .eunet.be; internet www.helsinki.fi/science/igu; f. 1922 to encourage the study of problems relating to geography, to promote and co-ordinate research requiring international co-operation, and to organize international congresses and commissions; mems: 83 countries, 11 associates; Pres. Prof. BRUNO MESSERLI (Switzerland); Sec.-Gen. Prof. ECKART EHLERS (Germany); publ. *IGU Bulletin* (2 a year).

International Mathematical Union—IMU: c/o Institute for Advanced Study (IAS), Einstein Drive, Princeton, NJ 08540, USA; e-mail imu@ias.edu; internet elib.zib.de/imu; f. 1952 to support and assist the International Congress of Mathematicians and other international scientific meetings or conferences and to encourage and support other international mathematical activities considered likely to contribute to the development of mathematical science—pure, applied or educational; mems: 63 countries; Pres. Prof. JACOB PALIS; Sec.-Gen. Prof. PHILLIP GRIFFITHS.

International Union for Physical and Engineering Sciences in Medicine—IUPESM: c/o Prof. G. Fullerton, UTHSCSA, Dept of Radiology, MSC 7800, 7703 Floyd Curl Drive, San Antonio, TX 78229-3900, USA; tel. (210) 567-5551; fax (210) 567-5549; e-mail fullerton@uthscsa.edu; internet www.iupesm.org; f. 1980 by its two constituent orgs (International Federation for Medical and Biological Engineering (see p. 361), and International Organization for Medical Physics, see p. 362); promotes international co-operation in health care science and technology and represents the professional interests of members; organizes seminars, workshops, scientific conferences; holds World Congress every three years (2003: Sydney, Australia); Sec.-Gen. Prof. GARY FULLERTON (USA); publs *IUPESM Newsletter* (2 a year), Congress proceedings.

International Union for Pure and Applied Biophysics—IUPAB: School of Biochemistry and Molecular Biology, University of Leeds, Leeds, LS2 9JT, United Kingdom; tel. (113) 2333023; fax (113) 2333167; e-mail a.c.t.north@leeds.ac.uk; internet www.iupab .org; f. 1961 to organize international co-operation in biophysics and promote communication between biophysics and allied subjects, to encourage national co-operation between biophysical societies, and to contribute to the advancement of biophysical knowledge; mems: 50 adhering bodies; Pres. I. PECHT (Israel); Sec.-Gen. Prof. A. C. T. NORTH (UK); publ. *Quarterly Reviews of Biophysics*.

International Union of Biochemistry and Molecular Biology—IUBMB: Institute for Biophysical Chemistry and Biochemistry, Technical University Berlin, Franklinstr. 29, 10587 Berlin, Germany; tel. (30) 31424205; fax (30) 31424783; e-mail kleinkauf@chem .tu-berlin.de; internet www.iubmb.unibe.ch; f. 1955 to sponsor the International Congresses of Biochemistry, to co-ordinate research and discussion, to organize co-operation between the societies of biochemistry and molecular biology, to promote high standards of biochemistry and molecular biology throughout the world and to contribute to the advancement of biochemistry and molecular biology in all its international aspects; mems: 65 bodies; Pres. W. WHELAN (USA); Gen. Sec. Prof. Dr H. KLEINKAUF (Germany).

International Union of Biological Sciences—IUBS: 51 blvd de Montmorency, 75016 Paris, France; tel. 1-45-25-00-09; fax 1-45-25-20-29; e-mail iubs@paris7.jussieu.fr; internet www.iubs.org; f. 1919; serves as an international forum for the promotion of biology; runs scientific programmes on subjects including biosystematics, bio-nomenclature, reproductive biology and aquaculture; carries out international collaborative research programmes; convenes General Assembly every 3 years; mems: 44 national bodies, 80 scientific bodies; Exec. Dir Dr T. YOUNES; publs *Biology International* (4 a year), *IUBS Monographs*, *IUBS Methodology*, *Manual Series*.

International Union of Crystallography: c/o M. H. Dacombe, 2 Abbey Sq., Chester, CH1 2HU, United Kingdom; tel. (1244) 345431; fax (1244) 344843; internet www.iucr.org; f. 1947 to facilitate the international standardization of methods, units, nomenclature and symbols used in crystallography; and to form a focus for the relations of crystallography to other sciences; mems: in 40 countries; Pres. Prof. W. L. DUAX (Netherlands); Gen. Sec. S. LARSEN (Denmark); Exec. Sec. M. H. DACOMBE; publs *IUCR Newsletter*, *Acta Crystallographica*, *Journal of Applied Crystallography*, *Journal of Synchroton Radiation*, *International Tables for Crystallography*, *World Directory of Crystallographers*, *IUCr/OUP Crystallographic Symposia*, *IUCr/OUP Monographs on Crystallography*, *IUCr/OUP Texts on Crystallography*.

International Union of Food Science and Technology: POB 61021, 511 Maplegrove Rd, Oakville, ON L6J 6X0, Canada; tel. (905) 815-1926; fax (905) 815-1574; e-mail iufost@ca.inter.net; internet home.inforamp.net/-iufost; f. 1970; sponsors international symposia and congresses; mems: 60 national groups; Pres. Prof. WALTER SPIESS (Germany); Sec.-Gen. JUDITH MEECH (Canada); publ. *IUFOST Newsline* (3 a year).

International Union of Geodesy and Geophysics—IUGC: Cires Campus Box 216, University of Colorado, Boulder, CO 80309, USA; tel. (303) 497-51-47; fax (303) 497-36-45; e-mail jjoselyn@cires .colorado.edu; internet www.iugg.org; f. 1919; federation of seven asscns representing Geodesy, Seismology and Physics of the Earth's Interior, Physical Sciences of the Ocean, Volcanology and Chemistry of the Earth's Interior, Hydrological Sciences, Meteorology and Atmospheric Physics, Geomagnetism and Aeronomy, which meet in committees and at the General Assemblies of the Union; organizes scientific meetings and sponsors various permanent services to collect, analyse and publish geophysical data; mems: in 66 countries; Pres. Prof. MASARU KONO (Japan); Sec.-Gen. Dr JOANN JOSELYN (USA); publs *IUGG Yearbook*, *Journal of Geodesy* (quarterly), *IASPEI Newsletter* (iregular), *Bulletin Volcanologique* (2 a year), *Hydrological Sciences Journal* (quarterly), *Bulletin de l'Association Internationale d'Hydrologie Scientifique* (quarterly), *IAMAP News Bulletin* (irregular).

International Union of Geological Sciences—IUGS: c/o Norges Geologiske Underskelse, N-7491 Trondheim, Norway; tel. 73-90-40-40; fax 73-50-22-30; e-mail iugs.secretariat.ngu.no; internet www .iugs.org/; f. 1961 to encourage the study of geoscientific problems, facilitate international and inter-disciplinary co-operation in geology and related sciences, and support the quadrennial International Geological Congress; organizes international meetings and co-sponsors joint programmes, including the International Geological Correlation Programme (with UNESCO); mems: in 114 countries; Pres. Prof. ED DE MULDER (Netherlands); Sec.-Gen. Prof. A. BORIANI (Italy).

International Union of Immunological Societies—IUIS: Executive Manager, IUIS Central Office, c/o Vienna Academy of Post-graduate Medical Education and Research, Alser Strasse 4, 1090 Vienna, Austria; tel. (1) 405-13-83-13; fax (1) 405-13-83-23; e-mail iuis-central-office@medacad.org; internet www.iuisonline.org; f. 1969; holds triennial international congress; mems: national societies in 50 countries and territories; Pres. PHILIPPA MARRACK; Sec.-Gen. Dr MOHAMED R. DAHA; Exec. Man. SYLVIA TRITTINGER.

International Union of Microbiological Societies—IUMS: c/o Prof. John S. Mackenzie, Dept of Microbiology, University of Queensland, Brisbane QLD 4072, Australia; tel. (7) 3365-4648; fax (7) 3365-6265; e-mail john.mackenzie@uq.edu.au; internet www .iums.org; f. 1930; mems: 106 national microbiological societies; Pres. Prof. JULIAN DAVIES (Canada); Sec.-Gen. Prof. JOHN S. MACKENZIE; publs *International Journal of Systematic Bacteriology* (quarterly), *International Journal of Food Microbiology* (every 2 months), *Advances in Microbial Ecology* (annually), Archives of Virology.

International Union of Nutritional Sciences—IUNS: c/o Dr Galal, UCLA School of Public Health, 10833 Le Conte Ave, POB 951772, Los Angeles, CA 90095-1772, USA; tel. (310) 2069639; fax (310) 7941805; e-mail ogalal@ucla.edu; internet www.iuns.org; f. 1946 to promote international co-operation in the scientific study of nutrition and its applications, to encourage research and exchange of scientific information by holding international congresses and issuing publications; mems: 69 organizations; Pres. Dr MARK

WHALQVIST; Sec.-Gen. Dr OSMAN GALAL; publs *Annual Report, IUNS Directory, Newsletter*.

International Union of Pharmacology: c/o Prof. Sue Piper Duckles, Dept of Pharmacology, College of Medicine, University of California, Irvine, CA 92697, USA; tel. (949) 824-4265; fax (924) 824-4855; e-mail spduckle@uci.edu; internet www.iuphar.org; f. 1963 to promote co-ordination of research, discussion and publication in the field of pharmacology, including clinical pharmacology, drug metabolism and toxicology; co-operates with WHO in all matters concerning drugs and drug research; holds international congresses; mems: 54 national and three regional societies; Pres. PAUL M. VANHOUTTE (France); Sec.-Gen. Prof. SUE PIPER DUCKLES; publ. *PI (Pharmacology International)*.

International Union of Physiological Sciences—IUPS: IUPS Secretariat, LGN, Bâtiment CERVI, Hôpital de la Pitié-Salpêtrière, 83 blvd de l'Hôpital, 75013 Paris, France; tel. 1-42-17-75-37; fax 1-42-17-75-75; e-mail suorsoni@infobiogen.fr; internet www.iups.org; f. 1955; mems: 50 national, six assoc., four regional, two affiliated and 14 special mems; Pres. Prof. ALAN W. COWLEY,, Jr (USA); Sec. Prof. OLE PETERSEN (UK).

International Union of Psychological Science: c/o Prof. P. L.-J. Ritchie, Ecole de psychologie, Université d'Ottawa, 145 Jean-Jacques-Lussier, CP 450, Succ. A, Ottawa, ON KIN 6N5, Canada; tel. (613) 562-5289; fax (613) 562-5169; e-mail pritchie@uottawa.ca; internet www.iupsys.org; f. 1951 to contribute to the development of intellectual exchange and scientific relations between psychologists of different countries; mems: 68 national and 12 affiliate orgs; Pres. Prof. M. DENIS (France); Sec.-Gen. Prof. P. L.-J. RITCHIE (Canada); publs *International Journal of Psychology* (quarterly), *The IUPsyS Directory* (irregular), *Psychology CD Rom Resource File* (annually).

International Union of Pure and Applied Chemistry—IUPAC: Bldg 19, 104 T. W. Alexander Dr., Research Triangle Park, POB 13757, NC 27709-3757, USA; tel. (919) 485-8700; fax (919) 485-8706; e-mail secretariat@iupac.org; internet www.iupac.org; f. 1919 to organize permanent co-operation between chemical asscns in the member countries, to study topics of international importance requiring standardization or codification, to co-operate with other international organizations in the field of chemistry and to contribute to the advancement of all aspects of chemistry; holds a biennial General Assembly; mems: in 43 countries; Pres. Prof. P. S. STEYN (South Africa); Sec.-Gen. Dr E. D. BECKER (USA); publs *Chemistry International* (2 a month), *Pure and Applied Chemistry* (monthly).

International Union of Pure and Applied Physics—IUPAP: c/o ESRF, BP 220, 38043 Grenoble Cédex, France; tel. 4-76-88-20-30; fax 4-76-88-24-18; e-mail petroff@esrf.fr; internet www.iupap.org; f. 1922 to promote and encourage international co-operation in physics and facilitate the world-wide development of science; mems: in 46 countries; Pres. Y. PETROFF; Sec.-Gen. Dr RENÉ TURLAY (France).

International Union of Radio Science: c/o INTEC, Ghent University, Sint-Pietersnieuwstraat 41, 9000 Ghent, Belgium; tel. (9) 264-33-20; fax (9) 264-42-88; e-mail ursi@intec.rug.ac.be; internet www.ursi.org; f. 1919 to stimulate and co-ordinate, on an international basis, studies, research, applications, scientific exchange and communication in the field of radio science; aims to encourage the adoption of common methods of measurement and the standardization of measuring instruments used in scientific work; represents radio science at national and international levels; there are 48 national committees; Pres. Prof. K. SCHLEGEL (Germany); Sec.-Gen. Prof. P. LAGASSE (Belgium); publs *The Radio Science Bulletin* (quarterly), *Proceedings of General Assemblies* (every 3 years), *Handbook on Radiopropagation related to Satellite Communications in Tropical and Subtropical Countries*, *Review of Radio Science* (every 3 years).

International Union of the History and Philosophy of Science: Division of the History of Science (DHS): Centre d'Histoire des Sciences et des Techniques, 5 quai Banning, 4000 Liège, Belgium; tel. (4) 366-94-79; fax (4) 366-94-47; e-mail chst@ulg.ac.be; Division of the History of Logic, Methodology and Philosophy of Science (DLMPS): 161 rue Ada, 34392 Montpellier, France; f. 1956 to promote research into the history and philosophy of science; DHS has 44 national committees and DLMPS has 35 committees; DHS Council: Pres. Prof. B. V. SUBBARAYAPPA (India); Sec. Prof. R. HALLEUX (Belgium); DLMPS Council: Pres. Prof. M. RABIN (Israel); Sec.-Gen. Prof. D. WESTERSTAHL (Sweden).

International Union of Theoretical and Applied Mechanics: c/o Prof. Dick H. van Campen, Dept of Mechanical Engineering, Eindhoven University of Technology, POB 513, 5600 Eindhoven, Netherlands; tel. (40) 2472768; fax (40) 2461418; e-mail sg@iutam.net; internet www.iutam.net; f. 1947 to form links between those engaged in scientific work (theoretical or experimental) in mechanics or related sciences; organizes international congresses of theoretical and applied mechanics, through a standing Congress Committee, and other international meetings; engages in other activities designed to promote the development of mechanics as a science; mems: from 49 countries; Pres. Prof. H. K. MOFFATT (UK); Sec.-Gen. Prof. D. H. VAN CAMPEN (Netherlands); publs *Annual Report, Newsletter*.

International Union of Toxicology: c/o Dept of Environmental and Occupational Health, Graduate School of Public Health, University of Pittsburgh, Pittsburgh, PA 15261, USA; tel. (412) 383-9473; fax (412) 624-3040; e-mail mhk@pitt.edu; internet www.iutox.org; f. 1980 to foster international co-operation among toxicologists and promote world-wide acquisition, dissemination and utilization of knowledge in the field; sponsors International Congresses and other education programmes; mems: 43 national societies; Sec.-Gen. MERYL H. KAROL; publs *IUTOX Newsletter*, Congress proceedings.

OTHER ORGANIZATIONS

Association for the Taxonomic Study of the Flora of Tropical Africa: National Botanic Garden of Belgium, Domein van Bouchout, 1860 Meise, Belgium; tel. (2) 260-09-28; fax (2) 260-08-45; e-mail rammeloo@br.fgov.be; f. 1950 to facilitate co-operation and liaison between botanists engaged in the study of the flora of tropical Africa south of the Sahara including Madagascar; maintains a library; mems: c. 800 botanists in 63 countries; Sec.-Gen. Prof. J. RAMMELOO; publs *AETFAT Bulletin* (annually), *Proceedings*.

Association of European Atomic Forums—FORATOM: 15–17 rue Belliard, 1040 Brussels, Belgium; tel. (2) 502-45-95; fax (2) 502-39-02; e-mail foratom@foratom.org; internet www.foratom.org; f. 1960; promotes the peaceful use of nuclear energy; provides information on nuclear energy issues to the EU, the media and the public; represents the nuclear industry within the EU institutions; holds periodical conferences; mems: atomic forums in 16 countries; Pres. FRANCIS TÉTREAU; Sec.-Gen. Dr PETER HAUG.

Association of Geoscientists for International Development—AGID: Institute of Geoscience, University of São Paulo, Rua do Lago 562, São Paulo, 05508-900 Brazil; tel. (11) 818-4206; fax (11) 210-4958; e-mail kmellito@usp.br; internet agid.igc.usp.br; f. 1974 to encourage communication and the exchange of knowledge between those interested in the application of the geosciences to international development; contributes to the funding of geoscience development projects; provides postgraduate scholarships; mems: 2,000 individual and institutional mems in over 120 countries; Pres. Dr S. D. LIMAYE (India); Sec. Dr A. J. REEDMAN (UK); publs *Geoscience and Developments* (2 or 3 a year), reports on geoscience and development issues.

Council for the International Congresses of Entomology: c/o FAO, POB 3700 MCPO, 1277 Makati, Philippines; tel. (2) 8134229; fax (2) 8127725; e-mail joliver@gasou.edu; f. 1910 to act as a link between quadrennial congresses and to arrange the venue for each congress; the committee is also the entomology section of the International Union of Biological Sciences; Chair. Dr M. J. WHITTAM (Australia); Sec. Dr J. OLIVER (USA).

European Association of Geoscientists and Engineers—EAGE: c/o EAGE Holdings, 3990 DB Houten, Netherlands; tel. (30) 6354055; fax (30) 6343524; e-mail eage@eage.nl; internet www.eage.nl; f. 1997 by merger of European Asscn of Exploration Geophysicists and Engineers (f. 1951) and the European Asscn of Petroleum Geoscientists and Engineers (f. 1988); these two organizations have become, respectively, the Geophysical and the Petroleum Divisions of the EAGE; aims to promote the applications of geoscience and related subjects and to foster co-operation between those working or studying in the fields; organizes conferences, workshops, education programmes and exhibitions; seeks global co-operation with organizations with similar objectives; mems: approx. 5,400 in 95 countries; Exec. Dir A. VAN GERWEN; publs *Geophysical Prospecting* (6 a year), *First Break* (monthly), *Petroleum Geoscience* (quarterly).

European Molecular Biology Organization—EMBO: Meyerhofstr. 1, Postfach 1022.40, 69012 Heidelberg, Germany; tel. (6221)8891-0; fax (6221) 8891-200; e-mail embo@embo.org; internet www.embo.org; f. 1962 to promote collaboration in the field of molecular biology and to establish fellowships for training and research; has established the European Molecular Biology Laboratory where a majority of the disciplines comprising the subject are represented; mems: 1,200; Exec. Dir Prof. FRANK GANNON; publ. *EMBO Journal* (24 a year); *EMBO Report* (monthly).

European Organization for Nuclear Research—CERN: European Laboratory for Particle Physics, 1211 Geneva 23, Switzerland; tel. (22) 7676111; fax (22) 7676555; internet www.cern.ch; f. 1954 to provide for collaboration among European states in nuclear research of a pure scientific and fundamental character, for peaceful purposes only; Council comprises two representatives of each member state; major experimental facilities: Proton Synchrotron (of 25–28 GeV), and Super Proton Synchrotron (of 450 GeV). Budget (1998) 875m. Swiss francs; mems: 20 European countries; observers: Israel,

Japan, Russia, Turkey, USA, European Commission, UNESCO; Dir-Gen. LUCIANO MAIANI (Italy); publs *CERN Courier* (monthly), *Annual Report*, *Scientific Reports*.

European-Mediterranean Seismological Centre: c/o LDG, BP 12, 91680 Bruyères-le-Châtel, France; tel. 1-69-26-78-14; fax 1-69-26-70-00; e-mail csem@mail.csem.fr; internet www.emsc-csem.org; f. 1976 for rapid determination of seismic hypocentres in the region; maintains data base; mems: institutions in 21 countries; Pres. C. BROWITT; Sec.-Gen. F. RIVIERE; publ. *Newsletter* (two a year).

Federation of Arab Scientific Research Councils: POB 13027, Al Karkh/Karadat Mariam, Baghdad, Iraq; tel. (1) 8881709; fax (1) 8866346; f. 1976 to encourage co-operation in scientific research, promote the establishment of new institutions and plan joint regional research projects; mems: national science bodies in 15 countries; Sec.-Gen. Dr TAHA AL-NUEIMI; publs *Journal of Computer Research*, *Journal of Environmental and Sustained Development*, *Journal of Biotechnology*.

Federation of Asian Scientific Academies and Societies—FASAS: c/o Malaysian Scientific Association (MSA), Room 1, 2nd Floor, Bangunan Sultan, Salahuddin Abdul Aziz Shah, 16 Jalan Utara, POB 48, 46700 Petaling Jaya, Malaysia; tel. (3)7954-1644; fax (3) 7957-8930; e-mail malsci@tm.net.my; f. 1984 to stimulate regional co-operation and promote national and regional self-reliance in science and technology, by organizing meetings, training and research programmes and encouraging the exchange of scientists and of scientific information; mems: national scientific academies and societies from Afghanistan, Australia, Bangladesh, People's Republic of China, India, Republic of Korea, Malaysia, Nepal, New Zealand, Pakistan, Philippines, Singapore, Sri Lanka, Thailand; Pres. Prof. TING-KUEH SOON (Philippines); Sec. Prof. INDIRA NATH (India).

Federation of European Biochemical Societies: c/o Institute of Cancer Biology and Danish Centre for Human Genome Research, Danish Cancer Society, Strandboulevarden 49, 2100 Copenhagen Ø, Denmark; tel. 3525-7363; fax 3525-7376; e-mail secretariat@febs.org; internet www.febs.org; f. 1964 to promote the science of biochemistry through meetings of European biochemists, advanced courses and the provision of fellowships; mems: 40,000 in 34 societies; Chair. Prof. G. DIRHEIMER; Sec.-Gen. Prof. JULIO E. CELIS; publs *European Journal of Biochemistry*, *FEBS Letters*, *FEBS Bulletin*.

Foundation for International Scientific Co-ordination (Fondation 'Pour la science', Centre international de synthèse): Revue de Synthèse, Centre International de Synthèse, CNRS UMS 2267 ACTA, 4 rue Lhomond, 75005, Paris, France; tel. 1-55-42-83-11; fax 1-55-42-83-19; e-mail revuedesynthese@ens.fr; internet www.ehess.fr/acta/synthese; f. 1925; Dirs MICHEL BLAY, ERIC BRIAN; publs *Revue de Synthèse*, *Revue d'Histoire des Sciences*, *Semaines de Synthèse*, *L'Evolution de l'Humanité*.

Intergovernmental Oceanographic Commission: UNESCO, 1 rue Miollis, 75732 Paris Cédex 15, France; tel. 1-45-68-39-83; fax 1-45-68-58-10; internet ioc.unesco.org/iocweb; f. 1960 to promote scientific investigation of the nature and resources of the oceans through the concerted action of its members; mems: 127 govts; Chair. SU JILAN (China); Exec. Sec. Dr PATRICIO BERNAL; publs *IOC Technical Series* (irregular), IOC *Manuals* and *Guides* (irregular), *IOC Workshop Reports* (irregular) and *IOC Training Course Reports* (irregular), annual reports.

International Academy of Astronautics—IAA: 6 rue Galilee, POB 1268–16, 75766 Paris Cédex 16, France; tel. 1-47-23-82-15; fax 1-47-23-82-16; internet www.iaanet.org; f. 1960; fosters the development of astronautics for peaceful purposes, holds scientific meetings and makes scientific studies, reports, awards and book awards; maintains 19 scientific cttees and a multilingual terminology data base (20 languages); mems: 681, and 382 corresponding mems, in basic sciences, engineering sciences, life sciences and social sciences, from 57 countries; Sec.-Gen. Dr JEAN-MICHEL CONTANT; publ. *Acta Astronautica* (monthly).

International Association for Biologicals—IABS: 8 chemin de la Gravière, 1227 Acacias, Geneva , Switzerland; tel. (22) 301-1036; fax (22) 301-1037; e-mail iabs@iabs.org; internet www.iabs.org; f. 1955 to connect producers and controllers of immunological products (sera, vaccines, etc.), for the study and development of methods of standardization; supports international organizations in their efforts to solve problems of standardization; mems: c. 500; Pres. J. PETRICCIANI (USA); Sec.-Gen. D. GAUDRY (France); publs *Newsletter* (quarterly), *Biologicals* (quarterly).

International Association for Earthquake Engineering: Kenchiku Kaikan, 3rd Floor, 5-26-20, Shiba, Minato-ku, Tokyo 108, Japan; tel. (3) 453-1281; fax (3) 453-0428; internet www.iaee.or.jp; f. 1963 to promote international co-operation among scientists and engineers in the field of earthquake engineering through exchange of knowledge, ideas and results of research and practical experience;

mems: national cttees in 49 countries; Pres. SHELDON CHERRY (Canada); Sec.-Gen. Dr TSUNEO KATAYAMA.

International Association for Ecology—INTECOL: Lunigiana Museum of Natural History, 54011 Aulla, Italy; tel. (0187) 400252; fax (0187) 420727; e-mail afarina@tamnet.it; internet www.intecol .org; f. 1967 to provide opportunities for communication between ecologists world-wide to co-operate with organizations and individuals having related aims and interests; to encourage studies in the different fields of ecology; affiliated to the International Union of Biological Sciences; mems: 35 national and international ecological societies, and 1,000 individuals; Pres. J. A. LEE (UK); Sec.-Gen. A. FARINA (Italy).

International Association for Mathematical Geology—IAMG: c/o T. A. Jones, POB 2189, Houston, TX 77252-2189, USA; tel. (713) 431-6546; fax (713) 431-6336; internet www.iamg.org; f. 1968 for the preparation and elaboration of mathematical models of geological processes; the introduction of mathematical methods in geological sciences and technology; assistance in the development of mathematical investigation in geological sciences; the organization of international collaboration in mathematical geology through various forums and publications; educational programmes for mathematical geology; affiliated to the International Union of Geological Sciences; mems: c. 600; Pres. Dr R. A. OLEA (USA); Sec.-Gen. Dr T. A. JONES (USA); publs *Mathematical Geology* (8 a year), *Computers and Geosciences* (10 a year), *Natural Resources Research* (quarterly), *Newsletter* (2 a year).

International Association for Mathematics and Computers in Simulation: c/o Free University of Brussels, Automatic Control, CP 165, 50 ave F. D. Roosevelt, 1050 Brussels, Belgium; tel. (2) 650-20-97; fax (2) 650-35-64; internet www.first.gmd.de/imacs97/imacs; f. 1955 to further the study of mathematical tools and computer software and hardware, analogue, digital or hybrid computers for simulation of soft or hard systems; mems: 1,100 and 27 assoc. mems; Pres. R. VICHNEVETSKY (USA); Sec. Prof. RAYMOND HANUS; publs *Mathematics and Computers in Simulation* (6 a year), *Applied Numerical Mathematics* (6 a year), *Journal of Computational Acoustics*.

International Association for the Physical Sciences of the Ocean—IAPSO: POB 820440, Vicksburg, MS 39182-0440, USA; tel. (601) 636-1363; fax (601) 629-9640; e-mail camfield@vicksburg .com; internet www.olympus.net/IAPSO; f. 1919 to promote the study of scientific problems relating to the oceans and interactions occurring at its boundaries, chiefly in so far as such study may be carried out by the aid of mathematics, physics and chemistry; to initiate, facilitate and co-ordinate research; and to provide for discussion, comparison and publication; affiliated to the International Union of Geodesy and Geophysics; mems: 81 member states; Pres. PAOLA RIZZOLI; Sec.-Gen. Dr FRED E. CAMFIELD (USA); publ. *Publications Scientifiques* (irregular).

International Association for Plant Physiology—IAPP: c/o Dr D. Graham, Div. of Food Science and Technology, CSIRO, POB 52, North Ryde, NSW, Australia 2113; tel. (2) 9490-8333; fax (2) 9490-3107; e-mail douglasgraham@dfst.csiro.au; f. 1955 to promote the development of plant physiology at the international level through congresses, symposia and workshops, by maintaining communication with national societies and by encouraging interaction between plant physiologists in developing and developed countries; affiliated to the International Union of Biological Sciences; Pres. Prof. S. MIYACHI; Sec.-Treas. Dr D. GRAHAM.

International Association for Plant Taxonomy—IAPT: Institute of Botany, University of Vienna, Rennweg 14, 1030 Vienna, Austria; tel. (1)-4277-54098; fax (1) 4277-54099; e-mail office@ iapt-taxon.org; internet www.botanik.univie.ac.at/iapt; f. 1950 to promote the development of plant taxonomy and encourage contacts between people and institutes interested in this work; affiliated to the International Union of Biological Sciences; mems: institutes and individuals in 85 countries; publs *Taxon* (quarterly), *Regnum vegetabile* (irregular).

International Association of Botanic Gardens—IABG: c/o Prof. J. E. Hernández-Bermejo, Córdoba Botanic Garden, Avda de Linneo, s/n, 14004 Córdoba, Spain; tel. (957) 200077; fax (957) 295333; e-mail jardinbotcord@telefonica.net; f. 1954 to promote co-operation between scientific collections of living plants, including the exchange of information and specimens to promote the study of the taxonomy of cultivated plants; and to encourage the conservation of rare plants and their habitats; affiliated to the International Union of Biological Sciences; Pres. Prof. H. E. SHANAN (People's Republic of China); Sec. Prof. J. ESTEBAN HERNÁNDEZ-BERMEJO (Spain).

International Association of Geodesy: Dept of Geophysics, Juliane Maries Vej 30, 2100 Copenhagen Oe, Denmark; tel. (45) 3532-0582; fax (45) 3536-5357; e-mail cct@gfy.ku.dk; internet www .gfy.ku.dk/niag; f. 1922 to promote the study of all scientific problems of geodesy and encourage geodetic research to promote and co-ordinate international co-operation in this field; to publish results; affiliated to the International Union of Geodesy and Geophysics;

mems: national committees in 73 countries; Pres. F. Sansó (Italy); Sec.-Gen. C. C. Tscherning (Denmark); publs *Journal of Geodesy, Travaux de l'AIG.*

International Association of Geomagnetism and Aeronomy—IAGA: c/o Dr JoAnn Joselyn, NOAA Space Environment Center, 325 Broadway, Boulder, CO 80303, USA; tel. (303) 497-5147; fax (303) 494-0980; e-mail jjoselyn@sec.noaa.gov; internet www.ngdc.noaa.gov/iaga; f. 1919 for the study of questions relating to geomagnetism and aeronomy and the encouragement of research; holds General and Scientific Assemblies every two years; affiliated to the International Union of Geodesy and Geophysics; mems: countries that adhere to the IUGG; Pres. M. Kono (Japan); Sec.-Gen. Dr JoAnn Joselyn; publs *IAGA Bulletin* (including annual *Geomagnetic Data*), *IAGA News* (annually).

International Association of Hydrological Sciences: Dept of Geography, Wilfrid Laurier Univ., Waterloo, ON N2L 3C5, Canada; tel. (519) 884-1970; fax (519) 846-0968; e-mail 44iahs@mach1.wlu.ca; internet www.wlu.ca/wwwiahs/index.html; f. 1922 to promote co-operation in the study of hydrology and water resources; Pres. Dr J. C. Rodda (UK); Sec.-Gen. Dr Gordon J. Young (Canada); publs *Journal* (every 2 months), *Newsletter* (3 a year).

International Association of Meteorology and Atmospheric Sciences—IAMAS: Dept of Physics, Univ. of Toronto, Toronto, ON M5S 1A7, Canada; internet iamas.org; f. 1919; maintains permanent commissions on atmospheric ozone, radiation, atmospheric chemistry and global pollution, dynamic meteorology, polar meteorology, clouds and precipitation, climate, atmospheric electricity, planetary atmospheres and their evolution, and meteorology of the upper atmosphere; holds general assemblies every four years, special assemblies between general assemblies; affiliated to the International Union of Geodesy and Geophysics; Pres. Prof. R. Duce (USA); Sec.-Gen. Prof. R. List (Canada).

International Association of Sedimentologists: c/o Prof. José-Pedro Calvo, Departamento de Petrologia y Geoquimica, Falcutad CC Geológicas, Universidad Complutense, 28040 Madrid, Spain; tel. (913) 944905; fax (915) 442535; e-mail jpcalvo@geo.ucm.es; internet www.blackwellpublishing.com/uk/society/ias; f. 1952; affiliated to the International Union of Geological Sciences; mems: 2,200; Pres. Prof. J. A. McKenzie (Switzerland); Gen. Sec. Prof. José-Pedro Calvo (Spain); publ. *Sedimentology* (every 2 months).

International Association of Theoretical and Applied Limnology (Societas Internationalis Limnologiae): Dept of Biology, University of Alabama, Tuscaloosa, AL 35487-0206, USA; tel. (205) 348-1793; fax (205) 348-1403; e-mail rwetzel@biology.as.ua.edu; internet www.limnology.org; f. 1922 for the study of physical, chemical and biological phenomena of lakes and rivers; affiliated to the International Union of Biological Sciences; mems: c. 3,200; Pres. G. E. Likens (USA); Gen. Sec. and Treas. Robert G. Wetzel (USA).

International Association of Volcanology and Chemistry of the Earth's Interior—IAVCEI: Geophysical Institute, University of Alaska Fairbanks, POB 757320, Fairbanks, AK 99775, USA; tel. (907) 474-7131; fax (907) 474-5618; f. 1919 to examine scientifically all aspects of volcanology; affiliated to the International Union of Geodesy and Geophysics; Pres. R. S. J. Sparks (UK); Sec.-Gen. S. R. McNutt (USA); publs *Bulletin of Volcanology, Catalogue of the Active Volcanoes of the World, Proceedings in Volcanology.*

International Association of Wood Anatomists: USDA Forest Service, Forest Products, Laboratory, 1 Gifford Pinchot Drive, Madison WI 53705-2398, USA; tel. (608) 231-9200; fax (608) 231-9508; f. 1931 for the purpose of study, documentation and exchange of information on the structure of wood; holds annual conference; mems: 650 in 68 countries; Exec. Sec. Regis B. Miller; publ. *IAWA Journal.*

International Astronautical Federation—IAF: 3–5 rue Mario-Nikis, 75015 Paris, France; tel. 1-45-67-42-60; fax 1-42-73-21-20; e-mail iaf@wanadoo.fr; internet www.iafastro.com; f. 1950 to foster the development of astronautics for peaceful purposes at national and international levels; the IAF has created the International Academy of Astronautics (IAA) and the International Institute of Space Law (IISL); mems: 165 national astronautical societies in 44 countries; Pres. Marcio Barbosa (Brazil); Deputy Exec. Dir. Annie Moulin.

International Biometric Society: c/o Prof. E. Baráth, Chair. of Statistics, 2103 Gödöllö, Hungary; tel. (28) 410-694; fax (28) 430-336; internet www.tibs.org; f. 1947 for the advancement of quantitative biological science through the development of quantitative theories and the application, development and dissemination of effective mathematical and statistical techniques; the Society has 16 regional organizations and 17 national groups, is affiliated with the International Statistical Institute and WHO, and constitutes the Section of Biometry of the International Union of Biological Sciences; mems: over 6,000 in more than 70 countries; Pres. Prof. Sue Wilson (Australia); Sec. Prof. E. Baráth (Hungary); publs *Biometrics* (quarterly), *Biometric Bulletin* (quarterly), *Journal of Agricultural, Biological and Environmental Statistics* (quarterly).

International Botanical Congress: c/o Dr Peter Hoch, Missouri Botanical Garden, PO Box 299, St Louis, MO 63166-0299, USA; tel. (314) 577-5175; fax (314) 577-9589; e-mail ibc16@mobot.org; f. 1864 to inform botanists of recent progress in the plant sciences; the Nomenclature Section of the Congress attempts to provide a uniform terminology and methodology for the naming of plants; other Divisions deal with developmental, metabolic, structural, systematic and evolutionary, ecological botany; genetics and plant breeding; 2005 Congress: Vienna, Austria; affiliated to the International Union of Biological Sciences; Sec. Dr Peter Hoch.

International Bureau of Weights and Measures (Bureau international des poids et mesures—BIPM): Pavillon de Breteuil, 92312 Sèvres Cédex, France; tel. 1-45-07-70-70; fax 1-45-34-20-21; e-mail info@bipm.org; internet www.bipm.org; f. 1875 works to ensure the international unification of measurements and their traceability to the International System of Unification; carries out research and calibration; organizes international comparisons of national measurement standards; mems: 51 member states and 10 associates; Pres. J. Kovalevsky (France); Sec. R. Kaarls (Netherlands); publs *Le Système International d'Unités* (in English and French), *Metrologia* (6 a year), scientific articles, reports and monographs, committee reports.

International Cartographic Association: 136 bis rue de Grenelle, 75700 Paris 07 SP, France; tel. 1-43-98-82-95; fax 1-43-98-84-00; internet www.icaci.org; f. 1959 for the advancement, instigation and co-ordination of cartographic research involving co-operation between different nations; particularly concerned with furtherance of training in cartography, study of source material, compilation, graphic design, drawing, scribing and reproduction techniques of maps; organizes international conferences, symposia, meetings, exhibitions; mems: 80 countries; Pres. Michael Wood; publ. *ICA Newsletter* (2 a year).

International Centre of Insect Physiology and Ecology: POB 30772, Nairobi, Kenya; tel. (20) 861680; fax (20) 803360; e-mail icipe@africaonline.co.ke; internet www.icipe.org; f. 1970; specializes in research and development of environmentally sustainable and affordable methods of managing tropical arthropod plant pests and disease vectors, and in the conservation and utilization of biodiversity of insects of commercial and ecological importance; organizes training programmes; Dir-Gen. Dr Hans Rudolph Herren; publs *Insect Science and its Application* (quarterly), *Annual Report*, training manuals, technical bulletins, newsletter.

International Commission for Optics—ICO: Institut d'Optique/CNRS, POB 147, 91403 Orsay Cédex, France; tel. 1-69-35-87-41; fax 1-69-35-87-00; e-mail Pierre.chavel@iota.u-psud.fr; internet www.ico-optics.org; f. 1948 to contribute to the progress of theoretical and instrumental optics, to assist in research and to promote international agreement on specifications; holds Gen. Assembly every three years; mems: committees in 42 territories, and four international societies; Pres. Prof. A. H. Gueuther (USA); Sec.-Gen. Dr P. Chavel (France); publ. *ICO Newsletter*.

International Commission for Plant-Bee Relationships: c/o Prof. I. Williams, Plant and Invertebrate Ecology Division, Rothamsted, Harpenden, Herts, AL5 2JQ, United Kingdom; e-mail ingrid.williams@bbsrc.ac.uk; f. 1950 to promote research and its application in the field of bee botany, and collect and spread information to organize meetings, etc., and collaborate with scientific organizations; affiliated to the International Union of Biological Sciences; mems: 240 in 41 countries; Pres. Prof. Ingrid Williams; Sec. Dr J. L. Osborne.

International Commission for the Scientific Exploration of the Mediterranean Sea (Commission internationale pour l'exploration scientifique de la mer Méditerranée—CIESM): 16 blvd de Suisse, 98000 Monaco; tel. 93-30-38-79; fax 92-16-11-95; e-mail fbriand@ciesm.org; internet www.ciesm.org; f. 1919 for scientific exploration of the Mediterranean Sea; organizes multilateral research investigations; includes 6 scientific committees; mems: 22 member countries, 2,500 scientists; Pres SAS Prince Albert of Monaco; Sec.-Gen. Prof. F. Doumenge; Dir-Gen. Prof. F. Briand; publs Congress reports, science and workshop series.

International Commission on Physics Education: c/o Prof. J. Barojas, POB 55534, 09340 México DF, Mexico; tel. (5) 686-35-19; internet www.physics.umd.edu/ripe/icpe; f. 1960 to encourage and develop international collaboration in the improvement and extension of the methods and scope of physics education at all levels; collaborates with UNESCO and organizes international conferences; mems: appointed triennially by the International Union of Pure and Applied Physics; Sec. Prof. J. Barojas.

International Commission on Radiation Units and Measurements—ICRU: 7910 Woodmont Ave, Suite 400, Bethesda, MD 20814, USA; tel. (301) 657-2652; fax (301) 907-8768; e-mail icru@icru

.org; internet www.icru.org; f. 1925 to develop internationally acceptable recommendations regarding: (1) quantities and units of radiation and radioactivity, (2) procedures suitable for the measurement and application of these quantities in clinical radiology and radiobiology, (3) physical data needed in the application of these procedures; makes recommendations on quantities and units for radiation protection (see below, International Radiation Protection Association); mems: from about 18 countries; Chair. A. WAMBERSIE; Sec. S. SELTZER; publs *Reports*.

International Commission on Zoological Nomenclature: c/o The Natural History Museum, Cromwell Rd, London, SW7 5BD, United Kingdom; tel. (20) 7942-5653; e-mail iczn@nhm.ac.uk; internet www.iczn.org; f. 1895; has judicial powers to determine all matters relating to the interpretation of the International Code of Zoological Nomenclature and also plenary powers to suspend the operation of the Code where the strict application of the Code would lead to confusion and instability of nomenclature; also responsible for maintaining and developing the Official Lists and Official Indexes of Names in Zoology; affiliated to the International Union of Biological Sciences; Pres. Dr N. L. EVENHUIS (USA); Exec. Sec. Dr A. WAKEHAM-DAWSON (UK); publs *Bulletin of Zoological Nomenclature* (quarterly), *International Code of Zoological Nomenclature, Official Lists and Indexes of Names and Works in Zoology, Towards Stability in the Names of Animals*.

International Council for Scientific and Technical Information: 51 blvd de Montmorency, 75016 Paris, France; tel. 1-45-25-65-92; fax 1-42-15-12-62; e-mail icsti@icsti.org; internet www.icsti.org; f. 1984 as the successor to the International Council of Scientific Unions Abstracting Board (f. 1952); aims to increase accessibility to scientific and technical information; fosters communication and interaction among all participants in the information transfer chain; mems: 50 organizations; Pres. KURT MOLHOLM (USA); Gen. Sec. MARIE WALLIN (Sweden).

International Council for the Exploration of the Sea—ICES: Palægade 2–4, 1261 Copenhagen K, Denmark; tel. 33-15-42-25; fax 33-93-42-15; e-mail ices.info@ices.dk; internet www.ices.dk; f. 1902 to encourage and facilitate research on the utilization and conservation of living resources and the environment in the North Atlantic Ocean and its adjacent seas; publishes and disseminate results of research; advises member countries and regulatory commissions; mems: 19 mem. countries and five countries or bodies with observer status; Gen. Sec. D. DE G. GRIFFITH; publs *ICES Journal of Marine Science, ICES Marine Science Symposia, ICES Fisheries Statistics, ICES Cooperative Research Reports, ICES Oceanographic Data Lists and Inventories, ICES Techniques in Marine Environmental Sciences, ICES Identification Leaflets for Plankton, ICES Identification Leaflets for Diseases and Parasites of Fish and Shellfish, ICES / CIEM Information*.

International Council of Psychologists: Dept of Psychology, Southwest Texas State University, San Marcos, TX 78666, USA; tel. (512) 245-7605; fax (512) 245-3153; internet www.geocities.com/icpsych; f. 1941 to advance psychology and the application of its scientific findings throughout the world; holds annual conventions; mems: 1,200 qualified psychologists; Sec.-Gen. Dr JOHN M. DAVIS; publs *International Psychologist* (quarterly), *World Psychology* (quarterly).

International Council of the Aeronautical Sciences—ICAS: c/o FOI, SE-17290 Stockholm, Sweden; tel. 5550-4229; e-mail secr.exec@icas.org; internet www.icas.org; f. 1957 to encourage free interchange of information on aeronautical science and technology; holds biennial Congresses; mems: national asscns in more than 30 countries; Pres. BILLY FREDRIKSSON (Sweden); Exec. Sec. ANDERS GUSTAFSSON (Sweden).

International Earth Rotation Service: Central Bureau, Paris Observatory, 61 ave de l'Observatoire, 75014 Paris, France; tel. 1-40-51-22-26; fax 1-40-51-22-91; e-mail iers@obspm.fr; internet hpiers.obspm.fr; f. 1988 (fmrly International Polar Motion Service and Bureau International de l'Heure); maintained by the International Astronomical Union and the International Union of Geodesy and Geophysics; defines and maintains the international terrestrial and celestial reference systems; determines earth orientation parameters (terrestrial and celestial co-ordinates of the pole and universal time) connecting these systems; monitors global geophysical fluids; organizes collection, analysis and dissemination of data; Pres. Directing Bd Prof. C. REIGBER.

International Federation for Cell Biology: c/o Dr Ivan Cameron, Dept of Cellular and Structural Biology, Univ. of Texas Health Science Center, 7703 Floyd Curl Drive, San Antonio, Texas 78229, USA; internet lonestar.texas.net/icameron/ifcb.htm; f. 1972 to foster international co-operation, and organize conferences; Pres. Dr JUDIE WALTON; Sec.-Gen. Dr IVAN CAMERON; publs *Cell Biology International* (monthly), reports.

International Federation of Operational Research Societies —IFORS: c/o Loretta Peregrina, Richard Ivey School of Business,

University of Western Ontario, London, ON N6A 3K7, Canada; tel. (519) 661-4220; fax (519) 661-3485; e-mail ifors@ivey.uwo.ca; internet www.ifors.org; f. 1959 for development of operational research as a unified science and its advancement in all nations of the world; mems: c. 30,000 individuals, 44 national societies, four kindred societies; Pres. Prof. PAOLO TOTH (Italy); Sec. LORETTA PEREGRINA; publs *International Abstracts in Operational Research, IFORS Bulletin, International Transactions in Operational Research*.

International Federation of Science Editors: School for Scientific Communication, Abruzzo Science Park, Via Antica Arischia 1, 67100 L'Aquila, Italy; tel. (0862) 3475308; fax (0862) 3475213; e-mail miriam.balaban@aquila.infn.it; f. 1978; links editors in different branches of science with the aim of improving scientific writing, editing, ethics and communication internationally; Pres. MIRIAM BALABAN (Italy).

International Federation of Societies for Electron Microscopy—IFSEM: Dept of Materials, Univ. of Oxford, Parks Rd, Oxford, OX1 3PH, United Kingdom; tel. (1865) 273654; fax (1865) 283329; e-mail david.cockayne@materials.ox.ac.uk; internet www.materials.ox.ac.uk/ifsem; f. 1955 to contribute to the advancement of all aspects of electron microscopy; promotes and co-ordinates research; sponsors meetings and conferences; holds International Congress every four years; mems: representative organizations of 40 countries; Pres. Prof. A. HOWIE (UK); Gen.-Sec. D. J. H. COCKAYNE (Australia).

International Food Information Service—IFIS: UK Office (IFIS Publishing), Lane End House, Shinfield Rd, Shinfield, Reading, RG2 9BB, United Kingdom; tel. (118) 988-3895; fax (118) 988-5065; e-mail ifis@ifis.org; internet www.ifis.org; f. 1968; board of governors comprises two members each from CAB-International (UK), Bundesministerium für Landwirtschaft, Ernährung und Forsten (represented by Deutsche Landwirtschafts-Gesellschaft e.V.) (Germany), the Institute of Food Technologists (USA), and the Centrum voor Landbouwpublikaties en Landbouwdocumentaties (Netherlands); collects and disseminates information on all disciplines relevant to food science, food technology and human nutrition; Man. Dir Prof. J. D. SELMAN; publ. *Food Science and Technology Abstracts* (monthly, also available via the internet and on CD-Rom).

International Foundation of the High-Altitude Research Stations Jungfraujoch and Gornergrat: Sidlerstrasse 5, 3012 Berne, Switzerland; tel. (31) 6314052; fax (31) 6314405; e-mail louise.wilson@phim.unibe.ch; internet www.ifjungo.ch; f. 1931; international research centre which enables scientists from many scientific fields to carry out experiments at high altitudes. Six countries contribute to support the station: Austria, Belgium, Germany, Italy, Switzerland, United Kingdom; Pres. Prof. E. FLÜCKIGER.

International Glaciological Society: Lensfield Rd, Cambridge, CB2 1ER, United Kingdom; tel. (1223) 355974; fax (1223) 336543; e-mail int_glaciol_soc@compuserve.com; internet www.spri.cam.ac.uk/igs/home.htm; f. 1936 to stimulate interest in and encourage research into the scientific and technical problems of snow and ice in all countries; mems: 850 in 30 countries; Pres. Dr ELIZABETH MORRIS; Sec.-Gen. C. S. L. OMMANNEY; publs *Journal of Glaciology* (quarterly), *Ice* (News Bulletin—3 a year), *Annals of Glaciology*.

International Hydrographic Organization—IHO: 4 quai Antoine 1er, BP 445, Monte Carlo, 98011 Monaco; tel. 93-10-81-00; fax 93-10-81-40; e-mail info@ihb.mc; internet www.iho.shom.fr; f. 1921 to link the hydrographic offices of member governments and co-ordinate their work, with a view to rendering navigation easier and safer; seeks to obtain, as far as possible, uniformity in charts and hydrographic documents; fosters the development of electronic chart navigation; encourages adoption of the best methods of conducting hydrographic surveys; encourages surveying in those parts of the world where accurate charts are lacking; provides IHO Data Centre for Digital Bathymetry; and organizes quinquennial conference; mems: 73 states; Directing Committee: Pres. Vice Adm. A. MARRATOS (Greece); Dirs Rear-Adm. K. BARBOR (USA;), Capt. H. GORZIGLIA (Chile); publs *International Hydrographic Bulletin* (3 a year), *IHO Yearbook*.

International Institute of Refrigeration: 177 blvd Malesherbes, 75017 Paris, France; tel. 1-42-27-32-35; fax 1-47-63-17-98; e-mail iifiir@iifiir.org; internet www.iifiir.org; f. 1908 to further the the science of refrigeration and its applications on a world-wide scale; to investigate, discuss and recommend any aspects leading to improvements in the field of refrigeration; maintains FRIDOC data-base (available via internet); mems: 61 national, 1,500 associates; Dir FRANÇOIS BILLIARD (France); publs *Bulletin* (every 2 months), *International Journal of Refrigeration* (8 a year), *Newsletter* (5 a year), books, proceedings, recommendations.

International Mineralogical Association: Institute of Mineralogy, University of Marburg, 3550 Marburg, Germany; tel. 28-5617; fax 285831; internet www.dst.unipi.it/ima; f. 1958 to further international co-operation in the science of mineralogy; affiliated to the

International Union of Geological Sciences; mems: national societies in 31 countries; Sec. Prof. S. S. HAFNER.

International Organization of Legal Metrology: 11 rue Turgot, 75009 Paris, France; tel. 1-48-78-12-82; fax 1-42-82-17-27; internet www.oiml.org; f. 1955 to serve as documentation and information centre on the verification, checking, construction and use of measuring instruments, to determine characteristics and standards to which measuring instruments must conform for their use to be recommended internationally, and to determine the general principles of legal metrology; mems: governments of 50 countries; Dir B. ATHANÉ (France); publ. *Bulletin* (quarterly).

International Palaeontological Association: c/o Prof. R. F. Maddocks , Room 336, Science and Research Bldg 1, Dept of Geosciences, Univ. of Houston, Houston, TX 77204-5503, USA, Paleontologisk Museum, Box 1172 Blindern, 0318 Oslo, Norway; tel. (713) 743-3429; fax (713) 748-7906; e-mail rmaddocks@uh.edu; internet ipa.geo.ukans.edu; f. 1933; affiliated to the International Union of Geological Sciences and the International Union of Biological Sciences; Pres. Dr J. TALENT (Australia); Sec.-Gen. Prof. ROSALIE F. MADDOCKS (Norway); publs *Lethaia* (quarterly), *Directory of Paleontologists of the World*, *Directory of Fossil Collectors of the World*.

International Peat Society: Vapaudenkatu 12, 40100 Jyväskylä, Finland; tel. (14) 3385440; fax (14) 3385410; e-mail ips@peatsociety.fi; internet www.peatsociety.fi; f. 1968 to encourage co-operation in the study and use of mires, peatlands, peat and related material, through international meetings, research groups and the exchange of information; mems: 18 Nat. Cttees, research institutes and other organizations, and individuals from 42 countries; Pres. GERRY HOOD (Canada); Sec.-Gen. RAIMO SOPO (Finland); publs *Peat News* (monthly electronic newsletter), *International Peat Journal* (annually).

International Phonetic Association—IPA: Dept of Linguistics, University of Victoria, POB 3045, Victoria, BC V8W 3P4, Canada; e-mail esling@uvic.ca; internet www.arts.gla.ac.uk/ipa/ipa.html; f. 1886 to promote the scientific study of phonetics and its applications; organizes International Congress of Phonetic Sciences every four years (2003: Barcelona, Spain); mems: 1,000; Pres. K. KOHLER (Germany); Sec. Prof. JOHN ESLING; publ. *Journal* (2 a year).

International Phycological Society: c/o Harbor Branch Oceanographic Institution, 5600 Old Dixie Highway, Fort Pierce, FL 34946, USA; fax (561) 468-0757; e-mail hanisak@hboi.edu; internet seaweed.ucg.ie/phycologia/ips.html; f. 1961 to promote the study of algae, the distribution of information, and international co-operation in this field; mems: about 1,000; Pres. C. J. BIRD; Sec. M. D. HANISAK; publ. *Phycologia* (every 2 months).

International Primatological Society: c/o Dr D. Fragaszy, Dept of Psychology, Univ. of Georgia, Athens, GA 30602, USA; tel. (706) 542-3036; fax (706) 542-3275; e-mail doree@arches.uga.edu; internet www.primate.wisc.edu/pin/ips.html; f. 1964 to promote primatological science in all fields; mems: about 1,500; Pres. Dr D. FRAGASZY; Sec.-Gen. Dr J. A. R. A. M. VAN HOOFF; publs *Bulletin*, *International Journal of Primatology*, *Codes of Practice*.

International Radiation Protection Association—IRPA: POB 662, 5600 AR Eindhoven, Netherlands; tel. (40) 247-33-55; fax (40) 243-50-20; e-mail irpa.exof@sbd.tue.nl; internet www.irpa.net; f. 1966 to link individuals and societies throughout the world concerned with protection against ionizing radiations and allied effects, and to represent doctors, health physicists, radiological protection officers and others engaged in radiological protection, radiation safety, nuclear safety, legal, medical and veterinary aspects and in radiation research and other allied activities; mems: 16,000 in 42 societies; Pres. Prof. K. DUFTSCMID (Austria); Sec.-Gen. C. J. HUYSKENS (Netherlands); publ. *IRPA Bulletin*.

International Society for General Semantics: POB 728, Concord, CA 94522, USA; tel. (925) 798-0311; e-mail isgs@generalsemantics.org; internet www.generalsemantics.org; f. 1943 to advance knowledge of and inquiry into non-Aristotelian systems and general semantics; mems: 2,000 individuals in 40 countries; Pres. CHARLES RUSSELL, Jr (USA); Exec. Dir PAUL D. JOHNSTON (USA).

International Society for Human and Animal Mycology—ISHAM: Mycology Unit, Women's and Children's Hospital, N. Adelaide 5006, Australia; tel. (8) 8204-7365; fax (8) 8204-7589; e-mail dellis@mad.adelaide.edu.au; internet www.leeds.ac.uk/isham; f. 1954 to pursue the study of fungi pathogenic for man and animals; holds congresses (2003 Congress: San Antonio, USA); mems: 1,100 in 70 countries; Pres. Prof. M. R. McGINNIS; Gen. Sec. Dr D. H. ELLIS; publ. *Medical Mycology* (6 a year).

International Society for Rock Mechanics: c/o Laboratório Nacional de Engenharia Civil, 101 Av. do Brasil, 1700-066 Lisboa , Portugal; tel. (21) 8443419; fax (21) 844302; e-mail isrm@lnec.pt; internet www.lnec.pt/isrm; f. 1962 to encourage and co-ordinate international co-operation in the science of rock mechanics; assists individuals and local organizations in forming national bodies; maintains liaison with organizations representing related sciences,

including geology, geophysics, soil mechanics, mining engineering, petroleum engineering and civil engineering; organizes international meetings; encourages the publication of research; mems: c. 6,000; Pres. Prof. MARC PANET; Sec.-Gen. JOSÉ DELGADO RODRIGUES; publ. *News Journal* (3 a year).

International Society for Stereology: c/o Dr Jens R. Nyengaard, Stereological Research Laboratory, Bartholin Bldg, Aarhus Univ., 8000 Århus C, Denmark; tel. 89-49-36-54; fax 89-49-36-50; e-mail stereo@svfcd.aau.dk; internet www.health.aau.dk/stereology/iss; f. 1962; an interdisciplinary society gathering scientists from metallurgy, geology, mineralogy and biology to exchange ideas on three-dimensional interpretation of two-dimensional samples (sections, projections) of their material by means of stereological principles; tenth Congress: Melbourne, Australia, 1999; mems: 300; Pres. BENTE PAKKENBERG; Treas. JENS R. NYENGAARD.

International Society for Tropical Ecology: c/o Botany Dept, Banaras Hindu University, Varanasi, 221 005 India; tel. (542) 368399; fax (542) 368174; e-mail tropecol@banaras.ernet.in; f. 1956 to promote and develop the science of ecology in the tropics in the service of humanity to publish a journal to aid ecologists in the tropics in communication of their findings; and to hold symposia from time to time to summarize the state of knowledge in particular or general fields of tropical ecology; mems: 500; Sec. Prof. J. S. SINGH (India); Editor Prof. K. P. SINGH; publ. *Tropical Ecology* (2 a year).

International Society of Biometeorology—IBS: c/o Dr M. Shibata, Dept of Biometeorology, Yamanashi Institute of Environmental Sciences, Fuji-Yoshida, Yamanashi 403-0005, Japan; tel. 555-72-6184; fax 555-72-6205; e-mail mshibata@yies.pref .yamanashi.jp; internet www.biometeorology.org; f. 1956 to unite all biometeorologists working in the fields of agricultural, botanical, cosmic, entomological, forest, human, medical, veterinarian, zoological and other branches of biometeorology; mems: 250 individuals, nationals of 46 countries; Pres. Dr IAN BURTON (Canada); Sec. Dr MASAKI SHIBATA (Japan); publs *Biometeorology* (Proceedings of the Congress of ISB), *International Journal of Biometeorology* (quarterly), *Biometeorology Bulletin*.

International Society of Criminology (Société internationale de criminologie): 4 rue Ferrus, 75014 Paris, France; tel. 1-45-88-00-23; fax 1-45-88-96-40; e-mail crim.sic@wanadoo.fr; f. 1934 to promote the development of the sciences in their application to the criminal phenomenon; mems: in 63 countries; Sec.-Gen. GEORGES PICCA; publ. *Annales internationales de Criminologie*.

International Union for Quaternary Research—INQUA: Dept of Soil and Water Sciences, Agricultural University of Norway, POB 3028, 1432, Aas, Norway; e-mail sylvi.haldorsen@ijvf.nlh.no; internet inqua.nlh.no; f. 1928 to co-ordinate research on the Quaternary geological era throughout the world; holds congress every four years (2003: Reno, USA); mems: in 38 countries and states; Sec.-Gen. Prof. SYLVI HALDORSEN (Norway); publs *Quarternary International*, *Quarternary Perspectives*.

International Union of Photobiology: c/o Dr Tom Dubbelman, POB 9503, 2300 RA Leiden, Netherlands; tel. (71) 5276053; fax (71) 5276125; e-mail t.m.a.r.dubbelman@mcb.medfac.leidenuniv.nl; internet www.pol.us.net/iupb; f. 1928 (frmly International Photobiology Asscn); stimulation of scientific research concerning the physics, chemistry and climatology of non-ionizing radiations (ultraviolet, visible and infra-red) in relation to their biological efffects and their applications in biology and medicine; 18 national committees represented; affiliated to the International Union of Biological Sciences. International Congresses held every four years; Pres. Prof. PILL SOON SONG; Sec.-Gen. Dr TOM DUBBELMAN.

International Water Association—IWA: Alliance House, 12 Caxton St, London SW1H OQS, United Kingdom; tel. (20) 7654-5500; fax (20) 7654-5555; e-mail water@iwahq.org.uk; internet www .iwahq.org.uk; f. 1999 by merger of the International Water Services Association and the International Association on Water Quality; aims to encourage international communication, co-operative effort, and exchange of information on water quality management, through conferences, electronic media and publication of research reports; mems: c. 9,000 in 130 countries; Pres. Prof. N. TAMBO (Japan); Exec. Dir ANTHONY MILBURN (UK); publs *Water Research* (monthly), *Water Science and Technology* (24 a year), *Water 21* (6 a year), *Yearbook*, *Scientific and Technical Reports*.

Pacific Science Association: 1525 Bernice St, POB 17801, Honolulu, HI 96817; tel. (808) 848-4139; fax (808) 847-8252; e-mail psa@bishop.bishop.hawaii.org; internet www.pacificscience.org; f. 1920 to promote co-operation in the study of scientific problems relating to the Pacific region, more particularly those affecting the prosperity and well-being of Pacific peoples; sponsors Pacific Science Congresses and Inter-Congresses; mems: institutional representatives from 35 areas, scientific societies, individual scientists. Tenth Inter-Congress: Guam, 2001; 20th Congress: Bangkok, Thailand, 2003; Pres. Dr R. GERARD WARD (Japan); Exec. Sec. Dr LUCIUS G. ELDREDGE; publ. *Information Bulletin* (2 a year).

Pan-African Union of Science and Technology: POB 2339, Brazzaville, Republic of the Congo; tel. 832265; fax 832185; f. 1987 to promote the use of science and technology in furthering the development of Africa; organizes triennial congress; Pres. Prof. EDWARD AYENSU; Sec.-Gen. Prof. LÉVY MAKANY.

Pugwash Conferences on Science and World Affairs: 63A Great Russell St, London, WC1B 3BJ, United Kingdom; tel. (20) 7405-6661; fax (20) 7831-5651; e-mail pugwash@qmw.ac.uk; internet www.pugwash.org; f. 1957 to organize international conferences of scientists to discuss problems arising from the development of science, particularly the dangers to mankind from weapons of mass destruction; mems: national Pugwash groups in 38 countries; Pres. Sir MICHAEL ATIYAH; Sec.-Gen. Prof. GEORGE RATHJENS; publs *Pugwash Newsletter* (quarterly), occasional papers, monographs.

Scientific, Technical and Research Commission—STRC: Nigerian Ports Authority Bldg, PMB 2359, Marina, Lagos, Nigeria; tel. (1) 2633430; fax (1) 2636093; e-mail oaustrc@rcl.nig.com; f. 1965 to succeed the Commission for Technical Co-operation in Africa (f. 1954); supervises the Inter-African Bureau for Animal Resources (Nairobi, Kenya), the Inter-African Bureau for Soils (Lagos, Nigeria) and the Inter-African Phytosanitary Commission (Yaoundé, Cameroon) and several joint research projects; provides training in agricultural man., and conducts pest control programmes; Exec. Sec. Dr ROBERT N. MSHANA.

Unitas Malacologica (Malacological Union): c/o Dr P. B. Mordan, The Natural History Museum, Science Depts, Zoology: Mollusca, Cromwell Rd, London, SW7 5BD, United Kingdom; tel. (20) 7938-9359; fax (20) 7938-8754; e-mail p.mordan@nhm.ac.uk; f. 1962 to further the study of molluscs; affiliated to the International Union of Biological Sciences; holds triennial congress; mems: 400 in over 30 countries; Pres. Dr F. WELLS (Australia); Sec. Dr PETER B. MORDAN (UK); publ. *UM Newsletter* (2 a year).

World Organisation of Systems and Cybernetics—WOSC (Organisation Mondiale pour la Systémique et la Cybernétique): c/o Prof. R. Vallée, 2 rue de Vouillé, 75015 Paris, France; tel. and fax 1-45-33-62-46; internet www.cybsoc.org/wosc; f. 1969 to act as clearing-house for all societies concerned with cybernetics and systems, to aim for the recognition of cybernetics as fundamental science, to organize and sponsor international exhibitions of automation and computer equipment, congresses and symposia, and to promote and co-ordinate research in systems and cybernetics; sponsors an honorary fellowship and awards a Norbert Wiener memorial gold medal; mems: national and international societies in 30 countries; Dir-Gen. Prof. R. VALLÉE (France); publs *Kybernetes*, *the International Journal of Cybernetics and Systems*.

Social Sciences

International Council for Philosophy and Humanistic Studies—ICPHS: Maison de l'UNESCO, 1 rue Miollis, 75732 Paris Cédex 15, France; tel. 1-45-68-26-85; fax 1-40-65-94-80; internet www.unesco.org/cipsh; f. 1949 under the auspices of UNESCO to encourage respect for cultural autonomy by the comparative study of civilization and to contribute towards international understanding through a better knowledge of humanity; works to develop international co-operation in philosophy, humanistic and kindred studies; encourages the setting up of international organizations; promotes the dissemination of information in these fields; sponsors works of learning, etc. mems: organizations (see below) representing 145 countries; Pres. JEAN D'ORMESSON (France); Sec.-Gen. TILO SCHABERT (Germany); publs *Bulletin of Information* (biennially), *Diogenes* (quarterly).

UNIONS FEDERATED TO THE ICPHS

International Association for the History of Religions—IAHR: c/o Prof. Armin W. Geertz, Institut for Religionsvidenskab, Aarhus Universitet, Taasingegade 3, 8000 Aarhus C, Denmark; tel. 89-42-23-06; fax 86-13-04-90; e-mail geertz@teologi.au.dk; internet www.iahr.dk; f. 1950 to promote international collaboration of scholars, to organize congresses and to stimulate research; mems: 33 countries; Pres. PETER ANTES; Sec.-Gen. Prof. ARMIN W. GEERTZ.

International Committee for the History of Art: 13 rue de Seine, 75006 Paris, France; e-mail philippe.senechal@inha.fr; internet www.esteticas.unam.mx/ciha; f. 1930 by the 12th International Congress on the History of Art, for collaboration in the scientific study of the history of art; holds international congress every four years, and at least two colloquia between congresses; mems: National Committees in 34 countries; Pres. Prof. STEPHEN BANN (United Kingdom); Sec. PHILIPPE SENECHAL (France); publ. *Bibliographie d'Histoire de l'Art. Bibliography of the History of Art* (quarterly).

International Committee of Historical Sciences: Département d'histoire, UQAM, CP 8888, Surcursale Centre-ville, Montréal, QC

H3C 3P8, Canada; e-mail cish@ihtp-cnrs.ens-cachan.fr; internet www.cish.org; f. 1926 to work for the advancement of historical sciences by means of international co-ordination; holds international congress every five years, 2005: Sydney, Australia; mems: 54 national committees, 28 affiliated international organizations and 12 internal commissions; Pres. JÜRGEN KOCKA (Germany); Sec.-Gen. JEAN-CLAUDE ROBERT (Canada); publ. *Bulletin d'Information du CISH*.

International Congress of African Studies: c/o International African Institute, School of Oriental and African Studies, Thornhaugh St, London, WC1H OXG, United Kingdom; tel. (20) 7898-4420; fax (20) 7898-4419; e-mail iai@soas.ac.uk; f. 1962.

International Federation for Modern Languages and Literatures: c/o D. A. Wells, Dept of German, Birkbeck College, Malet St, London, WC1E 7HX, United Kingdom; tel. (20) 7631-6103; fax (20) 7383-3729; e-mail d.wells@bbk.ac.uk; f. 1928 to establish permanent contact between historians of literature, to develop or perfect facilities for their work and to promote the study of modern languages and literature; holds Congress every three years; mems: 19 asscns, with individual mems in 98 countries; Sec.-Gen. D. A. WELLS (UK).

International Federation of Philosophical Societies: c/o I. Kuçuradi, Ahmet Rasim Sok. 8/4, Çankaya, 06550 Ankara, Turkey; tel. (312) 4407408; fax (312) 4410297; e-mail ioanna@fisp.org.tr; internet www.fisp.org.tr; f. 1948 under the auspices of UNESCO, to encourage international co-operation in the field of philosophy; holds World Congress of Philosophy every five years; mems: 110 societies from 50 countries; 27 international societies; Pres. IOANNA KUÇURADI (Turkey); Sec.-Gen. PETER KEMP (Denmark); publs *Newsletter*, *International Bibliography of Philosophy*, *Chroniques de Philosophie*, *Contemporary Philosophy*, *Philosophical Problems Today*, *Philosophy and Cultural Development*, *Ideas Underlying World Problems*,*The Idea of Values*.

International Federation of Societies of Classical Studies: c/o Prof. F. Paschoud, 6 chemin aux Folies, 1293 Bellevue, Switzerland; tel. (22) 7742656; fax (22) 7742734; e-mail zosime@bluewin.ch; f. 1948 under the auspices of UNESCO; mems: 79 societies in 44 countries; Pres. C. J. CLASSEN; Sec. Prof. F. PASCHOUD (Switzerland); publs *L'Année Philologique*, *Thesaurus linguae Latinae*.

International Musicological Society—IMS: CP 1561, 4001 Basel, Switzerland; fax (1) 9231027; e-mail imsba@swissonline.ch; internet www.ims-online.ch; f. 1927; holds international congresses every five years; Pres. LÁSZLÓ SOMFAI; Sec.-Gen. Dr DOROTHEA BAUMANN (Switzerland); publ. *Acta Musicologica* (2 a year).

International Union for Oriental and Asian Studies: Közraktar u. 12A 11/2, 1093 Budapest, Hungary; f. 1951 by the 22nd International Congress of Orientalists under the auspices of UNESCO, to promote contacts between orientalists throughout the world, and to organize congresses, research and publications; mems: in 24 countries; Sec.-Gen. Prof. GEORG HAZAI; publs *Philologiae Turcicae Fundamenta*, *Materialien zum Sumerischen Lexikon*, *Sanskrit Dictionary*, *Corpus Inscriptionum Iranicarum*, *Linguistic Atlas of Iran*, *Matériels des parlers iraniens*, *Turcology Annual*, *Bibliographie égyptologique*.

International Union of Academies—IUA (Union académique internationale—UAI): Palais des Académies, 1 rue Ducale, 1000 Brussels, Belgium; tel. (2) 550-22-00; fax (2) 550-22-05; e-mail info@uai-iua.org; internet www.uai-iua.org; f. 1919 to promote international co-operation through collective research in philology, archaeology, art history, history and social sciences; mems: academic institutions in 49 countries; Pres. S. SHAKED (Israel); Secs L HOUZIAUX, J.-L. DE PAEPE.

International Union of Anthropological and Ethnological Sciences—IUAES: c/o Dr P. J. M. Nas, Faculty of Social Sciences, Univ. of Leiden, Wassenaarseweg 52, POB 9555, 2300 RB Leiden, Netherlands; tel. (71) 5273992; fax (71) 5273619; e-mail nas@rulfsw.leidenuniv.nl; internet lucy.ukc.ac.uk/IUAES; f. 1948 under the auspices of UNESCO, to enhance exchange and communication between scientists and institutions in the fields of anthropology and ethnology; aims to promote harmony between nature and culture; organizes 22 international research commissions; mems: institutions and individuals in 100 countries; Pres. Prof. ERIC SUNDERLAND (UK); Sec.-Gen. Dr P. J. M. NAS (Netherlands); publ. *IUAES Newsletter* (3 a year).

International Union of Prehistoric and Protohistoric Sciences: c/o Prof. J. Bourgeois, Dept of Archaeology and Ancient History of Europe, University of Ghent, Blandijnberg 2, 9000 Ghent, Belgium; tel. (9) 264-41-06; fax (9) 264-41-73; e-mail jean.bourgeois@rug.ac.be; internet www.geocities.com/athens/ithaca/7152; f. 1931 to promote congresses and scientific work in the fields of pre- and proto-history; mems: 120 countries; Pres. Prof. P. BONENFANT (Belgium); Sec.-Gen. Prof. J. BOURGEOIS (Belgium).

Permanent International Committee of Linguists: Instituut voor Nederlandse Lexicologie, Matthias de Vrieshof 2, 2311 BZ

Leiden, Netherlands; tel. (71) 5141648; fax (71) 5272115; e-mail secretariaat@inl.nl; f. 1928; aims to further linguistic research, to co-ordinate activities undertaken for the advancement of linguistics, and to make the results of linguistic research known internationally; holds Congress every five years; mems: 34 countries and two international linguistic organizations; Pres. a.i. P. RAMAT (Italy); Sec.-Gen. P. G. J. VAN STERKENBURG (Netherlands); publ. *Linguistic Bibliography* (annually).

OTHER ORGANIZATIONS

African Social and Environmental Studies Programme: Box 4477, Nairobi, Kenya; tel. (20) 747960; fax (20) 740817; f. 1968; develops and disseminates educational material on social and environmental studies in eastern and southern Africa; mems: 18 African countries; Chair. Prof. WILLIAM SENTEZA-KAJUBI; Exec. Dir Prof. PETER MUYANDA MUTEBI; publs *African Social and Environmental Studies Forum* (2 a year), teaching guides.

Arab Towns Organization—ATO: POB 68160, Kaifan 71962, Kuwait; tel. 4849705; fax 4849322; e-mail ato@ato.net; internet www.ato.net; f. 1967; aims to promote co-operation and the exchange of expertise with regard to urban administration; works to improve the standard of municipal services and utilities in Arab towns and to preserve the character and heritage of Arab towns. Administers an Institute for Urban Development (AUDI), based in Riyadh, Saudi Arabia, which provides training and research for municipal officers; the Arab Towns Development Fund, to help member towns implement projects; and the ATO Award, to encourage the preservation of Arab architecture; mems: 413 towns; Dir-Gen. MOHAMMED ABDUL HAMID AL-SAQR; Sec.-Gen. ABD AL-AZIZ Y. AL-ADASANI; publ. *Al-Madinah Al-Arabiyah* (every 2 months).

Association for the Study of the World Refugee Problem—AWR: Piazzale di Porta Pia 121, 00198 Rome, Italy; tel. (06) 44250159; f. 1951 to promote and co-ordinate scholarly research on refugee problems; mems: 475 in 19 countries; Pres. FRANCO FOSCHI (Italy); Sec.-Gen. ALDO CLEMENTE (Italy); publs *AWR Bulletin* (quarterly, in English, French, Italian and German), treatises on refugee problems (17 vols).

Council for the Development of Social Science Research in Africa—CODESRIA: BP 3304, Dakar, Senegal; tel. 825-98-22; fax 824-12-89; e-mail codesria@sentoo.sn; internet www.codesria.org; f. 1973; promotes research, organizes conferences, working groups and information services; mems: research institutes and university faculties and researchers in African countries; Exec. Sec. ADEBAYO OLUKOSHI; publs *Africa Development* (quarterly), *CODESRIA Bulletin* (quarterly), *Index of African Social Science Periodical Articles* (annually), *African Journal of International Affairs* (2 a year), *African Sociological Review* (2 a year), *Afrika Zameni* (annually), *Identity, Culture and Politics* (2 a year), *Afro Arab Selections for Social Sciences* (annually), directories of research.

Council for Research in Values and Philosophy—CRVP: c/o Prof. G. F. McLean, School of Philosophy, Catholic University of America, Washington, DC 20064, USA; tel. and fax (202) 319-6089; e-mail cua-rvp@cua.edu; internet www.crvp.org; mems: 33 teams from 24 countries; Pres. Prof. KENNETH L. SCHMITZ (Canada); Sec.-Gen. Prof. GEORGE F. MCLEAN (USA); publ. *Cultural Heritage and Contemporary Change* series.

Eastern Regional Organisation for Planning and Housing: POB 10867, 50726 Kuala Lumpur, Malaysia; tel. (3) 718-7068; fax (3) 718-3931; f. 1958 to promote and co-ordinate the study and practice of housing and regional town and country planning; maintains offices in Japan, India and Indonesia; mems: 57 organizations and 213 individuals in 28 countries; Sec.-Gen. JOHN KOH SENG SIEW; publs *EAROPH News and Notes* (monthly), *Town and Country Planning* (bibliography).

English-Speaking Union of the Commonwealth: Dartmouth House, 37 Charles St, Berkeley Sq., London, W1J 5ED, United Kingdom; tel. (20) 7529-1550; fax (20) 7495-6108; e-mail esu@esu.org; internet www.esu.org; f. 1918 to promote international understanding between Britain, the Commonwealth, the United States and Europe, in conjunction with the ESU of the USA; mems: 70,000 (incl. USA); Chair. Lord ALAN WATSON; Dir-Gen. VALERIE MITCHELL; publ. *Concord.*

European Association for Population Studies—EAPS: POB 11676, 2502 AR The Hague, Netherlands; tel. (70) 3565200; fax (70) 3647187; e-mail contact@eaps.nl; internet www.eaps.nl; f. 1983 to foster research and provide information on European population problems; organizes conferences, seminars and workshops; mems: demographers from 40 countries; Exec. Sec. GYS BEETS; publ. *European Journal of Population/Revue Européenne de Démographie* (quarterly).

European Society for Rural Sociology: c/o C. Ray, Centre for Rural Economy, Univ. of Newcastle upon Tyne, NE1 7RU, United Kingdom; tel. (191) 222-6460; fax (191) 222-6720; e-mail christopher.ray@newcastle.ac.uk; internet cc.joensuu.fi/alma/esrs; f. 1957 to further research in, and co-ordination of, rural sociology and provide a centre for documentation of information; mems: 300 individuals, institutions and asscns in 29 European countries and nine countries outside Europe; Pres. Dr HILARY TOVEY (Ireland); Sec. CHRISTOPHER RAY (United Kingdom); publ. *Sociologia Ruralis* (quarterly).

Experiment in International Living: POB 595, Main St, Putney, VT 05346, USA; tel. (802) 387-4210; fax (802) 387-5783; e-mail federation@experiment.org; internet www.experiment.org; f. 1932 as an international federation of non-profit educational and cultural exchange institutions; works to create mutual understanding and respect among people of different nations, as a means of furthering peace; mems: organizations in 24 countries; Dir ILENE TODD.

International African Institute—IAI: School of Oriental and African Studies, Thornhaugh St, Russell Sq., London, WC1H 0XG, United Kingdom; tel. (20) 7898-4420; fax (20) 7898-4419; e-mail iai@soas.ac.uk; internet www.oneworld.org/iai; f. 1926 to promote the study of African peoples, their languages, cultures and social life in their traditional and modern settings; organizes an international seminar programme bringing together scholars from Africa and elsewhere; links scholars in order to facilitate research projects, especially in the social sciences; mems: 1,500 in 97 countries; Chair. Prof. V. Y. MUDIMBE; Dir Prof. PAUL SPENCER; publs *Africa* (quarterly), *Africa Bibliography* (annually).

International Association for Media and Communication Research: c/o Ole Prehn, Aalborg University, Kroghstr. 3, 9220 Aalborg East, Denmark; tel. 9635-9038; fax 9815-6869; e-mail prehn@hum.auc.dk; internet www.humfak.auc.dk/iamcr; f. 1957 (fmrly International Asscn for Mass Communication Research) to stimulate interest in mass communication research and the dissemination of information about research and research needs, to improve communication practice, policy and research and training for journalism, and to provide a forum for researchers and others involved in mass communication to meet and exchange information; mems: over 2,300 in c.70 countries; Pres. FRANK MORGAN; Sec.-Gen. OLE PREHN; publ. *Newsletter.*

International Association of Applied Linguistics (Association internationale de linguistique appliquée—AILA): c/o Susan M. Gass, Dept of Linguistics and German, Slavic, Asian and African Languages, Michigan State Univ., A-714 Wells Hall, East Langing, MI 48824; tel. (517) 353-0800; fax (517) 432-1149; e-mail gass@cal.msu.edu; internet www.aila.ac; f. 1964; organizes seminars on applied linguistics, and a World Congress every three years; mems: asscns in 38 countries; Pres. SUSAN M. GASS (USA); Sec.-Gen. Prof. KARLFRIED KNAPP (Germany); publs *AILA Review* (annually), *AILA News* (2 a year).

International Association of Metropolitan City Libraries—INTAMEL: c/o Frans Meijer, Bibliotheek Rotterdam, Hoogstraat 110, 3011 PV Rotterdam, Netherlands; tel. (10) 281-6140; fax (10)—281-6221; e-mail f.meijer@bibliotheek.rotterdam.nl; f. 1967; serves as a platform for libraries in cities of over 400,000 inhabitants or serving a wide and diverse geographical area; promotes the exchange of ideas and information on a range of topics including library networks, automation, press relations and research; mems: 98 libraries in 28 countries; Pres. FRANS MEIJER (Netherlands); publs *INTAMEL Metro* (2 a year), conference reports.

International Committee for Social Sciences Information and Documentation: c/o Dr A. F. Marks, Herengracht 410 (Swidoc), 1017BX Amsterdam, Netherlands; tel. (20) 6225061; fax (20) 6238374; internet www.unesco.org/most/icssd.htm; f. 1950 to collect and disseminate information on documentation services in social sciences, to help improve documentation, to advise societies on problems of documentation and to draw up rules likely to improve the presentation of documents; mems: from international asscns specializing in social sciences or in documentation, and from other specialized fields; Sec.-Gen. ARNAUD F. MARKS (Netherlands); publs *International Bibliography of the Social Sciences* (annually), *Newsletter* (2 a year).

International Council on Archives—ICA: 60 rue des Francs-Bourgeois, 75003 Paris, France; tel. 1-40-27-63-06; fax 1-42-72-20-65; e-mail ica@ica.cia.org; internet www.ica.org; f. 1948 to develop relationships between archivists in different countries; aims to protect and enhance archives, to ensure preservation of archival heritage; facilitates training of archivists and conservators; promotes implementation of a professional code of conduct; encourages ease of access to archives; has 12 regional branches; mems: 1,680 in 180 countries; Pres. ELISA DE SANTOS (Spain); Sec.-Gen. JOAN VAN ALBADA; publ. *Comma* (4 a year).

International Ergonomics Association—IEA: BP 2025, 3500 HA Utrecht, Netherlands; tel. (30) 35-44-55; fax (30) 35-76-39; internet www.iea.cc; f. 1957 to bring together organizations and persons interested in the scientific study of human work and its environment to establish international contacts among those specializing in this field, to co-operate with employers' asscns and trade unions in order to encourage the practical application of ergonomic sciences in industries, and to promote scientific research in this field; mems: 17 federated societies; Pres. ILKKA KUORINKA (Finland); Sec.-Gen. Prof. D. P. ROOKMAAKER; publ. *Ergonomics* (monthly).

International Federation for Housing and Planning—IFHP: Wassenaarseweg 43, 2596 CG The Hague, Netherlands; tel. (70) 3244557; fax (70) 3282085; e-mail info@ifhp.org; internet www.ifhp .org; f. 1913 to study and promote the improvement of housing and the theory and practice of town planning; holds world congress and international conference every 2 years; mems: 200 organizations and 300 individuals in 65 countries; Pres. IRENE WIESE-VON OFEN (Germany); Sec.-Gen. E. E. VAN HYLCKAMA VLIEG (Netherland); publ. *Newsletter* (quarterly).

International Federation of Institutes for Socio-religious Research: 1 pl. Montesquieu, bte 13, 1348 Louvain-la-neuve, Belgium; e-mail gendebien@anso.ucl.ac.be; f. 1958; federates centres engaged in scientific research in order to analyse and discover the social and religious phenomena at work in contemporary society; mems: institutes in 26 countries; Pres. Canon Fr HOUTART (Belgium); Sec. F. GENDEBIEN; publ. *Social Compass (International Review of Sociology of Religion)* (quarterly, in English and French).

International Federation of Social Science Organizations—IFSSO: Institute of Law, nardoni 18, 110 000 Prague 1, Czech Republic; tel. (2) 24913858; fax (2) 24913858; f. 1979 to assist research and teaching in the social sciences, and to facilitate co-operation and enlist mutual assistance in the planning and evaluation of programmes of major importance to members; mems: 31 national councils or academies in 29 countries; Pres. Prof. CARMEN-CITA T. AGUILAR; Sec.-Gen. Prof. J. BLAHOZ; publs *IFSSO Newsletter* (2 a year), *International Directory of Social Science Organizations*.

International Federation of Vexillological Associations: Box 580, Winchester, MA 01890, USA; tel. (781) 729-9410; fax (781) 721-4817; e-mail vexor@atthi.com; internet www.crwflags.com/fotw/flags/vex-fiav.html; f. 1967 to promote through its member organizations the scientific study of the history and symbolism of flags; sanctions international standards for scientific flag study; holds International Congresses every two years; mems: 42 institutions and asscns in 27 countries; Pres. Prof. MICHEL LUPANT (Belgium); Liaison Officer WHITNEY SMITH; publs *Recueil* (every 2 years), *The Flag Bulletin* (every 2 months), *Info FIAV* (every 4 months).

International Institute for Ligurian Studies: Via Romana 39, 18012 Bordighera, Italy; tel. (0184) 263601; fax (0184) 266421; e-mail istituto@üsl.it; internet www.üsl.it; f. 1947 to conduct research on ancient monuments and regional traditions in the northwest arc of the Mediterranean (France and Italy); maintains library of 80,000 vols. mems: in France, Italy, Spain, Switzerland; Dir Prof. CARLO VARALDO (Italy).

International Institute of Administrative Sciences—IIAS: 1 rue Defacqz, 1000 Brussels, Belgium; tel. (2) 538-91-65; fax (2) 537-97-02; e-mail iias@iiasiisa.be; internet www.iiasiisa.be; f. 1930 for the comparative examination of administrative experience; carries out research and programmes designed to improve administrative law and practices; maintains library of 15,000 vols; has consultative status with UN, UNESCO and ILO; organizes international congresses; mems: 46 mem. states, 55 national sections, nine international governmental organizations, 51 corporate mems, 13 individual members; Pres. IGNACIO PICHARDO PAGAZA (Mexico); Dir-Gen. GIANCARLO VILELLA (Italy); publs *International Review of Administrative Sciences* (quarterly), *Newsletter* (3 a year).

International Institute of Sociology—IIS: c/o Dr K. Cook, Dept of Sociology, Stanford University, Stanford CA 94305, USA; f. 1893 to enable sociologists to meet and to study sociological questions; mems: c. 300 in 47 countries; Pres. PAOLO AMMASSARI (Italy); Sec.-Gen. Dr KAREN COOK; publ. *The Annals of the IIS*.

International Numismatic Commission: Coins and Medals Dept, British Museum, London, WC1B 3DG, United Kingdom; tel. (20) 7323-8170; fax (20) 7323-8171; e-mail aburnett@thebritishmuseum.ac.uk; internet www.amnumsoc.org/inc; f. 1936; facilitates co-operation between scholars studying coins and medals; mems: numismatic organizations in 35 countries; Pres. A. BURNETT; Sec. M. AMANDRY.

International Peace Academy—IPA: 777 United Nations Plaza, New York, NY 10017, USA; tel. (212) 687-4300; fax (212) 983-8246; e-mail ipa@ipacademy.org; internet www.ipacademy.org; f. 1970 to promote the prevention and settlement of armed conflicts between and within states through policy research and development; educates government officials in the procedures needed for conflict resolution, peace-keeping, mediation and negotiation, through international training seminars and publications; off-the-record meetings are also conducted to gain complete understanding of a specific conflict; Chair. RITA E. HAUSER; Pres. OLARA A. OTUNNU; publs *Annual Report, Newsletter* (2 a year).

International Peace Research Association—IPRA: c/o Copenhagen Peace Research Institute, University of Copenhagen, Fredericiagade 18, 1310 Copenhagen, Denmark; tel. 3345-5052; fax 3345-5060; e-mail bmoeller@copn.dk; internet www.copn.dk/ipra/ipra .html; f. 1964 to encourage interdisciplinary research on the conditions of peace and the causes of war; mems: 150 corporate, five regional branches, 1,000 individuals, in 93 countries; Pres. URSULA OSWALD (Mexico); Sec.-Gen. BJOERN MOELLER (Denmark); publ. *IPRA Newsletter* (quarterly).

International Social Science Council—ISSC: Maison de l'UNESCO, 1 rue Miollis, 75732 Paris Cédex 15, France; tel. 1-45-68-25-58; fax 1-45-66-76-03; e-mail issclak@unesco.org; internet www .unesco.org/ngo/issc; f. 1952; aims to promote the advancement of the social sciences throughout the world and their application to the major problems of the world; encourages co-operation at an international level between specialists in the social sciences. ISSC has a Senior Board; and programmes on International Human Dimensions of Global Environmental Change (IHDP) and Comparative Research on Poverty (CROP); mems: 14 asscns (listed below), 17 national organizations, 16 associate member organizations; Pres. KURT PAWLIK (Germany); Sec.-Gen. LESZEK A. KOSINSKI (Canada).

Associations Federated to the ISSC:
(details of these organizations will be found under their appropriate category elsewhere in the International Organizations section)
International Association of Legal Sciences (see p. 355)
International Economic Association (see p. 343)
International Federation of Social Science Organizations (see p. 377)
International Geographical Union (see p. 369)
International Institute of Administrative Sciences (see p. 377)
International Law Association (see p. 356)
International Peace Research Association (see p. 377)
International Political Science Association (see p. 350)
International Sociological Association (see p. 377)
International Union for the Scientific Study of Population (see p. 378)
International Union of Anthropological and Ethnological Sciences (see p. 375)
International Union of Psychological Science (see p. 370)
World Association for Public Opinion Research (see p. 378)
World Federation for Mental Health (see p. 363)

International Society of Social Defence and Humane Criminal Policy—ISSD: c/o Centro nazionale di prevenzione e difesa sociale, Piazza Castello 3, 20121 Milan, Italy; tel. (02) 86460714; fax (02) 72008431; e-mail cnpds.ispac@iol.it; f. 1945 to combat crime, to protect society and to prevent citizens from being tempted to commit criminal actions; mems: in 43 countries; Pres. SIMONE ROZÈS (France); Sec.-Gen. EDMONDO BRUTI LIBERATI (Italy); publ. *Cahiers de défense sociale* (annually).

International Sociological Association: c/o Faculty of Political Sciences and Sociology, Universidad Complutense, 28223 Madrid, Spain; tel. (91) 3527650; fax (91) 3524945; e-mail isa@sis.ucm.es; internet www.ucm.es/info/isa; f. 1949 to promote sociological knowledge, facilitate contacts between sociologists, encourage the dissemination and exchange of information and facilities and stimulate research; has 53 research committees on various aspects of sociology; holds World Congresses every four years (15th Congress: Brisbane, Australia, 2002); Pres. A. MARTINELLI (Italy); Exec. Sec. IZABELA BARLINSKA; publs *Current Sociology* (3 a year), *International Sociology* (quarterly), *Sage Studies in International Sociology* (based on World Congress).

International Statistical Institute—ISI: POB 950, Prinses Beatrixlaan 428, 2270 AZ Voorburg, Netherlands; tel. (70) 3375737; fax (70) 3860025; e-mail isi@cbs.nl; internet www.cbs.nl/isi; f. 1885; devoted to the development and improvement of statistical methods and their application throughout the world; administers a statistical education centre in Calcutta, in co-operation with the Indian Statistical Institute; executes international research programmes; mems: 2,000 ordinary mems, 10 hon. mems, 110 *ex-officio* mems, 75 corporate mems, 45 affiliated organizations, 32 national statistical societies; Pres. DENNIS TREWIN; Dir Permanent Office M. P. R. VAN DEN BROECKE; publs *Bulletin of the International Statistical Institute* (proceedings of biennial sessions), *International Statistical Review* (3 a year), *Short Book Reviews* (3 a year), *Statistical Theory and Method Abstracts* (quarterly), *ISI Newsletter* (3 a year), *Membership Directory* (every 2 years).

International Studies Association—ISA: Social Science 324, Univ. of Arizona, Tucson, AZ 85721, USA; tel. (520) 621-7715; fax (520) 621-5780; e-mail isa@u.arizona.edu; internet www.isanet.org; f. 1959; links those whose professional concerns extend beyond their own national boundaries (government officials, representatives of business and industry, and scholars); mems: 3,500 in 60 countries; Pres. MICHAEL BRECHER; Exec. Dir THOMAS J. VOLGY; publs *International Studies Quarterly, International Studies Perspectives, International Studies Review, ISA Newsletter*.

International Union for the Scientific Study of Population— IUSSP: 34 rue des Augustins, 4000 Liège, Belgium; tel. (4) 222-40-80; fax (4) 222-38-47; e-mail iussp@iussp.org; internet www.iussp .org; f. 1928 to advance the progress of quantitative and qualitative demography as a science; mems: 1,917 in 121 countries; Pres. JoséÉ ALBERTO M. DE CARVALHO; publs *IUSSP Bulletin* and books on population.

Mensa International: 15 The Ivories, 6–8 Northampton St, London, N1 2HY, United Kingdom; tel. (20) 7226-6891; fax (20) 7226-7059; internet www.mensa.org/mensa-international; f. 1946 to identify and foster intelligence for the benefit of humanity; mems: individuals who score in a recognized intelligence test higher than 98% of people in general may become mems; there are 100,000 mems world-wide; Exec. Dir E. J. VINCENT (UK); publ. *Mensa International Journal* (monthly).

Third World Forum: 39 Dokki St, POB 43, Orman Giza, Cairo, Egypt; tel. (2) 7488092; fax (2) 7480668; e-mail 20sabry2@gega.net; internet www.egypt2020.org; f. 1973 to link social scientists and others from the developing countries, to discuss alternative development policies and encourage research; currently undertaking Egypt 2020 research project; maintains regional offices in Egypt, Mexico, Senegal and Sri Lanka; mems: individuals in more than 50 countries; Chair. ISMAIL-SABRI ABDALLA.

World Association for Public Opinion Research: c/o University of Nebraska-Lincoln, UNL Gallup Research Center, 200 N 11th St, Lincoln, NE 68588-0241, USA; tel. (402) 458-2030; fax (402) 458-2038; e-mail wapor@unl.edu; internet www.wapor.org; f. 1947 to establish and promote contacts between persons in the field of survey research on opinions, attitudes and behaviour of people in the various countries of the world; works to further the use of objective, scientific survey research in national and international affairs; mems: 450 from 72 countries; Man. Dir RENAE REIS; publs *WAPOR Newsletter* (quarterly), *International Journal of Public Opinion* (quarterly).

World Society for Ekistics: c/o Athens Center of Ekistics, 24 Strat. Syndesmou St, 106 73 Athens, Greece; tel. (1) 3623216; fax (1) 3629337; e-mail ekistics@otenet.gr; internet www.ekistics.org; f. 1965; aims to promote knowledge and ideas concerning human settlements through research, publications and conferences; mems: 170 individuals; Pres. ALEXANDER B. LEMAN; Sec.-Gen. P. PSOMO-POULOS; publs *Ekistics, The Problems and Science of Human Settlements, Ekistic Index of Periodicals*.

Social Welfare and Human Rights

African Commission on Human and People's Rights: Kairaba Ave, POB 673, Banjul, The Gambia; e-mail idoc@achpr.org; internet www.achpr.org; tel. 392962; fax 390764; f. 1987; mandated to monitor compliance with the African Charter on Human and People's Rights (ratified in 1986); investigates claims of human rights abuses perpetrated by govts that have ratified the Charter (claims may be brought by other African govts, the victims themselves, or by a third party); meets twice a year for 15 days in March and Oct. mems: 11; Sec. GERMAIN BARICAKO (Burundi).

Aid to Displaced Persons and its European Villages: 35 rue du Marché, 4500 Huy, Belgium; tel. (85) 21-34-81; fax (85) 23-01-47; e-mail aidepersdepl.huy@proximedia.be; internet www.proximedia .com/aideperso.html; f. 1957 to carry on and develop work begun by the Belgian asscn Aid to Displaced Persons; aims to provide material and moral aid for refugees; European Villages established at Aachen, Bregenz, Augsburg, Berchem-Ste-Agathe, Spiesen, Euskirchen, Wuppertal as centres for refugees; Pres. LUC DENYS (Belgium).

Amnesty International: 1 Easton St, London, WC1X 0DW, United Kingdom; tel. (20) 7413-5500; fax (20) 7956-1157; e-mail amnestyis@amnesty.org; internet www.amnesty.org/; f. 1961; an independent world-wide movement that campaigns impartially for the release of all prisoners of conscience, for fair and prompt trials for all political prisoners, for the abolition of torture and the death penalty and for an end to extrajudicial executions and 'disappearances'; also opposes abuses by opposition groups (hostage-taking, torture and arbitrary killings); financed by donations; mems: 1m. represented by 7,500 local, youth, student and other specialist groups, in more than 100 countries and territories; nationally organized sections in 56 countries; Sec.-Gen. IRENE KHAN (Bangladesh); publs *International Newsletter* (monthly), *Annual Report*, other country reports.

Anti-Slavery International: Thomas Clarkson House, The Stableyard, Broomgrove Rd, London, SW9 9TL, United Kingdom; tel. (20) 7501-8920; fax (20) 7738-4110; e-mail antislavery@antislavery.org; internet www.antislavery.org; f. 1839 to eradicate slavery and forced labour in all their forms, to generate awareness of such abuses, to promote the well-being of indigenous peoples, and to protect human rights in accordance with the Universal Declaration of Human Rights, 1948; mems: 1,800 members in 30 countries; Chair. REGGIE NORTON; Dir MIKE DOTTRIDGE; publs *Annual Report, Anti-Slavery Reporter* (quarterly), special reports on research.

Associated Country Women of the World—ACWW: Clutha House, 10 Storey's Gate, London, SW1P 3AY, United Kingdom; tel. (20) 7834-8635; internet www.acww.org.uk; f. 1933; aims to aid the economic and social development of countrywomen and homemakers of all nations, to promote international goodwill and understanding, and to work to alleviate poverty, and promote good health and education; Gen. Sec. ANNA FROST; publ. *The Countrywoman* (quarterly).

Association Internationale de la Mutualité—AIM (International Association of Mutual Health Funds): 50 rue d'Arlon, 1000 Brussels, Belgium; tel. (2) 234-57-00; fax (2) 234-57-08; e-mail aim .secretariat@aim-mutual.org; internet www.aim-mutual.org; f. 1950 as a grouping of autonomous health insurance and social protection bodies; aims to promote and reinforce access to health care by developing the sound management of mutualities; serves as a forum for exchange of information and debate; mems: 43 national federations in 31 countries; Pres. RON HENDRIKS (Netherlands); Dir WILLY PALM (Belgium); publs *AIMS* (newsletter), reports on health issues.

Aviation sans Frontières—ASF: Brussels National Airport, Brucargo 706, POB 7339, 1931 Brucargo, Belgium; tel. (2) 753-24-70; fax (2) 753-24-71; e-mail office@asfbelgium.org; internet www .asfbelgium.org; f. 1983 to make available the resources of the aviation industry to humanitarian organizations, for carrying supplies and equipment at minimum cost, both on long-distance flights and locally; Pres. PHILIPPE DEHENNIN; Gen. Man. XAVIER FLAMENT.

Co-ordinating Committee for International Voluntary Service—CCIVS: Maison de l'UNESCO, 1 rue Miollis, 75732 Paris Cédex 15, France; tel. 1-45-68-49-36; fax 1-42-73-05-21; e-mail ccivs@unesco.org; internet www.unesco.org/ccivs; f. 1948 to co-ordinate youth voluntary service organizations world-wide; Organizes seminars and conferences; publishes relevant literature; undertakes planning and execution of projects in collaboration with UNESCO, the UN, the EU etc; generates funds for member organizations' projects; Affiliated mems: 140 orgs in more than 90 countries; Pres. G. ORSINI; Dir S. COSTANZO-SOW; publs *News from CCIVS* (3 a year), *The Volunteer's Handbook*, other guides, handbooks and directories.

EIRENE (International Christian Service for Peace): 56503 Neuwied, Postfach 1322, Germany; tel. (2631) 83790; fax (2631) 31160; e-mail eirene-int@eirene.org; internet www.eirene.org; f. 1957; carries out professional training, apprenticeship programmes, agricultural work and work to support co-operatives in Africa and Latin America; runs volunteer programmes in co-operation with peace groups in Europe and the USA; Gen. Sec. ECKEHARD FRICKE.

European Federation of Older Persons—EURAG: Wielandgasse 9, 1 Stock, 8010 Graz, Austria; tel. (316) 81-46-08; fax (316) 81-47-67; e-mail eurag.europe@aon.at; internet www.eurag-europe.org; f. 1962 as the European Federation for the Welfare of the Elderly (present name adopted 2002); serves as a forum for the exchange of experience and practical co-operation among member organizations; represents the interests of members before international organizations; promotes understanding and co-operation in matters of social welfare; draws attention to the problems of old age; mems: organizations in 33 countries; Pres. EDMÉE MANGERS-ANEN (Luxembourg); Sec.-Gen. Dr ULLA HERFORT-WÖRNDLE (Austria); publs (in English, French, German and Italian) *EURAG Newsletter* (quarterly), *EURAG Information* (monthly).

Federation of Asia-Pacific Women's Associations—FAWA: Centro Escolar University, 9 Mendiola St, San Miguel, Manila, Philippines; tel. (2) 741-04-46; e-mail zmaustria@ceu.edu.ph; f. 1959 to provide closer relations, and bring about joint efforts among Asians, particularly women, through mutual appreciation of cultural, moral and socio-economic values; mems: 415,000; Pres. SUSY CHIA-ISAI (Singapore); Sec. WOO CHOON MEI (Singapore); publ. *FAWA News Bulletin* (quarterly).

Inclusion Europe: Galeries de la Toison d'Or, 29 ch. d'Ixelles, Ste 393/32, 1050 Brussels, Belgium; tel. (2) 502-28-15; fax (2) 502-80-10; e-mail secretariat@inclusion-europe.org; internet www .inclusion-europe.org; f. 1988 to advance the human rights and defend the interests of people with learning or intellectual disabilities, and their families, in Europe; mems: 40 societies in 28 European countries; Pres. FRANÇOISE JAN; Dir GEERT FREYHOFF; publs *INCLUDE* (in English and French), *Information Letter* (weekly online, in English and French), *Human Rights Observer* (in English and French), *Enlargement Update* (on-line every 2 weeks, in English and French), other papers and publs.

Interamerican Conference on Social Security (Conferencia Interamericano de Seguridad Social—CISS): Calle San Ramon s/n esq. Avda San Jerónimo, Unidad Independencia, Col. San Jerónimo Lídice, Deleg. Magdalena Contreras, CP 10100 México DF, Mexico;

tel. (55) 5595-0177; fax (55) 5683-8524; e-mail ciss@adetel.net; internet www.ciss.org.mx; f. 1942 to contribute to the development of social security in the countries of the Americas and to co-operate with social security institutions; CISS bodies are: the General Assembly, the Permanent Interamerican Committee on Social Security, the Secretariat General, six American Commissions of Social Security and the Interamerican Center for Social Security Studies; mems: 77 social security institutions in 38 countries; Pres. Dr SANTIAGO LEVY ALGAZI (Mexico); Sec.-Gen. Dr JOSÉ LUIS STEIN VELASCO (Mexico, acting); publs *Social Security Journal/Seguridad Social* (every 2 months), monographs, study series.

International Abolitionist Federation: Gasvaerksvej 24, 1656 Copenhagen V, Denmark; tel. 33-23-40-52; fax 33-23-40-51; e-mail iaf@iaf-online.org; f. 1875; aims to abolish traffic in persons, the exploitation of the prostitution of others, state regulation of prostitution, degradation, humiliation and marginalizing of women and children, all forms of discrimination based on gender, and all contemporary forms of slavery and slavery-like practices; holds international congress every three years and organizes regional conferences to raise awareness of the cultural, religious and traditional practices that affect adversely the lives of women and children; Affiliated organizations in 17 countries, corresponding mems in 40 countries; Pres. DORIS OTZEN (Denmark); Exec. Sec. BENOIT OMONT (France); publ. *IAF Information* (1-2 a year).

International Association for Education to a Life without Drugs (Internationaler Verband für Erziehung zu suchtmittelfreiem Leben—IVES): c/o Uljas Syväniemi, Haiharankatu 15 G 64, 33710 Tampere, Finland; e-mail uljas.syvaniemi@koti.tpo.ti; f. 1954 (as the International Association for Temperance Education) to promote international co-operation in education on the dangers of alcohol and drugs; collects and distributes information on drugs; maintains regular contact with national and international organizations active in these fields; holds conferences; mems: 77,000 in 10 countries; Pres. ULJAS SYVÄNIEMI; Sec. DAG MAGNE JOHANNESSEN.

International Association for Suicide Prevention: c/o Ms M. Campos, IASP Central Administrative Office, 1725 West Harrison St, Suite 955, Chicago, IL 60612, USA; tel. (312) 942-7208; fax (312) 942-2177; internet www.iasp1960.org; f. 1960; serves as a common platform for interchange of acquired experience, literature and information about suicide; disseminates information; arranges special training; encourages and carries out research; organizes the Biennial International Congress for Suicide Prevention; mems: 340 individuals and societies, in 55 countries of all continents; Pres. Dr DIEGO DE LEO; publ. *Crisis* (quarterly).

International Association of Children's International Summer Villages—CISV International Ltd: Mea House, Ellison Pl., Newcastle upon Tyne, NE1 8XS, United Kingdom; tel. (191) 232-4998; fax (191) 261-4710; e-mail international@cisv.org; internet www.cisv.org; f. 1950 to promote peace, education and cross-cultural friendship; conducts International Camps for children and young people mainly between the ages of 11 and 19; mems: c. 49,000; International Pres. CATHY KNOOP; Sec.-Gen. GABRIELLE MANDELL; publs *CISV News, Annual Review, Local Work Magazine, Interspectives* (all annually).

International Association of Schools of Social Work: c/o Dept of Social Work Studies, University of Southampton, Highfield, Southampton SO17 1BJ, United Kingdom; tel. (2380) 593054; fax (2380) 594800; e-mail ld@socsci.soton.ac.uk; internet www.iassw .soton.ac.uk; f. 1928 to provide international leadership and encourage high standards in social work education; mems: 1,600 schools of social work in 70 countries, and 25 national asscns of schools; Pres. LENA DOMINELLI (UK); Sec. BERTHA MARY RODRIGUEZ VILLA; publs *Newsletters* (in English, French and Spanish), *Directory of Schools of Social Work, Journal of International Social Work*, reports and case studies.

International Association of Workers for Troubled Children and Youth: 22 rue Halévy, 59000 Lille, France; tel. 3-20-93-70-16; fax 3-20-09-18-39; e-mail aieji@nordnet.fr; f. 1951 to promote the profession of specialized social workers for troubled children and youth; provides a centre of information about child welfare; encourages co-operation between members; 1997 Congress: Brescia, Italy; mems: national and regional public or private asscns from 22 countries and individual members in many other countries; Pres. GUSTAVO VELASTEGUI (France); Sec.-Gen. LARS STEINOV (Denmark).

International Catholic Migration Commission: CP 96, 37–39 rue de Vermont, POB 96, 1211 Geneva 20, Switzerland; tel. (22) 9191020; fax (22) 9191048; e-mail secretariat@icmc.dpn.ch; f. 1951; offers migration aid programmes; grants interest-free travel loans; assists refugees on a world-wide basis, helping with social and technical problems; mems: in 85 countries; Pres. Prof. STEFANO ZAMAGNI (Italy); Sec.-Gen. WILLIAM CANNY (USA); publ. *Annual Report*.

International Christian Federation for the Prevention of Alcoholism and Drug Addiction: 20A Ancienne Route, Apt. No 42,

1218 Grand-Saconnex, Geneva, Switzerland; tel. (22) 7888158; fax (22) 7888136; e-mail jonathan@iprolink.ch; f. 1960, reconstituted 1980 to promote world-wide education and remedial work through the churches and to co-ordinate Christian concern about alcohol and drug abuse, in co-operation with the World Council of Churches and WHO; Chair. KARIN ISRAELSSON (Sweden); Gen. Sec. JONATHAN N. GNANADASON.

International Civil Defence Organization—ICDO (Organisation internationale de protection civile—OIPC): POB 172, 10–12 chemin de Surville, 1213 Petit-Lancy 2, Geneva, Switzerland; tel. (22) 8796969; fax (22) 8796979; e-mail icdo@icdo.org; internet www .icdo.org; f. 1931, present statutes in force 1972; aims to contribute to the development of structures ensuring the protection of populations and the safeguarding of property and the environment in the face of natural and man-made disasters; promotes co-operation between civil defence organizations in member countries; Sec.-Gen. NAWAF B. S. AL SLEIBI (Jordan); publ. *International Civil Defence Journal* (quarterly, in Arabic, English, French, Russian and Spanish).

International Commission for the Prevention of Alcoholism and Drug Dependency: 12501 Old Columbia Pike, Silver Spring, MD 20904-6600, USA; tel. (301) 680-6719; fax (301) 680-6707; e-mail the_icpa@hotmail.com; internet www.adventist.org/icpa; f. 1952 to encourage scientific research on intoxication by alcohol, its physiological, mental and moral effects on the individual, and its effect on the community; 50th anniversary conference (eleventh World Congress): Bethesda, USA, 2002; mems: individuals in 120 countries; Exec. Dir Dr PETER N. LANDLESS; publ. *ICPA Quarterly*.

International Council of Voluntary Agencies—ICVA: 48 Chemin du Grand-Montfleury, 1290 Versoix, Switzerland; tel. (22) 9509600; fax (22) 9509609; e-mail secretariat@icva.ch; internet www .icva.ch; f. 1962 as a global network of human rights and humanitarian and development NGOs; focuses on information exchange and advocacy, primarily in the areas of humanitarian affairs and refugee issues; mems: 78 non-governmental organizations; Chair. ANDERS LADEKARL; Co-ordinator ED SCHENKENBERG VAN MIEROP; publ. *Talk Back* (newsletter; available on website).

International Council of Women—ICW (Conseil international des femmes—CIF): 13 rue Caumartin, 75009 Paris, France; tel. 1-47-42-19-40; fax 1-42-66-26-23; e-mail icw-cif@wanadoo.fr; internet www.icw-cif.org; f. 1888 to bring together in international affiliation Nat. Councils of Women from all continents, for consultation and joint action; promotes equal rights for men and women and the integration of women in development and decision-making; has five standing committees; mems: 59 national councils; Pres. PNINA HERZOG; Sec.-Gen. MARIE-CHRISTINE LAFARGUE; publ. *Newsletter*.

International Council on Alcohol and Addictions—ICAA: CP 189, 1001 Lausanne, Switzerland; tel. (21) 3209865; fax (21) 3209817; e-mail secretariat@icaa.ch; internet www.icaa.de; f. 1907; provides an international forum for all those concerned with the prevention of harm resulting from the use of alcohol and other drugs; offers advice and guidance in development of policies and programmes; organizes training courses, congresses, symposia and seminars in different countries; mems: affiliated organizations in 74 countries, as well as individual members; Pres. Dr IBRAHIM AL-AWAJI (Saudi Arabia); Exec. Dir Dr JÖRG SPIELDENNER (Germany); publs *ICAA News, Alcoholism* (2 a year).

International Council on Jewish Social and Welfare Services —INTERCO: World Jewish Relief, The Forum, 74–80 Camden St, London, NW1 OEG, United Kingdom; tel. (20) 7691-1771; fax (20) 7691-1780; e-mail wjr1@wjr.org.uk; f. 1961; functions include the exchange of views and information among member agencies concerning the problems of Jewish social and welfare services; represents views to governments and international organizations. mems: organizations in France, Switzerland, United Kingdom and the USA. Exec. Sec. CHERYL MARINER.

International Council on Social Welfare—ICSW: 380 St Antoine St West, Suite 3200, Montreal H2Y 3X7, Canada; tel. (514) 287-3280; fax (514) 287-9702; e-mail icsw@icsw.org; internet www .icsw.org; f. 1928 to provide an international forum for the discussion of social work and related issues and to promote interest in social welfare; holds international conference every two years; provides documentation and information services; mems: 45 national committees, 12 international organizations, 33 other organizations; Pres. JULIAN DISNEY (Australia); Exec. Dir STEPHEN KING (UK); publ. *Social Development Review* (quarterly).

International Dachau Committee: 2 rue Chauchat, 75009 Paris, France; tel. 1-45-23-39-99; fax 1-48-00-06-73; f. 1958 to perpetuate the memory of the political prisoners of Dachau to manifest the friendship and solidarity of former prisoners whatever their beliefs or nationality; to maintain the ideals of their resistance, liberty, tolerance and respect for persons and nations; and to maintain the former concentration camp at Dachau as a museum and international memorial; mems: national asscns in 20 countries; Pres. Gen.

ANDRÉ DELPECH; Sec.-Gen. JEAN SAMUEL; publ. *Bulletin Officiel du Comité International de Dachau* (2 a year).

International Federation of the Blue Cross: CP 6813, 3001 Bern, Switzerland; tel. (31) 3005860; fax (31) 3005869; e-mail ifbc .bern@bluewin.ch; internet www.eurocare.org/bluecross; f. 1877 to aid the victims of intemperance and drug addicts, and to take part in the general movement against alcoholism; Pres. Pastor RAYMOND BASSIN (Switzerland); Gen. Sec. HANS RÜTTIMAN.

International Federation of Educative Communities—FICE: Piazza S.S. Annunziale 12, 50122 Florence, Italy; tel. (055) 2469162; fax (055) 2347041; e-mail fice@lycosmail.com; f. 1948 under the auspices of UNESCO to co-ordinate the work of national asscns, and to promote the international exchange of knowledge and experience in the field of childcare; mems: national asscns from 21 European countries, India, Israel, Canada, Morocco, the USA and South Africa; Pres. ROBERT SOISSON (Luxembourg); Gen. Sec. GIANLUCA BARBANOTTI (Italy); publ. *Bulletin* (2 a year).

International Federation of Human Rights Leagues—FIDH: 17 passage de la Main d'Or, 75011 Paris, France; tel. 1-43-55-25-28; fax 1-43-55-18-80; e-mail fidh@csi.com; internet www.fidh.imaginet .fr; f. 1922; promotes the implementation of the Universal Declaration of Human Rights and other instruments of human rights protection; aims to raise awareness and alert public opinion to issues of human rights violations; undertakes investigation and observation missions; carries out training; uses its consultative and observer status to lobby international authorities; mems: 105 national leagues in over 86 countries; Pres. PATRICK BAUDOUIN; publs *Lettre* (2 a month), mission reports.

International Federation of Persons with Physical Disability —FIMITIC: Plittersdorfer Str. 103, 53173 Bonn, Germany; tel. (228) 9359-191; fax (228) 9359-192; e-mail fimitic@t-online.de; internet www.fimitic.org; f. 1953; brings together representatives of the disabled and handicapped into an international, non-profit, politically and religiously neutral organization under the guidance of the disabled themselves; focuses on ensuring equalization of opportunities and full participation of persons with disabilities; combats discrimination; mems: national groups from 25 European countries, corresponding mems from eight countries; Pres. MARIJA-LIDIJA STIGLIC (Germany); Gen. Sec. MARIJA ŠTIGLIC (Germany); publs *Bulletin, Nouvelles.*

International Federation of Social Workers—IFSW: POB 6875, Schwarztorstrasse 20, 3001 Bern, Switzerland; tel. (31) 3826015; fax (31) 3811222; e-mail secr.gen@ifsw.org; internet www .ifsw.org; f. 1928 as International Permanent Secretariat of Social Workers; present name adopted 1956; aims to promote social work as a profession through international co-operation on standards, training, ethics and working conditions; organizes international conferences; represents the profession at the UN and other international bodies; supports national asscns of social workers; mems: national asscns in 78 countries; Pres. IMELDA DODDS (Australia); Sec.-Gen. TOM JOHANNESEN (Switzerland); publs *Newsletter, IFSW update* (both available on-line), policy statements and manifestos.

International League against Racism and Antisemitism: CP 1754, 1211 Geneva 1, Switzerland; tel. (22) 7310633; fax (22) 7370634; e-mail licra@mnet.ch; internet www.licra.ch; f. 1927; mems in 17 countries; Pres. PIERRE AIDENBAUM (France).

International League for Human Rights: 823 UN Plaza Suite 717, New York, NY 10017, USA; tel. (212) 661-0480; fax (212) 661-0416; e-mail info@ilhr.org; internet www.ilhr.org; f. 1942 to implement political, civil, social, economic and cultural rights contained in the Universal Declaration of Human Rights adopted by the United Nations and to support and protect defenders of human rights worldwide; mems: individuals, national affiliates and correspondents throughout the world; Exec. Dir CATHERINE A. FITZPATRICK; publs various human rights reports.

International Planned Parenthood Federation—IPPF: Regent's College, Inner Circle, Regent's Park, London, NW1 4NS, United Kingdom; tel. (20) 7487-7900; fax (20) 7487-7950; e-mail info@ippf.org; internet www.ippf.org; f. 1952; aims to promote and support sexual and reproductive health and family planning services throughout the world, with a particular focus on the needs of young people; works to bring relevant issues to the attention of the media, parliamentarians, academics, governmental and non-governmental organizations, and the general public; mobilizes financial resources to fund programmes and information materials; offers technical assistance and training; collaborates with other international organizations. The International Medical Panel of the IPPF formulates guide-lines and statements on current medical and scientific advice and best practices; mems: independent family planning asscns in over 150 countries; Pres. ANGELA GÓMEZ; Dir-Gen. Dr STEVEN SINDING.

International Prisoners Aid Association: c/o Dr Ali, Department of Sociology, University of Louisville, Louisville, KY 40292,

USA; tel. (502) 588-6836; fax (502) 852-7042; f. 1950; works to improve prisoners' aid services, with the aim of promoting the rehabilitation of the individual and increasing the protection of society; mems: national federations in 29 countries; Pres. Dr WOLF-GANG DOLEISCH (Austria); Exec. Dir Dr BADR-EL-DIN ALI; publ. *Newsletter* (3 a year).

International Scout and Guide Fellowship—ISGF: 9 rue du Champ de Mars, bte 14, 1050 Brussels, Belgium; tel. (2) 511-46-95; fax (2) 511-84-36; e-mail isgf-aisg@euronet.be; internet www.isgf .org; f. 1953 to help adult scouts and guides to keep alive the spirit of the Scout and Guide Promise and Laws in their own lives and to bring that spirit into the communities in which they live and work; promotes liaison and co-operation between national organizations for adult scouts and guides; encourages the founding of an organization in any country where no such organization exists; mems: 90,000 in 46 mem. states; Chair. of Cttee NIELS ROSENBOM; Sec.-Gen. NAÏC PIRARD; publ. *World Gazette Mondiale* (quarterly).

International Social Security Association—ISSA: CP 1, 1211 Geneva 22, Switzerland; tel. (22) 7996617; fax (22) 7998509; e-mail issa@ilo.org; internet www.issa.int; f. 1927 to promote the development of social security throughout the world, mainly through the improvement of techniques and administration, in order to advance social and economic conditions on the basis of social equality; mems: 383 institutions in 147 countries; Pres. JOHAN VERSTRAETEN (Belgium); Sec.-Gen. DALMER D. HOSKINS (USA); publs *International Social Security Review* (quarterly, in English, French, German, Spanish), *Trends in Social Security* (quarterly, in English, French, German, Spanish), *Social Security Documentation* (African, Asian-Pacific and European series), *Social Security Worldwide* (CD Rom and internet), *Compendia of Conference Reports* (in English, French, German, Spanish), various news bulletins.

International Social Service—SSI (Service social international —SSI): 32 quai du Seujet, 1201 Geneva, Switzerland; tel. (22) 9067700; fax (22) 9067701; e-mail iss.gs@bluewin.ch; internet www .iss-ssi.org; f. 1921 to aid families and individuals whose problems require services beyond the boundaries of the country in which they live, and where the solution of these problems depends upon co-ordinated action on the part of social workers in two or more countries; studies from an international standpoint the conditions and consequences of emigration in their effect on individual, family, and social life; operates on a non-sectarian and non-political basis; mems: branches in 14 countries, five affiliated offices, and correspondents in some 100 other countries; Pres. Prof. Dr RAINER FRANK (Germany); Sec.-Gen. DAMIEN NGABONZIZA; publs *ISS Reports, Newsletter* (available on-line).

International Union of Family Organisations: 28 place Saint-Georges, 75009 Paris, France; tel. 1-48-78-07-59; fax 1-42-82-95-24; f. 1947 to bring together all organizations throughout the world working for family welfare; maintains commissions and working groups on issues including standards of living, housing, marriage guidance, rural families, etc. there are six regional organizations: the Pan-African Family Organisation (Rabat, Morocco), the North America organization (Montréal, Canada), the Arab Family Organisation (Tunis, Tunisia), the Asian Union of Family Organisations (New Delhi, India), the European regional organization (Berne, Switzerland) and the Latin American Secretariat (Curitiba, Brazil); mems: national asscns, groups and governmental departments in over 55 countries; Pres. MARIA TERESA DA COSTA MACEDO (Portugal).

International Union of Tenants: Box 7514, 10392 Stockholm, Sweden; tel. (8) 791-02-00; fax (8) 20-43-44; e-mail magnus .hammar@hyresgasterna.se; internet www.iut.nu; f. 1955 to collaborate in safeguarding the interests of tenants; participates in activities of UN-Habitat; has working groups for EC matters, eastern Europe, developing countries and for future development; holds annual council meeting and triennial congress; mems: national tenant organizations in 24 European countries, Australia, Benin, Canada, India, Kenya, New Zealand, Tanzania and Uganda; Chair. ELISABET LÖNNGREN; Sec.-Gen. MAGNUS HAMMAR; publ. *The Global Tenant* (quarterly).

Inter-University European Institute on Social Welfare— IEISW: 179 rue du Débarcadère, 6001 Marcinelle, Belgium; tel. (71) 44-72-67; fax (71) 47-11-04; e-mail ieiasmayence@hotmail.com; f. 1970 to promote, carry out and publicize scientific research on social welfare and community work; Pres. JOSEPH GILLAIN; Gen. Dir SERGE MAYENCE; publ. *COMM.*

Lions Clubs International: 300 West 22nd St, Oak Brook, IL 60523-8842, USA; tel. (630) 571-5466; fax (630) 571-8890; e-mail lions@lionsclubs.org; internet www.lionsclubs.org; f. 1917 to foster understanding among people of the world to promote principles of good government and citizenship and an interest in civic, cultural, social and moral welfare and to encourage service-minded people to serve their community without financial reward; mems: 1.4m. in over 44,500 clubs in 185 countries and geographic areas; Exec. Admin. WIN HAMILTON; publ. *The Lion* (10 a year, in 20 languages).

Médecins sans frontières—MSF: 39 rue de la Tourelle, 1040 Brussels, Belgium; tel. (2) 280-18-81; fax (2) 280-01-73; internet www.msf.org; f. 1971; independent medical humanitarian org composed of physicians and other members of the medical profession; aims to provide medical assistance to victims of war and natural disasters; operates longer-term programmes of nutrition, immunization, sanitation, public health, and rehabilitation of hospitals and dispensaries; awarded the Nobel peace prize in Oct. 1999; mems: national sections in 18 countries in Europe, Asia and North America; Pres. Dr NORTEN ROSTRUP; Sec.-Gen. RAFAEL VILASANJUAN; publ. *Activity Report* (annually).

Pan Pacific and South East Asia Women's Association—PPSEAWA: POB 119, Nuku'alofa, Tonga; tel. 24003; fax 41404; e-mail nanasi@kalianet.to; internet www.ppseawa.org; f. 1928 to foster better understanding and friendship among women in the region, and to promote co-operation for the study and improvement of social conditions; holds international conference every three years; mems: 19 national member organizations; Pres. HRH Princess NANASIPAU'U TUKU'AHO; publ. *PPSEAWA Bulletin*.

Rotary International: 1560 Sherman Ave, Evanston, IL 60201, USA; tel. (847) 866-3000; fax (847) 328-8554; e-mail wenerm@rotaryintl.org; internet www.rotary.org; f. 1905 to carry out activities for the service of humanity, to promote high ethical standards in business and professions and to further international understanding, goodwill and peace; mems: over 1,195,000 in 30,462 Rotary Clubs in 162 countries; Pres. RICHARD D. KING; Gen. Sec. EDWIN H. FUTA (USA); publs *The Rotarian* (monthly, English), *Rotary World* (5 a year, in 9 languages), *News Basket* (weekly).

Service Civil International (SCI): St-Jacobsmarkt 82, 2000 Antwerp, Belgium; tel. (3) 226-57-27; fax (3) 232-03-44; e-mail info@sciint.org; internet www.sciint.org; f. 1920 to promote peace and understanding through voluntary service projects; mems: 14,000 in 36 countries; Pres. I. DANCKAERTS; publ. *Action* (quarterly).

Society of Saint Vincent de Paul: 5 rue du Pré-aux-Clercs, 75007 Paris, France; tel. 1-53-45-87-53; fax 1-42-61-72-56; e-mail info@wfdnews.org; internet www.ozanet.org; f. 1833 to conduct charitable activities such as childcare, youth work, work with immigrants, adult literacy programmes, residential care for the sick, handicapped and elderly, social counselling and work with prisoners and the unemployed, through personal contact; mems: over 600,000 in 124 countries; Pres. JOSÉ RAMÓN DÍAZ TORREMOCHA; Sec.-Gen. YVES VERRÉ; publ. *Vincenpaul* (quarterly, in English, French and Spanish).

SOLIDAR: 22 rue de Commerce, 1000 Brussels, Belgium; tel. (2) 500-10-20; fax (2) 500-10-30; e-mail solidar@skynet.be; internet www.solidar.org; f. 1951 (fmrly International Workers' Aid); an asscn of independent development and social welfare agencies based in Europe, linked to the labour and democratic socialist movements; aims to contribute to the creation of radical models of economic and social development, and to advance practical solutions that enable people to have increased control over their future; mems: agencies in 90 countries; Sec.-Gen. GIAMPIERO ALHADEFF.

Soroptimist International: 87 Glisson Rd, Cambridge, CB1 2HG, United Kingdom; tel. (1223) 311833; fax (1223) 467951; e-mail sorophq@dial.pipex.com; internet www.sorop.org/; f. 1921 to strive for the advancement of the status of women, high ethical standards, human rights for all, equality and development of peace through international goodwill, understanding and friendship; convention held every 4 years; 2003: Sydney, Australia; mems: 95,000 in 3,000 clubs in 122 countries and territories; International Pres. IRHELI TORSSONEN (Finland); Exec. Officer JANET BILTON; publ. *International Soroptimist* (quarterly).

World Blind Union: c/o CBC ONCE, 18 La Coruña, 28020 Madrid, Spain; tel. (91) 5713675; fax (91) 5715777; e-mail umc@once.es; internet www.once.es/wbu; f. 1984 (amalgamating the World Council for the Welfare of the Blind and the International Federation of the Blind) to work for the prevention of blindness and the welfare of blind and visually-impaired people; encourages development of braille, talking book programmes and other media for the blind; organizes rehabilitation, training and employment; works on the prevention and cure of blindness in co-operation with the International Agency for the Prevention of Blindness; co-ordinates aid to the blind in developing countries; maintains the Louis Braille birthplace as an international museum; mems: in 146 countries; Pres. EUCLID HERIE (Canada); Sec.-Gen. PEDRO ZURITA (Spain); publ. *World Blind* (2 a year, in English, English Braille and on cassette, in Spanish and Spanish Braille and on cassette, and in French).

World Federation of the Deaf—WFD: POB 65, 00401 Helsinki, Finland; e-mail carol-lee.aquiline@wfdnews.org; internet www.wfdnews.org; f. 1951 to serve the interests of deaf people and their national organizations and represent these in international fora; works towards the goal of full participation by deaf people in society; encourages deaf people to set up and run their own organizations; priority is given to the promotion of the recognition and use of national sign languages, the education of deaf people and deaf people in the developing world; mems: 120 member countries; Pres. LIISA KAUPPINEN; Gen. Sec. CAROL-LEE AQUILINE; publ. *WFD News* (3 a year).

World ORT: ORT House, 126 Albert St, London, NW1 7NE, United Kingdom; tel. (20) 7446-8500; fax (20) 7446-8650; internet www.ort.org; f. 1880 for the development of industrial, agricultural and artisanal skills among Jews; now, a highly developed educational and training organization active in over 60 countries throughout the world; conducts vocational training programmes for adolescents and adults, including instructors' and teachers' education and apprenticeship training in more than 40 countries, including technical assistance programmes in co-operation with interested governments; mems: committees in over 40 countries; Dir-Gen. ROBERT SINGER; publs *Annual Report*, *Frontline News*, *World ORT Times*.

World Veterans Federation: 17 rue Nicolo, 75116 Paris, France; tel. 1-40-72-61-00; fax 1-40-72-80-58; e-mail fmacwvf@noos.fr; f. 1950 to maintain international peace and security by the application of the San Francisco Charter and work to help implement the Universal Declaration of Human Rights and related international conventions; aims to defend the spiritual and material interests of war veterans and war victims; promotes practical international co-operation in disarmament, legislation concerning war veterans and war victims, and development of international humanitarian law, etc; in 1986 established International Socio-Medical Information Centre (United Kingdom) for psycho-medical problems resulting from stress. Regional committees for Africa, Asia and the Pacific, and Europe and Standing Committee on Women; mems: national organizations in 84 countries, representing about 27m. war veterans and war victims; Pres. ABDUL HAMID IBRAHIM; Sec.-Gen. MAREK HAGMAJER (Poland); publs special studies (disarmament, human rights, rehabilitation).

Zonta International: 557 W. Randolph St, Chicago, IL 60661-2206, USA; tel. (312) 930-5848; fax (312) 930-0951; e-mail zontaint@zonta.org; internet www.zonta.org; f. 1919; links executives in business and the professions, with the aim of advancing the status of women world-wide; carries out local and international projects; supports women's education and leadership; makes fellowship awards in various fields; mems: 35,000 in 69 countries and areas; Pres. MARGIT WEBJORN; Exec. Dir JANET HALSTEAD; publ. *The Zontian* (quarterly).

Sport and Recreations

Arab Sports Confederation: POB 62997, Riyadh 11442, Saudi Arabia; tel. (1) 6482-1944; fax (1) 6482-3196; f. 1976 to encourage regional co-operation in sport; mems: 21 national Olympic Committees, 53 Arab sports federations; Sec.-Gen. OTHMAN M. AS-SAAD; publ. *Annual Report*.

Fédération Aéronautique Internationale—FAI (World Air Sports Federation): 24 ave Mon Repos, 1005 Lausanne, Switzerland; e-mail sec@fai.org; internet www.fai.org; f. 1905 to promote all aeronautical sports; organizes world championships; develops rules through Air Sports Commissions; endorses world aeronautical and astronautical records; mems: in 100 countries and territories; Pres. WOLFGANG WEINREICH; Sec.-Gen. MAX BISHOP; publ. *Air Sports International*.

General Association of International Sports Federations—GAISF (Association générale de fédérations internationales de sports): 4 blvd du Jardin Exotique, Monte Carlo, Monaco; tel. 97-97-65-10; fax 93-25-28-73; e-mail info@agfisonline.com; internet www.agfisonline.com; f. 1967 to act as a forum for the exchange of ideas and discussion of common problems in sport; collects and circulates information; and provides secretarial, translation, documentation and consultancy services for members; mems: 95 international sports organizations; Pres. Dr UN YONG KIM (Republic of Korea); Sec.-Gen. DON PORTER (USA); publs *Calendar of International Sports Competitions* (2 a year), *Sportvision Magazine* (quarterly, in English and French), *GAISF Calendar*, *Sport and Education* and *Sport and Media*.

International Amateur Athletic Federation—IAAF: 17 rue Princesse Florestine, BP 359, 98007 Monte Carlo Cédex, Monaco; tel. 93-10-88-88; fax 93-15-95-15; e-mail headquarters@iaaf.org; f. 1912 to ensure co-operation and fairness and to combat discrimination in athletics; compiles athletic competition rules and organizes championships at all levels; frames regulations for the establishment of World, Olympic and other athletic records; settles disputes between members; conducts a programme of development consisting of coaching, judging courses, etc. and affiliates national governing bodies; mems: national asscns in 210 countries and territories; Gen. Sec. ISTVÁN GYULAI (Hungary); publs *IAAF Handbook* (every 2 years), *IAAF Review* (quarterly), *IAAF Directory* (annually), *New Studies in Athletics* (quarterly).

International Amateur Boxing Association—AIBA: POB 76343, Atlanta, GA 30358, USA; tel. (770) 455-8350; fax (770) 454-6467; e-mail lbaker27@mindspring.com; internet www.aiba.net; f. 1946 as the world body controlling amateur boxing for the Olympic Games, continental, regional and inter-nation championships and tournaments in every part of the world; mems: 191 national asscns; Pres. Prof. A. CHOWDHRY (Pakistan); Sec.-Gen. LORING K. BAKER (USA); publ. *World Amateur Boxing Magazine* (quarterly).

International Amateur Radio Union: POB 310905, Newington, CT 06131-0905, USA; tel. (860) 594-0200; fax (860) 594-0259; internet www.iaru.org; f. 1925 to link national amateur radio societies and represent the interests of two-way amateur radio communication; mems: 150 national amateur radio societies; Pres. LARRY E. PRICE; Sec. DAVID SUMNER.

International Archery Federation (Fédération internationale de tir à l'arc—FITA): 135 ave de Cour, 1007 Lausanne, Switzerland; tel. (21) 6143050; fax (21) 6143055; e-mail info@archery.org; internet www.archery.org; f. 1931 to promote international archery; organizes world championships and Olympic tournaments; holds Biennial Congress (2003: New York, USA); mems: national amateur asscns in 130 countries; Pres. JAMES L. EASTON (USA); Sec.-Gen. GIUSEPPE CINNIRELLA (Italy); publs *Information FITA* (monthly), *The Arrow* (bulletin, quarterly), *The Target* (annually).

International Automobile Federation (Fédération internationale de l'automobile—FIA): 2 chemin de Blandonnet, CP 296, 1215 Geneva, Switzerland; tel. (22) 5444400; fax (22) 5444450; internet www.fia.com; f. 1904; manages world motor sport and organizes international championships; mems: 157 national automobile clubs and asscns in 119 countries; Pres. MAX MOSLEY; Sec.-Gen. (Sport) PIERRE DE CONINCK; Sec.-Gen. (Tourism) PETER DOGGWILER.

International Badminton Federation—IBF: Manor Park Place, Rutherford Way, Cheltenham, Gloucestershire, GL51 9TU, United Kingdom; tel. (1242) 234904; fax (1242) 221030; e-mail info@intbadfed.org; internet www.intbadfed.org; f. 1934 to oversee the sport of badminton world-wide; mems: affiliated national organizations in 147 countries and territories; Pres. LU SHENGRONG; Chief Exec. NEIL CAMERON (UK); publs *World Badminton* (available on internet), *Statute Book* (annually).

International Basketball Federation (Fédération internationale de basketball): POB 700607, 81306 Munich, Germany; tel. (89) 7481580; fax (89) 74815833; e-mail secretariat@office.fiba.com; internet www.fiba.com; f. 1932 as International Amateur Basketball Federation (present name adopted 1989); aims to promote, supervise and direct international basketball; organizes quadrennial congress; mems: affiliated national federations in 211 countries; Sec.-Gen. BORISLAV STANKOVIC; publs *FIBA Assist* (monthly), *FIBA Media Guide*.

International Canoe Federation: Calle de la Antracita 7, 4th Floor, 28045 Madrid, Spain; tel. (91) 506-11-50; fax (91) 506-11-55; e-mail message@canoeicf.com; internet www.canoeicf.com; f. 1924; administers canoeing at the Olympic Games; promotes canoe/kayak activity in general; mems: 114 national federations; Pres. ULRICH FELDHOFF; Sec.-Gen. JOSÉ PERURENA LOPEZ.

International Council for Health, Physical Education, Recreation, Sport and Dance—ICHPERSD: 1900 Association Drive, Reston, VA 20191, USA; tel. (800) 213-7193; internet www.ichpersd.org; f. 1958 to encourage the development of programmes in health, physical education, recreation, sport and dance throughout the world, by linking teaching professionals in these fields.

International Cricket Council: Lord's Cricket Ground, London, NW8 8QN, United Kingdom; tel. (20) 7266-1818; fax (20) 7266-1777; internet www.cricket.org; f. 1909 as the governing body for international cricket; holds an annual conference; mems: Australia, England, India, New Zealand, Pakistan, South Africa, Sri Lanka, West Indies, Zimbabwe, and 23 associate and 13 affiliate mems; Chief Exec. D. L. RICHARDS.

International Cycling Union (UCI): 37 route de Chavannes, 1860 Aigle, Switzerland; tel. (24) 468-5811; fax (24) 468-5812; e-mail admin@uci.ch; internet www.uci.ch; f. 1900 to develop, regulate and control all forms of cycling as a sport; mems: 160 federations; Pres. HEIN VERBRUGGEN (Netherlands); publs *International Calendar* (annually), *Velo World* (6 a year).

International Equestrian Federation: CP 157, ave Mon-Repos 24, 1000 Lausanne 5, Switzerland; tel. (21) 3104747; fax (21) 3104760; e-mail info@horsesport.org; internet www.horsesport.org; f. 1921; international governing body of equestrian sport recognized by the International Olympic Committee; establishes rules and regulations for conduct of international equestrian events, including on the health and welfare of horses; mems: 127 member countries; Sec.-Gen. Dr BO HELANDER.

International Federation of Associated Wrestling Styles: 17 ave Juste-Olivier, 1006 Lausanne, Switzerland; tel. (21) 3128426;

fax (21) 3236073; e-mail filalausanne@bluewin.ch; internet www.fila_wrestling.org; f. 1912 to encourage the development of amateur wrestling and promote the sport in countries where it is not yet practised and to further friendly relations between all members; mems: 142 federations; Pres. MILAN ERCEGAN; Sec.-Gen. MICHEL DUSSON; publs *News Bulletin, Wrestling Revue.*

International Federation of Association Football (Fédération internationale de football association—FIFA): FIFA House, Hitzigweg 11, POB 85, 8030 Zürich, Switzerland; tel. (1) 384-9595; fax (1) 384-9696; e-mail media@fifa.org; internet www.fifa.com; f. 1904 to promote the game of association football and foster friendly relations among players and national asscns to control football and uphold the laws of the game as laid down by the International Football Association Board; to prevent discrimination of any kind between players; and to provide arbitration in disputes between national asscns; organizes World Cup competition every four years; mems: 204 national asscns, six continental confederations; Pres. JOSEPH S. BLATTER (Switzerland); Gen. Sec. a.i. URS LINSI; publs *FIFA News* (monthly), *FIFA Magazine* (every 2 months) (both in English, French, German and Spanish), *FIFA Directory* (annually), *Laws of the Game* (annually), *Competitions' regulations and Technical Reports* (before and after FIFA competitions).

International Federation of Park and Recreation Administration—IFPRA: Globe House, Crispin Close, Caversham, Reading, Berks, RG4 7JS, United Kingdom; tel. and fax (118) 946-1680; e-mail ifpraworld@aol.com; internet www.ifpra.org; f. 1957 to provide a world centre for members of government departments, local authorities, and all organizations concerned with recreational services to discuss relevant matters; mems: 550 in over 50 countries; Gen. Sec. ALAN SMITH (UK); publ. *IFPRA Bulletin.*

International Fencing Federation (Fédération internationale d'escrime—FIE): ave Mon-Repos 24, CP 128, 1000 Lausanne 5, Switzerland; tel. (21) 3203115; fax (21) 3203116; e-mail contact@fie.ch; internet www.fie.ch; f. 1913; promotes development and co-operation between amateur fencers; determines rules for international events; organizes World Championships; mems: 109 national federations; Pres. RENÉ ROCH.

International Gymnastic Federation: rue des Oeuches 10, CP 359, 2740 Moutier 1, Switzerland; tel. (32) 4946410; fax (32) 4946419; e-mail gymnastics@fig.worldsport.org; f. 1881 to promote the exchange of official documents and publications on gymnastics; mems: in 122 countries and territories; Pres. BRUNO GRANDI; Gen. Sec. NORBERT BUECHE (Switzerland); publs *FIG Bulletin* (quarterly), *World of Gymnastics Magazine* (quarterly).

International Hockey Federation: 1 ave des Arts, Boîte 5, 1210 Brussels, Belgium; tel. (2) 219-45-37; fax (2) 219-27-61; e-mail info@fihockey.org; internet www.fihockey.org; f. 1924 to fix the rules of outdoor and indoor hockey for all affiliated national asscns to control the game of hockey and indoor hockey and to control the organization of international tournaments, such as the Olympic Games and the World Cup; mems: 120 national asscns; Pres. JUAN ANGEL CALZADO; Sec.-Gen. ELS VAN BREDA-VRIESMAN; publ. *World Hockey* (quarterly).

International Judo Federation: BP 333, El Menzah 1004, Tunis, Tunisia; tel. (71) 750-105; fax (71) 743-424; e-mail sgfij@gnet.tn; internet www.ijf.org; f. 1951 to promote cordial and friendly relations between members to protect the interests of judo throughout the world; to organize World Championships and the judo events of the Olympic Games; to develop and spread the techniques and spirit of judo throughout the world; and to establish international judo regulations; Pres. YONG SUNG PARK (Republic of Korea); Gen. Sec. Dr HEDI DHOUIB (Tunisia).

International Paralympic Committee: Adenauerallee 212–214, 53113 Bonn, Germany; tel. (228) 2097200; fax (228) 2097209; e-mail info@paralympic.org; internet www.paralympic.org; f. 1989; responsible for organizing the paralympic games for sportspeople with disabilities, which are held alongside the Olympic Games; mems: 161 national paralympic committees and 5 disability-specific international sports federations; Pres. PHILIP CRAVEN (UK); Chief Operating Officer a.i. XAVIER GONZALEZ (Germany); publ. *The Paralympian* (quarterly).

International Philatelic Federation: Jupiterstrasse 49, 9032 Zürich, Switzerland; tel. (1) 4223839; fax (1) 4223843; e-mail heiri@f-i-p.ch; internet www.f-i-p.ch/; f. 1926 to promote philately internationally; Pres. KNUD MOHR; Sec.-Gen. MARIE-LOUISE HEIRI.

International Rowing Federation (Fédération internationale des sociétés d'aviron—FISA): 135 ave de Cour, CP 18, 1000 Lausanne 3, Switzerland; tel. (21) 6178373; fax (21) 6178375; e-mail info@fisa.org; internet www.worldrowing.com; f. 1892 to establish contacts between rowers in all countries and to draw up racing rules; serves as the world controlling body of the sport of rowing; mems: 114 national federations; Pres. DENIS OSWALD; Sec.-Gen. and Exec.

Dir MATTHEW SMITH; publs *FISA Guide* (annually), *FISA World Rowing Magazine* (quarterly), *FISA Bulletins* (annually).

International Sailing Federation—ISAF: Ariadne House, Town Quay, Southampton, Hants, SO14 2AQ, United Kingdom; tel. (2380) 635111; fax (2380) 635789; e-mail sail@isaf.co.uk; internet www .sailing.org; f. 1907; serves as the controlling authority of sailing in all its forms throughout the world; establishes and amends international yacht racing rules; organizes the Olympic Sailing Regatta and other championships; mems: 117 national yachting federations; Pres. PAUL HENDERSON; Sec.-Gen. ARVE SUNDHEIM; Publ *Making Waves*.

International Shooting Sport Federation—ISSF: 80336 Munich, Bavariaring 21, Germany; tel. (89) 5443550; fax (89) 54435544; e-mail munich@issf-shooting.org; internet www .issf-shooting.org; f. 1907 to promote and guide the development of amateur shooting sports; organizes World Championships and controls the organization of continental and regional championships; supervises the shooting events of the Olympic and Continental Games under the auspices of the International Olympic Committee; mems: 151 federations in 146 countries; Pres. OLE-GARIO VÁZQUEZ-RAÑA (Mexico); Sec.-Gen. HORST G. SCHREIBER (Germany); publs *ISSF News, International Shooting Sport* (6 a year).

International Skating Union—ISU: chemin de Primerose 2, 1007 Lausanne, Switzerland; tel. (21) 6126666; fax (21) 6126677; e-mail info@isu.ch; internet www.isu.org; f. 1892; holds regular conferences; mems: 73 national federations in 57 countries; Pres. OTTAVIO CINQUANTA; Gen.-Sec. FREDI SCHMID; publs Judges' manuals, referees' handbooks, general and special regulations.

International Ski Federation (Fédération internationale de ski—FIS): 3653 Oberhofen am Thunersee, Switzerland; tel. (33) 2446161; fax (33) 2446171; internet www.fis-ski.com; f. 1924 to further the sport of skiing to prevent discrimination in skiing matters on racial, religious or political grounds; to organize World Ski Championships and regional championships and, as supreme international skiing authority, to establish the international competition calendar and rules for all ski competitions approved by the FIS, and to arbitrate in any disputes; mems: 100 national ski asscns; Pres. GIAN-FRANCO KASPER (Switzerland); Sec.-Gen. SARAH LEWIS (UK); publ. *FIS Bulletin* (quarterly).

International Swimming Federation (Fédération internationale de natation—FINA): POB 4, ave de l'Avant, 1005 Lausanne, Switzerland; tel. (21) 3126602; fax (21) 3126610; internet www.fina.org; f. 1908 to promote amateur swimming and swimming sports internationally; administers rules for swimming sports, competitions and for establishing records; organizes world championships and FINA events; runs a development programme to increase the popularity and quality of aquatic sports; mems: 180 federations; Pres. MUSTAPHA LARFAOUI (Algeria); Exec. Dir CORNEL MARCULESCU; publs *Handbook* (every 4 years), *FINA News* (monthly), *World of Swimming* (quarterly).

International Table Tennis Federation: ave Mon-Repos 30, 1005 Lausanne, Switzerland; tel. (21) 3407090; fax (21) 3407099; e-mail ittf@ittf.com; internet www.ittf.com; f. 1926; Pres. ADHAM SHARARA; Exec. Dir JORDI SERRA; publs *Table Tennis Illustrated, Table Tennis News* (both bimonthly), *Table Tennis Legends, Table Tennis Fascination, Table Tennis: The Early Years*.

International Tennis Federation: Bank Lane, Roehampton, London, SW15 5XZ, United Kingdom; tel. (20) 8878-6464; fax (20) 8878-7799; e-mail communications@itftennis.com; internet www .itftennis.com; f. 1913 to govern the game of tennis throughout the world, promote its teaching and preserve its independence of outside authority; produces the Rules of Tennis; promotes the Davis Cup Competition for men, the Fed. Cup for women, the Olympic Games Tennis Event, wheelchair tennis, 16 cups for veterans, the ITF Sunshine Cup and the ITF Continental Connelly Cup for players of 18 years old and under, the World Youth Cup for players of 16 years old and under, and the World Junior Tennis Tournament for players of 14 years old and under; mems: 141 full and 57 associate; Pres. FRANCESCO RICCI BITTI; publs *World of Tennis* (annually), *Davis Cup Yearbook, ITF World* (quarterly), *ITF This Week* (weekly).

International Volleyball Federation (Fédération internationale de volleyball—FIVB): ave de la Gare 12, 1001 Lausanne, Switzerland; tel. (21) 3453535; fax (21) 3453545; e-mail info@mail.fivb.ch; internet www.fivb.org; f. 1947 to encourage, organize and supervise the playing of volleyball, beach volleyball, and park volley; organizes biennial congress; mems: 218 national federations; Pres. Dr RUBÉN ACOSTA HERNÁNDEZ; Gen. Man. JEAN-PIERRE SEPPEY; publs *VolleyWorld* (every 2 months), *X-Press* (monthly).

International Weightlifting Federation—IWF: PF 614, 1374 Budapest, Hungary; tel. (1) 3530530; fax (1) 3530199; e-mail iwf@iwf .net; internet www.iwf.net; f. 1905 to control international weightlifting; draws up technical rules; trains referees; supervises World Championships, Olympic Games, regional games and international contests of all kinds; registers world records; mems: 167 national organizations; Pres. Dr THOMÁS AJAN (Hungary); Gen. Sec. YANNIS SGOUROS (Greece); publs *IWF Constitution and Rules* (every 4 years), *World Weightlifting* (quarterly).

International World Games Association: Ekeby House, Luiksesstraat 23, 2587 The Hague, Netherlands; tel. (70) 3512774; fax (70) 3509911; e-mail iwga@hetnet.nl; internet www.worldgames-iwga .org; f. 1980; organizes World Games every four years (2001: Akita, Japan), comprising 26 sports that are not included in the Olympic Games; Sec.-Gen. J. A. P. KOREN.

Union of European Football Associations—UEFA: route de Genève 46, 1260 Nyon 2, Switzerland; tel. (22) 9944444; fax (22) 9944488; internet www.uefa.com; f. 1954; works on behalf of Europe's national football asscns to promote football; aims to foster unity and solidarity between national asscns; mems: 51 national asscns; Pres. LENNART JOHANSSON; CEO GERHARD AIGNER; Publ *Magazine* (available on-line).

World Boxing Organization: c/o 100 West Randolph St, 9th Floor, Chicago, IL 60601, USA; tel. (312) 814-3145; fax (312) 814-2719; internet www.wbo-int.com; f. 1962; regulates professional boxing.

World Bridge Federation: 56 route de Vandoeuvres, 1253 Geneva, Switzerland; tel. (22) 7501541; fax (22) 7501620; internet www.bridge.gr; f. 1958 to promote the game of contract bridge throughout the world; federates national bridge asscns in all countries; conducts world championships competitions; establishes standard bridge laws; mems: 89 countries; Pres. ERNESTO D'ORSI (Brazil); publ. *World Bridge News* (quarterly).

World Chess Federation (Fédération internationale des echecs—FIDE): POB 166, 1000 Lausanne 4, Switzerland; tel. (21) 3103900; e-mail fide@fide.ch; internet www.fideonline.com; f. 1924; controls chess competitions of world importance and awards international chess titles; mems: national orgs in more than 160 countries; Pres. KIRSAN ILYUMZHINOV; publs (annually), *International Rating List* (2 a year).

World Squash Federation Ltd: 6 Havelock Rd, Hastings, East Sussex, TN34 1BP, United Kingdom; tel. (1424) 429245; fax (1424) 429250; e-mail wsf@worldsquash.org; internet www.worldsquash .org; f. 1966 to maintain quality and reputation of squash and increase its popularity; monitors rules and makes recommendations for change; trains, accredits and assesses international and world referees; sets standards for all technical aspects of squash; co-ordinates coaching training and awards; runs World Championships; mems: 119 national organizations; Exec. Dir EDWARD J. WALL-BUTTON.

World Underwater Federation: Viale Tiziano 74, 00196 Rome, Italy; tel. (06) 36858480; fax (02) 32110595; e-mail cmas@cmas2000 .org; internet www.cmas2000.org; f. 1959 to develop underwater activities to form bodies to instruct in the techniques of underwater diving; to perfect existing equipment, encourage inventions and experiment with newly marketed products; and to organize international competitions; mems: organizations in 100 countries; Pres. ACHILLE FERRERO (Italy); Sec. PIERRE DERNIER (Belgium); publs *International Year Book of CMAS, Scientific Diving: A Code of Practice*, manuals.

Technology

International Union of Technical Associations and Organizations (Union internationale des associations et organismes techniques—UATI): UNESCO House, 1 rue Miollis, 75015 Paris Cédex 15, France; tel. 1-45-68-27-70; fax 1-43-06-29-27; e-mail uati@unesco .org; internet www.unesco.org/uati; f. 1951 (fmrly Union of International Technical Associations) under the auspices of UNESCO; aims to promote and co-ordinate activities of member organizations and represent their interests; facilitates relations with international organizations, notably UN agencies; receives proposals and makes recommendations on the establishment of new international technical asscns; mems: 25 organizations; Chair. PHILIPPE AUSSOURD (France); publ. *Convergence* (3 a year).

MEMBER ORGANIZATIONS

Members of UATI include the following:

International Association of Hydraulic Engineering and Research—IAHR: Paseo Bajo Virgen del Puerto 3, 28005 Madrid, Spain; tel. (91) 3357908; fax (91) 3357935; e-mail iahr@iahr.org; internet www.iahr.org; f. 1935; promotes advancement and exchange of knowledge on hydraulic engineering; holds biennial congresses and symposia; mems: 1,850 individual, 300 corporate; Sec.-Gen. C. MATEOS (Spain); Publs *Journal of River Basin Management, IAHR Newsletter, Journal of Hydraulic Research, Proceedings of Biennial Conferences,, Fluvial Processes Monograph,, Fluvial Processes Solutions Manual*.

International Association of Lighthouse Authorities: 20 ter rue Schnapper, 78100 St Germain en Laye, France; tel. 1-34-51-70-01; fax 1-34-51-82-05; e-mail aismiala@easynet.fr; internet www .iala-aism.org; f. 1957; holds technical conference every four years; working groups study special problems and formulate technical recommendations, guide-lines and manuals; mems in 80 countries; Sec.-Gen. TORSTEN KRUUSE; publ. *Bulletin* (quarterly).

International Bridge, Tunnel and Turnpike Association: 1146 19th St, NW, Suite 800, Washington, DC 20036-3725, USA; tel. (202) 659-4620; fax (202) 659-0500; e-mail ibtta@ibtta.org; internet www .ibtta.org; f. 1932 to serve as a forum for sharing knowledge, with the aim of promoting toll-financed transportation services; mems: 240 mems in 22 countries; Exec. Dir. PATRICK D. JONES; publ. *Tollways* (monthly).

International Commission of Agricultural Engineering—CIGR: Institut für Landtechnik, Universität Bonn, Nussallee 5, 53 115 Bonn, Germany; tel. (228) 732389; fax (228) 739644; e-mail cigr@uni-bonn.de; internet www.cigr.org; f. 1930; aims to stimulate development of science and technology in agricultural engineering; encourages education, training and mobility of professionals; facilitates exchange of research; represents profession at international level; mems: asscns from more than 60 countries; Pres. Prof. A. MUNACK (Germany); Sec.-Gen. P. SCHULZE LAMMERS (Germany); Publs *Bulletin de la CIGR, Newsletter* (quarterly), technical reports.

International Commission on Glass: Stazione Sperimentale del Vetro, Via Briati 10, 30141 Murano, Venice, Italy; tel. (041) 739422; fax (041) 739420; e-mail spevetro@ve-nettuno.it; internet www .nettuno.it/fiera/spevetro; f. 1933 to co-ordinate research in glass and allied products, exchange information and organize conferences; mems: 30 organizations; Pres. D. PYE; Sec.-Gen. F. NICOLETTI.

International Commission on Irrigation and Drainage: 48 Nyaya Marg, Chanakyapuri, New Delhi 110 021, India; tel. (11) 26115679; fax (11) 26115962; e-mail icid@icid.org; internet www.icid .org; f. 1950; holds triennial congresses; mems: 70 national committees; Pres. .KEIZRUL BIN ABDULLAH (Malaysia); Sec.-Gen. C. D. THATTE (India); Publs *Journal* (quarterly), *World Irrigation, Multilingual Technical Dictionary, Historical Dams*, technical books.

International Federation for the Promotion of Mechanism and Machine Science: POB 4200, Univ. of Oulu, 90014 Oulu, Finland; tel. (8) 553-2050; fax (8) 553-2026; e-mail tatu@me.oulu.fi; internet www.caip.rutgers.edu/iftomm; f. 1969 to study robots, man-machine systems, etc. Pres. K. WALDRON; Sec.-Gen. T. LEINONEN; publ. *Mechanism and Machine Theory*.

International Federation of Automatic Control—IFAC: 2361 Laxenburg, Schlossplatz 12, Austria; tel. (2236) 71447; fax (2236) 72859; e-mail secr@ifac.co.at; internet www.ifac-control.org; f. 1957 to serve those concerned with the theory and application of automatic control and systems engineering; mems: 48 national asscns; Pres. Prof. YONG ZAI LU (People's Republic of China); Sec. G. HENCSEY; Publs *Automatica and Control Engineering Practice* (bi-monthly), *Newsletter* and affiliated journals.

International Gas Union: c/o N.V. Nederlandse Gasunie, POB 19, 9700 MA Groningen, Netherlands; tel. (50) 5212999; fax (50) 5255951; e-mail secr.igu@gasnie.nl; internet www.igu.org; f. 1931 to study all aspects and problems of the gas industry, with a view to promoting international co-operation and the general improvement of the industry; mems: national organizations in 59 countries; Pres. C. DÉTOURNÉ (France); Sec.-Gen. J. F. MEEDER (Netherlands).

International Institute of Welding: 90 rue des Vanesses, ZI Paris Nord II, 93420 Villepinte, France; tel. 1-49-90-36-08; fax 1-49-90-36-80; e-mail iiw@wanadoo.fr; internet www.iiw-iis.org; f. 1948; mems: 52 societies in 40 countries; Pres. Y. FUJITA (Japan); Chief Exec. M. BRAMAT (France); publ. *Welding in the World* (7 a year).

International Measurement Confederation—IMEKO: POB 457, 1371 Budapest 5, Hungary; tel. and fax (1) 353-1562; e-mail imeko.ime@mtesz.hu; internet www.imeko.org; f. 1958 as a federation of member organizations concerned with the advancement of measurement technology; aims to promote exchange of scientific and technical information in field of measurement and instrumentation and to enhance co-operation between scientists and engineers; holds World Congress every 3 years (2003: Dubrovnik; 2006: Rio de Janeiro); mems: 35 orgs; Pres. Prof. M. PETERS (Germany); Sec.-Gen. Dr TAMÁS KEMÉNY (Hungary); Publs *Acta IMEKO* (proccedings of World Congresses), *IMEKO TC Events Series, Measurement* (quarterly), *IMEKO Bulletin* (2 a year).

International Navigation Association: Graaf de Ferraris, 11e étage, bte 3, 156 blvd Roi Albert II, 1000 Brussels, Belgium; tel. (2) 553-71-60; fax (2) 553-71-55; e-mail navigation-aipcn-pianc@tornado .be; internet www.pianc-aicpn.org; f. 1885; fmrly Permanent International Assoc. of Navigation Congresses (PIANC); fosters progress in the construction, maintenance and operation of inland and maritime waterways, of inland and maritime ports and of coastal areas; holds Congresses every four years; mems: 40 governments, 2,780

others; Pres. Ir R. DE PAEPE; Sec.-Gen. C. VAN BEGIN; Publs *Bulletin* (quarterly), *Illustrated Technical Dictionary* (in 6 languages), technical reports, Congress papers.

International Union for Electricity Applications: Espace Elec. CNIT, BP 10, 2 place de la Défense, 92053 Paris, France; tel. 1-41-26-56-48; fax 1-41-26-56-49; e-mail uie@uie.org; internet www.uie .org; f. 1953, present title adopted 1994; aims to study all questions relative to electricity applications, except commercial questions; links national groups and organizes international congresses on electricity applications; mems: national committees, corporate associated and individual members in 18 countries; Pres. RONNIE BELMANS (Belgium); Gen. Sec. Prof. MICHEL MACHIELS; Publs UIE and Electra Collection of reports, UIE proceedings.

International Union of Air Pollution Prevention and Environmental Protection Associations: 44 Grand Parade, Brighton, BN2 2QA, United Kingdom; tel. (1273) 878772; fax (1273) 606626; e-mail iuappa@nsca.org.uk; internet www.iuappa.fsnet.co.uk; f. 1963; organizes triennial World Clean Air Congress and regional conferences for developing countries (several a year); undertakes policy development and research programmes on international environmental issues; Pres. Prof. M. LURIA (Israel); Dir-Gen. R. MILLS; Publs *IUAPPA Newsletter* (quarterly), *Clean Air around the World*.

International Union of Testing and Research Laboratories for Materials and Structures: Ecole Normale Supérieure, 61 ave du Président Wilson, 94235 Cachan Cédex, France; tel. 1-47-40-23-97; fax 1-47-40-01-13; e-mail sg@rilem.ens-cachan.fr; internet www .iabse.ethz.ch/lc/rilem.html; f. 1947 for the exchange of information and the promotion of co-operation on experimental research concerning structures and materials; studies research methods with a view to improvement and standardization; mems: laboratories and individuals in 73 countries; Pres. Dr JACQUES BRESSON (France); Sec.-Gen. M. BRUSIN (France); publ. *Materials and Structures—Testing and Research* (10 a year).

Union of the Electricity Industry—EURELECTRIC: Blvd de l'Impératrice 66, Box 2, 1000 Brussels, Belgium; tel. (2) 515-1000; fax (2) 510-1010; e-mail eurelectric@eurelectric.org; internet www .eurelectric.org; f. 1999 by merger of International Union of Producers and Distributors of Electrical Energy (UNIPEDE, f. 1925) and European Grouping of the Electricity Industry (EEIG, f. 1989); aims to study all questions relating to the production, transmission and distribution of electrical energy, and to promote the image of and defend the interests of the electricity supply industry; Pres. HANS HAIDER; Sec.-Gen. PAUL BULTEEL; publ. *Watt's New* (newsletter).

World Energy Council: 5th Floor, Regency House, 1–4 Warwick St, London, W1B 5LT, United Kingdom; tel. (20) 7734-5996; fax (20) 7734-5926; e-mail info@worldenergy.org; internet www.worldenergy .org; f. 1924 to link all branches of energy and resources technology and maintain liaison between world experts; holds congresses every three years; mems: 99 committees; Chair. ANTONIO DEL ROSARIO (Philippines); Sec.-Gen. GERALD DOUCET (Canada); Publs *Annual Report*, energy supply and demand projections, resources surveys, technical assessments, reports.

World Foundrymen Organization—WFO: National Metalforming Centre, 47 Birmingham Rd, West Bromwich, B70 6PY, United Kingdom; tel. (121) 601-6979; fax (121) 601-6981; e-mail secretary@thewfo.com; internet www.thewfo.com; Pres. MIKE CLIFFORD; Gen. Sec. Eng. A. TURNER.

World Road Association—PIARC: La Grande Arche, Paroi Nord, Niveau 8, 92055 La Défense Cédex, France; tel. 1-47-96-81-21; fax 1-49-00-02-02; e-mail piarc@wanadoo.fr; internet www.piarc.org; f. 1909 as the Permanent International Association of Road Congresses; aims to promote the construction, improvement, maintenance, use and economic development of roads; organizes technical committee and study sessions; mems: governments, public bodies, organizations and private individuals in 100 countries; Pres. O. MICHAUD (Switzerland); Sec.-Gen. J. F. CORTÉ (France); Publs *Bulletin, Technical Dictionary, Lexicon*, technical reports.

OTHER ORGANIZATIONS

African Organization of Cartography and Remote Sensing: 5 Route de Bedjarah, BP 102, Hussein Dey, Algiers, Algeria; tel. (2) 77-79-34; fax (2) 77-79-34; e-mail oact@wissal.dz; f. 1988 by amalgamation of African Association of Cartography and African Council for Remote Sensing; aims to encourage the development of cartography and of remote sensing by satellites; organizes conferences and other meetings, promotes establishment of training institutions; maintains four regional training centres (in Burkina Faso, Kenya, Nigeria and Tunisia); mems: national cartographic institutions of 24 African countries; Sec.-Gen. UNIS MUFTAH.

African Regional Centre for Technology: Imm. Fahd, 17th Floor, blvd Djilly Mbaye, BP 2435, Dakar, Senegal; tel. 823-77-12; fax 823-77-13; e-mail arct@sonatel.senet.net; f. 1977 to encourage the development of indigenous technology and to improve the terms of access to imported technology; assists the establishment of national centres; mems: govts of 31 countries; Exec. Di Dr OUSMANE KANE; Publs *African Technodevelopment, Alert Africa*.

AIIM International: 1100 Wayne Ave, Suite 1100, Silver Spring, USA; internet www.aiim.org; f. 1999 by merger of the Association for Information and Image Management (f. 1943) and the International Information Management Congress (f. 1962); serves as the international body of the document technologies industry; Chief Exec. JOHN H. MANCINI.

Bureau International de la Recupération et du Recyclage (Bureau of International Recycling): 24 ave Franklin Roosevelt, 1050 Brussels, Belgium; tel. (2) 627-57-70; fax (2) 627-57-73; e-mail bir@bir.org; internet www.bir.org; f. 1948 as the world federation of the reclamation and recycling industries; promotes international trade in scrap iron and steel, non-ferrous metals, paper, textiles, plastics and glass; mems: asscns and individuals in 53 countries; Dir-Gen. FRANCIS VEYS.

ECMA (Standardizing Information and Communication Systems): 114 rue de Rhône, 1204 Geneva, Switzerland; tel. (22) 8496000; fax (22) 8496001; e-mail helpdesk@ecma.ch; internet www.ecma.ch; f. 1961 to develop standards and technical reports, in co-operation with the appropriate national, European and international organizations, in order to facilitate and standardize the use of information processing and telecommunications systems; promulgates various standards applicable to the functional design and use of these systems; mems: 28 ordinary and 18 associate mems; Sec.-Gen. JAN VAN DEN BELD; Publs *ECMA Standards, ECMA Memento*.

EUREKA: 107 rue Neerveld, bte 5, 1200 Brussels, Belgium; tel. (2) 777-09-50; fax (2) 770-74-95; e-mail eureka.secretariat@es.eureka .be; internet www.eureka.be; f. 1985; aims to promote industrial collaboration between member countries on non-military research and development activities; enables joint development of technology; supports innovation and systematic use of standardization in new technology sectors; mems: 34 in 33 countries; Sec.-Gen. Dr HEIKKI KOTILAINEN; Publs *Annual Report, Eureka Bulletin*.

European Convention for Constructional Steelwork—ECCS: 32-36 ave des Ombrages, bte 20, 1200 Brussels, Belgium; tel. (2) 762-04-29; fax (2) 762-09-35; e-mail eccs@steelconstruct.com; internet www.steelconstruct.com; f. 1955 for the consideration of problems involved in metallic construction; mems: in 25 countries; Sec.-Gen. G. GENDEBEN; Publs Information sheets and documents, symposia reports, model codes.

European Federation of Chemical Engineering: c/o Institution of Chemical Engineers, Davis Bldg, 165–189 Railway Terrace, Rugby, Warwickshire, CV21 3HQ, United Kingdom; tel. (1788) 578214; fax (1788) 560833; internet www.icheme.org; f. 1953 to encourage co-operation between non-profit-making scientific and technical societies, for the advancement of chemical engineering and its application in the processing industries; mems: 65 societies in 25 European countries, 15 corresponding societies in other countries; Chief Exec. Dr T. J. EVANS.

European Federation of Corrosion: 1 Carlton House Terrace, London, SW1Y 5DB, United Kingdom; tel. (20) 7451-7336; fax (20) 8392-2289; e-mail paul.mcintyre@iom3.org; internet www.materials .org; f. 1955 to encourage co-operation in research on corrosion and methods of combating this; mems: societies in 24 countries; Pres. D. HARROP (UK); Hon. Secs J. P. BERGE (France), G. KREYSA (Germany), B. A. RICKINSON (UK); Scientific Sec. P. MCINTYRE (UK).

European Federation of National Engineering Associations (Fédération européenne d'associations nationales d'ingénieurs— FEANI): 21 rue du Beau Site, 1000 Brussels, Belgium; tel. (2) 639-03-90; fax (2) 639-03-99; e-mail rita.heissner@feani.org; internet www.feani.org; f. 1951 to affirm the professional identity of the engineers of Europe and to strive for the unity of the engineering profession in Europe; mems: 27 mem. countries; Pres. K. ALEXOPOULOS (Greece); Sec.-Gen. PHILIPPE WAUTERS (Belgium); Publs *FEANI News, INDEX*.

European Metal Union: Einsteinbaan 1, POB 2600, 3430 GA Nieuwegein, Netherlands; tel. (30) 605-33-44; fax (30) 605-31-15; e-mail info@metaalunie.nl; f. 1954 as International Union of Metal; liaises between national craft organizations and small and medium-sized enterprises in the metal industry; represents members' interests at a European level; provides for the exchange of information and ideas; mems: national federations from Austria, , Germany, Hungary, Luxembourg, Netherlands and Switzerland; Pres. PIET TOLSMA (Netherlands); Sec. HARM-JAN KEIJER (Netherlands).

European Organisation for the Exploitation of Meteorological Satellites—EUMETSAT: 64295 Darmstadt, Am Kavalleriesand 31, Germany; tel. (6151) 807377; fax (6151) 807304; e-mail ops@eumetsat.de; internet www.eumetsat.de; f. 1986; maintains and exploits European systems of meteorological satellites, including the Meteosat programme for gathering weather data; mems: 18 European countries and four co-operating states; Chair.

Dr HENRI MALCORPS (Belgium); Dir Dr TILLMANN MOHR; Publs *Annual Report, IMAGE Newsletter*, brochures, conference and workshop proceedings.

European Organization for Civil Aviation Equipment— EURO-CAE: 17 rue Hamelin, 75783 Paris Cédex 16, France; tel. 1-45-05-71-88; fax 1-45-05-72-30; e-mail eurocae@eurocae.com; internet www.eurocae.org; f. 1963; studies and advises on problems related to the equipment used in aeronautics; assists international bodies in the establishment of international standards; mems: 92 manufacturers, and regulatory and research bodies; Pres. TERRENCE KNIBB; Sec.-Gen. FRANCIS GRIMAL; Publs Reports, documents and specifications on civil aviation equipment.

Eurospace: 15-17 ave de Ségur, 75005 Paris, France; tel. 1-44-42-00-70; fax 1-44-42-00-79; e-mail letterbox@eurospace.org; internet www.eurospace.org; f. 1961 as an asscn of European aerospace industrial companies responsible for promotion of European Space activity; carries out studies on the legal, economic, technical and financial aspects of space activity; acts as an industrial adviser to the European Space Agency, in particular with regard to future space programmes and industrial policy matters; mems: 60 in 13 European countries; Pres. PASCALE SOURISSE (France); Sec.-Gen. ALAIN GAUBERT.

International Association for Bridge and Structural Engineering—IABSE: ETH—Hönggerberg, 8093 Zürich, Switzerland; tel. (1) 6332647; fax (1) 6331241; e-mail secretariat@iabse.ethz.ch; internet www.iabse.ethz.ch; f. 1929 to exchange knowledge and advance the practice of structural engineering world-wide; mems: 4,400 government departments, local authorities, universities, institutes, firms and individuals in over 100 countries; Pres. MANABU ITO (Japan); Exec. Dir A. GOLAY; Publs *Structural Engineering International* (quarterly), *Congress Report, IABSE Report, Structural Engineering Documents*.

International Association for Cybernetics (Association internationale de cybernétique): Palais des Expositions, ave Sergent Vrithoff 2, 5000 Namur, Belgium; tel. (81) 71-71-71; fax (81) 71-71-00; e-mail cyb@info.fundp.ac.be; internet pespmc1.vub.ac.be/iac .html; f. 1957 to ensure liaison between research workers engaged in various sectors of cybernetics; promotes the development of the science and its applications; disseminates information; mems: firms and individuals in 42 countries; Chair. J. RAMAEKERS; Gen. Sec. CARINE AIGRET; publ. *Cybernetica* (quarterly).

International Association of Technological University Libraries—IATUL: c/o Dr Judith Palmer, Radcliffe Science Library, Oxford University, Parks Rd, Oxford OX1 3QP, United Kingdom; tel. (1865) 272820; fax (1865) 272832; e-mail judith.palmer@bodley.ox .ac.uk; internet www.iatul.org; f. 1955 to promote co-operation between member libraries and stimulate research on library problems; mems: 202 university libraries in 41 countries; Pres. Dr MICHAEL BREAKS (UK); Sec. Dr JUDITH PALMER (UK); Publs *IATUL Proceedings, IATUL Newsletter* (electronic version only).

International Cargo Handling Co-ordination Association— ICHCA: Suite 2, 85 Western Rd, Romford, Essex RM1 3LS, United Kingdom; tel. (1708) 734787; fax (1708) 734877; e-mail info@ichca .org.uk; internet www.ichca.org.uk; f. 1952 to foster economy and efficiency in the movement of goods from origin to destination; mems: 2,000 in 90 countries; Pres. KEN HOGGAT; Chief Exec. GERRY ASKHAM; Publs *Cargo Tomorrow: Cargo Handling News* (bimonthly), *World of Cargo Handling* (annually), *Who's Who in Cargo Handling* (annually), technical publs and reviews.

International Colour Association: c/o Frank Rochow, LMT Lichtmesstechnik GmbH Berlin, Helmholtzstr. 9, 10587 Berlin, Germany; tel. (30) 3934028; fax (30) 3918001; f. 1967 to encourage research in colour in all its aspects, disseminate the knowledge gained from this research and promote its application to the solution of problems in the fields of science, art and industry; holds international congresses and symposia; mems: organizations in 28 countries; Pres. PAULA ALESSI (USA); Sec. and Treas. FRANK ROCHOW (Germany).

International Commission on Illumination—CIE: Kegelgasse 27, 1030 Vienna, Austria; tel. (1) 714-31-87-0; fax (1) 713-08-38-18; e-mail ciecb@ping.at; internet www.cie.co.at; f. 1900 as International Commission on Photometry, present name adopted 1913; aims to provide an international forum for all matters relating to the science and art of light and lighting; serves as a forum for the exchange of information; develops and publishes international standards and provides guidance in their application; mems: 40 national committees and 12 individuals; Gen. Sec. C. HERMANN; Publs standards, technical reports.

International Commission on Large Dams: 151 blvd Haussmann, 75008 Paris, France; tel. 1-40-42-68-24; fax 1-40-42-60-71; e-mail secretaire.general@icold-cigb.org; internet www.icold-cigb .org./; f. 1928; holds triennial congresses (2000 congress: Beijing, People's Republic of China); mems: in 80 countries; Pres. C. V. J.

VARMA (India); Sec.-Gen. JACQUES LECORNU; Publs *Technical Bulletin* (3 or 4 a year), *World Register of Dams, World Register of Mine and Industrial Wastes, Technical Dictionary on Dams,* studies.

International Committee on Aeronautical Fatigue—ICAF: c/o Prof. O. Buxbaum, Fraunhofer-Institut für Betriebsfestigkeit LBF, 64289 Darmstadt, Bartningstrasse 47, Germany; tel. (6151) 7051; fax (6151) 705214; internet www.icaf2003.com; f. 1951 for collaboration between aeronautical bodies and laboratories on questions of fatigue of aeronautical structures; organizes periodical conferences; mems: national centres in 13 countries; Sec. Prof. O. BUXBAUM (Germany).

International Council on Large High-Voltage Electric Systems (Conseil international des grands réseaux électriques—CIGRE): 21 rue d'Artois, 75008 Paris, France; tel. 1-53-89-12-90; fax 1-53-89-12-99; e-mail secretary-general@cigre.org; internet www.cigre.org; f. 1921 to facilitate and promote the exchange of technical knowledge and information in the general field of electrical generation and transmission at high voltages; holds general sessions (every 2 years) and symposia; mems: 5,000 in 80 countries; Pres. D. CROFT (Australia); Sec.-Gen. J. KOWAL (France); publ. *Electra* (every 2 months).

International Council for Research and Innovation in Building and Construction: Postbox 1837, 3000 BV Rotterdam, Netherlands; tel. (10) 4110240; fax (10) 4334372; e-mail secretariat@cibworld.nl; internet www.cibworld.nl; f. 1953 to encourage and facilitate co-operation in building research, studies and documentation in all aspects; mems: governmental and industrial organizations and qualified individuals in 70 countries; Pres. Dr S. A. BARAKAT (Canada); Sec.-Gen. W. J. P. BAKENS; Publs *Information Bulletin* (bi-monthly), conference proceedings and technical, best practice and other reports.

International Electrotechnical Commission—IEC: 3 rue de Varembé, POB 131, 1211 Geneva 20, Switzerland; tel. (22) 9190211; fax (22) 9190300; e-mail info@iec.ch; internet www.iec.ch; f. 1906 as the authority for world standards for electrical and electronic engineering: its standards are used as the basis for regional and national standards, and are used in the preparation of specifications for international trade; mems: national committees representing all branches of electrical and electronic activities in some 60 countries; Gen.-Sec. A. AMIT; Publs *International Standards and Reports, IEC Bulletin, Annual Report, Catalogue of Publications.*

International Special Committee on Radio Interference: British Electrotechnical Committee, British Standards Institution, 389 Chiswick High Rd, London, W4 4AL, United Kingdom; tel. (20) 8996-9000; fax (20) 8996-7400; e-mail chris_beckley@electricity.org.uk; f. 1934; special committee of the IEC, promoting international agreement on the protection of radio reception from interference by equipment other than authorized transmitters; recommends limits of such interference and specifies equipment and methods of measurement; mems: national committees of IEC and seven other international organizations; Sec. CHRISTOPHER BECKLEY.

International Federation for Information and Documentation: POB 90402, 2509 LK The Hague, Netherlands; tel. (70) 3140671; fax (70) 3140667; e-mail fid@fid.nl; internet www.fid.nl; f. 1895; aims to promote, and improve, through international co-operation, research in and development of information science, information management and documentation; maintains regional commissions for Latin America, North America and the Caribbean, Asia and Oceania, Western, Eastern and Southern Africa, North Africa and the Near East, and for Europe; mems: 62 national, five international, 330 institutional and individual mems; Pres. K. BRUNNSTEIN; Exec. Dir J. STEPHEN PARKER; Publs *FID Review* (every 2 months), *FID Directory* (every 2 years).

International Federation for Information Processing—IFIP: Hofstrasse 3, 2361 Laxenburg, Austria; tel. (2236) 73616; fax (2236) 736169; e-mail ifip@ifip.or.at; internet www.ifip.or.at; f. 1960 to promote information science and technology; encourages research, development and application of information processing in science and human activities; furthers the dissemination and exchange of information on information processing; mems: 45 organizations, 3 corresponding mems, 1 assoc. mem. and 11 affiliate mems; Pres. P. BOLLERSLEV (Denmark); Exec. Dir PLAMEN NEDKOV.

International Federation of Airworthiness—IFA: 14 Railway Approach, East Grinstead, West Sussex RH19 1BP, United Kingdom; tel. (1342) 301788; fax (1342) 317808; e-mail sec@ifairworthy.org; internet www.ifairworthy.org; f. 1964 to provide a forum for the exchange of international experience in maintenance, design and operations; holds annual conference; awards international aviation scholarship annually; mems: 120, comprising 50 airlines, 17 airworthiness authorities, 23 aerospace manufacturing companies, 17 service and repair organizations, three consultancies, six professional societies, two aviation insurance companies, one aircraft leasing company, and the Flight Safety Foundation (USA);

Pres. JOHN K LAUBER (USA); Exec. Dir J. W. SAULL (UK); publ. *IFA News* (quarterly).

International Federation of Automotive Engineering Societies—FISITA: 1 Birdcage Walk, London SW1H 9JJ, United Kingdom; tel. (20) 7973-1275; fax (20) 7973-1285; e-mail info@fisita.com; internet www.fisita.com; f. 1947 to promote the technical and sustainable development of all forms of automotive transportation; maintains electronic job centre for automotive engineers (www.fisitajobs.com); holds congresses every two years; mems: national orgs in 33 countries; Chief Exec. IAN DICKIE; publ. *Global Automotive Network.*

International Federation of Consulting Engineers (Fédération internationale des ingénieurs-conseils—FIDIC): POB 311, 1215 Geneva 15, Switzerland; tel. (22) 799-49-00; fax (22) 799-49-01; e-mail fidic@fidic.org; internet www.fidic.org; f. 1913 to encourage international co-operation and the establishment of standards for consulting engineers; mems: national asscns in 66 countries, comprising some 500,000 design professionals; Pres. EIGIL STEEN PEDERSEN; Publs *FIDIC Report, Annual Survey, Annual Review.*

International Federation of Hospital Engineering: 2 Abingdon House, Cumberland Business Centre, Northumberland Rd, Portsmouth, PO5 1DS, United Kingdom; tel. (2392) 823186; fax (2392) 815927l; e-mail ifhc@iheem.org.uk; f. 1970 to promote internationally standards of hospital engineering and to provide for the exchange of knowledge and experience in the areas of hospital and healthcare facility design, construction, engineering, commissioning, maintenance and estate management; mems: 50, in more than 30 countries; Pres. GUNNAR BÆKKEN (Norway); Gen. Sec. BERNARD SHAPIRO (South Africa); publ. *Hospital Engineering* (quarterly).

International Institute of Seismology and Earthquake Engineering—IISEE: Building Research Institute, 1 Tatehara, Tsukuba City, Ibaraki Pref., Japan; tel. (298) 79-0677; fax (298) 64-6777; e-mail iisee@kenken.go.jp; internet iisee.kenken.go.jp; f. 1962 to work on seismology and earthquake engineering for the purpose of reducing earthquake damage in the world; trains seismologists and earthquake engineers from the earthquake-prone countries; undertakes surveys, research, guidance and analysis of information on earthquakes and related matters; mems: 75 countries; Dir T. FUKUTA; Publs *Year Book, Bulletin* (annually), *Individual Studies* (annually).

International Institution for Production Engineering Research: 9 rue Mayran, 75009 Paris, France; tel. 1-45-26-21-80; fax 1-45-26-92-15; e-mail cirp@cirp.net; internet www.cirp.net; f. 1951 to promote by scientific research the study of the mechanical processing of all solid materials; carries out checks on efficiency and quality of work; mems: 510 in 40 countries; Pres. F. JOVANE (Italy); Sec.-Gen. D. DUMUR (France); publ. *Annals* (2 a year).

International Iron and Steel Institute—IISI: 120 rue Col Bourg, 1140 Brussels, Belgium; tel. (2) 702-89-00; fax (2) 702-88-99; e-mail steel@iisi.be; internet www.worldsteel.org; f. 1967 to promote the welfare and interests of the world's steel industries; undertakes research into all aspects of steel industries; serves as a forum for exchange of knowledge and discussion of problems relating to steel industries; collects, disseminates and maintains statistics and information; serves as a liaison body between international and national steel organizations; mems: in over 50 countries; Sec.-Gen. IAN CHRISTMAS; Publs *Worldsteel Newsletter,* policy statements and reports.

International Organization for Standardization: POB 56, 1 rue de Varembé, 1211 Geneva 20, Switzerland; tel. (22) 7490111; fax (22) 7333430; e-mail central@iso.org; internet www.iso.org; f. 1947 to reach international agreement on industrial and commercial standards; mems: national standards bodies of c. 145 countries; Pres. OLIVER R. SMOOT (USA); Sec.-Gen. ALAN BRYDEN; Publs *ISO International Standards, ISO Memento* (annually), *ISO Management Systems* (6 a year), *ISO Bulletin* (monthly), *ISO Catalogue* (annually, updated quarterly), *ISO Annual Report.*

International Research Group on Wood Preservation: Drottning Kristinas väg 33a, Stockholm, Sweden; tel. (8) 10-14-53; fax (8) 10-80-81; e-mail irg@sp.se; internet www.irg-wp.com; f. 1965 as Wood Preservation Group by OECD; independent since 1969; consists of five sections; holds plenary annual meeting; mems: 310 in 47 countries; Pres. Dr ALEX VALCKE (Belgium); Sec.-Gen. JÖRAN JERMER (Sweden); Publs technical documents.

International Rubber Research and Development Board—IRRDB: POB 10150, 50908 Kuala Lumpur, Malaysia; fax (3) 21620414; e-mail draziz@pop.jaring.my; internet www.irrdb.org; f. 1937; mems: 15 research institutes; Sec. Datuk Dr A. AZIZ.

International Society for Photogrammetry and Remote Sensing—ISPRS: c/o Ian Dowman, Dept of Geomatic Engineering, University College London, Gower St, London, WC1E 6BT, United Kingdom; fax (20) 7679-7226; e-mail idowman@ge.ucl.ac.uk; internet www.isprs.org/; f. 1910; holds congress every four years, and technical symposia; mems: 103 countries; Pres. JOHN C. TRINDER (Australia); Sec.-Gen. IAN DOWMAN (UK); Publs *Journal of Photogrammetry and Remote Sensing* (6 a year), *ISPRS Highlights* (quarterly), *International Archives of Photogrammetry and Remote Sensing* (every 2 years).

International Society for Soil Mechanics and Geotechnical Engineering: City University, Northampton Sq., London, EC1V 0HB, United Kingdom; tel. (20) 7040-8154; fax (20) 7040-8832; e-mail secretariat@issmge.org; internet www.issmge.org; f. 1936 to promote international co-operation among scientists and engineers in the field of geotechnics and its engineering applications; maintains 30 technical committees; holds quadrennial international conference, regional conferences and specialist conferences; mems: 17,000 individuals, 74 national societies, 23 corporate members; Pres. Prof. KENJI ISHIHARA; Sec.-Gen. Prof. W. F. VAN IMPE; Publs *ISSMGE News* (quarterly), *Lexicon of Soil Mechanics Terms* (in eight languages).

International Solar Energy Society: Wiesentalstrasse 50, 79115 Freiburg, Germany; tel. (761) 459060; fax (761) 4590699; e-mail hq@ises.org; internet www.ises.org; f. 1954; aims to bring recent developments in renewable energy, both in research and applications, to the attention of decision-makers and the general public, in order to increase the understanding and use of this non-polluting resource; holds international conferences; mems: c 30,000 in some 100 countries; Pres. Prof. ANNE GRETE HESTNES (Norway); Exec. Dir RIAN VAN STADEN (South Africa); Publs *Solar Energy Journal* (monthly), *Refocus Magazine* (6 a year), *Conference Proceedings* (annually).

International Solid Waste Association—ISWA: Overgaden Oven Vandet 48E, 1415 Copenhagen K, Denmark; tel. 32-96-15-88; fax 32-96-15-84; e-mail iswa@iswa.dk; internet www.iswa.org; f. 1970 to promote the exchange of information and experience in solid waste management, in order to protect human health and the environment; promotes research and development activities; provides advice; organizes conferences; Pres. CHRISTOPH SCHARFF (Austria); Man. Dir SUZANNE ARUP VELTZÉ (Denmark); Publs *Waste Management World*, *Waste Management and Research* (6 a year).

International Union for Vacuum Science, Technique and Applications—IUVSTA: 7 Mohawk Cres., Nepean, ON K2H 7G7, Canada; tel. (613) 829-5790; fax (613) 829-3061; e-mail bill@thinkfilms.ca; internet www.iuvsta.org; f. 1958; collaborates with the International Standards Organization in defining and adopting technical standards; holds triennial International Vacuum Congress, European Vacuum Conference, triennial International Conference on Thin Films, and International Conference on Solid Surfaces; administers the Welch Foundation scholarship for postgraduate research in vacuum science and technology; mems: organizations in 30 countries; Pres. Dr MARIE-GENEVIÈVE BARTHÉS-LABROUSSE (UK); Sec.-Gen. Dr W. D. WESTWOOD (Canada); publ. *News Bulletin* (twice a year).

International Water Resources Association—IWRA: University of New Mexico, 1915 Roma NE, Albuquerque, NM 87131-1436, USA; tel. (505) 277-9400; fax (505) 277-9405; e-mail iwra@unm.edu; internet www.iwra.siu.edu; f. 1972 to promote collaboration in and support for international water resources programmes; holds conferences; conducts training in water resources management; Pres. GLENN E. STOUT (USA); Sec.-Gen. VICTOR DE KOSINSKY (Belgium); publ. *Water International* (quarterly).

Latin-American Energy Organization (Organización Latinoamericana de Energía—OLADE): Avda Mariscal Antonio José de Sucre, No N58–63 y Fernándes Salvador, Edif. OLADE, Sector San Carlos, POB 17-11-6413 CCI, Quito, Ecuador; tel. (2) 598-122; fax (2) 531-691; e-mail oladel@olade.org.ec; internet www.olade.org.ec; f. 1973 to act as an instrument of co-operation in using and conserving the energy resources of the region; mems: 26 Latin-American and Caribbean countries; Exec. Sec. Dr JULIO HERRERA; publ. *Energy Magazine*.

Latin-American Iron and Steel Institute: Benjamín 2944, 5°, Las Condes, Santiago, Chile; tel. (2) 233-0545; fax (2) 233-0768; e-mail ilafa@entelchile.net; internet www.ilafa.org; f. 1959 to help achieve the harmonious development of iron and steel production, manufacture and marketing in Latin America; conducts economic surveys on the steel sector; organizes technical conventions and meetings; disseminates industrial processes suited to regional conditions; prepares and maintains statistics on production, end uses, prices, etc., of raw materials and steel products within this area; mems: 18 hon. mems; 63 mems; 68 assoc. mems; Chair. JULIO CÉSAR VILLARREAL; Sec.-Gen. ENRIQUE ALVAREZ; Publs *Acero Latinoamericano* (every 2 months), *Statistical Year Book*, *Directory of Latin American Iron and Steel Companies* (every 2 years).

Regional Centre for Mapping of Resources for Development: POB 18118, Nairobi, Kenya; tel. (20) 803320; fax (20) 802767; e-mail rcmrd@meteo.go.ke; internet www.rcmrd.org; f. 1975; present name adopted 1997; provides services for the professional techniques of map-making and the application of satellite and remote sensing data

in resource analysis and development planning; undertakes research and provides advisory services to African governments; mems: 14 signatory and 10 non-signatory governments; Dir-Gen. Prof. SIMON NDYETABULA.

Regional Centre for Training in Aerospace Surveys— RECTAS: PMB 5545, Ile-Ife, Nigeria; tel. (36) 230050; fax (36) 230481; e-mail rectas@oauife.edu.ng; f. 1972; provides practical and theoretical training in the field of geoinformatics; conducts seminars, workshops and short courses; undertakes studies and research; provides advisory and consultancy services in Africa; administered by the ECA; mems: eight governments; Dir O. KUFONIYI.

Regional Council of Co-ordination of Central and East European Engineering Organizations: c/o MTESZ, 1055 Budapest, Kossuth Lajos tér 6–8, Hungary; tel. (361) 353-4795; fax (361) 353-0317; e-mail mtesz@mtesz.hu; f. 1992; Hon. Pres. JÁNOS TÓTH.

World Association of Industrial and Technological Research Organizations—WAITRO: c/o SIRIM Berhad, 1 Persiaran Dato' Menteri, Section 2, POB 7035, 40911 Shah Alam, Malaysia; tel. 5544-6635; fax 5544-6735; e-mail info@waitro.sirim.my; internet www.waitro.org; f. 1970 by the UN Industrial Development Organization to organize co-operation in industrial and technological research; provides financial assistance for training and joint activities; arranges international seminars; facilitates the exchange of information; mems: 200 research institutes in 80 countries; Pres. BJORN LUNDBERG (Sweden); Contact MOSES MENGU; Publs *WAITRO News* (quarterly), *WAITRO News* (quarterly).

World Association of Nuclear Operators—WANO-CC: Kings Bldgs, 16 Smith Sq., London, SW1P 3JG, United Kingdom; tel. (20) 7828-2111; fax (20) 7828-6691; internet www.wano.org.uk; f. 1989 by operators of nuclear power plants; aims to improve the safety and operability of nuclear power plants through the exchange of operating experience; operates four regional centres (in France, Japan, Russia and the USA) and a co-ordinating centre in the UK; mems: in 34 countries; Dir (Co-ordinating Centre) V. J. MADDEN.

World Bureau of Metal Statistics: 27A High St, Ware, Herts, SG12 9BA, United Kingdom; tel. (1920) 461274; fax (1920) 464258; e-mail wbms@world-bureau.co.uk; internet www.world-bureau.com; f. 1949; produces statistics of production, consumption, stocks, prices and international trade in copper, lead, zinc, tin, nickel, aluminium and several other minor metals; Gen. Man. S. M. EALES; Publs *World Metal Statistics* (monthly), *World Tin Statistics* (monthly), *World Nickel Statistics* (monthly), *World Metal Statistics Yearbook*, *World Metal Statistics Quarterly Summary*, *World Stainless Steel Statistics* (annually), *World Wrought Copper Statistics* (annually).

World Federation of Engineering Organizations—WFEO: Maison de l'UNESCO, 1 rue Miollis, 75015 Paris, France; tel. 1-45-68-48-47; fax 1-43-06-29-27; e-mail peb.fmoi@unesco.org; internet www.unesco.org/wfeo; f. 1968 to advance engineering as a profession; fosters co-operation between engineering organizations throughout the world; undertakes special projects in co-operation with other international bodies; mems: 80 national mems, nine international mems; Pres. JOSÉ MEDEM SANJUAN (Spain); Exec. Dir PIERRE EDOUARD DE BOIGNE (France); publ. *WFEO Newsletter* (2 a year).

World Petroleum Congresses: 4th Floor, Suite 1, 1 Duchess St, London, W1N 3DE, United Kingdom; tel. (20) 7637-4958; e-mail pierce@world-petroleum.org; internet www.world-petroleum.org; f. 1933 to serve as a forum for petroleum science, technology, economics and management; undertakes related information and liaison activities; 2002 Congress: Rio de Janeiro, Brazil; mems: Permanent Council includes 59 mem. countries; Pres. Ir D. VAN DER MEER (Netherlands); Dir-Gen. Dr PIERCE W. F. RIEMER (UK).

Tourism

Alliance Internationale de Tourisme: 2 Chemin de Blandonnet, CP 111, 1215 Geneva 15, Switzerland; tel. (22) 5444501; fax (22) 5444550; e-mail webmaster@aitfia.ch; internet www.aitgva.ch; f. 1898, present title adopted 1919; represents motoring organizations and touring clubs around the world; aims to study all questions relating to international touring and to suggest reforms; mems: 140 asscns with 100m. members in 102 countries; Pres. B. DARBELNET (USA); Dir-Gen. P. DOGGWILER (Switzerland); publ. *AIT News*.

Asia Travel Marketing Association—ATMA: c/o Japan National Tourist Organization, 2-10-1 Yurakucho, Chiyoda-ku, Tokyo, Japan; tel. (3) 3216-1902; fax (3) 3216-1846; e-mail atma@jnto.go.jp; internet www.asiatravel.org; f. 1966 as East Asia Travel Association, present name adopted 1999; aims to promote tourism in the East Asian region, encourage and facilitate the flow of tourists to that region from other parts of the world, and to develop regional tourist industries by close collaboration among members; mems: six national tourist organizations and one travel asscn; Pres. ICHIRO TANAKA; Sec.-Gen. JOÃO MANUEL COSTA ANTUNES.

Caribbean Tourism Organization: Sir Frank Walcott Bldg, 2nd Floor, Culloden Farm Complex, St Michael, Barbados; tel. 427-5242; fax 429-3065; e-mail ctobar@caribsurf.com; internet www .onecaribbean.org; f. 1989, by merger of the Caribbean Tourism Association (f. 1951) and the Caribbean Tourism Research and Development Centre (f. 1974); aims to encourage tourism in the Caribbean region; organizes annual Caribbean Tourism Conference, Sustainable Tourism Development Conference and Tourism Investment Conference; conducts training and other workshops on request; maintains offices in New York, Canada and London; mems: 33 Caribbean governments, 400 allied mems; Sec.-Gen. JEAN HOLDER; publs *Caribbean Tourism Statistical News* (quarterly), *Caribbean Tourism Statistical Report* (annually).

European Travel Commission: 61 rue du Marché aux Herbes, 1000 Brussels, Belgium; tel. (2) 504-03-03; fax (2) 514-18-43; e-mail etc@planetinternet.be; internet www.etc-europe-travel.org; f. 1948 to promote tourism in and to Europe, to foster co-operation and the exchange of information, and to organize research; mems: national tourist organizations in 31 European countries; Exec. Dir WALTER LEU (Switzerland).

International Association of Scientific Experts in Tourism: Varnbüelstrasse 19, 9000 St Gallen, Switzerland; tel. (71) 2242530; fax (71) 2242536; e-mail aiest@unisg.ch; internet www.aiest.org; f. 1949 to encourage scientific activity in tourism, to support tourist institutions of a scientific nature and to organize conventions; mems: 400 from 40 countries; Pres. Prof. Dr PETER KELLER (Switzerland); Gen. Sec. Prof. Dr THOMAS BIEGER (Switzerland); publ. *The Tourism Review* (quarterly).

International Congress and Convention Association—ICCA: Entrada 121, 1096 EB Amsterdam, Netherlands; tel. (20) 398-19-19; fax (20) 699-07-81; e-mail icca@icca.nl; internet www.iccaworld.com; f. 1963 to establish world-wide co-operation between all involved in organizing congresses, conventions and exhibitions; mems: over 600 from 83 countries; Pres. CHRISTIAN MUTSCHLECHNER; CEO MARTIN SIRK; publ. *International Meetings News* (6 a year).

International Hotel and Restaurant Association: 251 rue du Faubourg St Martin, 75010 Paris, France; tel. 1-44-89-94-00; fax 1-40-36-73-30; e-mail members@ih-ra.com; internet www.ihra.com; f. 1946 to act as the authority on matters affecting the international hotel industry, to promote its interests and to contribute to its growth, profitability and quality; membership extended to restaurants in 1996; mems: 120 national hospitality asscns, 100 national and international hotel and restaurant chains; Dir and CEO ALAIN-PHILIPPE FEUTRÉ; publs *Hotels* (monthly), *Yearbook and Directory* (annually).

Latin-American Confederation of Tourist Organizations (Confederación de Organizaciones Turísticas de la América Latino—COTAL): Viamonte 640, 8°, 1053 Buenos Aires, Argentina; tel. (11) 4322-4003; fax (11) 4393-5696; e-mail cotal@cscom.com.ar; internet www.cotal.org.ar; f. 1957 to link Latin American national asscns of travel agents and their members with other tourist bodies around the world; mems: in 21 countries; Pres. ENZO U. FURNARI; publ. *Revista COTAL* (every 2 months).

Pacific Asia Travel Association—PATA: Unit B1, 28th floor, Siam Tower, 989 Rama 1 Rd, Pratumwan, Bangkok 10330, Thailand; tel. (2) 658-2000; fax (2) 658-2010; e-mail patabkk@pata.th .com; internet www.pata.org; f. 1951; aims to enhance the growth, value and quality of Pacific Asia travel and tourism for the benefit of PATA members; holds annual conference; divisional offices in Monaco, Sydney, USA; mems: more than 1,200 governments, carriers, tour operators, travel agents and hotels; publs *PATA Compass* (every 2 months), *Statistical Report* (quarterly), research reports, directories, newsletters.

South Pacific Tourism Organization: POB 13119, Suva, Fiji; tel. 3304177; fax 3301995; e-mail info@spto.org; internet www.tcsp.com; frmly the Tourism Council of the South Pacific; aims to foster regional co-operation in the development, marketing and promotion of tourism in the island nations of the South Pacific; receives EU funding and undertakes sustainable activities; mems: 13 countries in the South Pacific; Chief Exec. LISIATE AKOLO.

United Federation of Travel Agents' Associations—UFTAA: 1 ave des Castelans, Stade Louis II-Entrée H, 98000 Monaco; tel. 92-05-28-29; fax 92-05-29-87; e-mail uftaa@uftaa.org; internet www .uftaa.org; f. 1966 to unite travel agents' asscns; represents the interests of travel agents at the international level; helps in international legal differences; issues literature on travel; mems: regional and national asscns of travel agencies in 112 countries; Sec.-Gen. BIRGER BÄCKMAN; publs *UFTAA Newsletter*, *UFTAA Courier*, *Directory*.

World Association of Travel Agencies—WATA: 14 rue Ferrier, 1202 Geneva, Switzerland; tel. (22) 7314760; fax (22) 7328161;

e-mail wata@wata.net; internet www.wata.net; f. 1949 to foster the development of tourism, to help the rational organization of tourism in all countries, to collect and disseminate information and to participate in commercial and financial operations to foster the development of tourism; individual travel agencies may use the services of the world-wide network of 200 mems; Pres. ADEL ZAKI (Egypt); Sec.-Gen. MARCO AGUSTONI (Switzerland); publ. *WATA Gazette* (quarterly).

World Tourism Organization: Calle Capitán Haya 42, 28020 Madrid, Spain; tel. (91) 5678100; fax (91) 5713733; e-mail comm@ world-tourism.org; internet www.world-tourism.org; f. 1975 to promote travel and tourism; co-operates with member governments; secures financing for and carries out tourism development projects; provides training in tourism-related issues; works for sustainable and environmentally-friendly tourism development; encourages the liberalization of trade in tourism services; considers health and safety issues related to tourism; collects, analyses and disseminates data and operates a Documentation Centre; mems: governments of 138 countries and territories, also associate members, observers and over 300 affiliated mems; Sec.-Gen. FRANCESCO FRANGIALLI; publs *Yearbook of Tourism Statistics*, *Compendium of Tourism Statistics*, *Travel and Tourism Barometer*, *WTO News*, *Tourism Market Trends*, *Directory of Multilateral and Bilateral Sources of Financing for Tourism Development*, guide-lines and studies.

World Travel and Tourism Council—WTTC: 1–2 Queen Victoria Terrace, Sovereign Court, London, E1W 3HA, United Kingdom; tel. (870) 7279882; fax (870) 7289882; e-mail enquiries@wttc.org; internet www.wttc.org; f. 1989; promotes the development of the travel/tourism industry; analyses impact of tourism on employment levels and local economies and promotes greater expenditure on tourism infrastructure; administers a 'Green Globe' certification programme to enhance environmental management throughout the industry; mems: 57 global mems, five hon. mems; Pres. JEAN-CLAUDE BAUMGARTEN; Chair. Sir IAN PROSSER; publs *WTTC Backgrounder*, *Travel and Tourism Review*, *Viewpoint* (quarterly), regional and country reports.

Trade and Industry

African Regional Organization for Standardization: POB 57363, Nairobi, Kenya; tel. (20) 224561; fax (20) 218792; e-mail arso@bidii.com; internet www.arso-oran.org; f. 1977 to promote standardization, quality control, certification and metrology in the African region, to formulate regional standards, and to co-ordinate participation in international standardization activities; mems: 24 states; Sec.-Gen. Dr ADEBAYO O. OYEJOLA; publs *ARSO Bulletin* (2 a year), *ARSO Catalogue of Regional Standards* (annually), *ARSO Annual Report*.

Arab Iron and Steel Union—AISU: BP 4, Chéraga, Algiers, Algeria; tel. (21) 371580; fax (21) 371975; e-mail relex@solbarab .com; internet www.solbarab.com; f. 1972 to develop commercial and technical aspects of Arab steel production by helping member asscns commercialize their production in Arab markets, guaranteeing them high quality materials and intermediary products, informing them of recent developments in the industry and organizing training sessions; also arranges two annual symposia; mems: 80 companies in 15 Arab countries; Gen. Sec. MUHAMMAD LAID LACHGAR; publs *Arab Steel Review* (monthly), *Information Bulletin*, *News Steel World* (2 a month), *Directory* (annually).

Asian Productivity Organization: 2/F Hirakawa-cho Dai-ichi Seimei Bldg, 1-2-10, Hirakawa-cho, Chiyoda-ku, Tokyo 102–0093, Japan; tel. (3) 3408-7221; fax (3) 3408-7220; e-mail apo@gol.com; internet www.apo-tokyo.com; f. 1961 to strengthen the productivity movement in the Asian and Pacific regions and to disseminate technical knowledge on productivity; mems: 18 countries; Sec.-Gen. TAKASHI TAJIMA; publs *APO News* (monthly), *Annual Report*, *APO Productivity Journal* (2 a year), *Directory of National Productivity Organizations in APO member countries* (irregular), other related studies.

Association of African Trade Promotion Organizations— AATPO: Pavillion International, BP 23, Tangier, Morocco; tel. (9) 324465; fax (9) 943779; e-mail aoapc@mtds.com; f. 1975 under the auspices of the OAU (now AU) and the ECA to foster regular contact between African states in trade matters and to assist in the harmonization of their commercial policies, in order to promote intra-African trade; conducts research and training; organizes meetings and trade information missions; mems: 26 states; Sec.-Gen. Prof. ADEYINKA W. ORIMALADE; publs *FLASH: African Trade* (monthly), *Directory of African Consultants and Experts in Trade Promotion*, *Directory of Trade Information Contacts in Africa*, *Directory of Trade Information Sources in Africa*, *Directory of State Trading Organizations*, *Directory of Importers and Exporters of Food Products in Africa*, *Basic Information on Africa*, studies.

Association of European Chambers of Commerce and Industry—EUROCHAMBRES: 5 rue d'Archimède, 1000 Brussels, Belgium; tel. (2) 282-08-50; fax (2) 230-00-38; e-mail eurochambres@eurochambres.be; internet www.eurochambres.be; f. 1958 to promote the exchange of experience and information among its members and to bring their joint opinions to the attention of the institutions of the European Union; conducts studies and seminars; co-ordinates EU projects; mems: 15 full and 18 affiliated mems; Pres. JÖRG MITTELSTEN SCHEID (Germany); Sec.-Gen. ARNALDO ABRUZZINI (Italy).

Cairns Group: c/o Department of Foreign Affairs and Trade, GPO Box 12, Canberra, ACT 2601, Australia; tel. (2) 6263-2222; fax (2) 6261-3111; internet www.dfat.gov.au/trade/negotiations/cairns-group/index.html; f. 1986 by major agricultural exporting countries; aims to bring about reforms in international agricultural trade, including reductions in export subsidies, in barriers to access and in internal support measures; represents members' interests in WTO negotiations; mems: Argentina, Australia, Bolivia, Brazil, Canada, Chile, Colombia, Costa Rica, Fiji, Guatemala, Indonesia, Malaysia, New Zealand, Paraguay, Philippines, South Africa, Thailand, Uruguay; Chair. MARK VAILE (Australia).

Caribbean Association of Industry and Commerce—CAIC: POB 442, Trinidad Hilton and Conference Centre, Rooms 1238-1241, Lady Young Rd, St Ann's, Trinidad and Tobago; tel. (868) 623-4830; fax (868) 623-6116; e-mail sifill@wow.net; internet www.caic.wow.net; f. 1955; aims to encourage economic development through the private sector; undertakes research and training and gives assistance to small enterprises; encourages export promotion; mems: chambers of commerce and enterprises in 20 countries and territories; Exec. Dir SEAN IFILL; publ. *Caribbean Investor* (quarterly).

Committee for European Construction Equipment—CECE: c/o Diamont Bldg, blvd Reyers 80, 1030 Brussels, Belgium; tel. (2) 706-82-25; fax (2) 706-82-10; e-mail cece@skynet.be; internet www.cece-eu.org; f. 1959 to further contact between manufacturers, to improve market conditions and productivity and to conduct research into techniques; mems: representatives from 10 European countries; Sec.-Gen. RALF WEZEL.

Committee of Associations of European Foundries—CAEF: Sohnstrasse 70, D-40237 Düsseldorf, Germany; tel. (211) 687-1215; fax (211) 687-1205; e-mail info@caef-eurofoundry.org; internet www.caef-eurofoundry.org; f. 1953 to safeguard the common interests of European foundry industries and to collect and exchange information; mems: asscns in 17 countries; Sec.-Gen. Dr KLAUS URBAT; publ. *The European Foundry Industry* (annually).

Confederation of Asia-Pacific Chambers of Commerce and Industry—CACCI: 9th Floor, 3 Sungshou Rd, Taipei 110, Taiwan; tel. (2) 27255663; fax (2) 27255665; e-mail cacci@ttn.net; internet www.cacci.org.tw; f. 1966; holds biennial conferences to examine regional co-operation; liaises with governments to promote laws conducive to regional co-operation; serves as a centre for compiling and disseminating trade and business information; encourages contacts between businesses; conducts training and research; mems: national chambers of commerce and industry in 22 countries in the region, also affiliate and special mems; Dir-Gen. Dr WEBSTER KIANG; publs *CACCI Profile* (monthly), *CACCI Journal of Commerce and Industry* (2 a year).

Confederation of International Soft Drinks Associations—CISDA: 79 blvd St Michel, 1040 Brussels, Belgium; tel. (2) 743-40-50; fax (2) 732-51-02; e-mail mail@unesda-cisda.org; internet www.unesda-cisda.org; f. 1951 to promote co-operation among the national asscns of soft drinks manufacturers on all industrial and commercial matters, to stimulate the sales and consumption of soft drinks, to deal with matters of interest to all member asscns and to represent the common interests of member asscns; holds a congress every year; Gen. Sec. ALAIN BEAUMONT.

Consumers International: 24 Highbury Cres., London, N5 1RX, United Kingdom; tel. (20) 7226-6663; fax (20) 7354-0607; internet www.consumersinternational.org; f. 1960 as International Organization of Consumers' Unions—IOCU; links consumer groups worldwide through information networks and international seminars; supports new consumer groups and represents consumers' interests at the international level; maintains five regional offices; mems: 215 asscns in 93 countries; Dir-Gen. JULIAN EDWARDS; publs *Consumer Currents* (10 a year), *World Consumer* (quarterly), *Consumidores y Desarollo* (10 a year), *Consommation-Developpement* (quarterly).

Energy Charter Secretariat: blvd de la Woluwe 56, 1200 Brussels, Belgium; tel. (2) 775-98-00; fax (2) 775-98-01; e-mail info@encharter.org; internet www.encharter.org; f. 1995 under the provisions of the Energy Charter Treaty (1994); aims to promote trade and investment in the energy industries; mems: 51 signatory states; Sec.-Gen. RIA KEMPER (Germany); publs *Promoting Energy Efficiency*, *Trade in Energy*, *The Energy Charter Treaty - A Reader's Guide*, reports.

European Association of Advertising Agencies—EAAA: 152 blvd Brand Whitlock, 1200 Brussels, Belgium; tel. (2) 740-07-10; fax (2) 740-07-17; e-mail stig.carlson@eaaa.be; internet www.eaaa.be; f. 1960 to maintain and raise the standards of service to advertisers of all European advertising agencies to strive towards uniformity in fields where this would be of benefit; and to serve the interests of all agency members in Europe; mems: 18 national advertising agency asscns and 23 multinational agency groups; Pres. ALBERT WINNINGHOFF (Netherlands); Sec.-Gen. STIG CARLSON (Sweden); publ. *Next Steps* (monthly).

European Association of Electrical Contractors—AIE: 1 J. Chantraineplantsoen, 3070 Kortenberg, Belgium; tel. (2) 253-43222; fax (2) 253-6763; e-mail info@aie-elec.org; internet www.aie-elec.org; mems: national asscns in 18 countries and territories; Pres. AAGE KJAERGAARD; Gen. Sec. EVELYNE SCHELLEHAUS; publ. *AIE Brochure* (every 2 years).

European Association of Manufacturers of Radiators—EURORAD: Konradstr. 9, 8023 Zürich, Switzerland; tel. (1) 2719090; fax (1) 2719292; f. 1966 to represent the national asscns of manufacturers of radiators made of steel and cast iron, intended to be attached to central heating plants and which convey heat by natural convection and radiation without the need for casing; mems: in 15 countries; Pres. Dr H. GASSER (Belgium); Gen. Sec. K. EGLI (Switzerland).

European Association of National Productivity Centres—EANPC: 60 rue de la Concorde, 1050 Brussels, Belgium; tel. (2) 511-71-00; fax (2) 511-02-97; e-mail eanpc@skynet.be; internet www.eanpc.org; f. 1966 to enable members to pool knowledge about their policies and activities; mems: 19 European centres; Pres. PETER REHNSTRÖM; Sec.-Gen. A. C. HUBERT; publs *EPI* (quarterly), *Annual Report*.

European Brewery Convention: POB 510, 2380 BB Zoeterwoude, Netherlands; tel. (71) 545-60-47; fax (71) 541-00-13; e-mail secretariat@ebc-nl.com; internet www.ebc-nl.com; f. 1947, present name adopted 1948; aims to promote scientific co-ordination in malting and brewing; mems: national asscns in 22 European countries; Pres. E. PAJUNEN (Finland); Sec.-Gen. M. VAN WIJNGAARDEN (Netherlands); publs *Analytica*, *Thesaurus*, *Dictionary of Brewing*, monographs, conference proceedings, manuals of good practice.

European Chemical Industry Council: ave E. van Nieuwenhuyse 4, 1160 Brussels, Belgium; tel. (2) 676-72-11; fax (2) 676-73-00; e-mail mail@cefic.be; internet www.cefic.org; f. 1972; represents and defends the interests of the chemical industry in legal and trade policy, internal market, environmental and technical matters; liaises with intergovernmental organizations; provides secretariat for some 100 product sector groups; mems: 16 national federations; Dir-Gen. Dr HUGO LEVER; Sec.-Gen. JEAN-MARIE DEVOS.

European Committee for Standardization (Comité européen de normalisation—CEN): 36 rue de Stassart, 1050 Brussels, Belgium; tel. (2) 550-08-11; fax (2) 550-08-19; e-mail infodesk@cenorm.be; internet www.cenorm.be; f. 1961 to promote European standardization; works to eliminate obstacles caused by technical requirements, in order to facilitate the exchange of goods and services; mems: 22 national standards bodies, 7 associated and 11 affiliated bodies in central and eastern Europe and 4 partnership standardization bodies; Sec.-Gen. GEORG HONGLER; publs *Catalogue of European Standards*, *Work Programme* (both 2 a year), *CEN Networking* (newsletter, every 2 months), *Bulletin* (quarterly), *Directories and related standards* (in English, French and German), *Directions European Standardization in a Global Context*, *The Benefits of Standards*.

European Committee of Associations of Manufacturers of Agricultural Machinery: 19 rue Jacques Bingen, 75017 Paris, France; tel. 1-42-12-85-90; fax 1-40-54-95-60; e-mail cema@syma.org; f. 1959 to study economic and technical problems in field of agricultural machinery manufacture, to protect members' interests and to disseminate information; mems: 13 mem. countries; Pres. A. TASSINARI (Italy); Sec.-Gen. J. DEHOLLAIN (France).

European Committee of Textile Machinery Manufacturers—CEMATEX: POB 190, 2700-AD Zoetermeer, Netherlands; tel. (79) 531-100; fax (79) 531-365; f. 1952; promotes general interests of the industry; mems: organizations in eight European countries; Pres. Dr F. PAETZOLD (Germany); Gen. Sec. R. BICKER CAARTEN.

European Confederation of Iron and Steel Industries—EURO-FER: 211 rue du Noyer, 1000 Brussels, Belgium; tel. (2) 738-79-20; fax (2) 736-30-01; e-mail mail@eurofer.be; internet www.eurofer.org; f. 1976 as a confederation of national federations and companies in the European steel industry; aims to foster co-operation between the member federations and companies and to represent their common interests to the EU and other international organizations; mems: in 13 European countries, assoc. mems from central and eastern European countries; Dir-Gen. D. VON HÜLSEN.

European Confederation of Woodworking Industries: 5/4 Hof-Ter-Vleestdreef, 1070 Brussels, Belgium; tel. (2) 556-25-85; fax (2) 556-25-95; e-mail info@cei-bois.org; internet www.cei-bois.org; f. 1952 to liaise between national organizations, undertake research and defend the interests of the industry; mems: national federations in 19 European countries; Pres. Bo BORGSTRÖM (Finland); Sec.-Gen. Dr G. VAN STEERTEGEM; publ. *Brochure*.

European Council of Paint, Printing Ink and Artists' Colours Industry: ave E. van Nieuwenhuyse 4, 1160 Brussels, Belgium; tel. (2) 676-7480; fax (2) 676-7490; e-mail secretariat@cepe.org; internet www.cepe.org; f. 1951 to study questions relating to the paint and printing ink industries, to take or recommend measures for the development of these industries or to support their interests, and to exchange information; mems: national asscns in 17 European countries and 13 company members; Pres. N. PETERSEN; Gen. Sec. J. SCHODER; publs *Annual Review*, guidance documents.

European Federation of Associations of Insulation Enterprises: Kurfürstenstr. 129, 10785 Berlin, Germany; tel. (30) 212-86163; fax (30) 212-86160; e-mail bfa.wksb@bauindustrie.de; f. 1970; groups organizations in Europe representing insulation firms; aims to facilitate contacts between member asscns; studies problems of interest to the profession; works to safeguard the interests of the profession and represent it in international fora; mems: professional organizations in 16 European countries; Sec.-Gen. M. SCHMOLDT.

European Federation of Marketing Research Organisations —EFAMRO: Studio 38, Wimbledon Business Centre, Riverside Road, London, SW17 0BA, United Kingdom; tel. (20) 8879-0709; fax (20) 8947-2637; internet www.efamro.org; f. 1965 (frmly known as FEMRA) to facilitate contacts between researchers; maintains specialist divisions on European chemical marketing research, European technological forecasting, paper and related industries, industrial materials, automotives, textiles, methodology, and information technology; mems: 500; Pres. DAVID A. CLARK (Belgium).

European Federation of Management Consultants' Associations: 3–5 ave des Arts, 1210 Brussels, Belgium; tel. (2) 250-06-50; fax (2) 250-06-51; e-mail feaco@feaco.org; internet www.feaco.org; f. 1960 to bring management consultants together and promote a high standard of professional competence, by encouraging discussions of, and research into, problems of common professional interest; mems: 24 asscns; Pres. and Chair. GIL GIDRON; Exec. Man. ELSE GROEN; publs *Newsletter* (3 a year), *Annual Survey of the European Management Consultancy Market*.

European Federation of Materials Handling and Storage Equipment: Diamant Bldg, 80 blvd A. Reyers, 1030 Brussels, Belgium; tel. (2) 706-82-30; fax (2) 706-82-50; e-mail guy.vandoorslaer@orgalime.org; internet www.fem-eur.com; f. 1953 to facilitate contact between members of the profession, conduct research, standardize methods of calculation and construction and promote standardized safety regulations; mems: organizations in 12 European countries; Pres. STIG GUSTAVSON; Sec.-Gen. GUY VAN DOORSLAER.

European Federation of the Plywood Industry—FEIC: Allée Hof-ter-Vleest, bte 4, 1070 Brussels, Belgium; tel. (2) 556-25-84; fax (2) 556-25-95; e-mail info@europards.org; internet www.europlywood.org; f. 1957 to organize co-operation between members of the industry at the international level; mems: asscns in 15 European countries; Pres. N. RENI; Sec.-Gen. K. WŸNENDAELE.

European Federation of Tile and Brick Manufacturers: Obstgartenstrasse 28, 8035 Zürich, Switzerland; tel. (1) 3619650; fax (1) 3610205; e-mail office@tbe-euro.ch; internet www.tbe-euro.com; f. 1952 to co-ordinate research between members of the industry, improve technical knowledge and encourage professional training; mems: asscns in 23 European and east European countries; Chair. VITTORIO VITOLO; Dir Dr W. P. WELLER.

European Furniture Manufacturers Federation (Union européenne de l'ameublement—UEA): 35 chaussé de Haecht, 1210 Brussels; tel. (2) 218-18-89; fax (2) 219-27-01; e-mail secretariat@uea.be; internet www.ueanet.com; f. 1950 to determine and support the general interests of the European furniture industry and facilitate contacts between members of the industry; mems: organizations in 19 European countries; Pres. J. ENGELS; Sec.-Gen. B. DE TURCK; publs *UEA Newsletter* (bi-monthly), *Focus on Issues*, *Strategy Survey*.

European General Galvanizers Association—EGGA: Maybrook House, Godstone Rd, Caterham, Surrey, CR3 6RE, United Kingdom; tel. (1883) 331277; fax (1883) 331287; e-mail mail@egga.com; internet www.egga.com; f. 1955 to promote co-operation between members of the industry, especially in improving processes and finding new uses for galvanized products; mems: asscns in 17 European countries; Pres. FRAN THIEL (Netherlands).

European Glass Container Manufacturers' Committee: Northumberland Rd, Sheffield, S10 2UA, United Kingdom; tel. (114) 268-6201; fax (114) 268-1073; e-mail l.roe@britglass.co.uk; internet www.britglass.co.uk; f. 1951 to facilitate contacts between members of the industry and inform them of relevant legislation; mems: representatives from 15 European countries; Sec. Dr W. G. A. COOK.

European Organization for Quality—EOQ: 3 rue de Luxembourg, 1000 Brussels, Belgium; tel. (2) 501-07-35; fax (31) 501-07-36; e-mail bjouslin@compuserve.com; internet www.eoq.org; f. 1956 to encourage the use and application of quality management, with the aim of improving quality, lowering costs and increasing productivity; organizes the exchange of information and documentation; mems: organizations in 31 European countries; Sec.-Gen. BERTRAND JOUSLIN DE NORAY; publs *European Quality* (6 a year), *Annual Report*.

European Packaging Federation: c/o Institut Français de l'Emballage et du Conditionnement IFEC, 33 rue Louis Blanc, 93582 St-Ouen Cédex, France; tel. 1-40-11-22-12; fax 1-40-11-01-06; e-mail info@ifecpromotion.tm.fr; internet www.ifecpromotion.tm.fr/epf.htm; f. 1953 to encourage the exchange of information between national packaging institutes and to promote technical and economic progress; mems: organizations in 12 European countries; Pres. J. P. POTHET (France); Sec.-Gen. A. FREIDINGER-LEGAY (France).

European Panel Federation: Hof-ter-Vleestdreef 5, 1070 Brussels, Belgium; tel. (2) 556-25-89; fax (2) 556-25-94; e-mail info@europanels.org; internet www.europanels.org; f. 1958 as European Federation of Associations of Particle Board Manufacturers; present name adopted 1999; works to develop and encourage international co-operation in the particle board and MDF industry; Pres. F. DE COCK; Sec.-Gen. G. VAN STEERTEGEM (Belgium); publ. *Annual Report*.

European Patent Office—EPO: 80331 Munich, Erhardtstr. 27, Germany; tel. (89) 2399-0; fax (89) 23994560; internet www.european-patent-office.org; f. 1977 to grant European patents according to the Munich convention of 1973; conducts searches and examination of patent applications; mems: 25 European countries; Pres. INGO KOBER (Germany); Chair. Admin. Council ROLAND GROSSENBACHER; publs *Annual Report*, *Official Journal* (monthly), *European Patent Bulletin*, *European Patent Applications*, *Granted Patents*.

European Society for Opinion and Marketing Research—ESOMAR: Vondelstraat 172, 1054 GV Amsterdam, Netherlands; tel. (20) 664-21-41; fax (20) 664-29-22; e-mail email@esomar.nl; internet www.esomar.nl; f. 1948 to further professional interests and encourage high technical standards; mems: over 4,000 in 100 countries; Pres. JOHN KELLY (UK); Dir-Gen. JUERGEN SCHWOERER; publs *Research World* (monthly), *ESOMAR Directory* (annually).

European Union of Coachbuilders: 46 Woluwedal, bte 14, 1200 Brussels, Belgium; tel. (2) 778-62-00; fax (2) 778-62-22; e-mail mail@federauto.be; f. 1948 to promote research on questions affecting the industry, exchange information, and establish a common policy for the industry; mems: national federations in eight European countries; Pres. J. BLYWEERT (Belgium); Sec.-Gen. HILDE VANDER STICHELE (Belgium).

European Union of the Natural Gas Industry—EUROGAS: 4 ave Palmerston, 1000 Brussels, Belgium; tel. (2) 237-11-11; fax (2) 230-62-91; e-mail eurogas@eurogas.org; internet www.eurogas.org/; mems: organizations in 17 European countries; Pres. P. GADONNEIX (France); Gen. Sec. PETER CLAUS (Belgium).

Federación de Cámaras de Comercio del Istmo Centroamericano (Federation of Central American Chambers of Commerce): 10a Calle 3-80, Zona 1, 01001 Guatemala City, Guatemala; internet www.fecamco.com; f. 1961; plans and co-ordinates industrial and commercial exchanges and exhibitions; Pres. EMILIO BRUCE JIMÉNEZ (Costa Rica); Sec. JORGE E. BRIZ ABULARACH (Guatemala).

General Union of Chambers of Commerce, Industry and Agriculture for Arab Countries—GUCCIAAC: POB 11-2837, Beirut, Lebanon; tel. (1) 814269; fax (1) 862841; e-mail gucciaac@destination.com.lb; internet www.gucciaac.org.lb; f. 1951 to enhance Arab economic development, integration and security through the co-ordination of industrial, agricultural and trade policies and legislation; mems: chambers of commerce, industry and agriculture in 22 Arab countries; Sec. Gen. Dr ELIAS GHANTOUS; publs *Arab Economic Report*, *Al-Omran Al-Arabi* (every 2 months), economic papers, proceedings.

Global Crop Protection Federation—GCPF: ave Louise 143, 1050 Brussels, Belgium; tel. (2) 542-04-10; fax (2) 542-04-19; e-mail gcpf@pophost.eunet.be/; internet www.gcpf.org; f. 1960 as European Group of National Asscns of Pesticide Manufacturers, international body since 1967, present name adopted in 1996; aims to harmonize national and international regulations concerning crop protection products; supports the development of the industry; promotes observation of the FAO Code of Conduct on the Distribution and Use of Pesticides; holds an annual General Assembly; mems: 6 regional asscns covering Africa/Middle East, Asia-Pacific, Europe, Latin America, North America and Japan; Pres. WILLIAM J. MURRAY; Dir-Gen. K. P. VLAHODIMOS.

Gulf Organization for Industrial Consulting—GOIC: POB 5114, Doha, Qatar; tel. 4858888; fax 4831465; e-mail goic@goic.org.qa; internet www.goic.org.qa; f. 1976 by the Gulf Arab states to encourage industrial co-operation among Gulf Arab states, to pool industrial expertise and to encourage joint development of projects; undertakes feasibility studies, market diagnosis, assistance in policy-making, legal consultancies, project promotion, promotion of small and medium industrial investment profiles and technical training; maintains industrial data bank; mems: mem. states of the Gulf Co-operation Council; Sec.-Gen. MOHAMED BIN ALI BIN ABDULLAH AL-MUSALLAM; publs *GOIC Monthly Bulletin* (in Arabic), *Al Ta'awon al Sina'e* (quarterly, in Arabic and English).

Instituto Centroamericano de Administración de Empresas —INCAE (Central American Institute for Business Administration): Apdo 960, 4050 Alajuela, Costa Rica; tel. 443-0506; fax 433-9101; e-mail artauiar@mail.incae.ac.cr; internet www.incae.ac.cr; f. 1964; provides a postgraduate programme in business administration; runs executive training programmes; carries out management research and consulting; maintains a second campus in Nicaragua; libraries of 85,000 vols; Rector Dr ROBERTO ARTAUIA; publs *Alumni Journal* (in Spanish), *Bulletin* (quarterly), books and case studies.

Inter-American Commercial Arbitration Commission: OAS Administration Bldg, Rm 211, 19th and Constitution Ave, NW, Washington, DC 20006, USA; tel. (202) 458-3249; fax (202) 458-3293; f. 1934 to establish an inter-American system of arbitration for the settlement of commercial disputes by means of tribunals; mems: national committees, commercial firms and individuals in 22 countries; Dir-Gen. Dr ADRIANA POLANIA.

International Advertising Association Inc: 521 Fifth Ave, Suite 1807, New York, NY 10175, USA; tel. (212) 557-1133; fax (212) 983-0455; e-mail iaa@iaaglobal.org; internet www.iaaglobal.org; f. 1938 as a global partnership of advertisers, agencies, the media and other marketing communications professionals; aims to protect freedom of commercial speech and consumer choice; holds World Congress every 2 years (2004: China); mems: more than 3,600 in 99 countries; Pres. DAVID HANGER (UK); Dir-Gen. WALLY O'BRIEN (USA); publs *IAA Membership Directory and Annual Report, IAA World News*.

International Association of Buying and Marketing Groups: Vorgebirgsstr. 43, 53119 Bonn, Germany; tel. (228) 9858420; fax (228) 9858410; e-mail g.olesch@zgv-online.de; f. 1951 to research, document and compile statistics; holds annual conference; mems: 300 buying groups in 13 countries; Sec.-Gen. Dr GÜNTER OLESCH.

International Association of Department Stores: 4 rue de Rome, 75008 Paris, France; tel. 1-42-94-02-02; fax 1-42-94-02-04; e-mail iads@iads.org; internet www.iads.org; f. 1928 to conduct research and exchange information and statistics on management, organization and technical problems; maintains a documentation centre; mems: large-scale retail enterprises in 18 countries; Pres. JORGE ZONT (Spain); Gen. Sec. M. DE GROOT VAN EMBDEN (Netherlands); publ. *Retail News Letter* (monthly).

International Association of Scholarly Publishers: c/o Fred C. Bohm, Michigan State University Press, 1405 South Harrison Rd, East Lansing, MI 48823-5202, USA; tel. (517) 355-9543; fax (517) 432-2611; e-mail bohm@pilot.msu.edu; f. 1972 for the exchange of information and experience on scholarly and academic publishing by universities and others; assists in the transfer of publishing skills to developing countries; mems: over 140 in 38 countries; Pres. MICHAEL HUTER (Austria); Sec.-Gen. FRED C. BOHM (USA); publs *IASP Newsletter* (every 2 months), *International Directory of Scholarly Publishers*.

International Association of the Soap, Detergent and Maintenance Products Industry—AISE (Association internationale de la savonnerie, de la détergence et des produits d'entretien): 49 sq. Marie-Louise, 1000 Brussels, Belgium; tel. (2) 230-83-71; fax (2) 230-82-88; e-mail aise.main@aise-net.org; internet www.aise-net.org; f. 1967 to promote the manufacture and use of a wide range of cleaning products, polishes, bleaches, disinfectants and insecticides, to develop the exchange of statistical information and to study technical, scientific, economic and social problems of interest to its members; mems: 35 national asscns in 30 countries; Dir M. G. LABBERTON; publs *Annual Review*, technical documents and reports.

International Booksellers Federation—IBF: rue du Grand Hospice 34a, 1000 Belgium; tel. (2) 223-49-40; fax (2) 223-49-41; e-mail eurobooks@skynet.be; internet www.ibf-world.org; f. 1956 to promote the book trade and the exchange of information, and to protect the interests of booksellers when dealing with other international organizations; special committees deal with questions of postage, resale price maintenance, book market research, advertising, customs and tariffs, the problems of young booksellers, etc; mems: 200 in 22 countries; Pres. YVONNE STEINBERGER; Sec.-Gen. CHRISTIANE VUIDAR; publs *IBF-bulletin* (2 a year), *Booksellers International*.

International Bureau for the Standardization of Man-Made Fibres—BISFA: 4 ave van Nieuwenhuyse, 1160 Brussels, Belgium; tel. (2) 676-74-55; fax (2) 676-74-54; e-mail van@cirfs.org; internet www.bisfa.org; f. 1928 to examine and establish rules for the standardization, classification and naming of various categories of man-made fibres; mems: 49; Sec.-Gen. J. SPIJKERS.

International Butchers' Confederation: bte 10, 4 rue Jacques de Lalaing, 1040 Brussels, Belgium; tel. (2) 230-38-76; fax (2) 230-34-51; e-mail info@cibc.be; f. 1907; aims to defend the interests of small and medium-sized enterprises in the meat trading and catering industry; Pres. BRUNO KAMM; Sec.-Gen. INGOLF JAKOBI.

International Confederation for Printing and Allied Industries—INTERGRAF: 18 sq. Marie-Louise, bte 25, 1040 Brussels, Belgium; tel. (2) 230-86-46; fax (2) 231-14-64; internet www.intergraf.org; f. 1983 (frmly EUROGRAF, f. 1975) to defend the common interests of the printing and allied interests in mem. countries; mems: federations in 20 countries; Pres. MARTIN HANDGRAAF; Sec.-Gen. GEOFFREY WILSON.

International Confederation of Art Dealers: 33 rue Ernest-Allard, 1000 Brussels, Belgium; tel. (2) 511-67-77; internet www.cinoa.org; f. 1936 to co-ordinate the work of asscns of dealers in works of art and paintings and to contribute to artistic and economic expansion; mems: asscns in 24 countries; Pres. WALTER FEILCHENFELDT; Sec.-Gen. DORIS AMMANN.

International Co-operative Alliance—ICA: 15 route des Morillons, 1218 Grand-Saconnex, Geneva, Switzerland; tel. (22) 929-88-88; fax (22) 798-41-22; e-mail ica@coop.org; internet www.coop.org; f. 1895 for the pursuit of co-operative aims; a General Assembly and four Regional Assemblies meet every two years, on an alternating basis; a 20-member ICA Board controls the affairs of the organization between meetings of the General Assembly; specialized bodies have been established to promote co-operative activities in the following fields: agriculture, banking, fisheries, consumer affairs, energy, tourism, communications, co-operative research, health, human resources, wholesale distribution, housing, insurance, women's participation and industrial, artisanal and service producers' co-operatives; mems: 242 affiliated national orgs, with a total membership of more than 760m. individuals in 100 countries, and four int. orgs; Pres. IVANO BARBERINI (Italy); Dir-Gen. BRUCE THORDARSON (Canada); publs *Review of International Co-operation* (quarterly), *ICA News* (every 2 months), *Co-op Dialogue* (2 a year).

International Council of Societies of Industrial Design—ICSID: Erottajankatu 11A, 00130 Helsinki, Finland; tel. (9) 6962290; fax (9) 69622910; e-mail icsidsec@icsid.org; internet www.icsid.org; f. 1957 to encourage the development of high standards in the practice of industrial design; works to improve and expand the contribution of industrial design throughout the world; mems: 150 in 53 countries; Pres. PETER BUTENSCHON (Norway); Sec.-Gen. KAARINA POHTO; publs *ICSID News, World Directory of Design Schools*.

International Council of Tanners: Leather Trade House, Kings Park Rd, Moulton Park, Northampton, NN3 6JD, United Kingdom; tel. (1604) 679917; fax (1604) 679998; e-mail sec@tannerscouncilct.org; internet www.tannerscouncilct.org; f. 1926 to study all questions relating to the leather industry and maintain contact with national asscns; mems: national tanners' organizations in 33 countries; Pres. TONY MOSSOP (South Africa); Sec. PAUL PEARSON (UK).

International Emissions Trading Association: 20 Eglinton Ave West, Suite 1305, POB 2017, Toronto, Canada, ON M4R 1K8; tel. (416) 487-8591; fax (416) 481-2625; e-mail marcu@ieta.org; internet www.ieta.org; f. 1999; aims to establish a functional international framework for trading greenhouse gas emissions, in accordance with the objectives of the UN Framework Convention on Climate Change; serves as a specialized information centre on emissions trading and the greenhouse gas market; mems: 45 international companies from all sectors of the industry; Exec. Dir ANDREI MARCU.

International Exhibitions Bureau: 56 ave Victor Hugo, Paris 16e, France; tel. 1-45-00-38-63; fax 1-45-00-96-15; e-mail bie@bie-paris.org; internet www.bie-paris.org; f. 1931, revised by Protocol 1972, for the authorization and registration of international exhibitions falling under the 1928 Convention; mems: 88 states; Pres. GILLES NOGHES; Sec.-Gen. VICENTE GONZALES LOSCERTALES.

International Federation of Associations of Textile Chemists and Colourists—IFATCC: Postfach 403, 4153 Reinach 1, Switzerland; e-mail markus.krayer@cibasc.com; f. 1930 for liaison on professional matters between members and the furtherance of scientific and technical collaboration in the development of the textile finishing industry and the colouring of materials; mems: in 22 countries; Pres. LIONEL DUCROCQ (France); Sec. MARKUS KRAYER (Switzerland).

International Federation of Grocers' Associations—IFGA: Vakcentrum, Woerden, Netherlands; tel. (348) 419771; fax (348) 421801; f. 1927; initiates special studies and works to further the interests of members, with special regard to conditions resulting from European integration and developments in consuming and distribution; mems: 30 asscns representing 125,000 sales outlets.

International Federation of Insurance Intermediaries (Bureau international des producteurs d'assurances et de réassurances—BIPAR): 40 ave Albert-Elisabeth, 1200 Brussels, Belgium; tel. (2) 735-60-48; fax (2) 732-14-18; e-mail bipar@skynet.be; internet www.bipar.org; f. 1937 to represent, promote and defend the interests of national asscns of professional insurance agents and brokers at the international level; works to co-ordinate members' activities; mems: 43 asscns from 27 countries, representing approx. 250,000 brokers and agents; Pres. ANTONIO VILELA DA SILVA; Dir HARALD KRAUSS; publ. *BIPAR Intern* (quarterly).

International Federation of Pharmaceutical Manufacturers Associations—IFPMA: 30 rue de St Jean, POB 758, 1211 Geneva 13, Switzerland; tel. (22) 3383200; fax (22) 3383299; e-mail admin@ ifpma.org; internet www.ifpma.org; f. 1968 for the exchange of information and international co-operation in all questions of interest to the pharmaceutical industry, particularly in the field of health legislation, science and research; develops ethical principles and practices; co-operates with national and international organizations; mems: the national pharmaceutical asscn of 60 countries and one regional asscn (representing Latin America); Pres. Prof. ROLF KREBS (Germany); Dir-Gen. Dr HARVEY E. BALE, Jr (USA); publs *IPFMA Code of Pharmaceutical Marketing Practices*, action papers, occasional publications.

International Federation of the Phonographic Industry— IFPI: 54 Regent St, London, W1R 5PJ, United Kingdom; tel. (20) 7878-7900; fax (20) 7878-7950; e-mail info@ifpi.org; internet www .ifpi.org; f. 1933; represents the interests of record producers by campaigning for the introduction, improvement and enforcement of copyright and related rights legislation; co-ordinates the recording industry's anti-piracy activities; mems: 1,476 in 73 countries; Chair. and Chief Exec. JASON BERMAN.

International Fertilizer Industry Association: 28 rue Marbeuf, 75008 Paris, France; tel. 1-53-93-05-00; fax 1-53-93-05-45; e-mail ifa@fertilizer.org; internet www.fertilizer.org; Pres. C. E. CHILDERS; Sec.-Gen. L. M. MAENE.

International Fragrance Association—IFRA: 48 sq. Marie Louise, 1000 Brussels, Belgium; tel. (2) 2389904; fax (2) 2300265; e-mail secretariat@ifraorg.org; internet www.ifraorg.org; f. 1973 to collect and study scientific data on fragrance materials and to make recommendations on their safe use; mems: national asscns in 14 countries; Pres. J. BOYDEN; Exec. Dir M. WAGNER; publs *Code of Practice, Information Letters*.

International Fur Trade Federation: POB 495, Weybridge, KT13 8WD, United Kingdom; internet www.iftf.com; f. 1949 to promote and organize joint action by fur trade organizations in order to develop and protect the trade in fur skins and the processing of skins; mems: 33 organizations in 27 countries; Exec. Dir J. BAILEY.

International Meat Secretariat (Office international de la viande): 6 rue de la Victoire, 75009 Paris, France; tel. 1-45-26-68-97; fax 1-45-26-68-98; e-mail ims@wanadoo.fr; internet www.meat-ims .org; Pres. PHILIP M. SENG; Sec.-Gen. LAURENCE WRIXON.

International Organization of Motor Manufacturers (Organisation internationale des constructeurs d'automobiles—OICA): 4 rue de Berri, 75008 Paris; tel. 1-43-59-00-13; fax 1-45-63-84-41; e-mail oica@oica.net; internet www.oica.net; f. 1919 to co-ordinate and further the interests of the automobile industry, to promote the study of economic and other matters affecting automobile construction, and to control automobile manufacturers' participation in international exhibitions in Europe; mems: manufacturers' asscns of 16 European countries, China, Japan, the Republic of Korea and the USA; 40 assoc. mems; Gen. Sec. Y. VAN DER SRAATEN; publ. *Yearbook of the World's Motor Industry*.

International Organization of the Flavour Industry—IOFI: 49 sq. Marie Louise, 1000 Brussels, Belgium; tel. (2) 2389902; fax (2) 2300265; e-mail secretariat@iofiorg.org; f. 1969 to support and promote the flavour industry; active in the fields of safety evaluation and regulation of flavouring substances; mems: national asscns in 21 countries; Pres. M. DAVIS; Exec. Dir R. HONCY; publs *Documentation Bulletin, Information Letters, Code of Practice*.

International Publishers' Association: 3 ave de Miremont, 1206 Geneva, Switzerland; tel. (22) 3463018; fax (22) 3475717; e-mail secretariat@ipa-uie.org; internet www.ipa-uie.org; f. 1896 to defend the freedom of publishers, promote their interests and foster international co-operation; promotes the international trade in books; carries out work on international copyright; mems: 79 professional book publishers' organizations in 66 countries; Pres. PERE VICENS; Sec.-Gen. BENOÎT MÜLLER.

International Rayon and Synthetic Fibres Committee (Comité international de la rayonne et des fibres synthétique—CIRFS): 4 ave E. van Nieuwenhuyse, 1160 Brussels, Belgium; tel. (2) 676-74-55;

fax (2) 676-74-54; e-mail info@cirfs.org; internet www.cirfs.org; f. 1950 to improve the quality and promote the use of man-made fibres and products made from fibres; mems: individual producers in 24 countries; Pres. GIANCARLO BERTI; Dir-Gen. C. PURVIS (UK); publs *Statistical Booklet* (annually), market reports, technical test methods.

International Shopfitting Organisation: Gladbachstr. 80, 8044 Zürich, Switzerland; tel. (1) 2678100; fax (1) 2678150; e-mail petra .isenberg@vssm.ch; internet www.shopfitting.org; f. 1959 to promote the interchange of ideas between individuals and firms concerned with shopfitting; mems: companies in 13 countries; Pres. J. BREITENMOSER; Sec. PETRA ISENBERG.

International Textile Manufacturers Federation—ITMF: Am Schanzengraben 29, Postfach, 8039 Zürich, Switzerland; tel. (1) 2017080; fax (1) 2017134; e-mail secretariat@itmf.org; internet www .itmf.org; f. 1904, present title adopted 1978; aims to protect and promote the interests of its members, disseminate information, and encourage co-operation; mems: national textile trade asscns in c. 50 countries; Pres. HERBERT SCHMID (Brazil); Dir-Gen. Dr HERWIG STROLZ (Austria); publs *State of Trade Report* (quarterly), *Country Statements, Annual Conference Report, Directory*, various statistics, sectoral reports and publications.

International Union of Marine Insurance—IUMI: Gotthardstr. 3, POB 6304, Zug, Switzerland; tel. (41) 7293966; fax (41) 7293967; e-mail mail@iumi.com; internet www.iumi.com; f. 1873 to collect and distribute information on marine insurance on a world-wide basis; mems: 54 asscns; Pres. GEORG MEHL (Germany); Gen. Sec. STEFAN PELLER.

International Wool Textile Organisation—IWTO (Fédération lanière internationale—FLI): 4 rue de l'Industrie, 1000 Brussels, Belgium; tel. (2) 505-40-10; fax (2) 503-47-85; e-mail info@iwto.org; internet www.iwto.org; f. 1929 to link wool textile organizations in member-countries and represent their interests; holds annual International Wool Conference (2003: Buenos Aires); mems: in 23 countries; Pres. DIETER J. VOLLSTEDT (Germany); Sec.-Gen. W. H. LAKIN (UK); Gen. Man. HENRIK KUFFNER (UK); publs *Wool Statistics* (annually), *Global Wool Supplies and Wool Textile Manufacturing Activity* (annually), *Blue Book, Red Book*.

International Wrought Copper Council: 6 Bathurst St, Sussex Sq., London, W2 2SD, United Kingdom; tel. (20) 7724-7465; fax (20) 7724-0308; e-mail iwcc@coppercouncil.org; internet www .coppercouncil.org; f. 1953 to link and represent copper fabricating industries and represent the views of copper consumers to raw material producers; organizes specialist activities on technical work and the development of copper; mems: 17 national groups in Europe, Australia, Japan and Malaysia, 13 corporate mems; Chair. A. BAGRI; Sec.-Gen. SIMON PAYTON; publs *Annual Report*, surveys.

Liaison Group of the European Mechanical, Electrical, Electronic and Metalworking Industries—Orgalime: Diamant Bldg, 80 blvd Reyers, 1030 Brussels, Belgium; tel. (2) 511-34-84; fax (2) 512-99-70; e-mail secretariat@orgalime.be; internet www .orgalime.org; f. 1954 to provide a permanent liaison between the mechanical, electrical and electronic engineering, and metalworking industries of member countries; mems: 25 trade asscns in 16 European countries; Pres. ENRICO MASSIMO CARLE (Italy); Sec.-Gen. PATRICK KNOX-PEEBLES.

Union des Foires Internationales—UFI (Union of International Fairs): 35 bis, rue Jouffroy d'Abbans, 75017 Paris, France; tel. 1-42-67-99-12; fax 1-42-27-19-29; e-mail info@ufinet.org; internet www .ufinet.org; f. 1925; represents the show and fairground industry worldwide; works to increase co-operation between international trade fairs/exhibitions, safeguard their interests and extend their operations; imposes quality criteria and defines standards; mems: 191 organizers and managers with 621 approved events, 33 assoc. mems in 72 countries; Pres. SANDY ANGUS (UK); Man. Dir VINCENT GÉÉRARD (Belgium).

Union of Industrial and Employers' Confederations of Europe—UNICE: 40 rue Joseph II, 1000 Brussels, Belgium; tel. (2) 237-65-11; fax (2) 231-14-45; e-mail main@unice.be; internet www .unice.org; f. 1958; aims to ensure that European Union policy-making takes account of the views of European business; committees and working groups develop joint positions in fields of interest to business and submit these to the Community institutions concerned; the Council of Presidents (of member federations) lays down general policy; the Executive Committee (of Directors-General of member federations) is the managing body; and the Committee of Permanent Delegates, consisting of federation representatives in Brussels, ensures permanent liaison with mems; mems: 20 industrial and employers' federations from the EU member states, and 15 federations from non-EU countries, four observer federations; Pres. JÜRGEN STRUBE; publ. *UNICE@News* (monthly, by e-mail).

World Customs Organization—WCO: 30 rue du Marché, 1210 Brussels, Belgium; tel. (2) 209-92-11; fax (2) 209-92-92; e-mail info@

wcoomd.org; internet www.wcoomd.org; f. 1952 as Customs Co-operation Council; aims to enhance the effectiveness and efficiency of customs administrations in the areas of compliance with trade regulations, the protection of society and revenue collection; mems: governments of 161 countries; Chair. Dr PRAVIN GORDHAN (South Africa); Sec.-Gen. MICHEL DANET (France); publ. *WCO News* (quarterly).

World Federation of Advertisers: 120 ave Louise, 1050 Brussels; tel. (2) 502-57-40; fax (2) 502-56-66; e-mail info@wfanet.org; internet www.wfanet.org; f. 1953; promotes and studies advertising and its related problems; holds World Congress (2001: Tokyo, Japan); mems: asscns in 46 countries and 29 international companies; Pres. ROLF KREINER; Man. Dir STEPHAN HOERKE; publ. *EU Brief* (weekly).

World Packaging Organisation: POB 9, SE-164 93 Kista, Sweden; fax (8) 751-3889; e-mail carl.olsmats@packforsk.se; internet www.packaging-technology.com/wpo; f. 1967 to provide a forum for the exchange of knowledge of packaging technology and, in general, to create conditions for the conservation, preservation and distribution of world food production; holds annual congress and competition; mems: Asian, North American, Latin American, European and South African packaging federations; Pres. SERGIO HABERFELD (Brazil); Gen. Sec. CARL OLSMATS (Sweden).

World Trade Centers Association: 60 East 42nd St, Suite 1901, New York, NY 10165, USA; tel. (212) 432-2626; fax (212) 488-0064; internet www.wtca.org; f. 1968 to promote trade through the establishment of world trade centres, including education facilities, information services and exhibition facilities; operates an electronic trading and communication system (WTC On-Line); mems: trade centres, chambers of commerce and other organizations in 95 countries; Pres. GUY F. TOZZOLI; Chair. BRYAN MONTGOMERY; publ. *WTCA News* (monthly).

Transport

African Airlines Association: POB 20116, Nairobi, Kenya; tel. (20) 604925; fax (20) 601173; e-mail afraa@africaonline.co.ke; internet www.afraa.org; f. 1968 to give African air companies expert advice in technical, financial, juridical and market matters to improve air transport in Africa through inter-carrier co-operation; and to develop manpower resources; mems: 34 national carriers; publs *Newsletter*, reports.

Airports Council International—ACI: POB 16, 1215 Geneva 15-Airport, Switzerland; tel. (22) 7178585; fax (22) 7178888; e-mail aci@airports.org; internet www.airports.org; f. 1991, following merger of Airport Operators Council International and International Civil Airports Association; aims to represent and develop co-operation among airports of the world; mems: 554 mems operating more than 1,400 airports in 170 countries and territories; Chair. A. GHANEM AL-HAJRI; Dir-Gen. ROBERT J. AARONSON; Sec.-Gen. ALEXANDER STRAHL; publs *World Report* (6 a year), *Airport World Magazine*, *Policy Handbook*, reports.

Arab Air Carriers' Organization—AACO: PO Box 13-5468, Beirut, Lebanon; tel. (1) 861297; fax (1) 863168; e-mail info@aaco.org; internet www.aaco.org; f. 1965 to promote co-operation in the activities of Arab airline companies; mems: 22 Arab air carriers; Pres. ABDEL RAHMAN AL-BUSAEDI (Qatar); Sec.-Gen. ABDUL WAHAB TEFFAHA; publs *bulletins, reports and research documents*.

Association of Asia Pacific Airlines: 9th Floor, Kompleks Antarabangsa, Jalan Sultan Ismail, 50250 Kuala Lumpur, Malaysia; tel. (3) 2145-5600; fax (3) 2145-2500; e-mail info@aapa.org.my; internet www.aapairlines.org; f. 1966 as Orient Airlines Asscn; present name adopted in April 1997; represents the interests of Asia Pacific airlines; encourages the exchange of information and increased co-operation between airlines; seeks to develop safe, efficient, profitable and environmentally friendly air transport; mems: 17 scheduled international airlines; Dir.-Gen. RICHARD T. STIRLAND; publs *Annual Report*, *Annual Statistical Report*, *Monthly International Statistics*, *Orient Aviation* (10 a year).

Association of European Airlines: 350 ave Louise, bte 4, 1050 Brussels, Belgium; tel. (2) 639-89-89; fax (2) 639-89-90; e-mail aea.secretariat@aca.be; internet www.aea.be; f. 1954 to carry out research on political, commercial, economic and technical aspects of air transport; maintains statistical data bank; mems: 29 airlines; Chair. LEO H. VAN WIJK (Netherlands); Sec.-Gen. KARL-HEINZ NEUMEISTER (Germany).

Baltic and International Maritime Council—BIMCO: Bagsvaerdvej 161, 2880 Bagsvaerd, Denmark; tel. 44-36-68-00; fax 44-36-68-68; e-mail mailbox@bimco.dk; internet www.bimco.dk; f. 1905 to unite shipowners and other persons and organizations connected with the shipping industry; mems: in 122 countries, representing over 65% of world merchant tonnage; Pres. MICHAEL EVERARD (UK); Sec.-Gen. TRULS W. L'ORANGE; publs *BIMCO Review* (annually), *BIMCO Bulletin* (6 a year), *Vessel* (CD-ROM), manuals.

Central Commission for the Navigation of the Rhine: Palais du Rhin, Place de la République, 67000 Strasbourg, France; tel. 3-88-52-20-10; fax 3-88-32-10-72; e-mail ccmr@ccr-zkr.org; internet www.ccr-zkr.org; f. 1815 to ensure free movement of traffic and standard river facilities for ships of all nations; draws up navigational rules; standardizes customs regulations; arbitrates in disputes involving river traffic; approves plans for river maintenance work; there is an administrative centre for social security for boatmen; mems: Belgium, France, Germany, Netherlands, Switzerland; Sec.-Gen. JEAN-MARIE WOEHRLING (France); publs Guides, rules and directives (in French and German).

Danube Commission: Benczúr utca 25, 1068 Budapest, Hungary; tel. (1) 352-1835; fax (1) 352-1839; e-mail secretariat@danubecom-intern.org; internet www.danubecom-intern.org; f. 1948; ; supervises implementation of the Belgrade Convention on the Regime of Navigation on the Danube; approves projects for river maintenance; supervises a uniform system of traffic regulations on the whole navigable portion of the Danube and on river inspection; mems: Austria, Bulgaria, Croatia, Germany, Hungary, Moldova, Romania, Russia, Serbia and Montenegro, Slovakia, Ukraine; Pres. Dr S. NICK; Dir-Gen. Capt. D. NEDIALKOV; publs *Basic Regulations for Navigation on the Danube*, *Hydrological Yearbook*, *Statistical Yearbook*, proceedings of sessions.

European Civil Aviation Conference—ECAC: 3 bis Villa Emile-Bergerat, 92522 Neuilly-sur-Seine Cédex, France; tel. 1-46-41-85-44; fax 1-46-24-18-18; e-mail ecac@compuserve.com; internet www.ecac-ceac.org; f. 1955; aims to promote the continued development of a safe, efficient and sustainable European air transport system; mems: 41 European states; Pres. ALFREDO ROMA; Exec. Sec. RAYMOND BENJAMIN.

European Conference of Ministers of Transport—ECMT: 2 rue André Pascal, 75775 Paris Cédex 16, France; tel. 1-45-24-82-00; fax 1-45-24-97-42; e-mail ecmt.contact@oecd.org; internet www.oecd.org/cem; f. 1953 to achieve the maximum use and most rational development of European transport; aims to create a safe, sustainable, efficient, integrated transport system; provides a forum for analysis and discussion; holds round tables, seminars and symposia; shares Secretariat staff with OECD; mems: 41 member countries, 6 associate mems, 2 observer countries; Sec.-Gen. JACK SHORT; publs *Activities of the Conference* (annually), *ECMT News* (2 a year), *Catalogue of Publications*, various statistical publications and surveys.

European Organisation for the Safety of Air Navigation—EUROCONTROL: 96 rue de la Fusée, 1130 Brussels, Belgium; tel. (2) 729-90-11; fax (2) 729-90-44; internet www.eurocontrol.int; f. 1960; aims to develop a coherent and co-ordinated air traffic control system in Europe. A revised Convention was signed in June 1997, incorporating the following institutional structure: a General Assembly (known as the Commission in the transitional period), a Council (known as the Provisional Council) and an Agency under the supervision of the Director General; there are directorates, covering human resources and finance matters and a general secretariat. A special organizational structure covers the management of the European Air Traffic Management Programme. EUROCONTROL also operates the Experimental Centre (at Brétigny-sur-Orge, France), the Institute of Air Navigation Services (in Luxembourg), the Central Route Charges Office, the Central Flow Management Unit (both in Brussels) and the Upper Area Control Centre (in Maastricht, Netherlands); mems: 31 European countries; Dir-Gen. VÍCTOR M. AGUADO (Spain).

Forum Train Europe—FTE: Direction générale des chemins de fer fédéraux suisses, Hochschulstrasse 6, 3030 Bern, Switzerland; internet www.fte-rail.com; f. 1923 as the European Passenger Train Time-Table Conference to arrange international passenger connections by rail and water; since 1997 concerned also with rail freight; mems: rail and steamship companies and administrations. Administered by the Directorate of the Swiss Federal Railways; Pres. P. A. URECH.

Institute of Air Transport: 103 rue la Boétie, 75008 Paris, France; tel. 1-43-59-38-68; fax 1-43-59-47-37; e-mail contac@ita-paris.com; internet www.ita-paris.com; f. 1945 as an international centre of research on economic, technical and policy aspects of air transport, and on the economy and sociology of transport and tourism; acts as economic and technical consultant in research requested by members on specific subjects; maintains a data bank, a library and a consultation and advice service; organizes training courses on air transport economics; mems: organizations involved in air transport, production and equipment, universities, banks, insurance companies, private individuals and government agencies in 79 countries; Dir-Gen. JACQUES PAVAUX; publs (in French and English), *ITA Press* (2 a month), *ITA Studies and Reports* (quarterly), *Aviation Industry Barometer* (quarterly).

Intergovernmental Organization for International Carriage by Rail: Gryphenhübeliweg 30, 3006 Bern, Switzerland; tel. (31)

3591010; fax (31) 3591011; e-mail otif@otif.org; internet www.otif .org; f. 1893 as Central Office for International Carriage by Rail, present name adopted 1985; aims to establish and develop a uniform system of law governing the international carriage of passengers, luggage and goods by rail in member states; mems: 41 states; Dir-Gen. HANS RUDOLF ISLIKER; publ *Bulletin des Transports Internationaux ferroviaires* (quarterly, in English, French and German).

International Air Transport Association—IATA: 33 route de l'Aéroport, CP 416, 1215 Geneva 15, Switzerland; tel. (22) 7992525; fax (22) 7983553; e-mail information@iata.org; internet www.iata .org; f. 1945 to represent and serve the airline industry; Aims to promote safe, reliable and secure air services; to assist the industry to attain adequate levels of profitability while developing cost-effective operational standards; to promote the importance of the industry in global social and economic development; and to identify common concerns and represent the industry in addressing these at regional and international level; maintains regional offices in Amman, Brussels, Dakar, London, Nairobi, Santiago, Singapore and Washington, DC; mems: 258 airline cos; Dir-Gen. PIERRE JEANNIOT; Corporate Sec. LORNE CLARK; publ *Airlines International* (every 2 months).

IVR (International Association for the Rhine Vessels Register): Vasteland 12E 3011 BL Rotterdam (POB 23210, 3001 KE Rotterdam), Netherlands; tel. (10) 4116070; fax (10) 4129091; e-mail info@ivr.nl; internet www.ivr.nl; f. 1947 for the classification of Rhine ships, the organization and publication of a Rhine ships register, the unification of general average rules, and the harmonization of European inland navigation law; mems: shipowners and asscns, insurers and asscns, shipbuilding engineers, average adjusters and others interested in Rhine traffic; Gen. Sec. T. K. HACKSTEINER.

International Association of Ports and Harbors—IAPH: Kono Bldg, 1-23-9 Nishi-Shimbashi, Minato-ku, Tokyo 105, Japan; tel. (3) 3591-4261; fax (3) 3580-0364; e-mail iaph@msn.com; internet www .iaph.or.jp; f. 1955 to increase the efficiency of ports and harbours through the dissemination of information on port organization, management, administration, operation, development and promotion; encourages the growth of water-borne commerce; holds conference every two years; mems: 350 in 85 states; Pres. DOMINIC J. TADDEO (Canada); Sec.-Gen. SATOSHI INOUE (Japan); ; publs *Ports and Harbors* (10 a year), *Membership Directory* (annually).

International Association of Public Transport: 17 ave Herrmann-Debroux, 1160 Brussels, Belgium; tel. (2) 673-61-00; fax (2) 660-10-72; e-mail administration@uitp.com; internet www.uitp.com; f. 1885 to study all problems connected with the urban and regional public passenger transport industry; mems: 2,000 in 80 countries; Pres. JEAN-PAUL BAILLY (France); Sec.-Gen. HANS RAT; publs *Public Transport International* (every 2 months), *EUExpress*, *Mobility News* (monthly, electronic), statistics reports.

International Chamber of Shipping: Carthusian Court, 12 Carthusian St, London, EC1M 6EZ, United Kingdom; tel. (20) 7417-8844; fax (20) 7417-8877; e-mail ics@marisec.org; internet www .marisec.org; f. 1921 to co-ordinate the views of the international shipping industry on matters of common interest, in the policy-making, technical and legal fields of shipping operations; mems: national asscns representing free-enterprise shipowners and operators in 39 countries; Sec.-Gen. J. C. S. HORROCKS.

International Container Bureau: 167 rue de Courcelles, 75017 Paris, France; tel. 1-47-66-03-90; fax 1-47-66-08-91; f. 1933 to group representatives of all means of transport and activities concerning containers, to promote combined door-to-door transport by the successive use of several means of transport, to examine and bring into effect administrative, technical and customs advances, and to centralize data on behalf of mems; mems: 800; Sec.-Gen. JEAN REY; publ *Container Bulletin*.

International Federation of Freight Forwarders' Associations: Baumackerstr. 24, POB 8050 Zürich, Switzerland; tel. (1) 3116511; fax (1) 3119044; e-mail info@fiata.com; internet www.fiata .com; f. 1926 to protect and represent its members at international level; mems: 95 organizations and more than 2,500 associate members in 150 countries; Pres. ALDO DA ROS; Dir MARCO A. SANGALETTI; publ *FIATA Review* (every 2 months).

International Rail Transport Committee (Comité international des transports ferroviaires—CIT): Weltpoststr. 20, 3000 Bern 15, Switzerland; tel. (512) 202806; fax (512) 203457; e-mail info@cit-rail .org; internet www.cit-rail.org; f. 1902 for the development of international law relating to railway transport, on the basis of the Convention concerning International Carriage by Rail (COTIF) and its Appendices (CIV, CIM), and for the adoption of standard rules on other questions relating to international transport law; mems: 300 transport undertakings in 37 countries; Pres. M. WEIBEL (Switzerland); Sec. M. LEIMGRUBER (Switzerland).

International Railway Congress Association: Section 10, 85 rue de France, 1060 Brussels, Belgium; tel. (2) 520-78-31; fax (2) 525-40-84; e-mail secretariat@aiccf.org; internet www.aiccf.org; f. 1885 to facilitate the progress and development of railways; mems: governments, railway administrations, national and international organizations; Pres. E. SCHOUPPE; Sec.-Gen. A. MARTENS; publ *Rail International* (monthly).

International Road Federation—IRF: Washington office: 1010 Massachusetts Ave, NW, Suite 410, Washington, DC 20037, USA; Geneva Office: 2 chemin de Blandonnet 1214, Vernier, Geneva, Switzerland; tel. (202) 371-5544; fax (202) 371-5565; e-mail info@ irfnet.org; internet www.irfnet.org; tel. (22) 3060260; fax (22) 3060270; f. 1948 to encourage the development and improvement of highways and highway transportation; organizes IRF world and regional meetings; mems: 70 national road asscns and 500 individual firms and industrial asscns; Dir-Gen. (Washington) GERALD P. SHEA; Dir-Gen. (Geneva) M. W. WESTERHUIS; publs *World Road Statistics* (annually), *World Highways* (8 a year).

International Road Safety Association (La prevention routière internationale—PRI): Estrada da Luz, 90-1°, 1600-160 Lisbon, Portugal; tel. (21) 7222230; fax (21) 7222232; e-mail info@lapri.org; internet www.lapri.org; f. 1959 for exchange of ideas and material on road safety; organizes international action and congresses; assists non-member countries; mems: 74 national organizations; Pres. JOSÉ MIGUEL TRIGOSO (Portugal); Sec.-Gen. MARTINE PETERS;; publ *Newsletter* (6 a year).

International Road Transport Union—IRU: Centre International, 3 rue de Varembé, BP 44, 1211 Geneva, Switzerland; tel. (22) 9182700; fax (22) 9182741; e-mail iru@iru.org; internet www.iru.org; f. 1948 to study all problems of road transport, to promote unification and simplification of regulations relating to road transport, and to develop the use of road transport for passengers and goods; represents and promotes the industry at an international level; mems: 145 national asscns in 67 countries; Dir MARTIN MARMY;; publs studies, congress and conference reports, regulations and statistics.

International Shipping Federation: Carthusian Court, 12 Carthusian St, London, EC1M 6EZ, United Kingdom; tel. (20) 7417-8844; fax (20) 7417-8877; e-mail isf@marisec.org; internet www .marisec.org; f. 1909 to consider all personnel questions affecting the interests of shipowners; responsible for Shipowners' Group at conferences of the International Labour Organisation; represents shipowners at International Maritime Organization; mems: national shipowners' organizations in 34 countries; Pres. R. WESTFAL-LARSON (Norway); Sec.-Gen. J. C. S. HORROCKS; publs *Guide to International Shipping Registers*, conference papers, guidelines and training records.

International Union for Inland Navigation: 7 quai du Général Koenig, 67085 Strasbourg Cédex, France; tel. 3-88-36-28-44; fax 3-88-37-04-82; f. 1952 to promote the interests of inland waterways carriers; mems: national waterways organizations of Austria, Belgium, France, Germany, Italy, Luxembourg, Netherlands, Switzerland; Pres. P. GRULOIS (Belgium); Sec. M. RUSCHER; publs annual and occasional reports.

International Union of Railways (Union internationale des chemins de fer—UIC): 16 rue Jean-Rey, 75015 Paris, France; tel. 1-44-49-20-20; fax 1-44-49-20-29; e-mail communication@uic.asso.fr; internet www.uic.asso.fr; f. 1922 for the harmonization of railway operations and the development of international rail transport; aims to ensure international interoperability of the rail system; compiles information on economic, management and technical aspects of railways; co-ordinates research and collaborates with industry and the EU; organizes international conferences; mems: 160 railways in 87 countries; Pres. BENEDIKT WEIBEL; Chief Exec. PHILIPPE ROUMEGUÈRE; publs *Rail International*, jointly with the International Railway Congress Association (IRCA) (monthly, in English, French and German), *International Railway Statistics* (annually), *Activities Reports*, *UIC Panorama* (newsletter).

Northern Shipowners' Defence Club (Nordisk Skibsrederforening): Kristinelundv. 22, POB 33, Elisenberg, 0207 Oslo, Norway; tel. 22-13-56-00; fax 22-43-00-35; e-mail post@nordisk.no; internet www.nordisk.org; f. 1889 to assist members in disputes over charter parties, contracts and sale and purchase, taking the necessary legal steps on behalf of members and bearing the cost of such claims; mems: mainly Finnish, Swedish and Norwegian and some non-Scandinavian shipowners, representing about 1,800 ships and drilling rigs with gross tonnage of about 50m. Man. Dir GEORG SCHEEL; Chair. MORTEN WERRING; publ *A Law Report of Scandinavian Maritime Cases* (annually).

Organisation for the Collaboration of Railways: Hozà 63–67, 00681 Warsaw, Poland; tel. (22) 6573600; fax (22) 6573654; e-mail osjd@osjd.org.pl; f. 1956; aims to improve standards and co-operation in railway traffic between countries of Europe and Asia; promotes co-operation on issues relating to traffic policy and economic and environmental aspects of railway traffic; ensures enforcement of a number of rail agreements; aims to elaborate and standardize general principles for international transport law. Conference of Ministers of mem. countries meets annually; Conference of Gen. Dirs of Railways meets at least once a year; mems: ministries of transport of 27 countries world-wide; Chair. TADEUSZ SZOZDA;; publ *OSShD Journal* (every 2 months, in Chinese, German and Russian).

Pan American Railway Congress Association (Asociación del Congreso Panamericano de Ferrocarriles): Av. 9 de Julio 1925, 13°, 1332 Buenos Aires, Argentina; tel. (11) 4381-4625; fax (11) 4814-1823; e-mail acpf@nat.com.ar; f. 1907, present title adopted 1941; aims to promote the development and progress of railways in the American continent; holds Congresses every three years; mems: government representatives, railway enterprises and individuals in 21 countries; Pres. JUAN CARLOS DE MARCHI (Argentina); Gen. Sec. LUIS V. DONZELLI (Argentina); publ *Boletín ACPF* (5 a year).

Union of European Railway Industries—UNIFE: 221 ave Louise, 1050 Brussels, Belgium; tel. (2) 626-12-60; fax (2) 626-12-61; e-mail mail@unife.org; internet www.unife.org; f. 1975 to represent companies concerned in the manufacture of railway equipment in Europe to European and international organizations; mems: 140 companies in 14 countries; Chair. ROLF ECKRODT; Dir-Gen. DREWIN NIEUWENHUIS.

World Airlines Clubs Association—WACA: c/o IATA, 800 Pl. Victoria, POB 113, Montréal, Québec, QC H4Z 1M1, Canada; tel. (514) 874-0202; fax (514) 874-1753; e-mail info@waca.org; internet www.waca.org; f. 1966; holds a General Assembly annually, regional meetings, international events and sports tournaments; mems: clubs in 38 countries; Man. AUBREY WINTERBOTHAM; publs *WACA Contact*, *WACA World News*, annual report.

Youth and Students

AIESEC International: Teilingerstraat 126–128, 3032 Rotterdam, Netherlands; tel. (10) 443-43-83; fax (10) 265-13-86; e-mail info@ai .aiesec.org; internet www.aiesec.org; f. 1948 as International Association of Students in Economics and Management; works to develop leadership skills and socio-economic and international understanding among young people, through exchange programmes and related educational activities; mems: 50,000 students in more than 650 higher education institutions in 88 countries and territories; Pres. SAHIL KAUL; Vice-Pres. ANDREW SCHURGOTT; publ *Annual Report*.

Asia Students Association: 353 Shangai St, 14/F, Kowloon, Hong Kong; tel. 23880515; fax 27825535; e-mail asasec@netvigator.com; f. 1969; aims to promote students' solidarity in struggling for democracy, self-determination, peace, justice and liberation; conducts campaigns, training of activists, and workshops on human rights and other issues of importance. There are Student Commissions for Peace, Education and Human Rights; mems: 40 national or regional student unions in 25 countries and territories; Secretariat LINA CABAERO (Philippines), STEVEN GAN (Malaysia), CHOW WING-HANG (Hong Kong); publs *Movement News* (monthly), *ASA News* (quarterly).

Council on International Educational Exchange—CIEE: 205 East 42nd St, New York, NY 10017, USA; tel. (212) 661-1414; fax (212) 972-3231; e-mail strooboff@ciee.org; internet www.ciee.org; f. 1947; issues International Student Identity Card entitling holders to discounts and basic insurance; arranges overseas work and study programmes for students; co-ordinates summer work programme in the USA for foreign students; administers programmes for teachers and other professionals and sponsors conferences on educational exchange; operates a voluntary service programme; mems: 307 colleges, universities and international educational organizations; Pres. and CEO STEVAN TROOBOFF; publs include *Work, Study, Travel Abroad: The Whole World Handbook*, *Update*, *Volunteer!*, *High-School Student's Guide to Study, Travel and Adventure Abroad*.

European Law Students' Association—ELSA: 1 rue Defacqz, 1050 Brussels, Belgium; tel. (2) 534-56-79; fax (2) 534-65-86; internet www.elsa-online.org; f. 1981 to foster mutual understanding and promote social responsibility of law students and young laywers; publs *ELSA Law Review*, *Legal Studies in Europe*.

European Students' Forum (Association des états généraux des étudiants de l'Europe): 15 rue Nestor de Tiere, 1040 Brussels, Belgium; tel. (2) 245-23-00; fax (2) 245-62-60; e-mail info@aegee.org; internet www.aegee.org; promotes cross-border communication and integration between students; holds specialized conferences; mems: 17,000 students in 271 university cities in 40 countries.

European Youth Forum: 120 rue Joseph II, 1000 Brussels, Belgium; tel. (2) 286-94-12; fax (2) 233-37-09; e-mail youthforum@youthforum.org; internet www.europeanyouthforum.com; f. 1996; promotes development of a coherent and integrated youth policy; promotes the rights of young people, as well as understanding and

respect for human rights; consults with international organizations and governments on issues relevant to young people.

International Association for the Exchange of Students for Technical Experience—IAESTE: e-mail webmaster@iaeste.org; internet www.iaeste.org; f. 1948; mems: 63 national committees; publs *Activity Report*, *Annual Report*.

International Association of Dental Students—IADS: c/o FDI World Dental Federation, 7 Carlisle St, London, W1V 5RG, United Kingdom; tel. (20) 7935-7852; fax (20) 7486-0183; internet www.iads .ndirect.co.uk; f. 1951 to represent dental students and their opinions internationally, to promote dental student exchanges and international congresses; mems: 60,000 students in 45 countries, 15,000 corresponding mems; Pres. VALENTINA STERJOVA (UK); publ. *IADS Newsletter* (3 a year).

International Federation of Medical Students' Associations —IFMSA: Institute of Social Medicine, Academisch Medisch Centrum, Meibergdreef 15, 1105 Amsterdam, Netherlands; tel. (20) 5665366; fax (20) 6972316; e-mail f.w.hilhorst@amc.uva.nl; internet www.ifmsa.org; f. 1951 to promote international co-operation in professional treatment and the achievement of humanitarian ideals; provides forum for medical students; maintains standing committees on professional exchange, electives exchange, medical education, public health, refugees and AIDS; organizes annual General Assembly; mems: 57 asscns; Sec.-Gen. MIA HILHORST; publ. *IFMSA Newsletter* (quarterly).

International Pharmaceutical Students' Federation—IPSF: POB 84200, 2508 AE The Hague, Netherlands; tel. (70) 3021992; fax (70) 3021999; e-mail ipsf@fip.nl; internet www.pharmweb.net/ipsf .html; f. 1949 to study and promote the interests of pharmaceutical students and to encourage international co-operation; mems: 31 full mems from national organizations and 23 mems in assoc. from national or local organizations; Pres. GONÇALO SOUSA PINTO; Sec.-Gen. HELENA WESTERMARK; publ. *IPSF News Bulletin* (3 a year).

International Union of Students: POB 58, 17th November St, 110 01 Prague 01, Czech Republic; tel. (2) 312812; fax (2) 316100; internet www.stud.uni-hannover/delgruppen/ius; f. 1946 to defend the rights and interests of students and strive for peace, disarmament, the eradication of illiteracy and of all forms of discrimination; operates research centre, sports and cultural centre and student travel bureau; activities include conferences, meetings, solidarity campaigns, relief projects; awards 30–40 scholarships annually; mems: 140 organizations from 115 countries; Pres. JOSEF SKALA; Vice-Pres. MARTA HUBIČKOVÁ; Gen. Sec. GIORGOS MICHAELIDES (Cyprus); publs *World Student News* (quarterly), *IUS Newsletter*, *Student Life* (quarterly), *DE—Democratization of Education* (quarterly).

International Young Christian Workers: 4 ave G. Rodenbach, 1030 Brussels, Belgium; tel. (2) 242-18-11; fax (2) 242-48-00; e-mail jociycw@skynet.be; internet www.skynet.be/sky34197; f. 1925, on the inspiration of the Priest-Cardinal Joseph Cardijn; aims to educate young workers to take on present and future responsibilities in their commitment to the working class, and to confront all the situations which prevent them from fulfilling themselves; Pres. DESROSIERS JOSÉ (Canada); Sec.-Gen. LANGWIESNER GERTRAUD (Austria); publs *International INFO* (3 a year), *IYCW Bulletin* (quarterly).

International Youth and Student Movement for the United Nations—ISMUN: c/o Palais des Nations, 16 ave Jean-Tremblay, 1211 Geneva 10, Switzerland; tel. (22) 7985850; fax (22) 7334838; internet www.ismun.org; f. 1948 by the World Federation of United Nations Associations, independent since 1949; an international non-governmental organization of students and young people dedicated especially to supporting the principles embodied in the United Nations Charter and Universal Declaration of Human Rights; encourages constructive action in building economic, social and cultural equality and in working for national independence, social justice and human rights on a world-wide scale; maintains regional offices in Austria, France, Ghana, Panama and the USA; mems: asscns in 53 countries; Sec.-Gen. JAN LÖÖNN; publ. *ISMUN Newsletter* (monthly).

International Youth Hostel Federation: 1st floor, Fountain House, Parkway, Welwyn Garden City, Herts., AL8 6QW, United Kingdom; tel. (1707) 324170; fax (1707) 323980; e-mail iyhf@iyhf .org; internet www.iyhf.org; f. 1932; facilitates international travel by members of the various youth hostel asscns; advises and helps in the formation of youth hostel asscns in countries where no such organizations exist; records over 34m. overnight stays annually in around 4,300 youth hostels; mems: 58 national asscns with over 3.2m. national members and 1m. international guest members; 12 associated national organizations; Pres. Dr HARISH SAXENA (India); Sec.-Gen. ULRICH BUNJES (Germany); publs *Annual Report*, *Guidebook on World Hostels* (annually), *Manual*, *News Bulletin*.

Junior Chamber International (JCI), Inc.: 400 University Drive (POB 140-577), Coral Gables, FL 33114-0577, USA; tel. (305) 446-7608; fax (305) 442-0041; e-mail jciwhq@ix.netcom.com; internet www.juniorchamber.org; f. 1944 to encourage and advance international understanding and goodwill; aims to solve civic problems by arousing civic consciousness; Junior Chamber organizations throughout the world provide opportunities for leadership training and for the discussion of social, economic and cultural questions; mems: 400,000 in 90 countries; Pres. SALVADOR BATLLE (Spain); Sec.-Gen. BENNY ELLERBE; publ. *JCI News* (quarterly, in English and more than six other languages).

Latin American and Caribbean Confederation of Young Men's Christian Associations (Confederación Latinoamericana y del Caribe de Asociaciones Cristianas de Jóvenes): Culpina 272, 1406 Buenos Aires, Argentina; tel. (11) 4373-4156; fax (11) 4374-4408; e-mail clacj@wamani.apc.org; f. 1914; aims to encourage the moral, spiritual, intellectual, social and physical development of young men; to strengthen the work of national Asscns and to sponsor the establishment of new Asscns; mems: affiliated YMCAs in 25 countries (comprising 350,000 individuals); Pres. GERARDO VITUREIRA (Uruguay); Gen. Sec. MARCO ANTONIO HOCHSCHEIT (Brazil); publs *Diecisiete/21* (bulletin), *Carta Abierta*, *Brief*, technical articles and other studies.

Pan-African Youth Movement (Mouvement pan-africain de la jeunesse): 19 rue Debbih Chérif, BP 72, Didouch Mourad, 16000 Algiers, Algeria; tel. and fax (2) 71-64-71; f. 1962; aims to encourage the participation of African youth in socio-economic and political development and democratization; organizes conferences and seminars, youth exchanges and youth festivals; mems: youth groups in 52 African countries and liberation movements; publ. *MPJ News* (quarterly).

World Alliance of Young Men's Christian Associations: 12 clos. Belmont, 1208 Geneva, Switzerland; tel. (22) 8495100; fax (22) 8495110; e-mail office@ymca.int; internet www.ymca.int; f. 1855 to unite the National Alliances of Young Men's Christian Associations throughout the world; mems: national alliances and related asscns in 128 countries; Pres. CAESAR MOLEBATSI (South Africa); Sec.-Gen. SHAHA BARTHOLOMEW; publ. *YMCA World* (quarterly).

World Assembly of Youth: International Youth Centre, Jalan Tenteram, Bandar Tun Razak, 56000 Kuala Lumpur, Malaysia; tel. (3) 9732722; fax (3) 9736011; internet www.jaring.my/way; f. 1949 as co-ordinating body for youth councils and organizations; organizes conferences, training courses and practical development projects; Pres. Datuk ALI RUSTAM; Sec.-Gen. HEIKKI PAKARINEN; publs *WAY Information* (every 2 months), *Youth Roundup* (monthly), *WAY Forum* (quarterly).

World Association of Girl Guides and Girl Scouts—WAGGGS: World Bureau, Olave Centre, 12c Lyndhurst Rd, London, NW3 5PQ, United Kingdom; tel. (20) 7794-1181; fax (20) 7431-3764; e-mail wagggs@wagggsworld.org; internet www.wagggsworld.org; f. 1928 to enable girls and young women to develop their full potential as responsible citizens, toand support friendship and mutual understanding among girls and young women world-wide; World Conference meets every three years; mems: about 10m. individuals in 140 organizations; Chair. World Board GINNY RADFORD; Dir World Bureau LESLEY BULMAN; publs *Triennial Report, Annual Report, Trefoil Round the World* (every 3 years), *Our World News* (quarterly).

World Council of Service Clubs: POB 148, Wallaroo, South Australia 5556, Australia; e-mail kelly@kadina.mtx.net.au; internet www.woco.org; f. 1946 to provide a means for the exchange of information and news, with the aim of furthering international understanding and co-operation; aims to create in young people a sense of civic responsibility; works to facilitate the extension of service clubs; mems: over 3,000 clubs in 83 countries; Sec.-Gen. SHANE KELLY.

World Federation of Democratic Youth—WFDY: POB 147, 1389 Budapest, Hungary; tel. (1) 3502202; fax (1) 3501204; e-mail wfdy@mail.matav.hu; internet www.wfdy.org; f. 1945 to strive for peace, disarmament and joint action by democratic and progressive youth movements and for the creation of a new and more just international economic order; promotes national independence, democracy, social progress and youth rights; supports the liberation struggles in Asia, Africa and Latin America; mems: 152 members in 102 countries; Pres. IRAKLIS TSAVDARIDIS (Greece); publ. *WFDY News* (every 3 months, in English, French and Spanish).

World Organization of the Scout Movement: Case Postale 241, 1211 Geneva 4, Switzerland; tel. (22) 7051010; fax (22) 7051020; e-mail worldbureau@world.scout.org; internet www.scout.org; f. 1922 to promote unity and understanding of scouting throughout the world to develop good citizenship among young people by forming their characters for service, co-operation and leadership; and to provide aid and advice to members and potential member asscns. The World Scout Bureau (Geneva) has regional offices in Chile, Egypt, Kenya and the Philippines (the European Region has its offices in Brussels and Geneva); mems: over 25m. in 215 countries and territories; Sec.-Gen. Dr JACQUES MOREILLON (Switzerland); publs *Worldinfo Triennial Report*.

World Union of Jewish Students—WUJS: Rechov Alkalai 9, POB 4498, 91045 Jerusalem, Israel; tel. (2) 5610133; fax (2) 5610741; e-mail office@wujs.org.il; internet www.wujs.org.il; f. 1924 (by Albert Einstein); organization for national student bodies concerned with educational and political matters, where possible in co-operation with non-Jewish student organizations, UNESCO, etc. divided into six regions; organizes Congress every two years; mems: 52 national unions representing over 1,500,000 students; Chair. PELEG RESHEF; publs *The Student Activist Yearbook*, *Heritage and History*, *Forum*, *WUJS Report*.

World Young Women's Christian Association—World YWCA: 16 Ancienne Route, 1218 Grand-Saconnex, Geneva, Switzerland; tel. (22) 9296040; fax (22) 9296044; e-mail worldoffice@worldywca.org; internet www.worldywca.org; f. 1894 for the linking together of national YWCAs (now in 98 countries) for their mutual help and development and the initiation of work in countries where the Association does not yet exist; works for international understanding, for improved social and economic conditions and for basic human rights for all people; Pres. JANE WOLFE; Gen. Sec. MUSIMBI KANYORO; publs *Annual Report, Common Concern*.

Youth for Development and Co-operation—YDC: Rijswijk-strasse 141, 1062 HN Amsterdam, Netherlands; tel. (20) 6142510; fax (20) 6175545; e-mail ydc@geo2.geonet.de; aims to strengthen youth structures promoting co-operation between young people in the industrialized and developing worlds, in order to achieve development that is environmentally sustainable and socially just; holds seminars, conferences and campaigns on issues related to youth and development; mems: 51 organizations; Sec.-Gen. B. AUER; publ. *FLASH Newsletter* (irregular).

PART TWO
Afghanistan–Jordan

AFGHANISTAN

Introductory Survey

Location, Climate, Language, Religion, Flag, Capital

The Islamic State of Afghanistan is a land-locked country in south-western Asia. It is bordered by Turkmenistan, Uzbekistan and Tajikistan to the north, Iran to the west, the People's Republic of China to the north-east and Pakistan to the east and south. The climate varies sharply between the highlands and lowlands; the temperature in the south-west in summer reaches 49°C (120°F), but in the winter, in the Hindu Kush mountains of the north-east, it falls to −26°C (−15°F). Of the many languages spoken in Afghanistan, the principal two are Pashto (Pakhto) and Dari (a dialect of Farsi or Iranian). The majority of Afghans are Muslims of the Sunni sect; there are also minority groups of Shi'ite Muslims, Hindus, Sikhs and Jews. The state flag (proportions 1 by 2) has three equal vertical stripes from hoist to fly of black, red and green, bearing in the centre in gold and red the state arms and an inscription reading 'There is no God but Allah, and Muhammad is the Prophet of Allah' above the inscription 'God is Almighty', both in Arabic. The flag was first introduced in 1928, modified in 1964, and banned following the coup in 1978. The only differences featured in the current flag, introduced in June 2002, following the collapse of the Taliban, are the inscription bearing the word 'Afghanistan' and the Islamic date 1380. The capital is Kabul.

Recent History

The last King of Afghanistan, Mohammad Zahir Shah, reigned from 1933 to 1973. His country was neutral during both World Wars and became a staunch advocate of non-alignment. In 1953 the King's cousin, Lt-Gen. Sardar Mohammad Daud Khan, was appointed Prime Minister and, securing aid from the USSR, initiated a series of economic plans for the modernization of the country. In 1963 Gen. Daud resigned and Dr Mohammad Yusuf became the first Prime Minister not of royal birth. Dr Yusuf introduced a new democratic Constitution in the following year, which combined Western ideas with Islamic religious and political beliefs; the King, however, did not permit political parties to operate. Afghanistan made little progress under the succeeding Prime Ministers.

In July 1973, while King Zahir was in Italy, the monarchy was overthrown by a coup, in which the main figure was the former Prime Minister, Gen. Daud. The 1964 Constitution was abolished and Afghanistan was declared a republic. Daud renounced his royal titles and took office as Head of State, Prime Minister and Minister of Foreign Affairs and Defence.

A Loya Jirga (Grand National Council), appointed from among tribal elders by provincial governors, was convened in January 1977 and adopted a new Constitution, providing for presidential government and a one-party state. Daud was elected to continue as President for six years and the Loya Jirga was then dissolved. In March President Daud formed a new civilian Government, nominally ending military rule. However, during 1977 there was growing discontent with Daud, especially within the armed forces, and in April 1978 a coup, known (from the month) as the 'Saur Revolution', ousted the President, who was killed with several members of his family. Nur Mohammad Taraki, the imprisoned leader of the formerly banned People's Democratic Party of Afghanistan (PDPA), was released and installed as President of the Revolutionary Council and Prime Minister. The country was renamed the Democratic Republic of Afghanistan, the year-old Constitution was abolished and no political parties other than the communist PDPA were allowed to function. Afghanistan's already close relations with the USSR were further strengthened. However, opposition to the new regime led to armed insurrection, particularly by fiercely traditionalist Islamist rebel tribesmen (known, collectively, as the *mujahidin*), in almost all provinces, and the flight of thousands of refugees to Pakistan and Iran. In spite of purges of the army and civil service, Taraki's position became increasingly insecure, and in September 1979 he was ousted by Hafizullah Amin, an erstwhile Deputy Prime Minister and Minister of Foreign Affairs. Amin's imposition of rigorous communist policies proved unsuccessful and unpopular. In December he was killed in a coup, which was supported by the entry into Afghanistan of about 80,000 combat troops from the USSR. This incursion by Soviet armed forces into a traditionally non-aligned neighbouring country aroused world-wide condemnation. Babrak Karmal, a former Deputy Prime Minister under Taraki, was installed as the new Head of State, having been flown into Kabul by a Soviet aircraft from virtual exile in Eastern Europe.

Riots, strikes and inter-factional strife and purges continued into 1980 and 1981. Sultan Ali Keshtmand, hitherto a Deputy Prime Minister, replaced Karmal as Prime Minister in June 1981. In the same month the regime launched the National Fatherland Front (NFF), incorporating the PDPA and other organizations, with the aim of promoting national unity. Despite a series of government reorganizations carried out in the early 1980s, the PDPA regime continued to fail to win widespread popular support. Consequently, the Government attempted to broaden the base of its support: in April 1985 it summoned a Loya Jirga, which ratified a new Constitution for Afghanistan, and during the second half of 1985 and the first half of 1986 elections were held for new local government organs (it was claimed that 60% of those elected were non-party members) and several non-party members were appointed to high-ranking government posts (including the chairmanship of the NFF).

In May 1986 Dr Najibullah (the former head of the state security service, KHAD) succeeded Karmal as General Secretary of the PDPA. Karmal retained the lesser post of President of the Revolutionary Council. In the same month Najibullah announced the formation of a collective leadership comprising himself, Karmal and Prime Minister Keshtmand. In November, however, Karmal was relieved of all party and government posts. Haji Muhammad Chamkani, formerly First Vice-President (and a non-PDPA member), became Acting President of the Revolutionary Council, pending the introduction of a new constitution and the establishment of a permanent legislature.

In December 1986 an extraordinary plenum of the PDPA Central Committee approved a policy of national reconciliation, involving negotiations with opposition groups, and the proposed formation of a coalition government of national unity. In early January 1987 a Supreme Extraordinary Commission for National Reconciliation, led by Abd ar-Rahim Hatif (the Chairman of the National Committee of the NFF), was formed to conduct the negotiations. The NFF was renamed the National Front (NF), and became a separate organization from the PDPA. The new policy of reconciliation won some support from former opponents, but the seven-party *mujahidin* alliance (Ittehad-i-Islami Afghan Mujahidin, Islamic Union of Afghan Mujahidin—IUAM), which was based in Peshawar, Pakistan, refused to observe the cease-fire or to participate in negotiations, while continuing to demand a complete and unconditional Soviet withdrawal from Afghanistan.

In July 1987, as part of the process of national reconciliation, several important developments occurred: a law permitting the formation of other political parties (according to certain provisions) was introduced; Najibullah announced that the PDPA would be prepared to share power with representatives of opposition groups in the event of the formation of a coalition government of national unity; and the draft of a new Constitution was approved by the Presidium of the Revolutionary Council. The main innovations incorporated in the draft Constitution were: the formation of a multi-party political system, under the auspices of the NF; the formation of a bicameral legislature, called the Meli Shura (National Assembly), composed of a Sena (Senate) and a Wolasi Jirga (House of Representatives); the granting of a permanent constitutional status to the PDPA; the bestowal of unlimited power on the President, who was to hold office for seven years; and the reversion of the name of the country from the Democratic Republic to the Republic of Afghanistan. A Loya Jirga ratified the new Constitution in November.

Meanwhile, a considerable proportion of the successful candidates in local elections held throughout the country in August 1987 were reported to be non-PDPA members. On 30 September Najibullah was unanimously elected as President of the Revolutionary Council, and Haji Muhammad Chamkani resumed his former post as First Vice-President. In order to strengthen his position, Najibullah ousted all the remaining supporters of former President Karmal from the Central Committee and Politburo of the PDPA in October. In the following month a Loya Jirga unanimously elected Najibullah as President of the State.

In April 1988 elections were held to both houses of the new National Assembly, which replaced the Revolutionary Council. Although the elections were boycotted by the *mujahidin*, the Government left vacant 50 of the 234 seats in the House of Representatives, and a small number of seats in the Senate, in the hope that the guerrillas would abandon their armed struggle and present their own representatives to participate in the new administration. The PDPA itself won only 46 seats in the House of Representatives, but was guaranteed support from the NF, which secured 45, and from the various newly recognized left-wing parties, which won a total of 24 seats. In May Dr Muhammad Hasan Sharq (a non-PDPA member and a Deputy Prime Minister since June 1987) replaced Keshtmand as Prime Minister, and in June a new Council of Ministers was appointed.

On 18 February 1989, following the completion of the withdrawal of Soviet troops from Afghanistan (see below), Najibullah implemented a government reorganization, involving the replacement of non-communist ministers with loyal PDPA members. On the same day, Prime Minister Sharq (who had been one of the main promoters of the policy of national reconciliation) resigned from his post and was replaced by Keshtmand. Following the declaration of a state of emergency by Najibullah (citing allegations of repeated violations of the Geneva accords by Pakistan and the USA—see below) on 19 February, a PDPA-dominated 20-member Supreme Council for the Defence of the Homeland was established. The Council, which was headed by President Najibullah and was composed of ministers, members of the PDPA Politburo and high-ranking military figures, assumed full responsibility for the country's economic, political and military policies (although the Council of Ministers continued to function).

In early March 1990 the Minister of Defence, Lt-Gen. Shahnawaz Tanay, with the alleged support of the air force and some divisions of the army, led an unsuccessful coup attempt against Najibullah's Government. Najibullah subsequently enacted thorough purges of PDPA and army leaders and decided to revert rapidly to some form of constitutional civilian government. On 20 May the state of emergency was lifted; the Supreme Council for the Defence of the Homeland was disbanded; and a new Council of Ministers, under the premiership of Fazle Haq Khalikyar, was appointed. At the end of the month a Loya Jirga was convened in Kabul, which ratified constitutional amendments, greatly reducing Afghanistan's socialist orientation; ending the PDPA's and the NF's monopoly over executive power and paving the way for fully democratic elections; introducing greater political and press freedom; encouraging the development of the private sector and further foreign investment; lessening the role of the State and affording greater prominence to Islam. The extensive powers of the presidency were, however, retained. In addition, in late June the PDPA changed its name to the Homeland Party (HP—Hizb-i Watan), and dissolved the Politburo and the Central Committee, replacing them with an Executive Board and a Central Council, respectively. The party adopted a new programme, of which the hallmark was hostility to ideology. Najibullah was unanimously elected as Chairman of the HP. An important factor in Najibullah's decision to continue with, and to extend, the process of national reconciliation was the fact that the USSR's own internal problems meant that the Soviet administration was unwilling to sustain, for much longer, the supplies of weapons, goods and credits that were helping to support the Kabul regime.

Fighting between the *mujahidin* and Afghan army units had begun in the eastern provinces after the 1978 coup and was aggravated by the implementation of unpopular social and economic reforms by the new administrations. The Afghan army relied heavily upon Soviet military aid in the form of weapons, equipment and expertise, but morale and resources were severely affected by defections to the rebels' ranks: numbers fell from around 80,000 men in 1978 to about 40,000 in 1985. During 1984–89 the guerrilla groups, which had been poorly armed at first, received ever-increasing support (both military and financial) from abroad, notably from the USA (which began to supply them with sophisticated anti-aircraft weapons in 1986), the United Kingdom and the People's Republic of China. Despite the Government's decision to seal the border with Pakistan, announced in September 1985, and the strong presence of Soviet forces there, foreign weapons continued to reach the guerrillas

via Pakistan. Many of the guerrillas established bases in the North-West Frontier Province of Pakistan (notably in the provincial capital, Peshawar). From 1985 the fighting intensified, especially in areas close to the border between Afghanistan and Pakistan. There were many violations of the border, involving shelling, bombing and incursions into neighbouring airspace. The general pattern of the war, however, remained the same: the regime held the main towns and a few strategic bases, and relied on bombing of both military and civilian targets, and occasional attacks in force, together with conciliatory measures such as the provision of funds for local development, while the rebel forces dominated rural areas and were able to cause serious disruption.

The civil war brought famine to parts of Afghanistan, and there was a mass movement of population from the countryside to Kabul, and of refugees to Pakistan and Iran. In mid-1988 a UNHCR estimate assessed the number of Afghan refugees in Pakistan at 3.15m., and the number in Iran at 2.35m. Supply convoys were often prevented from reaching the cities, owing to the repeated severing of major road links by the guerrillas. Kabul, in particular, began to suffer from severe shortages of food and fuel, which were only partially alleviated by airlifts of emergency aid supplies. As a result of the increasing danger and hardship, a number of countries temporarily closed their embassies in the capital.

From 1980 extensive international negotiations took place to try to achieve the complete withdrawal of Soviet forces from Afghanistan. Between June 1982 and September 1987 seven rounds of indirect talks took place between the Afghan and Pakistani Ministers of Foreign Affairs in Geneva, under the auspices of the UN. In October 1986 the USSR made a token withdrawal of six regiments (6,000–8,000 men) from Afghanistan. As a result of the discussions in Geneva, an agreement was finally signed on 14 April 1988. The Geneva accords consisted of five documents: detailed undertakings by Afghanistan and Pakistan, relating to non-intervention and non-interference in each other's affairs; international guarantees of Afghan neutrality (with the USA and the USSR as the principal guarantors); arrangements for the voluntary and safe return of Afghan refugees; a document linking the preceding documents with a timetable for a Soviet withdrawal; and the establishment of a UN monitoring force, which was to oversee both the Soviet troop departures and the return of the refugees. The withdrawal of Soviet troops (numbering 100,000, according to Soviet figures, or 115,000, according to Western sources) commenced on 15 May.

Neither the *mujahidin* nor Iran played any role in the formulation of the Geneva accords, and, in spite of protests by Pakistan, no agreement was incorporated regarding the composition of an interim coalition government in Afghanistan, or the 'symmetrical' cessation of Soviet aid to Najibullah's regime and US aid to the *mujahidin*. Therefore, despite the withdrawal of the Soviet troops, the supply of weapons to both sides was not halted, and the fighting continued. Pakistan repeatedly denied accusations that it had violated the accords by continuing to harbour Afghan guerrillas and to act as a conduit for the supply of weapons. At the end of November 1988 Soviet officials held direct talks with representatives of the *mujahidin* in Peshawar, Pakistan, the first such meeting since the start of the 10-year conflict. High-level discussions were held in early December in Saudi Arabia between Prof. Burhanuddin Rabbani, the Chairman of the IUAM, and the Soviet ambassador to Afghanistan. These discussions collapsed, however, when the *mujahidin* leaders reiterated their demand that no members of Najibullah's regime should be incorporated in any future Afghan government, while the Soviet officials continued to insist on a government role for the PDPA. In spite of the unabated violence, the USSR, adhering to the condition specified in the Geneva accords, had withdrawn all of its troops from Afghanistan by mid-February 1989.

In mid-1988 the *mujahidin* had intensified their military activities, attacking small provincial centres and launching missiles against major cities. By the end of 1990 the *mujahidin* had failed to achieve any significant military successes and their control was confined to rural areas (including several small provincial capitals). The guerrillas also failed to make any important advances on the political front. Talks between the IUAM and the Iranian-based Hizb-i Wahadat-i Islami (Islamic Unity Party), an alliance of eight Shi'ite Afghan resistance groups, repeatedly failed to reach any agreement as to the composition of a broadly-based interim government. Consequently, in February 1989 the IUAM convened its own Shura

(Assembly) in Rawalpindi, Pakistan, at which an interim government-in-exile (known as the Afghan Interim Government, AIG) was elected. The AIG, however, was officially recognized by only four countries. It also failed to gain any substantial support or recognition from the guerrilla commanders, who were beginning to establish their own unofficial alliances inside the country. In March, however, the AIG received a form of diplomatic recognition, when it was granted membership of the Organization of the Islamic Conference (OIC). In addition, in June the US Government appointed a special envoy to the *mujahidin*, with the rank of personal ambassador. In mid-1989 the unity of the *mujahidin* forces was seriously weakened by an increase in internecine violence among the various guerrilla groups, while the AIG was riven by disputes between the moderates and the fundamentalists. The USA, Saudi Arabia and Pakistan began to reduce financial aid and military supplies to the IUAM in Peshawar, and to undertake the difficult task of delivering weapons and money directly to guerrilla commanders and tribal leaders inside Afghanistan.

Following extensive negotiations with the regional powers involved in the crisis, the UN Secretary-General made a declaration in May 1991, setting out five principles for a settlement, the main points of which were: recognition of the national sovereignty of Afghanistan; the right of the Afghan people to choose their own government and political system; the establishment of an independent and authorized mechanism to oversee free and fair elections to a broadly-based government; a UN-monitored cease-fire; and the donation of sufficient financial aid to facilitate the return of the refugees and internal reconstruction. The declaration received the approval of the Afghan and Pakistani Governments, but was rejected by the AIG.

Reflecting its disenchantment with the guerrilla cause, the US Government substantially reduced its aid to the *mujahidin* in 1991. New military campaigns had been launched by the *mujahidin* in the second half of 1990 in an attempt to impress their international supporters, disrupt the return of refugees and obstruct contacts between the Government and moderate guerrillas. At the end of March 1991, following more than two weeks of heavy fighting, the south-eastern city of Khost was captured by the *mujahidin*, representing the most severe reversal sustained by the Government since the Soviet withdrawal. The *mujahidin* also carried out attacks on Gardez, Jalalabad, Ghazni, Qandahar and Herat in 1991.

An unexpected breakthrough towards resolving the Afghan crisis occurred in mid-September 1991, when the USA and the USSR announced that they would stop supplying arms to the warring factions, and would encourage other countries (namely Pakistan, Saudi Arabia and Iran) to do likewise. Although both the Afghan Government and the *mujahidin* welcomed this pledge, neither side showed any sign of implementing the proposed cease-fire, and, indeed, the fighting intensified around Kabul. In February 1992, however, the peace process was given a major boost when Pakistan made it clear that, rather than continuing actively to encourage the *mujahidin*, through arms supplies and training, it was urging all the guerrilla factions to support the five-point UN peace plan (see above). In doing so, Pakistan was effectively abandoning its insistence on the installation of a fundamentalist government in Kabul. There were growing fears, none the less, that the peace process might be placed in jeopardy by an increase in ethnic divisions within both the government forces and a number of *mujahidin* groups, between the majority Pashtuns and minority groups such as the Tajiks and Uzbeks. As a result of a mutiny staged by Uzbek militia forces in the Afghan army, under the command of Gen. Abdul Rashid Dostam, the northern town of Mazar-i-Sharif was captured by the *mujahidin* in March.

On 16 April 1992 events took an unexpected turn when Najibullah was forced to resign by his own ruling party, following the capture of the strategically important Bagram air base and the nearby town of Charikar, only about 50 km north of Kabul, by the Jamiat-i Islami guerrilla group under the command of the Tajik general, Ahmad Shah Masoud. Najibullah went into hiding in the capital, under UN protection, while one of the Vice-Presidents, Abd ar-Rahim Hatif, assumed the post of acting President. Within a few days of Najibullah's downfall, every major town in Afghanistan was under the control of different coalitions of *mujahidin* groups co-operating with disaffected army commanders. Masoud was given orders by the guerrilla leaders in Peshawar to secure Kabul. On 25 April the forces of both Masoud and of Gulbuddin Hekmatyar, the leader of a rival guerrilla group, the Pashtun-dominated Hizb-i Islami

(Islamic Party), whose men were massed to the south of the capital, entered Kabul. The army surrendered its key positions, and immediately the city was riven by *mujahidin* faction-fighting. The military council that had, a few days earlier, replaced the Government relinquished power to the *mujahidin*. Having discarded the UN's proposal to form a neutral body, the guerrilla leaders in Peshawar agreed to establish a 51-member interim Islamic Jihad Council, composed of military and religious leaders, which was to assume power in Kabul. The leader of the small, moderate Jebha-i-Nejat-i-Melli (National Liberation Front), Prof. Sibghatullah Mojaddedi, was to chair the Islamic Jihad Council for two months, after which period a 10-member Leadership Council, comprising *mujahidin* chiefs and presided over by the head of the Jamiat-i Islami, Prof. Burhanuddin Rabbani, would be set up for a period of four months. Within the six months a special council was to meet to designate an interim administration which was to hold power for up to a year pending elections.

Mojaddedi arrived in Kabul on 28 April 1992 as the President of the new interim administration. The Islamic Jihad Council was not, however, supported by Hekmatyar, whose radical stance differed substantially from Mojaddedi's more tolerant outlook. At the end of the month Hekmatyar's forces lost control of their last stronghold in the centre of Kabul. Within a few weeks the Government of the newly proclaimed Islamic State of Afghanistan had won almost universal diplomatic recognition, and by early May about one-half of the Islamic Jihad Council had arrived in the capital. An acting Council of Ministers was formed, in which Masoud was given the post of Minister of Defence and the premiership was set aside for Ustad Abdol Sabur Farid, a Tajik commander from the Hizb-i Islami (Hekmatyar declined to accept the post). As part of the process of 'Islamization', the death penalty was introduced, alcohol and narcotics were banned and the wearing of strict Islamic dress by all women was enforced. Despite Mojaddedi's repeated pleas to Hekmatyar and his followers to lay down their arms, Hekmatyar, who was particularly angered by the presence of Gen. Dostam's Uzbek forces in the capital, continued to bombard Kabul with artillery and indiscriminate rocket launches from various strongholds around the city, killing and wounding scores of citizens.

On 28 June 1992 Mojaddedi surrendered power to the Leadership Council, which immediately offered Burhanuddin Rabbani the presidency of the country and the concomitant responsibility for the interim Council of Ministers for four months, as set forth in the Peshawar Agreement (see above). In early July Farid assumed the premiership, which had been held open for him since late April. On assuming the presidency Rabbani announced the adoption of a new Islamic flag, the establishment of an economic council, which was to address the country's severe economic problems, and the appointment of a commission to draw up a new Constitution. A Deputy President was appointed in late July. In early August the withdrawal of the members of the Hizb-i Islami faction led by Maulvi Muhammad Yunus Khalis from the Leadership Council revealed serious rifts within the Government. A further problem was the continuing inter-*mujahidin* violence in Kabul. Within days the violence had escalated into a full-scale ground offensive, launched by Hekmatyar's forces against the capital. The airport was closed, hundreds of people were killed or wounded, and tens of thousands of civilians fled Kabul. In response, President Rabbani expelled Hekmatyar from the Leadership Council and dismissed Prime Minister Farid. Hekmatyar demanded the expulsion of the 75,000 Uzbek militia from Kabul as a precondition to peace talks, alleging that Gen. Dostam was still closely allied to former members of the communist regime. At the end of the month a cease-fire agreement was reached between Rabbani and Hekmatyar and, after a few days of relative peacefulness, the airport was reopened. Sporadic fighting involving various *mujahidin* and militia groups (notably Gen. Dostam's Uzbek forces) continued, however, in Kabul itself and in the provinces throughout the remainder of the year. At the end of October the Leadership Council agreed to extend Rabbani's tenure of the presidency by two months. On 30 December a special advisory council, known as the Resolution and Settlement Council (Shura-e Ahl-e Hal wa Aqd), which was composed of 1,335 tribal leaders, was convened in Kabul. The Council elected Rabbani, who was the sole candidate, as President of the country for a period of a further two years. In early January 1993 200 members of the advisory council were selected to constitute the future membership of the country's legislature.

The establishment of the advisory council and the re-election of President Rabbani provoked yet further heavy fighting in Kabul and other provinces in early 1993. Owing to the worsening violence, all Western diplomats had left the capital by the end of January. In early March, however, President Rabbani, Hekmatyar, Mojaddedi and leaders of other major *mujahidin* factions held negotiations in Islamabad, at the end of which a peace accord was signed. Under the terms of the accord, an interim Government was to be established, which would hold power for 18 months; President Rabbani was to remain as Head of State, and Hekmatyar (or his nominee) was to assume the premiership of the acting Council of Ministers; a cease-fire was to be imposed with immediate effect; legislative elections were to be held within six months; a 16-member defence commission was to be formed, which would be responsible for the establishment of a national army; and all weaponry was to be seized from the warring factions in an attempt to restore peace and order. The peace accord was officially approved and signed by the Governments of Pakistan, Saudi Arabia and Iran.

Confronted with the difficult task of satisfying the demands of all the *mujahidin* groups, Hekmatyar was not able to present a new Council of Ministers until late May 1993 (it was sworn in the following month). Each *mujahidin* faction was allocated two ministerial posts, with further positions left vacant for other representatives (representatives from Gen. Dostam's group of predominantly Uzbek militiamen—known collectively as the National Islamic Movement (NIM) (Jonbesh-i Melli-i Islami)— were offered two posts in July). One of Hekmatyar's most noteworthy decisions in the formation of the new Council of Ministers was to remove one of his most powerful rivals, Ahmad Shah Masoud, from the crucial post of Minister of Defence. The new Prime Minister promised to hold a general election by October. The temporary headquarters of the Government were situated in Charasiab, Hekmatyar's military base, about 25 km south of Kabul.

Despite the signing of the Islamabad peace accord in March 1993, the violence between the various *mujahidin* groups did not cease, and hundreds of people continued to be killed and wounded. The interim Government was beset by internal dissension and proved rather ineffectual. Hekmatyar refused to co-operate with Rabbani, and frequently demanded the President's resignation. In September, however, it was reported that a new draft Constitution (known as the Basic Law) had been drawn up and approved by a special commission, in preparation for the holding of a general election. The fighting intensified in late December, when Gen. Dostam transferred his allegiance to his hitherto arch-enemy, Hekmatyar, and the supporters of the two combined to confront the forces of Rabbani and Masoud. The violence spread throughout the provinces, resulting in large numbers of military and civilian casualties and the internal displacement of thousands of people. Various unsuccessful attempts were made in 1994 by neighbouring countries and by international organizations, such as the UN and the OIC, to achieve a negotiated settlement between the main warring factions. In late June the Supreme Court ruled that Rabbani could retain the presidency for a further six months, but failed to grant a similar extension to Hekmatyar's premiership. Although President Rabbani's extended term in office expired at the end of December, he did not resign.

In the latter half of 1994, a new, hitherto unknown, militant grouping emerged in Afghanistan, known as the Taliban (the plural form of 'Talib', meaning 'seeker of religious knowledge'). The movement, which at the outset comprised an estimated 25,000 fighters (the majority of whom were reported to be young Pashtun graduates of fundamentalist Islamist schools established by Afghan refugees in Pakistan), advocated the adoption of extremist practices, including the complete seclusion of women from society. Although initially claiming that they had no interest in actually assuming power in Afghanistan, the Taliban, who were led by Mola Mohammad Omar, won a major victory in October, when they captured the city of Qandahar from the forces of Hekmatyar, which had hitherto dominated the southern provinces of the country. In February 1995 the Taliban routed Hekmatyar's men from their headquarters in Charasiab, and within a month they controlled 10 provinces, mostly in southern and south-eastern Afghanistan. However, the Taliban retreated from their advance on Kabul when Rabbani's troops launched a massive counter-offensive. By mid-1995, with both the Taliban and Hekmatyar's men held in check, President Rabbani and his supporters were enjoying an unprecedented level of authority and confidence in Kabul and its environs. This

was reflected in Rabbani's reneging on his earlier promise of standing down from the presidency in late March and in the growing number of countries that were considering reopening their embassies in the Afghan capital (the Indian embassy reopened in May). In mid-1995 talks were held between Rabbani and the Taliban, but relations between the two sides remained extremely strained. In early September the Taliban achieved a notable gain when they captured the key north-western city of Herat and the surrounding province from government forces. The resurgence of the Taliban apparently provoked an attack on the Pakistani embassy in Kabul by hundreds of pro-Government demonstrators protesting against Pakistan's alleged support for the student militia; the embassy was destroyed by fire, one employee was killed and a number wounded (including the ambassador himself). In response, the Afghan ambassador to Pakistan and six other Afghan diplomats were expelled from Islamabad. In October the Taliban launched a massive ground and air assault on Kabul, but by early January 1996 had failed to breach the capital's defences. The constant bombardment of the besieged city, however, resulted in hundreds of civilian deaths, and the road blockades around the capital caused serious shortages of vital supplies.

Despite the holding of exploratory negotiations between the Rabbani Government and major opposition parties in the first quarter of 1996, the fighting in and around Kabul intensified. The President's attempts at conciliation finally proved successful, however, in late May when, in a critical development (known as the Mahipar Agreement), he persuaded Hekmatyar to rejoin the Government. Hekmatyar's forces arrived in the capital during May to defend the city against the Taliban. In late June Hekmatyar resumed the post of Prime Minister and President Rabbani appointed a new Council of Ministers in early July, which was to hold power for a period of six–12 months pending the staging of a general election. In addition, under the terms of the Mahipar Agreement, a Constitution to cover the interim period was drawn up and published.

The political situation was radically altered in late September 1996 when, as a culmination of two weeks of sweeping military advances (including the capture of the crucial eastern city of Jalalabad), the Taliban seized control of Kabul following fierce clashes with government troops, who fled northwards together with the deposed Government. One of the Taliban movement's first actions in the captured capital was the summary execution of former President Najibullah and his brother. On assuming power, the Taliban declared Afghanistan a 'complete' Islamic state and appointed an interim Council of Ministers, led by Mola Mohammad Rabbani, to administer the country (of which it now controlled about two-thirds). Pakistan, which was widely suspected of actively aiding the Islamist militia, was the first country officially to recognize the new regime. (By mid-November, however, few other countries or international organizations had followed suit—neither the UN, India, Russia nor Iran had given official recognition to the Taliban administration.) The Taliban imposed a strict and intimidatory Islamic code—women were not permitted to enter employment or be formally educated beyond the age of eight; television, non-religious music, gambling and alcohol were all banned; amputations and public stonings were enforced as forms of punishment; compulsory attendance at mosques by all men was introduced; and women were ordered into purdah.

Taliban hopes that the opposition would remain divided were thwarted following the formation in October 1996 of a powerful military and logistical alliance by Gen. Dostam, the former Minister of Defence, Masoud, and the leader of the Shi'ite Hizb-i Wahadat-i Islami, Gen. Abdol Karim Khalili. Gen. Dostam, who controlled 10 northern provinces, apparently decided to establish this unlikely alliance after cease-fire talks between himself and the Taliban broke down. By late October the anti-Taliban forces, whose leaders were now collectively known as the Supreme Council for the Defence of Afghanistan (the headquarters of which were situated in Gen. Dostam's stronghold of Mazar-i-Sharif), had launched a concerted offensive against Kabul in the hope of ousting the Islamist militia. Despite repeated calls for a cease-fire from various foreign governments and the UN and despite complaints by the human rights organization Amnesty International regarding civilian casualties and abuses of human rights, the fighting between the Taliban and the allied opposition continued into January 1997. In mid-January, following the rapid collapse of UN-sponsored talks in Islamabad, the Taliban launched an unexpected offensive, advancing north and capturing Bagram air base and the provincial capital of Charikar. By late January the Taliban had made significant military gains and had pushed the front line to about 100 km north of Kabul. There was a dramatic development in mid-May when, following the defection of the Uzbek Gen. Abdul Malik and his men to the Taliban, the latter were able to capture the strategically important northern town of Mazar-i-Sharif with relatively little bloodshed. Gen. Dostam was reported to have fled to Turkey, and his position as leader of the NIM was assumed by Gen. Malik. The Taliban now controlled about 80% of the country, including all of the major towns and cities. Their position was also strengthened by Pakistan's decision to be the first country to accord formal recognition to the Taliban Government (closely followed by Saudi Arabia and the United Arab Emirates—UAE). Taliban control of Mazar-i-Sharif, however, was extremely brief, and within only three days of entering the town the movement was in full retreat. It appeared that Gen. Malik's tenuous alliance with the Taliban had collapsed almost immediately and his troops, together with Shi'ite militia, forced the newcomers out after ferocious fighting. The Taliban were soundly routed, and by early June their forces had retreated almost 200 km south of Mazar-i-Sharif. Taliban officials later alleged that, following the recapture of Mazar-i-Sharif, about 3,000 Taliban prisoners-of-war were summarily executed by their captors.

The regional aspect of the Afghan conflict was highlighted at the beginning of June 1997 by the Taliban decision to close down the Iranian embassy in Kabul; the Iranian Government was widely suspected of actively aiding the anti-Taliban northern alliance. The alliance was reported to have been expanded and strengthened in early June by the inclusion of the forces of Hekmatyar and of the Mahaz-i-Melli-i-Islami (National Islamic Front), led by Pir Sayed Ahmad Gailani. This new coalition, which superseded the Supreme Council for the Defence of Afghanistan, was known as the United National Islamic Front for the Salvation of Afghanistan, commonly known as the United Front and the Northern Alliance. The United Front was the military wing of the exiled government, the Islamic State of Afghanistan. Despite the arrival of thousands of reinforcements from training camps in Pakistan (many of whom, however, were inexperienced teenagers), the Taliban suffered a series of military defeats in northern Afghanistan, and by late July the United Front forces were within firing range of Kabul, having recaptured Charikar and the air base at Bagram. In the same month the UN Security Council demanded a cease-fire and an end to all foreign intervention in Afghanistan. In mid-1997 it was widely believed that the Taliban were supported by Pakistan and Saudi Arabia; on the opposing side, to various degrees, were ranged Iran, India, the Central Asian states (which feared the encroachment of Taliban fundamentalism) and Russia.

In mid-August 1997 it was reported that the United Front had appointed a new Government, based in Mazar-i-Sharif, with Rabbani continuing as President, Abdorrahim Ghafurzai as Prime Minister, Masoud as Minister of Defence and Gen. Malik as Minister of Foreign Affairs. The former Prime Minister in the anti-Taliban administration, Gulbuddin Hekmatyar, refused to recognize the new Government. Within a few days of its appointment, however, seven members of the new Government, including Prime Minister Ghafurzai, were killed in an aeroplane crash. In late August the anti-Taliban opposition alliance appointed Abdolghaffur Rawanfarhadi as new Prime Minister.

In September 1997 Gen. Dostam was reported to have returned to Mazar-i-Sharif from Turkey, and in the following month the member parties of the United Front re-elected him as commander of the forces of the alliance and appointed him as Vice-President of the anti-Taliban administration. However, there were reports of a bitter rivalry between Gen. Dostam and Gen. Malik and skirmishes between their respective forces. Dostam's battle for supremacy with his rival led him to make overtures to the Taliban, including offers of exchanges of prisoners-of-war. Gen. Dostam also accused Gen. Malik of having massacred about 3,000 Taliban prisoners earlier in the year. By late November Gen. Dostam had resumed the leadership of the NIM, ousting Gen. Malik. In late October the Taliban unilaterally decided to change the country's name to the Islamic Emirate of Afghanistan and altered the state flag, moves that were condemned by the opposition alliance and all of Afghanistan's neighbours except Pakistan. In late 1997 the World Food Programme (WFP) launched an emergency operation to help people facing starvation in the impoverished central region of Hazarajat (held by the Shi'ite Hizb-i Wahadat-i Islami), which had been blockaded by the Taliban since August. In January

1998, however, the UN was forced to suspend its airlifts of emergency supplies when Taliban aircraft bombed the area. Meanwhile, in mid-December 1997 the UN Security Council issued a communiqué expressing its concern at the alleged massacres of civilians and prisoners-of-war being perpetrated by various factions in Afghanistan. In May 1998 a UN exploratory mission visited the sites of alleged atrocities to assess the feasibility of a full-scale war-crimes investigation being carried out.

In late March 1998 the UN ceased operating aid programmes in the southern province of Qandahar (where the political headquarters of the Taliban were located) following attacks on staff and constant harassment by the Taliban. In the same month there were reports of factional fighting between rival members of the United Front in and around Mazar-i-Sharif, highlighting the fragile nature of the anti-Taliban alliance. In late April, following the launch of a major diplomatic initiative by the USA, the Taliban and the United Front held talks, sponsored by the UN and the OIC, in Islamabad, the first formal peace negotiations between the two opposing sides for more than a year. In early May, however, the talks broke down, and fighting resumed to the north of Kabul. One of the main reasons cited for the failure of the negotiations was the refusal of the Taliban to lift the blockade on Hazarajat, where thousands of people were reported to be at risk of imminent starvation.

Relations between the Taliban Government and the UN deteriorated in June 1998, as a result of the former's decision to close more than 100 private schools and numerous small, home-based vocational courses in Kabul, many of which were educating girls. The living conditions of the 1.2m. inhabitants of the capital were expected to worsen considerably as a result of the expulsion in July of almost all international aid agencies by the Taliban.

On 1 August 1998 the Taliban captured the northern city of Shiberghan, Gen. Dostam's new headquarters, after a number of his Uzbek commanders allegedly accepted bribes from the Taliban and switched allegiance. Gen. Dostam was reported to have fled to the Uzbek border and thence to Turkey. Following the recapture of Mazar-i-Sharif by the Taliban (who allegedly now included considerable numbers of extremist volunteers from various other Islamic countries, including Pakistan, Saudi Arabia, Algeria and Egypt) in early August, 10 Iranian diplomats and one Iranian journalist who were based in the city were reported to have been captured and killed by Taliban militia. The Taliban, however, initially denied any knowledge of the whereabouts of the Iranian nationals. In early September Afghanistan and Iran appeared to be on the verge of open warfare, as 70,000 Iranian troops were deployed on the mutual border, and it emerged that nine of the missing Iranian nationals had, in fact, been murdered by members of the Taliban as they stormed Mazar-i-Sharif. (It was later reported that 2,000–6,000 Shi'ite Hazara civilians had been systematically massacred by the guerrillas after recapturing the city.) Both Iran and Afghanistan massed more troops on the border; by mid-September 500,000 Iranian troops had reportedly been placed on full military alert. In mid-October, in an attempt to defuse the tension, the Taliban agreed to free all Iranian prisoners being held in Afghanistan and to punish those responsible for the killing of the nine Iranian diplomats (or military advisers, according to the Taliban). By the end of the year the situation appeared much calmer, with the Taliban having expressed regret for the deaths of the Iranian nationals and Iran having scaled down its border forces and having announced that it had no intention of invading Afghanistan.

Meanwhile, on 20 August 1998 the USA launched simultaneous air-strikes against alleged terrorist bases in eastern Afghanistan and Sudan, reportedly operated by the Saudi-born militant leader of the al-Qa'ida (Base) organization, Osama bin Laden (who was supported by the Taliban), in retaliation for the bombing of two US embassies in East Africa earlier that month. Many aid agencies withdrew their remaining expatriate staff from Afghanistan, fearing terrorist acts of vengeance. In September the Taliban suffered a considerable set-back when Saudi Arabia (one of only three countries officially to recognize the regime) withdrew its funding and political support and recalled its envoy from Kabul. The decision by the Saudi Government substantially to downgrade its relations with the Taliban appeared to have been prompted by its opposition to the reported brutality of the guerrilla authorities and to their sheltering of bin Laden. In the following month the Taliban stated that, although they were not willing to extradite the Saudi dissident, in the event of a lawsuit being filed against him, they would be prepared to place him on trial in Afghanistan. The Taliban also insisted that bin Laden (who had reportedly been resident in Afghanistan for at least two years) was under close supervision, with his activities and media access suitably restricted. In late November evidence submitted by the US Government to the Afghan Supreme Court was deemed by the latter as inadequate grounds for bin Laden's arrest.

In mid-September 1998 the Taliban captured the capital of Bamian Province, a Shi'ite stronghold; this victory meant that any substantial anti-Taliban opposition was effectively restricted to Masoud's stronghold in north-eastern Afghanistan. Taliban advances in the north alarmed Russia and the Central Asian states, which feared the unsettling potential of a militant Islamist army along their southern borders. In December the UN Security Council threatened the Taliban with the imposition of sanctions and called on the regime to commence negotiations with the opposition. Pakistan, on the other hand, demonstrated its diplomatic isolation with regard to the Afghan situation, by defending the Taliban and urging the other members of the UN to recognize their government.

In January 1999 it was reported that the United Front had established a multi-ethnic Supreme Military Council, under the command of Masoud, the aim of which was to give fresh impetus to the anti-Taliban movement and to co-ordinate manoeuvres against Taliban forces in northern Afghanistan. Despite a certain degree of optimism being raised by the holding of UN-monitored direct peace talks between representatives of the Taliban and the United Front in February, March and July, ultimately very little was achieved as a result of the negotiations. In March, however, the first UN personnel returned to Afghanistan since their evacuation in August 1998 (following the murder of three UN employees); this represented the beginning of a phased return of UN international staff to Afghanistan.

In July 1999, following reports that bin Laden was being sheltered in eastern Afghanistan, the USA imposed financial and economic sanctions on the Taliban regime in a further attempt to persuade it to hand over the militant leader (who the US authorities suspected of planning more atrocities) to stand trial in the USA. In response, the Taliban claimed that the sanctions would have very little impact and again refused to extradite bin Laden. In the following month 10 people were killed when a large bomb exploded outside the residence of the Taliban leader, Mola Mohammad Omar, in Qandahar. In late October the Taliban leader announced an extensive reorganization of key civilian, military and diplomatic posts, including changes in the Council of Ministers. Of especial note was the appointment of an English-speaking moderate, Wakil Ahmad Motawakkil, to the post of Minister of Foreign Affairs.

Meanwhile, following the collapse of the peace talks in Tashkent in July 1999, the Taliban launched a massive offensive against the United Front in the Panjshir Valley in early August; tens of thousands of (mainly Tajik) civilians were displaced in the fighting. Masoud rapidly instigated a devastating counter-attack, and the Taliban were forced into a swift retreat towards Kabul.

The Taliban continued to campaign for international recognition, to no avail. At the 1999 session of the UN General Assembly (held in September–November) the UN again rejected the Taliban request to represent Afghanistan; the seat remained under the control of President Rabbani, the leader of the 'Islamic State of Afghanistan'. In October 1999 the UN Secretary-General's Special Envoy to Afghanistan, Lakhdar Brahimi, announced his withdrawal from his mission, owing to the lack of progress (and particularly to the alleged negative attitude of the Taliban). In February 2000 Francesc Vendrell was appointed Head of the UN Special Mission to Afghanistan and Personal Representative of the UN Secretary-General, with the rank of Assistant Secretary-General. Relations between the UN and Afghanistan, however, remained tense, culminating in the UN's temporary withdrawal of its expatriate staff from Qandahar at the end of March, following an assault on UN offices by the Taliban.

In mid-November 1999 the UN Security Council imposed an embargo on all Taliban-controlled overseas assets and a ban on the international flights of the national airline, Ariana Afghan Airlines, as a result of the Afghan regime's continuing refusal to relinquish the suspected terrorist leader, bin Laden, to stand trial in the USA or in a third (possibly Islamic) country. Following the imposition of the sanctions, there were reports of large-scale demonstrations throughout Afghanistan, and inter-

national aid organizations once again came under attack. The impact of the sanctions was expected to be alleviated, however, by the reopening of key trade routes along the Afghan–Iranian border in late November. The Taliban Government expressed hopes that the trade with Iran would compensate for the significant decrease in imports of wheat and flour from Pakistan caused by the recent imposition of stricter border controls by the new military regime in Pakistan. Although the price of basic foodstuffs in Kabul and other towns duly declined dramatically as a result of renewed trade with Iran, the general economic circumstances in Kabul worsened. In February 2000 the UN relaxed the sanctions to permit the Taliban to operate flights to Mecca, in Saudi Arabia. In October an agreement was signed to allow weekly flights from Sharjah, in the UAE, to Qandahar, in southern Afghanistan.

In late December 1999 the Taliban attained some international standing when an Indian Airlines aircraft was hijacked by a group of Kashmiri separatists. The aeroplane, en route from Kathmandu (Nepal) to Delhi (India), eventually landed in Qandahar. Although initially the Taliban were prepared to attack the aircraft, they were deterred from doing so and eventually persuaded the hijackers to reduce their demands. Having released the passengers, the hijackers were allowed to leave Qandahar. In early February 2000 an Ariana Afghan Airlines civilian passenger aircraft on a domestic flight from Kabul to Mazar-i-Sharif was hijacked by a group of Afghan nationals. The aeroplane was diverted via Central Asia and Russia to Stansted airport in the United Kingdom. The hijackers surrendered, following several days of negotiations, during which they did not repeat their initial demand for the release of Ismail Khan (the anti-Taliban rebel leader and former governor of Herat, known as the 'Lion of Herat', imprisoned by the Taliban in Afghanistan). Some of the passengers returned to Afghanistan, while more than 70 sought asylum in the United Kingdom. In December 2001 nine men were convicted in the United Kingdom of hijacking, false imprisonment and possession of weapons.

During 2000 the Taliban and United Front suffered internal discord, with defections of senior officials occurring on both sides. In March a partial reorganization of the Taliban Interim Council of Ministers was announced. Heavy fighting, concentrated in the north of Kabul, resumed in early March. In the same month Ismail Khan escaped from prison in Qandahar and fled to Iran. The OIC hosted peace negotiations between representatives of the Taliban and the United Front in March and May, during which the two parties decided to exchange prisoners-of-war. No agreement, however, was reached on a ceasefire. In early June there was renewed fighting in northern and central Afghanistan, and by the end of July the Taliban had acquired more territory in the north of the country. As the fighting intensified throughout August, the Taliban became more confident of victory in the north, reopening training camps that had been previously closed down owing to international pressure. A minor reorganization of the Taliban Interim Council of Ministers was carried out in late August.

At the beginning of September 2000 the Taliban captured Taloqan, the capital of Takhar province in the north of Afghanistan and the headquarters of the United Front. This victory represented a serious military and political set-back for Masoud and the United Front. In December the Taliban and the United Front entered negotiations conducted by Francesc Vendrell. Meanwhile, the conflict exacerbated the effects of severe drought and famine, which the country had endured from early 2000.

Despite renewed attempts by the Taliban from September 2000 to end their diplomatic isolation, the UN continued to refute the Taliban claim to the Afghan seat at the UN. In early December Russia and the USA proposed a UN Security Council Resolution urging stricter sanctions against the Taliban. The possibility of tighter sanctions caused tension in Kabul, as a result of which the UN began to remove its foreign staff from the country. A few days later the UN Security Council passed a resolution, which stated that unless the Taliban surrendered bin Laden and closed down militant training camps by 19 January 2001, the international community would impose an arms embargo on the Taliban, tighten an existing embargo on flights and the 'freeze' on Taliban assets abroad, restrict the sale of chemicals used to produce heroin from poppies and close Ariana Afghan Airlines offices abroad. The weapons embargo would not affect the anti-Taliban forces. The Taliban refused to concede to the demands and, immediately after the UN's decision, shut down the UN special mission to Afghanistan and cancelled planned peace negotiations. By early January 2001 24 of the original 64 UN foreign workers had returned to Kabul. The sanctions were imposed in mid-January. Consequently, Francesc Vendrell's attempts to persuade the Taliban and their opposition to participate in open-ended negotiations collapsed.

In early January 2001 the Taliban reportedly detained and shot 300 male civilians, mainly Hazaras, in Yakaolang district. In mid-January the UN Secretary-General, Kofi Annan, expressed concern about reports of deliberate civilian killings and human rights violations and demanded a prompt investigation into the allegations. The Taliban, denying the claims, refused foreigners access to the town. However, United Front forces uncovered evidence of the massacre when they recaptured Bamian city, the provincial capital, in mid-February. A report by the human rights organization Human Rights Watch containing evidence given by eyewitnesses, confirmed that 170 men had been killed and that serious human rights violations had been committed. In mid-June the Taliban set fire to more than 4,500 houses and 500 shops and buildings in the town of Yakaolang, killing many Hazaras, after recapturing the area. On 26 February the Taliban ordered the destruction of all statues in Afghanistan depicting living creatures, including the world's tallest standing Buddhas in Bamian. Despite intense international opposition, destruction of Afghanistan's pre-Islamic cultural heritage was carried out in March. However, Hindu and Sikh statues, acknowledged as fundamental to the respective religious practices, were preserved. The order contravened a 1999 decree, which ordered the preservation of all ancient relics, thereby prompting speculation that members of bin Laden's al-Qa'ida had taken control of the Taliban, by ousting the more moderate leaders.

In mid-April 2001 the Chairman of the Taliban Interim Council of Ministers, and Gen. Commander of the Armed Forces of the Taliban, Mola Mohammad Rabbani, died, owing to illness. He was later replaced as Gen. Commander by his brother, Mola Ahmed. In May all UN political staff left Afghanistan in accordance with a Taliban order, a consequence of fresh sanctions imposed on the Taliban in January. At the end of the month the Taliban issued a decree commanding all non-Muslim minorities to display distinctive yellow badges or cloths as marks of identification. Sikhs were distinguished by their turbans and were thus not required to identify themselves. This pronouncement provoked international outrage; the Taliban defended their decision, claiming that they intended to prevent the unnecessary detention of non-Muslims for not conducting Muslim practices. At the end of June, however, the Taliban yielded to international pressure and withdrew their controversial decree. The militant policies of the Taliban caused increasing difficulties for humanitarian agencies. In June WFP threatened to close down its 130 bakeries in Kabul unless the Taliban withdrew their restriction on the employment of Afghan women to conduct an essential survey of food requirements in the capital. However, WFP was faced with a dilemma: although the employment of women was forbidden, male employees were not allowed direct contact with females. A compromise was reached to allow the bakeries to continue operating. In July the Taliban issued another set of controversial edicts: the use of the internet was outlawed; women were banned from visiting picnic areas; and items such as tape recorders, telephone sets, musical instruments and lipstick were proscribed as non-Islamic.

In early August 2001 eight foreign and 16 Afghan aid workers of a German-based Christian non-governmental organization were arrested by the Taliban on charges of Christian proselytization. A trial under the rules of *Shari'a* (Islamic religious law) of the foreign aid workers began in early September. Shortly afterwards the Taliban offer to release the detained humanitarian workers in return for the release of Sheikh Omar Abdul Rahman, an Egyptian militant Islamist sentenced to life imprisonment in the USA, was rejected. Meanwhile, the Taliban closed down two other Christian aid organizations and ordered the foreign staff to leave the country.

At the end of June 2001 the US ambassador to Pakistan issued a statement in which he warned the Taliban that they would be held accountable if bin Laden carried out an attack against US interests. In response, the Taliban Minister of Foreign Affairs stated that the regime was not responsible for safeguarding US security outside Afghanistan. In late July the UN Security Council adopted a resolution which reinforced the sanctions imposed in January. Some 15 UN officials were to be posted in and around Afghanistan to monitor the success of the existing arms embargo. The resolution was censured for

focusing solely on the Taliban and for failing to curb the United Front's arms supply.

Following the coup in Pakistan in October 1999, there were indications that relations between the Taliban and the new Pakistani administration, headed by Gen. Pervez Musharraf, might not prove as amicable as they had been since 1996. In his first major address to the Pakistani nation shortly after assuming power, Gen. Musharraf pledged to work for a 'truly representative government' in Afghanistan, and in the following month the State Bank of Pakistan complied with the UN sanctions in ordering a 'freeze' on all Taliban financial assets in Pakistan. In late January 2000, however, a delegation of the Islamic Emirate of Afghanistan, led by the Chairman of the Taliban Interim Council of Ministers, accepted a formal invitation to enter negotiations with Pakistani officials. Pakistan continued to offer economic aid and support to the Taliban and condemned the UN sanctions against Afghanistan. Although Gen. Musharraf strongly denied giving military assistance to the Taliban, allegations relating to the involvement of Pakistan's special forces in the Taliban campaign grew, following the latter's successful offensive in August–September 2000.

In the latter half of 1999 it was reported that the Taliban had moderated their original policy regarding female education by officially sanctioning the opening of about 13 schools for girls (up to the age of 12) in Kabul and its environs; the majority of the new schools were funded by international organizations. In May 2000, however, Amnesty International's annual report on human rights violations criticized the Taliban regime's alleged violation of women's rights. Two reports presented to the 56th session of the UN Commission on Human Rights, held in March/April, also censured the alleged human rights violations committed by the Taliban. A report published by Human Rights Watch in July 2001, however, stated that the Taliban were not solely responsible for the violence in Afghanistan. The report criticized the United Front and blamed Russia and Iran for contributing to the long-lasting conflict by donating significant military support to the opposition. The report also censured the Pakistani Government and its intelligence agencies for training and arming Taliban forces.

In 1998–99 the Taliban regime, which remained almost completely isolated in diplomatic and political terms world-wide, fostered relations with the People's Republic of China. China's investment in Afghanistan over this period was the highest among the country's limited foreign investors. The Taliban continued to encourage better relations with China in 2000; in mid-December a Chinese delegation was granted a rare meeting with the Taliban leader, Mola Mohammad Omar, during a visit to Afghanistan. In September 2001 the two parties signed a memorandum of understanding on economic co-operation. The Taliban Government's relations with Russia, however, deteriorated when the former officially recognized the separatist Islamic republic of Chechnya and allowed a so-called Chechen embassy to open in Kabul in January 2000. In mid-2000, furthermore, Russia threatened to use air-strikes against those Taliban bases in Afghanistan suspected of protecting and supporting Chechen rebels and Islamist militants from Central Asia.

On 9 September 2001 Masoud was seriously injured in an attack by suicide bombers; some six days later he died. His deputy, Gen. Muhammed Fahim, was appointed acting military leader of the United Front. Evidence that emerged from deserted al-Qa'ida camps following the fall of the Taliban in Kabul in mid-November indicated that the Arab suicide bombers were linked to bin Laden.

The situation in Afghanistan drastically changed as a result of the terrorist attacks on New York and Washington, DC, USA on 11 September 2001. Although bin Laden denied his involvement in the attacks, some two days after the events the US Secretary of State, Colin Powell, publicly identified bin Laden and his al-Qa'ida organization as principally responsible. The Taliban initially claimed that neither bin Laden nor Afghanistan had the means to carry out the attacks, warning that they would retaliate if the USA attacked Afghanistan. On 16 September the UN imposed diplomatic sanctions and an arms embargo on the Taliban. Meanwhile, the USA began to form an anti-terrorist coalition, with the assistance of the United Kingdom.

Pakistan, a supporter of the Taliban, under considerable pressure reversed its policy and agreed to co-operate with the US-led coalition. On 17 September 2001 a Pakistani delegation issued Taliban leaders with an ultimatum to surrender bin Laden or face retaliation from the USA. A few days later a *shura* (council) of Afghan clerics under the leadership of Mola Mohammad Omar issued an edict for bin Laden to leave Afghanistan voluntarily. The *shura* also demanded that the UN and OIC held independent investigations, and threatened to instigate a *jihad* (holy war) if the USA attacked Afghanistan. US officials, calling for unconditional surrender, considered the edict insufficient. At the same time US President George W. Bush warned that the Taliban would also be targeted if they refused to extradite bin Laden and the rest of al-Qa'ida. It remained highly improbable that the Taliban would surrender bin Laden, even though they reportedly asked to see evidence of the al-Qa'ida leader's involvement in the terrorist attacks, a request rejected by the USA. Al-Qa'ida had become increasingly involved in Taliban affairs: in late August bin Laden reportedly was appointed Commander-in-Chief of the Taliban forces.

In the mean time, the USA deployed aircraft around Afghanistan, in preparation for attack. Pakistan and Uzbekistan agreed to grant US forces access to their air bases for emergency operations; the latter would also allow search-and-rescue operations to take place from its bases. Tajikistan consented to its bases being used for humanitarian operations and Kyrgyzstan opened its airspace to military aircraft; two months later Tajikistan and Kyrgyzstan agreed to give the US-led coalition access to their military bases. Meanwhile, in September 2001 the UAE and Saudi Arabia severed diplomatic links with the Taliban. Pakistan closed its embassy, but maintained diplomatic relations. The US-led coalition was strengthened by Russia's offer of access to its airspace for humanitarian missions, of direct participation in search-and-rescue operations and of arms shipments to United Front forces. Saudi Arabia, however, refused to allow the USA to use its military bases, although it granted access to its airspace.

The Taliban responded to the developments with preparations for *jihad*. Tens of thousands of Taliban troops were reportedly mobilized. In a statement to Pakistani news agencies Mola Mohammad Omar defended the attacks on the USA, declaring that they were the result of the US Government's 'wrong policies'. He also repeated that bin Laden was incapable of such attacks and warned the USA that to eliminate terrorism it should withdraw from the Middle East and stop supporting Israel. On 26 September 2001 thousands of protesters set on fire the abandoned US embassy in Kabul. The next day Taliban officials announced that an edict had been delivered to bin Laden ordering him to leave the country. The US Government dismissed the edict and restated demands for the Taliban to surrender bin Laden to US authorities. The USA also rejected an offer by Mola Mohammad Omar to enter negotiations regarding the extradition of bin Laden. At the end of September US and British military officials confirmed that special military forces had entered Afghanistan to prepare for a planned offensive against al-Qa'ida and the Taliban. In the mean time, there were signs that discipline among the Taliban forces was declining; the religious police reportedly had deserted the streets of Kabul by the end of September.

The United Front suffered a serious set-back when Masoud was shot days before the terrorist attacks. However, speculation that the United Front would receive military assistance from the anti-terrorist coalition as a result of the likely military intervention in Afghanistan encouraged the anti-Taliban coalition, which reported military successes against the Taliban in late September 2001. On 1 October leaders of the United Front officially agreed with the former King of Afghanistan, Mohammad Zahir Shah, to establish a 120-member Supreme Council for National Unity, a *de facto* government to be in place until the convening of a Loya Jirga which would select a new government representing the various social and ethnic groups of Afghanistan. The Loya Jirga could also draw defectors from the Taliban, who were also members of the majority Pashtun ethnic group. The alliance received US approval; Pakistan, however, opposed the United Front and supported the inclusion of Taliban defectors and extremist Pashtuns in the new government. In early October there were reports that the USA was militarily assisting anti-Taliban groups within Afghanistan.

The Taliban reportedly repeated their request to enter negotiations with the US-led coalition in early October 2001, an offer rejected by the US President. Meanwhile, the Taliban continued forcibly to conscript men to bolster their army, which in early October numbered 40,000 fighters. There were reports that al-Qa'ida provided the Taliban with 10,000 fighters. On 2 October NATO declared that it had received evidence from the USA that confirmed bin Laden's responsibility for the terrorist attacks.

Some two days later the Pakistani Government announced that it had seen proof convincing enough to prosecute bin Laden in a court. The evidence also incriminated other members of al-Qa'ida and the Taliban regime.

A British journalist was arrested by the Taliban in late September 2001 on suspicion of spying while travelling undercover in Afghanistan without any official documents or permission and was released in early October and sent to Pakistan under the direct order of Mola Mohammad Omar. It was reported that a delegation from Pakistan had negotiated with the Taliban leader to secure the journalist's release. In the mean time, the trial of the foreign aid workers continued. On 6 October an offer by a Taliban official to release the detainees in exchange for the withdrawal of the US-led military threats was dismissed. In mid-November the aid workers were rescued by anti-Taliban fighters and flown by helicopter to Pakistan. On 9 October a French journalist and two Pakistani journalists were arrested by the Taliban on suspicion of spying. They were released in early November.

The events in Afghanistan were detrimental to the relief effort in the country. On 12 September 2001 the UN and other aid organizations began to remove their foreign staff from Afghanistan, owing to fears that the USA would launch retaliatory attacks against al-Qa'ida and the Taliban. Less than two weeks later the Taliban seized the UN Kabul office and shut down the Afghan communications network. At the same time, Taliban forces stole WFP's remaining 1,400 metric tons of food intended for internally displaced refugees, and disrupted the work of Afghan aid workers. The number of displaced people increased considerably; although accurate estimates of new refugees were not known, some reports estimated that 1.5m. Afghans had abandoned their homes in the latter half of September. Pakistan restricted entry to those at the border considered to be most in need of assistance. Thousands of refugees managed to enter Pakistan illegally, nevertheless. At the end of September communications were restored with Afghan humanitarian workers. WFP resumed emergency food deliveries to Kabul and Herat and northern Afghanistan on a trial basis; local aid workers were expected to distribute the aid. At the same time the Red Cross transported medical supplies to Kabul. In early October the US President announced a humanitarian aid programme for Afghans in order to undermine the Taliban and to show Muslim countries that the USA was planning war against terrorism and not Islam. However, the proposal to link humanitarian aid with a pending military operation concerned humanitarian organizations.

On the evening of 7 October 2001 US-led forces began the aerial bombardment of suspected al-Qa'ida camps and strategic Taliban positions in Afghanistan. In addition to military strikes, aircraft released food and medicine parcels to Afghan civilians near the southern border with Pakistan; leaflets were also dropped offering protection and a reward in return for information on the whereabouts of al-Qa'ida leaders. It was later announced that several hundred US troops were to be deployed at bases in Pakistan. The Taliban responded to the air-strikes by lifting communications restrictions on bin Laden, enabling him to carry out a 'war' against the USA. Mola Mohammad Omar appealed to all Muslims to help defend Afghanistan, and as a result several thousand pupils of *madrassas* (mosque schools) in Pakistan and some Arab countries arrived in Afghanistan during October. A pre-recorded videotape of bin Laden's response to the military strikes was broadcast by the Qatar-based satellite television company Al-Jazeera. In the recording bin Laden declared war on the 'infidels' and warned the USA that attacks against it would continue until it withdrew from the Middle East. Although he did not claim responsibility for the attacks, bin Laden's comments were widely seen to be an implicit admission of his organization's involvement. Bin Laden also encouraged Muslims in countries that had offered assistance to the anti-terrorist coalition to rebel against their Governments, thus provoking the sentiment that the US-led military strikes were against Afghanistan and Islam, as opposed to terrorism. One week after the military operation commenced a senior Taliban official offered to extradite bin Laden to a third country in return for an end to the bombing if the USA presented evidence of bin Laden's culpability. The US President rejected this offer, declaring the surrender of bin Laden and his closest colleagues to US authorities as 'non-negotiable'.

The US-led military operation, named 'Operation Enduring Freedom', achieved rapid results. Some two days after the bombing began it was reported that 40 Taliban commanders and

1,200 fighters had defected to the opposition. After 10 days President George W. Bush announced that the Taliban regime's air defences had been destroyed. The nature of the attack changed when US ground forces began an assault on Afghanistan on 20 October 2001. Some three days later it was announced that all of the identified al-Qa'ida training camps had been destroyed by air-strikes. The US-led military operation, however, also incurred failures, which resulted in civilian deaths. The Red Cross and UN buildings, as well as non-Taliban villages, were struck by stray missiles. Taliban claims of major casualties and widespread damage to civilian property were occasionally supported by civilians. According to the Taliban, about 1,000 civilians had been killed in the bombings in October, a claim refuted by the US-led coalition. Evidence of civilian casualties adversely affected support for the US-led military operation. Saudi Arabia, which had hitherto remained silent about the military strikes, voiced its discontent in mid-October. In addition, tension rose in Pakistan; thousands of pro-Taliban fighters attempted to cross the border into Afghanistan. The USA's strategy also concerned members of the United Front; the bombing had not transformed the military balance in Afghanistan and by the end of October the United Front forces were still outnumbered. Nevertheless, rival commanders in the United Front launched a joint assault against the Taliban to recapture Mazar-i-Sharif and Taloqan. US servicemen were also killed in the conflict. It was hoped that the bombing would uncover the location of bin Laden and his closest associates, but by the end of October the whereabouts of the Islamist fundamentalist leaders were still unknown.

Initially, the US-led coalition avoided targeting Kabul in order to prevent the fractious United Front from capturing the capital. There were fears that while no alternative transitional government existed, the defeat of the Taliban in Kabul and other major cities would leave a power vacuum, resulting in anarchy. Some members of the United Front also voiced their concerns over occupying Kabul without a mandate; however, others regarded this strategy as a US-Pakistani plot to prevent the anti-Taliban opposition from advancing on Kabul and began to plan an early assault. In the mean time, the USA, the United Kingdom, other UN Security Council members and countries neighbouring Afghanistan began discussions for a broad-based transitional government for Afghanistan. At a meeting of United Front leaders in mid-October 2001 it was decided that the alliance would postpone an attack on Kabul for at least one month. At the same time, a delegation headed by the moderate religious leader, Pir Sayed Ahmad Gailani, held negotiations with the former King, Zahir Shah, in Rome, Italy, during which Gailani agreed to create a council, to be led by the former King. However, a meeting of more than 1,000 exiled Afghan commanders and tribal elders, chaired by Gailani, in Pakistan in late October revealed deep divisions between rival opposition groups. Some warned against the inclusion of the United Front, which was mainly composed of Tajiks, Uzbeks and Hazaras, in a transitional government that was to represent a majority Pashtun population. Senior representatives of the United Front and the former King were absent from the assembly. The outcome of the meeting caused grave concern for Western Governments and the UN; many believed that Pakistan had sanctioned the conference in an attempt to encourage a resolute stand against support given by the West to the United Front. Plans to establish an alternative transitional council were hampered further by the capture and assassination of the Pashtun leader Abdul Haq by the Taliban. Haq entered Afghanistan on 21 October to attempt to mobilize Pashtuns to rebel against the Taliban; he was killed five days later.

The UN Secretary-General appointed a special representative for Afghanistan, Lakhdar Brahimi, to assist the formation of a transitional government. His first task was to negotiate an agreement between Afghanistan's neighbours regarding the council's composition. The USA had already requested the UN to supply a peace-keeping force that could secure Kabul; the UN refused, stating that it could not become involved while the war continued. Meanwhile, the humanitarian situation worsened. On 10 October 2001 the UN resumed food aid. On 12 October the UN High Commissioner for Human Rights called for a temporary halt to air-strikes to allow aid to reach up to 2m. civilians in Afghanistan. Other aid agencies repeated this call a few days later; however, the request was not heeded. Efforts to provide humanitarian and medical aid were occasionally thwarted by the theft of supplies, allegedly by the Taliban. At the same time, the number of Afghan refugees attempting to leave the country increased dramatically. Pakistan kept its frontier closed and refugees attempting to enter Pakistan were beaten back by guards, although those who bribed the guards often managed to cross the border. The UN attempted to form new camps in Pakistan to accommodate the influx of refugees, but the Pakistani Government ordered them to be located in remote areas to ensure that its towns and cities were not overwhelmed. The exact numbers of refugees trying to flee Afghanistan were not known; however, in early November UNHCR estimated that 135,000 refugees had entered Pakistan since the terrorist attacks on the USA.

In early November 2001 attacks against the Taliban in northern Afghanistan escalated. On 9 November the United Front captured Mazar-i-Sharif and continued to seize almost all of northern Afghanistan at an astonishing pace. The USA, United Kingdom and Pakistan advised the United Front not to enter Kabul until a leadership council was formed; however, on the night of 12 November the Taliban fled the capital and the next day, facing very little resistance, the United Front took over Kabul. There were also reports of defections of large groups of Taliban fighters, as morale among the Taliban declined. Although the United Front immediately requested assistance from the US-led coalition to create a transitional government, it was impossible to do so while the majority Pashtun ethnic group remained under-represented. The USA and Pakistan hitherto had failed to attract defectors from the Pashtun Taliban leadership to join the council; in addition, US-led forces had given little support to anti-Taliban Pashtun leaders attempting to capture southern Afghanistan. Commanders of the United Front were soon in disagreement over the running of provinces in northern Afghanistan. Anti-Taliban forces from all ethnic backgrounds quickly advanced on southern Afghanistan and by the end of November had captured the Taliban stronghold of Kunduz. Unlike the factions belonging to the United Front, these groups were not united under a political alliance.

On 27 November 2001 the UN hosted a conference of 28 Afghan leaders representing the United Front, the Rome Group led by Zahir Shah, the pro-Iranian Cyprus Process and the Pakistan-backed Peshawar process (composed of Pashtun exiles and headed by Gailani), as well as other leading figures, in Bonn, Germany. The conference faced many challenges; in particular, tension existed between ethnic groups as well as movements. Nevertheless, on 5 December the leaders signed the Agreement on Provisional Arrangements in Afghanistan Pending the Re-establishment of Permanent Government Institutions, also known as the Bonn Agreement, to establish a 30-member multi-ethnic Interim Authority to preside for six months from 22 December. It was decided that at the end of this transitional period an Emergency Loya Jirga chaired by former King Zahir Shah would appoint a Transitional Authority. At least 18 months later a Constitutional Loya Jirga in the style of a constituent assembly would adopt a constitution and prepare the country for democratic elections. A Pashtun tribal chief, Hamid Karzai, was named Chairman of the Interim Authority, which was to comprise 11 Pashtuns, eight Tajiks, five Hazaras, three Uzbeks and three members of smaller tribal and religious groups. The United Front received the most seats; three of the leading members, Younis Qanooni, Gen. Muhammed Fahim and Dr Abdullah Abdullah, were allocated the interior, defence and foreign affairs portfolios, respectively. Two female doctors were also granted posts in the executive council. Some leaders who were excluded from the government were dissatisfied with the outcome, including the former President Burhanuddin.

The Taliban regime's sole official contact with the outside world ended in late November 2001 when Pakistan severed all diplomatic links with the Taliban and closed their last remaining embassy. On 7 December the remaining members of the Taliban finally surrendered Qandahar and disappeared, marking the end of the Taliban regime. In the mean time, US ground forces were strengthened in an effort to find bin Laden and his supporters. Following unconfirmed reports that bin Laden and Mola Mohammad Omar were hiding in the Tora Bora caves with the rest of the Islamist forces, the US-led coalition and United Front intensified the air and ground assault on the cave complex. However, after much of the region had been destroyed, there was no sign of the two leaders and their close associates. Some unconfirmed reports suggested that bin Laden had fled to Pakistan. A new pre-recorded videotape featuring bin Laden was broadcast by Al-Jazeera in late December, supporting claims that the Islamist militant was still alive; it was impossible, however, to ascertain the date of the recording.

Meanwhile, the USA and its allies continued to search for remaining Taliban and al-Qa'ida forces in Afghanistan. On 9 December WFP began a massive aid distribution programme in Kabul. The reopening of the Friendship Bridge between Afghanistan and Uzbekistan on the same day was a momentous occasion and provided humanitarian agencies with a much-needed route by which to transport supplies. However, the poor weather conditions hampered the international relief campaign and most rural areas remained inaccessible, owing to safety concerns. Meanwhile, following the defeat of the Taliban regime, tens of thousands of refugees began to return to Afghanistan.

On 22 December 2001 the Interim Authority was inaugurated; Karzai was sworn in as Chairman. The country returned to the Constitution of 1964, which combined *Shari'a* with Western concepts of justice. The administration was expected to establish a central bank, a judicial system, a civil service and a human rights commission. The tasks for Karzai and his administration were immense: the leaders were required to unite a deeply divided country, destroyed by more than 20 years of war. Karzai was generally accepted as the most suitable unifying force. One of his first decisions was to appoint Gen. Dostam, who initially boycotted the Government in protest at his exclusion, as Vice-Chairman and Deputy Minister of Defence. At the end of December the UN Security Council authorized, as envisaged in the Bonn Agreement, the deployment of an International Security Assistance Force (ISAF) to help maintain security in Kabul over the next six months. Some 19 countries were authorized to form a 5,000-strong security force, led by the United Kingdom.

At the end of January 2002 US forces and Afghan soldiers raided a hospital in Qandahar and killed six al-Qa'ida fighters, thus ending a two-month siege of the hospital. In the same month the international community agreed to donate US $4,500m. over 2.5 years towards the reconstruction of Afghanistan; $1,800m. was to be made available for 2002 (this figure was later increased to more than $2,000m.). At the same time a 21-member Special Independent Commission for the Convening of the Emergency Loya Jirga (commonly known as the Loya Jirga Commission) was established to devise the selection process and conduct of the Emergency Loya Jirga. Deployment of the ISAF began in mid-January and remained confined to Kabul, despite Karzai's requests for the number of ISAF troops to be increased and the international force's mandate to be expanded to include security operations for the entire country. In May a UN Security Council Resolution approved the extension of the ISAF for six months beyond June. In June Turkey took over command of the security force. The ISAF participated in joint patrols with Afghan police and assisted in creating and training a new Afghan army. In early April the first 600-man battalion for an Afghan National Guard was inducted. It was envisaged that the Afghan National Guard would form the basis of a new Afghan National Army (ANA). US and French forces began training an initial set of recruits for the ANA in May. It was intended that the ANA would eventually be a force of some 60,000, supported by a border guard of 12,000 and an air force of 8,000. Meanwhile, however, regional military commanders continued to reorganize their own armies, preventing scarce resources from being sent to the ANA and making the task of creating a multi-ethnic national army even more difficult. In early 2002 reports were already emerging of fighting among ethnic groups. In mid-February the Minister of Civil Aviation and Tourism, Abdul Rahman, was assassinated by a rival faction within the Interim Authority. The murder of Rahman, a staunch supporter of Zahir Shah, was evidently an attempt to deter the former monarch from returning to Afghanistan. In early April the Interim Authority claimed to have prevented an attempt allegedly organized by Hekmatyar to assassinate Karzai. Government officials accused Hekmatyar of seeking to depose the Interim Authority and assume control. Some four days later the Minister of Defence, Gen. Fahim (self-promoted to Marshal later that month), escaped an apparent assassination attempt in Jalalabad. It was not clear who was responsible for the attack. Despite security concerns, former King Zahir Shah returned to Afghanistan as a 'private citizen' on 18 April. In late March the Loya Jirga Commission released the procedures by which members of the Emergency Loya Jirga should be selected.

In mid-January 2002 Afghanistan's main route connecting Kabul with the north, the Salang Pass, was reopened for the first time in 10 years, following a clearance operation by Russian and French teams. At the same time UN sanctions imposed on Ariana Afghan Airlines were lifted. The Interim Authority issued a decree banning poppy cultivation and the processing, trafficking and abuse of opiates. In February, however, reports were emerging that the large-scale planting of poppies had already taken place during the collapse of law and order in late 2001. In early April 2002 the Interim Administration introduced a radical programme to eradicate the crop. In accordance with the scheme, farmers would receive compensation for destroying their opium crops; those who refused would have their land seized by the Government and risk prosecution. However, the offer of compensation did not compare well with the lucrative sale of opium, and farmers carried out violent demonstrations throughout the country against the initiative. Despite attempts by the Government and the UN to curb the drugs trade, the annual survey conducted by the UN Office on Drugs and Crime (formerly the UN Office of Drug Control and Crime Prevention), published in October, reported that, owing to the planting of poppies in late 2001, Afghanistan had resumed its place as the world's biggest producer of opium. The UN urged the international community to provide greater assistance to the Afghan authorities in their anti-drugs campaign. Meanwhile, in late March an earthquake occurred in Nahrin (Baghlan province), killing around 1,800 people and leaving thousands homeless.

The number of refugees returning in 2002 surpassed all expectations. In early April UNHCR reported that more than 50,000 Afghan refugees were returning from Pakistan every week. In the same month UNHCR and the Iranian Government embarked on a joint voluntary repatriation programme to facilitate the return of more than 400,000 Afghans from Iran. By early December that target had almost been reached. At the end of 2002 UNHCR announced that more than 1.5m. refugees had returned from Pakistan. An estimated 4m. refugees remained outside Afghanistan, including 2m. in Iran and 1.5m. in Pakistan. In September, however, concerns were raised that Afghanistan was incapable of meeting the nutritional requirements of its population. Officials estimated that only 20%–30% of the country's land was cultivated in 2002, largely owing to the fourth successive year of drought. The crisis was exacerbated by the lack of sufficient humanitarian assistance from the international donor community. The rapid return of refugees placed an even greater strain on the humanitarian programme. Some 80% of the funds provided by the international agencies had been allocated to humanitarian aid, thus leaving only 20% available for the country's reconstruction programme. In mid-September Japan, Saudi Arabia and the USA announced a joint aid programme worth $180m. for the repair and improvement of roads throughout Afghanistan.

Internecine fighting escalated as tribal commanders attempted to consolidate territorial and political influence in preparation for the Loya Jirga. Human Rights Watch issued a report in March 2002 detailing a rise in incidents of violence, killing, rape and ethnic persecution in northern Afghanistan, particularly aimed at Pashtun villagers. Many of the commanders held responsible for the violence were supposed supporters of the Interim Authority. In April British members of the ISAF were fired at in an apparent attempt to destabilize Kabul. The USA and UN attempted to mediate between rival commanders as violent clashes between ethnic factions continued. In February the UN brokered an agreement between the leaders of the three feuding factions in northern and north-western Afghanistan, Gen. Dostam, Gen. Atta Mohammed and Mohammed Mohaqqeq, according to which a 600-strong security force was to be established in the region representing all three factions. However, factional fighting continued in the region and throughout Afghanistan. Meanwhile, in early May it was reported that the US Central Intelligence Agency (CIA) had unsuccessfully attempted to assassinate Hekmatyar.

In the mean time, the US-led coalition continued its search for the leaders of al-Qa'ida and the Taliban. In early February 2002 the former Taliban Minister of Foreign Affairs, Mawlawi Wakil Ahmad Motawakkil, surrendered himself to US forces in Qandahar. The search was often thwarted by the activities of regional Afghan (non-Taliban) military commanders. In early January, for example, the Interim Authority confirmed that seven senior Taliban members, who had surrendered to a local Afghan commander, had been released without the approval of the Interim Administration or the US-led coalition forces. 'Operation Anaconda', conducted by US-led forces against alleged Taliban and al-Qa'ida forces in the Shah-i Kot valley of Paktia province in March, was planned as a three-day assault, but developed into a 17-day conflict resulting in the deaths of coalition soldiers. Many al-Qa'ida and Taliban members fled to

Khost province. US forces depended heavily on information provided by military commanders regarding the whereabouts of militant Islamists. This tactic was often to the USA's detriment, as complex tribal allegiances and enmities regularly dictated the type of information given by tribal commanders. Indeed, it was largely believed that bin Laden had been allowed to escape from Tora Bora in December 2001 (see above) by Afghans who claimed to be US allies. The USA's policy of hiring and arming local soldiers in the hope of capturing Islamist militants at times compounded the unstable political situation. For example, Zadran, a supporter of the former King but opponent of the Karzai administration, was alleged to have given US forces false information, leading to the bombing in December of a convoy of tribal leaders travelling to Kabul to attend the opening ceremony for the Interim Authority. In March 2002 the funds provided by the US forces in return for the assistance of Afghan soldiers were reportedly used by various military commanders in their attempt to secure control of Khost province. In April the mission to find the remnants of al-Qa'ida and the Taliban became more dangerous and volatile. US-led and Afghan forces encountered considerable security threats. In mid-April British troops launched their first major military assault, joining US and Afghan soldiers in Paktia. US-led forces conducted several smaller operations in eastern Afghanistan in May–June, with the support of Afghan ground troops, with some success. The USA's military strategy came under severe criticism after a wedding party in Uruzgan province was bombed by mistake in early July. It appeared that US forces, not for the first time, had mistaken the traditional celebratory firing of weapons at an Afghan wedding for Taliban activity.

The election of 1,051 delegates to attend the Emergency Loya Jirga by district representatives took place in May–June 2002 under the monitoring of the UN and Loya Jirga Commission. International aid agencies, universities and other organizations chosen by the Commission appointed an additional 600 members to ensure that the assembly was balanced in terms of gender, geography, ethnicity and political beliefs. The Emergency Loya Jirga, due to commence on 10 June, was delayed by about 36 hours, largely owing to tension over the former King Zahir Shah's candidature for the presidency. Zahir Shah eventually withdrew his candidature, reportedly after pressure by the USA, and announced his support for Karzai. The former President, Burhanuddin Rabbani, also renounced his candidature and declared his support for Karzai. The Emergency Loya Jirga convened the following day, on 11 June, and was attended by an estimated 1,650 delegates. Karzai won the presidential election, with 1,295 of the approximately 1,575 votes cast. Massouda Jalal, a doctor and first woman ever to participate in an Afghan presidential election, came second with 171 votes; Mahfouz Nedai secured 109 votes. Some 83 voters abstained. The UN declared the elections flawed, with incidents of malpractice and intimidation of candidates, but fair. The Loya Jirga was also expected to choose the structure of the Transitional Authority and its principal staff; however, the decision-making took place largely outside the assembly tent. Debate in the assembly was reportedly obstructed by poor chairmanship and the lack of a clear agenda. Nevertheless, on 19 June the Loya Jirga approved (by a show of hands, as opposed to a formal written vote) the Transitional Authority cabinet, retaining most of the incumbent members of the Interim Authority. On the same day the Loya Jirga concluded with the ceremonial inauguration of President Karzai and Karzai's official appointment of his cabinet. The Loya Jirga failed to establish a Meli Shura (National Assembly). Instead, it was decided that a National Assembly Commission would be convened at a future date to discuss this issue. Karzai announced the creation of a number of other commissions to address the difficult issues facing the Transitional Administration, such as defence, human rights and internal security reform. A Constitutional Commission was proposed to draft a new constitution.

In late June 2002 the Afghan Supreme Court dismissed a blasphemy charge against the outgoing Interim Authority's Minister of Women's Affairs, Dr Sima Samar. Despite the outcome of the case, two days later President Karzai was forced by religious leaders to dismiss Dr Samar and appoint Habiba Sorabi as Minister of Women's Affairs of the Transitional Authority. In early July the Vice-President and Minister of Reconstruction, Haji Abdul Qadir, was assassinated, raising new concerns over the Transitional Authority's stability. Many observers held the remnants of the Taliban or al-Qa'ida responsible for the attack. Later that month US authorities declared

that they would provide armed guards for Karzai, in response to fears for the President's safety. An ISAF report published in mid-August on the assassination of Qadir stated that Afghan officials were inadequately protected and that it was unlikely that the assassins would be found, since the Afghan security agencies were ill-equipped to investigate the incident. Attacks by Islamist militants occurred throughout August. In early September Karzai escaped an assassination attempt in Qandahar; hours later a bomb explosion in Kabul killed 30 people and injured at least 160 others. Afghan officials and Western diplomats believed that Hekmatyar had joined forces with remnants of the Taliban and al-Qa'ida in south and east Afghanistan and had perpetrated the attacks in an attempt to depose the Transitional Authority. Hekmatyar had allegedly also held negotiations with other discontented regional leaders in an effort to form a wider alliance against the Afghan Government and US military presence in Afghanistan. Following the bomb attack some 800 additional ISAF troops were deployed across Kabul to carry out random searches of vehicles and to construct security checkpoints; police officers arrested more than 100 people in connection with the attack. In the mean time, reported incidents of factional fighting increased significantly in late June and July. In some parts of Afghanistan the fighting hindered humanitarian relief efforts. In mid-July Karzai announced the establishment of a UN-supported security commission, which would begin the disarming of rebel troops and precipitate the creation of a national army. Despite commanding little control outside Kabul, Karzai warned military commanders that their powers would be removed unless they denounced factional fighting and joined the Government. In early November the President dismissed more than 20 senior regional officials—including Gen. Abdul Hamid, the military commander of Mazar-i-Sharif—in an attempt to consolidate the Transitional Authority's jurisdiction outside Kabul. In the mean time, rival military commanders Gen. Dostam and Gen. Atta Mohammed eventually negotiated a cease-fire in October and agreed to support the security commission; however, violence was reportedly renewed in mid-November. The disarmament programme resumed after Gen. Dostam and Gen. Atta Mohammed agreed to co-operate; by mid-January 2003 thousands of weapons had been collected, but regional commanders remained as powerful as before. Meanwhile, fighting continued in Khost and Paktia provinces. At a conference focusing on Afghanistan's reconstruction in Germany in early December 2002, Karzai officially annouced the plan to build a 70,000–strong multi-ethnic army. Karzai also announced that all private armies would have to surrender their weapons and be centralized within the next 12 months. In January 2003 Karzai established four committees to accelerate the disarmament process and to recruit a national army.

In early September 2002 the Transitional Authority announced a currency reform programme designed to end the problem of hyperinflation and to stop regional commanders from printing their own banknotes to fund military operations. During a two-month period, commencing 7 October, old afghani notes were to be exchanged for new afghani notes at a rate of 1,000 old afghanis to one new afghani. The IMF-supported programme initially caused confusion and panic among currency traders. The Constitution Commission was inaugurated in early November. A final draft of a new Constitution was expected to be completed by October 2003 and submitted to the Constitutional Loya Jirga thereafter for endorsement. Discussions regarding a new judicial system were also under way in late 2002. At the end of October four girls' schools in remote villages south of Kabul were attacked by Islamist militants, as part of an apparent campaign against the education of girls. The perpetrators left letters at the scene of each attack urging Afghans to force out US forces who had 'occupied' Afghanistan and 'made our Afghan sisters their servants and slaves'. In mid-November Al-Jazeera broadcast an audiotape recording believed to have been made by bin Laden. The tape was considered by many as proof that bin Laden was still alive. Swiss scientists, however, believed the tape not to be authentic, while US officials thought the tape genuine, although they could not be certain owing to the poor quality of the recording. In late November Afghan authorities prevented an attempt to assassinate Marshal Fahim. Meanwhile, the search for the remnants of the Taliban and al-Qa'ida continued. In late 2002 US and British politicians urged their Governments to consider the expansion of the ISAF's activities beyond Kabul. At the end of November the UN Security Council approved the extension of the mandate of the ISAF for one year beyond 20 December; Germany and the Netherlands agreed to assume joint command of the force from Turkey. At the end of 2002 the USA was planning to shift its strategy in Afghanistan from a military focus to concentrating on the reconstruction of the country. Reconstruction had yet to begin in south and east Afghanistan, where Islamist militancy appeared to be growing. As long as Islamist attacks, factional fighting and the drugs trade continued to threaten the country's stability, the most serious challenge facing Afghanistan remained the lack of security. A minor cabinet reorganization was effected at the end of January 2003. The Minister of Mines and Industries, Juma Mohammad Mohammadi, was killed in an air crash in late February.

On 22 December 2002 the Governments of Afghanistan, China, Iran, Pakistan, Tajikistan, Turkmenistan and Uzbekistan signed the Kabul Declaration on Good-Neighbourly Relations in which they pledged never again to interfere in the affairs of Afghanistan. The agreement signalled a new era of regional co-operation. The reality, however, was different. Afghan officials claimed that Iranian Revolutionary Guards were continuing to provide financial and military assistance to Ismail Khan; Russia was reportedly supporting Marshal Fahim and his army; and certain Saudis allegedly had resumed sending financial assistance to the remnants of the Taliban in Pakistan. In addition, the Uzbek President had provided Uzbek Gen. Dostam with his own bodyguards. Normal relations with Pakistan had yet to be restored at the end of 2002. Publicly, the Pakistani President supported Karzai and the USA's campaign against al-Qa'ida; however, at the same time Pakistan's Inter-Services Intelligence was reportedly giving sanctuary to senior Taliban members and other anti-Government military commanders, such as Hekmatyar. In early 2003 Afghanistan's Minister of Defence stated his willingness to visit Pakistan to commence dialogue between the intelligence agencies of both countries.

Government

During 11–19 June 2002 an Emergency Loya Jirga, comprising an estimated 1,650 delegates, 1,051 of whom were elected by tribal representatives, with the remaining seats allocated to such groups as women and business leaders, appointed a head of state and the principal staff of a broad-based, gender-sensitive Transitional Authority. It was decided that a National Assembly Commission would convene at a later date to establish the structure of the legislature (Meli Shura). Within two years a Constitutional Loya Jirga styled on a constituent assembly was scheduled to adopt a new constitution and prepare the country for democratic elections.

Defence

Following the defeat of the Taliban in December 2001, an International Security Assistance Force (ISAF) was deployed in Kabul and at Bagram airbase to help maintain security in the area. In December 2002 Germany and the Netherlands assumed joint command of the force, which in late 2002 consisted of 4,800 members from 22 countries. The ISAF was also responsible for the training of the first battalion of the Afghan National Guard, which was operational in April. US and French forces began training the first set of recruits for a new multi-ethnic Afghan National Army (ANA) in May and by July a brigade was ready for deployment. In December President Karzai announced that the ANA would comprise 70,000 soldiers and ordered all private armies to disarm and merge into the ANA within one year. Four committees were established in January 2003 to accelerate the disarmament and army-building process. It was envisaged that the army would be supported by a border guard of 12,000. There was to be a paramilitary force, including police trained by Germany, numbering some 70,000.

Economic Affairs

According to the latest figures published by the US Central Intelligence Agency (CIA) on Afghanistan, the country's gross domestic product (GDP) has fallen substantially over the past 20 years or so, primarily owing to the loss of labour and capital, the collapse of agricultural production, the devastation caused to the infrastructure, and the disruption in the trade and transport sectors. It was estimated that in 2000 GDP in terms of purchasing-power parity totalled US $21,000m. (equivalent to $800 per head). According to the IMF, Afghanistan's GDP per caput (excluding the illegal cultivation of poppies and production of drugs) in the early 2000s was roughly estimated at $150–$180.

Agriculture (including hunting, forestry and fishing), according to UN estimates, contributed 64.4% of GDP in 1993. According to FAO, 66.6% of the economically active population were employed in the agricultural sector in 2001. Livestock plays an important role in the traditional Afghan economy and is normally a major source of income for the country's numerous nomadic groups. However, at the end of 2001 livestock herds in Afghanistan had been seriously depleted. In 1999 wheat production was estimated at 2.5m. metric tons. The principal commercial products of the sector were fruit and nuts (which accounted for around 39.7% of total export earnings, according to the IMF, in 1990/91), wool and cotton, and processed hides and skins. Total cereal output declined by 16% in 1999 to an estimated 3.26m. tons, owing to a shortage of irrigation water. The total cereal import requirement for the period June 1998–July 1999 was estimated by FAO at 740,000 tons, of which about 140,000 tons was to be wheat provided by the international aid community. Afghanistan continues to depend on food imports from abroad or in the form of aid. An international effort to replenish Afghanistan's seed stocks and to revive the country's farms, destroyed by years of war and three years of drought, began in 2002. However, the continuing drought, lack of sufficient humanitarian assistance and rapid return of refugees placed a strain on the programme and, according to official estimates, only 20%–30% of the country's land was cultivated in 2002. Nevertheless, following rainfall in some parts of Afghanistan in the latter half of 2002, the country was expected to produce 3.6m. tons of cereals in 2002.

According to UN estimates, the industrial sector (including mining, manufacturing, construction and power) contributed 20% of GDP in 1993, while the value of industrial output in that year decreased by 11.4%, compared with the previous year.

Mining and quarrying employed about 1.5% of the settled labour force in 1979. Natural gas was the major mineral export (accounting for about 23.6% of total export earnings, according to the IMF, in 1988/89). Salt, hard coal, copper, lapis lazuli, emeralds, barytes and talc are also mined. In addition, Afghanistan has small reserves of petroleum and iron ore. In 1998 the Taliban had claimed that monthly revenue from the allegedly renascent mining sector in Afghanistan totalled US $3.5m. (including revenue from the recently revived steel-smelting plant in Baghlan province). In 2002/03 the new Transitional Administration planned to rehabilitate the mining industry.

Manufacturing employed about 10.9% of the settled labour force in 1979. Afghanistan's major manufacturing industries included food products, cotton textiles, chemical fertilizers, cement, leather and plastic goods. In 1999 only one of the four existing cement plants in Afghanistan and about 10% of the textile mills remained in operation (prior to the Soviet invasion in 1979 there were about 220 state-owned factories operating in Afghanistan). The traditional handicraft sector has better survived the devastating effects of war, however, and carpets, leather, embroidery and fur products continued to be produced.

Energy is derived principally from petroleum (which is imported from Iran and republics of the former USSR, notably Turkmenistan) and coal. Afghanistan was estimated to have some 73m. metric tons of coal reserves. The pre-Taliban Government planned to increase internal sources of energy by establishing hydro- and thermal electric power stations. In early 1996 Afghanistan signed an agreement that could eventually lead to the construction of a high-pressure natural gas pipeline across the country, which would transport gas from Turkmenistan to Pakistan. In October 1997 the US petroleum company, Unocal, established a consortium which proposed to build a pipeline across Afghanistan. In March 1998, however, Unocal announced that the project was to be indefinitely postponed, owing to the continuing civil war; Unocal withdrew from the consortium in December. Following the establishment of the Afghan Interim Authority in late 2001, the plan was revived, and in May 2002 the leaders of Afghanistan, Pakistan and Turkmenistan formally agreed to facilitate the construction of one or more pipelines from Turkmenistan to Pakistan. However, the country's lack of infrastructure, concerns over the security situation and high global petroleum and gas prices appeared to deter investors. Furthermore, companies had already negotiated alternative routes with Central Asian states. None the less, Afghanistan, Pakistan and Turkmenistan signed a framework agreement in December to construct and operate a gas pipeline from the Dauletabad-Donmez gas field in Turkmenistan, across Afghanistan and Pakistan, and terminating eventually in India.

India refused to become involved in the project as Pakistan was a partner.

The negative trend in trade was apparent throughout the 1990s. The sharpest declines in both exports and imports occurred in 1992 and 1993. In 1996, following the Taliban accession to power, trade showed little sign of revival. In 1996/97, according to UN figures, total exports were estimated at $127m.; in 1999/2000 figures reached an estimated $150m. In 1996/97 the major export commodities included fruits and nuts, hand-woven carpets, wool, cotton, hides and pelts, and precious and semi-precious gems. The most important export markets in 1999 were Pakistan, Western Europe and the USA. In 1996/97, according to UN figures, total imports were estimated at $600m. and consisted mainly of food, petroleum products and other consumer goods. In 1999/2000 total imports were estimated at $600m. The principal sources of imports in 1999 were Pakistan, Japan and Western Europe. These official statistics do not, however, include illegal trade and smuggling. The trade deficit would be much lower if the illegal revenue from the export of opium were included. In the 1990s a World Bank study estimated that $2,500m. worth of goods were smuggled between Afghanistan and Pakistan each year. In late 1995 it was announced that trade tariffs were to be reduced between the member states of the Economic Co-operation Organization (ECO, see p. 192), which Afghanistan joined in late 1992. In January 2003 Afghanistan signed a number of favourable trade agreements with India and Iran. India, prohibited from trading with Afghanistan through Pakistan, also agreed to improve the road network linking Afghanistan with the Chabahar port in Iran. Afghanistan began to open trade routes with Central Asia in late 2002. Afghanistan is a member of the Colombo Plan (see p. 339), which seeks to promote economic and social development in Asia and the Pacific.

In 2000, according to UN figures, Afghanistan received US $88.2m. in bilateral official development assistance and $52.7m. in multilateral official development assistance. In 2002/03 Afghanistan was expected to receive $40.0m. in bilateral grants and $98.2m. in multilateral assistance.

It is difficult to provide an accurate economic profile of Afghanistan, owing to the civil war that afflicted the country for more than 20 years and the US-led military campaign against the Taliban and the al-Qa'ida (Base) organization. Population movements, communication problems and lack of reliable official statistics also make the task more problematic. The Transitional Authority is faced with the immense task of reviving the traditional economy, which, over the past 20 years or so, has been largely replaced by a criminal economy based on drugs and smuggling. In 2002 the Interim, and later Transitional, Administration began to address such problems as the severe food and fuel shortages, the lack of infrastructure and the difficulties of millions of refugees returning to their ravaged farms and fields studded with mines or devastated by air-strikes. In January the international donor community agreed to provide Afghanistan with financial assistance and strategic guidance and pledged US $4,500m. over 2.5 years towards the reconstruction of Afghanistan. The actual commitment and disbursement of assistance was slow to begin with, but by the end of 2002 some $2,000m. had been donated. The Afghan Government devised a National Development Framework for the reconstruction programme, which focused on security and human development, rebuilding the country's infrastructure and facilitating private economic activity. By the end of 2002 a number of infrastructure projects were under way or had reached completion. Central Asian countries and Iran agreed to supply electricity to some of Afghanistan's border regions. The humanitarian crisis, however, had placed a strain on the limited financial resources, thus delaying the reconstruction process. Nevertheless, in late 2002 the economy showed signs of recovery. The inflation rate declined significantly in the first quarter of 2002/03 to slightly more than 1%, much lower than the projected 4.5%. Efforts to rebuild the banking infrastructure also took place in 2002. Da Afghanistan Bank, Afghanistan's Central Bank, was revived. A currency reform programme devised to curb the problems of hyperinflation and to stop military regional commanders from printing their own banknotes (in early 2002 at least three local currencies circulated in Afghanistan) was announced in September. A new currency was introduced in October; by January 2003 old afghani notes had been replaced by new afghani notes at a rate of 1,000 old afghanis to one new afghani. Reconstruction of the education system was under way in 2002. Education became available to girls throughout the country. Women were also given equal employment rights. Owing to years of conflict and repression, many educated Afghans had fled the country. After the fall of the Taliban qualified Afghans living abroad were encouraged to return to Afghanistan to boost the rehabilitation process; by January 2003 about 400 Afghan professionals had returned. The restoration of telecommunications took place in 2002. A mobile cellular telephone system was launched in Kabul in April 2002 and covered four other cities by June; internet services were available in some parts of the country by early 2003.

The prevalent drugs trade remained a significant problem. Despite the introduction of a ban in January 2002 on poppy cultivation and the processing, trafficking and abuse of opiates, the large-scale planting of poppies during the collapse of law order in late 2001 had allowed Afghanistan to resume its place as the largest supplier of opium in the world. The Interim Administration introduced a programme in early April to eradicate the crop. Farmers were to receive compensation for destroying their opium crops; those who refused would have their land seized by the Government and could be prosecuted. Farmers, however, refusing to give up the lucrative drugs trade, reacted violently against the initiative. In the mean time, the return of refugees continued.

Education

The prolonged war resulted in a large-scale exodus of teachers, and some 3,600 school buildings were damaged or destroyed. In 1996/97 it was estimated that only about 600–650 primary and secondary schools were functioning.

Before the Taliban rose to power, primary education began at seven years of age and lasted for six years. Secondary education, beginning at 13 years of age, lasted for a further six years. As a proportion of the school-age population, the total enrolment at primary and secondary schools was equivalent to 36% (males 49%; females 22%) in 1995. Primary enrolment in that year was equivalent to an estimated 49% of children in the relevant age-group (boys 64%; girls 32%), while the enrolment ratio at general secondary schools was equivalent to 22% (boys 32%; girls 11%).

Higher education was disrupted by the departure of many teaching staff from Afghanistan during more than 20 years of civil war. In 1980 it was reported that up to 80% of university staff had fled their posts. In 1991 there were six institutions of higher education (including Kabul University, which was founded in 1932) in Afghanistan; a total of 17,000 students were enrolled in these institutions in that year.

Following their seizure of power in late September 1996, the Taliban banned education for girls over the age of eight, closed all the women's institutes of higher education and planned to draw up a new Islamic curriculum for boys' schools. In early 1998, however, there were still two co-educational universities functioning in Afghanistan (in areas not under Taliban control), one of which was situated in Bamian (with 300 students and 16 teachers). In mid-1998 the the Taliban decided to close more than 100 private schools and numerous small, home-based vocational courses in Kabul, many of which were educating girls. In 1999, however, the Taliban officially sanctioned the establishment of 13 schools for girls (up to the age of 12) in Kabul and its environs. According to Taliban figures, in September of that year 1,586,026 pupils were being educated by 59,792 teachers in 3,836 *madrassas* (mosque schools).

After the Taliban regime was defeated in late 2001, the Afghan Interim Administration, with the help of foreign governments and UN and humanitarian organizations, began to rehabilitate the education system. In late March 2002 more than 3m. boys and girls commenced a new academic year at more than 4,500 schools around the country, more than double the number anticipated. The enrolment of girls increased substantially, from 5% of total enrolment in 2001 to 30% in 2002. The World Food Programme embarked on a food-for-education programme; organizations world-wide supplied educational material, and tents were provided as temporary classrooms. More than 27,000 teachers were involved in education in 20 provinces in July, 36% of whom were women. In late 2002, however, the education authorities expressed concerns that some 1.5m. children could not attend classes, owing to a lack of schools and teachers. It was predicted that a further 1m. children would seek enrolment in March 2003. Although aid agencies had carried out the reconstruction of some 50 school buildings by mid-2002, more than 3,500 schools still required major repairs. Kabul University opened for men and women in March. Some 24,000 students enrolled at the higher education level. Foreign universities as well as governments and non-governmental organizations donated books and teaching materials. Universities in at least five other provinces were being rehabilitated.

In January 2003 UNESCO and the Afghan Transitional Administration launched a major project to boost literacy rates throughout Afghanistan.

Public Holidays

According to the Hejri solar calendar, the Afghan year 1382 runs from 21 March 2003 to 20 March 2004, and the year 1383 runs from 21 March 2004 to 20 March 2005.

2003: 11 February* (Arafat Day), 12 February* (Id al-Adha, Feast of the Sacrifice), 14 March* (Ashura, Martyrdom of Imam Husayn), 21 March (Nauroz: New Year's Day, Iranian calendar), 28 April (Loss of the Muslim Nation), 1 May (Workers' Day), 14 May* (Roze-Maulud, Birth of Prophet Muhammad), 19 August (Independence Day), 27 October* (first day of Ramadan), 26 November* (Id al-Fitr, end of Ramadan).

2004: 1 February* (Arafat Day), 2 February* (Id al-Adha, Feast of the Sacrifice), 2 March* (Ashura, Martyrdom of Imam Husayn), 21 March (Nauroz: New Year's Day, Iranian calendar), 28 April (Loss of the Muslim Nation), 1 May (Workers' Day), 2 May* (Roze-Maulud, Birth of Prophet Muhammad), 19 August (Independence Day), 15 October* (first day of Ramadan), 14 November* (Id al-Fitr, end of Ramadan).

* These holidays are dependent on the Islamic lunar calendar and may vary by one or two days from the dates given.

Weights and Measures

The metric system has been officially adopted but traditional weights are still used. One 'seer' equals 16 lb (7.3 kg).

Statistical Survey

Source (unless otherwise stated): Central Statistics Authority, Block 4, Macroraion, Kabul; tel. (93) 24883.

Area and Population

AREA, POPULATION AND DENSITY

Area (sq km)	652,225*
Population (census results)	
23 June 1979†	
Males	6,712,377
Females. . . .	6,338,981
Total	13,051,358
Population (official estimates at mid-year)‡	
1984	17,672,000
1985	18,136,000
1986	18,614,000
Density (per sq km) at mid-1986 .	28.5

* 251,773 sq miles.

† Figures exclude nomadic population, estimated to total 2,500,000. The census data also exclude an adjustment for underenumeration, estimated to have been 5% for the urban population and 10% for the rural population.

‡ These data include estimates for nomadic population (2,734,000 in 1983), but take no account of emigration by refugees. Assuming an average net outflow of 703,000 persons per year in 1980–85, the UN Population Division has estimated Afghanistan's total mid-year population (in '000) as: 14,519 in 1985; 14,529 in 1986; 14,709 in 1987. (Source: UN, *World Population Prospects: 1988*). At the end of 2002 UNHCR estimated that the total Afghan refugee population numbered 4m., of whom 2m. were living in Iran and 1.5m. in Pakistan.

Population (UN estimates, including nomads, at mid-year): 19,073,000 in 1995; 19,816,000 in 1996; 20,349,000 in 1997; 20,764,000 in 1998; 21,202,000 in 1999; 21,765,000 in 2000; 22,474,000 in 2001 (Source: UN, *World Population Prospects: The 2000 Revision*).

PROVINCES
(estimates, 2000)

	Area (sq km)	Population	Density (per sq km)	Capital
Kabul . . .	4,462	2,766,800	620.1	Kabul
Kapisa . .	1,842	429,600	233.2	Mahmud-e-Iraqi
Parvan . .	9,584	748,200	78.1	Charikar
Wardak* . .	8,938	347,100	38.8	Maidanshahr
Loghar*. .	3,880	306,100	78.9	Pul-i-Alam
Ghazni . .	22,915	1,023,700	44.7	Ghazni
Paktia . .	6,432	741,100	115.2	Gardez
Nangarhar .	7,727	1,370,700	177.4	Jalalabad
Laghman . .	3,843	631,100	164.2	Mehter Lam
Kunar . .	4,942	537,500	108.8	Asadabad
Badakhshan .	44,059	938,500	21.3	Faizabad
Takhar . .	12,333	735,000	59.6	Taloqan
Baghlan* . .	21,118	805,800	38.2	Baghlan
Kunduz . .	8,040	715,600	89.0	Kunduz
Samangan .	11,262	520,400	46.2	Aybak
Balkh . .	17,249	1,432,100	83.1	Mazar-i-Sharif
Jawzjan. .	11,798	676,000	57.3	Shiberghan
Faryab . .	20,293	868,500	42.8	Maymana
Badghis . .	20,591	626,800	30.4	Qaleh-ye-Now
Herat . .	54,778	1,273,100	23.2	Herat
Farah . .	48,471	421,900	8.7	Farah
Nimroz . .	41,005	203,800	5.0	Zaranj
Helmand . .	58,584	852,500	14.6	Lashgar Gah
Qandahar . .	54,022	1,367,600	25.3	Qandahar
Zabul . .	17,343	378,700	21.8	Qalat
Uruzgan . .	30,784	281,100	9.1	Terin Kowt
Ghor . .	36,479	592,400	16.2	Chaghcharan
Bamian . .	14,175	445,300	31.4	Bamian
Paktika . .	19,482	430,300	22.1	Sharan
Nuristan† .	9,225	n.a.	n.a.	Nuristan
Sar-e Pol‡ .	15,999	626,100	39.1	Sar-e Pol
Khost† . .	4,152	n.a.	n.a.	Khost
Total . .	645,807	23,093,400	35.8	

* By 1996 the capital of Loghar province had changed to Pul-i-Alam from Baraki Barak and the capital of Wardak province had moved to Maidanshahr from Kowt-i-Ashrow; it was reported that the capital of Baghlan province had moved to Pol-e-Khomri: this was yet to be confirmed.

† Nuristan province (formerly part of Kunar and Laghman provinces) and Khost province (formerly part of Paktia province) had been created by 1991 and 1995, respectively. Competing factions reportedly disagreed about whether they were legally created.

‡ Sar-e Pol province (formerly part of Balkh, Jawzjan and Samangan provinces) had been created by 1990.

Source: Gwillim Law, *Administrative Subdivisions of Countries*.

PRINCIPAL TOWNS

(estimated population at March 1982)

Kabul (capital)	1,036,407	Kunduz	57,112
Qandahar	191,345	Baghlan	41,240
Herat	150,497	Maymana	40,212
Mazar-i-Sharif	110,367	Pul-i-Khomri	32,695
Jalalabad	57,824	Ghazni	31,985

Estimated population at July 1988: Kabul 1,424,400; Qandahar 225,500; Herat 177,300; Mazar-i-Sharif 130,600 (Source: UN, *Demographic Yearbook*).

BIRTHS AND DEATHS

(UN estimates, annual averages)

	1985–90	1990–95	1995–2000
Birth rate (per 1,000)	49.0	48.0	47.6
Death rate (per 1,000)	23.8	22.5	22.0

Source: UN, *World Population Prospects: The 2000 Revision*.

Expectation of life (WHO estimates, years at birth): 42.3 (males 41.1; females 43.7) in 2001 (Source: WHO, *World Health Report*).

ECONOMICALLY ACTIVE POPULATION*

(ISIC Major Divisions, persons aged 8 years and over, 1979 census)

	Males	Females	Total
Agriculture, hunting, forestry and fishing	2,358,821	10,660	2,369,481
Mining and quarrying	57,492	1,847	59,339
Manufacturing	170,908	252,465	423,373
Electricity, gas and water	11,078	276	11,354
Construction	50,670	416	51,086
Wholesale and retail trade	135,242	2,618	137,860
Transport, storage and communications	65,376	867	66,243
Other services	716,511	32,834	749,345
Total	**3,566,098**	**301,983**	**3,868,081**

*Figures refer to settled population only and exclude 77,510 persons seeking work for the first time (66,057 males; 11,453 females).

Mid-2001 (estimates in '000): Agriculture, etc. 6,099; Total labour force 9,153 (Source: FAO).

Health and Welfare

KEY INDICATORS

Total fertility rate (children per woman, 2001)	6.8
Under-5 mortality rate (per 1,000 live births, 2000)	279
HIV/AIDS (% of persons aged 15–49, 1994)	<0.01
Physicians (per 1,000 head, 1997)	0.11
Hospital beds (per 1,000 head, 1990)	0.25
Health expenditure (2000): US $ per head (PPP)	9
Health expenditure (2000): % of GDP	1.0
Health expenditure (2000): public (% of total)	63.5
Access to water (% of persons, 2000)	13
Access to sanitation (% of persons, 2000)	12

For sources and definitions, see explanatory note on p. vi.

Agriculture

PRINCIPAL CROPS

('000 metric tons)

	1997	1998	1999
Wheat	2,711	2,834	2,499
Rice (paddy)	400	450	280
Barley	250	240	216
Maize	300	330	240
Millet*	22	22	22
Potatoes*	235	235	235
Pulses*	50	50	50
Sesame seed*	24	24	24
Cottonseed	66†	66*	66*
Cotton (lint)*	22	22	22
Vegetables*	612	632	652
Watermelons*	90	90	90
Cantaloupes and other melons*	22	22	22
Grapes	330†	330†	330*
Sugar cane*	38	38	38
Sugar beets*	1	1	1
Apples*	18	18	18
Peaches and nectarines*	14	14	14
Plums*	35	35	35
Oranges*	12	12	12
Apricots*	38	38	38
Other fruit*	230	230	230

* FAO estimate(s).
† Unofficial figure.

Source: FAO.

LIVESTOCK

('000 head, year ending 30 September)

	1997	1998	1999
Horses	100	100	104
Mules*	26	28	30
Asses	805	860	920
Cattle	2,895	3,008	2,600
Camels	242	265	290
Sheep	15,110	16,252	14,000
Goats	5,530	6,599	6,000
Chickens (million)	7	8	7

* FAO estimates.

Source: FAO.

LIVESTOCK PRODUCTS

('000 metric tons)

	1997	1998	1999
Beef and veal*	156	171	149
Mutton and lamb*	123	128	112
Goat meat	33	39	35
Poultry meat	14	15	14
Other meat*	12	12	12
Cows' milk*	1,593	1,825	1,560
Sheep's milk*	227	246	210
Goats' milk*	100	120	135
Cheese	23	26	25
Butter and ghee	37	42	36
Hen eggs*	18	18	18
Honey*	3	3	3
Wool: greasy*	20	20	20
Wool: scoured*	12	13	13
Cattle hides	17	19	17
Sheepskins	19	20	18
Goatskins	6	8	7

* FAO estimates.

Source: FAO.

Forestry

ROUNDWOOD REMOVALS

(FAO estimates, '000 cubic metres, excl. bark)

	1999	2000	2001
Sawlogs, veneer logs and logs for sleepers*	856	856	856
Other industrial wood	904	904	904
Fuel wood	1,210	1,279	1,314
Total	2,970	3,039	3,074

* Assumed to be unchanged from 1976.

Source: FAO.

SAWNWOOD PRODUCTION

(FAO estimates, '000 cubic metres, incl. railway sleepers)

	1974	1975	1976
Coniferous (softwood)	360	310	380
Broadleaved (hardwood)	50	20	20
Total	410	330	400

1977–2001: Annual production as in 1976 (FAO estimates).

Source: FAO.

Fishing

(FAO estimates, metric tons, live weight)

	1998	1999	2000
Total catch (freshwater fishes)	1,200	1,200	1,000

Source: FAO, *Yearbook of Fishery Statistics*.

Mining

(estimates, '000 metric tons, unless otherwise indicated)

	1998	1999	2000
Hard coal	190	200	200
Natural gas (million cu metres)*	2,600	3,000	3,000
Copper ore†	5	5	5
Salt (unrefined)	13	13	13
Gypsum (crude)	3	3	3

* Figures refer to gross output. Marketed production (estimates, million cubic metres) was: 2,200 in 1998; 2,500 in 1999; 2,500 in 2000.

† Figures refer to metal content.

Source: US Geological Survey.

Industry

SELECTED PRODUCTS

(year ending 20 March, '000 metric tons, unless otherwise indicated)

	1986/87	1987/88	1988/89
Margarine	3.5	3.3	1.8
Vegetable oil	4	n.a.	n.a.
Wheat flour*	187	203	166
Wine ('000 hectolitres)*	289	304	194
Soft drinks ('000 hectolitres)	8,500	10,300	4,700
Woven cotton fabrics (million sq metres)	58.1	52.6	32.1
Woven woollen fabrics (million sq metres)	0.4	0.3	0.3
Footwear—excl. rubber ('000 pairs)*	613	701	607
Rubber footwear ('000 pairs)*	2,200	3,200	2,200
Nitrogenous fertilizers†	56	57	55
Cement	103	104	70
Electric energy (million kWh)*‡	1,171	1,257	1,109

* Production in calendar years 1986, 1987 and 1988.

† Production in year ending 30 June.

‡ Provisional.

Wheat flour ('000 metric tons): 1,832 in 1994; 2,029 in 1995; 2,145 in 1996.

Nitrogenous fertilizers (provisional, year ending 30 June, '000 metric tons): 14 in 1994/95; 10 in 1995/96; 5 in 1996/97; 5 in 1998/99; 5 in 1999/2000.

Cement (provisional, '000 metric tons): 116 in 1998; 120 in 1999; 120 in 2000.

Electric energy (provisional, year ending 20 March, million kWh): 565 in 1996/97; 505 in 1997/98; 485 in 1998/99.

Sources: UN, *Industrial Commodity Statistics Yearbook* and *Statistical Yearbook for Asia and the Pacific*, FAO (Rome) and US Geological Survey.

Finance

CURRENCY AND EXCHANGE RATES

Monetary Units

100 puls (puli) = 2 krans = 1 afghani (Af)

Sterling, Dollar and Euro Equivalents (31 December 2002)

£1 sterling = 4,835.4 afghanis
US $1 = 3,000.0 afghanis
€1 = 3,146.1 afghanis
10,000 afghanis = £2.068 = $3.333 = €3.179

Exchange Rate: The foregoing information refers to the official exchange rate. The official rate was maintained at US $1 = 1,000 afghanis between 1 May 1995 and 30 April 1996. From 1 May 1996 a rate of US $1 = 3,000 afghanis has been in operation. However, this rate is applicable to only a limited range of transactions. There is also a market-determined rate, which was US $1 = 34,000 afghanis in March 2002. A new afghani, equivalent to 1,000 of the old currency, was introduced in October 2002. The new currency was to replace the old afghani after a transitional period expected to last eight weeks.

BUDGET

(projections, US $ million, year ending 20 March)

Revenue*	2002/03
Current revenue	83.0
Total	83.0

Expenditure†	2002/03
Defence, interior and national security	198.8
Subsidies to state-owned enterprises	34.1
Other wages and salaries	104.3
Other goods and services	60.7
Other social transfers	18.8
Other capital expenditure	14.4
Interest payments	6.6
Contingency	22.5
Total	460.3

* Excluding foreign grants ($138.2 million).
† Excluding clearance of wage arrears ($22.5 million).

Source: IMF, *Islamic State of Afghanistan: Report on Recent Economic Developments and Prospects, and the Role of the Fund in the Reconstruction Process.*

BANK OF AFGHANISTAN RESERVES
(US $ million at December)*

	1989	1990	1991
IMF special drawing rights . . .	10.63	9.02	6.67
Reserve position in IMF	6.41	6.97	7.01
Foreign exchange	226.65	250.41	221.22
Total	243.69	266.40	234.89

* Figures exclude gold reserves, totalling 965,000 troy ounces since 1980. Assuming a gold price of 12,850 afghanis per ounce, these reserves were officially valued at US $245.06 million in December of each year 1985–91.

IMF special drawing rights (US $ million at December): 4.37 in 1992; 2.76 in 1993; 1.40 in 1994.

Reserve position in IMF (US $ million at December): 6.78 in 1992; 6.77 in 1993; 7.19 in 1994; 7.33 in 1995; 7.09 in 1996; 6.65 in 1997; 6.94 in 1998; 6.77 in 1999; 6.42 in 2000; 6.19 in 2001; 6.70 in 2002.

Source: IMF, *International Financial Statistics.*

MONEY SUPPLY
(million afghanis at 21 December)

	1989	1990	1991
Currency outside banks	222,720	311,929	454,750
Private-sector deposits at Bank of Afghanistan	12,838	13,928	19,368
Demand deposits at commercial banks	11,699	18,217	n.a.

Source: IMF, *International Financial Statistics.*

COST OF LIVING
(retail price index, excluding rent; base: 1990 = 100)

	1988	1989	1991
All items	39.6	67.9	143.8

Source: UN, *Statistical Yearbook for Asia and the Pacific.*

NATIONAL ACCOUNTS
('000 million afghanis at constant 1978 prices)

Gross Domestic Product by Economic Activity

	1991	1992	1993
Agriculture, hunting, forestry and fishing	59.9	62.7	57.3
Mining and quarrying			
Manufacturing	29.2	14.3	12.3
Electricity, gas and water . . .			
Construction	7.0	5.8	5.5
Wholesale and retail trade, restaurants and hotels . . .	11.1	10.5	10.1
Transport, storage and communications	4.8	4.5	2.0
Finance, insurance, real estate and business services . . .	2.1	2.0	1.8
GDP in purchasers' values .	114.1	99.8	89.0

Source: UN, *Statistical Yearbook for Asia and the Pacific.*

BALANCE OF PAYMENTS
(US $ million)

	1987	1988	1989
Exports of goods f.o.b.	538.7	453.8	252.3
Imports of goods f.o.b.	−904.5	−731.8	−623.5
Trade balance	−365.8	−278.0	−371.2
Exports of services	35.6	69.6	8.2
Imports of services	−156.3	−120.0	−103.4
Balance on goods and services	−486.5	−328.4	−466.4
Other income received	19.2	23.3	20.1
Other income paid	−11.3	−11.5	−7.9
Balance on goods, services and income	−478.6	−316.6	−454.2
Current transfers received . . .	311.7	342.8	312.1
Current transfers paid	—	—	−1.2
Current balance	−166.9	26.2	−143.3
Investment liabilities	−33.9	−4.1	−59.6
Net errors and omissions . . .	211.6	−47.7	182.8
Overall balance	10.8	−25.6	−20.1

Source: IMF, *International Financial Statistics.*

OFFICIAL DEVELOPMENT ASSISTANCE
(US $ million)

	1998	1999	2000
Bilateral	88.5	104.2	88.2
Multilateral	65.7	38.3	52.7
Total	154.2	142.5	140.9
Grants	154.3	140.9	140.9
Loans	−0.1	1.6	—
Per caput assistance (US $) . .	7.4	6.7	6.5

Source: UN, *Statistical Yearbook for Asia and the Pacific.*

2002/03 (estimates, US $ million): Bilateral grants 40.0; Multilateral grants 98.2 (Source: IMF, *Islamic State of Afghanistan: Report on Recent Economic Developments and Prospects, and the Role of the Fund in the Reconstruction Process*).

External Trade

PRINCIPAL COMMODITIES
(US $ '000, year ending 20 March)

Imports c.i.f.	1980/81	1981/82	1983/84*
Wheat	798	18,100	38,251
Sugar	40,833	50,328	25,200
Tea	28,369	n.a.	23,855
Cigarettes	5,114	7,219	12,755
Vegetable oil	17,320	26,332	30,481
Drugs	4,497	4,195	3,768
Soaps	9,991	17,256	8,039
Tyres and tubes	16,766	12,764	28,823
Textile yarn and thread . . .	16,800	24,586	n.a.
Cotton fabrics	873	6,319	n.a.
Rayon fabrics	6,879	9,498	n.a.
Other textile goods . . .	52,546	49,036	n.a.
Vehicles and spare parts . .	89,852	141,062	n.a.
Petroleum products . . .	124,000	112,093	n.a.
Footwear (new)	2,058	5,275	5,317
Bicycles	2,042	488	1,952
Matches	1,171	1,542	1,793
Sewing machines	140	285	266
Electric and non-electric machines	2,333	765	n.a.
Chemical materials . . .	7,464	6,636	n.a.
Agricultural tractors . . .	1	8,280	n.a.
Fertilizers	8,325	3,300	3,904
Used clothes	2,523	1,875	5,334
Television receivers . . .	5,391	3,241	10,139
Other items	106,662	92,307	n.a.
Total	551,748	622,416	846,022

* Figures for 1982/83 are not available.

Exports f.o.b.	1988/89	1989/90	1990/91
Fruit and nuts	103,400	110,200	93,300
Karakul furskins	6,100	3,600	3,000
Natural gas	93,200	n.a.	n.a.
Wool	30,900	5,500	9,600
Carpets	39,100	38,000	44,000
Cotton	8,000	5,300	2,500
Total (incl. others)	394,700	235,900	235,100

Source: IMF, *International Financial Statistics*.

1991/92 (selected exports f.o.b., million afghanis, year ending 20 March): Dried fruit and nuts 165,770; Karakul furskins 4,303; Wool 19,953; Carpets and rugs 52,887 (Source: UN, *Statistical Yearbook for Asia and the Pacific*).

1992/93 (selected exports f.o.b., million afghanis, year ending 20 March): Dried fruit and nuts 33,259; Wool 7,585; Carpets and rugs 21,920 (Source: UN, *Statistical Yearbook for Asia and the Pacific*).

1995/96 (selected exports f.o.b., million afghanis, year ending 20 March): Dried fruit and nuts 19,282; Karakul furskins 27; Wool 122; Carpets and rugs 67,083 (Source: UN, *Statistical Yearbook for Asia and the Pacific*).

Total imports c.i.f. (US $ million, year ending 20 March): 347 in 1994/95; 359 in 1995/96; 621 in 1996/97; 570 in 1997/98; 498 in 1998/99; 600 in 1999/2000 (Source: UN, *Statistical Yearbook for Asia and the Pacific*).

Total exports f.o.b. (US $ million, year ending 20 March): 102 in 1994/95; 166 in 1995/96; 127 in 1996/97; 146 in 1997/98; 142 in 1998/99; 150 in 1999/2000 (Source: UN, *Statistical Yearbook for Asia and the Pacific*).

PRINCIPAL TRADING PARTNERS
(estimates, US $ million)

Imports	1997	1998	1999
ASEAN members	149	51	41
Indonesia	20	19	12
Malaysia	10	11	7
Singapore	101	14	14
Thailand	18	7	8
SAARC members	58	81	121
Bangladesh	10	10	1
India	25	26	27
Pakistan	21	42	90
Central Asian republics	39	46	41
Kazakhstan	9	13	8
Kyrgyzstan	4	3	3
Tajikistan	3	4	2
Turkmenistan	23	26	28
Other Asian countries			
China, People's Republic	36	27	18
Hong Kong	11	7	5
Japan	97	67	73
Turkey	7	24	n.a.
Western Europe	67	64	40
Russia	21	15	15
USA	13	8	20
Total (incl. others)	561	495	468

Exports	1997	1998	1999
ASEAN members	8	1	2
Singapore	7	—	1
SAARC members	35	34	46
India	3	8	9
Pakistan	30	25	36
Central Asian republics	6	9	4
Tajikistan	4	6	—
Turkmenistan	2	3	3
Other Asian countries			
China, People's Republic	1	n.a.	3
Japan	9	1	1
Western Europe	45	56	25
Russia	7	7	6
USA	10	16	8
Total (incl. others)	147	143	111

Source: UN, *Statistical Yearbook for Asia and the Pacific*.

Transport

ROAD TRAFFIC
('000 motor vehicles in use)

	1995	1996	1997
Passenger cars	1.6	4.1	4.6
Commercial vehicles	0.6	n.a.	n.a.

Passenger cars ('000 in use): 4.9 in 1998 (Source: UN, *Statistical Yearbook for Asia and the Pacific*).

CIVIL AVIATION
('000)

	1997	1998	1999
Kilometres flown	6,000	3,000	3,000
Passengers carried	90	53	140
Passenger-km	158,000	88,000	129,000
Freight ton-km	50,000	24,000	19,000

Source: UN, *Statistical Yearbook*.

Tourism

	1996	1997	1998
Tourist arrivals ('000)	4	4	4
Tourism receipts (US $ million)	1	1	1

Source: World Tourism Organization, *Yearbook of Tourism Statistics*.

Communications Media

	1995	1996	1997
Radio receivers ('000 in use)	2,400	2,550	2,750
Television receivers ('000 in use)	200	250	270
Main telephone lines ('000 in use)*†	29	29	29
Daily newspapers:			
Number	15*	12	n.a.
Average circulation ('000 copies)	200*	113	n.a.

* Estimate(s).

† 1998–2000: Number of main telephone lines in use assumed to be unchanged.

Television receivers ('000 in use): 290 in 1998; 300 in 1999.

Source: mainly UNESCO, *Statistical Yearbook* and UN, *Statistical Yearbook*.

Education

(1995/96)

	Institutions	Teachers	Pupils
Pre-primary	88	2,110	n.a.
Primary	2,146	21,869	1,312,200
Secondary*	n.a.	19,085	512,900
Higher	n.a.	n.a.	12,800

* Figures refer to general secondary education only, excluding vocational and teacher training.

Source: UN, *Statistical Yearbook for Asia and the Pacific*.

Adult literacy rate (UNESCO estimates): 36% in 1999 (Source: UN Development Programme, *Human Development Report*).

Directory

The Constitution

Immediately after the coup of 27 April 1978 (the Saur Revolution), the 1977 Constitution was abolished. Both Nur Mohammad Taraki (Head of State from April 1978 to September 1979) and his successor, Hafizullah Amin (September–December 1979), promised to introduce new constitutions, but these leaders were removed from power before any drafts had been prepared by special commissions which they had appointed. On 21 April 1980 the Revolutionary Council ratified the Basic Principles of the Democratic Republic of Afghanistan. These were superseded by a new Constitution ratified in April 1985. Another new Constitution was ratified during a meeting of a Loya Jirga (Grand National Council), held on 29–30 November 1987. This Constitution was amended in May 1990. The following is a summary of the Constitution as it stood in May 1990.

GENERAL PROVISIONS

The fundamental duty of the State is to defend the independence, national sovereignty and territorial integrity of the Republic of Afghanistan. National sovereignty belongs to the people. The people exercise national sovereignty through the Loya Jirga and the Meli Shura.

Foreign policy is based on the principle of peaceful co-existence and active and positive non-alignment. Friendship and co-operation are to be strengthened with all countries, particularly neighbouring and Islamic ones. Afghanistan abides by the UN Charter and the Universal Declaration of Human Rights and supports the struggle against colonialism, imperialism, Zionism, racism and fascism. Afghanistan favours disarmament and the prevention of the proliferation of nuclear and chemical weapons. War propaganda is prohibited.

Islam is the religion of Afghanistan and no law shall run counter to the principles of Islam.

Political parties are allowed to be formed, providing that their policies and activities are in accordance with the provisions of the Constitution and the laws of the country. A party that is legally formed cannot be dissolved without legal grounds. Judges and prosecutors cannot be members of a political party during their term of office.

Pashtu and Dari are the official languages.

The capital is Kabul.

The State shall follow the policy of understanding and co-operation between all nationalities, clans and tribes within the country to ensure equality and the rapid development of backward regions.

The family constitutes the basic unit of society. The State shall adopt necessary measures to ensure the health of mothers and children.

The State protects all forms of legal property, including private property. The hereditary right to property shall be guaranteed according to Islamic law.

For the growth of the national economy, the State encourages foreign investment in the Republic of Afghanistan and regulates it in accordance with the law.

RIGHTS AND DUTIES OF THE PEOPLE

All subjects of Afghanistan are equal before the law. The following rights are guaranteed: the right to life and security, to complain to the appropriate government organs, to participate in the political sphere, to freedom of speech and thought, to hold peaceful demonstrations and strikes, to work, to free education, to protection of health and social welfare, to scientific, technical and cultural activities, to freedom of movement both within Afghanistan and abroad, to observe the religious rites of Islam and of other religions, to security of residence and privacy of communication and correspondence, and to liberty and human dignity.

In criminal cases, an accused person is considered innocent until guilt is recognized by the court. Nobody may be arrested, detained or punished except in accordance with the law.

Every citizen is bound to observe the Constitution and the laws of the Republic of Afghanistan, to pay taxes and duties to the State in accordance with the provisions of the law, and to undertake military service, when and as required.

LOYA JIRGA

This is the highest manifestation of the will of the people of Afghanistan. It is composed of: the President and Vice-Presidents, members of the Meli Shura (National Assembly), the General Prosecutor, the Council of Ministers, the Attorney-General, his deputies and members of the Attorney-General's Office, the chairman of the Constitution Council, the heads of the provincial councils, representa-tives from each province, according to the number of their representatives in the Wolasi Jirga (House of Representatives), elected by the people by a general secret ballot, and a minimum of 50 people, from among prominent political, scientific, social and religious figures, appointed by the President.

The Loya Jirga is empowered: to approve and amend the Constitution; to elect the President and to accept the resignation of the President; to consent to the declaration of war and armistice; and to adopt decisions on major questions regarding the destiny of the country. The Loya Jirga shall be summoned, opened and chaired by the President. Sessions of the Loya Jirga require a minimum attendance of two-thirds of the members. Decisions shall be adopted by a majority vote. In the event of the dissolution of the Wolasi Jirga (House of Representatives), its members shall retain their membership of the Loya Jirga until a new Wolasi Jirga is elected. Elections to the Loya Jirga shall be regulated by law and the procedure laid down by the Loya Jirga itself.

THE PRESIDENT

The President is the Head of State and shall be elected by a majority vote of the Loya Jirga for a term of seven years. No person can be elected as President for more than two terms. The President is accountable, and shall report, to the Loya Jirga. The Loya Jirga shall be convened to elect a new President 30 days before the end of the term of office of the outgoing President. Any Muslim citizen of the Republic of Afghanistan who is more than 40 years of age can be elected as President.

The President shall exercise the following executive powers: the supreme command of the armed forces; the ratification of the resolutions of the Meli Shura; the appointment of the Prime Minister; the approval of the appointment of ministers, judges and army officials; the granting of citizenship and the commuting of punishment; the power to call a referendum, to proclaim a state of emergency, and to declare war (with the consent of the Loya Jirga). Should a state of emergency continue for more than three months, the consent of the Loya Jirga is imperative for its extension.

In the event of the President being unable to perform his duties, the presidential functions and powers shall be entrusted to the first Vice-President. In the event of the death or resignation of the President, the first Vice-President shall ask the Loya Jirga to elect a new President within one month. In the event of resignation, the President shall submit his resignation directly to the Loya Jirga.

MELI SHURA

The Meli Shura (National Assembly) is the highest legislative organ of the Republic of Afghanistan. It consists of two houses: the Wolasi Jirga (House of Representatives) and the Sena (Senate). Members of the Wolasi Jirga (representatives) are elected by general secret ballot for a legislative term of five years. Members of the Sena (senators) are elected and appointed in the following manner: two people from each province are elected for a period of five years; two people from each provincial council are elected by the council for a period of three years; and the remaining one-third of senators are appointed by the President for a period of four years.

The Meli Shura is vested with the authority: to approve, amend and repeal laws and legislative decrees, and to present them to the President for his signature; to interpret laws; to ratify and annul international treaties; to approve socio-economic development plans and to endorse the Government's reports on their execution; to approve the state budget and to evaluate the Government's report on its execution; to establish and make changes to administrative units; to establish and abolish ministries; to appoint and remove Vice-Presidents, on the recommendation of the President; and to endorse the establishment of relations with foreign countries and international organizations. The Wolasi Jirga also has the power to approve a vote of confidence or no confidence in the Council of Ministers or one of its members.

At its first session, the Wolasi Jirga elects, from among its members, an executive committee, composed of a chairman, two deputy chairmen and two secretaries, for the whole term of the legislature. The Sena elects, from among its members, an executive committee, composed of a chairman for a term of five years, and two deputy chairmen and two secretaries for a term of one year.

Ordinary sessions of the Meli Shura are held twice a year and do not normally last longer than three months. An extraordinary session can be held at the request of the President, the chairman of either house, or one-fifth of the members of each house. The houses of the Meli Shura can hold separate or joint sessions. Sessions require a minimum attendance of two-thirds of the members of each house and decisions shall be adopted by a majority vote. Sessions are open, unless the houses decide to meet in closed sessions.

The following authorities have the right to propose the introduction, amendment or repeal of a law in either house of the Meli Shura: the President, the standing commissions of the Meli Shura, at least one-tenth of the membership of each house, the Council of Ministers, the Supreme Court, and the office of the Attorney-General.

If the decision of one house is rejected by the other, a joint committee, consisting of an equal number of members from both houses, shall be formed. A decision by the joint committee, which will be agreed by a two-thirds majority, will be considered valid after approval by the President. If the joint committee fails to resolve differences, the matter shall be discussed in a joint session of the Meli Shura, and a decision reached by a majority vote. The decisions that are made by the Meli Shura are enforced after being signed by the President.

After consulting the chairman of the Wolasi Jirga, the chairman of the Sena, the Prime Minister, the Attorney-General and the chairman of the Constitution Council, the President can declare the dissolution of the Wolasi Jirga, stating his justification for doing so. Re-elections shall be held within 3 months of the dissolution.

COUNCIL OF MINISTERS

The Council of Ministers is composed of: a Prime Minister, deputy Prime Ministers and Ministers. The Council of Ministers is appointed by the Prime Minister. It is empowered: to formulate and implement domestic and foreign policies; to formulate economic development plans and state budgets; and to ensure public order.

The Council of Ministers is dissolved under the following conditions: the resignation of the Prime Minister, chronic illness of the Prime Minister, the withdrawal of confidence in the Council of Ministers by the Meli Shura, the end of the legislative term, or the dissolution of the Wolasi Jirga or the Meli Shura.

THE JUDICIARY

See section on the Judicial System.

THE CONSTITUTION COUNCIL

The responsibilities of this body are: to evaluate and ensure the conformity of laws, legislative decrees and international treaties with the Constitution; and to give legal advice to the President on constitutional matters. The Constitution Council is composed of a chairman, a vice-chairman and eight members, who are appointed by the President.

LOCAL ADMINISTRATIVE ORGANS

For the purposes of local administration, the Republic of Afghanistan is divided into provinces, districts, cities and wards. These administrative units are led, respectively, by governors, district administrators, mayors and heads of wards. In each province a provincial council and district councils are formed in accordance with the law. Provincial councils and district councils each elect a chairman and a secretary from among their members. The term of office of a provincial council and a district council is three years.

FINAL PROVISIONS

Amendments to the Constitution shall be made by the Loya Jirga. Any amendment shall be on the proposal of the President, or on the proposal of one-third and the approval of two-thirds of the members of the Meli Shura. Amendment to the Constitution during a state of emergency is not allowed.

Note: Following the downfall of Najibullah's regime in April 1992, a provisional *mujahidin* Government assumed power in Kabul. In July an acting executive body, known as the Leadership Council, appointed a special commission to draw up a new and more strictly Islamic Constitution. In September 1993 it was reported that a draft Constitution had been approved by the commission, in preparation for the holding of a general election.

In May 1996, following the signing of the Mahipar Agreement between President Burhanuddin Rabbani and Gulbuddin Hekmatyar, a Constitution to cover the interim period pending the holding of a general election was drawn up and published. The main provisions of the Constitution of the Interim Period were as follows:

General provision: Afghanistan is an Islamic country where all aspects of the life of the people shall be conducted according to the tenets of Shari'a.

President: The President is the Head of State and exercises the highest executive power; the President is the supreme commander of the armed forces and his approval is required for the appointment of all civil and military officials; the President is authorized to declare war or peace (on the advice of the Council of Ministers or an Islamic Shura), to approve death sentences or grant pardons, to summon and dismiss a Shura, and to sign international treaties. In the event of the President's death, the presidential functions and powers shall

be entrusted to the President of the Supreme Court until a new Head of State can be appointed.

Council of Ministers: The Council of Ministers, under the leadership of the Prime Minister, shall discuss and make decisions regarding government policy (both internal and external), the annual budget and administrative regulations, all of which shall be referred to the President for his assent.

According to the Agreement on Provisional Arrangements in Afghanistan Pending the Re-establishment of Permanent Government Institutions (also known as the Bonn Agreement) signed in December 2001, following the overthrow of the Taliban regime, Afghanistan reverted to the Constitution of 1964. (As long as the provisions were not inconsistent with those included in the Bonn Agreement; provisions relating to the monarchy, the executive body and legislature were excluded. In addition, existing laws could remain as long as they were consistent with the Bonn Agreement and the 1964 Constitution.) The Transitional Authority, with the assistance of the UN, established a Constitutional Drafting Commission in November 2002 to draw up a new constitution. A final draft was expected to be completed by October 2003 and submitted to the Constitutional Loya Jirga for adoption.

The Government

On 11–19 June 2002 an Emergency Loya Jirga, comprising approximately 1,650 delegates, 1,051 of whom were elected by tribal representatives, and the remainder selected by aid organizations, universities and other civil society bodies to ensure diverse representation, convened. The Loya Jirga appointed a broad-based, gender-sensitive Transitional Authority and a Head of State. At least 18 months later a Constitutional Loya Jirga, in the form of a constituent assembly, was scheduled to adopt a new constitution and prepare the country for democratic elections.

TRANSITIONAL AUTHORITY
(April 2003)

President: HAMID KARZAI.

Vice-Presidents: Marshal MUHAMMAD QASSIM FAHIM, ABDUL KARIM KHALILI, HEDAYAT AMIN ARSALA, NAMATULLAH SHAHRANI.

Special Adviser on Security: YOUNIS QANOONI.

Cabinet:

Minister of Defence: Marshal MUHAMMAD QASSIM FAHIM.

Minister of Foreign Affairs: Dr ABDULLAH ABDULLAH.

Minister of Finance: ASHRAF GHANI.

Minister of Interior Affairs: ALI AHMAD JALALI.

Minister of Planning: Haji MOHAMMAD MOHAQQEQ.

Minister of Communications: MASOOM STANAKZAI.

Minister of Border Affairs: ARIF NURZAI.

Minister of Refugees: INTAYATULLAH NAZERI.

Minister of Mines and Industries: (vacant).

Minister of Light Industries: MOHAMMAD ALIM RAZM.

Minister of Public Health: Dr SOHAILA SIDDIQI.

Minister of Commerce: SAYED MUSTAFA KASEMI.

Minister of Agriculture: SAYED HUSSAIN ANWARI.

Minister of Justice: ABBAS KARIMI.

Minister of Information and Culture: SAYED MAKHDOOM RAHIM.

Minister of Reconstruction: MOHAMMAD FAHIM FARHANG.

Minister of Haj and Mosques: MOHAMMAD AMIN NAZIRYAR.

Minister of Urban Affairs: YUSUF PASHTUN.

Minister of Public Works: ABDUL ALI.

Minister of Social Affairs: NOOR MOHAMMAD KARKIN.

Minister of Water and Power: AHMAD SHAKAR KARKAR.

Minister of Irrigation and the Environment: AHMAD YUSUF.

Minister of Martyrs and Disabled People: ABDULLAH WARDAK.

Minister of Higher Education: SHARIF FAIZ.

Minister of Civil Aviation and Tourism: Mir WAIS SADDIQ.

Minister of Transport: SAYED MOHAMMAD ALI JAWAD.

Minister of Education: YOUNIS QANOONI.

Minister of Rural Development: HANIF ASMAR.

Minister of Women's Affairs: HABIBA SORABI.

MINISTRIES

Office of the Council of Ministers: Shar Rahi Sedarat, Kabul; tel. (93) 26926.

Office of the Prime Minister: Prime Minister Compound, Kabul; tel. (20) 2102101.

Ministry of Agriculture: Jamal Mina, Kabul; tel. (93) 41151.

Ministry of Border Affairs: Shah Mahmud Ghazi Ave, Kabul; tel. (93) 21793.

Ministry of Civil Aviation and Tourism: POB 165, Ansari Wat, Kabul; tel. (93) 21015.

Ministry of Commerce: Darulaman Wat, Kabul; tel. (93) 2290090; fax (93) 2290089.

Ministry of Communications: Mohammad Jan Khan Wat, Kabul; fax (20) 290022; e-mail admin@af-com-ministry.org; internet www.af-com-ministry.org.

Ministry of Defence: Darulaman Wat, Kabul; tel. (93) 41232.

Ministry of Education: Mohammad Jan Khan Wat, Kabul; tel. and fax (20) 200000.

Ministry of Finance: Shar Rahi Pashtunistan, Kabul; tel. (93) 26041.

Ministry of Foreign Affairs: Shah Mahmud Ghazi St, Shar-i-Nau, Kabul; tel. (93) 25441.

Ministry of Haj and Mosques: Kabul.

Ministry of Higher Education: Jamal Mina, Kabul; tel. (93) 40041.

Ministry of Information and Culture: Mohammad Jan Khan Wat, Kabul; tel. and fax (20) 200000.

Ministry of Interior Affairs: Shar-i-Nau, Kabul; tel. (93) 32441.

Ministry of Irrigation and Environment: Kabul.

Ministry of Justice: Shar Rahi Pashtunistan, Kabul; tel. (93) 23404.

Ministry of Light Industries: Ansari Wat, Kabul; tel. (93) 41551.

Ministry of Martyrs and Disabled People: Kabul.

Ministry of Mines and Industries: Shar Rahi Pashtunistan, Kabul; tel. (93) 25841.

Ministry of Planning: Shar-i-Nau, Kabul; tel. (93) 21273.

Ministry of Public Health: Micro-Rayon, Kabul; tel. (93) 40851.

Ministry of Public Works: Kabul.

Ministry of Reconstruction: Micro-Rayon, Kabul; tel. (93) 63701.

Ministry of Refugees: Kabul.

Ministry of Rural Development: Kabul.

Ministry of Social Affairs: Kabul.

Ministry of Transport: Ansari Wat, Kabul; tel. (93) 25541.

Ministry of Water Resources Development and Irrigation: Darulaman Wat, Kabul; tel. (93) 40743.

Ministry of Urban Affairs: Kabul.

Ministry of Water and Power: Kabul.

Ministry of Women's Affairs: Kabul.

Legislature

A Meli Shura (National Assembly) was established in 1987 to replace the Revolutionary Council. It was composed of two houses: the Wolasi Jirga (House of Representatives) and the Sena (Senate). However, following the downfall of Najibullah's regime in April 1992, an interim *mujahidin* Government took power in Kabul and both houses were dissolved. A High State Council was formed under the chairmanship of the President. In September 1996 the Taliban took over Kabul and closed down the council. On assuming power, the regime adopted an Interim Council of Ministers to administer the country. After the Taliban regime collapsed in late 2001, an Interim Authority was installed. Owing to the failure of the Emergency Loya Jirga in June 2002 to agree on a future National Assembly, President Karzai announced that a National Assembly Commission would be established to address the composition and powers of a new legislature.

Political Organizations

Afghan Mellat Party (Afghan Social Democratic Party): e-mail ajmal.mirranay@afghanmellat.com; internet www.afghanmellat.com; Pres. Dr ANWAR-UL-HAQ AHADY.

Harakat-i Islami i Afghanistan (Islamic Movement of Afghanistan): Kabul; Leader Ayatollah MUHAMMED ASIF MUNSHI.

Hizb-i Islami Gulbuddin (Islamic Party Gulbuddin): e-mail info@hezb-e-islami.org; internet www.hezb-e-islami.org; Pashtun/Turkmen/Tajik; Leader GULBUDDIN HEKMATYAR; c. 50,000 supporters (estimate); based in Iran in 1998–99.

Hizb-i Islami Khalis (Islamic Party Khalis): Pashtun; Leader MAULVI MUHAMMAD YUNUS KHALIS; c. 40,000 supporters (estimate).

Hizb-i Wahadat i Islami (Islamic Unity Party): Kabul; coalition of Hazara groups; Leaders KARIM KHALILI, MOHAQQEQ.

Ittihad-i-Islami Bara i Azadi Afghanistan (Islamic Union for the Liberation of Afghanistan): Pashtun; Leader Prof. ABDUL RASUL SAYEF; Dep. Leader AHMAD SHAH AHMADZAY; c. 18,000 supporters (estimate).

Jamiat-i Islami (Islamic Society): internet www.jamiat.com; Turkmen/Uzbek/Tajik; Leaders Prof. BURHANUDDIN RABBANI, Marshal MUHAMMAD FAHIM; Sec.-Gen. ENAYATOLLAH SHADAB; c. 60,000 supporters (estimate).

Jebha-i-Nejat-i-Melli (National Liberation Front): Pashtun; Leader Prof. HAZRAT SIBGHATULLAH MOJADDEDI; Sec.-Gen. ZABIHOLLAH MOJADDEDI; c. 15,000 supporters (estimate).

Jonbesh-i Melli-i Islami (National Islamic Movement): f. 1992; formed mainly from troops of former Northern Command of the Afghan army; predominantly Uzbek/Tajik/Turkmen/Ismaili and Hazara Shi'ite; Leader Gen. ABDUL RASHID DOSTAM; 65,000–150,000 supporters.

Mahaz-i-Melli-i-Islami (National Islamic Front): Pashtun; Leader PIR SAYED AHMAD GAILANI; Dep. Leader HAMED GAILANI; c. 15,000 supporters (estimate).

Nizat-i-Milli: Kabul; f. 2002; Leader YOUNIS QANOONI.

Taliban: internet www.taleban.com; emerged in 1994; Islamist fundamentalist; mainly Sunni Pashtuns; in power 1996–2001; largely disbanded; Leader Mola MOHAMMAD OMAR.

Diplomatic Representation

EMBASSIES IN AFGHANISTAN

Austria: POB 24, Zarghouna Wat, Kabul; tel. (93) 32720.

Bangladesh: Kabul; tel. (93) 25783.

Bulgaria: Wazir Akbar Khan Mena, Kabul; tel. (93) 20683; Ambassador ANGEL URBETSOV.

China, People's Republic: Sardar Shah Mahmoud Ghazi Wai, Kabul; tel. (93) 20446; Ambassador SUN YUXI.

Cuba: Shar Rahi Haji Yaqub, opp. Shar-i-Nau Park, Kabul; tel. (93) 30863.

France: POB 62, Shar-i-Nau, Kabul; tel. (93) 23631; Chargé d'affaires a.i. JEAN-MARIN SCHUH.

Germany: Wazir Akbar Khan Mena, POB 83, Kabul; tel. (93) 22432; Ambassador RAINER EBERLE.

Hungary: POB 830, Sin 306–308, Wazir Akbar Khan Mena, Kabul; tel. (93) 24281.

India: Malalai Wat, Shar-i-Nau, Kabul; tel. (93) 30556; Ambassador VIVEK KATJU.

Indonesia: POB 532, Wazir Akbar Khan Mena, District 10, Zone 14, Road Mark Jeem House 93, Kabul; tel. (93) 20586.

Iran: Shar-i-Nau, Kabul; tel. (93) 26255; Ambassador MOHAMMAD IBRAHIM TAHERIAN.

Iraq: POB 523, Wazir Akbar Khan Mena, Kabul; tel. (93) 24797.

Italy: POB 606, Khoja Abdullah Ansari Wat, Kabul; tel. (93) 24624; Ambassador DOMENICO GIORGI.

Japan: POB 80, Wazir Akbar Khan Mena, Kabul; tel. (93) 26844; Ambassador KINICHI KOMANO.

Korea, Democratic People's Republic: Wazir Akbar Khan Mena, House 28, Sarak 'H' House 103, Kabul; tel. (93) 22161.

Kuwait: Kabul; Chargé d'affaires NASEER AHMED NOOR.

Libya: 103 Wazir Akbar Khan, Kabul; tel. (20) 25948; fax (20) 290160.

Mongolia: Wazir Akbar Khan Mena, Sarak 'T' House 8714, Kabul; tel. (93) 22138.

Pakistan: Kabul; tel. (91) 287464; fax (91) 287460; Ambassador RUSTAM SHAH MOHMAND.

Poland: Gozargah St, POB 78, Kabul; tel. (93) 42461.

Russia: Darulaman Wat, Kabul; tel. (93) 41541; Ambassador MIKHAIL KONAROVSKII.

Saudi Arabia: Kabul; Chargé d'affaires FAHD AL-QAHTANI.

Slovakia: Taimani Wat, Kala-i-Fatullah, Kabul; tel. (93) 32082.

Sudan: Kabul.

Sweden: Kabul; Ambassador PETER TEIJER.

Tajikistan: Kabul; Ambassador FARHOD MAHKAMOV.

Turkey: Shar-i-Nau, Kabul; tel. (93) 20072; Ambassador MUFIT OZDES.

Turkmenistan: Kabul; Ambassador AMANMAMMET YARANOW.

United Arab Emirates: Kabul; Ambassador ALI MUHAMMAD AL-SHAMSI.

United Kingdom: Karte Parwan, Kabul; tel. (93) 30512; Ambassador RONALD NASH.

USA: The Great Masoud Rd, Kabul; tel. (20) 290002; fax (20) 290153; Ambassador ROBERT FINN.

Uzbekistan: Kabul; Ambassador ALISHER AHMADJONOV.

Viet Nam: 3 Nijat St, Wazir Akbar Khan Mena, Kabul; tel. (93) 26596.

Judicial System

After 23 years of civil war, which ended in December 2001 with the defeat of the Taliban, there no longer existed a functioning national judicial system. In accordance with the Bonn Agreement, Afghanistan reverted to the Constitution of 1964, which combined *Shari'a* with Western concepts of justice. A new constitution was expected to be introduced in late 2003. In the mean time, a judicial commission was established in November 2002 to address the issues of judicial and legislative reform.

Chief Justice: FAZUL HADI SHINWARI.

Religion

The official religion of Afghanistan is Islam. Muslims comprise 99% of the population, approximately 84% of them of the Sunni and the remainder of the Shi'ite sect. There are small minority groups of Hindus, Sikhs and Jews.

ISLAM

The High Council of Ulema and Clergy of Afghanistan: Kabul; f. 1980; 7,000 mems; Chair. Mawlawi ABDOL GHAFUR SENANI.

The Press

Many newspapers and periodicals stopped appearing on a regular basis or, in a large number of cases, ceased publication during the civil war. Following the defeat of the Taliban in late 2001, a number of newspapers and periodicals resumed publication or were established for the first time.

PRINCIPAL DAILIES

Hewad (Homeland): Kabul; tel. (93) 26851; f. 1959; revived by the Taliban in 1998; Pashto; state-owned.

Kabul Times: POB 983, Ansari Wat, Kabul; tel. (93) 61847; f. 1962 as Kabul Times, renamed Kabul New Times in 1980; ceased publication in 2001; revived in 2002 under new management; English; state-owned.

Shari'at: Kabul.

PERIODICALS

Aamu: Aria Press, Kabul; quarterly; research; circ. 1,000.

Ambastagi: Aria Press, Kabul; weekly; circ. 1,000.

Anees: Kabul; weekly; government-supported; Editor AHMAD ZIA SYAMAK.

Kabul Weekly: Kabul; f. 1993; banned in 1997, revived in 2002; Dari, Pashto, English and French; weekly; independent; Editor-in-Chief FAHIM DASHTY; circ. c. 4,000.

Kilid (The Key): Kabul; weekly; current affairs.

Malalai: Kabul; f. 2002; monthly; women's; Chief Editor JAMILA MUJAHID.

Les Nouvelles de Kaboul (Kabul News): Kabul; f. 2002; monthly; Dari, Pashto and French; French-owned; Editor OLIVIER PUECH.

Payam-e-Mujahid: Panjshir; internet www.payamemujahid.com; weekly; Dari and Pashto; controlled by Burhanuddin Rabbani.

Roz (The Day): Kabul; f. 2002; monthly; women's; Dari, Pashto, French and English; Editor-in-Chief LAILOMA AHMADI.

Seerat (Character): Kabul; f. 2002; weekly; women's; circ. 1,000; Deputy Editor NAJIBA MURAM.

Women's Mirror: Kabul; f. 2002; weekly; independent; women's.

Zanbil e Gham: Kabul; monthly; satirical.

NEWS AGENCIES

Afghan Islamic Press: Peshawar, North-West Frontier Province, Pakistan.

Aria Press: Kabul; f. 1987; in Dushanbe, Tajikistan; independent; publishes three newsletters.

Bakhtar Information Agency (BIA): Ministry of Information and Culture, Mohammad Jan Khan Wat, Kabul; tel. and fax (20) 200000; f. 1939; Head Sultan AHMAD BAHEEN.

Reuters: POB 1069, Islamabad, Pakistan; tel. (51) 2274757; e-mail simon.denyer@reuters.com; Bureau Chief SIMON DENYER.

PRESS ASSOCIATIONS

Plans were under way in early 2003 to create an independent journalists' union in Kabul.

Afghanistan Women in Media Network: Kabul; f. 2002; association of female media staff; Pres. JAMILA MUJAHID.

Publishers

Some of the following publishers were forced to close down during the Taliban regime. Since the fall of the Taliban, publishers have been slowly reopening, with the help of the UN and other international aid agencies and foreign publishing houses.

Afghan Book: POB 206, Kabul; f. 1969; books on various subjects, translations of foreign works on Afghanistan, books in English on Afghanistan and Dari language textbooks for foreigners; Man. Dir JAMILA AHANG.

Afghanistan Today Publishers: POB 983, c/o The Kabul Times, Ansari Wat, Kabul; tel. (93) 61847; publicity materials; answers enquiries about Afghanistan.

Balhaqi Book Publishing and Importing Institute: POB 2025, Kabul; tel. (93) 26818; f. 1971 by co-operation of the Government Printing House, Bakhtar News Agency and leading newspapers; publishers and importers of books; Pres. MUHAMMAD ANWAR NUMYALAI.

Book Publishing Institute: Herat; f. 1970 by co-operation of Government Printing House and citizens of Herat; books on literature, history and religion.

Book Publishing Institute: Qandahar; f. 1970; supervised by Government Printing House; mainly books in Pashto language.

Educational Publications: Ministry of Education, Mohd Jan Khan Wat, Kabul; tel. and fax (20) 200000; textbooks for primary and secondary schools in the Pashto and Dari languages; also three monthly magazines in Pashto and in Dari.

Franklin Book Programs Inc: POB 332, Kabul.

Historical Society of Afghanistan: Kabul; tel. (93) 30370; f. 1931; mainly historical and cultural works and two quarterly magazines: *Afghanistan* (English and French), *Aryana* (Dari and Pashto); Pres. AHMAD ALI MOTAMEDI.

Institute of Geography: Kabul University, Kabul; geographical and related works.

International Center for Pashto Studies: Kabul; f. 1975 by the Afghan Govt with the assistance of UNESCO; research work on the Pashto language and literature and on the history and culture of the Pashto people; Pres. and Assoc. Chief Researcher J. K. HEKMATY; publs *Pashto* (quarterly).

Kabul University Press: Kabul; tel. (93) 42433; f. 1950; textbooks; two quarterly scientific journals in Dari and in English, etc.

Research Center for Linguistics and Literary Studies: Afghanistan Academy of Sciences, Akbar Khan Mena, Kabul; tel. (93) 26912; f. 1978; research on Afghan languages (incl. Pashto, Dari, Balochi and Uzbek) and Afghan folklore; Pres. Prof. MOHAMMED R. ELHAM; publs *Kabul* (Pashto), *Zeray* (Pashto weekly) and *Khurasan* (Dari).

Government Publishing House

Government Printing House: Kabul; tel. (93) 26851; f. 1870; under supervision of the Ministry of Information and Culture; Dir SAID AHMAD RAHAA.

Broadcasting and Communications

TELECOMMUNICATIONS

Afghan Wireless Communication Company (AWCC): Ministry of Communications Bldg, Mohammad Jan Khan Wat, Kabul; tel. and fax (93) 200000; e-mail info@afghanwireless.com; internet www.afghanwireless.com; f. 1999; jt venture between the Afghan Government and Telephone Systems International, Inc of the USA; reconstruction of Afghanistan's national and international telecommunications network; by June 2002 mobile and fixed-line telecommunications services covered Herat, Jalalabad, Kabul, Mazar-i-Sharif and Qandahar; the first centre providing internet services was opened in Kabul in July; CEO EHSAN BAYAT.

BROADCASTING

The media were severely restricted by the militant Taliban regime (1996–2001): television was banned and Radio Afghanistan was renamed Radio Voice of Shari'a. The overthrow of the Taliban in November–December 2001 led to the liberation of the media. On 13 November Radio Afghanistan was revived in Kabul; music was broadcast for the first time in five years. A few days later Kabul TV was resurrected, and a woman was employed as its newsreader.

Radio-Television Afghanistan: POB 544, Ansari Wat, Kabul; tel. (93) 20355; revived in 2001; programmes in Dari, Pashto, Turkmen and Uzbek; Gen. Dir MOHAMMAD ISAQ.

Radio Herat: Herat.

Radio Kabul: Kabul.

Voice of Freedom: Kabul; f. 2002; broadcasts one hour a day in Dari and Pashto; German-funded.

Kabul TV: Kabul; revived in 2001; broadcasts four hrs daily; Dir HUMAYUN RAWI.

TV Badakshan: Faizabad; f. 1987 as Faizabad TV, name changed in 2000; Pashto and Dari.

Balkh Radio and TV: Mazar-i-Sharif; Pashto and Dari; Chair. ABDORRAB JAHED.

Finance

(cap. = capital; auth. = authorized; p.u. = paid up; res = reserves; m. = million; brs = branches; amounts in afghanis unless otherwise stated)

BANKING

In June 1975 all banks were nationalized. There are no foreign banks operating in Afghanistan. The banking sector was under reconstruction in 2002, following the collapse of the Taliban regime.

Da Afghanistan Bank (Central Bank of Afghanistan): Ibne Sina Wat, Kabul; tel. (93) 24075; f. 1939; main functions: banknote issue, modernize the banking system, re-establish banking relations with international banks, create a financial market system, foreign exchange regulation, govt and private depository, govt fiscal agency; Gov. Dr ANWAR-UL-HAQ AHADY; 84 brs.

Agricultural Development Bank of Afghanistan: POB 414, Cineme Pamir Bldg, Jade Maiwand, Kabul; tel. (93) 24459; f. 1959; makes available credits for farmers, co-operatives and agro-business; aid provided by IBRD and UNDP; Chair. Dr M. KABIAR; Pres. Dr ABDULLAH NAQSHBANDI.

Banke Millie Afghan (Afghan National Bank): Jade Ibne-Sina, PO Box 522, Kabul; tel. (20) 2100311; fax (20) 2101801; f. 1933; Chair. Dr ANWAR-UL-HAQ AHADY; Pres. Prof. ABDUL QAYOOM ARIF; 19 brs in Afghanistan, 6 brs overseas.

Export Promotion Bank of Afghanistan: 24 Mohd Jan Khan Wat, Kabul; tel. (93) 24447; f. 1976; provides financing for exports and export-orientated investments; Pres. MOHAMMAD YAQUB NEDA; Vice-Pres. BURHANUDDIN SHAHIM.

Industrial Development Bank of Afghanistan: POB 14, Shar-i-Nau, Kabul; tel. (93) 33336; f. 1973; provides financing for industrial development; cap. 10,500m. (1996); Pres. Haji RAHMATULLAH.

Pashtany Tejaraty Bank (Afghan Commercial Bank): Mohd Jan Khan Wat, Kabul; tel. (93) 26551; f. 1954 to provide short-term credits, forwarding facilities, opening letters of credit, purchase and sale of foreign exchange; Chair. Dr BASIR RANJBAR; Pres. and CEO ZIR GUL WARDAK; 14 brs.

INSURANCE

There is one national insurance company:

Afghan National Insurance Co: National Insurance Bldg, Park, Shar-i-Nau, POB 329, Kabul; tel. (93) 33531; fax (762) 523846; f. 1964; mem. of Asian Reinsurance Corpn; marine, aviation, fire, motor and accident insurance; Pres. M. ABDULLAH MUDASIR; Claims Man. MEHRABUDDIN MATEEN.

No foreign insurance companies have been permitted to operate in Afghanistan.

Trade and Industry

GOVERNMENT AGENCIES

Board for the Promotion of Private Investment: Kabul.

Export Promotion Department: Ministry of Commerce, Darulaman Wat, Kabul; fax (93) 2290089; f. 1969; provides guidance for traders, collects and disseminates trade information, markets and performs quality control of export products.

High Commission for Combating Drugs: Kabul.

CHAMBERS OF COMMERCE AND INDUSTRY

Afghan Chamber of Commerce and Industry: Mohd Jan Khan Wat, Kabul; tel. (93) 26796; fax (93) 2290089; Head Mola MOHAMMAD DAUD ABED.

Federation of Afghan Chambers of Commerce and Industry: Darulaman Wat, Kabul; f. 1923; includes chambers of commerce and industry in Ghazni, Qandahar, Kabul, Herat, Mazar-i-Sharif, Fariab, Jawzjan, Kunduz, Jalalabad and Andkhoy.

INDUSTRIAL AND TRADE ASSOCIATIONS

Afghan Carpet Exporters' Guild: POB 3159, Darulaman Wat, Kabul; tel. (93) 41765; f. 1967; a non-profit-making, independent organization of carpet manufacturers and exporters; Pres. ZIAUDDIN ZIA; c. 1,000 mems.

Afghan Cart Company: POB 61, Zerghona Maidan, Kabul; tel. (20) 2201309; fax (20) 290238; f. 1988; the largest export/import company in Afghanistan; imports electrical goods, machinery, metal, cars, etc. exports raisins, medical herbs, wood, animal hides, etc; Pres. KABIR IMAQ.

Afghan Fruit Processing Co: POB 261, Industrial Estate, Puli Charkhi, Kabul; tel. (93) 65186; f. 1960; exports raisins, other dried fruits and nuts.

Afghan Raisin and Other Dried Fruits Institute: POB 3034, Sharara Wat, Kabul; tel. (93) 30463; exporters of dried fruits and nuts; Pres. NAJMUDDIN MUSLEH.

Afghan Wool Enterprises: Shar-i-Nau, Kabul; tel. (93) 31963.

Afghanistan Karakul Institute: POB 506, Puli Charkhi, Kabul; tel. (93) 61852; f. 1967; exporters of furs; Pres. G. M. BAHEER.

Afghanistan Plants Enterprise: POB 122, Puli Charkhi, Kabul; tel. (93) 31962; exports medicines, plants and spices.

Handicraft Promotion and Export Centre: POB 3089, Sharara Wat, Kabul; tel. (93) 32935; MOMENA RANJBAR.

Parapamizad Co Ltd: Jadai Nader Pashtoon, Sidiq Omar Market, POB 1911, Kabul; tel. (93) 22116; export/import co; Propr PADSHAH SARBAZ.

TRADE UNION

National Union of Afghanistan Employees (NUAE): POB 756, Kabul; tel. (93) 23040; f. 1978 as Central Council of Afghanistan Trade Unions, to establish and develop the trade union movement, including the formation of councils and organizational cttees in the provinces; name changed in 1990; composed of seven vocational unions; 300,000 mems; Pres. A. HABIB HARDAMSHAID; Vice-Pres. ASAD KHAN NACEIRY.

Transport

RAILWAYS

There is no railway system currently operating in Afghanistan.

ROADS

In 2001 there were an estimated 23,500 km of roads, of which more than 18,000 km were unpaved. All-weather highways link Kabul with Qandahar and Herat in the south and west, Jalalabad in the east and Mazar-i-Sharif and the Amu-Dar'ya river in the north. A massive reconstruction programme of the road system in Afghanistan began in early 2002. The Salang Highway was rehabilitated, thus reconnecting Kabul with the north. In November the first of five bridges across the River Pyanj on the Tajik–Afghan border was reopened for use.

Afghan International Transport Company: Kabul.

Afghan Container Transport Company Ltd: House No. 43, St No. 2, Left West of Charahe-Haji Yaqub, Shar-e-Naw, Kabul; tel. and fax (20) 2201392.

Afghan Transit Company: POB 530, Ghousy Market, Mohammad Jan Khan Wat, Kabul; tel. (93) 22654.

AFSOTR: Kabul; resumed operations in 1998; transport co; 90 vehicles.

Land Transport Company: Khoshal Mena, Kabul; tel. (93) 20345; f. 1943; commercial transport within Afghanistan.

The Milli Bus Enterprise: Ministry of Transport, Ansari Wat, Kabul; tel. (93) 25541; state-owned and -administered; 721 buses; Pres. Eng. Aziz Naghaban.

Salang-Europe International Transport and Transit: Kabul; f. 1991 as joint Afghan/Soviet co; 500 vehicles.

INLAND WATERWAYS

There are 1,200 km of navigable inland waterways, including the Amu-Dar'ya (Oxus) river, which is capable of handling vessels of up to about 500 dwt. River ports on the Amu-Dar'ya are linked by road to Kabul.

CIVIL AVIATION

In early 2002 there were international airports at Kabul and Qandahar, and almost 50 local airports were located throughout the country.

Ministry of Civil Aviation and Tourism: POB 165, Ansari Wat, Kabul; tel. (93) 21015.

Ariana Afghan Airlines: POB 76, Afghan Air Authority Bldg, Ansari Wat, Kabul; tel. (873) 762523844; fax (873) 762523846; e-mail flyariana@mail.com; internet www.flyariana.com; f. 1950; merged with Bakhtar Afghan Airlines Co Ltd in 1985; govt-owned; flights suspended in Nov. 1999–Jan. 2002, owing to UN sanctions; flights to India and United Arab Emirates resumed in March 2002; Pres. Capt. Jahed Azimi.

Tourism

Afghanistan's potential tourism attractions include: Bamian, with its thousands of painted caves; Bandi Amir, with its suspended lakes; the Blue Mosque of Mazar; Herat, with its Grand Mosque and minarets; the towns of Qandahar and Girishk; Balkh (ancient Bactria), 'Mother of Cities', in the north; Bagram, Hadda and Surkh Kotal (of interest to archaeologists); and the high mountains of the Hindu Kush. Furthermore, ruins of a Buddhist city dating from the second century were discovered in July 2002 in southern Afghanistan. The restoration of cultural heritage, sponsored by UNESCO, was under way in mid-2002. In 1998 an estimated 4,000 tourists visited Afghanistan and receipts from tourism amounted to around US $1m.

Afghan Tourist Organization (ATO): Ansari Wat, Shar-i-Nau, Kabul; tel. (93) 30323; f. 1958; Pres. Mohd Kazim Wardak (acting).

ALBANIA

Introductory Survey

Location, Climate, Language, Religion, Flag, Capital

The Republic of Albania lies in south-eastern Europe. It is bordered by Serbia and Montenegro to the north and north-east, by the former Yugoslav republic of Macedonia to the east, by Greece to the south and by the Adriatic and Ionian Seas (parts of the Mediterranean Sea) to the west. The climate is Mediterranean throughout most of the country. The sea plays a moderating role, although frequent cyclones in the winter months make the weather unstable. The average temperature is 14°C (57°F) in the north-east and 18°C (64°F) in the south-west. The language is Albanian, the principal dialects being Gheg (north of the Shkumbini river) and Tosk (in the south). An official ban on religious worship was in effect between 1967 and 1990. Before 1946 Islam was the predominant faith, and there were small groups of Christians (mainly Roman Catholic in the north and Eastern Orthodox in the south). The national flag (proportions 5 by 7) is red, with a two-headed black eagle in the centre. The capital is Tirana (Tiranë).

Recent History

On 28 November 1912, after more than 400 years of Turkish rule, Albania declared its independence under a provisional Government. Although the country was occupied by Italy in 1914, its independence was re-established in 1920. Albania was declared a republic in 1925 and Ahmet Beg Zogu was elected President; proclaimed King Zog in 1928, he reigned until he was forced into exile by the Italian occupation of Albania in April 1939. Albania was united with Italy for four years, before being occupied by German forces in 1943; the Germans withdrew one year later.

The communist-led National Liberation Front (NLF), established in 1941, was the most successful wartime resistance group and took power on 29 November 1944. Elections in December 1945 were contested by only communist candidates. The new regime was headed by Enver Hoxha, the leader of the Albanian Communist Party (ACP) since 1943. King Zog was declared deposed and the People's Republic of Albania was proclaimed on 11 January 1946. The ACP was renamed the Party of Labour of Albania (PLA) in 1948, the NLF having been succeeded by the Democratic Front of Albania (DFA) in 1945.

The communist regime developed close relations with Yugoslavia until the latter's expulsion from the Cominform (a Soviet-sponsored body co-ordinating the activities of European Communist parties) in 1948. Albania, fearing Yugoslav expansionism, became a close ally of the USSR and joined the Moscow-based Council for Mutual Economic Assistance (CMEA) in 1949. Hoxha resigned as Head of Government in 1954, but retained effective national leadership as First Secretary of the PLA. Albania joined the Warsaw Treaty Organization (Warsaw Pact) in 1955, but relations with the USSR deteriorated when Soviet leaders attempted a *rapprochement* with Yugoslavia. The Albanian leadership declared its support for the People's Republic of China in the Sino–Soviet ideological dispute, prompting the USSR to suspend relations with Albania in 1961. Albania established increasingly close relations with China, ended participation in the CMEA in 1962 and withdrew from the Warsaw Pact in 1968. However, following the improvement of relations between China and the USA after 1972, and the death of Mao Zedong, the Chinese leader, in 1976, Sino-Albanian relations progressively deteriorated. In 1978 Albania declared its support for Viet Nam in its dispute with China, prompting the Chinese Government to suspend all economic and military co-operation with Albania.

A new Constitution was adopted in December 1976, and the country was renamed the People's Socialist Republic of Albania. In December 1981 Mehmet Shehu, the Chairman of the Council of Ministers (Prime Minister) since 1954, died as a result of a shooting incident. Although officially reported to have committed suicide, there were suggestions of a leadership struggle with Hoxha, and subsequent allegations that he had been executed. Following the death of Shehu, a new Government, headed by Adil Çarçani, hitherto the First Deputy Chairman, was established. In November 1982 Ramiz Alia replaced Haxhi Lleshi as President of the Presidium of the People's Assembly (Head of State). A number of former state and PLA officials were reportedly executed in September 1983.

Enver Hoxha died in April 1985, and was succeeded as First Secretary of the PLA by Alia. In March 1986 Hoxha's widow, Nexhmije, was elected to the chairmanship of the General Council of the DFA. Alia was re-elected as First Secretary of the PLA and as President of the Presidium of the People's Assembly in November 1986 and February 1987, respectively. In the latter month Adil Çarçani was reappointed Chairman of the Council of Ministers.

In November 1989, on the 45th anniversary of Albania's liberation from Nazi occupation, an amnesty for certain prisoners (including some political prisoners) was declared. From December a number of anti-Government demonstrations were reportedly staged, particularly in the northern town of Shkodër. In late January, while continuing to deny the reports of internal unrest, Alia announced proposals for limited political and economic reform, including the introduction of a system of multi-candidate elections (although the leading role of the PLA was to be maintained). As part of a reorganization of the judicial system, approved by the People's Assembly in May, the Ministry of Justice was re-established, and the number of capital offences was considerably reduced. Although Albania was to remain a secular state, the practice of religion was henceforth to be tolerated. Furthermore, Albanians were to be granted the right to foreign travel, while the penalty for attempting to flee the country illegally was reduced. Following renewed unrest in July, in which anti-Government demonstrators in Tirana were violently dispersed by the security forces, more than 5,000 Albanians took refuge in foreign embassies, and were subsequently granted permission to leave the country. Meanwhile, the membership of both the Council of Ministers and the Political Bureau of the PLA had been reorganized; a number of prominent anti-reformists were among those replaced.

In November 1990, in response to increasing domestic pressure, Alia announced proposals for more radical political reforms, urging that the leading role of the PLA be redefined. In December it was announced that the establishment of independent political parties was to be permitted, prior to elections to the People's Assembly, scheduled to take place in February 1991. In mid-December 1990, however, anti-Government demonstrators clashed with the security forces in several cities. Nexhmije Hoxha resigned from the chairmanship of the General Council of the DFA, and was replaced by Çarçani (who was, in turn, replaced in mid-1991).

On 20 February 1991, following widespread anti-Government demonstrations, Alia declared presidential rule. An eight-member Presidential Council was established, and a provisional Council of Ministers was appointed. Çarçani was replaced as Chairman of the Council of Ministers by Fatos Nano, a progressive economist, who had been appointed Deputy Chairman at the end of January. In late February the unrest finally ended, owing, in part, to an increased use of force by the authorities.

Meanwhile, following opposition pressure, the elections had been postponed until the end of March 1991 to allow the newly established political organizations more time for preparation. Despite these concessions, an increasing number of ethnic Greek Albanians attempted to leave the country. In mid-March a general amnesty for all political prisoners was declared. The first round of the multi-party elections to the People's Assembly duly took place on 31 March, with second and third ballots on 7 and 14 April, respectively. The PLA and affiliated organizations won 169 of the 250 seats, while the Democratic Party of Albania (DPA) secured 75 seats, and the Democratic Union of the Greek Minority (OMONIA) obtained five seats. The victory of the PLA, amid allegations of electoral malpractice, prompted dismay in some urban areas, where support for the DPA had been strong. Widespread protests ensued, and in Shkodër security forces opened fire on demonstrators, killing four.

In late April 1991 an interim Constitution replaced that of 1976, pending the drafting of a new constitution. The country was renamed the Republic of Albania, and the post of executive

President, to be elected by two-thirds of votes cast in the People's Assembly, was created. Alia was subsequently elected to the new post, defeating the only other candidate, Namik Dokle, also of the PLA; all the opposition deputies abstained from voting. In early May Nano was reappointed Chairman of the Council of Ministers, and the Government was again reorganized. In accordance with the provisions of the interim Constitution, Alia resigned from the leadership of the PLA.

In early June 1991 the continuing general strike forced the resignation of Nano's administration. A Government of National Stability was subsequently formed, with Ylli Bufi (hitherto Minister of Food) as Chairman of the Council of Ministers. The coalition included representatives of the PLA, the DPA, the Albanian Republican Party (ARP), the Social Democratic Party (SDP) and the Agrarian Party (AP). Gramoz Pashko, a prominent member of the DPA, was appointed Deputy Chairman of the Council of Ministers and Minister of the Economy. At its 10th Congress, which took place later in June, the PLA was renamed the Socialist Party of Albania (SPA).

In August 1991, following a further seaborne exodus of migrants to Italy, the ports of Albania were placed under military control. Several vessels were refused entry by the Italian authorities, while many of the Albanians who had succeeded in disembarking were repatriated. Further opposition strikes and demonstrations were staged in subsequent weeks. In early December the Chairman of the DPA, Dr Sali Berisha, announced the withdrawal of party members from the coalition Government, despite opposition from other prominent DPA officials. The withdrawal of the seven DPA representatives, following the expulsion of three ARP ministers who had criticized the administration, forced Bufi's Government to resign. President Alia subsequently appointed an interim Government, principally comprising non-party 'technocrats', under a new Prime Minister, Vilson Ahmeti (hitherto Minister of Food); new elections were to take place in March 1992.

A new electoral law, approved by the People's Assembly in early February 1992, reduced the number of deputies in the Assembly from 250 to 140. Under provisions that defined legitimate political parties, OMONIA, as an organization representing an ethnic minority, was prohibited from contesting the forthcoming general election, prompting widespread protest from the Greek minority. At the general election, which was conducted in two rounds on 22 and 29 March, the DPA secured 92 of the 140 contested seats, while the SPA obtained 38 seats, the SDP seven seats, the Union for Human Rights Party (UHRP —supported by the minority Greek and Macedonian communities) two seats and the ARP one seat. According to official figures, 90% of the electorate participated. Following the defeat of the SPA, Alia resigned as President on 3 April. A few days later the new People's Assembly elected Berisha to the presidency. Berisha subsequently appointed a coalition Government, with Aleksander Meksi, a member of the DPA, as Prime Minister. The DPA held an additional 14 ministerial portfolios, while the SDP and ARP were allocated one portfolio each.

In July 1992 the Albanian Communist Party (which had been reconstituted in 1991) was banned. At the end of the month the DPA secured 43% of the total votes cast in the country's first multi-party local elections since the Second World War, while the SPA recovered some of the support that it had lost in the March general election, with 41% of the votes. In September divisions within the DPA resulted in the defection of a number of prominent party members, who had accused the Berisha administration of becoming increasingly right-wing and authoritarian, to form a new political grouping, the Democratic Alliance Party (DAP).

During 1992 a number of former communist officials were detained, including Nexhmije Hoxha, who was arrested on charges of corruption. In February 1993 the former Prime Minister, Vilson Ahmeti, was placed under house arrest, following charges of corruption; further allegations concerning abuse of power resulted in the arrest of another former Prime Minister, Fatos Nano (who was by this time President of the SPA), in July. Nexhmije Hoxha was imprisoned for nine years in January, having been convicted of embezzling state funds. (She was released in January 1997, after her term of imprisonment was twice reduced.) In August 1993 Alia was arrested on charges of abuse of power. Later that month Ahmeti was sentenced to two years' imprisonment. The trial of Nano commenced in April 1994, despite an international campaign on his behalf, organized by the SPA, and a European Parliament resolution appealing for his release. Nano was convicted of

misappropriation of state funds during his premiership in 1991, and was sentenced to 12 years' imprisonment. In July 1994 Alia, who had denied the charges against him, was sentenced to nine years' imprisonment for abuse of power and violating the rights of citizens. (In July 1995, however, under the terms of a general amnesty, Alia, and a further 30 political prisoners, were released.)

In October 1994 a draft Constitution was finally presented to Berisha, but failed to obtain the requisite two-thirds' majority approval in the People's Assembly, and was consequently submitted for endorsement at a national referendum. As a result of Berisha's personal campaign in support of the draft Constitution (which was to vest additional powers in the President, and reduce those of the legislature), the referendum was widely perceived as a vote of confidence in his leadership. At the referendum, which took place on 6 November, with the participation of 84.4% of the electorate, the draft Constitution was rejected by 53.9% of the voters, prompting demands for a general election (on the grounds that the administration lacked a popular mandate). In early December Berisha effected an extensive reorganization of the Council of Ministers. On the following day the ARP, which held only one seat in the People's Assembly, withdrew from the governing coalition. The SDP split into two factions; a new grouping, known as the Union of Social Democrats (USD—led by the Minister of Culture, Youth and Sport, Teodor Laco), remained in the coalition, and the SDP withdrew.

In March 1995 the Chairman of the DPA, Eduard Selami, was removed from his post at an extraordinary party congress, for opposing Berisha's efforts to organize a further referendum on the draft Constitution. Selami's accusations concerning Berisha's abuse of his position reinforced widespread discontent at the perceived corruption in the latter's administration. Public discontent at the slow pace of economic recovery in Albania was demonstrated by the continued flow of illegal immigrants to Italy, which, in May, deployed troops along its coast in an attempt to stem the influx.

In June 1995 Ilir Hoxha, the son of Enver Hoxha, was convicted on charges of inciting national hatred, after condemning leaders of the DPA in a newspaper interview. In September the People's Assembly adopted legislation prohibiting those in power under the former communist regime from holding public office until 2002 (thereby banning a large number of prospective candidates, including incumbent SPA deputies, from contesting legislative elections in 1996). In the same month the Minister of Justice dismissed three Supreme Court judges, owing to their alleged activities under the communist regime. The Chairman of the Supreme Court, Zef Brozi, challenged the Minister's authority to dismiss employees of the Court and refused to accept the decision. Following an ensuing ruling against Brozi by the Constitutional Court, which declared his previous suspension of lower court verdicts to be illegal, he was dismissed by the People's Assembly, and replaced by his deputy. The SPA deputies boycotted the People's Assembly, in protest at Brozi's dismissal and the Government's alleged infringement of the independence of the judiciary.

In November 1995 a parliamentary commission initiated an inquiry, following the discovery of a mass grave near the border town of Shkodër. Families of the deceased urged the prosecution service to initiate charges against former members of the communist regime, including Alia, who had allegedly been responsible for the killing by border guards of nationals attempting to flee the country in 1990–92. Also in November the People's Assembly approved legislation requiring senior civil servants to be investigated for their activities under the communist regime. In December 14 prominent former members of the communist regime were arrested on charges of involvement in the execution, internment and deportation of citizens for political reasons. (In May 1996 three of the former officials received death sentences, which were later commuted to terms of imprisonment, while the remaining defendants also received custodial terms in August and September.) In February Alia was detained in connection with the killing of demonstrators in Shkodër in April 1991 and the border incidents.

Following increasing division within the SPA, in March 1996 a liberal faction left the organization to form the Albanian New Socialist Party. The first round of the elections (which was preceded by SPA allegations of intimidation by the security forces) took place on 26 May; following alleged electoral irregularities, however, the principal opposition parties, including the SPA, the SDP and the DAP, withdrew from the poll and issued a statement rejecting the election results. A subsequent SPA demonstration held in protest at the alleged malpractice was violently dispersed by the security forces. The second round of the elections took place on 2 June; as a result of opposition demands for a boycott, only 59.4% of the electorate participated in the poll (compared with 89% in the first round). According to official results, the DPA secured 101 of the 115 directly elected seats (25 seats were to be allocated proportionately). However, international observers, who included representatives of the Organization for Security and Co-operation in Europe (OSCE, see p. 283), formerly the Conference on Security and Co-operation in Europe (CSCE), claimed that widespread malpractice and intimidation of voters had been perpetrated and urged the Government to conduct fresh elections, while SPA deputies initiated a hunger strike in an attempt to oblige Berisha to annul the results. Berisha rejected the allegations, and agreed to conduct further elections in only 17 constituencies. The principal opposition parties (which demanded that fresh elections be held, under international supervision, in all constituencies) continued their electoral boycott. Consequently, the DPA won all the seats contested in the partial elections, which took place on 16 June, thereby securing a total of 122 of the 140 seats in the People's Assembly. The SPA won 10 of the remaining seats, while the UHRP and the ARP each secured three and the National Front two. (The SPA, however, refused to recognize the new legislature and boycotted the inaugural session of the People's Assembly.) The OSCE subsequently issued a report, stating that the elections had failed to meet international legal standards. In early July Meksi, who had been reappointed to the office of Prime Minister, formed a new Council of Ministers.

In August 1996 the Government established a permanent Central Electoral Commission, prior to local government elections, which were scheduled to take place in October; the main opposition parties subsequently nominated a number of representatives to the Commission. Despite continued division within the SPA, Nano (who remained in prison) was re-elected as Chairman at a party congress in late August. In the local government elections, which took place in two rounds in late October, the DPA secured the highest number of votes in 58 of the 64 municipalities and in 267 of the 309 communes. Although the OSCE had withdrawn its observers, after Berisha claimed that one of its members was biased against the DPA, monitors from the Council of Europe (see p. 181) declared that, despite some irregularities, the elections had been conducted fairly.

In January 1997 the collapse of several popular 'pyramid' financial investment schemes (which had offered high rates of interest), resulting in huge losses of individual savings, prompted violent anti-Government demonstrations, particularly in Tirana and the southern town of Vlorë. It was widely believed that members of the Government were associated with the pyramid schemes, which had allegedly financed widespread illegal activities. The People's Assembly subsequently adopted legislation prohibiting the schemes. However, the Government increased efforts to suppress the protests (which were supported by a newly established opposition alliance, Forum for Democracy): large numbers of demonstrators were arrested and prominent opposition members were publicly assaulted by the security forces. At the end of January the People's Assembly granted Berisha emergency powers to mobilize special army units to restore order. It was reported that several people were killed in ensuing violent clashes between security forces and protesters (who continued to demand the resignation of Berisha and state reimbursement for the financial losses that they had incurred). On 3 March, however, Berisha, whose mandate was due to expire in April, was re-elected unopposed for a second five-year term (with the SPA continuing to boycott the People's Assembly).

Following an escalation in hostilities between insurgents (who seized armaments from military depots) and government troops in the south of the country, Berisha declared a national state of emergency at the beginning of March 1997, empowering security forces to shoot demonstrators and imposing total official censorship. However, insurgent groups gained control of the southern towns of Vlorë, Sarandë and Gjirokastër, and it was reported that large numbers of government forces had deserted or defected to join the rebels. Following negotiations with representatives of nine principal opposition parties, Berisha signed an agreement whereby an interim coalition government was to be installed, pending elections in June, and offered an amnesty to rebels who surrendered to the authorities. A former SPA mayor of Gjirokastër, Bashkim Fino, was appointed to the office of Prime Minister. Berisha subsequently approved the forma-

tion of a Government of National Reconciliation, which included representatives of eight opposition parties. (The DAP had withdrawn from the negotiations, after its proposal that the interior portfolio be allocated to an opposition member was rejected.) Despite these concessions, the insurgency continued, reaching the northern town of Tropojë and Tirana (where rebels seized the airport). All those detained in Tirana central prison, including Nano and Alia, were released; Nano was subsequently granted an official pardon by Berisha. The evacuation of western European and US nationals from Tirana and Durrës was impeded by the rebels, who exchanged fire with foreign troops effecting the evacuation. Extreme hardship and concern that the fighting would escalate into widespread civil conflict prompted thousands of Albanians to flee to Italy. Later in March, however, Italian naval authorities were ordered to intercept boats transporting Albanian refugees, in an effort to halt the exodus.

In late March 1997 it was reported that government forces had regained control of Tirana; the south of the country was controlled by insurgent groups opposed to the Government, while the north was largely held by paramilitary units loyal to Berisha. The Government of National Reconciliation requested military assistance in the restoration of civil order, and in late March Fino appealed to European Union (EU, see p. 199) foreign ministers for the establishment of a multinational force to supervise aid operations in Albania. At the end of March the UN Security Council endorsed an OSCE proposal that member states be authorized to contribute troops to the force. The 5,915-member Multinational Protection Force for Albania was established in April, with an official mission (known as Operation Alba) to facilitate the distribution of humanitarian assistance; the Italian contingent numbered 2,500, and the French 1,000, while Turkey, Greece, Spain, Romania, Austria and Denmark also contributed troops. The Force (which had a mandate to remain in the country for three months) was subsequently deployed in regions under government control in northern and central Albania. After negotiations between Italian forces and insurgents at Vlorë, the leader of the 'national committee for public salvation', Ekeren Osmani, announced that he would co-operate with the Italian troops.

At the beginning of April 1997 the SPA ended its boycott of the People's Assembly, which subsequently voted to end press restrictions that had been imposed under the state of emergency in March. Later in April the National Council of the DPA endorsed Berisha's leadership of the party and removed a number of dissident members who had demanded his resignation. The son of King Zog and claimant to the throne, Leka Zogu, returned to Albania in April, with the support of the pro-monarchist Legality Movement Party; the principal political parties had already agreed to conduct a referendum on the restoration of the monarchy. In early May the People's Assembly adopted legislation regulating the operation of pyramid investment schemes. Later in May the DPA submitted to the People's Assembly legislation on a new electoral system, which was approved, despite a further parliamentary boycott by SPA deputies; under the new legislation, the number of deputies in the People's Assembly was to be increased from 140 to 155, of whom 115 were to be directly elected and 40 elected on the basis of proportional representation. After discussions between the principal political parties, Franz Vranitzky, an OSCE special envoy, announced that further elections would take place on 29 June. The SPA and its allied parties agreed to participate in the elections, after Berisha complied with the stipulation that the Central Electoral Commission be appointed by the interim Government (rather than by himself).

Election campaigning was marred by violence, including a number of bomb explosions in Tirana. Leaders of the DPA and SPA signed an agreement in Rome, Italy, pledging to abide by the results of the election. On 29 June 1997 the first round of voting in the election to the People's Assembly took place; a referendum on the restoration of the monarchy was conducted on the same day. Despite the presence of the Multinational Protection Force (the mandate of which had been extended to mid-August), three people were reportedly killed in violent incidents during the voting. A further electoral ballot took place in 32 constituencies on 6 July. OSCE observers subsequently declared the electoral process to have been conducted satisfactorily. Later in July the Central Electoral Commission announced that the SPA had secured 101 seats in the People's Assembly, while the DPA had won 29 seats; the SPA and its allied parties (the SDP, the DAP, the AP and the UHRP) thereby secured the requisite two-thirds' majority for the approval of constitutional amendments that they had proposed earlier in the month. At the referendum, 66.7% of the electorate voted in favour of retaining a republic; at the end of August the Constitutional Court upheld the result, following a legal challenge by monarchists (who had accused the Central Electoral Commission of malpractice). On 24 July, following Berisha's resignation, the Secretary-General of the SPA, Dr Rexhep Mejdani, was elected President by the People's Assembly. Parliamentary deputies also voted to end the state of emergency imposed in March. The SPA proposed Nano to the office of Prime Minister, and a new Council of Ministers was appointed, which comprised representatives of the SPA and its allied parties, and retained Fino in the post of Deputy Prime Minister. At the end of July the new Government's programme for the restoration of civil order and economic reconstruction received a vote of confidence in the People's Assembly. The legislature also voted in favour of auditing existing pyramid schemes and investigating those that had been dissolved, in an attempt to reimburse lost savings.

In August 1997 the Government dispatched troops to the south of the country, in an effort to restore order in major towns that were under the control of rebel forces. It was subsequently announced that Vlorë had been recaptured and a number of rebel forces arrested; the Minister of the Interior ordered that all armaments looted during the unrest be surrendered to the authorities. By mid-August the Multinational Protection Force had left Albania, after the expiry of its mandate.

In early September 1997 the People's Assembly established a parliamentary commission, which was to draft a new constitution, in accordance with the amendments proposed by the SPA. Later in September an SPA member, Gafur Mazreku, shot and wounded an opposition deputy, following an acrimonious parliamentary session. Mazreku was subsequently charged with attempted murder, and the incident further exacerbated relations between the SPA and the DPA, which initiated a boycott of the People's Assembly. In October Berisha was re-elected Chairman of the DPA. In the same month Alia and three other former senior officials were acquitted of genocide by a Tirana court (upholding a ruling of the Supreme Court), on the grounds that the charge did not exist under the penal legislation of the former communist Government.

Violent unrest continued in early 1998, with numerous minor bomb attacks, one of which, in January, destroyed SPA offices in Gjirokastër. In February tensions in Shkodër precipitated an armed revolt by civilians and rebel members of the local security forces, who seized the town's police station and released a number of prisoners from custody. Government troops subsequently restored order in Shkodër; Berisha, however, attributed responsibility for the uprising to the Nano administration, and reiterated demands that further elections be organized.

In March 1998 the DPA announced that it was to end its boycott of the People's Assembly, in order to express support within the legislature for ethnic Albanians in Kosovo and Metohija, Yugoslavia (see below). At partial local government elections on 21 June a government electoral coalition, Alliance for the State, secured five of the seven contested municipalities and six of the nine contested communes, while a DPA-led opposition grouping, known as the Union for Democracy, won the remainder. Despite opposition claims of irregularities, OSCE observers declared that the elections had been conducted fairly. In early July a parliamentary commission, which had been established in October 1997 to investigate the unrest earlier that year, submitted a report recommending that several senior DPA officials, including Berisha, be charged in connection with the deployment of the armed forces to suppress the protests. Later in July 1998 Nano announced that the constitutional commission had presented draft legislation, which would be submitted for approval by the People's Assembly in October; the new Constitution was subsequently to be referred for endorsement at a national referendum.

In early September 1998 Azem Hajdari, a prominent DPA official and close associate of Berisha, was assassinated outside the party headquarters in Tirana. Berisha accused Nano of involvement in the killing, and demanded the resignation of the Government, and the DPA resumed its boycott of the People's Assembly. The incident prompted violent protests by DPA supporters, who seized government offices and occupied the state television and radio buildings. Government security forces subsequently regained control of the capital, after clashes with protesters, in which about seven people were reported to have been killed. Berisha denied government claims that the uprising constituted a coup attempt, and DPA supporters staged a dem-

onstration in his support in Tirana. Later in September the People's Assembly voted in favour of ending Berisha's parliamentary exemption from prosecution, thereby allowing him to be charged with attempting to overthrow the Government. An OSCE delegation, which mediated subsequent discussions between the political parties, condemned Berisha for inciting unrest, but also criticized Nano for the continued corruption within his administration. At the end of September the Minister of Public Order resigned, amid widespread criticism of the Government's failure to improve public security. Shortly afterwards Nano tended his resignation, following a meeting of the SPA leadership, having failed to reach agreement with the government coalition on the composition of a new Council of Ministers. Mejdani subsequently requested that the Secretary-General of the SPA, Pandeli Majko, who had been nominated by the party to the office of Prime Minister, form a new government. In early October a new coalition Council of Ministers, headed by Majko, was installed. Later that month the People's Assembly approved the draft Constitution (with the DPA and other deputies belonging to the Union for Democracy boycotting the vote). The new Constitution, which provided for the post-communist system of government, was submitted for endorsement at a national referendum, monitored by OSCE observers, on 22 November. The Government announced that 50.1% of the registered electorate had participated in the referendum, of whom 93.1% had voted in favour of adopting the draft Constitution. However, Berisha claimed that only 17% of the votes cast by a total of 35% of the electorate had been in favour of the new Constitution, and urged his supporters to stage further protests against the preliminary results of the referendum. The Government deployed additional security forces in Tirana in an effort to maintain public order. On 28 November Mejdani officially adopted the new Constitution. However, Berisha subsequently announced that the DPA would continue to refuse to recognize the Constitution. In July 1999 a DPA congress voted in favour of ending the boycott of the legislature.

At an SPA party congress in September 1999 Nano (who had resigned from the party chairmanship in January) was re-elected to the post, narrowly defeating Majko. In October Majko (who, consequently, no longer had the support of the SPA deputies in the People's Assembly) resigned from the office of Prime Minister. Mejdani subsequently nominated Ilir Meta (hitherto Deputy Prime Minister), who was supported by Nano, as Prime Minister. Berisha announced that the DPA would boycott a parliamentary motion to approve the new Council of Ministers formed by Meta, and that his supporters would stage mass protests following the return of Nano to the SPA leadership. In early November the new Government was formally approved in the People's Assembly (despite the opposition boycott).

In January 2000 the Union for Democracy criticized legislation governing the composition of the state electoral commission, on the grounds that the opposition coalition was not guaranteed equal representation on the body. In the same month Meta dismissed the Minister of Public Economy and Privatization, following controversy over the ministry's alleged contravention of legislation regulating the energy sector. In late February the Deputy Foreign Minister, Ben Blushi, who had allegedly revealed details of clandestine discussions between Meta and the US Secretary of State, Madeleine Albright, was also removed from office. Disagreement between Meta and Nano over the issue subsequently emerged at a meeting of the SPA leadership, after Meta refused a request to reinstate Blushi. In March President Mejdani announced the formal abolition of the death penalty. In July an extensive government reorganization was effected. A subsequent motion in the legislature to endorse the new Council of Ministers was boycotted by the DPA.

Local government elections took place, as scheduled, in October 2000, following the preparation of a new voters' register, with assistance from the United Nations Development Programme. The first round of the elections, which took place on 1 October, was won by the SPA, with about 43% of the votes cast. The DPA (which obtained about 34% of the votes) claimed that widespread electoral malpractice had been perpetrated and urged the party's supporters to boycott the second round. Nevertheless, OSCE observers, while reporting that irregularities had taken place, declared that they had not influenced the results of the poll. On 15 October about 50% of the electorate participated in the second round of voting for a number of mayoralties and local government councils where no candidates had obtained an absolute majority in the first round. Later that month the state electoral commission announced the official results, which indicated that the SPA had secured 252 seats on local government councils, while the DPA had won 118 seats. However, DPA supporters subsequently staged a series of protests against the election results, which the party continued to refuse to recognize. At the end of November, following continued DPA protests, anti-Government demonstrators attempted to seize the police station in the northern town of Bajram Curri; two protesters were killed in the suppression of the attack by security forces. In December, amid the continuing dispute over the local government elections, inter-party discussions over proposed amendments to the electoral regulations commenced, prior to elections to the People's Assembly, due to take place in June 2001. In February 2001 the DPA and SPA reached agreement on the adoption of a new electoral code.

In April 2001 President Mejdani announced that the first ballot of the legislative elections would take place on 24 June, with a second round in early July. A number of opposition parties, led by the DPA, subsequently formed an electoral alliance, known as Union for Victory. The first round of the elections to the People's Assembly (which was again reduced to number 140 deputies) took place as scheduled. Despite a number of minor violent incidents, the poll was judged by international observers to have been conducted satisfactorily. A second round took place on 8 July in 45 constituencies where no candidate had secured more than 50% of the votes cast. Ballots were repeated in four constituencies later in July, and in a further four in August, after opposition complaints of irregularities were upheld by the Constitutional Court. The Government subsequently announced that, according to provisional results, the SPA had retained its majority in the People's Assembly. Berisha protested that the Government had perpetrated widespread fraud, and announced the decision of the Union for Victory to reject the election results and boycott the People's Assembly. According to the final results, which were announced by the Central Electoral Commission on 21 August, the SPA won 73 of the 140 seats in the legislature (considerably fewer than it had obtained in 1997), and the Union for Victory secured 46 seats.

In late August 2001 Meta was re-elected to the office of Prime Minister by the General Steering Committee of the SPA, with a substantial majority, defeating two other candidates. Mejdani formally endorsed Meta's nomination as Prime Minister on 5 September. A reorganized Council of Ministers, nominated by Mejdani, was approved two days later. The new Government retained representatives of the SDP, notably the party Chairman, Skender Gjinushi, who was nominated to the post of Deputy Prime Minister and Minister of Labour and Social Affairs; the former Prime Minister, Pandeli Majko, became Minister of Defence. (Deputies belonging to the Union for Victory boycotted the new People's Assembly, which commenced sessions in early September, in continued protest at the outcome of the elections.) Following his inauguration, Meta announced that the country's rapid accession to the EU was to be a priority of the Government. A vote expressing confidence in the new Government, and its political and social programme, was adopted by 84 deputies in the People's Assembly (with six DAP representatives opposing the motion and the Union for Victory continuing to abstain).

In October 2001 the campaign by the Union for Victory to obtain international support for its allegations of malpractice in the legislative elections proved unsuccessful. OSCE observers maintained that the elections had been conducted successfully and urged the alliance to end its boycott of the People's Assembly. Later that month the Union for Victory agreed to enter the legislature, subject to several preconditions, which included the establishment of an inter-party parliamentary commission to rule on issues of contention. In December severe division emerged within the SPA, after Nano publicly accused Meta's Government of engaging in corrupt practices. At a meeting of the SPA's General Steering Committee early that month the Minister of Finance and the Minister of the Public Economy and Privatization (both of whom were party members) agreed to resign from the Government, after being personally implicated in the corruption allegations. Subsequently, two further SPA members also resigned their ministerial portfolios. Later in December Berisha was re-elected to the leadership of the DPA. At the end of that month attempts by Meta to appoint new ministers to the four vacant posts in the Government proved unsuccessful, since his nominees were repeatedly rejected by supporters of Nano in the People's Assembly. On 29

January 2002 Meta tendered his resignation, after the two SPA factions failed to reach agreement on a government reorganization. Majko (a compromise candidate, who was supported by Meta) was elected Prime Minister by the SPA; he was officially appointed to the office by Mejdani on 7 February. Following protracted negotiations between the two SPA factions and allied parties, the People's Assembly approved a new Council of Ministers, nominated by Majko, on 22 February. Portfolios were divided between supporters of Nano and Meta, with Kastriot Islami, a former Deputy Prime Minister who was favoured by Nano, becoming Minister of Finance.

Following the establishment of the new, transitional Council of Ministers, deputies from the DPA-led Union for Victory decided to resume participation in the People's Assembly, thereby ending their five-month boycott of the legislature. The SPA remained deeply divided, however, and a future split in the party remained a possibility. Meanwhile, as the end of Mejdani's term of office approached, it became apparent that Nano (who had announced his intention of contesting the presidency) would be unable to secure majority support in the People's Assembly, owing to strong opposition from Berisha. Following prolonged negotiations between the SPA and the DPA, Albania's ambassador to the EU, Artur Kuko, was selected as a compromise candidate for the presidency, but rejected the nomination. The parties subsequently agreed to nominate Alfred Moisiu, a retired general who had served in the Berisha administration. He was elected by 97 of the 140 deputies in the People's Assembly on 24 June 2002, and was inaugurated on 24 July (when Mejdani's tenure officially expired). On the following day Majko resigned as Prime Minister, after the SPA General Steering Committee decided that the party's Chairman should head the Government. Moisiu consequently appointed Nano to the premiership, and a new administration was approved at the end of the month, with Majko returning to his former post as Minister of Defence.

A security operation in August 2002 to suppress trafficking in drugs and illegal immigrants at Vlorë, in co-operation with the Italian, Greek and Yugoslav authorities, was declared to be highly successful; several senior police officers were subsequently charged with involvement in illegal activities. Also in August Moisiu removed the director of the national intelligence agency, following allegations of his complicity in organized crime and political assassinations. In October the authorities arrested several senior public officials, including the Deputy Minister of Public Order, on charges of embezzlement and abuse of office. (Required to address the issue of corruption as a precondition to consideration for EU membership, the Government had established the Anti-Corruption Coalition of Civil Society to examine the activities of public officials.)

The gradual relaxation of Albania's isolationist policies culminated in 1990, in a declaration of its intention to establish good relations with all countries, irrespective of their social system. Until 1990 Albania remained hostile to the USSR; in July of that year, however, Albania and the USSR formally agreed to restore diplomatic relations. Diplomatic relations between Albania and the USA were re-established in March 1991 (they had been suspended since 1946), and diplomatic links with the United Kingdom were restored in May. Albania was granted observer status at the 1990 CSCE summit meeting, and became a full member of the organization in June 1991. In May 1992 Albania and the European Community (now EU) signed a 10-year agreement on trade and co-operation. In June Albania, together with 10 other countries (including six of the former Soviet republics), signed a pact to establish the Black Sea Economic Co-operation (now the Organization of the Black Sea Economic Co-operation, see p. 294), which created a regional structure for economic co-operation. In December Albania was granted membership of the Organization of the Islamic Conference (OIC, see p. 295), and in the same month applied to join NATO, see p. 271, thus becoming the first former Warsaw Pact country formally to seek membership of the Western alliance. Albania joined NATO's 'Partnership for Peace' programme of military co-operation in April 1994. In July 1995 Albania was admitted to the Council of Europe, having agreed to adopt a new Constitution and to take measures to fulfil the Council's requirements concerning human rights. Prior to a NATO summit meeting in Prague, the Czech Republic, in November 2002, the Presidents of Albania, Croatia and the former Yugoslav republic of Macedonia (FYRM) agreed to adopt a common strategy for integration. Although those countries were not among the seven candidate nations invited at the summit to engage in accession discussions, NATO officials indicated that Albania's proposed entry would be considered in the future, subject to the implementation of further democratic and military reforms. Negotiations on the signature of an initial Stabilization and Association Agreement with the EU officially commenced at the end of January 2003.

Albania's relations with neighbouring Greece and Yugoslavia (now Serbia and Montenegro) have been strained. In August 1987 Greece formally ended the technical state of war with Albania that had been in existence since 1945. However, the status of the Greek minority in Albania, officially numbering some 59,000 at the 1989 census, but estimated to number some 300,000 by the Greek authorities, remained a sensitive issue. Relations between Albania and Greece deteriorated in 1993, owing to Greece's deportation of some 20,000 Albanian immigrants and to the alleged mistreatment of the Greek minority in southern Albania. Tensions were exacerbated further in April 1994, following a border incident in which two Albanian guards were killed by unidentified opponents; diplomatic expulsions ensued on both sides, and the border situation remained tense, with reports of minor skirmishes. In May six prominent members of the ethnic Greek organization, OMONIA, were arrested, following the alleged seizure by Albanian police of weapons and 'anti-constitutional' documents. Greece subsequently vetoed the provision of EU funds to Albania and increased deportations of illegal Albanian immigrants. In September five of the OMONIA detainees were convicted on charges including espionage and the illegal possession of weapons, and received custodial sentences. Following the verdict, Greece and Albania recalled their mutual ambassadors. In addition, the Greek Government submitted formal protests to the UN and the EU regarding Albania's perceived maltreatment of its ethnic Greek population and closed the Kakavija border crossing, which had hitherto been used by Albanian migrant workers. One of the OMONIA defendants was pardoned in December, after Greece withdrew its veto on EU aid to Albania in November. In February 1995 the four remaining OMONIA prisoners were released, allowing a subsequent improvement in bilateral relations. In June the Albanian Government approved a new education bill, which recognized the right of ethnic minorities to their own language and culture. In March 1996 the Greek President, Konstantinos Stefanopoulos, visited Albania, and a co-operation agreement was signed, apparently resolving outstanding issues of concern between the two nations. In August 1997 the Greek Government agreed to grant temporary work permits to illegal Albanian immigrants in Greece, in exchange for assistance from Albania in combating cross-border crime. In April 1998 the two countries signed a military co-operation agreement. A new border crossing between Albania and Greece was opened in May 1999. Nevertheless, relations between the Albanian authorities and the Greek minority became more tense during the controversial local government elections held in October 2000 (see above). In February 2001 Albania and Greece signed an agreement on increased bilateral economic and financial co-operation. The Greek Government subsequently provided extensive credit to the Albanian Government in a number of areas, and extended humanitarian aid during severe flooding in September 2002. In December Albania and Greece signed a defence co-operation agreement.

Relations with Yugoslavia deteriorated sharply in early 1989, when many ethnic Albanian demonstrators were killed during renewed unrest in the Yugoslav province of Kosovo and Metohija (where the population was principally composed of ethnic Albanian Muslims). Kosovo remained a focus of political and ethnic tension, and the insurgency in southern Albania in early 1997 (see above) prompted concern among western European Governments that armaments seized by the rebels might also be used to support an insurrection by ethnic Albanians in Kosovo. In November Prime Minister Nano and the Yugoslav President, Slobodan Milošević, met in an effort to improve relations between Albania and Yugoslavia. However, the Albanian Government condemned increased Serbian military activity against the ethnic Albanian majority in Kosovo in early 1998 (see chapter on Serbia and Montenegro); Nano urged international intervention to prevent widespread conflict in the region. In April clashes were reported on the Albanian border with Kosovo between Serbian troops and suspected members of the paramilitary Kosovo Liberation Army (KLA—Ushtria Çlirimtare e Kosovës). The Albanian administration initiated measures to prevent the illicit transportation of armaments from northern Albania to KLA forces in Kosovo. By mid-1998 some 10,000 ethnic Albanian refugees had fled to northern Albania, following continued Serbian military reprisals against the ethnic Albanian population in Kosovo.

In late March 1999, following the failure of diplomatic efforts to persuade Milošević to accede to NATO demands (see chapter on Serbia and Montenegro), NATO forces commenced an intensive aerial bombardment of Yugoslavia. The Albanian Government expressed support for NATO military action, and allowed Albania's air and sea facilities to be used for NATO operations. Further Albanian troops were deployed on the northern border with Serbia in preparation for a possible Serbian retaliatory offensive. The atrocities committed by Serbian forces in Kosovo precipitated a mass exodus of ethnic Albanian refugees from the province. NATO troops (which later numbered about 8,000, and became known as AFOR) were dispatched to Albania to support humanitarian aid operations. The Government appealed for international financial assistance in assisting the Kosovar refugee population, and requested a more rapid accession to NATO. It was reported that a number of ethnic Albanians had returned from abroad to join the KLA (which operated training camps in northern Albania). In early April Serbian forces bombarded Albanian border villages during heavy fighting with the KLA in Kosovo, increasing international concern that a broader regional conflict might develop. Later that month Serbian troops advanced into Albanian territory, but were repelled by members of the Albanian armed forces. Meanwhile, the KLA had succeeded in establishing a supply route for the transportation of armaments from bases in northern Albania to Kosovo. In early June Milošević finally accepted a peace plan for Kosovo (see chapter on Serbia and Montenegro). Following the deployment of a NATO-led peace-keeping Kosovo Force (KFOR) in the province, under the terms of the peace agreement, about one-half of the ethnic Albanian refugees returned to Kosovo from Albania and the FYRM later that month. Some 430,000 Kosovar refugees, who had fled to Albania during the conflict, were repatriated during 1999. In September NATO announced that AFOR, which had been gradually withdrawing from the country, was to be replaced by a contingent, to be known as Communications Zone West (COMMZ-W), which was mandated to maintain civil order in Albania and to support the KFOR mission in Kosovo. COMMZ-W (which was stationed in Durrës, under the command of KFOR) numbered some 1,200, and principally comprised Italian forces, although Greece, Turkey, the USA, France, Germany and Poland also contributed troops. (In November 2000 command of COMMZ-W was transferred from an Italian brigade to EUROFOR). Following the removal from power of Milošević in September 2000 (see the chapter on Serbia and Montenegro), Albania and Yugoslavia formally restored diplomatic relations in January 2001. Bilateral diplomatic relations were upgraded to ambassadorial level in September 2002. In December the principal Yugoslav airline resumed regular services to Albania (which had been suspended in 1981).

In February 1993 Albania refused to accept an application by the FYRM for membership of the CSCE, and it was only in April that Albania officially recognized the existence of the republic as an independent state. Albania was concerned at the oppression of the large ethnic Albanian minority in the FYRM, who constituted about 21% of the population and the majority of whom were Muslims. Relations between the two countries deteriorated in the course of the year, owing to a number of shooting incidents on the border. Following the civil unrest in Albania in early 1997 (see above), a number of incursions into FYRM territory by armed groups of Albanian rebels were reported; in September two members of the FYRM's security forces were killed in a clash with Albanians who had entered the country illegally. In October the Ministers of Defence of Albania and the FYRM signed an agreement providing for increased security at the joint border between the two countries.

The outbreak of conflict between government forces and ethnic Albanian rebels, known as the National Liberation Army (NLA), in the FYRM in February 2001, prompted large numbers of ethnic Albanian civilians to take refuge in Albania. Relations between Albania and the FYRM became strained, although the Albanian authorities maintained their opposition to the NLA's reported aim of creating a 'Greater Albania'. In August the FYRM Government and NLA leaders signed a peace agreement (which included constitutional amendments, adopted in November, according Albanian and other minority languages official status); however, the region remained unstable. In early September the Albanian ambassador to the FYRM was presented with a formal protest regarding the alleged involvement of Albanian nationals in rebel activities on Macedonian territory. Later that month the Albanian Government denied further claims by the FYRM that the NLA had established training bases in northern Albania. According to estimates by the office of the UN High Commissioner for Refugees, 7,626 refugees remained in Albania at the end of 2001. The replacement of the nationalist Government in the FYRM at elections in September 2002 was widely perceived to favour prospects for regional stability. In January 2003 the Governments of Albania and the FYRM announced that they planned to strengthen economic co-operation, in an effort to advance their applications for EU membership (see above).

Government

Under the Constitution adopted in November 1998, legislative power is vested in the unicameral People's Assembly. The People's Assembly, which is elected for a term of four years, comprises 140 deputies, of whom 100 are directly elected by a simple majority and the remainder on the basis of proportional representation. The President of the Republic is Head of State, and is elected by the People's Assembly for a term of five years. Executive authority is held by the Council of Ministers, which is led by the Prime Minister as Head of Government. The Prime Minister is appointed by the President. The Prime Minister appoints a Council of Ministers, which is then presented for approval to the People's Assembly. For the purposes of local government, Albania is divided into 36 districts (*rrethe*) and one municipality, the capital. The representative organs of the basic units of local government are councils, which are elected by general direct elections for a period of three years. The Council of Ministers appoints a Prefect in every region as its representative.

Defence

In 2002 the Albanian armed forces were undergoing a programme of reorganization, with assistance from European Governments and the USA. In August of that year the army numbered about 20,000, the air force 4,500 and the navy 2,500. Paramilitary forces comprised an internal security force, based in Tirana, and units in major towns, together with an estimated 500 border police. Military service is compulsory and lasts for 12 months. From September 1999 a NATO contingent, known as Communications Zone West (COMMZ-W), numbering about 1,200, was deployed in Albania to maintain civil order in the country and support the NATO-led international Kosovo Force (KFOR) in the province of Kosovo and Metohija. The budget for 2002 allocated some 6,300m. lekë to defence.

Economic Affairs

In 2001, according to World Bank estimates, Albania's gross national income (GNI), measured at average 1999–2001 prices, was US $4,236m., equivalent to $1,230 per head (or $3,880 on an international purchasing-power parity basis). During 1990–2001, it was estimated, the population increased at an average annual rate of 0.4%, while gross domestic product (GDP) increased, in real terms, by an average of 1.1% per year. Overall GDP increased, in real terms, at an average annual rate of 1.5% in 1990–2001; growth in 2001 was 6.5%.

Agriculture (including forestry and fishing) contributed an estimated 49.1% of GDP in 2001. Some 47.6% of the labour force were engaged in the sector in that year. An increasing degree of private enterprise was permitted from 1990, and agricultural land was subsequently redistributed to private ownership. The principal crops are wheat, sugar beet, maize, potatoes, barley and sorghum, and watermelons. Agricultural GDP increased at an average annual rate of 4.3%, in real terms, in 1990–2001; growth in the sector was 1.4% in 2001.

Industry (comprising mining, manufacturing, construction and utilities) accounted for an estimated 27.3% of GDP in 2001 and employed 22.5% of the labour force in 1989. Principal contributors to industrial output include mining, energy generation and food-processing. Construction was the fastest-growing sector in recent years, with GDP increasing at an average annual rate of 9.5% in 1990–2000 (rising by an estimated 17.9% in 2000). Industrial GDP declined at an average rate of 3.1% per year during 1990–2001; however, the GDP of the sector increased by 10.7% in 2001.

Albania is one of the world's largest producers of chromite (chromium ore), possessing Europe's only significant reserves (an estimated 37m. metric tons of recoverable ore, constituting about 5% of total world deposits). The mining sector has been centred on chromite and copper since the closure of nickel and iron ore operations, together with more than one-half of the

country's coal mines, in 1990. In 1999, however, chromite production declined by over 45%, to 79,445 tons. Albania has petroleum resources and its own refining facilities, and there has been considerable foreign interest in the exploration of both onshore and offshore reserves since 1991.

The manufacturing sector contributed an estimated 11.6% of GDP in 2001. The sector is based largely on the processing of building materials, agricultural products, minerals and chemicals. Manufacturing GDP declined at an average annual rate of 9.1% during 1990–2001; however, the GDP of the sector increased by 6.3% in 2001.

Hydroelectric generation accounted for some 97.1% of total electricity production in 1999. In 2000 imports of mineral fuels accounted for 8.9% of the value of total merchandise imports.

Services employed 21.5% of the labour force in 1989 and provided an estimated 23.6% of GDP in 2001. The combined GDP of the services sector increased, in real terms, by an average of 4.6% per year during 1990–2001; the GDP of the sector increased by 13.7% in 2001.

In 2001 Albania recorded a visible trade deficit of US $1,027.1m., and there was a deficit of $220.3m. on the current account of the balance of payments. In 2001 the principal source of imports (accounting for an estimated 33.3%) was Italy; the other major supplier was Greece. Italy was also the principal market for exports (taking an estimated 71.1% of the total); Greece and Germany were also important purchasers. The principal exports in 2001 were textiles, miscellaneous manufactured articles (particularly footwear) and base metals. The main imports in that year were machinery and mechanical appliances, mineral products, textiles, base metals, prepared foodstuffs and vegetable products.

Albania's overall budget deficit in 2000 was 48,835m. lekë (some 9.1% of GDP). At the end of 2000 Albania's total external debt was US $784.1m., of which $644.2m. was long-term public debt. In that year the cost of servicing the debt was equivalent to 2.0% of the value of exports of goods and services. In 1991–2001 the average annual rate of inflation was 31.1%; consumer prices increased by an estimated 3.1% in 2001. The rate of unemployment was estimated at 14.6% in 2001. Some 25.1% of the Albanian labour force were working abroad in 1996.

Having reversed its long-standing policy of economic self-sufficiency, in 1991 Albania became a member of the World Bank, the IMF and the newly established European Bank for Reconstruction and Development (EBRD, see p. 193). In 1992 Albania became a founder member of the Black Sea Economic Co-operation group (known as the Organization of the Black Sea Economic Co-operation from May 1999).

In 1992, in response to a serious economic crisis, a newly elected Government introduced an extensive programme of reforms, providing for the transfer to private ownership of farmland, state-owned companies and housing, and the abolition of trade restrictions and price controls. A strict programme of high interest rates, reduced subsidies, banking reforms and trade liberalization, supported by the IMF, was successful in reducing the large budget deficit and stabilizing the currency. Nevertheless, illicit trade continued to account for a high proportion of total revenue, and the country remained dependent on remittances from Albanian emigrants and foreign aid. The arrival of large numbers of refugees, following the NATO bombardment of Kosovo in March–June 1999 (see Recent History), placed great strain on the country's resources, which was, however, offset by large inflows of emergency relief aid from the international community. Consequently, the economic situation improved significantly in the second half of 1999. The Government's monetary policy resulted in further lowering inflation and reducing the fiscal deficit in 2000. Significant progress was also made in the privatization of state-owned enterprises, particularly in the telecommunications sector, and much-needed reform was initiated in the electricity sector, although supply shortages continued in 2001, as a result of low rainfall. The disbursement of funding under the IMF's Poverty Reduction and Growth Facility, which expired in July 2001, contributed to the restoration of high rates of growth, but poverty remained severe, particularly in rural areas. Albania's rapid accession to the European Union (EU) continued to be a main priority for the Government. The installation of a new President and the subsequent appointment of a new Council of Ministers in July 2002 eased longstanding political tension, and negotiations on the signature of an initial Stabilization and Association Agreement with the EU finally commenced in January 2003. However, the Government was required to address widespread corruption and organized crime, and to reform the security forces and judiciary, as a precondition to consideration for EU membership. The estimated rate of GDP growth for 2002 was the lowest in five years (principally owing to political dissension, continuing energy shortages and severe flooding at the end of September), and progress in privatization projects was adversely affected by the unfavourable state of the international economy. However, Albania was expected to benefit from the ratification of free trade agreements with the former Yugoslav republic of Macedonia (FYRM) and Croatia (and the signature of draft agreements with four further regional Governments) during 2002. Government strategy for 2003, which was supported by a new three-year credit arrangement with the IMF (reached in July 2002), laid particular emphasis on the liberalization of the energy sector and improvement in tax-collection methods. (Following a severe shortfall in revenue in 2002, which obliged the Government to reduce public investment, the reform of the tax and customs administration became the main priority for the authorities.) The IMF was expected to approve the disbursement of additional funds under a 'Stand-by Arrangement' at the end of February 2003.

Education

Education in Albania for children between the ages of six and 14 years is free and compulsory. Approximately 41.3% of children aged three to six years (boys 39.6%; girls 43.1%) attended pre-primary schools in 1999/2000. In that year 100% of children in the relevant age-group were enrolled at primary schools, while 71.5% of children in the appropriate age-group (boys 70.4%; girls 72.6%) attended secondary schools. In 2000 there were eight universities and two institutes of higher education in Albania. In 1999/2000 student enrolment in institutions of higher education was equivalent to 14.7% of the relevant age-group (males 11.5%; females 18.2%). The budget for 1999 allocated about 2.5% of projected government expenditure to education.

Public Holidays

2003: 1 January (New Year's Day), 11 January (Republic Day), 12 February* (Great Bayram, Feast of the Sacrifice), 18–21 April (Catholic Easter), 28 April (Orthodox Easter), 1 May (International Labour Day), 26 November* (Small Bayram, end of Ramadan), 28 November (Independence and Liberation Day), 25 December (Christmas Day).

2004: 1 January (New Year's Day), 11 January (Republic Day), 2 February* (Great Bayram, Feast of the Sacrifice), 9–12 April (Catholic Easter), 12 April (Orthodox Easter), 1 May (International Labour Day), 14 November* (Small Bayram, end of Ramadan), 28 November (Independence and Liberation Day), 25 December (Christmas Day).

* These holidays are dependent on the Islamic lunar calendar and may vary by one or two days from the dates given.

Weights and Measures

The metric system is in force.

Statistical Survey

Sources (unless otherwise indicated): Institute of Statistics (Instituti i Statistikës), POB 8194, Tirana; tel. (4) 2222411; fax (4) 2228300; e-mail root@ instat.gov.al; internet www.instat.gov.al; Bank of Albania (Banka e Shqipërisë), Sheshi Skënderbeu 1, Tirana; tel. (4) 2222752; fax (4) 2223558; e-mail public@bankofalbania.org; internet www.bankofalbania.org.

Area and Population

AREA, POPULATION AND DENSITY

Area (sq km)	
Land	27,398
Inland water	1,350
Total	28,748*
Population (census results)	
2 April 1989	3,182,417
1 April 2001 (preliminary)	
Males	1,539,980
Females	1,547,179
Total	3,087,159
Population (UN estimates at mid-year)†	
1999	3,131,000
2000	3,134,000
2001	3,145,000
Density (per sq km) at 1 April 2001	107.4

* 11,100 sq miles.

† Figures not revised to take account of 2001 census.

Source: UN, *World Population Prospects: The 2000 Revision.*

Ethnic Groups (census of 2 April 1989): Albanian 3,117,601; Greek 58,758; Macedonian 4,697; Montenegrin, Serb, Croat, etc. 100; others 1,261.

DISTRICTS
(census of 1 April 2001)

District (Rreth)	Area (sq km)	Population (preliminary)	Density (per sq km)	Capital
Berat	939	128,410	136.7	Berat
Bulqizë	469	42,985	91.6	Bulqizë
Delvinë	348	10,859	31.2	Delvinë
Devoll	429	34,744	81.1	Bilisht
Dibër	1,088	86,144	79.1	Peshkopi
Durrës	433	182,988	422.7	Durrës
Elbasan	1,372	224,974	163.9	Elbasan
Fier	785	200,154	254.9	Fier
Gjirokastër	1,137	55,991	49.2	Gjirokastër
Gramsh	695	35,723	51.4	Gramsh
Has	393	19,842	50.5	Krumë
Kavajë	414	78,415	189.3	Kavajë
Kolonjë	805	17,179	21.4	Ersekë
Korçë	1,752	143,499	81.9	Korçë
Krujë	333	64,357	193.3	Krujë
Kuçovë	84	35,571	423.0	Kuçovë
Kukës	938	64,054	68.3	Kukës
Kurbin	273	54,519	199.4	Laç
Lezhë	479	68,218	142.3	Lezhë
Librazhd	1,023	72,520	70.9	Librazhd
Lushnjë	712	144,351	202.6	Lushnjë
Malësi e Madhe	555	36,770	66.3	Koplik
Mallakastër	393	39,881	101.5	Ballsh
Mat	1,029	61,906	60.2	Burrel
Mirditë	867	37,055	42.7	Rrëshen
Peqin	109	32,920	302.9	Peqin
Përmet	930	25,837	27.8	Përmet
Pogradec	725	70,900	97.8	Pogradec
Pukë	1,034	34,454	33.3	Pukë
Sarandë	749	35,235	47.1	Sarandë
Shkodër	1,973	185,794	94.2	Shkodër
Skrapar	775	29,874	38.5	Çorovodë
Tepelenë	817	32,465	39.7	Tepelenë
Tiranë	1,238	523,150	422.7	Tiranë
Tropojë	1,043	28,154	27.0	Bajram Curri
Vlorë	1,609	147,267	91.5	Vlorë
Total	**28,748**	**3,087,159**	**107.4**	

PRINCIPAL TOWNS
(population at 2001 census)

Tiranë (Tirana, the capital) . . .	343,078	Korçë (Koritsa) . .	55,130
Durrës (Durazzo) .	99,546	Berat	40,112
Elbasan	87,797	Lushnjë	32,580
Shkodër (Scutari) .	82,455	Kavajë.	24,817
Vlorë (Vlonë or Valona) . . .	77,691	Pogradec . . .	23,843
Fier	56,297	Gjirokastër . . .	20,630

BIRTHS, MARRIAGES AND DEATHS*

	Registered live births		Registered marriages		Registered deaths	
	Number	Rate (per 1,000)	Number	Rate (per 1,000)	Number	Rate (per 1,000)
1986 . .	76,435	25.3	25,718	8.5	17,369	5.7
1987 . .	79,696	25.9	27,370	8.9	17,119	5.6
1988 . .	80,241	25.5	28,174	9.0	17,027	5.4
1989 . .	78,862	24.7	27,655	8.6	18,168	5.7
1990 . .	82,125	25.2	28,992	8.9	18,193	5.6
1991 . .	77,361	23.8	24,853	7.6	17,743	5.4

* From 1990 rates are based on unrevised estimates of mid-year population.

Registered births: 72,179 (20.3 per 1,000) in 1994; 72,081 (20.0 per 1,000) in 1995; 68,354 (18.7 per 1,000) in 1996; 61,739 (16.5 per 1,000) in 1997; 60,139 (15.9 per 1,000) in 1998.

Registered marriages (provisional): 25,260 (6.8 per 1,000) in 1997; 27,887 (7.4 per 1,000) in 1998.

Registered deaths: 17,238 (5.1 per 1,000) in 1992; 16,639 (4.8 per 1,000) in 1993; 18,342 (5.2 per 1,000) in 1994; 18,060 (5.0 per 1,000) in 1995; 17,600 (4.8 per 1,000) in 1996; 18,237 (4.9 per 1,000) in 1997; 18,250 (4.8 per 1,000) in 1998.

Sources: *Statistical Yearbook of the PSR of Albania, Statistical Yearbook of Albania*, UN, *Population and Vital Statistics Report* and UN, *Demographic Yearbook*.

Expectation of life (WHO estimates, years at birth): 69.5 (males 66.3; females 73.2) in 2001 (Source: WHO, *World Health Report*).

ECONOMICALLY ACTIVE POPULATION
(ISIC Major Divisions, 1989 census)

	Males	Females	Total
Agriculture, hunting, forestry and fishing	399,810	399,249	799,059
Mining and quarrying. . . . .⎫			
Manufacturing . . . . . .⎬	160,833	118,155	278,988
Electricity, gas and water. . .⎭			
Construction	41,979	7,312	49,291
Trade, restaurants and hotels . .	22,171	26,447	48,618
Transport, storage and communications	36,324	8,109	44,433
Financing, insurance, real estate and business services . . . .⎫			
Community, social and personal services . . . .⎬	119,279	100,905	220,184
Activities not adequately defined	10,293	6,798	17,091
Total employed	790,689	666,975	1,457,664

Source: ILO, *Yearbook of Labour Statistics*.

1997 (annual averages, '000 persons): Total domestic employment 1,107 (Agricultural sector 761); Unemployed 194; Domestic labour force 1,301 (males 794, females 507) (Source: IMF, *Albania: Selected Issues and Statistical Appendix* (July 2001)).

1998 (annual averages, '000 persons): Total domestic employment 1,085 (Agricultural sector 761); Unemployed 235; Domestic labour force 1,320 (males 803, females 517) (Source: IMF, *Albania: Selected Issues and Statistical Appendix* (July 2001)).

1999 (annual averages, '000 persons): Total domestic employment 1,065 (Agricultural sector 761); Unemployed 240; Domestic labour force 1,305 (males 791, females 514) (Source: IMF, *Albania: Selected Issues and Statistical Appendix* (July 2001)).

2000 (annual averages, '000 persons): Total domestic employment 1,067 (Agricultural sector 761); Unemployed 215; Domestic labour force 1,282 (males 779, females 503) (Source: IMF, *Albania: Selected Issues and Statistical Appendix* (July 2001)).

Mid-2001 (estimates in '000): Agriculture, etc. 748; Total labour force 1,573 (Source: FAO).

Health and Welfare

KEY INDICATORS

Total fertility rate (children per woman, 2001) . . .	2.4
Under-5 mortality rate (per 1,000 live births, 2001) . . .	30
HIV/AIDS (% of persons aged 15–49, 1999).	<0.01
Physicians (per 1,000 head, 1998)	1.29
Hospital beds (per 1,000 head, 1995)	3.19
Health expenditure (2000): US $ per head (PPP) . . .	129
Health expenditure (2000): % of GDP	3.4
Health expenditure (2000): public (% of total)	62.1
Human Development Index (2000): ranking	92
Human Development Index (2000): value	0.733

For sources and definitions, see explanatory note on p. vi.

Agriculture

PRINCIPAL CROPS
('000 metric tons)

	1999	2000	2001
Wheat and spelt	272.0	341.1	282.2
Barley	2.9	1.8	3.0
Maize	206.0	205.7	198.3
Rye	3.4	1.5	3.7
Oats	13.2	15.7	15.3
Sorghum*	14.5	14.7	14.7
Potatoes	161.9	161.0	163.7
Sugar beet	39.9	42.0	38.5
Dry beans	26.0	25.2	22.1
Tree-nuts*	3.0	3.0	3.0
Olives	42.0	36.2	39.6
Sunflower seed	2.7	2.9	2.7
Tomatoes	160.0	162.0	170.9
Other vegetables*	250.0	250.0	250.0
Oranges	2.2	2.2*	2.2*
Apples	11.8	12.0	15.8
Pears	2.4	2.8	3.5
Cherries	4.5	5.0	6.8
Peaches and nectarines	2.0	2.0	6.1
Plums	12.1	12.1	17.0
Grapes	70.4	79.3	85.1
Watermelons	220.0	250.0	277.0
Figs	12.1	13.1	22.8
Tobacco (leaves)	7.3	6.2	4.1

* FAO estimate(s).

Source: FAO.

LIVESTOCK
('000 head, year ending September)

	1999	2000	2001
Horses*	65	65	65
Mules*	25	25	25
Asses*	113	113	113
Cattle	720	728	708
Pigs	81	103	103
Sheep	1,941	1,939	1,906
Goats	1,120	1,106	1,027
Chickens	4,010	4,087	4,285

* FAO estimates.

Source: FAO.

LIVESTOCK PRODUCTS
('000 metric tons)

	1999	2000	2001
Beef and veal*	33.7	35.9	35.3
Mutton and lamb	11.7*	12.3*	12.3†
Goat meat	6.4*	7.2*	7.2
Pig meat	6.2*	6.8*	7.5†
Poultry meat	5.0	4.0	4.0
Cows' milk	761.0	807.0	840.0
Sheep's milk	73.0	70.0	72.0
Goats' milk	73.0	71.0	72.0
Cheese	11.4†	10.7	10.3
Butter†	1.6	1.7	1.7
Hen eggs	20.2	21.0	24.0
Wool: greasy	3.0	3.4	3.3
Cattle hides†	7.0	7.5	7.9
Sheep and lamb skins†	3.2	3.4	3.4
Goat and kid skins†	1.6	1.8	1.8

* Unofficial figure(s).
† FAO estimate(s).

Source: FAO.

Forestry

ROUNDWOOD REMOVALS
('000 cubic metres, excl. bark)

	1999	2000	2001
Sawlogs, veneer logs and logs for sleepers	39	119	131
Pulpwood	3	4*	4*
Other industrial wood	14	—	—
Fuel wood	174	324	324†
Total	230	447	459

* Unofficial figure.
† FAO estimate.

Source: FAO.

SAWNWOOD PRODUCTION
('000 cubic metres, incl. railway sleepers)

	1998	1999	2000
Coniferous (softwood)	9	15	47
Broadleaved (hardwood)	19	20	43
Total	28	35	90

2001: Figures assumed to be unchanged from 2000.

Source: FAO.

Fishing

(metric tons, live weight)

	1998	1999	2000
Capture	2,683	2,745	3,320
Common carp	230	216	230
Silver carp	104	130	140
Other cyprinids	229	227	300
Salmonoids	102	104	110
European hake	340	341	330
Bogue	220	220	220
Surmullets	143	145	140
Mullets	136	140	150
Jack and horse mackerels	85	92	90
Rays, stingrays and mantas	86	78	85
Common squids	93	93	90
Common octopus	93	90	85
Aquaculture	124	310	307
Mediterranean mussel	100	200	200
Total catch	2,807	3,055	3,627

Note: Figures exclude Sardinia coral (metric tons): 0.5 in 1998; 0.9 in 1999; 1.0 in 2000.

Source: FAO, *Yearbook of Fishery Statistics*.

Mining

('000 metric tons, unless otherwise indicated)

	1998	1999	2000
Lignite (brown coal)	49	33	21
Crude petroleum	365	323	314
Natural gas (million cu metres)	17	14	11
Copper (metric tons)*	3,200	900	900
Chromium ore (gross weight)	150	79	57

* Figures refer to estimated metal content.

Sources: IMF, *Albania: Selected Issues and Statistical Appendix* (July 2001), and US Geological Survey.

Industry

SELECTED PRODUCTS
('000 metric tons, unless otherwise indicated)

	1997	1998	1999
Wheat flour	68	83	n.a.
Wine ('000 hectolitres)	—	—	7
Cigarettes (million)	414	764	63
Veneer sheets ('000 cubic metres)*	10	10	10
Plywood ('000 cubic metres)	6	6	6
Mechanical wood pulp	2	2	2
Chemical wood pulp	14	14	14
Paper and paperboard*	44	44	8
Phosphatic fertilizers†	27	26	n.a.
Soap	2	2	n.a.
Motor spirit (petrol)	74	21	20
Kerosene	57	2	1
Gas-diesel (distillate fuel) oil	107	91	65
Residual fuel oils	39	39‡	n.a.
Petroleum bitumen (asphalt)‡	14	14	n.a.
Cement	100	84	107
Ferro-chromium	31	30	28
Crude steel	22	22	16
Copper (unrefined)	0.9	2.3	0.9
Electric energy (million kWh)	5,681	5,068	5,396

2000 ('000 metric tons, unless otherwise indicated): Motor spirit 24; Kerosene 2; Gas-diesel oil 72; Cement 180; Ferro-chromium 9; Electric energy (million kWh) 4,737.

* FAO estimate(s).
† Production in terms of phosphoric acid.
‡ Provisional or estimated production.

Sources: UN, *Industrial Commodity Statistics Yearbook*, and IMF, *Albania: Selected Issues and Statistical Appendix* (July 2001).

Finance

CURRENCY AND EXCHANGE RATES

Monetary Units

100 qindarka (qintars) = 1 new lek.

Sterling, Dollar and Euro Equivalents (29 November 2002)
£1 sterling = 214.0 lekë
US $1 = 137.9 lekë
€1 = 136.9 lekë
1,000 lekë = £4.673 = $7.253 = €7.306.

Average Exchange Rate (lekë per US $)
1999   137.69
2000   143.71
2001   143.49

STATE BUDGET
(million lekë)

Revenue*	1998	1999	2000
Counterpart sales revenue	137	155	—
Tax revenue	72,572	83,530	104,098
Turnover tax/value-added tax	28,771	29,794	38,107
Taxes on income and profits	6,400	10,331	14,346
Social security contributions	15,828	18,157	20,053
Import duties and export taxes	12,615	11,450	13,548
Excise taxes	4,910	6,961	9,153
Other revenue	20,806	24,124	16,490
Profit transfer from Bank of Albania	16,400	17,591	10,225
Income from budgetary institutions	3,326	5,352	4,841
Total	93,515	107,809	120,588

* Excluding privatization receipts (million lekë): 133 in 1998; 906 in 1999; 8,975 in 2000.

Expenditure	1998	1999	2000
Current expenditure	117,604	131,545	134,361
Wages	22,048	24,208	25,820
Social security contributions	6,288	6,976	7,420
Interest	36,086	34,938	29,572
Operational and maintenance	18,537	19,499	19,294
Subsidies	2,308	2,706	5,247
Social security	24,329	34,437	37,402
Unemployment insurance	1,621	1,450	1,919
Social assistance	6,168	6,360	6,661
Capital expenditure (investment)	23,789	34,127	35,062
Total	141,393	165,672	169,423

Source: IMF, *Albania: Selected Issues and Statistical Appendix* (July 2001).

INTERNATIONAL RESERVES
(US $ million at 31 December)

	1999	2000	2001
Gold*	34.50	30.40	30.70
IMF special drawing rights	76.95	76.00	81.52
Reserve position in IMF	4.60	4.37	4.22
Foreign exchange	287.50	271.85	276.80
Total	403.55	382.62	393.24

* Valued at market-related prices.

2002 (US $ million at 31 December): IMF special drawing rights 81.60; Reserve position in the IMF 4.56.

Source: IMF, *International Financial Statistics*.

MONEY SUPPLY
(million lekë at 31 December)

	1999	2000	2001
Currency outside banks	81,336	99,236	119,085
Demand deposits at deposit money banks	21,668	24,805	23,988
Total money	103,004	124,041	143,073

COST OF LIVING
(Consumer Price Index; base: 1992 = 100)

	1998	1999	2000
Food, beverages and tobacco	433.2	431.9	422.7
All items (incl. others)	444.1	446.1	446.5

Sources: ILO, *Yearbook of Labour Statistics*, and UN, *Monthly Bulletin of Statistics*.

NATIONAL ACCOUNTS
(million lekë at current prices)

Gross Domestic Product by Economic Activity

	1998	1999	2000*
Agriculture	250,705	266,270	273,519
Industry†	55,047	60,026	61,931
Construction	58,037	68,387	79,301
Transport	14,024	16,531	18,681
Other services	82,817	94,991	102,770
GDP in purchasers' values	460,631	506,205	536,203
GDP at constant 1990 prices	16,548	17,748	19,125

* Figures are provisional.
† Comprising mining, manufacturing, electricity, gas and water.

Source: IMF, *Albania: Selected Issues and Statistical Appendix* (July 2001).

2001 (million lekë, provisional): GDP: 657,030 at current prices; 20,508 at constant 1990 prices (Source: Ministry of Finance, Tirana).

BALANCE OF PAYMENTS
(US $ million)

	1999	2000	2001
Exports of goods f.o.b.	275.0	255.7	304.5
Imports of goods f.o.b.	−938.0	−1,070.0	−1,331.6
Trade balance	**−663.0**	**−814.3**	**−1,027.1**
Exports of services	269.4	447.8	534.3
Imports of services	−163.1	−429.3	−444.1
Balance on goods and services	**−556.7**	**−795.8**	**−936.9**
Other income received	85.5	115.9	162.5
Other income paid	−10.2	−9.3	−13.5
Balance on goods, services and income	**−481.4**	**−689.2**	**−787.9**
Current transfers received	508.9	629.0	647.5
Current transfers paid	−182.9	−96.1	−76.9
Current balance	**−155.4**	**−156.3**	**−217.3**
Capital account (net)	22.6	78.0	117.7
Direct investment from abroad	45.0	143.0	207.3
Portfolio investment assets	—	−25.0	−23.5
Other investment assets	−130.1	−40.2	−197.2
Other investment liabilities	122.6	110.6	123.4
Net errors and omissions	206.2	9.8	136.3
Overall balance	**107.1**	**119.9**	**146.7**

Source: IMF, *International Financial Statistics*.

External Trade

PRINCIPAL COMMODITIES
(US $ million)

Imports c.i.f.	1999	2000	2001
Live animals and animal products	41.4	30.3	28.9
Vegetable products	85.9	90.7	101.9
Prepared foodstuffs; beverages spirits and vinegar; tobacco and manufactured substitutes	108.8	97.6	108.2
Mineral products	81.3	141.7	184.6
Products of chemical or allied industries	51.4	60.4	71.9
Textiles and textile articles	118.1	128.5	138.6
Footwear, headgear, umbrellas walking-sticks, whips, etc.; prepared feathers; artificial flowers; articles of human hair	34.8	27.7	47.4
Articles of stone, plaster, cement asbestos, mica, etc.; ceramic products; glass and glassware	30.1	41.9	49.6
Base metals and articles thereof	75.8	83.8	118.2
Machinery and mechanical appliances; electrical equipment; sound and television apparatus	108.9	148.9	246.5
Vehicles, aircraft, vessels and associated transport equipment	70.6	80.1	70.9
Total (incl. others)	**943.0**	**1,079.3**	**1,337.5**

Exports f.o.b.	1999	2000	2001
Vegetable products	12.6	12.1	11.4
Prepared foodstuffs; beverages spirits and vinegar; tobacco and manufactured substitutes	12.7	13.7	14.1
Mineral products	17.5	7.4	5.9
Raw hides and skins, leather furskins and articles thereof; saddlery and harness; travel goods, handbags, etc.	7.0	8.3	10.9
Textiles and textile articles	98.3	108.7	113.8
Footwear, headgear, umbrellas walking-sticks, whips, etc.; prepared feathers; artificial flowers; articles of human hair	67.9	69.0	87.1
Base metals and articles thereof	14.6	21.5	24.4
Machinery and mechanical appliances; electrical equipment; sound and television receivers	12.4	4.4	7.1
Total (incl. others)	**274.4**	**255.9**	**304.6**

PRINCIPAL TRADING PARTNERS
(US $ million*)

Imports c.i.f.	1999	2000	2001
Austria	17	15	16
Belgium	10	6	9
Bulgaria	27	27	29
Croatia	8	13	18
Finland	2	7	26
France (incl. Monaco)	12	16	11
Germany	52	54	64
Greece	265	305	383
Italy	354	399	446
Macedonia, former Yugoslav republic	17	24	17
Netherlands	10	8	9
Romania	6	6	13
Slovenia	17	20	27
Spain	14	11	15
Turkey	52	59	82
United Kingdom	10	8	45
Total (incl. others)	**943**	**1,079**	**1,338**

Exports f.o.b.	1999	2000	2001
Austria	6	2	1
Denmark	3	3	1
Germany	17	17	17
Greece	40	31	40
Italy	184	182	217
Macedonia, former Yugoslav republic	4	2	5
Turkey	1	2	3
Yugoslavia†	3	7	9
Total (incl. others)	**274**	**256**	**305**

* Imports by country of origin; exports by country of destination.
† Now Serbia and Montenegro.

Transport

RAILWAYS
(traffic)

	1998	1999	2000
Passenger-km (million)	116	121	183
Freight ton-km (million)	25	26	28

Source: UN, *Statistical Yearbook*.

ROAD TRAFFIC
(motor vehicles in use at 31 December)

	1998	1999	2000
Passenger cars	90,766	99,220	114,532
Buses and coaches	9,227	10,316	16,806
Lorries and vans	34,378	37,880	43,301
Road tractors	2,731	3,018	2,274
Motorcycles and mopeds	4,109	4,061	3,808

Source: International Road Federation, *World Road Statistics*.

SHIPPING

Merchant Fleet
(registered at 31 December)

	1999	2000	2001
Number of vessels	33	34	33
Displacement ('000 gross registered tons)	21.4	23.9	25.2

Source: Lloyd's Register-Fairplay, *World Fleet Statistics*.

International Sea-borne Freight Traffic
('000 metric tons)

	1998	1999	2000
Goods loaded	108	120	132
Goods unloaded	1,536	2,040	2,424

2001 ('000 metric tons): Goods loaded 13.2 (Source: UN, *Monthly Bulletin of Statistics*).

CIVIL AVIATION
(traffic on scheduled services)

	1997	1998	1999
Passengers carried ('000) . . .	55	21	20
Passenger-km (million)	35	7	7
Total ton-km (million)	3	1	1

Source: UN, *Statistical Yearbook*.

Tourism

FOREIGN TOURIST ARRIVALS BY COUNTRY OF ORIGIN*

	1997	1998	1999
Austria.	751	805	1,515
Egypt	43	2,299	2,944
France	825	847	1,160
Germany	895	915	2,532
Greece	1,437	1,513	2,115
Italy	3,836	4,026	4,620
Netherlands	307	280	805
Turkey.	261	342	996
United Kingdom	1,198	1,960	1,400
USA	1,052	1,380	1,815
Yugoslavia†	661	820	320
Total (incl. others)	19,154	27,709	38,963

* Figures refer to arrivals in hotels.
† Now Serbia and Montenegro.

Tourism receipts (US $ million): 27 in 1997; 54 in 1998; 211 in 1999; 255 in 2000; 446 in 2001 (Sources: Bank of Albania; World Tourism Organization, *Yearbook of Tourism Statistics*; World Bank, *World Development Indicators*).

Communications Media

	1999	2000	2001
Television receivers ('000 in use) .	455	480	n.a.
Telephones ('000 main lines in use)	140.4	152.7	197.5
Facsimile machines ('000 in use) .	18.3	n.a.	n.a.
Mobile cellular telephones ('000 subscribers)	11.0	29.8	350.0
Personal computers ('000 in use) .	20	25	30
Internet users ('000)	2.5	3.5	10.0

Radio receivers ('000 in use): 810 in 1997.

Book production (1991): 381 titles (including 18 pamphlets).

Daily newspapers (1996): 5; Average circulation ('000 copies) 116.

Sources: UN, *Statistical Yearbook*; UNESCO, *Statistical Yearbook*; International Telecommunication Union.

Education
(1995/96, unless otherwise indicated)

	Institu-tions	Teachers	Students		
			Males	Females	Total
Pre-primary . . .	2,670	4,416	42,292	42,244	84,536
Primary . . .	1,782*	31,369	288,592	269,509	558,101
Secondary					
General . . .	162†	4,147	37,392	33,999	71,391
Vocational .	259†	2,174	12,758	5,746	18,504
Higher‡§	10‖	2,348	14,880	19,377	34,257
Universities, etc.	8‖	2,304	14,841	19,121	33,962
Other.	2‖	44	39	256	295

* 1994/95 figure.
† 1990 figure.
‡ Figures for students include those enrolled at distance-learning institutions.
§ 1996/97 figures.
‖ 1993/94 figure.

Sources: Ministry of Education, Tirana, and UNESCO, *Statistical Yearbook*.

Adult literacy rate (UNESCO estimates): 84.7% (males 92.1%; females 77.0%) in 2000 (Source: UN Development Programme, *Human Development Report*).

Directory

The Constitution

In October 1998 the People's Assembly approved a new Constitution, which had been drafted by a parliamentary commission. The Constitution was endorsed at a national referendum on 22 November, and was officially adopted on 28 November.

GENERAL PROVISIONS

Albania is a parliamentary republic. The Republic of Albania is a unitary state, with a system of government based on the separation and balancing of legislative, executive and judicial powers. Sovereignty is exercised by the people through their elected representatives. The Republic of Albania recognizes and protects the national rights of people who live outside the country's borders. Political parties are created freely, and are required to conform with democratic principles. The Republic of Albania does not have an official religion, and guarantees equality of religious communities. The economic system of the Republic of Albania is based on a market economy, and on freedom of economic activity, as well as on private and public property. The armed forces ensure the independence of the country, and protect its territorial integrity and constitutional order. Local government in the Republic of Albania is exercised according to the principle of decentralization of public power. The fundamental political, economic and social rights and freedoms of Albanian citizens are guaranteed under the Constitution.

LEGISLATURE

The People's Assembly comprises at least 140 deputies, and is elected for a term of four years. One hundred deputies are elected directly in single-member constituencies, while parties receiving more than 3% of votes cast nationally are allocated further deputies in proportion to the number of votes won. The Council of Ministers, every deputy and 20,000 voters each have the right to propose legislation. The People's Assembly makes decisions by a majority of votes, when more than one-half of the deputies are present. The 25-member Council of the Assembly is elected by the members of the People's Assembly at the beginning of the first session. The Council of the Assembly reviews preliminary draft laws, and gives opinions on specific issues.

PRESIDENT

The President of the Republic is the Head of State and represents the unity of the people. A candidate for President is proposed to the People's Assembly by a group of not less than 20 deputies. The President is elected by secret ballot by a majority of three-fifths of the members of the People's Assembly for a term of five years.

COUNCIL OF MINISTERS

The Council of Ministers comprises the Prime Minister, Deputy Prime Minister and ministers. The President of the Republic nominates as Prime Minister the candidate presented by the party or coalition of parties that has the majority of seats in the People's Assembly. The Prime Minister, within 40 days of his appointment, forms a Council of Ministers, which is presented for approval to the People's Assembly.

LOCAL GOVERNMENT

The units of local government are communes, municipalities, and regions. The representative organs of the basic units of local government are councils, which are elected by general direct elections for a period of three years. The executive organ of a municipality or commune is the Chairman. The Council of Ministers appoints a Prefect in every region as its representative.

JUDICIARY

Judicial power is exercised by the High Court, as well as by the Courts of Appeal and the Courts of First Instance. The Chairman and members of the High Court are appointed by the President of the Republic, with the approval of the People's Assembly, for a term of seven years. Other judges are appointed by the President upon the proposal of a High Council of Justice. The High Council of Justice comprises the Chairman of the High Court, the Minister of Justice, three members elected by the People's Assembly for a term of five years, and nine judges who are elected by a national judicial conference. The Constitutional Court arbitrates on constitutional issues, and determines the conformity of proposed legislation with the Constitution. The Constitutional Court comprises nine members, who are appointed by the President, with the approval of the People's Assembly, for a term of nine years.

The Government

HEAD OF STATE

President of the Republic: ALFRED MOISIU (elected 24 June 2002; took office 24 July 2002).

COUNCIL OF MINISTERS
(April 2003)

Prime Minister: FATOS NANO.

Deputy Prime Minister and Minister of Foreign Affairs: ILIR META.

Minister of Defence: PANDELI MAJKO.

Minister of Public Order: LUAN RAMA.

Minister of Justice: SPIRO PEÇI.

Minister of Transport: SPARTAK POÇI.

Minister of Finance: KASTRIOT ISLAMI.

Minister of Education and Science: LUAN MEMUSHI.

Minister of Culture, Youth and Sports: ARTA DADE.

Minister of Local Government and Decentralization: BEN BLUSHI.

Minister of the Environment: LUFTER XHUVELI.

Minister of Agriculture: AGRON DUKA.

Minister of Economic Co-operation and Trade: ARBEN MALAJ.

Minister of Health: MUSTAFA XHANI.

Minister of Industry and Energy: VIKTOR DODA.

Minister of Labour and Social Affairs: VALENTINA LESKAJ.

Minister of Territory Adjustment and Tourism: BESNIK DERIVISHI.

Minister of State, responsible for Integration: SOKOL NAKO.

Minister of State, responsible for Anti-corruption: BLENDI KLOSI.

MINISTRIES

Council of Ministers: Këshilli i Ministrave, Tirana; tel. (4) 228210; fax (4) 227888.

Ministry of Agriculture: Ministria e Bujqësisë dhe Ushqimit, Bulevardi Dëshmorët e Kombit, Tirana; tel. and fax (4) 232796.

Ministry of Culture, Youth and Sports: Ministria e Kulturës, Bulevardi Dëshmorët e Kombit, Tirana; tel. (4) 232488; fax (4) 227918; e-mail kabkult@mkrs.gov.al; internet www.mkrs.gov.al.

Ministry of Defence: Ministria e Mbrojtjes, Bulevardi Dëshmorët e Kombit, Tirana; tel. (4) 222103; fax (4) 228325; e-mail info@mod .gov.al; internet www.mod.gov.al.

Ministry of Economic Co-operation and Trade: Tirana; tel. (4) 234668; fax (4) 234658; internet www.mbet.gov.al.

Ministry of Education and Science: Ministria e Arsimit dhe Shkences, Rruga Durrësit 23, Tirana; tel. (4) 225987; fax (4) 232002; e-mail vqano@mash.gov.al; f. 1912.

Ministry of the Environment: Tirana.

Ministry of Finance: Ministria e Financave, Bulevardi Dëshmorët e Kombit, Tirana; tel. (4) 227937; fax (4) 228494; e-mail phida@ yahoo.com; internet www.minfin.gov.al.

Ministry of Foreign Affairs: Ministria e Punëve të Jashtme, Bulevardi Zhan D'Ark, Tirana; tel. (4) 262055; fax (4) 232971; e-mail dshtypi@abissnet.com.al; internet www.mfa.gov.al.

Ministry of Health: Ministria e Shendetesisë, Tirana; tel. and fax (4) 264632.

Ministry of Industry and Energy: Tirana.

Ministry of Justice: Ministria e Drejtësisë, Bulevardi Dëshmorët e Kombit, Tirana; tel. (4) 224041; fax (4) 228359; e-mail ministidre@ albaniaonline.net.

Ministry of Labour and Social Affairs: Ministria e Punës dhe Ndihmës Sociale, Rruga e Kavajes, Tirana; tel. (4) 240412; fax (4) 227779; e-mail molsa@icc-al.org; internet www.molsa.gov.al.

Ministry of Local Government and Decentralization: Bulevardi Dëshmorët e Kombit, Tirana; tel. (4) 233538.

Ministry of Public Order: Bulevardi Dëshmorët e Kombit, Tirana; tel. and fax (4) 224364.

Ministry of Territory Adjustment and Tourism: Bulevardi Dëshmorët e Kombit, Tirana; tel. and fax (4) 227879; e-mail militar@ albaniaonline.net.

Ministry of Transport: Abdi Toptani 4, Tirana; e-mail pmtrans@ icc-al.org.

Legislature

KUVENDI POPULLOR
(People's Assembly)

Tirana; e-mail mmyftiu@parliament.tirana.al; internet www .parlament.al.

President (Speaker): SERVET PELLUMBI.

Deputy President: MAKBULE CECO.

General Election, 24 June and 8 July 2001

Party	% of votes	Seats
Socialist Party of Albania	41.5	73
Union for Victory*	36.8	46
Democratic Alternative	5.1	6
Social Democratic Party of Albania	3.6	4
Union for Human Rights Party	2.6	3
Agrarian Party	2.6	3
Democratic Alliance Party	2.5	3
Independents	—	2
Others	5.3	—
Total	**100.0**	**140**

* Alliance comprising the Democratic Party of Albania, the Legality Movement, the Liberal Party, the National Front and the Republican Party.

Political Organizations

Agrarian Party (AP) (Partia Agrar Shqiptare): Rruga Budi 6, Tirana; tel. and fax (4) 227481; f. 1991; Chair. LUFTER XHUVELI.

Albanian Civil Party: Tirana; f. 1998; Chair. ROLAND VELKO; Sec. ETLEVA GJERMENI.

Albanian Communist Party: Tirana; f. 1991; granted legal recognition 1998; Chair. HYSNI MILLOSHI.

Albanian Conservative Party (Partia Konservatore Shqiptare): Tirana; Chair. ARMANDO RUCO.

Albanian Ecological Party (Partia Ekologjike Shqiptare): Rruga Aleksander Moissi 26, POB 135, Tirana; tel. (4) 222503; fax (4) 234413; f. 1991; environmental political party; Chair. Dr NAMIK VEHBI, FADILE HOTI.

Albanian Green Party (Partia e Blertë Shqiptare): POB 749, Tirana; tel. and fax (4) 233309; f. 1991; campaigns on environmental issues; Chair. NEVRUZ MALUKA; Sec. SHYQRI KONDI.

Albanian Helsinki Forum (Forum Shqiptar i Helsinkit): Tirana; f. 1990; mem. International Federation of Helsinki; Chair. Prof. ARBEN PUTO.

Albanian National Democratic Party (Partia Nacional Demokratike): Tirana; f. 1991; Chair. FATMIR ÇEKANI.

Albanian Nationalist Party: Tirana; f. 1993.

Albanian New Socialist Party: Tirana; f. 1996 by former mems of the SPA.

Albanian Republican Party (ARP) (Partia Republikane Shqiptare—PRS): Tirana; f. 1991; Gen. Council of 54 mems, Steering Commission of 21 mems; Chair. SABRI GODO; Vice-Chair. FATMIR MEDIU; Sec. CERCIZ MINGOMATAS.

Albanian Women's Federation (Forum i Grus Shqiptare): Tirana; tel. (4) 228309; f. 1991; independent organization uniting women from various religious and cultural backgrounds; Chair. DIANA ÇULI.

Albanian Workers' Movement Party (Partia Levizja e Punetoreve Shqiptare): Tirana; f. 2000; Chair. SOKOL QENDRO.

Çamëria Political and Patriotic Association (Shoqata Politike-Patriotike Çamëria): Tirana; supports the rights of the Çam minority (an Albanian people) in northern Greece; f. 1991; Chair. Dr ABAZ DOJAKA.

Christian Democratic Party of Albania (CDPA): Rruga Dëshmorët e 4 Shkurtit, Tirana; tel. (4) 2240574; fax (4) 2233024; e-mail zbushati@libero.it; f. 1991; Pres. ZEF BUSHATI; Gen.-Sec. SHPRESA PROSEKU.

Democratic Alliance Party (DAP): Tirana; internet www.aleanca.org; f. 1992 by former members of the DPA; Chair. NERITAN ÇEKA; Sec.-Gen. EDMOND DRAGOTI.

Democratic Alternative: Tirana; f. 1999 by breakaway faction of reformist members of the Democratic Party of Albania; Leader GENC POLLO.

Democratic Party of Albania (DPA) (Partia Demokratike e Shqipërisë—PDSH): Rruga Punetoret e Rilindjes; Tirana; tel. (4) 228091; fax (4) 223525; e-mail profsberisha@albaniaonline.net; internet www.albania.co.uk/dp; f. 1990; committed to centre-right democratic ideals and market economics; contested the legislative elections of June–July 2001 as part of the Union for Victory alliance; Chair. Prof. Dr SALI BERISHA; Sec.-Gen. DASHAMIR SHEHI BLERINA GJOKA.

Democratic Party of the Right: Tirana; Leader PETRIT KALAKULA.

Democratic Prosperity Party (Partia e Prosperitetit Demokratik): Tirana; f. 1991; Chair. YZEIR FETAHU.

Democratic Union of the Greek Minority (OMONIA) (Bashkimia Demokratik i Minoritet Grek): Tirana; f. 1991; Chair. JORGO LABOVITJADHI.

Democratic Unity Party (Partia e Bashkimit Demokratik): Tirana; Chair. XHEVDET LIBOHOVA.

Independent Party (Partia Indipendente): Tirana; f. 1991; Chair. EDMOND GJOKRUSHI.

Legality Movement (Partia Lëvizja e Legalitetit): Tirana; f. 1992; monarchist; contested the legislative elections of June–July 2001 as part of the Union for Victory alliance; Chair. GURI DUROLLARI.

Liberal Party (Partia Liberale): Tirana; f. 1991; contested the legislative elections of June–July 2001 as part of the Union for Victory alliance; Chair. VALTER FILE.

Movement for Democracy (Levizja per Democraci): Tirana; f. 1997 by former mems of the DPA; Leader DASHAMIR SHEHI.

National Committee of the War Veterans of the Anti-Fascist National Liberation War of the Albanian People (Komiteti Kombëtar i Veteranëve të Luftës Antifashiste Nacional Çlirimtare të Popullit Shqiptar): Rruga Dëshmorët e 4 Shkurtit, Tirana; f. 1957; Chair. PIRRO DODBIBA; Gen. Sec. QAMIL PODA.

National Front (Balli Kombëtar): c/o Kuvendi Popullor, Tirana; e-mail ilirians@hotmail.com; contested the legislative elections of June–July 2001 as part of the Union for Victory alliance; Chair. EKREM SPAHIA.

National Progress Party (Partia e Perparimit Kombëtar): Tirana; f. 1991; Chair. MYRTO XHAFERRI.

National Unity Party (Partia e Unitetit Kombëtar): Rruga Alqi Kondi, Tirana; tel. (4) 227498; fax (4) 223929; f. 1991; Chair. of Steering Cttee IDAJET BEQIRI.

New Democratic Party: Tirana; f. Feb. 2001 by former members of the DPA; Leader GENC POLLO.

New Party of Labour: Tirana; f. 1998; left-wing; defines itself as successor to the former communist Party of Labour of Albania.

People's Party (Partia Popullore): Tirana; f. 1991; aims to eradicate communism; Chair. BASHKIM DRIZA.

Republican Party (Partia Republika e Shqipërisë): Tirana; contested the legislative elections of June–July 2001 as part of the Union for Victory alliance; Chair. FATMIR MEDIU.

Right National Party: Tirana; f. 1998 by a breakaway faction of the National Front; Leader HYSEN SELFO.

Social Democratic Party of Albania (SDP) (Partia Social Demokratike e Shqipërisë—PSDS): Rruga Asim Vokshi 26, Tirana; tel. (4) 226540; fax (4) 227485; f. 1991; advocates gradual economic reforms and social justice; 100-member National Managing Council; Chair. SKENDER GJINUSHI; Gen. Sec. ENGJËLL BEJTAJ.

Social Justice Party (Partia e Drejtesise Shogerore): Tirana.

Social Labour Party of Albania (Partia Socialpuntore Shqiptare): Burrel; f. 1992; Pres. RAMADAN NDREKA.

Socialist Party of Albania (SPA) (Partia Socialiste e Shqipërisë—PSS): Tirana; tel. (4) 227409; fax (4) 227417; f. 1941 as Albanian Communist Party, renamed Party of Labour of Albania PLA in 1948, adopted present name in 1991; now rejects Marxism-Leninism and claims commitment to democratic socialism and a market economy; Managing Cttee of 81 mems, headed by Presidency of 15 mems; Chair. FATOS NANO; Sec.-Gen. GRAMOZ RUCI; 110,000 mems.

Union for Human Rights Party (UHRP) (Partia për Mbrojtjen e te Drejtave te Njeriut—PBDNj): Tirana; f. 1992; represents the Greek and Macedonian minorities; Chair. VASIL MELO; Sec.-Gen. THOMA MICO.

Union of Social Democrats (USD): Tirana; f. 1995; breakaway faction of the SDP; Leader TEODOR LACO.

Diplomatic Representation

EMBASSIES IN ALBANIA

Austria: Rruga Frederik Shiroka, Tirana; tel. (4) 233157; fax (4) 233140; e-mail tirana-ob@bmaa.gv.al; Ambassador HORST-DIETER RENNAU.

Bulgaria: Rruga Skënderbeu 12, Tirana; tel. (4) 233155; fax (4) 232272; Ambassador BOBI NIKOLOV BOBEV.

Canada: Rruga Brigada e Tete, Pall. 2, POB 47, Tirana; tel. (4) 257274; fax (4) 257273; e-mail canadalb@canada.gov.al; Ambassador STEPHEN MORAN.

China, People's Republic: Rruga Skënderbeu 57, Tirana; tel. (4) 232385; fax (4) 233159; e-mail chem@adanet.com.al; Ambassador TIAN CHANGCHUN.

Croatia: Rruga Abdyl Frashëri, Tirana; tel. (4) 228390; fax (4) 230578; Ambassador JOSIP JURAS.

Czech Republic: Rruga Skënderbeu 4, Tirana; tel. (4) 234004; fax (4) 232159; e-mail e-mail tirana@embassy.mzv.cz; Chargé d'affaires a.i. MIROSLAV ŠINDELÁŘ.

Denmark: Rruga Nikolla Tupe 1, POB 1743, Tirana; tel. (4) 257422; fax (4) 257420; e-mail tiaamb@um.dk; internet www.um.dk; Chargé d'affaires FINN THEILGAARD.

Egypt: Rruga Skënderbeu 43, Tirana; tel. (4) 233022; fax (4) 232295; Ambassador ATTIA QARAM.

France: Rruga Skënderbeu 14, Tirana; tel. (4) 234250; fax (4) 233763; e-mail ambcrtir@mail.adanet.com.al; Ambassador MICHEL MENACHEMOFF.

Germany: Rruga Skënderbeu 8, Tirana; tel. (4) 274505; fax (4) 233497; e-mail german.embassy@icc.al.eu.org; Ambassador HELMUTH SCHRÖDER.

Greece: Rruga Frederik Shiroka 3, Tirana; tel. (4) 234290; fax (4) 234443; Ambassador DIMITRIS ILIOLOPOULOS.

Holy See: Rruga e Durrësit 13, POB 8355, Tirana; tel. (4) 233516; fax (4) 232001; e-mail nunap-al@icc-al.org; Apostolic Nuncio Most Rev. GIOVANNI BULAITIS (Titular Archbishop of Narona).

Hungary: Rruga Skënderbeu 16, Tirana; tel. (4) 232238; fax (4) 233211; Ambassador SÁNDOR MESZAROS.

Iran: Rruga Mustafa Matohiti 20, Tirana; tel. (4) 227869; fax (4) 230409; Ambassador MOHAMMAD KAZEM BIGDELI SOLTANI.

Italy: Rruga Lek Dukagjini, Tirana; tel. (4) 234045; fax (4) 234276; e-mail ambittia@icc.al.eu.org; internet www.ambitalia-tirana.com; Ambassador MARIO BOVA.

Libya: Rruga Dëshmorët e 4 Shkurtit 48, Tirana; tel. (4) 228101; fax (4) 232098; Bureau Chief YOUSSEF ELTAEF SASSI.

Macedonia, former Yugoslav republic: Rruga Lek Dukagjini, Vila 2; tel. (4) 233036; fax (4) 232514; Ambassador ELEONORA KARANFILOVSKA.

Netherlands: Rruga e Vilave Gjermane 8, POB 1735, Tirana; tel. (4) 375111; fax (4) 375982; Ambassador FREDERIK LODEWIJK.

Norway: Rruga Dëshmorët e 4 Shkurtit 7/1; tel. and fax (4) 257035; Chargé d'affaires TOBIAS FRAMBE SVENNINGSEN.

Poland: Rruga e Durrësit 123, Tirana; tel. (4) 234190; fax (4) 233464; Ambassador ANDRZEJ CHODAKOWSKI.

Romania: Rruga Themistokli, Gjermeni 2, Tirana; tel. (4) 256071; fax (4) 256072; e-mail roemb@adanet.co.al; Ambassador CONSTANTIN EREMIA.

Russia: Rruga Asim Zeneli 5, Tirana; tel. (4) 256040; fax (4) 256046; Ambassador VLADIMIR N. TOKIN.

Saudi Arabia: Bulevardi Dëshmorët e Kombit; tel. (4) 248307; fax (4) 229982; Chargé d'affaires MOHAMMED LABANI.

Serbia and Montenegro: Tirana; Ambassador CAFO KAPETANOVIĆ.

Switzerland: Rruga e Elbasanit 81, Tirana; tel. (4) 234890; fax (4) 234889; e-mail swissemb@adanet.com.al; Ambassador FRANCIS COUSIN.

Turkey: Rruga Konferenca e Kavajes 31, Tirana; tel. (4) 233399; fax (4) 232719; e-mail turkemb@interalb.al; Ambassador MEHMET MURAT OĞUZ.

United Kingdom: Rruga Skënderbeu 12, Tirana; tel. (4) 234973; fax (4) 247697; Ambassador DAVID LANDSMAN.

USA: Rruga Labinoti 103, Tirana; tel. (4) 247285; fax (4) 232222; e-mail wm_tirana@pd.state.gov; internet www.usemb-tirana.rpo.al; Ambassador JAMES FRANKLIN JEFFREY.

Judicial System

The judicial structure comprises the High Court, the Courts of Appeal and the Courts of First Instance. The Chairman and members of the High Court are appointed by the President of the Republic, with the approval of the legislature, for a term of seven years. Other judges are appointed by the President upon the proposal of a High Council of Justice. The High Council of Justice comprises the Chairman of the High Court, the Minister of Justice, three members elected by the legislature for a term of five years, and nine judges of all levels who are elected by a national judicial conference.

The Constitutional Court

The Constitutional Court arbitrates on constitutional issues, and determines, *inter alia*, the conformity of proposed legislation with the Constitution. It is empowered to prohibit the activities of political organizations on constitutional grounds, and also formulates legislation regarding the election of the President of the Republic. The Constitutional Court comprises nine members, who are appointed by the President, with the approval of the legislature, for a term of nine years

Chairman of the Constitutional Court: FEHMI ABDIU.

Religion

All religious institutions were closed by the Government in 1967 and the practice of religion was prohibited. In May 1990, however, the prohibition on religious activities was revoked, religious services were permitted and, from 1991, mosques and churches began to be reopened. Under the Constitution of November 1998, Albania is a secular state, which observes freedom of religious belief. On the basis of declared affiliation in 1945, it is estimated that some 70% of the population are of Muslim background (mainly Sunni or adherents of the liberal Bektashi order), 20% Eastern Orthodox Christian (mainly in the south) and some 10% Roman Catholic Christian (mainly in the north).

ISLAM

Albanian Islamic Community (Bashkesia Islame e Shqipërisë): Rruga Puntoret e Rilindjes, Tirana; e-mail icalb@yahoo.com; f. 1991; Chair. HAFIZ H. SABRI KOÇI; Grand Mufti of Albania HAFIZ SELIM STAFA.

Bektashi Sect

World Council of Elders of the Bektashis: Tirana; f. 1991; Chair. RESHAT BABA BARDHI.

CHRISTIANITY

The Eastern Orthodox Church

Orthodox Autocephalous Church of Albania (Kisha Orthodhokse Autoqefale të Shqipërisë): Rruga Kavaja 151, Tirana; tel. (4) 234117; fax (4) 232109; e-mail orthchal@ocual.tirana.al; the Albanian Orthodox Church was proclaimed autocephalous at the Congress of Berat in 1922, its status was approved in 1929 and it was

recognized by the Ecumenical Patriarchate in İstanbul (Constantinople), Turkey, in 1936; Archbishop ANASTAS JANNOULATOS.

The Roman Catholic Church

Many Roman Catholic churches have been reopened since 1990, and in September 1991 diplomatic relations were restored with the Holy See. Albania comprises two archdioceses, four dioceses and one apostolic administration. At 31 December 2000 there were an estimated 512,601 adherents in the country, representing about 13.9% of the total population.

Bishops' Conference: Conferenza Episcopale dell'Albania, Rruga Don Bosco, Tirana; tel. and fax (4) 247159; e-mail cealbania@albnet.net; Pres. Most Rev. ANGELO MASSAFRA (Metropolitan Archbishop of Shkodër).

Archbishop of Durrës-Tirana: Most Rev. RROK K. MIRDITA, Arqipeshkvia, Bulevard Zhan d'Ark, Tirana; tel. (4) 232082; fax (4) 230727; e-mail arq@icc.al.org.

Archbishop of Shkodër: Most Rev. ANGELO MASSAFRA, Kryepeshkëvi, Sheshi Gijon Pali II, Shkodër; tel. (22) 42744; fax (22) 43673.

The Press

Until 1991 the Press was controlled by the Party of Labour of Albania, now the Socialist Party of Albania (SPA), and adhered to a strongly Marxist-Leninist line. From 1991 many new periodicals and newspapers were established by the newly emerging independent political organizations. In 2000 there were some 12 daily newspapers and 18 principal weekly periodicals in publication. The total daily circulation of all newspapers declined to less than 50,000 in 2000, compared with 65,000 in 1999.

PRINCIPAL DAILIES

Albania: POB 749, Tirana; tel. and fax (4) 233309; f. 1991; weekly; organ of the Albanian Green Party; environmental issues.

Albanian Daily News: Rruga Hile Mosi, 5, Tirana; tel. and fax (4) 227639; e-mail adn@icc.al.eu.org; internet www.albaniannews.com; f. 1995; weekly; English-language newspaper; Editor ARBEN LESKAJ.

Ekonomia: Bulevardi Zhan D'Ark, Tirana; tel. (4) 250766; fax (4) 250767; e-mail gazekonomia@albaniaonline.com.

Gazeta Shqiptare: Rruga e Dibres 370, Tirana; tel. (4) 262646; fax (4) 263885; e-mail gazesh@katamail.com.

Koha Jonë (Our Time): Sami Frasheri, Pallatet e Aviacionit, Tirana; tel. (4) 247004; fax (4) 247005; e-mail kohajone@albnet.net; internet www.kohajone.com; f. 1991; independent; Editor-in-Chief KICO BLUSHI; circ. 400,000.

Republika: Sami Frasheri, Pallatet e Aviacionit, Tirana; tel. and fax (4) 25988; e-mail republika@albaniaonline.net; internet www.pages.albaniaonline.net/republika; organ of the Republican Party; Editor-in-Chief YLLI RAKIPI.

Rilindja Demokratike (Democratic Revival): Rruga Punetoret e Rindjes 16, Tirana; tel. (4) 229609; fax (4) 242329; e-mail gazetard@albaniaonline.net; internet www.rilindjademokratike.com; f. 1991; organ of the DPA; Editor-in-Chief LORENC LIGORI; circ. 50,000.

Shekulli: Rruga Don Bosko, Vilat e Reja, Tirana; tel. (4) 251425; fax (4) 251424; e-mail webmaster@shekulli.com.al; internet www.shekulli.com.al; independent; Editor-in-Chief ZAMIR ALUSHI.

Tema: Rruga Xhorxhi Martini 10; tel. (4) 251069; fax (4) 251073; e-mail tema@albaniaonline.net.

Zëri i Popullit (The Voice of the People): Bulevardi Zhan D'Ark, Tirana; tel. (4) 222192; fax (4) 227813; e-mail zeri@zeripopullit.com; internet www.zeripopullit.com; f. 1942; daily, except Mon. organ of the SPA; Editor-in-Chief ERION BRACE; circ. 105,000.

PERIODICALS

Agrovizion: Rruga d'Istria, Tirana; tel. (4) 226147; f. 1992; 2 a week; agricultural economic policies, new technology in farming, advice for farmers; circ. 3,000.

Albanian Observer: Rruga Perlat Rexhepi Pall. 9, Shkurtit 1, Tirana; tel. and fax (4) 227419.

Bashkimi Kombëtar: Bulevardi Zhan D'Ark, Tirana; tel. (4) 228110; f. 1943; Editor-in-Chief QEMAL SAKAJEVA; circ. 30,000.

Blic: Rruga Fortuzi 44, Tirana; tel. (4) 234319; e-mail blici@juno.com; weekly; politics, information and culture; Editor ILIR YZEIRI.

Ditet Tona: Rruga Margaret Tutulani, Pall. 23, Shkurtit 1, Tirana; tel. (4) 230585.

Drita (The Light): Rruga Konferenca e Pezës 4, Tirana; tel. (4) 227036; f. 1960; weekly; publ. by Union of Writers and Artists of Albania; Editor-in-Chief BRISEIDA MEMA; circ. 31,000.

Fatosi (The Valiant): Tirana; tel. (4) 223024; f. 1959; fortnightly; literary and artistic magazine for children; Editor-in-Chief XHEVAT BEQARAJ; circ. 21,200.

Hosteni (The Goad): Tirana; f. 1945; fortnightly; political review of humour and satire; publ. by the Union of Journalists; Editor-in-Chief NIKO NIKOLLA.

The Hour of Albania: Rruga Dëshmorët e 4 Shkurtit, Tirana; tel. (4) 242042; fax (4) 234024; weekly; organ of the Christian Democratic Party of Albania; Editor-in-Chief Dr FAIK LAMA; circ. 3,000.

Identity: Rruga Daut Boriçi 874, Shköder; tel. (22) 41229; e-mail irsh@albnet.net.

Intervista: Rruga e Dibres 133, Tirana; tel. (4) 233164.

Klan: Rruga Myslym Shyri 8/1, Tirana; tel. (4) 240304; fax (4) 234424; e-mail klan@albnet.net.

Kombi (The Nation): Rruga Alqi Kondi, Tirana; tel. (4) 227498; fax (4) 223929; f. 1991; 2 a week; organ of the Party of National Unity; circ. 15,000.

Mbrojtja (The Defence): Bulevardi Dëshmorët e Kombit, Tirana; tel. (4) 226701; fax (4) 225726; e-mail tanct@al.pims.org; f. 1931; every 2 months; publ. by the Ministry of Defence; Editor-in-Chief ELMAZ LECI; circ. 1,500.

Official Gazette of the Republic of Albania: Kuvendi Popullore, Tirana; tel. (4) 228668; fax (4) 227949; f. 1945; occasional government review.

Pasqyra (The Mirror): Bulevardi Zogu I, Pall. A. Kelmendi, Tirana; tel. (4) 222956; fax (4) 229169; e-mail marketingu@pasqyra.com; internet www.pasqyra.com; f. 1991 to replace *Puna (Labour)*; f. 1945; weekly; organ of the Confederation of Albanian Trade Unions; Editor-in-Chief XHAFER SHATRI.

Progresi (Progress): Rruga Budi 6, Tirana; tel. (4) 227481; fax (4) 227481; f. 1991; 2 a week; organ of the Agrarian Party.

Revista Pedagogjike: Naim Frashëri St 37, Tirana; fax (4) 256441; f. 1945; quarterly; organ of the Institute of Pedagogical Studies; educational development, psychology, didactic; Editor BUJAR BASKA; circ. 4,000.

Shëndeti (Health): M. Duri 2, Tirana; tel. (4) 227803; fax (4) 227803; f. 1949; monthly; publ. by the National Directorate of Health Education; issues of health and welfare, personal health care; Editors-in-Chief KORNELIA GJATA, AGIM XHUMARI.

Shqiptarja e Re (The New Albanian Woman): Tirana; f. 1943; monthly; political and socio-cultural review; Editor-in-Chief VALENTINA LESKAJ.

Sindikalisti (Trade Unionists): Tirana; f. 1991; newspaper; organ of the Union of Independent Trade Unions of Albania; Editor-in-Chief VANGJEL KOZMAI.

Spektër (The Spectre): Tirana; e-mail redaksia@spekter.com.al; internet www.spekter.com.al; f. 1991; illustrated independent monthly; in Albanian and Italian.

Sporti Shquiptar: Rruga e Kavajës 23, Sheshi Ataturk, 2908 Tirana; tel. and fax (4) 220237; f. 1935; 3 a week; Editor BESNIK DIZDARI; circ. 10,000.

Tregtia e Jashtme Popullore (Albanian Foreign Trade): Rruga Konferenca e Pezës 6, Tirana; tel. (4) 222934; f. 1961; 6 a year; in English and French; organ of the Albanian Chamber of Commerce; Editor AGIM KORBI.

Tribuna e Gazetarit (The Journalist's Tribune): Tirana; 6 a year; publ. by the Union of Journalists of Albania; Editor NAZMI QAMILI.

Ushtria (Army): Bulevardi Dëshmorët e Kombit, Tirana; tel. (4) 224350; fax (4) 225726; f. 1945; weekly; publ. by the Ministry of Defence; Editor-in-Chief BARDHYL GOSNISHTI; circ. 3,200.

NEWS AGENCIES

Albanian Independent News Agency: Rruga 4 Dëshmorët 80, Tirana; tel. (4) 241727; fax (4) 233866.

Albanian Telegraphic Agency (ATA): Bulevardi Zhan D'Ark 23, Tirana; tel. (4) 222929; fax (4) 234230; e-mail hola@ata.tirana.al; internet www.ata-al.net; f. 1929; domestic and foreign news; brs in provincial towns and in Kosovo, Serbia and Montenegro; Dir-Gen. FRROK CUPI.

Enter: Shetitorja Dëshmorët e Kombit, Tirana; tel. (4) 240129; fax (4) 235916; internet www.Albania.co.uk/enter.

Foreign Bureau

Xinhua (New China) News Agency (People's Republic of China): Rruga Zef Jubani 3, Apt 903, Tirana; tel. (4) 233139; fax (4) 248019; e-mail xinhua-tirana@china.com; Bureau Chief LI JIYU.

PRESS ASSOCIATIONS

Albanian Media Institute: Rruga Gjin Bue Shpata 8, Tirana; tel. and fax (4) 229800; e-mail info@institutemedia.org.

Union of Journalists of Albania (Bashkimi i Gazetarëve të Shqipërisë): Tirana; tel. (4) 228020; f. 1949; Chair. MARASH HAJATI; Sec.-Gen. YMER MINXHOZI.

Publishers

Agjensia Qëndrore e Tregtimit të Librit Artistik dhe Shkencor (Central Agency of the Artistic and Scientific Book Trade): Tirana; tel. and fax (4) 227246.

Botime të Akademisë së Shkencave të RSH: Tirana; publishing house of the Albanian Academy of Sciences.

Botime te Universitetit Bujqësor të Tiranës: Kamzë, Tirana; publishing house of the Agricultural University of Tirana.

Botime të Shtëpisë Botuese 8 Nëntori: Tirana; tel. (4) 228064; f. 1972; books on Albania and other countries, political and social sciences, translations of Albanian works into foreign languages, technical and scientific books, illustrated albums, etc. Dir XHEMAL DINI.

Dituria Publishing House: Rruga Dervish Hima 32, Tirana; tel. and fax (4) 225882; f. 1991; dictionaries, calendars, encyclopaedias, social sciences, biographies, fiction and non-fiction; Gen. Dir PETRIT YMERI.

Drejtoria e Informacionit Agro-Ushqimor (Agriculture and Food Information Directory): Rruga S. Kosturi, Tirana; tel. (4) 226147; f. 1970; publishes various agricultural periodicals; Gen. Dir Prof. AGO NEZHA.

Fan Noli: Tirana; tel. (4) 242739; f. 1991; Albanian and foreign literature.

Shtëpia Botuese e Librit Shkollor: Tirana; tel. (4) 222331; f. 1967; educational books; Dir SHPËTIM BOZDO.

Shtëpia Botuese 'Libri Universitar': Rruga Dora d'Istria, Tirana; tel. (4) 225659; fax (4) 229268; f. 1988; publishes university textbooks on science, medicine, engineering, geography, history, literature, foreign languages, economics, etc. Dir MUSTAFA FEZGA.

Shtëpia Botuese e Lidhjes së Shkrimtarëve: Konferenca e Pezës 4, Tirana; tel. (4) 222691; fax (4) 225912; f. 1990; artistic and documentary literature; Dir ZIJA ÇELA.

Shtëpia Botuese Naim Frashëri: Tirana; tel. (4) 227906; f. 1947; fiction, poetry, drama, criticism, children's literature, translations; Dir GAQO BUSHAKA.

Union of Writers and Artists Publishing House: Tirana; f. 1991; fiction, poetry incl. foreign literature and works by the Albanian diaspora.

Broadcasting and Communications

TELECOMMUNICATIONS

State Department of Posts and Telecommunications: Rruga Myslym Shyri 42, Tirana; tel. (4) 227204; fax (4) 233772; e-mail kote@dshpt.tirana.al; Gen. Dir HYDAJET KOPANI; Man. Dir FREDERIK KOTE.

Albanian Mobile Communications (AMC): Rruga Gjergi Legisi, Laprake, Tirana; tel. (4) 234915; fax (4) 235157; e-mail agreva@amc.al; f. 1996; fmrly state-owned, bought by a Greek/Norwegian consortium in 2000; operates mobile-telephone network; Man. Dir STEFANOS OKTAPODAS.

Albanian Telecom (Telekomi Shqiptar): Rruga Myslym Shyri 42, Tirana; tel. (4) 232200; fax (4) 233323; internet www.atnet.com.al; scheduled for privatization in 20032; Dir-Gen. DHIMITRAQ RAFTI.

BROADCASTING

In 1991 state broadcasting was removed from political control and made subordinate to the Parliamentary Commission for the Media. By the end of 2000 the National Council of Radio and Television had licensed two national television stations, 45 local television stations, one national radio station and 31 local radio stations.

Regulatory Authority

National Council of Radio and Television (NCRT): Rruga Abdi Toptani, Tirana; tel. (4) 233326; fax (4) 226287; e-mail scela@kkrt .gov.al; internet www.kkrt.gov.al; f. 1998; Chair. SEFEDIN CELA.

Radio

Radio Televizioni Shqiptare: Rruga Ismail Qemali 11, Tirana; tel. (4) 228310; fax (4) 227745; e-mail dushiulp@yahoo.com; internet www.rtsh.sil.al; f. 1938 as Radio Tirana; two channels of domestic services (19 and five hours daily) and a third channel covering international broadcasting (two services in Albanian and seven in foreign languages); Chair. KASTRIST CAUSBI; Dir-Gen. EDUARD MAZI; Dir of Radio MARTIN LEKA.

Kontakt Radio: Rruga Muhamet Gjollesha, Kati i9, Tirana; tel. (4) 249474; fax (4) 257602; e-mail radiokontakt@albaniaonline.net; internet www.radiokontakt.com; independent radio station; commenced broadcasts Oct. 1997; Dir AGRON BALA.

Radio Klan: Rruga Myslim Shyri 8/1, Tirana; tel. (4) 240304; e-mail klan@albnet.net.

Top Albania Radio: International Centre of Culture, Bulevardi Dëshmorët e Kombit, Tirana; tel. (4) 247492; fax (4) 247493; e-mail topalbaniaradio@albaniaonline.net; internet www.pages .albaniaonline.net/topalbaniaradio.

Television

Radio Televizioni Shqiptare: Rruga Ismail Qemali 11, Tirana; tel. (4) 256056; fax (4) 256058; f. 1960; broadcasts range of television programmes; Chair. KASTRIST CAUSBI; Dir-Gen. EDUARD MAZI; Dir of Television VENA ISAK.

Alba Television: International Centre of Culture, Bulevardi Dëshmorët e Kombit, Tirana; tel. and fax (4) 234142; e-mail albatv@ albaniaonline.net; internet www.pages.albaniaonline.net/albatv; private television station; Dir PAULIN SHKJEZI.

Shijak TV: Rruga Kavajes, Sheshi Ataturk, Tirana; tel. and fax (4) 247135; e-mail shijaktv01@albaniaonline.net; internet www .shijaktv.com; Pres. GËZIM ISMAILI.

Teutar Televizion: Tirana; e-mail teutartv@albaniaonline.net; internet www.teutartv.com.

Finance

(cap. = capital; dep. = deposits; res = reserves; m. = million; brs = branches; amounts in lekë, unless otherwise stated)

BANKING

Central Bank

Bank of Albania (Banka e Shqipërisë): Sheshi Skënderbeu 1, Tirana; tel. (4) 222752; fax (4) 223558; e-mail public@bankofalbania .org; internet www.bankofalbania.org; f. 1992; cap. 750m., res 11,395m., dep. 41,491m. (Dec. 2001); Gov. SHKËLQIM CANI; 5 brs.

State Bank

Savings Bank of Albania: Rruga Dëshmorët e 4 Shkurtit 6, Tirana; tel. (4) 224972; fax (4) 223587; e-mail info@bkursimeve.com .al; internet www.bkursimeve.com.al; f. 1991; state-owned, scheduled for privatization in Dec. 2003; cap. 700m., res 2,109m., dep. 147,300m. (Dec. 2001); Gen. Man. ARDIAN KAMBERI; 37 brs.

Other Banks

American Bank of Albania (Banka Amerikanë e Shqipërisë): Rruga Ismail Qemali 27, POB 8319, Tirana; tel. (4) 248753; fax (4) 248762; e-mail americanbank@ambankalb.com; internet www .albambank.com; f. 1998; owned by Albanian-American Enterprise Fund USA; cap. US $5.1m. Chair. MICHAEL GRANOFF; Pres. and Chief Exec. LORENZO RONCARI.

Arab-Albanian Islamic Bank: Dëshmorët e Kombit 8, POB 128, Tirana; tel. (4) 227408; fax (4) 228460; e-mail aaib@albaniaonline .net; f. 1994; joint venture; cap. US $10.0m., res $1.1m., dep. $7.1m. (2001); Chair. SOLAIMAN ELKHEREIJI; Gen. Dir WAHEED ALAUI.

Fefad Bank: Rruga Ami Frasheri, POB 2395, Tirana; tel. (4) 220774; fax (4) 233481; e-mail fefad@icc.al.eu.org; internet www .fefadbank.com; f. 1996 as Foundation for Enterprise Finance and Development; name changed 1999; cap. 700.0m., res 56.7m., dep. 7,352.2m. (Dec. 2002); Gen. Man. EMMANUEL DECAMPS; 9 brs.

Italian-Albanian Bank (Banka Italo Shqiptare): Rruga e Barrikadave, Tirana; tel. (4) 235693; fax (4) 235700; e-mail biatia@adanet .com.al; f. 1993; cap. US $15.5m., res $0.9m., dep. $99.9m. Pres. EDMOND LEKA; Chair. GIOVANNI BOGANI.

National Commercial Bank of Albania: Bulevardi Zhan D'Ark, Tirana; tel. (4) 250955; fax (4) 250960; e-mail bkt@albmail.com; internet www.come.to.ncba; f. 1993; following merger of National Bank of Albania and Commercial Bank of Albania; privatized in 2000; cap. US $10.0m., res $2.8m., dep. $207.8m. (Dec. 2001); Chair. ILHAN NEBIOGLU; 30 brs.

Tirana Bank SA: Bulevardi Zogu I 55/1, Tirana; tel. (4) 233441; fax (4) 247140; e-mail tiranabank@icc.al.eu.org; f. 1996; cap. 1,040.5m., res 118.9m., dep. 17,127.7m. (Dec. 2001); Chair. STAVROS LEKAKOS.

INSURANCE

Insurance Institute of Albania (Instituti i Sigurimeve të Shqipërisë): Bulevardi Marcel Cachin, Tirana; tel. (4) 253407; fax (4) 233308; e-mail info@sigal.com.al; internet www.albaniainsurance .com; f. 1991; all types of insurance; Gen. Dir QEMAL DISHA; 12 brs.

STOCK EXCHANGE

Tirana Stock Exchange: Sheshi Skënderbeu 1, Tirana; tel. (4) 235568; fax (4) 223558; e-mail emeka@bankofalbania.org; internet www.asc.gov.al/tiranastock.html; f. 1996; Gen. Dir ELVIN MEKA (acting).

Trade and Industry

PRIVATIZATION AGENCY

National Agency for Privatization (NAP): Tirana; tel. and fax (4) 227933; govt agency under the control of the Council of Ministers; prepares and proposes the legal framework concerning privatization procedures and implementation; Dir NIKO GLOZHENI.

SUPERVISORY ORGANIZATIONS

Albanian Securities Commission (ASC): Bulevardi Dëshmorët e Kombit, Tirana; tel. and fax (4) 228260; e-mail asc@albaniaonline .net; internet www.asc.gov.al; Chair. ELISABETA GTONI.

Albkontroll: Rruga Skënderbeu 45, Durrës; tel. (52) 23377; fax (52) 22791; f. 1962; brs throughout Albania; independent control body for inspection of goods for import and export, means of transport, etc. Gen. Man. DILAVER MEZINI; 15 brs.

State Supreme Audit Control: Region Eurosai, Tirana; tel. and fax (4) 232491; e-mail klsh@albaniaonline.net; internet www.pages .albanianonline.net/klsh.

DEVELOPMENT ORGANIZATIONS

Albanian Centre for Economic Research: Rruga Frasheri 24, POB 2934, Tirana; tel. and fax (4) 225021; e-mail zefi@qske.tirana .al; internet www.arc.online.bq/ngos/albanian/acer.html; Pres. ZEF PREÇI.

Albanian Centre for Foreign Investment Promotion: Bulevardi Zhan D'Ark, Tirana; tel. (4) 228439; internet www.ipanet.net.

Albanian Development Fund: Rruga Durrësi, Tirana; tel. and fax (4) 2234885; e-mail eneida@a-d-f.org; Exec. Dir MAKS MITROJORGJI.

Albanian Economy Development Agency (AEDA): Bulevardi Zhan D'Ark, Tirana; tel. (4) 230133; fax (4) 228439; e-mail xhepa@ cpfi.tirana.al; internet www.aeda.gov.al; f. 1993; govt agency to promote foreign investment in Albania and to provide practical support to foreign investors; publishes Ekonomia; Chair. SELAMI XHEPA.

Business in Albania: Lagja Luigi Gurakuqi, Palliti 73, Elbasen; tel. and fax (54) 58994; e-mail gmaksuti@yahoo.com; provision of information on commerce and business in Albania; market research; Pres. TOM LODGE.

Enterprise Restructuring Agency (Agjensia e Ristrukturimit te Ndermarrjeve): Rruga e Durrësit 83, Tirana; tel. (4) 227878; fax (4) 225730; govt agency established to assist state-owned enterprises to become privately owned by offering enterprise sector surveys, strategic plans and consultations; provides technical assistance; Dir ADRIATIK BANKJA.

International Research And Exchange Board: Rruga Him Kolli 45, Tirana; tel. (4) 247543; fax (4) 247544; e-mail promedia@irex .tirana.al; internet www.irex.org.

Trade and Investment Promotion Support: Bulevardi Zhan D'Ark, Tirana; tel. and fax (4) 262067; e-mail besnik@tips.tirana.al; internet www.tips.eu.org/albania.

CHAMBERS OF COMMERCE

Union of Chambers of Commerce and Industry of Albania: Rruga Kavajes 6, Tirana; tel. and fax (4) 222934; f. 1958; Pres. ANTON LEKA.

Durrës Chamber of Commerce: Durrës; f. 1988; promotes trade with southern Italy.

Gjirokastër Chamber of Commerce: Gjirokastër; f. 1988; promotes trade with Greek border area.

Korçë Chamber of Commerce and Industry: Bulevardi Republika, Korçë; tel. and fax (82) 42457; e-mail dhtiko@icc.al.eu.org; internet www.albchamber.org; f. 1995.

Shkodër Chamber of Commerce: Shkodër; promotes trade with Yugoslav border area.

Tirana Chamber of Commerce and Industry: Rruga Kavajes 6, Tirana; tel. (4) 232448; fax (4) 229779; e-mail ccitr@abissnet.com.al; internet www.cci.gov.al; f. 1926; Chair. LUAN BREGASI.

There are also chambers of commerce in Kukës, Peshkopi, Pogradec, Sarandë and Vlorë.

UTILITIES

Electricity

State Electricity Corporation of Albania (Korporata Elektroenergjetike Shqiptare—KESH): Biloky 'Vasil Shanto', Tirana; tel. (4) 228434; fax (4) 232046; state corpn for the generation, transmission, distribution and export of electrical energy; govt-controlled; scheduled for reorganization in 2003, prior to transfer to private ownership; Chair. BASHKIM QATIPI; Gen. Dir Dr NAKO HOBDARI.

TRADE UNIONS

Until 1991 independent trade-union activities were prohibited, the official trade unions being represented in every work and production centre. During 1991, however, independent unions were established. The most important of these was the Union of Independent Trade Unions of Albania. Other unions were established for workers in various sectors of the economy.

Confederation of Albanian Trade Unions (Konfederata e Sindikatave të Shqipërisë—KSSh): Bulevardi Zogu I, Pall. A. Kelmendi, Tirana; tel. (4) 222956; fax (4) 229169; e-mail kssh@icc.al.eu.org; f. 1991 to replace the official Central Council of Albanian Trade Unions; f. 1945; includes 13 trade union federations representing workers in different sectors of the economy; Chair. of Man. Council KASTRIOT MUÇO.

Union of Independent Trade Unions of Albania (Bashkimi i Sindikatave të Pavarura të Shqipërisë——BSPSh): Tirana; f. 1991; Chair. (vacant).

Other Trade Unions

Agricultural Trade Union Federation (Federata Sindikale e Bujqesise): Tirana; f. 1991; Leaders ALFRED GJOMO, NAZMI QOKU.

Free and Independent Miners' Union (Sindikata e Lire dhe e Pavarur e Minatoreve): Tirana; f. 1991; Chair. GEZIM KALAJA.

Trade Union Federation of Employees and Pensioners of Albania: Bulevardi Dëshmorët e Kombit; tel. (4) 229169; Chair. PETRAQ TAPIA.

Union of Oil Industry Workers: Tirana; seceded from the Confederation of Albanian Trade Unions in 1991; represents workers in the petroleum and natural gas industry; Chair. MENPOR XHEMALI.

Transport

RAILWAYS

In 1994 there were approximately 720 km of railway track, with lines linking Tirana–Vlorë–Durrës, Durrës–Kavajë–Rrogozhinë-Elbasan–Librazhd–Prenjas–Pogradec, Rrogozhinë–Lushnjë–Fier-Ballsh, Milot–Rrëshen, Vlorë–Laç–Lezhë–Shkodër and Selenicë-Vlorë. There are also standard-gauge lines between Fier and Selenicë and between Fier and Vlorë. In 2000 projects were underway to rehabilitate the Rrogozhinë–Vlorë and Fier–Ballsh railway lines. The 50-km international freight link between Shkodër and Podgorica, Montenegro (Serbia and Montenegro), reopened in 2003, after a 10-year suspension of service.

Albanian Railways: Rruga Skënderbeg, Durrës; tel. and fax (52) 22037; internet www.pages.albaniaonline.net/hsh; Dir-Gen. L. BURNACI.

ROADS

In 2000 the road network comprised an estimated 18,000 km of classified roads, including 3,220 km of main roads and 4,600 km of secondary roads; 39% of the total network was paved. All regions are linked by the road network, but many roads in mountainous districts are unsuitable for motor transport. A three-year public investment plan, which was initiated in 1995, included substantial funds for the rehabilitation of the road network; the principal projects were the creation of east–west (Durrës–Kapshtice) and north–south highways. In 2000 investment projects concentrated on rehabilitating the north–south corridor, in an effort to encourage more goods' transport between Italy and Croatia. In December 2002 a 23.5 km road, linking Greece with southern Albania, was opened.

SHIPPING

At December 2001 Albania's merchant fleet had 33 vessels, with a total displacement of 25,170 grt. The chief ports are those in Durrës, Vlorë, Sarandë and Shëngjin. In 1996 the port of Himare, which was closed in 1991, was reopened. Ferry services have been established between Durrës and three Italian ports (Trieste, Bari and Ancona) and between Sarandë and the Greek island of Corfu. Services also connect Vlorë with the Italian ports of Bari and Brindisi. A new ferry terminal, financed by the EU, was under construction at Durrës in 2000. Furthermore, the World Bank and Italy's OPEC Fund were financing a US $23m. project to improve existing port facilities.

Adetare Shipping Agency Ltd: Durrës; tel. (52) 23883; fax (52) 23666.

Albanian State Shipping Enterprise: Durrës; tel. (52) 22233; fax (52) 229111.

CIVIL AVIATION

There is a small international airport at Rinas, 25 km from Tirana. Reconstruction of the airport was undertaken in the late 1990s. On average, 900,000 metric tons of goods were carried by air each year. A civil and military airport was constructed at Pish Poro, 29 km from Vlorë, under an agreement between the Ministries of Defence of Albania and Italy. The Government planned to increase the capacity of the international airport from an estimated 500,000 passengers in 2002 to 1m. by 2010.

General Directorate of Civil Aviation: Rruga e Kavajes, Perballe Xhamise, POB 205, Tirana; tel. and fax (4) 223969; e-mail dpac2@albanet.net.

Ada Air: Rruga Kemal Stafa 262, Tirana; tel. (4) 256111; fax (4) 226245; e-mail contact@adaair.com; internet www.adaair.com; f. 1991; operates passenger and cargo flights to Greece, Italy, Serbia and Montenegro and Switzerland; Pres. MARSEL SKENDO; Gen. Dir ILIR ZEKA.

Albanian Airlines SHPK: Rruga Mine Peza 2, Tirana; tel. and fax (4) 228461; e-mail tiadplvasita@msmail.com; f. 1992 as Albanian Airlines, a jt venture between the Albanian state-owned air agency, Albtransport, and the Austrian airline, Tyrolean Airways; acquired in 1995 by the Kuwaiti co, Aviation World Mak, and assumed present name; scheduled services to Germany, Italy and Turkey; Pres. FIKRY ABDUL WAHHAB; Man. Dir ASHRAF HASHEM.

Tourism

In 1999 there were some 38,963 international tourist arrivals at hotels in Albania. In that year receipts from tourism totalled about US $211m., compared with $54m. in 1998, and by 2001 tourism receipts amounted to $446m. The main tourist centres include Tirana, Durrës, Sarandë, Shkodër and Pogradec. The Roman amphitheatre at Durrës is one of the largest in Europe. The ancient towns of Apollonia and Butrint are important archaeological sites, and there are many other towns of historic interest. However, expansion of the tourist industry has been limited by the inadequacy of Albania's infrastructure and a lack of foreign investment in the development of new facilities. Regional instability, particularly during the NATO air offensive against Yugoslavia in early 1999, also inhibited tourist activity.

Albturist: Bulevardi Dëshmorët e Kombit, Hotel Dhajti, Tirana; tel. (4) 251849; fax (4) 234359; e-mail albturist.t.a@albnet.net; brs in main towns and all tourist centres;28 hotels throughout the country; Dir-Gen. BESNIK PELLUMBI.

Committee for Development and Tourism: Bulevardi Dëshmorët e Kombit 8, Tirana; tel. (4) 258323; fax (4) 258322; e-mail arskenderi@albaniaonline.com; govt body.

ALGERIA

Introductory Survey

Location, Climate, Language, Religion, Flag, Capital

The Democratic and People's Republic of Algeria lies in north Africa, with the Mediterranean Sea to the north, Mali and Niger to the south, Tunisia and Libya to the east, and Morocco and Mauritania to the west. The climate on the Mediterranean coast is temperate, becoming more extreme in the Atlas mountains immediately to the south. Further south is part of the Sahara, a hot and arid desert. Temperatures in Algiers, on the coast, are generally between 9°C (48°F) and 29°C (84°F), while in the interior they may exceed 50°C (122°F). Arabic is the official language, but French is widely used. Tamazight, the principal language of Algeria's Berber community, was granted 'national' status in 2002. Islam is the state religion, and almost all Algerians are Muslims. The national flag (proportions 2 by 3) has two equal vertical stripes, of green and white, with a red crescent moon and a five-pointed red star superimposed in the centre. The capital is Algiers (el-Djezaïr).

Recent History

Algeria was conquered by French forces in the 1830s and annexed by France in 1842. The territory was colonized with French settlers, and many French citizens became permanent residents. Unlike most of France's overseas possessions, Algeria was not formally a colony but was 'attached' to metropolitan France. However, the indigenous Muslim majority were denied equal rights, and political and economic power within Algeria was largely held by the settler minority.

On 1 November 1954 the principal Algerian nationalist movement, the Front de libération nationale (FLN), began a war for national independence, in the course of which about 1m. Muslims were killed or wounded. The French Government agreed to a cease-fire in March 1962, and independence was declared on 3 July 1962. In August the Algerian provisional Government transferred its functions to the Political Bureau of the FLN, and in September a National Constituent Assembly was elected (from a single list of FLN candidates) and a Republic proclaimed. A new Government was formed, with Ahmed Ben Bella, founder of the FLN, as Prime Minister.

A draft Constitution, providing for a presidential regime with the FLN as the sole party, was adopted by the Constituent Assembly in August 1963, and approved by popular referendum in September. Ben Bella was elected President, although real power remained with the bureaucracy and the army. In June 1965 the Minister of Defence, Col Houari Boumedienne, deposed Ben Bella in a bloodless coup and took control of the country as President of a Council of the Revolution, composed chiefly of army officers.

Boumedienne encountered considerable opposition from left-wing members of the FLN, but from 1971 the Government was confident enough to adopt a more active social policy. In 1975 Boumedienne announced a series of measures to consolidate the regime and enhance his personal power, including the drafting of a National Charter and a new Constitution, and the holding of elections for a President and National People's Assembly. The National Charter, which enshrined both the creation of a socialist system and the maintenance of Islam as the state religion, and a new Constitution (incorporating the principles of the Charter) were approved at referendums held in June and November 1976 respectively, and in December Boumedienne was elected President unopposed. The new formal structure of power was completed in February 1977 by the election of FLN members to the National People's Assembly.

President Boumedienne died in December 1978, and the eight-member Council of the Revolution took over the Government. In January 1979 the FLN adopted a new party structure, electing a Central Committee which was envisaged as the highest policy-making body both of the party and of the nation as a whole: this Committee was to choose a party Secretary-General, who would automatically become the sole presidential candidate. The Committee was also to elect an FLN Political Bureau (nominated by the Secretary-General). The Committee's choice of Col Ben Djedid Chadli, commander of Oran military district, as presidential candidate was endorsed by a refer-

endum in February. Unlike Boumedienne, Chadli appointed a Prime Minister, Col Muhammad Abd al-Ghani, anticipating constitutional changes approved by the National People's Assembly in June which included the obligatory appointment of a premier. In mid-1980 the FLN authorized Chadli to form a smaller Political Bureau, with more limited responsibilities, thereby increasing the power of the President.

At a presidential election held in January 1984 Chadli's candidature was endorsed by 95.4% of the electorate. Chadli subsequently appointed Abd al-Hamid Brahimi as Prime Minister. In 1985 Chadli initiated a public debate on Boumedienne's National Charter, resulting in the adoption of a new National Charter at a special FLN Congress in December. The revised Charter, which emphasized a state ideology based on the twin principles of socialism and Islam while encouraging the development of private enterprise, was approved by a referendum in January 1986. In July 1987 the National People's Assembly adopted legislation to permit the formation of local organizations without prior government approval: a ban remained, however, on associations that were deemed to oppose the policies of the Charter or to threaten national security.

During the second half of the 1980s opposition to the Government was increasingly manifest. In 1985 22 Berber cultural and human rights activists were imprisoned after being convicted of belonging to illegal organizations, and in 1986 there were riots at Constantine and Sétif, following student protests against inadequate facilities. In 1987 several leading activists of an Islamist group were killed by security forces, and some 200 of the group's members were given prison sentences. From mid-1988 severe unemployment, high prices, and shortages of essential supplies (resulting from economic austerity measures imposed in 1987 in response to a decline in world petroleum prices) provoked a series of strikes, and in early October rioting erupted in Algiers, spreading to Oran and Annaba. Chadli imposed a six-day state of emergency, and also proposed constitutional amendments that would allow non-FLN candidates to participate in elections and make the Prime Minister answerable to the National People's Assembly (rather than to the President). The reforms were approved by a referendum in November. In December Chadli was elected President for a third term of office, obtaining 81% of the votes cast.

In February 1989 a new Constitution, signifying the end of the one-party socialist state, was approved by referendum. The formation of political associations outside the FLN was henceforth permitted, while the armed forces were no longer allocated a role in the development of socialism. The executive, legislative and judicial functions of the State were separated and made subject to the supervision of a Constitutional Council. In July legislation permitting the formation of political parties entered force (although these were still required to be licensed by the Government): by mid-1991 a total of 47 political parties had been registered, including a radical Islamist group, the Front islamique du salut (FIS), the Mouvement pour la démocratie en Algérie (MDA), which had been founded by Ben Bella in 1984, the Parti d'avant-garde socialiste (renamed Ettahaddi in 1993), the Parti social-démocrate (PSD) and the Berber Rassemblement pour la culture et la démocratie (RCD). Other legislation adopted in July 1989 further reduced state control of the economy, allowed the expansion of investment by foreign companies, and ended the state monopoly of the press (while leaving the principal newspapers under FLN control). Nevertheless, strikes and riots persisted during 1989. In September Chadli appointed Mouloud Hamrouche (hitherto a senior official in the presidential office) as Prime Minister. A programme of economic liberalization was announced, and a new electoral law, adopted in March 1990, introduced a system of partial proportional representation for local elections.

At local elections held in June 1990 the principal Islamist party, the FIS, received some 55% of total votes cast, while the FLN obtained about 32%. In July, following disagreement within the FLN concerning the pace of economic and political reform, the Prime Minister and four other ministers resigned from the party's Political Bureau. In a reorganization of the

Council of Ministers in the same month the defence portfolio was separated from the presidency for the first time since 1965. Also in July Chadli acceded to the demands of the FIS for an early general election, announcing that polling would take place in early 1991. In December 1990 the National People's Assembly adopted a law whereby after 1997 Arabic would be Algeria's only official language and the use of French and Berber in schools and in official transactions would be punishable offences. More than 100,000 people demonstrated in Algiers against political and religious intolerance.

In April 1991 Chadli declared that Algeria's first multi-party general election would take place in late June. The FIS argued that a presidential election should be held simultaneously with, or shortly after, the general election, and in May organized an indefinite general strike and demonstrations to demand Chadli's resignation and changes in the electoral laws. Violent confrontations in June between Islamist activists and the security forces prompted Chadli to declare a state of emergency and postpone the general election; he also announced that he had accepted the resignation of the Prime Minister and his Government. The former Minister of Foreign Affairs, Sid-Ahmad Ghozali, was appointed premier, and he subsequently nominated a Council of Ministers consisting mainly of political independents.

Meanwhile, the FLN and the FIS reached a compromise whereby the strike was abandoned and legislative and presidential elections were to be held before the end of 1991. In late June, after further violent incidents between Islamists and security forces, Chadli resigned as Chairman of the FLN. Army units arrested some 700 Islamists in the following month and occupied the headquarters of the FIS. Among those arrested were the President of the FIS, Abbasi Madani, who had threatened to launch a *jihad* ('holy war') if the state of emergency was not ended, and the party's Vice-President, Ali Belhadj; both were charged with armed conspiracy against the State. The state of emergency was revoked in late September.

In October 1991, following revisions to the electoral code, Chadli formally announced that the first round of the multi-party general election to the newly enlarged 430-seat legislature would take place on 26 December, with a second round (in those constituencies where no candidate had secured an overall majority) scheduled for 16 January 1992. In all, 231 seats were won outright at the first round: the FIS took 188 seats (with 47.5% of the votes cast), the Front des forces socialistes (FFS) 25, the FLN just 15, and independents three. The FLN alleged widespread intimidation and electoral malpractice on the part of the FIS. On 11 January Chadli resigned as President, announcing that he had (one week earlier) dissolved the National People's Assembly. The following day the High Security Council (comprising the Prime Minister, three generals and two senior ministers) cancelled the second round of legislative voting, at which the FIS had been expected to consolidate its first-round victory, and on 14 January a five-member High Council of State (HCS) was appointed to act as a collegiate presidency until, at the latest, the expiry of Chadli's term of office in December 1993. The HCS was to be chaired by Muhammad Boudiaf, a veteran of the war of independence, but its most influential figure was believed to be Maj.-Gen. Khaled Nezzar, the Minister of Defence. The other members of the HCS were Ali Haroun (the Minister of Human Rights), Sheikh Tejini Haddam (the Rector of the Grand Mosque in Paris, France) and Ali Kafi (President of the war veterans' association, the Organisation nationale des moudjahidine—ONM); Ghozali was not included, although he remained premier. The constitutional legality of the HCS was disputed by all the political parties, including the FLN. The 188 FIS deputies who had been elected in December 1991 formed a 'shadow' assembly and demanded a return to legality.

In February 1992 the HCS declared a 12-month state of emergency and detention centres were opened in the Sahara; the FIS, which was officially dissolved by the Government in March, claimed that 150 people had been killed, and as many as 30,000 detained, since the military-sponsored take-over. In April Boudiaf, as Chairman of the HCS, announced the creation of a 60-member National Consultative Council (NCC), which was to meet each month in the building of the suspended Assembly, although it was to have no legislative powers. In June Boudiaf promised a constitutional review, the dissolution of the FLN and a presidential election. Moreover, despite continuing violence, he ordered the release from detention of 2,000 FIS militants.

On 29 June 1992 Boudiaf was assassinated while making a speech in Annaba. The HCS ordered an immediate inquiry into the assassination, for which the FIS denied all responsibility. Ali Kafi succeeded Boudiaf as Chairman of the HCS, and Redha Malek, the Chairman of the NCC, was appointed as a new member of the HCS. On 8 July Ghozali resigned in order to enable Kafi to appoint his own Prime Minister. He was replaced by Belaid Abd es-Salam, who had directed Algeria's post-independence petroleum and gas policy. Abd es-Salam appointed a new Council of Ministers later in the month.

In late July 1992 Madani and Belhadj were sentenced to 12 years' imprisonment for conspiracy against the State. Violent protests erupted in Algiers and quickly spread to other cities. Despite appeals by Abd es-Salam for a multi-party dialogue in an attempt to end civil strife, the Government attracted widespread criticism for reinforcing its emergency powers to repress any person or organization whose activities were deemed to represent a threat to stability.

Political manoeuvring and attempts at reconciliation continued against a background of escalating violence throughout the country. In February 1993 the state of emergency was renewed for an indefinite period. An assassination attempt shortly afterwards against Maj.-Gen. Nezzar was followed by a series of attacks on other senior government officials. In May large demonstrations were organized in Algiers, Constantine and Oran to protest against terrorism and to demand that there be no negotiation with its perpetrators. In June the HCS appealed for a 'general mobilization' against terrorism, although in the same month Abd es-Salam expressed his willingness to open a dialogue with the militants. None the less, violence continued unabated, with terrorist attacks increasingly targeting not only political officials but also prominent intellectual and civilian figures. In June the HCS announced that it would dissolve itself at the end of December, asserting that a modern democracy and free market economy would be created within three years of that date.

In July 1993 Liamine Zéroual (a retired general) succeeded Maj.-Gen. Nezzar as Minister of Defence, although Nezzar retained his post within the HCS. In August Redha Malek, who similarly remained a member of the HCS, was appointed to replace Abd es-Salam as Prime Minister. Malek, who appointed a new Council of Ministers in September, stated that the resolute stance against terrorism would be maintained, and rejected the possibility of dialogue with its perpetrators. In October the HCS appointed an eight-member National Dialogue Commission (NDC), which was charged with the preparation of a political conference to organize the transition to an elected and democratic form of government. In December it was announced that the HCS would not be disbanded until a new presidential body had been elected at the NDC conference in January 1994. However, all the main political parties (with the exception of the moderate Islamist Hamas) boycotted the conference. Liamine Zéroual (who retained the defence portfolio in the Council of Ministers) was inaugurated as President on 31 January for a three-year term, on the apparent recommendation of senior members of the military.

In February 1994 two senior members of the FIS, Ali Djeddi and Abdelkader Boukhamkham, were released from prison, and rumours circulated that divisions had occurred within the military as a result of contacts made by high-ranking members of the regime, including Zéroual, with imprisoned Islamist leaders. Malek, who was known to be opposed to any compromise with the Islamist militants, resigned as Prime Minister in April; Mokdad Sifi, hitherto Minister of Equipment, was appointed in his place. In May the President inaugurated a National Transition Council (NTC), an interim legislature of 200 appointed members, the aim of which was to provide a forum for debate pending legislative elections. Except for Hamas, most of the 21 parties that agreed to participate in the NTC were virtually unknown, and the 22 seats that were allocated to other major parties remained vacant. In the same month a group of six 'independent national figures', including former President Ben Bella, was commissioned by Zéroual to promote dialogue with Islamist militants and opposition groups.

It remained unclear whether the FIS actively supported the most prominent and radical Islamist militant group, the Groupe islamique armé (GIA) in its frequent attacks on members of the security forces, local government and the judiciary, as well as prominent public figures, intellectuals, journalists and ordinary civilians. In March 1994 an attack by Islamist militants on the high-security Tazoult prison, near Batna, resulted in the release of more than 1,000 political prisoners. Certain towns were virtually controlled by Islamist activists, and the deaths of a number of foreign nationals led several countries to advise their citizens to leave Algeria. In response to the rise in violence, the security forces intensified their campaign against armed Islamist groups, resorting to air attacks, punitive raids, torture and psychological warfare and killing thousands of militants.

In August 1994 members of the FLN, the Parti du renouveau algérien (PRA), the MDA, Nahdah and Hamas engaged in what was termed a national dialogue with the Government; the meetings were boycotted, however, by Ettahaddi, the FFS and the RCD. At further negotiations held in early September discussion focused on two letters sent to the President by Abbasi Madani, purportedly offering a 'truce'. Madani and Belhadj were released from prison in mid-September and placed under house arrest; however, the FIS did not participate in the next round of national dialogue later that month, declaring that negotiations could take place only after the granting of a general amnesty, the rehabilitation of the FIS and the repeal of the state of emergency. The GIA threatened reprisals if the FIS entered into dialogue with the regime, and intensified its campaign of violence against secular society by targeting educational institutions. In addition to the upheaval caused by Islamist violence, the Berber RCD urged a boycott of the start of the school year, and in September Berber activists in the Kabyle organized a general strike in protest at the exclusion of the Berber language, Tamazight, from the syllabus and at the prospect of the FIS entering the national dialogue. In May 1995 the RCD welcomed the establishment of a government body to oversee the teaching of Tamazight in schools and universities (commencing in October) and to promote its use in the official media.

In October 1994 Zéroual announced that a presidential election would be held before the end of 1995. However, the FIS and other opponents of the Algerian regime condemned the proposed organization of an election in the context of the ongoing civil conflict. In November 1994 representatives of several major Algerian parties, including the FIS, the FLN, the FFS and the MDA, attended a two-day conference in Rome, Italy, organized by the Sant' Egidio Roman Catholic community to foster discussion about the crisis in Algeria. The ensuing Sant' Egidio pact, endorsed by all the participants at a meeting in Rome in January 1995, rejected the use of violence to achieve or maintain power, and urged the Algerian regime to repeal the state of emergency and thereby facilitate negotiations between all parties. However, the pact was dismissed as a 'non-event' by the Government. In April Zéroual resumed discussions with the legalized opposition parties in preparation for the presidential election. Talks with the FLN and the FFS quickly collapsed, however, as both rejected the prospect of participating in an election from which the FIS was excluded. Subsequent dialogue between the Government and the FIS also proved unsuccessful.

Some 40 candidates announced their intention to contest the presidential election, the first round of which was scheduled for 16 November 1995, but only four were confirmed as having attained the required number of signatures (an electoral decree issued by the Government in May, and promulgated by the NTC in July, stipulated that presidential candidates must obtain the endorsement of 75,000 signatures from at least 25 provinces in order to qualify). Despite an appeal by the FLN, the FFS and the FIS for voters to boycott the election, official figures showed that some 75% of the electorate participated in the poll, in which Zéroual secured an outright victory, with 61.0% of the valid votes cast. Zéroual was inaugurated for a five-year term on 27 November. Shortly afterwards, despite the assassination of a high-ranking military official, the Government announced the closure of the last of seven detention centres (all of which had opened since February 1992), thereby releasing some 650 prisoners, many of whom were Islamist sympathizers. In late December Ahmed Ouyahia, a career diplomat, replaced Sifi as Prime Minister. Ouyahia's Government, named in early January 1996, included two members of Hamas and a dissident leader of the FIS.

In April 1996, in an attempt to foster national reconciliation, Zéroual held bilateral discussions with more than 50 influential individuals, including leaders of trade unions and opposition groups; the FIS was not invited to participate. In the following month Zéroual announced his intention to hold legislative elections in early 1997. In addition, he proposed that a referendum be held, prior to the elections, on amendments to the Constitution: these included measures to increase the powers of the President while limiting his tenure to a maximum of two con-

secutive mandates; the creation of a Council of the Nation as a second parliamentary chamber (one-third of the members of which would be chosen by the President); the establishment of a State Council (to regulate the administrative judiciary) and a High State Court; and, significantly, a ban on political parties that were based on religion, language, gender or regional differences. It was also suggested that the electoral law be revised to allow for a system of full proportional representation. Several opposition parties reiterated their demands that the Government resume negotiations with the FIS, and argued that constitutional reform should be undertaken only after legislative elections. Some 1,000 delegates, including representatives of the FLN, Nahdah and Hamas, attended a government-sponsored conference on national concord held in September. The conference was boycotted by the FFS, the RCD, Ettahaddi and the MDA. Owing to their lack of support, Zéroual subsequently withdrew his offer to include members of opposition parties in an expanded Council of Ministers and NTC. The proposed constitutional amendments were promulgated in December, having been approved by some 86% of the voters at a referendum held in November.

In January 1997 the Secretary-General of the FLN-affiliated Union Générale des Travailleurs Algériens (UGTA), Abd al-Hak Benhamouda, was shot dead in Algiers. Although an Islamist group claimed responsibility for the assassination, there was speculation that it may have been perpetrated by opponents within the regime. In February Zéroual announced that elections to the National People's Assembly would take place in late May or early June. Shortly afterwards the NTC adopted restrictive legislation concerning political parties in accordance with the amended Constitution; new electoral legislation replacing the majority system with proportional representation was also adopted. Later in February Abdelkader Bensalah, the President of the NTC, formed a centrist grouping, the Rassemblement national démocratique (RND), which was originally to have been led by Benhamouda. The RND received support from a wide range of organizations, including trade unions, anti-Islamist groups and the influential war veterans' ONM, and was closely linked with Zéroual and the Government. Several more political parties emerged in the months that followed, while certain existing parties changed their names to comply with the new legislation. Notably, Hamas became the Mouvement de la société pour la paix (MSP).

Some 39 political parties contested the elections to the National People's Assembly, held on 5 June 1997, although the FIS and Ettahaddi urged a boycott of the polls. As the preliminary results of the elections began to emerge, opposition leaders complained of irregularities during the electoral process, and accused officials of manipulating the results in favour of the RND. International observers were critical of the conduct of the elections, and commented that the rate of voter participation (officially estimated at 65.5% of the electorate) seemed unrealistically high. According to the final official results, the RND won 156 of the Assembly's 380 seats, followed by the MSP (69) and the FLN (62); Nahdah took 34 seats, the FFS 20, and the RCD 19. President Zéroual asked Ahmed Ouyahia to form a new Government, and later in June Ouyahia announced a new Council of Ministers, comprising members of the RND, the FLN and the MSP.

In July 1997 Abdelkader Hachani, a high-ranking member of the FIS, was formally sentenced to five years' imprisonment and three years' deprivation of his civil rights; he was released immediately, as he had been in custody for five years. Abbasi Madani was conditionally released shortly afterwards. The release of the two leaders was widely interpreted as a conciliatory gesture by the Government towards the Islamist opposition. However, in September Madani was once again confined to house arrest.

Following the RND's success at regional and municipal elections held in October 1997, the party's political dominance was consolidated with the appointment of the Council of the Nation in late December. Of the Council's 96 seats indirectly elected by regional and municipal authorities, 80 were won by the RND, 10 by the FLN, four by the FFS and two by the MSP; President Zéroual appointed the remaining 48 members. In the following month the authorities disbanded some 30 political groupings, including Ettahaddi and the PSD, for failing to satisfy the legal requirements concerning political associations.

There were violent protests in the Kabyle region in June 1998 following the assassination of Lounes Matoub, a popular Berber singer and an outspoken critic of both the Government and the fundamentalist Islamist movement. There were further protests in July when controversial legislation on the compulsory use of the Arabic language in public life (see above) came into effect. Berber activists in the Kabyle fiercely opposed the 'arabization' policy, demanding the recognition of Tamazight as an official language.

In September 1998 President Zéroual announced that a presidential election would be held before March 1999, nearly two years ahead of schedule. There was considerable speculation that the announcement had been prompted primarily by a power struggle within the regime between the faction loyal to the President and figures close to Lt-Gen. Muhammad Lamari, the Chief of Staff of the Army. Zéroual declared at the end of the following month that the presidential election would be postponed until April 1999 to allow political parties to prepare their campaigns. In December 1998 Ouyahia resigned; he was replaced as premier by Smail Hamdani, a widely respected senior politician and former diplomat.

A total of 47 candidates registered to contest the presidential election; however, the Constitutional Council declared only seven eligible to stand. Although the senior generals had decided not to nominate a member of the armed forces for the presidency, there was widespread cynicism regarding the military's assurances of its neutrality, and Abdelaziz Bouteflika was believed to have the support of the military establishment. Bouteflika also enjoyed the support of the four main political parties as well as that of the UGTA and several political associations.

On the eve of the election, which took place on 15 April 1999, Bouteflika's six rivals withdrew their candidacies after Zéroual refused to postpone the poll following allegations of massive electoral fraud in favour of Bouteflika. Voting papers were, nevertheless, distributed for all seven candidates, and no official boycott of the election was organized. The credibility of the poll was, however, seriously diminished, and Bouteflika announced that he would accept the presidency only if there were both a high rate of voter participation and a large majority in his favour. According to official results, Bouteflika won 73.8% of the votes cast (his closest rival, Ahmed Taleb Ibrahimi, a former Minister of Foreign affairs who was now supported by the outlawed FIS, secured 12.5%). However, this figure, together with the estimated official turn-out of more than 60%, was immediately disputed by his opponents, who maintained that only 23.3% of the registered electorate had participated, and that Bouteflika had received only 28% of the votes cast, compared with 20% for Ibrahimi. At his inauguration, on 27 April, Bouteflika emphasized the need for national reconciliation to end the civil conflict in Algeria, but pledged to continue the military campaign against terrorists and reaffirmed that the FIS would not be legalized.

Following clandestine negotiations between the Government and representatives of the FIS, in June 1999 the Armée islamique du salut (AIS, the armed wing of the FIS) announced the permanent cessation of its armed struggle against the Government. President Bouteflika's plans for a national reconciliation initiative were incorporated in a Law on Civil Concord, promulgated in July, whereby there was to be an amnesty for members of armed Islamist groups who surrendered within a six-month deadline and who were not implicated in mass killings, rape or bomb attacks on public places (perpetrators of such crimes would receive reduced sentences). The legislation was approved by 98.6% of those who voted (85% of the electorate) in a national referendum in September. Meanwhile, Bouteflika exhibited unprecedented candour, admitting in August that the civil conflict of the past seven years had resulted in the deaths of at least 100,000 people (hitherto the authorities had put the number of deaths at 30,000), as well as acknowledging that state monopolies were being abused by certain individuals. At the end of October Bouteflika pardoned 5,000 prisoners, bringing the total released since his installation as President to more than 14,500.

Abdelkader Hachani, the most senior member of the FIS at liberty, was assassinated in Algiers in November 1999. Hachani had favoured dialogue with all political interests, and was believed to have been involved in a secret political dialogue between the Government and the FIS. Although a member of the principal GIA faction was subsequently arrested and charged with the murder, several of Hachani's relatives claimed that the security forces, which had reportedly kept the FIS official under surveillance following his release from detention, had perpetrated the assassination.

Following a long delay Bouteflika finally named his Council of Ministers in December 1999. Led by Ahmed Benbitour, a former Minister of Finance, the new Government comprised members of the FLN, the MSP, Nahdah, the RCD, the Alliance nationale républicaine (ANR), the RND and the PRA, all of which had supported Bouteflika's presidential campaign. In February 2000 Bouteflika announced extensive changes to the military high command, which included the replacement of the commanders of four of the country's six military regions. The most senior positions, however, remained unaltered. In March Cherif Rahmani, the only regional governor (*wali*) to hold ministerial rank, was replaced as Governor of Algiers by Abdelmalek Nourani.

In early January 2000, following discussions between representatives of the Government, the army and the AIS, an agreement was reached whereby the AIS pledged to disband in return for the restoration of full civil and political rights to its former members. It was estimated that some 1,500–3,000 rebels were to be granted a full pardon under the agreement, some of whom were to be temporarily enlisted in an auxiliary unit to assist the security forces in apprehending members of the GIA and of a breakaway group from the GIA, the Groupe salafiste pour la prédication et le combat (GSPC, or Da'wa wal Djihad). In mid-January, following the expiry of the amnesty period specified under the Law on Civil Concord, the armed forces launched a concerted assault on rebel strongholds in the north-east and south-west of the country, in an attempt to eliminate remaining anti-Government factions. It was officially stated at this time that 80% of members of armed groups had surrendered. Meanwhile, the Government estimated that around 600 people (many of them civilians) had been killed between July 1999 and January 2000, mostly in incidents connected to the GIA and the GSPC.

Violence persisted following the expiry of the deadline for amnesty under the Law on Civil Concord; thousands of Islamist fighters remained at large, and fears were expressed in some quarters that the conflict between militant Islamist groups and the armed forces showed signs of escalating. In July 2000 an article in the daily *Jeune Indépendant*, citing unofficial sources, claimed that some 1,100 civilians and an estimated 2,000 terrorists had been killed in Algeria since the expiry of the general amnesty in January. However, following visits to Algeria in mid-2000 (the first by human rights organizations to be permitted by the Algerian authorities for some years) both Amnesty International and the Fédération internationale des ligues des droits de l'Homme (FIDH) reported that they had noted a significant decline in violence and a clear improvement in the country's human rights situation, although concern was expressed about the fate of an estimated 22,000 missing persons who had disappeared since 1992. In November 2000, at the end of a further visit to Algeria, representatives of Amnesty International expressed frustration at what they considered a lack of progress in investigating such issues as disappearances and secret detentions, stating notably that the authorities had made no response to requests for meetings with officers of the security forces.

Meanwhile, in May 2000 the Government announced its refusal to grant legal recognition to al-Wafa wa al-Adl (Wafa), a new political organization formed by Ahmed Taleb Ibrahimi, on the grounds that it was simply a reconstitution under another name of the outlawed FIS. In November the Minister of State for the Interior and Local Authorities ordered the closure of all offices of the Wafa party and confiscated all its documents.

In August 2000 Benbitour resigned the premiership and was replaced by Ali Benflis, a former Minister of Justice who had directed Bouteflika's presidential campaign. The composition of the new Government remained largely unchanged: most senior ministers retained their posts, a notable exception being the appointment as Minister of Foreign Affairs of Abdelaziz Belkadem, a former head of the legislature, in place of Youcef Yousfi, who now became Minister-delegate to the Prime Minister. At indirect elections in December 2000 for one-half of the 96 elective members of the Council of the Nation, the RND retained its comfortable majority, although its total number of seats was reduced from 80 to 74.

A sharp escalation in violence at the end of 2000 added weight to the arguments of those who believed that the amnesty under the Civil Concord had done little to quell unrest. Among more than 200 deaths recorded among Islamist fighters, government forces and civilians during the first three weeks of Ramadan were those of 16 pupils and their warden at a technical college in Médéa, who in mid-December were massacred in their dormitory by armed gunmen. The first killings of foreigners for almost two years were reported in early January 2001, when four Russian expatriate workers were killed in the Annaba region, and at least 190 deaths were reported as a result of continuing violence in that month. Meanwhile, there were persistent rumours of tensions between Bouteflika, the military high command and those parties opposed to any appeasement with militant fundamentalists

Violence continued unabated throughout 2001 with regular reports of incidents involving Islamists, the security forces and civilians resulting in large numbers of deaths on all sides. Reports in the Algerian press indicated that during April more than 150 people had been killed in attacks involving armed Islamist groups and that over 1,000 people, including more than 400 Islamists, had been killed since the beginning of the year. In June more than 110 people, including 40 members of the security forces, were killed by armed Islamists, and in August 34 people were injured in a bomb attack in Algiers—the first for more than two years. A renewed upsurge in violence during the holy month of Ramadan resulted in the deaths of some 50 people.

In early 2001 considerable media attention was given, particularly in France, to *La sale guerre*, a book written by Habib Souaida, a former lieutenant in the Algerian army, now living in France, who alleged Algerian army involvement in the torture and massacre of tens of thousands of civilians since the 1992 military take-over. This followed allegations made in a book, *Qui a tué à Bentalha?*, published in late 2000 by a survivor (now also living in France) of the massacre of almost 400 people in a suburb of Algiers in 1997: the killings had been attributed to Islamist extremists of the GIA, but the author implied that a special unit of the Algerian security forces had instigated the killings. Such allegations were refuted and condemned by senior members of the Algerian military, and in July 2002 the former Minister of Defence, Khaled Nezzar, commenced legal proceedings in France against Souaida for defamation, although his case was rejected by French judicial authorities. In April, meanwhile, Souaida had been sentenced *in absentia* in Algeria to 20 years' imprisonment after he was convicted of participating in efforts to undermine the morale of the army and of state security offences.

In May 2001 the National People's Assembly approved amendments to the penal code whereby authors of articles judged defamatory could be sentenced to up to three years' imprisonment and fines of AD 100,000, while fines to a maximum of AD 5m. could be imposed for offending the Head of State. Later that month 21 independent dailies cancelled their editions and more than 1,000 journalists marched in Algiers in protest against the new laws. Also in late May Bouteflika effected an extensive cabinet reorganization. Most notably, Mourad Medelci, hitherto Minister of Commerce, replaced Abdellatif Benachenou as Minister of Finance.

Violent clashes broke out in mid-April 2001 between protesters and security forces in several villages in the Kabyle following the death of a secondary school student (who had been apprehended for allegedly committing an assault during a robbery) in police custody at Beni Douala near the regional capital, Tizi Ouzou. Thousands of local inhabitants joined demonstrations, demanding a full inquiry into the incident and the withdrawal of paramilitary gendarmes from the Kabyle. Tensions were further fuelled by anger among Kabyles at the poor social and economic conditions in the region. Days after the student was killed the situation was further inflamed when three young Kabyles were assaulted by gendarmes near Béjaïa. The incidents coincided with demonstrations traditionally held to mark the anniversary of the so-called 'Berber Spring' protests of 1980, when Berber activism for cultural and linguistic rights had first taken form, and although the two major political parties in the Kabyle—the FFS and the RCD—appealed for calm, violence rapidly escalated throughout the area; the deaths of as many as 80 people had been reported by the end of the month. In a televised address, Bouteflika announced the creation of a national commission of inquiry, to be headed by Mohand Issad, a lawyer originating from the Kabyle, to investigate recent events in the region. Bouteflika also indicated that he planned revisions to the Constitution that would address the status of Tamazight, and revealed his intention to adopt a proposal making instruction in the Berber language compulsory in Tamazight-speaking areas. Furthermore, in his speech he accused unnamed groups both inside and outside the country of inciting extremism. Bouteflika's address was strongly criticized by the

main political groupings in the Kabyle, and the RCD withdrew from the coalition Government.

In early May 2001 an FFS-organized demonstration in Algiers, attended by some 10,000–30,000 people, proceeded peacefully; however, rallies in several Berber towns and villages were dispersed by riot police using tear gas. There followed a temporary lull in the violence in the Kabyle, but later in May rioting again intensified. In one protest, some 500,000 Berbers marched through the streets of Tizi Ouzou. Bouteflika again addressed the nation, urging rigorous sanctions against those who had instigated the events in the Kabyle and against all those responsible for the violence. In early June security forces dispersed a demonstration in Algiers by 3,000 Berbers, and a demonstration in Algiers the following week, organized by the Coordination des aarchs, dairas et communes (CADC—also known as the Coordination des comités de villages Kabyles), and which attracted more than 500,000 people, degenerated into violence after the protesters' intended route towards the presidential palace was blocked by security forces. Hundreds of protesters were injured and two journalists were killed as a result of the clashes. After further violent demonstrations in the Kabyle in mid-June, Prime Minister Benflis appeared on television to appeal for calm and all protests in Algiers were prohibited.

By the end of June 2001 unrest had spread beyond the Kabyle to the Aurès region, where rioting broke out in Khenchala and demonstrations were held in Batna, the provincial capital, as well as to Annaba and to Biskra in the south of the country. Official reports stated that 56 people had been killed, and 1,300 more injured, since the violence first erupted. Despite repeated calls in the independent press for his resignation, Bouteflika declared that he would not relinquish the presidency and again urged rioters not to participate in what he termed an external plot to undermine the security of the country. In early July the security forces prevented some 4,000–5,000 delegates of the CADC from entering Algiers, amid fears that a planned protest march would ignite a new round of rioting after a week of relative quiet. Later that month the Issad commission issued its preliminary report into the events in the Kabyle, in which it attached the blame for the rioting to the gendarmerie, maintaining that gendarmes had adopted a 'shoot-to-kill' policy and had acted in an illegal manner. However, the report failed to name those responsible for ordering the gendarmes' actions, and the commission complained of attempts, apparently on the part of vested interests within the security forces, to obstruct its investigations.

In August 2001 security forces blocked roads in order to prevent a large number of Berbers from marching on the capital, where they intended to present a list of 15 demands at the presidential palace. This 'el-Kseur Platform' (named after the Kabyle town in which it had been drawn up), notably requested the granting of official status to Tamazight without the holding of a referendum; the removal of all paramilitary gendarmes from the Kabyle; the annulment of legal proceedings against demonstrators; and the trial by civilian courts of all those who had ordered or perpetrated crimes and their dismissal from the security forces or the civil service.

In September 2001 President Bouteflika formally invited Berber community and tribal leaders, known as the *Aarouch*, to present their demands for social and political change, and designated premier Benflis to act as interlocutor between the authorities and the Berbers. Relations between the two sides were, however, complicated by divisions within the Berber movement, as some Berber leaders were unwilling to enter into any negotiations with the Government. The more radical *Aarouch*, angered by the prevention of three previous attempts to present the el-Kseur Platform to Bouteflika, rejected the President's offer and announced their intention to proceed with a rally planned for 5 October in the capital. Nevertheless, official reports claimed that a meeting took place on 3 October between Benflis and moderate *Aarouch* at which Benflis informed them that the President had decided to grant Tamazight the status of a national language in a forthcoming constitutional amendment. Other demands in the Berbers' el-Kseur manifesto were to be addressed at future meetings with Berber representatives. Radical Berbers, however, denied that such a meeting had taken place, rejected the proposals and reiterated their demand that Tamazight be granted equal status with Arabic as an official language. Ongoing dialogue between moderate Berber representatives and the Government resulted in the adoption, in January 2002, of a series of resolutions, including proposals for the establishment of a special ministerial council to implement the creation of decentralized government councils in the Kabyle at *wilaya* level. The Kabyles' demand that the gendarmerie be withdrawn from their region was, however, dismissed by Bouteflika as 'inconceivable'. The more radical Berber leaders voiced their disapproval of the resolutions, stating that the el-Kseur Platform was non-negotiable, and again insisted that the gendarmerie be withdrawn from the Kabyle.

In December 2001, meanwhile, the final report of the Issad commission had been published, confirming the initial findings that the gendarmerie had been to blame for the repression in the Kabyle, and also expressing deep pessimism about the immediate future of the region. Emphasizing the increasing authority of the military throughout the country since 1992, the report stated that the responsibilities of the civil and military authorities had become blurred and denounced the subtle slide from 'a state of emergency to a state of siege'. Issad also condemned the military's widespread abuse of its powers and the laws of the country.

In a televised address in early March 2002 Bouteflika officially announced that Tamazight would be recognized as a national language without, as had initially been intended, the issue first being put to a national referendum. Accordingly, on 7 April the National People's Assembly voted almost unanimously in favour of amending the Constitution to grant Tamazight the status of a national language. Nevertheless, Kabyle leaders urged a boycott of the forthcoming legislative elections, due to take place on 30 May, and unrest continued in the Kabyle: in mid-March 2002 five people were killed during clashes between security forces and Berber activists, and in early April the region was brought to a standstill by a series of strikes. In the period immediately preceding the elections, Kabyle leaders organized a five-day general strike, and there were reports of further violent disturbances during which protesters set light to ballot boxes, and security forces reportedly used tear gas to bring the situation under control.

In February 2002, meanwhile, the leader of the GIA, Antar Zouabri, was killed by security forces. Rachid Abou Tourab was subsequently named as Zouabri's successor. Zouabri's death precipitated an upsurge in violence between Islamists and security forces: 21 soldiers were killed by militant Islamists in early April, and in the first two weeks of May more than 50 people, among them 15 members of the armed forces, were killed. On the eve of the legislative elections 23 civilians were reported to have been killed in the village of Sedjas, 180 km west of Algiers, by Islamist militants in two separate incidents.

A total of 23 parties contested elections to the newly enlarged National People's Assembly held on 30 May 2002, although the polls were boycotted by the FFS and the RCD. According to official results, the FLN won 199 of the 389 available seats (compared with 64 in the outgoing, 380-member legislature), while the RND suffered a significant loss of support, with its parliamentary representation reduced from 155 seats to just 48. Sheikh Abdallah Djaballah's Mouvement pour la réforme nationale (MRN) took 43 seats, the MSP 38 (compared with 69 in 1997) and the Parti des travailleurs 21. Independent candidates took a total of 30 seats. The overall credibility of the election was, however, undermined by a low rate of voter participation: only 46.2% of the country's 18m. eligible voters cast their ballot. Voter abstention was particularly high in the Kabyle, with participation rates in Béjaïa and Tizi Ouzou recorded at just 2.6% and 1.8%, respectively. The FFS and the RCD demanded an annulment of the results, claiming that real voter turn-out had reached no more than 15%–20%.

Following the elections Bouteflika reappointed Benflis as Prime Minister, and in mid-June 2002 Benflis named a new, 39-member coalition Government, in which the majority of the key figures from the outgoing administration retained their posts. The most notable promotion was that of Muhammad Terbeche, hitherto Minister-delegate to the Minister of Finance, in charge of the Budget, who replaced Mourad Medelci as Minister of Finance. Former Prime Minister Ahmed Ouyahia was appointed Minister of State, Personal Representative of the President of the Republic. The new Government included five women, among them an outspoken campaigner for women's rights, Khalida Toumi-Messaoudi, who was appointed Minister for Communications and Culture and Government Spokesperson.

In early July 2002, as the country celebrated the 40th anniversary of independence from French rule, some 50 people were killed and more than 80 others were injured in a bomb attack in Larba, 25 km south of Algiers; this brought the total number of conflict-related deaths since the beginning of the year to more than 800. The attack came just days after the army Chief of Staff, Lt.-Gen. Lamari, had declared that the Government had won its campaign against the Islamist guerrillas. Some 150 people were estimated to have died in ongoing violence during July, among them Rachid Abou Tourab, who was reportedly killed, along with 15 other GIA militants, during a raid by security forces in the Tamezguida forest, south of the capital. A further 40 Islamists were killed in early August.

Prior to local elections in mid-October 2002, Bouteflika pardoned all detainees (numbering about 60) who had been sentenced for public order offences following the unrest in the Kabyle in 2001. The persistence of divisions within the Berber movement was highlighted when the RCD, supported by the CADC, announced that it would again boycott the polls. This was in direct contrast to the FFS, which was to present candidates in 40 of the country's 48 *wilayat*, maintaining that these would provide ordinary Kabyles with the possibility of attaining some form of political representation. At the elections the FLN won 668 of the 1,541 communes and thus secured control of 43 *wilayat*, although there were violent clashes in the Kabyle where demonstrators attempted to prevent voting from taking place. Voter turn-out was again low, particularly in the Kabyle.

There was a further escalation of violence in early January 2003 after some 60 people, including at least 43 soldiers, were killed in an ambush by GSPC fighters near Batna. Although Algerian officials maintained that fewer than 1,000 Islamist rebels remained in the country, there were continued reports of attacks on civilians and security forces by the GIA and the GSPC throughout the first months of the year.

In early May 2003 Bouteflika dismissed Benflis as Prime Minister, reportedly owing to 'far-reaching divergencies' between the two men. It was rumoured that Benflis intended to stand against Bouteflika in the presidential elections scheduled for 2004. The former Prime Minister, Ahmed Ouyahia, was subsequently appointed to succeed Benflis. Ouyahia announced a new coalition Government shortly afterwards, in which the majority of portfolios remained unchanged. Muhammad Terbeche was replaced as Minister of Finance by Abdelatif Benachenhou.

During the late 1970s and early 1980s the protracted struggle in Western Sahara embittered Algeria's relations with France, which supported the claims of Morocco. Algeria also criticized French military intervention elsewhere in Africa, while further grievances were the trade imbalance in favour of the former colonial power, and recurrent disputes over the price of Algerian exports of gas to France; the French Government's determination to reduce the number of Algerians residing in France was another source of contention. The Algerian military take-over in January 1992 was welcomed by the French Government, and French economic and political support for the Algerian regime increased in early 1993, following the appointment of Edouard Balladur as Prime Minister of France. Alleged Islamist militants residing in France continued to be prosecuted, and in August 1994, following the killing of five French embassy employees in Algiers, 26 suspected Algerian extremists were interned in northern France; 20 of them were subsequently expelled to Burkina Faso. In September the French embassy in Algiers confirmed that entry visas would be issued to Algerians only in exceptional cases. By November the number of French nationals killed by Islamist militants in Algeria had reached 21 and the French Government urged its citizens to leave Algeria. An Air France aircraft was hijacked in Algiers in December by members of the GIA, resulting in the deaths of three passengers and, later, in the killing of the hijackers by French security forces when the aircraft landed in France. A series of arrests made in early 1995 by French police in an attempt to dismantle support networks for Islamist militants in Algeria and Tunisia did not prevent an intensification of the GIA campaign of violence in France. The GIA claimed responsibility for numerous bomb attacks across France between July and November, in which seven people were killed and more than 160 injured. French nationals in Algeria continued to be the target of attacks by Islamist militants, and in May 1996 seven French clergymen who had been abducted by the GIA in March were killed, despite apparent efforts by the French authorities to negotiate their release. In July Hervé de Charette, the French Minister of Foreign Affairs, made an official visit to Algeria, the first ministerial-level visit for three years. However, the success of the visit was marred by the assassination in August of Pierre

Claverie, the French Roman Catholic Bishop of Oran, only hours after meeting de Charette. In December four people were killed and at least 45 were injured as a result of a bomb explosion on a passenger train in Paris, prompting speculation that the GIA had resumed its campaign of violence in France. The French authorities subsequently arrested numerous suspected Islamist activists. In early 1998 a French court sentenced 36 Islamist militants to terms of imprisonment of up to 10 years for providing logistical support for the bomb attacks in France in 1995. A further 138 people stood trial in France in September 1998, accused of criminal association with Algerian terrorists.

In June 1999 the French National Assembly voted unanimously to abandon the official claim that the eight-year struggle between Algerian nationalists and French troops, which began in November 1954, had been no more than 'an operation for keeping order' and thus admitted that France had indeed fought in the Algerian war of independence. Later in June the French Minister of Foreign Affairs, Hubert Védrine, visited Algeria and discussed with President Bouteflika plans to reopen the French consulates in Annaba and Oran. An apparent improvement in relations between Algeria and France was further signalled by a meeting in September between Bouteflika and the French President, Jacques Chirac, in New York (the first meeting between the leaders of the two countries since 1992). In November 1999 the President of the French Senate, Christian Poncelet, met Bouteflika in Algiers, and in January 2000 Algeria's Minister of Foreign Affairs, Youcef Yousfi, made the first official visit to France by an Algerian government member for six years. In mid-June Bouteflika made a full state visit to France—the first of its kind by an Algerian Head of State —during which he addressed the French National Assembly and held talks with both Chirac and the French Prime Minister, Lionel Jospin. Although the visit produced few tangible results, it was regarded as a success and an important step towards ending the diplomatic isolation imposed on Algeria following the military take-over in 1992.

Algeria's relations with France were placed under strain from late 2000 by a series of much-publicized revelations, mainly regarding occurrences during the war of independence. In November of that year Gen. Jacques Massu, who had commanded French troops during the Battle of Algiers in 1957, asserted in an interview with the French daily *Le Monde* that France should admit and condemn the use of torture by its forces during the conflict. In February 2001 the French Ministers of the Interior and of Defence held talks with their Algerian counterparts in Algiers. The meetings were, however, overshadowed by the recent publication of allegations of Algerian army involvement in the torture and massacre of civilians since 1992 (see above). Several Algerians resident in France initiated legal proceedings against former Minister of Defence Khaled Nezzar while he was visiting Paris in late April 2001. (Nezzar was reported to have left France immediately, before police could question him.) In his book *Services spéciaux Algérie 1955–57: Mon témoignage sur la torture*, published in May, a retired French general, Paul Aussarresses, admitted that he had, with the full knowledge and support of the French Government, personally tortured and killed 24 Algerian prisoners during the war of independence. In January 2002 Aussarresses, who had been deprived of his military rank, was convicted of 'apologizing for war crimes' and fined €7,500. Meanwhile, in August 2001 eight 'harkis'—Algerian Muslims who had served in the French army prior to independence—filed a formal complaint against the French Government for crimes and complicity in crimes against humanity. As many as 130,000 harkis were estimated to have been murdered by FLN troops following France's withdrawal from Algeria in 1962. In September 2001 President Chirac unveiled a plaque in Paris to commemorate those who were killed, and acknowledged his country's failure to halt the reprisals against the harkis.

Relations between the two countries improved markedly during 2002, and in late July Algeria's Minister of State for Foreign Affairs visited Paris for talks with his French counterpart. In early March 2003 Jacques Chirac became the first French President to visit Algeria since the former colony's independence in 1962; Bouteflika and Chirac signed the 'Declaration of Algiers', an agreement whereby both countries pledged to rebuild bilateral relations by holding annual meetings of their heads of state as well as twice-yearly talks between the two countries' ministers responsible for foreign affairs.

During the 1980s Algeria attempted to achieve a closer relationship with the other countries of the Maghreb region (Libya,

Mauritania, Morocco and Tunisia). The Maghreb Fraternity and Co-operation Treaty, signed by Algeria and Tunisia in March 1983 and by Mauritania in December of that year, established a basis for the creation of the long-discussed 'Great Arab Maghreb'. Relations with Morocco, however, continued to be affected by the dispute over Western Sahara. In May 1988 Algeria and Morocco restored diplomatic relations (severed in 1976) at ambassadorial level. Meeting in Algiers in June the five Heads of State of the Maghreb countries announced the formation of a Maghreb commission to examine areas of regional integration. In February 1989 the leaders signed a treaty establishing the Union du Maghreb arabe (UMA, see p. 342), with the aim of encouraging economic co-operation and eventually establishing a full customs union. The Algerian army's intervention in January 1992 to prevent victory by the FIS in the general election provoked relief, among the Maghreb countries, in Tunisia and Morocco that the establishment of a neighbouring fundamentalist state had been pre-empted. Elsewhere in the region, Egypt particularly welcomed the military's action.

Morocco imposed entry visas on Algerian nationals in August 1994, following the murder of two Spanish tourists in Morocco, allegedly by Algerian Islamist extremists. Algeria reciprocated by closing the border between the two countries and imposing entry visas on Moroccan nationals. Tensions eased slightly in September when Algeria announced the appointment of a new ambassador to Morocco, and in early 1995 negotiations commenced on the development of bilateral co-operation. However, in December King Hassan of Morocco expressed his disapproval at Algeria's alleged continuing support for the independence of Western Sahara, and demanded that UMA activities be suspended. A UMA summit meeting, scheduled for later that month, was subsequently postponed. Indications of an improvement in relations were apparently enhanced in August 1998, when Prime Minister Ahmed Ouyahia received his Moroccan counterpart, Abd ar-Rahman el-Youssoufi, for talks. Following his accession to the presidency, Bouteflika initially attempted further to improve bilateral relations in a visit to the Moroccan capital to attend the funeral of the Moroccan King, Hassan II. However, the *rapprochement* was halted in August 1999, on the day when the imminent reopening of the common border was announced, by the massacre by the GIA of 29 civilians in the border region of Bechar. Bouteflika's public allegation that Morocco was providing sanctuary for the perpetrators of the attack extended to accusations of drugs-trafficking and arms-dealing on the Algerian border. In September Bouteflika accused both Morocco and Tunisia of acting against the interests of the UMA by negotiating separate agreements with the European Union (EU, see p. 199). In February 2000 Algeria and Morocco both expressed their desire to improve bilateral relations, despite continued differences over the Western Sahara issue, and in April Bouteflika met with the new Moroccan ruler, King Muhammad VI, at the Africa-EU summit held in Cairo, Egypt. The two leaders agreed to establish joint committees in an attempt to reduce the number of violent incidents on their mutual border, and joint security operations involving the two countries' armed forces began along the border in May. In mid-March 2001 a meeting in Algiers of the UMA's council of ministers responsible for foreign affairs ended acrimoniously following disagreements between Moroccan and Algerian delegations. Relations between the two countries were further strained after Algeria announced its opposition to UN proposals for a settlement to the Western Sahara issue, as Algeria believed the plans unduly favoured Morocco and would inevitably lead to the formal integration of the disputed territory into Morocco.

In December 1996 the EU and Algeria began negotiations on Algeria's participation in a Euro-Mediterranean free-trade zone. In November 1999 an EU delegation visited Algiers, and negotiations on a trade partnership agreement resumed in April 2000. In January 2001 the President of the European Commission, Romano Prodi, visited Algeria, where he signed the financing protocols for a number of joint projects. In December negotiations for the EU-Algeria Euro-Mediterranean Association Agreement were concluded, and both parties formally signed the agreement in April 2002. The Agreement was to enter into force upon ratification by the respective legislatures of Algeria and of the member states of the EU and by the European Parliament.

The Algerian Government was swift to condemn the suicide attacks on New York and Washington, DC, on 11 September 2001, for which the USA held the al-Qa'ida (Base) organization of Osama bin Laden responsible, and to offer assistance for the

USA's proposed 'coalition against terror'. Later that month the Algerian authorities handed the US authorities a list containing the profiles of some 350 Islamist militants it believed had links to bin Laden and al-Qa'ida. In November President Bouteflika visited Washington, where he met with President George W. Bush and reiterated his support for the US-led campaign. Algeria continued to assist the USA with anti-terrorist operations, and in September 2002 Algerian security forces killed a senior al-Qa'ida operative, who was alleged to be liaising with the GSPC, in a raid near Batna. In December the US Administration announced that it had for the first time agreed to sell weaponry and other military equipment to Algeria as part of the USA's policy of intensifying security co-operation with Algeria.

In March 2003 four Algerians were sentenced to terms of imprisonment ranging from 10 to 12 years by a court in Frankfurt, Germany, after being convicted of conspiracy to commit murder, conspiracy to plant a bomb and of weapons violations. The four men had been arrested in December 2000 in Strasbourg, France, where, it was alleged, they had intended to detonate a series of bombs. Meanwhile, in January five Algerians were arrested in London, United Kingdom, and charged with being 'concerned in the development or production of a chemical weapon' and with having materials 'connected with the commission, preparation or instigation of an act of terrorism'. A number of Algerians were also detained following a series of police raids across the United Kingdom later that month.

Government

Under the 1976 Constitution (with modifications adopted by the National People's Assembly in June 1979 and with further amendments approved by popular referendum in November 1988, February 1989 and in November 1996), Algeria is a multi-party state, with parties subject to approval by the Ministry of the Interior. The Head of State is the President of the Republic, who is elected by universal adult suffrage for a five-year term, renewable once. The President presides over a Council of Ministers and a High Security Council. The President must appoint a Prime Minister as Head of Government, who appoints a Council of Ministers. The bicameral legislature consists of the 380-member National People's Assembly and the 144-member Council of the Nation. The members of the National People's Assembly are elected by universal, direct, secret suffrage for a five-year term. Two-thirds of the members of the Council of the Nation are elected by indirect, secret suffrage from regional and municipal authorities; the remainder are appointed by the President of the Republic. The Council's term in office is six years; one-half of its members are replaced every three years. Both the Head of Government and the parliamentary chambers may initiate legislation. Legislation must be deliberated upon respectively by the National People's Assembly and the Council of the Nation before promulgation. The country is divided into 48 departments (*wilayat*), which are, in turn, sub-divided into communes. Each *wilaya* and commune has an elected assembly.

Defence

In August 2002 the estimated strength of the armed forces was 136,700 (including 75,000 conscripts), comprising an army of 120,000, a navy of about 6,700 and an air force of 10,000. The defence budget for 2000 was estimated at AD 138,000m. Military service is compulsory for 18 months. There are paramilitary forces of 181,200, controlled by the Ministry of Defence and the Directorate of National Security, and an estimated 100,000 self-defence militia and communal guards.

Economic Affairs

In 2001, according to estimates by the World Bank, Algeria's gross national income (GNI), measured at average 1999–2001 prices, was US $50,355m., equivalent to $1,630 per head (or $5,150 on an international purchasing-power parity basis). During 1990–2001, it was estimated, the population increased at an average annual rate of 1.9%, while gross domestic product (GDP) per head declined, in real terms, at an average annual rate of 0.2%. Overall GDP increased, in real terms, at an average annual rate of 1.7% in 1990–2001; it grew by 2.4% in 2000, and by 1.9% in 2001.

Agriculture (including forestry and fishing) contributed 12.1% of GDP in 2001, and employed an estimated 24.1% of the labour force in that year. Domestic production of food crops is insufficient to meet the country's requirements. The principal crops are wheat, potatoes and tomatoes. Dates are Algeria's principal non-hydrocarbon export; olives, citrus fruits and grapes are also grown, and wine has been an important export since the French

colonial era. During 1990–2001 agricultural GDP increased at an average annual rate of 3.9%. Agricultural GDP increased declined by 5.0% in 2000, but increased by 7.0% in 2001.

Industry (including mining, manufacturing, construction and power) contributed 75.7% of GDP in 2000, and engaged 24.3% of the employed population in that year. During 1990–2001 industrial GDP increased at an average annual rate of 1.6%. Industrial GDP increased by 4.3% in 2000, and by 0.8% in 2001.

The mining sector provides almost all of Algeria's export earnings, although it engaged only 1.6% of the employed population in 1987. Petroleum and natural gas, which together contributed an estimated 43.0% of GDP in 2000, are overwhelmingly Algeria's principal exports, providing 98.1% of total export earnings in that year. Algeria's proven reserves of petroleum were 9,200m. barrels at the end of 2001, sufficient to maintain output at that year's levels—which averaged 1.56m. barrels per day (b/d)—for 18 years. With effect from February 2003 Algeria's production quota within the Organization of the Petroleum Exporting Countries (OPEC, see p. 298) was 735,000 b/d. Proven reserves of natural gas at the end of 2001 totalled 4,520,000m. cu m, sustainable at that year's production level (totalling 78,200m. cu m) for almost 58 years. Algeria currently transports natural gas through two pipelines to Spain and Italy, and feasibility studies were undertaken in 2001 regarding the possible construction of a further pipeline to supply other parts of Europe via Spain. Substantial reserves of iron ore, phosphates, barite (barytes), lead, zinc, mercury, salt, marble and industrial minerals are also mined, and the exploitation of gold reserves commenced in 2001. The GDP of the hydrocarbons sector increased by 6.1% in 1999 and by an estimated 4.9% in 2000, while that of other mining activities declined by 3.0% in 1999 but expanded by an estimated 6.5% in 2000.

Manufacturing engaged 12.2% of the employed population in 1987, and provided 10.3% of GDP in 2000. Measured by gross value of output, the principal branches of manufacturing in 1996 were food products, beverages and tobacco (which accounted for 52.3% of the total), metals, metal products, machinery and transport and scientific equipment (14.7%), non-metallic mineral products (10.2%), chemical, petroleum, coal, rubber and plastic products (8.6%), wood, paper and products (6.4%) and textiles and clothing (5.9%). During 1990–2000 the GDP of the manufacturing sector declined at an average annual rate of 0.1%. However, manufacturing GDP increased by 1.1% in 2000, and by 4.2% in 2001.

Energy is derived principally from natural gas (which contributed 94.3% of total electricity output in 1999). Algeria is a net exporter of fuels, with imports of energy products comprising only an estimated 1.4% of the value of merchandise imports in 2000.

Services engaged 60.0% of the employed labour force in 2000, and provided 12.2% of GDP in 2001. During 1990–2001 the combined GDP of the service sectors increased at an average annual rate of 1.7%. Services GDP increased by 1.7% in 2000, and by 3.0% in 2001.

In 2000 Algeria recorded a visible trade surplus of US $12,620m., while there was a surplus of $9,250m. on the current account of the balance of payments. France was the principal source of imports in 1997 (providing 23.6% of the total); other important suppliers were the USA, Italy, and Germany. Italy was the principal market for exports (20.1%) in that year; other major purchasers were the USA, France, Spain, the Netherlands, Brazil and Turkey. The principal exports in 2000 were, overwhelmingly, mineral fuels, lubricants, etc.; other exports included vegetables, tobacco, hides and dates. The principal imports in that year were machinery and transport equipment, food and live animals, and basic manufactures.

In 2000 Algeria recorded an overall budget surplus of AD 398,800m., equivalent to 9.9% of GDP. Algeria's total external debt at the end of 2000 amounted to US $25,002m., of which $23,062m. was long-term public debt. In that year the cost of debt-servicing was equivalent to 19.6% of the value of exports of goods and services. The annual rate of inflation averaged 15.4% in 1990–2001. Consumer prices decreased by an average of 0.6% in 2000, but increased by 3.5% in 2001. Some 29.8% of the labour force were unemployed in 2000.

Algeria is a member of the Union of the Arab Maghreb (UMA, see p. 342), which aims to promote economic integration of member states, and also of OPEC).

The initial optimism regarding Algeria's future economic prospects that had prevailed following Abdelaziz Bouteflika's inauguration as President in April 1999 had somewhat receded by early 2003. Despite the continuing privatization of state-owned enterprises and the further liberalization of the banking, energy, transport and telecommunications sectors, increasing social unrest, partially fuelled by high rates of unemployment and widespread poverty, was evident among large sections of the Algerian population. It did, however, appear that the ongoing civil conflict in the country had failed to deter major foreign investors—in particular those seeking to operate within the rapidly expanding hydrocarbons sector—from concluding valuable agreements with Algerian companies. In November 2002, notably, the state hydrocarbons company, SONATRACH, and BP agreed to commence a development project worth some US $1,800m., and the Algerian Government subsequently announced its intention further to develop natural gas production facilities and raise the export levels of that commodity to 85,000m. cu m per year by 2010. Meanwhile, it was planned to increase Algeria's oil production capacity from some 1.05m. b/d in mid-2002—already substantially in excess of agreed OPEC quotas—to 1.5m b/d by late 2004. The pending ratification of an association agreement with the EU was expected to facilitate additional overseas investment in the country, and negotiations regarding accession to the World Trade Organization were continuing. Algeria again recorded a sizeable budget surplus in 2002, enabling the funding of an Economic Recovery Programme, and overall GDP was forecast to rise by 3.0% in 2003. None the less, much higher growth and increased spending on infrastructural projects were required in order to reduce substantially the rate of unemployment and improve standards of living.

Education

Education, in the national language (Arabic), is officially compulsory for nine years between six and 15 years of age. Primary education begins at the age of six and lasts for six years. Secondary education begins at 12 years of age and lasts for up to six years (comprising two cycles of three years each). In 1996 the total enrolment at primary and secondary schools was equivalent to 86% of the school-age population (90% of boys; 82% of girls). Enrolment at primary schools in that year included 94% of children in the relevant age-group (97% of boys; 91% of girls), while enrolment at secondary schools included 56% of children in the relevant age-group (58% of boys; 54% of girls). Some 12.5% of total planned expenditure in the 1997 administrative budget was allocated to education and training. Priority is being given to teacher-training, to the development of technical and scientific teaching programmes, and to adult literacy and training schemes. In addition to the 10 universities, there are seven other *centres universitaires* and a number of technical colleges. In 1995/96 a total of 347,410 students were enrolled in higher education.

Public Holidays

2003: 1 January (New Year), 12 February* (Id al-Adha, Feast of the Sacrifice), 5 March* (Islamic New Year), 14 March* (Ashoura), 1 May (Labour Day), 14 May* (Mouloud, Birth of Muhammad), 19 June (Ben Bella's Overthrow), 5 July (Independence), 24 September* (Leilat al-Meiraj, Ascension of Muhammad), 27 October* (Ramadan begins), 1 November (Anniversary of the Revolution), 26 November* (Id al-Fitr, end of Ramadan).

2004: 1 January (New Year), 2 February* (Id al-Adha, Feast of the Sacrifice), 22 February* (Islamic New Year), 2 March* (Ashoura), 1 May (Labour Day), 2 May* (Mouloud, Birth of Muhammad), 19 June (Ben Bella's Overthrow), 5 July (Independence), 12 September* (Leilat al-Meiraj, Ascension of Muhammad), 15 October* (Ramadan begins), 1 November (Anniversary of the Revolution), 14 November* (Id al-Fitr, end of Ramadan).

*These holidays are dependent on the Islamic lunar calendar and may differ by one or two days from the dates given.

Weights and Measures

The metric system is in force.

Statistical Survey

Source (unless otherwise stated): Office National des Statistiques, 8 rue des Moussebiline, BP 55, Algiers; tel. (2) 64-77-90; e-mail ons@onssiege.ons.dz; internet www.ons.dz.

Area and Population

AREA, POPULATION AND DENSITY

Area (sq km)	2,381,741*
Population (census results)†	
20 April 1987	23,038,942
25 June 1998 (provisional)	
Males	14,471,318
Females.	14,801,025
Total	29,272,343
Population (official estimates at mid-year)	
1999	29,950,000
2000	30,386,000
2001	30,836,000
Density (per sq km) at mid-2001	12.9

* 919,595 sq miles.
† Excluding Algerian nationals residing abroad, numbering an estimated 828,000 at 1 January 1978.

POPULATION BY WILAYA (ADMINISTRATIVE DISTRICT)
(provisional, 1998 census)

	Area (sq km)	Population	Density (per sq km)
Adrar	439,700	311,615	0.7
Aïn Defla	4,897	660,342	134.9
Aïn Témouchent . . .	2,379	327,331	137.6
Algiers (el-Djezaïr) . .	273	2,562,428	9,386.2
Annaba	1,439	557,818	387.6
Batna	12,192	962,623	79.0
el-Bayadh	78,870	168,789	2.1
Béchar	162,200	225,546	1.4
Béjaïa	3,268	856,840	262.2
Biskra (Beskra) . . .	20,986	575,858	27.4
Blida (el-Boulaïda) . .	1,696	784,283	462.4
Borj Bou Arreridj. . .	4,115	555,402	135.0
Bouira	4,439	629,560	141.8
Boumerdes	1,591	647,389	406.9
Chlef (ech-Cheliff) . .	4,795	858,695	179.1
Constantine (Qacentina) .	2,187	810,914	370.8
Djelfa	66,415	797,706	12.0
Ghardaïa	86,105	300,516	3.5
Guelma	4,101	430,000	104.9
Illizi	285,000	34,108	0.1
Jijel	2,577	573,208	222.4
Khenchela.	9,811	327,917	33.4
Laghouat	25,057	317,125	12.7
Mascara (Mouaskar). .	5,941	676,192	113.8
Médéa (Lemdiyya) . .	8,866	802,078	90.5
Mila	9,375	674,480	71.9
Mostaganem	2,175	631,057	290.1
M'Sila	18,718	805,519	43.0
Naâma.	29,950	127,314	4.3
Oran (Ouahran) . . .	2,121	1,213,839	572.3

— continued

	Area (sq km)	Population	Density (per sq km)
Ouargla	211,980	445,619	2.1
el-Oued	54,573	504,401	9.2
Oum el-Bouaghi	6,768	519,170	76.7
Relizane (Ghilizane)	4,870	642,205	131.9
Saïda	6,764	279,526	41.3
Sétif	6,504	1,311,413	201.6
Sidi-bel-Abbès	9,096	525,632	57.8
Skikda	4,026	786,154	195.3
Souk Ahras	4,541	367,455	80.9
Tamanrasset (Tamanghest)	556,200	137,175	0.3
el-Tarf	3,339	352,588	105.6
Tébessa	14,227	549,066	38.6
Tiaret	20,673	725,853	35.1
Tindouf	159,000	27,060	0.2
Tipaza	2,166	506,053	233.6
Tissemsilt	3,152	264,240	83.8
Tizi Ouzou	3,568	1,108,708	310.7
Tlemcen	9,061	842,053	92.9
Total *	2,381,741	29,100,867	12.2

* Excluding Sahrawi refugees in camps (171,476 in 1998).

PRINCIPAL TOWNS

(provisional, population at 1998 census)

Algiers (el-Djezaïr capital)	1,519,570	Djelfa	154,265
		Tébessa (Tbessa)	153,246
Oran (Ouahran)	655,852	Blida (el-Boulaïda)	153,083
Constantine (Qacentina)	462,187	Skikda	152,335
Batna	242,514	Béjaïa	147,076
Annaba	215,083	Tiaret (Tihert)	145,332
Sétif (Stif)	211,859	Chlef	133,874
Sidi-bel-Abbès	180,260	el-Buni	133,471
Biskra (Beskra)	170,956	Béchar	131,010

BIRTHS, MARRIAGES AND DEATHS*

	Registered live births†		Registered marriages		Registered deaths†	
	Number	Rate (per 1,000)	Number	Rate (per 1,000)	Number	Rate (per 1,000)
1994	776,000	28.2	147,954	5.4	180,000	6.6
1995	711,000	25.3	152,786	5.5	180,000	6.4
1996	654,000	22.9	156,870	5.5	172,000	6.0
1997	654,000	22.5	157,831	5.4	178,000	6.1
1998	620,000	21.0	158,298	5.4	172,000	5.8
1999	605,000	21.2	163,126	5.5	168,000	5.6
2000	600,000	19.8	177,548	5.8	166,000	5.5
2001	631,000	20.5	194,273	6.3	168,000	5.4

* Figures refer to the Algerian population only. Birth registration is estimated to be at least 90% complete, but the registration of marriages and deaths is incomplete. According to UN estimates, the average annual rates per 1,000 in 1995–2000 were: births 25.9; deaths 7.5.

† Excluding live-born infants dying before registration of birth.

Expectation of life (WHO estimates, years at birth): 69.4 (males 67.7; females 71.1) in 2001 (Source: WHO, *World Health Report*).

ECONOMICALLY ACTIVE POPULATION

(1987 census)*

	Males	Females	Total
Agriculture, hunting, forestry and fishing	714,947	9,753	724,699
Mining and quarrying	64,685	3,142	67,825
Manufacturing	471,471	40,632	512,105
Electricity, gas and water	40,196	1,579	41,775
Construction	677,211	12,372	689,586
Trade, restaurants and hotels	376,590	14,399	390,990
Transport, storage and communications	207,314	9,029	216,343
Financing, insurance, real estate and business services	125,426	17,751	143,178
Community, social and personal services	945,560	234,803	1,180,364
Activities not adequately defined	149,241	83,718	232,959
Total employed	3,772,641	427,183	4,199,824
Unemployed	1,076,018	65,260	1,141,278
Total labour force	4,848,659	492,443	5,341,102

* Employment data relate to persons aged 6 years and over; those for unemployment relate to persons aged 16 to 64 years. Estimates have been made independently, so the totals may not be the sum of the component parts.

2000 (sample survey, '000 persons, July–September): Agriculture, hunting, forestry and fishing 898.0; Mining and quarrying, manufacturing, electricity, gas and water 720.9; Construction 669.8; Trade, restaurants and hotels 731.4; Government services 1,773.2; Other services 932.6; Total employed 5,725.9 (males 5,028.2, females 697.7); Unemployed 2,427.7 (males 2,132.7, females 295.0); Total labour force 8,153.6 (males 7,160.9, females 992.7). Figures refer to males aged 15 to 60 years and females aged 15 to 55 years.

Mid-2001 (estimates in '000): Agriculture, etc. 2,613; Total labour force 10,857 (Source: FAO).

Health and Welfare

KEY INDICATORS

Total fertility rate (children per woman, 2001)	2.9
Under-5 mortality rate (per 1,000 live births, 2001)	49
HIV/AIDS (% of persons aged 15–49, 1999)	0.10
Physicians (per 1,000 head, 1995)	0.85
Hospital beds (per 1,000 head, 1998)	2.1
Health expenditure (2000): US $ per head (PPP)	142
Health expenditure (2000): % of GDP	3.6
Health expenditure (2000): public (% of total)	82.2
Access to water (% of persons, 2000)	94
Access to sanitation (% of persons, 2000)	73
Human Development Index (2000): ranking	106
Human Development Index (2000): value	0.697

For sources and definitions, see explanatory note on p. vi.

Agriculture

PRINCIPAL CROPS
('000 metric tons)

	1999	2000	2001
Wheat	1,470	760	2,011*
Barley	510	163	574*
Oats	40	8	44*
Potatoes	996	1,208	1,200†
Broad beans, dry	22	13	15†
Chick-peas	13	7	8†
Almonds	26	26	26†
Olives	363	217	300†
Rapeseed†	100	100	100
Cabbages	22	19	20†
Artichokes	30	39	300†
Tomatoes	955	816	100†
Cauliflowers	40	44	44†
Pumpkins, squash and gourds	92	95	95†
Cucumbers and gherkins	46	53	53†
Aubergines (Eggplants)	34	38	38†
Chillies and green peppers	156	175	175†
Dry onions	382	316	320†
Garlic	30	36	35†
Green beans	26	26	25†
Green peas	45	47	48†
Green broad beans	119	78	80†
Carrots	135	149	148†
Other vegetables	263	246	245†
Oranges	307	300	300†
Tangerines, mandarins, clementines and satsumas	115	102	110†
Lemons and limes	29	29	29†
Apples	87	97	95†
Pears	82	74	75†
Apricots	74	56	60†
Peaches and nectarines	61	59	60†
Plums	25	26	27†
Grapes	178	204	200†
Watermelons	538	399	400†
Figs	51	54	55†
Dates	428	366	366†
Other fruits	57	61	119†
Pimento and allspice†	7	8	8
Tobacco (leaves)	6	7	7†

* Unofficial figure.
† FAO estimate(s).

Source: FAO.

LIVESTOCK
('000 head, year ending September)

	1999	2000	2001*
Sheep	18,200	19,500	19,300
Goats	3,400	3,400	3,500
Cattle	1,650	1,650	1,700
Horses	46	47	48
Mules*	50	50	50
Asses*	180	180	180
Camels	220	235	240
Chickens (million)	105	110	110

* FAO estimates.

Source: FAO.

LIVESTOCK PRODUCTS
('000 metric tons)

	1999	2000	2001*
Beef and veal	117	133	133
Mutton and lamb	163	164	165
Goat meat*	12	12	12
Poultry meat*	210	210	210
Rabbit meat*	7	7	7
Other meat	7	8	7
Cows' milk	1,040	1,170	1,150
Sheep's milk	220	180	200
Goats' milk	143	153	155
Poultry eggs*	125	144	145
Honey	2	2	2
Wool: greasy	23	24	25
Wool: scoured*	12	12	12
Cattle hides*	13	13	13
Sheepskins*	24	24	24
Goatskins*	2	2	2

* FAO estimates.

Source: FAO.

Forestry

ROUNDWOOD REMOVALS
(FAO estimates, '000 cubic metres, excl. bark)

	1998	1999	2000
Sawlogs, veneer logs and logs for sleepers	68	68	68
Pulpwood	85	85	85
Other industrial wood	291	298	298
Fuel wood	6,948	7,074	7,188
Total	7,392	7,525	7,639

Sawnwood production ('000 cubic metres, incl. railway sleepers): 13 per year (FAO estimates) in 1980–2001.

Source: FAO.

Fishing

('000 metric tons, live weight)

	1998	1999	2000*
Capture	92.3	102.4	100.0
Bogue	3.2	3.5	3.4
Jack and horse mackerels	4.8	6.2	6.0
Sardinellas	10.0	11.4	11.0
European pilchard (sardine)	49.3	56.7	55.0
European anchovy	3.5	3.1	3.0
Crustaceans and molluscs	3.6	3.3	3.3
Aquaculture	0.3	0.3	0.3
Total catch	92.6	102.7	100.3

* FAO estimates.

Source: FAO, *Yearbook of Fishery Statistics*.

Mining

('000 metric tons, unless otherwise indicated)

	1999	2000	2001*
Crude petroleum ('000 barrels)	457,158	476,288	465,000
Natural gas (million cu m)†	128,783	139,499	140,000
Iron ore:			
gross weight	1,336	1,645	1,500
metal content	680	n.a.	n.a.
Lead concentrates (metric tons)‡	1,215	818	900
Zinc concentrates (metric tons)‡	9,808	10,452	12,000
Mercury (metric tons)‡	240	216	220
Phosphate rock§	1,096	877	900
Barite (Barytes)	51	52	52
Salt (unrefined)	164	182	185
Gypsum (crude)*	1,316	1,341	1,350

* Provisional or estimated data.

† Figures refer to gross volume. Production on a dry basis (in million cu m) was: 97,151 in 1999; 100,092 in 2000; 105,000 in 2001.

‡ Figures refer to the metal content of ores or concentrates.

§ Figures refer to gross weight. The estimated phosphoric acid content (in '000 metric tons) was 340 in 1999; 265 in 2000; 280 in 2001.

Source: US Geological Survey.

Industry

SELECTED PRODUCTS

('000 metric tons, unless otherwise indicated)

	1997	1998	1999
Olive oil (crude)*	46	15	57
Refined sugar	68	58	48
Wine*	26	34	42
Beer ('000 hectolitres)	379	382	383
Soft drinks ('000 hectolitres)	599	375	315
Footwear—excl. rubber ('000 pairs)	2,542	1,249	1,167
Nitrogenous fertilizers (a)†	28‡	41‡	57
Phosphate fertilizers (b)†	118	183	201
Naphthas‡	4,043	3,855	n.a.
Motor spirit (petrol)	1,989	2,037‡	n.a.
Kerosene‡	325	317	n.a.
Jet fuel‡	1,197	970	n.a.
Gas-diesel (distillate fuel) oils	6,523	6,198‡	n.a.
Residual fuel oils	5,556	5,061‡	n.a.
Lubricating oils‡	98	104	n.a.
Petroleum bitumen (asphalt)‡	183	171	n.a.
Liquefied petroleum gas:			
from natural gas plants‡	6,186	7,089	n.a.
from petroleum refineries‡	477	466	n.a.
Cement	7,146	7,836	7,587
Pig-iron for steel-making§	526	757	807
Crude steel (ingots)§	361	581	675
Zinc—unwrought	31.4	23.7	24.9
Refrigerators for household use			
('000)	175	215	181
Telephones (million)	3	30	151
Television receivers ('000)	172	251	173
Buses and coaches—assembled			
(number)	264	307	529
Lorries—assembled (number)	1,293	1,798	1,583
Electric energy (million kWh)	21,489	23,615‡	n.a.

2000 ('000 metric tons*): Olive oil (crude) 30; Wine 42¶.

2001 (FAO estimates, '000 metric tons): Olive oil 45; Wine 42.

* Data from FAO.

† Production in terms of (a) nitrogen or (b) phosphoric acid.

‡ Provisional or estimated figure(s).

§ Data from the US Geological Survey.

¶ Unofficial figure.

Source: mainly UN, *Industrial Commodity Statistics Yearbook*.

Finance

CURRENCY AND EXCHANGE RATES

Monetary Units

  100 centimes = 1 Algerian dinar (AD)

Sterling, Dollar and Euro Equivalents (31 December 2002)

  £1 sterling = 128.50 dinars

  US \$1 = 79.72 dinars

  €1 = 83.61 dinars

  1,000 Algerian dinars = £7.782 = \$12.543 = €11.961

Average Exchange Rate (dinars per US \$)

  2000   75.260

  2001   77.215

  2002   79.682

BUDGET

('000 million AD)*

Revenue	1998	1999	2000
Hydrocarbon revenue	425.9	588.2	1,213.2
Export taxes	328.6	510.1	n.a.
Domestic receipts	50.0	50.0	n.a.
Dividends and entry rights	47.3	28.1	40.0
Other revenue	348.7	358.4	364.9
Tax revenue	329.8	314.8	349.5
Taxes on income and profits	88.1	72.2	82.0
Taxes on goods and services	154.9	149.7	165.0
Customs duties	75.5	80.2	86.3
Non-tax revenue	18.9	43.6	15.4
Total	**774.6**	**950.5**	**1,578.1**

Expenditure†	1998	1999	2000
Current expenditure	664.1	774.7	856.2
Personnel expenditure	268.6	286.1	289.6
War veterans' pensions	37.9	59.9	57.7
Material and supplies	47.5	53.6	54.6
Public services	75.2	81.9	92.0
Hospitals	28.8	31.2	33.0
Current transfers	124.1	166.8	200.0
Family allowances	42.5	36.2	29.0
Public works and social			
assistance	13.6	14.2	8.6
Food subsidies	0.2	0.4	0.5
Housing	19.0	14.5	8.6
Interest payments	110.8	126.4	162.3
Capital expenditure	211.9	187.0	321.9
Total	**875.7**	**961.7**	**1,178.1**

* Figures refer to operations of the central Government, excluding special accounts. The balance (revenue less expenditure) on such accounts (in '000 million AD) was: −6.9 in 1998; −5.6 in 1999; −0.7 in 2000.

† Excluding net lending by the Treasury ('000 million AD): 0.1 in 1998; −0.3 in 1999; 0.5 in 2000.

Source: IMF, *Algeria: Statistical Appendix* (September 2001).

2001 ('000 million AD): Total revenue 1,505.5; Total expenditure 1,334.5.

Source: IMF, *Government Finance Statistics Yearbook*..

CENTRAL BANK RESERVES

(US \$ million at 31 December)

	2000	2001	2002
Gold*	255	246	266
IMF special drawing rights	3	11	14
Reserve position in IMF	111	107	116
Foreign exchange	11,910	17,963	23,108
Total	**12,278**	**18,327**	**23,504**

* Valued at SDR 35 per troy ounce.

Source: IMF, *International Financial Statistics*.

MONEY SUPPLY
(million AD at 31 December)

	1999	2000	2001
Currency outside banks . . .	440,263	484,948	577,150
Demand deposits at deposit money banks	352,707	460,267	554,927
Checking deposits at post office .	87,428	89,090	96,998
Private sector demand deposits at treasury	9,384	7,066	9,435
Total money (incl. others) . . .	889,784	1,044,020	1,240,240

Source: IMF, *International Financial Statistics*.

COST OF LIVING
(Consumer Price Index; base: 1990 = 100)

	1999	2000	2001
Foodstuffs, beverages and tobacco	471.6	461.6	481.7
All items (incl. others) . . .	467.7	464.8	481.1

Source: UN, *Monthly Bulletin of Statistics*.

NATIONAL ACCOUNTS
(million AD at current prices)

National Income and Product

	1998	1999	2000
Compensation of employees . .	785,838.1	846,679.2	882,826.4
Operating surplus	1,289,716.7	1,544,284.9	2,085,199.8
Domestic factor incomes . .	2,075,554.8	2,390,964.1	2,968,026.2
Consumption of fixed capital .	218,993.4	262,852.8	357,371.6
Gross domestic product (GDP) at factor cost . .	2,294,548.2	2,653,816.9	3,325,397.8
Indirect taxes, *less* subsidies .	515,576.2	561,308.2	753,277.5
GDP in purchasers' values .	2,810,124.4	3,215,125.1	4,078,675.3
Factor income received from abroad	25,958.0	19,920.2	37,700.8
Less Factor income paid abroad	140,715.5	167,254.2	211,390.2
Gross national product . .	2,695,366.9	3,067,791.1	3,904,985.9
Less Consumption of fixed capital	218,993.4	262,852.8	357,371.6
National income in market prices	2,476,373.5	2,804,938.3	3,547,614.3
Other current transfers from abroad	97,071.0	101,473.8	106,247.8
Less Other current transfers paid abroad	3,152.6	3,423.8	29,201.3
National disposable income .	2,570,291.9	2,902,988.3	3,624,660.8

Expenditure on the Gross Domestic Product

	1998	1999	2000
Government final consumption expenditure	503,630.7	543,603.9	560,193.1
Private final consumption expenditure	1,555,370.7	1,667,199.8	1,713,206.5
Increase in stocks . . .	26,191.1	35,114.8	15,232.3
Gross fixed capital formation .	728,754.1	789,798.6	869,325.6
Total domestic expenditure .	2,813,946.6	3,035,717.1	3,157,957.5
Exports of goods and services .	652,257.3	918,889.0	1,748,978.7
Less Imports of goods and services	656,079.5	739,481.0	828,260.9
GDP in purchasers' values .	2,810,124.4	3,215,125.1	4,078,675.3

Gross Domestic Product by Economic Activity

	1998	1999	2000†
Agriculture, forestry and fishing	304,479.6	338,233.8	325,751.1
Hydrocarbons*	673,692.8	927,361.2	1,666,235.5
Mining (excl. hydrocarbons) .		4,710.7	5,021.6
Manufacturing (excl. hydrocarbons)	256,821.0	225,624.6	234,623.9
Electricity and water . . .		40,037.2	44,108.0
Construction	265,412.0	271,257.7	292,046.3
Wholesale and retail trade . . .	380,362.2	406,307.2	431,909.9
Hotels and restaurants . . .	38,795.5	46,384.6	46,930.0
Transport and communications .	206,470.2	238,856.0	272,696.8
Finance, real estate and business services	114,895.1	126,989.5	136,590.7
Government services . . .	333,092.8	353,930.8	359,744.4
Other services to households . .	48,003.1	51,731.2	58,106.6
Sub-total	2,622,024.3	3,031,424.4	3,873,764.8
Import duties	226,924.8	226,271.7	250,063.4
Less Imputed bank service charges	38,824.7	42,571.0	45,152.9
GDP in purchasers' values . .	2,810,124.4	3,215,125.1	4,078,675.3

* Extraction and processing of petroleum and natural gas, including related services and public works.

† Provisional.

BALANCE OF PAYMENTS
(US $ million)

	1998	1999	2000
Exports of goods f.o.b.	10,126	12,325	21,650
Imports of goods f.o.b.	-8,629	-8,960	-9,030
Trade balance	1,497	3,365	12,620
Exports of services	777	720	910
Imports of services	-2,311	-2,560	-2,360
Balance on goods and services .	-37	1,525	11,170
Other income received	340	220	380
Other income paid	-2,286	-2,510	-3,090
Balance on goods, services and income	-1,983	-765	8,460
Transfers (net)	1,064	790	790
Current balance	-919	25	9,250
Direct investment (net) . . .	505	460	420
Official capital (net)	-1,104	-1,957	-1,960
Short-term credit (net), net errors and omissions	352	-995	-147
Overall balance	-1,166	-2,467	7,563

Source: Ministry of Finance.

External Trade

Note: Data exclude military goods. Exports include stores and bunkers for foreign ships and aircraft.

PRINCIPAL COMMODITIES
(distribution by SITC, US $ million)

Imports c.i.f.	1998	1999	2000
Food and live animals	2,438.3	2,222.1	2,363.7
Dairy products and birds' eggs	481.8	437.9	429.6
Milk and cream	411.1	365.9	373.9
Cereals and cereal preparations	1,025.9	908.4	1,090.7
Wheat and meslin (unmilled)	691.2	660.8	803.9
Crude materials (inedible) except fuels	273.2	263.4	263.1
Animal and vegetable oils, fats and waxes	312.9	230.5	174.5
Chemicals and related products	1,051.0	1,073.7	1,042.9
Medicinal and pharmaceutical products	503.8	534.8	466.4
Medicaments (incl. veterinary)	468.9	499.9	428.9
Basic manufactures	1,681.8	1,666.6	1,598.1
Iron and steel	594.5	654.2	566.4
Tubes, pipes and fittings	191.5	301.7	169.1
Machinery and transport equipment	3,040.2	3,034.9	3,144.9
Power-generating machinery and equipment	296.4	255.2	266.2
Machinery specialized for particular industries	325.2	342.1	418.4
General industrial machinery, equipment and parts	800.7	859.6	729.7
Electrical machinery, apparatus, etc.	748.7	705.5	402.3
Telecommunications, sound recording and reproducing equipment	192.1	217.5	298.1
Road vehicles and parts*	648.8	666.1	604.6
Other transport equipment	59.3	32.3	275.3
Miscellaneous manufactured articles	422.7	459.6	397.5
Total (incl. others)	9,403.4	9,161.9	9,152.1

* Excluding tyres, engines and electrical parts.

Exports f.o.b.	1998	1999	2000
Mineral fuels, lubricants, etc.	9,544.0	12,167.2	21,609.8
Petroleum, petroleum products, etc.	5,502.1	6,940.0	12,591.0
Crude petroleum oils, etc.	4,084.2	4,975.1	9,254.4
Refined petroleum products	1,340.4	1,882.6	3,146.1
Gas oils (distillate fuels)	378.6	515.6	727.8
Residual fuel oils	390.9	596.3	1,120.3
Gas (natural and manufactured)	4,041.8	5,227.2	9,061.9
Liquefied petroleum gases	2,791.0	2,888.1	5,735.4
Petroleum gases, etc., in the gaseous state	1,250.8	2,339.2	3,281.5
Total (incl. others)	9,838.6	12,525.3	22,031.3

Source: UN, *International Trade Statistics Yearbook.*

2001 (US $ million): Total imports c.i.f. 9,910; Total exports f.o.b. 19,132.

PRINCIPAL TRADING PARTNERS
(US $ million)*

Imports c.i.f.	1998	1999	2000
Argentina	87.9	122.8	75.4
Austria	102.1	108.2	115.6
Belgium†	247.8	192.9	238.7
Brazil	57.7	104.8	56.3
Canada	523.2	385.8	349.9
China, People's Republic	211.7	229.5	212.7
Côte d'Ivoire	105.2	77.4	92.2
France (incl. Monaco)	2,241.3	2,086.1	2,159.4
Finland	81.5	97.4	96.6
Germany	645.1	678.7	709.6
Italy	845.8	907.4	811.1
Japan	205.7	356.6	273.1
Korea, Republic	209.4	308.8	185.5
Mexico	28.1	104.4	116.4
Netherlands	189.1	164.0	175.2
Russia	122.5	135.7	273.0
Spain	547.3	507.6	546.1
Sweden	105.0	75.4	55.6
Switzerland-Liechtenstein	105.3	107.8	110.4
Syria	135.8	65.4	25.9
Turkey	410.8	337.6	286.2
Ukraine	75.2	122.7	138.5
United Kingdom	250.4	218.6	210.1
USA	991.7	769.7	1,045.1
Total (incl. others)	9,403.4	9,161.9	9,152.1

Exports f.o.b.	1998	1999	2000
Belgium†	420.8	327.4	659.0
Brazil	632.2	964.0	1,502.7
Canada	358.9	405.0	779.7
France (incl. Monaco)	1,675.9	1,719.1	2,920.0
Germany	166.7	198.4	732.7
Italy	1,841.6	2,942.2	4,425.0
Netherlands	806.8	1,021.3	1,657.7
Portugal	61.5	154.0	249.5
Spain	960.3	1,329.0	2,329.1
Turkey	579.3	605.3	1,332.1
United Kingdom	258.4	233.2	647.7
USA	1,520.0	1,755.1	3,424.8
Total (incl. others)	9,838.6	12,525.3	22,031.3

* Imports by country of production; exports by country of last consignment.
† Figures for 1998 include trade with Luxembourg.

Source: UN, *International Trade Statistics Yearbook.*

Transport

RAILWAYS
(traffic)

	1997	1998	1999
Passengers carried ('000)	38,101	34,132	32,027
Freight carried ('000 metric tons)	7,927	8,292	7,842
Passenger-km (million)	1,360	1,163	1,069
Freight ton-km (million)	2,892	2,174	2,033

ROAD TRAFFIC
(motor vehicles in use at 31 December)

	1998	1999	2000
Passenger cars	1,634,394	1,676,784	1,692,148
Lorries	295,106	296,660	296,145
Vans	589,042	604,644	609,617
Buses and coaches	32,602	37,932	42,791
Motorcycles	9,025	9,119	9,198

SHIPPING

Merchant Fleet
(registered at 31 December)

	1999	2000	2001
Number of vessels	148	142	143
Total displacement ('000 grt) . .	1,004.7	960.8	963.9

Source: Lloyd's Register-Fairplay, *World Fleet Statistics*.

International Sea-borne Freight Traffic
('000 metric tons)

	1997	1998	1999
Goods loaded	74,300	75,500	77,900
Goods unloaded	15,200	16,000	16,600

Note: Figures are rounded to the nearest 100,000 metric tons.

CIVIL AVIATION
(traffic on scheduled services)

	1996	1997	1998
Kilometres flown (million) . . .	31	34	31
Passengers carried ('000) . . .	3,494	3,518	3,382
Passenger-km (million)	2,863	3,130	3,012
Total ton-km (million)	274	299	292

Source: UN, *Statistical Yearbook*.

Tourism

FOREIGN TOURIST ARRIVALS BY COUNTRY OF ORIGIN*

	1998	1999	2000
France	38,357	49,559	64,839
Germany	1,721	3,168	4,784
Italy	3,419	4,483	7,158
Libya	4,305	4,117	4,851
Mali	7,105	9,878	8,857
Morocco	2,399	2,949	3,805
Spain	5,518	4,652	7,048
Tunisia	20,056	22,779	32,481
Total (incl. others)	107,202	140,861	175,538

* Excluding arrivals of Algerian nationals resident abroad: 571,234 in 1998;
607,675 in 1999; 690,446 in 2000.

Source: World Tourism Organization, *Yearbook of Tourism Statistics*.

Tourism receipts (US $ million): 74 in 1998; 80 in 1999; 102 in 2000.

Communications Media

	1999	2000	2001
Television receivers ('000 in use)	3,300	3,400	n.a.
Telephones ('000 main lines in use)	1,600.0	1,761.3	1,880.0
Mobile cellular telephones			
(subscribers)	72	86	100
Personal computers ('000 in use)	180	200	220
Internet users ('000)	20	50	60

1990: Non-daily newspapers 37 (average circulation 1,409,000 copies);
Other periodicals 48 (average circulation 803,000 copies).

1996: Book production (titles)* 670; Daily newspapers 5 (average circulation 1,080,000 copies).

1997: Radio receivers ('000 in use): 7,100; Facsimile machines (number in use) 7,000.

* Excluding pamphlets.

Sources: UNESCO, *Statistical Yearbook* ; International Telecommunication Union.

Education

(1996/97, unless otherwise indicated)

	Institutions	Teachers	Pupils
Pre-primary	n.a.	1,333	33,503
Primary	15,426	170,956	4,674,947
Secondary:			
general	} 4,138 {	145,160	2,480,168
vocational		6,788	138,074
Higher:			
universities, etc.* . . .	n.a.	14,364	267,142
distance-learning			
institutions*	n.a.	3,213	60,095
other*	n.a.	2,333	20,173

* 1995/96.

Sources: UNESCO, *Statistical Yearbook* , and Ministère de l'Education nationale.

1998/99 (Pre-primary and primary): 15,729 institutions; 170,562 teachers;
4,843,313 pupils.

Adult literacy rate (UNESCO estimates): 66.7% (males 76.2%; females 57.1%) in 2000 (Source: UN Development Programme, *Human Development Report*).

Directory

The Constitution

A new Constitution for the Democratic and People's Republic of Algeria, approved by popular referendum, was promulgated on 22 November 1976. The Constitution was amended by the National People's Assembly on 30 June 1979. Further amendments were approved by referendum on 3 November 1988, on 23 February 1989, and on 28 November 1996. On 8 April 2002 the National People's Assembly approved an amendment, which granted Tamazight, the principal language spoken by the Berber population of the country, the status of a national language. The main provisions of the Constitution, as amended, are summarized below:

The preamble recalls that Algeria owes its independence to a war of liberation which led to the creation of a modern sovereign state, guaranteeing social justice, equality and liberty for all. It emphasizes Algeria's Islamic, Arab and Amazigh (Berber) heritage, and stresses that, as an Arab Mediterranean and African country, it forms an integral part of the Great Arab Maghreb.

FUNDAMENTAL PRINCIPLES OF THE ORGANIZATION OF ALGERIAN SOCIETY

The Republic

Algeria is a popular, democratic state. Islam is the state religion and Arabic and Tamazight are the official national languages.

The People

National sovereignty resides in the people and is exercised through its elected representatives. The institutions of the State consolidate national unity and protect the fundamental rights of its citizens. The exploitation of one individual by another is forbidden.

The State

The State is exclusively at the service of the people. Those holding positions of responsibility must live solely on their salaries and may not, directly or by the agency of others, engage in any remunerative activity.

Fundamental Freedoms and the Rights of Man and the Citizen

Fundamental rights and freedoms are guaranteed. All discrimination on grounds of sex, race or belief is forbidden. Law cannot operate retrospectively, and a person is presumed innocent until proved guilty. Victims of judicial error shall receive compensation from the State.

The State guarantees the inviolability of the home, of private life and of the person. The State also guarantees the secrecy of correspondence, the freedom of conscience and opinion, freedom of intellectual, artistic and scientific creation, and freedom of expression and assembly.

The State guarantees the right to form political associations (on condition that they are not based on differences in religion, language, race, gender or region), to join a trade union, the right to strike, the right to work, to protection, to security, to health, to leisure, to education, etc. It also guarantees the right to leave the national territory, within the limits set by law.

Duties of Citizens

Every citizen must respect the Constitution, and must protect public property and safeguard national independence. The law sanctions the duty of parents to educate and protect their children, as well as the duty of children to help and support their parents. Every citizen must contribute towards public expenditure through the payment of taxes.

The National Popular Army

The army safeguards national independence and sovereignty.

Principles of Foreign Policy

Algeria subscribes to the principles and objectives of the UN. It advocates international co-operation, the development of friendly relations between states, on the basis of equality and mutual interest, and non-interference in the internal affairs of states.

POWER AND ITS ORGANIZATION

The Executive

The President of the Republic is Head of State, Head of the Armed Forces and responsible for national defence. He must be of Algerian origin, a Muslim and more than 40 years old. He is elected by universal, secret, direct suffrage. His mandate is for five years, and is renewable once. The President embodies the unity of the nation. The President presides over meetings of the Council of Ministers. He decides and conducts foreign policy and appoints the Head of Government, who is responsible to the National People's Assembly. The Head of Government must appoint a Council of Ministers. He drafts, co-ordinates and implements his government's programme, which he must present to the Assembly for ratification. Should the Assembly reject the programme, the Head of Government and the Council of Ministers resign, and the President appoints a new Head of Government. Should the newly-appointed Head of Government's programme be rejected by the Assembly, the President dissolves the Assembly, and a general election is held. Should the President be unable to perform his functions, owing to a long and serious illness, the President of the Council of the Nation assumes the office for a maximum period of 45 days (subject to the approval of a two-thirds' majority in the National People's Assembly and the Council of the Nation). If the President is still unable to perform his functions after 45 days, the Presidency is declared vacant by the Constitutional Council. Should the Presidency fall vacant, the President of the Council of the Nation temporarily assumes the office and organizes presidential elections within 60 days. He may not himself be a candidate in the election. The President presides over a High Security Council which advises on all matters affecting national security.

The Legislature

The legislature consists of the Assemblée Populaire Nationale (National People's Assembly) and the Conseil de la Nation (Council of the Nation, which was established by constitutional amendments approved by national referendum in November 1996). The members of the lower chamber, the National People's Assembly, are elected by universal, direct, secret suffrage for a five-year term. Two-thirds of the members of the upper chamber, the Council of the Nation, are elected by indirect, secret suffrage from regional and municipal authorities; the remainder are appointed by the President of the Republic. The Council's term in office is six years; one-half of its members are replaced every three years. The deputies enjoy parliamentary immunity. The legislature sits for two ordinary sessions per year, each of not less than four months' duration. The commissions of the legislature are in permanent session. The two parliamentary chambers may be summoned to meet for an extraordinary session on the request of the President of the Republic, or of the Head of Government, or of two-thirds of the members of the National People's Assembly. Both the Head of Government and the parliamentary chambers may initiate legislation. Legislation must be deliberated upon respectively by the National People's Assembly and the Council of the Nation before promulgation. Any text passed by the Assembly must be approved by three-quarters of the members of the Council in order to become legislation.

The Judiciary

Judges obey only the law. They defend society and fundamental freedoms. The right of the accused to a defence is guaranteed. The Supreme Court regulates the activities of courts and tribunals, and the State Council regulates the administrative judiciary. The Higher Court of the Magistrature is presided over by the President of the Republic; the Minister of Justice is Vice-President of the Court. All magistrates are answerable to the Higher Court for the manner in which they fulfil their functions. The High State Court is empowered to judge the President of the Republic in cases of high treason, and the Head of Government for crimes and offences.

The Constitutional Council

The Constitutional Council is responsible for ensuring that the Constitution is respected, and that referendums, the election of the President of the Republic and legislative elections are conducted in accordance with the law. The Constitutional Council comprises nine members, of whom three are appointed by the President of the Republic, two elected by the National People's Assembly, two elected by the Council of the Nation, one elected by the Supreme Court and one elected by the State Council. The Council's term in office is six years; the President of the Council is appointed for a six-year term and one-half of the remaining members are replaced every three years.

The High Islamic Council

The High Islamic Council is an advisory body on matters relating to Islam. The Council comprises 15 members and its President is appointed by the President of the Republic.

Constitutional Revision

The Constitution can be revised on the initiative of the President of the Republic (subject to approval by the National People's Assembly and by three-quarters of the members of the Council of the Nation), and must be approved by national referendum. Should the Constitutional Council decide that a draft constitutional amendment does not in any way affect the general principles governing Algerian society, it may permit the President of the Republic to promulgate the amendment directly (without submitting it to referendum) if it has been approved by three-quarters of the members of both parliamentary chambers. Three-quarters of the members of both parliamentary chambers, in a joint sitting, may propose a constitutional amendment to the President of the Republic who may submit it to referendum. The basic principles of the Constitution may not be revised.

The Government

HEAD OF STATE

President and Minister of Defence: ABDELAZIZ BOUTEFLIKA (inaugurated 27 April 1999).

COUNCIL OF MINISTERS
(May 2003)

Prime Minister: AHMED OUYAHIA.

Minister of State for the Interior and Local Authorities: NOUREDINE YAZID ZERHOUNI.

Minister of State for Foreign Affairs: ABDELAZIZ BELKHADEM.

Minister of Justice and Attorney-General: MUHAMMAD CHARFI.

Minister of Commerce: NOUREDDINE BOUKROUH.

Minister of Energy and Mines: Prof. CHAKIB KHELIL.

Minister of Religious Affairs and Endowments: Prof. BOUABDELLAH GHLAMALLAH.

Minister of War Veterans: MUHAMMAD CHERIF ABBAS.

Minister of Town Planning and the Environment: Dr CHERIF RAHMANI.

Minister of Transport: ABDELMALEK SELLAL.

Minister of Youth and Sports: MUHAMMAD ALLALOU.

Minister of Agriculture and Rural Development: Dr SAÏD BERKAT.

Minister of Tourism: LAKHDAR DORBANI.

Minister of Public Works: Dr AMAR GHOUL.

Minister of Health, Population and Hospital Reform: Prof. ABDELHAMID ABERKANE.

Minister of Finance: ABDELATIF BENACHENHOU.

Minister of Communications and Culture, and Government Spokesperson: KHALIDA TOUMI-MESSAOUDI.

Minister of Water Resources: ADBELMADJID ATTAR.

Minister of Small and Medium-sized Enterprises and Handicrafts: MUSTAPHA BENBADA.

Minister of National Education: Prof. BOUBEKEUR BENBOUZID.

Minister of Higher Education and Scientific Research: Dr RACHID HARROUBIA.

Minister of Postal Services, Telecommunications and Information Technology: Prof. ZINE EDDINE YOUBI.

Minister of Vocational Training: Dr ABDELHAMID ABAD.

Minister of Housing and Urban Development: MUHAMMAD NADIR HAMIMID.

Minister of Industry: EL-HACHEMI DJAABOUB.

Minister of Labour and Social Security: TAYEB LOUH.

Minister of Employment and National Solidarity: TAYEB BELAIZ.

Minister in charge of Relations with Parliament: NOUREDDINE TALEB.

Minister of Fisheries and Marine Resources: Dr SMAIL MIMOUNE.

Minister-delegate to the Minister of State for Foreign Affairs, in charge of Maghreb and African Affairs: ABDELKADER MESSAHEL.

Minister-delegate to the Minister of State for the Interior and Local Authorities, responsible for Local Authorities: DAHO OULD KABLIA.

Minister-delegate to the Prime Minister, in charge of Family and Women's Affairs: Prof. BOUTHEINA CHERIET.

Minister-delegate to the Prime Minister, in charge of the Algerian Expatriate Community: FATMA ZOHRA BOUCHELMA.

Minister-delegate to the Prime Minister, in charge of Participation and Investment Promotion: KARIM DJOUDI.

Minister-delegate to the Minister of Town Planning and the Environment, in charge of Cities: BADREDINE BENZIOUECHE.

Minister-delegate to the Minister of Justice, in charge of Prison Reform: ABDELKADER SALLAT.

Minister-delegate to the Minister of Agriculture and Rural Development, in charge of Rural Development: Dr RACHID BENAISSA.

Minister-delegate to the Minister of Higher Education and Scientific Research, in charge of Scientific Research: Prof. LEILA HAMMOU BOUTLELIS.

Minister-delegate to the Minister of Finance, responsible for Financial Reform: FATIHA MENTOURI.

Secretary-General of the Government: AHMED NOUI.

MINISTRIES

Office of the President: Présidence de la République, el-Mouradia, Algiers; tel. (21) 69-15-15; fax (21) 69-15-95.

Office of the Prime Minister: rue Docteur Saâdane, Algiers; tel. (21) 73-23-40; fax (21) 71-79-27.

Ministry of Agriculture and Rural Development: 4 route des Quatre Canons, Algiers; tel. (21) 71-17-12; fax (21) 61-57-39; internet www.miniagri-algeria.org.

Ministry of Commerce: rue Docteur Saâdane, Algiers; tel. (21) 73-23-40; fax (21) 73-54-18; internet www.ministereducommerce-dz .org.

Ministry of Communications and Culture: Palais de la Culture, Les Annassers, BP 100, Kouba, Algiers; tel. (21) 29-12-28; fax (21) 29-20-89; e-mail info@mcc.gov.dz; internet www.mcc.gov.dz.

Ministry of Defence: Les Tagarins, el-Biar, Algiers; tel. (21) 71-15-15; fax (21) 64-67-26.

Ministry of Employment and National Solidarity: Route nationale 1, Les Vergers, BP 31, Bir Khadem, Algiers; tel. (21) 44-99-46; fax (21) 44-97-26; e-mail cellulemassn@massn.gov.dz; internet www .massn.gov.dz.

Ministry of Energy and Mines: 80 ave Ahmed Ghermoul, Algiers; tel. (21) 67-33-00; fax (21) 67-03-66; e-mail info@mem-algeria.org; internet www.mem-algeria.org.

Ministry of Finance: Immeuble Maurétania, place du Pérou, Algiers; tel. (21) 71-13-66; fax (21) 73-42-76; e-mail algeriafinance@ multimania.com; internet www.multimania.com/algeriafinance.

Ministry of Fisheries and Marine Resources: Route des Quatre Canons, Algiers; tel. (21) 43–31–81; fax (21) 21–43–31; e-mail mprh@wissal.dz; internet www.mprh-dz.com.

Ministry of Foreign Affairs: place Mohamed Seddik Benyahia, el-Mouradia, Algiers; tel. (21) 69-23-33; fax (21) 69-21-61; internet www.mae.dz.

Ministry of Health, Population and Hospital Reform: 125 rue Abd ar-Rahmane Laâla, el-Madania, Algiers; tel. (21) 68-29-00; fax (21) 66-24-13; internet www.ands.dz.

Ministry of Higher Education and Scientific Research: 11 rue Doudou Mokhtar, Algiers; tel. (21) 91-12-56; fax (21) 91-11-97; e-mail mesrs@ist.cerist.dz; internet www.mesrs.edu.dz.

Ministry of Housing and Urban Development: 135 rue Didouche Mourad, Algiers; tel. (21) 74-07-22; fax (21) 74-53-83; e-mail mhabitat@wissal.dz; internet www.mhu.gov.dz.

Ministry of Industry: Immeuble le Colisée, 4 rue Ahmed Bey, Algiers; tel. (21) 60-11-44; fax (21) 69-32-35; e-mail info@mir-algeria .org; internet www.mir-algeria.org.

Ministry of the Interior and Local Authorities: 18 rue Docteur Saâdane, Algiers; tel. (21) 73-23-40; fax (21) 73-43-67.

Ministry of Justice: 8 place Bir Hakem, el-Biar, Algiers; tel. (21) 92-41-83; fax (21) 92-25-60.

Ministry of Labour and Social Security: 40–44 blvd Mohamed Belouizdad, Algiers; tel. (21) 65-99-99; fax (21) 66-26-08; e-mail mtps@wissal.dz; internet www.mtss.gov.dz.

Ministry of National Education: 8 ave de Pékin, Algiers; tel. (21) 60-67-57; fax (21) 60-57-82; e-mail men@meducation.edu.dz; internet www.meducation.edu.dz.

Ministry of Participation and Investment Promotion: Chemin Ibn Badis el-Mouiz, El-Biar, Algiers; tel. (21) 92-98-85; fax (21) 92-17-55; internet www.mpcr-dz.com.

Ministry of Postal Services, Telecommunications and Information Technology: 4 blvd Krim Belkacem, Algiers; tel. (21) 71-12-20; fax (21) 71-92-71; internet www.barid.dz.

Ministry of Public Works: Algiers.

Ministry of Religious Affairs and Endowments: 4 rue de Timgad, Hydra, Algiers; tel. (21) 60-85-55; fax (21) 60-09-36.

Ministry of Small and Medium-sized Enterprises and Handicrafts: Immeuble le Colisée, 4 rue Ahmed Bey, Algiers; tel. (21) 69-73-63; fax (21) 23-00-94; internet www.pmepmi-dz.com.

Ministry of Tourism: 7 rue des Frères Ziata, el-Mouradia, 16000 Algiers; tel. (21) 60-33-55; fax (21) 59-13-15; internet www.tourisme .dz.

Ministry of Town Planning and the Environment: Algiers.

Ministry of Transport: 119 rue Didouche Mourad, Algiers; tel. (21) 74-06-99; fax (21) 74-33-95.

Ministry of Vocational Training: Algiers; e-mail abada@mfep .gov.dz; internet www.mfp.gov.dz.

Ministry of War Veterans: 2 ave du Lt. Med Benarfa, el-Biar, Algiers; tel. (21) 92-23-55; fax (21) 92-35-16.

Ministry of Water Resources: BP 86, Ex Grand Séminaire, Algiers; tel. (21) 68-95-00; fax (21) 58-63-64.

Ministry of Youth and Sports: 3 rue Mohamed Belouizdad, Place du 1er mai,Algiers; tel. (21) 65-55-55; fax (21) 68-41-71; e-mail mjsalgerie@mjs-dz.org; internet www.mjs.dz.

President and Legislature

PRESIDENT

Presidential Election, 15 April 1999

Candidate*	Votes	% of votes
Abdelaziz Bouteflika	7,445,045	73.76
Ahmed Taleb Ibrahimi	1,265,594	12.54
Sheikh Abdallah Djaballah	400,080	3.96
Hocine Aït Ahmed	321,179	3.18
Mouloud Hamrouche	314,160	3.11
Mokdad Sifi	226,139	2.24
Youcef Khateb	121,414	1.20
Total†	10,093,611	100.00

*Six of the seven presidential candidates withdrew prior to the election, leaving Abdelaziz Bouteflika as the only remaining official contestant.

† Excluding 559,012 invalid votes.

LEGISLATURE

National People's Assembly

President: Karim Younès.

General Election, 30 May 2002

	Votes	% of votes	Seats
Front de libération nationale (FLN)	2,618,003	35.28	199
Rassemblement national démocratique (RND)	610,461	8.23	47
Mouvement de la réforme nationale (MRN)	705,319	9.50	43
Mouvement de la société pour la paix (MSP)	523,464	7.05	38
Parti des travailleurs (PT)	246,770	3.33	21
Front national algérien	113,700	1.53	8
Nahdah	48,132	0.65	1
Parti du renouveau algérien (PRA)	19,873	0.27	1
Mouvement de l'entente nationale (MEN)	14,465	0.19	1
Independents	365,594	4.93	30
Others	2,155,056	29.04	—
Total	7,420,867	100.00	389

Council of the Nation

President: Abdelkader Bensalah.

Elections, 25 December 1997 and 30 December 2000*

	Seats*
Rassemblement national démocratique (RND)	74
Front de libération nationale (FLN)	15
Front des forces socialistes (FFS)	4
Mouvement de la société pour la paix (MSP)	3
Appointed by the President†	48
Total	144

* Deputies of the Council of the Nation serve a six-year term; one-half of its members are replaced every three years. Elected representatives are selected by indirect, secret suffrage from regional and municipal authorities.

† Appointed on 4 January 2001.

Political Organizations

Until 1989 the FLN was the only legal party in Algeria. The February 1989 amendments to the Constitution permitted the formation of other political associations, with some restrictions. The right to establish political parties was guaranteed by constitutional amendments in November 1996; however, political associations based on differences in religion, language, race, gender or region were proscribed. Some 39 political parties contested the legislative elections that took place in June 1997. The most important political organizations are listed below.

Alliance nationale républicaine (ANR): Algiers; f. 1995; anti-Islamist; Leader Redha Malek.

Congrès national algérien: Algiers; f. 1999; Leader Abdelkader Belhaye.

Front démocratique: Algiers; f. 1999; Leader Sid-Ahmed Ghozali.

Front des forces socialistes (FFS): 56 ave Souidani Boudjemaâ, 16000 Algiers; tel. (21) 59-33-13; fax (21) 59-11-45; internet www.f-f-s.com; f. 1963; revived 1990; Leader Hocine Aït Ahmed.

Front islamique du salut (FIS): Algiers; e-mail mail@fisalgeria.org; internet www.fisalgeria.org; f. 1989; aims to emphasize the importance of Islam in political and social life; formally dissolved by the Algiers Court of Appeal in March 1992; Leader Abbasi Madani.

Front de libération nationale (FLN): 7 rue du Stade, Hydra, Algiers; tel. (21) 59-21-49; f. 1954; sole legal party until 1989; socialist in outlook, the party is organized into a Secretariat, a Political Bureau, a Central Committee, Federations, Kasmas and cells; under the aegis of the FLN are various mass political organizations, including the Union Nationale de la Jeunesse Algérienne (UNJA) and the Union Nationale des Femmes Algériennes (UNFA); Sec.-Gen. Ali Benflis.

Front national algérien: Algiers; f. 1999; advocates eradication of poverty and supports the Govt's peace initiative; Pres. Moussa Touati.

Front national de renouvellement (FNR): Algiers; Leader Zineddine Cherifi.

Mouvement algérien pour la justice et le développement (MAJD): Villa Laibi, Lot Kapiot No. 5, Bouzaréah, Algiers; tel. (21) 60-58-00; fax (21) 78-78-72; f. 1990; reformist party supporting policies of fmr Pres. Boumedienne; Leader Moulay Habib.

Mouvement pour la démocratie et la citoyenneté (MDC): Tizi-Ouzou; f. 1997 by dissident members of the FFS; Leader Saïd Khelil.

Mouvement démocratique et social (MDS): Algiers; internet www.mds.pol.dz; f. 1998 by fmr mems of Ettahaddi; left-wing party; 4,000 mems; Sec.-Gen. Hachemi Cherif.

Mouvement pour la liberté: Algiers; f. 1999; in opposition to Pres. Bouteflika; Leader Mouloud Hamrouche.

Mouvement de la réforme nationale (MRN): Algiers; f. 1998; Leader Sheikh Abdallah Djaballah.

Mouvement de la société pour la paix (MSP): 163 Hassiba Ben Bouali, Algiers; e-mail bureau@hms-algeria.net; internet www.hms-algeria.net; f. as Hamas; adopted current name in 1997; moderate Islamic party, favouring the gradual introduction of an Islamic state; Leader Sheikh Mahfoud Nahnah.

Nahdah: Algiers; fundamentalist Islamist group; Sec.-Gen. Habib Adami.

Parti démocratique progressif (PDR): Algiers; f. 1990 as a legal party; Leader Saci Mabrouk.

Parti national pour la solidarité et le développement (PNSD): BP 110, Staouéli, Algiers; tel. and fax (21) 39-40-42; e-mail cherif_taleb@yahoo.fr; f. 1989 as Parti social démocrate; Leader Mohamed Cherif Taleb.

Parti du renouveau algérien (PRA): Algiers; tel. (21) 56-62-78; Sec.-Gen. Yacine Terkmane; Leader Noureddine Boukrouh.

Parti républicain progressif (PRP): 10 rue Ouahrani Abou-Mediène, Cité Seddikia, Oran; tel. (41) 35-79-36; f. 1990 as a legal party; Sec.-Gen. Slimane Cherif.

Parti des travailleurs (PT): Algiers; workers' party; Leader Louisa Hanoune.

Rassemblement pour la concorde nationale: Algiers; f. 2001 to support the policies of President Bouteflika; Chair. Sid Ahmed Abachi.

Rassemblement pour la culture et la démocratie (RCD): 40 rue Muhammad Chabane, el-Biar, Algiers; tel. (21) 92-50-76; fax (21) 92-51-01; internet www.rcd-algerie.org; f. 1989; secular party; advocates inclusion of Berber traditions into the Algerian identity; Pres. Saïd Saâdi.

Rassemblement national démocratique (RND): Algiers; f. 1997; centrist party; Sec.-Gen. Ahmed Ouyahia.

Union pour la démocratie et les libertés (UDL): Algiers; f. 1997; Leader Abdelkrim Seddiki.

Wafa wa al-Adl (Wafa): Algiers; f. 1999; Leader Ahmed Taleb Ibrahimi.

The following groups are in armed conflict with the Government:

Da'wa wal Djihad—Groupe salafiste pour la prédication et le combat (GSPC): f. 1998; breakaway group from the GIA; particularly active in the east of Algiers and in the Kabyle; responds to preaching by Ali Belhadj, the second most prominent member of the proscribed FIS; Leader Hassan Hattab.

Groupe islamique armé (GIA): the most prominent and radical Islamist militant group; Leader Rachid Abou Tourab.

Diplomatic Representation

EMBASSIES IN ALGERIA

Angola: 14 rue Marie Curie, el-Biar, Algiers; tel. (21) 92-54-41; fax (21) 79-74-41; Ambassador José César Augusto.

Argentina: 7 rue Hamami, 16000 Algiers; tel. (21) 71-86-83; fax (21) 64-38-43; e-mail emargentin@djazair-connect.com; Ambassador Jorge Alberto Rafael Vehils.

Austria: 17 chemin Abdel Kader Gadouche, 16035 Hydra, Algiers; tel. (21) 69-10-86; fax (21) 69-12-32; e-mail obalgier@mail.com; Ambassador Thomas Michael Baier.

Belgium: 22 chemin Youcef Tayebi, el-Biar, Algiers; tel. (21) 92-24-46; fax (21) 92-50-36; Ambassador Dirk Lettens.

Benin: 36 Lot du Stade, Birkhadem, Algiers; tel. (21) 56-52-71; Ambassador Leonard Adjin.

Brazil: 10 chemin Laroussi Messaoud Les Glycines, BP 186, Algiers; tel. (21) 74-95-75; fax (21) 74-96-87; Ambassador Sérgio Thompson-Flores.

Bulgaria: 13 blvd Col Bougara, Algiers; tel. (21) 23-00-14; fax (21) 23-05-33; Ambassador Peter Gradev.

Burkina Faso: 23 Lot el-Feth, Poirson, el-Biar, BP 212 Didouche Mourad, Algiers; tel. (21) 92-33-39; fax (21) 92-73-90; e-mail abf@wissal.dz; Ambassador Mamadou Serme.

Cameroon: 26 chemin Cheikh Bachir El-Ibrahimi, 16011 el-Biar, Algiers; tel. (21) 92-11-24; fax (21) 92-11-25; e-mail ambacam_alger@yahoo.fr; Chargé d'affaires Jean Missoup.

Canada: 18 rue Mustapha Khalef, Ben Aknoun, BP 48, 16000 Alger-Gare, Algiers; tel. (21) 91-49-51; fax (21) 91-49-73; e-mail alger@dfait-maeci.go.ca; Ambassador Richard Belliveau.

Chad: Villa No. 18, Cité DNC, chemin Ahmed Kara, Hydra, Algiers; tel. (21) 69-26-62; fax (21) 69-26-63; Ambassador El-Hadj Mahamoud Adji.

China, People's Republic: 34 blvd des Martyrs, Algiers; tel. (21) 69-27-24; fax (21) 69-29-62; Ambassador Wang Wangshen.

Congo, Democratic Republic: BP 302, Algiers; tel. (21) 59-12-27; Ambassador Ikaki Bomele Molingo.

Congo, Republic: 111 Parc Ben Omar, Kouba, Algiers; tel. (21) 58-68-00; Ambassador Pierre N'Gaka.

Côte d'Ivoire: Immeuble 'Le Bosquet', Le Paradou, BP 260 Hydra, Algiers; tel. (21) 69-23-78; fax (21) 69-30-32; e-mail acialg@yahoo.fr; Ambassador Largatton Gilbert Ouattara.

Cuba: 22 rue Larbi Alik, Hydra, Algiers; tel. (21) 69-21-48; fax (21) 69-32-81; Ambassador Rafael Polanco Brahojos.

Czech Republic: BP 358, Villa Koudia, 3 chemin Ziryab, Alger-Gare, Algiers; tel. (21) 23-00-56; fax (21) 23-01-03; e-mail algiers@embassy.mzv.cz; internet www.mzv.cz/algiers; Ambassador Jaromír Marek.

Denmark: 12 ave Emile Marquis, Lot Djenane el-Malik, 16035 Hydra, BP 384, 16000 Alger-Gare, Algiers; tel. (21) 69-27-55; fax (21) 69-28-46; e-mail ambadane@djazair-connect.com; Ambassador Bo Eric Weber.

Egypt: BP 297, 8 chemin Abdel-Kader Gadouche, 16300 Hydra, Algiers; tel. (21) 60-16-73; fax (21) 60-29-52; Ambassador Ibrahim Youssri.

Finland: BP 256, 16035 Hydra, Algiers; tel. (21) 69-29-25; fax (21) 69-16-37; e-mail finamb@wissal.dz.

France: chemin Abd al-Kader Gadouche, Hydra, Algiers; tel. (21) 69-24-88; fax (21) 69-13-69; Ambassador Daniel Bernard.

Gabon: BP 125, Rostomia, 21 rue Hadj Ahmed Mohamed, Hydra, Algiers; tel. (21) 69-24-00; fax (21) 60-25-46; Ambassador Yves Ongollo.

Germany: BP 664, Alger-Gare, 165 chemin Sfindja, Algiers; tel. (21) 74-19-56; fax (21) 74-05-21; e-mail info@allemagne-dj.org; Ambassador Hans Peter Schiff.

Ghana: 62 rue des Frères Benali Abdellah, Hydra, Algiers; tel. (21) 60-64-44; fax (21) 69-28-56; Ambassador George A. O. Kugblenu.

Greece: 60 blvd Col Bougara, Algiers; tel. (21) 92-34-91; fax (21) 69-16-55; Ambassador Ioannis Drakoularakos.

Guinea: 43 blvd Central Saïd Hamdine, Hydra, Algiers; tel. (21) 69-20-66; fax (21) 69-34-68; Ambassador Mamady Condé.

Guinea-Bissau: 17 rue Ahmad Kara, BP 32, Colonne Volrol, Hydra, Algiers; tel. (21) 60-01-51; fax (21) 60-97-25; Ambassador José Pereira Batista.

Holy See: 1 rue Noureddine Mekiri, 16021 Bologhine, Algiers (Apostolic Nunciature); tel. (21) 95-45-20; fax (21) 95-40-95; e-mail nuntiusalger@hotmail.com; Apostolic Nuncio Most Rev. Augustine Kasujja (Titular Archbishop of Caesarea in Numidia).

Hungary: BP 68, 18 ave des Frères Oughlis, el-Mouradia, Algiers; tel. (21) 69-79-75; fax (21) 69-81-86; e-mail huembalg@yahoo.com; Chargé d'affaires László Szabó.

India: 14 rue des Abassides, BP 108, el-Biar, 16030 Algiers; tel. (21) 92-04-11; fax (21) 92-32-88; e-mail indemb@wissal.dz; Ambassador (vacant).

Indonesia: BP 62, 16 chemin Abd al-Kader Gadouche, 16070 el-Mouradia, Algiers; tel. (21) 69-20-11; fax (21) 69-39-31; Ambassador Lillahi Grahana Sidharta.

Iraq: 4 rue Abri Arezki, Hydra, Algiers; tel. (21) 69-31-25; fax (21) 69-10-97; Ambassador Abd al-Karim al-Mulla.

Italy: 18 rue Muhammad Ouidir Amellal, el-Biar, 16030 Algiers; tel. (21) 92-23-30; fax (21) 92-59-86; e-mail ambitalgeri@ambitalgeri.org; Ambassador Romualdo Bettini.

Japan: 1 chemin el-Bakri, el-Biar, Algiers; tel. (21) 91-20-04; fax (21) 91-20-46; Ambassador Urabe Akira.

Jordan: 47 rue Ammani Belkalem, Hydra, Algiers; tel. (21) 60-20-31; e-mail jordan@wissal.dz; Ambassador Abdullah el-Ayyam.

Korea, Democratic People's Republic: 49 rue Hamlia, Bologhine, Algiers; tel. (21) 62-39-27; Ambassador Pak Ho Il.

Korea, Republic: BP 92, 17 chemin Abdelkader Gadouche, Hydra, Algiers; tel. (21) 69-36-20; fax (21) 69-16-03; Ambassador Heung-Sik Choi.

Kuwait: chemin Abd al-Kader Gadouche, Hydra, Algiers; tel. (21) 59-31-57; Ambassador Shamlan Abd-al-Aziz Muhammad ar-Rumi.

Lebanon: 9 rue Kaïd Ahmad, el-Biar, Algiers; tel. (21) 78-20-94; Ambassador Salhad Nasri.

Libya: 15 chemin Cheikh Bachir Ibrahimi, Algiers; tel. (21) 92-15-02; fax (21) 92-46-87; Ambassador Abdel-Moula el-Ghadhbane.

Madagascar: 22 rue Abd al-Kader Aouis, 16090 Bologhine, BP 65, Algiers; tel. (21) 95-03-89; fax (21) 95-17-76; Ambassador Laurent Radaody-Rakotondravao.

Mali: Villa 15, Cité DNC/ANP, chemin Ahmed Kara, Hydra, Algiers; tel. (21) 69-13-51; fax (21) 69-20-82; Ambassador Cheick S. Diarra.

Mauritania: 107 Lot Baranès, Aire de France, Bouzaréah, Algiers; tel. (21) 79-21-39; fax (21) 78-42-74; Ambassador Sid Ahmed Ould Babamine.

Mexico: BP 329, 21 rue du Commandant Amar Azzouz (ex rue Général Lapperine), el-Biar, 16030 Algiers; tel. (21) 92-40-23; fax (21) 92-34-51; e-mail mexiarl@ist.wissal.dz; Ambassador Franciso Correa Villalobos.

Morocco: 8 rue des Cèdres, el-Mouradia, Algiers; tel. (21) 69-14-08; fax (21) 69-29-00; Ambassador Abderrazak Doghmi.

Netherlands: BP 72, el-Biar, Algiers; tel. (21) 92-28-28; fax (21) 92-37-70; e-mail alg@minbuza.nl; Ambassador J. W. de Waal.

Niger: 54 rue Vercors Rostamia Bouzaréah, Algiers; tel. (21) 78-89-21; fax (21) 78-97-13; Ambassador Gourouza Oumarou.

Nigeria: BP 629, 27 bis rue Blaise Pascal, Algiers; tel. (21) 69-18-49; fax (21) 69-11-75; Ambassador Aliyu Mohammed.

Oman: 53 rue Djamel Eddine, El Afghani, Bouzaréah, Algiers; tel. (21) 94-13-10; fax (21) 94-13-75; Ambassador Hellal as-Siyabi.

Pakistan: BP 404, 62A Djenane el-Malik, Le Pardou, Hydra, Algiers; tel. (21) 69-37-81; fax (21) 69-22-12; e-mail parepalgiers@gwissal.dz; Ambassador M. Aslam Rizvi.

Poland: 37 ave Mustafa Ali Khodja, el-Biar, Algiers; tel. (21) 92-25-53; fax (21) 92-14-35; e-mail lupina@wissal.dz; Ambassador Andrzej Michal Lupina.

Portugal: 4 rue Mohamed Khoudi, el-Biar, Algiers; tel. (21) 92-53-13; fax (21) 92-54-14; e-mail portemdz@hotmail.com; Ambassador Eduardo Farinha Fernandes.

Qatar: BP 118, 7 chemin Doudou Mokhtar, Algiers; tel. (21) 92-28-56; fax (21) 92-24-15; Ambassador Hussain Ali ed-Dousri.

Romania: 24 rue Abri Arezki, Hydra, Algiers; tel. (21) 60-08-71; fax (21) 69-36-42; Ambassador Dumitru Olaru.

Russia: 7 chemin du Prince d'Annam, el-Biar, Algiers; tel. (21) 92-31-39; fax (21) 92-28-82; Ambassador Aleksandr Adsenyonok.

Saudi Arabia: 62 rue Med. Drafini, chemin de la Madeleine, Hydra, Algiers; tel. (21) 60-35-18; Ambassador HASAN FAQQI.

Senegal: BP 379, Alger-Gare, 1 chemin Mahmoud Drarnine, Hydra, Algiers; tel. (21) 69-16-27; fax (21) 69-26-84; Ambassador SAÏDOU NOUROU.

Serbia and Montenegro: BP 561, 7 rue des Frères Ben-hafid, Hydra, Algiers; tel. (21) 69-12-18; fax (21) 69-34-72; e-mail yuga@wissal.dz; Chargé d'affaires a.i. JOVAN DASIĆ.

Slovakia: BP 84, 7 chemin du Ziryab, Didouche Mourad, 16006 Algiers; tel. (21) 23-01-31; fax (21) 23-00-51; e-mail amb.slovaque .alger@centrum.sk; Chargé d'affaires a.i. Dr JÁN DÖMÖK.

South Africa: Sofitel Hotel, 172 rue Hassuba Ben Bouali, Algiers; tel. (21) 68-52-10; fax (21) 66-21-04.

Spain: 46 bis rue Mohamed Chabane, el-Biar, Algiers; tel. (21) 92-27-13; fax (21) 92-27-19; Ambassador EMILIO FERNÁNDEZ-CASTAÑO.

Sudan: Algiers; tel. (21) 56-66-23; fax (21) 69-30-19; Ambassador YOUCEF FADUL AHMED.

Sweden: rue Olof Palme, Nouveau Paradou, Hydra, Algiers; tel. (21) 69-23-00; fax (21) 69-19-17; Ambassador ANDREAS ADAHL.

Switzerland: BP 443, 2 rue Numéro 3, 16035 Hydra, Algiers; tel. (21) 60-04-22; fax (21) 60-98-54; Ambassador ANDRÉ VON GRAFFENINED.

Syria: Domaine Tamzali, 11 chemin Abd al-Kader Gadouche, Hydra, Algiers; tel. (21) 91-20-26; fax (21) 91-20-30; Ambassador HAMMADI SAID.

Tunisia: 11 rue du Bois de Boulogne, el-Mouradia, Algiers; tel. (21) 60-13-88; fax (21) 69-23-16; Ambassador MOHAMED EL FADHAL KHALIL.

Turkey: Villa dar el Ouard, chemin de la Rochelle, blvd Col Bougara, Algiers; tel. (21) 23-00-04; fax (21) 23-01-12; e-mail cezayir.be@mfa.gov.tr; Ambassador ATTILA UZER.

Ukraine: 199 rue des Frères Belhafid, Hydra, Algiers; tel. (21) 69-13-87; fax (21) 69-48-48; e-mail ekambas@gecos.net; Ambassador MYKHAILO DASHKEVYCH.

United Arab Emirates: BP 165, Alger-Gare, 14 rue Muhammad Drarini, Hydra, Algiers; tel. (21) 69-25-74; fax (21) 69-37-70; Ambassador HAMAD SAÏD AZ-ZAABI.

United Kingdom: BP 08, Alger-Gare, 16000 Algiers, 6 ave Souidani Boudjemaa, Algiers; tel. (21) 23-00-68; fax (21) 23-00-67; Ambassador GRAHAM HAND.

USA: BP 549, 4 chemin Cheikh Bachir Ibrahimi, 16000 Alger-Gare, Algiers; tel. (21) 60-11-86; fax (21) 60-39-79; e-mail amembalg@ist .cerist.dz; Ambassador JANET SANDERSON.

Venezuela: BP 297, 3 impasse Ahmed Kara, Algiers; tel. (21) 69-38-46; fax (21) 69-35-55; Ambassador EDUARDO SOTO ALVAREZ.

Viet Nam: 30 rue de Chenoua, Hydra, Algiers; tel. (21) 69-27-52; fax (21) 69-37-78; Ambassador TRAN XUAN MAN.

Yemen: Villa 19, Cité DNC, rue Ahmed Kara, Hydra, Algiers; tel. (21) 69-30-85; fax (21) 69-17-58; Ambassador GASSEM ASKAR DJEBRANE.

Judicial System

The highest court of justice is the Supreme Court (Cour suprême) in Algiers, established in 1963, which is served by 150 judges. Justice is exercised through 183 courts (tribunaux) and 31 appeal courts (cours d'appel), grouped on a regional basis. New legislation, promulgated in March 1997, provided for the eventual establishment of 214 courts and 48 appeal courts. The Cour des comptes was established in 1979. Algeria adopted a penal code in 1966, retaining the death penalty. In February 1993 three special courts were established to try suspects accused of terrorist offences; however, the courts were abolished in February 1995. Constitutional amendments introduced in November 1996 provided for the establishment of a High State Court (empowered to judge the President of the Republic in cases of high treason, and the Head of Government for crimes and offences), and a State Council to regulate the administrative judiciary. In addition, a Conflicts Tribunal is to be established to adjudicate in disputes between the Supreme Court and the State Council.

Supreme Court
ave du 11 décembre 1960, Ben Aknoun, Algiers; tel. and fax (21) 92-44-89.

President of Supreme Court: MUHAMMAD ZAGHLOUL BOUTERENE.

Attorney-General: MUHAMMAD CHARFI.

Religion

ISLAM
Islam is the official religion, and the whole Algerian population, with a few exceptions, is Muslim.

High Islamic Council
place Cheikh Abd al-Hamid ibn Badis, Algiers.

President of the High Islamic Council: (vacant).

CHRISTIANITY
The European inhabitants, and a few Arabs, are generally Christians, mostly Roman Catholics.

The Roman Catholic Church
Algeria comprises one archdiocese and three dioceses (including one directly responsible to the Holy See). In December 2000 there were an estimated 3,450 adherents in the country.

Bishops' Conference
Conférence des Evêques de la Région Nord de l'Afrique (CERNA), 13 rue Khélifa-Boukhalfa, 16000 Alger-Gare, Algiers; tel. (21) 63-35-62; fax (21) 63-38-42; e-mail seercerna@yahoo.fr.
f. 1985; Pres. Most Rev. HENRI TEISSIER (Archbishop of Algiers); Sec.-Gen. Fr BERNARD LEFEBVRE.

Archbishop of Algiers: Most Rev. HENRI TEISSIER, 22 Chemin d'Hydra, 16030 El Biar, Algiers; tel. (21) 92-56-67; fax (21) 92-55-76; e-mail evechealger@yahoo.fr.

Protestant Church

Protestant Church of Algeria: 31 rue Reda Houhou, 16000 Alger-Gare, Algiers; tel. and fax (21) 71-62-38; three parishes; 1,500 mems; Pastor Dr HUGH G. JOHNSON.

The Press

DAILIES

L'Authentique: Algiers; internet www.authentique-dz.com; French.

Ach-Cha'ab (The People): 1 place Maurice Audin, Algiers; e-mail ech-chaab@ech-chaab.com; internet www.ech-chaab.com; f. 1962; FLN journal in Arabic; Dir KAMEL AVACHE; circ. 24,000.

La Dépêche de Kabylie: f. 2002; Dir AMARA BENYOUNES.

Al-Djeza'ir El-Ghad (Algeria of Tomorrow): Algiers; f. 1999; Arabic; Editor MUSTAPHA HACINI.

Echourouk El Yaoumi: Algiers; f. 2000; Arabic.

L'Expression, Le Quotidien: Maison de la Presse, Kouba, Algiers; tel. (21) 23-37-97; fax (21) 23-25-80; e-mail direction@lexpressiondz .com; internet www.lexpressiondz.com; f. 2000; French; Editor AHMED FATTANI; circ. 70,000.

El Fedjr: Algiers; f. 2000; Arabic.

Horizons: 20 rue de la Liberté, Algiers; tel. (21) 73-47-25; fax (21) 73-61-34; e-mail admin@horizons-dz.com; internet www.horizons-dz .com; f. 1985; evening; French; circ. 35,000.

Le Jeune Indépendant: Algiers; tel. (21) 67-07-48; fax (21) 67-07-46; e-mail redaction@jeune-independant.com; internet www .jeune-independant.com; f. 1990; French; circ. 60,000.

Al-Joumhouria (The Republic): 6 rue Bensenouci Hamida, Oran; f. 1963; Arabic; Editor BOUKHALFA BENAMEUR; circ. 20,000.

Le Journal: Algiers; f. 1992; French.

El Khabar: Maison de Presse 'Abdelkader Safir', 2 rue Farid Zouioueche, Kouba, Algiers; tel. (21) 49-53-91; fax (21) 49-53-90; e-mail admin@elkhabar.com; internet www.elkhabar.com; f. 1990; Arabic; Dir-Gen. ALI DJERRI; circ. 450,000.

Liberté: 37 rue Larbi Ben M'Hidi, BP 178, Alger-Gare, Algiers; tel. (21) 69-25-88; fax (21) 69-35-46; e-mail webmaster@liberte-algeria .com; internet www.liberte-algerie.com; French; independent; Dir-Gen. ABROUS OUTOUDERT; circ. 20,000.

Al-Massa: Maison de la Presse, Abd al-Kader Safir, Kouba, Algiers; tel. (21) 59-54-19; fax (21) 59-64-57; f. 1977; evening; Arabic; circ. 45,000.

Le Matin: Maison de la Presse, 1 rue Bachir Attar, 16016 Algiers; tel. (21) 66-07-08; fax (21) 66-20-97; e-mail info@lematin-dz.com; internet www.lematin-dz.com; French; Dir MUHAMMAD BENCHICOU.

El-Moudjahid (The Fighter): 20 rue de la Liberté, Algiers; tel. (21) 73-70-81; fax (21) 73-90-43; e-mail redchef@elmoudjahid-dz.com; internet www.elmoudjahid-dz.com; f. 1965; govt journal in French and Arabic; Dir ABDELMAJID CHERBAL; circ. 392,000.

An-Nasr (The Victory): BP 388, Zone Industrielle, La Palma, Constantine; tel. (31) 93-92-16; f. 1963; Arabic; Editor ABDALLAH GUETTAT; circ. 340,000.

La Nouvelle République: Algiers; French.

Ouest Tribune: Oran; e-mail redact@ouest-tribune.com; internet www.ouest-tribune.com; French.

Le Quotidien d'Oran: 63 ave de l'ANP, BP 110, Oran; tel. (41) 32-63-09; fax (41) 32-51-36; internet www.quotidien-oran.com; French.

Le Soir d'Algérie: Algiers; e-mail info@lesoirdalgerie.com; internet www.lesoirdalgerie.com; f. 1990; evening; independent information journal in French; Editors ZOUBIR SOUISSI, MAAMAR FARRAH; circ. 80,000.

La Tribune: Algiers; e-mail latribune@latribune-online.com; internet www.latribune-online.com; f. 1994; current affairs journal in French; Editor BAYA GACEMI.

El Watan: Maison de la Presse, 1 rue Bachir Attar, 16016 Algiers; tel. (21) 68-21-83; fax (21) 68-21-87; e-mail infos@elwatan.com; internet www.elwatan.com; French; Dir OMAR BELHOUCHET.

El-Youm: 1 rue Bachir Attar, place du 1er mai, Algiers; tel. (21) 67-39-37; fax (21) 67-39-49; e-mail info@el-youm.com; internet www.el-youm.com; Arabic; circ. 54,000.

WEEKLIES

Algérie Actualité: 2 rue Jacques Cartier, 16000 Algiers; tel. (21) 63-54-20; f. 1965; French; Dir KAMEL BELKACEM; circ. 250,000.

Al-Hadef (The Goal): Algiers; tel. (21) 93-92-16; f. 1972; sports; French; Editor-in-Chief LARBI MOHAMED ABBOUD; circ. 110,000.

Libre Algérie: Algiers; French; organ of the FFS.

La Nation: 33 rue Larbi Ben M'hidi, Algiers; f. 1993; French; Editor SALIMA GHEZALI; circ. 35,000.

Révolution Africaine: Algiers; tel. (21) 59-77-91; fax (21) 59-77-92; current affairs journal in French; socialist; Dir FERRAH ABDELLALI; circ. 50,000.

El Wadjh al-Akhar (The Other Face): Algiers; Arabic.

OTHER PERIODICALS

Al-Acala: 4 rue Timgad, Hydra, Algiers; tel. (21) 60-85-55; fax (21) 60-09-36; f. 1970; published by the Ministry of Religious Affairs and Endowments; fortnightly; Editor MUHAMMAD AL-MAHDI.

Algérie Médicale: Algiers; f. 1964; publ. of Union médicale algérienne; 2 a year; circ. 3,000.

Alouan (Colours): 119 rue Didouche Mourad, Algiers; f. 1973; cultural review; monthly; Arabic.

Bibliographie de l'Algérie: Bibliothèque Nationale d'Algérie, BP 127, Hamma el-Annasser, 16000 Algiers; tel. (21) 67-18-67; fax (21) 67-29-99; f. 1963; lists books, theses, pamphlets and periodicals published in Algeria; 2 a year; Arabic and French; Dir-Gen. MOHAMED AÏSSA OUMOUSSA.

Ach-Cha'ab ath-Thakafi (Cultural People): Algiers; f. 1972; cultural monthly; Arabic.

Ach-Chabab (Youth): Algiers; journal of the UNJA; bi-monthly; French and Arabic.

Al-Djeich (The Army): Office de l'Armée Nationale Populaire, Algiers; f. 1963; monthly; Algerian army review; Arabic and French; circ. 10,000.

Journal Officiel de la République Algérienne Démocratique et Populaire: BP 376, Saint-Charles, Les Vergers, Bir Mourad Rais, Algiers; tel. (21) 54-35-06; fax (21) 54-35-12; f. 1962; French and Arabic.

Nouvelles Economiques: 6 blvd Amilcar Cabral, Algiers; f. 1969; publ. of Institut Algérien du Commerce Extérieur; monthly; French and Arabic.

Révolution et Travail: Maison du Peuple, 1 rue Abdelkader Benbarek, place du 1er mai, Algiers; tel. (21) 66-73-53; journal of UGTA (central trade union) with Arabic and French editions; monthly; Editor-in-Chief RACHIB AÏT ALI.

Revue Algérienne du Travail: Algiers; f. 1964; labour publication; quarterly; French.

Ath-Thakafa (Culture): 2 place Cheikh ben Badis, Algiers; tel. (21) 62-20-73; f. 1971; every 2 months; cultural review; Editor-in-Chief CHEBOUB OTHMANE; circ. 10,000.

NEWS AGENCIES

Agence Algérienne d'Information: Maison de la Presse Tahar Djaout, 1 rue Bachir Attar, place de 1er mai, Algiers; tel. (21) 67-52-34; fax (21) 67-07-32; e-mail redaction@aai-online.com; internet www.aai-online.com; f. 1999; Dir FILALI HOURIA.

Algérie Presse Service (APS): 2 rue Farid Zouioueche, Kouba, 16050 Algiers; tel. (21) 68-94-43; fax (21) 68-91-45; e-mail aps@wissal.dz; internet www.aps.dz; f. 1961; provides news reports in Arabic, English and French.

Foreign Bureaux

Agence France-Presse (AFP): 6 rue Abd al-Karim el-Khettabi, Algiers; tel. (21) 72-16-54; fax (21) 72-14-89; Chief MARC PONDAVEN.

Agencia EFE (Spain): 4 ave Pasteur, 15000 Algiers; tel. (21) 71-85-59; fax (21) 73-77-62; Chief MANUEL OSTOS LÓPEZ.

Agenzia Nazionale Stampa Associata (ANSA) (Italy): 4 ave Pasteur, Algiers; tel. (21) 63-73-14; fax (21) 61-25-84; Rep. CARLO DI RENZO.

Associated Press (AP) (USA): BP 769, 4 ave Pasteur, Algiers; tel. (21) 63-59-41; fax (21) 63-59-42; Rep. RACHID KHIARI.

Informatsionnoye Telegrafnoye Agentstvo Rossii—Telegrafnoye Agentstvo Suverennykh Stran (ITAR—TASS) (Russia): 21 rue de Boulogne, Algiers; Chief KONSTANTIN DUDAREV.

Rossiiskoye Informatsionnoye Agentstvo—Novosti (RIA—Novosti) (Russia): Algiers; Chief Officer YURII S. BAGDASAROV.

Xinhua (New China) News Agency (People's Republic of China): 32 rue de Carthage, Hydra, Algiers; tel. and fax (21) 69-27-12; Chief WANG LIANZHI.

Wikalat al-Maghreb al-Arabi (Morocco), the Middle East News Agency (Egypt) and Reuters (UK) are also represented.

Publishers

Entreprise Nationale du Livre (ENAL): 3 blvd Zirout Youcef, BP 49, Algiers; tel. and fax (21) 73-58-41; f. 1966 as Société Nationale d'Edition et de Diffusion, name changed 1983; publishes books of all types, and imports, exports and distributes printed material, stationery, school and office supplies; Pres. and Dir-Gen. HASSEN BENDIF.

Office des Publications Universitaires: 1 place Centrale de Ben Aknoun, Algiers; tel. (21) 78-87-18; publishes university textbooks.

Broadcasting and Communications

TELECOMMUNICATIONS

New legislation approved by the National People's Assembly in August 2000 removed the state's monopoly over the telecommunications sector and redefined its role to that of a supervisory authority. Under the legislation an independent regulator for the sector was created, and both the fixed-line and mobile sectors were opened to foreign competition.

Algérie Télécom: Route Nationale 5, Cinq Maisons Muhammadia, El-Harrech, Algiers; tel. (21) 82–38–38; fax (21) 82–38–39; e-mail at@postelecom.dz; internet www.postelecom.dz; f. 2001 to manage and develop telecommunications infrastructure.

Autorité de Régulation de la Poste et des Télécommunications (ARPT): 4 blvd Col Krim Belkacem, 16027 Algiers; e-mail arpt.lic@postelecom.dz; f. 2001; Dir-Gen. AHMAD GACEB.

Djezzy GSM: Orascom Telecom Algérie, Algiers; tel. (21) 54-00-53; e-mail souheila.battou@otalgerie.com; internet www.otalgerie.com; f. 2002; operates mobile cellular telephone network; Group Chair. NAGUIB SAWIRIS.

Entreprise Nationale des Télécommunications (ENTC): 1 ave du 1er novembre, Tlemcen; tel. (43) 20-76-71; fax (43) 26-39-51; f. 1978; national telecommunications org; jt venture with Sweden; Dir-Gen. SIBAWAGHI SAKER.

BROADCASTING

Radio

Arabic Network: transmitters at Adrar, Aïn Beïda, Algiers, Béchar, Béni Abbès, Djanet, El Goléa, Ghardaia, Hassi Messaoud, In Aménas, In Salah, Laghouat, Les Trembles, Ouargla, Reggane, Tamanrasset, Timimoun, Tindouf.

French Network: transmitters at Algiers, Constantine, Oran and Tipaza.

Kabyle Network: transmitter at Algiers.

Radiodiffusion Algérienne: 21 blvd des Martyrs, Algiers; tel. (21) 69-12-81; fax (21) 23-08-23; e-mail info@algerian-radio.dz; internet www.algerian-radio.dz; govt-controlled; Dir-Gen. ABDELKADER LALMI.

Television

The principal transmitters are at Algiers, Batna, Sidi-Bel-Abbès, Constantine, Souk-Ahras and Tlemcen. Television plays a major role in the national education programme.

Télévision Algérienne (ENTV): 21 blvd des Martyrs, Algiers; tel. (21) 60-23-00; fax (21) 60-19-22; internet www.entv.dz; Dir-Gen. HAMRAOUI HABIB CHAWKI.

Finance

(cap. = capital; res = reserves; dep. = deposits; brs = branches; m. = million; amounts in Algerian dinars)

BANKING

Central Bank

Banque d'Algérie: 38 ave Franklin Roosevelt, 16000 Algiers; tel. (21) 23-00-23; fax (21) 23-01-50; e-mail bacom@ist.cerist.dz; internet www.bank-of-algeria.dz; f. 1963 as Banque Centrale d'Algérie; present name adopted 1990; cap. 40m. bank of issue; Gov. MUHAMMAD LAKSACI; 50 brs.

Nationalized Banks

Banque Al-Baraka d'Algérie: Haï Bouteldja Houidef, Villa n°1 Rocades Sud, Ben Aknoun, Algiers; tel. (21) 91-64-50; fax (21) 91-64-57; e-mail info@albaraka-bank.com; internet www.albaraka-bank.com; f. 1991; cap. 500m., res 532.8m., dep. 9,771.3m. (Dec. 2000); Algeria's first Islamic financial institution; owned by the Jeddah-based Al-Baraka Investment and Development Co (50%) and the local Banque de l'Agriculture et du Développement Rural (BADR) (50%); Chair. ADNANE AHMAD YOUCEF; Gen. Man. MUHAMMAD SEDDIK HAFID.

Banque Extérieure d'Algérie (BEA): 11 blvd Col Amirouche, 16000, Algiers; tel. (21) 45-90-25; fax (21) 45-90-26; e-mail dircom@bea.dz; internet www.bea.dz; f. 1967; cap. 5,600m., res 12,417m., dep. 362,283m. (Dec. 1999); chiefly concerned with energy and maritime transport sectors; Chair. M. TERBECHE; Dir-Gen. HOCINE HANNACHI; 81 brs.

Banque du Maghreb Arabe pour l'Investissement et le Commerce: 7 rue de Bois, Hydra, Algiers; tel. (21) 59-07-60; fax (21) 59-02-30; owned by the Algerian Govt (50%) and the Libyan Govt (50%); Pres. M. HAKIKI; Dir-Gen. IBRAHIM ALBISHARY.

Banque Nationale d'Algérie (BNA): 8 blvd Ernesto Ché Guévara, 16000 Algiers; tel. (21) 71-55-64; fax (21) 71-47-59; e-mail dg-bna@bna.com.dz; internet www.bna.com.dz; f. 1966; cap. 8,000m., res 10,227m., dep. 68,920m. (Dec. 1995); specializes in industry, transport and trade sectors; Chair. and Man. Dir MUHAMMAD TERBECHE; 163 brs.

Crédit Populaire d'Algérie (CPA): BP 1031, 2 blvd Col Amirouche, 16000 Algiers; tel. (21) 63-56-84; fax (21) 63-57-13; e-mail cpadmc@gecos.net; internet www.cpa-bank.com; f. 1966; cap. 21,600m., total assets 342,045m. (Dec. 2000); specializes in light industry, construction and tourism; partial privatization pending; Chair. EL HACHEMI MEGHAOUI; Dir-Gen. FERHAT SAOUILI; 121 brs.

Development Banks

Banque de l'Agriculture et du Développement Rural (BADR): 17 blvd Col Amirouche, 16000 Algiers; tel. (21) 63-49-22; fax (21) 63-51-46; internet www.badr-dz.com; f. 1982; cap. 33,000m., res 1,473m., dep. 368,560m. (Dec. 1999); finance for the agricultural sector; Chair. and Man. Dir FAROUK BOUYAKOUB; 270 brs.

Banque Algérienne de Développement (BAD): Lot Mont-Froid, Zonka, Birkhadem, BP 36, 13336 Algiers; tel. (21) 55-22-89; fax (21) 55-48-63; e-mail bad@ist.cerist.dz; f. 1963; cap. 100m., total assets 152,082.0m. (Dec. 1999); a public establishment with fiscal sover-

eignty; aims to contribute to Algerian economic devt through long-term investment programmes; Chair. and Dir-Gen. SADEK ALILAT; 4 brs.

Banque de Développement Local (BDL): 5 rue Gaci Amar, Staouéli, Algiers; tel. (21) 39-37-55; fax (21) 39-37-57; f. 1985; regional devt bank; cap. 7,140m., dep. 108,708m. (2000); Pres. and Dir-Gen. AMAR DAOUDI; 15 brs.

Caisse Nationale d'Epargne et de Prévoyance (CNEP): 42 blvd Khélifa Boukhalfa, Algiers; tel. (21) 71-33-53; fax (21) 71-41-31; f. 1964; total assets 206,915.8m. (Dec. 1992); savings and housing bank; Pres. and Dir-Gen. ABDELKRIM NAAS.

Private Banks

Arab Algérie Leasing: Algiers; f. 2001.

Banque Commerciale et Industrielle d'Algérie (BCIA): 4 chemin Doudou Mokhtar, Ben Aknoun, 16030 Algiers; tel. (21) 91-30-06; fax (21) 91-17-13; internet www.bciabank.com; f. 1998; cap. and res 436.7m., dep. 2,768.8m. Pres. AHMED KHERROUBI; Chair. MUHAMMAD-ALI KHERROUBI; Gen. Man. BADREDDINE KHERROUBI.

BNP-Paribas El Djazair: 10 rue Abou Nouass, Hydr, Algiers; tel. (21) 60-39-42; fax (21) 60-39-29; f. 2001; cap 500m. Chair FATHI MESTIRI; Man. Dir JEAN-FRANÇOIS CHAZU.

EFG Hermes SPA: Algiers; f. 2000.

El Khalifa Bank: 61 Lot Ben Haddadi, Dar Diaf, Chéraga, 16800 Algiers; tel. (21) 36-97-70; fax (21) 36-98-04; e-mail ek_bank@ist.cerist.dz; internet www.elkhalifabank.com; f. 1998; cap. 125m., total assets 11,659.4m. (Dec. 1999); Pres. RAFIK ABDELMOUMENE KHELIFA.

El Mouna Bank: 22 rue Boudjellad Ahmad Hai el-Moudjahidine, Oran; tel. (41) 41-15-90; fax (41) 41-18-08; f. 1998; cap. 260m. Pres. AHMED BENSADOUN.

Al-Rayan Algerian Bank: 29 rue Ahmad Kara, Bir Mourad Rais, Algiers; tel. (21) 44-99-00; fax (21) 44-92-05; internet www.alrayan-bank.com; f. 2001.

Trust Bank: Algiers; f. 2001.

Union Bank: 5 bis chemin Mackley, el-Biar, 16030 Algiers; tel. (21) 91-45-49; fax (21) 91-45-48; internet www.ub-alger.com; f. 1995; cap. 250m., total assets 1,591m. (Dec. 1997); principal shareholder Brahim Hadjas; Pres. SELIM BENATA.

Foreign Banks

Arab Banking Corpn (Bahrain): 54 ave des Trois Frères Bouaddou, BP 367, Bir Mourad Rais, Algiers; tel. (21) 54-15-15; fax (21) 54-16-04; e-mail abcbank@ist.cerist.dz; total assets US $1,477.2m.

Natexis Al-Amana Banque (France): 62 chemin Drareni, Hydra, Algiers; tel. (21) 54-90-20; fax (21) 54-90-13; e-mail natexis@wissal.dz; f. 1999; owned by Natexis Banques Populaires; Man. Dir HOCINE MOUFFOK.

STOCK EXCHANGE

The Algiers Stock Exchange began trading in July 1999.

Commission d'Organisation et de Surveillance des Opérations de Bourse (COSOB): Algiers; tel. (21) 71-27-25; fax (21) 71-21-98; e-mail infos@cosob.com.dz; internet www.cosob.com.dz; Chair. BELKACEM IRATNI; Gen. Sec. ABDELHAKIM BERRAH.

INSURANCE

Insurance is a state monopoly; however, in 1997 regulations were drafted to permit private companies to enter the Algerian insurance market.

Caisse Nationale de Mutualité Agricole: 24 blvd Victor Hugo, Algiers; tel. (21) 73-46-31; fax (21) 73-34-79; f. 1972; Dir-Gen. YAHIA CHERIF BRAHIM; 47 brs.

Cie Algérienne d'Assurance et de Réassurance (CAAR): 48 rue Didouche Mourad, 16000 Algiers; tel. (21) 72-71-90; fax (21) 72-71-97; e-mail caaralg@caar.com.dz; internet www.caar.com.dz; f. 1963 as a public corpn; partial privatization pending; Pres. ALI DJENDI.

Cie Centrale de Réassurance (CCR): Lot No 1, Saïd-Hamdine-Bmr, Algiers; tel. (21) 54-69-33; fax (21) 54-75-06; f. 1973; general; Chair. DJAMEL-EDDINE CHOUAÏB CHOUITER.

Société Nationale d'Assurances (SNA): 5 blvd Ernesto Ché Guévara, Algiers; tel. (21) 71-47-60; fax (21) 71-22-16; f. 1963; state-sponsored co; Pres. KACI AISSA SLIMANE; Chair. and Gen. Man. LATROUS AMARQ.

Trust Algeria: 70 chemin Larbi Allik, Hydra, Algiers; tel. (21) 54-74-83; fax (21) 54-71-36; e-mail info@trust-algeria.com; internet www.trust-algeria.algeriainfo.com; f. 1997; 65% owned by Trust Insurance Co (Bahrain) and Qatar General Insurance and Reinsurance Co, 35% owned by CAAR; Gen. Man. HORI MOHD BOUZIANE.

Trade and Industry

GOVERNMENT AGENCIES

Centre Algérien pour la Promotion des Investissements (CALPI): Algiers; f. 1994 to promote investment; offices in the 48 administrative districts.

Conseil National des Participations de L'Etat (CNPE): Algiers; supervises state holdings; participants include the Prime Minister and reps of 16 govt ministries; Sec.-Gen. AHMED EL-ANTRI TIBAOUI.

DEVELOPMENT ORGANIZATIONS

Agence Nationale pour l'Aménagement du Territoire (ANAT): 30 ave Muhammad Fellah, Algiers; tel. (21) 58-48-12; fax (21) 68-85-03; f. 1980; Pres. and Dir-Gen. KOUIDER DJEBLI.

Engineering Environment Consult (EEC): BP 395, Alger-Gare, 50 rue Khélifa Boukhalfa, Algiers; tel. (21) 23-64-86; fax (21) 23-72-49; e-mail eec@wissal.dz; internet www.eec.com; f. 1982; Dir-Gen. MUHAMMAD BENTIR.

Institut National de la Production et du Développement Industriel (INPED): 126 rue Didouche Mourad, Boumerdès; tel. (21) 41-52-50.

Office Algérien de Promotion du Commerce Extérieur (PROMEX): RN 5, Muhammadia, Algiers; tel. (21) 52-20-82; fax (21) 52-11-26; e-mail promex@wissal.dz; internet www.promex.com .dz.

Office National de Recherche Géologique et Minière (ORGM): BP 102, 35000 Boumerdès, Algiers; tel. (24) 81–85–25; fax (24) 81–83–79; e-mail orgm@wissal.dz; internet www.orgm.com.dz.

CHAMBERS OF COMMERCE

Chambre Française de Commerce et d'Industrie en Algérie (CFCIA): 1 rue Lt Mohamed Touileb, Algiers; tel. (21) 73-28-28; fax (21) 63-75-33; internet www.cfcia.org; f. 1965; Pres. JEAN-PIERRE DEQUEKER; Dir JEAN-FRANÇOIS HEUGAS.

Chambre Algérienne de Commerce et d'Industrie (CACI): BP 100, Palais Consulaire, 6 blvd Amilcar Cabral C.P., 16003 Algiers; tel. (21) 57-55-55; fax (21) 57-70-25; e-mail caci@wissal.dz; internet www.caci.com.dz; f. 1980; Dir-Gen. MUHAMMAD CHAMI.

INDUSTRIAL AND TRADE ASSOCIATIONS

Association Nationale des Fabrications et Utilisateurs d'Emballages Métalliques: BP 245, rue de Constantine, Algiers; Pres. OTHMANI.

Centre National des Textiles et Cuirs (CNTC): BP 65, route du Marché, Boumerdès; tel. (21) 81-13-23; fax (21) 81-13-57.

Entreprise Nationale de Développement des Industries Alimentaires (ENIAL): RN 5, 16110 Bab Ezzouar, Algiers; tel. (21) 76-21-06; fax (21) 75-77-65; f. 1982; Dir-Gen. ARESKI LAKABI.

Entreprise Nationale de Développement des Industries Manufacturières (ENEDIM): 22 rue des Fusillés, El Anasser, Algiers; tel. (21) 68-13-43; fax (21) 67-55-26; f. 1983; Dir-Gen. FODIL.

Entreprise Nationale de Développement et de Recherche Industriels des Matériaux de Construction (ENDMC): BP 78, 35000 Algiers; tel. (21) 41-50-70; f. 1982; Dir-Gen. A. TOBBAL.

Groupement pour l'Industrialisation du Bâtiment (GIBAT): BP 51, 3 ave Col Driant, 55102 Verdun, France; tel. 29-86-09-76; fax 29-86-20-51; Dir JEAN MOULET.

Institut Algérien de la Propriété Industrielle (INAPI): 42 rue Larbi Ben M'hidi, 16000 Algiers; tel. (21) 73-23-58; fax (21) 73-55-81; e-mail info@inapi.org; internet www.inapi.org; f. 1973; Dir-Gen. M. BOUHNIK AMOR.

Institut National Algérien du Commerce Extérieur (COMEX): 6 blvd Anatole-France, Algiers; tel. (21) 62-70-44; Dir-Gen. SAAD ZERHOUNI.

Institut National des Industries Manufacturières (INIM): 35000 Boumerdès; tel. (21) 81-62-71; fax (21) 82-56-62; f. 1973; Dir-Gen. HOCINE HASSISSI.

State Trading Organizations

Since 1970 all international trading has been carried out by state organizations, of which the following are the most important:

Entreprise Nationale d'Approvisionnement en Bois et Dérivés (ENAB): BP 166, Alger-Gare, 2 blvd Muhammad V, Algiers; tel. (21) 63-75-35; fax (21) 63-77-17; e-mail info@enab-dz .com; internet www.enab-dz.com; import and distribution of wood and derivatives and other building materials; Dirs OMAR BENOUNICHE, OMAR SADAOUI, SMAÏL EL-ROBRINI.

Entreprise Nationale d'Approvisionnement en Outillage et Produits de Quincaillerie Générale (ENAOQ): 5 rue Amar Semaous, Hussein-Dey, Algiers; tel. (21) 23-31-83; fax (21) 47-83-33; tools and general hardware; Dir-Gen. SMATI BAHIDJ FARID.

Entreprise Nationale d'Approvisionnements en Produits Alimentaires (ENAPAL): Algiers; tel. (21) 76-10-11; f. 1983; monopoly of import, export and bulk trade in basic foodstuffs; brs in more than 40 towns; Chair. LAID SABRI; Man. Dir BRAHIM DOUAOURI.

Entreprise Nationale d'Approvisionnement et de Régulation en Fruits et Légumes (ENAFLA): BP 42, 12 ave des Trois Frères Bouadou, Bir Mourad Rais, Algiers; tel. (21) 54-10-10; fax (21) 56-79-59; f. 1983; division of the Ministry of Commerce; fruit and vegetable marketing, production and export; Man. Dir REDHA KHELEF.

Entreprise Nationale de Commerce: 6–9 rue Belhaffat-Ghazali, Hussein-Dey, Algiers; tel. (21) 77-43-20; Dir-Gen. MUHAMMAD LAÏD BELARBIA.

Office Algérien Interprofessionel des Céréales (OAIC): 5 rue Ferhat-Boussaad, Algiers; tel. (21) 73-26-01; fax (21) 73-22-11; f. 1962; monopoly of trade in wheat, rice, maize, barley and products derived from these cereals; Gen. Man. LAÏD TALAMALI.

Office National de la Commercialisation des Produits Viti-Vinicoles (ONCV): 112 Quai-Sud, Algiers; tel. (21) 73-72-75; fax (21) 73-72-97; e-mail info@oncv-dz.com; internet www.oncv-dz.com; f. 1968; monopoly of importing and exporting products of the wine industry; Man. Dir SAÏD MEBARKI.

UTILITIES

Commission de Régulation de l'Electricité et du Gaz: Algiers; f. 2002; regulatory authority.

Société Nationale de l'Electricité et du Gaz (SONELGAZ): 2 blvd Col Krim Belkacem, Algiers; tel. (21) 72-31-01; fax (21) 61-54-77; internet www.sonelgaz.com.dz; f. 1969; production, distribution and transportation of electricity and transportation and distribution of natural gas; Gen. Man. AÏSSA ABDELKRIM BENGHANEM.

Electricity

Entreprise de Travaux d'Electrification (KAHRIF): Villa Malwall, Ain d'Heb, Médéa; tel. (25) 50-26-96; fax (25) 58-31-14; e-mail kahrif@ixiissal.dz; f. 1982; study of electrical infrastructure; Pres. and Dir-Gen. HOCINE RAHMANI.

Gas

Entreprise Nationale de Production et de Distribution des Gaz Industriels (ENGI): 23 route de l'ALN, 16040 Hussein-Dey, Algiers; tel. (21) 49-85-99; fax (21) 49-71-94; e-mail boucherit@usa .net; internet www.gaz-ind.com; f. 1972; production and distribution of gas; Gen. Man. LAHOCINE BOUCHERIT.

Water

Agence Nationale de l'Eau Potable et Industrielle et de l'Assainissement (AGEP): rue Chemseddine Hafid-Kouba, 16000 Algiers; tel. (21) 28-30-96; fax (21) 28-30-33; f. 1985; state water co.

STATE HYDROCARBONS COMPANIES

Société Nationale pour la Recherche, la Production, le Transport, la Transformation et la Commercialisation des Hydrocarbures (SONATRACH): 10 rue du Sahara, Hydra, Algiers; tel. (21) 54-70-00; fax (21) 54-77-00; e-mail sonatrach@sonatrach.dz; internet www.sonatrach-dz.com; f. 1963; exploration, exploitation, transport and marketing of petroleum, natural gas and their products; Chair. ABDELMALEK ZITOUNI; Vice-Pres ALI HACHED (Marketing), ABDELHADI ZERGUINE (Transport), BACHIR ACHOUR (Liquefaction), DJAMEL EDINE KHENE (Exploration and Production).

Since 1980 the following associated companies have shared SONATRACH's functions:

Entreprise Nationale de Canalisation (ENAC): Muhammadia, rue Benyoucef Khattab, El Harrach, Algiers; tel. (21) 53-85-49; fax (21) 53-85-53; piping; Dir-Gen. RACHID HAMADOU.

Entreprise Nationale d'Engineering Pétrolier (ENEP): 2 blvd Muhammad V, Algiers; tel. (21) 64-08-37; fax (21) 63-71-83; design and construction for petroleum-processing industry; Gen. Man. MUSTAPHA MEKIDECHE.

Entreprise Nationale de Forage (ENAFOR): BP 211, 30500 Hassi Messaoud, Algiers; tel. (21) 73-71-35; fax (21) 73-22-60; drilling; Dir-Gen. ABD AR-RACHID ROUABAH.

Entreprise Nationale des Grands Travaux Pétroliers (ENGTP): BP 09, Zone industrielle, Reghaïa, Boumerdès; tel. (24)

80-06-80; fax (24) 85-14-70; f. 1980; major industrial projects; Dir-Gen. B. DRIAD.

Entreprise Nationale des Services aux Puits (ENSP): BP 83, 30500 Hassi Messaoud, Ouargla; tel. (29) 73-73-33; fax (29) 73-82-01; e-mail info@enspgroup.com; internet www.enspgroup.com; f. 1970; oil-well services; Dir-Gen. AZZEDINE GASMI.

Entreprise Nationale des Travaux aux Puits (ENTP): BP 206, 30500 Hassi Messaoud, Ouargla; tel. (29) 73-87-78; fax (29) 73-84-06; f. 1981; oil-well construction; Dir-Gen. ABD AL-AZIZ KRISSAT.

Groupe Industriel des Plastiques & Caoutchoucs: BP 452–453, Zone industrielle, 19000 Sétif; tel. (36) 90-75-45; fax (36) 93-05-65; e-mail grenpc@el-hidhab.cerist.dz; f. 1967; production and marketing of rubber and plastics products; Dir-Gen. BELKACEM SAMAT.

Société Nationale de Commercialisation et de Distribution des Produits Pétroliers (NAFTAL, SpA): BP 73, route des Dunes, Cheraga, Algiers; tel. (21) 36-09-69; fax (21) 36-07-86; e-mail naf-div-bp@wissal.dz; internet www.naftal-dz.com; f. 1987; international marketing and distribution of petroleum products; Gen. Man. NOREDINE CHEROUATI.

Société Nationale de Génie Civil et Bâtiments (CGB): BP 23, route de Corso, Boudouaou, Algiers; tel. (21) 84-65-26; fax (21) 84-60-09; civil engineering; Dir-Gen. ABD EL-HAMID ZERGUINE.

TRADE UNIONS

Union Générale des Travailleurs Algériens (UGTA): Maison du Peuple, place du 1er mai, Algiers; tel. (21) 66-89-47; f. 1956; 800,000 mems; Sec.-Gen. ABDELMADJID SIDI SAID.

There are 10 national 'professional sectors' affiliated to the UGTA:

Secteur Alimentation, Commerce et Tourisme (Food, Commerce and Tourist Industry Workers): Gen. Sec. ABD AL-KADER GHRIBLI.

Secteur Bois, Bâtiments et Travaux Publics (Building Trades Workers): Gen. Sec. LAIFA LATRECHE.

Secteur Education et Formation Professionnelle (Teachers): Gen. Sec. SAÏDI BEN GANA.

Secteur Energie et Pétrochimie (Energy and Petrochemical Workers): Gen. Sec. ALI BELHOUCHET.

Secteur Finances (Financial Workers): Gen. Sec. MUHAMMAD ZAAF.

Secteur Information, Formation et Culture (Information, Training and Culture).

Secteur Industries Légères (Light Industry): Gen. Sec. ABD AL-KADER MALKI.

Secteur Industries Lourdes (Heavy Industry).

Secteur Santé et Sécurité Sociale (Health and Social Security Workers): Gen. Sec. ABD AL-AZIZ DJEFFAL.

Secteur Transports et Télécommunications (Transport and Telecommunications Workers): Gen. Sec. EL-HACHEMI BEN MOUHOUB.

Al-Haraka al-Islamiyah lil-Ummal al-Jazarivia (Islamic Movement for Algerian Workers): Tlemcen; f. 1990; based on teachings of Islamic faith and affiliated to the FIS.

Ittahad as-Sahafiyin al-Jaza'iriyin (Algerian Journalists Union): Algiers; f. 2001.

Union Nationale des Paysans Algériens (UNPA): f. 1973; 700,000 mems; Sec.-Gen. AÏSSA NEDJEM.

Transport

RAILWAYS

Entreprise Métro d'Alger: 4 chemin de Wilaya 13, Kouba, Algiers; tel. (21) 28-94-64; fax (21) 28-01-83; construction of a 26.5-km metro railway line began in 1991; initial 12.5-km section (16 stations) scheduled to open in two stages, starting in 2006; Dir-Gen. A. MERKEBI.

Infrafer (Entreprise Publique Economique de Réalisation des Infrastructures Ferroviaires): BP 208, 35300 Rouiba; tel. (21) 85-27-47; fax (21) 85-17-55; f. 1987; responsible for construction and maintenance of track; Pres. and Dir-Gen. K. BENMAMI.

Société Nationale des Transports Ferroviaires (SNTF): 21–23 blvd Muhammad V, Algiers; tel. (21) 71-15-10; fax (21) 74-81-90; f. 1976 to replace Société Nationale des Chemins de Fer Algériens; 4,820 km of track, of which 304 km are electrified and 1,156 km are narrow gauge; daily passenger services from Algiers to the principal provincial cities and services to Tunisia and Morocco; Dir-Gen. ABD AL-ADIM BENALLEGUE.

ROADS

In 1996 there were an estimated 104,000 km of roads and tracks, of which 640 km were motorways, 25,200 km were main roads and 23,900 km were secondary roads. The French administration built a good road system (partly for military purposes), which, since independence, has been allowed to deteriorate in parts. New roads have been built linking the Sahara oil fields with the coast, and the Trans-Sahara highway is a major project. In 1996 it was estimated that the cost of renovating the national road system would amount to US $4,124m.

Société Nationale des Transports Routiers (SNTR): 27 rue des Trois Frères Bouadou, Bir Mourad Rais, Algiers; tel. (21) 54-06-00; fax (21) 54-05-35; e-mail dg-sntr@sntr-dz.com; internet www.groupe-sntr.com; f. 1967; holds a monopoly of goods transport by road; Chair. and Dir-Gen. ABDALLAH BENMAAROUF.

Société Nationale des Transports des Voyageurs (SNTV): Algiers; tel. (21) 66-00-52; f. 1967; holds monopoly of long-distance passenger transport by road; Man. Dir M. DIB.

SHIPPING

Algiers is the main port, with anchorage of between 23 m and 29 m in the Bay of Algiers, and anchorage for the largest vessels in Agha Bay. The port has a total quay length of 8,380 m and is expected to be able to handle 250,000 containers per year by 2005. There are also important ports at Annaba, Arzew, Béjaia, Djidjelli, Ghazaouet, Mostaganem, Oran, Skikda and Ténès. Petroleum and liquefied gas are exported through Arzew, Béjaia and Skikda. Algerian crude petroleum is also exported through the Tunisian port of La Skhirra. In December 2001 Algeria's merchant fleet totalled 143 vessels, with an aggregate displacement of 963,824 grt.

Cie Algéro-Libyenne de Transports Maritimes (CALTRAM): 19 rue des Trois Frères Bouadou, Bir Mourad Rais, Algiers; tel. (21) 57-17-00; fax (21) 54-21-04; e-mail caltram@wissal.dz; f. 1974; Man. Dir A. KERAMANE.

Entreprise Nationale de Réparation Navale (ERENAV): quai no. 12, Algiers; tel. (21) 42-37-83; fax (21) 42-30-39; internet www.erenav.com.dz; f. 1987; ship repairs; Dir-Gen. MUHAMMAD FARES.

Entreprise Nationale de Transport Maritime de Voyageurs—Algérie Ferries (ENTMV): BP 467, 5–6 rue Jawharlal Nehru, 16001 Algiers; tel. (21) 74-04-85; fax (21) 64-88-76; e-mail entmv@algerieferries.com; f. 1987 as part of restructuring of SNTM-CNAN; responsible for passenger transport; operates car ferry services between Algiers, Annaba, Skikda, Alicante (Spain), Marseille (France) and Oran; Dir-Gen. BOUDJEMA CHERIET.

Entreprise Portuaire d'Alger (EPAL): BP 16, 2 rue d'Angkor, Alger-Gare, Algiers; tel. (21) 71-54-39; fax (21) 71-54-52; e-mail portalg@ist.cerist.dz; internet www.portalger.com.dz; f. 1982; responsible for management and growth of port facilities and sea pilotage; Dir-Gen. ALI FERRAH.

Entreprise Portuaire d'Annaba (EPAN): BP 1232, Môle Cigogne-Quai nord, Annaba; tel. (38) 86-31-31; fax (38) 86-54-15; e-mail epan@annaba-port.com; internet www.annaba.port.com; Man. Dir DJILANI SALHI.

Entreprise Portuaire d'Arzew (EPA): BP 46, 7 rue Larbi Tebessi, Arzew; tel. (41) 37-24-91; fax (41) 47-49-90; Man. Dir CHAIB OUMER.

Entreprise Portuaire de Béjaia (EPB): 13 ave des Frères Amrani, BP 94, 06000 Béjaia; tel. (34) 21-18-07; fax (34) 22-03-46; e-mail portbj@wissal.dz; internet www.portdebejaia.com.dz; Man. Dir M. BOUMSILLA.

Entreprise Portuaire de Djen-Djen (EPJ): BP 87,18000 Jijel; tel. (34) 44-65-64; fax (34) 44-52-60; e-mail epjdjendjen@wissal.dz; internet www.djendjen-port.com.dz; f. 1984; Pres. MUHAMMAD ATMANE.

Entreprise Portuaire de Ghazaouet (EPG): BP 217, route du Phare, 13400 Ghazaouet; tel. (43) 32-32-20; fax (43) 32-32-55; e-mail portghztepg@maildz.com; f. 1982; Pres and Dir-Gen. ABDELMALEK BRAHIM.

Entreprise Portuaire de Mostaganem (EPM): BP 131, quai du Port, Mostaganem; tel. (45) 21-14-11; fax (45) 21-78-05; Dir-Gen. M. LAKEHAL.

Entreprise Portuaire d'Oran (EPO): 1 rue du 20 août, 31000 Oran; tel. (41) 33-24-41; fax (41) 33-24-98; e-mail webmaster@oran-port.com; internet oran-port.com; Man. Dir M. S. LOUHIBI.

Entreprise Portuaire de Skikda (EPS): BP 65, 46 ave Rezki Rahal, Skikda; tel. (38) 75-68-50; fax (38) 75-20-15; e-mail info@skikda-port.com; internet skikda-port.com; Man. Dir M. LEMRABET.

Entreprise Portuaire de Ténès (EPT): BP 18, 02200 Ténès; tel. (27) 76-72-76; fax (27) 76-61-77; Man. Dir K. EL-HAMRI.

NAFTAL Division Aviation Marine: BP 70, Aéroport Houari Boumedienne, Dar-el-Beïda, Algiers; tel. (21) 50-95-50; fax (21) 50-67-09; e-mail avm@ist.cerist.dz; Dir MESNOUS NOUREDINE.

Société Générale Maritime (GEMA): 2 rue J. Nehru, Algiers; tel. (21) 74-73-00; fax (21) 74-76-73; e-mail gemadg@gema-groupe.com; f. 1987 as part of restructuring of SNTM-CNAN; shipping, ship-handling and forwarding; Dir-Gen. BELKADI BOUALEM.

Société Nationale de Transport Maritime et Cie Nationale Algérienne de Navigation (SNTM-CNAN): BP 280, 2 quai no. 9, Nouvelle Gare Maritime, Algiers; tel. (21) 71-14-78; fax (21) 73-02-33; f. 1963; state-owned co which owns and operates fleet of freight ships; rep. office in Marseille (France) and rep. agencies in Antwerp (Belgium), Valencia (Spain) and the principal ports in many other countries; Gen. Man. ABDELHAMID KARA.

Société Nationale de Transports Maritimes des Hydrocarbures et des Produits Chimiques (SNTM-HYPROC): BP 60, Arzew, 31200 Oran; tel. (41) 47-48-55; fax (41) 47-34-45; e-mail hyproc@hyproc.com; internet www.hyproc.com; f. 1982; Pres. and Dir-Gen. MUSTAPHA ZENASNI.

CIVIL AVIATION

Algeria's principal international airport, Houari Boumedienne, is situated 20 km from Algiers. At Constantine, Annaba, Tlemcen and Oran there are also airports that meet international requirements. There are, in addition, 65 aerodromes, of which 20 are public, and a further 135 airstrips connected with the petroleum industry.

Air Algérie (Entreprise Nationale d'Exploitation des Services Aériens): BP 858, 1 place Maurice Audin, Immeuble el-Djazair, Algiers; tel. (21) 74-24-28; fax (21) 61-05-53; e-mail contact@airalgerie.dz; internet www.airalgerie.dz; f. 1953 by merger; state-owned from 1972; partial privatization pending; internal services and extensive services to Europe, North and West Africa, and the Middle East; Chair. and Dir-Gen. TAYEB BENOUIS; Sec.-Gen. NOUREDDINE MERROUCHE.

Desert Aviation Co: Touggourt; f. 1999; private co; internal flights; Exec. Dir CHOKRI MIAADI.

Ecoair International: 12 rue Branly, El Mouradia, Algiers; tel. (21) 69-82-00; f. 1998; private co operating domestic and international passenger flights to Europe and North Africa.

Khalifa Airways: chemin de la Petite Province, Lot 11 décembre 1960, Hydra, Algiers; tel. (21) 50-63-70; e-mail contact@khalifaairways-dz.com; internet www.khalifaairways-dz.com; f. 1999; private airline operating domestic and international passenger flights to destinations in Europe, Africa and the Middle East.

Saharan Airlines: BP 65 Cité Ezzahra, Touggourt; tel. (29) 68-31-91; fax (29) 68-13-12; e-mail shddz@yahoo.fr; f. 1999; domestic and international passenger services; CEO MIADI CHOUKRI.

Tassili Airlines: blvd Mustapha Ben Boulaid, 301 Hassi Messaoud; tel. (29) 73-84-25; fax (29) 73-84-24; f. 1997; jt venture between SONATRACH and Air Algérie; domestic passenger services.

Tourism

Algeria's tourist attractions include the Mediterranean coast, the Atlas mountains and the desert. In 2000 a total of 865,984 tourists visited Algeria, compared with 748,536 in 1999. Receipts from tourism totalled US $102m. in 2000.

Agence Nationale de Développement Touristique (ANDT): BP 151, Sidi Fredj Staoueli, Algiers; tourism promotion; Dir-Gen. ABDELKRIM BOUCETTA.

Office National du Tourisme (ONT): 2 rue Ismail Kerrar, Algiers; tel. (21) 71-30-60; fax (21) 71-30-59; e-mail ont@wissal.dz; internet www.ont.dz; f. 1988; state institution; oversees tourism promotion policy; Dir-Gen. ABDELÁADI TIR.

ONAT-TOUR (Opérateur National Algérien de Tourisme): 126 bis A, rue Didouche Mourod, 16000 Algiers; tel. (21) 74-44-48; fax (21) 74-32-14; e-mail onat@onat-dz.com; internet www.onat-dz.com; f. 1962; Dir-Gen. BELKACEMI HAMMOUCHE.

Société de Développement de l'Industrie Touristique en Algérie (SODITAL): 72 rue Asselah Hocine, Algiers; f. 1989; Dir-Gen. NOUREDDINE SALHI.

TCA-TOUR (Touring Club d'Algérie): BP 18, Birkhamden; rue Hacéne Benaamane, quartier les vergers, Algiers; tel. (21) 56-90-16; fax (21) 54-19-39; Dir-Gen. ABDERAHMANE ABD-EDDAIM.

ANDORRA

Introductory Survey

Location, Climate, Language, Religion, Flag, Capital

The Principality of Andorra lies in the eastern Pyrenees, bounded by France and Spain, and is situated roughly midway between Barcelona and Toulouse. The climate is alpine, with much snow in winter and a warm summer. The official language is Catalan, but French and Spanish are also widely spoken. Most of the inhabitants profess Christianity, and about 94% are Roman Catholics. The civil flag (proportions 2 by 3) has three equal vertical stripes, of blue, yellow and red. The state flag has, in addition, the state coat of arms (a quartered shield above the motto *Virtus unita fortior*) in the centre of the yellow stripe. The capital is Andorra la Vella.

Recent History

Owing to the lack of distinction between the authority of the General Council (Consell General) of Andorra and the Co-Princes (Coprínceps—the President of France and the Spanish Bishop of Urgel) who have ruled the country since 1278, the Andorrans encountered many difficulties in their attempts to gain international status for their country and control over its essential services.

Until 1970 the franchise was granted only to third-generation Andorran males who were more than 25 years of age. Thereafter, women, persons aged between 21 and 25, and second-generation Andorrans were allowed to vote in elections to the General Council. In 1977 the franchise was extended to include all first-generation Andorrans of foreign parentage who were aged 28 and over. The electorate remained small, however, when compared with the size of the population, and Andorra's foreign residents (who comprised 59.8% of the total population at December 2001) increased their demands for political and nationality rights. Immigration is on a quota system, being restricted primarily to French and Spanish nationals intending to work in Andorra.

Prior to 1993, political parties were not directly represented in the General Council, but there were loose groupings with liberal and conservative sympathies. The country's only political organization, the Partit Democràtic d'Andorra (PDA), was technically illegal, and in the 1981 elections to the General Council the party urged its supporters to cast blank votes.

In 1980, during discussions on institutional reform, representatives of the Co-Princes and the General Council agreed that an executive council should be formed, and that a referendum should be held on changes to the electoral system. In early 1981 the Co-Princes formally requested the General Council to prepare plans for reform, in accordance with these proposals. Following the December elections to the General Council, in January 1982 the new legislature elected Oscar Ribas Reig as Head of Government (Cap de Govern). Ribas Reig appointed an executive of six ministers, who expressed their determination to provide Andorra with a written constitution. The formation of the executive body, known as the Govern, constituted the separation of powers between an executive and a legislature, and represented an important step towards institutional reform.

Severe storm damage in November 1982, and the general effects of the world-wide economic recession, led to a controversial vote by the General Council, in August 1983, in favour of the introduction of income tax, in an effort to alleviate Andorra's budgetary deficit and to provide the Government with extra revenue for development projects. Subsequent government proposals for an indirect tax on bank deposits, hotel rooms and property sales encountered strong opposition from financial and tourism concerns, and prompted the resignation of the Government in April 1984. Josep Pintat Solans, a local business executive, was elected unopposed by the General Council as Head of Government in May. In August, however, the Ministers of Finance and of Industry, Commerce and Agriculture resigned, following disagreements concerning the failure to implement economic reforms (including the introduction of income tax).

At the December 1985 elections to the General Council the electorate was increased by about 27%, as a result of the newly-introduced lower minimum voting age of 18 years. The Council re-elected Pintat Solans as Head of Government in January 1986, when he won the support of 27 of its 28 members.

In September 1986 President François Mitterrand of France and the Bishop of Urgel, Dr Joan Martí Alanis (respectively the French and Spanish Co-Princes), met in Andorra to discuss the principality's status in relation to the European Community (EC, now European Union—EU, see p. 199), as well as the question of free exchange of goods between the members of the EC and Andorra, following Spain's admission to the Community in January of that year.

In April 1987 the Consejo Sindical Interregional Pirineos-Mediterráneo, a collective of French and Spanish trade unions, in conjunction with the Andorran Asociación de Residentes Andorranos, began to claim rights, including those of freedom of expression and association and the right to strike, on behalf of 20,000 of its members who were employed as immigrant workers in Andorra.

Further proposals for institutional reforms were approved by the General Council in October 1987. The transfer to the Andorran Government of responsibility for such matters as public order was proposed, while the authority of the Co-Princes in the administration of justice was recognized. The drafting of a constitution for Andorra was also envisaged. The implementation of the reforms was, however, dependent on the agreement of the Co-Princes.

Municipal elections were held in December 1987, at which 80% of the electorate voted; however, the number of citizens eligible to vote represented only 13% of Andorra's total population. For the first time, the election campaign involved the convening of meetings and the use of the media, in addition to traditional canvassing. Although Andorra then had no political parties as such, four of the seven seats were won by candidates promoting a conservative stance.

In April 1988 Andorra enacted legislation recognizing the Universal Declaration of Human Rights, adopted by the UN General Assembly in 1948. In June 1988 the first Andorran trade union was established by two French union confederations and by the Spanish Unión General de Trabajadores. (There were about 26,000 salaried workers in Andorra at this time, 90% of whom were of French or Spanish origin.) In the following month, however, the General Council rejected the formation of the union, as it did not recognize workers' right of association and prohibited the existence of any union.

Elections to the General Council took place in December 1989, at which more than 80% of the electorate participated. In January 1990 the new Council elected the reformist Ribas Reig as Head of Government, with the support of 22 members. In June the Council voted unanimously to establish a special commission to draft a constitution. The proposed document was to promulgate popular sovereignty and to constitutionalize the Co-Princes. In April 1991 representatives of the Co-Princes agreed to recognize popular sovereignty in Andorra and to permit the drafting of a constitution, which would be subject to approval by referendum. In September, however, Ribas Reig was threatened with a vote of 'no confidence' by traditionalist members of the Council. There followed a period of political impasse, during which no official budget was authorized for the principality. In January 1992, following small, but unprecedented, public demonstrations in protest against the political deadlock, Ribas Reig and the General Council resigned. A general election took place in April, at which 82% of the electorate (of 8,592 voters) voted. However, the result was inconclusive, necessitating a second round of voting one week later, following which supporters of Ribas Reig controlled 17 of the 28 seats. Accordingly, Ribas Reig was re-elected as Head of Government.

At a referendum held in March 1993, in which 75.7% of the electorate participated, 74.2% of those who voted approved the draft Constitution. The document was signed by the Co-Princes in April, and was promulgated on 4 May. Under its provisions, the Co-Princes remained as Heads of State, but with greatly reduced powers, while Andorran nationals were afforded full sovereignty and (together with foreigners who had lived in Andorra for at least 20 years) were authorized to form and to join political parties and trade unions. The Constitution provided for the establishment of an independent judiciary, and permitted the principality to formulate its own foreign policy and to join international organizations. The Co-Princes were to retain a right of veto over treaties with France and Spain that affected Andorra's borders or security.

The first general election under the terms of the new Constitution took place on 12 December 1993. One-half of the General Council's 28 members were directly elected from the single national constituency, the remainder being elected by Andorra's seven parishes (two for each parish). No party won an overall majority of seats, the largest number (eight) being secured by Ribas Reig's Agrupament Nacional Democràtic (AND–the successor to the PDA); Nova Democràcia (ND) and the Unió Liberal (UL) each won five seats. Some 80.8% of the electorate participated in the election. In January 1994 Ribas Reig was re-elected Head of Government, supported by the AND and the ND, together with the two representatives of the Iniciatíva Democràtica Nacional (IDN). Ribas Reig announced that it would be a priority of his administration to restore economic growth by means of financial reforms and infrastructural development. Opposition to Ribas Reig's proposed budget and tax legislation, however, led in November to the adoption of a motion of 'no confidence' in the Government. Ribas Reig immediately submitted his resignation; Marc Forné Molné, the leader of the UL, was subsequently elected Head of Government, and was inaugurated in late December.

Forné Molné's Government lacked an overall majority in the General Council; however, the support of councillors from regional political organizations enabled the Government to adopt more than 30 acts (between December 1994 and July 1996), including controversial legislation regarding foreign nationals (see Economic Affairs). Municipal elections, at which some 77.7% of the electorate voted, took place in December 1995. Bibiana Rossa (a former Minister of Health) became the first woman in Andorra to be elected to the office of mayor (of Canillo). After being censured twice in one year by the General Council, Forné Molné was obliged to announce that a general election would be held in early 1997. Elections to the Council took place on 16 February 1997, at which 81.6% of the registered electorate (of 10,837 voters) participated. The UL won an overall majority of seats (18 of 28); six seats were secured by the AND, while the ND and the IDN took two each. In April Forné Molné announced the formation of a new, expanded Government. The UL was subsequently renamed the Partit Liberal d'Andorra (PLA). In June 1998 Càndid Naudi Mora was appointed to the newly-created position of Minister of Territorial Development. In 2000 the AND split into two parties the Partit Socialdemocràta (PS) and the Partit Democràta (PD).

Elections to the General Council took place on 4 March 2001, at which 81.6% of the registered electorate (of some 13,342 voters) participated; however, the number of citizens eligible to vote represented only 20.7% of Andorra's total population. The PLA won an overall majority of seats (15 of 28), six seats were secured by the PS, the PD took five seats and the two remaining seats went to independent candidates. Forné Molné was re-elected Head of Government. On 9 April Forné Molné announced his new Government; the position of Minister for the Presidency was abolished, but there were otherwise few changes from the outgoing administration. A Ministry of Family Affairs was created in May. During early 2002, the position of Minister of Presidency was reintroduced; the Minister for Culture and Tourism, Enric Pujal Areny, was appointed to the post. While Pujal Areny retained responsibility for tourism, a separate Ministry of Culture was created, and Xavier Montané Atero was allocated the portfolio.

In late October 2002 the Government encountered controversy when it unexpectedly closed a waste incinerator in Lime Rosselló amid revelations that the plant had been emitting 1,000 times the amount of dioxins permitted by EU regulations. The Government had previously resisted demands from the opposition and ecological groups for the closure of the plant. Although Spain agreed to temporarily dispose of waste in the principality, in early November the Government approved a law permitting the construction of a new incinerator. However, this did not prevent Forné Molné facing the worst crisis of his mandate, with widespread discontent about the lack of information

Following the referendum of March 1993, Andorra formally applied for membership of the Council of Europe (see p. 181), gaining entry in October 1994. In June 1993 the Andorran

Government signed a treaty of co-operation with France and Spain, which explicitly recognized the sovereignty of Andorra. In the following month Andorra became the 184th member of the UN. In late 1993 France and Spain established embassies in Andorra, and Andorra subsequently opened embassies in Paris and Madrid. In September 1997 Jacques Chirac made his first official visit to Andorra in his capacity as President of France.

Government

Andorra is a co-principality, under the suzerainty of the President of France and the Spanish Bishop of Urgel. However, since May 1993, when the Constitution of the Principality of Andorra was promulgated, these positions have been almost purely honorary.

The General Council comprises 28 councillors, who are elected by universal suffrage for a four-year period. Two councillors are directly elected by each of the seven parishes of Andorra, and the remainder by a single national constituency. At its opening session the Council elects as its head the Speaker (Síndic General) and the Deputy Speaker (Subsíndic General), who cease to be members of the Council on their election. The General Council elects the Head of Government, who, in turn, appoints ministers to the Govern.

Andorra is divided into seven parishes, each of which is administered by a Communal Council. Communal councillors are elected for a four-year term by direct universal suffrage. At its opening session each Communal Council elects two consuls, who preside over it.

Defence

Andorra has no defence budget.

Economic Affairs

In 2000 Andorra's national revenue totalled an estimated US $1,275m., equivalent to $19,368 per head. Traditionally an agricultural country, Andorra's principal crops are tobacco and potatoes; livestock-rearing is also of importance. However, the agricultural sector (including forestry and fishing) accounted for only 0.4% of total employment in 2001, and Andorra is dependent on imports of foodstuffs to satisfy domestic requirements.

Industry in Andorra includes the manufacture of cigars and cigarettes, together with the production of textiles, leather goods, wood products and processed foodstuffs. Iron, lead, alum and stone are also produced. Including construction, industry provided 19.9% of total employment in 2001.

The country's hydroelectric power plant supplies only about one-quarter of domestic needs, and Andorra is dependent on imports of electricity and other fuels from France and Spain. Andorra's total electricity consumption in 2001 amounted to 439.8m. kWh.

After 1945 Andorra's economy expanded rapidly, as a result of the co-principality's development as a market for numerous European and overseas goods, owing to favourable excise conditions. The services sector engaged 73.9% of the employed labour force in 2001. The trade in low-duty consumer items and tourism are therefore the most important sources of revenue. An estimated 3.5m. tourists and 7.8m. day-trippers visited Andorra in 2001; tourism (excluding hotels) engaged 22.5% of the employed labour force in that year. The absence of income tax and other forms of direct taxation favoured the development of Andorra as a 'tax haven'. The banking sector makes a significant contribution to the economy.

Andorra's external trade is dominated by the import of consumer goods destined for sale to visitors. In 2001 imports were valued at €1,222.9m. and exports at €58.9m. Spain and France are Andorra's principal trading partners, respectively providing 57.6% and 27.5% of imports and taking 59.3% and 29.5% of exports in 2001.

In 1999 Andorra recorded a budgetary deficit of 1,800m. pesetas. For 2002 expenditure was projected at €260.8m. and revenue at €242.9m.. In the absence of direct taxation, the Government derives its revenue from levies on imports and on financial institutions, indirect taxes on petrol and other items, stamp duty and the sale of postage stamps. There is reportedly no unemployment in Andorra: the restricted size of the indigenous labour force necessitates high levels of immigration.

In March 1990 Andorra approved a trade agreement with the European Community (EC, now European Union—EU, see p. 199) which was effective from July 1991, allowing for the establishment of a customs union with the EC and enabling Andorran companies to sell non-agricultural goods to the EU market without being subject to the external tariffs levied on third countries. Andorra benefits from duty-free transit for goods imported via EU countries. In October 1997 Andorra's request to commence negotiations for membership of the World Trade Organization (WTO, see p. 323) was approved by the WTO General Council.

Notable impediments to growth in Andorra include the narrow economic base and the inability of the agricultural and manufacturing sectors to fulfil domestic needs. As part of initiatives to establish Andorra as a major financial centre, a law regulating financial services was approved in late 1993. In mid-1994 legislation was approved requiring banks to invest as much as 4% of their clients' deposits in a fund intended to alleviate the public debt. Controversial legislation was adopted in 1996 to allow certain foreign nationals to become 'nominal residents' (individuals who, for the purposes of avoiding taxation, establish their financial base in Andorra), on condition that they pay an annual levy of some 1m. pesetas, in addition to a deposit. The practice of granting this status (without the levy) had been suspended in 1992; however, in the mid-1990s those already accorded nominal residency were estimated to contribute 90% of Andorra's bank deposits. Concerns were expressed regarding the Andorran banking sector, following the publication in January 1993 of a report by the French Government, which stated that Andorra was being used for money 'laundering' (the passage of profits from criminal activities through the banking system in order to legitimize them). These concerns increased, as the impending conversion to the euro in 2002 led to substantial amounts of French and Spanish currency, which had been hoarded for tax purposes, being laundered in Andorra. In mid-2000, under its initiative to abolish 'harmful tax practices', the Organisation for Economic Co-operation and Development (OECD, see p. 277) identified a number of jurisdictions as 'tax havens' lacking financial transparency, and urged these to amend their national financial legislation. Many of the countries and territories identified agreed to follow a timetable for reform, with the aim of eliminating such practices by the end of 2005. Others at least entered into dialogue with OECD. A few did neither and have been designated by OECD as 'unco-operative tax havens'. In April 2002 OECD listed Andorra as one of seven states that remained 'unco-operative tax havens', which could be subject to financial sanctions by member states if non-compliance continued for a further year. The Government refuted OECD's allegations, claiming that the country's tax system was not designed to attract foreign capital. In mid-July, however, the prosecutor's office ordered a bank account to be 'frozen', following allegations that its contents, of €2m., were linked to a terrorist organization.

Education

Education is compulsory for children of between six and 16 years of age, and is provided free of charge by Catalan-, French- and Spanish-language schools. Six years of primary education are followed by four years of secondary schooling. University education is undertaken abroad, although there are two centres for vocational training in Andorra. In 1999/2000 there were a total of 7,658 pupils attending Andorra's 34 schools, while 3,186 students were in higher education. The 2003 budget allocated €45.5m. (16.8% of total expenditure) to education.

Public Holidays

2003: 1 January (New Year's Day), 6 January (Epiphany), 14 March (Constitution Day), 18 April (Good Friday), 21 April (Easter Monday), 1 May (Labour Day), 9 June (Whit Monday), 15 August (Assumption), 8 September (National Holiday), 1 November (All Saints' Day), 8 December (Immaculate Conception), 25 December (Christmas), 26 December (St Stephen's Day).

2004: 1 January (New Year's Day), 6 January (Epiphany), 15 March (for Constitution Day), 9 April (Good Friday), 12 April (Easter Monday), 3 May (for Labour Day), 20 May (Whit Monday), 15 August (Assumption), 8 September (National Holiday), 1 November (All Saints' Day), 8 December (Immaculate Conception), 25 December (Christmas), 26 December (St Stephen's Day).

Each Parish also holds its own annual festival, which is taken as a public holiday, usually lasting for three days, in July, August or September.

Weights and Measures

The metric system is in force.

Statistical Survey

Source (unless otherwise stated): Servei d'Estudis, Ministeri de Finances, Carrer Dr Vilanova 13, Edif. Davi, Esc. C5è, Andorra la Vella; tel. 865345; fax 867898; e-mail servest@andorra.ad; internet www.estadistica.ad.

AREA AND POPULATION

Area: 467.76 sq km (180.6 sq miles).

Population (December 2001): 66,334 (males 34,419; females 31,915); comprising 24,654 Andorrans, 26,251 Spanish, 6,708 Portuguese, 4,270 French and 4,451 others.

Density (December 2001): 141.8 per sq km.

Principal Towns (population at December 2001): Andorra la Vella (capital) 20,787; Escaldes-Engordany 15,519; Encamp 10,627; Sant Julià de Lòria 7,646; La Massana 6,375; Canillo 3,014; Ordino 2,366.

Births, Marriages and Deaths (2001): Registered live births 777; Registered marriages 213; Registered deaths 237.

Expectation of Life (WHO estimates, years at birth): 79.6 (males 76.2; females 82.9) in 2001. Source: WHO, *World Health Report*.

Employment (2001): Agriculture, forestry and fishing 143; Industry (incl. construction) 7,200; Services 26,755 (Food industry 1,443, Tourism 8,153, Hotels 5,185, Utilities 4,666, Finance and insurance 1,529, Administration 4,508); Other 2,906; Total 36,194.

HEALTH AND WELFARE

Key Indicators

Total Fertility Rate (children per woman, 2001): 1.3.

Under-5 Mortality Rate (per 1,000 live births, 2001): 7.

Physicians (per 1,000 head, 1998): 2.53.

Health Expenditure (2000): US $ per head (PPP): 1,639.

Health Expenditure (2000): % of GDP: 7.9.

Health Expenditure (2000): public (% of total): 86.5.

Access to Water (% of persons, 2000): 100.

Access to Sanitation (% of persons, 2000): 100.

For sources and definitions, see explanatory note on p. vi.

AGRICULTURE

Principal Crop (metric tons, 2000): Tobacco 324.

Livestock (2000/2001): Cattle 1,224; Sheep 2,053; Horses 982; Goats 402.

FINANCE

Currency and Exchange Rates: 100 cent = 1 euro. *Sterling and Dollar Equivalents* (31 December 2002): £1 sterling = 1.5370 euros; US $1 = 0.9536 euros; 100 euros = £65.06 = US $104.87. *Average Exchange Rate* (euros per US dollar): 1.0854 in 2000; 1.1175 in 2001; 1.0626 in 2002. Note: French and Spanish currencies were formerly in use. From the introduction of the euro, with French and Spanish participation, on 1 January 1999, fixed exchange rates of €1 = 6.55957 francs and €1 = 166.386 pesetas were in operation. Euro notes and coins were introduced on 1 January 2002. The euro and local currencies circulated alongside each other until 17 February (francs) or 28 February (pesetas), after which the euro became the sole legal tender. Some of the figures in this Survey are still in terms of pesetas.

Budget (preliminary figures, '000 euros, 2002): *Revenue:* Indirect taxes 190,821.8; Property income 34,752.5; Other taxes and income 17,025.6; Financial assets 216.8; Financial liabilities 131.1; Total 242,947.8. *Expenditure:* Current expenditure 125,644.6 (Personnel emoluments 51,423.6; Goods and services 29,150.2; Interest payments 4,913.8; Current transfers 40,157.1); Capital expenditure 135,022.7 (Fixed capital investment 95,279.6; Capital transfers 39,743.1); Financial assets 150.3; Financial liabilities 12.0; Total 260,829.6.

Cost of Living (2001; consumer price index base: 1998 = 100): Food, beverages and tobacco 112.5; Clothing and footwear 116.3; *All items* 110.9.

EXTERNAL TRADE

Principal Commodities (million euros, 2001): *Imports:* Live animals and animal products 59.3; Prepared foodstuffs; beverages, spirits and vinegar; tobacco and manufactured substitutes 155.3; Mineral products 64.1; Products of chemical or allied industries 116.7; Wood pulp, etc.; paper and paperboard and articles thereof 86.0; Textiles and textile articles 99.6; Base metals and articles thereof 44.5; Machinery and mechanical appliances; electrical equipment; sound and television apparatus 206.9; Vehicles, aircraft, vessels and associated transport equipment 104.4; Optical, photographic, cinematographic, precision and medical instruments, etc.; clocks and watches; musical instruments 66.1; Furniture, bed linen, etc.; lighting devices 68.6; Total (incl. others) 1,222.9. *Exports:* Prepared foodstuffs; beverages, spirits and vinegar; tobacco and manufactured substitutes 2.5; Products of chemical or allied industries 5.3; Wood pulp, etc.; paper and paperboard and articles thereof 5.4; Textiles and textile articles 3.2; Base metals and articles thereof 1.8; Machinery and mechanical appliances; electrical equipment; sound and television apparatus 12.6; Vehicles, aircraft, vessels and associated transport equipment 9.4; Optical, photographic, cinematographic, precision and medical instruments, etc.; clocks and watches; musical instruments 9.2; Furniture, bed linen, etc.; lighting devices 5.4; Total (incl. others) 58.9.

Principal Trading Partners (million pesetas, 2000): *Imports:* China, People's Republic 2,043; France 48,949; Germany 8,156; Italy 7,514; Japan 5,702; Netherlands 1,911; Spain 89,355; Switzerland 3,731; United Kingdom 4,569; USA 3,227; Total (incl. others) 184,024. *Exports:* France 2,152; Germany 128; Greece 138; Hong Kong 194; Russia 94; Spain 5,016; USA 98; Total (incl. others) 8,235.

TRANSPORT

Road Traffic (registered motor vehicles, 1999): Total 58,130. *1996:* Passenger cars 35,358; Commercial vehicles 4,238.

TOURISM

Tourist Arrivals (2001): Spanish 2,517,118; French 821,788; Others 177,355; Total 3,516,261.

COMMUNICATIONS MEDIA

Radio Receivers (1997): 16,000 in use.

Television Receivers (2000): 36,000 in use (Source: UNESCO).

Daily Newspapers (1999): 2 titles published.

Telephones (main lines in use, 2001): 34,505.

Facsimile Machines (number in use, 1998): 5,000 (Source: UN, *Statistical Yearbook*).

Mobile Cellular Telephones (subscribers, 2001): 28,605.

Internet Users (2000): 7,000.
Source: International Telecommunication Union.

EDUCATION

Pre-primary Enrolment (1999/2000): Andorran schools 665; French schools 807; Spanish schools* 678.

Primary and Secondary Enrolment (1999/2000): Andorran schools 1,229; French schools 2,136; Spanish schools* 2,143.

Non-university Higher Education Enrolment (1999/2000): 1,845.

University Enrolment (1999/2000): 1,341.
* Including congregational schools.
Source: Department of Education, Youth and Sports.

Directory

The Constitution

The Constitution of the Principality of Andorra came into force on 4 May 1993, having been approved by the Andorran people in a referendum on 14 March. The official name of the independent state is Principat d'Andorra. The Constitution asserts that Andorra is 'a Democratic and Social independent state abiding by the Rule of Law', defines the fundamental rights, freedoms and obligations of Andorran citizens and delineates the functions and competences of the organs of state.

In accordance with Andorran tradition, the Co-Princes (Coprínceps), respectively the Bishop of Urgel and the President of the French Republic, are titular Heads of State.

The legislature is the General Council (Consell General), one-half of whose members are elected from a single national constituency, the remainder being elected to represent Andorra's seven parishes (Parròquies); members are elected to the Consell General for four years. Elections are on the basis of direct universal adult suffrage. The ruling organ of the Consell General is the Sindicatura, headed by a Speaker (Síndic General).

The Govern (the executive organ of state) is directed by the Head of Government (Cap de Govern), who is elected by the Consell General (and formally appointed by the Co-Princes) and who must command the support of the majority of the legislature's members. The Head of Government nominates government ministers, who may not at the same time be members of the Consell General. The Head of Government is restricted to two consecutive full terms of office.

The Constitution defines the composition and powers of the judiciary, the highest organ of which is the Higher Court of Justice (Consell Superior de Justícia).

The Constitution defines the functions of the communal councils (Comuns), which are the organs of representation and administration of the parishes.

Revision of the Constitution shall require the approval of two-thirds of the members of the Consell General and ratification by a referendum. The Consell General is advised on constitutional matters by the Institució del Raonador del Ciutadà, an independent institution established in 1998, responsible for the application of the Constitution.

The Constitutional Court is the supreme interpreter of the Constitution. Its decisions are binding for public authorities and for individuals.

The Government

HEADS OF STATE

Episcopal Co-Prince: Dr JOAN MARTÍ ALANIS (Bishop of Urgel).
French Co-Prince: JACQUES CHIRAC.

GOVERNMENT
(April 2003)

Head of Government: MARC FORNÉ MOLNÉ.

Minister of Presidency and Tourism: ENRIC PUJAL ARENY.

Minister of Culture: XAVIER MONTANÉ ATERO.

Minister of Finance: MIREIA MAESTRE CORTADELLA.

Minister of Foreign Affairs: JULI MINOVES TRIQUELL.

Minister of Justice and the Interior: JORDI VISENT GUITART.

Minister of the Economy: MIQUEL ALVAREZ MARFANY.

Minister of Agriculture and the Environment: OLGA ADELLACH COMA.

Minister of Education, Youth and Sports: PERE CERVÓS CARDONA.

Minister of Territorial Development: JORDI SERRA MALLEU.

Minister of Welfare and Public Health: MÒNICA CODINA TORT.

MINISTRIES

Office of the Head of Government: Govern d'Andorra, Carrer Prat de la Creu 62–64, Andorra la Vella; tel. 875700; fax 822882; internet www.andorra.ad/govern/.

Ministry of Agriculture and the Environment: Carrer Prat de la Creu 62–64, Andorra la Vella; tel. 875700; fax 828906; internet www.mediambient.ad.

Ministry of Culture: 62–64 Carrer Prat de la Creu, Andorra la Vella.

Ministry of Education, Youth and Sports: Carrer Bonaventura Armengol 6, Edif. Crèdit Centre, Andorra la Vella; tel. 866585; fax 861229.

Ministry of Family Affairs: Carrer Prat de la Creu 62–64, Andorra la Vella.

Ministry of Finance: Carrer Prat de la Creu 62–64, Andorra la Vella; tel. 875700; fax 860962; internet www.finances.ad.

Ministry of Foreign Affairs: Carrer Prat de la Creu 62–64, Andorra la Vella; tel. 875700; fax 869559; e-mail exteriors.gov@andorra.ad.

Ministry of Justice and the Interior: Carrer Ciutat de Sabadell, Escaldes-Engordany; tel. 872080; fax 869250.

Ministry of Territorial Development: Carrer Prat de la Creu 62–64, Andorra la Vella; tel. 875701; fax 861313.

Ministry of Presidency and Tourism: Carrer Prat de la Creu 62–64, Andorra la Vella; tel. 875702; fax 860184; e-mail turisme@andorra.ad; internet www.turisme.ad.

Ministry of Welfare and Public Health: Avinguda Príncep Benlloch 26, Andorra la Vella; tel. 860345; fax 861933; internet www.salutibenestar.ad.

Legislature

CONSELL GENERAL
(General Council)

Síndic General (Speaker): FRANCESC ARENY CASAL (PLA).

Subsíndic General (Deputy Speaker): JOSEP ANGEL MORTÉS PONS.

General Election, 4 March 2001

Party	Votes cast	Seats
Partit Liberal d'Andorra	4,309	15
Partit Socialdemocràta	2,683	6
Partit Democràta	2,198	5
Independent candidates	1,702	2
Total	10,892	28

Political Organizations

The establishment of political parties was sanctioned under the Constitution that was promulgated in May 1993.

Iniciatíva Democràtica Nacional (IDN): Plaça Rebés 1, 2°, Andorra la Vella; tel. 866406; fax 866306; e-mail idn@andorra.ad; f. 1993; Leader VICENÇ MATEU ZAMORA.

Nova Democràcia (ND): Andorra la Vella; f. 1993; Leader JAUME BARTOMEU CASSANY.

Partit Democràta (PD): Avinguda del Fener 15–17, 1° C, Andorra la Vella; tel. 805777; fax 805779; e-mail partitdemocrata@andorra.ad; internet www.partitdemocrata.ad; f. 2000 after Agrupament Nacional Democràtic split into two parties; Leader JORDI MAS TORRES.

Partit Liberal d'Andorra (PLA): Edif. Eland, 4°, Avinguda del Fener 11, Andorra la Vella; tel. 869708; fax 869728; e-mail pla@andorra.ad; internet www.partitliberal.ad; f. 1992 as Unió Liberal; Leader MARC FORNÉ MOLNÉ.

Partit Socialdemocràta (PS): Carrer Verge del Pilar 5, 3°, Andorra la Vella; tel. 805262; fax 821746; e-mail ps@andorra.ad; internet www.psa.ad; Leader JAUME BARTUMEU CASSANY.

Other parties are the Bloc d'Acció Política, Democràcia Andorrana, Grup d'Opinió Liberal, Iniciatíva Andorrana d'Escaldes-Engordany, Partit Unió Laurediana and Unió Democràtica Andorrana.

Diplomatic Representation

EMBASSIES IN ANDORRA

France: POB 155, Carrer Sobrevia 7, Andorra la Vella; tel. 820809; fax 860132; e-mail ambaixada.de.franca@andorra.ad; internet www.ambafrance-ad.org; Ambassador DOMINIQUE LASSUS.

Spain: Carrer Prat de la Creu 34, Andorra la Vella; tel. 800030; fax 868500; e-mail embaspad@correo.mae.es; Ambassador CÉSAR GONZÁLEZ PALACIOS.

Judicial System

The 1993 Constitution guarantees the independence of the judiciary. Judicial power is vested, in the first instance, in the Magistrates' Courts (Batllia) and in the Judges' Tribunal (Tribunal de Batlles), the criminal-law courts (Tribunal de Corts) and the Higher Court of Justice (Tribunal Superior de la Justícia). The judiciary is represented, directed and administered by the Higher Council of Justice (Consell Superior de la Justícia), whose five members are appointed for single terms of six years. Final jurisdiction, in constitutional matters, is vested in the Constitutional Court (Tribunal Constitucional), whose four members hold office for no more than two consecutive eight-year terms.

The Press

7 DIES: Avinguda Riberaygua 39, Andorra la Vella; tel. 863700; fax 863800; weekly; local issues; Catalan; Pres. MARC VILA AMIGÓ; Dir ROSA MARI SORRIBES; circ. 27,000.

Butlletí Oficial de Principat d'Andorra: Andorra la Vella; tel. 861400; fax 864300; official govt gazette; weekly.

Correu Andorra: Avinguda Meritxell 144, Andorra la Vella; tel. 22500; fax 22938; weekly.

Diari d'Andorra: Avinguda Riberaygua 39, Andorra la Vella; tel. 863700; fax 863800; internet www.diariandorra.ad; f. 1991; daily; local issues; Catalan; Pres. MARC VILA AMIGÓ; Dir IGNASI PLANELL; circ. 3,500.

Món Diplomatic: Avda Santa Coloma, 36, Andorra la Vella; tel. (972) 911111; fax (872) 031000; e-mail redacció@mondiplomatic.com; internet www.mondiplomatic.com; Catalan edition of Le Monde Diplomatique; monthly.

El Periòdic d'Andorra: Parc de la Mola 10, Torre Caldea, Escaldes-Engordany; tel. 736200; fax 736210; internet www.elperiodico.es/andorra; daily; local issues; Catalan; Dir JOSEP ANTON ROSSELL PUJOL.

Broadcasting and Communications

TELECOMMUNICATIONS

Servei de Telecomunicacions d'Andorra (STA): Avinguda Meritxell 112, Andorra la Vella; tel. 875000; fax 860600; e-mail sta@sta.ad; internet www.sta.ad; provides national and international telecommunications services; Dir RAMÓN PLA.

BROADCASTING

In 2001 there were six radio stations and one television channel in Andorra. Andorra was also able to receive broadcasts from television stations in neighbouring countries.

Radio

Ràdio Nacional Andorra: Baixada del Molí, Andorra la Vella; tel. 873777; fax 864232; e-mail rtvasa@andorra.ad; internet www.rtvasa.ad; f. 1991 as an Andorran-owned commercial public broadcasting service to replace two stations that closed in 1981 following the expiry of their contracts with French and Spanish companies; two stations: Ràdio Andorra and Andorra Música; Dir ENRIC CASTELLET.

Ràdio Valira: Carrer del Parnal, 2,, Escaldes-Engordany; tel. 829600; fax 828273; e-mail radiovalira@radiovalira.ad; internet www.radiovalira.com; f. 1985; public commercial broadcasting service; Dirs GUALBERTO OSORIO, JOSÉ RABADA.

Television

Andorra Televisió: Baixada del Molí 24, Andorra la Vella; tel. 873777; fax 864232; e-mail rtvasa@andorra.ad; internet www.rtvasa.ad; f. 1995 as an Andorran-owned commercial public broadcasting service; Dir ENRIC CASTELLET.

Antena 7: Avinguda les Escoles 16, Escaldes-Engordany; tel. 824433; fax 826088; private co; in 1987 began to transmit one hour of Andorran-interest programmes from the Spanish side of the border.

Finance

(cap. = capital; res = reserves; dep. = deposits; m. = million; brs = branches; amounts in Spanish pesetas or euros—€)

PRINCIPAL BANKS

Andbanc—Grup Agricol Reig: C/. Manuel Cerqueda i Escaler, 6, Escaldes-Engordany; tel. 873315; fax 868050; e-mail info@andbanc.com; internet www.andbanc.com; f. 2002 by merger of Banca Reig and Banc Agricol i Comercial d'Andorra; cap. €68.1m., res €233.9m., dep. €1,862.6m. Chair. MANEL CERQUERDA; 13 brs.

Banc Internacional d'Andorra SA: POB 8, Avinguda Meritxell 32, Andorra la Vella; tel. 884488; fax 884499; e-mail bibm@bibm.ad; internet www.bibm.ad; f. 1958; 51% owned by Banco Bilbao Vizcaya Argentaria (Spain); cap. €42.4m., res €150.9m., dep. €2,054.2m. (Dec. 2001); Hon. Chair. JOAN MORA FONT; Chair. of Bd of Dirs JORDI ARISTOT MORA; 4 brs.

Banca Mora SA: POB 8, Plaça Coprínceps 2, Escaldes-Engordany; tel. 884488; fax 884499; e-mail bibm@bibm.ad; internet www.bibm.ad; f. 1952; subsidiary of Banc Internacional d'Andorra SA; cap. €30.1m., res €54.1m., dep. €873.8m. (Dec. 2001); Chair. FRANCESC MORA SAGUÉS; Dir JORDI ARISTOT MORA; 7 brs.

Banca Privada d'Andorra SA: POB 25, Avinguda Carlernany 119, Escaldes-Engordany; tel. 873500; fax 873520; e-mail bpa@bpa.ad; internet www.bpa.ad; f. 1962 as Banca Cassany SA; name changed to above in 1994; cap. €33.0m., res €10.9m., dep. €637.2m. (Dec. 2002); Pres. HIGINI CIERCO I GARCÍA; Gen. Man. JOAN PAU MIQUEL PRATS; 3 brs.

CaixaBank SA: POB 77F–2003E; Plaça Rebés 3, Andorra la Vella; tel. 874874; fax 829003; e-mail caixabank@andorra.ad; internet www.caixabank.ad; f. 1997; cap. 30m., res 44m., dep. 1,052m. (Dec. 2001); Chair. PERE ROQUET; Gen. Man. PERE CAMPISTOL.

Crèdit Andorrà: Avinguda Meritxell 80, Andorra la Vella; tel. 888000; fax 888001; e-mail ca@creditandorra.ad; internet www.creditandorra.ad; f. 1955; cap. €70.0m., res €298.3m., dep. €2,811.2m. (Dec. 2001); Chair. A. PINTAT; CEO J. PERALBA; 15 brs.

Trade and Industry

CHAMBER OF COMMERCE

Cambra de Comerç, Indústria i Serveis d'Andorra: Carrer Prat de la Creu 8, Edif. Le Mans, Despatx 204–205, Andorra la Vella; tel. 863232; fax 863233; e-mail ccis@andorra.ad; internet www.ccis.ad; Pres. RAMÓN CIERCO NOGUER.

UTILITIES

Electricity

Forces Elèctriques d'Andorra (FEDA): Andorra la Vella; f. 1988; imports, generates and distributes electricity.

Mútua Elèctrica Sant Julià de Lòria: Avinguda Francesc Cairat, Sant Julià de Lòria; tel. 841180; fax 843322; regional electricity distributor.

Sercensa: Avinguda Copríncep Francés 1, Encamp; tel. 832103; fax 833007; regional electricity distributor.

Transport

RAILWAYS

In 2001 construction began on a 40,000m.-peseta overhead train system, which was expected to alleviate traffic problems in Andorra la Vella. The 8 km-line was to link Sant Julià de Lòria and Escaldes-Engordany to the capital. Until completion of this network, the nearest stations are Ax-les-Thermes, L'Hospitalet and La Tour de Carol, in France (with trains from Toulouse and Perpignan), and Puigcerdá, in Spain, on the line from Barcelona. There is a connecting bus service from all four stations to Andorra.

ROADS

A good road connects the Spanish and French frontiers, passing through Andorra la Vella. In 1996 there were 279 national roads, 198 of which were tarmacked. The Envalira tunnel, between Andorra and France, was opened in September 2002.

CIVIL AVIATION

In late 2001 the Seo d'Urgel-Andorra airport, located in Spanish territory 10 km from the border, was under redevelopment as a one-runway international airport for Andorra, at an estimated cost of 2,000m. pesetas.

Tourism

Andorra has attractive mountain scenery, and winter sports facilities are available at six skiing centres. In 2001 the Government planned to promote Andorra as an up-market winter sports destination. By 2002 there were 174 ski slopes available. Tourists are also attracted by Andorra's duty-free shopping facilities. In 2001 there were 265 hotels and hostels in Andorra, with a total of 12,527 rooms. Around 3.5m. tourists visited Andorra in 2001.

Andorra Department of Tourism: Carrer Prat de la Creu 62–64, Andorra la Vella; tel. 875702; fax 860184; e-mail turisme@andorra.ad; internet www.turisme.ad.

Andorra Hotel Association: Antic Carrer Major 18, Andorra la Vella; tel. 820602; fax 861539; e-mail uhotelera@uha.ad; internet www.uha.ad; Pres. MARC ALEIX.

Sindicat d'Iniciatíva Oficina de Turisme: Carrer Dr Vilanova, Andorra la Vella; tel. 820214; fax 825823; e-mail sindicatdiniciativa@andorra.ad.

ANGOLA

Introductory Survey

Location, Climate, Language, Religion, Flag, Capital

The Republic of Angola lies on the west coast of Africa. The Cabinda district is separated from the rest of the country by the estuary of the River Congo and territory of the Democratic Republic of the Congo (DRC—formerly Zaire), with the Republic of the Congo lying to its north. Angola is bordered by the DRC to the north, Zambia to the east and Namibia to the south. The climate is tropical, locally tempered by altitude. There are two distinct seasons (wet and dry) but little seasonal variation in temperature. It is very hot and rainy in the coastal lowlands but temperatures are lower inland. The official language is Portuguese, but African languages (the most widely spoken being Umbundo, Lunda, Kikongo, Chokwe and Kwanyama) are also in common use. Much of the population follows traditional African beliefs, although a majority profess to be Christians, mainly Roman Catholics. The flag (proportions 2 by 3) has two equal horizontal stripes, of red and black; superimposed in the centre, in gold, are a five-pointed star, half a cog-wheel and a machete. The capital is Luanda.

Recent History

Formerly a Portuguese colony, Angola became an overseas province in 1951. African nationalist groups began to form in the 1950s and 1960s, including the Movimento Popular de Libertação de Angola (MPLA) in 1956, the Frente Nacional de Libertação de Angola (FNLA) in 1962 and the União Nacional para a Independência Total de Angola (UNITA) in 1966. Severe repression followed an unsuccessful nationalist rebellion in 1961, but, after a new wave of fighting in 1966, nationalist guerrilla groups were able to establish military and political control in large parts of eastern Angola and to press westward. Following the April 1974 *coup d'état* in Portugal, Angola's right to independence was recognized, and negotiations between the Portuguese Government and the nationalist groups began in September. After the formation of a common front by these groups, it was agreed that Angola would become independent in November 1975.

In January 1975 a transitional Government was established, comprising representatives of the MPLA, the FNLA, UNITA and the Portuguese Government. However, from March political differences led to violent clashes between the MPLA and the FNLA. By the second half of 1975 control of Angola was effectively divided between the three major nationalist groups, each aided by foreign powers. The MPLA (which held the capital) was supported by the USSR and Cuba, the FNLA by Zaire and Western powers (including the USA), while UNITA was backed by South African forces. The FNLA and UNITA formed a united front to fight the MPLA.

The Portuguese Government proclaimed Angola independent from 11 November 1975, transferring sovereignty to 'the Angolan people' rather than to any of the liberation movements. The MPLA proclaimed the People's Republic of Angola and the establishment of a government in Luanda under the presidency of the movement's leader, Dr Agostinho Neto. The FNLA and UNITA proclaimed the Democratic People's Republic of Angola and a coalition government, based in Nova Lisboa (renamed Huambo). By the end of February 1976, however, the MPLA, aided by Cuban technical and military expertise, had effectively gained control of the whole country. South African troops were withdrawn from Angola in March, but Cuban troops remained to assist the MPLA regime in countering guerrilla activity by the remnants of the defeated UNITA forces.

In May 1977 an abortive coup, led by Nito Alves (a former minister), resulted in a purge of state and party officials. In December the MPLA was renamed the Movimento Popular de Libertação de Angola—Partido do Trabalho (MPLA—PT), but further divisions became evident in December 1978, when President Neto abolished the post of Prime Minister and ousted several other ministers.

Neto died in September 1979, and José Eduardo dos Santos, hitherto the Minister of Planning, was elected party leader and President by the MPLA—PT Central Committee. Dos Santos continued to encourage strong links with the Soviet bloc and led campaigns to eliminate corruption and inefficiency. Elections to the National People's Assembly (Assembléia Popular Nacional), which replaced the Council of the Revolution (Conselho da Revolução), were first held in 1980. Fresh elections, due to be held in 1983, were postponed until 1986, owing to political and military problems.

The MPLA—PT Government's recovery programme was continually hindered by security problems. Although the FNLA rebel movement reportedly surrendered to the Government in 1984, UNITA conducted sustained and disruptive guerrilla activities, mainly in southern and central Angola, throughout the 1980s. In addition, forces from South Africa, which was providing UNITA with considerable military aid, made numerous armed incursions over the Angolan border with Namibia, ostensibly in pursuit of guerrilla forces belonging to the South West Africa People's Organisation (SWAPO), which was supported by the Angolan Government. Although the Government's military campaign against UNITA appeared to be increasingly successful during 1985, the rebels' position was strengthened in 1986, when US military aid began to arrive. (The US Government continued to provide covert military aid to UNITA until 1990.) Nevertheless, UNITA was excluded from a series of major peace negotiations, between Angola, Cuba and South Africa (with the unofficial mediation of the USA), which commenced in May 1988. By mid-July the participants had agreed to a document containing the principles for a peace settlement that provided for independence for Namibia, the discontinuation of South African military support for UNITA and the withdrawal of Cuban troops from Angola. In July and August Dr Jonas Savimbi, the President of UNITA, travelled to the USA and to several European and African capitals to seek support for UNITA's demands to be included in the negotiations. Although movement for a negotiated settlement between the MPLA—PT Government and UNITA gathered momentum, UNITA's position became vulnerable in August, when a cease-fire between Angola and South Africa was declared, and South African troops were withdrawn from Angola. UNITA refused to adhere to the cease-fire. Following the conclusion of the New York accords on Angola and Namibia in December, the US Government renewed its commitment to the rebels.

During late 1988 several African states (including Zaire) were involved in efforts, supported by the USA, to pressurize the Angolan Government into negotiating an internal settlement with UNITA. In December the UN Security Council established the UN Angola Verification Mission (UNAVEM) to verify the phased withdrawal of Cuban troops from Angola, which was completed in May 1991.

In February 1989 the Angolan Government offered a 12-month amnesty to UNITA members. UNITA, restating its aim of entering into a transitional coalition government with the MPLA—PT as a prelude to multi-party elections, responded by launching an offensive against government targets, which was halted following the intercession of President Houphouët-Boigny of Côte d'Ivoire. In March dos Santos announced that he was willing to attend a regional summit conference on the Angolan civil war; Savimbi, in turn, announced that he would honour a unilateral moratorium on offensive military operations until July. In May dos Santos presented a peace plan that envisaged the cessation of US aid to UNITA and offered the rebels reintegration into society; this was rejected by UNITA. Nevertheless, in June both dos Santos and Savimbi attended a conference at Gbadolite, Zaire, convened by the Zairean President, Mobutu Sese Seko. Mobutu succeeded in mediating a peace agreement between the Angolan Government and UNITA, in accordance with which a cease-fire came into effect on 24 June. The full terms of the accord were not, however, made public, and it subsequently became apparent that these were interpreted differently by each party. Within one week, each side had accused the other of violating the cease-fire, and in August Savimbi announced a resumption of hostilities.

In September 1989, after boycotting a conference of African Heads of State in Kinshasa, Zaire, at which the June peace accord had been redrafted, Savimbi announced a series of counter-proposals, envisaging the creation of an African peace-keeping force to supervise a renewed cease-fire and the commencement of negotiations between UNITA and the Angolan Government towards a settlement providing the foundation of a multi-party democracy in Angola. In October, following a meeting with President George Bush of the USA, Savimbi agreed to resume peace talks with the Angolan Government, with Mobutu acting as mediator. In December dos Santos proposed a peace plan that envisaged some political reform, but did not include provisions for a multi-party political system; the plan was rejected by UNITA.

In July 1990 the Central Committee of the MPLA—PT announced that the Government would allow Angola to 'evolve towards a multi-party system'. In October the Central Committee proposed a general programme of reform, including the replacement of the party's official Marxist-Leninist ideology with a commitment to 'democratic socialism', the legalization of political parties, the transformation of the army from a party institution to a state institution, the introduction of a market economy, a revision of the Constitution and the holding of multi-party elections in 1994, following a population census. These proposals were formally approved by the MPLA—PT in December. However, the Government and UNITA continued to disagree over the timing of elections and the status of UNITA pending the elections.

In March 1991 the Assembléia Popular approved legislation permitting the formation of political parties. On 1 May the Government and UNITA concluded a peace agreement in Estoril, Portugal, which provided for a cease-fire from 15 May, to be monitored by a joint political and military commission, with representatives from the MPLA—PT, UNITA, the UN, Portugal, the USA and the USSR. A new national army of 50,000 men was to be established, comprising equal numbers of government and UNITA soldiers. Free and democratic elections were to be held by the end of 1992. On 31 May the Government and UNITA signed a formal agreement in Lisbon, Portugal, ratifying the Estoril agreement. Meanwhile, all Cuban troops had been withdrawn from Angola, but the UN Security Council agreed to prolong the presence of the UN Angola Verification Mission (as UNAVEM II), with a mandate to ensure implementation of the peace accord. In July the Standing Commission of the Assembléia Popular approved a new amnesty law, under the terms of which amnesty would be granted for all crimes against state security as well as for military and common law offences committed before 31 May 1991.

A reshuffle of the Council of Ministers in July 1991 included the appointment of Fernando José França van-Dúnem to the post of Prime Minister, thus reintroducing the premiership to the Government. Supreme executive power remained, however, with the President.

In September 1991 Savimbi returned to Luanda for the first time since the civil war began in 1975, and UNITA headquarters were transferred to the capital from Jamba in October. In the following month dos Santos announced that legislative and presidential elections were to take place in September 1992, subject to the extension of state administration to areas still under UNITA control and the confinement of all UNITA forces to assembly points by mid-December 1991. In January 1992, on the recommendation of the joint political and military commission, a monitoring task group was established to oversee the implementation of the peace agreement. The creation of the group, which included members of the Government, UNITA and UNAVEM II, followed growing concern over the reported decline in the number of government and UNITA troops in confinement areas and the reoccupation of territory by UNITA forces.

Representatives of the Government and 26 political parties met in Luanda in January 1992 to discuss the transition to multi-party democracy. UNITA boycotted the meeting, but in February it held talks with the Government, at which it was agreed that the elections would be conducted on the basis of proportional representation, with the President elected for a five-year term, renewable for a maximum of three terms. The legislature would be a national assembly, elected for a four-year term. In April the Assembléia Popular adopted electoral legislation incorporating these decisions and providing for the creation of a National Assembly (Assembléia Nacional) comprising 223 members (90 to be elected in 18 provincial constituencies and the remainder from national lists).

In April 1992 the Supreme Court approved UNITA's registration as a political party. In May the MPLA—PT voted to enlarge the membership of the Central Committee to include prominent

dissidents who had returned to the party. The Central Committee recommended that the party's membership be further expanded with a view to broadening the party's support base. During the congress the delegates also voted to remove the suffix Partido do Trabalho (Party of Labour or Workers' Party) from the organization's official name. In August the legislature approved a further revision of the Constitution, removing the remnants of the country's former Marxist ideology, and deleting the words 'People's' and 'Popular' from the Constitution and from the names of official institutions. The name of the country was changed from the People's Republic of Angola to the Republic of Angola.

Increased tension and outbreaks of violence in the period preceding the general election seriously threatened to disrupt the electoral process. In early September 1992 in Cabinda province, the enclave that provides most of Angola's petroleum revenue, secessionist groups, notably the Frente de Libertação do Enclave de Cabinda (FLEC), intensified attacks on government troops. Also in that month, clashes took place between UNITA and government forces in Bié province.

On 27 September 1992 the government Forças Armadas Populares de Libertação de Angola (FAPLA) and the UNITA forces were formally disbanded, and the new national army, the Forças Armadas de Angola (FAA), was established. However, the process of training and incorporating FAPLA and UNITA troops into the new 50,000-strong national army had been hindered by delays in the demobilization programme. By 28 September fewer than 10,000 soldiers were ready to be sworn in as members of the FAA.

Presidential and legislative elections were held, as scheduled, on 29 and 30 September 1992. When preliminary results indicated victory for the MPLA in the elections to the new Assembléia Nacional, Savimbi accused the Government of electoral fraud, withdrew his troops from the FAA, and demanded the suspension of the official announcement of the election results until an inquiry into the alleged irregularities had been conducted. A second round of the presidential election was required to be held between dos Santos and Savimbi, as neither candidate had secured 50% of the votes cast in the first round. Savimbi, who had retreated to the UNITA-dominated province of Huambo, agreed to participate in this second round on the condition that it be conducted by the UN, while the Government insisted that the election should not take place until UNITA had satisfied the conditions of the Estoril peace agreement by transferring its troops to assembly points or to the FAA.

Following the announcement, on 17 October 1992, of the official results of the elections, which the UN had declared to have been free and fair, violence broke out between MPLA and UNITA supporters in the cities of Luanda and Huambo. By the end of October hostilities had spread throughout Angola, with the majority of UNITA's demobilized soldiers returning to arms. On 20 November, following negotiations with UN diplomats, Savimbi agreed to abide by the results of the September elections, although he maintained that the ballot had been fraudulent. Subsequently dos Santos announced that the Assembléia Nacional would be inaugurated on 26 November. On that day delegations from the Government and UNITA met in Namibe in an effort to resolve the crisis. A joint communiqué was issued, declaring full acceptance of the validity of the May 1991 Estoril peace agreement and the intention to implement immediately a nation-wide cease-fire. However, UNITA's 70 elected deputies failed to attend the inauguration of the Assembléia. On 27 November dos Santos announced the appointment of Marcolino José Carlos Moco, the Secretary-General of the MPLA, as Prime Minister. At the end of November, in violation of the recently signed Namibe accord, hostilities broke out in the north of the country. On 2 December a new Council of Ministers was announced, including minor ministerial positions for members of the FNLA and three other parties. In addition, one full and four deputy ministerial posts were reserved for UNITA, which was allowed one week to join the Government. UNITA subsequently nominated a number of its officials to the reserved posts. According to a statement by the Prime Minister, however, the appointment of UNITA officials to the Government was entirely dependent upon the implementation of the Estoril peace agreement.

In 1993–94 the UN continued its efforts to negotiate a permanent peace accord between the Government and UNITA. Meanwhile, civil war, in which both sides claimed military gains and suffered heavy losses, continued. Diplomatic moves to end the hostilities included talks in Addis Ababa, Ethiopia, in Abidjan,

Côte d'Ivoire, and in Lusaka, Zambia. In May 1993 the US President, Bill Clinton, announced that the USA was to recognize the Angolan Government. In September, following reports of an intensification of UNITA activity, the UN imposed an arms and petroleum embargo against the rebels, the 'freezing' of UNITA's foreign assets, and the expulsion of its representatives from Western capitals. However, in November UNITA agreed to withdraw its forces to UN-monitored confinement areas. In response, the UN agreed to delay the imposition of further sanctions against UNITA.

As a consequence of the Lusaka talks, by 10 December 1993 an agreement had reportedly been reached between UNITA and the Government on issues concerning the demobilization and confinement of UNITA troops, the surrender of UNITA weapons to the UN, and the integration of UNITA generals into the FAA, prompting the UN again to postpone additional sanctions against the rebels. The Lusaka talks resumed in January 1994, and agreement was reached on the formation, under UN supervision, of a national police force of 26,700 members, of which UNITA was to provide 5,500. Further talks culminated in the signing, on 17 February, of a document on national reconciliation. Acceptance of the September 1992 election results by both sides was also reaffirmed. However, progress at the Lusaka peace talks slowed as discussions advanced to the issue of the participation of UNITA in central and local government. Negotiations on the distribution of ministerial posts appeared to have reached an impasse in March 1994, although in May agreement was reached on the second round of the presidential election between dos Santos and Savimbi. Further talks, concerning UNITA's representation in the Council of Ministers and the status of Savimbi, reached a stalemate in May. Talks continued in Lusaka in late June, culminating in the signing of an 18-point document on national reconciliation.

In July 1994 President Mandela of South Africa hosted talks in Pretoria between the Presidents of Angola, Mozambique and Zaire. The discussions concentrated on allegations of Zairean support for UNITA and resulted in the re-establishment of a joint defence and security commission between Angola and Zaire, with the aim of curbing the supply of armaments to the rebels. In August UNITA acceded to government insistence that its officials be permitted to participate in government institutions only after the total demilitarization of the movement, and an 11-point procedural accord, enabling discussions on full reconciliation, was signed.

In early September 1994 UNITA reportedly accepted a proposal for the allocation to UNITA of government positions that included some 170 posts in central and local administration, but excluded the governorship of Huambo. In mid-September the Government and UNITA agreed on the general principles governing the mandate of a new UN Angola Verification Mission—UNAVEM III. At the end of that month, following successive extensions, the UN Security Council further extended the mandate of UNAVEM II until 31 October and urged both sides to sign a peace accord by 15 October. However, talks continued throughout October, concentrating on the issue of Savimbi's security and the replacement of the joint political and military commission with a new joint commission, which was to be chaired by the UN Secretary-General's special representative, Alioune Blondin Beye, and was to comprise representatives of the Government and UNITA and observers from the USA, Russia and Portugal. A peace accord was finally initialled on 31 October and formally signed on 20 November. However, hostilities continued beyond 22 November, when a permanent cease-fire was to have come into force, notably in Huambo and in Bié province.

In January 1995 a meeting took place at Chipipa, in Huambo province, between the Chief of General Staff of the FAA and his UNITA counterpart, at which agreement was reached on an immediate cessation of hostilities nation-wide. Nevertheless, the fighting continued. In February 1995 the UN Security Council adopted a resolution creating UNAVEM III. However, the deployment of the new peace-keeping mission remained conditional on the cessation of hostilities and the disengagement of government and UNITA forces.

In March 1995 both the Government and UNITA were criticized in a report made to the UN Security Council by the UN Secretary-General, Dr Boutros Boutros-Ghali, who accused the two sides of a lack of goodwill in implementing the peace process. The report set a deadline of 25 March for the two sides to demonstrate a genuine commitment to the peace process and appealed for preparations to be expedited to enable the prompt

transfer of UNITA troops into the FAA. In April the joint commission reported a significant reduction in violations of the cease-fire. However, at the same time Boutros-Ghali indicated that reports of military preparations, including the acquisition of arms from abroad, remained a serious concern.

In May 1995 dos Santos and Savimbi met in Lusaka for direct talks, which concluded with the ratification of the Lusaka peace accord. Notably, Savimbi recognized the status of dos Santos as President of Angola and pledged his full co-operation in the reconstruction of the nation. The two leaders agreed to accelerate the consolidation of the cease-fire, to create conditions for the deployment of UNAVEM III, to expedite the integration of UNITA troops into the FAA, and to establish a government of unity based on the provisions of the Lusaka accord (subsequent to the demobilization of the UNITA forces). Dos Santos requested that Savimbi immediately nominate the UNITA appointees to the new government.

In June 1995 the MPLA proposed a revision of the Constitution to create two new posts of Vice-President, of which one was to be offered to Savimbi, conditional upon the prior disbanding of UNITA forces. The other vice-presidency was to be assumed by van-Dúnem, the President of the Assembléia Nacional. Later that month Savimbi, who had publicly expressed his intention to accept the vice-presidency, declared the war in Angola to be at an end and appealed to neighbouring nations to prevent the traffic of arms to the country. In July the Assembléia approved the creation of the two new vice-presidential positions, and Boutros-Ghali announced that the deployment of UNAVEM III personnel would be completed by the end of August.

In September 1995 the joint commission expressed concern at continuing violations of the cease-fire. However, in the following month, figures issued by UNAVEM III revealed that recorded cease-fire violations had decreased by approximately 50% between July and September. In late September the Government signed a four-month cease-fire agreement with FLEC—Renovada (FLEC—R), a faction of FLEC. It was anticipated that the agreement, which followed an offensive by FLEC—R on Cabinda City in the previous month, would facilitate the negotiation, between the Government and all factions of FLEC, of a pact aimed at national reconciliation.

The cantonment of UNITA forces began officially in late November 1995. However, continued hostilities were reported that month, including confrontations in the diamond-producing areas of the north-east and in the Cabinda enclave. In December, following concerted military operations by government forces in Zaire province, UNITA suspended the confinement of its troops. In an effort to promote confidence in the peace process in advance of discussions to be conducted that month with US President Clinton, dos Santos introduced a number of conciliatory measures, including the withdrawal of government troops from positions seized in Zaire province, and the confinement of the paramilitary Rapid Intervention Force. In January 1996 UNITA resumed the process of confining its troops. By early February, however, only some 8,200 UNITA troops had been cantoned, prompting the UN Security Council to renew the mandate of UNAVEM III. In January, following discussions conducted in Brazzaville, Republic of the Congo, the Government and FLEC—R agreed to extend their cease-fire accord.

In March 1996 discussions between dos Santos and Savimbi, conducted in Libreville, Gabon, resulted in agreement on the establishment of a government of national unity, in accordance with the provisions of the Lusaka accord, by the end of July. Savimbi proposed the UNITA governmental nominees, while dos Santos formally invited Savimbi to assume the vice-presidency. (Later in March, however, Savimbi demanded the appointment of other opposition members to the government of national unity, presenting as a condition to his own participation the inclusion of the President of the FNLA, Holden Roberto.) Agreement was also reached in Libreville on the formation of a unified national army, which, it was envisaged, would be concluded in June. In subsequent talks it was agreed that 18 UNITA generals would be appointed to command posts in the new, unified FAA. It was also established that 26,300 of UNITA's total force of some 62,000 would be integrated into the FAA. In May agreement was reached on a programme to integrate UNITA troops into the FAA; selection of UNITA personnel was to begin on 1 June. During May Savimbi introduced further conditions for his acceptance of the vice-presidency and expressed his intention to retain control of diamond-producing areas in north-eastern Angola. In mid-May the Government and a Cabinda secessionist faction, FLEC—Forças Armadas Cabindesas (FLEC—FAC), signed an agreement outlining the principles of a cease-fire. However, following renewed fighting later that month between government troops and the secessionists, the leader of FLEC—FAC, Henrique N'zita Tiago, declared that a definitive cease-fire would only follow the withdrawal of the FAA from Cabinda.

In mid-1996 public protest at deteriorating economic conditions and the high level of corruption within the state apparatus placed increasing political pressure on dos Santos, who responded in June with the dismissal of the Moco administration. Moco was succeeded as Prime Minister by van-Dúnem. In August, following its party congress, UNITA issued a communiqué declining the appointment of Savimbi to the position of national Vice-President. UNITA did not propose the appointment of another of its officials to the post, and in September Beye confirmed that the offer of the vice-presidency had become void.

In October 1996 delays in the implementation of the provisions of the Lusaka accord prompted the UN Security Council to threaten the imposition of sanctions against UNITA unless it met certain requirements by 20 November, including the surrender of weapons and the designation of those UNITA troops to be integrated into the FAA. In the following month the Assembléia Nacional adopted a constitutional revision extending its mandate, which was due to expire that month, for a period of between two and four years, pending the establishment of suitable conditions for the conduct of free and fair elections. Despite assertions by UNITA that it had fully disarmed, UNAVEM III expressed concern in December that UNITA troops had deserted confinement areas, while UN sources reported the existence of a residual, well-armed UNITA force in central and north-eastern Angola. None the less, the Government announced that the UNITA deputies who had been elected in 1992 would join the Assembléia in mid-January 1997, and that a new government of national unity and reconciliation would be inaugurated on 25 January. However, following the failure of the UNITA deputies to join the Assembléia, the Government postponed the inauguration of the new administration. In February UNITA asserted that it would only send its deputies and government nominees to the capital, if the Government first agreed to negotiate a draft programme for the government of national unity and reconciliation. In March the Government conceded to UNITA's demand, and a basic programme was formulated. In April an agreement was reached to accord Savimbi the special status of official 'leader of the opposition'. Subsequent to the arrival of the full contingent of UNITA deputies and government nominees in Luanda, on 11 April the new Government of National Unity and Reconciliation was inaugurated. As envisaged, UNITA assumed a number of ministerial and deputy ministerial portfolios. Ten minor political parties were also represented in the Government.

In May 1997 the Angolan Government officially recognized the new Government of Laurent-Désiré Kabila in the Democratic Republic of the Congo (DRC, formerly Zaire). The Angolan Government had actively supported Kabila's rebels during the civil war in Zaire, while UNITA, which relied on Zaire as a conduit for exporting diamonds and importing arms, had reportedly sent some 2,000 troops to support President Mobutu. In the light of the defeat of UNITA's main ally, the Government subsequently launched a military offensive on UNITA strongholds in the north-eastern provinces of Lunda-Sul and Lunda-Norte in what appeared to be an attempt to eradicate UNITA as a military force.

On 30 June 1997 the UN Security Council unanimously approved the discontinuation of UNAVEM III, following numerous extensions to its mandate, and its replacement by a scaled-down observer mission, the UN Observer Mission in Angola (MONUA), with a seven-month mandate to oversee the implementation of the remaining provisions of the Lusaka accord. In late July the UN again condemned UNITA's failure to adhere to the Lusaka accord and threatened to impose further sanctions on the movement, including travel restrictions, if it did not take irreversible steps towards fulfilling its obligations. A deadline of 15 August was set by which date UNITA was to give a full account of its military strength and to allow for the disarmament of its troops and the extension of state administration into those areas under its control. UNITA failed to meet the requirements stipulated by the UN, which on 28 August unanimously adopted new sanctions. However, the implementation of the resolution was delayed until 30 Sep-

tember, and at the end of August UNITA announced that it intended to comply with the UN's demands. In September the restoration of state administration proceeded in several districts and, despite unsatisfactory progress in the demobilization of UNITA's residual force, was sufficient to prompt the UN Security Council, at the end of that month, to postpone the implementation of the sanctions for a further 30 days.

In July 1997 government delegations from Angola and the Republic of the Congo met in Cabinda to discuss the security situation along the border between the Angolan exclave and the Congo, following armed clashes between Angolan soldiers and FLEC separatists apparently operating from Congolese territory. The talks resulted in proposals to strengthen border security, including the establishment of a joint police force, comprising representatives from both countries and the UN High Commissioner for Refugees. However, in October it became evident that FAA troops were actively supporting the former Marxist ruler of the Congo, Gen. Denis Sassou-Nguesso, in his attempts to overthrow the Government of President Pascal Lissouba. Angola's involvement had been prompted by attacks on Cabinda by FLEC and UNITA forces operating from bases in the Congo provided by Lissouba. In mid-October Sassou-Nguesso's Cobra militia, with Angolan assistance, succeeded in securing his return to power in the Congo.

On 31 October 1997, as a result of UNITA's continued failure to meet its obligations under the peace accord, the UN Security Council finally ordered the implementation of additional sanctions against the movement. In November UNITA expressed its intention to continue to pursue a peaceful settlement, and during the ensuing months ceded further territory to state administration, including the important Cuango valley diamond mines in Lunda-Norte province.

In January 1998 a new schedule was agreed for the implementation of the Lusaka protocol, with a deadline of 28 February (later revised to 16 March) for UNITA demobilization. In early March UNITA announced the disbandment of its remaining forces, following which it received official recognition as a legally constituted party. Later that month the Government implemented the special status agreed for Savimbi, and legislation was adopted allowing him to retain a 400-strong personal guard. However, allegations persisted of preparations by UNITA for a resumption of hostilities. By June fighting had spread to 14 of the country's 18 provinces, displacing some 150,000 people. In July many members of UNITA were reported to have left Luanda, and a meeting of the joint commission had to be postponed owing to the temporary absence of UNITA's chief representative. In mid-August the Government threatened to suspend UNITA's representatives in the Government and the legislature unless it had disarmed fully and ceded all remaining territory under its control by 28 August. In late August UNITA accused the observer countries in the joint commission (Portugal, Russia and the USA) of bias in the Government's favour and declared that it would no longer negotiate with them. On 31 August the Government suspended UNITA's government and parliamentary representatives from office.

On 2 September 1998 a group of five UNITA moderates, who were based in the capital and led by the suspended Minister of Hotels and Tourism, Jorge Alicerces Valentim, issued a manifesto declaring the suspension of Savimbi and the introduction of an interim UNITA leadership, pending a general congress of the party. Although the group, which styled itself UNITA—Renovada (UNITA—R), commanded very limited support among UNITA's leaders in Luanda, the Government welcomed the development, recognizing UNITA—R as the sole and legitimate representative of UNITA in negotiations concerning the implementation of the Lusaka peace process. Dos Santos was supported in this decision by the Southern African Development Community, which passed a resolution denouncing Savimbi and recognizing the new group. The UN Security Council continued to seek a dialogue between dos Santos and Savimbi as the only solution to the conflict. In late September the Government revoked the suspension of UNITA's representatives in the Government and legislature, but dismissed UNITA's Minister of Geology and Mines, Marcos Samondo. In October the Assembléia Nacional revoked Savimbi's special status. In that month UNITA—R failed to impose its candidate to lead the UNITA parliamentary group when Abel Chivukuvuku was overwhelmingly re-elected as its Chairman. Chivukuvuku, while no longer claiming allegiance to Savimbi, was opposed to UNITA—R and subsequently formed his own wing of UNITA.

In November 1998, following increasingly frequent outbreaks of fighting, the UN Security Council demanded that UNITA withdraw immediately from territories that it had reoccupied through military action and complete the demilitarization of its troops. In the following month João Manuel Gonçalves Lourenço was elected Secretary-General of the MPLA, while dos Santos was re-elected unopposed as party President. The military situation deteriorated considerably in December, prompting the Government to approve the introduction of compulsory military service. In a report to the UN Security Council that month the UN Secretary-General, Kofi Annan, declared that Angola was once again at war and questioned whether the UN still had a role to play in the country. The UN also warned of a major humanitarian crisis in the country, where more than 400,000 people were reported to have abandoned their homes to escape the fighting.

In late January 1999 dos Santos reorganized the Council of Ministers in an effort to address the prevailing military and economic crisis. Notably, the premiership was assumed by dos Santos himself. In that month UNITA—R conducted its first congress in Luanda, at which Eugénio N'Golo 'Manuvakola' was elected leader of the faction. In a report to the UN Security Council issued in mid-January, Annan recommended the withdrawal of MONUA from Angola (after successive extensions to its mandate), declaring that conditions had deteriorated to such an extent that UN personnel were no longer able to function. Both the Government and UNITA had indicated that they favoured the withdrawal of the UN. In February the UN Security Council voted unanimously to end MONUA's mandate and withdraw its operatives by 20 March, although the UN expressed its intention to seek the Government's approval to maintain a presence in the country in the form of a 'follow-up' mission, intended to focus on issues concerning humanitarian assistance and human rights; in June the Government agreed in principle to the idea. In October it was agreed that the UN Office in Angola (UNOA) would comprise some 30 UN officials.

In October 1999, following a large-scale offensive by the FAA in northern, eastern and central Angola, the Government claimed to have made considerable gains, including, most notably, the capture of UNITA's headquarters in Andulo and Bailundo. While UNITA denied that the towns had fallen to the Government, there were reports that Savimbi had fled the area. In a letter to the Government received in late October, Savimbi warned that UNITA troops were approaching the capital and called for dialogue towards a 'national pact'. The Government, however, dismissed the possibility of further talks, demanding instead the full implementation of the Lusaka protocol.

During 1999 the UN increased its efforts to impose sanctions on UNITA, with the appointment of Canada's ambassador to the UN, Robert Fowler, as Chairman of the UN Sanctions Committee. In July the UN financed a six-month investigation into UNITA's funding of its war effort, the source of its armaments and the inefficacy of the sanctions imposed against it. A UN report published in June disclosed the contravention of UN sanctions by a number of African heads of state, including the Presidents of Togo and Burkina Faso, who were apparently involved in the trading of arms for UNITA-mined diamonds. (Angola threatened to boycott the Organization of African Unity summit, due to be held in Togo in June 2000, because of Togo's alleged involvement in the contravention of UN sanctions; Togo subsequently banned all sales of Angolan diamonds, except those bearing a certificate of origin.) In October 1999, following discussions with Fowler, the South African diamond company De Beers, which controls the majority of the international trade in diamonds, announced that it had placed a world-wide embargo on the purchase of all diamonds from Angola, except those whose acquisition was already under contract. The Angolan Government also attempted to stem the flow of illegal diamonds by introducing a strict regime of stone certification. In March 2000 a number of African leaders, as well as individuals in Belgium and Bulgaria, were criticized in a UN report for allegedly violating sanctions that had been imposed on UNITA following the discovery of the trade in illegally mined diamonds. In response, the Angolan Government announced the establishment of a state-owned company, the Sociedade de Comercialização de Diamantes, which was to be responsible for centralizing and regulating the country's diamond trade. All marketing was transferred to the newly created Angolan Selling Corporation. In December the new Canadian Head of the UN Angola Sanctions Committee, Paul Heinbecker, issued a further report on the smuggling of UNITA diamonds, which confirmed that sanctions had failed to prevent the movement's involvement in the diamond trade, and accused several countries of supporting the illegal trade.

At the end of June 2000 the Angolan Government and UNITA representatives were reported to have held secret talks, apparently prompted by a conference in Maputo, Mozambique, on the possible means of achieving peace in Angola. The conference was attended by the Angolan Deputy Minister of Foreign Affairs, George Chicoti, by Eugénio N'Golo 'Manuvakola' from UNITA—R and by Abel Chivukuvuku from UNITA. Furthermore, in August the Angolan Chief of Staff of the Armed Forces, Gen. João de Matos, announced that Savimbi would no longer be prosecuted for his failure to uphold the cease-fire imposed following the 1992 elections. However, he also stated that, although a position would be made available in the Assembléia Nacional for Savimbi, he would not be offered the vice-presidency.

In October 2000 UNITA put forward a 12-point peace plan, which proposed the formation of a 'broad consensus government', the depoliticization of the armed forces, the police and public administration, and the establishment of a national commission to monitor the use of public funds. The proposals were rejected by the Minister of Foreign Affairs, João Bernardo de Miranda. Nevertheless, UNITA reiterated its desire to negotiate with the Angolan Government, on condition that the current Portuguese, US and Russian observers be replaced by Angolan nationals, that the sanctions imposed on UNITA in 1993 be revoked, and that the second round of the 1992 presidential election be held. In November, however, UNITA admitted responsibility for shooting down an aircraft, allegedly carrying diamonds stolen from UNITA territory. Moreover, UNITA rejected an amnesty for all perpetrators of war crimes, which was declared by dos Santos in a speech marking the 25th anniversary of Angola's independence. Nevertheless, in December the Assembléia Nacional approved draft amnesty legislation, which had been proposed by the MPLA as a direct response to appeals for reconciliation in Angola.

In late 2000 and early 2001 strikes were held by civil servants, in protest at dos Santos' alleged participation in an arms-trafficking scandal involving a French company, Brenco International. The company, along with a number of prominent French politicians, including the son of a former French President, François Mitterrand, the former French Minister of the Interior, Charles Pasqua, and the former President of the European Bank for Reconstruction and Development, Jacques Attali, was alleged to have engaged in money-laundering and the unauthorized sales of arms to the dos Santos Government during the 1990s. (In June 2001 the case against Mitterrand's son was rejected by a French court on a technicality.)

Despite persistent fighting between UNITA and MPLA forces throughout early 2001, in March Savimbi announced his intention to abide by the Lusaka accord and called for the resumption of negotiations between the Government, UNITA and the UN. The Government refused to enter into further discussions with Savimbi, but declared its willingness to negotiate the terms of the Lusaka protocol with UNITA—R. In May dos Santos appealed for a cease-fire at an international conference on peace and democracy. Following Savimbi's request for mediation by the Roman Catholic Church in future peace negotiations, UNITA agreed to abide by a cease-fire, on condition that it was called by dos Santos.

In early June 2001, following an alleged declaration by Savimbi that UNITA forces had been conclusively defeated by the FAA, the Minister of Industry, Joaquim Duarte da Costa David, announced that the civil war had effectively ended. Nevertheless, sporadic fighting between both factions persisted throughout mid-2001, and in mid-June the Minister of Defence, Gen. Kundi Paihama, stated that civil war was the only means of securing peace in Angola. In August UNITA carried out an attack on a train in the government-controlled province of Cuanza Norte that was allegedly carrying munitions, although this was denied by the Government; the attack, in which some 260 people were killed, cast further doubts on both sides' commitment to peace. Also in that month, in an attempt to prevent further divisions within the MPLA, dos Santos stated his intention not to stand in the presidential election, which was scheduled to be held in 2002 or 2003.

In September 2001 the Church and civil movements in Angola launched an appeal for peace, calling for a cease-fire and the resumption of dialogue between the Government, UNITA and opposition parties. This appeal was supported by a coalition of

35 opposition parties, the Partidos da Oposição Civil, which advocated the establishment of a transitional government, to rule until such time as elections were held. Although UNITA continued to perpetrate attacks, in November dos Santos declared the civil war to be almost ended, on the grounds that UNITA had only a small number of troops remaining at its disposal.

On 22 February 2002 Savimbi was killed during an ambush by FAA soldiers in Moxico province. He was replaced as UNITA President by António Dembo; however, in early March it was reported that he, too, had died, possibly through FAA action, which the Government denied, or as a result of acute diabetes. On 13 March the Government halted military offensives against UNITA, and on 30 March, following talks between the Government and UNITA's Chief-of-Staff, Gen. Abreu 'Kamorteiro' Muengo, both parties signed a memorandum of understanding, aimed at ending the civil war. On 4 April a cease-fire agreement was ratified, in which UNITA accepted the Lusaka protocol and agreed to the cantonment of its soldiers. Some 5,000 UNITA soldiers were to be integrated into the FAA, and UNITA representatives were to take up positions in central, provincial and local government. In early May João Lourenço, the Secretary-General of the MPLA, announced that elections would take place in 2004.

By the end of July 2002 some 85,000 UNITA soldiers and an estimated 300,000 family members had registered in quartering camps, amid severe food shortages, but only 30,000 light arms had been turned over to the Government, provoking fears of incomplete disarmament of the rebels. Nevertheless, in early August UNITA announced that its military wing had been disbanded, following the integration of its soldiers into the FAA. Also in August, the UN Security Council established the UN Mission in Angola (UNMA) to succeed UNOA until 15 February 2003. On 23 August 2002 the Government and UNITA set a 45-day deadline for the full implementation of the Lusaka protocol, which was to be monitored by a UN-led joint commission, comprising representatives of the Government, UNITA and observer countries (Portugal, Russia and the USA). In October the inauguration of a new national political commission for UNITA, including former members of UNITA—R, marked the official reunification of the party; Gen. Paulo Lukamba 'Gato' was confirmed as interim leader of the party, pending a full congress.

In mid-September 2002 João Lourenço, the Secretary-General of the MPLA, admitted the possibility of limited autonomy for the Cabinda exclave, but ruled out independence. Meanwhile, fighting continued in Cabinda between FAA troops and FLEC—FAC rebels. An FAA offensive took FLEC—FAC headquarters in Kungo-Shonzo in late October, and armed conflict was reported in Buco-Zau in early November. At a meeting in Paris, France, in January 2003, between the Office of the President of Angola and the foreign mission of FLEC—FAC a proposed peace accord, providing for the integration of FLEC—FAC forces into the FAA and the establishment of both FLEC factions as political parties, was rejected by the rebel group. During February FLEC—R and FLEC—FAC forces in Cabinda were actively dispersed by the FAA, and 7,000 captured civilians were freed. Action against the Cabinda rebels was strengthened by a security pact between Angola, the Republic of the Congo and the DRC, which had been signed in January.

Meanwhile, in October 2002 the UN Development Programme reported that Angola was threatened with an 'extremely serious humanitarian crisis' as a result of the civil war, which had caused severe damage to political and economic structures and displaced some 4.3m. people. On 11 November, to mark the celebration of Angola's first peacetime Independence Day, UNITA declared its intention to accelerate the approval of new policies designed to aid the economy. Meanwhile, President dos Santos inaugurated several programmes for urban regeneration. The joint commission responsible for supervising the implementation of the Lusaka protocol was dissolved in late November, to be replaced by a joint UNITA-Government mechanism. Dos Santos confirmed the possibility of elections in 2004, dependent upon a stable political climate.

In early December 2002 Fernando (Nando) da Piedade Dias dos Santos, hitherto Minister of the Interior, was appointed as Prime Minister, a post that President dos Santos had himself held since January 1999. The Council of Ministers was subsequently reshuffled, with the inclusion of the four UNITA representatives; the appointment of Aguinaldo Jaime, hitherto Governor of the central bank, as Deputy Prime Minister was

also notable. Shortly afterwards the UN Security Council voted to lift all remaining sanctions on UNITA, having previously removed travel restrictions on officials of the former rebel group. Meanwhile, a Constitutional Commission (which had been established by the Assembléia Nacional in 1998) was considering proposals for a new draft constitution. Agreement was reached on a major point of contention in January 2003, when the Commission decided that the President of the Republic would remain Head of Government, as favoured by MPLA deputies; UNITA had advocated the devolvement of executive power to the Prime Minister. In mid-February UNMA withdrew from Angola, as scheduled. Later that month the Government announced that five of the 35 quartering camps had been closed, with the resettlement of 22,643 former UNITA fighters and 70,694 civilians.

In late 2002 the Angolan Government and the office of the UN High Commissioner for Refugees (UNHCR) established separate tripartite commissions with Zambia, the DRC and Namibia with the aim of facilitating the repatriation of Angolan refugees from these countries. In early 2003 there were an estimated 470,000 Angolan refugees in the region, including 210,000 in Zambia, 192,000 in the DRC and 24,000 in Namibia; UNHCR hoped to repatriate some 170,000 Angolan refugees in 2003. By February more than 90,000 Angolans were estimated to have returned to the country without assistance since April 2002.

Following the internal uprising in August 1998 against the Kabila regime in the DRC, the Angolan Government moved swiftly to provide Kabila with military support against the rebels. In September the number of FAA troops in the DRC was estimated at 5,000. In October, as the conflict escalated in the east of the DRC, Angola, in alliance with Namibia and Zimbabwe, stated that it would continue supporting Kabila until the rebels were defeated. Following the assassination of Kabila in January 2001, the Angolan Government announced its intention to allow its troops stationed in the DRC to remain there until further notice; moreover, several thousand additional Angolan troops were moved into that country later in January. In November, however, the Angolan Minister of Foreign Affairs, João Bernardo de Miranda, announced that a significant number of Angolan troops had been withdrawn from the DRC, and Angola's commitment to the successful implementation of the Lusaka peace accord, signed in July 1999 (see the chapter on the DRC), was reaffirmed. By the end of October 2002 Angola, Namibia and Zimbabwe had completed the withdrawal of their troops from the DRC.

Relations with Zambia became tense during 1999, following persistent allegations that it was actively supporting UNITA and allowing its territory to be used as a transit point for the provision of arms and supplies to the rebels. It was further alleged that senior ministers in the Zambian Government had been personally involved in contravening sanctions. In June, following co-operation talks between the respective governments, an agreement was signed putting aside past disputes. However, in May 2000 the Zambian Minister of Defence, Chitalu Sampa, accused the FAA of carrying out raids in Zambian territory and killing a Zambian soldier; the allegations were denied by Angola. However, both countries subsequently agreed to increase cross-border co-operation, and Zambian government officials confirmed that UNITA rebels would not be allowed to undertake any military incursions into Angola from Zambian territory. Meanwhile, clashes reportedly took place along the Namibian border with Angola, during which UNITA rebels were killed or arrested by the Namibian security forces.

In August 2002 one of the alleged leaders of the 1994 genocide in Rwanda (q.v.), Gen. Augustin Bizimungu, was discovered among UNITA soldiers in cantonment and transferred to the International Criminal Tribunal for Rwanda in Arusha, Tanzania. In September the Angolan Government denied that it was militarily involved in the defence of President Laurent Gbagbo's regime against rebel forces in Côte d'Ivoire, following a statement to that effect by the Ivorian defence minister.

In July 1996 Angola was among the five lusophone African countries that, together with Portugal and Brazil, formed the Comunidade dos Países de Língua Portuguesa (see p. 349), a Portuguese-speaking commonwealth seeking to achieve collective benefits from co-operation in technical, cultural and social matters.

Government

In March 1991 and in the first half of 1992 the Government of the Movimento Popular de Libertação de Angola—Partido do Trabalho (MPLA—PT) introduced a series of far-reaching amendments to the 1975 Constitution, providing for the establishment of a multi-party democracy (hitherto, no other political parties, apart from the ruling MPLA—PT, had been permitted). According to the amendments, legislative power was to be vested in the National Assembly (Assembléia Nacional), with 223 members elected for four years on the basis of proportional representation. Executive power was to be held by the President, who was to be directly elected for a term of five years (renewable for a maximum of three terms). As Head of State and Commander-in-Chief of the armed forces, the President was to govern with the assistance of an appointed Council of Ministers. Proposals for a new constitution were under consideration in early 2003.

For the purposes of local government, the country is divided into 18 provinces, each administered by an appointed Governor.

Legislative elections, held in September 1992, resulted in victory for the MPLA. However, in the presidential election, which was held at the same time, the MPLA's candidate and incumbent President, José Eduardo dos Santos, narrowly failed to secure the 50% of the votes necessary to be elected President. Following a resumption of hostilities between UNITA and government forces, the conduct of a second round of the presidential election was held in abeyance, with dos Santos remaining in the presidency. In accordance with the terms of the Lusaka peace accord of November 1994, in April 1997 a new Government of National Unity and Reconciliation was inaugurated in which UNITA held four portfolios. The second round of the presidential election having been abandoned, Savimbi was accorded the official title of 'leader of the opposition'. However, following a resumption of hostilities, in November 1998 Savimbi's 'special status' as 'leader of the opposition' was revoked. Following the ratification of a cease-fire agreement in April 2002, elections were expected to be held in 2004.

Defence

In accordance with the peace agreement concluded by the Government and the União Nacional para a Independência Total de Angola (UNITA) in May 1991 (see Recent History), a new 50,000-strong national army, the Forças Armadas de Angola (FAA), was established, comprising equal numbers of government forces, the Forças Armadas Populares de Libertação de Angola, and UNITA soldiers. Following elections in 1992, UNITA withdrew its troops from the FAA, alleging electoral fraud on the part of the Movimento Popular de Libertação de Angola, and hostilities resumed. After the signing of the Lusaka peace accord in November 1994, preparations for the confinement and demobilization of troops, and the integration of the UNITA contingent into the FAA, resumed. In 1995 the Government and UNITA reached agreement on the enlargement of the FAA to comprise a total of 90,000 troops, and discussions began concerning the potential formation of a fourth, non-combatant branch of the FAA, which would engage in public works projects. In mid-1997 the Government estimated that a residual UNITA force numbered some 25,000–30,000 troops, while UNITA claimed to have retained a force of only 2,963 'police'. In March 1998 UNITA issued a declaration announcing the complete demobilization of its forces. However, evidence of the existence of a large UNITA force became apparent with the escalation of widespread hostilities in Angola from mid-1998. Following the ratification of a peace agreement between UNITA and the Government in April 2002, some 5,000 former UNITA soldiers were incorporated into the FAA in mid-2002, while the movement's remaining troops (estimated at 80,000) were to be reintegrated into civilian life during 2003, following their demobilization.

In August 2002 the FAA had an estimated total strength of 100,000: army 90,000, navy 4,000 and air force 6,000. In addition, there was a paramilitary force numbering an estimated 10,000. The defence budget for 2000 was US $542m.

Economic Affairs

In 2001, according to estimates by the World Bank, Angola's gross national income (GNI), measured at average 1999–2001 prices, was US $6,707m., equivalent to $5,000 per head (or $1,550 per head on an international purchasing-power parity basis). During 1990–2001, it was estimated, Angola's population increased at an average annual rate of 3.2%, while gross domestic product (GDP) per head declined, in real terms, by an average of 2.1% per year. Overall GDP increased, in real terms, at an average annual rate of 1.0% per year in 1990–2001; growth in 2001 was 3.2%.

Agriculture, forestry and fishing contributed an estimated 8.0% of GDP in 2001. An estimated 71.6% of the total working population were employed in the agricultural sector in 2001. Coffee is the principal cash crop. The main subsistence crops are cassava, maize, sugar cane, bananas and sweet potatoes. Severe food shortages following a period of drought in late 2000 worsened in 2001, owing to continued low levels of agricultural productivity. During 1990–2001, according to the World Bank, agricultural GDP declined at an average annual rate of 1.1%. However, agricultural GDP increased by 17.9% in 2001.

Industry (including mining, manufacturing, construction and power) provided an estimated 66.8% of GDP in 2001, and employed an estimated 10.5% of the labour force in 1991. According to the World Bank, industrial GDP increased, in real terms, at an average annual rate of 3.1% in 1990–2001; growth in industrial GDP was 4.1% in 2001.

Mining contributed 70.3% of GDP in 1999. Petroleum production (including liquefied petroleum gas) accounted for 61.5% of GDP in that year. Angola's principal mineral exports are petroleum and diamonds. In addition, there are reserves of iron ore, copper, lead, zinc, gold, manganese, phosphates, salt and uranium.

The manufacturing sector provided an estimated 3.8% of GDP in 2001. The principal branch of manufacturing is petroleum refining. Other manufacturing activities include food-processing, brewing, textiles and construction materials. According to the World Bank, the GDP of the manufacturing sector increased at an average annual rate of 0.5% in 1990–2001; growth in manufacturing GDP was 10.1% in 2001.

Energy is derived mainly from hydroelectric power, which provided 67.0% of Angola's electricity production in 1999, while petroleum accounted for 33.0%. Angola's power potential exceeds its requirements.

Services accounted for an estimated 25.3% of GDP in 2001, and engaged an estimated 20.1% of the labour force in 1991. In real terms, the GDP of the services sector declined at an average annual rate of 2.4% in 1990–2001, according to the World Bank. Services GDP declined by 4.4% in 2001.

In 2001 Angola recorded an estimated visible trade surplus of US $3,355m., while there was an estimated deficit of $1,431m. on the current account of the balance of payments. In 1999 the principal source of imports (19%) was Portugal; other major suppliers were the USA (15%) and South Africa (12%). In that year the principal market for exports was the USA (60%); other notable purchasers were the People's Republic of China (8%) and Taiwan (8%). The principal exports in 2001 were crude petroleum, accounting for 87.1% of total export earnings, and diamonds (10.5%). The principal imports in 1985 were foodstuffs, transport equipment, electrical equipment and base metals.

In 1999 Angola recorded a budget surplus of 172m. kwanza (equivalent to 1.1% of GDP). Angola's total external debt at the end of 2000 was US $10,146m., of which $8,758m. was long-term public debt. In that year the cost of debt-servicing was equivalent to 15.1% of the value of exports of goods and services. The average annual rate of inflation was 445.4% in 1990–2002. Consumer prices increased by an average of 152.6% in 2001 and of 108.9% in 2002.

Angola is a member of both the Common Market for Eastern and Southern Africa (see p. 162) and the Southern African Development Community (see p. 311), which was formed with the aim of reducing the economic dependence of southern African states on South Africa.

Since independence, exploitation of Angola's extensive mineral reserves, hydroelectric potential and abundant fertile land has been severely impaired by internal conflict, as well as an acute shortage of skilled personnel. Following the ratification of a cease-fire agreement between the Government and UNITA in April 2002, Angola's prospects depended greatly on a definitive resolution of the civil strife, the successful reintegration of the displaced population and the rehabilitation of the country's devastated infrastructure. Despite civil conflict, the development of the petroleum sector continued apace in the late 1990s and early 2000s, although much petroleum revenue was used to finance the Government's military expenditure. National output of crude petroleum was projected to increase significantly by 2003, and in 2002 it was forecast that yields would reach 1.7m. barrels per day by 2006. In April 2000 an agreement was signed with the IMF, which aimed to encourage greater economic stability; it was hoped that the agreement would eventually lead to a long-term loan from the IMF. In February 2001, however, the IMF announced that Angola's reform programme was behind schedule. In August 2002 the IMF estimated that the Government had failed to account for some US $1,200m. of total petroleum revenues of $3,200m. in 2001 and declared its hesitancy at large-scale commitment in Angola without greater transparency. However, according to a report issued in September by the UN Conference on Trade and Development, Angola was the third largest recipient of foreign direct investment in the world in 2001, attracting some $1,100m., mostly in petroleum-related projects. In the budget for 2003, the Government allocated some $320m. towards the repair of infrastructure in the four provinces that had been most seriously damaged by the civil war. In November 2002 the UN appealed to international donors for some $386m. in humanitarian and development aid for Angola in 2003. GDP growth was forecast at 10.5% for 2002 and 7.0% for 2003.

Education

Education is officially compulsory for eight years, between seven and 15 years of age, and is provided free of charge by the Government. Primary education begins at six years of age and lasts for four years. Secondary education, beginning at the age of 10, lasts for up to seven years, comprising a first cycle of four years and a second of three years. As a proportion of the school-age population, the total enrolment at primary and secondary schools was 45% in 1991. According to UNESCO estimates, enrolment at primary schools in 1999/2000 included 27.3% of children in the relevant age-group (boys 29.2%; girls 25.4%), while secondary enrolment was equivalent to 15.5% of children in the relevant age-group (boys 17.5%; girls 13.4%). In 1997/98 the Agostinho Neto university, in Luanda, at that time the country's only university, had 8,337 students. In November 2002 the Government announced plans for the construction of seven provincial universities, five science and technology institutes, three medical schools and a nutrition research centre.

Much education is now conducted in vernacular languages rather than Portuguese. The 1999 budget allocated an estimated 430m. kwanza (4.8% of total expenditure) to education.

Public Holidays

2003: 1 January (New Year's Day), 6 January (for Martyrs' Day), 4 February (Anniversary of the outbreak of the armed struggle against Portuguese colonialism), 4 March (Carnival Day), 10 March (for International Women's Day), 27 March (Victory Day)*, 4 April (Peace and National Reconciliation Day), 14 April (Youth Day)*, 18 April (Good Friday), 21 April (Easter Monday), 1 May (Workers' Day), 25 May (Africa Day), 2 June (for International Children's Day), 1 August (Armed Forces' Day)*, 17 September (National Hero's Day, birthday of Dr Agostinho Neto), 3 November (for All Souls' Day), 11 November (Independence Day), 1 December (Pioneers' Day)*, 25 December (Christmas Day and Family Day).

2004: 1 January (New Year's Day), 5 January (for Martyrs' Day), 4 February (Anniversary of the outbreak of the armed struggle against Portuguese colonialism), 24 February (Carnival Day), 8 March (International Women's Day), 29 March (for Victory Day)*, 4 April (Peace and National Reconciliation Day), 9 April (Good Friday), 12 April (Easter Monday), 14 April (Youth Day)*, 3 May (for Workers' Day), 25 May (Africa Day), 1 June (International Children's Day), 2 August (for Armed Forces' Day)*, 17 September (National Hero's Day, birthday of Dr Agostinho Neto), 1 November (All Souls' Day), 11 November (Independence Day), 1 December (Pioneers' Day)*, 25 December (Christmas Day and Family Day).

*Although not officially recognized as public holidays, these days are popularly treated as such.

Weights and Measures

The metric system is in force.

Statistical Survey

Source (unless otherwise stated): Instituto Nacional de Estatística, Avda Ho Chi Minh, CP 1215, Luanda; tel. (2) 322776.

Area and Population

AREA, POPULATION AND DENSITY

Area (sq km)	1,246,700*
Population (census results)	
30 December 1960	4,480,719
15 December 1970	
Males	2,943,974
Females.	2,702,192
Total	5,646,166
Population (official estimates)†	
1998	13,766,000
1999	14,174,000
2000	14,602,000
Density (per sq km) at 2000	11.7

* 481,354 sq miles.
† Source: MINPLAN.

DISTRIBUTION OF POPULATION BY PROVINCE
(provisional estimates, mid-1995)

	Area (sq km)	Population	Density (per sq km)
Luanda	2,418	2,002,000	828.0
Huambo	34,274	1,687,000	49.2
Bié	70,314	1,246,000	17.7
Malanje	87,246	975,000	11.2
Huíla	75,002	948,000	12.6
Uíge	58,698	948,000	16.2
Benguela	31,788	702,000	22.1
Cuanza-Sul	55,660	688,000	12.4
Cuanza-Norte	24,110	412,000	17.1
Moxico	223,023	349,000	1.6
Lunda-Norte	102,783	311,000	3.0
Zaire	40,130	247,000	6.2
Cunene	88,342	245,000	2.8
Cabinda	7,270	185,000	25.4
Bengo	31,371	184,000	5.9
Lunda-Sul	56,985	160,000	2.8
Cuando-Cubango . .	199,049	137,000	0.7
Namibe	58,137	135,000	2.3
Total	**1,246,600**	**11,561,000**	**9.3**

PRINCIPAL TOWNS
(population at 1970 census)

Luanda (capital) . .	480,613*	Benguela	40,996
Huambo (Nova Lisboa)	61,885*	Lubango (Sá da Bandeira) . . .	31,674
Lobito	59,258*	Malanje	31,559

* Estimate for 2001, including suburbs: 2,819,000 (Source: UN, *World Urbanization Prospects: The 2001 Revision.*

Source: Direcção dos Serviços de Estatística.

BIRTHS AND DEATHS
(UN estimates, annual averages)

	1985–90	1990–95	1995–2000
Birth rate (per 1,000) . . .	51.5	51.0	51.0
Death rate (per 1,000) . . .	21.6	19.9	20.2

Source: UN, *World Population Prospects: The 2000 Revision*.

Expectation of life (WHO estimates, years at birth): 36.1 (males 34.1; females 38.3) in 2001 (Source: WHO, *World Health Report*).

ECONOMICALLY ACTIVE POPULATION
(estimates, '000 persons, 1991)

	Males	Females	Total
Agriculture, etc. . . .	1,518	1,374	2,892
Industry	405	33	438
Services	644	192	836
Total labour force . . .	2,567	1,599	4,166

Source: UN Economic Commission for Africa, *African Statistical Yearbook*.

Mid-2001 (estimates in '000): Agriculture, etc. 4,368; Total (incl. others) 6,104 (Source: FAO).

Health and Welfare

KEY INDICATORS

Total fertility rate (children per woman, 2001).	7.2
Under-5 mortality rate (per 1,000 live births, 2001) . .	260
HIV/AIDS (% of persons aged 15–49, 2001).	5.50
Physicians (per 1,000 head, 1997)	0.08
Hospital beds (per 1,000 head, 1990)	1.29
Health expenditure (2000): US $ per head (PPP) . . .	52
Health expenditure (2000): % of GDP	3.6
Health expenditure (2000): public (% of total) . . .	55.9
Access to water (% of persons, 2000). . . .	38
Access to sanitation (% of persons, 2000) . . .	44
Human Development Index (2000): ranking . . .	161
Human Development Index (2000): value	0.403

For sources and definitions, see explanatory note on p. vi.

Agriculture

PRINCIPAL CROPS
('000 metric tons)

	1999	2000	2001
Wheat*	4	4	4
Rice (paddy)*	16	16	16
Maize	428†	428*	429*
Millet	102†	102*	148*
Potatoes	19†	19*	27*
Sweet potatoes	182†	182*	353*
Cassava (Manioc)	3,130†	3,130*	5,394*
Sugar cane*	340	330	360
Dry beans	68†	68*	89*
Groundnuts (in shell) . . .	11†	11*	27*
Sunflower seed*	9	9	11
Oil palm fruit*	250	250	280
Cottonseed*	7	7	10
Tomatoes*	11	11	13
Onions and shallots (green)* . .	9	9	13
Other vegetables* . . .	220	220	271
Bananas*	290	290	300
Citrus fruit*	75	75	78
Pineapples*	32	32	40
Other fruits (excl. melons)*. . .	26	26	32
Coffee (green)	3†	4†	4*

* FAO estimate(s).
† Unofficial figure.

Source: FAO.

LIVESTOCK
('000 head, year ending September)

	1999	2000	2001
Cattle	3,900*	4,042*	4,042†
Pigs†	800	800	800
Sheep	336*	350*	350†
Goats†	2,000	2,150	2,150
Chickens†	6,650	6,400	6,800

* Unofficial figure.
† FAO estimate(s).

Source: FAO.

LIVESTOCK PRODUCTS
('000 metric tons)

	1999	2000	2001
Beef and veal*	85.0	85.0	85.0
Goat meat	9.0	9.7	9.7
Pig meat*	28.6	28.6	28.6
Chicken meat	7.6	7.6	7.7
Game meat*	7.5	7.5	7.5
Mutton and lamb. . . .	1.2	1.2	1.3
Cows' milk*	191.0	191.0	195.0
Cheese	1.2	1.2	1.2
Hen eggs	4.2	4.2	4.3
Honey*.	22.0	22.0	23.0
Beeswax*	2.2	2.2	2.3
Cattle hides	12.5	13.0	13.0

* FAO estimates.

Source: FAO.

Forestry

ROUNDWOOD REMOVALS
('000 cubic metres, excluding bark, FAO estimates)

	1999	2000	2001
Sawlogs, veneer logs and logs for sleepers*	66	66	66
Other industrial wood	1,050	1,050	1,050
Fuel wood	3,071	3,163	3,241
Total	4,187	4,279	4,357

* Annual output assumed to be unchanged since 1990.

Source: FAO.

SAWNWOOD PRODUCTION
('000 cubic metres, including railway sleepers, FAO estimates)

	1983	1984	1985
Total	6	2	5

1986–2001: Annual production as in 1985 (FAO estimates).

Source: FAO.

Fishing

('000 metric tons, live weight)

	1998	1999	2000
Freshwater fishes	6.0	6.0*	6.0*
West African croakers . . .	7.1	8.9	8.0
Dentex.	8.7	8.8	13.8
Cunene horse mackerel . .	39.7	47.7	53.2
Sardinellas	45.5	57.6	108.2
Total catch (incl. others) . . .	145.8	177.5	238.4

* FAO estimate.

Source: FAO, *Yearbook of Fishery Statistics*.

Mining

('000 metric tons, unless otherwise indicated)

	1998	1999	2000
Crude petroleum*	36,000	36,800	36,400
Natural gas (million cu metres) .	5,804	5,800	5,800
Salt (unrefined)	30	30	30
Diamonds ('000 carats):†			
Industrial	276	373	435
Gem	2,488	3,359	3,914

* Data from BP Amoco, *Statistical Review of World Energy, 2002*.
† Based on estimates of 90% of production at gem grade and 10% of production at industrial grade.

2001 ('000 metric tons): Crude petroleum 36,000 (Source: BP Amoco, *Statistical Review of World Energy, 2002*).

Source: mainly US Geological Survey.

Industry

SELECTED PRODUCTS
('000 metric tons, unless otherwise indicated)

	1997	1998	1999
Frozen fish	27.2	56.8	57.7
Wheat flour	52.0	46.0	57.5
Maize flour	134.1	113.5	n.a.
Yam flour	260.0	260.0	n.a.
Bread*	176.9	218.6	247.9
Beer ('000 hectolitres)* . . .	1,148.5	1,189.5	1,094.9
Jet fuels	292.3	285.0	338.5
Motor spirit (petrol) . . .	114.6	101.7	128.1
Kerosene	19.7	28.3	30.4
Distillate fuel oils . . .	466.3	485.7	493.0
Residual fuel oils	680.6	591.0	646.8
Butane gas	32.6	28.5	30.5
Cement*	201.3	296.5	182.4

* Source: MIND (Ministry of Industry).

Source: IMF, *Angola: Recent Economic Developments* (August 2000).

2000 (estimates, '000 hectolitres): Beer of barley 910; Beer of maize 216.5; Beer of millet 459.3; Palm oil ('000 metric tons) 56 (Source: FAO).

2001 (estimates, '000 hectolitres): Beer of barley 1,000; Beer of maize 214.2; Beer of millet 473.4; Palm oil ('000 metric tons) 56 (Source: FAO).

Finance

CURRENCY AND EXCHANGE RATES

Monetary Units
100 lwei = 1 kwanza

Sterling, Dollar and Euro Equivalents (31 December 2002)
£1 sterling = 94.56 kwanza
US $1 = 58.67 kwanza
€1 = 61.52 kwanza
1,000 kwanza = £10.58 = $17.05 = €16.25

Average Exchange Rate (kwanza per US $)
2000   10.041
2001   22.058
2002   43.530

Note: An official exchange rate of US $1 = 29.62 kwanza was introduced in 1976 and remained in force until September 1990. In that month the kwanza was replaced, at par, by the new kwanza. At the same time, it was announced that the currency was to be devalued by more than 50%, with the exchange rate adjusted to US $1 = 60 new kwanza, with effect from 1 October 1990. This rate remained in force until 18 November 1991, when a basic rate of US $1 = 90 new kwanza was established. The currency underwent further devaluation, by 50% in December 1991, and by more than 67% on 15 April 1992, when a basic rate of US $1 = 550 new kwanza was established. In February 1993 the currency was again devalued, when a basic rate of US $1 = 7,000 new kwanza was estab-lished. In April 1993 this was adjusted to US $1 = 4,000 new kwanza, and in October to US $1 = 6,500 new kwanza, a devaluation of 38.5%. Following a series of four devaluations in February and March 1994, a rate of US $1 = 35,000 new kwanza was established in late March. In April 1994 the introduction of a new method of setting exchange rates resulted in an effective devaluation, to US $1 = 68,297 new kwanza, and provided for an end to the system of multiple exchange rates. Further substantial devaluations followed, and in July 1995 a 'readjusted' kwanza, equivalent to 1,000 new kwanza, was introduced. The currency, however, continued to depreciate. Between July 1997 and June 1998 a fixed official rate of US $1 = 262,376 readjusted kwanza was in oper-ation. In May 1999 the Central Bank announced its decision to abolish the existing dual currency exchange rate system. In December 1999 the readjusted kwanza was replaced by a new currency, the kwanza, equivalent to 1m. readjusted kwanza. The former currency was to remain in circulation for a transitional period. Some of the figures in this Survey are still in terms of the readjusted kwanza.

BUDGET
(million kwanza)

Revenue	1997	1998	1999
Tax revenue	670	674	7,495
Income tax	445	360	5,676
Petroleum corporate tax . .	369	303	5,363
Petroleum transaction tax . .	52	4	50
Tax on goods and services . .	171	231	1,549
Petroleum sector . . .	144	170	1,221
Diamond sector	—	1	74
Taxes on foreign trade . .	34	56	224
Other taxes	20	27	46
Stamp tax	14	17	39
Non-tax revenue	9	11	45
Total	**679**	**685**	**7,540**

Expenditure*	1997	1998	1999
General public services . . .	174	194	1,440
Defence and public order . .	391	288	3,670
Peace process	6	—	10
Education	48	66	430
Health	31	35	250
Economic affairs and services . .	182	142	920
Interest payments	98	175	960
Total (incl. others)	**977**	**1,056**	**8,940**

* Including adjustments for unrecorded transactions. The data include lending minus repayments.

Source: IMF, *Angola: Recent Economic Developments* (August 2000).

INTERNATIONAL RESERVES
(US $ million at 31 December)

	2000	2001	2002
IMF special drawing rights	0.17	0.17	0.19
Foreign exchange	1,198.04	731.69	375.35
Total	1,198.21	731.87	375.55

Source: IMF, *International Financial Statistics*.

MONEY SUPPLY
(million kwanza at 31 December)

	2000	2001	2002
Currency outside banks	2,968.6	8,215.3	20,878.5
Demand deposits at banking institutions	2,037.0	5,449.5	11,146.0
Total (incl. others)	5,332.8	14,298.7	33,644.2

Source: IMF, *International Financial Statistics*.

COST OF LIVING
(Consumer Price Index for Luanda at December; base: 1994 average = 100)

	1997	1998	1999
Food	318,800	687,938	3,551,169
Clothing	420,563	1,250,460	5,808,275
Rent, fuel and light	4,572,243	5,647,634	12,901,550
All items (incl. others)	504,843	1,185,134	5,083,923

Source: IMF, *Angola: Recent Economic Developments* (August 2000).

All items (Consumer Price Index; base: 1995 = 100): 416,724 in 2000; 1,052,480 in 2001; 2,198,540 in 2002 (Source: IMF, *International Financial Statistics*).

NATIONAL ACCOUNTS

Composition of the Gross National Product
(US $ million)

	1987	1988	1989
Gross domestic product (GDP) at factor cost	6,482	6,877	7,682
Indirect taxes	94	95	117
Less Subsidies	189	122	93
GDP in purchasers' values	6,386	6,850	7,706
Net factor income from abroad	−402	−938	−1,079
Gross national product	5,984	5,912	6,627

Gross Domestic Product by Economic Activity
(million kwanza at current prices)

	1997	1998	1999
Agriculture, forestry and fishing	158	330	1,076
Mining	918	1,093	10,968
Manufacturing	77	160	554
Electricity and water	1	2	6
Construction	71	156	529
Trade	283	489	1,370
Other services	206	267	1,102
Sub-total	1,714	2,497	15,605
Import duties	41	35	37
GDP in purchasers' values	1,755	2,533	15,644

Source: IMF, *Angola: Recent Economic Developments* (August 2000).

BALANCE OF PAYMENTS
(US $ million)

	1999	2000	2001
Exports of goods f.o.b.	5,156.5	7,920.7	6,534.6
Imports of goods f.o.b.	−3,109.1	−3,039.5	−3,179.2
Trade balance	2,047.5	4,881.2	3,355.1
Exports of services	153.0	267.3	202.5
Imports of services	−2,594.6	−2,699.5	−3,518.1
Balance on goods and services	−394.1	2,449.0	39.5
Other income received	24.1	34.4	23.0
Other income paid	−1,396.2	−1,715.2	−1,584.0
Balance on goods, services and income	−1,766.2	768.2	−1,521.5
Current transfers received	154.2	123.5	208.3
Current transfers paid	−98.7	−96.0	−117.8
Current balance	−1,710.4	795.7	−1,430.9
Direct investment from abroad	2,471.5	878.6	2,145.5
Investment assets	−186.1	−702.1	−516.6
Investment liabilities	−545.7	−622.1	−678.9
Net errors and omissions	−78.9	−50.6	−308.6
Overall balance	−42.9	317.8	319.3

Source: IMF, *International Financial Statistics*.

External Trade

SELECTED COMMODITIES

Imports (million kwanza)	1983	1984	1985
Animal products	1,315	1,226	1,084
Vegetable products	2,158	3,099	2,284
Fats and oils	946	1,006	1,196
Food and beverages	2,400	1,949	1,892
Industrial chemical products	1,859	1,419	1,702
Plastic materials	431	704	454
Textiles	1,612	1,816	1,451
Base metals	1,985	3,730	2,385
Electrical equipment	3,296	2,879	2,571
Transport equipment	2,762	2,240	3,123
Total (incl. others)	20,197	21,370	19,694

Exports (US $ million)	1999	2000	2001
Crude petroleum	4,406	6,951	5,690
Diamonds	629	739	689
Total (incl. others)	5,157	7,921	6,534

Source: Banco Nacional de Angola.

Total imports (US $ million): 2,477 in 1997; 2,079 in 1998; 3,267 in 1999 (Source: IMF, *Angola: Recent Economic Developments* (August 2000)).

PRINCIPAL TRADING PARTNERS
(percentage of total trade)*

Imports c.i.f.	1997	1998	1999
Brazil	4.0	6.0	5.1
China, People's Repub	1.4	1.8	1.3
France	5.8	5.8	8.2
Germany	2.3	2.4	1.7
Italy	2.7	3.7	4.5
Netherlands	4.6	5.1	3.6
Portugal	22.4	20.3	18.8
South Africa	9.2	9.7	11.9
Spain	8.5	4.9	5.9
United Kingdom	6.4	3.4	6.2
USA	13.6	17.6	14.6

Exports f.o.b.	1997	1998	1999
China, People's Repub	13.2	4.0	8.2
France	3.9	2.9	2.1
Germany	0.7	1.7	2.4
Italy	0.4	1.4	1.4
Portugal	1.0	0.6	0.5
Spain	1.9	0.8	0.6
Taiwan	1.7	8.2	7.7
USA	64.9	63.8	59.5

* Data are compiled on the basis of reporting by Angola's trading partners.

Source: IMF, *Direction of Trade Statistics in Angola: Recent Economic Developments* (August 2000).

Transport

GOODS TRANSPORT
('000 metric tons)

	1988	1989	1990
Road	1,056.7	690.1	867.3
Railway	580.9	510.3	443.2
Water	780.8	608.6	812.1
Air	24.6	10.5	28.3
Total	2,443.0	1,819.5	2,150.9

Sources: Instituto Nacional de Estatística; Ministério de Transporte e Comunicações.

PASSENGER TRANSPORT
('000 journeys)

	1988	1989	1990
Road	12,699.2	32,658.7	48,796.1
Railway	6,659.7	6,951.2	6,455.8
Water	151.8	163.2	223.8
Air	608.9	618.4	615.9
Total	20,119.6	40,391.5	56,091.6

Sources: Instituto Nacional de Estatística; Ministério de Transporte e Comunicações.

ROAD TRAFFIC
(estimates, motor vehicles in use at 31 December)

	1994	1995	1996
Passenger cars	180,000	197,000	207,000
Lorries and vans	32,340	26,000	25,000
Total	212,340	223,000	232,000

Source: IRF, *World Road Statistics*.

SHIPPING

Merchant Fleet
(registered at 31 December)

	1999	2000	2001
Number of vessels . . .	124	125	123
Total displacement (grt) . . .	65,749	66,335	63,141

Source: Lloyd's Register-Fairplay, *World Fleet Statistics*.

International Sea-borne Freight Traffic
(estimates, '000 metric tons)

	1989	1990	1991
Goods loaded	19,980	21,102	23,288
Goods unloaded	1,235	1,242	1,261

Source: UN Economic Commission for Africa, *African Statistical Yearbook*.

CIVIL AVIATION
(traffic on scheduled services)

	1996	1997	1998
Kilometres flown (million) . . .	8	8	8
Passengers carried ('000) . . .	585	555	553
Passenger-km (million)	880	620	622
Total ton-km (million)	141	97	95

Source: UN, *Statistical Yearbook*.

Tourism

FOREIGN TOURIST ARRIVALS

Country of origin	1998	1999	2000
Brazil	2,835	2,192	3,272
France	4,335	3,543	4,577
Norway	447	995	520
Philippines	1,008	863	1,175
Portugal	19,412	15,528	15,601
Russia	1,648	1,365	1,243
South Africa	2,728	3,795	3,774
Spain	234	1,059	1,361
United Kingdom	3,440	2,857	3,648
USA	3,397	2,902	3,013
Total (incl. others)	52,011	45,477	50,765

Tourism receipts (US $ million): 8 in 1998; 13 in 1999; 18 in 2000.

Source: World Tourism Organization.

Communications Media

	1999	2000	2001
Television receivers ('000 in use)	190	250	n.a.
Telephones ('000 main lines in use)	67.2	69.7	80.0
Mobile cellular telephones ('000 subscribers)	24.0	25.8	86.5
Personal computers ('000 in use)	12	15	17
Internet users ('000)	10	30	60

Source: International Telecommunication Union.

Radio receivers ('000 in use, 1997): 630 (Source: UNESCO, *Statistical Yearbook*).

Daily newspapers (1996): 5 (average circulation 128,000 copies) (Source: UNESCO, *Statistical Yearbook*).

Book production (1995): 22 titles (all books) (Source: UNESCO, *Statistical Yearbook*).

Education

(1997/98)

	Teachers	Pupils
Pre-primary	n.a.	214,867*
Primary	31,062†	1,342,116
Secondary:		
general	5,138‡	267,399
teacher training	280§	10,772*
vocational	286‡	12,116*
Higher	776	8,337

* Figure for school year 1991/92.
† Figure for school year 1990/91.
‡ Figure for school year 1989/90.
§ Figure for school year 1987/88.

Source: mainly UNESCO, Institute for Statistics.

Adult literacy rate (UNESCO estimates): 41.7% (males 55.6%; females 28.5%) in 1990 (Source: UNESCO, *Statistical Yearbook*).

Directory

The Constitution

The MPLA regime adopted an independence Constitution for Angola in November 1975. It was amended in October 1976, September 1980, March 1991, April and August 1992, and November 1996. In early 2003 proposals for a new constitution were under consideration, following the ratification of a cease-fire agreement by the Government and UNITA in April 2002. The main provisions of the 1975 Constitution, as amended, are summarized below:

BASIC PRINCIPLES

The Republic of Angola shall be a sovereign and independent state whose prime objective shall be to build a free and democratic society of peace, justice and social progress. It shall be a democratic state based on the rule of law, founded on national unity, the dignity of human beings, pluralism of expression and political organization, respecting and guaranteeing the basic rights and freedoms of persons, whether as individuals or as members of organized social groups. Sovereignty shall be vested in the people, which shall exercise political power through periodic universal suffrage.

The Republic of Angola shall be a unitary and indivisible state. Economic, social and cultural solidarity shall be promoted between all the Republic's regions for the common development of the entire nation and the elimination of regionalism and tribalism.

Religion

The Republic shall be a secular state and there shall be complete separation of the State and religious institutions. All religions shall be respected.

The Economy

The economic system shall be based on the coexistence of diverse forms of property—public, private, mixed, co-operative and family—and all shall enjoy equal protection. The State shall protect foreign investment and foreign property, in accordance with the law. The fiscal system shall aim to satisfy the economic, social and administrative needs of the State and to ensure a fair distribution of income and wealth. Taxes may be created and abolished only by law, which shall determine applicability, rates, tax benefits and guarantees for taxpayers.

Education

The Republic shall vigorously combat illiteracy and obscurantism and shall promote the development of education and of a true national culture.

FUNDAMENTAL RIGHTS AND DUTIES

The State shall respect and protect the human person and human dignity. All citizens shall be equal before the law. They shall be subject to the same duties, without any distinction based on colour, race, ethnic group, sex, place of birth, religion, level of education, or economic or social status.

All citizens aged 18 years and over, other than those legally deprived of political and civil rights, shall have the right and duty to take an active part in public life, to vote and be elected to any state organ, and to discharge their mandates with full dedication to the cause of the Angolan nation. The law shall establish limitations in respect of non-political allegiance of soldiers on active service, judges and police forces, as well as the electoral incapacity of soldiers on active service and police forces.

Freedom of expression, of assembly, of demonstration, of association and of all other forms of expression shall be guaranteed. Groupings whose aims or activities are contrary to the constitutional order and penal laws, or that, even indirectly, pursue political objectives through organizations of a military, paramilitary or militarized nature shall be forbidden. Every citizen has the right to a defence if accused of a crime. Individual freedoms are guaranteed. Freedom of conscience and belief shall be inviolable. Work shall be the right and duty of all citizens. The State shall promote measures necessary to ensure the right of citizens to medical and health care, as well as assistance in childhood, motherhood, disability, old age, etc. It shall also promote access to education, culture and sports for all citizens.

STATE ORGANS

President of the Republic

The President of the Republic shall be the Head of State, Head of Government and Commander-in-Chief of the Angolan armed forces.

The President of the Republic shall be elected directly by a secret universal ballot and shall have the following powers:

to appoint and dismiss the Prime Minister, Ministers and other government officials determined by law;

to appoint the judges of the Supreme Court;

to preside over the Council of Ministers;

to declare war and make peace, following authorization by the Assembléia Nacional;

to sign, promulgate and publish the laws of the Assembléia Nacional, government decrees and statutory decrees;

to preside over the National Defence Council;

to decree a state of siege or state of emergency;

to announce the holding of general elections;

to issue pardons and commute sentences;

to perform all other duties provided for in the Constitution.

Assembléia Nacional

The Assembléia Nacional is the supreme state legislative body, to which the Government is responsible. The Assembléia shall be composed of 223 deputies, elected for a term of four years. The Assembléia shall convene in ordinary session twice yearly and in special session on the initiative of the President of the Assembléia, the Standing Commission of the Assembléia or of no less than one-third of its deputies. The Standing Commission shall be the organ of the Assembléia that represents and assumes its powers between sessions.

Government

The Government shall comprise the President of the Republic, the ministers and the secretaries of state, and other members whom the law shall indicate, and shall have the following functions:

to organize and direct the implementation of state domestic and foreign policy, in accordance with decision of the Assembléia Nacional and its Standing Commission;

to ensure national defence, the maintenance of internal order and security, and the protection of the rights of citizens;

to prepare the draft National Plan and General State Budget for approval by the Assembléia Nacional, and to organize, direct and control their execution.

The Council of Ministers shall be answerable to the Assembléia Nacional. In the exercise of its powers, the Council of Ministers shall issue decrees and resolutions.

Judiciary

The organization, composition and competence of the courts shall be established by law. Judges shall be independent in the discharge of their functions.

Local State Organs

The organs of state power at provincial level shall be the Provincial Assemblies and their executive bodies. The Provincial Assemblies shall work in close co-operation with social organizations and rely on the initiative and broad participation of citizens. The Provincial Assemblies shall elect commissions of deputies to perform permanent or specific tasks. The executive organs of Provincial Assemblies shall be the Provincial Governments, which shall be led by the Provincial Governors. The Provincial Governors shall be answerable to the President of the Republic, the Council of Ministers and the Provincial Assemblies.

National Defence

The State shall ensure national defence. The National Defence Council shall be presided over by the President of the Republic, and its composition shall be determined by law. The Angolan armed forces, as a state institution, shall be permanent, regular and non-partisan. Defence of the country shall be the right and the highest indeclinable duty of every citizen. Military service shall be compulsory. The forms in which it is fulfilled shall be defined by the law.

The Government

HEAD OF STATE

President: José Eduardo dos Santos (assumed office 21 September 1979).

COUNCIL OF MINISTERS
(April 2003)

Prime Minister: FERNANDO (NANDO) DA PIEDADE DIAS DOS SANTOS.

Deputy Prime Minister: AGUINALDO JAIME.

Minister of Defence: Gen. KUNDI PAIHAMA.

Minister of the Interior: OSVALDO DE JESUS SERRA VAN-DÚNEM.

Minister of Foreign Affairs: JOÃO BERNARDO DE MIRANDA.

Minister of Justice: Dr PAULO TJIPILIKA.

Minister of Territorial Administration: FERNANDO FAUSTINO MUTEKA.

Minister of Planning: ANA AFONSO DIAS LOURENÇO.

Minister of Finance: JOSÉ PEDRO DE MORAIS.

Minister of Petroleum: DESIDÉRIO DA GRAÇA VERÍSSIMO DA COSTA.

Minister of Fisheries: SALOMÃO LUHETO XIRIMBIMBI.

Minister of Industry: JOAQUIM DUARTE DA COSTA DAVID.

Minister of Agriculture and Rural Development: GILBERTO BUTA LUTUKUTA.

Minister of Geology and Mines: MANUEL ANTÓNIO AFRICANO.

Minister of Labour, Public Administration and Social Security: Dr ANTÓNIO DOMINGOS PITRA DA COSTA NETO.

Minister of Health: ALBERTINA JÚLIA HAMUKUAYA.

Minister of Education: ANTÓNIO BURITY DA SILVA NETO.

Minister of Culture: BOAVENTURA CARDOSO.

Minister of Science and Technology: JOÃO BAPTISTA NGANDAJINA.

Minister of Transport: ANDRÉ LUÍS BRANDÃO.

Minister of Posts and Telecommunications: LICÍNIO TAVARES RIBEIRO.

Minister of Family and the Promotion of Women: CÂNDIDA CELESTE DA SILVA.

Minister of Former Combatants and War Veterans: PEDRO JOSÉ VAN-DÚNEM.

Minister of Youth and Sports: JOSÉ MARCOS BARRICA.

Minister of Public Works: FRANCISCO HIGINO CARNEIRO.

Minister of Commerce: VITORINO DOMINGOS HOSSI.

Minister of Hotels and Tourism: JORGE ALICERCES VALENTIM.

Minister of Social Assistance and Reintegration: JOÃO BAPTISTA KUSSUMUA.

Minister of Social Communication: Dr PEDRO HENDRIK VAAL NETO.

Minister of Energy and Water: JOSÉ MARIA BOTELHO DE VASCONCELOS.

Minister of Urban Affairs and the Environment: VIRGÍLIO FERREIRA FONTES PEREIRA.

Ministers in the Office of the Presidency

Secretary of the Council of Ministers: JOSÉ DA COSTA E SILVA LEITÃO.

Diplomatic Affairs: CARLOS ALBERTO SARAIVA DE CARVALHO FONSECA.

Economic Affairs: AUGUSTO ARCHER DE SOUSA MANGUEIRA.

Military Affairs: MANUEL HELDER DIAS.

Legal Affairs: CARLOS MANUEL DOS SANTOS TEIXEIRA.

Regional Affairs: CARLOS MARIA DA SILVA FEIJO.

MINISTRIES

Office of the President: Protocolo de Estado, Futungo de Belas, Luanda; tel. (2) 350409.

Ministry of Agriculture and Rural Development: Avda Comandante Gika 2, CP 527, Luanda; tel. (2) 323593; fax (2) 323217.

Ministry of Commerce: Largo 4 de Fevereiro, Edif. Palácio de Vidro, CP 1242, Luanda; tel. (2) 338737; fax (2) 370804.

Ministry of Defence: Largo do Palácio do Povo, Luanda; tel. (2) 338156; fax (2) 392635.

Ministry of Education and Culture: Avda Comandante Gika, CP 1281, Luanda; tel. (2) 322797; fax (2) 321592.

Ministry of Energy and Water: Avda 4 de Fevereiro 105, CP 2229, Luanda; tel. (2) 393681; fax (2) 393687.

Ministry of the Family and the Promotion of Women: Largo 4 de Fevereiro, Palácio de Vidro, Luanda; tel. (2) 311728; fax (2) 330028; e-mail phildelgado@netangola.com; internet minfam .netangola.com.

Ministry of Finance: Avda 4 de Fevereiro 127, CP 592, Luanda; tel. (2) 332122; fax (2) 332069.

Ministry of Fisheries and the Environment: Avda 4 de Fevereiro 25, Edif. Atlântico, CP 83, Luanda; tel. (2) 390690; fax (2) 333814.

Ministry of Foreign Affairs: Avda Comandante Gika 8, CP 1500, Luanda; tel. (2) 323250; fax (2) 393246.

Ministry of Former Combatants and War Veterans: Avda Comandante Gika 2, CP 3828, Luanda; tel. (2) 330876.

Ministry of Geology and Mines: CP 1260, Luanda; tel. (2) 322766; fax (2) 321655.

Ministry of Health: Rua 17 de Setembro, CP 1201, Luanda; tel. (2) 396776; fax (2) 393579.

Ministry of Hotels and Tourism: Largo 4 de Fevereiro, Edif. Palácio de Vidro, Luanda; tel. (2) 331323; fax (2) 338211.

Ministry of Industry: Rua Cerqueira Lukoki 25, CP 594, Luanda; tel. (2) 334700; fax (2) 334700; e-mail info@mind-angola.com; internet www.mind-angola.com.

Ministry of the Interior: Avda 4 de Fevereiro 204, CP 2723, Luanda; tel. (2) 391049; fax (2) 395133.

Ministry of Justice: Rua 17 de Setembro, CP 2250, Luanda; tel. (2) 330327.

Ministry of Petroleum: Avda 4 de Fevereiro 105, CP 1279, Luanda; tel. (2) 337440; fax (2) 372373.

Ministry of Planning: Largo do Palácio do Povo, Luanda; tel. (2) 339529; fax (2) 339759.

Ministry of Posts and Telecommunications: Avda 4 de Fevereiro 42, 8° andar, Luanda; tel. (2) 337799; fax (2) 330776.

Ministry of Public Administration, Employment and Social Security: Rua 17 de Setembro 32, CP 1986, Luanda; tel. (2) 339654; fax (2) 339054.

Ministry of Public Works: Rua Ed Mutamba, 5° andar, CP 10611, Luanda; tel. (2) 336717; fax (2) 333814.

Ministry of Science and Technology: Isla de Luanda, Luanda; tel. (2) 331837.

Ministry of Social Communication: Avda Comandante Alódia, 1°–2° andares, CP 2608, Luanda; tel. (2) 343495; internet www .netangola.com/mcs.

Ministry of Social Assistance and Reintegration: Avda Hoji Ya Henda 117, CP 102, Luanda; tel. (2) 338124; fax (2) 342988.

Ministry of Territorial Administration: Avda Comandante Gika 8, Luanda; tel. (2) 320638; fax (2) 323272.

Ministry of Transport: Avda 4 de Fevereiro 42, CP 1250-C, Luanda; tel. (2) 337744; fax (2) 337687.

Ministry of Urban Affairs and the Environment: Luanda.

Ministry of Youth and Sports: Avda Comandante Gika, CP 5466, Luanda; tel. (2) 321117; fax (2) 323561.

PROVINCIAL GOVERNORS*

Bengo: EZELINO MENDES.

Benguela: DUMILDE DAS CHAGAS SIMÕES RANGEL.

Bié: JOSÉ AMARO TATI.

Cabinda: JOSÉ ANÍBAL LOPES ROCHA.

Cuando-Cubango: MANUEL GAMA.

Cuanza-Norte: MANUEL PEDRO PACAVIRA.

Cuanza-Sul: SERAFIM MARIA DO PRADO.

Cunene: PEDRO MUTINDE.

Huambo: PAULO KASSOMA.

Huíla: FRANCISCO JOSÉ RAMOS DA CRUZ.

Luanda: SIMÃO MATEUS PAULO.

Lunda-Norte: MANUEL FRANCISCO GOMES MAIATO.

Lunda-Sul: FRANCISCO TSCHIWISSA.

Malanje: CRISTOVÃO DA CUNHA.

Moxico: JOÃO ERNESTO DOS SANTOS.

Namibe: ÁLVARO MANUEL DE BOAVIDA NETO.

Uíge: CORDERO ERNESTO ZACUNDOMBA.

Zaire: LUDI KISSASSUNDA.

*All Governors are *ex-officio* members of the Government.

President and Legislature

PRESIDENT*

Presidential Election, 29 and 30 September 1992

	Votes	% of votes
José Eduardo dos Santos (MPLA)	1,953,335	49.57
Dr Jonas Malheiro Savimbi (UNITA)	1,579,298	40.07
António Alberto Neto (PDA)	85,249	2.16
Holden Roberto (FNLA)	83,135	2.11
Honorato Lando (PDLA)	75,789	1.92
Luís dos Passos (PRD)	59,121	1.47
Bengui Pedro João (PSD)	38,243	0.97
Simão Cacete (FPD)	26,385	0.67
Daniel Júlio Chipenda (Independent)	20,646	0.52
Anália de Victória Pereira (PLD)	11,475	0.29
Rui de Victória Pereira (PRA)	9,208	0.23
Total	3,940,884	100.00

*Under the terms of the electoral law, a second round of the presidential election was required to take place in order to determine which of the two leading candidates from the first round would be elected. However, a resumption of hostilities between UNITA and government forces prevented a second round from taking place. The electoral process was to resume only when the provisions of the Estoril peace agreement, concluded in May 1991, had been fulfilled. However, provision in the Lusaka peace accord of November 1994 for the second round of the presidential election was not pursued.

ASSEMBLÉIA NACIONAL

President: ROBERTO VÍCTOR DE ALMEIDA.

Legislative Election, 29 and 30 September 1992

	Votes	% of votes	Seats†
MPLA	2,124,126	53.74	129
UNITA	1,347,636	34.10	70
FNLA	94,742	2.40	5
PLD	94,269	2.39	3
PRS	89,875	2.27	6
PRD	35,293	0.89	1
AD Coalition	34,166	0.86	1
PSD	33,088	0.84	1
PAJOCA	13,924	0.35	1
FDA	12,038	0.30	1
PDP—ANA	10,620	0.27	1
PNDA	10,281	0.26	1
CNDA	10,237	0.26	—
PSDA	19,217	0.26	—
PAI	9,007	0.23	—
PDLA	8,025	0.20	—
PDA	8,014	0.20	—
PRA	6,719	0.17	—
Total	3,952,277	100.00	220

† According to the Constitution, the total number of seats in the Assembléia Nacional is 223. On the decision of the National Electoral Council, however, elections to fill three seats reserved for Angolans resident abroad were abandoned.

Political Organizations

Aliança Democrática de Angola: Leader SIMBA DA COSTA.

Angolan Democratic Coalition (AD Coalition): Pres. EVIDOR QUIELA (acting).

Convenção Nacional Democrata de Angola (CNDA): Leader PAULINO PINTO JOÃO.

Frente de Libertação do Enclave de Cabinda (FLEC): f. 1963; comprises several factions, claiming total forces of c. 5,000 guerrillas, seeking the secession of Cabinda province; mem. groups include:

> **Frente de Libertação do Enclave de Cabinda—Forças Armadas Cabindesas (FLEC—FAC):** www.cabinda .net (website of the proclaimed Federal Republic of Cabinda); Pres. HENRIQUES TIAGO N'ZITA (in exile in Paris, France); Chief-of-Staff (FAC) Commdr ESTANISLAU MIGUEL NGOMA.

> **Frente de Libertação do Enclave de Cabinda—Renovada (FLEC—R):** Pres. ANTÓNIO BENTO BEMBE; Sec.-Gen. ARTURO CHIBASA.

Frente Nacional de Libertação de Angola (FNLA): Champs Elysées 66, Immeuble D 75008, Paris, France; fax (331) 483900; e-mail fnla@ifrance.com; internet www.fnla.org; f. 1962; Pres. ALVARO HOLDEN ROBERTO; Sec.-Gen. NGOLA KABANGU.

Movimento de Defesa dos Interesses de Angola—Partido de Consciência Nacional (MDIA—PCN) (Movement for the Defence of Angolan Interests—National Conscience Party): f. 1991; Pres. FILIPE PINTO SUAMINA; Sec.-Gen. AFONSO MAYTUKA.

Movimento Popular de Libertação de Angola (MPLA) (People's Movement for the Liberation of Angola): Luanda; f. 1956; in 1961–74 conducted guerrilla operations against Portuguese rule; governing party since 1975; known as Movimento Popular de Libertação de Angola—Partido do Trabalho (MPLA—PT) (People's Movement for the Liberation of Angola—Workers' Party) 1977–92; in Dec. 1990 replaced Marxist-Leninist ideology with commitment to 'democratic socialism'; absorbed the Fórum Democrático Angolano (FDA) in 2002; Chair. JOSÉ EDUARDO DOS SANTOS; Sec.-Gen. JOÃO MANUEL GONÇALVES LOURENÇO.

Partido de Aliança de Juventude, Operários e Camponêses de Angola (PAJOCA) (Angolan Youth, Workers' and Peasants' Alliance Party): Leader MIGUEL JOÃO SEBASTIÃO.

Partido Angolano Independente (PAI): Leader ADRIANO PARREIRA.

Partido Democrático Angolano (PDA): Leader ANTÓNIO ALBERTO NETO.

Partido Democrático Liberal de Angola (PDLA): Leader HONORATO LANDO.

Partido Democrático para o Progresso—Aliança Nacional de Angola (PDP—ANA): Leader MFUFUMPINGA NLANDU VICTOR.

Partido Liberal Democrático (PLD): Rua Manuel Fernando Caldeira 3c, 3° andar, Esquerda Município de Ingombotas, CP 10199, Luanda; tel. (2) 396968; fax (2) 395966; e-mail pld@ebonet .net; internet www.pld.ebonet.net; Leader ANÁLIA DE VICTÓRIA PEREIRA.

Partido Nacional Democrata de Angola (PNDA): Sec.-Gen. PEDRO JOÃO ANTÓNIO.

Partido Reformador de Angola (PRA): Leader RUI DE VICTÓRIA PEREIRA.

Partido Renovador Democrático (PRD): Leader LUÍS DOS PASSOS.

Partido Renovador Social (PRS): Pres. EDUARDO KWANGANA.

Partido Social Democrata (PSD): Leader BENGUI PEDRO JOÃO.

Partido Social Democrata de Angola (PSDA): Leader ANDRÉ MILTON KILANDONOCO.

União Nacional para a Independência Total de Angola (UNITA): f. 1966 to secure independence from Portugal; later received Portuguese support to oppose the MPLA; UNITA and the Frente Nacional de Libertação de Angola conducted guerrilla campaign against the MPLA Govt with aid from some Western countries, 1975–76; supported by South Africa until 1984 and in 1987–88, and by USA after 1986; obtained legal status in March 1998, but hostilities between govt and UNITA forces resumed later that year; signed cease-fire agreement with the MPLA Govt in April 2002; joined the Govt in Dec. 2002; support drawn mainly from Ovimbundu ethnic group; Interim Leader Gen. PAULO LUKAMBA 'GATO'.

Diplomatic Representation

EMBASSIES IN ANGOLA

Algeria: Luanda; Ambassador HANAFI OUSSEDIK.

Belgium: Avda 4 de Fevereiro 93, CP 1203, Luanda; tel. (2) 336437; fax (2) 336438; e-mail luanda@diplobel.org; Ambassador MICHEL VANTROYEN.

Brazil: Rua Houari Boumedienne 132, CP 5428, Luanda; tel. (2) 344848; Ambassador PAULO DYRCEU PINHEIRO.

Bulgaria: Rua Fernão Mendes Pinto 35, CP 2260, Luanda; tel. (2) 321010; Chargé d'affaires a.i. LILO TOCHEV.

Cape Verde: Rua Alexandre Peres 29, Luanda; tel. (2) 333211; fax (2) 390989; Ambassador JOSÉ LUÍS JESUS.

China, People's Republic: Rua Houari Boumedienne 196, Luanda; tel. (2) 444685; fax (2) 444185; e-mail shiguan@netangola .com; Ambassador JIANG BEISAN.

Congo, Democratic Republic: Rua Cesario Verde 24, Luanda; tel. (2) 361953; Ambassador MUNDINDI DIDI KILENGO.

Congo, Republic: Rua 4 de Fevereiro 3, Luanda; Ambassador ANATOLE KHONDO.

Côte d'Ivoire: Rua Riyad 41–43, Luanda; tel. (2) 390150; fax (2) 333997; Ambassador ETIENNE MIEZAN EZO.

Cuba: Rua Che Guevara 42, Bairro Ingombotas, Luanda; tel. (2) 339165; Ambassador JUAN B. PUJOL-SÁNCHEZ.

Egypt: Rua Comandante Stona 247, Luanda; tel. (2) 321590; Ambassador ANWAR DAKROURY.

France: Rua Reverendo Pedro Agostinho Neto 31–33, Luanda; tel. (2) 334335; fax (2) 391949; Ambassador ALAIN RICHARD.

Gabon: Avda 4 de Fevereiro 95, Luanda; tel. (2) 372614; Ambassador RAPHAËL NKASSA-NZOGHO.

Germany: Avda 4 de Fevereiro 120, CP 1295, Luanda; tel. (2) 334516; fax (2) 334516; e-mail germanembassy.luanda@netangola.com; Ambassador Dr KLAUS-CHRISTIAN KRAEMER.

Ghana: Rua Vereador Castelo Branco 5, CP 1012, Luanda; tel. (2) 338239; fax (2) 338235; Ambassador KODJO ASIMENG WADEE.

Guinea: Luanda.

Holy See: Rua Luther King 123, CP 1030, Luanda (Apostolic Nunciature); tel. (2) 330532; fax (2) 332378; e-mail nunc.nuncio@multitel.co.ao; Apostolic Nuncio Most Rev. GIOVANNI ANGELO BECCIU (Titular Archbishop of Roselle).

Hungary: Luanda; tel. (2) 32313; fax (2) 322448; Ambassador Dr GÁBOR TÓTH.

India: Rua Marques das Minas 18A, Macalusso, CP 6040, Luanda; tel. (2) 392281; fax (2) 371094; e-mail indembluanda@ebonet.net; Ambassador RAVI MOHAN AGGARWAL.

Israel: Rua Rainha Ginga 34, 11° andar, Luanda; tel. (2) 397901; fax (2) 396366; internet www.israel.org.br/luanda; Ambassador TAMAR GOLA.

Italy: Rua dos Enganos 1, CP 6220, Luanda; tel. (2) 331245; fax (2) 333743; e-mail embitaly@ebonet.net; Ambassador PAOLO SANNELLA.

Korea, Democratic People's Republic: Luanda; tel. (2) 395575; fax (2) 332813; Ambassador HYON SOK.

Morocco: Rua Rainha Ginga, Edif. Siccal, 10° andar, Luanda; tel. (2) 393708; fax (2) 338847; Ambassador ABDELLAH AIT EL HAJ.

Mozambique: Luanda; tel. (2) 330811; Ambassador M. SALESSIO.

Namibia: Rua dos Cocqueiros, CP 953, Luanda; tel. (2) 395483; fax (2) 339234; e-mail embnam@netangola.com; Ambassador LINEEKELA MBOTI.

Netherlands: Edif. Secil, Avda 4 de Fevereiro 42–6/10, CP 3624, Luanda; tel. (2) 310686; fax (2) 310966; e-mail lua@minbuza.nl; internet www.angolanda.com; Ambassador J.E. VAN DEN BERG.

Nigeria: Rua Houari Boumedienne 120, CP 479, Luanda; tel. (2) 340084; Ambassador AGWOM GOKIR GOTIP.

Norway: Rua de Benguela, Bairro Patrice Lumumba, CP 3835, Luanda; tel. (2) 449936; fax (2) 446248; e-mail emb.luanda@mfa.no; internet ud55.mogul.no; Ambassador ARILD R. ØYEN.

Poland: Rua Comandante N'zaji 21–23, CP 1340, Luanda; tel. (2) 333655; fax (2) 390392; Ambassador EUGENIUSZ RZEWUSKI.

Portugal: Rua Karl Marx 50, CP 1346, Luanda; tel. (2) 333027; Ambassador FERNANDO MENDONÇA D'OLIVEIRA.

Romania: Ramalho Ortigão 30, Alvalade, Luanda; tel. and fax (2) 321076; Ambassador MARIN ILIESCU.

Russia: Rua Houari Boumedienne 170, CP 3141, Luanda; tel. (2) 445028; fax (2) 445320; e-mail rusemb@netangola.com; Ambassador ANDREI KEMARSKY.

São Tomé and Príncipe: Rua Armindo de Andrade 173–175, Luanda; tel. (2) 345677; Ambassador ARIOSTO CASTELO DAVID.

Serbia and Montenegro: Rua Comandante N'zaji 25–27, Luanda; tel. (2) 321421; fax (2) 321724; Chargé d'affaires a.i. BRANKO MARKOVIĆ.

Slovakia: Rua Amílcar Cabral 5, CP 2691, Luanda; tel. (2) 334456.

South Africa: Rua Manuel Fernandes Caldeira 6B, CP 6212, Luanda; tel. (2) 397391; fax (2) 339126; Ambassador T.S. MSIMANGA.

Spain: Avda 4 de Fevereiro 95, 1°, CP 3061, Luanda; tel. (2) 391187; fax (2) 332884; e-mail embespao@mail.mae.es; Ambassador MANUEL PRADAS ROMANÍ.

Sweden: Rua Garcia Neto 9, CP 1130, Miramar, Luanda; tel. (2) 440424; fax (2) 443460; Ambassador ROGER GARTOFT.

Tanzania: Luanda; tel. (2) 330536.

United Kingdom: Rua Diogo Cão 4, CP 1244, Luanda; tel. (2) 334583; fax (2) 333331; e-mail britemb.ang@ebonet.net; Ambassador CAROLINE M. T. ELMES.

USA: Rua Houari Boumedienne 32, Miramar, CP 6468, Luanda; tel. (2) 347028; fax (2) 346924; Ambassador CHRISTOPHER WILLIAM DELL.

Viet Nam: Rua Comandante N'zaji 66–68, CP 75, Luanda; tel. (2) 323388; Ambassador NGUYEN HUY LOI.

Zambia: Rua Rei Katyavala 106–108, CP 1496, Luanda; tel. (2) 331145; Ambassador BONIFACE ZULU.

Zimbabwe: Edif. Secil, Avda 4 de Fevereiro 42, CP 428, Luanda; tel. (2) 310125; fax (2) 311528; e-mail embzimbabwe@ebonet.net; Ambassador J. MANZOU.

Judicial System

There is a Supreme Court and Court of Appeal in Luanda. There are also civil, criminal and military courts.

Supreme Court: Rua 17 de Setembro, Luanda; fax (2) 335411; Pres. Dr CRISTIANO ANDRÉ.

Office of the Attorney-General: Rua 17 de Setembro, Luanda; tel. (2) 333171; fax (2) 333172; Attorney-General AUGUSTO DA COSTA CARNEIRO.

Religion

Much of the population follows traditional African beliefs, although a majority profess to be Christians, mainly Roman Catholics.

CHRISTIANITY

Conselho de Igrejas Cristãs em Angola (Council of Christian Churches in Angola): Rua Amílcar Cabral 182, 1° andar, CP 1659, Luanda; tel. (2) 330415; fax (2) 393746; f. 1977; 14 mem. churches; five assoc. mems; one observer; Pres. Rev. ALVARO RODRIGUES; Gen. Sec. Rev. AUGUSTO CHIPESSE.

Protestant Churches

Evangelical Congregational Church in Angola (Igreja Evangélica Congregacional em Angola—IECA): CP 1552, Luanda; tel. (2) 355108; fax (2) 350868; e-mail ieca.luanda@angonet.org; f. 1880; 350,000 mems; Gen. Sec. Rev. Dr JOSÉ BELO CHIPENDA.

Evangelical Pentecostal Church of Angola (Missão Evangélica Pentecostal de Angola): CP 219, Porto Amboim; 13,600 mems; Sec. Rev. JOSÉ DOMINGOS CAETANO.

United Evangelical Church of Angola (Igreja Evangélica Unida de Angola): CP 122, Uíge; 11,000 mems; Gen. Sec. Rev. A. L. DOMINGOS.

Other active denominations include the African Apostolic Church, the Church of Apostolic Faith in Angola, the Church of Our Lord Jesus Christ in the World, the Evangelical Baptist Church, the Evangelical Church in Angola, the Evangelical Church of the Apostles of Jerusalem, the Evangelical Reformed Church of Angola, the Kimbanguist Church in Angola and the United Methodist Church.

The Roman Catholic Church

Angola comprises three archdioceses and 12 dioceses. At 31 December 2000 an estimated 46.7% of the total population were adherents.

Bishops' Conference

Conferência Episcopal de Angola e São Tomé, CP 87, Luanda; tel. (2) 443686; fax (2) 445504.

f. 1967; Pres. Most Rev. ZACARIAS KAMWENHO (Archbishop of Lubango).

Archbishop of Huambo: Most Rev. FRANCISCO VITI, Arcebispado, CP 10, Huambo; tel. (41) 20130.

Archbishop of Luanda: Most Rev. DAMIÃO ANTÓNIO FRANKLIN, Arcebispado, Largo do Palácio, CP 87, 1230-C, Luanda; tel. (2) 331481; fax (2) 334433; e-mail arquidiocese@snet.co.ao.

Archbishop of Lubango: Most Rev. ZACARIAS KAMWENHO, Arcebispado, CP 231, Lubango; tel. (61) 20405; fax (61) 30140.

The Press

A free press was reinstituted in 1991, after 15 years of government control.

DAILIES

Diário da República: CP 1306, Luanda; official govt bulletin.

O Jornal de Angola: Rua Rainha Ginga 18–24, CP 1312, Luanda; tel. (2) 338947; fax (2) 333342; internet jornaldeangola.ebonet.net; f. 1923; Dir-Gen. LUÍS FERNANDO; mornings and Sun. circ. 41,000.

Newspapers are also published in several regional towns.

PERIODICALS

Actual: Rua Fernando Pessoa 103-A, Vila Alice, CP 6959, Luanda; tel. and fax (2) 325791; internet www.ebonet.net/actual; weekly; Editor JOAQUIM ALVES.

Agora: Rua Francisco A. Pinto 6, 2° andar, Luanda; tel. and fax (2) 323477; e-mail agora-es@ebonet.net; weekly; Dir ANGUEAR DOS SANTOS.

Angolense: Rua Cónego Manuel das Neves 83B, Luanda; tel. (2) 341501; fax (2) 340549; e-mail angolense@netangola.com; weekly.

Comércio Externo: Rua da Missão 81, CP 6375, Luanda; tel. (2) 334060; fax (2) 392216; e-mail com.actualidade@ebonet.net; f. 1993 as *Comércio Actualidade*; weekly; Editor VICTOR ALEIXO.

Correio de Semana: CP 1312, Luanda; Ed. JOÃO MELO.

Eme: Luanda; tel. (2) 321130; f. 1996; MPLA publ.

Folha 8: Rua Conselheiro Júlio de Vilhena 24, 5° andar, CP 6527, Luanda; tel. (2) 391943; fax (2) 392289; e-mail folha8@ebonet.net; internet www.folha8.com; two a week; Dir WILLIAM TONET.

Horizonte: Rua da Samba 144, 1° andar, Luanda.

Independente: Rua de Missão, 81, Luanda; tel. and fax (2) 343968; weekly.

Jornal de Benguela: CP 17, Benguela; two a week.

Jornal de Desportos: Rua da Rainha Ginga, 18–24, CP 1312, Luanda; tel. (2) 338947; fax (2) 333342.

Lavra & Oficina: CP 2767-C, Luanda; tel. (2) 322155; f. 1975; journal of the Union of Angolan Writers; monthly; circ. 5,000.

Notícias de Angola: Luanda; weekly.

Novembro: CP 3947, Luanda; tel. (2) 331660; monthly; Dir ROBERTO DE ALMEIDA.

O Planalto: CP 96, Huambo; two a week.

Tempos Novos: Avda Combatentes 244, 2° andar, CP 16088, Luanda; tel. (2) 349534; fax (2) 349534.

A Voz do Povo: Rua João de Deus 99–103, Vila Alice, Luanda.

A Voz do Trabalhador: Avda 4 de Fevereiro 210, CP 28, Luanda; journal of União Nacional de Trabalhadores Angolanos (National Union of Angolan Workers); monthly.

NEWS AGENCIES

ANGOP: Rua Rei Katiavala 120, CP 2181, Luanda; tel. (2) 346901; fax (2) 347342; internet www.angolapress-angop.ao; Dir-Gen. and Editor-in-Chief AVELINO MIGUEL.

Foreign Bureaux

Agence France-Presse (AFP): Prédio Mutamba, CP 2357, Luanda; tel. (2) 334939; Bureau Chief MANUELA TEIXEIRA.

Agência Lusa de Informação (Portugal): Luanda; Bureau Chief MIGUEL SOUTO.

Allgemeiner Deutscher Nachrichtendienst (ADN) (Germany): CP 3193, Luanda; Correspondent GUDRUN GROSS.

Informatsionnoye Telegrafnoye Agentstvo Rossii—Telegrafnoye Agentstvo Suverennykh Stran (ITAR—TASS) (Russia): Rua Marechal Tito 75, CP 3209, Luanda; tel. (2) 342524; Correspondent VLADIMIR BORISOVICH BUYANOV.

Inter Press Service (IPS) (Italy): c/o Centro de Imprensa Anibal de Melo, Rua Cequeira Lukoki 124, Luanda; tel. (2) 334895; fax (2) 393445; Correspondent CHRIS SIMPSON.

Prensa Latina (Cuba): Rua D. Miguel de Melo 92-2, Luanda; tel. (2) 336804; Chief Correspondent LUÍS MANUEL SÁEZ.

Reuters (UK): c/o Centro de Imprensa Anibal de Melo, Rua Cequeira Lukoki 124, Luanda; tel. (2) 334895; fax (2) 393445; Correspondent CRISTINA MULLER.

Rossiyskoye Informatsionnoye Agentstvo—Novosti (RIA—Novosti) (Russia): Luanda; Chief Officer VLADISLAV Z. KOMAROV.

Xinhua (New China) News Agency (People's Republic of China): Rua Karl Marx 57-3, andar E, Bairro das Ingombotas, Zona 4, Luanda; tel. (2) 332415; Correspondent ZHAO XIAOZHONG.

Publishers

Editorial Nzila: Rua Comandante Valódia 1, ao Largo do Kinaxixi, Luanda; tel. (2) 447137; e-mail edinzila@hotmail.com.

Empresa Distribuidora Livreira (EDIL), UEE: Rua da Missão 107, CP 1245, Luanda; tel. (2) 334034.

Neográfica, SARL: CP 6518, Luanda; publrs of *Novembro*.

Nova Editorial Angolana, SARL: CP 1225, Luanda; f. 1935; general and educational; Man. Dir POMBO FERNANDES.

Offsetográfica Gráfica Industrial Lda: CP 911, Benguela; tel. 32568; f. 1966; Man. FERNANDO MARTINS.

Government Publishing House

Imprensa Nacional, UEE: CP 1306, Luanda; f. 1845; Gen. Man. Dr ANTÓNIO DUARTE DE ALMEIDA E CARMO.

Broadcasting and Communications

TELECOMMUNICATIONS

Angola Telecom: Rua do I Congresso do MPLA 26, 2° andar, CP 625, Luanda; tel. (2) 631000; fax (2) 391688; e-mail info@angolatelecom.com; internet www.angolatelecom.com; international telecommunications.

Empresa Pública de Telecomunicações (EPTEL), UEE: Rua 1 Congresso 26, CP 625, Luanda; tel. (2) 392285; fax (2) 391688; state telecommunications company.

Instituto Angolano das Comunicações (INACOM): Avda. de Portugal, 92, 7° andar, CP 1459, Luanda; tel. (2) 338352; fax (2) 339356; e-mail incom@netangola.com; internet www.inacom.og.ao; f. 1999; monitoring and regulatory authority.

BROADCASTING

Radio

Rádio Nacional de Angola: Rua Comandante Gika, CP 1329, Luanda; tel. (2) 323172; fax (2) 324647; e-mail rna.dg@netangola.com; internet www.rna.ao; broadcasts in Portuguese, English, French, Spanish and vernacular languages (Chokwe, Kikongo, Kimbundu, Kwanyama, Fiote, Ngangela, Luvale, Songu, Umbundu); Dir-Gen. MANUEL RABELAIS.

Luanda Antena Comercial (LAC): Praceta Luther King 5, CP 3521, Luanda; tel. (2) 396229; fax (2) 396229; e-mail lac@ebonet.net; internet www.ebonet.net/lac.

Rádio 2000: CP 145, Lubango; tel. (61) 23935; fax (61) 23937; e-mail radio2000@netangola.com.

Rádio Ecclesia—Emissora Católica de Angola: Rua Comandante Bula 118, São Paulo, CP 3579, Luanda; tel. (2) 443041; fax (2) 443093; e-mail recclesia@recclesia.org; internet www.recclesia.org; f. 1955; Dir-Gen. ANTÓNIO JACA.

Rádio Morena Comercial: Avda Aires de Almeida Santos 537, Benguela; tel. (73) 32525; fax (73) 32731.

Television

Televisão Pública de Angola (TPA): Rua Ho Chi Minh, CP 2604, Luanda; tel. (2) 320025; fax (2) 323622; e-mail tpa.angola@netangola.com; internet www.tpa.ao; f. 1975; state-controlled; Man. Dir CARLOS CUNHA.

Finance

(cap. = capital; res = reserves; dep. = deposits; m. = million; brs = branches; amounts in kwanza (equivalent to 1m. readjusted kwanza), unless otherwise indicated)

BANKING

All banks were nationalized in 1975. In 1995 the Government authorized the formation of private banks.

Central Bank

Banco Nacional de Angola: Avda 4 de Fevereiro 151, CP 1298, Luanda; tel. (2) 332633; fax (2) 333717; e-mail cni@bna.ao; internet www.ebonet.net/bna; f. 1976; bank of issue; cap. 5m., res 1m., dep. 63.8m. (1997); Gov. AMADEU MAURÍCIO; 6 brs.

Commercial Banks

Banco Comercial Angolano (BCA): Avda Comandante Valódia 83A, CP 6900, Luanda; tel. (2) 349548; fax (2) 349516; e-mail bca@snet.co.ao; f. 1997; Pres. ANTÓNIO MOSQUITO; Gen. Man. MÁRIO PIZARRO.

Banco de Poupança e Crédito (BPC): Largo Saydi Mingas, CP 1343, Luanda; tel. and fax (2) 393790; 100% state-owned; cap.

16,118m. (Dec. 2000); Chair. Paixão António Júnior; brs throughout Angola.

Caixa de Crédito Agro-Pecuario e Pescas (CCAPP): Rua Rainha Ginga 83, Luanda; tel. (2) 392749; fax (2) 392225; f. 1991; assumed commercial operations of Banco Nacional de Angola in 1996.

Development Bank

Banco de Comércio e Indústria SARL: Avda 4 de Fevereiro 84–86, CP 1395, Luanda; tel. (2) 333819; fax (2) 334924; e-mail secretariado@bci.ebonet.net; internet www.angola.org/bci; f. 1991; 91% state-owned; due to be privatized in 2003; provides loans to businesses in all sectors; cap. 3.5m., res 7.3m., dep. 131.9m. (1999); Chair. Generoso Hermenegildo Gaspar de Almeida; 5 brs.

Investment Bank

Banco Africano de Investimentos SARL (BAI): Rua Major Kanhangulo 34, CP 6022, Luanda; tel. (2) 335127; fax (2) 335486; e-mail baisede@bainet.ebonet.net; f. 1997; 37.5% interest owned by Angolan shareholders; cap. 6.5m., res 1,240.7m., dep. 11,432.6m. (Dec. 2001); Pres. Dr Mário Abílio Palhares; 4 brs.

Foreign Banks

Banco BPI SA: Edif. BPC, 7°, Rua Dr Alfredo Troni, Luanda; tel. (2) 339198; fax (2) 339903; Gen. Man. Fernando Teles.

Banco Comercial Português SA: Largo Rainha Ginga 6/8, CP 5726, Luanda; tel. (2) 394897; fax (2) 397397.

Banco Totta de Angola SARL: Avda 4 de Fevereiro 99, CP 1231, Luanda; tel. (2) 332393; fax (2) 332333; e-mail bta.adm@multitel.co .ao; 99.8% owned by Banco Totta e Açores; cap. €15.3m., res €5.0m., dep. €146.7m. Man. Dir Dr Mário Nelson Maximino; 7 brs.

INSURANCE

Empresa Nacional de Seguros e Resseguros de Angola (ENSA), UEE: Avda 4 de Fevereiro 93, CP 5778, Luanda; tel. (2) 332990; fax (2) 332946; e-mail ensaio@ebonet.net; f. 1978; state-owned; Del. Admin. Bernardo L. Makombe.

Trade and Industry

GOVERNMENT AGENCIES

Gabinete de Redimensionamento Empresarial: Rua Cerqueira Lukoki 25, 9° andar, CP 594, Luanda; tel. (2) 390496; fax (2) 393381; privatization agency.

Instituto de Investimento Estrangeiro: Rua Cerqueira Lukoki, 25, 9° andar, Luanda; tel. (2) 333727; fax (2) 393381; foreign investment agency.

CHAMBER OF COMMERCE

Angolan Chamber of Commerce and Industry: Largo do Kinaxixi 14, 1° andar, CP 92, Luanda; tel. (2) 444506; fax (2) 444629; e-mail ccira@ebonet.net; internet www.ccia.ebonet.net; Pres. António João dos Santos.

INDUSTRIAL AND TRADE ASSOCIATIONS

Associação Comercial de Benguela: Rua Sacadura Cabral 104, CP 347, Benguela; tel. (72) 32441; fax (72) 33022; e-mail acbenguela@netangola.com; internet netangola.com/acb; f. 1907.

Associação Comercial e Industrial de Luanda (ACOMIL): Largo do Kinaxixi 14–30, Luanda; tel. (2) 335728.

Associação Comercial de Luanda (ASCANGOLA): CP 1275, 1° andar, Edif. Palácio de Comercio, Luanda; tel. (2) 332453.

STATE TRADING ORGANIZATIONS

Angomédica, UEE: Rua do Sanatório, Bairro Palanca, CP 2698, Luanda; tel. (2) 363765; fax (2) 362336; f. 1981 to import pharmaceutical goods; Gen. Dir Dr Fátima Saiundo.

Angolan Selling Corporation (ASCORP): Rua Tipografia Mama Tita, Edif. Soleil B, CP 3978, Ingombotas, Luanda; tel. (2) 396465; fax (2) 397615; e-mail ascorpadmin@ebonet.net; f. 1999; 51% state-owned diamond-trading co; Pres. Noe Baltazar.

Direcção dos Serviços de Comércio (Dept of Trade): Largo Diogo Cão, CP 1337, Luanda; f. 1970; brs throughout Angola.

Epmel, UEE: Rua Karl Marx 35–37, Luanda; tel. (2) 330943; industrial agricultural machinery.

Exportang, UEE: Rua dos Enganos 1A, CP 1000, Luanda; tel. (2) 332363; co-ordinates exports.

Importang, UEE: Calçada do Município 10, CP 1003, Luanda; tel. (2) 337994; f. 1977; co-ordinates majority of imports; Dir-Gen. Simão Diogo da Cruz.

Maquimport, UEE: Rua Rainha Ginga 152, CP 2975, Luanda; tel. (2) 339044; f. 1981 to import office equipment.

Mecanang, UEE: Rua dos Enganos, 1°–7° andar, CP 1347, Luanda; tel. (2) 390644; f. 1981 to import agricultural and construction machinery, tools and spare parts.

Sociedade de Comercialização de Diamantes de Angola, SARL (SODIAM): Rua Manuel Fernando Caldeira 6b-1, Luanda; tel. (2) 370217; fax (2) 370423; e-mail sodiama@hotmail.com; internet www.sodiam-angola.com; f. 2000; diamond trading organization.

STATE INDUSTRIAL ENTERPRISES

Companhia do Açúcar de Angola: Rua Direita 77, Luanda; production of sugar.

Companhia Geral dos Algodões de Angola (COTONANG): Avda da Boavista, Luanda; production of cotton textiles.

Empresa Abastecimento Técnico Material (EMATEC), UEE: Largo Rainha Ginga 3, CP 2952, Luanda; tel. (2) 338891; technical and material suppliers to the Ministry of Defence.

Empresa Açucareira Centro (OSUKA), UEE: Estrada Principal do Lobito, CP 37, Catumbela; tel. 24681; sugar industry.

Empresa de Construção de Edificações (CONSTROI), UEE: Rua Alexandre Peres, CP 2566, Luanda; tel. (2) 333930; construction.

Empresa de Obras Especiais (EMPROE): Rua Ngola Kiluange 183–185, Luanda; tel. (2) 382142; fax (2) 382143; undergoing privatization in 2003; building and civil engineering.

Empresa de Pesca de Angola (PESCANGOLA), UEE: Luanda; f. 1981; state fishing enterprise, responsible to Ministry of Fisheries and Environment.

Empresa de Rebenefício e Exportação do Café de Angola (CAFANGOL), UEE: Rua Robert Shields 4/6, CP 342, Luanda; tel. (2) 337916; fax (2) 334742; e-mail cafango@arrobasnet.co.ao; f. 1983; nat. coffee-processing and trade org; proposed transfer to private sector announced in 1991; Dir-Gen. Alvaro Faria.

Empresa de Tecidos de Angola (TEXTANG), UEE: Rua N'gola Kiluanji-Kazenga, CP 5404, Luanda; tel. (2) 381134; production of textiles.

Empresa dos Tabacos de Angola: CP 1238, Luanda; tel. (2) 336995; fax (2) 336921; manufacture of tobacco products; Gen. Man. K. Bittencourt.

Empresa Nacional de Cimento (ENCIME), UEE: CP 157, Lobito; tel. (711) 2325; undergoing privatization in 2003; cement production.

Empresa Nacional de Comercialização e Distribuição de Produtos Agrícolas (ENCODIPA): Luanda; central marketing agency for agricultural produce; numerous brs throughout Angola.

Empresa Nacional de Diamantes de Angola (ENDIAMA), UEE: Rua Major Kanhangulo 100, CP 1247, Luanda; tel. (2) 330377; fax (2) 337276; e-mail endiama@endiama-angola.com; internet www .endiama-angola.com; f. 1981; commenced operations 1986; diamond mining; Pres. Dr Manuel Arnaldo de Sousa Calado.

Empresa Nacional de Ferro de Angola (FERRANGOL): Rua João de Barros 26, CP 2692, Luanda; tel. (2) 373800; iron production; Dir Armando de Sousa.

Empresa Nacional de Manutenção (MANUTECNICA), UEE: Rua 7, Avda do Cazenga 10, CP 3508, Luanda; tel. (2) 383646; assembly of machines and specialized equipment for industry.

Geotécnica Unidad Económica Estatal: Rua Angola Kilmanse 389/393, Luanda; tel. (2) 381795; fax (2) 382730; f. 1978 for surveying and excavation; Man. P. M. M. Elvino Jnr; 500 employees.

NOVA CIMANGOLA, SARL: Avda 4 de Fevereiro 42, CP 2532, Luanda; tel. (2) 310190; fax (2) 311272; f. 1994; 51% state-owned; cement production; Man. Dir Frode Mauring.

Siderurgia Nacional, UEE: CP Zona Industrial do Forel das Lagostas, Luanda; tel. (2) 373028; f. 1963; nationalized 1980; steelworks and rolling mill plant.

Sociedade Nacional de Combustíveis de Angola (SONANGOL): Edif. DH, Avda 4 Fevereiro 214, CP 1316, Luanda; tel. (2) 396205; fax (2) 395998; f. 1976 for exploration, production and refining of crude petroleum, and marketing and distribution of petroleum products; sole concessionary in Angola, supervises on- and offshore operations of foreign petroleum cos; holds majority interest in jt ventures with Cabinda Gulf Oil Co (Cabgoc), Fina Petróleos de Angola and Texaco Petróleos de Angola; Man. Dir JOAQUIM DAVID.

Sociedade Unificada de Tabacos de Angola, Lda (SUT): Rua Deolinda Rodrigues 530/537, CP 1263, Luanda; tel. (2) 360180; fax (2) 362138; f. 1919; tobacco products; Gen. Man. Dr MANUEL LAMAS.

UTILITIES

Electricity

Empresa Nacional de Construções Eléctricas (ENCEL), UEE: Rua Comandante Che Guevara 185/7, CP 5230, Luanda; tel. (2) 446712; fax (2) 446759; e-mail encel@encel.co.ao; f. 1982; electricity generation; Dir.-Gen. DANIEL SIMAS.

Empresa Nacional de Electricidade (ENE), EP: Prédio Geominas, 6°–7° andar, CP 772, Luanda; tel. (2) 321529; fax (2) 323433; e-mail enedg@netangola.com; f. 1980; production and distribution of electricity; Pres. and Dir-Gen. Eng. EDUARDO GOMES NELUMBA.

TRADE UNIONS

Angolan General Independent and Free Trade Union Confederation: Chair. MANUEL DIFUILA.

União Nacional de Trabalhadores Angolanos (UNTA) (National Union of Angolan Workers): Avda 4 de Fevereiro, CP 28, Luanda; tel. (2) 334670; fax (2) 393590; e-mail untadis@netangola.com; f. 1960; Pres. MANUEL DIOGO DA SILVA NETO; Gen. Sec. MANUEL AUGUSTO VIAGE; 133,707 mems.

Transport

The transport infrastructure was severely dislocated by the civil war that ended in 2002.

RAILWAYS

The total length of track operated was 2,952 km in 1993. There are plans to extend the Namibe line beyond Menongue and to construct north–south rail links. Plans were announced in June 2002 to rebuild the Benguela railway, linking the port of Lobito to Beira in Mozambique.

Dirreção Nacional dos Caminhos de Ferro: Avda 4 de Fevereiro 42, CP 1250-C, Luanda; tel. (2) 339794; fax (2) 339976; f. 1975; nat. network operating four fmrly independent systems covering 2,952 track-km; Dir JULIO BANGO.

Amboim Railway: Porto Amboim; f. 1922; 123 track-km; Dir A. GUIA.

Benguela Railway (Companhia do Caminho de Ferro de Benguela): Praça 11 Novembro 3, CP 32, Lobito; tel. (711) 22645; fax (711) 22865; e-mail cfbeng@ebonet.net; f. 1903; line completed 1928; owned 90% by Tank Consolidated Investments (a subsidiary of Société Générale de Belgique), 10% by Govt of Angola; line carrying passenger and freight traffic from the port of Lobito across Angola, via Huambo and Luena, to the border of the Democratic Republic of the Congo (fmrly Zaire); 1,302 track-km; guerrilla operations by UNITA suspended all international traffic from 1975, with only irregular services from Lobito to Huambo being operated; the rehabilitation of the railway was a priority of a 10-year programme, planned by the Southern African Development Co-ordination Conference (SADCC), now the Southern African Development Community—SADC), to develop the 'Lobito corridor'; in 1997 an Italian company, Tor di Vale, began a US $450m.-programme of repairs to the railway; minimum repairs allowing the resumption of freight traffic were expected to take three years to complete, to be followed by further modernization; Pres. Dr GUILHERME PRATAS; Dir-Gen. DANIEL QUIPAXE.

Luanda Railway (Empresa de Caminho de Ferro de Luanda, UEE): CP 1250-C, Luanda; tel. (2) 370061; f. 1886; serves an iron, cotton and sisal-producing region between Luanda and Malanje; 536 track-km; Man. A. ALVARO AGANTE.

Namibe Railway: CP 130, Lubango; f. 1905; main line from Namibe to Menongue, via Lubango; br. lines to Chibia and iron ore mines at Cassinga; 899 track-km; Gen. Man. J. SALVADOR.

ROADS

In 1999 Angola had 51,429 km of roads, of which 7,944 km were main roads and 13,278 km were secondary roads. About 10.4% of roads were paved. In 1997 the state-owned road construction and maintenance company, the Instituto de Estradas de Angola, reported that 80% of the country's road network was in disrepair and that the cost of rebuilding the roads and bridges damaged during the civil conflict would total some US $4,000m.

SHIPPING

The main harbours are at Lobito, Luanda and Namibe. The first phase of a 10-year SADCC (now SADC) programme to develop the 'Lobito corridor', for which funds were pledged in January 1989, was to include the rehabilitation of the ports of Lobito and Benguela.

Agenang, UEE: Rua Engracia Fragoso, 47–49, Luanda; tel. (2) 336380; fax (2) 334392.

Angonave—Linhas Marítimas de Angola, UEE: Rua Serqueira 31, CP 5953, Luanda; tel. (2) 330144; shipping line; Dir-Gen. FRANCISCO VENÂNCIO.

Cabotang—Cabotagem Nacional Angolana, UEE: Avda 4 de Fevereiro 83A, Luanda; tel. (2) 373133; operates off the coasts of Angola and Mozambique; Dir-Gen. JOÃO OCTAVIO VAN-DÚNEM.

Empresa Portuária do Lobito, UEE: Avda da Independência, CP 16, Lobito; tel. (711) 2710; long-distance sea transport; Gen. Man. JOSÉ CARLOS GOMES.

Empresa Portuária de Moçâmedes—Namibe, UEE: Rua Pedro Benje 10A and 10C, CP 49, Namibe; tel. (64) 60643; long-distance sea transport; Dir HUMBERTO DE ATAIDE DIAS.

Orey Angola, Lda: Largo 4 de Fevereiro 3, 3° andar, CP 583, Luanda; tel. (2) 310850; fax (2) 310882; e-mail acarmona@oreylad.ebonet.net; internet www.orey.com/angola; international shipping, especially to Portugal; Dir Commdt A. CARMONA E COSTA.

Secil Marítima SARL, UEE: Avda 4 de Fevereiro 42, 1° andar, CP 5910, Luanda; tel. (2) 310950.

CIVIL AVIATION

Air Nacoia: Rua Comandante Che Guevara 67, 1° andar, Luanda; tel. and fax (2) 395477; f. 1993; Pres. SALVADOR SILVA.

TAAG—Linhas Aéreas de Angola: Rua da Missão 123, CP 79, Luanda; tel. (2) 332387; fax (2) 392229; internet www.taag-airlines.com; f. 1938; internal scheduled passenger and cargo services, and services from Luanda to destinations within Africa and to Europe and South America; Chair. JÚLIO SAMPAIO ALMEIDA; Pres. and CEO MIGUEL COSTA.

Angola Air Charter: Aeroporto Internacional 4 de Fevereiro, CP 3010, Luanda; tel. (2) 321290; fax (2) 320105; e-mail aacharter@independente.net; f. 1992; subsidiary of TAAG; CEO A. DE MATOS.

Transafrik International: 4th February International Airport, Luanda; tel. (2) 353714; fax (2) 354183; e-mail enquiries@transafrik.com; internet www.transafrik.com; f. 1986; operates contract cargo services mainly within Africa; Man. Dir ERICH F. KOCH; Gen. Man. PIMENTAL ARAUJO.

Tourism

National Tourist Agency: Palácio de Vidro, CP 1240, Luanda; tel. (2) 372750.

ANTARCTICA

Source: Scientific Committee on Antarctic Research, Scott Polar Research Institute, Lensfield Rd, Cambridge, CB2 1ER, United Kingdom; tel. (1223) 362061; fax (1223) 336550; e-mail execsec@scar.demon.co.uk; internet www.scar.org.

The Continent of Antarctica is estimated to cover 13,661,000 sq km. There are no indigenous inhabitants, but a number of permanent research stations have been established. W. S. Bruce, of the Scottish National Antarctic Expedition (1902–04), established a meteorological station on Laurie Island, South Orkney Islands, on 1 April 1903. After the expedition, this was transferred to the Argentine authorities (the British Government having declined to operate the station), who have maintained the observatory since 22 February 1904 (see Orcadas, below). The next permanent stations were established in 1944 by the United Kingdom, and then subsequently by other countries.

Tourism, which consists almost exclusively of 'eco-cruises', is promoted by the International Association of Antarctica Tour Operators (IAATO); the number of tourists visiting Antarctica totalled 15,325 in 2001 (compared with 4,800 in 1991). The dramatic increase in tourist numbers led to expressions of concern in the early 2000s regarding the environmental impact of the industry on the region. In 2003 the Antarctic and Southern Ocean Coalition, a consortium of 240 non-governmental organizations, appealed for quotas to be introduced to control tourist numbers and protect the continent's fragile environment.

Wintering Stations

(The following list includes wintering stations south of latitude 60° occupied during austral winter 2001)

	Latitude	Longitude
ARGENTINA		
General Belgrano II, Bertrab Nunatak, Luitpold Coast	77° 52′ S	34° 37′ W
Esperanza, Hope Bay	63° 23′ S	57° 00′ W
Teniente Jubany, King George Island	62° 14′ S	58° 39′ W
Vicecomodoro Marambio, Seymour Island	64° 14′ S	56° 39′ W
Orcadas, Laurie Island	60° 44′ S	44° 44′ W
General San Martín, Barry Island	68° 07′ S	67° 06′ W
AUSTRALIA		
Casey, Vincennes Bay, Budd Coast	66° 17′ S	110° 31′ E
Davis, Ingrid Christensen Coast	68° 34′ S	77° 58′ E
Mawson, Mac. Robertson Land	67° 36′ S	62° 52′ E
BRAZIL		
Comandante Ferraz, King George Island	62° 05′ S	58° 23′ W
CHILE		
Capitán Arturo Prat, Greenwich island	62° 30′ S	59° 41′ W
General Bernardo O'Higgins, Cape Legoupil	63° 19′ S	57° 54′ W
Presidente Eduardo Frei, King George Island	62° 12′ S	58° 57′ W
Professor Julio Escudero, King George Island	62° 12′ S	58° 57′ W
PEOPLE'S REPUBLIC OF CHINA		
Chang Cheng (Great Wall), King George Island	62° 13′ S	58° 58′ W
Zhongshan, Princess Elizabeth Land	69° 22′ S	76° 23′ E
FRANCE*		
Dumont d'Urville, Terre Adélie	66° 40′ S	140° 00′ E
GERMANY		
Neumayer, Ekström isen	70° 38′ S	8° 16′ W
INDIA		
Maitri, Schirmacheroasen	70° 46′ S	11° 44′ E
JAPAN		
Syowa, Ongul	69° 00′ S	39° 35′ E
REPUBLIC OF KOREA		
King Sejong, King George Island	62° 13′ S	58° 47′ W
NEW ZEALAND		
Scott Base, Ross Island	77° 51′ S	166° 46′ E
POLAND		
Henryk Arctowski, King George Island	62° 10′ S	58° 28′ W
RUSSIA		
Bellingshausen, King George Island	62° 11′ S	58° 57′ W
Mirnyy, Queen Mary Land	66° 33′ S	93° 00′ E
Molodezhnaya, Enderby Land	67° 40′ S	45° 51′ E
Novolazarevskaya, Prinsesse Astrid Kyst	70° 46′ S	11° 50′ E
Progress, Princess Elizabeth Land	69° 23′ S	76° 23′ E
Vostok, East Antarctica	78° 28′ S	106° 48′ E

	Latitude	Longitude
SOUTH AFRICA		
SANAE, Vesleskarvet	71° 40′ S	2° 49′ W
UKRAINE		
Vernadsky, Argentine Islands	65° 15′ S	64° 15′ W
UNITED KINGDOM		
Halley, Brunt Ice Shelf, Caird Coast	75° 36′ S	26° 32′ W
Rothera, Adelaide Island	67° 34′ S	68° 07′ W
USA		
McMurdo, Ross Island	77° 51′ S	166° 40′ E
Palmer, Anvers Island	64° 46′ S	64° 03′ W
Amundsen-Scott	South Pole†	
URUGUAY		
Artigas, King George Island	62° 11′ S	58° 54′ W

* A new research station, Concorde (at Dome C—75° 06′ S 123° 23′ E), was officially open for summer routine operations in December 1997 as a joint venture with Italy; the station was expected to be open year round from 2003.

† The precise co-ordinates of the location of this station are: 89° 59′ 51″ S, 139° 16′ 23″ E.

Territorial Claims

Territory	Claimant State
Antártida Argentina	Argentina
Australian Antarctic Territory	Australia
British Antarctic Territory	United Kingdom
Dronning Maud Land	Norway
Ross Dependency	New Zealand
Terre Adélie	France
Territorio Chileno Antártico	Chile

These claims are not recognized by the USA or Russia. No formal claims have been made in the sector of Antarctica between 90° W and 150° W.

See also Article 4 of the Antarctic Treaty, below.

Research

Scientific Committee on Antarctic Research (SCAR) of the **International Council for Science (ICSU):** Secretariat: Scott Polar Research Institute, Lensfield Rd, Cambridge, CB2 1ER, United Kingdom; tel. (1223) 362061; fax (1223) 336550; e-mail execsec@scar.demon.co.uk; internet www.scar.org; f. 1958 to initiate, promote and co-ordinate scientific research in the Antarctic, and to provide scientific advice to the Antarctic Treaty System; 26 full mems; six assoc. mems

President: Prof Dr Jörn Thiede (Germany).

Vice-Presidents: Dr R. Schlich (France), Prof Dr J. L. Lopez-Martínez (Spain), Dr C. H. Williams (New Zealand), Prof. C. G. Rapley (United Kingdom).

Executive Secretary: Dr P. D. Clarkson.

The Antarctic Treaty

The Treaty (summarized below) was signed in Washington, DC, on 1 December 1959 by the 12 nations co-operating in the Antarctic during the International Geophysical Year, and entered into force on 23 June 1961. The Treaty made provision for a review of its terms, 30 years after ratification; however, no signatory to the Treaty has requested such a review.

Article 1. Antarctica shall be used for peaceful purposes only.

Article 2. On freedom of scientific investigation and co-operation.

Article 3. On exchange of information and personnel.

Article 4. i. Nothing contained in the present Treaty shall be interpreted as:

(a) a renunciation by any Contracting Party of previously asserted rights of or claims to territorial sovereignty in Antarctica;

(b) a renunciation or diminution by any Contracting Party of any basis of claim to territorial sovereignty in Antarctica which it may have whether as a result of its activities or those of its nationals in Antarctica, or otherwise;

(c) prejudicing the position of any Contracting Party as regards its recognition or non-recognition of any other State's right of or claim or basis of claim to territorial sovereignty in Antarctica.

Article 4. ii. No acts or activities taking place while the present Treaty is in force shall constitute a basis for asserting, supporting or denying a claim to territorial sovereignty in Antarctica or create any rights of sovereignty in Antarctica. No new claim, or enlargement of an existing claim, to territorial sovereignty in Antarctica shall be asserted while the present Treaty is in force.

Article 5. Any nuclear explosions in Antarctica and the disposal there of radioactive waste material shall be prohibited.

Article 6. On geographical limits and rights on high seas.

Article 7. On designation of observers and notification of stations and expeditions.

Article 8. On jurisdiction over observers and scientists.

Article 9. On consultative meetings.

Articles 10–14. On upholding, interpreting, amending, notifying and depositing the Treaty.

ORIGINAL SIGNATORIES

Argentina	France	South Africa
Australia	Japan	USSR (former)
Belgium	New Zealand	United Kingdom
Chile	Norway	USA

ACCEDING STATES

Austria, Brazil, Bulgaria, Canada, the People's Republic of China, Colombia, Cuba, the Czech Republic, Denmark, Ecuador, Finland, Germany, Greece, Guatemala, Hungary, India, Italy, the Democratic People's Republic of Korea, the Republic of Korea, the Netherlands, Papua New Guinea, Peru, Poland, Romania, Slovakia, Spain, Sweden, Switzerland, Turkey, Ukraine, Uruguay, Venezuela.

Brazil, Bulgaria, the People's Republic of China, Ecuador, Finland, Germany, India, Italy, the Republic of Korea, the Netherlands, Peru, Poland, Spain, Sweden and Uruguay have achieved consultative status under the Treaty, by virtue of their scientific activity in Antarctica.

ANTARCTIC TREATY CONSULTATIVE MEETINGS

Meetings of representatives from all the original signatory nations of the Antarctic Treaty and acceding nations accorded consultative status (27 in 2002), are held every one to two years to discuss scientific, environmental and political matters. The 25th meeting was held in Warsaw, Poland, in September 2002. The representatives elect a Chairman and Secretary; Working Groups are established as required. The 26th meeting was scheduled to be held in Madrid, Spain, in June 2003.

Among the numerous measures that have been agreed and implemented by the Consultative Parties are several designed to protect the Antarctic environment and wildlife. These include Agreed Measures for the Conservation of Antarctic Flora and Fauna, the designation of Specially Protected Areas and Sites of Special Scientific Interest, a Convention for the Conservation of Antarctic Seals, and a Convention on the Conservation of Antarctic Marine Living Resources.

A Convention on the Regulation of Antarctic Mineral Resource Activities (the Wellington Convention) was adopted in June 1988 and was opened for signature in November. To enter into force, the Wellington Convention required the ratification of 16 of the Consultative Parties (then numbering 22). However, France and Australia opposed the Convention, which would permit mineral exploitation (under stringent international controls) in Antarctica, and proposed the creation of an Antarctic wilderness reserve. An agreement was reached at the October 1989 Consultative Meeting, whereby two extraordinary meetings were to be convened in 1990, one to discuss the protection of the environment and the other to discuss the issue of liability for environmental damage within the framework of the Wellington Convention. In September 1990 the Government of New Zealand, which had played a major role in drafting the Wellington Convention, reversed its policy, stating that it was no longer willing to ratify the Convention. At the same time, it introduced legislation in the New Zealand House of Representatives to ban all mining and prospecting activities from its territories

in Antarctica. At the special meeting held in Chile in November–December 1990, the Consultative Parties failed to reach an agreement regarding the protection of Antarctica's environment, although a draft protocol was approved that included provisions for elaborating the issue of liability for environmental damage. This formed the basis for a further meeting in Madrid, Spain, in April 1991. France, Australia and 16 other countries supported a permanent ban on mining, whereas the USA, the United Kingdom, Japan, Germany and four others were in favour of a moratorium. Subsequently, however, Japan and Germany transferred their allegiance to the Australian-French initiative, exerting considerable pressure on the USA and the United Kingdom. Agreement was eventually reached on a ban on mining activity for 50 years, and mechanisms for a review of the ban after 50 years, or before if all Parties agree. This agreement is embodied in Article 7 of the Protocol on Environmental Protection to the Antarctic Treaty, which was adopted by the original signatory nations in October 1991 immediately prior to the 16th Consultative Meeting. By late 1997 the Protocol had been ratified by all 26 of the then Consultative Parties, and it entered into force on 14 January 1998. Thus there can be mining in the Antarctic only with the consent of all the present Consultative Parties, and even then only when a regulatory regime is in place. The first four annexes to the Protocol, providing for environmental impact assessment, conservation of fauna and flora, waste disposal, and monitoring of marine pollution, entered into force with the Protocol, but the fifth annex, on area protection, agreed after the adoption of the Protocol, has yet to take effect. A sixth annex on environmental liability is under negotiation. At the 22nd Consultative Meeting, held in mid-1998, the Committee for Environmental Protection (CEP) was established, under the provisions of the Protocol on Environmental Protection, and held its first meeting. In January 1999 the first ever political meeting held in Antarctica took place at the US McMurdo Station on Ross Island, attended by representatives of 24 of the then 43 countries acceding to the Antarctic Treaty; all of the participants reaffirmed their commitment to the protection of the Antarctic environment under the terms of the Treaty. No Consultative Meeting took place in 2000, although the Netherlands hosted a session of the CEP, followed by a meeting at which parties to the Treaty adopted the CEP's recommendations.

At a meeting of the International Whaling Commission (see p. 332) held in Mexico in May 1994, it was agreed to establish a whale sanctuary around Antarctica below 40° S. The sanctuary, which was expected to protect about 80% of the world's remaining whales from commercial hunting, came into effect in December.

In late 1998 the New Zealand Government reported that the largest recorded hole in the ozone layer, covering more than 27m. sq km, had formed over Antarctica. In late 1999, however, the US National Aeronautics and Space Administration (NASA) reported that the ozone hole had decreased in size to 25.4m. sq km. In July 2001 the World Meteorological Organization (see p. 121) reported that record low ozone levels were recorded in 1999–2000. It is anticipated that reduced emissions of ozone-depleting gases will slowly improve the levels of stratospheric ozone over the next several decades, as long-lived chlorofluorocarbons (CFCs) are gradually removed from the atmosphere.

Substantial calving from ice shelves along the Antarctic Peninsula has fuelled speculation that this may be attributable to climate warming. In early 1995 the Larsen A ice shelf lost 1,300 sq km, and in 1998 the Larsen B and Wilkins ice shelves together lost 3,000 sq km. These calvings represented a much greater rate of loss than had been predicted. Climate records from stations on the western side of the Antarctic Peninsula show a warming trend of 1.09°C per decade during winter and 0.56°C per decade annually during the period 1951–2000. However, this trend is not definitive: whereas records at some stations suggest slight warming, others suggest slight cooling; furthermore, there are no data for large areas of the continent. Satellite measurements of the Antarctic ice sheet in the period 1992–96 have not indicated significant melting. The rise in global sea levels during the 21st century is predicted to be caused largely by factors such as thermal expansion of the oceans, rather than melting of the Antarctic ice sheet.

ANTIGUA AND BARBUDA

Introductory Survey

Location, Climate, Language, Religion, Flag, Capital

The country comprises three islands: Antigua (280 sq km—108 sq miles), Barbuda (161 sq km—62 sq miles) and the uninhabited rocky islet of Redonda (1.6 sq km—0.6 sq mile). They lie along the outer edge of the Leeward Islands chain in the West Indies. Barbuda is the most northerly (40 km—25 miles north of Antigua), and Redonda is 40 km south-west of Antigua. The French island of Guadeloupe lies to the south of the country, the United Kingdom Overseas Territory of Montserrat to the south-west and Saint Christopher and Nevis to the west. The climate is tropical, although tempered by constant sea breezes and the trade winds, and the mean annual rainfall of 1,000 mm (40 ins) is slight for the region. The temperature averages 27°C (81°F), but can rise to 33°C (93°F) during the hot season between May and October. English is the official language, but an English patois is commonly used. The majority of the inhabitants profess Christianity, and are mainly adherents of the Anglican Communion. The national flag consists of an inverted triangle centred on a red field; the triangle is divided horizontally into three unequal bands, of black, blue and white, with the black stripe bearing a symbol of the rising sun in gold. The capital is St John's, on Antigua.

Recent History

The British colonized Antigua in the 17th century. The island of Barbuda, formerly a slave stud farm for the Codrington family, was annexed to the territory in 1860. Until December 1959 Antigua and other nearby British territories were administered, under a federal system, as the Leeward Islands. The first elections under universal adult suffrage were held in 1951. The colony participated in the West Indies Federation, which was formed in January 1958 but dissolved in May 1962.

Attempts to form a smaller East Caribbean Federation failed, and most of the eligible colonies subsequently became Associated States in an arrangement that gave them full internal self-government while the United Kingdom retained responsibility for defence and foreign affairs. Antigua attained associated status in February 1967. A House of Representatives replaced the Legislative Council, the Administrator became Governor and the Chief Minister was restyled Premier.

In the first general election under associated status, held in February 1971, the Progressive Labour Movement (PLM) ousted the Antigua Labour Party (ALP), which had held power since 1946, by winning 13 of the 17 seats in the House of Representatives. George Walter, leader of the PLM, replaced Vere C. Bird, Sr, as Premier. However, a general election in February 1976 was won by the ALP, with 11 seats, while the seat representing Barbuda was won by an independent. Vere Bird, the ALP's leader, again became Premier, while Lester Bird, one of his sons, became Deputy Premier.

In 1975 the Associated States agreed to seek independence separately. In the 1976 elections the PLM campaigned for early independence while the ALP opposed it. In September 1978, however, the ALP Government declared that the economic foundation for independence had been laid, and a premature general election was held in April 1980, when the ALP won 13 of the 17 seats. There was strong opposition in Barbuda to gaining independence as part of Antigua, and at local elections in March 1981 the Barbuda People's Movement (BPM), which continued to campaign for secession from Antigua, won all the seats on the Barbuda Council. However, the territory finally became independent, as Antigua and Barbuda, on 1 November 1981, remaining within the Commonwealth. The grievances of the Barbudans concerning control of land and devolution of power were unresolved, although the ALP Government had conceded a certain degree of internal autonomy to the Barbuda Council. The Governor, Sir Wilfred Jacobs, became Governor-General, while the Premier, Vere Bird, Sr, became the country's first Prime Minister.

Following disagreements within the opposition PLM, George Walter formed his own political party, the United People's Movement (UPM), in 1982. In April 1984, at the first general election since independence, divisions within the opposition

allowed the ALP to win all of the 16 seats that it contested. The remaining seat, representing Barbuda, was retained by an unopposed independent (who subsequently formed the Barbuda National Party—BNP). A new opposition party, the National Democratic Party (NDP), was formed in Antigua in 1985. In April 1986 it merged with the UPM to form the United National Democratic Party (UNDP). Dr Ivor Heath, who had led the NDP, was elected leader of the new party.

In November 1986 controversy surrounding a rehabilitation scheme at the international airport on Antigua led to an official inquiry, which concluded that Vere Bird, Jr (a senior minister and the eldest son of the Prime Minister), had acted inappropriately by awarding part of the contract to a company with which he was personally involved. The affair divided the ALP, with eight ministers (including Lester Bird, the Deputy Prime Minister) demanding the resignation of Vere Bird, Jr, and Prime Minister Bird refusing to dismiss him. The rifts within the ALP and the Bird family continued into 1988, when new allegations of corruption implicated Lester Bird. At a general election in March 1989 the ALP remained the ruling party by retaining 15 of the 16 seats that it had held previously. The UNDP won more than 30% of the total votes, but only one seat. The Barbuda seat was won by the BPM.

In April 1990 the Government of Antigua and Barbuda received a diplomatic note of protest from the Government of Colombia regarding the sale of weapons to the Medellín cartel of drugs-traffickers in Colombia. The weapons had originally been sold by Israel to Antigua and Barbuda, but, contrary to regulation, were then immediately shipped on to Colombia in April 1989. The communication from the Colombian Government implicated Vere Bird, Jr, and the Prime Minister eventually agreed to establish a judicial inquiry. In October 1990 the Chamber of Commerce recommended the resignation of the Government. In the following month a news agency obtained a copy of the unpublished report of the inquiry, which accused Antigua and Barbuda of having become 'engulfed in corruption'. In addition, the report revealed the activities of a number of British mercenaries on Antigua, involved in the training of paramilitary forces employed by Colombian drugs-trafficking organizations. Also in November, acting upon the recommendations of the report, the Government of Antigua and Barbuda dismissed Vere Bird, Jr, and banned him for life from holding office in the Government. The head of the defence force, Col Clyde Walker, was also dismissed.

Discontent within the ALP (including dissatisfaction with the leadership of Vere Bird, Sr), provoked a serious political crisis in early 1991. The Minister of Finance, John St Luce, resigned in February, after claiming that the Prime Minister ignored his proposals for a restructuring of government. A subsequent cabinet reshuffle (in which Lester Bird lost his deputy premiership) provoked the immediate resignation of three ministers. In September, however, Lester Bird and John St Luce accepted invitations from the Prime Minister to rejoin the Cabinet.

In early 1992 further reports of corruption involving Vere Bird, Sr, provoked public unrest and demands for his resignation. In April the Antigua Caribbean Liberation Movement, the PLM and the UNDP consolidated their opposition to the Government by merging to form the United Progressive Party (UPP). In May Vere Bird, Sr, was re-elected ALP leader. In August further controversy arose when proposed anti-corruption legislation (which had been recommended following the Colombian arms scandal in 1991) was withdrawn as a result of legal intervention by the Prime Minister.

On 10 June 1993 James (later Sir James) Carlisle took office as Governor-General, replacing Sir Wilfred Jacobs. In September the ALP convened in order to hold further leadership elections. As a result of the vote, Lester Bird became leader of the party, while Vere Bird, Jr, was elected as Chairman.

At a general election in March 1994 the ALP remained the ruling party, although with a reduced majority, having secured 11 seats; the UPP won five and the BPM retained the Barbuda seat. Following the election, Lester Bird assumed the premiership. Despite some criticism, the election was generally thought to have been free and fair.

In February 1995 an ALP activist, Leonard Aaron, was charged with threatening to murder Tim Hector, editor of an opposition newspaper, *The Outlet*. It was reported that Hector's house had been burgled on several occasions, when material containing allegedly incriminating information relating to members of the Government had been stolen. Aaron was subsequently released, following the intervention of the Prime Minister. In May the Prime Minister's brother, Ivor Bird, was arrested following an incident in which he collected luggage at V. C. Bird International Airport from a Barbadian citizen from Venezuela, which contained 12 kg of cocaine. *The Outlet* claimed that such an exchange had occurred on at least three previous occasions. Ivor Bird's subsequent release from police custody, upon payment of a fine of EC $200,000, attracted considerable criticism. In an attempt to improve the country's worsening reputation as a centre for drugs-trafficking, the Government proposed legislation in 1996 which aimed to curb the illegal drugs trade. In the same year Wrenford Ferrance, a former financial controller at the Organisation of Eastern Caribbean States (OECS, see p. 341), was appointed to the newly-created position of Special Adviser to the Government on money-laundering and on the control of illicit drugs. However, a report published by the US Government in early 1998 found Antigua and Barbuda to be 'of primary concern' with regard to both of these illegal activities.

In May 1996 Vere Bird, Jr, who had been declared unfit for public office following a judicial inquiry in 1990 (see above), was controversially appointed to the post of Special Adviser to the Prime Minister. In September Molwyn Joseph resigned as Minister of Finance over allegations that he had used his position in order to evade the payment of customs duties on the import of a vintage motor car. His resignation followed an opposition protest, at which the UPP leader, Baldwin Spencer, and seven other party members, including Tim Hector, were arrested (charges brought against them were later dismissed). A further demonstration took place at the end of the month, when some 10,000 people demanded a full inquiry into the affair and an early general election. In early December 1997, however, Joseph was reinstated in the Cabinet, assuming the new post of Minister of Planning, Implementation and the Environment; the opposition vehemently condemned the appointment.

In March 1997 the opposition BPM defeated the ALP's ally, the New Barbuda Development Movement, in elections to the Barbuda Council, winning all five of the contested seats and thus gaining control of all the seats in the nine-member Council. In the same month the High Court upheld a constitutional motion presented by Baldwin Spencer seeking the right of expression for the opposition on state-owned radio and television (denied during the electoral campaign in March 1994). In May and June the UPP boycotted sittings of the House of Representatives (the first legislative boycotts in the country's history) during a parliamentary debate on a proposed US $300m. tourism development on Guiana Island, which was to be constructed by a Malaysian company. The opposition claimed that the Prime Minister had failed to publish the proposals for public discussion prior to the parliamentary debate and that the 2,000-room hotel project would have adverse effects on the island's ecology. The project was, none the less, endorsed by the legislature. In September Spencer applied to the High Court to have the hotel project agreement declared illegal and unconstitutional. However, his objections were overruled by the High Court in November, and a subsequent appeal, made to the Eastern Caribbean Court of Appeal, was also dismissed in April 1998. (The Prime Minister had rejected demands for a referendum on the controversial scheme in October 1997.) However, the Guiana Island project continued to provoke controversy. In December 1997 Vere Bird, Jr, was slightly wounded in a shooting incident on the same day as the Government agreed terms for the compulsory resettlement of the island's sole occupants, Cyril 'Taffy' Bufton and his wife. Bufton was subsequently charged with attempted murder, but was acquitted in October 1998. The UPP denied government allegations of its involvement in the attack.

Meanwhile, in August 1997 *The Outlet* published further allegations regarding government-supported drugs-trafficking, including a claim that a Colombian drug cartel had contributed US $1m. to the ALP's election campaign in 1994. In response, Prime Minister Lester Bird obtained a High Court injunction in early September prohibiting the newspaper from publishing further material relating to the allegations. In November the printing presses of *The Outlet* were destroyed by fire, two days after the newspaper's editor, Tim Hector, had publicly alleged that a large consignment of 'sophisticated' weaponry had entered Antigua. The Government denied allegations that it was responsible for the fire, and stated that a shipment of 'basic' arms had been imported for police use.

In August 1998 the House of Representatives approved an amendment to voting regulations, granting the right to vote to all citizens who had been born abroad (including non-Commonwealth citizens), but who had been resident in Antigua and Barbuda for more than three years. Opposition members accused the Government of enlarging the electoral register for political advantage; these allegations were strenuously denied.

At a general election held on 9 March 1999, the ALP increased its representation in the 17-seat House of Representatives from 11 to 12, at the expense of the UPP, which secured four seats; the BPM retained its single seat. Following the election, Lester Bird was reappointed Prime Minister, and a new Cabinet was duly appointed, which again controversially included Vere Bird, Jr, as Minister of Agriculture, Lands and Fisheries. The UPP subsequently filed electoral petitions alleging breaches of electoral law in six constituencies (all of which were either dismissed or withdrawn in July). Independent observers, meanwhile, declared the election to have been free, although they expressed reservations concerning its fairness, owing to the ALP's large-scale expenditure and use of the media during its electoral campaign.

Also in March 1999 the US Government published a report which claimed that recent Antiguan financial legislation had weakened regulations concerning money-laundering and increased the secrecy surrounding 'offshore' banks. It also advised US banks to scrutinize all financial dealings with Antigua and Barbuda, which was described as a potential 'haven for money-laundering activities'. In April the United Kingdom issued a similar financial advisory to its banks. In response, in July Antigua became the first Eastern Caribbean country to bring into force a treaty with the USA on extradition and mutual legal assistance. Furthermore, in September the Government established an independent body, the International Financial Sector Regulatory Body, to regulate 'offshore' banking. In November the authorities uncovered a significant money-laundering operation, run by a former Ukrainian prime minister. Although in 2000 Antigua and Barbuda's financial system was criticized by the Organisation for Economic Co-operation and Development (OECD, see p. 277) and by the Financial Action Task Force (FATF, see p. 343), in 2001 the FATF recognized the state as a 'fully co-operative jurisdiction against money laundering'. Furthermore, by July the country had satisfied the United Kingdom that its financial institutions no longer needed special attention and had conformed to the FATF rules on harmful tax practices and in the following month the US Treasury withdrew its financial advisory notice. In December the Government signed a tax information exchange agreement with the USA.

At the fourth convention of the UPP, held in November 1999, Vincent Derrick was re-elected as Chairman of the party, while Charlesworth Samuel was named deputy leader.

In January 2000 the Government established a commission, chaired by Sir Fred Philips, a former Governor of Saint Christopher and Nevis, to review the Constitution. The commission was to examine the role of the Government, political parties and non-governmental organizations, and was to focus on the maintenance of democracy and accountability. In addition, increased tensions between Antigua and Barbuda, and the latter's demands for autonomy, meant that constitutional change was a much discussed issue throughout 2001. The commission's recommendations, reported in February 2002, included the replacement of the Queen as head of state with a President chosen by the majority party in Parliament, and amalgamation of the Senate and House of Representatives into a unicameral legislature, as well as a bill of rights and integrity legislation.

In elections to the Barbuda Council in March 2001 the BPM retained control of all nine seats.

In May 2001 Dr Errol Cort, the Attorney-General, George 'Bacchanal' Walker, the Leader of Government Business in the Senate, and Bernard Percival, the former Minister of Health and head of the state-run Medical Benefits Scheme (MBS), were dismissed from their posts after the publication of a forensic audit into alleged fraud in the MBS. Although there was no evidence that either minister was involved in financial malpractice, Prime Minister Bird stated that both had shown a 'lapse of good judgement' regarding payments made to the Scheme. In the following month, bowing to pressure from non-governmental organizations and the general public, Bird announced that an independent Commission of Inquiry into the funding and practices of the MBS would be held. The Inquiry opened in December and, in late July 2002, recommended that a special prosecutor be appointed to examine charges against 12 people, including two former health ministers, implicated in abusing the scheme. The Inquiry also recommended the conversion of the MBS into a health insurance sheme run by an independent body, and stressed that the Government should not interfere with the scheme's operation. In April, following fraud allegations arising from the Inquiry, the Minister of Trade, Industry and Business Development, Hilroy Humphreys, resigned. The trade portfolio was passed to the Minister of Planning, Implementation and Public Service Affairs, Gaston Brown. In November the British Broadcasting Corporation (BBC) paid the Prime Minister libel damages of £50,000 over radio news reports relating to the MBS.

Also in April 2002 a further public dispute emerged, which prompted the Prime Minister to initiate a libel suit against leading members of the UPP, including Baldwin Spencer, as well as against an independent newspaper and radio station and a 15-year old girl. In early June the Prime Minister abandoned an initial attempt to obtain a court injunction against further repetition of the allegations, paying costs of EC $26,000 to his opponents. The libel case was scheduled to open in February 2003; however, Bird dropped the suit against the newspaper and radio journalists before proceedings began. The case against the 15-year old girl continued; however, she initiated civil proceedings against the Prime Minister.

In May 2002 an ALP Member of Parliament, Sherfield Bowen, called for the Prime Minister and his Chief of Staff to resign, to allow an independent investigation of allegations made against both of them. In September a demonstration organized by the UPP reportedly attracted several thousand marchers demanding the immediate resignation of the Prime Minister and a general election within six months. Also in September Robin Yearwood was appointed to the post of Deputy Prime Minister. The Prime Minister acknowledged that Yearwood, who continued to hold the position of Minister of Public Utilities, Aviation, Transport and Housing, was promoted in order to improve discipline within the Government following a series of corruption scandals, most notably that relating to the MBS.

In January 2003 two new political parties—the First Democratic Movement, led by Egbert Joseph, and the Organisation for National Development, founded by three erstwhile UPP members—were formed to contest the next general election, due to be held before March 2004.

In foreign relations the ALP Government follows a policy of non-alignment, although the country has strong links with the USA, and actively assisted in the US military intervention in Grenada in October 1983 as a member of the OECS. In September 2001 the Government established diplomatic relations with Libya, after that country announced a US $1m. aid package to Antigua. Antigua and Barbuda is also a member of the Caribbean Community and Common Market (CARICOM, see p. 155).

Government

Antigua and Barbuda is a constitutional monarchy. Executive power is vested in the British sovereign, as Head of State, and exercised by the Governor-General, who represents the sovereign locally and is appointed on the advice of the Antiguan Prime Minister. Legislative power is vested in Parliament, comprising the sovereign, a 17-member Senate and a 17-member House of Representatives. Members of the House are elected from single-member constituencies for up to five years by universal adult suffrage. The Senate is composed of 11 members (of whom one must be an inhabitant of Barbuda) appointed on the advice of the Prime Minister, four appointed on the advice of the Leader of the Opposition, one appointed at the discretion of the Governor-General and one appointed on the advice of the Barbuda Council. Government is effectively by the Cabinet. The Governor-General appoints the Prime Minister and, on the latter's recommendation, selects the other ministers. The Prime Minister must be able to command the support of a majority of the House, to which the Cabinet is responsible. The Barbuda Council has nine seats, with partial elections held every two years.

In July 2000 it was announced that there was to be public consultation on electoral reform, and in December a Common-

wealth review of the administration of Barbuda recommended the maintenance of the existing constitutional relationship between Barbuda and Antigua.

Defence

There is a small defence force of 170 men (army 125, navy 45). The US Government leases two military bases on Antigua. Antigua and Barbuda participates in the US-sponsored Regional Security System. The defence budget in 2002 was estimated at EC $12.0m.

Economic Affairs

In 2001, according to estimates by the World Bank, Antigua and Barbuda's gross national income (GNI), measured at average 1999–2001 prices, was US $621m., equivalent to $9,070 per head (or $9,870 per head on an international purchasing-power parity basis). During 1990–2001, it was estimated, the population increased at an average rate of 0.6% per year, while gross domestic product (GDP) per head increased, in real terms, by an average of 2.8% per year. Overall GDP increased, in real terms, at an average annual rate of 3.2% in 1990–2001. According to the Eastern Caribbean Central Bank (ECCB), real GDP increased by 2.5% in 2000 and by an estimated 1.5% in 2001.

Agriculture (including forestry and fishing) engaged 3.9% of the active labour force in 1991. The sector contributed 3.7% of GDP in 2000. According to the ECCB, agricultural GDP increased, in real terms, between 1994 and 2000 at an average rate of 0.8% per year. The agricultural sector increased, in real terms, by 4.2% in 1998, by 3.3% in 1999 and by 3.2% in 2000. The principal crops are cucumbers, pumpkins, sweet potatoes, mangoes, coconuts, limes, melons and the speciality 'Antigua Black' pineapple. In 2000 the Ministry of Agriculture, Lands and Fisheries announced a programme to encourage farmers to increase production. Lobster, shrimp and crab farms are in operation, and further projects to develop the fishing industry were undertaken in the 1990s.

Industry (comprising mining, manufacturing, construction and utilities) employed 18.9% of the active labour force in 1991 and provided 18.8% of GDP in 2000. The principal industrial activity is construction, accounting for 11.6% of total employment in 1991. Industrial GDP increased, in real terms, at an average rate of 7.0% per year during 1994–2000. It rose by 7.7% in 1998, by 7.9% in 1999 and by 6.5% in 2000.

Mining and quarrying employed only 0.2% of the active labour force in 1991 and contributed 1.6% of GDP in 2000. The real GDP of the mining sector increased at an average rate of 5.5% per year during 1994–2000. It rose by 8.0% in 1998, by 4.0% in 1999 and by 4.0% in 2000.

The manufacturing sector consists of some light industries producing garments, paper, paint, furniture, food and beverage products, and the assembly of household appliances and electrical components for export. Manufacturing contributed 2.1% of GDP in 2000, when construction provided 11.9%. In real terms, the GDP of the manufacturing sector increased at an average rate of 2.9% per year during 1994–2000. Real GDP in manufacturing increased by 4.0% in 1996, while construction activity increased by 12.0% (mainly owing to ongoing rehabilitation projects necessitated by 'Hurricane Luis'). Manufacturing GDP increased by 5.5% in 1998, by 4.5% in 1999, and by 3.0% in 2000. Over the same period construction growth was 10.0%, 8.0% and 6.5%, respectively.

Most of the country's energy production is derived from imported fuel. Imports of mineral fuels, lubricants and related materials accounted for 8.4% of total imports in 1998.

Services provided 70.2% of employment in 1991 and 77.6% of GDP in 2000. The combined GDP of the service sectors increased, in real terms, at an average rate of 3.2% per year during 1994–2000. It rose by 5.7% in 1998, by 4.3% in 1999 and by 1.3% in 2000. Tourism is the main economic activity, providing approximately 35% of employment in 1991, and accounting (directly and indirectly) for some 60% of GDP in the mid-1990s. By 1998 the industry showed significant signs of recovery, following the severe effects of 'Hurricane Luis' (despite suffering a minor set-back in September 1998, when 'Hurricane Georges' resulted in the closure of several hotels). Visitor arrivals increased from 470,975 in 1995 to 588,866 in 1999, to 675,517 in 2000; expenditure by tourists rose from EC $782.9m. in 1999 to $784.5m. in 2000, decreasing to $734.6m. in 2001 (according to preliminary figures). The real GDP of the hotels and restaurants sector decreased by 2.2% in 1998; it increased by 2.7% in 1999, but fell again in 2000, by 0.9%. Most stop-over tourists are from the United Kingdom (35%), the USA (31% in 1998), Canada (7%) and other Caribbean countries (16%). The decrease in US tourists following the terrorist attacks in the USA in September 2001 had an adverse affect on the sector; in 2001 tourist arrivals decreased to 193,176, compared with 206,871 in 2000. In November 2001 the Prime Minister, Lester Bird, announced financial aid for the hotel sector and there were also plans to attract more European tourists.

Antigua and Barbuda recorded a visible trade deficit in 2001 of US \$282.6m. and a deficit of US \$47.3m. on the current account of the balance of payments. The country's principal trading partners are the other members of the Caribbean Community and Common Market (CARICOM, see p. 155), the USA, the United Kingdom and Canada. In 1998 the USA provided 26.6% of total imports and was also one of the main markets for exports (mainly re-exports).

In 2001 there was an estimated budgetary deficit of EC \$118.5m. In 2000 debt-servicing costs were expected to account for EC \$102.5m. By the end of 2000 total external debt amounted to US \$401.1m. The annual average rate of inflation was 2.6% in 1993–99. Consumer prices rose by 3.3% in 1998 and by 1.1% in 1999. According to the Caribbean Development Bank, consumer prices rose by 0.7% in 2000 and by 0.1% in 2001. The rate of unemployment at the end of 2000 was reported to be 5% of the labour force.

Antigua and Barbuda is a member of CARICOM, the Organisation of Eastern Caribbean States (OECS), the Organization of American States (see p. 288), and is a signatory of the Cotonou Agreement (the successor agreement to Lomé Conventions) with the European Union (EU, see p. 199). Antigua and Barbuda is also a member of the Eastern Caribbean Securities Exchange (based in Saint Christopher and Nevis), established in 2001.

In the late 20th century the Government sought to diversify the economy, which is dominated by tourism. Despite a deceleration in economic growth in 1998 (largely as a result of infrastructural damage caused by 'Hurricane Georges'), the economy grew by 4.9% in 1999. In October 1999 it was reported that all but two of the country's external debts had been rescheduled and in August 2000 the United Kingdom agreed to cancel US \$9m. in debt and to reschedule a further \$6m. over 10 years. In the late 1990s the Government's attempts to develop the 'offshore' financial sector were restricted, following several cases of money-laundering (see History); however, following the implementation of legislation to encourage transparency, restrictions on the sector were lifted in 2001.

Economic expansion continued in 2000 (2.5%) and 2001 (1.5%), although at a slower rate. This was primarily owing to a weak performance in the tourism sector and an slowdown in the growth of the construction industry. In November 2001, in anticipation of the economic downturn that was expected following the terrorist attacks in the USA in September, the Government unveiled a five-point adjustment plan. The plan's aims included: a reduction in government expenditure through improved tax collection; the introduction of a two-year public-sector wage freeze in order to contain inflation; and stimulation of the tourism and financial-services sectors. Growth in 2002 was expected to continue at a similar level to the two previous years despite an expected further decline in the tourism sector. In particular, the economy was likely to have gained momentum from a buoyant construction industry. According to reports, growth in 2003 was expected to be around 2%, strengthened by an improved performance partly resulting from an expected increase in the number of tourist arrivals; however, the fiscal situation was likely to continue to worsen.

Education

Education is compulsory for 11 years between five and 16 years of age. Primary education begins at the age of five and normally lasts for seven years. Secondary education, beginning at 12 years of age, lasts for five years, comprising a first cycle of three years and a second cycle of two years. In 1987/88 there were 43 primary and 15 secondary schools; the majority of schools are administered by the Government. In 1996 some 11,596 primary school pupils and 4,730 secondary school pupils were enrolled. Teacher-training and technical training are available at the Antigua State College in St John's. An extra-mural department of the University of the West Indies offers several foundation courses leading to higher study at branches elsewhere. In November 2002 the EU agreed to provide funding for tertiary education worth EC \$2.6m. Current government expenditure on education in 1993/94 was projected at \$37.1m., equivalent to 12.8% of total budgetary expenditure.

Public Holidays

2003: 1 January (New Year's Day), 18 April (Good Friday), 21 April (Easter Monday), 5 May (Labour Day), 9 June (Whit Monday), 14 June (Queen's Official Birthday), 7 July (Vere Cornwall Bird, Sr Day), 4–5 August (Carnival), 1 November (Independence Day), 25–26 December (Christmas).

2004: 1 January (New Year's Day), 9 April (Good Friday), 12 April (Easter Monday), 3 May (Labour Day), 31 May (Whit Monday), 12 June (Queen's Official Birthday), 5 July (Vere Cornwall Bird, Sr Day), 2–3 August (Carnival), 1 November (Independence Day), 25–26 December (Christmas).

Weights and Measures

The imperial system is in use, but a metrication programme is being introduced.

Statistical Survey

Source (unless otherwise stated): Ministry of Finance, High St, St John's; tel. 462-4860; fax 462-1622.

AREA AND POPULATION

Area: 441.6 sq km (170.5 sq miles).

Population: 62,922 at census of 28 May 1991; 77,426 (provisional result, males 37,002, females 40,424) at census of 28 May 2001.

Density (May 2001): 175.3 per sq km.

Principal Town: St John's (capital), population 22,342 at 1991 census. *Mid-2001:* (UN estimate, incl. suburbs): St John's 24,000 (Source: UN, *World Urbanization Prospects: The 2001 Revision*).

Births, Marriages and Deaths (registrations): Live births (estimated, 2000) 1,528 (birth rate 23.5 per 1,000); Marriages (1995) 1,418 (marriage rate 21.0 per 1,000); Deaths (estimates, 2000) 451 (death rate 6.9 per 1,000). Source: UN, *Demographic Yearbook*.

Expectation of Life (WHO estimates, years at birth): 71.0 (males 68.7; females 73.5) in 2001. Source: WHO, *World Health Report*.

Employment (persons aged 15 years and over, census of 28 May 1991): Agriculture, forestry and fishing 1,040; Mining and quarrying 64; Manufacturing 1,444; Electricity, gas and water 435; Construction 3,109; Trade, restaurants and hotels 8,524; Transport, storage and communications 2,395; Finance, insurance, real estate and business services 1,454; Community, social and personal services 6,406; Activities not adequately defined 1,882; Total employed 26,753 (males 14,564, females 12,189). Source: ILO, *Yearbook of Labour Statistics*.

1998: Total active labour force (estimate) 30,000. Source: IMF *Antigua and Barbuda: Statistical Annex* (December 1999).

HEALTH AND WELFARE

Key Indicators

Total Fertility Rate (children per woman, 2001): 1.6.

Under-5 Mortality Rate (per 1,000 live births, 2001): 14.

Physicians (per 1,000 head, 1996): 1.14.

Hospital Beds (per 1,000 head, 1998): 3.88.

Health Expenditure (2000): US $ per head (PPP): 562.

Health Expenditure (2000): % of GDP: 5.5.

Health Expenditure (2000): public (% of total): 59.9.

Access to Water (% of persons, 2000): 91.

Access to Sanitation (% of persons, 2000): 96.

Human Development Index (2000): value: 0.800.
For sources and definitions, see explanatory note on p. vi.

AGRICULTURE, ETC.

Principal Crops (FAO estimates, '000 metric tons, 2001): Vegetables 1.8; Melons 0.7; Mangoes 1.4; Other fruits 7.2. Source: FAO.

Livestock (FAO estimates, '000 head, year ending September 2001): Asses 1.5; Cattle 13.6; Pigs 5.3; Sheep 18.0; Goats 34.5; Poultry 95. Source: FAO.

Livestock Products (FAO estimates, '000 metric tons, 2001): Beef and veal 0.5; Cows' milk 4.9. Source: FAO.

Fishing (metric tons, live weight, 2000): Total catch 1,481 (Marine fishes 1,164, Caribbean spiny lobster 275, Stromboid conchs 42). Source: FAO, *Yearbook of Fishery Statistics*.

INDUSTRY

Production (estimates, 1988): Rum 4,000 hectolitres; Wines and vodka 2,000 hectolitres; Electric energy (estimate, 1998) 99m. kWh. Source: UN, *Industrial Commodity Statistics Yearbook*.

FINANCE

Currency and Exchange Rates: 100 cents = 1 Eastern Caribbean dollar (EC $). *Sterling, US Dollar and Euro Equivalents* (31 December 2002): £1 sterling = EC $4.352; US $1 = EC $2.700; €1 = EC $2.831; EC $100 = £22.98 = US $37.04 = €35.32. *Exchange rate:* Fixed at US $1 = EC $2.700 since July 1976.

Budget (EC $ million, preliminary, 2001): *Revenue:* Tax revenue 316.5 (Taxes on income and profits 47.8, Taxes on domestic goods and services 67.1, Taxes on international transactions 195.6); Other current revenue 39.3; Capital revenue 1.4; Total 357.2, excluding grants received (7.7). *Expenditure:* Current expenditure 410.3 (Personal emoluments 220.0, Other goods and services 111.8, Interest payments 39.6, Transfers and subsidies 38.0); Capital expenditure 73.1; Total 483.4. Source: Eastern Caribbean Central Bank, *Report and Statement of Accounts*.

International Reserves (US $ million at 31 December 2002): IMF special drawing rights 0.01; Foreign exchange 87.64; Total 87.65. Source: IMF, *International Financial Statistics*.

Money Supply (EC $ million at 31 December 2002): Currency outside banks 88.20; Demand deposits at deposit money banks 246.98; Total money (incl. others) 335.19. Source: IMF, *International Financial Statistics*.

Cost of Living (Consumer Price Index; base: 1993 = 100): 111.9 in 1997; 115.6 in 1998; 116.9 in 1999. Source: ILO, *Yearbook of Labour Statistics*.

Expenditure on the Gross Domestic Product (EC $ million at current prices, 2000): Government final consumption expenditure 420.0; Private final consumption expenditure 780.1; Gross capital formation 862.4; *Total domestic expenditure* 2,062.5; Exports of goods and services 1,260.3; *Less* Imports of goods and services 1,536.2; *GDP in purchasers' values* 1,786.6. Source: IMF, *International Financial Statistics*.

Gross Domestic Product by Economic Activity (EC $ million at current prices, 2000): Agriculture, hunting, forestry and fishing 61.09; Mining and quarrying 26.77; Manufacturing 35.20; Electricity and water 52.42; Construction 199.21; Trade 169.89; Restaurants and hotels 178.61; Transport and communications 311.56; Finance, insurance, real estate and business services 248.19; Government services 269.18; Other community, social and personal services 118.06; Sub-total 1,670.18; *Less* Imputed bank service charges 124.02; *GDP at factor cost* 1,546.16. Source: Eastern Caribbean Central Bank, *National Accounts*.

Balance of Payments (US $ million, 2001): Exports of goods f.o.b. 38.62; Imports of goods f.o.b. −321.17; *Trade balance* −282.55; Exports of services 402.95; Imports of services −153.86; *Balance on goods and services* −33.46; Other income received 18.37; Other income paid −38.29; *Balance on goods, services and income* −53.38; Current transfers received 15.42; Current transfers paid −9.38; *Current balance* −47.34; Capital account (net) 18.39; Direct investment from abroad (net) 39.07; Portfolio investment assets −0.05; Portfolio investment liabilities −2.46; Other investment assets −3.86; Other investment liabilities −9.11; Net errors and omissions 21.56; *Overall balance* 16.20. Source: IMF, *International Financial Statistics*.

EXTERNAL TRADE

Total Trade (EC $ million): *Imports f.o.b.:* 946.1 in 1999; 913.4 in 2000; 904.3 in 2001 (preliminary figure). *Exports f.o.b.:* 42.6 in 1999; 44.1 in 2000; 45.5 in 2001 (preliminary figure). Source: Eastern Caribbean Central Bank, *Report and Statement of Accounts*.

Principal Commodities (EC $ million, estimates 1998): *Imports:* Food and live animals 89.2; Beverages and tobacco 27.1; Mineral fuels, lubricants, etc. 72.1; Chemicals and related products 50.0; Basic manufactures 252.1; Machinery and transport equipment 232.8; Miscellaneous manufactured articles 113.6. Total (incl. others) 854.6. *Exports:* Food and live animals 2.4; Mineral fuels, lubricants, etc. 13.7; Chemicals and related products 6.2; Basic manufactures 6.6; Machinery and transport equipment 22.6; Miscellaneous manufactured articles 25.1; Total (incl. others) 78.3. Source: OECS, *External Merchandise Trade Annual Report*.

Principal Trading Partners (EC $ million, estimates, 1998): *Imports:* Barbados 14.7; Canada 26.0; Trinidad and Tobago 26.6; United Kingdom 86.3; USA 227.5; Total (incl. others) 854.6. *Exports:* Barbados 7.4; Canada 1.4; French West Indies 1.3; Italy 1.8; Jamaica 1.6; Montserrat 2.5; Saint Christopher and Nevis 3.6; Saint Lucia 5.7; Trinidad and Tobago 5.7; United Kingdom 4.8, USA 1.4; Total (incl. others) 78.3. Source: OECS, *Digest of Trade Statistics*.

TRANSPORT

Road Traffic (registered vehicles, 1998): Passenger motor cars and commercial vehicles 24,000. Source: UN, *Statistical Yearbook*.

Shipping (international freight traffic, '000 metric tons, 1990): Goods loaded 28; Goods unloaded 113 (Source: UN, *Monthly Bulletin of Statistics*). *Merchant Fleet* (registered at 31 December): 840 vessels (total displacement 4,668,330 grt) in 2001. (Source: Lloyd's Register-Fairplay, *World Fleet Statistics*).

Civil Aviation (traffic on scheduled services, 1999): Kilometres flown (million) 11; Passengers carried ('000) 1,371; Passenger-km (million) 276; Total ton-km (million) 26. Source: UN, *Statistical Yearbook*.

TOURISM

Tourist Arrivals: 207,862 in 1999; 206,871 in 2000; 193,176 in 2001. Source: Antigua and Barbuda Dept of Tourism.

Visitor Expenditure (EC $ million, estimates): 782.9 in 1999; 784.5 in 2000; 734.6 in 2001 (preliminary figure). Source: Eastern Caribbean Central Bank, *Report and Statement of Accounts*.

COMMUNICATIONS MEDIA

Radio Receivers (1997): 36,000 in use*.

Television Receivers (1999): 33,000 in use*.

Telephones (2001): 37,300 main lines in use†.

Facsimile Machines (year ending 31 March 1997): 850 in use‡.

Mobile Telephones (2001): 25,000 subscribers†.

Internet Users (2000): 5,000†.

Daily Newspaper (1996): 1 (estimated circulation 6,000)*.

Non-daily Newspapers (1996): 4*.

* Source: UNESCO, *Statistical Yearbook*.
† Source: International Telecommunication Union.
‡ Source: UN, *Statistical Yearbook*.

EDUCATION

Pre-primary (1983): 21 schools; 23 teachers; 677 pupils.

Primary (1987/88): 43 schools; 446 teachers; 11,596 students (1996).

Secondary (1991/92): 15 schools (1987/88); 400 teachers (estimate); 4,730 students (1996).

Tertiary (1986): 2 colleges; 631 students.

Adult Literacy Rate: 86.6% in 2000 (Source: OECS).
Source: partly Caribbean Development Bank, *Social and Economic Indicators 2001*.

Directory

The Constitution

The Constitution, which came into force at the independence of Antigua and Barbuda on 1 November 1981, states that Antigua and Barbuda is a 'unitary sovereign democratic state'. The main provisions of the Constitution are summarized below

FUNDAMENTAL RIGHTS AND FREEDOMS

Regardless of race, place of origin, political opinion, colour, creed or sex, but subject to respect for the rights and freedoms of others and for the public interest, every person in Antigua and Barbuda is entitled to the rights of life, liberty, security of the person, the enjoyment of property and the protection of the law. Freedom of movement, of conscience, of expression (including freedom of the press), of peaceful assembly and association is guaranteed and the inviolability of family life, personal privacy, home and other property is maintained. Protection is afforded from discrimination on the grounds of race, sex, etc., and from slavery, forced labour, torture and inhuman treatment.

THE GOVERNOR-GENERAL

The British sovereign, as Monarch of Antigua and Barbuda, is the Head of State and is represented by a Governor-General of local citizenship.

PARLIAMENT

Parliament consists of the Monarch, a 17-member Senate and the House of Representatives composed of 17 elected members. Senators are appointed by the Governor-General: 11 on the advice of the Prime Minister (one of whom must be an inhabitant of Barbuda), four on the advice of the Leader of the Opposition, one at his own discretion and one on the advice of the Barbuda Council. The Barbuda Council is the principal organ of local government in that island, whose membership and functions are determined by Parliament. The life of Parliament is five years.

Each constituency returns one Representative to the House who is directly elected in accordance with the Constitution.

The Attorney-General, if not otherwise a member of the House, is an ex-officio member but does not have the right to vote.

Every citizen over the age of 18 is eligible to vote.

Parliament may alter any of the provisions of the Constitution.

THE EXECUTIVE

Executive authority is vested in the Monarch and exercisable by the Governor-General. The Governor-General appoints as Prime Minister that member of the House who, in the Governor-General's view, is best able to command the support of the majority of the members of the House, and other ministers on the advice of the Prime Minister. The Governor-General may remove the Prime Minister from office if a resolution of no confidence is passed by the House and the Prime Minister does not either resign or advise the Governor-General to dissolve Parliament within seven days.

The Cabinet consists of the Prime Minister and other ministers and the Attorney-General.

The Leader of the Opposition is appointed by the Governor-General as that member of the House who, in the Governor-General's view, is best able to command the support of a majority of members of the House who do not support the Government.

CITIZENSHIP

All persons born in Antigua and Barbuda before independence who, immediately prior to independence, were citizens of the United Kingdom and Colonies automatically become citizens of Antigua and Barbuda. All persons born outside the country with a parent or grandparent possessing citizenship of Antigua and Barbuda automatically acquire citizenship as do those born in the country after independence. Provision is made for the acquisition of citizenship by those to whom it would not automatically be granted.

The Government

Head of State: HM Queen ELIZABETH II (succeeded to the throne 6 February 1952).

Governor-General: Sir JAMES B. CARLISLE (took office 10 June 1993).

CABINET
(April 2003)

Prime Minister and Minister of Foreign Affairs, Caribbean Community Affairs, Defence and Security, Finance, Justice and Legal Affairs, Public Works, Telecommunications and Gaming, Legislature, Privatization, Printing and Electoral Affairs, and Merchant Shipping: LESTER BRYANT BIRD.

Deputy Prime Minister and Minister of Public Utilities, Aviation, Transport and Housing: ROBIN YEARWOOD.

Attorney-General: GERTEL THOM.

Minister of Health, Home Affairs, Urban Development and Renewal and Social Improvement: JOHN ST LUCE.

Minister of Tourism and the Environment: MOLWYN JOSEPH.

Minister of Education, Culture and Technology: Dr RODNEY WILLIAMS.

Minister of Agriculture, Lands and Fisheries: VERE BIRD, Jr.

Minister of Labour, Co-operatives and Public Safety: STEADROY BENJAMIN.

Minister of Planning, Implementation and Public Service Affairs, and of Trade, Industry and Business Development: GASTON BROWN.

Minister of Information and Public Broadcasting, Youth Affairs and Sports: Sen. GUY YEARWOOD.

Minister of State in the Office of the Prime Minister with responsibility for Finance: Sen. ASOT MICHAEL.

Minister of State in the Ministries of Information and Public Broadcasting, and Public Works: Sen. BERNARD WALKER.

MINISTRIES

Office of the Prime Minister: Queen Elizabeth Highway, St John's; tel. 462-4956; fax 462-3225; e-mail pmo@candw.ag; internet www.antiguabarbuda.net/pmo.

Ministry of Agriculture, Lands and Fisheries: Queen Elizabeth Highway, St John's; tel. 462-1543; fax 462-6104.

Ministry of Caribbean Community Affairs: St John's.

Ministry of Defence and Security: St John's.

Ministry of Education, Culture and Technology: Church St, St John's; tel. 462-4959; fax 462-4970.

Ministry of Finance: Govt Office Complex, Parliament Dr., St John's; tel. 462-5015; fax 462-4260; e-mail budget@candw.ag.

Ministry of Foreign Affairs: Queen Elizabeth Highway, St John's; tel. 462-1052; fax 462-2482; e-mail minforeign@candw.ag; internet www.antiguabarbuda.net/external.

Ministry of Health: St John's St, St John's; tel. 462-1600; fax 462-5003.

Ministry of Home Affairs, Urban Development and Renewal and Social Improvement: St John's.

Ministry of Information and Public Broadcasting: St John's.

Ministry of Justice and Legal Affairs, and Office of the Attorney-General: Hadeed Bldg, Redcliffe St, St John's; tel. 462-6037; fax 562-1879; e-mail legalaffairs@candw.ag; internet www.antiguabarbuda.net/ag.

Ministry of Labour, Co-operatives and Public Safety: Govt Office Complex, Queen Elizabeth's Highway, St John's; tel. 462-3331; fax 462-1595.

Ministry of Merchant Shipping: St John's.

Ministry of Planning, Implementation and Public Service Affairs: St John's.

Ministry of Printing and Electoral Affairs: St John's.

Ministry of Privatization: St John's.

Ministry of Public Utilities, Aviation, Transport and Housing: St John's St, St John's; tel. 462-0894; fax 462-1529.

Ministry of Public Works: St John's.

Ministry of Telecommunications and Gaming: St John's.

Ministry of Tourism and the Environment: Queen Elizabeth Highway, St John's; tel. 462-4625; fax 462-2836; e-mail mintourenv@candw.ag.

Ministry of Trade, Industry and Business Development: Redcliffe St, St John's; tel. 462-1543; fax 462-5003.

Ministry of Youth Affairs and Sports: St John's.

Legislature

PARLIAMENT

Senate

President: MILLICENT PERCIVAL.

There are 17 nominated members.

House of Representatives

Speaker: BRIDGETTE HARRIS.

Ex-Officio Member: The Attorney-General.

Clerk: L. DOWE.

General Election, 9 March 1999

Party	Votes cast	%	Seats
Antigua Labour Party . . .	17,417	52.6	12
United Progressive Party . .	14,817	44.8	4
Barbuda People's Movement .	418	1.3	1
Independents and others . . .	439	1.3	—
Total	33,091	100.0	17

Political Organizations

Antigua Labour Party (ALP): St Mary's St, POB 948, St John's; tel. 462-2235; f. 1968; Leader LESTER BRYANT BIRD; Chair. VERE BIRD, Jr.

Barbuda Independence Movement: Codrington; f. 1983 as Organisation for National Reconstruction, re-formed 1988; advocates self-government for Barbuda; Pres. ARTHUR SHABAZZ-NIBBS.

Barbuda National Party: Codrington; Leader ERIC BURTON.

Barbuda People's Movement (BPM): Codrington; campaigns for separate status for Barbuda; Parliamentary Leader THOMAS HILBOURNE FRANK; Chair. FABIAN JONES.

First Democratic Movement: St John's; f. 2003; Leader EGBERT JOSEPH.

National Movement for Change (NMC): St John's; f. 2002; Leader ALISTAIR THOMAS.

National Reform Movement (NRM): POB 1318, St John's.

New Barbuda Development Movement: Codrington; linked with the Antigua Labour Party.

Organisation for National Development: St John's; f. 2003.

United Progressive Party (UPP): Nevis St, St John's; tel. 462-1818; fax 462-5937; e-mail upp@candw.ag; f. 1992, by merger of the Antigua Caribbean Liberation Movement (f. 1979), the Progressive Labour Movement (f. 1970) and the United National Democratic Party (f. 1986); Leader BALDWIN SPENCER; Dep. Leader WILLMOTT DANIEL; Chair. Dr GEORGE DANIEL.

Diplomatic Representation

EMBASSIES AND HIGH COMMISSION IN ANTIGUA AND BARBUDA

China, People's Republic: Cedar Valley, POB 1446, St John's; tel. 562-0176; fax 462-6425; e-mail chinaemb_ag@mfa.gov.cn; Ambassador YANG SHIXIANG.

United Kingdom: British High Commission, Price Waterhouse Coopers Centre, 11 Old Parham Rd, POB 483, St John's; tel. 462-0008; fax 562-2124; e-mail britishc@candw.ag; High Commissioner JOHN WHITE (resident in Barbados).

Venezuela: Cross and Redcliffe Sts, POB 1201, St John's; tel. 462-1574; fax 462-1570; e-mail embaveneantigua@yahoo.es; Ambassador JOSÉ LAURENCIO SILVA MÉNDEZ.

Judicial System

Justice is administered by the Eastern Caribbean Supreme Court, based in Saint Lucia, which consists of a High Court of Justice and a Court of Appeal. One of the Court's Puisne Judges is resident in and responsible for Antigua and Barbuda, and presides over the Court of Summary Jurisdiction on the islands. There are also Magistrates' Courts for lesser cases.

Chief Justice: DENNIS BYRON.

Solicitor-General: LEBRECHT HESSE.

Attorney-General: GERTEL THOM.

Religion

The majority of the inhabitants profess Christianity, and the largest denomination is the Church in the Province of the West Indies (Anglican Communion).

CHRISTIANITY

Antigua Christian Council: POB 863, St John's; tel. 462-0261; f. 1964; five mem. churches; Pres. Rt Rev. DONALD J. REECE (Roman Catholic Bishop of St John's—Basseterre); Exec. Sec. EDRIS ROBERTS.

The Anglican Communion

Anglicans in Antigua and Barbuda are adherents of the Church in the Province of the West Indies. The diocese of the North Eastern Caribbean and Aruba comprises 12 islands: Antigua, Saint Christopher (St Kitts), Nevis, Anguilla, Barbuda, Montserrat, Dominica, Saba, St Maarten/St Martin, Aruba, St Bartholomew and St Eustatius; the total number of Anglicans is about 60,000. The See City is St John's, Antigua.

Bishop of the North Eastern Caribbean and Aruba: Rt Rev. LEROY ERROL BROOKS, Bishop's Lodge, POB 23, St John's; tel. 462-0151; fax 462-2090; e-mail dioceseneca@candw.ag.

The Roman Catholic Church

The diocese of St John's-Basseterre, suffragan to the archdiocese of Castries (Saint Lucia), includes Anguilla, Antigua and Barbuda, the British Virgin Islands, Montserrat and Saint Christopher and Nevis. At 31 December 2001 there were an estimated 15,233 adherents in the diocese. The Bishop participates in the Antilles Episcopal Conference (whose Secretariat is based in Port of Spain, Trinidad).

Bishop of St John's-Basseterre: Rt Rev. DONALD JAMES REECE, Chancery Offices, POB 836, St John's; tel. 461-1135; fax 462-2383; e-mail djr@candw.ag.

Other Christian Churches

Antigua Baptist Association: POB 277, St John's; tel. 462-1254; Pres. IVOR CHARLES.

Methodist Church: c/o POB 863, St John's; Superintendent Rev. ELOY CHRISTOPHER.

St John's Evangelical Lutheran Church: Woods Centre, POB W77, St John's; tel. 462-2896; e-mail lutheran@candw.ag; Pastor M. HENRICH, Pastor J. STERNHAGEN, Pastor T. SATORIUS.

There are also Pentecostal, Seventh-day Adventist, Moravian, Nazarene, Salvation Army and Wesleyan Holiness places of worship.

The Press

Antigua Sun: Woods Mall, POB W263, Friar's Hill Rd, St John's; tel. 480-5960; fax 480-5968; e-mail antiguasun@stanfordeagle.com; internet www.antiguanice.com/thesun; twice weekly; Publr ALLEN STANFORD.

Business Expressions: POB 774, St John's; tel. 462-0743; fax 462-4575; e-mail chamcom@candw.ag; monthly; organ of the Antigua and Barbuda Chamber of Commerce and Industry.

Daily Observer: Fort Rd, POB 1318, St John's; fax 462-5561; internet www.antiguaobserver.com; independent; Publr SAMUEL DERRICK; Editor WINSTON A. DERRICK; circ. 4,000.

The Nation's Voice: Public Information Division, Church St and Independence Ave, POB 590, St John's; tel. 462-0090; weekly.

National Informer: St John's; weekly.

The Outlet: Marble Hill Rd, McKinnons, POB 493, St John's; tel. 462-4410; fax 462-0438; e-mail outletpub@candw.ag; f. 1975; weekly; publ. by the Antigua Caribbean Liberation Movement (founder member of the United Progressive Party in 1992); Editor (vacant); circ. 5,000.

The Worker's Voice: Emancipation Hall, 46 North St, POB 3, St John's; tel. 462-0090; f. 1943; twice weekly; official organ of the Antigua Labour Party and the Antigua Trades and Labour Union; Editor NOEL THOMAS; circ. 6,000.

Publishers

Antigua Printing and Publishing Ltd: POB 670, St John's; tel. 462-1265; fax 462-6200.

Wadadli Productions Ltd: POB 571, St John's; tel. 462-4489.

Broadcasting and Communications

TELECOMMUNICATIONS

Most telephone services are provided by the Antigua Public Utilities Authority (see Trade and Industry).

Antigua Public Utilities Authority Personal Communications Services (APUA PCS): St John's; internet www.apuatel.com; f. 2000; digital mobile cellular telephone network; Man. JULIAN WILKINS.

Cable & Wireless (Antigua and Barbuda) Ltd: 42–44 St Mary's St, POB 65, St John's; tel. 480-4000; fax 480-4200; internet www.cwantigua.com; owned by Cable & Wireless PLC (United Kingdom).

RADIO

ABS Radio: POB 590, St John's; tel. 462-3602; internet www.cmattcomm.com/abs.htm; f. 1956; subsidiary of Antigua and Barbuda Broadcasting Services; (see Television, below); Programme Man. D. L. PAYNE.

Caribbean Radio Lighthouse: POB 1057, St John's; tel. 462-1454; fax 462-7420; e-mail cradiolight@candw.ag; internet www.mannelli.com/lighthouse; f. 1975; religious broadcasts; operated by Baptist Int. Mission Inc (USA); Dir CURTIS L. WAITE.

Caribbean Relay Co Ltd: POB 1203, St John's; tel. 462-0994; fax 462-0487; e-mail cm-crc@candw.ag; jtly operated by British Broadcasting Corpn and Deutsche Welle.

Observer Radio: f. 2002; independently-owned station.

Radio ZDK: Grenville Radio Ltd, POB 1100, St John's; tel. 462-1100; f. 1970; commercial; Programme Dir IVOR BIRD; CEO E. PHILIP.

Sun FM Radio: St John's; commercial.

TELEVISION

Antigua and Barbuda Broadcasting Service (ABS): Directorate of Broadcasting and Public Information, POB 590, St John's; tel. 462-0010; fax 462-4442; scheduled for privatization; Dir-Gen. HOLLIS HENRY; CEO DENIS LEANDRO.

ABS Television: POB 1280, St John's; tel. 462-0010; fax 462-1622; f. 1964; Programme Man. JAMES TANNY ROSE.

CTV Entertainment Systems: 25 Long St, St John's; tel. 462-0346; fax 462-4211; cable television co; transmits 33 channels of US television 24 hours per day to subscribers; Programme Dir K. BIRD.

Finance

(cap. = capital; res = reserves; dep. = deposits; brs = branches)

BANKING

The Eastern Caribbean Central Bank (see p. 343), based in Saint Christopher, is the central issuing and monetary authority for Antigua and Barbuda.

Antigua Barbuda Investment Bank Ltd: High St and Corn Alley, POB 1679, St John's; tel. 480-2723; fax 480-2750; e-mail aob@candw.ag; f. 1990; cap. EC $6.3m., res EC $2.3m., dep. EC $107.5m. (Sept. 1997); three subsidiaries: Antigua Overseas Bank Ltd, ABI Trust Ltd and AOB Holdings Ltd; Chair. EUSTACE FRANCIS; Man. Dir MCALISTER ABBOTT; 2 brs.

Antigua Commercial Bank: St Mary's and Thames Sts, POB 95, St John's; tel. 462-1217; fax 462-1220; internet www.actionline.com; f. 1955; auth. cap. EC $5m. Man. JOHN BENJAMIN; 2 brs.

Antigua and Barbuda Development Bank: 27 St Mary's St, POB 1279, St John's; tel. 462-0838; fax 462-0839; f. 1974; Man. S. ALEX OSBORNE.

Bank of Antigua: 1000 Airport Blvd, Coolidge, POB 315, St John's; tel. 462-4282; fax 462-4718; internet www.bankofantigua.com; f. 1981; Chair. ALLEN STANFORD; 2 brs.

Swiss American National Bank of Antigua Ltd: High St, POB 1302, St John's; tel. 462-4460; fax 462-0274; f. 1983; cap. US $1.0m., res US $2.1m., dep. US $31.9m. (Dec. 1993); Gen. Man. JOSEPH D. DASILVA; 3 brs.

Foreign Banks

Bank of Nova Scotia (Canada): High St, POB 342, St John's; tel. 480-1500; fax 480-1554; Man. LEN WRIGHT.

Caribbean Banking Corpn Ltd (Trinidad and Tobago): 45 High St, POB 1324, St John's; tel. 462-4217; fax 462-5040; e-mail hollings@candw.ag; Country Man. K. ARMSTRONG-HOLLINGSWORTH.

FirstCaribbean International Bank Ltd: St John's; internet www.firstcaribbeaninternational.com; adopted present name in 2002 following merger of Caribbean operations of CIBC and Barclays Bank PLC; Exec. Chair. MICHAEL MANSOOR; CEO CHARLES PINK.

Royal Bank of Canada: High and Market Sts, POB 252, St John's; tel. 480-1151; fax 480-1190; offers a trustee service.

At the beginning of 2002 there were 21 registered 'offshore' banks in Antigua and Barbuda.

Regulatory Body

Financial Services Regulatory Commission (FSRC): St John's; fmrly known as International Financial Sector Regulatory Authority, adopted current name in 2002; Chair. LEBRECHT HESSE; Admin. LEROY KING.

STOCK EXCHANGE

Eastern Caribbean Securities Exchange: e-mail info@ecseonline.com; internet www.ecseonline.com; based in Basseterre, Saint Christopher and Nevis; f. 2001; regional securities market designed to facilitate the buying and selling of financial products for the eight member territories—Anguilla, Antigua and Barbuda, Dominica, Grenada, Montserrat, Saint Christopher and Nevis, Saint Lucia and Saint Vincent and the Grenadines; Gen. Man. BALJIT VOHRA.

INSURANCE

Several foreign companies have offices in Antigua. Local insurance companies include the following

General Insurance Co Ltd: Upper Redcliffe St, POB 340, St John's; tel. 462-2346; fax 462-4482.

Sentinel Insurance Co Ltd: Coolidge, POB 207, St John's; tel. 462-4603.

State Insurance Corpn: Redcliffe St, POB 290, St John's; tel. 462-0110; fax 462-2649; f. 1977; Chair. Dr VINCENT RICHARDS; Gen. Man. ROLSTON BARTHLEY.

Trade and Industry

DEVELOPMENT ORGANIZATIONS

Barbuda Development Agency: St John's; economic development projects for Barbuda.

Development Control Authority: St John's; internet www.antiguagov.com/dca.

Industrial Development Board: Newgate St, St John's; tel. 462-1038; fax 462-1033; f. 1984 to stimulate investment in local industries.

St John's Development Corporation: Heritage Quay, POB 1473, St John's; tel. 462-2776; fax 462-3931; e-mail stjohnsdevcorp@candw.ag; internet www.firstyellow.com/stjohnsdev; f. 1986; manages the Heritage Quay Duty Free Shopping Complex, Vendors' Mall, Public Market and Cultural and Exhibition Complex.

CHAMBER OF COMMERCE

Antigua and Barbuda Chamber of Commerce and Industry Ltd: Redcliffe St, POB 774, St John's; tel. 462-0743; fax 462-4575; e-mail chamcom@candw.ag; f. 1944 as Antigua Chamber of Commerce Ltd; name changed as above in 1991, following the collapse of the Antigua and Barbuda Manufacturers' Asscn; Pres. CLARVIS JOSEPH.

INDUSTRIAL AND TRADE ASSOCIATIONS

Antigua Cotton Growers' Association: Dunbars, St John's; tel. 462-4962; Chair. FRANCIS HENRY; Sec. PETER BLANCHETTE.

Antigua Fisheries Corpn: St John's; e-mail fisheries@candw.ag; partly funded by the Antigua and Barbuda Development Bank; aims to help local fishermen.

Antigua Sugar Industry Corpn: Gunthorpes, POB 899, St George's; tel. 462-0653.

Private Sector Organization of Antigua and Barbuda: St John's.

EMPLOYERS' ORGANIZATION

Antigua Employers' Federation: Upper High Street, POB 298, St John's; tel. 462-0449; fax 462-0449; e-mail aempfed@candw.ag; f. 1950; 117 mems; Chair. PEDRO CORBIN; Exec. Sec. HENDERSON BASS.

UTILITIES

Antigua Public Utilities Authority (APUA): St Mary's St, POB 416, St John's; tel. 480-7000; fax 462-2782; generation, transmission and distribution of electricity; internal telecommunications; collection, treatment, storage and distribution of water; Gen. Man. PETER BENJAMIN.

Caribbean Power Ltd: supplies Barbuda with water and electricity services.

TRADE UNIONS

Antigua and Barbuda Meteorological Officers Association: c/o V. C. Bird International Airport, Gabatco, POB 1051, St John's; tel. and fax 462-4606; Pres. LEONARD JOSIAH.

Antigua and Barbuda Public Service Association (ABPSA): POB 1285, St John's; tel. 463-6427; fax 461-5821; e-mail abpsa@candw.ag; Pres. JAMES SPENCER; Gen. Sec. ELLOY DE FREITAS; 550 mems.

Antigua and Barbuda Union of Teachers: c/o Ministry of Education, Culture and Technology, Church St, St John's; tel. 462-2692; Pres. COLIN GREENE; Sec. FOSTER ROBERTS.

Antigua Trades and Labour Union (ATLU): 46 North St, POB 3, St John's; tel. 462-0090; fax 462-4056; e-mail atandlu@candw.ag; f. 1939; affiliated to the Antigua Labour Party; Pres. WIGLEY GEORGE; Gen. Sec. NATALIE PAYNE; about 10,000 mems.

Antigua Workers' Union (AWU): Freedom Hall, Newgate St, POB 940, St John's; tel. 462-2005; fax 462-5220; e-mail awu@candw.ag; f. 1967 following split with ATLU; not affiliated to any party; Pres. MAURICE CHRISTIAN; Gen. Sec. KEITHLYN SMITH; 10,000 mems.

Transport

ROADS

There are 384 km (239 miles) of main roads and 781 km (485 miles) of secondary dry-weather roads.

SHIPPING

The main harbour is the St John's Deep Water Harbour. It is used by cruise ships and a number of foreign shipping lines. There are regular cargo and passenger services internationally and regionally. At Falmouth, on the south side of Antigua, is a former Royal Navy dockyard in English Harbour. The harbour is now used by yachts and private pleasure craft.

Antigua and Barbuda Port Authority: Deep Water Harbour, POB 1052, St John's; tel. 462-4243; fax 462-2510; f. 1968; responsible to Ministry of Finance; Chair. LLEWELLYN SMITH; Port Man. LEROY ADAMS.

Joseph, Vernon, Toy Contractors Ltd: Nut Grove St, St John's.

Parenzio Shipping Co Ltd: Nevis St, St John's.

Vernon Edwards Shipping Co: Thames St, POB 82, St John's; tel. 462-2034; fax 462-2035; e-mail vedwards@candw.ag; cargo service to and from San Juan, Puerto Rico.

The West Indies Oil Co Ltd: Friars Hill Rd, POB 230, St John's; tel. 462-0140; fax 462-0543.

CIVIL AVIATION

Antigua's V. C. Bird (formerly Coolidge) International Airport, 9 km (5.6 miles) north-east of St John's, is modern and accommodates jet-engined aircraft. There is a small airstrip at Codrington on Barbuda. Antigua and Barbuda Airlines, a nominal company, controls international routes, but services to Europe and North America are operated by American Airlines (USA), Continental Airlines (USA), Lufthansa (Germany) and Air Canada. Antigua and Barbuda is a shareholder in, and the headquarters of, the regional airline, LIAT. Other regional services are operated by BWIA (Trinidad and Tobago) and Air BVI (British Virgin Islands).

LIAT (1974) Ltd: POB 819, V.C. Bird Int. Airport, St John's; tel. 480-5600; fax 480-5625; e-mail li.sales.mrkting@candw.ag; internet www.liatairline.com; f. 1956 as Leeward Islands Air Transport Services, jointly-owned by 11 regional Govts; privatized in 1995; shares are held by the Govts of Antigua and Barbuda, Montserrat, Grenada, Barbados, Trinidad and Tobago, Jamaica, Guyana, Dominica, Saint Lucia, Saint Vincent and the Grenadines and Saint Christopher and Nevis (30.8%), BWIA (29.2%), LIAT employees (13.3%) and private investors (26.7%); scheduled passenger and cargo services to 19 destinations in the Caribbean; charter flights are also undertaken; Chair. WILBUR HARRIGAN; CEO GARRY CULLEN.

Carib Aviation Ltd: V.C. Bird Int. Airport; tel. 462-3147; fax 462-3125; e-mail caribav@candw.ag; charter co; operates regional services.

Tourism

Tourism is the country's main industry. Antigua offers a reputed 365 beaches, an annual international sailing regatta and Carnival week, and the historic Nelson's Dockyard in English Harbour (a national park since 1985). Barbuda is less developed but is noted for its beauty, wildlife and beaches of pink sand. In 1986 the Government established the St John's Development Corporation to oversee the redevelopment of the capital as a commercial duty-free centre, with extra cruise-ship facilities. In 2001 there were 193,176 stop-over visitors, as well as 471,700 cruise-ship passengers. In that year some 32% of stop-over visitors came from the USA. Expenditure by visitors was an estimated EC $734.6m. in 2001.

Antigua and Barbuda Department of Tourism: Nevis St and Friendly Alley, POB 363, St John's; tel. 462-0029; fax 462-2483; e-mail info@antigua-barbuda.org; internet www.antigua-barbuda.org; Dir-Gen. SHIRLENE NIBBS; Asst Man. IRMA TOMLINSON.

Antigua Hotels and Tourist Association (AHTA): Island House, Newgate St, POB 454, St John's; tel. 462-3703; fax 462-3702; e-mail ahta@candw.ag; internet www.antiguahotels.org; Acting Chair. DANIEL CADET; Exec. Dir CYNTHIA G. SIMON.

ARGENTINA

Introductory Survey

Location, Climate, Language, Religion, Flag, Capital

The Argentine Republic occupies almost the whole of South America south of the Tropic of Capricorn and east of the Andes. It has a long Atlantic coastline stretching from Uruguay and the River Plate to Tierra del Fuego. To the west lie Chile and the Andes mountains, while to the north are Bolivia, Paraguay and Brazil. Argentina also claims the Falkland Islands (known in Argentina as the Islas Malvinas), South Georgia, the South Sandwich Islands and part of Antarctica. The climate varies from sub-tropical in the Chaco region of the north to sub-arctic in Patagonia, generally with moderate summer rainfall. Temperatures in Buenos Aires are usually between 5°C (41°F) and 29°C (84°F). The language is Spanish. The great majority of the population profess Christianity: more than 90% are Roman Catholics and about 2% Protestants. The national flag (proportions 14 by 9) has three equal horizontal stripes, of light blue (celeste), above white, above light blue. The state flag (proportions 1 by 2) has the same design with, in addition, a gold 'Sun of May' in the centre of the white stripe. The capital is Buenos Aires.

Recent History

During the greater part of the 20th century, government in Argentina tended to alternate between military and civilian rule. In 1930 Hipólito Yrigoyen, a member of the reformist Unión Cívica Radical (UCR), who in 1916 had become Argentina's first President to be freely elected by popular vote, was overthrown by an army coup, and the country's first military regime was established. Civilian rule was restored in 1932, only to be supplanted by further military intervention in 1943. A leading figure in the new military regime, Col (later Lt-Gen.) Juan Domingo Perón Sosa, won a presidential election in 1946. As President, he established the Peronista party in 1948 and pursued a policy of extreme nationalism and social improvement, aided by his second wife, Eva ('Evita') Duarte de Perón, whose popularity (particularly among industrial workers and their families) greatly enhanced his position and contributed to his re-election as President in 1951. In 1954, however, his promotion of secularization and the legalization of divorce brought him into conflict with the Roman Catholic Church. In September 1955 President Perón was deposed by a revolt of the armed forces. He went into exile, eventually settling in Spain, from where he continued to direct the Peronist movement.

Following the overthrow of Perón, Argentina entered another lengthy period of political instability. Political control continued to pass between civilian (mainly Radical) and military regimes during the late 1950s and the 1960s. This period was also characterized by increasing guerrilla activity, particularly by the Montoneros, a group of left-wing Peronist sympathizers, and urban guerrillas intensified their activities in 1971 and 1972.

Congressional and presidential elections were conducted in March 1973. The Frente Justicialista de Liberación, a Peronist coalition, secured control of the Congreso Nacional (National Congress), while the presidential election was won by the party's candidate, Dr Héctor Cámpora, who assumed the office in May. However, Cámpora resigned in July, to enable Gen. Perón, who had returned to Argentina in June, to contest a fresh presidential election. In September Perón was returned to power, with more than 60% of the votes. He took office in October, with his third wife, María Estela ('Isabelita') Martínez de Perón, as Vice-President.

Gen. Perón died in July 1974 and was succeeded as President by his widow. The Government's economic austerity programme and the soaring rate of inflation led to widespread strike action, dissension among industrial workers, and demands for the resignation of 'Isabelita' Perón. In March 1976 the armed forces, led by Gen. Jorge Videla (Commander of the Army), overthrew the President and installed a three-man junta: Gen. Videla was sworn in as President. The junta made substantial alterations to the Constitution, dissolved the Congreso Nacional, suspended all political and trade union activity and removed most government officials from their posts. Several hundred people were arrested, while 'Isabelita' Perón was detained and later went into exile.

The military regime launched a successful, although ferocious, offensive against left-wing guerrillas and opposition forces. The imprisonment, torture and murder of suspected left-wing activists by the armed forces provoked domestic and international protests against violations of human rights. Repression eased in 1978, after all armed opposition had been eliminated.

In March 1981 Gen. Roberto Viola, a former member of the junta, succeeded President Videla and made known his intention to extend dialogue with political parties as a prelude to an eventual return to democracy. Owing to ill health, he was replaced in December by Lt-Gen. Leopoldo Galtieri, the Commander-in-Chief of the Army, who attempted to cultivate popular support by continuing the process of political liberalization initiated by his predecessor.

In April 1982, in order to distract attention from an increasingly unstable domestic situation, and following unsuccessful negotiations with the United Kingdom in February over Argentina's long-standing sovereignty claim, President Galtieri ordered the invasion of the Falkland Islands (Islas Malvinas) (see chapter on the Falkland Islands, q.v.). The United Kingdom recovered the islands after a short conflict, in the course of which about 750 Argentine lives were lost. Argentine forces surrendered in June 1982, but no formal cessation of hostilities was declared until October 1989. Humiliated by the defeat, Galtieri was forced to resign, and the members of the junta were replaced. The army, under the control of Lt-Gen. Cristino Nicolaides, installed a retired general, Reynaldo Bignone, as President in July 1982. The armed forces were held responsible for the disastrous economic situation, and the transfer of power to a civilian government was accelerated. Moreover, in 1983 a Military Commission of Inquiry into the Falklands conflict concluded in its report that the main responsibility for Argentina's defeat lay with members of the former junta, who were recommended for trial. Galtieri was sentenced to imprisonment, while several other officers were put on trial for corruption, murder and insulting the honour of the armed forces. Meanwhile, in August 1983 the regime approved the Ley de Pacificación Nacional, an amnesty law which granted retrospective immunity to the police, the armed forces and others for political crimes that had been committed over the previous 10 years.

In February 1983 the Government announced that general and presidential elections would be held on 30 October. At the elections, the UCR defeated the Peronist Partido Justicialista (PJ), attracting the votes of many former Peronist supporters. The UCR won 317 of the 600 seats in the presidential electoral college, and 129 of the 254 seats in the Cámara de Diputados (Chamber of Deputies), although the PJ won a narrow majority of provincial governorships. Dr Raúl Alfonsín, the UCR candidate, took office as President on 10 December. President Alfonsín promptly announced a radical reform of the armed forces, which led to the immediate retirement of more than one-half of the military high command. In addition, he repealed the Ley de Pacificación Nacional and ordered the court martial of the first three military juntas to rule Argentina after the 1976 coup, for offences including abduction, torture and murder. Public opposition to the former military regime was reinforced by the discovery and exhumation of hundreds of bodies from unmarked graves throughout the country. (It was believed that 15,000–30,000 people 'disappeared' during the so-called 'dirty war' between the former military regime and its opponents in 1976–83.) In December the Government announced the formation of the National Commission on the Disappearance of Persons to investigate the events of the 'dirty war'. The trial of the former leaders began in April 1985. Several hundred prosecution witnesses gave testimonies which revealed the systematic atrocities and the campaign of terror perpetrated by the former military leaders. In December four of the accused were acquitted, but sentences were imposed on the remaining five, including sentences of life imprisonment for Gen. Videla and Adm. Eduardo Massera. The court martial of the members of the junta that had held power during the Falklands conflict was conducted concurrently with the trial of the former military leaders. In May 1986 all three members of the junta were found guilty of negligence and received prison sentences, including a term of 12 years for Galtieri.

In late 1986 the Government sought approval for the Punto Final ('Full Stop') Law, whereby civil and military courts were to begin new judicial proceedings against members of the armed forces accused of violations of human rights, within a 60-day period ending on 22 February 1987. The pre-emptive nature of the legislation provoked widespread popular opposition but was, nevertheless, approved by the Congreso Nacional in December 1986. However, in May 1987, following a series of minor rebellions at army garrisons throughout the country, the Government announced new legislation, known as the Obediencia Debida ('Due Obedience') law, whereby an amnesty was to be declared for all but senior ranks of the police and armed forces. Therefore, under the new law, of the 350–370 officers hitherto due to be prosecuted for alleged violations of human rights, only 30–50 senior officers were now to be tried. The legislation provoked great controversy, and was considered to be a decisive factor in the significant gains made by the PJ at gubernatorial and legislative elections conducted in September. The UCR's defeat was also attributed to its imposition, in July, of an unpopular economic programme of austerity measures.

In January 1989 the army quickly repelled an attack by 40 left-wing activists on a military base at La Tablada, in which 39 lives were lost. Many of the guerrilla band were identified as members of the Movimiento Todos por la Patria.

In the campaign for the May 1989 elections, Carlos Saúl Menem headed the Frente Justicialista de Unidad Popular (FREJUPO) electoral alliance, comprising his own PJ grouping, the Partido Demócrata Cristiano (PDC) and the Partido Intransigente (PI). On 14 May the Peronists were guaranteed a return to power, having secured, together with the two other members of the FREJUPO alliance, 48.5% of the votes cast in the presidential election and 310 of the 600 seats in the electoral college. The Peronists were also victorious in the election for 127 seats (one-half of the total) in the Cámara de Diputados, winning 45% of the votes and 66 seats, in contrast to the 29% (41 seats) obtained by the UCR. The failure of attempts by the retiring and incoming administrations to collaborate, and the reluctance of the Alfonsín administration to continue in office with the prospect of further economic embarrassment, left the nation in a political vacuum. Although Menem was scheduled to take office as President on 10 December 1989, the worsening economic situation compelled Alfonsín to resign five months early, and Menem assumed the presidency on 8 July.

Rumours of a possible amnesty, agreed between the newly elected Government and military leaders, prompted the organization of a massive demonstration in Buenos Aires in support of human rights in September 1989. In October, however, the Government issued decrees whereby 210 officers, NCOs and soldiers who had been involved in the 'dirty war', the governing junta during the Falklands conflict (including Gen. Galtieri) and leaders of three recent military uprisings (including Lt-Col Rico and Col Seineldín) were pardoned.

Economic affairs dominated the latter half of 1989 and much of 1990. The Minister of the Economy, Nestór Rapanelli, introduced several measures, including the devaluation of the austral, but these failed to reverse the trend towards hyperinflation, and Rapanelli resigned in December 1989. His successor, Antonio Erman González, introduced a comprehensive plan for economic readjustment, incorporating the expansion of existing plans for the transfer to private ownership of many state-owned companies, the rationalization of government-controlled bodies, and the restructuring of the nation's financial systems. In August 1990 Erman González appointed himself head of the Central Bank and assumed almost total control of the country's financial structure. Public disaffection with the Government's economic policy was widespread. Failure to contain the threat of hyperinflation led to a loss in purchasing power, and small-scale food riots and looting became more frequent. The Government's rationalization programme proved unpopular with public-sector employees, and resulted in industrial action and demonstrations, organized from within the sector with the support of trade unions, political opposition parties and human rights groups.

Widespread public concern at the apparent impunity of military personnel increased following President Menem's suggestion that a further military amnesty would be granted before the end of 1990, and was exacerbated by rumours of escalating military unrest (which were realized in December 1990 when 200–300 rebel soldiers staged a swiftly suppressed uprising at the Patricios infantry garrison in Buenos Aires). A second round of presidential pardons was announced in late December. More than 40,000 demonstrators gathered in Buenos Aires to protest against the release of former military leaders, including Gen. Videla, Gen. Viola and Adm. Massera. Critics and political opponents dismissed Menem's claims that such action was essential for the effective 'reconciliation' of the Argentine people. In mid-1991 it was announced that the number of armed forces personnel was to be reduced by some 20,000 men; military spending was also to be restricted.

In January 1991 Menem was obliged to reorganize the Cabinet, following allegations that government ministers and officials had requested bribes from US businessmen during the course of commercial negotiations. Later in the month, the President was forced to implement a second cabinet reshuffle when his economic team, led by Erman González, resigned following a sudden spectacular decline in the value of the austral in relation to the US dollar.

In the first two rounds of voting in gubernatorial and congressional elections, the Peronists were unexpectedly successful, wresting the governorship of San Juan from the provincial Bloquista party in August 1991, and securing control of nine of the 12 contested provinces (including the crucial province of Buenos Aires) in September. The third and fourth rounds of voting, in October and December, respectively, proved less successful for the PJ. Overall, however, the Peronists secured control of 14 of the 24 contested territories and increased their congressional representation by seven seats, compared with a five-seat reduction in the congressional representation of the UCR.

The success of the Peronist campaign was widely attributed to the popularity of the Minister of the Economy, Domingo Cavallo, and the success of the economic policies that he had implemented since succeeding Erman González. New economic measures included the abolition of index-linked wage increases and, most dramatically, the implementation of the 'Convertibility Plan', which linked the austral to the US dollar, at a fixed rate of exchange. This initiative soon achieved considerable success in reducing inflation, and impressed international finance organizations sufficiently to secure the negotiation of substantial loan agreements. In October 1991 the President issued a comprehensive decree ordering the removal of almost all of the remaining bureaucratic apparatus of state regulation of the economy, and in November the Government announced plans to accelerate the transfer to private ownership of the remaining public-sector concerns. Continuing economic success in 1992 helped to secure agreements for the renegotiation of repayment of outstanding debts with the Government's leading creditor banks and with the 'Paris Club' of Western creditor governments. However, in November the Confederación General del Trabajo (CGT—General Confederation of Labour) organized a one-day general strike, in protest at the Government's continuing economic austerity programme. The strike was precipitated by revelations that senior government officials were to receive pay increases of as much as 200%.

Meanwhile, President Menem sought to consolidate his own position and to increase the popularity of his party in the months preceding legislative elections scheduled for 3 October 1993, at which the Peronists hoped to make significant gains in order to facilitate Menem's wish to effect a constitutional amendment that would allow him to pursue a second, consecutive presidential term. The elections to renew 127 seats in the Cámara de Diputados were won convincingly by the ruling PJ party, with 42.3% of the votes, while the UCR obtained 30% of the votes.

An unexpected development in November 1993 was the return to political prominence of former President Alfonsín. While UCR opposition to Menem's presidential ambitions had remained vociferous, several opposition leaders, notably Alfonsín, feared that the UCR would be excluded from negotiations on constitutional reform, should the unorthodox political manoeuvring of the Peronists, largely orchestrated by the President of the Senado (Senate), Menem's brother Eduardo, succeed in propelling the reform proposal through the legislature. Alfonsín, also anxious to avoid another humiliating defeat for the UCR at a national referendum which Menem had elected to organize in late 1993 on the question of constitutional reform, entered into a dialogue with the President, which resulted in a declaration, in November, that a framework for constitutional reform had been negotiated, apparently in return for Menem's postponement of the referendum and acceptance of modified reform proposals. In December the UCR national convention endorsed the terms of the agreement, which included the possibility of re-election of the President for one consecutive term, a reduction in the presidential term (to four years), the abolition of the presidential electoral college, the delegation of some presidential powers to a Chief of Cabinet, an increase in the number of seats in the Senado and a reduction in the length of the mandate of all senators, a reform of the procedure for judicial appointments, the removal of religious stipulations from the terms of eligibility for presidential candidates, and the abolition of the President's power to appoint the mayor of the federal capital. The need for constitutional reform was approved by the Congreso later in the month, and Menem immediately declared his intention to seek re-election in 1995.

Elections to the Constituent Assembly took place in April 1994. While the Peronists won the largest share of the vote (37.8%—136 seats), they failed to secure an absolute majority in the Assembly. The UCR won only 19.9% of the votes, equivalent to 75 seats in the Assembly, while a centre-left coalition, Frente Grande, emerged unexpectedly as the third political force (with 12.5% of the votes and 31 seats), having campaigned against institutionalized corruption. The Assembly was inaugurated in May, and on 24 August a new Constitution, containing 19 new articles, 40 amendments to existing articles and a new chapter on civil rights and guarantees, was duly promulgated. An electoral timetable was also established, with presidential, legislative and provincial elections all scheduled for May 1995. In December 1994 the Senado approved the new electoral code providing for the direct election of a president and a vice-president and for a second round of voting for the first- and second-placed candidates in the event of a closely contested election.

In January 1995 Carlos Ruckauf, the Minister of the Interior, was named as President Menem's running mate for the new post of vice-president. Menem's campaign for re-election concentrated on the economic success of his previous administration and, despite the increasingly precarious condition of the economy, was sufficiently successful to secure 49.9% of the votes at the presidential election of 14 May, thereby avoiding a second ballot. José Octavio Bordón, the candidate of the Frente del País Solidario (Frepaso—a centre-left alliance of socialist, communist, Christian Democrat and dissident Peronist groups) was second with 29.3% of the votes, ahead of the UCR candidate, Horacio Massaccesi, who received 17.0% of the votes. The Peronists were also successful in nine of the 14 gubernatorial contests; however, Frepaso won the largest share of the 130 contested seats in the Cámara de Diputados at legislative elections conducted concurrently, and significantly increased its representation in the Senado (as did the Peronists) largely at the expense of the UCR. Menem was inaugurated as President for a four-year term on 8 July. The composition of a largely unaltered Cabinet was announced simultaneously, led by Eduardo Bauzá, in the new post of Cabinet Chief. The Peronists performed well at gubernatorial elections conducted in late 1995, but suffered an unexpected defeat at senatorial elections in the capital in October at which the Peronist candidate was beaten into third place by the Frepaso and UCR candidates, respectively.

Meanwhile, the Government's ongoing programme of economic austerity continued to provoke violent opposition, particularly from the public sector, where redundancies and a 'freeze' on salaries had been imposed in many provinces. However, in August 1994 a 12-month moratorium on appointments in the public sector was announced, as were plans to privatize several more state enterprises. In March 1995 the Government presented an economic consolidation programme aimed at protecting the Argentine currency against devaluation and supporting the ailing banking sector, which had been adversely affected by the financial crisis in Mexico in late 1994. Subsequent austerity measures adopted by provincial governments, together with a dramatic increase in the rate of unemployment, provoked widespread social unrest in the city of Córdoba and in the province of Río Negro in 1995.

In June 1996 the Government suffered a serious political defeat when a UCR candidate, Fernando de la Rúa, won almost 40% of the votes cast in the first direct elections for the Mayor of the Federal District of Buenos Aires; a Frepaso candidate secured 26.5% of the votes, while the incumbent Peronist Mayor, Jorge Domínguez, received only 18% of the ballot. The PJ also fared badly in concurrent elections to the 60-member Constituent Assembly (which was charged with drafting a con-

stitution for the newly autonomous Federal District of Buenos Aires); Frepaso candidates secured 25 seats, the UCR 19, the PJ 11 and the recently formed Nueva Dirigencia (ND, led by a former Peronist, Gustavo Béliz) five. In July the Government was again undermined by the resignations of Rodolfo Barra, the Minister of Justice, and that of Oscar Camilión, the Minister of Defence, whose parliamentary immunity was to be removed to allow investigations in connection with the illegal sale of armaments to Ecuador and Croatia. More significant was the dismissal of Cavallo from the post of Minister of the Economy, following months of bitter dispute with the President and other cabinet members. Roque Fernández, hitherto President of the Central Bank, assumed the economy portfolio. Cavallo became increasingly vociferous in his attacks against the integrity of certain cabinet members, and, in October, as Menem launched a well-publicized campaign against corruption after the discovery of wide-scale malpractice within the customs service, he accused the Government of having links with organized crime.

Industrial unrest continued during 1996, and in August a 24-hour general strike, organized by the CGT, the Congreso de los Trabajadores Argentinos (CTA) and the Movimiento de Trabajadores Argentinos (MTA), received widespread support. A 36-hour strike in September was also widely observed. None the less, in that month taxation and austerity measures secured congressional approval, albeit with significant amendments. In October relations between the Government and the trade unions deteriorated, following the submission to the Congreso of controversial labour reform legislation. In December, owing to the slow pace at which debate on the bill was progressing in the legislature, President Menem introduced part of the reforms by decree. Although three decrees were signed, radically altering labour contracts, in January 1997 a court declared that they were unconstitutional.

In March 1997 Eduardo Alberto Duhalde, the Peronist Governor of the province of Buenos Aires, initiated a radical reorganization of the provincial police in an attempt to divert attention from the politically sensitive issue of corruption, with which the PJ was increasingly associated. Nevertheless, in June Elías Jassan, the Minister of Justice, tendered his resignation after admitting maintaining links with Alfredo Yabrán, a controversial businessman whom Cavallo had accused of corruption, having previously denied that he had ever met him.

The popularity of the PJ was undermined further by an upsurge in social and industrial unrest during 1997, which was primarily the result of widespread discontent with proposed labour reforms, reductions in public expenditure and the high level of unemployment. In May violent protests erupted across Argentina as police clashed with thousands of demonstrators who had occupied government buildings and blockaded roads and bridges. In July some 30,000 people demonstrated in the capital to protest at the high level of unemployment, then estimated at more than 17%. A general strike in August, organized by the MTA and the CTA, was only partially observed.

In March 1997 Cavallo founded his own political party, Acción por la República (AR), and in July he and Béliz of the ND formed an alliance to contest the forthcoming congressional elections. In the following month the leaders of Frepaso and the UCR confirmed that they had agreed to an electoral pact, known as the Alianza por el Trabajo, la Justicia y la Educación (ATJE), in order to present joint lists in certain constituencies, notably in the province of Buenos Aires, and to remain in alliance subsequently.

At the mid-term congressional elections, held in October 1997, the UCR and Frepaso (in both separate and joint lists) won 45.6% of the votes and 61 of the 127 seats contested, in contrast to the 36.3% (51 seats) obtained by the PJ; of the remaining 15 seats, three were secured by AR—ND. The PJ thus lost its overall majority in the Cámara de Diputados (its total number of seats being reduced to 118), while the UCR and Frepaso together increased their representation to 110 seats. More significant was the PJ's poor performance in the critical constituency of the province of Buenos Aires, where it received only 41.3% of the votes, compared with the ATJE's 48.3%.

In December 1997 President Menem appointed Erman González as Minister of Labour and Social Security, following the resignation of Armando Caro Figueroa, who had been criticized for failing to introduce labour reforms. Legislation concerning labour reforms, including the elimination of short-term contracts and a reduction in redundancy payments, was finally approved by the legislature in September 1998.

Preparations for the 1999 presidential election gained momentum in April 1998 with the UCR's selection of Fernando de la Rúa as the party's candidate. In a nation-wide primary in November, de la Rúa was elected as the ATJE presidential candidate, defeating Graciela Fernández Meijide, the highly regarded Frepaso nominee. In December Carlos 'Chacho' Alvarez of Frepaso was formally nominated as de la Rúa's running mate, while Fernández Meijide was to contest the governorship of Buenos Aires. In July President Menem abandoned a controversial campaign to amend the Constitution in order to allow him to contest the presidency for a third consecutive term of office. The campaign was vociferously opposed by the leading PJ contender, Eduardo Duhalde, who had threatened to hold a provincial plebiscite on the issue. Duhalde's main rival for the PJ presidential nomination was Ramón 'Palito' Ortega, a former Governor of Tucumán, who had been appointed Secretary of Social Development in April. The popularity of the PJ remained low, not least because of the corruption scandals that had beset the Menem administration, and in November the President was accused of seeking to undermine the independence of the judiciary when he demanded the investigation of a prosecutor probing allegations of government involvement in the sale of armaments to Ecuador and Croatia. In September a judge had ordered that Erman González, who had held the defence portfolio at the time of the alleged incidents, be summoned to testify in the investigation. Guido di Tella, the Minister of Foreign Affairs, and Menem's brother-in-law, Emir Yoma, a former presidential adviser, were also implicated in the case. An agreement reached by Duhalde and Ortega to run jointly in the PJ presidential primary seemed to restore some unity to the party, although it was apparent that Menem had not entirely abandoned the idea of a re-election bid. In March 1999, however, the Supreme Court rejected appeals for Menem to be allowed to stand in the October elections.

In June 1999 Duhalde officially received the PJ presidential nomination after the only other contender, Adolfo Rodríguez Saá, the Governor of San Luis, withdrew from the contest. Duhalde's candidacy was publicly endorsed by Menem. Meanwhile, social unrest escalated in several provinces, as economic recession led to rising levels of unemployment and non-payment of public-sector salaries. At the presidential election, conducted on 24 October, de la Rúa (with 48.5% of the votes) defeated Duhalde (who secured 38.1%), thereby ending 10 years of Menem's Peronist rule. The ATJE also performed well in concurrent elections to renew 130 of the 257 seats in the Cámara de Diputados, winning 63 seats, while the PJ secured 50 seats and Cavallo's AR won nine. The ATJE's total number of seats in the Cámara increased to 127—only two short of an absolute majority—in contrast to the PJ, whose representation was reduced to 101 seats. However, in gubernatorial elections held on the same day, the ATJE candidate, Graciela Fernández Meijide, failed to secure the critical province of Buenos Aires, where Carlos Ruckauf, the outgoing Vice-President, was elected. As a result of the elections the PJ controlled 14 of the 24 provincial administrations, while the ATJE held only six. In November de la Rúa formally announced the composition of his new Cabinet, which significantly comprised a large number of economists. De la Rúa took office as President on 10 December, with Carlos Alvarez as his Vice-President. Later that month the new Congreso Nacional approved an austerity budget that reduced public expenditure by US $1,400m., as well as a major tax reform programme and a federal revenue-sharing scheme.

In April 2000 the Senado approved a controversial major revision of employment law. The legislation met with public criticism and led to mass demonstrations by public-sector workers and, subsequently, to two 24-hour national strikes organized by the CGT. In May the ruling ATJE candidate, Aníbal Ibarra, was elected Mayor of the Federal District of Buenos Aires. Later that year the Government came under intense pressure after it was alleged that some senators had received bribes from government officials to pass the employment legislation. In September the Senado voted to end the immunity that protected lawmakers, judges and government ministers from criminal investigation in order to allow an inquiry into the corruption allegations. The political crisis intensified on 6 October when Alvarez resigned as Vice-President, one day after a cabinet reorganization, in which two ministers implicated in the bribery scandal were not removed. One of these, former labour minister Alberto Flamarique, who was appointed Presidential Chief of Staff in the reshuffle, resigned later the same day. The other, Fernando de Santibáñez, head of the state intelligence service (SIDE),

resigned from the Government in late October. Earlier that month the President of the Senado, José Genoud, also resigned after he too was implicated in the bribery allegations.

The economic situation continued to deteriorate in 2000 and 2001. In November 2000 thousands of unemployed workers blocked roads throughout the country to demand jobs, welfare programmes and improvements in standards of living. In the same month the country was paralysed by a 36-hour national strike, organized in response to the Government's proposed introduction of an IMF-backed economic recovery package that included a five-year freeze on federal and provincial spending. Additional measures included a reform of the pension system and an increase in the female retirement age. In December the Congreso approved the reforms and, later in the month, the IMF agreed a package, worth an estimated US $20,000m., to meet Argentina's external financing requirement for 2001.

The resignation of the Minister of the Economy, José Luis Machinea, precipitated another political crisis in March 2001. The announcement by his successor, Ricardo López Murphy, of major reductions in public expenditure, resulted in several ministerial resignations. As a consequence, in late March a second reshuffle occurred, in which the most notable appointee was Domingo Cavallo as the new Minister of the Economy. In June Cavallo announced a series of measures designed to ease the country's financial situation. The most controversial of these was the introduction of a complex trade tariff system that created multiple exchange rates (based on the average of a euro and a US dollar); this was, in effect, a devaluation of the peso for external trade, although the dollar peg remained in operation for domestic transactions. As Argentina's debt crisis intensified and fears of a default increased, a further emergency package, the seventh in 19 months, was unveiled in July. A policy of 'zero-deficit' was announced, whereby neither the federal Government nor any province would be allowed to spend more than it collected in taxes. In order to achieve this, state salaries and pensions were to be reduced by 13%. Despite mass protests and a one-day national strike, the measures were granted congressional approval at the end of July. Nevertheless, the economic situation continued to deteriorate throughout 2001. There were protests against the austerity measures in August and following the introduction of one-year bonds, known as 'patacones', as payment to 160,000 public-sector workers. Meanwhile, the Government encountered difficulties in effecting economic policies: negotiations with the opposition Peronists, who controlled the majority of Argentina's provincial governments, on lower monthly tax transfers (essential to achieving a 'zero-deficit') were repeatedly stalled in late 2001.

The impoverished state of the economy contributed to the ATJE's poor performance in the legislative elections, held in October 2001. The PJ won control of the Cámara de Diputados, with 37.4% of the votes cast, and increased its representation in the lower house to 116 seats overall. In comparison, the ATJE obtained 23.1% of the votes cast and 88 seats (UCR 71 seats; Frepaso 17). In the Senado, which for the first time was directly elected by popular vote, the PJ increased its majority, winning 40 seats and 40.0% of the ballot, while the ATJE secured 23.3% of the vote and 25 seats (UCR 24 seats; Frepaso one seat). The elections were marred by a high percentage of spoiled ballots (21.1%—in some provinces the number of spoiled ballots was higher than that for the winning candidate) and a high rate of abstention, about 28%, in a country where voting is obligatory.

In December 2001, as the economic situation deteriorated and the possibility of a default on the country's debt increased considerably, owing to the IMF's refusal to disburse more funds to Argentina, the Government introduced restrictions on bank account withdrawals and appropriated private pension funds. These measures proved to be extremely unpopular and resulted in two days of rioting and demonstrations nation-wide, in which at least 27 people died. On 20 December Cavallo resigned as Minister of the Economy and, following further rioting on the same day, President de la Rúa submitted his resignation. The newly appointed President of the Senado, Ramón Puerta, became acting President of the Republic but was succeeded two days later by the Peronist Adolfo Rodríguez Saá. He, in turn, resigned one week later after protests against his proposed economic reforms (including the introduction of a new currency and the suspension of debt repayments) resulted in further unrest. On 1 January 2002 the former Peronist presidential candidate and recently elected Senator for the Province of Buenos Aires, Eduardo Alberto Duhalde, was elected President by the Congreso Nacional; he took office the following day. He was Argentina's fifth President in less than two weeks. (The President of the Cámara de Diputados, Eduardo Camaño, was acting President from 31 December 2001 to 2 January 2002 following the resignation of Puerta as President of the Senado.) On 3 January Argentina officially defaulted on its loan repayments, reportedly the largest ever debt default, and on 6 January the Senado gave authorization to the Government to set the exchange rate, thus officially ending the 10-year-old-parity between the US dollar and the peso.

In February 2002 the Supreme Court ruled (by a margin of six to three) that the restrictions imposed on bank withdrawals (the 'corralito') were unconstitutional. Some accounts were freed from the restrictions but, in order to forestall the complete collapse of the financial system, the Government decreed a six-month ban on legal challenges to the remainder of the bank withdrawal regime. Numerous bank holidays were also decreed to prevent another run on the banks and a further devaluation of the currency. A constitutional crisis ensued as the Congreso initiated impeachment proceedings against the unpopular Supreme Court Justices (see below). Later that month the Government signed a new tax-sharing pact with the provincial Governors, linking the monthly amount distributed to the provinces to tax collections, as recommended by the IMF. However, in late April Jorge Remes Lenicov resigned as Minister of the Economy, following the Senado's refusal to support an emergency plan to exchange 'frozen' bank deposits for government bonds, despite an uncompromising message from the IMF that no further help would be available unless drastic reforms were forthcoming. He was replaced by Roberto Lavagna (the sixth Argentine economy minister in 12 months) and, following more ministerial resignations, a partial cabinet reshuffle was effected in May. The most notable appointments were those of Alfredo Néstor Atanasof as Cabinet Chief and Jorge Rubén Matzkin as Minister of the Interior.

Meanwhile, the economy achieved mixed progress during 2002. While the number of deposits in Argentine banks increased, indicating a healthier economy, Argentina still defaulted on an US $805m. loan instalment that was owed to the World Bank in November, thus jeopardizing Argentina's last remaining source of external finance. The situation was aggravated by disagreements between the Minister of the Economy and the President of the Central Bank over the 'corralito' restrictions. Public anger against the Government and at the state of the economy did not subside, and in June 2002 two people were killed and dozens more injured when protesters demanding jobs and food clashed with the police. The next day thousands of anti-Government protesters marched in front of the Congreso while teachers and public-sector workers went on strike.

In the latter half of 2002 congressional efforts to impeach the Supreme Court Justices for incompetence were repeatedly frustrated. The Cámara de Diputados failed to achieve quorum to begin the impeachment debate on five occasions but, in October, and after calls from the IMF for political consensus between the judiciary and the legislature, the impeachment bid was voted down in the Cámara. Nevertheless, later that month one Supreme Court judge resigned. Contentious decisions taken by the Supreme Court included ruling against the 'corralito', pay and pensions reductions for public-sector workers and public utility price increases.

In July 2002 President Duhalde announced that presidential elections would take place six months earlier than planned, on 30 March 2003, and that a new administration would take office on 25 May. It was hoped that this move would reduce political pressures on the Government during its ongoing negotiations with the IMF. In November, following negotiations between the Government, legislators and provincial Governors, agreement was reached to postpone the presidential elections until 27 April 2003, with a run-off vote (if necessary) scheduled for 18 May. Internal rivalries within the ruling PJ, most notably between Duhalde (who supported the candidacy of the Santa Cruz provincial Governor, Néstor Kirchner) and former President Carlos Menem, resulted in a bitter argument regarding the election of a Peronist candidate. Eventually, in late January 2003, the PJ congress voted to allow all three Peronist aspirants (namely Menem, Kirchner and Adolfo Rodríguez Saá) to contest the presidential election, despite a court order (obtained by Menem) ordering that a primary election be held.

In the first round of the presidential election, on 27 April 2003, Menem won 24% of the votes cast, according to preliminary results, followed by Kirchner, with 22% of the ballot. Ricardo López Murphy gained 16% of the votes, while Elisa Carrió of the Alternativa por una República de Iguales and Rodríguez Sáa each won 14% of the ballot. As no candidate gained a majority of votes, a run-off election was to be held on 18 May.

Carlos Menem had been the subject of a number of scandals in 2001 and 2002. In June 2001 he was arrested on charges of illegal arms-trafficking during his terms in office, and in July was formally charged with selling arms to Croatia (in violation of international embargoes in the early 1990s) and Ecuador (when Argentina was a guarantor of a peace treaty that ended a border conflict between Ecuador and Peru, and was thus obliged to remain neutral). In November the Supreme Court dismissed the charges against Menem and he was released from house arrest. In the previous month two Swiss bank accounts belonging to Menem were 'frozen' while an investigation was launched to trace the origins of the funds. In August 2002 it was alleged that Menem had accepted a US $10m. bribe, deposited in one of the Swiss bank accounts (of which he only acknowledged the existence of in July), to cover up evidence of Iranian involvement in a bomb attack on a Jewish social centre in Buenos Aires in 1994, which resulted in 86 fatalities. Both Menem and the Iranian Government vigorously denied the allegations. Menem declared that the $650,000 held in a Swiss bank account was compensation that he had been awarded for being imprisoned during the military dictatorship, and he accused the Duhalde Peronist faction of trying to sabotage his bid for a third presidential term.

Despite the public expressions of regret (in 1995) by the heads of the navy, the army and the air force for crimes committed by the armed forces during 1976–83, issues concerning the 'dirty war' remained politically sensitive at the beginning of the 21st century. In January 1998 Alfredo Astiz, a notorious former naval captain, was deprived of his rank and pension after he defended the elimination of political opponents during the dictatorship. In the following month the Swiss authorities revealed that they had discovered a number of Swiss bank accounts belonging to former Argentine military officials, including Astiz and Antonio Domingo Bussi, then Governor of Tucumán. It was rumoured that the accounts contained funds stolen by the military regime from Argentines who had been detained or 'disappeared'. (In July 2001 Astiz was arrested at the request of an Italian court on the grounds of his involvement in the murder of three Italian citizens during the 'dirty war'. He was released the following month.) In March the Congreso approved legislation repealing the Punto Final and Obediencia Debida laws (adopted in 1986 and 1987, respectively); however, the new legislation was not retrospective and would not affect those who had already received an amnesty. In June Gen. Videla was arrested in connection with the abduction and illegal adoption of children whose parents had 'disappeared' during the dictatorship. As many as 300 infants born in special holding centres during the 'dirty war' were believed to have been abducted by the military. In the following months further arrests were made in connection with the alleged kidnappings, including that of former President Reynaldo Bignone, former army chief Lt-Gen. Cristino Nicolaides and former navy chief Vice-Adm. Rubén Oscar Franco. In April 2000 a mass grave was discovered in Lomas de Zamora, containing the remains of about 90 victims of the 'dirty war'. In July 2001 Videla was arrested, pending an inquiry into his role in 'Plan Condor', an alleged scheme among right-wing dictators in Argentina, Chile, Uruguay and Bolivia to eradicate leftist political opponents living in exile during the 1970s. In September he was ordered to stand trial for the abduction of 72 foreigners who were taken as part of 'Plan Condor'. In July 2002 former dictator Gen. Galtieri was arrested, along with at least 30 others, on charges relating to the kidnapping and murder of opponents during the 'dirty war'. Specifically, the charges concerned the torture and murder of 20 members of the Montoneros guerrilla group in 1980. In September he was imprisoned, along with 24 other former military officers, pending trial. (Galtieri remained under house arrest until his death in January 2003.)

In May 1985 a treaty was formally ratified by representatives of the Argentine and Chilean Governments, concluding the territorial dispute over three small islands in the Beagle Channel, south of Tierra del Fuego. The islands were awarded to Chile, while Argentine rights to petroleum and other minerals in the disputed waters were guaranteed. In August 1991 Argentina and Chile reached a settlement regarding claims to territory in the Antarctic region; however, the sovereignty of the territory remained under dispute, necessitating the signing of an additional protocol in late 1996. In December 1998 the Presidents of the two countries signed a new agreement on the border demarcation of the contested 'continental glaciers' territory in the Antarctic region (despite the 1991 treaty); the accord became effective in June 1999 following ratification by the Argentine and Chilean legislatures. Meanwhile, the two countries' navies held joint exercises for the first time in August 1998. In February 1999, during a meeting held in Ushuaia, southern Argentina, President Menem and the Chilean President, Eduardo Frei Ruiz-Tagle, signed a significant defence agreement and issued a joint declaration on both countries' commitment to the consolidation of their friendship.

Full diplomatic relations were restored with the United Kingdom in February 1990, following senior-level negotiations in Madrid, Spain. The improvement in relations between Argentina and the United Kingdom prompted the European Community (now European Union, see p. 199) to sign a new five-year trade and co-operation agreement with Argentina in April. In November Argentina and the United Kingdom concluded an agreement for the joint administration of a comprehensive protection programme for the lucrative South Atlantic fishing region. Subsequent agreements to regulate fishing in the area were made in 1992 and 1993. A diplomatic accord, signed in September 1991, significantly reduced military restrictions in the region, which the United Kingdom had imposed on Argentina following the Falklands conflict. The question of sovereignty over the disputed islands was not resolved. The results of preliminary seismic investigations (published in late 1993), which indicated rich petroleum deposits in the region, were expected to further complicate future negotiations. Although a comprehensive agreement on exploration was signed by both countries in New York, USA, in September 1995, negotiations on fishing rights in the region remained tense. In 1996 the Argentine Government suggested, for the first time, that it might consider shared sovereignty of the Falkland Islands with the United Kingdom. The proposal was firmly rejected by the British Government and by the Falkland Islanders, who reiterated their commitment to persuading the UN Special Political and Decolonization Committee to adopt a clause allowing the Islanders the right to self-determination. Anglo-Argentine relations improved in November 1996 when Lt-Gen. Martín Balza, the Chief of Staff of the Argentine Army, became the first high-ranking Argentine military official to visit the United Kingdom since 1982. Relations between Argentina and the United Kingdom were consolidated further in January 1997 when the two countries agreed to resume negotiations on a long-term fisheries accord. Moreover, in October 1998 President Menem made an official visit to the United Kingdom, during which he held talks with the British Prime Minister, Tony Blair, on issues including the arms embargo, defence, trade and investment. Notably, Menem paid tribute to the British servicemen who died during the 1982 conflict, while he also appealed for an 'imaginative' solution to the Falkland Islands sovereignty issue. Earlier in 1998 relations with the United Kingdom had been strained by the presentation of draft legislation to the Argentine Congress on the imposition of sanctions on petroleum companies and fishing vessels operating in Falkland Island waters without Argentine authorization. In late 1998 the United Kingdom partially lifted its arms embargo against Argentina. In May 1999 formal negotiations were held between the British and Argentine Governments and members of the Falkland Islands' legislature. Following further talks in July, an agreement was reached providing for an end to the ban on Argentine citizens visiting the Falkland Islands and for the restoration of air links between the islands and South America, with stopovers in Argentina to be introduced from October. In September Argentine and British government officials reached an understanding on co-operation against illegal fishing in the South Atlantic, and naval forces from both countries held joint exercises in the region in November. In August 2001 Tony Blair became the first British Prime Minister to make an official visit to Argentina; however, the issue of the sovereignty of the Falkland Islands was not discussed.

In March 1991 the Presidents of Argentina, Brazil, Paraguay and Uruguay signed the Asunción treaty in Paraguay, thereby confirming their commitment to the creation of a Southern Common Market, Mercosur (Mercado Común del Sur, see p. 316). Mercosur duly came into effect on 1 January 1995. While a complete common external tariff was not expected until 2006, customs barriers on 80%–85% of mutually exchanged goods were removed immediately. The effects of economic recession and the devaluation of the Brazilian currency in January 1999 provoked a series of trade disputes within Mercosur during that year, particularly between Argentina and Brazil, the two largest members.

In late 1997, following a visit to Argentina by the then US President, Bill Clinton, the US Congress declared Argentina a 'special non-NATO ally', affording the country privileged access to US surplus defence supplies and certain military funding. Chile and Brazil criticized the granting of the special status, claiming it would lead to a regional imbalance. In January 1999, during a visit by President Menem to Washington, DC, a number of US-Argentine defence agreements were signed, which aimed to enhance military co-operation between the two countries.

In 1996 a criminal investigation was begun in Spain regarding the torture, disappearance and killing of several hundred Spanish citizens in Argentina during 1976–83. A parallel investigation was instigated into the abduction of 54 children of Spanish victims during this period. In October 1997 Adolfo Scilingo, a former Argentine military official, was arrested in Madrid after admitting to his involvement in the 'dirty war'. During that year a Spanish High Court judge issued international arrest warrants for several other Argentine officers, including Adm. Massera and Gen. Galtieri. Following further investigations, in November 1999 international arrest warrants on charges of genocide, terrorism and torture were issued for 98 of those accused. Shortly afterwards Scilingo, now in prison in Spain awaiting trial, retracted his earlier confession, claiming that he had been pressured to lie under oath. In December the Spanish magistrate Baltasar Garzón issued international arrest warrants for 49 people, including former military presidents Videla and Galtieri, effectively confining them to Argentine territory. However, in January 2000 a federal judge refused to extradite them.

Government

For administrative purposes Argentina comprises 1,617 municipalities located in 22 provinces, the Federal District of Buenos Aires, and the National Territory of Tierra del Fuego.

Legislative power is vested in the bicameral Congress (Congreso): the Chamber of Deputies (Cámara de Diputados) has 257 members, elected by universal adult suffrage for a term of four years (with approximately one-half of the seats renewable every two years). In accordance with the amended Constitution, promulgated in August 1994, from 1995 legislative elections provided for an expanded Senate (Senado), which was eventually to have 72 members, with three members drawn from each of the 22 provinces, the Federal District of Buenos Aires and the National Territory of Tierra del Fuego. From 2001 all members of the expanded Senate were directly elected for a six-year term. The President is directly elected for a four-year term, renewable once. Each province has its own elected Governor and legislature, concerned with all matters not delegated to the federal Government.

Defence

Conscription was ended on 1 April 1995. The total strength of the regular armed forces in August 2002 was 69,900, comprising a 41,400-strong army, a 16,000-strong navy and an air force of 12,500 men. There were also paramilitary forces numbering 31,240 men. The defence budget for 2002 put defence expenditure at 3,300m. new pesos.

Economic Affairs

In 2001, according to estimates by the World Bank, Argentina's gross national income (GNI), measured at average 1999–2001 prices, was US $260,994m., equivalent to $6,960 per head (or $11,690 on an international purchasing-power parity basis). During 1990–2001, it was estimated, Argentina's population increased at an average rate of 1.3% per year, while gross domestic product (GDP) per head increased, in real terms, by an average of 2.5% per year. Overall GDP increased, in real terms, at an average annual rate of 3.8% in 1990–2001. Real GDP decreased by 0.8% in 2000, and by a further 4.5% in 2001.

Agriculture (including forestry and fishing) contributed an estimated 4.8% of GDP in 2001, and, in mid-2001, employed an estimated 9.5% of the labour force. The principal cash crops are wheat, maize, sorghum and soybeans. Beef production is also important. During 1990–2000 agricultural GDP increased at an average annual rate of 3.0%. The GDP of the sector increased by 1.6% in 1999, but declined by 2.5% in 2000.

Industry (including mining, manufacturing, construction and power) engaged 25.3% of the employed labour force in 1991 and provided an estimated 26.6% of GDP in 2001. During 1990–2000 industrial GDP increased, in real terms, at an estimated average annual rate of 3.8%.

Mining contributed an estimated 2.6% of GDP in 2001, and employed 0.4% of the working population in 1991. Argentina has substantial deposits of petroleum and natural gas, as well as steam coal and lignite. The GDP of the mining sector increased, in real terms, at an average rate of 7.3% per year during 1993–98; growth of 2.3% was recorded in 1998.

Manufacturing contributed an estimated 17.0% of GDP in 2001, and employed 17.3% of the working population in 1991. In 1993 the most important branches of manufacturing, measured by gross value of output, were food products and beverages (accounting for 26.4% of the total), chemical products (10.5%), transport equipment (9.9%) and petroleum refineries. During 1990–2000 manufacturing GDP increased, in real terms, at an estimated average annual rate of 2.8%. However, manufacturing GDP decreased by 7.7% in 1999, and by a further 3% in 2000.

Energy is derived principally from natural gas (responsible for the production of 55.1% of total primary energy consumption in 2000) and oil. In 2000 almost 3% of Argentina's total energy requirements were produced by its two nuclear power-stations. In 2001 imports of mineral fuels comprised 3.9% of the country's total imports.

Services engaged 62.7% of the employed labour force in 1991 and accounted for an estimated 68.6% of GDP in 2001. The combined GDP of the service sectors increased, in real terms, at an estimated average rate of 4.7% per year during 1990–2000; sectoral GDP decreased by 1.5% in 1999, but increased by 0.5% in 2000.

In 2001 Argentina recorded a visible trade surplus of US $7,451m., and there was a deficit of $4,554m. on the current account of the balance of payments. In 2001 (according to provisional figures) the principal source of imports (26%) was Brazil, followed by the USA (18%). Brazil also accounted for 23.5% of exports, a 3.5% decrease on the previous year. Other major trading partners in 2001 were the People's Republic of China, Chile and Spain. The principal exports in that year were food and live animals, machinery and transport equipment, mineral products and animal and vegetable oils and fats. The principal imports were machinery and transport equipment, chemical and mineral products, and basic manufactures.

In 2001 there was a budget deficit of 8,919.7m. new Argentine pesos, equivalent to 3.3% of GDP. Argentina's total external debt was US $146,172m. at the end of 2000, of which $86,599m. was long-term public debt. In that year, the total cost of debt-servicing was equivalent to 71.3% of revenue from exports of goods and services. The annual rate of inflation averaged 13.4% in 1990–2001; however, following deflation of 0.9% in 2000 and 1.1% in 2001, consumer prices once again increased in 2002, by 25.9%. The national unemployment rate, despite a slight decrease in 2001, reached a new record high of 2.8m. workers in May 2002 (equivalent to 21.4% of the labour force).

During 1986–90 Argentina signed a series of integration treaties with neighbouring Latin American countries, aimed at increasing bilateral trade and establishing the basis for a Latin American economic community. Argentina is a member of ALADI, see p. 259 and of Mercosur (see p. 316).

Economic growth in Argentina in the 1980s was hampered primarily by massive external debt obligations, limited access to financial aid and a scarcity of raw materials. The success of new economic measures introduced by the Government in the early 1990s (including a programme of privatization), drastically reduced inflation and helped to secure agreements to reschedule debt repayments and the disbursement of loans from international financial organizations. From mid-1998, however, the economy began to contract, with both trade and budget deficits widening, as international prices for certain commodities fell, adversely affecting exports. Exports declined further in 1999 following the devaluation of the Brazilian currency in January, and the economy entered recession; annual GDP declined by 3.4% in 1999. Further decreases in the price of commodity exports, as well as an uncompetitive US dollar (to which the peso was tied), and higher international interest rates, increased the debt burden, leading GDP to contract by 0.5% in 2000. As economic prospects continued to deteriorate, the Argentine Gov-

ernment agreed terms for a US $40,000m. loan from the IMF in December 2000. However, throughout 2001 fears of an imminent debt crisis deepened, in spite of an effective devaluation of the peso for foreign trade and renewed attempts to impose fiscal discipline. A series of austerity measures, culminating in a freeze on bank deposits in December, met with sustained popular opposition. Faced with declining tax revenues, the Government failed to secure any further IMF funding, and in January 2002 a major default on the country's sovereign debt (estimated at $155,000m.) and a 30% devaluation of the peso inevitably ensued. The de la Rúa administration collapsed, initiating a period of political, civil and economic turmoil. In November 2002 the Government of Eduardo Duhalde announced its intention to default on payment obligations to the World Bank and the Inter—American Development Bank (IDB), in the absence of a new agreement with the IMF. Both institutions ceased to disburse funds with immediate effect. However, in January 2003 a breakthrough was achieved following the signing of a new $6,700m. bridging agreement with the IMF, following the Government's decision to authorize repayments to creditor institutions from its international reserves. The deal also established closely-monitored economic performance targets, upon which disbursement would be conditional in mid-2003. In the same month the Central Bank announced the relaxation of exchange controls, the ending of which had also been an IMF condition. This followed the announcement, in November 2002, of the ending of the 'corralito' (the restrictions imposed on bank withdrawals), in force since December 2001. There had been fears that the end of the restrictions would result in a massive withdrawal of funds from the banking system. However, bank deposits had been increasing since the middle of the year and such fears were not realized.

In 2002 GDP contracted by an estimated 11.7%. However, by early 2003, despite domestic inflationary pressures and a slowdown in world trade, the economy had returned to growth, albeit meagre, and an increase in GDP of 2.0% was forecast for the year, with further growth of 5.0% predicted for 2004. Nevertheless, the economic situation remained precarious, and recovery was largely dependent on the maintenance of political stability, particularly in the months following the presidential elections that were scheduled to be held in April 2003.

Education

Education from pre-school to university level is available free of charge. Education is officially compulsory for all children at primary level, between the ages of six and 14 years. Secondary education lasts for between five and seven years, depending on the type of course: the normal certificate of education (bachillerato) course lasts for five years, whereas a course leading to a technical or agricultural bachillerato lasts for six years. Technical education is supervised by the Consejo Nacional de Educación Técnica. The total enrolment at primary and secondary schools in 1996 was estimated at 99.4% and 67.2% of the school-age population, respectively. Non-university higher education, usually leading to a teaching qualification, is for three or four years, while university courses last for four years or more. There are 36 state universities and 48 private universities. Government expenditure on education, culture, science and technology in 2000 was 3,747.1m. new pesos (7.6% of total public expenditure).

Public Holidays

2003: 1 January (New Year's Day), 18 April (Good Friday), 1 May (Labour Day), 25 May (Anniversary of the 1810 Revolution), 9 June (for Occupation of the Islas Malvinas), 23 June (for Flag Day), 9 July (Independence Day), 18 August (for Death of Gen. José de San Martín), 13 October (for Columbus Day), 25 December (Christmas).

2004: 1 January (New Year's Day), 9 April (Good Friday), 1 May (Labour Day), 25 May (Anniversary of the 1810 Revolution), 8 June (for Occupation of the Islas Malvinas), 21 June (for Flag Day), 9 July (Independence Day), 16 August (for Death of Gen. José de San Martín), 11 October (for Columbus Day), 25 December (Christmas).

Weights and Measures

The metric system is in force.

Statistical Survey

Sources (unless otherwise stated): Instituto Nacional de Estadística y Censos, Avda Julio A. Roca 609, 1067 Buenos Aires; tel. (11) 4349-9613; fax (11) 4349-9601; e-mail okace@indec.mecon.ar; internet www.indec.mecon.ar; and Banco Central de la República Argentina, Reconquista 266, 1003 Buenos Aires; tel. (11) 4394-8111; fax (11) 4334-5712; internet www.bcra.gov.ar.

Area and Population

AREA, POPULATION AND DENSITY

Area (sq km)	2,780,400*
Population (census results)†	
15 May 1991	32,615,528
17–18 November 2001 (provisional results)	
Males	17,667,874
Females.	18,556,073
Total	36,223,947
Population (official estimates at mid-year)‡	
1999	36,578,358
2000	37,031,802
2001	37,486,938
Density (per sq km) at 2001 census	13.0

* 1,073,518 sq miles. The figure excludes the Falkland Islands (Islas Malvinas) and Antarctic territory claimed by Argentina.
† Figures exclude adjustment for underenumeration, estimated to have been 0.9% at the 1991 census.
‡ Not revised to take account of 2001 census.

PROVINCES

(2001, provisional census results)

	Area (sq km)	Population	Density (per sq km)	Capital
Buenos Aires— Federal District .	200	2,768,772	13,843.9	
Buenos Aires— Province . .	307,571	13,818,677	44.9	La Plata
Catamarca . .	102,602	333,661	3.3	San Fernando del Valle de Catamarca
Chaco . .	99,633	983,087	9.9	Resistencia
Chubut . .	224,686	413,240	1.8	Rawson
Córdoba . .	165,321	3,061,611	18.5	Córdoba
Corrientes . .	88,199	929,236	10.5	Corrientes
Entre Ríos . .	78,781	1,156,799	14.7	Paraná
Formosa . .	72,066	485,700	6.7	Formosa
Jujuy . .	53,219	611,484	11.5	San Salvador de Jujuy
La Pampa . .	143,440	298,460	2.1	Santa Rosa
La Rioja . .	89,680	289,820	3.2	La Rioja
Mendoza . .	148,827	1,576,585	10.6	Mendoza
Misiones . .	29,801	963,869	32.3	Posadas
Neuquén . .	94,078	473,315	5.0	Neuquén
Río Negro . .	203,013	552,677	2.7	Viedma
Salta . .	155,488	1,079,422	6.9	Salta
San Juan . .	89,651	622,094	6.9	San Juan
San Luis . .	76,748	366,900	4.8	San Luis
Santa Cruz . .	243,943	197,191	0.8	Río Gallegos
Santa Fe . .	133,007	2,997,376	22.5	Santa Fe
Santiago del Estero	136,351	806,347	5.9	Santiago del Estero
Tucumán . .	22,524	1,336,664	59.3	San Miguel de Tucumán
Territory				
Tierra del Fuego .	21,571	100,960	4.7	Ushuaia
Total . .	2,780,400	36,223,947	13.0	Buenos Aires

Population (revised census results for 2001): Buenos Aires—Federal District 2,776,138; Chaco 984,446; Chubut 413,237; Corrientes 930,991; Formosa 486,104; Jujuy 611,888; Mendoza 1,579,651; La Pampa 299,294; La Rioja 289,983; Misiones 965,522; Neuquén 474,155; Rio Negro 552,822; Salta 1,079,051; Santa Cruz 196,958; Tierra del Fuego 101,079.

PRINCIPAL TOWNS

(population at 1991 census)*

Buenos Aires (capital). . .	2,965,403	San Isidro. . . .	299,023
Córdoba . . .	1,157,507	Vicente López . .	289,505
San Justo		Moreno . . .	287,715
(La Matanza) . .	1,121,298	Esteban Echeverría	275,793
Rosario . . .	907,718	Bahía Blanca . .	260,096
General Sarmiento .	652,969	Corrientes. . . .	258,103
Morón	643,553	Tigre	257,922
Lomas de		Florencio Varela . .	254,997
Zamora . . .	574,330	Berazategui . .	244,929
La Plata . . .	521,936	Resistencia . . .	229,212
Mar del Plata . .	512,880	Paraná . . .	207,041
Quilmes . . .	511,234	Posadas . . .	201,273
San Miguel de		Villa Nueva	
Tucumán . .	470,809	(Guaymallén) . .	200,595
Lanús . . .	468,561	Santiago del Estero	189,947
Almirante Brown .	450,698	Godoy Cruz . .	179,588
General San		San Salvador de	
Martín . . .	406,809	Jujuy	178,748
Merlo	390,858	Neuquén . . .	167,296
Salta	367,550	Formosa . . .	147,636
Santa Fe . . .	353,063	Las Heras. . . .	145,823
Caseros . . .	349,376	San Fernando . .	141,063
Avellaneda . . .	344,991	Río Cuarto . .	134,355

* In each case the figures refer to the city proper. At the 1991 census the population of the Buenos Aires agglomeration was 11,298,030.

2001 (revised census result): Buenos Aires (capital) 2,776,138.

BIRTHS AND DEATHS

	Registered live births		Registered deaths	
	Number	Rate (per 1,000)	Number	Rate (per 1,000)
1993	667,518	19.8	267,286	7.9
1994	707,869	20.7	260,245	7.6
1995	658,735	18.9	268,997	7.7
1996	675,437	19.2	268,715	7.6
1997	692,357	19.4	270,910	7.6
1998	683,301	18.9	280,180	7.8
1999	686,748	18.8	289,543	7.9
2000*	701,878	19.0	277,148	7.5

* Provisional figures.
Source: mainly UN, *Demographic Yearbook* and *Population and Vital Statistics Report*.

Marriages: 158,805 (marriage rate 4.6 per 1,000) in 1995; 148,721 (4.2 per 1,000) in 1996.

Expectation of life (WHO estimates, years at birth): 73.9 (males 70.1; females 77.7) in 2001 (Source: WHO, *World Health Report*).

ECONOMICALLY ACTIVE POPULATION

(persons aged 14 years and over, census of 15 May 1991)

	Males	Females	Total
Agriculture, hunting, forestry and fishing	1,142,674	222,196	1,364,870
Mining and quarrying	43,905	3,525	47,430
Manufacturing	1,590,713	546,090	2,136,803
Electricity, gas and water	92,469	11,318	103,787
Construction	818,831	17,617	836,448
Wholesale and retail trade restaurants and hotels	1,730,600	808,702	2,539,302
Transport, storage and communication	583,938	54,024	637,962
Finance, insurance, real estate and business services	432,264	222,757	655,021
Community, social and personal services	1,459,492	2,464,552	3,924,044
Activities not adequately described	81,013	41,648	122,661
Total employed	7,975,899	4,392,429	12,368,328
Unemployed	447,488	386,384	833,872
Total labour force	8,423,387	4,778,813	13,202,200

1995 (provisional figures, sample survey, persons aged 15 years and over): Total active population 14,345,171 (males 9,087,075; females 5,258,096) (Source: ILO, *Yearbook of Labour Statistics*).

Mid-2001 (estimates in '000): Agriculture, etc. 1,462; Total labour force 15,335 (Source: FAO).

Health and Welfare

KEY INDICATORS

Total fertility rate (children per woman, 2001)	2.5
Under-5 mortality rate (per 1,000 live births, 2001)	19
HIV (% of persons aged 15–49, 2001)	0.69
Physicians (per 1,000 head, 1992)	2.68
Hospital beds (per 1,000 head, 1996)	3.29
Health expenditure (2000): US $ per head (PPP)	1,091
Health expenditure (2000): % of GDP	8.6
Health expenditure (2000): public (% of total)	55
Access to water (% of persons, 2000)	79
Access to sanitation (% of persons, 2000)	85
Human Development Index (2000): ranking	34
Human Development Index (2000): value	0.844

For sources and definitions, see explanatory note on p. vi.

Agriculture

PRINCIPAL CROPS

('000 metric tons)

	1999	2000	2001
Wheat	15,479	16,147	15,300
Rice (paddy)	1,658	904	859
Barley	420	717	722
Maize	13,504	16,817	15,365
Rye	116	125	108
Oats	554	644	644
Sorghum	3,222	3,351	2,905
Potatoes	2,700	2,221	2,050*
Sweet potatoes	335	254	335*
Cassava (Manioc)*	175	170	170
Sugar cane†	16,700	16,000	15,000
Dry beans	340	297	270
Soybeans (Soya beans)	20,000	20,207	26,737
Groundnuts (in shell)	486	600	563
Olives*	85	95	95
Cottonseed†	337	223	257
Sunflower seed	7,125	6,070	3,179
Linseed	86	47	22
Artichokes*	85	85	85
Tomatoes	720	675	700*
Pumpkins, squash and gourds	327	321	325*
Chillies and green peppers	126	121	121*
Dry onions	850	660	673*
Garlic	145	143	131
Carrots	222	218*	220*
Other vegetables*	720	720	720
Bananas	175*	175	175*
Oranges	706	787	861†
Tangerines, mandarins, clementines and satsumas	346	438	474†
Lemons and limes	1,043	1,171	1,180†
Grapefruit and pomelos	205	218	191†
Apples	1,116	833	1,428
Pears	537	514	585
Peaches and nectarines	240	205	252
Plums	78	75	105
Grapes	2,425	2,191†	2,458†
Watermelons*	125	125	125
Cantaloupes and other melons	67	63	64*
Tea (made)	56	52	50*
Mate	270	272	285*
Tobacco (leaves)	113	115	101†
Cotton (lint)*	196	130	160

* FAO estimate(s).
† Unofficial figure(s).

Source: FAO.

LIVESTOCK

('000 head, year ending September)

	1999	2000*	2001
Horses*	3,600	3,600	3,600
Mules*	180	180	180
Asses*	95	95	95
Cattle	49,057	48,674	50,167†
Pigs*	4,200	4,200	4,200
Sheep	13,703	13,562	13,500*
Goats	3,403	3,490	3,500*
Chickens*	107,000	109,000	110,000
Ducks*	2,300	2,300	2,300
Geese*	130	130	130
Turkeys*	2,800	2,800	2,850

* FAO estimate(s).
† Unofficial figure.

Source: FAO.

LIVESTOCK PRODUCTS

('000 metric tons)

	1999	2000	2001
Beef and veal	2,720	2,683	2,640
Mutton and lamb	45*	50†	50†
Pig meat	215	214	214†
Horse meat†	55	55	55
Poultry meat	983	1,000	971
Cows' milk	10,649	9,933	9,500*
Butter	55*	60†	60†
Cheese*	445	468	420
Hen eggs	319	325	325†
Honey	93	98	90*
Wool: greasy	65	58	58*
Wool: scoured	36*	32*	32†
Cattle hides (fresh)† . . .	364	369	369
Sheepskins (fresh)† . . .	23	23	23

* Unofficial figure(s).
† FAO estimate(s).

Source: FAO.

Forestry

ROUNDWOOD REMOVALS

('000 cubic metres, excl. bark)

	1998	1999	2000
Sawlogs, veneer logs and logs for sleepers	735	3,547	2,091
Pulpwood	3,784	2,944	3,794
Other industrial wood . . .	119	161	120
Fuel wood	1,103	3,950	3,965
Total	5,741	10,602	9,970

2001: Production as in 2000 (FAO estimates).

Source: FAO.

SAWNWOOD PRODUCTION

('000 cubic metres, incl. railway sleepers)

	1998	1999	2000
Coniferous (softwood) . . .	744	686	619
Broadleaved (hardwood) . . .	633	722	202
Total	1,377	1,408	821

2001: Production as in 2000 (FAO estimates).

Source: FAO.

Fishing

('000 metric tons, live weight)

	1998	1999	2000
Capture	1,138.7*	1,037.8*	917.7
Southern blue whiting . .	71.6	55.1	61.3
Argentine hake . . .	458.4	312.0	193.9
Patagonian grenadier . . .	96.2	117.6	123.6
Argentine red shrimp . . .	23.2	15.9	36.8
Patagonean scallop . . .	3.5	4.7	36.9
Argentine shortfin squid . .	291.2	342.7	279.0
Aquaculture	1.0*	1.2	1.7
Total catch	1,139.7*	1,039.0*	919.5

* FAO estimate.

Note: The data exclude aquatic plants (metric tons, capture only): 500 in 1998 (FAO estimate); 100 in 1999 (FAO estimate); 3 in 2000. Also excluded are aquatic mammals, recorded by number rather than by weight. The number of toothed whales caught was 15 in 1998 and 445 in 2000.

Source: FAO, *Yearbook of Fishery Statistics*.

Mining

('000 metric tons, unless otherwise indicated)

	1999	2000*	2001*
Crude petroleum ('000 cu metres) .	46,507	44,679	45,174
Natural gas (million cu metres) .	42,414	44,870	45,917
Lead ore†	14.3	14.1	12.3
Zinc ore†	34.2	34.9	39.7
Silver ore (kilograms)† . . .	73,785	78,271	152,802
Uranium ore (metric tons)† . . .	4	—	—
Gold ore (kilograms)†	38,515	25,954	30,630

* Estimates.
† Figures refer to the metal content of ores and concentrates.
Source: mainly US Geological Survey.

Industry

SELECTED PRODUCTS

('000 metric tons, unless otherwise indicated)

	1999	2000	2001
Wheat flour	3,605	3,595	3,537
Beer (sales, '000 hectolitres) . .	12,503	12,090	12,390
Cigarettes (million units) . .	1,996	1,843	739
Paper and paper products . .	1,130	1,214	1,229*
Rubber tyres for motor vehicles ('000)	8,250	8,636	8,037
Portland cement	7,187	6,114	5,545
Distillate fuel oils . . .	12,727	12,309	12,224
Residual fuel oils	1,692	1,537	1,782
Motor spirit (petrol) ('000 cu metres)	7,867	7,245	7,160
Kerosene ('000 cu metres) . .	171	n.a.	n.a.
Passenger motor vehicles ('000 units)	225	239	170
Refrigerators ('000 units) . . .	354*	325	246*
Washing machines ('000 units) . .	279	317	308
Television receivers ('000) . . .	1,335	1,556	1,201*
Electric energy (million kWh) . .	78,493*	n.a.	n.a.

* Provisional figure.

Finance

CURRENCY AND EXCHANGE RATES

Monetary Units
  100 centavos = 1 nuevo peso argentino (new Argentine peso).

Sterling, Dollar and Euro Equivalents (31 December 2002)
  £1 sterling = 5.351 nuevos pesos
  US $1 = 3.320 neuvos pesos
  €1 = 3.482 neuvos pesos
  100 nuevos pesos = £18.69 = $30.12 = €28.72.

Average Exchange Rate (nuevos pesos per US $)
  2002   3.0633
Note: From April 1996 to December 2001 the official exchange rate was fixed at US $1 = 99.95 centavos. In January 2002 the Government abandoned this exchange rate and devalued the peso: initially there was a fixed official exchange rate of US $1 = 1.40 nuevos pesos for trade and financial transactions, while a free market rate was applicable to other transactions. In February, however, a unified 'floating' exchange rate system, with the rate to be determined by market conditions, was introduced.

BUDGET
(million new pesos)*

Revenue	1999	2000	2001
Tax revenue	35,387.8	36,785.4	33,511.1
Taxes on income and profits	6,434.5	6,866.2	6,655.2
Social security contributions	9,654.9	9,437.5	8,455.4
Taxes on property	541.8	1,284.2	3,432.8
Taxes on goods and services	16,497.6	17,179.1	13,337.4
Taxes on international trade and transactions	2,210.6	1,971.7	1,586.1
Other current revenue	4,330.0	3,507.8	3,508.5
Property income	1,510.0	1,461.4	1,460.3
Fees and charges	2,601.4	1,772.8	1,750.9
Capital revenue	47.4	52.8	74.3
Total	37,765.2	40,346.0	37,093.9

Expenditure†	1999	2000	2001
General public services	5,118.7	4,422.5	4,028.6
Defence	2,044.2	1,907.1	1,757.6
Public order and safety	1,458.3	1,448.3	1,386.2
Education	3,023.4	3,029.7	2,632.4
Health	1,045.5	904.4	818.7
Social security and welfare	23,280.3	23,369.0	22,009.2
Housing and community amenities	900.5	1,015.3	752.4
Recreational, cultural and religious affairs and services	114.5	100.1	65.0
Economic affairs and services	2,806.3	2,264.8	2,172.4
Transport and communications	1,503.5	1,251.2	1,145.1
Other expenditures	8,324.5	9,798.6	10,433.6
Sub-total	48,116.2	48,259.8	46,056.1
Adjustment	−59.6	−35.1	−42.7
Total	48,056.6	48,224.7	46,013.4
Current‡	44,986.3	45,332.6	43,548.1
Capital	3,070.3	2,892.1	2,465.3

* Budget figures refer to the consolidated accounts of the central Government.

† Excluding lending minus repayments (million new pesos): −111.8 in 1999; −1,410.7 in 2000; −44.1 in 2001.

‡ Including interest payments (million new pesos): 8,200.6 in 1999; 9,617.7 in 2000; 10,170.0 in 2001.

Source: IMF, *Government Finance Statistics Yearbook*.

INTERNATIONAL RESERVES
(US $ million at 31 December)

	2000	2001	2002
Gold*	7	3	3
IMF special drawing rights	733	11	94
Foreign exchange	24,414	14,542	10,395
Total	25,154	14,556	10,492

* National valuation.

Source: IMF, *International Financial Statistics*.

MONEY SUPPLY
(million new pesos at 31 December)

	2000	2001	2002
Currency outside banks	12,571	9,081	16,657
Demand deposits at commercial banks	7,267	6,763	12,026
Total money	19,838	15,844	28,683

Source: IMF, *International Financial Statistics*.

COST OF LIVING
(Consumer Price Index for Buenos Aires metropolitan area; annual averages; base: 1999 = 100)

	1998	2000	2001
Food and beverages	105.6	99.1	97.2
Clothing	105.3	97.0	92.6
Housing	98.5	99.7	99.2
All items (incl. others)	102.0	99.9	98.8

NATIONAL ACCOUNTS
(million new pesos at current prices)

National Income and Product

	1999	2000	2001
Gross domestic product (GDP) at market prices	283,523	284,204	268,697
Net primary income from abroad	−7,472	−7,372	−8,094
Gross national income (GNI)	276,051	276,832	260,603

Source: IMF, *International Financial Statistics*.

Expenditure on the Gross Domestic Product

	1999	2000	2001
Final consumption expenditure	237,777	236,219	223,201
Households*	198,869	197,044	185,164
General government	38,908	39,175	38,037
Gross capital formation	50,696	49,786	42,153
Gross fixed capital formation	51,074	46,020	38,099
Changes in inventories	−378	3,766	4,054
Total domestic expenditure	288,473	286,005	265,354
Exports of goods and services	27,751	30,937	30,700
Less Imports of goods and services	32,702	32,738	27,358
Gross domestic product (GDP) in market prices	283,523	284,204	268,697
GDP at constant 1993 prices	278,369	276,173	263,870

* Including non-profit institutions serving households (NPISHs).

Source: IMF, *International Financial Statistics*.

Gross Domestic Product by Economic Activity

	1999	2000*	2001*
Agriculture, hunting and forestry	12,080	12,725	11,565
Fishing	559	575	711
Mining and quarrying	4,674	7,098	6,657
Manufacturing	48,090	46,877	43,242
Electricity, gas and water supply	6,133	6,584	6,332
Construction	15,368	13,308	11,597
Wholesale and retail trade	37,662	36,110	32,831
Hotels and restaurants	7,966	7,796	7,309
Transport, storage and communications	23,485	24,137	22,873
Financial intermediation	11,518	11,517	13,762
Real estate, renting and business activities	44,511	44,501	42,697
Public administration and defence†	17,503	17,803	17,117
Education, health and social work	23,184	24,067	24,052
Other community, social and personal service activities‡	14,174	14,451	14,232
Sub-total	266,906	267,550	254,976
Value-added tax	18,771	19,009	16,233
Import duties	2,278	1,976	1,575
Less Imputed bank service charge	4,432	4,331	4,087
GDP in purchasers' values	283,523	284,204	268,697

* Provisional figures.

† Including extra-territorial organizations and bodies.

‡ Including private households with employed persons.

BALANCE OF PAYMENTS
(US $ million)

	1999	2000	2001
Exports of goods f.o.b.	23,309	26,410	26,610
Imports of goods f.o.b.	−24,103	−23,852	−19,159
Trade balance	**−795**	**2,558**	**7,451**
Exports of services	4,556	4,704	4,310
Imports of services	−8,662	−9,011	−8,403
Balance on goods and services	**−4,901**	**−1,749**	**3,357**
Other income received	6,160	7,520	5,660
Other income paid	−13,558	−14,892	−13,755
Balance on goods, services and income	**−12,298**	**−9,121**	**−4,738**
Current transfers received	704	601	572
Current transfers paid	−307	−360	−389
Current balance	**−11,902**	**−8,879**	**−4,554**
Capital account (net)	86	87	101
Direct investment abroad	−1,175	−1,018	123
Direct investment from abroad	23,988	11,657	3,214
Portfolio investment assets	−2,128	−1,060	2,019
Portfolio investment liabilities	−4,780	−1,331	−9,516
Other investment assets	−2,817	−1,764	−3,940
Other investment liabilities	1,838	2,287	−5,490
Net errors and omissions	−1,098	−1,154	−3,361
Overall balance	**2,013**	**−1,176**	**−21,405**

Source: IMF, *International Financial Statistics*.

External Trade

PRINCIPAL COMMODITIES
(provisional, US $ million)

Imports c.i.f.	1999	2000	2001
Prepared foodstuffs; beverages, spirits and vinegar; tobacco and manufactured substitutes	614.7	618.4	629.4
Mineral products	875.4	1,170.9	1,002.2
Mineral fuels, mineral oils and products of their distillation	676.0	927.8	794.6
Products of chemical or allied industries	3,915.9	3,935.6	3,614.4
Organic chemicals	1,342.9	1,429.8	1,319.9
Pharmaceutical products	646.8	647.6	638.6
Plastics, rubber and articles thereof	1,555.6	1,681.0	1,393.9
Plastics and articles thereof	1,133.1	1,220.6	1,035.6
Paper-making material; paper and paperboard and articles thereof	1,119.1	1,112.7	923.6
Paper and paperboard; articles of paper pulp, of paper or of paperboard	811.6	810.8	681.0
Textiles and textile articles	926.7	989.6	813.9
Base metals and articles thereof	1,609.3	1,453.8	1,305.6
Machinery and mechanical appliances; electrical equipment; sound and television apparatus	8,135.3	8,158.3	6,083.5
Nuclear reactors, boilers machinery and mechanical appliances	4,792.9	4,172.8	3,521.9
Electrical machinery and equipment and parts; sound and television apparatus, parts and accessories	3,342.3	3,985.5	2,561.6
Vehicles, aircraft, vessels and associated transport equipment	3,795.9	3,121.3	2,123.6
Vehicles other than railway or tramway rolling-stock, and parts and accessories	2,959.4	2,715.4	1,877.4
Optical, photographic cinematographic measuring, precision and medical apparatus; clocks and watches; musical instruments	784.6	779.0	620.3
Total (incl. others)	25,508.2	25,242.9	20,311.6

Exports f.o.b.	1999	2000	2001
Live animals and animal products	1,934.3	1,880.7	1,509.8
Fish, crustaceans, molluscs, etc.	780.7	822.5	896.0
Vegetable products	3,895.9	4,315.5	4,796.7
Cereals	2,062.9	2,414.2	2,434.9
Oil seeds and oleaginous fruits; miscellaneous grains, seeds and fruit; industrial or medicinal plants; straw and fodder	869.5	1,013.5	1,373.7
Animal or vegetable fats, oils and waxes	2,331.5	1,677.3	1,654.7
Prepared foodstuffs; beverages, spirits and vinegar; tobacco and manufactured substitutes	3,343.3	3,641.1	3,807.0
Residues and waste from food industries; prepared animal fodder	2,049.3	2,432.4	2,621.0
Mineral products	3,331.3	5,123.6	5,036.8
Mineral fuels, mineral oils and products of their distillation	2,828.7	4,678.9	4,495.8
Products of chemical or allied industries	1,504.9	1,519.6	1,566.2
Raw hides and skins, leather furskins and articles thereof; saddlery and harness; travel goods, handbags, etc	834.6	884.2	912.3
Raw hides and skins (other than furskins) and leather	752.2	809.9	814.7
Base metals and articles thereof	1,076.6	1,406.6	1,432.3
Machinery and mechanical appliances; electrical equipment; sound and television apparatus	1,052.5	1,097.8	1,138.6
Nuclear reactors, boilers machinery and mechanical appliances	786.8	807.1	805.8
Vehicles, aircraft, vessels and associated transport equipment	1,751.4	2,267.3	2,202.9
Vehicles other than railway or tramway rolling-stock, and parts and accessories	1,628.1	1,949.2	2,007.9
Total (incl. others)	23,332.7	26,409.5	26,655.2

PRINCIPAL TRADING PARTNERS
(provisional, US $ million)*

Imports c.i.f.	1999	2000	2001
Belgium	259.2	216.0	168.2
Brazil†	5,599.0	6,478.4	5,277.4
Canada	290.1	307.1	201.5
Chile†	638.5	608.1	505.7
China, People's Republic	992.1	1,156.7	1,065.3
France (incl. Monaco)	1,503.8	994.6	737.2
Germany	1,409.4	1,261.8	1,051.3
Italy (incl. San Marino)	1,354.7	1,014.3	839.7
Japan	1,068.4	1,006.1	767.2
Korea, Republic	563.8	533.2	409.2
Mexico	490.7	583.3	434.9
Paraguay	304.1	294.8	302.8
Spain	999.9	903.6	712.9
Sweden	311.7	314.7	173.9
Switzerland	294.5	227.8	186.8
Taiwan	299.3	278.8	230.3
United Kingdom	542.6	449.2	407.2
USA	4,941.6	4,731.7	3,737.1
Uruguay†	395.8	426.1	328.4
Total (incl. others)	25,508.2	25,242.9	20,311.6

Exports f.o.b.	1999	2000	2001
Belgium	309.6	311.0	285.1
Bolivia	321.3	266.4	260.0
Brazil†	5,689.6	6,991.3	6,272.5
Canada	239.3	283.1	241.6
Chile†	1,869.0	2,670.6	2,780.3
China, People's Republic	507.9	796.2	1,109.2
Egypt	386.3	348.8	344.1
France (incl. Monaco)	349.5	536.9	261.9
Germany	629.1	608.4	464.1
India	436.8	442.5	446.3
Iran	155.3	348.5	419.3
Italy (incl. San Marino)	688.7	731.9	843.3
Japan	527.5	398.8	384.5
Korea, Republic	181.3	165.5	429.5
Malaysia	221.1	242.8	301.0
Mexico	281.6	325.7	488.9
Netherlands	1,013.0	745.9	792.0
Paraguay	563.1	592.2	487.5
Peru	212.7	293.4	394.7
South Africa	308.4	243.0	321.2
Spain	962.0	914.7	1,089.7
Thailand	169.7	187.9	310.5
United Kingdom	263.4	261.5	304.2
USA	2,628.3	3,110.8	2,849.6
Uruguay†	818.6	818.3	752.4
Venezuela	247.0	217.6	236.2
Total (incl. others)	23,332.7	26,409.5	26,655.2

* Imports by country of origin; exports by country of destination.
† Including free-trade zones.

Transport

RAILWAYS
(traffic)

	1998	1999	2000
Passengers carried (million)	480	481	n.a.
Freight carried ('000 tons)	18,828	17,489	n.a.
Passenger-km (million)	9,652	9,102	8,939
Freight ton-km (million)	9,824	9,101	8,696

Source: UN, *Statistical Yearbook*.

ROAD TRAFFIC
(motor vehicles in use)

	1996	1997	1998
Passenger cars	4,783,908	4,901,265	5,047,630
Buses and coaches	38,434	40,191	43,232
Lorries and vans	1,248,527	1,332,344	1,453,335
Motorcycles and mopeds	35,640	n.a.	n.a.

Source: International Road Federation, *World Road Statistics*.

SHIPPING

Merchant Fleet
(registered at 31 December)

	1999	2000	2001
Number of vessels	493	493	478
Total displacement ('000 grt)	477.3	464.3	421.6

Source: Lloyd's Register-Fairplay, *World Fleet Statistics*.

International Sea-borne Freight Traffic
('000 metric tons)

	1996	1997	1998
Goods loaded	52,068	58,512	69,372
Goods unloaded	16,728	19,116	19,536

Source: UN, *Monthly Bulletin of Statistics*.

CIVIL AVIATION
(traffic on scheduled services)

	1997	1998	1999
Kilometres flown (million)	155	157	170
Passengers carried ('000)	8,603	8,623	9,192
Passenger-km (million)	14,348	14,379	14,024
Total ton-km (million)	1,566	1,597	1,559

Source: UN, *Statistical Yearbook*.

Tourism

TOURISM ARRIVALS BY REGION
('000)

	1998	1999	2000†
Europe	341.4	336.7	354.0
USA	263.9	249.8	280.0
South America:			
Bolivia	145.2	101.7	95.1
Brazil	466.1	451.8	466.0
Chile	527.6	541.2	568.0
Paraguay	478.3	515.9	499.8
Uruguay	544.9	513.7	488.0
Total (incl. others)*	2,969.8	2,898.4	2,949.1

* Excluding nationals residing abroad.
† Preliminary figures.

Tourism receipts (US $ million): 2,888 in 1998; 2,812 in 1999; 2,903 in 2000 (Source: World Tourism Statistics).

Communications Media

	1999	2000	2001
Television receivers ('000 in use)*	10,900	11,200	n.a.
Telephones ('000 main lines in use)	7,356.8	7,894.2	8,108.0
Mobile cellular telephones ('000 subscribers)	4,434.0	6,050.0	6,974.9
Personal computers ('000 in use)*	1,700	1,900	2,000
Internet users ('000)*	500	2,500	3,000

* Estimates.

Radio receivers ('000 in use): 24,300 in 1997.

Facsimile machines (estimate, '000 in use): 87 in 1998.

Book production: 13,149 titles in 2000.

Daily newspapers: 34 in 1998.

Sources: mainly UNESCO, *Statistical Yearbook* , and International Telecommunication Union.

Education

(1999)

	Institutions	Students	Teachers
Pre-primary	15,946	1,180,733	77,103
Primary	22,283	4,609,077	307,874
Secondary	21,492	3,281,512	127,718
Universities*	36	945,790	113,797
Colleges of higher education	1,708	391,010	12,427

* 1998 figures for state universities only.

Source: Ministerio de Cultura y Educación.

Adult literacy rate (UNESCO estimates): 96.8% (males 96.8%; females 96.8%) in 2000 (Source: UN Development Programme, *Human Development Report*).

Directory

The Constitution

The return to civilian rule in 1983 represented a return to the principles of the 1853 Constitution, with some changes in electoral details. In August 1994 a new Constitution was approved, which contained 19 new articles, 40 amendments to existing articles and the addition of a chapter on New Rights and Guarantees. The Constitution is summarized below:

DECLARATIONS, RIGHTS AND GUARANTEES

Each province has the right to exercise its own administration of justice, municipal system and primary education. The Roman Catholic religion, being the faith of the majority of the nation, shall enjoy state protection; freedom of religious belief is guaranteed to all other denominations. The prior ethnical existence of indigenous peoples and their rights, as well as the common ownership of lands they traditionally occupy, are recognized. All inhabitants of the country have the right to work and exercise any legal trade; to petition the authorities; to leave or enter the Argentine territory; to use or dispose of their properties; to associate for a peaceable or useful purpose; to teach and acquire education, and to express freely their opinion in the press without censorship. The State does not admit any prerogative of blood, birth, privilege or titles of nobility. Equality is the basis of all duties and public offices. No citizens may be detained, except for reasons and in the manner prescribed by the law; or sentenced other than by virtue of a law existing prior to the offence and by decision of the competent tribunal after the hearing and defence of the person concerned. Private residence, property and correspondence are inviolable. No one may enter the home of a citizen or carry out any search in it without his consent, unless by a warrant from the competent authority; no one may suffer expropriation, except in case of public necessity and provided that the appropriate compensation has been paid in accordance with the provisions of the laws. In no case may the penalty of confiscation of property be imposed.

LEGISLATIVE POWER

Legislative power is vested in the bicameral Congreso (Congress), comprising the Cámara de Diputados (Chamber of Deputies) and the Senado (Senate). The Chamber of Deputies has 257 directly-elected members, chosen for four years and eligible for re-election; approximately one-half of the membership of the Chamber shall be renewed every two years. Until October 1995 the Senate had 48 members, chosen by provincial legislatures for a nine-year term, with one-third of the seats renewable every three years. Since October 1995 elections have provided for a third senator, elected by provincial legislatures. From 2001 all members of the expanded Senate were directly elected for a six-year term.

The powers of Congress include regulating foreign trade; fixing import and export duties; levying taxes for a specified time whenever the defence, common safety or general welfare of the State so requires; contracting loans on the nation's credit; regulating the internal and external debt and the currency system of the country; fixing the budget and facilitating the prosperity and welfare of the nation. Congress must approve required and urgent decrees and delegated legislation. Congress also approves or rejects treaties, authorizes the Executive to declare war or make peace, and establishes the strength of the Armed Forces in peace and war.

EXECUTIVE POWER

Executive power is vested in the President, who is the supreme head of the nation and controls the general administration of the country. The President issues the instructions and rulings necessary for the execution of the laws of the country, and himself takes part in drawing up and promulgating those laws. The President appoints, with the approval of the Senate, the judges of the Supreme Court and all other competent tribunals, ambassadors, civil servants, members of the judiciary and senior officers of the Armed Forces and bishops. The President may also appoint and remove, without reference to another body, his cabinet ministers. The President is Commander-in-Chief of all the Armed Forces. The President and Vice-President are elected directly for a four-year term, renewable only once.

JUDICIAL POWER

Judicial power is exercised by the Supreme Court and all other competent tribunals. The Supreme Court is responsible for the internal administration of all tribunals. In April 1990 the number of Supreme Court judges was increased from five to nine.

PROVINCIAL GOVERNMENT

The 22 provinces, the Federal District of Buenos Aires and the National Territory of Tierra del Fuego retain all the power not delegated to the Federal Government. They are governed by their own institutions and elect their own governors, legislators and officials.

The Government

HEAD OF STATE

President of the Republic: EDUARDO ALBERTO DUHALDE (took office 2 January 2002).

CABINET
(April 2003)

Cabinet Chief: ALFREDO NÉSTOR ATANASOF.

Minister of the Interior: JORGE RUBÉN MATZKIN.

Minister of Foreign Affairs, International Trade and Worship: CARLOS FEDERICO RUCKAUF.

Minister of Education: GRACIELA MARÍA GIANNETTASIO.

Minister of Defence: JOSÉ HORACIO JAUNARENA.

Minister of the Economy: ROBERTO LAVAGNA.

Minister of Labour, Employment and Social Security: GRACIELA CAMAÑO.

Minister of Production: ANÍBAL DOMINGO FERNÁNDEZ.

Minister of Health: GINEÉS GONZÁLEZ GARCÍA.

Minister of Justice, Human Rights and Internal Security: JUAN JOSÉ ALVAREZ.

Minister of Social Development and the Environment: MARÍA NÉLIDA DOGA.

MINISTRIES

General Secretariat to the Presidency: Balcarce 50, 1064 Buenos Aires; tel. (11) 4344-3662; fax (11) 4344-3789; e-mail secgral@presidencia.net.ar.

Ministry of Defence: Azopardo 250, 1328 Buenos Aires; tel. (11) 4346-8800; e-mail mindef@mindef.gov.ar; internet www.mindef.gov.ar.

Ministry of the Economy: Hipólito Yrigoyen 250, 1310 Buenos Aires; tel. (11) 4349-5000; e-mail ministrosecpriv@mecon.gov.ar; internet www.mecon.gov.ar.

Ministry of Education: Pizzurno 935, 1020 Buenos Aires; tel. (11) 4129-1000; e-mail info@me.gov.ar; internet www.me.gov.ar.

Ministry of Foreign Affairs, International Trade and Worship: Esmeralda 1212, 1007 Buenos Aires; tel. (11) 4819-7000; e-mail web@mrecic.gov.ar; internet www.mrecic.gov.ar.

Ministry of Health: 9 de Julio 1925, 1332 Buenos Aires; tel. (11) 4381-8911; fax (11) 4381-2182; e-mail consultas@msal.gov.ar; internet www.msal.gov.ar.

Ministry of the Interior: Balcarce 50, 1064 Buenos Aires; tel. (11) 446-9841; fax (11) 4331-6376; e-mail secretariaprivada@mininterior.gov.ar; internet www.mininterior.gov.ar.

Ministry of Justice, Human Rights and Internal Security: Sarmiento 329, 1041 Buenos Aires; tel. (11) 4328-3015; internet www.jus.gov.ar.

Ministry of Labour, Employment and Social Security: Leandro N. Alem 650, 1001 Buenos Aires; tel. (11) 4311-2913; fax (11) 4312-7860; e-mail consultas@trabajo.gov.ar; internet www.trabajo.gov.ar.

Ministry of Production: Avda Julio A. Roca 651, 1067 Buenos Aires; tel. (11) 4349-3000; e-mail webmaster@minproduccion.gov.ar; internet www.minproduccion.gov.ar.

Ministry of Social Development and the Environment: Avda 9 de Julio 1925, 14°, 1332 Buenos Aires; tel. (11) 4379-3600; e-mail desarrollosocial@desarrollosocial.gov.ar; internet www.desarrollosocial.gov.ar.

President and Legislature

PRESIDENT

Election, First Round, 27 April 2003*

Candidates	Votes	% votes cast
Carlos Menem (PJ)	4,686,675	24.36
Néstor C. Kirchner (PJ)	4,232,188	22.00
Ricardo López Murphy (MFRC) . . .	3,144,532	16.34
Elisa M. A. Carrió (ARI)	2,720,696	14.14
Adolfo Rodríguez Sáa (PJ) . . .	2,715,822	14.12
Total (incl. others)	19,239,674	100.00

* Provisional results.

CONGRESO

Cámara de Diputados
(Chamber of Deputies)

President: EDUARDO OSCAR CAMAÑO.

The Chamber has 257 members, who hold office for a four-year term, with approximately one-half of the seats renewable every two years.

Distribution of Seats, November 2001*

	Seats
Partido Justicialista (PJ)	116
Alianza para el Trabajo, la Justicia y la Educación ATJE†	88
Alternativa por una República de Iguales (ARI) . .	17
Acción por la República (AR)	9
Polo Social	4
Izquierda Unida	3
Others	20
Total	257

*The table indicates the distribution of the total number of seats, following the elections for 127 seats on 14 October 2001.
† Alliance comprising Frente del País Solidario and the Unión Cívica Radical.

Senado
(Senate)

President: JUAN CARLOS MAQUEDA.

Legislative Elections, 14 October 2001*

	Seats
Partido Justicialista (PJ)	40
Unión Cívica Radical (UCR)	24
Frente del País Solidario (Frepaso)	1
Alternativa por una República de Iguales (ARI) . . .	1
Provincial parties	6
Total	72

*From October 1995 the Senate comprised 72 members, directly elected (three members from each region) for a six-year term of office. Until 2001 one-third of these seats were renewable every two years. In 2001 the entire Senate was renewed.

PROVINCIAL ADMINISTRATORS
(April 2003)

Mayor of the Federal District of Buenos Aires: ANÍBAL IBARRA.

Governor of the Province of Buenos Aires: FELIPE SOLÁ.

Governor of the Province of Catamarca: OSCAR CASTILLO.

Governor of the Province of Chaco: ANGEL ROZAS.

Governor of the Province of Chubut: JOSÉ LUIS LIZURUME.

Governor of the Province of Córdoba: JOSÉ MANUEL DE LA SOTA.

Governor of the Province of Corrientes: HORACIO RICARDO COLOMBI.

Governor of the Province of Entre Ríos: SERGIO MONTIEL.

Governor of the Province of Formosa: GILDO INSFRÁN.

Governor of the Province of Jujuy: EDUARDO FELLNER.

Governor of the Province of La Pampa: RUBÉN HUGO MARÍN.

Governor of the Province of La Rioja: ANGEL EDUARDO MAZA.

Governor of the Province of Mendoza: ROBERTO IGLESIAS.

Governor of the Province of Misiones: CARLOS ROVIRA.

Governor of the Province of Neuquén: JORGE OMAR SOBISCH.

Governor of the Province of Río Negro: PABLO VERANI.

Governor of the Province of Salta: JUAN CARLOS ROMERO.

Governor of the Province of San Juan: ALFREDO AVELÍN.

Governor of the Province of San Luis: MARÍA ALICIA LEMME.

Governor of the Province of Santa Cruz: NÉSTOR CARLOS KIRCHNER.

Governor of the Province of Santa Fe: CARLOS REUTEMANN.

Governor of the Province of Santiago del Estero: CARLOS ARTURO JUÁREZ.

Governor of the Province of Tucumán: JULIO MIRANDA.

Governor of the Territory of Tierra del Fuego: CARLOS MANFREDOTTI.

Political Organizations

Acción por la República—Nueva Dirigencia (AR—ND): Buenos Aires; f. 1997; electoral alliance; Leaders CARO FIGUEROA.

Acción por la República (AR): Buenos Aires; e-mail accionrepublic@geocities.com; internet www.ar-partido.com.ar; f. 1997; right-wing; Leader CARO FIGUEROA.

Nueva Dirigencia (ND): Buenos Aires; internet www.nuevadirigencia.org.ar; f. 1996; centre-right; Leader GUSTAVO BÉLIZ.

Alternativa por una República de Iguales (ARI): Buenos Aires; f. 2001; progressive party; Leader ELISA CARRIÓ.

Alianza para el Trabajo, la Justicia y la Educación (ATJE): Buenos Aires; f. 1997; electoral alliance comprising the UCR and Frepaso.

Frente del País Solidario (Frepaso): Buenos Aires; tel. (11) 4370-7100; e-mail frepaso@sion.com; internet www.frepaso.org.ar; f. 1994; centre-left coalition of socialist, communist and Christian Democrat groups; Leader CARLOS ALVAREZ.

Unión Cívica Radical (UCR): Alsina 1786, 1088 Buenos Aires; tel. and fax (11) 4375-2000; e-mail info@ucr.org.ar; internet www.ucr.org.ar; moderate; f. 1890; Pres. (vacant); 2.9m. mems.

Frente para el Cambio: Buenos Aires; Leader ALICIA CASTRO.

Movimiento por la Dignidad y la Independencia (Modin): Buenos Aires; f. 1991; right-wing; Leader Col ALDO RICO.

Movimiento Federal para Recrear al Crecimiento (MFRC): Buenos Aires; Leader RICARDO LÓPEZ MURPHY.

Movimiento de Integración y Desarrollo (MID): Buenos Aires; f. 1963; Leader ARTURO FRONDIZI; 145,000 mems.

Movimiento al Socialismo (MAS): Chile 1362, 1098 Buenos Aires; tel. (11) 4381-2718; fax (11) 4381-2976; e-mail mas@giga.com.ar; internet www.wp.com/mas; Leaders RUBÉN VISCONTI, LUIS ZAMORA; 55,000 mems.

Partido Comunista de Argentina: Buenos Aires; f. 1918; Leader PATRICIO ECHEGARAY; Sec.-Gen. ATHOS FAVA; 76,000 mems.

Partido Demócrata Cristiano (PDC): Combate de los Pozos 1055, 1222 Buenos Aires; fax (11) 426-3413; f. 1954; Leader ESIO ARIEL SILVEIRA; 85,000 mems.

Partido Demócrata Progresista (PDP): Chile 1934, 1227 Buenos Aires; Leader RAFAEL MARTÍNEZ RAYMONDA; 97,000 mems.

Partido Intransigente: Buenos Aires; f. 1957; left-wing; Leaders Dr OSCAR ALENDE, LISANDRO VIALE; Sec. MARIANO LORENCES; 90,000 mems.

Partido Justicialista (PJ): Buenos Aires; internet www.pj.org.ar; Peronist party; f. 1945; Pres. CARLOS SAÚL MENEM; 3m. mems; three factions within party.

Frente Renovador, Justicia, Democracia y Participación—Frejudepa: f. 1985; reformist wing; Leaders CARLOS SAÚL MENEM, ANTONIO CAFIERO, CARLOS GROSSO.

Movimiento Nacional 17 de Octubre: Leader HERMINIO IGLESIAS.

Oficialistas: Leaders JOSÉ MARÍA VERNET, LORENZO MIGUEL.

Partido Nacional de Centro: Buenos Aires; f. 1980; conservative; Leader RAÚL RIVANERA CARLES.

Partido Nacionalista de los Trabajadores (PNT): Buenos Aires; f. 1990; extreme right-wing; Leader ALEJANDRO BIONDINI.

Partido Obrero: Ayacucho 444, Buenos Aires; tel. (11) 4953-3824; fax (11) 4953-7164; internet www.po.org.ar; f. 1982; Trotskyist; Leaders JORGE ALTAMIRA, CHRISTIAN RATH; 61,000 mems.

Partido Popular Cristiano: Leader JOSÉ ANTONIO ALLENDE.

Partido Socialista Democrático: Rivadavia 2307, 1034 Buenos Aires; Leader AMÉRICO GHIOLDI; 39,000 mems.

Partido Socialista Popular: f. 1982; Leaders GUILLERMO ESTÉVEZ BOERO, EDGARDO ROSSI; 60,500 mems.

Partido Unidad Federalista (PaUFe): Buenos Aires; internet www.paufe.org.ar; Leader LUIS PATTI.

Política Abierta para la Integridad Social (PAIS): Buenos Aires; f. 1994 following split with the PJ.

Polo Social: Echeverría 441, 1878 Quilmes, Buenos Aires; tel. and fax (11) 4253-0971; e-mail polosocial@cscom.com.ar; internet www .polosocial.org; f. 1999; Leader Father LUIS FARINELLO.

Unión del Centro Democrático (UCeDé): Buenos Aires; f. 1980 as coalition of eight minor political organizations to challenge the 'domestic monopoly' of the populist movements; Leader ÁLVARO ALSOGARAY.

Unión para la Nueva Mayoría: Buenos Aires; f. 1986; centre-right; Leader JOSÉ ANTONIO ROMERO FERIS.

The following political parties and groupings also contested the 2001 legislative elections: Autodeterminación y Libertad, Cruzada Renovadora (San Juan), Frente Partido Nuevo, Fuerza Republicana (Tucumán), Izquierda Unida, Movimiento Popular Neuquino, Movimiento Popular Feuguiño, Partido Humanista, Partido Autonomista (Corrientes), the Partido de Trabajadores por el Socialismo, Partido de la Unidad Bonaerense and Renovador de Salta.

Other parties and groupings include: Afirmación Peronista, Alianza Socialista, Confederación Socialista Argentina, Frente Cívica y Socialista (Catamarca), Movimiento Línea Popular, Movimiento Patriótico de Liberación, Movimiento Peronista, Movimiento Popular (Tierra del Fuego), Partido Bloquista de San Juan, Partido Conservador Popular, Partido Izquierda Nacional, Partido Liberal (Corrientes), Partido Obrero Comunista Marxista-Leninista and Partido Socialista Unificado.

The following political parties and guerrilla groups are illegal:

Intransigencia y Movilización Peronista: Peronist faction; Leader NILDA GARRES.

Movimiento Todos por la Patria (MTP): left-wing movement.

Partido Peronista Auténtico (PPA): f. 1975; Peronist faction; Leaders MARIO FIRMENICH, OSCAR BIDEGAIN, RICARDO OBREGÓN CANO.

Partido Revolucionario de Trabajadores: political wing of the Ejército Revolucionario del Pueblo (ERP); Leader LUIS MATTINI.

Triple A—Alianza Anticomunista Argentina: extreme right-wing; Leader ANÍBAL GORDON (in prison).

Diplomatic Representation

EMBASSIES IN ARGENTINA

Albania: Avda del Libertador 946, 4°, 1001 Buenos Aires; tel. (11) 4812-8366; fax (11) 4815-2512; e-mail ambasada.bue@fibertel.com .ar; Ambassador EDMOND TRAKO.

Algeria: Montevideo 1889, 1021 Buenos Aires; tel. (11) 4815-1271; fax (11) 4815-8837; e-mail argelia@peoples.com.ar; Ambassador NOURREDINE AYADI.

Angola: Buenos Aires; Ambassador FERNANDO DITO.

Armenia: Avda Roque S. Peña 570, 3°, 1035 Buenos Aires; tel. (11) 4345-2051; fax (11) 4343-2467; e-mail armenia@teletel.com.ar; Ambassador ARA AIVAZIAN.

Australia: Villanueva 1400, 1426 Buenos Aires; tel. (11) 4777-6580; fax (11) 4776-3349; e-mail dima-buenos_aires@dfait.gov.au; internet www.australia.org.ar; Ambassador SHARYN MINAHAN.

Austria: French 3671, 1425 Buenos Aires; tel. (11) 4802-7195; fax (11) 4805-4016; e-mail botschaft@austria.org.ar; internet www .austria.org.ar; Ambassador YURI STANDENAT.

Belarus: Cazadores 2166, 1428 Buenos Aires; tel. (11) 4788-9394; fax (11) 4788-2322; Ambassador VADIM LAZERKO.

Belgium: Defensa 113, 8°, 1065 Buenos Aires; tel. (11) 4331-0066; fax (11) 4311-0814; e-mail buenosaires@diplobel.org; internet www .diplobel.org/argentina/default.htm; Ambassador RONAL DE LANGHE.

Bolivia: Avda Corrientes 545, 2°, 1043 Buenos Aires; tel. (11) 4394-6042; Ambassador FERNANDO BEDOYA BALLIVIAN.

Bosnia and Herzegovina: Miñones 2445, Buenos Aires; tel. (11) 4896-0284; fax (11) 4896-0351; Ambassador DUŠKO LADAN.

Brazil: Arroyo 1142, 1007 Buenos Aires; tel. (11) 444-0035; fax (11) 4814-4085; e-mail embras@embrasil.org.ar; internet www.brasil.org .ar; Ambassador SEBASTIÃO DO REGO BARROS NETTO.

Bulgaria: Mariscal A. J. de Sucre 1568, 1428 Buenos Aires; tel. (11) 4781-8644; fax (11) 4786-6273; e-mail embular@sinectis.com.ar; internet www.sinectis.com.ar/u/embular; Ambassador ATRANAS I. BUDEV.

Canada: Tagle 2828, 1425 Buenos Aires; tel. (11) 4805-3032; fax (11) 4806-1209; internet www.dfait-maeci.gc.ca/bairs; Ambassador THOMAS MACDONALD.

Chile: Tagle 2762, 1425 Buenos Aires; tel. (11) 4802-7020; fax (11) 4804-5927; Ambassador JUAN GABRIEL VALDES.

China, People's Republic: Avda Crisólogo Larralde 5349, 1431 Buenos Aires; tel. (11) 4543-8862; fax (11) 4545-1141; Ambassador ZHANG SHAYING.

Colombia: Carlos Pellegrini 1363, 3°, 1010 Buenos Aires; tel. (11) 4325-0494; fax (11) 4322-9370; e-mail emargent@internet.siscotel .com; Ambassador NELSON POLO HERNÁNDEZ.

Congo, Democratic Republic: Callao 322, 2°, Buenos Aires; tel. (11) 4373-7565; fax (11) 4374-9865; Chargé d'affaires a.i. YEMBA LOHAKA.

Costa Rica: Avda Callao 1103, 9°I, 1023 Buenos Aires; tel. (11) 4815-8160; fax (11) 4815-8159; e-mail embarica@infovia.com.ar; Ambassador EDUARDO FRANCISCO OTOYA BOULANGER.

Croatia: Gorostiaga 2104, 1426 Buenos Aires; tel. (11) 4777-6409; fax (11) 4777-9159; e-mail embajadadecroacia@velocom.com.ar; Ambassador RIKARD ROSSETTI.

Cuba: Virrey del Pino 1810, 1426 Buenos Aires; tel. (11) 4782-9049; fax (11) 4786-7713; e-mail embcuba@arnet.com.ar; Ambassador ALEJANDRO J. GONZÁLEZ GALIANO.

Czech Republic: Villanueva 1356, 2° Buenos Aires; tel. (11) 4777-0435; fax (11) 4771-0075; e-mail buenosaires@embassy.mzv.cz; internet www.mfa.cz/buenosaires; Ambassador EDITA HRDÁ.

Denmark: Avda Leandro N. Alem 1074, 9°, 1001 Buenos Aires; tel. (11) 4312-6901; fax (11) 4312-7857; e-mail ambadane@ambadane .org.ar; Ambassador JENS PETER LARSEN.

Dominican Republic: Avda Santa Fe 1206, 2°c, 1059 Buenos Aires; tel. (11) 4811-4669; fax (11) 4804-3902; Ambassador CIRILO J. CASTELLANOS ARAÚJO.

Ecuador: Quintana 585, 9° y 10°, 1129 Buenos Aires; tel. (11) 4804-0073; fax (11) 4804-0074; e-mail embecu@ciudad.com.ar; Ambassador HARRY KLEIN MANN.

Egypt: Olleros 2140, 1425 Buenos Aires; tel. (11) 4899-0300; fax (11) 4899-0803; e-mail embegypt@fibertel.com.ar; Ambassador HAZEM TAHER.

El Salvador: Esmeralda 1066, 7°, 1059 Buenos Aires; tel. (11) 4311-1864; fax (11) 4314-7628; Ambassador RAFAEL ALFONSO QUIÑÓNEZ MEZA.

Finland: Avda Santa Fe 846, 5°, 1059 Buenos Aires; tel. (11) 4312-0600; fax (11) 4312-0670; e-mail embajadafinlandia@arnet.com.ar; internet www.finembue.com.ar; Ambassador RISTO KAARLO VELTHEIM.

France: Cerrito 1399, 1010 Buenos Aires; tel. (11) 4819-2930; fax (11) 4393-1235; e-mail ambafr@impsat1.com.ar; internet www .embafrancia-argentina.org; Ambassador PAUL DIJOUD.

Germany: Villanueva 1055, 1426 Buenos Aires; tel. (11) 4778-2500; fax (11) 4778-2550; e-mail info@embajada-alemana.org.ar; internet www.embjada-alemana.org.ar; Ambassador HANS ULRICH D. SPOHN.

Greece: Avda Roque S. Peña 547, 4°, 1035 Buenos Aires; tel. (11) 4342-4598; fax (11) 4342-2838; Ambassador GEORGES GEORGIOU.

Guatemala: Avda Santa Fe 830, 5°, 1059 Buenos Aires; tel. (11) 4313-9160; fax (11) 4313-9181; e-mail embargentina@minex.gob.gt; Ambassador (vacant).

Haiti: Avda Figueroa Alcorta 3297, 1425 Buenos Aires; tel. (11) 4802-0211; fax (11) 4802-3984; e-mail embahaiti@interar.com.ar; Ambassador EDRIS SAINT-AMAND.

Holy See: Avda Alvear 1605, 1014 Buenos Aires; tel. (11) 4813-9697; fax (11) 4815-4097; Apostolic Nuncio Most Rev. SANTOS ABRIL Y CASTELLÓ (Titular Archbishop of Tamada).

Honduras: Avda Libertador 1146, 1112 Buenos Aires; tel. (11) 4804-6181; fax (11) 4804-3222; e-mail honduras@ciudad.com.ar; Ambassador NAPOLEÓN ALVAREZ ALVARADO.

Hungary: Coronel Díaz 1874, 1425 Buenos Aires; tel. (11) 4822-0767; fax (11) 4805-3918; e-mail hungria@escape.com.ar; Ambassador FERENC SZÖNYI.

India: Córdoba 950, 4°, 1054 Buenos Aires; tel. (11) 4393-4001; fax (11) 4393-4063; e-mail indembarg@infomatic.com.ar; internet www .indembarg.org.ar; Ambassador NIGAM PRAKASH.

Indonesia: Mariscal Ramón Castilla 2901, 1425 Buenos Aires; tel. (11) 4807-2211; fax (11) 4802-4448; e-mail emindo@tournet.com.ar; Ambassador ACHMAD SURYADI.

Iran: Avda Figueroa Alcorta 3229, 1425 Buenos Aires; tel. (11) 4802-1470; fax (11) 4805-4409; Chargé d'affaires a.i. MOHAMED ALÍ TABATA-BAEI HASAN.

Ireland: Suipacha 1380, 2°, 1011 Buenos Aires; tel. (11) 4325-8588; fax (11) 4325-5572; e-mail info@irlanda.org.ar; internet irlgov.ie/iveagh; Ambassador PAULA SLATTERY.

Israel: Avda. de Mayo 701, 10°, 1084 Buenos Aires; tel. (11) 4338-2500; internet www.israel-embassy.org.ar/embajada.html; Ambassador BENJAMIN ORON.

Italy: Billinghurst 2577, 1425 Buenos Aires; tel. (11) 4802-0071; fax (11) 4804-4914; e-mail stampa@ambitalia-bsas.org.ar; internet www .ambitalia-bsas.org.ar; Ambassador ROBERTO NIGIDO.

Japan: Bouchard 547, 17°, Buenos Aires; tel. (11) 4318-8200; fax (11) 4318-8210; Ambassador TOSHIO WATANABE.

Korea, Republic: Avda del Libertador 2395, 1425 Buenos Aires; tel. (11) 4802-8062; fax (11) 4803-6993; e-mail embcorea@cscom.com .ar; internet www.mofat.go.kr/argentina.htm; Ambassador SEUNG-YOUNG KIM.

Kuwait: Uruguay 739, 1015 Buenos Aires; tel. (11) 4374-7202; fax (11) 4374-8718; e-mail kuwait@microstar.com.ar; internet www .kuwait.com.ar; Ambassador SALEM G. AZ-ZAMANAN.

Lebanon: Avda del Libertador 2354, 1425 Buenos Aires; tel. (11) 4802-4492; fax (11) 4802-2909; e-mail embajada@ellibano.com.ar; Ambassador HICHAM SALIM HAMDAN.

Libya: 3 de Febrero 1358, 1426 Buenos Aires; tel. (11) 4788-3760; fax (11) 4788-9394; Chargé d'affaires a.i. SSIED H. KHALFALLAH.

Malaysia: Villanueva 1040-1048, 1062 Buenos Aires; tel. (11) 4776-0504; e-mail mwbaires@cvtci.com.ar; Ambassador DATO M. SANTHA-NANABAN.

Mexico: Larrea 1230, 1117 Buenos Aires; tel. (11) 4821-7172; fax (11) 4821-7251; e-mail embamexarg@intlink.com.ar; Ambassador ROSARIO G. GREEN MACÍAS.

Morocco: Mariscal Ramón Castilla 2952, 1425 Buenos Aires; tel. (11) 4801-8154; fax (11) 4802-0136; e-mail sifamabueno@tournet .com.ar; internet www.embajadamarruecos.org.ar; Ambassador MOHAMED MAA EL-AININ.

Netherlands: Avda de Mayo 701, 19°, 1084 Buenos Aires; tel. (11) 4334-4000; fax (11) 4334-2717; e-mail nlgovbue@informatic.com.ar; Ambassador JAN EDWARD CRAANEN.

New Zealand: Carlos Pellegrine 1427, 5°, 1010; Buenos Aires; tel. (11) 4328-0747; fax (11) 4328-0757; e-mail kiwiargentina@ datamarkets.com.ar; Ambassador CARL ROBINSON WORKER.

Nicaragua: Avda Corrientes 2548, 4°I, 1426 Buenos Aires; tel. (11) 4951-3463; fax (11) 4952-7557; e-mail embanic@overnet.com.ar; Ambassador EMILIO J. SOLÍS BERMÚDEZ.

Nigeria: Rosales 2674, 1636 Olivos, Buenos Aires; tel. (11) 4771-6541; fax (11) 4790-7564; Ambassador MOHAMMAD A. WALI.

Norway: Esmeralda 909, 3°B, 1007 Buenos Aires; tel. (11) 4312-2204; fax (11) 4315-2831; e-mail embajada.noruega@way.net.ar; Ambassador SISSEL BREIE.

Pakistan: Gorostiaga 2176, 1426 Buenos Aires; tel. (11) 4782-7663; fax (11) 4776-1186; e-mail parepbaires@sinectis.com.ar; Ambassador SAEED KHALID.

Panama: Avda Santa Fe 1461, 5°, 1060 Buenos Aires; tel. (11) 4811-1254; fax (11) 4814-0450; e-mail epar@ba.net; Ambassador MER-CEDES ALFARO CHAPMAN DE LÓPEZ.

Paraguay: Avda Las Heras 2545, 1425 Buenos Aires; tel. (11) 4802-3826; fax (11) 4801-0657; Ambassador CARLOS ALBERTO GONZÁLEZ GARABELLI.

Peru: Avda del Libertador 1720, 1425 Buenos Aires; tel. (11) 4802-2000; fax (11) 4802-5887; Ambassador HUGO DE ZELA MARTÍNEZ.

Philippines: Juramento 1945, 1428 Buenos Aires; tel. (11) 4781-4173; fax (11) 4783-8171; e-mail phba@peoples.com.ar; Ambassador CARLOS A. VILLA ABRILLE.

Poland: Alejandro M. de Aguado 2870, 1425 Buenos Aires; tel. (11) 4802-9681; fax (11) 4802-9683; e-mail polemb@datamarkets.com.ar; Ambassador SLAWOMIR RATAJSKI.

Portugal: Córdoba 315, 3°, 1054 Buenos Aires; tel. (11) 4311-2586; fax (11) 4311-2586; Ambassador JOSÉ A. BAPTISTA LÓPEZ E SEABRA.

Romania: Arroyo 962-970, 1007 Buenos Aires; tel. and fax (11) 4322-2630; e-mail embarombue@fibertel.com.ar; Ambassador CRIS-TIAN LÁZÁRESCU.

Russia: Rodríguez Peña 1741, 1021 Buenos Aires; tel. (11) 4813-1552; fax (11) 4812-1794; Ambassador YEVGENII M. ASTAKHOV.

Saudi Arabia: Alejandro M. de Aguado 2881, 1425 Buenos Aires; tel. (11) 4802-4735; Ambassador ADNAN B. BAGHDADI.

Serbia and Montenegro: Marcelo T. de Alvear 1705, 1060 Buenos Aires; tel. (11) 4811-2860; fax (11) 4812-1070; e-mail snovak@ipm .net; Ambassador GOJKO CELEBIĆ.

Slovakia: Avda Figueroa Alcorta 3240, 1425 Buenos Aires; tel. (11) 4786-0692; fax (11) 4786-0938; Ambassador JAN JURISTA.

Slovenia: Suipacha 1380, 3°, 1001 Buenos Aires; tel. (11) 4393-2067; fax (11) 4326-0829; Ambassador BOJAN GROBOVŠEK.

South Africa: Marcelo T. de Alvear 590, 8°, 1058 Buenos Aires; tel. (11) 4317-2900; fax (11) 4317-2951; e-mail saemba@sicoar.com; Ambassador MLUNGIS WASHINGTON MAKALIMA.

Spain: Mariscal Ramón Castilla 2720, 1425 Buenos Aires; tel. (11) 4802-6031; fax (11) 4802-0719; Ambassador MANUEL ALABART.

Sweden: Casilla 3599, Correo Central 1000, Buenos Aires; tel. (11) 4311-3088; fax (11) 4311-8052; e-mail swedemb@infovia.com.ar; Ambassador MADELEINE STRÖJE-WILKENS.

Switzerland: Avda Santa Fe 846, 10°, 1059 Buenos Aires; tel. (11) 4311-6491; fax (11) 4313-2998; e-mail vertretung@bue.rep.admin .ch; Ambassador ARMIN RITZ.

Syria: Calloa 956, 1023 Buenos Aires; tel. (11) 4813-2113; fax (11) 4814-3211; Chargé d'affaires a.i. MASSOUN KASSAWAT.

Thailand: Virrey del Pino 2458, 6°, 1426 Buenos Aires; tel. (11) 4785-6504; fax (11) 4785-6548; e-mail thbsemb@tournet.com.ar; Chargé d'affaires a.i. SIRILAK SRISUKHO.

Tunisia: Ciudad de la Paz 3086, 1429 Buenos Aires; tel. (11) 4544-2618; fax (11) 4545-6369; e-mail embtun@peoples.com.ar; Ambassador GHAZI JOMAA.

Turkey: 11 de Setiembre 1382, 1426 Buenos Aires; tel. (11) 4788-3239; fax (11) 4784-9179; e-mail iyihava@ba.net; Ambassador ERHAN YIGITBASIOGLU.

Ukraine: Lafinur 3057, 1425 Buenos Aires; tel. (11) 4802-7316; fax (11) 4802-3864; e-mail embucra@embucra.com.ar; internet www .embucra.com.ar; Ambassador OLEKSANDR MAIDANNYK.

United Kingdom: Dr Luis Agote 2412/52, 1425 Buenos Aires; tel. (11) 4803-7070; fax (11) 4806-5713; e-mail ukembarg@starnet.net .ar; internet www.britain.org.ar; Ambassador Sir ROBIN CHRISTOPHER.

USA: Avda Colombia 4300, 1425 Buenos Aires; tel. (11) 4774-7611; fax (11) 4775-4205; internet usembassy.state.gov/baires_embassy; Ambassador JAMES D. WALSH.

Uruguay: Avda Las Heras 1907, 1127 Buenos Aires; tel. (11) 4803-6030; fax (11) 4807-3050; e-mail embarou@impsat1.com.ar; Ambassador ALBERTO C. VOLONTÉ BERRO.

Venezuela: Virrey Loreto 2035, 1428 Buenos Aires; tel. (11) 4788-4944; fax (11) 4784-4311; e-mail venargs@peoples.com.ar; internet www.la-embajada.com.ar; Ambassador EDMUNDO GONZÁLEZ URRUTIA.

Viet Nam: 11 de Septiembre 1442, 1426 Buenos Aires; tel. (11) 4783-1802; fax (11) 4782-0078; e-mail sqvnartn@teletel.com.ar; Ambassador HOAN TRAN-QUANG.

Judicial System

SUPREME COURT

Corte Suprema

Talcahuano 550, 4°, 1013 Buenos Aires; tel. (11) 440-0837; fax (11) 440-2270; internet www.pjn.gov.ar/corte.htm.

The nine members of the Supreme Court are appointed by the President, with the agreement of at least two-thirds of the Senate. Members are dismissed by impeachment.

President: JULIO SALVADOR NAZARENO.

Vice-President: EDUARDO MOLINÉ O'CONNOR.

Justices: CARLOS SANTIAGO FAYT, AUGUSTO CÉSAR BELLUSCIO, ENRIQUE SANTIAGO PETRACCHI, ADOLFO VÁZQUEZ, ANTONIO BOGGIANO, GUILLERMO A. F. LÓPEZ, GUSTAVO A. BOSSERT.

OTHER COURTS

Judges of the lower, national or further lower courts are appointed by the President, with the agreement of the Senate, and are dismissed by impeachment. From 1999, however, judges were to retire on reaching 75 years of age.

The Federal Court of Appeal in Buenos Aires has three courts: civil and commercial, criminal, and administrative. There are six other courts of appeal in Buenos Aires: civil, commercial, criminal, peace, labour, and penal-economic. There are also federal appeal courts in: La Plata, Bahía Blanca, Paraná, Rosario, Córdoba, Mendoza, Tucumán and Resistencia. In August 1994, following constitutional amendments, the Office of the Attorney-General was established as an independent entity and a Council of Magistrates was envisaged. In December 1997 the Senate adopted legislation to create the Council.

The provincial courts each have their own Supreme Court and a system of subsidiary courts. They deal with cases originating within and confined to the provinces.

Attorney-General: Oscar Luján Fappiano.

Religion

CHRISTIANITY

More than 90% of the population are Roman Catholics and about 2% are Protestants.

Federación Argentina de Iglesias Evangélicas (Argentine Federation of Evangelical Churches): José María Moreno 873, 1424 Buenos Aires; tel. and fax (11) 4922-5356; e-mail faie@faie.com.ar; internet www.cristianet.com/faie; f. 1938; 29 mem. churches; Pres. Rev. Emilio Monti (Methodist Evangelical Church); Exec. Sec. Rev. Florencia Himitian.

The Roman Catholic Church

Argentina comprises 14 archdioceses, 50 dioceses (including one each for Uniate Catholics of the Ukrainian rite, of the Maronite rite and of the Armenian rite) and three territorial prelatures. The Archbishop of Buenos Aires is also the Ordinary for Catholics of Oriental rites, and the Bishop of San Gregorio de Narek en Buenos Aires is also the Apostolic Exarch of Latin America and Mexico for Catholics of the Armenian rite.

Bishops' Conference: Conferencia Episcopal Argentina, Suipacha 1034, 1008 Buenos Aires; tel. (11) 4328-0993; fax (11) 4328-9570; e-mail seccea@cea.org.ar; internet www.cea.org.ar; f. 1959; Pres. Mgr Eduardo Vicente Mirás (Archbishop of Rosario).

Armenian Rite

Bishop of San Gregorio de Narek en Buenos Aires: Vartan Waldir Boghossian, Charcas, 3529, 1425 Buenos Aires; tel. (11) 4824-1613; fax (11) 4827-1975; e-mail exarmal@pcn.net; internet www.fast.to/exarcado.

Latin Rite

Archbishop of Bahía Blanca: Rómulo García, Avda Colón 164, 8000 Bahía Blanca; tel. (291) 455-0707; fax (291) 452-2070; e-mail arzobispado@bblanca.com.ar.

Archbishop of Buenos Aires: Cardinal Jorge Bergoglio, Rivadavia 415, 1002 Buenos Aires; tel. (11) 4343-3925; fax (11) 4334-8373; e-mail arzobispado@arzbaires.org.ar.

Archbishop of Córdoba: Carlos José Náñez, Hipólito Yrigoyen 98, 5000 Córdoba; tel. (351) 422-1015; fax (351) 425-5082.

Archbishop of Corrientes: Domingo Salvador Castagna, 9 de Julio 1543, 3400 Corrientes; tel. and fax (3783) 422436; e-mail arzctes@arnet.com.ar.

Archbishop of La Plata: Héctor Aguer, Calle 14, 1009, 1900 La Plata; tel. (221) 425-1656; e-mail arzolap@satlink.com.ar; internet www.arzolap.org.ar.

Archbishop of Mendoza: José María Arancibia, Catamarca 98, 5500 Mendoza; tel. (261) 423-3862; fax (261) 429-5415; e-mail arzobispadomza@supernet.com.ar.

Archbishop of Mercedes-Luján: Rubén Héctor di Monte, Calle 22, No 745, 6600 Mercedes, Buenos Aires; tel. (2324) 432-412; fax (2324) 432-104; e-mail arzomerce@yahoo.com.

Archbishop of Paraná: Mgr Estanislao Esteban Karlic, Monte Caseros 77, 3100 Paraná; tel. (343) 431-1440; fax (343) 423-0372; e-mail arzparan@satlink.com.ar.

Archbishop of Resistencia: Carmelo Juan Giaquinta, Bartolomé Mitre 363, Casilla 35, 3500 Resistencia; tel. and fax (3722) 434573; e-mail arzobrcia@lared.com.ar.

Archbishop of Rosario: Eduardo Vicente Mirás, Córdoba 1677, 2000 Rosario; tel. (341) 425-1298; fax (341) 425-1207; e-mail arzobros@lidernet.com.ar; internet www.delrosario.org.ar.

Archbishop of Salta: Mario Antonio Cargnello, España 596, 4400 Salta; tel. (387) 421-4306; fax (387) 421-3101; e-mail arzobisposalta@infovia.com.ar.

Archbishop of San Juan de Cuyo: Alfonso Delgado Evers, Bartolomé Mitre 250 Oeste, 5400 San Juan de Cuyo; tel. (264) 422-2578; fax (264) 427-3530; e-mail arzobispadosanjuan@infovia.com.ar.

Archbishop of Santa Fe de la Vera Cruz: Edgardo Gabriel Storni, Avda General López 2720, 3000 Santa Fe; tel. (342) 459-5791; fax (342) 459-4491; e-mail arzobs@infovia.com.ar.

Archbishop of Tucumán: Luis Héctor Villalba, Avda Sarmiento 895, 4000 San Miguel de Tucumán; tel. (381) 422-6345; fax (381) 431-0617; e-mail arztuc@arnet.com.ar.

Maronite Rite

Bishop of San Charbel en Buenos Aires: Charbel Merhi, Eparquía Maronita, Paraguay 834, 1057 Buenos Aires; tel. (11) 4311-7299; fax (11) 4312-8348; e-mail mcharbel@hotmail.com.

Ukrainian Rite

Bishop of Santa María del Patrocinio en Buenos Aires: Rt Rev. Miguel Mykycej, Ramón L. Falcón 3950, Casilla 28, 1407 Buenos Aires; tel. (11) 4671-4192; fax (11) 4671-7265; e-mail pekrov@ciudad.com.ar.

The Anglican Communion

The Iglesia Anglicana del Cono Sur de América (Anglican Church of the Southern Cone of America) was formally inaugurated in Buenos Aires in April 1983. The Church comprises seven dioceses: Argentina, Northern Argentina, Chile, Paraguay, Peru, Bolivia and Uruguay. The Primate is the Bishop of Northern Argentina.

Bishop of Argentina: Rt Rev. Gregory Venables, 25 de Mayo 282, 1002 Buenos Aires; Casilla 4293, Correo Central 1000, Buenos Aires; tel. (11) 4342-4618; fax (11) 4331-0234; e-mail diocesisanglibue@arnet.com.ar.

Bishop of Northern Argentina: Rt Rev. Maurice Sinclair, Casilla 187, 4400 Salta; tel. (387) 431-1718; fax (387) 431-2622; e-mail sinclair@salnet.com.ar; jurisdiction extends to Jujuy, Salta, Tucumán, Catamarca, Santiago del Estero, Formosa and Chaco.

Protestant Churches

Convención Evangélica Bautista Argentina (Baptist Evangelical Convention): Virrey Liniers 42, 1174 Buenos Aires; tel. and fax (11) 4864-2711; e-mail ceba@sion.com; f. 1909; Pres. Carlos A. Caramutti.

Iglesia Evangélica Congregacionalista (Evangelical Congregational Church): Perón 525, 3100 Paraná; tel. (43) 21-6172; f. 1924; 100 congregations, 8,000 mems, 24,000 adherents; Supt Rev. Reynoldo Horstt.

Iglesia Evangélica Luterana Argentina (Evangelical Lutheran Church of Argentina): Ing. Silveyra 1639-41, 1607 Villa Adelina, Buenos Aires; tel. (11) 4766-7948; fax (11) 4766-7948; f. 1905; 30,000 mems; Pres. Waldomiro Maili.

Iglesia Evangélica del Río de la Plata (Evangelical Church of the River Plate): Mariscal Sucre 2855, 1428 Buenos Aires; tel. (11) 4787-0436; fax (11) 4787-0335; e-mail presidente@ierp.org.ar; f. 1899; 40,000 mems; Pres. Federico Hugo Sch.

Iglesia Evangélica Metodista Argentina (Methodist Church of Argentina): Rivadavia 4044, 3°, 1205 Buenos Aires; tel. (11) 4982-3712; fax (11) 4981-0885; e-mail iema@iema.com.ar; internet www.iema.com.ar; f. 1836; 6,040 mems, 9,000 adherents, seven regional superintendents; Bishop Aldo M. Etchegoyen; Exec. Sec.-Gen. Bd Daniel A. Favaro.

JUDAISM

Delegación de Asociaciones Israelitas Argentinas (DAIA) (Delegation of Argentine Jewish Associations): Pasteur 633, 7°, 1028 Buenos Aires; tel. and fax (11) 4378-3200; e-mail daia@daia.org.ar; internet news.daia.org.ar; f. 1935; there are about 250,000 Jews in Argentina, mostly in Buenos Aires; Pres. Dr José Hercman; Sec.-Gen. Dr Julio Toker.

The Press

PRINCIPAL DAILIES

Buenos Aires

Ambito Financiero: Avda Paseo Colón 1196, 1063 Buenos Aires; tel. (11) 4349-1500; fax (11) 4349-1505; e-mail correo@ambito.com.ar; internet www.ambitoweb.com.ar; f. 1976; morning (Mon.–Fri.); business; Dir Julio A. Ramos; circ. 115,000.

Buenos Aires Herald: Azopardo 455, 1107 Buenos Aires; tel. (11) 4342-1535; fax (11) 4334-7917; e-mail info@buenosairesherald.com;

internet www.buenosairesherald.com; f. 1876; English; morning; independent; Editor-in-Chief ANDREW GRAHAM YOOLL; circ. 20,000.

Boletín Oficial de la República Argentina: Suipacha 767, 1008 Buenos Aires; tel. (11) 4322-3982; fax (11) 4322-3982; f. 1893; morning (Mon.–Fri.); official records publication; Dir RUBÉN ANTONIO SOSA; circ. 15,000.

Clarín: Piedras 1743, 1140 Buenos Aires; tel. (11) 4309-7500; fax (11) 4309-7559; e-mail lectores@www.clarin.com; internet www .clarin.com; f. 1945; morning; independent; Dir ERNESTINA L. HERRERA DE NOBLE; circ. 616,000 (daily), 1.0m. (Sunday).

Crónica: Avda Juan de Garay 40, 1063 Buenos Aires; tel. (11) 4361-1001; fax (11) 4361-4237; f. 1963; morning and evening; Dir MARIO ALBERTO FERNÁNDEZ (morning); RICARDO GANGEME (evening); circ. 330,000 (morning), 190,000 (evening), 450,000 (Sunday).

El Cronista: Honduras 5663, 1414 Buenos Aires; tel. (11) 4778-6789; fax (11) 4778-6727; e-mail cronista@sadei.org.ar; f. 1908; morning; Dir NÉSTOR SCIBONA; circ. 65,000.

Diario Popular: Beguiristain 142, 1872 Sarandí, Avellaneda, Buenos Aires; tel. (11) 4204-2778; fax (11) 4205-2376; e-mail redacpop@inea.net.ar; f. 1974; morning; Dir ALBERTO ALBERTENGO; circ. 145,000.

La Gaceta: Beguiristain 182, 1870 Avellaneda, Buenos Aires; Dir RICARDO WEST OCAMPO; circ. 35,000.

La Nación: Bouchard 551, 1106 Buenos Aires; tel. (11) 4319-1600; fax (11) 4319-1969; e-mail cescribano@lanacion.com.ar; internet www.lanacion.com.ar; f. 1870; morning; independent; Dir BARTOLOMÉ MITRE; circ. 184,000.

Página 12: Avda Belgrano 671, 1092 Buenos Aires; tel. (11) 4334-2334; fax (11) 4334-2335; e-mail lectores@pagina12.com.ar; internet www.pagina12.com.ar; f. 1987; morning; independent; Dir ERNESTO TIFFEMBERG; Editor FERNANDO SOKOLOWICZ; circ. 280,000.

La Prensa: Azopardo 715, 1107 Buenos Aires; tel. (11) 4349-1000; fax (11) 4349-1025; e-mail laprensa@interlink.com; internet www .interlink.com.ar/laprensa; f. 1869; morning; independent; Dir FLORENCIO ALDREY IGLESIAS; circ. 100,000.

La Razón: Río Cuarto 1242, 1168 Buenos Aires; tel. and fax (11) 4309-6000; e-mail larazon@arnet.com.ar; internet www.larazon.com .ar; f. 1992; evening; Dir OSCAR MAGDALENA; circ. 62,000.

El Sol: Hipólito Yrigoyen 122, Quilmes, 1878 Buenos Aires; tel. and fax (11) 4257-6325; e-mail elsol@elsolquilmes.com.ar; internet www .elsolquilmes.com.ar; f. 1927; Dir RODRIGO GHISANI; circ. 25,000.

Tiempo Argentino: Buenos Aires; tel. (11) 428-1929; Editor Dr TOMÁS LEONA; circ. 75,000.

PRINCIPAL PROVINCIAL DAILIES

Catamarca

El Ancasti: Sarmiento 526, 1°, 4700 Catamarca; tel. and fax (3833) 431385; e-mail ancasti@satlink.com; f. 1988; morning; Dir ROQUE EDUARDO MOLAS; circ. 8,000.

Chaco

Norte: Carlos Pellegrini 744, 3500 Resistencia; tel. (3722) 428204; fax (3722) 426047; e-mail prensanorte@diarionorte.com.ar; f. 1968; Dir MIGUEL A. FERNÁNDEZ; circ. 14,000.

Chubut

Crónica: Impresora Patagónica, Namuncurá 122, 9000 Comodoro Rivadavia; tel. (297) 447-1200; fax (297) 447-1780; e-mail cronica@ arnet.com.ar; f. 1962; morning; Dir Dr DIEGO JOAQUÍN ZAMIT; circ. 15,000.

Córdoba

Comercio y Justicia: Mariano Moreno 378, 5000 Córdoba; tel. and fax (351) 422-0202; e-mail sistemas@powernet.com.ar; internet www.powernet.com.ar/cyj; f. 1939; morning; economic and legal news; Editor PABLO EGUÍA; circ. 5,800.

La Voz del Interior: Monseñor P. Cabrera 6080, 5008 Córdoba; tel. (351) 4757000; fax (351) 4757247; e-mail lavoz@lavozdelinterior.com .ar; internet www.lavozdelinterior.com.ar; f. 1904; morning; independent; Dir Dr CARLOS HUGO JORNET; circ. 68,000.

Corrientes

El Litoral: Hipólito Yrigoyen 990, 3400 Corrientes; tel. and fax (3783) 422227; e-mail el-litoral@compunort.com.ar; internet www .corrientes.com.ar/el-litoral; f. 1960; morning; Dir CARLOS A. ROMERO FERIS; circ. 25,000.

El Territorio: Avda Quaranta 4307, 3300 Posadas; tel. and fax (3752) 452100; e-mail elterritorio@elterritorio.com.ar; internet www

.elterritorio.com.ar; f. 1925; Dir GONZALO PELTZER; circ. 22,000 (Mon.–Fri.), 28,000 (Sunday).

Entre Ríos

El Diario: Buenos Aires y Urquiza, 3100 Paraná; tel. (343) 423-1000; fax (343) 431-9104; e-mail saer@satlink.com; internet www .eldiario.com.ar; f. 1914; morning; democratic; Dir Dr LUIS F. ETCHEVEHERE; circ. 25,000.

El Heraldo: Quintana 42, 3200 Concordia; tel. (345) 421-5304; fax (345) 421-1397; e-mail heraldo@infovia.com.ar; internet www .elheraldo.com.ar; f. 1915; evening; Editor Dr CARLOS LIEBERMANN; circ. 10,000.

Mendoza

Los Andes: Avda San Martín 1049, 5500 Mendoza; tel. (261) 449-1280; fax (261) 449-1217; e-mail havila@losandes.com.ar; internet www.losandes.com.ar; f. 1982; morning; Dir GERARDO HEIDEL; circ. 60,000.

Provincia de Buenos Aires

El Atlántico: Bolívar 2975, 7600 Mar del Plata; tel. (223) 435462; f. 1938; morning; Dir OSCAR ALBERTO GASTIARENA; circ. 20,000.

La Capital: Avda Champagnat 2551, 7600 Mar del Plata; tel. (223) 478-8490; fax (223) 478-1038; e-mail diario@lacapitalnet.com.ar; internet www.lacapitalnet.com.ar; f. 1905; Dir FLORENCIO ALDREY IGLESIAS; circ. 32,000.

El Día: Avda A. Diagonal 80, 817-21, 1900 La Plata; tel. (221) 425-0101; fax (221) 423-2996; e-mail redaccion@eldia.com; f. 1884; morning; independent; Dir RAÚL E. KRAISELBURD; circ. 54,868.

Ecos Diarios: Calle 62, No 2486, 7630 Necochea; tel. (2262) 430754; fax (2262) 424114; e-mail ecosdiar@satlink.com; internet www .ecosdiarios.com; f. 1921; morning; independent; Dir GUILLERMO IGNACIO; circ. 6,000.

La Nueva Provincia: Rodríuez 55, 8000 Bahía Blanca; tel. (291) 459-0000; fax (291) 459-0001; e-mail info@lanueva.com; internet www.lanueva.com.ar; f. 1898; morning; independent; Dir DIANA JULIO DE MASSOT; circ. 22,000 (Mon.–Fri.), 30,000 (Sunday).

La Voz del Pueblo: Avda San Martín 991, 7500 Tres Arroyos; tel. (2983) 430680; fax (2938) 430682; e-mail redaccion@lavozdelpueblo .com.ar; f. 1902; morning; independent; Dir ALBERTO JORGE MACIEL; circ. 8,500.

Río Negro

Río Negro: 9 de Julio 733, 8332, Gen. Roca, Río Negro; tel. (2941) 439300; fax (2941) 430517; e-mail rnredaccion@rionet.rionegro.com .ar; internet www.rionegro.com.ar; f. 1912; morning; Editor NÉLIDA RAJNERI DE GAMBA.

Salta

El Tribuno: Avda Ex Combatientes de Malvinas 3890, 4400 Salta; tel. (387) 424-0000; fax (387) 424-1382; e-mail tribuno@salnet.com .ar; internet www.eltribuno.com.ar; f. 1949; morning; Dir ROBERTO EDUARDO ROMERO; circ. 25,000.

San Juan

Diario de Cuyo: Mendoza 380 Sur, 5400 San Juan; tel. (264) 429-0038; fax (264) 429-0063; e-mail fbmontes@infovia.com.ar; f. 1947; morning; independent; Dir FRANCISCO B. MONTES; circ. 20,000.

San Luis

El Diario de La República: Junín 741, 5700 San Luis; tel. (2623) 422037; fax (2623) 428770; e-mail paynesa@infovia.com.ar; f. 1966; Dir ZULEMA A. RODRÍGUEZ SAA DE DIVIZIA; circ. 12,000.

Santa Fe

La Capital: Sarmiento 763, 2000 Rosario; tel. (341) 420-1100; fax (341) 420-1114; e-mail elagos@lacapital.com.ar; f. 1867; morning; independent; Dir CARLOS MARÍA LAGOS; circ. 65,000.

El Litoral: Avda 25 de Mayo 3536, 3000 Santa Fe; tel. (342) 450-2500; fax (342) 450-2530; e-mail litoral@litoral.com.ar; internet www.litoral.com.ar; f. 1918; morning; independent; Dir GUSTAVO VÍTTORI; circ. 37,000.

Santiago del Estero

El Liberal: Libertad 263, 4200 Santiago del Estero; tel. (385) 422-4400; fax (385) 422-4538; e-mail liberal@teletel.com.ar; internet www.sdnet.com.ar; f. 1898; morning; Exec. Dir JOSÉ LUIS CASTIGLIONE; Editorial Dir Dr JULIO CÉSAR CASTIGLIONE; circ. 20,000.

Tucumán

La Gaceta: Mendoza 654, 4000 San Miguel de Tucumán; tel. (381) 431-1111; fax (381) 431-1597; e-mail redaccion@lagaceta.com.ar; internet www.lagaceta.com.ar; f. 1912; morning; independent; Dir ALBERTO GARCÍA HAMILTON; circ. 70,000.

WEEKLY NEWSPAPER

El Informador Público: Uruguay 252, 3°F, 1015 Buenos Aires; tel. (11) 4476-3551; fax (11) 4342-2628; f. 1986.

PERIODICALS

Aeroespacio: Casilla 37, Sucursal 12B, 1412 Buenos Aires; tel. and fax (11) 4514-1562; e-mail info@aeroespacio.com.ar; internet www .aeroespacio.com.ar; f. 1940; every 2 months; aeronautics; Dir JORGE A. CUADROS; circ. 24,000.

Billiken: Azopardo 579, 1307 Buenos Aires; tel. (11) 4342-7071; fax (11) 4343-7040; e-mail artebilliken@atlantida.com.ar; f. 1919; weekly; children's magazine; Dir JUAN CARLOS PORRAS; circ. 240,000.

Casas y Jardines: Sarmiento 643, 1382 Buenos Aires; tel. (11) 445-1793; f. 1932; every 2 months; houses and gardens; publ. by Editorial Contémpora SRL; Dir NORBERTO M. MUZIO.

Chacra y Campo Moderno: Editorial Atlántida, SA, Azopardo 579, 1307 Buenos Aires; tel. (11) 4331-4591; fax (11) 4331-3272; f. 1930; monthly; farm and country magazine; Dir CONSTANCIO C. VIGIL; circ. 35,000.

Claudia: Avda Córdoba 1345, 12°, Buenos Aires; tel. (11) 442-3275; fax (11) 4814-3948; f. 1957; monthly; women's magazine; Dir ANA TORREJÓN; circ. 150,000.

El Economista: Avda Córdoba 632, 2°, 1054 Buenos Aires; tel. (11) 4322-7360; fax (11) 4322-8157; f. 1951; weekly; financial; Dir Dr D. RADONJIC; circ. 37,800.

Fotografía Universal: Buenos Aires; monthly; circ. 39,500.

Gente: Azopardo 579, 3°, 1307 Buenos Aires; tel. (11) 433-4591; f. 1965; weekly; general; Dir JORGE DE LUJÁN GUTIÉRREZ; circ. 133,000.

El Gráfico: Paseo Colón 505, 2°, 1063 Buenos Aires; tel. (11) 5235-5100; fax (11) 5235-5137; e-mail elgrafico@elgrafico.com.ar; internet www.elgrafico.com.ar; f. 1919; weekly; sport; Editor MARTIN MAZUR; circ. 127,000.

Guía Latinoamericana de Transportes: Florida 8287 esq. Portinari, 1669 Del Viso (Ptdo de Pilar), Provincia de Buenos Aires; tel. (11) 4320-7004; fax (11) 4307-1956; f. 1968; every 2 months; travel information and timetables; Editor Dr ARMANDO SCHLECKER HIRSCH; circ. 7,500.

Humor: Venezuela 842, 1095 Buenos Aires; tel. (11) 4334-5400; fax (11) 411-2700; f. 1978; every 2 months; satirical revue; Editor ANDRÉS CASCIOLI; circ. 180,000.

Legislación Argentina: Talcahuano 650, 1013 Buenos Aires; tel. (11) 4371-0528; e-mail jurispru@lvd.com.ar; f. 1958; weekly; law; Dir RICARDO ESTÉVEZ BOERO; circ. 15,000.

Mercado: Rivadavia 877, 2°, 1002 Buenos Aires; tel. (11) 4346-9400; fax (11) 4343-7880; e-mail mdiez@mercado.com.ar; internet www .mercado.com.ar; f. 1969; monthly; business; Dir MIGUEL ANGEL DIEZ; circ. 28,000.

Mundo Israelita: Pueyrredón 538, 1°B, 1032 Buenos Aires; tel. (11) 4961-7999; fax (11) 4961-0763; f. 1923; weekly; Editor Dr JOSÉ KESTELMAN; circ. 15,000.

Nuestra Arquitectura: Sarmiento 643, 5°, 1382 Buenos Aires; tel. (11) 445-1793; f. 1929; every 2 months; architecture; publ. by Editorial Contémpora SRL; Dir NORBERTO M. MUZIO.

Para Ti: Azopardo 579, 1307 Buenos Aires; tel. (11) 4331-4591; fax (11) 4331-3272; f. 1922; weekly; women's interest; Dir ANÍBAL C. VIGIL; circ. 104,000.

Pensamiento Económico: Avda Leandro N. Alem 36, 1003 Buenos Aires; tel. (11) 4331-8051; fax (11) 4331-8055; e-mail cac@cac.com.ar; internet www.cac.com.ar; f. 1925; quarterly; review of Cámara Argentina de Comercio; Dir Dr CARLOS L. P. ANTONUCCI.

La Prensa Médica Argentina: Junín 845, 1113 Buenos Aires; tel. (11) 4961-9793; fax (11) 4961-9494; e-mail presmedarg@hotmail .com; f. 1914; monthly; medical; Editor Dr P. A. LÓPEZ; circ. 8,000.

Prensa Obrera: Ayacucho 444, Buenos Aires; tel. (11) 4953-3824; fax (11) 4953-7164; f. 1982; weekly; publication of Partido Obrero; circ. 16,000.

La Semana: Sarmiento 1113, 1041 Buenos Aires; tel. (11) 435-2552; general; Editor DANIEL PLINER.

La Semana Médica: Arenales 3574, 1425 Buenos Aires; tel. (11) 4824-5673; f. 1894; monthly; Dir Dr EDUARDO F. MELE; circ. 7,000.

Siete Días Ilustrados: Avda Leandro N. Alem 896, 1001 Buenos Aires; tel. (11) 432-6010; f. 1967; weekly; general; Dir RICARDO CÁMARA; circ. 110,000.

Técnica e Industria: Buenos Aires; tel. (11) 446-3193; f. 1922; monthly; technology and industry; Dir E. R. FEDELE; circ. 5,000.

Visión: French 2820, 2°A, 1425 Buenos Aires; tel. (11) 4825-1258; fax (11) 4827-1004; e-mail edlatin@visionmag.com.ar; f. 1950; fortnightly; Latin American affairs, politics; Editor LUIS VIDAL RUCABADO.

Vosotras: Avda Leandro N. Alem 896, 3°, 1001 Buenos Aires; tel. (11) 432-6010; f. 1935; women's weekly; Dir ABEL ZANOTTO; circ. 33,000; Monthly supplements:

Labores: circ. 130,000.

Modas: circ. 70,000.

NEWS AGENCIES

Agencia TELAM, SA: Bolívar 531, 1066 Buenos Aires; tel. (11) 4339-0315; fax (11) 4339-0316; e-mail telam@sinectis.com.ar; internet www.telam.com.ar; Dir RODOLFO POUSÁ.

Diarios y Noticias (DYN): Avda Julio A. Roca 636, 8°, 1067 Buenos Aires; tel. (11) 4342-3040; fax (11) 4342-3043; e-mail info@dyn.com .ar; internet www.dyn.com.ar; Editor SANTIAGO GONZÁLEZ.

Noticias Argentinas, SA (NA): Suipacha 570, 3°b, 1008 Buenos Aires; tel. (11) 4394-7522; fax (11) 4394-7648; f. 1973; Dir LUIS FERNANDO TORRES.

Foreign Bureaux

Agence France-Presse (AFP): Avda Corrientes 456, 3°, Of. 34/37, 1366 Buenos Aires; tel. (11) 4394-8169; fax (11) 4393-9912; e-mail afp-baires@tournet.com.ar; internet www.afp.com; Bureau Chief JEAN VIREBAYRE.

Agencia EFE (Spain): Guido 1770, 1016 Buenos Aires; tel. (11) 4812-9596; fax (11) 4815-8691; Bureau Chief AGUSTÍN DE GRACIA.

Agenzia Nazionale Stampa Associata (ANSA) (Italy): San Martín 320, 6°, 1004 Buenos Aires; tel. (11) 4394-7568; fax (11) 4394-5214; e-mail ansabairestec@infovia.com.ar; Bureau Chief ANTONIO CAVALLARI.

Associated Press (AP) (USA): Bouchard 551, 5°, Casilla 1296, 1106 Buenos Aires; tel. (11) 4311-0081; fax (11) 4311-0082; Bureau Chief WILLIAM H. HEATH.

Deutsche Presse-Agentur (dpa) (Germany): Buenos Aires; tel. (11) 4311-5311; e-mail msvgroth@ba.net; Bureau Chief Dr HENDRIK GROTH.

Informatsionnoye Telegrafnoye Agentstvo Rossii-Telegrafnoye Agentstvo Suverennykh Stran (ITAR-TASS) (Russia): Avda Córdoba 652, 11°E, 1054 Buenos Aires; tel. (11) 4392-2044; Dir ISIDORO GILBERT.

Inter Press Service (IPS) (Italy): Buenos Aires; tel. (11) 4394-0829; Bureau Chief RAMÓN M. GORRIARÁN; Correspondent GUSTAVO CAPDEVILLA.

Magyar Távirati Iroda (MTI) (Hungary): Marcelo T. de Alvear 624, 3° 16, 1058 Buenos Aires; tel. (11) 4312-9596; Correspondent ENDRE SIMÓ.

Prensa Latina (Cuba): Buenos Aires; tel. (11) 4394-0565; Correspondent MARIO HERNÁNDEZ DEL LLANO.

Reuters (United Kingdom): Avda Eduardo Madero 940, 25°, 1106 Buenos Aires; tel. (11) 4318-0600; fax (11) 4318-0698; Dir CARLOS PÍA MANGIONE.

Xinhua (New China) News Agency (People's Republic of China): Tucumán 540, 14°, Apto D, 1049 Buenos Aires; tel. (11) 4313-9755; Bureau Chief JU QINGDONG.

The following are also represented: Central News Agency (Taiwan), Interpress (Poland), Jiji Press (Japan).

PRESS ASSOCIATION

Asociación de Entidades Periodísticas Argentinas (ADEPA): Chacabuco 314, 3°, 1069 Buenos Aires; tel. and fax (11) 4331-1500; e-mail adepa@ciudad.com.ar; internet www.adepa.com.ar; f. 1962; Pres. GUILLERMO IGNACIO.

Publishers

Editorial Abril, SA: Moreno 1617, 1093 Buenos Aires; tel. (11) 4331-0112; f. 1961; fiction, non-fiction, children's books, textbooks; Dir ROBERTO M. ARES.

Editorial Acme, SA: Santa Magdalena 635, 1277 Buenos Aires; tel. (11) 4328-1508; f. 1949; general fiction, children's books, agriculture, textbooks; Man. Dir EMILIO I. GONZÁLEZ.

Aguilar, Altea, Taurus, Alfaguara, SA de Ediciones: Beazley 3860, 1437 Buenos Aires; tel. (11) 4912-7220; fax (11) 4912-7440; internet www.santillana.com.ar; f. 1946; general, literature, children's books; Pres. ESTEBAN FERNÁNDEZ ROSADO; Gen. Man. DAVID DELGADO DE ROBLES.

Editorial Albatros, SACI: Torres Las Plazas, J Salguero 2745, 5°, 1425 Buenos Aires; tel. (11) 4807-2030; fax (11) 4807-2010; e-mail info@albatros.com.ar; internet www.albatros.com.ar; f. 1945; technical, non-fiction, social sciences, sport, children's books, medicine and agriculture; Pres. ANDREA INÉS CANEVARO.

Amorrortu Editores, SA: Paraguay 1225, 7°, 1057 Buenos Aires; tel. (11) 4393-8812; fax (11) 4325-6307; f. 1967; anthropology, religion, economics, sociology, philosophy, psychology, psychoanalysis, current affairs; Man. Dir HORACIO DE AMORRORTU.

Angel Estrada y Cía, SA: Bolívar 462-66, 1066 Buenos Aires; tel. (11) 4331-6521; fax (11) 4331-6527; e-mail edito@estrada.com.ar; f. 1869; textbooks, children's books; Gen. Man. OSCAR DOMECQ.

Editorial Atlántida, SA: Azopardo 579, 1307 Buenos Aires; tel. (11) 4346-0100; fax (11) 4331-3272; internet www.atlantida.com; f. 1918; fiction and non-fiction, children's books; Exec. Dir ALFREDO VERCELLI.

Ediciones La Aurora: Buenos Aires; tel. and fax (11) 4941-8940; f. 1925; general, religion, spirituality, theology, philosophy, psychology, history, semiology, linguistics; Dir Dr HUGO O. ORTEGA.

Az Editora, SA: Paraguay 2351, 1121 Buenos Aires; tel. (11) 961-4036; fax (11) 961-0089; f. 1976; social sciences and medicine; Pres. DANTE OMAR VILLALBA.

Biblioteca Nacional de Maestros: c/o Ministry of Education, Pizzurno 935, planta baja, 1020 Buenos Aires; tel. (11) 4129-1272; fax (11) 4129-1268; e-mail gperrone@me.gov.ar; internet www.bnm.me.gov.ar; f. 1884; Dir GRACIELA PERRONE.

Centro Editor de América Latina, SA: Tucumun 1736, 1050 Buenos Aires; tel. (11) 4371-2411; f. 1967; literature, history; Man. Dir JOSÉ B. SPIVACOW.

Editorial Claretiana: Lima 1360, 1138 Buenos Aires; tel. (11) 427-9250; fax (11) 427-4015; e-mail editorial@editorialclaretiana.com.ar; internet www.editorialclaretiana.com.ar; f. 1956; Catholicism; Man. Dir DOMINGO ANGEL GRILLIA.

Editorial Claridad, SA: Viamonte 1730, 1°, 1055 Buenos Aires; tel. (11) 4371-5546; fax (11) 4375-1659; e-mail editorial@heliasta.com.ar; internet www.heliasta.com.ar; f. 1922; literature, biographies, social science, politics, reference, dictionaries; Pres. Dra ANA MARÍA CABANELLAS.

Club de Lectores: Avda de Mayo 624, 1084 Buenos Aires; tel. (11) 4342-6251; f. 1938; non-fiction; Man. Dir MERCEDES FONTENLA.

Editorial Columba, SA: Sarmiento 1889, 5°, 1044 Buenos Aires; tel. (11) 445-4297; f. 1953; classics in translation, 20th century; Man. Dir CLAUDIO A. COLUMBA.

Editorial Contémpora, SRL: Sarmiento 643, 5°, 1382 Buenos Aires; tel. (11) 445-1793; architecture, town-planning, interior decoration and gardening; Dir NORBERTO C. MUZIO.

Cosmopolita, SRL: Piedras 744, 1070 Buenos Aires; tel. (11) 4361-8925; fax (11) 4361-8049; f. 1940; science and technology; Man. Dir RUTH F. DE RAPP.

Depalma, SA: Talcahuano 494, 1013 Buenos Aires; tel. (11) 4371-7306; fax (11) 4371-6913; e-mail info@ed-depalma.com; internet www.ed-depalma.com; f. 1944; periodicals and books covering law, politics, sociology, philosophy, history and economics; Man. Dir ROBERTO SUARDIAZ.

Editorial Difusión, SA: Sarandi 1065–67, Buenos Aires; tel. (11) 4941-0088; f. 1937; literature, philosophy, religion, education, textbooks, children's books; Dir DOMINGO PALOMBELLA.

Edicial, SA: Rivadavia 739, 1002 Buenos Aires; tel. (11) 4342-8481; fax (11) 4343-1151; e-mail edicial@ssdnet.com.ar; internet www.ssdnet.com.ar/edicial; f. 1931; education; Man. Dir J. A. MUSSET.

Emecé Editores, SA: Alsina 2062, 1090 Buenos Aires; tel. (11) 4954-0105; fax (11) 4953-4200; e-mail editorial@emece.com.ar; internet www.emece.com.ar; f. 1939; non-fiction, biographies, history, art, essays; Pres. ALFREDO DEL CARRIL.

Espasa Calpe Argentina, SA: Avda Independencia 1668, 1100 Buenos Aires; tel. (11) 4382-4043; fax (11) 4383-3793; f. 1937; literature, science, dictionaries; publ. *Colección Austral*; Dir GUILLERMO SCHAVELZON.

EUDEBA (Editorial Universitaria de Buenos Aires): Rivadavia 1573, 1033 Buenos Aires; tel. (11) 4383-8025; fax (11) 4383-2202; e-mail eudeba@eudeba.com.ar; internet www.eudeba.com.ar; f.

1958; university text books and general interest publications; Pres. Dr LUIS YANES.

Fabril Editora, SA: Buenos Aires; tel. (11) 421-3601; f. 1958; non-fiction, science, arts, education and reference; Editorial Man. ANDRÉS ALFONSO BRAVO; Business Man. RÓMULO AYERZA.

Editorial Glem, SACIF: Avda Caseros 2056, 1264 Buenos Aires; tel. (11) 426-6641; f. 1933; psychology, technology; Pres. JOSÉ ALFREDO TUCCI.

Editorial Guadalupe: Mansilla 3865, 1425 Buenos Aires; tel. (11) 4826-8587; fax (11) 4823-6672; e-mail ventas@editorialguadalupe.com.ar; internet www.editorialguadalupe.com.ar; f. 1895; social sciences, religion, anthropology, children's books, and pedagogy; Man. Dir LORENZO GOYENECHE.

Editorial Heliasta, SRL: Viamonte 1730, 1°, 1055 Buenos Aires; tel. (11) 4371-5546; fax (11) 4375-1659; e-mail editorial@heliasta.com.ar; internet www.heliasta.com.ar; f. 1944; literature, biography, dictionaries, legal; Pres. Dra ANA MARÍA CABANELLAS.

Editorial Hispano-Americana, SA (HASA): Alsina 731, 1087 Buenos Aires; tel. (11) 4331-5051; f. 1934; science and technology; Pres. Prof. HÉCTOR OSCAR ALGARRA.

Editorial Inter-Médica, SAICI: Junín 917, 1°, 1113 Buenos Aires; tel. (11) 4961-9234; fax (11) 4961-5572; e-mail info@inter-medica.com.ar; internet www.inter-medica.com.ar; f. 1959; medicine, dentistry, psychology, psychiatry, veterinary; Pres. JORGE MODYEIEVSKY.

Editorial Inter-Vet, SA: Avda de los Constituyentes 3141, Buenos Aires; tel. (11) 451-2382; f. 1987; veterinary; Pres. JORGE MODYEIEVSKY.

Kapelusz Editora, SA: San José 831, 1076 Buenos Aires; tel. (11) 4342-7400; fax (11) 4331-8020; e-mail empresa@kapelusz.com.ar; internet www.kapelusz.com.ar; f. 1905; textbooks, psychology, pedagogy, children's books; Vice-Pres. RAFAEL PASCUAL ROBIES.

Editorial Kier, SACIFI: Avda Santa Fe 1260, 1059 Buenos Aires; tel. (11) 4811-0507; fax (11) 4811-3395; e-mail info@kier.com.ar; internet www.kier.com.ar; f. 1907; Eastern doctrines and religions, astrology, parapsychology, tarot, I Ching, occultism, cabbala, freemasonry and natural medicine; Pres. HÉCTOR S. PIBERNUS; Mans SERGIO PIBERNUS, OSVALDO PIBERNUS.

Ediciones Librerías Fausto: Avda Corrientes 1316, 1043 Buenos Aires; tel. (11) 4476-4919; fax (11) 4476-3914; f. 1943; fiction and non-fiction; Man. RAFAEL ZORRILLA.

Carlos Lohlé, SA: Tacuarí 1516, 1139 Buenos Aires; tel. (11) 427-9969; f. 1953; philosophy, religion, belles-lettres; Dir FRANCISCO M. LOHLÉ.

Editorial Losada, SA: Moreno 3362/64, 1209 Buenos Aires; tel. (11) 4863-8608; fax (11) 4864-0434; f. 1938; general; Pres. JOSÉ JUAN FERNÁNDEZ REGUERA.

Ediciones Macchi, SA: Alsina 1535/37, 1088 Buenos Aires; tel. (11) 446-2506; fax (11) 446-0594; e-mail info@macchi.com.ar; internet www.macchi.com; f. 1947; economic sciences; Pres. RAÚL LUIS MACCHI; Dir JULIO ALBERTO MENDONÇA.

Editorial Médica Panamericana, SA: Marcelo T. de Alvear 2145, 1122 Buenos Aires; tel. (11) 4821-5520; fax (11) 4825-5006; e-mail info@medicapanamericana.com.ar; internet www.medicapanamericana.com.ar; f. 1962; medicine and health sciences; Pres. HUGO BRIK.

Ediciones Nueva Visión, SAIC: Tucumán 3748, 1189 Buenos Aires; tel. (11) 4864-5050; fax (11) 4863-5980; e-mail ednuevavision@ciudad.com.ar; f. 1954; psychology, education, social sciences, linguistics; Man. Dir HAYDÉE P. DE GIACONE.

Editorial Paidós: Defensa 599, 1°, 1065 Buenos Aires; tel. (11) 4331-2275; fax (11) 4345-6769; e-mail paidos@internet.siscotel.com; f. 1945; social sciences, medicine, philosophy, religion, history, literature, textbooks; Man. Dir MARITA GOTTHEIL.

Plaza y Janés, SA: Buenos Aires; tel. (11) 486-6769; popular fiction and non-fiction; Man. Dir JORGE PÉREZ.

Editorial Plus Ultra, SA: Callao 575, 1022 Buenos Aires; tel. (11) 4374-2953; e-mail plusultra@epu.virtual.ar.net; f. 1964; literature, history, textbooks, law, economics, politics, sociology, pedagogy, children's books; Man. Editors RAFAEL ROMÁN, LORENZO MARENGO.

Editorial Santillana: Buenos Aires; f. 1960; education; Pres. JESÚS DE POLANCO GUTÉRREZ.

Schapire Editor, SRL: Uruguay 1249, 1016 Buenos Aires; tel. (11) 4812-0765; fax (11) 4815-0369; f. 1941; music, art, theatre, sociology, history, fiction; Dir MIGUEL SCHAPIRE DALMAT.

Editorial Sigmar, SACI: Belgrano 1580, 7°, 1093 Buenos Aires; tel. (11) 4383-3045; fax (11) 4383-5633; e-mail editorial@sigmar.com.ar; f. 1941; children's books; Man. Dir ROBERTO CHWAT.

Editorial Sopena Argentina, SACI e I: Maza 2138, 1240 Buenos Aires; tel. (11) 4912-2383; fax (11) 4912-2383; f. 1918; dictionaries, classics, chess, health, politics, history, children's books; Dir MARTA A. J. OLSEN.

Editorial Stella: Viamonte 1984, 1056 Buenos Aires; tel. (11) 4374-0346; fax (11) 4374-8719; general non-fiction and textbooks; owned by Asociación Educacionista Argentina.

Editorial Sudamericana, SA: Humberto 545, 1°, 1103 Buenos Aires; tel. (11) 4300-5400; fax (11) 4362-7364; e-mail info@edsudamericana.com.ar; internet www.edsudamericana.com.ar; f. 1939; general fiction and non-fiction; Gen. Man. OLAF HANTEL.

Editorial Troquel, SA: Pichincha 967, 1219 Buenos Aires; tel. (11) 4941-7943; e-mail troquel@ba.net; f. 1954; general literature and textbooks; Pres. GUSTAVO A. RESSIA.

PUBLISHERS' ASSOCIATION

Cámara Argentina de Publicaciones: Reconquista 1011, 6°, 1003 Buenos Aires; tel. (11) 4311-6855; f. 1970; Pres. AGUSTÍN DOS SANTOS; Man. LUIS FRANCISCO HOULIN.

Broadcasting and Communications

Secretaría de Comunicaciones: Sarmiento 151, 4°, 1000 Buenos Aires; tel. (11) 4318-9410; fax (11) 4318-9432; co-ordinates 30 stations and the international service; Sec. Dr GERMÁN KAMMERATH.

Subsecretaría de Planificación y Gestión Tecnológica: Sarmiento 151, 4°, 1000 Buenos Aires; tel. (11) 4347-9970; Under-Sec. Ing. ALEJANDRA CABALLERO.

Subsecretaría de Radiocomunicaciones: Sarmiento 151, 4°, 1000 Buenos Aires; tel. (11) 4311-5909; Under-Sec. Ing. ALFREDO R. PARODI.

Subsecretaría de Telecomunicaciones: Sarmiento 151, 4°, 1000 Buenos Aires; tel. (11) 4311-5909; Under-Sec. JULIO I. GUILLÁN.

Comité Federal de Radiodifusión (COMFER): Suipacha 765, 9°, 1008 Buenos Aires; tel. (11) 4320-4900; fax (11) 4394-6866; e-mail mlagier@comfer.gov.ar; f. 1972; controls various technical aspects of broadcasting and transmission of programmes; Head GUSTAVO LÓPEZ.

TELECOMMUNICATIONS

Cámara de Informática y Comunicaciones de la República Argentina (CICOMRA): Avda Córdoba 744, 2°, 1054 Buenos Aires; tel. (11) 4325-8839; fax (11) 4325-9604; e-mail cicomra@starnet.net.ar.

Comisión Nacional de Comunicaciones (CNC): Perú 103, 9°, 1067 Buenos Aires; tel. (11) 4347-9242; fax (11) 4347-9244; Pres. Dr ROBERTO CATALÁN.

Cía Ericsson SACI: Avda Madero, 1020 Buenos Aires; tel. (11) 4319-5500; fax (11) 4315-0629; Dir-Gen. Ing. ROLANDO ZUBIRÁN.

Cía de Radiocomunicaciones Móviles SA: Tucumán 744, 9°, 1049 Buenos Aires; tel. (11) 4325-5006; fax (11) 4325-5334; mobile telecommunications co; Pres. Lic. MAURICIO E. WIOR.

Movicom: Tucumán 744, 2°, 1049 Buenos Aires; tel. (11) 4978-4773; fax (11) 4978-7373; e-mail rree@movi.com.ar; internet www.movi.com.ar; telecommunications services, including cellular phones, trunking, paging and wireless access to the internet; Pres. Lic. MAURICIO WIOR.

Telecom Argentina: Alicia Moreau de Justo 50, 1107 Buenos Aires; tel. (11) 4968-4000; fax (11) 4968-1420; e-mail inversores@intersrv.telecom.com.ar; internet www.telecom.com.ar; provision of telecommunication services in the north of Argentina; Pres. JUAN CARLOS MASJOAN.

Telecomunicaciones Internacionales de Argentina, SA (TELINTAR): 25 de Mayo 457, 7°, 1002 Buenos Aires; tel. (11) 4318-0500; fax (11) 4313-4924; e-mail mlamas@telintar.com.ar; internet www.telintar.com.ar; Sec.-Gen. Dr MARCELO MIGUEL LAMAS.

Telefónica de Argentina, SA (TASA): Tucumán 1, 17°, 1049 Buenos Aires; tel. (11) 4345-5772; fax (11) 4345-5771; e-mail gabello@telefonica.com.ar; internet www.telefonica.com.ar; provision of telecommunication services in the south of Argentina; Pres. CARLOS FERNÁNDEZ PRIDA.

RADIO

There are three privately-owned stations in Buenos Aires and 72 in the interior. There are also 37 state-controlled stations, four provincial, three municipal and three university stations. The principal ones are Radio Antártida, Radio Argentina, Radio Belgrano, Radio Ciudad de Buenos Aires, Radio Excelsior, Radio Mitre, Radio El Mundo, Radio Nacional, Radio del Plata, Radio Rivadavia and Radio Splendid, all in Buenos Aires.

Radio Nacional: Maipú 555, 1006 Buenos Aires; tel. (11) 4325-4590; fax (11) 4325-4313; e-mail secretariansor@sion.com; Dir MARIO ANDRÉS CELLA.

Cadena Argentina de Radiodifusión (CAR): Avda Entre Ríos 149, 3°, 1079 Buenos Aires; tel. (11) 4325-9100; fax (11) 4325-9433; groups all national state-owned commercial stations which are operated directly by the Subsecretaría Operativa.

LRA Radio Nacional de Buenos Aires: Maipú 555, 1006 Buenos Aires; tel. and fax (11) 4325-9433; e-mail rna@mecon.ar; f. 1937; Dir PATRICIA IVONE BARRAL.

Radiodifusión Argentina al Exterior (RAE): Maipú 555, 1006 Buenos Aires; tel. (11) 4325-6368; fax (11) 4325-9433; e-mail rna@mecon.ar; f. 1958; broadcasts in eight languages to all areas of the world; Dir-Gen. PERLA DAMURI.

Asociación de Radiodifusoras Privadas Argentinas (ARPA): Juan D. Perón 1561, 8°, 1037 Buenos Aires; tel. (11) 4382-4412; f. 1958; an association of all but three of the privately-owned commercial stations; Pres. DOMINGO F. L. ELÍAS.

TELEVISION

There are 42 television channels, of which 29 are privately owned and 15 are owned by provincial and national authorities. The national television network is regulated by the Comité Federal de Radiodifusión (see above).

The following are some of the more important television stations in Argentina: Argentina Televisora Color LS82 Canal 7, LS83 (Canal 9 Libertad), LS84 (Canal 11 Telefé), LS85 Canal 13 ArTeAr SA, LV80 Telenueva, LU81 Teledifusora Bahiense SA, LV81 Canal 12 Telecor SACI, Dicor Difusión Córdoba, LV80 TV Canal 10 Universidad Nacional Córdoba, and LU82 TV Mar del Plata SA.

Asociación de Teleradiodifusoras Argentinas (ATA): Avda Córdoba 323, 6°, 1054 Buenos Aires; tel. (11) 4312-4208; fax (11) 4315-4681; e-mail info@ata.org.ar; internet www.ata.org.ar; f. 1959; asscn of 22 private television channels; Pres. CARLOS FONTAN BALESTRA.

ATC (Argentina Televisora Color LS82 TV Canal 7): Avda Figueroa Alcorta 2977, 1425 Buenos Aires; tel. (11) 4802-6001; fax (11) 4802-9878; e-mail presidencia@canal7argentina.com.ar; internet www.canal7argentina.com.ar; state-controlled channel; Dir MARIO ANDRÉS CELLA.

Azul Televisión—LS83 (Canal 9 Libertad): Dorrego 1708, Buenos Aires; tel. (11) 777-2321; fax (11) 777-9620; e-mail noticias@azultv.com; internet www.azultv.com; private channel; Dir ALEJANDRO RAMAY.

LS84 (Canal 11 Telefé): Pavón 2444, 1248 Buenos Aires; tel. (11) 4941-9549; fax (11) 4942-6773; leased to a private concession in 1992; Pres. PEDRO SIMONCINI.

LS85: Canal 13 (ArTeAr SA): Avda San Juan 1170, 1147 Buenos Aires; tel. (11) 4305-0013; fax (11) 4307-0315; e-mail webmaster@webtv.artear.com; internet www.webtv.artear.com.ar; f. 1989; leased to a private concession in 1992; Dir-Gen. LUCIO PAGLIARO.

Finance

(cap. = capital; res = reserves; dep. = deposits; m. = million; amounts in nuevos pesos argentinos—$, unless otherwise stated)

BANKING

In September 2001 there were two public banks, 11 municipal banks, 33 domestic private banks, 39 foreign private banks and two co-operative banks.

Central Bank

Banco Central de la República Argentina: Reconquista 266, 1003 Buenos Aires; tel. (11) 4348-3500; fax (11) 4348-3955; e-mail sistema@bcra.gov.ar; internet www.bcra.gov.ar; f. 1935 as a central reserve bank; it has the right of note issue; all capital is held by the State; cap. and res $3,837.5m., dep. $992.3m. (Dec. 1999); Pres. ADOLFO PRAT-GAY.

Government-owned Commercial Banks

Banco de la Ciudad de Buenos Aires: Florida 302, 1313 Buenos Aires; tel. (11) 4329-8600; fax (11) 4112-098; e-mail bcdad39@sminter.com.ar; internet www.bancociudad.com.ar; municipal bank; f. 1878; cap. $169.5m., res $109.8m., dep. $3,109.4m. (Dec. 2001); Chair. ROBERTO J. FELETTI; Gen. Man. HUGO HARLEY ARBARELLO; 42 brs.

Banco de Inversión y Commercio Exterior, SA (BICE): 25 de Mayo 526, 1002 Buenos Aires; tel. (11) 4313-9546; fax (11) 4315-4097; e-mail rcancel@bice.com.ar; internet www.bice.com.ar; f. 1991; cap. \$489.2m., res \$17.8m., dep. \$121.8m. (Dec. 2000); Pres. DIEGO YOFRE; Gen. Man. SUSANA OLGIATI.

Banco de la Nación Argentina: Bartolomé Mitre 326, 1036 Buenos Aires; tel. (11) 4347-6000; fax (11) 4347-6316; e-mail gerencia@bna.com.ar; internet www.bna.com.ar; f. 1891; national bank; cap. \$381.0m., res \$1,531.4m., dep. \$16,732.0m. (Dec. 1999); Pres. HORACIO ERNESTO PERICOLI; 617 brs.

Banco de la Pampa: Carlos Pellegrini 255, 6300 Santa Rosa; tel. (2954) 433008; fax (2954) 433196; internet www.blp.com.ar; f. 1958; cap. \$6.9m., res \$136.2m., dep. \$873.6m. (June 1999); Pres. LUIS E. ROLDÁN; Gen. Man. NORBERTO RAÚL CANTERO; 112 brs.

Banco de la Provincia de Buenos Aires: Avda San Martín 137, 1004 Buenos Aires; tel. (11) 4347-0000; fax (11) 4347-0229; e-mail baprocri@internet.siscotel.com; internet www.bpba.com; f. 1822; provincial bank; cap. \$1,250.0m., res \$207.3m., dep. \$12,274.2m. (Dec. 2000); Pres. RICARDO GUTIÉRREZ; Gen. Man. MARIO MALATINI; 313 brs.

Banco de la Provincia de Córdoba: San Jerónimo 166, 5000 Córdoba; tel. (351) 420-7200; fax (351) 422-9718; e-mail gcomexterior@bancocordoba.com; internet www.bancocordoba.com; f. 1873; provincial bank; cap. \$47.6m., res \$142.8m., dep. \$1,036.1 (Dec. 1994); Pres. LUIS ENRIQUE GRUNHAUT; 150 brs.

Banco de la Provincia del Neuquén: Avda Argentina 41/45, 8300 Neuquén; tel. (299) 434221; fax (299) 4480439; internet www.bpn.com.ar; f. 1960; dep. \$232.8m., total assets \$388.6m. (March 1995); Pres. LUIS ALBERTO MANGANARO; Gen. Man. JOSÉ MANUEL OSER; 22 brs.

Banco de la Provincia de San Luis: Rivadavia 602, 5700 San Luis; tel. (2623) 425013; fax (2623) 424943; dep. \$88.8m., total assets \$107.8m. (May 1995); Principal Officer SALVADOR OMAR CAMPO.

Banco de la Provincia de Santa Cruz: Avda General Roca 802, 9400 Río Gallegos; tel. (2966) 420845; dep. \$211.7m., total assets \$382.1m. (June 1995); Govt Admin. EDUARDO LABOLIDA.

Banco de la Provincia de Santiago del Estero: Avda Belgrano 529 Sur, 4200 Santiago del Estero; tel. (385) 422-2300; dep. \$69.9m., total assets \$101.6m. (Jan. 1995); Pres. AMÉRICO DAHER.

Banco de la Provincia de Tucumán: San Martín 362, 4000 San Miguel de Tucumán; tel. (381) 431-1709; dep. \$164.7m., total assets \$359.5m. (March 1995); Govt Admin. EMILIO APAZA.

Banco Provincial de Salta: España 550, 4400 Salta; tel. (387) 422-1300; fax (387) 431-0020; f. 1887; dep. \$40.7m., total assets \$125.0m. (June 1995); Pres. Dr REYNALDO ALFREDO NOGUEIRA; 19 brs.

Banco Social de Córdoba: 27 de Abril 185, 1°, 5000 Córdoba; tel. (351) 422-3367; dep. \$187.3m., total assets \$677.3m. (June 1995); Pres. Dr JAIME POMPAS.

Banco de Tierra del Fuego: Maipú 897, 9410 Ushuaia; tel. (2901) 441600; e-mail entradas@bancotdf.com.ar; internet www.bancotdf.com.ar; national bank; cap. and res \$21.8m., dep. \$54.2m. (June 1992); Pres. GUSTAVO LOFIEGO; Gen. Man. MIGUEL LANDERRECHE; 4 brs.

Nuevo Banco de la Rioja, SA: Rivadavia 702, CP 5300, 5300 La Rioja; tel. (3822) 430575; fax (3822) 430618; f. 1994; provincial bank; Pres. ELIAS SAHAD; 2 brs.

Nuevo Banco de Santa Fé, SA: Tucumán 2545, 2°, 3000 Santa Fe; tel. (342) 450-4700; fax (342) 455-4543; e-mail bobbiom@bancobsf.com.ar; internet www.bancobsf.com.ar; f. 1847; as Banco Provincial de Santa Fe, adopted current name in 1998; provincial bank; cap. \$60.0m., res \$31.1m., dep. \$643.5m. (Dec. 1998); Chair. JOSÉ ENRIQUE ROHM; 103 brs.

Private Commercial Banks

Banco BI Creditanstalt, SA: Bouchard 547, 24° y 25°, 1106 Buenos Aires; tel. (11) 4319-8400; fax (11) 4319-8230; e-mail bicreditanstalt.com.ar; internet www.bicreditanstalt.com.ar; f. 1971 as Banco Interfinanzas, name changed as above in 1997; cap. \$38.3m., res \$9.2m., dep. \$474.5m. (Dec. 2000); Pres. Dr MIGUEL ANGEL ANGELINO.

Banco Bansud, SA: Sarmiento 447, 1041 Buenos Aires; tel. (11) 5222-6500; fax (11) 5222-6624; internet www.bansud.com; f. 1995; after merger of Banesto Banco Shaw, SA and Banco del Sud, SA; cap. \$64.4m., res \$114.6m., dep. \$881.0m. (Dec. 2001); Pres. JORGE HORACIO BRITO; 39 brs.

Banco Caja de Ahorro, SA: Avda Corrientes 629, 1324 Buenos Aires; tel. (11) 4323-5000; fax (11) 4323-5073; internet www.lacaja.com.ar; f. 1923 as Banco Mercantil Argentino, SA, adopted current name in 1999 following merger with Banco Caja de Ahorro, SA; cap. \$0.1m., res \$61.5m., dep. \$587.3m. (Dec. 1997); Pres. NOEL WERTHEIN.

Banco CMF, SA: Macacha Güemes 555, Puerto Madero, 1106 Buenos Aires; tel. (11) 4318-6800; fax (11) 4318-6812; f. 1978 as

Corporación Metropolitana de Finanzas, SA, adopted current name in 1999; cap. \$49.0m., res \$6.7m., dep. \$445.1m. (Dec. 2000); Pres. JOSÉ P. BENEGAS LYNCH.

Banco COMAFI: Avda Roque Sáenz Peña 660, 1035 Buenos Aires; tel. (11) 4347-0400; fax (11) 4347-0404; e-mail contactenos@comafi.com.ar; internet www.comafi.com.ar; f. 1984; assumed control of 65% of Scotiabank Quilmes in April 2002; Pres. GUILLERMO CERVIÑO; Vice-Pres. EDUARDO MASCHWITZ.

Banco Comercial Israelita, SA: Bartolomé Mitre 702, 2000 Rosario; tel. (341) 420-0557; fax (341) 420-0517; f. 1921; cap. \$4.3m., res \$20.5m., dep. \$232.0m. (June 1998); Pres. Ing. DAVID ZCARNY; 4 brs.

Banco de Corrientes: 9 de Julio 1099, esq. San Juan, 3400 Corrientes; tel. (3783) 479200; fax (3783) 479283; internet www.elbancodecorrientes; f. 1951 as Banco de la República de Corrientes; adopted current name in 1993, after transfer to private ownership; cap. and res \$38.5m., dep. \$126.7m. (June 1995); Pres. PEDRO DOMINGO GOIDA; 33 brs.

Banco Crédito Provincial SA: Calle 7, esq. 50, Casilla 54, 1900 La Plata; tel. and fax (221) 429-2000; f. 1911; cap. \$2.5m., res \$40.5m., dep. \$160.5m. (June 1995); Pres. ANTONIO R. FALABELLA; 47 brs.

Banco de Entre Ríos SA: Monte Caseros 128, 3100 Paraná; tel. (343) 423-1200; fax (343) 421-1221; e-mail bersaext@satlink.com; f. 1935; provincial bank; transferred to private ownership in 1995; cap. \$55.2m., res \$3.2m., dep. \$680.5m. (June 2000); Pres. CARLOS ALBERTO CELAÁ; 29 brs.

Banco Florencia, SA: Reconquista 353, 1003 Buenos Aires; tel. (11) 4325-5949; fax (11) 4325-5849; f. 1984; cap. and res \$8.8m., dep. \$11.8m. (Dec. 1993); Chair. ALBERTO BRUNET; Vice-Chair. JORGE GONZÁLEZ.

Banco de Galicia y Buenos Aires SA: Juan D. Perón 407, Casilla 86, 1038 Buenos Aires; tel. (11) 4394-7080; fax (11) 4393-1603; e-mail bancogalicia@bancogalicia.com.ar; internet www.bancogalicia.com.ar; f. 1905; cap. \$405.4m., res \$516.0m., dep. \$11,640.3m. (June 1999); Chair. EDUARDO J. ESCASANY; 165 brs.

Banco Israelita de Córdoba, SA: Ituzaingó 60, 5000 Córdoba; tel. (351) 420-3200; fax (351) 424-3616; f. 1942; cap. \$9.0m., res \$18.3m., dep. \$160.5m. (June 1995); Pres. JUAN MACHTEY; 20 brs.

Banco Macro, SA: Sarmiento 735, 1041 Buenos Aires; tel. (11) 4325-9511; fax (11) 4325-2330; e-mail bmmholding@inea.com.ar; internet www.grupomarco.com.ar; f. 1997 by merger of Banco Macro, SA (f. 1988) and Banco de Misiones, SA; adopted current name in 1991 following merger with Banco de Salta, SA; cap. \$35.5m., res \$25.7m., dep. \$463.2m. (Dec. 2001); Pres. JORGE HORACIO BRITO.

Banco Mariva, SA: Sarmiento 500, 1041 Buenos Aires; tel. (11) 4331-7571; fax (11) 4321-2222; e-mail tecnol@mariva.com.ar; f. 1980; cap. \$30.0m., res \$10.0m., dep. \$206.3m. (Dec. 1994); Pres. RICARDO MAY.

Banco Patagonia, SA: 25 de Mayo 544, 1002 Buenos Aires; tel. (11) 4317-4500; fax (11) 4317-4848; e-mail capfed@bancopatagonia.com.ar; internet www.bancopatagonia.com.ar; f. 1979 as Cambio Mildesa; following merger with Banco Río Negro, name changed to Banco de Río Negro, SA; adopted current name in 2000; cap. \$42.6m., res \$3.6m., dep. \$301.8m. (June 2001); Pres. JORGE G. STUART MILNE.

Banco Río de la Plata, SA: Bartolomé Mitre 480, 1036 Buenos Aires; tel. (11) 4341-1000; fax (11) 4341-1554; internet www.bancorio.com.ar; f. 1908; cap. \$335.3m., res \$787.9m., dep. \$12,292.7m. (June 2000); Pres. JOSÉ LUIS ENRIQUE CRISTOFANI; 266 brs.

Banco Suquía, SA: 25 de Mayo 160, 5000 Córdoba; tel. (351) 420-0200; fax (351) 420-0443; internet www.bancosuquia.com.ar; f. 1961 as Banco del Suquía, SA; adopted current name in 1998; dep. \$2,051.0m. (June 2000); Pres. JOSÉ P. PORTA; Gen. Man. RAÚL FERNÁNDEZ; 100 brs.

Banco de Valores, SA: Sarmiento 310, 1041 Buenos Aires; tel. (11) 4323-6900; fax (11) 4334-1731; e-mail info@banval.sba..com.ar; internet www.bancodevalores.com; f. 1978; cap. \$10.0m., res \$6.7m., dep. \$143.9m. (Dec. 2000); Pres. JULIO A. MACCHI; 1 br.

Banco Velox, SA: San Martín 298, 1004 Buenos Aires; tel. (11) 4320-0200; fax (11) 4393-7672; f. 1991; cap. \$101.1m., dep. \$404.2m. (Dec. 2000); Pres. JUAN PEIRANO; 7 brs.

Banex: San Martín 136, 1004 Buenos Aires; tel. (11) 4340-3000; fax (11) 4334-4402; e-mail infocra@banex.com.ar; internet www.banex.com.ar; f. 1998; by merger of Exprinter Banco with Banco San Luis, SA; cap. \$29.1m., res \$18.8m., dep. \$196.6m. (Dec. 1999); Pres. MARÍA DEL CARMEN ALGORTA DE SUPERVIELLE; 25 brs.

BBVA Banco Francés, SA: Reconquista 199, 1003 Buenos Aires; tel. (11) 4346-4000; fax (11) 4346-4320; internet www.bancofrances

.com; f. 1886 as Banco Francés del Río de la Plata, SA; changed name to Banco Francés, SA in 1998 following merger with Banco de Crédito Argentino; adopted current name in 2000; cap. $209.6m., res $575.5m., dep. US $6,973.4m. (Dec. 2001); Chair. GERVÁSIO COLLAR ZAVALETA; CEO and Gen. Man. ANTONIO MARTINEZ-JORQUERA; 308 brs.

HSBC Bank Argentina, SA: 25 de Mayo 701, 27°, 1084 Buenos Aires; tel. (11) 4344-3333; fax (11) 4334-6404; internet www.hsbc.com.ar; f. 1978 as Banco Roberts, SA; name changed to HSBC Banco Roberts, SA in 1998; adopted current name in 1999; cap. $237.4m., res $85.5m., dep. $4,697.6m. (June 2000); Chair. and CEO MICHAEL SMITH; 68 brs.

Nuevo Banco del Chaco, SA: Güemes 40, 3500 Resistencia; tel. (3722) 424888; f. 1958 as Banco del Chaco; transferred to private ownership and adopted current name in 1994; cap. $10.5m., dep. $45.4m. (June 1995); 28 brs.

Nuevo Banco de Formosa: 25 de Mayo 102, 3600 Formosa; tel. (3717) 426030; transferred to private ownership in 1995; dep. $145.3m., total assets $235.7m. (May 1995); Pres. JOSÉ MANUEL PABLO VIUDES.

Co-operative Banks

Banco Almafuerte Cooperativo Ltdo: Corrales Viejos 64, 1437 Buenos Aires; tel. (11) 4911-5153; fax (11) 4911-6887; f. 1978; cap. $18.3m., res $38.1m., dep. $378.4m. (Dec. 1997); Pres. Dr ELIAS FARAH; 27 brs.

Banco Credicoop Cooperativo Ltdo: Reconquista 484, 1003 Buenos Aires; tel. (11) 4320-5000; fax (11) 4324-5891; e-mail credicoop@rcc.com.ar; internet www.credicoop.com.ar; f. 1979; cap. $0.7m., res $251.1m., dep. $1,910.4m. (June 2001); Pres. RAÚL GUELMAN.

Banco Mayo Cooperativo Ltdo: Sarmiento 706, 1041 Buenos Aires; tel. (11) 4329-2400; fax (11) 4326-8080; f. 1978; cap. $83.4m., res $32.4m., dep. $904.2m. (June 1997); Chair. RUBÉN E. BERAJA; 106 brs.

Banco Roco Cooperativo Ltdo: 25 de Mayo 122, 1002 Buenos Aires; tel. (11) 4342-0051; fax (11) 4331-6596; f. 1961; cap. and res $10.8m., dep. $58.1m. (Dec. 1992); Pres. ALFREDO B. ARREGUI.

Other National Bank

Banco Hipotecario Nacional: Reconquista 151, 5°, 1003 Buenos Aires; tel. (11) 4347-5470; fax (11) 4347-5416; e-mail info@hipotecario.com.ar; internet www.hipotecario.com.ar; f. 1886; partially privatized in Jan. 1999; mortgage bank; cap. and res $322.4m., dep. $83.6m. (April 1992); Pres. MIGUEL KIGUEL; 23 brs.

Foreign Banks

ABN Amro Bank N.V. (Netherlands): Florida 361, Casilla 171, 1005 Buenos Aires; tel. (11) 4320-0600; fax (11) 4322-0839; f. 1914; cap. and res $37.7m., dep. $94.5m. (June 1992); Gen. Man. CÉSAR A. DEYMONNAZ; 7 brs.

Banca Nazionale del Lavoro, SA (BNL) (Italy): Florida 40, 1005 Buenos Aires; tel. (11) 4323-4400; fax (11) 4323-4689; internet www.bnl.com.ar; cap. $272m., dep. $2,306m. (June 1999); took over Banco de Italia y Río de la Plata in 1987; Pres. ADEMARO LANZARA; Gen. Man. NICCOLO PANDOLFIU; 136 brs.

Banco do Brasil, SA (Brazil): Sarmiento 487, Casilla 2684, 1041 Buenos Aires; tel. (11) 4394-0939; fax (11) 4394-9577; f. 1960; cap. and res $33.9m., dep. $2.0m. (June 1992); Gen. Man. HÉLIO TESTONI.

Banco do Estado de São Paulo (Brazil): Tucumán 821, Casilla 2177, 1049 Buenos Aires; tel. (11) 4325-9533; fax (11) 4325-9527; cap. and res $11.7m., dep. $6.7m. (June 1992); Gen. Man. CARLOS ALBERTO BERGAMASCO.

Banco Europeo para América Latina (BEAL), SA: Juan D. Perón 338, 1038 Buenos Aires; tel. (11) 4331-6544; fax (11) 4331-2010; e-mail bealbsa@interprov.com; f. 1914; cap. and res $60m., dep. $121m. (Nov. 1996); Gen. Mans JEAN PIERRE SMEETS, KLAUS KRÜGER.

Banco Itaú Buen Ayre, SA (Brazil): 25 de Mayo 476, 2°, 1002 Buenos Aires; tel. (11) 4325-6698; fax (11) 4394-1057; internet www.itau.com.ar; fmrly Banco Itaú Argentina, SA, renamed as above following purchase of Banco del Buen Ayre, SA, in May 1998; cap. and res $20.2m., dep. $1.2m. (June 1992); Dir-Gen. ANTONIO CARLOS B. DE OLIVEIRA; 94 brs.

Banco Société Générale, SA (France): Reconquista 330, 1003 Buenos Aires; tel. (11) 4329-8000; fax (11) 4329-8080; e-mail info@ar.socgen.com; internet www.ar.socgen.com.ar; f. 1887 as Banco Supervielle de Buenos Aires, SA, adopted current name in 2000; cap. $50.5m., res $56.8m., dep. $820.6m. (Dec. 2001); Chair. and Gen. Man. MARC-EMMANUEL VIVES; 64 brs.

Banco Sudameris Argentina, SA: Juan D. Perón 500, 1038 Buenos Aires; tel. (11) 4329-5200; fax (11) 4331-2793; e-mail marketing@sudameris.com.ar; internet www.sudameris.com.ar; f. 1912; cap. $89.0m., res $11.5m., dep. $977.2m. (Dec. 1998); Exec. Dir CARLOS GONZÁLEZ TABOADA.

Bank of Tokyo-Mitsubishi, Ltd (Japan): Avda Corrientes 420, 1043 Buenos Aires; tel. (11) 4348-2001; fax (11) 4322-6607; f. 1956; cap. and res $20m., dep. $81m. (Sept. 1994); Gen. Man. KAZUO OMI.

BankBoston NA (USA): Florida 99, 1005 Buenos Aires; tel. (11) 4346-2000; fax (11) 4346-3200; f. 1784; cap. $456.8m., dep. $4,012m. total assets $8,677m. (Sept. 1998); Pres. Ing. MANUEL SACERDOTE; 139 brs.

Banque Nationale de Paris, SA (France): 25 de Mayo 471, 1002 Buenos Aires; tel. (11) 4318-0318; fax (11) 4311-1368; f. 1981; cap. and res $29.4m., dep. $86.7m. (June 1992); Gen. Man. CHISLAIN DE BEAUCÉ.

Chase Manhattan Bank (USA): Arenales 707, 5°, 1061 Buenos Aires; tel. (11) 4319-2400; fax (11) 4319-2416; f. 1904; cap. and res $46.3m., dep. $12,387m. (Sept. 1992); Gen. Man. MARCELO PODESTÁ.

Citibank, NA (USA): Colón 58, Bahía Blanca, 8000 Buenos Aires; tel. (11) 4331-8281; f. 1914; cap. and res $172.8m., dep. $660.8m. (June 1992); Pres. RICARDO ANGLES; Vice-Pres. GUILLERMO STANLEY; 16 brs.

Deutsche Bank Argentina, SA (Germany): Bartolomé Mitre 401, Casilla 995, 1036 Buenos Aires; tel. (11) 4343-2510; fax (11) 4343-3536; f. 1960; cap. and res $123.6m., dep. $801.0m. (June 1994); Gen. Man. GERARDO GREISER; 47 brs.

Lloyds Bank (Bank of London and South America) Ltd (United Kingdom): Tronador 4890, 13°, Casilla 128, 1003 Buenos Aires; tel. (11) 4335-3551; fax (11) 4342-7487; f. 1862; subsidiary of Lloyds Bank TSB Group; cap. and res $108.1m., dep. $583.4m. (Sept. 1997); Gen. Man. for Argentina COLIN J. MITCHELL; 31 brs.

Morgan Guaranty Trust Co of New York (USA): Avda Corrientes 411, 1043 Buenos Aires; tel. and fax (11) 4325-8046; cap. and res $29.1m., dep. $11.6m. (June 1992); Gen. Man. JOSÉ McLOUGHLIN.

Republic National Bank of New York (USA): Bartolomé Mitre 343, 1036 Buenos Aires; tel. (11) 4343-0161; fax (11) 4331-6064; cap. and res $17.2m., dep. $13.6m. (March 1994); Gen. Man. ALBERTO MUCHNICK.

Bankers' Associations

Asociación de Bancos del Interior de la República Argentina (ABIRA): Avda Corrientes 538, 4°, 1043 Buenos Aires; tel. (11) 4394-3439; fax (11) 4394-5682; f. 1956; Pres. Dr JORGE FEDERICO CHRISTENSEN; Dir RAÚL PASSANO; 30 mems.

Asociación de Bancos Públicos y Privados de la República Argentina (ABAPPRA): Florida 470, 1°, 1005 Buenos Aires; tel. (11) 4322-6321; fax (11) 4322-6721; e-mail info@abappra.com.ar; internet www.abappra.com; f. 1959; Pres. ENRIQUE OLIVERA; Man. LUIS B. BUCAFUSCO; 31 mems.

Federación de Bancos Cooperativos de la República Argentina (FEBANCOOP): Maipú 374, 9°/10°, 1006 Buenos Aires; tel. (11) 4394-9949; f. 1973; Pres. OMAR C. TRILLO; Exec. Sec. JUAN CARLOS ROMANO; 32 mems.

STOCK EXCHANGES

Mercado de Valores de Buenos Aires, SA: 25 de Mayo 367, 8°–10°, 1002 Buenos Aires; tel. (11) 4313-6021; fax (11) 4313-4472; internet www.merval.sba.com.ar; Pres. EUGENIO DE BARY.

There are also stock exchanges at Córdoba, Rosario, Mendoza and La Plata.

Supervisory Authority

Comisión Nacional de Valores (CNV): 25 de Mayo 175, 1002 Buenos Aires; tel. (11) 4342-4607; fax (11) 4331-0639; e-mail gharte@mecon.ar; internet www.cnv.gob.ar; monitors capital markets; Pres. GUILLERMO HARTENECK.

INSURANCE

Superintendencia de Seguros de la Nación
Avda Julio A. Roca 721, 5°, 1067 Buenos Aires; tel. (11) 4331-8733; fax (11) 4331-9821.

f. 1938; Superintendent Dr IGNACIO WARNES
In March 2001 there were 222 insurance companies operating in Argentina, of which 121 were general insurance companies. The following is a list of those offering all classes or a specialized service.

La Agrícola, SA: Buenos Aires; tel. (11) 4394-5031; f. 1905; associated co La Regional; all classes; Pres. LUIS R. MARCO; First Vice-Pres. JUSTO J. DE CORRAL.

Aseguradora de Créditos y Garantías, SA: Avda Corrientes 415, 4°, 1043 Buenos Aires; tel. (11) 4394-4037; fax (11) 4394-0320; e-mail acgtias@infovia.com.ar; internet www.acg.com.ar; f. 1965; Pres. Lic. HORACIO SCAPPARONE; Exec. Vice-Pres. Dr ANÍBAL E. LÓPEZ.

Aseguradora de Río Negro y Neuquén: Avda Alem 503, Cipolletti, Río Negro; tel. (299) 477-2725; fax (299) 477-0321; f. 1960; all classes; Gen. Man. ERNESTO LÓPEZ.

Aseguradores de Cauciones, SA: Paraguay 580, 1057 Buenos Aires; tel. (11) 4318-3700; fax (11) 4318-3799; e-mail directorio@ caucion.com.ar; internet www.caucion.com.ar; f. 1968; all classes; Pres. JOSÉ DE VEDIA.

Aseguradores Industriales, SA: Juan D. Perón 650, 6°, 1038 Buenos Aires; tel. (11) 4326-8881; fax (11) 4326-3742; f. 1961; all classes; Exec. Pres. Dir LUIS ESTEBAN LOFORTE.

La Austral: Buenos Aires; tel. (11) 442-9881; fax (11) 4953-4459; f. 1942; all classes; Pres. RODOLFO H. TAYLOR.

Colón, Cía de Seguros Generales, SA: San Martín 548–550, 1004 Buenos Aires; tel. (11) 4320-3800; fax (11) 4320-3802; f. 1962; all classes; Gen. Man. L. D. STSCK.

Columbia, SA de Seguros: Juan D. Perón 690, 1038 Buenos Aires; tel. (11) 4325-0208; fax (11) 4326-1392; f. 1918; all classes; Pres. MARTA BLANCO; Gen. Man. HORACIO H. PETRILLO.

El Comercio, Cía de Seguros a Prima Fija, SA: Avda Corrientes 415, 3° y 5°, 1043 Buenos Aires; tel. (11) 4394-1300; fax (11) 4393-1311; internet www.bristolgroup.com.ar; f. 1889; all classes; Pres. HORACIO SCAPPARONE; Vice-Pres. EDUARDO MARTELLI.

Cía Argentina de Seguros de Créditos a la Exportación, SA: Corrientes 345, 7°, 1043 Buenos Aires; tel. (11) 4313-3048; fax (11) 4313-2919; f. 1967; covers credit and extraordinary and political risks for Argentine exports; Pres. LUIS ORCOYEN; Gen. Man. Dr MARIANO A. GARCÍA GALISTEO.

Cía Aseguradora Argentina, SA: Avda Roque S. Peña 555, 1035 Buenos Aires; tel. (11) 430-1571; fax (11) 430-5973; f. 1918; all classes; Man. GUIDO LUTTINI; Vice-Pres. ALBERTO FRAGUIO.

La Continental, Cía de Seguros Generales SA: Avda Corrientes 655, 1043 Buenos Aires; tel. (11) 4393-8051; fax (11) 4325-7101; f. 1912; all classes; Pres. RAÚL MASCARENHAS.

La Franco-Argentina, SA: Buenos Aires; tel. (11) 430-3091; f. 1896; all classes; Pres. Dr GUILLERMO MORENO HUEYO; Gen. Man. Dra HAYDÉE GUZIAN DE RAMÍREZ.

Hermes, SA: Edif. Hermes, Bartolomé Mitre 754/60, 1036 Buenos Aires; tel. (11) 4331-4506; fax (11) 4343-5552; e-mail hermes@mbox .servicenet.com.ar; f. 1926; all classes; Pres. DIONISIO KATOPODIS; Gen. Man. FRANCISCO MARTÍN ZABALO.

India, Cía de Seguros Generales SA: Avda Roque S. Peña 728/36, 1035 Buenos Aires; tel. (11) 4328-6001; fax (11) 4328-5602; f. 1950; all classes; Pres. ALFREDO JUAN PRIESSE; Vice-Pres. Dr RAÚL ALBERTO GUARDIA.

Instituto Italo-Argentino de Seguros Generales, SA: Avda Roque S. Peña 890, 1035 Buenos Aires; tel. (11) 4320-9200; fax (11) 4320-9229; f. 1920; all classes; Pres. ALEJANDRO A. SOLDATI.

La Meridional, Cía Argentina de Seguros SA: Juan D. Perón 646, 1038 Buenos Aires; tel. (11) 4909-7000; fax (11) 4909-7274; e-mail meridi@starnet.net.ar; f. 1949; life and general; Pres. GUILLERMO V. LASCANO QUINTANA; Gen. Man. PETER HAMMER.

Plus Ultra, Cía Argentina de Seguros, SA: San Martín 548–50, 1004 Buenos Aires; tel. (11) 4393-5069; f. 1956; all classes; Gen. Man. L. D. STSCK.

La Primera, SA: Blvd Villegas y Oro, Trenque Lauquén, Prov. Buenos Aires; tel. (11) 4393-8125; all classes; Pres. ENRIQUE RAÚL U. BOTTINI; Man. Dr RODOLFO RAÚL D'ONOFRIO.

La Rectora, SA: Avda Corrientes 848, 1043 Buenos Aires; tel. (11) 4394-6081; fax (11) 4394-3251; f. 1951; all classes; Pres. PEDRO PASCUAL MEGNA; Gen. Man. ANTONIO LÓPEZ BUENO.

La República Cía Argentina de Seguros Generales, SA: San Martín 627/29, 1374 Buenos Aires; tel. (11) 4314-1000; fax (11) 4318-8778; e-mail ccastell@republica.com.ar; f. 1928; group life and general; Pres. JOSÉ T. GUZMAN DUMAS; Gen. Man. EDUARDO ESCRIÑA.

Sud América Terrestre y Marítima Cía de Seguros Generales, SA: Florida 15, 2°, Galería Florida 1, 1005 Buenos Aires; tel. (11) 4340-5100; fax (11) 4340-5380; f. 1919; all classes; Pres. EMA SÁNCHEZ DE LARRAGOITI; Vice-Pres. ALAIN HOMBREUX.

La Unión Gremial, SA: Mitre 665/99, 2000 Rosario, Santa Fe; tel. (341) 426-2900; fax (341) 425-9802; f. 1908; general; Gen. Man. EDUARDO IGNACIO LLOBET.

La Universal: Buenos Aires; tel. (11) 442-9881; fax (11) 4953-4459; f. 1905; all classes; Pres. RODOLFO H. TAYLOR.

Zurich-Iguazú Cía de Seguros, SA: San Martín 442, 1004 Buenos Aires; tel. (11) 4329-0400; fax (11) 4322-4688; f. 1947; all classes; Pres. RAMÓN SANTAMARINA.

Reinsurance

Instituto Nacional de Reaseguros: Avda Julio A. Roca 694, 1067 Buenos Aires; tel. (11) 4334-0084; fax (11) 4334-5588; f. 1947; reinsurance in all branches; Pres. and Man. REINALDO A. CASTRO.

Insurance Associations

Asociación Argentina de Cías de Seguros (AACS): 25 de Mayo 565, 2°, 1002 Buenos Aires; tel. (11) 4312-7790; fax (11) 4312-6300; e-mail secret@aacsra.org.ar; internet www.aacsra.org.ar; f. 1894; 60 mems; Pres. ROBERTO F. E. SOLLITTO.

Asociación de Entidades Aseguradoras Privadas de la República Argentina (EAPRA): Esmeralda 684, 4°, 1007 Buenos Aires; tel. (11) 4393-2268; fax (11) 4393-2283; f. 1875; asscn of 12 foreign insurance cos operating in Argentina; Pres. Dr PIERO ZUPPELLI; Sec. BERNARDO VON DER GOLTZ.

Trade and Industry

GOVERNMENT AGENCIES

Cámara de Exportadores de la República Argentina: Avda Roque S. Peña 740, 1°, 1035 Buenos Aires; tel. (11) 4394-4351; fax (11) 4328-1003; e-mail contacto@cera.org.ar; internet www.cera.org .ar; f. 1943 to promote exports; 700 mems.

Consejo Federal de Inversiones: San Martín 871, 1004 Buenos Aires; tel. (11) 4313-5557; fax (11) 4313-4486; federal board to co-ordinate domestic and foreign investment and provide technological aid for the provinces; Sec.-Gen. Ing. JUAN JOSÉ CIÁCERA.

Dirección de Forestación (DF): Avda Paseo Colón 982, anexo jardin, 1063 Buenos Aires; tel. (11) 4349-2124; fax (11) 4349-2102; e-mail bfores@sagpya.minproduccion.gov.ar; assumed the responsibilities of the national forestry commission (Instituto Forestal Nacional—IFONA) in 1991, following its dissolution; supervised by the Secretaría de Agricultura, Ganadería y Pesca; maintains the Centro de Documentación e Información Forestal; Library Man. NILDA E. FERNÁNDEZ.

Instituto de Desarrollo Económico y Social (IDES): Araoz 2838, 1425 Buenos Aires; tel. (11) 4804-4949; fax (11) 4804-5856; e-mail ides@ides.org.ar; internet www.ides.org.ar; f. 1960; investigation into social sciences and promotion of social and economic devt; 700 mems; Pres. ADRIANA MARSHALL; Sec. LUIS BECCARIA.

Junta Nacional de Granos: Avda Paseo Colón 359, 1063 Buenos Aires; tel. (11) 430-0641; national grain board; supervises commercial practices and organizes the construction of farm silos and port elevators; Pres. JORGE CORT.

Organismo Nacional de Administración de Bienes (ONABE): 1302 Avda J. M. Ramos Mejia, Of. 1104, Buenos Aires; tel. (11) 4318-3458; responsible for overseeing privatization of state property.

Secretaría de Agricultura, Ganadería, Pesca y Alimentación: Avda Paseo Colón 922, 1°, Of. 146, 1063 Buenos Aires; tel. (11) 4349-2291; fax (11) 4349-2292; e-mail mpelle@sagpya.mecon.gov.ar; internet www.sagpya.mecon.gov.ar; f. 1871; undertakes regulatory, promotional, advisory and administrative responsibilities on behalf of the meat, livestock, agriculture and fisheries industries; Sec. MIGUEL A. PAULON.

Sindicatura General de Empresas Públicas: Lavalle 1429, 1048 Buenos Aires; tel. (11) 449-5415; fax (11) 4476-4054; f. 1978 to exercise external control over wholly- or partly-owned public enterprises; Pres. ALBERTO R. ABAD.

DEVELOPMENT ORGANIZATIONS

Instituto Argentino del Petróleo y Gas: Maipú 645, 3°, 1006 Buenos Aires; tel. (11) 4325-8008; fax (11) 4393-5494; e-mail informa@iapg.org.ar; internet www.iapg.org.ar; f. 1958; established to promote the devt of petroleum exploration and exploitation; Pres. Ing. E. J. ROCCHI.

Secretario de Programación Económica: Hipólito Yrigoyen 250, 8°, Of. 819, Buenos Aires; tel. (11) 4349-5710; fax (11) 4349-5714; f. 1961 to formulate national long-term devt plans; Sec. Dr JUAN JOSÉ LACH.

Sociedad Rural Argentina: Florida 460, 1005 Buenos Aires; tel. (11) 4324-4700; fax (11) 4324-4774; f. 1866; private org. to promote the devt of agriculture; Pres. ENRIQUE C. CROTTO; 9,400 mems.

CHAMBERS OF COMMERCE

Cámara Argentina de Comercio: Avda Leandro N. Alem 36, 1003 Buenos Aires; tel. (11) 4331-8051; fax (11) 4331-8055; e-mail gerencia@cac.com.ar; internet www.cac.com.ar; f. 1924; Pres. JORGE LUIS DI FIORI.

Cámara de Comercio, Industria y Producción de la República Argentina: Florida 1, 4°, 1005 Buenos Aires; tel. (11) 4331-0813; fax (11) 4331-9116; f. 1913; Pres. José Chediek; Vice-Pres. Dr Faustino S. Diéguez, Dr Jorge M. Mazalan; 1,500 mems.

Cámara de Comercio Exterior de Rosario: Avda Córdoba 1868, 2000 Rosario, Santa Fe; tel. and fax (341) 425-7147; e-mail ccer@commerce.com.ar; internet www.commerce.com.ar; f. 1958; deals with imports and exports; Pres. Juan Carlos Retamero; Vice-Pres. Eduardo C. Salvatierra; 150 mems.

Similar chambers are located in most of the larger centres and there are many foreign chambers of commerce.

INDUSTRIAL AND TRADE ASSOCIATIONS

Asociación de Importadores y Exportadores de la República Argentina: Avda Belgrano 124, 1°, 1092 Buenos Aires; tel. (11) 4342-0010; fax (11) 4342-1312; e-mail aiera@aiera.org.ar; internet www.aiera.org.ar; f. 1966; Pres. Héctor Marcello Vidal; Man. Adriano de Fina.

Asociación de Industriales Textiles Argentinos: Buenos Aires; tel. (11) 4373-2256; fax (11) 4373-2351; f. 1945; textile industry; Pres. Bernardo Abramovich; 250 mems.

Asociación de Industrias Argentinas de Carnes: Buenos Aires; tel. (11) 4322-5244; meat industry; refrigerated and canned beef and mutton; Pres. Jorge Borsella.

Asociación Vitivinícola Argentina: Güemes 4464, 1425 Buenos Aires; tel. (11) 4774-3370; f. 1904; wine industry; Pres. Luciano Cotumaccio; Man. Lic. Mario J. Giordano.

Cámara de Sociedades Anónimas: Florida 1, 3°, 1005 Buenos Aires; tel. (11) 4342-9013; fax (11) 4342-9225; Pres. Dr Alfonso de la Ferrere; Man. Carlos Alberto Perrone.

Centro de Exportadores de Cereales: Bouchard 454, 7°, 1106 Buenos Aires; tel. (11) 4311-1697; fax (11) 4312-6924; f. 1943; grain exporters; Pres. Raúl S. Loeh.

Confederaciones Rurales Argentinas: México 628, 2°, 1097 Buenos Aires; tel. (11) 4261-1501; Pres. Arturo J. Navarro.

Coordinadora de Actividades Mercantiles Empresarias: Buenos Aires; Pres. Osvaldo Cornide.

Federación Lanera Argentina: Avda Paseo Colón 823, 5°, 1063 Buenos Aires; tel. (11) 4300-7661; fax (11) 4361-6517; e-mail info@flasite.com; internet www.flasite.com; f. 1929; wool industry; Pres. Julio Aisenstein; Pres. Richard von Gerstenberg; Sec. Julio Aisenstein; 80 mems.

EMPLOYERS' ORGANIZATION

Unión Industrial Argentina (UIA): Avda Leandro N. Alem 1067, 11°, 1001 Buenos Aires; tel. (11) 4313-4474; fax (11) 4313-2413; e-mail uia01@act.net.ar; internet www.uia.org.ar; f. 1887; re-established in 1974 with the fusion of the Confederación Industrial Argentina (CINA) and the Confederación General de la Industria; following the dissolution of the CINA in 1977, the UIA was formed in 1979; asscn of manufacturers, representing industrial corpns; Pres. Osvaldo Rial; Sec.-Gen. Dr José I. de Mendiguren.

UTILITIES

Regulatory Authorities

Ente Nacional Regulador de la Electricidad (ENRE): Avda Eduardo Madero 1020, 10°, 1106 Buenos Aires; tel. (11) 4314-5805; fax (11) 4314-5416; internet www.enre.gov.ar.

Ente Nacional Regulador del Gas (ENARGAS): Suipacha 636, 10°, 1008 Buenos Aires; tel. (11) 4325-9292; fax (11) 4348-0550; internet www.enargas.gov.ar.

Electricity

CAPEX: Melo 630, Vicente López, 1638 Buenos Aires; tel. (11) 4796-6000; e-mail info@capex.com.ar; internet www.capex.com; f. 1988; electricity generation; Chair. Enrique Götz; Vice-Chair. Alejandro Götz.

Central Costanera, SA (CECCO): Avda España 3301, 1107 Buenos Aires; tel. (11) 4307-3040; fax (11) 4307-1706; generation, transmission, distribution and sale of thermal electric energy; Chair. Jaime Bauzá Bauzá.

Central Puerto, SA (CEPU): Avda Tomás Edison 2701, 1104 Buenos Aires; tel. (11) 4317-5000; fax (11) 4317-5099; electricity generating co; CEO Antonio Büchi Buć.

Comisión Nacional de Energía Atómica (CNEA): Avda del Libertador 8250, 1429 Buenos Aires; tel. (11) 4704-1384; fax (11) 4704-1176; e-mail freijo@cnea.edu.ar; internet www.cnea.gov.ar; f.

1950; scheduled for transfer to private ownership; nuclear energy science and technology; Pres. Jacobo Dan Beninson.

Comisión Técnica Mixta de Salto Grande (CTMSG): Avda Leandro N. Alem 449, 1003 Buenos Aires; operates Salto Grande hydroelectric station, which has an installed capacity of 650 MW; joint Argentine-Uruguayan project.

Dirección de Energía de la Provincia de Buenos Aires: Calle 55, No. 570, La Reja, 1900 Buenos Aires; tel. (11) 4415-000; fax (11) 4216-124; f. 1957; electricity co for province of Buenos Aires; Dir Agustín Núñez.

Empresa Distribuidora y Comercializadora Norte, SA (EDENOR): Azopardo 1025, 1107 Buenos Aires; tel. (11) 4348-2121; fax (11) 4334-0805; e-mail ofitel@edenor.com.ar; internet www.edenor.com.ar; distribution of electricity.

Empresa Distribuidora Sur, SA (EDESUR): San José, 140, 1076 Buenos Aires; tel. (11) 4381-8981; fax (11) 4383-3699; internet www.edesur.com.ar; f. 1992; distribution of electricity; Gen. Man. Ing. José María Rovira.

Entidad Binacional Yacyretá: Avda Eduardo Madero 942, 21°–22°, 1106 Buenos Aires; tel. (11) 4510-7500; e-mail rrpp@eby.org.ar; internet www.yacyreta.org.ar; operates the hydroelectric dam at Yacyretá on the Paraná river; owned jointly by Argentina and Paraguay; Completed in 1998, it is one of the world's largest hydroelectric complexes; consisting of 20 generators with a total generating capacity of 2,700 MW.

Hidronor Ingenieria y Servicios, SA (HISSA): Hipólito Yrigoyen 1530, 6°, 1089 Buenos Aires; tel. and fax (11) 4382-6316; e-mail info@hidronor.com; formerly HIDRONOR, SA, the largest producer of electricity in Argentina; responsible for developing the hydroelectric potential of the Limay and neighbouring rivers; transferred to private ownership in 1992 and divided into the following companies.

> **Central Hidroeléctrica Alicurá, SA:** Avda Leandro N. Alem 712, 7°, 1001 Buenos Aires.
>
> **Central Hidroeléctrica Cerros Colorados, SA:** Avda Leandro N. Alem 690, 12°, 1001 Buenos Aires.
>
> **Central Hidroeléctrica El Chocón, SA:** Suipacha 268, 9°, Of. A, Buenos Aires.
>
> **Hidroeléctrica Piedra del Aguila, SA:** Avda Tomás Edison 1251, 1104 Buenos Aires; tel. (11) 4315-2586; fax (11) 4317-5174; Pres. Dr Uriel Federico O'Farrell; Gen. Man. Ignacio J. Rosner.
>
> **Transener, SA:** Avda Paseo Colón 728, 6°, 1063 Buenos Aires; tel. (11) 4342-6925; fax (11) 4342-7147; energy transmission co.

Pérez Companc, SA (PECOM): Maipú 1, 22°, 1084 Buenos Aires; tel. (11) 4331-8393; fax (11) 4331-8369; internet www.pecom.com.ar; f. 1946; operates the hydroelectric dam at Pichi Picún Leufu; Chair. Jorge Gregorio Pérez Companc.

Servicios Eléctricos del Gran Buenos Aires, SA (SEGBA): Balcarce 184, 1002 Buenos Aires; tel. (11) 4331-1901; Principal Officer Carlos A. Mattausch.

Gas

Distribuidora de Gas del Centro, SA: Avda Hipólito Yrigoyen 475, 5000 Córdoba; tel. (351) 4688-100; fax (351) 4681-568; state-owned co; distributes natural gas.

Gas Natural Ban, SA: Isabel la Católica 939, 1269 Buenos Aires; tel. (11) 4303-1380; internet www.gasnaturalban.com.ar; distribution of natural gas; Gen. Man. Antoni Peris Mingot.

Metrogás, SA: Avda Montes de Oca 1120, 1271 Buenos Aires; tel. (11) 4309-1000; fax (11) 4309-1366; internet www.metrogas.com; gas distribution; Dir-Gen. William Adamson.

Transportadora de Gas del Norte, SA: Don Bosco 3672, 3°, 1206 Buenos Aires; tel. (11) 4959-2000; fax (11) 4959-2253; state-owned co; distributes natural gas; Gen. Man. Freddy Cameo.

Transportadora de Gas del Sur, SA (TGS): Don Bosco 3672, 5°, 1206 Buenos Aires; tel. (11) 4865-9050; fax (11) 4865-9059; e-mail totgs@tgs.com.ar; internet www.tgs.com.ar; processing and transport of natural gas; 47% owned by Pérez Companc; Gen. Dir Eduardo Ojea Quintana.

Water

Aguas Argentinas: Buenos Aires; distribution of water in Buenos Aires; privatized in 1993; Dir-Gen. Jean-Louis Chaussade.

TRADE UNIONS

Congreso de los Trabajadores Argentinos (CTA): Buenos Aires; dissident trade union confederation; Leader Víctor de Genaro.

Confederación General del Trabajo (CGT) (General Confederation of Labour): Buenos Aires; f. 1984; Peronist; represents approx. 90% of Argentina's 1,100 trade unions; Sec.-Gen. Hugo Moyano.

Movimiento de Trabajadores Argentinos (MTA): Buenos Aires; dissident trade union confederation.

Transport

Comisión Nacional de Regulación del Transporte (CNRT): Maipú 88, 1084, Buenos Aires; tel. (11) 4819-3000; e-mail msenet@mecon.gov.ar; internet www.cnrt.gov.ar; regulates domestic and international transport services; part of Ministry of Infrastructure and Housing.

Secretaría de Obras Públicas y Transporte: Hipólito Yrigoyen 250, 12°, 1310 Buenos Aires; tel. (11) 4349-7254; fax (11) 4349-7201; Sec. Ing. Armando Guibert.

Secretaría de Transporte Metropolitano y de Larga Distancia: Hipólito Yrigoyen 250, 12°, 1310 Buenos Aires; tel. (11) 4349-7162; fax (11) 4349-7146; Under-Sec. Dr Armando Canosa.

Secretaría de Transporte Aero-Comercial: Hipólito Yrigoyen 250, 12°, 1310 Buenos Aires; tel. (11) 4349-7203; fax (11) 4349-7206; Under-Sec. Arq. Fermín Alarcia.

Dirección de Estudios y Proyectos: Hipólito Yrigoyen 250, 12°, 1310 Buenos Aires; tel. (11) 4349-7127; fax (11) 4349-7128; Dir Ing. José Luis Jagodnik.

RAILWAYS

Lines: General Belgrano (narrow-gauge), General Roca, General Bartolomé Mitre, General San Martín, Domingo Faustino Sarmiento (all wide-gauge), General Urquiza (medium-gauge) and Línea Metropolitana, which controls the railways of Buenos Aires and its suburbs. There are direct rail links with the Bolivian Railways network to Santa Cruz de la Sierra and La Paz; with Chile, through the Las Cuevas–Caracoles tunnel (across the Andes) and between Salta and Antofagasta; with Brazil, across the Paso de los Libres and Uruguayana bridge; with Paraguay (between Posadas and Encarnación by ferry-boat); and with Uruguay (between Concordia and Salto). In 1999 there were 35,753 km of tracks. In the Buenos Aires commuter area 270.4 km of wide-gauge track and 52 km of medium gauge track are electrified.

Plans for the eventual total privatization of Ferrocarriles Argentinos (FA) were initiated in 1991, with the transfer to private ownership of the Rosario–Bahía Blanca grain line and with the reallocation of responsibility for services in Buenos Aires to the newly-created Ferrocarriles Metropolitanos, prior to its privatization.

In early 1993 central government funding for the FA was suspended and responsibility for existing inter-city passenger routes was devolved to respective provincial governments. However, owing to lack of resources, few provinces have successfully assumed the operation of services, and many trains have been suspended. At the same time, long-distance freight services were sold as six separate 30-year concessions (including lines and rolling stock) to private operators. By late 1996 all freight services had been transferred to private management, with the exception of Ferrocarril Belgrano Cargas, SA, which was in the process of undergoing privatization. In the mid-1990s the FA was replaced by Ente Nacional Administrador de los Bienes Ferroviaros (Enabief), which assumed responsibility for railway infrastructure and the rolling stock not already sold off. The Buenos Aires commuter system was divided into eight concerns (one of which incorporates the underground railway system) and was offered for sale to private operators as 10- or 20-year (subsidized) concessions. The railway network is currently regulated by the National Commission for Transport Regulation (CNRT—see above).

Ente Nacional de Administración de Bienes Ferroviarios (ENABIEF): Avda Raqmos Mejía 1302, 6°, Buenos Aires; tel. (11) 4318-3594.

Ferrocarriles Metropolitanos, SA (FEMESA): Bartolomé Mitre 2815, Buenos Aires; tel. (11) 4865-4135; fax (11) 4861-8757; f. 1991 to assume responsibility for services in the capital; 820 km of track; Pres. Matías Ordóñez; concessions to operate services have been awarded to the following companies.

Ferrovías: Avda Ramos Mejia 1430, 1104 Buenos Aires; tel. (11) 4314-1444; fax (11) 3311-1181; operates northern commuter line in Buenos Aires; Pres. B. G. Romero.

Metropolitano: Avda Santa Fe 4636, 1425 Buenos Aires; tel. (11) 4778-5800; fax (11) 4778-5878; e-mail eltren@metropolitano.co.ar; f. 1993; operates three commuter lines; Pres. J. C. Loustau Bidaut.

Metrovías (MV): Bartolomé Mitre 3342, 1201 Buenos Aires; tel. (11) 4959-6800; fax (11) 4866-3037; e-mail info@metrovias.com.ar; internet www.metrovias.com; f. 1994; operates subway (Subterráneos de Buenos Aires—see below) and two commuter lines; Pres. A. Verra.

Trenes de Buenos Aires, SA (TBA): Avda Ramos Mejia 1358, 1104 Buenos Aires; tel. (11) 4317-4400; fax (11) 4317-4409; e-mail prensa@tbanet.com.ar; took over operations of two commuter lines from state in 1995; Pres. S. C. Cirigliano.

Cámara de Industriales Ferroviarios: Alsina 1609, 1°, Buenos Aires; tel. (11) 4371-5571; private org. to promote the devt of Argentine railway industries; Pres. Ing. Ana María Guibaudi.

The following consortia were awarded 30-year concessions to operate rail services, in the 1990s:

Ferrobaires (Unidad Ejecutora del Programa Ferroviario Provincial) (UEPFP): General Hornos 11, 4°, 1084 Buenos Aires; tel. (11) 4305-5174; fax (11) 4305-5933; f. 1993; operates long-distance passenger services; Pres. G. Crespo.

Ferrocarril Buenos Aires al Pacífico/San Martín (BAP): Avda Santa Fe 4636, 3°, Buenos Aires; tel. (11) 4778-2486; fax (11) 4778-2493; operates services on much of the San Martín line, and on 706 km of the Sarmiento line; 6,106 km of track; bought by Brazil's America Latina Logistica, SA, in 1999; Pres. N. Silva.

Ferrocarril Belgrano Cargas, SA (FCGB): Maipú 88, 1084 Buenos Aires; tel. (11) 4343-7220; fax (11) 4343-7229; f. 1993; operates freight services; Pres. Dr Ignacio A. Ludveña.

Ferrocarril Mesopotámico General Urquiza (FMGU): Avda Santa Fe 4636, 3°, 1425 Buenos Aires; tel. (11) 4778-2425; fax (11) 4778-2493; operates freight services on the Urquiza lines; 2,272 km of track; bought by Brazil's America Latina Logistica, SA, in 1999; Pres. N. Silva.

Ferroexpreso Pampeano (FEPSA): Bouchard 680, 9°, 1106 Buenos Aires; tel. (11) 4318-4900; fax (11) 4510-4945; operates services on the Rosario–Bahía Blanca grain lines; 5,193 km of track; Pres. H. Masoero.

Ferrosur Roca (FR): Bouchard 680, 8°, 1106 Buenos Aires; tel. (11) 4319-3900; fax (11) 4319-3901; e-mail ferrosur@impsat1.com.ar; operator of freight services on the Roca lines since 1993; 3,000 km of track; Gen. Man. Sergio do Rego.

Nuevo Central Argentino (NCA): Avda Alberdi 50, 2000 Rosario; tel. (341) 437-6561; fax (341) 439-2377; operates freight services on the Bartolomé Mitre lines since 1993; 5,011 km of track; Pres. M. Acevedo.

Buenos Aires also has an underground railway system:

Subterráneos de Buenos Aires: Bartolomé Mitre 3342, 1201 Buenos Aires; tel. (11) 4862-6844; fax (11) 4864-0633; f. 1913; became completely state-owned in 1951; fmrly controlled by the Municipalidad de la Ciudad de Buenos Aires; responsibility for operations was transferred, in 1993, to a private consortium (Metrovías) with a 20-year concession; five underground lines totalling 36.5 km, 63 stations, and a 7.4 km light rail line with 13 stations, which was inaugurated in 1987; Pres. A. Verra.

ROADS

In 2000 there were 215,434 km of roads, of which 29.5% were paved. Four branches of the Pan-American highway run from Buenos Aires to the borders of Chile, Bolivia, Paraguay and Brazil. In 1996 9,932 km of main roads were under private management. Construction work on a 41-km bridge across the River Plate (linking Punta Lara in Argentina with Colonia del Sacramento in Uruguay) was scheduled to begin in the late 1990s.

Dirección Nacional de Vialidad: Avda Julio A. Roca 378, Buenos Aires; tel. (11) 4343-2838; fax (11) 4343-7292; controlled by the Secretaría de Transportes; Gen. Man. Ing. Elio Vergara.

Asociación Argentina de Empresarios Transporte Automotor (AAETA): Bernardo de Irigoyen 330, 6°, 1072 Buenos Aires; e-mail aaeta@sei.com.ar; internet www.aaeta.org.ar; Gen. Man. Ing. Marcelo González.

Federación Argentina de Entidades Empresarias de Autotransporte de Cargas (FADEAC): Avda 25 de Mayo 1370, 3°, 1372 Buenos Aires; tel. (11) 4383-3635; Pres. Rogelio Cavalieri Iribarne.

There are several international passenger and freight services including:

Autobuses Sudamericanos, SA: Buenos Aires; tel. (11) 4307-1956; fax (11) 4307-1956; f. 1928; international bus services; car and bus rentals; charter bus services; Pres. Armando Schlecker Hirsch; Gen. Man. Miguel Angel Ruggiero.

INLAND WATERWAYS

There is considerable traffic in coastal and river shipping, mainly carrying petroleum and its derivatives.

Dirección Nacional de Construcciones Portuarias y Vías Navegables: Avda España 221, 4°, Buenos Aires; tel. (11) 4361-5964; responsible for the maintenance and improvement of waterways and dredging operations; Dir Ing. ENRIQUE CASALS DE ALBA.

SHIPPING

There are more than 100 ports, of which the most important are Buenos Aires, Quequén and Bahía Blanca. There are specialized terminals at Ensenada, Comodoro Rivadavia, San Lorenzo and Campana (petroleum); Bahía Blanca, Rosario, Santa Fe, Villa Concepción, Mar del Plata and Quequén cereals); and San Nicolas and San Fernando (raw and construction materials). In 2001 Argentina's merchant fleet totalled 478 vessels, amounting to 421,604 grt.

Administración General de Puertos: Avda Ing. Huergo 431, 1°, Buenos Aires; tel. (11) 4343-2425; fax (11) 4331-0298; e-mail institucionales@puertobuenosaires.gov.ar; internet www .puertobuenosaires.gov.ar; f. 1956; state enterprise for direction, administration and exploitation of all national sea- and river-ports; scheduled for transfer to private ownership; Pres. RICARDO HORACIO DEL VALLE.

Capitanía General del Puerto: Avda Julio A. Roca 734, 2°, 1067 Buenos Aires; tel. (11) 434-9784; f. 1967; co-ordination of port operations; Port Captain Capt. PEDRO TARAMASCO.

Administración General de Puertos (Santa Fe): Duque 1 Cabacera, Santa Fe; tel. (42) 41732.

Consorcio de Gestión del Puerto de Bahía Blanca: Avda Dr Mario M. Guido s/n, 8103 Provincia de Buenos Aires; tel. (91) 57-3213; Pres. JOSÉ E. CONTE; Sec.-Gen. CLAUDIO MARCELO CONTE.

Terminales Portuarias Argentinas: Buenos Aires; operates one of five recently privatized cargo and container terminals in the port of Buenos Aires.

Terminales Río de la Plata: Buenos Aires; operates one of five recently privatized cargo and container terminals in the port of Buenos Aires.

Empresa Líneas Marítimas Argentinas, SA (ELMA): Avda Corrientes 389, 1327 Buenos Aires; tel. (11) 4312-9245; fax (11) 4311-7954; f. 1941; as state-owned org. transferred to private ownership in 1994; operates vessels to northern Europe, the Mediterranean, west and east coasts of Canada and the USA, Gulf of Mexico, Caribbean ports, Brazil, Pacific ports of Central and South America, Far East, northern and southern Africa and the Near East; Pres. PABLO DOMINGO DE ZORZI.

Other private shipping companies operating on coastal and overseas routes include:

Antártida Pesquera Industrial: Moreno 1270, 5°, 1091 Buenos Aires; tel. (11) 4381-0167; fax (11) 4381-0519; Pres. J. M. S. MIRANDA; Man. Dir J. R. S. MIRANDA.

Astramar Cía Argentina de Navegación, SAC: Buenos Aires; tel. (11) 4311-3678; fax (11) 4311-7534; Pres. ENRIQUE W. REDDIG.

Bottacchi SA de Navegación: Maipú 509, 2°, 1006 Buenos Aires; tel. (11) 4392-7411; fax (11) 411-1280; Pres. ANGEL L. M. BOTTACCHI.

Maruba S. en C. por Argentina: Maipú 535, 7°, 1006 Buenos Aires; tel. (11) 4322-7173; fax (11) 4322-3353; Chartering Man. R. J. DICKIN.

Yacimientos Petrolíferos Fiscales (YPF): Avda Roque S. Peña 777, 1364 Buenos Aires; tel. (11) 446-7271; privatization finalized in 1993; Pres. NELLS LEÓN.

CIVIL AVIATION

Argentina has 10 international airports (Aeroparque Jorge Newbery, Córdoba, Corrientes, El Plumerillo, Ezeiza, Jujuy, Resistencia, Río Gallegos, Salta and San Carlos de Bariloche). Ezeiza, 35 km from Buenos Aires, is one of the most important air terminals in Latin America. More than 30 airports were scheduled for transfer to private ownership.

Aerolíneas Argentinas: Bouchard 547, 9°, 1106 Buenos Aires; tel. (11) 4317-3000; fax (11) 4320-2116; internet www.aerolineas.com.ar; f. 1950; transfer to private ownership initiated in 1990; acquired by the Spanish company AirComet Marsans in 2001; services to North and Central America, Europe, the Far East, New Zealand, South Africa and destinations throughout South America; the internal network covers the whole country; passengers, mail and freight are carried; Pres. ANTONIO MATA.

Austral Líneas Aéreas (ALA): Corrientes 485, 9°, 1398, Buenos Aires; tel. (11) 4317-3600; fax (11) 4317-3777; internet www.austral .com.ar; f. 1971; domestic flights linking 27 cities in Argentina; Pres. MANUEL CASERO.

CATA Líneas Aéreas S.A.C.I.F.I.: Cerrito 1320, 3°, 1010 Buenos Aires; tel. (11) 4812-3390; fax (11) 4811-2966; e-mail cataaer@ satlink.com; internet www.webs.satlink.com/usuarios/c/cataaer; f. 1978; domestic passenger flights; Pres. ROQUE PUGLIESE.

Líneas Aéreas Entre Ríos: Salvador Caputo, Paraná , Entre Ríos; tel. (343) 436-2013; fax (343) 436-2177; e-mail contable@laer.com.ar; internet www.laer.com.ar; f. 1988; scheduled domestic passenger services; Gen. Man. LUIS VARISCO.

Líneas Aéreas del Estado (LADE): Perú 710, 1068 Buenos Aires; tel. (11) 4362-1853; fax (11) 4300-0031; e-mail director@lade.com.ar; Dir GUILLERMO JOSÉ TESTONI.

Líneas Aéreas Privadas Argentinas (LAPA): Avda Santa Fe 1970, 2°, 1123 Buenos Aires; tel. (11) 4812-0953; fax (11) 4814-2100; e-mail gcaputi@lapa.com.ar; f. 1976; domestic scheduled passenger services, and international routes to Uruguay; Pres. GUSTAVO ANDRÉS DEUTSCH.

Transporte Aéreo Costa Atlántica (TACA): Bernardo de Yrigoyen 1370, 1°, Ofs 25–26, 1138 Buenos Aires; tel. (11) 4307-1956; fax (11) 4307-8899; f. 1956; domestic and international passenger and freight services between Argentina and Bolivia, Brazil and the USA; Pres. Dr ARMANDO SCHLECKER HIRSCH.

Transportes Aéreos Neuquén: Diagonal 25 de Mayo 180, 8300 Neuquén; tel. (299) 4423076; fax (299) 4488926; e-mail tancentr@ satlink.com.ar; domestic routes; Pres. JOSÉ CHALÉN; Gen. Man. PATROCINIO VALVERDE MORAIS.

Valls Líneas Aéreas: Río Grande, Tierra del Fuego; f. 1995; operates three routes between destinations in southern Argentina, Chile and the South Atlantic islands.

Tourism

Argentina's superb tourist attractions include the Andes mountains, the lake district centred on Bariloche (where there is a National Park), Patagonia, the Atlantic beaches and Mar del Plata, the Iguazú falls, the Pampas and Tierra del Fuego. Tourist arrivals in Argentina in 2000 totalled an estimated 2,949,000. In the same year tourist receipts were US $2,903m.

Secretaría de Turismo de la Nación: Suipacha 1111, 20°, 1368 Buenos Aires; tel. (11) 4312-5611; fax (11) 4313-6834; e-mail info@ turismo.gov.ar; internet www.sectur.gov.ar.

Asociación Argentina de Agencias de Viajes y Turismo (AAAVYT): Viamonte 640, 10°, 1053 Buenos Aires; tel. (11) 4325-4691; fax (11) 4322-9641; e-mail secretaria@aaavyt.org.ar; f. 1951; Pres. MARCO A. PALACIOS; Gen. Man. GERARDO BELO.

ARMENIA
Introductory Survey

Location, Climate, Language, Religion, Flag, Capital

The Republic of Armenia is situated in south-west Transcaucasia, on the north-eastern border of Turkey. Its other borders are with Iran to the south, Azerbaijan to the east, and Georgia to the north. The Nakhichevan Autonomous Republic, an Azerbaijani territory, is situated to the south, separated from the remainder of Azerbaijan by Armenian territory. The climate is typically continental: dry, with wide temperature variations. Winters are cold, the average January temperature in Yerevan being −3°C (26°F), but summers can be very warm, with August temperatures averaging 25°C (77°F), although high altitude moderates the heat in much of the country. Precipitation is low in the Yerevan area (annual average 322 mm), but much higher in the mountains. The official language is Armenian, the sole member of a distinct Indo-European language group. It is written in the Armenian script. Kurdish is used in broadcasting and publishing for some 56,000 Kurds inhabiting Armenia. Most of the population are adherents of Christianity, the largest denomination being the Armenian Apostolic Church. There are also Russian Orthodox, Protestant, Islamic and Yazidi communities. The national flag (approximate proportions 2 by 3) consists of three equal horizontal stripes, of red, blue and orange. The capital is Yerevan.

Recent History

Although Armenia was an important power in ancient times, for much of its history it was ruled by foreign states. In 1639 Armenia was partitioned, with the larger, western part being annexed by Turkey and the eastern region becoming part of the Persian Empire. In 1828, after a period of Russo–Persian conflict, eastern Armenia was ceded to the Russian Empire by the Treaty of Turkmanchai, and subsequently became a province of the Empire. At the beginning of the 20th century Armenians living in western, or Anatolian, Armenia, under Ottoman rule, were subject to increasing persecution by the Turks. As a result of brutal massacres and deportations (particularly in 1915), the Anatolian lands were largely emptied of their Armenian population, and it was estimated that during 1915–22 some 1.5m. Armenians perished. After the collapse of Russian imperial power in 1917, Russian Armenia joined the anti-Bolshevik Transcaucasian Federation, which included Georgia and Azerbaijan. This collapsed when threatened by Turkish forces, and on 28 May 1918 Armenia was proclaimed an independent state. Without Russian protection, however, the newly formed republic was almost defenceless against Turkish expansionism and was forced to cede the province of Kars and other Armenian lands to Turkey. Armenia was recognized as an independent state by the Allied Powers and by Turkey in the Treaty of Sèvres, signed on 10 August 1920. However, the rejection of the Treaty by the new Turkish ruler, Mustafa Kemal, left Armenia vulnerable to renewed Turkish threats. In September Turkish troops attacked Armenia, but they were prevented from establishing full control over the country by the invasion of Armenia, from the east, by Russian Bolshevik troops, and the founding, on 29 November, of a Soviet Republic of Armenia. In December 1922 the republic became a member, together with Georgia and Azerbaijan, of the Transcaucasian Soviet Federative Socialist Republic (TSFSR), which, in turn, became a constituent republic of the USSR. In 1936 the TSFSR was dissolved and Armenia became a full union republic of the USSR.

Many Armenians suffered under communist rule, but advances were made in economic and social development. During the period of tsarist rule Russian Armenia had been an underdeveloped region of the Empire, with very little infrastructure; however, in the Armenian Soviet Socialist Republic (SSR), the authorities implemented a policy of forced modernization, which expanded communications and introduced industrial plants. Literacy and education were also improved. A programme to collectivize agriculture, initiated on a voluntary basis in 1928, engendered little enthusiasm; collectivization was enforced in 1930, and many thousands of peasants who opposed it were deported. Armenians experienced further suffering during the Stalinist purges of the late 1930s, in which thousands

of people were executed or imprisoned. During the Second World War (1939–45), Armenia avoided occupation by German forces, despite their invasion of the USSR in June 1941. Consequently, the republic provided an essential source of labour for the Soviet economy, and as many as 600,000 Armenians served in the Soviet armies (of whom an estimated 350,000 were killed). In the immediate post-war period the Soviet Government gave priority to developing the industrial sector in Armenia, while expanding the agricultural collectivization programme. In the late 1940s an estimated 150,000 Armenians of the diaspora returned to the republic.

The Soviet leader Mikhail Gorbachev's policies of *perestroika* (restructuring) and *glasnost* (openness), introduced following his accession to power in 1985, had little initial impact in Armenia. The first manifestations of the new policies were campaigns against corruption in the higher echelons of the Communist Party of Armenia (CPA). On a more public level, environmental problems became a focus for popular protest. The first demonstrations against ecological degradation took place in September 1987, but the demands of protesters soon began to include the redress of historical and political grievances. The most significant of the historical and ethnic issues discussed from late 1987 concerned the status of Nagornyi Karabakh, an autonomous oblast (region) within neighbouring Azerbaijan, largely populated by (non-Muslim) Armenians, control of which had been ceded to Azerbaijan in 1921 (see chapter on Azerbaijan). In February 1988 as many as 1m. people took part in demonstrations in Yerevan, the Armenian capital, in support of demands from within the enclave for the incorporation of Nagornyi Karabakh into the Armenian SSR. The demonstrations were organized by Yerevan intellectuals, who formed a group known as the Karabakh Committee. In response to increased unrest within Armenia, many Azerbaijanis began to leave the republic. Reports of ill-treatment of the refugees led to anti-Armenian riots in Sumgait, Azerbaijan, in late February, in which 26 Armenians died. This event provoked further Armenian anger, which was compounded by the decision of the Presidium of the USSR's Supreme Soviet (legislature) not to transfer Nagornyi Karabakh to Armenia. Strikes and rallies continued under the leadership of the officially outlawed Karabakh Committee, and the inability of the local authorities to control the unrest led to the dismissal, in May, of the First Secretary (leader) of the CPA. In December, however, the issue of Nagornyi Karabakh was temporarily subordinated to the problem of overcoming the effects of a severe earthquake, which had struck northern Armenia. Some 25,000 people were reported to have been killed and many thousands more were made homeless. Following the earthquake members of the Karabakh Committee were arrested, ostensibly for interfering in relief work. They were released only in May 1989, after huge demonstrations took place, protesting against their continued internment. Meanwhile, in January the Soviet Government had formed a Special Administration Committee of the Council of Ministers to preside over Nagornyi Karabakh, although the enclave remained under formal Azerbaijani jurisdiction.

Throughout 1989 *glasnost* allowed a much fuller examination of Armenian history and culture, and several unofficial groups, concerned with both cultural and political issues, were formed. In May the *yerakuyn*, the national flag of independent Armenia, was flown again, and 28 May, the anniversary of the establishment of independent Armenia, was declared a national day. However, internal politics remained dominated by events in Nagornyi Karabakh, and unrest continued both in Armenia and within the enclave. In September Azerbaijan implemented an economic blockade against Armenia, seriously affecting the reconstruction programme required after the 1988 earthquake. In November the Special Administration Committee was disbanded, and Azerbaijan resumed control over Nagornyi Karabakh. This prompted the Armenian Supreme Soviet to declare the enclave part of a 'unified Armenian Republic'. In January 1990 this was declared unconstitutional by the USSR's Supreme Soviet; the Armenian Supreme Soviet responded by granting itself the power to veto any legislation approved by the central authorities.

The increasing disillusionment with the Soviet Government was apparently responsible for the low level of participation in the elections to the Armenian Supreme Soviet, which took place in May–July 1990. No party achieved an overall majority, but the Armenian Pan-National Movement (APNM), the successor to the Karabakh Committee, was the largest single party, with some 35% of the seats in the legislature. Supported by other non-communist groups, Levon Ter-Petrossian, a leader of the APNM, defeated Vladimir Movsissian, the First Secretary of the CPA, in elections to the chairmanship of the Supreme Soviet. Vazgen Manukian, also an APNM leader, was appointed Prime Minister. On 23 August the legislature adopted a declaration of sovereignty, including a claim to the right to maintain armed forces and a demand for international recognition that the Turkish massacres of Armenians in 1915 constituted genocide. The Armenian SSR was renamed the Republic of Armenia. The new Government began to establish political and commercial links with the Armenian diaspora, and several prominent exiles returned to the republic. In late November 1990, after much debate, the CPA voted to become an independent organization within the Communist Party of the Soviet Union (CPSU).

The Armenian Government refused to enter into the negotiations between Soviet republics on a new treaty of union, which took place in late 1990 and early 1991, and officially boycotted the referendum on the renewal of the USSR, which was held in March 1991 in nine republics. Instead, the legislature decided to conduct a referendum on Armenian secession from the USSR, to be held in September. Initially, it was planned that the referendum would be conducted under the Soviet law on secession, adopted in April by the all-Union Supreme Soviet, which provided for a transitional period of at least five years before full independence could be achieved.

In late April 1991 there was an escalation of tension in Nagornyi Karabakh. The Armenian Government continued to deny any direct involvement in the violence, claiming that the attacks were outside its control, being organized by units of the ethnic Armenian 'Nagornyi Karabakh self-defence forces'. However, Azerbaijan countered that Armenia was, in fact, playing an aggressive role in the conflict, and made reference to 'Armenian expeditionary forces'. In a further complication, Armenia suggested that the Soviet leadership was supporting Azerbaijan, following the latter's agreement to sign the new union treaty, and punishing Armenia for its moves towards independence, for its refusal to take part in discussions on the union treaty and for its nationalization of CPA property.

The moderate policies of the new APNM-led Government, especially in developing relations with Turkey, attracted criticism from more extreme nationalist groups, notably the Union for National Self-Determination (UNS), which continued to seek the recovery of lands lost to Turkey after the First World War. The CPA attacked the Government for its willingness to promote relations with Turkey, as did the Armenian Revolutionary Federation (ARF, or Dashnaktsutiun, which had formed the Government of independent Armenia during 1918–20). The CPA also strongly opposed the idea of secession, while the ARF advocated a more gradual process towards independence. The UNS campaigned for immediate secession, which was in breach of the constitutional procedure.

The attempted coup in the Soviet and Russian capital, Moscow, and subsequent events of August 1991 forced the Government to accelerate progress towards secession, and provided further support for those advocating complete independence for Armenia. The referendum on independence took place, as scheduled, on 21 September. According to the official results, 94.4% of the electorate took part, of whom 99.3% supported Armenia's reconstitution as 'an independent, democratic state outside the Union'. On 23 September, instead of conforming to the Soviet law on secession, the Supreme Soviet declared Armenia to be, thenceforth, a fully independent state. Meanwhile, in early September a congress of the CPA voted to dissolve the party.

The independence declaration was followed, on 16 October 1991, by an election to the post of President of the Republic. Six candidates participated in the poll, which was won by the incumbent, Ter-Petrossian (with some 87% of the votes cast). The President continued to demand international recognition of Armenia, but on 18 October, with the leaders of seven other Soviet republics, he signed a treaty to establish an economic community, stressing, however, that it did not encroach on

Armenia's political independence, and refusing to sign a new treaty on political union. The Armenian leadership did, nevertheless, join the Commonwealth of Independent States (CIS, see p. 172), and signed the founding Almaty (Alma-Ata) Declaration on 21 December. In early 1992 Armenia was admitted to the Conference on Security and Co-operation in Europe (CSCE), which was renamed the Organization for Security and Co-operation in Europe (OSCE, see p. 283) in December 1994 and the UN.

In 1992 economic conditions in Armenia deteriorated, and there were widespread shortages of foodstuffs and fuel. The situation was exacerbated not only by the continuing conflict in Nagornyi Karabakh (see below), but also by fighting in neighbouring Georgia (which impeded supplies to Armenia), and the ongoing economic blockade by Azerbaijan (and its ally, Turkey). Compounding the economic crisis was the enormous influx of refugees from Nagornyi Karabakh and Azerbaijan. There were also increasing indications of public dissatisfaction with the Ter-Petrossian administration, and in mid-August and in February 1993 mass rallies were staged in Yerevan to demand the President's resignation. Earlier in February Ter-Petrossian had dismissed the Prime Minister, Khosrov Haroutunian, following disagreements over economic and social policy, and a new Council of Ministers was subsequently announced, headed by Hrant Bagratian, who was widely known as an economic reformist. However, the economic crisis intensified, and hundreds of thousands of Armenians were reported to have emigrated. In the latter half of 1994 thousands of people participated in anti-Government protests, which were organized at regular intervals by an association of opposition groups, known as the Union of Civic Accord (UCA). The assassination in December of a former mayor of Yerevan prompted the Government to effect a number of measures aimed at eliminating terrorism, the most radical of which was the suspension in late December of the leading opposition party, the ARF. Anti-Government forces condemned the measures, and monthly rallies were organized by the UCA in early 1995 in protest at official harassment of opposition activists.

Armenia's first post-Soviet legislative elections were held in July 1995. Thirteen parties and organizations contested the 190 seats of the new National Assembly under a mixed system of voting (with 150 seats to be filled by majority vote and the remainder by proportional representation on the basis of party lists). Nine parties, including the ARF, were barred from participation. The Republican bloc (an alliance of six groups, led by the APNM) won a majority of the seats in the Assembly (119). Eight seats were won by the Shamiram Women's Party, the revived CPA secured seven and the UNS took three. Forty-five independent candidates won representation in the Assembly. Some irregularities were reported by OSCE observers, and opposition parties contested the authenticity of the election results. In late July President Ter-Petrossian appointed a new Government, in which Hrant Bagratian remained as Prime Minister. A referendum on the new Armenian Constitution (under discussion from late 1992) was held simultaneously with the general election. Of the 56% of the electorate who participated in the plebiscite, some 68% voted in favour of the Constitution, which granted wide-ranging executive authority to the President and provided for a smaller, 131-member Assembly (effective from the next general election).

A presidential election was held on 22 September 1996. Ter-Petrossian was the candidate of the Republican bloc, while five opposition parties united to support Vazgen Manukian, the Chairman of the National Democratic Union (NDU). Although preliminary results indicated that Ter-Petrossian had been re-elected, the opposition made allegations of widespread electoral malpractice, and thousands staged protest rallies in Yerevan, to demand the President's resignation. International observers reported serious irregularities in the electoral proceedings, which cast doubt on the validity of the result. On 25 September supporters of Manukian stormed the National Assembly, injuring, among others, the Chairman and his deputy. A temporary ban on rallies was consequently imposed, and large numbers of opposition supporters were arrested. According to the final election results, Ter-Petrossian received 51.8% of the votes cast, and Manukian secured 41.3% (although he received significantly more votes than Ter-Petrossian in Yerevan). Opposition parties continued to demand fresh elections, and some boycotted the elections to the new bodies of local government, established by the Constitution in 1995, which were held in November 1996. The resignation of Bagratian as Prime Minister, allegedly in response to opposition to his programme of economic reforms, was announced in November; he was replaced by Armen Sarkissian. The latter resigned in March 1997 on grounds of ill health, and was replaced by Robert Kocharian, hitherto the President of Nagornyi Karabakh, in what was regarded as an attempt by Ter-Petrossian to reduce pressure from opposition parties.

Following the unexpected resignation of Ter-Petrossian on 3 February 1998, owing to government controversy over his support of an OSCE plan for a progressive settlement in Nagornyi Karabakh (see below), a presidential election was held on 16 and 30 March. In the second round of voting, Kocharian, the acting President, achieved victory over the former Soviet-era CPA leader, Karen Demirchian, obtaining 59.5% of the votes cast. The results were declared valid, despite some OSCE reports of electoral irregularities, and Kocharian was inaugurated as President on 9 April. On the following day Kocharian appointed Armen Darbinian, the erstwhile Minister of Finance and the Economy, as Prime Minister. In early May Kocharian relegalized the ARF, and appointed two further members of the party, including its leader, Vahan Hovhanissian, to positions in the Government (an ARF member had been included in the Government on its appointment the previous month). Meanwhile, in early July it was announced that, as part of a major reform of the judicial and legal system, the Supreme Court was to be replaced by a Court of Cassation. A controversial new law on electoral procedure, approved by the National Assembly in November, which provided for a 131-member legislature (composed of 75 deputies elected by majority vote through single-mandate constituencies, with the remainder chosen under a system of proportional representation, on the basis of party lists), was fully adopted in February 1999; shortly afterwards it was announced that legislative elections were to be held on 30 May. In April the Republican Party of Armenia (RPA) and the People's Party of Armenia (PPA) formed an electoral alliance, the Unity bloc (Miasnutiun), which won 55 seats in the National Assembly. The CPA secured 11 seats and the ARF obtained nine, while the Law and Unity bloc, the Law-governed Country Party and the NDU each won six seats; the APNM, the Armenian Democratic Party, the Mission Party and the National Unity Party each secured one seat, and independents accounted for the remainder. On 11 June Darbinian (who had been demoted to the post of Minister of the Economy), was replaced as Prime Minister by Vazgen Sarkissian, the unofficial leader of the RPA and, hitherto, Minister of Defence. At the first session of the new National Assembly, which was held a few days later, Karen Demirchian, by this time head of the PPA, was elected Chairman of the legislature.

In February 1999 the legislature, under threat of dissolution, endorsed a petition by the Prosecutor-General for permission to arrest the Chairman of the APNM and former Minister of the Interior, Vano Siradeghian (thereby removing his parliamentary immunity), who was alleged to have been involved in a number of politically motivated murders in the mid-1990s. Siradeghian (who had left the country earlier in the year) was placed under arrest on his return to Armenia in May; however, although his trial commenced in January 2000, Siradeghian fled the country in April. Meanwhile, in February 1999 the Deputy Minister of the Interior and National Security and commander of Armenia's internal troops, Maj.-Gen. Artsrun Makarian, was found shot dead; Makarian's bodyguards were subsequently charged with murder, amid speculation that he had been killed to prevent him from giving evidence against Siradeghian.

On 27 October 1999 Armenia was thrown into political turmoil when five gunmen besieged the National Assembly, killing eight people, including Prime Minister Sarkissian, Karen Demirchian and his two deputies, and a cabinet minister. The gunmen (who claimed no political affiliation) announced that they were seeking revenge against the 'corrupt political elite'. On their surrender, following overnight negotiations with President Kocharian, the assailants were charged with murder and terrorist offences; their trial commenced in February 2001. In the aftermath of the attack, the Ministers of the Interior and of National Security tendered their resignations. At the beginning of November 1999 the National Assembly held an extraordinary sitting, at which Armen Khachatrian, of the PPA, was elected Chairman of the legislature. On the following day President Kocharian appointed Aram Sarkissian, the younger brother of the murdered premier, and a political novice, as Prime Minister, on the recommendation of members of the Unity bloc.

Impeachment proceedings against President Kocharian, initiated in April 2000 by the majority Unity bloc following his decision not to allow the Military Prosecutor-General to testify in a parliamentary hearing concerning the shootings of October 1999, were cancelled, when it was ruled that the President had not acted in contravention of the Constitution. In early May 2000 the Prime Minister was dismissed by Kocharian, who cited his inability to work with Sarkissian's Government. Andranik Markarian, the leader of the RPA, was appointed premier on 12 May, and a cabinet reshuffle took place later that month. Both the President and the new Prime Minister pledged to bring to an end the conflict between their respective posts and the legislature.

In September 2000 Armen Khachatrian resigned as Chairman of the National Assembly, owing to conflict between the two constituent factions of the Unity bloc. However, he was reinstated, after the Constitutional Court declared Khachatrian's resignation to have been unconstitutional. In July 2001 Khachatrian resigned from the PPA, amid claims that the party had deviated from its founding principles. The PPA left the Unity bloc in early September, urging that fresh legislative elections be held. In late October the PPA, together with Republic (Hanrapetutiun—founded by former members of the RPA and the Yerkrapah Union of Volunteers in early 2001) and the National Unity Party, organized a rally to demand the impeachment of the President, whom they accused, *inter alia*, of precipitating a socio-economic crisis in the country, acting in contravention of the Constitution and condoning terrorism. Meanwhile, in mid-September Gagik Pogossian, an aide to Prime Minister Markarian and a former Minister of State Revenues, was killed as a result of a bomb attack; he had been involved in the investigation of fraud and corruption.

A number of government changes took place in 2001. In July two ministers exchanged portfolios: Andranik Manukian became Minister of Transport and Communications, and Yervand Zakharian became Minister of State Revenues. Vardan Aivazian, hitherto leader of the Stability Party (renamed the Agro-industrial People's Association in the same month) was appointed Minister of Environmental Protection. In November Levon Mkrtchian, a senior member of the ARF, was appointed Minister of Education and Science, becoming the second ARF member in the Government. Armen Movsissian was appointed Minister of Energy in early December. A minor government reorganization took place at the end of January 2002. David Zadoian, hitherto Minister of Industrial Infrastructure, was appointed Minister of Agriculture, and the portfolio of the Minister of Regional Government, Hovik Abrahamian, was expanded to include the co-ordination of infrastructure.

In April 2002 thousands of people participated in protests against the closure of the independent television station, A1+, which opposition parties claimed to be politically motivated, and demands were made for the President's resignation. In June parliamentary proceedings were temporarily suspended when Armen Khachatrian (who remained Chairman of the National Assembly) refused to accept an opposition motion proposing Kocharian's impeachment. In the same month legislation was adopted abolishing the death penalty, although the new law was not to apply to those found guilty of terrorist offences or paedophilia prior to its introduction (and, notably, would enable those found guilty of the parliamentary killings of October 1999 to be sentenced to death). In September 2002, however, the Council of Europe (see p. 181) threatened Armenia with expulsion from the organization, unless it agreed to the unconditional abolition of capital punishment by June 2003.

At the beginning of August 2002 a controversial law was signed into law, which restored the number of deputies elected by majority vote through single-mandate constituencies to 56 (it had been reduced to 37 as part of electoral reform enacted in December 2000); opposition deputies argued that the amendment would serve to benefit the ruling RPA in the legislative election due to be held in May 2003. The composition of the Central Electoral Commission was also reorganized, with three of its nine members to be presidential appointments. In late August 2002 16 opposition parties, including Republic, the PPA and the National Unity Party, formed the People's Patriotic Union (PPU), with the intention of nominating a joint candidate for the forthcoming presidential election, scheduled to take place on 19 February 2003. However, the RPA confirmed its political dominance in the local elections held on 20 October 2002, and in the following month a number of parties detached themselves from the PPU and declared their intention to nominate separate candidates for the presidential election.

In mid-December 2002 the Ministry of Internal Affairs and the Ministry of National Security were restructured as non-ministerial institutions, and renamed the Police of the Republic of Armenia and the National Security Service. Although the respective former ministers remained part of the Government, some observers interpreted the measure as reinforcing legislation passed earlier in the year, which had increased presidential control over the country's security framework. In late December Tigran Naghdalian, the Chairman of the board of Armenian Public Television and Radio and a supporter of the President, was assassinated; it was reported that there had been a political motivation for the killing.

The National Assembly failed to reconvene in early February 2003, following a one-month recess, owing to the lack of a quorum, prompting opposition deputies to claim that the pro-Government majority was seeking deliberately to stall debate until after the presidential election. Ultimately, nine candidates participated in the election, which took place on 19 February, as scheduled. Robert Kocharian received 49.5% of the votes cast, fewer than the 50% required to secure an outright victory. A second round was consequently scheduled for 5 March, contested by Kocharian and PPA leader Stepan Demirchian (the son of the murdered parliamentary Chairman, Karen Demirchian), who had received 28.2% of the votes cast in the first round. Kocharian was re-elected as President in the second round, receiving 67.5% of the votes cast. However, monitors from both the OSCE and the Council of Europe recorded 'serious irregularities' in electoral procedure, and thousands of people took part in protests against the results, which were, none the less, declared valid by the Constitutional Court in mid-April. A referendum on a number of proposed constitutional amendments (including the right to hold dual citizenship) was scheduled to take place on the same day as the legislative election, on 25 May.

The proclamation of Armenia's independence in September 1991 led to an escalation of hostilities in the disputed enclave of Nagornyi Karabakh. In that month the territory declared itself an independent republic, and violence intensified following the dissolution of the USSR in December. In January 1992 the President of Azerbaijan, Ayaz Mutalibov, placed the region under direct presidential rule; in the same month Azerbaijani forces surrounded and attacked Stepanakert, the capital of Nagornyi Karabakh, while the Armenians laid siege to Shusha, a town with a mainly Azerbaijani population. In May the Nagornyi Karabakh self-defence forces (which the Armenian Government continued to claim was operating without its military support) captured Shusha, thereby gaining complete control of the enclave and ending the bombardment of Stepanakert. With the capture of the strategically-important Lachin valley, the Armenian militia succeeded in opening a 'corridor' inside Azerbaijan, linking Nagornyi Karabakh with Armenia proper.

In June 1992 Azerbaijani forces launched a sustained counter-offensive in Nagornyi Karabakh, recapturing villages both inside and around the enclave, and expelling several thousand inhabitants, thus exacerbating the already urgent refugee crisis. In early August Azerbaijani forces resumed the bombardment of Stepanakert. In response to the escalation of attacks and ensuing military gains by Azeri forces, the Nagornyi Karabakh legislature declared a state of martial law, and a state defence committee, in close alignment with the Ter-Petrossian administration, replaced the enclave's government.

In early 1993 the military situation in Nagornyi Karabakh was reversed, as Armenian forces undertook a series of successful offensives, regaining territory that they had lost in 1992 and also taking control of large areas of Azerbaijan surrounding the enclave. With the capture of the Kelbajar district of Azerbaijan in April 1993, the Armenians succeeded in creating a second corridor linking the enclave with Armenia and effectively securing the whole swath of Azerbaijani territory extending south to the Lachin corridor. Many thousands of Azeris fled or were expelled from their homes. The Armenian position was only strengthened by the growing political turmoil in Azerbaijan in mid-1993 (q.v.), and by late June Armenian forces had secured full control of Nagornyi Karabakh.

The Armenian seizure of Azerbaijani territory prompted widespread international condemnation, particularly by neighbouring Turkey and Iran, the latter fearing a massive influx of refugees from south-western Azerbaijan. UN Security Council Resolutions 822 and 853, demanding the withdrawal of Arme-

nian forces from Azerbaijan, went unheeded; hostilities reintensified, and more than 20% of Azerbaijan's total territory was reported to have been captured by the Nagornyi Karabakh Armenian forces, who had extended their operations as far south as the Azerbaijan–Iran border. Azeri forces launched a major new counter-offensive in December, recapturing some of the territory that they had lost during the year. In February 1994 it was reported that as many as 18,000 people had been killed since 1988, with a further 25,000 wounded. The number of displaced Azeris was believed to have exceeded 1m.

A series of fragile cease-fire agreements was reached in the first half of 1994, and in early May, following protracted mediation by the CSCE and Russia, a new cease-fire agreement was signed by the Ministers of Defence of Armenia and Azerbaijan and representatives of Nagornyi Karabakh. The agreement was formalized in July. Ter-Petrossian held talks with the President of Azerbaijan, Heydar Aliyev, in Moscow, in early September. Although agreement was reached on some key provisions of a future peace treaty, Aliyev stated that his willingness to negotiate such an accord depended on the unconditional withdrawal of Armenian forces from occupied Azerbaijani territory. Negotiations were held at regular intervals throughout 1995 under the aegis of the 'Minsk Group' of the OSCE. However, progress towards a political settlement was hampered by Azerbaijan's demand for the return of Lachin and Shusha regions, as well as by its apparent unwillingness to recognize the Nagornyi Karabakh leadership as an equal party in the negotiations. Nevertheless, the cease-fire continued to be observed, with only sporadic violations reported, and in May the three sides carried out a large-scale exchange of prisoners of war. Direct discussions between Armenia and Azerbaijan, which were held in conjunction with the OSCE negotiations, were initiated in December.

Ter-Petrossian and Aliyev met, together with President Eduard Shevardnadze of Georgia, in April 1996 in Luxembourg, where they signed an agreement on partnership and co-operation with the European Union (EU, see p. 199) and affirmed their commitment to the 1994 cease-fire. A further exchange of prisoners of war occurred in May 1996. Elections to the post of President of Nagornyi Karabakh, held in November, were condemned by Azerbaijan and criticized by the Minsk Group as a hindrance to the peace process. Robert Kocharian, the incumbent President, was re-elected with some 86% of the votes cast. In December Ter-Petrossian and Aliyev attended an OSCE summit meeting in Lisbon, Portugal. Following demands by Azerbaijan, the OSCE Chairman issued a statement recommending three principles that would form the basis of a future political settlement in the enclave: the territorial integrity of Armenia and Azerbaijan; the legal status of Nagornyi Karabakh, which would be granted broad autonomy within Azerbaijan; and security guarantees for the population of Nagornyi Karabakh. Armenia, however, refused to accept the terms of the statement.

Relations between the two countries deteriorated in early 1997, with mutual accusations of the stockpiling of weapons in preparation for the renewal of military conflict in Nagornyi Karabakh. Negotiations under the auspices of the OSCE continued, however. Fresh elections to the post of President of Nagornyi Karabakh in early September, which were scheduled following the appointment of Kocharian as Prime Minister of Armenia, were won by Arkadii Ghukassian, with some 90% of the votes, but were criticized by the international community. Ghukassian reportedly rejected the OSCE peace settlement on the grounds that the proposals presupposed Azerbaijan's sovereignty over the enclave. However, in late September it was reported that Armenia had accepted, in principle, the OSCE's plan for a stage-by-stage settlement of the conflict, which entailed the withdrawal of Armenian forces from six districts around Nagornyi Karabakh, to be followed by a decision on the status of the Shusha and Lachin corridors, and on the status of Nagornyi Karabakh itself. A statement by President Ter-Petrossian that Nagornyi Karabakh could hope neither to gain full independence, nor to be united with Armenia, appeared to indicate a significant change in policy, and the President's moderate approach to the crisis, which provoked much government disapproval, led to his resignation in early February 1998. His replacement, Kocharian, who was born in Nagornyi Karabakh, was expected to adopt a more nationalistic stance towards resolving the situation in the disputed enclave. In late November the Armenian Government accepted new proposals put forward by the Minsk Group for a settlement of the conflict in Nagornyi Karabakh, which were based on the principle of a 'common state'; they were, however, rejected by Azerbaijan. Following an escalation in hostilities in mid-1999, each side accused the other of attempting to abrogate the 1994 cease-fire agreement. Meanwhile, in June 1999 Ghukassian dismissed the Government of Zhirayr Pogossian (who had replaced Leonard Petrossian as the enclave's Prime Minister in June 1998); Anushavan Danielian was appointed to head a new administration. In July Pogossian was arrested and charged with illegally possessing arms and ammunition, and with losing a state document. In March 2000 President Ghukassian sustained serious injuries following an attack by gunmen in Stepanakert. Among those arrested in connection with the assassination attempt was the former Minister of Defence of Nagornyi Karabakh, Samuel Babaian, who was gaoled for 14 years in February 2001. Despite several meetings between Presidents Kocharian and Aliyev in 2000–02 , no substantive progress was made towards reaching a final resolution of the Nagornyi Karabakh conflict.

In April 1997 the Armenian legislature ratified a treaty, which allowed Russia to maintain military bases in Armenia for a period of 25 years. The ties between Russia and Armenia were reinforced by a declaration of alliance and co-operation, and a number of bilateral agreements were concluded in September 2000. A further 10-year economic co-operation agreement was signed in September 2001, during a visit to Armenia by the Russian President, Vladimir Putin. Armenia's close diplomatic and military links with Russia from the late 1990s (including reports of large supplies of Russian armaments to Armenia) were met with disapproval and suspicion on the part of the Azerbaijani Government. Armenia's relations with Georgia were furthered by a visit by Georgian President Shevardnadze in May 1997, during which several co-operation agreements were signed. President Kocharian expressed concern in 2001 over the increasing political tension in Georgia, the territory of which represented an important trade route for Armenian exports, and which was home to a significant ethnic Armenian minority. Relations with Turkey remained uneasy, and in June 2000 an Armenian delegation, invited to Turkey to attend a peace forum for the Caucasus, was expelled. Turkey also refused to allow the demarcation of its border with Armenia, owing to the presence of Russian border guards in that country. In September 2001 the first meeting of a Turkish-Armenian Reconciliation Commission (TARC), composed of members from both countries, was held in İstanbul, Turkey; at a second meeting, held in New York, USA, it was agreed to ask the New York-based International Centre for Transitional Justice to establish whether the Turkish massacre of Armenians in 1915–22 had constituted 'genocide'. In mid-December 2001 the Commission suspended its work, as a result of internal disagreement. None the less, in 2002 meetings took place between the Armenian Minister of Foreign Affairs, Vardan Oskanian, and his Turkish counterpart, İsmail Cem, and in May a tripartite meeting was held, attended by the Ministers of Foreign Affairs of Armenia, Azerbaijan and Turkey. The TARC reconvened in July. In February 2003 it was reported that the International Centre for Transitional Justice had concluded that the massacres of 1915–22 could be interpreted as genocide, according to international criteria.

In June 2000 the Parliamentary Assembly of the Council of Europe voted to admit both Armenia and Azerbaijan to that organization; they became full members in January 2001.

Government

Under the Constitution of 1995, the President of the Republic is Head of State and Supreme Commander-in-Chief of the armed forces, but also holds broad executive powers. The President is directly elected for a term of five years (and for no more than two consecutive terms of office). The President appoints the Prime Minister and, on the latter's recommendation, the members of the Government. Legislative power is vested in the 131-member National Assembly, which is elected for a four-year term by universal adult suffrage. For administrative purposes, Armenia is divided into 11 regions (*marzer*), including the capital, Yerevan. The regions are subdivided into communities (*hamaynker*).

Defence

Following the dissolution of the USSR in December 1991, Armenia became a member of the Commonwealth of Independent States and its collective security system. The country also began to establish its own armed forces, which numbered some

44,610 in August 2002, including an army of 38,900. Military service is compulsory and lasts for two years (a law was passed in 2000, however, allowing for the exemption from military service of university graduates and those engaged in certain professions). There is also a paramilitary force of an estimated 1,000. In August 2002 there were approximately 2,900 Russian troops stationed on Armenian territory. In October 1994 Armenia joined NATO's (see p. 271) 'Partnership for Peace' programme of military co-operation. The budget for 2002 allocated an estimated US $62m. to defence; the 2003 budget provided for an increase in defence expenditure of over 20%.

Economic Affairs

In 2001, according to estimates by the World Bank, Armenia's gross national income (GNI), measured at average 1999–2001 prices, was US $2,127m., equivalent to $560 per head (or $2,880 on an international purchasing-power parity basis). During 1990–2001, it was estimated, the population increased at an average rate of 0.6% per year, while gross domestic product (GDP) per head decreased, in real terms, by an annual average of 3.3%. Over the same period, Armenia's overall GDP decreased, in real terms, by an average of 2.7% annually. However, real GDP increased by 6.0% in 2000 and by 9.6% in 2001.

According to the World Bank, agriculture and forestry contributed 25.9% of GDP in 2001 and, according to official figures, employed 45.5% of the working population. However, the FAO estimated the proportion of the working population employed in agriculture at 24.0% in that year. The principal crops are potatoes and other vegetables, cereals and fruit. Private farms accounted for some 98% of agricultural production in 1998. During 1990–2001, according to estimates by the World Bank, agricultural GDP increased, in real terms, at an average annual rate of 0.1%. The GDP of the sector decreased by 2.4% in 2000, but increased by 2.5% in 2001.

According to the World Bank, in 2001 industry (including mining, manufacturing, construction and power) contributed 34.1% of GDP. The sector (excluding utilities) employed 16.8% of the working population in that year, according to official figures. World Bank estimates indicated that during 1990–2001 industrial GDP declined by an average of 9.6% annually. However, the GDP of the sector increased by 8.2% in 2000 and by 5.4% in 2001.

Armenia's mining sector has not yet been extensively developed. Copper, molybdenum, gold, silver and iron are extracted on a small scale, and there are reserves of lead and zinc. There are also substantial, but largely unexploited, reserves of mineral salt, calcium oxide and carbon, although in 2001 there were plans for a British company to commence mineral production in Armenia, within the framework of the EU's programme of Technical Assistance to the Commonwealth of Independent States (TACIS, see p. 227). Production of gold decreased significantly in the 1990s, but the Government hoped to encourage a recovery in the industry, following the conclusion of an agreement with a Canadian company to develop new extraction facilities, which went into production in 1998.

In 2001, according to the World Bank, the manufacturing sector provided 23.4% of Armenia's GDP. According to IMF figures, in that year the principal branches of manufacturing, measured by gross value of output, were food-processing and beverages (accounting for 55.0% of the total), base metals and fabricated metal (12.4%), and jewellery and related articles (8.4%). According to the World Bank, during 1990–2001 the GDP of the manufacturing sector declined, in real terms, at an average annual rate of 5.1%. However, real sectoral GDP increased by 6.5% in 2000 and by 5.8% in 2001.

Armenia is heavily dependent on imported energy, much of which is supplied by Russia (petroleum and derivatives) and Turkmenistan (natural gas); there are also plans to build a natural gas pipeline to Armenia from Iran. It is, however, thought probable that Armenia has significant reserves of petroleum and natural gas. The country's sole nuclear power station, at Medzamor, was closed following the earthquake of 1988. However, in late 1995, in view of Armenia's worsening energy crisis, the station's second generating unit resumed operations, following restoration work. (In 1996 proposals were made for the construction of a new nuclear power plant, scheduled for completion in 2010.) By 2001 nuclear power contributed 35.6% of the country's electricity supply, thermoelectric power produced 47.3%, and hydroelectric power provided 17.1% of the total (compared with 63.1% in 1994). By July 1999 Armenia had a surplus of electricity, some of which was exported to Georgia; a new high-voltage electricity line opened between the two countries in December 2000. In September 1999 Armenia signed an agreement with the EU on shutting down the Medzamor power station by 2004. The agreement was, however, dependent on the construction of adequate alternative energy facilities. In February 2003 Armenia agreed to transfer responsibility for the financial management of the Medzamor plant to Russia, in return for the settlement of its fuel arrears. Imports of mineral fuels comprised 21.3% of the value of merchandise imports in 2001.

The services sector contributed 40.0% of GDP in 2001, according to the World Bank, and official figures indicated that the sector (including utilities) engaged 37.7% of the employed labour force in that year. According to the World Bank, during 1990–2001 the GDP of the sector increased by an average of 7.7% annually, in real terms. Real services GDP increased by 11.0% in 2000 and by 11.1% in 2001.

In 2001 Armenia recorded a visible trade deficit of US $420.2m., while the deficit on the current account of the balance of payments was $200.5m. In that year the principal source of imports, according to official statistics, was Russia, which provided 19.8% of the total; other main sources were the United Kingdom (10.4%), the USA (9.6%), Iran (8.9%) and the United Arab Emirates (5.4%). In the same year Russia was also the main market for exports, accounting for 17.7% of the total. Other important purchasers were the USA (15.3%), Belgium (13.6%), Israel (9.8%), Iran (9.3%) and the United Kingdom (5.9%). The principal exports in 2001 were pearls, precious and semi-precious stones, precious metals, imitation jewellery and coins; prepared foodstuffs, beverages and tobacco; base metals; mineral products; machinery and electrical equipment; and textiles. The principal imports in that year were mineral products; pearls, precious and semi-precious stones, precious metals, imitation jewellery and coins; machinery and electrical equipment; vegetable products; prepared foodstuffs, beverages and tobacco; and chemicals.

In 2001, according to IMF figures, there was a budgetary deficit of 45,100m. drams (equivalent to 3.8% of GDP). At the end of 2000 Armenia's total external debt was US $897.5m. (equivalent to 46.5% of GNI), of which $658.1m. was long-term public debt. In that year the cost of debt-servicing was equivalent to 7.6% of the value of exports of goods and services. Inflation increased at an average annual rate of 95.0% in 1993–2000. Consumer prices increased by 3.1% in 2001. At the end of November 2002 an estimated 155,500 people were officially registered as unemployed, giving an unemployment rate of 9.2%.

Armenia is a member of the IMF, the World Bank and the European Bank for Reconstruction and Development (EBRD, see p. 193), and it is also a member of the Organization of the Black Sea Economic Co-operation (BSEC, see p. 294). In February 2003 Armenia became a member of the World Trade Organization (WTO, see p. 322).

The collapse of the Soviet central planning system and internal trading structures, together with the severe effects of the earthquake in 1988 and of the conflict in Nagornyi Karabakh, exacerbated an already critical economic situation in Armenia. The economic blockade of Armenia by Azerbaijan and, subsequently, Turkey, as well as the civil war in Georgia, resulted in widespread shortages of food and fuel, and a concomitant decline in industrial production. A wide-ranging programme of economic reforms was initiated in the early 1990s, which included price liberalization, the promotion of privatization and a rationalization of the taxation system, and the first signs of economic recovery were observed by 1994. Although the privatization programme was well advanced by late 1998, the economy was adversely affected by that year's economic crisis in Russia. This problem was compounded by the political upheaval that followed the assassination in October 1999 of the Armenian Prime Minister and seven other government officials. However, by 2001 Armenia had recorded a significant improvement in economic performance, despite a decline in foreign investment, (partly owing to the negative impact on investment in the Caucasus region that resulted from the large-scale suicide attacks on the USA in September, and the subsequent military action in Afghanistan—see US chapter). In 2001 two consecutive attempts to privatize the country's four regional energy-distribution networks failed, although the privatization of other enterprises continued successfully, and a list was drawn up in late 2001 of over 900 state-owned enterprises to be privatized by 2004. In March 2002 the electricity-distribution networks were merged to form a single entity, an 81% stake in which was finally divested in August. In November an agreement was signed with Russia, under the terms of which five Armenian state-owned enterprises were to come under Russian ownership, as a means of repaying arrears amounting to some US $98m. Meanwhile, in 2001 the World Bank approved a $50m. Structural Adjustment Credit, and the IMF was to provide a further $90m. under its Poverty Reduction and Growth Facility, although the disbursement of funding was repeatedly delayed, owing to the Government's failure to meet tax-collection targets. However, tax revenues increased significantly in 2002, and in December 2002 the National Assembly adopted legislation, which sought further to enhance tax-collection methods. In that year economic growth was estimated at over 12% (the highest level of GDP growth recorded in more than a decade), the rate of consumer-price inflation was estimated at some 2%, and the level of external debt was reduced. However, one-half of the population continued to subsist below the World Bank's national poverty level and unemployment remained high. Moreover, export trade remained severely hampered by the lack of transport links with Azerbaijan and Turkey. It was anticipated, however, that membership of the WTO from February 2003 would be of substantial benefit to the economy.

Education

Education is free and compulsory at primary and secondary levels. Until the early 1990s the general education system conformed to that of the centralized Soviet system, but extensive changes were subsequently introduced, with greater emphasis placed on Armenian history and culture. Primary education usually began at seven years of age and lasted for four years. Secondary education, beginning at 11 years of age, comprised a first cycle of four years and a second of two years. In 2001/02, however, Armenia introduced an 11-year system of schooling. In 2000 total enrolment at pre-school establishments was equivalent to 17.2% of the relevant age-group. In 1999 combined enrolment at primary, secondary and tertiary establishments was equivalent to 79% of the female school-age population, and 75% for males. In 1996 primary enrolment was equivalent to 86% of children in the relevant age-group, and the comparable ratio for secondary enrolment was 88%. Most instruction in higher institutions is in Armenian, although Russian is widely taught as a second language. In 2000/01 98.4% of students in general education schools were taught in Armenian, and 1.3% were mainly taught in Russian. In the same year 43,600 students were enrolled in establishments of higher education, of whom 22,400 attended the country's seven universities. Current expenditure on education by all levels of government, according to preliminary figures, was 8,717m. drams in 2000.

Public Holidays

2003: 1–2 January (New Year), 6 January (Christmas), 8 March (Women's Day), 18–20 April (Easter), 24 April (Armenian Genocide Commemoration Day), 9 May (Victory Day), 28 May (Declaration of the First Armenian Republic Day), 5 July (Constitution Day), 21 September (Independence Day), 7 December (Day of Remembrance of the 1988 Earthquake), 31 December (New Year's Eve).

2004: 1–2 January (New Year), 6 January (Christmas), 8 March (Women's Day), 9–11 April (Easter), 24 April (Armenian Genocide Commemoration Day), 9 May (Victory Day), 28 May (Declaration of the First Armenian Republic Day), 5 July (Constitution Day), 21 September (Independence Day), 7 December (Day of Remembrance of the 1988 Earthquake), 31 December (New Year's Eve).

Weights and Measures

The metric system is in force.

Statistical Survey

Principal source: National Statistical Service of the Republic of Armenia, 375010 Yerevan, Republic Sq., Government House 3; tel. (1) 52-42-13; fax (1) 52-19-21; e-mail armstat@sci.am; internet www.armstat.am.

Area and Population

AREA, POPULATION AND DENSITY

Area (sq km)	29,743*
Population (census results)†	
12 January 1989	
Males.	1,619,308
Females	1,685,468
Total	3,304,776
10 October 2001 (provisional)	3,210,606
Population (official estimates at 1 January)‡	
2000	3,803,400
2001	3,802,400
2002	3,800,000
Density (per sq km) at 1 January 2002	127.8

* 11,484 sq miles.

† Figures refer to *de jure* population. The *de facto* total was 3,287,677 in 1989 and 3,000,807 in 2001.

‡ The figures, which include persons temporarily absent (475,200 at 1 January 1999), have not been adjusted to take account of the October 2001 census results.

POPULATION BY NATIONALITY
(permanent inhabitants, 1989 census)

	%
Armenian	93.3
Azerbaijani	2.6
Kurdish	1.7
Russian	1.5
Others	0.9
Total	100.0

MARZER (PROVINCES)
(1 January 2001)

Marz (Province)	Area (sq km)*	Estimated Population†	Density (per sq km)	Capital
Yerevan . . .	227	1,246,100	5,489.4	Yerevan
Aragatsotn . .	2,753	168,100	61.1	Ashtarak
Ararat . . .	2,096	311,400	148.6	Artashat
Armavir . . .	1,242	323,300	260.3	Armavir
Gegharkunik .	5,348	278,600	67.8	Gavar
Kotaik . . .	2,089	328,900	157.4	Hrazdan
Lori	3,789	392,300	103.5	Vanadzor
Shirak . . .	2,681	3621,400	134.8	Gyumri
Syunik . . .	4,506	164,000	36.4	Kapan
Tavush . . .	2,704	156,500	57.9	Ijevan
Vayots Dzor. .	2,308	69,400	30.1	Yeghegnadzor
Total	29,743	3,800,000	127.8	

* Including inland water, totalling 1,278 sq km.

† Provisional figures, including persons temporarily absent from the country.

PRINCIPAL TOWNS
(estimated population at 1 January 2001)

Yerevan (capital).	1,246,100		Vagarshapat	
			(Echmiadzin) . .	65,700
Gyumri* . . .	210,100		Hrazdan (Razdan) .	63,400
Vanadzor† . . .	170,800		Abovian . . .	60,600

* Known as Leninakan between 1924 and 1991.

† Known as Kirovakan between 1935 and 1992.

BIRTHS, MARRIAGES AND DEATHS*

	Registered live births		Registered marriages		Registered deaths	
	Number	Rate (per 1,000)	Number	Rate (per 1,000)	Number	Rate (per 1,000)
1994 . .	51,143	13.7	17,118	4.6	24,652	6.6
1995 . .	48,960	13.0	15,911	4.2	24,842	6.6
1996 . .	48,134	12.8	14,234	3.8	24,936	6.6
1997 . .	43,929	11.6	12,521	3.3	23,985	6.3
1998 . .	39,366	10.4	11,365	3.0	23,210	6.1
1999 . .	36,502	9.6	12,459	3.3	24,087	6.3
2000 . .	34,276	9.0	10,986	2.9	24,025	6.3
2001† . .	32,065	8.4	12,302	3.2	24,003	6.3

* Rates are calculated from unrevised population estimates.

† Figures are provisional.

Expectation of life (WHO estimates, years at birth): 69.7 (males 66.2; females 73.0) in 2001 (Source: WHO, *World Health Report*).

ECONOMICALLY ACTIVE POPULATION
(annual averages, '000 persons)

	1998	1999	2000†
Material sphere	987	956	946
Agriculture	566	560	554
Forestry	2	2	2
Industry*	209	195	193
Construction	57	54	53
Transport and communications .	28	26	26
Trade and catering . . .	113	109	108
Other activities	12	10	10
Non-material sphere	349	340	335
Education, culture and art . .	155	153	152
Science	17	16	16
Health, physical culture and social welfare	78	77	76
Housing and personal services .	43	38	38
General administration . . .	29	28	28
Other activities . . .	27	28	25
Total employed	1,337	1,298	1,283
Registered unemployed . . .	139	164	170
Total labour force	1,476	1,462	1,453

* Principally mining, manufacturing, electricity, gas and water.

† Preliminary figures.

Source: IMF, *Republic of Armenia: Recent Economic Developments and Selected Issues* (May 2001).

2000 ('000 persons, annual averages): Agriculture 564.6; Forestry 2.1; Industry (including construction) 226.2; Transport and communications 46.6; Trade and catering 106.9; Education, culture and art 153.9; Other services 167.3; Activities not adequately defined 10.1; Registered unemployed 169.5; Total labour force 1,447.2.

2001 ('000 persons, annual averages): Agriculture 567.9; Forestry 2.1; Industry (including construction) 210.8; Transport and communications 44.2; Trade and catering 110.5; Education, culture and art 155.2; Other services 162.8; Activities not adequately defined 11.4; Registered unemployed 146.8; Total labour force 1,411.7.

Health and Welfare

KEY INDICATORS

Total fertility rate (children per woman, 2001)	1.2
Under-five mortality rate (per 1,000 live births, 2001) . .	35
HIV (% of persons aged 15–49, 2001)	0.15
Physicians (per 1,000 head, 1998)	3.16
Hospital beds (per 1,000 head, 1996)	7.2
Health expenditure (1998): US $ per head (PPP)	174
Health expenditure (2000): % of GDP	7.5
Health expenditure (2000): public (% of total)	42.3
Human Development Index (2000): ranking	76
Human Development Index (2000): value	0.754

For sources and definitions, see explanatory note on p. vi.

Agriculture

PRINCIPAL CROPS
('000 metric tons)

	1999	2000	2001
Wheat	214.4	177.8	241.7
Barley	65.1	32.9	107.4
Maize	11.4	5.9	9.9
Other cereals	6.5	4.5*	2.1*
Potatoes	414.1	290.3	363.8
Pulses	3.7	3.9	3.1
Cabbages	94.0	51.5	80.4
Tomatoes	151.4	143.7	158.3
Cauliflowers	2.4	2.2	3.8
Cucumbers and gherkins . .	55.3*	30.0	49.6*
Dry Onions	40.5	31.3	33.0
Garlic	7.0	6.1	6.7
Peas (green)	0.1	1.2	0.7
Carrots	18.3	6.6	14.1
Other vegetables*	80.0	103.0	120.0
Apples	23.5	23.2	35.4
Pears	16.5	16.3	9.8
Apricots	15.4	36.7	10.8
Peaches and nectarines . .	11.5	26.8	16.0
Plums	7.7	11.8	10.5
Grapes	114.8	115.8	116.5
Watermelons†	88.5	52.8	54.8

* Unofficial figure(s).
† Including melons, pumpkins and squash.

Source: FAO.

LIVESTOCK
('000 head, year ending September)

	1999	2000	2001
Horses	12	12	11
Asses*	3	2	3
Cattle	469	479	485
Pigs	86	71	69
Sheep	508	497	540
Goats	12	11	10
Rabbits*	5	5	5
Chickens	3,190	4,255	4,300
Turkeys*	175	170	170

* FAO estimates.

Source: FAO.

LIVESTOCK PRODUCTS
('000 metric tons)

	1999	2000	2001
Beef and veal	32	33	32
Mutton and lamb	5	6	7
Pig meat	8	6	6
Poultry meat	3	3	3
Cows' milk	452	462	450
Sheep's milk	11	10	10
Cheese*	3	3	3
Hen eggs	18†	22†	19
Wool: greasy	1	1	1
Wool: scoured*	1	1	1

* FAO estimates.
† Unofficial figure.

Source: FAO.

Forestry

ROUNDWOOD REMOVALS
('000 cubic metres, excluding bark)

	2000	2001
Total (all fuel wood)	57	42

Source: FAO.

Fishing

(metric tons, live weight)

	1998	1999	2000
Capture	698	1,111	1,105
Crucian carp	42	26	38
Whitefishes	605	922	881
Aquaculture	437	901	902
Common carp	101	352	381
Silver carp	19	59	51
Rainbow trout	308	445	439
Total catch	1,135	2,012	2,007

Source: FAO, *Yearbook of Fishery Statistics*.

Mining

	1998	1999	2000
Copper concentrates (metric tons)*†	9,200	9,600	14,000
Molybdenum concentrates (metric tons)*	2,500†	5,403	6,044
Silver ores (kg)*	1,000	1,200†	1,300
Gold ores (kg)*	350†	400	400
Salt ('000 metric tons) . . .	25	27	30

* Figures refer to the metal content of ores and concentrates.
† Estimated production.

Source: US Geological Survey.

Industry

SELECTED PRODUCTS
('000 metric tons, unless otherwise indicated)

	1999	2000	2001
Wheat flour	148	152	112
Wine ('000 hectolitres)	48	26	60
Beer ('000 hectolitres)	84	79	100
Mineral water ('000 hectolitres)	106	180	197
Soft drinks ('000 hectolitres)	222	216	284
Cigarettes (million)	3,132	2,109	1,623
Wool yarn—pure and mixed (metric tons)	24	46	34
Cotton yarn—pure and mixed (metric tons)	55	80	60
Woven cotton fabrics ('000 sq metres)	157	219	147
Silk fabrics ('000 sq metres)	21	16	n.a.
Woven woollen fabrics ('000 sq metres)	9	48	28
Carpets ('000 sq metres)	18	19	18
Leather footwear ('000 pairs)	24	n.a.	n.a.
Rubber tyres ('000)*	5	n.a.	n.a.
Rubber footwear ('000 pairs)	12	n.a.	n.a.
Cement	287	219	276
Electric energy (million kWh)‡	5,717	5,958	5,744

* For road motor vehicles.
‡ Source: IMF, *Republic of Armenia: Statistical Annex* (October 2002).

Finance

CURRENCY AND EXCHANGE RATES

Monetary Units
100 louma = 1 dram

Sterling, Dollar and Euro Equivalents (31 December 2002)
£1 sterling = 942.7 drams
US $1 = 584.9 drams
€1 = 613.4 drams
1,000 drams = £1.061 = $1.710 = €1.630

Average Exchange Rate (drams per US $)
2000   539.53
2001   555.08
2002   573.35

Note: The dram was introduced on 22 November 1993, replacing the Russian (formerly Soviet) rouble at a conversion rate of 1 dram = 200 roubles. The initial exchange rate was set at US $1 = 14.3 drams, but by the end of the year the rate was $1 = 75 drams. After the introduction of the dram, Russian currency continued to circulate in Armenia. The rouble had been withdrawn from circulation by March 1994.

STATE BUDGET
(million drams)*

Revenue	1999	2000	2001†
Tax revenue	190,469	182,526	200,700
Value-added tax	68,270	67,491	79,500
Excises	21,677	25,403	31,000
Enterprise profits tax	21,499	20,320	16,300
Personal income tax	18,835	14,777	11,200
Land tax	1,471	1,473	1,700
Customs duties	8,051	8,672	9,800
Payroll taxes	25,085	23,480	26,600
Other taxes	25,582	20,909	24,400
Other revenue	18,813	12,897	17,000
Grants	15,100	6,582	18,500
Total	224,383	202,005	236,100

Expenditure	1999	2000	2001†
Current expenditure	224,149	211,491	218,400
Wages	34,394	36,603	37,100
Subsidies	14,183	8,306	6,600
Interest	19,845	17,320	14,200
Transfers	72,978	66,273	73,000
Pensions	32,434	32,035	38,500
Family allowances	21,391	19,717	16,600
Other transfers	19,153	14,520	17,900
Goods and services	82,749	82,988	87,200
Health	14,257	14,576	n.a
Education	7,654	8,717	n.a.
Other	60,838	59,695	n.a.
Capital expenditure	46,285	40,313	46,700
Net lending	26,686	15,607	16,000
Total	297,120	267,411	281,200

* Figures refer to the consolidated accounts of republican and local authorities, including the operations of the Pension and Employment Fund.
† Figures rounded to the nearest 100 million drams.

Sources: IMF, *Republic of Armenia: Recent Economic Developments and Selected Issues* (May 2001) and *Republic of Armenia: Statistical Appendix* (October 2002).

INTERNATIONAL RESERVES
(US $ million at 31 December)

	2000	2001	2002
Gold*	11.79	12.41	15.68
IMF special drawing rights	21.55	10.24	30.10
Foreign exchange	296.77	310.58	394.92
Total	330.11	333.23	440.70

* National valuation.

Source: IMF, *International Financial Statistics*.

MONEY SUPPLY
(million drams at 31 December)

	1999	2000	2001
Currency outside banks	42,610	59,486	65,037
Demand deposits at commercial banks	9,553	11,743	12,073
Total money (incl. others)	52,227	71,395	77,297

Source: IMF, *International Financial Statistics*.

COST OF LIVING
(Consumer Price Index; base: 1994 = 100)

	1999	2000	2001
Food (incl. non-alcoholic beverages)	362.4	340.9	357.0
Electricity, gas and other fuels	643.5	650.2	649.0
Clothing (incl. footwear)	231.5	222.8	220.3
Rent	12,391.6	12,447.3	12,464.5
All items (incl. others)	408.2	405.1	417.7

Source: ILO.

NATIONAL ACCOUNTS
(million drams at current prices)

Expenditure on the Gross Domestic Product

	1999	2000	2001
Government final consumption expenditure.	117,591	123,512	125,777
Private final consumption expenditure.	951,565	985,821	1,107,600
Increase in stocks	19,085	15,439	19,438
Gross fixed capital formation . .	162,134	182,394	199,577
Total domestic expenditure. .	1,250,375	1,307,166	1,452,392
Exports of goods and services .	204,976	241,856	300,781
Less Imports of goods and services	491,769	524,932	540,120
Sub-total	963,582	1,024,090	1,213,053
Statistical discrepancy* . . .	23,862	9,236	−37,564
GDP in purchasers' values . .	987,444	1,033,330	1,175,490

* Referring to the difference between the sum of the expenditure components and official estimates of GDP, compiled from the production approach.

Source: IMF, *International Financial Statistics*.

Gross Domestic Product by Economic Activity

	1998	1999	2000
Agriculture and forestry . . .	295,628	251,147	231,908
Industry*	207,452	212,883	226,898
Construction	80,936	93,360	112,743
Transport and communications .	48,528	73,978	71,698
Trade and catering	82,401	87,809	94,878
Other services	243,847	268,897	294,331
Total	958,791	988,074	1,032,455

* Principally mining, manufacturing, electricity, gas and water.

Source: IMF, *Republic of Armenia: Recent Economic Developments and Selected Issues* (May 2001).

BALANCE OF PAYMENTS
(US $ million)

	1999	2000	2001
Exports of goods f.o.b. . . .	247.3	309.9	353.1
Imports of goods f.o.b. . . .	−721.3	−773.4	−773.3
Trade balance	−474.0	−463.5	−420.2
Exports of services	135.8	136.9	186.5
Imports of services	−197.9	−192.7	−204.3
Balance on goods and services	−536.1	−519.3	−438.0
Other income received . . .	93.6	103.7	103.1
Other income paid	−38.6	−50.8	−39.6
Balance on goods, services and income	−481.2	−466.4	−374.5
Current transfers received . .	200.6	208.5	200.8
Current transfers paid . . .	−26.5	−20.5	−26.8
Current balance	−307.1	−278.4	−200.5
Capital account (net)	12.6	28.3	30.1
Direct investment from abroad. .	122.0	104.2	69.9
Portfolio investment assets . .	0.1	−19.1	−5.8
Portfolio investment liabilities . .	1.6	0.3	−0.1
Other investment assets . . .	3.0	−9.5	−18.2
Other investment liabilities . .	159.5	174.0	131.1
Net errors and omissions . .	13.1	17.0	12.1
Overall balance	4.8	16.9	18.6

Source: IMF, *International Financial Statistics*.

External Trade

PRINCIPAL COMMODITIES
(US $ '000)

Imports c.i.f.	1999	2000	2001
Live animals and animal products	41,485	33,612	30,816
Meat and edible meat offal . . .	25,937	20,477	20,940
Vegetable products	75,684	99,124	85,151
Cereals.	47,297	64,425	48,170
Prepared foodstuffs; beverages, spirits and vinegar; tobacco and manufactured substitutes	76,991	69,802	76,889
Tobacco and manufactured tobacco substitutes	30,435	29,580	29,923
Mineral products	176,039	179,251	188,191
Mineral fuels, mineral oils and products of their distillation; bituminous substances; mineral waxes	175,037	178,516	187,201
Products of chemical or allied industries	71,353	82,386	65,135
Pharmaceutical products . . .	32,441	42,290	28,945
Textiles and textile articles . .	30,040	32,058	35,963
Natural or cultured pearls, precious or semi-precious stones, precious metals and articles thereof; imitation jewellery; coins	86,712	113,247	106,771
Base metals and articles thereof	23,835	24,363	36,056
Machinery and mechanical appliances; electrical equipment; sound and television apparatus . . .	81,403	117,234	88,366
Nuclear reactors, boilers, machinery and mechanical appliances; parts thereof . . .	49,215	50,130	48,529
Electrical machinery, equipment and parts; sound and television apparatus, and parts and accessories	32,188	67,104	39,836
Vehicles, aircraft, vessels and associated transport equipment.	33,146	23,202	25,897
Vehicles other than railway or tramway rolling-stock, and parts and accessories thereof . . .	30,945	21,859	24,619
Optical, photographic, measuring and medical instruments and apparatus; clocks and watches; musical instruments	12,959	12,342	26,953
Total (incl. others)	811,268	884,674	877,434

Exports f.o.b.	1999	2000	2001
Prepared foodstuffs; beverages, spirits and vinegar; tobacco and manufactured substitutes	15,917	27,334	47,978
Beverages, spirits and vinegar	9,792	22,473	39,119
Mineral products	30,996	37,194	37,885
Ores, slag and ash	7,752	15,241	20,493
Mineral fuels, mineral oils and products of their distillation; bituminous substances; mineral waxes	19,154	20,658	17,158
Plastics, rubber and articles thereof	9,110	9,049	13,068
Rubber and articles thereof	8,898	8,802	12,405
Textiles and textile articles	13,585	13,184	24,288
Non-knitted clothing and accessories	10,980	9,029	15,543
Natural or cultured pearls, precious or semi-precious stones, precious metals and articles thereof; imitation jewellery; coins	99,879	121,452	122,848
Base metals and articles thereof	24,952	44,203	43,445
Iron and steel	8,454	10,790	9,582
Copper and articles thereof	5,448	15,999	12,882
Aluminium and articles thereof	9,155	14,366	17,865
Machinery and mechanical appliances; electrical equipment; sound and television apparatus	17,488	31,020	28,474
Nuclear reactors, boilers, machinery and mechanical appliances; parts thereof	8,644	9,657	15,081
Electrical machinery, equipment and parts; sound and television apparatus, and parts and accessories	8,843	21,363	13,394
Total (incl. others)	231,669	300,487	341,836

PRINCIPAL TRADING PARTNERS
(US $ '000)

Imports c.i.f.	1999	2000	2001
Belgium	85,192	84,372	41,783
Bulgaria	12,082	7,216	6,424
Canada	10,024	5,396	6,929
France	12,340	17,559	12,048
Georgia	26,856	19,801	18,503
Germany	34,244	36,487	33,962
Greece	13,029	54,003	13,579
Iran	78,450	82,328	78,121
Israel	2,425	19,378	27,593
Italy	23,725	25,711	29,635
Lebanon	9,355	4,572	5,984
Netherlands	5,123	12,427	6,958
Panama	23,581	20,957	19,331
Russia	149,878	137,158	173,648
Switzerland	16,415	22,920	26,516
Turkey	40,152	40,462	33,756
Ukraine	7,926	12,342	22,102
United Arab Emirates	40,196	41,728	47,422
United Kingdom	67,031	59,481	91,225
USA	85,669	102,675	84,153
Total (incl. others)	811,268	884,733	877,434

Exports f.o.b.	1999	2000	2001
Belgium	84,227	75,051	46,489
Georgia	11,100	15,989	12,413
Germany	10,201	12,918	11,122
Iran	34,161	30,089	31,870
Israel	2,225	17,300	33,391
Italy	1,443	2,683	6,065
Russia	33,856	44,560	60,501
Switzerland	3,749	8,830	8,937
Turkmenistan	6,069	5,544	813
Ukraine	2,096	3,271	10,983
United Arab Emirates	2,612	5,479	7,277
United Kingdom	9,444	10,099	20,116
USA	16,008	37,861	52,268
Total (incl. others)	231,669	300,487	341,836

Transport

RAILWAYS
(traffic)

	1998	1999	2000
Passenger journeys ('000)	1,612.4	1,323.5	1,086.6
Passenger-km (million)	52.4	46.4	46.8
Freight carried ('000 metric tons)	1,730.8	1,389.3	1,423.2
Freight ton-km (million)	418.5	323.9	353.6

2001: Passenger journeys ('000) 1,165.7; Freight carried ('000 metric tons) 1,394.3.

CIVIL AVIATION
(traffic)

	1998	1999	2000
Kilometres flown (million)	9*	n.a.	n.a.
Passengers carried ('000)	600†	630	611
Passengers-km (million)	888.8	646.2	579.2
Cargo ton-kilometres ('000)	15.2	12.8	9.6

* On scheduled services only.
† Figure rounded.

2001: Passengers carried ('000) 768.6.

Tourism

ARRIVALS BY NATIONALITY

	1998	1999	2000
CIS countries*	13,525	16,326	15,000
France	2,280	3,046	3,724
Germany	1,025	1,195	1,209
Greece	768	847	954
Iran	1,104	4,653	8,573
Lebanon	894	1,406	1,574
Turkey	714	823	427
United Kingdom	1,636	919	1,021
USA	3,804	5,151	6,804
Total (incl. others)	31,837	40,745	45,222

* Comprising Azerbaijan, Belarus, Georgia, Kazakhstan, Kyrgyzstan, Moldova, Russia, Tajikistan, Turkmenistan, Ukraine and Uzbekistan.

Tourism receipts (US $ million): 10 in 1998; 27 in 1999; 45 in 2000.

Sources: World Tourism Organization, *Yearbook of Tourism Statistics*, and World Bank, *World Development Indicators*.

Tourist arrivals: 123,263 in 2001; 162,089 in 2002.

Source: National Statistical Service of the Republic of Armenia..

Communications Media

	1998	1999	2000
Television receivers ('000 in use)	840	850	860
Telephones ('000 main lines in use)	557	547.3	533.4
Facsimile machines (number in use)	n.a.	1,000*	n.a.
Mobile cellular telephones ('000 subscribers).	7.0	8.1	17.4
Personal computers ('000 in use)	15	20	n.a.
Internet users ('000).	30	30	50
Book production†:			
Titles	535	571	657
Copies ('000)	392	754	460
Newspapers:			
Titles	126	102	91
Total circulation ('000 copies) .	207	150	302
Periodicals:			
Titles	75	64	44
Total circulation ('000 copies) .	220	230	115

* Estimate.
† Including brochures.

2001: Telephones ('000 main lines in use) 529.3; Mobile cellular telephones ('000 subscribers) 25.0; Personal computers ('000 in use) 30.

Source: partly International Telecommunication Union.

Education

(2000/01, unless otherwise indicated)

	Institutions	Teachers	Students
Pre-primary	769*	7,585†	46,600*
General.	1,433	56,300	572,200
Gymnasia and lyceums .	48	n.a.	8,800
Vocational	56	n.a.	5,100
Other specialized schools .	75	n.a.	26,900
State higher schools (incl. universities).	19	4,420*	60,700

* Dec. 2000.
† 1998/99.

Source: partly UN, *Statistical Yearbook for Asia and the Pacific*.

Adult literacy rate (UNESCO estimates): 98.4% (males 99.3%; females 97.6%) in 2000 (Source: UN Development Programme, *Human Development Report*).

Directory

The Constitution

The Constitution was approved by some 68% of the electorate in a national referendum, held on 5 July 1995. It replaced the amended Soviet Constitution of 1978. The following is a summary of the new Constitution's main provisions:

GENERAL PROVISIONS OF CONSTITUTIONAL ORDER

The Republic of Armenia is an independent democratic state; its sovereignty is vested in the people, who execute their authority through free elections, referendums and local self-government institutions and officials, as defined by the Constitution. Referendums, as well as elections of the President of the Republic, the National Assembly and local self-government bodies, are carried out on the basis of universal, equal, direct suffrage by secret ballot. Through the Constitution and legislation, the State ensures the protection of human rights and freedoms, in accordance with the principles and norms of international law. A multi-party political system is guaranteed. The establishment of political parties is a free process, but the activities of political parties must not contravene the Constitution and the law. The right to property is recognized and protected. Armenia conducts its foreign policy based on the norms of international law, seeking to establish neighbourly and mutually beneficial relations with all countries. The State ensures the protection of the environment, and historical and cultural monuments, as well as cultural values. The official language is Armenian.

FUNDAMENTAL HUMAN AND CIVIL RIGHTS AND FREEDOMS

The acquisition and loss of citizenship are prescribed by law. A citizen of the Republic of Armenia may not be simultaneously a citizen of another country. The rights, liberties and duties of citizens of Armenia, regardless of nationality, race, sex, language, creed, political or other convictions, social origin, property and other status, are guaranteed. No one shall be subject to torture or cruel treatment. Every citizen has the right to freedom of movement and residence within the republic, as well as the right to leave the republic. Every citizen has the right to freedom of thought, speech, conscience and religion. The right to establish or join associations, trade unions, political organizations, etc., is guaranteed, as is the right to strike for protection of economic, social and labour interests. Citizens of the republic who have attained 18 years of age are entitled to participate in state government through their directly elected representatives or by expression of free will.

Every citizen has the right to social insurance in the event of old age, disability, sickness, widowhood, unemployment, etc. Every citizen has the right to education. Education is provided free at elementary and secondary state educational institutions. Citizens belonging to national minorities have the right to preserve their traditions and to develop their language and culture. Everyone charged with a penal offence has the right to be presumed innocent until proved guilty. The advocacy of national, racial and religious hatred, and the propagation of violence and war, are prohibited.

THE PRESIDENT OF THE REPUBLIC

The President of the Republic of Armenia ensures the observance of the Constitution and the effective operation of the legislative, executive and juridical authorities. The President is the guarantor of the independence, territorial integrity and security of the republic. He/she is elected by citizens of the republic for a period of five years. Any person who has the right to participate in elections, has attained the age of 35 years, and has been a resident citizen of Armenia for the preceding 10 years is eligible for election to the office of President. No person may be elected to the office for more than two successive terms.

The President signs and promulgates laws adopted by the National Assembly, or returns draft legislation to the National Assembly for reconsideration; may dismiss the National Assembly and declare special elections to it, after consultation with the Prime Minister and the Chairman of the National Assembly; appoints and dismisses the Prime Minister; appoints and dismisses the members of the Government, upon the recommendation of the Prime Minister; appoints civil service officials; establishes deliberation bodies; represents Armenia in international relations, co-ordinates foreign policy, concludes international treaties, signs international treaties ratified by the National Assembly, and ratifies agreements between governments; appoints and recalls diplomatic representatives of Armenia to foreign countries and international organizations, and receives the credentials of diplomatic representatives of foreign countries; appoints the Procurator-General, as nominated by the Prime Minister; appoints members and the Chairman of the Constitutional Court; is the Supreme Commander-in-Chief of the Armed Forces; takes decisions on the use of the Armed Forces; grants titles of honour; and grants amnesties to convicts.

THE NATIONAL ASSEMBLY

Legislative power in the Republic of Armenia is executed by the National Assembly. The Assembly comprises 131 deputies, elected for a four-year term. Any person who has attained the age of 25 years and has been a permanent resident and citizen of Armenia for the preceding five years is eligible to be elected a deputy.

The National Assembly deliberates and enacts laws; has the power to express a vote of 'no confidence' in the Government; confirms the state budget, as proposed by the Government; supervises the implementation of the state budget; elects its Chairman (Speaker) and two Deputy Chairmen; appoints the Chairman and Deputy Chairman of the Central Bank, upon the nomination of the President; and appoints members of the Constitutional Court.

At the suggestion of the President of the Republic, the National Assembly declares amnesties; ratifies or declares invalid international treaties; and declares war. Upon the recommendation of the Government, the National Assembly confirms the territorial and administrative divisions of the republic.

THE GOVERNMENT

Executive power is realized by the Government of the Republic of Armenia, which is composed of the Prime Minister and the Ministers. The Prime Minister is appointed by the President; upon the recommendation of the Prime Minister, the President appoints the remaining Ministers. The Prime Minister directs the current activities of the Government and co-ordinates the activities of the Ministers.

The Government presents the programme of its activities to the National Assembly for approval; presents the draft state budget to the National Assembly for confirmation, ensures implementation of the budget and presents a report on its implementation to the National Assembly; manages state property; ensures the implementation of state fiscal, loan and tax policies; ensures the implementation of state policy in the spheres of science, education, culture, health care, social security and environmental protection; ensures the implementation of defence, national security and foreign policies; and takes measures to strengthen adherence to the laws, to ensure the rights and freedoms of citizens, and to protect public order and the property of citizens.

JUDICIAL POWER*

In the Republic of Armenia the courts of general competence are the tribunal courts of first instance, the review courts and the courts of appeal. There are also economic, military and other courts. The guarantor of the independence of judicial bodies is the President of the Republic. He/she is the Head of the Council of Justice. The Minister of Justice and the Procurator-General are the Deputy Heads of the Council of Justice. Fourteen members appointed by the President of the Republic for a period of five years are included in the Council. The Constitutional Court is composed of nine members, of whom the National Assembly appoints five and the President of the Republic appoints four. The Constitutional Court, *inter alia*, determines whether decisions of the National Assembly, decrees and orders of the President, and resolutions of the Government correspond to the Constitution; decides, prior to ratification of an international treaty, whether the obligations created in it correspond to the Constitution; resolves disputes relating to referendums and results of presidential and legislative elections; and decides on the suspension or prohibition of the activity of a political party.

TERRITORIAL ADMINISTRATION AND LOCAL SELF-GOVERNMENT

The administrative territorial units of the Republic of Armenia are regions and communities. Regions are comprised of rural and urban communities. Local self-government takes place in the communities. Bodies of local self-government, community elders and the community head (city mayor or head of village) are elected for a three-year period to administer community property and solve issues of community significance. State government is exercised in the regions. The Government appoints and dismisses regional governors, who carry out the Government's regional policy and co-ordinate the performance of regional services by state executive bodies. The city of Yerevan has the status of a region.

* The new judicial system came into force in January 1999. The Supreme Court was replaced by the Court of Cassation, and Appellate Courts were to operate in the place of People's Courts. Members of the Court of Cassation were to be appointed by the President, for life.

The Government

HEAD OF STATE

President: ROBERT KOCHARIAN (acting from 3 February 1998, elected 30 March, inaugurated 9 April; re-elected 5 March 2003).

GOVERNMENT
(April 2003)

Prime Minister: ANDRANIK MARKARIAN.

Minister of Foreign Affairs: VARDAN OSKANIAN.

Minister of Defence: SERGE SARKISSIAN.

Minister of Finance and the Economy: VARDAN KHACHATRIAN.

Minister of Justice: DAVID HAROUTUNIAN.

Minister of Energy: ARMEN MOVSSISSIAN.

Minister of Regional Government and the Co-ordination of Infrastructure: HOVIK ABRAHAMIAN.

Minister of Urban Planning: DAVID LOKIAN.

Minister of Social Welfare: RAZMIK MARTIROSSIAN.

Minister of Health: ARARAT MKRTCHIAN.

Minister of Agriculture: DAVID ZADOIAN.

Minister of the Environment: VARDAN AYVAZIAN.

Minister of Trade and Economic Development: KAREN CHSHMARITIAN.

Minister of Education and Science: LEVON MKRTCHIAN.

Minister of Culture, Youth Affairs and Sport: ROLAND SHAROIAN.

Minister of Transport and Communications: ANDRANIK MANUKIAN.

Minister of State Property: DAVID VARDANIAN.

Minister of State Revenue: YERVAND ZAKHARIAN.

Cabinet Chief of Staff: MANOOK TOPUZIAN.

Head of the Police of the Republic of Armenia: Lt-Gen. HAIK HAROUTUNIAN.

Head of the National Security Service: Lt-Gen. KARLOS PETROSSIAN.

Mayor of Yerevan: RUBEN NAZARIAN.

MINISTRIES

Office of the President: 375077 Yerevan, Marshal Baghramian St 26; tel. (1) 52-02-04; fax (1) 52-15-51; internet www.president.am.

Office of the Prime Minister: 375010 Yerevan, Republic Sq. 1, Govt House; tel. (1) 52-03-60; fax (1) 15-10-35; internet www.gov.am/am/gov/premier.

Ministry of Agriculture: 375010 Yerevan, Nalbandian St 48; tel. (1) 52-46-41; fax (1) 15-10-86.

Ministry of Culture, Youth Affairs and Sport: 375010 Yerevan, Tumanian St 5; tel. (1) 52-93-49; fax (1) 52-39-22.

Ministry of Defence: Yerevan, Proshian Settlement, G. Shaush St 60; tel. (1) 28-94-52; fax (1) 28-16-74.

Ministry of Education and Science: 375010 Yerevan, Movses Khorenatsi St 13; tel. (1) 52-66-02; fax (1) 58-04-03; internet www.edu.am/mes.

Ministry of Energy: 375010 Yerevan, Republic Sq. 2, Govt House 2; tel. (1) 52-19-64; fax (1) 15-16-87.

Ministry of the Environment: 375002 Yerevan, Moskovian St 35; tel. (1) 53-49-82; fax (1) 53-81-87; e-mail infocenter@nature.am; internet www.nature.am.

Ministry of Finance and the Economy: 375010 Yerevan, Melik-Adamian St 1; tel. (1) 52-70-82; fax (1) 52-37-45; e-mail staff@mf.gov.am.

Ministry of Foreign Affairs: 375010 Yerevan, Republic Sq. 1, Govt House 2; tel. (1) 54-40-41; fax (1) 54-39-25; e-mail info@armeniaforeignministry.com; internet www.armeniaforeignministry.am.

Ministry of Health: 375001 Yerevan, Tumanian St 8; tel. (1) 58-24-13; fax (1) 15-10-97; internet www.armhealth.am.

Ministry of Justice: 375010 Yerevan, Khorhrdaranayin St 8; tel. (1) 58-21-57; fax (1) 58-24-49.

Ministry of Regional Government and the Co-ordination of Infrastructure: Yerevan.

Ministry of Social Welfare: 375025 Yerevan, Terian St 69; tel. (1) 52-68-31; fax (1) 15-19-20.

Ministry of State Property: 375010 Yerevan, Republic Sq. 2, Govt House; tel. (1) 52-42-13; fax (1) 52-65-57; e-mail tender@privatization.am; internet www.privatization.am.

Ministry of State Revenue: 375015 Yerevan, Movses Khorenatsi St 3; tel. (1) 53-91-95; fax (1) 53-82-26; internet www.taxservice.am.

Ministry of Trade and Economic Development: 375008 Yerevan, Hanrapetoutioun St 5; tel. (1) 52-61-34; fax (1) 15-16-75.

Ministry of Transport and Communications: 375010 Yerevan, Nalbandian St 28; tel. (1) 52-38-62; fax (1) 54-59-79; e-mail traceca@arminco.am.

Ministry of Urban Planning: 375010 Yerevan, Republic Sq., Govt House; tel. (1) 58-90-80; fax (1) 52-32-00.

National Security Service: Yerevan.

Office of the Cabinet Chief of Staff: 375010 Yerevan, Republic Sq., Govt House; tel. (1) 53-16-12; fax (1) 15-10-36.

Office of the Mayor of Yerevan: Yerevan, Grigor Lusavorichi St; tel. (1) 52-58-47.

Police of the Republic of Armenia: 375025 Yerevan, Nalbandian St 104; tel. (1) 56-09-08; fax (1) 57-84-40.

President and Legislature

PRESIDENT

Presidential Election, First Ballot, 19 February 2003

Candidates	% of votes
Robert Kocharian	49.48
Stepan Demirchian	28.22
Artashes Geghamian	17.66
Aram Karapetian	2.95
Others	1.68
Total	**100.00**

Second Ballot, 5 March 2003

Candidates	% of votes
Robert Kocharian	67.48
Stepan Demirchian	32.52
Total	**100.00**

NATIONAL ASSEMBLY

375095 Yerevan, Marshal Baghramian St 19; tel. (1) 58-82-25; fax (1) 52-98-26; internet www.parliament.am.

Chairman: ARMEN KHACHATRIAN.

Deputy Chairmen: TIGRAN TOROSSIAN, GAGIK ASLANIAN.

General Election, 30 May 1999

Parties and blocs	% of votes for seats by proportional representation	Total seats
Unity bloc*	41.2	55
Communist Party of Armenia	12.1	11
Armenian Revolutionary Federation	7.7	9
Law and Unity bloc	8.0	6
Law-governed Country Party of Armenia	5.3	6
National Democratic Union	5.2	6
Armenian Pan-National Movement	1.2	1
Armenian Democratic Party	1.0	1
Mission Party	0.8	1
National Unity Party	—	1
Independents	—	32
Total (incl. others)	**100.0**	**131†**

*A coalition of the Republican Party of Armenia and the People's Party of Armenia.

† Results were annulled in two constituencies; the subsequent by-elections, which were held in July, were won by independents.

Political Organizations

At 1 January 2002 there were 107 political parties registered with the Ministry of Justice.

Agro-industrial People's Association: Yerevan; f. 2000; changed name from Stability Party in 2001; Leader AMAIAK OVANESSIAN.

Armenian Christian Democratic Union: Yerevan; tel. (1) 52-62-49; e-mail pride@freenet.am; Chair. ANAIDA MARTIROSSIAN.

Armenian Democratic Party: Yerevan, Koriun St 14; tel. (1) 52-52-73; f. 1992 by elements of Communist Party of Armenia; Chair. ARAM SARKISSIAN.

Armenian Pan-National Movement (APNM) (Haiots Hamazgaien Sharjoum–HHSh): 375019 Yerevan, Khanjian St 27; tel. (1) 57-04-70; f. 1989; absorbed the 21st Century Party in March 2002; Pres. LEVON TER-PETROSSIAN; Chair. ALEKSANDR ARZUMANIAN.

Armenian Renewed Communist Party: Yerevan; f. 2001; socialist, revolutionary; First Sec. YURI MANUKIAN.

Armenian Revolutionary Federation (ARF) (Hai Heghapokhakan Dashnaktsutyun): 375025 Yerevan, Miasniak Ave 2; internet www.arf.am; f. 1890; formed the ruling party in independent Armenia, 1918–20; prohibited under Soviet rule, but continued its activities in other countries; permitted to operate legally in Armenia from 1991; suspended in December 1994; legally reinstated 1998; 40,000 mems; Chair. RUBEN HAGOBIAN, VAHAN HOVHANISSIAN.

Armenian Social Democratic Party (Hunchakian): Yerevan, Aghbiur Serob St 7; tel. (1) 27-33-15; internet www.hunchak.org.au; Chair. ERNEST SOGOMONIAN.

Communist Party of Armenia (CPA) (HHK): Yerevan, Marshal Baghramian St 10; tel. (1) 56-79-33; fax (1) 53-38-55; f. 1920; dissolved 1991, relegalized 1992; c. 50,000 mems; Chair. VLADIMIR DARBINIAN.

Hayastan: Yerevan; Chair. MIASNIK ALKHASIAN.

Law-Governed Country Party of Armenia (Orinats Yerkir): Yerevan; f. 1998; centrist; also known as the Legal State Party; 1,100 mems; Head ARTUR BAGDASARIAN.

Liberal Democratic Party (Ramgavar Azadagan): 375009 Yerevan, Koriun St 19A; tel. and fax (1) 52-64-03; f. 1991; joined the Union of Social Democratic Forces in 2000; Leader ROUBEN MIRZAKHANIAN; 1,100 mems.

Liberal Democratic Union of Armenia: Yerevan; f. 2001 following the division of the National Democratic Union; also known as the People's Liberal Union; Leader SEYRAN AVAKIAN; 7,000 mems.

National Democratic Party: Yerevan, Abovian St 12; tel. and fax (1) 56-31-88; e-mail adjm@arminco.com; f. 2001 following the division of the National Democratic Union; Leader SHAVARSH KOCHARIAN.

National Unity Party: c/o National Assembly, 375095 Yerevan, Marshal Baghramian St 19; f. 1998; Leaders GARNIK ISAGULIAN, IGOR MURADIAN, GRANT KHACHATRIAN.

People's Democratic Party: Yerevan; f. 2001 following the split in the PPA; centrist; Leader GAGIK ASLANIAN; 1,250 mems.

People's Party of Armenia (PPA) (HzhK): Yerevan; f. 1998; contested the general election of May 1999 as part of the Unity (Miasnutiun) bloc, together with the RPA (see below); it left the coalition in Sept. 2001; Leader STEPAN DEMIRCHIAN.

Republic (Hanrapetutiun): Yerevan; f. 2001 by members of the Yerkrapah Union of Volunteers and former members of the Republican Party of Armenia; Leader ALBERT BAZEIAN.

Republican Party of Armenia (RPA) (HHK): Yerevan; tel. (1) 58-00-31; fax (1) 56-60-34; f. 1990 following a split in the UNS (see below); contested the general election of May 1999 as part of the Unity bloc, together with the PPA (see above), the PPA left the coalition in Sept. 2001; 13 territorial orgs; 5,500 mems; Chair. ANDRANIK MARKARIAN.

Shamiram Women's Party: Yerevan; f. 1995.

Union of National Democrats: Yerevan; f. 2001 following a split in the National Democratic Union; Leader ARSHAK SADOIAN.

Union for National Self-Determination (UNS): 375013 Yerevan, Grigor Lusavorichi St 15; tel. (1) 52-55-38; Chair. PARUIR HAIRIKIAN.

Union of Right Forces: Yerevan; f. 2000 as an alliance of the Hazatutiun (Freedom) Party, the 21st Century Party (Democratic National Party), the Liberal Democratic Party and the Armat (Root) Party.

Union of Social Democratic Forces: Yerevan; f. 2000.

Union of Socialist Forces: Yerevan; f. 1997; left-wing; Leader ASHOT MANUCHARIAN.

Diplomatic Representation

EMBASSIES IN ARMENIA

Belarus: 375009 Yerevan, Abovian St 23–6; tel. (1) 56–70–18; e-mail armenia@arminco.com; Ambassador MARINA DOLGOPOLOVA.

Bulgaria: Yerevan, Nor Aresh 11 St, h. 85; tel. (1) 45–82–33; fax (1) 45-46-02; e-mail bularm@arminco.com; Ambassador IVAN IVANSHEV.

China, People's Republic: Yerevan, Marshal Baghramian St 12; tel. (1) 56-00-67; fax (1) 54-57-61; e-mail chiemb@mbox.amilink.net; Ambassador ZUO XUELIANG.

Egypt: Yerevan, Sepuhi St 6A; tel. (1) 22-67-55; fax (1) 28-11-62; e-mail egyemb@arminco.com; Ambassador SAID IMAM MAHMOUD SAID.

France: 375015 Yerevan, Grigor Lusavorichi St 8; tel. (1) 56-11-03; fax (1) 15-11-05; e-mail secretar@ambafran.arminco.com; internet www.ambafran.am; Ambassador HENRI CUNY.

Georgia: Yerevan, Arami St 42; tel. (1) 56-43-57; fax (1) 56-41-83; e-mail georgia@arminco.com; Ambassador NIKOLOZ NIKOLOZISHVILI.

Germany: 375025 Yerevan, Charents St 29; tel. (1) 52-32-79; fax (1) 52-47-81; e-mail germemb@arminco.com; internet www .deutschebotschaft-eriwan.am; Ambassador HANS-WULF BARTELS.

Greece: Yerevan, Proshian St 12; tel. (1) 53-00-51; fax (1) 15-11-70; e-mail grembarm@arminco.com; Ambassador ANTONIOS VLAVIANOS.

India: 375019 Yerevan 19, Pionerakan St 50/2; tel. (1) 53-82-88; fax (1) 53-39-84; e-mail inemyr@arminco.com; Ambassador DEEPAK VOHRA.

Iran: Yerevan, Budaghian St 1; tel. (1) 28-04-57; fax (1) 23-00-52; e-mail info@iranembassy.am; internet www.iranembassy.am; Ambassador MOHAMMAD FARHAD KOLEINI.

Iraq: Yerevan, Sevastopolian St 24; tel. (1) 27-51-45; fax (1) 26-13-22; Chargé d'affaires ABBAS MUZHAR AL-BADRY.

Italy: 375010 Yerevan, Italia St 5; tel. (1) 54-23-35; fax (1) 54-23-41; e-mail ambitaly@arminco.com; internet www.ambitarm.am; Ambassador PAOLO ANDREA TRABALZA.

Lebanon: Yerevan, Vardanants St 7; tel. (1) 52-65-40; fax (1) 15-11-28; e-mail libarm@arminco.am; Chargé d'affaires a.i. SAAD ZAKHIA.

Poland: Yerevan, Hanrapetutiun St 44A; tel. (1) 54-24-93; fax (1) 54-24-98; e-mail polemb@arminco.com; Chargé d'affaires PIOTR IWASZ-KIEWICZ.

Romania: Yerevan, Sepuhi St 3; tel. (1) 27-47-01; fax (1) 54-41-44; e-mail ambrom@netsys.am; Chargé d'affaires a.i. DORIN CIMPOEŞU.

Russia: 375015 Yerevan, Grigor Lusavorichi St 13A; tel. (1) 56-74-27; fax (1) 56-71-97; e-mail rossia@arminco.com; internet www .armenia.mid.ru; Ambassador ANATOLII DRYUKOV.

Syria: Yerevan, Marshal Baghramian St 14; tel. (1) 52-40-28; fax (1) 52-40-58; e-mail syria.em.arm@netsys.am; Chargé d'affaires a. i. HAMED HASAN.

Turkmenistan: Yerevan, Dzorapi St 72, Hotel Hrazdan; tel. (1) 53-05-12; fax (1) 52-52-35; e-mail serdar@arminco.com; Ambassador TOILY KURBANOV.

Ukraine: 375033 Yerevan, Yerznkian St 58; tel. (1) 58-68-56; fax (1) 22-82-96; e-mail ukremb@arminco.com; internet www.erevan.am/ ukrembassy; Ambassador VOLODOMYR TYAGLO.

United Kingdom: Yerevan, Charents St 28; tel. (1) 55-30-81; fax (1) 54-38-20; e-mail britemb@arminco.com; Ambassador THORHILDA (THORDA) ABBOTT-WATT.

USA: Yerevan, Marshal Baghramian St 18; tel. (1) 52-46-61; fax (1) 52-08-00; e-mail usinfo@arminco.com; internet www.usa.am/index .html; Ambassador JOHN M. ORDWAY.

Judicial System

A new judicial and legal system came into force in January 1999. The Supreme Court was replaced by the Court of Cassation, and Appellate Courts were to operate in the place of People's Courts. Members of the Court of Cassation were to be appointed by the President, for life.

Constitutional Court

375019 Yerevan, Marshal Baghramian St 10; tel. (1) 58-81-40; fax (1) 52-99-91; e-mail armlaw@concourt.am; internet www.concourt .am. f. 1996; Chair. GAGIK HAROUTUNIAN.

Chairman of the Court of Cassation: TARIEL K. BARSEGIAN.

Prosecutor-General: ARAM TAMAZIAN.

Religion

The major religion is Christianity. The Armenian Apostolic Church is the leading denomination and was widely identified with the movement for national independence. There are also Russian Orthodox and Islamic communities, although the latter lost adherents as a result of the departure of large numbers of Muslim Azeris from the republic. Most Kurds are also adherents of Islam, although some are Yazidis. In 2002 51 religious organizations were registered in Armenia, after legislative amendments were adopted, which increased the number of adherents required for registration from 50 to 200. (The Jehovah's Witness community was estimated to number 12,000, but failed to qualify for registration as its statutes were deemed to be in contravention of the Constitution.)

GOVERNMENT AGENCY

Council for the Affairs of the Armenian Church: 375001 Yerevan, Abovian St 3; tel. (1) 56-46-34; fax (1) 56-41-81.

Religious Council: Yerevan; f. 2002 as a consultative council, to advise the Government on religious affairs; was to comprise representatives of the Government, the Office of the Prosecutor-General, the Armenian Apostolic Church, and the Catholic and Protestant Churches.

CHRISTIANITY

Armenian Apostolic Church: Vagharshapat, Monastery of St Etchmiadzin; tel. (1) 28-57-37; fax (1) 15-10-77; e-mail holysee@ etchmiadzin.am; internet www.holyetchmiadzin.com; nine dioceses in Armenia, four in other ex-Soviet republics and 25 dioceses and bishoprics in the rest of the world; 7m. members world-wide (some 4m. in Armenia); 15 monasteries and three theological seminaries in Armenia; Supreme PATRIARCH KAREKIN II (Catholicos of All Armenians).

The Roman Catholic Church

Armenian Rite

Armenian Catholics in Eastern Europe are under the jurisdiction of an Ordinary (equivalent to a bishop with direct authority). At 31 December 2000 there were an estimated 220,000 adherents within this jurisdiction.

Ordinary: Most Rev. NERSES DER-NERSESSIAN (Titular Archbishop of Sebaste), Gyumri, Atarbekian St 82; tel. (41) 22-115; fax (41) 34-959; e-mail armorda@shirak.am.

Latin Rite

The Apostolic Administrator of the Caucasus is the Apostolic Nuncio (Ambassador of the Holy See) to Georgia, Armenia and Azerbaijan, who is resident in Tbilisi, Georgia.

The Press

PRINCIPAL NEWSPAPERS

In 2000 91 newspaper titles were published in Armenia, 74 of which were in Armenian. Those listed below are in Armenian except where otherwise stated.

Ankakhutiun (Independence): 375013 Yerevan, Grigor Lusavorichi St 15; tel. (1) 58-18-64; daily; organ of the Union for National Self-Determination; Editor PARUIR HAIRIKIAN.

Aravot: 375023 Yerevan, Arshakuniats Ave 2, 15th Floor; tel. (1) 56-89-68; fax (1) 52-87-52; e-mail news@aravot.am; internet www .aravot.am; daily; Editor A. ABRAMIAN.

Avangard: 375023 Yerevan, Arshakuniats Ave 2; f. 1923; 3 a week; organ of the Youth League of Armenia; Editor M. K. ZOHRABIAN.

Azg (The Nation): 375010 Yerevan, Hanrapetoutioun St 47; tel. (1) 52-16-35; e-mail azg2@arminco.com; internet www.azg.am; f. 1990; Editor HAGOP AVETIKIAN.

Bravo: Yerevan, Abovian St 12, Hotel Yerevan; tel. (1) 55-44-05; weekly; Editor K. KAZARIAN.

Delovoi Express: Yerevan, Zarian St 22, 2nd Floor; tel. (1) 25-26-83; fax (1) 25-90-23; e-mail eis@arminco.com; f. 1992; weekly; Editor E. NAGDALIAN.

Epokha (Epoch): 375023 Yerevan, Arshakuniats Ave 2; f. 1938; fmrly *Komsomolets*; weekly; Russian; organ of the Youth League of Armenia; Editor V. S. GRIGORIAN.

Golos Armenii (The Voice of Armenia): 375023 Yerevan, Arshakuniats Ave 2, 7th Floor; tel. (1) 52-77-23; e-mail root@goloss .arminco.com; f. 1934 as *Kommunist*; 3 a week; in Russian; Editor F. NASHKARIAN.

Grakan Tert (Literary Paper): 375019 Yerevan, Marshal Baghramian St 3; tel. (1) 52-05-94; f. 1932; weekly; organ of the Union of Writers; Editor F. H. MELOIAN.

Haiastan (Armenia): 375023 Yerevan, Arshakuniats Ave 2; tel. (1) 52-84-50; f. 1920; 6 a week; in Russian; Editor G. ABRAMIAN.

Haik (Armenia): Yerevan; tel. (1) 52-77-01; e-mail root@hayk .arminco.com; weekly; organ of the Armenian Pan-National Movement; Editor V. DAVTIAN; circ. 30,000.

Haiots Ashkhar: Yerevan, Tumanian St 38; tel. (1) 53-32-11; fax (1) 53-88-65; e-mail hayashkh@armnico.com; f. 1997; Editor G. MKRTCHIAN; circ. 3,500.

Hanrapetakan: Yerevan; tel. (1) 58-00-31; fax (1) 56-60-34; organ of the Republican Party of Armenia.

Hazatamart (The Battle for Freedom): 375070 Yerevan, Atarbekian 181; organ of the Armenian Revolutionary Federation (ARF); Editor M. MIKAYELIAN.

Hnchak Haiastani (The Bell of Armenia): Yerevan; weekly;

Marzakan Haiastan: 375023 Yerevan, Arshakuniats Ave 5; tel. (1) 52-62-41; weekly; Editor S. MOURADIAN.

Molorak: 375023 Yerevan, Arshakuniats Ave 5; tel. (1) 52-62-12; daily; Editor H. GHAGHRINIAN.

Respublika Armenia: 375023 Yerevan, Arshakuniats Ave 2, 9th Floor; tel. (1) 52-69-69; e-mail root@ra.arminco.com; government publication; Editor A. KHANBABIAN.

Ria Taze (New Way): Yerevan; 2 a week; Kurdish.

Vozny (Hedgehog): 375023 Yerevan, Arshakuniats Ave 2, 12th Floor; tel. (1) 52-63-83; f. 1954; Editor A. SAHAKIAN.

Yerevanian Orer (Yerevan Days): Yerevan; Editor M. AIRAPETIAN.

Yerkir (Country): 375070 Yerevan, Zavarian St 181; tel. (1) 57-10-95; e-mail erkir@arminco.com; f. 1991; daily; organ of the ARF; publication temporarily suspended in January 2000.

Yerokoian Yerevan (Evening Yerevan): 375023 Yerevan, Arshakuniats Ave 2, 10th Floor; tel. (1) 52-97-52; weekly; organ of Yerevan City Council; Editor N. YENGIBARIAN.

Yeter: Yerevan, Manukian St 5; tel. (1) 55-34-13; weekly; Editor G. KAZARIAN.

Zroutsakits: 375023 Yerevan, Arshakuniats Ave 2, 2nd Floor; tel. (1) 52-84-30; weekly; Editor M. MIRIDJANIAN.

PRINCIPAL PERIODICALS

In 2000 44 periodicals were published, of which 32 were in Armenian.

Aghbiur (Source): Yerevan; f. 1923, fmrly *Pioner*; monthly; for teenagers; Editor T. V. TONOIAN.

Armenian Kommersant: Yerevan, Koriuni St 19A; tel. (1) 52-79-77; monthly; Editor M. VARTANIAN.

Aroghchapautiun (Health): 376001 Yerevan, Tumanian St 8; tel. (1) 52-35-73; e-mail mharut@dmc.am; f. 1956; quarterly; journal of the Ministry of Health; Editor M. A. MURADIAN; circ. 2,000–5,000.

Arvest (Art): 375001 Yerevan, Tumanian St 5; f. 1932, fmrly *Sovetakan Arvest* (Soviet Art); monthly; publ. by the Ministry of Culture, Youth Affairs and Sports; Editor G. A. AZAKELIAN.

Chetvertaya Vlast: Yerevan, Abovian St 12, Rm 105, Hotel Yerevan 105; tel. (1) 59-73-81; monthly; Editor A. GEVORKIAN.

Ekonomika (Economics): Yerevan, Vardanants St 2; tel. (1) 52-27-95; f. 1957; monthly; government organ; Editor R. H. SHAKHKULIAN; circ. 1,500–2,000.

Garoun (Spring): 375015 Yerevan, Grigor Lusavorichi St 15; tel. (1) 56-29-56; e-mail garoun@garoun.am; f. 1967; monthly; independent; fiction, poetry and socio-political issues; Editor V. S. AYOUZIAN; circ. 1,500.

Gitutyun ev Tekhnika (Science and Technology): 375048 Yerevan, Komitasa Ave 49/3; tel. (1) 23-37-27; f. 1963; quarterly; journal of the Research Institute of Scientific-Technical Information and of Technological and Economic Research; Dir M.B. YEDILIAN; Editor M. A. CHUGURIAN; circ. 1,000.

Hayastani Ashkhatavoruhi (Working Women of Armenia): Yerevan; f. 1924; monthly; Editor A. G. CHILINGARIAN.

Hayreniky Dzayn (Voice of the Motherland): Yerevan; f. 1965; weekly; organ of the Armenian Committee for Cultural Relations with Compatriots Abroad; Editor L. H. ZAKARIAN.

Iravunk: 375002 Yerevan, Yeznik Koghbatsu St 50A; tel. (1) 53-27-30; fax (1) 53-41-92; e-mail info@iravunk.com; internet www.iravunk.com; f. 1989; weekly; Editor HAIK BABUKHANIAN; circ. 45,000.

Literaturnaya Armeniya (Literature of Armenia): 375019 Yerevan, Marshal Baghramian St 3; tel. (1) 56-36-57; f. 1958; monthly; journal of the Union of Writers; fiction; Russian; Editor A. M. NALBANDIAN.

Nork: Yerevan; f. 1934; fmrly *Sovetakan Grakanutyun* (Soviet Literature); monthly; journal of the Union of Writers; fiction; Russian; Editor R. G. OVSEPIAN.

Novoye Vremya: 375023 Yerevan, Arshakuniats Ave 2, 3rd Floor; tel. (1) 52-69-46; fax (1) 52-73-62; e-mail nvremya@arminco.com; f. 1992; 3 a week; Editor R. A. SATIAN; circ. 5,000.

Veratsnvats Haiastan (Reborn Armenia): Yerevan; f. 1945 as *Sovetakan Hayastan* (Soviet Armenia); monthly; journal of the Armenian Committee for Cultural Relations with Compatriots Abroad; fiction; Editor V. A. DAVITIAN.

Yerevan Times: 375009 Yerevan, Isaahakian St 28, 3rd Floor; tel. (1) 52-82-70; fax (1) 15-17-38; e-mail yertime@armpress.arminco.com; weekly; English; Editor T. HAKOBIAN.

NEWS AGENCIES

Arka News Agency: 375010 Yerevan, Pavstos Byuzand St 1/3; tel. (1) 52-21-52; fax (1) 52-40-80; e-mail arka@arminco.com; internet www.arka.am; f. 1996; economic, financial and political news; Russian and English.

Armenpress (Armenian News Agency): 375009 Yerevan, Isaahakian St 28, 4th Floor; tel. (1) 52-67-02; fax (1) 52-57-98; e-mail contact@armenpress.am; internet www.armenpress.am; f. 1922 as state information agency, transformed into state joint-stock company in 1997; Armenian, English and Russian; Dir H. ZORIAN.

Arminfo: 375009 Yerevan, Isaahakian St 28, 2nd Floor; tel. (1) 52-20-34; fax (1) 54-31-72; e-mail news@arminfo.am; internet www.arminfo.am; f. 1991 as Snark; name changed as above in 2001; Dir EMMANUIL MKRTCHIAN; Editor ALEKSANDR AVANISOV.

Mediamax (Armenian Press Agency): Yerevan, Marshal Baghramian St 31A; tel. (1) 22-87-86; fax (1) 27-11-56; e-mail media@arminco.com; internet www.mediamax.am; Dir ARA TADEVOSIAN; Editor-in-Chief DAVID ALAVERDIAN.

Noyan Tapan (Noah's Ark): 375009 Yerevan, Isaahakian St 28, 3rd Floor; tel. (1)56-59-65; fax (1) 52-42-79; e-mail contact@noyan-tapan.am; internet www.nt.am; also broadcaster, advertising agency, publisher and printing agency; Dir TIGRAN HAROUTUNIAN.

Publishers

Academy of Sciences Publishing House: 375019 Yerevan, Marshal Baghramian St 24G; Dir KH.H. BARSEGHIAN.

Anait: Yerevan; art publishing.

Arevik Publishing House: 375009 Yerevan, Terian St 91; tel. (1) 52-45-61; fax (1) 52-05-36; e-mail arevikp@freenet.am; f. 1986; closed joint-stock co; political, scientific, fiction for children, textbooks; Pres. DAVID HOVHANNES; Exec. Dir ASTGHIK STEPANIAN.

Hayastan (Armenia Publishing House): 375009 Yerevan, Isaahakian St 28; tel. (1) 52-85-20; e-mail nunjan@hragir.aua.am; f. 1921; political and fiction; Dir VAHAGN SARKISSIAN.

Haikakan Hanragitaran Hratarakchutioun (Armenian Encyclopaedia Publishing House): 375001 Yerevan 1, Tumanian St 17; tel. (1) 52-43-41; fax (1) 52-06-67; e-mail encyclop@sci.am; internet www.encyclopedia.am; f. 1967; encyclopedias and other reference books; Editor H. M. AIVAZIAN.

  Hanragitaran—Armenica (Encyclopaedia—Armenica LLC): 375001 Yerevan 1, Tumanian St 17; tel. (1) 52-43-41; fax (1) 52-06-67; e-mail e-armenica@yahoo.com; internet www.e_armenica.am; f. 1995; encyclopaedias, other reference books; Dir S. A. KEROBIAN.

Louys Publishing House: 375009 Yerevan, Isaahakian St 28; fax (1) 56-55-07; e-mail louys@arminco.com; internet www.spyur.am/luys.htm; f. 1955; textbooks; Dir H. Z. HAROUTUNIAN.

Nairi Ltd: Yerevan, Terian St 91; tel. and fax (1) 56-58-54; e-mail nairi_hrat@rambler.ru; f. 1991; fiction; Pres. HRACHIA TAMRAZIAN.

Broadcasting and Communications

TELECOMMUNICATIONS

ArmenTel: Yerevan, Azatutiun Ave 24; tel. (1) 54-91-00; fax (1) 28-98-88; internet www.armentel.com; transferred to private ownership in 1998; 10% state-owned, 90% owned by Hellenic Telecommunications Organization (Greece); Chief Exec. NIKOLAOS GEORGOULAS; Chair. VASSILIS MAGLARAS; 7,159 employees (Dec. 2001).

Arminco Global Telecommunications: 375009 Yerevan, Isaahakian St 28, POB 10; tel. (1) 52-43-51; fax (1) 28-50-82; internet www.arminco.com; internet service provider; Gen. Dir ANDRANIK ALEKSANDRIAN.

Netsys LLC: Yerevan, Abovian St 38; tel. (1) 54-00-91; fax (1) 54-00-21; e-mail info@netsys.am; internet www.netsys.am; US-Armenian jt venture; internet service provider.

BROADCASTING

Radio

Armenian Radio: 375070 Yerevan, Vardanants 28, apt 34; tel. (1) 55-33-43; fax (1) 55-46-00; e-mail armen@armradio.am; internet www.mediaconcern.am; three programmes; broadcasts inside the republic in Armenian, Russian and Kurdish; external broadcasts in Armenian, Russian, Kurdish, Azeri, Arabic, English, French, Spanish and Farsi; transformed into state joint-stock co in 1997; Dir-Gen. ARMEN AMIRIAN.

Television

Armenian Public Television: 375047 Yerevan, Hovsepian St 26; tel. (1) 56-95-74; fax (1) 56-24-60; internet www.armtv.com; broadcasts in Armenian, and occasionally in Russian and English; transformed into state joint-stock co in 1997; Chair. of Council ALEKSAN HAROUTUNIAN; Exec. Dir ARMEN ARZUMANIAN.

Finance

(cap. = capital; res = reserves; dep. = deposits; m. = million; brs = branches; amounts in drams, unless otherwise stated)

BANKING

Central Bank

Central Bank of the Republic of Armenia: 375010 Yerevan, V. Sarkissian St 6; tel. (1) 58-38-41; fax (1) 52-38-52; e-mail cba@cba .am; internet www.cba.am; f. 1993 as successor to the Armenian Republic Bank; state-owned; cap. 100.0m., res 16,748.9m., dep. 26,588.5m. (Dec. 2001); Chair. Dr TIGRAN SARKISSIAN.

Commercial Banks

In October 2002 there were 28 commercial banks in operation in Armenia. Some of the most influential of these are listed below:

Agricultural Co-operative Bank of Armenia: 375009 Yerevan, Byron St 1; tel. (1) 56-85-58; fax (1) 15-17-55; e-mail acba@arminco .com; internet www.acba.am; f. 1996; cap. 825m., res 2,300m., dep. 5,437m; Gen. Man. STEPAN GISHIAN.

Ardshinbank (ASHB): 375010 Yerevan, Deghatan St 3; tel. (1) 52-85-13; fax (1) 56-74-86; e-mail international@ashb.am; internet www.ardshin.bank.am; f. 1922, reorganized as joint-stock commercial bank, Bank for Industry and Construction, in 1992; restructured 1997; merged with Adana bank in Feb. 2002; second largest bank in Armenia; cap. 1,305.0m., res 412.8m., dep. 21,279.6m. (Dec. 2001); Chair. of Council ARAM VARDANIAN; Head of Admin. ARTASHES DAVTIAN; 29 brs.

Armagrobank OJSC: 375015 Yerevan, M. Khorenatsi St 7A; tel. (1) 53-43-42; fax (1) 53-09-97; e-mail agrobank@agrobank.am; internet www.agrobank.am; f. 1991, incorporated as joint-stock co in 1992; cap. 1,394.6m. (June 2001); Chair. GRIGOR GHONJEIAN; 36 brs.

Armenian Development Bank: 375015 Yerevan, Paronian St 21/1; tel. (1) 53-88-41; fax (1) 53-32-33; e-mail info@armdb.com; internet www.armdb.com; f. 1990; cap. US $3.0m., res $0.6m., dep. $12.2m. (2002); Chair. ALEKSANDR GRIGORIAN.

Armenian Economy Development Bank (Armeconombank): 375002 Yerevan, Amirian St 23/1; tel. (1) 56-27-05; fax (1) 53-89-04; e-mail bank@aeb.am; internet www.aeb.am; incorporated as joint-stock co in 1992; corporate banking; cap. 1,200m., res 29.8m., dep. 9,136.8m. (Dec. 2001); Chair. of Bd SARIBEK SUKIASSIAN; Chief Exec. ASHOT OSSIPIAN; 23 brs.

Armenian Import-Export Bank CJSC (Armimpexbank): 375010 Yerevan, Vazgen Sarkissian St 2; tel. (1) 58-99-06; fax (1) 56-48-87; e-mail office@impexbank.am; internet www.impexbank.am; f. 1992 by reorganization of Armenian br. of the Vneshekonombank of the former USSR; joint-stock co with foreign shareholding; cap. US $3.1m., dep. $14m. (Sept. 1999); Chair. of Bd B. ASATRIAN; 5 brs.

Arminvestbank CJSC: 375010 Yerevan, Vardanants St 13; tel. (1) 52-39-29; fax (1) 54-58-35; e-mail ibank@dolphin.am; f. 1992; cap. US $1.9m., res $0.3m., dep. $3.3m. Chair. of Bd VAROUZHAN AMIRAGHIAN.

Bank Mellat CJSC: 375010 Yerevan, Amirian St 6, POB 24; tel. (1) 58-13-54; fax (1) 54-08-85; e-mail mellat@netsys.am; cap. and res 1,001.0m., dep. 6,418.4m. (Dec. 1999); Chair. ESSA GHAREMANI CHABOCK.

Converse Bank Corpn: 375051 Yerevan, Vazgen Sarkissian St 26; tel. (1) 56-92-48; fax (1) 54-09-20; e-mail post@cb.aic.net; internet www.cb.aic.net; f. 1994; reorganized in 1997; cap. 1,296.4m., res 195.2m., dep. 15,282.7m. (Dec. 2002); Pres. KHORI MODALAL; Gen. Dir SMBAT NASIBIAN.

Credit-Yerevan Joint-Stock Commercial Bank: 375010 Yerevan, Amirian St 2/8; tel. (1) 58-90-65; fax (1) 15-18-20; e-mail garik@ mail.creyer.am; f. 1993; cap. US $2.1m. (Nov. 1998); Pres. MARTIN HOVHANNISIAN.

HSBC Bank of Armenia cjsc: 375010 Yerevan, Vazgen Sarkissian St 9; tel. (1) 56-32-29; fax (1) 52-69-49; e-mail hsbc@arminco.com; internet www.hsbc.com; f. 1996; cap. 2,438m., res 1,922m., dep. 33,156m. (July 2002); Chief Exec. CHARLES B. GREGORY; 2 brs.

Prometey Bank LLC: 375010 Yerevan, Hanrapetoutioun St 44/2; tel. (1) 56-20-36; fax (1) 54-57-19; e-mail office@prometeybank.am;

internet www.prometeybank.am; f. 1990 as Prometheus Commercial Bank; name changed as above 2001; cap. 2,482.9m., res 52.1m., dep. 8,530.9m. (Dec. 2001); Chair. of Bd EMIL SOGHOMONIAN.

Unibank CJSC: 375001 Yerevan, Amiryan St 12; tel. (1) 53-98-70; fax (1) 53-30-52; e-mail unibank@unibank.am; internet www .unibank.am; f. 2001; Russian-owned; cap. US $5.0m., dep. $6.6m. (2002); Exec. Dir VARDAN G. ATAIAN; Chair. GAGIK ZAKARIAN; 3 brs.

United Bank OJSC: 375004 Yerevan, Spendiarov St 4; tel. (1) 53–90–41; fax (1) 53-69-055; e-mail ubank@netsys.am; internet www .ubank.am; f. 1996, as Haysnund, by merger; cap. 1,510m., res 221.2m., dep. 17,052.9m. (Dec. 1999); Chair. BENIK HAROUTUNIAN; Exec. Dir HOVSEP GALSTIAN.

Savings Bank

Armsavingsbank (Armsberbank): 375010 Yerevan, Nalbandian St 46; tel. (1) 58-04-51; fax (1) 56-55-78; e-mail headoffice@asb.am; internet www.asb.am; reorganized 1996; privatized in 2001; cap. 444.4m., res 138.6m., dep. 3,320.1m. (Nov. 1998); Chair. of Bd MIKHAIL BAGDASAROV; Exec. Dir SEDA PETROSSIAN; 97 regional brs.

Banking Union

Union of Banks of Armenia: 375009 Yerevan, Koriun St 19A; tel. (1) 52-77-31; fax (1) 56-75-86; e-mail root@tsark.arminco.com; internet www.bank.am; Pres. ARMEN YEGIAZARIAN.

COMMODITY AND STOCK EXCHANGES

Armenian Stock Exchange (Armex): Yerevan, Mher Mkrtchyan St 5B , 6th Floor; tel. (1) 54-33-21; fax (1) 55-3324; e-mail info@armex .am; internet www.armex.am; Man. Dir A. G. MELIKYAN.

Gyumri Stock Exchange: 375504 Gyumri, Abovian St 244; tel. (41) 2-31-09; fax (41) 2-10-23; f. 1995; Dir SISAK MCHITARIAN.

Yerevan Commodity and Raw Materials Exchange 'Adamand': Yerevan, Mkrtchian St 5; tel. (1) 56-31-15; fax (1) 56-30-51; e-mail ycre@cornet.am; internet www.yercomex.am; Dir GRIGOR VARDIKIAN.

Yerevan Stock Exchange: 375010 Yerevan, Hanrapetoutioun St 5; tel. (1) 52-32-01; fax (1) 15-15-48; internet www.yse.am; f. 1993; Pres. Dr SEDRAK SEDRAKIAN.

INSURANCE

Armenian Financial Insurance Co (AFIC): 375010 Yerevan, Hanrapetoutioun St 5; tel. (1) 52-77-93; fax (1) 15-15-48; e-mail imamik@yse.armenia.su; f. 1996; Exec. Man. LEVON MAMIKONIAN.

Asco-Pro Insurance Co Ltd: Yerevan, Ghazar Parpetsi St 15, apt 3; tel. (1) 53-93-70; fax (1) 53-93-72; e-mail asco_pro@netsys.am; Dir G. AGHAJANIAN.

Prime Insurance Co Ltd: Yerevan, Charents St 1, 4th Floor; tel. (1) 57-51-18; fax (1) 55-94-73; e-mail prime@netsys.am; f. 1995; cargo, vehicle, aviation, construction, medical, property, and business-interruption insurance; Gen. Dir H. I. KARAPETIAN.

Resolution Consultants Ltd: Yerevan, Sayat Nova Ave 37, apt 60; tel. and fax (1) 55-79-37; e-mail recon@arminco.com; internet www .recon.am; f. 2000; Pres. JONATHAN STARK.

State Insurance Armenia CJSC: Yerevan, Zeytun, Karapet Ulnetsu St 31; tel. and fax (1) 24-94-83; e-mail petap@netsys.am; Russian-Armenian joint venture; Man. Dir V. H AVETISSIAN.

Trade and Industry

CHAMBER OF COMMERCE

Chamber of Commerce and Industry of the Republic of Armenia: 375001 Yerevan, Sayat-Nova Ave 29/1; tel. (1) 56-54-38; fax (1) 56-50-71; e-mail chamber@arminco.com; f. 1959; Chair. SAMUEL SHARBATIAN.

EMPLOYERS' ORGANIZATIONS

Armenian Business Forum: Yerevan; tel. (1) 52-75-43; fax (1) 52-43-32; f. 1991; promotes joint ventures, foreign capital investments; Pres. VAHE JAZMADARIAN.

Armenian Union of Industrialists and Entrepreneurs: Yerevan; Chair. ARSEN KAZARIAN.

UTILITIES

Armenian Energy Commission: Yerevan; Chair. VARDAN MOVSISIAN.

Electricity

In March 2002 Armenia's four state-owned regional electricity-distribution networks were merged to create a single entity, an 81.1% stake in which was divested to Midland Resources Holding (based in the United Kingdom) in August of that year.

Armenian Nuclear Power Plant (ANPP) Co: 377766 Medzamor, Armavir; tel. (1) 28-18-80; fax (1) 28-06-69; e-mail anpp@lx2.yerphi.am; WWER-440 (V–270) pressurized water-reactor, with a 407.5 MW operating capacity; agreement on the transfer of financial management to Unified Energy Systems (Russia) signed in Feb. 2003; Gen. Dir GAGIK MARKOSIAN.

Gas

Armgazprom: Yerevan, Tbilisskoe St 43; tel. (1) 28-60-70; fax (1) 28-65-31; state gas company; Dir ROLAND ADONTS.

Armrusgazprom CJSC: Yerevan; f. 1997; Armenian-Russian joint-stock co; Gen. Dir KAREN KARAPETIAN.

Water

Yerevan Water and Sewer CJSC: Yerevan.

TRADE UNIONS

At 1 January 2002 159 trade-union organizations were registered with the Ministry of Justice.

Confederation of Trade Unions of Armenia: 375010 Yerevan, Nalbandian St 26; tel. (1) 52-36-82; fax (1) 54-33-82; e-mail boris@xar.am; Chair. MARTIN HAROUTUNIAN.

Agrarian Union of Armenia: Yerevan; Chair. HRACHIK BERBERIAN.

Transport

RAILWAYS

In 2000 there were 711 km of railway track. There are international lines to Iran and Georgia; lines to Azerbaijan and Turkey remained closed in 2002, as a result of those countries' continuing economic blockade of Armenia.

Armenia Railways: 375005 Yerevan, Tigran Mets St 50; tel. (1) 52-04-28; e-mail arway@mbox.amilink.net; f. 1992 following the dissolution of the former Soviet Railways; Pres. A. V. KHRIMIAN.

Metropolitan Railway

An initial 10-km route, with nine stations, opened in 1981, and a 10-km extension, with two stations, was under construction. A second line was planned, and proposals envisaged the installation of a 47-km network.

Yermetro: 375033 Yerevan, Marshal Baghramian St 76; tel. (1) 27-45-43; fax (1) 27-24-60; e-mail papiev@netsys.am; f. 1981; Gen. Man. P. YAYLOIAN.

ROADS

In 2000 there were an estimated 15,918 km of roads in Armenia (including 7,527 km of motorways, 3,360 km of highways and 4,167 km of secondary roads); 96.3% of roads were paved. In 1996 plans were made to upgrade existing roads, and to construct some 1,400 km of new roads over the next four years, with financial assistance from various international organizations. As a result of the economic blockade imposed in 1989 by Azerbaijan (and subsequently reinforced by Turkey), the Kajaran highway linking Armenia with Iran emerged as Armenia's most important international road connection; in December 1995 a permanent road bridge over the Araks (Aras) river was opened, strengthening this link. In mid-1997 a bus route to Syria was opened—the first overland route between the two countries.

CIVIL AVIATION

Armenian Airlines: 375042 Yerevan, Zvarnots Airport; tel. (1) 22-54-47; fax (1) 15-13-93; f. 1993; operates scheduled and charter passenger services to countries of the CIS, Europe and the Middle East; privatization project approved by the Govt in 1997; Man. Dir VYACHESLAV YARALOV.

Yer-Avia: 375010 Yerevan, 1–3 Busand St; tel. (1) 58-01-21; fax (1) 56-75-11; f. 1992; international and domestic passenger and cargo services; Chief Exec. ARSEN ASLANIAN.

National Aviation Union of Armenia: Yerevan; Chair. DMITRI ATBASHIAN.

Tourism

Prior to secession from the USSR in 1991, Armenia attracted a number of tourists from the other Soviet republics. Following its independence, however, tourism severely declined, although by the late 1990s some European firms were beginning to introduce tours to the country. According to the World Tourism Organization, tourism receipts increased from about US $5m. in 1995 to $7m. in 1997. Receipts, according to the World Bank, increased rapidly thereafter, reaching $27m. in 1999 and $45m. in 2000. Armenia received an estimated 162,089 tourist arrivals in 2002. The major tourist attractions were the capital, Yerevan; Artashat, an early trading centre on the 'Silk Road'; and medieval monasteries. There was, however, little accommodation available outside the capital.

Directorate of Trade, Tourism and Services: Ministry of Industry and Trade, 375008 Yerevan, Hanrapetoutioun St 5; tel. (1) 58-94-94; fax (1) 56-61-23; e-mail garnikn@yahoo.com; Dir ARTAK DAVTIAN.

Armenia Association of Tourism: Yerevan; tel. (1) 53-45-01; fax (1) 56-39-27; e-mail nta@freenet.am; Chair. ARTUR VOSKANIAN.

Tourism Armenia: 375010 Yerevan, 15 Khanjian St 15; tel. (1) 57-80-01; fax (1) 57-83-51.

AUSTRALIA

Introductory Survey

Location, Climate, Language, Religion, Flag, Capital

The Commonwealth of Australia occupies the whole of the island continent of Australia, lying between the Indian and Pacific Oceans, and its offshore islands, principally Tasmania to the south-east. Australia's nearest neighbour is Papua New Guinea, to the north. In the summer (November–February) there are tropical monsoons in the northern part of the continent (except for the Queensland coast), but the winters (July–August) are dry. Both the north-west and north-east coasts are liable to experience tropical cyclones between December and April. In the southern half of the country, winter is the wet season; rainfall decreases rapidly inland. Very high temperatures, sometimes exceeding 50°C (122°F), are experienced during the summer months over the arid interior and for some distance to the south, as well as during the pre-monsoon months in the north. The official language is English; 170 indigenous languages are spoken by Aboriginal and Torres Strait Islander peoples. At the census of 1996 70.9% of the population professed Christianity (of whom 27.0% were Roman Catholic and 22.0% Anglican). The national flag (proportions 1 by 2) is blue, with a representation of the United Kingdom flag in the upper hoist, a large seven-pointed white star in the lower hoist and five smaller white stars, in the form of the Southern Cross constellation, in the fly. The capital, Canberra, lies in one of two enclaves of federal territory known as the Australian Capital Territory (ACT).

Recent History

Since the Second World War, Australia has played an important role in Asian affairs, and has strengthened its political and economic ties with Indonesia and the other countries of South-East Asia, and with Japan. The country co-operates more closely than formerly with the USA (see ANZUS, see p. 348), and has given much aid to Asian and Pacific countries.

At the election of December 1949 the ruling Australian Labor Party (ALP) was defeated by the Liberal Party, in coalition with the Country Party. In January 1966 Sir Robert Menzies resigned after 16 years as Prime Minister, and was succeeded by Harold Holt, who was returned to office at elections in December of that year. However, Holt died in December 1967. His successor, Senator John Gorton, took office in January 1968 but resigned, after losing a vote of confidence, in March 1971. William McMahon was Prime Minister from March 1971 until December 1972, when, after 23 years in office, the Liberal-Country Party coalition was defeated at a general election for the House of Representatives. The ALP, led by Gough Whitlam, won 67 of the 125 seats in the House. Following a conflict between the Whitlam Government and the Senate, both Houses of Parliament were dissolved in April 1974, and a general election was held in May. The ALP was returned to power, although with a reduced majority in the House of Representatives. However, the Government failed to gain a majority in the Senate, and in October 1975 the Opposition in the Senate obstructed legislative approval of budget proposals. The Government was not willing to consent to a general election over the issue, but in November the Governor-General, Sir John Kerr, intervened and took the unprecedented step of dismissing the Government. A caretaker Ministry was installed under Malcolm Fraser, the Liberal leader, who formed a coalition Government with the Country Party. This coalition gained large majorities in both Houses of Parliament at a general election in December 1975, but the majorities were progressively reduced at general elections in December 1977 and October 1980.

Fraser's coalition Government was defeated by the ALP at a general election in March 1983. Robert (Bob) Hawke, who had replaced William (Bill) Hayden as Labor leader in the previous month, became the new Prime Minister and immediately organized a meeting of representatives of government, employers and trade unions to reach agreement on a prices and incomes policy (the 'Accord') that would allow economic recovery. Hawke called a general election for December 1984, 15 months earlier than necessary, and the ALP was returned to power with a reduced majority in the House of Representatives. The opposition coalition between the Liberal Party and the National Party (formerly

known as the Country Party) collapsed in April 1987, when 12 National Party MPs withdrew from the agreement and formed the New National Party (led by the right-wing Sir Johannes Bjelke-Petersen, the Premier of Queensland), while the remaining 14 National Party MPs continued to support their leader, Ian Sinclair, who wished to remain within the alliance. Parliament was dissolved in June, in preparation for an early general election in July. The election campaign was dominated by economic issues. The ALP was returned to office with an increased majority, securing 86 of the 148 seats in the House of Representatives. The Liberal and National Parties announced the renewal of the opposition alliance in August. Four months later, Bjelke-Petersen was forced to resign as Premier of Queensland, under pressure from National Party officials.

During 1988 the Hawke Government suffered several defeats at by-elections, seemingly as a result of a decline in living standards and an unpopular policy of wage restraint. The ALP narrowly retained power at state elections in Victoria, but was defeated in New South Wales, where it had held power for 12 years. In May 1989 the leader of the Liberal Party, John Howard, was replaced by Andrew Peacock, and Charles Blunt succeeded Ian Sinclair as leader of the National Party. In July a commission of inquiry into alleged corruption in Queensland published its report. The Fitzgerald report documented several instances of official corruption and electoral malpractice by the Queensland Government, particularly during the administration of Bjelke-Petersen. Following the publication of the report, support for the National Party within Queensland declined once more, and in December the ALP defeated the National Party in the state election (the first time that it had defeated the National Party in Queensland since 1957). By the end of 1991 four former members of the Queensland Cabinet and the former chief of the state's police force had received custodial sentences. The trial of Bjelke-Petersen, initially on charges of perjury and corruption but subsequently of perjury alone, resulted in dismissal of the case, when the jury failed to reach a verdict.

In February 1990 Hawke announced that a general election for the House of Representatives and for 40 of the 76 seats in the Senate was to be held on 24 March. The Government's position in the period preceding the election had been strengthened by the ALP's victory in Queensland in December 1989, the removal of an unpopular Labor leadership in Western Australia and its replacement by the first female Premier, Dr Carmen Lawrence, and by the support that it secured from environmental groups as a result of its espousal of 'green' issues. Although the opposition parties won the majority of the first-preference votes in the election for the House of Representatives, the endorsement of the environmental groups delivered a block of second-preference votes to the ALP, which was consequently returned to power, albeit with a reduced majority, securing 78 of the 148 seats. Following its defeat, Peacock immediately resigned as leader of the Liberal Party and was replaced by Dr John Hewson, a former professor of economics. Blunt lost his seat in the election and was succeeded as leader of the National Party by Timothy Fischer.

In September 1990, at a meeting of senior ALP members, government proposals to initiate a controversial programme of privatization were endorsed, effectively ending almost 100 years of the ALP's stance against private ownership. In October plans for constitutional and structural reform were approved in principle by the leaders of the six state and two territory governments. The proposed reforms envisaged the creation of national standards in regulations and services. They also aimed to alleviate the financial dependence of the states and territories on the Federal Government. These suggested reforms, however, encountered strong opposition from sections of the public services, the trade unions and the business community. In July 1991 the leaders of the federal and state Governments finally agreed to reforms in the country's systems of marketing, transport, trade and taxation, with the aim of creating a single national economy from 1992.

In April 1991, as a result of preliminary investigations by a Royal Commission into the financial dealings of the Labor

Government of Western Australia in the 1980s, Brian Burke, the former state Premier, resigned as Australia's ambassador to Ireland and the Holy See. Owing to the alleged irregularities, more than $A1,000m. of public funds were believed to have been lost. In May the Premier of New South Wales called a state election, 10 months earlier than was necessary, in an attempt to take advantage of the problems of Labor administrations at federal and state level. However, the Liberal-National Party Government lost its overall majority and was able to retain power only with the support of independent members of the state legislature.

In June 1991, following months of divisions within the ALP, Hawke narrowly defeated a challenge to his leadership from Paul Keating, the Deputy Prime Minister and Treasurer, who accused the Prime Minister of reneging on a promise to resign in his favour before the next general election. This cast doubt on Hawke's credibility, as he had assured Parliament and the public in 1990 that he would continue as leader for the whole of the parliamentary term. Following his defeat, Keating resigned. In December Hawke dismissed John Kerin, Keating's replacement as Treasurer, following a series of political and economic crises. Hawke called another leadership election, but, on this occasion, he was defeated by Keating, who accordingly became Prime Minister. A major reorganization of the Cabinet followed. John Dawkins, a staunch supporter of Keating, was appointed Treasurer.

Following the ALP's defeat in state elections in Tasmania, the party encountered further embarrassment in April 1992, when a by-election in Melbourne to fill the parliamentary seat vacated by Bob Hawke was won by a local football club coach, standing as an independent candidate. In May the Prime Minister suffered another set-back, when Graham Richardson, the Minister for Transport and Communications, resigned, owing to his implication in a scandal involving a relative who was alleged to have participated in an illegal scheme whereby Taiwanese investors were able to secure US residency rights via the Marshall Islands. Meanwhile, Brian Burke, the former Premier of Western Australia, had been arrested. It was alleged that, during his term of office, he had misappropriated more than $A17,000 from a parliamentary expense account. In October 1992 the conclusions of the inquiry into the ALP's alleged involvement in corrupt practices in Western Australia were released. The Royal Commission was highly critical of the improper transactions between successive governments of Western Australia and business entrepreneurs. The conduct of Brian Burke drew particular criticism. (In July 1994 Burke received a prison sentence of two years upon conviction on four charges of fraud; he was released in February 1995, but was sentenced to three years' imprisonment in February 1997 for the theft of $A122,000 from ALP funds.) Furthermore, in February 1995 Ray O'Connor, Premier of Western Australia between 1982 and 1983, received a prison sentence of 18 months, having been found guilty of the theft in 1984 of $A25,000, intended as a donation to the Liberal Party. He was released in August 1995.

In September 1992 John Bannon became the seventh state Premier since 1982 to leave office in disgrace. The resignation of the ALP Premier of South Australia was due to a scandal relating to attempts to offset the heavy financial losses incurred by the State Bank of South Australia. At state elections in Queensland in mid-September, the ALP administration of Wayne Goss was returned to power. In the following month, however, the ruling ALP was defeated in state elections in Victoria. Furthermore, in November a new financial scandal emerged: the federal Treasurer was alleged to have suppressed information pertaining to the former ALP Government of Victoria which, in a clandestine manner prior to the state elections, was believed to have exceeded its borrowing limits.

By late 1992, therefore, the ALP's prospects of being returned to office at the forthcoming general election appeared to have been seriously damaged. Proposals for radical tax and economic reforms that were advocated by the federal opposition leader, Dr John Hewson, attracted much attention. At state elections in Western Australia in February 1993, the incumbent Labor Government was defeated. Dr Carmen Lawrence was replaced as Premier by Richard Court of the Liberal-National coalition.

Nevertheless, at the general election, held on 13 March 1993, the ALP was unexpectedly returned to office for a fifth consecutive term, having secured 80 of the 147 seats in the House of Representatives. In January 1994 the Government was embarrassed by the resignation of the Minister of Industry, Technology and Regional Development, Alan Griffiths, as a result of

allegations that public funds and ALP resources had been misappropriated in order to meet the private business debts incurred by his Melbourne sandwich shop. In the following month Ros Kelly, the Minister for Environment, Sport and Territories and close associate of the Prime Minister, yielded to pressure to resign, owing to a scandal relating to the alleged use of community sports grants to attempt to influence voters in vulnerable ALP-held constituencies prior to the 1993 general election. In May 1994 Dr John Hewson was replaced as leader of the Liberal Party by Alexander Downer, a supporter of the monarchy. Downer was therefore expected to lead the campaign against Paul Keating's proposal that Australia become a republic (see below). In January 1995, however, Downer resigned. The party leadership was resumed by John Howard, also a monarchist.

At state elections in New South Wales in March 1995 the ALP defeated the ruling Liberal-National coalition. Robert (Bob) Carr was appointed Premier. At a federal by-election in Canberra, however, the ALP suffered a serious reverse when, for the first time in 15 years, the seat fell to the Liberal Party. In July, at state elections in Queensland, the ALP Government of Wayne Goss was narrowly returned to office, only to be ousted following a by-election defeat in February 1996. In June 1995, meanwhile, the Deputy Prime Minister, Brian Howe, who intended to retire at the next general election, announced his resignation from the Cabinet. He was replaced by the Minister for Finance, Kim Beazley.

At the general election held on 2 March 1996 the Liberal-National coalition achieved a decisive victory, securing a total of 94 of the 148 seats in the House of Representatives. The ALP won only 49 seats. In the Senate the minor parties and independent members retained the balance of power. John Howard of the Liberal Party became Prime Minister, and immediately promised to give priority to the issues of industrial relations, the transfer to partial private ownership of the state telecommunications company, Telstra, and to expanding relations with Asia. The leader of the National Party, Tim Fischer, was appointed Deputy Prime Minister and Minister for Trade. Paul Keating was replaced as leader of the ALP by Kim Beazley.

In August 1996, in an unprecedented display of violence, demonstrators protesting against proposed budget cuts stormed the Parliament building in Canberra. Clashes between the police and the protesters resulted in many injuries. Meanwhile, fears for Australia's tradition of racial tolerance continued to grow. In October Pauline Hanson, a newly-elected independent member of the House of Representatives, aroused much controversy when, in a speech envisaging 'civil war', she reiterated her demands for the ending of immigration from Asia and for the elimination of special funding for Aboriginal people. The Prime Minister attracted criticism for his failure to issue a direct denunciation of the views of Pauline Hanson, a former member of the Liberal Party. The increasingly bitter debate also damaged Australia's image in the countries of Asia, a vital source of investment and of tourist revenue. In March 1997, moreover, the One Nation Party was established by Pauline Hanson and rapidly attracted support. In May, while attending a fundraising rally in Perth, Pauline Hanson was besieged by more than 1,000 opponents. Larger protests against her policies followed in Melbourne and Canberra. Meanwhile, after his initial weak response, the Prime Minister condemned the views of the founder of the One Nation Party. In August, as fears for Australian revenue from Asian investment, trade and tourism grew, the Government issued a document on foreign policy, in which Pauline Hanson's views were strongly repudiated and in which Australia's commitment to racial equality was reiterated. In order to counter the negative impact of the activities of the One Nation Party, a special diplomatic unit was established. In November 1997, furthermore, former Prime Ministers Keating, Hawke and Whitlam published a statement denouncing Pauline Hanson.

In early 1998 the long-standing tension between the National Farmers' Federation and the powerful Maritime Union of Australia (MUA) developed into a bitter dispute over trade unionists' rights when farmers established their own non-unionized stevedoring operation in Melbourne to handle their exports, in protest at high dockside costs and alleged inefficiency. The confrontation escalated in April, when Patrick Stevedores, a major cargo-handling company based in Sydney, dismissed its entire unionized work-force of 1,400 dockers, with the intention of replacing them with secretly-trained contract workers. As part of its campaign to break the MUA monopoly (the offensive being supported by the Government), Patrick Stevedores drafted in hundreds of security guards to its 14 terminals around Australia, in an operation to lock out the dockers. The Federal Court, however, subsequently ruled that Patrick Stevedores had acted illegally and ordered the company to reinstate the 1,400 trade unionists. Following the rejection of an appeal to the High Court by Patrick Stevedores and the return to work of the dockers in May, the Prime Minister nevertheless pledged to press ahead with waterfront reform. Although the majority of Australians appeared to support the reform of labour practices in the country's ports, the Government's handling of the dispute had attracted much criticism.

Meanwhile, in December 1997 the New One Nation Party was established by former supporters of Pauline Hanson, who had apparently become disillusioned with her autocratic style of leadership. In June 1998, at state elections in Queensland, the One Nation Party won 23% of first-preference votes, thus unexpectedly securing 11 of the 89 seats in the legislature and leading to renewed concern among tourism and business leaders. In August it was announced that an early general election was to be held in October. As the campaign commenced, former Prime Ministers Whitlam, Fraser, Hawke and Keating signed an open letter urging citizens not to support racist candidates at the forthcoming election.

At the election, conducted on 3 October 1998, the Liberal-National coalition was narrowly returned to office, winning a total of 80 of the 148 seats in the House of Representatives. The ALP increased its representation to 67 seats. Contrary to expectations, the One Nation Party failed to win any representation in the lower house, the controversial Pauline Hanson losing her Queensland seat. (The one seat secured by the One Nation Party in the Senate was subsequently subjected to a legal challenge, owing to the candidate's apparent failure to meet citizenship requirements—see below.) In a referendum held on the same day, the electorate of the Northern Territory unexpectedly rejected a proposal for the territory's elevation to full statehood. In mid-October the Prime Minister announced the composition of his new Cabinet; most senior ministers retained their portfolios. Changes included the establishment of a special portfolio (transport and regional services) to focus on rural issues, in response to the ruling coalition's poor electoral performance in rural areas. John Howard also created a new Ministry of Financial Services and Regulation.

In February 1999 Pauline Hanson was re-elected leader of the One Nation Party, despite a series of defections, including the departure from the party of several of the 11 One Nation members of the Queensland legislature. At state elections in New South Wales in March, at which the ALP was returned to power, the One Nation Party won two seats in the 42-member upper chamber. In June a court ruled that the One Nation Senator was ineligible to occupy her seat in the federal upper house, owing to her failure to renounce her British citizenship prior to the general election. She was subsequently replaced by another member of the One Nation Party. In January 2000 police officers in Queensland and New South Wales raided premises belonging to the One Nation Party, seizing hundreds of documents relating to the party's membership and its financial structure. In April the Queensland Electoral Commission ruled that the party had been fraudulently registered by the falsification of significant sections of its 200-name membership list, in order to qualify for public funding in Queensland. Consequently, the party was ordered to repay some $A0.5m. of state funds which it had received. As the sole signatory on the registration papers, Pauline Hanson found herself personally responsible for the repayment. Hanson repaid the funds after a successful appeal for public donations, and she re-registered the One Nation Party in January 2001 to contest the forthcoming Queensland state elections (see below).

Meanwhile, following a protracted debate, in June 1999 the Senate narrowly approved the Government's proposal to dispose of a further 16.6% of the assets of Telstra (to bring the total transferred to the private sector to 49.9%). Two independent Senators, including the veteran Brian Harradine of Tasmania, had initially opposed the plan, but reversed their stance in exchange for commitments of additional funding for their respective regions. Kim Beazley, leader of the opposition ALP, denounced the arrangement as 'shameful'. The Treasurer, however, maintained that the sale of a further tranche of the telecommunications corporation would permit the Government drastically to reduce public debt. In October 2000 the Government was forced to delay its plan to sell its remaining 51% stake

in Telstra after a report was released condemning the state of Australia's rural telecommunications services. A year later Treasurer Peter Costello announced a new plan fully to privatize Telstra in the financial year 2003/04. Following several modifications prior to its final approval by the Senate, the controversial GST was implemented in mid-2000.

Following state elections in Victoria in September 1999, the Liberal-National Premier, Jeffrey Kennett, was replaced by Stephen Bracks of the ALP. The defeat of the Liberal-National coalition was regarded as a set-back to the Federal Government's programme of economic reform, the transfer of public utilities to the private sector having been particularly unpopular among the voters of Victoria.

In September 2000 Australia hosted the Olympic Games in Sydney. The event was widely perceived as having been successful and of particular benefit to the local economy. However, the fact that security forces were given emergency powers to shoot on sight anyone thought likely to pose a threat to security at the Games caused some controversy, with civil rights groups expressing concern that the draconian anti-terrorist measures might persist after the conclusion of the event. In the same month a series of violent confrontations occurred between demonstrators and security personnel in Melbourne at a three-day summit meeting of the World Economic Forum. The demonstrators, several of whom were injured in the clashes, were protesting against capitalism and economic globalization.

A marked increase in illegal immigration during 1999 and 2000 prompted the introduction of new legislation empowering Australian police to board vessels in international waters. In 1999 almost 2,000 illegal immigrants were intercepted by the authorities and transferred to detention centres in Australia, while many others were believed to have died in the attempt to enter the country. In April 2000 more than 250 people, mostly from Iran and Iraq, died when their three boats sank in rough seas while trying to enter Australia illegally. The issue of alleged maltreatment of illegal immigrants captured in Australia was highlighted by a series of protests at a privately-run detention centre in Woomera, South Australia. Moreover, in November the Government ordered an inquiry into allegations that children at the centre had been subjected to systematic sexual abuse. Campaigners, who had repeatedly appealed for more humane treatment of illegal immigrants, claimed that the Government had suppressed evidence of abuse at Woomera and other detention centres.

Australia's handling of immigration problems provoked international condemnation in August 2001 when the Prime Minister refused to admit 433 refugees, stranded on an overcrowded Norwegian cargo ship off Christmas Island, onto the Australian mainland. The Government, faced with a high court challenge, swiftly enacted new legislation empowering the navy to prevent migrants coming ashore and excluding remote Australian island territories from the definition of official landfall. The situation was eventually resolved when New Zealand, Nauru and Papua New Guinea agreed to accommodate the asylum-seekers whilst their applications were processed. In the interim, however, traffic in illegal immigrants attempting to reach Australia's outlying territories—the majority via Indonesia—continued to increase; according to government figures, 1,823 'boat people' departed for Australia in September and October 2001. The Government proposed its so-called 'Pacific solution', whereby neighbouring South Pacific nations could agree to host asylum-seekers during their processing on a continuing basis in exchange for substantial aid. Nauru signed an agreement to take up to 1,200 refugees at any one time, whilst Papua New Guinea prevaricated on the possibility of accommodating a further 1,000 people. Concerns about Australia's immigration policy again focused on the Woomera detention centre in January 2002, when 259 detainees began a hunger strike in protest at poor living conditions there and at the long delays in the processing of their applications; 64 inmates had stitched together their lips. Neville Roach, the Chairman of the Council for Multicultural Australia, resigned in protest. In February the Australian Government announced that a representative of the UN High Commissioner for Human Rights and other observers would be permitted to inspect the camp between May and August.

A state election in Western Australia in February 2001 resulted in defeat for the governing Liberal-National coalition and the replacement of Premier Richard Court by the state's Labor leader, Geoffrey Gallop. Ongoing anxieties regarding illegal immigration were reflected in the unexpected success of the One Nation Party, which secured almost 10% of votes at the poll. At the state election in Queensland in the same month, the ALP Government, led by Peter Beattie, was decisively re-elected. The One Nation Party garnered 9% of the total votes.

A federal election took place on 10 November 2001. The Liberal-National coalition won 82 of the 150 seats in the House of Representatives, thus narrowly securing a third consecutive term of office. Despite its successes at state and territorial elections in Western Australia and the Northern Territory earlier in the year, the ALP, winning 65, took two fewer seats than at the previous federal election. Many political commentators attributed the coalition's apparent reversal of fortune to Howard's controversial handling of immigration issues, which had led to a surge in his popularity. Kim Beazley resigned as leader of the ALP and was replaced by Simon Crean, formerly the Shadow Treasurer. The One Nation Party won no seats in either the House of Representatives or the Senate. (In December Pauline Hanson resigned as leader of the One Nation Party to concentrate on contesting charges of electoral fraud brought against her in July 2001.)

John Howard announced the composition of his third Ministry in late November 2001, appointing six new cabinet ministers. Changes included the incorporation of the Department of Reconciliation and Aboriginal and Torres Strait Islander Affairs into the new portfolio of Immigration and Multicultural and Indigenous Affairs. The Department of Industry, Science and Resources became that of Industry, Tourism and Resources, emphasizing the tourism sector's growing importance to the Australian economy. Wilson Tuckey was appointed Minister for Regional Services, Territories and Local Government, despite being the subject of a police investigation into issues associated with the charter of aircraft in Western Australia. At a state election in South Australia in February 2002, the ruling Liberal-National coalition was defeated. Michael Rann of the ALP was appointed Premier.

In mid-February 2002 the leader of the ALP accused the Prime Minister of having lied during the previous year's election campaign to boost his coalition's chances of victory, after it emerged that government claims that refugees in a ship intercepted by the Australian navy had thrown their children into the sea were false. John Howard, nevertheless, withstood a censure motion introduced in the House of Representatives. In mid-March the Prime Minister requested Senator Bill Heffernan to resign from his post as parliamentary secretary after he issued false allegations about Justice Michael Kirby in an attempt to ruin the judge's career. A motion to censure John Howard for his handling of the affair was defeated in the House of Representatives. Opposition parties instigated a further three unsuccessful censure motions against the Prime Minister in February–March. Senator Natasha Stott Despoja, leader of the Australian Democrats, resigned in August; she was replaced by Andrew Bartlett two months later. In late November the ruling ALP, led by Stephen Bracks, won a state election in Victoria. The Labor Government in New South Wales was re-elected in March 2003 for an unprecedented third term; Bob Carr was reappointed Premier. Meanwhile, in February the Senate passed a 'no-confidence' motion on John Howard over the Government's unilateral decision to deploy troops to the Middle East in preparation for a possible US-led military campaign to remove the regime of Saddam Hussein in Iraq. Although it had no legal impact, the motion—the first to be carried against a government in 102 years—was considered symbolic. Public demonstrations against Australia's anticipated involvement in the war took place throughout the month.

Protesters against the Government's mandatory detention of all asylum-seekers stormed the Woomera detention centre in late March 2002. Most of the approximately 50 asylum-seekers who managed to escape were recaptured; about 11, however, disappeared into the desert. In April riots took place at detention centres in Curtin and Port Hedland, Western Australia. In late May the Government offered financial incentives to almost 1,000 Afghan asylum-seekers in detention centres throughout Australia and Nauru of $A2,000 each (with a limit of $A10,000 per family) if they returned to Afghanistan. The Government gave the detainees 28 days (from the day their asylum review process ended) to decide whether to accept the offer, which also included counselling, air fares and vocational training. International aid agencies criticized the scheme, stating that Afghanistan was not stable enough for asylum-seekers to return. By mid-July only 76 Afghans had accepted the offer. Concerns about the alleged maltreatment of asylum-seekers were raised

again after supporters helped 34 detainees to escape from Woomera detention centre in late June. At the same time more than 120 inmates began a hunger strike in protest at poor living conditions and at the long delays in the processing of their applications. In late July a representative of the UN High Commissioner for Human Rights issued a report on the condition of Australia's detention camps criticizing the indefinite mandatory detention of asylum-seekers and claiming that the Australian Government was breaching international treaties on human rights and the rights of the child. The Australian Government rejected the report as inaccurate and biased. In the mean time, Australia's controversial efforts to deter refugees appeared to have been effective: the number of 'boat people' seeking asylum in Australia had declined significantly. In early December the Minister for Immigration and Multicultural and Indigenous Affairs, Philip Ruddock, announced plans to expand a programme to allow women and children asylum-seekers to live in the community rather than in the detention camps. The authorities employed tighter security measures at detention centres following riots at Woomera, Baxter, Port Hedland and on Christmas Island in late December. In mid-March 2003 Ruddock announced that Woomera detention centre would be closed down in mid-April, for reasons of cost. Families faced being separated after it was agreed that fathers and husbands would be moved to the Baxter detention centre near Port Augusta, while women and children would have to continue to live in the community in Woomera. The Government, however, stated that discussions to establish a residential housing programme for women and children at Port Augusta would continue.

In mid-May 2002 the Government expressed its regret for the 'suffering and injustice' experienced by some 3,500 child migrants taken from British children's homes after the Second World War. The migrants, many of whom suffered serious physical, psychological and sexual abuse after being sent to Australia, were offered a $A3.8m. reparation package, mainly to assist them to trace their families. In June Roman Catholic Archbishop George Pell came under pressure to resign after he publicly admitted to offering compensation payments to the family of two girls who had been sexually abused by a priest. Pell denied claims that the payments included secrecy clauses; however, a lawyer representing the Church later confirmed that confidentiality terms were attached to the payments, adding that bishops appeared to have been unaware of the conditions. Some two months later Pell faced an inquiry into allegations that as a trainee priest in 1961 he had sexually abused a boy. Pell denied the allegations, but agreed to step down temporarily during the investigations. The inquiry cleared Pell of the allegations in mid-October.

On 12 October 2002 88 Australians were killed in a bomb explosion in a night-club on the Indonesian island of Bali. The Islamist militant Jemaah Islamiah was held principally responsible for the attack, which killed almost 200 people in total. The Australian Government proscribed the organization, which was suspected of having links with the al-Qa'ida (Base) network, and successfully led a campaign to have Jemaah Islamiah listed as a terrorist organization by the UN. In an attempt to prevent retaliatory attacks against Muslims in Australia, the Prime Minister publicly declared that Islam was not responsible for the attack. However, a mosque and an Islamic school in Sydney were attacked in mid-October, prompting the Premier of New South Wales, Bob Carr, to establish a community harmony reference group to ease tensions. In early November the Government was accused of harassing Muslims, following a series of high-profile armed raids on the homes of Indonesian-born Muslims suspected of having connections with Jemaah Islamiah. Although the authorities denied the accusations, the raids antagonized the Muslim community and adversely affected relations with Indonesia. In mid-November Jack Roche, a British-born Muslim convert, was charged with devising bomb attacks on the Israeli embassy in Canberra and the Israeli consulate in Sydney. Roche, who had earlier admitted to having met Osama bin Laden, the Saudi-born leader of al-Qa'ida, and Riduan Isamuddin, the suspected operations chief of Jemaah Islamiah, denied the charges. In late 2002 the number of reported attacks against Australian Muslims increased.

In March 1986, meanwhile, Australia's constitutional links with the United Kingdom were reduced by the Australia Act, which abolished the British Parliament's residual legislative, executive and judicial controls over Australian state law. In February 1992, shortly after a visit by Queen Elizabeth, Paul

Keating caused a furore by accusing the United Kingdom of abandoning Australia to the Japanese threat during the Second World War. Following a visit to the United Kingdom in September 1993, Keating announced that Australia was to become a republic by the year 2001, subject to approval by referendum. Sir William Deane succeeded William Hayden as Governor-General in February 1996, the former's term of office being scheduled to expire at the end of the year 2000. Although John Howard personally favoured the retention of the monarchy, in 1996 the new Prime Minister announced plans for a constitutional convention, prior to the holding of a referendum on the issue if necessary. In an unexpected development in January 1997, the Deputy Prime Minister put forward proposals for the removal from the Constitution of all references to the monarch and for the transfer of the Queen's functions to Australia's Chief Justice.

Voluntary postal voting to select, from among 609 candidates, 76 delegates who were to attend the constitutional convention (scheduled for February 1998) commenced in November 1997. The complex system of preferential voting, however, appeared to give rise to much confusion, particularly in New South Wales where a total of 174 candidates were contesting 20 places at the forthcoming convention. In addition to the official groupings, the Australian Republican Movement (ARM) and Australians for a Constitutional Monarchy (ACM), numerous other republican and monarchist, as well as individual, candidates were standing for election. Only 42.6% of registered voters were reported to have returned their ballot papers, the participation rate in New South Wales being only 39.9%. In February 1998, following nine days of debate, a majority of the 152 delegates (a further 76 having been appointed by the Government) endorsed proposals to adopt a republican system and to replace the British monarch as Head of State. Although the Constitutional Convention was dominated by Republicans, delegates were divided over the method of election of a future head of state.

In December 1998 it was confirmed that a referendum on the republican issue would be held in late 1999. In August 1999 the Federal Parliament gave approval to the wording of the question to be posed to the electorate, which was to be asked if support was forthcoming for an 'act to alter the Constitution to establish the Commonwealth of Australia as a republic with the Queen and Governor-General being replaced by a President appointed by a two-thirds' majority of the members of the Commonwealth Parliament'. At the referendum, conducted on 6 November 1999, 55% of voters favoured the retention of the monarchy. Moreover, some 61% of voters expressed opposition to a proposal to include a preamble to the Constitution, recognizing Aborigines as 'the nation's first people'. Although the result was regarded as a victory for Howard, who had campaigned for the retention of the monarchy, many observers interpreted the result as a rejection of the particular republican system offered, opinion polls having indicated that more than two-thirds of Australians would support the introduction of a republican system of government if the President were to be directly elected. Howard extended Sir William Deane's tenure as Governor-General by six months, allowing Deane to participate in an official capacity in the events commemorating Australia's centenary of Federation. In April 2001 the Anglican Archbishop of Brisbane, Peter Hollingworth, was named as Deane's successor; he was sworn in in June. In February 2002, as the Queen commenced a golden jubilee visit to Australia, the Governor-General refused to yield to pressure to resign over claims that he had deliberately concealed alleged cases of child abuse by the clergy in Queensland. The Prime Minister rejected calls to dismiss the Governor-General. In May 2003 Hollingworth temporarily relinquished his post, pending the investigation of rape allegations against him. The Governor-General strongly denied the charge against him, which dated back to the 1960s. Sir Guy Green, the Governor of Tasmania, was appointed acting Governor-General.

In May 1987 Australia and the United Kingdom began a joint operation to ascertain the extent of plutonium contamination resulting from British nuclear weapons testing at Maralinga in South Australia between 1956 and 1963. Many Australians were highly critical of the United Kingdom's apparent disregard for the environmental consequences of the tests and of the British authorities' failure to make adequate arrangements to protect the local Aboriginal people, who were now campaigning for a thorough decontamination of their traditional lands. In June 1993 Australia announced its acceptance of $A45m. in compensation from the British Government for the cost of the decontamination. In December 1994 the displaced Aboriginal

people and the federal Government reached agreement on a compensation settlement of $A13.5m., to be spent on health, employment and infrastructural projects. In January 1999, furthermore, it was announced that the Australian and British Governments were to conduct separate inquiries into research linking the nuclear tests to the numerous cases of a rare form of cancer in servicemen who had witnessed the explosions. In March 2000 it was announced that a joint decontamination programme effected by the British and Australian Governments had been completed. However, the Australian Government issued a report in May 2000 stating that, despite the removal of 300,000 cu m of plutonium-contaminated topsoil during the operation, some 120 sq km of the territory was still considered too contaminated for permanent habitation, permitting only limited access to it. In March 2003, furthermore, the former head of the Maralinga Rehabilitation Committee declared the decontamination operation to have been a failure. In mid-September 2002 the Government's nuclear safety body authorized the construction in 2005 of a new nuclear research reactor in Sydney to replace an existing reactor.

The sensitive issue of Aboriginal land rights was addressed by the Government in August 1985, when it formulated proposals for legislation that would give Aboriginal people inalienable freehold title to national parks, vacant Crown land and former Aboriginal reserves, in spite of widespread opposition from state governments (which had previously been responsible for their own land policies), from mining companies and from the Aboriginal people themselves, who were angered by the Government's withdrawal of its earlier support for the Aboriginal right to veto mineral exploitation. In October 1985 Ayers Rock, in the Northern Territory, was officially transferred to the Mutijulu Aboriginal community, on condition that continuing access to the rock (the main inland tourist attraction) be guaranteed. In 1986, however, the Government abandoned its pledge to impose such federal legislation on unwilling state governments, and this led to further protests from Aboriginal leaders. In June 1991 the Government imposed a permanent ban on mining at an historical Aboriginal site in the Northern Territory.

An important precedent was established in June 1992, when the High Court overruled the concept of *terra nullius* (unoccupied land) by recognizing the existence of land titles that predated European settlement in 1788 in cases where a close association with the land in question had been continued; however, land titles legally acquired since 1788 were to remain intact. As a result of the 'Mabo' decision of 1992 (named after the Aboriginal claimant, Eddie Mabo), in December 1993 Parliament approved the Native Title Act, historic legislation granting Aboriginal people the right to claim title to their traditional lands. Despite the Prime Minister's personal involvement in the issue, the legislation aroused much controversy, particularly in Western Australia (vast areas of the state being vacant Crown land) where rival legislation to replace native title rights with lesser rights to traditional land usage, such as access for ceremonial purposes only, had been enacted. In March 1995 the High Court declared the Native Title Act to be valid, rejecting as unconstitutional Western Australia's own legislation. The ruling was expected to have widespread implications for the mining industry.

In October 1996, following protracted delays in the development of a valuable zinc mine in Queensland owing to Aboriginal land claims, the Howard Government announced proposals to amend the Native Title Act to permit federal ministers to overrule Aboriginal concerns if a project of 'major economic benefit' to Australia were threatened. Other proposed amendments included the simplification of the process of negotiation between potential developers and Aboriginal claimants. In December the Larrakia people of the Northern Territory presented a claim under the Native Title Act. The area in question incorporated the city of Darwin and was thus the first such claim to encompass a provincial capital. The claim reached the Federal Court in September 2002. Meanwhile, in October 1996 the federal High Court upheld an appeal by two Aboriginal communities in Queensland (including the Wik people of Cape York) against an earlier ruling that prevented them from submitting a claim to land leased by the state Government to cattle and sheep farmers. The Court's decision, known as the Wik judgment, was expected to encourage similar challenges to 'pastoral' leases, which covered 40% of Australia. Vociferous protests from farmers, who were strongly opposed to the co-existence of native title and pastoral leases, followed.

In April 1997 the first native title deed to be granted on mainland Australia was awarded to the Dunghutti people of New South Wales. In the same month the Prime Minister announced the introduction of legislation to clarify the issue of land tenure; a 10-point plan was to be drawn up in consultation with state governments and with representatives of the Aboriginal community. In September the Government introduced the Wik Native Title Bill, which was subsequently passed by the House of Representatives. In November, however, the Senate questioned the constitutional validity of the proposed legislation, whereby pastoralists' rights and activities would prevail over, but not extinguish (as had been assumed), the Aboriginal people's rights to Native Title. In December the Government refused to accept the Senate's proposed amendments to the legislation, thus raising the possibility of an early general election dominated by Aboriginal issues. In April 1998 the Senate rejected the legislation for a second time. Finally, in July, following a protracted and acrimonious debate, the Senate narrowly approved the Native Title Amendment Bill, thereby restricting the Aboriginal people's rights to claim access to Crown land leased to farmers. The passage of the controversial legislation was immediately denounced by Aboriginal leaders, who threatened to enlist international support for their cause. In the same month, however, the federal court of Darwin granted communal (but not exclusive or commercial) native title to the waters and sea-bed around Croker Island in the Northern Territory to five Aboriginal groups. With about 140 similar claims over Australian waters pending, the historic ruling represented the first recognition of native title rights over the sea. However, the area's traditional owners launched an appeal against the decision, insisting on the commercial right to negotiate on fishing and pearling activities. In March 1999, in a conciliatory gesture that settled a land claim case outstanding since 1845, the Tasmanian Government relinquished the site of a mission station at Wybellena, where 200 Aboriginal people had been forcibly resettled; most had subsequently died of disease and maltreatment. The land rights movement suffered a set-back in August 2002 when the High Court in Canberra rejected a claim by the Miriuwung-Gajerrong people to territory in Western Australia and the Northern Territory that contained the Argyle diamond mine owned by the Anglo-Australian mining company, Rio Tinto. The decision to give precedence to mining and petroleum leases over Aboriginal land rights appeared to reverse earlier court rulings that supported the land rights movement. In September, however, Rio Tinto offered to close the Jabiluka uranium mine in the Northern Territory following opposition to the project from the indigenous Mirrar people (the owners of the land) and environmental groups. The Mirrar people welcomed the proposal. Later that month the state Government of Western Australia agreed to return about 13.7m. ha of land to the Martu people. In December the Australian High Court rejected the Aboriginal Yorta Yorta people's claim to territory along the River Murray on the border of Victoria and New South Wales.

In November 1987 an official commission of inquiry into the cause of the high death rate among Aboriginal prisoners recommended immediate government action, and in July 1988 it was announced that 108 cases remained to be investigated. In August 1988 a UN report accused Australia of violating international human rights in its treatment of the Aboriginal people. In November the Government announced an inquiry into its Aboriginal Affairs Department, following accusations from the opposition coalition of nepotism and misuse of funds. The commission of inquiry published its first official report in February 1989. Following the report's recommendations, the Government announced the creation of a $A10m. programme to combat the high death rate among Aboriginal prisoners. In October an unofficial study indicated that Aboriginal people, although accounting for only 1% of the total population of Australia, comprised more than 20% of persons in prison. In May 1991 the report of the Royal Commission into Aboriginal Deaths in Custody was published, after three years of investigation. The report outlined evidence of racial prejudice in the police force and included more than 300 recommendations for changes in policies relating to Aboriginal people, aimed at improving relations between the racial groups of Australia and granting Aboriginal people greater self-determination and access to land ownership. In June Parliament established a Council for Aboriginal Reconciliation. In March 1992, Aboriginal deaths in custody having continued, radical plans for judicial, economic and social reforms, aimed at improving the lives of Aboriginal

people, were announced. The Government made an immediate allocation of $A150m.; a total of $A500m. was to be made available over the next 10 years. In February 1993 the human rights organization, Amnesty International, issued a highly critical report on the prison conditions of Aboriginal people. In March 1996 Amnesty International claimed that Australia had made little progress with regard to its treatment of Aboriginal prisoners. In March 2000 the UN Committee on Elimination of Racial Discrimination issued a report denouncing Australia's treatment of its indigenous people. The report was particularly critical of the mandatory prison sentences for minor property offences in force in the Northern Territory and Western Australia, which appeared to target juvenile Aborigines. In July a legal case was initiated against the Australian Government accusing it of breaching the human rights of Aboriginal people with these harsh mandatory sentencing laws. In August 2001 the Australian Bureau of Statistics published its biannual survey of indigenous health, based on 1997–99 figures. It found the average life expectancy of Aboriginal men and women to be, respectively, 20 and 19 years less than that of other Australians. The Government claimed that $A220m. was being spent on Aboriginal health services in that year, to be increased to $A260m. by 2004.

In July 1996 the Roman Catholic Church issued an apology for its role in the forcible removal from their parents of tens of thousands of Aboriginal children, in a controversial practice of placement in white foster homes, where many were abused. This policy of assimilation had continued until the late 1960s. In August 1996 the new Governor-General, Sir William Deane, urged all state parliaments to affirm their support for reconciliation with the Aboriginal people. The legislature of South Australia was the first to do so, in November. In May 1997 the publication of the findings of a two-year inquiry into the removal of as many as 100,000 Aboriginal children from their families had profound political repercussions. The author of the report, a distinguished former judge and President of the Human Rights and Equal Opportunities Commission, urged the Government to issue a formal apology to the 'stolen generation'. At a conference on reconciliation at the end of the month, the Prime Minister made an unexpected personal apology. The Government, however, repudiated the commission's assertion that the policy of assimilation had been tantamount to genocide and rejected recommendations that compensation be paid to victims. In December the Government reaffirmed that it would not issue a formal apology to the 'stolen generation'. A $A63m. programme to help reunite divided Aboriginal families was nevertheless announced. In February 1998 the Anglican Church apologized unreservedly for its part in the removal of Aboriginal children from their families. In May 2000, when 250,000 citizens took part in a march across Sydney Harbour Bridge, the Prime Minister refused to involve himself fully in the campaign for reconciliation between White and Aboriginal Australia, and ruled out any notion of a treaty. Two separate UN reports, released in March and July 2000, were highly critical of Australia's treatment of the Aboriginal population. The findings of the UN Committee on Elimination of Racial Discrimination (see above), and subsequently of the UN Human Rights Committee, were strongly rejected by the Australian Government. In August 2000, at the conclusion of a test case brought in the Northern Territory by two members of the 'stolen generation', who hoped to win compensation for the trauma occasioned by their removal from their families, the Federal Court ruled that the Government was not obliged to pay punitive damages to the two Aboriginal claimants, on the grounds of insufficient evidence. As many as 30,000 similar cases had been pending. In December some 300,000 people took part in demonstrations in Melbourne and Perth in support of reconciliation between the white and indigenous communities, and the Prime Minister was subject to renewed pressure to apologize for the treatment of Aboriginal people by white settlers. A Senate committee recommended issuing an apology to the 'stolen generation' and establishing a reparations tribunal to deal with compensation claims. However, the Government strongly rejected the recommendations. In August 2001, at a human rights conference in Sydney, various indigenous and legal groups finalized a new proposal for a reparations tribunal; again the Government rejected it, insisting that its own $A60m. programme of practical assistance was sufficient. In November 2001 Pope John Paul II apologized to Australia's Aboriginal community for what he called the 'shameful injustices' of the past, asking for forgiveness for the

Catholic Church's role in forcibly removing Aboriginal children from their families.

In foreign affairs, the Hawke and Keating Governments placed greater emphasis on links with South-East Asia. This policy was continued by John Howard, who pledged to expand relations with Asia. In January 1989 Hawke proposed the creation of an Asia-Pacific Economic Co-operation forum (APEC, see p. 139) to facilitate the exchange of services, tourism and direct foreign investment in the region. The inaugural APEC conference took place in Canberra in November 1989.

Australian relations with Indonesia, which had been strained since the Indonesian annexation of the former Portuguese colony of East Timor in 1976, improved in August 1985, when Hawke made a statement recognizing Indonesian sovereignty over the territory, but subsequently deteriorated, following the publication in a Sydney newspaper, in April 1986, of an article containing allegations of corruption against the Indonesian President, Gen. Suharto. Relations between Australia and Indonesia improved in December 1989, when they signed an accord regarding joint exploration for petroleum and gas reserves in the Timor Gap, an area of sea forming a disputed boundary between the two countries. Portugal, however, withdrew its ambassador from Canberra in protest, and in February 1991 instituted proceedings against Australia at the International Court of Justice. In June 1995 the Court refused to invalidate the exploration treaty. In April 1992 Paul Keating's visit to Indonesia, the new Prime Minister's first official overseas trip, aroused controversy, owing to the repercussions of the massacre of unarmed civilians in East Timor by Indonesian troops in November 1991. In July 1995, owing to strong opposition in Australia, Indonesia was obliged to withdraw the appointment as ambassador to Canberra of Lt-Gen. (retd) Herman Mantiri, a former Chief of the General Staff of the Armed Forces and an apparent supporter of the November 1991 Dili massacre. Nevertheless, in December 1995 Australia and Indonesia unexpectedly signed a joint security treaty. In March 1996 a new Indonesian ambassador took up his appointment in Canberra, and in September, following a visit to Jakarta by John Howard, Indonesia accepted Australia's ambassador-designate.

Meanwhile, the investigation into the deaths of six Australia-based journalists (including two Britons) in East Timor in 1975 had been reopened, and in June 1996 a government report concluded that they had been murdered by Indonesian soldiers. In October 1996, as Canberra continued to fail to denounce the Suharto Government's violations of human rights, Australian senators from all parties urged the Government to withdraw its recognition of Indonesian sovereignty over East Timor. In March 1997 Australia and Indonesia signed a treaty defining their seabed and 'economic zone' boundaries. The political unrest in Indonesia in early 1998, culminating in President Suharto's replacement in May, caused deep concern in Australia. In August the International Commission of Jurists, the Geneva-based human-rights organization, reported that five of the six journalists had been murdered in an East Timorese village in October 1975 in an attempt to conceal the invasion of the territory, while the sixth man was killed in Dili in December of that year. Furthermore, it was claimed that the Australian embassy in Jakarta had been aware of the forthcoming invasion of East Timor but had failed to give adequate warning to the journalists. In October 1998, as newly-emerging evidence continued to suggest that the truth had been suppressed and as interest in the matter was renewed in the United Kingdom, the Indonesian Government declared that it would not open an inquiry into the deaths of the two British journalists, maintaining that they and their colleagues had been killed in crossfire. Australia, however, announced that its judicial inquiry was to be reopened. Government documents declassified in late 2000 proved conclusively that Australian officials had prior knowledge of Indonesia's plans to invade East Timor.

In January 1999, in a significant shift in its policy, Australia announced that henceforth it would support eventual self-determination for East Timor. (Australia had been the only developed nation to recognize Indonesia's annexation of the territory.) In late January, furthermore, Australia welcomed the Indonesian Government's declaration of its willingness to consider the possibility of full independence, if proposals for autonomy were rejected by the East Timorese people. During 1999, however, Australia became increasingly concerned at the deteriorating security situation in East Timor. The announcement of the result of the referendum on the future of East Timor, held in late August, at which the territory's people voted overwhelmingly in

favour of independence (see the chapter on Indonesia) led to a rapid escalation of the violence. As pro-Jakarta militias embarked upon a campaign of murder and arson against innocent civilians, most of whom were forced to flee their homes, thousands of refugees were airlifted to safety in northern Australia. With a commitment of 4,500 troops in its largest operation since the Viet Nam War, Australia took a leading role in the deployment of a multinational peace-keeping force, the first contingent of which landed in East Timor on 20 September 1999. Several Asian countries, however, in particular Malaysia and Thailand, along with Indonesia itself (which earlier in the month had suspended its security pact with Australia), were critical of Australia's bias towards pro-independence groups and of the country's apparent aggressive approach to its role in the operation, which some observers considered would have been more appropriately led by the Association of South East Asian Nations (ASEAN). A deterioration in relations between the two countries led President Abdurrahman Wahid of Indonesia to postpone an official visit to Australia in mid-2000. A series of postponements or cancellations of ministerial meetings followed.

In a further demonstration of anti-Australian feeling, the Canberra's ambassador to Indonesia was assaulted by a pro-Jakarta mob in Makassar, Sulawesi, in November 2000. In the same month the Australian Government agreed to help create an East Timor defence force, contributing some US $26m. over five years and providing training for police officers and border guards. Abdurrahman Wahid made a long-postponed official visit to Australia in June 2001, the first Indonesian President to do so in 26 years. In turn, John Howard was the first foreign leader to meet the next President of Indonesia, Megawati Sukarnoputri, when he visited the country in August. He affirmed that Australia would encourage the international community's support for Indonesia. However, the increasing numbers of immigrants, the majority from the Middle East, attempting to enter Australia by boat via Indonesia during 2000–01 proved contentious. Indonesia disclaimed responsibility for the many boatloads of asylum-seekers on the grounds that they had entered Indonesia illegally. The situation prompted senior-level talks between Australian and Indonesian officials in September 2001 which, however, failed to resolve the problem. Discussions resumed in November, when the Indonesian Minister of Foreign Relations visited Canberra. At an international forum on the issue of people-smuggling in February 2002, delegates agreed to pursue a 12-month programme, which included imposing stricter law enforcement and better information and intelligence-sharing, to combat smuggling and illegal immigration. In late February officials from Australia, Indonesia and Timor-Leste (formerly East Timor) held the first ever trilateral talks on future co-operation issues in Denpasar, on the Indonesian island of Bali. In September three Indonesians were convicted of attempting to smuggle 'illegal immigrants' into Australia in October 2001; they were sentenced to five years' imprisonment. Relations between Australia and Indonesia were strained as a result of Australia's treatment of Indonesian-born Muslims suspected of having links with the banned Islamist militant organization, Jemaah Islamiah, in the aftermath of the bomb attack on Bali in October 2002 (see above). In mid-December Timor-Leste's Parliament ratified a treaty with Australia on production, profit-sharing and royalty and tax distribution from oil and gas reserves.

A crisis in Australia's relations with Malaysia arose in late 1993, when Paul Keating described the Malaysian Prime Minister as a 'recalcitrant' for his failure to attend the APEC summit meeting in Seattle, USA, in November. Relations subsequently improved, however, manifest in such initiatives as the Malaysia-Australia Dialogue (MAD), established in 1995 to encourage the long-term bilateral relationship at government-to-government level in education, business, the media and other sectors. In January 1996 Keating paid the first official visit to Malaysia by an Australian Prime Minister since 1984 and the ministerial-level Joint Trade Committee (JTC) talks were inaugurated. These led to the signing of a new trade and investment agreement, which took effect in January 1998. During 1999 Australia was critical of the continued detention and the trials of Anwar Ibrahim, the former Deputy Prime Minister and Minister of Finance (see the chapter on Malaysia). In early October 2002 the Australian Minister for Foreign Affairs met Myanma government officials and Myanma opposition leader Aung Sang Suu Kyi for discussions, during the first visit to Myanmar by an Australian minister for nearly 20 years.

The Howard Government's more aggressive stance towards South-East Asia in late 2002 led to a deterioration in relations with the region. In early December the Prime Minister stated that he would be prepared to conduct pre-emptive strikes on militant organizations in neighbouring countries suspected of planning terrorist attacks on Australia. Malaysia warned Australia that any incursion into Malaysia would be considered as an act of war.

Australia's relations with the People's Republic of China, meanwhile, continued to be strained by the issue of China's nuclear-testing programme, and deteriorated further in September 1996 when the Dalai Lama, the exiled spiritual leader of Tibet, was received in Sydney by the Prime Minister. In March 1997, however, the Australian Prime Minister began a six-day official visit to China, where he had discussions with Premier Li Peng. In July 1999, during a visit to Beijing by the Australian Minister of Foreign Affairs, Australia endorsed China's bid for membership of the World Trade Organization (WTO). The two countries also signed a bilateral trade pact. In September, however, President Jiang Zemin's visit to Australia was disrupted by pro-Tibet and Taiwan activists. Political and economic relations with China improved in the early 2000s, partly owing to Australia's refraining from criticizing China's human rights record. Australia's relations with Japan were strained in the late 1990s by a fishing dispute relating to the latter's failure to curb its catches of the endangered southern bluefin tuna, as agreed in a treaty of 1993, of which New Zealand was also a signatory. In August 1999, however, an international tribunal ruled in favour of Australia and New Zealand.

In May 2000 diplomatic relations between Australia and the Democratic People's Republic of Korea, which had been severed in 1975, were restored. Discussions between the two nations, initiated by the North Korean Government in April 1999, had been dominated by the International Atomic Energy Agency's concerns over nuclear facilities and long-range missile testing. The Australian Minister of Foreign Affairs paid an official two-day visit to Pyongyang in November 2000. He confirmed that six North Korean officials were expected to participate in a nuclear-safeguards training course in Australia. An Australian trade mission organized by Austrade, Australia's trade and investment promotion agency, visited North Korea in December; discussions were held with North Korean officials regarding problems in the country's energy sector. Australia and North Korea agreed to establish, within two years, embassies in their respective capitals when North Korea's Minister of Foreign Affairs paid Australia a reciprocal visit in June 2001. Furthermore, a Memorandum of Understanding was signed to facilitate co-operation between Australian and North Korean scientists in agricultural research, including the participation of North Korean scientists in research programmes and on-the-job training activities in Australian research institutes. Plans to open an embassy in North Korea were deferred in late 2002, however, owing to North Korea's efforts to reactivate its nuclear weapons programme.

The viability of the ANZUS military pact, which was signed in 1951, linking Australia, New Zealand and the USA, was disputed by the US Government following the New Zealand Government's declaration, in July 1984, that vessels which were believed to be powered by nuclear energy, or to be carrying nuclear weapons, would be barred from the country's ports. Hawke did not support the New Zealand initiative, and Australia continued to participate with the USA in joint military exercises from which New Zealand had been excluded. However, the Hawke Government declined directly to endorse the US action against New Zealand, and in 1986 stated that Australia regarded its 'obligations to New Zealand as constant and undiminishing'. In September 1990 Australia and New Zealand signed an agreement to establish a joint venture to construct as many as 12 naval frigates to patrol the South Pacific. In February 1994 the USA announced its decision to resume senior-level contacts with New Zealand. In July 1996 Australia and the USA upgraded their defence alliance. In 1999 Australia's trading relations with the USA were strained by the latter's imposition of tariffs on imports of Australian lamb. In October Australia urged that the dispute be settled by means of a WTO panel; in December 2000 the WTO upheld the complaint, ruling that the tariffs violated global trade rules. Meanwhile, in July 2000 the US Secretary of Defense made an official visit to Australia, following which he re-emphasized the importance of bilateral defence ties; and the Ministers for Foreign Affairs and Defence participated in the Australia-US Leadership Dialogue

in Washington. In September 2001 Prime Minister John Howard condemned the terrorist attacks suffered by the USA and promised Australia's full support for the offensive in Afghanistan. In 2002 John Howard expressed his support for the USA's 'war on terrorism' and in early 2003 deployed some 2,000 troops to the Middle East in preparation for the US-led military campaign to oust the regime of Saddam Hussein in Iraq, which commenced in March.

Owing to Australian opposition to French test explosions of nuclear weapons at Mururoa Atoll (French Polynesia) in the South Pacific Ocean, a ban on uranium sales to France was introduced in 1983. However, in August 1986 the Government announced its decision to resume uranium exports. In December Australia ratified a treaty declaring the South Pacific area a nuclear-free zone. France's decision, in April 1992, to suspend its nuclear-testing programme was welcomed by Australia. In June 1995, however, the French President's announcement that the programme was to be resumed provoked outrage throughout the Pacific region. The Australian ambassador to France was recalled, and the French consulate in Perth was destroyed in an arson attack. Further widespread protests followed the first of the new series of tests in September. Australia's relations with the UK were strained by the British Government's refusal to join the condemnation of France's policy. The final test was conducted in January 1996. On an official visit to Paris in September, the Australian Minister for Foreign Affairs adopted a conciliatory stance (which drew much criticism from anti-nuclear groups). A ban on new contracts for the supply of uranium to France, imposed in September 1995, was removed in October 1996. Meanwhile, Australia remained committed to achieving the elimination of all nuclear testing. In August, following a veto of the draft text by India and Iran at the UN Conference on Disarmament in Geneva, Australia took the initiative in leading an international effort to secure the passage of the Comprehensive Test Ban Treaty. In an unusual procedure, the Treaty was referred to the UN General Assembly, which voted overwhelmingly in its favour in September.

Relations with neighbouring Pacific island states were strained in mid-1997. In July Australia was embarrassed by the unauthorized publication of a secret official document in which certain regional politicians were described as corrupt and incompetent. At a meeting of the South Pacific Forum in September, the member countries failed to reach agreement on a common policy regarding mandatory targets for the reduction of emissions of the so-called 'greenhouse gases'. The low-lying nation of Tuvalu was particularly critical of Australia's refusal to compromise, the Australian Prime Minister declaring that the Pacific islands' concerns over rising sea levels were exaggerated. In July 2001 Australia declined Tuvalu's request to take in more Tuvaluan nationals. The Australian Government, committed to its 'Pacific solution', nevertheless made a verbal request of shelter for some of its many asylum-seekers to Tuvalu in November.

Australia's relations with Papua New Guinea were strained in early 1997 as a result of the latter's decision to engage the services of a group of mercenaries in the Government's operations against secessionists on the island of Bougainville. Fearing for the stability of the South Pacific region, the Australian Prime Minister denounced the use of foreign forces as unacceptable. In January 1998 a permanent cease-fire agreement between the Papua New Guinea Government and the Bougainville secessionists, which was to take effect in April, was signed in New Zealand. Australia reaffirmed its commitment to the provision of a peace-monitoring force. Since 1998 both Canberra and Townsville, in Queensland, had provided a neutral platform for rounds of negotiations regarding Bougainville's secession, and in August 2001 the Minister for Foreign Affairs, Alexander Downer, signed the Bougainville Peace Agreement as a witness. In October the Government concluded a deal with Papua New Guinea for it to house 223 asylum-seekers in exchange for $A1m.

Australia played a leading role in the events following a coup in Solomon Islands, which took place in June 2000. The Australian Navy dispatched a warship to assist in the evacuation of Australian and other nationals from the islands, while a similar ship anchored offshore served as a venue for negotiations between the two warring ethnic militias. The Australian Minister for Foreign Affairs led an international delegation with the aim of facilitating discussions between the factions. In October a peace agreement was signed in Townsville, which ended the two-year conflict; it was qualified and complemented by the

Marau Peace Agreement, signed in February 2001. The Australian Government subsequently led an International Peace Monitoring Team, in an attempt to ensure continued stability in the islands. In September Australia contributed $A1.6m. towards financing democratic elections, and technical support was provided by the Australian Electoral Commission.

Government

Australia comprises six states and three territories. Executive power is vested in the British monarch and exercised by the monarch's appointed representative, the Governor-General, who normally acts on the advice of the Federal Executive Council (the Ministry), led by the Prime Minister. The Governor-General appoints the Prime Minister and, on the latter's recommendation, other Ministers.

Legislative power is vested in the Federal Parliament. This consists of the monarch, represented by the Governor-General, and two chambers elected by universal adult suffrage (voting is compulsory). The Senate has 76 members (12 from each state and two each from the Northern Territory and the Australian Capital Territory), who are elected by a system of proportional representation for six years when representing a state, with half the seats renewable every three years, and for a term of three years when representing a territory. The House of Representatives has 150 members, elected for three years (subject to dissolution) from single-member constituencies. The Federal Executive Council is responsible to Parliament.

Each state has a Governor, representing the monarch, and its own legislative, executive and judicial system. The state governments are essentially autonomous, but certain powers are placed under the jurisdiction of the Federal Government. All states except Queensland have an Upper House (the Legislative Council) and a Lower House (the Legislative Assembly or House of Assembly). The chief ministers of the states are known as Premiers, as distinct from the Federal Prime Minister. The Northern Territory (self-governing since 1978) and the Australian Capital Territory (self-governing since 1988) have unicameral legislatures, and each has a government led by a Chief Minister. The Jervis Bay Territory is not self-governing.

Defence

Australia's defence policy is based on collective security, and it is a member of the British Commonwealth Strategic Reserve and of ANZUS, with New Zealand and the USA. Australia also participates in the Five-Power Defence Arrangements, with New Zealand, Malaysia, Singapore and the United Kingdom. In August 2002 Australia's armed forces numbered 50,920 (army 25,150, navy 12,570, air force 13,200). Defence expenditure for 2001/02 was budgeted at $A12,017m. Service in the armed forces is voluntary. In September 1999 Australia committed 4,500 troops to the peace-keeping operation in East Timor, where 1,315 remained in August 2002. In December 2000 the Government announced an increase in defence expenditure of some $A 13,000m. over the next decade. In October 2001 Australia committed 1,550 Australian servicemen and women to the International Coalition against Terrorism.

Economic Affairs

In 2001, according to estimates by the World Bank, Australia's gross national income (GNI), measured at average 1999–2001 prices, was US $383,291m., equivalent to US $19,770 per head (or US $25,780 per head on an international purchasing-power parity basis). During 1990–2001, it was estimated, the population increased at an average annual rate of 1.2%, while gross domestic product (GDP) per head increased, in real terms, by an average of 2.4%. Overall GDP increased, in real terms, at an average annual rate of 3.6% in 1990–2001. GDP expanded by 1.9% in 2000 and by 2.4% in 2001. GDP was forecast to increase by 3.7% in 2002.

Agriculture (including forestry, hunting and fishing) contributed 3% of GDP in 2002, and engaged 4.7% of the employed labour force in 2001. The principal crops are wheat, fruit, sugar and cotton. Australia is the world's leading producer of wool. Export earnings from greasy wool rose from $A2,103m. in 2000 to $A2,304m. in 2001. The export of wine is of increasing importance, rising from 10m. litres in 1986 to 471m. litres in 2002. The value of wine exports increased by 30% in 2002 to $A2,287m. Australia had thus become the world's fourth largest wine exporter. Beef production is also important, beef being Australia's leading meat export and contributing an estimated 15% of the value of gross farm output in 2001/02. Between 1990 and 1999 agricultural GDP increased at an average annual rate

of 3.0%, but it declined by 0.5%, compared with the previous year, in 1997, before rising by 7.5% in 1998. In 2002 agricultural production was severely affected by one of Australia's worst droughts in 100 years. By late October some 40,000 employees of the agricultural sector had lost their jobs, and in January 2003 Australia was forced to import grain for the first time since 1995. Wheat production was forecast to decline by almost 60% in 2002/03, to about 10m. metric tons. The recurrent problem of bush fires was exacerbated from late 2001 by the prolonged drought.

Industry (comprising mining, manufacturing, construction and utilities) employed 21.5% of the working population in 2001, and provided 25.7% of GDP in 1999/2000. Industrial GDP increased at an average rate of 2.8% per year between 1990 and 1999, growing by 4.0% in 1997 and by 1.9% in 1998.

The mining sector employed 0.9% of the working population in 2001, and contributed 4.9% of GDP in 2000/01. Australia is one of the world's leading exporters of coal. Earnings from coal and related products in 2000/01 reached $A10,840m., accounting for 9.1% of total export receipts in that year. The other principal minerals extracted are iron ore, gold, silver, petroleum and natural gas. Bauxite, zinc, copper, titanium, nickel, tin, lead, zirconium and diamonds are also mined. Between 1989/90 and 1996/97 the GDP of the mining sector increased at an average annual rate of 2.9%. Compared with the previous year, mining GDP rose by 9.8% in 1999/2000.

Manufacturing contributed 11.2% of GDP in 2000/01. The sector employed 12.5% of the working population in 2001. Measured by the value of sales, the principal branches of manufacturing in 1999/2000 were food, beverages and tobacco (22.1%), equipment and machinery (19.2%), metal products (17.9%), petroleum, coal and chemical products (15.6%), printing, publishing and recording (7.5%) and wood and paper products (6.1%). The manufacturing sector's GDP grew at an average annual rate of 2.0% between 1990 and 1999, increasing by 0.4% in 1997 and by 2.4% in 1998. Compared with the previous year, in 2000/01 the manufacturing sector's GDP grew by 5.0%.

Energy is derived principally from petroleum, natural gas and coal. Production of petroleum declined from 33,931m. litres in 1997/98 to 30,306m. litres in 1998/99, before increasing to 43,264m. litres in 2000/01. The production of black coal increased from 226.8m. tons in 1997/98 to 322m. tons in 2000/01.

The services sector provided 71.0% of GDP in 1999/2000, and engaged 73.7% of the employed labour force in 2001. The tourism industry has become Australia's second largest source of foreign-exchange earnings. The number of visitor arrivals increased from 4.5m. in 1999 to 4.8m. in 2002. Tourist receipts, however, declined from $A19,800m. in 2000 to an estimated $A15,344m. in 2001. It was estimated that in 2001 the tourism sector contributed 4.7% of GDP and accounted for 6.3% of total employment in 2000/01. The GDP of the services sector increased at an average annual rate of 4.3% between 1990 and 1998, rising by 5.2% in 1997 and by 5.3% in 1998.

In 2001 Australia recorded a visible trade surplus of US $1,874m., and there was a deficit of US $8,722m. on the current account of the balance of payments. In the year ending 30 June 2001 the principal source of imports was the USA (18.9%), followed by Japan (13.0%). Japan was the principal market for exports in that year (19.6%), followed by the USA (9.7%) and the Republic of Korea (7.7%). Other major trading partners are New Zealand, the United Kingdom, Singapore, Taiwan and the People's Republic of China. The principal exports were metalliferous ores (sales of gold being of increasing significance), coal, machinery, non-ferrous metals, textile fibres (mainly wool), and meat (mainly beef). The principal imports were machinery (mainly road vehicles and transport equipment), basic manufactures, and chemicals and related products.

In the 2001/02 financial year a budgetary deficit of about $A1,300m. was recorded. In mid-2002 Australia's net external debt stood at $A330,457m. An estimated average of 6.2% of the labour force were unemployed in December 2002. The annual rate of inflation averaged 2.4% in 1990–2001. Consumer prices rose by 1.5% in 1999, by 4.5% in 2000 and by 4.3% in 2001.

Australia is a member of the Asian Development Bank (ADB, see p. 143), the Pacific Islands Forum (see p. 306), the Pacific Community (see p. 304) (formerly the South Pacific Commission) and the Colombo Plan (see p. 339). In 1989 Australia played a major role in the creation of the Asia-Pacific Economic Co-operation group (APEC, see p. 139), which aimed to stimulate economic development in the region. Australia is also a member of the Organisation for Economic Co-operation and Development (OECD, see p. 277), of the Cairns Group (see p. 389) and of the International Grains Council (see p. 336).

Upon taking office in March 1996, the Howard Government confirmed its determination to achieve fiscal balance. One of the principal aims of the administration's programme was the transfer to the private sector of Telstra, the state-owned telecommunications company. The sale of one-third of the company's assets took place in November 1997, raising revenue of $A14,300m. and representing the most successful Australian flotation to date. In late 1999 a further 16.6% of Telstra's assets were sold. The Government also remained committed to the deregulation of the labour market. The 1999/2000 budget allocated additional funding (of $A800m.) to the biotechnology industry, the sector being regarded as a significant source of future economic growth. The 2000/01 budget provided for additional funding for rural communities. A total of $A1,800m. (of which $A562m. was to be allocated to regional health programmes) was to be released over the next four years. The budget also provided for personal tax cuts worth $A12,000m., which took effect in July 2000. In the same month the Government introduced the controversial 10% goods-and-services tax (GST). During 2000 Australia experienced a sharp increase in earnings from its commodity exports owing to a decline in the Australian dollar, which fell to its lowest level against the US dollar since its flotation in 1983. The economic benefits of this situation, however, were tempered by extensive damage to crops (most significantly the wheat crop) caused by drought in late 2000, followed by heavy rains and severe flooding. Between January and December 2001 the value of the Australian currency decreased by more than 8% against the US dollar. For the first time in six years, the Government announced a budget deficit in 2001/02, largely owing to the global economic slowdown, lower tax revenues and spending on the housing and deportation of 'illegal immigrants'. Despite the weak global economy and poor performance of the agricultural sector, as a result of drought, the Australian economy continued to expand. Tax reductions introduced by the 2001/02 budget contributed to a rise in disposable income; private consumption and the property sector also expanded. By the end of 2001 the Reserve Bank of Australia's rate of interest had been reduced to its lowest level for 28 years, standing at 4.25%, before rising to 4.75% in the second half of 2002. Employment experienced positive growth, and the rate of unemployment declined in 2002. The trend in employment growth was expected to continue in 2003, although at a slower pace. The Government predicted a budgetary surplus in 2002/03. The budget also introduced further tax relief schemes for families, as well as increased expenditure on defence, protecting Australia's borders, domestic security, health, aged care and welfare reform. The central bank estimated that the Australian economy had grown by an annualized rate of 3.7% in the year ending September 2002 and predicted

that in 2003 the rate of inflation would remain at a similar level to that reached in 2002. The economy was expected to grow by an average 3.75% in 2002/03. Meanwhile, the stagnation in international growth led to a deceleration in Australia's export trade. Tourist arrivals, furthermore, were badly affected by the repercussions of the terrorist attacks on the USA in September 2001 and on Bali in October 2002, and also by the outbreak of Severe Acute Respiratory Syndrome (SARS) in East Asia in early 2003, receipts declining sharply as a result.

Education

Education is the responsibility of each of the states and the Federal Government. It is compulsory, and available free of charge, for all children from the ages of six to 15 years (16 in Tasmania). Primary education generally begins at six years of age and lasts for six years. Secondary education, beginning at the age of 12, usually lasts for five years. As a proportion of children in the relevant age-groups, the enrolment ratios in 1997 were 95% in primary schools and 89% in 1996 in secondary schools. In 2000 there were 1,386,000 children enrolled in government primary schools and 862,500 in secondary schools, while 998,834 children were attending private schools (517,861 primary and 480,973 secondary). Special services have been developed to fulfil the requirements of children living in the remote 'outback' areas, notably Schools of the Air, using two-way receiver sets. A system of one-teacher schools and correspondence schools also helps to satisfy these needs. Under a major reform programme initiated in 1988, the binary system of universities and colleges of advanced education was replaced by a unified national system of fewer and larger institutions. In 2000 there were 42 publicly-funded institutions of higher education. In the same year students totalled 735,500. Most courses last from three to six years. Public expenditure on education in the financial year 2001/02 was $A11,761m. and was expected to provide for 5,500 more university places for information and communications technology, maths and science; and over 1,800 places in regional universities.

Public Holidays*

2003: 1 January (New Year's Day), 26 January (Australia Day), 18–21 April (Easter), 25 April (Anzac Day), 9 June (Queen's Official Birthday, except Western Australia), 25–26 December (Christmas Day, Boxing Day).

2004: 1 January (New Year's Day), 26 January (Australia Day), 9–12 April (Easter), 25 April (Anzac Day), 14 June (Queen's Official Birthday, except Western Australia), 25–26 December (Christmas Day, Boxing Day).

*National holidays only. Some states observe these holidays on different days. There are also numerous individual state holidays.

Weights and Measures

The metric system is in force.

Statistical Survey

Source (unless otherwise stated): Australian Bureau of Statistics, POB 10, Belconnen, ACT 2616; tel. (2) 6252-7911; fax (2) 6251-6009; internet www.abs .gov.au.

Area and Population

AREA, POPULATION AND DENSITY

Area (sq km)	7,692,030*
Population (census results)†	
6 August 1996	17,892,423
7 August 2001	
Males	9,362,021
Females	9,610,329
Total	18,972,350
Population (official estimates at mid-year)†	
1999	18,937,200
2000	19,157,100
2001	19,386,700
Density (per sq km) at mid-2001	2.5

* 2,969,909 sq miles.

† Census results exclude, and estimates include, an adjustment for under-enumeration, estimated to have been 1.9% in 1991. Estimates also exclude overseas visitors in Australia and include Australian residents temporarily overseas. The estimates shown above have not been revised to take account of the August 2001 census result. The adjusted estimate for mid-2001 is 19,485,278 (density 2.5 per sq km).

STATES AND TERRITORIES

(30 June 2001)

	Area (sq km)	Estimated Population	Density (per sq km)
New South Wales (NSW) . .	800,640	6,609,304	8.3
Victoria	227,420	4,822,663	21.2
Queensland	1,730,650	3,635,121	2.1
South Australia . . .	983,480	1,514,854	1.5
Western Australia . . .	2,529,880	1,906,114	0.8
Tasmania	68,400	472,931	6.9
Northern Territory . . .	1,349,130	200,019	0.1
Australian Capital Territory (ACT) . .	2,360	321,680	136.3
Jervis Bay Territory . . .	70	n.a.	n.a.
Total	7,692,030	19,485,278*	2.5

* Includes populations of Jervis Bay Territory, Christmas Island and the Cocos (Keeling) Islands.

PRINCIPAL TOWNS

(estimated population at 30 June 2000)*

Canberra (national capital) . . .	310,500	Gold Coast-Tweed . .	404,300
Sydney (capital of NSW) . .	4,085,600	Wollongong . . .	264,400
Melbourne (capital of Victoria) . .	3,466,000	Hobart (capital of Tasmania) . .	194,200
Brisbane (capital of Queensland) .	1,626,900	Sunshine Coast . .	178,000
Perth (capital of W Australia) . .	1,381,100	Geelong . . .	157,900
Adelaide (capital of S Australia) . .	1,096,100	Townsville . . .	130,000
Newcastle . . .	483,300	Cairns . . .	115,600

* Figures refer to metropolitan areas, each of which normally comprises a municipality and contiguous urban areas.

BIRTHS, MARRIAGES AND DEATHS*

	Registered live births		Registered marriages		Registered deaths	
	Number	Rate (per 1,000)	Number	Rate (per 1,000)	Number	Rate (per 1,000)
1993 . .	260,229	14.7	113,255	6.4	121,599	6.9
1994 . .	258,051	14.5	111,174	6.2	126,692	7.1
1995 . .	256,190	14.2	109,386	6.1	125,133	6.9
1996 . .	253,834	13.9	106,103	5.8	128,719	7.0
1997 . .	251,842	13.5	106,735	5.8	129,350	6.9
1998 . .	249,616	13.3	110,598	5.9	127,202	6.8
1999 . .	248,870	13.1	114,316	6.0	128,102	6.8
2000 . .	249,636	13.0	113,400†	5.9	128,300†	6.7

* Data are tabulated by year of registration rather than by year of occurrence.

† Figures are rounded.

Expectation of life (WHO estimates, years at birth): 80.0 (males 77.4; females 82.6) in 2001 (Source: WHO, *World Health Report*).

IMMIGRATION AND EMIGRATION

(year ending 30 June)*

	1998/99	1999/2000	2001/02†
Permanent immigrants	84,143	92,272	88,900
Permanent emigrants	35,181	41,078	48,241

* Figures refer to persons intending to settle in Australia, or Australian residents intending to settle abroad.

† Figures for 2000/01 not yet available.

Source: Department of Immigration and Multicultural and Indigenous Affairs, Belconnen.

ECONOMICALLY ACTIVE POPULATION

(annual averages, '000 persons aged 15 years and over, excluding armed forces)

	1999	2000*	2001*
Agriculture, forestry and fishing .	431.9	437.5	428.8
Mining	76.4	78.2	78.3
Manufacturing	1,073.0	1,113.1	1,129.8
Electricity, gas and water supply .	64.6	64.5	65.7
Construction	663.1	695.4	681.3
Wholesale trade	522.1	494.9	438.7
Retail trade	1,322.5	1,324.6	1,331.2
Accommodation, cafés and restaurants	417.6	432.8	469.0
Transport and storage . . .	414.3	407.3	421.2
Communication services . . .	154.6	169.3	182.6
Finance and insurance . . .	315.3	327.5	337.3
Property and business services . .	961.5	988.7	1,081.0
Government administration and defence	349.5	345.8	365.8
Education	612.2	609.3	621.1
Health and community services .	814.5	828.1	874.8
Cultural and recreational services .	212.5	217.1	225.2
Personal and other services . .	341.9	352.3	342.5
Total employed	8,747.4	8,886.5	9,074.3
Unemployed	684.4	661.4	625.5
Total labour force (incl. others)	9,467.1	9,577.9	9,755.4
Males	5,359.6	5,398.6	5,471.8
Females	4,107.5	4,179.3	4,283.6

* Year ending June.

Source: *ABS Labour Force Australia*.

Health and Welfare

KEY INDICATORS

Total fertility rate (children per woman, 2001)	1.8
Under-5 mortality rate (per 1,000 live births, 2000) . . .	7
HIV/AIDS (% of persons aged 15–49, 2001)	0.07
Physicians (per 1,000 head, 1998)	2.40
Hospital beds (per 1,000 head, 1998)	8.5
Health expenditure (2000): US $ per head (PPP) . . .	2,213
Health expenditure (2000): % of GDP	8.3
Health expenditure (2000): public (% of total)	72.4
Access to water (% of persons, 2000)	100
Access to sanitation (% of persons, 2000)	100
Human Development Index (2000): ranking	5
Human Development Index (2000): value	0.939

For sources and definitions, see explanatory note on p. vi.

Agriculture

PRINCIPAL CROPS

('000 metric tons)

	1999	2000	2001
Wheat	25,012	22,190	23,760
Rice (paddy)	1,390	1,101	1,760
Barley	5,043	6,819	7,459
Maize	338	406	355
Oats	1,118	1,131	1,222
Millet	43*	57	60*
Sorghum	1,891	2,116	2,107
Triticale (wheat-rye hybrid) . .	764	764	532
Potatoes	1,327	1,200	1,250*
Sugar cane	38,534	38,165	31,228
Dry broad beans	226	253	200*
Dry peas	357	401	416
Chick-peas	230	146	258
Lentils	103	163	180*
Vetches	53	24	24*
Lupins	1,968	800	1,104
Soybeans (Soya beans) . . .	109	105	62
Sunflower seed	209	147	170
Rapeseed	2,426	1,905	172†
Cottonseed	1,047	1,124	968
Cabbages	59	69	60*
Lettuce.	131	152	145*
Tomatoes	394	414	425*
Cauliflower	113	116	120*
Pumpkins, squash and gourds . .	107	124	115*
Chillies and green peppers . .	41	44	50*
Dry onions	224	247	250*
Green peas	66	67	65*
Carrots	257	283	265*
Green corn	57	45	55*
Watermelons	66	85	86*
Cantaloupes and other melons .	101	87	87*
Grapes.	1,266	1,343	1,551
Apples	334	320	290†
Pears	157	156	175†
Peaches and nectarines . .	93	86	90*
Oranges	446	510	624
Tangerines, mandarins, clementines and satsumas . .	78	85	116
Pineapples	131	139	140*
Bananas	225	257	275*
Cotton (lint)	741	795	684

* FAO estimate.
† Unofficial figure.

Source: FAO.

LIVESTOCK

('000 head at 31 March)

	1999	2000	2001
Horses*	220	220	220
Cattle	26,578	27,588	28,768
Pigs	2,626	2,433	2,763
Sheep	115,456	118,552	116,200
Goats*	220	220	200
Chickens	91,472	85,000	98,000*
Ducks*	400	400	400
Turkeys*	1,300	1,300	1,300

* FAO estimate(s).

Source: FAO.

LIVESTOCK PRODUCTS

('000 metric tons)

	1999	2000	2001
Beef and veal	2,010.5	1,987.9	2,119.0
Mutton and lamb. . . .	628.4	680.0	715.0
Goat meat*	8.1	10.6	8.1
Pig meat	369.9	362.9	365.2
Horse meat*	21.3	21.3	21.3
Chicken meat	575.0	610.0	630.0
Duck meat	7.7	8.0	8.2*
Turkey meat*	22.8	22.8	22.8
Cows' milk	10,490†	11,183	10,875
Butter	176	170	151
Cheese	335.4	369.2	376.0
Hen eggs†	173.4	143.0	180.0
Honey	18.9	21.4	21.4*
Wool: greasy	671	652	587
Wool: scoured	437†	437*	437*
Cattle hides (fresh)* . . .	230	230	230
Sheepskins (fresh)* . . .	140.4	149.1	158.7

* FAO estimate(s).
† Unofficial figure(s).
Note: Figures for meat and milk refer to the 12 months ending 30 June of the year stated.

Source: FAO.

Forestry

ROUNDWOOD REMOVALS

('000 cubic metres, excl. bark)

	1999	2000	2001
Sawlogs, veneer logs and logs for sleepers	10,043	11,005	10,727
Pulpwood	9,840	12,345	12,814
Other industrial wood . . .	704	692	667
Fuel wood*	5,974	6,333	6,707
Total	26,561	30,375	30,915

* FAO estimates.

Source: FAO.

SAWNWOOD PRODUCTION

('000 cubic metres, incl. railway sleepers)

	1999	2000	2001
Coniferous (softwood) . . .	2,338	2,637	2,351
Broadleaved (hardwood). . .	1,335	1,346	1,174
Total	3,673	3,983	3,525

Source: FAO.

Fishing

('000 metric tons, live weight, year ending 30 June)

	1997/98	1998/99	1999/2000
Capture	205.4	216.3	211.4
Blue grenadier	4.8	6.2	9.4
Orange roughy	12.3	12.3	9.2
Skipjack tuna	3.1	9.6	7.4
Sharks, rays, skates, etc.	10.5	10.2	8.8
Australian spiny lobster	10.4	15.8	17.3
Penaeus shrimps	24.4	24.5	20.3
Scallops	9.9	11.6	10.9
Aquaculture	28.1	33.7	39.9
Atlantic salmon	7.1	9.2	10.9
Southern bluefin tuna	5.1	6.4	7.8
Total catch	233.5	250.1	251.3

Note: Figures exclude aquatic plants ('000 metric tons, capture only): 20.8 in 1998; 20.8 in 1999; 13.7 in 2000. Also excluded are crocodiles, recorded by number rather than by weight. The number of Estuarine crocodiles caught was: 9,896 in 1998; 5,048 in 1999; 13,296 in 2000. The number of Australian crocodiles caught was: 309 in 1998; 44 in 1999; 10 in 2000. Also excluded are pearl oyster shells (FAO estimates, metric tons): 250 in 1998; 250 in 1999; 250 in 2000.

Source: FAO, *Yearbook of Fishery Statistics*.

Mining

('000 metric tons, unless otherwise indicated)

	1998	1999	2000
Hard coal	285,000	293,000	301,000
Lignite	63,900	66,000	65,000
Crude petroleum ('000 barrels)	225,935	226,665	208,472
Natural gas (million cu metres)	30,364	30,743	30,794
Iron ore: gross weight	155,731	151,558	170,999
Iron ore: metal content	99,418	93,807	106,232
Copper ore*	607	739	830
Nickel ore (metric tons)*	143,513	127,000	168,300
Bauxite	44,553	48,416	53,802
Lead ore*	619	681	678
Zinc ore*	1,066	1,163	1,410
Tin ore (metric tons)*	10,174	10,011	9,146
Manganese ore (metallurgical): gross weight	1,500	1,900	1,613
Manganese ore (metallurgical): metal content	729	929	787
Chromite	80	70	90
Ilmenite	2,425	1,989	2,156
Leucoxene	31	31	27
Rutile	243	190	237
Tantalum and niobium (columbium) concentrates (metric tons)‡	1,150	1,230	1,600
Zirconium concentrates	369	359	373
Antimony ore (metric tons)*	1,800†	1,679	1,511
Cobalt ore (metric tons)*†	4,000	7,000	5,100
Silver (metric tons)*	1,474	1,720	2,060
Uranium (metric tons)*§	4,885	5,979	7,578
Gold (kilograms)*	310,070	301,070	296,410
Limestone†	12,000	12,000	12,000
Bertonite and bentonitic clay†	104	180	180
Kaolin and ball clay†	180	200	220
Brick clay and shale†	8,000	8,000	8,000
Magnesite (metric tons)	360,115	280,505	349,783
Phosphate rock‖	1†	1†	805
Barite (Barytes)†	13	18	20
Salt (unrefined)	9,033	10,022	8,798
Gypsum (crude)†	1,900	2,500	3,800
Talc (metric tons)¶	199,315	190,037	178,545
Pyrophyllite (metric tons)¶	702	347	1,727
Diamonds ('000 carats): gem	18,379	16,381	14,656
Diamonds ('000 carats): industrial	22,464	13,403	11,992

* Figures refer to the metal content of ores and concentrates.

† Estimated production.

‡ The estimated metal content (in metric tons) was: Niobium (Columbium) 140 in 1998, 140 in 1999, 160 in 2000; Tantalum 330 in 1998, 350 in 1999, 485 in 2000.

§ Data from the World Nuclear Association (London, United Kingdom).

‖ The estimated phosphoric acid content (in '000 metric tons) was 28% in 2000.

¶ Production during 12 months ending 30 June of the year stated.

Source (unless otherwise indicated): US Geological Survey.

Industry

SELECTED PRODUCTS
(year ending 30 June, '000 metric tons, unless otherwise indicated)

	1997/98	1998/99	1999/2000
Pig-iron	7,928	7,453	6,489
Blooms and slabs from continuous casting	8,356	7,698	6,742
Aluminium—unwrought*	1,589	1,686	1,742
Copper—unwrought	286	313	477
Lead—unwrought*	185	199	233
Zinc—unwrought*	304	323	405
Tin—unwrought (metric tons)*	650	595	600
Motor spirit (petrol—million litres)	18,592	18,705	18,652
Fuel oil (million litres)	1,673	1,634	1,839
Diesel-automotive oil (million litres)	13,183	12,968	12,737
Aviation turbine fuel (million litres)	5,423	5,219	5,538
Clay bricks (million)	1,532	1,594	1,735
Woven cotton fabrics (incl. towelling, '000 sq metres)†	62,000	56,000	n.a.
Woven woollen fabrics (incl. blanketing, '000 sq metres)†	6,600	6,300	n.a.
Electricity (million kWh)	176,212	179,630	184,790
Cement	7,236	7,704	7,937
Concrete—ready-mixed ('000 cu m)	17,412	18,601	20,597
Newsprint	402	400	381
Wheat flour†	1,762	1,857	n.a.
Beer (million litres)	1,757	1,729	1,768
Tobacco and cigarettes (metric tons)	21,257	21,045	20,688

* Primary refined metal only.
† Source: UN, *Industrial Commodity Statistics Yearbook*.

2001/02: Wine (million litres) 1,174 (Source: Australian Wine and Brandy Corporation).

Finance

CURRENCY AND EXCHANGE RATES

Monetary Units
100 cents = 1 Australian dollar ($A)

Sterling, US Dollar and Euro Equivalents (31 December 2002)
£1 sterling = $A2.8467
US $1 = $A1.7662
€1 = $A1.8522
$A100 = £35.13 = US $56.62 = €53.99

Average Exchange Rate (US $ per Australian dollar)
2000   0.5823
2001   0.5176
2002   0.5439

COMMONWEALTH GOVERNMENT BUDGET
($A million, year ending 30 June)

Revenue	1999/2000	2000/01	2001/02
Tax revenue	152,457	151,156	149,848
Direct taxes	113,687	120,861	119,032
Individuals	83,161	76,599	86,422
Companies	23,982	35,136	27,133
Indirect taxes, etc.	33,534	25,601	25,634
Non-tax revenue	17,465	10,369	12,540
Total	169,921	161,526	162,388

Expenditure	1999/2000	2000/01	2001/02
Defence	9,956	11,360	12,017
Education	10,587	10,966	11,761
Health	23,540	25,242	27,614
Social security and welfare	57,129	66,898	69,081
Economic services	7,924	9,940	12,971
General public services	19,131	11,923	12,097
Public-debt interest	9,493	5,836	4,995
Total (incl. others)	160,408	156,783	166,482

Source: Reserve Bank of Australia, *Bulletin*.

OFFICIAL RESERVES
(US $ million at 31 December)

	2000	2001	2002
Gold*	699	709	878
IMF special drawing rights	94	109	136
Reserve position in IMF	1,243	1,412	1,934
Foreign exchange	16,782	16,434	18,618
Total	18,817	18,664	21,567

* Valued at market-related prices.

Source: IMF, *International Financial Statistics*.

MONEY SUPPLY
($A million at 31 December)

	1999	2000	2001
Currency outside banks	24,604	26,928	28,471
Demand deposits at trading and savings banks	101,179	110,660	138,456
Total money (incl. others)	125,945	137,720	167,035

Source: IMF, *International Financial Statistics*.

COST OF LIVING
(Consumer Price Index*; base 1990 = 100)

	1999	2000	2001
Food	126.4	129.5	138.0
Electricity, gas and other fuels†	120.0	126.2	133.3
Clothing	103.7	106.8	109.3
Rent‡	94.7	101.2	106.0
All items (incl. others)	119.1	124.4	129.8

* Weighted average of eight capital cities.
† From September 1998 including water and sewerage.
‡ Including expenditure on maintenance and repairs of dwellings; from September 1998 excluding mortgage interest charges and including house purchase and utilities.

Source: ILO.

NATIONAL ACCOUNTS
($A million, year ending 30 June)

National Income and Product
(at current prices)

	1997/98	1998/99	1999/2000
Compensation of employees	270,267	286,761	303,134
Operating surplus	143,093	146,791	159,384
Domestic factor incomes	413,360	433,552	462,518
Consumption of fixed capital	87,621	91,509	97,531
Gross domestic product (GDP) at factor cost	500,981	525,061	560,049
Indirect taxes *Less* Subsidies	64,900	70,356	72,093
GDP in purchasers' values	565,881	595,417	632,141
Net factor income from abroad	−17,955	−18,328	−18,591
Gross national product	547,926	577,089	613,550
Less Consumption of fixed capital	87,621	91,509	97,531
National income in market prices	460,305	485,580	516,019

Expenditure on the Gross Domestic Product
(at current prices)

	1997/98	1998/99	1999/2000
Government final consumption expenditure	103,045	108,733	117,773
Private final consumption expenditure	333,407	353,757	373,313
Increase in stocks	960	5,307	2,062
Gross fixed capital formation	133,215	142,230	151,103
Statistical discrepancy	—	—	2,739
Total domestic expenditure	570,627	610,027	644,251
Exports of goods and services	113,829	111,843	125,774
Less Imports of goods and services	118,575	126,453	140,954
GDP in purchasers' values	565,881	595,417	631,810

Gross Domestic Product by Economic Activity
(provisional, at constant prices)

	1997/98*	1998/99†	1999/2000‡
Agriculture, hunting, forestry and fishing	16,668	19,044	19,005
Mining and quarrying	23,769	23,873	26,183
Manufacturing	65,878	73,800	75,560
Electricity, gas and water . . .	14,292	13,496	11,314
Construction	30,003	34,334	34,434
Wholesale and retail trade . .	61,519	62,366	66,679
Transport, storage and communications	49,129	50,317	54,049
Finance, insurance, real estate and business services . .	92,060	97,243	114,389
Ownership of dwellings . .	49,169	52,961	55,603
Public administration and defence	23,185	22,906	22,702
Other community, recreational and personal services (incl. restaurants and hotels) . .	88,849	96,419	95,079
Sub-total	514,522	546,759	574,997
Taxes on products . . . }	42,734	42,680	48,303
Less subsidies on products . }			
Statistical discrepancy . .	−333	2,107	−2,347
GDP in purchasers' values .	556,923	591,546	620,963

* At constant 1996/97 prices.

† At constant 1997/98 prices.

‡ At constant 1998/99 prices.

BALANCE OF PAYMENTS
(US $ million)

	1999	2000	2001
Exports of goods f.o.b. . . .	56,096	64,052	63,676
Imports of goods f.o.b. . . .	−65,826	−68,752	−61,802
Trade balance	−9,730	−4,699	1,874
Exports of services . . .	17,354	18,536	16,355
Imports of services . . .	−18,304	−18,100	−16,722
Balance on goods and services .	−10,680	−4,263	1,507
Other income received . . .	6,909	8,988	7,981
Other income paid	−19,211	−19,800	−18,232
Balance on goods, services and income	−22,983	−15,075	−8,743
Current transfers received . .	3,003	2,622	2,242
Current transfers paid . . .	−3,032	−2,669	−2,221
Current balance	−23,012	−15,123	−8,722
Capital account (net) . . .	819	615	591
Direct investment abroad . .	2,989	−732	−11,024
Direct investment from abroad . .	5,699	12,697	4,232
Portfolio investment assets . .	−6,443	−12,369	−9,107
Portfolio investment liabilities . .	17,224	15,000	18,616
Financial derivatives assets . .	247	−1,213	195
Financial derivatives liabilities .	1,054	390	277
Other investment assets . .	−2,907	−4,223	126
Other investment liabilities . .	10,105	2,399	4,384
Net errors and omissions . .	929	1,194	1,529
Overall balance	6,705	−1,365	1,096

Source: IMF, *International Financial Statistics*.

External Trade

PRINCIPAL COMMODITIES
($A million, year ending 30 June)

Imports f.o.b.	1998/99	1999/2000	2000/01
Food and live animals . .	3,760	3,954	4,236
Mineral fuels, lubricants, etc. .	4,621	7,680	10,473
Petroleum, petroleum products, etc.	4,524	7,516	10,295
Chemicals and related products	11,435	12,497	14,200
Medicinal and pharmaceutical products.	3,041	3,520	4,371
Basic manufactures . . .	12,855	13,654	14,055
Machinery and transport equipment	45,418	51,442	53,492
Machinery specialized for particular industries . . .	4,234	4,153	3,835
General industrial machinery, equipment and parts . .	5,770	5,398	5,729
Office machines and automatic data-processing machines . .	7,104	7,589	8,317
Telecommunications and sound-recording and reproducing apparatus and equipment . .	4,926	6,773	7,938
Other electrical machinery, apparatus, appliances and parts	5,870	6,213	6,782
Road vehicles (incl. air-cushion vehicles) and parts* . . .	11,904	12,784	14,346
Other transport equipment and parts*	2,848	5,432	3,409
Miscellaneous manufactured articles	14,463	15,479	16,804
Total (incl. others)	97,611	110,078	118,264

* Data on parts exclude tyres, engines and electrical parts.

Exports f.o.b.	1998/99	1999/2000	2000/01
Food and live animals . . .	15,453	16,892	20,115
Meat and meat preparations . .	4,000	4,467	5,772
Cereals and cereal preparations .	5,041	4,940	5,405
Crude materials (inedible) except fuels	17,219	18,381	23,592
Textile fibres and waste* . .	4,070	4,299	5,590
Metalliferous ores and metal scrap	10,665	11,314	14,761
Mineral fuels, lubricants, etc. .	14,162	18,083	25,211
Coal, coke and briquettes . . .	9,302	8,337	10,840
Petroleum, petroleum products, etc.	3,133	7,145	10,868
Chemicals and related products	3,575	4,195	5,146
Basic manufactures . . .	10,117	12,328	14,011
Non-ferrous metals	5,399	7,395	9,398
Machinery and transport equipment	10,324	11,619	13,408
Road vehicles (incl. air-cushion vehicles) and parts† . . .	2,091	2,808	3,833
Miscellaneous manufactured articles	3,447	3,826	4,455
Non-monetary gold (excl. gold ores and concentrates) . .	6,335	5,031	5,110
Total (incl. others)	85,991	97,286	119,602

* Excluding wool tops.

† Data on parts exclude tyres, engines and electrical parts.

PRINCIPAL TRADING PARTNERS
($A million, year ending 30 June)

Imports f.o.b.	1998/99	1999/2000	2000/01
Canada	1,547	1,848	1,866
China, People's Republic	6,106	7,515	9,881
France	2,202	2,228	2,478
Germany	6,082	5,791	6,174
Hong Kong	1,228	1,280	1,367
Indonesia	3,275	2,701	3,277
Ireland	1,000	937	1,140
Italy	2,916	3,043	3,259
Japan	13,587	14,110	15,371
Korea, Republic	3,894	4,311	4,710
Malaysia	2,845	3,765	4,177
New Zealand	3,950	4,372	4,565
Papua New Guinea	781	1,353	1,457
Saudi Arabia	532	1,002	1,613
Singapore	2,944	4,359	3,898
Sweden	1,575	1,646	1,624
Switzerland	1,092	1,279	1,171
Taiwan	2,978	3,244	3,327
Thailand	1,902	2,422	2,780
United Kingdom	5,545	6,350	6,321
USA	20,893	22,135	22,356
Viet Nam	972	1,726	2,431
Total (incl. others)	97,611	110,078	118,264

Exports f.o.b.	1998/99	1999/2000	2000/01
Belgium-Luxembourg	1,085	1,089	1,003
Canada	1,274	1,175	1,768
China, People's Republic	3,748	4,959	6,846
France	914	871	1,079
Germany	1,409	1,245	1,490
Hong Kong	3,071	3,211	3,904
India	1,837	1,588	2,086
Indonesia	2,199	2,408	3,119
Italy	1,564	1,575	2,100
Japan	16,566	18,822	23,479
Korea, Republic	6,320	7,615	9,209
Malaysia	1,859	2,141	2,506
Netherlands	866	1,378	1,738
New Zealand	5,838	6,739	6,872
Papua New Guinea	1,014	927	1,050
Philippines	1,208	1,304	1,495
Saudi Arabia	1,060	1,334	2,196
Singapore	3,417	4,855	5,997
South Africa	943	1,039	1,296
Taiwan	4,202	4,696	5,871
Thailand	1,306	1,703	2,219
United Kingdom	4,473	4,158	4,639
USA	7,983	9,602	11,654
Total (incl. others)	85,991	97,286	119,602

Transport

RAILWAYS
(traffic)

	1997/98	1998/99	1999/2000
Passengers carried (million)	587.7	595.2	629.2
Freight carried (millon metric tons)	487.5	492.0	508.0
Freight ton-km ('000 million)	125.2	127.4	134.2

* Traffic on government railways only.

ROAD TRAFFIC
('000 vehicles registered at 31 October)

	1997	1998	1999
Passenger vehicles	9,206.2	9,526.7	9,719.9
Light commercial vehicles	1,632.2	1,686.4	1,721.2
Trucks	418.4	426.9	427.8
Buses	61.1	64.0	65.9
Motorcycles	313.1	328.8	333.8

SHIPPING

Merchant Fleet
(registered at 31 December)

	1999	2000	2001
Number of vessels	621	631	622
Total displacement ('000 grt)	2,084.2	1,912.1	1,887.8

Source: Lloyd's Register-Fairplay, *World Fleet Statistics*.

International Sea-borne Traffic
('000 metric tons, year ending 30 June)

	1998/99	1999/2000	2000/01
Goods loaded	438,816	487,500	497,436
Goods unloaded	57,612	54,180	56,316

Source: UN, *Monthly Bulletin of Statistics*.

CIVIL AVIATION
(traffic)*

	1997	1998	1999
International services:			
Passenger arrivals	7,090,979	7,153,514	7,540,535
Passenger departures	7,010,931	7,084,655	7,442,226
Freight carried (metric tons)	649,371	631,908	680,458
Mail carried (metric tons)	21,975	23,437	25,316
Domestic services†:			
Passengers carried	23,375,317	23,574,788	24,375,906
Passenger-km ('000)	26,357,069	26,774,140	27,842,795
Freight and mail carried (metric tons)	190,680	192,770	192,326

* Includes Christmas Island and Norfolk Island.
† Year ending 30 June.

Tourism

VISITOR ARRIVALS BY COUNTRY OF ORIGIN*

	2000	2001	2002
China, People's Republic	120,300	158,000	190,000
Germany	143,300	147,600	134,800
Hong Kong	154,100	154,200	150,900
Indonesia	98,100	97,900	89,400
Japan	721,000	673,600	715,500
Korea, Republic	157,400	175,600	189,700
Malaysia	152,100	149,400	159,000
New Zealand	817,000	814,900	790,100
Singapore	285,700	296,000	286,900
Taiwan	134,300	110,100	97,400
United Kingdom	580,400	617,200	642,700
USA	488,100	446,400	434,500
Total (incl. others)	4,931,400	4,855,700	4,841,200

* Visitors intending to stay for less than one year.

Receipts from tourism ($A million): 17,000 in 1999; 19,800 in 2000.

Source: Australian Tourist Commission, Sydney.

Communications Media

	1999	2000	2001
Television receivers ('000 in use) .	13,400	14,129	n.a.
Telephones ('000 main lines in use)	9,760	10,050	10,060
Mobile cellular telephones ('000 subscribers).	6,315	8,562	11,169
Personal computers ('000 in use) .	7,900	8,900	10,000
Internet users ('000).	5,600	6,600	7,200

Source: International Telecommunication Union.

Radio receivers ('000 in use, 1997): 25,500.

Facsimile machines ('000 in use, 1997): 900.

Book production (1994): 10,835 titles.

Newspapers (1996): 65 dailies (estimated combined circulation 5,370,000); 98 non-dailies (circulation 383,000).

Source: mainly UNESCO, *Statistical Yearbook*.

Education

(August 2001)

	Institutions	Teaching staff	Students ('000)
Government schools	6,942	152,138*	2,248.2†
Non-government schools . .	2,654	69,789*	1,019.9
Higher educational institutions	47‡	78,228	726.4

* Full-time teaching staff and full-time equivalent of part-time teaching staff.

† Comprising 1,384,866 primary and 863,353 secondary students.

‡ Public institutions only.

Directory

The Constitution

The Federal Constitution was adopted on 9 July 1900 and came into force on 1 January 1901. Its main provisions are summarized below:

PARLIAMENT

The legislative power of the Commonwealth of Australia is vested in a Federal Parliament, consisting of HM the Queen (represented by the Governor-General), a Senate, and a House of Representatives. The Governor-General may appoint such times for holding the sessions of the Parliament as he or she thinks fit, and may also from time to time, by proclamation or otherwise, prorogue the Parliament, and may in like manner dissolve the House of Representatives. By convention, these powers are exercised on the advice of the Prime Minister. After any general election Parliament must be summoned to meet not later than 30 days after the day appointed for the return of the writs.

THE SENATE

The Senate is composed of 12 senators from each state, two senators representing the Australian Capital Territory and two representing the Northern Territory. The senators are directly chosen by the people of the state or territory, voting in each case as one electorate, and are elected by proportional representation. Senators representing a state have a six-year term and retire by rotation, one-half from each state on 30 June of each third year. The term of a senator representing a territory is limited to three years. In the case of a state, if a senator vacates his or her seat before the expiration of the term of service, the houses of parliament of the state for which the senator was chosen shall, in joint session, choose a person to hold the place until the expiration of the term or until the election of a successor. If the state parliament is not in session, the Governor of the state, acting on the advice of the state's executive council, may appoint a senator to hold office until parliament reassembles, or until a new senator is elected.

The Senate may proceed to the dispatch of business notwithstanding the failure of any state to provide for its representation in the Senate.

THE HOUSE OF REPRESENTATIVES

In accordance with the Australian Constitution, the total number of members of the House of Representatives must be as nearly as practicable double that of the Senate. The number in each state is in proportion to population, but under the Constitution must be at least five. The House of Representatives is composed of 150 members, including two members for the Australian Capital Territory and two members for the Northern Territory.

Members are elected by universal adult suffrage and voting is compulsory. Only Australian citizens are eligible to vote in Australian elections. British subjects, if they are not Australian citizens or already on the rolls, have to take out Australian citizenship before thay can enrol and before they can vote.

Members are chosen by the electors of their respective electorates by the preferential voting system.

The duration of the Parliament is limited to three years.

To be nominated for election to the House of Representatives, a candidate must be 18 years of age or over, an Australian citizen, and entitled to vote at the election or qualified to become an elector.

THE EXECUTIVE GOVERNMENT

The executive power of the Federal Government is vested in the Queen, and is exercisable by the Governor-General, advised by an Executive Council of Ministers of State, known as the Federal Executive Council. These ministers are, or must become within three months, members of the Federal Parliament.

The Australian Constitution is construed as subject to the principles of responsible government and the Governor-General acts on the advice of the ministers in relation to most matters.

THE JUDICIAL POWER

See Judicial System, below.

THE STATES

The Australian Constitution safeguards the Constitution of each state by providing that it shall continue as at the establishment of the Commonwealth, except as altered in accordance with its own provisions. The legislative power of the Federal Parliament is limited in the main to those matters that are listed in section 51 of the Constitution, while the states possess, as well as concurrent powers in those matters, residual legislative powers enabling them to legislate in any way for 'the peace, order and good Government' of their respective territories. When a state law is inconsistent with a law of the Commonwealth, the latter prevails, and the former is invalid to the extent of the inconsistency.

The states may not, without the consent of the Commonwealth, raise or maintain naval or military forces, or impose taxes on any property belonging to the Commonwealth of Australia, nor may the Commonwealth tax state property. The states may not coin money.

The Federal Parliament may not enact any law for establishing any religion or for prohibiting the exercise of any religion, and no religious test may be imposed as a qualification for any office under the Commonwealth.

The Commonwealth of Australia is charged with protecting every state against invasion, and, on the application of a state executive government, against domestic violence.

Provision is made under the Constitution for the admission of new states and for the establishment of new states within the Commonwealth of Australia.

ALTERATION OF THE CONSTITUTION

Proposed laws for the amendment of the Constitution must be passed by an absolute majority in both Houses of the Federal Parliament, and not less than two or more than six months after its passage through both Houses the proposed law must be submitted in each state to the qualified electors.

In the event of one House twice refusing to pass a proposed amendment that has already received an absolute majority in the other House, the Governor-General may, notwithstanding such refusal, submit the proposed amendment to the electors. By convention, the Governor-General acts on the advice of the Prime Minister. If in a majority of the states a majority of the electors voting approve the proposed law and if a majority of all the electors voting also approve, it shall be presented to the Governor-General for Royal Assent.

No alteration diminishing the proportionate representation of any state in either House of the Federal Parliament, or the minimum number of representatives of a state in the House of Representatives, or increasing, diminishing or altering the limits of the state, or in any way affecting the provisions of the Constitution in relation thereto, shall become law unless the majority of the electors voting in that state approve the proposed law.

STATES AND TERRITORIES

New South Wales

The state's executive power is vested in the Governor, appointed by the Crown, who is assisted by an Executive Council composed of cabinet ministers.

The state's legislative power is vested in a bicameral Parliament, composed of the Legislative Council and the Legislative Assembly. The Legislative Council consists of 42 members directly elected for the duration of two parliaments (i.e. eight years), 21 members retiring every four years. The Legislative Assembly consists of 93 members and sits for four years.

Victoria

The state's legislative power is vested in a bicameral Parliament: the Upper House, or Legislative Council, of 44 members, elected for two terms of the Legislative Assembly; and the Lower House, or Legislative Assembly, of 88 members, elected for a minimum of three and maximum of four years. One-half of the members of the Council retires every three–four years.

In the exercise of the executive power the Governor is assisted by a cabinet of responsible ministers. Not more than six members of the Council and not more than 17 members of the Assembly may occupy salaried office at any one time.

The state has 88 electoral districts, each returning one member, and 22 electoral provinces, each returning two Council members.

Queensland

The state's executive power is vested in the Governor, appointed by the Crown, who is assisted by an Executive Council composed of Ministers. The state's legislative power is vested in the Parliament comprising the Legislative Assembly (composed of 89 members who are elected at least every three years to represent 89 electoral districts) and the Governor, who assents to bills passed by the Assembly. The state's Constitution anticipates that Ministers are also members of the Legislative Assembly and provides that up to 18 members of the Assembly can be appointed Ministers.

South Australia

The state's Constitution vests the legislative power in a Parliament elected by the people and consisting of a Legislative Council and a House of Assembly. The Council is composed of 22 members, one-half of whom retires every three years. Their places are filled by new members elected under a system of proportional representation, with the whole state as a single electorate. The executive has no authority to dissolve this body, except in circumstances warranting a double dissolution.

The 47 members of the House of Assembly are elected for four years from 45 electoral districts.

The executive power is vested in a Governor, appointed by the Crown, and an Executive Council consisting of 10 responsible ministers.

Western Australia

The state's administration is vested in the Governor, a Legislative Council and a Legislative Assembly.

The Legislative Council consists of 34 members, two of the six electoral regions returning seven members on a proportional representation basis, and four regions returning five members. Election is for a term of four years.

The Legislative Assembly consists of 57 members, elected for four years, each representing one electorate.

Tasmania

The state's executive authority is vested in a Governor, appointed by the Crown, who acts upon the advice of his premier and ministers, who are elected members of either the Legislative Council or the House of Assembly. The Council consists of 15 members who sit for six years, retiring in rotation. The House of Assembly has 25 members elected for four years.

Northern Territory

On 1 July 1978, the Northern Territory was established as a body politic with executive authority for specified functions of government. Most functions of the Federal Government were transferred to the Territory Government in 1978 and 1979, major exceptions being Aboriginal affairs and uranium mining.

The Territory Parliament consists of a single house, the Legislative Assembly, with 25 members. The first Parliament stayed in office for three years. As from the election held in August 1980, members are elected for a term of four years.

The office of Administrator continues. The Northern Territory (Self-Government) Act provides for the appointment of an Administrator by the Governor-General charged with the duty of administering the Territory. In respect of matters transferred to the Territory Government, the Administrator acts with the advice of the Territory Executive Council; in respect of matters retained by the Commonwealth, the Administrator acts on Commonwealth advice.

Australian Capital Territory

On 29 November 1988 the Australian Capital Territory (ACT) was established as a body politic. The ACT Government has executive authority for specified functions, although a number of these were to be retained by the Federal Government for a brief period during which transfer arrangements were to be finalized.

The ACT Parliament consists of a single house, the Legislative Assembly, with 17 members. The first election was held in March 1989. Members are elected for a term of three years.

The Federal Government retains control of some of the land in the ACT for the purpose of maintaining the Seat of Government and the national capital plan.

Jervis Bay Territory

Following the attainment of self-government by the ACT (see above), the Jervis Bay Territory, which had formed part of the ACT since 1915, remained a separate Commonwealth Territory, administered by the then Department of the Arts, Sport, the Environment and Territories. The area is governed in accordance with the Jervis Bay Territory Administration Ordinance, issued by the Governor-General on 17 December 1990.

The Government

Head of State: HM Queen Elizabeth II (succeeded to the throne 6 February 1952).

Governor-General: Sir Guy Stephen Montague Green (assumed office on an acting basis, 11 May 2003).

THE MINISTRY
(April 2003)

Cabinet Ministers

Prime Minister: John Howard.

Deputy Prime Minister and Minister for Transport and Regional Services: John Anderson.

Minister for Foreign Affairs: Alexander Downer.

Treasurer: Peter Costello.

Minister for Trade: Mark Vaile.

Minister for Defence and Leader of the Government in the Senate: Senator Robert Hill.

Minister for Communications, Information Technology and the Arts: Senator Richard Alston.

Minister for Employment and Workplace Relations: Tony Abbott.

Minister for Education, Science and Training: Dr Brendan Nelson.

Minister for Health and Ageing: Senator Kay Patterson.

Minister for Industry, Tourism and Resources: Ian Macfarlane.

Minister for the Environment and Heritage: Dr David Kemp.

Minister for Finance and Administration: Senator Nicholas Minchin.

Minister for Family and Community Services: Amanda Vanstone.

Minister for Agriculture, Fisheries and Forestry: Warren Truss.

Minister for Immigration and Multicultural and Indigenous Affairs: Phillip Ruddock.

Attorney-General: Daryl Williams.

Other Ministers

Minister for Regional Services, Territories and Local Government: Wilson Tuckey.

Minister for Revenue and Assistant Treasurer: Senator HELEN COONAN.

Minister for Small Business and Tourism: JOE HOCKEY.

Minister for Fisheries, Forestry and Conservation: Senator IAN MACDONALD.

Minister for Science: PETER MCGAURAN.

Minister for Employment Services: MAL BROUGH.

Minister for Children and Youth Affairs: LAWRENCE ANTHONY.

Minister Assisting the Minister for Defence and Minister for Veterans' Affairs: DANNA VALE.

Minister for Ageing: KEVIN ANDREWS.

Special Minister of State: Senator ERIC ABETZ.

Minister for Justice and Customs: Senator CHRISTOPHER ELLISON.

Minister for the Arts and Sport: Senator ROD KEMP.

Minister for Citizenship and Multicultural Affairs: GARY HARD-GRAVE.

DEPARTMENTS

Department of the Prime Minister and Cabinet: 3–5 National Circuit, Barton, ACT 2600; tel. (2) 6271-5111; fax (2) 6271-5414; internet www.dpmc.gov.au.

Aboriginal and Torres Strait Islander Commission: Lovett Tower, Woden Town Centre, Phillip, ACT 2606; tel. (2) 6121-4000; fax (2) 6121-4621; internet www.atsic.gov.au.

Department of Agriculture, Fisheries and Forestry: GPOB 858, Canberra, ACT 2601; tel. (2) 6272-3933; fax (2) 6272-3008; internet www.affa.gov.au.

Attorney-General's Department: Robert Garran Offices, Barton, ACT 2600; tel. (2) 6250-6666; fax (2) 6250-5900; internet www.law .gov.au.

Department of Communications, Information Technology and the Arts: GPOB 2154, Canberra, ACT 2601; tel. (2) 6271-1000; fax (2) 6271-1901; internet www.dcita.gov.au.

Department of Defence: Russell Offices, Russell Drive, Campbell, Canberra, ACT 2600; tel. (2) 6265-9111; e-mail webmaster@cbr .defence.gov.au; internet www.defence.gov.au.

Department of Education, Science and Training: GPOB 9880, Canberra, ACT 2601; tel. (2) 6240-8111; fax (2) 6240-8571; e-mail library@dest.gov.au; internet www.dest.gov.au.

Department of Employment and Workplace Relations: GPOB 9879, Canberra, ACT 2601; tel. (2) 6121-6000; fax (2) 6121-7542; e-mail webmaster@dewrsb.gov.au; internet www.dewrsb.gov.au.

Department of the Environment and Heritage: GPOB 787, Canberra, ACT 2601; tel. (2) 6274-1111; fax (2) 6274-1123; internet www.ea.gov.au.

Department of Family and Community Services: Box 7788, Canberra Mail Centre, ACT 2610; tel. (2) 6244-7788; fax (2) 6244-5540; e-mail facs.internet@facs.gov.au; internet www.facs.gov.au.

Department of Finance and Administration: John Gorton Bldg, King Edward Tce, Parkes, ACT 2600; tel. (2) 6263-2222; fax (2) 6273-3021; internet www.dofa.gov.au.

Department of Foreign Affairs and Trade: GPOB 12, Canberra City, ACT 2601; tel. (2) 6261-1111; fax (2) 6261-3959; internet www .dfat.gov.au.

Department of Health and Ageing: GPOB 9848, Canberra, ACT 2601; tel. (2) 6289-1555; fax (2) 6281-6946; internet www.health.gov .au.

Department of Immigration and Multicultural and Indigenous Affairs: Benjamin Offices, Chan St, Belconnen, ACT 2617; tel. (2) 6264-1111; fax (2) 6264-2670; internet www.immi.gov.au.

Department of Industry, Tourism and Resources: GPOB 9839, Canberra, ACT 2601; tel. (2) 6213-6000; fax (2) 6213-7000; e-mail customerrelation@industry.gov.au; internet www.industry.gov.au.

Department of Transport and Regional Services: GPOB 594, Canberra, ACT 2601; tel. (2) 6274-7111; fax (2) 6257-2505; e-mail publicaffairs@dotrs.gov.au; internet www.dotrs.gov.au.

Department of the Treasury: Langton Crescent, Parkes, ACT 2600; tel. (2) 6263-2111; fax (2) 6273-2614; internet www.treasury .gov.au.

Department of Veterans' Affairs: POB 21, Woden, ACT 2606; tel. (2) 6289-1111; fax (2) 6289-6025; internet www.dva.gov.au.

Legislature

FEDERAL PARLIAMENT

Senate

President: Senator MARGARET REID.

Election, 10 November 2001

Party	Seats*
Liberal Party of Australia	31
Australian Labor Party	28
Australian Democrats Party	8
National Party of Australia	3
Greens	2
Independents	3
One Nation	1
Total	**76**

* The election was for 36 of the 72 seats held by state senators and for all four senators representing the Northern Territory and the Australian Capital Territory (See The Constitution). The figures for seats refer to the totals held from 1 July 2002.

House of Representatives

Speaker: NEIL ANDREW.

Election, 10 November 2001

Party	Seats
Liberal Party of Australia	69
Australian Labor Party	65
National Party of Australia	13
Independents	3
Total	**150**

State and Territory Governments

(April 2003)

NEW SOUTH WALES

Governor: MARIE BASHIR, Level 3, Chief Secretary's Bldg, 121 Macquarie St, Sydney, NSW 2000; tel. (2) 9242-4200; fax (2) 9242-4266; internet www.nsw.gov.au.

Premier: ROBERT (BOB) J. CARR (Labor), Level 40, Governor Macquarie Tower, 1 Farrer Place, Sydney, NSW 2000; tel. (2) 9228-5239; fax (2) 9228-3935; e-mail bob.carr@nsw.gov.au.

VICTORIA

Governor: JOHN LANDY, Government House, Melbourne, Vic 3004; tel. (3) 9655-4211; fax (3) 9654-8430; internet www.governor.vic.gov .au.

Premier: STEPHEN P. BRACKS (Labor), 1 Treasury Place, Vic 3000; internet www.premier.vic.gov.au.

QUEENSLAND

Governor: Maj.-Gen. PETER M. ARNISON, Government House, Brisbane, Qld 4001; tel. (7) 3858-5700; fax (7) 3858-5701; e-mail govhouse@govhouse.qld.gov.au; internet www.govhouse.qld.gov.au.

Premier: PETER D. BEATTIE (Labor), Executive Bldg, 100 George St, Brisbane, Qld 4002; tel. (7) 3224-2111; fax (7) 3229-2990; internet www.premiers.qld.gov.au.

SOUTH AUSTRALIA

Governor: MARJORIE JACKSON-NELSON, Government House, North Terrace, Adelaide, SA 5000; tel. (8) 8203-9800; fax (8) 8203-9899; e-mail govthsesa@saugov.sa.gov.au; internet www.sa.gov.au.

Premier: MICHAEL (MIKE) RANN (Labor), 200 Victoria Square, Adelaide, SA 5001; tel. and fax (8) 8463-3166; e-mail premier@saugov.sa .gov.au; internet www.ministers.sa.gov.au.

WESTERN AUSTRALIA

Governor: Lt-Gen. JOHN MURRAY SANDERSON, Government House, Perth, WA 6000; tel. (8) 9429-9199; fax (8) 9325-4476; e-mail enquiries@govhouse.wa.gov.au; internet www.wa.gov.au.

Premier: GEOFFREY GALLOP (Labor), 24th Floor, 197 St George's Terrace, Perth, WA 6000; tel. (8) 9222-9888; fax (8) 9322-1213; e-mail wa-government@mpc.wa.gov.au; internet www.premier.wa .gov.au.

TASMANIA

Governor: Sir GUY STEPHEN MONTAGUE GREEN, Government House, Hobart, Tas 7000; tel. (3) 6234-2611; fax (3) 6234-2556; internet www.tas.gov.au.

Premier: JAMES A. BACON (Labor), GPOB 123B, Hobart, Tas 7001; tel. (3) 6233-3464; fax (3) 6234-1572; e-mail premier@dpac.tas.gov .au; internet www.premier.tas.gov.au.

NORTHERN TERRITORY

Administrator: JOHN ANICTOMATIS, GPOB 497, Darwin, NT 0801; tel. (8) 8999-7103; fax (8) 8981-5521; e-mail john.anictomatis@nt.gov .au; internet www.nt.gov.au/administrator.

Chief Minister: CLARE MARTIN (Labor), GPOB 3146, Darwin, NT 0801; tel. (8) 8901-4000; fax (8) 8901-4099; e-mail chiefminister.nt@ nt.gov.au; internet www.nt.gov.au/ministers.

AUSTRALIAN CAPITAL TERRITORY

Chief Minister: JONATHAN STANHOPE (Labor), Legislative Assembly Bldg, Civic Square, London Circuit, Canberra, ACT 2601; tel. (2) 6205-0104; fax (2) 6205-0399; e-mail canberraconnect@.act.gov.au; internet www.act.gov.au.

Political Organizations

Australians for Constitutional Monarchy (ACM): GPOB 9841, Sydney, NSW 2001; tel. (2) 9231-2200; fax (2) 9231-2359; e-mail acmhq@norepublic.com.au; internet www.norepublic.com.au; f. 1992; also known as No Republic; Exec. Dir KERRY JONES.

Australian Democrats Party: Victorian Division, G1/Eastbourne House, 62 Wellington Pde, East Melbourne, Vic 3002; tel. (3) 9419-5808; fax (3) 9419-5697; e-mail senator.bartlett@democrats.org.au; internet www.democrats.org.au; f. 1971; comprises the fmr Liberal Movement and the Australia Party; Leader Senator ANDREW BARTLETT.

Australian Greens: GPOB 1108, Canberra, ACT 2601; e-mail frontdesk@greens.org.au; internet www.greens.org.au; f. 1992; Leader Senator BOB BROWN.

Australian Labor Party (ALP): Centenary House, 19 National Circuit, Barton, ACT 2600; tel. (2) 6120-0800; fax (2) 6120-0801; e-mail natsect@alp.org.au; internet www.alp.org.au/; f. 1891; advocates social democracy; trade unions form part of its structure; Fed. Parl. Leader SIMON CREAN; Nat. Pres. GREG SWORD; Nat. Sec. GEOFF WALSH.

Australian Republican Movement (ARM): POB A870, Sydney South, NSW 1235; tel. (2) 9267-8022; fax (2) 9267-8155; e-mail republic@ozemail.com.au; internet www.republic.org.au; Chair. GREG BARNS; Nat. Dir JAMES TERRIE.

Communist Party of Australia: 65 Campbell St, Surry Hills, NSW 2010; tel. (2) 9212-6855; fax (2) 9281-5795; e-mail cpa@cpa.org .au; internet www.cpa.org.au; f. 1971; fmrly Socialist Party; advocates public ownership of the means of production, working-class political power; Pres. Dr H. MIDDLETON; Gen. Sec. P. SYMON.

Liberal Party of Australia: Federal Secretariat, Cnr Blackall and Macquarie Sts, Barton, ACT 2600; tel. (2) 6273-2564; fax (2) 6273-1534; e-mail libadm@liberal.org.au; internet www.liberal.org.au; f. 1944; advocates private enterprise, social justice, individual liberty and initiative; committed to national development, prosperity and security; Fed. Dir BRIAN LOUGHNANE; Fed. Parl. Leader JOHN HOWARD.

National Party of Australia: John McEwen House, National Circuit, Barton, ACT 2600; tel. (2) 6273-3822; fax (2) 6273-1745; e-mail federal@nationalparty.org; internet www.nationalparty.org; f. 1916 as the Country Party of Australia; adopted present name in 1982; advocates balanced national development based on free enterprise, with special emphasis on the needs of people outside the major metropolitan areas; Fed. Pres. HELEN DICKIE; Fed. Parl. Leader JOHN ANDERSON; Fed. Dir ANDREW HALL.

One Nation Party: GPOB 812, Ipswich, Qld 4304; e-mail pauline@ onenation.com.au; internet www.onenation.com.au; f. 1997; opposes globalization, high immigration and special funding for Aboriginal people, advocates public ownership of major services; Pres. (vacant); Vice-Pres. JOHN FISHER.

Diplomatic Representation

EMBASSIES AND HIGH COMMISSIONS IN AUSTRALIA

Afghanistan: Deakin, ACT 2600; Ambassador MAHMOUD SAIKAL.

Argentina: POB 4835, Kingston, ACT 2604; tel. (2) 6273-9111; fax (2) 6273-0500; e-mail eaust@canberra.teknet.net.au; internet www .argentina.org.au; Ambassador NÉSTOR E. STANCANELLI.

Austria: POB 3375, Manuka, ACT 2603; tel. (2) 6295-1533; fax (2) 6239-6751; e-mail austria@bigpond.net.au; internet www .austriaemb.org.au/; Ambassador Dr OTMAR KOLER.

Bangladesh: POB 5, Red Hill, ACT 2603; tel. (2) 6295-3328; fax (2) 6295-3351; e-mail bdoot.canberra@cyberone.com.au; High Commissioner MIRZA SHAMSUZZAMAN.

Belgium: 19 Arkana St, Yarralumla, ACT 2600; tel. (2) 6273-2501; fax (2) 6273-3392; e-mail canberra@diplobel.org; Ambassador LUK DARRAS.

Bosnia and Herzegovina: 5 Beale Crescent, Deakin, ACT 2600; tel. (2) 6232-4646; fax (2) 6232-5554; e-mail embaucbr@webone.com .au; internet www.bosnia.webone.com.au; Ambassador Dr RADOMIR DAVIDOVIĆ.

Brazil: GPOB 1540, Canberra, ACT 2601; tel. (2) 6273-2372; fax (2) 6273-2375; e-mail brazil@connect.net.au; internet brazil.org.au; Ambassador ANTÔNIO AUGUSTO DAYRELL DE LIMA.

Brunei: 10 Beale Crescent, Deakin, ACT 2603; tel. (2) 6285-4500; fax (2) 6285-4545; High Commissioner Haji ZAKARIA Haji AHMAD (acting).

Cambodia: 5 Canterbury Crescent, Deakin, ACT 2600; tel. (2) 6273-1259; fax (2) 6273-1053; e-mail cambodianembassy@ozemail.net.au; internet www.embassyofcambodia.org.nz/au; Ambassador HOR NAMBORA.

Canada: Commonwealth Ave, Canberra, ACT 2600; tel. (2) 6270-4000; fax (2) 6273-3285; internet www.canada.org.au; High Commissioner JEAN T. FOURNIER.

Chile: POB 69, Red Hill, ACT 2603; tel. (2) 6286-2430; fax (2) 6286-1289; e-mail chilemb@embachile-australia.com; internet www .embachile-australia.com; Ambassador CRISTÓBAL VALDÉS.

China, People's Republic: 15 Coronation Drive, Yarralumla, ACT 2600; tel. (2) 6273-4780; fax (2) 6273-4878; Ambassador WU TAO.

Colombia: GPOB 2892, Canberra City, ACT 2601; tel. (2) 6257-2027; fax (2) 6257-1448; e-mail emaustralia@iprimus.com.au; internet www.embacol.org.au; Ambassador JUAN SANTIAGO URIBE.

Croatia: 14 Jindalee Crescent, O'Malley, ACT 2606; tel. (2) 6286-6988; fax (2) 6286-3544; e-mail croemb@bigpond.com; Ambassador Dr MLADEN IBLER.

Cyprus: 30 Beale Crescent, Deakin, ACT 2600; tel. (2) 6281-0832; fax (2) 6281-0860; e-mail cyphicom@iprimus.com.au; High Commissioner SOTOS LIASSIDES.

Czech Republic: 8 Culgoa Circuit, O'Malley, ACT 2606; tel. (2) 6290-1386; fax (2) 6290-0006; e-mail canberra@embassy.mzv.cz; Ambassador JOSEF SLÁDEK.

Denmark: 15 Hunter St, Yarralumla, ACT 2600; tel. (2) 6273-2196; fax (2) 6273-3864; e-mail dkembact@dynamite.com.au; Ambassador JENS OSTENFELD.

Ecuador: 1st Floor, Law Society Bldg of Canberra, 11 London Circuit, ACT 2601; tel. (2) 6262-5282; fax (2) 6262-5285; e-mail embecu@hotkey.net.au; Ambassador Dr ABELARDO POSSO-SERRANO.

Egypt: 1 Darwin Ave, Yarralumla, ACT 2600; tel. (2) 6273-4437; fax (2) 6273-4279; Ambassador ASSEM AHMED MEGAHED.

Fiji: POB 159, Deakin West, ACT 2600; tel. (2) 6260-5115; fax (2) 6260-5105; e-mail fhc@cyberone.com.au; High Commissioner JIOJI KONROTE.

Finland: 12 Darwin Ave, Yarralumla, ACT 2600; tel. (2) 6273-3800; fax (2) 6273-3603; e-mail finland@austarmetro.com.au; internet www.finland.org.au; Ambassador ANNELI PUURA-MÁRKÄLÄ.

France: 6 Perth Ave, Yarralumla, ACT 2600; tel. (2) 6216-0100; fax (2) 6216-0127; e-mail embassy@france.net.au; internet www .embafrance-au.org; Ambassador PIERRE VIAUX.

Germany: 119 Empire Circuit, Yarralumla, ACT 2600; tel. (2) 6270-1911; fax (2) 6270-1951; e-mail embgerma@bigpond.net.au; internet www.germanembassy-canberra.com; Ambassador Dr KLAUS-PETER KLAIBER.

Greece: 9 Turrana St, Yarralumla, ACT 2600; tel. (2) 6273-3011; fax (2) 6273-2620; e-mail greekemb@greekembassy-au.org; Ambassador FOTIOS-JEAN XYDAS.

Holy See: POB 3633, Manuka, ACT 2603 (Apostolic Nunciature); tel. (2) 6295-3876; Apostolic Nuncio Most Rev. Francesco Canalini (Titular Archbishop of Valeria).

Hungary: 17 Beale Crescent, Deakin, ACT 2600; tel. (2) 6282-3226; fax (2) 6285-3012; e-mail hungcbr@ozemail.com.au; Ambassador Dr István Gyürk.

India: 3–5 Moonah Place, Yarralumla, ACT 2600; tel. (2) 6273-3999; fax (2) 6273-1308; e-mail hciisi@cyberone.com.au; High Commissioner C. P. Ravindranathan.

Indonesia: 8 Darwin Ave, Yarralumla, ACT 2600; tel. (2) 6273-8600; fax (2) 6250-6017; e-mail embindo@cyberone.com.au; Ambassador Sudjadnan Parnohadiningrat.

Iran: POB 3219, Manuka, ACT 2603; tel. (2) 6290-2427; fax (2) 6290-2431; internet www.embassyiran.org.au; Ambassador Dr Gholamali Khoshroo.

Iraq: 48 Culgoa Circuit, O'Malley, ACT 2606; tel. (2) 6286-1333; fax (2) 6290-1788; Ambassador (vacant).

Ireland: 20 Arkana St, Yarralumla, ACT 2600; tel. (2) 6273-3022; fax (2) 6273-3741; e-mail irishemb@cyberone.com.au; Ambassador Declan M. Kelly.

Israel: 6 Turrana St, Yarralumla, ACT 2600; tel. (2) 6273-1309; tel. 62224; fax (2) 6273-4273; e-mail israelembassy@israemb.org; internet www.mfa.gov.il; Ambassador Gabby Levy.

Italy: 12 Grey St, Deakin, ACT 2600; tel. (2) 6273-3333; fax (2) 6273-4223; e-mail embassy@ambitalia.org.au; internet www.ambitalia.org.au; Ambassador Dino Volpicelli.

Japan: 112 Empire Circuit, Yarralumla, ACT 2600; tel. (2) 6273-3244; fax (2) 6273-1848; e-mail embofjpn@ozemail.com.au; internet www.japan.org.au; Ambassador Atsushi Hatakanaka.

Jordan: 20 Roebuck St, Red Hill, ACT 2603; tel. (2) 6295-9951; fax (2) 6239-7236; Ambassador Dr Khaldoun Tharwat Talhouni.

Kenya: GPOB 1990, Canberra, ACT 2601; tel. (2) 6247-4788; fax (2) 6257-6613; e-mail kenrep@dynamite.com.au; High Commissioner Steven A. Loyatum.

Korea, Republic: 113 Empire Circuit, Yarralumla, ACT 2600; tel. (2) 6270-4100; fax (2) 6273-4839; e-mail embassy-au@mofat.go.kr; internet www.mofat.go.kr; Ambassador Song Young-Shik.

Laos: 1 Dalman Crescent, O'Malley, ACT 2606; tel. (2) 6286-4595; fax (2) 6290-1910; e-mail clao@cyberone.com.au; Ambassador Vichit Xindavong.

Lebanon: 27 Endeavour St, Red Hill, ACT 2603; tel. (2) 6295-7378; fax (2) 6239-7024; Ambassador Michel Bitar.

Malaysia: 7 Perth Ave, Yarralumla, ACT 2600; tel. (2) 6273-1544; fax (2) 6273-2496; e-mail malcnbera@kln.gov.my; High Commissioner M. H. Arshad.

Malta: 38 Culgoa Circuit, O'Malley, ACT 2606; tel. (2) 6290-1724; fax (2) 6290-2453; e-mail maltahc@bigpond.com; High Commissioner Dr Ivan Fsadni.

Mauritius: 2 Beale Crescent, Deakin, ACT 2600; tel. (2) 6281-1203; fax (2) 6282-3235; e-mail mhccan@cyberone.com.au; High Commissioner Patrice Curé.

Mexico: 14 Perth Ave, Yarralumla, ACT 2600; tel. (2) 6273-3905; fax (2) 6273-1190; e-mail embamex@mexico.org.au; internet www.embassyofmexicoinaustralia.org; Ambassador Raphael Steger-Cataño.

Myanmar: 22 Arkana St, Yarralumla, ACT 2600; tel. (2) 6273-3811; fax (2) 6273-4357; Ambassador Mr Aye.

Netherlands: 120 Empire Circuit, Yarralumla, ACT 2600; tel. (2) 6220-9400; fax (2) 6273-3206; e-mail can@minbuza.nl; internet www.netherlands.org.au; Ambassador H. H. M. Sondaal.

New Zealand: Commonwealth Ave, Canberra, ACT 2600; tel. (2) 6270-4211; fax (2) 6273-3194; e-mail nzhccba@austarmetro.com.au; internet www.nzembassy.com/australia; High Commissioner Kate Lackey.

Nigeria: POB 241, Civic Square, ACT 2608; tel. (2) 6282-7411; fax (2) 6282-8471; e-mail chancery@nigeria-can.org.au; internet www.nigeria-can.org.au; High Commissioner Dr Rufai A. O. Soule.

Norway: 17 Hunter St, Yarralumla, ACT 2600; tel. (2) 6273-3444; fax (2) 6273-3669; e-mail emb.canberra@mfa.no; Ambassador Ove Thorsheim.

Pakistan: POB 684, Mawson, ACT 2607; tel. (2) 6290-1676; fax (2) 6290-1073; e-mail parepcanberra@actonline.com.au; High Commissioner Khizar Hayat Khan Niazi.

Papua New Guinea: POB E432, Queen Victoria Terrace, Kingston, ACT 2604; tel. (2) 6273-3322; fax (2) 6273-3732; High Commissioner Renagi R. Lohia.

Peru: POB 106, Red Hill, ACT 2603; tel. (2) 6273-8752; fax (2) 6273-8754; e-mail embassy@embaperu.org.au; internet www.embaperu.org.au; Ambassador José Luis Garaycochea.

Philippines: 1 Moonah Place, Yarralumla, Canberra, ACT 2600; tel. (2) 6273-2535; fax (2) 6273-3984; e-mail cbrpe@philembassy.au.com; internet www.philembassy.au.com; Ambassador Delia Domingo-Albert.

Poland: 7 Turrana St, Yarralumla, ACT 2600; tel. (2) 6273-1208; fax (2) 6273-3184; e-mail ambpol@clover.com.au; Ambassador Dr Tadeusz Szumowski.

Portugal: 23 Culgoa Circuit, O'Malley, ACT 2606; tel. (2) 6290-1733; fax (2) 6290-1957; e-mail sab@mail2me.com.au; Ambassador Dr José Vieira Branco.

Romania: 4 Dalman Crescent, O'Malley, ACT 2606; tel. (2) 6286-2343; fax (2) 6286-2433; e-mail roembcbr@cyberone.com.au; internet www.roembau.org.au; Ambassador Manuela Vulpe.

Russia: 78 Canberra Ave, Griffith, ACT 2603; tel. (2) 6295-9033; fax (2) 6295-1847; e-mail rusembassy@lightningpl.net.au; Ambassador Leonid Moiseev.

Samoa: POB 3274, Manuka, ACT 2603; tel. (2) 6286-5505; fax (2) 6286-5678; e-mail samoahcaussi@netspeed.com.au; High Commissioner Leiataua Dr Kilifoti S. Eteuati.

Saudi Arabia: POB 63, Garran, ACT 2605; tel. (2) 6282-6999; fax (2) 6282-8911; e-mail saudiemb@hotmail.com; Ambassador Mohamad I. al-Hejailan.

Serbia and Montenegro: POB 728, Mawson, ACT 2607; tel. (2) 6290-2630; fax (2) 6290-2631; Ambassador Radomir Jergić.

Singapore: 17 Forster Crescent, Yarralumla, ACT 2600; tel. (2) 6273-3944; fax (2) 6273-9823; e-mail shc.cbr@u030.aone.net.au; internet www.mfa.gov.sg/canberra; High Commissioner Joseph K. H. Koh.

Slovakia: 47 Culgoa Circuit, O'Malley, ACT 2606; tel. (2) 6290-1516; fax (2) 6290-1755; e-mail slovak@cyberone.com.au; internet www.slovakemb-aust.org; Ambassador Dr Anna Tureničová.

Slovenia: POB 284, Civic Square, Canberra, ACT 2608; tel. (2) 6243-4830; fax (2) 6243-4827; e-mail vca@mzz-dkp.gov.si; internet slovenia.webone.com.au; Chargé d'affaires Bojan Bertoncelj.

Solomon Islands: POB 256, Deakin West, ACT 2600; tel. (2) 6282-7030; fax (2) 6282-7040; e-mail info@solomon.emb.gov.au; High Commissioner Milner Tozaka.

South Africa: cnr State Circle and Rhodes Place, Yarralumla, ACT 2600; tel. (2) 6273-2424; fax (2) 6273-3543; e-mail info@rsa.emb.gov.au; internet www.rsa.emb.gov.au; High Commissioner Zolile Magugu.

Spain: POB 9076, Deakin, ACT 2600; tel. (2) 6273-3555; fax (2) 6273-3918; e-mail embespau@mail.mae.es; internet www.embaspain.com; Ambassador José Ramón Baranaño.

Sri Lanka: 35 Empire Circuit, Forrest, ACT 2603; tel. (2) 6239-7041; fax (2) 6239-6166; e-mail slhc@atrax.net.au; internet slhccanberra.webjump.com; High Commissioner Maj.-Gen. Janaka Perera.

Sweden: 5 Turrana St, Yarralumla, ACT 2600; tel. (2) 6270-2700; fax (2) 6270-2755; e-mail sweden@austarmetro.com.au; Ambassador Lars-Erik Wingren.

Switzerland: 7 Melbourne Ave, Forrest, ACT 2603; tel. (2) 6273-3977; fax (2) 6273-3428; e-mail vertretung@can.rep.admin.ch; Ambassador André Faivet.

Thailand: 111 Empire Circuit, Yarralumla, ACT 2600; tel. (2) 6273-1149; fax (2) 6273-1518; e-mail rtecanberra@mfa.go.th; Ambassador Sawanit Kongsiri.

Timor-Leste: Canberra; Ambassador Jorge Teme.

Turkey: 60 Mugga Way, Red Hill, ACT 2603; tel. (2) 6295-0227; fax (2) 6239-6592; e-mail turkembs@bigpond.net.au; internet www.turkishembassy.org.au; Ambassador Tansu Okandan.

United Arab Emirates: 36 Culgoa Circuit, O'Malley, ACT 2606; tel. (2) 6286-8802; fax (2) 6286-8804; e-mail uaeembassy@bigpond.com; internet www.users.bigpond.com/uaeembassy; Ambassador Khalifa Mohammed Bakhit al-Falasi.

United Kingdom: Commonwealth Ave, Canberra, ACT 2600; tel. (2) 6270-6666; fax (2) 6273-3236; e-mail BHC.Canberra@uk.emb.gov.au; internet www.uk.emb.gov.au; High Commissioner Sir Alastair Goodlad.

USA: Moonah Place, Yarralumla, ACT 2600; tel. (2) 6214-5600; fax (2) 6214-5970; Ambassador Edward W. Gnehm.

Uruguay: POB 5058, Kingston, ACT 2604; tel. (2) 6273-9100; fax (2) 6273-9099; e-mail urucan@austarmetro.com.au; Ambassador Pedro Mó Amaro.

Venezuela: 5 Culgoa Circuit, O'Malley, ACT 2606; tel. (2) 6290-2968; fax (2) 6290-2911; e-mail embaustralia@venezuela-emb-org.au; internet www.venezuela-emb.org.au; Ambassador LIONEL VIVAS.

Viet Nam: 6 Timbarra Crescent, O'Malley, ACT 2606; tel. (2) 6286-6059; fax (2) 6286-4534; e-mail vnembassy@webone.com.au; internet www.au.vnembassy.org; Ambassador VU CHI CONG.

Zimbabwe: 11 Culgoa Circuit, O'Malley, ACT 2606; tel. (2) 6286-2700; fax (2) 6290-1680; e-mail zimbabwe1@austarmetro.com.au; High Commissioner FLORENCE L. CHITAURO.

Judicial System

The judicial power of the Commonwealth of Australia is vested in the High Court of Australia, in such other Federal Courts as the Federal Parliament creates, and in such other courts as it invests with Federal jurisdiction.

The High Court consists of a Chief Justice and six other Justices, each of whom is appointed by the Governor-General in Council, and has both original and appellate jurisdiction.

The High Court's original jurisdiction extends to all matters arising under any treaty, affecting representatives of other countries, in which the Commonwealth of Australia or its representative is a party, between states or between residents of different states or between a state and a resident of another state, and in which a writ of mandamus, or prohibition, or an injunction is sought against an officer of the Commonwealth of Australia. It also extends to matters arising under the Australian Constitution or involving its interpretation, and to many matters arising under Commonwealth laws.

The High Court's appellate jurisdiction has, since June 1984, been discretionary. Appeals from the Federal Court, the Family Court and the Supreme Courts of the states and of the territories may now be brought only if special leave is granted, in the event of a legal question that is of general public importance being involved, or of there being differences of opinion between intermediate appellate courts as to the state of the law.

Legislation enacted by the Federal Parliament in 1976 substantially changed the exercise of Federal and Territory judicial power, and, by creating the Federal Court of Australia in February 1977, enabled the High Court of Australia to give greater attention to its primary function as interpreter of the Australian Constitution. The Federal Court of Australia has assumed, in two divisions, the jurisdiction previously exercised by the Australian Industrial Court and the Federal Court of Bankruptcy and was additionally given jurisdiction in trade practices and in the developing field of administrative law. In 1987 the Federal Court of Australia acquired jurisdiction in federal taxation matters and certain intellectual property matters. In 1991 the Court's jurisdiction was expanded to include civil proceedings arising under Corporations Law. Jurisdiction has also been conferred on the Federal Court of Australia, subject to a number of exceptions, in matters in which a writ of mandamus, or prohibition, or an injunction is sought against an officer of the Commonwealth of Australia. The Court also hears appeals from the Court constituted by a single Judge, from the Supreme Courts of the territories, and in certain specific matters from State Courts, other than a Full Court of the Supreme Court of a state, exercising Federal jurisdiction.

In March 1986 all remaining categories of appeal from Australian courts to the Queen's Privy Council in the UK were abolished by the Australia Act.

FEDERAL COURTS

High Court of Australia
POB E435, Kingston, Canberra, ACT 2604; tel. (2) 6270-6811; fax (2) 6270-6868; internet www.hcourt.gov.au.

Chief Justice: ANTHONY MURRAY GLEESON.

Justices: MARY GENEVIEVE GAUDRON, MICHAEL HUDSON MCHUGH, WILLIAM MONTAGUE CHARLES GUMMOW, MICHAEL DONALD KIRBY, KENNETH MADISON HAYNE, IAN DAVID FRANCIS CALLINAN.

Federal Court of Australia
Chief Justice: MICHAEL ERIC JOHN BLACK.

In 2003 there were 46 other judges.

Family Court of Australia
Chief Justice: ALISTAIR BOTHWICK NICHOLSON.

In 2003 there were 50 other judges.

NEW SOUTH WALES
Supreme Court
Chief Justice: JAMES JACOB SPIGELMAN.
President: KEITH MASON.
Chief Judge in Equity: PETER WOLSTENHOME YOUNG.
Chief Judge at Common Law: JAMES ROLAND TOMSON WOOD.

VICTORIA
Supreme Court
Chief Justice: JOHN HARBER PHILLIPS.
President of the Court of Appeal: JOHN SPENCE WINNEKE.

QUEENSLAND
Supreme Court
Chief Justice: PAUL DE JERSEY.
President of the Court of Appeal: MARGARET MCMURDO.
Senior Judge Administrator, Trial Division: MARTIN PATRICK MOYNIHAN.

Central District (Rockhampton)
Resident Judge: PETER RICHARD DUTNEY.

Northern District (Townsville)
Resident Judge: KEIRAN ANTHONY CULLINANE.

Far Northern District (Cairns)
Resident Judge: STANLEY GRAHAM JONES.

SOUTH AUSTRALIA
Supreme Court
Chief Justice: JOHN JEREMY DOYLE.

WESTERN AUSTRALIA
Supreme Court
Chief Justice: DAVID KINGSLEY MALCOLM.

TASMANIA
Supreme Court
Chief Justice: WILLIAM JOHN ELLIS COX.

AUSTRALIAN CAPITAL TERRITORY
Supreme Court
Chief Justice: (vacant).

NORTHERN TERRITORY
Supreme Court
Chief Justice: BRIAN FRANK MARTIN.

Religion

CHRISTIANITY
According to the provisional results of the population census of August 2001, Christians numbered 12,764,342.

National Council of Churches in Australia: Locked Bag 199, QVB PO, Sydney, NSW 1230; tel. (2) 9299-2215; fax (2) 9262-4514; e-mail christianworldservice@ncca.org.au; internet www.ncca.org.au; f. 1946; 14 mem. churches; Pres. Archbishop JOHN BATHERSBY; Gen. Sec. Rev. DAVID GILL.

The Anglican Communion
The constitution of the Church of England in Australia, which rendered the church an autonomous member of the Anglican Communion, came into force in January 1962. The body was renamed the Anglican Church of Australia in August 1981. The Church comprises five provinces (together containing 22 dioceses) and the extra-provincial diocese of Tasmania. At the 2001 population census there were an estimated 3,881,162 adherents.

National Office of the Anglican Church

General Synod Office, Box Q190, QVB PO, Sydney, NSW 1230; tel. (2) 9265-1525; fax (2) 9264-6552; e-mail gsoffice@anglican.org.au; internet www.anglican.org.au.

Gen. Sec. Rev. Dr B. N. KAYE.

Archbishop of Adelaide and Metropolitan of South Australia: Most Rev. IAN G. C. GEORGE, Bishop's Court, 45 Palmer Place, North Adelaide, SA 5006; fax (8) 8305-9399; e-mail Igeorge.churchoffice@ anglicare-sa.org.au.

Archbishop of Brisbane and Metropolitan of Queensland: Dr PHILLIP JOHN ASPINALL, Bishopsbourne, GPOB 421, Brisbane, Qld 4001; tel. (7) 3835-2218; fax (7) 3832-5030; e-mail archbishop@ anglicanbrisbane.org.au; internet www.anglicanbrisbane.gil.com .au.

Archbishop of Melbourne and Metropolitan of Victoria: Most Rev. PETER R. WATSON, Bishopscourt, 120 Clarendon St, East Melbourne, Vic 3002; tel. (3) 9653-4220; fax (3) 9650-2184; e-mail archbishop@melbourne.anglican.com.au.

Archbishop of Perth and Metropolitan of Western Australia, Primate of Australia: Most Rev. Dr PETER F. CARNLEY, GPOB W2067, Perth, WA 6846; tel. (8) 9325-7455; fax (8) 9325-6741; e-mail abcsuite@perth.anglican.org; internet www.perth.anglican.org.

Also has jurisdiction over Christmas Island and the Cocos (Keeling) Islands.

Archbishop of Sydney and Metropolitan of New South Wales: Most Rev. Dr PETER F. JENSEN, POB Q190, QVB Post Office, Sydney, NSW 1230; tel. (2) 9265-1521; fax (2) 9265-1504; e-mail archbishop@ sydney.anglican.asn.au; internet www.sydney.anglican.asn.au.

The Roman Catholic Church

Australia comprises five metropolitan archdioceses, two archdioceses directly responsible to the Holy See and 25 dioceses, including one diocese each for Catholics of the Maronite, Melkite and Ukrainian rites, and one military ordinariate. At the census of 1996 there were 4.8m. adherents in the country.

Australian Catholic Bishops' Conference

GPOB 368, Canberra, ACT 2601; tel. (2) 6201-9845; fax (2) 6247-6083; e-mail gensec@catholic.org.au; internet www.catholic.org.au. f. 1979; Pres. Most Rev. FRANCIS PATRICK CARROLL (Archbishop of Canberra and Goulburn); Sec. Rev. BRIAN LUCAS.

Archbishop of Adelaide: Most Rev. PHILIP WILSON, GPOB 1364, Adelaide, South Australia 5001; tel. (8) 8210-8108; fax (8) 8223-2307.

Archbishop of Brisbane: Most Rev. JOHN A. BATHERSBY, Archbishop's House, 790 Brunswick St, New Farm, Brisbane, Qld 4005; tel. (7) 3224-3364; fax (7) 3358-1357; e-mail archbishop@bne.catholic .net.au.

Archbishop of Canberra and Goulburn: Most Rev. FRANCIS PATRICK CARROLL, GPOB 89, Canberra, ACT 2601; tel. (2) 6248-6411; fax (2) 6247-9636.

Archbishop of Hobart: Most Rev. ADRIAN DOYLE, GPOB 62, Hobart, Tas 7001; tel. (3) 6225-1920; fax (3) 6225-3865; e-mail archbishop .hobart@cdftas.com; internet www.hobart.catholic.org.au.

Archbishop of Melbourne: Most Rev. DENIS HART, GPOB 146, East Melbourne, Vic 3002; tel. (3) 9926-5677; fax (3) 9926-5613.

Archbishop of Perth: Most Rev. BARRY J. HICKEY, St Mary's Cathedral, 17 Victoria Sq., Perth, WA 6000; tel. (8) 9223-1350; fax (8) 9221-1716; e-mail archsec@perth.catholic.org.au; internet www.perth .catholic.org.au.

Archbishop of Sydney: Most Rev. GEORGE PELL, St Mary's Cathedral, Sydney, NSW 2000; tel. (2) 9390-5100; fax (2) 9261-8312.

Orthodox Churches

Greek Orthodox Archdiocese of Australia: 242 Cleveland St, Redfern, Sydney, NSW 2016; tel. (2) 9698-5066; fax (2) 9698-5368; f. 1924; 700,000 mems; Primate His Eminence Archbishop STYLIANOS. The Antiochian, Coptic, Romanian, Serbian and Syrian Orthodox Churches are also represented.

Other Christian Churches

Baptist Union of Australia: POB 377, Hawthorn, Vic 3122; tel. (3) 9818-0341; fax (3) 9818-1041; e-mail bua@baptistvic-asn.au; f. 1926; 64,159 mems; 883 churches; Nat. Pres. Rev. TIM COSTELLO; Nat. Sec. C. K. MOSS.

Churches of Christ in Australia: POB 55, Helensburgh, NSW 2508; tel. (2) 4294-1913; fax (2) 4294-1914; e-mail bobsmith@ozemail

.com.au; internet www.churchesofchrist.org.au; 36,000 mems; Pres. Rev. PETER OVERTON; Co-ordinator Rev. ROBERT SMITH.

Lutheran Church of Australia: National Office, 197 Archer St, North Adelaide, SA 5006; tel. (8) 8267-7300; fax (8) 8267-7310; e-mail president@lca.org.au; internet www.lca.org.au; f. 1966; 98,191 mems; Pres. Rev. M. P. SEMMLER.

United Pentecostal Church of Australia: GPOB 1434, Springwood, Qld, 4127; tel. (7) 3806-1817; fax (7) 3806-0029; e-mail homemissions@powerup.com.au; internet www.upca.org.au; 174,720 adherents in 1996.

Uniting Church in Australia: POB A2266, Sydney South, NSW 1235; tel. (2) 8267-4428; fax (2) 8267-4222; e-mail assysec@nat.uca .org.au; internet nat.uca.org.au; f. 1977 with the union of Methodist, Presbyterian and Congregational Churches; 1.4m. mems; Pres. Rev. Prof. JAMES HAIRE; Gen. Sec. Rev. TERENCE CORKIN; Other active denominations include the Armenian Apostolic Church, the Assyrian Church of the East and the Society of Friends (Quakers).

JUDAISM

The Jewish community numbered an estimated 83,993 at the census of August 2001.

Great Synagogue: 166 Castlereagh St, Sydney, NSW; tel. (2) 9267-2477; fax (2) 9264-8871; e-mail admin@greatsynagogue.org.au; internet www.greatsynagogue.org.au; f. 1828; Sr Minister Rabbi RAYMOND APPLE.

OTHER FAITHS

According to the August 2001 census, Muslims numbered an estimated 281,578, Buddhists 357,813 and Hindus 95,473.

The Press

The total circulation of Australia's daily newspapers is very high, but in the remoter parts of the country weekly papers are even more popular. Most of Australia's newspapers are published in sparsely populated rural areas where the demand for local news is strong. The only newspapers that may fairly claim a national circulation are the dailies *The Australian* and *Australian Financial Review*, and the weekly magazines *The Bulletin*, *Time Australia* and *Business Review Weekly*, the circulation of most newspapers being almost entirely confined to the state in which each is produced.

ACP Publishing Pty Ltd: 54–58 Park St, Sydney, NSW 2000; tel. (2) 9282-8000; fax (2) 9264-4541; internet www.acp.com.au; publishes *Australian Women's Weekly*, *The Bulletin with Newsweek*, *Cleo*, *Cosmopolitan*, *Woman's Day*, *Dolly*, *Belle*, *Wheels*, *Motor* and more than 60 other magazines; Chief Exec. JOHN ALEXANDER.

APN News and Media Ltd: 10th Floor, 300 Ann St, Brisbane, Qld 4000; tel. (7) 3307-0300; fax (7) 3307-0307; Chair. L. P. HEALY; Chief Exec. VINCENT CROWLEY.

John Fairfax Holdings Ltd: POB 506, Sydney, NSW 2001; tel. (2) 9282-2833; fax (2) 9282-3133; e-mail rvictor@mail.fairfax.com.au; internet www.fairfax.com.au; f. 1987; Chair. DEAN WILLS; Chief Exec. FREDERICK G. HILMER; publs include *The Sydney Morning Herald*, *The Australian Financial Review* and *Sun-Herald* (Sydney), *The Age* and *BRW Publications* (Melbourne); also provides online and interactive services.

The Herald and Weekly Times Ltd: POB 14999, Melbourne MC, Vic 8001; tel. (3) 9292-2000; fax (3) 9292-2002; e-mail newspapers@ hwt.newsltd.com.au; internet www.heraldsun.com.au; acquired by News Ltd in 1987; Chair. JANET CALVERT-JONES; Man. Dir JULIAN CLARKE; publs include *Herald Sun*, *Sunday Herald Sun*, *The Weekly Times*, *MX*.

The News Corporation: 2 Holt St, Surry Hills, Sydney, NSW 2010; tel. (2) 9288-3000; fax (2) 9288-2300; internet www.newscorp.com; Chair. and CEO K. RUPERT MURDOCH; controls *The Australian* and *The Weekend Australian* (national), *Daily Telegraph*, *Sunday Telegraph* (Sydney), *The Herald Sun* and *Sunday Herald Sun* (Victoria), *Northern Territory News* (Darwin), *Sunday Times* (Perth), *Townsville Bulletin*, *Courier Mail*, *Sunday Mail* (Queensland), *The Mercury* (Tasmania), *The Advertiser*, *Sunday Mail* (South Australia).

Rural Press Ltd: 159 Bells Line of Road, North Richmond, NSW 2754; tel. (2) 4570-4444; fax (2) 4570-4663; e-mail cosec@rpl.com.au; internet www.rpl.com.au; Chair. JOHN B. FAIRFAX; Man. Dir B. K. McCARTHY.

West Australian Newspapers Holdings Ltd: Newspaper House, 50 Hasler Rd, Osborne Park, WA 6017; tel. (8) 9482-3111; fax (8) 9482-9080; Chair. W. G. KENT; Man. Dir I. F. LAW.

Other newspaper publishers include Federal Capital Press (K. Stokes).

NEWSPAPERS

Australian Capital Territory

The Canberra Times: 9 Pirie St, Fyshwick, ACT 2609; POB 7155, Canberra Mail Centre, ACT 2610; tel. (2) 6280-2122; fax (2) 6280-2282; internet www.canberratimes.com; f. 1926; daily and Sun. morning; Editor-in-Chief JACK WATERFORD; circ. 38,694 (Mon.–Fri.), 72,080 (Sat.), 39,075 (Sun.).

New South Wales

Dailies

The Australian: News Ltd, 2 Holt St, Surry Hills, NSW 2010, POB 4245; tel. (2) 9288-3000; fax (2) 9288-3077; f. 1964; edited in Sydney, simultaneous edns in Sydney, Melbourne, Perth, Townsville, Adelaide and Brisbane; Editor-in-Chief DAVID ARMSTRONG; Editor CAMPBELL REID; circ. 122,500 (Mon.–Fri.); *The Weekend Australian* (Sat.) 311,000.

Australian Financial Review: 201 Sussex St, GPOB 506, Sydney, NSW 2000; tel. (2) 9282-2512; fax (2) 9282-3137; f. 1951; Mon.–Fri. distributed nationally; Publr/Editor-in-Chief MICHAEL GILL; Editor GLEN BURGE; circ. 92,500 (Mon.–Fri.), 92,000 (Sat.).

The Daily Telegraph: 2 Holt St, Surry Hills, NSW 2010; tel. (2) 9288-3000; fax (2) 9288-2300; f. 1879; merged in 1990 with Daily Mirror (f. 1941); 24-hour tabloid; CEO LACHLAN MURDOCH; circ. 442,000.

The Manly Daily: 26 Sydney Rd, Manly, NSW 2095; tel. (2) 9977-3333; fax (2) 9977-2831; e-mail manlydailynews@cng.newsltd.com.au; f. 1906; Tue.–Sat. Editor STEVE STICKNEY; circ. 89,326.

The Newcastle Herald: 28–30 Bolton St, Newcastle, NSW 2300; tel. (2) 4979-5000; fax (2) 4979-5888; f. 1858; morning; 6 a week; Editor-in-Chief ALAN OAKLEY; circ. 53,456.

The Sydney Morning Herald: 201 Sussex St, GPOB 506, Sydney, NSW 2001; tel. (2) 9282-2822; fax (2) 9282-3253; internet www.smh.com.au; f. 1831; morning; Editor-in-Chief and Publr ALAN REVELL; circ. 231,508 (Mon.–Fri.), 400,000 (Sat.).

Weeklies

Bankstown Canterbury Torch: Nabberly House, Cnr Marion St and Airport Ave, Bankstown, NSW 2200; tel. (2) 9795-0000; fax (2) 9795-0096; f. 1920; Wed. Editor CHARLES ELIAS; circ. 86,577.

Northern District Times: 79 Rowe St, Eastwood, NSW 2122; tel. (2) 9858-1766; fax (2) 9804-6901; f. 1921; Wed. Editor D. BARTOK; circ. 55,302.

The Parramatta Advertiser: 142 Macquarie St, Parramatta, NSW 2150; tel. (2) 9689-5370; fax (2) 9689-5353; Wed. Editor LES POBJIE; circ. 96,809.

St George and Sutherland Shire Leader: 182 Forest Rd, Hurstville, NSW 2220; tel. (2) 9598-3999; fax (2) 9598-3987; f. 1960; Tue. and Thur. Editor PETER ALLEN; circ. 143,595.

Sun-Herald: Level 24, 201 Sussex St, GPOB 506, Sydney, NSW 2001; tel. (2) 9282-2822; fax (2) 9282-2151; e-mail shnews@mail.fairfax.com.au; internet www.sunherald.com.au; f. 1953; Sun. Editor PHILIP McLEAN; circ. 580,000.

Sunday Telegraph: 2 Holt St, Surry Hills, NSW 2010; tel. (2) 9288-3000; fax (2) 9288-3311; f. 1938; Editor JENI COOPER; circ. 720,000.

Northern Territory

Daily

Northern Territory News: Printers Place, POB 1300, Darwin, NT 0801; tel. (8) 8944-9900; fax (8) 8981-6045; f. 1952; Mon.–Sat. Gen. Man. D. KENNEDY; circ. 24,470.

Weekly

Sunday Territorian: Printers Place, GPOB 1300, Darwin, NT 0801; tel. (8) 8944-9900; fax (8) 8981-6045; Sun. Editor DAVID COREN; circ. 26,437.

Queensland

Daily

Courier-Mail: 41 Campbell St, Bowen Hills, Brisbane, Qld 4006; tel. (7) 3252-6011; fax (7) 3252-6696; f. 1933; morning; Editor-in-Chief C. MITCHELL; circ. 250,875.

Weekly

Sunday Mail: 9th floor, 41 Campbell St, Bowen Hills, Brisbane, Qld 4006; tel. (7) 3666-8000; fax (7) 3666-6692; e-mail porterk@qnp.newsltd.com.au; f. 1953; Editor KAREN PORTER; circ. 590,423.

South Australia

Daily

The Advertiser: 121 King William St, Adelaide, SA 5001; tel. (8) 8206-2220; fax (8) 8206-3669; e-mail tiser@adv.newsltd.com.au; f. 1858; morning; Editor MELVIN MANSELL; circ. 203,440 (Mon.–Fri.), 274,045 (Sat.).

Weekly

Sunday Mail: 9th Floor, 121 King William St, Adelaide, SA 5000; tel. (8) 8206-2000; fax (8) 8206-3646; e-mail porterk@adv.newsltd.com.au; internet www.sundaymail.com.au; f. 1912; Editor KAREN PORTER; circ. 345,036.

Tasmania

Dailies

The Advocate: POB 63, Burnie 7320; tel. (3) 6440-7405; fax (3) 6440-7461; e-mail letters.advocate@harrisgroup.com.au; f. 1890; morning; Editor PETER DWYER; circ. 25,623.

Examiner: 71–75 Paterson St, POB 99A, Launceston, Tas 7250; tel. (3) 6336-7111; fax (3) 6334-7328; e-mail mail@examiner.com.au; internet www.examiner.com.au/examiner/; f. 1842; morning; independent; Editor R. J. SCOTT; circ. 38,721.

Mercury: 91–93 Macquarie St, Hobart, Tas 7000; tel. (3) 6230-0622; fax (3) 6230-0711; e-mail mercuryedletter@dbl.newsltd.com.au; internet www.news.com.au; f. 1854; morning; Man. Dir REX GARDNER; Editor I. McCAUSLAND; circ. 52,815.

Weeklies

Sunday Examiner: 71–75 Paterson St, Launceston, Tas 7250; tel. (3) 6336-7111; fax (3) 6334-7328; e-mail mail@examiner.com.au; f. 1924; Editor R. J. SCOTT; circ. 42,000.

Sunday Tasmanian: 91–93 Macquarie St, Hobart, Tas 7000; tel. (3) 6230-0622; fax (3) 6230-0711; e-mail e-mailsuntas.news@dbl.newsltd.com.au; f. 1984; morning; Man. Dir REX GARDNER; Editor IAN McCAUSLAND; circ. 58,325.

Victoria

Dailies

The Age: 250 Spencer St (cnr Lonsdale St), Melbourne, Vic 3000; tel. (3) 9600-4211; fax (3) 9601-2598; e-mail newsdesk@theage.fairfax.com.au; internet www.theage.com.au; f. 1854; independent; morning, incl. Sun. Publr and Editor-in-Chief MICHAEL GAWENDA; circ. 196,000 (Mon.–Fri.), 330,000 (Sat.), 197,000 (Sun.).

Herald Sun: HWT Tower, 40 City Rd, Southbank, Vic 3006; tel. (3) 9292-2000; fax (3) 9292-2112; e-mail news@heraldsun.com.au; internet www.heraldsun.com.au; f. 1840; Editor-in-Chief PETER BLUNDEN; circ. 548,764.

Weeklies

Progress Press: 360 Burwood Rd, Hawthorn, Vic 3122; tel. (3) 9818-0555; fax (3) 9818-0029; e-mail editor@ldr.newsltd.com.au; f. 1960; Tue. Editor LYNNE KINSEY; circ. 74,829.

Sunday Herald Sun: HWT Tower, 40 City Rd, Southbank, Vic 3006; tel. (3) 9292-2000; fax (3) 9292-2080; e-mail sundayhs@heraldsun.com.au; f. 1991; Editor ALAN HOWE; circ. 550,000.

Western Australia

Daily

The West Australian: POB D162, Perth, WA 6001; tel. (8) 9482-3111; fax (8) 9482-3399; e-mail editor@wanews.com.au; f. 1833; morning; Editor BRIAN ROGERS; circ. 214,000 (Mon.–Fri.), 386,000 (Sat.).

Weekly

Sunday Times: 34–42 Stirling St, Perth, WA 6000; tel. (8) 9326-8326; fax (8) 9326-8316; e-mail editorial@sundaytimes.newsltd.com.au; f. 1897; Man. Dir DAVID MAGUIRE; Editor BRETT McCARTHY; circ. 346,014.

PRINCIPAL PERIODICALS

Weeklies and Fortnightlies

Aussie Post: 35-51 Mitchell St, McMahon's Point, NSW 2060; tel. (2) 9464-3129; fax (2) 9464-3169; e-mail aussiepost@pacpubs.com.au; f. 1864; factual, general interest, Australiana; Mon. Editor GILL CHALMERS; circ. 24,500.

Australian Journal of Mining: Informa Australia Pty Ltd, Level 2, 120 Sussex St, Sydney, NSW 2000; e-mail charles.macdonald@

informa.com.au; internet www.theajmonline.com; f. 1986; fortnightly; mining and exploration throughout Australia and South Pacific; Editor CHARLES MCDONALD; circ. 6,771.

The Bulletin: 54 Park St, Sydney, NSW 2000; tel. (2) 9282-8227; fax (2) 9267-4359; e-mail cclegg@acp.com.au; f. 1880; Wed. Editor-in-Chief PAUL BAILEY; circ. 70,000.

Business Review Weekly: Level 2, 469 La Trobe St, Melbourne, Vic 3000; tel. (3) 9603-3888; fax (3) 9670-4328; f. 1981; Chair. and Editorial Dir ROBERT GOTTLIEBSEN; Editor ROSS GREENWOOD; circ. 75,166.

The Countryman: 219 St George's Terrace, Perth, WA 6000; GPOB D162, Perth 6001; tel. (8) 9482-3322; fax (8) 9482-3324; e-mail countryman@wanews.com.au; f. 1885; Thur. farming; Editor GARY MCGAY; circ. 13,444.

The Medical Journal of Australia: Locked Bag 3030, Strawberry Hills, NSW 2012; tel. (2) 9954-8666; fax (2) 9954-8699; e-mail mja@ampco.com.au; internet www.mja.com.au; f. 1914; fortnightly; Editor Dr MARTIN VAN DER WEYDEN; circ. 27,318.

New Idea: 35–51 Mitchell St, McMahons Point, NSW 2060; tel. (2) 9464-3200; fax (2) 9464-3203; e-mail newidea@pacpubs.com.au; weekly; women's; Editor JENNI GILBERT; circ. 471,000.

News Weekly: POB 186, North Melbourne, Vic 3051; tel. (3) 9326-5757; fax (3) 9328-2877; e-mail freedom@connexus.net.au; f. 1943; publ. by National Civic Council; fortnightly; Sat. political, social, educational and trade union affairs; Editor PETER WESTMORE; circ. 12,000.

People: 54 Park St, Sydney, NSW 2000; tel. (2) 9282-8743; fax (2) 9267-4365; e-mail sbutler-white@acp.com.au; weekly; Editor SIMON BUTLER-WHITE; circ. 70,000.

Picture: GPOB 5201, Sydney, NSW 2001; tel. (2) 9288-9686; fax (2) 9267-4372; e-mail picture@acp.com.au; weekly; men's; Editor TOM FOSTER; circ. 110,000.

Queensland Country Life: POB 586, Cleveland, Qld 4163; tel. (7) 3826-8200; fax (7) 3821-1236; f. 1935; Thur. Editor MARK PHELPS; circ. 33,900.

Stock and Land: 10 Sydenham St, Moonee Ponds, Vic 3039; tel. (3) 9287-0900; fax (3) 9370-5622; e-mail stockland@ruralpress.com; internet www.stockandland.com; f. 1914; weekly; agricultural and rural news; Editor JOHN CARSON; circ. 16,000.

That's Life!: 35–51 Mitchell St, McMahons Point, NSW 2060; tel. (2) 9464-3300; fax (2) 9464-3480; e-mail thatslife@pacpubs.com.au; f. 1994; weekly; features; Editor BEV HADGRAFT; circ. 465,500 (incl. New Zealand).

Time Australia Magazine: GPOB 3873, Sydney, NSW 2001; tel. (2) 9925-2646; fax (2) 9954-0828; e-mail time.letters@time.com.au; internet www.time.com.au; Editor STEVE WATERSON; circ. 111,000.

TV Week: 54 Park St, Sydney, NSW 2000; tel. (2) 9288-9611; fax (2) 9283-4849; e-mail tvweek@acp.com.au; internet www.tvweek .ninemsn.com.au; f. 1957; Wed. colour national; Editor EMMA NOLAN; circ. 364,044.

The Weekly Times: POB 14999, Melbourne City MC, Vic 8001; tel. (3) 9292-2000; fax (3) 9292-2697; e-mail wtimes@hwt.newsltd.com .au; internet www.news.com.au; f. 1869; farming, regional issues, country life; Wed. Editor PETER FLAHERTY; circ. 78,900.

Woman's Day: 54–58 Park St, POB 5245, Sydney, NSW 1028; tel. (2) 9282-8000; fax (2) 9267-4360; e-mail Womansday@acp.com.au; weekly; circulates throughout Australia and NZ; Editor-in-Chief PHILIP BARKER; circ. 765,170.

Monthlies and Others

Architectural Product News: Architecture Media Pty Ltd, Level 3, 4 Princes St, Port Melbourne, Vic 3207; tel. (3) 9646-4760; fax (3) 9646-4918; e-mail apn@archmedia.com.au; internet www .archmedia.com.au; 6 a year; Editor SUE HARRIS; circ. 24,871.

Architecture Australia: Architecture Media Pty Ltd, Level 3, 4 Princes St, Port Melbourne, Vic 3207; tel. (3) 9646-4760; fax (3) 9646-4918; e-mail aa@archmedia.com.au; internet www.archmedia.com .au; f. 1904; 6 a year; Editor IAN CLOSE; circ. 14,266.

Australian Hi-Fi: POB 5555, St Leonards, NSW 1590; tel. (2) 9901-6100; fax (2) 9901-6198; e-mail hifi@horwitz.com.au; f. 1970; every 2 months; consumer tests on hi-fi and home theatre equipment; Editor GREG BORROWMAN; circ. 11,800.

Australian Home Beautiful: 35–51 Mitchell St, McMahons Point, NSW 2060; tel. (2) 9464-3218; fax (2) 9464-3263; e-mail homebeaut@pacpubs.com.au; internet www.homebeautiful.com.au; f. 1925; monthly; Editor ANDREA JONES; circ. 83,808.

Australian House and Garden: 54 Park St, Sydney, NSW 2000; tel. (2) 9282-8456; fax (2) 9267-4912; e-mail h&g@acp.com.au; f.

1948; monthly; design, decorating, renovating, gardens, food and travel; Editor ANNY FRIIS; circ. 110,000.

Australian Journal of Pharmacy: 100 Harris St, Pyrmont, NSW 2009; tel. (2) 8587-7000; fax (2) 8587-7100; f. 1886; monthly; journal of the associated pharmaceutical orgs; Man. Editor DAVID WESTON; circ. 6,443.

Australian Law Journal: 100 Harris St, Pyrmont, NSW 2009; tel. (2) 8587-7000; fax (2) 8587-7104; f. 1927; monthly; Editor Justice P. W. YOUNG; circ 4,500.

Australian Photography: POB 606, Sydney, NSW 2001; tel. (2) 9281-2333; fax (2) 9281-2750; e-mail robertkeeley@yaffa.com.au; monthly; Editor ROBERT KEELEY; circ. 9,010.

The Australian Women's Weekly: 54–56 Park St, Sydney, NSW 2000; tel. (2) 9282-8000; fax (2) 9267-4459; e-mail FDaniele@acp.com .au; internet www.ninemsn.com.au/aww; f. 1933; monthly; Editor DEBORAH THOMAS; circ. 701,088.

Belle: 54 Park St, Sydney, NSW 2000; tel. (2) 9282-8000; fax (2) 9267-8037; e-mail belle@acp.com.au; f. 1975; every 2 months; Editor ERIC MATTHEWS; circ. 44,663.

Better Homes and Gardens: 45 Jones St, Ultimo, NSW 2007; tel. (2) 9692-2000; fax (2) 9692-2264; e-mail philippah@mm.com.au; f. 1978; 13 a year; Editor TONI EATTS; circ. 340,133.

Cleo: 54 Park St, Sydney, NSW 2000; POB 4088, Sydney, NSW 2001; tel. (2) 9282-8617; fax (2) 9267-4368; f. 1972; women's monthly; Editor DEBORAH THOMAS; circ. 263,353.

Commercial Photography: GPOB 606, Sydney, NSW 1041; tel. (2) 9281-2333; fax (2) 9281-2750; e-mail yaffa@flex.com.au; every 2 months; journal of the Professional Photographers Asscn of Australia and Photographic Industry Marketing Asscn of Australia; Editor SAIMA MOREL; circ. 3,835.

Cosmopolitan: 54 Park St, Sydney, NSW 2000; tel. (2) 9282-8039; fax (2) 9267-4457; e-mail cosmo@acp.com.au; internet www .cosmopolitan.com.au; f. 1973; monthly; Editor MIA FREEDMAN; circ. 203,058.

Dolly: 54–58 Park St, Sydney, NSW 1028; tel. (2) 9282-8437; fax (2) 9267-4911; e-mail dolly@ninemsn.com.au; internet www.ninemsn .com.au/dolly; f. 1970; monthly; for young women; Editor VIRGINIA KNIGHT; circ. 177,268.

Ecos: CSIRO, POB 1139, Collingwood, Vic 3066; tel. (3) 9662-7500; fax (3) 9662-7555; internet www.publish.csiro.au; f. 1974; quarterly; reports of CSIRO environmental research findings for the non-specialist reader; Editor BRYONY BENNETT; circ. 8,000.

Electronics Australia: POB 199, Alexandria, NSW 1435; tel. (2) 9353-0620; fax (2) 9353-0613; e-mail electaus@fpc.com.au; internet www.electronicsaustralia.com.au; f. 1922; monthly; technical, radio, television, microcomputers, hi-fi and electronics; Editor GRAHAM CATTLEY; circ. 20,900.

Elle: 54 Park St, Sydney, NSW 2000; tel. (2) 9282-8790; fax (2) 9267-4375; f. 1990; monthly; Editor MARINA GO; circ. 68,154.

Family Circle: Pier 8/9, 23 Hickson Rd, Millers Point, NSW 2000; tel. (2) 8220-2000; fax (2) 8220-2111; e-mail family_circle@mm.com .au; 13 a year; circ. 235,860.

Gardening Australia: POB 199, Alexandria, NSW 1435; tel. (2) 9353-6666; fax (2) 9317-4615; f. 1991; monthly; Editor BRODIE MYERS-COOKE; circ. 87,000.

Houses: Architecture Media Pty Ltd, Level 3, 4 Princes St, Port Melbourne, Vic 3207; tel. (3) 9646-4760; fax (3) 9646-4918; e-mail houses@archmedia.com.au; internet www.archmedia.com.au; f. 1989; 4 a year; Editor JULIE DILLAN; Man. Editor SUE HARRIS; circ. 23,768.

HQ: 54 Park St, Sydney, NSW 1028; tel. (2) 9282-8260; fax (2) 9267-3616; e-mail hq@publishing.acp.com.au; internet www.hq.ninemsn .com.au; f. 1989; every 2 months; Publr JOHN ALEXANDER; Editor KATHY BAIL; circ. 32,837.

Manufacturers' Monthly: Level 1/28 Riddell Parade, Elsternwick, Vic 3185; tel. (3) 9245-7777; fax (3) 9245-7750; f. 1961; Editor GREG VIDEON; circ. 15,188.

Modern Boating: The Federal Publishing Co Pty Ltd, Unit 2, 160 Bourke Rd, Alexandria, NSW 2015; tel. (2) 9353-6666; fax (2) 9353-0935; e-mail imacrae@fpcpower.com.au; internet www .modernboating.com.au; f. 1965; every 2 months; Editor IAN MACRAE; circ. 11,000.

Motor: Locked Bag 12, Oakleigh, Vic 3166; tel. (3) 9567-4200; fax (3) 9563-4554; e-mail motor@acpaction.com.au; f. 1954; monthly; Editor GED BULMER; circ. 41,414.

New Woman: Murdoch Magazines, 45 Jones St, Ultimo, NSW 2007; tel. (2) 9692-2000; fax (2) 9692-2488; monthly; Editor-in-Chief GAY BRYANT; circ. 108,444.

The Open Road: L27, 388 George St, Sydney, NSW 2000; tel. (2) 9292-9275; fax (2) 9292-9069; f. 1927; every 2 months; journal of National Roads and Motorists' Asscn (NRMA); Editor Steve Fraser; circ. 1,555,917.

Personal Investor: Level 2, 469 La Trobe St, Melbourne, Vic 3000; tel. (3) 9603-3888; fax (3) 9670-4328; e-mail pieditor@brw.fairfax.com.au; internet www.personalinvestor.com.au; monthly; Editor Robin Bowerman; circ. 61,016.

Reader's Digest: 26–32 Waterloo St, Surry Hills, NSW 2010; tel. (2) 9690-6111; fax (2) 9690-6211; monthly; Editor-in-Chief Bruce Heilbuth; circ. 508,142.

Street Machine: Locked Bag 756, Epping, NSW 2121; tel. (2) 9868-4832; fax (2) 9869-7390; e-mail streetmachine@acpaction.com.au; Editor Mark Oastler; circ. 55,000.

TV Hits: Private Bag 9900, North Sydney, NSW 2059; tel. (2) 9464-3300; fax (2) 9464-3508; f. 1988; monthly; circ. 114,509.

TV Soap: 55 Chandos St, St Leonards, NSW 2065; tel. (2) 9901-6100; fax (2) 9901-6166; f. 1983; monthly; Editor Ben Mitchell; circ. 103,000.

Vogue Australia: Level 2, 170 Pacific Highway, Greenwich, NSW 2065; tel. (2) 9964-3888; fax (2) 9964-3879; f. 1959; monthly; fashion; Editor Juliet Ashworth; circ. 54,705.

Wheels: GPOB 4088, Sydney, NSW 2001; tel. (2) 9263-9700; fax (2) 9263-9702; internet www.carpoint.com.au; f. 1953; monthly; international motoring magazine; circ. 60,286.

Wildlife Research: CSIRO Publishing, 150 Oxford St, POB 1139, Collingwood, Vic 3066; tel. (3) 9662-7622; fax (3) 9662-7611; e-mail publishing.wr@_csiro.au; internet www.publish.csiro.au/journals/wr; f. 1974; 6 a year; Man. Editor D. W. Morton; circ. 1,000.

Your Garden: 35–51 Mitchell St, McMahons Point, NSW 2060; tel. (2) 9464-3586; fax (2) 9464-3487; e-mail yg@pacpubs.com.au; internet www.yourgarden.com.au; monthly; Editor Maree Tredinnick; circ. 60,246.

NEWS AGENCIES

AAP Information Services: Locked Bag 21, Grosvenor Place, Sydney, NSW 2000; tel. (2) 9322-8000; fax (2) 9322-8888; f. 1983; owned by major daily newspapers of Australia; Chair. and CEO C. L. Casey.

Foreign Bureaux

Agence France-Presse (AFP): 7th Floor, 259 George St, Sydney, NSW 2000; tel. (2) 9251-1544; fax (2) 9251-5230; e-mail afpsyd@afp.com; internet www.afp.com; Bureau Chief David Millikin.

Agenzia Nazionale Stampa Associata (ANSA) (Italy): Suite 4, 2 Grosvenor St, Bondi Junction, NSW 2022; tel. (2) 9369-1427; fax (2) 9369-4351; e-mail ansasyd@ozemail.com.au; Bureau Chief Claudio Marcello.

Deutsche Presse-Agentur (dpa) (Germany): 36 Heath St, Mona Vale, NSW 2103; tel. (2) 9979-8253; fax (2) 9997-3154; e-mail hofman@zip.com.au; Correspondent Alexander Hofman.

Jiji Press (Australia) Pty Ltd (Japan): GPOB 2584, Sydney, NSW 2001; tel. (2) 9230-0020; fax (2) 9230-0024; e-mail jijiaust@bigpond.com; Bureau Chief Nobotushi Kobayashi.

Kyodo News Service (Japan): Level 7, 9 Lang St, Sydney, NSW 2000; tel. (2) 9251-5240; fax (2) 9251-4980; e-mail jumper8@attglobal.net; Bureau Chief Masato Ishii.

Reuters Australia Pty Ltd: Level 30, 60 Margaret St, Sydney, NSW 2031; e-mail Sydney.newsroom@reuters.com; internet www.reuters.com; Bureau Chief Phil Smith.

Xinhua (New China) News Agency (People's Republic of China): 50 Russell St, Hackett, Canberra, ACT 2602; tel. (2) 6248-6369; fax (2) 6257-4706; Chief Correspondent Lin Zhenxi.

The Central News Agency (Taiwan) and the New Zealand Press Association are represented in Sydney, and Antara (Indonesia) is represented in Canberra.

PRESS ASSOCIATIONS

Australian Press Council: Suite 303, 149 Castlereagh St, Sydney, NSW 2000; tel. (2) 9261-1930; fax (2) 9267-6826; e-mail info@presscouncil.org.au; internet www.presscouncil.org.au; Chair. Prof. Ken McKinnon.

Community Newspapers of Australia Pty Ltd: POB Q1527, QVB, NSW 1230; tel. (2) 9248-7300; fax (2) 9299-0087; e-mail robyn@printnet.com.au; Sec. Robyn Baker.

Country Press Association of SA Incorporated: 198 Greenhill Rd, Eastwood, SA 5063; tel. (8) 8373-6533; fax (8) 8373-6544; f. 1912;

represents South Australian country newspapers; Pres. B. Price; Exec. Dir M. R. Townsend.

Country Press Australia: POB Q182, Queen Victoria Bldg, Sydney, NSW 2000; tel. (2) 9299-4658; fax (2) 9299-1892; f. 1906; Exec. Dir D. J. Sommerlad; 420 mems.

Queensland Country Press Association: POB 103, Paddington, Qld 4064; tel. (7) 3356-0033; Pres. M. Hodgson; Sec. N. D. McLary.

Tasmanian Press Association Pty Ltd: 71–75 Paterson St, Launceston, Tas 7250; tel. (3) 6336-7111; Sec. Tom O'Meara.

Victorian Country Press Association Ltd: 33 Rathdowne St, Carlton, Vic 3053; tel. (3) 9662-3244; fax (3) 9663-7433; e-mail vcpa@vcpa.com.au; f. 1910; Pres. G. Kelly; Exec. Dir J. E. Ray; 114 mems.

Publishers

Allen and Unwin Pty Ltd: 83 Alexander St, Crows Nest, NSW 2065; tel. (2) 8425-0100; fax (2) 9906-2218; e-mail info@allenandunwin.com; internet www.allenandunwin.com; fiction, trade, academic, children's; Man. Dir Patrick A. Gallagher.

Australasian Medical Publishing Co Pty Ltd: Level 2, 26-32 Pyrmont Bridge Road, Pyrmont, NSW 2009; tel. (2) 9562-6666; fax (2) 9562-6600; e-mail ampco@ampco.com.au; internet www.ampco.com.au; f. 1913; scientific, medical and educational; CEO Dr Martin van der Weyden.

Britannica.com.au: Locked Bag 927, North Sydney, NSW 2060; tel. (2) 9923-5600; fax (2) 9929-3753; e-mail sales@Britannica.com.au; internet www.britannica.com.au; reference, education, art, science and commerce; Man. Dir David Campbell.

Butterworths: Tower 2, 475 Victoria Ave, Chatswood, NSW 2067; tel. (2) 9422-2222; fax (2) 9422-2444; internet www.lexisnexis.com.au; f. 1910; div. of Reed International Books Australia Pty Ltd; legal and commercial; Man. Dir Max Piper.

Cambridge University Press (Australia): 10 Stamford Road, Oakleigh, Melbourne, Vic 3166; tel. (3) 9568-0322; fax (3) 9569-9292; e-mail info@cup.edu.au; internet www.cup.edu.au; scholarly and educational; Dir Sandra McComb.

Commonwealth Scientific and Industrial Research Organisation (CSIRO PUBLISHING): 150 Oxford St, POB 1139, Collingwood, Vic 3066; tel. (3) 9662-7500; fax (3) 9662-7555; e-mail publishing@csiro.au; internet www.publish.csiro.au; f. 1926; scientific and technical journals, books, magazines, videos, CD-ROMs; Gen. Man. P. W. Reekie.

Doubleday Australia Pty Ltd: 91 Mars Rd, Lane Cove, NSW 2066; tel. (2) 9427-0377; fax (2) 9427-6973; educational, trade, nonfiction, Australiana; Man. Dir Barry MacMullen.

Elsevier Australia (a division of Reed International Books Australia Pty Ltd): 30–52 Smidmore St, Marrickville, NSW 2204; tel. (2) 9517-8999; fax (2) 9517-2249; e-mail service@elsevier.com.au; internet www.elsevier.com.au; health sciences, science and medicine; Man. Dir Fergus Hall.

Harcourt Education Australia: POB 460, Port Melbourne, Vic 3207; tel. (3) 9245-7111; fax (3) 9245-7333; e-mail admin@harcourteducation.com.au; internet www.hi.com.au; primary, secondary and tertiary educational; division of Reed International; Man. Dir David O'Brien.

Harlequin Enterprises (Australia) Pty Ltd: Unit 2, 3 Gibbes St, Chatswood, NSW 2067; tel. (2) 9415-9200; fax (2) 9415-9292; internet www.eHarlequin.com.au; Man. Dir Michelle Laforest.

Hodder Headline Australia Pty Ltd: Level 22, 201 Kent, Sydney, NSW 2000; tel. (2) 8248-0800; fax (2) 8248-0810; e-mail auspub@hha.com.au; internet www.hha.com.au; fiction, general, technical, children's; Man. Dir Malcolm Edwards.

Hyland House Publishing Pty Ltd: POB 122, Flemington, Vic 3031; tel. and fax (3) 9376-4461; e-mail hyland3@netspace.net.au; f. 1976; trade, general, gardening, pet care, Aboriginal, Asian-Pacific public policy, fiction; Rep. Michael Schoo.

Lansdowne Publishing: Level 1, 18 Argyle St, The Rocks, NSW 2000; tel. (2) 9240-9222; fax (2) 9241-4818; e-mail steven@lanspub.com.au; cookery, gardening, health, history, pet care; Chief Exec. Steven Morris.

LBC Information Services: 100 Harris St, Pyrmont, NSW 2009; tel. (2) 8587-7000; fax (2) 8587-7100; e-mail lbccustomer@thomson.com.au; legal and professional; Man. Dir E. J. Costigan.

Lothian Books: Level 5, 132 Albert Rd, South Melbourne, Vic 3205; tel. (3) 9694 4900; fax (3) 9645-0705; e-mail books@lothian.com.au; internet www.lothian.com.au; f. 1888; gardening, health, sport, business, New Age, self-help, general non-fiction, young adult fiction and children's picture books; Man. Dir Peter Lothian.

McGraw-Hill Australia Pty Ltd: 4 Barcoo St, Roseville, Sydney, NSW 2069; tel. (2) 9415-9899; fax (2) 9417-8872; e-mail cservice_sydney@mcgraw-hill.com; internet www.mcgraw-hill.com .au; educational, professional and technical; Man. Dir FIRGAL ADAMS.

Melbourne University Press: 268 Drummond St, Carlton South, Vic 3053; tel. (3) 9347-0300; fax (3) 9342-0399; e-mail info@mup .unimelb.edu.au; internet www.mup.com.au; f. 1922; scholarly non-fiction, Australian history and biography; Chair. Prof. BARRY SHEEHAN; Dir JOHN MECKAN.

Murdoch Books: GPOB 1203, Sydney, NSW 2001; tel. (2) 8220-2000; fax (2) 8220-2558; e-mail incaw@mm.com.au; cooking, gardening, DIY, children's; CEO JULIET ROGERS; Publr KAY SCARLETT.

National Library of Australia: Parkes Place, Canberra, ACT 2600; tel. (2) 6262-1111; fax (2) 6273-4493; e-mail phetheri@nla.gov .au; internet www.nla.gov.au; f. 1960; national bibliographic service, etc. Publications Dir PAUL HETHERINGTON.

Nelson Thomson Learning: 102 Dodds St, South Melbourne, Vic 3205; tel. (3) 9685-4111; fax (3) 9685-4199; e-mail customerservice@ nelson.com.au; internet www.nelsonitp.com; educational; Man. Dir G. J. BROWNE.

Oxford University Press: 253 Normanby Rd, South Melbourne, Vic 3205; tel. (3) 9934-9123; fax (3) 9934-9100; f. 1908; general non-fiction and educational; Man. Dir MAREK PALKA.

Pan Macmillan Australia Pty Ltd: Level 18, St Martin's Tower, 31 Market St, Sydney, NSW 2000; tel. (2) 9285-9100; fax (2) 9285-9190; e-mail pansyd@macmillan.com.au; general, reference, children's, fiction, non-fiction; Chair. R. GIBB.

Pearson Education Australia Pty Ltd: 95 Coventry St, South Melbourne, Vic 3205; tel. (3) 9697-0666; fax (3) 9699-2041; e-mail longman.sales@pearsoned.com.au; internet www.pearsoned.com .au; f. 1957; mainly educational, academic, computer, some general; Man. Dir DAVID BARNETT.

Penguin Books Australia Ltd: POB 701, Hawthorn, Vic 3122; tel. (3) 9811-2400; fax (3) 9811-2620; internet www.penguin.com.au; f. 1946; general; Man. Dir PETER FIELD; Publishing Dir ROBERT SESSIONS.

Random House Australia Pty Ltd: 20 Alfred St, Milsons Point, NSW 2061; tel. (2) 9954-9966; fax (2) 9954-4562; e-mail random@ randomhouse.com.au; internet www.randomhouse.com.au; fiction, non-fiction, children's and illustrated; Man. Dir MARGARET SEALE.

Reader's Digest (Australia) Pty Ltd: POB 4353, Sydney, NSW 2000; tel. (2) 9690-6111; fax (2) 9699-8165; general; Man. Dir WILLIAM B. TOOHEY.

Scholastic Australia Pty Ltd: Railway Crescent, Lisarow, POB 579, Gosford, NSW 2250; tel. (2) 4328-3555; fax (2) 4323-3827; internet www.scholastic.com.au; f. 1968; educational and children's; Man. Dir KEN JOLLY.

Schwartz Publishing (Victoria) Pty Ltd: 45 Flinders Lane, Melbourne, Vic 3000; tel. (3) 9654-2000; fax (3) 9650-5418; fiction, non-fiction; Dir MORRY SCHWARTZ.

Simon and Schuster Australia: 20 Barcoo St, POB 507, East Roseville, NSW 2069; tel. (2) 9415-9900; fax (2) 9417-4292; general fiction, non-fiction, cooking, gardening, craft, parenting, health, history, travel and biography; Man. Dir JON ATTENBOROUGH.

Thames and Hudson (Australia) Pty Ltd: 11 Central Boulevard, Portside Business Park, Fishermans Bend, Vic 3207; tel. (3) 9646-7788; fax (3) 9646-8790; e-mail thaust@thaust.com.au; art, history, archaeology, architecture, photography, design, fashion, textiles, lifestyle; Man. Dir PETER SHAW.

Thorpe-Bowker: C3, 85 Turner St (Locked Bag 20) Port Melbourne, Vic 3207; tel. (3) 8645-0300; fax (3) 8645-0333; e-mail customer.service@thorpe.com.au; internet www.thorpe.com.au; bibliographic, library and book trade reference; Gen. Man. RICHARD SIEGERSYA.

Time Life Australia Pty Ltd: Level 12, 33 Berry St, North Sydney, NSW 2060; tel. (2) 8925-3800; fax (2) 9957-4227; general and educational; Man. Dir ROBERT HARDY.

UNSW Press Ltd: UNSW, Sydney, NSW 2052; tel. (2) 9664-0999; fax (2) 9664-5420; e-mail info.press@unsw.edu.au; f. 1961; scholarly, general and tertiary texts; Man. Dir Dr ROBIN DERRICOURT.

University of Queensland Press: POB 6042, St Lucia, Qld 4067; tel. (7) 3365-2127; fax (7) 3365-7579; e-mail uqp@uqp.uq.edu.au; internet www.uqp.uq.edu.au; f. 1948; scholarly and general cultural interest, incl. South Australian writers, adult and children's fiction; Gen. Man. LAURIE MULLER.

University of Western Australia Press: c/o University of Western Australia, WA 6009; tel. (8) 9380-3670; fax (8) 9380-1027; e-mail uwap@cyllene.uwa.edu.au; internet www.uwapress.uwa.edu .au; f. 1954; natural history, history, literary studies, Australiana, children's, general non-fiction; Dir Dr JENNY GREGORY.

John Wiley & Sons Australia, Ltd: POB 1226, Milton, Qld 4064; tel. (7) 3859-9755; fax (7) 3859-9715; e-mail brisbane@johnwiley.com .au; internet www.johnwiley.com.au; f. 1954; educational, reference and trade; Man. Dir PETER DONOUGHUE.

Government Publishing House

AusInfo: GPOB 1920, Canberra, ACT 2601; tel. (2) 6275-3442; fax (2) 6275-3682; internet www.ausinfo.gov.au; f. 1970; fmrly Australian Govt Publishing Service; Assistant Sec. MICHELLE KINNANE.

PUBLISHERS' ASSOCIATION

Australian Publishers Association Ltd: 60/89 Jones St, Ultimo, NSW 2007; tel. (2) 9281-9788; fax (2) 9281-1073; e-mail apa@ publishers.asn.au; internet www.publishers.asn.au; f. 1948; 115 mems; Pres. GREG BROWNE; Chief Exec. SUSAN BRIDGE.

Broadcasting and Communications

TELECOMMUNICATIONS

By March 2003, 112 licensed telecommunication carriers were in operation.

AAPT Ltd: AAPT Centre, 9 Lang St, Sydney, NSW 2000; tel. (2) 9377-7000; fax (2) 9377-7133; internet www.aapt.com.au; f. 1991; long-distance telecommunications carrier; Chair C. L. CASEY; CEO and Man. Dir L. WILLIAMS.

Cable & Wireless Optus Ltd: POB 1, North Sydney, NSW 2059; tel. (2) 9342-7800; fax (2) 9342-7100; internet www.cwo.com.au; f. 1991; general and mobile telecommunications, data and internet services, pay-TV; Chair. Sir RALPH ROBINS; Chief Exec. CHRIS ANDERSON.

Matrix Telecommunications Services: 1st Floor, 24 Artamon Rd, Willoughby, NSW 2068; tel. (2) 9290-4111; fax (2) 9262-2574; f. 1985; mobile communication services; Chair. MARK CARNEGIE; Pres. and CEO JOSEPH YANG.

One.Tel Ltd: Level 28, 9 Castlereagh St, Sydney, NSW 2000; tel. (2) 9777-8111; fax (2) 9777-8199; internet www.onetel.com.au; telecommunication services; Chair. JOHN GREAVES.

Telstra Corpn Ltd: Level 14, 231 Elizabeth St, Sydney, NSW 2000; tel. (2) 9287-4677; fax (2) 9287-5869; internet www.telstra.com.au; general and mobile telecommunication services; Man. Dir and Chief Exec. ZIGGY SWITKOWSKI.

Vodafone Pacific Pty Ltd: Tower A, 799 Pacific Highway, Chatswood, NSW 2067; tel. (2) 9878-7000; fax (2) 9878-7788; internet www .vodafone.com.au; mobile telecommunication services.

Regulatory Authority

Australian Communications Authority (ACA): POB 78, Belconnen, ACT 2616; tel. (3) 9963-6800; fax (3) 9963-6899; e-mail candinfo@aca.gov.au; internet www.aca.gov.au; f. 1997; Commonwealth regulator for telecommunications and radiocommunications; Chair. TONY SHAW.

BROADCASTING

Many programmes are provided by the non-commercial statutory corporation, the Australian Broadcasting Corporation (ABC). Commercial radio and television services are provided by stations operated by companies under licences granted and renewed by the Australian Broadcasting Authority (ABA). They rely for their income on the broadcasting of advertisements. In mid-1993 there were 166 commercial radio stations in operation, and 44 commercial television stations.

In 1997 there were an estimated 25.5m. radio receivers. The number of television receivers in use totalled 14,129 in 2000.

Australian Broadcasting Corporation (ABC): 700 Harris St, Ultimo, POB 9994, Sydney, NSW 2001; tel. (1) 9333-1500 (radio); fax (2) 9333-2603 (radio), (2) 9950-3050 (television); e-mail comments@ your.abc.net.au; internet www.abc.net.au; f. 1932 as Australian Broadcasting Commission; became corporation in 1983; one national television network operating on about 700 transmitters and six radio networks operating on more than 6,000 transmitters; Chair. DONALD McDONALD; Man. Dir RUSSELL BALDING.

Radio Australia: international service broadcast by short wave and satellite in English, Indonesian, Standard Chinese, Khmer, Tok Pisin and Vietnamese.

Radio

Federation of Australian Radio Broadcasters Ltd: Level 5, 88 Foveaux street, Surry Hills, NSW 2010; tel. (2) 9281-6577; fax (2) 9281-6599; e-mail mail@commercialradio.com.au; internet www

.commercialradio.com; asscn of privately-owned Australian commercial stations; CEO JOAN WARNER.

Major Commercial Broadcasting Station Licensees

5AD Broadcasting Co Pty Ltd: 201 Tynte St, Nth Adelaide, SA 5006; tel. (8) 8300-1000; fax (8) 8300-1020; internet www.5adfm.com.au; also operates 5DN and Mix102.3; Gen. Man. GRAEME TUCKER.

Associated Communications Enterprises (ACE) Radio Broadcasters Pty Ltd: POB 7515, Melbourne, Vic 3004; tel. (3) 9645-9877; fax (3) 9645-9886; operates six stations; Man. Dir S. EVERETT.

Austereo Pty Ltd: Ground Level, 180 St Kilda Rd, St Kilda, Vic 3182; tel. (3) 9230-1051; fax (3) 9593-9007; e-mail pharvie@austereo.com.au; internet www.austereo.com.au; operates 14 stations; Exec. Chair. PETER HARVIE.

Australian Radio Network Pty Ltd: Level 8, 99 Mount St, North Sydney, NSW 2060; tel. (2) 9464-1000; fax (2) 9464-1010; operates nine stations; CEO NEIL MOUNT.

Australian Regional Broadcasters: 1 June Rd, Gooseberry Hill, WA 6076; tel. (8) 9472-8900; fax (8) 9472-8911; operates three stations; Man. Dir NICK RINGROSE.

Bass Radio: 109 York St, Launceston, Tas 7250; tel. (3) 6331-4844; fax (3) 6334-5858; operates five radio stations and part of RG Capital Radio; Man. DAVE HILL.

Capital Radio: 28 Sharp St, Cooma, NSW 2630; tel. (2) 6452-1521; fax (2) 6452-1006; operates four stations; Man. Dir KEVIN BLYTON.

DMG Regional Radio Pty Ltd: Level 5, 33 Saunders St, Pyrmont, NSW 2009; tel. (2) 9564 9888; fax (2) 9564 9867; e-mail sydoff@dmgradio.com.au; internet www.dmgradio.com.au; operates 59 stations; Gen. Mans KEN GANNAWAY (Western Group), DAVID SCOPELLITI (Northern Group), GARRY LEDDIN (Southern Group); Chair. PAUL THOMPSON.

Grant Broadcasting: 63 Minimbah Rd, Northbridge, NSW 2063; tel. (2) 9958-7301; fax (2) 9958-6906; operates seven stations; Gen. Man. JANET CAMERON.

Greater Cairns Radio Ltd: Virginia House, Abbott St, Cairns, Qld 4870; tel. (7) 4050-0800; fax (7) 4051-8060; e-mail cnssales@dmgradio.com.au; Gen. Man. J. ELLER.

Macquarie Radio Network Pty Ltd: POB 4290, Sydney, NSW 2001; tel. (2) 9269-0646; fax (2) 9287-2772; operates 2GB and 2CH; CEO GEORGE BUSCHMAN.

Moree Broadcasting and Development Company Ltd: 87–89 Balo St, Moree, NSW 2400; tel. (2) 6752-1155; fax (2) 6752-2601; operates two stations; Man. KEN BIRCH.

Radio 2SM Gold 1269: 186 Blues Point Rd, North Sydney, NSW 2060; tel. (2) 9922-1269; fax (2) 9954-3117; f. 1931; CEO and Chair. C. M. MURPHY.

RadioWest Hot FM: POB 10067, Kalgoorlie, WA 6430; tel. (8) 9021-2666; fax (8) 9091-2209; e-mail radio6KG@gold.net.au; f. 1931.

Regional Broadcasters (Australia) Pty: McDowal St, Roma, Qld 4455; tel. (7) 4622-1800; fax (7) 4622-3697; Chair. G. McVEAN.

RG Capital Radio Pty Ltd: Level 2, Seabank Bldg, 12–14 Marine Parade, Southport, Qld 4215; tel. (7) 5591-5000; fax (7) 5591-2869; operates 34 stations; Man. Dir RHYS HOLLERAN.

Rural Press Ltd: Cnr Pine Mt Rd and Hill St, Raymonds Hill, Qld 4305; tel. (7) 3201-6000; fax (7) 3812-3060; internet www.rpl.com.au; f. 1911; operates five stations; Gen. Man. RICHARD BURNS.

SEA FM Pty Ltd: POB 5910, Gold Coast Mail Centre, Bundall, Qld 4217; tel. (7) 5591-5000; fax (7) 5591-6080; operates 28 stations; Man. Dir RHYS HOLLERAN.

Southern Cross Broadcasting (Australia) Ltd: see under Television.

Supernetwork Radio Pty Ltd: POB 97, Coolangatta, Qld 4225; tel. (7) 5524-4497; fax (7) 5554-3970; operates 15 stations; Chair. W. CARALIS.

Tamworth Radio Development Company Pty Ltd: POB 497, Tamworth, NSW 2340; tel. (2) 6765-7055; fax (2) 6765-2762; operates five stations; Man. W. A. MORRISON.

Tasmanian Broadcasting Network (TBN): POB 665G, Launceston, Tas 7250; tel. (3) 6431-2555; fax (3) 6431-3188; operates three stations; Chair. K. FINDLAY.

Wesgo Ltd: POB 234, Seven Hills, NSW 2147; tel. (2) 9831-7611; fax (2) 9831-2001; operates eight stations; CEO G. W. RICE.

Television

Federation of Australian Commercial Television Stations (FACTS): 44 Avenue Rd, Mosman, NSW 2088; tel. (2) 9960-2622; fax (2) 9969-3520; internet www.facts.org.au; f. 1960; represents all commercial television stations; Chair. JUDITH STACK; CEO JULIE FLYNN.

Commercial Television Station Licensees

Amalgamated Television Services Pty Ltd: Mobbs Lane, Epping, NSW 2121; tel. (2) 9877-7777; fax (2) 9877-7888; f. 1956; originating station for Seven Network TV programming; Exec. Chair. KERRY STOKES.

Australian Capital Television Pty Ltd (Ten Capital): Private Bag 10, Dickson, ACT 2602; tel. (2) 6242-2400; fax (2) 6241-7230; f. 1962; Gen. Man. ERIC PASCOE.

Broken Hill Television Ltd: POB 472, Rocky Hill, Broken Hill, NSW 2880; tel. (8) 8087-6013; fax (8) 8087-8492; internet www.centralonline.com.au; f. 1968; operates one station; Chair. PETER STORROCK; Chief Exec. D. WESTON.

Channel 9 South Australia Pty Ltd: 202 Tynte St, North Adelaide 5006; tel. (8) 8267-0111; fax (8) 8267-3996; f. 1959; Gen. Man. M. COLSON.

Channel Seven Adelaide Pty Ltd: 45–49 Park Terrace, Gilberton, SA 5081; tel. (8) 8342-7777; fax (8) 8342-7717; f. 1965; operates SAS Channel 7; mem. of Seven Network; Man. Dir MAX WALTERS.

Channel Seven Brisbane Pty Ltd: GPOB 604, Brisbane, Qld 4001; tel. (7) 3369-7777; fax (7) 3368-2970; f. 1959; operates one station; mem. of Seven Network; Man. Dir L. M. RILEY.

Channel Seven Melbourne Pty Ltd: 119 Wells St, Southbank, Vic 3006; tel. (3) 9697-7777; fax (3) 9697-7888; e-mail daspinall@seven.com.au; f. 1956; operates one station; Chair. KERRY STOKES; Man. Dir DAVID ASPINALL.

Channel Seven Perth Pty Ltd: POB 77, Tuart Hill, WA 6939; tel. (8) 9344-0777; fax (8) 9344-0670; f. 1959; Chair. C. S. WHARTON.

General Television Corporation Pty Ltd: 22–46 Bendigo St, POB 100, Richmond, Vic 3121; tel. (3) 9429-0201; fax (3) 9429-3670; internet www.nine.msn.com.au; f. 1957; operates one station; Man. Dir GRAEME YARWOOD.

Golden West Network: POB 5090, Geraldton, WA 6531; tel. (8) 9921-4422; fax (8) 9921-8096.

Golden West Network Pty Ltd: POB 1062, West Perth, WA 6872; tel. (8) 9481-0050; fax (8) 9321-2470; f. 1967; operates three stations (SSW10, VEW and WAW); Gen. Man. W. FENWICK.

Imparja Television Pty Ltd: POB 52, Alice Springs, NT 0871; tel. (8) 8950-1411; fax (8) 8953-0322; e-mail imparja@ozemailimparja.com.au; internet www.imparja.com.au; CEO CORALLIE FERGUSON.

Independent Broadcasters of Australia Pty Ltd: POB 285, Sydney, NSW 2001; tel. (2) 9264-9144; fax (2) 9264-6334; fmrly Regional Television Australia Pty Ltd; Chair. GRAEME J. GILBERTSON; Sec. JEFF EATHER.

Mt Isa Television Pty Ltd: 110 Canooweal St, Mt Isa, Qld 4825; tel. (7) 4743-8888; fax (7) 4743-9803; f. 1971; operates one station; Station Man. LYALL GREY.

NBN Ltd: Mosbri Crescent, POB 750L, Newcastle, NSW 2300; tel. (2) 4929-2933; fax (2) 4926-2936; f. 1962; operates one station; Man. Dir DENIS LEDBURY.

Network Ten Ltd: GPOB 10, Sydney, NSW 2001; tel. (2) 9650-1010; fax (2) 9650-1170; operates Australian TV network and commercial stations in Sydney, Melbourne, Brisbane, Perth and Adelaide; CEO JOHN McALPINE.

Nine Network Australia Pty Ltd: POB 27, Willoughby, NSW 2068; tel. (2) 9906-9999; fax (2) 9958-2279; internet www.ninemsn.com.au; f. 1956; division of Publishing and Broadcasting Ltd; operates three stations: TCN Channel Nine Pty Ltd (Sydney), Queensland Television Ltd (Brisbane) and General Television Corporation Ltd (Melbourne); CEO DAVID LECKIE.

Northern Rivers Television Pty Ltd: Peterson Rd, Locked Bag 1000, Coffs Harbour, NSW 2450; tel. (2) 6652-2777; fax (2) 6652-3034; f. 1965; CEO GARRY DRAFFIN.

Prime Television Group: Level 6, 1 Pacific Highway, North Sydney, NSW 2060; tel. (2) 9965-7700; fax (2) 9965-7729; e-mail primetv@primetv.com.au; internet www.primetv.com.au; Chair. PAUL RAMSAY; CEO BRENT HARMAN.

Prime Television (Northern) Pty Ltd: POB 2077, Elermore Vale, NSW 2287; tel. (2) 4952-0500; fax (2) 4952-0502; internet www.primetv.com.au; Gen. Man. BRAD JONES.

Prime Television (Southern) Pty Ltd: POB 465, Orange, NSW 2800; tel. (2) 6361-6888; fax (2) 6363-1889; Gen. Man. D. EDWARDS.

Prime Television (Victoria) Pty Ltd: Sunraysia Highway, Ballarat, Vic 3350; tel. (3) 5337-1777; fax (3) 5337-1700; e-mail primetv.ballarat@primetv.com.au; Gen. Man. CRAIG WHITFIELD.

Queensland Television Ltd: POB 72, GPO Brisbane, Qld 4001; tel. (7) 3214-9999; fax (7) 3369-3512; f. 1959; operates one station; Gen. Man. IAN R. MÜLLER.

Seven Network Ltd: Level 13, 1 Pacific Highway, North Sydney, NSW 2060; tel. (2) 9967-7903; fax (2) 9967-7972; internet www .seven.com.au; owns Amalgamated Television Services Pty Ltd (Sydney), Brisbane TV Ltd (Brisbane), HSV Channel 7 Pty Ltd (Melbourne), South Australian Telecasters Ltd (Adelaide) and TVW Enterprises Ltd (Perth); Exec. Chair. KERRY STOKES.

Australia Television: international satellite service; broadcasts to more than 30 countries and territories in Asia and the Pacific.

Seven Queensland: 140–142 Horton Parade, Maroochydore, Qld 4558; tel. (7) 5430-1777; fax (7) 5430-1767; f. 1965; fmrly Sunshine Television Network Ltd.

Southern Cross Broadcasting (Australia) Ltd: 41–49 Bank St, South Melbourne, Vic 3205; tel. (3) 9243-2100; fax (3) 9690-0937; internet www.scbnetwork.com.au; f. 1932; operates four TV and four radio stations; Man. Dir A. E. BELL.

Southern Cross Television (TNT9) Pty Ltd: Watchorn St, Launceston, Tas 7250; tel. (3) 6344-0202; fax (3) 6343-0340; f. 1962; operates one station; Gen. Man. BRUCE ABRAHAM.

Special Broadcasting Service (SBS): Locked Bag 028, Crows Nest, NSW 1585; tel. (2) 9430-2828; fax (2) 9430-3700; e-mail sbs .com.au; internet www.sbs.com.au; f. 1980; national multi-cultural broadcaster of TV and radio; Man. Dir NIGEL MILAN.

Spencer Gulf Telecasters Ltd: POB 305, Port Pirie, SA 5540; tel. (8) 8632-2555; fax (8) 8633-0984; e-mail dweston@centralonline.com .au; internet www.centralonline.com.au; f. 1968; operates two stations; Chair. P. M. STURROCK; Chief Exec. D. WESTON.

Swan Television & Radio Broadcasters Pty Ltd: POB 99, Tuart Hill, WA 6939; tel. (8) 9449-9999; fax (8) 9449-9900; Gen. Man. P. BOWEN.

Telecasters Australia Ltd: Level 8, 1 Elizabeth Plaza, North Sydney, NSW 2060; tel. (2) 9922-1011; fax (2) 9922-1033; internet www.telecasters.com.au; operates commercial TV services of TEN Queensland, TEN Northern NSW, Seven Central and Seven Darwin.

Territory Television Pty Ltd: POB 1764, Darwin, NT 0801; tel. (8) 8981-8888; fax (8) 8981-6802; f. 1971; operates one station; Gen. Man. A. G. BRUYN.

WIN Television Griffith Pty Ltd: 161 Remembrance Driveway, Griffith, NSW 2680; tel. (2) 6962-4500; fax (2) 6962-0979; e-mail mtntv@ozemail.com.au; fmrly MTN Television; Man. Dir RAY GAMBLE.

WIN Television Loxton SA Pty Ltd: Murray Bridge Rd, POB 471, Loxton, SA 5333; tel. (8) 8584-6891; fax (8) 8584-5062; f. 1976; operates one station; Exec. Chair. E. H. URLWIN; Gen. Man. W. L. MUDGE.

WIN Television Mildura Pty Ltd: 18 Deakin Ave, Mildura, Vic 3500; tel. (3) 5023-0204; fax (3) 5022-1179; f. 1965; Chair. JOHN RUSHTON; Man. NOEL W. HISCOCK.

WIN Television NSW Network: Television Ave, Mt St Thomas, Locked Bag 8800, South Coast Mail Centre, NSW 2521; tel. (2) 4223-4199; fax (2) 4227-3682; internet www.wintv.com.au; f. 1962; Man. Dir K. KINGSTON; CEO JOHN RUSHTON.

WIN Television Qld Pty Ltd: POB 568 Rockhampton, Qld 4700; tel. (7) 4930-4499; fax (7) 4930-4490; Station Man. R. HOCKEY.

WIN Television Tas Pty Ltd: 52 New Town Rd, Hobart, Tas 7008; tel. (3) 6228-8999; fax (3) 6228-8991; e-mail wintas@win.com.au; internet www.wintv.com.au; f. 1959; Gen. Man. GREG RAYMENT.

WIN Television Vic Pty Ltd: POB 464, Ballarat, Vic 3353; tel. (3) 5320-1366; fax (3) 5333-1598; internet www.winnet.com.au; f. 1961; operates five stations; Gen. Man. MICHAEL TAYLOR.

Satellite, Cable and Digital Television

Digital television became available in metropolitan areas in January 2001 and was to be available in all major regional areas by 2004.

Austar United Communications: Level 29, AAP Centre, 259 George St, Sydney, NSW 2000; tel. (2) 9251-6999; fax (2) 9251-61361812; e-mail austar@austarunited.com.au; internet www .austarunited.com.au; began operations in 1995; 42.7m. subscribers (Sept. 2001); CEO JOHN C. PORTER.

Foxtel: Foxtel Television Centre, Pyrmont, Sydney; internet www .foxtel.com.au; owned by the News Corpn, Telstra Corpn and PBL; 800,100 subscribers (Aug. 2002).

Optus Vision: Tower B, Level 15, 16 Zenith Centre, 821–841 Pacific Highway, Chatswood, NSW 2067; commenced cable services on 11 channels in 1995; 210,000 subscribers (March 1999).

Regulatory Authority

Australian Broadcasting Authority: POB Q500, QVB Post Office, NSW 1230; tel. (2) 9334-7700; fax (2) 9334-7799; e-mail info@ aba.gov.au; internet www.aba.gov.au; regulates radio and TV broadcasting, and internet content; Chair. Prof. DAVID FLINT.

Finance

(cap. = capital; p.u. = paid up; res = reserves; dep. = deposits; m. = million; brs = branches; amounts in Australian dollars)

Radical reforms of the financial sector, were introduced in 1998. The banking system was opened up to greater competition. The licensing and regulation of deposit-taking institutions was supervised by the new Australian Prudential Regulation Authority, while consumer protection was the responsibility of the Australian Corporations and Financial Services Commission.

Australian Prudential Regulation Authority (APRA): GPOB 9836, Sydney, NSW 2000; tel. (2) 9210-3000; fax (2) 9210-3411; e-mail APRAinfo@apra.gov.au; internet www.apra.gov.au; responsible for regulation of banks, insurance cos, superannuation funds, credit unions, building societies and friendly societies; CEO GRAEME THOMPSON.

BANKING

Central Bank

Reserve Bank of Australia: GPOB 3947, Sydney, NSW 2001; tel. (2) 9551-8111; fax (2) 9551-8000; e-mail rbainfo.@rba.gov.au; internet www.rba.gov.au; f. 1911; responsible for monetary policy, financial system stability, payment system development; cap. 40m., res 9,470m., dep. 13,992m., total assets 60,128m., notes on issue 31,930m. (June 2002); Gov. IAN MACFARLANE.

Development Bank

Primary Industry Bank of Australia Ltd: GPOB 4577, Sydney, NSW 1042; tel. (2) 9234-4200; fax (2) 9221-6218; internet www.piba .com.au; f. 1978; cap. 123.2m., res 2.5m. Chair. H. G. GENTIS; 21 brs.

Trading Banks

ABN AMRO Australia Ltd: Level 29, ABN AMRO Tower, 88 Phillip St, Sydney, NSW 2000; tel. (2) 8259-5000; fax (2) 8259-5444; internet www.abnamro.com.au; f. 1971; cap. 70m., res 590,000 (Dec. 2000); CEO STEVE CRANE.

Arab Bank Australia Ltd: GPOB N645, Grosvenor Place, 200 George St, Sydney, NSW 2000; tel. (2) 9377-8900; fax (2) 9221-5428; internet www.arabbank.com.au; cap. 55.0m., dep. 464.9m. (Dec. 2000); Chair. KHALID SHOMAN; Man. Dir JACK BEIGHTON.

Australia and New Zealand Banking Group Ltd: GPOB 537E 100 Queen St, Melbourne, Vic 3000; tel. (3) 9273-5555; fax (3) 9658-2484; internet www.anz.com; f. 1835; present name adopted in 1970; cap. 5,402.0m., res 786.0m., dep. 112,849.0m. (2000); 871 brs; Chair. C. B. GOODE; CEO JOHN MCFARLANE.

Bank of America Australia Ltd: Level 63, MLC Centre, 19–29 Martin Place, Sydney, NSW 2000; tel. (2) 9931-4200; fax (2) 9221-1023; f. 1964; cap. 150.3m. (Dec. 1998); Man. Dir JOHN LILES.

Bank of Melbourne: 360 Collins St, Melbourne, Vic 3000; tel. (3) 9608-3222; fax (3) 9608-3700; division of Westpac Banking Corpn; f. 1989; cap. 752m., dep. 8,706m. (1997); Chair. CHRIS STEWART; CEO MATTHEW SLATTER; 129 brs.

Bank of Queensland Ltd: 229 Elizabeth St, POB 898, Brisbane, Qld 4001; tel. (7) 3212-3333; fax (7) 3212-3399; internet www.boq .com.au; f. 1874; cap. 189.9m., res 1.0m., dep. 3,699.0m. (Aug. 2001); Chair. NEIL ROBERTS; Man Dir DAVID P. LIDDY; 97 brs.

Bank of Tokyo-Mitsubishi (Australia) Ltd: Level 26, Gateway, 1 Macquarie Place, Sydney, NSW 2000; tel. (2) 9296-1111; fax (2) 9247-4266; e-mail btmacorp@btma.com.au; cap. 152.9m., res 33,000m., dep. 1,910.8m. (Dec. 2000); f. 1985; Chair. R. NICOLSON; Man. Dir H. KOJIMA.

Bank of Western Australia Ltd (BankWest): Level 7, BankWest Tower, 108 St George's Terrace, POB E237, Perth, WA 6001; tel. (8) 9449-7000; fax (8) 9449-7050; e-mail finmkts@bankwest.com.au; internet www.bankwest.com.au; f. 1895 as Agricultural Bank of Western Australia, 1945 as Rural and Industries Bank of Western Australia; present name adopted in 1994; cap. 715.9m., res 6m., dep. 12,753.2m. (Feb. 2001); Chair. IAN C. R. MACKENZIE; Man. Dir TERRY C. BUDGE; 109 brs.

Bankers' Trust Australia Ltd: GPOB H4, Australia Sq., Sydney, NSW 2000; tel. (2) 9259-3555; fax (2) 9259-9800; internet www.btal

.com.au; f. 1986; cap. 273.3m., dep. 6,266.8m. (Dec. 1997); Man. Dir R. A. FERGUSON; 5 brs.

The Chase Manhattan Bank: GPOB 9816, NSW 2001; tel. (2) 9250-4111; fax (2) 9250-4554; internet www.chase.com; Man. Dir W. SCOTT REID.

Citibank Ltd: GPOB 40, Sydney, NSW 1027; tel. (2) 9239-9100; fax (2) 9239-9110; internet www.citibank.com.au; f. 1954; cap. 457m., res 1m., dep. 5,619m. (Dec. 1998); Country Corporate Officer WILLIAM W. FERGUSON; Chair. THOMAS MCKEAN.

Commonwealth Bank of Australia: Level 1, 48 Martin Place, Sydney, NSW 1155; tel. (2) 9378-2000; fax (2) 9378-3317; internet www.commbank.com.au; f. 1912; cap. 12,521.0m., res 3,265.0m., dep. 142,509.0m. (June 2000); Chair. J. T. RALPH; CEO and Man. Dir D. V. MURRAY; more than 1,500 brs world-wide; merged with Colonial Ltd in 2000.

HSBC Bank Australia Ltd: Level 10, 1 O'Connell Street, Sydney, NSW 2000; tel. (2) 9255-2888; fax (2) 9255-2332; internet www.hsbc .com.au; f. 1985; fmrly Hongkong Bank of Australia; cap. 560.0m., res 100,000., dep. 5,052.8m. (Dec. 2000); Chair D. J. SAY; CEO STUART DAVIS; 18 brs.

IBJ Australia Bank Ltd: Level 21, Colonial Centre, 52 Martin Place, Sydney, NSW 2000; tel. (2) 9377-8888; fax (2) 9377-8884; internet www.ibj.com.au; f. 1985; subsidiary of Mizuho Holdings Inc; cap. 104.0m., res 40.0m., dep. 1,336.0m. (Dec. 2000); Chair. M. J. PHILLIPS; Man. Dir YOSHIMICHI KAWASAKI.

ING Bank (Australia) Ltd: Level 13, 140 Sussex St, Sydney, NSW 2000; tel. (2) 9028-4000; fax (2) 9028-4708; f. 1994; cap. 60m., res 1.3m., dep. 1,015.4m. (Dec. 1998); Gen. Man. JULIE BROWN.

Macquarie Bank Ltd: 1 Martin Place, Sydney, NSW 2000; tel. (2) 8232-3333; fax (2) 8232-3350; internet www.macquarie.com.au; f. 1969 as Hill Samuel Australia Ltd; present name adopted in 1985; cap. 2,020m. dep. 13,954m. (March 2002). Chair. DAVID S. CLARKE; Man. Dir ALLAN E. MOSS; 2 brs.

National Australia Bank Ltd: 500 Bourke St, Melbourne, Vic 3000; tel. (3) 8641-3500; fax (3) 8641-4912; internet www.national .com.au/; f. 1858; cap. 9,855m., res 2,006m., dep. 244,661m. (Sept. 2000); Chair. MARK RAYNER; Exec. Dir FRANK CICUTTO; 2,349 brs.

N. M. Rothschild & Sons (Australia) Ltd: Level 16, 1 O'Connell St, Sydney, NSW 2000; tel. (2) 9323-2000; fax (2) 9323-2323; internet www.rothschild.com.au; f. 1967 as International Pacific Corpn; cap. 130.0m., dep. 978.1m. (March 1999); Chair. PHILIP BRASS; Chief Exec. RICHARD LEE.

SG Australia Ltd: Level 21, 400 George St, Sydney, NSW 2000; tel. (2) 9210-8000; fax (2) 9235 3941; internet www.au.sg-ib.com; f. 1981; fmrly Société Générale Australia Ltd; cap. 21.5m., res 208m., dep. 5,656m. (Dec. 1999); CEO MICHEL L. MACAGNO.

St George Bank Ltd: Locked Bag 1, PO, Kogarah, NSW 2217; tel. (2) 9952-1311; fax (2) 9952-1000; e-mail stgeorge@stgeorge.com.au; internet www.stgeorge.com.au; f. 1937 as building society; cap. 3,174m., res 130m., dep. 35,047m. (Sept. 2000); Chair. F. J. CONROY; CEO and Man. Dir GAIL KELLY; 421 brs.

Standard Chartered Bank Australia Ltd: Level 11, 345 George St, Sydney, NSW 2000; tel. (2) 9232-9333; fax (2) 9232-9345; f. 1986; cap. 226.2m., dep. 667.8m. (Dec. 1999); Chair. RICHARD NETTLETON; CEO EUGENE ELLIS.

Toronto Dominion Australia Ltd: Level 34, Rialto South Tower, 525 Collins St, Melbourne, Vic 3000; tel. (3) 9993-1344; fax (3) 9614-0083; internet www.tdbank.ca; f. 1970; cap. 191.5m., res 6.0m., dep. 3,435.4m. (Oct. 1997); Man. Dir STEVE FRYER.

Westpac Banking Corporation: 60 Martin Place, Sydney, NSW 2000; tel. (2) 9226-3311; fax (2) 9226-4128; e-mail westpac@westpac .com.au; internet www.westpac.com.au; f. 1817; cap. 2,258m., res 4,892m., dep. 113,169m. (Sept. 2000); Chair. L. A. DAVIS; Man. Dir DAVID MORGAN.

Foreign Banks

Bank of China (People's Republic of China): 39–41 York St, Sydney, NSW 2000; tel. (2) 9267-5188; fax (2) 9262-1794; e-mail bocsyd@bigpond.com.au; Gen. Man. GAO JI LU.

Bank of New Zealand: 9th Floor, BNZ House, 333–339 George St, Sydney, NSW 2000; tel. (2) 9290-6666; fax (2) 9290-3414; Chief Operating Officer G. ARMBRUSTER.

BNP Paribas (France): 60 Castlereagh St, Sydney, NSW 2000; POB 269, Sydney, NSW 2001; tel. (2) 9232-8733; fax (2) 9221-3026; e-mail bnp@bnp.com.au; internet www.bnp.com.au; CEO JEAN-FRANÇOIS VARLET; 4 brs.

Deutsche Bank AG (Germany): GPOB 7033, Sydney, NSW 1170; tel. (2) 9258-1234; fax (2) 9241-2565; internet www.australia.db .com; CEO CHUM DARVALL.

STOCK EXCHANGE

Australian Stock Exchange Ltd (ASX): Level 9, 20 Bridge St, Sydney, NSW 2000; tel. (2) 9227-0000; fax (2) 9227-0885; e-mail info@asx.com.au; internet www.asx.com.au; f. 1987 by merger of the stock exchanges in Sydney, Adelaide, Brisbane, Hobart, Melbourne and Perth, to replace the fmr Australian Associated Stock Exchanges; demutualized and listed Oct. 1998; Chair. MAURICE NEWMAN; Man. Dir and CEO RICHARD HUMPHRY.

Supervisory Body

Australian Securities and Investments Commission (ASIC): GPOB 4866, Sydney, NSW 1042; tel. (2) 9911-2000; fax (2) 9911-2030; e-mail infoline@asic.gov.au; internet www.asic.gov.au; f. 1990; corporations and financial products regulator; Chair. DAVID KNOTT.

PRINCIPAL INSURANCE COMPANIES

Allianz Australia Ltd: 2 Market St, Sydney, NSW 2000; tel. (2) 9390-6222; fax (2) 9390-6425; internet www.allianz.com.au; f. 1914; workers' compensation; fire, general accident, motor and marine; Chair. J. S. CURTIS; Man. Dir T. TOWELL.

AMP Ltd: AMP Bldg, 33 Alfred St, Sydney, NSW 2000; tel. (2) 9257-5000; fax (2) 9257-7886; internet www.amplimited.com.au; f. 1849; fmrly Australian Mutual Provident Society; life insurance; Chair. STAN WALLIS; Man. Dir (vacant).

AMP General Insurance Ltd: 10 Loftus St, Sydney Cove, NSW 2000; tel. (2) 9257-2500; fax (2) 9257-2199; internet www.amp.com .au; f. 1958; Chair. GREG COX; Man. Dir GAVIN PEACE.

Australian Guarantee Corpn Ltd: 130 Phillip St, Sydney, NSW 2000; tel. (2) 9234-1122; fax (2) 9234-1225; f. 1925; Chair. J. A. UHRIG; Man. Dir R. THOMAS.

Australian Unity General Insurance Ltd: 114 Albert Rd, South Melbourne, Vic 3205; tel. (3) 9697-0219; fax (3) 9690-5556; e-mail webmaster@austunity.com.au; internet www.austunity.com.au; f. 1948; Chair. LEON HICKEY; Chief Exec. M. W. SIBREE.

Catholic Church Insurances Ltd: 324 St Kilda Rd, Melbourne, Vic 3004; tel. (3) 9334-3000; fax (3) 9934-3460; f. 1911; Chair. Most Rev. KEVIN MANNING (Bishop of Parramatta); Gen. Man. PETER RUSH.

CGU Insurance Ltd: CGU Centre, 485 La Trobe St, Melbourne, Vic 3000; tel. (3) 9601-8222; fax (3) 9601-8366; f. 1960; fire, accident, marine; Chair. HUGH FLETCHER; Man. Dir I. M. BALFE.

The Copenhagen Reinsurance Co Ltd: 60 Margaret St, Sydney, NSW 2000; tel. (2) 9247-7266; fax (2) 9235-3320; e-mail david .kennedy@copre.com; internet www.copre.com; reinsurance; Gen. Man. DAVID KENNEDY.

FAI Insurances Ltd: FAI Insurance Group, 333 Kent St, Sydney, NSW 1026; tel. (2) 9274-9000; fax (2) 9274-9900; internet www.fai .com.au; f. 1953; Chair. JOHN LANDERER; CEO RODNEY ADLER.

Fortis Australia Ltd: 464 St Kilda Rd, Melbourne, Vic 3004; tel. (3) 9869-0300; fax (3) 9820-8537; CEO R. B. WILLING.

GeneralCologne Re Australia Ltd: Level 13, 225 George St, Sydney, NSW 2000; tel. (2) 9336-8100; fax (2) 9251-1665; f. 1961; reinsurance, fire, accident, marine; Chair. F. A. MCDONALD; Man. Dir G. C. BARNUM.

GIO Australia Holdings Ltd: Level 39, Governor Phillip Tower, 1 Farrer Place, Sydney, NSW 2000; tel. (2) 9255-8090; fax (2) 9251-2079; e-mail emailus@gio.com.au; internet www.gio.com.au; f. 1926; CEO PETER CORRIGAN.

Guild Insurance Ltd: Guild House, 40 Burwood Rd, Hawthorn, Vic 3122; tel. (3) 9810-9820; fax (3) 9819-5670; f. 1963; Man. Dir W. K. BASTIAN.

HIH Insurance Ltd: AMP Centre, 50 Bridge St, Sydney, NSW 2000; tel. (2) 9650-2000; fax (2) 9650-2030; internet www.hih.com .au; f. 1968; Chair. G. A. COHEN; CEO R. R. WILLIAMS.

Lumley General Insurance Ltd: Lumley House, 309 Kent St, Sydney, NSW 1230; tel. (2) 9248-1111; fax (2) 9248-1122; e-mail general@lumley.com.au; Man. Dir D. M. MATCHAM.

Mercantile Mutual Holdings Ltd: 347 Kent St, Sydney, NSW; tel. (2) 9234-8111; fax (2) 9299-3979; internet www.mercantilemutual .com.au; f. 1878; Chair. A. R. BERG; Man. Dir R. J. ATFIELD.

The National Mutual Life Association of Australasia Ltd: 447 Collins St, Melbourne, Vic 3000; tel. (3) 9618-4920; fax (3) 9616-3445; e-mail investor.relations@axa.com.au; internet www.axa.com .au; f. 1869; life insurance, superannuation, income protection; Chair. R. H. ALLERT; Group CEO A. L. OWEN.

NRMA Insurance Ltd: 151 Clarence St, Sydney, NSW 2000; tel. (2) 9292-9222; fax (2) 9292-8472; f. 1926; CEO IAN BROWN (acting).

NZI Insurance Australia Ltd: 9th Floor, 10 Spring St, Sydney, NSW 2000; tel. (2) 9551-5000; fax (2) 9551-5865; Man. Dir H. D. SMITH.

QBE Insurance Group Ltd: 82 Pitt St, Sydney, NSW 2000; tel. (2) 9375-4444; fax (2) 9235-3166; internet www.qbe.com; f. 1886; general insurance; Chair. E. J. CLONEY; Man. Dir F. M. O'HALLORAN.

RAC Insurance Pty Ltd: 228 Adelaide Terrace, Perth, WA 6000; tel. (8) 9421-4444; fax (8) 9421-4593; f. 1947; Gen. Man. TONY CARTER.

RACQ Insurance: POB 4, Springwood, Qld 4127; tel. (7) 3361-2444; fax (7) 3841-2995; e-mail inorris@gio.com.au; internet www.racqinsurance.com.au; f. 1971; CEO I. W. NORRIS.

RACV: 550 Princes Highway, Noble Park, Vic 3174; tel. (3) 9790-2211; fax (3) 9790-3091.

RSA Insurance Australia Ltd: 465 Victoria Ave, Chatswood, NSW 2067; tel. (2) 9978-9000; fax (2) 9978-9807; fire, accident and marine insurance; Gen. Man. E. KULK.

Suncorp-Metway Ltd: Level 18, 36 Wickham Tce, Brisbane, Qld 4000; tel. (7) 3835-5355; fax (7) 3836-1190; e-mail direct@suncorp.co.au; internet www.suncorp.com.au; f. 1996; Man. Dir STEVE JONES.

Swiss Re Australia Ltd: 363 George St, Sydney, NSW 2000; tel. (2) 8295-9500; fax (2) 8295-9804; f. 1962; Man. Dir R. G. WATTS.

Wesfarmers Federation Insurance Ltd: 184 Railway Parade, Bassendean, WA 6054; tel. (8) 9273-5770; fax (8) 9273-5290; e-mail mel.rom@wfi.wesfarmers.com.au; internet www.wfi.com.au; Gen. Man. R. J. BUCKLEY.

Westpac Life Ltd: 35 Pitt St, Sydney, NSW 2000; tel. (2) 9220-4768; f. 1986; CEO DAVID WHITE.

World Marine & General Insurances Ltd: 600 Bourke St, Melbourne, Vic 3000; tel. (3) 9609-3333; fax (3) 9609-3634; f. 1961; Chair. G. W. MCGREGOR; Man. Dir A. E. REYNOLDS.

Zurich Financial Services Australia Ltd: 5 Blue St, North Sydney, NSW 2060; tel. (2) 9391-1111; fax (2) 9922-4630; CEO MALCOLM M. JONES.

Insurance Associations

Australian Insurance Association: GPOB 369, Canberra, ACT 2601; tel. (2) 6274-0609; fax (2) 6274-0666; f. 1968; Pres. RAYMOND JONES; Exec. Sec. P. M. MURPHY.

Australian and New Zealand Institute of Insurance and Finance: Level 17, 31 Queen St, Melbourne, Vic 3000; tel. (3) 9629-4021; fax (3) 9629-4204; e-mail ceo@theinstitute.com.au; internet www.theinstitute.com.au; f. 1919; Pres. JOHN RICHARDSON; CEO JOAN FITZPATRICK; 11,984 mems.

Insurance Council of Australia Ltd: Level 3, 56 Pitt St, Sydney, NSW 2000; tel. (2) 9253-5100; fax (2) 9253-5111; internet www.ica.com.au; f. 1975; CEO ALAN MASON.

Investment and Financial Services Association (IFSA): Suite 1, Level 24, 44 Market St, Sydney, NSW 2000; tel. (2) 9299-3022; fax (2) 9299-3198; e-mail ifsa@ifsa.com.au; f. 1996; fmrly Life, Investment and Superannuation Asscn of Australia Inc; Chair. ANDREW MOHL; CEO RICHARD GILBERT.

Trade and Industry

GOVERNMENT AGENCY

Austrade: GPOB 5301, Sydney, NSW 2001; e-mail managing.director@austrade.gov.au; internet www.austrade.gov.au; trade and investment facilitation agency; Chair. ROSS ADLER; Man. Dir CHARLES JAMIESON.

CHAMBERS OF COMMERCE

Australian Chamber of Commerce and Industry (ACCI): POB E14, Kingston, ACT 2604; tel. (2) 6273-2311; fax (2) 6273-3286; e-mail acci@acci.asn.au; internet www.acci.asn.au; Pres. Dr JOHN KENIRY; CEO MARK PATERSON.

Chamber of Commerce and Industry of Western Australia (CCIWA): POB 6209, East Perth, WA 6892; tel. (8) 9365-7555; fax (8) 9365-76167550; e-mail whitakerinfo@cciwa.com; internet www.cciwa.com; f. 1890; 6,000 mems; Chief Exec. LYNDON ROWE; Pres. TONY HOWARTH.

Commerce Queensland: Industry House, 375 Wickham Terrace, Brisbane, Qld 4000; tel. (7) 3842-2244; fax (7) 3832-3195; e-mail info@commerceqld.com.au; internet www.commerceqld.com.au; f. 1868; operates World Trade Centre, Brisbane; 5,500 mems; CEO ANDREW CRAIG.

South Australian Employers' Chamber of Commerce and Industry Inc: Enterprise House, 136 Greenhill Road, Unley, SA 5061; tel. (8) 8300-0000; fax (8) 8300-0001; e-mail enquiries@business-sa.com; internet www.business-sa.com; f. 1839; 4,700 mems; CEO P. VAUGHAN.

State Chamber of Commerce (New South Wales): Level 12, 83 Clarence St, GPO 4280, Sydney, NSW 2001; tel. (2) 9350-8100; fax (2) 9350-8199; e-mail worldtradecentre@thechamber.com.au; internet www.thechamber.com.au; operates World Trade Centre, Sydney; Man. Trade Development JANETTE SHOMAR.

Tasmanian Chamber of Commerce and Industry: GPOB 793H, Hobart, Tas 7001; tel. (3) 6234-5933; fax (3) 6231-1278; CEO TIM ABEY.

Victorian Employers' Chamber of Commerce and Industry: Employers' House, 50 Burwood Rd, Hawthorn, Vic 3122; tel. (3) 9251-4333; fax (3) 9819-3826; e-mail itd@vecci.org.au; f. 1885; CEO N. FEELY.

AGRICULTURAL, INDUSTRIAL AND TRADE ASSOCIATIONS

Australian Business Ltd: Private Bag 938, North Sydney, NSW 2059; tel. (2) 9458-7500; fax (2) 9923-1166; e-mail member.services@australianbusiness.com.au; internet www.australianbusiness.com.au; f. 1885; fmrly Chamber of Manufactures of NSW; CEO MARK BETHWAITE.

Australian Dairy Corporation: Locked Bag 104, Flinders Lane, Vic 8009; tel. (3) 9694-3777; fax (3) 9694-3888; e-mail adcenquiries@adc.aust.com; internet www.dairycorp.com.au; provides services to industry in areas of trade policy and market access, domestic and export market devt, and export agency national marketing, international trade development, regulatory activity, industry relations; Chair. DES NICHOLL; Man. Dir ALEXANDER MURDOCH.

Australian Manufacturers' Export Council: POB E14, Queen Victoria Terrace, ACT 2600; tel. (2) 6273-2311; fax (2) 6273-3196; f. 1955; Exec. Dir G. CHALKER.

Australian Wine and Brandy Corporation (AWBC): POB 2733, Kent Town Business Centre, Kent Town, SA 5071; tel. (8) 8228-2000; fax (8) 8228-2022; e-mail awbc@awbc.com.au; internet www.awbc.com.au; Chief Exec. SAM TOTLEY.

Australian Wool Services Ltd: Wool House, 369 Royal Parade, Parkville, Vic 3052; tel. (3) 9341-9111; fax (3) 9341-9273; internet www.wool.com.au; f. 2001 following the privatization of the Australian Wool Research and Promotion Organisation; operates two subsidiaries, Australian Wool Innovation which manages wool levy funds and invests in research and development, and The Woolmark Company responsible for commercial development; Chair. RODNEY PRICE.

AWB Ltd: Ceres House, 528 Lonsdale St, Melbourne, Vic 3000; tel. (3) 9209-2000; fax (3) 9670-2782; e-mail awb@awb.com.au; internet www.awb.com.au; f. 1939; fmrly Australian Wheat Board; national and international marketing of grain, financing and marketing of wheat and other grains for growers; 12 mems; Chair. TREVOR FLUGGE; CEO ANDREW LINDBERG.

Business Council of Australia: 15th Floor, 10 Queens Rd, Melbourne, Vic 3004; tel. (3) 9274-7777; fax (3) 9274-7744; public policy research and advocacy; governing council comprises chief execs of Australia's major cos; Pres. STAN WALLIS; Exec. Dir DAVID BUCKINGHAM.

Cotton Australia: Level 2, 490 Crown St, Surry Hills, NSW 2010; tel. (2) 9360-8500; fax (2) 9360-8555; e-mail talktous@cottonaustralia.com.au; internet www.cottonaustralia.com.au; Chair. CHARLES WILSON.

Meat and Livestock Australia: Level 1, 165 Walker St, North Sydney, NSW 2060; tel. 1800-023-100; fax (2) 9463-9393; internet www.mla.com.au; producer-owned co; represents, promotes, protects and furthers interests of industry in both the marketing of meat and livestock and industry-based research and devt activities; Chair. DAVID CROMBIE.

National Farmers' Federation: POB E10, Kingston, ACT 2604; tel. (2) 6273-3855; fax (2) 6273-2331; e-mail nff@nff.org.au; internet www.nff.org.au; Pres. PETER CORISH; CEO ANNA CRONIN.

Natural Resources Management Ministerial Council (NRMC): Dept of Agriculture, Fisheries and Forestry—Australia, Barton, Canberra, ACT 2600; tel. (2) 6272-5216; fax (2) 6272-4772; internet www.mincos.gov.au; f. 2002 to replace the Agricultural and Resource Management Council of Australia and New Zealand to promote the conservation and sustainable use of Australia's natural resources; mems comprising the Commonwealth/state/territory and New Zealand ministers responsible for environment, water and natural resources.

Primary Industries Ministerial Council (PIMC): Dept of Agriculture, Fisheries and Forestry—Australia, Barton, Canberra, ACT 2600; tel. (2) 6272-5216; fax (2) 6272-4772; internet www.mincos.gov .au; f. 2002 to replace the Agricultural and Resource Management Council of Australia and New Zealand to develop and promote sustainable, innovative and profitable agriculture, fisheries, food and forestry industries; mems comprising the Commonwealth/state/territory and New Zealand ministers responsible for agriculture, fisheries, food and forestry.

Trade Policy Advisory Council (TPAC): c/o Dept of Foreign Affairs and Trade, R. G. Casey Bldg, John McEwen Cres., Barton, ACT 2600; tel. (2) 6262-2125; fax (2) 6261-2465; e-mail diane .johnstone@dfat.gov.au; advises the Minister for Trade on policy issues; Chair. GEOFF ALLEN.

WoolProducers: POB E10, Kingston, Canberra, ACT 2604; tel. (2) 6273-2531; fax (2) 6273-1120; e-mail woolproducers@nff.org.au; internet www.woolproducers.com; fmrly Wool Council Australia; comprises 20 mems; represents wool-growers in dealings with the Federal Govt and industry; Pres. SIMON CAMPBELL.

EMPLOYERS' ORGANIZATIONS

Australian Co-operative Foods Ltd: Level 12, 168 Walker St, North Sydney, NSW 2060; tel. (2) 9903-5222; fax (2) 9957-3530; e-mail exports@dairyfarmers.com.au; f. 1900; Man. Dir A. R. TOOTH.

Australian Industry Group: 51 Walker St, North Sydney, NSW 2060; tel. (2) 9466-5566; fax (2) 9466-5599; e-mail louisep@aignsw .aigroup.asn.au; internet www.aigroup.asn.au; f. 1998 through merger of MTIA and ACM; 11,500 mems; Nat. Pres. G. J. ASHTON; CEO ROBERT N. HERBERT; 11,500 mems.

National Meat Association: 25–27 Albany St, Crows Nest, NSW 2065; POB 1208, Crows Nest, NSW 1585; tel. (2) 9906-7767; fax (2) 9906-8022; e-mail lmigachov@nmaa.org.au; internet www.nmaa.org .au; f. 1928; Pres. GARY HARDWICK; CEO KEVIN COTTRILL (acting).

NSW Farmers' Association: GPOB 1068, Sydney, NSW 1041; tel. (2) 8251-1700; fax (2) 8251-1750; e-mail emailus@nswfarmers.org .au; internet www.nswfarmers.org.au; f. 1978; CEO JONATHAN MCKEOWN; Pres. MAL PETERS.

UTILITIES

Australian Gas Association (AGA): GPOB 323, Canberra, ACT 2601; tel. (2) 6272-1555; fax (2) 6272-1566; e-mail canberra@gas.asn .au; internet www.gas.asn.au; 1,000 mems, incl. more than 300 corporate mems; Chair. OLLIE CLARK; Chief Exec. BILL NAGLE.

Australian Institute of Energy: POB 268, Toukley, NSW 2263; tel. 1800-629-945; fax (2) 4393-1114; e-mail aie@tpgi.com.au; internet www.aie.org.au.

Electricity Supply Association of Australia: POB A2492, Sydney South, NSW 1235; tel. (2) 9261-0141; fax (2) 9261-3153 internet www.esaa.com.au; Man. Dir KEITH ORCHISON.

Electricity Companies

Actew AGL: GPOB 366, Canberra City, ACT 2601; tel. (2) 6248-3111; e-mail webmaster@actewagl.com.au; internet www.actewagl .com.au; f. 2000 by amalgamation of ACTEW Corpn Ltd and AGL; supplier of electricity, gas, water and wastewater services; Chief Exec. PAUL PERKINS.

Delta Electricity: POB Q863, QVB, NSW 1230; tel. (2) 9285-2700; fax (2) 9285-2777; internet www.de.com.au; f. 1996; Chief Exec. JIM HENNESS.

ENERGEX: GPOB 1461, Brisbane, Qld 4001; tel. (7) 3407-4000; fax (7) 3407-4609; e-mail enquiries@energex.com.au; internet www .energex.com.au; spans Queensland and New South Wales; CEO GREG MADDOCK.

EnergyAustralia: 145 Newcastle Rd, Wallsend, NSW 2287; tel. (2) 4951-9346; fax (2) 4951-9351; e-mail energy@energy.com.au; internet www.energy.com.au; supplies customers in NSW; CEO PETER HEADLEY; Man. Dir PAUL BROAD.

Ergon Energy: POB 107, Albert St, Brisbane, Qld 4002; tel. (7) 3228-8222; fax (7) 3228-8118; internet www.ergon.com.au; national retailer of electricity.

Generation Victoria Corpn—Ecogen Energy: 5th Floor, 416 Collins St, Melbourne, Vic 3000; tel. (3) 9679-4600; fax (3) 9679-4619; internet www.ecogen-energy.com.au/; f. 1994; CEO GERRY BASTEN.

Great Southern Energy: Level 1, Citilink Plaza, Morriset St, Queanbeyan, NSW 2620; tel. (2) 6214-9600; fax (2) 6214-9860; e-mail mail@gsenergy.com.au; internet www.gsenergy.com.au; state-owned electricity and gas distributor; Chair. BRUCE RODELY.

Powercor Australia Ltd: 40 Market St, Melbourne, Vic 3000; tel. (3) 9683-4444; fax (3) 9683-4499; e-mail info@powercor.com.au;

internet www.powercor.com.au; Chair. WILLIAM SHURNIAK; CEO C. T. WAN.

Snowy Mountains Hydro-electric Authority: POB 332, Cooma, NSW 2630; tel. (2) 6452-1777; fax (2) 6452-3794; e-mail info@ snowyhydro.com.au; internet www.snowyhydro.com.au.

United Energy Ltd: Level 13, 101 Collins St, Melbourne, Vic 3000; fax (3) 9222-8588; e-mail info@mail.ue.com.au; internet www.ue .com.au; f. 1994 following division of State Electricity Commission of Victoria; transferred to private sector; distributor of electricity and gas.

Western Power Corpn: GPOB L921, Perth, WA 6842; tel. (8) 9326-4911; fax (8) 9326-4595; e-mail info@wpcorp.com.au; internet www .wpcorp.com.au; f. 1995; principal supplier of electricity in WA; Chair. HECTOR STEBBINS (acting); Man. Dir DAVID EISZELE.

Gas Companies

AlintaGas: GPOB W2030, Perth, WA 6846; internet www.alintagas .com.au; f. 1995; CEO ROBERT BROWNING.

Allgas Energy Ltd: 150 Charlotte St, Brisbane, Qld 4000; tel. (7) 3404-1822; fax (7) 3404-1821; e-mail corporate@allgas.com.au; internet www.allgas.com.au; f. 1885; Chief Exec. TOM BLOXSOM.

Australian Gas Light Co: AGL Centre, Corner Pacific Highway and Walker St, North Sydney, NSW 2060; tel. (2) 9922-0101; fax (2) 9957-3671; e-mail aglmail@agl.com.au; internet www.agl.com.au; f. 1837; Chair. M. J. PHILLIPS; Man. Dir. GREG MARTIN.

Envestra: 10th Floor, 81 Flinders St, Adelaide, SA 5000; tel. (8) 8227-1500; fax (8) 8277-1511; e-mail des.petherick@envestra.com .au; internet www.envestra.com.au; f. 1997 by merger of South Australian Gas Co, Gas Corpn of Queensland and Centre Gas Pty Ltd; purchased Victorian Gas Network in 1999; Chair. J. G. ALLPASS; Man. Dir O. G. CLARK.

Epic Energy: GPOB 657, Brisbane, Qld 4001; tel. (2) 6200-1600; fax (7) 3218-1650; internet www.epicenergy.com.au; f. 1996; privately-owned gas transmission co; CEO SUE ORTENSTONE.

Origin Energy: GPOB 5376, Sydney, NSW 2001; tel. (2) 9220-6400; fax (2) 9235-1661; internet www.origin.energy@originenergy.com .au; Man. Dir GRANT KING.

TXU: Level 19, East Tower, 40 City Road, Southbank, Vic 3006; tel. (3) 9299-2666; fax (3) 9299-2777; e-mail enq@txu.com.au; internet www.txu.com.au.

TRADE UNIONS

Australian Council of Trade Unions (ACTU): Level 2, 393 Swanston St, Melbourne, Vic 3000; tel. (3) 9663-5266; fax (3) 9663-4051; e-mail mailbox@actu.asn.au; internet www.actu.asn.au; f. 1927; br. in each state, generally known as a Trades and Labour Council; 46 affiliated trade unions; Pres. SHARAN BURROW; Sec. GREGORY COMBET.

Principal Affiliated Unions

Ansett Pilots Association (APA): 19 Napier St, Essendon, Vic 3040; tel. (3) 9375-1941; fax (3) 9375-7405; Pres. HENRY OTTO; Sec. JOHN DOGGETT.

Association of Professional Engineers, Scientists & Managers, Australia (APESMA): POB 1272L, Melbourne, Vic 3001; tel. (3) 9695-8800; fax (3) 9696-9312; e-mail info@apesma.asn.au; internet www.apesma.asn.au; Pres. ROB J. ALLEN; Sec. GREG SUTHERLAND; 24,000 mems.

Australasian Meat Industry Employees' Union (AMIEU): 377 Sussex St, Sydney, NSW 2000; tel. (2) 9264-2279; fax (2) 9261-1970; e-mail amieu_fed@bigpond.com; internet www.amieu.asn.au; Fed. Pres. ROSS RICHARDSON; Fed. Sec. T. R. HANNAN; 23,100 mems.

Australian Airline Flight Engineers Association (AAEA): Aspect House, 3/87 Buckley St, Essendon, Vic 3040; tel. (3) 9375-7590; fax (3) 9375-7590; e-mail aeu@aeufederal.org.au; internet www.aeufederal.org.au; f. 1984; Fed. Pres. JEFF SEABURN; Fed. Sec. RON HARE.

Australian Collieries Staff Association (ACSA): POB 21, Merewether, NSW 2291; tel. (02) 4963-5656; fax (02) 4963-3425; e-mail acsa@acsa.org.au; internet www.acsa.org.au; Gen. Pres. MICK BURGESS; Gen. Sec. WENDY CLEWS.

Australian Education Union (AEU): 120 Clarendon St, Southbank, Vic 3006; tel. (3) 9693-1800; fax (3) 9254-1805; e-mail aeu@ aeufederal.org.au; internet www.aeufederal.org.au; f. 1984; Fed. Pres. DENIS FITZGERALD; Fed. Sec. ROBERT DURBRIDGE; 155,000 mems.

Australian Manufacturing Workers' Union (AMWU): POB 160, Granville, NSW 2142; tel. (2) 9897-9133; fax (2) 9897-9274; e-mail amwu2@amwu.asn.au; internet www.amwu.asn.au; Nat. Pres. JULIUS ROE; Nat. Sec. DOUG CAMERON; 170,000 mems.

Australian Services Union (ASU): Ground Floor, 116 Queensberry St, Carlton South, Vic 3053; tel. (3) 9342-1400; fax (3) 9342-1499; e-mail asunatm@asu.asn.au; internet www.asu.asn.au; f. 1885; amalgamated, in present form in 1993; Nat. Sec. PAUL SLAPE; 140,000 mems.

Australian Workers' Union (AWU): 685 Spencer St, West Melbourne, Vic 3003; tel. (2) 9329-8733; fax (2) 9329-2871; e-mail awu@alphalink.net.au; internet www.awu.net.au; f. 1886; Nat. Pres. GRAHAM ROBERTS; Nat. Sec. BILL SHORTEN; 130,000 mems.

Communications, Electrical, Electronic, Energy, Information, Postal, Plumbing and Allied Services Union of Australia (CEPU): POB 812, Rockdale, NSW 2216; tel. (2) 9597-4499; fax (2) 9597-6354; e-mail edno@nat.cepu.asn.au; internet www.cepu.asn.au; Nat Pres. BRIAN BAULK; Nat. Sec. PETER TIGHE; 180,000 mems.

Community and Public Sector Union (CPSU): Level 5, 191–199 Thomas St, Haymarket, NSW 2000; tel. (2) 9334-9200; fax (2) 8204-6902; e-mail cpsu@cpsu.org; internet www.cpsu.org; Nat. Pres. MATTHEW REYNOLDS; Nat. Sec. WENDY CAIRD; 200,000 mems.

Construction, Forestry, Mining and Energy Union (CFMEU): Box Q235, Queen Victoria Bldg, Sydney, NSW 1230; tel. (2) 9267-3393; fax (2) 9267-2460; internet www.cfmeu.asn.au; f. 1992 by amalgamation; Pres. TREVOR SMITH; Sec. JOHN MAITLAND; 120,000 mems.

Finance Sector Union of Australia (FSU): GPOB 2829AA, 341 Queen St, Melbourne, Vic 3001; tel. (3) 9261-5300; fax (3) 9670-2950; e-mail fsuinfo@fsunion.org.au; internet www.fsunion.org.au; f. 1991; Nat. Pres. JOY BUCKLAND; Nat. Sec. TONY BECK; 61,000 mems.

Health Services Union of Australia (HSUA): 171 Drummond St, Carlton, Vic 3053; tel. (3) 9376-8242; fax (3) 9376-8243; e-mail union@hsua.asn.au; internet www.hsua.asn.au; Nat. Pres. MICHAEL WILLIAMSON; Nat. Sec. ROBERT ELLIOTT; 90,000 mems.

Independent Education Union of Australia (IEU): POB 1301, South Melbourne, Vic 3205; tel. (3) 9254-1830; fax (3) 9254-1835; e-mail ieu@ieu.org.au; internet www.ieu.org.au; Fed. Sec. LYNNE ROLLEY; Fed. Pres. RICHARD SHEARMAN; 45,000 mems.

Liquor, Hospitality and Miscellaneous Workers Union (LHMU): Locked Bag 9, Haymarket, NSW 1240; tel. (2) 8204-7200; fax (2) 9281-4480; e-mail lhmu@lhmu.org.au; internet www.lhmu.org.au; f. 1992; Nat. Pres. HELEN CREED; Nat. Sec. JEFF LAWRENCE; 143,800 mems.

Maritime Union of Australia (MUA): 2nd floor, 365 Sussex St, Sydney, NSW 2000; tel. (2) 9267-9134; fax (2) 9261-3481; e-mail muano@mua.org.au; internet www.mua.org.au; f. 1993; Nat. Sec. PADDY CRUMLIN; 10,012 mems.

Media, Entertainment & Arts Alliance (MEAA): POB 723, Strawberry Hills, NSW 2012; tel. (2) 9333-0999; fax (2) 9333-0933; e-mail mail@alliance.org.au; internet www.alliance.org.au; Fed. Sec. CHRISTOPHER WARREN; 30,000 mems.

National Union of Workers (NUW): POB 343, North Melbourne, Vic 3051; tel. (3) 9287-1850; fax (3) 9287-1818; e-mail nuwnat@nuw.org.au; internet www.nuw.org.au; Gen. Sec. GREG SWORD; Gen. Pres. LLOYD FREEBURN; 100,000 mems.

Rail, Tram and Bus Union (RTBU): 83–89 Renwick St, Redfern, NSW 2016; tel. (2) 9310-3966; fax (2) 9319-2096; e-mail rtbu@magna.com.au; internet www.rtbu-nat.asn.au; Nat. Pres. R. HAYDER; Nat. Sec. ROGER JOWETT; 35,000 mems.

Shop, Distributive & Allied Employees Association (SDA): 5th Floor, 53 Queen St, Melbourne, Vic 3000; tel. (3) 9629-2299; fax (3) 9629-2646; e-mail sdanat@c031.aone.net.au; internet www.sda.org.au; f. 1908; Nat. Pres. DON FARRELL; Nat. Sec. JOE DE BRUYN; 209,708 mems.

Textile, Clothing and Footwear Union of Australia (TCFUA): Ground Floor, 28 Anglo Rd, Campsie, NSW 2194; tel. (2) 9789-4188; fax (2) 9789-6510; e-mail tcfua@tcfua.org.au; f. 1919; Pres. BARRY TUBNER; Nat. Sec. TONY WOOLGAR; 21,354 mems.

Transport Workers' Union of Australia (TWU): POB 211, Carlton South, Vic 3053; tel. (3) 9347-0099; fax (3) 9347-2502; e-mail twu@twu.com.au; internet www.twu.com.au; Fed. Pres. HUGHIE WILLIAMS; Fed. Sec. JOHN ALLAN; 82,000 mems.

Transport

Australian Transport Council: POB 594, Canberra, ACT 2601; tel. (2) 6274-7851; fax (2) 6274-7703; e-mail atc@dotrs.gov.au; internet www.atcouncil.gov.au; f. 1993; mems include: Federal Minister for Transport and Regional Services, State, Territory and New Zealand Ministers responsible for transport; Sec. D. JONES.

State Transit Authority of New South Wales: 100 Miller St, North Sydney, NSW 2060; tel. (2) 9245-5777; fax (2) 9245-5710; internet www.sta.nsw.gov.au; operates government buses and ferries in Sydney and Newcastle metropolitan areas; Chair. DAVID HERLIHY; CEO JOHN STOTT.

TransAdelaide (South Australia): GPOB 2351, Adelaide, SA 5001; tel. (8) 8218-2200; fax (8) 8218-4399; e-mail info@transadelaide.sa.gov.au; internet www.transadelaide.com.au; f. 1994; fmrly State Transport Authority; operates metropolitan train, bus, tram and Busway services; Gen. Man. SUE FILBY.

RAILWAYS

In June 2001 there were 39,844 km of railways in Australia (including tram and light rail track).

National Rail Corporation Ltd: POB 1419, Parramatta, NSW 2124; tel. (2) 9685-2555; fax (2) 9687-1804; e-mail information@nrc.com.au; internet www.nationalrail.com.au; freight; Chair. P. YOUNG; Man. Dir V. J. GRAHAM.

Public Transport Corporation (Victoria): Level 15, 589 Collins St, Melbourne, Vic 3000; tel. (3) 9619-4222; fax (3) 9619-4911; e-mail j.barry@ptc.vic.gov.au; f. 1989; Exec. Dir JOHN R. BARRY.

QR (Queensland Rail): POB 1429, Brisbane, Qld 4001; tel. (7) 3235-2222; fax (7) 3235-1799; internet www.qr.com.au; Chief Exec. BOB SCHEUBER.

State Rail Authority of New South Wales: POB K349, Haymarket, NSW 1238; tel. (2) 9379-3000; fax (2) 9379-2090; internet www.staterail.nsw.gov.au; f. 1980; responsible for passenger rail and associated coach services in NSW; Chief Exec. LUCIO DE BARTOLOMEO (acting).

Western Australian Government Railways (Westrail): POB 8125, Perth 6849, WA; tel. (8) 9326-2000; fax (8) 9326-2500; internet www.wagr.wa.gov.au; statutory authority competing in the freight, passenger and related transport markets in southern WA; operates 1,029 main line route-km of track; Commr REECE WALDOCK (acting).

ROADS

In June 2001 there were 808,294 km of roads open for general traffic. In 1996 this included 1,000 km of freeways, a further 103 km of toll roads, 45,889 km of highways, 77,045 km of arterial and major roads and 30,596 of secondary tourist and other roads. Local roads in urban areas account for 93,677 km of the network and those in rural localities for 537,278 km.

Austroads Inc: POB K659, Haymarket, NSW 2000; tel. (2) 9264-7088; fax (2) 9264-1657; e-mail austroads@austroads.com.au; internet www.austroads.com.au; f. 1989; asscn of road transport and traffic authorities.

SHIPPING

In December 2001 the Australian merchant fleet comprised 622 vessels, with a total displacement of 1,887,808 grt.

Adsteam Marine Ltd: Level 22, 6 O'Connell St, Sydney, NSW 2000; tel. (2) 9232-3955; fax (2) 9232-3988; e-mail info@adsteam.com.au; f. 1875; fmrly Adelaide Steamship Co; Man. Dir DAVID RYAN; Chief Exec. CLAY FREDERICK.

ANL Ltd (Australian National Line): GPOB 2238T, Melbourne, Vic 3004; tel. (3) 9257-0613; fax (3) 9257-0517; e-mail anl@anl.com.au; f. 1956; shipping agents; coastal and overseas container shipping and coastal bulk shipping; container management services; overseas container services to Hong Kong, Taiwan, the Philippines, Korea, Singapore, Malaysia, Thailand, Indonesia and Japan; extensive transhipment services; Chair. E. G. ANSON; Man. Dir MALCOLM TURNBULL.

BHP Transport Pty Ltd: 27th Level, 600 Bourke St, POB 86A, Melbourne, Vic 3001; tel. (3) 9609-3333; fax (3) 9609-2400; Chair. D. ARGUS; Man. Dir P. ANDERSEN.

William Holyman and Sons Pty Ltd: No. 3 Berth, Bell Bay, Tas 7253; tel. (3) 6382-2383; fax (3) 6382-3391; coastal services; Chair. R. J. HOY.

Howard Smith Ltd: POB N364, Grosvenor Place, Sydney, NSW 2000; tel. (2) 9230-1777; fax (2) 9251-1190; e-mail info@hst.com.au; internet www.howardsmith.com.au; harbour towage and other services; Chair. FRANCIS JOHN CONROY; CEO KENNETH JOHN MOSS.

CIVIL AVIATION

Eastern Australia Airlines: POB 538, Mascot, Sydney, NSW 2020; tel. (2) 9691-2333; fax (2) 9693-2715; internet www.qantas.com.au; subsidiary of Qantas; domestic flights; Gen. Man. ASHLEY KILROY.

Impulse Airlines: Eleventh St, Sydney Kingsford-Smith Airport, Mascot, NSW 2020; tel. (2) 9317-5400; fax (2) 9317-3440; e-mail info@ImpulseAirlines.com.au; internet www.impulseairlines.com

.au; f. 1992; domestic services; Chief Exec./Chair. GERRY MCGOWAN; Exec. Dir SUE MCGOWAN.

National Jet Systems: Adelaide Airport, 28 James Schofield Drive SA 5000; tel. (8) 8238-7200; fax (8) 8238-7238; internet www .nationaljet.com.au; f. 1989; domestic services; Man. Dir DANIELA MARSILLI; Group Gen. Man. Commdr ROBERT BIRKS.

Qantas Airways Ltd: Qantas Centre, 203 Coward St, Mascot, NSW 2020; tel. (2) 9691-3636; fax (2) 9691-3339; internet www.qantas .com.au; f. 1920 as Queensland and Northern Territory Aerial Services; Australian Govt became sole owner in 1947; merged with Australian Airlines in Sept. 1992; British Airways purchased 25% in March 1993; remaining 75% transferred to private sector in 1995; services throughout Australia and to 34 countries, including destinations in Europe, Africa, the USA, Canada, South America, Asia, the Pacific and New Zealand; Chair. MARGARET JACKSON; CEO GEOFF DIXON.

Spirit Airlines: Level 9, 580 St Kilda Rd, Melbourne, Vic 3004; fax (3) 9510-4095; e-mail info@spiritairlines.com.au; internet www .spiritairlines.com.au/; f. 1998; domestic services; CEO MIKE DIXON.

Sunstate Airlines: Lobby 3, Level 3, 153 Campbell St, Bowen Hills, Qld 4006; tel. (7) 3308-9022; fax (7) 3308-9088; e-mail edalessio@ qantas.com.au; f. 1982; wholly owned by Qantas; operates passenger services within Queensland and to Newcastle (NSW) and Lord Howe Island; Gen. Man. ELSA D'ALESSIO.

Virgin Blue: Centenary Place, Level 7, 100 Wickham St, Brisbane, Qld; tel. (7) 3295-3000; e-mail customercare@virginblue.com.au; internet www.virginblue.com.au; domestic services; CEO BRETT GODFREY.

Tourism

The main attractions are the cosmopolitan cities, the Great Barrier Reef, the Blue Mountains, water sports and also winter sports in the Australian Alps, notably the Snowy Mountains. The town of Alice Springs, the Aboriginal culture and the sandstone monolith of Ayers Rock (Uluru) are among the attractions of the desert interior. Much of Australia's wildlife is unique to the country. Australia received 4,841,200 foreign visitors in 2002. The majority of visitors came from New Zealand, Japan, the United Kingdom and the USA. Receipts totalled $A19,800m. in 2000. The 2000 Olympic Games were held in Sydney in September.

Australian Tourist Commission: GPOB 2721, Sydney, NSW 1006; Level 4, 80 William St, Woolloomooloo, Sydney, NSW 2011; tel. (2) 9360-1111; fax (2) 9331-6469; internet www.atc.australia.com; f. 1967 for promotion of international inbound tourism; 13 offices overseas; Chair. NICK EVERS; Man. Dir KEN BOUNDY.

AUSTRALIAN EXTERNAL TERRITORIES

CHRISTMAS ISLAND

Introduction

Christmas Island lies 360 km south of Java Head (Indonesia) in the Indian Ocean. The nearest point on the Australian coast is North West Cape, 1,408 km to the south-east. Christmas Island has no indigenous population. The population was 1,508 at the 2001 census (compared with 1,906 in 1996), comprising mainly ethnic Chinese (some 70%), but there were large minorities of Malays (about 10%) and Europeans (about 20%). A variety of languages are spoken, but English is the official language. The predominant religious affiliation is Buddhist (55% in 1991). The principal settlement and only anchorage is Flying Fish Cove.

Following annexation by the United Kingdom in 1888, Christmas Island was incorporated for administrative purposes with the Straits Settlements (now Singapore and part of Malaysia) in 1900. Japanese forces occupied the island from March 1942 until the end of the Second World War, and in 1946 Christmas Island became a dependency of Singapore. Administration was transferred to the United Kingdom on 1 January 1958, pending final transfer to Australia, effected on 1 October 1958. The Australian Government appointed Official Representatives to the Territory until 1968, when new legislation provided for an Administrator, appointed by the Governor-General. Responsibility for administration lies with the Minister for Regional Services, Territories and Local Government. In 1980 an Advisory Council was established for the Administrator to consult. In 1984 the Christmas Island Services Corporation was created to perform those functions that are normally the responsibility of municipal government. This body was placed under the direction of the Christmas Island Assembly, the first elections to which took place in September 1985. Nine members were elected for one-year terms. In November 1987 the Assembly was dissolved, and the Administrator empowered to perform its functions. The Corporation was superseded by the Christmas Island Shire Council in 1992.

In May 1994 an unofficial referendum on the island's status was held concurrently with local government elections. At the poll, sponsored by the Union of Christmas Island Workers, the islanders rejected an option to secede from Australia, but more than 85% of voters favoured increased local government control. The referendum was prompted, in part, by the Australian Government's plans to abolish the island's duty-free status (which had become a considerable source of revenue).

Since 1981 all residents of the island have been eligible to acquire Australian citizenship. In 1984 the Australian Government extended social security, health and education benefits to the island, and enfranchised Australian citizens resident there. Full income-tax liability was introduced in the late 1980s.

During the late 1990s an increasing number of illegal immigrants travelling to Australia landed on Christmas Island. In January 2001 Australian government officials denied claims by Christmas Islanders that some 86 illegal immigrants who had arrived at the island from the Middle East via Indonesia were being detained in inhumane conditions. Local people claimed that the detainees were sleeping on concrete floors and were being denied adequate food and medical care.

International attention was focused on Christmas Island in August 2001 when the *MV Tampa*, a Norwegian container ship carrying 433 refugees whom it had rescued from a sinking Indonesian fishing boat, was refused permission to land on the island. As the humanitarian crisis escalated, the Australian Government's steadfast refusal to admit the mostly Afghan refugees prompted international condemnation and led to a serious diplomatic dispute between Australia and Norway. The office of the United Nations High Commissioner for Refugees (UNHCR) and the International Organization for Migration (IOM) expressed grave concern at the situation. Hundreds of Christmas Island residents attended a rally urging the Australian Government to reconsider its uncompromising stance. In September the refugees were transferred (via Papua New Guinea and New Zealand) to Nauru, where their applications for asylum were to be processed. In the same month the Senate in Canberra approved new legislation, which excised Christmas Island and other outlying territories from Australia's official migration zone. The new legislation also imposed stricter criteria for the processing of asylum-seekers and the removal of their right to recourse to the Australian court system. Meanwhile, increasing numbers of asylum-seekers continued to attempt to reach Christmas Island via Indonesia. Among the many controversial incidents that occurred in the waters of Christmas Island in September–December 2001 was that of 186 Iraqis who jumped into the sea when ordered to leave Australian waters in October. They were temporarily housed on Christmas Island before being transferred to Nauru. According to Australian Immigration Department figures, 146 asylum-seekers were turned away from Christmas Island and Ashmore Reef in December 2001. In January 2002 211 asylum-seekers remained on Christmas Island awaiting transferral. In March the Government announced plans to establish a permanent detention centre on the island, the construction of which was expected to cost more than $A150m. The Government was thus preparing to accommodate an anticipated total of 18,000 illegal immigrants who were expected to arrive at Christmas Island during 2002–06. However, plans to scale down the project were announced in February 2003.

The economy has been based on the recovery of phosphates. During the year ending 30 June 1984 about 463,000 metric tons were exported to Australia, 332,000 tons to New Zealand and 341,000 tons to other countries. Reserves were estimated to be sufficient to enable production to be maintained until the mid-1990s. In November 1987 the Australian Government announced the closure of the phosphate mine, owing to industrial unrest, and mining activity ceased in December. In 1990, however, the Government allowed private operators to recommence phosphate extraction, subject to certain conditions such as the preservation of the rainforest. A total of 220,000 metric tons of phosphates were produced in 1995. In 2001 the mine employed some 180 workers. The owner of the mine, Phosphate Resources Ltd (trading as Christmas Island Phosphates), was thus the island's largest employer. A total of 570,000 metric tons of phosphate dust were exported in 2001/02, and phosphate exports were worth $A43.8m. in 1997/98. A new 21-year lease, drawn up by the Government and Phosphate Resources Ltd, took effect in February 1998. The agreement incorporated environmental safeguards and provided for a conservation levy, based on the tonnage of phosphate shipped, which was to finance a programme of rainforest rehabilitation.

Efforts have been made to develop the island's considerable potential for tourism. In 1989, in an attempt to protect the natural environment and many rare species of flora and fauna (including the Abbott's Booby and the Christmas frigate bird), the National Park was extended to cover some 70% of the island. A hotel and casino complex, covering 47 ha of land, was opened in November 1993. In 1994 revenue from the development totalled $A500m. A 50-room extension to the complex was constructed in 1995. In early 1997, however, fears for the nascent industry were expressed, following the decision by Ansett Australia to discontinue its twice-weekly air service to the island from September of that year. Despite the subsequent commencement of a weekly flight from Perth, Australia, operated by National Jet Systems, the complex was closed down in April 1998 and some 350 employees were made redundant. In July the resort's casino licence was cancelled and a liquidator was appointed to realize the complex's assets. The closure of the resort had serious economic and social repercussions for the island. An audit of tourist accommodation, conducted in May 2000, counted approximately 140 beds on the island.

Between 1992 and 1999 the Australian Government invested an estimated $A110m. in the development of Christmas Island's infrastructure as part of the Christmas Island Rebuilding Programme. The main areas of expenditure under this programme were a new hospital, the upgrading of ports facilities, school extensions, the construction of housing, power, water supply and sewerage, and the repair and construction of roads. In 2000 further improvements to marine facilities and water supply were carried out, in addition to the construction of new housing to relocate islanders away from a major rockfall risk area. The cost of the island's imports from Australia increased from $A13m. in 1998/99 to $A17m. in 1999/2000 and declined to $A16m. in 2000/01 when the Territory's exports to that country earned $A7m. In 1998/99 imports from New Zealand cost $NZ9m. Although Christmas Island purchased no imports from New Zealand in 2000/01, exports to that country were worth $NZ4m. An estimated 7.5% of the island's population were unemployed in 1996.

Proposals for the development of a communications satellite launching facility on the island were under consideration in 1998. An assessment of the environmental impact was subsequently undertaken, and the scheme received government approval in May 2000. Following an agreement between the Governments of Australia and Russia in May 2001, preparations for the establishment of a space control centre on Christmas Island commenced. Australia and Russia were to contribute up to US $100m. towards the project, the total cost of which was expected to be US $425m. The Christmas Island site was to be developed by the Asia Pacific Space Centre, an Australian company. Construction began in November 2001, with the first rocket launch being planned for 2004. The space centre was expected to become the world's first wholly privately-owned land-based launch facility, with an operational lifespan of 15–20 years. Asia Pacific planned to launch 10–12 satellites annually by 2005. Although the project would create many employment opportunities on the island (an estimated 400 new jobs during construction and 550 during operation) and lead to substantial infrastructural improvements, environmentalists continued to express concern.

Statistical Survey

AREA AND POPULATION

Area: 135 sq km (52 sq miles).

Population: 1,906 (males 1,023, females 883) at census of 30 June 1996; 1,508 (males 850, females 658) at census of 7 August 2001; 1,506 (official estimate) at August 2002. *Ethnic Groups* (census of 30 June 1981): Chinese 1,587; Malay 693; European 336; Total (incl. others) 2,871. Source: mainly UN, *Demographic Yearbook*.

Density (2002): 11.2 per sq km.

Births and Deaths (1985): Registered live births 36 (birth rate 15.8 per 1,000); Registered deaths 2.

Labour Force (1996): 971 (employed 898, unemployed 73).

MINING

Natural Phosphates (official estimates, '000 metric tons): 285 in 1994; 220 in 1995.

FINANCE

Currency and Exchange Rates: Australian currency is used, see p. 562.

EXTERNAL TRADE

Principal Trading Partners (phosphate exports, '000 metric tons, year ending 30 June 1984)): Australia 463; New Zealand 332; Total (incl. others) 1,136.

2000/01 ($A million): *Imports:* Australia 16. *Exports:* Australia 7. Source: Australian Bureau of Statistics, *Year Book Australia*.

2000/01 ($NZ million): *Exports:* New Zealand 4. Source: Ministry of Foreign Affairs and Trade, New Zealand.

TRANSPORT

International Sea-borne Shipping (estimated freight traffic, '000 metric tons, 1990): Goods loaded 1,290; Goods unloaded 68. Source: UN, *Monthly Bulletin of Statistics*.

TOURISM

Visitor Arrivals and Departures by Air: 14,513 in 1996; 3,895 in 1997; 2,712 in 1998. Source: *Year Book Australia*.

COMMUNICATIONS MEDIA

Radio Receivers (1997): 1,000 in use.

Television Receivers (1997): 600 in use.

Personal Computers (home users, 2001): 506.

Internet Users (2001): 1,450.

EDUCATION

Pre-primary (2002): 37 pupils.

Primary (2002): 217 pupils.

Secondary (2002): 124 pupils.
Source: Education Department of Western Australia.

Directory

The Government

The Administrator, appointed by the Governor-General of Australia and responsible to the Minister for Regional Services, Territories and Local Government, is the senior government representative on the island.

Administrator: WILLIAM TAYLOR.

Administration Headquarters: POB 863, Christmas Island 6798, Indian Ocean; tel. (8) 9164-7901; fax (8) 9164-8524.

Shire of Christmas Island: George Fam Centre, POB 863, Christmas Island 6798, Indian Ocean; tel. (8) 9164-8300; fax (8) 9164-8304; e-mail soci@pulau.cx.

Judicial System

The judicial system comprises the Supreme Court, District Court, Magistrate's Court and Children's Court.

Supreme Court

c/o Govt Offices, Christmas Island 6798, Indian Ocean; tel. (8) 9164-7911; fax (8) 9164-8530.

Judges (non-resident) ROBERT SHERATON FRENCH, MALCOLM CAMERON LEE.

Managing Registrar: JEFFERY LOW, Govt Offices, Christmas Island 6798, Indian Ocean; tel. (8) 9164-7911; fax (8) 9164-8530.

Religion

According to the census of 1991, of the 1,275 residents of Christmas Island, some 55% were Buddhists, 10% were Muslims, and 15% were Christians. Within the Christian churches, Christmas Island lies in the jurisdiction of both the Anglican and Roman Catholic Archbishops of Perth, in Western Australia.

The Press

The Islander: Shire of Christmas Island, George Fam Centre, POB 863, Christmas Island 6798, Indian Ocean; tel. (8) 9164-8300; fax (8) 9164-8304; newsletter; fortnightly; Editor TENG BOON EIANG.

Broadcasting and Communications

Telecommunications

Indian Ocean Communications: Christmas Island; tel. (8) 9164-8505; e-mail mobiles@pulau.cx; provides stand-alone mobile cellular telephone network.

Broadcasting

Radio

Christmas Island Community Radio Service: f. 1967; operated by the Administration since 1991; daily broadcasting service by Radio VLU-2 on 1422 KHz and 102 MHz FM, in English, Malay, Cantonese and Mandarin; Station Man. WILLIAM TAYLOR.

Christmas Island Radio VLU2–FM: POB 474, Christmas Island 6798, Indian Ocean; tel. (8) 9164-8316; fax (8) 9164-8315; daily broadcasts on 102.1FM and 105.3FM in English, Malay, Cantonese and Mandarin; Chair. and Station Manager TONY SMITH.

Television

Christmas Island Television: POB AAA, Christmas Island 6798, Indian Ocean.

Finance

BANKING

Commercial Bank

Westpac Banking Corpn (Australia): Flying Fish Cove, Christmas Island, Indian Ocean; tel. (8) 9164-8221; fax (8) 9164-8241.

Trade and Industry

In April 2001 there were 67 small businesses in operation.

Administration of Christmas Island: POB 868, Christmas Island 6798, Indian Ocean; tel. (8) 9164-7901; fax (8) 9164-8524; operates power, airport, seaport, health services, public housing, local courts; Director of Finance JEFFERY TAN.

Christmas Island Chamber of Commerce: Christmas Island 6798, Indian Ocean; tel. (8) 9164-8249; Pres. DON O'DONNELL; Vice Pres. PHILLIP OAKLEY.

Shire of Christmas Island: George Fam Centre, POB 863, Christmas Island 6798, Indian Ocean; tel. (8) 9164-8300; fax (8) 9164-8304; e-mail soci@iocomm.com.au; f. 1992 by Territories Law Reform Act to replace Christmas Island Services Corpn; provides local govt services; manages tourism and economic development; Pres. DAVID McLANE; CEO DAVID PRICE.

Union of Christmas Island Workers (UCIW): Poon Saan Rd, POB 84, Christmas Island 6798, Indian Ocean; tel. (8) 9164-8471; fax (8) 9164-8470; e-mail uciw@pulau.cx; fmrly represented phosphate workers; Pres. FOO KEE HENG; Gen. Sec. GORDON THOMSON; 800 mems.

Transport

There are good roads in the developed areas. National Jet Systems operate a twice-weekly flight from Perth, via the Cocos (Keeling) Islands, and a private Christmas Island-based charter company operates services to Jakarta, Indonesia. In 1998 arrivals and departures by air in Christmas Island totalled 2,712 (compared with 3,895 in the previous year). The Australian National Line (ANL) operates ships to the Australian mainland. Cargo vessels from Fremantle deliver supplies to the island every four to six weeks. The Joint Island Supply System, established in 1989, provides a shipping service for Christmas Island and the Cocos Islands. The only anchorage is at Flying Fish Cove.

Tourism

Tourism is a growing sector of the island's economy. Visitors are attracted by the unique flora and fauna, as well as the excellent conditions for scuba-diving and game-fishing. In 2000 there were approximately 90 hotel rooms on the island.

Christmas Island Tourism Association/Christmas Island Visitor Information Centre: POB 63, Christmas Island 6798, Indian Ocean; tel. (8) 9164-8382; fax (8) 9164-8080; e-mail cita@christmas .net.au; internet www.christmas.net.au; Tourism Co-ordinator TERESA HENDREN.

Christmas Island Tours and Travel: Christmas Island 6798, Indian Ocean; tel. (8) 9164-7168; fax (8) 9164-7169; e-mail xch@ citravel.com.au; Dir TAN SIM KIAT.

Island Bound Travel: tel. (8) 9381-3644; fax (8) 9381 2030; e-mail info@islandbound.com.au.

Parks Australia: Christmas Island 6798, Indian Ocean; tel. (8) 9164-8700; fax (8) 9164-8755.

COCOS (KEELING) ISLANDS

Introduction

The Cocos (Keeling) Islands are 27 in number and lie 2,768 km north-west of Perth, in the Indian Ocean. The islands form two low-lying coral atolls, densely covered with coconut palms. The climate is equable, with temperatures varying from 21°C (69°F) to 32°C (88°F), and rainfall of 2,000 mm per year. In 1981 some 58% of the population were of the Cocos Malay community, and 26% were Europeans. The Cocos Malays are descendants of the people brought to the islands by Alexander Hare and of labourers who were subsequently introduced by the Clunies-Ross family (see below). English is the official language, but Cocos Malay and Malay are also widely spoken. Most of the inhabitants are Muslims (56.8% in 1981). Home Island, which had a population of 446 in mid-1992, is where the Cocos Malay community is based. The only other inhabited island is West Island, with a population of 147 in mid-1992, and where most of the European community lives, the administration is based and the airport is located. The total population of the islands was 621 at the census of August 2001.

The islands were uninhabited when discovered by Capt. William Keeling, of the British East India Company, in 1609, and the first settlement was not established until 1826, by Alexander Hare. The islands were declared a British possession in 1857 and came successively under the authority of the Governors of Ceylon (now Sri Lanka), from 1878, and the Straits Settlements (now Singapore and part of Malaysia), from 1886. Also in 1886 the British Crown granted all land on the islands above the high-water mark to John Clunies-Ross and his heirs and successors in perpetuity. In 1946, when the islands became a dependency of the Colony of Singapore, a resident administrator, responsible to the Governor of Singapore, was appointed. Administration of the islands was transferred to the Commonwealth of Australia on 23 November 1955. The agent of the Australian Government was known as the Official Representative until 1975, when an Administrator was appointed. The Minister for Regional Services, Territories and Local Government is responsible for the governance of the islands. The Territory is part of the Northern Territory Electoral District.

In June 1977 the Australian Government announced new policies concerning the islands, which resulted in its purchase from John Clunies-Ross of the whole of his interests in the islands, with the exception of his residence and associated buildings. The purchase for $A6.5m. took effect on 1 September 1978. An attempt by the Australian Government to acquire Clunies-Ross' remaining property was deemed by the Australian High Court in October 1984 to be unconstitutional.

In July 1979 the Cocos (Keeling) Islands Council was established, with a wide range of functions in the Home Island village area (which the Government transferred to the Council on trust for the benefit of the Cocos Malay community) and, from September 1984, in the greater part of the rest of the Territory.

On 6 April 1984 a referendum to decide the future political status of the islands was held by the Australian Government, with UN observers present. A large majority voted in favour of integration with Australia. As a result, the islanders were to acquire the rights, privileges and obligations of all Australian citizens. In July 1992 the Cocos (Keeling) Islands Council was replaced by the Cocos (Keeling) Islands Shire Council, modelled on the local government and state law of Western Australia.

In September 2001, following an increase in the numbers of illegal immigrants reaching Australian waters (see the chapter on Christmas Island), legislation was passed removing the Cocos Islands and other territories from Australia's official migration zone. In October of that year the Australian Government sent contingency supplies to the islands as a precaution, should it be necessary to accommodate more asylum-seekers. This development provoked concern among many Cocos residents that the former quarantine station used as a detention centre might become a permanent asylum-processing facility under the order of the Australian Government. In December 123 Sri Lankan and Vietnamese asylum-seekers were housed at the station, which was built to accommodate only 40.

Following unsuccessful investment in a shipping venture, the Clunies-Ross family was declared bankrupt in mid-1993, and the Australian Government took possession of its property.

Although local fishing is good, some livestock is kept and domestic gardens provide vegetables, bananas and papayas (pawpaws), the islands are not self-sufficient, and other foodstuffs, fuels and consumer items are imported from mainland Australia. A Cocos postal service (including a philatelic bureau) came into operation in September 1979, and revenue from the service is used for the benefit of the community.

Coconuts, grown throughout the islands, are the sole cash crop: total output was an estimated 7,625 metric tons in 2001. Total exports of coconuts in 1984/85 were 202 metric tons. The cost of the islands' imports from Australia increased from $A5m. in 1999/2000 to $A11m. in 2000/01. Exports to Australia totalled $A2m. in 1996/97. Some 8% of the population were unemployed in 1996. The conversion of a disused quarantine station into a business centre was under consideration in 2001. Meanwhile, the islands' internet domain name suffix, '.cc' was sold to Clear Channel, a US radio group, thus providing additional revenue.

Primary education is provided at the schools on Home and West Islands. Secondary education is provided to the age of 16 years on West Island. A bursary scheme enables Cocos Malay children to continue their education on the Australian mainland.

Statistical Survey

AREA AND POPULATION

Area: 14.2 sq km (5.5 sq miles).

Population: 655 (males 338, females 317): at census of 30 June 1996; 621 (males 334, females 287) at census of 7 August 2001. *Ethnic Groups* (census of 30 June 1981): Cocos Malay 320; European 143; Total (incl. others) 555. Source: mainly UN, *Demographic Yearbook.*

Density (2001): 43.7 per sq km.

Births and Deaths (1986): Registered live births 12 (birth rate 19.8 per 1,000); Registered deaths 2.

Labour Force (2001): 270 (employed 218, unemployed 52). Source: Indian Ocean Group Training.

AGRICULTURE

Production (FAO estimates, metric tons, 2001): Coconuts 7,625; Copra 1,000. Source: FAO.

FINANCE

Currency and Exchange Rates: Australian currency is used, see p. 562.

EXTERNAL TRADE

Principal Commodities (metric tons, year ending 30 June 1985): *Exports*: Coconuts 202. *Imports*: Most requirements come from Australia. The trade deficit is offset by philatelic sales and Australian federal grants and subsidies.

2000/01 ($A '000): *Imports*: Australia 11,000.
Source: *Year Book Australia.*

COMMUNICATIONS MEDIA

Radio Receivers (1992): 300 in use.

Personal Computers (home users, 2001): 142.

Internet Users (2001): 618.

EDUCATION

Pre-primary (2002): 23 pupils.

Primary (2002): 84 pupils.

Secondary (2002): 31 pupils.

Teaching Staff (2002): 18.
Source: Education Department of Western Australia.

Directory

The Government

The Administrator, appointed by the Governor-General of Australia and responsible to the Minister for Regional Services, Territories and Local Government, is the senior government representative in the islands.

Administrator: WILLIAM TAYLOR (non-resident).

Administrative Offices: POB 1093, West Island, Cocos (Keeling) Islands 6799, Indian Ocean; tel. (8) 9162-6615; fax (8) 9162-6697.

Cocos (Keeling) Islands Shire Council: POB 94, Home Island, Cocos (Keeling) Islands 6799, Indian Ocean; tel. (8) 9162-6649; fax (8) 9162-6668; e-mail info@shire.cc; f. 1992 by Territories Law Reform Act; Pres. MOHAMMED SAID CHONGKIN; CEO BOB JARVIS.

Judicial System

Supreme Court, Cocos (Keeling) Islands: West Island Police Station, Cocos (Keeling) Islands 6799, Indian Ocean; tel. (8) 9162-6615; fax (8) 9162-6697; Judge ROBERT SHERATON FRENCH; Additional Judge MALCOLM CAMERON LEE.

Magistrates' Court, Cocos (Keeling) Islands
Special Magistrate (vacant).

Managing Registrar: ROBYN JENKINS, Cocos (Keeling) Islands 6799, Indian Ocean; tel. (8) 9162-6615; fax (8) 9162-6697.

Religion

According to the census of 1981, of the 555 residents, 314 (some 57%) were Muslims and 124 (22%) Christians. The majority of Muslims live on Home Island, while most Christians are West Island residents. The Cocos Islands lie within both the Anglican and the Roman Catholic archdioceses of Perth (Western Australia).

Broadcasting and Communications

BROADCASTING

Radio

Radio VKW Cocos: POB 33, Cocos (Keeling) Islands 6799, Indian Ocean; tel. (8) 9162-6666; e-mail vkw@kampong.cc; non-commercial; daily broadcasting service in Cocos Malay and English; 200 listeners; Station Man. CATHERINE CLUNIES-ROSS.

Television

A television service, broadcasting Indonesian, Malaysian and Australian satellite television programmes and videotapes of Australian television programmes, began operating on an intermittent basis in September 1992.

Industry

Cocos (Keeling) Islands Co-operative Society Ltd: Home Island, Cocos (Keeling) Islands 6799, Indian Ocean; tel. (8) 9162-6702; fax (8) 9162-6764; f. 1979; conducts the business enterprises of the Cocos Islanders; activities include boat construction and repairs, copra and coconut production, sail-making, stevedoring and airport operation; owns and operates a supermarket and tourist accommodation; Chair. MOHAMMED SAID BIN CHONGKIN; Gen. Man. RONALD TAYLOR.

Transport

National Jet Systems operate a twice-weekly service from Perth, via Christmas Island, for passengers, supplies and mail to and from the airport on West Island. Cargo vessels from Singapore and Perth deliver supplies, at intervals of four to six weeks.

Cocos Trader: Cocos (Keeling) Islands 6799, Indian Ocean; tel. (8) 9162-6612; fax (8) 9162-6568; e-mail manpower@kampong.cc; shipping agent.

Tourism

Cocos Island Tourism Association: POB 30, Cocos (Keeling) Islands 6799, Indian Ocean; tel. (8) 9162-6790; fax (8) 9162-6696; e-mail info@cocos-tourism.cc.

NORFOLK ISLAND

Introductory Survey

Location, Climate, Language, Religion, Capital

Norfolk Island lies off the eastern coast of Australia, about 1,400 km east of Brisbane, to the south of New Caledonia and 640 km north of New Zealand. The Territory also comprises uninhabited Phillip Island and Nepean Island, 7 km and 1 km south of the main island respectively. Norfolk Island is hilly and fertile, with a coastline of cliffs and an area of 34.6 sq km (13.3 sq miles). It is about 8 km long and 4.8 km wide. The climate is mild and subtropical, and the average annual rainfall is 1,350 mm, most of which occurs between May and August. The resident population, which numbered 1,772 in August 1996, consists of 'islanders' (descendants of the mutineers from HMS *Bounty*, evacuated from Pitcairn Island, who numbered 683 in 1996) and 'mainlanders' (originally from Australia, New Zealand or the United Kingdom). English is the official language, but a local Polynesian dialect (related to Pitcairnese) is also spoken. Most of the population (70.4% at the 1996 census) adhere to the Christian religion. The capital of the Territory is Kingston.

Recent History and Economic Affairs

The island was uninhabited when discovered in 1774 by a British expedition, led by Capt. James Cook. Norfolk Island was used as a penal settlement from 1788 to 1814 and again from 1825 to 1855, when it was abandoned. In 1856 it was resettled by 194 emigrants from Pitcairn Island, which had become overpopulated. Norfolk Island was administered as a separate colony until 1897, when it became a dependency of New South Wales. In 1913 control was transferred to the Australian Government. Norfolk Island has a continuing dispute with the Australian Government concerning the island's status as a territory of the Commonwealth of Australia. There have been successive assertions of Norfolk Island's right to self-determination, as a distinct colony.

Under the Norfolk Island Act 1979, Norfolk Island is progressing to responsible legislative and executive government, enabling the Territory to administer its own affairs to the greatest practicable extent. Wide powers are exercised by the nine-member Legislative Assembly and by the Executive Council, comprising the executive members of the Legislative Assembly who have ministerial-type responsibilities. The Act preserves the Australian Government's responsibility for Norfolk Island as a territory under its authority, with the Minister for Regional Services, Territories and Local Government as the responsible minister. The Act indicated that consideration would be given within five years to an extension of the powers of the Legislative Assembly and the political and administrative institutions of Norfolk Island. In 1985 legislative and executive responsibility was assumed by the Norfolk Island government for public works and services, civil defence, betting and gaming, territorial archives and matters relating to the exercise of executive authority. In 1988 further amendments empowered the Legislative Assembly to select a Norfolk Island government auditor (territorial accounts were previously audited by the Commonwealth Auditor-General). The office of Chief Minister was replaced by that of the President of the Legislative Assembly. David Ernest Buffett was reappointed to this post following the May 1992 general election. A lack of consensus among members of the Executive Council on several major issues prompted early legislative elections in April 1994. The newly-elected seventh Legislative Assembly was significant in having three female members. Following elections in April 1997, in which 22 candidates contested the nine seats, George Smith was appointed President (subsequently reverting to the title of Chief Minister) of the eighth Legislative Assembly. At legislative elections in February 2000 three new members were elected to the Assembly, and Ronald Nobbs was subsequently appointed Chief Minister. Geoffrey Gardner, hitherto Minister for Health, replaced Nobbs as Chief Minister following the elections of November 2001. The incoming Assembly included four new members.

In December 1991 the population of Norfolk Island overwhelmingly rejected a proposal, made by the Australian Government, to include the island in the Australian federal electorate. The outcome of the poll led the Australian Government, in June 1992, to announce that it had abandoned the plan. Similarly, in late 1996 a proposal by the Australian Government to combine Norfolk Island's population with that of Canberra for record-keeping purposes was strongly opposed by the islanders.

In late 1997 the Legislative Assembly debated the issue of increased self-determination for the island. Pro-independence supporters argued that the Territory could generate sufficient income by exploiting gas- and oilfields in the island's exclusive economic zone.

In August 1998 a referendum proposing that the Norfolk Island electoral system be integrated more closely with that of mainland Australia (initiated in Canberra by the Minister for Regional Development, Territories and Local Government) was rejected by 78% of the Territory's electorate. A similar referendum in May 1999 was opposed by 73% of voters.

Frustration with the Australian Government's perceived reluctance to facilitate the transfer of greater powers to the Territory (as outlined in the Norfolk Island Act of 1979, see above) led the island's Legislative Assembly in mid-1999 to vote by seven members to one in favour of full internal self-government. Negotiations regarding the administration of crown land on the island, which continued in 2000, were seen as indicative of the islanders' determination to pursue greater independence from Australia.

In April 2002 a hotel worker from Sydney, Australia, was murdered. This was the first murder to occur on Norfolk Island in more than 150 years. As part of its investigation, the police force took fingerprints of the entire adult population in August. The Australian authorities announced in April 2003 that they were no closer to solving the crime.

Legislation was approved in late March 2003 to amend the requirements to vote in Norfolk Island elections. Under the new system Australian, New Zealand and British citizens were to be allowed to vote after a residency period of 12 months (reduced from 900 days). The amendments, which followed a series of occasionally acrimonious discussions with the Australian Government, provoked concern among islanders who feared that succumbing to Australian pressure to reform the Norfolk Island Act would result in the effective removal of authority over electoral matters from island control.

Despite the island's natural fertility, agriculture is no longer the principal economic activity. About 400 ha of land are arable. The main crops are Kentia palm seed, cereals, vegetables and fruit. Cattle and pigs are farmed for domestic consumption. Development of a fisheries industry is restricted by the lack of a harbour. Some flowers and plants are grown commercially. The administration is increasing the area devoted to Norfolk Island pine and hardwoods. Seed of the Norfolk Island pine is exported. Potential oil- and gas-bearing sites in the island's waters may provide a possible future source of revenue. A re-export industry has been developed to serve the island's tourist industry. In early 1999 the Norfolk Island Legislative Assembly announced plans to seek assistance from the Australian Government to establish an offshore financial centre on the island.

In 2000/01 imports from Australia cost $A19m. (compared with almost $A23m. in the previous year). In 1998/99 exports to Australia earned $A1m. In 1999/2000 imports from New Zealand totalled $A9.3m. (compared with $A9.0m. in the previous year). In 2000/01 the total cost of imports reached $A41.3m. (compared with $A59.1m. in 1999/2000), while revenue from exports amounted to $A2.7m.(compared with almost $A2.8m. in the previous year) The authorities receive revenue from customs duties (some $A3.9m., equivalent to 34.3% of total revenue in 2000/01) and the sale of postage stamps, but tourism is the island's main industry. In 2000/01 there were 40,221 tourist arrivals on the island. In 1985 and 1986 the Governments of Australia and Norfolk Island jointly established the 465-ha Norfolk Island National Park. This was to protect the remaining native forest, which is the habitat of several unique species of flora (including the largest fern in the world) and fauna (such as the Norfolk Island green parrot, the guavabird and the boobook owl). Conservation efforts include the development of Phillip Island as a nature reserve.

Education

Education is free and compulsory for all children between the ages of six and 15. Pupils attend the government school from infant to secondary level. A total of 335 pupils were enrolled at infant, primary and secondary levels in 2000/01. Students wishing to follow higher education in Australia are eligible for bursaries and scholarships. The budgetary allocation for education was $A1,846,000 in 2000/01 (equivalent to 18.1% of total expenditure).

Weights and Measures

The metric system is in force.

Statistical Survey

Source: The Administration of Norfolk Island, Administration Offices, Kingston, Norfolk Island 2899; tel. 22001; fax 23177; internet www.norfolk.gov.nf.

AREA AND POPULATION

Area: 34.6 sq km (13.3 sq miles).

Population: 2,181, including 409 visitors, at census of 6 August 1996; 2,601 (males 1,257, females 1,344), including 564 visitors, at census of 7 August 2001.

Density (2001): 75.2 per sq km.

Births, Marriages and Deaths (2000/01): Live births 17; Marriages 32 (1999/2000); Deaths 28.

Economically Active Population (persons aged 15 years and over, 2001 census): 1,609 (males 849, females 760).

FINANCE

Currency and Exchange Rates: Australian currency is used, see p. 562.

Budget (year ending 30 June 2001): Revenue $A11,499,600 (Customs duties $A3,948,541); Expenditure $A10,199,300 (Education $A1,846,000).

EXTERNAL TRADE

2000/01 (year ending 30 June): *Imports:* $A41,260,213, mainly from Australia and New Zealand. *Exports:* $A2,708,120.

Trade with Australia ($A million, 2000/01): *Imports* 19.

Trade with New Zealand ($NZ million, 2000/01): *Imports* 6.7; *Exports* 0.04.

TOURISM

Visitors (year ending 30 June): 36,514 in 1998/99; 38,298 in 1999/2000; 40,221 in 2000/01.

COMMUNICATIONS MEDIA

Radio Receivers (1996): 2,500 in use.

Television Receivers (1996): 1,200 in use.

Non-daily Newspaper (2002): 1 (estimated circulation 1,400).

EDUCATION

Institution (2002): 1 state school incorporating infant, primary and secondary levels.

Teachers (2001/02): 20.

Students (1999/2000): Infants 79; Primary 116; Secondary 119.

Directory

The Constitution

The Norfolk Island Act 1979 constitutes the administration of the Territory as a body politic and provides for a responsible legislative and executive system, enabling it to administer its own affairs to the greatest practicable extent. The preamble of the Act states that it is the intention of the Australian Parliament to consider the further extension of powers.

The Act provides for an Administrator, appointed by the Australian Government, who shall administer the government of Norfolk Island as a territory under the authority of the Commonwealth of Australia. The Administrator is required to act on the advice of the Executive Council or the responsible Commonwealth Minister in those matters specified as within their competence. Every proposed law passed by the Legislative Assembly must be effected by the assent of the Administrator, who may grant or withhold that assent, reserve the proposed law for the Governor-General's pleasure or recommend amendments.

The Act provides for the Legislative Assembly and the Executive Council, comprising the executive members of the Assembly who have ministerial-type responsibilities. The nine members of the Legislative Assembly are elected for a term of not more than three years under a cumulative method of voting: each elector is entitled to as many votes (all of equal value) as there are vacancies, but may not give more than four votes to any one candidate. The nine candidates who receive the most votes are declared elected.

The Government

The Administrator, who is the senior representative of the Commonwealth Government, is appointed by the Governor-General of Australia and is responsible to the Minister for Regional Services, Territories and Local Government. A form of responsible legislative and executive government was extended to the island in 1979, as outlined above.

Administrator: ANTHONY J. MESSNER (assumed office on 4 August 1997).

EXECUTIVE COUNCIL
(April 2003)

Chief Minister and Minister for Intergovernment Relations: GEOFFREY R. GARDNER.

Minister for Finance: GRAEME DONALDSON.

Minister for Tourism and Community Services: GEORGE SMITH.

Minister for Land and the Environment: IVENS BUFFETT.

MINISTRIES

All Ministries are located at: Old Military Barracks, Kingston, Norfolk Island 2899; tel. 22003; fax 23378; e-mail executives@ assembly.gov.nf.

GOVERNMENT OFFICES

Office of the Administrator: New Military Barracks, Norfolk Island 2899; tel. 22152; fax 22681.

Administration of Norfolk Island: Administration Offices, Kingston, Norfolk Island 2899; tel. 22001; fax 23177; e-mail rmurdoch@admin.gov.nf; internet www.norfolkisland.gov.nf; all govt depts; CEO ROBYN MURDOCH.

Legislature

LEGISLATIVE ASSEMBLY

Nine candidates are elected for not more than three years. The most recent general election was held on 29 November 2001.

Speaker: DAVID ERNEST BUFFETT.

Deputy Speaker: CHLOE NICHOLAS.

Other Members: RONALD C. NOBBS, GEOFFREY R. GARDNER, IVENS BUFFETT, GEORGE SMITH, GRAEME DONALDSON, VICKY JACK, JOHN T. BROWN.

Judicial System

Supreme Court of Norfolk Island
Kingston.

Appeals lie to the Federal Court of Australia.

Chief Magistrate: RON CAHILL.

Judges: BRYAN ALAN BEAUMONT (Chief Justice), MURRAY RUTLEDGE WILCOX.

Religion

The majority of the population professes Christianity (70.4%, according to the census of 1996), with the principal denominations being the Church of England (38%), the Uniting Church (14%) and the Catholic Church (11%).

The Press

Norfolk Island Government Gazette: Kingston, Norfolk Island 2899; tel. 22001; fax 23177; weekly.

Norfolk Islander: Greenways Press, POB 150, Norfolk Island 2899; tel. 22159; fax 22948; e-mail news@islander.nf; f. 1965; weekly; Co-Editors TOM LLOYD, TIM LLOYD; circ. 1,350.

Broadcasting and Communications

TELECOMMUNICATIONS

Norfolk Telecom: Kingston; internet www.telecom.gov.nf; Man. KIM DAVIES.

BROADCASTING

Radio

Norfolk Island Broadcasting Service: New Cascade Rd, POB 456, Norfolk Island 2899; tel. 22137; fax 23298; e-mail 2niradio@ni.net.nf; govt-owned; non-commercial; broadcasts 112 hours per week; relays television and radio programmes from Australia; Broadcast Man. ROGER NEWMAN.

Radio VL2NI: New Cascade Rd, POB 456, Norfolk Island 2899; tel. 22137; fax 23298; e-mail 2niradio@ni.net.nf; internet www.users.nf/nfradio/.

Television

Norfolk Island Broadcasting Service: see Radio.

Norfolk Island Television Service: f. 1987; govt-owned; relays programmes of Australian Broadcasting Corpn, Special Broadcasting Service Corpn and Central Seven TV by satellite.

TV Norfolk (TVN): locally operated service featuring programmes of local events and information for tourists.

Finance

BANKING

Commonwealth Bank of Australia (Australia): Taylors Rd, Norfolk Island 2899; tel. 22144; fax 22805.

Westpac Banking Corpn Savings Bank Ltd (Australia): Burnt Pine, Norfolk Island 2899; tel. 22120; fax 22808.

Trade

Norfolk Island Chamber of Commerce Inc: POB 370, Norfolk Island 2899; tel. 22317; fax 23221; e-mail photopress@ni.net.nf; f. 1966; affiliated to the Australian Chamber of Commerce; 60 mems; Pres. GARY ROBERTSON; Sec. MARK MCGUIRE.

Norfolk Island Gaming Authority: POB 882, Norfolk Island 2899; tel. 22002; fax 22205; e-mail secgameauth@norfolk.net.nf; Dir KEVIN LEYSHON.

Transport

ROADS

There are about 100 km of roads, including 85 km of sealed road.

SHIPPING

Norfolk Island is served by the three shipping lines, Neptune Shipping, Pacific Direct Line and Roslyndale Shipping Company Pty Ltd. A small tanker from Nouméa (New Caledonia) delivers petroleum products to the island and another from Australia delivers liquid propane gas.

CIVIL AVIATION

Norfolk Island has one airport, with two runways (of 1,900 m and 1,550 m), capable of taking medium-sized jet-engined aircraft. Air New Zealand operates a twice-weekly direct service between Christchurch and Norfolk Island (via Auckland). Charter flights from Lord Howe Island and occasionally from New Caledonia also serve the island. The cessation of scheduled services from Australia by Ansett Australia in 1997 had an adverse effect on the island's important tourist industry. As a consequence, Norfolk Jet Express was established to provide a weekly service to Australia. In February 1999 Air Nauru began to operate a weekly charter flight service to Norfolk Island from Sydney, under contract with Norfolk Jet Express. In mid-2002 services from Brisbane and Sydney were also being provided by Alliance Airlines.

Tourism

Visitor arrivals totalled 40,221 in 2000/01.

Norfolk Island Visitors Information Centre: Taylors Rd, Burnt Pine, POB 211, Norfolk Island 2899; tel. 22147; fax 23109; e-mail info@norfolkisland.com.au; internet www.norfolkisland.com.au; Gen. Man. JOANNE LIBLINE.

OTHER TERRITORIES

Territory of Ashmore and Cartier Islands

The Ashmore Islands (known as West, Middle and East Islands) and Cartier Island are situated in the Timor Sea, about 850 km and 790 km west of Darwin respectively. The Ashmore Islands cover some 93 ha of land and Cartier Island covers 0.4 ha. The islands are small and uninhabited, consisting of sand and coral, surrounded by shoals and reefs. Grass is the main vegetation. Maximum elevation is about 2.5 m above sea-level. The islands abound in birdlife, sea-cucumbers (*bêches-de-mer*) and, seasonally, turtles.

The United Kingdom took formal possession of the Ashmore Islands in 1878, and Cartier Island was annexed in 1909. The islands were placed under the authority of the Commonwealth of Australia in 1931. They were annexed to, and deemed to form part of, the Northern Territory of Australia in 1938. On 1 July 1978 the Australian Government assumed direct responsibility for the administration of the islands, which rests with a parliamentary secretary appointed by the Minister for Regional Services, Territories and Local Government. Periodic visits are made to the islands by the Royal Australian Navy and aircraft of the Royal Australian Air Force, and the Civil Coastal Surveillance Service makes aerial surveys of the islands and neighbouring waters. The oilfields of Jabiru and Challis are located in waters adjacent to the Territory.

In August 1983 Ashmore Reef was declared a national nature reserve. An agreement between Australia and Indonesia permits Indonesian traditional fishermen to continue fishing in the territorial waters and to land on West Island to obtain supplies of fresh water. In 1985 the Australian Government extended the laws of the Northern Territory to apply in Ashmore and Cartier, and decided to contract a vessel to be stationed at Ashmore Reef during the Indonesian fishing season (March–November) to monitor the fishermen.

During 2000–01 increasing numbers of refugees and asylum-seekers attempted to land at Ashmore Reef, hoping to gain residency in Australia. The majority had travelled from the Middle East via Indonesia, where the illegal transport of people was widespread. Consequently, in late 2000 a vessel with the capacity to transport up to 150 people was chartered to ferry unauthorized arrivals to the Australian mainland. In September 2001 the Australian Government introduced an item of legislation to Parliament excising Ashmore Reef and other outlying territories from Australia's migration zone.

Australian Antarctic Territory

The Australian Antarctic Territory was established by Order in Council in February 1933 and proclaimed in August 1936, subsequent to the Australian Antarctic Territory Acceptance Act (1933). It consists of the portion of Antarctica (divided by the French territory of Terre Adélie) lying between 45°E and 136°E, and between 142°E and 160°E. The Antarctic Division of the Department of the Environment, Sport and Territories (subsequently renamed the Department of the Environment and Heritage) was established in 1948 as a permanent agency, and to administer and provide support for the Australian National Antarctic Research Expeditions (ANARE), which maintains three permanent scientific stations (Mawson, Davis and Casey) in the Territory. The area of the Territory is estimated to be 5,896,500 sq km (2,276,650 sq miles), and there are no permanent inhabitants, although there is a permanent presence of scientific personnel. Environmentalists expressed alarm at proposals in the late 1990s to encourage tourism in the Territory, which, they claimed, could damage the area's sensitive ecology. In November 2001 an international team of scientists commenced Australia's largest ever scientific expedition, to gather data on the influence of the Southern Ocean on the world's climate and the global carbon cycle. In January 2002 Australia attempted to expel Japanese whaling ships from the 200-nautical-mile exclusive economic zone it claimed to be under the jurisdiction of the Australian Antarctic Territory. The Government allocated $A102.3m. to its Antarctic Programme in 2002/03. The Territory is administered by the Antarctic Division of the Department of the Environment and Heritage. Australia is a signatory to the Antarctic Treaty, see p. 492

Coral Sea Islands Territory

The Coral Sea Islands became a Territory of the Commonwealth of Australia under the Coral Sea Islands Act of 1969. The Territory lies east of Queensland, between the Great Barrier Reef and longitude 156° 06′E, and between latitude 12°S and 24°S, and comprises several islands and reefs. The islands are composed largely of sand and coral, and have no permanent fresh water supply, but some have a cover of grass and scrub. The area has been known as a notorious hazard to shipping since the 19th century, the danger of the reefs being compounded by shifting sand cays and occasional tropical cyclones. The Coral Sea Islands have been acquired by Australia by numerous acts of sovereignty since the early years of the 20th century.

Spread over a sea area of approximately 780,000 sq km (300,000 sq miles), all the islands and reefs in the Territory are very small, totalling only a few sq km of land area. They include Cato Island, Chilcott Islet in the Coringa Group, and the Willis Group. In 1997 the Coral Sea Islands Act was amended to include Elizabeth and Middleton Reefs. A meteorological station, operated by the Commonwealth Bureau of Meteorology and with a staff of four, has provided a service on one of the Willis Group since 1921. The other islands are uninhabited. There are eight automatic weather stations (on Cato Island, Flinders Reef, Frederick Reef, Holmes Reef, Lihou Reef, Creal Reef, Marion Reef and Gannet Cay) and several navigation aids distributed throughout the Territory.

The Act constituting the Territory did not establish an administration on the islands, but provides means of controlling the activities of those who visit them. The Lihou Reef and Coringa-Herald National Nature Reserves were established in 1982 to provide protection for the wide variety of terrestrial and marine wildlife, which include rare species of birds and sea turtles (one of which is the largest, and among the most endangered, of the world's species of sea turtle). The Australian Government has concluded agreements for the protection of endangered and migratory birds with Japan and the People's Republic of China. The Governor-General of

Australia is empowered to make ordinances for the peace, order and good government of the Territory and, by ordinance, the laws of the Australian Capital Territory apply. The Supreme Court and Court of Petty Sessions of Norfolk Island have jurisdiction in the Territory. The Territory is administered by a parliamentary secretary appointed by the Minister for Regional Services, Territories and Local Government, and the area is visited regularly by the Royal Australian Navy.

Territory of Heard Island and the McDonald Islands

These islands are situated about 4,000 km (2,500 miles) south-west of Perth, Western Australia. The Territory, consisting of Heard Island, Shag Island (8 km north of Heard) and the McDonald Islands, is almost entirely covered in ice and has a total area of 369 sq km (142 sq miles). Sovereignty was transferred from the United Kingdom to the Commonwealth of Australia on 26 December 1947, following the establishment of a scientific research station on Heard Island (which functioned until March 1955). The islands are administered by the Antarctic Division of the Australian Department of the Environment and Heritage. There are no permanent inhabitants. However, in 1991 evidence emerged of a Polynesian community on Heard Island some 700 years before the territory's discovery by European explorers. The island is of considerable scientific interest, as it is believed to be one of the few Antarctic habitats uncontaminated by introduced organisms. Heard Island is about 44 km long and 20 km wide and possesses an active volcano, named Big Ben. In January 1991 an international team of scientists travelled to Heard Island to conduct research involving the transmission of sound waves, beneath the surface of the ocean, in order to monitor any evidence of the 'greenhouse effect' (melting of polar ice and the rise in sea-level as a consequence of pollution). The pulses of sound, which travel at a speed largely influenced by temperature, were to be received at various places around the world, with international co-operation. Heard Island was chosen for the experiment because of its unique location, from which direct paths to the five principal oceans extend. The McDonald Islands, with an area of about 1 sq km (0.4 sq miles), lie some 42 km west of Heard Island. In late 1997 Heard Island and the McDonald Islands were accorded World Heritage status by UNESCO in recognition of their outstanding universal significance as a natural landmark. In 1999 concern was expressed that stocks of the Patagonian toothfish in the waters around the islands were becoming depleted as a result of over-exploitation, mainly by illegal operators. In 2001 the Australian Government's Antarctic Division conducted a five-month scientific expedition to Heard Island. It claimed that glacial cover had retreated by 12% since 1947 as a result of global warming. In October 2002 the Australian Government declared the establishment of the Heard Island and McDonald Islands Marine Reserve. The world's largest reserve protected the conservation values of the islands themselves, the territorial sea and a marine protected area. Scientific research and environmental monitoring were allowed in the Marine Reserve.

AUSTRIA

Introductory Survey

Location, Climate, Language, Religion, Flag, Capital

The Republic of Austria lies in central Europe, bordered by Switzerland and Liechtenstein to the west, by Germany and the Czech Republic to the north, by Hungary and Slovakia to the east, and by Italy and Slovenia to the south. The mean annual temperature lies between 7°C and 9°C (45°F and 48°F). The population is 99% German-speaking, with small Croat- and Slovene-speaking minorities. The majority of the inhabitants profess Christianity: about 70% are Roman Catholics and about 5% are Protestants. The national flag (proportions 2 by 3) consists of three equal horizontal stripes, of red, white and red. The state flag has, in addition, the coat of arms (a small shield, with horizontal stripes of red separated by a white stripe, superimposed on a black eagle, wearing a golden crown and holding a sickle and a hammer in its feet, with a broken chain between its legs) in the centre. The capital is Vienna (Wien).

Recent History

Austria was formerly the centre of the Austrian (later Austro-Hungarian) Empire, which comprised a large part of central Europe. The Empire, under the Habsburg dynasty, was dissolved in 1918, at the end of the First World War, and Austria proper became a republic. The first post-war Council of Ministers was a coalition led by Dr Karl Renner, who remained Chancellor until 1920, when a new Constitution introduced a federal form of government. Many of Austria's inhabitants favoured union with Germany, but this was forbidden by the post-war peace treaties. In March 1938, however, Austria was occupied by Nazi Germany's armed forces and incorporated into the German Reich, led by the Austrian-born Adolf Hitler.

After Hitler's defeat in Austria, a provisional Government, under Dr Renner, was established in April 1945. In July, following Germany's surrender to the Allied forces, Austria was divided into four zones, occupied respectively by forces of the USA, the USSR, the United Kingdom and France. At the first post-war elections to the 165-seat Nationalrat (National Council), held in November 1945, the conservative Österreichische Volkspartei (ÖVP, Austrian People's Party) won 85 seats and the Sozialistische Partei Österreichs (SPÖ, Socialist Party of Austria) secured 76. The two parties formed a coalition Government. In December Dr Renner became the first Federal President of the second Austrian Republic, holding office until his death in December 1950. However, it was not until May 1955 that the four powers signed a State Treaty with Austria, ending the occupation and recognizing Austrian independence, effective from 27 July; occupation forces left in October.

More than 20 years of coalition government came to an end in April 1966 with the formation of a Council of Ministers by the ÖVP alone. Dr Josef Klaus, the Federal Chancellor since April 1964, remained in office. The SPÖ achieved a relative majority in the March 1970 general election and formed a minority Government, with Dr Bruno Kreisky (a former Minister of Foreign Affairs, who had been party leader since 1967) as Chancellor. In April 1971 the incumbent President, Franz Jonas of the SPÖ, was re-elected, defeating the ÖVP candidate, Dr Kurt Waldheim, a former Minister of Foreign Affairs (who subsequently served two five-year terms as UN Secretary-General, beginning in January 1972). The SPÖ won an absolute majority of seats in the Nationalrat at general elections in October 1971 (when the number of seats was increased from 165 to 183) and October 1975. President Jonas died in April 1974, and the subsequent presidential election, held in June, was won by Dr Rudolf Kirchschläger, who had been the Minister of Foreign Affairs since 1970. He was re-elected for a second six-year term in 1980.

In November 1978 a government proposal to commission Austria's first nuclear power plant was defeated in a national referendum. Despite expectations that Chancellor Kreisky would resign, he received the full support of the SPÖ and emerged in an apparently even stronger position. At the general election in May 1979 the SPÖ increased its majority in the Nationalrat. The general election of April 1983, however, marked the end of the 13-year era of one-party government: the

SPÖ lost its absolute majority in the Nationalrat and Kreisky, unwilling to participate in a coalition, resigned as Chancellor. The reduction in the SPÖ's representation was partly attributed to the emergence of two environmentalist 'Green' parties, both founded in 1982. The two parties together received more than 3% of the total votes cast, but failed to win any seats. Kreisky's successor, Dr Fred Sinowatz (the former Vice-Chancellor and Minister of Education), took office in May, leading a coalition of the SPÖ and the right-of-centre Freiheitliche Partei Österreichs (FPÖ, Freedom Party of Austria). The new Government continued the social welfare policy that had been pursued by its predecessor, in addition to maintaining Austria's foreign policy of 'active neutrality'.

A presidential election was held in May 1986 to choose a successor to Kirchschläger. The SPÖ candidate was Dr Kurt Steyrer (the Minister of Health and Environment), while Dr Waldheim stood as an independent candidate, although with the support of the ÖVP. The campaign was dominated by allegations that Waldheim, a former officer in the army of Nazi Germany, had been implicated in atrocities committed by the Nazis in the Balkans during 1942–45; the ensuing controversy divided the country and brought unexpected international attention to the election. Waldheim won a run-off ballot in June 1986, with 54% of the votes cast. The defeat of the SPÖ presidential candidate led Chancellor Sinowatz and four of his ministers to resign. Dr Franz Vranitzky, hitherto the Minister of Finance, became the new Chancellor. In September the FPÖ elected a controversial new leader, Dr Jörg Haider, who represented the far right wing of his party. This precipitated the end of the partnership between the SPÖ and the FPÖ, and the general election for the Nationalrat, scheduled for April 1987, was brought forward to November 1986. No party won an absolute majority: the SPÖ took 80 seats, the ÖVP 77, the FPÖ 18 and an alliance of three 'Green' parties eight. Following several weeks of negotiations, a 'grand coalition' of the SPÖ and the ÖVP, with Vranitzky as Chancellor, was formed in January 1987.

Waldheim's election to the presidency was controversial both domestically and internationally, and Austria's relations with Israel and the USA, in particular, were severely strained. In February 1988 a specially-appointed international commission of historians concluded that Waldheim must have been aware of the atrocities that had been committed. Waldheim refused to resign, but in June 1991 he announced that he would not seek a second presidential term.

At the general election held in October 1990 the SPÖ retained its position as the largest single party, increasing its number of seats in the Nationalrat by one, to 81 of the 183 seats, while the ÖVP obtained only 60 seats, a decline of 17; the FPÖ increased its representation by 15 seats, to 33. The FPÖ's success was attributed, in large part, to its support for restrictions on immigration, especially from eastern Europe. The Grüne Alternative Liste (GAL, Green Alternative List), an informal electoral alliance comprising Die Grüne Alternative (The Green Alternative) and the Vereinte Grüne Österreichs (United Green Party of Austria), increased 'Green' representation by one seat, to nine. In December, following several weeks of negotiations, the SPÖ and the ÖVP formed a new coalition Government, again led by Vranitzky.

A congress of the SPÖ held in June 1991 voted to revert to the party's original name, the Sozialdemokratische Partei Österreichs (SPÖ, Social-Democratic Party of Austria). In the same month the FPÖ leader, Dr Haider, was dismissed as Governor of Carinthia (Kärnten) after publicly praising Hitler's employment policies. In December the Nationalrat approved government legislation whereby Austria became the only country in Europe able to reject asylum requests from individuals without identity papers. Following the imprisonment, in January 1992, of a prominent right-wing activist for demanding the restoration of the Nazi party, and the subsequent fire-bombing of a refugee hostel by neo-Nazis in northern Austria, the Nationalrat voted unanimously in February to amend anti-Nazi legislation. The minimum prison sentence for Nazi agitation was reduced from five years to one year (in order to increase the number of successful prosecutions) and denial of the Nazi Holocaust was made a criminal offence.

At the presidential election held in April 1992 the two main candidates were Dr Rudolf Streicher (hitherto the Minister of Public Economy and Transport), for the SPÖ, and Dr Thomas Klestil (a former ambassador to the USA), representing the ÖVP. No candidate achieved the required 50% of the vote at the first ballot, but in the second run-off ballot, held in May, Klestil received almost 57% of the votes cast; he assumed the presidency in July.

In January 1993 the FPÖ organized a national petition seeking to require the Nationalrat to debate the introduction of legislation that would halt immigration into Austria and impose stricter controls on foreign residents in the country (the estimated number of whom had increased from 350,000 to 600,000 since 1989). Although the petition was signed by 7.4% of the electorate (417,000 signatures, compared with the constitutional requirement of 100,000 to force parliamentary debate), the result was considered disappointing by the FPÖ. The initiative was strongly opposed by a broad coalition of politicians, church leaders and intellectuals. In February 1993 five FPÖ deputies in the Nationalrat left the party, partly in protest at the petition on immigration, and formed a new political organization, the Liberales Forum (LiF, Liberal Forum), under the leadership of Dr Heide Schmidt, hitherto the Vice-President of the FPÖ. In December four campaigners for tolerance towards immigrant and refugee communities, including the Mayor of Vienna, were injured by letter-bombs. In March 1999 a lone right-wing extremist was sentenced to life imprisonment, having been found guilty of perpetrating these and other bomb attacks during the 1990s against members and supporters of ethnic minorities, including an assault in February 1995 that killed four gypsies. In late September 2001, purportedly as part of a plan to combat international terrorism following the devastating terrorist attacks in the USA, Dr Haider, whose party (the FPÖ) now shared power with the ÖVP in a coalition Government (see below), asserted that refugees from continents other than Europe seeking asylum within the European Union (EU, see p. 199) should no longer be granted residence in Europe while their requests were being processed. The FPÖ's parliamentary leadership supported Dr Haider's standpoint. The FPÖ also suggested the introduction of 'biometric' identification methods (namely, fingerprinting), a fortnightly 'control' of all asylum-seekers and the immediate expulsion of any foreigners suspected of being involved in criminal activities. Furthermore, the FPÖ proposed the introduction of a so-called *Integrationsvertrag* ('integration contract') for immigrant workers and their families, including those who were already living in the country. Under this contract immigrants would be obliged to attend, and pass, 'integration' courses in German language and citizenship; those who did not comply within four years would have their social security benefits gradually reduced, and, in extreme cases, would face expulsion from the country. The controversial propositions provoked fierce criticism from political leaders and human rights groups both within Austria and throughout the EU. The ÖVP initially distanced itself from the proposals of its partner in government and condemned Dr Haider's views. Chancellor Wolfgang Schüssel (of the ÖVP) intervened to state that, contrary to Dr Haider's wishes, Austria would remain open to all refugees and asylum-seekers. Nevertheless, in early October the ÖVP endorsed the FPÖ's recommendations regarding asylum-seekers and immigrants (with the exception of the proposal to deny asylum-seekers the right of temporary residence). Despite strong opposition from the SPÖ and the 'Greens', the proposed measures, including the introduction of the 'integration contract', were approved by the legislature and came into force on 1 January 2003. Moreover, in late 2001 the Minister of the Interior, Dr Ernst Strasser, announced that it would no longer be possible to claim asylum through Austria's consulates overseas; Austria had been the only EU country to offer this facility.

Meanwhile, in late 1993 an ongoing debate over Austria's future in Europe intensified when the EU set a deadline of 1 March 1994 by which time the conditions of Austria's entry into the Union (pending a national referendum) were to be agreed. Austria strongly defended its right to preserve its neutrality, to uphold higher environmental standards and to impose restrictions on the transit of road-freight traffic through the Austrian Alps. Eventually a number of compromises were reached, including an extension of the existing limit on lorry transit traffic until 2001. At the ensuing national referendum on the

terms of Austria's membership of the EU, held in June 1994, some two-thirds of voters (66.4%) supported Austria's entry into the Union. Following the referendum Austria announced plans to sign NATO's Partnership for Peace programme (see p. 273). Austria was formally admitted to the EU on 1 January 1995. Observer status at the Western European Union (see p. 318) was subsequently granted.

At the general election held in October 1994 the ruling coalition lost its two-thirds' majority in the Nationalrat. The SPÖ obtained 66 of the 183 seats in the legislature (winning 35% of the votes cast), the ÖVP took 52 seats (with 28% of the votes cast), and the FPÖ (which had campaigned against Austria's accession to the EU) increased its share of the votes cast by 6%, to 23%, securing 42 seats. The GAL and the LiF also made gains, winning 13 and 10 seats respectively. The success of the FPÖ's populist campaign, which had concentrated on countering corruption and immigration and had advocated referendum-based rather than parliamentary-based governance, unsettled the Austrian political establishment after years of relative consensus. At the end of November, following protracted negotiations, the SPÖ and ÖVP finally agreed to form a new coalition Government, with Vranitzky remaining as Chancellor.

The new SPÖ-ÖVP coalition was beleaguered by disagreements, mainly concerning differences in approach to the urgent need to reduce the annual budgetary deficit in compliance with Austria's commitment, as a member of the EU, to future economic and monetary union (EMU). In early 1995 five ministers, including the Vice-Chancellor, Dr Erhard Busek, resigned. Busek was simultaneously replaced as Chairman of the ÖVP by Dr Wolfgang Schüssel. In October a deepening rift between the SPÖ and ÖVP regarding the means of curtailing the 1996 budgetary deficit proved irreconcilable, culminating in the collapse of the coalition. Consequently a new general election was held in December 1995. The SPÖ improved upon its disappointing performance at the previous election, receiving 38.1% of the votes cast and winning 71 of the 183 seats in the Nationalrat. The ÖVP secured 28.3% of the votes cast (obtaining 53 seats), the FPÖ (which had been popularly restyled Die Freiheitlichen in January 1995) 21.9% (40 seats), the LiF 5.5% (10 seats) and the GAL 4.8% (nine seats). In early March 1996, following lengthy negotiations, the SPÖ and ÖVP agreed an economic programme and formed a new coalition Government, with Vranitzky remaining as Chancellor. However, in mid-January 1997 Vranitzky unexpectedly resigned as Chancellor. Viktor Klima, the Minister of Finance, was appointed as his successor, both as Chancellor and as Chairman of the SPÖ, and the Council of Ministers was reorganized.

In March 1998, following months of debate, the Government announced that Austria would not apply to join NATO, and would thereby preserve its traditional neutrality (as favoured by the SPÖ, but opposed by the ÖVP). Nevertheless, in early April 1999 Austria, in conjunction with the three other officially neutral EU member states, signed an EU declaration stating that the ongoing bombing of Serbia by NATO forces was 'both necessary and warranted'. In the aftermath of the terrorist attacks on the USA in September 2001, Chancellor Schüssel stated, in early November, that Austria might consider abandoning its policy of neutrality and joining NATO at some time in the future.

At the presidential election held in April 1998 Klestil was re-elected emphatically, winning 63.5% of the votes cast. The FPÖ made significant gains at regional elections in March 1999, becoming the dominant party in Dr Haider's home province of Carinthia; Haider was subsequently elected Governor of Carinthia (having previously been dismissed from that post in 1991—see above). The general election held in October 1999 resulted in unprecedented success for the FPÖ, which, by a narrow margin of 415 votes, took second place ahead of the ÖVP. The SPÖ won 65 of the 183 seats in the Nationalrat (with 33.2% of the votes cast), while the FPÖ and ÖVP both secured 52 seats (each with 26.9% of the votes cast). The GAL took 14 seats (7.4%). The FPÖ had campaigned on a programme that included a halt to immigration, the obstruction of the projected eastwards expansion of the EU, the radical deregulation of the business sector and the introduction of a uniform low rate of income tax and of hugely increased child allowances for Austrian citizens. Dr Haider appeared to have inflamed popular fears that the planned admission to the EU of Austria's eastern neighbours would flood the domestic market with cheap labour, thereby causing the level of unemployment to rise. During the FPÖ campaign Haider allegedly revived nationalist terminology previously employed by the Nazi regime; nevertheless, he consistently denied embracing neo-Nazi ideology. The election result was most widely regarded as a protest against the 12-year old 'grand' SPÖ-ÖVP coalition, which had acquired a reputation for unwieldy bureaucracy and for sanctioning politically-motivated appointments to public companies.

Following the election, protracted negotiations took place with a view to forming a new administration. In late January 2000, after a failed attempt to reconstruct the SPÖ-ÖVP coalition, the SPÖ announced that it would not attempt to form a minority government. At the beginning of February President Klestil reluctantly presided over the inauguration of an ÖVP-FPÖ coalition Government, with the ÖVP leader, Dr Schüssel, as Chancellor. Dr Haider elected not to participate directly in the new administration, which included an FPÖ Vice-Chancellor, Dr Susanne Riess-Passer, and five FPÖ ministers (including those responsible for finance, justice and defence). Although the new coalition had committed itself to respecting human rights and had adopted a relatively moderate political programme, the participation in government of the FPÖ provoked strong opposition both within Austria (where numerous demonstrations were organized) and abroad. Israel and the USA immediately recalled their ambassadors from Vienna, pending a reassessment of bilateral relations, while Austria's 14 fellow EU member states each suspended bilateral political co-operation, maintaining diplomatic relations at a 'technical' level, pending the removal of the FPÖ from the coalition. In late February Dr Haider announced that he was to resign as leader of the FPÖ, stating that he would concentrate instead on his position as Governor of Carinthia; few people, however, doubted that he would remain the *de facto* leader of the party.

In February 2000 Klima resigned as Chairman of the SPÖ and was replaced by Dr Alfred Gusenbauer. In April Gusenbauer apologized on behalf of his party for decades of political opportunism and acknowledged that the SPÖ had erred in embracing and promoting former Nazis after the Second World War in its efforts to become Austria's most powerful political force. He later established a commission of independent historians to investigate the matter. Gusenbauer's initiative was expected to put pressure on the coalition Government to launch similar projects, but officials from both constituent parties claimed they had already dealt with the issue and had no plans to follow suit. However, in June Ernest Windholz, the newly elected head of the FPÖ in Lower Austria (Niederösterreich), provoked controversy by using a Nazi-era slogan to honour long-serving members of his party. The slogan ('Unsere Ehre heisst Treue'—'our honour is called loyalty') was a motto of the armed SS wing of Hitler's Nazi party. The incident was thought to have harmed Austria's chances of having the diplomatic sanctions (see above) lifted at a forthcoming EU summit meeting, the last such meeting before the rotating EU presidency was to be assumed by France, which had pressed for the introduction of the sanctions following the FPÖ's accession to power. Prospects improved, however, at the end of June when Chancellor Schüssel agreed to the nomination by the President of the Court of Human Rights of a three-person EU delegation to examine the Austrian Government's commitment to common European values (with particular regard to the rights of minority groups, immigrants and refugees and to the political philosophy of the FPÖ). Following the publication of the delegation's report, the 14 members of the EU were to reassess the necessity for sanctions. Schüssel, however, declined to abandon a referendum, which he had announced in May, and which was scheduled to take place in October/November, in which Austrian voters would be invited to express their views on sanctions and future policy towards the EU. The Austrian Government also warned that the continuation of sanctions could affect EU decisions on constitutional reform and the accession of new member states. The delegation visited Austria in late July, and issued its report in September. A report by the European Commission against Racism and Intolerance (ECRI), which expressed deep concern about racist propaganda in Austria and criticized the FPÖ in particular, was 'leaked' to the press shortly before the EU delegation was due to make its decision regarding sanctions against Austria. The delegation recommended, however, that the sanctions be lifted on the grounds that they were counter-productive and tended to generate increased nationalist sentiment. Although the report did criticize the xenophobic tendencies of the FPÖ, it confirmed that Austria's treatment of minorities was superior to that of many EU member states and that incidences of violence against foreigners were less frequent in Austria than in other EU

countries. The report also criticized the FPÖ for trivializing Nazism and threatening press freedom by using libel suits to silence criticism. Concurrently, economic analysts reported that upholding the sanctions against Austria could adversely affect the euro, which had reached a record low against the US dollar (EU ministers responsible for finance were meeting in the same week to discuss the euro's future). As a result, the EU lifted its sanctions in September, but at the same time warned that it would continue to monitor closely the influence of the FPÖ, and Dr Haider, upon government policies. The decision represented a defeat for France, which had strongly supported the retention of sanctions, and was condemned by the Israeli Government.

Shortly after the lifting of EU sanctions in September 2000, Dr Haider attended a reunion of veterans of the Third Reich where he made a speech in which he praised those gathered as good citizens and reiterated comments that survivors of the Second World War had been maligned. He also demanded justice for German and Austrian citizens who had lost property after the war. Haider provoked further criticism when he spent more than 1m. Schilling on the restoration of Nazi frescoes, previously housed in the Carinthian parliament building, for display in a museum.

The end of 2000 was a troubled time for the FPÖ, whose influence and popularity (which had, rather perversely, benefited from the imposition of EU sanctions) was beginning to wane. The party fared badly in regional elections in Styria (Steiermark) and Burgenland; the decline in support was widely attributed to the FPÖ losing its appeal as a 'protest party' upon entering into government. In November the Minister of Science and Transport, Michael Schmid, resigned from the coalition Government, citing the FPÖ's poor electoral performance in Styria. He was the third FPÖ minister to resign since the formation of the Government in February, provoking accusations that the party was unfit to govern. Schmid subsequently resigned from the FPÖ after refusing to pay one-half of his government pension into a party fund. Poor electoral results, instability and repeated indiscretions linking the party with Nazism were, however, overshadowed by the emergence of a major political scandal. In October the FPÖ was accused of illicitly obtaining police files to discredit opponents, including the former Minister of Finance, Caspar Einem. The allegations surfaced as a result of a book published by a former police officer, Josef Kleindienst, in which he confessed to securing such documents and testified that many other police officers had done so for financial reward. A formal investigation was launched into 18 members of the FPÖ, including Haider and the Minister of Justice, Dr Dieter Böhmdorfer, who for many years had been Dr Haider's lawyer. Böhmdorfer, who had been deemed unfit for office by the EU delegation in September, was accused of using illegally obtained police documents when representing Haider in court. He rejected calls from the opposition and the judges' union to resign, and in October survived a vote of 'no confidence', the third such vote in his short ministerial career. By November the number of FPÖ members under investigation had risen to 67. Officials from the prosecutor's office raided the homes of FPÖ officials, including the party leader in Vienna, Hilmar Kabas, and Dr Haider's bodyguard, a police-officer named Horst Binder. The raid on Binder's home uncovered a note, allegedly from him to Dr Haider, which suggested that Binder had sent confidential police files to Dr Haider following requests for information from several senior FPÖ members. Both parties claimed that the note was a forgery. Eleven police-officers were suspended in connection with the scandal.

In March 2001 the FPÖ performed poorly in local elections in Vienna, and in May the German Federal Chancellor, Gerhard Schröder, refused to meet with any members of the FPÖ during an official visit to Austria. Also in May the head of Vienna's Jewish community, Dr Ariel Muzicant, won a lawsuit against Dr Haider, barring him from repeating comments in which he branded Muzicant as dirty and mocked his first name (also the name of a household detergent). After the ruling, Muzicant stated that he would seek to establish whether Dr Haider could be found guilty of anti-Semitism. Days earlier the World Jewish Congress had strongly criticized the FPÖ for its anti-Semitism and racism, including the adoption of Nazi slogans, and had alleged that anti-Semitism had increased in Austria since the entry of the FPÖ into government.

In early May 2001 Böhmdorfer presented draft legislation under which journalists would face prosecution and up to six months' imprisonment for divulging information drawn from judicial inquiries. The proposed legislation was strongly condemned by journalists' unions as an attack on press freedom.

The ÖVP-FPÖ coalition was characterized by periods of drive and reform intermittently supplanted by bouts of internecine strife. It was an internal power struggle within the FPÖ that, in early September 2002, led to the resignation of a number of moderate FPÖ ministers, including the Vice-Chancellor and party Chairwoman, Dr Susanne Riess-Passer. Hitherto, Schüssel had succeeded in persuading these moderate FPÖ ministers to eschew the more extremist elements of their party's credo, while himself adopting some of the FPÖ's more reasonable policies. Haider, believing that his party's influence was thus being undermined, had reverted to populist tactics in an effort to restore the FPÖ's perceived credentials as an 'anti–establishment' party. In February he had lost the support of many Austrians and had been severely criticized by the opposition for making an unofficial visit to the Iraqi President, Saddam Hussein, in Baghdad. Haider's renewed bouts of invective against foreigners, the EU and even against Schüssel himself, did nothing to improve his political standing or that of the FPÖ. With this increasing instability in his party's junior coalition partner, Schüssel had little option but to dissolve the legislature on 20 September pending an early general election. On the same day Mathias Reichhold was elected as the new Chairman of the FPÖ, following Haider's refusal to stand for the post. When Reichhold resigned from the leadership of the FPÖ later that year owing to ill health, he was replaced by a staunch ally of Haider, Herbert Haupt.

At the general election, which was held on 24 November 2002, the ÖVP received 42.3% of the votes cast, securing 79 of the 183 seats in the legislature (the party's largest single share of the votes in more than 30 years, mainly at the expense of the FPÖ, which obtained only 10.0% of the votes cast (18 seats), compared with 26.9% in 1999. The SPÖ received 36.5% of the votes cast (69 seats) and the 'Greens' 9.5% (17 seats). A few days after his party's poor performance in the election Haider's political profile was further diminished when he announced his decision to resign as Governor of Carinthia, only to retract his statement the following day. Although the ÖVP was the party with the largest representation in the legislature, it did not have a sufficient number of seats to form a majority government. The 'Greens', many of whom were still mistrustful of Schüssel after his earlier co-operation with Haider, had already ruled out any coalition agreement with the ÖVP; many members of the SPÖ, too, were unwilling to form a coalition with the ÖVP in which their party would be the junior partner; finally, the FPÖ, much weakened and still riven by factional infighting, was initially no longer viewed as a suitable coalition partner. Such were the difficulties facing Schüssel that, by mid-February 2003, he had still not managed to form a Government. At the end of the month, however, and with some apparent reluctance, Schüssel invited the FPÖ to form another coalition administration with the ÖVP; a new Council of Ministers was sworn in on 28 February. The new Government notably included only three ministers from the FPÖ, compared with five in the previous administration.

During the late 1990s a number of lawsuits were filed by US interests against several Austrian banks, which were accused of having profited during the Second World War from handling stolen Jewish assets. In November 1999 Bank Austria AG agreed to pay US $33m. as compensation to Holocaust survivors and, furthermore, to establish a humanitarian fund to assist survivors resident in Austria. Similar lawsuits were also filed against the Government, and in February 2000 Chancellor Schüssel appointed a former President of Bank Austria AG, Maria Schaumayer, as the co-ordinator in charge of Nazi-era compensation claims. In July the legislature approved the establishment of a €438m. fund, which was to be financed by unspecified contributions from the Government and from Austrian businesses (that had profited from slave labour), to compensate an estimated 150,000 concentration camp inmates, who had been forced into slave labour by the Nazis. However, doubts subsequently arose as to whether Austrian businesses would agree to pay for their share of the compensation fund. Another potential problem facing the settlement of the slave-labourers' claims was that 'class-action' lawyers were threatening not to drop their claims unless the agreement contained a firm commitment to a similarly extensive solution for the restitution of Jewish property. In January 2001, however, Austria signed an agreement with the USA to pay US $500m. to compensate Jews for property lost when the Nazis took power, in return for the

dismissal of survivors' lawsuits. The agreement, which allowed for the first payments to take place in March/April, was strongly criticized by Haider.

The Heads of Government of Austria, Hungary and Slovakia met on several occasions during the late 1990s in order to pursue co-operation on security and economic issues. In September 1999, however, Austria threatened to hinder Slovakia's entry into the EU, in protest at the alleged inadequacy of that country's nuclear safety standards. There were protests throughout 2000 against the proposed activation of a Soviet-designed nuclear reactor in Temelín in the Czech Republic, 48 km from the border with Austria; both Austria and Germany claimed that the reactor was dangerously flawed. An agreement was signed in December under which the reactor would not operate until a full evaluation of the plant's safety and environmental impact was completed by a joint Austro-Czech safety commission. Demonstrations against the activation of the plant, however, continued into 2001. In January 2002 the FPÖ launched a petition demanding the closure of the plant and stated that it intended to block attempts by the Czech Republic to join the EU unless the reactor (which was due to become fully operational in 2003) was closed down. This initiative caused a rift within the Austrian coalition Government, since the ÖVP opposed the petition on the grounds that it could damage the country's international standing and isolate it within the EU. Testing on the plant was still incomplete in early 2003, and Austrian opposition to its activation remained strong. Relations between Austria and the Czech Republic were further marred by the latter's refusal to abolish the so-called Beneš Decrees—legislation enacted at the end of the Second World War, which provided for the expulsion of ethnic Sudeten Germans from the Czech Republic without recourse to compensation. Austria repeatedly threatened to block the Czech Republic's anticipated accession to the EU in 2004 unless the Decrees were anulled; the EU authorities, however, did not regard their abolition as a prerequisite for entry.

Government

Austria is a federal republic, divided into nine provinces, each with its own provincial assembly and government. Legislative power is held by the bicameral Federal Assembly. The first chamber, the Nationalrat (National Council), has 183 members, elected by universal adult suffrage for four years (subject to dissolution) on the basis of proportional representation. The second chamber, the Bundesrat (Federal Council), has 64 members, elected for varying terms by the provincial assemblies. The Federal President, elected by popular vote for six years, is the Head of State, and normally acts on the advice of the Council of Ministers, which is led by the Federal Chancellor, and which is responsible to the Nationalrat.

Defence

After the ratification of the State Treaty in 1955, Austria declared its permanent neutrality. To protect its independence, the armed forces were instituted. Austria reaffirmed its neutrality in March 1998, having evaluated the possibility of joining NATO. Military service is compulsory and normally consists of seven months' initial training, followed by a maximum of 30 days' reservist training over eight years (officers, non-commissioned officers and specialists undergo 60–90 days' reservist training); alternatively, military service may entail eight months' training, with no further reservist training. In August 2002 the total armed forces numbered some 34,600 (including an estimated 17,200 conscripts). The air force (numbering 6,850, of whom an estimated 2,240 were conscripts) is an integral part of the army. Total reserves numbered 72,000, compared with 100,700 in August 1999 and 200,000 in June 1992. The defence budget for 2002 amounted to an estimated €1,629m.

Economic Affairs

In 2001, according to estimates by the World Bank, Austria's gross national income (GNI), measured at average 1999–2001 prices, was US $194,463m., equivalent to $23,940 per head (or $27,080 per head on an international purchasing-power parity basis). During 1990–2001 the population grew at an estimated average rate of only 0.4% per year, while gross domestic product (GDP) per head increased, in real terms, at an average annual rate of 1.7%. Overall GDP grew, in real terms, at an average annual rate of 2.2% in 1990–2001; growth was 3.5% in 2000 and 0.7% in 2001.

The contribution of agriculture (including hunting, forestry and fishing) to GDP was 2.3% in 2001. In 2001, according to the

ILO, some 5.6% of the employed labour force were engaged in the agricultural sector. Austrian farms produce more than 90% of the country's food requirements, and surplus dairy products are exported. The principal crops are wheat, barley, maize and sugar beet. The GDP of the agricultural sector increased, in real terms, at an average annual rate of 0.4% in 1990–99; it increased by 2.5% in 1998, but declined by 3.1% in 1999.

Industry (including mining and quarrying, manufacturing, construction and power) contributed 30.5% of GDP in 2001; according to the ILO, the sector engaged 29.8% of the employed labour force in that year. Industrial GDP increased, in real terms, at an average annual rate of 1.9% in 1990–99; it increased by 3.7% in 1998 and by 2.5% in 1999.

In 2001 mining and quarrying contributed 0.4% of GDP; according to the ILO, the sector employed 0.2% of the employed labour force in that year. The most important indigenous mineral resource is iron ore (1.9m. metric tons, with an iron content of 30%, were mined in 2000). Austria also has deposits of petroleum, lignite, magnesite, lead and some copper. The GDP of the mining sector declined, in real terms, at an average rate of 2.6% per year during 1990–99; it declined by 2.7% in 1998, but increased by 4.4% in 1999.

Manufacturing contributed 20.6% of GDP in 2001; according to the ILO, the sector engaged 19.6% of the employed labour force in that year. Measured by the value of output, the principal branches of manufacturing in 1998 were metals and metal products (accounting for 13.9% of the total), electrical machinery and telecommunications equipment (13.0%), food products (10.2%), wood and paper products (9.4%), and non-electrical machinery (9.2%). The production of non-metallic mineral products, beverages, chemicals and road vehicles are also important activities. The GDP of the manufacturing sector increased, in real terms, at an average annual rate of 2.8% during 1990–99; it grew by 4.5% in 1998 and by 2.4% in 1999.

Hydroelectric power resources provide the major domestic source of energy, accounting for 68.4% of total electricity production in 1999, followed by gas (14.7%), coal (9.1%) and petroleum (4.7%). By 2000 hydroelectric power contributed 70% of total electricity output. Austria is heavily dependent on imports of energy, mainly from eastern Europe. Net imports of energy for commercial use were equivalent to 71% of the total in 1997. Imports of mineral fuels and lubricants (including electrical current) accounted for 7.0% of the total cost of imports in 2001.

The services sector contributed 67.3% of GDP in 2001; according to the ILO, the sector engaged 64.4% of the employed labour force in that year. Tourism has traditionally been a leading source of revenue, providing receipts of €11,297m. in 2001. The GDP of the services sector increased, in real terms, at an average annual rate of 2.1% in 1990–99; it grew by 3.1% in 1998 and by 1.6% in 1999.

In 2001, according to the IMF, Austria recorded a visible trade deficit of US $1,328m., and the current account of the balance of payments showed a deficit of $4,103m. Much of Austria's trade is conducted with other member countries of the European Union (EU, see p. 199), which accounted for 65.4% of Austria's imports and 60.8% of exports in 2001. In that year the principal source of imports (40.5%) was Germany; other major suppliers were Italy (7.2%), the USA (5.3%) and France (4.1%). Germany was also the principal market for exports (32.5%); other significant purchasers were Italy (8.5%), the USA (5.3%) and Switzerland (5.2%). The principal exports in 2001 were machinery and transport equipment (accounting for 43.3% of total export revenue) and basic manufactures (23.1%). The principal imports were also machinery and transport equipment (particularly road vehicles and electrical machinery) and basic manufactures (accounting, respectively, for 40.2% and 16.9% of total import costs).

The federal budget for 2001 produced a deficit of €1,415m., equivalent to 0.7% of GDP. The central Government's debt was 1,623,361m. Schilling at 31 December 1999, equivalent to 59.9% of annual GDP. The average annual rate of inflation was 2.3% in 1990–99. According to the IMF, consumer prices increased by 2.4% in 2000, by 2.7% in 2001 and by 1.8% in 2002. In 2000 some 3.5% of the labour force were unemployed.

Austria joined the EU in January 1995. The country is also a member of the Organisation for Economic Co-operation and Development (OECD, see p. 277).

Overall, Austria's economy continues to be characterized by a high level of productivity and an unemployment level considerably lower than the European average. When the ÖVP-FPÖ coalition Government assumed power in 2000 it began the implementation of reforms not undertaken under previous Social Democratic coalitions and challenged powerful institutional interests, most notably the state holding company, the Österreichische Industrieholding AG (ÖIAG). Professional business executives replaced party appointees, and the privatization programme (which had proceeded lamentably slowly under previous administrations) was accelerated. In just over a year the ÖIAG's debt was reduced from €6,300m. to €3,200m. through the sale of the Österreichischer Postsparkasse AG (the Postal Savings Bank), the Dorotheum auction house, Austria Tabak and part of Telekom Austria AG. This last sale, however, proved a failure: the company was put on the market before it was ready for such a move, and its share price soon collapsed. The privatization programme was further hindered by the onset of a lengthy period of adverse market conditions and renewed political interference. In 2001 Austria produced its first balanced budget for 30 years; previous governments had consistently been burdened with budgetary deficits and had proved incapable of adopting effective measures to resolve the situation. However, by the time the Government was dissolved in late 2002, Austria was experiencing its worst economic downturn for more than a decade. Bank Austria predicted GDP growth of just 0.7% for that year, and 1.4% in 2003, while Wifo (Austria's main economic research institute) predicted 0.9% and 2.2% respectively. While Austria was no longer the most heavily indebted European country, its ratio of government debt to GDP was still higher than the European average, at 61.8%; moreover the country's tax burden, already equivalent to 45.7% of GDP, rose during 2001. The challenges facing Austria's incoming Government in late February 2003, in addition to reducing taxes and renewing the privatization programme, also included reforming the country's pension system to meet its commitment to a balanced budget. Austria currently has one of the most generous pension systems in Europe, and a rapidly ageing population. The new ÖVP-FPÖ coalition Government was faced with an unpopular decision that would have to be made in the near future—either to raise the retirement age or to reduce pension benefits. Opportunities for increased economic prosperity do exist, however, largely owing to Austria's proximity to prospective EU members in Central and Eastern Europe (where the Austrian banking sector is already profiting greatly), although whether this will be enough to compensate for the impact of slow growth rates in Austria's main trading partner, Germany, remains to be seen.

Education

The central controlling body is the Federal Ministry of Education, Science and Cultural Affairs. Provincial boards (Landesschulräte) supervise school education in each of the nine federal provinces. Budgetary expenditure on education in 2001 was estimated at €5,650m. (equivalent to 2.7% of GDP).

Education is free and compulsory between the ages of six and 15 years. In 1999/2000 enrolment at pre-primary level was equivalent to 81.4% of those in the relevant age-group, enrolment at primary level included 90.8% of children in the relevant age-group (males 90.3%; females 91.3%), and enrolment at secondary level included an estimated 88.8% of children in the relevant age-group (males 89.0%; females 88.5%). Children undergo four years' primary education at a Volksschule, after which they choose between two principal forms of secondary education. This may be a Hauptschule, which, after four years, may be followed by one of a variety of schools offering technical, vocational and other specialized training, some of which provide a qualification for university. Alternatively, secondary education may be obtained in an Allgemeinbildende höhere Schule, which provides an eight-year general education covering a wide range of subjects, culminating in the Reifeprüfung or Matura. This gives access to all Austrian universities. In addition, all Austrian citizens over the age of 24, and with professional experience, may attend certain university courses in connection with their professional career or trade.

Opportunities for further education exist at six universities as well as 13 colleges of technology, all of which have university status, and schools of art and music. Institutes of adult education (Volkshochschulen) are found in all provinces, as are other centres operated by public authorities, church organizations and the Austrian Trade Union Federation. In 1999/2000 enrolment at tertiary level was equivalent to 56.2% of those in the relevant age-group (males 53.6%; females 58.8%).

Public Holidays

2003: 1 January (New Year's Day), 6 January (Epiphany), 28 April (Easter Monday), 1 May (Labour Day), 5 June (Ascension Day), 16 June (Whit Monday), 19 June (Corpus Christi), 15 August (Assumption), 26 October (National Holiday), 1 November (All Saints' Day), 8 December (Immaculate Conception), 25 December (Christmas Day), 26 December (St Stephen's Day).

2004: 1 January (New Year's Day), 6 January (Epiphany), 12 April (Easter Monday), 1 May (Labour Day), 20 May (Ascension Day), 31 May (Whit Monday), 10 June (Corpus Christi), 15 August (Assumption), 26 October (National Holiday), 1 November (All Saints' Day), 8 December (Immaculate Conception), 25 December (Christmas Day), 26 December (St Stephen's Day).

Weights and Measures

The metric system is in force.

Statistical Survey

Sources (unless otherwise stated): Statistik Austria, Hintere Zollamtsstr. 2b, 1033 Vienna; tel. (1) 711-28-76-55; fax (1) 711-28-77-28; e-mail info@statistik.gv.at; internet www.statistik.at; Austrian National Bank, Postfach 61, Otto-Wagner-Pl. 3, 1090 Vienna; tel. (1) 404-20-0; fax (1) 404-20-66-96; e-mail oenb.info@oenb.co.at; internet www.oenb.at.

Area and Population

AREA, POPULATION AND DENSITY

Area (sq km)	83,871*
Population (census results)†	
15 May 1991	7,795,786
15 May 2001	
Males	3,889,189
Females	4,143,737
Total	8,032,926
Population (official estimates at mid-year)‡	
1998	8,078,449
1999	8,092,254
2000	8,110,244
Density (per sq km) at 15 May 2001 . . .	95.8

* 32,383 sq miles.

† Figures include all foreign workers.

‡ Figures refer to annual averages. The estimated population at 30 June 2000 was 8,108,700. The data have not been revised to take account of the 2001 census results.

PROVINCES

(census of 15 May 2001)

	Area (sq km)*	Population	Density (per sq km)	Capital (with population)
Burgenland . . .	3,965.5	277,569	70.0	Eisenstadt (11,334)
Kärnten (Carinthia) .	9,536.0	559,404	58.7	Klagenfurt (90,141)
Niederösterreich (Lower Austria) .	19,177.8	1,545,804	80.6	Sankt Pölten (49,121)
Oberösterreich (Upper Austria) .	11,981.7	1,376,797	114.9	Linz (183,504)
Salzburg . . .	7,154.2	515,327	72.0	Salzburg (142,662)
Steiermark (Styria) .	16,391.9	1,183,303	72.2	Graz (226,244)
Tirol (Tyrol) . .	12,647.7	673,504	53.3	Innsbruck (113,392)
Vorarlberg . . .	2,601.5	351,095	135.0	Bregenz (121,123)
Wien (Vienna) . .	414.7	1,550,123	3,737.9	
Total . . .	83,871.0	8,032,926	95.8	

* According to the reorganization of Länder boundaries in 2002.

PRINCIPAL TOWNS

(population at census of 15 May 2001)

Wien (Vienna, the capital) . . .	1,550,123	Klagenfurt . .	90,141
Graz . . .	226,244	Villach . . .	57,497
Linz . . .	183,504	Wels . . .	56,478
Salzburg . . .	142,662	Sankt Pölten . .	49,121
Innsbruck . . .	113,392	Dornbirn . . .	42,301

BIRTHS, MARRIAGES AND DEATHS*

	Registered live births		Registered marriages		Registered deaths	
	Number	Rate (per 1,000)	Number	Rate (per 1,000)	Number	Rate (per 1,000)
1994 . .	92,415	11.5	43,284	5.4	80,684	10.0
1995 . .	88,669	11.0	42,946	5.3	81,171	10.1
1996 . .	88,809	10.9	42,298	5.2	80,790	9.9
1997 . .	84,045	10.4	41,394	5.1	79,432	9.8
1998 . .	81,233	10.1	39,143	4.8	78,339	9.7
1999 . .	78,138	9.7	39,485	4.9	78,200	9.7
2000 . .	78,268	9.7	39,228	4.8	76,780	9.5
2001 . .	75,458	9.3	34,213	4.2	74,767	9.2

* Rates prior to 2001 are based on unrevised population estimates.

Expectation of life (WHO estimates, years at birth): 79.0 (males 75.9; females 81.8) in 2001 (Source: WHO, *World Health Report*).

ECONOMICALLY ACTIVE POPULATION*

('000 persons aged 15 years and over)

	1999	2000	2001
Agriculture, hunting and forestry	230.3	217.7	218.8
Fishing	0.3	0.3	0.2
Mining and quarrying . . .	11.2	9.6	9.7
Manufacturing	763.3	763.9	773.6
Electricity, gas and water supply .	31.2	29.9	31.7
Construction	336.4	339.3	361.1
Wholesale and retail trade; repair of motor vehicles, motorcycles and personal and household goods	592.8	593.7	630.0
Hotels and restaurants . . .	212.2	214.0	222.2
Transport, storage and communications	254.4	245.6	262.7
Financial intermediation . .	141.8	138.5	135.2
Real estate, renting and business activities	240.6	269.4	305.2
Public administration and defence; compulsory social security . .	247.7	253.0	260.2
Education	220.2	225.5	227.2
Health and social work . . .	301.3	299.9	317.1
Other community, social and personal service activities . .	161.6	159.4	160.1
Private households with employed persons	12.3	11.8	13.4
Extra-territorial organizations and bodies	4.8	5.0	4.8
Not classifiable by economic activity	—	—	7.1
Total employed	3,762.3	3,776.5	3,940.3
Unemployed	146.7	138.8	142.5
Total labour force	3,909.0	3,915.3	4,082.8
Males	2,221.4	2,219.4	2,295.6
Females	1,687.7	1,695.9	1,787.2

* Yearly averages, based on the results of quarterly sample surveys. The figures include members of the armed forces, except conscripts not employed before their military service.

Source: ILO.

Health and Welfare

KEY INDICATORS

Total fertility rate (children per woman, 2001) . . .	1.3
Under-5 mortality rate (per 1,000 live births, 2001) . . .	5
HIV/AIDS (% of persons aged 15–49, 2001)	0.24
Physicians (per 1,000 head, 1998)	3.02
Hospital beds (per 1,000 head, 1998)	8.9
Health expenditure (2000): US $ per head (PPP) . . .	2,171
Health expenditure (2000): % of GDP	8.0
Health expenditure (2000): public (% of total) . . .	69.7
Access to water (% of persons, 2000)	100
Access to sanitation (% of persons, 2000)	100
Human Development Index (2000): ranking	15
Human Development Index (2000): value	0.926

For sources and definitions, see explanatory note on p. vi.

Agriculture

PRINCIPAL CROPS
('000 metric tons)

	1999	2000	2001
Wheat	1,416.2	1,313.0	1,508.3
Barley	1,152.8	854.7	1,012.4
Maize	1,699.6	1,851.7	1,771.1
Rye	218.2	182.8	213.5
Oats	152.4	117.6	128.3
Triticale (wheat-rye hybrid) . .	120.0	134.8	157.0
Mixed grain	47.0	35.8	36.6
Potatoes	711.7	694.6	694.6
Soybeans (Soya beans) . . .	50.4	32.8	33.9
Sunflower seed	64.1	55.0	50.6
Rapeseed	192.4	125.4	146.5
Cabbages	78.4	71.3	74.4
Lettuce	53.9	60.5	60.5
Cucumbers and gherkins . .	44.5	42.8	43.8
Onions (dry)	134.6	117.1	95.7
Carrots	75.9	60.0	65.0
Grapes	364.4	303.9	330.0
Sugar beet	3,216.7	2,559.6	2,773.5
Apples	409.7	490.4	409.7
Pears	114.0	130.2	108.6
Plums	44.9	57.3	75.0
Cherries (incl. sour) . . .	29.5	35.1	37.7

Source: FAO.

LIVESTOCK
('000 head at December)

	1999	2000	2001
Horses	81.6	n.a.	n.a.
Cattle	2,152.8	2,155.4	2,118.5
Pigs	3,433.0	3,347.9	3,440.4
Sheep	352.3	339.2	320.5
Goats	58.0	56.1	59.5
Chickens	13,797.8	11,077.3	11,905.1
Ducks, geese and guinea-fowl . }	700.3 {	120.8	n.a.
Turkeys . . . . }		588.5	547.2

LIVESTOCK PRODUCTS
('000 metric tons)

	1999	2000	2001
Beef and veal	203.3	203.5	215.2
Mutton and lamb	6.0	7.5	7.2
Pig meat*	684.1	624.0	613.8
Poultry meat	104.9	111.2	113.0
Cows' milk	3,349.9	3,340.1	3,299.6
Sheep's milk	7.3	7.4	7.6
Goats' milk	16.1	16.8	16.5
Cheese	136.8	145.4	164.8
Butter	36.8	37.1	36.9
Hen eggs	92.1	86.1	86.1
Honey	9.3	8.7	8.7†
Cattle hides (fresh)†	22.0	21.5	22.3

* Unofficial figures.

† FAO estimate(s).

Source: FAO.

Forestry

ROUNDWOOD REMOVALS
('000 cubic metres, excl. bark)

	1999	2000	2001
Sawlogs, veneer logs and logs for sleepers	8,067	8,033	8,057
Pitprops (mine timber), pulpwood, and other industrial wood . . .	2,921	2,383	2,505
Fuel wood	3,095	2,860	2,905
Total	14,083	13,276	13,467

Source: FAO.

SAWNWOOD PRODUCTION
('000 cubic metres, incl. railway sleepers)

	1999	2000	2001
Coniferous (softwood)	9,400	10,150	10,011
Broadleaved (hardwood)	228	240	216
Total	9,628	10,390	10,227

Source: FAO.

Fishing

(metric tons, live weight)

	1998	1999	2000
Capture	451	432	859
Common carp	451	432	439
European whitefish	n.a.	n.a.	400
Aquaculture	2,911	3,070	2,847
Common carp	565	595	620
Sea trout	104	104	61
Rainbow trout	1,997	2,097	1,950
Brook trout	195	191	162
Total catch	3,362	3,502	3,706

Source: FAO, *Yearbook of Fishery Statistics*.

Mining

('000 metric tons, unless otherwise indicated)

	1999	2000	2001
Brown coal (incl. lignite) . . .	1,137.4	1,254.6	1,194.0
Crude petroleum	1,063.5	1,056.2	n.a.
Iron ore:			
gross weight	1,752	1,850	1,800
metal content*	553	590	575
Magnesite (crude)	748.6	725.8	680.5
Tungsten, concentrate (metric tons)*†	1,610	1,600 ‡	1,600
Gypsum and anhydrite (crude). .	999.2	946.0	929.2
Kaolin	152.5	118.5	89.6
Basalt	5,200.8	4,933.2	4,689.8
Dolomite	7,968.1	7,152.2	6,172.0
Limestone and marble . . .	26,408.6	23,823.5	23,799.7
Quartz and quartzite* . . .	409	372	375
Natural gas (million cu metres) .	1,740.7	1,804.7	1,954.4

* Data from the US Geological Survey.

† Figures refer to metal content.

‡ Estimated production.

Industry

SELECTED PRODUCTS

('000 metric tons, unless otherwise indicated)

	1997	1998	1999
Wheat flour	277	278	293
Raw sugar*	529	533	545
Wine ('000 hectolitres) . . .	1,802	2,703	2,803
Beer ('000 hectolitres) . . .	9,303	8,837	8,884
Cotton yarn—pure and mixed (metric tons)	21,849	24,829	n.a.
Woven cotton fabrics—pure and mixed ('000 sq metres) . .	100,076	101,133	74,000†
Wool yarn—pure and mixed (metric tons)	2,692	n.a.	n.a.
Woven woollen fabrics—pure and mixed ('000 sq metres) . .	22,279	26,594	n.a.
Mechanical wood pulp . . .	378	376	369
Chemical and semi-chemical wood pulp	1,097	1,116	1,152
Newsprint.	397	376	394
Other printing and writing paper .	1,826	2,002	2,067
Other paper and paperboard . .	1,593	1,630	1,681
Plastics and resins	1,035	1,074	n.a.
Motor spirit (petrol)	2,410	2,158	2,142
Jet fuel	505	533	n.a.
Distillate fuel oils	3,916	3,892	3,677
Residual fuel oils.	1,540	1,347	1,308
Cement	3,944	3,958	n.a.
Crude steel‡	5,196	5,298	5,213
Refined copper—unwrought (metric tons): secondary‡ . . .	74,000	71,000	77,573
Refined lead—unwrought (metric tons): secondary‡	22,700	23,100	24,500
Passenger motor cars (number) .	97,774	97,774	123,586
Motorcycles, etc. (number) . .	17,007	19,832	21,647
Construction: new dwellings completed (number) . . .	58,029	57,489	59,447
Electric energy (million kWh) . .	56,854	57,437	60,351
Manufactured gas (terajoules)§ .	30,132	30,076	n.a.

* Provisional figures.

† To nearest million sq metres.

‡ Data from the US Geological Survey.

§ Production of blast-furnace gas and coke-oven gas.

Sources: mainly Austrian Central Statistical Office, Vienna; FAO, *Yearbook of Forest Products*; UN, *Industrial Commodity Statistics Yearbook* and *Monthly Bulletin of Statistics*; International Road Federation, *World Road Statistics*.

Finance

CURRENCY AND EXCHANGE RATES

Monetary Units

100 cent = 1 euro (€)

Sterling and Dollar Equivalents (31 December 2002)

£1 sterling = 1.5370 euros

US $1 = 0.9536 euros

100 euros = £65.06 = $104.87

Average Exchange Rate (euros per US $)

2000 1.0854

2001 1.1175

2002 1.0626

Note: The national currency was formerly the Schilling. From the introduction of the euro, with Austrian participation, on 1 January 1999, a fixed exchange rate of €1 = 13.7603 Schilling was in operation. Euro notes and coins were introduced on 1 January 2002. The euro and local currency circulated alongside each other until 28 February, after which the euro became the sole legal tender. Some of the figures in this Survey are still in terms of Schilling.

FEDERAL BUDGET

(million euros)

Revenue	2000	2001*	2002†
Total taxes and levies (net) . . .	33,041	37,933	37,978
Gross tax revenue	50,387	56,210	56,776
Tax on wages and salaries. .	14,468	15,672	17,078
Tax on assessed income . .	2,818	3,987	3,343
Withholding tax	1,473	1,616	1,744
Corporate income tax . . .	3,865	6,235	4,760
Turnover tax.	17,056	17,354	18,459
Tobacco tax	1,197	1,234	1,257
Mineral oils tax	2,726	2,880	2,798
Other taxes and levies . .	6,784	7,232	7,337
Transfers to provinces, municipalities, etc. . . .	−15,257	−16,285	−16,400
Transfers to European Union .	−2,088	−1,992	−2,398
Social insurance contributions . .	6,903	7,224	7,373
Other revenue	15,449	13,831	13,195
Total	**55,393**	**58,988**	**58,546**

Expenditure	2000	2001*	2002†
Education	5,563	5,650	5,624
Research and science . . .	2,387	2,484	2,477
Health	839	748	867
Social welfare.	15,764	16,890	16,943
Housing construction . . .	1,819	1,812	1,816
Transport	6,501	7,353	6,744
Agriculture and forestry . .	1,771	1,729	1,662
Defence	1,690	1,628	1,629
Security and law enforcement .	2,166	2,231	2,154
Debt-servicing and currency swaps	9,240	8,195	8,715
Total (incl. others)	**58,247**	**60,403**	**59,374**

* Provisional.

† Forecast.

Source: Federal Ministry of Finance, Vienna.

NATIONAL BANK RESERVES

(US $ million at 31 December)

	2000	2001	2002
Gold*	3,331	3,089	3,499
IMF special drawing rights . .	134	233	185
Reserve position in IMF. . .	692	833	959
Foreign exchange.	13,492	11,444	8,540
Total	**17,649**	**15,599**	**13,183**

* Valued at market prices.

Source: IMF, *International Financial Statistics*.

MONEY SUPPLY
(million euros at 31 December)

	2000	2001	2002
Currency in circulation . . .	14,541	10,685	11,007*
Demand deposits at banking institutions	45,055	51,045	54,084

* Currency put into circulation by the Oesterreichische Nationalbank was 18,411 million euros.

Source: IMF, *International Financial Statistics*.

COST OF LIVING
(Consumer Price Index; base: 1996 = 100)

	1999	2000	2001*
Food and beverages	103.4	104.5	103.3
Rent (incl. maintenance and repairs)	106.9	109.1	102.9
Fuel and power	101.0	107.6	103.2
Clothing and footwear . . .	99.9	100.1	101.6
All items (incl. others) . . .	102.8	105.2	102.7

* Base: 2000 = 100.

All items (base:1995=100): 107.2 in 2000; 110.0 in 2001; 112.0 in 2002 (Source: IMF, *International Financial Statistics*).

NATIONAL ACCOUNTS
(million euros at current prices)

National Income and Product

	1999	2000	2001
Gross domestic product (GDP) in market prices	197,154	207,037	211,857
Primary incomes received from abroad	13,520	14,361	15,043
Less Primary incomes paid abroad . .	16,557	17,625	19,114
Gross national income (GNI)	194,117	203,773	207,786
Less Consumption of fixed capital .	28,226	29,631	31,145
Net national income	165,890	174,142	176,640
Current transfers from abroad . .	1,967	2,197	2,678
Less Current transfers paid abroad	3,110	3,080	3,310
Net national disposable income	164,747	173,259	176,008

Expenditure on the Gross Domestic Product

	1999	2000	2001
Final consumption expenditure .	151,034	157,245	162,124
Gross capital formation . . .	48,354	50,267	49,121
Total domestic expenditure.	199,388	207,512	211,245
Exports of goods and services . .	89,632	103,913	111,124
Less Imports of goods and services	91,327	105,178	111,186
Statistical discrepancy	−539	791	673
GDP in market prices .	197,154	207,037	211,857
GDP at constant 1995 prices .	190,617	197,352	198,674

Gross Domestic Product by Economic Activity

	1999	2000	2001
Agriculture, hunting, forestry and fishing	4,281	4,322	4,513
Mining and quarrying. . . .	625	709	806
Manufacturing	37,474	40,365	41,335
Electricity, gas and water. . .	4,759	4,395	4,244
Construction	14,863	15,148	14,746
Wholesale and retail trade . .	23,319	24,905	25,141
Restaurants and hotels . . .	7,339	7,934	8,557
Transport, storage and communications	12,925	13,392	13,905
Finance and insurance . . .	11,745	13,215	13,146
Real estate and business services*	29,122	31,423	33,814
Public administration and defence	12,222	12,504	12,752
Other services	25,344	26,529	27,473
Sub-total	184,018	194,842	200,394
Less Imputed bank service charges	8,361	9,603	10,293
GDP at basic prices . . .	175,657	185,239	190,101
Taxes on products . . . . }	21,496	21,799	21,757
Less Subsidies on products . . }			
GDP in purchasers' values	197,154	207,037	211,857

* Including imputed rents of owner-occupied dwellings.

BALANCE OF PAYMENTS
(US $ million)

	1999	2000	2001
Exports of goods f.o.b. . . .	64,422	64,684	66,899
Imports of goods f.o.b. . . .	−68,051	−67,421	−68,227
Trade balance	−3,629	−2,737	−1,328
Exports of services	31,306	31,342	32,896
Imports of services	−29,421	−29,653	−31,535
Balance on goods and services.	−1,745	−1,048	33
Other income received . . .	12,673	11,992	12,297
Other income paid	−15,552	−14,456	−15,292
Balance on goods, services and income	−4,624	−3,512	−2,962
Current transfers received . .	2,925	2,914	3,264
Current transfers paid . . .	−4,956	−4,267	−4,404
Current balance	−6,655	−4,864	−4,103
Capital account (net) . . .	−265	−432	−514
Direct investment abroad . .	−3,306	−5,599	−3,046
Direct investment from abroad.	3,008	8,523	5,898
Portfolio investment assets . .	−29,216	−27,145	−11,867
Portfolio investment liabilities . .	26,364	30,360	16,583
Financial derivatives assets . .	−517	441	−394
Financial derivatives liabilities . .	100	254	96
Other investment assets . . .	−11,592	−16,334	−6,172
Other investment liabilities . .	19,948	13,790	712
Net errors and omissions . . .	−40	1,143	919
Overall balance	−2,172	−746	−1,888

Source: IMF, *International Financial Statistics*.

External Trade

Note: Austria's customs territory excludes Mittelberg im Kleinen Walsertal (in Vorarlberg) and Jungholz (in Tyrol). The figures also exclude trade in silver specie and monetary gold.

PRINCIPAL COMMODITIES
(distribution by SITC, million euros)

Imports c.i.f.	1999*	2000	2001
Food and live animals . . .	47,163.3	3,552.5	3,937.1
Crude materials (inedible) except fuels	34,219.6	3,013.9	2,930.0
Mineral fuels, lubricants, etc. (incl. electric current) . . .	39,643.2	4,898.6	5,500.3
Petroleum, petroleum products, etc.	26,844.0	3,397.3	3,277.4
Chemicals and related products	92,871.3	7,571.5	8,229.2
Medicinal and pharmaceutical products.	30,660.2	2,141.4	2,639.7
Basic manufactures . . .	153,219.0	12,501.5	13,264.5
Other metal manufactures .	37,439.5	2,964.6	3,252.1
Machinery and transport equipment. . . .	370,801.0	30,818.4	31,612.2
Machinery specialized for particular industries . . .	27,209.1	2,268.6	2,298.1
General industrial machinery, equipment and parts . . .	46,924.7	3,846.6	4,252.6
Office machines and automatic data-processing machines .	32,588.8	2,497.7	2,658.6
Telecommunications and sound equipment	35,749.1	3,032.2	2,526.9
Other electrical machinery, apparatus, etc.. . . .	67,823.1	5,894.0	6,238.0
Road vehicles and parts (excl. tyres, engines and electrical parts) .	108,882.8	8,610.8	9,021.9
Passenger motor cars (excl. buses).	52,908.9	3,954.8	4,098.0
Parts for cars, buses, lorries, etc.	32,231.6	2,694.4	3,108.9
Miscellaneous manufactured articles. . . .	151,974.6	11,813.7	12,430.8
Clothing and accessories (excl. footwear)	39,300.4	2,925.5	3,126.9
Total (incl. others) . . .	898,760.9	74,935.2	78,691.6

Exports f.o.b.	1999*	2000	2001
Food and live animals . . .	31,776.8	2,478.5	2,803.3
Crude materials (inedible) except fuels	29,475.9	2,396.1	2,387.6
Chemicals and related products	77,820.6	6,427.1	7,077.4
Medicinal and pharmaceutical products.	n.a.	1,981.8	2,296.6
Basic manufactures . . .	198,687.6	16,363.1	17,187.3
Paper, paperboard and manufactures	39,066.3	3,240.0	3,381.7
Paper and paperboard (not cut to size or shape)	27,815.9	2,336.6	2,352.4
Iron and steel.	35,068.3	2,959.1	3,182.4
Other metal manufactures .	40,279.9	3,098.6	3,309.3
Machinery and transport equipment. . . .	357,518.7	30,611.7	32,137.5
Power-generating machinery and equipment	46,387.4	3,641.6	3,981.7
Internal combustion piston engines and parts . . .	33,567.4	2,790.3	2,963.7
Machinery specialized for particular industries . . .	44,847.9	3,789.1	4,041.2
General industrial machinery, equipment and parts . . .	49,788.5	3,936.9	4,269.7
Telecommunications and sound equipment	28,099.9	2,482.1	2,378.0
Other electrical machinery, apparatus, etc.. . . .	67,186.7	6,102.3	6,519.6
Road vehicles and parts (excl. tyres, engines and electrical parts) .	82,688.1	6,869.2	7,316.5
Passenger motor cars (excl. buses).	38,354.8	2,974.8	3,189.3
Parts for cars, buses, lorries, etc.	26,359.0	2,146.9	2,150.8
Miscellaneous manufactured articles. . . .	114,727.5	9,089.4	9,909.9
Total (incl. others) . . .	829,276.5	69,692.3	74,251.5

* Figures in million Schilling.

PRINCIPAL TRADING PARTNERS
(million euros)*

Imports c.i.f.	1999	2000	2001
Belgium-Luxembourg . . .	1,405.9	1,475.4	1,620.2
China, People's Republic . .	916.8	1,243.2	1,359.5
Czech Republic.	1,625.6	1,921.1	2,118.9
Finland	671.4	816.0	789.3
France	3,291.1	3,312.3	3,198.1
Germany	27,379.8	30,534.0	31,901.1
Hungary	2,176.1	2,604.7	2,688.0
Italy	4,958.6	5,354.0	5,642.6
Japan	1,633.6	2,015.3	1,757.9
Netherlands	2,081.3	2,285.1	2,299.1
Poland	594.4	756.9	938.3
Russia	706.2	1,237.8	1,146.0
Slovakia.	764.3	1,042.3	1,113.1
Spain	960.8	1,047.7	1,088.0
Sweden	874.8	1,130.1	1,041.7
Switzerland-Liechtenstein .	2,230.0	2,279.7	2,527.7
United Kingdom	2,025.5	2,092.0	2,081.3
USA	3,490.0	4,107.8	4,209.9
Total (incl. others) . . .	65,315.5	74,935.2	78,692.0

Exports f.o.b.	1999	2000	2001
Belgium-Luxembourg	987.4	1,168.6	1,448.9
China, People's Republic	390.8	490.5	844.5
Croatia	578.3	666.8	886.6
Czech Republic	1,698.0	1,999.4	2,151.3
France	2,671.2	3,078.3	3,391.1
Germany	21,054.8	23,244.0	24,160.0
Hungary	2,966.3	3,466.3	3,316.0
Italy	5,064.8	6,046.1	6,323.2
Japan	730.3	913.8	908.6
Netherlands	1,392.3	1,585.7	1,764.0
Poland	953.2	1,109.8	1,215.3
Russia	468.1	655.4	941.2
Slovakia	672.0	767.8	946.0
Slovenia	1,051.0	1,229.0	1,282.8
Spain	1,750.1	1,852.1	1,853.8
Sweden	697.7	813.4	845.2
Switzerland-Liechtenstein	3,616.0	4,422.7	3,862.4
United Kingdom	2,650.5	3,038.4	3,467.0
USA	2,750.4	3,498.0	3,932.9
Total (incl. others)	60,265.9	69,692.3	74,251.0

* Imports by country of production; exports by country of consumption.

Transport

RAILWAYS
(traffic, Federal Railways only)

	1999	2000	2001
Passenger-km (millions)	7,997.0	8,206.0	n.a.
Freight net ton-km (millions)	15,556.2	17,109.6	17,386.6
Freight tons carried ('000)	78,017.8	84,738.8	86,411.0

ROAD TRAFFIC
(motor vehicles in use at 31 December)

	1999	2000	2001
Passenger cars	4,009,604	4,097,145	4,182,027
Buses and coaches	9,834	9,918	9,902
Goods vehicles	318,757	326,784	331,394
Motorcycles	263,297	279,728	294,843
Mopeds and motor scooters	359,630	352,984	346,591

SHIPPING

Merchant Fleet
(registered at 31 December)

	1999	2000	2001
Number of vessels	22	24	8
Total displacement ('000 grt)	71.1	89.6	35.3

Source: Lloyd's Register-Fairplay, *World Fleet Statistics*.

International Freight Traffic on the Danube
('000 metric tons, excl. transit traffic)

	1999	2000	2001
Goods loaded	1,263.0	1,190.9	1,257.6
Goods unloaded	5,172.5	5,449.9	5,607.0

CIVIL AVIATION
(Austrian Airlines, '000)

	1999	2000	2001
Kilometres flown	69,769	70,411	66,316
Passenger ton-km	817,454	914,870	846,385
Cargo ton-km	214,030	284,533	252,406
Mail ton-km	14,257	11,635	12,539

Tourism

FOREIGN TOURIST ARRIVALS
(by country of origin)*

	1998	1999	2000
Belgium	347,963	351,808	349,391
France	511,837	455,240	386,828
Germany	9,696,521	9,844,027	9,990,133
Italy	965,741	956,015	911,030
Netherlands	1,054,177	1,110,755	1,185,856
Switzerland-Liechtenstein	699,751	696,947	736,877
United Kingdom	564,396	595,988	666,616
USA	670,075	630,105	781,455
Total (incl. others)	17,352,477	17,466,714	17,982,204

* Arrivals at accommodation establishments.

Source: World Tourism Organization, *Yearbook of Tourism Statistics*.

2001: Total arrivals 18,180,100.

Receipts from tourism (million euros): 10,058 in 1998; 10,354 in 1999; 10,752 in 2000; 11,297 in 2001 (Source: Austrian National Bank).

Communications Media

	1999	2000	2001
Telephones ('000 lines in use)	3,202	2,929	3,810*
Radio licences issued	2,766,612	2,755,126	2,808,948
Television licences issued	2,670,743	2,712,352	2,779,279
Book titles produced	18,719	20,283	20,192
Daily newspapers	17	16	16
Weekly newspapers	159	191	197
Other periodicals	2,774	2,783	2,788

* Source: International Telecommunication Union.

Facsimile machines ('000 in use): 210.0 in 1993; 240.0 in 1994; 284.7 in 1995 (Source: UN, *Statistical Yearbook*).

Mobile cellular telephones ('000 subscribers): 4,250.4 in 1999; 6,252.8 in 2000; 6,566 in 2001 (Source: International Telecommunication Union).

Personal computers ('000 in use): 1,900 in 1998; 2,100 in 1999; 2,270 in 2000 (Source: International Telecommunication Union).

Internet users ('000): 1,250 in 1999; 2,100 in 2000; 2,600 in 2001 (Source: International Telecommunication Union).

Education

(2001/02)

	Institutions	Staff	Students
Pre-primary	4,849	25,892	218,439
Primary	3,309	33,814	387,408
General secondary and upper primary	1,891	75,317	581,006
Compulsory vocational*	178	4,621	132,613
Technical and vocational	721	n.a.	64,940
Teacher training:			
second level	47	1,443	8,996
third level	35	2,674	13,664
Universities*	19	16,099	242,598
Tertiary vocational*	67	229	11,743

* 2000/01 figures.

Directory

The Constitution

The Austrian Constitution of 1920, as amended in 1929, was restored on 1 May 1945. Its main provisions, with subsequent amendments, are summarized below:

Austria is a democratic republic, having a Federal President (Bundespräsident), elected directly by the people, and a bicameral legislature, the Federal Assembly (Bundesversammlung), consisting of the National Council (Nationalrat) and the Federal Council (Bundesrat). The republic is organized on the federal system, comprising the nine federal provinces (Bundesländer) of Burgenland, Carinthia (Kärnten), Lower Austria (Niederösterreich), Upper Austria (Oberösterreich), Salzburg, Styria (Steiermark), Tyrol (Tirol), Vorarlberg and Vienna (Wien). There is universal suffrage for men and women who are more than 18 years of age.

The Nationalrat consists of 183 members, elected by universal direct suffrage, according to a system of proportional representation. It functions for a maximum period of four years.

The Bundesrat represents the Bundesländer. Lower Austria sends 12 members, Vienna and Upper Austria 11 each, Styria 10, Carinthia and Tyrol five each, Salzburg four, and Burgenland and Vorarlberg three each, making 64 in total. The seats are divided between the parties according to the number of seats that they control in each Provincial Assembly (Landtag) and are held during the life of the provincial government (Landesregierung) that they represent. Each Land, in turn, provides the Chairman of the Bundesrat for six months.

The Bundesversammlung meets for certain matters of special importance, for example to witness the swearing-in of the President. It can also be convened to declare war or to demand a referendum on the deposition of the President, if demanded by the Nationalrat.

The Federal President, elected by popular vote, is the Head of State and holds office for a term of six years. The President is eligible for re-election only once in succession. Although invested with special emergency powers, the President normally acts on the authority of the Council of Ministers, which is responsible to the Nationalrat for governmental policy.

The Federal Government consists of the Federal Chancellor, the Vice-Chancellor and the other ministers and state secretaries, who may vary in number. The Chancellor is chosen by the President, usually from the party with the strongest representation in the newly elected Nationalrat, and the other ministers are then selected by the President on the advice of the Chancellor.

If the Nationalrat adopts an explicit motion expressing 'no confidence' in the Federal Government or individual members thereof, the Federal Government or the federal minister concerned is removed from office.

All new legislative proposals must be read and submitted to a vote in both chambers of the Bundesversammlung. A new draft law is presented first to the Nationalrat, where it usually has three readings, and secondly to the Bundesrat, where it can be delayed, but not vetoed.

The Constitution also provides for appeals by the Government to the electorate on specific points by means of referendum. If a petition supported by 100,000 electors or more is presented to the Government, the Government must submit it to the Nationalrat.

The Landtag exercises the same functions in each province as the Nationalrat does in the State. The members of the Landestag elect the Landesregierung, consisting of a provincial governor (Landeshauptmann) and his or her councillors (Landesräte). They are responsible to the Landtag.

The spheres of legal and administrative competence of both national and provincial governments are clearly defined. The Constitution distinguishes four groups:

1. Law-making and administration are the responsibility of the State: e.g. foreign affairs, justice and finance.

2. Law-making is the responsibility of the State, administration is the responsibility of the provinces: e.g. elections, population matters and road traffic.

3. The State formulates the rudiments of the law, the provinces enact the law and administer it: e.g. charity, rights of agricultural workers, land reform.

4. Law-making and administration are the responsibility of the provinces in all matters not expressly assigned to the State: e.g. municipal affairs.

The Government

HEAD OF STATE

Federal President: Dr Thomas Klestil (sworn in 8 July 1992; re-elected 19 April 1998).

COUNCIL OF MINISTERS
(April 2003)

A coalition of the Freiheitliche Partei Österreichs (FPÖ) and the Österreichische Volkspartei (ÖVP).

Federal Chancellor: Dr Wolfgang Schüssel (ÖVP).

Vice-Chancellor and Minister of Social Security and Generations: Herbert Haupt (FPÖ).

Minister of Foreign Affairs: Dr Benita Ferrero-Waldner (ÖVP).

Minister of Economic Affairs and Labour: Dr Martin Bartenstein (ÖVP).

Minister of Health and Women's Issues: Maria Rauch-Kallat (ÖVP).

Minister of Finance: Karl-Heinz Grasser (FPÖ).

Minister of the Interior: Dr Ernst Strasser (ÖVP).

Minister of Justice: Dr Dieter Böhmdorfer (FPÖ).

Minister of Defence: Günther Platter (ÖVP).

Minister of Agriculture, Forestry, Environment and Water Management: Josef Pröll (ÖVP).

Minister of Education, Science and Cultural Affairs: Elisabeth Gehrer (ÖVP).

Minister of Transport, Innovation and Technology: Hubert Gorbach (FPÖ).

Secretaries of State in the Federal Chancellery: Franz Morak (ÖVP), Karl Schweitzer (FPÖ).

Secretary of State in the Ministry of Finance: Dr Alfred Finz (ÖVP).

Secretary of State in the Ministry of Health and Women's Issues: Reinhart Waneck (FPÖ).

Secretary of State in the Ministry of Social Security and Generations: Ursula Haubner (FPÖ).

Secretary of State in the Ministry of Transport, Innovation and Technology: Helmut Kukacka (ÖVP).

MINISTRIES

Office of the Federal President: Hofburg, 1010 Vienna; tel. (1) 534-22-0; fax (1) 535-65-12; internet www.hofburg.at.

Office of the Federal Chancellor: Ballhauspl. 2, 1014 Vienna; tel. (1) 531-15-0; fax (1) 535-03-380; e-mail praesidium@bka.gv.at; internet www.bka.gv.at.

Ministry of Agriculture, Forestry, Environment and Water Management: Stubenring 1, 1010 Vienna; tel. (1) 711-00-0; fax (1) 710-32-54; e-mail office@bmlfuw.gv.at; internet www.lebensministerium.at.

Ministry of Defence: Dampfschiffstr. 2, 1030 Vienna; tel. (1) 5200-0; fax (1) 520-17033; e-mail buergsrv@bmlv.gv.at; internet www.bundesheer.at.

Ministry of Economic Affairs and Labour: Stubenring 1, 1011 Vienna; tel. (1) 711-00-0; fax (1) 713-79-95; e-mail service@bmwa.gv.at; internet www.bmwa.gv.at.

Ministry of Education, Science and Cultural Affairs: Minoritenpl. 5, 1014 Vienna; tel. (1) 531-20-00; fax (1) 531-20-30-99; e-mail ministerium@bmbwk.gv.at; internet www.bmbwk.gv.at.

Ministry of Finance: Himmelpfortgasse 4–8b, 1015 Vienna; tel. (1) 514-33-0; fax (1) 512-78-69; internet www.bmf.gov.at.

Ministry of Foreign Affairs: Ballhauspl. 2, 1014 Vienna; tel. (1) 531-15-0; fax (1) 535-45-30; e-mail presse@bmaa.gv.at; internet www.bmaa.gv.at.

Ministry of Health and Women's Issues: Radetzkystr. 2, 1030 Vienna; tel. (1) 711-00-0; internet www.bmgf.gv.at.

Ministry of the Interior: Herrengasse 7, 1014 Vienna; tel. (1) 531-26-0; fax (1) 531-26-39-10; e-mail ministerbuero@bmi.gv.at; internet www.bmi.gv.at.

Ministry of Justice: Museumstr. 7, 1016 Vienna; tel. (1) 521-52-0; fax (1) 521-52-72-7; internet www.bmj.gv.at.

Ministry of Public Affairs and Sports: Minoritenpl. 3, 1014 Vienna; tel. (1) 531-15-0; e-mail post@bmols.gv.at; internet www .bmols.gv.at.

Ministry of Social Security and Generations: Stubenring 1, 1010 Vienna; tel. (1) 711-00; fax (1) 711-00-64-69; e-mail einlaufstelle@bmsg.gv.at; internet www.bmsg.gv.at.

Ministry of Transport, Innovation and Technology: Radetz-kystr. 2, 1030 Vienna; tel. (1) 711-62-0; fax (1) 531-20-4499; internet www.bmvit.gv.at.

President and Legislature

PRESIDENT

Presidential Election, 19 April 1998

Candidates	Votes	%
Dr Thomas Klestil (ÖVP)	2,626,860	63.5
Gertraud Knoll (Independent)	559,943	13.5
Dr Heide Schmidt (FPÖ)	458,491	11.1
Richard Lugner (Independent)	411,378	9.9
Karl Walter Novak (Independent)	80,741	2.0
Total	4,137,413	100.0

FEDERAL ASSEMBLY

Nationalrat
(National Council)

President of the Nationalrat: Prof. Dr ANDREAS KOHL.

General Election, 24 November 2002

	Votes	% of total	Seats
Sozialdemokratische Partei Österreichs (SPÖ)	1,792,499	36.51	69
Österreichische Volkspartei (ÖVP)	2,076,833	42.30	79
Freiheitliche Partei Österreichs (FPÖ)	491,328	10.01	18
Die Grünen—Die Grüne Alternative	464,980	9.47	17
Others	84,005	1.71	—
Total	4,909,645	100.00	183

Bundesrat
(Federal Council)
(April 2003)

Chairman of the Bundesrat: HERWIG HÖSELE (Dec. 2002–July 2003).

Provinces	SPÖ	ÖVP	FPÖ	Die Grünen	Total seats
Burgenland	2	1	—	—	3
Carinthia (Kärnten)	1	1	2	—	4
Lower Austria (Niederösterreich)	5	5	2	—	12
Upper Austria (Oberösterreich)	3	6	2	—	11
Salzburg	1	2	1	—	4
Styria (Steiermark)	3	5	1	—	9
Tyrol (Tirol)	1	3	1	—	5
Vorarlberg	—	2	1	—	3
Vienna (Wien)	6	2	2	1	11
Total	22	27	12	1	62

Political Organizations

Freiheitliche Partei Österreichs (FPÖ/Die Freiheitlichen) (Freedom Party): Esslingasse 14–16, 1010 Vienna; tel. (1) 512-35-35; fax (1) 513-35-35-9; internet www.fpoe.at; f. 1955; partially succeeding the Verband der Unabhängigen (League of Independents, f. 1949); popularly known as Die Freiheitlichen; populist right-wing party advocating the participation of workers in management, stricter immigration controls and deregulation in the business sector; opposes Austria's membership of the EU; Chair. HERBERT HAUPT; Vice-Chair. MAGDA BLECKMANN, MAXIMILIAN WALCH; Gen. Sec. KARL SCHWEITZER.

Die Grünen–Die Grüne Alternative (Greens–Green Alternative): Lindengasse 40, 1071 Vienna; tel. (1) 521-25-0; fax (1) 526-91-10; e-mail bundesbuero@gruene.at; internet www.gruene.at; f. 1986; campaigns for environmental protection, peace and social justice; Chair. and Leader of Parliamentary Group Prof. Dr ALEXANDER VAN DER BELLEN.

Kommunistische Partei Österreichs (KPÖ) (Communist Party of Austria): Weyringergasse 33/5, 1040 Vienna; tel. (1) 503-65-80; fax (1) 503-65-80-411; e-mail bundesvorstand@kpoe.at; internet www .kpoe.at; f. 1918; strongest in the industrial centres and trade unions; advocates a policy of strict neutrality and opposes Austria's membership of the EU; Chair. WALTER BAIER.

Liberales Forum (LiF) (Liberal Forum): Nikolsdorfer Gasse 42/2–5, 1050 Vienna; tel. (1) 503-06-67; fax (1) 503-06-67-20; e-mail office@lif.at; internet www.lif.at; f. 1993 by fmr mems of Freiheitliche Partei Österreichs; Leader ALEXANDER ZACH.

Österreichische Volkspartei (ÖVP) (Austrian People's Party): Lichtenfelsgasse 7, 1010 Vienna; tel. (1) 401-26; fax (1) 401-26-32-9; e-mail email@oevp.at; internet www.oevp.at; f. 1945; Christian-Democratic party; advocates an ecologically orientated social market economy; Chair. Dr WOLFGANG SCHÜSSEL; Sec.-Gen. MARIA RAUCH-KALLAT.

Sozialdemokratische Partei Österreichs (SPÖ) (Social-Democratic Party of Austria): Löwelstr. 18, 1014 Vienna; tel. (1) 534-27-0; fax (1) 535-96-83; e-mail spoe@spoe.at; internet www.spoe.at; f. as the Social-Democratic Party in 1889, subsequently renamed the Socialist Party, reverted to its original name in 1991; advocates democratic socialism and Austria's permanent neutrality; 500,000 mems; Chair. Dr ALFRED GUSENBAUER; Secs ANDREA KUNTZL, DORIS BURES.

Die Unabhängigen (DU) (Independents): Gablenzgasse 11, 1015 Vienna; tel. (1) 981-40-202; fax (1) 981-40-99; e-mail service@ldu.at; f. 1999; Chair. RICHARD LUGNER.

Diplomatic Representation

EMBASSIES IN AUSTRIA

Afghanistan: Kaiserstr. 84/1/3, 1070 Vienna; tel. (1) 524-78-06; fax (1) 524-78-07; Chargé d'affaires FARID A. AMIN.

Albania: An den langen Lüssen 1, 1190 Vienna; tel. (1) 328-86-56; fax (1) 328-86-58; Ambassador ALBERT SEJDIAJ.

Algeria: Rudolfinergasse 16–18, 1190 Vienna; tel. (1) 369-88-53; fax (1) 369-88-56; Ambassador TAOUS FEROUKITI.

Angola: Seilerstätte 15/10, 1010 Vienna; tel. (1) 718-74-88; fax (1) 718-74-86; e-mail embangola.vienna@embangola.at; Ambassador Dr FIDELINO LOY DE JESUS FIGUEIREDO.

Argentina: Goldschmiedgasse 2/1, 1010 Vienna; tel. (1) 533-85-77; fax (1) 533-87-97; Ambassador (vacant).

Armenia: Neubaugasse 12–14/1/16, 1070 Vienna; tel. (1) 522-74-79; fax (1) 522-74-81; Chargé d'affaires SAMUEL MKRTCHIAN.

Australia: Mattiellistr. 2, 1040 Vienna; tel. (1) 506-74-0; fax (1) 504-11-78; internet www.australian-embassy.at; Ambassador MAX WILLIAM HUGHES.

Azerbaijan: Strozzigasse 10, 1080 Vienna; tel. (1) 403-13-22; fax (1) 403-13-23; e-mail azerembvienna@csi.com; Ambassador VAQIF SADIQOV.

Belarus: Hüttelbergstr. 6, 1140 Vienna; tel. (1) 419-96-30; fax (1) 416-96-30-30; e-mail austria@belembassy.org; Ambassador VIKTAR GAISENAK.

Belgium: Wohllebengasse 6, 1040 Vienna; tel. (1) 502-07; fax (1) 502-07-11; Ambassador MICHEL ADAM.

Bolivia: Waaggasse 10/4, 1040 Vienna; tel. (1) 587-46-75; fax (1) 586-68-80; e-mail embol.austria@chello.at; Ambassador JAIME NIÑO DE GUZMÁN QUIROZ.

Bosnia and Herzegovina: Tivoligasse 54, 1120 Vienna; tel. (1) 811-85-55; fax (1) 811-85-69; Ambassador Prof. Dr EMINA KEĆO-ISAKOVIĆ.

Brazil: Lugeck 1/V/15, 1010 Vienna; tel. (1) 512-06-31; fax (1) 513-50-56; e-mail ausbrem@xpoint.at; Ambassador AFFONSO CELSO DE OURO-PRETO.

Bulgaria: Schwindgasse 8, 1040 Vienna; tel. (1) 505-64-44; fax (1) 505-14-23; e-mail bulgembassy@eunet.at; Ambassador Dr ELENA KIRTCHEVA.

Burkina Faso: Prinz-Eugen-Str. 18/3A, 1040 Vienna; tel. (1) 503-82-64; fax (1) 503-82-64-20; Ambassador BÉATRICE DAMIBA.

Canada: Laurenzerberg 2, 1010 Vienna; tel. (1) 531-38-30-00; fax (1) 531-38-39-05; internet www.kanada.at; Ambassador INGRID HALL.

Cape Verde: Schwindgasse 20, 1040 Vienna; tel. (1) 503-87-27; fax (1) 503-87-29; e-mail embcviena@chello.at; Ambassador ALIRIO VICENTE SILVA.

Chile: Lugeck 1/III/10, 1010 Vienna; tel. (1) 512-23-53; fax (1) 512-92-08-33; e-mail echileat@netway.at; Ambassador OSVALDO PUCCIO HUIDOBRO.

China, People's Republic: Metternichgasse 4, 1030 Vienna; tel. (1) 714-31-49-48; fax (1) 713-68-16; Ambassador LIU CHANGYE.

Colombia: Stadiongasse 6–8, 1010 Vienna; tel. (1) 406-44-46; fax (1) 408-83-03; e-mail embcol@atnet.at; Ambassador HÉCTOR CHARRY SAMPER.

Costa Rica: Vienna; tel. (1) 804-05-37; fax (1) 804-90-71; e-mail aviram@aktiv.co.at; Chargé d'affaires STELLA AVIRAM NEUMAN.

Croatia: Heuberggasse 10, 1170 Vienna; tel. (1) 485-95-24; fax (1) 480-29-42; e-mail vlprhbec@reinprecht.at; Ambassador Prof. DRAŽEN VUKOV COLIĆ.

Cuba: Postfach 36; Himmelhofgasse 40A–C, 1130 Vienna; tel. (1) 877-81-98; fax (1) 877-81-98-30; Ambassador JOSÉ R. CABANAS RODRIGUEZ.

Cyprus: Parkring 20, 1010 Vienna; tel. (1) 513-06-30; fax (1) 513-06-32; e-mail embassy2@cyprus.vienna.at; Ambassador STAVROS A. EPAMINONDAS.

Czech Republic: Penzingerstr. 11–13, 1140 Vienna; tel. (1) 894-21-25; fax (1) 894-12-00; e-mail vienna@embassy.mzv.cz; Ambassador JIŘÍ GRUŠA.

Denmark: Postfach 298, Führichgasse 6, 1015 Vienna; tel. (1) 512-79-04-0; fax (1) 513-81-20; Ambassador HENRIK WÖHLK.

Ecuador: Goldschmiedgasse 10/2/24, 1010 Vienna; tel. (1) 535-32-08; fax (1) 535-08-97; e-mail mecaustria@chello.at; Ambassador PATRICIO PALACIOS.

Egypt: Hohe Warte 52, 1190 Vienna; tel. (1) 370-81-04; fax (1) 370-81-04-27; e-mail egyptembassyvienna@egyptembassyvienna.at; Ambassador Dr SAMEH SHOUKAY.

Estonia: Wohllebengasse 9/13, 1040 Vienna; tel. (1) 503-77-61; fax (1) 503-77-61-20; Ambassador Dr MART LAANEMÄE.

Ethiopia: Zaunergasse 1–3, 1030 Vienna; tel. (1) 710-21-68; fax (1) 710-21-71; e-mail ethiopia@eunet.at; Ambassador MENBERE ALEMAYEHU.

Finland: Gonzagagasse 16, 1010 Vienna; tel. (1) 531-59-0; fax (1) 535-57-03; Ambassador TOM CARL ERNST GRÖNBERG.

France: Technikerstr. 2, 1040 Vienna; tel. (1) 505-75-0; fax (1) 505-75-168; e-mail france@netway.at; internet www.ambafrance-at.org; Ambassador JEAN CADET.

Georgia: Marokkanergasse 16, 1030 Vienna; tel. (1) 710-36-11; fax (1) 710-36-10; Ambassador GIORGI ARSENISHVILI.

Germany: Metternichgasse 3, 1030 Vienna; tel. (1) 711-54; fax (1) 713-83-66; internet www.deubowien.magnet.at; Ambassador URSULA SEILER-ALBRING.

Greece: Argentinierstr. 14, 1040 Vienna; tel. (1) 505-57-91; fax (1) 505-62-17; e-mail grembat@aon.at; Ambassador CHRISTOS ALEXANDRIS.

Guatemala: Salesianergasse 25/1/5, 1030 Vienna; tel. (1) 714-35-70; fax (1) 714-35-70-15; Ambassador FEDERICO ADOLFO URRUELA PRADO.

Guinea-Bissau: Vienna; tel. (1) 328-80-62; fax (1) 328-80-63; Chargé d'affaires EDUARD W. BURGE.

Holy See: Theresianumgasse 31, 1040 Vienna; tel. (1) 505-13-27; fax (1) 505-61-40; e-mail nuntius@nuntiatur.at; internet www.nuntiatur.at; Apostolic Nuncio Most Rev. GEORG ZUR.

Hungary: Bankgasse 4–6, 1010 Vienna; tel. (1) 537-80-300; fax (1) 535-99-40; e-mail kom@huembvie.at; Ambassador ETEEKA BARSI-PATAKY.

India: Kärntner Ring 2A, 1015 Vienna; tel. (1) 505-86-66-69; fax (1) 505-92-19; Ambassador YOGESH MOHAN TIWARI.

Indonesia: Gustav-Tschermak-Gasse 5–7, 1180 Vienna; tel. (1) 479-05-37; fax (1) 479-05-57; Ambassador RHOUSDY SOERIATMADJA.

Iran: Jaurèsgasse 9, 1030 Vienna; tel. (1) 712-26-57; fax (1) 713-57-33; e-mail oftab123@chello.at; Ambassador EBRAHIM RAHIM POUR.

Iraq: Johannesgasse 26, 1010 Vienna; tel. (1) 713-81-95; fax (1) 713-67-20; e-mail botschaft_von_irak@utanet.at; Chargé d'affaires KHALID A. NASIR.

Ireland: Rotenturmstr. 16–18, 5th Floor, 1010 Vienna; tel. (1) 715-42-46; fax (1) 713-60-04; e-mail vienna@iveagh.irlgov.ie; Ambassador RONAN MURPHY.

Israel: Anton-Frank-Gasse 20, 1180 Vienna; tel. (1) 470-47-41; fax (1) 470-47-46; Ambassador (vacant) (withdrawn in Feb. 2000).

Italy: Rennweg 27, 1030 Vienna; tel. (1) 712-51-21; fax (1) 713-97-19; e-mail ambitalviepress@via.at; Ambassador Dr PIER LUIGI RACHELE.

Japan: Hessgasse 6, 1010 Vienna; tel. (1) 531-92-0; fax (1) 532-05-90; internet www.embjapan.at; Ambassador YUSHU TAKASHIMA.

Jordan: Doblhoffgasse 3/2, 1010 Vienna; tel. (1) 405-10-25; fax (1) 405-10-31; Ambassador Dr MAZEN ARMOUTI.

Kazakhstan: Vienna; tel. (1) 367-91-75; fax (1) 367-91-74; Ambassador RAKHAT ALIYEV.

Kenya: Neulinggasse 29/8, 1030 Vienna; tel. (1) 712-39-19; fax (1) 712-39-22; e-mail kenyarep-vienna@aon.at.

Korea, Democratic People's Republic: Beckmanngasse 10–12, 1140 Vienna; tel. (1) 894-23-11; fax (1) 894-31-74; Ambassador KIM KWANG SOP.

Korea, Republic: Gregor-Mendel-Str. 25, 1180 Vienna; tel. (1) 478-19-91; fax (1) 478-10-13; e-mail mail@koreaemb.at; Ambassador SONG-DUK CHOI.

Kuwait: Universitätsstr. 5/2, 1010 Vienna; tel. (1) 405-56-46; fax (1) 405-564-639; e-mail kuwaitem@eunet.at; Ambassador NABEELA AL-MULLA.

Kyrgyzstan: Naglergasse 25/5, 1010 Vienna; tel. (1) 535-03-78; fax (1) 535-03-79-131; e-mail kyrbot@kyrbotwien.or.at; Ambassador KAMIL BAIALINOV.

Latvia: Stefan Esders Pl. 4, 1190 Vienna; tel. (1) 403-31-12; fax (1) 403-311-227; e-mail lettbox@netway.at; Ambassador ELITA KUZMA.

Lebanon: Oppolzergasse 6/3, 1010 Vienna; tel. (1) 533-88-21; fax (1) 533-49-84; e-mail ambassade.liban@vienna.telecom.at; Ambassador SAMIR CHAMMA.

Libya: Blaasstr. 33, 1190 Vienna; tel. (1) 367-76-39; fax (1) 367-76-01; Secretary of People's Bureau Dr SAID ABDULAATI MUHAMMAD.

Liechtenstein: Löwelstr. 8/7, 1010 Vienna; tel. (1) 535-92-11; fax (1) 535-92-114; e-mail liechtenstein.embassy.vienna@bvie.li; Ambassador MARIA-PIA KOTHBAUER Princess of Liechtenstein.

Lithuania: Löwengasse 47/4, 1030 Vienna; tel. (1) 718-54-67; fax (1) 718-54-69; e-mail chancery@mail.austria.eu.net; Ambassador JONAS RUDALEVIČIUS.

Luxembourg: Sternwartestr. 81, 1180 Vienna; tel. (1) 478-21-42; fax (1) 478-21-44; Ambassador PAUL FABER.

Macedonia, former Yugoslav republic: Maderstr. 1/10, 1070 Vienna; tel. (1) 524-87-56; fax (1) 524-87-53; e-mail macembassy@24on.cc; Ambassador OGNEN MALESKI.

Malaysia: Prinz-Eugen-Str. 18, 1040 Vienna; tel. (1) 505-10-42-0; fax (1) 505-79-42; e-mail mwvienna@utanet.at; Ambassador HUSSEIN HANIFF.

Malta: Opernring 5/1, 1010 Vienna; tel. (1) 586-50-10; fax (1) 586-50-109; e-mail noboso@aon.at; Ambassador Dr NOEL BUTTIGIEG-SCICLUNA.

Mexico: Vienna; tel. (1) 310-73-83; fax (1) 310-73-87; e-mail embamex@embamex.or.at; Ambassador ROBERTA LAJOUS.

Moldova: Taborstr. 24A, 1020 Vienna; tel. (1) 216-60-03; fax (1) 214-19-97; e-mail amda@netway.at; Ambassador Dr NATALIA GHERMAN.

Morocco: Opernring 3–5/I/4, 1010 Vienna; tel. (1) 586-66-50; fax (1) 586-76-67; e-mail emb-pmissionvienna@morocco.at; Ambassador Dr TAJEDDINE BADDOU.

Namibia: Strozigasse 10/15, 1080 Vienna; tel. (1) 402-93-74; fax (1) 402-93-70; e-mail nam.emb.vienna@eunet.at; Ambassador HINYANGERWA P. ASHEEKE.

Netherlands: Postfach 190, Opernring 5, 1010 Vienna; tel. (1) 589-39; fax (1) 589-39-265; e-mail nlgovwen@eunet.at; internet www.netherlands-embassy.at; Ambassador JAAP RAMAKER.

Nicaragua: Ebendorferstr. 10/3/12, 1010 Vienna; tel. (1) 403-18-38; fax (1) 403-27-52; e-mail 113350.2341@compuserve.com; Ambassador SUYAPA INDIANA PADILLA TERCERO.

Nigeria: Postfach 183, Rennweg 25, 1030 Vienna; tel. (1) 712-66-85; fax (1) 714-14-02; Ambassador ABDULKADER BIN RIMDAP.

Norway: Reisnerstr. 55–57, 1030 Vienna; tel. (1) 715-66-92; fax (1) 712-65-52; e-mail emb.vienna@mfa.no; internet www.norway.at; Ambassador ARNE WALTHER.

Oman: Währingerstr. 2–4/24–25, 1090 Vienna; tel. (1) 310-86-43; fax (1) 310-72-68; Ambassador SALIM M. AR-RIYAMI.

Pakistan: Hofzeile 13, 1190 Vienna; tel. (1) 368-73-81; fax (1) 368-73-76; e-mail parep.vienna@telecom.at; Ambassador (vacant).

Panama: Elisabethstr. 4–5/4/10, 1010 Vienna; tel. (1) 587-23-47; fax (1) 586-30-80; e-mail mail@empanvienna.co.at; Ambassador Dr JORGE ENRIQUE HALPHEN PÉREZ.

Paraguay: Vienna; tel. (1) 715-56-08; fax (1) 715-56-09; e-mail embapar@abacus.at; Chargé d'affaires MARÍA CRISTINA ACOSTA-ALVAREZ.

Peru: Gottfried-Keller-Gasse 2/8, 1030 Vienna; tel. (1) 713-43-77; fax (1) 712-77-04; e-mail embperu.austria@peru.jet2web.at; Ambassador JAVIER PAULINICH.

Philippines: Laurenzerberg 2, 1010 Vienna; tel. (1) 533-24-01; fax (1) 533-24-01-24; e-mail ph.vienna@magnet.at; Ambassador VICTOR G. GARCIA III.

Poland: Hietzinger Hauptstr. 42c, 1130 Vienna; tel. (1) 870-15-804; fax (1) 870-15-331; e-mail oscemis.pl@eunet.at; Ambassador Dr HENRYK SZLAJFER.

Portugal: Opernring 3/1, 1010 Vienna; tel. (1) 586-75-36; fax (1) 586-75-36-99; e-mail portugal@portembassy.at; Ambassador (vacant).

Qatar: Vienna; tel. (1) 479-98-03; fax (1) 478-49-66; Chargé d'affaires SALEH ABDULLAH AL-BOUANIN.

Romania: Prinz-Eugen-Str. 60, 1040 Vienna; tel. (1) 505-32-27; fax (1) 504-14-62; e-mail ambrimviena@nextra.at; Ambassador Dr TRAIAN CHEBELEU.

Russia: Reisnerstr. 45–47, 1030 Vienna; tel. (1) 712-12-29; fax (1) 712-33-88; e-mail rusemb@chello.at; Ambassador ALEXANDR W. GOLOVIN.

San Marino: Getreidemarkt 12, 1010 Vienna; tel. (1) 586-21-80; fax (1) 586-22-35; Ambassador GIOVANNI VITO MARCUCCI.

Saudi Arabia: Parkring 10, 5. Stock, 1010 Vienna; tel. (1) 368-23-16; fax (1) 368-25-60; Ambassador OMAR MUHAMMAD KURDI.

Serbia and Montenegro: Rennweg 3, 1030 Vienna; tel. (1) 713-25-95; fax (1) 713-25-97; e-mail yuambaus@ins.at; Ambassador Dr RADOS SMILJKOVIĆ.

Slovakia: Armbrustergasse 24, 1190 Vienna; tel. (1) 318-90-55-201; fax (1) 318-90-55-208; e-mail zuwien.pol@aon.at; internet www.slovak-trade.at; Ambassador LUBOR BYSTRICKÝ.

Slovenia: Nibelungengasse 13/3, 1010 Vienna; tel. (1) 586-13-09; fax (1) 586-12-65; Ambassador IVO VAJGL.

South Africa: Sandgasse 33, 1190 Vienna; tel. (1) 320-64-93; fax (1) 320-64-93-51; e-mail saembvie@aon.at; internet www.southafrican-embassy.at; Ambassador Prof. ALFRED TOKOLLO MOLEAH.

Spain: Argentinierstr. 34, 1040 Vienna; tel. (1) 505-57-88; fax (1) 505-57-88-25; Ambassador RAIMUNDO PÉREZ-HERNÁNDEZ Y TORRA.

Sri Lanka: Rainergasse 1/2/5, 1040 Vienna; tel. (1) 503-79-88; fax (1) 503-79-93; e-mail embassy@srilanka.at; internet www.embassy.srilanka.at; Ambassador ANIL MOONESINGHE.

Sudan: Reisnerstr. 29/5, 1030 Vienna; tel. (1) 710-23-43; fax (1) 710-23-46; e-mail sudan-embassy-vienna@aon.at; internet www.members.aon.at/sudanivienna; Ambassador ABD EL-GHAFFAR ABD ER-RAHMAN HASSAN.

Sweden: Obere Donaustr. 49–51, 1025 Vienna; tel. (1) 217-53-200; fax (1) 217-53-370; e-mail ambassaden.wien@foreign.ministry.se; Ambassador GABRIELLE LINDHOLM.

Switzerland: Daffingerstr. 4, 1030 Vienna; tel. (1) 533–46–33–5; fax (1) 533–46–33–32; e-mail vienna-embassy@syrianembassy.jet2web.at; Ambassador SAFWAN GHANEM.

Syria: Wallnerstr. 8, 1010 Vienna; tel. (1) 533-46-33; fax (1) 533-46-32; Ambassador Dr RIAD SIAGE.

Tajikistan: Wallnergasse 8, 1090 Vienna; tel. and fax (1) 409-82-66; Ambassador KHAMROKHON ZARIPOV.

Thailand: Cottagegasse 48, 1180 Vienna; tel. (1) 478-27-97; fax (1) 478-29-07; e-mail thai.vn@embthai.telecom.at; Ambassador SORAYOUTH PROMPOJ.

Tunisia: Opernring 5/3, 1010 Vienna; tel. (1) 581-52-81; fax (1) 581-55-92; Ambassador ABDELAZIZ CHAABANE.

Turkey: Prinz-Eugen-Str. 40, 1040 Vienna; tel. (1) 505-73-38-0; fax (1) 505-36-60; e-mail tuerkische-botschat@chello.at; Ambassador A. MITHAT BALKAN.

Turkmenistan: Argentinierstr. 22/11/EG, 1040 Vienna; tel. (1) 503-64-70; fax (1) 503-64-73; e-mail turkmen.del.osce@chello.at; Ambassador VLADIMIR KADYROV.

Ukraine: Naaffgasse 23, 1180 Vienna; tel. (1) 479-71-72; fax (1) 479-71-72-47; e-mail ukremb@netway.at; Ambassador MYKOLA P. MAKAREVYCH.

United Arab Emirates: Peter-Jordan-Str. 66, 1190 Vienna; tel. (1) 368-14-55; fax (1) 368-44-85; Chargé d'affaires AHMAD RASHED AD-DOSARI.

United Kingdom: Jaurèsgasse 12, 1030 Vienna; tel. (1) 716-13-0; fax (1) 716-13-69-00; e-mail info@britishembassy.at; internet www.britishembassy.at; Ambassador ANTONY FORD.

USA: Boltzmanngasse 16, 1090 Vienna; tel. (1) 313-39–0; fax (1) 310-06-82; e-mail embassy@embassy.at; internet www.usembassy.at; Ambassador LYONS BROWN.

Uruguay: Palais Esterhazy, Wallnerstr. 4/3/17, 1010 Vienna; tel. (1) 535-66-36; fax (1) 535-66-18; e-mail uruvien@embuy.or.at; Ambassador FRUCTUOSO PITTALUGA.

Uzbekistan: Porzellangasse 32/5, 1090 Vienna; tel. (1) 315-39-94; fax (1) 315-39-93; e-mail botschaft.usbekistan@aon.at; Chargé d'affaires YAKUBDJAN IRGASHEV.

Venezuela: Marokkanergasse 22, 1030 Vienna; tel. (1) 712-26-38; fax (1) 715-32-19; Ambassador Prof. Dr DEMETRIO BOERSNER.

Viet Nam: Félix-Mottl-Str. 20, 1190 Vienna; tel. (1) 368-07-55; fax (1) 368-07-54; e-mail embassyofvietnam@netway.at; Ambassador NGUYEN XUAN HONG.

Yemen: Karolinengasse 5/7, 1040 Vienna; tel. (1) 503-29-30; fax (1) 505-31-59; e-mail vienna@yemen-embassy.at; Ambassador Dr HASSAN MUHAMMAD MAKKI.

Zimbabwe: Strozzigasse 10/15, 1080 Vienna; tel. (1) 407-92-36; fax (1) 407-92-38; e-mail z.vien@chello.at; Ambassador TIRIVAFI JOHN KANGAI.

Judicial System

The Austrian legal system is based on the principle of a division between legislative, administrative and judicial power. There are three supreme courts (Verfassungsgerichtshof, Verwaltungsgerichtshof and Oberster Gerichtshof). The judicial courts are organized into about 200 local courts (Bezirksgerichte), 17 provincial and district courts (Landes- und Kreisgerichte), and four higher provincial courts (Oberlandesgerichte) in Vienna, Graz, Innsbruck and Linz.

SUPREME ADMINISTRATIVE COURTS

Verfassungsgerichtshof (Constitutional Court): Judenpl.11, 1010 Vienna; tel. (1) 531-22-0; fax (1) 531-22-499; e-mail vfgh@vfgh.gv.at; internet www.vfgh.gv.at; f. 1919; deals with matters affecting the Constitution, examines the legality of legislation and administration; Pres. Prof. Dr KARL KORINEK; Vice-Pres. Dr BRIGITTE BIERLEIN.

Verwaltungsgerichtshof (Administrative Court): Judenpl. 11, 1010 Vienna; tel. (1) 531-11; fax (1) 531-11-135; internet www.vwgh.gv.at; deals with matters affecting the legality of administration; Pres. Prof. Dr CLEMENS JABLONER; Vice-Pres. Prof. Dr WOLFGANG PESENDORFER.

SUPREME JUDICIAL COURT

Oberster Gerichtshof: Schmerlingpl. 10–11, 1016 Vienna; tel. (1) 521-52-0; fax (1) 521-52-37-10; Pres. Dr ERWIN FELZMANN; Vice-Pres Dr HORST SCHLOSSER; Hon. Prof. Dr KONRAD BRUSTBAUER.

Religion

CHRISTIANITY

Ökumenischer Rat der Kirchen in Österreich (Ecumenical Council of Churches in Austria): Fleischmarkt 13, 1010 Vienna; tel. (1) 533-29-65; fax (1) 533-38-89; f. 1958; 14 mem. Churches, 11 observers; Hon. Pres. Bishop MICHAEL STAIKOS (Greek Orthodox Church); Vice-Pres Dr JOHANNES DANTINE (Protestant Church of the Augsburgian Confession); Mother Superior CHRISTINE GLEIXNER (Roman Catholic Church); Sec. Superintendent HELMUT NAUSNER (United Methodist Church).

The Roman Catholic Church

Austria comprises two archdioceses, seven dioceses and the territorial abbacy of Wettingen-Mehrerau (directly responsible to the Holy See). The Archbishop of Vienna is also the Ordinary for Catholics of the Byzantine rite in Austria (totalling an estimated 5,000). At 31 December 2000 there were an estimated 5,872,737 adherents (about 73% of the population).

Bishops' Conference

Österreichische Bischofskonferenz, Wollzeile 2, 1010 Vienna; tel. (1) 516-11-32-80; fax (1) 516-11-34-36; e-mail sekretariat@bischofskonferenz.at; internet www.bischofskonferenz.at. f. 1849; Pres. Cardinal Dr CHRISTOPH SCHÖNBORN (Archbishop of Vienna); Gen. Sec. Mgr Dr ÄGIDIUS ZSIFKOVICS.

Archbishop of Salzburg: Most Rev. Dr GEORG EDER, Postfach 62, 5020 Salzburg, Kapitelpl. 2; 5020 Salzburg; tel. (662) 80-47-100; fax (662) 80-47-75; e-mail ordinariat.sbg@kirchen.net; internet www.kirchen.net.

Archbishop of Vienna: Cardinal Dr CHRISTOPH SCHÖNBORN, Wollzeile 2, 1010 Vienna; tel. (1) 515-52-0; fax (1) 515-52-37-28.

Orthodox Churches

The Armenian Apostolic Church and the Bulgarian, Coptic, Greek, Romanian, Russian, Serbian and Syrian Orthodox Churches are active in Austria.

The Anglican Communion

Within the Church of England, Austria forms part of the diocese of Gibraltar in Europe. The Bishop is resident in London, United Kingdom.

Archdeacon of the Eastern Archdeaconry: Ven. JEREMY PEAKE, Thugutstr. 2/12, 1020 Vienna; tel. and fax (1) 663-92-09-264.

Protestant Churches

Bund der Baptistengemeinden in Österreich (Fed. of Baptist Communities): Krummgasse 7/4, 1030 Vienna; tel. (1) 713-68-28; fax (1) 713-68-28-4; Pres. ANTON KORB.

Evangelische Kirche Augsburgischen Bekenntnisses in Österreich (Protestant Church of the Augsburgian Confession): Severin-Schreiber-Gasse 3, 1180 Vienna; tel. (1) 479-15-23; fax (1) 479-15-23-110; e-mail bischof@okr-evang.at; internet www.evang.at; 330,880 mems; Bishop Mag. HERWIG STURM.

Evangelische Kirche HB (Helvetischen Bekenntnisses) (Protestant Church of the Helvetic Confession): Dorotheergasse 16, 1010 Vienna; tel. (1) 513-65-64; fax (1) 512-44-90; e-mail kirche-hb@evang.at; 13,994 mems (2002); Landessuperintendent Hofrat Pfarrer Mag. PETER KARNER.

Evangelisch-methodistische Kirche (United Methodist Church): Sechshauser Str. 56, 1150 Vienna; tel. and fax (1) 604-53-47; e-mail info@emk.at; internet www.emk.at; Superintendent LOTHAR PÖLL.

Other Christian Churches

Altkatholische Kirche Österreichs (Old Catholic Church in Austria): Schottenring 17, 1010 Vienna; tel. (1) 317-83-94; fax (1) 317-83-94-9; e-mail bischof.heitz@altkatholiken.at; internet www.altkatholiken.at; c. 18,000 mems; Bishop BERNHARD HEITZ.

JUDAISM

There are about 10,000 Jews in Austria.

Israelitische Kultusgemeinde (Jewish Community): Seitenstettengasse 4, 1010 Vienna; tel. (1) 531-04-0; fax (1) 531-04-109; e-mail office@ikg-wien.at; internet www.ikg-wien.at; Pres. Dr ARIEL MUZICANT.

The Press

Austria's first newspaper was published in 1605. The *Wiener Zeitung*, founded in 1703, is the world's oldest daily newspaper. Restrictions on press freedom are permissible only within the framework of Article 10 (2) of the European Convention on Human Rights.

The Austrian Press Council (Presserat), founded in 1961, supervises the activities of the press. Vienna is the focus of newspaper and periodical publishing, although there is also a strong press in some provinces. The three highest circulation dailies are the *Neue Kronen-Zeitung* the *Kurier* and the *Kleine Zeitung* (Graz).

PRINCIPAL DAILIES

Bregenz

Neue Vorarlberger Tageszeitung: Arlbergstr. 117, 6901 Bregenz; tel. (5574) 40-90; fax (5574) 40-93-00; f. 1972; morning; independent; Editor (vacant); circ. 20,136.

Vorarlberger Nachrichten: Gutenbergstr. 1, 6858 Schwarzach; tel. (5572) 501-0; fax (5572) 501-227; internet www.vmh.at; morning; Editor EUGEN A. RUSS; circ. 74,948.

Graz

Kleine Zeitung: Schönaugasse 64, 8011 Graz; tel. (316) 87-50; fax (316) 87-54-03-4; internet www.kleine.co.at; f. 1904; independent; Chief Editor Dr ERWIN ZANKEL; circ. 177,050.

Innsbruck

Tiroler Tageszeitung: Ing.-Etzel-Str. 30, 6020 Innsbruck; tel. (512) 53-54-0; fax (512) 57-59-24; e-mail redaktion@tt.com; internet www.tirol.com/tt; morning; independent; Chief Editor CLAUS REITAN; circ. 112,690.

Klagenfurt

Kärntner Tageszeitung: Viktringer Ring 28, 9020 Klagenfurt; tel. (463) 58-66-0; fax (463) 58-66-32-1; f. 1946; morning except Monday; Socialist; Chief Editor Dr HELLWIG VALENTIN.

Kleine Zeitung: Funderstr. 1A, 9020 Klagenfurt; tel. (463) 200-58-00; fax (463) 56-50-0; independent; Editor Dr HORST PIRKER; circ. 99,380.

Linz

Neues Volksblatt: Hafenstr. 1–3, 4010 Linz; tel. (732) 76-06-0; fax (732) 77-92-42; e-mail volksblatt@volksblatt.at; internet www.volksblatt.at; f. 1869; organ of Austrian People's Party; Chief Editor Dr FRANZ ROHRHOFER.

Oberösterreichische Nachrichten: Promenade 23, 4010 Linz; tel. (732) 78-05-41-0; fax (732) 78-05-21-7; internet www.oon.at; f. 1865; morning; independent; Chief Editor Dr HANS KÖPPL; circ. 123,470.

Salzburg

Salzburger Nachrichten: Karolingerstr. 40, 5021 Salzburg; tel. (662) 83-73-0; fax (662) 83-73-39-9; e-mail service@salzburg.com; internet www.salzburg.com; f. 1945; morning; independent; Editor-in-Chief RONALD ARAZON; circ. 99,123.

Salzburger Volkszeitung: Bergstr. 12, 5020 Salzburg; tel. (662) 87-94-91; fax (662) 87-94-91-13; e-mail suz-redaktion@sbg.at; organ of Austrian People's Party; Editor HELMUT MÖDLHAMMER; circ. weekdays 12,030.

Vienna

Kurier: Seidengasse 11, 1072 Vienna; tel. (1) 521-00; fax (1) 521-00-22-63; e-mail leser@kurier.at; internet www2.kurier.at; f. 1954; independent; Chief Editor PETER RABL; circ. weekdays 334,204, Sunday 545,700.

Neue Kronen-Zeitung: Muthgasse 2, 1190 Vienna; tel. (1) 360-10; fax (1) 369-83-85; internet www.krone.at; f. 1900; independent; Editor HANS DICHAND; circ. weekdays 510,226, Sunday 751,296.

Die Presse: Parkring 12A, 1015 Vienna; tel. (1) 514-14; fax (1) 514-14-400; e-mail chefredaktion@diepresse.com; internet www.diepresse.com; f. 1848; morning; independent; Editor JULIUS KAINZ; circ. Mon.–Wed. 105,000, Thur.–Fri. 115,000, Sat. 195,000.

Der Standard: Herrengasse 19–21, 1014 Vienna; tel. (1) 531-70; fax (1) 531-70-13-1; e-mail documentation@derstandard.at; internet www.derstandard.at; f. 1988; independent; Editors-in-Chief OSCAR BRONNER, Dr GERFRIED SPERL; circ. 104,050.

Wiener Zeitung: Wiedner Gürtel 10, 1040 Vienna; tel. (1) 206-99-0; fax (1) 206-99-733; e-mail redaktion@wienerzeitung.at; internet www.wienerzeitung.at; f. 1703; morning; official govt paper; Editors PETER BOCHSKAN, HANZ FAHNLER; circ. 20,020.

PRINCIPAL WEEKLIES

Blickpunkt: E.-Bodem-Gasse 6, 6020 Innsbruck; tel. (512) 32-00; fax (512) 32-01-20; Editor OTTO STEIXNER.

Die Furche: Vienna; tel. (1) 512-52-61; fax (1) 512-82-15; f. 1945; Catholic; Editor Dr GOTTFRIED MOIK.

Die Ganze Woche: Ignaz-Köck-Str. 17, 1210 Vienna; tel. (1) 391-60-0; fax (1) 391-60-06-4; circ. 582,060.

IW-Internationale Wirtschaft: Nikolsdorfer Gasse 7–11, 1051 Vienna; tel. (1) 546-64-346; fax (1) 546-64-342; economics; Editor NIKOLAUS GERSTMAYER; circ. 13,430.

Kärntner Nachrichten: Stauderpl. 5, 9020 Klagenfurt; tel. (463) 511515; fax (463) 511515-51; e-mail office@abc-werbeagentur.at; f. 1954; Editors ARMIN HORDESCH, HELMUT PRASCH.

Die Neue Wirtschaft: Nikolsdorfer Gasse 7–11, 1051 Vienna; tel. (1) 546-64-24-7; fax (1) 546-64-34-7; economics; circ. 25,650.

Neue Wochenschau: J. N. Bergerstr. 2, 7210 Mattersburg; tel. and fax (2622) 67-47-3; f. 1908; Editor HELMUT WALTER; circ. 128,500.

NFZ (Neue Freie Zeitung): Postfach 81, 1013 Vienna; Esslinggasse 14–16, 1010 Vienna; tel. (1) 512-35-35-311; fax (1) 512-35-35-412; e-mail redaktion.nfz@fpoe.at; organ of Freedom Party; Chief Editor MICHAEL A. RICHTER; circ. 70,000.

Niederösterreichische Nachrichten: Gutenbergstr. 12, 3100 St Pölten; tel. (2742) 80-20; fax (2742) 80-21-48-0; e-mail chefredaktion@noen.at; internet www.noen.at; Editor HARALD KNABL; circ. 158,972.

Oberösterreichische Rundschau: Hafenstr. 1–3, 4010 Linz; tel. (732) 76-16-0; fax (732) 76-16-30-7; Editor-in-Chief RUDOLF CHMELIR; circ. 284,650.

Der Österreichische Bauernbündler: Vienna; tel. (1) 533-16-76-16; fax (1) 533-16-76-45; Editor Prof. PAUL GRUBER; circ. 70,000.

Präsent: Exlgasse 20, 6020 Innsbruck; tel. (512) 22-33; fax (512) 22-33-50-1; f. 1892; independent Catholic; Chief Editor PAUL MVIGG.

Samstag: Vienna; tel. (1) 795-94-13-5; e-mail samstag@heroldwien .at; f. 1951; weekly; independent; Chief Editor GERLINDE KOLANDA; circ. 41,000.

Tiroler Bauernzeitung: Brixner Str. 1, 6021 Innsbruck; tel. (512) 59-90-00; fax (1) 59-90-03-1; publ. by Tiroler Bauernbund; Chief Dir GEORG KEUSCHNIGG; circ. 23,000.

Volksstimme: Weyringergasse 35/DG, 1040 Vienna; tel. (1) 503-68-28; fax (1) 503-66-38; e-mail redaktion@volksstimme.at; f. 1994; Chief Editor WALTER BAIER.

POPULAR PERIODICALS

Agrar Post: Schulstr. 64, 2103 Langenzersdorf; tel. (2244) 46-47; f. 1924; monthly; agriculture.

Austria-Ski: Olympiastr. 10, 6020 Innsbruck; tel. (512) 335-01-0; fax (512) 361-99-8; 6 a year; official journal of Austrian Skiing Asscn; Editor JOSEF SCHMID.

Auto Touring: Tauchnergasse 5, 3400 Klosterneuburg; tel. (2243) 40-40; fax (2243) 40-43-72-1; e-mail elisabeth.pechmann@oeamtc.at; monthly; official journal of the Austrian Automobile Organizations; Editor-in-Chief ELISABETH PECHMANN; circ. 1,240,000.

Bunte Österreich: Vienna; tel. (1) 712-95-10; fax (1) 712-95-59; illustrated weekly.

Frauenblatt: Faradaygasse 6, 1032 Vienna; tel. (1) 795-94-13-5; e-mail samstag@heroldwien.at; women's weekly; Editor KURT MAR-KARITZER; circ. 22,300.

Die Neue Sportzeitung: Vienna; tel. (1) 405-55-88; fax (1) 402-49-60; e-mail redaktion@sportzeitung.at; internet www.sportzeitung .at; f. 1949; weekly sports illustrated; Editor HORST HÖTSCH; circ. 28,330.

News: Praterstr. 31, 1020 Vienna; tel. (1) 213-12-0; fax (1) 213-12-30-0; weekly; illustrated; Editor WOLFGANG FELLNER; circ. 342,244.

Profil: Lindengasse 52, 1070 Vienna; tel. (1) 534-70-0; fax (1) 535-32-50; e-mail redaktion@profil.at; internet www.profil.at; f. 1970; weekly; political, general; independent; circ. 100,000.

RZ (Wochenschau): Lilienbrumgasse 7–9, 1020 Vienna; tel. (1) 553-55-0; fax (1) 553-55-10-11; f. 1936; weekly illustrated; Chief Editor PAUL WEISS.

Trend: Marc-Aurel-Str. 10–12, 1010 Vienna; tel. (1) 534-70; monthly; economics.

TV Media: Taborstr. 1–3, 1020 Vienna; tel. (1) 213-120; weekly; illustrated; Editor WOLFGANG FELLNER; circ. 210,150.

Vídeňské svobodné listy: Margaretenpl. 7/2, 1050 Vienna; tel. (1) 587-83-08; fortnightly for Czech and Slovak communities in Austria; Editor HEINRICH DRAZDIL.

Welt der Frau: Lustenauerstr. 21, 4020 Linz; tel. (732) 77-00-01-11; fax (732) 77-00-01-24; women's monthly magazine; circ. 73,530.

Wiener: Lifestyle Zeitschriften Verlag GmbH, Davidgasse 79, A-1100 Vienna; tel. (1) 601–17–249; fax (1) 601–17–350; monthly; Chief Editor PETER MOSSER; circ. 85,000.

SPECIALIST PERIODICALS

Eurocity: Leberstr. 122, 1110 Vienna; tel. (1) 740-95-46-4; fax (1) 740-95-49-1; e-mail karp.zv@bohmann.at; internet www.eurocity.at; f. 1928; every 2 months; Editor-in-Chief GEORG KARP; circ. 70,000.

Forum: Vienna; tel. (1) 932-73-3; fax (1) 938-36-8; f. 1954; every 2 months; international magazine for cultural freedom, political equality and labour solidarity; Editor-in-Chief GERHARD OBERSCHLICK.

Itm Praktiker: ZB-Verlag, Marochallpl. 23/1/21, 1125 Vienna; tel. (1) 804-04-74; fax (1) 804-44-39; technical hobbies; Chief Editor GERHARD K. BUCHBERGER; circ. 18,800.

Juristische Blätter (mit Beilage 'Wirtschaftsrechtliche Blätter'): Springer Verlag, Sachsenpl. 4, 1201 Vienna; tel. (1) 330-24-15-

0; fax (1) 330-24-26; internet www.springer.at/jbl; f. 1872; monthly; nine editors.

Die Landwirtschaft: Wiener Str. 64, 3100 St Pölten; tel. (2742) 259-93-00; e-mail presse@lk-noe.at; internet www.lk-noe.at; f. 1923; monthly; agriculture and forestry; owned and publ. by Österreichischer Agrarverlag; Editor GERD RITTENAUER.

Liberale Zeichen: Vienna; tel. (1) 503-06-67; fax (1) 503-06-67-20; e-mail office@lif.at; internet www.lif.at; 4 a year; organ of Liberal Forum.

Literatur und Kritik: Otto-Müller-Verlag, Ernest-Thun-Str. 11, 5020 Salzburg; tel. (662) 88-19-74; fax (662) 87-23-87; e-mail email otto.muellerverlag@salzburg.co.at; f. 1966; 5 a year; Austrian and European literature and criticism; Editor KARL-MARKUS GAUSS.

Monatshefte für Chemie: Sachsenpl. 4–6, 1201 Vienna; tel. (1) 330-24-15-0; fax (1) 330-24-26; e-mail journals@springer.at; internet www.springer.at/mochem; f. 1880; monthly; chemistry; Man. Editor H. FALK.

Oeffentliche Sicherheit: Herrengasse 7, 1014 Vienna; tel. (1) 531-26-0; fax (1) 531-26-39-10; 6 a year; published by the Ministry of the Interior; circ. 15,000.

Österreichische Ärztezeitung: Weihburggasse 9, 1010 Vienna; tel. (1) 512-44-86; fax (1) 512-44-86-24; e-mail presse.verlags@oak .at; f. 1945; 21 a year; organ of the Austrian Medical Board; Editor MARTIN STICKLER.

Österreichische Ingenieur- und Architekten-Zeitschrift (ÖIAZ): Eschenbachgasse 9, 1010 Vienna; tel. (1) 587-35-36-0; fax (1) 587-35-36-5; e-mail office@oiav.at; internet www.oiav.at; f. 1849; 6 a year; Editor Dr GEORG WIDTMANN; circ. 3,000.

Österreichische Monatshefte: Lichtenfelsgasse 7, 1010 Vienna; tel. (1) 401-26-53-2; f. 1945; monthly; organ of Austrian People's Party; Editor GERHARD WILFLINGER.

Österreichische Musikzeitschrift: Hegelgasse 13, 1010 Vienna; tel. (1) 512-68-69; fax (1) 512-68-69-9; e-mail order@musikzeit.at; internet internet www.musikzeit.at; f. 1946; monthly; Editor Dr M. DIEDERICHS-LAFITE; circ. 5,000.

Reichsbund-Aktuell mit SPORT: Laudongasse 16, 1080 Vienna; tel. and fax (1) 405-54-06; e-mail info@amateurfussball.at; internet www.amateurfussball.at; f. 1917; monthly; Catholic; organ of Reichsbund, Bewegung für christliche Gesellschaftspolitik und Sport; Editor WALTER RAMING; circ. 12,000.

Welt der Arbeit: Altmannsdorferstr. 154–156, 1230 Vienna; tel. (1) 662-32-96; socialist industrial journal; Editor WALTER KRATZER; circ 64,350.

Wiener Klinische Wochenschrift: Sachsenpl. 4–6, 1201 Vienna; tel. (1) 330-24-15; fax (1) 330-24-26; e-mail journals@springer.at; internet www.springer.at/wkw; f. 1888; medical bi-weekly; Editors W. DRUML, H. SINZINGER.

Die Zukunft: Löwelstr. 18, 1014 Vienna; tel. (1) 534-27-20-6; fax (1) 535-96-83; monthly; organ of Social-Democratic Party of Austria; Editor ALBRECHT K. KONECNY; circ. 15,000.

NEWS AGENCIES

APA (Austria Presse-Agentur): Internationales Pressezentrum (IPZ), Gunoldstr. 14, 1199 Vienna; tel. (1) 360-60-0; fax (1) 360-60-30-99; e-mail marketing@apa.at; internet www.apa.at; f. 1946; co-operative agency of the Austrian Newspapers and Broadcasting Co (private co); 37 mems; Man. Dir Dr WOLFGANG VYSLOZIL; Chief Editor WOLFGANG MAYR.

Foreign Bureaux

Agence France-Presse (AFP) (France): Vienna; tel. (1) 368-31-87; fax (1) 368-31-88-20; e-mail afpvie@afp.com; Bureau Chief PATRICK RAHIR.

Agenzia Nazionale Stampa Associata (ANSA) (Italy): IPZ, Gunoldstr. 14, 1199 Vienna; tel. (1) 368-13-00; fax (1) 368-79-35; Bureau Chief ROBERTO PAPI.

Associated Press (AP) (USA): IPZ, Gunoldstr. 14, 1199 Vienna; tel. (1) 368-41-56; fax (1) 369-15-58; Bureau Chief ROBERT REID.

Central News Agency (CNA) (Taiwan): Vienna; tel. (1) 799-17-02; fax (1) 798-45-98; Bureau Chief OU CHUN-LIN.

Česká tisková kancelář (ČTK) (Czech Republic): Vienna; tel. and fax (1) 439-21-8.

Deutsche Presse-Agentur (dpa) (Germany): IPZ, Gunoldstr. 14, 1199 Vienna; tel. (1) 368-21-58; fax (1) 369-85-49.

Informatsionnoye Telegrafnoye Agentstvo Rossii–Telegrafnoye Agentstvo Suverennykh Stran (ITAR–TASS) (Russia): Grosse Neugasse 28, 1040 Vienna; tel. (1) 810-43-1; fax (1) 566-53-6; Correspondent ALEKSANDR S. KUZMIN.

Jiji Tsushin (Japan): IPZ, Gunoldstr. 14, 1199 Vienna; tel. (1) 369-17-97; fax (1) 369-10-52; Bureau Chief NOBUYUKI SATO.

Kyodo Tsushin (Japan): IPZ, Gunoldstr. 14/130, 1199 Vienna; tel. (1) 368-15-20; fax (1) 369-92-52-2; e-mail kyodowien@apanet.at; internet www.kyodo.co.jp; Bureau Chief MASATOSHI NAGATA.

Magyar Távirati Iroda (MTI) (Hungary): Vienna; tel. and fax (1) 876-69-94; Correspondent ZSÓFIA FÜLEP.

Reuters (UK): Börsegasse 11, 1010 Vienna; tel. (1) 531-12-0; fax (1) 531-12-5; e-mail marketing@reuters.at; internet www.reuters.at; Bureau Chief RICHARD MURPHY.

Xinhua (New China) News Agency (People's Republic of China): Reisnerstr. 15/8, 1030 Vienna; tel. (1) 713-41-40; fax (1) 714-14-57; Chief Correspondent YANG HUANQIN.

PRESS ASSOCIATIONS

Österreichischer Zeitschriften- und Fachmedien-Verband (Asscn of Periodical Publrs): Renngasse 12/6, 1010 Vienna; tel. and fax (1) 319-70-01; e-mail oezv@oezv.or.at; internet www.oezv.or.at; f. 1946; 176 mems; Pres. Dr RUDOLF BOHMANN; Man. Dir Dr WOLFGANG BRANDSTETTER.

Verband Österreichischer Zeitungen (Newspaper Asscn of Austria): Renngasse 12, 1010 Vienna; tel. (1) 533-79-79-0; fax (1) 533-79-79-22; e-mail gs@voez.at; internet www.voez.at; f. 1946; 16 daily and most weekly papers are mems; Pres. FRANZ IVAN; Sec.-Gen. Dr WALTER SCHAFFELHOFER.

Publishers

Akademische Druck- und Verlagsanstalt: Postfach 598, Auersperggasse 12, 8010 Graz; tel. (316) 36-44; fax (316) 36-44-24; e-mail info@adeva.com; internet www.adeva.com; f. 1949; scholarly reprints and new works, facsimile editions of Codices, fine art facsimile editions; Dir Dr URSULA STRUZL.

Alekto Verlag GmbH: Klagenfurt; tel. (463) 515230; fax (463) 503351; e-mail bali@bali.co.at; literature; Man. Dir STEFAN ZEFFERER.

Betz, Annette, Verlag GmbH: Alser Str. 24, 1091 Vienna; tel. (1) 404-44-0; fax (1) 404-44-5; internet www.annettebetz.com; f. 1962; Man. Dir Dr JOHANNA RACHINGER.

Blackwell Wissenschafts-Verlag GmbH: Firmiangasse 7, 1130 Vienna; tel. (1) 877-93-51-0; fax (1) 877-93-51-24; e-mail verlag@ blackwell.at; internet www.blackwell.de; f. 1989; medicine, medical journals; Dir WILLIAM ANTHONY ATTWOOD.

Böhlau Verlag GmbH & Co KG: Sachsenpl. 4–6, 1201 Vienna; tel. (1) 330-24-27; fax (1) 330-24-32; e-mail boehlau@boehlau.at; internet www.boehlau.at; f. 1947; history, law, philology, the arts, sociology; Dirs Dr PETER RAUCH, RUDOLF SIEGLE.

Bohmann Fachbuch im Verlag Jugend & Volk: Universitätsstr. 11, 1010 Vienna; tel. (1) 407-27-07; fax (1) 407-27-07-22; e-mail verlag@jugendvolk.at; internet www.jugendvolk.at; f. 1936; trade, technical and educational books.

Christian Brandstätter, Verlag und Edition: Schwarzenbergstr. 5, 1010 Vienna; tel. (1) 512-15-43-233; fax (1) 512-15-43-231; e-mail cbv@oebv.co.at; f. 1982; art books; Chair. Dr CHRISTIAN BRANDSTÄTTER.

Wilhelm Braumüller Universitätsverlagsbuchhandlung, GmbH: Servitengasse 5, 1092 Vienna; tel. (1) 319-11-59; fax (1) 310-28-05; e-mail office@braumueller.at; internet www.braumueller.at; f. 1783; sociology, politics, history, law, ethnology, linguistics, journalism, communications, psychology, philosophy, literature and theatre; university publrs; Dirs BRIGITTE PFEIFER, KONSTANZE WEBER.

Czernin Verlag GmbH: Piaristengasse 1, 1080 Vienna; tel. (1) 512-01-32; fax (1) 512-01-32-15; e-mail office@czernin-verlag.com; internet www.czernin-verlag.com.

Franz Deuticke Verlagsgesellschaft mbH: Hegelgasse 21, 1010 Vienna; tel. (1) 512-15-44-281; fax (1) 512-15-44-289; e-mail info@ deuticke.at; internet www.deuticke.at; f. 1878; culture, literature, non-fiction; Dirs Dr ROBERT SEDLACZEK, Dr MARTINA SCHMIDT.

Ludwig Doblinger Musikhaus-Musikverlag: Dorotheergasse 10, 1010 Vienna; tel. (1) 515-03-0; fax (1) 515-03-51; e-mail music@ doblinger.co.at; internet www.doblinger.at; f. 1876; music; Dir HELMUTH PANY.

Edition Ergo Sum: Kaltenleutgeben, f. as Anna Pichler Verlag GmbH; present name adopted 2000.

Freytag-Berndt und Artaria KG Kartographische Anstalt: Brunnerstr. 69, 1231 Vienna; tel. (1) 869-90-90; fax (1) 869-88-55; e-mail sales@freytag-berndt.at; internet www.freytag-berndt.at; f. 1879; 1770—Artaria; geography, maps and atlases; Chair. Dr CHRISTIAN HALBWACHE.

Gerold & Co: Vienna; tel. (1) 533-50-14; fax (1) 533-50-14-18; f. 1867; philology, literature, eastern Europe, sociology and philosophy; Dir PETER NEUSSER.

Jugend and Volk GmbH: Universitätsstr. 11, 1016 Vienna; tel. (1) 407-27-07; fax (1) 407-27-07-22; e-mail verlag@jugendvolk.at; internet www.jugendvolk.at; f. 1921; pedagogics, textbooks.

Kunstverlag Wolfrum: Augustinerstr. 10, 1010 Vienna; tel. (1) 512-53-98-0; fax (1) 512-53-98-57; e-mail wolfrum@utanet.at; f. 1919; art; Dir HUBERT WOLFRUM.

Leykam Verlag: Stempfergasse 3, 8011 Graz; tel. (316) 80-76; fax (316) 80-76-39; f. 1585; art, literature, academic, law; Dir Dr KLAUS BRUNNER.

Linde Verlag Wien: Scheydgasse 24, 1211 Vienna; tel. (1) 278-05-26; fax (1) 278-05-26-23; e-mail office@lindeverlag.at; internet www .lindeverlag.at; f. 1925; business; Man. Dir ANDREAS JENTZSCH.

Manz'sche Verlags- und Universitätsbuchhandlung GmbH: Kohlmarkt 16, 1014 Vienna; tel. (1) 531-61-0; fax (1) 531-61-181; e-mail verlag@manz.at; f. 1849; law, political and economic sciences; textbooks and school-books; Chief Execs Dr KRISTIN HANUSCH-LINSER, LUCAS SCHNEIDER-MANNS-AU.

Wilhelm Maudrich: Spitalgasse 21A, 1096 Vienna; tel. (1) 408-58-92; fax (1) 408-50-80; e-mail medbook@maudrich.com; internet www .maudrich.com; f. 1909; medical; Man. Dir GERHARD GROIS.

Molden Verlag GmbH: Stadiongasse 6–8, 1010 Vienna; tel. (1) 403-94-09; fax (1) 402-17-55.

Otto Müller Verlag: Ernest-Thun-Str. 11, 5020 Salzburg; tel. (662) 88-19-74; fax (662) 87-23-87; e-mail info.otto_mueller@tera.net; f. 1937; general; Man. ARNO KLEIBEL.

Öbv & hpt Verlagsgesellschaft mbH: Frankgasse 4, 1090 Vienna; tel. (1) 401-36; fax (1) 401-36-185; e-mail office@oebvhpt.at.

Pinguin Verlag Pawlowski GmbH: Lindenbühelweg 2, 6021 Innsbruck; tel. (512) 28-11-83; fax (512) 29-32-43; f. 1945; illustrated books; Dir OLAF PAWLOWSKI.

Residenz Verlag GmbH: Gaisbergstr. 6, 5020 Salzburg; tel. (662) 64-19-86; fax (662) 64-35-48; e-mail info@residenzverlag.at; internet www.residenzverlag.at; f. 1956; Dir Dr MARTINA SCHMIDT.

Anton Schroll & Co: Spengergasse 37, 1051 Vienna; tel. (1) 544-56-41; fax (1) 544-56-41-66; f. 1884; also in Munich; art; Man. F. GEYER.

Springer-Verlag KG: Sachsenpl. 4–6, 1201 Vienna; tel. (1) 330-24-15; fax (1) 330-24-26; e-mail springer@springer.at; internet www .springer.at; f. 1924; medicine, science, technology, law, sociology, economics, architecture, art, periodicals; Man. Dir RUDOLF SIEGLE.

Leopold Stocker Verlag: Hofgasse 5, 8011 Graz; tel. (316) 82-16-36; fax (316) 83-56-12; f. 1917; history, nature, hunting, fiction, agriculture, textbooks; Dir WOLFGANG DVORAK-STOCKER.

Carl Ueberreuter Verlag: Alserstr. 24, 1091 Vienna; tel. (1) 404-44-0; fax (1) 404-44-5; e-mail office@vcu.ueberreuter.com; internet www.ueberreuter.at; non-fiction, children's; Chief Exec. JOHANNA RACHINGER.

Universal Edition: Brucknerstr. 6, 1040 Vienna; tel. (1) 337-23-0; fax (1) 337-23-40-0; e-mail office@universaledition.com; internet www.universaledition.com; f. 1901; music; Dir Dr J. JURANEK; Dir. MARION VON HARTLIEB.

Urban & Schwarzenberg GmbH: Frankgasse 4, 1096 Vienna; tel. (1) 405-27-31; fax (1) 405-27-24-41; f. 1866; science, medicine; Dir GUNTER ROYER.

Verlag Kerle im Verlag Herder & Co: Wollzeile 33, 1010 Vienna; tel. (1) 512-14-13; fax (1) 512-14-13-60; f. 1886; children's books, juvenile.

Verlag Kremayr & Scheriau: Ungargasse 45/13, 1030 Vienna; tel. (1) 713-87-70-0; fax (1) 713-87-70-20; f. 1951; non-fiction, history.

Verlag Oldenbourg: Neulinggasse 26/12, 1030 Vienna; tel. (1) 712-62-58; fax (1) 712-62-58-19; e-mail gala@oldenbourg.co.at; f. 1959; Dir Dr THOMAS CORNIDES.

Verlag Orac: Graben 17, 1010 Vienna; tel. (1) 534-52; fax (1) 534-52-14-1; e-mail bestellung@orac.at; internet www.orac.at; f. 1946; Dir Dr DIETRICH SCHERF.

Verlag Styria: Schönaugasse 64, 8011 Graz; tel. (316) 80-63-0; fax (316) 80-63-70-04; e-mail skaiser@styria.co.at; f. 1869; literature, history, theology, philosophy; Chair. Dr REINHARD HABER-FELLNER.

Verlagsanstalt Tyrolia GmbH: Postfach 220, Exlgasse 20, 6020 Innsbruck; tel. (512) 22-33-202; fax (512) 22-33-206; e-mail buchverlag@tyrolia.at; internet www.tyrolia.at; f. 1888; geography, history, science, children's, religion, fiction; Chair. Dr GOTTFRIED KOMPATSCHER.

Verlagsbuchhandlung Brüder Hollinek und Co GmbH: Luisenstr. 20, 3002 Purkersdorf; tel. and fax (2231) 673-65; f. 1872;

science, law and administration, printing, reference works, dictionaries; Dir RICHARD HOLLINEK.

Paul Zsolnay Verlag GmbH: Prinz-Eugen-Str. 30, 1041 Vienna; tel. (1) 505-76-61; fax (1) 505-76-61-10; e-mail info@zsolnay.at; internet www.zsolnay.at; f. 1923; fiction, non-fiction; Dirs MICHAEL KRÜGER, STEPHAN D. JOSS.

Government Publishing House

Verlag Österreich (Austrian Publishing House): Rennweg 16, 1037 Vienna; tel. (1) 797-89-407; fax (1) 797-89-419; e-mail verlag-oesterreich@verlag.oesd.co.at; f. 1804; law, CD-ROMs.

PUBLISHERS' ASSOCIATION

Hauptverband des Österreichischen Buchhandels (Asscn of Austrian Publrs and Booksellers): Grünangergasse 4, 1010 Vienna; tel. (1) 512-15-35; fax (1) 512-84-82; e-mail sekretariat@hvb.at; internet www.buecher.at; f. 1859; Pres. Dr ANTON C. HILSCHER; 605 mems.

Broadcasting and Communications

TELECOMMUNICATIONS

Rundfunk und Telekom Regulierungs GmbH: Mariahilferstr. 77–79, 1060 Vienna; tel. (1) 580-58-0; fax (1) 580-58-91-91; e-mail rtr@rtr.at; internet www.rtr.at; f. 1997 as Telekom-Control GmbH; regulatory body for the broadcasting and telecommunications sector.

Telekom Austria AG: Schwarzenbergpl. 3, 1010 Vienna; tel. and fax (1) 590-59-1; e-mail kundenservice@telekom.at; internet www.telekom.at; f. 1998; Dir-Gen. HEINZ SUNDT.

Connect Austria Gesellschaft für Telekommunikation GmbH: Brunnerstr. 52, 1210 Vienna; tel. (1) 277-28-0; internet www.connectaustria.at; Chair. FRANZ GEIGER.

Max.mobil Telekommunikation Service GmbH: Kelsenstr. 5–7, 1030 Vienna; tel. (1) 795-85-0; fax (1) 795-85-53-2; internet www.maxmobil.at; Chair. Dr STEPHAN HUXOLD.

Mobilkom Austria AG & Co KG: Obere Donaustr. 29, 1020 Vienna; tel. (1) 331-61-0; internet www.mobilkom.at.

Tele.ring Telekom Service GmbH & Co KG: Hainburgerstr. 33, 1030 Vienna; tel. (1) 931-01-20; e-mail info@telering.co.at; internet www.telering.at; 54% owned by Mannesmann AG (Germany).

RADIO AND TELEVISION

The state-owned Österreichischer Rundfunk (ORF) provides three national and nine regional radio channels, as well as an overseas service. The ORF also has two terrestrial television channels, and operates a satellite station in conjunction with German and Swiss companies. While the ORF retains a monopoly over television broadcasting in Austria, the provision of radio services was liberalized in 1998, when a number of commercial radio stations were launched.

Österreichischer Rundfunk (ORF) (Austrian Broadcasting Company): Würzburggasse 30, 1136 Vienna; tel. (1) 87878-0; fax (1) 878-78-12250; e-mail kundendienst@orf.at; internet www.orf.at; f. 1924; state-owned; Dir-Gen. Dr MONIKA LINDNER; Dirs Dr REINHARD DRAXLER (Television), KURT RAMMERSTORFER (Radio).

Finance

(cap. = capital; res = reserves; dep. = deposits; m. = million; brs = branches; amounts in Schilling or euros—€)

BANKS

Banks in Austria, apart from the National Bank, belong to one of five categories. The first category comprises banks that are organized as corporations (i.e. joint-stock and private banks), and special-purpose credit institutions; the second category comprises savings banks; and the third category comprises co-operative banks. Co-operative banks include rural credit co-operatives (Raiffeisenbanken) and industrial credit co-operatives (Volksbanken). The remaining two categories comprise the mortgage banks of the various Austrian Länder, and the building societies. The majority of Austrian banks (with the exception of the building societies) operate on the basis of universal banking, although certain categories have specialized. Banking operations are governed by the Banking Act of 1993 (Bankwesengesetz–BWG).

Central Bank

Oesterreichische Nationalbank (Austrian National Bank): Postfach 61, Otto-Wagner-Pl. 3, 1090 Vienna; tel. (1) 404-20-0; fax (1) 404-20-66-96; e-mail oenb.info@oenb.co.at; internet www.oenb.at; f. 1922; 50% state-owned; cap. €12m., res €4,235m., dep. €7,957m. (Dec. 2001); Pres. ADOLF WALA; Gov. Dr KLAUS LIEBSCHER; 8 brs.

Commercial Banks

Adria Bank AG: Gumzagagasse 16, 1010 Vienna; tel. (1) 514-09; fax (1) 514-09-43; e-mail headoffice@adriabank.at; f. 1980; cap. 170m., res 242m., dep. 2,414m. (Dec. 2001); Chair. JURIJ DETICEK; Mans CIRIL KRPAC, Dr ALFRED SCHERHAMMER.

Bank Austria Creditanstalt AG: Vordere Zollamtsstr. 13, 1030 Vienna; tel. (1) 711-91-0; fax (1) 711-91-28-72; e-mail inter.contact@bankaustria.com; internet www.bankaustria.com; f. 1991 as Bank Austria AG by merger of Österreichische Länderbank and Zentralsparkasse und Kommerzialbank; merged with HypoVereinsbank AG of Germany in mid-2001; present name adopted 2002; cap. €829m., res €1,898m., dep. €131,500m. (Dec. 2001); Pres. and Chair. Bd of Man. Dirs ALBRECHT SCHMIDT; Group CEO GERHARD RANDA; 381 brs.

Bank Austria Creditanstalt International AG: Am Hof 2, 1010 Vienna; tel. (1) 536-36-0; fax (1) 536-36-61-0; e-mail info@at.bacai.com; f. 1998; through merger of international business of Bank Austria AG (see above) with Creditanstalt AG (f. 1855); wholly owned by Bank Austria AG.

Bank Austria Handelsbank AG: Postfach 83, Operngasse 6, 1015 Vienna; tel. (1) 514-40-0; fax (1) 512-66-01; f. 1935; present name adopted 1994; cap. 331m., res 160m., dep. 5,192m. (Dec. 1999); Chair. KARL SAMSTAG.

Bank für Arbeit und Wirtschaft AG (BAWAG): Seitzergasse 2–4, 1010 Vienna; tel. (1) 534-53-0; fax (1) 534-53-2840; e-mail bawag@bawag.com; internet www.bawag.com; f. 1947; present name adopted 1963; purchased PSK, the state-owned postal bank in Aug. 2000; cap. €125m., res €863m., dep. €36,946m. (Dec. 2001); Chair. and CE O. HELMUT ELSNER; 155 brs.

Bank Gutmann AG: Schwarzenbergpl. 16, 1010 Vienna; tel. (1) 502-20-0; fax (1) 502-201-99; internet www.gutmann.at; f. 1970 as Bank Gebrüd AG, present name adopted 1995; 83% owned by Gutmann Holding AG, 17% owned by partners; cap. €12m., res €10m., dep. €253m. (Dec. 2001); Gen. Man. Dr RUDOLF F. STAHL.

Bank Winter und Co AG: Singerstr. 10, 1011 Vienna; tel. (1) 515-04-0; fax (1) 515-04-21-3; e-mail contact@bankwinter.com; f. 1959; cap. 650m., res 1,059m., dep. 23,364m. (June 2001); Chair. and CEO THOMAS MOSKOVICS; 1 br.

Bankhaus Schelhammer und Schattera AG: Postfach 618, 1011 Vienna; Goldschmiedgasse 3, 1010 Vienna; tel. (1) 534-34; fax (1) 534-34-64; e-mail bank.office@schelhammer.at; internet www.schelhammer.at; f. 1832; cap. €34.5m., res €28.0m., dep. €363.7m. (Dec. 2001); Chair. Dr HEINZ BURGMANN; 1 br.

Citibank International PLC (Austria): Schwarzenbergpl. 3, 1010 Vienna; tel. (1) 717-17-0; fax (1) 713-92-06; f. 1959 as Internationale Investitions- und Finanzierungs Bank AG; present name adopted 1978; wholly-owned subsidiary of Citibank Overseas Investment Corpn; Gen. Man. HELMUT GOTTLIEB.

Deutsche Bank (Austria) AG: Hohenstaufengasse 4, 1010 Vienna; tel. (1) 531-81-0; fax (1) 533-94-59; f. 1989; cap. 250m., res 386m., dep. 10,200m. (Dec. 1994); Man. Dirs Dr WILFRIED AMANSHAUSER, KARL-FRIEDRICH SCHALLER, CHRISTOPH BREWKA.

Donau-Bank AG: Postfach 1451, Parkring 6, 1011 Vienna; tel. (1) 515-35; fax (1) 515-35-29-7; e-mail general@donau-bank.at; internet www.donau-bank.at; f. 1974; 85% owned by Bank for Foreign Trade (Russia), 15% owned by Central Bank of the Russian Federation; cap. €72m., res €107m., dep. €586m. (Dec. 2001); Chair. and Gen. Dir ANDREI E. TCHETYRKIN.

Kathrein und Co Privatgeschäftsbank AG: Postfach 174, Wipplingerstr. 25, 1013 Vienna; tel. (1) 534-51-0; fax (1) 534-51-221; e-mail privatgeschaeftsbank.ag@kathrein.at; internet www.kathrein.at; f. 1924; 100% owned by Raiffeisen Zentralbank Österreich AG; cap. 440m., res 77m., dep. 3,493m. (Dec. 2000); Chair. Dr CHRISTOPH KRAUS.

Meinl Bank AG: Postfach 99, Bauernmarkt 2, 1015 Vienna; tel. (1) 531-88; fax (1) 531-88-44; e-mail servicecentre@meinlbank.com; internet www.meinlbank.com; f. 1922; cap. €9m., res €32m., dep. €346m. (Dec. 2001); Chair. Dr ANTON OSOND; 2 brs.

SKWB Schoellerbank AG: Renngasse 1–3, 1010 Vienna; tel. (1) 534-71-0; fax (1) 534-71-635; e-mail info@skwbschoellerbank.at; internet www.skwbschoellerbank.at; f. 1998 by merger of Schoellerbank AG (f. 1833) and Salzburger Kredit-und Wechsel-Bank AG (f. 1922); cap. €34m., res €71m., dep. €2,001m. (Dec. 2001); Chair. JÜRGEN DANZMAYR.

VakifBank International (Wien) AG: Kärntner Ring 17, 1010 Vienna; tel. (1) 512-35-20; fax (1) 512-35-20-22; e-mail office@ vakifbank.at; internet www.vakifbank.at; cap. 220m., res 66m., dep. 1,202m. (Dec. 2000); Pres. IRFAN ERCIYAS.

Regional Banks

Allgemeine Sparkasse Oberösterreich Bank AG: Postfach 92, Promenade 11–13, 4041 Linz; tel. (732) 73-91-0; fax (732) 73-91-28-01; e-mail ebusiness@sparkasse-ooe.at; internet www.sparkasse-ooe .at; f. 1849; cap. 783m., res 3,259m., dep. 83,011m. (Dec. 2001); Chair. Dr MARKUS LIMBERGER; 148 brs.

Bank für Kärnten und Steiermark AG: St. Veiter Ring 43, 9020 Klagenfurt; tel. (463) 58-58; fax (463) 58-58-94-3; e-mail bks@bks.at; internet www.bks.at; f. 1922; cap. €34m., res €161m., dep. €3,287m. (Dec. 2001); Pres. Dr HEINRICH TREICHL; 6 brs.

Bank für Tirol und Vorarlberg AG: Langer Weg 11, 6020 Innsbruck; tel. (512) 53-33-0; fax (512) 533-31-408; e-mail btv@btv.at; internet www.btv.at; f. 1904; cap. €36m., res €200m., dep. €3,389m. (Dec. 2001); Chair. PETER GAUGG; 35 brs.

Bank Styria, Steiermärkische Bank und Sparkassen AG: Postfach 844, Sparkassenpl. 4, 8011 Graz; tel. (316) 80-33-0; fax (316) 80-33-30; e-mail bankstyria@bank-styria.at; internet www .bank-styria.at; f. 1825 as Steyermärkischer Spar-Casse Graz; present name adopted 1992; cap. 1,732m., res 3,593m., dep. 73,112m. (Dec. 2000); CEO JOSEPH KASSLER; Dirs Dr HEINZ HOFER, AUGUST JOST, Dr GERHARD FABISCH; 122 brs.

Bankhaus Carl Spängler und Co AG: Postfach 41, 5024 Salzburg; Schwarzstr. 1, 5020 Salzburg; tel. (662) 86-86; fax (662) 86-86-15-8; e-mail bankhaus@spaengler.co.at; internet www.spaengler.co .at; f. 1828; cap. €11m., res €21m., dep. €484m. (Dec. 2001); Gen. Man. HEINRICH SPANGLER; 10 brs.

Bankhaus Krentschker und Co AG: Am Eisernen Tor 3, 8010 Graz; tel. (316) 80-30-0; fax (316) 80-30-94-9; e-mail mail@ krentschker.at; internet www.krentschker.at; f. 1924; cap. 475m., res 395m., dep. 11,494m. (Dec. 2001); Chair. Dr JÖRG BRUCKBAUER; 3 brs.

Hypo Alpe-Adria-Bank AG: Postfach 517, Alpe-Adria-Pl. 1, 9020 Klagenfurt; tel. (463) 58-60; fax (463) 58-60-50; e-mail austria@ hypo-alpe-adria.com; internet www.hypo-alpe-adria.com; f. 1896 as Kärntner Landes- und Hypothekenbank AG; present name adopted 1999; cap. €109m., res €206m., dep. €46,866m. (Dec. 2001); Chair Dr HERBERT KOCH; Man. Dirs Dr WOLFGANG KULTERER, Dr JÖRG SCHUSTER; 78 brs.

Hypo Tirol Bank AG: Postfach 524, Meranerstr. 8, 6020 Innsbruck; tel. (512) 59-11-0; fax (512) 59-11-21-21; e-mail office@ hypotirol.at; internet www.hypotirol.at; f. 1901 as Landes-Hypothekenbank Tirol AG, present name adopted 2000; cap. €17m., res €204m., dep. €5,559m. (Dec. 2001); Pres. Dr JOSEF PRADER; 23 brs.

Niederösterreichische Landesbank-Hypothekenbank AG: Kremsergasse 20, 3100 St Pölten; tel. (2742) 49-20; fax (2742) 49-20-14-44; e-mail hypobank@hypobank.co.at; internet www.hypobank .co.at; f. 1889; cap. €48m., res €128m., dep. €4,177m. (Dec. 2001); Pres. and Chair. HERBERT FICHTA; Gen. Man. WERNER SCHMITZER; 26 brs.

Oberbank AG: Hauptpl. 10–11, 4020 Linz; tel. (732) 78-02-0; fax (732) 78-58-04; e-mail tre@oberbank.at; internet www.oberbank.at; f. 1869 as Bank für Oberösterreich und Salzburg; present name adopted 1998; cap. €60m., res €365m., dep. €8,375m. (Dec. 2001); Chair. Dr FRANZ GASSELSBERGER; 100 brs and sub-brs.

Oberösterreichische Landesbank AG: Landstr. 38, 4020 Linz; tel. (70) 76-39-0; fax (70) 76-39-20-5; e-mail innovationsservice@ hypo-ooe.at; internet www.hypo.at; f. 1891; cap. €66m., res €128m., dep. €3,892m. (Dec. 2000); Pres. Dr WOLFGANG STAMPFL; Gen. Man. Dr WOLFGANG LANGBAUER; 14 brs.

Privatinvest Bank AG: Postfach 16, Griesgasse 11, 5010 Salzburg; tel. (662) 80-48-0; fax (662) 80-48-33-3; e-mail piag@piag.at; internet www.privatinvestbank.com; f. 1885 as Bankhaus Daghofer & Co; present name adopted 1990; cap. €6m., res €5m., dep. €132m. (Dec. 2001); Chair. HANS-WERNER ZESCHKY.

Salzburger Landes-Hypothekenbank AG: Postfach 136, Residenzpl. 7, 5010 Salzburg; tel. (662) 804-60; fax (662) 804-65-69-2; e-mail office@hypobank.sbg.at; internet www.hypobank.sbg.at; cap. €15m., res €68m., dep. €2,663m. (Dec. 2001); Gen. Man. Dr REINHARD SALHOFER; 24 brs.

Tiroler Sparkasse-Bankaktiengesellschaft Innsbruck: Sparkassenpl. 1, 6020 Innsbruck; tel. (512) 59-10-2; fax (512) 59-10-45-00; f. 1822 as Sparkasse der Stadt Innsbruck; present name adopted 1990, following merger in 1975; cap. 2,100m., res 1,827m., dep. 40,658m. (Dec. 1999); Pres. ANDREAS TREICHL; Chair. and Gen. Man. ANDREAS TREICHL; 49 brs.

Volkskreditbank AG: Postfach 116, Rudigierstr. 5–7, 4010 Linz; tel. (70) 76-37-0; fax (70) 76-37-60-0; e-mail international@vkb-bank .at; internet www.vkb-bank.at; f. 1872; cap. €33m., res €127m., dep. €1,564m. (Dec. 2001); Gen. Man. Dr GERNOT KRENNER; 46 brs.

Vorarlberger Landes- und Hypothekenbank AG: Hypo-Passage 1, 6900 Bregenz; tel. (5574) 414-0; fax (5574) 414-45-7; e-mail info@hypovbg.at; internet www.hypovbg.at; f. 1899; cap. €125m., res €267m., dep. €5,526m. (Dec. 2001); Chair. Dr KURT RUPP; 25 brs.

Specialized Banks

Kommunalkredit Austria AG: Türkenstr. 9, 1092 Vienna; tel. (1) 316-31-0; fax (1) 316-31-50-0; e-mail kommunal@kommunalkredit .at; internet www.kommunalkredit.at; f. 1958; total assets €6,901m. (June 2002); CEO Dr REINHARD PLATZER; Mans GERHARD GANGL, PATRICK GIACOBBI.

Oesterreichische Kontrollbank AG: Postfach 70, Am Hof 4, 1011 Vienna; tel. (1) 531-27-0; fax (1) 531-27-5698; e-mail public .relations@oekb.at; internet www.oekb.at; f. 1946; export financing, stock exchange clearing, organization and administration of domestic bond issues, central depository for securities and settlement of off-floor transactions, money market operations; cap. €100m., res €105m., dep. €475m. (Dec. 2001); Mans Dr JOHANNES ATTEMS, Dr RUDOLF SCHOLTEN.

Savings Banks

Dornbirner Sparkasse: Postfach 199, Bahnhofstr. 2, 6850 Dornbirn; tel. (5572) 381-10; fax (5572) 381-14; e-mail service@dornbirn .sparkasse.at; internet www.dornbirn.sparkasse.at; cap. 204m., res 1,711m., dep. 17,209m. (Dec. 2001); Chair. WOLFGANG RÜMMELE; 15 brs.

Erste Bank der öesterreichischen Sparkassen AG (Erste Bank) (First Austrian Savings Bank): Postfach 162, Graben 21, 1010 Vienna; tel. (1) 531-00-0; fax (1) 531-00-22-72; e-mail service .center@erstebank.at; internet www.erstebank.at; f. 1819; present name adopted 1997; dep. €75,568m., total assets €86,033m. (Dec. 2001); Chair. and CEO ANDREAS TREICHL; 279 brs.

Kärntner Sparkasse AG: Neuerpl. 14, 9020 Klagenfurt; tel. (463) 588-80; fax (463) 588-82-91; e-mail info@kaerntnersparkasse.co.at; internet www.kaerntnersparkasse.at; f. 1835; cap. 1,235m., res 1,399m., dep. 30,072m. (Dec. 2000); Pres. Dr HANS KOSTWERN; Chair. and Gen. Man. ALOLS HOCHEGGER; 55 brs.

Österreichische Postsparkasse AG (PSK): Georg-Coch Pl. 2, 1018 Vienna; tel. (1) 51-40-00; fax (1) 514-00-17-00; e-mail kundenservice@mail.psk.co.at; internet www.psk.at; f. 1883; sold to BAWAG in Aug. 2000; cap. €128m., res €604m., dep. €20,224m. (Dec. 2000); Chair. STEPHAN KOREN.

Salzburger Sparkasse Bank AG: Postfach 5000, Alter Markt 3, 5021 Salzburg; tel. (662) 80-40-0; fax (662) 80-40-81; internet www .salzburger-sparkasse.co.at; f. 1855; cap. €97m., res €143m., dep. €3,122m. (Dec. 2001); Gen. Man. WALTER SCHWIMBERSKY; 79 brs.

Co-operative Banks

Österreichische Volksbanken-AG: Peregringasse 3, 1090 Vienna; tel. (1) 313-40-37-89; fax (1) 313-40-31-70; e-mail infomail@ oevag.volksbank.at; internet www.oevag.volksbank.at; f. 1922; cap. and res €742m.; dep. and bonds €18,854m. (Dec. 2001); Chair. and CEO Dr KLAUS THALHAMMER; 85 brs.

Raiffeisen Centrobank AG: Postfach 272, Tegetthoffstr. 1, 1015 Vienna; tel. (1) 515-20-0; fax (1) 513-43-96; e-mail general@ centrobank.com; internet www.centrobank.com; f. 1973; cap. 655m., res 246m., dep. 8,600m. (Dec. 2000); Chair. Dr GERHARD VOGT.

Raiffeisen Zentralbank Österreich AG (RZB-Austria): Am Stadtpark 9, 1030 Vienna; tel. (1) 717-07-0; fax (1) 717-07-17-15; internet www.rzb.at; f. 1927; core cap. €1,726m., dep. €35,176m. (Dec. 2001); central institute of the Austrian Raiffeisen banking group; Chair. Supervisory Bd Dr CHRISTIAN KONRAD; Chair. Bd of Management Dr WALTER ROTHENSTEINER.

Raiffeisenlandesbank Kärnten-Rechenzentrum und Revisionsverband rGmbH: St.-Veiter-Ring 53, 9020 Klagenfurt; tel. (463) 581-52-7-0; fax (463) 581-53-6; internet www.raiffeisen.at/ktn; cap. €5m., res €59m., dep. €1,496m. (Dec. 2001); Chair. Dr KLAUS PEKAREK; 48 brs.

Raiffeisenlandesbank Niederösterreich-Wien rGmbH: Friedrich-Wilhelm-Raiffeisen-Pl. 1, Raiffeisenhaus, 1020 Vienna; tel. (1) 21-13-60; fax (1) 21-13-62-22-3; internet www.rlbnoew.at; f. 1898; cap. €199m., res €337m., dep. €9,241m. (Dec. 2001); Chair. Dr CHRISTIAN KONRAD.

Raiffeisenlandesbank Oberösterreich rGmbH: Postfach 455, Europapl. 1A, 4021 Linz; tel. (732) 6596-3150; fax (732) 6596-3155; e-mail cb@rlbooe.at; internet www.rlbooe.at; f. 1900; cap. €461m., res €447m., dep. €9,818m. (Dec. 2001); Chair. Dr LUDWIG SCHARINGER; 21 brs.

Raiffeisenlandesbank Steiermark rGmbH: Kaiserfeldgasse 5–7, 8010 Graz; tel. (316) 80-36-0; fax (316) 80-36-17-11-3; internet www.ribstmk.at; f. 1927; cap. €96m., res €260m., dep. €4,257m. (Dec. 2001); Chair. JOSEF RIEGLER.

Raiffeisenlandesbank Vorarlberg Waren-und Revisions Verbank rGmbH: Rheinstr. 11, 6900 Bregenz; tel. (5574) 4050; fax (5574) 405-333; internet www.vol.at/raiffeisen; cap. €25m., res €81m., dep. €2,332m. (Dec. 2001); Chair. Dr KARL WALTLE; Dirs KARLHEINZ WAIBEL, WILFRIED HOPFNER.

Raiffeisenverband Salzburg reg Gen mbH: Schwarzstr. 13–15, 5024 Salzburg; tel. (662) 88860; fax (662) 888-65-24; e-mail friedrich.buchmueller@rvs.at; internet www.salzburg.raiffeisen.at; f. 1905; present name adopted 1949; cap. €37m., res €164m., dep. €2,919m. (Dec. 2001); Chair. MANFRED HOLZTRATTNER.

Bankers' Organization

Verband österreichischer Banken und Bankiers (Asscn of Austrian Banks and Bankers): Postfach 132, Börsegasse 11, 1013 Vienna; tel. (1) 535-17-71; fax (1) 535-17-71/38; e-mail voebb@voebb.at; internet www.voebb.at; f. 1945; Pres. HELMUT ELSNER; Gen. Sec. FRANZ OVESNY; 55 mems and 23 extraordinary mems.

STOCK EXCHANGES

Wiener Börse (Vienna Stock Exchange): Postfach 192, Strauchagasse 1–3, 1014 Vienna; tel. (1) 531-65-0; fax (1) 532-97-40; e-mail communications@vienna-stock-exchange.at; internet www.wbag.at; f. 1771; 50% state-owned; two sections: Stock Exchange, Commodity Exchange; Pres. GERHARD REIDLINGER; Gen. Sec. Dr ULRICH KAMP.

Österreichische Termin- und Optionenbörse (Austrian Futures and Options Exchange): Postfach 192, Walluerstr. 8, 1014 Vienna; tel. (1) 531-65-0; fax (1) 532-97-40; f. 1991 by appointment to the Vienna Stock Exchange, provides a fully automated screen-based trading system, the Austrian Traded Index (ATX), and acts as clearing house for options and futures; trades futures on the Austrian index and options on 17 Austrian stocks listed on the Vienna Stock Exchange; Chief Execs Dr ERICK OBERSTEINER, Dr STEFAN ZAPOTOCKY.

INSURANCE COMPANIES

Allgemeine Pechtsschutz Versicherungs-AG (ARAG): Heinrichsgasse 4, 1013 Vienna; tel. (1) 531-02-0; fax (1) 531-02-923; e-mail info@arag.at; internet info@arag.at; Man. Dr HERBERT KITTINGER.

Allianz Elementar Lebensversicherung-AG: Hietzinger Kai 101–105, 1130 Vienna; tel. (1) 878-07-0; fax (1) 878-07-27-03; e-mail office@allianz.at; internet www.allianz.at; life insurance; Gen. Man. Dr ALEXANDER HOYOS.

Allianz Elementar Versicherungs-AG: Hietzinger Kai 101–105, 1130 Vienna; tel. (1) 878-07-0; fax (1) 878-07-53-90; e-mail office@allianz.at; internet www.allianz.co.at; f. 1860; all classes except life insurance; Gen. Man. Dr ALEXANDER HOYOS.

AXA Nordstern Colonia Versicherungs-AG: Uraniastr. 2, 1010 Vienna; tel. (1) 711-50-0; fax (1) 711-50-212; e-mail kundendienst@axa-versicherung.at; internet www.axa-versicherung.at; Gen. Man. DAVID FURTWÄNGLER.

Donau Allgemeine Versicherungs-AG: Schottenring 15, 1010 Vienna; tel. (1) 313-11; fax (1) 310-77-51; e-mail donau@donauversicherung.at; internet www.donauversicherung.at; f. 1867; all classes; Gen. Man. HANS RAUWAUF.

Generali Versicherung AG: Landskrongasse 1–3, 1011 Vienna; tel. (1) 534-01; fax (1) 534-01/12-26; e-mail headoffice@generali.at; internet www.generali.co.at; f. 1882 as Erste Österreichische Allgemeine Unfall-Versicherungs-Gesellschaft; Gen. Man. Dr HANS PEER.

Grazer Wechselseitige Versicherung: Herrengasse 18–20, 8011 Graz; tel. (316) 80-37-0; fax (316) 80-37-41-4; f. 1828; all classes; Gen. Man. Dr OTHMAR EDERER.

Interunfall Versicherungs-AG: Tegetthoffstr. 7, 1011 Vienna; tel. (1) 514-03-0; fax (1) 514-03-4590; e-mail z-v@interunfall.at; internet www.interunfall.at; all classes of insurance (including reinsurance); Man. Dr HANS PEER.

Raiffeisen-Versicherung AG: Untere Donaustr. 25, 1021 Vienna; tel. (1) 211-19-0; fax (1) 211-19-11-34; e-mail kommunikation@raiffeisen-versicherung.at; internet www.raiffeisen-versicherung.at; Dir Dr PETER EICHLER.

Salzburger Landes-Versicherung AG: Auersperstr. 9, 5021 Salzburg; tel. (662) 899-98-0; fax (662) 889-98-109; e-mail sekretariat@slv.co.at; internet www.slv.co.at; Gen. Man. Dr JOSEF GLASER.

Sparkassen Versicherung AG: Wipplingerstr. 36–38, 1011 Vienna; tel. (1) 313-81-0; fax (1) 313-81-300; e-mail sag@s-versicherung.co.at; internet www.s-versicherung.co.at; Gen. Man. Dr MICHAEL HARRER.

Uniqa Versicherungen AG: Praterstr. 1–7, 1021 Vienna; tel. (1) 211-11-0; fax (1) 214-33-36; e-mail kommunikation@uniqa.at; internet www.uniqa.at; present name adopted 1999, fmrly Versicherungsanstalt der österreichischen Bundesländer Versicherungs-AG; Chair. Dr KONSTANTIN KLIEN.

Wiener Städtische Allgemeine Versicherung AG: Schottenring 30, Ringturm, 1010 Vienna; tel. (1) 531-39-0; fax (1) 535-34-37; e-mail mail-us@wr.staedtische.co.at; internet www.staedtische.co.at; f. 1824; all classes; Chief Exec. Dr SIEGFRIED SELLITSCH.

Wüstenrot Versicherungs-AG: Alpenstr. 61, 5033 Salzburg; tel. (662) 6386-0; fax (662) 6386-623; e-mail versicherung@wuestenrot.at; internet www.wuestenrot.at; Gen. Man. HELMUT GEIER.

Zürich Kosmos Versicherungen AG: Schwarzenbergpl. 15, 1015 Vienna I; tel. (1) 501-25-0; fax (1) 505-04-85; internet www.zuerichkosmos.at; f. 1910; all classes; Gen. Man. FRANZ WIPFLI.

Insurance Organization

Verband der Versicherungsunternehmen Österreichs (Asscn of Austrian Insurance Cos): Schwarzenbergpl. 7, 1030 Vienna; tel. (1) 711-56-0; fax (1) 711-56-27-0; e-mail versver@ibm.net; internet www.vvo.at; f. 1945; Pres. Dr ALEXANDER HOYOS; Gen. Sec. HERBERT RETTER; 86 mems.

Trade and Industry

GOVERNMENT AGENCIES

Austrian Business Agency (ABA): Opernring 3, 1010 Vienna; fax (1) 586-86-59; e-mail office@aba.gv.at; internet www.aba.gv.at; Man. Dir RENÉ SIEGL.

Österreichische Industrieholding AG (ÖIAG): Postfach 99, Kantgasse 1, 1015 Vienna; tel. (1) 711-14-0; fax (1) 711-14-37-8; f. 1970; Mans. KARL HOLLWEGER, Dr ERICH BECKER.

CHAMBERS OF COMMERCE

All Austrian enterprises must by law be members of the Economic Chambers. The Federal Economic Chamber promotes international contacts and represents the economic interests of trade and industry on a federal level. Its Foreign Trade Organization includes about 90 offices abroad.

Wirtschaftskammer Österreich (Austrian Federal Economic Chamber): Wiedner Hauptstr. 63, 1045 Vienna; tel. (1) 501-05; fax (1) 502-06-25-0; e-mail mservice@wkoe.wk.or.at; f. 1946; six depts: Commerce, Industry, Small-scale Production, Banking and Insurance, Transport and Tourism; these divisions are subdivided into branch asscns; Local Economic Chambers with divisions and branch asscns in each of the nine Austrian provinces; Pres. CHRISTOPH LEITL; Sec.-Gen. GÜNTER STUMMVOLL; c. 300,000 mems.

INDUSTRIAL AND TRADE ASSOCIATIONS

Wirtschaftskammer Österreich—Bundessparte Industrie: Wiedner Hauptstr. 63, 1045 Vienna; tel. (1) 501-05-34-20; fax (1) 501-05-27-3; e-mail bsi@wko.at; internet www.wko.at/bsi; f. 1896 as Zentralverband der Industrie Österreichs (Central Fed. of Austrian Industry), merged into present org. 1947; Chair. Dr WERNER TESSMAR-PFOHL; Dir WOLFGANG DAMIANISCH; comprises the following industrial feds:

Fachverband der Audiovisions-und Filmindustrie Österreichs (Film): Postfach 327, Wiedner Hauptstr. 63, 1045 Vienna; tel. (1) 501-05-30-10; fax (1) 501-05-27-6; e-mail film@fafo.at; internet www.fafo.at; Chair. MICHAEL WOLKENSTEIN; 1,700 mems.

Fachverband der Bauindustrie (Building): Karlsgasse 5, 1040 Vienna; tel. (1) 504-15-51; fax (1) 504-15-55; e-mail sekretariat@bauindustrie.at; internet www.bauindustrie.at; Chair. Ing. ERNST NUSSBAUMER; Dir Dr JOHANNES SCHENK; 150 mems.

Fachverband der Bekleidungsindustrie (Clothing): Schwarzenbergpl. 4, 1030 Vienna; tel. (1) 712-12-96; fax (1) 713-92-04; e-mail pitnik@fashion-industry.at; internet www.fashion-industry.at; Chair. WILHELM EHRLICH; Dir FRANZ J. PITNIK; 280 mems.

Fachverband der Bergwerke und Eisenerzeugenden Industrie (Mining and Steel Production): Postfach 300, Goethegasse 3, 1015 Vienna; tel. (1) 512-46-01; fax (1) 512-46-01-20; e-mail fvil@wkoesk.wk.or.at; internet www.wko.at/bergbau-stahl; Chair. Gen. Dir FRANZ STRUZL; Sec. Ing. HERMANN PRINZ; 39 mems.

Fachverband der Chemischen Industrie (Chemicals): Postfach 325, Wiedner Hauptstr. 63, 1045 Vienna; tel. (1) 501-05-280; fax (1) 502-06-28-0; e-mail office@fcio.wko.at; internet www.fcio .at; Pres. Dr Wolfgang Frank; Gen. Dir Dr Wolfgang Eickhoff; 530 mems.

Fachverband der Elektro- und Elektronikindustrie Oesterreichs (Electrical): Mariahilfer Str. 37–39, 1060 Vienna; tel. (1) 58839-0; fax (1) 5866971; e-mail info@feel.at; internet www.feel .at; Pres. Albert Hochleitner; Man. Dir Lothar Roitner; 558 mems.

Fachverband der Fahrzeugindustrie (Vehicles): Wiedner Hauptstr. 63, 1045 Vienna; tel. (1) 501-05-48-01; fax (1) 501-05-28-9; Pres. Bruno Krainz; Gen. Sec. Walter Linszbauer; 224 mems.

Fachverband der Gas- und Wärmeversorgungsunternehmungen (Gas and Heating): Schubertring 14, 1010 Vienna; tel. (1) 513-15-88; fax (1) 513-15-88-25; e-mail fv@fv-ovgw.or.at; internet www.gaswaerme.at; Gen. Dir Dr Karl Skyba.

Fachverband der Giessereiindustrie (Foundries): Postfach 339, Wiedner Hauptstr. 63, 1045 Vienna; tel. (1) 501-05-34-63; fax (1) 501-05-27-9; e-mail giesserei@wko.at; Chair. Michael Zimmermann; Dir Ing. Dr Hansjörg Dichtl; 60 mems.

Fachverband der Glasindustrie (Glass): Wiedner Hauptstr. 63, 1045 Vienna; tel. (1) 501-05/3428; fax (1) 501-05/281; e-mail office@fvglas.at; Chair. Rudolf Schraml; Dir Alexander Krissmanek; 65 mems.

Fachverband der Holzindustrie Österreichs (Wood): Postfach 123, Schwarzenbergpl. 4, 1037 Vienna; tel. (1) 712-26-01-0; fax (1) 712-26-01-19; e-mail office@saege.at; internet www .holzindustrie.at; f. 1947 as Fachverband der Sägeindustrie Österreichs; present name adopted 2000; Chair. Dr Erich Wiesner; Dir Dr Gerhard Altrichter; 1,800 mems.

Fachverband der Holzverarbeitenden Industrie (Wood Processing): Postfach 123, Schwarzenbergpl. 4, 1037 Vienna; tel. (1) 712-26-01; fax (1) 713-03-09; e-mail office@holzindustrie.at; f. 1946; Chair. Dr Erich Wiesner; Dir Dr Claudius Kollmann; 360 mems.

Fachverband der Ledererzeugenden Industrie (Leather Production): Postfach 312, Wiedner Hauptstr. 63, 1045 Vienna 4; tel. (1) 501-05-34-53; fax (1) 501-05-278; e-mail fvleder@wko.at; f. 1945; Chair. Helmut Schmidt; Dir Peter Kovacs; 8 mems.

Fachverband der Lederverarbeitenden Industrie (Leather Processing): Postfach 313, Wiedner Hauptstr. 63, 1045 Vienna; tel. (1) 501-05-3453; fax (1) 501-05-278; e-mail fvleder@wko.at; internet www.shoes-leather.at; f. 1945; Chair. Joseph Lorenz; Dir Peter Kovacs; 45 mems.

Fachverband der Maschinen- und Stahlbauindustrie (Machinery and Steel Construction): Wiedner Hauptstr. 63, 1045 Vienna; tel. (1) 502-25; fax (1) 505-10-20; e-mail machinen@fms.at; internet www.fms.at; Pres. Dr Clemens Malina-Altzinger; Dir Johann Zoder; 850 mems.

Fachverband der Metallwarenindustrie Österreichs (Metal Goods): Postfach 335, Wiedner Hauptstr. 63, 1045 Vienna; tel. (1) 501-05; fax (1) 505-09-28; internet www.fmwi.at; f. 1908; Chair. Ing. Wolfgang Welser; Gen. Man. Dr Wolfgang Locker; 800 mems.

Fachverband der NE-Metallindustrie (Metals): Postfach 338, Wiedner Hauptstr. 63, 1045 Vienna; tel. (1) 501-05-33-09; fax (1) 501-05-33-78; e-mail nemetall@wko.at; f. 1946; Chair. Ing. Gerhard Eschner; Dir Dr Günter Greil; 69 mems.

Fachverband der Mineralölindustrie (Petroleum): Erdbergstr. 72, 1031 Vienna; tel. (1) 713-23-48; fax (1) 713-05-10; e-mail office@oil-gas.at; internet www.oil-gas.at; f. 1947; Gen. Dirs Dr Richard Schenz, Dr Rudolf Merten; 20 mems.

Fachverband der Nahrungs- und Genussmittelindustrie (Provisions): Zaunergasse 1-3, Vienna; tel. (1) 712-21-21; fax (1) 713-18-02; Chair. Dr Erwin Bundschuh; Dir Dr Michael Blass; 674 mems.

Fachverband der Papier und Pappe verarbeitenden Industrie (Paper and Board Processing): Brucknerstr. 8, 1041 Vienna; tel. (1) 505-53-82-0; fax (1) 505-90-18; e-mail ppv@ppv.at; internet www.ppv.at; Chair. Gustav Glöckler; 134 mems.

Fachverband der Papierindustrie (Paper): Gumpendorferstr. 6, 1061 Vienna; tel. (1) 588-86-0; fax (1) 588-86-22-2; e-mail austropapier@austropapier.at; internet www.austropapier.at; Chair. Dr Veit Sorger; Dir Dr Gerolf Ottawa; 30 mems.

Fachverband der Stein- und keramischen Industrie (Stone and Ceramics): Postfach 329, Wiedner Hauptstr. 63, 1045 Vienna; tel. (1) 501-05-35-31; fax (1) 505-62-40; e-mail steine@wko.at; internet www.baustoffindustrie.at; f. 1946; Chair. Dr Carl Hennrich; Pres. Dr Erhard Schaschl; 400 mems.

Fachverband der Textilindustrie (Textiles): Rudolfspl. 12, 1013 Vienna; tel. (1) 533-37-26-0; fax (1) 533-37-26-40; e-mail fvtextil@fvtextil.wk.or.at; internet www.textilindustrie.at; Pres. Dr Peter Pfneisl; Dir Dr Wolfgang Zeyringer; 265 mems.

UTILITIES

Electricity

Burgenländische Elektrizitätswirtschafts-AG: Kasemenstr. 9, 7001 Eisenstadt; tel. (2682) 900-01-02-1; fax (2682) 900-01-91-0; e-mail guenther.ofner@bewag.co.at; Chair. Dr Günther Ofner.

Energie-Versorgung-Niederösterreich AG (EVN): Johann-Steinboeck-Str. 1, 2344 Maria Enzersdorf; tel. (2742) 80-00; fax (2742) 80-03-60; Chair. Dr Rudolf Gruber.

Kärntner Elektrizitäts-AG: Arnulfpl. 2, 9020 Klagenfurt; tel. (463) 52-50; fax (463) 52-51-59-6; Chair. Dr Günther Bresitz.

Oberösterreichische Kraftwerke AG: Böhmerwaldstr. 3, 4020 Linz; tel. (732) 65-93-0; fax (732) 65-93-36-00; Chair. Dr Leopold Windtner.

Österreichische Elektrizitätswirtschafts-AG: Am Hof 6a, 1010 Vienna; tel. (1) 531-13-0; fax (1) 531-13-41-91; e-mail info@pol .verbund.co.at; internet www.verbund.co.at/verbund; federal electricity authority; operates national grid, wholesales electricity to the nine regional operators; Dir Hans Haider.

Salzburg AG für Energie, Verkehr und Telekommunikation: Bayerhamerstr. 16, 5021 Salzburg; tel. (662) 88-84-0; fax (662) 88-84-17-0; e-mail offic@salzburg-ag.at; internet www.salzburg-ag.at.

Steirische Wasserkraft- und Elektrizitäts-AG: Leonhardgurtel 10, 8011 Graz; tel. (316) 3870; fax (316) 387290; Chair. Dr Oswin Kois.

Tiroler Wasserkraftwerke AG: Landhauspl., 6010 Innsbruck; tel. (512) 50-60; fax (512) 50-62-12-6; Chair. Dr Helmut Mayr.

Vorarlberger Kraftwerke AG: Weidachstr. 6, 6900 Bregenz; tel. (5574) 601-0; fax (5574) 60-15-00; e-mail energie@vkw.at; internet www.vkw.at; Chair. Dr Leo Wagner, Dr Otto Waibel.

WienStrom GmbH: Mariannegasse 4, 1095 Vienna; tel. (1) 400-43-00-00; fax (1) 400-43-00-99; e-mail vavra@wienstrom.co.at; internet www.wienstrom.co.at; f. 1902; Chair. Helmut Kastl.

Gas

BEGAS (Burgenländische Erdgasversorgungs-AG): Kasernenstr. 10, 7000 Eisenstadt; tel. (2682) 70-9; fax (2682) 70-91-74; Chair. Heribert Artinger.

Oberösterreichische Ferngas-AG: Neubauzeile 99, 4030 Linz; tel. (732) 38-83; fax (732) 37-72-19; Chair. Max Dobruckt.

Steirische Ferngas-AG: Gaslaternenweg 4, 8041 Graz; tel. (316) 476-0; fax (316) 476-28-000; e-mail info@steirische.ferngas.at; internet www.steirische.ferngas.at; Chair. Dominique Bayen, Peter Köberl, Max Pölzl.

Water

Österreichischer Wasser- und Abfallwirtschaftsverband (ÖWAV) (Austrian Water and Refuse Board): Marc-Aurel-Str. 5, 1010 Vienna; tel. (1) 535-57-20; fax (1) 535-40-64; e-mail randl@ oewav.at; internet www.oewav.at.

TRADE UNIONS

Österreichischer Gewerkschaftsbund (ÖGB) (Austrian Trade Union Fed.): Hohenstaufengasse 10–12, 1010 Vienna; tel. (1) 534-44; fax (1) 534-44-20-4; e-mail oegb@oegb.or.at; internet www.oegb.or .at; non-party union org. with voluntary membership; f. 1945; org. affiliated with ICFTU and the European Trade Union Confederation (ETUC); Pres. Friedrich Verzetnitsch; Exec. Sec. Roswitha Bachner; 1,428,409 mems (Sept. 2001); comprises the following 13 trade unions.

Gewerkschaft Agrar-Nahrung-Genuss (Agricultural, Food, Beverage and Tobacco Workers): Albertgasse 35, 1081 Vienna; tel. (1) 401-49; fax (1) 401-49-20; e-mail ang@ang.oegb.or.at; Chair. Dr Leopold Simperl; 40,113 mems (1989).

Gewerkschaft Bau-Holz (Building Workers and Woodworkers): Ebendorferstr. 7, 1010 Vienna; tel. (1) 401-47; fax (1) 401-47-314; e-mail sonja.schmid@gbh.oegb.or.at; Chair. Johann Driemer; 171,000 mems (1997).

Gewerkschaft der Chemiearbeiter (Chemical Workers): Stumpergasse 60, 1060 Vienna; tel. (1) 597-15-01; fax (1) 597-21-01-23; Chair. Gerhard Linner; 51,172 mems (1993).

Gewerkschaft Druck, Journalismus und Papier (Printing, Journalism and Paper Trade Workers): Postfach 91, Seidengasse 15–17, 1070 Vienna; tel. (1) 523-82-31; fax (1) 523-81-32-28; e-mail gewdu@netway.at; f. 1842; Chair. Franz Bittner; 18,023 mems (1999).

Gewerkschaft der Eisenbahner (Railwaymen): Margaretenstr. 166, 1051 Vienna; tel. (1) 546-41-50-0; fax (1) 546-41-50-4; e-mail gde@gde.oegb.or.at; Chair. Wilhelm Haberzettl; 100,000 mems (2000).

Gewerkschaft der Gemeindebediensteten (Municipal Employees): Maria-Theresien-Str. 11, 1090 Vienna; tel. (1) 313-16-83; fax (1) 313-16-7701; e-mail gdg@gdg.oegb.or.at; internet www.gdg.at; Chair. Rudolf Hundstorfer; 174,677 mems (2001).

Gewerkschaft Handel, Transport, Verkehr (Workers in Commerce and Transport): Teinfaltstr. 7, 1010 Vienna; tel. (1) 534-54; fax (1) 534-54-32-5; f. 1904; Chair. Willibald Steinkellner; 37,846 mems (1989).

Gewerkschaft Hotel, Gastgewerbe, Persönlicher Dienst (Hotel and Restaurant Workers): Hohenstaufengasse 10, 1013 Vienna; tel. (1) 534-44; fax (1) 534-44-50-5; e-mail hgpd@cahgpd .oegb.or.at; f. 1906; Chair. Rudolf Kaske; 50,977 mems (1997).

Gewerkschaft Kunst, Medien, Sport, freie Berufe (Musicians, Actors, Artists, Journalists, etc.): Maria-Theresien-Str. 11, 1090 Vienna; tel. (1) 313-16; fax (1) 313-16-77-00; e-mail sekretariat@kmsfb.oegb.or.at; f. 1945; Chair. Peter Paul Skrepek; Sec.-Gen. Dr Herbert Stegmüller; 15,700 mems (2000).

Gewerkschaft Metall-Textil (Metal Workers, Miners and Power Supply Workers and Textile, Leather and Garment Industry Workers): Plösslgasse 15, 1041 Vienna; tel. (1) 501-46-0; fax (1) 501-46-13-30-0; e-mail gmbe@metaller.at; internet www .metaller.at; following merger of Gewerkschaft Metall-Bergbau-Energie (f. 1890) and Gewerkschaft Textil, Bekleidung, Leder (f. 1945); Chair. Rudolf Nürnberger; 216,000 mems (2000).

Gewerkschaft Öffentlicher Dienst (Public Employees): Teinfaltstr. 7, 1010 Vienna; tel. (1) 534-54-0; fax (1) 534-54-207; e-mail goed@goed.at; internet www.goed.at; f. 1945; Chair. Fritz Neugebauer; Gen. Secs Dr Manfred Mögele, Gerhard Neugebauer, Erich Rudolf; 230,000 mems (2002).

Gewerkschaft der Post- und Fernmeldebediensteten (Postal and Telegraph Workers): Postfach 343, Biberstr. 5, 1010 Vienna; tel. (1) 512-55-11; fax (1) 512-55-11/52; e-mail gpf@gpf .oegb.or.at; Chair. Fritz Gerhard; 71,137 mems (2001).

Gewerkschaft der Privatangestellten (Commercial, Clerical and Technical Employees): Deutschmeisterpl. 2, 1013 Vienna; tel. and fax (1) 313-93; e-mail gpa@gpa.at; internet www.gpa.at; Chair. Hans Sallmutter; 301,046 mems (1997).

Bundesfraktion Christlicher Gewerkschafter im Österreichischen Gewerkschaftsbund (Christian Trade Unionists' Section of the Austrian Trade Union Fed.): Hohenstaufengasse 12, 1010 Vienna; tel. (1) 534-44; organized in Christian Trade Unionists' Sections of the above 13 trade unions; affiliated to WCL; Sec.-Gen. Karl Klein.

Transport

RAILWAYS

Österreichische Bundesbahnen (ÖBB—Austrian Federal Railways) operates more than 90% of all the railway routes in Austria. In 2000 there were 6,281 km of track, of which ÖBB operated 5,683 km; all main lines were electrified.

Österreichische Bundesbahnen (ÖBB) (Austrian Federal Railways): Head Office: Elisabethstr. 9, 1010 Vienna; tel. (1) 58-00-0; fax (1) 58-00/25-00-1; Gen. Dir Dr Helmut Draxler.

Innsbruck Divisional Management: Claudiastr. 2, 6020 Innsbruck; tel. (512) 50-33-00-0; fax (512) 50-35-00-5; Dir Johann Lindenberger.

Linz Divisional Management: Bahnhofstr. 3, 4021 Linz; tel. (732) 69-09-0; fax (732) 69-09-18-33; Dir Helmuth Aflenzer; Vice-Dir Klaus Seebacher.

Vienna Divisional Management: Nordbahnstr. 50, 1020 Vienna; tel. (1) 580-05-00-00; fax (1) 580-02-56-01; Dir Franz Polzer.

Villach Divisional Management: 10-Oktober-Str. 20, 9501 Villach; tel. (4242) 20-20-32-00; fax (4242) 20-20-32-29; e-mail

willibald.schicho@gv.oebb.at; internet www.railcargo.at; Dir Willibald Schicho.

Other railway companies include: Achenseebahn AG, AG der Wiener Lokalbahnen, Graz-Köflacher Eisenbahn- und Bergbau GmbH, Lokalbahn, Montafonerbahn AG, Raab-Oedenburg-Ebenfurter Eisenbahn, Salzburger Stadtwerke AG-Verkehrsbetriebe, Steiermarkische Lokalbahnen, Stern & Hafferl Verkehrs GmbH, Zillertaler Verkehrsbetriebe AG.

ROADS

At 1 January 2001 Austria had 106,058 km of classified roads, of which 1,633 km were modern motorways, 10,280 km main roads, 23,086 km secondary roads and 71,059 km other roads.

INLAND WATERWAYS

The Danube (Donau) is Austria's only navigable river. It enters Austria from Germany at Passau and flows into Slovakia near Hainburg. The length of the Austrian section of the river is 351 km. Danube barges carry up to 1,800 metric tons, but loading depends on the water level, which varies considerably throughout the year. Cargoes are chiefly petroleum and derivatives, coal, coke, iron ore, iron, steel, timber and grain. Transport on the Danube was severely disrupted by the NATO bombing of Serbian bridges in early 1999. The Rhine-Main-Danube Canal opened in 1992. A passenger service is maintained on the Upper Danube and between Vienna and the Black Sea. Passenger services are also provided on Bodensee (Lake Constance) and Wolfgangsee by Austrian Federal Railways, and on all the larger Austrian lakes.

CIVIL AVIATION

The main international airport is located at Schwechat, near Vienna. There are also international flights from Graz, Innsbruck, Klagenfurt, Linz and Salzburg, and internal flights between these cities.

Principal Airlines

Austrian Airlines (Österreichische Luftverkehrs AG): Fontanastr. 1, 1107 Vienna; tel. (1) 517-66; fax (1) 688-55-05; e-mail public .relations@aua.com; internet www.aua.com; f. 1957; 39.7% state-owned; serves 116 cities in 64 countries world-wide; Chair. Rainer Wieltsch; Pres. Vagn Sörensen.

Austrian Airtransport (AAT): Postfach 50, Fontanastr. 1, 1107 Vienna; tel. (1) 688-16-91; fax (1) 688-11-91; f. 1964; 80% owned by Austrian Airlines, from which it leases most of its aircraft; operates scheduled and charter flights for passengers and cargo, and tour services; Man. Dir Dr Herbert Koschier.

Lauda Air Luftfahrt AG: Postfach 56, Lauda Air Bldg, 1300 Vienna-Schwechat; tel. (1) 7000-0; fax (1) 7000-790-15; e-mail office@laudaair.com; internet www.laudaair.com; f. 1979; became a scheduled carrier 1987; 47% owned by Austrian Airlines; operates scheduled passenger services and charter flights to Europe, Australia, the Far East and the USA; Chair. Ferdinand Schmidt.

Tiroler Luftfahrt GmbH (Tyrolean Airways): Postfach 98, Fürstenweg 176, 6026 Innsbruck; tel. (512) 22-2-0; fax (512) 22-22-90-05; internet www.tyrolean.at; f. 1958 as Aircraft Innsbruck; adopted present name 1980; operates scheduled services and charter flights within Austria and to other European countries; Pres. and Chief Exec. Fritz Feitl; Man. Dir Johann Messner.

Tourism

Tourism plays an important part in the Austrian economy. Following a decline in the number of foreign visitors and the consequent decrease in tourism receipts during the mid-1990s, the sector showed signs of recovery in the late 1990s. In 2001 Austria received 18.2m. foreign visitors at accommodation establishments (compared with 18.0m. in 2000) and receipts from the tourism sector rose by 5.1% to reach €11,297m. The country's mountain scenery attracts visitors in both summer and winter, while Vienna and Salzburg, hosts to a number of internationally-renowned art festivals, are important cultural centres.

Österreich Werbung (Austrian National Tourist Office): Margaretenstr. 1, 1040 Vienna; tel. (1) 588-66-0; fax (1) 588-66-20; internet www.austria-tourism.at; f. 1955.

AZERBAIJAN

Introductory Survey

Location, Climate, Language, Religion, Flag, Capital

The Azerbaijan Republic is situated in eastern Transcaucasia, on the western coast of the Caspian Sea. To the south it borders Iran, to the west Armenia, to the north-west Georgia, and to the north the Republic of Dagestan, in Russia. The Nakhichevan Autonomous Republic is part of Azerbaijan, although it is separated from the rest of Azerbaijan by Armenian territory. Azerbaijan also includes the Nagorno-Karabakh Autonomous Oblast (Nagornyi Karabakh), which is largely populated by Armenians but does not legally constitute part of Armenia. The Kura plain has a dry, temperate climate with an average July temperature of 27°C (80°F) and an average January temperature of 1°C (34°F). Average annual rainfall on the lowlands is 200 mm–300 mm, but the Lenkoran plain normally receives between 1,000 mm and 1,750 mm. The official language is Azerbaijani, one of the South Turkic group of languages; although in 1992 the Latin script was to have replaced the Cyrillic alphabet (which had been in use since 1939), the use of Cyrillic for official and business purposes was not formally abolished until August 2001. Religious adherence corresponds largely to ethnic origins: almost all ethnic Azerbaijanis are Muslims, some 70% being Shi'ite and 30% Sunni. There are also Christian communities, mainly representatives of the Russian Orthodox and Armenian Apostolic denominations. The national flag (proportions 1 by 2) consists of three equal horizontal stripes, of pale blue, red and green, with a white crescent moon framing a white eight-pointed star on the central red stripe. The capital is Baku (Baki).

Recent History

An independent state in ancient times, Azerbaijan was dominated for much of its subsequent history by foreign powers. Under the Treaty of Turkmanchai of 1828, Azerbaijan was divided between Persia (now Iran, which was granted southern Azerbaijan) and Russia (northern Azerbaijan). During the latter half of the 19th century petroleum was discovered in Azerbaijan, and by 1900 the region had become one of the world's leading petroleum producers. Immigrant Slavs began to dominate Baku and other urban areas.

After the October Revolution of 1917 in Russia, there was a short period of pro-Bolshevik rule in Baku before a nationalist Government took power and established an independent state on 28 May 1918, with Gyanja (formerly Elisavetpol, but renamed Kirovabad in 1935) as the capital. Independent Azerbaijan was occupied by troops of both the Allied and Central Powers; after their withdrawal, it was invaded by the Red Army in April 1920, and on 28 April a Soviet Republic of Azerbaijan was established. In December 1922 the republic became a member of the Transcaucasian Soviet Federative Socialist Republic (TSFSR), which entered the USSR as a constituent republic on 31 December. The TSFSR was disbanded in 1936, and Azerbaijan became a full union republic, the Azerbaijan Soviet Socialist Republic (SSR).

Following the Soviet seizure of power in 1920, many nationalist and religious leaders and their followers were persecuted or killed. Religious intolerance was particularly severe in the 1930s, and many mosques and religious sites were destroyed. In 1930–31 forced collectivization of agriculture led to peasant uprisings, which were suppressed by Soviet troops. The purges of 1937–38, under the Soviet leader, Stalin (Iosif V. Dzhugashvili), involved the execution or imprisonment of many members of the Communist Party of Azerbaijan (CPA), including Sultan Mejit Efendiyev, the republic's leader, and two republican premiers. In 1945 the Soviet Government attempted to unite the Azerbaijani population of northern Iran with the Azerbaijan SSR, by providing military support for a local 'puppet' government in Iran; Soviet troops were forced to withdraw from northern Iran in the following year by US-British opposition.

The most influential of Azerbaijan's communist leaders in the period following the Second World War was Heydar Aliyev, who was installed as First Secretary of the CPA in 1969. He greatly increased the all-Union sector of the economy at the expense of republican industry, while retaining popularity with his liberal attitude to local corruption. Attempts to address corruption in the CPA were made after Mikhail Gorbachev became leader of the USSR in 1985. Aliyev was dismissed in October 1987, but popular dissatisfaction became more vocal. Unlike most Soviet republics, Azerbaijan had an annual trade surplus with the rest of the USSR, and yet its income per head was the lowest outside Central Asia. Public grievances over economic mismanagement and the privileges enjoyed by the party leadership were expressed at demonstrations in November 1988. Protesters occupied the main square in Baku, the capital, for 10 days, before being dispersed by troops, who arrested the leaders of the demonstrations.

The initial impetus, however, for the demonstrations was the debate on the status of Nagornyi Karabakh (an autonomous region within Azerbaijan) and Nakhichevan (an autonomous republic of Azerbaijan, separated from it by Armenian land). Both territories were claimed by Armenia, on historical grounds, and Nagornyi Karabakh had an overwhelming majority of (non-Muslim) Armenians in its population. Nakhichevan, despite the apparent surrender of Azerbaijan's claims to the territory in 1920, never became part of Soviet Armenia. The Soviet-Turkish Treaty of March 1921 included a clause guaranteeing Azerbaijani jurisdiction over Nakhichevan. The 45%–50% of the republic's population that had been ethnically Armenian in 1919 was reduced to less than 5% by 1989. Nagornyi Karabakh had been a disputed territory during the period of Armenian and Azerbaijani independence (1918–20), but in June 1921 the Bureau for Caucasian Affairs (the Kavburo) voted to unite Nagornyi Karabakh with Armenia. However, some days after the Kavburo vote, following an intervention by Stalin, the decision was reversed. In 1923 the territory was declared an autonomous oblast (region) within the Azerbaijan SSR. There were attempts to challenge Azerbaijan's jurisdiction over the region, including two petitions by the inhabitants of Nagornyi Karabakh in the 1960s, but they were strongly opposed by the Soviet and Azerbaijani authorities.

Conflict over the territory re-emerged in February 1988, when the Nagornyi Karabakh regional soviet (council) requested the Armenian and Azerbaijani Supreme Soviets to agree to the transfer of the territory to Armenia. The Soviet and Azerbaijani authorities rejected the request, thus provoking huge demonstrations by Armenians, not only in Nagornyi Karabakh, but also in the Armenian capital, Yerevan. Azerbaijanis began leaving Armenia, and reports that refugees had been attacked led to three days of anti-Armenian violence in the Azerbaijani town of Sumgait. According to official figures, 32 people died, 26 of whom were Armenians. Disturbances over the issue of Nagornyi Karabakh continued throughout 1988, leading to a large-scale exodus of refugees from both Armenia and Azerbaijan.

In January 1989, in an attempt to end the tension, the Soviet Government suspended the activities of the local authorities in Nagornyi Karabakh and established a Special Administration Committee (SAC), responsible to the USSR Council of Ministers. Although it was stressed that the region would formally retain its status as an autonomous oblast within Azerbaijan, the decision was widely viewed by Azerbaijanis as an infringement of the country's territorial integrity. This imposition of 'direct rule' from Moscow and the dispatch of some 5,000 Soviet troops did little to reduce tensions within Nagornyi Karabakh, where Armenians went on strike from May until September.

In mid-1989 the nationalist Popular Front of Azerbaijan (PFA) was established. Following sporadic strikes and demonstrations throughout August, the PFA organized a national strike in early September and demanded discussion on the issue of sovereignty, the situation in Nagornyi Karabakh, the release of political prisoners and official recognition of the PFA. After one week, the Azerbaijan Supreme Soviet agreed to concessions to the PFA, including official recognition. In addition, draft laws on economic and political sovereignty were published, and on 23 September the Supreme Soviet adopted the 'Constitutional Law on the Sovereignty of the Azerbaijan SSR', effectively a declaration of sovereignty. The conflict with Armenia continued, with the imposition by Azerbaijan of an economic blockade of Armenia.

In November 1989 the Soviet Government transferred control of Nagornyi Karabakh from the SAC to an Organizing Committee, dominated by ethnic Azerbaijanis. This decision was denounced by the Armenian Supreme Soviet, which declared Nagornyi Karabakh to be part of a 'unified Armenian republic', prompting further outbreaks of violence in Nagornyi Karabakh and along the Armenian–Azerbaijani border. Growing unrest within Azerbaijan, exacerbated by the return of refugees from Armenia to Baku, was directed both at the local communist regime and at ethnic Armenians.

In January 1990 radical members of the PFA led assaults on CPA and government buildings in Baku and other towns. Border posts were attacked on the Soviet–Iranian border, and nationalist activists seized CPA buildings in Nakhichevan and declared its secession from the USSR. In addition, renewed violence against Armenians, with some 60 people killed in rioting in Baku, led to a hasty evacuation of the remaining non-Azerbaijanis, including ethnic Russians, from the city. On 19 January a state of emergency was declared in Azerbaijan, and Soviet troops were ordered into Baku, where the PFA was in control. According to official reports, 131 people were killed, and some 700 wounded, during the Soviet intervention. The inability of the CPA to ensure stability in the republic led to the dismissal of Abdul Vezirov as First Secretary of the party; he was replaced by Ayaz Mutalibov.

Despite the arrest of leading members of the PFA and the outlawing of other radical nationalist organizations, continuing unrest caused the election to the republic's Supreme Soviet (held in most of the other Soviet republics in February 1990) to be postponed, and it eventually took place in September–October. Although the CPA won an overall majority, the opposition Democratic Alliance (which included the PFA) questioned the election's validity. In addition, the continuing state of emergency, which prohibited large public meetings, severely disrupted campaigning by the opposition. When the new Supreme Soviet convened in February 1991, some 80% of its deputies were members of the CPA. The small group of opposition deputies united as the Democratic Bloc of Azerbaijan.

Unlike the other Caucasian republics (Armenia and Georgia), Azerbaijan declared a willingness to sign a new Union Treaty and participated in the all-Union referendum on the preservation of the USSR, which took place in March 1991. Official results of the referendum demonstrated a qualified support for the preservation of the USSR, with 75.1% of the electorate participating, of whom 93.3% voted for a 'renewed federation'. In Nakhichevan, however, only some 20% of eligible voters approved President Gorbachev's proposal. Opposition politicians also contested the results of the referendum, claiming that only 15%–20% of the electorate had actually participated.

In August 1991, when the State Committee for the State of Emergency seized power in Moscow, Mutalibov issued a statement that appeared to demonstrate support for the coup. Despite denials that he had supported the coup leaders, large demonstrations took place, demanding his resignation, the declaration of Azerbaijan's independence, the repeal of the state of emergency, and the postponement of the presidential election, scheduled for 8 September. The opposition was supported by Heydar Aliyev, by this time Chairman of the Supreme Majlis (legislature) of Nakhichevan, who had become increasingly critical of Mutalibov's leadership. Mutalibov responded by ending the state of emergency and resigning as First Secretary of the CPA; on 30 August the Azerbaijani Supreme Soviet voted to 'restore the independent status of Azerbaijan'. The election to the presidency proceeded, although it was boycotted by the opposition, with the result that Mutalibov was the only candidate. According to official results, he won 84% of the total votes cast. At a congress of the CPA, held later in September, it was agreed to dissolve the party.

Independence was formally restored on 18 October 1991. The Supreme Soviet voted not to sign the treaty to establish an economic community, which was signed by the leaders of eight other Soviet republics on the same day. In a further move towards full independence, the Supreme Soviet adopted legislation allowing for the creation of national armed forces, and Azerbaijani units began to take control of the Soviet Army's military facilities in the republic. However, Azerbaijan did join the Commonwealth of Independent States (CIS, see p. 172), signing the Almaty (Alma-Ata) Declaration on 21 December.

Following the dissolution of the USSR, hostilities intensified in Nagornyi Karabakh. In March 1992 President Mutalibov resigned, owing to military reverses suffered by Azeri forces. He was replaced, on an interim basis, by Yagub Mamedov, the Chairman of the Milli Majlis, or National Assembly (which had replaced the Supreme Soviet following its suspension in late 1991), pending a presidential election in June. However, further military reverses prompted the Majlis to reinstate Mutalibov as President in mid-May. His immediate declaration of a state of emergency and the cancellation of the forthcoming presidential election outraged the opposition PFA, which organized a large-scale protest rally in Baku. The demonstrators occupied both the Majlis building and the presidential palace, and succeeded in deposing Mutalibov, who had held office for only one day. (He subsequently took refuge in Russia.) The PFA's effective take-over was consolidated in the following month, when the party's leader, Abulfaz Elchibey, was elected President of Azerbaijan by direct popular vote, defeating four other candidates by a substantial margin. Meanwhile, the Government had to contend with a steadily deteriorating economic situation, largely the result of the continuing conflict in Nagornyi Karabakh and the collapse of the former Soviet economic system. Severe shortages of food and fuel were reported throughout the country, and the Government's failure to provide adequate support for an estimated 500,000 refugees prompted protest actions in Baku from mid-1992.

The background of military defeats and continuing economic decline severely undermined the Government and led to divisions within the PFA in early 1993. In June a rebel army, led by Col Surat Husseinov (the former Azerbaijani military commander in Nagornyi Karabakh), seized the city of Gyanja and advanced towards the capital, with the apparent intention of deposing Elchibey. In an attempt to bolster his leadership, Elchibey summoned Heydar Aliyev to Baku; in mid-June Aliyev was elected Chairman of the legislature. Following Elchibey's subsequent flight from the capital, Aliyev announced that he had assumed the powers of the presidency. There ensued what appeared to be a power struggle between Aliyev and Husseinov, following the bloodless capture of Baku by the rebel forces. However, in late June virtually all presidential powers were transferred, on an acting basis, to Aliyev by the Milli Majlis (which had voted to impeach Elchibey), and Husseinov was appointed Prime Minister, with control over the security services.

A referendum of confidence in Elchibey (who had taken refuge in Nakhichevan and still laid claim to the presidency) was held in late August 1993; of the 92% of the electorate that participated, 97.5% voted against him. The Milli Majlis endorsed the result and announced the holding of a direct presidential election, which took place on 3 October. Aliyev was elected President of Azerbaijan, defeating two other candidates, with 98.8% of the votes cast. In the months preceding the election there was an escalation of opposition harassment, particularly of the PFA, which boycotted the election in protest.

The domestic political situation remained tense during 1994. There was an increase in organized crime (drugs-trafficking, in particular) as well as political violence. Opponents of President Aliyev and his New Azerbaijan Party (NAP) were subject to increasing harassment, and their media activities were severely restricted. In February over 40 PFA members were arrested at a regional party conference. In the following month police raided the PFA headquarters in Baku, arresting more than 100 people; the PFA, it was claimed, had been planning to overthrow the Government. The signature, in May, of a cease-fire agreement in Nagornyi Karabakh (see below) led to further unrest in Azerbaijan. Nationalist opposition leaders claimed that the cease-fire would result in humiliating concessions by Azerbaijan and would be followed by the deployment of Russian troops as peace-keepers. Large-scale, anti-Government demonstrations were organized by the PFA in Baku in May and September.

A new political crisis arose in late September 1994 when the Deputy Chairman of the Milli Majlis and Aliyev's security chief were assassinated; three members of the special militia (known as OPON) attached to the Ministry of Internal Affairs were subsequently arrested. In early October some 100 OPON troops, led by Rovshan Javadov (a Deputy Minister of Internal Affairs), stormed the office of the Procurator-General, taking him and his officials hostage and securing the release of the three OPON members in custody. President Aliyev described the incident as an attempted coup and declared a state of emergency in Baku and Gyanja.

In the immediate aftermath of these events, other forces mutinied in Baku and elsewhere in Azerbaijan. In Gyanja, rebel forces, reportedly led by a relative of Surat Husseinov, occupied government and strategic buildings, although troops loyal to Aliyev quickly re-established control. Despite Husseinov's assurances of allegiance to Aliyev, he was dismissed as Prime Minister, and replaced, on an acting basis, by Fuad Kuliyev. However, Aliyev stated that he would head the Government for the immediate future, and initiated a series of purges of senior members of the Government and the armed forces. In mid-October 1994 the Milli Majlis voted unanimously to remove Husseinov's parliamentary immunity from prosecution, so that he could be arrested on charges of treason (he was, however, believed to have fled to Russia).

Further political turmoil arose in March 1995, following a decree by the Government to disband the OPON militia (which had remained under the control of Javadov). OPON forces seized government and police buildings in Baku and in north-western Azerbaijan, and many casualties were reported, as government forces clashed with the OPON units. The rebellion was crushed when government troops stormed the OPON headquarters near Baku; Javadov and many of his men were killed, and some 160 rebels were arrested. Aliyev accused former President Elchibey and Surat Husseinov of collusion in the attempted coup. In the aftermath of the unrest the PFA was also accused of involvement, and the party was banned. In early April Aliyev extended the state of emergency in Baku until June, although the state of emergency in Gyanja was lifted. In May Fuad Kuliyev was confirmed as Prime Minister. The latter half of 1995 was dominated by preparations for Azerbaijan's first post-Soviet legislative election. However, unrest continued: in late July a new plot to overthrow Aliyev was allegedly uncovered, linked to Elchibey, Husseinov and other anti-Aliyev forces based in exile in Moscow. The harassment of opposition parties in Azerbaijan intensified, prompting protest actions in Baku.

The election of the new, 125-member Milli Majlis took place, as scheduled, on 12 November 1995. Of Azerbaijan's 31 officially registered parties, as few as eight were, in the event, permitted to participate; of these, only two were opposition parties—the PFA (recently relegalized) and the National Independence Party (NIP). Almost 600 independent candidates were barred from participation. The election was held under a mixed system of voting: 25 seats were to be filled by proportional representation and the remaining 100 by majority vote in single-member constituencies. These included the constituencies of Nagornyi Karabakh and of the other Armenian-occupied territories (refugees from those regions voted in areas under Azerbaijani control, in anticipation of the eventual restoration of the country's territorial integrity). The result demonstrated widespread support for President Aliyev's NAP, which won 19 of the 25 party seats (with the PFA and the NIP receiving three seats each). The NAP and independent candidates supporting Aliyev won an overwhelming majority of single-constituency seats. Of the remaining 28 seats in the Majlis, 27 were filled at 'run-off' elections held in late November 1995 and in February 1996, while one seat remained vacant. Some international observers monitoring the election declared that it had not been free and fair and that 'serious electoral violations' had occurred. On the same occasion as the election of the Milli Majlis, Azerbaijan's new Constitution was approved by an overwhelming majority of the electorate (officially, 91.9%) in a national referendum. The Constitution, which replaced the 1978 Soviet version, provided for a secular state, headed by the President, who was accorded wide-ranging executive powers.

In early 1996 supporters of Surat Husseinov and former President Elchibey received lengthy custodial sentences for their involvement in the alleged coup attempts of October 1994 and March 1995. In February 1996 two former government members were sentenced to death on charges of treason and several others were sentenced to death on conspiracy charges in the following months. Former President Mutalibov, whom Aliyev had accused of conspiring with Javadov, was arrested in Russia in April. However, he remained in Moscow for medical treatment, and the Russian authorities later refused to extradite him, on the grounds of insufficient evidence.

Repressive measures against the opposition continued, with the seizure by the police of the PFA headquarters in April 1996. Several members of the party were later arrested, one for an alleged attempt to assassinate Aliyev in 1993, and the others on charges of establishing illegal armed groups. In July 1996 Aliyev criticized the Cabinet of Ministers for failing to implement economic reforms, and dismissed several senior government officials for corruption. Fuad Kuliyev resigned from the office of Prime Minister, officially on grounds of ill health, after he was accused by Aliyev of hindering the process of reform; Artur Rasizade, hitherto first Deputy Prime Minister, was appointed Prime Minister, initially in an acting capacity. In September the Chairman of the Milli Majlis, Rasul Kuliyev, who had been criticized by the NAP, resigned. Murtuz Aleskerov, a staunch supporter of Aliyev, was elected in his place.

In January 1997 the Azerbaijani authorities released details of an abortive coup in October 1996, which had reportedly been organized by, among others, Mutalibov and Surat Husseinov. Charges were subsequently brought against some 40 alleged conspirators; in early 1997 many people, including 31 former members of the Baku police force, received prison sentences for their part in the attempted coups of October 1994 and March 1995. Husseinov was extradited from Russia in March 1997, and his trial, on charges of treason, began in July 1998. (In February 1999 he was sentenced to life imprisonment.) Meanwhile, in February 1997 four leading members of the opposition Islamic Party of Azerbaijan, including its Chairman, Ali Akram Aliyev, went on trial on charges of espionage on behalf of Iran (which denied any involvement). The four men received lengthy terms of imprisonment in April. In the same month President Aliyev established a Security Council, the creation of which was stipulated in the 1995 Constitution. Also in April 1997 the formation of an informal alliance of 10 parties (including the ruling NAP) to support Aliyev's policies and his candidacy in the 1998 presidential election, was criticized as unrepresentative by the opposition PFA. Meanwhile, in May 1997 former President Elchibey was elected Chairman of the Democratic Congress, an opposition alliance.

In January 1998 the Azerbaijani authorities accused Rasul Kuliyev (who was resident in the USA), of organizing a conspiracy to depose President Aliyev. In April Kuliyev, who denied the accusations, was charged *in absentia* with alleged abuses of power while Chairman of the Milli Majlis. In May legislation was passed creating a 24-member Central Electoral Commission, 12 members of which were to be directly appointed by the President, and 12 by the legislature. A law regarding presidential elections was approved in June, which required candidates to collect 50,000 signatures to stand, and set a minimum level of voter participation of 50%, although this was reduced to 25% in July. Each voter was allowed to endorse more than one candidate. The opposition protested that the law favoured Aliyev's re-election, and launched a series of demonstrations to demand the cancellation of the election, which was scheduled to be held in October. In mid-September police and demonstrators clashed violently in Baku, resulting in a number of arrests. Subsequent demonstrations were conducted peacefully following the imposition of new restrictions on public protests. Meanwhile, in August Aliyev issued a decree dismantling the General Directorate of State Secrets, thereby effectively abolishing media censorship, although harassment of the independent media continued.

The presidential election was held, as planned, on 11 October 1998; according to official results, Heydar Aliyev was re-elected with 77.6% of the votes cast. Five other candidates contested the election, which was criticized by the Organization for Security and Co-operation in Europe (OSCE, see p. 283)—known as the Conference on Security and Co-operation in Europe (CSCE) until December 1994—and the Council of Europe (see p. 181) for failing to meet international standards. Unrest continued, owing to the opposition's dissatisfaction with the validity of the results, and in November the Prosecutor-General announced that criminal proceedings would be instigated against a number of opposition leaders for sedition. The Cabinet of Ministers resigned shortly after the presidential election, as required by the Constitution. In late October the majority of ministers, including Prime Minister Rasizade, were reconfirmed in their positions by President Aliyev. In late December the Milli Majlis approved a revised Constitution for Nakhichevan, which defined the enclave as an 'autonomous state' within Azerbaijan. The amended Constitution had earlier been endorsed by the Nakhichevan legislature. The revisions were opposed by some deputies, on the grounds that the enclave's redefined status as a state within a state could set an undesirable precedent. In November the Movement for Democratic Elections and Electoral Reform, an alliance composed of 23 opposition groups, was established, with the aim of campaigning for the annulment of the recent presidential election.

In the first half of 1999 President Aliyev's poor health caused fears of instability and reports circulated that Aliyev was preparing his son Ilham (the Vice-Chairman of the State Oil Company of the Azerbaijan Republic) to assume the presidency. Following medical treatment in the USA in April, however, the President's health improved, and in the following months he made a number of cabinet changes and announced, in September, that he was prepared to stand for a third term; none the less, Ilham Aliyev's political profile continued to be raised, and he was elected Chairman of the pro-Aliyev NAP in December. Meanwhile, in April the Democratic Congress, which comprised, among other parties, the PFA and the Civic Solidarity Party (CSP—some 17 deputies in total), began a boycott of the Milli Majlis, on the grounds that the Government had violated the rights of opposition deputies by refusing to discuss draft laws on municipal elections. The boycott was ended in late June following negotiations with the Government, and Azerbaijan's first municipal elections since independence were held in December, thereby fulfilling a prerequisite for membership of the Council of Europe. However, mass electoral violations were observed and in March 2000 repeat elections were held to 75 municipal councils where the vote had been deemed invalid. Although there were reports of numerous infringements of press freedoms in 2000, including the suspension of several publications and the arrests of journalists, President Aliyev made continued concessions towards Council of Europe membership, such as the granting of amnesties to political prisoners.

In April 2000 a demonstration, attended by up to 20,000 people, was organized by the Democratic Congress, which demanded the introduction of measures to ensure that the legislative election due to be held in November would be free and fair. Many arrests were made, and the security forces were accused of using excessive force. In mid-May the Milli Majlis passed a draft law on the composition of the Central Electoral Commission, which was endorsed by the Government and rejected by opposition parties. The death, in August, of former President Abulfaz Elchibey, prompted divisions to emerge within both the PFA and the Democratic Congress. The PFA divided into traditionalist and reformist factions, with separate Supreme Councils; the Central Electoral Commission recognized only the reformist wing, led by Ali Kerimov (Kerimli). The Democratic Congress was forced to restructure when five parties, including the reformist branch of the PFA, left in October. Shortly afterwards the traditionalist faction of the PFA, led by Murmahmud Fattayev, reached agreement with Musavat to co-operate in the election. Meanwhile, in September the Central Electoral Commission refused to register eight opposition parties. Although the Commission's decision was revoked, following strong criticism from the US Government, a number of political parties (largely those that had initially been prevented from registering) decided to boycott the election, which they condemned as undemocratic. In October a warrant was issued for the arrest of Rasul Kuliyev (who remained in exile in the USA), on charges of having attempted to organize a coup in March, although there were allegations that the warrant was politically motivated. In January 2001 seven people were convicted of having collaborated with Kuliyev in the coup attempt.

The legislative election, held, as scheduled, on 5 November 2000, was condemned by the OSCE for the falsification of results and intimidatory practices, and country-wide protests followed. Of the 25 seats filled by proportional representation, 17 were obtained by the NAP and four by the PFA, while the CPA and the CSP each secured two seats in the legislature. Of the 99 seats contested in single-mandate constituencies, 62 were obtained by the NAP and 26 by independent candidates; the election results were invalidated in 11 constituencies and repeat elections were held on 7 January 2001, despite demands that the Court of Appeal declare the election to have been invalid. Several parties chose, once again, to boycott the repeat elections. Ultimately, the reformist faction of the PFA reversed an earlier decision to reject the legitimacy of the legislature and took up its seats in the Milli Majlis, as did the CSP.

The suppression of press freedoms remained prevalent in 2001, as several publications were closed down, amid accusations of official harassment. A number of newspapers were also penalized for acting in contravention of a presidential decree, which, from 1 August, introduced the Latin, rather than the Cyrillic, script for official and business purposes. Divisions within the NAP became more evident during 2001, with the emergence of a faction known as the '91st' group, the members of which were largely excluded from the party's political council,

following a party congress held in November. The congress re-elected Aliyev as Chairman of the NAP and his son, Ilham Aliyev, was elected to the newly established post of First Deputy Chairman. In June 2002 President Aliyev confirmed his intention to stand for re-election in 2003.

In early June 2002 government troops used armed force against inhabitants of the village of Nardaran, on the outskirts of Baku, who were protesting over deteriorating socio-economic conditions. As a result of the clashes, one person was killed and 18 protesters, including the village's chief elder, were detained in custody indefinitely, thereby exacerbating tensions. Demonstrations continued to take place thereafter. In January 2003 the trials commenced of 15 protesters, including Alikram Aliyev, the leader of the Islamic Party of Azerbaijan, and the Chairman of the Association of Baku Villages. In early February the security forces launched a further assault on the village, and several people were detained.

Meanwhile, in early August 2002 Ziya Mammedov was appointed to the newly created post of Minister of Transport. On 24 August a referendum was held on 39 proposed amendments to the Constitution, among the most notable of which were proposals for executive power to be transferred to the (presidentially appointed) prime minister, rather than the elected chairman of the Milli Majlis, in the event of the president's inability to govern; and for the outcome of the presidential election to be determined by a straightforward majority of the votes cast, rather than the existing pre-requisite of two-thirds. According to the official results of the plebiscite, 96% of votes (cast by 84% of the electorate) were in favour of the constitutional amendments, although demonstrations followed, after reports by both opposition parties and observers from the OSCE and the USA of fraud and procedural violations. The amendments were subsequently approved by the Council of Europe, but large-scale protest rallies took place from September, to demand the annulment of the results of the referendum, the holding of free and fair elections, and the resignation of President Aliyev; several members of the opposition were arrested. Further political controversy arose towards the end of the year over proposed revisions to the electoral code, and in late December opposition parties boycotted OSCE-mediated negotiations on the foundation of a conciliation commission, to be composed of government and opposition representatives, which aimed to reach consensus on the issue.

In January 2003 the Ministry of Justice annulled the registration of the 'reformist' faction of the PFA, in favour of a third successor group, founded in August 2002 and led by Gudrat Hasankuliyev, who had been expelled from the 'reformist' wing of the party in April. The two original factions condemned the registration of the new grouping as an attempt by the Government to hinder their activity prior to the presidential election, and President Aliyev subsequently overturned the Ministry's ruling. Meanwhile, in January 2003 the Editor-in-Chief of the leading opposition newspaper, Yeni Müsavat, and 11 other journalists began a hunger strike, in protest at legal action against the publication by representatives of the Government, and physical assaults on its staff. In the previous month several hundred people had taken part in a protest rally against the perceived repression of the media. Large-scale protest demonstrations convened by the Democratic Party of Azerbaijan to demand Aliyev's resignation continued into early 2003.

At the time of the disintegration of the USSR in late 1991, the leadership of Nagornyi Karabakh declared the enclave to be an independent republic. Azerbaijan refused to accept the territory's attempts to secede, and in January 1992 Nagornyi Karabakh was placed under direct presidential rule. International efforts to negotiate a peace settlement foundered, owing to Azerbaijan's insistence that the conflict was a domestic problem. Military successes by the ethnic Armenian forces of Nagornyi Karabakh in early 1992 culminated in the creation, in May, of a 'corridor' through Azerbaijani territory to link Nagornyi Karabakh with Armenia proper. Despite a successful Azerbaijani counter-offensive in late 1992, ethnic Armenian forces were able to open a second corridor in early 1993, following which they extended their operations into Azerbaijan itself, apparently in an attempt to create a secure zone around Nagornyi Karabakh. By August some 20% of Azerbaijan's territory had been seized by Armenian units, while all of Nagornyi Karabakh had already come under their control. The Armenian military gains prompted mounting alarm among the Azeri population, and there was a massive new movement of refugees fleeing from Armenian-occupied territory. The Armenian offensive in Azerbaijan continued, despite widespread international condemnation. Although it did not directly accuse Armenia itself of aggression, the UN Security Council adopted a series of resolutions demanding an immediate cease-fire and the withdrawal of all Armenian units from Azerbaijan. There were also strong protests by Turkey and Iran, both of which mobilized troops in regions bordering Armenia and Azerbaijan in September. In December Azeri forces launched a new counter-offensive in Nagornyi Karabakh, recapturing some areas that they had lost to Armenian control, although suffering heavy casualties. Meanwhile, international efforts to halt the conflict continued, led by the 'Minsk Group', which had been established by the CSCE in 1992 to provide a framework for peace negotiations. However, all cease-fire agreements were quickly violated. In early 1994 it was estimated that, since the conflict began in 1988, some 18,000 people had been killed and a further 25,000 had been wounded. The number of Azeri refugees was believed to have exceeded 1m.

However, in early May 1994 a major breakthrough was achieved, with Azerbaijan's signature of the so-called Bishkek Protocol, which had been adopted several days previously at a meeting of the CIS Inter-Parliamentary Assembly, with the approval of representatives of both Armenia and Nagornyi Karabakh. The Protocol, although not legally binding, was regarded as an expression of willingness by the warring factions to negotiate a lasting peace accord. On 8 May the Nagornyi Karabakh leadership ordered its forces to cease hostilities, in accordance with the Protocol. Although isolated violations were subsequently reported, the cease-fire remained in force. In the latter half of the year efforts were made to co-ordinate the separate peace proposals of the CSCE 'Minsk Group' and Russia. However, Azerbaijan refused either to negotiate a peace settlement or to discuss the future status of Nagornyi Karabakh until Armenian forces were withdrawn entirely from occupied Azerbaijani territory and Azerbaijani refugees had returned to their homes. Azerbaijan also insisted that international peace-keeping forces be deployed in Nagornyi Karabakh (as opposed to the Russian- and CIS-led force favoured by Armenia). In December, at a summit meeting of the CSCE (subsequently known as the OSCE), delegates agreed in principle to deploy a 3,000-strong multinational peace-keeping force in Nagornyi Karabakh; Russia was to contribute not more than 30% of the peacekeepers. In May 1995 the exchange of prisoners of war and other hostages was commenced. In April–June a new, 33-seat republican legislature was elected in Nagornyi Karabakh (replacing the 81-member Supreme Soviet). Robert Kocharian, hitherto Chairman of the State Defence Committee, was appointed to the new office of an executive presidency. The election to the office of President of Nagornyi Karabakh was held in November 1996, despite earlier criticism from the OSCE and condemnation by Azerbaijan, and Kocharian was re-elected with more than 85% of votes cast. Azeri refugees from the enclave staged protests in Baku, while Azerbaijan declared that it would not recognize the election results.

Negotiations to reach a political settlement continued throughout 1996. Aliyev, who met President Ter-Petrossian of Armenia on several occasions, continued to affirm his commitment to Azerbaijan's territorial integrity, reiterating that Nagornyi Karabakh could be granted autonomy within Azerbaijan, but not full independence. In December Aliyev and Ter-Petrossian attended a summit meeting of the OSCE, in Lisbon, Portugal. Following demands by Azerbaijan, a statement was released by the OSCE Chairman, recommending three principles that would form the basis of a political settlement to the conflict: the territorial integrity of Armenia and Azerbaijan; legal status for Nagornyi Karabakh, which would be granted self-determination within Azerbaijan; and security guarantees for the population of Nagornyi Karabakh. However, Armenia refused to accept the terms of the statement.

Relations between Azerbaijan and Armenia deteriorated in February 1997, when Azerbaijan condemned the provision of weapons to Armenia by several countries, including Russia, as a violation of the Conventional Forces in Europe (CFE) Treaty. Armenia retaliated by accusing Azerbaijan of preparing for a military offensive against Nagornyi Karabakh to regain the territory. The admission by the Russian Minister of Defence that weapons had been delivered to Armenia in 1994–96 without the authorization, or knowledge, of the Russian Government, resulted in a deterioration in relations between Russia and Azerbaijan, particularly since Russia, as a participant in the 'Minsk Group', was expected to act as an impartial mediator.

Azerbaijan demanded that the issue be investigated by the signatories to the CFE Treaty. Negotiations under the auspices of the OSCE resumed in Moscow in April, but later that month a series of clashes, which left many people killed or wounded, occurred on the Armenian–Azerbaijani border, with each side accusing the other of initiating the hostilities.

In late May 1997 a draft peace settlement for the disputed enclave was presented by the 'Minsk Group'. Although the proposals were initially rejected, a revised plan, issued in July, received the qualified support of President Aliyev. The proposals provided for a stage-by-stage settlement of the conflict: Nagornyi Karabakh would receive autonomous status within Azerbaijan, and the withdrawal of Armenian forces from the enclave was to be followed by the deployment of OSCE peace-keeping troops, which would guarantee freedom of movement through the Lachin corridor linking Armenia with Nagornyi Karabakh. The appointment of Robert Kocharian, who was born in Nagornyi Karabakh, as Prime Minister of Armenia in March, and the proposed presidential election in Nagornyi Karabakh, scheduled for September, were severely criticized by Aliyev; the Azerbaijani authorities also expressed concern at the conclusion of a partnership treaty between Armenia and Russia, fearing that a strengthening of relations between the two countries was a hindrance to the peace process.

The election of Arkadii Ghukassian to the post of President of Nagornyi Karabakh in September 1997 was not recognized by the international community and threatened to hamper further progress on reaching a settlement, owing to his outright dismissal of the OSCE proposals; it was reported later in that month, however, that both Azerbaijan and Armenia had accepted the revised plan drawn up by the 'Minsk Group'. In addition, in an apparently significant change in policy, President Ter-Petrossian of Armenia publicly admitted that Nagornyi Karabakh could expect neither to gain full independence, nor to be united with Armenia. Moreover, the Azerbaijani authorities indicated that they would be willing to discuss with the leadership of Nagornyi Karabakh the level of autonomy to be granted to the enclave, providing that the principles of the Lisbon statement were accepted, having previously refused to recognize the Nagornyi Karabakh administration as an equal party in the negotiations.

Ter-Petrossian's cautious and moderate approach to the Nagornyi Karabakh crisis provoked much government disapproval and led to the President's resignation in early February 1998. His replacement, Kocharian, was expected to adopt a more belligerent and nationalistic stance towards resolving the situation in the disputed enclave. In June Leonard Petrossian, who had been appointed in 1996, resigned as Prime Minister of Nagornyi Karabakh; he was replaced by Zhirayr Pogossian. In late November the Armenian Government announced that, despite some reservations, it officially accepted the latest proposals put forward by the 'Minsk Group' regarding a settlement of the conflict in Nagornyi Karabakh, which were based on the principle of a 'common state' (comprising Azerbaijan and Nagornyi Karabakh). The Azerbaijani Government, however, rejected the proposals, claiming that they threatened the territorial integrity of Azerbaijan.

An escalation in hostilities in mid-1999 prompted mutual accusations by Azerbaijan and Armenia that the other was attempting to abrogate the 1994 cease-fire agreement. Presidents Kocharian and Aliyev met on several occasions in the latter half of 1999, but no substantive progress was made. Meanwhile, in June President Ghukassian dismissed the Government of Nagornyi Karabakh for failing to remedy the enclave's economic problems; at the end of that month Anushavan Danielian was appointed to head a new administration. In July former Prime Minister Zhirayr Pogossian was arrested and charged with the illegal possession of arms and ammunition, and with responsibility for the loss of a state document. Samuel Babaian, Minister of Defence until June and an ally of Pogossian, who opposed Ghukassian's political stance, was subsequently dismissed as army commander. Following an assassination attempt against President Ghukassian in late March 2000, Babaian was charged with organizing the attack, as part of a purported coup. (He was sentenced to 14 years' imprisonment in February 2001.) A legislative election was held in Nagornyi Karabakh on 18 June 2000. Five parties contested the election to the 33-seat legislature; the pro-Presidential Democratic Artsakh Party secured the most seats, with 13. Direct talks between the Armenian and Azerbaijani Presidents continued in 2000–02, but little progress was made towards reaching a final solution to the crisis. On 11 August 2002 Arkadii Ghukassian was re-elected as President of Nagornyi Karabakh, receiving over 88% of the votes cast.

Although it signed the Almaty Declaration in December 1991, Azerbaijan's subsequent attitude towards its membership of the CIS was equivocal. Indeed, the Milli Majlis failed to ratify the Commonwealth's founding treaty, and in October 1992 it voted overwhelmingly against further participation in the CIS. However, with the overthrow of the nationalist PFA Government and the accession to power of Heydar Aliyev, the country's position regarding the CIS was reversed, and in September 1993 Azerbaijan was formally admitted to full membership of the body. None the less, Azerbaijan did not renew its membership of the CIS Collective Security Treaty in 1999, because of the continued occupation of Nagornyi Karabakh by Armenian troops, and in protest against Russia's continuing supply of armaments to Armenia. In October relations with Russia were further strained, when it was reported that a Russian military aircraft had accidentally bombed a village in northern Azerbaijan. However, a visit to Azerbaijan by the Russian President, Vladimir Putin, in January 2001, and the signature of a number of co-operation agreements, appeared to signal a new stage in relations between the two countries. A reciprocal visit to Russia by President Aliyev took place in late January 2002, at which a 10-year economic co-operation plan was agreed. Furthermore, in late September a bilateral agreement was signed on the delimitation of the Caspian Sea, according to which the seabed would be divided into national sectors, and the surface be used in common; a similar agreement had already been reached with Kazakhstan. Meanwhile, in 1997 a dispute with Turkmenistan concerning ownership of the Kyapaz (known as Serdar by Turkmenistan) offshore oilfield threatened the conclusion of a contract with Russia to develop the area. Relations remained strained, and in June 2001 Turkmenistan closed its embassy in Baku, ostensibly owing to financial reasons. However, in December 2002 an Azerbaijani ambassador was accredited to Turkmenistan for the first time.

The strengthening of relations with Turkey, which had been cultivated by successive leaderships following independence in 1991, continued under Aliyev. Throughout the conflict over Nagornyi Karabakh, Azerbaijan was supported by Turkey, which provided humanitarian and other aid, and reinforced Azerbaijan's economic blockade of Armenia. An intergovernmental agreement in support of the construction of a petroleum pipeline from the Azerbaijani oilfields to the Turkish port of Ceyhan via Tbilisi, Georgia, was signed in October 1998; a further agreement was signed by the Azerbaijani Government with the State Oil Company of the Azerbaijan Republic (SOCAR) and a number of petroleum companies in October 2000. The large Azeri minority in neighbouring Iran (numbering an estimated 20m.) was regarded as a potential source of tension. In early 1995 it was reported that Azeri organizations in northern areas of Iran had established a 'national independence front' in order to achieve unification with Azerbaijan. Nevertheless, official relations between Iran and Azerbaijan remained amicable, and bilateral trade increased significantly in the 1990s, with Iran becoming one of Azerbaijan's largest trading partners by 1997. Relations deteriorated in 1999, however, following Azerbaijani allegations, which were denied by Iran, that Iranian spies had been operating in Azerbaijan to supply Armenia with military intelligence and that Islamist guerrillas had been trained in Iran as part of a plot against the Azerbaijani Government. Tensions also arose over the status of the Caspian Sea, together with Azerbaijan's increasing involvement with international petroleum companies. In July 2001 an Iranian military patrol boat ordered Azerbaijani survey vessels leased by the US-based petroleum company BP to leave the disputed Sharg-Araz-Alov (known as Alborz to Iran) area of the Sea. As a result, BP suspended its petroleum-exploration operations in the southern Caspian, pending a resolution of the dispute. There were subsequent reports of violations of Azerbaijani airspace by Iranian aircraft, although these allegations were strongly denied by Iran. None the less, in May 2002 President Aliyev paid a long-scheduled visit to Iran, signing a number of accords on bilateral co-operation, which were expected significantly to stimulate trade; a further agreement on economic co-operation was signed in October, which included plans for the construction of a pipeline to carry natural gas from Iran to Nakhichevan, at a cost of some US $13.8m., and improved transit links and customs procedures between the two countries. By January 2003 the two countries were also reported to be closer to reaching consensus over the division of the Caspian Sea.

Relations with the USA developed significantly in the mid-1990s, and in July 1997 President Aliyev visited the USA, the first visit by an Azerbaijani Head of State since the country regained its independence. An agreement on military co-operation was signed between the two countries, and four contracts between SOCAR and US petroleum companies to develop off-shore oilfields in the Caspian Sea were also concluded. The USA assumed co-chairmanship of the 'Minsk Group' in early 1997, together with Russia and France. New contracts for the development of the petroleum industry, worth US $10m., were signed during a visit to Washington, DC, by Aliyev in April 1999. The USA also expressed its support for a proposed pipeline to carry petroleum from Baku to Ceyhan (see above), and a financial agreement on its construction was signed in Washington in April 2000. Following the initiation of a US-led anti-terrorism campaign in late 2001 (see USA chapter), the US Government agreed to halt the provision of financial assistance to Nagornyi Karabakh and commit funds to Azerbaijan, through the temporary suspension of Amendment 907 to the Freedom Support Act of 1992 (establishing a foreign assistance programme to the countries of the former USSR), which prevented the donation of aid to Azerbaijan while that country's blockade of the Armenian border remained in place. The waiver was renewed for a further year in January 2003.

In March 1992 Azerbaijan was admitted to the UN; it subsequently became a member of the CSCE. In April 1996, together with Armenia and Georgia, Azerbaijan signed a co-operation agreement with the European Union (see p. 199). Azerbaijan was awarded observer status at NATO in June 1999, and in the following month it sent 30 troops to form part of the NATO peace-keeping force in the province of Kosovo and Metohija, the Federal Republic of Yugoslavia. Azerbaijan was finally inaugurated as a full member of the Council of Europe on 25 January 2001 (as was Armenia).

Government

Under the Constitution of November 1995, the President of the Azerbaijan Republic is Head of State and Commander-in-Chief of the armed forces. The President, who is directly elected for a five-year term of office, holds supreme executive authority in conjunction with the Cabinet of Ministers, which is appointed by the President and is headed by the Prime Minister. Supreme legislative power is vested in the 125-member Milli Majlis (National Assembly), which is directly elected (under a mixed system of voting) for a five-year term. Azerbaijan is divided into 64 administrative districts, in addition to an autonomous oblast, Nagornyi Karabakh, and an autonomous republic, the exclave of Nakhichevan.

Defence

After gaining independence in 1991, Azerbaijan began the formation of national armed forces. In August 2002 these numbered 72,100: an army of 62,000, a navy of 2,200 and an air force of 7,900. Military service is for 17 months (but may be extended for ground forces). The Ministry of Internal Affairs controls a militia of some 10,000 and a border guard of an estimated 5,000. As a member of the CIS, Azerbaijan's naval forces operate under CIS (Russian) control. In May 1994 Azerbaijan became the 15th country to join NATO's (see p. 271) 'Partnership for Peace' programme of military co-operation. The 2002 budget allocated an estimated US $118m. to defence.

Economic Affairs

In 2001, according to World Bank estimates, Azerbaijan's gross national income (GNI), measured at average 1999–2001 prices, was US $5,283m., equivalent to $650 per head (or $3,020 per head on an international purchasing-power parity basis). During 1993–2001, it was estimated, the population increased at an average rate of 1.0% per year, while gross domestic product (GDP) per head increased, in real terms, at an average annual rate of 0.1%. Overall GDP increased, in real terms, at an average annual rate of 1.0% in 1993–2001. Real GDP increased by 11.1% in 2000 and by 9.0% in 2001.

Agriculture (including fishing) contributed 19.8% of GDP in 2001, when some 40.0% of the working population were employed in the sector. The principal crops are grain, apples, watermelons and other fruit, vegetables and cotton. By mid-1999 some 80% of state-owned agriculture had passed into private ownership, and by the end of 2001 all collective farms had been privatized. During 1993–2001, according to World

Bank estimates, agricultural GDP increased, in real terms, at an average annual rate of 1.4%. Real agricultural GDP increased by 11.9% in 2000 and by 9.1% in 2001.

Industry (including mining, manufacturing, construction and power) contributed 38.3% of GDP in 2001, according to World Bank figures. In that year, according to official sources, 10.8% of the working population were employed in the sector. According to the World Bank, during 1993–2001 industrial GDP declined, in real terms, by an annual average of 5.0%, although sectoral GDP increased by 6.7% in 2000 and by an estimated 5.8% in 2001. Those sectors associated with the petroleum industry, such as construction, have tended to experience steady growth, whereas non-petroleum-based industries have demonstrated a significant decline.

Azerbaijan is richly endowed with mineral resources, the most important of which is petroleum. The country's known reserves of petroleum were estimated to total 1,000m. metric tons at the end of 2001, mainly located in offshore fields in the Caspian Sea. In September 1994 the Azerbaijani Government and a consortium of international petroleum companies, the Azerbaijan International Operating Company (AIOC), concluded an agreement to develop the offshore oilfields. By mid-2000 the State Oil Company of the Azerbaijan Republic (SOCAR) had signed 19 production-sharing agreements with international partners, largely for the exploration of new fields. Production of 'early' oil began in October 1997 and accounted for a 50% increase in overall petroleum extraction over the following two years. The petroleum was transported to the Russian Black Sea port of Novorossiisk, via Chechnya, although technical problems with the pipeline and the conflict in Chechnya caused regular closures; a new section of the pipeline, avoiding Chechnya, was completed in March 2000. A further pipeline, transporting petroleum from Baku to the Georgian port of Supsa, opened in April 1999. In October 2000 the Government of Azerbaijan signed an agreement with SOCAR and a consortium of petroleum companies on the construction of a pipeline from Baku, via Tbilisi (Georgia), to Ceyhan in Turkey. Azerbaijan also has substantial reserves of natural gas, most of which are located offshore. In July 1999 a massive gasfield was discovered at Shah Deniz in the Caspian Sea, with reserves estimated at more than 400,000m. cu m., and there were plans to construct a gas pipeline to transport natural gas to Erzerum (Turkey), via Tbilisi. The new gas pipeline was scheduled for completion in 2005, with an initial anticipated capacity of 2,000m. cu m per year. Other minerals extracted include gold, silver, iron ore, copper concentrates, alunite (alum-stone), iron pyrites, barytes, cobalt and molybdenum.

Manufacturing accounted for some 5.3% of GDP in 2001. In 1996 the principal branches of manufacturing, measured by gross value of output, were petroleum refineries (accounting for 47.6% of the total), textiles (13.0%), chemicals (3.2%) and food products and beverages (1.3%). The GDP of the sector declined, in real terms, at an annual average rate of 8.1% in 1993–2001. However, sectoral GDP increased by 15.1% in 2000 and by 8.5% in 2001.

In 1992 only around 6% of Azerbaijan's supply of primary energy was provided by petroleum and petroleum products, but by 1999 72.0% of electricity generation was derived from petroleum, while natural gas accounted for 19.8% of production, and the remainder was provided by hydroelectric stations. Fuels accounted for just 4.9% of merchandise imports in 2000.

In 2001, according to the World Bank, the services sector provided an estimated 41.9% of GDP, and in the same year it accounted for 49.2% of employment. From the mid-1990s retail trade, restaurants and hotels gained in importance, concomitantly with the petroleum industry. During 1993–2001, the GDP of the services sector increased, in real terms, at an average annual rate of 13.4%. Sectoral GDP increased by 11.9% in 2000 and by an estimated 8.9% in 2001.

In 2001 Azerbaijan recorded a visible trade surplus of US $613.9m., but there was a deficit of $51.8m. on the current account of the balance of payments. In that year the principal source of imports was Russia (11.6%). Other major sources of imports were Turkey, Switzerland, Germany, Kazakhstan, the USA, Iran and the United Kingdom. The main market for exports was Italy (31.2%). Other important purchasers were Israel, Germany, Turkey and France. The major exports in 2001 were mineral products (accounting for 91.5% of the total). The principal imports in that year were machinery and electrical equipment (24.7%), mineral products, vehicles and transport equipment, base metals and vegetable products.

Azerbaijan's budget deficit for 2001 was some 113,000m. manats (equivalent to some 0.4% of GDP). At the end of 2000 the country's total external debt was estimated to be US $1,184.2m., of which $593.5m. was long-term public debt. The cost of debt-servicing in that year was equivalent to 8.0% of the value of exports of goods and services. Inflation increased by an average of 158.2% per year during 1991–2001. Consumer prices increased by an average of 1,664.5% in 1994, but the rate of inflation declined to 19.8% in 1996, and deflation was recorded in 1998–99. The average annual rate of inflation increased to 1.8% in 2000, and was 1.5% in 2001. Some 48,446 people were registered as unemployed in 2001, although the actual rate of unemployment was thought to be much higher.

Azerbaijan became a member of the IMF and the World Bank in 1992. It also joined the Islamic Development Bank (see p. 257), the European Bank for Reconstruction and Development (EBRD, see p. 193), the Economic Co-operation Organization (ECO, see p. 192) and the Black Sea Economic Co-operation group (known as the Organization of the Black Sea Economic Co-operation (see p. 294) from May 1999). In February 2000 Azerbaijan became a member of the Asian Development Bank (see p. 143).

The dissolution of the USSR in 1991, the conflict in Nagornyi Karabakh and the disruption of trade routes through Georgia and Chechnya all caused significant economic problems in Azerbaijan. However, owing to its enormous mineral wealth, Azerbaijan's prospects for eventual economic prosperity were considered to be favourable. Agreements were concluded with international consortia from the mid-1990s, and the development of export routes for the country's petroleum and natural gas reserves was expected greatly to improve Azerbaijan's economic situation. The Government's stabilization and reform programme, adopted in early 1995, had achieved considerable success by 1998, and the easing of monetary and exchange-rate policies in the latter half of 1999 helped to restore confidence in the manat, after the adverse impact of the Russian financial crisis of 1998. A new Ministry of Fuel and Energy was established in 2001, to assume some of the regulatory responsibility for the petroleum sector, and in September progress was made towards the planned natural gas pipeline to Turkey, via Georgia, with the signature of an agreement on terms for the transit of gas through the latter country. The pipeline was to be laid alongside the Baku–Ceyhan petroleum pipeline, on which construction work was scheduled to commence in April 2003. Although foreign investment increased significantly in 2002, owing to the increased international interest in the country's hydrocarbons resources, in August the international organization Transparency International identified Azerbaijan as among the world's most corrupt countries (of a total of 102 countries, it was rated 95th). Moreover, the disbursement of funding under the IMF's Poverty Reduction and Growth Facility was suspended in September, owing to the Government's failure to withdraw subsidies on sales of imported gas and petroleum and to increase domestic energy prices to world levels. Further negotiations with the IMF failed in December, primarily owing to concerns over the Government's continued separation of the operations of the State Oil Fund from the state budget. However, by March 2003 the Government had begun to comply with the IMF's recommendations. Meanwhile, the continued disparity between the level of investment and growth recorded in the petroleum sector and the relative lack of development in the remaining sectors of the economy represented a serious cause for concern, leading to widespread poverty and underemployment in the non-petroleum sector, particularly outside the capital.

Education

In the early 1990s the education system was reorganized, as part of overall economic and political reforms. Education is officially compulsory between the ages of six and 17 years. Primary education begins at six years of age and lasts for four years. Secondary education, beginning at the age of 10, comprises a first cycle of five years and a second cycle of two years. In 1998 total net enrolment at primary schools was equivalent to 96% of school-age population, and enrolment at secondary schools was equivalent to 82%. Almost all secondary schools use Azerbaijani as the medium of instruction, although some 6% use Russian. There are 25 state-supported institutions of higher education and 15 private universities; courses of study for full-time students last between four and five years. Higher education institutes include Baku State University, which specializes in the sciences, and the State Petroleum Academy, which trains engineers for the petroleum industry. In 2000/01 there were 120,500 students enrolled in institutes of higher education. Government expenditure on education totalled 909,200m. manats in 2000 (representing 23.8% of total state expenditure).

Public Holidays

2003: 1 January (New Year), 20 January (Martyrs' Day), 12 February* (Kurban Bayramy, Sacrifice Day), 8 March (International Women's Day), 22 March (Noruz Bayrami, Festival of Spring), 1 May (Labour Day), 9 May (Victory Day), 28 May (Republic Day), 15 June (Day of Liberation of the Azerbaijani People), 9 October (Day of the Armed Services), 18 October (Day of Statehood), 12 November (Constitution Day), 17 November (Day of National Survival), 26 November* (Ramazan Bayramy, end of Ramadan), 31 December (Day of Azerbaijani Solidarity World-wide).

2004: 1 January (New Year), 20 January (Martyrs' Day), 2 February* (Kurban Bayramy, Sacrifice Day), 8 March (International Women's Day), 22 March (Noruz Bayrami, Festival of Spring), 1 May (Labour Day), 9 May (Victory Day), 28 May (Republic Day), 15 June (Day of Liberation of the Azerbaijani People), 9 October (Day of the Armed Services), 18 October (Day of Statehood), 12 November (Constitution Day), 14 November* (Ramazan Bayramy, end of Ramadan), 17 November (Day of National Survival), 31 December (Day of Azerbaijani Solidarity World-wide).

*These holidays are dependent on the Islamic lunar calendar and may vary by one or two days from the dates given.

Weights and Measures

The metric system is in force.

Statistical Survey

Source (unless otherwise stated): State Statistical Committee of Azerbaijan Republic, 370136 Baku, Inshatchilar St; tel. (12) 38-64-98; fax (12) 38-24-42; e-mail ssc@azstat.org; internet www.azstat.org.

Area and Population

AREA, POPULATION AND DENSITY

Area (sq km)	86,600*
Population (census results)†	
12 January 1989 . . .	7,021,178
27 January 1999 (provisional)	
Males	3,883,155
Females. . . .	4,070,283
Total	7,953,438
Population (official estimates at 1 January)	
2000	8,016,200
2001	8,081,000
2002	8,141,400
Density (per sq km) at 1 January 2002	94.0

* 33,400 sq miles.

† Figures refer to *de jure* population. The *de facto* total at the 1989 census was 7,037,867.

Source: partly UN, *Population and Vital Statistics Report*.

ETHNIC GROUPS

(permanent inhabitants, 1999 census)

	Number ('000)	%
Azeri	7,205.5	90.6
Lazs (Lezghi)	178.0	2.2
Russian	141.7	1.8
Armenian.	120.7	1.5
Talish.	76.8	1.0
Avar	50.9	0.6
Turkish	43.4	0.5
Tatar	30.0	0.4
Ukrainian	29.0	0.4
Sakhur	15.9	0.2
Georgian	14.9	0.2
Kurd	13.1	0.2
Tat	10.9	0.1
Jewish	8.9	0.1
Udin	4.2	0.1
Others	9.5	0.1
Total	7,953.4	100.0

PRINCIPAL TOWNS

(estimated population at 1 January 2002)

Baki (Baku, the capital) . . .	1,817,900	Mingachevir (Mingechaur) . .	94,600
Nakhichevan . .	364,500	Ali Bayramli . .	70,900
Gyanja* . . .	301,400	Khankendi (Stepanakert) . .	54,600

* Known as Kirovabad between 1935 and 1989.

BIRTHS, MARRIAGES AND DEATHS

	Registered live births		Registered marriages		Registered deaths	
	Number	Rate (per 1,000)	Number	Rate (per 1,000)	Number	Rate (per 1,000)
1994 . .	159,761	21.4	47,147	6.3	54,921	7.3
1995 . .	143,315	18.9	43,130	5.7	50,828	6.7
1996 . .	129,247	16.9	38,572	5.1	48,242	6.3
1997 . .	132,052	17.1	46,999	6.1	46,962	6.1
1998 . .	123,996	15.9	40,851	5.2	46,299	5.9
1999 . .	117,539	14.9	37,382	4.8	46,295	5.9
2000 . .	116,994	14.8	39,611	5.0	46,701	5.9
2001 . .	110,356	13.8	41,861	5.2	45,284	5.7

Expectation of life (WHO estimates, years at birth): 63.6 (males 60.7; females 66.6) in 2001 (Source: WHO, *World Health Report*).

ECONOMICALLY ACTIVE POPULATION

(ISIC Major Divisions, annual average, '000 persons)

	1999	2000	2001
Agriculture, hunting and forestry	1,566.3	1,517.2	1,482.0
Fishing	0.5	2.0	2.3
Mining and quarrying . . .	39.6	39.6	39.0
Manufacturing . . .	180.6	169.3	169.0
Electricity, gas and water supply	38.8	40.5	39.0
Construction	154.7	153.6	155.0
Wholesale and retail trade; repair of motor vehicles, motorcycles and household goods . . .	576.4	626.1	659.5
Hotels and restaurants . . .	9.8	9.8	11.0
Transport, storage and communications . . .	168.4	167.0	167.5
Financial intermediation . . .	15.2	13.5	13.0
Real estate, renting and business activities . . .	98.7	98.0	97.0
Public administration and defence; compulsory social security . .	260.2	257.7	267.3
Education	299.6	317.9	318.0
Health and social work . . .	168.2	168.9	170.0
Other community, social and personal service activities . .	125.5	123.2	125.0
Extra-territorial organizations and bodies . . .	0.3	0.2	0.4
Total employed	3,702.8	3,704.5	3,715.0
Unemployed	45.2	43.7	48.4
Total labour force	3,748.0	3,748.2	3,763.4

Health and Welfare

KEY INDICATORS

Total fertility rate (children per woman, 2001)	1.6
Under-five mortality rate (per 1,000 live births, 2001) . .	105
HIV (% of persons aged 15–49, 2001)	<0.10
Physicians (per 1,000 head, 1998)	3.60
Hospital beds (per 1,000 head, 1996)	9.69
Health expenditure (2000): US $ per head (PPP)	57
Health expenditure (2000): % of GDP	2.1
Health expenditure (2000): public (% of total)	44.2
Human Development Index (2000): ranking	88
Human Development Index (2000): value	0.741

For sources and definitions, see explanatory note on p. vi.

Agriculture

PRINCIPAL CROPS

('000 metric tons)

	1999	2000	2001
Wheat	865.7	1,150.3	1,500.0
Rice (paddy)	15.9	22.2	19.0
Barley	102.3	219.5	360.0
Maize	100.3	103.5	116.4
Potatoes	394.1	469.0	605.3
Sugar beet.	42.2	46.7	40.8
Pulses	12.4	15.6	21.1*
Hazelnuts	12.6	13.3	15.0†
Other nuts†	10.4	13.0	12.0
Cottonseed	59.1	54.9	52.2†
Cabbages	58.1	72.4	78.6*
Tomatoes	329.3	337.4	445.3*
Cucumbers and gherkins . .	70.7	80.5	95.6*
Dry onions	75.0	88.8	101.4*
Garlic	14.5	17.1	19.6*
Other vegetables*	123.3	152.1	166.7
Oranges*	30.0	40.0	41.7
Apples*	268.0	286.3	298.6
Pears	28.5*	33.4	34.8*
Apricots	14.0*	13.0	14.0*
Peaches and nectarines* . . .	32.0	40.0	41.7
Plums	17.4	18.1	18.8*
Grapes	112.5	76.8	63.1
Watermelons‡	206.3	261.0	290.5
Other fruits*	35.2	46.3	47.9
Tobacco (leaves)	8.6	17.3	12.8
Cotton (lint)	33.9	32.0	32.0*

* Unofficial figure(s).
† FAO estimate(s).
‡ Including melons, pumpkins and squash.

Source: FAO.

LIVESTOCK

('000 head, year ending September)

	1999	2000	2001
Horses	56	61	64
Asses	33	36	38
Cattle	1,913	1,961	2,022
Buffaloes	297	299	306
Pigs	26	20	19
Sheep	5,131	5,280	5,553
Goats	381	494	533
Chickens*	13,443	14,269	14,298
Turkeys*	431	442	442

* Unofficial figures.

Source: FAO.

LIVESTOCK PRODUCTS

('000 metric tons)

	1999	2000	2001
Beef and veal	52.0	574.0	56.6
Mutton and lamb.	34.8	36.1	37.9
Pig meat	1.5	1.6	1.6
Poultry meat	16.3	16.9	17.7
Cows' milk	993.4	1,031.1	1,073.4
Cheese	10.5	10.3*	10.8*
Butter	4.9	4.9	5.0
Hen eggs†	29.4	30.2	30.9
Wool: greasy	10.5	10.9	11.4
Wool: scoured	6.3	6.6	6.9
Cattle hides (fresh)*	8.9	9.3	9.7
Sheepskins (fresh)*	3.9	4.1	4.3

* FAO estimate(s).
† Unofficial figures.

Source: FAO.

Forestry

ROUNDWOOD REMOVALS

('000 cubic metres, excl. bark)

	1998	1999	2000
Sawlogs, veneer logs and logs for sleepers*	3,200	3,200	3,500
Pulpwood*.	3,200	3,200	3,500
Other industrial wood	—	—	100*
Fuel wood*	6,200	6,200	6,400
Total	12,600	12,600	13,500

* Unofficial figure(s).

Source: FAO.

Fishing

(metric tons, live weight)

	1998	1999	2000
Capture	4,678	20,861	18,797
Freshwater bream. . . .	314	52	55
Azov sea sprat	4,043	20,460	18,520
Aquaculture	211	235	120
Total catch	4,889	4,935	18,917

Source: FAO, *Yearbook of Fishery Statistics*.

Mining

	1999	2000	2001
Crude petroleum ('000 metric tons)	13,652	13,869	14,775
Natural gas (million cu metres) .	5,997	5,642	5,534

Source: Asian Development Bank, *Key Indicators of Developing Asian and Pacific Countries*.

Industry

SELECTED PRODUCTS

('000 metric tons, unless otherwise indicated)

	1997	1998	1999
Margarine	0.4	0.0	0.9
Wheat flour	90	79	52
Ethyl alcohol ('000 hectolitres)	15	1	0
Wine ('000 hectolitres)	49	26	47
Beer ('000 hectolitres)	16	12	69
Mineral water ('000 hectolitres)	16	18	16
Soft drinks ('000 hectolitres)	495	569	326
Cigarettes	827	241	416
Wool yarn—pure and mixed (metric tons)	100	200	100
Cotton yarn—pure and mixed (metric tons)	8,600	2,600	900
Woven cotton fabrics ('000 metres)	17,600	7,400	800
Silk fabrics ('000 sq metres)	49	0	0
Woollen woven fabrics ('000 sq metres)	0	100	100
Leather footwear ('000 pairs)	313	315	54
Aluminium plates, sheets, strip and foil	0.6	0.3	0
Steel	25	8	n.a.
Cement	303	201	171
Potassic fertilizers*	5	0	0
Sulphuric acid	53	24	26
Caustic soda (Sodium hydroxide)	23	21	21
Bricks (million)	11	14	10
Television receivers ('000)	1	3	0
Electric energy (million kWh)	16,836	17,985	n.a.
Jet fuels	450	526	n.a.
Motor spirit (petrol)	800	630	n.a.
Kerosene	150	178	n.a.
Gas-diesel (distillate fuel) oil	1,900	2,057	n.a.
Lubricants	128	82	n.a.
Residual fuel oil (Mazout)	3,900	4,028	n.a.

* Production in terms of potassium oxide.

Source: partly UN, *Industrial Commodity Statistics Yearbook*.

1999 (million kWh): Electric energy 18,176.

2000 ('000 metric tons): Cement 249; Wheat flour 295; Sulphuric acid 38; Caustic soda (Sodium hydroxide) 25; Bricks (million) 11; Electric energy (million kWh) 18,699 (Source: partly Asian Development Bank, *Key Indicators of Developing Asian and Pacific Countries*).

2001 ('000 metric tons): Cement 523; Wheat flour 394; Sulphuric acid 9; Caustic soda (Sodium hydroxide) 22; Bricks (million) 12; Electric energy (million kWh) 18,970 (Source: partly Asian Development Bank, *Key Indicators of Developing Asian and Pacific Countries*).

Finance

CURRENCY AND EXCHANGE RATES

Monetary Units

100 gopik = 1 Azerbaijani manat

Sterling, Dollar and Euro Equivalents (31 December 2002)

£1 sterling = 7,886.5 manats
US $1 = 4,893.0 manats
€1 = 5,131.3 manats
10,000 manats = £1.268 = $2.044 = €1.949

Average Exchange Rate (Azerbaijani manats per US $)

2000   4,474.2
2001   4,656.6
2002   4,860.8

Note: The Azerbaijani manat was introduced in August 1992, initially to circulate alongside the Russian (formerly Soviet) rouble, with an exchange rate of 1 manat = 10 roubles. In December 1993 Azerbaijan left the rouble zone, and the manat became the country's sole currency.

STATE BUDGET

('000 million manats)

Revenue	1999	2000	2001
Tax revenue	2,338.9	2,872.2	3,570.4
Other current revenue	397.4	589.6	321.8
Capital revenue	61.3	114.4	27.7
Total	2,797.6	3,576.2	3,919.9

Expenditure	1999	2000	2001
General public services	252.6	260.8	303.8
Education	795.1	909.2	n.a.
Health	186.2	204.7	210.1
Social security and welfare	603.9	696.7	730.7
Economic services	331.3	447.2	516.0
Agriculture	144.2	157.4	159.1
Other purposes	1,088.1	1,301.2	1,344.2
Total	3,257.2	3,819.8	4,032.9

Source: Asian Development Bank, *Key Indicators of Developing Asian and Pacific Countries*.

INTERNATIONAL RESERVES

(US $ million at 31 December)

	2000	2001	2002
IMF special drawing rights	6.60	2.49	0.70
Reserve position in IMF	0.01	0.01	0.01
Foreign exchange	672.99	894.20	720.80
Total	679.61	896.70	721.51

Source: IMF, *International Financial Statistics*.

MONEY SUPPLY

('000 million manats at 31 December)

	2000	2001	2002
Currency outside banks	1,349.81	1,468.99	1,668.73
Demand deposits at commercial banks	218.21	218.73	292.74
Total money (incl. others)	1,569.81	1,693.10	1,967.27

Source: IMF, *International Financial Statistics*.

COST OF LIVING

(Consumer Price Index; base: 1993 = 100)

	1999	2000	2001
Food	9,630.3	9,853.0	10,117.3
All items (incl. others)	10,182.1	10,365.9	10,526.3

Source: UN, *Monthly Bulletin of Statistics*.

NATIONAL ACCOUNTS

('000 million manats at current prices)

Expenditure on the Gross Domestic Product

	1999	2000	2001
Government final consumption expenditure	1,396.0	1,401.8	1,287.0
Private final consumption expenditure	15,854.2	17,367.0	18,120.0
Increase in stocks	−380.3	−581.0	−75.9
Gross fixed capital formation	5,381.5	5,458.1	5,649.2
Total domestic expenditure	22,251.4	23,645.9	24,980.3
Exports of goods and services	5,279.4	9,476.8	11,294.1
Less Imports of goods and services	7,900.4	9,053.6	10,002.7
Statistical discrepancy	−755.0	−478.6	348.0
GDP in purchasers' values	18,875.4	23,590.5	26,619.8

Source: Asian Development Bank, *Key Indicators of Developing Asian and Pacific Countries*.

Gross Domestic Product by Economic Activity

	1999	2000	2001
Agriculture and fishing . . .	3,439.5	3,755.1	4,171.9
Mining	3,493.0	6,522.5	7,522.1
Manufacturing	1,140.4	1,248.2	1,294.4
Electricity, gas and water . .	693.8	724.0	643.9
Construction	2,053.4	1,539.6	1,630.4
Trade	1,336.4	1,574.9	1,786.3
Transport and communications	2,022.5	2,835.8	3,268.6
Finance	140.3	219.1	246.5
Public administration . .	371.5	480.3	539.4
Other	3,438.7	3,235.0	3,455.9
GDP at factor cost . . .	18,129.5	22,134.5	24,559.4
Indirect taxes *less* subsidies . .	745.9	1,456.0	2,060.4
GDP in purchasers' values . .	18,875.4	23,590.5	26,619.8

Source: Asian Development Bank, *Key Indicators of Developing Asian and Pacific Countries*.

BALANCE OF PAYMENTS
(US $ million)

	1999	2000	2001
Exports of goods f.o.b.	1,025.2	1,858.3	2,078.9
Imports of goods f.o.b.	−1,433.4	−1,539.0	−1,465.1
Trade balance	−408.2	319.3	613.9
Exports of services . . .	256.8	259.8	289.8
Imports of services . . .	−485.1	−484.5	−664.9
Balance on goods and services	−636.5	94.6	238.8
Other income received . . .	11.0	55.9	41.5
Other income paid	−56.0	−391.4	−408.7
Balance on goods, services and income	−681.5	−240.9	−128.4
Current transfers received . .	134.5	135.0	176.5
Current transfers paid . . .	−52.8	−62.0	−99.9
Current balance	−599.7	−167.8	−51.8
Direct investment from abroad. .	510.3	129.1	226.5
Other investment assets . . .	−81.0	−114.2	−394.0
Other investment liabilities . .	260.9	478.4	293.5
Net errors and omissions . .	42.4	—	−0.1
Overall balance	132.9	325.6	73.4

Source: IMF, *International Financial Statistics*.

External Trade

PRINCIPAL COMMODITIES
(US $ million)

Imports c.i.f.	1999	2000	2001
Vegetable products	116.6	119.5	116.8
Prepared foodstuffs, beverages, spirits and vinegar; tobacco and manufactured substitutes . .	52.4	59.5	69.7
Mineral products	89.9	115.2	248.0
Products of chemical or allied industries	57.6	84.1	68.7
Base metals and articles thereof	111.5	123.4	132.1
Machinery and mechanical appliances; electrical equipment; sound and television apparatus .	342.6	362.8	353.8
Vehicles, aircraft, vessels and associated transportation equipment	90.4	100.0	198.6
Optical, photographic, measuring and medical instruments and apparatus; clocks and watches; musical instruments . . .	20.2	35.8	35.9
Total (incl. others)	1,035.9	1,172.1	1,430.9

Exports f.o.b.	1999	2000	2001
Prepared foodstuffs; beverages, spirits and vinegar; tobacco and manufactured substitutes . .	33.5	24.2	31.6
Mineral products	730.6	1,485.3	2,117.9
Machinery and mechanical appliances; electrical equipment; sound and television apparatus .	35.4	31.1	38.1
Total (incl. others)	929.2	1,745.3	2,314.3

Source: Asian Development Bank, *Key Indicators of Developing Asian and Pacific Countries*.

PRINCIPAL TRADING PARTNERS
(US $ million)

Imports c.i.f.	1999	2000	2001
Bulgaria	7.6	11.8	n.a.
China, People's Repub.	13.7	23.1	n.a.
France	24.9	19.0	n.a.
Germany	46.3	67.6	95.9
Iran	47.4	56.8	66.2
Italy	8.3	28.1	n.a.
Japan	55.5	16.4	n.a.
Kazakhstan	24.9	57.6	90.3
Korea, Republic . . .	14.7	5.1	n.a.
Netherlands	14.2	18.9	n.a.
Norway	37.0	6.0	n.a.
Poland	n.a.	20.7	n.a.
Russia	226.5	249.3	143.1
Singapore	41.3	13.2	n.a.
Switzerland	3.5	56.2	108.9
Turkey.	143.0	128.5	128.5
Turkmenistan	12.9	9.6	n.a.
Ukraine	38.5	35.8	35.8
United Arab Emirates . .	12.3	19.9	27.5
United Kingdom	67.1	58.9	62.9
USA	83.0	117.7	71.0
Total (incl. others)	1,035.7	1,172.1	1,237.3

Exports f.o.b.	1999	2000	2001
France	58.1	205.2	112.2
Georgia	71.7	74.7	n.a.
Germany	7.6	8.3	143.5
Greece	13.2	22.7	n.a.
Iceland.	n.a.	31.5	n.a.
Iran	22.7	7.7	7.7
Israel	56.9	135.2	270.3
Italy	313.1	762.5	547.6
Malta	n.a.	25.4	n.a.
Netherlands	4.4	26.2	n.a.
Russia	83.1	98.3	66.0
Switzerland	36.8	45.8	54.9
Tajikistan	10.8	19.6	n.a.
Turkey.	69.1	105.0	140.9
Ukraine	24.0	23.6	23.6
United Kingdom	11.0	18.8	16.3
USA	29.8	8.0	n.a.
Total (incl. others)	929.2	1,745.3	1,757.1

Source: mainly Asian Development Bank, *Key Indicators of Developing Asian and Pacific Countries*.

Transport

RAILWAYS

	1999	2000	2001
Passengers carried ('000) . . .	4,050	4,250	4,646
Passenger-km (million)	422	493	537
Freight carried (million metric tons)	14.2	15.9	15.4
Freight ton-km (million) . . .	5,052	5,770	6,141

ROAD TRAFFIC
(vehicles in use at 31 December)

	1998	1999	2000
Passenger cars	281,320	306,993	332,026
Buses	13,666	14,941	16,756
Lorries and vans	79,934	69,685	78,566
Motorcycles and mopeds	9,271	9,269	8,016

Source: International Road Federation, *World Road Statistics*.

SHIPPING

Merchant Fleet
(registered at 31 December)

	1999	2000	2001
Number of vessels	286	284	283
Total displacement ('000 grt)	654.2	647.0	641.2

Source: Lloyd's Register-Fairplay, *World Fleet Statistics*.

International Sea-borne Freight Traffic
('000 metric tons)

	1997	1998	1999
Goods loaded	7,128	7,812	7,176

Source: UN, *Monthly Bulletin of Statistics*.

CIVIL AVIATION
(traffic on scheduled services)

	1999	2000	2001
Kilometres flown (million)	21	17	9
Passengers carried ('000)	697	701	701
Passenger-km (million)	835	798	827
Total ton-km (million)	112	102	76

Kilometres flown (million): 21 in 1996; 17 in 1997; 9 in 1998 (Source: UN, *Statistical Yearbook*).

Tourism

FOREIGN TOURIST ARRIVALS

Country of residence	1999	2000	2001
CIS countries*	431,151	346,482	320,229
Iran	121,604	242,354	321,882
Turkey	10,390	20,961	8,493
Total (incl. others)	602,047	681,000	766,992

* Comprising Armenia, Belarus, Georgia, Kazakhstan, Kyrgyzstan, Moldova, Russia, Tajikistan, Turkmenistan, Ukraine and Uzbekistan.

Tourism receipts (US $ million): 125 in 1998; 81 in 1999; 81 in 2000 (Sources: World Tourism Organization, *Yearbook of Tourism Statistics*, and World Bank, *World Development Indicators*).

Communications Media

	1999	2000	2001
Television receivers ('000 in use)	1,980	2,000	n.a.
Telephones ('000 main lines in use)	730	801	865.5
Mobile cellular telephones ('000 subscribers)	180.0	430.0	620
Internet users ('000)	8	12	25
Book production (including pamphlets): titles	400	400	n.a.

1994: Facsimile machines (number in use) 2,500.

1996: Daily newspapers (number) 6; Non-daily newspapers (number) 251.

Sources: UN, *Statistical Yearbook*, UNESCO, *Statistical Yearbook*, and International Telecommunication Union.

Education

(2000/01, unless otherwise indicated)

	Institutions	Teachers	Students*
Pre-primary	1,794	11,500†	111,400
Primary	446	39,780	13,000
Secondary	3,149	109,600†	1,516,000
General	923	88,822	125,000
Special needs schools	20	n.a.	4,789
Vocational	69	n.a.	49,200†
Higher	40	11,216‡	120,500

* Figures are rounded to the nearest 100.
† 1999/2000.
‡ Excluding non-state institutions.

Source: partly UN, *Statistical Yearbook for Asia and the Pacific*.

Adult literacy rate (UNESCO estimates): 99.6% (males 99.7%; females 99.5%) in 1995 (Source: UNESCO, *Statistical Yearbook*).

Directory

The Constitution

The new Constitution was endorsed by 91.9% of the registered electorate in a national referendum, held on 12 November 1995. It replaced the amended Soviet Constitution of 1978. The following is a summary of the 1995 Constitution's main provisions:

GENERAL PROVISIONS

The Azerbaijan Republic is a democratic, secular and unitary state. State power is vested in the people, who implement their sovereign right through referendums and their directly elected representatives. No individual or organization has the right to usurp the power of the people. State power is exercised on the principle of the division of powers between the legislature, the executive and the judiciary. The supreme aim of the state is to ensure human and civil rights and freedoms. The territory of the Azerbaijan Republic is inviolable and indivisible. Azerbaijan conducts its foreign policy on the basis of universally accepted international law. The state is committed to a market economic system and to freedom of entrepreneurial activity.

Three types of ownership—state, private and municipal—are recognized; natural resources belong to the Azerbaijan Republic. The state promotes the development of art, culture, education, medical care and science, and defends historical, material and spiritual values. All religions are equal by law; the spread of religions that contradict the principles of humanity is prohibited. The state language is Azerbaijani, although the republic guarantees the free use of other languages. The capital is Baku (Baki).

MAJOR RIGHTS, FREEDOMS AND RESPONSIBILITIES

Every citizen has inviolable, undeniable and inalienable rights and freedoms. Every person is equal before the law and the courts, regardless of sex, race, nationality, religion, origin, property and other status, and political or other convictions. Every person has the right to life. Any person charged with a penal offence is considered innocent until proven guilty. Capital punishment as an extreme measure of punishment, while still in force, can be applied for grave crimes. Every person has the right to freedom of thought, speech, conscience and religion. Everyone has the right to protect their national and ethnic affiliation. No one is to be subject to torture or the degradation of human dignity. The mass media are free, and censorship is prohibited. Every person has the right to freedom of movement and residence within the republic, and the right to leave the republic. The right to assemble publicly is guaranteed, and every person has the right to establish a political party, trade union or other organization; the activity of unions that seek to overthrow state power is prohibited. Citizens of the Azerbaijan Republic have the right to participate in the political life of society and the state, and the right to elect and to be elected to government bodies, and to participate in referendums. Every person has the right to health protection and medical aid, and the right to social security in old age, sickness, disability, unemployment, etc. The state guarantees the right to free secondary education.

THE LEGISLATIVE

The supreme legislative body is the 125-member Milli Majlis (National Assembly). Deputies are elected by universal, equal, free, direct suffrage, and by secret ballot, for a five-year term. Any citizen who has reached the age of 25 years is eligible for election, with the exception of those possessing dual citizenship, those performing state service, and those otherwise engaged in paid work, unless employed in the creative, scientific and education sectors. The instigation of criminal proceedings against a deputy, and his or her detention or arrest, are only permitted on the decision of the Milli Majlis, on the basis of a recommendation by the Prosecutor-General. The Milli Majlis passes legislation, constitutional laws and resolutions; ratifies or denunciates treaties, agreements and conventions; ratifies the state budget; gives consent to declare war, on the recommendation of the President of the Republic; confirms administrative and territorial divisions; and declares amnesties. Upon the nomination of the President, the Milli Majlis is authorized to approve the appointment of the Prime Minister and the Prosecutor-General; appoint and dismiss members of the Constitutional Court and Supreme Court; and appoint and dismiss the Chairperson of the National Bank. It also has the power to express a vote of 'no confidence' in the Government; to call a referendum; to initiate impeachment proceedings against the President, on the recommendation of the Constitutional Court; and to introduce draft legislation and other issues for parliamentary discussion.

EXECUTIVE POWER

The President, who is directly elected for a term of five years, is Head of State and Commander-in-Chief of the Armed Forces. Executive power is held by the President, who acts as guarantor of the independence and territorial integrity of the republic. Any university graduate aged 35 years or over, who has the right to vote, has been a resident of the republic for the preceding 10 years, has never been tried for a major crime, and who is exclusively a citizen of the Azerbaijan Republic, is eligible for election to the office of President. The President appoints and dismisses the Cabinet of Ministers, headed by the Prime Minister, which is the highest executive body.

The President calls legislative elections; concludes international treaties and agreements, and submits them to the Milli Majlis for ratification; signs laws or returns draft legislation to the Milli Majlis for reconsideration; proposes candidates for the Constitutional Court, the Supreme Court and the Economic Court, and nominates the Prosecutor-General and the Chairman of the National Bank; appoints and recalls diplomatic representatives of Azerbaijan to foreign countries and international organizations, and receives the credentials of diplomatic representatives; may declare a state of emergency or martial law; and grants titles of honour.

The President enjoys immunity from prosecution during his or her period in office. In the event that the President commits a grave crime, he may be removed from office on the recommendation of the Supreme Court and the Constitutional Court, and with the approval of the Milli Majlis.

THE JUDICIARY

Judicial power is implemented only by the courts. Judges are independent and are subordinate only to the Constitution and the law; they are immune from prosecution. Trials are held in public, except in specialized circumstances.

The Constitutional Court is composed of nine members, appointed by the Milli Majlis on the recommendation of the President. It determines, among other things, whether presidential decrees, resolutions of the Milli Majlis and of the Cabinet of Ministers, laws of the Nakhichevan Autonomous Republic, and international treaties correspond to the Constitution; and decides on the prohibition of the activities of political parties. The Supreme Court is the highest judicial body in administrative, civil and criminal cases; the Economic Court is the highest legal body in considering economic disputes.

AUTONOMOUS REPUBLIC OF NAKHICHEVAN

The Nakhichevan Autonomous Republic is an autonomous republic forming an inalienable part of the Azerbaijan Republic. It has its own Constitution, which must not contravene the Constitution and laws of Azerbaijan. Legislative power in Nakhichevan is vested in the 45-member Ali Majlis (Supreme Assembly), which serves a five-year term, and executive power is vested in the Cabinet of Ministers. The Ali Majlis elects a Chairman from among its members, as the highest official in the Republic of Nakhichevan. The Ali Majlis is responsible for the budget, the approval of economic and social programmes; and the approval of the Cabinet of Ministers. The Ali Majlis may dismiss its Chairman and express 'no confidence' in the Cabinet of Ministers, which is appointed by the Ali Majlis on the recommendation of the Prime Minister of Nakhichevan (the Chairman of the Cabinet of Ministers). The Prime Minister of Nakhichevan is, likewise, appointed by the Ali Majlis on the nomination of the President of Azerbaijan. Heads of local executive power in Nakhichevan are appointed by the President of Azerbaijan, after consultation with the Chairman of the Ali Majlis and the Prime Minister of Nakhichevan. Justice is administered by the courts of the Republic of Nakhichevan.

In December 1998 the Milli Majlis approved a revised Constitution for Nakhichevan, which defined the enclave as an 'autonomous state' within Azerbaijan.

LOCAL SELF-GOVERNMENT

Local government in rural areas and towns, villages and settlements is exercised by elected municipalities.

RIGHTS AND LAW

The Constitution has supreme legal force. Amendments and additions may only be introduced following a referendum.

The Government

HEAD OF STATE

President: HEYDAR ALIRZA OGLU ALIYEV (elected by direct popular vote, 3 October 1993; inaugurated on 10 October 1993; re-elected 11 October 1998; inaugurated on 18 October 1998).

CABINET OF MINISTERS
(April 2003)

Prime Minister: ARTUR TAHIR OGLU RASIZADE.

First Deputy Prime Ministers: ABBAS A. ABBASSOV, YAQUB ABDULLA OGLU AYYUBOV.

Deputy Prime Ministers: ELCHIN ILYAS OGLU EFENDIYEV, ABID QOCA OGLU SHARIFOV, ALI SAMIL OGLU HASANOV, HACIBALA IBRAHIM OGLU ABUTALIBOV.

Minister of Public Health: ALI BINNET OGLU INSANOV.

Minister of Foreign Affairs: VILAYAT MUKHTAR OGLU KULIYEV.

Minister of Agriculture and Produce: IRSHAD NADIR OGLU ALIYEV.

Minister of Internal Affairs: Col RAMIL IDRIS OGLU USUBOV.

Minister of Culture: POLAD OGLU BYUL-BYUL.

Minister of Education: MISIR CUMAYIL OGLU MARDANOV.

Minister of Communications: NADIR ALI OGLU AKHMEDOV.

Minister of Finance: AVAZ AKBAR OGLU ALEKPEROV.

Minister of Justice: FIKRET FARRUKH OGLU MAMMADOV.

Minister of Labour and Social Protection: ALI TEYMUR OGLU NAGIYEV.

Minister of National Security: Lt-Gen. NAMIG RASID OGLU ABBASOV.

Minister of Defence: Col-Gen. SAFAR AKHUNDBALA OGLU ABIYEV.

Minister of Fuel and Energy: MAJID KARIMOV.

Minister of Youth, Sport and Tourism: ABULFAZ MURSAL OGLU KARAYEV.

Minister of Economic Development: FARKHAD SOKHRAT OGLU ALIYEV.

Minister of Ecology and Natural Resources: HUSSEIN BAGHIROV.

Minister of Transport: ZIYA MAMMEDOV.

Chairmen of State Committees

Chairman of the State Tax Inspection Committee: FAZIL MAMMADOV.

Chairman of the State Committee for Securities: HEYDAR BABAYEV.

Chairman of the State Committee for Construction and Architectural Affairs: Abid G. Sharifov.

Chairman of the State Committee for Anti-monopoly Policy and Enterprise Support: Rahib Guliyev.

Chairman of the State Committee for Statistics: Arif A. Veliyev.

Chairman of the State Committee for Religious Affairs: Dr Rafik Aliyev.

Chairman of the State Committee for Geology and Mineral Resources: Islam Tagiyev.

Chairman of the State Committee for Supervision of Safety at Work in Industry and Mining: Yagub Eyyubov.

Chairman of the State Committee for Material Resources: Hulmammad Javadov.

Chairman of the State Committee for Specialized Machinery: Sabir Alekperov.

Chairman of the State Committee for Science and Technology: Azad Mirzajanzade.

Chairman of the State Land and Mapping Committee: Harib Mammadov.

Chairman of the State Customs Committee: Kamaleddin Heydarov.

Chairman of the State Committee for Veterinary Affairs: Mirsaleh Husseinov.

Chairman of the State Committee for Hydrometeorology: Zulfugar Musayev.

Chairman of the State Committee for the Protection and Refurbishment of Historical and Cultural Monuments: Fakhreddin Miraliyev.

Chairman of the State Committee for Refugees and Involuntary Migrants: Ali Hasanov.

Chairman of the State Committee for Improvements of Soil and Water Economy: Ahmed Ahmedzade.

Chairman of the State Committee for Women's Issues: Zahra Guliyeva.

MINISTRIES

Office of the President: 370066 Baku, Istiklal St 19; tel. (12) 92-17-26; fax (12) 92-35-43; e-mail office@apparat.gov.az; internet www.president.az.

Office of the Prime Minister: 370066 Baku, Lermontov St 63; tel. (12) 92-66-23; fax (12) 92-91-79.

Ministry of Agriculture and Produce: 370016 Baku, Azadliq Sq. 1, Govt House; tel. (12) 93-53-55.

Ministry of Communications: 370139 Baku, Azerbaijan Ave 33; tel. (12) 93-00-04; fax (12) 98-79-12; e-mail mincom@azerin.com; internet www.azmincom.com.

Ministry of Culture: 370016 Baku, Azadliq Sq. 1, Govt House; tel. (12) 93-43-98; fax (12) 93-56-05; internet www.culture.az/minist:8101.

Ministry of Defence: 370139 Baku, Azerbaijan Ave; tel. (12) 39-41-89; fax (12) 92-92-50.

Ministry of Ecology and Natural Resources: Baku; tel. (12) 92-59-07.

Ministry of Economic Development: 370016 Baku, Azadliq Sq. 1, Govt House; tel. (12) 93-61-62; fax (12) 93-20-25; e-mail office@economy.gov.az; internet economy.gov.az.

Ministry of Education: 370016 Baku, Azadliq Sq. 1, Govt House; tel. (12) 93-72-66; fax (12) 98-75-69; e-mail edu_min@azeri.com; internet www.min.edu.az.

Ministry of Finance: 370022 Baku, Samed Vurghun St 83; tel. (12) 93-30-12; fax (12) 98-79-69; e-mail ferho@aznetmail.com.

Ministry of Foreign Affairs: 370004 Baku, Ghanjlar meydani 3; tel. (12) 92-68-56; fax (12) 92-56-06.

Ministry of Fuel and Energy: Baku; tel. (12) 47-05-84; internet www.mfe.az.

Ministry of Internal Affairs: 370005 Baku, Gusi Hajiyev St 7; tel. (12) 92-57-54; fax (12) 98-22-85; internet www.mia.gov.az.

Ministry of Justice: 370601 Baku, Bul-Bul Ave 13; tel. (12) 93-97-85; fax (12) 98-49-41.

Ministry of Labour and Social Protection: 370016 Baku, Azadliq Sq. 1, Govt House; tel. (12) 93-05-42; fax (12) 93-94-72; e-mail mlspp@azerin.com.

Ministry of National Security: 370602 Baku, Parliament Ave 2; tel. (12) 95-01-63; fax (12) 95-04-91.

Ministry of Public Health: 370014 Baku, Malaya Morskaya St 4; tel. (12) 93-29-77; fax (12) 93-76-47; e-mail webmaster@mednet.az; internet www.mednet.az.

Ministry of Transport: Baku.

Ministry of Youth, Sport and Tourism: 370072 Baku, Olympiya St 4; tel. (12) 90-64-42; fax (12) 90-64-38; e-mail mys@azeri.com; internet www.myst.azeri.com.

President and Legislature

PRESIDENT

Presidential Election, 11 October 1998

Candidates	Votes	% of votes
Heydar Aliyev (New Azerbaijan Party)	2,556,059	77.61
Etibar Mamedov (National Independence Party)	389,662	11.83
Nizami Suleymanov (Independent Azerbaijan Party)	270,709	8.22
Firudin Hasanov (Communist Party of Azerbaijan-2)	29,244	0.89
Ashraf Mehdiyev (Association of Victims of Illegal Political Repressions)	28,809	0.87
Khanhusein Kazymly (Social Welfare Party)	8,254	0.25
Blank or spoiled	10,910	0.33
Total	3,293,647	100.00

MILLI MAJLIS

Milli Majlis
(National Assembly)
370152 Baku, Mehti Hussein St 2; tel. (12) 92-79-45; fax (12) 98-02-42.

Chairman (Speaker): Murtuz Aleskerov.

First Deputy Chairman: Arif Rahimzade.

Elections to Azerbaijan's new 125-member Milli Majlis were held on 5 November 2000. The electoral law of August 1995 provided for a mixed system of voting: 25 seats to be filled by proportional representation, according to party lists, the remaining 100 deputies to be elected in single-member constituencies. The latter included the constituencies of Armenian-held Nagornyi Karabakh and other occupied territories: refugees from those regions cast their votes in other parts of Azerbaijan (in anticipation of the eventual return of occupied areas to Azerbaijani jurisdiction). All 25 party seats were filled: the New Azerbaijan Party (NAP) obtained 17 seats, the Popular Front of Azerbaijan (PFA) four, and the Civic Solidarity Party (CSP) and independent candidates each secured two. Of the 88 constituency seats filled, 62 were reported to have been taken by the NAP and 26 by independent candidates. A further round of voting was held on 7 January 2000, in order to elect members for 11 vacant seats. The NAP obtained five seats, and five other parties and an independent candidate each obtained one seat. Thus, following all the rounds of voting, only one seat in the Majlis remained vacant (representing the Khankendi-Khojali-Khojavend constituency in Nagornyi Karabakh).

Political Organizations

Adalat Party (Justice Party): f. 2001; Leader Ilyas Ismailov; 21,000 mems.

Alliance for Azerbaijan Party: Baku; f. 1994; Leader Abutalyb Samadov.

Azerbaijan Democratic Independence Party: Baku; tel. (12) 98-78-23; in 1997 merged with Vahdat Party and one-half of the People's Freedom Party; Chair. Leyla Yunusova; Leader Vagif Kerimov.

Azerbaijan National Democratic Party: Baku; tel. (12) 94-89-37; fmrly the Grey Wolves Party (Boz Gurd); Leader Iskandar Hamidov.

Azerbaijan National Equality Party: Baku; tel. (12) 60-05-21; Leader Fahraddin Aydayev.

Azerbaijani Democratic Left Party: Baku; f. 1999; Chair. Mehman Amiraliyev.

Azerbaijani Salvation Party (Milly Qutulush): Baku, Nizami St 86; tel. (12) 98-73-96; f. 1999; nationalist; supports a united Azerbaijan; Chair. ELDAR GARADAGLY.

Azerbaijan Social Democratic Party (ASDP): 370014 Baku, 28 May St 3–11; tel. (12) 98-04-21; fax (12) 98-79-03; e-mail asdp@ bakililar.az; internet www.soc-dem.org; f. 1989; formed a union with the Islamic Party of Azerbaijan and the Vahdat (Unity) Party in April 2000, as the Union of Pro-Azerbaijanist Forces; Chair. ARAZ ALIZADEH, ZARDUSHT ALIZADE; Dep. Chair. SEYRAN MIRZOYEV, KHANHUSEIN ALIYEV, RENA GAVADOVA; 5,672 mems (2002).

Civic Solidarity Party (CSP) (Vatandash Hamrailiyi): Baku; tel. (12) 92-67-47; f. 1992; Chair. SABIR RUSTAMKHANLY.

Civic Unity Party of Azerbaijan (CUPA): Baku; Sec.-Gen. SABIR HAJIYE; Chair. AYAZ MUTALLIBOV.

Communist Party of Azerbaijan (CPA): Baku; tel. (12) 94-89-37; disbanded Sept. 1991, re-established Nov. 1993; Chair. RAMIZ AHMADOV.

Communist Workers' Party of Azerbaijan: Baku; fmrly the United Communist Party of Azerbaijan; Leader SAYYAD SAYYADOV.

Democratic Development Party: Baku; f. 1999; Leader SABUHI ABDINOV.

Democratic Party of Azerbaijan: Baku, M. Huseinov St 5; tel. (12) 66-79-71; f. 1994; unregistered; merged with the Democratic Way Party in 2000; Chair. RASUL KULIYEV; Gen. Sec. SARDAR JALALOGLU.

Heyrat Party: Baku; Sec.-Gen. ASHRAF MEHDIYEV.

Independent Azerbaijan Party: Baku, A. Abbaszale 17; tel. (12) 39-30-96; fax (12) 39-53-55; Chair. NIZAMI SULEYMANOV.

Islamic Party of Azerbaijan: Baku; tel. (12) 93-72-61; f. 1992; forms part of the Union of Pro-Azerbaijanist Forces; Chair. ROVSAN AGAYEV; Leader ALI AKRAM ALIYEV (imprisoned 1997 on charges of treason, but pardoned in 1999; subsequently imprisoned in June 2002 for inciting public disorder); 50,000 mems (1997).

Labour Party of Azerbaijan: Baku; Leader SABUTAY MARNEDOV.

Liberal Democratic Party: Baku; divisions emerged in Nov. 2000.

Liberal Party of Azerbaijan: Baku, Azerbaijan Ave; tel. (12) 98-00-95; pro-Russian; Chair. LALA SHOVKAT HAJIYEVA.

Modern Turan Party (Chagdash-Turan): Baku; tel. (12) 73-16-79; Chair. ARIF ISLAM TAGIEV.

Motherland Party (Ana Vatan): Baku; tel. (12) 93-82-97; Leader FAZAIL AGAMALIYEV.

Musavat (Equality): Baku, Azerbaijan Ave 37; tel. (12) 47-46-56; fax (12) 47-43-75; e-mail ilkin@turgut.baku.az; f. 1911; in exile from 1920; re-established 1992; joined the United Opposition Movement (comprising 25 political parties) in Jan. 2002; Chair. ISA GAMBAR; Gen. Sec. VURGUN EYYUB.

Namus Party (Dignity): Baku; f. 1999; Chair. TOGRUL IBRAHIMOV.

National Congress Party: Baku; f. 1997 by disaffected members of Musavat; Chair. IHTIYAR SHIRINOV.

National Independence Party (NIP) (Milli Istiklal): Baku, Azadliq Ave 179; internet www.amip.info; f. 1992; Chair. ETIBAR MAMEDOV.

National Statehood Party: Baku; tel. (12) 67-71-74; f. 1994; unregistered from 1997; Chair. SABIR TARIVERDIYEV.

New Azerbaijan Party (NAP) (Yeni Azerbaijan): 370000 Baku, Bul-Bul Ave 13; tel. (12) 93-84-25; fax (12) 98-59-71; e-mail yap@ bakinter.net; internet www.yap.org.az; f. 1992; internal divisions were reported to have emerged in 2001; Co-Chair. HEYDAR ALIYEV; First Dep. Chair. ILHAM ALIYEV; Dep. Chair. ALI NAGIYEV (Minister of Labour and Social Protection), MURTUZ ALESKEROV (Chairman of Milli Majlis), SIRUS TABRIZLI.

Party for National Reconciliation: Baku; f. 2000 by breakaway faction of the Liberal Democratic Party.

People's Freedom Party (Halg Azadliq): Baku, Khagani St 22; tel. (12) 98-31-45; Leader PANAH SHAHSEVENLI.

People's Party of Azerbaijan: Baku; f. 1998; Chair. PANAH HUSSEINOV.

Popular Front of Azerbaijan (PFA) (Azerbaijan Xalq Cabhasi): c/o Milli Majlis, 370152 Baku, Mehti Hussein St 2; tel. (12) 98-07-94; f. 1989; divided into reformist and conservative factions; the reformist faction was registered for the legislative election held in Nov. 2000, while the conservative faction entered into co-operation with Musavat; in Jan. 2002 the conservative faction of the PFA joined the United Opposition Movement, comprising a total of 25 parties; Chair. (reformist) ALI KERIMLI; Chair. (traditionalist) MURMAHMUD FATTAYEV.

Progress Party (Taraqqi): Baku; Chair. CHINGIZ SADIKHOV.

Reformist Communist Party of Azerbaijan (CPA-2): Baku; tel. (12) 94-89-37; f. 1998 as Communist Party of Azerbaijan 2; name changed 2001; Chair. FIRUDIN HASANOV.

Republican Party: Baku, Azadliq St 161; tel. (12) 61-98-19; f. 1999; Chair. RUFIZ GONAGOV.

Social Justice Party: Baku; Leader MATLAB MUTALLIMOV.

Social Welfare Party: Baku; Chair. KHANHUSEIN KAZYMLY.

Socialist Party of Azerbaijan: Baku; f. 1997; Co-Chair. SHAPUR GASIMI, MUBARIZ IBADOV; 2,000 mems.

Turkic Nationalist Party: Baku; Leader VUGAR BEYTURAN.

Umid Party (Hope Party): Baku; tel. (12) 38-57-35; f. 1993; socialist; Chair. IQBAL AGAZADA; Leader ABULFAR AHMADOV; 5,000 mems (1998).

Vahdat Party (Unity Party): Baku, Azerbaijan Ave, Dom 23, Rm 52/54; tel. (12) 98-00-44; e-mail vahdat@box.az; f. 1995; a splinter faction, the Unity Party II, emerged in April 2000 and subsequently merged with the PFA in December; member of the Union of Pro-Azerbaijanist Forces; Chair. TAHIR KARIMLI; 17,500 mems (2000).

Workers' Party of Azerbaijan: Sumgait; f. 1999; socialist; Chair. AKIF HASANOGLU.

Yurdash Party (Compatriot Party): Baku; tel. (12) 32-10-47; f. 1991; Chair. MAIS SAFARLI.

Other political groups include the Democratic Enlightenment Party, the Modern Musavat Party, the People's Democratic Party and the National Movement Party. The Azerbaijan Patriots' Party was founded in July 2000 and Alim Babayev was elected as its Chair.

Diplomatic Representation

EMBASSIES IN AZERBAIJAN

China, People's Republic: 370010 Baku, Khagani St 67; tel. (12) 98-62-57; fax (12) 98-00-10; e-mail chinaemb@azeurotel.com; Ambassador ZHANG XIYUN.

Egypt: Baku, Moscow Ave 50, 3rd Floor; tel. (12) 98-79-06; fax (12) 98-79-54; e-mail emb.egypt@azeuro.net; Ambassador JIHAN AMIN MEHMET ALI.

France: 370000 Baku, Rassoul Reza St 7, POB 36; tel. (12) 92-89-77; fax (12) 98-92-53; e-mail ambafranbakou@azerin.com; internet www .ambafranbakou.com; Ambassador CHANTAL POIRET.

Georgia: Baku, Asaf Zeynalli St 24; tel. (12) 97-45-58; fax (12) 97-45-61; e-mail emb@georgian.baku.az; Ambassador ZURAB GUMBERIDZE.

Germany: 370000 Baku, Mamedaliyev St 15; tel. (12) 98-78-19; fax (12) 98-54-19; e-mail post@botschaftbaku.de; internet www .botschaftbaku.de; Ambassador Prof. Dr KLAUS W. GREWLICH.

Greece: 370004 Baku, Icheri Sheher, Kichik Gala St 86/88; tel. (12) 92-46-80; fax (12) 92-48-35; e-mail greekemb@azeri.com; Ambassador Dr MERCOURIOS B. KARAFOTIAS.

India: 370069 Baku, Narimanov District, Oktay Karimov St 31/39; tel. (12) 47-41-86; fax (12) 47-25-72; e-mail eibaku@adanet.az; Ambassador JYOTE SVARUP PANDE.

Iran: Baku, B. Sadarov St 4; tel. (12) 92-64-53; fax (12) 98-07-33; e-mail iranemb@azerin.com; Ambassador AHAD QAZAIE.

Iraq: 370000 Baku, Khagani St 9; tel. (12) 98-14-47; fax (12) 98-14-37; e-mail iraqya@azeri.com.

Israel: 370073 Baku, Bakikhanov St 1, Hyatt Complex, 7th Floor; tel. (12) 38-52-82; fax (12) 98-92-83; e-mail israel.embassy@isfr.baku .az; Ambassador EITAN NA'EH.

Italy: 370004 Baku, Kichic Gala St 44; tel. (12) 97-51-33; fax (12) 97-52-02; e-mail ambbaku@azeuro.net; internet www.ambitalbaku .com; Ambassador MARGHERITA COSTA.

Japan: Baku, 1033 Izmir St, Hyatt Tower 3, 5th Floor; tel. (12) 90-78-18; fax (12) 90-78-20; e-mail japan@emb.baku.az; Ambassador TOSHIYUKI FUJIVARA.

Kazakhstan: Baku, Inglab St 889/82; tel. (12) 90-62-48; fax (12) 90-62-49; e-mail embassy@adanet.az; Ambassador ANDAR SHUKPUTOV.

Korea, Democratic People's Republic: Baku; Ambassador LI CHOL-GWANG.

Libya: Baku, Husein Javid Ave 520/20; tel. (12) 93-23-65; fax (12) 98-12-47; Ambassador N. M. ABDUSSAMI.

Norway: 370004 Baku, Vagif Mustafazade St 6–10; tel. (12) 97-43-25; fax (12) 97-37-98; e-mail emb.baku@mfa.no; Ambassador STEINAR GIL.

Pakistan: Baku, Atatürk Ave 30; tel. (12) 90-68-39; fax (12) 90-68-41; e-mail parepbaku@artel.net.az; Ambassador FAIZ MOHAMMED KHOSO.

Poland: 370069 Baku, Atatürk St 30; tel. (12) 61-22-42; fax (12) 41-09-57; Ambassador MARCIN NAWROT.

Romania: 370069 Baku, Tariverdiyev St 9A; tel. (12) 62-04-29; fax (12) 40-77-00; e-mail rom_amb_baku@azdata.net; Ambassador TASIN GEMIL.

Russia: 370022 Baku, Bakikhanov St 17; tel. (12) 98-60-16; fax (12) 97-36-08; e-mail embrus@embrus.baku.az; internet intrans.baku.az/embrus; Ambassador NIKOLAI RYABOV.

Saudi Arabia: Wellington Heights, Shahbazi St 8, Apt 203; tel. (12) 97-23-05; fax (12) 97-23-02; Ambassador ALI HASAN JAFAR.

Turkey: 370000 Baku, Khagani St 27; tel. (12) 98-81-33; fax (12) 98-83-49; e-mail bakube@artel.net.az; Ambassador AHMET UNAL CEVIKOZ.

Ukraine: 37069 Baku, U. Vezizov St 49; tel. (12) 41-27-06; fax (12) 98-27-42; e-mail ukremb@azeurotel.com; internet www.ukremb.azeriland.com; Ambassador BORIS G. ALEKSENKO.

United Kingdom: 370065 Baku, Izmir St 2; tel. (12) 97-51-88; fax (12) 97-24-74; e-mail office@britemb.baku.az; internet www.britishembassy.az; Ambassador ANDREW TUCKER.

USA: 370007 Baku, Azadliq Ave 83; tel. (12) 98-03-36; fax (12) 98-37-55; internet www.usembassybaku.org; Ambassador ROSS WILSON.

Uzbekistan: Baku, Atatürk Ave 46; tel. (12) 97-25-49; fax (12) 97-25-48; e-mail embuzb@azeri.com; Ambassador ABDULGARUF ADU-DRAKHMANOV.

Judicial System

Constitutional Court

Baku; internet www.constitutional-court-az.org.

Comprises a Chairman and eight judges, who are nominated by the President and confirmed in office by the Milli Majlis for a term of office of 10 years. Only the President, the Milli Majlis, the Cabinet of Ministers, the Procurator-General, the Supreme Court and the legislature of the Autonomous Republic of Nakhichevan are permitted to submit cases to the Constitutional Court.

Chairman of the Constitutional Court and of the Supreme Court: KHANLAR HAJIYEV.

Prosecutor-General: ZAKIR BEKIR OGLU GARALOV.

Religion

ISLAM

The majority (some 70%) of Azerbaijanis are Shi'ite Muslims; most of the remainder are Sunni (Hanafi school). The Spiritual Board of Muslims of the Caucasus is based in Baku. It has spiritual jurisdiction over the Muslims of Armenia, Georgia and Azerbaijan. The Chairman of the Directorate is normally a Shi'ite, while the Deputy Chairman is usually a Sunni.

Spiritual Board of Muslims of the Caucasus: Baku; Chair. Sheikh ALLASHUKUR PASHEZADE.

CHRISTIANITY

The Roman Catholic Church

The Church is represented in Azerbaijan by a Mission, established in October 2000. There were an estimated 120 adherents at 31 December 2000.

Superior: Rev. JOZEF DANIEL PRAVDA, 370069 Baku, Teimur Aliyev St 69b/1; tel. (12) 62-36-15; fax (12) 62-22-55; e-mail parish@catol.baku.az.

The Press

In 1996 there were 257 newspaper titles, and in 1995 49 periodicals were officially registered in Azerbaijan. Owing to financial, political and technical difficulties, many publications reportedly suffered a sharp decrease in circulation. In August 1998 President Aliyev signed a decree abolishing censorship and ordering government bodies to provide support to the independent media.

PRINCIPAL NEWSPAPERS

In Azerbaijani, except where otherwise stated.

Adabiyat: 370146 Baku, Metbuat Ave, Block 529; tel. (12) 39-50-37; organ of the Union of Writers of Azerbaijan.

Ayna-Zerkalo: 370138 Baku, Sharifzadeh St 1; tel. and fax (12) 97-71-23; e-mail gazeta@zerkalo.az; internet www.zerkalo.az; f. 1990; daily; independent; Editor-in-Chief ELCIN SIXLINSKI; circ. 4,500 (daily).

Azadliq (Liberty): 370000 Baku, Khaqani St 33; tel. (12) 98-90-81; fax (12) 47-45-60; e-mail mail@azadliq.az; internet www.azadliq.az; f. 1989; weekly; independent; organ of the Popular Front of Azerbaijan; in Azerbaijani and Russian; Editor-in-Chief BAHADDIN HAZIYEV; circ. 9,034.

Azerbaijan: Baku, Metbuat Ave, Block 529; tel. (12) 39-44-91; fax (12) 39-43-23; e-mail azerbaijan_newspaper@azdata.net; internet www.azerbaijan.news.az; f. 1991; 5 a week; publ. by the Milli Majlis; in Azerbaijani and Russian; Editor-in-Chief BAKHTIYAR SADIGOV; circ. 10,242 (Azerbaijani), 3,040 (Russian).

Azernews: 370002 Baku, S. Askerova St 85, 3 et. tel. (12) 94-93-73; fax (12) 95-85-37; e-mail azernews@azeurotel.com; internet www.azernews.net; f. 1997; weekly; Azeri, English and Russian; in association with AssA-Irada news agency; Editor-in-Chief FAZIL ABBASOV; circ. 5,000–6,000.

Bakinskii Rabochii (Baku Worker): 370146 Baku, Metbuat Ave, Block 529; tel. (12) 38-00-29; e-mail bakrab@azerin.com; internet www.br.az; f. 1906; 5 a week; govt newspaper; in Russian; Editor I. VEKILOVA; circ. 4,776.

Baku Today: 370000 Baku, A. Guliyev St 133, apt 23; tel. and fax (12) 98-68-69; e-mail editor@bakutoday.net; internet www.bakutoday.net; first online newspaper in English to cover the Caucasus and Caspian region; Azeri version on www.xeber.net; Editor-in-Chief MAHIR ISKENDER; circ. 1,500–3,000 daily.

Baku Sun: 370073 Baku, Inshaatchilar Ave 2, Office 42; tel. (12) 97-55-31; e-mail editor@bakusun.baku.az; internet www.bakusun.az; f. 1998; weekly; free; in English.

Bizim Asr: 370141 Baku, A. Alakbarov 83/23; tel. (12) 97-88-99; fax (12) 97-88-98; e-mail bizim_asr@media-az.com; internet bizmasr.media-az.com; f. 1999; owned by Media Holding.

Echo: Baku; tel. (12) 97-51-74; fax (12) 47-41-50; internet www.echo-az.com.

Ezhednevniye Novosti (Daily News): Baku, Bratia Alibekovy St 43; tel. and fax (12) 92-12-24; e-mail alpha@azeri.com; internet www.alpha.azeri.com; in Russian; Editor EMIL ASADOV.

525 Gazet: 370033 Baku, S. Mustafayev St 27/121; tel. (12) 66-67-89; fax (12) 66-25-20; internet www.525ci.com; f. 1992; 5 days a week; Azerbaijani, English and Russian; Editor-in-Chief RASHAD MAJID.

Hayat (Life): 370146 Baku, Metbuat Ave, Block 529; f. 1991; 5 a week; publ. by the Milli Majlis; Editor-in-Chief A. H. ASKEROV.

Hurriyet (Liberty): Baku; tel. (12) 67-53-22; fax (2) 98-82-27; organ of the Democratic Party of Azerbaijan; Editor-in-Chief AYDYN GULIEV.

Intibakh (Revival): Baku; independent; 3 a week; Editor-in-Chief MUSTAFA HAJIBEILI; circ. 10,000.

Istiklal (Independence): 370014 Baku, 28 May St 3–11; tel. (12) 93-33-78; fax (12) 98-75-55; e-mail istiklal@ngonet.baku.az; 4 a month; organ of the Azerbaijan Social Democratic Party; Editor ZARDUSHT ALIZADEH; circ. 5,000.

Khalg Gazeti: Baku; tel. (12) 93-02-80; fax (12) 98-85-29; f. 1919; fmrly *Kommunist*; 6 a week; organ of the office of the President; Editor HASAN HASANOV.

Millat: Baku; organ of the National Independence Party.

Molodezh Azerbaijana (Youth of Azerbaijan): 370146 Baku, Metbuat Ave, Block 529, 8th Floor; tel. (12) 39-00-51; f. 1919; weekly; in Russian; Editor V. EFENDIYEV; circ. 7,000.

Respublika (Republic): 370146 Baku, Metbuat Ave, Block 529; tel. (12) 38-01-14; fax (12) 38-01-31; f. 1996; daily; govt newspaper; Editor-in-Chief T. AHMADOV; circ. 5,500.

Sharg: Baku; tel. (12) 39-00-73; fax (12) 39-00-79; e-mail info@sherq.com; internet www.sherq.com.

Veten Sesi (Voice of the Motherland): 370146 Baku, Metbuat Ave, Block 529; f. 1990; weekly; publ. by the Society of Refugees of Azerbaijan; in Azerbaijani and Russian; Editor-in-Chief T. A. AHMEDOV.

Vyshka (Oil derrick): 370146 Baku, Metbuat Ave, Block 529; tel. and fax (12) 39-96-97; e-mail vyshka@azeurotel.com; internet www.vyshka.com; f. 1928; weekly; independent social-political newspaper; in Russian; Editor M. E. GASANOVA.

Yeni Azerbaijan: Baku; tel. (12) 39-82-27; fax (12) 97-53-04; internet www.yeniazerbaycan.com; f. 1993; weekly; organ of the New Azerbaijan Party; Editor ALGYSH MUSAYEV; circ. 2,493.

Yeni Müsavat: Baku; tel. (12) 98-00-61; fax (12) 98-20-88; internet www.yenimusavat.com; independent; opposition; Editor-in-Chief RAUF ARIFOGLU.

Yeni Yuzil (New Century): Baku; f. 2001 by the founder of Azadliq (q.v.); Editor-in-Chief GUNDUZ TAHIRLI.

PRINCIPAL PERIODICALS

Azerbaijan: Baku; tel. (12) 92-59-63; f. 1923; monthly; publ. by the Union of Writers of Azerbaijan; recent works by Azerbaijani authors; Editor-in-Chief YUSIF SAMEDOGLU.

Azerbaijan Gadyny (Woman of Azerbaijan): Baku; f. 1923; monthly; illustrated; Editor H. M. HASILOVA.

Dialog (Dialogue): Baku; f. 1989; fortnightly; in Azerbaijani and Russian; Editor R. A. ALEKPEROV.

Iki Sahil: Baku, Nobel Ave 64; f. 1965; weekly; organ of the New Baku Oil-Refining Plant; Editor-in-Chief V. RAHIMZADEH; circ. 2,815.

Kend Khayaty (Country Life): Baku; f. 1952; monthly; journal of the Ministry of Agriculture and Produce; advanced methods of work in agriculture; in Azerbaijani and Russian; Editor D. A. DAMIRLI.

Kirpi (Hedgehog): Baku; f. 1952; fortnightly; satirical; Editor A. M. AIVAZOV.

Literaturnyi Azerbaijan (Literature of Azerbaijan): 370001 Baku, Khagani St 25; tel. (12) 93-51-00; e-mail sima@azeri.com; f. 1931; monthly; journal of the Union of Writers of Azerbaijan; fiction; in Russian; Editor-in-Chief M. F. VEKILOV.

Monitor: f. 2002; independent; Editor-in-Chief ELMAR HUSEINOV.

Ulus: Baku; tel. (12) 92-27-43; internet www.ulus-az.com; 2 a week; Editor TOFIK DADASHEV.

NEWS AGENCIES

AssA-Irada: 370002 Baku, S. Askerova St 85, 3 et. tel. (12) 94-93-73; fax (12) 95-85-37; e-mail azernews@azeurotel.com; internet www .azernews.net; f. 1991; Azeri, English and Russian.

Azadinform Information Agency: 370000 Baku, F. Amirov St 1; tel. (12) 98-48-59; fax (12) 98-47-60; e-mail azadinform@azerin.com; internet www.azadinform.baku-az.com; f. 1998; independent information agency; Chief Editor ASEF HAJIYEV.

AzerTag (Azerbaijan State News Agency): 370000 Baku, Bul-Bul Ave 18; tel. (12) 93-59-29; fax (12) 93-62-65; e-mail azertac@azdata .net; internet www.azertag.net; f. 1920; Gen. Dir SHAMIL MAMMAD OGLU SHAHMAMMADOV.

Baku Telegraph: see section on Telecommunications.

Bilik Dunyasi: Baku; tel. (12) 94-28-80.

Media-Press: 370141 Baku, A. Alakbarov 83/23; tel. (12) 97-07-05; fax (12) 97-88-98; e-mail news@mediapress.media-az.com; internet mediapress.media-az.com; f. 1999; owned by Media Holding; independent.

Midiya Press Agency (MPA): 370000 Baku, Bashir Safaroglu St 191/28; tel. (12) 97-42-45; fax (12) 97-33-59; e-mail agency@mpa .baku.az; internet www.az/mpa/; Azerbaijani, English and Russian.

Sharg News Agency: 370001 Baku, Mirza Shafi 6; tel. (12) 92-69-80; fax (12) 92-46-23; e-mail sharg@azeri.com; internet www .azsharg.com; f. 1994; Correspondent K. MUSTAFAYEVA.

Trend Information-Analytical Agency: 370601 Baku, Fizuli St 69; tel. (12) 97-30-89; fax (12) 97-30-89; e-mail infotrend@azeurotel .com; internet web.az:8101/trend/; f. 1995; Russian and Turkish; Correspondent E. HUSSEINOV.

Turan News Agency: 370000 Baku, Khagani St 33; tel. (12) 98-42-26; fax (12) 98-38-17; e-mail root@turan.baku.az; internet www .turaninfo.com; f. 1990; independent news agency; Azerbaijani, English and Russian; Dir MEHMAN ALIYEV.

Foreign Bureaux

Agence France-Presse (AFP): Baku, Zargar Palan 128; tel. and fax (12) 47-07-18.

Interfax (Russia): Baku; f. 2002.

PRESS ASSOCIATION

Central Asian and Southern Caucasus Freedom of Expression Network: 370105 Baku, A. Haqverdiyev St 3A/5; tel. and fax (12) 38-32-56; e-mail azeri@ajip.baku.az; based in the office of the Trade Union of Journalists; members include the Azerbaijan National Committee of the International Press Institute, the Independent Association of Georgian Journalists, the Public Association of Journalists from Kyrgyzstan, the National Association of Independent Mass Media of Tajikistan and Union of Independent Journalists of Uzbekistan; Co-ordinator AZER H. HASRET.

Publishers

Azerbaijan Ensiklopediyasy (Azerbaijan Encyclopedia): 370004 Baku, Boyuk Gala St 41; tel. (12) 92-87-11; fax (12) 92-77-83; e-mail azenciklop@ctc.net.az; f. 1965; encyclopedias and dictionaries; Gen. Dir I. O. VELIYEV.

Azerneshr (State Publishing House): 370005 Baku, Gusi Hajiyev St 4; tel. (12) 92-50-15; f. 1924; various; Dir A. MUSTAFAZADE; Editor-in-Chief A. KUSEINZADE.

Elm (Azerbaijani Academy of Sciences Publishing House): 370073 Baku, Narimanov Ave 37; scientific books and journals.

Gyanjlik (Youth): 370005 Baku, Gusi Hajiyev St 4; books for children and young people; Dir E. T. ALIYEV.

Ishyg (Light): 370601 Baku, Gogol St 6; posters, illustrated publs; Dir G. N. ISMAILOV.

Maarif (State Publishing House of Educational Literature): 370111 Baku, A. Mageramov St 4; tel. and fax (12) 31-58-27; f. 1959; educational literature and materials; Dir ABAS ALI GIZI ALIYEVA SEVDA.

Madani-maarif Ishi (Education and Culture): 370146 Baku, Metbuat Ave, Block 529; tel. (12) 32-79-17; Editor-in-Chief ALOVSAT ATAMALY OGLU BASHIROV.

Medeniyyat (Publishing House of the 'Culture' Newspaper): 370146 Baku, Metbuat Ave 146; tel. (12) 32-98-38; Dir SHAKMAR AKPER OGLU AKPERZADE.

Sada, Literaturno-Izdatelskyi Centr: 370004 Baku, Bolshaya Krepostnaya St 28; tel. (12) 92-75-64; fax (12) 92-98-43; reference.

Shur: Baku; tel. (12) 92-93-72; f. 1992; Dir GASHAM ISA OGLU ISABEYLI.

Yazychy (Writer): 370005 Baku, Natavan St 1; fiction; Dir F. M. MELIKOV.

Broadcasting and Communications

TELECOMMUNICATIONS

Azercell Telecom JV: 370139 Baku, Tbilisi Ave 61A; tel. (12) 96-70-07; fax (12) 30-05-68; internet www.azercell.com; f. 1996; provides communication services with integrated voice and data transfer and internet services (Azeronline); joint-venture co between the Ministry of Communications and Fintur Holdings B.V. (Netherlands); 83.6% market share of mobile cellular telephone subscribers; Gen. Dir ESRA TAN; 295 employees.

AzEuroTel JV: 370001 Baku, B. Sardarov St 1; tel. (12) 97-07-07; fax (12) 97-01-01; e-mail aet@azeurotel.com; internet rus.azeurotel .com; f. 1995; established by the Ministry of Communications and LUKoil Europe Ltd (Russia) as a joint venture with the United Kingdom; digital, wireless, trunking and satellite communications and internet provider; Gen. Dir NURI AGAMIRZA AKHMEDOV.

Baku Telegraph Joint-Stock Co: 370000 Baku, Azerbaijan Ave 41; tel. (12) 93-61-42; fax (12) 98-55-25; f. 1932; operates international telegraph, fax and telex services, and provides independent news services; Dir SABIRA AGARZAEVA.

RADIO AND TELEVISION

National Television and Radio Council: Baku; f. 2003; nine-member regulatory body.

Radio and Television Company of Azerbaijan: 370011 Baku, Mehti Hussein St 1; tel. (12) 92-72-53; fax (12) 39-54-52; f. 1956; state-owned; Dir NIZAMI MANAF OGLU KHUDIYEV; 2,490 employees.

Azerbaijan National Television: tel. (12) 39-77-72; fax (12) 97-20-20; internet www.aztv.az; f. 1956; programmes in Azerbaijani, English and Russian (14 hours a day); one regional channel and one national channel.

Azerbaijan State Radio: tel. (12) 92-87-68; fax (12) 39-72-48; f. 1926; broadcasts in Azerbaijani, Arabic, English and Turkish; two channels and one international broadcasting studio; Head MOVLUD SULEIMAN.

ANS Independent Broadcasting and Media Co: internet www .ans-dx.com; f. 1999; joint-stock co, independent; Pres. VAHID MUSTAFAYEV.

ANS TV: tel. (12) 97-72-67; fax (12) 98-94-98; f. 1990.

ANS-CHM Radio: f. 1994; broadcasts in Azerbaijani, English, Russian and Turkish.

Lider TV: 370141 Baku, A. Alakbarov 83/23; tel. (12) 97-88-99; fax (12) 97-87-77; e-mail mail@media-az.com; internet www.lidertv .com; f. 2000; owned by Media Holding.

Lider 107 FM: 370141 Baku, A. Alakbarov 83/23; tel. (12) 97-07-05; fax (12) 97-88-98; e-mail lider@lider.fm; internet www.lider.fm; owned by Media Holding.

Sara-TV: Baku; entertainment programmes.

Space TV and Radio: 370073 Baku, H. Javid Ave 8; tel. (12) 33-00-66; fax (12) 92-76-65; e-mail info@space-az.com; internet www.space-az.com; f. 1997 (radio broadcasts commenced in 2001); Chair. ETIBAR ADIL BABAYEV.

Finance

(cap. = capital; res = reserves; dep. = deposits; m. = million; brs = branches; amounts in manats, unless otherwise stated)

BANKING

Central Bank

National Bank of Azerbaijan: 370014 Baku, R. Behbutov St 32; tel. (12) 93-11-22; fax (12) 93-55-41; e-mail mail@nba.az; internet www.nba.az; f. 1992 as central bank and supervisory authority; cap. 26,685m., res 395,263m., dep. 935,087m. (Dec. 2000); Chair. ELMAN ROUSTAMOV.

State-owned Banks

International Bank of Azerbaijan: 370005 Baku, Nizami St 67; tel. (12) 93-00-91; fax (12) 93-40-91; e-mail ibar@ibar.az; internet www.ibar.az; f. 1992 to succeed br. of USSR Vneshekonombank; 50.2% owned by the Ministry of Finance, 9.24% owned by employees; carries out all banking services; cap. 50,000m., res 260,000m., dep. 382,000m. (Dec. 2002); Chair. of Bd JAHANGIR HAJIYEV; First Dep. Chair. RAUF RZAYEV; 32 brs.

United Joint-Stock Bank: Baku; f. 2000 by merger of Agroprombank (Agricultural bank), Prominvest (Industrial Investment Bank) and the Savings Bank; commenced operations 1 April; Pres. ZAKIR ZEYNALOV.

Other Banks

In January 2000 there were 70, mainly small, registered commercial banks operating in Azerbaijan, some of the most prominent of which are listed below:

Azerbaijan Central Republican Bank: 370088 Baku, Fizuli St 71; tel. (12) 93-05-61; fax (12) 93-94-89; Chair. HUSEYN SAFROV.

Azerbaijan Industrial Bank: 370010 Baku, Fizuli St 71; tel. (12) 93-17-01; fax (12) 93-12-66; f. 1992; joint-stock commercial bank; Chair. ORUJ H. HEYDAROV; 40 brs.

Azerbaijan-Turkish Commercial Bank (Azer-Turk): 370005 Baku, Islam Seferli St 5; tel. (12) 97-43-16; fax (12) 98-37-02; e-mail azerturk@artel.net.az; internet www.azerturkbank.in-baku.com; f. 1995; cap. 8,435.0m., res 1,696.4m., dep. 19,636.8m. (Dec. 2000); Chair. MEMET MUSAYEV QURBANOĞLU; Gen. Man. MURAT AKSOY.

Azerdemiryolbank: 370008 Baku, Garabag St 31; tel. (12) 40-24-29; fax (12) 96-09-77; e-mail damir@azerdemiryolbank.am; internet www.azerdemiryolbank.am; f. 1989; largest private commercial bank; operates mainly in transport sector; cap. 12,717.2m., dep. 82,216.5m. (Dec. 2001); Chair. of Bd ROMAN AMIRDJANOV; 10 brs.

Azerigazbank: 370073 Baku, Inshaatchylar Ave 3; tel. (12) 97-50-17; fax (12) 39-26-03; e-mail damir@azerdemiryolbank.com; internet www.azerdemiryolbank.com; f. 1992; joint-stock investment bank; Chair. AZER MOVSUMOV; 10 brs.

Bakcoopbank (Baku Co-operative Bank): Baku; tel. (12) 67-45-46; Gen. Dir ALIM I. AZIMOV.

Baybank: 370000 Baku, S. Vurgun St 14; tel. (12) 93-50-07; fax (12) 98-57-76; e-mail baybank@artel.net.az; f. 1995; joint-stock bank, carries out all banking services; cap. US $1.5m., dep. $2.3m. (Dec. 1998); Pres., Gen. Man. and Chief Exec. T. SERDAR ERZURUMLU; Chair. HUSEYN BAYRAKTAR.

Günay Bank: 370095 Baku, Rasul Rza St 4/6; tel. (12) 98-04-55; fax (12) 98-14-39; e-mail gunaybank@azerin.com; internet www.gunaybank.com; f. 1992; first privately owned bank in Azerbaijan; cap. 15,100m., res 2,200m., dep. 19,000m. Chair. of Bd SHAKIR ABDULLAYEV; 2 brs.

Rabitabank: 370001 Baku, B. Sardarov St 1; tel. (12) 92-57-61; fax (12) 92-61-57; e-mail rbtbank@azevt.com; f. 1993; joint-stock commercial bank; operates mainly in telecommunications sector; Chair. ZAKIR NURIYEV; 4 brs.

Ruzubank: 370055 Baku, Istiglaliyat St 27; tel. (12) 92-42-58; fax (12) 92-78-12; f. 1992; joint-stock bank; cap. 216m., res 30.4m., dep. 1,834m. Pres. S. A. ALIYEV; Chair. of Bd V. N. MUSAYEV.

Trustbank JS Bank: 370143 Baku, Firuddin Agayev St 9; tel. (12) 93-14-01; fax (12) 93-12-16; e-mail root@trustbank.baku.az; f. 1994; commercial bank; cap. 9,531m., res 592m. (1998), dep. 991m. (Jan. 2003); Pres. AZER AKHMEDOVICH ALIYEV; Chair. BAKHRAM ASLAN OGLU SULTANOV.

United Universal JS Bank: 370014 Baku, Fizuli St 71; tel. (12) 41-41-07; fax (12) 41-41-19; e-mail aibbank@artel.net.az; f. 1992 to replace br. of USSR Sberbank; changed name from Amanatbank in 2000; Chair. ZAKIR H. ZEYNALOV; 88 brs.

Universal Commercial Bank: 370002 Baku, B. Megidov St 44/46; tel. (12) 97-30-34; fax (12) 97-30-29; e-mail bank@usal.baku.az; f. 1998; cap. 6,000m., res 620m., dep. 1,404m. (Dec. 2000); Pres. HEYDAR R. IBRAHIMOV.

Vostochniy Bank: 370070 Baku, Kirova Ave 19; tel. (12) 93-22-47; fax (12) 93-11-81; Gen. Dir RAGIMOV A. ABBAL.

Association

Azerbaijan Association of Banks: Baku, B. Sardarov St 1; tel. (12) 97-58-29; fax (12) 97-15-15; e-mail bank_assoc@azeurotel.com; f. 1990; co-ordinates banking activity; Pres. ZAKIR NURIYEV; 49 mems.

INSURANCE

In January 2002 there were 38 insurance companies operating in Azerbaijan.

Azergarant Joint-Stock Insurance Company: 370001 Baku, Istiglaliyat St 31; tel. (12) 92-72-49; fax (12) 92-54-71; e-mail info@azerinvest.baku.az; f. 1993; Pres. Dr ALEKPER MAMEDOV; Gen. Dir FAIG HUSSEINOV.

Azersigorta: Baku.

Günay Anadolu Sigorta JV: 370005 Baku, Terlan Aliyarbekov St 3; tel. (12) 98-13-56; fax (12) 98-13-60; e-mail gunaysigorta@azdata.net; internet insurancegunayanadolu.com; f. 1992; serves major international cos operating in Azerbaijan; Gen. Man. ALOVSET GOJAYEV.

Shafag: Baku; f. 1998; medical insurance.

Trade and Industry

CHAMBER OF COMMERCE

Chamber of Commerce and Industry: 370601 Baku, Istiglaliyat St 31/33; tel. (12) 92-89-12; fax (12) 98-93-24; e-mail expo@chamber.baku.az; internet www.exhibition.azeri.com; Pres. SULEYMAN BAYRAM OGLU TATLIYEV.

INDUSTRIAL AND TRADE ASSOCIATIONS

Azerbintorg: 370004 Baku, Nekrasov St 7; tel. (12) 93-71-69; fax (12) 98-32-92; imports and exports a wide range of goods (90.4% of exports in 1995); Dir E. M. HUREYNOV.

Azerkontract: 370141 Baku, A. Alekperov St 83/23; tel. (12) 39-42-96; fax (12) 39-91-76.

Azertijaret: 370004 Baku, Genjler Sq. 3; tel. (12) 92-66-67; fax (12) 98-07-56; e-mail aztij@azeri.com; Dir R. SH. ALIYEV.

MIT International Trade Co: 370148 Baku, Mehti Hussein St, Hotel Anba; tel. (12) 98-45-20; fax (12) 98-45-19; f. 1993; food products and consumer goods; Dir TAHIR RAMAZAN OGLU ASADOV.

UTILITIES

Electricity

AzerEnerji JSC: Baku; Pres. ETIBAR PIRVERDIYEV.

Gas

AzeriGaz CJSC: 370025 Baku, Yusif Safarov St 23; tel. (12) 67-74-47; fax (12) 65-12-01; f. 1992; transport, distribution, sale, compression and storage of natural gas; Chair. ALIHUSEIN JAMALOV; 13,000 employees.

STATE HYDROCARBONS COMPANIES

Azerbaijan International Operating Company (AIOC): 370003 Baku, Villa Petrolea, Neftchilar Ave 2; tel. (12) 91-21-02; fax (12) 75-96-02; e-mail bayatltf@bp.com; f. 1994 as a consortium of: SOCAR (q.v.), British Petroleum and Ramco of the United Kingdom, Amoco, Exxon and Unocal of the USA, Itocha of Japan, LUKoil of Russia, Statoil of Norway, Türkiye Petrolleri of Turkey and Delta Nimir of Saudi Arabia; exploration and development of Azerbaijani offshore petroleum reserves; Pres. DAVID WOODWARD.

State Committee for Geology and Mineral Resources of Azerbaijan: 370073 Baku, Bakhram Agayeb St 100A; tel. (12) 38-04-31; fax (12) 39-84-32; f. 1932; prospecting, research and surveys; Chair. ISLAM TAGIEV.

State Oil Company of the Azerbaijan Republic (SOCAR): 370004 Baku, Neftchilar Ave 73; tel. (12) 92-07-45; fax (12) 97-11-67; e-mail akhmedo@aiocaz.com; internet www.socar-cc.com; f. 1992, following a merger of the two state petroleum companies, Azerineft and Azneftkhimiya; conducts production and exploration activities, oversees refining and capital construction activities; Pres. NATIK ALIYEV; Vice-Pres. ILHAM ALIYEV; Exec. Dir SAMIR RAUF OGLU SHARIFOV; 67,000 employees.

TRADE UNIONS

Association of Independent Workers of Azerbaijan: Baku; Chair. NEYMAT PANAKHLI.

Confederation of Azerbaijan Trade Unions: Baku; tel. and fax (12) 92-72-68; Chair. SATTAR MEHBALIYEV.

Free Trade Union of Teachers: Baku; Chair. SEYRAN SEYRANOV.

Trade Union of Journalists (JuHI): 370000 Baku, Khagani St 33; tel. (50) 335-27-95; fax (12) 98-78-18; e-mail juhi@juhiaz.org; internet www.juhiaz.org; f. 1998; registered by Govt in March 2000; 654 mems; Chair. AZER HASRET.

Trade Union of Oil and Gas Industry Workers: 370033 Baku, Aga Neymatulla St 39; tel. (12) 67-69-53; fax (12) 47-15-85; e-mail oilunion@online.az; f. 1906; mems belong to 210 local organizations in the petroleum and gas sectors; 71,500 mems; Chair. JAHANGIR ALIYEV.

Transport

RAILWAYS

In 2000 there were 2,116 km of railway track, of which 1,269 km were electrified. The overwhelming majority of total freight traffic is carried by the railways. Railways connect Baku with Tbilisi (Georgia), Makhachkala (Dagestan, Russia) and Yerevan (Armenia). In 1997 passenger rail services between Moscow and Baku were resumed, and a service to Kiev (Ukraine) was inaugurated. The rail link with Armenia runs through the Autonomous Republic of Nakhichevan, but is currently disrupted, owing to Azerbaijan's economic blockade of Armenia. From Nakhichevan an international line links Azerbaijan with Tabriz (Iran). In 1991 plans were agreed with the Iranian Government for the construction of a rail line between Azerbaijan and Nakhichevan, which would pass through Iranian territory, thus bypassing Armenia. There is an underground railway in Baku (the Baku Metro); initially comprising two lines (total length 28 km), with 19 stations, a further 4.1 km, with three stations, was under construction.

Azerbaijani Railways (AZ): 370010 Baku, Dilara Aliyeva St 230; tel. (12) 98-44-67; fax (12) 98-85-47; f. 1992, following the dissolution of the former Soviet Railways; First Dep. Pres. and Chief Eng. M. M. MEHTIYEV.

Baku Metropolitan: 370602 Baku, H. Javid Ave 33A; tel. (12) 90-00-00; fax (12) 97-53-96; internet www.metro.gov.az:8101; f. 1967; Gen. Man. T. AKHMEDOV.

ROADS

In 2000 the total length of roads in Azerbaijan was 24,981 km, of which 6,897 km were main roads; 92.3% of the road network was paved.

SHIPPING

Shipping services on the Caspian Sea link Baku with Astrakhan (Russia), Turkmenbashi (Turkmenistan) and the Iranian ports of Bandar Anzali and Bandar Nowshar. At 31 December 2001 the Azerbaijani merchant fleet comprised 283 vessels, with a combined displacement of 641,184 grt. The total included 38 petroleum tankers (175,431 grt).

Shipowning Company

Caspian Shipping Company (Caspar): 370005 Baku, Mammademin Resulzade St 5; tel. (12) 93-20-58; fax (12) 93-53-39; f. 1858; nationalized by the Govt in 1991; transports crude petroleum and petroleum products; operates cargo and passenger ferries; Pres. A. A. BASHIROV.

CIVIL AVIATION

There are five airports in Azerbaijan, of which Baku (www.airport-baku.com) is the largest. A new air terminal was commissioned for the Bina-Baku airport in 1999. Nakhichevan also has its own airport.

Civil Aviation Administration: 370000 Baku, Azadliq Ave 11; tel. (12) 93-44-34; fax (12) 98-52-37; e-mail azal_coordpt@azerin.com; internet www.azaviation.com; Chief Inspector ILHAM G. AMIROV.

Azerbaijan Airlines (AZAL) (Azerbaijan Hava Yollari): 370000 Baku, Azadliq Ave 11; tel. (12) 93-44-34; fax (12) 98-52-37; e-mail azal@azal.baku.az; internet www.azal.az; f. 1992; formerly Azalavia; state airline operating scheduled and charter passenger services to Africa, the CIS, Europe, South-East Asia and the Middle East; Gen. Dir JAHANGIR ASKEROV.

Cargo Air Company (CAC): 370109 Baku, Bina Airport; tel. and fax (12) 97-16-71; e-mail office@azavcar.baku.az; internet www.cacazal.com; state-owned; Dir YASHAR HASANOV.

IMAIR Airlines: 370000 Baku, Hazi Aslanov St 115; tel. (12) 93-41-71; fax (12) 93-27-77; e-mail root@imair.com; internet www.imair.com; f. 1995; independent airline operating international regular passenger and charter passenger and cargo services, mainly within the CIS region; Chair. and Pres. FIZOULI ALEKPEROV.

Turan Air: 370022 Baku, 102 Mardanov Bros St; tel. (12) 98-94-31; fax (12) 98-94-34; internet www.turan.com; f. 1994; operates scheduled and charter passenger and cargo services, mainly within the former USSR.

Tourism

Tourism is not widely developed. However, there are resorts on the Caspian Sea, including the Ganjlik international tourist centre, on the Apsheron Peninsula, near Baku, which has four hotels as well as camping facilities. There were 766,992 tourist arrivals in 2001.

Council for Foreign Tourism: 370004 Baku, Neftchilar Ave 65; tel. (12) 92-87-13; fax (12) 98-03-68; e-mail ff-com@azdata.net; under the Cabinet of Ministers.

THE BAHAMAS

Introductory Survey

Location, Climate, Language, Religion, Flag, Capital

The Commonwealth of the Bahamas consists of about 700 islands and more than 2,000 cays and rocks, extending from east of the Florida coast of the USA to just north of Cuba and Haiti, in the West Indies. The main islands are New Providence, Grand Bahama, Andros, Eleuthera and Great Abaco. Almost 70% of the population reside on the island of New Providence. The remaining members of the group are known as the 'Family Islands'. A total of 29 of the islands are inhabited. The climate is mild and sub-tropical, with average temperatures of about 30°C (86°F) in summer and 20°C (68°F) in winter. The average annual rainfall is about 1,000 mm (39 ins). The official language is English. Most of the inhabitants profess Christianity, the largest denominations being the Anglican, Baptist, Roman Catholic and Methodist Churches. The national flag comprises three equal horizontal stripes, of blue, gold and blue, with a black triangle at the hoist, extending across one-half of the width. The capital is Nassau, on the island of New Providence.

Recent History

A former British colonial territory, the Bahamas attained internal self-government in January 1964, although the parliamentary system dates back to 1729. The first elections under universal adult suffrage were held in January 1967 for an enlarged House of Assembly. The Progressive Liberal Party (PLP), supported mainly by Bahamians of African origin and led by Lynden (later Sir Lynden) Pindling, won 18 of the 38 seats, as did the ruling United Bahamian Party (UBP), dominated by those of European origin. With the support of another member, the PLP formed a Government and Pindling became Premier (he was restyled Prime Minister in September 1968). At the next elections, in April 1968, the PLP won 29 seats and the UBP only seven.

Following a constitutional conference in September 1968, the Bahamas Government was given increased responsibility for internal security, external affairs and defence in May 1969. In the elections of September 1972, which were dominated by the issue of independence, the PLP maintained its majority. Following a constitutional conference in December 1972, the Bahamas became an independent nation, within the Commonwealth, on 10 July 1973. Pindling remained Prime Minister. The PLP increased its majority in the elections of July 1977 and was again returned to power in the June 1982 elections, with 32 of the 43 seats in the enlarged House of Assembly. The remaining 11 seats were won by the Free National Movement (FNM), which had reunited for the elections after splitting into several factions over the previous five years.

Trading in illicit drugs, mainly for the US market, has become a major problem for the country, since many of the small islands and cays are used by drugs-traffickers in their smuggling activities. In 1983 allegations of widespread corruption, and the abuse of Bahamian bank secrecy laws by drugs-traffickers and US tax evaders, led Pindling to appoint a Royal Commission to investigate thoroughly the drugs trade in the Bahamas. The Commission's hearings revealed the extent to which money deriving from this trade had permeated Bahamian social and economic affairs. Evidence presented to the Commission led to the resignation, in October 1984, of two cabinet ministers, and by November 1985 a total of 51 suspects had been indicted, including the assistant police commissioner. The Commission also revealed that Pindling had received several million dollars in gifts and loans from business executives, although it found no evidence of a link to the drugs trade. After unsuccessfully demanding Pindling's resignation, the Deputy Prime Minister, Arthur Hanna, resigned, and two other ministers, Perry Christie and Hubert Ingraham, were dismissed.

Although the issue of the illegal drugs trade and of drugs-related corruption within the Government dominated the general election campaign, the PLP was returned to power for a fifth consecutive term in June 1987, winning 31 of the 49 seats in the enlarged House of Assembly. The FNM won 16 seats, while the remaining two seats were secured by Christie and Ingraham as independents.

In February 1988 new claims of official corruption were made at the trial in Florida, USA, of a leading Colombian drugs-trafficker. Pindling and the Deputy Prime Minister were alleged to have accepted bribes, but this was vehemently denied. In March 1990 the Minister of Agriculture, Trade and Industry, Ervin Knowles, resigned, following allegations of nepotism and the misuse of public funds. He was replaced by Christie, who rejoined the PLP. The other independent member, Ingraham, subsequently joined the FNM and became its leader in May, upon the death of Sir Cecil Wallace-Whitfield.

The general election campaign in mid-1992 was disrupted by industrial unrest in the country's telephone and electricity companies, and by the continuing problems of the state airline, Bahamasair. Despite predictions of a PLP victory, the FNM won the general election on 19 August, securing 33 seats, while Pindling's party won the remaining 16. Ingraham replaced Pindling as Prime Minister, and announced a programme of measures aimed at increasing the accountability of government ministers, combating corruption and revitalizing the economy. Acknowledging responsibility for his party's defeat in the election, Pindling resigned as leader of the PLP, but, at the party's annual convention in January 1993, agreed to continue in office.

The resignation of Orville Turnquest, the Deputy Prime Minister, Minister of Foreign Affairs and Attorney-General, in January 1995, in order to assume the post of Governor-General, prompted an extensive cabinet reorganization.

A marked increase in violent crime in parts of New Providence led the Government to announce the creation, in March 1995, of a special police unit to tackle the problem. Meanwhile, the trade in illegal drugs remained widespread in the country, and in late 1995 several local business leaders, as well as close relatives of a member of Parliament, were arrested in connection with a large seizure of cocaine. In October of that year the Prime Minister introduced further legislation that aimed to prevent the abuse of Bahamian banks by drugs-traffickers, and thus improve the reputation of the country's financial sector, particularly in the USA.

The decision in March 1996 to hang a man convicted of murder in early 1991 was controversial, owing to the fact that the period spent awaiting execution had exceeded five years. In recognition of a prisoner's suffering in anticipation of execution, previous cases had held five years to constitute the maximum term after which the case should be subject to review with a possible commutation to life imprisonment. However, in October 1996 the Judicial Committee of the Privy Council ruled that to await execution for more than three and a half years would amount to inhuman punishment, and that all such cases should be commuted. The ruling was believed to affect 22 of the 39 prisoners under sentence of death in the Bahamas at that time.

At a general election held on 14 March 1997, in which 91.7% of the electorate participated, the FNM won 34 of the 40 seats in a reduced House of Assembly, and the PLP six. The FNM's overwhelming victory in the election was attributed both to the Prime Minister's success in reversing the economic decline and the involvement of the PLP in various financial scandals. Most notably, Pindling was implicated in February in the findings of a public inquiry (instituted in 1993) to investigate alleged corruption and misappropriation of funds in the three principal state corporations. Following the election, Pindling, who had retained his seat in the House of Assembly, resigned as leader of the PLP and was replaced by Christie. In July Pindling announced his retirement from parliamentary politics (he died in August 2000), and his seat was won by the FNM at a by-election in September. The PLP was further damaged in January 2000 by the resignation of its deputy leader, Bernard Nottage, who subsequently formed a rival party, the Coalition for Democratic Reform (CDR).

In the late 1990s and early 2000s violent crime continued to be of major concern to Bahamians. In April 1998 the Government signed a convention drawn up by the Organization of American States to ban illegal guns, amid a disturbing increase in gun-related crime. In September 1998, following the murders of several tourists, the Prime Minister increased security in tourist areas, and announced plans to limit the right of appeal against death sentences (17 prisoners had had their sentences commuted in January). The hanging in October of two convicted murderers caused controversy, despite growing public demand for execution as a deterrent against crime. In carrying out the executions, the Government rejected a last-minute plea for clemency from the European Union (EU), on the grounds that both men had appeals pending at the Inter-American Commission on Human Rights (IACHR) in Washington, DC, USA. In August 1999 the Bahamian authorities were strongly criticized by human-rights groups, after they announced their intention to execute another two convicted murderers who had also submitted petitions to the IACHR. The Government justified its decision, however, by referring to a 1998 court ruling that executions could be carried out if appeals had been pending at the IACHR for more than 18 months. Despite attempts to reduce levels of crime, the murder rate increased in 1999 and 2000, reaching 72 in the latter year. However, two important drugs-trafficking organizations were uncovered in the first five months of 2001, with eight major participants arrested. Partly as a result of these successes, there was a dramatic decrease in the murder rate in 2001, which fell sharply to 43. Cocaine seizures in 2001 totalled 2.67 metric tons. Surveillance equipment detected 100 suspected drugs transhipment incidents, a decrease on the 2000 figure of 14; however, the decline was, in part, attributable to the withdrawal of some US detection and monitoring aircraft following the terrorist attacks on the USA in September 2001.

In 2000 the Bahamas was listed by the Financial Action Task Force (FATF) as a non-co-operative jurisdiction, and by the Organisation for Economic Co-operation and Development (OECD) as a tax 'haven'. The Bahamas also received the lowest grade of a bank supervision report by the Financial Stability Forum, a group of international regulators, and remained classified as a 'Country of Primary Concern' in the US International Narcotics Control Strategy Report, partly because of its banking secrecy laws and the size of its 'offshore' financial sector. The Government responded by establishing, in October 2000, a Financial Intelligence Unit and by adopting legislation intended to encourage transparency in the sector. As a result, in August 2001 the FATF removed the Bahamas from their blacklist. In January 2002 an agreement to share information on tax matters with the USA was signed, while in March the OECD accepted the country's commitment to improve the transparency of its financial sector.

The Bahamas suffered considerable damage in September 1999 when 'Hurricane Floyd' struck the islands; one person died and at least 2,000 were made homeless as a result of the storm. In the following month 'Hurricane Irene' caused another four deaths and inflicted further structural damage on the Bahamas. In November 2001 'Hurricane Michelle' caused an estimated B \$120m.–\$150m.-worth of damage to the islands.

In mid-1999 there was vigorous public opposition in the Bahamas to the proposed privatization of the state-owned telecommunications company, BaTelCo (which was proceeding in early 2003). In December the Attorney-General and Minister of Justice, Tennyson Wells, announced his resignation from both positions, in order to challenge Ingraham for the leadership of the FNM. This announcement prompted the Prime Minister, in January 2000, to effect a cabinet reorganization. Eight ministers retained their portfolios unchanged, while the Minister of Foreign Affairs, Janet Bostwick, also assumed that of Attorney-General. Several ministries were restructured, leading to the creation of new ministries, including a Ministry of Commerce, Agriculture and Industry, aimed at the promotion of small business.

In July 2001 Prime Minister Ingraham announced his retirement from politics following the next general election, to be held by mid-2002.

In 1997 the FNM proposed establishing a commission to give detailed consideration to constitutional reforms, the first since the Constitution had come into existence, in 1973. Progress, however, was slow. In December 2001 the House of Assembly approved legislation to end discriminatory constitutional provisions relating to inheritance. The Government also proposed reforms to the electoral system, including the establishment of an independent Boundaries Commission. All constitutional amendments were subject to approval by referendum.

At the general election of 3 May 2002 the PLP secured a surprise landslide victory over the FNM, winning 29 of the 40 seats (and 50.8% of the vote) in the House of Assembly. The

FNM secured seven seats (and 41.1% of the ballot). Independent candidates won the remaining four seats. The tourism minister and FNM leader-designate, Tommy Turnquest, failed to regain his seat, as did several other cabinet ministers. Later the same month Christie announced his Cabinet, which included the appointment of Allyson Maynard-Gibson to the newly-created post of Minister of Financial Services and Investments. James Smith, the former Governor of the Central Bank, was appointed Minister of State in the Ministry of Finance.

The Bahamas' traditionally close relationship with the USA was strained in the 1990s by the increasingly aggressive attitude of the US Government towards the bank secrecy laws and the drugs-smuggling in the islands. Bilateral relations were damaged in August 1997, when an incendiary device exploded at a travel agency in Nassau commonly used by US tourists. Nevertheless, the USA and the Bahamas collaborated in a series of operations to intercept drugs-traffickers, and in 1998 the USA commended the Bahamian authorities for their efforts to curb this illegal trade. In late 2002, however, the relationship worsened after the US Ambassador to the Bahamas, J. Richard Blankenship, claimed that the judicial system did not penalize drugs-traffickers severely enough, and urged a thorough reform of the Royal Bahamian Defence Force.

Relations with the Bahamas' other neighbours, Haiti and Cuba, were strained by the influx of large numbers of illegal immigrants from both countries. In June 1998 the Bahamian Government agreed to inform Cuba of the arrival of illegal Cuban immigrants within 72 hours of their discovery, while Cuba agreed to their repatriation within 15 days. In 1998 many Cubans were deported from the Bahamas, despite an offer by Nicaragua of temporary asylum for 200 detainees. In the first four months of 2002 1,428 migrants were intercepted between Haiti and the Bahamas. In May of that year at least 12 Haitian migrants died when their boat capsized off the coast of the Bahamas.

In November 2001 the Governor-General, Orville Turnquest, resigned after seven years in office. Dame Ivy Dumont, the Bahamas' first female Governor-General, succeeded him in an interim capacity. She was confirmed in this post in January 2002.

Government

Legislative power is vested in the bicameral Parliament. The Senate has 16 members, of whom nine are appointed by the Governor-General on the advice of the Prime Minister, four by the Leader of the Opposition and three after consultation with the Prime Minister. The House of Assembly has 40 members, elected for five years (subject to dissolution) by universal adult suffrage. Executive power is vested in the British monarch, represented by a Governor-General, who is appointed on the Prime Minister's recommendation and who acts, in almost all matters, on the advice of the Cabinet. The Governor-General appoints the Prime Minister and, on the latter's recommendation, selects the other ministers. The Cabinet is responsible to the House of Assembly.

Defence

The Royal Bahamian Defence Force, a paramilitary coastguard, is the only security force in the Bahamas, and numbered 860 (including 70 women) in August 2002. Defence expenditure in 2002 was budgeted at B \$26m.

Economic Affairs

In 2000, according to estimates by the World Bank, the Bahamas' gross national income (GNI), measured at average 1998–2000 prices, was US \$4,533m., equivalent to US \$14,960 per head (or US \$16,400 per head on an international purchasing-power parity basis). During 1990–2001, it was estimated, the population increased at an average annual rate of 1.7%. In 1990–2000 gross domestic product (GDP) per head increased, in real terms, by an annual average of 0.1%. Overall GDP increased, in real terms, at an average rate of 1.8% per year in 1990–2000; growth in 2000 was 4.5%.

Agriculture, hunting, forestry and fishing, which together accounted for only 3.4% of GDP in 1992 and engaged an estimated 4.0% of the employed labour force in 1999, were developed by the Government in the 1990s in an attempt to reduce dependence on imports (80% of food supplies were imported in the 1980s). In 1998, however, agricultural production accounted for only 1.0% of total land area. By the late 1990s, according to official estimates, agriculture contributed less than 3% of GDP. The increase in agricultural output has resulted in the export of certain crops, particularly of cucumbers, tomatoes, pineapples, papayas, avocados, mangoes, limes and other citrus fruits. The development of commercial fishing has concentrated on conchs and crustaceans. In 1998 exports of Caribbean spiny lobster (crawfish) provided 19.1% of all export earnings, and accounted for 74.6% of the fishing total. There is also some exploitation of pine forests in the northern Bahamas.

Industry (comprising mining, manufacturing, construction and utilities) employed an estimated 16.6% of the working population in 1999 (construction accounted for 11.4%) and provided 10.8% of GDP in 1992.

Mining and manufacturing together contributed only 4.0% of GDP in 1992. Mining provided an estimated 1.2% of employment, and manufacturing 4.1%, in 1999. The islands' principal mineral resources are salt (which provided 14.5% of domestic export earnings in 1995) and aragonite. In late 2002 the Government granted a licence to an international oil company to explore for petroleum in Bahamian waters. The Government was due to receive over US $4m. during the exploration stage, in addition to 18% of any revenues should oil be discovered.

The manufacturing sector contributed some 10% of GDP in 1982, since when it has declined, owing to the closure, in 1985, of the country's petroleum refinery. In 1992 the sector contributed 4.0% of GDP. In 1998 the principal branches of manufacturing, based on the value of output, were beverages, chemicals and printing and publishing. Exports of rum accounted for US $12.2m., or 8.8% of domestic export earnings. Petroleum transhipment on Grand Bahama remains an important activity (petroleum products accounted for about 11% in 1988). The construction sector experienced much activity in the latter part of the 20th century, owing to hotel-building and harbour developments. In the late 1990s and early 2000s several major projects guaranteed strong growth in the sector.

Most of the energy requirements of the Bahamas are fulfilled by the petroleum that Venezuela and, particularly, Mexico provide under the San José Agreement (originally negotiated in 1980), which commits both the petroleum producers to selling subsidized supplies, on favourable terms, to the developing countries of the region. Excluding transhipments of petroleum, imports of mineral fuels accounted for 6.2% of total imports in 1998.

Service industries constitute the principal sectors of the economy, providing 85.3% of GDP in 1992 and about 78.9% of total employment in 1999. The Bahamas established its own shipping registry in 1976, and by 1983 had one of the largest 'open-registry' fleets in the world. In 1999 an international container-transhipment was completed at Freeport, Grand Bahama, capable of handling 950,000 container units per year. It was to act as an intercontinental hub port serving North America, the Caribbean and South America. At the end of 2001 a total of 1,312 vessels were registered under the Bahamian flag. With a combined displacement of 33.4m. grt, the fleet was the third largest in the world.

Banking is the second most important economic activity in the Bahamas and there is a large 'offshore' financial sector. In May 1999 the Government introduced legislation to establish an insurance fund to protect bank depositors, following the suspension of the Gulf Union Bank's banking licence. In May 2000 a stock exchange, which planned to develop trading in global depository receipts for overseas companies, began trading; by 2002 it was trading the shares of 18 local companies. However, with market turnover low, commission income was not sufficient to cover running costs, and by early 2002 the exchange was in severe financial difficulty.

Despite increasing competition, the Bahamas continues to be the principal tourist destination of the Caribbean. Tourism is the predominant sector of the economy, directly accounting for 15% of GDP in 1998, and employing some 30% of the working population in 1994. In 1998 travel receipts covered 78% of the cost of goods imported. According to the World Tourism Organization, in 2000 81.8% of visitor arrivals were from the USA, although attempts are being made to attract visitors from other countries and improve air access to resorts. In the same year some 8.0% of visitors came from Europe and 5.7% came from Canada. Tourist arrivals increased steadily during the 1980s, and by 1991 amounted to some 3.7m. Figures declined somewhat during the 1990s, as a result of recession in the important US market, an increase in the incidence of crime in the islands and competition from alternative destinations. However, following tourist-related investment totalling US $1,500m.–$2,000m., the sector experienced a recovery at the end of the

decade. In 2000 tourist arrivals were 4.2m., an increase of 15.2% on the previous year. Total arrivals remained at about the same level in 2001. Hotel-room occupancy in Nassau increased from 52% in 1992 to 72.8% in 2000, in spite of an increase in the number of hotel rooms. The Sun International Atlantis resort on Paradise Island completed the second stage of its expansion in December 1998, providing 2,355 rooms and employment for 5,600 people—equivalent to 4% of national employment: further expansion, which included a US $100m. condominium-marina project, began in 2001. The Bahamas received more cruise-ship arrivals than any other Caribbean destination. Receipts from tourism rose in 1999 to B $1,583m., compared with B $1,354m. in 1998. Receipts rose further in 2000, to approximately B $1,814m.

In 2001 the Bahamas recorded a visible trade deficit of US $1,150.6m., and there was a deficit of US $348.0m. on the current account of the balance of payments. The USA is the principal trading partner of the Bahamas, providing 90.8% of non-petroleum imports and taking 77.1% of total exports in 1997. Excluding the trade in petroleum and its products, the principal exports (including re-exports) in 1998 were machinery and transport equipment (26.0% of the total), food and live animals (25.1%), and chemicals (22.3%). In that year the principal imports were machinery and transport equipment (30.6% of the total), basic manufactures (19.7%), food and live animals (14.3%) and miscellaneous manufactured articles (14.2%).

In 2001 there was a budgetary deficit of B $44.1m. At 31 December 1998 the external debt of the central Government was B $85.0m. and in 1999 foreign-currency debt servicing cost US $69.5m., equivalent to 8.0% of the recurrent revenue of US $868.9m. The debt-service ratio, however was just 3.2% of the value of goods and services in the same year, down from 5.5% in 1997. The annual rate of inflation averaged 1.4% during 1995–2001; consumer prices increased by 2.0% in 2001. The rate of unemployment declined from 13.3% of the labour force in April 1994 to some 8% in 2001.

The Bahamas is a member of the Caribbean Community and Common Market (CARICOM, see p. 155) and the Organization of American States (OAS, see p. 288), the Association of Caribbean States (see p. 338) and is a signatory of the Cotonou Agreement (see p. 234) with the EU (this replaced the Lomé Convention, which expired in February 2000).

Economic expansion through foreign investment continued to be restricted by fears of widespread corruption and instability, caused by the activities of illegal drugs-trafficking networks in the islands, although investor confidence was reported to have increased in the late 1990s. In spite of measures, taken from 1989, to combat corruption in the financial sector and thus improve the reputation of the country's economic institutions, in mid-2000 the Bahamas was listed by the Financial Action Task Force (FATF) as a non-co-operative jurisdiction and by the Organisation for Economic Co-operation and Development (OECD) as tax 'haven'. Following the introduction of further legislation in late 2000, in 2001 the FATF removed the country from its blacklist, and the OECD followed suit in March 2002. However, legal challenges were made against various aspects of the new financial legislation in late 2001 and early 2002, and the incoming Progressive Liberal Party (PLP) Government, elected in May 2002, pledged to review the recent financial legislation. By 2000 all but one of the state-owned hotels had been transferred to private ownership, under a privatization programme launched in 1993, with a number of foreign companies investing in large-scale projects. The divestment of the state telecommunications and electricity companies, though delayed, was expected during the PLP administration. In addition, the loss-making Bahamasair Holdings was scheduled for privitization from September 2002. In September 2001 the IMF praised the Government's economic policies, in particular its fiscal discipline and infrastructural improvements. Recent enhancements in the supervision of the offshore financial sector also met with IMF approval. In 2001 and 2002 economic growth was expected to decrease to 1.0%; the Central Bank blamed the stagnation of real GDP on the problems in the tourism industry since the terrorism attacks on the USA in September 2001. In addition, in November 2002, the reduction in tourism-sector revenues led the Prime Minister to announce a freeze in public-sector recruitment, in order to protect the fiscal position.

Education

Education is compulsory between the ages of five and 16 years, and is provided free of charge in government schools. There are several private and denominational schools. Primary education begins at five years of age and lasts for six years. Secondary education, beginning at the age of 11, also lasts for six years and is divided into two equal cycles. In 1997 97% of children in the relevant age-group were enrolled at primary level. In the same year 85% of children in the relevant age-group were enrolled at secondary level. The University of the West Indies has an extramural department in Nassau, offering degree courses in hotel management and tourism. The Bahamas Hotel Training College was established in 1992. The Bahamas Law School, part of the University of the West Indies, opened in 1998. Technical, teacher-training and professional qualifications can be obtained at the two campuses of the College of the Bahamas.

Government expenditure on education in 2001 was B $187.3m. (or 19.4% of total spending from the General Budget).

Public Holidays

2003: 1 January (New Year's Day), 18 April (Good Friday), 21 April (Easter Monday), 1 June (Labour Day), 9 June (Whit Monday), 10 July (Independence Day), 2 August (Emancipation Day), 12 October (Discovery Day/Columbus Day), 25–26 December (Christmas).

2004: 1 January (New Year's Day), 9 April (Good Friday), 12 April (Easter Monday), 31 May (Whit Monday), 7 June (Labour Day), 10 July (Independence Day), 5 August (Emancipation Day), 12 October (Discovery Day/Columbus Day), 25–26 December (Christmas).

Weights and Measures

The imperial system is used.

Statistical Survey

Source (unless otherwise stated): Central Bank of the Bahamas, Frederick St, POB N-4868, Nassau; tel. 322-2193; fax 322-4321; e-mail cbob@centralbankbahamas.com; internet www.centralbankbahamas.com.

AREA AND POPULATION

Area: 13,939 sq km (5,382 sq miles).

Population: 255,095 at census of 2 May 1990; 304,913 (males 147,804, females 157,109) at census of 1 May 2000 (provisional results); 308,000 (estimate) at mid-2001. *By island* (1990): New Providence 172,196 (including the capital, Nassau); Grand Bahama 40,898; Andros 8,187; Eleuthera 10,586. Source: partly UN, *Population and Vital Statistics Report*.

Density (mid-2001): 22.1 per sq km.

Principal Towns (population, 2000): Nassau (capital) 210,832; Freeport 26,910. Source: Thomas Brinkhoff, *City Population* (internet www.citypopulation.de).

Births, Marriages and Deaths (1996): Registered live births 5,873 (birth rate 20.7 per 1,000); Registered marriages 2,628 (marriage rate 9.3 per 1,000); Registered deaths 1,537 (death rate 5.4 per 1,000). *1999:* Registered deaths 1,567 (death rate 5.3 per 1,000); Registered births 6,367 (birth rate 21.4 per 1,000). Sources: UN, *Demographic Yearbook* and *Population and Vital Statistics Report*.

Expectation of Life (WHO estimates, years at birth): 71.9 (males 68.8; females 75.0) in 2001. Source: WHO, *World Health Report*.

Economically Active Population (sample survey, persons aged 15 years and over, excl. armed forces, April 1999): Agriculture, hunting, forestry and fishing 5,835; Mining, quarrying, electricity, gas and water 1,745; Manufacturing 5,910; Construction 16,540; Wholesale and retail trade 19,955; Hotels and restaurants 23,300; Transport, storage and communications 10,305; Finance, insurance, real estate and business services 13,350; Community, social and personal services 47,780; Activities not adequately defined 630; *Total employed* 145,350 (males 77,245, females 68,105); Unemployed 12,290 (males 4,955, females 7,335); *Total labour force* 157,640 (males, 82,200, females 75,440). Source: ILO Caribbean Office.

HEALTH AND WELFARE

Key Indicators

Total Fertility Rate (children per woman, 2001): 2.3.

Under-5 Mortality Rate (per 1,000 live births, 2001): 16.

HIV/AIDS (% of persons aged 15–49, 2001): 3.50.

Physicians (per 1,000 head, 1996): 1.52.

Hospital Beds (per 1,000 head, 1996): 3.94.

Health Expenditure (2000): US $ per head (PPP): 880.

Health Expenditure (2000): % of GDP: 8.0.

Health Expenditure (2000): public (% of total): 55.5.

Access to Water (% of persons, 2000): 96.

Access to Sanitation (% of persons, 2000): 93.

Human Development Index (2000): ranking: 41.

Human Development Index (2000): value: 0.826.
For sources and definitions, see explanatory note on p. vi.

AGRICULTURE, ETC.

Principal Crops ('000 metric tons, 2001): Roots and tubers 1.0*; Sugar cane 50.0*; Tomatoes 3.4; Other vegetables 18.2*; Bananas 3.3; Lemons and limes 8.5*; Grapefruit and pomelos 12.5*. * FAO estimate. Source: FAO.

Livestock ('000 head, year ending September 2001): Cattle 0.7; Pigs 4.9; Sheep 6.3; Goats 13.9; Poultry 3,450 (estimate). Source: FAO.

Livestock Products ('000 metric tons, 2000): Chicken meat 6.9; Cows' milk 0.6*; Goats' milk 1.0*; Hen eggs 0.9. * FAO estimate. Source: FAO.

Forestry (FAO estimates, '000 cubic metres, 2001): Roundwood removals (excl. bark): Sawlogs and veneer logs 17 (output assumed to be unchanged since 1992); Sawnwood production (incl. railway sleepers): Coniferous (softwood) 1 (output assumed to be unchanged since 1970).
Source: FAO.

Fishing (FAO estimates, metric tons, live weight, 2000): Capture 10,500 (Nassau grouper 381, Snappers 866, Caribbean spiny lobster 8,225, Stromboid conchs 472); Aquaculture 2; *Total catch* 10,502. Figures exclude marine shells (4* metric tons) and sponges (6* tons). * FAO estimate. Source: FAO, *Yearbook of Fishery Statistics*.

MINING

Production (estimates, '000 metric tons, 2000): Unrefined salt 900; Aragonite 1,200. Source: US Geological Survey.

INDUSTRY

Production (estimate, million kWh, 1998): Electric energy 1,227.

FINANCE

Currency and Exchange Rates: 100 cents = 1 Bahamian dollar (B $). *Sterling, US Dollar and Euro Equivalents* (31 December 2002): £1 sterling = B $1.6118; US $1 = B $1.0000; €1 = B $1.0487; B $100 = £62.04 = US $100.00 = €95.36. *Exchange Rate*: Since February 1970 the official exchange rate, applicable to most transactions, has been US $1 = B $1, i.e., the Bahamian dollar has been at par with the US dollar. There is also an investment currency rate, applicable to certain capital transactions between residents and non-residents and to direct investments outside the Bahamas. Since 1987 this exchange rate has been fixed at US $1 = B $1.225.

General Budget (B $ million, 2001): *Revenue:* Taxation 820.1 (Taxes on property 73.4, Taxes on international trade and transactions 514.8); Other current revenue 100.1 (Entrepreneurial and property income 21.6); Capital revenue 0.1; Total 920.3. *Expenditure:* General public services 146.6; Defence 28.1; Public order and safety 107.3; Education 187.3; Health 156.7; Social security and welfare 61.5; Economic affairs and services 164.0 (Transport and communication 22.8); Interest payments 103.5; Total (incl. other) 964.4 (current 865.9; capital 98.5). Source: IMF, *Government Finance Statistics Yearbook*.

International Reserves (US $ million at 31 December 2002): Reserve position in IMF 8.5; Foreign exchange 372.1; Total 380.6. Source: IMF, *International Financial Statistics*.

Money Supply (B $ million at 31 December 2002): Currency outside banks 155; Demand deposits at deposit money banks 644; Total money (incl. others) 811. Source: IMF, *International Financial Statistics.*

Cost of Living (consumer price index; base: 1995 = 100): 104.6 in 1999; 106.3 in 2000; 108.4 in 2001. Source: IMF, *International Financial Statistics.*

Gross Domestic Product (US $ million at current prices): 3,451 in 1997; 3,670 in 1998; 3,994 in 1999. Source: UN, *Statistical Yearbook.*

Expenditure on the Gross Domestic Product (B $ million at current prices, 1995): Government final consumption expenditure 483.9; Private final consumption expenditure 2,077.4; Increase in stocks 13.8; Gross fixed capital formation 698.5; *Total domestic expenditure* 3,273.6; Exports of goods and services 1,680.1; *Less* Imports of goods and services 1,819.6; Statistical discrepancy –64.7; *GDP in purchasers' values* 3,069.4. Source: IMF, *International Financial Statistics.*

Gross Domestic Product by Economic Activity (B $ million at current prices, 1992): Agriculture, hunting, forestry and fishing 89; Manufacturing (incl. mining and quarrying) 105; Electricity, gas and water 88; Construction 91; Trade, restaurants and hotels 705; Transport, storage and communications 227; Finance, insurance, real estate and business services 610; Government services 336; Other community, social and personal services 310; Other services 55; Statistical discrepancy 13; *Sub-total* 2,629; Import duties 268; Other indirect taxes 162; *GDP in purchasers' values* 3,059. Source: UN, *National Accounts Statistics.*

Balance of Payments* (US $ million, 2001): Exports of goods f.o.b. 614.1; Imports of goods f.o.b. –1,764.7; *Trade balance* –1,150.6; Exports of services 1,889.7; Imports of services –939.1; *Balance on goods and services* –200.0; Other income received 94.0; Other income paid –283.8; *Balance on goods, services and income* –389.8; Current transfers received 52.7; Current transfers paid –10.9; *Current balance* –348.0; Capital account (net) –20.3; Direct investment from abroad (net) 100.8; Other investment assets –25,411.7; Other investment liabilities 25,590.7; Net errors and omissions –58.6; *Overall balance* –29.9. Source: IMF, *International Financial Statistics.*
*The figures for merchandise imports and exports exclude petroleum and petroleum products, except imports for local consumption.

EXTERNAL TRADE*

Principal Commodities (US $ million, 1998): *Imports c.i.f.*: Food and live animals 260.1; Mineral fuels, lubricants etc. 112.7; Chemicals 160.5; Basic manufactures 358.7; Machinery and transport equipment 555.8; Miscellaneous manufactured articles 257.7; Total (incl. others) 1,816.4. *Exports f.o.b.*: Food and live animals 75.3; Beverages and tobacco 12.8; Crude materials (inedible) except fuels 28.4; Chemicals 67.0; Basic manufactures 26.1; Machinery and transport equipment 78.2; Miscellaneous manufactured articles 12.4; Total (incl. others) 300.3

1999 (B $ million): Total imports c.i.f. 1,772; Total exports f.o.b. 532.

2000 (B $ million): Total imports c.i.f. 1,764; Total exports f.o.b. 805.

2001 (B $ million): Total imports c.i.f. 1,797; Total exports f.o.b. 614. Source: IMF, *International Financial Statistics.*

Principal Trading Partners (US $ million, 1997): *Imports c.i.f.*: USA 1,472.8; Total (incl. others) 1,621.6. *Exports f.o.b.*: Canada 3.9; France 20.9; Mexico 3.5; United Kingdom 3.8; USA 139.9; Total (incl. others) 181.4. Source: UN, *International Trade Statistics Yearbook.*
*The data exclude imports and exports of crude petroleum and residual fuel oils that are brought into the Bahamas for storage on behalf of foreign companies abroad. Also excluded is trade in certain chemical products.

TRANSPORT

Road Traffic (vehicles in use, 1998): 67,400 passenger cars; 16,800 commercial vehicles. Source: Auto and Truck International (Illinois), *World Automotive Market Report.*

Shipping: *Merchant fleet* (displacement, '000 grt at 31 December): 29,483 in 1999; 31,445 in 2000; 33,386 in 2001. (Source: Lloyd's Register-Fairplay, *World Fleet Statistics*). *International sea-borne freight traffic* (estimates, '000 metric tons, 1990): Goods loaded 5,920; Goods unloaded 5,705. (Source: UN, *Monthly Bulletin of Statistics.*).

Civil Aviation (1999): Kilometres flown (million) 6.8; Passengers carried ('000) 1,719.4; Passenger-km (million) 366.2; Total ton-km of freight (million) 1.5. Source: UN Economic Commission for Latin America and the Caribbean, *Statistical Yearbook.*

TOURISM

Visitor Arrivals: 3,648,291 in 1999; 4,203,831 in 2000; 4,188,281 (1,439,020 by air, 2,749,251 by sea) in 2001.

Tourism Receipts (B $ million): 1,354 in 1998; 1,583 in 1999; 1,814 in 2000.

COMMUNICATIONS MEDIA

Radio Receivers (1997): 215,000 in use.

Television Receivers (1999): 73,000 in use.

Telephones (2001): 123,300 main lines in use.

Facsimile Machines (1996): 500 in use.

Mobile Cellular Telephones (2001): 60,600 subscribers.

Internet Users (2001): 16,900.

Daily Newspapers (1996): 3 titles (total circulation 28,000 copies). Sources: UN, *Statistical Yearbook*; UNESCO, *Statistical Yearbook*; International Telecommunication Union.

EDUCATION

Pre-primary (1996/97): 20 schools; 76 teachers; 1,094 pupils.

Primary (1996/97): 113 schools; 1,792 teachers; 33,141 pupils (1998).

Secondary: 37 junior/senior high schools (1990); 2,097 teachers (1996/97); 24,450 students (1998).

Tertiary (1987): 249 teachers; 5,305 studentsIn 2002 there were 3,463 students registered at the College of the Bahamas. Sources: UNESCO, *Statistical Yearbook*, UN, Economic Commission for Latin America and the Caribbean, *Statistical Yearbook* and Caribbean Development Bank, *Social and Economic Indicators 2001.*

Adult Literacy Rate (UNESCO estimates): 95.4% (males 96.3%; females 94.5%) in 1999 (Source: UN Development Programme, *Human Development Report*).

Directory

The Constitution

A representative House of Assembly was first established in 1729, although universal adult suffrage was not introduced until 1962. A new Constitution for the Commonwealth of the Bahamas came into force at independence, on 10 July 1973. The main provisions of the Constitution are summarized below.

Parliament consists of a Governor-General (representing the British monarch, who is Head of State), a nominated Senate and an elected House of Assembly. The Governor-General appoints the Prime Minister and, on the latter's recommendation, the remainder of the Cabinet. Apart from the Prime Minister, the Cabinet has no fewer than eight other ministers, of whom one is the Attorney-General. The Governor-General also appoints a Leader of the Opposition.

The Senate (upper house) consists of 16 members, of whom nine are appointed by the Governor-General on the advice of the Prime Minister, four on the advice of the Leader of the Opposition and three on the Prime Minister's advice after consultation with the Leader of the Opposition. The House of Assembly (lower house) has 40 members. A Constituencies Commission reviews numbers and boundaries at intervals of not more than five years and can recommend alterations for approval of the House. The life of Parliament is limited to a maximum of five years.

The Constitution provides for a Supreme Court and a Court of Appeal.

The Government

Head of State: HM Queen ELIZABETH II (succeeded to the throne 6 February 1952).

Governor-General: Dr Dame IVY DUMONT (took office 1 January 2002).

THE CABINET
(April 2003)

Prime Minister and Minister of Finance: PERRY G. CHRISTIE.

Deputy Prime Minister and Minister of National Security: CYNTHIA A. PRATT.

Attorney-General and Minister of Justice and of Education: ALFRED M. SEARS.

Minister of Agriculture, Fisheries and Local Government: V. ALFRED GRAY.

Minister of Financial Services and Investments: ALLYSON MAYNARD-GIBSON.

Minister of Foreign Affairs and Public Service: FRED A. MITCHELL.

Minister of Health and Environmental Services: Dr MARCUS C. BETHEL.

Minister of Housing and National Insurance: D. SHANE GIBSON.

Minister of Labour and Immigration: VINCENT A. PEET.

Minister of Public Works and Utilities: BRADLEY B. ROBERTS.

Minister of Social Services and Community Development: MELANIE S. GRIFFIN.

Minister of Tourism: OBEDIAH 'OBIE' H. WILCHCOMBE.

Minister of Trade and Industry: LESLIE O. MILLER.

Minister of Transport and Aviation: GLENNYS M. E. HANNA-MARTIN.

Minister of Youth, Sports and Culture: NEVILLE W. WISDOM.

Minister of State in the Ministry of Finance: JAMES H. SMITH.

MINISTRIES

Attorney-General's Office and Ministry of Justice: Post Office Bldg, East Hill St, POB N-3007, Nassau; tel. 322-1141; fax 356-4179.

Office of the Prime Minister: Sir Cecil V. Wallace-Whitfield Centre, West Bay St, POB CB-10980, Nassau; tel. 327-5826; fax 327-5806; e-mail info@opm.gov.bs; internet www.opm.gov.bs.

Office of the Deputy Prime Minister: Churchill Bldg, Bay St, POB N-3217, Nassau; tel. 356-6792; fax 356-6087.

Ministry of Agriculture and Fisheries: Levy Bldg, East Bay St, POB N-3028, Nassau; tel. 325-7502; fax 322-1767.

Ministry of Education: Collins House, Shirley St, POB N-3913, Nassau; tel. 322-8140; fax 322-8491.

Ministry of Finance: Cecil V. Wallace-Whitfield Centre, West Bay St, POB N-3017, Nassau; tel. 327-1530; fax 327-1618.

Ministry of Financial Services and Investments: Sir Cecil V. Wallace-Whitfield Centre, West Bay St, POB CB-10980, Nassau; tel. 327-5826; fax 327-5806.

Ministry of Foreign Affairs and Public Service: East Hill St, POB N-3746, Nassau; tel. 322-7624; fax 328-8212; e-mail mfabahamas@batelnet.bs.

Ministry of Health and Environmental Services: Royal Victoria Gardens, Shirley St, POB N-3730, Nassau; tel. 322-7425; fax 322-7788.

Ministry of Housing and National Insurance: National Insurance Bldg, Baillou Rd, POB N-7508, Nassau; tel. 502-1500; fax 323-3048.

Ministry of Labour and Immigration: Post Office Bldg, East Hill St, POB N-3008, Nassau; tel. 323-7814; fax 325-1920.

Ministry of National Security: Churchill Bldg, Bay St, POB N-3217, Nassau; tel. 356-6792; fax 356-6087.

Ministry of Social Services and Community Development: Frederick House, Frederick St, POB N-3206, Nassau; tel. 356-0765; fax 323-3883.

Ministry of Public Works and Utilities: John F. Kennedy Dr., POB N-8156, Nassau; tel. 322-4830; fax 326-7344.

Ministry of Tourism: British Colonial Hilton Hotel, Bay St, POB N-3701, Nassau; tel. 322-7500; fax 328-0945; e-mail tourism@bahamas.com; internet www.bahamas.com.

Ministry of Trade and Industry: Manx Bldg, West Bay St, POB N-4849, Nassau; tel. 328-2700; fax 328-1324.

Ministry of Transport, Aviation and Local Government: Pilot House Complex, POB N-10114, Nassau; tel. 394-0445; fax 394-5920.

Ministry of Youth, Sports and Culture: 7th Floor, Post Office Bldg, East Hill St, POB N-4891, Nassau; tel. 322-6250; fax 322-6546.

Legislature

PARLIAMENT

Senate

President: SHARON R. WILSON.
There are 16 nominated members.

House of Assembly

Speaker: OSWALD INGRAHAM.
The House has 40 members.

General Election, 3 May 2002

Party	Seats
Progressive Liberal Party (PLP)	29
Free National Movement (FNM)	7
Independents	4
Total	**40**

Political Organizations

Bahamas Freedom Alliance (BFA): Nassau; formed Coalition Plus Labour alliance with CDR and PLM to contest 2002 legislative elections; Leader D. HALSTON MOULTRIE.

Coalition for Democratic Reform (CDR): Nassau; f. 2000; centrist, formed Coalition Plus Labour alliance with BFA and PLM to contest 2002 legislative elections; Leader BERNARD NOTTAGE.

Free National Movement (FNM): POB N-10713, Nassau; tel. 393-7863; fax 393-7914; f. 1972; Leader ORVILLE ALTON THOMPSON (TOMMY) TURNQUEST; Chair. DWIGHT SAWYER.

People's Labour Movement (PLM): Nassau; formed Coalition Plus Labour alliance with BFA and CDR to contest 2002 legislative elections.

Progressive Liberal Party (PLP): East Sunrise Highway, Grand Bahama; tel. 325-2900; e-mail eightmr@bahamiansfirst.com; internet www.bahamiansfirst.com; f. 1953; centrist party; Leader PERRY G. CHRISTIE; Chair. OBIE WILCHCOMBE.

Diplomatic Representation

EMBASSIES AND HIGH COMMISSION IN THE BAHAMAS

China, People's Republic: 3rd Orchard Terrace, Village Rd, POB CB-10996, Nassau; tel. 393-1415; fax 393-0733; e-mail chinemb@batel.net; Ambassador WU CHANGSHENG.

Haiti: Sears House, Shirley St, POB N-666, Nassau; tel. 326-0325; Chargé d'affaires JOSEPH J. ETIENNE.

United Kingdom: Ansbacher Bldg, 3rd Floor, East St, POB N-7516, Nassau; tel. 325-7471; fax 323-3871; High Commissioner RODERICK GEMMELL.

USA: Mosmar Bldg, Queen St, POB N-8197, Nassau; tel. 322-1181; fax 328-7838; e-mail embnas@state.gov; internet usembassy.state.gov/nassau/wwwhmain.html; Ambassador J. RICHARD BLANKENSHIP.

Judicial System

The Judicial Committee of the Privy Council (based in the United Kingdom), the Bahamas Court of Appeal, the Supreme Court and the Magistrates' Courts are the main courts of the Bahamian judicial system.

All courts have both a criminal and civil jurisdiction. The Magistrates' Courts are presided over by professionally qualified Stipendiary and Circuit Magistrates in New Providence and Grand Bahama, and by Island Administrators sitting as Magistrates in the Family Islands.

Whereas all magistrates are empowered to try offences that may be tried summarily, a Stipendiary and Circuit Magistrate may, with the consent of the accused, also try certain less serious indictable offences. The jurisdiction of magistrates is, however, limited by law.

The Supreme Court consists of the Chief Justice, two Senior Justices and six Justices. The Supreme Court also sits in Freeport, with two Justices.

Appeals in almost all matters lie from the Supreme Court to the Court of Appeal, with further appeal in certain instances to the Judicial Committee of the Privy Council.

Supreme Court of the Bahamas

Parliament Sq., POB N-8167, Nassau; tel. 322-3315; fax 323-6895. Chief Justice Sir BURTON HALL.

Court of Appeal

POB N-8167, Nassau; tel. 322-3315; fax 325-6895.
Pres. Dame JOAN SAWYER.

Magistrates' Courts

POB N-421, Nassau; tel. 325-4573; fax 323-1446.
15 magistrates and a circuit magistrate.

Registrar of the Supreme Court: ESTELLE EVANS, POB N-167, Nassau; tel. 322-4348; fax 325-6895.

Attorney-General: ALFRED M. SEARS.

Office of the Attorney-General

Post Office Bldg, East Hill St, POB N-3007, Nassau; tel. 322-1141; fax 356-4179.

Dir of Legal Affairs RHONDA BAIN; Dir of Public Prosecutions BERNARD TURNER (acting).

Registrar-General: STERLING QUANT, 50 Shirley St, POB N-532, Nassau; tel. 322-3316; fax 322 553.

Religion

Most of the population profess Christianity, but there are also small communities of Jews and Muslims.

CHRISTIANITY

According to the census of 1990, there were 79,465 Baptists (31.2% of the population), 40,894 Roman Catholics (16.0%) and 40,881 Anglicans (16.0%). Other important denominations include the Pentecostal Church (5.5%), the Church of Christ (5.0%) and the Methodists (4.8%).

Bahamas Christian Council: East–West Highway, POB 4394, Nassau; tel. and fax 393-3946; e-mail newcovenantbaptistchurch@coralworld.com; f. 1948; 27 mem. churches; Pres. Bishop SIMEON B. HALL.

The Roman Catholic Church

The Bahamas comprises the single archdiocese of Nassau. At 31 December 2001 there were an estimated 47,688 adherents in the Bahamas. The Archbishop participates in the Antilles Episcopal Conference (whose Secretariat is based in Port of Spain, Trinidad). The Turks and Caicos Islands are also under the jurisdiction of the Archbishop of Nassau.

Archbishop of Nassau: Most Rev. LAWRENCE A. BURKE, The Hermitage, West St, POB N-8187, Nassau; tel. 322-8919; fax 322-2599; e-mail rcchancery@grouper.batelnet.bs.

The Anglican Communion

Anglicans in the Bahamas are adherents of the Church in the Province of the West Indies. The diocese also includes the Turks and Caicos Islands.

Archbishop of the West Indies, and Bishop of Nassau and the Bahamas: Most Rev. DREXEL GOMEZ, Bishop's Lodge, POB N-7107, Nassau; tel. 322-3015; fax 322-7943.

Other Christian Churches

Bahamas Conference of The Methodist Church: POB SS-5103, Nassau; tel. 393-3726; fax 393-8135; e-mail bcmc@bahamas.net; Pres. Rev. CHARLES SWEETING.

Bahamas Conference of Seventh-day Adventists: Harrold Rd, POB N-356, Nassau; tel. 341-4021; fax 341-4088; internet www.bahamasconference.org.

Bahamas Evangelical Church Association: Carmichael Rd, POB N-1224, Nassau; tel. 362-1024.

Greek Orthodox Church: Church of the Annunciation, West St, POB N-823, Nassau; tel. 322-4382; f. 1928; part of the Archdiocese of North and South America, based in New York (USA); Priest Rev. THEOPHANIS KULYVAS.

Methodist Church Conference in the Bahamas (MCCA): POB N-3702, Nassau; tel. 373-1888; Conference Pres. Rev. LIVINGSTON MALCOLM.

Other denominations include African Methodist Episcopal, the Assemblies of Brethren, Christian Science, the Jehovah's Witnesses, the Salvation Army, Pentecostal, Presbyterian, Seventh Day Adventist, Baptist, Lutheran and Assembly of God churches.

BAHÁ'Í FAITH

Bahá'í National Spiritual Assembly: Nassau; tel. 326-0607; e-mail nsabaha@mail.com.

OTHER RELIGIONS

Islam

There is a small community of Muslims in the Bahamas.

Islaamic Centre: Carmichael Rd, POB N-10711, Nassau; tel. 341-6612.

Islaamic Centre Jamaat Ul-Islam: 13 Davies St, Oakes Field, POB N-10711, Nassau; tel. 325-0413.

Judaism

Most of the Bahamian Jewish community are based on Grand Bahama. There were 126 Jews, according to the 1990 census.

Bahamas Jewish Congregation Synagogue: POB CB-11003, Cable Beach Shopping Centre, Nassau; tel. 327-2064.

The Press

NEWSPAPERS

Bahama Journal: Media House, POB N-8610, Nassau; tel. 325-3082; fax 356-7256; internet www.love97fm.com/journal.htm; daily; circ. 5,000.

Freeport News: Cedar St, POB F-40007, Freeport; tel. 352-8321; fax 352-3449; f. 1961; daily; Gen. Man. DORLAN COLLIE; Editor ROBYN ADDERLEY; circ. 6,000.

The Nassau Guardian: 4 Carter St, Oakes Field, POB N-3011, Nassau; tel. 323-5654; fax 328-8943; e-mail nasguard@bahamainfo.com; internet www.thenassauguardian.com; f. 1844; daily; Gen. Man. PATRICK WALKES; Editor ANTHONY CAPRON; circ. 12,277.

The Punch: POB N-4081, Nassau; tel. 322-7112; fax 323-5268; twice weekly; Editor IVAN JOHNSON; circ. 25,000.

The Tribune: Shirley St, POB N-3207, Nassau; tel. 322-1986; fax 328-2398; e-mail tribune@100jamz.com; f. 1903; daily; Publr and Editor EILEEN DUPUCH CARRON; circ. 13,500.

PERIODICALS

The Bahamas Financial Digest: Miramar House, Bay and Christie Sts, POB N-4271, Nassau; tel. 356-2981; fax 356-7118; e-mail michael.symonette@batelnet.bs; f. 1973; 4 a year; business and investment; Publr and Editor MICHAEL A. SYMONETTE; circ. 15,890.

Bahamas Tourist News: Baypar Bldg, Parliament St, POB N-4855, Nassau; tel. 322-4528; fax 322-4527; e-mail starpub@batelnet.bs; f. 1962; monthly; Editor BOBBY BOWER; circ. 371,000 (annually).

Nassau City Magazine: Miramar House, Bay and Christie Sts, POB N-4824, Nassau; tel. 356-2981; fax 326-2849.

Official Gazette: c/o Cabinet Office, POB N-7147, Nassau; tel. 322-2805; weekly; publ. by the Cabinet Office.

What's On Magazine: Woodes Rogers Wharf, POB CB-11713, Nassau; tel. 323-2323; fax 322-3428; e-mail info@whatsonbahamas.com; internet www.whatsonbahamas.com; monthly; Publr NEIL ABERLE.

Publishers

Bahamas Free Press Ltd: POB CB-13309, Nassau; tel. 323-8961.

Etienne Dupuch Jr Publications Ltd: 51 Hawthorne Rd, POB N-7513, Nassau; tel. 323-5665; fax 323-5728; e-mail dupuch@bahamasnet.com; internet www.dupuch.com; f. 1959; publishes

Bahamas Handbook, Trailblazer maps, *What To Do* magazines, *Welcome Bahamas, Tadpole* (educational colouring book) series and *Dining and Entertainment Guide*; Dirs ETIENNE DUPUCH, Jr, S. P. DUPUCH.

Media Enterprises Ltd: 31 Shirley Park Ave, POB N-9240, Nassau; tel. 325-8210; fax 325-8065; e-mail info@bahamasmedia .com; internet www.bahamasmedia.com; Pres. and Gen. Man. LARRY SMITH; Publishing Dir NEIL E. SEALEY.

Printing Tours and Publishing: Miramar House, Bay and Christie Sts, POB N-4846, Nassau; tel. 356-2981; fax 356-7118.

Sacha de Frisching Publishing: POB N-7776, Nassau; tel. 362-6230; fax 362-6274; children's books.

Star Publishers Ltd: POB N-4855, Nassau; tel. 322-3724; fax 322-4537; e-mail starpub@bahamas.net.bs; internet www.supermaps .com.

Broadcasting and Communications

TELECOMMUNICATIONS

The telecommunications sector was to be opened up to competition in 2002–03.

Bahamas Telecommunications Co (BaTelCo): POB N-3048, John F. Kennedy Dr., Nassau; tel. 302-7000; fax 326-7474; e-mail info@batelnet.bs; internet www.batelnet.bs; f. 1966; state-owned; scheduled for partial privatization in 2003; Chair. RENO BROWN; Gen. Man. MICHAEL SYMONETTE.

Cable Bahamas Ltd: POB CB-13050, Nassau; tel. 356-2200; fax 356-8997; e-mail info@cablebahamas.com; internet www .cablebahamas.com; f. 1995; provides cable television and internet services; Pres. RICHARD PARDY.

BROADCASTING

Radio

Broadcasting Corporation of the Bahamas: 3rd Terrace, POB N-1347, Centreville, New Providence; tel. 322-4623; fax 322-6598; f. 1936; govt-owned; commercial; Chair. MICHAEL D. SMITH; Gen. Man. EDWIN LIGHTBOURNE.

Radio Bahamas: internet www.univox.com/radio/zns.html; f. 1936; broadcasts 24 hours per day on four stations: the main Radio Bahamas ZNS1, Radio New Providence ZNS2, which are both based in Nassau, Radio Power 104.5 FM, and the Northern Service (ZNS3—Freeport); f. 1973; Station Man. Anthony Forster; Programme Man. TANYA PINDER.

Cool 96 FM: POB F-40773, Freeport, Grand Bahama; tel. 353-7440; fax 352-8709.

Love 97 FM: Bahamas Media House, East St North, POB N-3909, Nassau; tel. 356-2555; fax 356-2555; e-mail twilliams@ jonescommunications.com; internet www.love97fm.com.

More 95.9 FM: POB CR-54245, Nassau; tel. 361-2447; fax 361-2448; e-mail morefm94.9@batelnet.bs.

Tribune Radio Ltd (One Hundred JAMZ): Shirley and Deveaux St, POB N-3207, Nassau; tel. 328-4771; fax 356-5343; e-mail michelle@ 100jamz.com; internet www.100jamz.com; Gen. Man. STEPHEN HAUGHEY; Programme Dir ERIC WARD.

Television

Broadcasting Corporation of the Bahamas: see Radio.

Bahamas Television: f. 1977; broadcasts for Nassau, New Providence and the Central Bahamas; transmitting power of 50,000 watts; full colour; Programme Man. CARL BETHEL.

US television programmes and some satellite programmes can be received. Most islands have a cable-television service.

Finance

In recent years the Bahamas has developed into one of the world's foremost financial centres (there are no corporation, income, capital gains or withholding taxes or estate duty), and finance has become a significant feature of the economy. At December 2001 there were 356 banks and trust companies operating in the Bahamas. 199 banks and trust companies had a physical presence in the islands at June 1999.

BANKING

(cap. = capital; dep. = deposits; res = reserves; m. = million; brs = branches)

Central Bank

The Central Bank of the Bahamas: Frederick St, POB N-4868, Nassau; tel. 322-2193; fax 322-4321; e-mail cbob@ centralbankbahamas.com; internet www.centralbankbahamas.com; f. 1973; bank of issue; cap. B \$3.0m., res B \$88.0m., dep. B \$168.4m. (Dec. 2000); Gov. and Chair. JULIAN W. FRANCIS; Dep. Gov. WENDY M. CRAIGG.

Development Bank

The Bahamas Development Bank: Cable Beach, West Bay St, POB N-3034, Nassau; tel. 327-5780; fax 327-5047; e-mail info@ bahamasdevelopmentbank.com; internet www .bahamasdevelopmentbank.com; f. 1978 to fund approved projects and channel funds into appropriate investments; Chair. MACGREGOR N. ROBERTSON; Man. Dir GEORGE E. RODGERS; 2 brs.

Principal Bahamian-based Banks

Bank of the Bahamas Ltd: Shirley St, POB N-7118, Nassau; tel. 326-2560; fax 325-2762; f. 1970; name changed as above in 1988, when Bank of Montreal Bahamas Ltd became; jointly owned by Govt and Euro Canadian Bank; 50% owned by Govt, 50% owned by c. 4,000 Bahamian shareholders; cap. B \$10.0m., res B \$1.2m., dep. B \$204.6m. (June 2000); Chair. HUGH G. SANDS; Man. Dir P.M. ALLEN-DEAN; 7 brs.

Commonwealth Bank Ltd: 610 Bay St, POB SS-5541, Nassau; tel. 394-7373; fax 394-5807; f. 1960; Pres. WILLIAM SANDS; 8 brs.

Private Investment Bank Ltd: Devonshire House, Queen St, POB N-3918, Nassau; tel. 302-5950; fax 302-5970; f. 1984 as Bank Worms and Co International Ltd; renamed in 1990, 1996 and 1998; in 2000 merged with Geneva Private Bank and Trust (Bahamas) Ltd; cap. US \$3.0m., res US \$12.0m., dep. US \$163.0m. (Dec. 2000); Chair. and Dir FRANÇOIS ROUGE.

Principal Foreign Banks

Banco Internacional de Costa Rica Ltd (BICSA): Bank Lane, POB N-7768, Nassau; fax 326-5020; e-mail bicsacr@racsa.co.cr; internet www.bisca.com; f. 1976; 55% owned by Banco Nacional de Costa Rica, 20% owned by Banco de Costa Rica, 10% owned by Banco Crédito de Agrícola de Cartago; cap. US \$57.7m., res US \$2.4m., dep. US \$463.5m. (Dec. 2000); Chair. OSCAR E. BARAHONA; CEO THELMO VARGAS M.

BNP Paribas (Bahamas) Ltd: Beaumont House, 3rd Floor, Bay St, POB N-4883, Nassau; tel. 326-5935; fax 3265871; internet www .bnpgroup.com; Man. Dir ANDRÉ LAMOTHE.

BSI Overseas (Bahamas) Ltd (Italy): Bayside Executive Park, West Bay St, POB N-7130, Nassau; tel. 702-1200; fax 702-1250; f. 1990; wholly-owned subsid. of BSI AG (Switzerland); cap. US \$10.0m., res US \$66.1m., dep. US \$1,103.4m. (Dec. 2001); Chair. RETO KESSLER; Man. Dir MARTIN HUTTER.

Canadian Imperial Bank of Commerce (CIBC) (Canada): 4th Floor, 308 East Bay St, POB N-8329, Nassau; tel. 393-4710; fax 393-4280; internet www.cibc.com; Area Man. TERRY HILTS; 9 brs.

Citibank NA (USA): 4th Floor, Citibank Bldg, Thompson Blvd, Oakes Field, POB N-8158, Nassau; tel. 302-8859; fax 302-8625; internet www.citibank.com; Gen. Man. ALISON JOHNSTON; 2 brs.

Credit Suisse (Bahamas) Ltd (Switzerland): Bahamas Financial Centre, Shirley and Charlotte Sts, POB N-4928, Nassau; tel. 356-8100; fax 326-6589; f. 1968; subsidiary of Credit Suisse Zurich; portfolio and asset management, offshore company management, trustee services; cap. US \$12.0m., res US \$20.0m., dep. US \$500.7m. (Dec. 1997); Man. Dir GREGOR MAISSEN.

FirstCaribbean International Bank Ltd: Roseau; internet www .firstcaribbeaninternational.com; f. 2002 following merger of Caribbean operations of Barclays Bank PLC and CIBC; Exec. Chair. MICHAEL MANSOOR; CEO CHARLES PINK.

Handelsfinanz-CCF Bank International Ltd (Switzerland): Third Floor, Maritime House, Frederick St, POB N-10441, Nassau; tel. 328-8644; fax 328-8600; e-mail hfccfint@bahamas.net.bs; f. 1971; cap. US \$5.0m., res US \$15.5m., dep. US \$581.3m. (Dec. 1999); Chair. MARC DE GUILLEBON; Gen. Man. IVANO ALLIATA.

Lloyds TSB Bank and Trust (Bahamas) Ltd (United Kingdom): Bolam House, King and George Sts, POB N-1262, Nassau; tel. 302-3000; fax 322-8719; e-mail lloyd.pb@batelnet.bs; f. 1977; cap. US \$15.0m., dep. US \$305.1 (Dec. 1998); Principal Man. and Dir GRAHAM S. JOHNS.

National Bank of Canada (International) Ltd: Charlotte House, Charlotte St, POB N-3015, Nassau; tel. 322-4024; fax 323-8086;

e-mail nabkint@batelnet.bs; f. 1978; 100% owned by Natcan Holdings International Ltd; Gen. Man. JACQUES LATENDRESSE.

Overseas Union Bank and Trust (Bahamas) Ltd (Switzerland): 250 Bay St, POB N-8184, Nassau; tel. 322-2476; fax 323-8771; f. 1980; cap. US $5.0m., res US $6.2m., dep. US $97.9m. (Dec. 1997); Chair. Dr CARLO SGANZINI; Gen. Man. URS FREI.

Pictet Bank and Trust Ltd (Switzerland): Bayside Executive Park, Bldg Number One, POB N-4837, Nassau; tel. 322-3938; fax 323-7986; e-mail pbtbah@bahamas.net.bs; internet www.pictet.com/nassau.htm; f. 1978; cap. US $1.0m., res US $10.0m., dep. US $126.2m. (Dec. 1995); Chair. CHRISTIAN MALLET.

Royal Bank of Canada Ltd (Canada): 4th Floor, Royal Bank House, East Hill St, POB N-7549, Nassau; tel. 356-8500; fax 328-7145; internet www.royalbank.com; f. 1869; Chair. ALLAN TAYLOR; Vice-Pres. MICHAEL F. PHELAN; 16 brs.

Scotiabank (Bahamas) Ltd (Canada): Scotiabank Bldg, Rawson Sq., POB N-7518, Nassau; tel. 356-1400; fax 322-7989; e-mail scotiabank@batelnet.bs; internet www.scotiabank.com; Man. Dir ANTHONY C. ALLEN; Pres. BRUCE BIRMINGHAM; 18 brs.

UBS (Bahamas) Ltd (Switzerland): UBS House, East Bay St, POB N-7757, Nassau; tel. 394-9300; fax 394-9333; internet www.ubs.com/bahamas; f. 1968 as Swiss Bank Corpn (Overseas) Ltd, name changed as above 1998; cap. US $4.0m., dep. US $420.2m. (Dec. 1997); Chair. MARTIN LIECHTI; CEO ERIC TSCHIRREN.

Principal Bahamian Trust Companies

Ansbacher (Bahamas) Ltd: Ansbacher House, Bank Lane, POB N-7768, Nassau; tel. 322-1161; fax 326-5020; e-mail info@ansbacher.bs; internet www.ansbacher.com; incorporated 1957 as Bahamas International Trust Co Ltd, name changed 1994; cap. B $1.0m., res B $9.7m., dep. B $190.3m. (Sept. 1998); Man. Dir DAVID L. E. FAWKES.

Bahamas International Trust Co Ltd: Bitco Bldg, Bank Lane, Nassau; tel. 322-1161; security brokers and dealers; Man. Dir J.M. KNOTT.

Bank of Nova Scotia Trust Company (Bahamas) Ltd: Scotiabank Bldg, Rawson Sq., POB N-3016, Nassau; tel. 356-1500; fax 328-8473; e-mail bahamas@scotiatrust.com; internet www.scotiabank.com; wholly owned by the Bank of Nova Scotia International Ltd; Man. Dir DOUGLAS H. STEWART.

Chase Manhattan Trust Corpn: Shirley and Charlotte Sts, POB N-3708, Nassau; tel. 356-1305; fax 325-1706; Gen. Man. KEN BROWN; 4 brs.

Leadenhall Bank and Trust Co Ltd: IBM Bldg, East Bay and Church Sts, POB N-1965, Nassau; tel. 325-5508; fax 328-7030; e-mail drounce@leadentrust.com; f. 1976; Man. Dir DAVID J. ROUNCE.

MeesPierson (Bahamas) Ltd: POB SS-5539, Nassau; tel. 393-8777; fax 393-0582; internet www.mpbahamas.com; f. 1987; subsidiary of MeesPierson International AG of Zug, Switzerland; Chair. IAN D. FAIR; Man. Dir DAVID E. RICHARDSON.

Oceanic Bank and Trust: POB AP-59203, Nassau; tel. 502-8822; fax 502-8840; f. 1969; Man. Dir BRUCE BELL.

Winterbotham Trust Co Ltd: Bolam House, King and George Sts, POB N-3026, Nassau; tel. 356-5454; fax 356-9432; e-mail nassau@winterbotham.com; internet www.winterbotham.com; cap. US $3.8m. CEO GEOFFREY HOOPER; 2 brs.

Bankers' Organizations

Association of International Banks and Trust Companies in the Bahamas: POB N-7880, Nassau; tel. 356-3898; Chair. ANDREW LAW.

Bahamas Institute of Bankers: Royal Palm Mall, Mackey St, POB N-3202, Nassau; tel. 393-0456; fax 394-3503; Pres. KIM BODIE.

Financial Services Promotion Board: Nassau; f. 1998; jt govt/private initiative responsible for overseas marketing of financial services.

STOCK EXCHANGE

Bahamas International Securities Exchange (BISX): British Colonial Centre of Commerce, 1 Bay St, POB EE-15672, Nassau; e-mail info@bisxbahamas.com; internet www.bisxbahamas.com; f. 2000; 18 local companies listed at Dec. 2002; Chair. IAN FAIR.

INSURANCE

The leading British and a number of US, Canadian and Caribbean companies have agents in Nassau and Freeport. Local insurance companies include the following:

Allied Bahamas Insurance Co Ltd: 93 Collins Ave, POB N-1216, Nassau; tel. 326-5439; fax 356-5472; general, aviation and marine.

Bahamas First General Insurance Co Ltd: 93 Collins Ave, POB N-1216, Nassau; tel. 326-5439; fax 326-5472; Man. Dir PATRICK G. W. WARD.

Colina Insurance Co Ltd: 12 Village Rd, POB N-4728, Nassau; tel. 393-2224; fax 393-1710; scheduled to merge with Global Life Assurance Bahamas in 2002.

The Family Guardian Insurance Co Ltd (FamGuard): East Bay St, POB SS-6232, Nassau; tel. 393-1023; fax 394-1631; f. 1965.

Global Life Assurance Bahamas Ltd: 308 East Bay St, POB N-4937, New Providence; tel. 393-5433; fax 394-5645; e-mail phermanns@mail.global-life-bahamas.com; scheduled to merge with Colina Insurance Co Ltd in 2002; Pres. PATRICIA HERMANNS.

Association

Bahamas General Insurance Association: POB N-860, Nassau; tel. 323-2596; fax 328-4354; e-mail bgia@bahamas.net.bs; Co-ordinator ROBIN B. HARDY.

Trade and Industry

DEVELOPMENT ORGANIZATIONS

Bahamas Agricultural and Industrial Corpn (BAIC): Levy Bldg, East Bay St, POB N-4940, Nassau; tel. 322-3740; fax 322-2133; internet www.bahamasb2b.com/baic; f. 1981 as an amalgamation of Bahamas Development Corpn and Bahamas Agricultural Corpn for the promotion of greater co-operation between tourism and other sectors of the economy through the development of small and medium-sized enterprises; Exec. Chair. ALVIN SMITH.

Bahamas Financial Service Board: 4th Floor, Euro-Canadian Centre, POB N-1764; tel. 356-2985; fax 326-7007; e-mail info@bsfb-bahamas.com; internet www.bfsb-bahamas.com; CEO and Exec. Dir WENDY C. WARREN; Chair. MICHAEL PATON.

Bahamas Investment Authority: Cecil V. Wallace-Whitfield Centre, POB CB-10980, Nassau; tel. 327-5970; fax 327-5907; e-mail info@opm.gov.bs; internet www.opm.gov.bs/bia.php; Deputy Dir PHILIP MILLER.

Bahamas Light Industries Development Council: POB SS-5599, Nassau; tel. 394-1907; Pres. LESLIE MILLER.

Nassau Paradise Island Promotion Board: Dean's Lane, Fort Charlotte, POB N-7799, Nassau; tel. 322-8381; fax 325-8998; f. 1970; Chair. GEORGE R. MYERS; Sec. MICHAEL C. RECKLEY; 30 mems.

CHAMBER OF COMMERCE

Bahamas Chamber of Commerce: Shirley St and Collins Ave, POB N-665, Nassau; tel. 322-2145; fax 322-4649; internet www.bahamasb2b.com/bahamaschamber; f. 1935 to promote, foster and protect trade, industry and commerce; Pres. D. NEIL McKINNEY; 450 mems.

EMPLOYERS' ASSOCIATIONS

Bahamas Association of Land Surveyors: POB N-10147, Nassau; tel. 322-4569; Pres. DONALD THOMPSON; Vice-Pres. GODFREY HUMES; 30 mems.

Bahamas Boatmen's Association: POB ES-5212, Nassau; f. 1974; Pres. and Sec. FREDERICK GOMEZ.

Bahamas Contractors' Association: POB N-8170, Nassau; Chair. GODFREY E. LIGHTBOURN; Sec. ROBERT E. MYERS.

Bahamas Employers' Confederation: POB N-166, Nassau; tel. 393-5613; fax 322-4649; f. 1963; Pres. BRIAN NUTT.

Bahamas Hotel Employers' Association: SG Hambros Bldg, West Bay St, POB N-7799, Nassau; tel. 322-2262; fax 502-4221; f. 1958; Pres. J. BARRIE FARRINGTON; Exec. Vice-Pres. MICHAEL C. RECKLEY; 26 mems.

Bahamas Institute of Chartered Accountants: Star Plaza, Mackey St, POB N-7037, Nassau; tel. 394-3439; fax 394-3629; f. 1971; Pres. L. EDGAR MOXEY.

Bahamas Institute of Professional Engineers: Nassau; tel. 322-3356; fax 323-8503; Pres. ANTHONY DEAN.

Bahamas Motor Dealers' Association: POB N-3919, Nassau; tel. 328-7671; fax 328-1922; Pres. HARRY ROBERTS.

Bahamas Real Estate Association: Bahamas Chamber Bldg, POB N-8860, Nassau; tel. 325-4942; fax 322-4649; Pres. PATRICK STRACHAN.

UTILITIES

Electricity

The Bahamas Electricity Corpn (BEC): Big Pond and Tucker Rds, POB N-7509, Nassau; tel. 325-4101; fax 323-6852; internet www.bahamaselectricity.com; f. 1956; state-owned; scheduled for privatization in 2002; provides 70% of the islands' power-generating capacity; Chair. AL JARRETT; Gen. Man. BRADLEY S. ROBERTS.

Freeport Power Co Ltd: Mercantile Bldg, Cedar St, POB F-888, Freeport; tel. 352-6611; f. 1962; privately-owned; Pres. ALBERT J. MILLER.

Gas

Caribbean Gas Storage and Terminal Ltd: POB N-9665, Nassau; tel. 327-5587; fax 362-5006; e-mail info@caribbeangas.com; internet www.caribbeangas.com; f. 1992; Man. Dir PETER T. NEWELL.

Tropigas: Nassau; tel. 322-2404.

Water

Bahamas Water and Sewerage Corpn (WSC): 87 Thompson Blvd, POB N-9440, Nassau; tel. 302-5500; fax 356-7152; e-mail wcexcoff@batelnet.bs; internet www.wsc.com.bs; f. 1960; Chair. MICHAEL L. BARNETT; Man. GEORGE MOSS.

TRADE UNIONS

All Bahamian unions are members of one of the following:

Commonwealth of the Bahamas Trade Union Congress: Congress House, 3 Warwick St, POB CB-10992, Nassau; tel. 394-6301; fax 394-7401; e-mail tuc@bahamas.net.bs; Pres. OBIE FERGUSON Jr; 12,500 mems.

National Congress of Trade Unions: Horseshoe Dr., POB GT-2887, Nassau; tel. 356-7459; fax 356-7457; Pres. LEROY (DUKE) HANNA; Gen. Sec. KINGSLEY L. BLACK; 20,000 mems.

The main unions are as follows

Bahamas Airport, Airline and Allied Workers' Union: Workers' House, Harold Rd, POB N-3364, Nassau; tel. 323-4491; fax 323-7086; f. 1958; Pres. FRANKLYN CARTER; Gen. Sec. PATRICIA TYNES; 550 mems.

Bahamas Brewery, Distillers Union: POB N-838, Nassau; tel. 362-1412; fax 362-1415; f. 1968; Pres. JOSEPH MOSS; Gen. Sec. RAFAEL HOLMES; 140 mems.

Bahamas Communications and Public Officers' Union: Farrington Rd, POB N-3190, Nassau; tel. 322-1537; fax 323-8719; e-mail prebcpou@batelnet.bs; f. 1973; Pres. D. SHANE GIBSON; Sec.-Gen. ROBERT A. FARQUHARSON; 2,100 mems.

Bahamas Doctors' Union: Nassau; Pres. Dr EUGENE NEWERY; Gen. Sec. GEORGE SHERMAN.

Bahamas Electrical Workers' Union: East West Highway, POB GT-2535, Nassau; tel. 393-1838; fax 356-7383; Pres. CHARLES ROLLE; Gen. Sec. PATRICIA JOHNSON.

Bahamas Hotel Catering and Allied Workers' Union: Harold Rd, POB GT-2514, Nassau; tel. 323-5933; fax 325-6546; f. 1958; Pres. PATRICK BAIN; Gen. Sec. LEO DOUGLAS; 6,500 mems.

Bahamas Maritime Port and Allied Workers' Union: Prince George Docks, POB FF-6501, Nassau; tel. 322-2049; fax 322-5445; Pres. FREDERICK N. RODGERS; Sec.-Gen. LEON WALLACE.

Bahamas Musicians' and Entertainers' Union: Horseshoe Dr., POB N-880, Nassau; tel. 322-3734; fax 323-3537; f. 1958; Pres. LEROY (DUKE) HANNA; Gen. Sec. PORTIA NOTTAGE; 410 mems.

Bahamas Public Services Union: Wulff Rd, POB N-4692, Nassau; tel. 325-0038; fax 323-5287; f. 1959; Pres. WILLIAM McDONALD; Sec.-Gen. SYNIDA DORSETT; 4,247 mems.

Bahamas Taxi-Cab Union: Nassau St, POB N-1077, Nassau; tel. 323-5818; fax 326-2919; Pres. FELTON COX; Gen. Sec. ROSCOE WEECH.

Bahamas Union of Teachers: 104 Bethel Ave, Stapledon Gardens, POB N-3482, Nassau; tel. 323-4491; fax 323-7086; f. 1945; Pres. KINGSLEY L. BLACK; Sec.-Gen. HELLENA O. CARTWRIGHT; 2,600 mems.

Eastside Stevedores' Union: POB N-2167, Nassau; tel. 322-4069; fax 364-7437; f. 1972; Pres. CURTIS TURNQUEST; Gen. Sec. TREVOR CAREY.

Bahamas Utility Services and Allied Workers' Union: Nassau; Pres. HUEDLEY MOSS.

Grand Bahama Construction, Refinery, Maintenance and Allied Workers' Union: 33A Kipling Bldg, POB 42397, Freeport; tel. 352-2476; fax 351-7009; f. 1971; Pres. NEVILLE SIMMONS; Gen. Sec. MCKINLEY JONES.

United Brotherhood of Longshoremen's Union: Wulff Rd, POB N-7317, Nassau; f. 1959; Pres. JOSEPH McKINNEY; Gen. Sec. DEGLANVILLE PANZA; 157 mems.

Transport

ROADS

There are about 966 km (600 miles) of roads in New Providence and 1,368 km (850 miles) in the Family Islands, mainly on Grand Bahama, Cat Island, Eleuthera, Exuma and Long Island. In 1999 57.4% of roads were paved. In 2001 the Government began a US $66m. road-improvement programme, partly funded by a $42.5m. loan from the Inter-American Development Bank and scheduled for completion in 2003.

SHIPPING

The principal seaport is at Nassau (New Providence), which can accommodate the very largest cruise ships. Passenger arrivals exceed two million annually. The other main ports are at Freeport (Grand Bahama), where a container terminal opened in 1997, and Matthew Town (Inagua). There are also modern berthing facilities for cruise ships at Potters Cay (New Providence), Governor's Harbour (Eleuthera), Morgan's Bluff (North Andros) and George Town (Exuma).

The Bahamas converted to free-flag status in 1976, and by 1983 possessed the world's third-largest open-registry fleet. The fleet's displacement was 33,385,713 grt in December 2001 (the third-largest national fleet in the world).

There is a weekly cargo and passenger service to all the Family Islands.

Bahamas Maritime Authority: POB N-4679, Nassau; tel. 323-3130; fax 323-2119; internet www.bahamasmaritime.com; e-mail nassau@bahamasmaritime.com; f. 1995; promotes ship registration and co-ordinates maritime administration.

Freeport Harbour Co Ltd: POB F-42465, Freeport; tel. 352-9651; fax 352-6888; e-mail fhcol@batelnet.bs; Gen. Man. MICHAEL J. POWER.

Nassau Port Authority: Prince George Wharf, POB N-8175, Nassau; tel. 356-7354; fax 322-5545; regulates principal port of the Bahamas; Port Dir ANTHONY ALLENS.

Principal Shipping Companies

Cavalier Shipping: Arawak Cay, POB N-8170, New Providence; tel. 328-3035.

Dockendale Shipping Co Ltd: Dockendale House, West Bay St, POB N-10455, Nassau; tel. 325-0448; fax 328-1542; e-mail dockship@dockendale.com; f. 1973; ship management; Man. Dir L. J. FERNANDES; Tech. Dir K. VALLURI.

Eleuthera Express Shipping Co: POB N-4201, Nassau.

Grand Master Shipping Co: POB N-4208, Nassau.

Grenville Ventures Ltd: 43 Elizabeth Ave, POB CB-13022, Nassau.

HJH Trading Co Ltd: POB N-4402, Nassau; tel. 392-3939; fax 392-1828.

Gladstone Patton: POB SS-5178, Nassau.

Pioneer Shipping Ltd: Union Wharf, POB N-3044, Nassau; tel. 325-7889; fax 325-2214.

Teekay Shipping Corporation: TK House, Bayside Executive Park, West Bay St & Blake Rd, POB AP-59212, Nassau; tel. 502-8820; fax 502-8840; internet www.teekay.com; Pres. and CEO BJORN MOLLER.

Tropical Shipping Co Ltd: POB N-8183, Nassau; tel. 322-1012; fax 323-7566.

United Shipping Co Ltd: POB F-42552, Freeport; tel. 352-9315; fax 352-4034; e-mail info@unitedship.com; internet www.unitedship.com.

CIVIL AVIATION

Nassau International Airport (15 km (9 miles) outside the capital) and Freeport International Airport (5 km (3 miles) outside the city, on Grand Bahama) are the main terminals for international and internal services. There are also important airports at West End (Grand Bahama) and Rock Sound (Eleuthera) and some 50 smaller airports and landing strips throughout the islands. A $30m. airport improvement programme was under way in 2002.

Bahamasair Holdings Ltd: Coral Harbour Rd, POB N-4881, Nassau; tel. 377-8451; fax 377-7409; e-mail astuart@bahamasair.com; internet www.bahamasair.com; f. 1973; state-owned, scheduled for privatization; scheduled services between Nassau, Freeport, destinations within the USA and 20 locations within the Family Islands; Chair. ANTHONY MILLER; Man. Dir PAT ROLLE (acting).

Tourism

The mild climate and beautiful beaches attract many tourists. In 2001 tourist arrivals decreased by 9.2%, compared with the previous year, to 4,188,281 (including 2,749,251 by sea). The majority of stop-over arrivals (83% in 1999) were from the USA. Receipts from the tourist industry stood at B $1,814m. in 2000. In September 1999 there were 223 hotels in the country, with a total of 14,080 rooms.

Ministry of Tourism: British Colonial Hilton Hotel, Bay St, POB N-3701, Nassau; tel. 322-7500; fax 328-0945; e-mail tourism@ bahamas.com; internet www.bahamas.com; Dir-Gen. VINCENT VANDERPOOL-WALLACE.

Bahamas Hotel Association: Dean's Lane, Fort Charlotte, POB N-7799, Nassau; tel. 322-8381; fax 326-5346; e-mail bhainfo@ batelnet.bs; Pres. BARBARA HANNAH COX; Exec. Vice-Pres. BASIL H. SMITH.

Bahamas Tourism and Development Authority: POB N-4740, Nassau; tel. 326-0992; fax 323-0993; e-mail linkages@batelnet.bs; f. 1995; Exec. Dir FRANK J. COMITO.

Hotel Corporation of the Bahamas: West Bay St, POB N-9520, Nassau; tel. 327-8395; fax 327-6978; Chair. GEOFFREY JOHNSTONE; Chief Exec. WARREN ROLLE.

BAHRAIN

Introductory Survey

Location, Climate, Language, Religion, Flag, Capital

The Kingdom of Bahrain consists of a group of some 36 islands, situated midway along the Persian (Arabian) Gulf, approximately 24 km (15 miles) from the east coast of Saudi Arabia (to which it is linked by a causeway), and 28 km from the west coast of Qatar. The construction of a causeway linking eastern Bahrain to Qatar (the Friendship Bridge) is planned. There are six principal islands in the archipelago, the largest of these being Bahrain itself, which is about 50 km long, and between 13 km and 25 km wide. To the north-east of Bahrain island, and linked to it by a causeway and road, lies Muharraq island, which is approximately 6 km long. Another causeway links Bahrain island with Sitra island. The climate is temperate from December to the end of March, with temperatures ranging from 19°C to 25°C, but becomes very hot and humid during the summer months. In August and September temperatures can rise to 40°C. The official language is Arabic, but English is also widely spoken. Almost all Bahraini citizens are Muslims, divided into two sects: Shi'ites (almost 60%) and Sunnis (more than 40%). Non-Bahrainis comprised 37.6% of the total population at the census of April 2001. The national flag (proportions 3 by 5) is red, with a vertical white stripe at the hoist, the two colours being separated by a serrated line forming five white triangles. The capital is Manama, on Bahrain island.

Recent History

Bahrain, a traditional Arab monarchy, became a British Protected State in the 19th century. Under this arrangement, government was shared between the ruling Sheikh and his British adviser. Following a series of territorial disputes in the 19th century, Persia (now Iran) made renewed claims to Bahrain in 1928. This disagreement remained unresolved until May 1970, when Iran accepted the findings of a UN-commissioned report showing that the inhabitants of Bahrain overwhelmingly favoured complete independence, rather than union with Iran.

Sheikh Sulman bin Hamad al-Khalifa, who became ruler of Bahrain in 1942, was succeeded upon his death in November 1961 by his eldest son, Sheikh Isa bin Sulman al-Khalifa. Extensive administrative and political reforms were implemented in January 1970, when a supreme executive authority, the 12-member Council of State, was established, representing the first formal derogation of the ruler's powers. Sheikh Khalifa bin Sulman al-Khalifa, the ruler's eldest brother, was appointed President of the Council.

Meanwhile, in January 1968 the United Kingdom had announced its intention to withdraw British military forces from the area by 1971. In March 1968 Bahrain joined the nearby territories of Qatar and the Trucial States (now the United Arab Emirates—UAE), which were also under British protection, in the Federation of Arab Emirates. It was intended that the Federation should become fully independent, but the interests of Bahrain and Qatar proved to be incompatible with those of the smaller sheikhdoms, and both seceded from the Federation. Bahrain thus became a separate independent state on 15 August 1971, when a new treaty of friendship was signed with the United Kingdom. Sheikh Isa took the title of Amir, while the Council of State became the Cabinet, with Sheikh Khalifa as Prime Minister. A Constituent Assembly, convened in December 1972, formulated a new Constitution providing for a National Assembly to be comprised of 14 cabinet ministers and 30 elected members. The Constitution came into force on 6 December 1973, and elections to the new Assembly were conducted the following day. In the absence of political parties, candidates sought election as independents. In August 1975 the Prime Minister submitted his resignation, complaining that the National Assembly was obstructing the Government's initiatives for new legislation, particularly regarding national security. However, Sheikh Khalifa was reappointed and, at his request, the Assembly was dissolved by Amiri decree. New elections were to be held following minor changes to the Constitution and to the electoral law, but there were few subsequent signs that the National Assembly would be reconvened. With no elected legislative body, the ruling family continued to exercise near-abso-

lute power. On 16 January 1993 a 30-member Consultative Council (Majlis ash-Shoura)—appointed by the ruling authorities and comprising a large number of business executives and some members of the old National Assembly—held its inaugural meeting. The Council was to act in a purely advisory capacity, with no legislative powers.

In March 1981 Bahrain was one of the six founder members of the Co-operation Council for the Arab States of the Gulf (or Gulf Co-operation Council—GCC, see p. 175), which was established in order to co-ordinate defence strategy and to promote freer trading and co-operative economic protection among Gulf states.

For many years there have been indications of tension between Shi'a Muslims, who form a slender majority in Bahrain (and many of whom are of Iranian descent), and the dominant Sunni Muslims, to which sect the ruling family belongs. During the 1980s two plots to overthrow the Government, one of which was alleged to have Iranian support, were uncovered, as was a plan to sabotage Bahrain's petroleum installations, in which Iran was also alleged to be implicated. In December 1993 the human rights organization Amnesty International published a report criticizing the Bahraini Government's treatment of Shi'ite Muslims, some of whom had been forcibly exiled. In March 1994, apparently in response to this criticism, the Amir issued a decree pardoning 64 Bahrainis who had been in exile since the 1980s and permitting them to return to Bahrain. In December 1994, however, Sheikh Ali Salman Ahmad Salman, a Muslim cleric, was arrested following his criticism of the Government and his public appeal for reform, particularly the restoration of the National Assembly. Widespread rioting ensued throughout Bahrain, especially in Shi'ite districts, and large-scale demonstrations were held in Manama in support of Sheikh Salman's demands and to petition for his release. Civil unrest continued despite the Amir's pledge to extend the powers of the Consultative Council; 12 people died and some 2,500 demonstrators were arrested in clashes with the security forces during December and in early January 1995. Sheikh Salman was deported in January and sought asylum in the United Kingdom. The unprecedented scale of the protests was widely attributed to a marked deterioration in socio-economic conditions in Bahrain, and in particular to a high level of unemployment.

There were further anti-Government demonstrations in Shi'ite districts in March and April 1995, following a police search of the property of an influential Shi'ite cleric, Sheikh Abd al-Amir al-Jamri, who was subsequently placed under house arrest and later imprisoned. In May and July several people received custodial sentences, ranging from one year's detention to life imprisonment, for damaging public installations, and one Bahraini was sentenced to death for the murder of a police-officer in March. In June, in an apparent attempt to appease Shi'ite opposition leaders, the Prime Minister announced the first major cabinet reshuffle for 20 years, although the strategic portfolios of the interior, defence, foreign affairs and of finance and national economy remained unchanged.

In August 1995 the Government initiated talks with Shi'ite opposition leaders in an effort to foster reconciliation. In the same month the Amir issued a decree pardoning 150 people detained since the unrest. However, a report issued by Amnesty International in September indicated that as many as 1,500 demonstrators remained in detention in Bahrain, and that two prisoners (including a young student) had died in police custody following torture. Talks between the Government and opposition leaders collapsed in mid-September, but more than 40 political prisoners, among them Sheikh al-Jamri, were none the less released later in the month. In late October al-Jamri and six other opposition figures began a hunger strike in protest at the Government's refusal to concede to their demands, which included the release of all political prisoners and the restoration of the National Assembly. In early November, following a large demonstration to mark the end of the hunger strike, the Government announced that it would take 'necessary action' to prevent future 'illegal' gatherings. In December the Amir declared an amnesty for nearly 150 prisoners, mostly people arrested during the recent disturbances. There were large-scale demonstrations in late December and in early January 1996, in protest at the heavy deployment of security forces in Shi'ite districts and at the closure of two mosques. Opposition activists strongly criticized the use of tear gas and plastic bullets to disperse protesters, and also suggested that Saudi Arabian and Indian security officers had been dispatched to reinforce the Bahrain police. In mid-January eight opposition leaders, including Sheikh al-Jamri, were arrested on charges of inciting unrest. In February Ahmad ash-Shamlan, a noted lawyer and writer, became the first prominent Sunni to be detained in connection with the disturbances, following his distribution of a statement accusing the Government of authoritarianism. A number of bomb explosions in February and early March culminated in an arson attack on a restaurant in Sitra, in which seven Bangladeshi workers died. Also in March jurisdiction with regard to a number of criminal offences was transferred from ordinary courts to the High Court of Appeal, acting in the capacity of State Security Court. This move effectively accelerated court proceedings, while removing the right of appeal and limiting the role of the defence. In late March Isa Ahmad Hassan Qambar was executed by firing squad, having been condemned to death for killing a police-officer during the unrest of March 1995 (see above). The execution—the first to take place in Bahrain since 1977—provoked mass protests within Bahrain, while international human rights organizations challenged the validity of Qambar's confession and trial.

Civil disturbances continued during 1996, and tensions were exacerbated by the Government's announcement, in April, of the creation of a Higher Council of Islamic Affairs (to be appointed by the Prime Minister and headed by the Minister of Justice and Islamic Affairs) to supervise all religious activity (including that of the Shi'ite community) in Bahrain. In June, however, the Amir sought to appease the demands of opposition reformers by announcing the future expansion of the Consultative Council from 30 to 40 members: a new 40-member Council was duly appointed by the Amir in September. In July the State Security Court imposed death sentences on three of the eight Bahrainis convicted of the arson attack in Sitra, while four men were sentenced to life imprisonment. The death sentences provoked widespread domestic protests and international criticism. In response the Government agreed to allow an appeal against the ruling. In October the Court of Cassation ruled that it had no jurisdiction to overturn the verdict, and the fate of the three men seemed likely to be decided by the Amir. Towards the end of the year government plans to close a number of Shi'ite mosques resulted in further riots. Demonstrators gathered at the Ras Roman mosque in central Manama became involved in a violent confrontation with the security forces, during which police fired tear gas on worshippers. As unrest continued into early 1997, there were rumours of division within the ruling family concerning the use of force in response to the crisis. In January 1997 a National Guard was created, to provide support for the Bahraini Defence Force and the security forces of the Ministry of the Interior. The Amir's son, Hamad, was appointed to command the new force, prompting speculation that its primary duty would be to protect the ruling family. In March a week of anti-Government protests marked the first anniversary of the execution of Isa Ahmad Hassan Qambar. It was reported that since the outbreak of civil unrest at the end of 1994 some 28 people had been killed and 220 imprisoned in connection with the protests. In July and August 1997 two human rights groups produced reports criticizing the Bahrain police for allegedly making arbitrary arrests, using torture, and arresting children as young as seven years of age. The Government rejected these reports, claiming that they were based on dishonest sources. It did, however, appear to respond to the allegations when, in November, the trial *in absentia* of eight prominent exiled activists (including Sheikh Ali Salman Ahmad Salman) resulted in the imposition of prison sentences of between five and 15 years. Although the activists claimed not to have been summoned to stand trial, their sentences were considered lenient in view of the severity of the offences with which they were charged, which included attempting to overthrow the regime. Furthermore, during 1997 publishing restrictions were relaxed, and in December the Amir announced plans to enlarge further the Consultative Council and to allow greater media coverage of its activities. In February 1998 opposition groups welcomed the appointment of Khalid bin Muhammad al-Khalifa as the new head of the State Security Investigation Directorate (the previous, long-serving, incumbent was a British national) and

urged the continuing 'Bahrainization' of the security apparatus as a precondition for the initiation of dialogue between the regime and the opposition.

Sheikh Isa died on 6 March 1999. He was succeeded as Amir by his son, Crown Prince Sheikh Hamad bin Isa al-Khalifa, hitherto Commander-in-Chief of the Bahrain Defence Force and National Guard; Sheikh Hamad's eldest son, Sheikh Salman bin Hamad al-Khalifa, became Crown Prince and also assumed his father's military command. Initially, opposition groups welcomed Sheikh Hamad's accession, which raised expectations of political change. In his first months in office Sheikh Hamad permitted Shi'ites to join the armed forces, allowed an investigation by Amnesty International into alleged brutality by the Sunni security forces, and released more than 300 Shi'ite prisoners being held on security-related charges. However, the opposition claimed that 1,200–1,500 political prisoners remained in detention, and Sheikh Hamad was regarded as having failed to initiate prompt negotiations to end political unrest. At the end of May he announced a limited cabinet reorganization in which three new ministers were appointed, including the former Governor of the Bahrain Monetary Agency, Abdullah Hassan Saif, as Minister of Finance. Despite evident tension in relations between the new Amir and the uncompromising Sheikh Khalifa, the Prime Minister retained his position. In July Sheikh al-Jamri, who was brought to trial in February, having been detained since 1996 under the terms of the State Security Act (which allows the imprisonment of suspects without trial for a period of up to three years), was sentenced to 10 years' imprisonment for spying and inciting anti-Government unrest; a substantial fine was also imposed. Following intense international pressure Sheikh Hamad granted him an official pardon the following day, although Sheikh al-Jamri remained effectively under house arrest. In August 1999 Bahrain's longest serving political prisoner, As-Sayed Jafar al-Alawi, was released from detention; he was one of 72 people convicted in 1981 for plotting against the Government, and had been sentenced to 25 years' imprisonment. In November–December 1999 the Amir ordered the release of some 345 detainees. In October, meanwhile, Sheikh Hamad issued a decree ordering the Consultative Council to establish a human rights committee. None the less, Amnesty International asserted in November 2000 that while the human rights situation in Bahrain had improved since 1998 (the organization cited the release of hundreds of prisoners, the creation of the human rights body and ratification, in March 1998, of the UN Convention against Torture and Other Cruel, Inhuman or Degrading Treatment or Punishment), the mechanisms that had facilitated past human rights violations remained in place.

In May 2000 the Prime Minister stated that municipal elections, on the basis of universal suffrage, would be held in early 2001 and that parliamentary elections would take place in 2004. At the end of September 2000 four women, as well as a number of non-Muslims, were appointed for the first time to the Consultative Council. The Amir announced in late November that a 46-member Supreme National Committee (SNC) had been formed to prepare a National Action Charter (NAC), which would outline the future evolution of Bahrain's political system. Among the SNC's recommendations, submitted in late December, were that there should be a transition from an emirate to a constitutional monarchy, comprising a directly elected bicameral parliament (with women permitted both to vote and to seek election), a consultative chamber that would be appointed by the Government from all sections of society, and an independent judiciary. Critics of the Bahrain regime dismissed the proposed transition to a monarchy as a pretext for the continuation of autocratic rule. Meanwhile, a Supreme Council for Economic Development (subsequently restyled the Economic Development Board) was established in April, under the chairmanship of the Prime Minister.

The new Charter was submitted for approval in a national referendum held on 14–15 February 2001 (at which Bahraini women were permitted to vote for the first time), and was duly endorsed by 98.4% of participating voters. Two committees were formed by Sheikh Hamad later that month. The tasks of the first committee, the Committee for the Activation of the National Charter, headed by the Crown Prince, were to implement the NAC and to define the respective roles of the legislature and the monarchy. The second committee, chaired by the Minister of Justice and Islamic Affairs, was required to oversee amendments to the Constitution. The 1974 Decree Law on State Security Measures and the State Security Court were both abolished at this time. Prior to the referendum all political prisoners, including the Shi'ite cleric Sheikh al-Jamri, were reportedly released by the Amir. Moreover, following the removal of travel restrictions for members of the opposition, by March 2001 at least 100 political exiles had returned to Bahrain, among them Sheikh Ali Salman, the Muslim cleric deported in 1995. Also in March 2001, prior to a visit by representatives of Amnesty International, the Government granted a licence to the independent Bahrain Human Rights Society (BHRS).

A government reorganization was effected in April 2001. Although the key portfolios remained unaltered, several ministries were restructured and five new ministers were appointed to the Cabinet. The formation of a Supreme Council for Women in Bahrain, to be chaired by the wife of the Amir, was announced in August.

On 14 February 2002 Sheikh Hamad announced the establishment of a constitutional monarchy in Bahrain, proclaiming himself King. The new monarch approved the amendments to the Constitution outlined in the NAC and dissolved the Consultative Council. Municipal elections were held on 9 May (with run-off voting one week later); female candidates—for the first time permitted to stand for public office—failed to win any seats on the five new regional councils.

Meanwhile, it was announced that Bahrain's first legislative elections for 27 years would take place, earlier than had previously been indicated, on 24 October 2002. In preparation for the elections, in late June the Government approved a draft electoral law. The new legislation was criticized by opposition groups on the grounds that it barred all trade unions and overtly political organizations from participating in the ballot; in September, however, King Hamad removed restrictions on campaigning by political groups. Opposition activists expressed strong concern, furthermore, that the unelected Consultative Council would have the same rights as the elected House of Representatives in the bicameral parliament, and stated that they would boycott the polls. Meanwhile, in early July the King ordered the establishment of an independent financial auditing court, with far-reaching powers to monitor state spending. Later in that month the creation of a Constitutional Court was also approved by the Government. Legislation allowing the establishment of independent trade unions was enacted in late September.

At the elections to the House of Representatives, which proceeded as scheduled on 24 October 2002, 21 of the 40 seats were won by independents and 'moderate' Sunni candidates, with the remaining 19 seats taken by more radical Islamists. The rate of participation by voters was, according to official figures, 53.2% of the registered electorate. Reformists expressed their view that the newly elected legislature would not reflect the structure of Bahraini society, since a large proportion of the Shi'ite majority had boycotted the elections and female candidates had failed to win any seats (there had been eight women among a total of 174 candidates). Opposition groups, both leftist and Islamist, also complained that international human rights groups had not been permitted to monitor the elections. On 17 November the new Consultative Council, headed by Dr Faisal Radhi al-Mousawi, hitherto Minister of Health, was sworn in by the King: the new body comprised 40 appointed members, including four women. Earlier in the same month King Hamad named an expanded Cabinet, in which Dr Khalil bin Ibrahim Hassan succeeded al-Mousawi as Minister of Health. Other notable changes included the appointment of two Shi'ites, Dr Majid bin Hassan al-Alawi and Sheikh Jawad bin Salem al-Oraid, as Minister of Labour and Social Affairs and Minister of Justice, respectively. In addition, for the first time two deputy prime ministers were appointed; Sheikh Abdullah bin Khalid al-Khalifa, who also held the position of Minister of Islamic Affairs, and Sheikh Muhammad bin Mubarak, who retained the foreign affairs portfolio. The legislation permitting the establishment of independent trade unions was ratified in November; the King also declared 1 May, international Labour Day, as an official holiday.

Although relations between Bahrain and Iran were upgraded to ambassadorial level in late 1990, the situation between the two countries began to deteriorate in the mid-1990s. While there was sufficient evidence to suggest largely domestic motivation for the recent increase in popular disaffection, the Bahraini authorities continued to imply that the disturbances were fomented by Iranian-backed militant Shi'ite fundamentalists seeking to destabilize the country. These allegations were frequently dismissed by Iran. In June 1996 the Bahraini Government announced that it had uncovered details of a plot, initiated in 1993 with support from fundamentalist Shi'ite groups in Iran, to oust the Government and ruling family in Bahrain and replace them with a pro-Iranian administration. It was claimed that a previously unknown Shi'ite group, Hezbollah Bahrain, had been established and financed by Iran's Revolutionary Guard. Young Bahraini Shi'ites were alleged to have received military training in Iran and at guerrilla bases in Lebanon, in preparation for a terrorist offensive in Bahrain, which had culminated in the unrest of the previous 18 months. Within days of the Government's announcement more than 50 Bahrainis had been arrested in connection with the alleged plot. Many of the detainees, including six who made televised confessions, admitted membership of Hezbollah Bahrain. The Iranian authorities denied any involvement in the planned insurrection, but bilateral relations were severely undermined by the unprecedented directness of the Bahrain Government's accusations; the two countries' respective ambassadors were withdrawn, and diplomatic relations were downgraded. During June 1996 more than 30 Bahrainis received prison sentences of between one and 13 years—for offences connected to the disturbances—from the State Security Court (and were therefore denied the right of appeal). In March 1997 59 Bahraini Shi'ites accused of belonging to Hezbollah Bahrain were brought to trial; similar charges had been made against a further 22 Shi'ites who, according to the Bahrain Government, were to be tried *in absentia*. The State Security Court sentenced 37 of the defendants to terms of imprisonment ranging from three to 15 years, and acquitted the others. There was a period of *détente* in relations between most countries of the GCC and Iran following the election of Muhammad Khatami to the Iranian presidency in May of that year, and in December 1999 relations at ambassadorial level were formally restored between Bahrain and Iran. In March 2000 the Ministers of Foreign Affairs of the two countries met in Manama to discuss regional security as well as political and economic co-operation; a bilateral economic commission held its first meeting in that month. In early 2001 it was announced that Shi'ite Muslims of Iranian descent and whose families had lived in Bahrain for several generations were to be granted full Bahraini citizenship.

In common with other Gulf states, Bahrain consistently expressed support for Iraq at the time of the Iran–Iraq war (1980–88). However, following the Iraqi invasion of Kuwait in August 1990, Bahrain firmly supported the implementation of UN economic sanctions against Iraq and permitted the stationing of US troops and combat aircraft in Bahrain. (Military co-operation with the USA had been close for many years.) In June 1991, following the liberation of Kuwait in February, it was confirmed that Bahrain would remain a regional support base for the USA, and later in the year the two countries signed a defence co-operation agreement. In January 1994 Bahrain signed further accords of military co-operation with the USA and the United Kingdom. Relations with Iraq remained strained, and in October hopes of improved relations receded when Iraqi forces were again deployed in the Iraq–Kuwait border area. In response, Bahrain deployed combat aircraft and naval units to join GCC and US forces in the defence of Kuwait. In late 1995 Bahrain agreed to the temporary deployment on its territory of US fighter aircraft, in order to deter any possible military threat from Iraq. In February 1998 Bahrain strongly advocated a diplomatic solution to the ongoing dispute between Iraq and the UN weapons inspectors (see the chapter on Iraq), and refused to allow US military aircraft to launch attacks on Iraq from Bahraini bases. In June, as part of a wider US effort to reduce its military presence in the region, US military aircraft were withdrawn from Bahrain. In December a further US-led military campaign against Iraq was supported by the Bahraini authorities (the operation was centred in Manama, where the US Fifth Fleet is based), although Bahrain refrained from any public endorsement of the air-strikes. In August 1999 it was reported that Bahrain desired a further reduction of the US military presence in Bahrain, particularly that of the Fifth Fleet. Bahrain joined the other GCC states in condemning the suicide attacks on New York and Washington, DC, on 11 September 2001, and pledged to co-operate with the USA's attempts to forge an international 'coalition against terror', notably by 'freezing' the financial assets of individuals or organizations allegedly linked to the fundamentalist Islamist al-Qa'ida (Base) network of Osama bin Laden, held by the USA to be principally responsible for the attacks. Nevertheless, in the aftermath of the suicide attacks, small demonstrations and 'bomb-scare' telephone calls to US companies based in Bahrain indicated renewed antipathy towards the USA in some quarters. As in the other Gulf states, there was concern in Bahrain that US-led military action, which began in Afghanistan in early October, should not be directed against any Muslim target in the Middle East. In April 2002 anti-US slogans featured prominently in a large demonstration organized in support of the Palestinians during Israeli military incursions into Palestinian-controlled territories. As the momentum towards a US-led military campaign to oust the regime of Saddam Hussain in Iraq grew, anti-war riots broke out with increasing frequency in Bahrain, and in February 2003 police opened fire on a 2,000-strong violent demonstration outside the US embassy in Manama. Although in the same month King Hamad expressed hope that a diplomatic solution to the crisis could be found, Bahrain announced that it would contribute a frigate and an unspecified number of troops to the defence of Kuwait from possible Iraqi retaliation should the US-led campaign proceed. In March the Bahrain Government lent its support to an appeal by the UAE for Saddam Hussain to go into exile in order to save his country from the consequences of the US pursuit of 'regime change', and offered him asylum in Bahrain. Following the commencement, later in March, of US-led military action in Iraq, in April Bahrain ordered the expulsion of an Iraqi diplomat who was alleged to be linked to an explosion outside the Fifth Fleet base.

In April 1986 Qatari military forces raided the island of Fasht ad-Dibal, which had been artificially constructed on a coral reef (submerged at high tide), situated midway between Bahrain and Qatar; both countries claimed sovereignty over the island. Following GCC mediation, in May the two Governments agreed to destroy the island. Other areas of dispute between the two states were Zubarah (which was part of Bahraini territory until the early 20th century), in mainland Qatar, and the Hawar islands, the region of which is believed to contain potentially valuable reserves of petroleum and natural gas. In July 1991 Qatar instituted proceedings at the International Court of Justice (ICJ) in The Hague, Netherlands, regarding the issue of the Hawar islands (in 1939 a British judgment had awarded sovereignty of the islands to Bahrain), Fasht ad-Dibal and Qit'at Jaradah (over which the British Government had recognized Bahrain's 'sovereign rights' in 1947), together with the delimitation of the maritime border between Qatar and Bahrain. The question of sovereignty was further complicated in April 1992, when the Government of Qatar issued a decree redefining its maritime borders to include territorial waters claimed by Bahrain, and tensions were exacerbated by Qatar's persistent rejection of Bahrain's insistence that the two countries should seek joint recourse to the ICJ. Moreover, Bahrain had reportedly attempted to widen the issue to include its claim to the Zubarah region. Qatar applied unilaterally to the Court, and in February 1995 the ICJ ruled that it was competent to adjudicate in the dispute. Relations between Bahrain and Qatar deteriorated following the Bahrain Government's decision, in September, to construct a tourist resort on the Hawar islands, and remained tense subsequently, with the Bahraini Government advocating a regional solution to the dispute in preference to ICJ jurisdiction. In December 1996 Bahrain boycotted the GCC annual summit convened in Doha, Qatar, at which it was decided to establish a quadripartite committee (comprising those GCC members not involved in the dispute) to facilitate a solution. The committee reportedly made some progress, and following senior-level ministerial meetings between Bahrain and Qatar in London, United Kingdom, and in Manama in early 1997, it was announced that diplomatic relations at ambassadorial level were to be established between the two countries. Qatar, however, was alone in nominating its diplomatic representative shortly after. Regional efforts failed to find a solution to the territorial dispute, and the announcement of Bahraini construction plans on the Hawar islands (which, in addition to the opening of an hotel in mid-1997, included a housing complex and a causeway linking the islands to Bahrain) did little to further bilateral relations. Bahrain emphasized that it would disregard any ruling on the issue by the ICJ, and also dismissed as a forgery a series of documents, submitted to the ICJ by the Qatar Government, supporting the Qatari claim. In September 1998 Qatar presented a report to the ICJ in support of the legitimacy of the documents, although it subsequently agreed to withdraw them from evidence. At the end of 1999 the Amir of Qatar made his first official visit to Manama, during which it was agreed that a joint committee, headed by the Crown Princes of Bahrain and Qatar, would be established to encourage bilateral co-operation. Qatar also agreed to withdraw its petition from the ICJ in the event of the joint committee's reaching a solution to the territorial disputes. Senior-level contacts were furthered in January 2000, upon the first visit of the new Amir of Bahrain, Sheikh Hamad, to Qatar, and the two countries agreed to hasten the opening of embassies in Manama and Doha. In February, following the first meeting of the Bahrain-Qatar Supreme Joint Committee, it was announced that the possibility of constructing a causeway to link the two states was to be investigated; Qatar officially named its ambassador to Bahrain on the same day. In May, however, Bahrain unilaterally suspended the Supreme Joint Committee pending the ruling of the ICJ. Hearings by the Court began later that month and were completed by the end of June. A verdict was issued in March 2001, whereby Bahrain was found to have sovereignty over the Hawar islands and Qit'at Jaradah, while Qatar held sovereignty over Zubarah, Janan island and the low-tide elevation of Fasht ad-Dibal; the Court drew a single maritime boundary between the two states. Both Bahrain and Qatar accepted the ICJ ruling. Later in March, following a high-profile visit by Sheikh Hamad to Doha, the two sides announced that meetings of the Supreme Joint Committee would resume. In September a Danish consortium was appointed to carry out a feasibility study for the construction of the planned causeway linking Bahrain to Qatar (the Friendship Bridge), with an anticipated completion date of 2006. From early 2002 international oil companies were invited to submit bids to drill for oil and gas off the Hawar islands. Meanwhile, Sheikh Hamad renewed pledges to transform the area into a major tourist resort.

Government

A National Action Charter, drafted in late 2000 by a Supreme National Committee and approved in a national referendum held in February 2001, envisaged a transition from an emirate to a constitutional monarchy. The Amir proclaimed himself King in February 2002. Subsequently, a bicameral legislature, comprising a directly elected legislative body and an appointed consultative chamber, was instituted. Elections to a 40-member House of Representatives took place in October 2002, and a new Consultative Council, comprising 40 appointed members, was sworn in by the King in November of that year.

Defence

Military service is voluntary. In August 2002 the active Bahraini Defence Force consisted of 10,700 men (8,500 army, 1,000 navy, 1,200 air force). There were also paramilitary forces of an estimated 10,160 men (9,000 police, some 900 national guard, 260 coastguard). The defence budget for 2001 was estimated at BD 140m.

Economic Affairs

In 1999, according to estimates by the World Bank, Bahrain's gross national income (GNI), measured at average 1997–99 prices, was US $6,247m., equivalent to $9,370 per head (or $14,410 per head on an international purchasing-power parity basis). During 1990–2001, it was estimated, the population increased at an average annual rate of 3.2%, while gross domestic product (GDP) per head increased, in real terms, by an average of 2.3% per year during 1990–99. Overall GDP increased, in real terms, at an average annual rate of 4.6% per year in 1990–2000; growth in 2001 was 4.8%.

Agriculture (including hunting, forestry and fishing) engaged an estimated 1.0% of the labour force in 2001, and contributed 0.7% of GDP in that year. The principal crops are dates, tomatoes, onions and cabbages. Livestock production is also important. Agricultural GDP increased at an average annual rate of 4.6% in 1990–2000. The GDP of the sector decreased by an estimated 7.1% in 2001.

Industry (comprising mining, manufacturing, construction and utilities) engaged 28.2% of the employed labour force in 1991, and provided 38.8% of GDP in 2001. During 1990–2000 industrial GDP increased by an average of 5.4% per year. Industrial GDP increased by an estimated 4.1% in 2001.

Mining and quarrying engaged 1.7% of the employed labour force in 1991, and contributed 22.8% of GDP in 2001. The major mining activities are the exploitation of petroleum and natural gas, which in 2001 accounted for 22.5% of GDP. At the beginning of 2002 Bahrain's proven published reserves of crude petroleum were estimated to be only 100m. barrels, sufficient to maintain production (at 2001 levels) for just four years. Including production from the Abu Saafa oilfield, situated between Bahrain and Saudi Arabia, all revenues from which have since 1996 been allocated to Bahrain, production for the whole of 2000 averaged 102,000 b/d. Bahrain's reserves of natural gas at the end of 2001 were put at 90,000m. cu m, sufficient to maintain production (at 2001 levels) for 10.3 years. Mining GDP increased by an annual average of 6.4% in 1990–2000. The sector's GDP decreased by an estimated 12.0% in 2001.

In 1991 manufacturing engaged 12.6% of the employed labour force, and the sector provided 11.0% of GDP in 2001. Important industries include the petroleum refinery at Sitra, aluminium (Bahrain is the region's largest producer) and aluminium-related enterprises, shipbuilding, iron and steel, and chemicals. Since the mid-1980s the Government has encouraged the development of light industry. During 1990–2000 manufacturing GDP increased at an average annual rate of 6.1%. Manufacturing GDP increased by an estimated 4.4% in 2001.

Industrial expansion has resulted in energy demand that threatens to exceed the country's 1,126-MW total installed generating capacity, particularly as not all of the installed capacity is operational, owing to the advanced age of a number of stations. (It was reported in 2000 that energy demands were increasing by more than 5% per year.) A programme of refurbishment and expansion, which included private-sector funding, had begun by 1999. Despite these improvements, and an agreement with Aluminium Bahrain to provide an additional 275 MW annually until 2004, it was estimated that a further 560 MW would be required by 2006.

The services sector contributed 60.6% of GDP in 2001. The financial services industry, notably the operation of 'offshore' banking units (OBUs), is a major source of Bahrain's prosperity. At the end of 2002 there were 51 registered OBUs. Bahrain has developed as a principal centre for Islamic banking and other financial services. In January 2002 Bahrain became the first country to publish a full set of regulations, including requirements in terms of capital adequacy, risk management, asset quality, liquidity management and corporate governance, for its Islamic banking sector. The first International Islamic Financial Market, with a liquidity management centre and Islamic ratings agency based in Bahrain, was inaugurated in August of that year. During 1999–2000 the services sector showed an average GDP increase of 4.2% per year. The GDP of the sector increased by an estimated 2.2% in 2001.

In 2001 Bahrain recorded a visible trade surplus of US $1,536.4m., and there was a surplus of $157.2m. on the current account of the balance of payments. In 2001 the principal sources of non-petroleum imports were Australia (accounting for 10.0% of the total), Saudi Arabia (9.0%), Japan, the USA, the United Kingdom and Germany. Saudi Arabia also provided most of Bahrain's petroleum imports (and accounted for 50.8% of all imports in 1990). The USA was the principal customer for Bahrain's non-petroleum exports (24.8% of the total) in 2001; other important markets were Saudi Arabia (14.8%) and Taiwan (10.2%). The principal exports are petroleum, petroleum products and aluminium. Sales of petroleum and petroleum products provided 67.8% of total export earnings in 2001. The principal import is crude petroleum (for domestic refining), accounting for 36.6% of total imports in 2001. The main category of non-petroleum imports (18.6% in 2001) is machinery and mechanical appliances, electrical, sound and television equipment.

In 2001 there was a budgetary deficit of BD 180.3m. (equivalent to 6.0% of GDP). The average annual rate of inflation was 0.6% in 1990–2000; consumer prices decreased by an annual average of 0.7% in 2000, and by a further 1.2% in 2001. About 63% of the labour force were expatriates in 1999. The official rate of unemployment was 5.6% in late 2001, although unofficial sources estimated unemployment to be in excess of 15%.

Bahrain is a member of the Co-operation Council for the Arab States of the Gulf (Gulf Co-operation Council—GCC, see p. 175). The GCC's six members established a unified regional customs tariff in January 2003, and agreed to create a single market and currency no later than January 2010. The country is also a member of the Organization of Arab Petroleum Exporting Countries (OAPEC, see p. 292), the Arab Monetary Fund (see p. 138) and the Islamic Development Bank (see p. 257).

In recognition of the fact that Bahrain's reserves of petroleum and natural gas are nearing exhaustion, the Government has introduced measures both to diversify the country's industrial base and to attract wider foreign investment: non-petroleum exports reportedly increased by 125% between 1992 and 2001, although petroleum and related products still accounted for some two-thirds of total export earnings in the latter year.

During the 1990s the Government continued to encourage the greater participation of the private sector in economic development, and indicated that it would adopt a gradual approach to the privatization of state enterprises (excluding the petroleum sector), and would prioritize employment opportunities for Bahraini nationals. In late 2001 five committees were established by the Ministry of Labour and Social Affairs in order to tighten the regulations governing non-Bahraini employees and to create about 24,000 jobs for Bahrainis. By late 2000 only 14 state enterprises had been part-privatized, and the World Trade Organization (see p. 323), of which Bahrain is a member, urged the Government to accelerate economic liberalization by increasing private investment in the petroleum and telecommunications sectors. In April 2003 the Government ended the monopoly of the state-owned Bahrain Telecommunications Company over the rapidly expanding mobile phone services market by granting a second GSM (Global System for Mobile Communications) licence. Several important construction projects made progress in 2001, as Bahrain's economy benefited from sustained buoyancy in world petroleum markets. Among the tourism projects initiated in that year was a scheme to develop infrastructure on the Hawar islands, following the settlement of Bahrain's long-standing territorial dispute with Qatar. In May 2002 plans were announced for the US $130m. Fanar Beach tourism complex on the western side of the man-made Amwaj islands, as the first phase of real estate development covering a 2.8m. sq m plot at Ghalali, north-east of Muharraq island. Meanwhile, the dramatic recovery in international petroleum prices in 1999 improved Bahrain's economic prospects markedly, with annual GDP growth of some 5% projected for the early years of the 21st century, combined with regular budget surpluses. Despite a decline in oil prices and fears of a global economic recession in late 2001, growth was sustained in that year, and investor confidence was enhanced by moves towards political liberalization in Bahrain. GDP growth was again reported to be in the region of 5% in 2002, and was expected to continue at a similar level in 2003. In late 2002, however, intervention by the Bahrain Monetary Agency to prevent the failure of two investment banks, prompted fears that the threat of a US-led military campaign to oust the regime of Saddam Hussein in Iraq would undermine confidence in regional economies, including in Bahrain's 'offshore' banking sector.

Education

Although education is not compulsory, it is provided free of charge up to the secondary level. The education system is composed of three different stages: primary and intermediate schooling, which together form 'basic education', and secondary schooling. Primary education lasts from six to 11 years of age; it is divided into two cycles, each comprising three years. Intermediate education lasts for three years, between the ages of 12 and 14. Entry to secondary education, which comprises three years between the ages of 15 and 17, is conditional on obtaining the Intermediate School Certificate or its equivalent. Students choose to follow one of the following curriculums: general (science or literary), commercial, technical or vocational. Private and religious education are also available. The University of Bahrain, established by Amiri decree in 1986, comprises five colleges: the College of Engineering, the College of Arts, the College of Science, the College of Education and the College of Business Administration. About 9,665 students were enrolled at the University in 1999. The Arabian Gulf University (AGU), funded by seven Arab governments, also provides higher education. In 1999 it comprised two colleges: the College of Medicine and Medical Sciences and the College of Graduate Studies. The University campus is due to be completed at the end of 2006, and will accommodate 5,000 students. In 1999 569 students were enrolled at the AGU. Higher education is also provided by the College of Health Sciences, which was attended by 610 students in 1999. In 1996 enrolment at primary, intermediate and secondary levels was 97.8% (males 97.6%; females 97.9%), 96.0% (males 96.4%; females 95.5%) and 95.0% (males 90.2%; females 99.9%), respectively, of the relevant age-groups. Budget forecasts for 2001 allocated BD 93.1m. (11.3% of total government expenditure) to education.

Public Holidays

2003: 1 January (New Year's Day), 12 February* (Id al-Adha, Feast of the Sacrifice), 5 March* (Muharram, Islamic New Year), 14 March* (Ashoura), 1 May (Labour Day), 14 May*

(Mouloud, Birth of the Prophet), 26 November* (Id al-Fitr, end of Ramadan), 16 December (National Day).

2004: 1 January (New Year's Day), 2 February* (Id al-Adha, Feast of the Sacrifice), 22 February* (Muharram, Islamic New Year), 2 March* (Ashoura), 1 May (Labour Day), 2 May* (Mou-

loud, Birth of the Prophet), 14 November* (Id al-Fitr, end of Ramadan), 16 December (National Day).

*These holidays are dependent on the Islamic lunar calendar and may vary by one or two days from the dates given.

Weights and Measures

The metric system is being introduced.

Statistical Survey

Sources (unless otherwise stated): Central Statistics Organization, POB 5835, Manama; tel. 725725; fax 728989; e-mail cso@bahrain.gov.bh; Bahrain Monetary Agency, POB 27, Bldg 96, Block 317, Rd 1702, Manama; tel. 547777; fax 534170; e-mail bmalbr@batelco.com.bh; internet www.bma.gov.bh; Ministry of Finance and National Economy, POB 333, Diplomatic Area, Manama; tel. 530800; fax 532853; e-mail mofne@batelco.com.bh; internet www.mofne.gov.bh.

AREA AND POPULATION

Area (2001): 711.9 sq km (274.9 sq miles).

Population: 508,037 at census of 16 November 1991; 650,604 (males 373,649; females 276,955), comprising 405,667 Bahrainis (males 204,623; females 201,044) and 244,937 non-Bahraini nationals (males 169,026; females 75,911), at census of 7 April 2001.

Density (2001): 913.9 per sq km.

Principal Towns (estimated populations at 2001 census): Manama (capital) 135,000; Rifa'a 79,985; Muharraq Town 56,000; Hammad 52,718; Madinat Isa 36,833. Source: Thomas Brinkhoff, *City Population* (internet www.citypopulation.de).

Births, Marriages and Deaths (2000): Registered live births 13,947 (birth rate 20.2 per 1,000); Registered marriages 3,963 (marriage rate 5.7 per 1,000); Registered deaths 2,045 (death rate 3.0 per 1,000).

Expectation of Life (WHO estimates, years at birth): 72.7 (males 72.2; females 73.4) in 2001. Source: WHO, *World Health Report*.

Economically Active Population (persons aged 15 years and over, 1991 census): Agriculture, hunting, forestry and fishing 5,108; Mining and quarrying 3,638; Manufacturing 26,618; Electricity, gas and water 2,898; Construction 26,738; Trade, restaurants and hotels 29,961; Transport, storage and communications 13,789; Financing, insurance, real estate and business services 17,256; Community, social and personal services 83,944; Activities not adequately defined 2,120; *Total employed* 212,070 (males 177,154; females 34,916); Unemployed 14,378 (males 9,703; females 4,675); *Total labour force* 226,448 (males 186,857; females 39,591), comprising 90,662 Bahrainis (males 73,118; females 17,544) and 135,786 non-Bahraini nationals (males 113,739; females 22,047). *Mid-2001* (estimates): Agriculture, etc. 3,000; Total 307,000 (Source: FAO).

HEALTH AND WELFARE

Key Indicators

Total Fertility Rate (children per woman, 2001): 2.4.

Under-5 Mortality Rate (per 1,000 live births, 2001): 16.

HIV/AIDS (% of persons aged 15–49, 2001): 0.26.

Physicians (per 1,000 head, 2000): 1.53.

Hospital Beds (per 1,000 head, 2000): 2.6.

Health Expenditure (2000): US $ per head (PPP): 611.

Health Expenditure (2000): % of GDP: 4.1.

Health Expenditure (2000): public (% of total): 69.1.

Human Development Index (2000): ranking: 39.

Human Development Index (2000): value: 0.831.

For sources and definitions, see explanatory note on p. vi.

AGRICULTURE, ETC.

Principal Crops ('000 metric tons, 2001): Tomatoes 3.4; Dry onions 1.3; Other vegetables 5.6*; Lemons and limes 1.0*; Dates 16.5; Other fruits (excl. melons) 4.2*.
*FAO estimate. Source: FAO.

Livestock (FAO estimates, '000 head, year ending September 2001): Cattle 11.0; Sheep 17.5*; Goats 16.3*.
*FAO estimate. Source: FAO.

Livestock Products ('000 metric tons, 2001): Mutton and lamb 5.5*; Goat meat 1.8*; Poultry meat 5.4†; Cows' milk 14.0*; Hen eggs 3.0†.
*FAO estimate.
† Unofficial figure. Source: FAO.

Fishing (metric tons, live weight, 2000): Capture 11,718 (Groupers 670, Emperors 1,403, Porgies and seabreams 591, Spinefeet 2,114, Carangids 414, Portunus swimcrabs 2,380, Penaeus shrimps 2,104); Aquaculture 12; Total catch 11,730. Source: FAO, *Yearbook of Fishery Statistics*.

MINING

Production (estimates, 2001): Crude petroleum 13,656,000 barrels; Natural gas 9,285 million cubic metres. Source: US Geological Survey.

INDUSTRY

Production ('000 barrels, 2000, unless otherwise indicated): Liquefied petroleum gas 346; Naphtha 12,899; Motor spirit (Gasoline) 7,090; Kerosene and jet fuel 18,445; Fuel oil 21,278; Diesel oil and gas oil 32,389; Petroleum bitumen (asphalt) 1,078; Electric energy (2001) 6,779.3 million kWh; Aluminium (unwrought, 2001) 514,347 metric tons.

FINANCE

Currency and Exchange Rates: 1,000 fils = 1 Bahraini dinar (BD). *Sterling, Dollar and Euro Equivalents* (31 December 2002): £1 sterling = 606.0 fils; US $1 = 376.0 fils; €1 = 394.3 fils; 100 Bahraini dinars = £165.01 = $265.96 = €253.61. *Exchange Rate:* Fixed at US $1 = 376.0 fils (BD 1 = $2.6596) since November 1980.

Budget (BD million, 2001): *Revenue:* Taxation 215.0 (Taxes on income and profits 44.4, Social security contributions 76.5, Domestic taxes on goods and services 19.0, Import duties 57.3); Entrepreneurial and property income 716.3; Other current revenue 37.5; Capital revenue 0.5; Total 969.3, excl. grants from abroad (37.6). *Expenditure:* General public services 243.6; Defence 125.9; Public order and safety 101.3; Education 110.2; Health 64.4; Social security and welfare 62.4; Housing and community amenities 30.3; Recreational, cultural and religious affairs and services 4.4; Economic affairs and services 32.5 (Transport and communications 22.5); Interest payments 51.6; Total 826.6 (Current 653.8, Capital 172.8). *2002 (forecasts, BD million):* Revenue 675; Expenditure 835. Source: IMF, *Government Finance Statistics Yearbook*.

International Reserves (US $ million at 31 December 2002): Gold (valued at $44 per troy oz) 6.6; IMF special drawing rights 1.1; Reserve position in IMF 93.3; Foreign exchange 1,631.4; Total 1,732.4. Source: IMF, *International Financial Statistics*.

Money Supply (BD million at 31 December 2002): Currency outside banks 142.0; Demand deposits at commercial banks 505.2; Total money 647.2. Source: IMF, *International Financial Statistics*.

Cost of Living (Consumer Price Index; base: 1994–95 = 100): 102.8 in 1999; 102.1 in 2000; 100.9 in 2001.

Expenditure on the Gross Domestic Product (provisional, BD million, 2001): Government final consumption expenditure 550.62; Private final consumption expenditure 1,415.70; Increase in stocks –23.26; Gross fixed capital formation 397.72; *Total domestic expenditure* 2,340.78; Exports of goods and services 2,407.80; *Less* Imports of goods and services 1,765.10; *GDP in purchasers' values* 2,983.49.

Gross Domestic Product by Economic Activity (provisional, BD million at current prices, 2001): Agriculture, hunting, forestry and fishing 21.7; Mining and quarrying 739.9; Manufacturing 358.1; Electricity and water 42.8; Construction 119.4; Trade, restaurants and hotels 319.6; Transport, storage and communications 224.2; Finance, insurance, real estate and business services 842.7; Government services 505.7; Other community, social and personal services 77.6; *Sub-total* 3,251.6; *Less* Imputed bank service charge 325.8; *GDP at factor cost* 2,925.8; Import duties 57.6; *GDP in purchasers' values* 2,983.4.

Balance of Payments (US $ million, 2001): Exports of goods f.o.b. 5,544.7; Imports of goods f.o.b. –4,008.2; *Trade balance* 1,536.4; Exports of services 950.3; Imports of services –743.9; *Balance on goods and services* 1,742.8; Other income received 3,794.4; Other income paid –4,116.0; *Balance on goods, services and income* 1,421.3; Current transfers received 22.9; Current transfers paid –1,287.0; *Current balance* 157.2; Capital account (net) 100.0; Direct investment abroad –216.0; Direct investment from abroad 80.3; Portfolio investment assets –1,448.1; Portfolio investment liabilities –30.6; Other investment assets 5,623.4; Other investment liabilities –4,426.1; Net errors and omissions 283.3; *Overall balance* 123.5. Source: IMF, *International Financial Statistics.*

EXTERNAL TRADE

Total Trade (BD million): *Imports c.i.f.:* 1,390.3 in 1999; 1,742.2 in 2000; 1,602.8 in 2001. *Exports:* 1,556.8 in 1999; 2,144.5 in 2000; 2,084.8 in 2001. Source: IMF, *International Financial Statistics.*

Principal Commodities (BD million, 2001): *Imports c.i.f.:* Live animals and animal products 47.3; Vegetable products 55.6; Prepared foodstuffs; beverages, spirits and vinegar; tobacco and manufactured substitutes 76.6; Mineral products 66.9; Products of chemical or allied industries 146.4; Plastics, rubber and articles thereof 32.3; Textiles and textile articles 93.9; Articles of stone, plaster, cement, asbestos, mica, etc.; ceramic products; glass and glassware 33.4; Base metals and articles thereof 59.5; Machinery and mechanical appliances; electrical equipment; sound and television apparatus 189.3; Vehicles, aircraft, vessels and associated transport equipment 108.8; Miscellaneous manufactured articles 31.0; Total (incl. others) 1,015.8. *Exports f.o.b.:* Mineral products 90.8; Products of chemicals and allied industries 40.9; Textiles and textile articles 158.2; Base metals and articles of base metal 313.3; Total (incl. others) 662.2, excl. re-exports (27.8). Note: Figures exclude trade in petroleum (BD million): Imports 587.0; Exports 1,394.8.

Principal Trading Partners (BD million, 2001): *Imports c.i.f.:* Argentina 11.8; Australia 101.4; Belgium 15.6; Brazil 25.1; China, People's Repub. 51.2; France 36.2; Germany 61.4; India 40.9; Italy 33.3; Japan 84.3; Korea, Repub. 24.0; Malaysia 14.7; Netherlands 19.0; Pakistan 18.2; Saudi Arabia 91.2; Spain 12.3; Sweden 10.2; Switzerland 22.5; Thailand 13.2; United Arab Emirates 40.2; United Kingdom 64.7; USA 79.4; Total (incl. others) 1,015.8. *Exports f.o.b.:* Algeria 9.5; China, People's Repub. 12.5; India 29.1; Indonesia 19.1; Iran 17.7; Italy 21.5; Japan 22.5; Korea, Repub. 8.1; Kuwait 13.9; Malaysia 30.0; Netherlands 13.6; Oman 6.9; Qatar 24.2; Saudi Arabia 97.8; Taiwan 67.4; United Arab Emirates 21.9; USA 164.1; Total (incl. others) 662.2. Note: Figures exclude trade in petroleum.

TRANSPORT

Road Traffic (registered motor vehicles, 31 December 2000): Passenger cars 176,261; Buses and coaches 5,473; Lorries and vans 30,758; Motorcycles 2,159. *2001:* Registered vehicles 229,780.

Shipping (international sea-borne freight traffic, '000 metric tons, 1990): *Goods loaded:* Dry cargo 1,145; Petroleum products 12,140. *Goods unloaded:* Dry cargo 3,380; Petroleum products 132. (Source: UN, *Monthly Bulletin of Statistics*). *Merchant Fleet* (31 December 2001): Registered vessels 121; Total displacement 338,091 grt. (Source: Lloyd's Register-Fairplay, *World Fleet Statistics*).

Civil Aviation (1999): Kilometres flown (million) 21; Passengers carried ('000) 1,307; Passenger-km (million) 2,836; Total ton-km (million) 387. Figures include an apportionment (equivalent to one-quarter) of the traffic of Gulf Air, a multinational airline with its headquarters in Bahrain. Source: UN, *Statistical Yearbook.*

TOURISM

Tourist Arrivals (2000): 3,868,738*.

Tourist Receipts (2001): BD 130.3 million.

*Figure refers to arrivals at frontiers of visitors from abroad (excluding Bahraini nationals residing abroad).
Source: partly World Tourism Organization, *Yearbook of Tourism Statistics.*

COMMUNICATIONS MEDIA

Radio Receivers ('000 in use, 1997): 338.

Television Receivers ('000 in use, 2000): 275.

Telephones ('000 main lines in use, 2001): 173.9.

Facsimile Machines (1999): 6,928 in use.

Mobile Cellular Telephones ('000 subscribers, 2001): 299.6.

Personal Computers ('000 in use, 2001): 100.

Internet Users ('000, 2001): 140.

Book Production (1996, titles, first editions only): 40.

Daily Newspapers (1996): 4 (circulation 67,000 copies).

Non-daily Newspapers (1993): 5 (circulation 17,000 copies).

Other Periodicals (1993): 26 (circulation 73,000 copies).
Source: mainly UNESCO, *Statistical Yearbook,* and International Telecommunication Union.

EDUCATION

Pre-primary: 90 schools (1996/97); 449 teachers (1995/96); 12,308 pupils (1996/97) (Source: UNESCO, *Statistical Yearbook*).

Primary (2000/01): 62,917 pupils* (males 31,374; females 31,543).

Intermediate (2000/01): 28,972 pupils* (males 14,211; females 14,761).

General Secondary (2000/01): 11,974 pupils (males 3,941; females 8,033).

Commercial Secondary (2000/01): 7,870 pupils (males 3,622; females 4,248).

Technical Secondary (2000/01): 2,566 pupils.

Vocational Secondary (2000/01): 956 pupils.

*Figures refer to government schools only and exclude pupils of religious education.
Source: Ministry of Education.

Adult Literacy Rate (UNESCO estimates): 87.6% (males 90.9%; females 82.6%) in 2000 (Source: UN Development Programme, *Human Development Report*).

Directory

The Constitution

A 108-article Constitution was ratified in June 1973. It states that 'all citizens shall be equal before the law' and guarantees freedom of speech, of the press, of conscience and of religious beliefs. Other provisions include the outlawing of the compulsory repatriation of political refugees. The Constitution also states that the country's financial comptroller should be responsible to the legislature and not to the Government, and allows for national trade unions 'for legally justified causes and on peaceful lines'. Compulsory free primary education and free medical care are also laid down in the Constitution. The Constitution, which came into force on 6 December 1973, also provided for a National Assembly, composed of 14 members of the Cabinet and 30 members elected by popular vote, although this was dissolved in August 1975.

A National Action Charter was approved in a nation-wide referendum held on 14–15 February 2001. The Charter had been prepared by a Supreme National Committee, created by Amiri decree in late 2000 with the task of outlining the future evolution of Bahrain's political system. Principal among the Committee's recommendations were that there should be a transition from an emirate to a constitutional monarchy (the Amir proclaimed himself King on 14 February 2002), with a bicameral parliament (comprising a directly elected legislature and an appointed consultative chamber). Bahraini women were to be permitted for the first time to hold public office and to vote in elections. Direct elections to the 40-member House of Representatives took place on 24 October 2002, and the new Consultative Council (Majlis ash-Shoura), also comprising 40 members, was appointed by the King on 17 November. Members of both chambers are appointed for terms of four years. Members of the lower house are required to be Bahraini nationals of at least 30 years of age, while those of the appointed chamber—who must also be Bahraini citizens—are to be aged at least 35.

The Government

HEAD OF STATE

King: HM Sheikh HAMAD BIN ISA AL-KHALIFA (acceded as Amir 6 March 1999; proclaimed King 14 February 2002).

Crown Prince and Commander-in-Chief of Bahraini Defence Force: Sheikh SALMAN BIN HAMAD AL-KHALIFA.

CABINET
(April 2003)

Prime Minister: Sheikh KHALIFA BIN SALMAN AL-KHALIFA.

Deputy Prime Minister and Minister of Islamic Affairs: Sheikh ABDULLAH BIN KHALID AL-KHALIFA.

Deputy Prime Minister and Minister of Foreign Affairs: Sheikh MUHAMMAD BIN MUBARAK AL-KHALIFA.

Minister of the Interior: Sheikh MUHAMMAD BIN KHALIFA AL-KHALIFA.

Minister of Transport: Sheikh ALI BIN KHALIFA AL-KHALIFA.

Minister of Justice: Sheikh JAWAD BIN SALEM AL-ORAID.

Minister of the Prime Minister's Court: Sheikh KHALID BIN ABDULLAH AL-KHALIFA.

Minister of Municipalities and Agriculture: Dr MUHAMMAD ALI AS-SITRI.

Minister of Public Works and Housing: FAHMI BIN ALI AL-JOUDER.

Minister of Finance and National Economy: ABDULLAH BIN HASSAN SAIF.

Minister of Defence: Maj.-Gen. Sheikh KHALIFA BIN AHMAD AL-KHALIFA.

Minister of Cabinet Affairs: MUHAMMAD BIN IBRAHIM AL-MUTAWA.

Minister of Information: NABIL BIN YAQUB AL-HAMER.

Minister of Oil: Sheikh ISA BIN ALI AL-KHALIFA.

Minister of Commerce: ALI BIN SALEH AS-SALEH.

Minister of Industry: Dr HASSAN BIN ABDULLAH FAKHRO.

Minister of Education: Dr MAJID BIN ALI AL-NO'AIMI.

Minister of Health: Dr KHALIL BIN IBRAHIM HASSAN.

Minister of Electricity and Water: Sheikh ABDULLAH BIN SALMAN AL-KHALIFA.

Minister of Labour and Social Affairs: Dr MAJID BIN HASSAN AL-ALAWI.

Minister of Royal Court Affairs: Sheikh ALI BIN ISA AL-KHALIFA.

Ministers of State: Brig.-Gen. ABD AL-AZIZ MUHAMMAD AL-FADHIL (Consultative Council Affairs), Dr MUHAMMAD BIN ABD AL-GHAFFAR ABDULLAH (Foreign Affairs), Sheikh KHALID BIN AHMAD AL-KHALIFA (Royal Court Affairs), ABD AL-HUSSAIN BIN ALI MIRZA, ABD AN-NABI BIN ABDULLAH ASH-SHO'ALA.

MINISTRIES

Royal Court: POB 555, Riffa Palace, Manama; tel. 666666; fax 663070.

Office of the Prime Minister: POB 1000, Government House, Government Rd, Manama; tel. 253361; fax 533033.

Ministry of Cabinet Affairs: POB 26613, Manama; tel. 223366.

Ministry of Commerce: POB 5479, Diplomatic Area, Manama; tel. 531531; fax 534547; e-mail drmansoor@commerce.gov.bh; internet www.commerce.gov.bh.

Ministry of Defence: POB 245, West Rifa'a; tel. 653333; fax 663923.

Ministry of Education: POB 43, Isa Town; tel. 685558; fax 680161; e-mail info@batelco.com.bh; internet www.education.gov.bh.

Ministry of Electricity and Water: POB 2, Manama; tel. 533133; fax 533035.

Ministry of Finance and National Economy: POB 333, Diplomatic Area, Manama; tel. 530800; fax 532853; e-mail mofne@batelco.com.bh; internet www.mofne.gov.bh.

Ministry of Foreign Affairs: POB 547, Government House, Government Rd, Manama; tel. 227555; fax 212603.

Ministry of Health: POB 12, Sheikh Sulman Rd, Manama; tel. 255555; fax 252569; e-mail webmaster@health.gov.bh; internet www.moh.gov.bh.

Ministry of Industry: PO Box 1435, Manama; tel. 291511; fax 290157.

Ministry of Information: POB 572, Manama; tel. 781111; fax 682777; e-mail brtcnews@batelco.com.bh; internet www.moi.gov.bh.

Ministry of the Interior: POB 13, Police Fort Compound, Manama; tel. 272111; fax 262169.

Ministry of Islamic Affairs: POB 450, Diplomatic Area, Manama; tel. 531333; fax 536343.

Ministry of Justice: PO Box 450, Diplomatic Area, Manama; tel. 5313333; fax 536343.

Ministry of Labour and Social Affairs: POB 32333, Isa Town; tel. 687800; fax 686954; e-mail jamalq@bah-molsa.com; internet www.bah-molsa.com.

Ministry of Municipalities and Agriculture: POB 26909, Manama; tel. 293693; fax 293694.

Ministry of Oil: POB 1435, Manama; tel. 291511; fax 293007.

Ministry of Public Works and Housing: POB 5, Muharraq Causeway Rd, Manama; tel. 535222; fax 533095.

Ministry of Transport: POB 10325, Diplomatic Area, Manama; tel. 534534; fax 534041.

Legislature

The National Assembly provided for in the 1973 Constitution was dissolved in August 1975. Among the recommendations of the National Action Charter, approved in a referendum in February 2001, was that there should be a bicameral parliament, comprising a directly elected legislature and an appointed consultative chamber. Elections to a 40-member legislature (House of Representatives) were subsequently held on 24 October 2002; 21 seats were taken by independent candidates, with the remaining 19 seats taken by Islamist candidates. On 17 November a new 40-seat Consultative Council (Majlis ash-Shoura) was also established, with members appointed by the King.

Political Organizations

Political parties are still prohibited in Bahrain. However, several political and civic societies (many of which were previously in exile) are now active in the country, and a number of new groups have been established since 2001. Restrictions on campaigning by political groups were revoked prior to the elections to the new House of Representatives, held in October 2002, although the principal opposition organizations boycotted the polls.

Diplomatic Representation

EMBASSIES IN BAHRAIN

Algeria: POB 26402, Villa 579, Rd 3622, Adliya, Manama; tel. 713669; fax 713662; e-mail abdemyh@hotmail.com; Ambassador MUHAMMAD MELLOUH.

Bangladesh: POB 26718, House 2280, Rd 2757, Area 327, Adliya, Manama; tel. 714717; fax 710031; e-mail bangla@batelco.com.bh; Chargé d'affaires KHANDAKAR ABDUS SATAR.

Brunei: Manama; Chargé d'affaires Haji MULOK BIN Haji JUMAT.

China, People's Republic: POB 3150, Bldg 158, Road 382, Juffair Ave, Block 341, Manama; tel. 723800; fax 727304; Ambassador YANG HONGLIN.

Egypt: POB 818, Adliya, Manama; tel. 720005; fax 721518; e-mail jawad1eg@yahoo.com; Ambassador MAHMOUD ABD AL-JAWAD.

France: POB 11134, Road 1901, Building 51, Block 319, Diplomatic Area, Manama; tel. 291734; fax 293655; e-mail consulfr@batelco.com.bh; Ambassador ANITA LIMIDO.

Germany: POB 10306, Al-Hasan Bldg, Sheikh Hamad Causeway, Manama; tel. 530210; fax 536282; Ambassador WOLFGANG LERKE.

India: POB 26106, Bldg 182, Rd 2608, Area 326, Adliya, Manama; tel. 712785; fax 715527; e-mail indemb@batelco.com.bh; internet www.indianembassy-bah.com; Ambassador BHASKAR KUMAR MITRA.

Iran: POB 26365, Entrance 1034, Rd 3221, Area 332, Mahooz, Manama; tel. 722400; fax 722101; Ambassador MUHAMMAD FARAZMAND.

Iraq: POB 26477, Ar-Raqib Bldg, No 17, Rd 2001, Comp 320, King Faysal Ave, Manama; tel. 741472; fax 720756; Chargé d'affaires ABDULLAH AL-JABURI.

Italy: PO Box 397, Manama; tel. 252424; Ambassador ANGELO LA MARTE.

Japan: POB 23720, 55 Salmaniya Ave, Manama Tower 327, Manama; tel. 716565; fax 715059; e-mail embjap@batelco.com.bh; Ambassador ONO YASUAKI.

Jordan: POB 5242, Villa 43, Rd 915, Area 309, Hoora, Manama; tel. 291019; fax 291980; e-mail jordemb@batelco.com.bh; Ambassador LUAY MUHAMMAD ALKHASHMAN.

Kuwait: POB 786, Rd 1703, Diplomatic Area, Manama; tel. 534040; fax 530278; Ambassador JASSIM MUBARAK AL-MUBARAKI.

Lebanon: POB 32474, Manama; tel. 786994; fax 784998; Ambassador MUHAMMAD SHAKEEB AL-HAIJAR.

Libya: Manama; Chargé d'affaires EL-MEHDI SALEH EL-MEJRBI.

Morocco: POB 26229, Manama; tel. 740566; fax 740178; Ambassador ABDELKADER ZAOUI.

Oman: POB 26414, Bldg 37, Rd 1901, Diplomatic Area, Manama; tel. 293663; fax 293540; Ambassador SALIM ALI OMAR BAYAQOOB.

Pakistan: POB 563, Bldg 261, Rd 2807, Block 328, Segeiya, Manama; tel. 244113; fax 255960; e-mail parep@batelco.com.bh; Chargé d'affaires NISARULLAH BALUCH.

Philippines: POB 26681, Manama; tel. 710200; fax 710300; e-mail ambaphil_manama@hotmail.com; Ambassador RODOLFO I. DUMAPIAS.

Qatar: Manama; Ambassador Sheikh ABDULLAH BIN THAMIR ATH-THANI.

Russia: POB 26612, House 877, Rd 3119, Block 331, Zinj, Manama; tel. 725222; fax 725921; e-mail rusemb@batelco.com.bh; Ambassador VALERII VLASOV.

Saudi Arabia: POB 1085, Bldg 1450, Rd 4043, Area 340, Juffair, Manama; tel. 537722; fax 533261; Chargé d'affaires ABDULLAH BIN ABDUL AZIZ AL-ABDULKAREEM.

Sudan: POB 5438, Villa 690, Rd 1219, Block 312, Manama; tel. 252558; fax 252594; e-mail sudanimanama@hotmail.com; Ambassador SALAH ALDIN KARAR.

Syria: Manama; Chargé d'affaires MUHAMMAD SHAKAR AL-KHAYAT.

Thailand: Manama; Chargé d'affaires ATTAPONG PANTRAT.

Tunisia: POB 26911, House 54, Rd 3601, Area 336, Manama; tel. 714149; fax 715702; e-mail tunisemb@batelco.com.bh; Ambassador MUHAMMAD AOUITI.

Turkey: POB 10821, 5th Floor, Sehl Center, Bldg 81, Rd 1702, Area 317, Manama; tel. 533448; fax 536557; e-mail tcbahrbe@batelco.com.bh; Ambassador HILAL BASKAL.

Ukraine: Manama; Ambassador I. V. TYMOFYEYEV.

United Arab Emirates: POB 26505, Manama; tel. 723737; fax 727343; Ambassador SULTAN AL-QARTASI AN-NUAIMI.

United Kingdom: POB 114, 21 Government Ave, Area 306, Manama; tel. 534404; fax 536109; e-mail britemb@batelco.com.bh; internet www.ukembassy.gov.bh; Ambassador PETER FORD.

USA: POB 26431, Bldg 979, Rd 3119, Block 331, Zinj, Manama; tel. 273300; fax 272594; e-mail consularmanama@state.gov; internet www.usembassy.com.bh; Ambassador RONALD E. NEUMANN.

Yemen: POB 26193, House 1048, Rd 1730, Area 517, Saar; tel. 277072; fax 262358; Ambassador AHMAD MUHAMMAD AL-MUTAWAKL.

Judicial System

Since the termination of British legal jurisdiction in 1971, intensive work has been undertaken on the legislative requirements of Bahrain. The Criminal Law is at present contained in various Codes, Ordinances and Regulations. All nationalities are subject to the jurisdiction of the Bahraini courts, which guarantee equality before the law irrespective of nationality or creed. The 1974 Decree Law on State Security Measures and the State Security Court were both abolished in February 2001. A Constitutional Court and independent financial auditing court are both to be established.

Directorate of Courts: POB 450, Government House, Government Rd, Manama; tel. 531333.

Religion

At the November 1991 census the population was 508,037, distributed as follows: Muslims 415,427; Christians 43,237; others 49,373.

ISLAM

Muslims are divided between the Sunni and Shi'ite sects. The ruling family is Sunni, although the majority of the Muslim population (estimated at almost 60%) are Shi'ite.

CHRISTIANITY

The Anglican Communion

Within the Episcopal Church in Jerusalem and the Middle East, Bahrain forms part of the diocese of Cyprus and the Gulf. There are two Anglican churches in Bahrain: St Christopher's Cathedral in Manama and the Community Church in Awali. The congregations are entirely expatriate. The Bishop in Cyprus and the Gulf is resident in Cyprus, while the Archdeacon in the Gulf is resident in Qatar.

Provost: Very Rev. KEITH W. T. W. JOHNSON, St Christopher's Cathedral, POB 36, Al-Mutanabi Ave, Manama; tel. 253866; fax 246436; e-mail decani@batelco.com.bh; internet www.stchcathedral.org.bh.

Roman Catholic Church

A small number of adherents, mainly expatriates, form part of the Apostolic Vicariate of Arabia. The Vicar Apostolic is resident in the United Arab Emirates.

The Press

DAILIES

Akhbar al-Khaleej (Gulf News): POB 5300, Manama; tel. 620111; fax 624312; e-mail editor@akhbar-alkhaleej.com; internet www.akhbar-alkhaleej.com; f. 1976; Arabic; Chair. IBRAHIM AL-MOAYED; Chair. and Editor-in-Chief ANWAR ABD AR-RAHMAN; circ. 42,000.

Al-Ayam (The Days): POB 3232, Manama; tel. 727111; fax 729009; e-mail alayam@batelco.com.bh; internet www.alayam.com; f. 1989; Arabic; publ. by Al-Ayam Establishment for Press and Publications; Editor-in-Chief ISA ASH-SHAYGI; circ. 21,000.

Bahrain Tribune: POB 3232, Manama; tel. 827111; fax 827222; e-mail tribune@batelco.com.bh; internet www.bahraintribune.com; f. 1997; English; Editor-in-Chief JALIL OMAR; circ. 12,500.

Gulf Daily News: POB 5300, Manama; tel. 620222; fax 622141; e-mail gdnl@batelco.com.bh; internet www.gulf-daily-news.com; f. 1978; English; Chair. ANWAR ABD AR-RAHMAN; Editor-in-Chief GEORGE WILLIAMS; circ. 50,000.

Khaleej Times: POB 26707, City Centre Bldg, Suite 403, 4th Floor, Government Ave, Manama; tel. 213911; fax 211819; f. 1978; English; circ. 72,565.

WEEKLIES

Al-Adhwaa' (Lights): POB 250, Old Exhibition Rd, Manama; tel. 290942; fax 293166; f. 1965; Arabic; publ. by Arab Printing and Publishing House; Chair. RAID MAHMOUD AL-MARDI; Editor-in-Chief MUHAMMAD QASSIM SHIRAWI; circ. 7,000.

Al-Bahrain ath-Thaqafia: POB 2199, Manama; tel. 290210; fax 292678; e-mail aqaqeel@batelco.com.bh; internet www.al-thaqafia.com; Arabic; publ. by the Ministry of Information; Editor MAI BINT MUHAMMAD AL-KHALIFA.

BAPCO News: Bahrain Refinery, Sitra; tel. 755049; fax 755047; e-mail kathleen_croes@bapco.net.bh; bi-weekly; English and Arabic; publ. by the Bahrain Petroleum Co BSC; Editors KATHLEEN CROES, KHALID F. MEHMAS; circ. 4,000.

Gulf Economic Monitor: POB 224, Exhibition Ave, Manama; tel. 293131; fax 293400; e-mail hilalmag@tradearabia.net; English; publ. by Al-Hilal Publishing and Marketing Group; Man. Dir RONNIE MIDDLETON.

Huna al-Bahrain (Here is Bahrain): POB 26005, Isa Town; tel. 731888; fax 681292; f. 1957; Arabic; publ. by the Ministry of Information; Editor HAMAD AL-MANNAI; circ. 3,000.

Al-Mawakif (Attitudes): POB 1083, Manama; tel. 231231; fax 271720; f. 1973; Arabic; general interest; Editor-in-Chief MANSOOR M. RADHI; circ. 6,000.

Oil and Gas News: POB 224, Bldg 149, Exhibition Ave, Manama; tel. 293131; fax 293400; e-mail hilalmag@batelco.com.bh; f. 1983; English; publ. by Al-Hilal Publishing and Marketing Co; Editor-in-Chief CLIVE JACQUES; circ. 5,000.

Sada al-Usbou (Weekly Echo): POB 549, Manama; tel. 291234; fax 290507; f. 1969; Arabic; Owner and Editor-in-Chief ALI ABDULLAH SAYYAR; circ. 40,000 (in various Gulf states).

OTHER PERIODICALS

Arab Agriculture: POB 10131, Manama; tel. 213900; fax 211765; e-mail fanar@batelco.com.bh; f. 1984; annually; English and Arabic; publ. by Fanar Publishing WLL; Editor-in-Chief ABD AL-WAHED ALWANI; Gen. Man. FAYEK AL-ARRAYED; circ. 13,000.

Arab World Agribusiness: POB 10131, Manama; tel. 213900; fax 211765; e-mail fanar@batelco.com.bh; f. 1985; nine per year; English and Arabic; publ. by Fanar Publishing WLL; Editor-in-Chief ABD AL-WAHED ALWANI; Gen. Man. FAYEK AL-ARRAYED; circ. 16,618.

Bahrain This Month: POB 20461, Manama; tel. 244455; fax 242229; e-mail redhouse@batelco.com.bh; internet www .bahrainthismonth.com; f. 1997; monthly; English; Publ. Dir GEORGE F. MIDDLETON; Editor ROY KIETZMAN; circ. 9,948.

Discover Bahrain: POB 10704, Manama; tel. 534587; fax 531296; f. 1988; English; publ. by G. and B. Media Ltd; Publr and Editor ROBERT GRAHAM.

Gulf Construction: POB 224, Exhibition Ave, Manama; tel. 293131; fax 293400; e-mail editor@gulfconstructiononline.com; internet www.gulfconstructionworldwide.com; f. 1980; monthly; English; publ. by Al-Hilal Publishing and Marketing Group; Editor BINA PRABHU GOVEAS; circ. 12,485.

Gulf Industry: POB 224, Manama; tel. 293131; fax 293400; e-mail salvador.almeida@tradearabia.net; English; journal of industry and transport; publ. By Al-Hilal Publishing and Marketing Group; Editor SALVADOR ALMEIDA.

Gulf Panorama: POB 3232, Manama; tel. 727111; fax 727552; f. 1983; monthly; Arabic; Editor IBRAHIM BASHMI; circ. 10,000.

Al-Hayat at-Tijariya (Commerce Review): POB 248, Manama; tel. 229555; fax 224985; e-mail bahcci@batelco.com.bh; monthly; English and Arabic; publ. by Bahrain Chamber of Commerce and Industry; Editor KHALIL YOUSUF; circ. 7,500.

Al-Hidayah (Guidance): POB 450, Manama; tel. 727100; fax 729819; f. 1978; monthly; Arabic; publ. by Ministry of Justice and Islamic Affairs; Editor-in-Chief ABD AR-RAHMAN BIN MUHAMMAD RASHID AL-KHALIFA; circ. 5,000.

Middle East Expatriate: POB 224, Manama; tel. 293131; fax 292400; e-mail info@middleeastexpatonline.com; internet www .middleeastexpatonline.com; monthly; English; publ. by Al-Hilal Publishing and Marketing Group; Editor BABU KALYANPUR; circ. 16,816.

Al-Mohandis (The Engineer): POB 835, Manama; e-mail mohandis@batelco.com.bh; internet www.mohandis.org; f. 1972; quarterly; Arabic and English; publ. by Bahrain Society of Engineers; Editor ISA ALI JANAHI.

Al-Musafir al-Arabi (Arab Traveller): POB 10131, Manama; tel. 213900; fax 211765; e-mail fanar@batelco.com.bh; f. 1984; six per year; Arabic; publ. by Fanar Publishing WLL; Editor-in-Chief ABD AL-WAHED ALWANI; Gen. Man. FAYEK AL-ARRAYED.

Profile: POB 10243, Manama; tel. 291110; fax 294655; f. 1992; monthly; English; publ. by Bahrain Market Promotions; Editor ISA KHALIFA AL-KHALIFA.

Al-Quwwa (The Force): POB 245, Manama; tel. 291331; fax 659596; f. 1977; monthly; Arabic; publ. by Bahrain Defence Force; Editor-in-Chief Maj. AHMAD MAHMOUD AS-SUWAIDI.

Travel and Tourism News Middle East: POB 224, Exhibition Ave, Manama; tel. 293131; fax 293400; e-mail hilalmag@tradearabia .net; internet www.ttnonline.com; f. 1983; monthly; English; travel trade; publ. by Al-Hilal Publishing and Marketing Group; Editorial Man. KAMLESHKUMAR DESAI; circ. 6,621.

NEWS AGENCIES

Bahrain News Agency (BNA): Ministry of Information, POB 26613, Government House, Government Rd, Manama; f. 2001.

Gulf News Agency (GNA): POB 5421, Manama; tel. 689044; fax 683825; e-mail brtcnews@batelco.com.bh; internet www.gna.gov.bh; f. 1978; transmits news to the Gulf region in Arabic and English; Chief Editor KHALID ABDULLAH AZ-ZAYANI.

Foreign Bureaux

Agence France-Presse (AFP): POB 5890, Kanoo Tower, Phase 3, Tijaar Ave, Manama; tel. and fax 403446; Dir JEAN-PIERRE PERRIN.

Associated Press (AP) (USA): POB 26940, Mannai Bldg, Manama; tel. 530101; fax 530249.

Deutsche Presse-Agentur (dpa) (Germany): POB 26695, Manama; tel. 716655; fax 714119.

Reuters (United Kingdom): POB 1030, UGB Bldg, 6th Floor, Diplomatic Area, Manama; tel. 536111; fax 536192; Bureau Man. KENNETH WEST.

PRESS ASSOCIATION

Bahrain Journalists' Association (BJA): Manama; f. 2000; Chair. NABIL YAQUB AL-HAMER; 250 mems.

Publishers

Arab Communicators: POB 551, 6th Floor, Almoayyed Bldg, Government Ave, Manama; tel. 534664; fax 531837; f. 1981; publrs of annual Bahrain Business Directory; Dirs AHMAD A. FAKHRI, HAMAD A. ABUL.

Fanar Publishing WLL: POB 10131, Manama; tel. 213900; fax 211765; e-mail fanar@batelco.com.bh.

Gulf Advertising: POB 5518, Manama; tel. 226262; fax 228660; e-mail gulfad@batelco.com.bh; f. 1974; advertising and marketing communications; Chair. and Man. Dir KHAMIS AL-MUQLA.

Al-Hilal Publishing and Marketing Group: POB 224, Exhibition Ave, Manama; tel. 293131; fax 293400; e-mail hilalpmg@tradearabia .net; f. 1977; specialist magazines and newspapers of commercial interest; Chair. A. M. ABD AR-RAHMAN; Man. Dir R. MIDDLETON.

Manama Publishing Co WLL: POB 1013, Manama; tel. 213223; fax 211548.

Al-Masirah Journalism, Printing and Publishing House: POB 5981, Manama; tel. 258882; fax 276178; e-mail almasera@batelco .com.bh.

Tele-Gulf Directory Publications, WLL: POB 2738, 3rd Floor, Bahrain Tower, Manama; tel. 213301; fax 210503; e-mail telegulf@ batelco.com.bh; f. 1977; publrs of annual *Gulf Directory* and *Arab Banking and Finance.*

Government Publishing House

Directorate of Publications: POB 26005, Manama; tel. 689077; Dir MUHAMMAD AL-KHOZAI.

Broadcasting and Communications

TELECOMMUNICATIONS

Regulatory Authority

Telecommunications Regulatory Authority (TRA): POB 10353, Manama; tel. 540120; fax 532125; e-mail contact@tra.org.bh; internet www.tra.org.bh; f. 2002; Chair. and Gen. Dir Dr MUHAMMAD J. K. ALGHATAM.

Principal Operator

Bahrain Telecommunications Co BSC (BATELCO): POB 14, Manama; tel. 884557; fax 611898; e-mail batelco@btc.com.bh; internet www.batelco.com.bh; f. 1981; cap. BD 100m; 80% owned by Government of Bahrain, financial institutions and public of Bahrain, 20% by Cable and Wireless PLC (United Kingdom); launched mobile cellular telecommunications service, Sim Sim, in 1999; Chair. Sheikh ALI BIN KHALIFA BIN SALMAN AL-KHALIFA; CEO TONY HART.

BROADCASTING

Radio

Bahrain Radio and Television Corpn: POB 702, Manama; tel. 781888; fax 681544; internet www.gna.gov.bh/brtc/radio.html; f. 1955; state-owned and -operated enterprise; two 10-kW transmitters; programmes are in Arabic and English, and include news, drama and discussions; Dir of Broadcasting ABD AR-RAHMAN ABDULLAH.

Radio Bahrain: POB 702, Manama; tel. 871585; fax 780911; e-mail skhalid@bahrainradio.com; f. 1977; commercial radio station in English language; Head of Station SALAH KHALID.

Television

Bahrain Radio and Television Corpn: POB 1075, Manama; tel. 686000; fax 681544; e-mail ceobrtc@batelco.bh; internet www.gna .gov.bh/brtc/bah-tv.html; commenced colour broadcasting in 1973; broadcasts on five channels, of which the main Arabic and the main English channel accept advertising; covers Bahrain, eastern Saudi Arabia, Qatar and the UAE; an Amiri decree in early 1993 established the independence of the Corpn, which was to be controlled by a committee; Dir H. AL-UMRAN.

Finance

(cap. = capital; res = reserves; dep. = deposits; m. = millions;
brs = branches; amounts in Bahraini dinars unless otherwise stated)

BANKING

Central Bank

Bahrain Monetary Agency (BMA): POB 27, Bldg 96, Block 317, Rd 1702, Manama; tel. 547777; fax 534170; e-mail bmalbr@batelco .com.bh; internet www.bma.gov.bh; f. 1973; in operation from January 1975; controls issue of currency, regulates exchange control and credit policy, organization and control of banking and insurance systems, bank credit and stock exchange; cap. and res 290.9m., dep. 136.0m. (May 2000); Gov. Sheikh AHMAD BIN MUHAMMAD AL-KHALIFA.

Locally-incorporated Commercial Banks

Ahli United Bank BSC (AUB): Manama; e-mail info@ahliunited .com; internet www.ahliunited.com; f. 2001; by merger of Al-Ahli Commercial Bank and Commercial Bank of Bahrain; cap. US $450.0m., res US $114.3m., dep. US $3,145.2m. (Dec. 2001); Chair. FAHAD AR-RAJAAN; Gen. Man. ADEL EL-LABBAN.

Bahrain Islamic Bank BSC: POB 5240, Government Rd, Manama; tel. 535888; fax 535808; e-mail bahisl@batelco.com.bh; internet www.bahisl.com.bh; f. 1979; cap. 23.0m., res 14.1m., dep. 151.0m. (Dec. 2001); Chair. MOHD ABDULLAH AL-ZAMIL; CEO ABD AL-LATIF ABD AR-RAHIM JANAHI; 5 brs.

Bahraini Saudi Bank BSC (BSB): POB 1159, As-Saddah Bldg, Government Ave, Manama; tel. 211010; fax 210989; e-mail bsbbahr@batelco.com.bh; internet www.bahrainisaudibank.com; f. 1983; commenced operations in early 1985; licensed as a full commercial bank; cap. 20.0m., res 10.2m., dep. 181.2m. (Dec. 2001); Chair. Sheikh IBRAHIM BIN HAMAD AL-KHALIFA; Gen. Man. MANSOOR A. AS-SAYED; 5 brs.

Bank of Bahrain and Kuwait BSC (BBK): POB 597, 43 Government Ave, Manama 309; tel. 207400; fax 210636; e-mail monaa@ bbkonline.com; internet www.bbkonline.com; f. 1971; cap. 56.9m., res 35.6m., dep. 958.2m. (Dec. 2001); Chair. HASSAN KHALIFA AL-JALAHMA; Gen. Man. and CEO MURAD ALI MURAD; 20 brs.

National Bank of Bahrain BSC (NBB): POB 106, Government Ave, Manama; tel. 228800; fax 228998; e-mail nbb@nbbonline.com; internet www.nbbonline.com; f. 1957; 49% govt-owned; cap. 40.0m., res 94.1m., dep. 923.3m. (Dec. 2001); Chair. ABDULLAH ALI KANOO; Gen. Man. ABD AR-RAZAK A. HASSAN; 25 brs.

Shamil Bank of Bahrain EC (SBB): POB 3005, Chamber of Commerce Bldg, King Faysal Rd, Manama; tel. 227040; fax 224872; e-mail alshamil@shamilbank.com.bh; internet shamilbank.com.bh; f. 1982 as Massraf Faysal Al-Islami of Bahrain EC; renamed Faysal Islamic Bank of Bahrain in 1987 and as above in 2000; cap. US $100.0m., res US $15.7m., dep. US $162.0m. (Dec. 1999); Chair. MUHAMMAD AL-FAISAL AS-SAUD; CEO SAEED AL-MARTAN; 3 brs.

Foreign Commercial Banks

Arab Bank PLC (Jordan): POB 395, Government Rd, Manama; tel. 229988; fax 210443; internet www.arabbank.com; Chair. ABD AL-MAJEED SHOMAN; 4 brs.

Bank Melli Iran: POB 785, Government Rd, Manama; tel. 229910; fax 224402; e-mail bmibah@batelco.com.bh; Gen. Man. MOHAMMAD TAGHI TAVAKULI; 2 brs.

Bank Saderat Iran: POB 825, 106 Government Rd, Manama; tel. 210003; fax 210398; Man. MUHAMMAD JAVAD NASSIRI; 2 brs.

Banque du Caire, SAE (Egypt): POB 815, Government Ave, Manama; tel. 227454; fax 213704; Man. MOUSTAFA ES-SAYED ED-DOKMAWEY.

Citibank NA (USA): POB 548, Bab al-Bahrain Bldg, Government Rd, Manama; tel. 223344; fax 211323; internet www.citibank.com/ bahrain; Gen. Man. MUHAMMAD ASH-SHROOGI; 1 br.

Habib Bank Ltd (Pakistan): POB 566, Government Ave, Manama; tel. 224746; fax 224749; e-mail maziz@batelco.com.bh; f. 1941; Exec. Vice-Pres. and Gen. Man. ASHRAF BIDIWALA; 5 brs.

HSBC Bank Middle East (United Kingdom): POB 57, 93 Al-Khalifa Ave, Manama 304; tel. 224555; fax 226822; e-mail hsbcmnm@batelco.com.bh; internet www.banking.middleeast.hsbc .com; CEO SALEH AL-KOWARY; 4 brs.

Rafidain Bank (Iraq): POB 607, Heaya House Bldg, Government Rd, Manama; tel. 275796; fax 255656; f. 1969; Man. IBTISAM NAJEM ABOUD; 1 br.

Standard Chartered Bank (United Kingdom): POB 29, Government Rd, Manama; tel. 223636; fax 225001; internet www

.standardchartered.com/bh/index.html; f. in Bahrain 1920; Man. PETER RAWLINGS; 5 brs.

United Bank Ltd (Pakistan): POB 546, Government Rd, Manama; tel. 224030; fax 224099; e-mail ublbah@batelco.com.bh; Gen. Man. M. A. RAUF; 3 brs.

Specialized Financial Institutions

Bahrain Development Bank (BDB): POB 20501, Manama; tel. 537007; fax 534005; f. 1992; invests in manufacturing, agribusiness and services; cap. 10.0m., res 0.3m., dep. 0.1m. (Dec. 2001); Chair. Sheikh IBRAHIM BIN KHALIFA AL-KHALIFA; Gen. Man. NEDHAL S. AL-AUJAN.

The Housing Bank: POB 5370, Diplomatic Area, Manama; tel. 534443; fax 533437; f. 1979; provides housing loans for Bahraini citizens and finances construction of commercial properties. Chair. Sheikh KHALID BIN ABDULLAH BIN KHALID AL-KHALIFA; Gen. Man. ISA SULTAN ADH-DHAWADI.

'Offshore' Banking Units

Bahrain has been encouraging the establishment of 'offshore' banking units (OBUs) since 1975. An OBU is not permitted to provide local banking services, but is allowed to accept deposits from governments and large financial organizations in the area and make medium-term loans for local and regional capital projects. At the end of 2002 there were 51 OBUs in operation in Bahrain.

Allied Banking Corporation (Philippines): POB 20493, Bahrain Tower, 11th Floor, Govt Ave, Manama; tel. 224707; fax 210506; e-mail ally3540@batelco.com.bh; f. in Bahrain 1980; Chair. LUCIO C. TAN; Gen. Man. RAMON R. LANDINGIN.

Alubaf Arab International Bank EC: POB 11529, UGB Tower, Diplomatic Area, Manama; tel. 531212; fax 523100; f. 1982; cap. US $50.0m., res US $0.6m., dep. US $4.6m. (Dec. 2001); Chair. RASHID AZ-ZAYANI.

Arab Bank PLC (Jordan): POB 813, Manama; tel. 549000; fax 541116; e-mail cib@arabbank.com.bh; f. 1930; Senior Vice-Pres. and Man. HANI FADAYEL.

Arab Banking Corporation BSC: POB 5698, ABC Tower, Diplomatic Area, Manama; tel. 543000; fax 533062; e-mail webmaster@ arabbanking.com; internet www.arabbanking.com; f. 1980; cap. US $1,000m., res US $389m., dep. US $21,544m. (Dec. 2001); Chair. KHALIFA MOHAMED AL-KINDI; Pres. and CEO GHAZI ABD AL-JAWAD.

Arab Investment Co. S.A.A. (Saudi Arabia): POB 5559, Bldg 2309, Rd 2830, As-Seef District 428, Manama; tel. 588888; fax 588885; e-mail taicone@batelco.com.bh; Dir-Gen. Dr SALEH AL-HUMAIDAN.

Bahrain International Bank EC: POB 5016, As-Salam Tower, Government Ave, Manama; tel. 538777; fax 535141; internet www .dilmun.com; f. 1982; cap. US $182.1m., res US $14.4m., dep. US $441.5m. (Dec. 2001); Chair. and CEO FAISAL YOUSUF AL-MAR-ZOUK; Vice-Chair. SAMI SALMAN KAIKSOW.

Bank of Tokyo-Mitsubishi, Ltd. (Japan): POB 5850, Government Ave, Manama; tel. 227518; fax 225013; Regional and Gen. Man. KAN SATOH.

Banque de Commerce et de Placements (Switzerland): POB 11720, BDB Bldg, Diplomatic Area, Manama; tel. 530500; fax 532400; e-mail bcpsa@batelco.com.bh; Man. WAQAR AL-ISLAM.

Banque Française de l'Orient (France): POB 5820, Zina Complex, Tijar Rd, Manama; tel. 229995; fax 229994; Regional Man. HERMAN DOM.

BNP Paribas (France): POB 5253, UGB Bldg, 10th Floor, Diplomatic Area, Manama; tel. 531152; fax 531237; e-mail jean-christophe.durand@mideastbnpparibas.com; Regional Man. JEAN-CHRISTOPHE DURAND.

Chase Manhattan Bank N.A. (USA): POB 368, 368 Sheraton Complex, Government Ave, Manama; tel. 535388; fax 535135; Man. STEVEN J. FULLENKAMP.

Crédit Agricole Indosuez (France): POB 5410, Manama; tel. 531345; fax 531476; Reg. Man. MUHAMMAD SALEH.

Gulf International Bank BSC (GIB): POB 1017, Ad-Duwali Bldg, 3 Palace Ave, Manama 317; tel. 534000; fax 522633; e-mail info@ gibbah.com; internet www.gibonline.com; cap. US $1,000m., res US $141.9m., dep. US $12,494.7m. (Dec. 2001); Chair. Sheikh IBRAHIM BIN KHALIFA AL-KHALIFA; CEO Dr KHALID AL-FAYEZ.

Korea Exchange Bank (Repub. of Korea): POB 5767, Manama; tel. 229333; fax 225327; e-mail kebbn002@batelco.com.bh; Gen. Man. JONG-HO YOON.

Korfezbank (Turkey): POB 1937, UNITAG House, 6th Floor, Govt Ave, Manama; tel. 216161; fax 214477.

Mashreq Bank PSC (UAE): POB 20654, Manama Centre, Govt Ave, Manama; tel. 211241; fax 213516; Branch Man. ADEL AL-MANNAI.

Muslim Commercial Bank Ltd (Pakistan): POB 10164, Dipl. Area, Manama; tel. 533306; fax 533308; Gen. Man. FAQIR EIAZ ASGHER.

National Bank of Abu Dhabi (UAE): POB 5886, Manama 304; tel. 214450; fax 210086.

National Bank of Kuwait S.A.K.: POB 5290, Bahrain BMB Centre, Dipl. Area, Manama; tel. 532225; fax 530658; e-mail nbkbah@batelco.com.bh; Gen. Man. ALI Y. FARDAN.

National Commercial Bank (Saudi Arabia): POB 10363, Manama; tel. 531182; fax 530657; Man. SALEH HUSSEIN.

Pamukbank T.A.S. (Turkey): POB 11378, BDB Bldg, Dipl. Area, Manama; tel. 537711; fax 535463.

Standard Chartered Bank PLC (United Kingdom): POB 29, Manama; tel. 223636; fax 225001; CEO RUPERT KEELEY.

State Bank of India: POB 5466, Bahrain Tower, Govt Ave, Manama; tel. 224956; fax 224692; CEO ASHWINI KUMAR SHARMA.

Woori Bank (Repub. of Korea): POB 1151, Government Rd, Manama; tel. 223503; fax 224429; e-mail bahrain@wooribank.com; internet www.wooribank.com; formerly Hanvit Bank; Gen. Man. OK YOUNG KANG.

Yapi ve Kredi Bankasi A.S (Turkey): POB 10615, c/o Bahrain Development Bank, Dipl. Area, Manama; tel. 530313; fax 530311; Dir TURAN UNGOR.

Investment Banks

Al-Baraka Islamic Bank BSC (EC): POB 1882, Diplomatic Area, Manama; tel. 535300; fax 533993; e-mail baraka@batelco.com.bh; internet www.barakaonline.com; f. 1984 as Al-Baraka Islamic Investment Bank BSC (EC); current name adopted in 1998; cap. US $50.0m., res US $4.1m., dep. US $63.4m. (Dec. 2001); Chair. SALEH JAMEEL MALAIKAH; Gen. Man. SALAH AHMAD ZAINDABEDIN; 4 brs.

ANZ Investment Bank: POB 5793, 14th Floor, Al-Jasra Tower, Bldg 95, Road 1702, Block 317, Diplomatic Area, Manama; tel. 549292; fax 532319; Regional Man. GEOFFREY BIRON.

BMB Investment Bank: POB 797, BMB Centre, Diplomatic Area, Manama; tel. 532345; fax 530526; e-mail corpcom@bmb.com.bh; internet www.bmb.com.bh; formerly Bahrain Middle East Bank EC; cap. US $90.8m., res US $–47.6m., dep. US $458.2m. (Dec. 2001); Chair. Sheikh ALI JARRAH AS-SABAH; CEO ALBERT KITTANEH.

INVESTCORP Bank EC: POB 5340, Investcorp House, Diplomatic Area, Manama; tel. 532000; fax 530816; e-mail info@investcorp.com; internet www.investcorp.com; f. 1982 as Arabian Investment Banking Corpn (INVESTCORP) EC, current name adopted in 1990; cap. US $298.6m., res US $–5.6m., dep. US $669.1m. (Dec. 2001); Pres. and CEO NEMIR A. KIRDAR; Chair. ABD AR-RAHMAN SALIM AL-ATEEQI.

Nomura Investment Banking (Middle East) EC: POB 26893, 7th Floor, BMB Centre, Diplomatic Area, Manama; tel. 530531; fax 530365; f. 1982; cap. US $25m., res US $107.9m., dep. US $15.4m. (Dec. 2001); Chair. TAKUMI SHIBATA.

TAIB Bank EC: POB 20485, Sehl Centre, 81 Rd 1702, Diplomatic Area, Manama 317; tel. 533334; fax 533174; e-mail taib@taib.com; internet www.taib.com; f. 1979 as Trans-Arabian Investment Bank EC; current name adopted in 1994; cap. US $100.2m., res US $44.9m., dep. US $262.7m. (Dec. 2001); Chair. ABD AR-RAHMAN AL-JERAISY; Vice-Chair. and CEO IQBAL G. MAMDANI.

United Gulf Bank (BSC) EC: POB 5964, UGB Tower, Diplomatic Area, Manama; tel. 533233; fax 533137; e-mail ugbbah@batelco.com.bh; internet www.ugbbh.com; f. 1980; cap. US $182.9m., res US $17.7m., dep. US $443.3m. (Dec. 2001); Chair. FAISAL HAMAD M. AL-AYYAR; CEO WILLIAM KHOURI.

Other investment banks operating in Bahrain include the following: ABC Islamic Bank EC, Amex (Middle East) EC, Arab Financial Services Co EC, Bahrain Investment Bank BSC, Bahrain Islamic Investment Co BSC, Capital Union EC, Daiwa Middle East EC, Faysal Investment Bank of Bahrain EC, First Islamic Investment Bank EC, Man-Ahli Investment Bank EC, Merrill Lynch Int. Bank Ltd, Nikko Europe PLC, Okasan Int. (Middle East) EC, Turk-Gulf Merchant Bank EC.

STOCK EXCHANGE

Bahrain Stock Exchange (BSE): POB 3203, Manama; tel. 261260; fax 256362; e-mail info@bahrainstock.com; internet www.bahrainstock.com; f. 1989; 36 listed companies at Dec. 2001; linked to Muscat Securities Market (Oman) in 1995, and to Amman Financial Market (Jordan) in 1996; Dir-Gen. Sheikh AHMAD BIN MUHAMMAD AL-KHALIFA.

INSURANCE

Abdullah Yousuf Fakhro Corpn: POB 39, Government Ave, Manama; tel. 275000; fax 256999; internet www.fakhro.com; general; Man. Dir ADEL FAKHRO.

Al-Ahlia Insurance Co BSC: POB 5282, 4th Floor, Chamber of Commerce Bldg, King Faysal Rd, Manama; tel. 225860; fax 224870; e-mail alahlia@alahlia.com; internet www.alahlia.com; f. 1976; Chair. ABDULLATIF MUHAMMAD SHARIF AR-RAYES; Gen. Man. YAHYA NOORUDDIN.

Arab Insurance Group BSC (ARIG): POB 26992, Arig House, Diplomatic Area, Manama; tel. 544444; fax 531155; e-mail info@arig.com.bh; internet www.arig.com.bh; f. 1980; owned by Governments of Kuwait, Libya and the UAE (49.5%), and other shareholders; reinsurance and insurance; Chair. NASSER M. AL-NOWAIS; CEO UDO KRUEGER.

Arab International Insurance Co EC (AIIC): POB 10135, Manama; tel. 295935; fax 294059; f. 1981; non-life reinsurance; Chair. and Man. Dir Sheikh KHALID J. AS-SABAH.

Bahrain Kuwait Insurance Co BSC: POB 10166, Diplomatic Area, Manama; tel. 542222; fax 530799; e-mail bkicbah@batelco.com.bh; internet www.bkic.com; f. 1975; CEO A. HAMEED AN-NASSER; Gen. Man. SAMEER E. AL-WAZZAN.

Bahrain National Insurance (BNI): POB 843, Manama; tel. 227800; fax 224385; e-mail gm@bnigroup.com; internet www.bnigroup.com; f. 1998; by merger of Bahrain Insurance Co and National Insurance Co; all classes including life insurance; Chair. QASSIM MUHAMMAD FAKHRO; Gen. Man. PATRICK IRWIN.

Gulf Union Insurance and Reinsurance Co: POB 10949, Ground Floor, Manama Centre, Manama; tel. 215622; fax 215421; e-mail guirco@batelco.com.bh; internet www.gulfunion-bah.com; Chair. Sheikh IBRAHIM BIN HAMAD AL-KHALIFA.

Trade and Industry

GOVERNMENT AGENCIES

Economic Development Board (EDB): POB 11299, Manama; tel. 583311; fax 583322; e-mail edb@bahrainedb.com; internet www.bahrainedb.com; f. 2000; assumed duties of Bahrain Promotions and Marketing Board (f. 1993) and Supreme Council for Economic Development (f. 2000) in 2001; provides national focus for Bahraini marketing initiatives; attracts inward investment; encourages development and expansion of Bahraini exports; Chair. Sheikh SALMAN BIN HAMAD AL-KHALIFA; CEO JAMAL ALI AL-HAZEEM.

Supreme Oil Council: Manama; formulates Bahrain's petroleum policy; Chair. (vacant) (Prime Minister).

CHAMBER OF COMMERCE

Bahrain Chamber of Commerce and Industry: POB 248, Manama; tel. 229555; fax 224985; e-mail bahcci@batelco.com.bh; f. 1939; 7,300 mems (1996); Chair. KHALID MUHAMMAD KANOO; Sec.-Gen. JASSIM MUHAMMAD ASH-SHATTI.

STATE HYDROCARBONS COMPANIES

Bahrain National Gas Co BSC (BANAGAS): POB 29099, Rifa'a; tel. 756222; fax 756991; e-mail bng@banagas.com.bh; internet www.banagas.com.bh; f. 1979; responsible for extraction, processing and sale of hydrocarbon liquids from associated gas derived from onshore Bahraini fields; ownership is 75% Government of Bahrain, 12.5% Caltex and 12.5% Arab Petroleum Investments Corpn (APICORP); produced 202,955 metric tons of LPG and 189,803 tons of naphtha in 1996; Chair. Sheikh HAMAD BIN IBRAHIM AL-KHALIFA; Gen. Man. Dr Sheikh MUHAMMAD BIN KHALIFA AL-KHALIFA.

Bahrain Petroleum Co BSC (BAPCO): POB 25555, Awali; tel. 704040; fax 704070; e-mail info@bapco.net; f. 2000 by merger of Bahrain National Oil Co (f. 1976) and Bahrain Petroleum Co (f. 1980); fully integrated co responsible for exploration, drilling and production of oil and gas; supply of gas to power-generating plants and industries, refining crude oil, international marketing of crude oil and refined petroleum products, supply and sale of aviation fuel at Bahrain International Airport, and local distribution and marketing of petroleum products; Pres. and Man. Dir MUHAMMAD SALEH SHEIKH ALI; CEO JOHANN LUBBE.

Gulf Petrochemical Industries Co BSC (GPIC): POB 26730, Sitra; tel. 731777; fax 731047; f. 1979 as a joint venture between the Governments of Bahrain, Kuwait and Saudi Arabia, each with one-third equity participation; a petrochemical complex at Sitra, inaugurated in 1981; produces 1,200 metric tons of both methanol and ammonia per day (1990); Chair. Sheikh ISA BIN ALI AL-KHALIFA; Gen. Man. MUSTAFA AS-SAYED.

UTILITIES

Ministry of Electricity and Water: see Ministries, above; provides electricity and water throughout Bahrain.

Electricity

Directorate of Electricity: POB 2, King Faysal Rd, Manama; tel. 533133; supplies domestic and industrial power and street lighting.

Water

Directorate of Water Supply: POB 326, Manama; tel. 727009; responsible for water supply to all areas except Awali.

TRADE UNIONS

There are currently no trade unions in Bahrain. However, in September 2002 legislation was enacted to permit the establishment of independent trade unions.

Transport

RAILWAYS

There are no railways in Bahrain.

ROADS

In 2000 Bahrain had 3,261 km of roads, including 421 km of highways, main or national roads, 410 km of secondary or regional roads and 1,650 km of other roads; about 78% of roads were paved. A modern network of dual highways is being developed, and a 25-km causeway link with Saudi Arabia was opened in 1986. A three-lane dual carriageway links the causeway to Manama. Other causeways link Bahrain with Muharraq island and with Sitra island. In March 1997 the Government approved the construction of the Sheikh Khalifa bin Sulman Causeway, linking Hidd on Muharraq island with the port of Mina Salman; the new causeway was scheduled to be completed in 2003. A second, 2.5-km Manama-to-Muharraq causeway was opened in early 1997. It is planned to construct a causeway (the Friendship Bridge) linking eastern Bahrain with Qatar by 2006.

Directorate of Roads: POB 5, Manama; tel. 545555; fax 532565; responsible for traffic engineering and planning, traffic control and safety, bridges, road design, maintenance and construction supervision; Dir WALEED Y. AS-SAIE.

SHIPPING

Numerous shipping services link Bahrain and the Gulf with Europe, the USA, Pakistan, India, the Far East and Australia.

The deep-water harbour of Mina Salman was opened in 1962; it has 13 conventional berths, two container terminals (one of which has a 400-m quay—permitting two 180-m container ships to be handled simultaneously) and a roll-on roll-off berth. Two nearby slipways can accommodate vessels of up to 1,016 tons and 73 m in length, and services are available for ship repairs afloat. During 2000 906 vessels called at Mina Salman, and in that year the port handled 1,954,396 tons of cargo.

By 1999 work had begun on the construction of a new port and industrial zone at Hidd, on Muharraq island. The port, Mina Khalifa bin Salman, which is scheduled to become operational in 2005 (at an estimated cost of US $330m.), is to have an annual handling capacity of 234,000 TEUs and to include a general cargo berth and two container berths with roll-on roll-off facilities.

Directorate of Customs and Ports: (Customs) POB 15, Manama; (Ports) POB 453, Manama; tel. 725333; fax 727556; e-mail customs@batelco.com.bh; internet www.bahraincustoms.com.bh; tel. 725555; fax 725534; internet www.bahrainports.com.bh; responsible for customs activities and acts as port authority; Pres. of Customs and Ports EID ABDULLAH YOUSUF; Dir-Gen. of Ports Capt. MAHMOOD Y. AL-MAHMOOD; Dir-Gen. of Customs JASSIM JAMSHEER.

Arab Shipbuilding and Repair Yard Co (ASRY): POB 50110, Hidd; tel. 671111; fax 670236; e-mail asryco@batelco.com.bh; internet www.asry.net; f. 1974 by OAPEC members; 500,000-ton dry dock opened 1977; two floating docks in operation since 1992; repaired 104 ships in 2001; Chair. EID ABDULLAH YOUSUF; CEO MUHAMMAD M. AL-KHATEEB.

Principal Shipping Agents

Bahrain Enterprises Co Ltd: POB 2661, Manama; tel. 731224.

Dilmun Shipping Co Ltd E.C.: POB 11664, Manama; tel. 534530; fax 531287; e-mail dilmunbh@batelco.com.bh; Chair. Capt. PHILIP G. CARR.

The Gulf Agency Co (Bahrain) WLL: POB 412, Manama; tel. 827927; fax 827928; e-mail bahrain.ops@gulfagencycompany.com; internet www.gacbahrain.com; f. 1957; Man. Dir Capt. BJORN SVANHOLM.

Al-Jazeera Shipping Co WLL: POB 302, Manama; tel. 728837; fax 728217; Dir ALI HASSAN MAHMOUD.

Abdullah Ahmad Nass: POB 669, Manama; tel. 254856.

Ash-Sharif Group: POB 1322, Manama; tel. 530535; fax 537637; e-mail general@bahragents.com; Dirs ALI ABD AR-RASOOL ASH-SHARIF, KHALID ABD AR-RASOOL ASH-SHARIF.

UCO Marine Contracting WLL: POB 1074, Manama; tel. 5730816; fax 5732131; e-mail ucomarin@batelco.com.bh; Man. Dirs BADER A. KAIKSOW, HASSAN AS-SABAH, ALI AL-MUSALAM.

Yusuf bin Ahmad Kanoo: POB 45, Al-Khalifa Ave, Manama; tel. 220800; fax 229122; e-mail kanoomgt@batelco.com.bh; air and shipping cargo services, commercial and holiday services; Chair. and CEO ABDULLAH ALI KANOO.

CIVIL AVIATION

Bahrain International Airport (BIA) has a first-class runway, capable of taking the largest aircraft in use. In 2000 there were 60,072 flights to and from the airport, and some 3.9m. passengers were carried. Extension work to the airport's main terminal building was undertaken during the 1990s, in order to increase the airport's cargo-handling facilities. Construction of a new terminal is planned, to give BIA an annual passenger capacity of 8m. by 2005.

Department of Civil Aviation Affairs: POB 586, Bahrain International Airport, Muharraq; tel. 321000; fax 325757; e-mail caainfo@bahrainairport.com; internet www.bahrainairport.com; Under-Sec. IBRAHIM ABDULLAH AL-HAMER.

Gulf Air Co GSC (Gulf Air): POB 138, Manama; tel. 322200; fax 338033; e-mail gfpr@batelco.com.bh; internet www.gulfairco.com; f. 1950; jointly owned by Govts of Bahrain, Oman and Abu Dhabi (part of the United Arab Emirates) since 1974; services to the Middle East, South-East Asia, the Far East, Australia, Africa and Europe; Chair. Sheikh HAMDAN BIN MUBARAK AN-NAHYAN (UAE); Pres. and CEO JAMES HOGAN.

Tourism

There are several archaeological sites of importance in Bahrain, which is the site of the ancient trading civilization of Dilmun. There is a wide selection of hotels and restaurants, and a new national museum opened in 1989. The Government is currently promoting Bahrain as a destination for sports and leisure activities. In 2000 Bahrain received 3.9m. foreign visitors (excluding Bahraini nationals residing abroad). Income from tourism totalled BD 130.3m. in 2001.

Bahrain Tourism Co (BTC): POB 5831, Manama; tel. 530530; fax 530867; e-mail btc@alseyaha.com; internet www.alseyaha.com; Chair. MUHAMMAD YOUSUF JALAL.

Tourism Affairs: Ministry of Information, POB 26613, Manama; tel. 201203; fax 229787; e-mail btour@bahraintourism.com; internet www.bahraintourism.com; Asst Under-Sec. for Tourism Dr KADHIM RAJAB.

BANGLADESH

Introductory Survey

Location, Climate, Language, Religion, Flag, Capital

The People's Republic of Bangladesh lies in southern Asia, surrounded by Indian territory except for a short south-eastern frontier with Myanmar (formerly Burma) and a southern coast fronting the Bay of Bengal. The country has a tropical monsoon climate and suffers from periodic cyclones. The average temperature is 19°C (67°F) from October to March, rising to 29°C (84°F) between May and September. The average annual rainfall in Dhaka is 188 cm (74 ins), of which about three-quarters occurs between June and September. About 95% of the population speak Bengali, the state language, while the remainder mostly use tribal dialects. More than 85% of the people are Muslims, Islam being the state religion, and there are small minorities of Hindus, Buddhists and Christians. The national flag (proportions 3 by 5) is dark green, with a red disc slightly off-centre towards the hoist. The capital is Dhaka (Dacca).

Recent History

Present-day Bangladesh was formerly East Pakistan, one of the five provinces into which Pakistan was divided at its initial creation, when Britain's former Indian Empire was partitioned in August 1947. East Pakistan and the four western provinces were separated by about 1,000 miles (1,600 km) of Indian territory. East Pakistan was created from the former Indian province of East Bengal and the Sylhet district of Assam. Although the East was more populous, government was based in West Pakistan. Dissatisfaction in East Pakistan at its dependence on a remote central government flared up in 1952, when Urdu was declared Pakistan's official language. Bengali, the main language of East Pakistan, was finally admitted as the joint official language in 1954, and in 1955 Pakistan was reorganized into two wings, east and west, with equal representation in the central legislative assembly. However, discontent continued in the eastern wing, particularly as the region was under-represented in the administration and armed forces, and received a disproportionately small share of Pakistan's development expenditure. The leading political party in East Pakistan was the Awami League (AL), led by Sheikh Mujibur (Mujib) Rahman, who demanded autonomy for the East. A general election in December 1970 gave the AL an overwhelming victory in the East, and thus a majority in Pakistan's National Assembly. Sheikh Mujib should therefore have been appointed Prime Minister, but Pakistan's President, Gen. Yahya Khan, would not accept this, and negotiations on a possible constitutional compromise broke down. The convening of the new National Assembly was postponed indefinitely in March 1971, leading to violent protests in East Pakistan. The AL decided that the province should unilaterally secede from Pakistan, and on 26 March Sheikh Mujib proclaimed the independence of the People's Republic of Bangladesh ('Bengal Nation').

Civil war immediately broke out. President Yahya Khan outlawed the AL and arrested its leaders. By April 1971 the Pakistan army dominated the eastern province. In August Sheikh Mujib was secretly put on trial in West Pakistan. Resistance continued, however, from the Liberation Army of East Bengal (the Mukhti Bahini), who launched a major offensive in November. As a result of the conflict, an estimated 9.5m. refugees crossed into India. On 4 December India declared war on Pakistan, with Indian forces intervening in support of the Mukhti Bahini. Pakistan surrendered on 16 December, and Bangladesh became independent. Pakistan was thus confined to its former western wing. In January 1972 Sheikh Mujib was freed by Pakistan's new President, Zulfiqar Ali Bhutto, and became Prime Minister of Bangladesh. Under a provisional Constitution, Bangladesh was declared to be a secular state and a parliamentary democracy. The new nation quickly achieved international recognition, causing Pakistan to withdraw from the Commonwealth in January 1972. Bangladesh joined the Commonwealth in April. The members who had been elected from the former East Pakistan for the Pakistan National Assembly and the Provincial Assembly in December 1970 formed the Bangladesh Constituent Assembly. A new Constitution was approved by this Assembly in November 1972 and

came into effect in December. A general election for the country's first Jatiya Sangsad (Parliament) was held in March 1973. The AL received 73% of the total votes and won 292 of the 300 directly elective seats in the legislature. Bangladesh was finally recognized by Pakistan in February 1974. Internal stability, however, was threatened by opposition groups which resorted to terrorism and included extremists such as Islamist fundamentalists and Maoists. In December a state of emergency was declared and constitutional rights were suspended. In January 1975 parliamentary government was replaced by a presidential form of government. Sheikh Mujib became President, assuming absolute power, and created the Bangladesh Peasants' and Workers' Awami League. In February Bangladesh became a one-party state.

In August 1975 Sheikh Mujib and his family were assassinated in a right-wing coup, led by a group of Islamist army officers. Khandakar Mushtaq Ahmed, the former Minister of Commerce, was installed as President; martial law was declared, and political parties were banned. A counter-coup on 3 November brought to power Brig. Khalid Musharaf, the pro-Indian commander of the Dhaka garrison, who was appointed Chief of Army Staff; on 7 November a third coup overthrew Brig. Musharaf's brief regime, and power was assumed jointly by the three service chiefs, under a non-political President, Abusadet Mohammed Sayem, the Chief Justice of the Supreme Court. A neutral non-party Government was formed, in which the reinstated Chief of Army Staff, Major-Gen. Ziaur Rahman (Gen. Zia), took precedence over his colleagues. Political parties were legalized again in July 1976.

An early return to representative government was promised, but in November 1976 elections were postponed indefinitely and, in a major shift of power, Gen. Zia took over the role of Chief Martial Law Administrator from President Sayem, assuming the presidency also in April 1977. He amended the Constitution, making Islam, instead of secularism, its first basic principle. In a national referendum held in May 99% of voters affirmed their confidence in President Zia's policies, and in June 1978 the country's first direct presidential election resulted in a clear victory for Zia, who formed a Council of Ministers to replace his Council of Advisers. Parliamentary elections followed in February 1979: in an attempt to persuade opposition parties to participate in the elections, Zia met some of their demands by repealing 'all undemocratic provisions' of the 1974 constitutional amendment, releasing political prisoners and withdrawing press censorship. Consequently, 29 parties contested the elections, in which Zia's Bangladesh Nationalist Party (BNP) received 49% of the total votes and won 207 of the 300 contested seats in the Jatiya Sangsad. In April 1979 a new Prime Minister was appointed, and martial law was repealed. The state of emergency was revoked in November.

Political instability recurred, however, when Gen. Zia was assassinated on 30 May 1981 during an attempted military coup, allegedly led by Maj.-Gen. Mohammad Abdul Manzur, an army divisional commander who was himself later killed in unclear circumstances. The Vice-President, Justice Abdus Sattar, assumed the role of acting President, but was confronted by strikes and demonstrations in protest against the execution of several officers who had been involved in the coup, and by pressure from opposition parties to reschedule the date of the presidential election. As the only person acceptable to the different groups within the BNP, Sattar was none the less nominated as the party's presidential candidate, and secured an overwhelming victory at the November election. President Sattar announced his intention of continuing the policies of the late Gen. Zia. He found it increasingly difficult, however, to retain civilian control over the country, and in January 1982 formed a National Security Council, which included military personnel, led by the Chief of Army Staff, Lt-Gen. Hossain Mohammad Ershad. On 24 March Gen. Ershad seized power in a bloodless coup, claiming that political corruption and economic mismanagement had become intolerable. The country was placed under martial law, with Ershad as Chief Martial Law Administrator (redesignated Prime Minister in October), aided by a mainly military Council of Advisers. Ershad nominated a retired judge, Justice Abul Chowdhury, as President. Political activities were banned, and several former ministers were later tried and imprisoned on charges of corruption.

Although the Government's economic policies achieved some success and gained a measure of popular support for Ershad, there were increasing demands in 1983 for a return to democratic government. The two principal opposition groups that emerged were an eight-party alliance headed by the AL under Sheikh Hasina Wajed (daughter of the late Sheikh Mujib), and a seven-party group led by the BNP under former President Sattar (who died in 1985) and Begum Khaleda Zia (widow of Gen. Zia). In September 1983 the two groups formed an alliance, the Movement for the Restoration of Democracy (MRD), and jointly issued demands for an end to martial law, for the release of political prisoners and for the holding of parliamentary elections before any other polls. In November the resumption of political activity was permitted, and it was announced that a series of local elections between December 1983 and March 1984 were to precede a presidential election and parliamentary elections later in the year. A new political party, the Jana Dal (People's Party), was formed in November 1983 to support Ershad as a presidential candidate. Following demonstrations demanding civilian government, the ban on political activity was reimposed at the beginning of December, only two weeks after it had been rescinded, and leading political figures were detained. On 11 December Ershad declared himself President.

Strikes and political demonstrations occurred frequently during 1984. Local elections, planned for March, were postponed, as the opposition objected to their taking place prior to the presidential and parliamentary elections, on the grounds that Ershad was trying to strengthen his power-base. The presidential and parliamentary elections, scheduled for May, were also postponed until December, in response to persistent opposition demands for the repeal of martial law and for the formation of an interim neutral government to oversee a fair election. In October an offer by Ershad to repeal martial law if the opposition would participate in the elections was met with an appeal for a campaign of civil disobedience, which led to the indefinite postponement of the elections.

In January 1985 it was announced that parliamentary elections would be held in April, to be preceded by a partial relaxation of martial law: the Constitution was to be fully restored after the elections. The announcement was followed by the formation of a new Council of Ministers, composed entirely of military officers and excluding all members of the Jana Dal, in response to demands by the opposition parties for a neutral government during the pre-election period. Once more, the opposition threatened to boycott the elections, as President Ershad would not relinquish power to an interim government, and in March the elections were abandoned and political activity was again banned. This was immediately followed by a referendum, held in support of the presidency, in which Ershad reportedly received 94% of the total votes. Local elections were held in May, without the participation of the opposition, following which Ershad claimed that 85% of the elected council chairmen were his supporters, although not necessarily of his party. In September a new five-party political alliance, the National Front (comprising the Jana Dal, the United People's Party, the Gonotantrik Party, the Bangladesh Muslim League and a breakaway section of the BNP), was established to promote government policies.

In January 1986 the 10-month ban on political activity was ended. The five components of the National Front formally became a single pro-Government entity, named the Jatiya Dal (National Party). In March President Ershad announced that parliamentary elections were to be held (under martial law) at the end of April. He relaxed martial law, however, by removing all army commanders from important civil posts and by abolishing more than 150 military courts and the martial law offices. These concessions fulfilled some of the opposition's demands, and candidates from the AL alliance (including Sheikh Hasina Wajed herself), the Jamaat-e-Islami Bangladesh and other smaller opposition parties thus participated in the parliamentary elections—which eventually proceeded in May. However, the BNP alliance, led by Begum Khaleda Zia, boycotted the polls, which were characterized by allegations of extensive fraud, violence and intimidation. The Jatiya Dal won 153 of the 300 directly elective seats in the Jatiya Sangsad. In addition, 30 seats reserved for women were filled by nominees of the Jatiya Dal. In July a mainly civilian Council of Ministers was sworn in.

Mizanur Rahman Chowdhury, former General Secretary of the Jatiya Dal, was appointed Prime Minister.

In order to be eligible to stand as a candidate in the forthcoming presidential election, Ershad retired as Chief of Army Staff in August 1986, while remaining Chief Martial Law Administrator and Commander-in-Chief of the Armed Forces. In early September Ershad officially joined the Jatiya Dal, whereupon he was elected as Chairman of the party and nominated as its presidential candidate. The presidential election, held in October, was boycotted by both the BNP and the AL, and resulted in an overwhelming victory for Ershad over his 11 opponents.

In November 1986 the Jatiya Sangsad approved indemnity legislation, effectively legitimizing the military regime's actions since March 1982. Ershad repealed martial law and restored the 1972 Constitution. The opposition alliances criticized the indemnity law, stating that they would continue to campaign for the dissolution of the Jatiya Sangsad and the overthrow of the Ershad Government. In December 1986, in an attempt to curb increasing dissent, President Ershad formed a new Council of Ministers, including four AL members of the legislature. The Minister of Justice, Justice A. K. M. Nurul Islam, was appointed Vice-President.

Opposition groups continued to organize anti-Government strikes and demonstrations during 1987, often with the support of trade unions and student groups. In July the Jatiya Sangsad approved a bill enabling army representatives to participate alongside elected representatives in the district councils. The adoption of this controversial legislation provoked widespread and often violent strikes and demonstrations, organized by the opposition groups, which perceived the measure as an attempt by the President to entrench military involvement in the governing of the country despite the ending of martial law in November 1986. Owing to the intensity of public opposition, President Ershad was forced to withdraw the legislation in August 1987 and return it to the Jatiya Sangsad for reconsideration. Political events were subsequently overshadowed somewhat by the widespread devastation caused in August and September by the most severe floods in the region for 40 years. In November, in a renewed effort to oust President Ershad, opposition groups combined forces and organized further protests. Thousands of activists were detained, but demonstrations and strikes continued, leading to numerous clashes between police units and protesters and causing considerable economic disruption. In an attempt to forestall another general strike, President Ershad declared a nation-wide state of emergency on 27 November, suspending political activity and civil rights and banning all anti-Government protests. Disturbances persisted, despite the imposition of curfews on the main towns. In December, as about 6,000 activists remained in detention, opposition parties in the Jatiya Sangsad announced that their representatives intended to resign their seats. After 12 opposition members had withdrawn and the 73 AL members had agreed to do likewise, President Ershad dissolved the Jatiya Sangsad. In January 1988 the President announced that parliamentary elections would be held on 28 February, but leaders of the main opposition parties declared their intention to boycott the proposed poll while Ershad remained in office. Local elections, held throughout Bangladesh in February, were not boycotted by the opposition but were marred by serious outbreaks of violence. The parliamentary elections (postponed until 3 March) were also characterized by widespread violence, as well as by alleged fraud and malpractice. The opposition's appeal for a boycott of the polls was widely heeded, with the actual level of participation by the electorate appearing to have been considerably lower than the Government's estimate of 50%. As expected, the Jatiya Dal won a large majority of the seats.

A radical reshuffle of the Council of Ministers later in March 1988 included the appointment of a new Prime Minister, Moudud Ahmed, a long-time political ally of Ershad and hitherto the Minister of Industry and a Deputy Prime Minister, in place of Mizanur Rahman Chowdhury. In response to an abatement in the opposition's anti-Government campaign, Ershad repealed the state of emergency in April. Despite strong condemnation by the political opposition and sections of the public, a constitutional amendment establishing Islam as Bangladesh's state religion was approved by an overall majority in the Jatiya Sangsad in June. By early September, however, political events had been completely overshadowed by new monsoon floods, which began in August and proved to be the most severe in the area's recorded history. Bangladesh suffered further flooding in

December 1988 and January 1989, following a devastating cyclone in late November. At the end of 1988 the Government established a national Disaster Prevention Council.

In July 1989 the Jatiya Sangsad approved legislation limiting the tenure of the presidency to two electoral terms of five years each and creating the post of a directly elected Vice-President (an appointment hitherto in the gift of the President). In August Ershad appointed Moudud Ahmed as Vice-President to replace Justice A. K. M. Nurul Islam, who was dismissed following charges of inefficiency. Kazi Zafar Ahmed, formerly the Minister of Information and a Deputy Prime Minister, was in turn promoted to the post of Prime Minister. Local elections held in March 1990 were officially boycotted by the opposition parties, although many members participated on an individual basis. In April Ershad announced that he would present himself as a candidate in the presidential election, which was scheduled for mid-1991.

Opposition groups, with the support of thousands of students, co-operated to intensify their anti-Government campaign in late 1990. In October at least eight demonstrators were shot dead by riot police, more than 500 people were arrested, and Ershad announced the closure of Dhaka University and other educational institutions. Violent incidents also occurred in Chittagong and in several other towns in southern and central Bangladesh. On 27 November President Ershad proclaimed a nation-wide state of emergency for the second time in three years, suspending civil rights, imposing strict press censorship and enforcing an indefinite curfew throughout the country. On the following day, however, army units were summoned to impose order in the capital as thousands of protesters defied the curfew and attacked police. The death toll in resultant clashes between the troops and demonstrators was variously estimated at between 20 and 70. Under increasing pressure from the opposition groups, Ershad resigned on 4 December and declared that parliamentary elections would be held before the presidential election; the state of emergency was revoked, and the Jatiya Sangsad was dissolved. Following his nomination by the opposition, Justice Shahabuddin Ahmed, the Chief Justice of the Supreme Court, was appointed Vice-President. He assumed the responsibilities of acting President and was appointed to lead a neutral interim Government pending fresh parliamentary elections. Shahabuddin Ahmed undertook a comprehensive reorganization of personnel in financial institutions, local government and the civil service in an effort to remove Ershad's appointees from important posts. The opposition parties welcomed these developments and abandoned their protest campaigns. They also demanded that Ershad be tried for alleged corruption and abuse of power. Ershad was placed under house arrest, and was later sentenced to 20 years' imprisonment for illegal possession of firearms and other offences. (In June 1995 the former President was acquitted of illegally possessing firearms, and his sentence was halved. In the following month, however, Ershad was sentenced to a further three years' imprisonment for criminal misconduct.)

The BNP alliance won an overall majority at parliamentary elections held in February 1991. Following discussions with the Jamaat-e-Islami, as a result of which the BNP was ensured a small working majority in the Jatiya Sangsad, Begum Khaleda Zia assumed office as Prime Minister. In May the Government was faced with the immense problems created by a devastating cyclone, which caused the deaths of as many as 250,000 people and wrought massive economic damage. In August the Jatiya Sangsad approved a constitutional amendment ending 16 years of presidential rule and restoring the Prime Minister as executive leader (under the previous system, both the Prime Minister and the Council of Ministers had been responsible to the President). The amendment, which was approved by national referendum in the following month, reduced the role of the President, who was now to be elected by the Jatiya Sangsad for a five-year term, to that of a titular Head of State. Accordingly, a new President was elected by the Jatiya Sangsad in October. The successful candidate was the BNP nominee, former Speaker of the Jatiya Sangsad Abdur Rahman Biswas. In September the BNP had secured an absolute majority in the Jatiya Sangsad as a result of the party's success in a number of by-elections. In November, despite strong protest from the opposition parties, the Government abolished the *upazilla* (sub-district) system of rural administration, introduced by Ershad in 1982. Henceforth, all public functions at *upazilla* level were to be performed through executive orders of the central Government, pending the introduction of a new system of rural administration. To this end, the

Government established a special committee to review all aspects of local government.

In early 1992 measures to transfer public-sector industries to private ownership and to curb endemic labour unrest led to strong political resistance from the opposition. In April, in an apparent attempt to destabilize the Government, accusations were made against the leader of the Jamaat-e-Islami, Golam Azam, of complicity in Pakistani war crimes in 1971 and of having remained a Pakistani citizen while participating in Bangladesh politics. AL representatives boycotted the Jatiya Sangsad over the issue, demanding that Azam be tried immediately by a special tribunal. A compromise was reached in June 1992 whereby charges were to be brought against Azam, but only through the highly dilatory regular courts. In August the Government defeated a parliamentary motion of 'no confidence' introduced by the AL. The opposition accused the Government of failing to curb the increasing lawlessness in the country, notably amongst university students. Anti-terrorism measures introduced in November were, however, widely criticized as being excessively harsh and undemocratic. Subsequently, the opposition parties sank their differences in pursuit of a common demand that the general election due in 1996 be held under the auspices of a neutral, caretaker government.

From late 1993 and into 1994 mass anti-Government demonstrations were organized by the opposition, which initiated a boycott of parliamentary proceedings in February 1994. In January the AL had won the mayoralties of Dhaka and Chittagong, but a by-election success in March revealed the continuing strength of the BNP elsewhere. The number of strikes and violent protests staged by the opposition multiplied in the latter half of 1994, and culminated in the resignation of all the opposition members from the Jatiya Sangsad in December. In spite of the political chaos, compounded by the holding of further general strikes by the opposition, the Prime Minister pledged to use her party's parliamentary majority to maintain constitutional government.

The opposition co-ordinated further nation-wide strikes in September–October 1995, which were, at times, marked by outbreaks of violence. In response to the intensification of the anti-Government campaign, and in an attempt to break the political impasse caused by the refusal of the opposition parties to take part in forthcoming by-elections, the Jatiya Sangsad was dissolved in November at the request of the Prime Minister, pending the holding of a general election in early 1996. Despite opposition demands for a neutral interim government to oversee the election, the President requested that Begum Khaleda Zia's administration continue in office in an acting capacity. Strikes and demonstrations aimed at obstructing the electoral process were organized by the opposition throughout December 1995 and into January 1996. All of the main opposition parties boycotted the general election, which was held in mid-February, and independent monitors estimated the turn-out at only about 10%–15% of the registered electorate. Of the 207 legislative seats declared by the end of February, the BNP had won 205 (a partial repoll had been ordered in most of the 93 remaining constituencies where violence had disrupted the electoral process). The opposition refused to recognize the legitimacy of the polls, and announced the launch of a 'non-co-operation' movement against the Government. Renewed street protests rendered the country virtually ungovernable, and Begum Khaleda Zia eventually agreed to the holding of fresh elections under neutral auspices. The Prime Minister and her Government duly resigned on 30 March, and the Jatiya Sangsad was dissolved. President Biswas appointed former Chief Justice Muhammad Habibur Rahman as acting Prime Minister, and requested that a fresh general election be held, under the auspices of an interim neutral government, within three months. At the general election, held on 12 June, the AL won 146 of the 300 elective seats in the Jatiya Sangsad, the BNP 116, the Jatiya Dal 32 and the Jamaat-e-Islami three. An understanding was rapidly reached between the AL and the Jatiya Dal, the latter's major interest being the release of Ershad, who had secured a legislative seat from within prison. (The former President was released on bail in January 1997.) Sheikh Hasina Wajed was sworn in as Prime Minister on 23 June 1996. Her Council of Ministers incorporated one member from the Jatiya Dal; it also included a number of retired officials and army officers.

Meanwhile, an unsuccessful military coup attempt on 20 May 1996 indicated the continuing fragility of the country's institutions. The Chief of Army Staff, Lt-Gen. Abu Saleh Mohammed Nasim, had objected to the action of the President (who retained direct control of the armed forces during the period prior to the general election) in dismissing some senior officers for political activity, and endeavoured to seize power, but was unable to mobilize sufficient support. Lt-Gen. Nasim was immediately replaced.

On 23 July 1996 the AL's presidential nominee, retired Chief Justice and former acting President Shahabuddin Ahmed, was elected unopposed as Bangladesh's Head of State. In early September the AL won eight of the 15 seats contested in by-elections; this result gave the AL, which was also allocated 27 of the 30 nominated women's parliamentary seats in July, an absolute majority in the Jatiya Sangsad.

On assuming power, Sheikh Hasina Wajed had vowed to bring to justice those responsible for the assassination of her father, Sheikh Mujibur Rahman, in 1975. In November 1996 the Jatiya Sangsad voted unanimously to repeal the indemnity law enacted in 1975 to protect the perpetrators of the military coup in that year; the BNP and the Jamaat-e-Islami, however, boycotted the vote. The trial of 19 people accused of direct involvement in Sheikh Mujib's assassination began in March 1997, with 14 of the defendants being tried *in absentia*.

Agitation persisted throughout 1997; in March the opposition launched a campaign to protest against the Government's agreement with India with regard to the sharing of the Ganga (Ganges) waters (see below), and during an anti-Government strike held at the end of the month one person was killed and many were injured. The opposition organized further general strikes in July and August in protest at the Government's imposition of higher taxes and the increase in fuel prices. Despite a subsequent government ban on street rallies and processions, a series of strikes and demonstrations, organized by the BNP in conjunction with Islamist and right-wing groups, ensued. In addition to the disruption caused by such actions (which frequently involved violent clashes between demonstrators and police), the efficacy of the Jatiya Sangsad was undermined by several boycotts of parliamentary proceedings organized by BNP deputies. In mid-1998 the opposition organized public demonstrations in protest at problems of law and order and at power failures. The BNP's foremost demand was the holding of fresh elections, reiterating the AL's earlier campaign. The AL, however, strengthened its position through a series of by-election victories. Thus the departure of the Jatiya Dal from the coalition in March had little effect on the ruling party's hold on power. In June and August Begum Khaleda Zia was indicted on charges of corruption and abuse of power, allegedly perpetrated during her tenure as premier.

In August 1998 the Government appealed for international aid following devastating floods (the worst since 1988), which had caused more than 500 deaths (this figure later rose to more than 1,500) and infrastructural damage estimated at about US $220m. By late August more than 60% of the country was submerged, including large parts of the capital, and the flooding lasted an unprecedented 11 weeks.

In September 1998 the controversial feminist writer Taslima Nasreen was reported to have secretly returned to Bangladesh after four years in self-imposed exile. (Nasreen, whose allegedly anti-Islamic public stance and statements had made her the target of a campaign of vilification by fundamentalist Islamist groups in Bangladesh, had—with the apparent complicity of government officials—fled the country in August 1994 and been granted refuge in Sweden, shortly after a warrant had been issued for her arrest on blasphemy-related charges.) On her return, a fresh warrant for the writer's arrest on charges of blasphemy was issued by a Dhaka court. Islamist extremists organized street protests, reiterating their demand for Nasreen's immediate arrest and execution. In November 1998 Nasreen voluntarily surrendered herself before the High Court in Dhaka, where she was granted bail. In January 1999 the author again left Bangladesh for Sweden, following renewed death threats from Islamist extremists. The sale of her third novel was authorized in Bangladesh in 2001; however, her fourth book was banned by the Bangladeshi authorities in August 2002. In October a court outside Dhaka sentenced Nasreen *in absentia* to one year's imprisonment on charges of blasphemy.

Also in September 1998 three former government ministers, including the former Deputy Prime Minister, Shah Moazzem Hossain, and a prominent member of the BNP, K. M. Obaidur Rahman, were arrested in connection with the murder in 1975 of four former government ministers, who were shot dead in Dhaka two months after the assassination of Bangladesh's founder, Sheikh Mujib. In October 2000 they were indicted on charges of murder. Of a total of 22 defendants, 14 had fled the country. In November 1998 a Dhaka court sentenced to death 15 of the 19 people accused of Mujib's assassination, acquitting the others. Only four of those convicted, however, were in custody in Bangladesh; the 11 others remained fugitives abroad. In April 2000 the Chief Justice established a two-judge bench to review the sentences. In December, after a 64-day appeal hearing and High Court review of the sentences, the two judges confirmed the death sentence against 10 of the accused, but announced a split verdict on the sentences of five defendants. The case was to be referred to a third judge.

The BNP organized a three-day, nation-wide general strike in November 1998, in protest at alleged government repression. At least two people were killed and many injured when the police clashed with protesters in Dhaka (the tension was exacerbated by the BNP's disapproval of the death sentences imposed on Mujib's assassins). The Government, in response, accused the opposition of disrupting vital post-flood rehabilitation work. In mid-December at least 100 people were injured in Dhaka in further violent clashes between police and opposition activists protesting against what was claimed to be electoral fraud on the part of the Government during a recent by-election. Later in the month the opposition was strengthened by a decision by the BNP and the Jamaat-e-Islami to accept Ershad and the Jatiya Dal in the anti-Government movement without any condition. The Minister of Home Affairs was forced to resign in March 1999, following an escalation in violence and political instability, culminating in two bomb explosions in Jessore as a result of which 11 people died.

In July 1999 the opposition condemned as too costly and unnecessary government proposals to spend US $115m. on eight Russian fighter aircraft. The announcement in the following month of plans to permit the transhipment of Indian goods through Bangladesh to the remote states in north-eastern India provoked further protests and strikes by the opposition, which claimed that the transit proposals would pose a threat to Bangladesh's sovereignty and would allow India to transport troops across Bangladesh's borders to suppress separatists in the adjacent Indian states. In retaliation, the Government asserted that the transhipment plans could earn Bangladesh $400m. per year and enhance the status of the port of Chittagong. The Government was also criticized in August for its plans to evict thousands of people from Dhaka's slums in response to the increasing environmental risks and rising levels of crime; a major rehabilitation programme was to be instigated for those displaced.

Unrest continued throughout the latter half of 1999 and into 2000. The opposition parties boycotted parliamentary proceedings from January 2000, and persisted in their demands for the holding of early elections. The situation remained tense, despite the efforts of influential business leaders to negotiate an arrangement between the Prime Minister and the opposition parties. Street demonstrations resumed in February. The announcement in the same month of the introduction of the controversial Public Safety Act, which permitted detention without trial for up to 90 days, provoked a three-day nation-wide strike. A further opposition-led strike at the end of the month caused two days of serious disruption. The opposition parties suspended their boycott of the Jatiya Sangsad in June in order to avoid disqualification (which would take effect after an absence of 90 working days from the legislature without the Speaker's approval). However, following accusations that the Government was conspiring to change the Constitution, opposition members promptly resumed their boycott, claiming that they were not allowed to address the legislature (an allegation denied by the Speaker). Political unrest and strikes continued; in early August an assassination attempt on the Prime Minister was foiled. (The trial commenced in June 2001 of 15 people accused of involvement in the attempt.)

In August 2000 the High Court in Dhaka reduced the sentence imposed by a lower court on Ershad to five years' imprisonment, and stipulated the payment of a fine of 54m. taka and the confiscation of a property, the Janata Tower, for misappropriating funds during his tenure of power between 1983 and 1990. In accordance with the Constitution, Ershad was deprived of his parliamentary seat. Following an appeal in November, and shortly after Ershad had begun his term of imprisonment, the Supreme Court reduced the sentence to three years and seven months; the former President was released on bail in April 2001, owing to illness. In May 2002 Ershad was sentenced to six months' imprisonment for attempting to influence the proceedings in a corruption case. In early September 2000 the opposition leader, Begum Khaleda Zia, was accused by the anti-corruption unit of financial irregularities.

Intermittent opposition-led strikes in early 2001 caused serious disruption and adversely affected the economy. Discontent with the Government was often manifested violently: in mid-June, for example, 22 people were killed as a result of a bomb explosion at a local office of the AL. It was alleged that militant Islamist groups were involved, although none claimed responsibility.

Sheikh Hasina Wajed announced at the end of June 2001 that a general election would take place in September: she was the first Prime Minister in the history of Bangladesh to complete a five-year term of office. In July the Government failed to obtain sufficient votes to pass a constitutional amendment to permit an increase in the number of female members of parliament. In mid-July the Government resigned, and the Jatiya Sangsad was dissolved in order to allow an interim neutral administration to prepare for the general election, to be held within three months. The interim administration was established shortly afterwards under the leadership of former Chief Justice Latifur Rehman. The election campaign was reportedly the most violent in the country's history, and Rehman ordered the deployment of more than 50,000 troops to curb the violence. A bomb explosion at an election rally of the AL in Bagerhat in late September resulted in eight deaths. The total number of people killed during the campaign was more than 150; thousands more were injured.

The general election proceeded on 1 October 2001, although voting was postponed in several constituencies owing to violence. The AL claimed that voting had been manipulated as it became clear that the opposition alliance, led by the BNP, had won an overwhelming majority of the 300 directly elective seats in the Jatiya Sangsad; however, international monitors declared the poll to be free and fair. Immediately after the election the BNP leader, Begum Khaleda Zia, asserted, in an apparent effort to allay national and international concerns regarding the presence of two fundamentalist Islamist parties in the four-party alliance, that Bangladesh would not become an Islamic state. Following elections on 9 October in 15 of those constituencies where voting had been delayed, the BNP-led alliance controlled a total 214 of the directly elective seats, the AL 62 and the Jatiya Dal 14; two smaller parties held one seat each, and independents a total of six. Meanwhile, the AL, refusing to accept the election results, boycotted the ceremony at which newly elected members of the legislature were sworn in. On 10 October Begum Khaleda Zia was sworn in as Prime Minister, and a new Cabinet was appointed the following day. At the end of October newly elected members of Parliament representing the opposition AL took the oath of office, but refused to join the opening session of the Jatiya Sangsad, in continuing protest against what they considered a rigged election; the opposition party also condemned violence allegedly perpetrated by the BNP-led alliance against AL members and religious minority groups, stating that it would not attend the Jatiya Sangsad until the Government demonstrated a greater commitment to curb the alleged violence. Reports of attacks, particularly against the Hindu minority, increased markedly after the victory of the BNP-led coalition. Hindus either sought refuge in AL offices or fled the country to neighbouring India. The Government admitted that some of the assertions were true, while dismissing reports of widespread attacks as overstated, and announced that an investigation would be conducted into alleged violent acts against religious minorities and into reports that Hindus had left the country. In December Shahriar Kabir, a journalist and human rights activist, was arrested on charges of treason after visiting Kolkata (Calcutta), India, to interview Hindus who had fled Bangladesh claiming religious persecution; he was released on bail one month later. In May 2002 the human rights organization Amnesty International issued a report stating that the Bangladesh Government had failed to take effective measures to curb attacks allegedly perpetrated by supporters of the BNP-led coalition, before, during and after the October 2001 election, against the Hindu community, other minorities and women. The report also claimed that the police had failed to protect the minorities and that custodial torture by members of the police and armed forces had taken place during and after the general election. The Government rejected the charges; while admitting to some of the incidents, the BNP-led coalition held its political opponents responsible for the criminal acts. In the mean time, the Goverment had not provided any information regarding an official investigation into the alleged attacks. In August 2002 the Chief of the Hindu Unity Council warned that unless demands for the restoration of a secular Constitution, as originally devised immediately after Bangladesh's independence, were met, Hindus would remain 'second-class citizens' in the country.

Meanwhile, elections took place on 12 November 2001 in the remaining two constituencies where voting had not taken place in October. On the same day Prof. A. Q. M. Badrudozza Chowdhury, a former Minister of Foreign Affairs, was declared President after his only nominated opponent, Mohammad Rowshan Ali, withdrew. Prof. Chowdhury immediately resigned from the BNP, and was sworn into office two days later. The AL (which had refused to participate in the presidential election) boycotted the oath-taking ceremony. In December the Jatiya Sangsad repealed the Father of the Nation Family Security Act. The Security Act, which had been approved in June under the AL administration, guaranteed lifelong security for Sheikh Hasina Wajed and her sister. The AL considered the safety of the daughters of Sheikh Mujib to be at risk because several convicted assassins of the latter remained at large; however, the act was strongly criticized by the BNP, which considered its founder, Gen. Zia, to be the 'father of the nation'. In March 2002 the AL demonstrated against the repealing of the Father of the Nation's Portrait Display and Preservation Act, which made it mandatory for government officials to display portraits of Sheikh Mujib in their offices.

AL members of Parliament continued their boycott of the Jatiya Sangsad until June 2002. The party also refused to take part in civic elections in April and carried out a policy of agitation, organizing a series of strikes in protest against higher taxes, crime and rises in fuel prices. In response to the opposition's campaign, the Government filed two corruption charges against Sheikh Hasina Wajed and other AL members in December 2001, in relation to an arms contract with Russia signed in 1999. Meanwhile, a corruption case against Begum Khaleda Zia, filed under Sheikh Hasina Wajed's Government in 1998, was quashed.

In mid-June 2002 the President yielded to pressure from the BNP to resign from office after he failed to visit Gen. Zia's grave on the anniversary of the latter's assassination. The resignation was considered unconstitutional by many observers. Some two days later Begum Khaleda Zia appointed her son, Tarique Rahman, to the post of Secretary-General of the BNP, prompting claims that the Prime Minister intended eventually to relinquish power to Rahman. In early September the BNP candidate, Iajuddin Ahmed, was declared President by the Election Commission after it was established that the nomination papers of the two other candidates were invalid.

In late September 2002 bomb explosions at a cinema and circus in the south-western town of Satkhira occurred, killing at least 10 people and seriously injuring 150. Islamist militant groups were suspected to have carried out the attack, although none claimed responsibility. In mid-October the Government launched a campaign to curb crime; some 40,000 members of the armed forces had been enlisted to assist the police. The AL claimed that the Government was using this campaign as a guise for the harrassment of opposition members. By the end of the month almost 3,500 people had been arrested, including two former AL ministers. A former Minister of Industry and AL member was detained in November and released in January 2003; no charges were brought against him. Concerns were raised over the unusually high number of people who had died in army custody. In early January the Government approved a law granting the armed forces legal immunity for any actions carried out during the three-month operation against crime. A number of journalists were also detained during the campaign. Meanwhile, in December 2002 bomb explosions at four cinemas in the town of Mymensingh occurred, killing at least 18 people and injuring some 300. The Prime Minister rejected suggestions that the Islamist militant al-Qa'ida (Base) organization was involved in the attack. However, it was claimed that Bangladeshi Islamist militant groups had collaborated with South-East Asian Islamist groups connected with al-Qa'ida since 1999. In January–March 2003 almost 50 people were killed and 6,000 injured in violent attacks during staggered local elections.

Floods in mid-2002 submerged 33% of the country, as a result of which more than 140 people died and some 6m. were displaced.

In foreign affairs, Bangladesh has traditionally maintained a policy of non-alignment. Relations with Pakistan improved in

1976: ambassadors were exchanged, and trade, postal and tele-communication links were resumed. In September 1991 Pakistan finally agreed to initiate a process of phased repatriation and rehabilitation of some 250,000 Bihari Muslims (who supported Pakistan in Bangladesh's war of liberation in 1971) still remaining in refugee camps in Bangladesh. The first group of Bihari refugees returned to Pakistan from Bangladesh in January 1993, but the implementation of the repatriation process has since been very slow. Relations with Pakistan deteriorated in September 2000 when, at the UN Millennium Summit in New York, the Prime Minister Sheikh Hasina Wajed condemned Pakistan's military leadership, ostensibly as part of a general request for the UN to take action against undemocratic changes of government. A diplomatic row ensued over who was responsible for the events during Bangladesh's war of liberation, culminating in the withdrawal of the Pakistani Deputy High Commissioner to Bangladesh. In late July 2002 Pakistani President Pervez Musharraf paid a visit to Bangladesh, during which he expressed regret for the atrocities committed by Pakistani troops during the 1971 war.

Relations with India have been strained over the questions of cross-border terrorism (especially around the area of the Chittagong Hill Tracts, where Buddhist tribal rebels, the Shanti Bahini, waged a lengthy guerrilla campaign against the Bangladeshi police and Bengali settlers—see below) and of the Farrakka barrage, which was constructed by India on the Ganga river in 1975, so depriving Bangladesh of water for irrigation and river transport during the dry season. In December 1996, however, Indo-Bangladesh relations were given a major boost following the signing of an historic 30-year water-sharing agreement. In January 1997 the Indian Prime Minister paid an official visit to Bangladesh, the first Indian premier to do so for 20 years. In June 1999, during a visit to Dhaka by the Indian Prime Minister, Atal Bihari Vajpayee, to celebrate the inauguration of the first direct passenger bus service between Bangladesh and India, Vajpayee promised Bangladesh greater access to Indian markets and announced that India would give its neighbour US $50m. in credits over three years to help develop its transport and industrial infrastructure. In August the Bangladeshi Government was criticized by the opposition for its approval of proposals to permit the transhipment of Indian goods through Bangladesh to the north-eastern states of India by Bangladeshi transport companies (see above).

In June 1992 the Indian Government, under the provisions of an accord signed with Bangladesh in 1974, formally leased the Tin Bigha Corridor (a small strip of land covering an area of only 1.5 ha) to Bangladesh for 999 years. India maintained sovereignty over the corridor, but the lease gave Bangladesh access to its enclaves of Dahagram and Angarpota. In September 1997 India granted Nepal a transit route through a 60-km corridor in the Indian territory joining Nepal and Bangladesh, thus facilitating trade between those two countries. Despite the 1992 border agreement between Bangladesh and India, the issue of territorial rights to pockets of land or enclaves along the irregular border remained a source of dispute, and occasional efforts to resolve this problem failed to prevent intermittent clashes between border guards. The worst fighting between the two countries since 1976 took place in April 2001 on the Bangladeshi border with the Indian state of Meghalaya. Some 16 members of the Indian Border Security Forces and three members of the Bangladesh Rifles were killed. The situation was brought under control, and the two sides entered border negotiations in June and July as a result of which two joint working groups were established to review the undemarcated section of the border.

Relations with India deteriorated in November 2002 as a result of accusations by India's Deputy Prime Minister and Minister of Home Affairs, Lal Krishna Advani, that al-Qa'ida had increased its activities in Bangladesh since the BNP-led coalition's assumption of power in October 2001. Advani also claimed that Bangladesh was covertly assisting al-Qa'ida and Pakistan's Inter-Services Intelligence Agency, and was providing refuge for Indian separatist groups. The Bangladeshi Government strongly denied the allegations. In January 2003 the Indian Government announced plans to deport some 16m. Bangladeshis who it claimed were working and living in India illegally, because they were perceived to be a security threat. The Bangladeshi Government rejected the claim as groundless.

In 1989 the Government attempted to suppress the Shanti Bahini insurgency in the Chittagong Hill Tracts by introducing concessions providing limited autonomy to the region in the form of three new semi-autonomous hill districts. Voting to elect councils for the districts took place relatively peacefully in June, despite attempts at disruption by the Shanti Bahini, who continued to demand total autonomy for the Chakma tribals. The powers vested in the councils were designed to give the tribals sufficient authority to regulate any further influx of Bengali settlers to the districts (the chief complaint of the tribals since Bengalis were settled in the Chittagong Hill Tracts, as plantation workers and clerks, by the British administration in the 19th century). Despite these concessions, violence continued unabated, and refugees continued to flee across the border into India (the number of refugees living in camps in Tripura reached about 56,000). In May 1992 Bangladesh and India negotiated an agreement intended to facilitate the refugees' return. However, the refugees, fearing persecution by the Bangladesh security forces, proved reluctant to repatriate. Following the conclusion of a successful round of negotiations in early 1994, the process of phased repatriation commenced, although by August only about 2,000 refugees had returned. In December 1997 the Bangladeshi Government signed a peace agreement with the political wing of the Shanti Bahini ending the insurgency in the Chittagong Hill Tracts. The treaty offered the rebels a general amnesty in return for the surrender of their weapons and gave the tribal people greater powers of self-governance through the establishment of three new elected district councils (to control the area's land management and policing) and a regional council (the chairman of which was to enjoy the rank of a state minister). The peace agreement, which was strongly criticized by the opposition for representing a 'sell-out' of the area to India and a threat to Bangladesh's sovereignty, was expected to accelerate the process of repatriating the remaining refugees from Tripura (who totalled about 31,000 at the end of December 1997). According to official Indian sources, only about 5,500 refugees remained in Tripura by early February 1998. By the end of 2000 most of the Chakma refugees had been repatriated, the district and regional councils were in operation, and a land commission had been established. The transitional period was scheduled to end in early 2001, with the withdrawal of the army from the region and its replacement by the Bangladesh Rifles. In early 2001 a tribal group in Tripura threatened forcibly to repatriate remaining refugees if India failed to deport them. In June it was reported that rioting in the Chittagong area had caused a new flow of refugees to Tripura. Following the accession to power of the BNP-led alliance in October, there were reports of thousands of members of Buddhist, Christian and Hindu minorities fleeing to Tripura.

Bangladesh security forces were put on alert in late 2000, as tension along the border with Myanmar increased following reports that Myanmar was laying landmines and that Myanma troops had been deployed in the border area. In January 2001 border guards exchanged fire, amid rising tension over a controversial dam project on the Naaf river, which Bangladesh claimed would cause flooding in its territory; the shooting took place after work began in Myanmar on the construction of an embankment. The Myanma authorities agreed to suspend the project. Shortly afterwards Myanmar alleged that Bangladesh had violated the two countries' 1979 border agreement by cultivating shrimps in the area, an accusation denied by the Bangladeshi Government. Border negotiations took place subsequently, but collapsed after the Myanma authorities refused to sign the minutes. In early February 2001, however, Myanmar agreed permanently to halt construction of the dam. In January 2002 the World Food Programme launched an appeal for US $2.1m. in assistance for 21,500 Myanma Rohingya Muslim refugees who remained in two camps in south-eastern Bangladesh. Some 250,000 Rohingyas had fled Myanmar's Northern Rakhine state in 1991–92. Myanmar had in August 1997 suspended a programme of voluntary repatriations agreed by the Bangladeshi and Myanma authorities in 1992, under which about 230,000 refugees had returned to Myanmar, although smaller-scale repatriations had resumed in late 1998 following intervention by the office of the UN High Commissioner for Refugees (UNHCR). According to UNHCR data, 16,000 of the Rohingyas remaining in Bangladesh were considered by the Government of Myanmar to be ineligible for repatriation, since they had not been authorized for return prior to August 1997, and 5,000 were unwilling to return owing to protection concerns; however, the Bangladeshi Government continued to favour repatriation of the refugees.

In September 2001 Bangladesh's interim administration agreed, with the support of the AL and BNP, to offer the USA use of Bangladeshi airspace and ports in the event of military action against Afghanistan, where the Taliban leadership was believed to be harbouring Osama bin Laden and al-Qa'ida—held principally responsible by the USA for that month's suicide attacks against New York and Washington, DC.

Bangladesh is a member of the South Asian Association for Regional Co-operation (SAARC, see p. 310), formally constituted in 1985, with Bhutan, India, Maldives, Nepal, Pakistan and Sri Lanka. Included in SAARC's charter are pledges of non-interference by members in each other's internal affairs and a joint effort to avoid 'contentious' issues whenever the association meets. The SAARC Preferential Trading Arrangement (SAPTA) was signed in April 1993 and came into effect in December 1995. It was also agreed that members should work towards the objective of establishing a South Asian Free Trade Area (SAFTA) by 2005.

Government

The role of the President, who is elected by the Jatiya Sangsad (Parliament) for a five-year term, is essentially that of a titular Head of State. Executive power is held by the Prime Minister, who heads the Council of Ministers. The President appoints the Prime Minister and, on the latter's recommendation, other ministers. The Jatiya Sangsad comprises 330 members, 300 of whom are elected by universal suffrage: an additional 30 female members are appointed by the elective members. The Jatiya Sangsad serves a five-year term, subject to dissolution.

For purposes of local government, the country is divided into 64 administrative districts.

Defence

Military service is voluntary. In August 2002 the armed forces numbered 137,000: an army of 120,000, a navy of 10,500 and an air force of 6,500. The paramilitary forces totalled 63,200, and included the Bangladesh Rifles (border guard) of 38,000. Budget expenditure on defence was estimated at 39,000m. taka for 2002.

Economic Affairs

In 2001, according to estimates by the World Bank, Bangladesh's gross national income (GNI), measured at average 1999–2001 prices, was US $49,882m., equivalent to $370 per head (or $1,680 per head on an international purchasing-power parity basis). During 1990–2001, it was estimated, the population increased at an average annual rate of 1.8%, while gross domestic product (GDP) per head increased, in real terms, by an average of 3.0% per year. Overall GDP increased at an average annual rate of 4.8% in 1990–2001. GDP grew by 5.9% in 2000, and by 5.2% in 2001. GDP was projected to increase by 4.8% in 2001/02.

Agriculture (including hunting, forestry and fishing) contributed an estimated 23.3% of total GDP in 2001. In 1999/2000 64.8% of the employed labour force were engaged in that sector. The principal sources of revenue in the agricultural sector are jute, tea, shrimps and fish. Raw jute and jute goods accounted for 5.1% of total export earnings in 2001/02. Despite severe flooding in 2000, Bangladesh achieved self-sufficiency in basic foods in 2000/01, mainly owing to increased rice production. The output of foodgrains declined in 2001/02; nevertheless, self-sufficiency in foodgrains was maintained. Widespread flooding in mid-2002 was expected adversely to affect agricultural production in 2002/03. Agricultural GDP expanded at an average annual rate of 3.2% in 1990–2001. Following growth estimated at 7.4% in 1999/2000, growth in the agriculture and forestry sector was 5.0% in 2000/01, according to the Asian Development Bank (ADB).

Industry (including mining, manufacturing, power and construction) employed 10.7% of the working population in 1999/2000. The industrial sector contributed an estimated 25.0% of total GDP in 2001. During 1990–2001 industrial GDP increased at an average annual rate of 7.5%. According to official figures, growth in the industrial sector declined to 3.2% in 1998/99, owing to floods, although by 2000/01 the rate of growth was estimated to have reached 8.6%.

Bangladesh's proven reserves of natural gas totalled 300,000m. cu m at the end of 2001, although recent discoveries indicate that actual reserves may be considerably larger. Production of natural gas increased from 8,300m. cu m in 1999 to 10,800m. cu m in 2001. It is envisaged that an exportable surplus of natural gas may eventually be produced. Bangladesh possesses substantial deposits of coal (estimated at more than 1,000m. metric tons), although difficulties of exploitation continue to make coal imports necessary, and petroleum.

Manufacturing contributed an estimated 15.0% of GDP in 2001. The sector employed 7.6% of the working population in 1999/2000. Based on a census of establishments engaged in manufacturing (excluding hand-loom weaving), the principal branches of the sector, measured by value of output, in 1991/92 were textiles (accounting for 23.8% of the total), food products (20.4%), wearing apparel (excluding footwear) (13.6%) and chemicals (11.4%). During 1990–2001 manufacturing GDP increased at an average annual rate of 6.8%. According to official figures, the GDP of the manufacturing sector grew by an estimated 4.3% in 1999/2000.

Energy is derived principally from natural gas (which contributed 85.0% of total electricity output in 1999). Imports of petroleum products and crude petroleum comprised 8.5% of the cost of total imports in 2001/02.

The services sector accounted for 51.7% of total GDP in 2001. In 1999/2000 24.5% of the employed labour force were engaged in the sector. The GDP of the services sector increased at an average annual rate of 4.6% during 1990–2001. According to the ADB, the sector's GDP expanded by an estimated 5.3% in 2000/01, largely owing to significant progress in the transport, communications and financial sectors.

In 2001, according to the IMF, Bangladesh recorded a visible trade deficit of US $2,048.7m., and there was a deficit of $535.4m. on the current account of the balance of payments. In 2001 the principal source of imports was India (which contributed 11.9% of the total), while the USA was the principal market for exports (accounting for 29.7% of the total). Other major trading partners were Singapore, Japan, the People's Republic of China and Germany. The principal exports in 2001/02 were ready-made garments (accounting for an estimated 52.2% of export revenue), knitwear and hosiery products, raw jute and jute goods, and frozen shrimp and fish. The principal imports were capital goods (an estimated 30.6% of the total), textiles, petroleum products and yarn.

In 2002/03 the overall budgetary deficit was projected to amount to 117,700m. taka, equivalent to 4% of GDP. Bangladesh's total external debt was US $15,609m. at the end of 2000, of which $15,098m. was long-term public debt. In that year the cost of debt-servicing was equivalent to 9.1% of total revenue from exports of goods and services. The annual rate of inflation averaged 5.3% in 1990–2000. Consumer prices increased by an average of 8.9% in 1999, although the annual inflation rate slowed to an average of 3.9% in 2000, before declining again, to 1.7%, in 2001. About 3.3% of the total labour force were unemployed in 1999/2000.

Bangladesh is a member of the Asian Development Bank (ADB, see p. 143), of the South Asian Association for Regional Co-operation (SAARC, see p. 310) and of the Colombo Plan (see p. 339). Bangladesh is also a member of the International Jute Organization, which is based in Dhaka.

The problems of developing Bangladesh include widespread poverty, malnutrition and underemployment, combined with an increasing population and a poor resource base—this last making the country particularly vulnerable to adverse climatic conditions and to fluctuations in international prices for its export commodities. Despite the frequency of natural disasters, food security has improved somewhat in recent years, as have efforts to enhance production methods (notably through subsidies and the increased use of high-yielding variety crops), storage and distribution facilities. The birth rate has decreased considerably, owing to a successful nation-wide birth-control campaign. In the 1990s high rates of growth were achieved in exports of non-traditional items, particularly ready-made garments and knitwear. Furthermore, recent discoveries of huge reserves of natural gas appear to offer opportunities both in terms of domestic fuel self-sufficiency and, in the longer term, export potential. Nevertheless, the increasing fiscal deficit, exacerbated by the heavy losses incurred by state-owned enterprises, continues to cause concern, as does Bangladesh's heavy dependence on foreign aid: total disbursed aid in 2000/01 amounted to US $1,369m. The country's balance-of-payments position was adversely affected in 2000/01 by a decline of some 3% in remittances from nationals working abroad (which are the country's second largest source of foreign revenue, after ready-made garments), to an estimated $1,882m., as the global economic slowdown resulted in reduced demand for Bangladeshi labour overseas. In 2001/02 real GDP growth slowed to the lowest rate in six years, owing to a deceleration in all sectors of the economy. In particular, the global economic slowdown had led to a decline in textile exports; more than 1,000 textile factories closed down, resulting in almost 500,000 workers losing their jobs. In 2002/03, however, exports appeared to be rising, the textile industry was showing signs of recovery and the level of remittances from Bangladeshis working abroad was maintained. Despite the adverse impact of devastating floods on the agricultural sector, the Government predicted high abundant yields of rice. According to the ADB, the predicted GDP growth rate of 5.2% for 2002/03, however, was short of the 8% growth rate required for the country to meet its poverty-reduction target of 50% by 2010. Bangladesh needed to address the deteriorating law and order situation and the problem of corruption in order to attract greater foreign investment. The coalition Government led by the Bangladesh Nationalist Party (BNP), which came into power in October 2001, pledged to reform the banking sector and expressed its commitment to privatization. (The Awami League (AL) Government (1996–2001) attempted to rehabilitate the banking sector and, despite resistance from trade unionists, accelerate the privatization process; however, it attracted criticism from sections of the international financial community for failing to accelerate the implementation of economic reforms.) The BNP-led Government successfully managed to reduce the fiscal deficit in 2001/02. The Government also expressed its intention to export natural gas, particularly to India. This was in contrast to the policy of the previous AL administration, which considered that Bangladesh should meet its domestic requirements before commencing exports.

Education

The Government provides free schooling for children of both sexes for eight years. Primary education, which is compulsory, begins at six years of age and lasts for five years. Secondary education, beginning at the age of 11, lasts for up to seven years, comprising a first cycle of five years and a second cycle of two further years. In 1997 an estimated 75.1% of children (80.6% of boys; 69.6% of girls) in the relevant age-group attended primary schools, while the enrolment ratio at secondary schools was 21.6% of children (27.6% of boys; 15.6% of girls) in the relevant age-group. Secondary schools and colleges in the private sector vastly outnumber government institutions. There are seven state universities, including one for agriculture, one for Islamic studies and one for engineering. The Government launched an

Open University Project in 1992 at an estimated cost of US $34.3m. The 2000/01 budget allocated 33,440m. taka to education (equivalent to 17.0% of total government expenditure).

Public Holidays

2003: 1 January (New Year's Day), 12 February* (Id al-Adha, Feast of the Sacrifice), 21 February (Shaheed Day), 5 March* (Muharram, Islamic New Year), 17 March (Birth of the Father of the Nation), 26 March (Independence Day), 14 April (Bengali New Year), 1 May (May Day), 14 May* (Birth of the Prophet), 16 May* (Buddha Purinama), 7 July (First Monday in July), 15 August (National Mourning Day), 20 August* (Janmashtami), 24 September (Shab-i Bharat, Ascension of the Prophet), 5 October* (Durga Puja), 7 November (National Revolution Day), 26 November* (Id al-Fitr, end of Ramadan), 16 December (Victory Day), 25 December (Christmas), 26 December (Boxing Day), 31 December (Bank Holiday).

2004: 1 January (New Year's Day), 2 February* (Id al-Adha, Feast of the Sacrifice), 21 February (Shaheed Day), 22 February* (Muharram, Islamic New Year), 17 March (Birth of the Father of the Nation), 26 March (Independence Day), 14 April (Bengali New Year), 1 May (May Day), 2 May* (Birth of the Prophet), 4 May* (Buddha Purinama), 5 July (First Monday in July), 15 August (National Mourning Day), 6 September* (Janmashtami), 12 September* (Shab-i Bharat, Ascension of the Prophet), 22 October* (Durga Puja), 7 November (National Revolution Day), 14 November* (Id al-Fitr, end of Ramadan), 16 December (Victory Day), 25 December (Christmas), 26 December (Boxing Day), 31 December (Bank Holiday).

* Dates of certain religious holidays are subject to the sighting of the moon, and there are also optional holidays for different religious groups.

Weights and Measures

The imperial system of measures is in force, pending the introduction of the metric system. The following local units of weight are also used:

  1 maund = 82.28 lb (37.29 kg).

  1 seer = 2.057 lb (932 grams).

  1 tola = 180 grains (11.66 grams).

Statistical Survey

Source (unless otherwise stated): Bangladesh Bureau of Statistics, Statistics Division, Ministry of Planning, E- 27/A, Agargaon, Sher-e-bangla Nagar, Dhaka 1207; tel. (2) 9118045; fax (2) 9111064; e-mail ndbp@bangla.net; internet www.bbstats.org.

Area and Population

AREA, POPULATION AND DENSITY

Area (sq km)	147,570*
Population (census results)	
11 March 1991†	111,455,185
23 January 2001†‡	
Males	62,735,988
Females.	60,415,258
Total	123,151,246
Population (official estimates at mid-year)§	
1999	128,100,000
2000	129,800,000
2001	131,500,000
Density (per sq km) at January 2001	834.5

* 56,977 sq miles.

† Including adjustment for underenumeration, estimated to have been 3.08% at 1991 census.

‡ Provisional results.

§ Not adjusted to take account of the 2001 census results.

ADMINISTRATIVE DIVISIONS
(1991 census)*

Division	Area (sq km)	Population ('000)†	Density (per sq km)
Barisal.	13,297	7,757	583.4
Chittagong	33,771	21,865	647.4
Dhaka	31,119	33,940	1,090.7
Khulna.	22,274	13,243	594.5
Rajshahi	34,513	27,500	796.8
Sylhet	12,596	7,150	567.6
Total	**147,570**	**111,455**	**755.3**

* Data refer to the local government structure resulting from reorganizations subsequent to the census date, whereby the divisions of Barisal (formerly part of Khulna) and Sylhet (formerly part of Chittagong) were created.

† Including adjustments for net underenumeration.

PRINCIPAL TOWNS
(population at 1991 census)*

Dhaka (capital) .	3,612,850	Comilla	135,313
Chittagong . . .	1,392,860	Nawabganj . . .	130,577
Khulna	663,340	Dinajpur	127,815
Rajshahi	294,056	Bogra	120,170
Narayanganj . . .	276,549	Sylhet	114,300
Sitakunda . . .	274,903	Brahmanbaria . .	109,032
Rangpur	191,398	Tangail	106,004
Mymensingh			
(Nasirabad) . .	188,713	Jamalpur	103,556
Barisal (Bakerganj) .	170,232	Pabna	103,277
Tongi (Tungi) . .	168,702	Naogaon	101,266
Jessore	139,710	Sirajganj	99,669

* Figures in each case refer to the city proper. The population of the largest urban agglomerations at the 1991 census was: Dhaka 6,487,459 (including Narayanganj and Tongi); Chittagong 2,079,968 (including Sitakunda); Khulna 921,365; Rajshahi 507,435; Mymensingh 273,350; Sylhet 225,541; Comilla 225,259; Rangpur 208,294; Barisal 202,746; Jessore 169,349; Bogra 161,155.

BIRTHS AND DEATHS*

	Registered live births (rate per 1,000)	Registered deaths (rate per 1,000)
1990	32.8	11.4
1991	31.6	11.2
1992	30.8	11.0
1993	28.8	10.0
1994	27.8	9.0
1995	26.5	8.4
1996	25.6	8.1

* Registration is incomplete. According to UN estimates, the average annual rates per 1,000 were: Births 35.1 in 1990–95, 31.4 in 1995–2000; Deaths 11.4 in 1990–95, 9.8 in 1995–2000 (Source: UN, *World Population Prospects: The 2000 Revision*).

1997 (provisional): Registered live births 3,057,000 (birth rate 24.6 per 1,000); Registered deaths 958,000 (death rate 7.7 per 1,000) (Source: UN, *Population and Vital Statistics Report*).

Expectation of life (WHO estimates, years at birth): 61.8 (males 61.9; females 61.7) in 2001 (Source: WHO, *World Health Report*).

ECONOMICALLY ACTIVE POPULATION*
(sample survey, '000 persons aged 15 years and over, year ending June 2000)

	Males	Females	Total
Agriculture, hunting, forestry and fishing	17,256	14,914	32,171
Mining and quarrying	107	188	295
Manufacturing	2,346	1,436	3,783
Electricity, gas and water . .	116	18	134
Construction	999	100	1,099
Trade, restaurants and hotels . .	5,769	506	6,275
Transport, storage and communications	2,432	77	2,509
Financing, insurance, real estate and business services . . .	357	46	403
Community, social and personal services	1,243	1,726	2,969
Activities not adequately defined	1,744	384	2,126
Total employed	32,369	19,395	51,764
Unemployed	1,083	666	1,750
Total labour force	33,452	20,061	53,514

* Figures exclude members of the armed forces.

Note: totals may not be equal to sum of components owing to rounding.

Source: ILO, *Yearbook of Labour Statistics*.

Mid-2001 (estimates in '000): Agriculture, etc. 39,023; Total labour force 71,395 (Source: FAO).

Health and Welfare

KEY INDICATORS

Total fertility rate (children per woman, 2001)	3.6
Under-five mortality rate (per 1,000 live births, 2001) . . .	77
HIV/AIDS (% of persons aged 15–49, 2001)	<0.10
Physicians (per 1,000 head, 1997)	0.20
Hospital beds (per 1,000 head, 1994)	0.3
Health expenditure (2000): US $ per head (PPP)	47
Health expenditure (2000): % of GDP	3.8
Health expenditure (2000): public (% of total)	36.4
Access to water (% of persons, 2000)	97
Access to sanitation (% of persons, 2000)	53
Human Development Index (2000): ranking	145
Human Development Index (2000): value	0.478

For sources and definitions, see explanatory note on p. vi.

Agriculture

PRINCIPAL CROPS
('000 metric tons, year ending 30 June)

	1998/99	1999/2000	2000/01
Wheat	1,908	1,840	1,673
Rice (paddy)	34,601	37,628	38,500*
Millet	55	55	57†
Potatoes	2,762	2,933	3,216
Sweet potatoes	383	378	357
Sugar cane	6,951	6,910	6,742
Other sugar crops	332	292	300
Beans (dry)	54	57	54
Chick-peas	15	14	14
Lentils	131	128	126
Other pulses	183	187	174
Groundnuts (in shell) . . .	42	32	30*
Areca nuts (betel)† . . .	29	30	30
Rapeseed	253	249	238
Sesame seed*	49	49	49
Linseed	46	48*	50*
Cottonseed*	28	27	30
Coconuts	89	89	89
Cabbages	115	112	115
Lettuce	52	53	35
Spinach	25	26	27
Tomatoes	98	100	100
Cauliflower	80	80	79
Pumpkins, squash and gourds . .	187	198	206
Dry onions	131	134	127
Garlic	38	40	39
Beans (green)	49	49	50
Other vegetables	913	931	931
Cantaloupes and other melons . .	97	79	85
Mangoes	187	187	188
Pineapples	146	148	152
Bananas	562	572	606
Papayas	40	41	44
Other fruits and berries . . .	405	413	417
Tea (made)	56	46	52
Tobacco (leaves)	29	35	37
Pimento and allspice† . . .	54	55	56
Ginger	38	38	42
Other spices	46	51	51†
Jute	711	821	859

* Unofficial figure(s).
† FAO estimate(s).

Source: FAO.

LIVESTOCK
(FAO estimates, '000 head, year ending September)

	1999	2000	2001
Cattle	23,652	23,900	23,900
Buffaloes	828	830	830
Sheep	1,121	1,132	1,132
Goats	33,800	34,100	34,100
Chickens	139,300	140,000	140,000
Ducks	13,000	13,000	13,000

Source: FAO.

LIVESTOCK PRODUCTS
(FAO estimates, '000 metric tons)

	1999	2000	2001
Beef and veal	170	172	172
Buffalo meat	3.5	3.5	3.5
Mutton and lamb	2.6	2.7	2.7
Goat meat	127	129	129
Chicken meat	98.5	98.7	98.7
Duck meat	13	13	13
Cows' milk	755	763	763
Buffalo milk	22.4	22.4	22.4
Sheeps' milk	22.4	22.6	22.6
Goats' milk	1,296	1,304	1,304
Ghee	16.4	16.4	16.6
Hen eggs	131.5	133.0	133.0
Other poultry eggs	26	26	26
Cattle and buffalo hides	31.8	32.1	32.1
Goatskins	38.0	38.4	38.4

Source: FAO.

Forestry

ROUNDWOOD REMOVALS
(FAO estimates, '000 cubic metres, excl. bark)

	1999	2000	2001
Sawlogs, veneer logs and logs for sleepers	174	174	174
Pulpwood*	69	69	69
Other industrial wood	380	380	380
Fuel wood	27,843	27,836	27,799
Total	28,466	28,459	28,422

* Annual output assumed to be unchanged since 1986.

Source: FAO.

SAWNWOOD PRODUCTION
(FAO estimates, '000 cubic metres, incl. railway sleepers)

	1993	1994	1995
Total (all broadleaved)	79	79	70

1996–2001: Annual production as in 1995 (FAO estimates).
Source: FAO.

Fishing

('000 metric tons, live weight)

	1998	1999	2000
Capture	839.1	959.2	1,004.3
Freshwater fishes	457.1	575.6	591.3
Hilsa shad	205.7	214.5	219.5
Marine fishes	145.3	137.3	162.0
Aquaculture	514.8	620.1	657.1
Roho labeo	95.0	112.0	126.0
Catla	77.0	91.0	102.0
Silver carp	95.0	112.0	126.0
Penaeus shrimps	66.1	81.1	58.2
Total catch	1,353.9	1,579.3	1,661.4

Source: FAO, *Yearbook of Fishery Statistics*.

Mining

(million cubic feet, year ending 30 June)

	1999/2000	2000/01	2001/02*
Natural gas	331,247	372,690	387,630

* Estimate.

Source: IMF, *Bangladesh: Selected Issues and Statistical Appendix* (June 2002).

Industry

SELECTED PRODUCTS
('000 metric tons, unless otherwise indicated; year ending 30 June)

	1998/99	1999/2000	2000/01
Refined sugar	152.6	123.4	96.3
Cigarettes (million)	19,558	19,732	20,052*
Cotton yarn ('000 bales)	304†	325†	326*
Woven cotton fabrics ('000 metres)	11,155	12,410	14,307*
Jute fabrics‡	365.3	335.2	325.6
Newsprint	21.6	17.9	11.2
Other paper	38.3	37.0	40.0
Fertilizers	1,799.4	1,904.0	2,073.7

* Provisional figure.
† 1 bale = 180 kg.
‡ Production of jute mills.

Source: Bangladesh Bank.

Finance

CURRENCY AND EXCHANGE RATES

Monetary Units
100 poisha = 1 taka

Sterling, Dollar and Euro Equivalents (31 December 2002)
£1 sterling = 93.32 taka
US $1 = 57.90 taka
€1 = 60.72 taka
1,000 taka = £10.72 = $17.27 = €16.47

Average Exchange Rate (taka per US $)
2000   52.142
2001   55.807
2002   57.888

BUDGET
(million taka, year ending 30 June)

Revenue	1999/2000*	2000/01†	2001/02‡
Taxation	158,400	191,100	220,200
Customs duties	41,600	48,300	53,500
Income and profit taxes	23,300	30,700	41,000
Excise duties	—	—	3,000
Value-added tax	81,600	96,800	108,300
Other revenue	45,300	37,000	54,300
Total	203,700	228,100	274,600

Expenditure	1999/2000*	2000/01†	2001/02‡
Goods and services	92,500	97,200	94,000
Pay and allowances	56,000	63,100	61,400
Operations and maintenance	7,900	8,900	9,500
Works	2,700	2,700	3,000
Interest payments	37,600	40,500	45,600
Domestic	30,800	31,900	35,900
Foreign	6,900	8,600	9,700
Subsidies and current transfers	46,700	49,300	63,100
Unallocated	7,500	10,200	19,900
Gross current expenditure	184,300	197,200	222,600

* Revised figures.
† Estimates.
‡ Forecasts.

Source: IMF, *Bangladesh: Selected Issues and Statistical Appendix* (June 2002).

2002/03 (forecasts, million taka): Total revenue 330,840; Total expenditure 448,540 (Source: Ministry of Finance (Economic Relations Division)).

PUBLIC-SECTOR DEVELOPMENT EXPENDITURE
(estimates, million taka, year ending 30 June)

	1997/98	1998/99‡	1999/2000§
Agriculture	6,000	6,100	8,400
Rural development	9,000	12,700	16,000
Water and flood control	10,400	8,800	10,200
Industry	1,200	1,000	2,000
Power, scientific research and natural resources	18,800	21,000	26,100
Transport*	22,600	22,500	24,700
Communications	3,900	3,900	5,000
Physical planning and housing	6,000	6,700	10,200
Education	14,900	16,900	19,600
Health	5,300 }	10,200	15,300
Family planning	6,300 }		
Social welfare†	1,600	1,700	2,200
Other sectoral	200	—	400
Total sectoral allocations	106,400	111,400	140,100
Block allocations	10,900	8,700	9,200
Food for Work	5,700	5,300	2,400
Technical assistance	3,000	3,200	3,200
Domestic self-financing	1,700	1,800	2,500
Total development expenditure	122,000	125,100	155,000

* Includes Jamuna Bridge.
† Includes employment.
‡ Revised figures.
§ Estimates.

Source: Ministry of Planning (Implementation, Monitoring and Evaluation Division).

INTERNATIONAL RESERVES
(US $ million at 31 December)

	2000	2001	2002
Gold*	29.6	30.6	n.a.
IMF special drawing rights	0.4	1.2	2.2
Reserve position in IMF	0.2	0.2	0.3
Foreign exchange	1,485.3	1,273.6	1,680.7
Total	1,515.6	1,305.6	n.a.

* Valued at market-related prices.

Source: IMF, *International Financial Statistics*.

MONEY SUPPLY
(million taka at 31 December)

	1999	2000	2001
Currency outside banks	93,870	116,877	127,863
Demand deposits at deposit money banks*	91,055	102,074	114,572
Total money (incl. others)	184,925	218,951	242,437

* Comprises the scheduled banks plus the agricultural and industrial development banks.

Source: IMF, *International Financial Statistics*.

COST OF LIVING
(Consumer Price Index, year ending 30 June; base: 1985/86 = 100)

	1999/2000	2000/01	2001/02
Food, beverages and tobacco	239.1	241.4	244.4
Rent, fuel and lighting	235.9	241.1	251.8
Household requisites	204.7	209.2	216.9
Clothing and footwear	178.6	183.8	189.8
Miscellaneous	220.9	226.1	232.4
All items	235.1	238.8	244.4

Source: Bangladesh Bank.

NATIONAL ACCOUNTS
(rounded figures, million taka at current prices, year ending 30 June)

Expenditure on the Gross Domestic Product

	1999/2000	2000/01	2001/02
Government final consumption expenditure	108,390	114,250	120,430
Private final consumption expenditure	1,838,530	1,964,930	2,105,130
Gross capital formation	545,870	585,360	628,460
Statistical discrepancy	2,470	26,050	20,630
Total domestic expenditure	2,495,260	2,690,590	2,874,650
Exports of goods and services	331,450	390,000	458,050
Less Imports of goods and services	455,850	545,130	618,560
GDP in purchasers' values	2,370,860	2,535,460	2,714,140
GDP at constant 1995/96 prices	2,049,320	2,157,350	2,260,890

Source: IMF, *International Financial Statistics*.

Gross Domestic Product by Economic Activity

	1999/2000*	2000/01	2001/02*
Agriculture and forestry	446,920	456,310	473,680
Fishing	136,740	134,060	137,490
Mining and quarrying	23,110	26,400	29,250
Manufacturing	348,370	382,340	412,450
Electricity, gas and water	30,720	33,460	36,530
Construction	176,220	193,340	210,110
Trade, hotels and restaurants	306,670	340,690	372,570
Transport, storage and communications	197,430	221,290	241,410
Financial, real estate and business services	247,870	262,760	281,840
Public administration and defence	62,340	66,950	72,290
Other services	311,220	332,390	354,570
Sub-total	2,287,610	2,449,990	2,622,200
Import duties	83,250	85,470	91,950
GDP in purchasers' values	2,370,860	2,535,460	2,714,140

* Provisional figures.

Source: Bangladesh Bank.

BALANCE OF PAYMENTS
(US $ million)

	1999	2000	2001
Exports of goods f.o.b.	5,458.3	6,399.2	6,084.7
Imports of goods f.o.b.	−7,535.5	−8,052.9	−8,133.4
Trade balance	−2,077.2	−1,653.7	−2,048.7
Exports of services	777.7	815.1	752.2
Imports of services	−1,396.7	−1,620.2	−1,521.5
Balance on goods and services	−2,696.3	−2,458.9	−2,818.0
Other income received	94.3	78.4	76.6
Other income paid	−258.5	−344.8	−361.9
Balance on goods, services and income	−2,860.4	−2,725.3	−3,103.3
Current transfers received	2,501.4	2,426.5	2,572.8
Current transfers paid	−5.3	−7.0	−4.9
Current balance	−364.4	−305.8	−535.4
Capital account (net)	364.1	248.7	235.4
Direct investment abroad	−0.1	—	n.a.
Direct investment from abroad	179.7	280.4	78.5
Portfolio investment assets	−0.2	—	0.1
Portfolio investment liabilities	−1.1	1.3	−3.5
Other investment assets	−1,143.7	−1,246.8	−433.8
Other investment liabilities	518.4	709.1	620.7
Net errors and omissions	258.0	282.4	−106.0
Overall balance	−189.2	−30.7	−143.9

Source: IMF, *International Financial Statistics*.

FOREIGN AID DISBURSEMENTS
(US $ million, year ending 30 June)

	1998/99	1999/2000	2000/01
Bilateral donors	638	785	706
Canada	27	28	19
China, People's Republic	—	18	26
Denmark	33	29	5
Germany	37	21	43
India	7	4	20
Japan	235	390	316
Kuwait	6	8	36
Netherlands	43	28	19
Norway	10	19	17
Sweden	22	20	16
United Kingdom	52	61	53
USA	69	92	39
Multilateral donors	898	790	663
Asian Development Bank	218	283	236
International Development Association	477	354	299
European Union	39	5	32
International Fund for Agricultural Development	11	15	—
UN Development Programme	37	7	17
World Food Programme	81	68	1
UNICEF	19	27	49
Islamic Development Bank	12	16	16
Total aid disbursements	1,536	1,575	1,369

Source: Ministry of Finance (Economic Relations Division).

External Trade

PRINCIPAL COMMODITIES
(US $ million, year ending 30 June)

Imports	1999/2000	2000/01	2001/02
Wheat	266.0	177.0	171.0
Edible oil	256.0	218.0	251.0
Petroleum products	406.0	566.0	481.0
Crude petroleum	232.0	273.0	242.0
Chemicals	278.0	339.0	335.0
Cotton	277.0	360.0	312.0
Yarn	300.0	322.0	283.0
Textiles	1,153.0	1,291.0	1,063.0
Iron and steel	393.0	464.0	413.0
Capital goods	2,133.0	2,515.0	2,617.0
Total (incl. others)	8,403.0	9,335.0	8,540.0

Exports	1999/2000	2000/01	2001/02
Raw jute	72.0	67.0	61.0
Jute goods (excl. carpets)	263.0	229.0	242.0
Leather and leather products	195.0	254.0	207.0
Frozen shrimp and fish	344.0	363.0	276.0
Ready-made garments	3,083.0	3,364.0	3,125.0
Knitwear and hosiery products	1,270.0	1,496.0	1,459.0
Total (incl. others)	5,762.0	6,476.0	5,986.0

Source: Bangladesh Bank.

PRINCIPAL TRADING PARTNERS
(US $ million)

Imports c.i.f.	1999	2000	2001
Australia	213	175	194
China, People's Republic	534	667	882
Hong Kong	441	470	493
India	1,024	945	1,186
Indonesia	159	193	201
Japan	559	850	581
Korea, Republic	291	348	625
Singapore	659	761	901
United Kingdom	280	239	173
USA	446	214	297
Total (incl. others)	8,352	8,993	9,959

Exports f.o.b.	1999	2000	2001
Belgium	146	175	182
Canada	77	97	100
France	263	289	301
Germany	450	608	624
Hong Kong	62	87	98
Italy	200	228	263
Japan	71	67	64
Netherlands	187	234	253
United Kingdom	364	440	500
USA	1,411	1,779	1,754
Total (incl. others)	4,520	5,590	5,908

Source: Asian Development Bank, *Key Indicators of Developing Asian and Pacific Countries.*

Transport

RAILWAYS
(traffic, year ending 30 June)

	1994/95	1995/96	1996/97
Passenger-kilometres (million)	4,037	3,333	3,754
Freight ton-kilometres (million)	760	689	782

Source: Bangladesh Railway.

ROAD TRAFFIC
(motor vehicles in use at 31 December)

	1997*	1998*	1999†
Passenger cars	54,784	57,068	60,846
Buses and coaches	29,310	30,361	32,371
Lorries and vans	40,084	42,425	45,234
Road tractors	2,769	2,813	2,999
Motorcycles and mopeds	125,259	145,259	147,205
Total	252,206	277,926	288,655

* Revised figures.
† Estimates.

Source: International Road Federation, *World Road Statistics.*

SHIPPING

Merchant Fleet
(registered at 31 December)

	1999	2000	2001
Number of vessels	306	310	317
Total displacement ('000 grt)	377.8	370.1	387.6

Source: Lloyd's Register-Fairplay, *World Fleet Statistics.*

International Sea-borne Freight Traffic
('000 metric tons)

	1999	2000	2001
Total goods loaded	528	n.a.	868
Total goods unloaded	3,612	n.a.	13,631

Source: UN, *Monthly Bulletin of Statistics.*

CIVIL AVIATION
(traffic on scheduled Biman Bangladesh services)

	1997	1998	1999
Kilometres flown (million)	20	20	21
Passengers carried ('000)	1,315	1,162	1,215
Passenger-km (million)	3,233	3,422	3,515
Total ton-km (million)	494	524	545

Source: UN, *Statistical Yearbook.*

Tourism

TOURIST ARRIVALS BY COUNTRY OF NATIONALITY

	1998	1999	2000
China, People's Republic . . .	4,379	5,208	5,901
India	57,937	62,935	74,268
Japan	7,808	7,055	8,006
Korea, Republic	6,154	6,596	6,746
Malaysia	2,857	2,890	3,827
Nepal	4,799	4,733	4,481
Pakistan	12,087	7,894	10,637
United Kingdom	19,605	22,510	29,106
USA	11,358	9,557	11,924
Total (incl. others) . . .	171,961	172,781	199,211

Tourism receipts (US $ million): 51 in 1998; 50 in 1999; 59 in 2000 (estimate).

Source: World Tourism Organization, *Yearbook of Tourism Statistics*.

Hotel rooms (including rooms of similar establishments): 4,166 in 1996; 4,249 in 1997; 4,461 in 1998 (Source: UN, *Statistical Yearbook for Asia and the Pacific*).

Hotel beds: 8,386 in 1996; 8,552 in 1997; 9,407 in 1998 (Source: UN, *Statistical Yearbook for Asia and the Pacific*).

Communications Media

	1998	1999	2000
Television receivers ('000 in use) .	920	940	960
Telephones ('000 main lines in use)	412.7	433.0	491.3
Facsimile machines (number in use)*†	75,000	n.a.	n.a.
Daily newspapers:			
Number of titles . . .	233	n.a.	n.a.
Average circulation ('000) . .	6,658†	n.a.	n.a.
Non-daily newspapers and other periodicals:			
Number of titles . . .	509	n.a.	n.a.
Average circulation ('000) . .	9,256†	n.a.	n.a.
Books published (number of titles)	483	n.a.	n.a.
Mobile cellular telephones ('000 subscribers)*	75	149	205
Personal computers ('000 in use) .	120	130	200
Internet users ('000)	5	50	100

* Twelve months ending 30 June of year stated.
† Provisional figure(s).

Radio receivers ('000 in use): 6,150 in 1997.

2001: Telephones ('000 main lines in use) 514.0; Mobile cellular telephones ('000 subscribers) 520; Personal computers ('000 in use) 250; Internet users ('000)150.

Sources: UNESCO, *Statistical Yearbook*; UN, *Statistical Yearbook*; International Telecommunication Union; Bangladesh Bureau of Statistics.

Education

(1997/98*)

	Institutions	Teachers	Students
Primary schools	66,235	250,990	17,627,000
Secondary schools	13,419	161,141	6,289,000
Universities (government) . . .	11	4,334	105,598,000

Technical colleges and institutes (government, 1990/91†): 141 institutions, 23,722 students.

* Provisional figures.
† In addition to government-owned and managed institutes, there are many privately administered vocational training centres.

Adult literacy rate (UNESCO estimates): 41.3% (males 52.3%; females 29.9%) in 2000 (Source: UN Development Programme, *Human Development Report*).

Directory

The Constitution

The members who were returned from East Pakistan (now Bangladesh) for the Pakistan National Assembly and the Provincial Assembly in the December 1970 elections formed the Bangladesh Constituent Assembly. A new Constitution for the People's Republic of Bangladesh was approved by this Assembly on 4 November 1972 and came into effect on 16 December 1972. Following the military coup of 24 March 1982, the Constitution was suspended, and the country was placed under martial law. On 10 November 1986 martial law was repealed and the suspended Constitution was revived. The main provisions of the Constitution, including amendments, are listed below.

SUMMARY

Fundamental Principles of State Policy

The Constitution was initially based on the fundamental principles of nationalism, socialism, democracy and secularism, but in 1977 an amendment replaced secularism with Islam. The amendment states that the country shall be guided by 'the principles of absolute trust and faith in the Almighty Allah, nationalism, democracy and socialism'. A further amendment in 1988 established Islam as the state religion. The Constitution aims to establish a society free from exploitation in which the rule of law, fundamental human rights and freedoms, justice and equality are to be secured for all citizens. A socialist economic system is to be established to ensure the attainment of a just and egalitarian society through state and co-operative ownership as well as private ownership within limits prescribed by law. A universal, free and compulsory system of education shall be established. In foreign policy the State shall endeavour to consolidate, preserve, and strengthen fraternal relations among Muslim countries based on Islamic solidarity.

Fundamental Rights

All citizens are equal before the law and have a right to its protection. Arbitrary arrest or detention, discrimination based on race, age, sex, birth, caste or religion, and forced labour are prohibited. Subject to law, public order and morality, every citizen has freedom of movement, of assembly and of association. Freedom of conscience, of speech, of the press and of religious worship are guaranteed.

GOVERNMENT

The President

The President is the constitutional Head of State and is elected by Parliament (Jatiya Sangsad) for a term of five years. He is eligible for re-election. The supreme control of the armed forces is vested in the President. He appoints the Prime Minister and other Ministers as well as the Chief Justice and other judges.

The Executive

Executive authority shall rest in the Prime Minister and shall be exercised by him either directly or through officers subordinate to him in accordance with the Constitution.

There shall be a Council of Ministers to aid and advise the Prime Minister.

The Legislature

Parliament (Jatiya Sangsad) is a unicameral legislature. It comprises 300 members and an additional 30 women members elected by the other members. Members of Parliament, other than the 30 women members, are directly elected on the basis of universal adult franchise from single territorial constituencies. Persons aged 18 and over are entitled to vote. The parliamentary term lasts for five years. War can be declared only with the assent of Parliament. In the case of actual or imminent invasion, the President may take whatever action he may consider appropriate.

THE JUDICIARY

The Judiciary comprises a Supreme Court with High Court and an Appellate Division. The Supreme Court consists of a Chief Justice and such other judges as may be appointed by the President. The High Court division has such original appellate and other jurisdiction and powers as are conferred on it by the Constitution and by other law. The Appellate Division has jurisdiction to determine appeals from decisions of the High Court division. Subordinate courts, in addition to the Supreme Court, have been established by law.

ELECTIONS

An Election Commission supervises elections, delimits constituencies and prepares electoral rolls. It consists of a Chief Election Commissioner and other Commissioners as may be appointed by the President. The Election Commission is independent in the exercise of its functions. Subject to the Constitution, Parliament may make provision as to elections where necessary.

The Government

HEAD OF STATE

President: Prof. IAJUDDIN AHMED (took office 6 September 2002).

COUNCIL OF MINISTERS
(April 2003)

Prime Minister and Minister of the Armed Forces Division, of Defence, of the Cabinet Division, of Power, Energy and Mineral Resources, of Chittagong Hill Tracts Affairs, of the Primary and Mass Education Division, and of the Establishment: Begum KHALEDA ZIA.

Minister of Foreign Affairs: M. MORSHED KHAN.

Minister of Home Affairs: ALTAF HUSSAIN CHOWDHURY.

Minister of Local Government, Rural Development and Co-operatives: ABDUL MANNAN BHUIYAN.

Minister of Finance and of Planning: M. SAIFUR RAHMAN.

Minister of Education: Dr OSMAN FARUQUE.

Minister of Labour and Employment: LUTFAR RAHMAN KHAN AZAD.

Minister of Water Resources: Eng. L. K. SIDDIQI.

Minister of Commerce: AMIR KHASRU MAHMUD CHOWDHURY.

Minister of Industry: M. K. ANWAR.

Minister of Post and Telecommunications: MOHAMMAD AMINUL HAQUE.

Minister of Information: TARIQUL ISLAM.

Minister of Jute: Maj. (retd) HAFIZUDDIN AHMED.

Minister of Agriculture: MATIUR RAHMAN NIZAMI.

Minister of Food: ABDULLAH AL-NOMAN.

Minister of Housing and Public Works: MIRZA ABBAS.

Minister of Law, Justice and Parliamentary Affairs: MOUDUD AHMED.

Minister of Communications: NAZMUL HUDA.

Minister of Women's and Children's Affairs: KHURSHID JAHAN HAQ.

Minister of Health and Family Welfare: Dr KHANDAKER M. HOSSAIN.

Minister of Social Welfare: ALI AHSAN MUHAMMAD MUJAHID.

Minister of the Environment and Forests: SHAHJAHAN SIRAJ.

Minister for Fisheries and Livestock: SADEQ HOSSAIN KHOKA.

Minister of Textiles: ABDUL MATIN CHOWDHURY.

Minister of Land: M. SHAMSUL ISLAM.

Minister of Disaster Management and Relief: KAMAL IBNE YUSUF.

Minister of Shipping: Lt-Col (retd) AKBAR HOSSAIN.

Minister of Science and Technology: Dr ABDUL MOYEEN KHAN.

Minister without Portfolio: HARUNUR RASHID KHAN MUNNU.

There are also 29 Ministers of State and three Deputy Ministers.

MINISTRIES

Prime Minister's Office: Old Sangsad Bhaban, Tejgaon, Dhaka; tel. (2) 815100; fax (2) 813244; e-mail pm@pmo.bdonline.com; internet www.bangladeshgov.org/pmo.

Ministry of Agriculture: Bangladesh Secretariat, Bhaban 4, 2nd 9-Storey Bldg, Dhaka; tel. (2) 832137; internet www.bangladeshgov.org/moa.

Ministry of Chittagong Hill Tracts Affairs: Dhaka; internet www.bangladeshgov.org/mochta.

Ministry of Civil Aviation and Tourism: Bangladesh Secretariat, Bhaban 6, 19th Floor, Dhaka 1000; tel. (2) 866485.

Ministry of Commerce: Bangladesh Secretariat, Bhaban 3, Dhaka 1000; tel. (2) 862826; fax (2) 865741.

Ministry of Communications: Bangladesh Secretariat, Bhaban 7, 1st 9-Storey Bldg, 8th Floor, Dhaka 1000; tel. (2) 868752; fax (2) 866636.

Ministry of Cultural Affairs: Dhaka; tel. (2) 402133.

Ministry of Defence: Old High Court Bldg, Dhaka; tel. (2) 259082.

Ministry of Disaster Management and Relief: Dhaka; tel. (2) 866262.

Ministry of Education: Bangladesh Secretariat, Bhaban 7, 2nd 9-Storey Bldg, 6th Floor, Dhaka; tel. (2) 404162.

Ministry of Energy and Mineral Resources: Bangladesh Secretariat, Bhaban 6, First Floor, Dhaka 1000; tel. (2) 865918; fax (2) 861110.

Ministry of Finance: Bangladesh Secretariat, Bhaban 7, 1st 9-Storey Bldg, 3rd Floor, Dhaka 1000; tel. (2) 8690202; fax (2) 865581.

Ministry of Fisheries and Livestock: Dhaka; tel. (2) 862430.

Ministry of Food: Dhaka; e-mail mof@bttb.net.bd; internet www.bangladeshgov.org/mof.

Ministry of Foreign Affairs: Segunbagicha, Dhaka 1000; tel. (2) 9569129; fax (2) 9562163; e-mail pspmo@bangla.net; internet www.bangladeshonline.com/gob/mofa.

Ministry of Health and Family Welfare: Bangladesh Secretariat, Main Bldg, 3rd Floor, Dhaka; tel. (2) 832079.

Ministry of Home Affairs: Bangladesh Secretariat, School Bldg, 2nd and 3rd Floors, Dhaka; tel. (2) 404142.

Ministry of Housing and Public Works: Bangladesh Secretariat, Bhaban 5, Dhaka; tel. (2) 834494; fax (2) 861290.

Ministry of Industry: Shilpa Bhaban, 91 Motijheel C/A, Dhaka 1000; tel. (2) 9564250; fax (2) 860588.

Ministry of Information: Bangladesh Secretariat, 2nd 9-Storey Bldg, 8th Floor, Dhaka; tel. (2) 235111; fax (2) 834535; internet www.moi-gob.org.

Ministry of Jute: Bangladesh Secretariat, Bhabhan 6, 7th Floor, Dhaka 1000; tel. (2) 8612250; fax (2) 8618766; e-mail jutebd@bangla.net; internet www.bangladeshgov.org/jute/jute_information.htm.

Ministry of Labour and Employment: Bangladesh Secretariat, 1st 9-Storey Bldg, 4th Floor, Dhaka; tel. (2) 404106; fax (2) 813420.

Ministry of Land: Bangladesh Secretariat, Bhaban 4, 2nd 9-Storey Bldg, 3rd Floor, Dhaka.

Ministry of Local Government, Rural Development and Co-operatives: Bangladesh Secretariat, Bhaban 7, 1st 9-Storey Bldg, 6th Floor, Dhaka.

Ministry of Planning: Block No. 7, Sher-e-Bangla Nagar, Dhaka; tel. (2) 815142; fax (2) 822210.

Ministry of Post and Telecommunications: Bangladesh Secretariat, Bhaban 7, 6th Floor, Dhaka 1000; tel. (2) 864800; fax (2) 865775.

Ministry of Religious Affairs: Dhaka; tel. (2) 404346.

Ministry of Science and Technology: Bangladesh Secretariat, Bhaban 6, Dhaka; tel. (2) 8616144; fax (2) 8619606; e-mail most@bangla.net; internet www.most-bd.org.

Ministry of Shipping: Bangladesh Secretariat, Bhaban 6, 8th Floor, Dhaka 1000; tel. (2) 861275.

Ministry of Social Welfare and Women's Affairs: Bangladesh Secretariat, Bhaban 6, New Bldg, Dhaka; tel. (2) 402076.

Ministry of Textiles: Bangladesh Secretariat, Bhaban 6, 11th Floor, Dhaka 1000; tel. (2) 862051; fax (2) 860600.

Ministry of Youth and Sports: Dhaka; tel. (2) 407670.

President and Legislature

PRESIDENT

On 5 September 2002 the Bangladesh Nationalist Party's presidential candidate, Prof. IAJUDDIN AHMED, was declared elected unopposed by the Election Commission as Bangladesh's new Head of State.

JATIYA SANGSAD
(Parliament)

Speaker: JAMIRUDDIN SIRCAR.

General Election, 1 and 9 October 2001

	Seats
Bangladesh Jatiyatabadi Dal (Bangladesh Nationalist Party—BNP)	199*
Awami League (AL)	62
Jamaat-e-Islami Bangladesh	17
Jatiya Dal	14†
Jatiya Dal (Manju)	1
Bangladesh Krishak Sramik Party	1
Independents	6
Total	**300**

In addition to the 300 directly-elected members, a further 30 seats are reserved for women members.

*Includes six seats won by the Jatiya Dal (Naziur-Firoz) and the Islami Jatiya Oikya Jote.

†Includes several seats won by the Islami Jatiya Oikya Front.

Political Organizations

Awami League (AL): 23 Bangabandhu Ave, Dhaka; f. 1949; supports parliamentary democracy; advocates socialist economy, but with a private sector, and a secular state; pro-Indian; 28-member central executive committee, 15-member central advisory committee and a 13-member presidium; Pres. Sheikh HASINA WAJED; Gen.-Sec. ZILLUR RAHMAN; c. 1,025,000 mems.

Bangladesh Jatiya League: 500A Dhanmandi R/A, Rd 7, Dhaka; f. 1970 as Pakistan National League, renamed in 1972; supports parliamentary democracy; Leader ATAUR RAHMAN KHAN; c. 50,000 mems.

Bangladesh Jatiyatabadi Dal (Bangladesh Nationalist Party—BNP): 29 Minto Rd, Dhaka; f. 1978 by merger of groups supporting Ziaur Rahman, including Jatiyatabadi Gonotantrik Dal (Jagodal—Nationalist Democratic Party); right of centre; favours multi-party democracy and parliamentary system of govt; Chair. Begum KHALEDA ZIA; Sec.-Gen. ABDUL MANNAN BHUIYAN, TARIQUE RAHMAN.

Bangladesh Khelafat Andolon: 314/2 Lalbagh Kellar Morr, Dhaka 1211; tel. (2) 8612465; fax (2) 9881436; e-mail khelafat@cimabd.com; Supreme Leader SHAH AHMADULLAH ASHRAF IBN HAFEZZEE; Sec.-Gen. Maulana MUHAMMAD ZAFRULLAH KHAN.

Bangladesh Krishak Sramik Party (Peasants' and Workers' Party): Sonargaon Bhavan, 99 South Kamalapur, Dhaka 1217; tel. (2) 834512; f. 1914; renamed 1953; supports parliamentary democracy, non-aligned foreign policy, welfare state, guarantee of fundamental rights for all religions and races, free market economy and non-proliferation of nuclear weapons; 15-mem. exec. council; Pres. A. S. M. SULAIMAN; Sec.-Gen. RASHEED KHAN MEMON; c. 125,000 mems.

Bangladesh Muslim League: Dhaka; Sec.-Gen. Alhaj MOHAMMAD ZAMIR ALI.

Bangladesh People's League: Dhaka; f. 1976; supports parliamentary democracy; Leader KHANDAKER SABBIR AHMED; c. 75,000 mems.

Communist Party of Bangladesh: 21/1 Purana Paltan, Dhaka 1000; tel. (2) 9558612; fax (2) 837464; e-mail manzur@bangla.net; f. 1948; Pres. SHAHIDULLAH CHOWDHURY; Gen. Sec. MUJAHIDUL ISLAM SELIM; c. 22,000 mems.

Democratic League: 68 Jigatola, Dhaka 9; tel. (2) 507994; f. 1976; conservative; Leader ABDUR RAZZAK.

Freedom Party: f. 1987; Islamic; Co-Chair. Lt-Col (retd) SAID FARUQ RAHMAN, Lt-Col (retd) KHANDAKAR ABDUR RASHID.

Gonoazadi League: 30 Banagran Lane, Dhaka.

Islami Jatiya Oikya Front: Dhaka.

Islami Jatiya Oikya Jote: Dhaka; mem. of the BNP-led alliance; Chair. Maulana AZIZUL HAQ; Sec.-Gen. Mufti FAZLUL HAQ AMINI.

Islamic Solidarity Movement: 84 East Tejturi Bazar, Tejgaon, Dhaka 1215; tel. (2) 325886; fmrly known as Islamic Democratic League; renamed as above in 1984; Chair. HAFIZ MUHAMMAD HABIBUR RAHMAN.

Jamaat-e-Islami Bangladesh: 505 Elephant Rd, Bara Maghbazar, Dhaka 1217; tel. (2) 401581; f. 1941; Islamic fundamentalist; mem. of the BNP-led alliance; Chair. Prof. GHULAM AZAM; Sec.-Gen. ALI AHSAN MUHAMMAD MUJAHID; Asst Sec.-Gen. MUHAMMAD QUAMARUZZAMAN.

Jatiya Dal (National Party): c/o Jatiya Sangsad, Dhaka; f. 1983 as Jana Dal; reorg. 1986, when the National Front (f. 1985), a five-party alliance of the Jana Dal, the United People's Party, the Gonotantrik Dal, the Bangladesh Muslim League and a breakaway section of the Bangladesh Nationalist Party, formally converted itself into a single pro-Ershad grouping; advocates nationalism, democracy, Islamic ideals and progress; Chair. Lt-Gen. HOSSAIN MOHAMMAD ERSHAD; Sec.-Gen. NAZIUR RAHMAN MONZUR; in April 1999 a group of dissidents, led by MIZANUR RAHMAN CHOWDHURY and ANWAR HUSSAIN MANJU, formed a rival faction; a rival faction, led by KAZI FIROZ RASHID, was also formed.

Jatiya Samajtantrik Dal (Rab): breakaway faction of JSD; Pres. A. S. M. ABDUR RAB; Gen. Sec. HASANUL HAQUE INU.

Jatiya Samajtantrik Dal (JSD—(S)) (National Socialist Party): 23 DIT Ave, Malibagh Choudhury Para, Dhaka; f. 1972; left-wing; Leader SHAJAHAN SIRAJ; c. 5,000 mems.

Jatiyo Gonotantrik Party (JAGPA): Purana Paltan, Dhaka; Jt Gen. Secs AZIZUR RAHMAN, SARDAR SHAHJAHAN.

Jatiyo Janata Party: Janata Bhaban, 47A Toyenbee Circular Rd, Dhaka 1000; tel. (2) 9667923; f. 1976; social democratic; Chair. NURUL ISLAM KHAN; Gen. Sec. MUJIBUR RAHMAN HERO; c. 35,000 mems.

National Awami Party—Bhashani (NAP): Dhaka; f. 1957; Maoist; Leader NAZRUL ISLAM; Gen. Sec. ABDUS SUBHANI.

National Awami Party—Muzaffar (NAP—M): 21 Dhanmandi Hawkers' Market, 1st Floor, Dhaka 5; f. 1957; reorg. 1967; Pres. MUZAFFAR AHMED; Sec.-Gen. PANKAJ BHATTACHARYA; c. 500,000 mems.

Parbattya Chattagram Jana Sanghati Samity: f. 1972; political wing of the Shanti Bahini; represents interests of Buddhist tribals in Chittagong Hill Tracts; Leader JATINDRA BODDHIPRIYA ('SHANTU') LARMA.

Samyabadi Dal: Dhaka; Maoist; Leader MOHAMMAD TOAHA.

Zaker Party: f. 1989; supports sovereignty and the introduction of an Islamic state system; Leader SYED HASMATULLAH; Mem. of the Presidium MUSTAFA AMIR FAISAL.

Diplomatic Representation

EMBASSIES AND HIGH COMMISSIONS IN BANGLADESH

Afghanistan: House CWN(C), 2A Gulshan Ave, Gulshan Model Town, Dhaka 1212; tel. (2) 603232.

Australia: 184 Gulshan Ave, Gulshan Model Town, Dhaka 1212; tel. (2) 8813105; fax (2) 8811125; e-mail ahcdhaka@agni.com; internet www.aushighcomdhaka.org; High Commissioner LORRAINE BARKER.

Bhutan: House No. SE(N) 12, 107 Gulshan Ave, Dhaka 1212; tel. (2) 8827160; fax (2) 8823939; e-mail kutshab@bdmail.net; Ambassador LHATU WANGCHUK.

Canada: House 16A, Rd 48, Gulshan Model Town, POB 569, Dhaka 1212; tel. (2) 607071; fax (2) 883043; High Commissioner JON SCOTT.

China, People's Republic: Plot NE(L) 6, Rd 83, Gulshan Model Town, Dhaka 1212; tel. (2) 884862; Ambassador HU QIANWEN.

Czech Republic: Dhaka; tel. (2) 601673.

Denmark: House NW(H) 1, Rd 51, Gulshan Model Town, POB 2056, Dhaka 1212; tel. (2) 8821799; fax (2) 8823638; e-mail dandhaka@mail.citechco.net; internet www.citechco.net/dandhaka; Ambassador NIELS SEVERIN MUNK.

Egypt: House NE(N) 9, Rd 90, Gulshan Model Town, Dhaka 1212; tel. (2) 882766; fax (2) 884883; Ambassador OSSAMA MOHAMED TAWFIK.

France: House 18, Rd 108, Gulshan Model Town, POB 22, Dhaka 1212; tel. (2) 8813812; Ambassador MICHEL LUMMAUX.

Germany: 178 Gulshan Ave, Gulshan Model Town, POB 108, Dhaka 1212; tel. (2) 8824735; fax (2) 8823141; e-mail aadhaka@ citecho.net; Ambassador DIETRICH ANDREAS.

Holy See: Lake Rd 2, Diplomatic Enclave, Baridhara Model Town, POB 6003, Dhaka 1212; tel. (2) 8822018; fax (2) 8823574; e-mail ve@ bdonline.com; Apostolic Nuncio Most Rev. PAUL TSCHANG IN-NAM (Titular Archbishop of Amantia).

Hungary: 80 Gulshan Ave, Dhaka; tel. (2) 608101; fax (2) 883117; Chargé d'affaires a.i. I. B. BUDAY.

India: House 2, Rd 142, Gulshan-I, Dhaka; tel. (2) 8820243; fax (2) 8817487; internet www.hcidhaka.org; High Commissioner MANI LAL TRIPATHI.

Indonesia: CWS(A) 10, 75 Gulshan Ave, Gulshan Model Town, Dhaka 1212; tel. (2) 600131; fax (2) 885391; Ambassador HADI A. WAYARABI ALHADAR.

Iran: CWN(A), 12 Kamal Ataturk Ave, Gulshan Model Town, Dhaka 1212; tel. (2) 601432; Ambassador MOHAMMAD SADEQ FAYAZ.

Iraq: House 8, Rd 59, Gulshan 2, Dhaka 1212; tel. (2) 600298; fax (2) 8823277; Ambassador NAHED ALI AJAJ.

Italy: Plot No. 2 & 3, Rd 74/79, Gulshan Model Town, POB 6062, Dhaka 1212; tel. (2) 882781; fax (2) 882578; e-mail ambdhaka@ citechco.net; internet www.citechco.net/italydhaka; Ambassador MARIO FILIPPO PINI.

Japan: 5 & 7, Dutabash Rd, Baridhara, Dhaka; tel. (2) 870087; fax (2) 886737; Ambassador YOSHIKAZU KANEKO.

Korea, Democratic People's Republic: House 6, Rd 7, Baridhara Model Town, Dhaka; tel. (2) 601250; Ambassador RI SANG IL.

Korea, Republic: 4 Madani Ave, Diplomatic Enclave, Baridhara, Dhaka; tel. (2) 872088; fax (2) 883871; e-mail rokdhaka@bangla.net; Ambassador LEE KYU-HUNG.

Kuwait: Plot 39, Rd 23, Block J, Banani, Dhaka 13; tel. (2) 600233; Ambassador AHMAD MURSHED AL-SULIMAN.

Libya: NE(D), 3A Gulshan Ave (N), Gulshan Model Town, Dhaka 1212; tel. (2) 600141; Sec. of People's Committee MUSBAH ALI A. MAIMOON (acting).

Malaysia: House 4, Rd 118, Gulshan Model Town, Dhaka 1212; tel. (2) 887759; fax (2) 883115; High Commissioner Dato' ZULKIFLY IBRAHIM bin ABDUR RAHMAN.

Myanmar: NE(L) 3, Rd 84, Gulshan, Dhaka 1212; tel. (2) 601915; fax (2) 8823740; Ambassador U OHN THWIN.

Nepal: United Nations Rd, Rd 2, Diplomatic Enclave, Baridhara, Dhaka; tel. (2) 601790; fax (2) 8826401; e-mail rnedhaka@bdmail .net; Ambassador MADHU RAMAN ACHARYA.

Netherlands: House 49, Rd 90, Gulshan Model Town, POB 166, Dhaka 1212; tel. (2) 882715; fax (2) 883326; e-mail nlgovdha@ citechco.net; internet www.citechco.net/Netherlands; Ambassador J. L. IJZERMANS.

Pakistan: House NE(C) 2, Rd 71, Gulshan Model Town, Dhaka 1212; tel. (2) 885388; High Commissioner KARAM ELAHI.

Philippines: House NE(L) 5, Rd 83, Gulshan Model Town, Dhaka 1212; tel. (2) 605945; Ambassador CESAR C. PASTORES.

Poland: House 12A, Rd 86, Gulshan 2, POB 6089, Dhaka 1212; tel. (2) 8825895; fax (2) 8827568; e-mail pl_dhaka@citechco.net; Chargé d'affaires a.i. ZBIGNIEW SMUGA.

Qatar: House 23, Rd 108, Gulshan Model Town, Dhaka 1212; tel. (2) 604477; Chargé d'affaires a.i. ABDULLAH AL-MUTAWA.

Romania: House 33, Rd 74, Gulshan Model Town, Dhaka 1212; tel. (2) 601467; Chargé d'affaires a.i. ALEXANDRU VOINEA.

Russia: NE(J) 9, Rd 79, Gulshan Model Town, Dhaka 1212; tel. (2) 8828147; fax (2) 8823735; e-mail rusemb@citechco.net; Ambassador NIKOLAI G. SHEVCHENKO.

Saudi Arabia: House 12, Rd 92, Gulshan (North), Dhaka 1212; tel. (2) 889124; fax (2) 883616; Ambassador ABDULLAH OMAR BARRY.

Sri Lanka: House NW 15, Rd 50, Gulshan 2, Dhaka; tel. (2) 882790; fax (2) 883971; e-mail slhc@citechco.net; High Commissioner S. B. ATUGODA.

Sweden: House 1, Rd 51, Gulshan, Dhaka 1212; tel. (2) 884761; fax (2) 883948; Ambassador ANDERS JOHNSON.

Thailand: House NW(D) 4, Rd 58–62, Gulshan Model Town, Dhaka 1212; tel. (2) 8812795; fax (2) 8823588; Ambassador PITHAYA POO-KAMAN.

Turkey: House 7, Rd 62, Gulshan Model Town, Dhaka 1212; tel. (2) 8823536; fax (2) 8823873; e-mail dakkabe@citechco.net; Ambassador FERIT ERGIN.

United Arab Emirates: POB 6014, Dhaka 1212; tel. (2) 9882244; fax (2) 8823225; e-mail info@uaeembassydhaka.com; internet www .uaeembassydhaka.com; f. 1978; Chargé d'affaires a.i. ABDUL RAZAK HADI.

United Kingdom: United Nations Rd, Baridhara, POB 6079, Dhaka 1212; tel. (2) 8822705; fax (2) 8826181; e-mail ukcomsec@ bolonline.com; internet www.ukinbangladesh.org; High Commissioner Dr DAVID CARTER.

USA: Diplomatic Enclave, Madani Ave, Baridhara, POB 323, Dhaka 1212; tel. (2) 8824700; fax (2) 8823744; e-mail ustc@bangla.net; internet www.usembassy-dhaka.org; Ambassador MARY ANN PETERS.

Judicial System

A judiciary, comprising a Supreme Court with High Court and Appellate Divisions, is in operation (see under Constitution).

Supreme Court

Dhaka 2; tel. (2) 433585.

Chief Justice: MUSTAFA KAMAL.

Attorney-General: MAHMUDUL ISLAM.

Deputy Attorney-General: A. M. FAROOQ.

Religion

The results of the 1991 census classified 88.3% of the population as Muslims, 10.5% as caste Hindus and scheduled castes, and the remainder as Buddhists, Christians and tribals.

Freedom of religious worship is guaranteed under the Constitution but, under the 1977 amendment to the Constitution, Islam was declared to be one of the nation's guiding principles and, under the 1988 amendment, Islam was established as the state religion.

BUDDHISM

World Federation of Buddhists Regional Centre: Buddhist Monastery, Kamalapur, Dhaka 14; Leader Ven. VISUDDHANANDA MAHATHERO.

CHRISTIANITY

Jatiyo Church Parishad (National Council of Churches): 395 New Eskaton Rd, Moghbazar, Dhaka 2; tel. (2) 402869; f. 1949 as East Pakistan Christian Council; four mem. churches; Pres. Dr SAJAL DEWAN; Gen. Sec. M. R. BISWAS.

Church of Bangladesh—United Church

After Bangladesh achieved independence, the Diocese of Dacca (Dhaka) of the Church of Pakistan (f. 1970 by the union of Anglicans, Methodists, Presbyterians and Lutherans) became the autonomous Church of Bangladesh. In 1986 the Church had an estimated 12,000 members. In 1990 a second diocese, the Diocese of Kushtia, was established.

Bishop of Dhaka: Rt Rev. BARNABAS DWIJEN MONDAL, St Thomas's Church, 54 Johnson Rd, Dhaka 1100; tel. (2) 7116546; fax (2) 7118218; e-mail cbdacdio@bangla.net.

Bishop of Kushtia: Rt Rev. MICHAEL BAROI, Church of Bangladesh, 94 N.S. Rd, Thanapara, Kushtia; tel. (71) 3603.

The Roman Catholic Church

For ecclesiastical purposes, Bangladesh comprises one archdiocese and five dioceses. At 31 December 2000 there were an estimated 263,595 adherents in the country.

Catholic Bishops' Conference: Archbishop's House, 1 Kakrail Rd, Ramna, POB 3, Dhaka 1000; tel. (2) 9358247; fax (2) 8314993; e-mail archbp@bangla.net; f. 1978; Pres. Most Rev. MICHAEL ROZARIO (Archbishop of Dhaka).

Secretariat

CBCB Centre, 24C Asad Ave, Mohammadpur, Dhaka 1207; tel. and fax (2) 9127339; e-mail cbcbsec@bdcom.com.

Sec.-Gen. Rt Rev. THEOTONIUS GOMES (Titular Bishop of Zucchabar).

Archbishop of Dhaka: Most Rev. MICHAEL ROZARIO, Archbishop's House, 1 Kakrail Rd, Ramna, POB 3, Dhaka 1000; tel. (2) 9358247; e-mail secabdac@aitlbd.net.

Other Christian Churches

Bangladesh Baptist Sangha: 33 Senpara, Parbatta, Mirpur 10, Dhaka 1216; tel. (2) 8012967; fax (2) 9005842; e-mail bbsangha@ bdmail.net; f. 1922; 33,232 mems (2000); Pres. SUSANTA ADHIKARI; Gen. Sec. Rev. ROBERT SARKAR.

In early 2000 there were about 48 denominational churches active in the country, including the Bogra Christian Church, the Evangelical Christian Church, the Garo Baptist Union, the Reformed Church of Bangladesh and the Sylhet Presbyterian Synod. The Baptist Sangha was the largest Protestant Church.

The Press

PRINCIPAL DAILIES

Bengali

Ajker Kagoj: Dhaka; tel. (2) 9138245; fax (2) 9139859; e-mail ajkkagoj@hotmail.com; internet www.ajkerkagoj.com; circ. 9,139,848.

Azadi: 9 C.D.A. C/A, Momin Rd, Chittagong; tel. (31) 224341; f. 1960; Editor Prof. MOHAMMAD KHALED; circ. 13,000.

Banglar Bani: 81 Motijheel C/A, Dhaka 1000; tel. (2) 237548; e-mail bani@bangla.net; f. 1972; Editor Sheikh FAZLUL KARIM SALIM; circ. 20,000.

Dainik Bangla: Dhaka; f. 1964; Editor AHMED HUMAYUN; circ. 65,000.

Dainik Bhorer Kagoj: 8 Link Rd, Banglamotor, Dhaka; tel. (2) 868802; fax (2) 868801; e-mail bkagoj@bangla.net; Editor MATIUR RAHMAN; circ. 50,000.

Dainik Birol: 26 R. K. Mission Rd, Motijheel C/A, Dhaka 1203; tel. (2) 7121620; fax (2) 8013721; Chair. of Editorial Bd ABDULLAH AL-NASER.

Dainik Inqilab: 2/1 Ramkrishna Mission Rd, Dhaka 1203; tel. (2) 9563162; fax (2) 9552881; e-mail inqilab@bttb.net; internet www .dailyinqilab.com; Editor A. M. M. BAHAUDDIN; circ. 180,025.

Dainik Ittefaq: 1 Ramkrishna Rd, Dhaka 1203; tel. (2) 256075; e-mail ittefaqnews@bangla.net; internet www.ittefaq.com; f. 1953; Propr/Editor ANWAR HUSSAIN MANJU; circ. 200,000.

Dainik Jahan: 3/B Shehra Rd, Mymensingh; tel. (91) 5677; f. 1980; Editor MUHAMMAD HABIBUR RAHMAN SHEIKH; circ. 4,000.

Dainik Janakantha (Daily People's Voice): Globe Janakantha Shilpa Paribar, Janakantha Bhaban, Dhaka 1000; tel. (2) 9347780; fax (2) 9351317; e-mail janakantha@citechco.net; internet www .janakantha.net; f. 1993; Man. Editor TOAB KHAN; Exec. Editor BORHAN AHMED; circ. 100,000.

Dainik Janata: 24 Aminbagh, Shanti Nagar, Dhaka 1217; tel. (2) 400498; Editor Dr M. ASADUR RAHMAN.

Dainik Janmobhumi: 110/1 Islampur Rd, Khulna; tel. (41) 721280; fax (41) 724324; f. 1982; Editor HUMAYUN KABIR; circ. 30,000.

Dainik Karatoa: Chalkjadu Rd, Bogra; tel. (51) 3660; fax (51) 5898; f. 1976; Editor MOZAMMEL HAQUE LALU; circ. 40,000.

Dainik Khabar: 137 Shanti Nagar, Dhaka 1217; tel. (2) 406601; f. 1985; Editor MIZANUR RAHMAN MIZAN; circ. 18,000.

Dainik Millat: Dhaka; tel. (2) 242351; Editor CHOWDHURY MOHAMMAD FAROOQ.

Dainik Nava Avijan: Lalkuthi, North Brook Hall Rd, Dhaka; tel. (2) 257516; Editor A. S. M. REZAUL HAQUE; circ. 15,000.

Dainik Patrika: 85 Elephant Rd, Maghbazar, Dhaka 1217; tel. (2) 415057; fax (2) 841575; e-mail patrika@citechco.net; Publr and Chief Editor MIA MUSA HOSSAIN; Editor M. FAISAL HASSAN HASSAN (acting).

Dainik Probaha: 3 KDA Ave, Khulna; tel. (41) 722552; f. 1977; Editor ASHRAF-UL-HAQUE; circ. 11,400.

Dainik Purbanchal: 38 Iqbal Nagar Mosque Lane, Khulna 9100; tel. (41) 22251; fax (41) 21432; f. 1974; Editor LIAQUAT ALI; circ. 42,000.

Dainik Rupashi Bangla: Abdur Rashid Rd, Natun Chowdhury Para, Bagicha Gaon, Comilla 3500; tel. (81) 76689; f. 1972; a weekly until 1979; Editor Prof. ABDUL WAHAB; circ. 10,000.

Dainik Sangram: 423 Elephant Rd, Baramaghbazar, Dhaka 1217; tel. (2) 9346448; fax (2) 9330579; e-mail dsangram@bttb.net; f. 1970; Chair. ALI AHSAN MUHAMMAD MUJAHID; Editor ABUL ASAD; circ. 50,000.

Dainik Sphulinga: Amin Villa, P-5 Housing Estate, Jessore 7401; tel. (421) 6433; f. 1971; Editor Mian ABDUS SATTAR; circ. 14,000.

Dainik Uttara: Bahadur Bazar, Dinajpur Town, Dinajpur; tel. (531) 4326; f. 1974; Editor Prof. MUHAMMAD MOHSIN; circ. 8,500.

Ganakantha: Dhaka; f. 1979; morning; Editor JAHANGIR KABIR CHOWDHURY; Exec. Editor SAIYED RABIUL KARIM; circ. 15,000.

Janabarta: 5 Babu Khan Rd, Khulna; tel. (41) 21075; f. 1974; Editor SYED SOHRAB ALI; circ. 4,000.

Jugabheri: Sylhet; tel. (821) 5461; f. 1931; Editor FAHMEEDA RASHEED CHOWDHURY; circ. 6,000.

Manav Jomeen (Human Land): Dhaka; f. 1998; tabloid.

Naya Bangla: 101 Momin Rd, Chittagong; tel. (31) 206247; f. 1978; Editor ABDULLAH AL-SAGIR; circ. 12,000.

Protidin: Ganeshtola, Dinajpur; tel. (531) 4555; f. 1980; Editor KHAIRUL ANAM; circ. 3,000.

Runner: Pyari Mohan Das Rd, Bejpara, Jessore; tel. (421) 6943; f. 1980; circ. 2,000.

Sangbad: 36 Purana Paltan, Dhaka 1000; tel. (2) 9558147; fax (2) 9562882; e-mail sangbad@bangla.net; f. 1952; Editor AHMADUL KABIR; circ. 71,050.

Swadhinata: Chittagong; tel. (31) 209644; f. 1972; Editor ABDULLAH AL-HARUN; circ. 4,000.

English

Bangladesh Observer: Observer House, 33 Toyenbee Circular Rd, Motijheel C/A, Dhaka 1000; tel. (2) 235105; e-mail observer@shapla .net; internet www.thebangladeshobserver.com; f. 1949; morning; Editor S. M. ALI; circ. 75,000.

The Bangladesh Times: Dhaka; tel. (2) 233195; f. 1975; morning; Editor MAHBUB ANAM; circ. 35,000.

Daily Evening News: 26 R. K. Mission Rd, Motijheel C/A, Dhaka 1203; tel. (2) 7121619; fax (2) 8013721; Chair. of Editorial Bd ABDULLAH AL-NASER.

Daily Rupali: 28/A/3 Toyenbee Circular Rd, Dhaka 1000; tel. (2) 235542; fax (2) 9565558; e-mail network@bangla.net; Editor MAFUZUR RAHMAN MITA.

Daily Star: 19 Karwan Bazar, Dhaka 1215; tel. (2) 8124944; fax (2) 8125155; e-mail dseditor@gononet.com; internet www .dailystarnews.com; f. 1991; Publr and Editor MAHFUZ ANAM; circ. 30,000.

Daily Tribune: 38 Iqbal Nagar Mosque Lane, Khulna 9100; tel. (41) 21944; fax (41) 22251; f. 1978; morning; Editor FERDOUSI ALI; circ. 22,000.

Financial Express: 28/1 Toyenbee Circular Rd, 2nd Floor, POB 2526, Dhaka 1000; tel. (2) 9568154; fax (2) 9567049; e-mail tfe@ bangla.net; internet www.financial-express.com; f. 1994; Editor-in-Chief REAZUDDIN AHMED.

The Independent: Beximco Media Complex, 32 Kazi Nazrul Islam Ave, Karwan Bazar, Dhaka 1215; tel. (2) 9129938; fax (2) 9127722; e-mail ind@gononet.com; internet www.independent-bangladesh .com; f. 1995; Editor MAHBUBUL ALAM.

New Nation: 1 Ramkrishna Mission Rd, Dhaka 1203; tel. (2) 256071; fax (2) 245536; e-mail newnation@nation-online.com; internet www.nation-online.com; f. 1981; Editor ALAMGIR MOHIUDDIN; circ. 15,000.

People's View: 102 Siraj-ud-Daulla Rd, Chittagong; tel. (31) 227403; f. 1969; Editor SABBIR ISLAM; circ. 3,000.

PERIODICALS

Bengali

Aachal: Dhaka; weekly; Editor FERDOUSI BEGUM.

Adhuna: 1/3 Block F, Lalmatia, Dhaka 1207; tel. (2) 812353; fax (2) 813095; e-mail adab@bdonline.com; f. 1974; quarterly; publ. by the Asscn of Devt Agencies in Bangladesh (ADAB); Exec. Editor MINAR MONSUR; circ. 10,000.

Ahmadi: 4 Bakshi Bazar Rd, Dhaka 1211; tel. (2) 7300808; fax (2) 7300925; e-mail amgb@bol-online.com; f. 1925; fortnightly; Editor-in-Chief M. A. S. MAHMOOD; Exec. Editor MOHAMMAD M. RAHMAN.

Alokpat: 166 Arambagh, Dhaka 1000; tel. (2) 413361; fax (2) 863060; fortnightly; Editor RABBANI JABBAR.

Amod: Chowdhury Para, Comilla 3500; tel. (81) 5193; f. 1955; weekly; Editor SHAMSUN NAHAR RABBI; circ. 6,000.

Ananda Bichitra: Dhaka; tel. (2) 241639; f. 1986; fortnightly; Editor SHAHADAT CHOWDHURY; circ. 32,000.

Begum: 66 Loyal St, Dhaka 1; tel. (2) 233789; f. 1947; women's illustrated weekly; Editor NURJAHAN BEGUM; circ. 25,000.

Bichitra: Dhaka; tel. (2) 232086; e-mail bchitra@bangla.net; f. 1972; weekly; Editor SHAHADAT CHOWDHURY; circ. 42,000.

Chakra: 242A Nakhalpara, POB 2682, Dhaka 1215; tel. (2) 604568; social welfare weekly; Editor HUSNEARA AZIZ.

Chitra Desh: 24 Ramkrishna Mission Rd, Dhaka 1203; weekly; Editor HENA AKHTAR CHOWDHURY.

Chitrali: Observer House, 33 Toyenbee Circular Rd, Motijheel C/A, Dhaka 1000; tel. (2) 9550938; fax (2) 9562243; f. 1953; film weekly; Editor PRODIP KUMAR DEY; circ. 25,000.

Ekota: 15 Larmini St, Wari, Dhaka; tel. (2) 257854; f. 1970; weekly; Editor MATIUR RAHMAN; circ. 25,000.

Fashal: 28J Toyenbee Circular Rd, Motijheel C/A, Dhaka 1000; tel. (2) 233099; f. 1965; agricultural weekly; Chief Editor ERSHAD MAZUMDAR; circ. 8,000.

Ispat: Majampur, Kushtia; tel. (71) 3676; f. 1976; weekly; Editor WALIUR BARI CHOUDHURY; circ. 3,000.

Jaijaidin: 15 New Bailey Rd, Dhaka 1000; tel. (2) 8316448; fax (2) 9568598; e-mail jajadi@aitlbd.net; internet www.jaijaidin.com; f. 1984; weekly; Editor SHAFIK REHMAN; circ. 100,000.

Jhorna: 4/13 Block A, Lalmatia, Dhaka; tel. (2) 415239; Editor MUHAMMAD JAMIR ALI.

Kalantar: 87 Khanjahan Ali Rd, Khulna; tel. (41) 61424; f. 1971; weekly; Editor NOOR MOHAMMAD; circ. 12,000.

Kankan: Nawab Bari Rd, Bogra; tel. (51) 6424; f. 1974; weekly; Editor SUFIA KHATUN; circ. 6,000.

Kirajagat: National Sports Control Board, 62/63 Purana Paltan, Dhaka; f. 1977; weekly; Editor ALI MUZZAMAN CHOWDHURY; circ. 7,000.

Kishore Bangla: Observer House, Motijheel C/A, Dhaka 1000; juvenile weekly; f. 1976; Editor RAFIQUL HAQUE; circ. 5,000.

Moha Nagar: 4 Dilkusha C/A, Dhaka 1000; tel. (2) 255282; Editor SYED MOTIUR RAHMAN.

Moshal: 4 Dilkusha C/A, Dhaka 1000; tel. (2) 231092; Editor MUHAMMAD ABUL HASNAT; circ. 3,000.

Muktibani: Toyenbee Circular Rd, Motijheel C/A, Dhaka 1000; tel. (2) 253712; f. 1972; weekly; Editor NIZAM UDDIN AHMED; circ. 35,000.

Natun Bangla: 44/2 Free School St Bylane, Hatirpool, Dhaka 1205; tel. (2) 866121; fax (2) 863794; e-mail mujib@bangla.net; f. 1971; weekly; Editor MUJIBUR RAHMAN.

Natun Katha: 31E Topkhana Rd, Dhaka; weekly; Editor HAJERA SULTANA; circ. 4,000.

Nipun: 520 Peyarabag, Magbazar, Dhaka 11007; tel. (2) 312156; monthly; Editor SHAJAHAN CHOWDHURY.

Parikrama: 65 Shanti Nagar, Dhaka; tel. (2) 415640; Editor MOMTAZ SULTANA.

Prohar: 35 Siddeswari Rd, Dhaka 1217; tel. (2) 404206; Editor MUJIBUL HUQ.

Protirodh: Dept of Answar and V.D.P. Khilgoan, Ministry of Home Affairs, School Bldg, 2nd and 3rd Floors, Bangladesh Secretariat, Dhaka; tel. (2) 405971; f. 1977; fortnightly; Editor ZAHANGIR HABIBULLAH; circ. 20,000.

Purbani: 1 Ramkrishna Mission Rd, Dhaka 1203; tel. (2) 256503; f. 1951; film weekly; Editor KHONDKER SHAHADAT HOSSAIN; circ. 22,000.

Robbar: 1 Ramkrishna Mission Rd, Dhaka; tel. (2) 256071; e-mail robbar@nation-online.com; internet www.robbar.com; f. 1978; weekly; Editor ABDUL HAFIZ; circ. 20,000.

Rokshena: 13B Avoy Das Lane, Tiktuli, Dhaka; tel. (2) 255117; Editor SYEDA AFSANA.

Sachitra Bangladesh: 112 Circuit House Rd, Dhaka 1000; tel. (2) 402129; f. 1979; fortnightly; Editor A. B. M. ABDUL MATIN; circ. 8,000.

Sachitra Sandhani: 68/2 Purana Paltan, Dhaka; tel. (2) 409680; f. 1978; weekly; Editor GAZI SHAHABUDDIN MAHMUD; circ. 13,000.

Sandip Bhabhan: 28/A/3 Toyenbee Circular Rd, Dhaka; tel. (2) 235542; fax (2) 9565558; e-mail network@bangla.net; weekly; Editor MAFUZUR RAHMAN MITA.

Shishu: Bangladesh Shishu Academy, Old High Court Compound, Dhaka 1000; tel. (2) 230317; f. 1977; children's monthly; Editor GOLAM KIBRIA; circ. 5,000.

Sonar Bangla: 423 Elephant Rd, Mogh Bazar, Dhaka 1217; tel. (2) 400637; f. 1961; Editor MUHAMMED QAMARUZZAMAN; circ. 25,000.

Swadesh: 19 B.B. Ave, Dhaka; tel. (2) 256946; weekly; Editor ZAKIUDDIN AHMED; circ. 8,000.

Tarokalok: Tarokalok Complex, 25/3 Green Rd, Dhaka 1205; tel. (2) 506583; fax (2) 864330; weekly; Editor AREFIN BADAL.

Tide: 56/57 Motijheel C/A, Dhaka; tel. (2) 259421; Editor ENAYET KARIM.

Tilotwoma: 14 Bangla Bazar, Dhaka; Editor ABDUL MANNAN.

English

ADAB News: 1/3, Block F, Lalmatia, Dhaka 1207; tel. (2) 327424; f. 1974; 6 a year; publ. by the Asscn of Devt Agencies in Bangladesh (ADAB); Editor-in-Chief AZFAR HUSSAIN; circ. 10,000.

Bangladesh: 112 Circuit House Rd, Dhaka 1000; tel. (2) 402013; fortnightly; Editor A. B. M. ABDUL MATIN.

Bangladesh Gazette: Bangladesh Government Press, Tejgaon, Dhaka; f. 1947; name changed 1972; weekly; official notices; Editor M. HUDA.

Bangladesh Illustrated Weekly: Dhaka; tel. (2) 23358; Editor ATIQUZZAMAN KHAN; circ. 3,000.

Cinema: 81 Motijheel C/A, Dhaka 1000; Editor SHEIKH FAZLUR RAHMAN MARUF; circ. 11,000.

Detective: Polwell Bhaban, Naya Paltan, Dhaka 2; tel. (2) 402757; f. 1960; weekly; also publ. in Bengali; Editor SYED AMJAD HOSSAIN; circ. 3,000.

Dhaka Courier: Cosmos Centre, 69/1 New Circular Rd, Malibagh, Dhaka 1217; tel. (2) 408420; fax (2) 831942; e-mail cosmos@citecho.net; internet www.dhakacourier.com; weekly; Editor ENAYETULLAH KHAN; circ. 18,000.

Holiday: Holiday Bldg, 30 Tejgaon Industrial Area, Dhaka 1208; tel. (2) 9122950; fax (2) 9127927; e-mail holiday@bangla.net; internet www.weekly-holiday.net; f. 1965; weekly; independent; Editor-in-Chief ENAYETULLAH KHAN; circ. 18,000.

Motherland: Khanjahan Ali Rd, Khulna; tel. (41) 61685; f. 1974; weekly; Editor M. N. KHAN.

Tide: 56/57 Motijheel C/A, Dhaka; tel. (2) 259421; Editor ENAYET KARIM.

Voice From the North: Dinajpur Town, Dinajpur; tel. (531) 3256; f. 1981; weekly; Editor Prof. MUHAMMAD MOHSIN; circ. 5,000.

NEWS AGENCIES

Bangladesh Sangbad Sangstha (BSS) (Bangladesh News Agency): 68/2 Purana Paltan, Dhaka 1000; tel. (2) 235036; Man. Dir and Chief Editor MAHBUBUL ALAM; Gen. Man. D. P. BARUA.

Eastern News Agency (ENA): Dhaka; tel. (2) 234206; f. 1970; Man. Dir and Chief Editor GOLAM RASUL MALLICK.

Islamic News Society (INS): 24 RK Mission Rd, Motijheel C/A, Dhaka 1203; tel. (2) 7121619; fax (2) 8013721; Editor ABDULLAH AL-NASER.

United News of Bangladesh: Dhaka.

Foreign Bureaux

Agence France-Presse (AFP): Shilpa Bank Bldg, 5th Floor, 8 DIT Ave, nr Dhaka Stadium, Dhaka 1000; tel. (2) 242234; Bureau Chief GOLAM TAHABOOR.

Associated Press (AP) (USA): 69/1 New Circular Rd, Dhaka 1217; tel. (2) 833717; Representative HASAN SAEED FARID HOSSAIN.

Inter Press Service (IPS) (Italy): c/o Bangladesh Sangbad Sangstha, 68/2 Purana Paltan, Dhaka 1000; tel. (2) 235036; Correspondent A. K. M. TABIBUL ISLAM.

Reuters Ltd (UK): POB 3993, Dhaka; tel. (2) 864088; fax (2) 832976; Bureau Chief ATIQUL ALAM.

United Press International (UPI) (USA): Dhaka; tel. (2) 233132.

PRESS ASSOCIATIONS

Bangladesh Press Council: Dhaka; f. 1974; established under an act of Parliament to preserve the freedom of the press and maintain and develop standards of newspapers and news agencies.

Bangladesh Sangbadpatra Karmachari Federation (Newspaper Employees' Fed.): Dhaka; tel. (2) 235065; f. 1972; Pres. RAFIQUL ISLAM; Sec.-Gen. MIR MOZAMMEL HOSSAIN.

Bangladesh Sangbadpatra Press Sramik Federation (Newspaper Press Workers' Federation): 1 Ramkrishna Mission Rd, Dhaka 1203; f. 1960; Pres. M. ABDUL KARIM; Sec.-Gen. BOZLUR RAHMAN MILON.

Dhaka Union of Journalists: National Press Club, Dhaka; f. 1947; Pres. ABEL KHAIR; Gen.-Sec. ABDUL KALAM AZAD.

Overseas Correspondents' Association of Bangladesh (OCAB): 18 Topkhana Rd, Dhaka 1000; e-mail naweed@bdonline.com; f. 1979; Pres. ZAGLUL A. CHOWDHURY; Gen. Sec. NADEEM QADIR; 60 mems.

Press Institute of Bangladesh: 3 Circuit House Rd, Dhaka 1000; tel. (2) 412130; fax (2) 416569; e-mail pib@bdonline.com; f. 1976; trains journalists, conducts research, operates a newspaper library and data bank.

Publishers

Academic Publishers: 2/7 Nawab-Habibullah Rd, Dhaka 1000; tel. (2) 507355; fax (2) 863060; f. 1982; social sciences and sociology; Jt Man. Dir HABIBUR RAHMAN.

Agamee Prakashani: 36 Bangla Bazar, Dhaka 1100; tel. (2) 7111332; fax (2) 7123945; e-mail agamee@bdonline.com; internet www.agameeprakashani-bd.com; f. 1986; fiction and academic; Chief Exec. OSMAN GANI.

Ahmed Publishing House: 7 Zindabahar 1st Lane, Dhaka 1; tel. (2) 36492; f. 1942; literature, history, science, religion, children's, maps and charts; Man. Dir KAMALUDDIN AHMED; Man. MESBAHUDDIN AHMED.

Ankur Prakashani: 38/4 Bangla Bazar, Dhaka 1100; tel. (2) 9564799; e-mail ankur@agnionline.com; f. 1986; academic and general.

Ashrafia Library: 4 Hakim Habibur Rahman Rd, Chawk Bazar, Dhaka 1000; Islamic religious books, texts, and reference works of Islamic institutions.

Asiatic Society of Bangladesh: 5 Old Secretariat Rd, Ramna, Dhaka; tel. (2) 9560500; f. 1952; periodicals on science, Bangla and humanities; Pres. Prof. WAKIL AHMED; Admin. Officer MD ABDUL AWAL MIAH.

Bangla Academy (National Academy of Arts and Letters): Burdwan House, 3 Kazi Nazrul Islam Ave, Dhaka 1000; tel. (2) 869577; f. 1955; higher education textbooks in Bengali, research works in language, literature and culture, language planning, popular science, drama, encyclopaedias, translations of world classics, dictionaries; Dir-Gen. Prof. MONSUR MUSA.

Bangladesh Books International Ltd: Ittefaq Bhaban, 1 Ramkrishna Mission Rd, POB 377, Dhaka 3; tel. (2) 256071; f. 1975; reference, academic, research, literary, children's in Bengali and English; Chair. MOINUL HOSSEIN; Man. Dir ABDUL HAFIZ.

Bangladesh Publishers: 45 Patuatully Rd, Dhaka 1100; tel. (2) 233135; f. 1952; textbooks for schools, colleges and universities, cultural books, journals, etc. Dir MAYA RANI GHOSAL.

Gatidhara: 38/2-Ka Bangla Bazar, Dhaka 1100; tel. (2) 247515; fax (2) 956600; f. 1988; academic, general and fiction.

Gono Prakashani: House 14/E, Rd 6, Dhanmondhi R/A, Dhaka 1205; tel. (2) 8617208; fax (2) 8613567; e-mail gk@citechco.net; f. 1978; science and medicine; Man. Dir SHAFIQ KHAN; Editor BAZLUR RAHIM.

International Publications: 8 Baitul Mukarram, 1st Floor, GPO Box 45, Dhaka 1000.

Muktadhara: 74 Farashganj, Dhaka 1100; tel. (2) 231374; e-mail muktadhara1971@yahoo.com; f. 1971; educational, literary and general; Bengali and English; Dir J. L. SAHA; Man. Dir C. R. SAHA.

Mullick Brothers: 3/1 Bangla Bazar, Dhaka 1100; tel. (2) 232088; fax (2) 833983; educational.

Osmania Book Depot: 30/32 North Brook Hall Rd, Dhaka 1100.

Puthighar Ltd: 74 Farashganj, Dhaka 1100; tel. (2) 7111374; e-mail muktadhara1971@yahoo.com; f. 1951; educational; Bengali and English; Dir J. L. SAHA; Man. Dir C. R. SAHA.

Rahman Brothers: 5/1 Gopinath Datta, Kabiraj St, Babu Bazar, Dhaka; tel. (2) 282633; educational.

Royal Library: Ispahani Bldg, 31/32 P. K. Roy Rd, Bangla Bazar, Dhaka 1; tel. (2) 250863.

Shahitya Prakash: 51 Purana Paltan, Dhaka 1000; tel. (2) 9560485; fax (2) 9565506; f. 1970; Prin. Officer MOFIDUL HOQUE.

University Press Ltd: Red Crescent Bldg, 114 Motijheel C/A, POB 2611, Dhaka 1000; tel. (2) 9565444; fax (2) 9565443; e-mail upl@bangla.net; internet www.uplbooks.com; f. 1975; educational, academic and general; Man. Dir MOHIUDDIN AHMED.

Government Publishing Houses

Bangladesh Bureau of Statistics: Parishankhan Bhaban, E-27/A, Agargaon, Sher-e-Bangla Nagar, Dhaka 1207; tel. (2) 9133378; fax (2) 9111064; internet www.bbsgov.org; f. 1971; statistical year book and pocket book, censuses, surveys, agricultural year book, special reports, etc. Jt Dir S. M. TAJUL ISLAM; Sec. BADIUR RAHMAN.

Bangladesh Government Press: Tejgaon, Dhaka 1209; tel. (2) 606316; f. 1972.

Department of Films and Publications: 112 Circuit House Rd, Dhaka 1000; tel. (2) 402263.

Press Information Department: Bhaban 6, Bangladesh Secretariat, Dhaka 1000; tel. (2) 400958.

PUBLISHERS' ASSOCIATIONS

Bangladesh Publishers' and Booksellers' Association: 3rd Floor, 3 Liaquat Ave, Dhaka 1; f. 1972; Pres. JANAB JAHANGIR MOHAMMED ADEL; 2,500 mems.

National Book Centre of Bangladesh: 67A Purana Paltan, Dhaka 1000; f. 1963 to promote the cause of 'more, better and cheaper books'; organizes book fairs, publs a monthly journal; Dir FAZLE RABBI.

Broadcasting and Communications

TELECOMMUNICATIONS

Bangladesh Telegraph and Telephone Board: Central Office, Telejogajog Bhaban, 37/E Eskaton Garden, Dhaka 1000; tel. (2) 831500; fax (2) 832577; Chair. M.A. MANNAN CHOWDHURY; Dir (International) MD HASSANUZZAMAN.

Grameen Telecom: Dhaka; f. 1996 by Grameen Bank to expand cellular telephone service in rural areas; Head NAJMUL HUDA.

BROADCASTING

Radio

Bangladesh Betar: NBA House, 121 Kazi Nazrul Islam Ave, Shahabag, Dhaka 1000; tel. (2) 865294; fax (2) 862021; e-mail dgradio@drik.bgd.toolnet.org; f. 1971; govt-controlled; regional stations at Dhaka, Chittagong, Khulna, Rajshahi, Rangpur, Sylhet, Rangamati and Thakurgaon broadcast a total of approximately 160 hours daily; transmitting centres at Lalmai and Rangamati; external service broadcasts 8 transmissions daily in Arabic, Bengali, English, Hindi, Nepalese and Urdu; Dir-Gen. M.I. CHOWDHURY; Dep. Dir-Gen. (Programmes) ASHFAQUR RAHMAN KHAN.

Television

Bangladesh Television (BTV): Television House, Rampura, Dhaka 1219; tel. (2) 866606; fax (2) 832927; f. 1964; govt-controlled; daily broadcasts on one channel from Dhaka station for 10 hours; transmissions also from nationwide network of 14 relay stations; Dir-Gen. SAYED SALAHUDDIN ZAKI; Gen. Man. NAWAZISH ALI KHAN.

Finance

(cap. = capital; res = reserves; dep. = deposits; m. = million; brs = branches; amounts in taka)

BANKING

Central Bank

Bangladesh Bank: Motijheel C/A, POB 325, Dhaka 1000; tel. (2) 9555000; fax (2) 9566212; e-mail banglabank@bangla.net; internet www.bangladesh-bank.org; f. 1971; cap. 30m., res 9,117.9m., dep. 85,313.0m. (June 2000); Gov. Dr MOHAMMED FARASHUDDIN; 9 brs.

Nationalized Commercial Banks

Agrani Bank: Agrani Bank Bhaban, Motijheel C/A, POB 531, Dhaka 1000; tel. (2) 9566160; fax (2) 9563662; f. 1972; 100% state-owned; cap. 2,484m., res 324m., dep. 101,795m. (Dec. 1999); Chair. Dr MOHAMMAD SOHRAB UDDIN; Man. Dir M. A. YOUSOOF; 903 brs.

Janata Bank: 110 Motijheel C/A, POB 468, Dhaka 1000; tel. (2) 9565041; fax (2) 9564644; e-mail id-obd@janatabank-bd.com; internet www.janatabank-bd.com; f. 1972; 100% state-owned; cap. 2,594m., res 540m., dep. 103,846m. (Dec. 2000); Chair. M. AYUBUR RAHMAN; Man. Dir MURSHID KULI KHAN; 894 brs in Bangladesh, 4 brs in the UAE.

Rupali Bank Ltd: Rupali Bhaban, 34 Dilkusha C/A, POB 719, Dhaka 1000; tel. (2) 9564122; fax (2) 9564148; e-mail rblhocom@bdcom.com; f. 1972; 94% state-owned, 6% by public; cap. 1,250m., res 2,862.5m., dep. 39,637.8m. (Dec. 1999); Chair. Dr MOMTAZ UDDIN AHMED; Man. Dir MOHAMMAD YEASIN ALI; 513 brs in Bangladesh, 1 br. in Pakistan.

Sonali Bank: 35–44 Motijheel C/A, POB 3130, Dhaka 1000; tel. (2) 9550426; fax (2) 9561410; f. 1972; 100% state-owned; cap. 3,272.2m., res 2,036.0m., dep. 170,960.7m. (Dec. 1999); Chair. MUHAMMED ALI; Man. Dir M. ENAMUL HAQ CHOWDHURY; 1,313 brs in Bangladesh, 6 brs in United Kingdom and 1 br. in India.

Private Commercial Banks

Al-Arafah Islami Bank Ltd: Rahman Mansion, 161 Motijheel C/A, Dhaka; tel. (2) 9560198; f. 1995; 100% owned by 23 sponsors; cap. 101.2m., res 10m., dep. 534.4m. (Aug. 1996); Chair. A. Z. M. SHAMSUL ALAM; Man. Dir M. M. NURUL HAQUE.

Al-Baraka Bank Bangladesh Ltd: Kashfia Plaza, 35c Naya Paltan (VIP Rd), POB 3467, Dhaka 1000; tel. (2) 410050; fax (2) 834943; f. 1987; on Islamic banking principles; 34.68% owned by Al-Baraka Group, Saudi Arabia, 5.78% by Islamic Development Bank, Jeddah, 45.91% by local sponsors, 5.75% by Bangladesh Govt, 7.8% by general public; cap. 259.6m., res 14.9m., dep. 4,898.1m. (June 1996); Chair. Dr SALEH J. MALAIKAH; Man. Dir ANOWAR AHMED; 33 brs.

Arab Bangladesh Bank Ltd: BCIC Bhaban, 30–31 Dilkusha C/A, POB 3522, Dhaka 1000; tel. (2) 9560312; fax (2) 9564122; e-mail abbank@citecho.net; f. 1981; 95% owned by Bangladesh nationals and 5% by Bangladesh Govt; cap. 409.9m., res 354.8m., dep. 13,899.7m. (Dec. 1999); Chair. M. MORSHED KHAN; Pres. and Man. Dir C. M. KOYES SAMI; 62 brs, 1 br. in India.

City Bank Ltd: Jiban Bima Tower, 10 Dilkusha C/A, POB 3381, Dhaka 1000; tel. (2) 9565925; fax (2) 9562347; e-mail cbl@citechco.net; internet www.thecitybank.com; f. 1983; 50% owned by sponsors and 50% by public; cap. 160.0m., res 263.1m., dep. 17,184.0m. (Dec. 2001); Chair. DEEN MOHAMMAD; Man. Dir ABBAS UDDIN AHMED; 76 brs.

Dhaka Bank Ltd: 1st Floor, Biman Bhaban, 100 Motijheel C/A, Dhaka 1000; tel. (2) 9554514; fax (2) 9556584; e-mail dhakabnk@bdonline.com; internet www.dhakabankltd.com; f. 1995; cap. 303.5m., res 202.2m., dep. 15,085.8m. (Dec. 2001); Chair. A. T. M. HAYATUZZAMAN KHAN; Man. Dir MOHAMMAD MOKHLESUR RAHMAN; 11 brs.

Eastern Bank Ltd: Jiban Bima Bhaban, 2nd Floor, 10 Dilkusha C/A, POB 896, Dhaka 1000; tel. (2) 9556360; fax (2) 9562364; e-mail ebank@bdcom.com; f. 1992; appropriated assets and liabilities of fmr Bank of Credit and Commerce International (Overseas) Ltd; 83% owned by public, 17% owned by government and private commercial banks; cap. 720m., res 2,322m., dep. 13,277m. (Dec. 2001); Chair. M. GHAZIUL HAQUE; Man. Dir K. MAHMOOD SATTAR; 22 brs.

International Finance Investment and Commerce Bank Ltd (IFICB): BSB Bldg, 17th–19th Floors, 8 Rajuk Ave, POB 2229, Dhaka 1000; tel. (2) 9563020; fax (2) 9562015; e-mail ificmd@citechco.net; f. 1983; 40% state-owned; cap. 279.4m., res 311.1m., dep. 17,229.5m. (Dec. 1998); Chair. MANZURUL ISLAM; Man. Dir ATAUL HAQ; 52 brs in Bangladesh, 2 brs in Pakistan.

Islami Bank Bangladesh Ltd (IBBL): Head Office, Islami Bank Tower, 40 Dilkusha C/A, POB 233, Dhaka 1000; tel. (2) 9563046; fax (2) 9564532; e-mail ibbl@ncll.com; internet www.islamibankbd.com; f. 1983 on Islamic banking principles; cap. 640.0m., res 2,097.6m., dep. 47,555.5m. (June 2002); Chair. SHAH ABDUL HANNAN; Exec. Pres. and CEO ABDUR RAQUIB; 122 brs.

National Bank Ltd: 18 Dilkusha C/A, POB 3424, Dhaka 1000; tel. (2) 9557045; fax (2) 9563953; e-mail nblid@bdonline.com; internet www.nblbd.com; f. 1983; 50% owned by sponsors, 45% by general public and 5% by Govt; cap. 430.3m., res 742.7m., dep. 24,946.8m. (June 2002); Chair. ABU TAHER MIAH; Man. Dir RAFIQUL ISLAM KHAN; 76 brs.

National Credit and Commerce Bank Ltd: 7–8 Motijheel C/A, POB 2920, Dhaka 1000; tel. (2) 9561902; fax (2) 9566290; e-mail nccbl@bdmail.net; internet www.nccbank-bd.com; f. 1993; 50% owned by sponsors, 50% by general public; cap. 429m., res 375m., dep. 12,500m. (Dec. 2001); Chair. NURUL ISLAM; Man. Dir ANWAR AHMED; 30 brs.

Prime Bank Ltd: Adamjee Court Annex Bldg No. 2, 119–20 Motijheel C/A, Dhaka 1000; tel. (2) 9567265; fax (2) 9567230; e-mail primebnk@bangla.net; internet www.prime-bank.com; f. 1995; cap. 500m., res 366.1m., dep. 13,259.9m. (Dec. 2001); Chair. MOHAMMAD AMINUL HAQUE; Man. Dir M. SHAHJAHAN BHUIYAN; 26 brs.

Pubali Bank Ltd: Pubali Bank Bhaban, 26 Dilkusha C/A, POB 853, Dhaka 1000; tel. (2) 9551614; fax (2) 9564009; e-mail pubali@bdmail.net; f. 1959 as Eastern Mercantile Bank Ltd; name changed to Pubali Bank in 1972; 95% privately-owned, 5% state-owned; cap. 160m., res 644.2m., dep. 25,200.6m. (Dec. 1999); Chair. EMADUDDIN AHMED CHAUDHURY; Man. Dir MOHAMMAD QAMRUL HUDA; 350 brs.

Social Investment Bank: 15 Dilkusha C/A, Dhaka 1000; tel. (2) 9554855; fax (2) 9559013; e-mail sibl@bdonline.com; internet www.siblbd.com; f. 1995; cap. 200.0m., res 16.8m., dep. 3,899.7m. (Dec. 1999); Chair. AHMED AKBAR SOBHAN; Man. Dir GOLAM MUSTAFA; 5 brs.

Southeast Bank Ltd: 3rd Floor, 1 Dilkusha C/A, Dhaka 1000; tel. (2) 9550081; fax (2) 9563102; e-mail seastbk@citecho.net; internet www.southeastbank-bangladesh.com; f. 1995; cap. 300m., res 261.5m., dep. 8,569.7m. (Dec. 2000); Chair. YUSSUF ABDULLAH HAROON; Pres. and Man. Dir SHAH MOHAMMAD NURUL ALAM; 12 brs.

United Commercial Bank Ltd: Federation Bhaban, 60 Motijheel C/A, POB 2653, Dhaka 1000; tel. (2) 9560585; fax (2) 9560587; f. 1983; 50% owned by sponsors, 45% by general public and 5% by Govt; cap. 230.2m., res 334.8m., dep. 10,102.0m. (Dec. 1999); Chair. ZAFAR AHMED CHOWDHURY; 79 brs.

Uttara Bank Ltd: 90 Motijheel C/A, POB 818, Dhaka 1000; tel. (2) 9560021; fax (2) 8613529; e-mail ublmis@citecho.net; f. 1965 as Eastern Banking Corpn Ltd; name changed to Uttara Bank in 1972 and to Uttara Bank Ltd in 1983; 5% state-owned; cap. 99.8m., res 702.4m., dep. 26,375.1m. (Dec. 2000); Chair. AZHARUL ISLAM; Man. Dir and CEO M. AMINUZAMMAN; 198 brs.

Foreign Commercial Banks

American Express Bank Ltd (USA): ALICO Bldg, 18–20 Motijheel C/A, POB 420, Dhaka 1000; tel. (2) 9561751; fax (2) 9561722; e-mail amexbd@gononet.com; res 537.5m., dep. 6,236.5m. (Dec. 1995); Chair. RICHARD HOLMES; Gen. Man. JOHN A. SMETANKA; 8 brs.

ANZ Grindlays Bank Ltd (UK): 2 Dilkusha C/A, POB 502, Dhaka 1000; tel. (2) 9550181; fax (2) 9562332; e-mail choudhun@anz.com; res 60.5m., dep. 20,060m. (1999); Gen. Man. MUHAMMAD A. ALI; 9 brs.

Citibank, NA (USA): 122–124 Motijheel C/A, POB 1000, Dhaka 1000; tel. (2) 9550060; fax (2) 642611; f. 1995; cap. 209.5m., res 5.5m., dep. 648.8m. (July 1996); Chair. JOHN S. REED; Man. Dir S. SRIDHAR; 1 br.

Crédit Agricole Indosuez (France): 47 Motijheel C/A, POB 3490, Dhaka 1000; tel. (2) 9566566; fax (2) 9465707; res 591m., dep. 5,302m. (Dec. 1997); Country Man. FRANCIS DUBUS; Chief Operating Officer S. R. VATOVEY; 2 brs.

Habib Bank Ltd (Pakistan): 53 Motijheel C/A, POB 201, Dhaka 1000; tel. (2) 9563043; fax (2) 9561784; e-mail hbldhaka@bdonline.com; cap. 80.5m., res 14.3m., dep. 578.6m. (Dec. 1996); Country Man. GHAZANFAR ALI; 2 brs.

The Hongkong and Shanghai Banking Corpn Ltd (Hong Kong): 5th Floor, Anchor Tower, 1/1B Sonargaon Rd, Dhaka, 1205; tel. (2) 9660536; fax (2) 9660554; CEO for Bangladesh DAVID HUMPHREYS.

Muslim Commercial Bank Ltd (Pakistan): 4 Dilkusha C/A, POB 7213, Dhaka 1000; tel. (2) 9568871; fax (2) 860671; cap. 100m., res 4m., dep. 650.3m. (July 1996); Gen. Man. AHMED KARIM; 2 brs.

Standard Chartered Bank (UK): ALICO Bldg, 18–20 Motijheel C/A, POB 536, Dhaka 1000; tel. (2) 9561465; fax (2) 9561758; internet www.standardchartered.com; cap. 215m., dep. 5,850m. (Dec. 1995); Chief Exec. (Bangladesh) GEOFF WILLIAMS; 3 brs.

State Bank of India: 24–25 Dilkusha C/A, POB 981, Dhaka 1000; tel. (2) 9559935; fax (2) 9563991; e-mail sbibd@bangla.net; cap. 190.4m., dep. 557.1m. (March 1997); CEO ASHITAVA GHOSH; 1 br.

Development Finance Organizations

Bangladesh House Building Finance Corpn (BHBFC): HBFC Bldg, 22 Purana Paltan, POB 2167, Dhaka 1000; tel. (2) 9562767; f. 1952; provides low-interest credit for residential house-building; 100% state-owned; cap. 972.9m., total investment 23,255.3m. (Dec. 1999); Chair. S. M. ATIUR RAHMAN; Man. Dir S. M. MONIAM HOSSEIN; 9 zonal offices, 13 regional offices and 6 camp offices.

Bangladesh Krishi Bank (BKB): 83–85 Motijheel C/A, POB 357, Dhaka 1000; tel. (2) 9553028; fax (2) 9561211; e-mail bkb@citechco.net; f. 1961 as the Agricultural Development Bank of Pakistan, name changed as above in 1973; provides credit for agricultural and rural devt; also performs all kinds of banking; 100% state-owned; cap. 1,250.0m., res 820.4m., dep. 40,380.0m. (June 2002); Chair. Dr MUHAMMAD AHBAB AHMED; Man. Dir A. K. M. SAJEDUR RAHMAN; 921 brs.

Bangladesh Samabaya Bank Ltd (BSBL): 'Samabaya Sadan', 9D Motijheel C/A, POB 505, Dhaka 1000; tel. (2) 9564628; f. 1948; provides credit for agricultural co-operatives; cap. 31.6m., res 558m., dep. 22m. (June 1996); Chair. Dr ABDUL MOYEEN KHAN; Gen. Man. MD ABDUL WAHED.

Bangladesh Shilpa Bank (BSB) (Industrial Development Bank): 8 Rajuk Ave, POB 975, Dhaka 1000; tel. (2) 9555151; fax (2) 9562061; e-mail bsblink@citechco-net; f. 1972; fmrly Industrial Devt Bank; provides long- and short-term financing for industrial devt in the private and public sectors; also provides underwriting facilities and equity support; 51% state-owned; cap. 1,320.0m., res 778.3m., dep. 571.0m. (June 2000); Chair. Dr AHSRAF UDDIN CHOWDHURY; 15 brs.

Bangladesh Shilpa Rin Sangstha (BSRS) (Industrial Loan Agency): BIWTA Bhaban, 5th Floor, 141-143 Motijheel C/A, POB 473, Dhaka 1000; tel. (2) 9565046; fax (2) 9567057; f. 1972; 100% state-owned; cap. 700m., res 462.8m. (June 1996); Chair. Dr M. FARASHUDDIN; Man. Dir AL-AMEEN CHAUDHURY; 4 brs.

Bank of Small Industries and Commerce Bangladesh Ltd (BASIC): Suite 601/602, Sena Kalyan Bhaban, 6th Floor, 195 Motijheel C/A, Dhaka 1000; tel. (2) 956430; fax (2) 9564829; f. 1988; 100% state-owned; cap. 80m., res 106m., dep. 2,738m. (Dec. 1995); Chair. A. M. AKHTER; Man. Dir ALAUDDIN A. MAJID; 19 brs.

Grameen Bank: Head Office, Mirpur-2, POB 1216, Dhaka 1216; tel. (2) 801138; fax (2) 803559; e-mail grameen.bank@grameen.net; internet www.grameen.com; f. 1976; provides credit for the landless rural poor; 6.97% owned by Govt; cap. 258.1m., res 188.2m., dep. 6,063.2m. (Dec. 1998); Chair. REHMAN SOBHAN; Man. Dir Dr MUHAMMAD YUNUS; 1,140 brs.

Infrastructure Development Co Ltd (IDCOL): Dhaka; f. 1999; state-owned.

Investment Corpn of Bangladesh (ICB): BSB Bldg, 12th–15th Floors, 8 DIT Ave, POB 2058, Dhaka 1000; tel. (2) 9563455; fax (2) 9563313; e-mail icb@agni.com; internet www.invest-corp.bangladesh.com; f. 1976; provides investment banking services; 28.97% owned by Govt; cap. 466.04m., res 525.08m. (June 2002); Chair. MUHAMMAD HASINUR RAHMAN; Man. Dir MUHAMMAD ZIAUL HAQUE KHONDKER; 7 brs.

Rajshahi Krishi Unnayan Bank: Sadharan Bima Bhaban, Kazihata, Greater Rd, Rajshahi 6000; tel. (721) 775759; fax (721) 775947; f. 1987; 100% state-owned; cap. 980m., res 208.4m., dep. 2,622.7m. (June 1996); Chair. MD EMRAN ALI SARKAR; Man. Dir SHAHIDUL HAQ KHAN.

STOCK EXCHANGES

Chittagong Stock Exchange: CSE Bldg, 1080 Sk Mujib Rd, Agrabad, Chittagong; tel. (31) 714100; fax (31) 714101; e-mail maroof@csebd.com; internet www.csebd.com; CEO WALI-UL-MAROOF MATIN.

Dhaka Stock Exchange Ltd: 9F Motijheel C/A, Dhaka 1000; tel. (2) 9564601; fax (2) 9564727; e-mail dse@bol-online.com; internet www.dsebd.org; f. 1960; 196 listed cos; Chair. RAKIBUR RAHMAN.

Regulatory Authority

Bangladesh Securities and Exchange Commission: Jiban Bima Tower, 15th–16th Floors, 10 Dilkusha C/A, Dhaka 1000; tel. (2) 9568101; fax (2) 9563721; CEO M. ABU SAYEED.

INSURANCE

Bangladesh Insurance Association: Hadi Mansion, 7th Floor, 2 Dilkusha C/A, Dhaka; tel. (2) 237330; Chair. MAYEEDUL ISLAM.

Department of Insurance: 74 Motijheel C/A, Dhaka 1000; attached to Ministry of Commerce; supervises activities of domestic and foreign insurers; Controller of Insurance SHAMSUDDIN AHMAD.

In 1973 the two corporations below were formed, one for life insurance and the other for general insurance:

Jiban Bima Corpn: 24 Motijheel C/A, POB 346, Dhaka 1000; tel. (2) 9552047; fax (2) 868112; state-owned; comprises 37 national life insurance cos; life insurance; Man. Dir A. K. M. MOSTAFIZUR RAHMAN.

Sadharan Bima Corpn: 33 Dilkusha C/A, POB 607, Dhaka 1000; tel. (2) 9566108; state-owned; general insurance; Man. Dir M. LUTFAR RAHMAN.

Trade and Industry

GOVERNMENT AGENCIES

Board of Investment: Jiban Bima Tower, 19th Floor, 10 Dilkusha C/A, Dhaka 1000; tel. (2) 9563570; fax (2) 9562312; e-mail ec@boi.bdmail.net; Exec. Chair. FAROOQ SOBHAN; Dep. Dir LUTFUR RAHMAN BHUIYA.

Export Promotion Bureau: 122–124 Motijheel C/A, Dhaka 1000; tel. (2) 9552245; fax (2) 9568000; e-mail epb.tic@pradeshta.net; internet www.epbbd.com; f. 1972; attached to Ministry of Commerce; regional offices in Chittagong, Khulna and Rajshahi; brs in Comilla, Sylhet, Barisal and Bogra; Dir-Gen. MOHAMMAD ABU ZAFAR; Vice-Chair. SHAFIQUL ISLAM.

Petrobangla, Bangladesh Oil, Gas and Mineral Corporation: Petrocenter Bhaban, 3 Kawran Bazar C/A, POB 849, Dhaka 1205; tel. (2) 814936; fax (2) 811613; explores and develops gas, petroleum and mineral resources, manages Bangladesh Petroleum Exploration Co Ltd and Sylhet Gas Fields Ltd; Chair. S. K. MOHAMMAD ABDULLAH.

Planning Commission: Planning Commission Secretariat, G.O. Hostel, Sher-e-Bangla Nagar, Dhaka; f. 1972; govt agency responsible for all aspects of economic planning and development including the preparation of the five-year plans and annual development programmes (in conjunction with appropriate govt ministries), promotion of savings and investment, compilation of statistics and evaluation of development schemes and projects.

Privatization Board: Jiban Bima Tower, 14th Floor, 10 Dilkusha C/A, Dhaka 1000; tel. (2) 9563723; fax (2) 9563766; e-mail pb@

bdonline.com; internet www.bangladeshonline.com/pb; f. 1993; Chair. KAZI ZAFRULLAH; Sec. A. M. M. NASIR UDDIN.

Trading Corpn of Bangladesh: 1–2 Kawranbazar, Dhaka 1215; tel. (2) 8111515; fax (2) 8113582; e-mail tcb@bdonline.com; f. 1972; imports, exports and markets goods through appointed dealers and agents; Chair. A. K. M. A. B. SIDDIQUE; Sec. MOHAMMAD SHAHJAHAN MIAH.

DEVELOPMENT ORGANIZATIONS

Bangladesh Chemical Industries Corpn: BCIC Bhaban, 30–31 Dilkusha C/A, Dhaka; tel. (2) 955280; fax (2) 9564120; e-mail bciccomp@bangla.net; internet www.bangla.net/bcic; Chair. A. K. M. MOSHARRAF HOSSAIN.

Bangladesh Export Processing Zones Authority: 222 New Eskaton Rd, Dhaka 1000; tel. (2) 8312553; fax (2) 8314967; e-mail bepza@bdmail.net; internet www.bangladesh-epz.com; f. 1983 to plan, develop, operate and manage export processing zones (EPZs) in Bangladesh; in mid-2000 two state-owned EPZs (one in Chittagong and the other in Dhaka) were in operation, and another four EPZs were at the implementation stage; Exec. Chair. Brig M. A. B. SIDDIQUE TALUKDER.

Bangladesh Fisheries Development Corpn: 24–25 Dilkusha C/A, Dhaka 1000; tel. (2) 9552689; fax (2) 9563990; e-mail bfdc@citechco.net; f. 1964; under Ministry of Fisheries and Livestock; development and commercial activities; Chair. Brig.-Gen. (retd) CHOWDHURY KHALEQUZZAMAN; Sec. A. K. M. SHAHIDUL ISLAM.

Bangladesh Forest Industries Development Corpn: Dhaka; Chair. M. ATIKULLAH.

Bangladesh Jute Mills Corpn: Adamjee Court (Annexe), 115–120 Motijheel C/A, Dhaka 1000; tel. (2) 861980; fax (2) 863329; f. 1972; operates 35 jute mills, incl. 2 carpet mills; world's largest manufacturer and exporter of jute goods; bags, carpet backing cloth, yarn, twine, tape, felt, floor covering, etc. Chair. MANIRUDDIN AHMAD; Man. (Marketing) MD JAHIRUL ISLAM.

Bangladesh Small and Cottage Industries Corpn (BSCIC): 137/138 Motijheel C/A, Dhaka 1000; tel. (2) 9565612; fax 9550704; e-mail cbscic@aitlbd.net; internet www.bscic-bd.org; f. 1957; Chair. MUHAMMAD SIRAJUDDIN.

Bangladesh Steel and Engineering Corpn (BSEC): BSEC Bhaban, 102 Kazi Nazrul Islam Ave, Dhaka 1215; tel. (2) 814616; fax (2) 812846; 16 industrial units; sales US $83m. (1994); cap. US $52m. Chair. A. I. M. NAZMUL ALAM; Gen. Man. (Marketing) ASHRAFUL HAQ; 8,015 employees.

Bangladesh Sugar and Food Industries Corpn: Shilpa Bhaban, Motijheel C/A, Dhaka 1000; tel. (2) 258084; f. 1972; Chair. M. NEFAUR RAHMAN.

Bangladesh Textile Mills Corpn: Dhaka; tel. (2) 252504; f. 1972; Chair. M. NURUNNABI CHOWDHURY.

CHAMBERS OF COMMERCE

Federation of Bangladesh Chambers of Commerce and Industry (FBCCI): Federation Bhaban, 60 Motijheel C/A, 4th Floor, POB 2079, Dhaka 1000; tel. (2) 9560102; fax (2) 863213; f. 1973; comprises 135 trade asscns and 58 chambers of commerce and industry; Pres. YUSUF ABDULLAH HAROON.

Barisal Chamber of Commerce and Industry: Asad Mansion, 1st Floor, Sadar Rd, Barisal; tel. (431) 3984; Pres. Qazi ISRAIL HOSSAIN.

Bogra Chamber of Commerce and Industry: Chamber Bhaban, 2nd Floor, Kabi Nazrul Islam Rd, Jhawtola, Bogra 5800; tel. (51) 4138; fax (51) 6257; f. 1963; Pres. AMJAD HOSSAIN TAJMA; Sr Vice-Pres. Alhaj ABUL KALAM AZAD.

Chittagong Chamber of Commerce and Industry: Chamber House, Agrabad C/A, POB 481, Chittagong; tel. (31) 713366; fax (31) 710183; e-mail ccci@globalctg.net; f. 1959; 4,000 mems; Pres. FARID AHMED CHOWDHURY; Sec. OSMAN GANI CHOWDHURY.

Comilla Chamber of Commerce and Industry: Rammala Rd, Ranir Bazar, Comilla; tel. (81) 5444; Pres. AFZAL KHAN.

Dhaka Chamber of Commerce and Industry: Dhaka Chamber Bldg, 1st Floor, 65–66 Motijheel C/A, POB 2641, Dhaka 1000; tel. (2) 9552562; fax (2) 9560830; e-mail dcci@bangla.net; f. 1958; 5,000 mems; Pres. AFTAB UL ISLAM; Sr Vice-Pres. AM MUBASH-SHAR.

Dinajpur Chamber of Commerce and Industry: Chamber Bhaban, Maldhapatty, Dinajpur 5200; tel. (531) 3189; Pres. KHAIRUL ANAM.

Faridpur Chamber of Commerce and Industry: Chamber House, Niltuly, Faridpur; tel. (631) 3530; Pres. KHANDOKER MOHSIN ALI.

Foreign Investors' Chamber of Commerce and Industry: 'Mahbub Castle', 4th Floor, 35/A Purana Paltan Line, Inner Circular Rd, GPO Box 4086, Dhaka 1000; tel. (2) 8319448; fax (2) 8319449; e-mail ficci@bangla.net; f. 1963 as Agrabad Chamber of Commerce and Industry, name changed as above in 1987; Pres. WALI R. BHUIYAN; Sec. JAHANGIR BIN ALAM.

Khulna Chamber of Commerce and Industry: 5, KDA C/A, Khulna; tel. (41) 24135; e-mail kcci@bttb.net.bd; f. 1934; Pres. S. M. NAZRUL ISLAM.

Khustia Chamber of Commerce and Industry: 15, S Rd, Kushtia; tel. (71) 54068; e-mail kushcham@kushtia.com; Pres. MOHAMMAD MOZIBAR RAHMAN.

Metropolitan Chamber of Commerce and Industry: Chamber Bldg, 4th Floor, 122–124 Motijheel C/A, Dhaka 1000; tel. (2) 9565208; fax (2) 9565212; e-mail sg@citechco.net; internet www .mccibd.org; f. 1904; 310 mems; Sec.-Gen. C. K. HYDER.

Noakhali Chamber of Commerce and Industry: Noakhali Pour-shara Bhaban, 2nd Floor, Maiydee Court, Noakhali; tel. (321) 5229; Pres. MOHAMMAD NAZIBUR RAHMAN.

Rajshahi Chamber of Commerce and Industry: Chamber Bhaban, Station Rd, P.O. Ghoramara, Rajshahi 6100; tel. (721) 772115; fax (721) 772412; f. 1960; 800 mems; Pres. OMAR FARUK CHOWDHURY.

Sylhet Chamber of Commerce and Industry: Chamber Bldg, Jail Rd, POB 97, Sylhet 3100; tel. (821) 714403; fax (821) 715210; e-mail scci@btsnet.net; Pres. MOHD SAFWAN CHOUDHURY.

INDUSTRIAL AND TRADE ASSOCIATIONS

Bangladesh Frozen Foods Exporters Association: Dhaka; tel. and fax (2) 837531; e-mail bffea@drik.dgd.toolnet.org; Pres. SALA-HUDDIN AHMED.

Bangladesh Garment Manufacturers and Exporters Association: 7–9 Karwanbazar, BTMC Bhaban, Dhaka 1215; tel. (2) 815597; fax (2) 813951; e-mail bgmea@bgmea.agni.co; Pres. KUTU-BUDDIN AHMED; Vice-Pres. NURUL HAQ SIKDAR.

Bangladesh Jute Association: BJA Bldg, 77 Motijheel C/A, Dhaka; tel. (2) 9552916; fax (2) 9560137; Chair. M.A. MANNAN; Sec. S. H. PRODHAN.

Bangladesh Jute Exporters Association: Nahar Mansion, 2nd Floor, 150 Motijheel C/A, Dhaka 1000; tel. (2) 9561102.

Bangladesh Jute Goods Association: 2nd Floor, Nahar Mansion, 150 Motijheel C/A, Dhaka 1000; tel. (2) 253640; f. 1979; 17 mems; Chair. M. A. KASHEM; Haji MOHAMMAD ALI.

Bangladesh Jute Mills Association: Adamjee Court, 4th Floor, 115–120 Motijheel C/A, Dhaka 1000; tel. (2) 9560071; fax (2) 9566472; Chair. A. M. ZAHIRUDDIN KHAN.

Bangladesh Jute Spinners Association: 55 Purana Paltan, 3rd Floor, Dhaka 1000; tel. (2) 9551317; fax (2) 9562772; f. 1979; 50 mems; Chair. AHMED HOSSAIN; Sec. SHAHIDUL KARIM.

Bangladesh Tea Board: 171–172 Baizid Bostami Rd, Nasirabad, Chittagong; tel. (31) 682903; fax (31) 682863; e-mail btb@spnetctg .com; internet bdteaboard.com; f. 1951; regulates, controls and promotes the cultivation and marketing of tea, both in Bangladesh and abroad; Contact ALI OHIDUZ ZAMAN.

Bangladesh Textile Mills Association: Moon Mansion, 6th Floor, Block M, 12 Dilkusha C/A, Dhaka 1000; tel. (2) 9552799; fax 9563320; e-mail btma@citechco.net.

Bangladeshiyo Cha Sangsad (Tea Association of Bangladesh): 'Dar-e-Shahidi', 3rd Floor, 69 Agrabad C/A, POB 287, Chittagong 4100; tel. (31) 501009; f. 1952; Chair. QUAMRUL CHOWDHURY; Sec. G. S. DHAR.

UTILITIES

Electricity

Bangladesh Atomic Energy Commission (BAEC): 4 Kazi Nazrul Islam Ave, POB 158, Dhaka 1000; tel. (2) 502600; fax (2) 863051; f. 1964 as Atomic Energy Centre of the fmr Pakistan Atomic Energy Comm. in East Pakistan; reorg. 1973; operates an atomic energy research establishment and a 3-MW research nuclear reactor (inaugurated in January 1987) at Savar, an atomic energy centre at Dhaka, etc. Chair. M. A. QUAIYUM; Sec. RAFIQUL ALAM.

Bangladesh Power Development Board: WAPDA Bldg, Motijheel, Dhaka; tel. (2) 9562154; fax (2) 9564765; e-mail chbpdb@ bol-online.com; internet www.bd-pdb.org; f. 1972; under Ministry of Power, Energy and Mineral Resources; generation, transmission and distribution of electricity; installed capacity 4,710 MW (2002); Chair. SYED ABDUL MAYEED.

Dhaka Electric Supply Authority: Dhaka; under Ministry of Energy and Mineral Resources.

Powergrid Company of Bangladesh: Dhaka; f. 1996; responsible for power transmission throughout Bangladesh.

Rural Electrification Board: Dhaka; under Ministry of Energy and Mineral Resources.

Water

Chittagong Water Supply and Sewerage Authority: Dampara, Chittagong; tel. (31) 621606; fax (31) 610465; f. 1963; govt corpn; Chair. SULTAN MAHMUD CHOWDHURY.

Dhaka Water Supply and Sewerage Authority: 98 Kazi Nazrul Islam Ave, Kawran Bazar, Dhaka 1215; tel. (2) 8116792; fax (2) 8112109; e-mail mddwasa@bangla.net; f. 1963; govt corpn; Man. Dir K. AZHARUL HAQ.

TRADE UNIONS

In 2001 only 4.3% of the non-agricultural labour force was unionized. There were about 4,200 registered unions, organized mainly on a sectoral or occupational basis. There were 23 national trade unions to represent workers at the national level.

Bangladesh Free Trade Union Congress (BFTUC): 6-A 1–19 Mirpur, Dhaka 1216; tel. (2) 8017001; fax (2) 8015919; e-mail bftuc@ agni.com; Gen. Sec. M. R. CHOWDHURY; 115,000 mems.

Bangladesh Jatio Sramik League (BJSL): POB 2730, Dhaka; tel. (2) 282063; fax (2) 863470; 62,000 mems.

Transport

RAILWAYS

In July 2000 Bangladesh Railway and the Indian Railway Board signed an agreement to resume rail services on the Benapole–Petrapole route. The service opened fully in January 2001. In December regular rail services between Bangabandhu and Kolkata (India) resumed.

Bangladesh Railway: Rail Bhaban, Abdul Ghani Rd, Dhaka 1000; tel. (2) 9561200; fax (2) 9563413; e-mail systcan@citechco.net; f. 1862; supervised by the Railway and Road Transport Division of the Ministry of Communications; divided into East and West zones, with HQ at Chittagong (tel. (31) 711294) and Rajshahi (tel. (721) 761576; fax (721) 761982); total length of 2,734 route km (June 1999); 451 stations; Dir-Gen. M. A. RAHIM; Gen. Man. (East Zone) A. Z. M. SAZZADUR RAHMAN; Gen. Man. (West Zone) MD NURUL AMINKHAN.

ROADS

In 1999 the total length of roads in use was 207,486 km (19,775 km of highways, 17,297 km of secondary roads and 170,413 km of other roads), of which 9.5% were paved. In 1992 the World Bank approved Bangladesh's US $700m. Jamuna Bridge Project. The construction of the 4.8-km bridge, which was, for the first time, to link the east and the west of the country with a railway and road network, was begun in early 1994. The bridge, which was renamed the Banga-bandhu Jamuna Multipurpose Bridge, was officially opened in June 1998.

In June 1999 the first direct passenger bus service between Bangladesh (Dhaka) and India (Kolkata) was inaugurated.

Bangladesh Road Transport Corpn: Paribhaban, DIT Ave, Dhaka; f. 1961; state-owned; operates transport services, incl. truck division; transports govt foodgrain; Chair. AZMAN HOSSAIN CHOWD-HURY.

INLAND WATERWAYS

In Bangladesh there are some 8,433 km of navigable waterways, which transport 70% of total domestic and foreign cargo traffic and on which are located the main river ports of Dhaka, Narayanganj, Chandpur, Barisal and Khulna. A river steamer service connects these ports several times a week. Vessels of up to 175-m overall length can be navigated on the Karnaphuli river.

Bangladesh Inland Water Transport Corpn: 5 Dilkusha C/A, Dhaka 1000; tel. (2) 257092; f. 1972; 273 vessels (1986).

SHIPPING

The chief ports are Chittagong, where the construction of a second dry-dock is planned, and Chalna. A modern seaport is being developed at Mongla.

Atlas Shipping Lines Ltd: Atlas House, 7 Sk. Mujib Rd, Agrabad C/A, Chittagong 2; tel. (31) 504287; fax (31) 225520; Man. Dir S. U. CHOWDHURY; Gen. Man. M. KAMAL HAYAT.

Bangladesh Shipping Corpn: BSC Bhaban, Saltgola Rd, POB 641, Chittagong 4100; tel. (31) 713277; fax (31) 710506; e-mail bsc–ctg@spnetctg.com; f. 1972; maritime shipping; 15 vessels, 210,672 dwt capacity (1999); Chair. MOFAZZAL HOSSAIN CHOWDHURY MAYA; Man. Dir ZULFIQAR HAIDAR CHAUDHURY.

Bengal Shipping Line Ltd: Palm View, 100A Agrabad C/A, Chittagong 4100; tel. (31) 714800; fax (31) 710362; e-mail bsl@mkrgroup.com; Chair. MOHAMMED ABDUL AWWAL; Man. Dir MOHAMMED ABDUL MALEK.

Blue Ocean Lines Ltd: 1st Floor, H.B.F.C. Bldg, 1D Agrabad C/A, Agrabad, Chittagong; tel. (31) 501567; fax (31) 225415.

Broadway Shipping Line: Hafiz Estate, 65 Shiddeswari Rd, Dhaka; tel. (2) 404598; fax (2) 412254.

Chittagong Port Authority: POB 2013, Chittagong 4100; tel. (31) 505041; f. 1887; provides bunkering, ship repair, towage and lighterage facilities as well as provisions and drinking water supplies; Chair. MD SHAHADAT HUSSAIN.

Continental Liner Agencies: 3rd Floor, Facy Bldg, 87 Agrabad C/A, Chittagong; tel. (31) 721572; fax (31) 710965; Man. SAIFUL AHMED; Dir (Technical and Operations) Capt. MAHFUZUL ISLAM.

Nishan Shipping Lines Ltd: 1st Floor, Monzoor Bldg, 67 Agrabad C/A, Chittagong; tel. (31) 710855; fax (31) 710044; Dir Capt. A. K. M. ALAMGIR.

CIVIL AVIATION

There is an international airport at Dhaka (Zia International Airport) situated at Kurmitola, with the capacity to handle 5m. passengers annually. There are also airports at all major towns. In 1997 the civil aviation industry was deregulated to permit domestic competition to Biman Bangladesh Airlines. Plans were under way in 2002 to privatize 49% of the national airline.

Biman Bangladesh Airlines: Head Office, Balaka, Kurmitola, Dhaka 1229; tel. (2) 8917400; fax (2) 8913005; internet www.bimanair.com/; f. 1972; 100% state-owned; domestic services to seven major towns; international services to the Middle East, the Far East, Europe, and North America; Chair. Minister of Civil Aviation and Tourism; Man. Dir Air Cmmdre M. KHUSRUL ALAM.

GMG Airlines: ABC House, 9th Floor, 8 Kamal Ataturk Ave, Banani, Dhaka 1213; tel. (2) 8825845; fax (2) 8826115; e-mail gmgairlines@gmggroup.com; internet www.gmgairlines.com; f. 1997; private, domestic airline; Dir (Flight Operations) Capt. HABIBUR RAHMAN; Man. Dir SHAHAB SATTAR.

Tourism

Tourist attractions include the cities of Dhaka and Chittagong, Cox's Bazar—which has the world's longest beach (120 km)—on the Bay of Bengal, and Teknaf, at the southernmost point of Bangladesh. Tourist arrivals totalled 199,211 in 2000. Earnings from tourism in 2000 reached an estimated US $59m. in the same year. The majority of visitors are from India, Japan, Pakistan, the United Kingdom and the USA.

Bangladesh Parjatan Corpn (National Tourism Organization): 233 Airport Rd, Tejgaon, Dhaka 1215; tel. (2) 8117855; fax (2) 8117235; internet www.parjatan.org; there are four tourist information centres in Dhaka, and one each in Bogra, Chittagong, Cox's Bazar, Dinajpur, Khulna, Kuakata, Rangamati, Rangpur, Rajshahi and Sylhet; Chair. MD ABU SALEH; Man. (Public Relations Division) MOHAMMAD AHSAN ULLAH.

BARBADOS

Introductory Survey

Location, Climate, Language, Religion, Flag, Capital

Barbados is the most easterly of the Caribbean islands, lying about 320 km (200 miles) north-east of Trinidad. The island has a total area of 430 sq km (166 sq miles). There is a rainy season from July to November and the climate is tropical, tempered by constant sea winds, during the rest of the year. The mean annual temperature is about 26°C (78°F). Average annual rainfall varies from 1,250 mm (49 ins) on the coast, to 1,875 mm (74 ins) in the interior. The official language is English. Almost all of the inhabitants profess Christianity, but there are small groups of Hindus, Muslims and Jews. The largest denomination is the Anglican church, but about 90 other Christian sects are represented. The national flag (proportions 2 by 3) has three equal vertical stripes, of blue, gold and blue; superimposed on the centre of the gold band is the head of a black trident. The capital is Bridgetown.

Recent History

Barbados was formerly a British colony. The Barbados Labour Party (BLP) won a general election in 1951, when universal adult suffrage was introduced, and held office until 1961. Although the parliamentary system dates from 1639, ministerial government was not established until 1954, when the BLP's leader, Sir Grantley Adams, became the island's first Premier. He was subsequently Prime Minister of the West Indies Federation from January 1958 until its dissolution in May 1962.

Barbados achieved full internal self-government in October 1961. The Democratic Labour Party (DLP), formed in 1955 by dissident members of the BLP, won an election in December. The DLP's leader, Errol Barrow, became Premier, succeeding Dr Hugh Cummins of the BLP. When Barbados achieved independence on 30 November 1966, Barrow became the island's first Prime Minister, following another electoral victory by his party earlier in the month.

The DLP retained power in 1971, but in the general election of September 1976 the BLP, led by J. M. G. M. ('Tom') Adams (Sir Grantley's son), ended Barrow's 15-year rule. The BLP successfully campaigned against alleged government corruption, winning a large majority over the DLP. At a general election in June 1981 the BLP was returned to office with 17 of the 27 seats in the newly-enlarged House of Assembly. The DLP won the remainder of the seats. Adams died suddenly in March 1985 and was succeeded as Prime Minister by his deputy, Bernard St John, a former leader of the BLP.

At a general election in May 1986 the DLP won a decisive victory, receiving 59.4% of the total votes and winning 24 seats in the House of Assembly. Bernard St John and all except one of his cabinet ministers lost their seats, and Errol Barrow returned as Prime Minister after 10 years in opposition. In June it was announced that Barrow was to review Barbados' participation in the US-supported Regional Security System (RSS), the defence force that had been established soon after the US invasion of Grenada in October 1983. Under Adams Barbados was one of the countries whose troops had supported the invasion. In June 1987 Barrow died suddenly. He was succeeded by L. Erskine Sandiford (hitherto the Deputy Prime Minister), who pledged to continue Barrow's economic and social policies. In September 1987, however, the Minister of Finance, Dr Richard (Richie) Haynes, resigned, accusing Sandiford of failing to consult him over financial appointments. Sandiford assumed the finance portfolio, but acrimony over government policy continued to trouble the DLP. In February 1989 Haynes and three other members of Parliament resigned from the DLP and announced the formation of the National Democratic Party (NDP). Haynes was subsequently appointed as leader of the parliamentary opposition.

At a general election in January 1991 the DLP won 18 of the 28 seats in the enlarged House of Assembly, while the BLP secured the remaining 10. The creation of a Ministry of Justice and Public Safety by the new Government, and the reintroduction of flogging for convicted criminals, reflected widespread concern over increased levels of violent crime on the island.

Moreover, as a result of serious economic problems, a series of austerity measures were proposed in September. However, the proposals resulted in public unrest, which continued in 1992, as large numbers of civil servants and agricultural workers were made redundant. In 1993 and 1994 the increasing unpopularity of Sandiford's premiership provoked continued demands for his resignation, culminating, in June 1994, in his narrow defeat in a parliamentary motion of confidence. Despite intense speculation that he would resign, Sandiford remained in office, but announced the dissolution of Parliament in preparation for a general election, which was to take place in September.

A general election took place on 6 September 1994, at which the BLP won a decisive victory, securing 19 seats in the House of Assembly, compared with the DLP's eight and the NDP's one. Owen Arthur was subsequently appointed as Prime Minister.

In May 1995 Arthur announced the formation of a 10-member commission to advise the Government on possible reforms of the country's Constitution and political institutions. In July 1996 the commission was asked to consider, in particular, the continuing role of the British monarch as Head of State in Barbados. The commission's report, published in December 1998, recommended, as expected, the replacement of the British monarch with a ceremonial President. It also proposed changes in the composition of the Senate and the substitution of a jointly-administered Caribbean Court for the existing highest judicial body, the Privy Council. In February 2001 Caribbean leaders agreed to establish such a court by 2002. However, in early 2003, the court had yet to be established.

In December 1996 the DLP retained a seat in a by-election. This development resulted in renewed pressure for the reunification of the DLP and the NDP, which together secured more votes (though fewer seats) than the BLP in the general election. In mid-1997 two prominent members of the NDP (including the influential General Secretary of the National Union of Public Workers, Joseph Goddard) rejoined the DLP. The NDP lost a further electoral candidate to the ruling BLP in November, and in September two candidates (one of whom subsequently joined the DLP) resigned from the BLP, attributing their decision to the Prime Minister's lack of control over the party. In September 1998 Hamilton Lashley, a prominent DLP member of the House of Assembly, accepted the post of consultant to the Prime Minister on matters of poverty alleviation. In October Lashley transferred political allegiance to the governing BLP.

A general election was held on 20 January 1999, which the BLP won comfortably. The BLP received 64.8% of the total votes cast, winning 26 of the 28 seats in the House of Assembly, while the DLP received 35.1% of the votes and won only two seats (the NDP did not contest the election). The result represented an even greater defeat for the DLP than the BLP had itself experienced in the elections of 1986 (see above), and was largely attributed to the Government's recent successes in reviving the Barbadian economy, particularly in reducing unemployment. On 24 January the Prime Minister announced an expanded 14-member Cabinet, including the new post of Minister of Social Transformation (to which Lashley was appointed), whose major concern was to be poverty alleviation. Arthur promised to create a 'new and unprecedented prosperity' in Barbados, and declared his Government's commitment to transforming Barbados into a republic (although he simultaneously pledged to keep the country within the Commonwealth).

In April 1999 Trafalgar Square, in the centre of Bridgetown, was renamed National Heroes Square, and the decision was made to replace the statue of the British Admiral Lord Horatio Nelson which stood there, with one of Errol Barrow, the country's first Prime Minister. These developments, which reinforced existing differences between Barbados' two main ethnic communities, were seen as evidence that the country was beginning its transformation into a republic. With the aim of resolving any growing divisions, the Government organized a day of national reconciliation in July, while a 13-member Committee for National Reconciliation was also established. In August 2000 Arthur announced that there would be a referendum on the replacement of the monarchy with a republic, a move which had the clear support of all political parties. A series of sharp political controversies in neighbouring Trinidad and Tobago over the constitutional powers of the President in 2000–02 led to an enhanced appreciation in Barbados of the need for careful consideration of the relationship between an elected Government and a ceremonial President. Nevertheless, in early 2002 the Deputy Prime Minister and Minister of Foreign Affairs and Foreign Trade, Billie Miller, announced that new constitutional legislation would be drafted by the end of the year.

In August 2001, following the retirement from politics of David Simmons, the Prime Minister appointed Mia Motley, hitherto Minister of Education, Youth Affairs and Culture, to the post of Attorney-General and Minister of Home Affairs. In the following month a further reallocation of government portfolios took place. Notably, Elizabeth Thompson was reappointed to the Cabinet, as Minister for Physical Development and the Environment. Rudolph Greenidge, previously Minister of Labour, Sports and the Public Sector, assumed responsibility for the education, youth and sport portfolios, while Rawle Eastmond moved from the Ministry of the Environment, Energy and Natural Resources to become Minister of Labour and Social Security.

In late September 2001, following the defeat of the DLP in a by-election, David Thompson resigned as party leader. Clyde Mascoll, a former Central Bank economist, was elected as his successor in November.

In late 2002 and early 2003 media reports suggested that a general election could be called for mid-2003. During this period, condemnation of the Government's use of public money to pay off the debts of a financially-troubled tourist resort—known as Gems of Barbados—intensified. Despite this criticism, and the continuing economic slump, in the early part of 2003 the incumbent BLP enjoyed a commanding lead in opinion polls and would enter legislative elections as strong favourites. In contrast, the DLP were in disarray, with reports of a serious rift between the party's two legislative deputies. In late April Arthur announced that a general election was to take place on 21 May. It was also announced that the Electoral and Boundaries Commission Review of 2002 would come into effect, dividing the island into 30 constituencies, two more than under the previous system.

In late 1997 the Government established a committee to examine alternative methods of punishing offenders, following a report which found Barbados' only prison to be grossly overcrowded. In October 1998, owing to a recent significant increase in the number of violent crimes involving firearms, the Government announced a temporary amnesty for individuals surrendering illegally-owned weapons; tougher penalties for unlawful possession were introduced as part of new firearms-control legislation enacted in November. Amid a further escalation in violent crime and fears that the country's tourism industry might be affected, it was announced in October 1999 that an anti-firearms unit was to be established in the police force. In July 2001 the Inter-American Development Bank approved a US $8.75m. loan to help Barbados modernize and strengthen its justice and penal system. Furthermore, in September 2001 the Government announced plans to build a modern maximum-security prison, capable of housing 500 inmates. In November 2002 the Government established a National Commision on Law and Order to help develop a plan of action to combat the rising crime rate on the island.

In November 1990 the Government of Barbados signed a bilateral fishing agreement with the Government of Trinidad and Tobago; the two countries also agreed, in late 1999, to draft a boundary delimitation treaty and to establish a negotiating mechanism to resolve trade disputes. Relations between the two countries were temporarily strained in late 2001 after several Barbadian fishermen were arrested in Trinidad and Tobago's waters; however, fears that the dispute could escalate receded in January 2002 after discussions on the issue were held between the Prime Minister and the Minister of Foreign Affairs of Trinidad and Tobago. Negotiations on a new fishing agreement were due to recommence at the end of that month. In late 1996 Barbados signed an agreement with the USA to co-operate with a regional initiative to combat the illegal drugs trade. In March 1998 Barbados began negotiations with the Organisation of Eastern Caribbean States (OECS, see p. 341) concerning the country's eventual membership in a confederation, and possible political union, of Eastern Caribbean states. Areas under discussion included health, education, diplomatic representation and the judiciary. A 14-member joint 'task force' had been appointed in February to discuss the possible incorporation of

Barbados into the OECS. An inaugural meeting of the discussion group took place in April, when it was suggested that a working confederation could be instituted within 2–3 years. Although monetary union was not to be a prior condition to membership, OECS spokesmen described the adoption of a single currency as highly desirable. In June 2000 Barbados officially declared its acceptance of the compulsory jurisdiction of the Inter-American Court of Human Rights, an institution of the Organization of American States (OAS, see p. 288).

Government

Executive power is vested in the British monarch, represented by a Governor-General, who acts on the advice of the Cabinet. The Governor-General appoints the Prime Minister and, on the latter's recommendation, other members of the Cabinet. Legislative power is vested in the bicameral Parliament, comprising a Senate of 21 members, appointed by the Governor-General, and a House of Assembly with 28 members, elected by universal adult suffrage for five years (subject to dissolution) from single-member constituencies. The Cabinet is responsible to Parliament. In 1969 elected local government bodies were abolished in favour of a division into 11 parishes, all of which are administered by the central Government. In April 2003 it was announced that the number of seats in the House of Assembly would be increased to 30 for the 21 May general election.

Defence

The Barbados Defence Force was established in 1978. The total strength of the Barbados armed forces in August 2002 was estimated at 610; the army consisted of 500 members and the navy (coastguard) 110. There was also a reserve force of 430. The defence budget for 2002 was estimated at Bds $26m.

Economic Affairs

In 2000, according to estimates by the World Bank, the island's gross national income (GNI), measured at average 1998–2000 prices, was US $2,469m., equivalent to US $9,250 per head (or US $15,020 on an international purchasing-power parity basis). Between 1990 and 2001 the population increased at an average rate of 0.3% per year. Barbados' gross domestic product (GDP) per head, increased, in real terms, at an average rate of 1.2% per year during 1990–2000. Overall GDP increased, in real terms, at an average annual rate of 1.6% in 1990–2000. According to the Central Bank, real GDP increased by 2.8% in 1999 and by 3.1% in 2000, before decreasing by 2.3% in 2001; the economy was expected to contract by 1.1% in 2002.

Agriculture (including hunting, forestry and fishing) contributed 6.3% of GDP in 2000 and engaged an estimated 4.2% of the employed labour force in 2001. Sugar remains the main commodity export, earning US $26.7m. in 2000, when output was an estimated 55,000 tons. Production, however, fell by an estimated 14% in 2001. The sugar industry was faced by increased pressure to reform from the 1990s, particularly as further liberalization of international trade was likely to make the island less competitive. In 2000, according to the UN, sugar accounted for 10.1% of total exports. Sea-island cotton, once the island's main export crop, was revived in the mid-1980s. The other principal crops, primarily for local consumption, are sweet potatoes, carrots, yams and other vegetables and fruit. Fishing was also developed in the late 20th century. The GDP of the agricultural sector declined, in real terms, at an average rate of 0.4% per year during 1990–2000. Agricultural GDP fell by 13.0% in 1998, but was estimated to have increased by 7.0% in 1999 and by 6.5% in 2000.

In 2000 industry accounted for 21.0% of GDP, and an estimated 19.8% of the working population were employed in all industrial activities (manufacturing, construction, quarrying and utilities) in 2001. In real terms, industrial GDP increased at an average rate of 1.9% annually in 1990–2000. Real industrial GDP rose by 10.4% in 1998, by 2.2% in 1999 and by 0.5% in 2000.

Owing to fluctuations in international prices, the production of crude petroleum declined substantially from its peak in 1985, to 328,000 barrels in 1997. In late 1996 the Barbados National Oil Company signed a five-year agreement with a US company to intensify exploration activity, with the aim of increasing petroleum production from 1,000 barrels per day (b/d) to 10,000 b/d by 2001. As a result of an onshore drilling programme begun in 1997, production increased dramatically in 1998 and 1999, reaching 579,636 and 708,500 barrels, respectively, before falling to 559,675 barrels in 2000 and 463,699 barrels in 2001. After a temporary suspension in drilling as a result of low international oil prices, drilling was again resumed in October

2000. Production of natural gas decreased from 46.9m. cu m in 1998 to 38m. cu m in 1999 and 2000, and 35m. cu m in 2001. Imports of mineral fuels accounted for 11.5% of total imports in 2000. Mining and construction contributed 9.0% of GDP in 2000 and employed an estimated 11.4% of the working population in 1999.

Manufacturing contributed 9.0% of GDP in 2000 and employed an estimated 7.2% of the working population in 2001. Excluding sugar factories and refineries, the principal branches of manufacturing, measured by the value of output, in 1994 were chemical, petroleum, rubber and plastic products (accounting for 27.3% of the total), food products (26.9%), and beverages and tobacco (15.0%). Manufacturing GDP increased, in real terms, at an average rate of 0.1% per year during 1990–2000; it rose by 3.7% in 1998, but fell by 3.0% in 1999, remaining at the same level in 2000.

Service industries are the main sector of the economy, accounting for 72.8% of GDP in 2000 and 76.0% of employment in 2001. The combined GDP of the service sectors increased, in real terms, at an average rate of 1.2% per year during 1990–2000. In 1999 the sector grew by 2.3% and, in 2000, by 3.8%. Business and general services contributed an estimated 16.9% of GDP in 1999. The Government has encouraged the growth of 'offshore' financial facilities, particularly through the negotiation of double taxation agreements with other countries. At the end of 2000 there were 4,038 international business companies and 2,981 foreign sales corporations operating in the country. It was estimated that the 'offshore' sector contributed US $122m. in foreign earnings in 1995. In the following year the Government announced a series of proposals which aimed to expand the industry. Barbados has an active anti-money-laundering regime, which was further strengthened by new legislation in 1998, although the island remained classified by the USA as a 'country of concern' with regard to money-laundering. Moreover, in May 2000 the Organisation for Economic Co-operation and Development (OECD) placed Barbados on a list of tax 'havens' which faced counter-measures from February 2002 if they failed to modify tax regimes in line with OECD requirements. However, Barbados escaped inclusion on a list of non-co-operating jurisdictions drawn up by the Financial Action Task Force on Money Laundering in September 2001, and was removed from the OECD list in January 2002.

Tourism made a direct contribution of an estimated 15% to GDP in 1999, and it employed an estimated 10.7% of the working population in 2001. Receipts from the tourist industry almost doubled between 1980 and 1988, and in 2000 totalled US $711.3m., falling to $703.5m. in 2001. Partly because of the reduction in the number of US tourists following the terrorist attacks in the USA of September 2001, stop-over tourist arrivals decreased from 545,027 in 2000 to 507,086 in 2001, while cruise-ship passenger arrivals also decreased, by 1.1%, to 527,597. In 2000 some 41.6% of stop-over arrivals were from the United Kingdom.

In 2001 Barbados recorded an estimated visible trade deficit of US $681.1m. and there was an estimated deficit of $94.4m. on the current account of the balance of payments. In 2000 the USA was both the principal source of imports (41.6%) and the largest single recipient of exports (15.8%). The United Kingdom accounted for 8.1% of imports and 13.2% of exports. Other major trading partners included the CARICOM countries (see below), especially Trinidad and Tobago. The principal commodity exports in 2000 were petroleum products (22.1% of total exports), machinery and transport equipment (14.0%) and chemicals (13.6%). The principal imports were machinery and transport equipment and basic manufactures.

For the financial year ending 31 March 2002 there was an estimated total budgetary deficit of Bds $182.9m. At December 1999 the total external debt of Barbados was US $468.8m. In that year the cost of foreign debt-servicing was equivalent to 7.7% of the value of exports of goods and services. The average annual rate of inflation was 2.5% in 1995–2001. Average consumer prices rose by 2.4% in 2000 and by 2.6% in 2001. By the end of September 2000 unemployment was estimated to have fallen to 9.3% of the labour force, compared with 11.1% at the beginning of 1999. However, by December 2001 the unemployment rate had increased slightly to 9.8%.

Barbados is a member of the Caribbean Community and Common Market (CARICOM, see p. 155), of the Inter-American Development Bank (IDB, see p. 239), of the Latin American Economic System (SELA, see p. 340) and of the Association of Caribbean States (see p. 338).

Political stability and consensus have contributed to the economic strengths of Barbados. Tourism dominates the economy but 'offshore' banking and sugar production are also important. The closure of major hotels for refurbishment in 1999 (until 2003) brought about a marginal temporary decline in tourism earnings. Furthermore, following the terrorist attacks of 11 September 2001 in the USA, the Barbados tourist industry suffered a significant decrease in bookings. A US $20m.–$25m. government plan to subsidize the industry and other affected sectors was proposed in the same month. The 2000/2001 budget proposals, announced in October 2000, contained plans to end the British company Cable & Wireless' monopoly of the telecommunications sector. A phased liberalization of this market commenced at the end of 2000 and was to be completed by April 2003. The proposed privatization of the Barbados National Bank and the Insurance Company of Barbados were also announced (the latter was transferred to the private sector in December 2000). The year 2000 was the eighth successive year of economic expansion, with real GDP growth of 3.1%; however, there was a decrease in real GDP of 2.3% in 2001 and an estimated further contraction of 1.1% in 2002. Nevertheless, third-quarter growth of 1.4% in 2002, compared with the same period in 2001, engendered some optimism that the economy would emerge from its recession in 2003; the Central Bank predicted growth for 2003 to be 1.5%–2.5%, although there were fears that the US-led war against the Iraqi regime of Saddam Hussain could lead to another year of reduced tourism receipts and a further contraction in real GDP. The budget for the fiscal year 2002/03, presented in October 2002 after a year of decline in government revenue (a decrease of 6.4% since the beginning of 2002), aimed to stimulate economic growth. It provided for an increase in national insurance contributions and an increase in the retirement age, from 65 to 67, but also introduced reductions in the rate of corporation tax and the basic rate of personal income tax.

Education

Education is compulsory for 12 years, between five and 16 years of age. Primary education begins at the age of five and lasts for seven years. Secondary education, beginning at 12 years of age, lasts for five years. In 2002 enrolment of children in the primary age-group was 99.1% (males 99.8%, females 98.5%), and in the secondary-school age-group enrolment was 98% (males 97.4%, females 98.6%). Tuition at all government schools is free. In the same year enrolment at tertiary level was some 48% of the relevant age-group (males 38.5%; females 57.5%). In 1998 7,538 students were enrolled at universities or similar institutions. Degree courses in arts, law, education, natural sciences and social sciences are offered at the Cave Hill campus of the University of the West Indies. A two-year clinical-training programme for medical students is conducted by the School of Clinic Medicine and Research of the University, while an in-service training programme for teachers is provided by the School of Education. The Government announced in September 2000 that it expected to realize its ambition of providing universal pre-school education by the academic year 2002. In 2002 80% of children aged three and four attended school. Current expenditure on education by the central Government in 2001/02 totalled some Bds $375m. (equivalent to about 19.5% of total expenditure). According to the 2002 budget address, government expenditure on education in 2002/03 would equal Bds $396m., representing 17.2% of total expenditure. A US $200m. programme for curriculum reform and the introduction of technology into education, known as Edutech 2000, was scheduled for completion by 2007.

Public Holidays

2003: 1 January (New Year's Day), 21 January (Errol Barrow Day), 18 April (Good Friday), 21 April (Easter Monday), 28 April (National Heroes' Day), 1 May (Labour Day), 9 June (Whit Monday), 1 August (Emancipation Day), 4 August (Kadooment Day), 30 November (Independence Day), 25–26 December (Christmas).

2004: 1 January (New Year's Day), 21 January (Errol Barrow Day), 9 April (Good Friday), 12 April (Easter Monday), 28 April (National Heroes' Day), 1 May (Labour Day), 31 May (Whit Monday), 1 August (Emancipation Day), 2 August (Kadooment Day), 30 November (Independence Day), 25–26 December (Christmas).

Weights and Measures

The metric system is used.

Statistical Survey

Sources (unless otherwise stated): Barbados Statistical Service, National Insurance Bldg, 3rd Floor, Fairchild St, Bridgetown; tel. 427-7841; fax 435-2198; e-mail barstats@caribsurf.com; internet www.bgis.gov.bb/stats; Central Bank of Barbados, Spry St, POB 1016, Bridgetown; tel. 436-6870; fax 427-1431; e-mail cbb.libr@caribsurf.com; internet www.centralbank.org.bb.

AREA AND POPULATION

Area: 430 sq km (166 sq miles).

Population: 252,029 (males 119,665, females 132,364) at census of 12 May 1980; 257,082 (provisional) at census of 2 May 1990; 268,000 (estimate) at mid-2001. Source: partly UN, *Population and Vital Statistics Report.*

Density (mid-2001): 623.3 per sq km.

Ethnic Groups (*de jure* population, excl. persons resident in institutions, 1990 census): Black 228,683; White 8,022; Mixed race 5,886; Total (incl. others) 247,288.

Principal Town: Bridgetown (capital), population 5,928 at 1990 census. *Mid-2001:* (UN estimate, incl. suburbs): Bridgetown 136,000 (Source: UN, *World Urbanization Prospects: The 2001 Revision*).

Births, Marriages and Deaths (provisional, 2000): Live births 3,762 (birth rate 14.1 per 1,000); Marriages (1997) 3,377 (marriage rate 12.7 per 1,000); Deaths, 2,367 (death rate 8.8 per 1,000). Source: partly UN, *Population and Vital Statistics Report.*

Expectation of Life (WHO estimates, years at birth): 74.4 (males 70.5; females 78.2) in 2001. Source: WHO, *World Health Report.*

Economically Active Population* (provisional figures, labour force sample survey, '000 persons aged 15 years and over, excl. armed forces, 2001): Agriculture, forestry and fishing 5.4; Manufacturing 9.2; Electricity, gas and water 2.0; Construction and quarrying 14.2; Wholesale and retail trade 18.9; Tourism 13.7; Transport, storage and communications 5.9; Financing, insurance, real estate and business services 10.4; Community, social and personal services 48.8; Activities not adequately defined 0.2; Total employed 128.7 (males 67.6, females 58.5); Unemployed 14.1 (males 6.1, females 7.5); Total labour force 142.8 (males 73.7, females 66.0). * Figures for totals may not add up owing to rounding. Source: ILO Caribbean Office.

HEALTH AND WELFARE

Key Indicators

Total Fertility Rate (children per woman, 2001): 1.5.

Under-5 Mortality Rate (per 1,000 live births, 2001): 14.

HIV/AIDS (% of persons aged 15–49, 1999): 1.20.

Physicians (per 1,000 head, 1993): 1.25.

Hospital Beds (per 1,000 head, 1996): 7.56.

Health Expenditure (2000): US $ per head (PPP): 606.

Health Expenditure (2000): % of GDP: 6.4.

Health Expenditure (2000): public (% of total): 64.8.

Access to Water (% of persons, 2000): 100.

Access to Sanitation (% of persons, 2000): 100.

Human Development Index (2000): ranking: 31.

Human Development Index (2000): value: 0.871.
For sources and definitions, see explanatory note on p. vi.

AGRICULTURE, ETC.

Principal Crops (FAO estimates, '000 metric tons, 2001): Maize 2; Sweet potatoes 5; Cassava 1; Yams 1; Pulses 1; Coconuts 2; Cabbages 1; Tomatoes 1; Pumpkins 1; Cucumbers 1; Chillies and peppers 1; String beans 1; Carrots 1; Other vegetables 5; Sugar cane 450; Bananas 1; Other fruits 3. Source: FAO.

Livestock (FAO estimates, '000 head, year ending September 2001): Horses 1; Mules 2; Asses 2; Cattle 20; Pigs 35; Sheep 42; Goats 5; Poultry 3,500. Source: FAO.

Livestock Products (FAO estimates, '000 metric tons, 2001): Beef and veal 1; Pig meat 4; Poultry meat 12; Cows' milk 9; Hen eggs 1. Source: FAO.

Forestry (FAO estimates, '000 cubic metres): Roundwood removals 5 in 1999; 5 in 2000; 5 in 2001. Source: FAO.

Fishing (metric tons, live weight, 2000): Total catch 3,100 (Yellowfin tuna 155, Flyingfishes 1,916, Common dolphinfish 728). Source: FAO, *Yearbook of Fishery Statistics.*

MINING

Production (2001): Natural gas 35.0m. cu m; Crude petroleum 463,699 barrels.

INDUSTRY

Selected Products (official estimates, 1999): Raw sugar (unofficial figure, 2000) 55,000 metric tons; Rum 9,600,000 litres; Beer 7,600,000 litres; Cigarettes (1995) 65 metric tons; Batteries (1998) 17,165; Electric energy (1998) 715m. kWh. Source: partly UN, *Industrial Commodity Statistics Yearbook.*

FINANCE

Currency and Exchange Rates: 100 cents = 1 Barbados dollar (Bds $). *Sterling, US Dollar and Euro Equivalents* (31 December 2002): £1 sterling = Bds $3.224; US $1 = Bds $2.000; €1 = Bds $2.097; Bds $100 = £31.02 = US $50.00 = €47.68. *Exchange Rate:* Fixed at US $1 = Bds $2.000 since 1986.

Budget (estimates, Bds $ million, year ending 31 March 2002): *Revenue:* Tax revenue 1,634.0 (Direct taxes 739.9, of which Personal income tax 315.9, Corporate taxes 250.6, Taxes on property 108.1); Indirect taxes 894.1 (Value-added tax 488.3, Excises 154.6, Import duties 131.5, Other indirect taxes 102.5); Non-tax revenue 111.0; Total 1,745.0. *Expenditure:* Current 1,612.3 (Wages and salaries 643.2, Other goods and services 197.9, Interest payments 276.8, Transfers and subsidies 494.4); Capital (incl. net lending 19.9) 295.7; Total 1,927.9 Note: Budgetary data refer to current and capital budgets only and exclude operations of the National Insurance Fund and other central government units with their own budgets.

International Reserves (US $ million at 31 December 2002): IMF special drawing rights 0.06; Reserve position in IMF 6.60; Foreign exchange 644.42; Total 651.07. Source: IMF, *International Financial Statistics.*

Money Supply (Bds $ million at 31 December 2002): Currency outside banks 337.5; Demand deposits at commercial banks 842.3; Total money (incl. others) 1,173.7. Source: IMF, *International Financial Statistics.*

Cost of Living (Index of Retail Prices; base: 1995 = 100): 110.6 in 1999; 113.3 in 2000; 116.2 in 2001. Source: IMF, *International Financial Statistics.*

Expenditure on the Gross Domestic Product (Bds $ million at current prices, 2001): Government final consumption expenditure 1,129.0; Private final consumption expenditure 3,286.3; Gross fixed capital formation 825.0; *Total domestic expenditure* 5,240.3; Exports of goods and services 2,592.8; Less Imports of goods and services 2,735.3; *GDP in purchasers' values* 5,097.8. Source: Caribbean Development Bank, *Social and Economic Indicators 2001.*

Gross Domestic Product by Economic Activity (Bds $ million at current prices, 1998): Agriculture, hunting, forestry and fishing 158.1; Mining and quarrying 20.1; Manufacturing 243.5; Electricity, gas and water 126.4; Construction 240.6; Wholesale and retail trade 702.2; Tourism 482.2; Transport, storage and communications 381.7; Finance, insurance, real estate and business services 715.7; Government services 674.5; Other community, social and personal services 179.8; *GDP at factor cost* 3,924.8; Indirect taxes, *less* subsidies 852.1; *GDP in purchasers' values* 4,776.9.

Balance of Payments (US $ million, 2001): Exports of goods f.o.b. 271.2; Imports of goods f.o.b. –952.3; *Trade balance* –681.1; Exports of services 1,085.2; Imports of services –498.5; *Balance on goods and services* –94.4; Other income received 73.0; Other income paid –166.4; *Balance on goods, services and income* –187.8; Current transfers received 125.6; Current transfers paid –32.3; *Current balance* –94.4; Capital account (net) 1.3; Direct investment abroad –1.1; Direct investment from abroad 18.6; Portfolio investment assets –30.5; Portfolio investment liabilities 150.2; Other investment assets –56.7; Other investment liabilities 202.6; Net errors and omissions 32.6; *Overall balance* 222.4. Source: IMF, *International Financial Statistics.*

EXTERNAL TRADE

Principal Commodities (US $ million, 2000): *Imports c.i.f.:* Food and live animals 139.3; Crude materials (inedible) except fuels 37.9; Mineral fuels, lubricants, etc. 133.3 (Refined petroleum products 127.9); Chemicals and related products 105.0; Basic manufactures 201.0; Machinery and transport equipment 320.8 (General industrial machinery and equipment 46.3, Telecommunications and sound equipment 43.8, Other electrical machinery, apparatus, etc. 57.1, Road vehicles and parts 88.5); Miscellaneous manufactured articles 182.1; Total (incl. others) 1,155.5. *Exports f.o.b.:* Food and live animals 57.3 (Raw sugar 26.7, Margarine 7.7); Beverages and tobacco 16.2 (Alcoholic beverages 14.5); Mineral fuels, lubricants, etc. 60.4 (Petroleum, petroleum products, etc. 60.4); Chemicals and related products 37.1 (Medicinal and pharmaceutical products 15.4, Disinfectants, insecticides, fungicides, etc. 10.0); Basic manufactures 34.8 (Non-metallic mineral manufactures 11.0; Metal manufactures 13.0); Machinery and transport equipment 38.1 (Electrical machinery, apparatus, etc. 21.0); Miscellaneous manufactured articles 22.8 (Printed matter 10.8); Total (incl. others) 272.8. Source: UN, *International Trade Statistics Yearbook*.

Principal Trading Partners (US $ million, 2000): *Imports:* Brazil 19.0; Canada 47.8; China, People's Republic 16.13; France 16.7; Germany 18.3; Japan 60.0; Netherlands 11.9; New Zealand 12.6; Trinidad and Tobago 190.1; United Kingdom 93.3; USA 480.2; Total (incl. others) 1,155.5.3. *Exports:* Antigua and Barbuda 6.9; Belize 2.7; Canada 5.6; Dominica 5.0; Grenada 7.2; Guyana 7.1; Jamaica 19.2; Netherlands Antilles 3.0; Saint Lucia 14.5; Saint Kitts and Nevis 6.2; Saint Vincent and the Grenadines 9.1; Suriname 3.5; Trinidad and Tobago 36.1; United Kingdom 35.9; USA 43.1; Total (incl. others) 272.8. Source: UN, *International Trade Statistics Yearbook*.

TRANSPORT

Road Traffic (motor vehicles in use, 1999): Private cars 60,826; Buses and coaches 1,262; Lorries and vans 8,316; Motorcycles and mopeds 1,410; Road tractors 768. Source: International Road Federation, *World Road Statistics*.

Shipping (estimated freight traffic, '000 metric tons, 1990): Goods loaded 206; Goods unloaded 538. (Source: UN, *Monthly Bulletin of Statistics*.) *Total goods handled* ('000 metric tons, 1997): 1,095. (Source: Barbados Port Authority.) *Merchant Fleet* (vessels registered at 31 December 2001): Number of vessels 68; Total displacement 687,331 grt. (Source: Lloyd's Register-Fairplay, *World Fleet Statistics*).

Civil Aviation (1994): Aircraft movements 36,100; Freight loaded 5,052.3 metric tons; Freight unloaded 8,548.3 metric tons.

TOURISM

Tourist Arrivals: *Stop-overs:* 517,869 in 1999; 545,027 in 2000; 507,086 in 2001. *Cruise-ship passengers:* 445,821 in 1999; 533,278 in 2000; 527,597 in 2001.

Visitor arrivals by country ('000 persons, 2000): Canada 60.0; Guyana 13.5; Netherlands Antilles 13.5; Trinidad and Tobago 23.2; United Kingdom 226.8; USA 112.2; Total (incl. others) 545.0. Source: World Tourism Organization, *Yearbook of Tourism Statistics*.

Tourism Receipts (US $ million): 666.3 in 1999; 711.3 in 2000; 703.5 in 2001. Source: Caribbean Development Bank, *Social and Economic Indicators 2001*.

COMMUNICATIONS MEDIA

Radio Receivers (1999): 175,000 in use.

Television Receivers (2000): 83,000 in use.

Telephones (2000): 123,800 main lines in use.

Facsimile Machines (year ending 31 March 1997): 1,800 in use.

Mobile Cellular Telephones (2000): 28,500 subscribers.

Personal Computers (2001): 25,000 in use.

Internet Users (2000): 10,000.

Newspapers: *Daily* (1996): 2 (circulation 53,000). *Non-daily* (1990): 4 (estimated circulation 95,000).
Sources: partly UNESCO, *Statistical Yearbook*, UN, *Statistical Yearbook*, and International Telecommunication Union.

EDUCATION

Pre-primary (1995/96): 84 schools; 529 teachers; 4,689 pupils.

Primary (2002): 109 schools; 1,823 teachers; 29,502 pupils.

Secondary (2002): 32 schools; 1,389 teachers; 21,436 pupils.

Tertiary (2002): 4 schools; 339 teachers; 11,226 students.

Adult Literacy Rate: 97.0% in 2002.
Source: Ministry of Education, Youth Affairs and Sport.

Directory

The Constitution

The parliamentary system has been established since the 17th century, when the first Assembly sat, in 1639, and the Charter of Barbados was granted, in 1652. A new Constitution came into force on 30 November 1966, when Barbados became independent. Under its terms, protection is afforded to individuals from slavery and forced labour, from inhuman treatment, deprivation of property, arbitrary search and entry, and racial discrimination; freedom of conscience, of expression, assembly, and movement are guaranteed.

Executive power is nominally vested in the British monarch, as Head of State, represented in Barbados by a Governor-General, who appoints the Prime Minister and, on the advice of the Prime Minister, appoints other ministers and some senators.

The Cabinet consists of the Prime Minister, appointed by the Governor-General as being the person best able to command a majority in the House of Assembly, and not fewer than five other ministers. Provision is also made for a Privy Council, presided over by the Governor-General.

Parliament consists of the Governor-General and a bicameral legislature, comprising the Senate and the House of Assembly. The Senate has 21 members: 12 appointed by the Governor-General on the advice of the Prime Minister, two on the advice of the Leader of the Opposition and seven as representatives of such interests as the Governor-General considers appropriate. The House of Assembly has (since January 1991) 28 members, elected by universal adult suffrage for a term of five years (subject to dissolution). The House of Assembly was to increase to 30 members following the May 2003 general election. The minimum voting age is 18 years.

The Constitution also provides for the establishment of Service Commissions for the Judicial and Legal Service, the Public Service, the Police Service and the Statutory Boards Service. These Commissions are exempt from legal investigation; they have executive powers relating to appointments, dismissals and disciplinary control of the services for which they are responsible.

The Government

Head of State: HM Queen ELIZABETH II (succeeded to the throne 6 February 1952).

Governor-General: Sir CLIFFORD HUSBANDS (appointed 1 June 1996).

THE CABINET
(April 2003)

Prime Minister and Minister of Finance, Defence and Security: OWEN S. ARTHUR.

Deputy Prime Minister and Minister of Foreign Affairs and Foreign Trade: BILLIE A. MILLER.

Attorney-General and Minister of Home Affairs: MIA A. MOTTLEY.

Minister of Education, Youth Affairs and Sport: RUDOLPH N. GREENIDGE.

Minister of Health: Dr JEROME WALCOTT.

Minister of Physical Development and the Environment: ELIZABETH THOMPSON.

Minister of Agriculture and Rural Development: ANTHONY P. WOOD.

Minister of Social Transformation: HAMILTON F. LASHLEY.

Minister of Tourism and International Transport: NOEL A. LYNCH.

Minister of Housing and Lands: GLINE A. CLARKE.

Minister of Commerce, Consumer Affairs and Business Development: RONALD TOPPIN.

Minister of Economic Development, Industry and International Business: REGINALD R. FARLEY.

Minister of Labour and Social Security: RAWLE C. EASTMOND.

Minister of Public Works and Transport: ROMMEL MARSHALL.

Minister of State in the Office of the Prime Minister and the Ministry for the Civil Service (with responsibility for Information): GLYNE S.H. MURRAY.

Minister of State in the Ministry of Education, Youth Affairs and Sport: CYNTHIA FORDE.

MINISTRIES

Office of the Prime Minister: Government Headquarters, Bay St, St Michael; tel. 436-6435; fax 436-9280; e-mail info@primeminister.gov.bb; internet www.primeminister.gov.bb.

Ministry of Agriculture and Rural Development: Graeme Hall, POB 505, Christ Church; tel. 428-4150; fax 420-8444; internet www.barbados.gov.bb/minagri.

Ministry for the Civil Service: Roebuck Plaza, 20–23 Roebuck St, Bridgetown; tel. 426-2390; fax 228-0093.

Ministry of Commerce, Consumer Affairs and Business Development: Government Headquarters, Bay St, St Michael; tel. 427-5270.

Ministry of Defence and Security: Government Headquarters, Bay St, St Michael; tel. 436-1970.

Ministry of Economic Development, Industry and International Business: The Business Centre, Upton, St Michael; tel. 430-2200; fax 429-6849; e-mail mtbbar@caribsurf.com.

Ministry of Education, Youth Affairs and Sport: Elsie Payne Complex, Constitution Rd, Bridgetown; tel. 430-2700; fax 436-2411; e-mail mined1@caribsurf.com; internet www.edutech2000.gov.bb.

Ministry of Finance and Economic Affairs: Government Headquarters, Bay St, St Michael; tel. 436-6435; fax 429-4032.

Ministry of Foreign Affairs and Foreign Trade: 1 Culloden Rd, St Michael; tel. 436-2990; fax 429-6652; e-mail barbados@foreign.gov.bb; internet www.foreign.gov.bb.

Ministry of Health: Jemmott's Lane, St Michael; tel. 426-5080; fax 426-5570.

Ministry of Home Affairs: General Post Office Bldg, Level 5, Cheapside, Bridgetown; tel. 228-8961; fax 437-3794; e-mail mha@caribsurf.com.

Ministry of Housing and Lands: Culloden Rd, St Michael; tel. 431-7600; fax 435-0174; e-mail psmhl@caribsurf.com.

Ministry of International Transport: Port Authority Bldg, University Row, Bridgetown; tel. 426-9144; fax 429-3809.

Ministry of Labour and Social Security: National Insurance Bldg, 5th Floor, Fairchild St, Bridgetown; tel. 436-6320; fax 426-8959; internet www.labour.gov.bb.

Minister of Physical Development and the Environment: Frank Walcott Bldg, Culloden Rd, St Michael; tel. 431-7692.

Ministry of Public Works and Transport: The Pine, St Michael; tel. 429-2191; fax 437-8133; internet www.publicworks.gov.bb.

Ministry of Social Transformation: Nicholas House, Broad St, Bridgetown; tel. 228-5878.

Ministry of Tourism: Sherbourne Conference Centre, Two Mile Hill, St Michael; tel. 430-7500; fax 436-4828.

Office of the Attorney-General: Sir Frank Walcott Bldg, Culloden Rd, St Michael; tel. 431-7750; fax 228–5433; e-mail attygen@caribsurf.com.bb.

Legislature

PARLIAMENT

Senate

President: Sir FRED GOLLOP.
There are 21 members.

House of Assembly

Speaker: ISHMAEL ROETT.

General Election, 20 January 1999

Party	Votes	%	Seats
Barbados Labour Party (BLP) . .	83,085	64.85	26
Democratic Labour Party (DLP)	44,974	35.10	2
Others	64	0.05	—
Total	128,123	100.00	28

Political Organizations

Barbados Labour Party: Grantley Adams House, 111 Roebuck St, Bridgetown; tel. 429-1990; e-mail hq@blp.org.bb; internet www.blp.org.bb; f. 1938; moderate social democrat; Leader OWEN S. ARTHUR; Chair. REGINALD FARLEY; Gen. Sec. MIA A. MOTTLEY.

Democratic Labour Party: George St, Belleville, St Michael; tel. 429-3104; fax 429-3007; e-mail dlp@dlpbarbados.bb; internet www.dlpbarbados.org; f. 1955; Pres. CLYDE MASCOLL.

National Democratic Party: 'Sueños', 3 Sixth Ave, Belleville; tel. 429-6882; f. 1989 by split from Democratic Labour Party; Leader Dr RICHARD (RICHIE) HAYNES.

Diplomatic Representation

EMBASSIES AND HIGH COMMISSIONS IN BARBADOS

Australia: Bishops Court Hill, Pine Rd, St Michael; tel. 435-2834; High Commissioner W. PEPPINCK.

Brazil: Sunjet House, 3rd Floor, Fairchild St, Bridgetown; tel. 427-1735; fax 427-1744; e-mail brembarb@sunbeach.net; Ambassador ORLANDO GALVÊAS OLIVEIRA.

Canada: Bishops Court Hill, Pine Rd, POB 404, St Michael; tel. 429-3550; fax 429-3780; High Commissioner SANDELLE S. SCRIMSHAW.

China, People's Republic: 17 Golf View Terrace, Rockley, Christ Church; tel. 435-6890; fax 435-8300; Ambassador YANG ZHIKUAN.

Costa Rica: Omega Bldg, Suite 4, 1st Floor, Dayreels Rd, Christ Church; tel. 431-0250; fax 431-0261; e-mail embcr@sunbeach.net; Chargé d'affaires a.i. JORGE REVOLLO FRANCO.

Cuba: Palm View, Erdiston Dr., St Michael; tel. 435-2769; fax 435–2734; e-mail embajadadecuba@sunbeach.net; Ambassador JOSÉ JOAQUÍN ALVAREZ PORTELA.

United Kingdom: Lower Collymore Rock, POB 676, St Michael; tel. 430-7800; fax 430-7826; e-mail britishhc@sunbeach.net; internet www.britishhc.org; High Commissioner JOHN WHITE.

USA: Canadian Imperial Bank of Commerce Bldg, Broad St, POB 302, Bridgetown; tel. 436-4950; fax 429-5246; Ambassador EARL N. PHILLIPS, Jr.

Venezuela: Hastings, Main Rd, Christ Church; tel. 435-7619; fax 435-7830; e-mail jesusmachin@sunbeach.net; Ambassador MARIA CORINA RUSSIAN FRONTADO.

Judicial System

Justice is administered by the Supreme Court of Judicature, which consists of a High Court and a Court of Appeal. Final appeal lies with the Judicial Committee of the Privy Council, in the United Kingdom. There are Magistrates' Courts for lesser offences, with appeal to the Court of Appeal.

Supreme Court: Judiciary Office, Coleridge St, Bridgetown; tel. 426-3461; fax 246-2405.

Chief Justice: Sir DAVID SIMMONS.

Justices of Appeal: G.C.R. MOE; ERROL DA COSTA CHASE; COLIN A. WILLIAMS.

Judges of the High Court: FREDERICK A. WATERMAN; MARIE A. MACCORMACK; E. GARVEY HUSBANDS; CARLISLE PAYNE; SHERMAN MOORE; LIONEL DACOSTA GREENIDGE.

Registrar of the Supreme Court: SANDRA MASON.

Office of the Attorney-General: Sir Frank Walcott Bldg, Culloden Rd, St Michael; tel. 431-7750; fax 228–5433; e-mail attygen@caribsurf.com.bb; Dir of Public Prosecutions CHARLES LEACOCK (cbleacock@inaccs.com.bb).

Religion

More than 100 religious denominations and sects are represented in Barbados, but the vast majority of the population profess Christianity. According to the 1980 census, there were 96,894 Anglicans (or some 40% of the total population), while the Pentecostal (8%) and Methodist (7%) churches were next in importance. There are also small groups of Hindus, Muslims and Jews.

CHRISTIANITY

The Anglican Communion

Anglicans in Barbados are adherents of the Church in the Province of the West Indies, comprising eight dioceses. The Archbishop of the Province is the Bishop of Nassau and the Bahamas, resident in Nassau, the Bahamas. In Barbados there is a Provincial Office (St George's Church, St George) and an Anglican Theological College (Codrington College, St John).

Bishop of Barbados: Rt Rev. Rufus Theophilus Broome, Leland, Philip Dr., Pine Gardens, St Michael; fax 426-0871; e-mail mandeville@sunbeach.com.

Barbados Christian Council

Caribbean Conference of Churches Bldg, George St and Collymore Rock, St Michael; tel. 426-6014.

The Roman Catholic Church

Barbados comprises a single diocese (formed in January 1990, when the diocese of Bridgetown-Kingstown was divided), which is suffragan to the archdiocese of Port of Spain (Trinidad and Tobago). At 31 December 2001 there were an estimated 10,750 adherents in the diocese. The Bishop participates in the Antilles Episcopal Conference (currently based in Port of Spain, Trinidad and Tobago).

Bishop of Bridgetown: Rt Rev. Malcolm Patrick Galt, St Patrick's Presbytery, Jemmott's Lane, POB 1223, Bridgetown; tel. 426-3510; fax 429-6198; e-mail rcbishopbgi@caribnet.com.

Protestant Churches

Baptist Churches of Barbados: National Baptist Convention, President Kennedy Dr., Bridgetown; tel. 429-2697.

Church of God (Caribbean Atlantic Assembly): St Michael's Plaza, St Michael's Row, POB 1, Bridgetown; tel. 427-5770; Pres. Rev. Victor Babb.

Church of Jesus Christ of Latter-day Saints (Mormons)— West Indies Mission: Bridgetown; tel. 435-8595; fax 435-8278.

Church of the Nazarene: District Office, Eagle Hall, Bridgetown; tel. 425-1067.

Methodist Church: Bethel Church Office, Bay St, Bridgetown; tel. and fax 426-2223; e-mail methodist@caribsurf.com.

Moravian Church: Roebuck St, Bridgetown; tel. 426-2337; Superintendent Rev. Errol Connor.

Seventh-day Adventists (East Caribbean Conference): Brydens Ave, Brittons Hill, POB 223, St Michael; tel. 429-7234; fax 429-8055.

Wesleyan Holiness Church: General Headquarters, Bank Hall; tel. 429-4864.

Other denominations include the Abundant Life Assembly, the African Orthodox Church, the Apostolic Church, the Assemblies of Brethren, the Berean Bible Brethren, the Bethel Evangelical Church, Christ is the Answer Family Church, the Church of God the Prophecy, the Ethiopian Orthodox Church, the Full Gospel Assembly, Love Gospel Assembly, the New Testament Church of God, the Pentecostal Assemblies of the West Indies, the People's Cathedral, the Salvation Army, Presbyterian congregations, the African Methodist Episcopal Church, the Mt Olive United Holy Church of America and Jehovah's Witnesses.

ISLAM

In 1996 there were an estimated 2,000 Muslims in Barbados.

Islamic Teaching Centre: Harts Gap, Hastings; tel. 427-0120.

JUDAISM

Jewish Community: Nidhe Israel and Shaara Tzedek Synagogue, Rockley New Rd, POB 651, Bridgetown; tel. 437-1290; fax 437-1303; there were 60 Jews in Barbados in 1997; Pres. Rachelle Altman; Sec. Sharon Oran.

Caribbean Jewish Congress: POB 1331, Bridgetown; tel. 436-8163; fax 437-4992; e-mail waw@sunbeach.net; f. 1994; aims to foster closer relations between Jewish communities in the region and to promote greater understanding of the Jewish faith; Dir-Gen. W. A. Winston Ben Zebedee.

HINDUISM

Hindu Community: Hindu Temple, Roberts Complex, Government Hill, St Michael; tel. 434-4638; there were 411 Hindus at the census of 1980.

The Press

Barbados Advocate: POB 230, St Michael; tel. 467-2000; fax 434-1000; e-mail advocate@sunbeach.net; internet www.barbadosadvocate.com; f. 1895; daily; Editor Reudon Eversley; circ. 11,413.

The Beacon: 111 Roebuck St, Bridgetown; organ of the Barbados Labour Party; weekly; circ. 15,000.

The Broad Street Journal: Plantation Complex, St Lawrence Main Rd, Christ Church; tel. 420-6245; fax 420-5477; e-mail bsj@sunbeach.net; internet www.broadstreetjournal.com; f. 1993; weekly; business; Editor Patrick Hoyos.

Caribbean Week: Lefferts Place, River Rd, St Michael; tel. 436-1906; fax 436-1904; e-mail cweek@sunbeach.net; internet www.cweek.com; f. 1989; fortnightly; Editor-in-Chief John E. Lovell; Publr Timothy C. Forsyth; circ. 56,200.

The Nation: Nation House, Fontabelle, St Michael; tel. 430-5400; fax 427-6968; e-mail nationnews@sunbeach.net; internet www.nationnews.com; f. 1973; daily; Pres. and Editor-in-Chief Harold Hoyte; circ. 23,144 (weekday), 33,084 (weekend).

Official Gazette: Government Printing Office, Bay St, St Michael; tel. 436-6776; Mon. and Thur.

Sunday Advocate: POB 230, St Michael; tel. 467-2000; fax 434-1000; e-mail advocate@sunbeach.net; internet www.barbadosadvocate.com; f. 1895; Editor Reudon Eversley; circ. 17,490.

The Sunday Sun: Fontabelle, St Michael; tel. 436-6240; fax 427-6968; e-mail subs@sunbeach.net; f. 1977; Dir Harold Hoyte; circ. 42,286.

Weekend Investigator: POB 230, St Michael; tel. 434-2000; circ. 14,305.

NEWS AGENCIES

Caribbean Media Corporation (CMC): Culloden View, Beckles Rd, St Michael; tel. 467-1000; fax 429-4355; e-mail admin@cananews.com; internet www.cananews.com; by merger of Caribbean News Agency CANA and Caribbean Broadcasting Union; COO Gary Allen.

Foreign Bureaux

Inter Press Service (IPS) (Italy): POB 697, Bridgetown; tel. 426-4474; Correspondent Marva Cossy.

Xinhua (New China) News Agency (People's Republic of China): Christ Church; Chief Correspondent Ding Baozhong.

Agence France-Presse (AFP) is also represented.

Publishers

The Advocate Publishing Co Ltd: POB 230, St Michael; tel. 434-2000; fax 434-2020.

Business Tutors: POB 800e St Michael; tel. 428-5664; fax 429-4854; e-mail pchad@caribsurf.com; business, management, computers.

Carib Research and Publications Inc: POB 556, Bridgetown; tel. 438-0580; f. 1986; regional interests; CEO Dr Farley Braithwaite.

Nation Publishing Co Ltd: Nation House, Fontabelle, St Michael; tel. 436-6240; fax 427-6968.

Broadcasting and Communications

TELECOMMUNICATIONS

Cable & Wireless (Barbados) Ltd: POB 32, Wildey, St Michael; tel. 292-6000; fax 427-5808; e-mail bdsinfo@caribsurf.com; internet www.candwbet.com.bb; f. 1984; fmrly Barbados External Telecommunications Ltd; became Cable & Wireless BET Ltd, which merged with Barbados Telephone Co Ltd (BARTEL), Cable & Wireless

Caribbean Cellular and Cable & Wireless Information Systems in 2002; provides international telecommunications services; owned by Cable & Wireless PLC (United Kingdom); Chair. STEPHEN EMTAGE; Gen. Man. VINCENT YEARWOOD.

BROADCASTING

Regulatory Authority

Caribbean Broadcasting Corporation (CBC): The Pine, POB 900, Bridgetown; tel. 429-2041; fax 429-4795; e-mail cbc@caribsurf .com; f. 1963; Chair. FOLZO BREWSTER.

Radio

Barbados Broadcasting Service Ltd: Astoria St George, Bridgetown; tel. 437-9550; fax 437-9554; f. 1981; FM station. Faith 102 FM; religious broadcasting.

Barbados Rediffusion Service Ltd: River Rd, Bridgetown; tel. 430-7300; fax 429-8093; f. 1935; public company; Gen. Man. VIC FERNANDES; HOTT FM, at River Rd, Bridgetown; f. 1998; is a commercial station; Voice of Barbados, at River Rd, Bridgetown; f. 1981; is a commercial station covering Barbados and the eastern Caribbean; YESS Ten-Four FM, at River Rd, Bridgetown; f. 1988; is a commercial station.

CBC Radio: POB 900, Bridgetown; tel. 429-2041; fax 429-4795; e-mail CBC@CaribNet.Net; f. 1963; commercial; Programme Man. W. CALLENDER; CBC Radio 900; f. 1963; broadcasts 21 hours daily; Radio Liberty FM; f. 1984; broadcasts 24 hours daily.

Television

CBC TV: POB 900, Bridgetown; tel. 429-2041; fax 429-4795; f. 1964; Channel Eight is the main national service, broadcasting 24 hours daily; a maximum of 30 subscription channels are available through Multi Choice; Gen. Man. MELBA SMITH; Programme Man. HILDA COX.

Finance

In December 2001 there were 4,038 international business companies and 2,981 foreign sales corporations registered in Barbados. In May 2002 87 offshore banks were licensed.

BANKING

(cap. = capital; auth. = authorized; dep. = deposits; res = reserves; brs = branches; m. = million; amounts in Barbados dollars unless otherwise indicated)

Central Bank

Central Bank of Barbados: Tom Adams Financial Centre, POB 1016, Spry St, Bridgetown; tel. 436-6870; fax 427-9559; e-mail cbb .libr@caribsurf.com; internet www.centralbank.org.bb; f. 1972; bank of issue; cap. 2.0m., res 10.0m., dep. 733.8m. (Dec. 2001); Gov. MARION V. WILLIAMS; Deputy Gov. DARCY W. BOYCE.

Commercial Banks

Caribbean Commercial Bank Ltd: Lower Broad St, POB 1007c, Bridgetown; tel. 431-2500; fax 431-2530; f. 1984; cap. 25.0m., res 4.5m., dep. 178.5m. (Dec. 2000); Chair. DAVID C. STOREY; Pres. and CEO MARIANO R. BROWNE; 4 brs.

FirstCaribbean International Bank Ltd: Warrens, St Michael; tel. 367-2500; fax 424-8977; internet www.firstcaribbeanbank.com; f. 2002; previously known as CIBC West Indies Holdings, adopted present name following merger of CIBC West Indies and Caribbean operations of Barclays Bank PLC; Chair. MICHAEL K. MANSOOR; CEO CHARLES PINK; 9 brs.

Mutual Bank of the Caribbean Inc: Trident House, Lower Broad Stc, Bridgetown; tel. 436-8335; fax 429-5734; 4 brs.

Regional Development Bank

Caribbean Development Bank: Wildey, POB 408, St Michael; tel. 431-1600; fax 426-7269; e-mail info@caribank.org; internet www .caribank.org; f. 1970; cap. US $149.5m., res US $14.1m. (Dec. 2001); Pres. Dr COMPTON BOURNE.

National Bank

Barbados National Bank (BNB): 2 Broad St, POB 1002, Bridgetown; tel. 431-5739; fax 426-5037; internet www.bnbbarbados.com; f. 1978; by merger; cap 48m., res 38.7m., dep. 864.1m., total assets 519.5m. (Dec. 2001); scheduled for privatization; Chair. KENNETH HEWITT; Man. Dir and CEO LOUIS GREENIDGE; 5 brs.

Foreign Banks

Bank of Nova Scotia (Canada): Broad St, POB 202, Bridgetown; tel. 431-3000; fax 228-8574; e-mail peter.vanschie@scotiabank.com; f. 1956; Gen. Man. PETER F. VAN SCHIE; 6 brs.

Royal Bank of Canada: Second Floor, Bldg 2, Chelston Park, Collymore Rock, POB 986, St Michael; tel. 431-6680; fax 436-9675; e-mail roycorp@caribsurf.com; f. 1911; 1 br.

Victoria Bank (Canada): c/o David King and Co, First Floor, Trident House, Broad St, Bridgetown; tel. 427-3174; fax 436-5973; f. 1873; opened April 2001.

Trust Companies

Bank of Nova Scotia Trust Co (Caribbean) Ltd: Bank of Nova Scotia Bldg, Broad St, POB 1003b, Bridgetown; tel. 431-3120; fax 426-0969.

Barbados International Bank and Trust Co: The Financial Services Centre, Bishop's Court Hill, POB 111, St Michael; tel. 436-7000; fax 436-7057; f. 1981.

Clico Mortgage & Finance Corporation: C L Duprey Financial Centre, Walrond St, Bridgetown; tel. 431-4719; fax 426-6168; e-mail cmfc@sunbeach.net.

Ernst & Young Trust Corporation: Bay St, POB 261, St Michael; tel. 430-3900; fax 435-2079.

FirstCaribbean International Trust and Merchant Bank (Barbados) Ltd: Warren, St Michael; tel. 367-2324; fax 421-7178; internet www.firstcaribbeaninternational.com; known as CIBC Trust and Merchant Bank until 2002.

Royal Bank of Canada Financial Corporation: 2nd Floor, Bldg 2, Chelston Park, Collymore Rock, POB 986, St Michael; tel. 431-6580; fax 429-3800; e-mail roycorp@caribsurf.com; Man. N.L. SMITH.

St Michael Trust Corpn: c/o PriceWaterhouseCoopers, Collymore Rock, St Michael; tel. 436-7000; fax 429-3747; e-mail bb@fiscglobal .com; internet www.fiscglobal.com; f. 1987.

STOCK EXCHANGE

Securities Exchange of Barbados (SEB): Tom Adams Financial Centre, 5th Floor, Church Village, Bridgetown; tel. 436-9871; fax 429-8942; e-mail sebd@caribsurf.com; f. 1987; in 1989 the Govts of Barbados, Trinidad and Tobago and Jamaica agreed to link exchanges; cross-trading began in April 1991; Chair. NEVILLE LEROY SMITH; Gen. Man. VIRGINIA MAPP.

INSURANCE

The leading British and a number of US and Canadian companies have agents in Barbados. At the end of 2001 there were 447 exempt insurance and insurance management companies were registered in the country. Local insurance companies include the following

Barbados Fire & Commercial Insurance Co: Beckwith Place, Broad St, POB 150, Bridgetown; tel. 431-2800; fax 426-0752; e-mail bf&c@caribsurf.com; f. 1996; following merger of Barbados Commercial Insurance Co. Ltd and Barbados Fire and General Insurance Co; f. 1880; Man. Dir. DAVID DEAN.

Barbados Mutual Life Assurance Society (BMLAS): Collymore Rock, St Michael; tel. 431-7000; fax 436-8829; e-mail info@ themutual.com; internet www.themutual.com; f. 1840; Chair. COLIN G. GODDARD; Pres. J. ARTHUR L. BETHELL.

Insurance Corporation of Barbados (ICB): Roebuck St, Bridgetown; tel. 427-5590; fax 426-3393; e-mail icb@icbbarbados.com; internet www.icbbarbados.com; f. 1978; cap. Bds $3m. Chair. Dr JOHN MAYERS; Man. Dir WISMAR GREAVES; Gen. Man. MONICA SKINNER.

Life of Barbados Ltd (LOB): Wildey, POB 69, St Michael; tel. 426-1060; fax 436-8835; internet www.lifeofbarbados.com; f. 1971; purchased by Barbados Mutual Life Assurance Society in May 2002; cap. Bds $41.3m. (1998); Pres. and CEO STEPHEN M.C. ALLEYNE.

United Insurance Co Ltd: United Insurance Centre, Lower Broad St, POB 1215, Bridgetown; tel. 430-1900; fax 436-7573; e-mail united@caribsurf.com; f. 1976; Man. Dir DAVE A. BLACKMAN.

Insurance Association

Insurance Association of the Caribbean Inc: IAC Bldg, Collymore Rock, St Michael; tel. 427-5608; fax 427-7277; e-mail info@ iac-caribbean.com; internet www.iac-caribbean.com; regional asscn.

Trade and Industry

GOVERNMENT AGENCY

Barbados Agricultural Management Co Ltd: Warrens, POB 719c, St Michael; tel. 425-0010; fax 425-0007; e-mail bamc@cariaccess.com; Chair. R. CARL SYLVESTER; Gen. Man. E. LEROY ROACH.

DEVELOPMENT ORGANIZATIONS

Barbados Agriculture Development and Marketing Corpn: Fairy Valley, Christ Church; tel. 428-0250; fax 428-0152; f. 1993; by merger; programme of diversification and land reforms; Chair. TYRONE POWER; CEO E. LEROY ROACH.

Barbados Investment and Development Corpn: Pelican House, Princess Alice Highway, Bridgetown; tel. 427-5350; fax 426-7802; e-mail bidc@bidc.org; internet www.bidc.com; f. 1992; by merger; facilitates the devt of the industrial sector, especially in the areas of manufacturing, information technology and financial services; offers free consultancy to investors; provides factory space for lease or rent; administers the Fiscal Incentives Legislation; Chair. TREVOR CLARKE; CEO ERROL HUMPHREY.

Department for International Development in the Caribbean: Collymore Rock, POB 167, St Michael; tel. 436-9873; fax 426-2194; Head BRIAN THOMSON.

CHAMBER OF COMMERCE

Barbados Chamber of Commerce and Industry: Nemwil House, 1st Floor, Lower Collymore Rock, POB 189, St Michael; tel. 426-2056; fax 429-2907; e-mail bdscham@caribsurf.com; internet www.bdscham.com; f. 1825; 200 mem. firms, 321 reps; Pres. ROBERT FOSTER; Exec. Dir RUALL HARRIS.

INDUSTRIAL AND TRADE ASSOCIATIONS

Barbados Agricultural Society: The Grotto, Beckles Rd, St Michael; tel. 436-6683; fax 435-0651; e-mail heshimu@sunbeach.net; Pres. TYRONE POWER.

Barbados Association of Medical Practitioners: BAMP Complex, Spring Garden, St Michael; tel. 429-7569; fax 435-2328; e-mail bamp@sunbeach.net; Pres. Dr MARGARET O'SHEA.

Barbados Association of Professional Engineers: POB 666, Bridgetown; tel. 425-6105; fax 425-6673; f. 1964; Pres. GLYNE BARKER; Sec. PATRICK CLARKE.

Barbados Hotel and Tourism Association: Fourth Ave, Belleville, St Michael; tel. 426-5041; fax 429-2845; e-mail bhta@maccs.com.bb; internet www.funbarbados.com/bhta; Pres. ALAN BANFIELD; Exec. Vice-Pres. SUSAN SPRINGER.

Barbados Manufacturers' Association: Bldg 1, Pelican Industrial Park, St Michael; tel. 426-4474; fax 436-5182; e-mail bmex-products@sunbeach.net; internet www.bma.org.bb; f. 1964; Pres. RICHARD COZIER; Exec. Dir CLIFTON E. MAYNARD; 100 mem. firms.

EMPLOYERS' ORGANIZATION

Barbados Employers' Confederation: Nemwil House, 1st Floor, Collymore Rock, St Michael; tel. 426-1574; fax 429-2907; e-mail bcon@sunbeach.net; internet www.barbadosemployers.com; f. 1956; Pres. HARCOURT SANDIFORD; 235 mems (incl. associate mems).

UTILITIES

Electricity

Barbados Light and Power Co (BL & P): POB 142, Garrison Hill, St Michael; tel. 436-1800; fax 429-6000; f. 1911; electricity generator and distributor; operates three stations with a combined capacity of 209,500 kW; Chair. F. O. MCCONNEY; Man. Dir ANDREW GITTENS.

Public Utilities Board: cnr Pine Plantation Rd, Collymore Rock, St Michael; tel. 427-5693; fax 437-3542; e-mail ftchq@caribsurf.com; f. 1955; utility regulator, merged with Fair Trading Comm. in 2001.

Gas

Barbados National Oil Co Ltd (BNOCL): POB 175, Woodbourne, St Philip; tel. 423-0918; fax 423-0166; e-mail ronhewitt@bnocl.com; internet www.bnocl.com; f. 1979; extraction of petroleum and natural gas; state-owned, scheduled for privatization; Chair. HARCOURT LEWIS; 166 employees.

National Petroleum Corporation: Wildey, St Michael; tel. 430-4000; fax 426-4326; gas production and distribution; Gen. Man. KEN LINTON (acting).

Water

Barbados Water Authority: The Pine, St Michael; tel. 427-3990.

TRADE UNIONS

Principal unions include:

Barbados Secondary Teachers' Union: Ryeburn, Eighth Ave, Belleville, St Michael; tel. and fax 429-7676; e-mail bstumail@caribsurf.com; f. 1949; Pres. WAYNE WILLOCK; Gen. Sec. PHIL PERRY; 388 mems.

Barbados Union of Teachers: Merry Hill, Welches, POB 58, St Michael; tel. 427-8510; fax 426-9890; e-mail but4@hotmail.com; f. 1974; Pres. UNDENE WHITTAKER; Gen. Sec. HERBERT GITTENS; 2,000 mems.

Barbados Workers' Union (BWU): Solidarity House, Harmony Hall, POB 172, St Michael; tel. 426-3492; fax 436-6496; e-mail bwu@caribsurf.com; internet www.bwu-bb.org; f. 1941; operates a Labour College; Gen. Sec. LEROY TROTMAN; 20,000 mems.

National Union of Public Workers: Dalkeith House, Dalkeith Rd, POB 174, St. Michael; tel. 426-1764; fax 436-1795; e-mail nupwbarbados@sunbeach.net; f. 1944; Pres. CECIL W. DRAKES; Gen. Sec. JOSEPH E. GODDARD; 6,000 mems.

Transport

ROADS

Ministry of Public Works and Transport: The Pine, St Michael; tel. 429-2191; fax 437-8133; internet www.publicworks.gov.bb; maintains a network of 1,793 km (1,114 miles) of roads, of which 1,703 km (1,058 miles) are paved; US $40m. road-paving programme was announced in August 2001; Chief Tech. Officer C.H. ARCHER.

SHIPPING

Bridgetown harbour has berths for eight ships and simultaneous bunkering facilities for five. The Pierhead project, a US $600m. plan to extend and modernize the harbour, was expected to start in July 2002.

Barbados Port Authority: University Row, Bridgetown Harbour; tel. 430-4700; fax 429-5348; e-mail administrator@barbadosport.com; internet www.barbadosport.com; f. 1979; Chair. LARRY TATEM; Gen. Man. EVERTON WALTERS; Port Dir Capt. H. L. VAN SLUYTMAN.

Shipping Association of Barbados: Trident House, 2nd Floor, Broad St, Bridgetown; tel. 427-9860; fax 426-8392; e-mail shasba@caribsurf.com.

Principal Shipping Companies

Barbados Shipping and Trading Co Ltd (B.S. and T.): Musson Bldg, Hincks St, POB 1227c, Bridgetown; tel. 426-3844; fax 427-4719; e-mail info@bsandtco.com; internet www.bsandtco.com; f. 1920; Chair. C. D. BYNOE; Man. Dir A. C. FIELDS.

Bernuth Agencies: Bridgetown; tel. 431-3343.

Carlisle Shipping Ltd: Carlisle House, Bridgetown; tel. 430-4803.

DaCostas Ltd: Carlisle House, Hincks St, POB 103, Bridgetown; tel. 426-3451; fax 429-5445; shipping company; Man. Dir JOHN WILKINSON.

T. Geddes Grant Bros: White Park Rd, Bridgetown; tel. 431-3300.

Hassell, Eric and Son Ltd: Carlisle House, Hincks St, Bridgetown; tel. 436-6102; fax 429-3416; e-mail info@erichassell.com; internet www.erichassell.com; shipping agent, stevedoring contractor and cargo fowarder.

Maersk: James Fort Bldg, Hincks St, Bridgetown; tel. 430-4816.

Tropical Shipping Kensington: Fontabelle Rd, St Michael; tel. 426-9990; fax 426-7750; internet www.tropical.com.

Windward Lines Ltd: Brighton Warehouse Complex, Black Rock, St Michael; tel. 425-7402.

CIVIL AVIATION

The principal airport is Grantley Adams International Airport, at Seawell, 18 km (11 miles) from Bridgetown. A Bds $140m. contract to build a new arrivals terminal was awarded in late 2001. The project was expected to be completed by October 2004.

Tourism

The natural attractions of the island consist chiefly of the warm climate and varied scenery. In addition, there are many facilities for outdoor sports of all kinds. Revenue from tourism increased from Bds \$13m. in 1960 to some \$1,415m. in 2000, before decreasing slightly in 2001, to \$1,407m. The number of stop-over tourist arrivals was 507,086 in 2001, while the number of visiting cruise-ship passengers was 527,597. There were some 6,000 hotel rooms on the island in 1999.

Barbados Tourism Authority: Harbour Rd, POB 242, Bridgetown; tel. 427-2623; fax 426-4080; e-mail btainfo@barbados.org; internet www.barbados.org; f. 1993 to replace Barbados Board of Tourism; offices in London, New York, Los Angeles, Miami, Toronto, Frankfurt, Milan, Paris and Stockholm; Chair. HUDSON HUSBANDS; Pres. and CEO OLIVER JORDAN.

BELARUS

Introductory Survey

Location, Climate, Language, Religion, Flag, Capital

The Republic of Belarus is a land-locked state in north-eastern Europe. It is bounded by Lithuania and Latvia to the north-west, by Ukraine to the south, by Russia to the east, and by Poland to the west. The climate is of a continental type, with an average January temperature, in Minsk, of −5°C (23°F) and an average for July of 19°C (67°F). Average annual precipitation is between 560 mm and 660 mm. The official languages of the republic are Belarusian and Russian. The major religion is Christianity—the Roman Catholic Church and the Eastern Orthodox Church being the largest denominations. There are also small Muslim and Jewish communities. The national flag (proportions 1 by 2) consists of two unequal horizontal stripes, of red over light green, with a red-outlined white vertical stripe at the hoist, bearing in red a traditional embroidery pattern. The capital is Minsk (Miensk).

Recent History

Following periods of Lithuanian and Polish rule, Belarus became a part of the Russian Empire in the late 18th century. During the 19th century there was a growth of national consciousness in Belarus and, as a result of industrialization, significant migration from rural to urban areas. After the February Revolution of 1917 in Russia, Belarusian nationalists and socialists formed a rada (council), which sought a degree of autonomy from the Provisional Government in Petrograd (St Petersburg). In November, after the Bolsheviks had seized power in Petrograd, Red Army troops were dispatched to Minsk, and the rada was dissolved. However, the Bolsheviks were forced to withdraw by the invasion of the German army. The Treaty of Brest-Litovsk, signed in March 1918, assigned most of Belarus to Germany. On 25 March Belarusian nationalists convened to proclaim a Belarusian National Republic, but it achieved only limited autonomy. After the Germans had withdrawn, the Bolsheviks easily reoccupied Minsk, and the Belarusian Soviet Socialist Republic (BSSR) was declared on 1 January 1919.

In February 1919 the BSSR was merged with neighbouring Lithuania in a Lithuanian-Belarusian Soviet Republic (known as 'Litbel'). In April, however, Polish armed forces entered Lithuania and Belarus, and both were declared part of Poland. In July 1920 the Bolsheviks recaptured Minsk, and in August the BSSR was re-established; Lithuania became an independent state. However, the BSSR comprised only the eastern half of the lands populated by Belarusians. Western Belarus was granted to Poland by the Treaty of Riga, signed on 18 March 1921. The Treaty also assigned Belarus's easternmost regions to Russia, but they were returned to the BSSR in 1924 and 1926. Meanwhile, the BSSR, with Ukraine and Transcaucasia, had joined with Russia to establish the Union of Soviet Socialist Republics (USSR) in December 1922.

The Soviet leadership's New Economic Policy of 1921–28, which permitted some liberalization of the economy, brought a measure of prosperity, and there was significant cultural and linguistic development, with the use of the Belarusian language officially encouraged. This period ended in 1929 with the emergence of Stalin (Iosif V. Dzhugashvili) as the dominant figure in the USSR. In that year Stalin began a campaign to collectivize agriculture, which was strongly resisted by the peasantry. In Belarus, as in other parts of the USSR, there were riots and rebellions in rural areas, and many peasants were deported or imprisoned. The purges of the early 1930s were initially targeted against Belarusian nationalists and intellectuals, but by 1936–38 they had widened to include all sectors of the population.

After the invasion of Poland by German and Soviet forces in September 1939, the BSSR was enlarged by the inclusion of the lands that it had lost to Poland and Lithuania in 1921. Between 1941 and 1944 the BSSR was occupied by Nazi German forces; an estimated 2.2m. people died, including most of the republic's large Jewish population. At the Yalta conference, in February 1945, the Allies agreed to recognize the 'Curzon line' as the western border of the BSSR, thus endorsing the unification of western and eastern Belarus. As a result of the Soviet demand for more voting strength in the UN, the Western powers permitted the BSSR to become a member of the UN in its own right.

The immediate post-war period was dominated by the need to rehabilitate the republic's infrastructure. The reconstruction programme's requirements and the local labour shortage led to an increase in Russian immigration into the republic, thus discouraging use of the Belarusian language. During the 1960s and 1970s the process of 'russification' continued; there was a decline in the use of Belarusian in schools and in the media. The republic was, however, one of the most prosperous in the USSR, with a wider variety of consumer goods available than in other republics. This relative prosperity was one reason why the ruling Communist Party of Belarus (CPB) was initially able to resist implementing the economic and political reforms that were proposed by the Soviet leader, Mikhail Gorbachev, from 1985. By 1987, however, the press had become critical of the CPB's stance on cultural and ecological issues. Intellectuals and writers campaigned for the greater use of Belarusian in education. Campaigners also demanded more information about the consequences of the explosion of April 1986 at the Chornobyl (Chernobyl) nuclear power station in Ukraine, which had affected large areas of southern Belarus. The two most important unofficial groups to emerge in the late 1980s were the Belarusian Language Association and the Belarusian Ecological Union.

There was, however, little opportunity for overt political opposition. A Belarusian Popular Front (BPF) was established in October 1988, but the CPB severely restricted its activities and banned republican media reports about the new group. The BPF did have some success in the elections to the all-Union Congress of People's Deputies, which took place in March 1989, persuading voters to reject several leading officials of the CPB. However, the inaugural congress of the BPF took place in Vilnius, Lithuania, in June, the Front having been refused permission to meet in Minsk. None the less, in early 1990, in anticipation of the elections to the republican Supreme Soviet, or Supreme Council (legislature), the CPB adopted some of the BPF's policies regarding the Belarusian language. In January the authorities approved a law declaring Belarusian to be the state language, effective from 1 September. (However, Russian was reinstated as a second state language, following the adoption of a new Constitution in November 1996.) The BPF was not officially permitted to participate in the elections to the Belarusian Supreme Council, which took place in March 1990. Instead, its members joined other pro-reform groups in a coalition known as the Belarusian Democratic Bloc (BDB). The BDB secured about one-quarter of the 310 seats that were decided by popular election; most of the remainder were won by CPB members loyal to the republican leadership. The opposition won most seats in the large cities, notably Gomel (Homiel) and Minsk, where Zyanon Paznyak, the leader of the BPF, was elected to the Supreme Council. When it first convened in May the BDB deputies immediately demanded the adoption of a declaration of sovereignty. The CPB initially opposed such a move, but on 27 July, apparently after consultations with the leadership of the Communist Party of the Soviet Union in Moscow, a Declaration of State Sovereignty of the BSSR was adopted unanimously by the Supreme Council. The declaration asserted the republic's right to maintain armed forces, to establish a national currency and to exercise full control over its domestic and foreign policies. On the insistence of the opposition, the declaration included a clause stating the republic's right to compensation for the damage caused by the nuclear accident at Chornobyl, and the issue united both communist and opposition deputies. The Belarusian Government appealed to the all-Union Government for a minimum of 17,000m. roubles to address the consequences of the disaster, but was offered only 3,000m. roubles in compensation.

The Belarusian Government took part in the negotiation of a new Treaty of Union and signed the protocol to the draft treaty on 3 March 1991. The all-Union referendum on the preservation of the USSR took place in the BSSR on 17 March; of the 83% of the electorate who participated, 83% voted in favour of Gorbachev's proposals for a 'renewed federation of equal sovereign republics'. Members of the BPF conducted a campaign advocating rejection of Gorbachev's proposals, but complained that they were denied the opportunity to present their views to the public.

On 10 April 1991 a general strike took place, and an estimated 100,000 people attended a demonstration in Minsk. The Government agreed to certain economic concessions, including high wage increases, but the strikers' political demands, including the resignation of the Belarusian Government and the depoliticization of republican institutions, were rejected. Some 200,000 workers were estimated to have taken part in a second general strike on 23 April, in protest at the legislature's refusal to reconvene. The CPB-dominated Supreme Council was eventually convened in May, although the authority of the conservative CPB was threatened by increased internal dissent. In June 33 deputies joined the opposition as a 'Communists for Democracy' faction, led by Alyaksandr Lukashenka.

The Belarusian leadership did not strongly oppose the attempted *coup d'état* in Moscow in August 1991. The Presidium of the Supreme Council released a neutral statement on the last day of the coup, but the Central Committee of the CPB declared its unequivocal support. Following the failure of the coup, an extraordinary session of the Supreme Council was convened. Mikalay Dzemyantsei, the Chairman of the Supreme Council (republican head of state), was forced to resign; he was replaced by Stanislau Shushkevich, a respected centrist politician, pending an election to the office. In addition, the Supreme Council agreed to nationalize all CPB property, to prohibit the party's activities in law-enforcement agencies, and to suspend the CPB, pending an investigation into its role in the coup. (In February 1993 the suspension was lifted and the CPB was permitted to re-establish itself.) On 25 August 1991 the legislature voted to grant constitutional status to the July 1990 Declaration of State Sovereignty, and declared the political and economic independence of Belarus.

On 19 September 1991 the Supreme Council voted to rename the BSSR the Republic of Belarus, and also elected Shushkevich as its Chairman. Shushkevich demonstrated his strong support for the continuation of some form of union by signing, in October, a treaty to establish an economic community and by agreeing, in November, to the first draft of the Treaty on the Union of Sovereign States. On 8 December Shushkevich, with the Russian and Ukrainian Presidents, signed the Minsk Agreement, establishing a new Commonwealth of Independent States (CIS, see p. 172), which was to have its headquarters in Minsk. On 21 December the leaders of 11 former Soviet republics confirmed this decision by the Almaty (Alma-Ata) Declaration.

By comparison with other former Soviet republics, Belarus experienced relative stability in 1992, attributed to the country's more favourable social and economic policies, and to the comparatively homogenous nature of the population. The BPF campaigned insistently for a referendum to be held to assess the electorate's confidence in the Supreme Council and the Government, but in October the Council voted against the holding of a referendum, owing to alleged irregularities in the collection of signatures by the BPF.

In March 1993 the CPB formed, with 17 other parties and groups opposed to Belarusian independence, an informal coalition, the Popular Movement of Belarus. Divisions between the various branches of government became more pronounced during that year, and a major source of controversy was the drafting of Belarus's new Constitution. Shushkevich and the BPF strongly opposed the establishment of Belarus as a presidential republic; nevertheless, the new Constitution, which provided for a presidential system, was adopted in March 1994. A further point of dispute was whether Belarus should adopt closer relations with Russia and the CIS (as advocated by the Supreme Council). Shushkevich and the BPF were opposed to Belarus's signing the Collective Security Treaty (concluded by six other CIS states in May 1992), on the grounds that this would contravene the Declaration of State Sovereignty, which defined Belarus as a neutral state, and lead to renewed Russian domination. None the less, in April 1994 the Supreme Council voted to sign the Treaty. Three months later the legislature passed a vote of 'no confidence' in Shushkevich, in response to his continued opposition to the Treaty; he remained in office, however, until a second vote of confidence, held in January 1994, voted overwhelmingly in favour of his dismissal, on charges of

corruption. He was replaced by Mechislau Gryb, formerly a senior police official.

Further allegations of corruption, against the premier, Vyacheslau Kebich, and leading members of the Cabinet of Ministers, coupled with the worsening economic situation, culminated in a BPF-led general strike in Minsk in February 1994, which forced Gryb to bring forward the presidential election to mid-1994. Six candidates stood for election, including Kebich, Shushkevich, Paznyak and Lukashenka, who, as head of the Supreme Council's anti-corruption committee, had been responsible for bringing the corruption charges against Shushkevich. In the first ballot, held in late June, no candidate secured an overall majority, although Lukashenka, with 47% of the valid votes, led by a considerable margin. In the second ballot, contested by Lukashenka and Kebich and held in early July, Lukashenka received 85% of the votes cast, and he was inaugurated as the first President of Belarus on 20 July. Mikhail Chigir, an economic reformist, became Chairman of a new Cabinet of Ministers.

In early 1995 there were repeated confrontations between President Lukashenka and the Supreme Council over constitutional issues. In late January the Council voted for a second time to adopt legislation whereby the President could be removed by a two-thirds' quorum in the Council. In March Lukashenka announced that, simultaneously with the legislative election scheduled to take place in May, a referendum would be held on four policy questions. In early April, following the Council's rejection of all but one of the proposed questions (on closer integration with Russia), Lukashenka threatened to dissolve the legislature. A number of opposition deputies (including Paznyak) were forcibly evicted from the Supreme Council building, where they had declared a hunger strike in protest at the referendum. Shortly after this action, deputies voted in favour of the inclusion in the referendum of the remaining three questions: to give the Russian language equal status with Belarusian as an official language; to abandon the state insignia and flag of independent Belarus in favour of a modified Soviet-era version; and to amend the Constitution in order to empower the President to suspend the Supreme Council in the event of unconstitutional acts. Some 65% of the electorate participated in the referendum, held on 14 May, at which all four questions received overwhelming popular support.

On the same day, Belarus's first post-Soviet legislative election was held. However, owing to stringent electoral regulations, only 18 of the 260 seats in the Supreme Council were filled. A further 101 deputies were elected at 'run-off' elections held on 28 May 1995, but the necessary two-thirds' quorum was only achieved after two further rounds of voting, held on 29 November and 10 December, brought the total membership of the Supreme Council to 198. The CPB emerged with the largest number of seats in the new legislature (42), followed by the Agrarian Party (AP—33), the United Civic Party of Belarus and the Party of People's Accord. Independent candidates accounted for 95 seats. The BPF failed to win representation in the Council, as the 62 seats remaining vacant, largely owing to low electoral participation, were mostly in areas where the BPF commanded its strongest support. The Supreme Council held its inaugural session in early January 1996. Syamyon Sharetski, the leader of the AP, was appointed Chairman of the Council, replacing Mechislau Gryb.

Relations between the Constitutional Court and President Lukashenka deteriorated in early 1996, and the Court declared the observance of constitutional law in 1995 to have been unsatisfactory. Lukashenka extended his authority over the security services and the state-owned media, giving control of editorial appointments to the Cabinet of Ministers. Despite strong opposition and protests against government proposals to sign a new union treaty with Russia, President Lukashenka and the Russian President, Boris Yeltsin, signed the Treaty on the Formation of a Community of Sovereign Republics (CSR) in Moscow on 2 April 1996. Although it did not establish a single state, the Treaty included extensive provisions covering military, economic and political co-operation. Following the Treaty's endorsement, confrontation between Lukashenka and the opposition parties increased. A warrant was issued in April for the arrest of Paznyak, who was accused of organizing the anti-Union treaty demonstrations; he fled the country and later applied for political asylum in the USA. Several activists were arrested, and riot police clashed with demonstrators. Unauthorized rallies, organized by the opposition movement, were held in Minsk at the end of the month to commemorate the 10th anniversary of the disaster at the Chornobyl nuclear power station. The rallies, which the demonstrators used to express publicly their dissatisfaction with the Government and the formation of the CSR, were reportedly brutally dispersed by the police, and numerous arrests were made.

Lukashenka, seeking to enhance his powers, scheduled another national referendum for 24 November 1996 (with polling stations to be open from 9 November for those unable to vote on the later date), which was to consider, *inter alia*, proposed amendments to the 1994 Constitution. Elections for the remaining vacant seats in the Supreme Council were due to be held on the same day. Relations between Lukashenka and the Constitutional Court deteriorated in November, when the Court ruled that the approval of amendments to the Constitution would not be legally binding. The revocation of this decision by presidential decree provoked fierce criticism.

The referendum ballot papers contained seven questions, four of which were proposed by Lukashenka: that amendments be made to the Constitution to extend the President's term of office from 1999 to 2001, to enable the President to issue decrees that would carry legal force, and to grant him extensive powers of appointment both to the judiciary and to the envisaged bicameral National Assembly, which would replace the Supreme Council; that Belarusian Independence Day be moved from 27 July (the anniversary of the Declaration of State Sovereignty) to 3 July (the anniversary of the liberation from the Nazis); that there be an unrestricted right to purchase and sell land; and that the death penalty be abolished. The remaining three questions were submitted by the Supreme Council in an attempt to curtail the President's powers, and proposed that there be a significant reduction in the powers of the President (in effect, virtually abolishing the presidency); that the Supreme Council be allowed to elect heads of local administration (hitherto appointed by the President); and that state institutions be funded from the budget, instead of from a non-budgetary fund controlled by the President.

Despite the inclusion of questions concerning proposed constitutional changes, copies of the draft Constitution were not available to the public by the time that voting began. The Chairman of the Central Electoral Commission, Viktar Ganchar, stated that he would not approve the results of the voting, owing to this and other electoral violations, and was subsequently dismissed by Lukashenka. The crisis worsened in mid-November 1996, when the Chairman of the Cabinet of Ministers, Mikhail Chigir, resigned, urging that the referendum be cancelled; he was replaced, in an acting capacity, by Syarhey Ling, who was confirmed in the appointment in February 1997. Some 10,000 people attended an anti-Government rally in Minsk, protesting at the restrictions on their freedom of expression. Radio stations and newspapers came under renewed government pressure, and widespread violations of the law were reported by parliamentary electoral observers. The Organization for Security and Co-operation in Europe (OSCE, see p. 283) refused to send observers to monitor the referendum, and the Council of Europe (see p. 181) declared that the presidential draft of the amended Constitution did not comply with European standards. Meanwhile, 75 deputies in the Supreme Council submitted a motion to the Constitutional Court to begin impeachment proceedings against the President; although the Court had already found 17 decrees issued by Lukashenka to be unconstitutional, it was forced to abandon the motion, as deputies subsequently retracted their support.

The referendum results revealed considerable support for the President, but their accuracy was disputed. According to official figures, some 84% of the electorate took part, 70.5% of whom voted for the President's constitutional amendments; only 7.9% voted for those of the Supreme Council. The amended Constitution was published on 27 November 1996 and came into immediate effect.

Following the referendum, the Supreme Council divided into two factions. More than 100 deputies declared their support for Lukashenka, and adopted legislation abolishing the Supreme Council and establishing a 110-member House of Representatives, the lower chamber of the new National Assembly. Some 50 other deputies denounced the referendum as invalid and declared themselves to be the legitimate legislature. The House of Representatives convened shortly afterwards and elected Anatol Malafeyeu as its Chairman. Deputies were granted a four-year mandate, while the term of office of those opposed to the new legislature was curtailed to two months. Deputies elected in the by-elections held simultaneously with the refer-

endum were denied registration. Legislation governing the formation of the upper house of the National Assembly, the 64-member Council of the Republic, was approved by Lukashenka in early December 1996: eight members were appointed by the President and the remaining 56 were elected by regional councils. In the event, no deputies from the former Supreme Council participated in the Council of the Republic, which convened for the first time in mid-January 1997, and elected Pavel Shypuk as its Chairman. Meanwhile, in protest at the constitutional amendments introduced by the referendum, the Chairman of the Constitutional Court, Valery Tsikhinya, and several other judges announced their resignations.

In January 1997 the Public Coalition Government–National Economic Council, a form of 'shadow' cabinet, was formed, chaired by Genadz Karpenka. Structural changes to the Government were implemented by Lukashenka, with the Chairmen of State Committees henceforth to be included in the Cabinet of Ministers. Doubts about the legitimacy of the referendum were expressed by international organizations, including the Council of Europe, which suspended Belarus's 'guest status', and the Permanent Council of the Parliamentary Assembly of the OSCE, which recognized the right of a delegation from the former Supreme Council, rather than members of the new House of Representatives, officially to represent Belarus at that organization.

The signing with Russia of the Treaty of Union, and initialling of the Charter of the Union on 2 April 1997, by Presidents Lukashenka and Yeltsin (see below) prompted an anti-Union demonstration in Minsk, which was forcibly suppressed by the police, resulting in many arrests. Charges of violating the presidential decree (which had entered into force in the previous month) restricting the right to demonstrate were subsequently brought against opposition members. Nevertheless, support for the union treaty appeared to be widespread, and some 15,000 people participated in a pro-Union rally in Minsk in mid-May. The Charter of the Union was signed in Moscow on 23 May. The Treaty and Charter were ratified shortly afterwards by the respective legislatures, and came into effect in mid-June.

Negotiations mediated by the Council of Europe and the European Union (EU, see p. 199) to end the confrontation between the former Supreme Council and the new legislature began in June 1997, but collapsed in July, following disagreement over which constitution was to form the basis of the discussions. Negotiations were subsequently postponed indefinitely. In October Lukashenka issued a presidential decree providing for more severe measures to combat terrorism and violent crime, following the death in a bomb attack of a senior law-enforcement official in the Mogilev (Mahilou) region. In the following month the opposition launched a petition movement, Charter-97 (Khartyya-97—a title reminiscent of the Czechoslovak Charter-77 pro-democracy movement), which called for greater democracy in Belarus and for presidential elections to be held in 1999 as demanded by the 1994 Constitution. However, later in November *Svaboda*, the largest independent newspaper, was closed, following its publication of an article advocating Lukashenka's resignation. A number of senior BPF members were arrested in April 1998 during an unauthorized rally to protest against the Treaty of Union, held on the anniversary of the signature of the Treaty. A further 30 demonstrators were arrested later in the month at a rally led by former members of the disbanded Supreme Council, urging Lukashenka's resignation for mismanaging the economy and destroying national culture; Lukashenka's campaign to institutionalize the use of the Russian language had successfully marginalized Belarusian, which had become widely associated with the opposition. Throughout 1998 the opposition remained without access to the media or representation in public institutions. Moreover, in June legislation was approved that rendered defamation of the President an offence punishable by up to five years' imprisonment.

In November 1998 Lukashenka decreed the formation of a special economic committee, to be known as the National Headquarters, which was to supersede the Cabinet of Ministers in economic policy; he expanded the role of the Ministry of Foreign Affairs in the following month. Meanwhile, in September about 30 left-wing and centrist parties, including the CPB and the Liberal Democratic Party of Belarus, formed a new alliance to promote further integration with Russia and to support Lukashenka's candidacy in the presidential election scheduled for 2001. The alliance elected the CPB leader, Viktar Chykin, as its Executive Secretary and declared its intention to contest future legislative elections as a single bloc. A new law on local elections was approved by the House of Representatives in December 1998, effectively banning those with a police record or fine from standing in the local elections that were to be held in April 1999, thereby excluding numerous opposition candidates. In the event, the opposition organized an electoral boycott, and the majority of the seats in the elections were each contested by a single candidate. International observers noted irregularities in the voting procedure, in particular with regard to the participation rate, which was believed to be much lower than the officially reported 66.9% of the electorate.

Meanwhile, in January 1999 the Central Electoral Commission of the former Supreme Council scheduled a presidential election for 16 May. In March the Commission's Chairman, Viktar Ganchar, was arrested and charged with the offence of 'appointing oneself as an official', but was released on health grounds after a 10-day hunger strike. Nevertheless, during March the Commission registered two presidential candidates, the exiled Paznyak and the former Chairman of the Cabinet of Ministers, Mikhail Chigir. The latter was arrested in April and charged with embezzlement and abuse of office (the embezzlement charges were later dropped), prompting speculation that his arrest was politically motivated. Following the death of Genadz Karpenka in April, Mechislau Gryb was elected Chairman of the Public Coalition Government–National Economic Council in November. In May the Central Electoral Commission of the Supreme Council was unable to organize fixed polling stations for the presidential election, which was not recognized by the Government or by the international community. Paznyak withdrew his candidacy in mid-May, stating that the voting procedure had violated the law. The election results were declared invalid later in the month, owing to alleged irregularities, despite a reported participation rate of 53%. In July the Chairman of the Supreme Council, Syamyon Sharetski, fled to Lithuania, anticipating his imminent arrest in Belarus, following his appointment by the Supreme Council as acting President of the country (according to the 1994 Constitution Lukashenka's legitimate term of office expired in mid-July 1999).

In January 1999 Lukashenka had decreed that political parties, trade unions and other organizations were required to re-register by 1 July; those failing to do so were to be disbanded. By September only 17 of the 28 existing official parties had been re-registered. In late September Paznyak's supporters formed a breakaway faction, known as the Conservative Christian Party of the BPF, with Paznyak as Chairman. At the end of October Vintsuk Vyachorka was elected Chairman of the 'rump' BPF, which changed its name to BPF—'Revival' (BPF—'Adradzhennye') in December, in order to comply with legislation banning the use of certain words in the names of non-governmental organizations. In early September OSCE-mediated negotiations commenced between the Government and the opposition, concerning the legislative elections to be held in 2000; however, further rounds of talks were subject to government-proposed postponements, and opposition frustration was such that when talks resumed in March 2000 its participation was much reduced. Although stricter security measures were implemented in 1999, and the independent press sector also came under greater scrutiny, the Government made a statement in August, committing itself to a number of measures to defend and improve human rights in Belarus. Meanwhile, however, a number of outspoken critics of the President disappeared, in unexplained circumstances. In May a former Minister of the Interior and campaigner for Chigir, Yuriy Zakharenka, went missing. His disappearance was followed in the next months by those of Tamara Vinnikava, a former head of the central bank, who had been under house arrest since January 1997, an independent publisher, and Viktar Ganchar; it was officially claimed that the four had voluntarily gone into hiding to attract attention to their political cause.

In October 1999 15,000 people were estimated to have taken part in an anti-Government 'Freedom March' in Minsk (this constituted the largest opposition demonstration to have taken place in Belarus since April 1996). One of the protesters' demands was the release of political prisoners. Chigir was released in late November pending trial, which began in January 2000; he received a three-year suspended sentence in May, and a substantial fine, prompting criticism of the verdict by the EU. In June two opposition activists, Mikalai Statkevich (the leader of the Belarusian Social Democratic Party) and Valery Shchukin, received suspended sentences of two years and one year, respec-

tively, for organizing the demonstration of October 1999. In August 2000, however, their convictions were overturned and a retrial was ordered. Statkevich subsequently decided to maintain his candidacy in the forthcoming elections to the National Assembly.

In February 2000 Syarhey Ling resigned as Chairman of the Cabinet of Ministers, and was replaced by Uladzimir Yermoshin, hitherto the Governor of Minsk City. Also in February the opposition agreed to boycott the parliamentary elections due to take place in October, in protest at not having been consulted about the preparation of a new draft electoral code. This decision appeared to prompt increased repression of both the unofficial media and opposition political parties. The peaceful staging, in mid-March, of a second Freedom March, resulted in the prohibition of demonstrations in the centre of the capital. A further demonstration, to commemorate the creation of the Belarusian National Republic in 1918, which took place later that month, in contravention of the ban, was brutally suppressed by the security forces and resulted in 272 arrests. Many of those detained were journalists and international observers, and Lukashenka subsequently issued an apology. In the following month the Minister of Internal Affairs, Yuriy Sivakov, resigned, ostensibly for health reasons. In September the offices of *Rabochy*, an opposition publication, were raided by the authorities, and later that month the headquarters of the Belarusian Social Democratic Party were broken into, in what was suspected to have been a politically motivated attack.

A large-scale anti-election rally by opposition activists preceded the elections to the National Assembly that took place on 15 October 2000. Voting was declared invalid in 13 of the 110 constituencies, necessitating a further round of voting on 29 October. The OSCE denounced the elections as neither free nor fair, and numerous irregularities were reported. The official rate of participation, at 60.6%, was widely believed to have been exaggerated, and the international community refused to recognize the validity of the elections. In early December the Central Election Commission announced that repeat elections, to fill the 56 seats that had remained vacant in the invalid constituencies after the first round of voting, were to take place on 18 March 2001.

In late November 2000 Lukashenka made a number of changes to government and security-service personnel. Notably, Ural Latypaw, hitherto Deputy Prime Minister and Minister of Foreign Affairs, was appointed State Secretary of the Security Council; he was replaced by Mikhail Khvastov. Leanid Yeryn was appointed Chairman of the State Security Committee, replacing Uladzimir Matskevich, and the Procurator General, Alec Bazhelka, was dismissed, and later replaced by Viktar Sheyman. The new appointments, which were allegedly linked to the lack of progress made in investigating the disappearance of public figures, resulted in a transfer of power from ethnic Belarusians to ethnic Russians. In February 2001 a minor reshuffle of the Cabinet of Ministers and of security officials took place; Mikhail Rusy was appointed Minister of Agriculture and Food, Uladzimir Gancharenka as Minister of Communications, and Lyavontsy Kharouzhyk as Minister for Natural Resources and the Environment. At the end of March the Minister of Defence, Col-Gen. Alyaksandr Chumakow, was replaced by Lt-Gen. (later Col-Gen.) Leanid Maltsaw, who had held the position in 1995–96.

In early January 2001 tax officials seized equipment from a publishing company that printed several major newspapers critical of the Government, prompting concern among the opposition media that the authorities intended further to suppress press freedom ahead of the presidential election, due to take place in September. Meanwhile, Alyaksandr Chigir, a son of Mikhail Chigir, was arrested in February, and charged with selling stolen goods; the former premier claimed that the arrest was an attempt to discredit his candidacy for the presidency. (Alyaksandr Chigir was sentenced to seven years' imprisonment in March 2002.)

In mid-March 2001 President Lukashenka signed a decree, which imposed severe restrictions on the use of foreign financial assistance by both individuals and national organizations. The decree required all foreign aid to be officially registered, and prohibited the use of such aid for political campaigning or for the organization of strikes and rallies, prompting fears by opposition activists that the decree would prevent the deployment of observers at the presidential election, which was to have been funded by the OSCE. Repeat elections were held on 18 March and 1 April to fill the vacant seats remaining in the House of

Representatives. The opposition held a third Freedom March in Minsk on 25 March, at which demonstrators protested against Lukashenka's regime and urged that the forthcoming presidential election be free and fair; a small number of arrests were made, including that of the leader of BPF—'Revival', Vintsuk Vyachorka. In early May the five main opposition candidates for the presidency announced their intention to select a joint candidate, in order to avoid dividing the votes cast against Lukashenka between several candidates. The candidates comprised Mikhail Chigir; a former Chairman of the Regional Executive Committee of Grodno Oblast, Syamyon Domash; the leader of the Party of Communists of Belarus, Syarhey Kalyakin; the Chairman of the Federation of Trade Unions of Belarus, Uladzimir Gancharyk; and a former Minister of Defence, Pavel Kazlovsky. In the same month the opposition, which pledged its commitment to improving living standards and human rights, to combating crime and corruption, and to bringing an end to Belarus's international isolation, formed a new, popular movement, known as 'For a New Belarus', to support the candidacy of a democratic presidential candidate.

In June 2001 two former investigators at the Procuracy, who had been granted exile in the USA, claimed that senior government officials had organized the assassinations of political opponents to Lukashenka's regime, and alleged them to be responsible for the deaths of the missing opposition figures, Viktar Ganchar and Yuriy Zakharenka, as well as a cameraman for Russian television, Dmitrii Zavadski, who had been missing since July 2000. The allegations were supported by Gancharyk, who revealed documents in mid-July 2001 that apparently linked the Procurator General and former State Secretary of the Security Council, Viktar Sheyman, and the former Minister of Internal Affairs, Yuriy Sivakow, with the murders of Ganchar and Zakharenka.

In late July 2001 the opposition selected Gancharyk as its candidate for the presidency; his election campaign focused on continuing allegations of the government-sanctioned assassination of opposition figures. In late August two state security agents released to the media a recorded testimony, in which they supported claims that Ganchar, together with a business associate, had been kidnapped and killed in September 1999 by a special police unit, attached to the Ministry of Internal Affairs. Meanwhile, media outlets came under increased pressure to withdraw their support for Gancharyk, as a number of police raids took place throughout the month.

The presidential election was held, as scheduled, on 9 September 2001, although a constitutional provision had permitted some voting to begin on 4 September. This provision was criticized by the opposition, which asserted that it made the election more difficult to monitor. Lukashenka was re-elected with 75.7% of the valid votes cast; Gancharyk received 15.7% of the votes, and the only other candidate, the leader of the Liberal Democratic Party of Belarus, Syarhey Gaydukevich, received just 2.5%. The election was described as fundamentally flawed by the OSCE, and Gancharyk urged the public to protest against Lukashenka's victory; however, a popular uprising failed to materialize, and observers noted that voters, particularly in the rural areas where Lukashenka drew much of his support, feared that the election of a new, reformist leader might lead to increased economic hardship.

Following Lukashenka's inauguration on 20 September 2001, the Prime Minister, Uladzimir Yermoshin, tendered the resignation of his Government. Lukashenka subsequently reshuffled the Cabinet of Ministers, reducing the number of ministries to 28. In the same month, Ural Latypaw was appointed to head the presidential administration; his former post as State Secretary of the Security Council was filled by Lt-Gen. Genadz Nyavyhlas. At the beginning of October Lukashenka nominated former Deputy Prime Minister Genadz Navitski as premier, and the appointment was approved by the House of Representatives on 10 October. In late 2001 and early 2002 a number of state officials and managers of state enterprises were arrested, as part of an anti-corruption campaign initiated by the President; among those arrested was Viktar Rakhmanko, a member of the Council of the Republic, and hitherto head of Belarusian State Railways; Rakhmanko was succeeded by Vasil Hapeyeu in early February 2002. The opposition media claimed the arrests to be politically motivated, and linked them to criticism of Lukashenka's economic policies. Meanwhile, in late December 2001 Uladzimir Gancharyk resigned the chairmanship of the Federation of Trade Unions, citing differences with the Government.

In early July 2002 President Lukashenka effected a minor reorganization of the Cabinet of Ministers, elevating Deputy Prime Minister Syarhey Sidorsky to the new post of First Deputy Prime Minister, and appointing Deputy Prime Minister Andrey Kabyakow to serve concurrently as Minister of the Economy; a fifth Deputy Prime Minister, Anatol Tsyutsyunow, was also appointed. Lydmila Pastayalka was appointed Minister of Health Care, replacing Uladzimir Astapenka, who had been dismissed in April. In mid-July Lukashenka's position was strengthened when the Deputy Head of the Presidential Administration, Leanid Kozik, was elected Chairman of the Federation of Trade Unions, replacing Frants Vitko (who had been Gancharyk's deputy). Kozik's appointment was expected to reverse the Federation's association with opposition forces. In mid-September the Federation of Trade Unions held a congress, at which it confirmed Kozik as Chairman, and changed its name to the Trade Union Federation of Belarus.

The opposition came under renewed pressure in 2002. At the beginning of March several opposition leaders and journalists were detained at the border, before being permitted to enter Lithuania to attend a political conference in that country's capital, Vilnius. Later that month two former police officers were sentenced to life imprisonment, having been found guilty of kidnapping the Russian cameraman Dmitrii Zavadski (whose body had not been found) in July 2000. However, there were claims that the charges had been fabricated to divert attention from the involvement of more senior government officials. In late May 2002 the first sentences were awarded to the state-enterprise officials arrested from late 2001, and in the following month three opposition journalists were given quasi-labour sentences after publishing articles criticizing Lukashenka. In July 2002 Mikhail Chigir was awarded a three-year, suspended prison sentence, following his trial on charges of tax evasion while working for a German company in Moscow in the late 1990s; Chigir declared the case to have been politically motivated. In August 2002 two opposition newspapers were closed down: *Svobodnye Novosti* was forced to close owing to a lack of funds, and the other, *Nasha Svaboda*, had its assets confiscated after losing a libel case. In mid-September the Editor-in-Chief of the independent newspaper *Rabochy* was sentenced to two years' corrective labour after accusing the President of having profited from illicit arms sales. In January 2003 six journalists were dismissed from the newspaper of the Trade Union Federation of Belarus, *Belaruski Chas*, amid allegations of a political motivation; the newspaper's editor had already been dismissed. The Government also undertook dramatically to reduce the re-broadcast of Russian programmes, which were often critical of President Lukashenka; to this end all radio and television companies were required to re-register by June 2003.

Fears over the future of religious freedom in Belarus were heightened from early October 2002, when the National Assembly adopted a new law on religion, which imposed severe restrictions on the practise of minority faiths. The law prohibited meetings of fewer than 20 people and meetings in private homes, and banned those religions that had become active after 1982 from establishing missions and producing written material. All religions were compelled to re-register and conform to the new regulations, which required religious literature to be submitted to the Government for state approval. Officially, the law, which came into effect on 16 November, was introduced to prevent the spread of cults, but, in practice, it was expected to serve to guarantee the dominance of the Belarusian Orthodox Church.

By late 2002 there were reports that President Lukashenka planned to schedule a referendum on proposed amendments to the Constitution, which would allow him to stand for a third term of office in 2006. In January 2003 Yuriy Sivakow, the controversial former Minister of Internal Affairs, was appointed Minister of Sports and Tourism, and in March Syarhey Martynow was appointed as Minister of Foreign Affairs. Local elections were held in two rounds in March, amid opposition allegations of electoral irregularities. Many constituencies registered only one candidate for the ballot, and a substantial number of opposition candidates were reported to have been denied registration.

Following the dissolution of the USSR in 1991, Belarus's closest relations continued to be with member states of the CIS, in particular neighbouring Russia. In April 1993 Belarus signed the CIS Collective Security Treaty (see above), and accords on closer economic co-operation with CIS states followed. In April 1994 Belarus and Russia concluded an agreement on eventual monetary union. In March 1996 Belarus, Kazakhstan, Kyrgyzstan and Russia signed the Quadripartite Treaty, which envisaged a common market and a customs union between the four countries, as well as joint transport, energy and communications systems. (Tajikistan signed the Treaty in 1998.)

In April 1996 Belarus and Russia concluded the far-reaching and controversial Treaty on the Formation of a Community of Sovereign Republics, providing for closer economic, political and military integration. On 2 April 1997 a further Treaty of Union was signed by Yeltsin and Lukashenka in Moscow, and a Charter of the Union, detailing the process of integration, was also initialled. The stated aim of the Union was the 'voluntary unification of the member states', including the development of a common infrastructure, a single currency and a joint defence policy. The Union's ruling body was to be a Supreme Council, chaired alternately by the President of each country, and comprising the Heads of State and Government, the leaders of the legislatures and the Chairman of the Executive Committee. The Executive Committee was to be appointed by the Supreme Council. The Parliamentary Assembly (provision for which had been made in the 1996 Treaty and which had convened in March) comprised 36 members from the legislature of each country. The Charter was submitted for nation-wide discussion in both countries, before being signed in Moscow on 23 May. Ratification of the documents by the respective co-legislatures took place in June, and the first official session of the Parliamentary Assembly followed shortly afterwards, with the Assembly adopting the anthem of the former USSR.

In November 1998 the Parliamentary Assembly of the Russia-Belarus Union voted for the creation of a unified parliament, to consist of two chambers. The upper chamber was to include deputies delegated by the legislatures of the two countries, and the lower chamber, comprising 25 Belarusian and 75 Russian deputies, was to be elected by direct universal suffrage. On 25 December, at a meeting in Moscow, Presidents Lukashenka and Yeltsin signed a document providing for equal rights for their citizens in Russia and Belarus and the creation of a union state within one year. A treaty on unification was to be drafted and submitted for national discussion by mid-1999. Provisions were to include the formation of the necessary governing bodies and a mechanism for pursuing a common policy in international affairs and defence and security matters, as well as further progress towards economic integration. The opposition in Belarus criticized the agreement as representing a loss of sovereignty. Agreements on enhanced military co-operation between Belarus and Russia were signed in April 1999. Lukashenka's hopes for the formation of a single state, which were much contested by the Belarusian opposition, were also not shared by Russia, and the draft treaty on unification, which was submitted for public inspection in October, did not fully satisfy the wishes of the Belarusian President. In addition, the Russian Prime Minister, Vladimir Putin, warned that implementation might take several years. The signature of the treaty took place in Moscow on 8 December, having been postponed from November. The treaty was ratified by the two countries' respective legislatures and by Lukashenka later in December and by Putin, who had replaced Yeltsin as the President of Russia, on 3 January 2000. The treaty came into force on 26 January, when Lukashenka was appointed Chairman of the High State Council of the Union. In April Gennadii Seleznev was elected Chairman of the Parliamentary Assembly of the Union of Russia and Belarus. A union budget was passed at a session of the Parliamentary Assembly in May. Although progress towards a full union appeared to be advancing steadily, Putin remained more pragmatic than did Lukashenka, in particular in his attitude towards the formation of joint armed forces, a measure that the Belarusian President strongly favoured. On 30 November, during a CIS summit meeting in Minsk, an agreement on the introduction of a single currency was signed; the agreement, according to which the Russian rouble was to be adopted as the union currency from 1 January 2005, and a new currency was to be adopted three years later, was ratified by the National Assembly in April 2001. Both Heads of State declared that a single currency would compel Russia and Belarus to share sovereignty, but Putin remained anxious not to rush the process of full integration. In November it was announced that Belarus and Russia were finally to merge their air-defence systems, and a draft constitution of the Russia-Belarus Union was made public.

During 2002, however, relations between with Russia notably worsened, owing to disagreements over the nature of the planned union, and partly as a result of Russia's re-orientation towards the West, following the large-scale terrorist attacks on the USA in September 2001 (see chapters on the Russian Federation and the USA). In mid-March 2002 Belarus and Russia reached agreement on the harmonization of customs and tax laws and the removal of trade barriers, but in late June, at a meeting held in St Petersburg, Russia, Putin publicly criticized Lukashenka's union plans. Subsequently, in mid-August, at a summit meeting held in Moscow, Putin presented Lukashenka with a new unification plan, which effectively provided for the absorption of Belarus's seven regions into the Russian Federation. According to Putin's proposal, both countries would hold referendums on unification in May 2003, followed by elections to a common parliament in December; Belarus would then adopt the Russian rouble in January 2004 (rather than January 2005), and presidential elections to the new state would be held in early 2004. However, Lukashenka denounced the plan as unacceptable and as an insult to Belarus's sovereignty. In late October 2002 the Belarusian authorities refused to permit Boris Nemtsov, a prominent member of the Russian State Duma, to enter the country, accusing him of co-operating with opposition figures to overthrow Lukashenka, owing to his intention to participate in an opposition-organized conference on alternative approaches to bilateral integration. However, in late November Lukashenka attended another meeting with Putin in Moscow, at which the two Presidents were reported to have reached agreement on further integration; Lukashenka was believed to have become more conciliatory towards Russia, after the deterioration of relations with the EU and the USA earlier in the month (see below).

In June 1998 a diplomatic scandal resulted from the enforced eviction, for 'essential repairs', of 22 diplomatic families from their residences outside Minsk. This violation of the Vienna Convention, guaranteeing the inviolability of diplomatic residences, led to the recall from Belarus of the ambassadors from EU countries, a number of other European states and the USA and Japan. In a retaliatory act, Belarusian envoys were expelled from the EU in June, and in the following month Belarusian officials (including the President) were barred from entering its member states. The ban was subsequently adopted by several other European countries and the USA. In December, however, Belarus undertook compensation procedures for those families that had been forced to relocate and Lukashenka gave assurances that, henceforth, he would comply with international agreements. All heads of diplomatic missions accredited to Belarus, with the exception of the US ambassador, returned to Minsk in January 1999. The EU ban on Belarusian officials entering its territory was repealed in February, and the US ambassador returned to Minsk in September. Relations with the USA remained uneasy during 2000, and the USA urged the Belarusian opposition to boycott the legislative elections of October. Tensions were particularly evident during the presidential election campaign of 2001, when the US State Department described as 'credible' allegations of the government-sponsored assassination of opposition figures. The USA did not recognize the results of the presidential election, held in September, and the US ambassador refused to attend Lukashenka's inauguration ceremony. From late 2001 the USA expressed increasing concern over the alleged illegal sale of arms to states accused of supporting terrorist activity. Notably, Belarus had developed close economic and military relations with Iraq, and was reported to have helped to upgrade Iraq's air defence systems, although the Belarusian Government denied having acted in contravention of UN sanctions.

International organizations, including the OSCE, had continued to recognize the former Supreme Council as the legitimate legislature of Belarus. However, an OSCE Advisory and Monitoring Group commenced operations in Minsk in February 1998, with the aim of encouraging democratization, promoting a dialogue between the Government and the opposition and monitoring human rights. The OSCE described the 2001 presidential election as flawed, but warned against the pursuit of a policy that might serve to strengthen Belarus's international isolation. Relations with the OSCE deteriorated severely during 2002, and in mid-April the acting head of the Advisory and Monitoring Group, Michel Rivollier of France, was forced to leave the country, when the authorities refused to renew his visa. An OSCE delegation visited Belarus in late May and met members of the National Assembly, as well as relatives of missing opposition leaders. However, the Advisory and Monitoring Group was not permitted to resume its work, and was accused of attempting to further Western interests in the country. The new acting head of the mission, British diplomat Andrew Carpenter, was forced to leave Belarus in June, and in September its First Secretary was also expelled. The final OSCE representative left Belarus in late October, upon the expiry of her visa. Meanwhile, in September the Council of Europe refused to renew Belarus's special guest status at the Council of Europe (suspended since January 1997), owing to its continuing record of human rights abuses. In mid-November 2002 the Czech Government denied an entry visa to President Lukashenka, thereby preventing him from attending a meeting of NATO's Euro-Atlantic Partnership Council in the capital, Prague, later that month. Fourteen EU member states subsequently agreed to impose a visa ban on Lukashenka and seven other senior Belarusian officials, and in late November the USA also prohibited Lukashenka from entering the country, in protest at his country's poor record on human rights, and the expulsion of the OSCE Advisory and Monitoring Group. (The bans were not lifted until April 2003.) However, following negotiations between the Belarusian Government and the OSCE in Vienna, Austria, in December 2002, an agreement was reached for the establishment of a new OSCE mission in Belarus in January 2003. In late February the OSCE Parliamentary Assembly voted to recognize the legitimacy of the National Council of Belarus, despite a negative assessment of the country's democratic progress by an OSCE delegation.

With the dissolution of the USSR in December 1991, Belarus effectively became a nuclear power, with approximately 80 SS-25 intercontinental ballistic missiles stationed on its territory. However, the Government consistently stressed Belarus to be, under the Declaration of State Sovereignty of July 1990, a neutral and non-nuclear state. Accordingly, in May 1992 Belarus signed the Lisbon Protocol to the Treaty on the Non-Proliferation of Nuclear Weapons (see the International Atomic Energy Agency, see p. 80), under which it pledged to transfer all nuclear missiles to Russia by 1999. In February 1993 the Supreme Council ratified the first Strategic Arms' Reduction Treaty (START 1—for further details, see chapter on the USA). Substantial amounts of financial and technical aid were pledged by the USA to help Belarus dismantle its nuclear arsenal. The last remaining nuclear warhead was transported to Russia in late November 1996. In 1998 Belarus signed the International Convention on Nuclear Safety, adopted in June 1994 in Vienna. In September 2000 Belarus became a permanent member of the Non-aligned Movement (see p. 350).

Government

Under the Constitution of March 1994, which was amended in November 1996, legislative power is vested in the bicameral National Assembly. The lower chamber, the 110-member House of Representatives, is elected by universal adult suffrage for a term of four years. The upper chamber, the Council of the Republic, comprises 64 members: 56 members elected by organs of local administration, and eight members appointed by the President. The President is the Head of State, and is elected by popular vote for five years. Executive authority is exercised by the Cabinet of Ministers, which is led by the Chairman (Prime Minister) and is responsible to the National Assembly. For administrative purposes, Belarus is divided into six regions (*oblasts*) and the capital city of Minsk; the regions are divided into districts (*rayons*).

Defence

In August 2002 the total strength of Belarus's armed forces was 79,800, comprising an army of 29,300, an air force of 22,000 (including air defence of 10,200), as well as 28,500 in centrally controlled units and Ministry of Defence staff. There is also a border guard numbering 12,000, which is controlled by the Ministry of Internal Affairs. Military service is compulsory and lasts for between nine and 12 months. In October 1994 it was announced that two Russian non-nuclear military installations were to remain in Belarus. In late 2001 it was reported that the armed forces were to be reduced to 65,000 personnel, including 50,000 servicemen, by 2006. Defence expenditure totalled 229,930m. readjusted roubles in 2001. The defence budget for 2002 was projected at 321,300m. readjusted roubles. In January 1995 Belarus joined NATO's (see p. 271) 'Partnership for Peace' programme of military co-operation.

Economic Affairs

In 2001, according to estimates by the World Bank, Belarus's gross national income (GNI), measured at average 1999–2001

prices, was US $11,892m., equivalent to $1,190 per head. In terms of purchasing power parity, GNI in that year was equivalent to $8,030 per head. During 1990–2001 the population declined at an average annual rate of 0.2%, while gross domestic product (GDP) per head increased, in real terms, by an average of 0.5% per year. Over the same period, overall GDP declined, in real terms, by an average of 0.7% annually. However, real GDP increased by 5.8% in 2000 and by 4.1% in 2001.

Agriculture contributed an estimated 15.7% of GDP in 2001, according to World Bank estimates, and 12.6% of the employed labour force were engaged in the sector, according to FAO. The principal crops are potatoes, grain and sugar beet. Large areas of arable land (some 1.6m. ha) are still unused after being contaminated in 1986, following the accident at the Chornobyl nuclear power station in Ukraine. The Belarusian authorities have largely opposed private farming, and by 1999 collective and state farms still accounted for some 83% of agricultural land. However, private farms produced the majority of Belarus's potatoes, fruit and vegetables, as well as a significant proportion of total livestock-product output. In 1998, according to the IMF, 49.8% of total crop output was produced by the private sector. During 1990–2001, according to World Bank estimates, real agricultural GDP decreased at an average annual rate of 3.0%. According to official figures, agricultural output increased by 9.3% in 2000, its first year of positive growth since 1996, and by an estimated 1.8% in 2001.

Industry (comprising mining, manufacturing, construction and power) provided 41.9% of GDP in 2001, according to World Bank estimates, and engaged 34.7% of the employed labour force in 2000. According to the World Bank, industrial GDP decreased, in real terms, at an average annual rate of 0.8% during 1990–2001. However, industrial output increased by 5.9% in 2001 and by 4.3% in 2002, according to official figures.

Belarus has relatively few mineral resources, although there are small deposits of petroleum and natural gas, and important peat reserves. Peat extraction, however, was severely affected by the disaster at Chornobyl, since contaminated peat could not be burned. Belarus produced 50% of the former USSR's output of potash. However, production of potash declined in the 1990s. In 1994 only 0.6% of the labour force were engaged in mining and quarrying.

According to the World Bank, the manufacturing sector contributed an estimated 34.9% of GDP in 2001, and employed 26.5% of the labour force in 1994. Machine-building, power generation and chemicals are the principal branches of the sector. During 1990–2001 manufacturing GDP increased, in real terms, at an average annual rate of 0.1%, according to World Bank estimates. Overall sectoral GDP increased, in real terms, by 7.2% in 2000 and by 3.0% in 2001.

In 1999 much of Belarus's supply of energy was provided by natural gas (90.0%), with petroleum and petroleum products accounting for almost all of the remainder. In that year the country imported 86% of its crude-oil consumption, 98% of its natural-gas consumption and 30% of its electricity consumption. Energy products comprised 29.2% of the total value of imports in 2000. There are two large petroleum refineries, at Novopolotsk and Mozyr. In 2000 Belarus's principal gas supplier, the Russian company, Gazprom, announced plans to construct two new natural gas pipelines across Belarus, in order to halt the alleged misappropriation of supplies from existing pipelines in Ukraine. However, from the latter half of the 1990s Gazprom repeatedly threatened to reduce gas supplies to Belarus, owing to that country's mounting energy arrears. Belarus's debts continued to increase, although Gazprom subsidized the price of gas, a concession viewed to result from the signature of the Russia-Belarus Union Treaty. In November 2002 Gazprom reduced its supply of natural gas to Belarus by around 50%. The Belarusian Government consequently agreed to authorize the privatization of the domestic natural gas importer, Beltransgaz, reportedly enabling Gazprom to acquire a stake in the company, in return for the partial settlement of Belarus's arrears.

The services sector accounted for 50.5% of total employment in 2000 and, according to the World Bank, provided 42.4% of GDP in 2001. The sector is led by transport and communications and trade and catering, which accounted for an estimated 13.5% and 10.6% of GDP, respectively, in 2000. According to World Bank estimates, during 1990–2001 the GDP of the services sector increased, in real terms, at an average annual rate of 3.8%. Sectoral GDP increased, in real terms, by 4.2% in 2000 and by 58.5% in 2001.

In 2001 Belarus recorded a visible trade deficit of US $806.9m., and there was a deficit of $285.2m. on the current account of the balance of payments. Trading partners outside the CIS accounted for 30.8% of Belarus's imports and 44.9% of its exports in 2002. However, the efforts of a number of neighbouring countries to achieve membership of the European Union from 2004, were expected to have a negative impact on Belarusian foreign trade, as additional border and trade controls were imposed by candidate countries. In 2002 Belarus's principal trading partners among countries constituting the former USSR were Russia (which accounted for some 65.1% of total imports and 50.1% of exports), Ukraine and Latvia; outside the former USSR its most important trading partners were Germany and the United Kingdom. In 2000 the principal exports were machinery and metalworking, petroleum and gas, chemical and petroleum products, and light manufactures. The principal imports were petroleum and gas, machinery and metalworking, chemical and petroleum products, and metallurgy.

The 2001 state budget registered a deficit of 235,680m. re-adjusted roubles (equivalent to 2.5% of GDP). Belarus's total external debt was US $851m. at the end of 2000, of which $692m. was long-term public debt. In that year the cost of debt-servicing was equivalent to 2.9% of the value of exports of goods and services. During 1992–2001 consumer prices increased at an average rate of 283.3% per year. The average annual rate of inflation was 168.6% in 2000 and 61.1% in 2001. In January 2003 3.1% of the economically active population were registered as unemployed. However, the true rate of unemployment was believed to be far higher, as many people were unwilling to register, owing to the low level of official benefits.

Belarus joined the IMF and the World Bank in 1992. It also became a member of the European Bank for Reconstruction and Development (EBRD, see p. 193). Belarus was pursuing membership of the World Trade Organization (WTO, see p. 322), although its failure to introduce market economic principles made the prospect of early accession unlikely.

Following the dissolution of the USSR, Belarus experienced serious economic problems and a severe contraction in output in all sectors. Economic policy was influenced by the country's aim of integration with Russia, as envisaged in a number of treaties and agreements signed from the mid-1990s. On 1 January 2000 a redenominated rouble, equivalent to 1,000 new roubles, was introduced, and in September a single rouble exchange rate replaced the previous multiple exchange-rate system. In December 2000 the Government of Belarus and the National Bank agreed to fix a reference rate for the Belarusian currency in relation to the Russian rouble from 1 January 2001, with an established fluctuation margin of 3.0%, which was later to decline to 2.5%. It was hoped that these measures would help to stabilize the currency, which had depreciated considerably in 1998–99. However, the Government's reliance on Russia for favourably-priced energy resources and bilateral barter trade had ensured that the economy was protected from serious decline. In April 2001 the legislature ratified a currency accord with Russia, under which the Russian rouble was to be adopted as the Belarusian currency from 2005, and a new single currency was to be introduced in 2008. The ratification of the agreement entitled Belarus to a Russian stabilization loan, worth some US $100m., the first tranche of which was disbursed in August 2001. Moreover, in 2001 both the IMF and the World Bank resumed relations with Belarus, suspended since the mid-1990s. The World Bank recommenced lending in June, but the IMF resumed relations at an evaluative level only and the re-election of President Lukashenka in September, amid strong criticism from election observers, served to undermine the strength of Belarus's future relations with the international lending institutions. In November 2002 Lukashenka denounced Gazprom's decision to reduce gas supplies to Belarus (see above) as politically motivated, and despite the legislature's subsequent vote in favour of removing a legal ban on the privatization of Beltransgaz, thereby permitting its partial acquisition by Gazprom, the incident emphasized the fact that relations between Belarus and Russia were also becoming increasingly uneasy. In early 2003 the IMF praised the maintenance of economic growth (of some 4.7%) in 2002 and the development of price liberalization measures in a number of sectors, but drew attention to the continuing high rate of annual inflation, the increasing wage and tax arrears of domestic enterprises, and the slow pace of privatization. Although Belarus announced terms for the privatization of several major petrochemical enterprises in February 2003, they were criticized as being unattractive to potential investors.

Education

Education is officially compulsory for nine years. Generally, education lasts for 11 years from six to 17 years of age. In 2001 the total enrolment at pre-primary level was equivalent to 70.8% of children in the relevant age group. Primary education usually begins at six years of age and lasts for four years (Grades 1–4). In 2001 the total enrolment at primary level was equivalent to 91.5% of the school-age population (males 91.8%; females 91.2%). Secondary education, beginning at the age of 10, lasts for a further seven years (Grades 5–11), comprising a first cycle of five years and a second of two years. In 2001 enrolment at Grades 5–9 was equivalent to 93.9% of those in the relevant age group (males 93.9%; females 93.9%). Enrolment at Grades 10–11 was equivalent to 54.6% of those aged 16–17 years, while a further 21% were enrolled at vocational schools. Enrolment at specialized institutions of secondary education was equivalent to 36.8% of those aged 18–23 years in 2001. From 1998 a transition began to be made towards introducing compulsory education for 10 years and general education for 12 years. In 2001/02 27.7% of all pupils were taught in Belarusian, and 72.2% were taught in Russian (0.1% were taught in Polish). Higher education institutions include 26 universities, as well as nine academies, 15 institutes, five higher colleges, one higher technical school, and two theological seminaries. In 2001/02 301,753 students were enrolled in higher education (equivalent to 302 per 10,000 inhabitants). Research is co-ordinated by the National Academy of Sciences of Belarus. Budgetary expenditure on education by all levels of government was 201,600m. readjusted roubles (equivalent to 2.1% of GDP) in 2001.

Public Holidays

2003: 1 January (New Year's Day), 7 January (Orthodox Christmas), 8 March (International Women's Day), 21 April (Catholic Easter), 28 April (Orthodox Easter), 1 May (Labour Day), 6 May (Radunitsa, Remembrance Day), 9 May (Victory Day), 11 May (State Flag Day), 3 July (Independence Day), 7 November (October Revolution Day), 25 December (Catholic Christmas).

2004: 1 January (New Year's Day), 7 January (Orthodox Christmas), 8 March (International Women's Day), 12 April (Catholic and Orthodox Easter), 1 May (Labour Day), 6 May (Radunitsa, Remembrance Day), 9 May (Victory Day and State Flag Day), 3 July (Independence Day), 7 November (October Revolution Day), 25 December (Catholic Christmas).

Weights and Measures

The metric system is in force.

Statistical Survey

Source: mainly Ministry of Statistics and Analysis, 220070 Minsk, pr. Partizanski 12; tel. (17) 249-42-78; fax (17) 249-22-04; e-mail minstat@mail.belpak .by; internet www.president.gov.by/Minstat/en/main.html.

Area and Population

AREA, POPULATION AND DENSITY

Area (sq km)	207,595*
Population (census results)†	
12 January 1989	10,151,806
16 February 1999	
Males	4,717,621
Females.	5,327,616
Total	10,045,237
Population (official estimates at 1 January)	
1999	10,019,480
2000	9,990,435
2001	9,950,900
Density (per sq km) at 1 January 2001 . . .	47.9

* 80,153 sq miles.

† Figures refer to the *de jure* population. The *de facto* total was 10,199,709 in 1989.

POPULATION BY NATIONALITY

(1999 census)

	%
Belarusian	81
Russian	11
Polish	4
Ukrainian	2
Others	2
Total	100

PRINCIPAL TOWNS*

(estimated population at 1 January 2001)

Minsk (Miensk, capital)	1,699,100	Borisov (Barysau) .	150,900
Gomel (Homiel) .	480,000	Pinsk . . .	131,100
Mogilev (Mahiloŭ) . .	360,600	Orsha (Vorsha) . .	124,000
Vitebsk (Viciebsk) . .	341,500	Mozyr (Mazyr) . .	110,700
Grodno (Horadnia) . .	307,100	Novopolotsk . .	102,100
Brest (Bieraście)† . .	291,400	Soligorsk . .	101,900
Bobruysk (Babrujsk) .	221,400	Lida . . .	100,000
Baranovichi			
(Baranavichy) . .	168,800		

* The Belarusian names of towns, in Latin transliteration, are given in parentheses after the more widely used Russian names.

† Formerly Brest-Litovsk.

BIRTHS, MARRIAGES AND DEATHS

	Registered live births		Registered marriages		Registered deaths	
	Number	Rate (per 1,000)	Number	Rate (per 1,000)	Number	Rate (per 1,000)
1994 . .	110,599	10.7	75,540	7.3	130,003	12.6
1995 . .	101,144	9.8	77,027	7.5	133,775	13.0
1996 . .	95,798	9.3	63,677	6.2	133,422	13.0
1997 . .	89,586	8.8	69,735	6.8	136,653	13.4
1998 . .	92,645	9.1	71,354	7.0	137,296	13.5
1999 . .	92,975	9.3	72,994	7.3	142,027	14.2
2000 . .	93,691	9.4	62,485	6.2	134,867	13.5
2001* . .	91,700	9.2	68,700	6.9	140,300	14.1

* Figures are provisional.

Expectation of life (WHO estimates, years at birth): 68.5 (males 62.9; females 74.2) in 2001.

EMPLOYMENT

(annual averages, '000 persons)

	1998	1999	2000
Agriculture	695.3	659.5	625.1
Forestry	28.7	29.7	32.5
Industry*	1,221.0	1,231.0	1,226.7
Construction	329.5	330.5	312.3
Trade and communications .	321.4	323.5	318.3
Trade and public catering† . . .	483.2	493.3	532.3
Housing, public utilities and			
personal services	193.4	202.5	208.1
Health care	262.0	266.1	269.9
Physical culture and social security	51.6	56.3	56.2
Education	454.5	460.6	463.7
Culture and arts	73.9	77.0	80.2
Science.	43.7	43.9	42.2
Credit and insurance . . .	53.2	55.7	58.4
Other activities	205.2	212.4	215.1
Total	**4,416.6**	**4,442.0**	**4,441.0**
Males	2,146.5	2,127.8	2,113.9
Females	2,270.1	2,314.2	2,327.1

* Comprising manufacturing (except printing and publishing), mining and quarrying, electricity, gas, logging and fishing.

† Including material and technical supply and procurement.

Unemployment ('000 persons registered at December): 95.8 (males 37.6, females 58.2) in 2000; 102.9 (males 40.8, females 62.1) in 2001; 130.5 (males 47.8, females 82.7) in 2002.

2002 ('000 persons): Total labour force (annual average) 4,459.0 (males 2,087.0, females 2,372.0).

Health and Welfare

KEY INDICATORS

Total fertility rate (children per woman, 2001).	1.2
Under-5 mortality rate (per 1,000 live births, 2001) . .	20
HIV/AIDS (% of persons aged 15–49, 2001). . . .	0.27
Physicians (per 1,000 head, 1998)	4.43
Hospital beds (per 1,000 head, 1996)	12.23
Health expenditure (2000): US $ per head (PPP) . .	430
Health expenditure (2000): % of GDP	5.7
Health expenditure (2000): public (% of total) . . .	82.8
Access to water (% of persons, 2000).	100
Human Development Index (2000): ranking	56
Human Development Index (2000): value	0.788

For sources and definitions, see explanatory note on p. vi.

Agriculture

PRINCIPAL CROPS
('000 metric tons)

	1999	2000	2001
Wheat	711.4	949.0*	1,050.0*
Barley	1,180.7	1,574.0*	1,750.0*
Maize	9.9	13.0*	15.7*
Rye	928.9	1,239.0*	1,300.0*
Oats	368.5	491.0*	600.0*
Buckwheat	8.8	12.0*	12.0*
Triticale (wheat-rye hybrid)	203.6	270.0*	198.0*
Potatoes	7,491.0	8,717.8	7,767.6
Sugar beet	1,186.5	1,473.6	1,682.1
Dry beans*	101	135	100
Dry peas*	130	173	127
Walnuts†	12	12	12
Sunflower seed†	19	22	18
Rapeseed	57.2	68.0†	58.0†
Linseed	12.6	22.0†	18.0†
Cabbages	446.3	525.0*	538.0*
Tomatoes	76.6	125.0*	130.0*
Cucumbers and gherkins	178.5	128.0*	150.0*
Dry onions	63.5	66.1*	70.0*
Carrots	200.2	185.0*	171.0*
Other vegetables†	207	177	229
Apples	123*	144†	160†
Pears	8*	10†	16†
Plums	28*	32†	43†
Sour cherries	17*	18†	30†
Cherries	10*	12†	16†
Other fruits and berries†	6	8	6
Flax fibre	20.9	37.2	31.5

* Unofficial figure(s).
† FAO estimate(s).

Source: FAO.

LIVESTOCK
('000 head at 1 January)

	1999	2000	2001
Horses	229	221	217
Cattle	4,686	4,326	4,221
Pigs	3,698	3,556	3,431
Sheep	106	92	89
Goats	56	58	61*
Chickens	30,000*	30,000*	32,000†

* Unofficial figure.
† FAO estimate.

Source: FAO.

LIVESTOCK PRODUCTS
('000 metric tons)

	1999	2000	2001
Beef and veal	262.1	269.4*	283.0*
Mutton and lamb*	3.0	2.6	2.7
Pig meat	311.0	256.0*	270.0*
Poultry meat	70.0	65.0*	68.0*
Other meat	6.2	6.2†	6.0
Cows' milk	4,740.8	4,489.6	4,834.1
Cheese	56.8	56.6	62.5
Butter	62.6	65.1	65.9
Hen eggs*	188.3	182.3	174.0
Honey	3.2	2.4†	3.2†
Cattle hides (fresh)†	29.4	29.7	31.2
Sheepskins (fresh)†	95.7	83.2	86.4

* Unofficial figure(s).
† FAO estimate(s).

Source: FAO.

Forestry

ROUNDWOOD REMOVALS
('000 cubic metres, excl. bark)

	1999	2000	2001
Sawlogs, veneer logs and logs for sleepers	2,995	3,168	3,202
Pulpwood	893	991	1,114
Other industrial wood	1,530	1,049	1,035
Fuel wood	1,144	928	923
Total	6,561	6,136	6,274

Source: FAO.

SAWNWOOD PRODUCTION
('000 cubic metres, incl. railway sleepers)

	1999	2000	2001
Coniferous (softwood)	1,457	1,211	1,153
Broadleaved (hardwood)	718	597	568
Total	2,175	1,808	1,721

Source: FAO.

Fishing

(metric tons, live weight)

	1998	1999	2000
Capture	457	514	553
Aquaculture	4,727	5,289	6,716
Common carp	3,254	4,088	5,867
Crucian carp	410	354	396
Silver carp	1	125	358
Northern pike	1,062	477	40
Total catch	5,184	5,809	7,269

Source: FAO, *Yearbook of Fishery Statistics*.

Mining

('000 metric tons, unless otherwise indicated)

	1998	1999	2000
Crude petroleum	1,830	1,840	1,841
Natural gas (million cu metres)	252	256	257
Chalk	79	78	114
Gypsum (crude)	17	27	30
Peat: for fuel	2,035	3,090	2,023
Peat: for agriculture	107	308	188

Industry

SELECTED PRODUCTS

('000 metric tons, unless otherwise indicated)

	1998	1999	2000
Refined sugar.	476	501	565
Margarine.	15.0	22.4	20.8
Wheat flour	1,153	1,134	924
Ethyl alcohol ('000 hectolitres) .	1,046	982	1,035
Wine ('000 hectolitres) .	5,832	5,467	6,917
Beer ('000 hectolitres)	2,603.7	2,728.4	2,370.6
Mineral water ('000 hectolitres)	1,082.5	1,453.4	1,532.5
Soft drinks ('000 hectolitres) .	2,196.3	1,870.3	1,861.4
Cigarettes (million)	7,296	9,259	10,356
Cotton yarn (pure and mixed) .	18.6	15.1	16.8
Flax yarn .	17.4	16.6	10.2
Wool yarn (pure and mixed) .	16.3	16.4	15.7
Woven cotton fabrics (million sq metres) .	67.1	50.6	66.6
Woven woollen fabrics (million sq metres) .	9.5	9.3	9.3
Linen fabrics (million sq metres) .	50.1	49.4	33.1
Woven fabrics of cellulosic fibres (million sq metres)	77.2	71.5	62.4
Carpets ('000 sq metres) .	8,145	9,155	8,744
Footwear (excluding rubber, '000 pairs) .	16,223	16,538	15,388
Plywood ('000 cu metres) .	139	140	126
Paper .	45	53	44
Paperboard .	150	162	176
Benzene (Benzol).	16.7	23.4	51.7
Ethylene (Ethene) .	108.1	115.4	114.7
Propylene (Propene) .	70.5	74.2	70.7
Xylenes (Xylol) .	—	7.5	38.0
Sulphuric acid (100%) .	640	614	584
Nitrogenous fertilizers (a)[1]	559	615	597
Phosphate fertilizers (b)[1]	130	120	87
Potash fertilizers (c)[1]	3,451	3,613	3,372
Non-cellulosic continuous fibres .	66.2	66.8	72.7
Cellulosic continuous filaments .	14.3	13.0	11.7
Soap .	26.3	33.7	38.6
Rubber tyres ('000)[2] .	2,324	2,263	2,440
Rubber footwear ('000 pairs) .	5,036	4,797	3,348
Quicklime .	684	663	586
Cement .	2,035	1,998	1,847
Concrete blocks ('000 cu metres) .	2,130	1,759	1,752
Crude steel .	1,412	1,449	1,623
Tractors ('000) .	26.9	27.4	22.5
Refrigerators ('000) .	802	802	812
Domestic washing machines ('000)	90.8	92.2	88.1
Television receivers ('000) .	468	516	532
Radio receivers ('000) .	114	195	101
Lorries (number) .	12,799	13,370	14,656
Motorcycles ('000) .	20.4	24.4	36.6
Bicycles ('000).	452	508	586
Cameras ('000) .	5	8	4
Watches ('000) .	4,848	5,218	5,602
Electric energy (million kWh) .	23,492	26,516	26,095

[1] Production in terms of (a) nitrogen; (b) phosphoric acid; or (c) potassium oxide.

[2] For lorries and farm vehicles.

2001 ('000 metric tons, unless otherwise indicated): Paper 51; Cement 1,803; Tractors ('000) 22.7; Electric energy (million kWh) 25,100.

2002 ('000 metric tons, unless otherwise indicated): Paper 52; Cement 2,171; Tractors ('000) 24.3; Electric energy (million kWh) 26,400.

Finance

CURRENCY AND EXCHANGE RATES

Monetary Units

100 kopeks = 1 readjusted Belarusian rouble (rubel)

Sterling, Dollar and Euro Equivalents (31 December 2002)

£1 sterling = 3,094.7 readjusted roubles
US $1 = 1,920.0 readjusted roubles
€1 = 2,013.5 readjusted roubles
10,000 readjusted Belarusian roubles = £3.231 = $5.208 = €4.966

Average Exchange Rate (readjusted Belarusian roubles per US $)

2000	876.750
2001	1,390.000
2002	1,790.920

Note: The Belarusian rouble was introduced in May 1992, initially as a coupon currency, to circulate alongside (and at par with) the Russian (formerly Soviet) rouble. The parity between Belarusian and Russian currencies was subsequently ended, and the Belarusian rouble was devalued. In August 1994 a new Belarusian rouble, equivalent to 10 old roubles, was introduced. On 1 January 1995 the Belarusian rouble became the sole national currency, while the circulation of Russian roubles ceased. On 1 January 2000 a readjusted Belarusian rouble, equivalent to 1,000 of the former units, was introduced. Some of the figures in this survey are still in terms of new roubles prior to redenomination.

STATE BUDGET

('000 million roubles)*

Revenue	1999	2000	2001
Tax revenue .	802.38	2,447.22	4,568.97
Taxes on income, profits and capital gains .	93.15	287.01	468.62
Social security contributions .	297.86	928.75	1,863.39
Payroll taxes .	23.93	73.10	154.54
Domestic taxes on goods and services .	329.42	1,016.56	1,782.42
General sales, turnover or value-added taxes .	176.79	544.30	936.15
Excises .	66.44	183.40	323.06
Taxes on international trade and transactions .	58.01	141.80	300.00
Other current revenue .	66.46	172.47	321.30
Capital revenue .	7.39	26.33	47.93
Total .	876.23	2,646.02	4,938.20

Expenditure†	1999	2000	2001
General public services .	43.71	121.25	228.04
Defence .	37.96	113.06	229.93
Public order and safety .	35.25	111.12	228.59
Education .	32.16	102.17	201.60
Health .	32.64	92.77	178.76
Social security and welfare .	311.38	1,008.17	2,233.09
Recreation, cultural and religious affairs and services .	12.14	40.95	74.68
Economic affairs and services .	135.42	399.28	711.79
Agriculture, forestry, fishing and hunting .	64.61	219.53	344.89
Transport and communications .	34.08	89.50	247.57
Other purposes .	291.93	650.60	992.95
Total (incl. others) .	933.88	2,639.80	5,080.21
Current expenditure .	723.35	2,197.84	4,440.63
Capital expenditure .	210.53	441.96	639.58

* Figures are in terms of the readjusted rouble, introduced on 1 January 2000 and equivalent to 1,000 of the former units. The data represent a consolidation of the operations of central government bodies.

† Excluding lending minus repayments ('000 million roubles) : 2.58 in 1999; −0.99 in 2000; 93.67 in 2001.

Source: IMF, *Government Finance Statistics Yearbook*.

INTERNATIONAL RESERVES

(US $ million at 31 December)

	1999	2000	2001
IMF special drawing rights .	0.42	0.18	0.40
Reserve position in IMF .	0.03	0.03	0.03
Foreign exchange.	293.82	350.29	390.26
Total .	294.27	350.50	390.68

Source: IMF, *International Financial Statistics*.

MONEY SUPPLY
(million roubles at 31 December)*

	1999	2000	2001
Currency outside banks	86,852	238,796	512,211
Demand deposits at deposit money banks	140,714	259,602	376,038
Total money (incl. others)	233,415	508,432	889,553

* Figures are in terms of the readjusted rouble, introduced on 1 January 2000 and equivalent to 1,000 of the former units.

Source: IMF, *International Financial Statistics*.

COST OF LIVING
(Consumer price index; base: 1992 = 100)

	1999	2000	2001
Food (incl. beverages)	5,264.1	13,945.7	21,871.1
Fuel and light	4,297.4	22,462.4	60,457.4
Clothing (incl. footwear)	1,508.6	3,369.5	4,939.0
Rent	10,789.0	41,576.4	85,797.1
All items (incl. others)	4,130.5	11,094.6	17,877.8

Source: partly ILO.

NATIONAL ACCOUNTS

Expenditure on the Gross Domestic Product
('000 million roubles at current prices)*

	1999	2000	2001
Government final consumption expenditure	590.2	1,779.1	3,496.6
Private final consumption expenditure	1,774.6	5,198.8	9,891.2
Increase in stocks	−79.3	18.0	14.2
Gross fixed capital formation	796.7	2,301.9	3,738.5
Total domestic expenditure	3,082.2	9,297.8	17,140.5
Exports of goods and services	1,791.5	6,321.6	11,475.0
Less Imports of goods and services	1,865.0	6,612.7	12,073.3
Statistical discrepancy	17.4	127.8	370.4
GDP in purchasers' values	3,026.1	9,133.8	16,912.6

* Figures are in terms of the readjusted rouble, introduced on 1 January 2000 and equivalent to 1,000 of the former units.

Source: IMF, *International Financial Statistics*.

Gross Domestic Product by Economic Activity
('000 million new roubles at current prices)

	1998	1999	2000*
Agriculture	80,461.9	368,551.9	1,155.6
Forestry	4,231.5	15,775.3	41.9
Industry†	203,708.6	836,333.3	2,354.9
Construction	40,921.5	175,733.9	516.3
Transport	59,348.5	297,289.2	938.6
Communications	10,125.9	48,595.9	139.5
Trade and catering	66,148.3	289,678.5	844.1
Material supply	8,739.3	41,175.1	123.2
Procurement	1,683.9	7,271.9	20.6
Housing	27,644.0	82,626.4	273.6
Public utilities	10,340.0	45,131.2	153.4
Health care	21,678.4	93,608.3	294.4
Education	30,758.2	131,271.8	388.7
Culture and science	6,883.7	34,391.4	86.0
Banks and insurance	14,433.0	81,497.4	226.7
Public administration and defence	22,438.4	87,552.6	276.2
Other services	11,294.0	51,210.1	162.5
Sub-total	620,839.1	2,687,694.2	7,996.2
Less Imputed bank service charge	10,314.9	62,885.3	177.3
GDP at factor cost	610,524.2	2,624,808.9	7,818.9
Indirect taxes, *less* subsidies	91,636.9	401,254.8	1,306.7
GDP in purchasers' values	702,161.1	3,026,063.7	9,125.6

* Preliminary figures, in terms of the readjusted rouble.

† Principally mining, manufacturing, electricity, gas and water.

BALANCE OF PAYMENTS
(US $ million)

	1999	2000	2001
Exports of goods f.o.b.	5,646.4	6,640.5	7,256.2
Imports of goods f.o.b.	−6,216.4	−7,524.6	−8,063.1
Trade balance	−570.0	−884.1	−806.9
Exports of services	753.3	1,015.6	1,013.1
Imports of services	−438.8	−562.6	−602.7
Balance on goods and services	−255.5	−431.1	−396.5
Other income received	20.8	25.7	27.0
Other income paid	−62.8	−72.4	−69.8
Balance on goods, services and income	−297.5	−477.8	−439.3
Current transfers received	137.0	177.1	202.6
Current transfers paid	−33.2	−22.4	−48.5
Current balance	−193.7	−323.1	−285.2
Capital account (net)	60.4	69.4	56.3
Direct investment abroad	−0.8	−0.2	−0.3
Direct investment from abroad	444.0	118.8	95.8
Portfolio investment assets	−15.4	−5.7	10.5
Portfolio investment liabilities	−5.2	50.1	−45.4
Other investment assets	−36.7	41.7	−139.2
Other investment liabilities	13.6	−64.6	328.6
Net errors and omissions	−246.3	238.9	−99.6
Overall balance	19.9	125.3	−78.5

Source: IMF, *International Financial Statistics*.

External Trade

PRINCIPAL COMMODITIES
('000 million new roubles at domestic prices*)

Imports	1998	1999	2000†
Industrial products	414,175	1,682,403	5,772
Petroleum and gas	86,540	361,776	1,784
Metallurgy	53,195	240,737	719
Chemical and petroleum products	65,749	262,317	814
Machinery and metalworking	112,650	419,624	1,233
Wood and paper products	12,756	53,590	194
Light industry	21,889	96,514	307
Food and beverages	39,081	166,818	474
Agricultural products (unprocessed)	11,565	73,858	255
Total (incl. others)	431,447	1,779,247	6,117
USSR (former)‡	277,518	1,146,268	4,380
Other countries	153,929	632,979	1,738

Exports	1998	1999	2000†
Industrial products	358,398	1,535,208	5,176
Petroleum and gas	27,761	142,750	1,047
Metallurgy	27,371	104,504	306
Chemical and petroleum products	78,228	350,334	1,010
Machinery and metalworking	118,053	536,793	1,532
Wood and paper products	24,517	102,658	320
Construction materials	9,967	33,164	125
Light industry	36,364	147,838	460
Food and beverages	34,900	110,083	350
Total (incl. others)	367,897	1,574,700	5,360
USSR (former)‡	259,282	968,077	3,272
Other countries	108,615	606,623	2,088

* Figures relating to trade with Russia are compiled from enterprise surveys, while data on trade with other countries are calculated on the basis of customs declarations.

† Figures in terms of the readjusted rouble.

‡ Excluding trade with Estonia, Latvia and Lithuania.

PRINCIPAL TRADING PARTNERS
(US $ million)

Imports c.i.f.	2000	2001	2002
Brazil	n.a.	n.a.	104.5
Germany	587.6	589.2	692.7
Italy	162.6	163.9	215.2
Lithuania	n.a.	107.3	109.4
Netherlands	79.5	79.3	84.0
Poland	215.8	199.5	219.6
Russia	5,549.7	5,230.6	5,842.5
Ukraine	340.6	277.4	290.7
United Kingdom	106.3	61.3	67.7
USA	138.7	131.3	103.1
Total (incl. others)	8,646.0	8,046.0*	8,980.0*

Exports f.o.b.	2000	2001	2002
Brazil	n.a.	76.7	89.4
China, People's Republic	148.4	143.1	217.4
Estonia	147.4	129.2	63.4
Germany	231.7	241.0	348.0
Hungary	n.a.	75.4	70.8
Italy	n.a.	85.4	130.1
Latvia	467.3	492.3	520.1
Lithuania	348.8	275.8	256.7
Netherlands	130.3	125.8	279.0
Poland	276.8	248.0	273.3
Russia	3,715.7	4,037.6	4,053.9
Ukraine	559.7	421.8	271.6
United Kingdom	95.9	222.9	493.7
USA	97.0	77.1	91.3
Total (incl. others)	7,326.0	7,525.0*	8,098.0*

* Figure rounded.

2001 (US $ million, revised figures): Total imports c.i.f. 8,178; Total exports f.o.b. 7,448.

Transport

RAILWAYS
(traffic)

	2000	2001	2002
Passenger-km (million)	17,722	15,264	14,349
Freight ton-km (million)	31,425	29,727	34,169

ROAD TRAFFIC
(motor vehicles in use at 31 December)

	1998	1999	2000
Passenger cars	1,279,208	1,356,611	1,448,491
Buses and coaches	8,768	8,452	8,273
Motorcycles and mopeds	558,251	533,658	523,613

Source: partly IRF, *World Road Statistics*.

CIVIL AVIATION
(traffic on scheduled services)

	2000	2001	2002
Passengers carried ('000)	216	n.a.	n.a.
Passenger-km (million)	513	546	553
Total ton-km (million)	18	28	37

Tourism

FOREIGN TOURIST ARRIVALS

Country of Nationality	1996	1997	1998
Germany	12,740	12,155	15,822
Italy	5,004	4,916	7,030
Latvia	4,078	3,969	4,610
Lithuania	6,747	5,870	8,652
Moldova	2,359	1,866	4,308
Poland	30,216	9,802	12,955
Russia	112,678	145,018	211,171
Ukraine	15,115	15,183	29,129
United Kingdom	9,024	10,095	11,182
USA	6,870	8,218	8,358
Total (incl. others)	234,226	254,023	355,342

Tourism receipts (US $ million): 55 in 1996; 23 in 1997; 22 in 1998; 13 in 1999; 17 in 2000.

Sources: World Tourism Organization, *Yearbook of Tourism Statistics*, and World Bank.

Communications Media

	1998	1999	2000
Television receivers ('000 in use)	3,300	3,400	3,500
Telephones ('000 main lines in use)	2,489.9	2,638.5	2,751.9
Facsimile machines (number in use)	19,472	23,847	26,925
Mobile cellular telephones (subscribers)	12,155	23,457	49,353
Internet users ('000)	7.5	50.0	180.0
Book production (incl. pamphlets):			
titles	6,073	6,064	7,686
copies ('000)	60,022	63,305	61,627
Daily newspapers:			
number	20	12	10
average circulation ('000)	1,559	1,094	1,101
Non-daily newspapers:			
number	560	578	600
average circulation ('000)	8,973	10,094	10,339
Other periodicals:			
number	318	331	354
average circulation ('000)	1,687	1,498	1,381

Radio receivers ('000 in use): 3,020 in 1997 (Source: UNESCO, *Statistical Yearbook*).

2001: Telephones ('000 main lines in use) 2,857.9; Mobile cellular telephones ('000 subscribers) 138.3; Internet users ('000) 422.2.

Source: partly International Telecommunication Union.

Education
(2001/02)

	Institutions	Teachers	Students
Pre-primary	4,423	52,524	390,812
Primary (Grades 1–4) } Secondary (Grades 5–11) }	4,709	138,744	1,473,950
Vocational and technical	248	14,772	138,593
Specialized secondary	156	12,748	155,352
Higher	58	21,684	301,753
Institutions offering post-graduate studies	377	9,000	570,000

Source: Ministry of Education, Minsk.

Adult literacy rate (UNESCO estimates): 99.6% (males 99.7%; females 99.4%) in 2000 (Source: UN Development Programme, *Human Development Report*).

Directory

The Constitution

A new Constitution came into effect on 30 March 1994. An amended version of the 1994 Constitution became effective on 27 November 1996, following a referendum held on 24 November. The following is a summary of its main provisions:

PRINCIPLES OF THE CONSTITUTIONAL SYSTEM

The Republic of Belarus is a unitary, democratic, social state based on the rule of law. The people are the sole source of state power and the repository of sovereignty in the Republic of Belarus. The people shall exercise their power directly through representative and other bodies in the forms and within the bounds specified by the Constitution. Democracy in the Republic of Belarus is exercised on the basis of diversity of political institutions, ideologies and opinions. State power in the Republic of Belarus is exercised on the principle of division of powers between the legislature, executive and judiciary, which are independent of one another. The Republic of Belarus is bound by the principle of supremacy of law; it recognizes the supremacy of the universally acknowledged principles of international law and ensures that its laws comply with such principles. Property may be the ownership of the State or private. The mineral wealth, waters and forests are the sole and exclusive property of the State. Land for agricultural use is the property of the State. All religions and creeds are equal before the law. The official languages of the Republic of Belarus are Belarusian and Russian. The Republic of Belarus aims to make its territory a neutral, nuclear-free state. The capital is Minsk.

THE INDIVIDUAL, SOCIETY AND THE STATE

All persons are equal before the law and entitled without discrimination to equal protection of their rights and legitimate interests. Every person has the right to life. Until its abolition, the death penalty may be applied in accordance with the verdict of a court of law as an exceptional penalty for especially grave crimes. The State ensures the freedom, inviolability and dignity of the individual. No person may be subjected to torture or cruel, inhuman or humiliating treatment or punishment. Freedom of movement is guaranteed. Every person is guaranteed freedom of opinion and beliefs and their free expression. The right to assemble publicly is guaranteed, as is the right to form public associations, including trade unions. Citizens of the Republic of Belarus have the right to participate in the solution of state matters, both directly and through freely elected representatives; the right to vote freely and to be elected to state bodies on the basis of universal, equal, direct or indirect suffrage by secret ballot. The State shall create the conditions necessary for full employment. The right to health care is guaranteed, as is the right to social security in old age, in the event of illness, disability and in other instances. Each person has the right to housing and to education. Everyone has the right to preserve his or her ethnic affiliation, to use his or her native language and to choose the language of communication. Payment of statutory taxes and other levies is obligatory. Every person is guaranteed the protection of his or her rights and freedom by a competent, independent and impartial court of law, and every person has the right to legal assistance.

THE ELECTORAL SYSTEM AND REFERENDUMS

Elections and referendums are conducted by means of universal, free, equal and secret ballot. Citizens of the Republic of Belarus who have reached the age of 18 years are eligible to vote. Deputies are elected by direct ballot. Referendums may be held to resolve the most important issues of the State and society. National referendums may be called by the President of the Republic of Belarus, by the National Assembly or by no fewer than 450,000 citizens eligible to vote. Local referendums may be called by local representative bodies or on the recommendation of no less than 10% of the citizens who are eligible to vote and resident in the area concerned. Decisions adopted by referendum may be reversed or amended only by means of another referendum.

THE PRESIDENT

The President of the Republic of Belarus is Head of State, the guarantor of the Constitution of the Republic of Belarus, and of the rights and freedoms of its citizens. The President is elected for a term of five years by universal, free, equal, direct and secret ballot for no more than two terms.

The President calls national referendums; calls elections to the National Assembly and local representative bodies; dissolves the chambers of the National Assembly, as determined by the Con-

stitution; appoints six members to the Central Electoral Commission; forms, dissolves and reorganizes the Administration of the President, as well as other bodies of state administration; appoints the Chairman of the Cabinet of Ministers (Prime Minister) of the Republic of Belarus with the consent of the House of Representatives; determines the structure of the Government, appoints and dismisses Ministers and other members of the Government, and considers the resignation of the Government; appoints, with the consent of the Council of the Republic, the Chairman of the Constitutional, Supreme and Economic Courts, the judges of the Supreme and Economic Courts, the Chairman of the Central Electoral Commission, the Procurator General, the Chairman and members of the board of the National Bank, and dismisses the aforementioned, having notified the Council of the Republic; appoints six members of the Constitutional Court, and other judges of the Republic of Belarus; appoints and dismisses the Chairman of the State Supervisory Committee; reports to the people of the Republic of Belarus on the state of the nation and on domestic and foreign policy; may chair meetings of the Government of the Republic of Belarus; conducts negotiations and signs international treaties, appoints and recalls diplomatic representatives of the Republic of Belarus; in the event of a natural disaster, a catastrophe or unrest involving violence or the threat of violence that may endanger people's lives or jeopardize the territorial integrity of the State, declares a state of emergency; has the right to abolish acts of the Government and to suspend decisions of local councils of deputies; forms and heads the Security Council of the Republic of Belarus, and appoints and dismisses the Supreme State Secretary of the Security Council; is the Commander-in-Chief of the Armed Forces and appoints and dismisses the Supreme Command of the Armed Forces; imposes, in the event of military threat or attack, martial law in the Republic of Belarus; issues decrees and orders which are mandatory in the Republic of Belarus. In instances determined by the Constitution, the President may issue decrees which have the force of law. The President may be removed from office for acts of state treason and other grave crimes, by a decision of the National Assembly.

THE NATIONAL ASSEMBLY

The National Assembly is a representative and legislative body of the Republic of Belarus, consisting of two chambers: the House of Representatives and the Council of the Republic. The term of the National Assembly is four years. The House of Representatives comprises 110 deputies. Deputies are elected by universal, equal, free, direct suffrage and by secret ballot. The Council of the Republic is a chamber of territorial representation with 64 members, consisting of eight deputies from every region and from Minsk, elected by deputies of local councils. Eight members of the Council of the Republic are appointed by the President. Any citizen who has reached the age of 21 years may become a deputy of the House of Representatives. Any citizen who has reached the age of 30 years, and who has been resident in the corresponding region for no less than five years, may become a member of the Council of the Republic. The chambers of the National Assembly elect their Chairmen.

The House of Representatives considers draft laws concerning amendments and alterations to the Constitution; domestic and foreign policy; the military doctrine; ratification and denunciation of international treaties; the approval of the republican budget; the introduction of national taxes and levies; local self-government; the administration of justice; the declaration of war and the conclusion of peace; martial law and a state of emergency; and the interpretation of laws. The House of Representatives calls elections for the presidency; grants consent to the President concerning the appointment of the Chairman of the Cabinet of Ministers; accepts the resignation of the President; together with the Council of the Republic, takes the decision to remove the President from office.

The Council of the Republic approves or rejects draft laws adopted by the House of Representatives; consents to appointments made by the President; elects six judges of the Constitutional Court and six members of the Central Electoral Commission; considers charges of treason against the President; takes the decision to remove the President from office; considers presidential decrees on the introduction of a state of emergency, martial law, and general or partial mobilization.

Any proposed legislation is considered initially in the House of Representatives and then in the Council of the Republic. On the proposal of the President, the House of Representatives and the Council of the Republic may adopt a law, delegating to him legislative powers to issue decrees which have the power of a law.

However, he may not issue decrees making alterations or addenda to the Constitution or to policy laws.

THE GOVERNMENT

Executive power in the Republic of Belarus is exercised by the Cabinet of Ministers. The Government is accountable to the President and responsible to the National Assembly. The Chairman of the Cabinet of Ministers is appointed by the President with the consent of the House of Representatives. The Government of the Republic of Belarus formulates and implements domestic and foreign policy; submits the draft national budget to the President; and issues acts that have binding force.

THE JUDICIARY

Judicial authority in the Republic of Belarus is exercised by the courts. Justice is administered on the basis of adversarial proceedings and equality of the parties involved in the trial. Supervision of the constitutionality of enforceable enactments of the State is exercised by the Constitutional Court, which comprises 12 judges (six of whom are appointed by the President and six are elected by the Council of the Republic).

LOCAL GOVERNMENT AND SELF-GOVERNMENT

Citizens exercise local and self-government through local councils of deputies, executive and administrative bodies and other forms of direct participation in state and public affairs. Local councils of deputies are elected by citizens for a four-year term, and the heads of local executive and administrative bodies are appointed and dismissed by the President of the Republic of Belarus.

THE PROCURATOR'S OFFICE AND THE STATE SUPERVISORY COMMITTEE

The Procurator's office exercises supervision over the implementation of the law. The Procurator General is appointed by the President with the consent of the Council of the Republic, and is accountable to the President. The Supervisory Authority monitors the implementation of the national budget and the use of public property. The State Supervisory Committee is formed by the President, who appoints the Chairman.

APPLICATION OF THE CONSTITUTION AND THE PROCEDURE FOR AMENDING THE CONSTITUTION

The Constitution has supreme legal force. Amendments and supplements to the Constitution are considered by the chambers of the National Assembly on the initiative of the President, or of no fewer than 150,000 citizens of the Republic of Belarus who are eligible to vote. The Constitution may be amended or supplemented via a referendum.

The Government

HEAD OF STATE

President: ALYAKSANDR R. LUKASHENKA (elected 10 July 1994; inaugurated 20 July; re-elected 9 September 2001; inaugurated 20 September).

CABINET OF MINISTERS
(April 2003)

Prime Minister: GENADZ V. NAVITSKY.

First Deputy Prime Minister: SYARHEY S. SIDORSKY.

Deputy Prime Minister and Minister of the Economy: ANDREY U. KABYAKOW.

Deputy Prime Ministers: ULADZIMIR N. DRAZHYN, ALYAKSANDR A. PAPKOW, ANATOL D. TSYUTSYUNOW.

Minister of Agriculture and Food: MIKHAIL I. RUSY.

Minister of Architecture and Construction: GENADZ F. KURACHKIN.

Ministry of Communications: ULADZIMIR I. GANCHARENKO.

Minister of Culture: LEANID N. HULYAKA.

Minister of Defence: Col-Gen. LEANID S. MALTSAW.

Minister of Education: Prof. PYOTR BRIGADIN.

Minister for Emergency Situations: VALERY P. ASTAPOU.

Minister of Energy: ULADZIMIR SYMASHKA.

Minister of Finance: NIKOLAY P. KORBUT.

Minister of Foreign Affairs: SYARHEY MARTYNOW.

Minister of Health Care: LYDMILA A. PASTAYALKA.

Minister of Housing and Municipal Services: ALYAKSANDR A. MILKOTA.

Minister of Industry: ANATOL D. KHARLAP.

Minister of Information: MIKHAIL V. PADHAYNY.

Minister of Internal Affairs: ULADZIMIR U. NAUMAU.

Minister of Justice: VIKTAR G. GOLOVANOU.

Minister of Labour and Social Protection: ANTONINA P. MOROVA.

Minister for Natural Resources and Environmental Protection: LYAVONTSY I. KHAROUZHYK.

Minister of Revenue: KONSTANTIN A. SUMAR.

Minister of Sports and Tourism: YURIY SIVAKOW.

Minister of Statistics and Analysis: ULADZIMIR I. ZINOVSKY.

Minister of Trade: ALYAKSANDR M. KULICHKOW.

Minister of Transport and Communications: MIKHAIL I. BOROVOY.

Head of the Presidential Administration: URAL R. LATYPAW.

MINISTRIES

Office of the President: 220016 Minsk, vul. K. Marksa 38, Dom Urada; tel. (17) 222-60-06; internet www.president.gov.by.

Office of the Prime Minister and Deputy Prime Ministers: 220010 Minsk, vul. Savetskaya 11; tel. (17) 222-61-05; fax (17) 222-66-65.

Cabinet of Ministers of the Republic of Belarus: 220010 Minsk, pl. Nezalezhnasti, Dom Pravitelstva; tel. (17) 222-69-05; fax (17) 222-66-65; e-mail cm@mail.belpak.by; internet www.president.gov .by.

Ministry of Agriculture and Food: 220050 Minsk, vul. Kirava 15; tel. (17) 227-37-51; fax (17) 227-42-96; e-mail kanc@mshp.minsk.by; internet mshp.minsk.by.

Ministry of Architecture and Construction: 220050 Minsk, vul. Myasnikova 39; tel. (17) 227-26-42; fax (17) 220-74-24.

Ministry of Post and Telecommunications: 220050 Minsk, pr. F. Skaryny 10; tel. (17) 227-21-57; fax (17) 226-08-48; e-mail mpt@ belpak.by; internet www.mpt.gov.by.

Ministry of Culture: 220004 Minsk, pr. Masherava 11; tel. (17) 223-75-74; fax (17) 223-90-45.

Ministry of Defence: 220034 Minsk, vul. Kamunistychnaya 1; tel. (17) 239-23-79; fax (17) 289-19-74; internet www.mod.mil.by.

Ministry of the Economy: 220050 Minsk, vul. Stankevicha 14; tel. (17) 222-60-48; fax (17) 220-37-77; e-mail gen@plan.minsk.by.

Ministry of Education: 220010 Minsk, vul. Savetskaya 9; tel. (17) 227-47-36; fax (17) 220-80-57; e-mail root@minedu.unibel.by; internet www.minedu.unibel.by.

Ministry for Emergency Situations: 220050 Minsk, vul. Revolutsionnaya 5; tel. (17) 206-54-25; fax (17) 206-51-91; e-mail mcs@ infonet.by; internet www.rescue01.gov.by.

Ministry of Energy: 220050 Minsk, vul. K. Marksa 14; tel. (17) 229-83-59; fax (17) 229-84-68.

Ministry of Finance: 220010 Minsk, vul. Savetskaya 7; tel. (17) 222-61-37; fax (17) 222-66-40; e-mail mofb@office.un.minsk.by; internet www.ncpi.gov.by/minfin.

Ministry of Foreign Affairs: 220030 Minsk, vul. Lenina 19; tel. (17) 227-29-22; fax (17) 227-45-21; internet www.mfa.gov.by.

Ministry of Health Care: 220095 Minsk, vul. Myasnikova 39; tel. (17) 222-60-33; fax (17) 222-62-97.

Ministry of Housing and Municipal Services: 220050 Minsk, vul. Bersana 16; tel. (17) 220-15-45; fax (17) 220-38-94.

Ministry of Industry: 220033 Minsk, pr. Partizansky 2, kor. 4; tel. (17) 224-95-95; fax (17) 224-87-84; e-mail minprom@ntc.niievm .minsk.by; internet www.niievm.minsk.by/minprom/minprom.htm.

Ministry of Information: 220048 Minsk, pr. Masherava 11; tel. (17) 223-92-31; fax (17) 223-34-35.

Ministry of Internal Affairs: 220050 Minsk, Gorodskoy Val 4; tel. (17) 229-78-08; fax (17) 226-12-47; internet mvd.belarus.nsys.by.

Ministry of Justice: 220004 Minsk, vul. Kalektarnaya 10; tel. (17) 220-97-55; fax (17) 220-86-94; e-mail dep07@minjust.belpak.minsk .by; internet www.ncpi.gov.by/minjust.

Ministry of Labour and Social Protection: 220004 Minsk, pr. Masherava 23, kor. 2; tel. (17) 206-37-97; fax (17) 206-38-84; e-mail mintrud@mail.belpak.by; internet www.ssf.gov.by.

Ministry for Natural Resources and Environmental Protection: 220048 Minsk, vul. Kalektarnaya 10; tel. (17) 220-66-91; fax

(17) 220-55-83; e-mail minproos@mail.belpak.by; internet www .president.gov.by/minpriroda.

Ministry of Revenue and Taxes: 220010 Minsk, vul. Savetskaya 9; tel. (17) 222-68-90; fax (17) 222-64-50; internet www.nalog.by.

Ministry of Sports and Tourism: 220600 Minsk, vul. Kirava 8, kor. 2; tel. (17) 227-72-37; fax (17) 227-30-31; e-mail inter.sport@solo .by; internet www.mst.by.

Ministry of Statistics and Analysis: 220033 Minsk, pr. Partizansky 12; tel. (17) 249-52-00; fax (17) 249-22-04; e-mail minstat@ mail.belpak.by; internet www.president.gov.by/Minstat/en/main .html.

Ministry of Trade: 220050 Minsk, vul. Kirava 8, kor. 1; tel. (17) 227-08-97; fax (17) 227-24-80.

Ministry of Transport and Communications: 220029 Minsk, vul. Chicherina 21; tel. (17) 234-11-52; fax (17) 239-42-26; e-mail mail@mintrans.by; internet www.mintrans.by.

President and Legislature

PRESIDENT

Presidential Election, 9 September 2001

Candidates		Votes	%
Alyaksandr Lukashenka	. . . . . .	4,666,680	75.65
Uladzimir Gancharyk	. . . . . .	965,261	15.65
Syarhey Gaydukevich	. . . . . .	153,199	2.48
Invalid votes	. . . .	383,947	6.22
Total	. . . .	6,169,087	100.00

NATIONAL ASSEMBLY*

Council of the Republic

Chairman: ALYAKSANDR VAYTOVICH.

The Council of the Republic is the upper chamber of the legislature and comprises 64 deputies. Of the total, 56 deputies are elected by regional councils and eight deputies are appointed by the President.

House of Representatives

Chairman: VADZIM PAPOW.

Deputy Chairman: ULADZIMIR KANAPLYOW.

The House of Representatives is the lower chamber of the legislature and comprises 110 deputies elected by universal, equal, free, direct electoral suffrage and by secret ballot. In the first round of voting in the legislative election of 15 October 2000, 41 seats were filled and 13 constituencies were declared invalid. A second round of voting for the remaining 56 seats took place on 29 October. Owing to the high incidence of electoral violations, however, repeat elections in the invalid constituencies took place on 18 March and 1 April 2001.
* The National Assembly was formed following a referendum held on 24 November 1996. Deputies who had been elected to the Supreme Council at the general election held in late 1995 were invited to participate in the new legislative body. However, many deputies regarded the new National Assembly as unconstitutional and declared themselves to be the legitimate legislature. A form of 'shadow' cabinet, the Public Coalition Government—National Economic Council, chaired by Genadz Karpenka, was established in January 1997 by opposition deputies. Following Karpenka's death in April 1999, the chairmanship of the Council was assumed by Mechislau Gryb (he was officially elected to the post in November).

Political Organizations

Following the Government's imposition of stringent measures for re-registration in January 1999, in September of that year there were only 17 political parties officially registered with the Ministry of Justice (28 had previously been registered).

Agrarian Party (AP) (Agrarnaya Partya): 220050 Minsk, vul. Kazintsa 86–2; tel. (17) 220-38-29; fax (17) 249-50-18; f. 1992; Leader SYAMYON SHARETSKY.

Belarusian Christian-Democratic Party (Belaruskaya Khryst-siyanska-Demakratychnaya Partya): Minsk, vul. Bagdanovicha 7A; f. 1994; Leader MIKALAI KRUKOUSKY.

Belarusian Christian-Democratic Union (Belaruskaya Khryst-siyanska-Demakratychnaya Zluchnasts): 220065 Minsk, vul. Avakyana 38–59; tel. and fax (17) 229-67-56; f. 1991; nationalist, reformist; Leader PETR SILKO.

Belarusian Ecological Green Party: Minsk; tel. (17) 220-11-16; fax (17) 256-82-72; f. 1998 by the merger of the Belarusian Ecological Party (f. 1993) and the Green Party of Belarus (f. 1992).

Belarusian Green Party (Belaruskaya Partya Zyaleny): 246023 Gomel, vul. Brestskaya 6; tel. (23) 247-08-08; fax (23) 247-96-96; f. 1994 as Belarusian Greenpeace Party, present name adopted 1999; Leaders OLEG GROMYKA, NICK LEKUNOVICH.

Belarusian National Party (Belaruskaya Natsiyanalnaya Partya): 220094 Minsk, vul. Plekhanava 32–198; tel. (17) 227-43-76; f. 1994; Leader ANATOL ASTAPENKA.

Belarusian Party of Labour (Belaruskaya Partya Pratsy): 220126 Minsk, pr. Masherava 21; tel. (17) 223-82-04; fax (17) 223-97-92; e-mail acmbel2@mail.belpak.by; f. 1993; Leader LEANID LEMYA-SHONAK.

Belarusian Party of Women 'Hope' (Belaruskaya Partya Zhanchyn 'Nadzeya'): 220126 Minsk, pr. Masherov 21; tel. (17) 223-89-57; fax (17) 223-90-40; e-mail zmn@sfpb.belpak.minsk.by; internet www .nadzeya.org; f. 1994; Pres. VALENTINA POLEVIKOVA.

Belarusian Patriotic Party (Belaruskaya Patryatychnaya Partya): Minsk; tel. (17) 220-27-57; f. 1994; Leader ANATOL BAR-ANKEVICH.

Belarusian Peasant Party (Belaruskaya Syalyanskaya Partya): 220068 Minsk, vul. Gaya 38-1; tel. (17) 277-19-05; fax (17) 277-96-51; f. 1991; advocates agricultural reforms; 7,000 mems; Leader YAUGEN M. LUGIN.

Belarusian People's Patriotic Union: Minsk; f. 1998; a pro-Lukashenka alliance supportive of further integration with Russia, comprising 30 left-wing and centrist organizations, incl. the CPB, the Belarusian Patriotic Party, the Liberal Democratic Party of Belarus, the White Rus Slavonic Council and the Union of Reserve Officers; Exec. Sec. VIKTAR CHYKIN.

Belarusian Popular Party (Belaruskaya Narodnaya Partya): 220050 Minsk, vul. K. Marksa 18; tel. (17) 227-89-52; fax (17) 227-13-30; e-mail imi@imibel.belpak.minsk.by; f. 1994; Leader VIKTAR TERESCHENKO.

Belarusian Republican Party (Belaruskaya Respublikanskaya Partya): 220100 Minsk, vul. Kulman 13–71; tel. (17) 234-07-49; f. 1994; Leaders VALERY ARTYSHEUSKY, ULADZIMIR RAMANAU.

Belarusian Social Democratic Assembly (Belaruskaya Satsyal-demakratychnaya Hramada): 220035 Minsk, vul. Drozda 8–52; tel. and fax (17) 226-74-37; e-mail bsdggramada@tut.by; f. 1998; Leader STANISLAU SHUSHKEVICH.

Belarusian Social Democratic Party: Minsk; f. 2001 by defectors from the Belarusian Social Democratic Party (National Assembly); Leader ALYAKSEY KAROL.

Belarusian Social Democratic Party (National Assembly) (Belaruskaya Satsyal-demakratychnaya Partya—Narodnaya Hramada): 220114 Minsk, pr. F. Skaryny 153/2/107; tel. and fax (17) 263-37-48; e-mail bsdp@infonet.by; f. 1903, re-established 1991; merged with Party of People's Accord (f. 1992) in 1996; centrist; Leader MIKALAI STATKEVICH; c. 2,500 mems.

Belarusian Socialist Party (Belaruskaya Satsyalistychnaya Partya): Minsk; tel. (17) 229-37-38; f. 1994; aims for a civilized society, where rights and freedoms are guaranteed for all; Leader MIKHAIL PADGAINY.

Belarusian Social-Sports Party (Belaruskaya Satsyalna-Spartyunaya Partya): 220000 Minsk, pr. Partizanskaya 89A; tel. (17) 226-93-15; f. 1994; Leader ULADZIMIR ALYAKSANDROVICH.

BPF—'Revival' (BPF—'Adradzhennye'): 220005 Minsk, vul. Varvasheni 8; tel. (17) 231-48-93; fax (17) 233-50-12; e-mail bpf@bpf .minsk.by; internet pages.prodigy.net/dr_fission/bpf; fmrly the Belarusian Popular Front, name changed as above Dec. 1999; f. 1988; anti-communist movement campaigning for democracy, genuine independence for Belarus and national and cultural revival; Chair. VINTSUK VYACHORKA; Exec. Sec. ANATOL KRYVAROT.

Christian-Democratic Choice (Khrystsiyanska-Demakratychny Vybar): 220050 Minsk, vul. Leningradskaya 3–1; tel. (17) 237-28-86; f. 1995; Leader VALERY SAROKA.

Communist Party of Belarus (CPB) (Kamunistychnaya Partya Belarusi): 220007 Minsk, vul. Varanyanskaga 52; tel. (17) 226-64-22; fax (17) 232-31-23; Leader VIKTAR CHYKIN.

Conservative Christian Party of the BPF: Minsk; f. 1999 as a breakaway faction of the BPF; Chair. ZYANON PAZNYAK; Dep. Chair. MIKALAI ANTSIPOVICH, YURIY BELENKI, SYARHEY PAPKOW, ULADZIMIR STARCHANKA.

Liberal Democratic Party of Belarus (Liberalna-Demakratych-naya Partya Belarusi): 220071 Minsk, vul. Platonava 22, 12th Floor; tel. and fax (17) 231-63-31; e-mail ldpb@infonet.by; f. 1994; advocates continued independence of Belarus, increased co-operation with other European countries and eventual membership of the European Union, and expansion of the private sector; Leader SYARHEY GAYDUKEVICH; over 45,000 mems (2002).

National Democratic Party of Belarus (Natsyanalna-Demakratychnaya Partya Belarusi): Minsk, vul. Labanka 97–140; tel. (17) 271-95-16; fax (17) 236-99-72; f. 1990; Leader VIKTAR NAVUMENKA.

Party of Common Sense (Partya Zdarovaga Sensu): 220094 Minsk, pr. Rakasouskaga 37–40; tel. (17) 247-08-68; f. 1994; Leader IVAN KARAVAYCHYK.

Party of Communists of Belarus (Partya Kamunistau Belaruskaya): 220005 Minsk, pr. F. Skaryny 46A; tel. (17) 232-25-73; fax (17) 231-80-36; e-mail ck_pkb@anitex.by; f. 1991; Leader SYARHEY KALYAKIN.

Republican Party (Respublikanskaya Partya): 220000 Minsk, vul. Pershamayskaya 18; tel. (17) 236-50-71; fax (17) 236-32-14; f. 1994; aims to build a neutral, independent Belarus; Leader ULADZIMIR BELAZOR.

Republican Party of Labour and Justice (Respublikanskaya Partya Pratsy i Spravyadlivasti): 220004 Minsk, vul. Amuratarskaya 7; tel. (17) 223-93-21; fax (17) 223-86-41; f. 1993; Leader ANATOL NYATYLKIN.

Social-Democratic Party of Popular Accord (Satsiyal-Demakratychnaya Partya Narodnay Zgody): 220050 Minsk, vul. K. Marksa 10; tel. (17) 286-35-65; f. 1992; Leader SYARHEY ERMAK.

United Civic Party of Belarus (UCP) (Abyadnanaya Hramadzyanskaya Partya Belarusi): 220050 Minsk, vul. Kamsamolskaya 11, Office 216; tel. (17) 227-75-49; fax (17) 211-02-79; e-mail ucpb@ucpb.org; internet www.ucpb.org; f. 1990; liberal-conservative; Chair. ANATOL U. LIABEDZKA; Hon. Chair. STANISLAU A. BAHDANKEVICH; Dep. Chair. PAVEL DANEIKA, ALYAKSANDR A. DABRAVOLSKY, JAROSLAU ROMANCHUK, VASILY SHLYNDZIKAV.

White Rus Slavonic Council (Slavyansky Sabor 'Belaya Rus'): 220088 Minsk, vul. Pershamayskaya 24/1/80; tel. (17) 239-52-32; fax (17) 270-09-28; f. 1992; Leader MIKALAY SYARHEY.

Diplomatic Representation

EMBASSIES IN BELARUS

Armenia: 220050 Minsk, vul. Kirava 17; tel. and fax (17) 227-09-36; Ambassador SUREN HAROUTUNIAN.

Bulgaria: 220030 Minsk, pl. Svabody 11, 1st Floor; tel. (17) 206-65-58; fax (17) 206-65-59; Chargé d'affaires a.i. BOYKO KOSEV BOEV.

China, People's Republic: 220071 Minsk, vul. Berestyanskaya 22; tel. (17) 285-36-82; fax (17) 285-36-83; e-mail zbesg@telecom.by; Ambassador YU ZHENQI.

Cuba: 220071 Minsk, vul. Krasnozviozdnaya 13; tel. (17) 220-03-83; fax (17) 220-23-45; e-mail embacuba@belsonet.net; Ambassador FÉLIX LEÓN CARBALLO.

Czech Republic: 220030 Minsk, Muzykalny per. 1/2; tel. (17) 226-52-43; fax (17) 211-01-37; Chargé d'affaires a.i. ALES FOJTIK.

France: 220030 Minsk, pl. Svabody 11; tel. (17) 210-28-68; fax (17) 210-25-48; Ambassador STÉPHANE CHMELEWSKY.

Germany: 220034 Minsk, vul. Zakharava 26; tel. (17) 288-17-52; fax (17) 236-85-52; e-mail germanembassy@mail.belpak.by; internet www.germanembassy.org.by; Ambassador HELMUT FRICK.

Greece: 220030 Minsk, vul. Engelsa 13, Hotel Oktyabrskaya, Room 515; tel. (17) 227-27-60; fax (17) 226-08-05; Ambassador PANAYOTIS GOUMAS.

Holy See: Minsk, vul. Valadarskaga 6, 3rd Floor; tel. (17) 289-15-84; fax (17) 289-15-17; Apostolic Nuncio IVAN JURKOVIČ (Archbishop of Corbavia).

India: 220090 Minsk, vul. Kaltsova 4, kor. 5; tel. (17) 262-93-99; fax (17) 262-97-99; e-mail indembminsk@indiatimes.com; Ambassador BHARATH RAJ MUTHU KUMAR.

Iran: 220049 Minsk, vul. Suvorava 2; tel. (17) 207-66-99; fax (17) 207-61-99; Ambassador MUHAMMAD MOUSSA HASHEMI GOLPAYEGANI.

Iraq: Minsk; tr. Smorgovsky 68B; tel. (17) 213-44-99; fax (17) 213-38-99; Ambassador SALMAN ZEIDAN.

Israel: 220033 Minsk, pr. Partizansky 6A; tel. (17) 230-44-44; fax (17) 210-52-70; Ambassador MARTIN PELED-FLAX.

Italy: 220030 Minsk, vul. K. Marksa 37; tel. (17) 229-29-69; fax (17) 234-30-46; e-mail ambitminsk@belsonet.net; Ambassador STEFANO BENAZZO.

Japan: 220004 Minsk, pr. Masherova 23, kor. 1, 8th Floor; tel. (17) 223-60-37; fax (17) 210-41-80; Chargé d'affaires a.i. NAOTAKE YAMASHITA.

Kazakhstan: 220029 Minsk, vul. Kuibysheva 12; tel. (17) 213-30-26; fax (17) 234-96-50; e-mail tem@kazemb.belpak.minsk.by; Ambassador GAZIZ ALDAMZHAROV.

Kyrgyzstan: 220002 Minsk, vul. Staravilenskaya 57; tel. (17) 234-91-17; fax (17) 234-16-02; e-mail manas@nsys.minsk.by; Ambassador RYSBEK KACHKEYEV.

Latvia: 220013 Minsk, vul. Doroshevicha 6A; tel. (17) 284-93-93; fax (17) 284-73-34; e-mail daile@belsonet.net; Ambassador EGONS NEIMANIS.

Libya: Minsk, vul. Nyajdanavay 41; tel. (17) 268-66-01; fax (17) 234-70-88; Chargé d'affaires a.i. ABDALLA AL MAGRAVI.

Lithuania: 220088 Minsk, vul. Zakharova 68; tel. (17) 285-24-48; fax (17) 285-33-37; e-mail lt.embassy@belsonet.net; Ambassador JONAS PASLAUSKAS.

Moldova: 220030 Minsk, vul. Belaruskaya 2; tel. (17) 289-14-41; fax (17) 289-11-47; Ambassador ILIE VANCEA.

Peru: 220082 Minsk, vul. Pritytskogo 34; tel. and fax (17) 216-91-14.

Poland: 220034 Minsk, vul. Rumyantsava 6; tel. (17) 2188-23-13; fax (17) 236-49-92; e-mail ambminsk@nsys.by; internet www.embassypoland.nsys.bg; Ambassador TADEUSZ PAWŁAK.

Romania: 220035 Minsk, per. Moskvina 4; tel. (17) 223-77-26; fax (17) 210-40-85; Chargé d'affaires a.i. MIHAI PUYU.

Russia: 220002 Minsk, vul. Staravilenskaya 48; tel. (17) 234-54-97; fax (17) 250-36-64; e-mail karp@rusamb.belpak.minsk.by; Ambassador ALEKSANDR BLOKHIN.

Serbia and Montenegro: 220012 Minsk, vul. Surganova 28A; tel. (17) 239-39-90; fax (17) 232-51-54; e-mail embassies@smip.sv.gov.yu; Ambassador NIKOLA PEJAKOVICH.

Slovakia: 220050 Minsk, vul. Valadarskaga 6; tel. (17) 206-57-78; fax (17) 206-57-76; Chargé d'affaires a.i. JOSEF BOZHEK.

Tajikistan: 220050 Minsk, vul. Kirava 17; tel. (17) 222-37-98; fax (17) 227-76-13; Chargé d'affaires OLIM RAKHIMOV.

Turkey: 220050 Minsk, vul. Valadarskaga 6, 4th Floor; tel. (17) 227-13-83; fax (17) 227-27-46; e-mail dtmin@comco.belpak.minsk.by; Ambassador ALI VURAL ÖKTEM.

Turkmenistan: 220050 Minsk, vul. Kirava 17; tel. (17) 222-34-27; fax (17) 222-33-67; Ambassador ILYA VELDJANOV.

Ukraine: 220002 Minsk, vul. Staravilenskaya 51; tel. (17) 283-19-90; fax (17) 283-19-80; e-mail slavutych@anitex.by; Ambassador ANATOLII DRON.

United Kingdom: 220030 Minsk, vul. K. Marksa 37; tel. (17) 210-59-20; fax (17) 229-23-06; e-mail pia@bepost.belpak.minsk.by; Ambassador BRIAN BENNETT.

USA: 220002 Minsk, vul. Staravilenskaya 46; tel. (17) 210-12-83; fax (17) 234-78-53; e-mail webmaster@usembassy.minsk.by; internet www.usembassy.minsk.by; Ambassador GEORGE KROL.

Judicial System

In May 1999 there were 154 courts in Belarus, employing some 200 judges.

Supreme Court: 220030 Minsk, vul. Lenina 28; tel. (17) 226-12-06; fax (17) 227-12-25; Chair. VALENTIN SUKALO; Dep. Chair. VALERY VYSHKEVICH.

Supreme Economic Court: 220050 Minsk, vul. Valadarskaga 8; tel. and fax (17) 227-16-41; fax (17) 229-20-85; e-mail bxc@court.by; internet www.court.by; Chair. VIKTAR KAMYANKOW.

Procuracy: 220050 Minsk, vul. Internatsionalnaya 22; tel. (17) 226-43-57; fax (17) 226-42-52; Procurator General VIKTAR SHEYMAN.

Constitutional Court: 220016 Minsk, vul. K. Marksa 32; tel. and fax (17) 227-80-12; e-mail ksrb@user.unibel.by; f. 1994; 12 mem. judges; Chair. RYHOR VASILEVICH; Dep. Chair. ALYAKSANDR MARYSKYN.

Religion

CHRISTIANITY

The major denomination is the Eastern Orthodox Church, but there are also an estimated 1.1m. adherents of the Roman Catholic Church. Of these, some 25% are ethnic Poles and there is a significant number of Uniates or 'Greek Catholics'. There is also a growing number of Baptist churches.

The Eastern Orthodox Church

In 1990 Belarus was designated an exarchate of the Russian Orthodox Church, thus creating the Belarusian Orthodox Church.

Belarusian Orthodox Church: 220004 Minsk, vul. Osvobozhdeniya 10; tel. and fax (17) 223-25-05; e-mail orthobel@gin.by; f. 922 AD; Metropolitan of Minsk and Slutsk, Patriarchal Exarch of All Belarus His Eminence FILARET.

The Roman Catholic Church

Although five Roman Catholic dioceses, embracing 455 parishes, had officially existed since the Second World War, none of them had a bishop. In 1989 a major reorganization of the structure of the Roman Catholic Church in Belarus took place. The dioceses of Minsk and Mogilev (Mahilou) were merged, to create an archdiocese, and two new dioceses were formed, in Grodno (Horadnia) and Pinsk. The Eastern-rite, or Uniate, Church was abolished in Belarus in 1839, but was re-established in the early 1990s. At 31 December 2000 the Roman Catholic Church had an estimated 1,059,000m. adherents in Belarus (about 10.6% of the population).

Latin Rite

Archdiocese of Minsk and Mogilev: 220030 Minsk, pl. Svabody 9; tel. (17) 223-65-41; fax (17) 226-90-92; Archbishop Cardinal KAZIMIERZ ŚWIĄTEK.

Byzantine Rite

Belarusian Greek Catholic (Uniate) Church: 224014 Brest, vul. Dvornikova 63; tel. and fax (16) 224-74-82; e-mail bgkc_carkva@tut.by; Dean Protopresbyter VIKTAR DANILAU.

Protestant Churches

Union of Evangelical Christian Baptists of Belarus: 220093 Minsk, POB 108; tel. (17) 253-92-67; fax (17) 253-82-49; e-mail beluecb@belsonet.net; internet www.gospel-web.org.

ISLAM

There are small communities of Azeris and Tatars, who are adherents of Islam. In 1994 the supreme administration of Muslims in Belarus, which had been abolished in 1939, was reconstituted. In mid-1998 there were some 4,000 Muslims and four mosques.

Muslim Society: 220004 Minsk, vul. Zaslavskaya 11, kor. 1, kv. 113; tel. (17) 226-86-43; f. 1991; Chair. ALI HALEMBEK.

JUDAISM

Before Belarus was occupied by Nazi German forces, in 1941–44, there was a large Jewish community, notably in Minsk. There were some 142,000 Jews at the census of 1989, but many have since emigrated.

Jewish Religious Society: 220030 Minsk, pr. F. Skaryny 44A.

The Press

In 2000 954 periodicals were published in Belarus. Of the 878 periodicals published in 1998, 116 were in Belarusian and 295 in Russian, and 447 were in both Belarusian and Russian. Most daily newspapers are government-owned.

PRINCIPAL DAILIES

In Russian, except where otherwise stated.

Belaruskaya Niva (Belarusian Cornfield): 220013 Minsk, vul. B. Hmyalnitskaga 10A; tel. (17) 268-26-20; fax (17) 268-26-43; e-mail belniva@yandex.ru; internet belniva.chat.ru; f. 1921; 5 a week; organ of the Cabinet of Ministers; in Belarusian and Russian; Editor E. SEMASHKO; circ. 65,000 (2000).

Narodnaya Hazeta (The People's Newspaper): 220013 Minsk, vul. B. Hmyalnitskaga 10A; tel. (17) 268-28-70; fax (17) 268-25-29; e-mail info@ng.press.net.by; f. 1990; 5–6 a week; in Belarusian and Russian; Editor-in-Chief M. SHIMANSKY; circ. 90,000 (2000).

Respublika (Republic): 220013 Minsk, vul. B. Hmyalnitskaga 10A; tel. (17) 268-26-15; fax (17) 268-26-12; e-mail info@respublika.info; internet www.respublika.info; 5 a week; in Belarusian; Editor ANATOLI LEMIASHONAK; circ. 120,000 (2002).

Sovetskaya Belorussiya (Soviet Belorussia): 220013 Minsk, vul. B. Hmyalnitskaga 10A; tel. and fax (17) 232-14-32; e-mail admin@sb.press.net.by; internet sb.press.net.by; 5 a week; Editor-in-Chief PAVEL YAKUBOVICH; circ. 435,000 (2000).

Vechernii Minsk (Evening Minsk): 220805 Minsk, pr. F. Skaryny 44; tel. (17) 213-30-54; fax (17) 213-48-35; e-mail omp@nsys.minsk.by; internet www.belarus.net/minsk-evl; Editor S. SVERKUNOU; circ. 93,000 (2000).

Znamya Yunosti (Banner of Youth): 220013 Minsk, vul. B. Hmyalnitskaga 10A; tel. and fax (17) 268-26-84; f. 1938; 5 a week; organ of the Cabinet of Ministers; Editor-in-Chief ELENA PHILIPTCHIK; circ. 9,000 (2000).

Zvyazda (Star): 220013 Minsk, vul. B. Hmyalnitskaga 10A; tel. (17) 268-29-19; fax (17) 268-27-79; f. 1917 as Zvezda; 5 a week; organ of the Cabinet of Ministers; in Belarusian; Editor ULADZIMIR B. NARKEVICH; circ. 90,000 (1998).

PRINCIPAL PERIODICALS

In Belarusian, except where otherwise stated.

Advertisements Weekly: 220805 Minsk, pr. F. Skaryny 44; tel. and fax (17) 213-45-25; e-mail omp@bm.belpak.minsk.by; Editor T. ANANENKO; circ. 21,500 (1997).

Alesya: 220013 Minsk, pr. F. Skaryny 77; tel. and fax (17) 232-20-51; e-mail magalesya@mail.ru; f. 1924; monthly; Editor TAMARA BUNTO; circ. 10,500 (2003).

Belarus: 220005 Minsk, vul. Zakharava 19; tel. (17) 284-80-01; f. 1930; monthly; publ. by the State Publishing House; journal of the Union of Writers of Belarus and the Belarusian Society of Friendship and Cultural Links with Foreign Countries; fiction and political essays; in Belarusian, English and Russian; Editor-in-Chief A. A. SHABALIN.

Belaruskaya Krinitsa: 220065 Minsk, vul. Avakyana 38–59; tel. and fax (17) 229-67-56; f. 1991; monthly; journal of the Belarusian Institute of Social Development and Co-operation; Editor-in-Chief MIKHAIL MALKO; circ. 5,000.

Byarozka (Birch Tree): 220013 Minsk, pr. F. Skaryny 77; tel. (17) 232-94-66; f. 1924; monthly; fiction; illustrated; for 10–15-year-olds; Editor-in-Chief UL. I. JAGOUDZIK.

Chyrvonaya Zmena (Red Rising Generation): 220013 Minsk, vul. B. Hmyalnitskaga 10A; tel. and fax (17) 232-21-03; e-mail czm@mail.ru; internet czm.press.net.by; f. 1921; weekly; Editor A. KARLUKIEVICH; circ. 5,000 (2000).

Gramadzyanin: Minsk; tel. (17) 229-08-34; fax (17) 272-95-05; publ. by the United Civic Party of Belarus.

Holas Radzimy (Voice of the Motherland): 220005 Minsk, pr. F. Skaryny 44; tel. (17) 288-17-82; fax (17) 288-11-97; e-mail golas_radzimy@tut.by; f. 1955; weekly; articles of interest to Belarusians in other countries; Editor-in-Chief NATALIA SALUK.

Krynitsa (Spring): 220807 Minsk, vul. Kiseleva 11; tel. (17) 236-60-71; fax (17) 236-61-42; e-mail www.krynitsa@open.by; f. 1988; monthly; publ. by the state media holding, Literatura i Mastatstva; literary and cultural; in Belarusian; Editor ALA KANAPELKA; circ. 2,100 (2001).

Litaratura i Mastatstva (Literature and Arts): 220005 Minsk, vul. Zakharava 19; tel. (17) 284-84-61; f. 1932; weekly; publ. by the state media holding, Literatura i Mastatstva; Editor ALYAKSANDR PISMENKOV; circ. 5,000 (1998).

Maladosts (Youth): 220013 Minsk, vul. B. Hmyalnitskaga 10A; tel. (17) 268-27-54; f. 1953; monthly; publ. by the state media holding, Literatura i Mastatstva; novels, short stories, essays, translations, etc., for young people; Editor-in-Chief G. DALIDOVICH.

Mastatstva (Art): 220029 Minsk, vul. Chicherina 1; tel. (17) 289-34-67; fax (17) 276-94-67; e-mail masta@ibamedia.com; internet www.ibamedia.com; monthly; illustrated; Editor-in-Chief ALYAKSEY DUDARAU; circ. 1,000–1,200 (2001).

Narodnaya Asveta (People's Education): 220023 Minsk, vul. Makaenka 12; tel. (17) 264-62-68; f. 1924; publ. by the Ministry of Education; Editor-in-Chief N. I. KALESNIK.

Neman (The River Nieman): 220005 Minsk, pr. F. Skaryny 39; tel. (17) 213-40-72; fax (17) 213-44-61; f. 1945; monthly; publ. by the state media holding, Literatura i Mastatstva; literary; fiction; in Russian; Editor-in-Chief A. ZHOUK.

Polymya (Flame): 220005 Minsk, vul. Zakharava 19; tel. (17) 284-80-12; f. 1922; monthly; publ. by the state media holding, Literatura i Mastatstva; literary; fiction; Editor-in-Chief S. I. ZAKONNIKOU.

Tovarisch: 220005 Minsk, pr. F. Skaryny 46A; tel. (17) 202-08-14; fax (17) 231-80-36; e-mail ck_pkb@anitex.by; internet pkb.promedia.minsk.by; f. 1994; weekly newspaper of the Party of Communists of Belarus; Editor-in-Chief SYARGEY. V. VOZNYAK; circ. 6,000 (2001).

Vozhyk (Hedgehog): 220013 Minsk, pr. F. Skaryny 77; tel. and fax (17) 232-12-40; f. 1941; fortnightly; satirical; Editor-in-Chief MIKHAIL POZDNYAKOV; circ. 12,000 (1998).

Vyaselka (Rainbow): 220617 Minsk, vul. Kalektarnaya 10; tel. (17) 220-92-61; fax (17) 236-62-67; f. 1957; monthly; popular; for 5–10-year-olds; Editor-in-Chief V. S. LIPSKY; circ. 30,000 (1999).

PRESS ASSOCIATIONS

Belarusian Association of Journalists: Minsk; tel. (17) 227-05-58; internet www.baj.unibel.by; f. 1995; Pres. ZHANNA LITVINA.

Belarusian Union of Journalists: 220005 Minsk, vul. Rumyantsava 3; tel. and fax (17) 236-51-95; 3,000 mems; Pres. L. EKEL.

NEWS AGENCY

BelTa (Belarusian News Agency): 220030 Minsk, vul. Kirava 26; tel. (17) 227-19-92; fax (17) 227-13-46; e-mail coper@belta.minsk.by; internet www.belta.minsk.by; f. 1921; Dir DMITRIY ZHUK.

Publishers

In 2000 there were 7,686 titles published in Belarus (62m. copies).

Belarus: 220600 Minsk, pr. F. Skaryny 79; tel. (17) 223-87-42; fax (17) 223-87-31; f. 1921; social, political, technical, medical and musical literature, fiction, children's, reference books, art reproductions, etc. Dir MIKHALAY KAVALEVSKY; Editor-in-Chief ELENA ZAKONNIKOVA.

Belaruskaya Entsiklopediya (Belarusian Encyclopaedia): 220072 Minsk, vul. Akademicheskaya 15A; tel. (17) 284-17-67; fax (17) 284-09-83; f. 1967; encyclopedias, dictionaries, directories and scientific books; Editor-in-Chief G. P. PASHKOV.

Belaruskaya Navuka (Science and Technology Publishing House): 220067 Minsk, vul. Zhodinskaya 18; tel. (17) 263-76-18; f. 1924; scientific, technical, reference books, educational literature and fiction in Belarusian and Russian; Dir LUDMILA PIETROVA.

Belarusky Dom Druku (Belarusian House of Printing): 220013 Minsk, pr. F. Skaryny 79; tel. (17) 268-27-03; fax (17) 231-67-74; e-mail dom.pechati@bdp.minsk.by; f. 1917; social, political, children's and fiction in Belarusian, Russian and other European languages; Dir BARYS KUTAVY.

Belblankavyd: 220035 Minsk, vul. Timirazeva 2; tel. (17) 226-71-22; reference books in Belarusian and Russian; Dir VALENTINA MILOVANOVA.

Mastatskaya Litaratura (Art Publishing House): 220600 Minsk, pr. Masherava 11; tel. (17) 223-48-09; f. 1972; fiction in Belarusian and Russian; Dir GEORGE MARCHUK.

Narodnaya Asveta (People's Education Publishing House): 220600 Minsk, pr. Masherava 11; tel. and fax (17) 223-61-84; e-mail igpna@asveta.belpak.minsk.by; f. 1951; scientific, educational, reference literature and fiction in Belarusian, Russian and other European languages; Dir IGAR N. LAPTSYONAK.

Polymya (Flame Publishing House): 220004 Minsk, pr. Masherava 11; tel. and fax (17) 223-52-85; f. 1950; social, political, scientific, technical, religious, children's and fiction; Dir MIKHAIL A. IVANOVICH.

Uradzhay (Harvest Publishing House): 220048 Minsk, pr. Masherava 11; tel. (17) 223-64-94; fax (17) 223-80-23; f. 1961; scientific, technical, educational, books and booklets on agriculture; in Belarusian and Russian; Dir YAUGEN MALASHEVICH.

Vysheyshaya Shkola (Higher School Publishing House): 220048 Minsk, pr. Masherava 11; tel. and fax (17) 223-54-15; e-mail vsh@solo.by; internet www.vsh.h1.ru; f. 1954; textbooks and science books for higher educational institutions; in Belarusian, Russian and other European languages; absorbed the Universitetskae publishing house in 2002; Dir ANATOL A. ZHADAN; Editor-in-Chief T. K. MAIBORODA.

Yunatstva (Youth Publishing House): 220600 Minsk, pr. Masherava 11; tel. (17) 223-24-30; fax (17) 223-31-16; f. 1981; fiction and children's books; Dir ALYAKSANDR KOMAROVSKY; Vice-Dir MIKHAIL POZDNIAKOV.

Broadcasting and Communications

TELECOMMUNICATIONS

Belcel: 22005 Minsk, vul. Zolotaya Gorka 5; tel. (17) 276-01-00; fax (17) 276-03-33; e-mail belcel@cpen.minsk.by; internet www.cplc.com/business/euremaf/eastern/units; 50% owned by Cable and Wireless (United Kingdom); mobile telecommunications services; Gen. Man ULADZIMIR GETMANOV.

Beltelecom: 220030 Minsk, vul. Engelsa 6; tel. (17) 217-10-05; fax (17) 227-44-22; e-mail info@main.beltelecom.by; internet www.beltelecom.by; f. 1995; national telecommunications operator; Dir-Gen. NIKOLAY KRUKOVSKY.

BROADCASTING

At the beginning of 2003 there were 183 radio and television companies registered in Belarus; however, all such companies were required to re-register by mid-2003.

National State Television and Radio Company of Belarus: 220807 Minsk, vul. A. Makayenka 9; tel. (17) 263-13-20; fax (17) 264-81-82; internet www.tvr.by; f. 1925; Chair. EGOR RYBAKOV.

Belarusian Television: 220807 Minsk, vul. A. Makayenka 9; tel. (17) 233-45-01; fax (17) 264-81-82; f. 1956; Pres. A. R. SITYLAROU.

Belarusian Radio: 220807 Minsk, vul. Chyrvonaya 4; tel. (17) 239-58-30; fax (17) 284-85-74; e-mail radio-minsk@tvr.by; internet www.tvr.by; Gen. Dir A. P. SALAMAHA.

Television

Television Broadcasting Network (TBN): 220072 Minsk, pr. F. Skaryny 15A; tel. and fax (17) 239-41-71; e-mail mmc@glas.apc.org; comprises 12 private television cos in Belarus's largest cities.

Minsk Television Company: Minsk; private; broadcasts to the CIS, Western Europe and North America.

ONT: f. 2002; 51% state-owned; the country's second nation-wide television channel; Chair. RYHOR KISEL.

Finance

(cap. = capital; dep. = deposits; res = reserves; m. = million; brs = branches; amounts in readjusted Belarusian roubles, unless otherwise indicated)

BANKING

At January 2003 there were 28 commercial banks registered in Belarus.

Central Bank

National Bank of Belarus: 220008 Minsk, pr. F. Skaryny 20; tel. (17) 219-23-03; fax (17) 227-48-79; e-mail k.badulin@nbrb.by; internet www.nbrb.by; f. 1990; cap. 41,673.9m. roubles (Dec. 2000), res 48,237,703m., dep. 129,402,309m. (Dec. 1999); Chair. PYOTR P. PRAKAPOVICH; 46 brs.

Commercial Banks

Absolutbank: 220023 Minsk, pr. F. Skaryny 115, POB 9; tel. (17) 237-07-02; fax (17) 264-60-43; e-mail root@absolutbank.by; f. 1993; cap. 39,234m. (Dec. 1997); total assets 6,865m. (June 2001); Chair. ULADZIMIR SHCHERBO; 1 br.

Bank Poisk: 220090 Minsk, vul. Gamarnik 9/4; tel. (17) 228-32-49; fax (17) 228-32-48; f. 1974 (as a regional branch of Gosbank of the USSR); renamed Housing and Communal Bank (ZhilSotsBank) in 1989; present name adopted in 1992; cap. 672m., res 535m., dep. 14,184m. (Dec. 2000); Chair. ALGERDAS TABATADZE; 4 brs.

BELAGROPROMBANK: 220073 Minsk, vul. Olshevskaga 24; tel. (17) 228-55-13; fax (17) 228-53-19; e-mail bapb@bapb.minsk.by; internet www.belapb.com; f. 1991; cap. 89,730m., res 67,284m., dep. 315,187m. (Dec. 2001); Chair. ALYAKSANDR A. GAVRUSHEV; 132 brs.

Belarusbank: 220050 Minsk, vul. Myasnikova 32; tel. (17) 220-18-31; fax (17) 226-47-50; e-mail info@belarusbank.minsk.by; internet www.belarusbank.minsk.by; f. 1995 following merger with Sberbank (Savings Bank; f. 1922); cap. 100,695m., res 71,958m., dep. 1,473,323m. (Dec. 2001); Chair. NADEZHDA A. YERMAKOVA; 160 brs.

Belarusian Joint-Stock Commercial Bank for Industry and Construction (BELPROMSTROIBANK): 220071 Minsk, Blvd Lunacharskogo 6; tel. (17) 210-13-14; fax (17) 210-03-42; e-mail teletype@belpsb.by; internet www.belpsb.by; f. 1991; provides credit to enterprises undergoing privatization and conversion to civil production; cap. 10,901m., dep. 237,140m. (Dec. 2001); Gen. Dir GALINA P. KUKHARENKO.

Belarusky Narodnyi Bank: 220004 Minsk, vul. Tankovaya 1A; tel. and fax and fax (17) 223-84-57; e-mail bnb@bnb.by; internet www.bnb.by; f. 1992; cap. 593.4m., res 3,610.1m., dep. 7,663.9m. (Dec. 2001); Chair. of Bd ANDREY S. TARATUKHIN; 1 br.

Belgazprombank: 220121 Minsk, vul. Pritytsky 60/2; tel. (17) 259-40-24; fax (17) 259-45-25; e-mail telecom@bgpb.minsk.by; internet www.belgazprombank.by; f. 1990; cap. 17,415.2m., dep. 27,321.4m. (Aug. 2002); Chair. of Bd VIKTAR D. BABARIKO; 7 brs.

Belinvestbank JSC: 220002 Minsk, vul. Varvasheniy 81; tel. (17) 289-35-42; fax (17) 289-36-70; e-mail corr@belinvestbank.by; internet www.belinvestbank.by; f. 2001, by merger of Belbusinessbank JSC and the Belarusian Bank of Development; cap. US $40.0m. (Jan. 2003); Chair. of Bd ALYAKSANDR E. RUTKOVSKY; 52 brs.

OJSC Belvnesheconombank: 220050 Minsk, vul. Myasnikova 32; tel. (17) 238-12-15; fax (17) 226-48-09; e-mail office@bveb.minsk.by; internet www.bveb.by; f. 1991; merged with Belkoopbank in March 2001; cap. 17,158.0m., res 1,983.6m., dep. 220,948.2m. (Jan. 2002); Chair. of Bd GEORGIY YEGOROV; 28 brs.

Djembank: 220012 Minsk, vul. Surganava 28; tel. (17) 219-84-44; fax (17) 219-84-90; e-mail main@djem.com.by; internet www.djem

.com.by; f. 1991; cap. 20,390.9m. (Jan. 2003); Gen. Dir ALYAKSANDR V. TATARINTSEV.

Foreign Bank Moskva-Minsk: 220002 Minsk, vul. Kommunis-ticheskaya 49; tel. (17) 288-63-01; fax (17) 288-63-02; e-mail mmb@mmbank.minsk.by; f. 2000; wholly owned by Moscow Municipal Bank — Bank of Moscow (Russia); cap. US $1.8m., res $1.9m., dep. $9.1m. Dir ALYAKSANDR RAKOVETS.

Golden Taler Bank (Bank Zolotoy Taler): 220035 Minsk, vul. Tatarskaya 3; tel. (17) 206-44-26; fax (17) 210-55-32; e-mail office@gtbank.gtp.by; internet www.gtbank.gtp.by; f. 1994; cap. 801.4m., res 2,472.2m., dep. 14,571.8m. (Jan. 2003); Chair. of Bd ALYAKSANDR A. ZHILINSKY.

Infobank: 220035 Minsk, vul. Ignatenka 11; tel. and fax (17) 250-43-88; e-mail root@infobank.by; f. 1994; cap. 6,748m., res 6,664m., dep. 17,255m. (Dec. 2001); Chair. ALYAKSANDR OSMOLOVSKIY; 4 brs.

ITI Bank (International Trade and Investment Bank): 2200530 Minsk, vul. Sovetskaya 12; tel. (17) 220-68-80; fax (17) 220-17-00; e-mail iti_bank@tut.by; f. 1999; Chair. GENNADY ALEINIKOV.

Minski Tranzitnyi Bank (JSC Minsk Transit Bank): 220033 Minsk, pr. Partizansky 6A; tel. (17) 213-29-00; fax (17) 213-29-09; e-mail cor@mtb.minsk.by; f. 1994; cap. US $10.2m., res $0.6m., dep. $3.2m. (Jan. 2003); Chair. of Bd ANNA G. GRINKEVICH; 5 brs.

Priorbank JSC: 220002 Minsk, vul. V. Khoruzhey 31A; tel. (17) 269-09-64; fax (17) 234-15-54; e-mail root@priorbank.by; internet www.priorbank.by; f. 1989, present name since 1992; cap. US $26,137m. (July 2002), res 2,432m., dep. 256,023m. (Dec. 2001); Pres. SYARHEY A. KOSTYUCHENKA; 219 brs.

Slavneftebank: 220007 Minsk, vul. Fabritsius 8; tel. (17) 222-07-09; fax (17) 222-07-52; e-mail snb@snbank.by; internet www.snbank .by; f. 1996; cap. and res US $7.9m., dep. $14.3m. (Aug. 2002); Pres. IVAN BAMBIZA; Chair. of Bd ULADZIMIR V. IVANOV; 6 brs.

Technobank: 220002 Minsk, vul. Krapotkina 44; tel. (17) 283-27-27; fax (17) 283-15-10; e-mail info@technobank.com.by; internet www.technobank.com.by; f. 1994; total assets 27,086m. (June 2001); Chair. of Bd VIKTAR I. KHLOPITSKY; 2 brs.

Trade and Industrial Bank SA (Torgovo-Promishlenny Bank): 220141 Minsk, vul. Russiyanov 8; tel. and fax (17) 268-03-45; e-mail tib_sa@anitex.by; f. 1994 as Novokom; cap. 1,141,435m. new roubles (Nov. 1999); Chair. FELIKS I. CHERNYAVSKY.

BANKING ASSOCIATION

Association of Belarusian Banks: 220071 Minsk, vul. Smolyach-kova 9; tel. (17) 227-78-90; fax (17) 227-58-41; e-mail root@abbank .minsk.by; Chair. NIKOLAY POZNIAK.

COMMODITY AND STOCK EXCHANGES

Belagroprambirzha (Belarusian Agro-Industrial Trade and Stock Exchange): 220108 Minsk, vul. Kazintsa 86, kor. 2; tel. (17) 277-07-26; fax (17) 277-01-37; f. 1991; trade in agricultural products, indus-trial goods, shares; 900 mems; Pres. ANATOL TIBOGANOU; Chair. of Bd ALYAKSANDR P. DECHTYAR.

Belarusian Currency and Stock Exchange: 220004 Minsk, vul. Melnikaite 2; tel. (17) 276-91-21; fax (17) 229-25-66; f. 1991; Gen. Dir VYACHESLAV A. KASAK.

Belarusian Universal Exchange (BUE): 220099 Minsk, vul. Kazintsa 4; tel. (17) 278-11-21; fax (17) 278-85-16; f. 1991; Pres. ULADZIMIR SHEPEL.

Gomel Regional Commodity and Raw Materials Exchange (GCME): 246000 Gomel, vul. Savetskaya 16; tel. (232) 55-73-28; fax (232) 55-70-07; f. 1991; Gen. Man. ANATOL KUZILEVICH.

INSURANCE

Belarusian Insurance Co: 220141 Minsk, vul. Zhodinskaya 1–4; tel. (17) 263-38-57; fax (17) 268-80-17; e-mail reklama@belinscosc .belpak.minsk.by; f. 1992; Dir-Gen. LEANID M. STATKEVICH.

Belgosstrakh (Belarusian Republican Unitary Insurance Co): 220036 Minsk, vul. K. Libknekht 70; tel. (17) 259-10-21; fax (17) 213-08-05; e-mail bgs@belsonet.net; internet www.belgosstrakh.by; Dir-Gen. VIKTAR I. SHOUST; 145 brs.

Belingosstrakh: 220078 Minsk, pr. Masherava 19; tel. and fax (17) 226-98-04; f. 1977; non-life, property, vehicle and cargo insurance; Dir-Gen. YURI A. GAVRILOV.

GARIS: 220600 Minsk, vul. Myasnikova 32; tel. (17) 220-37-01.

Polis: 220087 Minsk, pr. Partizansky 81; tel. (17) 245-02-91; Dir DANUTA I. VORONOVICH.

SNAMI: 220040 Minsk, vul. Nekrasova 40A; tel. and fax (17) 231-63-86; f. 1991; Dir S. N. SHABALA.

Trade and Industry

CHAMBERS OF COMMERCE

Belarusian Chamber of Commerce and Industry: 220035 Minsk, pr. Masherava 14; tel. (17) 226-91-27; fax (17) 226-98-60; e-mail mbox@cci.by; internet www.cci.by; f. 1952; brs in Brest, Gomel, Grodno, Mogilev and Vitebsk; Pres. ULADZIMIR N. BOBROV.

Minsk Branch: 220113 Minsk, vul. Kolasa 65; tel. (17) 266-04-73; fax (17) 266-26-04; Man. Dir P. A. YUSHKEVICH.

EMPLOYERS' ORGANIZATION

Belarusian Union of Industrialists and Entrepreneurs: 220004 Minsk, vul. Kalvaryskaya 1-608; tel. (17) 222-47-96; fax (17) 222-47-94; e-mail buee@nsys.by; internet vyales.nysys.by; f. 1990; business association; Pres. GEORGY BADEY.

UTILITIES

Electricity

In November 1999 an agreement was signed on the unification of Russia's and Belarus' energy systems (including a power-grid merger).

Institute of Nuclear Energy: 223061 Minsk, Sosny Settlement; tel. (17) 246-77-12.

Gas

Belnaftagaz: Minsk; tel. (17) 233-06-75.

Beltopgaz: distributes natural gas to end-users.

Beltransgaz: legislation enabling its privatization approved in Nov. 2002; imports natural gas; acts as holding co for regional trans-mission and storage enterprises.

TRADE UNIONS

Belarusian Congress of Democratic Trade Unions: 220005 Minsk, vul. Zaharova 24; tel. (17) 233-31-82; fax (17) 210-15-00; f. 1993; alliance of four independent trade unions; Pres. ALYAKSANDR YARASHUK; 18,000 mems.

Free Trade Union of Belarus: 220005 Minsk, vul. Zakharova 24; tel. (17) 284-31-82; fax (17) 284-59-94; e-mail spb@user.unibel .by; internet www.praca.by; f. 1992; Chair. GENADZ BYKOU; Vice-Chair. NIKOLAY KANAH; 6,000 mems.

Independent Trade Union of Belarus: 223710 Soligorsk, vul. Lenina 42; tel. and fax (17) 102-00-59; e-mail sol_sn@inbox.ru; f. 1991; Chair. VIKTAR BABAYED; Sec. NIKOLAY ZIMIN; 10,000 mems.

Belarusian Organization of Working Women: 220030 Minsk, pl. Svabody 23; tel. (17) 227-57-78; fax (17) 227-13-16; f. 1992; 7,000 mems.

Belarusian Peasants' Union (Syalansky Sayuz): 220199 Minsk, vul. Brestskaya 64-327; tel. (17) 277-99-93; Chair. KASTUS YARMO-LENKA.

Independent Association of Industrial Trade Unions of Belarus: 220013 Minsk, vul. Kulman 4; tel. (17) 223-80-74; fax (17) 223-82-04; f. 1992; Chair. ALYAKSANDR I. BUKHVOSTOU, G. F. FEDYNICH; 380,000 mems; derecognized by Govt in 1999.

Trade Union Federation of Belarus: Minsk; Chair. LEANID KOZIK.

Union of Electronic Industry Workers: Minsk; Leader G. F. FEDYNICH.

Union of Motor Car and Agricultural Machinery Construc-tion Workers: Minsk; largest industrial trade union in Belarus; Leader ALYAKSANDR I. BUKHVOSTOU; 200,000 mems.

Union of Small Ventures: 220010 Minsk, vul. Sukhaya 7; tel. (17) 220-23-41; fax (17) 220-93-41; f. 1990; legal, business; Gen. Dir VIKTAR F. DROZD.

Transport

RAILWAYS

In 2000 the total length of railway lines in use was 5,512 km. Minsk is a major railway junction, situated on the east–west line between Moscow and Warsaw, and north–south lines linking the Baltic countries and Ukraine. There is an underground railway in Minsk, the Minsk Metro, which has two lines (total length 23 km), with 19 stations.

Belarusian State Railways: 220745 Minsk, vul. Lenina 17; tel. (17) 225-44-00; fax (17) 227-56-48; f. 1992, following the dissolution of the former Soviet Railways; Pres. VASIL HAPEYEU.

ROADS

At 31 December 2000 the total length of roads in Belarus was 74,385 km (including 15,345 km of main roads and 59,040 km of secondary roads). Some 89.0% of the total network was hard-surfaced. In September 1999 it was estimated that more than 28,000 km of Belarus' road network was in need of repair.

CIVIL AVIATION

Minsk has two airports, one largely for international flights and one for domestic connections.

Belair Belarussian Airlines: Minsk; tel. (17) 222-57-02; fax (17) 222-75-09; f. 1991; operates regional and domestic charter services.

Belavia: 220004 Minsk, vul. Nemiga 14; tel. (17) 229-24-24; fax (17) 229-23-83; e-mail info@belavia.by; internet www.belavia.by; f. 1993

from former Aeroflot division of the USSR; became state national carrier in 1996; operates services in Europe and selected destinations in Asia, the CIS and the Middle East; Gen. Dir ANATOLY GUSAROV.

Gomel Air Detachment: 246011 Gomel, Gomel Airport; tel. (23) 251-14-07; fax (23) 253-14-15; f. 1944; Chief Exec. VALERY N. KULAKOUSKY.

Tourism

BELINTOURIST: 220004 Minsk, pr. Masherava 19; tel. (17) 226-98-40; fax (17) 223-11-43; e-mail office@belintourist.by; internet www.belintourist.by; f. 1992; leading tourist org. in Belarus; Dir-Gen. ULADZIMIR S. KHOMICH.

BELGIUM

Introductory Survey

Location, Climate, Language, Religion, Flag, Capital

The Kingdom of Belgium lies in north-western Europe, bounded to the north by the Netherlands, to the east by Luxembourg and Germany, to the south by France, and to the west by the North Sea. The climate is temperate. Temperatures in the capital, Brussels, are generally between 0°C (32°F) and 23°C (73°F). Flemish (closely related to Dutch), spoken in the north (Flanders), and French, spoken in the south (Wallonia), are the two main official languages. Brussels (which is situated in Flanders) has bilingual status. Nearly 60% of the population are Flemish-speaking, about 40% are French-speaking and less than 1% have German as their mother tongue. The majority of the inhabitants profess Christianity, and about four-fifths are Roman Catholics. The national flag (proportions 13 by 15) consists of three equal vertical stripes, of black, yellow and red.

Recent History

Since the Second World War, Belgium has promoted international co-operation in Europe. It is a founder member of many important international organizations, including the North Atlantic Treaty Organization (NATO, see p. 271), the Council of Europe (see p. 181), the European Union (EU, see p. 199) and the Benelux Economic Union (see p. 339).

In the latter half of the 20th century linguistic divisions were exacerbated by the political and economic polarization of Flemish-speaking Flanders in the north and francophone Wallonia in the south. The faster-growing and relatively prosperous population of Flanders has traditionally supported the conservative Flemish Christelijke Volkspartij (CVP—Christian People's Party) and the nationalist Volksunie—Vlaamse Vrije Democraten (VU—People's Union—Flemish Free Democrats), while Wallonia has traditionally been a stronghold of socialist political sympathies. Most major parties have both French and Flemish sections, as a result of a trend away from centralized administration towards greater regional control. Moderate constitutional reforms, introduced in 1971, were the first steps towards regional autonomy; in the following year further concessions were made, with the German-speaking community being represented in the Cabinet for the first time, and in 1973 linguistic parity was assured in central government. Provisional legislation, adopted in 1974, established separate Regional Councils and Ministerial Committees. The administrative status of Brussels remained contentious: the majority of the city's inhabitants are francophone, but the Flemish parties were, until the late 1980s, unwilling to grant the capital equal status with the other two regional bodies (see below).

In June 1977 the Prime Minister, Leo Tindemans, formed a coalition composed of the CVP and the francophone Parti Social Chrétien (PSC—Christian Social Party), which were collectively known as the Christian Democrats, the Socialists, the Front Démocratique des Francophones (FDF—French-speaking Democratic Front) and the VU. The Cabinet, in what became known as the Egmont Pact, proposed the abolition of the virtually defunct nine-province administration, and devolution of power from the central Government to create a federal Belgium, comprising three political and economic regions (Flanders, Wallonia and Brussels), and two linguistic communities. However, these proposals were not implemented. Tindemans resigned in October 1978 and the Minister of Defence, Paul Vanden Boeynants, was appointed Prime Minister in a transitional Government. Legislative elections in December caused little change to the distribution of seats in the Chamber of Representatives. Four successive Prime Minister-designates failed to form a new government, the main obstacle being the future status of Brussels. The six-month crisis was finally resolved when a new coalition Government was formed in April 1979 under Dr Wilfried Martens, the President of the CVP.

During 1980 the linguistic conflict worsened, sometimes involving violent incidents. Legislation was formulated, under the terms of which Flanders and Wallonia were to be administered by regional assemblies, with control of cultural matters, public health, roads, urban projects and 10% of the national budget, while Brussels was to retain its three-member executive.

Belgium suffered severe economic difficulties during the late 1970s and early 1980s, and internal disagreement over Martens' proposals for their resolution resulted in the formation of four successive coalition Governments between April 1979 and October 1980. Proposed austerity measures, including a 'freeze' on wages and reductions in public expenditure at a time of high unemployment, provoked demonstrations and lost Martens the support of the Socialist parties. Martens also encountered widespread criticism over plans to install NATO nuclear missiles in Belgium. In April 1981 a new Government was formed, comprising a coalition of the Christian Democrats and the Socialist parties and led by Mark Eyskens (of the CVP), hitherto Minister of Finance. However, lack of parliamentary support for his policies led to Eyskens' resignation in September. In December Martens formed a new centre-right Government, comprising the Christian Democrats and the two Liberal parties. In 1982 Parliament granted special powers for the implementation of economic austerity measures; these were effective until 1984, and similar powers were approved in March 1986. Opposition to reductions in public spending was vigorous, with public-sector trade unions undertaking damaging strike action throughout the 1980s.

In November 1983 the Chamber of Representatives debated the controversial proposed installation of 48 US 'cruise' nuclear missiles on Belgian territory, deferring a final decision on the issue until 1985. A series of bombings, directed against NATO-connected targets, occurred during 1984. Responsibility for the attacks was claimed by an extreme left-wing organization. In March 1985 the Chamber finally adopted a majority vote in favour of the cruise sitings, and 16 missiles were installed at Florennes. Further terrorist attacks against NATO targets were perpetrated in 1985, before a number of arrests were made. The missiles were removed in December 1988, under the terms of the Intermediate-range Nuclear Forces treaty concluded by the USA and the USSR in December 1987.

In May 1985 a riot at a football match between English and Italian clubs at the Heysel Stadium in Brussels, which resulted in 39 deaths, precipitated demands for the resignation of the Minister of the Interior, Charles-Ferdinand Nothomb, over accusations of inefficient policing. In July the resignation, in connection with the issue, of six Liberal cabinet members (including the Deputy Prime Minister, Jean Gol) led to the collapse of the coalition. Martens offered the resignation of his Government, but this was 'suspended' by King Baudouin pending a general election, which was called for October. Meanwhile, however, controversy regarding educational reform provoked a dispute between the two main linguistic groups and caused the final dissolution of Parliament in September. The general election returned the Christian Democrats-Liberal alliance to power, and in November Martens formed his sixth Cabinet.

The Government collapsed in October 1987, as a result of continuing division between the French- and Flemish-speaking parties of the coalition. At the ensuing general election in December, the CVP sustained significant losses in Flanders, while the French-speaking Parti Socialiste (PS—Socialist Party) gained seats in Wallonia, and the Socialists became the largest overall grouping in the Chamber of Representatives. No party, however, had a clear mandate for power, and negotiations for a new coalition lasted 146 days. During this time, Martens assumed a caretaker role, while a series of mediators, appointed by the King, attempted to reach a compromise. In May 1988 Martens was sworn in at the head of his eighth administration, after agreement was finally reached by the French- and Flemish-speaking wings of both the Christian Democrats and Socialist parties and by the VU.

The five-party coalition agreement committed the new Government to a programme of further austerity measures, together with tax reforms and increased federalization. In August 1988 Parliament approved the first phase of the federalization plan, intended ultimately to lead to a constitutional amendment, whereby increased autonomy would be granted to the country's Communities and Regions in several areas of jurisdiction, including education and socio-economic policy. It was also agreed that Brussels would have its own Regional Council, with an executive responsible to it, giving the city equal status with Flanders and Wallonia. In January 1989 Parliament approved the second phase of the federalization programme, allocating the public funds necessary to give effect to the regional autonomy that had been approved in principle in August 1988. The federal Constitution formally came into effect in July 1989.

A brief constitutional crisis in 1990 provoked widespread demands for a review of the powers of the Monarch, as defined by the Constitution. In March proposals for the legalization of abortion (in strictly-controlled circumstances) completed their passage through Parliament. However, King Baudouin had previously stated that his religious convictions would render him unable to give royal assent to any such legislation. A compromise solution was reached in early April, whereby Article 82 of the Constitution, which makes provision for the Monarch's 'incapacity to rule', was invoked. Baudouin thus abdicated for 36 hours, during which time the new legislation was promulgated. A joint session of Parliament was then convened to declare the resumption of Baudouin's reign. However, the incident prompted considerable alarm within Belgium: it was widely perceived as setting a dangerous precedent for the reinterpretation of the Constitution.

The Government was weakened by the resignation of both VU ministers in September 1991 and by the resultant loss of its two-thirds' parliamentary majority, necessary for the implementation of the third stage of the federalization programme. Further linguistic conflict between the remaining coalition partners led to Martens' resignation as Prime Minister in October and the subsequent collapse of the Government. However, King Baudouin rejected the resignations of Martens and the Cabinet. The Government remained in office until the next general election, which took place in November. The results of the election reflected a significant decline in popular support for all five parties represented in the outgoing Government. The Socialist parties remained the largest overall grouping in the Chamber of Representatives, although they sustained the highest combined loss of seats (nine). Following the election, the political parties conducted protracted negotiations, during which Martens' interim Cabinet continued in office. In early March 1992 four of the five parties that had composed the previous Government, the CVP, the PSC, the Socialistische Partij (SP) and the PS (which together controlled 120 seats in the 212-member Chamber of Representatives), agreed to form a new administration; a leading member of the CVP, Jean-Luc Dehaene, was appointed Prime Minister. The new Government committed itself to the completion of the constitutional reforms that had been initiated under Martens' premiership. For several months, however, the coalition partners repeatedly failed to reach agreement, both on proposals for the implementation of the third stage of the federalization programme and on amendments to the 1993 budget. A compromise on both issues was eventually reached at the end of September 1992.

In July 1992 the Chamber of Representatives voted, by 146 to 33, in favour of ratifying the Treaty on European Union, agreed by the heads of government of member states of the European Community (now EU) at Maastricht, in the Netherlands, in December 1991. The Senate approved ratification in November 1992.

In February 1993 (in accordance with the constitutional reforms agreed in September 1992) Parliament voted to amend the Constitution to create a federal state of Belgium, comprising the largely autonomous regions of Flanders, Wallonia and (bilingual) Brussels. The three regions, and the country's three linguistic groups, were to be represented by the following directly-elected administrations: a combined administration for Flanders and the Flemish-speaking community, regional administrations for Wallonia and Brussels, and separate administrations for French- and German-speakers. The regional administrations were to assume sole responsibility for the environment, housing, transport and public works, while the language community administrations were to supervise education policy and culture. Legislation to implement the reforms was enacted in July 1993.

In July 1993 King Baudouin died; he was succeeded by his brother, hitherto Prince Albert of Liège, in August.

In January 1994 three government ministers who were members of the PS (including a Deputy Prime Minister, Guy Coëme)

resigned from their posts, following allegations that they had been involved in a bribery scandal concerning the apparently illegal receipt by the SP (the Flemish section of the party) of a substantial sum of money in connection with the award, in 1988, of a defence contract to an Italian helicopter company. The PS (the Walloon section of the party) was subsequently implicated in a similar scandal involving a French aviation company. In April 1996 Coëme and seven others were found guilty of fraud and abuse of public office; Coëme, who received a two-year suspended prison sentence, subsequently resigned from the Chamber of Representatives. The scandal also led to the suicide in March 1995 of a retired Chief of Staff of the Air Force, the resignation in the same month of Frank Vandenbroucke, a Deputy Prime Minister and the Minister of Foreign Affairs, (who claimed that he had participated unwittingly in the affair) and the resignation of Willy Claes, a prominent SP official and former Deputy Prime Minister and Minister of Foreign Affairs, as Secretary-General of NATO, and his eventual conviction in February 1999 on charges of corruption, fraud and forgery; he received a three-year suspended prison sentence.

At a general election held in May 1995 the ruling centre-left coalition retained significant support, securing a total of 82 seats in the Chamber of Representatives (membership of which had been reduced from 208 to 150), despite the ongoing investigation into allegedly illegal activities by officials of the two Socialist parties. The performance of the extreme right-wing Vlaams Blok (Flemish Bloc) was not as strong as had been anticipated (the party having performed well in the mid-1994 elections to the European Parliament): although the Vlaams Blok won nearly 28% of the votes cast in Antwerp, Belgium's second largest city, it received only 12% of the votes overall in Flanders. Elections to the regional assemblies took place concurrently with the national legislative elections. Following an unusually short period of negotiations, the CVP-PSC-PS-SP coalition was reformed and in mid-June a new Cabinet was appointed, with Dehaene remaining as Prime Minister. The Government, which continued to be strongly committed to meeting the economic targets for future European economic and monetary union, introduced several strict economic austerity measures in late 1995; public-sector trade unions responded by organizing protest strike action. In April 1996 the Government, employers and trade unions agreed measures that aimed to reduce the high level of unemployment. The agreement was, however, short-lived, owing to the subsequent withdrawal of one of the main trade unions, on the grounds that the proposals for job creation were not sufficiently detailed. In the following month Parliament granted the Dehaene administration special emergency powers to implement economic austerity measures by decree.

The latter half of 1996 was dominated by extreme public concern over allegations of endemic official corruption, following the discovery, in August, of an international paedophile network based in Belgium, and subsequent widespread speculation (fuelled by the arrests in early September of several police-officers) that this had received protection from the police force and from senior figures in the judicial and political establishment, who were allegedly implicated in the activities of organized crime syndicates. During September King Albert promised a thorough investigation of the network and, in an unprecedented gesture, demanded a review of the judicial system. In October, however, allegations of a judicial and political conspiracy to impede the progress of the investigation were prompted by the removal from the case of Jean-Marc Connerotte, a widely-respected senior investigating judge. The prevailing mood of national crisis was heightened by the arrests, during September, of Alain van der Biest of the PS (a former federal Minister of Pensions) and four others, on charges connected with the assassination in 1991 of a former Deputy Prime Minister, André Cools. It was alleged that PS colleagues had ordered Cools' murder, in order to prevent him from disclosing corruption within the party. In June 1998 a Tunisian court found two Tunisian citizens guilty of the murder; however, the background to the assassination remained unclear. Although the motive remained elusive, in December 2001 van der Biest, in addition to eight members of his entourage, was charged with murder for his part in the killing; his trial was expected to take place in 2003.

Meanwhile, in March 1997 Guy Spitaels (a former Deputy Prime Minister and an erstwhile President of the PS), having resigned in the previous month as President of the Walloon regional assembly, was indicted on bribery charges relating to the political scandals of 1994–95 (see above). In April 1997 a parliamentary committee, which had been established in October 1996 to investigate allegations of official corruption and mismanagement, issued a report that claimed that rivalry between the country's various police and judicial divisions often prevented their effective co-operation; it recommended the establishment of a single integrated national police force. However, the committee found little evidence that paedophile networks had received official protection. In February 1998 the Government announced that, in place of the recommended integrated national police force, efforts would be made to facilitate 'voluntary co-operation contracts' between the various law enforcement services.

In April 1998 Marc Dutroux, a convicted paedophile whose arrest in August 1996 on charges of child kidnapping and murder had prompted the ongoing scrutiny of Belgium's national institutions, briefly escaped from police custody. (In June 2000 Dutroux was sentenced to five years' imprisonment for his escape, but had not yet been tried for his role in the murder of at least two children.) The incident incited renewed public anger and precipitated the resignations of several high-ranking figures, including the commander of the national gendarmerie and the Ministers of the Interior and of Justice. A proposed vote of 'no confidence' in the Dehaene Government, also ensuing from Dutroux's escape, was defeated in the Chamber of Representatives. Dehaene immediately reaffirmed his commitment to restructuring the police and judiciary. However, in May 2002, the parents of one of Dutroux's alleged child victims declared a lack of confidence in the competence of the authorities and withdrew from the criminal investigation. Their principal complaint was the alleged obstruction of attempts to broaden the inquiry to include an investigation into allegations of Dutroux's involvement in a potential paedophile network that extended into the political and judicial establishment. The police completed their inquiry in August but it appeared unlikely that the trial of Dutroux would begin until the third quarter of 2003.

In mid-June 1998 a reorganization of the Cabinet included the appointment of a new (Socialist) Minister of Finance. In late September Louis Tobback, who had been appointed Deputy Prime Minister and Minister of the Interior in April, resigned, following protests at the death of a Nigerian woman during an attempt forcibly to deport her from Belgium. Two police-officers were subsequently charged with involuntary manslaughter, and the Government suspended the forced repatriation of asylum-seekers, pending further investigations.

Preparations for the general election scheduled to be held in mid-June 1999 were overshadowed by the public announcement in late May that animal feed contaminated with industrial oil containing dioxin (a carcinogenic chemical) had been supplied to farms throughout Belgium from a factory near Ghent. Following the announcement, many Belgian food products, particularly poultry and egg-based products, were withdrawn from sale in Belgium and elsewhere in Europe, while production was suspended at farms across Belgium. There was widespread public anger that, although veterinary inspectors had identified a problem as early as mid-March, it was not until May that the Ministry of Agriculture had suspended sales from the affected animal-feed suppliers, and had informed government officials in neighbouring countries. On 1 June Karel Pinxten, the Minister of Agriculture and Small and Medium-sized Enterprises, and Marcel Colla, the Minister of Consumer Affairs, Public Health and the Environment, who had been jointly blamed for the delay in informing the public of the contamination, resigned from their posts. In early June the EU announced that it was to demand the removal from sale, and subsequent destruction, of poultry, pork and cattle products from farms whose feed had been contaminated with dioxin. The Belgian Government subsequently introduced a total ban on the slaughter and transportation of all poultry, cattle and pigs until it could confirm which farms had received the affected feed. On 7 June Dehaene took the unprecedented step of halting his electoral campaign, and announced an official parliamentary inquiry into the contamination. On 10 June, in an apparent attempt to assuage farmers who were losing large amounts of income on a daily basis and demanding compensation, the Government announced that slaughtering and exports could resume at farms that had not received the contaminated feed, despite the lack of a definitive list of dioxin-free farms. This relaxation of the temporary ban on production contravened the advice of the European Commission, which had recommended that the ban should remain in place while there continued to be uncertainty

about which farms had received the contaminated feed. It was alleged that the Government had believed that, for political reasons, it could not wait for the convening of the Commission's scientific and veterinary committee, whose meeting was scheduled to take place after the Belgian general election. Confusion, however, remained within Belgium as to the identification of the affected farms, and Belgian farmers blocked the roads into the country from France and the Netherlands, in an attempt to prevent agricultural imports. The Commission later announced that it was to initiate legal proceedings against the Belgian Government over its handling of the crisis, which had led to imports of European food products being banned by many non-European countries (including the USA). The Commission announced in June 2001 that it had dropped legal action against Belgium.

At the general election, which was held on 13 June 1999, the Christian Democrats suffered heavy losses, mainly at the hands of the Liberals and the ecologist parties. The Vlaams Blok also showed significant gains, winning more than 10% of the vote in many areas. The Vlaamse Liberalen en Demokraten—Partij van de Burger (VLD—Flemish Liberals and Democrats—Citizens' Party) emerged as the largest single party, with 23 seats in the 150-member Chamber of Representatives (having received 14.3% of the total votes cast), while the ecologist parties, Anders Gaan Leven (Agalev) and the Ecologistes Confédérés pour l'Organisation des Luttes Originales (Ecolo), almost doubled their representation, to 20 seats (with 14.4%), and the Vlaams Blok became the fifth largest party in the lower house, with 15 seats (9.9%). The CVP secured 22 seats (14.1% of the total votes) and the PSC won 10 seats (5.9%), while the Socialist parties obtained a combined total of 33 seats (19.8%). The VLD also performed well in the elections to the Senate, which (together with elections to the assemblies for the regions and linguistic communities) were held on the same day as the elections to the Chamber of Representatives; the VLD won the largest number of votes in the polling for the 40 directly-elective seats in the upper house (with 15.4% of the total votes). The defeat of the outgoing coalition in the general election was largely attributed to public anger at the authorities' perceived incompetence in their response to the dioxin scandal (which compounded general disquiet over the earlier corruption and paedophile scandals). Dehaene, who had held the premiership for eight years, tendered his resignation on 14 June and announced that he was considering leaving national politics. On 23 June the King asked the President of the VLD, Guy Verhofstadt, to form a new government. Following intensive negotiations, a new six-party coalition Government, comprising the VLD, the francophone Parti Réformateur Libéral (PRL), the two Socialist parties and the two ecologist parties, was sworn in on 12 July. The new administration was of historic note in that it was the first Belgian Government in 40 years not to include the Christian Democrats, the first to include the ecologist parties, and the first to be headed by a Liberal Prime Minister since 1884. Reflecting the right-wing programme of the Liberal parties, the new Government promised to reduce the social charges payable by employers and to reduce levels of public debt through the privatization of state assets. It also committed itself to the gradual abandonment of nuclear power (prompted by the greatly strengthened ecologist lobby), the further liberalization of the electricity sector and greater investment in the railway network. In response to the scandals that beset the previous Government, the new administration also planned to restructure Belgium's inefficient bureaucracy, making it more accountable to the public (and ending the practice of political appointments), to reform the police service and ease the tension between the Flemish and Walloon regions by granting them greater fiscal autonomy, with limited discretion to raise or lower local taxes.

Despite demonstrations staged by farmers (many of whom were reportedly on the brink of bankruptcy) in late June and in early July 1999, in protest at the authorities' handling of the dioxin crisis, the new Government announced that it was to add a further 400 farms to the list of 800 already forbidden to sell their produce. The Government also announced that it was to buy back and destroy some 80,000 metric tons of pork. In early August, in response to recommendations made by scientific advisers from the European Commission, the Belgian Government agreed to add beef to the list of livestock exports that were banned until definitively cleared of contamination. A few days later the Government promulgated a decree banning the export of food products containing more than 2% animal fat (except dairy products) that did not have a certificate guaranteeing their safety. Although the Minister of Consumer Affairs, Public Health and the Environment described the decree as unnecessarily harsh, representatives of the agricultural industry subsequently persuaded her that stringent procedures were required in order to regain consumer confidence and to avoid the imposition of a total ban on all Belgian agricultural exports by the EU. The Government, none the less, announced that, while it would comply with EU directives, it would mount a legal challenge in the hope of reducing their severity.

In October 1999 the Government announced that legislation was to be introduced, aimed at reforming the procedure of applying for asylum. The new procedure was to take no longer than one month, including the appeals process, and those applicants not granted asylum were to be repatriated without delay. The Government also announced that all outstanding asylum applications would be processed within one year. In a temporary amnesty in January 2000 asylum-seekers resident in Belgium for five years and illegal immigrants resident in Belgium for six years were granted legal status. In November, in an attempt to address the growing number of asylum-seekers (which had increased from 35,778 in 1999 to more than 40,000 in 2000, many of whom were from Eastern Europe), the Government proposed the introduction of border controls to slow down the inflow of immigrants and an accelerated procedure for deporting those whose claims were without foundation.

The general popularity of the new Government was slightly undermined by the results of the local elections that took place in early October 2000. Although the government parties performed well, their achievements were overshadowed by the success of the Vlaams Blok, which had campaigned against immigration and in favour of independence for Flanders. The Vlaams Blok made significant advances in Flanders, particularly in Antwerp where it won 33% of the votes cast, securing 20 of the 55 seats on Antwerp's municipal council. It also performed well in Ghent and Mechelen, and most surprisingly in Brussels, where its share of the vote doubled, to about 9%, in several districts, compared with the previous election. The Vlaams Blok remained unrepresented in any municipal government, owing to the refusal of any other party to co-operate with the group, but there were fears nevertheless that its extremist positions were altering political debate in Belgium. In September 2002 the Court of Appeal ruled that two human rights groups could begin legal proceedings seeking the dissolution of the Vlaams Blok, on the grounds that its xenophobic and racist views were in contravention of equal rights legislation.

In January 2001 the federal Cabinet approved a directive for the decriminalization, subject to parliamentary approval, of cannabis. The following October, the Senate approved legislation which enabled the legalization of euthanasia. In May 2002, the Chamber of Representatives endorsed a law which permitted adult patients suffering extreme physical or psychological pain resulting from an accident or terminal illness, to seek the right to die. Despite opposition from the Roman Catholic Church, the law was promulgated in September. Legislation providing for marriage between homosexual couples was approved by the Senate in November and by the Chamber of Representatives in January 2003; it was due to enter into force in May.

In mid-August 2002 an agreement secured by the Minister of Foreign Affairs, Louis Michel, for the supply of 5,500 automatic rifles to the Government of Nepal caused divisions within the coalition Government. While Michel maintained that the sale would help the Nepalese administration counter Maoist rebel attempts to establish a communist dictatorship in the country, opponents led by Agalev claimed that the deal broke EU directives against the sale of weapons to countries engaged in civil war. On 26 August the Agalev Minister of Consumer Affairs, Health, and the Environment, Magda Aelvoet, resigned in protest at the deal; she was replaced by fellow Agalev member, Jef Tavernier. On 31 August the Government won a parliamentary vote of confidence by 87 votes to 38, although Verhofstadt was obliged to accede to a number of minor concessions concerning the deal to secure the support of all the coalition partners. The first consignment of weapons arrived in Nepal in January 2003.

In late November 2002 the murder of a man of Moroccan origin, allegedly by a white man, provoked rioting in Antwerp; police arrested some 160 people of North African origin in the city. Among the detainees was Abu Jahjah, the leader of an Arab militant group, the Arab European League (AEL). Originally from Lebanon, Jahjah had previously fought for the Islamist extremist group, Hezbollah (Party of God) and rejected the assimilation of Arabs into Belgian society, demanding separate schools and the creation of self-governing Arab areas. He was subsequently charged with conspiracy to foment disorder. A week before the rioting began, members of the AEL had been pursuing police with video recorders to compile evidence of what they claimed was racist behaviour by the authorities. The Vlaams Blok demanded that organization be banned. Also in November a member of the Islamist Al-Qa'eda terrorist group confessed that he had planned to attack a US air force installation in eastern Belgium, which was believed to contain nuclear warheads.

In December 2002 the Chamber of Representatives voted to close all seven nuclear power plants, which supplied about 57.8% of Belgian electricity requirements in 2001) by 2025. The legislation, which provided incentives for the use of altenative energy sources, was expected to be endorsed by the Senate.

In January 2003 Verhofstadt announced that a general election would take place a month earlier than scheduled, on 18 May. Verhofstadt was obliged to reorganize the Cabinet in early May, following the withdrawal from the six-party coalition Government of Ecolo. The Deputy Prime Minister and Minister of Mobility and Transport, Isabelle Durant, and the State Secretary for Energy and Sustainable Development, Olivier Deleuze, resigned after Durant had been deprived of responsibility for the transport portfolio following her refusal to implement a recently negotiated compromise on night flights over Brussels. The dispute over flight routes reflected Belgium's language divide as the proposed route change would affect the predominantly French-speaking population of the city whereas the previous arrangement caused greater disturbance to the Flemish-speaking residents. (Durant and Deleuze represented the French-speaking Ecolo, whereas Verhofstadt's VLD was Flemish-speaking.) The transport portfolio was allocated to the PS Deputy Prime Minister and Minister of Employment, Laurette Onkelinx, while responsibility for energy and sustainable development was awarded to a PRL government official, Alain Zenner.

Belgium's international profile was raised in 2003 by its Government's public opposition to the USA's policy of a preemptive military attack against Iraq, owing to its alleged failure to disarm in compliance with a resolution by the UN. The Belgian position, which was shared by the French and German Governments, also created a crisis in NATO as the three countries used their veto to reject US-supported defensive aid to Turkey in preparation for a potential war with Iraq. France, Germany and Belgium argued that the timing was inappropriate and that military planning by NATO would undermine continuing diplomatic attempts to prevent a war with Iraq. While opposition from Germany and France was successfully circumvented, the Belgian Government, which was under considerable pressure from domestic anti-war public opinion prior to a general election (which had been scheduled for 18 May), remained isolated. The issue was resolved by the inclusion of Belgian amendments to the agreement to provide military aid to Turkey, notably the addition of an explicit reference to the framework of the UN for the peaceful solution of the crisis.

From late 1988 Belgium's hitherto cordial relations with its former colonies underwent considerable strain. Proposals that Prime Minister Martens made in November 1988 regarding the relief of public and commercial debts owed to Belgium by Zaire (formerly the Belgian Congo, renamed the Democratic Republic of the Congo—DRC— in 1997) provoked allegations in the Belgian press of corruption within the Zairean Government and of the misappropriation of development aid. President Mobutu Sese Seko of Zaire responded by ordering the withdrawal of all Zairean state-owned businesses from Belgium and by demanding that all Zairean nationals resident in Belgium remove their assets from, and leave, their host country. In July 1989 the situation was apparently resolved following meetings between Martens and Mobutu, at which a new debt-servicing agreement was signed. However, relations again deteriorated when, in May 1990, the Mobutu regime refused to accede to demands for an international inquiry into the alleged massacre of as many as 150 students by the Zairean security forces. Mobutu accused Belgium of interfering in his country's internal affairs, and ordered the expulsion from Zaire of some 700 Belgian technical workers, together with the closure of three of Belgium's four consular offices. Following the collapse of public order in Zaire in September 1991, the Belgian Government dispatched 1,000 troops to Zaire for the protection of the estimated 11,000 Belgian nationals resident there. By the end of 1991 all the troops had been withdrawn and about 8,000 Belgian nationals had been evacuated. Prospects for the normalization of relations improved following the establishment of a transitional Government in Zaire in July 1992 and the removal of Zairean sanctions against Belgium. Relations deteriorated again, however, in January 1993, when, in response to rioting by troops loyal to President Mobutu, Belgium dispatched 520 troops to evacuate the remaining 3,000 Belgian nationals in Zaire. In October 1994 the Belgian Government pledged to resume humanitarian aid to Zaire. In August 1997, following the deposition of Mobutu's regime in May by the forces of Laurent-Désiré Kabila, it was announced that normal relations between Belgium and the DRC (as Zaire was now renamed) would be gradually restored. In October 1999 a high-level Belgian delegation visited the capital of the DRC, Kinshasa, to express the willingness of the Belgian Government to mediate in the ongoing crisis in the troubled African state.

In October 1990 the Martens Government dispatched 600 troops to protect some 1,600 Belgian nationals resident in Rwanda (part of the former Belgian territory of Ruanda-Urundi), when exiled opponents of the incumbent regime invaded that country. The Belgian Government insisted that the deployment was a purely humanitarian action, and stated that it would not agree to a request from the Rwandan Government for military assistance, citing unacceptable violations of human rights by the authorities. In late October a cease-fire agreement came into effect, and in early November Belgian forces were withdrawn from Rwanda. Nevertheless, the conflict in Rwanda continued during 1991–94. Following the signing of a peace accord in August 1993, some 420 Belgian troops were redeployed as part of a UN peace-keeping force; this was, however, unable to prevent an outbreak of extreme violence, beginning in April 1994, which resulted in the deaths of many hundreds of thousands of people. Following the execution of 10 Belgian troops in April, the Belgian Government withdrew its peace-keeping contingent. It also dispatched some 800 paratroopers to Rwanda to co-ordinate the evacuation of the estimated 1,500 Belgian expatriates remaining in the country, as well as other foreign nationals. In October 1998 three Belgian army officers were demoted, having been found negligent in not preventing the 10 troop fatalities in April 1994.

The election of a new Government in Belgium in June 1999 led to an improvement in relations between Belgium and the DRC. The new Belgian Minister of Foreign Affairs, Louis Michel, was determined to develop a new strategy towards the central African countries with which Belgium has historical ties. Following the assassination of the DRC's President Kabila in January 2001, the Belgian Government intensified its attempts to relaunch the peace initiative in the region. During a visit to Belgium by the new DRC President, Kabila's son, Joseph, as part of a tour to meet those instrumental in the DRC peace efforts, the Belgian Prime Minister urged Kabila to commit to peace negotiations under the auspices of the UN. Michel also aimed to add an 'ethical' dimension to Belgian foreign policy. Initiatives that reflected this new approach included Belgium's leading role, together with France, in demanding that the EU suspend bilateral ties with Austria following the latter's inclusion of the far-right Freiheitliche Partei Österreichs (Freedom Party) in the government coalition; efforts to have the former Chilean dictator, Gen. Augusto Pinochet, extradited from the United Kingdom to stand trial for human rights abuses; and an apology for Belgium's role in the Rwandan genocide (see above) and the provision of funding in Rwanda for an AIDS control programme. Moreover, in February 2002 Belgium apologized for its role in the murder of the Belgian Congo's first Prime Minister, Patrice Lumumba, in 1961. Although a report had found no direct link between the killing and the Belgian Government, it did conclude that ministers at the time bore a 'moral responsibility' by failing to prevent it. In July 2002 the state-funded Royal Museum for Central Africa announced that it had commissioned a review of Belgium's colonial past. This followed allegations by a US author, Adam Hochschild, in his book published in translation in Belgium in 1999, that 10m. Congolese had been killed as a result of policies adopted during the colonial rule of King Leopold II (1885–1908). The investigators were expected to present their findings in 2004.

In 2000 Belgium was criticized in a UN report on sanctions against diamonds used to fund anti-Government rebels in Angola for 'extremely lax controls and regulations governing the Antwerp market'. The new Government protested, however,

that it had already agreed a certification scheme with Angola to ensure that it did not sell diamonds from rebel-held areas.

In June 2001 a Belgian court convicted four Rwandan nationals of war crimes for their role in the ethnic violence in Rwanda in 1994. The case was the first to be successfully conducted under legislation introduced in 1993, which endowed Belgian courts with universal jurisdiction in human rights cases. (Three of the four subsequently filed an appeal against their convictions.) In February 2002, however, the International Court of Justice ruled that Belgium did not have the right to try suspects who were protected by diplomatic immunity. In mid-May 2002, the final hearing began in a Belgian appeals court for a case brought against the Israeli Prime Minister, Ariel Sharon, for war crimes allegedly committed against Palestinian refugees in 1982, when he was the Israeli Minister of Defence. However, in June judges ruled that the case could not be brought to trial since according to the Belgian criminal code, alleged crimes committed outside the country required subjects to be on Belgian territory to be investigated and tried. Another human rights case against President Laurent Gbagbo of Côte d'Ivoire was similarly dismissed. In early February, however, the Supreme Court reversed the earlier ruling but recognized Sharon's diplomatic immunity so that proceedings against him were inadmissible whilst he remained the Israeli premier. However, the court ruled that proceedings against members of the Israeli defence forces, who served as senior commanders during the conflict in Lebanon, could begin. Israel responded by recalling its ambassador from Belgium.

Government

Belgium is a constitutional and hereditary monarchy, consisting of a federation of the largely autonomous regions of Brussels, Flanders and Wallonia and of the Flemish-, French- and German-speaking language communities. The central legislature consists of a bicameral Parliament (the Chamber of Representatives and the Senate). The Chamber has 150 members, all directly elected for a term of four years by universal adult suffrage, on the basis of proportional representation. The Senate has 71 normal members, of whom 40 are directly elected at intervals of four years, also by universal suffrage on the basis of proportional representation, 21 are appointed by the legislative bodies of the three language communities (see below), and 10 are co-opted by the elected members. In addition, children of the King are entitled to honorary membership of the Senate from 18 years of age and acquire voting rights at the age of 21. Members of both Houses serve for up to four years. Executive power, nominally vested in the King, is exercised by the Cabinet. The King appoints the Prime Minister and, on the latter's advice, other Ministers. The Cabinet is responsible to the Chamber of Representatives. The three regions and three linguistic communities are represented by the following directly-elected legislative administrations: a combined administration for Flanders and the Flemish-speaking community, regional administrations for Wallonia and Brussels, and separate administrations for French- and German-speakers. The regional administrations have sole responsibility for the environment, housing, transport and public works, while the language community administrations supervise education policy and culture. Under a constitutional amendment approved by the Chamber of Representatives in June 2001, the regions were also granted greater autonomy over taxation and public expenditure, agriculture, and policies regarding foreign aid and trade. In April 2002 a further set of reforms was agreed in principle. It was proposed that the Senate would become the assembly of the regions and communities and the Chamber of Representatives the sole federal representative body.

Defence

Belgium is a member of NATO. In August 2002 the total strength of the armed forces was 39,260 (including 1,860 in the Medical Service), comprising an army of 26,400, a navy of 2,400 and an air force of 8,600. The defence budget for 2002 was estimated at €5.2m. Compulsory military service was abolished in 1995. In 1996 the Belgian and Netherlands navies came under a joint operational command, based at Den Helder, the Netherlands. In November 2000 Belgium committed 1,000 troops to a proposed joint EU rapid reaction force, which was to be ready and able to be deployed by 2003.

Economic Affairs

In 2001, according to estimates by the World Bank, Belgium's gross national income (GNI), measured at average 1999–2001 prices, was US $239,779m., equivalent to $23,340 per head (or $28,210 per head on an international purchasing-power parity basis). During 1990–2001, it was estimated, the population increased at an average annual rate of 0.3% per year, while gross domestic product (GDP) per head increased, in real terms, by an average of 1.7% per year. Overall GDP increased, in real terms, at an average annual rate of 2.0% during 1990–2001; it rose by 3.7% in 2000 and by 0.8% in 2001.

Agriculture (including hunting, forestry and fishing) contributed 1.4% of GDP in 2000 and engaged 0.8% of the employed labour force in 2001. The principal agricultural products are sugar beet, cereals and potatoes. Pig meat, beef and dairy products are also important. Exports of live animals and animal and vegetable products accounted for 5.7% of Belgium's total export revenue in 1998, and for 5.2% in 1999, despite the adverse effects of the dioxin contamination scandal (see Recent History). According to World Bank estimates, agricultural GDP increased, in real terms, at an average annual rate of 3.9% in 1990–2000; it increased by 11.3% in 1999 before declining by 1.0% the following year.

Industry (including mining and quarrying, manufacturing, power and construction) contributed 26.6% of GDP and engaged 24.3% of the employed labour force in 2001. According to World Bank estimates, real industrial GDP increased at an average rate of 1.6% per year in 1990–2000; it rose by 2.2% in 1999 and by 3.9% in 2000.

Belgium has few mineral resources, and the country's last coal mine closed in 1992. In 2000 extractive activities accounted for only 0.2% of GDP and engaged only 0.1% of the employed labour force in 2001. Belgium is, however, an important producer of copper, zinc and aluminium, smelted from imported ores. The sector's GDP declined at an average rate of 2.5% per year during 1995–99. It declined by 3.1% in 1998, but increased by 0.7% in 1999.

Manufacturing contributed 18.9% of GDP in 2000 and engaged 17.9% of the employed labour force in 2001. In 2001 the main branches of manufacturing, in terms of value added, were chemicals, chemical products and man-made fibres (accounting for 20.0% of the total), basic metals and fabricated metal products (13.6%) and food products (13.1%). According to World Bank estimates, during 1995–99 manufacturing GDP increased at an average annual rate of 3.1%; it rose by 1.4% in 1998 and by 1.2% in 1999.

Belgium's seven nuclear reactors accounted for 57.8% of total electricity generation in 2001 (one of the highest levels in the world). Coal-fired and natural gas power stations produced 40.0% of Belgium's total electricity output in the same year. The country's dependence on imported petroleum and natural gas has increased since 1988, following the announcement by the Government in that year of the indefinite suspension of its nuclear programme and of the construction of a gas-powered generator. In December 2002 a bill was approved by the Chamber of Representatives to phase out the use of nuclear power by 2025, with the first nuclear power station scheduled to be closed in 2015. Imports of mineral fuels comprised an estimated 8.6% of the value of Belgium's total imports in 2001.

The services sector contributed 72.0% of GDP in 2000 and engaged 74.9% of the employed labour force in 2001. The presence in Belgium of the offices of many international organizations and businesses is a significant source of revenue. In September 2000 Euronext was formed from the merger of the stock exchanges of Brussels (Brussels Exchanges), Amsterdam (Amsterdam Exchanges) and Paris (Paris Bourse). According to World Bank estimates, the GDP of the services sector increased at an average annual rate of 2.0% in 1990–2000; it increased by 2.2% in 1999 and by 4.4% in 2000. Tourism is an expanding industry in Belgium, and in 2001 an estimated 6.5m. foreign tourists visited the country. Tourism receipts totalled US $7,039m. in 1999 (including receipts from Luxembourg).

In 2001 the Belgo-Luxembourg Economic Union (BLEU) recorded a visible trade surplus of US $3,668m., and there was a surplus of $13,534m. on the current account of the balance of payments. In 2001 Belgium's principal source of imports was the Netherlands (providing 17.1% of the total); other major suppliers were Germany (16.3%), France (13.5%), the United Kingdom (8.0%) and the USA (7.0%). The principal market for exports in that year was Germany (accounting for 18.1% of the total); other major purchasers were France (17.4%), the Netherlands (12.2%) and the United Kingdom (10.1%). The principal exports in 2001 were machinery and transport equipment, basic manufactures (including gem diamonds and iron and steel),

chemicals and related products, food and live animals, and miscellaneous manufactured articles. The principal imports in that year were machinery and transport equipment, basic manufactures, chemicals and related products, miscellaneous manufactured articles and food and live animals.

In 1995 there was a budget deficit of BF 259,100m., equivalent to 3.2% of GDP. By means of strict austerity measures, however, the budget deficit had decreased to 0.5% of GDP by 1999, a balanced budget was achieved in 2000 and in 2001 there was a budget surplus equivalent to 0.4% of GDP. The country's total external debt was BF 11,295,700m. in 1999, equivalent to 116.1% of GDP. The annual rate of inflation averaged 2.1% in 1990–2001. Consumer prices increased by an annual average of 2.5% in 2001 and by 1.6% in 2002. At November 2000 8.6% of the labour force were unemployed; there was, however, a discrepancy between the more affluent Flanders, where, according to national statistics, the rate of unemployment stood at 6.5% in March 2000, and Wallonia, where unemployment was 16.1%.. In 2001 the average annual unemployment rate was 10.8% of the labour force.

Belgium is a member of the European Union (EU, see p. 199), including the European Monetary System (EMS), and of the Benelux Economic Union (see p. 339). Belgium is also a member of the European System of Central Banks (ESCB), which was inaugurated in 1998 (see European Central Bank).

Belgium's economic priorities were dominated in the late 1990s by the need to reduce the large budget deficit and chronic public-sector debt in order to qualify for the final stage of economic and monetary union (EMU) within the EU. The reduction of the budget deficit to the equivalent of 0.9% of GDP and the level of public debt to 116.1% of GDP by 1999 (from 7% and 135%, respectively, in 1993) enabled Belgium to participate in the introduction of the European single currency, the euro, which came into effect on 1 January 1999 (in 11 participating countries). Despite the damage to the economy caused by the food contamination scandal in mid-1999, greater fiscal consolidation, allied to a general economic recovery in Europe, permitted the Verhofstadt Government, which acceded to power in June, to reduce the social charges payable by employers (the highest in Europe) and to inaugurate a youth employment programme. The percentage of the population in work improved from 57% in 1998 to 60% in 2001; further progress was considered essential for the long-term prospects of the economy, as social security and pension payments remained a serious burden on public finances. The privatization programme, which had partly financed Belgium's progress towards EMU membership, was to be accelerated under the new Government. However, in September 2001 the European Commission announced that it intended to indict the Belgian authorities over their failure to implement legislation to liberalize the Belgian energy sector. The Verhofstadt administration, which presided over strong growth in the economy, continued to reduce the budget deficit and public indebtedness: reducing thet deficit to only 0.1% in 2000 and achieving the first budget surplus for 50 years (of 0.4%) in 2001; while public debt was expected to fall to below 100% of GDP by the end of 2003. The government surplus was to be used to finance tax reductions (the total burden of taxation and other social contributions was 45% of GDP in 2001, one of the highest such rates in the EU), which were announced in a Fiscal Reform Plan in October 2000. The reforms which were to contribute to a 15% reduction in income tax between 2001 and 2006, included the removal of the two highest bands of taxation and plans to phase out the 3% 'crisis surcharge', which had been introduced to ensure Belgium met the criteria for monetary union. Corporate taxation reforms in 2002 included the reduction of corporate tax from 40% to 34%, with a lower rate of 25% for small and medium-sized enterprises of 25%. In June 2001 the Government also attempted to address the imbalances in the performances of the regional economies, granting greater fiscal control to the regions (long a demand of the more affluent Flanders), with the discretion to raise or lower local taxes. On 1 January 2002 euro notes and coins were introduced and on 28 February the Belgian franc ceased to be legal tender, although the currency could still be exchanged at banks. No major problems were reported regarding the adoption of the new currency, although it was widely believed that retailers had taken the opportunity to increase their prices. In September 2002 the Minister of Finance, Didier Reynders, criticized the decision of the European Commission (EC) to extend by two years to 2006 the deadline for France, Germany, Italy and Portugal to reduce their budget deficits to the amount permitted for members of the

EMU. Supported by Austria, the Netherlands and Finland, Belgium accused the EC of treating the larger countries in the EMU more favourably than the smaller ones. The Government predicted that the economy would grow by 2.1% in 2003.

Education

Legislation granting responsibility for the formulation of education policy to the administrations of the Flemish-, French- and German-speaking communities came into effect in 1993. Education may be provided by the Communities, by public authorities or by private interests. All educational establishments, whether official or 'free' (privately-organized), receive most of their funding from the Communities. Roman Catholic schools constitute the greatest number of 'free' establishments.

Full-time education in Belgium is compulsory between the ages of six and 16 years. Thereafter, pupils must remain in part-time education for a further two-year period. About 90% of infants attend state-financed nursery schools. Elementary education begins at six years of age and consists of three courses of two years each. Secondary education, beginning at the age of 12, lasts for six years and is divided into three two-year cycles or, in a few cases, two three-year cycles. According to UNESCO, enrolment at primary schools in 1999/2000 included 100% of children in the relevant age-group, while the comparable ratio at secondary schools was 95.0% (males 94.6%; females 95.5%).

The requirement for university entrance is a pass in the 'examination of maturity', taken after the completion of secondary studies. Courses are divided into 2–3 years of general preparation followed by 2–3 years of specialization. The French Community controls four universities, while the Flemish Community controls three such institutions; in addition, there are 11 university centres or faculties (six French, five Flemish). In 2000/01 a total of 116,710 students were enrolled in university-level establishments. Non-university institutions of higher education provide arts education, technical training and teacher training; in 2000/01 a total of 176,930 students were enrolled in such institutions. In 1995 enrolment at tertiary level was equivalent to 56% of those in the relevant age-group (males 55%; females 57%). A national study fund provides grants where necessary and almost 20% of students receive scholarships.

Expenditure on education by all levels of government was BF 439,608m. in 1994 (equivalent to 10.2% of total government spending).

Public Holidays

2003: 1 January (New Year's Day), 21 April (Easter Monday), 1 May (Labour Day), 29 May (Ascension Day), 9 June (Whit Monday), 11 July (Flemish-speaking Community), 21 July (Independence Day), 15 August (Assumption), 27 September (French-speaking Community), 1 November (All Saints' Day), 11 November (Armistice Day), 15 November (German-speaking Community), 25 December (Christmas Day).

2004: 1 January (New Year's Day), 12 April (Easter Monday), 1 May (Labour Day), 20 May (Ascension Day), 31 May (Whit Monday), 11 July (Flemish-speaking Community), 21 July (Independence Day), 15 August (Assumption), 27 September (French-speaking Community), 1 November (All Saints' Day), 11 November (Armistice Day), 15 November (German-speaking Community), 25 December (Christmas Day).

Weights and Measures

The metric system is in force.

Statistical Survey

Source: mainly Institut National de Statistique, 44 rue de Louvain, 1000 Brussels; tel. (2) 548-62-11; fax (2) 548-63-67; e-mail info@statbel.mineco.fgov .be; internet www.statbel.fgov.be.

Area and Population

AREA, POPULATION AND DENSITY

Area (sq km)	30,528*
Population (census results)†	
1 March 1981	9,848,647
1 March 1991	
Males	4,875,982
Females.	5,102,699
Total	9,978,681
Population (official estimates at 1 January)†	
2000	10,239,085
2001	10,263,414
2002	10,309,725
Density (per sq km) at 1 January 2002	337.7

* 11,787 sq miles.

† Population is *de jure*.

PROVINCES
(1 January 2002)

	Area (sq km)	Population	Density (per sq km)	Capital (with population)
Flemish region . .	13,521	5,952,781	440.3	
Antwerp . . .	2,867	1,6652,450	576.4	Antwerp (448,709)*
Brabant (Flemish) .	2,106	1,022,821	485.7	Leuven (89,152)
Flanders (East) .	2,982	1,366,652	458.3	Ghent (226,220)
Flanders (West) .	3,144	1,132,275	360.1	Brugge (116,836)
Limburg . . .	2,422	798,583	329.7	Hasselt (68,771)
Walloon region . .	16,845	3,358,560	199.4	
Brabant (Walloon) .	1,091	355,297	325.7	Wavre (31,526)
Hainaut. . . .	3,786	1,281,042	338.4	Mons (90,953)
Liège . . .	3,862	1,020,130	264.1	Liège (185,131)
Luxembourg . .	4,440	250,406	56.4	Arlon (25,261)
Namur . . .	3,666	447, 775	122.1	Namur (105,393)
Brussels (capital) .	162	978,384	6,039.4	—
Total	30,528	10,309,725	337.7	—

* Including Deurne and other suburbs.

PRINCIPAL TOWNS
(population at 1 January 2002)

Bruxelles (Brussel, Brussels—capital).	978,384*	Leuven (Louvain) .	89,152
Antwerpen (Anvers, Antwerp) . .	448,709†	Aalst (Alost) . .	76,382
Gent (Gand, Ghent) .	226,220	Mechelen (Malines) .	75,946
Charleroi . . .	200,578	Kortrijk (Courtrai) .	74,558
Liège (Luik) . .	185,131	Hasselt . . .	68,771
Brugge (Bruges) . .	116,836	Sint-Niklaas (Saint-Nicolas) . .	68,473
Namur (Namen) . .	105,393	Oostende (Ostende, Ostend) . .	67,574
Mons (Bergen) . .	90,953	Tournai (Doornik) .	67,232

* Including Schaerbeek (population 107,736), Anderlecht (90,134) and other suburbs.
† Including Deurne and other suburbs.

BIRTHS, MARRIAGES AND DEATHS

	Registered live births		Registered marriages*		Registered deaths†	
	Number	Rate (per 1,000)	Number	Rate (per 1,000)	Number	Rate (per 1,000)
1994 . .	116,449	11.5	51,962	5.1	104,894	10.4
1995 . .	115,638	11.4	51,402	5.1	105,933	10.5
1996 . .	115,214	11.3	50,552	5.0	104,140	10.3
1997 . .	115,864	11.4	47,759	4.7	103,802	10.2
1998 . .	114,276	11.2	44,393	4.4	104,583	10.3
1999 . .	113,469	11.1	44,171	4.3	104,904	10.2
2000 . .	114,883	11.2	45,123	4.4	104,903	10.2
2001 . .	114,014	11.1	42,110	4.1	103,447	10.1

* Including marriages among Belgian armed forces stationed outside the country and alien armed forces in Belgium, unless performed by local foreign authority.
† Including Belgian armed forces stationed outside the country, but excluding alien armed forces stationed in Belgium.

Expectation of life (WHO estimates, years at birth): 78.0 (males 74.8; females 81.2) in 2001 (Source: WHO, *World Health Report*).

EMPLOYMENT
(estimates, '000 persons aged 15 and over, yearly averages)

	1999	2000	2001
Agriculture, hunting and forestry	28.6	27.9	27.7
Fishing	0.8	0.7	0.7
Mining and quarrying . .	3.6	3.5	3.5
Manufacturing	618.1	621.2	622.0
Electricity, gas and water supply	27.4	26.8	26.7
Construction	181.0	185.7	189.4
Wholesale and retail trade; repair of motor vehicles, motorcycles and personal and household goods	423.7	435.2	446.3
Hotels and restaurants . .	96.9	95.9	98.5
Transport, storage and communications . . .	247.2	254.3	260.7
Financial intermediation . .	131.1	132.9	134.5
Real estate, renting and business activities	323.3	355.3	367.7
Public administration and defence; compulsory social security .	411.9	418.1	419.8
Education	333.0	334.2	333.1
Health and social work . .	309.4	322.6	345.6
Other community, social and personal service activities .	101.2	102.8	105.0
Private households with employed persons	81.5	82.9	84.4
Total in home employment . .	3318.6	3399.9	3465.7
Persons working abroad (net) .	49.0	50.1	50.0
Total employed	3367.6	3450.0	3515.7

Unemployment ('000 persons aged 15 years and over, yearly averages): 395 in 1999; 374 in 2000; 360 in 2001.

Source: Service Statistiques financières et économiques, Banque Nationale de Belgique.

Health and Welfare

KEY INDICATORS

Total fertility rate (children per woman, 2001). . . .	1.5
Under-5 mortality rate (per 1,000 live births, 2001) . .	6
HIV/AIDS (% of persons aged 15–49, 2001). . . .	0.16
Physicians (per 1,000 head, 1998)	3.95
Hospital beds (per 1,000 head, 1997)	7.2
Health expenditure (2000): US $ per head (PPP) . .	1,936
Health expenditure (2000): % of GDP	8.7
Health expenditure (2000): public (% of total) . . .	71.2
Human Development Index (2000): ranking	4
Human Development Index (2000): value	0.939

For sources and definitions, see explanatory note on p. vi.

Agriculture
(Figures include totals for Luxembourg)

PRINCIPAL CROPS
('000 metric tons)

	1999	2000	2001
Wheat and spelt	1,528	1,634	1,442
Barley	388	387	423
Maize	405	399	439
Oats	49	47	42
Triticale (wheat-rye hybrid) . .	50	76	51
Potatoes	3,007	3,033	2,497
Rapeseed*	29	34	33
Cabbages	101	143	110
Lettuce.	189	172	180
Spinach	58	124	90
Tomatoes	292	216	250†
Cauliflowers	95	126	90†
Leeks and other alliaceous vegetables	228	180	172
Beans (green).	99	153	140†
Peas (green)†	150	165	144
Carrots	150*	166	150†
Mushrooms	45	44	45†
Chicory roots	638	731	600
Other vegetables	362	393	395
Sugar beet.	7,112	5,311	5,300*
Apples	562	512	340*
Pears	165	183	90*
Strawberries	49	48†	48†
Other fruits and berries . . .	37	34	33*

* Unofficial figure(s).
† FAO estimate(s).

Source: FAO.

LIVESTOCK
('000 head, year ending September)

	1999	2000	2001
Horses*	67	75	75
Cattle	3,395	3288	3,245
Pigs	7,632	7,404	7,394
Sheep	158†	126	167
Goats	13	14	17
Rabbits*	180	180	180
Chickens	48,635	55,000*	52,000*
Ducks	35	40*	40*
Geese	10	10*	10*
Turkeys	376	250*	250*

* FAO estimate(s).
† Unofficial figure.

Source: FAO.

LIVESTOCK PRODUCTS
('000 metric tons)

	1999	2000	2001
Beef and veal	281	274	296
Mutton and lamb	5	4	5*
Pig meat	1,005	1,065	1,082
Horse meat	5	6	5†
Poultry meat	369	407	387
Other meat	26	28	27
Cows' milk	3,649	3,689	3,694
Butter	117	125	120†
Cheese	65*	59*	59
Hen eggs	226	194	184
Cattle hides*	26	25	27

* Unofficial figure(s).
† FAO estimate.

Source: FAO.

Forestry

ROUNDWOOD REMOVALS
('000 cubic metres, excluding bark)

	1999	2000	2001
Sawlogs, veneer logs and logs for sleepers	2,550	2,660	2,630
Pulpwood	1,200	1,200*	910†
Other industrial wood	100	100*	100*
Fuel wood	550	550*	550*
Total	4,400	4,510	4,190

* FAO estimate.
† Unofficial estimate.

Source: FAO.

SAWNWOOD PRODUCTION
('000 cubic metres, including railway sleepers)

	1999	2000*	2001*
Coniferous (softwood)	892	950	1,075
Broadleaved (hardwood)	164	200	225
Total	1,056	1,150	1,300

* FAO estimates.

Source: FAO.

Fishing

('000 metric tons, live weight)

	1998	1999	2000
Capture	30.8	29.9	29.8
European plaice	7.4	8.2	9.1
Common dab	1.0	1.0	0.9
Lemon sole	1.3	1.0	1.1
Common sole	4.1	4.5	4.5
Atlantic cod	6.9	4.5	3.7
Haddock	1.0	0.6	0.5
Whiting	0.9	1.1	8.2
Angler (Monk)	1.0	0.8	1.0
Rays	1.2	1.4	1.2
Common shrimp	0.4	1.1	0.6
Aquaculture	0.8	1.6	1.6
Total catch	31.7	31.5	31.4

Source: FAO, *Yearbook of Fishery Statistics*.

Mining

('000 metric tons, unless otherwise indicated)

	1996	1997	1998
Lignite	560	427	n.a.
Uranium (metric tons)	28	27	15
Kaolin*	300	300	300
Chalk	2,139	2,071	2,099
Barite (Barytes)*	30	30	40

* Estimates.

1999 (estimates, '000 metric tons): Kaolin 300; Barite (Barytes) 30; Chalk 2,096.

2000 (estimates, '000 metric tons): Kaolin 300; Barite (Barytes) 30; Chalk 1,963.

2001 (estimates, '000 metric tons): Kaolin 300; Barite (Barytes) 30.

Source: partly US Geological Survey and UN, *Industrial Commodity Statistics Yearbook*.

Industry

SELECTED PRODUCTS
('000 metric tons, unless otherwise indicated)

	1998	1999	2000
Wheat flour[1]	1,332	1,417	1,281
Raw sugar	994	926	1,070
Margarine	305.0	298.7	315.3
Beer ('000 hectolitres)	14,662.7	15,056.6	15,470.7
Cigarettes (million)	17,518.2	14,712.7	n.a.
Cotton yarn—pure and mixed (metric tons)	20,375	22,221	23,482
Woven cotton fabrics—pure and mixed (metric tons)[2]	39,347	38,093	37,317
Flax yarn (metric tons)[3]	3,027	2,867	2,697
Wool yarn—pure and mixed (metric tons)	14,889	14,434	14,959
Woven woollen fabrics—pure and mixed (metric tons)[2]	3,051	3,023	2,644
Woven rayon and acetate fabrics—pure and mixed (metric tons)[4]	173	196	196
Mechanical wood pulp[5]	207	196*	196*
Chemical and semi-chemical wood pulp[5]	225	235	235
Newsprint[5]	105	124*	124*
Other paper and paperboard[5]	1,725.5	1,603.0*	1,603.0*
Ethyl alcohol—Ethanol ('000 hectolitres)	102.4	n.a.	n.a.
Sulphuric acid (100%)	626.6	682.4	741.6
Nitric acid (100%)	55.7	56.0	55.9
Residual fuel oil	6,957.7	5,821.0	6,658.6
Petroleum bitumen (asphalt)	797.4	766.5	552.5
Coke-oven coke	3,400	3,400	3,400
Cement	9,875	9,248.7	8,600.8
Pig-iron[6]	8,619	8,431	8,472
Crude steel[6]	11,617	10,931	11,635
Refined copper—unwrought (metric tons)[7]	623,350	652,357	678,043
Refined lead—unwrought (metric tons)	111,858	125,243	156,215
Tin: secondary (metric tons)[6]	2,500	8,100	8,500
Passenger motor cars ('000)[8]	974.9	935.9	923.1
Commercial motor vehicles ('000)[8]	97.7	83.5	109.9

Liquefied petroleum gas ('000 metric tons): 605 in 1996; 578 in 1997; 598 in 1998.

Naptha ('000 metric tons): 1,148 in 1996; 1,407 in 1997; 1,524 in 1998.

Motor spirit (petrol) ('000 metric tons): 5,947 in 1996; 6,103 in 1997; 6,431 in 1998.

Kerosene ('000 metric tons): 100 in 1996; 113 in 1997; 128 in 1998.

White spirit ('000 metric tons): 112 in 1996; 164 in 1997; 157 in 1998.

Jet fuel ('000 metric tons): 1,739 in 1996; 1,644 in 1997; 2,067 in 1998.

Distillate fuel oils ('000 metric tons): 12,619 in 1996; 12,250 in 1997; 12,447 in 1998.

Electric energy (million kWh): 76,147.4 in 1996; 78,891.7 in 1997; 79,492.4 in 1998.

Manufactured gas (million cu metres): 1,510 in 1996; 1,366 in 1997; 1,334 in 1998.

[1] Industrial production only.
[2] Including blankets and carpets.
[3] Including yarn made from tow.
[4] Including fabrics of natural silk and blankets and carpets of cellulosic fibres.
[5] Data for 1998 include production in Luxembourg. Source: FAO, *Yearbook of Forest Products*.
[6] Estimated production. Source: US Geological Survey.
[7] Including alloys and the processing of refined copper imported from the Democratic Republic of the Congo.
[8] Assembled wholly or mainly from imported parts.
* Unofficial or FAO estimate.

Finance

CURRENCY AND EXCHANGE RATES

Monetary Units

100 cent = 1 euro (€)

Sterling and Dollar Equivalents (31 December 2002)

£1 sterling = 1.5366 euros
US $1 = 0.9536 euros
100 euros = £65.06 = $104.87

Average Exchange Rate (euros per US $)

2000	1.0854
2001	1.1175
2002	1.0626

Note: The national currency was formerly the Belgian franc. From the introduction of the euro, with Belgian participation, on 1 January 1999, a fixed exchange rate of €1 = 40.3399 Belgian francs was in operation. Euro notes and coins were introduced on 1 January 2002. The euro and local currency circulated alongside each other until 28 February, after which the euro became the sole legal tender. Some of the figures in this Survey are still in terms of Belgian francs.

BUDGET

('000 million Belgian francs)*

Revenue†	1996	1997	1998
Tax revenue	3,571.2	3,758.5	3,909.6
Taxes on income, profits and capital gains	1,293.0	1,382.1	1,465.0
Social security contributions . .	1,229.1	1,274.4	1,313.0
Taxes on property	102.0	115.6	135.0
Domestic taxes on goods and services	950.8	991.0	1,005.0
General sales, turnover or value-added taxes . . .	581.7	605.9	786.0
Excises	202.6	210.4	219.0
Other current revenue	95.0	57.7	64.6
Entrepreneurial and property income	52.4	28.4	21.8
Capital revenue	19.0	3.9	11.9
Total	3,685.2	3,820.1	3,896.1

Expenditure‡	1996	1997	1998
Current expenditure	3,731.7	3,839.1	3,937.4
Expenditure on goods and services	739.0	769.7	800.0
Wages and salaries . . .	527.7	543.5	558.8
Interest payments	682.7	664.5	663.8
Subsidies and other current transfers	2,310.0	2,404.9	2,473.6
Subsidies	157.7	126.2	129.0
Transfers to other levels of national government . . .	240.3	239.2	246.5
Transfers to non-profit institutions and households	1,859.7	1,979.7	2,030.9
Capital expenditure	177.8	193.2	214.9
Capital transfers	117.2	127.2	149.0
Total	3,909.5	4,032.3	4,152.3

* Figures refer to the consolidated transactions of the central Government. In addition to the general budget, the data include the operations of social security funds, government agencies and other extrabudgetary funds.
† Excluding grants received ('000 million Belgian francs): 5.0 in 1996; 20.3 in 1997; 6.8 in 1998.
‡ Excluding lending minus repayments ('000 million Belgian francs): −9.1 in 1996; −26.8 in 1997; 2.7 in 1998.

Source: IMF, *Government Finance Statistics Yearbook*.

INTERNATIONAL RESERVES

(US $ million at 31 December)*

	2000	2001	2002
Gold†‡	2,262	2,294	2,843
IMF special drawing rights . . .	307	472	554
Reserve position in IMF . . .	1,699	2,051	2,392
Foreign exchange‡	8,298	8,297	8,294
Total	12,566	13,114	14,083

* From January 1999 figures were adjusted to accord with the Euro-system's definition of reserves.
† Valued at market-related prices.
‡ Figures for gold and foreign exchange refer to the monetary association between Belgium and Luxembourg and exclude deposits made with the European Monetary Institute (now the European Central Bank).

Source: IMF, *International Financial Statistics*.

MONEY SUPPLY

(million euros at 31 December)

	2000	2001	2002
Currency outside banks	13,496	9,081	12,715*
Demand deposits at commercial banks	58,499	61,397	62,294

* Currency put into circulation by the Banque Nationale de Belgique was 7,888 million euros.

Source: IMF, *International Financial Statistics*.

COST OF LIVING

(Consumer Price Index; base: 1990 = 100)

	1999	2000	2001
Food (incl. beverages) . . .	109.3	110.2	114.9
Fuel and light	106.7	118.9	122.3
Clothing (incl. footwear) . . .	116.5	117.2	118.3
Rent	132.0	133.9	136.5
All items (incl. others) . . .	119.5	122.5	125.6

All items (base: 1995=100): 108.6 in 2000; 111.3 in 2001; 113.1 in 2002 (Source: IMF, *International Financial Statistics*).

NATIONAL ACCOUNTS

National Income and Product
(million euros at current prices)

	1999	2000	2001
Compensation of employees. . .	121,294.4	126,847.0	133,381.1
Operating surplus	52,032.1	54,454.5	52,803.4
Domestic factor incomes. .	173,326.5	181,301.5	186,184.5
Consumption of fixed capital . .	33,428.9	35,815.8	38,240.1
Gross domestic product (GDP)			
at factor cost	206,755.4	217,117.3	224,424.6
Indirect taxes.	33,191.0	34,767.2	34,592.0
Less Subsidies	4,314.4	4,415.7	4,734.2
GDP in purchasers' values . .	235,632.0	247,468.8	254,282.4
Factor income received from abroad	30,060.5	34,241.8	40,027.6
Less Factor income paid abroad	24,037.3	27,374.2	33,697.9
Subsidies received from abroad . .	857.6	694.2	733.6
Less Indirect taxes paid abroad	2,186.2	2,395.1	2,476.5
Gross national product (GNP) .	240,326.6	252,635.5	258,869.2
Less Consumption of fixed capital .	33,428.9	35,815.8	38,240.1
National income in market			
prices	206,897.8	216,819.7	220,629.1
Other current transfers from			
abroad	3,071.4	3,344.0	3,631.8
Less Other current transfers paid			
abroad	5,529.5	5,660.0	5,801.3
National disposable income. .	204,439.6	214,503.7	218,459.6

Source: Service Statistiques financières et économiques, Banque Nationale de Belgique.

Expenditure on the Gross Domestic Product
(million euros at current prices)

	1999	2000	2001
Government final consumption			
expenditure.	49,957	52,362	55,103
Private final consumption			
expenditure.	126,608	133,834	138,457
Increase in stocks	−568	944	−1,132
Gross fixed capital formation . .	49,308	52,377	52,897
Total domestic expenditure. .	225,305	239,517	245,325
Exports of goods and services . .	178,290	211,594	217,055
Less Imports of goods and services	167,963	203,642	208,096
GDP in purchasers' values . .	235,632	247,469	254,282
GDP at constant 1995 prices .	223,124	231,433	233,216

Source: Service Statistiques financières et économiques, Banque Nationale de Belgique.

Gross Domestic Product by Economic Activity
(million euros at current prices)

	1999	2000	2001
Agriculture, hunting and forestry .	2,826.7	3,082.0	3,354.4
Fishing	59.8	52.4	59.4
Mining and quarrying	337.2	350.2	346.8
Manufacturing	41,437.8	43,400.9	43,174.2
Electricity, gas and water supply .	5,859.0	5,997.4	5,942.3
Construction	10,794.3	11,501.6	11,879.8
Wholesale and retail trade; repair			
of motor vehicles, motorcycles			
and personal and household			
goods	25,538.8	26,222.3	27,617.2
Hotels and restaurants	3,519.8	3,789.3	3,867.0
Transport, storage and			
communications	15,021.7	15,568.7	16,307.3
Financial intermediation . .	14,254.5	13,431.9	12,814.3
Real estate, renting and business			
activities*	47,069.2	50,611.9	53,298.3
Public administration and defence;			
compulsory social security . .	17,324.3	17,948.6	18,701.2
Education	14,035.9	14,501.0	15,094.7
Health and social work	13,952.3	15,004.1	16,289.5
Other community, social and			
personal service activities . .	5,414.4	5,657.2	5,804.8
Private households with employed			
persons	1,162.0	1,199.8	1,265.0
Sub-total	218,607.7	228,319.3	235,816.2
Less Financial intermediation			
services indirectly measured . .	−8,792.9	−8,304.6	−8,446.7
GDP at basic prices	209,814.8	220,014.7	227,369.4
Taxes on products	28,569.2	30,113.2	29,728.7
Less Subsidies on products . . .	2,752.0	2,659.1	2,815.7
GDP in purchasers' values . .	235,632.0	247,468.8	254,282.4

* Including imputed rents of owner-occupied dwellings.

Source: Service Statistiques financières et économiques, Banque Nationale de Belgique.

BALANCE OF PAYMENTS
(US $ million)*

	1999	2000	2001
Exports of goods f.o.b.	161,263	164,677	163,498
Imports of goods f.o.b.	−154,237	−162,086	−159,790
Trade balance	7,027	2,592	3,707
Exports of services	45,292	44,008	44,480
Imports of services	−39,167	−41,868	−43,316
Balance on goods and services	13,151	10,512	10,705
Other income received	71,892	75,673	78,906
Other income paid	−66,125	−70,625	−75,999
Balance on goods, services and			
income	18,918	15,560	13,612
Current transfers received . .	7,064	7,014	7,316
Current transfers paid . . .	−11,872	−11,193	−11,535
Current balance	14,086	11,381	9,392
Capital account (net)	−78	−213	26
Direct investment abroad . . .	−121,722	−229,355	−66,376
Direct investment from abroad. .	130,010	206,962	86,092
Portfolio investment assets . . .	−161,521	−122,814	−125,068
Portfolio investment liabilities . .	135,837	132,547	140,588
Financial derivatives assets . .	884	−3,653	−5,089
Financial derivatives liabilities . .	1,142	1,252	942
Other investment assets . . .	−58,713	−39,033	−70,053
Other investment liabilities . .	56,210	14,999	62,158
Net errors and omissions . . .	−2,410	−2,891	3
Overall balance	−1,867	−959	1,442

* Data refer to the Belgium-Luxembourg Economic Union and exclude transactions between the two countries.

Source: IMF, *International Financial Statistics*.

External Trade

PRINCIPAL COMMODITIES
(distribution by SITC, million euros)

Imports c.i.f.	1999	2000	2001*
Food and live animals	12,056.0	12,867.2	13,852.3
Crude materials (inedible) except fuels	5,877.1	7,503.0	6,670.2
Mineral fuels, lubricants, etc.	8,850.4	17,077.2	17,007.9
Petroleum, petroleum products, etc.	6,597.3	13,272.2	12,646.9
Chemicals and related products	25,344.3	31,426.6	36,420.9
Organic chemicals	7,664.5	9,250.4	10,682.8
Medicinal and pharmaceutical products	4,718.0	6,072.0	10,215.7
Basic manufactures	32,217.3	39,445.6	37,853.4
Non-metallic mineral manufactures	12,340.4	15,733.5	14,750.0
Machinery and transport equipment	49,392.2	60,367.4	62,170.3
General industrial machinery, equipment and parts	5,800.4	6,855.2	6,948.2
Office machines and automatic data-processing machines	4,662.8	5,971.9	6,018.4
Electrical machinery, apparatus, etc.	10,715.4	14,729.0	14,369.0
Road vehicles (incl. air-cushion vehicles) and parts[†]	19,141.4	22,417.7	24,656.0
Miscellaneous manufactured articles	18,015.4	20,627.4	21,156.1
Clothing and accessories (excl. footwear)	4,707.2	5,227.7	5,570.3
Total (incl. others)	154,635.1	192,194.9	198,624.1

Exports f.o.b.	1999	2000	2001*
Food and live animals	14,567.4	15,931.0	17,099.3
Mineral fuels, lubricants, etc.	4,879.8	9,699.2	8,503.1
Petroleum, petroleum products, etc.	4,151.6	8,419.3	7,639.2
Chemicals and related products	34,174.8	41,504.1	44,838.7
Organic chemicals	7,459.8	9,236.7	9,402.9
Medicinal and pharmaceutical products	6,046.1	7,419.8	10,491.1
Plastics in primary forms	7,349.5	9,351.0	9,307.3
Basic manufactures	40,066.2	48,090.4	46,054.1
Textile yarn, fabrics, etc.	6,286.2	6,833.0	6,757.9
Non-metallic mineral manufactures	14,089.7	17,214.0	15,941.0
Iron and steel	6,802.3	8,617.5	7,968.0
Machinery and transport equipment	50,561.9	61,165.2	65,375.1
General industrial machinery, equipment and parts	5,373.4	6,675.7	6,858.4
Electrical machinery, apparatus, etc.	9,674.3	13,260.2	13,279.7
Road vehicles (incl. air-cushion vehicles) and parts[†]	23,745.6	26,834.5	31,103.6
Miscellaneous manufactured articles	16,966.4	19,390.5	20,728.9
Total (incl. others)	168,091.3	203,953.2	211,168.3

* Figures are provisional.
† Data on parts exclude tyres, engines and electrical parts.

PRINCIPAL TRADING PARTNERS
(million euros)*

Imports c.i.f.	1999	2000	2001
China, People's Repub.	2,952.3	4,010.7	4,315.7
France‡	21,255.2	24,349.9	26,867.0
Germany	27,006.7	31,542.3	32,427.6
Ireland	3,374.4	4,300.9	5,592.2
Israel	1,600.2	2,373.0	2,160.7
Italy	5,992.9	7,514.6	8,519.9
Japan	4,786.2	5,948.9	5,713.2
Netherlands	25,850.0	33,575.0	34,139.4
Norway	939.3	1,962.7	2,185.9
Spain	3,129.6	3,486.2	3,894.7
Sweden	3,890.1	4,393.8	4,656.0
United Kingdom	13,242.5	16,501.0	15,496.6
USA	11,640.1	14,391.6	13,940.0
Total (incl. others)	154,635.1	192,194.9	199,491.6

Exports f.o.b.	1999	2000	2001
Austria	1,896.2	2,095.5	2,307.1
France‡	30,033.3	35,843.9	36,955.8
Germany	29,795.4	34,541.5	38,526.2
India	3,072.5	3,467.1	3,017.4
Israel	3,020.4	3,804.8	3,071.1
Italy	9,366.0	11,286.4	12,266.0
Japan	1,990.5	2,420.0	2,197.4
Luxembourg	3,411.9	4,143.1	4,176.3
Netherlands	21,453.0	25,758.5	25,892.9
Spain	6,646.0	7,342.7	8,203.9
Sweden	2,636.3	3,195.2	2,959.5
Switzerland	2,435.9	3,080.9	3,067.8
United Kingdom	16,914.9	20,239.4	21,375.7
USA	8,751.9	11,918.7	11,823.8
Total (incl. others)	168,091.2	203,953.3	212,538.7

* Imports by country of production; exports by country of last consignment.
† Figures are provisional.
‡ Including trade with Overseas Departments (French Guiana, Guadeloupe, Martinique and Réunion).

Transport

RAILWAYS
(traffic)

	1999	2000	2001
Passenger journeys ('000)	147,291	153,300	160,300
Passenger-km (million)	6,737	7,732	8,038
Freight carried ('000 metric tons)	59,149	61,279	57,050
Freight ton-km (million)	7,287	7,674	7,080

Source: SNCB Railways.

ROAD TRAFFIC
(motor vehicles in use)

	1999	2000	2001
Passenger cars	4,583,615	4,678,376	4,739,850
Buses and coaches	14,588	14,673	14,722
Lorries and vans	480,033	502,979	526,334
Road tractors	44,055	45,452	46,302
Motorcycles and mopeds	260,567	277,838	293,630

SHIPPING

Merchant Fleet
(registered at 31 December)

	1999	2000	2001
Number of vessels	184	182	185
Displacement ('000 grt)	132.1	143.9	151.0

Source: Lloyd's Register-Fairplay, *World Fleet Statistics*.

Freight Traffic
('000 metric tons)

	1999	2000	2001
Sea-borne shipping:			
goods loaded	63,393	68,801	67,706
goods unloaded.	102,647	111,082	107,135
Inland waterways:			
goods loaded	56,776	n.a.	n.a.
goods unloaded.	72,013	n.a.	n.a.

Source: partly Ministère des Communications et de l'Infrastructure.

CIVIL AVIATION
(traffic)

	1996	1997	1998
Kilometres flown ('000)	118,218	121,556	167,464
Passenger-km ('000)	9,099,901	11,273,577	16,971,798
Ton-km ('000).	818,990	1,014,622	1,527,490
Mail ton-km ('000)	16,231	13,090	n.a.

Figures refer to SABENA Belgian Airlines.

Source: Ministère des Communications et de l'Infrastructure.

Tourism

TOURIST ARRIVALS BY COUNTRY OF ORIGIN*

Country of residence	1998	1999	2000
France	834,757	868,086	837,525
Germany	867,193	883,505	816,207
Italy	211,510	215,336	216,675
Japan	153,719	160,616	169,097
Netherlands	1,468,188	1,559,142	1,573,140
Spain	175,167	177,060	178,661
United Kingdom	1,022,218	1,086,845	1,198,097
USA	325,576	337,631	347,794
Total (incl. others). . . .	6,179,254	6,369,030	6,457,325

* Non-residents staying in accommodation establishments.

Tourism receipts (US $ million, incl. Luxembourg): 5,443 in 1998; 7,039 in 1999.

Source: World Tourism Organization, mainly *Yearbook of Tourism Statistics*.

2001 (provisional, '000 arrivals): France 835; Germany 783; Netherlands 1,657; United Kingdom 1,254; USA 326; Total (incl. others) 6,451.

Communications Media

	1999	2000	2001
Television receivers ('000 in use)	5,400	5,500	n.a.
Telephones ('000 main lines in use)	5,142.1	5,060.9	5,074.0
Mobile cellular telephones ('000 subscribers).	3,186.6	5,577.0	7,690.0
Personal computers ('000 in use)	3,200	3,500	n.a.
Internet users ('000)	1,200	2,000	2,881

Source: International Telecommunication Union.

Facsimile machines ('000 in use): 180 in 1995; 190 in 1996.

Radio receivers ('000 in use): 8,000 in 1995; 8,050 in 1996; 8,075 in 1997.

Daily newspapers: *Titles*: 31 in 1995; 30 in 1996. *Average circulation* ('000 copies): 1,628 in 1995; 1,625 in 1996.

Sources: mainly UN, *Statistical Yearbook*; UNESCO, *Statistical Yearbook*.

Education

(1996/97)

	Institutions		Students	
	French*	Flemish	French*	Flemish
Pre-primary . . .	1,932	2,175	171,478	253,043
Primary	2,023	2,378	320,454	417,369
Secondary	648	1,079	349,170	447,775
Non-university higher education . . .	105	29	73,359	94,140
University level . .	9	8	62,300	n.a.

* Figures for 1995/96.

1999/2000 (estimates): Total students: Pre-primary 399,000; Primary 778,000; Secondary 779,000; Non-university higher education 170,000; University level 128,000.

2000/01: Total students: Pre-primary 400,790; Primary 771,690; Secondary 783,960; Non-university higher education 176,930; University level 116,710.

Teachers: French (1995/96): Pre-primary and primary 38,150; Secondary 57,555; Higher education 20,927. Flemish (1996/97): Pre-primary and primary 44,018; Secondary 57,707; Higher education 17,087.

Students: French (2001/02): Pre-primary 158,695; Primary 327,137; Secondary 354,348; Non-university higher education 78,831; University 61,611. Flemish (1997/98): Pre-primary 247,515; Primary 424,110; Secondary 441,876; Non-university higher education 97,780; University 56,902.

Directory

The Constitution

The Belgian Constitution has been considerably modified by amendments since its creation in 1831. Belgium is a constitutional monarchy. The central legislature consists of a bicameral Parliament (the Chamber of Representatives—Chambre des Représentants/Kamer van Volksvertegenwoordigers and the Senate —Sénat/Senaat). In July 1993 the Constitution was amended to provide for a federation of the largely autonomous regions of Brussels, Flanders and Wallonia and of the Flemish-, French- and German-speaking language communities. Article 1 of the Constitution states 'Belgium is a federal state which consists of communities and regions'. The three regions and three linguistic groups are represented by the following directly-elected legislative bodies: a combined administration for Flanders and the Flemish-speaking community, regional administrations for Wallonia and Brussels, and separate community administrations for French- and German-speakers. Each body is elected for a term of four years. The regional administrations have sole responsibility for the local economy, the environment, housing, transport and public works, while the language community administrations supervise education policy and culture. In addition, in June 2001 a constitutional amendment was passed by Parliament granting the regions greater responsibility for taxation and public expenditure, agriculture, and issues relating to foreign aid and trade.

ELECTORAL SYSTEM

Members of Parliament must be 25 years of age, and they are elected by secret ballot according to a system of proportional representation. Suffrage is universal for citizens of 18 years or over, and voting is compulsory.

The Chamber of Representatives consists of 150 members, who are elected for four years unless the Chamber is dissolved before that time has elapsed. The Senate comprises 71 normal members, of whom 40 are directly elected, usually at intervals of four years, 21 are appointed by the legislative bodies of the three language communities (10 each from the Flemish- and French-speaking communities and one from the German-speaking community), and 10 are co-opted by the elected members. Children of the King are entitled to honorary membership of the Senate from 18 years of age and acquire voting rights at the age of 21.

THE CROWN

The King has the right to veto legislation, but, in practice, he does not exercise it. The King is nominally the supreme head of the executive, but, in fact, he exercises his control through the Cabinet, which is responsible for all acts of government to the Chamber of Representatives. According to the Constitution, the King appoints his own ministers, but in practice, since they are responsible to the Chamber of Representatives and need its confidence, they are generally the choice of the Representatives. Similarly, the royal initiative is in the control of the ministry.

LEGISLATION

Legislation is introduced either by the federal Government or the members in the two Houses, and as the party complexion of both Houses is generally almost the same, measures passed by the Chamber of Representatives are usually passed by the Senate. Each House elects its own President at the beginning of the session, who acts as an impartial Speaker, although he is a party nominee. The Houses elect their own committees, through which all legislation passes. They are so well organized that through them the Legislature has considerable power of control over the Cabinet. Nevertheless, according to the Constitution (Article 68), certain treaties must be communicated to the Chamber only as soon as the 'interest and safety of the State permit'. Further, the Government possesses an important power of dissolution which it uses; a most unusual feature is that it may be applied to either House separately or to both together (Article 71).

Revision of the Constitution is to be first settled by an ordinary majority vote of both Houses, specifying the article to be amended. The Houses are then automatically dissolved. The new Chambers thereupon determine the amendments to be made, with the provision that in each House the presence of two-thirds of the members is necessary for a quorum, and a two-thirds' majority of those voting is required.

The Government

HEAD OF STATE

King of the Belgians: HM King ALBERT II (succeeded to the throne 9 August 1993).

THE CABINET
(May 2003)

A coalition of Vlaamse Liberalen en Demokraten—Partij van de Burger (VLD), the Parti Réformateur Libéral (PRL), the Parti Socialiste (PS), the Socialistische Partij (SP) and Anders Gaan Leven (Agalev). The Ecologistes Confédérés pour l'Organisation des Luttes Originales (Ecolo) resigned from the coalition on 5 May 2003.

Prime Minister: GUY VERHOFSTADT (VLD).

Deputy Prime Minister, Minister of Employment and Minister of Mobility and Transport: LAURETTE ONKELINX (PS).

Deputy Prime Minister and Minister of Foreign Affairs: LOUIS MICHEL (PRL).

Deputy Prime Minister and Minister of the Budget, Social Integration and Social Economy: JOHAN VANDE LANOTTE (SP).

Minister of the Interior: ANTOINE DUQUESNE (PRL).

Minister of Social Affairs and Pensions: FRANK VANDENBROUCKE (SP).

Minister of the Civil Service and Modernization of Public Administration: LUC VAN DEN BOSSCHE (SP).

Minister of Defence: ANDRÉ FLAHAUT (PS).

Minister of Justice: MARK VERWILGHEN (VLD).

Minister of Finance: DIDIER REYNDERS (PRL).

Minister of Telecommunications, Public Enterprises and Participation, responsible for the Self-employed: RIK DAEMS (CVD).

Minister of Economic Affairs and Scientific Research, responsible for Urban Policy: CHARLES PICQUE (PS).

Minister, attached to the Minister of Foreign Affairs, responsible for Agriculture: ANNEMIE NEYTS-UYTTEBROECK (VLD).

Minister of Consumer Affairs, Health and the Environment: JEF TAVERNIER (Agalev).

State Secretary for Development Co-operation, attached to the Minister of Foreign Affairs: EDDY BOUTMANS (Agalev).

State Secretary for Energy and Sustainable Development, attached to the Minister of Mobility and Transport: ALAIN ZENNER (PRL).

MINISTRIES

Office of the Prime Minister: 16 rue de la Loi, 1000 Brussels; tel. (2) 501-02-11; fax (2) 512-69-53; internet verhofstadt.fgov.be.

Ministry of the Budget, Social Integration and Social Economy: 180 rue Royale, 1000 Brussels; tel. (2) 210-19-11; fax (2) 217-33-28; internet www.begroting.be.

Ministry of Consumer Affairs, Health and the Environment: 6–9 ave des Arts, 1210 Brussels; tel. (2) 220-20-11; fax (2) 220-20-67.

Ministry of Defence: 8 rue Lambermont, 1000 Brussels; tel. (2) 550-28-11; fax (2) 550-29-19; e-mail cabinet@mod.mil.be; internet mod.fgov.be.

Ministry of Economic Affairs and Scientific Research: 23 square de Meeûs, 1000 Brussels; tel. (2) 506-51-11; fax (2) 511-46-83; e-mail cpicque@picque.skynet.be; internet www.mineco.fgov.be.

Ministry of Employment and Equal Opportunities: 76–80 rue du Commerce, 1040 Brussels; tel. (2) 233-51-11; fax (2) 230-10-67; e-mail vdplaets@meta.fgov.be; internet meta.fgov.be.

Ministry of Finance: 12 rue de la Loi, 1000 Brussels; tel. (2) 233-81-11; fax (2) 233-80-03; e-mail contact@ckfin.minfin.be; internet www.minfin.fgov.be.

Ministry of Foreign Affairs: 15 rue des Petits Carmes, 1000 Brussels; tel. (2) 501-82-11; fax (2) 511-63-85; e-mail cab.ae@diplobel.org; internet diplobel.fgov.be.

Ministry of the Interior: 60–62 rue Royale, 1000 Brussels; tel. (2) 504-85-11; fax (2) 504-85-00; e-mail cab.affint@mibz.fgov.be; internet mibz.fgov.be.

Ministry of Justice: 115 blvd de Waterloo, 1000 Brussels; tel. (2) 542-79-11; fax (2) 538-07-67; internet www.just.fgov.be.

Ministry of Mobility and Transport: 65 rue de la Loi, 1040 Brussels; tel. (2) 237-67-11; fax (2) 230-18-24; e-mail cabinet.durant@vici.fgov.be.

Ministry of Social Affairs and Pensions: 62 rue de la Loi, 1040 Brussels; tel. (2) 238-28-11; fax (2) 230-38-95; e-mail cabinetas@minsoc.fed.be; internet www.vandenbroucke.fgov.be.

Ministry of Telecommunications, Public Enterprises and Participation: 87 ave de la Toison d'or, 1060 Brussels; tel. (2) 250-03-03; fax (2) 219-09-14; internet www.telcobel.be.

Federal Public Service of Personnel and Organization: Copernicus Building, 51 Wetstraat-Rue de la Loi, 1040 Brussels; tel. (2) 790-58.00; fax (2) 790-58-99; e-mail info@p-o.be; internet www.p-o.be.

Legislature

CHAMBRE DES REPRÉSENTANTS/KAMER VAN VOLKSVERTEGENWOORDIGERS
(Chamber of Representatives)

General Election, 13 June 1999

	% of votes	Seats
VLD	14.3	23
CVP	14.1	22
PS	10.2	19
PRL-FDF	10.1	18
Vlaams Blok	9.9	15
SP	9.6	14
Ecolo	7.4	11
PSC	5.9	10
Agalev	7.0	9
VU-ID21	5.6	8
FN	1.5	1
Total (incl. others)	100.0	150

SÉNAT/SENAAT

General Election, 13 June 1999

	% of votes	Seats
VLD	15.4	6
CVP	14.7	6
PRL-FDF	10.6	5
PS	9.7	4
Vlaams Blok	9.4	4
SP	8.9	4
Ecolo	7.4	3
Agalev	7.1	3
PSC	6.0	3
VU-ID21	5.1	2
Total (incl. others)	100.0	40

In addition, the Senate has 21 members appointed by the legislative bodies of the three language communities and 10 members co-opted by the elected members. Children of the King are entitled to honorary membership of the Senate from 18 years of age and acquire voting rights at the age of 21.

Advisory Councils

Conseil Central de l'Economie/Centrale Raad voor het Bedrijfsleven: 17–21 ave de la Joyeuse entrée, 1040 Brussels; tel. (2) 233-88-11; fax (2) 233-89-12; e-mail mail@ccecrb.fgov.be; internet www.ccecrb.fgov.be; f. 1948; representative and consultative body; advises the authorities on economic issues; 50 mems; Pres. Baron ROBERT TOLLET.

Conseil d'Etat/Raad van Staat: 33 rue de la Science, 1040 Brussels; tel. (2) 234-96-11; e-mail webmaster@raadvst-consetat.be; internet www.raadvst.consetat.be; f. 1946; advisory body on legislative and regulatory matters; supreme administrative court; hears complaints against the actions of the legislature; 38 mems; Pres. JEAN-JACQUES STRYCKMANS.

Regional and Community Administrations

Belgium is a federal state, and considerable power has been devolved to the regional administrations of Brussels, Wallonia and Flanders, and to the French-, German- and Flemish-speaking communities. The regional authorities have sole responsibility for the environment, housing, transport and public works, and for certain aspects of social welfare, while the community administrations are primarily responsible for cultural affairs and for education. In addition, in June 2001 Parliament granted the regions greater responsibility for taxation and public expenditure, agriculture, and matters relating to foreign aid and trade. The administrations of Flanders and of the Flemish-speaking community are homologous.

REGION OF FLANDERS AND THE FLEMISH-SPEAKING COMMUNITY

Minister-President: PATRICK DEWAEL (VLD).

Vlaams Parlement (Flemish Parliament): 27 Leuvensweg, 1011 Brussels; tel. (2) 552-11-11; fax (2) 552-11-22; internet www.vlaamsparlement.be; f. 1980; 124 mems.

Vlaamse Overheid (Flemish Authority): 19 Martelaarsplein, 1000 Brussels; tel. (2) 553-29-11; fax (2) 553-29-05; e-mail kabinet.dewael@vlaanderen.be; internet www.vlaanderen.be.

REGION OF WALLONIA

Minister-President: JEAN-CLAUDE VAN CAUWENBERGHE (PS).

Le Parlement Wallon (Walloon Parliament): 24 rue Saint-Nicolas, 5000 Namur; tel. (81) 23-10-36; fax (2) 23-12-20; internet www.parlement-wallon.be; elects Government of Wallonia; 75 mems.

Gouvernement Wallon (Walloon Government): 1 Place de la Wallonie, Bât 2, 5100 Namur; tel. (81) 33-31-60; fax (81) 33-31-66; e-mail dircom@mrw.wallonie.be; internet www.wallonie.be; 9 mems.

REGION OF BRUSSELS-CAPITAL

Minister-President: FRANÇOIS-XAVIER DE DONNEA (PRL).

Conseil de la Région de Bruxelles-Capitale/Brusselse Hoofdstedelijke Raad (Council of the Region of Brussels-Capital): 1005 Brussels; tel. (2) 549-62-11; fax (2) 549-62-12; e-mail Parlement@parlbru.irisnet.be; internet www.parlbru.irisnet.be.

Gouvernement de la Région de Bruxelles-Capitale/Brusselse Hoofdstedelijke Regering (Government of Brussels-Capital): 7–9 rue Ducale, 1000 Brussels; tel. (2) 506-32-11; fax (2) 514-40-22; internet www.bruxelles.irisnet.be.

FRENCH-SPEAKING COMMUNITY

Minister-President: HERVÉ HASQUIN (PRL).

Parlement de la Communauté française de Belgique (Parliament of the French-speaking Community): 6 rue de la Loi, 1000 Brussels; tel. (2) 506-38-11; fax (2) 506-39-78; internet www.pcf.be; comprises mems of the Walloon Parliament and the 19 francophone mems of the Council of the Region of Brussels-Capital; 94 mems.

Gouvernement de la Communauté française Wallonie-Bruxelles (Government of the French-speaking Community): 15–17 place Surlet de Chokier, 1000 Brussels; tel. (2) 227-32-11; fax (2) 227-33-53; internet www.cfwb.be.

GERMAN-SPEAKING COMMUNITY

Minister-President: KARL-HEINZ LAMBERTZ (PS).

Rat der Deutschsprachigen Gemeinschaft Belgiens (Council of the German-speaking Community): 8 Kaperberg, 4700 Eupen; tel.

and fax (87) 55-59-70; e-mail rdg@euregio.net; internet www.euregio.net/rdg.

Regierung der Deutschsprachigen Gemeinschaft Belgiens (Government of the German-speaking Community): 32 Klötzerbahn, 4700 Eupen; tel. (87) 59-64-00; fax (87) 74-02-58; e-mail kab.lamberty@dgov.be; internet www.dglive.be.

Political Organizations

Anders Gaan Leven (Agalev) (Ecologist Party—Flemish-speaking): Segeant De Bruynestraat 78–82, 1070 Anderlecht; tel. (2) 219-19-19; fax (2) 223-10-90; e-mail agalev@agalev.be; internet www.agalev.be; f. 1982; Gen. Sec. LUC LEMIENGRE.

Le Centre Démocrate Humaniste (CDH) (Christian Democrats): 41 rue des Deux-Eglises, 1000 Brussels; tel. (2) 238-01-11; fax (2) 238-01-29 ; e-mail info@lecdh.be; internet www.lecdh.be; f. 1945; founded as the Parti Social Chrétien/Christelijke Volkspartij (PSC/CVP), the PSC separated from the CVP by 1972, name changed as above in May 2002; Pres. JOËLLE MILQUET; Vice-Pres ANDRÉ ANTOINE, BENOIT CEREXHE.

Christen-Democratisch en Vlaams Partij (CD&V): 89 Wetstraat, 1040 Brussels; tel. (2) 238–38–11; fax (2) 230–43–60; e-mail inform@cdenv.be; internet www.cdenv.be; f. 1945; founded as Parti Social Chrétien/Christelijke Volkspartij (PSC/CVP), CVP separated from PSC by 1972, renamed as above in 2001; Pres. STEFAAN DE CLERCK.

Ecologistes Confédérés pour l'Organisation des Luttes Originales (Ecolo) (Ecologist Party—French-speaking): 8 rue du Séminaire, 5000 Namur; tel. (8) 122-78-71; fax (8) 230-06-03; e-mail info@ecolo.be; internet www.ecolo.be; Fed. Secs JACQUES BAUDUIN, PHILIPPE DEFEYT, BRIGITTE ERNST.

Front Démocratique des Francophones (FDF) (French-speaking Democratic Front): 127 chaussée de Charleroi, 1060 Brussels; tel. (2) 538-83-20; fax (2) 539-36-50; e-mail fdf@fdf.be; internet www.fdf.be; f. 1964; aims to preserve the French character of Brussels; has co-operation agreement with the PRL; Pres. OLIVIER MAINGAIN; Sec.-Gen. CAROLINE PERSOONS.

Front National (FN): 12 clos du Parnasse, 1050 Brussels; tel. (2) 511-75-77; e-mail daniel.feret@frontnational.be; internet www.frontnational.be; f. 1985; extreme right-wing nationalist party; Pres. DANIEL FERET.

Mouvement des Citoyens pour le Changement (MCC): 50 rue de la Vallée, 1000 Brussels; tel. (2) 642-29-99; fax (2) 642-29-90; e-mail info@lemcc.be; internet www.lemcc.be; member of the Mouvement Réformateur alliance with the FDF and the PRL; Pres. NATHALIE DE T'SERCLAES.

Nieuw-Vlaamse Alliantie (N-VA) (New-Flemish Alliance): 12 Barrikadenplein, 1000 Brussels; tel. (2) 219-49-30; fax (2) 217-35-10; e-mail info@n-va.be; internet www.n-va.be; f. 1954 as Volksunie—Vlaamse Vrije Democraten, name changed, as above, 2001; Flemish nationalist party supporting national and European federalism; Pres. GEERT BOURGEOIS; Sec. KRIS VAN DIJCK; 11,000 mems.

Partei der Deutschsprachigen Belgier (PDB) (Party of German-speaking Belgians): 6 Kaperberg, 4700 Eupen; tel. (87) 55-59-87; fax (87) 55-59-84; internet www.pju-pdb.be; f. 1971; promotes equality for the German-speaking minority; Pres. GUIDO BREUER.

Parti Communiste (PC) (Communist Party): 4 rue Rouppe, 1000 Brussels; tel. (2) 548-02-90; fax (2) 548-02-95; internet www.kp-online.be; f. 1921 as Parti Communiste de Belgique–Kommunistische Partij van België, name changed 1990; Pres. PIERRE BEAUVOIS; 5,000 mems.

Parti de la Liberté du Citoyen/Parti Libéral Chretien/Partij der Liberale Christenen (PLC): 46 ave de Scheut, 1070 Brussels; tel. (2) 524-39-66; fax (2) 521-60-71; Pres LUC EYKERMAN, PAUL MOORS.

Parti Humaniste de Belgique: 131 rue du Noyer, 1000 Brussels; tel. (2) 427-71-43; fax (2) 426-03-78; e-mail parti.humaniste@chello.be; internet www.multimania.com/phum; f. 1994; promotes social equality and human rights.

Parti Réformateur Libéral (PRL) (Liberal Party—French-speaking wing): 41 rue de Naples, 1050 Brussels; tel. (2) 500-35-11; fax (2) 500-35-00; e-mail prl@prl.be; internet www.prl.be; f. 1846 as Parti Libéral; member of the Mouvement Réformateur alliance with the FDF and MCC; Pres. DANIEL DUCARME; 50,000 mems.

Parti Socialiste (PS) (Socialist Party—French-speaking wing): Maison du PS, 13 blvd de l'Empereur, 1000 Brussels; tel. (2) 548-32-11; fax (2) 548-33-80; e-mail secretariat@ps.be; internet www.ps.be; f. 1885 as the Parti Ouvrier Belge; split from the Flemish wing 1979; Pres. ELIO DI RUPO; Sec. JEAN-POL BARAS.

Parti Wallon (PW) (Walloon Party): 14 rue du Faubourg, 1430 Quenast; tel. (6) 767-00-19; f. 1985 by amalgamation of the Rassemblement Wallon (f. 1968), the Rassemblement Populaire Wallon and the Front Indépendantiste Wallon; left-wing socialist party advocating an independent Walloon state; Pres. JEAN-CLAUDE PICCIN.

Partij van de Arbeid van België (PvdA)/Parti du Travail de Belgique (PTB) (Worker's Party of Belgium): 171 blvd M. Lemonnier, 1000 Brussels; tel. (2) 504-01-10; fax (2) 513-98-31; e-mail wpb@wpb.be; internet www.wpb.be; f. 1979; Marxist-Leninist; Gen. Sec. NADINE ROSA-ROSSO.

Sociaal Progressief Alternatief (SP.A) (Socialist Party—Flemish wing): 105/37 Grasmarkt, 1000 Brussels; tel. (2) 552-02-00; fax (2) 552-02-55; e-mail info@s-p-a.be; internet www.s-p-a.be; f. 1885; fmrly Socialistische Partij Anders, renamed as above in 2001; Chair. PATRICK JANSSENS; Sec. ALAIN ANDRÉ.

Spirit (Sociaal, Progressif, Internationaal, Regionalistisch, Integraal-democratisch en Toekomstgericht): Woeringenstraat 19, 1000 Brussels; tel. (2) 513-20-63; fax (2) 513-85-75; e-mail info@meerspirit .be; internet www.meerspirit.be; f. 1998 as ID 21; Chair. ELS VAN WEERT.

Vlaams Blok (Flemish Bloc): 8 Madouplein, bus 9, 1210 Brussels; tel. (2) 219-60-09; fax (2) 219-72-74; e-mail info@vlaams-blok.be; internet www.vlaamsblok.be; f. 1979 as a breakaway party from the Volksunie; advocates Flemish separatism and is anti-immigration; Chair. FRANK VANHECKE; Chief Officer LUK VAN NIEUWENHUYSEN.

Vlaamse Liberalen en Demokraten—Partij van de Burger (VLD) (Flemish Liberals and Democrats—Citizens' Party: Liberal Party—Flemish-speaking wing): 34 Melsensstraat, 1000 Brussels; tel. (2) 549-00-20; fax (2) 512-60-25; e-mail vld@vld.be; internet www .vld.be; f. 1961 as Partij voor Vrijheid en Vooruitgang; name changed, as above, 1992; Pres. KAREL DE GUCHT; Sec.-Gen. LIEVE DECOCK; 80,000 mems.

Diplomatic Representation

EMBASSIES IN BELGIUM

Albania: 30 rue Tenbosch ,1000 Brussels; tel. (2) 640-14-22; fax (2) 640-28-58; e-mail amba.brux@brutele.be; Ambassador IPRIZ BASHA.

Algeria: 209 ave Molière, 1060 Brussels; tel. (2) 343-50-78; fax (2) 343-51-68; Ambassador MISSOUM SBIH.

Andorra: 10 rue de la Montagne, 1000 Brussels; tel. (2) 513-28-06; fax (2) 513-07-41; e-mail meritxell.mateu@andorra.be; internet www .andorra.be; Ambassador MERITXELL MATEU.

Angola: 182 rue Franz Merjay, 1050 Brussels; tel. (2) 346-18-72; fax (2) 344-08-94; e-mail angola.embassy.brussels@skynet.be; internet www.embargentina.be; Ambassador ARMANDO MATEUS CADETE.

Argentina: 225 ave Louise, bte 3, 1050 Brussels; tel. (2) 647-78-12; fax (2) 647-93-19; e-mail febelg@mrecic.gov.ar; Ambassador EDUARDO M. DE L. AIRALDI.

Armenia: 157 rue Franz Merjay, 1050 Brussels; tel. and fax (2) 346-56-67; e-mail armembel@wanadoo.be; internet www .armenian-embassy.be; Ambassador V. TCHITETCHIAN.

Australia: 6–8 rue Guimard, 1040 Brussels; tel. (2) 286-05-00; fax (2) 230-68-02; e-mail austemb.brussels@dfat.gov.au; Ambassador JOANNA HEWITT.

Austria: 5 place du Champs de Mars, 1050 Brussels; tel. (2) 289-07-00; fax (2) 513-66-41; e-mail botschaft.brussel@brutele.be; Ambassador THOMAS MAYR-HARTING.

Azerbaijan: 464 ave Molière, 1050 Brussels; tel. (2) 345-26-60; fax (2) 345-91-58; e-mail azbeigamba@skynet.be; Ambassador MIR-HAMZA EFENDIEV.

Bangladesh: 29–31 rue Jacques Jordaens, 1000 Brussels; tel. (2) 640-55-00; fax (2) 646-59-98; Ambassador A. S. M. KHAIRHUL ANAM.

Barbados: 100 ave Franklin Roosevelt, 1050 Brussels; tel. (2) 732-17-37; fax (2) 732-32-66; e-mail brussels@foreign.gov.bb; internet www.foreign.gov.bb; Ambassador ERROL HUMPHREY.

Belarus: 192 ave Molière, 1050 Brussels; tel. (2) 340-02-70; fax (2) 340-02-87; e-mail embbel@skynet.be; Ambassador SERGEI N. MARTYNOV.

Belize: Brand Witlocklaan 136, 1200 Brussels; tel. (2) 732-62-04; fax (2) 732-62-46; e-mail embel.bru@pophost.eunet.be.

Benin: 5 ave de l'Observatoire, 1180 Brussels; tel. (2) 374-91-92; fax (2) 375-83-26; e-mail ambassade.du.benin@skynet.be; Ambassador EULOGE HINVI.

Bolivia: 176 ave Louise, bte 6, 1050 Brussels; tel. (2) 627-00-10; fax (2) 647-47-82; e-mail embajada.bolivia@embolbrus.be; Ambassador ARTURO SUAREZ VARGAS.

Bosnia and Herzegovina: 34 rue Tenbosch, 1000 Brussels; tel. (2) 644-20-08; fax (2) 644-16-98; Ambassador ZDENKO MARTINOVIĆ.

Botswana: 169 ave de Tervueren, 1150 Brussels; tel. (2) 735-20-70; fax (2) 735-63-18; e-mail embassyofbotswana@ub.yahoo.com; internet www.gov.bw; Ambassador SASARA CHASALA GEORGE.

Brazil: 350 ave Louise, bte 5, 1050 Brussels; tel. (2) 640-20-15; fax (2) 640-81-34; e-mail brasbruxelas@beon.be; Ambassador MARCIO DE OLIVEIRA DIAS.

Brunei: 238 ave F. D. Roosevelt, 1050 Brussels; tel. (2) 675-08-78; fax (2) 672-93-58; e-mail kedutaan-brunei.brussels@skynet.be; Ambassador Pengiran MASHOR AHMAD.

Bulgaria: 58 ave Hamoir, 1180 Brussels; tel. (2) 374-59-63; fax (2) 374-84-94; e-mail embassy@bulgaria.be; Ambassador EMILE VALIEV.

Burkina Faso: 16 place Guy d'Arezzo, 1180 Brussels; tel. (2) 345-99-12; fax (2) 345-06-12; e-mail ambassade.burkina@skynet.be; Ambassador KADRÉ DÉSIRÉ OUEDRAOGO.

Burundi: 46 square Marie-Louise, 1000 Brussels; tel. (2) 230-45-35; fax (2) 230-78-83; e-mail ambassade.burundi@skynet.be; Ambassador JONATHAS NIYUNGEKO.

Cameroon: 131–133 ave Brugmann, 1190 Brussels; tel. (2) 345-18-70; fax (2) 344-57-35; Ambassador ISABELLE BASSONG.

Canada: 2 ave de Tervueren, 1040 Brussels; tel. (2) 741-06-11; fax (2) 741-06-43; e-mail bru@dfait-maeci.gc.ca; internet www .dfait-maeci.gc.ca/brussels; Ambassador JACQUES BILODEAU.

Cape Verde: 29 ave Jeanne, 1050 Brussels; tel. (2) 646-62-70; fax (2) 646-33-85; e-mail emb.caboverde@skynet.be; Ambassador FERNANDO WAHNON.

Central African Republic: 416 blvd Lambermont, 1030 Brussels; tel. (2) 242-28-80; fax (2) 215-13-11; e-mail ambassade.centrafrique@ skynet.be; Chargé d'affaires a.i. JEAN-PIERRE MBAZOA.

Chad: 52 blvd Lambermont, 1030 Brussels; tel. (2) 215-19-75; fax (2) 216-35-26; e-mail ambassade.tchad@chello.be; Ambassador ABDERAHIM Y. NDIAYE.

Chile: 40 rue Montoyer, 1000 Brussels; tel. (2) 280-16-20; fax (2) 280-14-81; e-mail embachili.belgica@skynet.be; Ambassador RICARDO BRODSKY BAUDET.

China, People's Republic: 443–445 ave de Tervueren, 1150 Brussels; tel. (2) 771-33-09; fax (2) 779-28-95; internet www .chinaembassy-org.be; e-mail bangongshi@skynet.be; Ambassador GUAN CHENYUAN.

Colombia: 96A ave F. D. Roosevelt, 1050 Brussels; tel. (2) 649-56-79; fax (2) 646-54-91; e-mail colombia@emcolbru.org; internet www .emcolbru.org; Ambassador ROBERTO ARENAS BONILLA.

Congo, Democratic Republic: 30 rue Marie de Bourgogne, 1040 Brussels; tel. (2) 513-66-10; fax (2) 514-04-03; Ambassador RACHEL ALBERT KISONGA MAZAKAZA.

Congo, Republic: 16–18 ave F. D. Roosevelt, 1050 Brussels; tel. (2) 648-38-56; fax (2) 648-42-13; e-mail ambassade.congobrazza@skynet .be; Ambassador JACQUES OBIA.

Costa Rica: 489 ave Louise, bte 13, 1050 Brussels; tel. (2) 640-55-41; fax (2) 648-31-92; e-mail ambcrbel@coditel.net; Chargé d'affaires a.i. MICHEL CHARITIER.

Côte d'Ivoire: 234 ave F. D. Roosevelt, 1050 Brussels; tel. (2) 672-23-57; fax (2) 672-04-91; Ambassador MARIE GOSSET.

Croatia: 50 ave des Arts, 1000 Brussels; tel. (2) 500-09-30; fax (2) 646-56-64; Ambassador VLADIMIR DROBNJAK.

Cuba: 77 rue Roberts-Jones, 1180 Brussels; tel. (2) 343-00-20; fax (2) 344-96-91; e-mail mision@embacuba.be; Ambassador RODRIGO MALMIERCA DIAZ.

Cyprus: 51 rue de la Vallée, 1000 Brussels; tel. (2) 650-06-10; fax (2) 650-06-20; e-mail ambassade.cyprus@skynet.be; Ambassador KALLIOPI AVRAAM.

Czech Republic: 143 ave Adolphe Buyl,1050 Brussels; tel. (2) 641-89-30; fax (2) 640-77-94; e-mail brussels@embassy.mzw.cz; Ambassador KATEŘINA LUKEŠOVÁ.

Denmark: 73 rue d'Arlon, 1040 Brussels; tel. (2) 233-09-00; fax (2) 233-09-30; e-mail bruamb@um.dk; Ambassador ALF JÖNSSON.

Djibouti: Brugmannlaan 410, 1180 Brussels; tel. (2) 347-69-67; fax (2) 347-69-63.

Dominican Republic: 12 ave Bel Air, 1180 Brussels; tel. (2) 346-49-35; fax (2) 346-51-52; e-mail embajadombelgica@euronet.be; Ambassador CLARA JOSELYN QUIÑONES DE LONGO.

Eastern Caribbean States: 42 rue de Livourne, 1000 Brussels; tel. (2) 534-26-11; fax (2) 539-40-09; e-mail ecs.embassies@skynet.be; internet www.caribisles.org; Ambassador EDWIN PONTIEN JOSEPH LAURENT.

Ecuador: 363 ave Louise, 1050 Brussels; tel. (2) 644-30-50; fax (2) 644-28-13; e-mail ecuador@skypro.be; Ambassador ALFREDO PINOAR-GOTE CEVALLOS.

Egypt: 19 ave de l'Uruguay, 1000 Brussels; tel. (2) 663-58-00; fax (2) 675-58-88; e-mail embassy.egypt@skynet.be; Ambassador SOLIMAN AWAAD.

El Salvador: 171 ave de Tervueren, 1050 Brussels; tel. (2) 733-04-85; fax (2) 735-02-11; Ambassador JOAQUÍN RODEZNO MUNGUIA.

Equatorial Guinea: Jupiterlaan 17, 1190 Brussels; tel. (2) 346-25-09; fax (2) 346-33-09; Chargé d'affaires MARI CRUZ EVUNA ANDEME.

Eritrea: Wolvendaellaan 15–17, 1180 Brussels; tel. (2) 374-44-34; fax (2) 372-07-30; e-mail andatw@hotmail.com; Ambassador ANDER-BRHAN WELDEGIORGIS.

Estonia: 1 ave Isidore Gérard, 1160 Brussels; tel. (2) 779-07-55; fax (2) 779-28-17; e-mail embassy@estemb.be; Ambassador SULEV KAN-NIKE.

Ethiopia: 231 ave de Tervueren, 1150 Brussels; tel. (2) 771-32-94; fax (2) 771-49-14; Ambassador Dr PETER GABRIEL ROBLEH.

Fiji: 66 ave Kortenberg, bte 7, 1000 Brussels; tel. (2) 736-66-07; fax (2) 736-14-58; e-mail ingo@fijiembassy.be; internet www.fijiembassy.be; Ambassador ISIKELI U. MATAITOGA.

Finland: 58 ave des Arts, 1000 Brussels; tel. (2) 287-12-12; fax (2) 287-12-00; e-mail bry@formin.fi; Ambassador ANTTI SIERLA.

France: 65 rue Ducale, 1000 Brussels; tel. (2) 548-87-11; fax (2) 548-87-32; internet www.ambafrance.be; Ambassador JACQUES RUMMEL-HARDT.

Gabon: 112 ave Winston Churchill, 1180 Brussels; tel. (2) 340-62-10; fax (2) 346-46-69; Ambassador RENÉ MAKONGO.

Gambia: 126 ave F. D. Roosevelt, 1050 Brussels; tel. (2) 640-10-49; fax (2) 646-32-77; e-mail bs175335@skynet.be; Ambassador A. M. NGUM.

Georgia: 58 ave Orban, 1150 Brussels; tel. (2) 761-11-91; fax (2) 761-11-99; e-mail mdgade@skynet.be; Ambassador K. ZALDASTANISH-VILI.

Germany: 190 ave de Tervueren, 1150 Brussels; tel. (2) 774-19-11; fax (2) 772-36-92; e-mail zreg@bruedip.auswaertiges-amt.de; Ambassador PETER VON BUTLER.

Ghana: blvd Général Wahis, 1030 Brussels; tel. (2) 705-82-20; fax (2) 705-66-53; e-mail head@ghembassy.arc.be; Ambassador KOBINA WUDU.

Greece: 2 ave F. D. Roosevelt, 1050 Brussels; tel. (2) 648-17-30; fax (2) 647-45-25; e-mail ambagre@skynet.be; Ambassador IOANNIS CAM-BOUS.

Grenada: 123 Laekenstraat, 1000 Brussels; tel. (2) 223-73-03; fax (2) 223-73-07; e-mail embassyofgrenadabxl@skynet.be; Chargé d'affaires a.i. JOAN-MARIE COUTAIN.

Guatemala: 185 ave Winston Churchill, 1180 Brussels; tel. (2) 345-90-47; fax (2) 344-64-99; e-mail obguab@euronet.be; Ambassador EDMOND MULET-LESIEUR.

Guinea: 75 ave Roger Vandendriessche, 1150 Brussels; tel. (2) 771-01-26; fax (2) 762-60-36; Ambassador NABY MOUSSA SOUMAH.

Guinea-Bissau: 70 ave F. D. Roosevelt, 1050 Brussels; tel. (2) 647-13-51; fax (2) 640-43-12; Chargé d'affaires JOSÉ FONSECA.

Guyana: 12 ave du Brésil, 1000 Brussels; tel. (2) 675-62-16; fax (2) 675-55-98; e-mail embassy.guyana@skynet.be; Chargé d'affaires GALE LEE.

Haiti: 139 Chaussee de Charleroi, 1060 Brussels; tel. (2) 649-73-81; fax (2) 640-60-80; Ambassador YOLETTE AZOR-CHARLES.

Holy See: 9 ave des Franciscains, 1150 Brussels (Apostolic Nuncia-ture); tel. (2) 762-20-05; fax (2) 762-20-32; e-mail nonciature.apostolique@euronet.be; Apostolic Nuncio Most Rev.

Honduras: 3 ave des Gaulois (5e étage), 1040 Brussels; tel. (2) 734-00-00; fax (2) 735-26-26; e-mail ambassade.Honduras@chello.be; Ambassador TEODOLINDA BANEGAS DE MAKRIS.

Hungary: 41 rue Edmond Picard, 1050 Brussels; tel. (2) 348-18-00; fax (2) 347-60-28; e-mail huembbxl@huembbxl.be; Ambassador LÁSZLÓ TRÓCSÁNYI.

Iceland: 74 rue de Trèves, 1040 Brussels; tel. (2) 286-17-00; fax (2) 286-17-70; e-mail icemb.brussel@utn.stjr.is; internet www.iceland.org/be; Ambassador KJARTAN JÓHANSSON.

India: 217 chaussée de Vleurgat, 1050 Brussels; tel. (2) 640-91-40; fax (2) 648-96-38; e-mail eoibru@mail.interpac.be; Ambassador P. K. SINGH.

Indonesia: 294 ave de Tervueren, 1150 Brussels; tel. (2) 771-20-14; fax (2) 771-22-91; e-mail email kbribxl@brutele.be; Ambassador SULAIMAN ABDULMANAN.

Iran: 415 ave de Tervueren, 1150 Brussels; tel. (2) 762-37-45; fax (2) 762-39-15; e-mail eiri.bxl@skynet.be; Ambassador ABOLGHASEM DELFI.

Iraq: 23 ave des Aubépines, 1180 Brussels; tel. (2) 374-59-92; fax (2) 374-76-15; e-mail abassade.irak@skynet.be; Chargé d'affaires a.i. Dr RIADH I. AL-WEYES.

Ireland: 89 rue Froissard, 1040 Brussels; tel. (2) 230-53-37; fax (2) 230-53-12; Ambassador PADRAIC CRADOCK.

Israel: 40 ave de l'Observatoire, 1180 Brussels; tel. (2) 373-55-00; fax (2) 373-56-17; Ambassador JEHUDI KINAR.

Italy: 28 rue Emile Claus, 1050 Brussels; tel. (2) 643-38-50; fax (2) 648-54-85; e-mail ambitbxl@ambitaliabruxelles.org; internet www.ambitaliabruxelles.org; Ambassador GAETANO CORTESE.

Jamaica: 2 ave Palmerston, 1000 Brussels; tel. (2) 230-11-70; fax (2) 230-37-09; e-mail emb.jam.brussels@skynet.be; Ambassador EVADNE COYE.

Japan: 58 ave des Arts, bte 17/18, 1000 Brussels; tel. (2) 513-23-40; fax (2) 513-15-56; e-mail kobun1@amb-jpn.be; internet www.amb-jpn.be; Ambassador JUNICHI NAKAMURA.

Jordan: 104 ave F. D. Roosevelt, 1050 Brussels; tel. (2) 640-77-55; fax (2) 640-27-96; e-mail jordan.embassy@skynet.be; Ambassador Dr ALIA BOURAN.

Kazakhstan: 30 ave Van Bever, 1180 Brussels; tel. (2) 374-95-62; fax (2) 374-50-91; Ambassador AKHMETZHAN S. YESIMOV.

Kenya: 208 ave Winston Churchill, 1180 Brussels; tel. (2) 340-10-40; fax (2) 340-10-62; e-mail kenbrussels@hotmail.com; Ambassador PETER O. NKURAIYIA.

Korea, Republic: 173–175 chaussée de la Hulpe, 1170 Brussels; tel. (2) 662-23-03; fax (2) 675-52-21; e-mail eukorea@skynet.be; Ambassador PARK YANG-CHUN.

Kuwait: 43 ave F. D. Roosevelt, 1050 Brussels; tel. (2) 647-79-50; fax (2) 646-12-98; e-mail embassy.kwt@euronet.be; Ambassador ABDULAZEEZ AL-SHARIKH.

Kyrgyzstan: 47 Abdijstraat, 1050 Brussels; tel. (2) 640-18-68; fax (2) 640-01-31; e-mail aitmatov@infonie.be; Ambassador CHINGIZ TOR-EKULOVITCH AITMATOV.

Laos: 19–21 ave de la Brabançonne, 1000 Brussels; tel. (2) 734-16-66; fax (2) 734-16-66.

Latvia: 158 ave Molière, 1050 Brussels; tel. (2) 344-16-82; fax (2) 344-74-78; e-mail lvembassybenelux@arcadis.be; Ambassador AIVARS GROZA.

Lebanon: 2 rue Guillaume Stocq, 1050 Brussels; tel. (2) 645–77–60; fax (2) 645–77–69; Ambassador JIHAD MORTADA.

Lesotho: 45 blvd Général Wahis, 1030 Brussels; tel. (2) 705-39-76; fax (2) 705-67-79; e-mail lesothobrussels@hotmail.com; Ambassador M. A. MATLANYANE.

Liberia: 50 ave du Château, 1080 Brussels; tel. (2) 411-01-12; fax (2) 411-09-12; Ambassador Dr CECIL T. O. BRANDY, Sr.

Libya: 28 ave Victoria, 1050 Brussels; tel. (2) 647-37-37; fax (2) 640-90-76; Sec. of People's Bureau HAMED AHMED ELHOUDERI.

Liechtenstein: 1 place du Congrès, 1000 Brussels; tel. (2) 229-39-00; fax (2) 219-35-45; e-mail ambassade.liechtenstein@bbru.llv.li; Ambassador Prince NIKOLAUS VON LIECHTENSTEIN.

Lithuania: 48 rue Maurice Liétart, 1150 Brussels; tel. (2) 772-27-50; fax (2) 772-17-01; Chargé d'affaires AUDRIUS NAVIKAS.

Luxembourg: 75 ave de Cortenbergh, 1000 Brussels; tel. (2) 737-57-00; fax (2) 737-57-10; Ambassador JOSEPH WEYLAND.

Macedonia, former Yugoslav republic: 128 ave Tervuren, 1050 Brussels; tel. (2) 732-91-08; fax (2) 732-91-11; e-mail mk.mission@brutele.be; Ambassador STEFKOV SAŠKO.

Madagascar: 276 ave de Tervueren, 1150 Brussels; tel. (2) 770-17-26; fax (2) 772-37-31; e-mail beriziky.jean.omer@ambassademadagascar.be; Ambassador JEAN OMER BERIZIKY.

Malawi: 15 rue de la Loi, 1040 Brussels; tel. (2) 231-09-80; fax (2) 231-10-66; e-mail embassy.malawi@pi.de; Ambassador JULIE NANYONI MPHANDE.

Malaysia: 414A ave de Tervueren, 1150 Brussels; tel. (2) 776-03-40; e-mail mwbrusel@euronet.be; fax (2) 762-50-49; Ambassador Dato DEVA M. RIDZAM.

Mali: 487 ave Molière, 1050 Brussels; tel. (2) 345-74-32; fax (2) 344-57-00; e-mail ambassade.mali@skynet.be; Ambassador (vacant).

Malta: 44 rue Jules Lejeune, 1050 Brussels; tel. (2) 343-01-95; fax (2) 343-01-06; e-mail victor.camilleri@magnet.mt; Ambassador VICTOR CAMILLERI.

Mauritania: 6 ave de la Colombie, 1000 Brussels; tel. (2) 672-47-47; fax (2) 672-20-51; e-mail amb.bxl.mauritanie@skynet.be; Ambassador MOHAMED SALEM OULD LEKHAL.

Mauritius: 68 rue des Bollandistes, 1040 Brussels; tel. (2) 733-99-88; fax (2) 734-40-21; e-mail ambmaur@skynet.be; Ambassador SUTIAWAN GUNESSEE.

Mexico: 94 ave F. D. Roosevelt, 1050 Brussels; tel. (2) 629-07-77; fax (2) 646-87-68; e-mail embamexbel@pophost.eunet.be; Ambassador PORFIRIO MUÑOZ LEDO.

Moldova: Tenboschstraat 154, 1050 Brussels; tel. (2) 732-96-59; fax (2) 732-96-60; e-mail molda@skynet.be; Ambassador ION CAPATINA.

Monaco: 17 place Guy d'Arezzo, bte 7, 1180 Brussels; tel. (2) 347-49-87; fax (2) 343-49-20; e-mail ambassade.monaco@skynet.be; Ambassador JEAN ANDRÉ GRÉTHER.

Mongolia: 18 ave Besme, 1190 Brussels; tel. (2) 344-69-74; fax (2) 344-32-15; e-mail brussels.mn.embassy@chello.be; Ambassador ONON SODOV.

Morocco: 29 bd Saint-Michel, 1040 Brussels; tel. (2) 626-34-10; fax (2) 626-34-34; e-mail mission.maroc@skynet.be; Ambassador AICHA BELARBI.

Mozambique: 97 blvd St-Michel, 1040 Brussels; tel. (2) 736-25-64; fax (2) 735-62-07; e-mail embamoc.bru@skynet.be; Ambassador ALVARO O. DA SILVA.

Namibia: 454 ave de Tervueren, 1150 Brussels; tel. (2) 771-14-10; fax (2) 771-96-89; e-mail nam.emb@brutele.be; Ambassador Dr ZEDEKIA J. NGAVIRUE.

Nepal: 58 ave Winston Churchill, 1180 Brussels; tel. (2) 346-26-58; fax (2) 344-13-61; e-mail rne.bru@skynet.be; Ambassador KEDAR BHAKTA SHRESTHA.

Netherlands: 48 ave Hermann Debroux, 1160 Brussels; tel. (2) 679-17-11; fax (2) 679-17-75; Ambassador A. F. VAN DONGEN.

New Zealand: 1 Meeussquare, 1000 Brussels; tel. (2) 512-10-40; fax (2) 513-48-56; e-mail nzemb.brussels@skynet.be; Ambassador DELL HIGGIE.

Nicaragua: 55 ave de Wolvendael, 1180 Brussels; tel. (2) 375-65-00; fax (2) 375-71-88; e-mail sky77706@skynet.be; Ambassador MARIO BLANDÓN LANZAS.

Niger: 78 ave F. D. Roosevelt, 1050 Brussels; tel. (2) 648-61-40; fax (2) 648-27-84; Ambassador HOUSSEINI ABDOU-SALEYE.

Nigeria: 288 ave de Tervueren, 1150 Brussels; tel. (2) 762-52-00; fax (2) 762-37-63; Ambassador GABRIEL SAM AKUNWAFOR.

Norway: 17 rue Archimède (3e étage), 1000 Brussels; tel. (2) 646-07-80; fax (2) 646-28-82; e-mail emb.brussels@mfa.no; Ambassador JOHN BJØRNEBYE.

Pakistan: 57 ave Delleur, 1170 Brussels; tel. (2) 673-80-07; fax (2) 675-83-94; e-mail parepbrussels@skynet.be; Ambassador TARIQ FATEMI.

Panama: 390–392 ave Louise, 1050 Brussels; tel. (2) 647-07-29; fax (2) 648-92-16; e-mail embajada.panama@skynet.be; Ambassador ROLANDO A. GUEVARA ALVARADO.

Papua New Guinea: 430 ave de Tervueren, 1150 Brussels; tel. (2) 779-08-26; fax (2) 772-70-88; Ambassador GABRIEL KOIBA PEPSON.

Paraguay: 475 ave Louise, 1050 Brussels; tel. (2) 649-90-55; fax (2) 647-42-48; e-mail embapar.belgica@skynet.be; Ambassador MANUEL M. CÁCERES.

Peru: 179 ave de Tervueren, 1150 Brussels; tel. (2) 733-33-19; fax (2) 733-48-19; e-mail comunicaciones@embassy-of-peru.be; Ambassador JOSÉ URRUTIA.

Philippines: 297 ave Molière, 1050 Brussels; tel. (2) 340-33-77; fax (2) 345-64-25; e-mail Brusselspe@brutele.be; Ambassador CLEMENCIO F. MONTESA.

Poland: 29 ave des Gaulois, 1040 Brussels; tel. (2) 739-01-00; fax (2) 736-18-81; e-mail polambbxl@skynet.net; Ambassador JAN W. PIE-KARSKI.

Portugal: 55 ave de la Toison d'Or, 1060 Brussels; tel. (2) 533-07-00; fax (2) 539-07-73; Ambassador FRANCISCO PESSANHA DE QUEVEDO CRESPO.

Romania: 105 rue Gabrielle, 1180 Brussels; tel. (2) 345-26-80; fax (2) 346-23-45; e-mail amrobel@belgacom.net; Ambassador VIRGIL N. CONSTANTINESCU.

Russia: 66 ave de Fré, 1180 Brussels; tel. (2) 374-34-00; fax (2) 374-26-13; e-mail amrusbel@skynet.be; Ambassador SERGEI KISLYAK.

Rwanda: 1 ave des Fleurs, 1150 Brussels; tel. (2) 763-07-05; fax (2) 763-07-53; e-mail ambarwanada@skynet.be; internet www.ambarwanda.be; Ambassador IMANZI KAYITANA.

Samoa: 123 ave F. D. Roosevelt, bte 14, 1050 Brussels; tel. (2) 660-84-54; fax (2) 675-03-36; e-mail samoa.emb.bxl@skynet.be; Ambassador TAU'ILI'ILI UILI MEREDITH.

San Marino: 62 ave F. D. Roosevelt, 1050 Brussels; tel. (2) 644-22-24; fax (2) 644-20-57; e-mail ambrsm.bxl@coditel.net; Ambassador SAVINA ZAFFERANI.

São Tomé and Príncipe: 175 ave de Tervueren, 1150 Brussels; tel. (2) 734-89-66; fax (2) 734-88-15; e-mail ambassade.sao.tome@skynet .be; Chargé d'affaires a.i. ANTÓNIO DE LIMA VIEGAS.

Saudi Arabia: 45 ave F. D. Roosevelt, 1050 Brussels; tel. (2) 649-20-44; fax (2) 647-24-92; Ambassador NASSER ASSAF HUSSEIN AL-ASSAF.

Senegal: 196 ave F. D. Roosevelt, 1050 Brussels; tel. (2) 673-00-97; fax (2) 675-04-60; e-mail senegal.ambassade.coditel.net; Ambassador SALIOU CISSE.

Serbia and Montenegro: 11 ave Emile de Mot, 1000 Brussels; tel. (2) 647-57-81; fax (2) 647-29-41; e-mail ambayougoslavie@skynet.be; Ambassador ZORAN POPOVIĆ.

Sierra Leone: 410 ave de Tervueren, 1150 Brussels; tel. (2) 771-00-53; fax (2) 771-82-30; e-mail slembassy-brussels@email.com; internet www.sierra-leone.org; Ambassador FODE M. DABOR.

Singapore: 198 ave F. D. Roosevelt, 1050 Brussels; tel. (2) 660-29-79; fax (2) 660-86-85; e-mail amb.eu@singembbru.be; internet www .mfa.gov.sg/brussels; Ambassador A. SELVERAJAH.

Slovakia: 195 ave Molière, 1050 Brussels; tel. (2) 346-40-45; fax (2) 346-63-85; e-mail ambassade.slovaque@euronet.be; Ambassador FRANTIŠEK LIPKA.

Slovenia: 179 ave Louise, 1050 Brussels; tel. (2) 646-90-99; fax (2) 646-36-67; e-mail vbr@mzz-dkp.gov.si; Ambassador MARIJA ADANJA.

Solomon Islands: 17 ave Edouard Lacomble, 1040 Brussels; tel. (2) 732-70-85; fax (2) 732-68-85; Ambassador ROBERT SISILO.

South Africa: 26 rue de la Loi, bus 7–8, 1040 Brussels; tel. (2) 285-44-00; fax (2) 285-44-02; e-mail embassy@southafrica.be; Ambassador JERRY MATTHEWS MATJILA.

Spain: 19 rue de la Science, 1040 Brussels; tel. (2) 230-03-40; fax (2) 230-93-80; e-mail ambespbe@mail.mae.es; Ambassador FRANCISCO FERNÁNDEZ FÁBREGAS.

Sri Lanka: 27 rue Jules Lejeune, 1050 Brussels; tel. (2) 344-53-94; fax (2) 344-67-37; e-mail sri.lanka@euronet.be; Ambassador G. R. JAYASINGHE.

Sudan: 124 ave F. D. Roosevelt, 1050 Brussels; tel. (2) 647-94-94; fax (2) 648-34-99; Ambassador ABDELRAHIM AHMED KHALIL.

Suriname: 379 ave Louise, 1050 Brussels; tel. (2) 640-11-72; fax (2) 646-39-62; e-mail sur.amb.bru@online.be; Ambassador GERHARD O. HIWAT.

Swaziland: 188 ave Winston Churchill, 1180 Brussels; tel. (2) 347-47-71; fax (2) 347-46-23; Ambassador Dr THEMBAYENA ANNASTASIA DLAMINI.

Sweden: 3 rue de Luxembourg, 1000 Brussels; tel. (2) 289-57-60; fax (2) 289-57-90; e-mail ambassaden.bryssel@foreign.ministry.se; Ambassador ANDERS OLJELUND.

Switzerland: 26 rue de la Loi, bte 9, 1040 Brussels; tel. (2) 285-43-50; fax (2) 230-37-81; e-mail vertretung@bru.rep.admin.ch; Ambassador ANTON THALMANN.

Syria: 3 ave F. D. Roosevelt, 1050 Brussels; tel. (2) 648-01-35; fax (2) 646-40-18; Ambassador Dr HANI HABEEB.

Tanzania: 363 ave Louise (7e étage), 1050 Brussels; tel. (2) 640-65-00; fax (2) 640-80-26; e-mail tanzania@skynet.be; Ambassador ALI ABEID KARUME.

Thailand: 2 square du Val de la Cambre, 1050 Brussels; tel. (2) 640-68-10; fax (2) 648-30-66; e-mail thaibxl@pophost.eunet.be; internet www.waw.be/rte/be; Ambassador SURAPONG POSAYANOND.

Togo: 264 ave de Tervueren, 1150 Brussels; tel. (2) 770-55-63; fax (2) 771-50-75; Ambassador FOLLY-GLIDJITO AKAKPO.

Trinidad and Tobago: 14 ave de la Faisanderie, 1150 Brussels; tel. (2) 762-94-00; fax (2) 772-27-83; e-mail information@ttm.eunet.be; Chargé d'affaires S. N. GORDON.

Tunisia: 278 ave de Tervueren, 1150 Brussels; tel. (2) 771-73-95; fax (2) 771-94-33; e-mail amb.detunisie@brutele.be; Ambassador SLA-HEDDINE BEN M'BAREK.

Turkey: 4 rue Montoyer, 1000 Brussels; tel. (2) 513-40-95; fax (2) 514-07-48; e-mail tcbrukselbe@yucom.be; Ambassador TEMEL ISKIT.

Turkmenistan: 106 ave F. D. Roosevelt, 1050 Brussels; tel. (2) 648-18-74; fax (2) 648-19-06; e-mail turkmenistan@skynet.be.

Uganda: 317 ave de Tervueren, 1150 Brussels; tel. (2) 762-58-25; fax (2) 763-04-38; e-mail ugembrus@brutele.be; Chargé d'affaires a.i. LEWIS D. BALINDA.

Ukraine: 30–32 ave Lancaster, 1180 Brussels; tel. (2) 379-21-01; fax (2) 379-21-79; e-mail embassy@ukraine.be; internet www.ukraine .be; Ambassador VOLODYMYR KHANDOGIY.

United Arab Emirates: 73 ave F. D. Roosevelt, 1050 Brussels; tel. (2) 640-60-00; fax (2) 646-24-73; e-mail emirates.bxl@infonie.be; Ambassador ABDULHADI AL-KHAJAH.

United Kingdom: 85 rue d'Arlon, 1040 Brussels; tel. (2) 287-62-11; fax (2) 287-63-55; e-mail ppa@britain.be; internet www .british-embassy.be; Ambassador GAVIN HEWITT.

USA: 27 blvd du Régent, 1000 Brussels; tel. (2) 508-21-11; fax (2) 511-27-25; e-mail SniderPW@state.gov; internet www.usinfo.be; Ambassador STEPHEN F. BRAUER.

Uruguay: 22 ave F. D. Roosevelt, 1050 Brussels; tel. (2) 640-11-69; fax (2) 648-29-09; e-mail uruemb@euronet.be; Ambassador JORGE TALICE.

Uzbekistan: 99 ave F. D. Roosevelt, 1050 Brussels; tel. (2) 672-88-44; fax (2) 672-39-46; e-mail embassy@uzbekistan.be; internet corporate.skynet.be/uzbekistan; Ambassador ALISHER SHAYKHOV.

Venezuela: 10 ave F. D. Roosevelt, 1050 Brussels; tel. (2) 639-03-40; fax (2) 647-88-20; e-mail embajada@venezuela-eu.org; Chargé d'affaires a.i. LUISA ROMERO.

Viet Nam: 130 ave de la Floride, 1080 Brussels; tel. (2) 374-91-33; fax (2) 374-93-76; Ambassador HUYNH ANH DZUNG.

Yemen: 114 ave F. D. Roosevelt, 1050 Brussels; tel. (2) 646-52-90; fax (2) 646-29-11; Ambassador A. K. AL-AGHBARI.

Zambia: 469 ave Molière, 1050 Brussels; tel. (2) 343-56-49; fax (2) 347-43-33; e-mail zambiansbrussels@skynet.be; Ambassador GRIFFIN K. NYIRONGO.

Zimbabwe: 11 square Joséphine Charlotte, 1200 Brussels; tel. (2) 762-58-08; fax (2) 762-96-05; e-mail zimbrussels@skynet.be; Ambassador KELEBERT NKOMANI.

Judicial System

The independence of the judiciary is based on the constitutional division of power between the legislative, executive and judicial bodies, each of which acts independently. Judges are appointed by the crown for life, and cannot be removed except by judicial sentence. The judiciary is organized on four levels, from the judicial canton to the district, regional and national courts. The lowest courts are those of the Justices of the Peace and the Police Tribunals. Each district has one of each type of district court, including the Tribunals of the First Instance, Tribunals of Commerce, and Labour Tribunals, and there is a Court of Assizes in each province. There are Courts of Appeal and Labour Courts in each region. The highest courts are the national civil and criminal Courts of Appeal, Labour Courts and the Supreme Court of Justice. The Military Court of Appeal is in Brussels.

COUR DE CASSATION/HOF VAN CASSATIE
(SUPREME COURT OF JUSTICE)

First President: PIERRE MARCHAL.

President: I. VEROUGSTRAETE.

Counsellors: D. BATSELÉ, R. BOES, C. PARMENTIER, P. ECHEMENT, CHR. STORCK, P. MATHIEU, C. MATRAY, S. VELU, E. WAUTERS, G. SUETENS-BOURGEOIS, G. LONDERS, E. DIRIX, STASSIJNS, A FETTWEIS, G. DHAEYER, E. GOETHALS, P. MAFFEI, D. DEBRUYNE, J. DE CODT, F. CLOSE, D. PLAS, M. LAHOUSSE, F. FISCHER, D. MATHIEU, B. DEJEMEPPE, E. FORRIER L. HUYBRECHTS, J.-P. FRÈRE, L. VAN HOOGENBEMT.

Attorney-General: J. DU JARDIN.

First Advocate-General: J.-F. LECLERCQ.

Advocates-General: X. DE RIEMAECKER, J. SPREUTELS, A. HENKES, R. LOOP, M. TIMPERMAN, M. DE SWAEFF, G. BRESSELEERS, A. DE RAEVE, G. DUBRULLE, P. DUINSLAEGER, TH. WERQUIN.

COURS D'APPEL/HOVEN VAN BEROEP
(CIVIL AND CRIMINAL HIGH COURTS)

Antwerp: First Pres. Y. LIEGEOIS, Attorney-Gen. CHRISTINE DEKKERS.

Brussels: First Pres. JACQUELINE COPPIN, Attorney-Gen. ANDRÉ VAN OUDENHOVE.

Ghent: First Pres. LUC DECLERCQ, Attorney-Gen. FRANK SCHINS.

Liège: First Pres. ANDRÉE SPRIESTERBACH, Attorney-Gen. ANNE THILY.

Mons: First Pres. CHRISTIAN JASSOGNE, Attorney-Gen. GASTON LADRIÈRE.

COURS DU TRAVAIL/ARBEIDSHOVEN
(LABOUR COURTS)

Antwerp: First Pres. RENILDE VAN STRYDONCK.

Brussels: First Pres. WILFRIED DECROCK.

Ghent: First Pres. PATRICK BRICOURT.

Liège: First Pres. JOEL HUBIN.

Mons: First Pres. JOSEPH GILLAIN.

Religion

CHRISTIANITY

The Roman Catholic Church

Belgium comprises one archdiocese and seven dioceses. At 31 December 1999 there were an estimated 8,180,088 adherents (some 80% of the total population).

Bishops' Conference

Bisschoppenconferentie van België/Conférence Episcopale de Belgique, 1 rue Guimard, 1040 Brussels; tel. (2) 509-96-93; fax (2) 509-96-95; e-mail ce.belgica@catho.kerknet.be; internet www.kerknet .be.

f. 1981; Pres. Cardinal GODFRIED DANNEELS (Archbishop of Mechelen-Brussels).

Archbishop of Mechelen-Brussels: Cardinal GODFRIED DANNEELS, Aartsbisdom, 15 Wollemarkt, 2800 Mechelen; tel. (15) 21-65-01; fax (15) 20-94-85; e-mail aartsbisdom@kerknet.be.

Protestant Churches

Belgian Evangelical Lutheran Church: Brussels; tel. (2) 511-92-47; f. 1950; 425 mems; Pres. C. J. HOBUS.

Church of England: Holy Trinity Pro-Cathedral, 29 rue Capitaine Crespel, 1050 Brussels; tel. (2) 511-71-83; fax (2) 511-10-28; e-mail holy.trinity@arcadis.be; internet www.holytrinitybrussels.com; Rev. Canon NIGEL WALKER (Chaplain and Chancellor of the Pro-Cathedral of the Holy Trinity, Brussels).

Eglise Protestante Unie de Belgique: 5 rue du Champ de Mars, 1050 Brussels; tel. (2) 510-61-66; fax (2) 510-61-64; e-mail belpro .epub@skynet.be; internet www.protestanet.be; Pres. Rev. DANIEL VANESCOTE; Sec. Mrs B. SMETRYNS-BAETENS; 45,000 mems.

Mission Evangélique Belge: 158 blvd Lambermont, 1030 Brussels; tel. (2) 241-30-15; fax (2) 245-79-65; e-mail information@b-e-m .org; internet www.b-e-m.org; f. 1919; Pres. JOHAN LUKASSE; Dirs WILFRIED GOOSSENS, ERIC ZANDER; c. 12,000 mems.

Union of Baptists in Belgium (UBB): 85 A. Liebaertstraat, 8400 Ostend; tel. (59) 32-46-10; fax (59) 32-46-10; e-mail 106466.3510@ compuserve.com; f. 1922 as Union of Protestant Baptists in Belgium; Pres. SAMUEL VERHAEGHE; Sec. EMMANUEL MUKWEGE.

ISLAM

There are some 350,000 Muslims in Belgium. In December 1998 the Belgian Islamic community elected an Islamic representative body.

Leader of the Islamic Community: Imam Prof. SALMAN AL-RAHDI.

JUDAISM

There are about 35,000 Jews in Belgium.

Consistoire Central Israélite de Belgique (Central Council of the Jewish Communities of Belgium): 2 rue Joseph Dupont, 1000 Brussels; tel. (2) 512-21-90; fax (2) 512-35-78; e-mail consis@online .be; internet www.jewishcom.be; f. 1808; Chair. Prof. JULIEN KLENER; Sec. Gen. MICHEL LAUB.

The Press

Article 25 of the Belgian Constitution states: 'The Press is free; no form of censorship may ever be instituted; no cautionary deposit may be demanded from writers, publishers or printers. When the author is known and is resident in Belgium, the publisher, printer or distributor may not be prosecuted.'

There were an estimated 30 general information dailies in 1996, with an estimated combined circulation of 1,625,000 copies per issue.

There is a trend towards concentration. The Rossel ('Le Soir') group and the Médiabel group control the majority of francophone newspapers, while the principal publisher of Flemish newspapers is the VUM ('De Standaard') group. The Roularta media group is an important publisher of regional newspapers and periodicals, and the Mediaxis group is an important magazine publisher.

The most widely-circulating dailies in French in 1995 were: *Le Soir* (182,520), *L'Avenir de Luxembourg/Vers l'Avenir* (139,960) and *La Capitale (formerly La Lanterne), La Meuse, La Wallonie* (129,840). (*La Wallonie* was subsequently superseded by *Le Matin*.) The corresponding figures for Flemish-language dailies were: *De Standaard/Nieuwsblad/De Gentenaar* (372,410) and *Het Laatste Nieuws/De Nieuwe Gazet* (306,240). The major weeklies include *De Bond, Flair, Humo* and *Télémoustique*. Some periodicals are printed in both French and Flemish.

PRINCIPAL DAILIES

Antwerp

De Financieel Economische Tijd: Franklin Bldg, 3 Posthoflei, 2600 Berchem; tel. (3) 286-02-11; fax (3) 286-02-10; e-mail tijd@tijd .be; internet www.tijd.be; f. 1968; economic and financial; Gen. Man. HANS MAERTENS; circ. 51,700.

Gazet van Antwerpen: 2 Katwilgweg, 2050 Antwerp; tel. (3) 210-02-10; fax (3) 219-40-41; e-mail webmaster@gva.be; internet www .gva.be; f. 1891; Christian Democrat; Man. Dir MARC VANGEEL; Editor LUC VAN LOON; circ. 123,000.

De Lloyd/Le Lloyd: 18 Vleminckstraat, 2000 Antwerp; tel. (3) 234-05-50; fax (3) 234-25-93; internet www.anlloyd.be; f. 1858; Flemish and French edns, with supplements in English; shipping, commerce, industry, finance; Dir GUY DUBOIS; Editor BERNARD VAN DEN BOSSCHE; circ. 10,600.

De Nieuwe Gazet: Berchem; tel. (3) 286-89-30; fax (3) 286-89-40; e-mail peterverbruggen@persgroep.be; f. 1897; liberal; Chief Editor PETER VERBRUGGEN.

Arlon

L'Avenir du Luxembourg: 38 rue des Déportés, 6700 Arlon; tel. (63) 23-10-20; fax (63) 23-42-89; e-mail info@belmail.com; f. 1897; Catholic; Chief Editor JEAN-LUC HENQUINET; circ. 139,960 (with *Vers l'Avenir*).

Brussels

La Capitale: 120 rue Royale, 1000 Brussels; tel. (2)225-56-00; fax (2)225-59-13; e-mail red.lacapitale@sudpresse.be; f. 1944; independent; Dir-Gen. M. THIBAUT; Chief Editor DIDIER HAMANN.

La Dernière Heure/Les Sports: 127 blvd Emile Jacqmain, 1000 Brussels; tel. (2) 211-28-88; fax (2) 211-28-70; e-mail dhbelgique@ saipm.com; internet www.dhnet.be; f. 1906; independent Liberal; Dir FRANÇOIS LE HODEY; Chief Editor MICHEL MARTEAU; circ. 73,130.

L'Echo: 131 rue de Birmingham, 1070 Brussels; tel. (2) 526-55-11; fax (2) 526-55-26; e-mail redaction@echonet.be; f. 1881; economic and financial; Dir R. WATSON; Editor F. MELAET; circ. 22,230.

Het Laatste Nieuws: 347 Brusselsesteenweg, 1730 Asse-Kobbegem; tel. (2) 454-22-11; fax (2) 454-28-22; e-mail redactie.hln@ persgroep.be; f. 1888; Flemish; independent; Dir-Gen. R. BERTELS; Editors JAAK SMEETS, PAUL DAENEN; circ. 306,279.

La Libre Belgique: 127 blvd Emile Jacqmain, 1000 Brussels; tel. (2) 211-27-77; fax (2) 211-28-32; e-mail llb.redaction@saipm.com; internet www.lalibre.be; f. 1884; European; independent; Chief Editor JEAN-PAUL MARTHOZ; circ. 80,000 (with *La Libre Belgique—Gazette de Liège*).

De Morgen: 54 Brogniezstraat, 1070 Brussels; tel. (2) 556-68-11; fax (2) 520-35-15; e-mail info@demorgen.be; Dir-Gen. KOEN CLEMENT; Editor YVES DESMET; circ. 35,000.

Het Nieuwsblad: 30 Gossetlaan, 1702 Groot Bijgaarden; tel. (2) 467-22-11; fax (2) 466-30-93; e-mail nieuwsblad@vum.be; internet www.vum.be; f. 1923; Dir-Gen. JO VAN CROONENBOZCH; Chief Editors GUIDO VAN LIEFFERIUGE, LUC SAUS; circ. 320,000 (with *Het Volk* and *De Gentenaar*).

Le Soir: 120 rue Royale, 1000 Brussels; tel. (2) 225-54-32; fax (2) 225-59-10; e-mail journal@lesoir.be; internet www.lesoir.com; f. 1887; independent; Chief Editor BEATRICE DELVAUX; circ. 178,569.

De Standaard: 28 Gossetlaan, 1702 Groot Bijgaarden; tel. (2) 467-22-11; fax (2) 466-30-93; e-mail standaard@vum.be; internet www .standaard.be; f. 1914; Dir-Gen. GUIDO VERDEYEN; Chief Editor PIETER VANDERMEERSCH; circ. 77,000.

Charleroi

La Nouvelle Gazette (Charleroi, La Louvière, Philippeville, Namur, Nivelles); La Province (Mons): 2 quai de Flandre, 6000 Charleroi; tel. (71) 27-64-11; fax (71) 27-65-67; e-mail gazette@ charline.be; internet www.nouvellegazette.be; f. 1878; Man. Dir PATRICK HURBAIN; Editor M. FROHONT.

Le Rappel: 16 rue Charles Dupret, 6000 Charleroi; tel. (71) 20-00-60; fax (71) 31-43-61; f. 1900; Dir-Gen. JACQUES DE THYSEBAERT; Chief Editor BRUNO MALTER.

Eupen

Grenz-Echo: 8 Marktplatz, 4700 Eupen; tel. (87) 59-13-00; fax (87) 74-38-20; e-mail info@grenzecho.be; internet www.grenzecho.be; f. 1927; German; independent Catholic; Dir A. KÜCHENBERG; Chief Editor HEINZ WARNY; circ. 12,040.

Ghent

De Gentenaar: 102 Lousbergskaai, 9000 Ghent; tel. (9) 265-68-51; fax (9) 265-68-50; e-mail gentenaar@vum.be; internet www.vum.be; f. 1879; Catholic; Dir-Gen. GUIDO VERDEYEN; Chief Editor RIK VAN WALLEGHEN; circ. 366,665 (with *Het Nieuwsblad* and *De Standaard*).

Het Volk: Ghent; tel. (9) 265-61-11; fax (9) 225-35-27; e-mail redactie.gent@hetvolk.be; internet www.hetvolk.be; f. 1891; Catholic; Dir-Gen. GUIDO VERDEYEN; Chief Editor JAKI LOUAGE; circ. 114,473.

Hasselt

Het Belang van Limburg: 10 Herckenrodesingel, 3500 Hasselt; tel. (11) 87-81-11; fax (11) 87-82-04; e-mail hbvlredactie@rug.be; internet www.hbvl.be; f. 1879; Dir MARC VANGEEL; Editors LUC VAN LOON, IVO VANDEKERCKHOVE, RICHARD SWARTENBROEKX; circ. 100,980.

Liège

La Libre Belgique—Gazette de Liège: 26 blvd d'Avroy, 4000 Liège; tel. (4) 223-19-33; fax (4) 222-41-26; e-mail llb.redaction@ saipm.com; internet www.lalibre.be; f. 1840; Dir-Gen. F. LE HODEY; Editor FRÉDÉRIC VAN VLODORP; circ. 80,000 (with *La Libre Belgique—Brussels*).

Le Matin: Liège; tel. (4) 230-56-56; fax (4) 223-31-17; e-mail redaction@lematin.be; f. 1998; progressive; Dir JOSÉ VERDIN; Editor FABRICE JACQUEMART; circ. 8,000.

La Meuse: 8–12 blvd de la Sauvenière, 4000 Liège; tel. (4) 220-08-11; fax (4) 220-08-40; e-mail lameuse@mail.interpac.be; internet www.lameuse.be; f. 1855; independent; Editor-in-Chief MARC DURAND; circ. 129,840 (with *La Lanterne*).

Mons

La Province: 29 rue des Capucins, 7000 Mons; tel. (65) 31-71-51; fax (65) 33-84-77; internet www.nouvellegazette.be; Dir PHILIPPE DAUTEZ; Chief Editor JEAN GODIN.

Namur

Editions de l'Avenir: 12 blvd Ernest Mélot, 5000 Namur; tel. (81) 24-88-11; fax (81) 22-60-24; e-mail va@verslavenir.be; f. 1918; Editor PASCAL BELPAIRE; circ. 130,000 (with *L'Avenir du Luxembourg*).

Tournai

Le Courrier de l'Escaut: 10 rue de Paris, 7500 Tournai; tel. (69) 88-96-20; fax (69) 88-96-61; e-mail courrier.escaut@skynet.be; f. 1829; Chief Editor WILLY THOMAS.

Verviers

Le Jour/Le Courrier: 14 rue du Brou, 4800 Verviers; tel. (87) 32-20-70; fax (87) 31-67-40; f. 1894; independent; Dir JACQUES DE THYSEBAERT; Chief Editor THIERRY DEGIVES.

WEEKLIES

Atlas Weekblad: 89 Condédreef, 8500 Kortrijk; tel. (56) 26-10-10; fax (56) 21-35-93; e-mail atlas@atlasweekblad.be; internet www .atlasweekblad.be; classified advertising, regional news and sports.

Boer en Tuinder: 8 Minderbroedersstraat, 3000 Leuven; tel. (16) 24-21-60; fax (16) 24-21-68; internet www.boerenbond.be; f. 1891; agriculture and horticulture; circ. 38,000.

De Bond: 170 Langestraat, 1150 Brussels; tel. (2) 779-00-00; fax (2) 779-16-16; e-mail com@publicarto.be; f. 1921; general interest; circ. 314,420.

Brugsch Handelsblad: 20 Sint-Jorisstraat, 8000 Brugge; tel. (50) 44-21-55; fax (50) 44-21-66; e-mail redactie.bhblad@roularta.be; f. 1906; local news; includes *De Krant van West-Vlaanderen* as a supplement; Dir EDDY BROUCKAERT; Editor-in-Chief HEDWIG DACQUIN; circ. 40,000.

Ciné Télé Revue: 101 ave Reine Marie-Henriette, 1190 Brussels; tel. (2) 345-99-68; fax (2) 343-12-72; e-mail redaction@cinetelerevue .be; internet www.cinetelerevue.be; f. 1944 as Theatra Ciné Revue, current name adopted 1984; TV listings, celebrity news, family issues; circ. 2m.

La Cité: 26 rue St Laurent, 1000 Brussels; tel. (2) 217-23-90; fax (2) 217-69-95; f. 1950 as daily, weekly 1988; Christian Democrat; Editor Jos Schoonbroodt; circ. 20,000.

European Voice: 17–19 rue Montoyer, 1000 Brussels; tel. (2) 540-90-90; fax (2) 540-90-71; e-mail info@europeanvoice.com; internet www.europeanvoice.com; f. 1995; EU policy-making, politics and business; Editor Dennis Abbott; circ 18,000.

Femmes d'Aujourd'hui: 109 rue Neewald, 1200 Brussels; tel. (2) 776-28-53; fax (2) 776-23-99; e-mail editeur@femmesaujourdhui.be; internet www.femmesaujourdhui.com; f. 1933; women's magazine; Chief Editor Robert Malies; circ. 160,000.

Flair: 82 Uitbreidingsstraat, 2600 Berchem; tel. (3) 290-13-92; fax (3) 290-13-94; e-mail flairsec@sanomamagazines.be; internet www.flair.be; Flemish; women's magazine; weekly; Chief Editor A. Brouckmans; circ. 157,955.

Humo: 109 Neerveldstraat, 1200 Brussels; tel. (2) 776-24-20; fax (2) 776-23-24; e-mail humo@sanoma-magazines.be; internet www.humo.be; general weekly and TV and radio guide in Flemish; Chief Editor Guy Mortier; circ. 277,863.

Joepie TV Plus: 2 Brandekensweg, 2627 Schelle; tel. (3) 880-84-65; fax (3) 844-61-52; f. 1973; teenagers' interest; Chief Editor Guido van Liefferinge; circ. 144,841.

Kerk en Leven: 92 Halewijnlaan, 2050 Antwerp; tel. (3) 210-08-40; fax (3) 210-08-36; e-mail redactie.kerkenleven@kerknet.be; internet www.kerknet.be; f. 1942; Catholic; five regional edns; circ. 620,000.

Knack: 50 Raketstraat, 1130 Brussels; tel. (2) 702-46-51; fax (2) 702-46-52; e-mail knack@knack.be; internet www.knack.be; f. 1971; news magazine; Dir and Chief Editor Rik van Cauwelaert; circ. 140,000.

Kontakt Lier: 14 Centrale Weg, 2560 Nijlen; tel. (3) 481-89-58; fax (3) 481-71-22; f. 1967; Antwerp local news.

De Kortrijks Handelsblad: 83b Doorniksewijk, 8500 Kortrijk; tel. (56) 27-00-30; fax (56) 27-00-39; e-mail khblad@roularta.be; regional news; owned by Roularta Media Group; includes *De Krant van West-Vlaanderen* as a supplement; Chief Editor Luc Demiddele.

De Krant van West-Vlaanderen: 33 Meiboomlaan, 8800 Roeselare; tel. (51) 26-61-11; fax (51) 26-65-87; e-mail kvwvl@roularta.be; internet www.kw.be; regional news and sport; owned by Roularta Media Group; 11 different edns; included as a supplement with titles *De Weekbode, Het Wekelijks Nieuws, De Zeewacht, Brugsch Handelsbad, De Kortrijks Handelsbad*; Dir Eddy Brouckaert; Chief Editor Noël Maes; circ. 424,000.

Kwik: 347 Brusselsesteenweg, 1730 Kobbegem; tel. (2) 454-25-01; fax (2) 454-28-28; f. 1962; men's interest; Dir Christian van Thillo; Editor Frank Schraets; circ. 55,000.

Landbouwleven/Le Sillon Belge: 92 ave Léon Grosjean, 1140 Brussels; tel. (2) 730-33-00; fax (2) 726-91-34; e-mail erulu@euronet.be; f. 1952; agriculture; Gen. Dir P. Callebaut; Editorial Man. André de Mol; circ. 37,300.

Libelle : 82 Uitbreidingstraat, 2600 Berchem; tel. (3) 290-14-42; fax (3) 290-14-44; e-mail libelle@sanoma-magazines.be; f. 1945; Flemish; women's interest; Dir Jan Vandenwyngaerden; Chief Editor Liliane Senepart; circ. 250,668.

Le Soir Magazine: 120 rue Royale, 1000 Brussels; tel. (2) 225-55-55; fax (2) 225-59-11; e-mail ned.enione@lesoirmagazine.com; internet www.lesoirmagazine.com; f. 1928; independent illustrated; Chief Editor Steve Polus; circ. 90,000.

Spirou/Robbedoes: 52 rue Jules Deserée, 6001 Marcinelle; tel. (71) 60-05-00; children's interest; circ. 80,000.

Sport/Foot Magazine and Sport/Voetbal Magazine: 50 Raketstraat, 1130 Brussels; tel. (2) 702-45-71; fax (2) 702-45-72; e-mail sportmagazine@roularta.be; internet www.sportmagazine.be; Flemish and French; football; Chief Editors J. Sys, J. Baete.

Story: 82 Uitbreidingsstraat, 2600 Berchem; tel. (3) 290-15-13; fax (3) 290-15-14; e-mail story@mediaxis.be; f. 1975; Flemish; women's interest; Dir J. Vandenwyngaerden; Chief Editor Hilde Debisschop; circ. 175,111.

Télé Moustique: Brussels; tel. (2) 776-25-20; fax (2) 776-23-14; f. 1924; radio and TV; Dir Jan Vandenwyngaerden; Editor Patrick Weber; circ. 170,000.

Télépro/Telepro: 31 rue Saint Remacle, 4800 Verviers; tel. (87) 30-70-24; fax (87) 31-35-37; f. 1954; TV listings; owned by Roularta Media Group; Chief Editor Guy Darrenougué; circ. 185,000.

TeVe-Blad: 82 Uitbreidingsstraat, 2600 Berchem; tel. (3) 290-14-81; fax (3) 290-14-82; e-mail teveblad@sanoma-magazines.be; f. 1981; TV listings; illustrated; Chief Editor Rob Jans.

Trends: 50 Raketstraat, bus 4, 1130 Brussels; tel. (2) 702-48-01; fax (2) 702-48-02; e-mail trends@trends.be; internet www.trends.be;

economic analysis and business news; owned by Roularta Media Group; Dir Frans Crols; Chief Editor Piet Depuydt; circ. 43,514.

TV Ekspres: 82 Uitbreidingsstraat, 2600 Berchem; tel. (3) 290-14-81; fax (3) 290-14-82; e-mail tvexpres@mediaxis.be; Chief Editor Rob Jans; circ. 95,000.

Le Vif/L'Express: Roularta Media Group NV, Research Park, Zellik, De Haak, 1731 Zellik; tel. (2) 467-56-11; fax (2) 467-57-57; f. 1971; current affairs; owned by Roularta Media Group; Dir-Gen. Patrick de Borchgrave; Chief Editors Jacques Gevers, Stéphane Renard; circ. 83,816.

De Weekbode: 33 Meiboomlaan, 8800 Roeselare; tel. (51) 26-61-11; fax (51) 26-65-87; regional news; owned by Roularta Media Group; includes *De Krant van West-Vlaanderen* as a supplement; Chief Editor Noël Maes.

De Weekkrant: 10 Herckenrodesingel, 3500 Hasselt; tel. (11) 87-83-70; fax (11) 87-85-09; e-mail weekkrant@rug.be; f. 1949; Brabant and Limburg local news; circ. 370,000.

Het Wekelijks Nieuws: 5 Nijverheidslaan, 8970 Poperinge; tel. (57) 33-67-21; fax (57) 33-40-18; Christian news magazine; Dir Wim Wauters; Editor Herman Sansen; circ. 56,000.

Het Wekelijks Nieuws Kust: 52–54 Torhoutsesteenweg, 8400 Ostend; tel. (59) 56-02-21; fax (59) 56-02-22; e-mail sandra.rosseel@roularta.be; Furnes, Dixmude and Belgian West coast local news; owned by Roularta Media Group; includes *De Krant van West-Vlaanderen* as a supplement.

De Zeewacht: 52–54 Torhoutsesteenweg, 8400 Ostend; tel. (59) 56-02-21; fax (59) 56-02-22; e-mail kris.carlier@roularta.be; Ostend local news; owned by Roularta Media Group; includes *De Krant van West-Vlaanderen* as a supplement.

ZIE-Magazine: Antwerp; tel. (3) 231-47-90; fax (3) 234-34-66; f. 1930; illustrated; Dir Jan Merckx; Chief Editor Rob Jans.

Zondag Nieuws: 2 Brandekensweg, 2627 Schelle; tel. (2) 220-22-11; fax (2) 217-98-46; f. 1958; general interest; Dir Rik Duyck; Chief Editor Luc Vandriessche; circ. 113,567.

Zondagsblad: 22 Forelstraat, 9000 Ghent; tel. (9) 265-68-02; fax (9) 223-16-77; f. 1949; Gen. Man. Wim Schaap; Editor Jef Nijs; circ. 75,000.

SELECTED OTHER PERIODICALS

Alternative Libertaire: BP 3, 4000 Lege; internet www.anarchie.be/AL; 11 a year; radical social criticism and debate.

Axelle: 170 Langestraat, 1150 Brussels; tel. (2) 799-00-00; fax (2) 799-16-16; e-mail com@publicarto.be; f. 1917; monthly; women's interest; circ. 40,677.

Le Cri du Citoyen: BP 1607, 1000 Brussels 1; tel. and fax (2) 217-48-31; e-mail redaction@lecriducitoyen.com; internet www.chez.com/lecriducitoyen; social comment; 10 a year; Editor Francesco Paolo Catania.

Eigen Aard: 170 Langestraat, 1150 Brussels; tel. (2) 799-00-00; fax (2) 799-16-16; e-mail com@publicarto.be; f. 1911; monthly; women's interest; circ. 131,986.

International Engineering News: 100 rue des Palais, 1030 Brussels; tel. (2) 240-26-58; fax (2) 245-75-82; e-mail p.alvenius@ien-online.com; internet www.ien-online.com; f. 1975; 10 a year; Man. Dir J. Michael Clement; circ. 55,000.

Jet Limburg: 10 Herckenrodesingel, 3500 Hasselt; tel. (11) 87-84-85; fax (11) 87-84-84; fortnightly; general interest; circ. 292,000.

Marie Claire: Neerveldstraat 109, 1200 Brussels; tel. (2) 776-22-11; fax (2) 776–23–99; e-mail marieclaire@sanoma-magazines.be; monthly; women's interest; circ. 80,000.

Le Moniteur Belge/Belgisch Staatsblad: 40–42 rue de Louvain, 1000 Brussels; tel. (2) 552-24-59; fax (2) 511-01-84; internet moniteur.be; legislation and official documents; up to 5 a week.

Le Moniteur de l'Automobile: 56 ave Général Dumonceau, 1190 Brussels; tel. (2) 333-32-20; fax (2) 333-32-10; e-mail contacT.mab@lemoniteurautomobile.be; internet www.lemoniteurautomobile.be; fortnightly; motoring; Editor Étienne Visart; circ. 85,000.

Notre Temps/Onze Tijd: 33 rue de la Concorde, 1050 Brussels; tel. (2) 514-24-24; fax (2) 514-22-44; e-mail Redaction.NT@bayard-presse.be; senior citizen's interests; monthly; circ. 96,672.

Passie/Passion: T & M, place du Congrès, 4020 Luik; tel. (4) 343-50-50; fax (4) 342-70-00; e-mail tindnees.m@swmj.be; 4 a year; luxury goods; owned by Roularta Media Group; Dir and Chief Editor Jocelyn Dumont; circ. 20,000.

PC World Belgium: 70 rue Rederbachstraat, 1190 Brussels; tel. (2) 346-48-50; fax (2) 346-43-65; internet www.best.be; f. 1998; monthly; Pres. Jean de Gheldere; circ. 35,000.

Santé: Drogenbos; tel. (2) 331-06-13; fax (2) 331-23-33; monthly; popular health, diet, fitness; circ. 200,000.

Sélection du Reader's Digest: 20 blvd Paepsem, 1070 Brussels; tel. (2) 526-81-85; fax (2) 526-81-89; f. 1947; monthly; general; Man. Dir CAREL ROG; circ. 80,000.

Vrouw & Wereld: 170 Langestraat, 1150 Brussels; tel. (2) 799-00-00; fax (2) 799-16-16; e-mail com@publicarto.be; f. 1920; monthly; women's interest; circ. 161,042.

NEWS AGENCIES

Agence Belga (Agence Télégraphique Belge de Presse SA)—Agentschap Belga (Belgisch Pers-telegraafagentschap NV): 8B rue F. Pelletier, 1030 Brussels; tel. (2) 743-23-11; fax (2) 735-18-74; internet www.belga.be; f. 1920; largely owned by daily newspapers; Chair. L. NEELS; Gen. Man. E. HANS.

Agence Europe SA: 36 rue de la Gare, 1040 Brussels; tel. (2) 737-94-94; fax (2) 736-37-00; internet www.agenceurope.com; f. 1952; daily bulletin on EU activities.

Centre d'Information de Presse (CIP): 199 blvd du Souverain, 1160 Brussels; tel. (2) 675-25-79; f. 1946; Dir T. SCHOLTES.

Foreign Bureaux

Agence France-Presse (AFP): Europe Center, 17/3 rue Archimède, 1000 Brussels; tel. (2) 230-83-94; fax (2) 230-23-04; e-mail afp.bru@euronet.be; internet www.afp.com; Dir PHILIPPE VALAT.

Agencia EFE (Spain): 1 blvd Charlemagne, bte 20, 1041 Brussels; tel. (2) 285-48-30; internet www.efe.com; Dir JOSÉ MANUEL SANZ MINGOTE.

Agenzia Nazionale Stampa Associata (ANSA) (Italy): 1 blvd Charlemagne, bte 7, 1040 Brussels; tel. (2) 230-81-92; fax (2) 230-60-82; internet www.ansa.it; Dir LUIGI MAYER.

Algemeen Nederlands Persbureau (ANP) (Netherlands): 1 blvd Charlemagne, bte 6, 1041 Brussels; tel. (2) 230-11-88; fax (2) 231-18-04; internet www.anp.nl; Correspondents TON VAN LIEROP, KEES PIJNAPPELS, WILMA VAN MELEREN.

Associated Press (AP) (USA): 1 blvd Charlemagne, bte 49, 1041 Brussels; tel. (2) 230-52-49; internet www.ap.org; Dir ROBERT WIELAARD.

Česká Tisková Kancelář (ČTK) (Czech Republic): 2 rue des Egyptiens, bte 6, 1050 Brussels; tel. (2) 648-01-33; fax (2) 640-31-91; e-mail karol.bartak@skynet.be; internet www.ctk.cz; Correspondent M. BARTAK.

DDP Nachrichtenagentur GmbH (ddp) (Germany): Brussels.

Deutsche Presse-Agentur (dpa) (Germany): 1 blvd Charlemagne, bte 17, 1041 Brussels; tel. (2) 230-36-91; fax (2) 230-98-96; e-mail dpa@dpa.be; internet www.dpa.de; Dir THOMAS SPIEKER.

Informatsionnoye Telegrafnoye Agentstvo Rossii-Telegrafnoye Agentstvo Suverennykh Stran (ITAR-TASS) (Russia): 103 rue Général Lotz, bte 10, 1180 Brussels; tel. (2) 343-86-70; fax (2) 344-83-76; e-mail tassfoto@noos.fz; internet www.itar-tass.com; Correspondents ALEKSANDR KONDRASHEV, MSTISLAV KONDRASHEV.

Inter Press Service-Vlaanderen (IPS) (Italy): 21 Inquisitiestraat, 1000 Brussels; tel. (2) 732-69-16; fax (2) 735-20-89; e-mail ips@ngonet.be; internet www.ips.ngonet.be; Dirs PETER DHONDT, MAARTEN MESSIAEN.

Jiji Tsushin (Japan): 1 blvd Charlemagne, bte 26, 1041 Brussels; tel. (2) 285-09-48; fax (2) 230-14-50; Dir HIROSHI MASUDA.

Kyodo News Service (Japan): 1 blvd Charlemagne, bte 37, 1041 Brussels; tel. (2) 285-09-10; fax (2) 230-53-34; internet www.kyodo.co.jp; Dir ONISHI SHIRO.

Magyar Távirati Iroda Rt. (MTI) (Hungary): 41 rue Jean Chapelié, 1050 Brussels; tel. and fax (2) 343-75-35; internet www.mti.hu; Correspondents JENÖ ERDÉSZ, BALÁZS LÁSZLÓ.

Reuters (United Kingdom): 61 rue de Trèves, 1040 Brussels; tel. (2) 287-66-11; fax (2) 230-55-40; internet www.reuters.com; Man. Dir PETER KAYER.

Rossiyskoye Informatsionnoye Agentstvo—Novosti (RIA-Novosti) (Russia): 74 rue du Merlo, 1180 Brussels; tel. (2) 332-24-35; fax (2) 332-17-29; e-mail novosti@skynet.be; internet www.rian.ru; Dir VIKTOR ONOUTCHKO.

Xinhua (New China) News Agency (People's Republic of China): 32 square Ambiorix, Résidence le Pavois, bte 4, 1040 Brussels; tel. (2) 230-32-54; internet www.xinhua.org; Chief Correspondent LE ZUDE.

PRESS ASSOCIATIONS

Association belge des Editeurs de Journaux/Belgische Vereniging van de Dagbladuitgevers: 22 blvd Paepsem, bte 7, 1070 Brussels; tel. (2) 558-97-60; fax (2) 558-97-68; e-mail abej.bvdu@pressorg.be; f. 1964; 17 mems; Pres P.-H. FALLY; Gen. Secs ALEX FORDYN (Flemish), MARGARET BORIBON (French).

Association générale des Journalistes professionnels de Belgique/Algemene Vereniging van de Beroepsjournalisten in België: Résidence Palace, Bloc C, Rue de la Loi 155, 1040 Brussels; tel. (2) 229-14-60; fax (2) 223-02-72; e-mail info@ajp.be; f. 1978 by merger; 4,000 mems; affiliated to IFJ (International Federation of Journalists); Pres. PHILIPPE LERUTH; Vice-Pres. LUS STANDAERTS.

Fédération Belge des Magazines/Federatie van de Belgische Magazines: 22/8 blvd Paepsemlaan, 1070 Brussels; tel. (2) 558-97-50; fax (2) 558-97-58; e-mail magazines@febelma.be; internet www.febelma.be; f. 1956; Pres. PATRICK DE BORCHGRAVE; Sec.-Gen. ALAIN LAMBRECHTS.

Fédération de la Presse Périodique de Belgique/Federatie van de periodieke pers van België (FPPB): 54 rue Charles Martel, 1000 Brussels; tel. (2) 230-09-99; fax (2) 231-14-59; e-mail ajpp@euronet.be; f. 1891; Pres. CLAUDE MOYLS.

Principal Publishers

Acco CV: 153 Brusselsestraat, 3000 Leuven; tel. (16) 62-80-00; fax (16) 62-80-01; e-mail rob.berrevoets@acco.be; f. 1960; general reference, scientific books, periodicals; Dir ROB BERREVOETS.

Uitgeverij Altiora Averbode NV (Publishing Dept): 1 Abdijstraat, bte 54, 3271 Averbode; tel. (13) 78-01-82; fax (13) 78-01-79; e-mail averbode.publ@verbode.be; internet www.averbode.com; f. 1993; educational, religious; Business Unit Man. P. HERMANS.

De Boeck & Larcier SA: 39 rue des Minimes, 1000 Brussels; tel. (10) 48-25-11; fax (10) 48-26-50; e-mail deboeck.larcier@deboeck.be; internet www.deboeck.be; f. 1795; school, technical and university textbooks, youth, nature, legal publs and documentaries; Dirs CHR. DE BOECK, G. HOYOS.

De Boeck Uitgevery: 8 Nijverheidsstraat, 2390 Malle; tel. (3) 309-13-30; fax (3) 311-77-39; e-mail informatie@deboeck.be; internet www.deboeck.be; f. 1919 as De Sikkel, name changed (as above) 2001; educational books and magazines; Dir L. CAMPS.

Brepols Publishers NV: 67 Begijnhof, 2300 Turnhout; tel. (14) 44-80-20; fax (14) 42-89-19; e-mail info@brepols.net; internet www.brepols.net; f. 1796; humanities; Dir PAUL DE JONGH.

Casterman SA: 132 rue Royale, bte 2, 1000 Brussels; tel. (2) 209-83-00; fax (2) 209-83-01; internet www.casterman.com; f. 1780; fiction, encyclopaedias, education, history, comic books and children's books; Man. Dir LOUIS DELAS.

D2H Didier Hatier-Hachette Education SA: 2 place Baudouin, 5004 Bouge; tel. (81) 21-37-00; fax (81) 21-23-72; e-mail d2h@euronet.be; internet www.groupeerasme.be; f. 1979; school books; Dir I. PONET.

Davidsfonds vzw: 79–81 Blijde Inkomststraat, 3000 Leuven; tel. (16) 31-06-00; fax (16) 31-06-08; e-mail informatie@davidsfonds.be; internet www.davidsfonds.be; f. 1875; general, reference, textbooks; Dir N. D'RULST.

Editions Dupuis SA: 52 rue Jules Destrée, 6001 Marcinelle; tel. (71) 60-50-00; fax (71) 60-05-99; internet www.dupuis.com; f. 1898; children's fiction, periodicals and comic books for children and adults, multimedia and audiovisual; Dir PHILIPPE BUCK.

Etablissements Emile Bruylant: 67 rue de la Régence, 1000 Brussels; tel. (2) 512-98-45; fax (2) 511-72-02; e-mail info@bruylant.be; internet www.bruylant.be; f. 1838; law; Chief Man. Dir J. VANDEVELD.

Halewijn NV: 92 Halewijnlaan, 2050 Antwerp; tel. (3) 210-08-11; fax (3) 210-08-36; e-mail Jo.Cornille@kerknet.be; f. 1953; general, periodicals; Dir-Gen. J. CORNILLE.

Editions Hemma SA: 106 rue de Chevron, 4987 Chevron; tel. (86) 43-01-01; fax (86) 43-36-40; e-mail hemma@hemma.be; internet www.hemma.be; f. 1956; juveniles, educational books and materials; Dir ALBERT HEMMERLIN.

Houtekiet NV: 33 Vrijheidstraat, 2000 Antwerp; tel. (3) 238-12-96; fax (3) 238-80-41; e-mail info@houtekiet.com; internet www.houtekiet.com; f. 1983; Dir L. DE HAES.

Die Keure NV: 108 Oude Gentweg, 8000 Brugge; tel. (50) 47-12-72; fax (50) 34-37-68; e-mail die.keure@pophost.eunet.be; internet www.diekeure.be; f. 1948; textbooks, law, political and social sciences; Dirs J. P. STEEVENS (education), R. CARTON (law).

Uitgeverij De Klaproos: 4 Hostenstraat, 8670 Koksijde; tel. (58) 51-85-30; fax (58) 51-29-42; internet www.klaproos.be; f. 1992; historical works.

Kritak NV: 249 Diestsestraat, 3000 Louvain; tel. (16) 23-12-64; fax (16) 22-33-10; f. 1976; art, law, social sciences, education, humanities, literature, periodicals; Dir ANDRÉ VAN HALEWIJCK.

Editions Labor: 29 Quai du Commerce, 1000 Brussels; tel. (2) 250-06-70; fax (2) 217-71-97; e-mail labor@labor.be; internet www.labor .be; f. 1925; general; *L'Ecole 2000* (periodical); Gen. Man. MARIE-PAULE ESKÉNAZI.

Uitgeverij Lannoo NV: 97 Kasteelstraat, 8700 Tielt; tel. (51) 42-42-11; fax (51) 40-11-52; e-mail lannoo@lannoo.be; internet www .lannoo.com; f. 1909; general, reference.

Editions du Lombard SA: 1–11 ave Paul-Henri Spaak, 1070 Brussels; tel. (2) 526-68-11; f. 1946; juveniles, games, education, geography, history, religion; Man. Dir ROB HARREU.

Imprimerie Robert Louis Editions: 35–43 rue Borrens, 1050 Brussels; tel. (2) 640-10-40; fax (2) 640-07-39; f. 1952; science and technical; Man. PIERRE LOUIS.

Manteau: 147A Belgiëlei, 2018 Antwerp; tel. (3) 285-72-26; fax (3) 285-72-99; e-mail info@standaarduitgeverij.be; internet www .standaarduitgeverij.be; f. 1932; literature; Publr WIM VERHELJE.

Mercatorfonds: 85 Meir, 2000 Antwerp; tel. (3) 202-72-60; fax (3) 231-13-19; f. 1965; art, ethnography, literature, music, geography and history; Dir JAN MARTENS.

Nouvelles Editions Marabout SA: 30 ave de l'Energie, 4432 Alleur; tel. (41) 246-38-63; fax (41) 263-88-63; f. 1977; paperbacks; Man. Dir J. FIRMIN; Dir JEAN ARCACHE.

Peeters pvba: 153 Bondgenotenlaan, 3000 Louvain; tel. (16) 23-51-70; fax (16) 22-85-00; f. 1970; general, reference; Dir M. PEETERS-LISMOND.

Uitgeverij Pelckmans NV: 222 Kapelsestraat, 2950 Kapellen; tel. (3) 664-53-20; fax (3) 655-02-63; f. 1893 as De Nederlandsche Boekhandel, name changed (as above) 1988; school books, scientific, general; Dirs J PELCKMANS, R. PELCKMANS.

Roularta Books: 33 Meiboomlaan, 8800 Roeselare; tel. (51) 26-63-32; fax (51) 26-64-87; e-mail roulartabooks@roularta.be; f. 1988; owned by Roularta Media Group; Publr JAN INGELBEEN.

Snoeck-Ducaju en Zoon NV: 464 Begijnhoflaan, 9000 Ghent; tel. (9) 23-48-97; fax (9) 23-68-30; f. 1948; art books, travel guides; Pres. SERGE SNOECK.

Sanoma Magazines Belgium: Neerveldstraat 109, 1200 Brussels (Walouwe); tel. (2) 776-22-11; fax (2) 776-23-99; e-mail info@ sanoma-magazines.be; periodicals; Dir CLAUDE CUVELIER.

Standaard Uitgeverij NV: 147A Belgiëlei, 2018 Antwerp; tel. (3) 285-72-00; fax (3) 285-72-99; e-mail info@standaard.com; internet www.standaard.com; f. 1924; general, fiction, non-fiction, comics, dictionaries and professional literature; Dirs ERIC WILLEMS, JOHAN DE KONING, DIANE DEVRIENDT, HERMAN CAUWELS.

Vlaamse Uitgeversmaatschappij (VUM): 30 Gossetlaan, 1702 Groot-Bijgaarden; tel. (2) 467-22-11; internet www.vum.be; f. 1976; newspaper and magazine publishing group; Man. Dir JO VAN CROONENBORCH.

Wolters Kluwer Belgie NV: 30 Motstraat, 2800 Mechelen; tel. (1) 536-11-87; fax (1) 536-11-91; e-mail herman.jongeling@wkb.be; internet www.wkb.be; law, business, scientific; Dir H. JONGELING.

Wolters Plantyn: 21–25 Santvoortbeeklaan, 2100 Deurne; tel. (3) 360-03-37; fax (3) 360-03-30; e-mail info@woltersplantyn.be; internet www.woltersplantyn.be; f. 1959; education; Dir JACQUES GERMONPREZ.

Zuidnederlandse Uitgeverij NV: 7 Vluchtenburgstraat, 2630 Aartselaar; tel. (3) 887-14-64; fax (3) 877-21-15; f. 1956; general fiction and non-fiction, children's books; Dir J. VANDE VELDEN.

PUBLISHERS' ASSOCIATIONS

Association des Editeurs Belges (ADEB): 140 blvd Lambermont, 1030 Brussels; tel. (2) 241-65-80; fax (2) 216-71-31; internet www .adeb.irisnet.be; f. 1922; asscn of French-language book publrs; Dir BERNARD GÉRARD.

Cercle Belge de la Librairie: 35 rue de la Chasse Royale, 1160 Brussels; tel. (2) 640-52-41; f. 1883; assen of Belgian booksellers and publrs; 205 mems; Pres. M. DESTREBECQ.

Vlaamse Uitgevers Vereniging: 17 hof ter Schrieclaan, 2600 Berchem, Antwerp; tel. (3) 230-89-23; fax (3) 281-22-40; e-mail jan .vanderheyden@boek.be; internet www.boek.be; assen of Flemish-language book publrs; Sec. JAN VANDERHEYDEN.

Broadcasting and Communications

TELECOMMUNICATIONS

In January 1998 the Belgian telecommunications sector was fully opened to private-sector competition. More than 300 private companies have subsequently registered as service providers.

Regulatory Authority

Institut Belge des Services Postaux et de Télécommunications (IBPT)/Belgisch Instituut voor Postdiensten en Telecommunicatie (BIPT): 14 ave de l'Astronomie, 1210 Brussels; tel. (2) 226-88-88; fax (2) 223-24-77; e-mail info@bipt.be; internet www .bipt.be; Administrator-Gen. ERIC VAN HEESVELDE.

Major Service Providers

BASE: 115 rue Colonel Bourg, 1140 Brussels; tel. (2) 486-19-1999; fax (2) 702-42-01; mobile cellular telephone operator owned by KPN Belgium.

Belgacom: 27 blvd Emile Jacqmain, 1030 Brussels; tel. (2) 202-41-11; fax (2) 203-54-93; e-mail about@is.belgacom.be; internet www .belgacom.be; 50% plus 1 share state owned; total service operator; Pres and CEOs (acting) MICHEL DUSSENNE; RAY STEWART.

Belgacom Mobile SA: 177 blvd Emile Jacqmain, 1130 Brussels; tel. (2) 205-40-00; fax (2) 205-40-40; 75% owned by Belgacom, 25% by AirTouch; mobile cellular telephone operator.

BT (Worldwide) Ltd: Zaventem; tel. (2) 718-22-11; e-mail olivier .servais@bt.be; internet www.bt.be.

Cable & Wireless Belgium SA: 331–333 ave Louise, 1050 Brussels; tel. (2) 627-34-00; fax (2) 627-34-01; e-mail eveline.verdonck@ cw.com; internet www.cw.com.

Esprit Telecom Belgium BV: Zaventem; tel. (2) 720-35-45; fax (2) 720-01-02; e-mail belgiuminfo@esprittele.com; internet www .esprittele.com; f. 1995.

Mobistar: 149 rue Colonel Bourg, 1140 Brussels; tel. (2) 745-71-11; fax (2) 745-70-00; internet www.mobistar.be; f. 1995; 51% owned by FTMI group; mobile cellular telephone and fixed-line operator; Pres. J. CORDIER; Dir-Gen. B. GHILLEBAERT.

Telenet Operaties NV: 4 Liersesteenweg, 2800 Mechelen; tel. (1) 533-30-00; e-mail communicatie@telenet.be; internet www.telenet .be; f. 1996; telecommunications and cable service provider; CEO DUCO SICKINGHE.

KPN Belgium: 50 Medialaan, 1800 Vilvoorde; tel. (2) 275-33-11; fax (2) 275-33-33; internet www.eunet.be; formerly Unisource Belgium NV; Man. Dir PIERRE VERBRUGEN.

Versatel Belgium NV: 166 Koningin Astridlaan, 1780 Wemmel; e-mail info@versatel.be; internet www.versatel.be; f. 1995.

WorldCom NV: 37 Wetenschapstraat, 1040 Brussels; tel. (2) 400-80-00; fax (2) 400-84-00; e-mail worldcom.info@wcom.be; internet www.worldcom.be; subsidiary of WorldCom.Inc; telecom operator.

STATE BROADCASTING ORGANIZATIONS

Flemish

Vlaamse Radio- en Televisieomroep NV (VRT): 52 Auguste Reyerslaan, 1043 Brussels; tel. (2) 741-31-11; fax (2) 734-93-51; e-mail info@vrt.be; internet www.vrt.be; f. 1998; shares held by Flemish Community; operates five radio stations and three television stations; Pres. of Bd of Dirs GUY PEETERS; Man. Dir TONY MARY; Dir of Radio Programmes FRANS IEVEN; Dir of Television Programmes and COO CHRISTINA VON WACKERBARTH.

French

Radio-Télévision Belge de la Communauté Française (RTBF): 52 blvd Auguste Reyers, 1044 Brussels; tel. (2) 737-21-11; fax (2) 737-25-56; internet www.rtbf.be; operates five radio stations and two television stations; Chair. MARIE-HÉLÈNE CROMBE-BERTON; Admin-Gen. JEAN-PAUL PHILIPPOT; Dir of Radio CLAUDE DELACROIX; Dir of Television GERARD LOVERIUS.

German

Belgisches Rundfunk- und Fernsehzentrum der Deutschsprachigen Gemeinschaft (BRF): 11 Kehrweg, 4700 Eupen; tel. (87) 59-11-11; fax (87) 59-11-09; e-mail direktion@brf.be; internet www.brf.be; Dir H. ENGELS.

COMMERCIAL, CABLE AND PRIVATE BROADCASTING

Canal Plus Belgique: 656 chaussée de Louvain, 1030 Brussels; tel. (2) 730-02-11; fax (2) 730-03-79; internet www.canalplus.be; f. 1989;

42% owned by Canal Plus Europe; broadcasts to Brussels region and Wallonia.

Regionale TV Media: Brussels; tel. (2) 467-58-77; fax (2) 467-56-54; e-mail contact@rtvm.be; internet www.rtvm.be; group of 11 regional news broadcasters within Flanders; commercial.

Télévision Indépendante (TVI): 1 ave Ariane, 1201 Brussels; tel. (2) 778-68-11; fax (2) 778-68-12; commercial station; broadcasts in French.

Vlaamse Media Maatschappij: 1 Medialaan, 1800 Vilvoorde; tel. (2) 255-32-11; fax (2) 252-37-87; f. 1987; commercial; broadcasts in Flemish; Gen. Man. ERIC CLAEYS.

Finance

(cap. = capital; m. = million; res = reserves; dep. = deposits; brs = branches; amounts in euros, unless otherwise indicated)

BANKING

Commission bancaire et financière/Commissie voor het Bank- en Financiewezen: 99 ave Louise, 1050 Brussels; tel. (2) 535-22-11; fax (2) 535-23-23; internet www.cbf.be; f. 1935 to supervise the application of legislation relating to the legal status of credit institutions and to the public issue of securities; Chair. E. WYMEERSCH; CEOs P. PRAET, R. BONTE, M. DE WACHTER; Sec.-Gen. A. NIESTEN.

Central Bank

Banque Nationale de Belgique: 14 blvd de Berlaimont, 1000 Brussels; tel. (2) 221-21-11; fax (2) 221-31-01; e-mail secretariat@nbb.be; internet www.bnb.be; f. 1850; bank of issue; cap. 9,9116,000, res 1,449.8m., total assets 31,20.0m. (Dec. 2001); Gov. GUY QUADEN; Vice-Gov. MARCIA DE WACHTER; Exec. Dirs J.-P. PAUWELS, JAN SMETS, JEAN HILGERS, FRANÇOISE MASAI, PETER PRAET; 2 brs.

Development Bank

Investeringsmaatschappij voor Vlaanderen (GIMV): 37 Karel Oomsstraat, 2018 Antwerp; tel. (3) 290-21-00; fax (3) 290-21-05; e-mail receptie@gimv.be; internet www.gimv.com; f. 1980; promotes creation, restructuring and expansion of private cos; cap. 220m. (2001); Chair. HERMAN DAEMS; Dir-Gen. DIRK BOOGMANS.

Major Commercial Banks

ABN AMRO Bank NV: 53 Regentlaan, 1000 Brussels; tel. (2) 546-04-60; fax (2) 546-04-23; e-mail postbox@abnamro.be; internet www.abnamro.be; cap. BF 1,050m., res BF 1,887m., dep. BF 106,649m. (Dec. 1996); Chair. R. W. J. GROENINK; Dir J. J. W. ZWEEGERS; 7 brs.

Antwerpse Diamantbank NV/Banque Diamantaire Anversoise SA/Antwerp Diamond Bank NV: 54 Pelikaanstraat, 2018 Antwerp; tel. (3) 204-72-04; fax (3) 233-90-95; e-mail adia.be; f. 1934; cap. 34.4m., res 65.9m., dep. 1,305.7m. (Dec. 2000); Chair. JAN VANHEVEL; Man. Dir and Chair. of Exec. Cttee PAUL C. GORIS.

AXA Bank Belgium NV: 214 Grotesteenweg, 2600 Antwerp; tel. (3) 286-22-11; fax (3) 286-24-07; e-mail contact@axa-bank.be; internet www.axa.be; f. 1881 as ANHYP Bank NV, present name adopted 2000; cap. 6.2m., res 285.7m., dep 6,472.2m. (Dec. 2001); Chair. of Bd of Dirs ALFRED BOUCKAERT; Chair. of Exec. Cttee GÉRARD FIÉVET.

Banca Monte Paschi Belgio SA/NV: 24 rue Joseph II, 1000 Brussels; tel. (2) 220-72-11; fax (2) 203-83-91; internet www.montepaschi.be; f. 1947 as Banco di Roma (Belgique), name changed 1992; cap. 26.0m., res 33.0m., dep. 1,693.6m. (Dec. 2000); Pres. of Exec. Cttee and Man. Dir MARIO GAETANO MAZZARINO; 6 brs.

Bank J. van Breda & Co NV: 295 Plantin en Moretuslei, 2140 Borgerhout; tel. (3) 217-51-11; fax (3) 235-37-84; e-mail mail@bankvanbreda.be; internet www.bankvanbreda.be; f. 1930; cap. 17.5m., res 98.0m., dep. 1,660.1m. (Dec. 2001); Gen. Man. CARLO HENRIKSEN; 32 brs.

Bank Brussels Lambert/Banque Brussels Lambert (BBL): 24 ave Marnix, 1000 Brussels; tel. (2) 547-21-11; fax (2) 547-38-44; e-mail info@bbl.be; internet www.bbl.be; f. 1975; taken over by ING Bank NV (the Netherlands) Jan. 1998; cap. 850m., res 2,732.9m., dep. 116,309.7m. (Dec. 2001); Chair. of Bd MICHEL TILMANT; Pres. and CEO LUC VANDEWALLE; 953 brs.

Bank Degroof SA/Banque Degroof SA: 44 rue de l'Industrie, 1040 Brussels; tel. (2) 287-91-11; fax (2) 230-67-00; e-mail info@degroof.be; internet www.degroof.be; f. 1871; present name adopted 1998; cap. 35.0m., res 105.6m., dep. 1,068.6m. (Sept. 2001); Man. Dir and Chair. of Bd ALAIN PHILIPPSON.

Banque Belgolaise SA/Belgolaise Bank: 1 Cantersteen, bte 807, 1000 Brussels; tel. (2) 551-72-11; fax (2) 551-75-15; e-mail belgolaise.brussels@belgolaise.com; internet www.belgolaise.com; f. 1960 as Banque Belgo-Congolaise SA, present name adopted 1991; cap. 25,000m., res 59,507m., dep. 2,019,288m. (Dec. 2001); Chair. MARC YVES BLANPAIN; Vice-Chair. FILIP DIERCKX; 1 br.

Banque Delen NV/SA: 184 Jan van Rijswijcklaan, 2020 Antwerp; tel. (3) 244-55-66; fax (3) 216-04-91; e-mail info@delen.be; internet www.delen.be; f. 1928; cap. 40.0m., res 2.3m., dep. 731.0m. (Dec. 2001); Pres. JACQUES DELEN; Chair. JAN SUYKENS; 2 brs.

Banque Européenne pour l'Amérique Latine (BEAL) SA: 166 chaussée de la Hulpe, 1170 Brussels; tel. (2) 663-69-00; fax (2) 663-69-59; e-mail head-office_bealbrussels@bankbeal.com; internet www.westlb.com/beals; f. 1974; cap. 80.0m., res 40.6m., dep. 3,122.0m. (Dec. 2001); Chair. ANDREAS SEIBERT; Man. Dirs PHILIP WYKES, HORST R. MAGIERA.

Banque Nagelmackers 1747 SA: 23 ave de l'Astronomie, 1210 Brussels; tel. (2) 229-76-00; fax (2) 229-76-99; e-mail koen.troosters@nagelmackers.be; internet www.nagelmackers.be; f. 1747; cap. 46.0m., res 54.3m., dep. 1,877.5m. (Dec. 2000); Pres. Exec. Cttee PIET VERBRUGGE; 62 brs.

Byblos Bank Europe SA: 10B rue Montoyer, 1000 Brussels; tel. (2) 551-00-20; fax (2) 513-05-26; e-mail byblosbank.europe@byblosbankeur.com; f. 1976; cap. 20.0m., res 6.4m., dep. 433.7m. (Dec. 2001); Chair. ALBERT S. NASSAR; Man. Dir and Pres. NAJAH L. SALEM.

Caisse Privée Banque SA/Private Kas Bank NV: 2 place du Champ de Mars, 1050 Brussels; tel. (2) 518-92-11; fax (2) 513-58-94; f. 1923; cap. 25.4m., res 8.0m., dep. 943.0m. (Dec. 2001); Chair. and Gen. Man. ERIC ORLANS; 9 brs.

CBC Banque SA: 5 Grand-Place, 1000 Brussels; tel. (2) 547-12-15; fax (2) 547-13-12; e-mail info@cbc.be; internet www.cbc.be; f. 1958; name changed as above 1998; cap. 89.6m., res 136.3m., dep. 7,609.6m. (Dec. 2001); Chair. BARON HUYGHEBAERT; 136 brs.

Citibank Belgium NV/SA: 263 blvd Général Jacques, 1050 Brussels; tel. (2) 626-51-11; fax (2) 626-55-84; internet www.citibank.be; f. 1919; present name adopted 1992; cap. 44.9m., res 11.0m., dep. 1,950.0m. (Dec. 2000); Gen. Man. JACK WRIGHT.

Crédit Agricole SA/Landbouwkrediet NV: 251 blvd Sylvain Dupuis, 1070 Brussels; tel. (2) 558-71-11; fax (2) 558-76-23; f. 1937; cap. 193.3m., res 101.1m., dep. 5,115.5m. (Dec. 2001); Pres. JACQUES ROUSSEAUX.

Crédit à l'Industrie/Krediet aan de Nijverheid: 14 ave de l'Astronomie, 1210 Brussels; tel. (2) 214-12-11; fax (2) 218-04-78; f. 1919; owned by Fortis Bank; cap. BF 4,500m., res BF 7,554m., dep. BF 511,133m. (Dec. 1995); Chair. FRED RAMPEN; 4 brs.

Crédit Professionnel SA/Beroepskrediet NV: 6–9 ave des Arts, 1210 Brussels; tel. (2) 289-87-06; fax (2) 289-89-97; e-mail info@bkcp.be; internet www.bkcp.be; f. 1992 as Caisse Nationale de Crédit Professionnel SA; name changed as above 1997; cap. 53m., res 1.3m., dep. 781.5m. (Dec. 2000); Chair. of Supervisory Bd GUIDO VERHAEGEN; Chair. of Exec. Cttee THIERRY FAUT.

Delta Lloyd Bank NV: 46 Parklaan, 2300 Turnhout; tel. (14) 44-32-00; fax (14) 42-78-51; internet www.dlbank.be; f. 1966; cap. 22.8m., res 10.9m., dep. 762.5m. (Dec. 1999); Chair. LEENDERT KEEMINK; CEO PIET VERBRUGGE.

Deutsche Bank SA/NV: 13 ave Marnix, 1000 Brussels; tel. (2) 551-65-11; fax (2) 551-66-66; internet www.deutschebank24.be; f. 1893 as Banque de Commerce SA (Handelsbank NV), renamed Crédit Lyonnais Belgium 1989, bought by Deutsche Bank 1999; cap. BF 6,587m., res BF 3,847m., dep. BF 406,231m. (Dec. 1997); Chair. H. J. LAMBERT; Chief Exec. YVES DELACOLLETTE; 26 brs.

Dexia Bank Belgium SA: 44 Pachécolaan, 1000 Brussels; tel. (2) 222-11-11; fax (2) 222-31-23; internet www.dexia.be; f. 1860 as Crédit Communal de Belgique SA, present name adopted 2000; cap. 2,891.0m., res 2,463.0m., dep. 187,732.0m. (Dec. 2001); Chair. LUC ONCLIN.

Europabank NV: 170 Burgstraat, 9000 Ghent; tel. (9) 224-73-11; fax (9) 223-34-72; e-mail europabank@village.uunet.be; f. 1964; owned by Staal Bank NV, The Hague; cap. 1.6m., res 39.5m., dep. 17,302.7m. (Dec. 2001); Chair. of Supervisory Bd ALBERT VAN HOUTTE; 25 brs.

Fortis Bank NV/Fortis Banque SA: 3 Montagne du Parc, 1000 Brussels; tel. (2) 565-11-11; fax (2) 565-42-22; e-mail info@fortisbank.com; internet www.fortisbank.com; f. 1999; by merger of Generale Bank/Générale de Banque and ASLK-CGER Bank/Banque with the Fortis Group; banking, insurance and investments; cap. 3,111.8m., res 6,303.4m., dep. 288,768.6m. (Dec. 2000); Chair. of Bd of Dirs ANTON VAN ROSSUM; Chair. of Exec. Cttee HERMAN VERWILST; 2,500 brs.

Goffin Bank NV (HBM Bank NV): 120 Verlorenbroodstraat, 9820 Merelbeke; tel. (9) 261-02-00; fax (9) 261-02-01; f. 1955; cap. 6.5m., res 1.1m., dep. 211.1m. (Dec. 2001); Pres. ANTOON VAN COILIE; Chair. WALTER VANDERBREKEN.

KBC Bank NV: 2 Havenlaan, 1080 Brussels 8; tel. (2) 429-11-11; fax (2) 429-81-31; e-mail kbc.telecenter@kbc.be; internet www.kbc.be; f. 1935 as Kredietbank NV; merged with Bank von Roeselare NV and CERA Investment Bank NV in 1998; cap. 3,558.7m., res 3,448.6, dep. 172,431.5m. (Dec. 2001); Pres. REMI VERMEIREN.

Parfibank SA: 40 blvd du Régent, 1000 Brussels; tel. (2) 513-90-20; fax (2) 512-73-20; e-mail rudi.sneyers@artesia.be; f. 1976 as Nippon European Bank SA, present name adopted 1996; cap. 75.0m., res 32.9m., dep. 1,275.7m. (Dec. 2001); Chair. RENAUD GREINDL; Man. Dir RUDI SNEYERS.

RealBank (Bank voor Koophandel van Brussel NV): 1 rue des Colonies, 1000 Brussels; tel. (2) 503-30-00; fax (2) 503-11-11; f. 1905; cap. 7.9m., res 2.5m., dep. 223.6m. (Dec. 2000); Gen. Man. CLAUDE PIQUEUR.

Santander Central Hispano Benelux SA/NV: 227 rue de la Loi, 1040 Brussels; tel. (2) 286-54-11; fax (2) 230-09-40; f. 1914 as Société Hollandaise de Banque, present name adopted 2001; cap. 39.6m., res 0.6m., dep. 976.8m. (Dec. 2001); Man. Dir MIGUEL SÁNCHEZ TÓVAR.

Banking Association

Association Belge des Banques/Belgische Vereniging van Banken (ABB): 36 rue Ravenstein, 1000 Brussels; tel. (2) 507-68-11; fax (2) 512-58-61; e-mail abb-bvb@abb-bvb.be; f. 1936; 137 mems; affiliated to Fédération des Entreprises de Belgique and Fédération Bancaire de l'UE; Pres. KAREL DE BOECK; Dir-Gen. GUIDO RAVOET.

STOCK EXCHANGE

In September 2000 Euronext was formed from the merger of the stock exchanges of Brussels (Brussels Exchanges), Amsterdam (Amsterdam Exchanges) and Paris (Paris Bourse).

Euronext Brussels: Palais de la Bourse, 1000 Brussels; tel. (2) 509-12-11; fax (2) 509-12-12; e-mail info@euronext.com; internet www.euronext.com; Sec.-Gen. O. LEFEBVRE.

HOLDING COMPANY

Société Générale de Belgique: 30 rue Royale, 1000 Brussels; tel. (2) 507-02-11; fax (2) 512-18-95; f. 1822; investment and holding co with substantial interests in banking and finance, industry, mining and energy; CEO PHILIPPE LIOTIER.

INSURANCE

In 1998 there were 234 registered insurance companies active in Belgium, of which 150 were Belgian-owned.

Regulatory Authority

Office de Contrôle des Assurances/Controledienst voor de Verzekeringen: 61 ave de Cortenbergh, 1000 Brussels; tel. (2) 737-07-11; fax (2) 736-88-17; e-mail diederik.vandendriessche@cdv-oca.be; internet www.cdv-oca.be; f. 1975; supervises insurance and mortgage cos, pension funds, and insurance intermediaries; Chair. WILLY P. LENAERTS; Dir-Gen. GUIDO VERNAILLEN.

Principal Insurance Companies

Aviabel, Compagnie Belge d'Assurances Aviation, SA: 10 ave Brugmann, 1060 Brussels; tel. (2) 349-12-11; fax (2) 349-12-99; e-mail insurance@aviabel.be; internet www.aviabel.be; f. 1935; aviation, insurance, reinsurance; Chair. P. GERVY; Gen. Man. J. VERWILGHEN.

AXA Royale Belge: 25 blvd du Souverain, 1170 Brussels; tel. (2) 678-61-11; fax (2) 678-93-40; e-mail webmaster@axa-royalebelge.be; internet www.axa-royalebelge.be; f. 1853; member of the AXA group; all branches; Pres. Comte JEAN-PIERRE DE LAUNOIT; Man. Dir ALFRED BOUCKAERT.

Belgamar, Compagnie Belge d'Assurances Maritimes SA: 66 Mechelsesteenweg, 2018 Antwerp; tel. (3) 247-36-11; fax (3) 247-35-90; f. 1945; marine insurance; Chair. P. H. SAVERYS; Man. Dir A. THIÈRY.

Compagnie d'Assurance de l'Escaut: 10 rue de la Bourse, Antwerp; f. 1821; fire, accident, life, burglary, reinsurance; Man E. DIERCXSENS.

Compagnie de Bruxelles 1821 SA d'Assurances: Brussels; tel. (2) 237-12-11; fax 237-12-16; f. 1821; fire, life, general; Pres. C. BASECQ.

DVV Verzekeringen NV/Les AP Assurances SA: 6 ave Livingston, 1000 Brussels; tel. (2) 286-61-11; fax (2) 286-15-15; internet www.dvv.be; f. 1929; all branches; 82% owned by Artesia Banking Corporation.

EULER-COBAC Belgium SA/NV: 15 rue Montoyer, 1000 Brussels; tel. (2) 289-31-11; fax (2) 289-32-99; e-mail Cobacbe@eulergroup.com; internet www.eulergroup.com; f. 1929 as Compagnie Belge d'Assurance-Crédit; present name adopted 1998; CEO JEAN LUC LOUIS.

Fortis AG: 53 blvd Emile Jacqmain, 1000 Brussels; tel. (2) 220-81-11; fax (2) 220-81-50; e-mail info@fortis.com; internet www.fortisag.be; f. 1990; owned by the Fortis Group; CEO JOZEF DE MEY.

Generali Belgium SA: 149 ave Louise, 1050 Brussels; tel. (2) 403-81-11; fax (2) 403-88-99; internet www.generali.be; fire, accident, marine, life, reinsurance; Pres. G. BECKERS; Dir-Gen. T. DELVAUX.

KBC SA/NV: Havenlaan 2, 1080 Brussels; tel. (2) 429-71-11; fax (2) 429-81-31; e-mail kbc.telecenter@kbc.be; internet www.kbc.be; f. 1998.

Mercator & Noordstar NV: 302 Kortrijksesteen Weg, 9000 Ghent; tel. (9) 242-37-11; fax (9) 242-36-36; e-mail info@mercator.be; internet www.mercator.be; all branches.

Société Mutuelle des Administrations Publiques (SMAP): 24 rue des Croisiers, 4000 Liège; tel. (4) 220-31-11; internet www.smap.be; f. 1919; institutions, civil service employees, public administration and enterprises; CEO GUY BURTON.

Victoire, Société Anonyme Belge d'Assurances: Brussels; tel. (2) 286-24-11; fax (2) 230-94-73; life and non-life; Chair. M. P. DE COURCEL; Gen. Man. G. DUPIN.

Insurance Associations

Fédération des Producteurs d'Assurances de Belgique (FEPRABEL): 40 ave Albert-Elisabeth, 1200 Brussels; tel. (2) 743-25-60; fax (2) 735-44-58; e-mail info@feprabel.be; internet www.feprabel.be; f. 1934; Pres. RÉGINALD VAN INGELGEM; 500 mems.

Union Professionnelle des Entreprises d'Assurances Belges et Etrangères Opérant en Belgique/Beroepsvereniging der Belgische en in België werkzame Buitenlandse Verzekeringsondernemingen: 29 square de Meeûs, 1000 Brussels; tel. (2) 547-56-11; fax (2) 547-56-00; e-mail pdg@upea.be; internet www.upea.be; f. 1921; affiliated to Fédération des Entreprises de Belgique; Pres. C DESSEILLE; Man. Dir MICHEL BAECKER; 95 mems.

Trade and Industry

GOVERNMENT AGENCIES

Investeren in Vlaanderen–Flanders Foreign Investment Office: 4 Leuvenseplein, 1000 Brussels; tel. (2) 227-53-11; fax (2) 227-53-10; e-mail flanders@ffio.be; internet www.ffio.com; f. 1988; promotes investment in Flanders; Man. Dir POL VERHAEGEN.

Société de Développement de la Région de Bruxelles (SDRB): 6 rue Gabrielle Petit, 1080 Brussels; tel. (2) 422-51-11; fax (2) 422-51-12; e-mail info@brda.irisnet.be; internet www.brda.be; f. 1974; promotes economic development in the capital; Chair. C. PAELINCK.

Société Régionale d'Investissement de Wallonie: 13 ave Destenay, 4000 Liège; tel. (4) 221-98-11; fax (4) 221-99-99; e-mail sriw@sriw.be; internet www.sriw.be; f. 1979; promotes private enterprise in Wallonia; Pres. JEAN-CLAUDE DEHOVRE.

PRINCIPAL CHAMBERS OF COMMERCE

There are chambers of commerce and industry in all major towns and industrial areas.

Kamer van Koophandel en Nijverheid van Antwerpen: 12 Markgravestraat, 2000 Antwerp; tel. (3) 232-22-19; fax (3) 233-64-42; e-mail info@kkna.be; internet www.kknaw.be; f. 1969; Pres. JOHN STOOP; Gen. Man. LUC LUWEL.

Chambre de Commerce et d'Industrie de Bruxelles: 500 ave Louise, 1050 Brussels; tel. (2) 648-50-02; fax (2) 640-93-28; f. 1875; Pres. YVAN NUYGHEBAERT.

Chambre de Commerce et d'Industrie de Liège: Palais des Congrès, 2 Esplanade de l'Europe, 4020 Liège; tel. (43) 43-92-92; fax (43) 43-92-67; e-mail info@ccilg.be; internet www.ccilg.be; f. 1866; Pres. JACQUES THOMAS.

INDUSTRIAL AND TRADE ASSOCIATIONS

Fédération des Entreprises de Belgique (Federation of Belgian Companies): 4 rue Ravenstein, 1000 Brussels; tel. (2) 515-08-11; fax (2) 515-09-99; e-mail red@vbo-feb.be; internet www.vbo-feb.be; f. 1895; federates all the main industrial and non-industrial asscns; Pres. KAREL BOONE; CEO TONY VANDEPUTTE; 35 full mems.

Agoria—Fédération Multisectorielle de l'Industrie Technologique (Multisector Federation for the Technology Industry): 80 blvd Auguste Reyers, 1030 Brussels; tel. (2) 706-78-00; fax (2)

706-78-01; e-mail info@agoria.be; internet www.agoria.be; f. 1946 as Fédération des Enterprises de l'Industrie des Fabrications Métalliques, Mécaniques, Electriques, Electroniques et de la Transformation des Matières Plastiques (FABRIMETAL), present name adopted 2000; more than 1,200 mem. cos; Pres. JOHN CORDIER; CEO PAUL SOETE.

ASBL Fédération des Producteurs de Pierre Bleue—Petit Granit (Limestone): 1 chemin de Carrières, 7063 Neufvilles; tel. (67) 34-68-00; fax (67) 34-68-01; f. 1948; Pres. F. GALER.

Association Belge des Banques/Belgische Vereniging van Banken (ABB): see Finance above.

Association des Fabricants de Pâtes, Papiers et Cartons de Belgique (COBELPA) (Paper): 306 Louizalaan, bus 11, 1050 Brussels; tel. (2) 646-64-50; fax (2) 646-82-97; e-mail general@cobelpa.be; internet www.cobelpa.be; f. 1940; Pres. PIERRE MACHARIS.

 Brasseurs Belges (Breweries): Maison des Brasseurs, 10 Grand' Place, 1000 Brussels; tel. (2) 511-49-87; fax (2) 511-32-59; e-mail belgian.brewers@beerparadise.be; internet www.beerparadise.be; f. 1971; Pres. YANNICK BOES.

Confédération Nationale de la Construction (CNC) (Civil Engineering, Road and Building Contractors and Auxiliary Trades): 34–42 rue du Lombard, 1000 Brussels; tel. (2) 545-56-00; fax (2) 545-59-00; e-mail info@confederatiebouw.be; internet www.cnc.be; f. 1946; Pres. ROB LENAERS.

Confédération Professionnelle du Sucre et de ses Dérivés (Sugar): 182 ave de Tervueren, 1150 Brussels; tel. (2) 775-80-69; fax (2) 775-80-75; e-mail info@subel.be; f. 1938; mems: 10 groups, 66 cos; Pres. E. KESSELS; Dir-Gen. M. ROSIERS.

Fédération Belge de la Brique (Bricks): 13 rue des Poissonniers, bte 22, 1000 Brussels; tel. (2) 511-25-81; fax (2) 513-26-40; e-mail info@brique.be; internet www.brique.be; f. 1947; Pres. GILBERT DE BAERE.

Fédération Belge des Dragueurs de Gravier et de Sable (BELBAG-DRAGBEL) (Quarries): Hasselt; tel. (89) 56-73-45; fax (89) 56-45-42; f. 1967; Pres. CHARLES LECLUYSE.

Fédération Belge des Entreprises de la Transformation du Bois (FEBELBOIS) (Wood): 5 Hof-ter-Vleest, bte 1, 1070 Brussels; tel. (2) 556-25-55; fax (2) 556-25-70; e-mail dir@febehout.be; internet www.febelhout.be; Pres. GUSTAAF NEYT.

Fédération Belge des Industries Graphiques (FEBELGRA) (Graphic Industries): 20 rue Belliard, bte 16, 1040 Brussels; tel. (2) 512-36-38; fax (2) 513-56-76; e-mail info@febelgra.be; internet www.febelgra.be; f. 1978.

Fédération Belge des Industries de l'Habillement (Clothing): 24 rue Montoyer, 1040 Brussels; tel. (2) 238-10-11; fax (2) 230-10-10; e-mail roggeman@belgianfashion.be; internet www.belgianfashion.be; f. 1946; Pres. ALAIN CHAUVEHEID.

Fédération Belgo-Luxembourgeoise de l'Industrie du Tabac (FEDETAB) (Tobacco): 251 ave Louise, 1000 Brussels; tel. (2) 646-04-20; fax (2) 646-22-13; e-mail tobacco@fedetab.be; f. 1947; Pres. G. VANDERMARLIÈRE.

Fédération Charbonnière de Belgique (Coal): Brussels; tel. (2) 230-37-40; fax (2) 230-88-50; f. 1909; Pres. YVES SLEUWAEGEN; Dir JOS VAN DEN BROECK.

Fédération d'Employeurs pour le Commerce International, le Transport et les Branches d'Activité Connexes (Employers' Federation of International Trade, Transport and Related Activities): 33 Brouwersvliet, bus 7, 2000 Antwerp; tel. (3) 221-99-90; fax (3) 221-99-09; e-mail cepa@cepa.be; f. 1937; Pres. FRANÇOIS VAN GEEL; Dir RENÉ DE BROUWER.

Fédération de l'Industrie Alimentaire/Federatie Voedingsindustrie (FEVIA) (Food and Agriculture): 172 Kortenberglaan, bte 7, 1040 Brussels; tel. (2) 743-08-00; fax (2) 733-94-26; e-mail info@fevia.be; internet www.fevia.be; f. 1937; Pres. ERIC SWENDEN; Dir-Gen. CHRIS MORIS.

Fédération de l'Industrie du Béton (FEBE) (Precast Concrete): 12 rue Volta, 1050 Brussels; tel. (2) 735-80-15; fax (2) 734-77-95; e-mail mail@febe.be; internet www.febe.be; f. 1936; Pres. P. DECLERCK; Dir EDDY DANO.

Fédération des Industries Chimiques de Belgique (FEDICHEM) (Chemical Industries): 49 square Marie-Louise, 1000 Brussels; tel. (2) 238-97-11; fax (2) 231-13-01; e-mail postmaster@fedichem.be; internet www.fedichem.be; f. 1919; Pres. ANTOON DIEUSAERT; Man. Dir JEAN-MARIE BIOT.

Fédération de l'Industrie Cimentière Belge (FEBELCEM) (Cement): 8 rue Volta, 1050 Brussels; tel. (2) 645-52-11; fax (2) 640-06-70; e-mail febelcem@febelcem.be; internet www.febelcem.be; f. 1949; Pres. BERNARD KUENG; Dir-Gen. JEAN-PIERRE JACOBS.

Fédération des Industries Extractives et Transformatrices de Roches non Combustibles (FEDIEX) (Extraction and processing of non-fuel rocks): 61 rue du Trône, 1050 Brussels; tel. (2) 511-61-73; fax (2) 511-12-84; e-mail fediex@fediex.be; f. 1942 as Union des Producteurs Belges de Chaux, Calcaires, Dolomies et Produits Connexes, name changed (as above) 1990; co-operative society; CEO YVES DE LESPINAY; Chair. ROBERT GOFFIN.

Fédération de l'Industrie du Gaz (FIGAZ) (Gas): 4 ave Palmerston, 1000 Brussels; tel. (2) 237-11-11; fax (2) 230-44-80; e-mail figaz@figaz.be; f. 1946; Pres. WALTER PEERAER; Sec. Gen. FERDINAND DE LICHTERVELDE.

Fédération de l'Industrie Textile Belge (FEBELTEX) (Textiles): 24 rue Montoyer, bte 1, 1000 Brussels; tel. (2) 287-08-11; e-mail info@febeltex.be; internet www.febeltex.be; f. 1945; Pres. PHILIPPE VLERICK; Dir-Gen. JEAN-FRANÇOIS QUIX; 500 mems.

Fédération des Industries Transformatrices de Papier et Carton (FETRA) (Paper and Cardboard): 715 chaussée de Waterloo, BP 25, 1180 Brussels; tel. (2) 344-19-62; fax (2) 344-86-61; f. 1976; Pres. PAUL PISSENS.

Fédération de l'Industrie du Verre (Glass): 89 ave Louise, 1050 Brussels; tel. (2) 542-61-20; fax (2) 542-61-21; e-mail info@vgi-fiv.be; internet www.vgi-fiv.be; f. 1947; Pres. L. WILLAME; Man. Dir ROLAND DERIDDER.

Fédération Patronale des Ports Belges (Port Employers): 33 Brouwersvliet, bus 7, 2000 Antwerp; tel. (3) 221-99-85; fax (3) 226-83-77; e-mail cepa@cepa.be; f. 1937; Pres. FRANÇOIS VAN GEEL; Secs RENÉ DE BROUWER, GUY VANKRUNKELSVEN.

Fédération Pétrolière Belge (Petroleum): 39 ave des Arts, bt 2, 1040 Brussels; tel. (2) 508-30-00; fax (2) 511-05-91; e-mail fpb-bpf@petrolfed.be; internet www.petrolfed.be; f. 1926; Pres. M. BRYKMAN; Sec.-Gen. G. VAN DE WERVE.

Groupement des Sablières (Sand and Gravel): 49 Quellinstraat, 2018 Antwerp; tel. (3) 223-66-83; fax (3) 223-66-47; e-mail pdn@sibelco.be; f. 1937; Pres. A. SPECKAERT; Sec. PAUL DE NIE.

Groupement de la Sidérurgie (Iron and Steel): 47 rue Montoyer, 1000 Brussels; tel. (2) 509-14-11; fax (2) 509-14-00; e-mail gsv@steelbel.be; internet www.steelbel.be; f. 1953; Pres. PAUL MATTHYS.

Industrie des Huiles Minérales de Belgique (IHMB—IMOB) (Mineral Oils): 49 square Marie-Louise, 1000 Brussels; tel. (2) 238-97-11; fax (2) 230-03-89; f. 1921; Pres. J. VERCHEVAL; Sec. D. DE HEMPTINNE; 65 mems.

Union des Armateurs Belges (Shipowners): 33 Brouwersvliet, 2000 Antwerp; tel. (3) 232-72-32; fax (3) 831-39-97; e-mail info@brv.be; internet www.brv.be; Chair. NICOLAS SAVERYS; Man. Dir M. NVYTEMANS.

Union des Carrières et Scieries de Marbres de Belgique (UCSMB) (Marble): 8 Heideveld, 1654 Huizingen; tel. (2) 361-36-81; fax (2) 361-31-55; Pres. P. STONE.

Union des Exploitations Electriques et Gazières en Belgique (UEGB) (Electricity and Gas): 8 blvd du Régent, 1000 Brussels; tel. (2) 518-61-11; fax (2) 518-64-58; f. 1911; Pres. ANTOINE DECLOEDT.

Union Professionnelle des Producteurs de Fibres-Ciment (Fibre-Cement): 114 Aerschotstraat, 9100 Sint-Niklaas; tel. (3) 760-49-45; fax (3) 777-47-84; f. 1941; Pres. MARC VANDEN BOSCH; Sec. GEORGES SANDERS.

Union de la Tannerie et de la Mégisserie Belges (UNITAN) (Tanning and Tawing): c/o 140 rue des Tanneurs, 7730 Estaimbourg; tel. (69) 36-23-23; fax (69) 36-23-10; f. 1962; Pres. BRUNO COLLE; Sec. ANNE VANDEPUTTE; 4 mems.

UTILITIES

Electricity

Electrabel: 8 Regentlaan, 1000 Brussels; tel. (2) 518-61-11; fax (2) 518-64-00; internet www.electrabel.com; f. 1905; 44% owned by Tractebel; CEO WILLY BOSMANS.

Gas

Distrigas: 10 rue de l'Industrie, 1000 Brussels; tel. (2) 557-31-11; fax (2) 557-31-12; e-mail info@distri.be; internet www.distrigas.be; supply and sale of natural gas; f. 2001.

Fluxys: 31 Kunstlaan, 1040 Brussels; tel. (2) 282-78-33; fax (2) 282-71-50; natural gas transportation services.

Water

Société Wallonne des Eaux: 41 rue de la Concorde, 4800 Verviers; tel. (87) 34-28-11; fax (87) 34-28-00; e-mail relex@swde.be; internet www.swde.be; f. 1986; Dir-Gen. MARC DECONINCK.

Vlaamse Maatschappij voor Watervoorziening: 73 Belliard-straat, 1040 Brussels; tel. (2) 238-94-11; fax (2) 230-97-98; e-mail info@vmw.be; internet www.vmw.be.

TRADE UNIONS

Fédération Générale du Travail de Belgique (FGTB)/Algemeen Belgisch Vakverbond (ABVV): 42 rue Haute, 1000 Brussels; tel. (2) 506-82-11; fax (2) 506-82-29; internet www .abvv.be; f. 1899; affiliated to ICFTU; Pres. MIA DE VITS; Gen. Sec. ANDRÉ MORDANT; an association of seven branch unions, three inter-regional organizations and 21 regional organizations with an esti-mated total membership of 1.2m. (2000).

Affiliated unions:

Belgische Transportarbeidersbond/Union Belge des Ouv-riers du Transport (Belgian Transport Workers' Union): 66 Paardenmarkt, 2000 Antwerp; tel. (3) 224-34-11; fax (3) 224-34-49; f. 1913; Pres. IVAN VICTOR; 29,091 mems (2001).

La Centrale Générale/De Algemene Centrale (Central Union, building, timber, glass, paper, chemicals and petroleum indus-tries): 26–28 rue Haute, 1000 Brussels; tel. (2) 549-05-49; fax (2) 514-16-91; e-mail info@accg.be; internet www.accg.be; Pres. MAURICE CORBISIER; Sec.-Gen. ALAIN CLAUWAERT; 300,000 mems (1998).

Centrale Générale des Services Publics/Algemene Centrale der Openbare Diensten (Public-Service Workers): Maison des Huit Heures, 9–11 place Fontainas, 1000 Brussels; tel. (2) 508-58-11; fax (2) 508-59-02; e-mail algemeen@acod.be; internet www .acod.be; f. 1945; Pres. HENRI DUJARDIN; Vice-Pres. F. FERMON.

Centrale de l'Industrie du Métal de Belgique/Centrale der Metaalindustrie van België (Metal Workers): 17 rue Jacques Jordaens, 1000 Brussels; tel. (2) 627-74-11; fax (2) 627-74-90; f. 1887; Pres. HERWIG JORISSEN; 185,570 mems (1993).

Centrale Voeding-Horeca-Diensten (Catering and Hotel Workers): 18 rue des Alexiens, 1000 Brussels; tel. (2) 512-97-00; fax (2) 512-53-68; e-mail jean.paschenkol@horval.be; internet users.skynet.be/sky90351/horval; f. 1912; Pres. F. DE MEY; Nat. Sec. J. PASCHENKO.

FGTB—Textile, Vêtement, et Diamant/ABVV—Textiel, Kleding – Diamant (Textile, Clothing and Diamond Workers): 143 Opvoedingstraat, 9000 Ghent; tel. (9) 242-86-86; fax (9) 242-86-96; e-mail abvvtkd.fgtbtvd@glo.be; f. 1994; Pres. DONALD WIT-TEVRONGEL; 60,000 mems (1999).

Syndicat des Employés, Techniciens et Cadres de Belgique/Bond der Bedienden, Technici en Kaders van België (Employees, Technicians, Administrative Workers, Graphical and Paper Workers): 42 rue Haute, 1000 Brussels; tel. (2) 512-52-50; fax (2) 511-05-08; e-mail nationaal@setca-fgtb.be; internet www.bbtk.org; f. 1891; Pres. CHRISTIAN ROLAND; Gen. Sec. ROBERT WITTEBROUCK.

Les Cadets: an organization for students and school pupils. also affiliated to the FGTB/ABVV.

Confédération des Syndicats Chrétiens (ACV-CSC): 579 Haachtsesteenweg, POB 10, 1031 Brussels; tel. (2) 246-36-00; fax (2) 246-30-10; e-mail international@acv-csc.be; internet www.acv-csc .be; Pres. LUC CORTEBEECK; 16 affiliated unions with an estimated total membership of 1,652,854 (2000).

Affiliated unions:

CSC Bâtiment et Industrie (Building and Industrial Workers): 31 rue de Trèves, 1040 Brussels; tel. (2) 285-02-11; fax (2) 230-74-43; e-mail bouw_industrie@acv-csc.be; internet www.cscbi.be; Pres. J. JACKERS; Sec.-Gen. JEAN-PAUL GHEYSEN; 225,000 mems (1999).

Centrale Chrétienne de l'Alimentation et des Services (Food and Service Industries): 70 Kartuizersstraat, 1000 Brussels; tel. (2) 500-28-11; fax (2) 500-28-99; e-mail ccvd-ccas@acv-csc.be; f. 1919; Pres. W. VIJVERMAN; Sec.-Gen. F. BOCKLANDT.

Centrale Chrétienne des Métallurgistes de Belgique (Metal Workers): 127 rue de Heembeek, 1120 Brussels; tel. (2) 244-99-11; fax (2) 244-99-90; e-mail ccmb@acv-csc.be; Pres. T. JANSSEN.

CSC Energie-Chimie (Chemical and Energy Workers): 52 ave de Cortenbergh, 1000 Brussels; tel. (2) 739-45-45; e-mail a .depotter@acv-csc.be; internet www.csc-energie-chimie.be; f. 1912; Pres. A. DE POTTER; Gen. Sec. I. RODOMONTI; 63,155 mems (1993).

Centrale Chrétienne des Ouvriers du Textile et du Vête-ment de Belgique (Textile and Clothing Workers): 27 Koning Albertlaan, 9000 Ghent; tel. (9) 222-57-01; fax (9) 220-45-59; e-mail acvtextiel@acv-csc.be; f. 1886; Pres. JACQUES JOURET; Gen. Sec. DIRK VITTENHOUG.

Centrale Chrétienne du Personnel de l'Enseignement Technique (Teachers in Technical Education): 16 rue de la Vic-toire, 1060 Brussels; tel. (2) 542-09-00; fax (2) 542-09-08; e-mail ccpet-uceo@acv-csc.be; Sec.-Gen. PROSPER BOULANGE; 8,500 mems (2001).

Centrale Chrétienne des Professeurs de l'Enseignement Moyen et Normal Libre (Lay Teachers in Secondary and Teacher-Training Institutions): 16 rue de la Victoire, 1060 Brus-sels; tel. (2) 543-68-00; fax (2) 543-68-10; e-mail cemnl@acv-csc.be; Pres. WILLEM MILLER.

Centrale Chrétienne des Services Publics—Christelijke Centrale van de Openbare Diensten (Public-Service Workers): 26–32 ave d'Auderghem, 1040 Brussels; tel. (2) 231-00-90; fax (2) 230-45-62; e-mail ccod@acv-csc.be; f. 1921; Pres. FILIP WIEERS; Sec.-Gen. GUY RASNEUR.

Centrale Nationale des Employés (CNE) (Private-Sector Workers): 46 rue Pépin, 5000 Namur; tel. (81) 22-02-22; fax (81) 22-50-47; Sec.-Gen. PIERRA PRAVATA; 120,000 mems (2000).

Christelijke Centrale van Diverse Industrieen (Miscella-neous): 26–32 Oudergemselaan, 1040 Brussels; tel. (2) 238-72-11; fax (2) 238-73-12; Pres. LEO DUSOLEIL; Nat. Secs FRANÇOIS LICATA, LEON VAN HAUDT.

Christelijke Onderwijs Centrale (COC) (Teachers): 31–33 Tri-erstraat, 1040 Brussels; tel. (2) 285-04-40; fax (2) 230-28-83; e-mail coc.brussel@acv-csc.be; internet www.coc.be; f. 1993 as a result of a merger of the Flemish wings of three teachers' unions; Chair. ERIC DOLFEN; Gen. Sec. GUST VAN DONGEN.

Christelijk Onderwijzersverbond van België (Schoolteach-ers): 203 Koningsstraat, 1210 Brussels; tel. (2) 227-41-11; fax (2) 219-47-61; e-mail cov@acv-csc.be; internet www.cov.be; f. 1893; Pres. G. BOURDEAUD'HUI; Sec.-Gen. R. MAES; 41,000 mems (1999).

CSC—Transcom (Confédération des Syndicats Chrétiens) (Christian Trade Union Confederation; railway, post, telecommu-nications, water, transport, shipping, civil aviation, radio, tele-vision and cultural workers): Galerie Agora, 105 rue Marché aux Herbes, bte 40, 1000 Brussels; tel. (2) 549-07-60; fax (2) 512-95-91; e-mail acv-transcom@acv-csc.be; f. 1919; Pres. M. BOVY; Vice-Pres. P. BERTIN.

Fédération des Instituteurs Chrétiens (Schoolteachers): 16 rue de la Victoire, 1060 Brussels; tel. (2) 539-00-01; fax (2) 534-13-36; internet www.fic.be; f. 1893; publishes twice monthly period-ical 'L'éducateur'; Sec.-Gen. R. DOHOGNE; 17,100 mems (2001).

Sporta-vsb (Sport): 70 Kaltuizersstraat, 1000 Brussels; tel. (2) 500-28-30; fax (2) 500-28-39; e-mail sporta@acv-csc.be; Nat. Sec. DIRK DE VOS.

Union Chrétienne des Membres du Personnel de l'Enseignement Officiel: 16 rue de la Victoire, 1060 Brussels; tel. (2) 542-09-00; fax (2) 542-09-08; e-mail ccpet-uceo@acv-csc.be; Sec.-Gen. P. BOULANGE.

Centrale Générale des Syndicats Libéraux de Belgique (CGSLB) (General Federation of Liberal Trade Unions of Belgium): 95 Koning Albertlaan, 9000 Ghent; tel. (9) 222-57-51; fax (9) 221-04-74; e-mail cgslb@cgslb.be; internet www.cgslb.be; f. 1891; Nat. Pres. GUY HAAZE; 227,657 mems.

Fédération Wallonie de l'Agriculture (FWA): 47 chaussée de Namur, 5030 Gembloux; tel. (81) 60-00-60; fax (81) 60-04-46; e-mail fwa@fwa.be; Pres L. FRANC, S. SKA; Sec.-Gen. J. P. CHAMPAGNE.

Landelijke Bediendencentrale-Nationaal Verbond voor Kaderpersoneel (LBC-NVK) (Employees): 5 Sudermanstraat, 2000 Antwerp; tel. (3) 220-87-11; fax (3) 220-87-33; e-mail lbc-nvk .fwyckmans@acv-csc.be; internet www.lbc-nvk.be; f. 1912; Sec.-Gen. FERRE WYCKMANS; 280,000 mems (2000).

Nationale Unie der Openbare Diensten (NUOD)/Union Natio-nale des Services Publics (UNSP): 25 rue de la Sablonnière, 1000 Brussels; tel. (2) 219-88-02; fax (2) 223-38-36; f. 1983; Pres. GÉRALD VAN ACKER; Sec.-Gen. FRANCIS SACRE.

Transport

RAILWAYS

The Belgian railway network is one of the densest in the world. The main lines are operated by the Société Nationale des Chemins de Fer Belges (SNCB) under lease from the State Transport Administra-tion. Construction of the Belgian section of a high-speed railway network for northern Europe, which will eventually link Belgium, France, Germany, the Netherlands and the United Kingdom, is expected to be completed by 2005. A high-speed link between Brus-sels and Paris was completed in 1997. In March 2001 the Govern-ment announced a €16,000m. programme to modernize the network.

Société Nationale des Chemins de Fer Belges (SNCB)/Nationale Maatschappij der Belgische Spoorwegen (NMBS): 85 rue de France, 1060 Brussels; tel. (2) 525-21-11; fax (2) 525-40-45; internet www.sncb.be; f. 1926; 143.6m. passengers were carried in 2000; 3,422 km of lines, of which 2,507 km are electrified; Chair. MICHEL DAMAR; Man. Dir ETIENNE SCHOUPPE.

ROADS

In 2000 there were 1,726.7 km of motorways and some 12,600 km of other main or national roads. There were also 1,349 km of secondary or regional roads and an additional 132,540 km of minor roads.

Société Régionale Wallonne du Transport: 96 ave Gouverneur Bovesse, 5100 Namur; tel. (81) 32-27-11; fax (81) 32-27-10; f. 1991; operates light railways, buses and trams; Dir-Gen. JEAN-CLAUDE PHLYPO.

Société des Transports Intercommunaux de Bruxelles: 15 ave de la Toison d'or, 1050 Brussels; tel. (2) 515-20-00; fax (2) 515-32-84; e-mail flauscha@stib.irisnet.be; internet www.stib.be; operates a metro service, buses and trams; Dir-Gen. A. FLAUSCH.

VVM-De Lijn: 1 Hendrik Consciencestraat, 2800 Mechelen; tel. (15) 44-07-11; fax (15) 44-07-09; internet www.delijn.be; f. 1991; public transport; Dir-Gen. HUGO VAN WESEMAEL.

INLAND WATERWAYS

There are over 1,520 km of inland waterways in Belgium, of which 660 km are navigable rivers and 860 km are canals.

In 1989 waterways administration was divided between the Flemish region (1,055 km), the Walloon region (450 km) and the Brussels region (15 km):

Flemish region:

Departement Leefmilieu en Infrastructuur Administratie Waterwegen en Zeewezen: Graaf de Ferraris-Gebouw, 20 Koning Albert II-laan, bte 5, 1000 Brussels; tel. (2) 553-77-11; fax (2) 553-77-05; e-mail awz@lin.vlaanderen.be; internet www.lin.vlaanderen.be; Dir-Gen. JAN STRUBBE.

Walloon region:

Direction Générale des Voies Hydrauliques: Centre administratif du MET, 8 blvd du Nord, 5000 Namur; tel. (81) 77-29-94; fax (81) 77-37-80; e-mail jlaurent@met.wallonie.be; internet voies-hydrauliques.wallonie.be; Dir-Gen. J. LAURENT.

Brussels region:

Haven van Brussel: 6 place des Armateurs, 1000 Brussels; tel. (2) 420-67-00; fax (2) 420-69-74; e-mail havenvanbrussel@haven.irisnet.be; internet www.havenvanbrussel.irisnet.be; f. 1993; Chair. OLIVER MAINGAIN VANACKERE; Gen. Man. CHARLES HUYGENS.

SHIPPING

The modernized port of Antwerp is the second biggest in Europe and handles about 80% of Belgian foreign trade by sea and inland waterways. It is also the largest railway port and has one of the largest petroleum refining complexes in Europe. Antwerp has 98 km of quayside and 17 dry docks. Other ports include Zeebrugge, Ostend, Ghent, Liège and Brussels.

Ahlers Logistic and Maritime Services: 139 Noorderlaan, 2030 Antwerp; tel. (3) 543-72-11; fax (3) 542-00-23; e-mail info@ahlers.com; internet www.ahlers.com; services to Finland, Poland, Latvia, Morocco; Man. Dir (Belgium) ALBERT WEYNEN.

ESSO Belgium: POB 100, 2060 Antwerp; tel. (3) 543-31-11; fax (3) 543-34-95; internet www.esso.be; refining and marketing of petroleum products; Pres. K. O. GILJE.

De Keyser Thornton: 38 Huidevettersstraat, 2000 Antwerp; tel. (3) 205-31-00; fax (3) 234-27-86; e-mail info@multimodal.be; internet www.dekeyserthornton.com; f. 1853; shipping agency, forwarding and warehousing services; President PHILIP VAN TILBURY.

Northern Shipping Service NV: 54 St Katelijnevest, 2000 Antwerp; tel. (3) 204-78-78; fax (3) 231-30-51; e-mail sales@northern-shipping.be; internet www.northern-shipping.be; forwarding, customs clearance, liner and tramp agencies, chartering, Rhine and inland barging, multi-purpose bulk/bags fertilizer, minerals and agri-bulk terminal; Man. Dirs ALAIN AUDET, DIRK VERCRUYSSEN.

P&O North Sea Ferries Ltd: Leopold II Dam, 13, 8380 Zeebrugge; tel. (50) 54-34-11; fax (50) 54-68-35; internet www.ponsf.com; roll-on/roll-off ferry services between Zeebrugge, Felixstowe, Hull and Middlesbrough; Dirs P. V. D. BROMDHOF, R. B. LOUGH.

TotalFinaElf SA: 52 rue de l'Industrie, 1040 Brussels; tel. (2) 288-94-49; fax (2) 288-34-45; integrated petroleum co active in exploration and production, transportation and petroleum refining, petrochemicals, etc., marketing of petroleum products and research; Vice-Chair. and Man. Dir FRANÇOIS CORNELIS.

CIVIL AVIATION

The main international airport is at Brussels, with a direct train service from the air terminal. A major programme of expansion, more than doubling the airport's passenger-handling capacity, was completed in 1994. Further expansion work was to include the construction of a new concourse by 2002. There are also international airports at Antwerp, Liège, Charleroi and Ostend. Following the collapse of the Belgian state airline, SABENA, in late 2001, the latter's regional subsidiary, Delta Air Transport, was reorganized as SN Brussels Airlines in February 2002.

SN Brussels Airlines: Airport Bldg 117, 1820 Melsbroek; tel. (2) 754-19-00; fax (2) 754-19-99; internet www.brussels-airlines.com; f. 1966; formerly Delta Air Transport NV, reorganized under current name Feb. 2002; scheduled and charter services within Europe and to Africa; CEO PETER DAVIES.

Sobelair (Société Belge de Transports par Air) NV: Bldg 45, Brussels National Airport, 1930 Zaventem; tel. (2) 754-12-11; fax (2) 754-12-88; f. 1946; 99% owned by Belgian World Airlines; operates charter flights; CEO LUC HELLAERSS.

Virgin Express: Airport Bldg 116, 1820 Melsbroek; tel. (2) 752-05-11; fax (2) 752-05-06; f. 1991 as EuroBelgium Airlines, name changed as above 1996; 51% owned by Virgin Group (UK), scheduled and charter services to European destinations; Chair. DAVID HOARE; Man. Dir NEIL BURROWS.

Tourism

Belgium has several towns of rich historic and cultural interest, such as Antwerp, Bruges, Brussels, Durbuy, Ghent, Liège, Namur and Tournai. The country's seaside towns attract many visitors. The forest-covered Ardennes region is renowned for hill-walking and gastronomy. In 2001 tourist arrivals totalled an estimated 6,451,000.

Brussels Tourism (Bi-Tc): Hôtel de Ville, Grand-Place, 1000 Brussels; tel. (2) 513-89-40; fax (2) 513-83-20; e-mail info@brusselstourism.com; internet bxltour.combiz.be; Dir G. RENDERS.

Office de Promotion du Tourisme Wallonie–Bruxelles: 61 rue Marché-aux-Herbes, 1000 Brussels; tel. (2) 504-02-00; fax (2) 513-69-50; e-mail info@qot.be; e-mail info@opt.be; internet www.belgique-tourisme.net; f. 1981; promotion of tourism in French-speaking Belgium; Dir-Gen. VIVIANE JACOBS.

Tourist Office for Flanders: 63 Grasmarkt, 1000 Brussels; tel. (2) 504-03-00; fax (2) 504-03-77; e-mail info@toerismvlaanderen.be; internet www.visitflanders.com; f. 1985; official promotion and policy body for tourism in Flemish region of Belgium; Gen. Commissioner URBAIN CLAEYS.

BELIZE

Introductory Survey

Location, Climate, Language, Religion, Flag, Capital

Belize lies on the Caribbean coast of Central America, with Mexico to the north-west and Guatemala to the south-west. The climate is sub-tropical, tempered by trade winds. The temperature averages 24°C (75°F) from November to January, and 27°C (81°F) from May to September. Annual rainfall ranges from 1,290 mm (51 ins) in the north to 4,450 mm (175 ins) in the south. The average annual rainfall in Belize City is 1,650 mm (65 ins). Belize is ethnically diverse, the population (according to the 2000 census) consisting of 49% Mestizos (Maya-Spanish), 25% Creoles (those of predominantly African descent), 11% Amerindian (mainly Maya), 6% Garifuna ('Black Caribs', descendants of those deported from the island of Saint Vincent in 1797) and communities of Asians, Portuguese, German Mennonites and others of European descent. English is the official language and an English Creole is widely understood. Spanish is the mother-tongue of some 15% of the population but is spoken by many others. There are also speakers of Garifuna (Carib), Maya and Ketchi, while the Mennonites speak a German dialect. Most of the population profess Christianity, with about 58% being Roman Catholics in 1997. The national flag (proportions usually 3 by 5) is dark blue, with narrow horizontal red stripes at the upper and lower edges; at the centre is a white disc containing the state coat of arms, bordered by an olive wreath. The capital is Belmopan.

Recent History

Belize, known as British Honduras until June 1973, was first colonized by British settlers (the 'Baymen') in the 17th century, but was not recognized as a British colony until 1862. In 1954 a new Constitution granted universal adult suffrage and provided for the creation of a legislative assembly. The territory's first general election, in April 1954, was won by the only party then organized, the People's United Party (PUP), led by George Price. The PUP won all subsequent elections until 1984. In 1961 Price was appointed First Minister under a new ministerial system of government. The colony was granted internal self-government in 1964, with the United Kingdom retaining responsibility for defence, external affairs and internal security. Following an election in 1965, Price became Premier and a bicameral legislature was introduced. In 1970 the capital of the territory was moved from Belize City to the newly-built town of Belmopan.

Much of the recent history of Belize has been dominated by the territorial dispute with Guatemala, particularly in the years prior to Belize's independence (see below). This was achieved on 21 September 1981, within the Commonwealth, and with Price becoming Prime Minister. However, the failure of the 1981 draft treaty with Guatemala, and the clash of opposing wings within the ruling party, undermined the dominance of the PUP. Internal disputes within the PUP intensified during 1983, although Price succeeded in keeping the factions together. However, at the general election held in December 1984 the PUP's 30 years of rule ended when the United Democratic Party (UDP) received 53% of the total votes and won 21 of the 28 seats in the enlarged House of Representatives. The UDP's leader, Manuel Esquivel, was appointed Prime Minister. The new Government pledged to revive Belize's economy through increased foreign investment.

A general election was held in September 1989. At the election the PUP obtained almost 51% of the total valid votes cast, and won 15 seats in the 28-member House of Representatives. The UDP received 49% of the votes and retained 13 seats, although one of their members subsequently joined the PUP. Price was again appointed Prime Minister.

A general election was held in June 1993. The UDP formed an alliance with the National Alliance for Belizean Rights (NABR) to contest the election, and their campaign concentrated on concern about the security situation in the light of the imminent withdrawal of British troops and the prevailing political crisis in neighbouring Guatemala (see below). The PUP had called the election 15 months before it was constitutionally due, following recent successes at local and by-elections. However, at the election the PUP secured only 13 seats in the House of Repre-

sentatives, despite obtaining more than 51% of the votes. The UDP/NABR alliance received 48.7% of the votes but secured 16 seats (the total number of seats having been increased from 28 to 29). Esquivel was appointed Prime Minister. In November, at Esquivel's request, Dame Minita Gordon, who had been the Governor-General since independence, resigned her position. She was replaced by Dr (later Sir) Colville Young, formerly President of the University College of Belize.

In June 1994 the sale of citizenship, of which many Hong Kong Chinese had taken advantage, was officially ended, following criticism that the system was open to abuse. However, a revised 'economic citizenship' programme, including mechanisms to prevent corruption, received government approval in early 1995. In June the Minister of Human Resources, Community and Youth Development, Culture and Women's Affairs, Phillip S. W. Goldson, was relieved of responsibility for immigration and nationality affairs, following allegations implicating him in the sale of false residence and visitor permits to nationals of the People's Republic of China and the Republic of China (Taiwan). Reportedly some 5,000 such permits had been issued over the previous 12-month period, and the recipients then smuggled into the USA. In August the Judicial Committee of the Privy Council in the United Kingdom (the final court of appeal for Belize) issued stays of execution for two convicted murderers. The ruling, which came amid growing concern at rising crime in Belize, prompted widespread criticism of the British court, which was considered to be undermining the authority of the Belizean judiciary, and demands for a revision of the appeals system.

In mid-1996 the UDP established a bipartisan committee to discuss political reform. However, the committee made little progress and, in October 1997, PUP members withdrew from it. In the following month the PUP presented its own proposals for reform, which included the establishment of a republican form of government, with the Governor-General to be replaced by a president elected by the National Assembly. The PUP leader, Said Musa, pledged that, should his party gain power at the forthcoming general election (due to be held in August 1998), preliminary proposals for political reform would be introduced within 100 days of taking office. At the general election of August 1998 the PUP won an overwhelming victory, securing 26 of the 29 seats in the House of Representatives. The UDP obtained the remaining three seats. The result reflected popular discontent with the outgoing Government's structural-adjustment policies, including the introduction of value-added tax (VAT), which the PUP had pledged to repeal. The PUP had also promised to create 15,000 new jobs, to build 10,000 new houses and to reduce public utility tariffs. Following the defeat of his party, Esquivel, who had lost his seat in the House of Representatives, resigned as leader of the UDP. He was succeeded by Dean Barrow. On 1 September Said Musa was sworn in as Prime Minister.

In July 1999 Musa issued a statement rejecting allegations, published in the British press, that Michael Ashcroft, a businessman with dual British/Belizean nationality, who had extensive business and banking interests in Belize and was its ambassador to the UN, had used improper influence in Belizean affairs and was involved in money-laundering. In March 2000 Ashcroft resigned his UN post after receiving a life peerage in the British House of Lords. In the same year the British Government commissioned an investigation, by KPMG accountants, into Belize's financial system, including the regulation of the 'offshore' sector and the impact of tax concessions on the level of poverty. The British Government had previously suspended debt relief to Belize, pending the completion of the audit. However, following the conclusion of the investigation in late 2000, it requested that the inquiry be expanded to investigate public investment companies operating from Belize, including Ashcroft's Carlisle Holdings. In December 2001 it was announced that the Government had refused the United Kingdom's offer of £10m. of debt relief in exchange for a reform of its financial regime and an end to tax relief given to Carlisle Holdings and another company.

On 5 April 2000 Belize became the eighth country to ratify the Rome Statute of the International Criminal Court, which was to be established following its ratification by 60 states. On 14 February 2001, following legislative approval in November 2000, the leaders of 11 Caribbean countries, including Belize, signed an agreement to establish a Caribbean Court of Justice, based in Trinidad and Tobago. The Court was to replace the British Privy Council as the final court of appeal, and would allow the execution of convicted criminals. In August the Government announced that although it supported the foundation of the Caribbean Court of Justice, the British Privy Council would continue to handle final appeal cases in Belize. However, in August 2002 the Government announced its intention to ratify the agreement establishing the regional Court.

In late October 2002 the Attorney-General, Godfrey Smith, defended before a panel of the Inter-American Commission on Human Rights a proposed amendment to the Constitution that would prevent prisoners sentenced to death from appealing to the Privy Council in the United Kingdom. This followed a petition to the Commission by a group of prisoners who claimed that the amendment was incompatible with the Government's obligations to an Organization of American States (OAS) treaty on human rights. The proposed amendment would establish the Court of Appeals as the final court of appeal. It would also allow the National Assembly to approve either the establishment of a higher court of appeal or to declare the proposed Caribbean Court of Justice as the highest appellate court. The Attorney-General maintained that Belize had the right to legislate in its own domestic affairs.

In October 2001 'Hurricane Iris' struck Belize, killing 19 tourists and causing an estimated US $250m.-worth of damage. Some 12,000 people were left homeless, crops were destroyed and the power and communications infrastructures were damaged. On 12 October the Minister of National Security and of Economic Development, Jorge Espat, resigned his post, after criticizing the Government. Three days later Musa undertook a reorganization of the Cabinet, in an attempt to resolve the economic crisis and the damage resulting from the hurricane. In January 2002 Assad Shoman, hitherto High Commissioner to the United Kingdom, assumed the foreign affairs, foreign trade and co-operation portfolio, held by Musa since October.

In February 2002 the policy of economic citizenship was formally abolished. However, a report produced in late July by the Ministry of Foreign Affairs substantiated claims that the immigration authorities had apparently continued the practice illegally until that month. As a result, the Director of Immigration, Paulino Castellano, was suspended and replaced by Col Peter Parchue. In early August Maxwell Samuels, hitherto Minister of Home Affairs, was appointed Minister of Public Utilities, Transport and Communications. At the same time, Musa announced that a Commission of Inquiry into the economic citizenship affair would ensue. Samuels' move precipitated a cabinet reorganization, in which responsibility for the Department of Immigration was transferred from the Ministry of Home Affairs to the Ministry of Foreign Affairs, Foreign Trade and Co-operation. The Minister of Budget Management, Investment and Head of the Central Bank, Ralph Fonseca, was also appointed Minister of Home Affairs and the Deputy Prime Minister, John Briceño, assumed the trade and industry portfolio from Musa. In addition, Vildo Marin was made Minster of Works and Development and the Minister of Tourism and Culture, Mark Espat, also became Minister of Broadcasting and Information. In late November the Commission of Inquiry into the economic citizenship programme reported that while no person was granted Belizean citizenship under the programme following its annulment in February, over 1,000 applications were approved during the first seven months of 2002 and a number of irregularities had been detected.

In late September 2002 a proposed High Seas Fishing Act was under discussion by the Government. Under the Act, the activities of fishing boats operating under the Belizean flag would be monitored by satellite. In 2001 the Government had been accused of allowing illegal fishing to be carried out by foreign vessels using the Belizean flag as a so-called 'flag of convenience'.

In a general election on 5 March 2003, the PUP won 53.2% of valid votes cast and 22 seats in the House of Representatives; the UDP secured 45.6% of votes cast and increased its legislative representation to seven seats (from three). Musa became the country's first Prime Minister to be sworn in for a second term in office. He subsequently formed a new Cabinet.

The frontier with Guatemala was agreed by a convention in 1859 but this was declared invalid by Guatemala in 1940. Guatemalan claims to sovereignty of Belize date back to the middle of the 19th century and were written into Guatemala's Constitution in 1945. In November 1975 and July 1977 British troops and aircraft were sent to protect Belize from the threat of Guatemalan invasion, and a battalion of troops and a detachment of fighter aircraft remained in the territory. Negotiations between the United Kingdom and Guatemala began in 1977. In 1980 the United Kingdom warned that it might unilaterally grant independence to Belize if no settlement with Guatemala were forthcoming, and later that year the British Government finally excluded the possibility of any cession of land to Guatemala, although offering economic and financial concessions. In November the UN General Assembly overwhelmingly approved a resolution urging that Belize be granted independence (similar resolutions having been adopted in 1978 and 1979), and the United Kingdom decided to proceed with a schedule for independence. A tripartite conference in March 1981 appeared to produce a sound basis for a final settlement, with Guatemala accepting Belizean independence in exchange for access to the Caribbean Sea through Belize and the use of certain offshore cayes and their surrounding waters. A constitutional conference began in April. Further tripartite talks in May and July collapsed, however, as a result of renewed claims by Guatemala to Belizean land. With Belizean independence imminent, Guatemala made an unsuccessful appeal to the UN Security Council to intervene, severing diplomatic relations with the United Kingdom and sealing its border with Belize on 7 September. However, on 21 September, as scheduled, Belize achieved independence. Guatemala alone refused to recognize Belize's new status, and during 1982 requested the reopening of negotiations with the United Kingdom, alleging that Belize was not legally independent. Tripartite talks in January 1983 collapsed when Belize rejected Guatemala's proposal that Belize should cede the southern part of the country. This claim was subsequently suspended. Belize is a member of the Caribbean Community and Common Market (CARICOM, see p. 155), whose summit conferences have consistently expressed support for Belize's territorial integrity against claims by Guatemala.

At independence the United Kingdom had agreed to leave troops as protection and for training of the Belize Defence Force 'for an appropriate time'. In 1984 Prime Minister Esquivel was given renewed assurances from the British Government as regards its commitment to keep British troops in Belize until the resolution of the territorial dispute with Guatemala. Discussions with Guatemala resumed in February 1985, with greater optimism shown by all three parties. In July the new draft Guatemalan Constitution omitted the previous unconditional claim to Belize, while Esquivel had previously acknowledged Guatemala's right of access to the Caribbean Sea, but no settlement was forthcoming. In January 1986 Dr Marco Vinicio Cerezo was inaugurated as the elected President of Guatemala, representing a change from military to civilian government. In August the United Kingdom and Guatemala renewed diplomatic relations at consular level, and in December the restoration of full diplomatic relations was announced. In March 1987 the first Guatemalan trade delegation since independence visited Belize, and in April renewed discussions were held between Guatemala, the United Kingdom and Belize (although Belize was still regarded by Guatemala as being only an observer at the meetings). Tripartite negotiations continued, and in May 1988 the formation of a permanent joint commission (which, in effect, entailed a recognition of the Belizean state by Guatemala) was announced.

In September 1991 Belize and Guatemala signed an accord under the terms of which Belize pledged to legislate to reduce its maritime boundaries and to allow Guatemala access to the Caribbean Sea and use of its port facilities. In return, President Jorge Serrano Elías of Guatemala officially announced his country's recognition of Belize as an independent state and established diplomatic relations. In January 1992 the Maritime Areas Bill was approved in the Belizean House of Representatives. The legislation, however, had caused serious divisions within the UDP, leading to the formation, in December 1991, of the Patriotic Alliance for Territorial Integrity (PATI) by certain members of the party to co-ordinate opposition to the bill. Further disagreement between PATI activists and the leaders of the UDP resulted in the expulsion or resignation of five UDP members (including two members of Parliament) in January 1992. In February these members formed a new organization, the NABR (see above), led by the former UDP Deputy Leader and Minister of Transport, Derek Aikman. In November 1992 the Guatemalan legislature voted to ratify Serrano's decision to recognize Belize. Serrano, however, indicated that the accord was not definitive and that Guatemala maintained its territorial claim over Belize.

In April 1993 Belize and Guatemala signed a non-aggression pact, affirming their intent to refrain from the threat or use of force against each other, and preventing either country from being used as a base for aggression against the other. Relations between the two countries were jeopardized when, in June, President Serrano was ousted following an attempt to suspend certain articles of the Constitution and dissolve Congress. However, in June the new Guatemalan President, Ramiro de León Carpio, announced that Guatemala would continue to respect Belize's independence. In July the Belizean Prime Minister, Manuel Esquivel, reportedly suspended the September 1991 accord, which had been signed by the previous administration and had still not been formally ratified, stating that it involved too many concessions on the part of Belize and that the issue should be put to a referendum.

On 1 January 1994 responsibility for the defence of Belize was transferred to the Belize Defence Force, and all of the British troops were withdrawn by October, with the exception of some 180 troops, who remained to organize training for jungle warfare.

In March 1994, in a letter to the UN Secretary-General, Guatemala formally reaffirmed its territorial claim to Belize, prompting the Belizean Minister of Foreign Affairs to seek talks with the British Government regarding assistance with national defence. Concern was also expressed by the Standing Committee of CARICOM Ministers of Foreign Affairs, which reaffirmed its support for Belizean sovereignty. In mid-1994 Esquivel accused Guatemala of employing destabilizing tactics against Belize by encouraging Guatemalans to occupy and settle in areas of Belizean forest. In September 1996 the Ministers of Foreign Affairs of Belize and Guatemala conducted preliminary talks in New York concerning a resumption of negotiations on the territorial dispute. Further such discussions, involving representatives of the Governments and armed forces of both countries, were conducted in Miami, Florida, in February 1997. In November 1998, at a meeting of ambassadors and officials of both countries, conducted in Miami, agreement was reached on the establishment of a joint commission to deal with immigration, cross-border traffic and respect for the rights of both countries' citizens.

In January 2000 Belizean security guards shot and killed a Guatemalan civilian in what was claimed to be an act of self-defence. In February Guatemalan forces captured three members of the Belizean border patrol, who later escaped; the men were assisted in their escape by the Belizean ambassador, who was expelled from Guatemala as a result. Bilateral talks resumed in May and in August a panel of negotiators was installed at the headquarters of the OAS. In November the two countries signed an agreement to initiate joint patrols of the unofficial common border and to hold quarterly meetings between operational commanders. On 23 November 2001 two Guatemalans were killed, following their attack on a Belize Defence Force patrol, close to the border of the two countries.

In June 2002 the Minister of Foreign Affairs, Assad Shoman, and his Guatemalan counterpart, Gabriel Orellana Rojas, met to discuss the border dispute issue. The meeting was mediated by the OAS. Relations appeared to have improved further when Musa attended a ceremony in Guatemala City in late July, marking the twinning of Belmopan with the Guatemalan capital. At the same time, during a visit by Pope John Paul II to Guatemala, a member of the papal delegation, Cardinal Angelo Sodano, mediated in further talks between Shoman and Orellana. Following further, OAS-mediated, negotiations in August, in early September proposals were outlined for a solution to the dispute. These included the provision that Guatemala would recognize Belize's land boundary as laid out in the treaty of 1859 and the creation of a model settlement, complete with modern amenities, for peasants and landless farmers in the border area. Guatemalan farmers occupying land within the Belizean border were to have priority rights of residency on this settlement. There was also provision for the establishment of a Free Trade Agreement between the two countries and a Development Trust Fund, to be managed by the Inter-American Development Bank, with the money being used to alleviate poverty in the border region. In addition, Guatemala would be granted a 200 sq mile

Exclusive Economic Zone in the Gulf of Honduras, although Belize and Honduras would retain fishing rights and 50% of any mineral resources discovered in the sea-bed. A Commission comprising Belize, Guatemala and Honduras would oversee the establishment and management of an Ecological Marine Park in coastal areas and a separate Tripartite Regional Fisheries Management Commission would manage fishing in the Gulf of Honduras. The details of the agreement were concluded on 30 September and the two countries agreed to hold simultaneous public referendums by the end of November. However, in early October, the Guatemalan legislature approved a resolution recommending the establishment of temporary military outposts on the Belizean border. This followed the shooting and killing of a Guatemalan farmer in the border area and the alleged arrest of three Guatemalans by Belizean soldiers. Musa subsequently declared that the deadline for the holding of the referendums would have to be extended. Further discussions were held in January 2003.

Government

Belize is a constitutional monarchy, with the British sovereign as Head of State. Executive authority is vested in the sovereign and is exercised by the Governor-General, who is appointed on the advice of the Prime Minister, must be of Belizean nationality, and acts, in almost all matters, on the advice of the Cabinet. The Governor-General is also advised by an appointed Belize Advisory Council. Legislative power is vested in the bicameral National Assembly, comprising a Senate (eight members appointed by the Governor-General) and a House of Representatives (29 members elected by universal adult suffrage for five years, subject to dissolution). The Governor-General appoints the Prime Minister and, on the latter's recommendation, other ministers. The Cabinet is responsible to the House of Representatives.

Defence

The Belize Defence Force was formed in 1978 and was based on a combination of the existing Police Special Force and the Belize Volunteer Guard. Military service is voluntary. Provision has been made for the establishment of National Service if necessary to supplement normal recruitment. In August 2002 the regular armed forces totalled an estimated 1,050, with some 700 militia reserves. In 1994 all British forces were withdrawn from Belize and in 2002 some 30 troops remained to organize training for jungle warfare. The defence budget for 2002 was an estimated BZ $37m.

Economic Affairs

In 2001, according to estimates by the World Bank, the country's gross national income (GNI), measured at average 1999–2001 prices, was US $718m., equivalent to US $2,910 per head (or $5,350 per head on an international purchasing-power parity basis). During 1990–98, it was estimated, GNI per head increased, in real terms, at an annual average rate of 0.5%. During 1991–2000 Belize's population grew at an average rate of 2.7% per year. Belize's gross domestic product (GDP) increased, in real terms, at an average rate of 4.4% per year in 1990–2001; GDP increased by 11.0% in 2000 and by 3.3% in 2001. GDP was expected to increase by 3.7% in 2002.

Although 38% of the country is considered suitable for agriculture, only an estimated 6.1% of total area was used for agricultural purposes in 1999. Nevertheless, in 2000 agriculture, hunting, forestry and fishing employed an estimated 30.4% of the working population and contributed an estimated 16.3% of GDP. The principal cash crops are citrus fruits (citrus concentrates accounted for an estimated 20% of total domestic exports in 2001), sugar cane (sugar and molasses accounted for an estimated 15.4%) and bananas (an estimated 10.8%). Maize, red kidney beans and rice are the principal domestic food crops, and the development of other crops, such as cocoa, coconuts and soybeans (soya beans), is being encouraged. The country is largely self-sufficient in fresh meat and eggs. Belize has considerable timber reserves, particularly of tropical hardwoods, and the forestry sector is being developed. In 2001 fishing provided export earnings of an estimated US $31.9m. (16.1% of total domestic export revenue). According to UN estimates, the real GDP of the agricultural sector increased at an average annual rate of 6.0% during 1990–2000. According to IMF estimates, real agricultural GDP increased by 4.2% in 2000 and by 12.2% in 2001.

Industry (including mining, manufacturing, construction, water and electricity) employed 17.0% of the working population in 1999 and contributed an estimated 24.1% of GDP in 2000. Manufacturing alone, particularly of clothing, accounted for an estimated 13.3% of GDP in 2000 and employed 9.4% of the working population in 1999. The processing of agricultural products is important, particularly sugar cane (for sugar and rum). New ventures in the industrial sector included the manufacture of hot pepper sauces, worth US $206,000 in 1998, and coffee, grown organically and hand-picked for a niche market, mostly in the USA and Singapore. Investment was being sought for the expansion of the meat processing and dried fruit sectors. A small-scale industry existed for the production of items of wood and conch shell for the tourist market. According to the UN, industrial GDP increased at an average annual rate of 4.4% during 1990–2000; according to the IMF, real industrial GDP increased by an estimated 17.% in 2000 and by 3.7% in 2001. Manufacturing GDP increased at an average rate of 4.6% per year during 1990–2000; according to IMF estimates the sector increased by 19.5% in 2000 and by 2.0% in 2001. Mining and quarrying accounted for an estimated 0.7% of GDP 2000 and only 0.4% of employment in 1999.

Belize has no indigenous energy resources other than wood. Exploration for petroleum in the interior of Belize continued in the 1990s, despite increasing concern for the impact of such activity on the environment. Imports of mineral fuels accounted for 8.2% of the total cost of retained imports in 2001. Hydroelectric power was developed in the 1990s; in the late 1990s the Mollejón hydroelectric station, on the Macal River, began operations. Financed by the International Finance Corporation and the Caribbean Development Bank, the project attracted criticism over its cost and efficiency. In 2001 construction, by the Canadian company Fortis, of a controversial second hydroelectric dam at Chalillo on the Macal River began; upon completion, the dam would be operated by Fortis until it reverted to state ownership in 2031. However, environmentalists claimed that the dam would destroy the habitat of some 40 species of rare animals and birds, including the endangered scarlet macaw. In March 2002 the non-government organization the Belize Alliance of Conservation (BACONGO) instigated proceedings to seek a judicial review of the Government's approval of the project. In December the Chief Justice ordered that work on the dam be halted while a series of public hearings was held. However, the ruling did not reverse government approval of construction and subsequently BACONGO announced that it intended to take its case to the Court of Appeal.

The services sector employed 55.5% of the working population in 1999 and contributed 59.7% of GDP in 2000. Tourist development is concentrated on promoting 'eco-tourism', based on the attraction of Belize's natural environment, particularly its rain forests and the barrier reef, the second largest in the world. Tourist arrivals totalled an estimated 326,642 in 2000, which represented an increase of 13.4% compared with the previous year. However, arrivals declined by 40% in 2001, to an estimated 195,955, mainly owing to a sharp decrease in overland visitors. In the first half of 2002 cruise-ship arrivals were estimated to have increased by almost 40% and tourism authorities hoped that a new air service to Montego Bay, Jamaica, operated by Air Jamaica, would increase the number of tourist arrivals in 2002. According to UN estimates, the GDP of the services sector increased, in real terms, at an average rate of 4.0% per year during 1990–2000; according to the IMF, real GDP increased by 10.5% in 2000 and by 2.0% in 2001. Belize's 'offshore' financial centre opened in 1996 and by 2000 there were more than 10,000 registered 'offshore' companies.

In 2000 Belize recorded a trade deficit of US $191.4m., and a deficit of US $139.5m. on the current account of the balance of payments. In 2001 the principal source of imports was the USA (accounting for 48.0% of the total). The USA was also the principal export market, accounting for 53.8% of total exports, followed by the United Kingdom (23.0%). Mexico is another important trading partner. The principal exports in 2001 were food and live animals (89.0%). The principal imports in that year were basic manufactures, machinery and transport equipment and food and live animals.

For the financial year 2001/02 there was a budgetary deficit of BZ $174.8m. Belize's total external debt was US $499.0m. in 2000, of which US $449.0m. was long-term public debt, in that year equivalent to 16.1% of GDP. The annual rate of inflation averaged 1.7% in 1990–2001. Consumer prices increased by 0.6% in 2000 and by 1.2% in 2001. In 1999 12.8% of the economically active population were unemployed. Many Belizeans, however, work abroad, and remittances to the country

from such workers are an important source of income. Emigration, mainly to the USA, is offset by the number of immigrants and refugees from other Central American countries, particularly El Salvador.

Belize is a member of the Caribbean Community and Common Market (CARICOM, see p. 155), and in 1991 acceded to the Organization of American States (OAS, see p. 288). In September 1992 Belize was granted membership of the Inter-American Development Bank (IDB, see p. 239).

Agriculture is the dominant sector of the Belizean economy. As a member of the Commonwealth, Belize enjoys low tariffs on its exports to the European Union (EU) under the Cotonou Agreement (see p. 234) (which replaced the Lomé Convention in June 2000), and tariff-free access to the USA under the Caribbean Basin Initiative. The development of tourism and the availability of foreign investment have been hindered by the uncertainties arising from the territorial dispute with Guatemala. In an effort to develop service industries, an international shipping register was established in 1989 and legislation on 'offshore' financial services was introduced in 1990. The withdrawal of British troops from Belize in 1994 had serious economic repercussions, with the loss of an estimated BZ $60m. annually to the economy. As part of a reform of the tax system, value-added tax (VAT), at a basic rate of 15%, was introduced with effect from April 1996. High interest rates and low commodity prices were reflected in the lack of real GDP growth in 1998/99. However, the economy grew by 5.6% in 1999. On taking office in September 1998 the Musa administration inherited an extremely weak fiscal position, including a public-sector deficit of some BZ $51m. (equivalent to 4.0% of GDP). Despite this the new Government proceeded to implement its manifesto pledges, including a restructuring of the tax system: in April 1999 VAT was replaced with a broad-based 8% sales tax. Plans for a large-scale public investment programme were also initiated. By the end of 1999 prospects for economic growth had improved, based on the moderation of interest rates, expanded market opportunities for bananas (despite the phasing out of the EU preferential market for Caribbean bananas, see below) and increased investment in the tourism sector. GDP increased by 11.1% in 2000. The country was adversely affected by both 'Hurricane Keith', which struck in October 2000, causing an estimated BZ $523m.-worth of damage, and by 'Hurricane Iris', which struck in October 2001, causing an estimated US $250m.-worth of damage. As a result, growth in the economy slowed in 2001, to 5.1%.

On 11 April 2001, following an EU-USA agreement regarding banana imports, the EU preferential market for Caribbean bananas ended. From 1 July a transitional system, issuing licences according to historical trade patterns, was implemented, while the definitive tariff-only system was to be in place by 1 January 2006. This was expected to adversely affect banana revenue. In May Central American countries, including Belize, reached agreement with Mexico on regional integration through the 'Plan Puebla-Panamá', a series of joint projects intended to integrate the transport, industry and tourism of the countries involved. On 8 June the Government approved a Sugar Industry Bill intended to reform the sector, reducing the State's role, while encouraging outside investment.

In September 2001 the Government announced that the 15-year exclusive licence held by Belize Telecommunications Ltd (BTL) would not be renewed, and that the telecommunications sector would be liberalized. In April 2002 BTL was granted a judicial review into contracts subsequently awarded to a rival company, INTELCO. BTL sought to have the contracts declared null and void, alleging that it had not been properly informed of the awarding of the contract. However, this claim was rejected by the Supreme Court in November. In August 2002 the Government made an inaugural bond issue of US $125m. on the international capital markets to help pay off short-term debts. In November the IMF expressed concern at the country's current-account deficit, which was equivalent to an estimated 20% of GDP in 2001. It urged the Government to reduce the fiscal deficit to 5.0% of GDP in the 2002/03 financial year and advised against proposals for a government-subsidized national health service and affordable housing scheme.

Education

Education is compulsory for all children for a period of 10 years between the ages of five and 14 years. Primary education, beginning at five years of age and lasting for eight years, is provided free of charge, principally through subsidized denominational schools under government control. There were 54,616 pupils enrolled at 284 primary schools in 1998/99. Secondary education, beginning at the age of 13, lasts for four years. There were 11,724 students enrolled in 34 general secondary schools in 1998/99. In 1997 primary enrolment included an estimated 99.9% of children in the relevant age-group (males 99.9%; females 99.9%), while secondary enrolment in that year was equivalent to 63.6% (males 64.6%; females 62.6%).

In 1997/98 there were 2,853 students enrolled in 12 other educational institutions, which included technical, vocational and teacher-training colleges. There is an extra-mural branch of the University of the West Indies in Belize. In 2000 the University of Belize was formed through the amalgamation of five higher education institutions, including the University College of Belize and Belize Technical College. In 1999 the combined enrolment of primary, secondary and tertiary education was an estimated 73% (males 73%; females 72%). Budgetary expenditure on education in the financial year 1997/98 was projected at BZ $74.2m., representing 20.5% of total spending by the central Government.

Public Holidays

2003: 1 January (New Year's Day), 10 March (Baron Bliss Day), 18–21 April (Easter), 1 May (Labour Day), 26 May (for Commonwealth Day), 10 September (St George's Caye Day), 22 September (for Independence Day), 13 October (for Columbus Day, anniversary of the discovery of America), 19 November (Garifuna Settlement Day), 25–26 December (Christmas).

2004: 1 January (New Year's Day), 9 March (Baron Bliss Day), 9–12 April (Easter), 3 May (for Labour Day), 24 May (Commonwealth Day), 10 September (St George's Caye Day), 21 September (Independence Day), 12 October (Columbus Day, anniversary of the discovery of America), 19 November (Garifuna Settlement Day), 25–26 December (Christmas).

Weights and Measures

Imperial weights and measures are used, but petrol and paraffin are measured in terms of the US gallon (3.785 litres).

Statistical Survey

Source (unless otherwise stated): Central Statistical Office, Ministry of Finance, 2nd Floor, New Administration Bldg, Belmopan; tel. 822-2207; fax 822-3206; e-mail csogob@blt.net.

AREA AND POPULATION

Area: 22,965 sq km (8,867 sq miles).

Population: 189,774 at census of 12 May 1991; 240,204 (males 121,278, females 118,926) at census of 12 May 2000; 257,310 at mid-2001 (official estimate).

Density (mid-2001): 11.2 per sq km.

Districts (official estimates at mid-2001): Belize 76,370; Cayo 55,950; Orange Walk 40,725; Corozal 33,750; Stann Creek 26,000; Toledo 24,515.

Principal Towns (population at census of 12 May 2000): Belize City (former capital) 49,050; Orange Walk 13,483; San Ignacio/Santa Elena 13,260; Dangriga (formerly Stann Creek) 8,814; Belmopan (capital) 8,130; Corozal 7,888; Benque Viejo 5,088; San Pedro 4,499; Punta Gorda 4,329.

Births, Marriages and Deaths (1998): Registered live births 5,986 (birth rate 25.1 per 1,000); Registered marriages 1,374 (marriage rate 5.8 per 1,000); Registered deaths 1,350 (death rate 5.7 per 1,000). Source: UN, *Demographic Yearbook.*

Expectation of Life (WHO estimates, years at birth): 70.0 (males 67.7; females 72.7) in 2001. Source: WHO, *World Health Report.*

Economically Active Population (labour force survey, 1999): Agriculture, hunting, forestry and fishing 21,360; Mining and quarrying 300; Manufacturing 7,305; Electricity, gas and water 1,025; Construction 4,580; Trade, restaurants and hotels 17,775; Transport, storage and communications 4,230; Financing, insurance, real estate and business services 2,940; Community, social and personal services 15,165; Private households 2,855; Other 220; Total employed 77,755; Total unemployed 11,455; Total labour force 89,210. Source: ILO. *2001 (estimates in '000):* Agriculture, etc. 25; Total 82 (Source: FAO).

HEALTH AND WELFARE

Key Indicators

Total Fertility Rate (children per woman, 2001): 3.0.

Under-5 Mortality Rate (per 1,000 live births, 2001): 40.

HIV/AIDS (% of persons aged 15–49, 2001): 2.0.

Physicians (per 1,000 head, 1996): 0.55.

Hospital Beds (per 1,000 head, 1996): 2.13.

Health Expenditure (2000): US $ per head (PPP): 273.

Health Expenditure (2000): % of GDP: 4.6.

Health Expenditure (2000): public (% of total): 45.5.

Access to Water (% of persons, 2000): 76.

Access to Sanitation (% of persons, 2000): 42.

Human Development Index (2000): ranking: 58.

Human Development Index (2000): value: 0.784.
For sources and definitions, see explanatory note on p. vi.

AGRICULTURE, ETC.

Principal Crops (FAO estimates, '000 metric tons, 2001): Rice (paddy) 12.1; Maize 36.7; Sugar cane 1,207.4; Dry beans 5.8; Fresh vegetables 5.9; Bananas 58.5; Plantains 26.3; Oranges 234.1; Grapefruit and pomelos 53.0; Mangoes 1.2; Other fresh fruit 10.8. Source: FAO.

Livestock (FAO estimates, '000 head, year ending September 2001): Horses 5; Mules 4; Cattle 59; Pigs 28; Sheep 4; Goats 2; Chickens 1,350. Source: FAO.

Livestock Products (FAO estimates, '000 metric tons, 2001): Beef and veal 1.5; Chicken meat 10.3; Pig meat 1.1; Cows' milk 1.3; Hen eggs 1.3. Source: FAO.

Forestry (1995): *Roundwood removals* ('000 cubic metres, excl. bark): Sawlogs, veneer logs and logs for sleepers 62, Fuel wood 126, Total 188. *Sawnwood* ('000 cubic metres, incl. railway sleepers): Coniferous (softwood) 5, Broadleaved (hardwood) 30, Total 35. *1996–2001:* Annual production as in 1995 (FAO estimates). Source: FAO.

Fishing ('000 metric tons, live weight, 2000): Capture 61.0 (Patagonian grenadier 1.7; Porgies and seabreams 2.2, Sardinellas 5.5, European anchovy 6.7, Skipjack tuna 5.9, Yellowfin tuna 1.4, Jack and horse mackerels 7.6, Chub mackerel 4.9, Penaeus shrimps 3.7, Cuttle fish and bobtail squids 4.9; Argentine shortfin squid 4.1; Octopuses 1.2); Aquaculture 2.6 (Whiteleg shrimp 2.6); *Total catch* 63.6. Source: FAO, *Yearbook of Fishery Statistics.*

INDUSTRY

Production (2001): Raw sugar 103,862 long tons; Molasses 34,291 long tons; Cigarettes 88 million; Beer 2,385,000 gallons; Batteries 5,397; Flour 26,122,000 lb; Fertilizers 23,749 short tons; Garments 1,507,000 items; Citrus concentrate 6,503,000 gallons; Soft drinks 1,346,000 cases. Source: IMF, *Belize: Statistical Appendix* (October 2002).

FINANCE

Currency and Exchange Rates: 100 cents = 1 Belizean dollar (BZ $). *Sterling, US Dollar and Euro Equivalents* (31 December 2002): £1 sterling = BZ $3.224; US $1 = BZ $2.000; €1 = BZ $2.097; BZ $100 = £31.02 = US $50.00 = €47.68. *Exchange rate:* Fixed at US $1 = BZ $2.000 since May 1976.

Budget (BZ $ million, year ending 31 March 2002): *Revenue:* Taxation 331.0 (Taxes on income, profits, etc. 77.0, Domestic taxes on goods and services 117.0, Import duties 134.2); Other current revenue 36.1; Capital revenue 10.4; Total 377.5, excl. grants (22.0). *Expenditure:* Current expenditure 326.2 (Wages and salaries 162.7, Pensions 23.6, Expenditure on goods and services 62.6, Interest payments 51.6, Subsidies and current transfers 25.7); Capital expenditure 263.3; Statistical discrepancy –15.2; Total 574.3. Source: IMF, *Belize: Statistical Appendix* (October 2002).

International Reserves (US $ million at 31 December 2002): IMF special drawing rights 2.01; Reserve position in the IMF 5.76; Foreign exchange 106.74; Total 114.51. Source: IMF, *International Financial Statistics.*

Money Supply (BZ $ million at 31 December 2002): Currency outside banks 106.80; Demand deposits at commercial banks 214.13; Total money (incl. others) 328.47. Source: IMF, *International Financial Statistics*.

Cost of Living (Consumer Price Index; base: 1995 = 100): 105.3 in 1999; 105.9 in 2000; 107.2 in 2001. Source: IMF, *International Financial Statistics*.

Expenditure on the Gross Domestic Product (BZ $ million at current prices, 2001): Government final consumption expenditure 263.0; Private final consumption expenditure 1,155.7; Increase in stocks 52.7; Gross fixed capital formation 497.1; *Total domestic expenditure* 1,968.5; Exports of goods and service 887.3; *Less* Imports of goods and services 1,193.2; Statistical discrepancy –52.7; *GDP in purchasers' values* 1,609.9. Source: IMF, *International Financial Statistics*.

Gross Domestic Product by Economic Activity (BZ $ million at current prices, 2000): Agriculture, hunting, forestry and fishing 220.3; Mining and quarrying 9.0; Manufacturing 180.3; Electricity, gas and water 43.0; Construction 93.4; Wholesale and retail trade, restaurants and hotels 282.9; Transport, storage and communications 129.5; Finance, insurance, real estate and business services 170.7; Community, social and personal services 224.5; *Sub-total* 1,353.7; *Less* Imputed bank service charges 46.4; *GDP at factor cost* 1,307.3; *GDP at constant 1984 prices* 896.9. Source: UN Economic Commission for Latin America and the Caribbean, *Statistical Yearbook*.

Balance of Payments (US $ million, 2000): Exports of goods f.o.b. 212.3; Imports of goods c.i.f. –403.7; *Trade balance* –191.4; Exports of services 172.4; Imports of services –119.8; *Balance on goods and services* –138.8; Other income received 4.8; Other income paid –58.9; *Balance on goods, services and income* –192.9; Current transfers received 56.6; Current transfers paid –3.2; *Current balance* –139.5; Capital account (net) 0.5; Direct investment from abroad 17.7; Portfolio investment liabilities 26.9; Other investment assets –39.4; Other investment liabilities 83.3; Net errors and omissions 7.3; *Overall balance* –43.3. Source: IMF, *International Financial Statistics*.

EXTERNAL TRADE

Principal Commodities (US $ million, 2001): *Imports c.i.f.*: Food and live animals 59.6; Mineral fuels, lubricants, etc. 31.9; Chemicals and related products 35.2; Miscellaneous manufactured articles 120.6; Machinery and transport equipment 118.8; Total (incl. others) 389.0. *Exports f.o.b.*: Food and live animals 143.5 (Sugar 30.3,); Miscellaneous manufactures 15.3; Total (incl. others) 161.3. Note: Figures refer to retained imports and domestic exports. The data exclude re-exports. Source: IMF, *Belize: Statistical Appendix* (October 2002).

Principal Trading Partners (US $ million, 2001): *Imports c.i.f.*: Mexico 49.8; United Kingdom 11.9; USA 216.3; Total (incl. others) 450.5. *Exports f.o.b.* (excl. re-exports): United Kingdom 37.0; USA 86.6; Total (incl. others) 161.0. Source: IMF, *Belize: Statistical Appendix* (October 2002).

TRANSPORT

Road Traffic ('000 vehicles in use, 1998): Passenger cars 9,929; Buses and coaches 416; Lorries and vans 11,339; Motorcycles and mopeds 270. (Source: IRF, *World Road Statistics*). *2000* ('000 vehicles in use): Passenger cars 21.5; Commercial vehicles 3.9 (Source: UN, *Statistical Yearbook*).

Shipping (sea-borne freight traffic, '000 metric tons, 1996): Goods loaded 255.4; Goods unloaded 277.1. *Merchant Fleet* (vessels registered at 31 December 2001): Number of vessels 1,516; Total displacement 1,828,190 grt. (Source: Lloyd's Register of Shipping, *World Fleet Statistics*).

Civil Aviation (2001): Passenger arrivals 174,201. Source: IMF, *Belize: Statistical Appendix* (October 2002).

TOURISM

Tourist Arrivals: 288,098 (cruise-ship passengers 34,130; by air 115,089) in 1999; 326,642 (cruise-ship passengers 58,131; by air 131,634) in 2000; 195,955 (cruise-ship passengers 48,116; by air 133,775) in 2001.

Tourist Receipts (US $ million): 111.5 in 1999; 121.1 in 2000; 120.5 in 2001.

Hotels: 390 in 1999; 391 in 2000; 418 in 2001. Source: Belize Tourist Board.

COMMUNICATIONS MEDIA

Radio Receivers (1997): 133,000 in use*.

Television Receivers (2000): 44,000 in use†.

Telephones (2001): 35,200 main lines in use†.

Facsimile Machines (1996): 500 in use‡.

Mobile Cellular Telephones (2001): 28,200 subscribers†.

Personal Computers (2001): 33,000 in use†.

Internet Users (2001): 18,000†.

Book Production (1996): 107 titles*.

Non-daily Newspapers (1996): 6 (circulation 80,000)*.
* Source: UNESCO, *Statistical Yearbook*.
† Source: International Telecommunication Union.
‡ Source: UN, *Statistical Yearbook*.

EDUCATION

Pre-primary* (1994/95): 90 schools, 190 teachers, 3,311 students.
Primary (1998/99): 284 schools, 2,064 teachers, 54,616 students.
Secondary (1998/99): 34 schools, 754 teachers, 11,724 students.
Higher (1997/98): 12 institutions, 228 teachers, 2,853 students.
* Source: UNESCO, *Statistical Yearbook*.
Source: Ministry of Education Planning Unit.

Adult Literacy Rate (UNESCO estimates): 93.2% (males 93.3%; females 93.2%) in 2000. (Source: UN Development Programme, *Human Development Report*).

Directory

The Constitution

The Constitution came into effect at the independence of Belize on 21 September 1981. Its main provisions are summarized below:

FUNDAMENTAL RIGHTS AND FREEDOMS

Regardless of race, place of origin, political opinions, colour, creed or sex, but subject to respect for the rights and freedoms of others and for the public interest, every person in Belize is entitled to the rights of life, liberty, security of the person, and the protection of the law. Freedom of movement, of conscience, of expression, of assembly and association and the right to work are guaranteed and the inviolability of family life, personal privacy, home and other property and of human dignity is upheld. Protection is afforded from discrimination on the grounds of race, sex, etc., and from slavery, forced labour and inhuman treatment.

CITIZENSHIP

All persons born in Belize before independence who, immediately prior to independence, were citizens of the United Kingdom and Colonies automatically become citizens of Belize. All persons born outside the country having a husband, parent or grandparent in possession of Belizean citizenship automatically acquire citizenship, as do those born in the country after independence. Provision is made which permits persons who do not automatically become citizens of Belize to be registered as such. (Belizean citizenship was also offered, under the Belize Loans Act 1986, in exchange for interest-free loans of US $25,000 with a 10-year maturity. The scheme was officially ended in June 1994, following sustained criticism of alleged corruption on the part of officials. However, a revised economic citizenship programme, offering citizenship in return for a minimum investment of US $75,000, received government approval in early 1995.)

THE GOVERNOR-GENERAL

The British monarch, as Head of State, is represented in Belize by a Governor-General, a Belizean national.

Belize Advisory Council

The Council consists of not less than six people 'of integrity and high national standing', appointed by the Governor-General for up to 10 years upon the advice of the Prime Minister. The Leader of the Opposition must concur with the appointment of two members and be consulted about the remainder. The Council exists to advise the

Governor-General, particularly in the exercise of the prerogative of mercy, and to convene as a tribunal to consider the removal from office of certain senior public servants and judges.

THE EXECUTIVE

Executive authority is vested in the British monarch and exercised by the Governor-General. The Governor-General appoints as Prime Minister that member of the House of Representatives who, in the Governor-General's view, is best able to command the support of the majority of the members of the House, and appoints a Deputy Prime Minister and other Ministers on the advice of the Prime Minister. The Governor-General may remove the Prime Minister from office if a resolution of 'no confidence' is passed by the House and the Prime Minister does not, within seven days, either resign or advise the Governor-General to dissolve the National Assembly. The Cabinet consists of the Prime Minister and other Ministers.

The Leader of the Opposition is appointed by the Governor-General as that member of the House who, in the Governor-General's view, is best able to command the support of a majority of the members of the House who do not support the Government.

THE LEGISLATURE

The Legislature consists of a National Assembly comprising two chambers: the Senate, with eight nominated members; and the House of Representatives, with 29 elected members. The Assembly's normal term is five years. Senators are appointed by the Governor-General: five on the advice of the Prime Minister; two on the advice of the Leader of the Opposition or on the advice of persons selected by the Governor-General; and one after consultation with the Belize Advisory Council. If any person who is not a Senator is elected to be President of the Senate, he or she shall be an ex-officio Senator in addition to the eight nominees.

Each constituency returns one Representative to the House, who is directly elected in accordance with the Constitution.

If a person who is not a member of the House is elected to be Speaker of the House, he or she shall be an ex-officio member in addition to the 29 members directly elected. Every citizen older than 18 years is eligible to vote. The National Assembly may alter any of the provisions of the Constitution.

The Government

Head of State: HM Queen Elizabeth II (succeeded to the throne 6 February 1952).

Governor-General: Sir Colville Young (appointed 17 November 1993).

THE CABINET
(April 2003)

Prime Minister and Minister of Education and of Public Service: Said Musa.

Minister in the Office of Prime Minister: Francis Fonseca.

Deputy Prime Minister and Minister of Natural Resources and the Environment and of Commerce, Trade and Industry: John Briceño.

Minister of Defence and National Emergency Management: Sylvia Flores.

Attorney-General and Minister of Foreign Affairs and Co-operation: Godfrey Smith.

Minister of Finance and Home Affairs: Ralph Fonseca.

Minister of Health: José Coye.

Minister of Human Development and of Labour and Local Government: Marcial Mes.

Minister of Agriculture and Fisheries: Servulo Baeza.

Minister of Housing: Cordel Hyde.

Minister of Economic Development, Tourism and Culture: Mark Espat.

Minister of Investment and Foreign Trade: Eamon Courtenay.

Minister of Works and of Transport and Communications: Vildo Marin.

Ambasssador with ministerial rank and Chief Foreign Affairs Representative of the Government of Belize: Assad Shoman.

MINISTRIES

Office of the Prime Minister: New Administration Bldg, Belmopan; tel. 822-2346; fax 822-0071; e-mail prime-minister@belize.gov.bz.

Ministry of Agriculture and Fisheries: 2nd Floor, West Block Bldg, Belmopan; tel. 822-2241; fax 822-2409; e-mail mafpaeu@btl.net.

Ministry of the Attorney-General: Belmopan; tel. 822-2504; fax 822-3390; e-mail atgenmin@btl.net.

Ministry of Investment and Foreign Trade: New Administration Bldg, Belmopan; tel. 822-2345; fax 822-2195.

Ministry of Commerce, Trade and Industry: East Block Bldg, Belmopan; tel. 822-2153.

Ministry of Defence and National Emergency Management: Curl Osmond Thompson Bldg, Belmopan; tel. 822-2225; fax 822-2615; e-mail mnsi@btl.net.

Ministry of Works: New Administration Bldg, Belmopan; tel. 822-2526.

Ministry of Education: West Block Bldg, Belmopan; tel. 822-3380; fax 822-3389; e-mail educate@btl.net.

Ministry of Finance: New Administration Bldg, Belmopan; tel. 822-2169; fax 822-3317; e-mail finsecmof@btl.net.

Ministry of Foreign Affairs and Co-operation: POB 174, New Administration Bldg, Belmopan; tel. 822-2167; fax 822-2854; e-mail belizemfa@btl.net.

Ministry of Health: New Administration Bldg, Belmopan; tel. 822-2325; fax 822-2942.

Ministry of Home Affairs: East Block Bldg, Belmopan; tel. 822-2016; fax 822-3337.

Ministry of Housing: East Block Bldg, Belmopan; tel. 822-2016; fax 822-3337.

Ministry of Human Development: West Block, Independence Hill, Belmopan; tel. 822-2161; fax 822-3175.

Ministry of Information and Broadcasting: East Block Bldg, Belmopan; tel. 822-0094.

Ministry of Natural Resources and the Environment: Market Sq., Belmopan; tel. 822-2249; fax 822-2333; e-mail lincenbze@btl.net.

Ministry of Public Service: Belmopan.

Ministry of Rural Development: East Block, Belmopan; tel. 822-2444; fax 822-0317; e-mail ruraldev@btl.net.

Ministry of Labour and Local Government: 3rd Floor, Diamond Bldg, Constitution Dr., Belmopan; tel. 822-3990; fax 822-3365; e-mail msillg@belize.gov.bz.

Ministry of Economic Development, Tourism and Culture: Constitution Dr., Belmopan; tel. 822-3393; fax 822-3815; e-mail tourismmdpt@btl.net.

Ministry of Transport and Communications: Power Lane, Belmopan; tel. 822-2136; fax 822-3282; e-mail peumow@btl.net.

Legislature

NATIONAL ASSEMBLY

The Senate

President: Elizabeth Zabaneh.

There are eight nominated members.

House of Representatives

Speaker: Sylvia Flores.

Clerk: Jesus Ken.

General Election, 5 March 2003

	Votes cast	% of total	Seats
People's United Party (PUP) .	52,934	53.2	22
United Democratic Party (UDP)	45,415	45.6	7
Others	1,211	1.2	—
Total	99,560	100.00	29

Political Organizations

National Alliance for Belizean Rights (NABR): Belize City; f. 1992 by UDP members opposed to compromise over territorial dispute with Guatemala; Chair. (vacant); Co-ordinator Philip S. W. Goldson.

People's United Party (PUP): 3 Queen St, Belize City; tel. 223-2428; fax 223-3476; internet www.pupbelize.org; f. 1950; based on organized labour; merged with Christian Democratic Party in 1988; Leader SAID MUSA; Chair. JORGE ESPAT; Deputy Leaders MAXWELL SAMUELS, JOHN BRICEÑO.

United Democratic Party (UDP): South End Bel-China Bridge, POB 1898, Belize City; tel. 227-2576; fax 227-6441; e-mail info@udp .org.bz; internet www.udp.org.bz; f. 1974 by merger of People's Development Movement, Liberal Party and National Independence Party; conservative; Leader DEAN BARROW; Chair. ELODIO ARAGON.

Diplomatic Representation

EMBASSIES AND HIGH COMMISSION IN BELIZE

China (Taiwan): 20 North Park St, POB 1020, Belize City; tel. 227-8744; fax 223-3082; e-mail embroc@btl.net; Ambassador TASI ERH-HUANG.

Costa Rica: 11AHandy Side St, POB 1820, Belize City; tel. 223-6525; fax 223-6523; e-mail cremb@btl.net; Ambassador FERNANDO BORBÓN.

Cuba: 6048 Manatee Dr., Buttonwood Bay, POB 1775, Belize City; tel. 223-5345; fax 223-1105; e-mail embacub@btl.net; Ambassador REGLA C. DÍAZ HERNÁNDEZ.

El Salvador: 49 Nanche St, POB 215, Belmopan; tel. 822-3404; fax 822-3569; Ambassador MANUEL ANTONIO VÁSQUEZ MENA.

Guatemala: 8 'A' St, POB 1771, Belize City; tel. 223-3314; fax 223-5140; e-mail guatemb.bz@btl.net; Ambassador RAFAEL AGUILAR.

Honduras: 91 North Front St, POB 285, Belize City; tel. 224-5889; fax 223-0562; Chargé d'affaires a.i. JOSE RIGOBERTO ARRIAGA.

Mexico: 20 North Park St, POB 754, Belize City; tel. 223-0193; fax 227-8742; e-mail embamexbze@btl.net; Ambassador JOSÉ ARTURO TREJO NAVA.

United Kingdom: Embassy Sq., POB 91, Belmopan; tel. 822-2146; fax 822-2761; e-mail brithicom@btl.net; internet www.bhcbelize.org; High Commissioner PHILIP J. PRIESTLEY.

USA: 29 Gabourel Lane, POB 286, Belize City; tel. 227-7161; fax 223-0802; e-mail embbelize@state.gov; internet www.usemb-belize .gov; Ambassador RUSSELL F. FREEMAN.

Venezuela: 18–20 Unity Blvd, POB 49, Belmopan; tel. 822-2384; fax 822-2022; e-mail embaven@btl.net; Ambassador AMINTA GUACARAN TORREABLA.

Judicial System

Summary Jurisdiction Courts (criminal jurisdiction) and District Courts (civil jurisdiction), presided over by magistrates, are established in each of the six judicial districts. Summary Jurisdiction Courts have a wide jurisdiction in summary offences and a limited jurisdiction in indictable matters. Appeals lie to the Supreme Court, which has jurisdiction corresponding to the English High Court of Justice and where a jury system is in operation. From the Supreme Court further appeals lie to a Court of Appeal, established in 1967, which holds an average of four sessions per year. Final appeals are made to the Judicial Committee of the Privy Council in the United Kingdom.

Supreme Court: Supreme Court Bldg, Belize City; tel. 227-7256; fax 227-0181; internet www.belizelaw.org/supreme_court.html; Registrar RAYMOND A. USHER; Chief Justice Dr ABDULAI OSMAN CONTEH.

Magistrate's Court: Paslow Bldg, Belize City; tel. 227-7164; Chief Magistrate HERBERT LORD.

Religion

CHRISTIANITY

Most of the population are Christian, the largest denomination being the Roman Catholic Church (62% of the population, according to the census of 1980). The other main groups were the Anglican (12% in 1980), Methodist (6%), Mennonite (4%), Seventh-day Adventist (3%) and Pentecostal (2%) churches.

Belize Council of Churches: 149 Allenby St, POB 508, Belize City; tel. 227-7077; f. 1957 as Church World Service Committee, present name adopted 1984; eight mem. Churches, four assoc. bodies; Pres. Maj. ERROL ROBATEAU (Salvation Army); Gen. Sec. SADIE VERNON.

The Roman Catholic Church

Belize comprises the single diocese of Belize City-Belmopan, suffragan to the archdiocese of Kingston in Jamaica. In December 2000 it was estimated that there were 132,940 adherents in the diocese. The Bishop participates in the Antilles Episcopal Conference (whose secretariat is based in Port of Spain, Trinidad and Tobago).

Bishop of Belize City-Belmopan: OSMOND PETER MARTIN, Bishop's House, 144 North Front St, POB 616, Belize City; tel. 227-2122; fax 223-1922.

The Anglican Communion

Anglicans in Belize belong to the Church in the Province of the West Indies, comprising eight dioceses. The Archbishop of the Province is the Bishop of North Eastern Caribbean and Aruba, resident in St John's, Antigua.

Bishop of Belize: Rt Rev. SYLVESTRE DONATO ROMERO-PALMA, Bishopthorpe, 25 Southern Foreshore, POB 535, Belize City; tel. 227-3029; fax 227-6898; e-mail bzediocese@btl.net.

Protestant Churches

Methodist Church (Belize/Honduras District Conference): 88 Regent St, POB 212, Belize City; tel. 227-7173; fax 227-5870; f. 1824; c. 2,620 mems; District Pres. Rev. Dr LESLEY G. ANDERSON.

Mennonite Congregations in Belize: POB 427, Belize City; tel. (8) 30137; fax (8) 30101; f. 1958; four main Mennonite settlements: at Spanish Lookout, Shipyard, Little Belize and Blue Creek; Bishop J. B. LOEWEN, Bishop J. K. BARKMAN, Bishop P. THIESSEN, Bishop H. R. PENNER, Bishop CORNELIUS ENNS.

Other denominations active in the country include the Seventh-day Adventists, Pentecostals, Presbyterians, Baptists, Moravians, Jehovah's Witnesses, the Church of God, the Assemblies of Brethren and the Salvation Army.

OTHER RELIGIONS

There are also small communities of Hindus (106, according to the census of 1980), Muslims (110 in 1980), Jews (92 in 1980) and Bahá'ís.

The Press

Amandala: Amandala Press, 3304 Partridge St, POB 15, Belize City; tel. (2) 24476; fax (2) 24702; e-mail amandala@btl.net; internet www.amandala.bz; f. 1969; weekly; independent; Editor EVAN X. HYDE; circ. 45,000.

The Belize Times: 3 Queen St, POB 506, Belize City; tel. (2) 45757; fax 223-1940; e-mail editor@belizetimes.com; internet www .belizetimes.com; f. 1956; weekly; party political paper of PUP; Editor ANDREW STEINHAUER; circ. 6,000.

Belize Today: Belize Information Service, East Block, POB 60, Belmopan; tel. 822-2159; fax 822-3242; monthly; official; Editor MIGUEL H. HERNÁNDEZ Jr; circ. 17,000.

Government Gazette: Government Printery, 1 Power Lane, Belmopan; tel. 822-2127; fax 822-3367; e-mail info@gazette.gov.bz; internet www.gazette.gov.br; official; weekly; Editor L. J. NICHOLAS.

The People's Pulse: 7 Tanoomah St, Belize City; tel. 227-7035; fax 227-6012.

The Reporter: 147 cnr Allenby and West Sts, POB 707, Belize City; tel. 227-2503; f. 1968; weekly; Editor HARRY LAWRENCE; circ. 6,500.

The San Pedro Sun: POB 35, San Pedro Town, Ambergris Caye; fax 226-2905; e-mail sanpedrosun@btl.net; internet www .ambergriscaye.com; weekly; Editor DAN JAMISON, EILEEN JAMISON.

NEWS AGENCY

Agencia EFE (Spain): c/o POB 506, Belize City; tel. 224-5757; Correspondent AMALIA MAI.

Publisher

Government Printery: 1 Power Lane, Belmopan; tel. 822-2293; f. 1871; responsible for printing, binding and engraving requirements of all govt depts and ministries; publications include annual govt estimates, govt magazines and the official Government Gazette.

www.europaworldonline.com

Broadcasting and Communications

TELECOMMUNICATIONS

In September 2001 the Government announced that the telecommunications sector was to be liberalized. Following the expiry of the 15-year exclusive licence held by Belize Telecommunications Ltd in December 2002, the Goverment issued a general licence to the International Telecommunications Co. (INTELCO). Intelco's services were expected to become fully operational in April 2003.

Belize Telecommunications Ltd: Esquivel Telecom Centre, St Thomas St, POB 603, Belize City; tel. 223-2868; fax 223-2096; e-mail educ@btl.net; internet www.btl.net; f. 1987; owned by Carlisle Holdings; Chair. MICHAEL A. ASHCROFT; CEO EDBERTO TESECUM.

International Telecommunications Co (Intelco): 121/2 Miles Northern Highway, Boom Cut-Off Road, Belize City; tel. 225-4128; fax 225-4130; CEO JUAN MCKENZIE.

Office of Telecommunications: Administration Complex, Mahogany St Extension, Belize City; tel. 222-4938; fax 222-4939; Dir CLIFFORD SLUSHER.

RADIO

Broadcasting Corporation of Belize (BCB): Albert Cattouse Bldg, Regent St, POB 89, Belize City; tel. 227-2468; fax 227-5040; e-mail rbgold@btl.net; f. 1937; privatized in 1998; broadcasts in English (75%) and Spanish; also transmits programmes in Garifuna and Maya; Gen. Man. RUTH STAINE-DAWSON.

Love FM: 33 Freetown Rd, Belize City; tel. 223-2098; fax 223-0529; e-mail lovefm@btl.net; internet www.lovefm.com; f. 1992; purchased Friends FM in 1998; Man. Dir RENE VILLANUEVA.

Radio Krem Ltd: 3304 Partridge St, POB 15, Belize City; tel. 227-5929; fax 227-4079; commercial; purchased Radio Belize in 1998; Man. EVA S. HYDE.

Other private radio stations broadcasting in Belize include: Estereo Amor, My Refuge Christian Radio, Radio 2000 and Voice of America.

TELEVISION

In 1986 the Belize Broadcasting Authority issued licences to eight television operators for 14 channels, which mainly retransmit US satellite programmes, thus placing television in Belize on a fully legal basis for the first time.

Baymen Broadcasting Network (CTV-Channel 9): 27 Baymen Ave, Belize City; tel. (2) 44400; fax 223-1242; commercial; Man. MARIE HOARE.

Channel 5 Belize: POB 679, Belize City; tel. 227-3146; fax 227-4936; e-mail gbtv@btl.com; internet www.channel5belize.com; f. 1991.

Tropical Vision (Channels 7 and 11): 73 Albert St, Belize City; tel. 227-7246; fax 227-5040; e-mail tvseven@btl.net; commercial; Man. NESTOR VASQUEZ.

Finance

(cap. = capital; res = reserves; dep. = deposits; brs = branches; amounts in BZ $, unless otherwise indicated)

BANKING

Central Bank

Central Bank of Belize: Gabourel Lane, POB 852, Belize City; tel. 223-6194; fax 223-6226; e-mail governor@cenbank.gov.bz; f. 1982; cap. 10m., res 12.2m., dep. 148.0m. (2001); Head RALPH FONSECA; Gov. and Chair. JORGE MELITON AUIL.

Development Bank

Development Finance Corporation: Bliss Parade, Belmopan; tel. 822-3360; fax 822-3096; e-mail dfc@btl.net; internet www.dfcbelize.org; f. 1972; issued cap. 10m. Chair. GLENN GODFREY; Gen. Man. ROBERTO BAUTISTA; 5 brs.

Other Banks

Alliance Bank of Belize Ltd: 106 Princess Margaret Dr., Belize City; tel. 223-6783; fax 223-6785; e-mail alliance@btl.net; f. 2001; total assets 113.7m.; deposits 6,876m.

Atlantic Bank Ltd: Cnr Freetown Rd and Cleghorn St, POB 481, Belize City; tel. 223-4123; fax 223-3907; e-mail atlantic@btl.net; internet www.atlabank.com; f. 1971; total assets 191.9m., dep. 161.0m. (2001); Chair. Dr GUILLERMO BUESO; 8 brs.

Bank of Nova Scotia (Scotiabank) (Canada): Albert St, POB 708, Belize City; tel. 227-7027; fax 227-7416; e-mail bns.belize@scotiabank.com; Gen. Man. C. E. MARCEL; 5 brs.

Barclays Bank PLC (United Kingdom): 21 Albert St, POB 363, Belize City; tel. 227-7211; fax 227-8572; Man. TILVAN KING; 3 brs.

Belize Bank Ltd: 60 Market Sq., POB 364, Belize City; tel. 227-7132; fax 227-2712; e-mail bzbnk@btl.net; internet www.belizebank.com; cap. $4.3m., res $4.3m., dep. $280.1m. (April 1997); Chair. Sir EDNEY CAIN; Senior Vice-Pres. and Gen. Man. LOUIS ANTHONY SWASEY; 9 brs.

Provident Bank and Trust of Belize: 35 Barrack Rd, POB 1867, Belize City; tel. 223-5698; fax 223-0368; e-mail provident@btl.net; internet www.providentbelize.com; f. 1998; cap. $2.6m., dep. $88.8m. (2001); Chair. RICARDO ESCALANTE; Man. LEOPOLDO WAIGHT.

There is also a government savings bank. In late 2001 the Government amended the exchange control regulations to allow foreign currency exchange bureaux.

INSURANCE

General insurance is provided by local companies, and British, US and Jamaican companies are also represented.

Trade and Industry

STATUTORY BODIES

Banana Control Board: c/o Dept of Agriculture, West Block, Belmopan; management of banana industry; in 1989 it was decided to make it responsible to growers, not an independent executive; Head LALO GARCIA.

Belize Beef Corporation: c/o Dept of Agriculture, West Block, Belmopan; f. 1978; semi-governmental organization to aid development of cattle-rearing industry; Dir DEEDIE RUNKEL.

Belize Marketing Board: 117 North Front St, POB 633, Belize City; tel. 227-7402; fax 227-7656; f. 1948 to encourage the growing of staple food crops; purchases crops at guaranteed prices, supervises processing, storing and marketing intelligence; Chair. SILAS C. CAYETANO.

Belize Sugar Board: 7, 2nd St South, Corozal Town; tel. 422-2005; fax 422-2672; f. 1960 to control the sugar industry and cane production; includes representatives of the Government, sugar manufacturers, cane farmers and the public sector; Chair. ORLANDO PUGA; Exec. Sec. MARIA PUERTO.

Citrus Control Board: c/o Dept of Agriculture, West Block, Belmopan; tel. 822-2199; f. 1966; determines basic quota for each producer, fixes annual price of citrus; Chair. C. SOSA.

DEVELOPMENT ORGANIZATIONS

Belize Reconstruction and Development Corporation: 36 Trinity Blvd, POB 1, Belmopan; tel. 822-2271; fax 822-3992; e-mail recondev@btl.net; Gen. Man. ALOYSIUS PALACIO.

Belize Trade and Investment Development Service: 14 Orchid Garden St, Belmopan; tel. 822-3737; fax 822-0595; e-mail beltraide@belize.gov.bz; internet www.belizeinvest.org.bz; f. 1986; as a joint government and private-sector institution to encourage export and investment; Gen. Man. PETER USHER.

Department of Economic Development: Ministry of Budget Planning, Economic Development, Investment and Trade, New Administrative Bldg, Belmopan; tel. 822-2526; fax 822-3111; administration of public and private-sector investment and planning; statistics agency; Head HUMBERTO PAREDES.

CHAMBER OF COMMERCE

Belize Chamber of Commerce and Industry: 63 Regent St, POB 291, Belize City; tel. 227-3148; fax 227-4984; e-mail bcci@btl.net; internet www.belize.org; f. 1920; Pres. YOLANDA CROMBIE; Gen. Man. KEVIN HERRERA; 300 mems.

EMPLOYERS' ASSOCIATIONS

Banana Growers' Association: Big Creek, Independence Village, Stann Creek District; tel. 523-2001; fax 523-2112; e-mail banana@btl.net.

Belize Cane Farmers' Association: 34 San Antonio Rd, Orange Walk; tel. 322-2005; fax 322-3171; f. 1959 to assist cane farmers and negotiate with the Sugar Board and manufacturers on their behalf; Chair. PABLO TUN; 16 district brs.

Belize Livestock Producers' Association: 47.5 miles Western Highway, POB 183, Belmopan; tel. 822-3202; fax 822-3886; e-mail blpa@btl.net; Chair. PETE LIZARRAGA.

Citrus Growers' Association: 9 miles Stann Creek Valley Rd, POB 7, Stann Creek District; tel. 522-3585; fax 522-2686; e-mail cga@btl.net; f. 1966; CEO BRIDGET COLLERTON.

UTILITIES

Electricity

Office of Electricity Supply: Mahogany St, POB 1846, Belize City; tel. 222-4995; fax 222-4994; f. 1992; Dir-Gen. HERMAN CHARLES-WORTH.

Belize Electricity Co Ltd (BECOL): 115 Barrack Rd, POB 327, Belize City; tel. 227-0954; fax 223-0891; e-mail bel@btl.net; 95% owned by Fortis Inc (Canada); operates Mollejón hydroelectric plant, which supplies electricity to Belize Electricity Ltd (BEL—see below); Chair. NESTOR VASQUEZ; CEO LUIS LUE.

Belize Electricity Ltd (BEL): 2.5 miles Northern Highway, POB 327, Belize City; tel. 227-0954; fax 223-0891; e-mail pr@bel.com.bz; internet www.bel.com.bz; fmrly Belize Electricity Board, changed name upon privatization in 1992; Govt held 51% of shares until 1999; 67% owned by Fortis Inc (Canada); Pres. and CEO LYNN R. YOUNG; Chair. ROBERT USHER.

Water

Belize Water Services Ltd: POB 150, Central American Blvd, Belize City; tel. 222-4757; fax 222-4759; f. 1971 as Water and Sewerage Authority (WASA); changed name upon privatization in March 2001; 82.7% owned by Cascal, BV (United Kingdom/Netherlands); CEO RICHARD POPE.

TRADE UNIONS

National Trades Union Congress of Belize (NTUCB): POB 2359, Belize City; tel. 227-1596; fax 227-2864; e-mail ntucb@wgs1 .btl.net; Pres. DORENE QUIROS; Gen. Sec. ANTONIO GONZÁLEZ.

Principal Unions

Belize Communications Workers' Union: POB 1291, Belize City; tel. 223-4213; fax 224-3809; e-mail ahoare@btl.net; Pres. ISAAC WILLIAMS; Gen. Sec. DORENE QUIROS.

Belize Energy Workers' Union: c/o Belize Electricity Board, POB 1066, Belize City; tel. 227-0954; Pres. COLVILLE YOUNG; Gen. Sec. FLOYD HERRERA.

Belize National Teachers' Union: Racecourse St, POB 382, Belize City; tel. 227-2857; Pres. JOHN PINELO; Sec. LOIS BARBER; 1,000 mems.

Belize Workers' Union: Tate St, Orange Walk Town; tel. 822-2327; Pres. EDWARDO MELÉNDEZ.

Christian Workers' Union: 107BCemetery Rd, POB 533, Belize City; tel. 227-2150; fax 227–8470; e-mail cwu@btl.net; f. 1962; general; Pres. ANTONIO GONZÁLEZ; Gen. Sec. JAMES MCFOY; 1,000 mems.

Democratic Independent Union: Belize City; Pres. CYRIL DAVIS; 1,250 mems.

Public Service Union of Belize: 2 Mayflower St, POB 458, Belmopan; tel. 822-0282; fax 822-0283; e-mail belizepsu@btl.net; f. 1922; public workers; Pres. MARGARET VENTURA; Sec.-Gen. HUBERT ENRÍQUEZ; 1,400 mems.

United Banners Banana Workers' Union: Dangriga; f. 1995; Pres. MARCIANA FUNEZ.

United General Workers' Union: 1259 Lakeland City, Dangriga; tel. 522-2105; f. 1979 by amalgamation of the Belize General Development Workers' Union and the Southern Christian Union; three branch unions affiliated to the central body; affiliated to ICFTU; Pres. FRANCIS SABAL; Gen. Sec. CONRAD SAMBULA.

Transport

Department of Transport: Forest Dr., Belmopan; tel. 822-2417; fax 822-3379; Commissioner PHILLIP BRACKETT.

RAILWAYS

There are no railways in Belize.

ROADS

There are 2,710 km of roads, of which 500 km were paved. There are 2,210 km of unpaved roads, including 1,600 km of gravel roads, 300 km of improved earth roads and 310 km of unimproved earth roads. In 2000 the World Bank approved a loan of US $13m. for road construction. In 2002 the European Union approved a grant of BZ $3.6m. towards the construction of a bridge over the New Sibun River. The Government was to provide BZ $1m. in funding and the project was expected to be completed by late 2004.

SHIPPING

There is a deep-water port at Belize City and a second port at Commerce Bight, near Dangriga (formerly Stann Creek), to the south of Belize City. There is a port for the export of bananas at Big Creek and additional ports at Corozol and Punta Gorda. Nine major shipping lines operate vessels calling at Belize City, including the Carol Line (consisting of Harrison, Hapag-Lloyd, Nedlloyd and CGM).

Belize Port Authority: Caesar Ridge Rd, POB 633, Belize City; tel. 227-2439; fax 227-3571; e-mail portbz@btl.net; f. 1980; Chair. KAY MENZIES; Ports Commr ALFRED B. COYE.

Belize Lines Ltd: 37 Regent St, Belize City.

CIVIL AVIATION

Phillip S. W. Goldson International Airport, 14 km (9 miles) from Belize City, can accommodate medium-sized jet-engined aircraft. The runway was extended in 2000. There are 37 airstrips for light aircraft on internal flights near the major towns and offshore islands.

Department of Civil Aviation: POB 367, Belize City; e-mail aviation@btl.net; Dir EFRAÍN GÓMEZ.

Maya Island Air: San Pedros Town, Ambergris Caye; tel. 223-1140; fax 223-5371; e-mail miaspr@btl.net; internet www.ambergriscaye .com/islandair; f. 1997 as merger between Maya Airways Ltd and Island Air; operated by Belize Air Group; internal services, centred on Belize City, and charter flights to neighbouring countries; Exec. Dir TREVOR ROE; Gen. Man. ROSITA MENZIES.

Tropical Air Services (Tropic Air): San Pedro, POB 20, Ambergris Caye; tel. 226-2012; fax 226-2338; e-mail djonsson@btl.net; internet www.tropicair.com; f. 1979; operates internal services and services to Mexico and Guatemala; Chair. CELI MCCORKLE; Man. Dir JOHN GREIF.

Tourism

The main tourist attractions are the beaches and the barrier reef, diving, fishing and the Mayan archaeological sites. There are nine major wildlife reserves (including the world's only reserves for the jaguar and for the red-footed booby), and government policy is to develop 'eco-tourism', based on the attractions of an unspoilt environment and Belize's natural history. The country's wildlife also includes howler monkeys and 500 species of birds, and its barrier reef is the second largest in the world. However, in May 2000 scientists reported that the high sea temperatures recorded in 1998, caused by the El Niño phenomenon and global warming, had resulted in extensive damage to the coral population. There were some 418 hotels in Belize in 2001. In the same year there were an estimated 195,955 tourist arrivals and tourist receipts totalled an estimated US $120.5m. In February 1996 the Mundo Maya Agreement was ratified, according to which Belize, El Salvador, Guatemala, Honduras and Mexico would co-operate in the management of Mayan archaeological remains. In February 2000 the Belize Tourist Board announced that all tour operators and guides needed to obtain a licence. In June the Inter-American Development Bank approved a loan of US $11m. towards the Government's tourism development plan.

Belize Tourism Board: Level 2, New Central Bank Bldg, POB 325, Gabourel Lane, Belize City; tel. 223-1913; fax 223-1943; e-mail info@ travelbelize.org; internet www.travelbelize.org; f. 1964; fmrly Belize Tourist Bureau; eight mems; Chair. PATTY ARCEO; Dir TRACY TAEGAR.

Belize Tourism Industry Association (BTIA): 10 North Park St, POB 62, Belize City; tel. 227-5717; fax 227-8710; e-mail btia@btl.net; internet www.btia.org; Exec. Dir ANDREW GODOY.

BENIN

Introductory Survey

Location, Climate, Language, Religion, Flag, Capital

The Republic of Benin is a narrow stretch of territory in West Africa. The country has an Atlantic coastline of about 100 km (60 miles), flanked by Nigeria to the east and Togo to the west; its northern borders are with Burkina Faso and Niger. Benin's climate is tropical, and is divided into three zones: the north has a rainy season between July and September, with a hot, dry season in October–April; the central region has periods of abundant rain in May–June and in October; and there is year-round precipitation in the south, the heaviest rains being in May–October. Average annual rainfall in Cotonou is 1,300 mm. French is the official language, but each of the indigenous ethnic groups has its own language. Bariba and Fulani are the major languages in the north, while Fon and Yoruba are widely spoken in the south. It is estimated that 35% of the people follow traditional beliefs and customs; about 35% are Christians, mainly Roman Catholics, and the majority of the remainder are Muslims. The national flag (proportions 2 by 3) has a vertical green stripe at the hoist, with equal horizontal stripes of yellow over red in the fly. The administrative capital is Porto-Novo, but most government offices and other state bodies are presently in the economic capital, Cotonou.

Recent History

Benin, called Dahomey until 1975, was formerly part of French West Africa. It became a self-governing republic within the French Community in December 1958, and an independent state on 1 August 1960. The early years of independence were characterized by chronic political instability and by periodic regional unrest, fuelled by long-standing rivalries between north and south.

Elections in December 1960 were won by the Parti dahoméen de l'unité, whose leader, Hubert Maga (a northerner), became the country's first President. In October 1963, following riots by workers and students, Maga was deposed in a coup led by Col (later Gen.) Christophe Soglo, Chief of Staff of the Army. Soglo served as interim Head of State until January 1964, when Sourou-Migan Apithy, a southerner who had been Vice-President under Maga, was elected President. Another southerner, Justin Ahomadegbé, became Prime Minister. In November 1965, following a series of political crises, Gen. Soglo forced Apithy and Ahomadegbé to resign. A provisional Government was formed, but the army intervened again in December, and Soglo assumed power at the head of a military regime. In December 1967 industrial unrest, following a ban on trade-union activity, precipitated another coup, led by Maj. (later Lt-Col) Maurice Kouandété. Lt-Col Alphonse Alley, hitherto Chief of Staff, became interim Head of State, and Kouandété Prime Minister.

A return to civilian rule was attempted in 1968. A new Constitution was approved by referendum in March, and a presidential election followed in May. All former Heads of State and other leading politicians, banned from contesting the presidency, urged their supporters to boycott the election. Only about 26% of the electorate voted, with the abstention rate reaching 99% in the north. The election was declared void, and in June the military regime nominated Dr Emile-Derlin Zinsou, a former Minister of Foreign Affairs, as President; he was confirmed in office by referendum in July. In December 1969 Zinsou was deposed by Lt-Col Kouandété, then Commander-in-Chief of the Army, and a three-member military Directoire assumed power.

In March 1970 a presidential election was abandoned when counting revealed roughly equal support for the three main candidates—Ahomadegbé, Apithy and Maga—to whom the Directoire ceded power in May: it was intended that each member of this Presidential Council would act as Head of State, in rotation, for a two-year period. Maga was the first to hold this office (a concession to the north) and was succeeded in May 1972 by Ahomadegbé. In October, however, the civilian leadership was deposed by Maj. (later Brig.-Gen.) Mathieu Kérékou, Deputy Chief of Staff of the armed forces. Kérékou, a northerner, asserted that his military regime would be based on equal representation between northern, central and southern regions. In September 1973 a Conseil national révolutionnaire (CNR), comprising representatives from each of these regions, was established.

Strategic sectors and financial institutions were acquired by the State, under Kérékou's regime, which pursued Marxist-based policies. In late 1975 the Parti de la révolution populaire du Bénin (PRPB) was established as the sole party, and Dahomey was renamed the People's Republic of Benin.

In January 1977 an airborne attack on Cotonou, led by a French mercenary, Col Robert Denard, was repelled by the armed forces. In August the CNR adopted a *Loi fondamentale* decreeing new structures in government. Elections to a new 'supreme authority', the Assemblée nationale révolutionnaire (ANR), took place in November 1979, when a single list of 336 'People's Commissioners' was approved by 97.5% of voters. At the same time a Comité exécutif national (CEN) was established to replace the CNR. The PRPB designated Kérékou as the sole candidate for President of the Republic, and in February 1980 he was unanimously elected to this office by the ANR. In April 1981 it was announced that Ahomadegbé, Apithy and Maga, imprisoned following the coup of 1972, had been released from house arrest. A gradual moderation in Benin's domestic policies followed, and both the extreme left and the army, whose officers were by now outnumbered by civilians in the Government, gradually lost influence.

In February 1984 the ANR increased the mandates of People's Commissioners and of the President from three years to five, while reducing the number of Commissioners to 196. At legislative elections in June 98% of voters approved the single list of People's Commissioners, and in July the ANR re-elected Kérékou, again the sole candidate, as President. Kérékou subsequently consolidated his position, reducing the membership of the CEN and effectively depriving southern communities of influence in government.

In January 1987 Kérékou resigned from the army to become a civilian Head of State. Concern among army officers at perceived corruption within Kérékou's civilian Government, together with opposition to the proposed establishment of a Court of State Security, were the apparent catalysts for a coup attempt in March 1988; almost 150 officers, including members of the Presidential Guard, were reportedly arrested.

Chronic economic difficulties caused Benin to seek stronger ties with the West in the late 1980s. In June 1989 economic adjustment measures were agreed with the IMF and the World Bank, prompting fears of further austerity measures. At elections to the ANR in that month a relative decline in support for the single list of PRBP-approved candidates (which was endorsed by 89.6% of voters) was attributed to dissatisfaction with the economic situation, and labour and academic unrest, which had provoked strike action earlier in the year, continued.

In August 1989 the ANR re-elected Kérékou (the sole candidate) as President. A reorganization of the CEN included the appointment of several known proponents of reform. At the end of the year Kérékou yielded to domestic pressure and to demands made by France and other external creditors, instituting radical political changes and abandoning Marxism-Leninism as the official ideology of the State.

In February 1990 delegates at a conference of the 'active forces of the nation' voted to abolish the *Loi fondamentale* and its institutions; all resolutions adopted by the conference were incorporated in a 'national charter' that was to form the basis of a new constitution. An Haut conseil de la République (HCR) was appointed to assume the functions of the ANR pending the appointment of a new legislature. Among the members of the HCR were former Presidents Ahomadegbé, Maga and Zinsou, all of whom had returned to Benin to lead opposition parties. Presidential and legislative elections, to be held in the context of a multi-party political system, were scheduled for early 1991. A former official of the World Bank (who had briefly been Minister of Finance and Economic Affairs in the mid-1960s), Nicéphore Soglo, was designated interim Prime Minister, and Kérékou subsequently relinquished the defence portfolio to Soglo. The conference also voted to change the country's name to the Republic of Benin.

In March 1990 an amnesty was announced for all political dissidents. The HCR was inaugurated, and Soglo appointed a transitional, civilian Government. Of the previous administration, only Kérékou remained in office. In May civilian administrators replaced the provincial military prefects, prior to an extensive restructuring of the armed forces. Legislation permitting the registration of political parties was promulgated in August. (The PRPB had itself been succeeded by a new party, the Union des forces du progrès, in May.)

After considerable delay, a national referendum on the draft Constitution was conducted on 2 December 1990. Voters were asked to choose between two proposed documents, one of which incorporated a clause stipulating upper and lower age-limits for presidential candidates, and would therefore prevent the candidatures of Ahomadegbé, Maga and Zinsou. It was reported that 95.8% of those who voted approved one or other of the versions, with 79.7% of voters favouring the age-restriction clause.

Some 24 political parties contested the legislative elections on 17 February 1991. The largest grouping in the new 64-member Assemblée nationale was an alliance of three pro-Soglo parties, which secured 12 seats.

Kérékou and Soglo were among 13 candidates at the first round of the presidential election on 10 March 1991. Soglo, who won 36.2% of the total votes cast, received his greatest support in the south of the country, while Kérékou, who received 27.3% of the overall vote, was reported to have secured the support of more than 80% of voters in the north. Soglo and Kérékou proceeded to a second round of voting, which was conducted two weeks later, amid violence and allegations of electoral malpractice. Soglo was elected President, obtaining 67.7% of the total votes cast. In late March, prior to its dissolution, the HCR granted Kérékou immunity from any legal proceedings connected with actions committed since the *coup d'état* of October 1972.

Soglo was inaugurated as President on 4 April 1991, and shortly afterwards he relinquished the defence portfolio. As President, Soglo furthered attempts to address Benin's economic problems and to recover state funds allegedly embezzled by former members of the Kérékou regime. None the less, the new administration's inability to pay public-sector salary arrears provoked intermittent labour unrest. There was, moreover, considerable opposition in the Assemblée nationale to elements of the Government's programme of economic reform, notably the sale of former state-owned enterprises to foreign interests. Tensions between the executive and legislature eased somewhat following the formation, in June, of a 34-member pro-Soglo grouping, styled Le Renouveau, in the Assemblée nationale, although Soglo's economic policies continued to be a source of domestic disquiet.

In May 1992, meanwhile, several army officers were arrested following an incident outside the presidential palace in Cotonou. In August it was reported that some of the detainees, including their leader, Capt. Pascal Tawes (formerly deputy commander of the now-disbanded Presidential Guard), had escaped from custody and that Tawes was leading a mutiny at an army camp in the north. The rebellion was quickly suppressed, but Tawes was among those who evaded arrest. (In September 1994 Tawes and 15 others were sentenced *in absentia* to life imprisonment with hard labour, having been convicted of plotting to overthrow the Government.) In March 1993 more than 100 prisoners, including several soldiers who were implicated in the previous year's disturbances, escaped from detention in Ouidah, in the south-west. The dismissal, shortly afterwards, of the armed forces Chief of Staff and of other senior members of the security forces prompted the Minister at the Office of the President, responsible for Defence, to resign, protesting that Soglo had acted unconstitutionally by unilaterally making new military appointments. In October 15 assembly members withdrew from Le Renouveau, alleging that Soglo was consistently excluding the legislature from the decision-making process. In July Soglo, who had previously asserted his political neutrality, had made public his membership of the (Parti de la) renaissance du Bénin (RB), formed by his wife, Rosine Soglo, in 1992; he was appointed leader of the RB in July 1994.

Social tensions re-emerged following the 50% devaluation of the CFA franc in January 1994. After a period of severe labour unrest, in May the Government announced salary increases of 10% for all state employees, as well as the reintroduction of housing allowances (abolished in 1986) and an end to the eight-year freeze on promotions within the civil service. The payment of salary arrears from 1983–91 began in November 1994.

In November 1994 the Assemblée nationale voted to establish an independent electoral supervisory body, the Commission électorale nationale autonome (CENA), despite resistance from Soglo, who also opposed a planned increase in the number of deputies from 64 to 83. Some 31 political organizations participated in the legislative elections, which took place on 28 March 1995. In mid-April the Constitutional Court annulled the results of voting for 13 seats on the grounds of irregularities. Following by-elections in May, the RB held 20 seats in the Assemblée nationale, and other supporters of Soglo 13. Opposition parties held 49 seats, the most prominent being the Parti du renouveau démocratique (PRD), with 19 seats, and the Front d'action pour le renouveau et le développement—Alafia (FARD—Alafia), which had attracted considerable support from Kérékou supporters in the north (although the former President had not actively campaigned in the election), with 10. In June 1995 Bruno Amoussou, the leader of the opposition Parti social-démocrate (PSD), was elected President of the Assemblée nationale. Later that month the RB formed a new Government.

In late 1995 rumours circulated of a coup plot and of attempts to sabotage a conference of Heads of State and Government of the Conseil permanent de la francophonie, which was due to take place in Cotonou in December. Tensions escalated following a rocket attack in November on the newly built conference centre at which the summit was to take place.

The success of supporters of Kérékou at the 1995 parliamentary elections prompted speculation that Kérékou might again contest the presidency in 1996, and in January of that year he announced his candidature. While Soglo's economic policies had earned his administration the respect of the international financial community, there was internal disquiet that growth had been achieved at the expense of social concerns and that the regime had become increasingly authoritarian.

In December 1995 the Assemblée nationale voted to delay ratification of the third phase of Benin's structural adjustment programme, the most contentious element of which was the planned restructuring of the state company responsible for the distribution of petroleum products, the Société nationale de commercialisation des produits pétroliers (SONACOP). Deputies rejected ratification of a modified programme twice during January 1996, and also rejected the Government's draft budget for that year, prompting Soglo to implement the budget and adjustment programme by decree.

The first round of the presidential election, on 3 March 1996, was contested by seven candidates. Some 22.8% of the votes cast were invalidated by the Constitutional Court prior to the announcement of the official results, whereby Soglo secured 35.7% of the valid votes and Kérékou 33.9%, followed by the leader of the PRD, Adrien Houngbédji, (19.7%) and Amoussou (7.8%). The rate of participation by voters was 86.9%. Most of the defeated candidates quickly expressed their support for Kérékou, among them Houngbédji, who had, in 1975, been sentenced *in absentia* to death for his part in a plot to overthrow Kérékou's military regime.

On 24 March 1996 the Constitutional Court issued the official results of the second round of voting, held on 18 March, announcing Kérékou's election, with 52.5% of the valid votes. Some 78.1% of those eligible had voted, and less than 3% of the votes had been disallowed. Kérékou won the support of a majority of voters in four of the country's six provinces, although Soglo performed strongly in Cotonou and in his native Zou province, in central Benin. On 1 April the Court confirmed Kérékou's victory, and Soglo conceded defeat on the following day.

Having sought authorization by the Constitutional Court for the appointment of a Prime Minister (provision for such a post is not stipulated in the Constitution), in April 1996 Kérékou named Houngbédji as premier and assumed personal responsibility for defence. The new Government's stated priorities were to strengthen the rule of law, to combat corruption, and to promote economic revival and social development.

In September 1997 the Assemblée nationale approved an amnesty for electoral and media crimes and all acts seeking to undermine state security committed between January 1990 and June 1996. The amnesty, which, most notably, benefited members of the military and civilians implicated in the events of late 1995, provoked protests by the RB, which warned that the measure would exacerbate ethnic and regional divisions. The law was promulgated by Kérékou shortly afterwards, but in

October 1997 the Constitutional Court invalidated the amnesty legislation, on the grounds that the failure of the Government to consult the Supreme Court rendered such legislation unconstitutional.

In late 1997 proposals to end automatic promotions within the civil service, which had prompted strke action by state employees, were rejected by the legislature, forcing the Government to revise its budgetary provisions for 1998. From early 1998 the Government's failure to pay civil servants salary arrears that had accumulated since 1992 provoked further discontent, culminating in a general strike in mid-May. Meanwhile, Houngbédji, who was apparently dissatisfied at his exclusion from the drafting of the 1998 budget and concerned that an impending government reshuffle would result in a loss of influence for himself and the PRD, resigned the premiership. Kérékou named a new Government in which there was no Prime Minister, the most senior minister being Pierre Osho (hitherto Minister of Foreign Affairs and Co-operation) as Minister-delegate to the Presidency, in charge of Defence and Relations with the Institutions.

In March 1999 six people were sentenced to prison terms of between two and 12 years, having been convicted on charges related to proposed electoral fraud, in advance of legislative elections scheduled for later in the month; charges in connection with similar offences remained against some 40 defendants. Polling proceeded on 30 March, with more than 2,900 candidates, representing 35 parties and alliances, contesting the 83 seats in the Assemblée nationale. International monitors reported that the elections had been conducted peacefully and democratically. Official results, issued by the CENA on 3 April and confirmed by the Constitutional Council one week later, indicated that the combined opposition parties had won a slender majority in the legislature, with 42 seats. The RB won the largest number of seats, with 27, principally in the south and centre (including eight of Cotonou's nine seats). FARD—Alafia (10 seats), the PSD (nine seats) and other parties loyal to the President performed strongly in the north and west. The PRD, which won 11 seats, was, however, strongly challenged in the east, particularly by the pro-Kérékou Mouvement africain pour la démocratie et le progrès, which won six seats overall. The rate of participation by voters was in excess of 70%. Both the presidential group and the new parliamentary majority expressed optimism regarding the forthcoming period of institutional 'cohabitation'. Houngbédji was elected Speaker of the new assembly, defeating Amoussou. In June Kérékou effected a government reshuffle, increasing the number of parties represented in the Council of Ministers from seven to 10, in an apparent effort to consolidate his support in the Assemblée nationale.

The findings of a commission of inquiry into official corruption in Benin, which had been established by Kérékou following his election in 1996, were published in July 1999. The commission revealed that public funds valued at more than 70,000m. francs CFA had been embezzled in the three years to April 1999. At the end of July the Government instituted a code of ethics that excluded those convicted of corruption from public office and obliged the disclosure of all payments made during tendering for state projects.

In October 1999 an estimated 32,000 civil servants undertook a three-day strike after public-sector unions and the Government failed to reach agreement on the payment of salary arrears (valued by the unions at some 18,000m. francs CFA) and the abolition of the new meritocratic system of promotion. Although the Government pursued negotiations with workers' representatives, in November some unions began further industrial action, claiming that offers made by the Government were unsatisfactory. Agreement was subsequently reached on the creation of a bipartite commission to investigate a new system of remuneration and promotion for the civil service, and on the payment of salary arrears. None the less, one trade-union federation resumed strike action the following week, demanding the immediate implementation of the provisions of the agreement.

In January 2000 the President imposed the annual budget by decree, after the legislative opposition had rejected its provisions. In the same month members of the armed forces demonstrated in Cotonou against the non-payment of bonuses due to them for their service in West African peace-keeping missions; the Government later admitted that sums of money due to the troops had been misappropriated by senior military figures. Kérékou subsequently announced that he suspected the armed forces and certain opposition parties of preparing a *coup d'état*,

although he presented no evidence to substantiate these allegations. In early 2000 Soglo and Houngbédji formed a new alliance of 10 opposition parties, which condemned the perceived corruption of the Kérékou administration, particularly in relation to the privatization of SONACOP and the Government's reputed manipulation of the media.

In late January 2001 the 25-member CENA was belatedly convened; two previous attempts by the Assemblée nationale to nominate a majority of candidates from the parliamentary opposition to the electoral commission had been rejected by the Constitutional Court as unrepresentative of the political composition of the assembly.

In the period preceding the presidential election Soglo was widely regarded as the sole credible challenger to Kérékou. Corruption became a leading issue, as allegations emerged of fraudulent behaviour by both Kérékou and Soglo involving large parastatal companies. Early results of the first round of the election, which was held on 4 March 2001 and contested by 17 candidates, indicated that Kérékou had gained the largest share of the vote, with Soglo in second place, but had failed to secure an absolute majority; a second round was scheduled for 18 March.

As campaigning by supporters of Soglo and Kérékou proceeded, the Constitutional Court conducted a review of the election results declared by the CENA. Revised provisional results gave Kérékou 45.42% of the votes cast, Soglo 27.12%, Adrien Houngbédji 12.62% and Bruno Amoussou (who had originally been placed fifth) 8.59%. Following the declaration of the revised results, which indicated an increase in the electoral roll by some 300,000 and a participation rate of around 80%, Houngbédji endorsed the candidature of Soglo, while Amoussou encouraged his supporters to vote for Kérékou, who stated that he would form a broad-based government of national unity, if re-elected.

Meanwhile, there were calls for a boycott of the second round of voting, owing to alleged irregularities in the conduct of the first round. Soglo appealed to the Constitutional Court to annul the disputed results, and to rerun the election, either in those constituencies, or on a nation-wide basis. On 16 March 2001 Soglo, having had his appeal rejected, withdrew his candidature. The Government postponed the second round of the election, which was thus to be contested by Kérékou and Houngbédji, firstly until 19 March and subsequently until 22 March. However, on 19 March Houngbédji also declared his dissatisfaction with the conduct of the election and withdrew from the second round. Consequently, Amoussou, who had previously declared his support for Kérékou, was now to challenge him for the presidency. Nine opposition members of the CENA resigned in protest at the conduct of the election, alleging that a small group close to both Kérékou and Amoussou had effectively manipulated the commission to their own ends.

The second round of the presidential election duly took place on 22 March 2001. Voter participation, at about 55%, was significantly lower than in the first round. Two days after polling the CENA announced that Kérékou had won 84.06% of valid votes cast. Kérékou was declared President for a further term, in spite of allegations that the depleted CENA was not qualified to organize the election.

In April 2001 Benin attracted widespread international attention following reports that a ship, the Nigerian-registered MV *Etireno*, which was believed to be illicitly trafficking more than 200 child workers from various West African countries, was to dock at Cotonou, having been refused entry to ports in Gabon and Cameroon. Although only 43 of the 139 passengers found on board the vessel on its arrival in Cotonou were minors (aged under 24 years), a report issued jointly by the UN Children's Fund and the Government at the end of the month confirmed that the *Etireno* had been involved in the clandestine transport of minors and other workers. As the issue of child-trafficking gained increasing prominence in the region, a regime of mandatory authorization for minors leaving Benin was introduced in September, and in March 2002 Benin, Burkina Faso, Côte d'Ivoire, Mali, Niger and Togo announced the introduction of more stringent controls and monitoring of the transport of minors.

Meanwhile, in May 2001 Kérékou announced the formation of his new Government, which included eight new appointees among the 21 ministers. Amoussou retained a senior position in the Council of Ministers, as Minister of State, responsible for the Co-ordination of Government Action, Future Planning and Development, and became the sole representative of the PSD in the new Government. In June the Assemblée nationale adopted legislation that granted amnesty to those who had committed various crimes during the period surrounding the presidential election. One of the stated priorities of the new administration was to combat corruption, and the Government announced the implementation of what it termed a strategic plan to that end. In July it was announced that proposed municipal elections, initially scheduled to be held in 2000, had been cancelled, as a result of overspending on the presidential election.

In August 2001 dissent within the RB became apparent, when 10 of the party's deputies, led by the party's Vice-Chairman, Nathaniel Bah, formed a separate grouping within the Assemblée nationale. Despite the expulsion of Bah from the RB in mid-August, his supporters announced his assumption of the party chairmanship (displacing Rosine Soglo) at an extraordinary congress in early September. In January 2002, however, a congress of the RB reinstated Rosine Soglo as the party Chairman.

In early February 2002 the President was again obliged to implement the state budget by decree, following the failure of the Assemblée nationale to adopt the proposed draft. In late 2001 and early 2002 up to 32,000 civil servants and workers, primarily in the health and education sectors, participated in a series of nation-wide strikes, in support of demands for higher salaries and the withdrawal of proposals to introduce promotion on grounds of merit within the public sector. In early March 2002 the Government reached agreement with six of the seven trade unions that had organized the strikes; wage arrears were to be paid and an increase in civil servants' salaries granted, while the question of procedures for promotions was to be referred to the Assemblée nationale. Meanwhile, in mid-February Abdoulaye Bio Tchané stepped down as Minister of Finance and the Economy, to take the position of Director of the African Department at the IMF; he was replaced by Grégoire Laourou. In late April riot police used tear gas to disperse a banned demonstration by members of the RB, who were protesting against the refusal of the Ministry of the Interior, Security and Decentralization to recognize Rosine Soglo as the party's Chairman.

In November 2002 it was announced that legislative elections would be held on 30 March 2003. Meanwhile, the delayed municipal and local elections were held in two rounds in December 2002 and January 2003. Some 5,700 candidates, comprising independents and representatives of five parties, contested the 1,199 seats nation-wide; although supporters of Kérékou, who formed an electoral alliance known as the Union pour le Bénin du futur (UBF), were the most successful grouping overall, the RB gained the majority of seats in Cotonou, where Nicéphore Soglo was elected mayor, while the PRD secured control of Porto-Novo.

The legislative elections, which were held, as scheduled, on 30 March 2003, resulted in the establishment of a clear pro-presidential majority in the Assemblé nationale for the first time since the introduction of multi-party elections in Benin, with supporters of Kérékou securing 52 of the 83 elective seats. The UBF emerged as the largest single party, with 31 seats, and the pro-presidential Mouvement africain pour la démocratie et le progrès (MADEP), led by Séfou Fagbohoun, a business executive, won nine seats. The representation of the RB, the largest party in the outgoing assembly, was reduced from 27 to 15 seats. On 10 April Houngbédji announced that the PRD, which secured 11 seats in the elections, would, henceforth, support the Government, as a result of which the pro-presidential bloc in the Assemblée held 63 seats. Eight other parties or alliances won representation in the legislature in the elections, which were contested by 1,162 candidates, representing 14 political groups.

In late April 2003 Amoussou and seven other ministers who had recently been elected as deputies resigned from the Government, in order to assume their legislative responsibilities, as required by the Constitution. At the end of the month Antoine Idji Kolawolé of the MADEP, hitherto Minister of Foreign Affairs and African Integration, was elected as President of the Assemblée nationale, defeating Rosine Soglo. The formation of a new Government was expected to be announced in May.

Benin has in recent years played an active role in efforts to co-ordinate regional peace-keeping and humanitarian assistance operations, contributing troops to peace-keeping operations undertaken by the Economic Community of West African States in Guinea-Bissau from late 1998 until mid-1999 (when the force was withdrawn, following the *coup d'état* in that country) and in Côte d'Ivoire from early 2003. Benin maintains generally good

relations with neighbouring countries and joined the Community of Sahel-Saharan States (see p. 339) in March 2002. None the less, in mid-2000 a long-term dispute between Benin and Niger, over the ownership of various small islands in the Niger river, erupted after Nigerien soldiers reportedly sabotaged the construction of a Beninois administrative building on Lété Island. Meetings between representatives of the two Governments and arbitration by the Organization of African Unity (now the African Union (see p. 130) failed to resolve the dispute, and in April 2002 the two countries officially ratified an agreement (signed in 2001) to refer the dispute to the International Court of Justice at The Hague, Netherlands, for arbitration. Following concerns about cross-border crime, and the reputed import of small arms from Benin into Nigeria, the two countries launched joint police patrols along their common border in August 2001.

Government

The Constitution of the Republic of Benin, which was approved in a national referendum on 2 December 1990, provides for a civilian, multi-party political system. Executive power is vested in the President of the Republic, who is elected by direct universal adult suffrage with a five-year mandate, renewable only once. The legislature is the 83-member Assemblée nationale, which is similarly elected, for a period of four years, by universal suffrage. The President of the Republic appoints the Council of Ministers, subject to formal parliamentary approval.

For the purposes of local administration, Benin is divided into 12 departments, each administered by a civilian prefect. These departments are further divided into a total of 77 communes.

Defence

In August 2002 the Beninois Armed Forces numbered an estimated 4,550 in active service (land army 4,300, navy about 100, air force 150). Paramilitary forces comprised a 2,500-strong gendarmerie. Military service is by selective conscription, and lasts for 18 months. The estimated defence budget for 2002 was 34,000m. francs CFA.

Economic Affairs

In 2001, according to estimates by the World Bank, Benin's gross national income (GNI), measured at average 1999–2001 prices, was US $2,349m., equivalent to $360 per head (or $1,030 on an international purchasing-power parity basis). During 1990–2001, it was estimated, the population increased at an average annual rate of 2.9% per year, while gross domestic product (GDP) per head increased, in real terms, by an average of 1.9% per year. Overall GDP increased, in real terms, at an average annual rate of 4.9% per year in 1990–2001; growth in 2001 was 5.0%, according to the IMF.

Agriculture (including forestry and fishing) contributed 38.6% of GDP in 2001. In that year an estimated 53.0% of the labour force were employed in the sector. The principal cash crops are cotton (exports of which accounted for an estimated 84.6% of total exports in 2000, according to the World Bank) and oil palm. Benin is normally self-sufficient in basic foods; the main subsistence crops are yams, cassava and maize. The World Bank estimated that agricultural GDP increased at an average annual rate of 5.8% in 1990–2001; growth in 2001 was 5.1%.

Industry (including mining, manufacturing, construction and power) contributed 15.7% of GDP in 2001, and engaged 10.4% of the employed labour force at the time of the 1992 census. According to the World Bank, industrial GDP increased at an average annual rate of 4.8% in 1990–2001; growth in 2001 was 8.5%.

Mining contributed only 0.2% of GDP in 2001, and engaged less than 0.1% of the employed labour force in 1992. Petroleum extraction at Sémé was terminated on the grounds of unprofitability in 1998, contributing to a 82.2% decline in mining GDP in the following year, although a contract signed between Benin and the multinational Zetah Oil Company in October 1999 envisaged the exploitation of Sémé's remaining petroleum reserves, estimated at some 22m. barrels. Marble and limestone are also exploited commercially. There are also deposits of gold, phosphates, natural gas, iron ore, silica sand, peat and chromium. The GDP of the mining sector declined at an average annual rate of 28.6% in 1994–2001; growth in mining GDP was negligible in 2001.

The manufacturing sector, which contributed 10.0% of GDP in 2001, engaged 7.8% of the employed labour force in 1992. The sector is based largely on the processing of primary products (principally cotton-ginning and oil-palm processing). Construction materials and some simple consumer goods are also produced for the domestic market. According to the World Bank, manufacturing GDP increased at an average annual rate of 6.2% in 1990–2001; growth in 2001 was 6.8%.

Benin is at present highly dependent on imports of electricity from Ghana (which supplied some 85% of total available production in 1996). It is envisaged that a hydroelectric installation on the Mono river, constructed and operated jointly with Togo, will reduce Benin's dependence on imported electricity, and a second such installation is under construction downstream. In 1999 95.7% of Benin's electricity production was derived from petroleum. In 2000 the construction of a further electricity line, to run from Lagos, Nigeria, to Togo, through Benin, was proposed by the Governments of the three countries. A pipeline to supply natural gas from Nigeria to Benin, Togo and Ghana was expected to come on stream in 2005, three years later than initially planned. Imports of mineral fuels and lubricants accounted for 20.8% of the value of total imports in 1998.

The services sector contributed 45.7% of GDP in 2001, and engaged 31.8% of the employed labour force in 1992. The port of Cotonou is of considerable importance as an entrepôt for regional trade: re-exports comprised an estimated 38.5% of the value of total exports in 1997. According to the World Bank, the GDP of the services sector increased at an average annual rate of 4.1% per year in 1990–2001; growth in 2001 was 5.6%.

In 2000 Benin recorded a visible trade deficit of US $123.7m., while there was a deficit of $111.0m. on the current account of the balance of payments. In 1999 the principal source of imports (22.0%) was France; other major sources were Côte d'Ivoire, Togo, the People's Republic of China, the USA and the Netherlands. The principal market for exports in that year was Brazil (19.8%); other important purchasers were India, Indonesia and Thailand. The principal exports in 1998 were raw cotton (providing 46.3% of total exports) and ores and concentrates of uranium and thorium. The main imports in 1998 were refined petroleum products (accounting for 19.1% of total imports), textile yarn and fabrics, cereals and cereal preparations, and road vehicles and parts.

In 2001 Benin recorded an overall budget deficit of an estimated 24,600m. francs CFA (equivalent to 1.4% of GDP). The country's total external debt at the end of 2000 was US $1,599m., of which $1,443m. was long-term public debt. In that year the cost of debt-servicing was equivalent to 12.6% of the value of exports of goods and services. The annual rate of inflation, which had been negligible prior to the 50% devaluation of the CFA franc in January 1994, increased to 38.5% in 1994, but slowed to an average of 3.8% per year in 1995–2001. Consumer prices increased by 4.0% in 2001. About one-quarter of the urban labour force was estimated to be unemployed in 1997.

Benin is a member of the Economic Community of West African States (ECOWAS, see p. 187), of the West African organs of the Franc Zone (see p. 238), of the African Petroleum Producers' Association (APPA, see p. 335), of the Conseil de l'Entente (see p. 339) and of the Niger Basin Authority (see p. 341).

Benin has experienced considerable economic growth since the early 1990s, with significant success achieved in strengthening public finances, improving the external balance-of-payments position and in reforming the financial sector. A three-year Enhanced Structural Adjustment Facility (ESAF) was agreed with the IMF in August 1996. The renewal of co-operation with the IMF ensured debt-relief measures, notably along concessionary terms by the 'Paris Club' of official creditors. The Government's slow progress in the privatization of a number of major state enterprises and in the reform of the civil service led the IMF to suspend disbursements during 1998, although the facility was resumed in January 1999. In July 2000, as part of the Heavily Indebted Poor Countries (HIPC) initiative, the IMF and the World Bank cancelled some US $460m. of Benin's debt and announced a further three-year enhanced HIPC programme for 2000–03. Also in that month the IMF approved funding of some $35.7m., under its Poverty Reduction and Growth Facility

(PRGF, the successor to ESAF), in support of the Government's economic programme for 2000–03. However, proposed restructuring and divestiture programmes were only implemented sporadically. Although the primary marketing of the important crop of seed cotton was transferred, in January 2001, from the parastatal Société Nationale pour la Promotion Agricole (SONAPRA) to the private sector, the privatization of SONAPRA itself, initially intended to occur in 2002, was postponed. None the less, by the early 2000s the country's cotton sector was one of the most liberalized in western or central Africa, and programmes to open the water and electricity sectors to private-sector involvement were being developed; it was also intended that the telecommunications and postal operations of the Office des Postes et des Télécommunications be separated, with the former transferred to private management by late 2003. GDP growth of 5.3% was projected for 2002, as an increase in cotton production partly compensated for a sharp decline in international prices for that commodity. In July 2002 the IMF announced that the PRGF arrangement agreed in 2000 was to be extended until 2004, and additional debt relief, amounting to $5m., was also granted under the HIPC initiative. The Government intended to increase real GDP growth to 6.8% by 2004, while reducing the annual rate of inflation to less than 3.0%.

Education

The Constitution of Benin obliges the state to make a quality compulsory primary education available to all children. All public primary and secondary schools in Benin finance themselves through school fees. Primary education begins at six years of age and lasts for six years. Secondary education, beginning at 12 years of age, lasts for up to seven years, comprising a first cycle of four years and a second of three years. Primary enrolment in 1999/2000 included 70.3% of children in the appropriate age-group (males 83.2%; females 57.3%), according to UNESCO estimates. Enrolment at secondary schools in that year included 17.4% of children in the appropriate age group (males 23.8%; females 11.0%). In the 1990s the Government sought to extend the provision of education. In 1993 girls in rural areas were exempted from school fees, and in 1999 the Government created a 500m. francs CFA fund to increase female enrolment. The Université Nationale du Bénin, at Cotonou, was founded in 1970 and had a student population of approximately 9,000 in 1999/2000. A second university, in Parakou, with a student capacity of approximately 3,000, opened in 2001. In 2001 public expenditure on education totalled 71,100m. francs CFA.

Public Holidays

2003: 1 January (New Year's Day), 10 January (Vodoun national holiday), 16 January (Martyrs' Day, anniversary of mercenary attack on Cotonou), 12 February* (Id al-Adha, Feast of the Sacrifice), 1 April (Youth Day), 18 April (Good Friday), 21 April (Easter Monday), 1 May (Workers' Day), 29 May (Ascension Day), 9 June (Whit Monday), 1 August (Independence Day), 15 August (Assumption), 26 October (Armed Forces Day), 1 November (All Saints' Day), 26 November* (Id al-Fitr, end of Ramadan), 30 November (National Day), 25 December (Christmas Day), 31 December (Harvest Day).

2004: 1 January (New Year's Day), 10 January (Vodoun national holiday), 16 January (Martyrs' Day, anniversary of mercenary attack on Cotonou), 2 February* (Id al-Adha, Feast of the Sacrifice), 1 April (Youth Day), 9 April (Good Friday), 12 April (Easter Monday), 1 May (Workers' Day), 20 May (Ascension Day), 31 May (Whit Monday), 1 August (Independence Day), 15 August (Assumption), 26 October (Armed Forces Day), 1 November (All Saints' Day), 14 November* (Id al-Fitr, end of Ramadan), 30 November (National Day), 25 December (Christmas Day), 31 December (Harvest Day).

*These holidays are dependent on the Islamic lunar calendar and may vary by one or two days from the dates given.

Weights and Measures

The metric system is in force.

Statistical Survey

Source (unless otherwise stated): Institut National de la Statistique et de l'Analyse Economique, BP 323, Cotonou; tel. and fax 30-82-46; e-mail insae@ planben.intnet.bj.

Area and Population

AREA, POPULATION AND DENSITY

Area (sq km)	112,622*
Population (census results)	
20–30 March 1979	3,331,210
15–29 February 1992	
Males	2,390,336
Females	2,525,219
Total	4,915,555
Population (official estimates at mid-year)	
1999	5,990,000
2000	6,169,000
2001	6,420,000
Density (per sq km) at mid-2001	57.0

* 43,484 sq miles.

ETHNIC GROUPS

1995 (percentages): Fon 25.2; Yoruba 13.2; Bariba 11.6; Gun 11.6; Somba 6.9; Aizo 4.2; Mina 2.8; Dendi 1.9; Others 22.6 (Source: La Francophonie).

PROVINCES
(1992 census)

Province	Area (sq km)*	Population	Capital	Population of capital
Atacora	31,200	649,308	Natitingou	57,173
Atlantique . . .	3,222	1,066,373	Cotonou	536,827
Borgou . . .	51,000	827,925	Parakou	127,347
Mono . . .	3,800	676,377	Lokossa	54,260
Ouémé . . .	4,700	876,574	Porto-Novo	179,138
Zou . . .	18,700	818,998	Abomey	66,595
Total	112,622	4,915,555		

* Figures are rounded.

Note: In July 1998 the six provinces listed above were replaced by 12 administrative departments: Alibori (area 25,683 sq km), Atacora (20,459 sq km), Atlantique (3,233 sq km), Borgou (25,310 sq km), Collines (13,561 sq km), Couffo (2,404 sq km), Donga (10,691 sq km), Littoral (79 sq km), Mono (1,396 sq km), Ouémé (2,835 sq km), Plateau (1,865 sq km) and Zou (5,106 sq km).

PRINCIPAL TOWNS
(Localities, 1992 census)

Cotonou	536,827	Natitingou . .	57,153
Porto-Novo (capital) .	179,138	Djougou	49,769
Parakou . . .	103,577	Save	45,403
Abomey . . .	66,595	Bohicon . . .	43,453

Source: Thomas Brinkoff, *City Population* (internet www .citypopulation.de).

BIRTHS AND DEATHS
(UN estimates, annual averages)

	1985–90	1990–95	1995–2000
Birth rate (per 1,000)	49.0	45.6	42.8
Death rate (per 1,000)	16.3	14.4	13.1

Source: UN, *World Population Prospects: The 2000 Revision.*

Expectation of life (WHO estimates, years at birth): 52.1 (males 51.0; females 53.3) in 2001 (Source: WHO, *World Health Report*).

ECONOMICALLY ACTIVE POPULATION
(persons aged 10 years and over, 1992 census)

	Males	Females	Total
Agriculture, hunting, forestry and fishing	780,469	367,277	1,147,746
Mining and quarrying	609	52	661
Manufacturing	93,157	67,249	160,406
Electricity, gas and water . . .	1,152	24	1,176
Construction	50,959	696	51,655
Trade, restaurants and hotels . .	36,672	395,829	432,501
Transport, storage and communications	52,228	609	52,837
Finance, insurance, real estate and business services	2,705	401	3,106
Community, social and personal services	126,122	38,422	164,544
Activities not adequately defined .	25,579	12,917	38,496
Total employed	1,169,652	883,476	2,053,128
Unemployed	26,475	5,843	32,318
Total labour force	1,196,127	889,319	2,085,446

Source: ILO, *Yearbook of Labour Statistics.*

Mid-2001 (estimates in '000): Agriculture, etc. 1,548; Total labour force 2,920 (Source: FAO).

Health and Welfare

KEY INDICATORS

Total fertility rate (children per woman, 2001)	5.8
Under-5 mortality rate (per 1,000 live births, 2001) . . .	158
HIV/AIDS (% of persons aged 15–49, 2001)	3.61
Physicians (per 1,000 head, 1995)	0.06
Hospital beds (per 1,000 head, 1994)	0.23
Health expenditure (2000): US $ per head (PPP) . . .	27
Health expenditure (2000): % of GDP	3.2
Health expenditure (2000): public (% of total)	50.0
Access to water (% of persons, 2000)	63
Access to sanitation (% of persons, 2000)	23
Human Development Index (2000): ranking	158
Human Development Index (2000): value	0.420

For sources and definitions, see explanatory note on p. vi.

Agriculture

PRINCIPAL CROPS
('000 metric tons)

	1999	2000	2001
Rice (paddy)	34.0	49.2	54.9
Maize	783.0	750.4	685.9
Millet	29.5	36.4	35.0
Sorghum	126.4	155.3	165.3
Sweet potatoes . . .	68.3	65.6	57.0
Cassava (Manioc) . . .	2,113.0	2,350.2	2,703.5
Yams	1,647.0	1,742.0	1,701.0
Sugar cane	43.5*	52.1	73.4
Pulses	17.5	18.1	15.7
Dry beans	74.2	85.6	78.4
Cashew nuts*	26	26	26
Groundnuts (in shell) . .	101.9	121.2	125.4
Coconuts*	20	20	20
Oil palm fruit* . . .	220	220	220
Karité nuts (Sheanuts)* .	15	15	15
Cottonseed	225.4	190.2	216.1
Tomatoes	124.4	139.2	117.6
Chillies and green peppers .	54.6	33.3	29.3
Okra	54.6	59.0	58.1
Other vegetables* . . .	106.7	107.0	107.0
Pineapples	78.4	53.0	57.1
Other fruit*	143	143	143
Cotton (lint)†	122.6	152.0	141.0
Pimento and allspice* . .	14	14	14

* FAO estimate(s).
† Unofficial figures.

Source: FAO.

LIVESTOCK
('000 head, year ending September)

	1999	2000	2001*
Horses*	6	6	6
Cattle	1,438	1,500	1,520
Pigs*	470	460	460
Sheep	645	650*	655
Goats	1,183	1,190*	1,195
Poultry*	29,000	30,000	30,000

* FAO estimate(s).

Source: FAO.

LIVESTOCK PRODUCTS
(FAO estimates, '000 metric tons)

	1999	2000	2001
Beef and veal	21.1	21.5	21.7
Mutton and lamb . . .	2.4	2.4	2.4
Goat meat	3.9	3.9	4.0
Pig meat	6.0	5.8	5.8
Poultry meat	33.0	34.1	34.1
Game meat	6.0	6.0	6.0
Cows' milk	20.8	23.4	23.7
Goats' milk	6.2	6.2	6.3
Poultry eggs	20.9	21.6	21.6
Cattle hides	3.5	3.5	3.6

Source: FAO.

Forestry

ROUNDWOOD REMOVALS
('000 cubic metres, excl. bark)

	1999	2000*	2001*
Sawlogs, veneer logs and logs for sleepers	35	35	35
Other industrial wood* . . .	297	297	297
Fuel wood*	5,896	5,910	5,937
Total	6,228	6,242	6,269

* FAO estimates.

Source: FAO.

SAWNWOOD PRODUCTION
('000 cubic metres, incl. railway sleepers)

	1997	1998	1999
Total (all broadleaved) . . .	12	13	13

2000–01: Annual production as in 1999 (FAO estimates).

Source: FAO.

Fishing

('000 metric tons, live weight)

	1998	1999	2000
Tilapias	11.5*	11.6	9.6*
Black catfishes . . .	1.5*	1.5	1.3*
Torpedo-shaped catfishes . .	1.7*	1.5	1.3*
Mullets	2.0*	2.2	1.8*
Bonga shad	1.8*	1.8	1.5*
Freshwater crustaceans* . .	4.9	5.0	4.2
Penaeus shrimps . . .	2.7*	2.6	2.1*
Total catch (incl. others) . .	42.1	40.4	32.3

* FAO estimate(s).
Note: Figures exclude catches by Beninois canoes operating from outside the country.

Source: FAO, *Yearbook of Fishery Statistics*.

Mining

('000 barrels)

	1997	1998	1999
Crude petroleum	455.1	355.9	—

Source: Banque centrale des états de l'Afrique de l'ouest.

Industry

SELECTED PRODUCTS
('000 metric tons, unless otherwise indicated)

	1999	2000	2001
Cement* †	450	450	n.a.
Beer of barley†	25.5	25.5	35.0
Beer of sorghum† . . .	26.3	32.8	35.0
Palm oil†	15	15	15
Palm kernel oil	9.7‡	9.7‡	9.7†

* Data from the US Geological Survey.
† Estimate(s).
‡ Unofficial figure.

Electric energy (million kWh): 6 in 1998.

Salted, dried or smoked fish ('000 metric tons): 2.0 in 1997.

Sources: mainly UN, *Industrial Commodity Statistics Yearbook*; FAO.

Finance

CURRENCY AND EXCHANGE RATES

Monetary Units

100 centimes = 1 franc de la Communauté financière africaine (CFA)

Sterling, Dollar and Euro Equivalents (31 December 2002)

£1 sterling = 1,008.17 francs CFA
US $1 = 625.50 francs CFA
€1 = 655.96 francs CFA
10,000 francs CFA = £9.992 = $15.957 = €15.245

Average Exchange Rate (francs CFA per US $)

2000	711.98
2001	733.04
2002	696.99

Note: An exchange rate of 1 French franc = 50 francs CFA, established in 1948, remained in force until January 1994, when the CFA franc was devalued by 50%, with the exchange rate adjusted to 1 French franc = 100 francs CFA. This relationship to French currency remained in effect with the introduction of the euro on 1 January 1999. From that date, accordingly, a fixed exchange rate of €1 = 655.957 francs CFA has been in operation.

BUDGET

('000 million francs CFA)

Revenue*	1999	2000	2001†
Tax revenue	200.8	234.1	247.1
Taxes on income and profits	46.4	51.7	59.3
Individual	17.2	22.6	23.3
Corporate	25.6	26.0	33.0
Taxes on payroll and workforce	3.1	3.5	3.9
Taxes on property	3.5	3.2	2.8
Domestic taxes on goods and services	41.0	48.9	47.9
Turnover taxes	22.3	27.8	31.6
Excises	6.7	7.4	4.4
Taxes on international trade and transactions	106.8	126.7	133.2
Customs duties	25.6	39.2	42.6
Value-added tax	66.8	69.2	71.0
Non-tax revenue	34.1	32.1	33.9
Total	234.9	266.2	281.0

Expenditure‡	1999	2000	2001
Salaries	66.2	74.8	80.7
Pensions and scholarships	18.3	19.3	20.5
Current transfers	20.5	26.8	41.5
Investment	92.8	122.5	135.3
Budgetary contribution	28.0	35.0	55.4
Financed from abroad	64.8	87.4	79.8
Interest due	13.5	14.1	15.2
Domestic debt	1.9	1.6	1.8
External debt	11.6	12.4	13.5
Capital expenditure	42.4	64.7	59.6
Total	253.5	322.2	352.8

* Excluding grants received ('000 million francs CFA): 51.1 in 1999; 27.0 in 2000; 46.0 in 2001.

† Estimates.

‡ Excluding net lending ('000 million francs CFA): 4.5 in 1999; 0.3 in 2000; 0.4 in 2001.

Sources: IMF, *Benin: 2002 Article IV Consultation, Third Review Under the Poverty Reduction and Growth Facility, and Requests for an Extension of the Poverty Reduction and Growth Facility Arrangement and for an Additional Interim Assistance Under the Enhanced Initiative for Heavily Indebted Poor Countries—Staff Report; Public Information Notice and News Brief on the Executive Board Discussion* (August 2002), *Benin: Statistical Appendix* (August 2002).

INTERNATIONAL RESERVES

(US $ million at 31 December)

	1999	2000	2001
Gold*	3.3	n.a.	n.a.
IMF special drawing rights	0.2	0.1	0.4
Reserve position in IMF	3.0	2.9	2.7
Foreign exchange	396.9	455.2	574.9
Total	403.4	n.a.	n.a.

* Valued at market-related prices.

Source: IMF, *International Financial Statistics*.

MONEY SUPPLY

(million francs CFA at 31 December)

	1999	2000	2001
Currency outside banks	160,302	211,789	222,336
Demand deposit at deposit money banks	104,246	146,655	167,199
Checking deposits at post office	5,114	5,840	9,596
Total money (incl. others)	270,613	365,401	401,761

Source: IMF, *International Financial Statistics*.

COST OF LIVING

(Consumer price index; base: 1995 = 100)

	1999	2000	2001
All items	115.2	120.0	124.7

Source: IMF, *International Financial Statistics*.

NATIONAL ACCOUNTS

('000 million francs CFA at current prices)

Expenditure on the Gross Domestic Product

	1999	2000	2001
Government final consumption expenditure	147.3	185.6	202.4
Private final consumption expenditure	1,251.7	1,323.5	1,423.8
Gross fixed capital formation	257.4	303.9	333.5
Total domestic expenditure	1,656.4	1,813.1	1,959.6
Exports of goods and services	237.3	243.7	264.0
Less Imports of goods and services	423.7	451.4	485.0
GDP in purchasers' values	1,469.9	1,605.4	1,738.6

Source: IMF, *Benin: Statistical Appendix* (August 2002).

Gross Domestic Product by Economic Activity

	1999	2000	2001
Agriculture, livestock, forestry, hunting and fishing	556.3	586.5	617.7
Mining and petroleum	3.3	3.7	4.0
Manufacturing and handicrafts	127.2	140.8	159.7
Water, gas and electricity	12.6	14.3	16.6
Construction and public works	58.2	64.2	70.7
Trade	261.8	292.7	318.0
Transport and communications	100.9	122.1	139.8
Public administration	94.4	100.2	106.8
Other services	144.4	154.2	167.5
GDP at factor cost	1,359.1	1,478.6	1,600.8
Indirect taxes, *less* subsidies	110.8	126.8	137.8
GDP in purchasers' values	1,469.9	1,605.4	1,738.6
GDP at constant 1985 prices	740.0	782.6	821.9

Source: IMF, *Benin: Statistical Appendix* (August 2002).

BALANCE OF PAYMENTS

(US $ million)

	1998	1999	2000
Exports of goods f.o.b.	414.3	421.5	392.4
Imports of goods f.o.b.	−572.6	−635.2	−516.1
Trade balance	−158.3	−213.7	−123.7
Exports of services	142.3	176.9	136.1
Imports of services	−191.4	−215.3	−191.7
Balance on goods and services	−207.4	−252.2	−179.4
Other income received . . .	27.8	27.7	28.0
Other income paid	−41.2	−39.1	−40.3
Balance on goods, services and income	−220.8	−263.6	−191.6
Current transfers received . .	102.0	87.1	91.3
Current transfers paid . . .	−32.7	−14.9	−10.7
Current balance	−151.5	−191.4	−111.0
Capital account (net) . . .	66.6	69.9	73.3
Direct investment abroad . . .	−1.9	1.4	−8.1
Direct investment from abroad. .	34.7	39.3	64.3
Portfolio investment assets . .	1.2	−1.4	5.7
Portfolio investment liabilities .	1.2	2.0	0.1
Financial derivatives assets . .	n.a.	−0.1	—
Financial derivatives liabilities .	—	8.6	—
Other investment assets . .	−9.6	−58.3	25.1
Other investment liabilities . .	−34.4	36.8	−76.2
Net errors and omissions . .	7.1	7.3	6.7
Overall balance	−86.7	−88.7	−20.3

Source: IMF, *International Financial Statistics*.

External Trade

PRINCIPAL COMMODITIES

(US $ million)

Imports c.i.f.	1996	1997	1998
Food and live animals . . .	169.7	130.2	148.1
Cereals and cereal preparations	110.4	66.8	54.7
Rice	89.5	46.9	34.4
Rice, semi-milled or milled (unbroken)	n.a.	n.a.	31.6
Beverages and tobacco . . .	25.2	55.6	39.2
Tobacco, manufactured . . .	14.8	46.0	26.4
Cigarettes	n.a.	n.a.	24.5
Crude materials (inedible) except fuels	33.9	44.8	46.8
Old clothing and other old textile articles; rags.	27.8	36.5	39.7
Bulk textile waste, old clothing traded in bulk or in bales	27.8	36.5	39.2
Mineral fuels, lubricants, etc.	53.0	131.8	167.7
Petroleum, petroleum products, etc.	52.8	130.9	155.8
Petroleum products, refined . .	33.0	116.2	153.8
Gasoline and other light oils	32.9	116.1	—
Petroleum bitumen, petroleum coke, bituminous mixtures	19.8	14.6	1.9
Chemicals and related products	74.9	71.0	63.9
Medicinal and pharmaceutical products	13.0	23.2	22.8
Fertilizers, manufactured . .	22.2	21.3	17.4
Disinfectants, insecticides, fungicides, etc.	20.0	11.9	9.3
Basic manufactures	161.6	150.0	155.5
Textile yarn, fabrics, etc.. . .	74.1	75.3	74.6
Cotton fabrics, woven (not incl. narrow or special fabrics) .	35.6	45.9	51.0
Woven fabrics with 85% or more of grey cotton, not mercerized	35.6	45.9	13.1
Cotton fabrics, woven, bleached, dyed or otherwise finished . .	n.a.	n.a.	35.9
Woven fabrics with 85% or more of cotton, bleached, etc., finished	n.a.	n.a.	31.5
Fabrics, woven, of man-made fibres (not narrow or special fabrics).	32.8	24.3	21.1
Woven fabrics with 85% or more of discontinuous synthetic fibres	31.4	24.2	9.9
Non-metallic mineral manufactures	25.0	23.1	22.2
Lime, cement and fabricated construction materials . .	19.5	17.7	15.3
Iron and steel	23.0	17.5	13.7
Machinery and transport equipment	93.4	95.9	138.7
Power-generating machinery and equipment	5.8	6.1	24.4
Electric machinery, apparatus and appliances, and parts . .	19.7	18.1	21.0
Road vehicles and parts* . . .	34.2	39.5	44.5
Passenger motor vehicles (excl. buses).	28.0	31.6	29.1
Miscellaneous manufactured articles	29.9	30.4	34.4
Total (incl. others)	649.7	714.6	807.0

* Excluding tyres, engines and electrical parts.

Exports f.o.b.	1996	1997	1998
Food and live animals . . .	19.8	16.8	12.7
Beverages and tobacco . . .	16.9	42.6	21.5
Tobacco, manufactured . . .	15.7	42.2	20.6
Cigarettes	n.a.	n.a.	20.5
Crude materials (inedible)			
except fuels	348.6	280.6	275.7
Oil seeds and oleaginous fruit .	13.4	10.3	18.0
Seeds and oleaginous fruit, whole			
or broken, for 'soft' fixed oil. .	13.4	10.3	14.0
Cotton seeds	n.a.	n.a.	14.0
Raw cotton, excl. linters, not carded			
or combed	203.8	145.5	154.2
Metalliferous ores and metal scrap	128.6	122.3	99.6
Roasted iron pyrites . .	128.5	122.2	—
Ores and concentrates of			
uranium and thorium. . .	—	—	99.5
Basic manufactures . . .	14.4	10.5	6.1
Total (incl. others)	420.4	370.8	332.9

Source: UN, *International Trade Statistics Yearbook.*

PRINCIPAL TRADING PARTNERS
(US $ million)

Imports c.i.f.	1997	1998	1999
Belgium-Luxembourg . . .	11.1	14.5	n.a.
Brazil	6.3	11.7	4.6
Cameroon	19.1	12.9	8.8
China, People's Repub. . . .	37.7	40.4	43.4
Côte d'Ivoire	44.7	90.2	88.3
France (incl. Monaco) . . .	168.8	167.3	185.4
Germany	27.5	24.7	28.3
Ghana	15.5	12.5	23.0
Hong Kong	13.0	9.5	7.1
India	11.4	26.0	15.7
Italy	22.3	36.6	32.9
Japan	27.9	35.6	29.0
Korea, Repub..	10.4	7.1	5.3
Netherlands	34.5	41.0	40.3
Nigeria.	13.8	3.6	8.5
Pakistan	13.8	6.9	5.6
Romania	2.7	16.7	4.7
Senegal	12.5	17.4	23.4
Southern African Customs Union*	2.1	16.8	0.8
Spain	29.5	18.2	31.6
Thailand	21.7	9.7	22.6
Togo	0.0	0.0	47.2
United Kingdom	55.8	57.1	32.6
USA	36.0	47.8	42.8
Viet Nam	8.3	1.5	3.1
Total (incl. others)	714.6	807.0	843.2

Exports f.o.b.	1997	1998	1999
Bangladesh	1.2	4.5	9.8
Belgium-Luxembourg . . .	2.1	4.3	n.a.
Brazil	21.6	54.6	41.0
China, People's Repub. . . .	0.6	2.8	2.9
Côte d'Ivoire	2.0	1.8	2.4
Denmark	1.8	7.6	0.7
France (incl. Monaco) . . .	60.5	65.1	3.0
Germany	4.4	8.4	1.9
India	1.2	11.2	32.1
Indonesia	4.8	13.5	20.8
Italy	5.0	8.5	8.0
Mali	10.3	6.3	0.6
Morocco	9.0	10.0	4.2
Niger	28.8	29.0	5.4
Nigeria.	12.6	15.0	0.4
Pakistan	0.0	0.1	8.7
Portugal	3.6	6.1	5.5
Saudi Arabia	0.5	2.3	2.2
Spain	2.4	7.8	7.4
Switzerland-Liechtenstein . .	1.2	6.0	3.6
Thailand	5.2	16.2	11.0
Turkey.	0.0	1.6	5.8
United Kingdom	5.4	13.6	1.6
USA	0.4	2.5	8.7
Total (incl. others)	370.8	332.9	207.1

* Comprising Botswana, Lesotho, Namibia, South Africa and Swaziland.

Source: UN, *International Trade Statistics Yearbook.*

Transport

RAILWAYS
(traffic)

	1998	1999	2000
Passengers carried ('000) . . .	699.8	n.a.	n.a.
Passenger-km (million) . . .	112.0	82.2	156.6
Freight ton-km (million) . . .	218.7	269.0	153.2

Source: mainly IMF, *Benin: Statistical Appendix* (August 2002).

ROAD TRAFFIC
(motor vehicles in use)

	1994	1995	1996
Passenger cars	26,507	30,346	37,772
Buses and coaches	353	405	504
Lorries and vans	5,301	6,069	7,554
Road tractors	2,192	2,404	2,620
Motorcycles and mopeds . . .	220,800	235,400	250,000

Source: IRF, *World Road Statistics.*

Passenger cars ('000 in use): 7.3 in 1997; 7.3 in 1998 (Source: UN, *Statistical Yearbook*).

Commercial vehicles ('000 in use): 6.0 in 1997; 6.2 in 1998 (Source: UN, *Statistical Yearbook*).

SHIPPING

Merchant Fleet
(registered at 31 December)

	1999	2000	2001
Number of vessels	7	7	6
Total displacement ('000 grt) . .	1.1	1.1	1.0

Source: Lloyd's Register-Fairplay, *World Fleet Statistics.*

International Sea-borne Freight Traffic
(at Cotonou, including goods in transit, '000 metric tons)

	1999	2000	2001
Goods loaded	360.4	398.7	384.1
Goods in transit.	5.3	4.9	6.5
Goods unloaded	2,236.2	2,674.8	2,941.5
Goods in transit.	507.2	839.6	984.9

Source: IMF, *Benin: Statistical Appendix* (August 2002).

CIVIL AVIATION
(traffic on scheduled services)*

	1997	1998	1999
Kilometres flown (million) . . .	3	3	3
Passengers carried ('000) . . .	86	91	84
Passenger-km (million)	242	258	235
Total ton-km (million)	38	38	36

* Including an apportionment of the traffic of Air Afrique.

Source: UN, *Statistical Yearbook.*

Tourism

	1996	1997	1998
Tourist arrivals ('000)	143	148	152
Tourism receipts (US $ million). .	29	31	33

Source: World Tourism Organization.

Communications Media

	1999	2000	2001
Television receivers ('000 in use)	263	272	n.a.
Telephones ('000 main lines in use)	43.7	51.6	59.3
Mobile cellular telephones ('000 subscribers)	7.3	55.5	125.0
Personal computers ('000 in use)	9	10	11
Internet users ('000)	10	15	25

Facsimile machines (number in use, 1996): 1,064.

Source: International Telecommunication Union.

Radio receivers ('000 in use, 1999): 2,661 (Source: UNESCO, *Statistical Yearbook*).

Daily newspapers (1996): 1 (average circulation 12,000 copies) (Source: UNESCO, *Statistical Yearbook*).

Non-daily newspapers (1996): 4 (average circulation 66,000 copies) (Source: UNESCO, *Statistical Yearbook*).

Periodicals (1999): 106 (average circulation 110,000 copies) (Source: UNESCO, *Statistical Yearbook*).

Book production (first editions, 1994): 84 titles (42,000 copies) (Source: UNESCO, *Statistical Yearbook*).

Education

(1996/97)

	Institutions	Teachers	Students Males	Students Females	Students Total
Pre-primary	283*	622	9,106	8,335	17,441
Primary†	4,178	17,710	557,802	374,622	932,424
Secondary					
General	145‡	5,352	102,011	44,124	146,135
Vocational‡	14	283	3,553	1,320	4,873
Higher	9	962§	11,398¶	2,657¶	14,055¶

* 1995/96.
† 1999/2000.
‡ 1993/94.
§ 1995.
¶ 1996.

Source: mainly UNESCO, *Statistical Yearbook*.

1998/99: *Secondary:* 174,450 students; *Higher:* 16,304 students.

Adult literacy rate (UNESCO estimates): 37.4% (males 52.1%; females 23.6%) in 2000 (Source: UN Development Programme, *Human Development Report*).

Directory

The Constitution

A new Constitution was approved in a national referendum on 2 December 1990. Its main provisions are summarized below:

PREAMBLE

The Beninois People reaffirm their opposition to any political regime founded on arbitrariness, dictatorship, injustice and corruption, reassert their attachment to the principles of democracy and human rights, as defined in the United Nations Charter, the Universal Declaration of Human Rights and the African Charter of the Rights of Man and Peoples, proclaim their attachment to the cause of African Unity and solemnly adopt this new Constitution as the supreme Law of the State.

I. THE STATE AND SOVEREIGNTY

Articles 1–6: The State of Benin is an independent, sovereign, secular, democratic Republic. The capital is Porto-Novo. The official language is French. The principle of the Republic is 'government of the People, by the People and for the People'. National sovereignty belongs to the People and is exercised through elected representatives and by referendums. Political parties operate freely, as determined by the Charter of Political Parties, and must respect the principles of national sovereignty, democracy, territorial integrity and the secular basis of the State. Suffrage is universal, equal and secret.

II. RIGHTS AND DUTIES OF THE INDIVIDUAL

Articles 7–40: The State is obliged to respect and protect the sacred and inviolable rights of the individual, and ensures equal access to health, education, culture, information, vocational training and employment. Primary education is compulsory. The State progressively assures the provision of free public education. Private schools are permitted. Torture and the use of cruel or degrading punishment are prohibited, and detention is subject to strict limitations. All persons have the right to property ownership, to freedom of conscience and expression. The State guarantees the freedoms of movement and association. All are equal before the law. The State recognizes the right to strike. Military service is compulsory.

III. THE EXECUTIVE

Articles 41–78: The President of the Republic is the Head of State. Candidates for the presidency must be of Beninois nationality by birth or have been naturalized for at least 10 years, and must be aged 40–70 years. The President is elected for a mandate of five years, renewable only once, by an absolute majority of votes cast. If no candidate receives an absolute majority, a second round is to be held between the two highest-placed candidates. The Constitutional Court oversees the regularity of voting and announces the results. No President may serve more than two mandates.

The President of the Republic holds executive power. Following consultation with the Bureau of the Assemblée nationale, he names the members of the Government, who may not hold any parliamentary mandate. The President of the Republic chairs the Council of Ministers and has various defined powers of appointment.

The President of the Republic promulgates laws adopted by the Assemblée nationale, and may demand the resubmission of a law to the Assemblée nationale prior to its promulgation. In the event that the President of the Republic fails to promulgate a law, the Constitutional Court may, in certain circumstances, declare the law as binding.

After consultation with the President of the Assemblée nationale and the President of the Constitutional Court, the President of the Republic may call a referendum on matters pertaining to human rights, sub-regional or regional integration or the organization of public powers. The President of the Republic is the Supreme Chief of the Armed Forces.

The President of the Republic may delegate certain specified powers to ministers. The President of the Republic or any member of his Government may be called to account by the Assemblée nationale.

IV. THE LEGISLATURE

i. The Assemblée Nationale

Articles 79–93: Parliament exercises legislative power and controls the activities of the Government. Deputies of the Assemblée nationale, who must be civilians, are elected by direct universal suffrage for four years, and may be re-elected. The Assemblée nationale elects its President and a Bureau. Deputies enjoy various conditions of immunity from prosecution.

ii. Relations between the Assemblée Nationale and the Government

Articles 94–113: Members of the Government may attend sessions of the Assemblée nationale. Laws are approved by a simple majority, although organic laws require an absolute majority and approval by the Constitutional Court. The Assemblée nationale authorizes any declaration of war. States of siege and of emergency are declared in the Council of Ministers, although the Assemblée nationale must approve the extension of any such state beyond 15 days.

Deputies may, by a three-quarters' majority, decide to submit any question to referendum. If the Assemblée nationale has not approved a balanced budget by 31 December of any year, the measures foreseen by the finance law may be implemented by ordinance.

V. THE CONSTITUTIONAL COURT

Articles 114–124: The Constitutional Court is composed of seven members, of which four are named by the Bureau of the Assemblée nationale and three by the President of the Republic, each for a mandate of five years, renewable only once. The President of the Constitutional Court is elected by his peers for a period of five years and is a senior magistrate or lawyer. The decisions of the Constitutional Court are not subject to appeal.

VI. THE JUDICIARY

Articles 125–130: The judiciary is independent of the legislature and of the executive. It consists of the Supreme Court, and other courts and tribunals created in accordance with the Constitution. Judges may not be removed from office. The President of the Republic appoints magistrates and is the guarantor of the independence of the judiciary, assisted by the Higher Council of Magistrates, the composition, attributes, organization and function of which are fixed by an organic law.

i. The Supreme Court

Articles 131–134: The Supreme Court is the highest jurisdiction of the State in administrative and judicial matters, and with regard to the accounts of the State and to local elections. The decisions of the Court are not subject to appeal. The President of the Supreme Court is appointed for five years by the President of the Republic. The President of the Supreme Court may not be removed from office during his mandate, which is renewable only once.

ii. The High Court of Justice

Articles 135–138: The High Court of Justice comprises the members of the Constitutional Court (other than its President), six deputies of the Assemblée nationale and the President of the Supreme Court. The High Court of Justice elects a President from among its members and is competent to try the President of the Republic and members of the Government in cases of high treason, crimes committed during the exercise of their functions and plots against state security. In the event of an accusation of high treason or of contempt of the Assemblée nationale, and in certain other cases, the President of the Republic and members of the Government are to be suspended from their functions. In the case of being found guilty of such charges, they are dismissed from their responsibilities.

VII. THE ECONOMIC AND SOCIAL COUNCIL

Articles 139–141: The Economic and Social Council advises on proposed laws, ordinances or decrees that are submitted to it. Proposed laws of an economic or social nature must be submitted to the Council.

VIII. THE HIGH AUTHORITY FOR BROADCASTING AND COMMUNICATION

Articles 142–143: The High Authority for Broadcasting and Communication assures the freedom of the press and all other means of mass communication. It oversees the equitable access of political parties, associations and citizens to the official means of communication and information.

IX. INTERNATIONAL TREATIES AND ACCORDS

Articles 144–149: The President of the Republic negotiates and ratifies international treaties and accords. Peace treaties, those relating to international organization or territorial changes and to certain other matters must be ratified by law.

X. LOCAL AUTHORITIES

Articles 150–153: The local authorities of the Republic are created by law and are freely administered by elected councils. Their development is overseen by the State.

XI. ON REVISION

Articles 154–156: The initiative for the revision of the Constitution belongs jointly to the President of the Republic, after a decision has been taken in the Council of Ministers, and to the Assemblée nationale, given a majority vote of three-quarters of its members. A revision requires approval by referendum, unless it is supported by a majority of four-fifths of the members of the Assemblée nationale. The republican and secular basis of the State may not be the subject of any revision.

XII. TRANSITIONAL AND FINAL DISPOSITIONS

Articles 157–160: This new Constitution must be promulgated within eight days of its adoption by referendum. The President of the Republic must assume office and the Assemblée nationale convene by 1 April 1991. The Haut Conseil de la République and the transitional Government will continue to exercise their functions until the installation of the new institutions.

The Government

HEAD OF STATE

President: Gen. (retd) Mathieu Kérékou (took office 4 April 1996; re-elected 22 March 2001).

COUNCIL OF MINISTERS
(April 2003)

President: Gen. (retd) Mathieu Kérékou.

Minister of State, responsible for the Co-ordination of Government Action, Future Planning and Development: (vacant).

Minister of State, responsible for National Defence: Pierre Osho.

Minister of Finance and the Economy: Grégoire Laourou.

Minister of Foreign Affairs and African Integration: (vacant).

Minister of Mining, Energy and Water Resources: (vacant).

Minister of Communication and the Promotion of Information Technology: Gaston Zossou.

Minister of Culture, Handicrafts and Tourism: Amos Elegbe.

Minister of Primary and Secondary Education: Jean Bio Tchabi Orou.

Minister of Technical Education and Professional Training: Dominique Codjo K. Sohounhloue.

Minister of Higher Education and Scientific Research: Dorothé Cossi Sossa.

Minister of Youth, Sport and Leisure: (vacant).

Minister of Industry, Trade and the Promotion of Employment: (vacant).

Minister of the Family, Social Protection and Solidarity: Claire Ayémona Hougan.

Minister of the Environment, Housing and Town Planning: Luc-Marie Constant Gnacadja.

Minister of Public Works and Transport: Joseph Sourou Attin.

Minister of Public Health: Yvette Céline Seignon Kandissounon.

Minister of the Interior, Security and Decentralization: (vacant).

Minister of the Civil Service, Labour and Administrative Reform: Ousmane Batoko.

Minister of Justice, Legislation and Human Rights: Joseph Gnonlonfoun.

Minister of Agriculture, Stockbreeding and Fishing: (vacant).

Minister, responsible for Relations with the Institutions, Civil Society and Benin Nationals Abroad: (vacant).

MINISTRIES

Office of the President: BP 1288, Cotonou; tel. 30-00-90; fax 30-06-36; internet www.gouv.bj.

Ministry of Agriculture, Stockbreeding and Fishing: 03 BP 2900, Cotonou; tel. 30-40-10; fax 30-03-26; e-mail sg@agriculture.gouv.bj; internet www.agriculture.gouv.bj.

Ministry of the Civil Service, Labour and Administrative Reform: BP 907, Cotonou; tel. 31-26-18; fax 31-06-29; e-mail mfptra@gouv.bj.

Ministry of Communication and the Promotion of Information Technology: BP 120, Cotonou; tel. 31-22-27; fax 31-59-31; e-mail sg@communication.gouv.bj.

Ministry for the Co-ordination of Government Action, Future Planning and Development: BP 342, Cotonou; tel. 30-00-30; fax 30-16-60; e-mail sg@planben.gouv.bj; internet www.planben.gouv.bj.

Ministry of Culture, Handicrafts and Tourism: 01 BP 2037, Guincomey, Cotonou; tel. 30-70-10; fax 30-70-31; e-mail sg@tourisme.gouv.bj.

Ministry of the Environment, Housing and Town Planning: 01 BP 3621, Cotonou; tel. 31-55-96; fax 31-50-81; e-mail sg@environnement.gouv.bj; internet www.environnement.gouv.bj.

Ministry of the Family, Social Protection and Solidarity: 01 BP 2802, Cotonou; tel. 31-67-08; fax 31-64-62; e-mail mfpss@gouv.bj.

Ministry of Finance and the Economy: BP 302, Cotonou; tel. 30-02-81; fax 31-18-51; e-mail sg@finance.gouv.bj.

Ministry of Foreign Affairs and African Integration: Zone Résidentielle, route de l'Aéroport, BP 318, Cotonou; tel. 30-04-00; fax

30-19-64; e-mail sg@etranger.gouv.bj; internet www.etranger.gouv
.bj.

Ministry of Higher Education and Scientific Research: BP
348, Cotonou; tel. 30-06-81; fax 30-68-20; e-mail sg@recherche.gouv
.bj.

**Ministry of Industry, Trade and the Promotion of Employ-
ment:** BP 363, Cotonou; tel. 30-76-46; fax 30-30-24; e-mail micpe@
gouv.bj.

Ministry of the Interior, Security and Decentralization: BP
925, Cotonou; tel. 30-11-06; fax 30-01-59; e-mail misd@gouv.bj.

Ministry of Justice, Legislation and Human Rights: BP 967,
Cotonou; tel. 31-31-46; fax 31-34-48; e-mail mjldh@gouv.bj.

Ministry of Mining, Energy and Water Resources: 04 BP 1412,
Cotonou; tel. 31-29-07; fax 31-35-46; e-mail mmeh@gouv.bj.

Ministry of National Defence: BP 2493, Cotonou; tel. 30-08-90;
fax 30-18-21; e-mail sg@defense.gouv.bj.

Ministry of Primary and Secondary Education: 01 BP 10,
Cotonou; tel. 21-52-23; fax 21-50-11; e-mail sg@enseignement.gouv
.bj.

Ministry of Public Health: Immeuble ex–MCAT, 01 BP 2802,
Cotonou; tel. 33-21-63; fax 33-04-64; e-mail msp@gouv.bj; internet
www.sante.gouv.bj.

Ministry of Public Works and Transport: BP 351, Cotonou; tel.
31-46-33; fax 31-06-17; e-mail mtpt@gouv.bj.

**Ministry of Relations with the Institutions, Civil Society and
Benin Nationals Abroad:** 01 BP 406, Cotonou; tel. 30-60-93; fax
30-78-94; e-mail sg@exterieur.gouv.bj; internet www.exterieur.gouv
.bj.

Ministry of Technical Education and Professional Training:
BP 348, Cotonou; tel. 30-56-15; e-mail sg@formation.gouv.bj.

Ministry of Youth, Sport and Leisure: 03 BP 2103, Cotonou; tel.
30-36-14; fax 30-21-36; e-mail mjsl@gouv.bj.

President and Legislature

PRESIDENT

Presidential Election, First Ballot, 4 March 2001

Candidate	Votes	% of votes
Mathieu Kérékou (Ind.)	1,127,200	45.42
Nicéphore Soglo (RB)	672,927	27.12
Adrien Houngbédji (PRD)	313,186	12.62
Bruno Amoussou (PSD)*	213,136	8.59
Others	155,080	6.25
Total	2,481,529	100.00

* Parti social démocrate, which was absorbed into the UBF in late
2002.

Second Ballot, 22 March 2001*

Candidate	Votes	% of votes
Mathieu Kérékou	1,286,465	84.06
Bruno Amoussou	244,032	15.94
Total	1,530,497	100.00

* Following the withdrawals of Nicéphore Soglo and Adrien Houngbédji, the second-round ballot took place, in accordance with the
Constitution, between Bruno Amoussou and Mathieu Kérékou.

ASSEMBLÉE NATIONALE

Assemblée nationale: BP 371, Porto-Novo; tel. 21-22-19; fax 21-51-
61; e-mail assemblee.benin@syfed.bj.refer.org.

President: ANTOINE IDJI KOLAWOLÉ.

Elections, 30 March 2003

Party	Seats
Union pour le Bénin du futur (UBF)	31
La renaissance du Bénin (RB)	15
Parti du renouveau démocratique (PRD)	11
Mouvement africain pour la démocratie et le progrès (MADEP)	9
Force clé	5
Alliance étoile	3
Alliance MDC-PS-CPP	2
La nouvelle alliance (LNA)	2
Alliance impulsion pour le progrès et la démocratie (Alliance IPD)	2
Alliance des forces du progrès (AFP)	1
Rassemblement pour la démocratie et le panafricanisme (RDP)	1
Mouvement pour le développement et la solidarité (MDS —Alo de Alome)	1
Total	83

Advisory Council

Economic and Social Council (CES): ave Jean-Paul II, 08 BP
679, Cotonou; tel. 30-03-99; fax 30-03-13; e-mail dasoul@cma.inbox
.as; internet www.ces.gouv.bj; f. 1994; 30 mems,representing the
executive, legislature and 'all sections of the nation'; reviews all
legislation relating to economic and social affairs; competent to
advise on proposed economic and social legislation, as well as to
recommend economic and social reforms; Pres. RAPHIOU TOUKOUROU.

Political Organizations

The registration of political parties commenced in August 1990. In
mid-2002 there were more than 160 registered parties. The following
parties and alliances gained representation in the legislative elections of March 2003:

Alliance étoile: f. 2002; opposes Govt of Pres. Kérékou; Leader
SACCA LAFIA.

    Union pour la démocratie et la solidarité nationale (UDS):
BP 1761, Cotonou; tel. 31-38-69; Pres. SACCA LAFIA.

    Les verts du Bénin—Parti ecologiste du Bénin: 06 BP 1336,
Cotonou; tel. and fax 35-19-47; e-mail greens_benin@yahoo.fr;
internet lesvertsdubenin.be.tf; Pres. TOUSSAINT HINVI; Sec. PIERRE
AHOUANOZIN.

Alliance des forces du progrès (AFP): Cotonou; supports Pres.
Kérékou; Leader VALENTIN ADITI HOUDÉ.

**Alliance impulsion pour le progrès et la démocratie (Alliance
IPD):** 04 BP 0812, Cotonou; tel. 33-11-45; f. 1999; supports Govt of
Pres. Kérékou; Leaders BERTIN BORNA, THÉOPHILE NATA.

Alliance MDC-PS-CPP: Cotonou; Leader DAMIEN ZINSOU MODÉRAN
ALAHASSA.

    Congrès du peuple pour le progrès (CPP): quartier Houéyiho,
villa 061, cité BCEAO, Cotonou; Leader SÉDÉGNON ADANDE-KINTI.

    Mouvement pour le développement par la culture (MDC):
Cotonou; Pres. CODJO ACHODÉ.

    Parti du salut (PS): 06 BP 11, Cotonou; tel. 36-02-56; f. 1994;
Leader DAMIEN MODÉRAN ZINSOU ALAHASSA.

Force clé: carré 315, Scoa Gbéto, 01 BP 1435, Cotonou; tel. 35-09-
36; f. 2003 on basis of Mouvement pour une alternative du peuple;
supports Pres. Kérékou; Leader LAZARE SÈHOUÉTO.

**Mouvement africain pour la démocratie et le progrès
(MADEP):** Cotonou; tel. 31-31-22; f. 1997; supports Pres. Kérékou;
Leader SÉFOU L. FAGBOHOUN.

**Mouvement pour le développement et la solidarité (MDS—
Alo de Alome):** Cotonou; Leader SACCA MOUSSÉDIKOU FIKARA.

La Nouvelle Alliance (LNA): Cotonou; opposes Govt of Pres.
Kérékou; Leader SOULÉ DANKORO.

    Union pour le progrès et la démocratie (UPD—Gamèsu):
Cotonou; f. 2002 by mems of fmr Parti social démocrate; Pres.
JEAN-CLAUDE HOUNKPONOU.

Parti du renouveau démocratique (PRD): BP 281, Cotonou; tel.
33-94-88; fax 33-94-89; f. 1990; Leader ADRIEN HOUNGBÉDJI.

**Rassemblement pour la démocratie et le panafricanisme
(RDP):** 03 BP 4073, Cotonou; tel. 32-02-83; f. 1995; Leaders DOMI-
NIQUE O. HOUNGNINOU, GILLES AUGUSTE MINONTIN.

La renaissance du Bénin (RB): BP 2205, Cotonou; tel. 31-40-89; f. 1992; Hon. Pres. Nicéphore Soglo; the chairmanship of the party was disputed between Nathaniel Bah and Rosine Vieyra Soglo in early 2003; Nat. Exec. Sec. Candide Azannaï.

Union pour le Bénin du futur (UBF): 04 BP 0772, Cotonou; tel. 33-12-23; e-mail amoussou@avu.org; f. 2002 by supporters of Pres. Kérékou; Co-ordinator Bruno Amoussou.

Diplomatic Representation

EMBASSIES IN BENIN

China, People's Republic: 2 route de l'Aéroport, 01 BP 196, Cotonou; tel. 30-07-65; fax 30-08-41; e-mail prcbenin@serv.eit.bj; Ambassador Wang Xinshi.

Congo, Democratic Republic: Carré 221, Ayélawadjè, Cotonou; tel. 30-00-01.

Cuba: ave de la Marina, face Hôtel du Port, 01 BP 948, Cotonou; tel. 31-52-97; fax 31-65-91; e-mail ecubabtn@leland.bj; Ambassador Gabriel Tiel Capote.

Denmark: Carré 08, Les Cocotiers, 04 BP 1223, Cotonou; tel. 30-38-62; fax 30-38-60; e-mail cooamb@cooamb.um.dk; Chargé d'affaires a.i. Johnny Flentø.

Egypt: Carré 26, route de l'Aéroport, BP 1215, Cotonou; tel. 30-08-42; fax 30-14-25; Ambassador Amina Gomaa.

France: ave Jean-Paul II, BP 966, Cotonou; tel. 30-02-25; fax 30-15-47; e-mail ambafrance.cotonou@diplomatie.fr; internet www.ambafrance-bj.org; Ambassador François Mimin.

Germany: 7 ave Jean-Paul II, BP 504, Cotonou; tel. 31-29-67; fax 31-29-62; Ambassador Hans-Burkhard Sauerteig.

Ghana: route de l'Aéroport, Lot F, Les Cocotiers, BP 488, Cotonou; tel. 30-07-46; fax 30-03-45; e-mail ghaemb02@leland.bj; Ambassador Timothy E. K. Amesimeku.

Holy See: blvd de France, quartier Awhouanléko/Djoméhountin, Zone des Ambassades, Cotonou; tel. 30-03-57; fax 30-03-10; Apostolic Nuncio Pierre Nguyên Van Tot (Titular Bishop of Rusticiana).

Libya: Carré 36, Cotonou; tel. 30-04-52; fax 30-03-01; Ambassador Toufik Ashour Adam.

Netherlands: ave Jean-Paul II, 08 BP 0783, Cotonou; tel. 30-41-52; fax 30-41-50; e-mail cot@minbuza.nl; Chargé d'affaires Saskia N. Bakker.

Niger: derrière l'Hôtel de la Plage, BP 352, Cotonou; tel. 31-56-65; Ambassador Mahaman Bachir Zadaa.

Nigeria: ave de France, Marina, BP 2019, Cotonou; tel. 30-11-42; fax 30–18–79; Ambassador F. O. Oladeji.

Russia: BP 2013, Cotonou; tel. 31-28-34; fax 31-28-35; e-mail benamrus@leland.bj; Ambassador Yurii Tchepik.

USA: Carré 125, rue Caporal Anani Bernard, 01 BP 2012, Cotonou; tel. 30-06-50; fax 30-06-70; e-mail amemb.coo@intnet.bj; internet usembassy.state.gov/benin; Ambassador Wayne Neill (designate).

Judicial System

The Constitution of December 1990 establishes the judiciary as an organ of state whose authority acts as a counterbalance to that of the executive and of the legislature.

Constitutional Court: BP 2050, Cotonou; tel. 31-16-10; fax 32-37-12; e-mail constitut_sg@netcourrier.com; f. 1990; inaug. 1993; seven mems; four appointed by the Assemblée nationale, three by the President of the Republic; exercises highest jurisdiction in constitutional affairs; determines the constitutionality of legislation, oversees and proclaims results of national elections and referendums, responsible for protection of individual and public rights and obligations, charged with regulating functions of organs of state and authorities; Pres. Conceptia L.-Denis-Ouinsou; Sec.-Gen. Marcelline-Claire Gbeha Afouda.

High Court of Justice: Cotonou; comprises the six members of the Constitutional Court (other than its President), six deputies of the Assemblée nationale and the First President of the Supreme Court; competent to try the President of the Republic and members of the Government in cases of high treason, crimes committed in, or at the time of, the exercise of their functions, and of plotting against state security; Pres. Maurice Ahanhanzo Glele.

Supreme Court: Ganhi, 01 BP 330, Cotonou; tel. 31-50-47; fax 31-54-92; e-mail info@coursupreme.gouv.bj; internet www.bj.refer.org/cop/cs; f. 1960; highest juridical authority in administrative and judicial affairs and in matters of public accounts; competent in disputes relating to local elections; advises the executive on jurisdiction and administrative affairs; comprises a First President (appointed by the President of the Republic, after consultation with the President of the Assemblée nationale, senior magistrates and jurists), presidents of the component chambers, a public prosecutor, four assistant procurators-fiscal, counsellors and clerks; First Pres. Me Saliou Aboudou; Attorney-Gen. Nestor Dako; Pres. of the Judicial Chamber Edwige Boussari; Pres. of the Administrative Chamber G. Gregoire Alaye; Pres. of the Chamber of Accounts Djimenou Firmin; Chief Clerk Françoise Quenum.

Religion

At the time of the 1992 census it was estimated that some 35% of the population held animist beliefs; another 35% were Christians (mainly Roman Catholics) and the remainder were mostly Muslims. Religious and spiritual cults, which were discouraged under Kérékou's military regime, re-emerged as a prominent force in Beninois society during the 1990s.

CHRISTIANITY

The Roman Catholic Church

Benin comprises two archdioceses and eight dioceses. At 31 December 2000 there were an estimated 1.5m. Roman Catholics (about 23.1% of the population), mainly in the south of the country.

Bishops' Conference

Conférence Episcopale du Bénin, Archevêché, 01 BP 491, Cotonou; tel. 30-66-48; fax 30-07-07; e-mail cepiscob@intnet.bj.

Pres. Most Rev. Nestor Assogba (Archbishop of Cotonou).

Archbishop of Cotonou: Most Rev. Nestor Assogba, Archevêché, 01 BP 491, Cotonou; fax 30-07-07; e-mail cotonou@cef.fr.

Archbishop of Parakou: Most Rev. Fidèle Agbatchi, Archevêché, BP 75, Parakou; tel. 61-02-54; fax 61-01-99; e-mail archeveche@borgou.net.

Protestant Church

There are an estimated 257 Protestant mission centres in Benin.

Eglise Protestante Méthodiste en République du Bénin: 54 ave Mgr Steinmetz, BP 34, Cotonou; tel. 31-11-42; fax 31-25-20; f. 1843; Pres. Rev. Dr Moïse Sagbohan; Sec. Rev. Mathieu D. Olodo; 95,827 mems (1996).

VODOUN

The origins of the traditional *vodoun* religion can be traced to the 14th century. Its influence is particularly strong in Latin America and the Caribbean, owing to the shipment of slaves from the West African region to the Americas in the 18th and 19th centuries.

Communauté Nationale du Culte Vodoun (CNCV): Ouidah; Pres. Adan Yossi Guédêhoungué.

ISLAM

Union Islamique du Bénin: Cotonou.

BAHÁ'Í FAITH

National Spiritual Assembly: BP 1252, Cotonou; e-mail ntirandaz@aol.com.

The Press

In early 2001 there were 18 daily newspapers and 37 periodicals published in Benin.

DAILIES

L'Araignée: Immeuble du Projet VINOTIC, rue de la Francophonie, 01 BP 1357, Cotonou; tel. 30-12-30; e-mail relation@laraignee.org; internet www.laraignee.org; online only; politics, public affairs, culture.

L'Aurore: face Clinique Boni, 05 BP 464, Cotonou; tel. 33-70-43; e-mail laurorebenin1@yahoo.fr; internet www.webfirstplus.com/laurore; Dir Patrick Adjamonsi; circ. 1,500.

Bénin-Presse Info: 01 BP 72, Cotonou; tel. 31-26-55; bulletin of Agence Bénin-Presse; Dir Yaovi Hounkponou; Editor-in-Chief Josèphe Vodounon.

Les Echos du Jour: Carré 136, Sodjatimè, 08 BP 718, Cotonou; tel. 33-18-33; fax 33-17-27; e-mail echos@netcourrier.com; independent; Dir Maurice Chabi; Editor-in-Chief Michel Tchanou; circ. 3,000.

Fraternité: Cadjèhoun, Von Forum, 05 BP 907, Cotonou; tel. 30-42-06; fax 30-73-44; e-mail fraternite@altern.org; internet www.webfirstplus.com/fraternite; Dir-Gen. MALICK SEIBOU GOMINA; Editor-in-Chief BRICE U. HOUSSOU.

L'Informateur: Etoile Rouge, Bâtiment Radio Star, Carré 1072c, 01 BP 5421, Cotonou; tel. and fax 32-66-39; f. 2001; Dir CLÉMENT ADÉCHIAN; Editor-in-Chief BRICE GUÈDÈ.

Le Matin: Carré 54, Tokpa Hoho, 06 BP 2217, Cotonou; tel. 31-10-80; fax 33-42-62; e-mail lematinonline@moncourrier.com; internet www.lematin.bj; f. 1994; independent; Dir MOÏSE DATO; Editorial Dir PIERRE MATCHOUDO.

Le Matinal: Carré 153–154, Atinkanmey, 06 BP 1989, Cotonou; tel. 31-49-20; fax 31-49-19; e-mail lematinal@h2com.com; internet nt7.h2com.com; Dir-Gen. CHARLES TOKO; Editor-in-Chief NAPOLÉON MAFORIKAN.

La Nation: Cadjèhoun, 01 BP 1210, Cotonou; tel. 30-02-99; fax 30-34-63; e-mail la.nation@elodia.intnet.bj; f. 1990; official newspaper; Dir INNOCENT M. ADJAHO; Editor-in-Chief ALFRED AHOUNOU; circ. 4,000.

L'Oeil du Peuple: Carré 743, rue PTT, Gbégamey, 01 BP 5538, Cotonou; tel. 30-22-07; e-mail loeildupeuple@yahoo.fr; Dir CELESTIN ABISSI; Editor-in-Chief PAUL AGBOYIDOU.

Le Point au Quotidien: 332 rue du Renouveau, 05 BP 934, Cotonou; tel. 32-50-55; fax 32-25-31; e-mail lepointq@leland.bj; independent; Dir VINCENT FOLY; Editor-in-Chief FERNANDO HESSOU; circ. 2,000.

Le Républicain: Carré 630, Tanto, 05 BP 1230, Cotonou; tel. 33-83-04; fax 33-98-03; e-mail lerepublicain@lerepublicain.org; internet www.lerepublicain.org; independent; Editor-in-Chief ISIDORE ZINSOU.

Le Soleil: Carré 850, Sikècodji, 02 BP 8187, Cotonou; tel. 32-69-96; Dir MAURILLE GNANSOUNOU; Editor-in-Chief MATINI MARCOS.

PERIODICALS

Afrique Identité: ave du Canada, Lot 1069 T, 02 BP 1215, Cotonou; Dir ANGELO AHOUANMAGMA; Editorial Dir SERGE AUGUSTE LOKO.

Agri-Culture: 03 BP 0380, Cotonou; tel. and fax 36-05-46; e-mail agriculture@uva.org; f. 1999; monthly; Editor-in-Chief JOACHIM SAÏZONOU; circ. 1,000.

L'Autre Gazette: 02 BP 1537, Cotonou; tel. 32-59-97; e-mail collegi@beninweb.org; Editor-in-Chief WILFRIED AYIBATIN.

L'Avenir: Carré 911, 02 BP 8134, Cotonou; tel. 32-21-23; fortnightly; political analysis; Dir CLAUDE FIRMIN GANGBE.

Bénin Hebdo: 03 BP 2332, Cotonou; tel. 92-24-09; Dir SANGARÉ NOUHOUN; Editor-in-Chief DENIS CHAUMEREUIL.

Bénin Info: 06 BP 590, Cotonou; tel. 32-52-64; fortnightly; Dir ROMAIN TOI.

Bénin Santé: 06 BP 1905, Cotonou; tel. 33-26-38; fax 33-18-23; fortnightly.

Le Canard du Golfe: Carré 240, Midombo, Akpakpa, 06 BP 59, Cotonou; tel. 32-72-33; e-mail lecanardugolfe@yahoo.fr; satirical; weekly; Dir. F. L. TINGBO; Editor-in-Chief EMMANUEL SOTIKON.

Le Continental: BP 4419, Cotonou; Editor-in-Chief ARNAULD HOUNDETE.

La Croix du Bénin: Centre Paul VI, 01 BP 105, Cotonou; tel. and fax 32-12-07; e-mail lacroixbenin@excite.fr; f. 1946; fortnightly; Roman Catholic; Dir BARTHÉLÉMY ASSOGBA CAKPO.

La Dernière Barque—Creuset de la Jeunesse Chrétienne Céleste: 06 BP 446, Cotonou; tel. 33-04-07; fax 33-42-14.

Emotion: 06 BP 1404, Cotonou; tel. 40-17-07; fax 32-50-83; e-mail e.houannou@caramail.com; f. 1998; monthly; women's interest; Editor-in-Chief ERIC SESSINOU HOUANNOU; circ. 3,000.

L'Enjeu: 04 BP 0454, Cotonou; tel. 35-19-93; Editor-in-Chief MATHURIN ASSOGBA.

La Flamme: 01 BP 2582, Cotonou; tel. 30-69-03; Editor-in-Chief PHILIPPE NOUDJENOUME.

La Gazette du Golfe: Immeuble La Gazette du Golfe, Carré 902E Sikècodji, 03 BP 1624, Cotonou; tel. 32-68-44; fax 32-52-26; e-mail gazettedugolfe@serv.eit.bj; f. 1987; weekly; Dir ISMAËL Y. SOUMANOU; Editor MARCUS BONI TEIGA; circ. 18,000 (nat. edn), 5,000 (international edn).

Le Gongonneur: 04 BP 1432, Cotonou; tel. 39-23-74; fax 35-04-22; e-mail dahoun@yahoo.com; Dir MATHIAS C. SOSSOU; Editor-in-Chief EUSTACHE YAOVI HAKPONDE.

Le Heraut: 03 BP 3417, Cotonou; tel. 36-00-64; e-mail heraut@syfed.bj.refer.org; monthly; current affairs; analysis; produced by students at Université nationale du Bénin; Dir GEOFFREY GOUNOU N'GOYE; Editor-in-Chief GABRIEL DIDEH.

Initiatives: 01 BP 2093, Cotonou; tel. 31-44-47; fax 31-59-50; e-mail cepepe@firstnet.bj; 6 a year; journal of the Centre de Promotion et d'Encadrement des Petites et Moyennes Entreprises.

Journal Officiel de la République du Bénin: BP 59, Porto-Novo; tel. 21-39-77; f. 1890; present name adopted 1990; official govt bulletin; fortnightly; Dir AFIZE DÉSIRÉ ADAMO.

Labari: BP 816, Parakou; tel. and fax 61-69-10; f. 1997; weekly; Dir DRAMANE AMI-TOURE; circ. 3,000.

La Lumière de l'Islam: Carré 163, 01 BP 4022, Cotonou; tel. and fax 31-34-59; monthly; Dir MOHAMED BACHIROU SOUMANOU.

Le Magazine de l'Entreprise: BP 850, Cotonou; tel. 30-80-79; fax 30-47-77; e-mail oliviergat@hotmail.com; f. 1999; monthly; business; Dir A. VICTOR FAKÈYÈ.

Nouvel Essor: Carré 497, Jéricho, 06 BP 1182, Cotonou; tel. 32-43-13; monthly; Editor-in-Chief JEAN-BAPTISTE HOUNKONNOU.

Opérateur Économique: ave du Général de Gaulle, 01 BP 31, Cotonou; tel. 31-20-81; fax 31-22-99; monthly; published by Chambre de Commerce et d'Industrie du Bénin; Dir WASSI MOUFTAOU.

Le Perroquet: Carré 478, Bar Tito, 03 BP 880, Cotonou; tel. 32-18-54; e-mail perroquet@uva.org; f. 1995; 2 a month; independent; news and analysis; Dir DAMIEN HOUESSOU; Editor-in-Chief SEPTIME ATCHEKPE; circ. 3,500 (2002).

Le Piment: Carré 1965, Zogbo, 07 BP 0665, Cotonou; tel. 30-26-01; fax 31-25-81; 2 a month; independent; Editor-in-Chief JOACHIM GBOYOU.

Le Radical: 03 BP 0408, Cotonou; Dir ALASSANE BAWA.

Le Recadaire: 02 BP 308, Cotonou; tel. 22-60-11; e-mail lerecadaire@yahoo.com; Dir GUTEMBERT HOUNKANRIN.

La Région: Carré 1030, 05 BP 708, Cotonou; Editor-in-Chief ROMAIN CODJO.

La Réplique: BP 1087, Porto-Novo; tel. and fax 21-45-77; Dir EMILE ADECHINA; Editor-in-Chief JERÔME AKLAMAVO.

La Sirène: Carré 357, Sènadé, 01 BP 122, Cotonou; tel. 33-40-17; Dir ETIENNE HOUSSOU.

Le Télégramme: 06 BP 1519, Cotonou; tel. 33-04-18; fortnightly; Editor-in-Chief RENÉ NANA.

Le Temps: Kouhounou, 04 BP 43, Cotonou; tel. 30-55-06; 2 a month; Dir YAYA YOLOU; Editor-in-Chief GUY CONDÉ.

Le Tribune de l'Economie: BP 31, Cotonou; tel. 31-20-81; fax 31-32-99; monthly; Editor-in-Chief MOUFTAOU WASSI.

Press Association

Union des Journalistes de la Presse Privée du Bénin (UJPB): blvd de la République, près Cadmes Plus, 03 BP 383, Cotonou; tel. 32-52-73; e-mail ujpb@h2com.com; internet www.h2com.com/ujpb; f. 1992; assocn of independent journalists; Pres. AGAPIT N. MAFORIKAN.

NEWS AGENCIES

Agence Bénin-Presse (ABP): BP 72, Cotonou; tel. and fax 31-26-55; e-mail abpben@intnet.bj; f. 1961; national news agency; section of the Ministry of Communication and the Promotion of Information Technology; Dir YAOVI R. HOUNKPONOU.

Associated Press (USA) is also represented in Benin.

Publishers

Editions de l'ACACIA: 08 BP 271, Cotonou; tel. and fax 35-04-72; fax 94-66-28; e-mail joachimomega@yahoo.fr; f. 1989; fmrly Editions du Flamboyant; literary fiction, history, popular science; Dir OSCAR DE SOUZA.

Editions des Diasporas: 04 BP 792, Cotonou; e-mail lawin@club-internet.fr; poetry, essays; Dir CAMILLE AMOURO.

Editions Ruisseaux d'Afrique: 04 BP 1154, Cotonou; tel. and fax 94-79-25; e-mail ruisseau@nakayo.leland.bj; f. 1992; children's literature; Dir BÉATRICE GBADO.

Graphitec: 04 BP 825, Cotonou; tel. and fax 30-46-04; e-mail lewado@yahoo.com; internet www.wado.net/graphitec.

Imprimerie Notre Dame: BP 109, Cotonou; tel. 32-12-07; fax 32-11-19; e-mail lacroixbenin@excite.fr; f. 1974; Roman Catholic publications; Dir BARTHÉLÉMY ASSOGBA CAKPO.

Société Tunde: 06 BP 1925, Cotonou; tel. 30-15-68; fax 30-42-86; f. 1997; economics, management; Pres. BABATOUNDÉ RASAKI OLLOFINDJI.

Government Publishing House

Office National d'Imprimerie et de Presse: 01 BP 1210, Cotonou; tel. 30-02-99; fax 30-34-63; f. 1975; Dir-Gen. INNOCENT ADJAHO.

Broadcasting and Communications

TELECOMMUNICATIONS

Office des Postes et des Télécommunications (OPT): 01 BP 5959, Cotonou; tel. 31-20-45; fax 31-38-43; e-mail info@intnet.bj; internet www.opt.bj; f. 1959; state-owned; Dir-Gen. SABI SOUMANOU SANNI.

Bell Benin Communications (BCOM): Cotonou; f. 2002; mobile cellular telephone operator; Chief Exec. ISSA SALIFOU.

Libercom: blvd Saint-Michel, face Hall des Arts et de la Culture, 01 BP 5959, Cotonou; tel. 31-68-01; fax 31-68-00; internet www.test.bj/libercom; f. 2000; mobile cellular telephone operator in Cotonou and Porto-Novo; jt venture between the OPT, Alcatel (France) and Titan Corpn (USA); 23,000 subscribers (2001).

Spacetel Bénin-BéninCell: 01 BP 5293, Cotonou; tel. 31-66-41; internet www.spacetelbenin.com; f. 2000; mobile cellular telephone operator in Cotonou, Porto-Novo and Parakou; affiliate of Spacetel (United Kingdom); 6,000 subscribers (2001).

Telecel Bénin: Cotonou; tel. 31-66-60; internet www.telecel.com; f. 2000; mobile cellular telephone operator in Cotonou, Porto-Novo, Abomey, Lokossa, additional regions of southern Benin and in Parakou; subsidiary of Telecel International (Switzerland); 15,000 subscribers (Jan. 2001).

In July 2000 proposals to divide OPT into separate postal and telecommunications companies were announced; the latter, to be known as Société Béninoise des Télécommunications (SOBÉTEL), was to be privatized in the early 2000s.

BROADCASTING

Since 1997 the HAAC has issued licences to private radio and television stations.

Haute Autorité de l'Audiovisuel et de la Communication (HAAC): 01 BP 3567, Cotonou; tel. 31-17-43; fax 31-17-42; e-mail haac@planben.intnet.bj; f. 1992 as the highest authority for the media; Pres. TIMOTHÉE ADANLIN; Sec.-Gen. HOSPICE NOUDEHOU.

Radio

In early 2002 there were nine commercial radio stations, 17 non-commercial stations and five rural or local stations broadcasting in Benin.

Office de Radiodiffusion et de Télévision du Bénin (ORTB): 01 BP 366, Cotonou; tel. 30-10-96; fax 30-04-48; e-mail ortb@intnet.bj; internet www.ortb.bj; state-owned; radio programmes broadcast from Cotonou and Parakou in French, English and 18 local languages; Dir-Gen. JEAN N'TCHA; Dir of National Radio PELU C. DIOGO; Dir of Television MAMA SOUMAILA.

Atlantic FM: 01 BP 366, Cotonou; tel. 30-30-41; Dir JOSEPH OGOUNCHI.

Radio Cotonou: 01 BP 306, Cotonou; tel. 30-04-81; Dir PELU CHRISTOPHE DIOGO.

Radio Régionale de Parakou: BP 128, Parakou; tel. 61-07-73; Dir DIEUDONNÉ METOZOUNVÉ.

Radio Afrique Espoir: Carré 123, 03 BP 203, Porto-Novo; tel. 21-34-55; fax 21-32-63; e-mail afespoir@intnet.bj; Dir RAMANOU KOUFERIDJI.

Bénin-Culture: BP 21, Association pour l'Institutionnalisation de la Mémoire et de la Pensée Intellectuelle Africaine, BP 21, Porto-Novo; tel. 22-28-83; Dir MAURILLE AGBOKOU.

Radio FM-Ahémé: BP 66, Bopa, Mono; tel. 05-58-18; f. 1997; informative, cultural and civic education broadcasts; Dir AMBROISE COKOU MOUSSOU.

Radio Carrefour: BP 440, Bohicon; tel. 51-16-03; fax 51-16-55; e-mail radiocar@intnet.bj; f. 1999; Dir CHRISTOPHE DAVAKAN.

Golfe FM-Magic Radio: 03 BP 1624, Cotonou; tel. 32-42-08; fax 32-52-26; e-mail golfefm@serv.eit.bj; internet www.eit.bj/golfefm.htm; Dir ISMAËL SOUMANOU.

Radio Immaculée Conception: BP 88, Allada; tel. 37-10-23; operated by the Roman Catholic Church of Benin; broadcasts to Abomey, Allanda, Cotonou, Dassa-Zoume, Djougou and Parakou; Dir Fr ALFONSO BRUNO.

Radio Maranatha: 03 BP 4113, Cotonou; tel. and fax 32-58-82; e-mail radiocepeb@yahoo.fr; operated by the Conseil des Eglises Protestantes Evangéliques du Bénin; Dir Rev. CLOVIS ALFRED KPADE.

Radio Planète: 02 BP 1528, Immeuble Master Soft, Cotonou; tel. 30-30-30; fax 30-24-51; e-mail janvier@planetefm.com; internet www.planetefm.com; Dir JANVIER YAHOUEDEHOU.

Radio Solidarité FM: BP 135, Djougou; tel. 80-11-29; fax 80-15-63; Dir DAOUDA TAKPARA.

La Voix de la Lama: BP 21, Porto-Novo; tel. 31-11-61; Dir SÉRAPHINE DADY.

La Voix de l'Islam: 08 BP 134, Cotonou; tel. 31-11-34; fax 31-51-79; e-mail islamben@leland.bj; operated by the Communauté musulmane de Zongo; Dir El Hadj MAMAN YARO.

Radio Wêkê: 05 BP 436, Cotonou; tel. 21-38-40; fax 21-37-14; e-mail radioweke@bimyns.com; Promoter ISSA BADAROU-SOULÉ.

Benin also receives broadcasts from Africa No. 1, the British Broadcasting Corporation World Service and Radio France International.

Television

ORTB: (see radio); Dir of Television MAMA SOUMAÏLA.

ATVS: BP 7101, Cotonou; tel. 31-43-19; owned by African Television System-Sobiex; Dir JACOB AKINOCHO.

La Cellule 2 (LC2): 05 BP 427, Cotonou; tel. 33-47-49; fax 33-46-75; e-mail lc2@intnet.bj; commenced broadcasts 1997; Dir CHRISTIAN ENOCK LAGNIDÉ.

Telco: 44 ave Delorme, 01 BP 1241, Cotonou; tel. 31-37-72; e-mail telco@serv.eit.bj; internet www.eit.bj/telco.htm; relays five international channels; Dir JOSEPH JÉBARA.

TV+ International: 01 BP 2376, Cotonou; tel. 31-53-54; Dir CLAUDE KARAM.

Finance

(cap. = capital; res = reserves; m. = million; br. = branch; amounts in francs CFA)

BANKING

Central Bank

Banque Centrale des Etats de l'Afrique de l'Ouest (BCEAO): ave Jean-Paul II, BP 325, Cotonou; tel. 31-24-66; fax 31-24-65; e-mail akangni@bceao.int; internet www.bceao.int; HQ in Dakar, Senegal; f. 1962; bank of issue for the mem. states of the Union économique et monétaire ouest-africaine (UEMOA, comprising Benin, Burkina Faso, Côte d'Ivoire, Guinea-Bissau, Mali, Niger, Senegal and Togo); cap. and res 850,500m., total assets 5,157,700m. (Dec. 2001); Gov. CHARLES KONAN BANNY; Dir in Benin IDRISS LYASSOU DAOUDA; br. at Parakou.

Commercial Banks

Bank of Africa—Bénin (BOAB): ave Jean-Paul II, 08 BP 0879, Cotonou; tel. 31-32-28; fax 31-31-17; e-mail boabe.dg@bkofafrica.com; internet www.bkofafrica.net; f. 1990; 35.2% owned by African Financial Holding; cap. 4,200m., res 6,896m., dep. 199,601m. (Dec. 2001); Pres. FRANÇOIS ODJO TANKPINOU; Man. Dir RENÉ FORMEY DE SAINT LOUVENT; 9 brs.

Banque Internationale du Bénin (BIBE): carrefour des Trois Banques, ave Giran, 03 BP 2098, Jéricho, Cotonou; tel. 31-55-49; fax 31-23-65; e-mail bibe@intnet.bj; f. 1989; owned by Nigerian commercial interests; cap. 9,000m., res –400.0m., dep. 47,079m. (Dec. 2001); Pres. Chief Dr RUFUS FOLUSO GIWA; Man. Dir JEAN-PAUL K. AIDDO; 4 brs.

Continental Bank—Bénin: ave Jean-Paul II, carrefour des Trois Banques, 01 BP 2020, Cotonou; tel. 31-24-24; fax 31-51-77; e-mail contibk@intnet.bj; internet www.ad-net.fr/cbb; f. 1995 to assume activities of Crédit Lyonnais Bénin; 25% state-owned; cap. and res 7,250m., total assets 42,195m. (Dec. 1999); Pres. WASSI MOUFTAOU; Man. Dir CLAUDE ACAKPO; 1 br.

Ecobank—Bénin SA: rue Gouverneur Bayol, 01 BP 1280, Cotonou; tel. 31-40-23; fax 31-33-85; e-mail ecobankbj@ecobank.com; internet www.ecobank.com; f. 1989; 84% owned by Ecobank Transnational Inc (operating under the auspices of the Economic Community of West African States); cap. 3,500m., res 3,333m., dep. 105,070m. (Dec. 2001); Pres. GILBERT MEDJE; Gen. Man. CHRISTOPHE JOCKTANE; 7 brs.

Financial Bank Bénin (FBB): Immeuble Adjibi, rue Decoeur, 01 BP 2700, Cotonou; tel. and fax 31-31-02; e-mail financialbank@finadev.rr.nu; f. 1996; 85% owned by Financial BC (Switzerland);

cap. and res 2,440m. (Dec. 1999), total assets 52,479m. (Dec. 2000); Pres. and Man. Dir RÉMY BAYSSET; 8 brs.

Savings Bank

Caisse Nationale d'Epargne: Cadjèhoun, route Inter-Etat Cotonou-Lomé, Cotonou; tel. 30-18-35; fax 31-38-43; state-owned; cap. and res 736m., total assets 15,738m. (Dec. 1997); Pres. MARCELLIN DOSSOU KPANOU; Dir ANDRÉ H. AFFEDJOU.

Credit Institutions

Crédit du Bénin: 08 BP 0936, Cotonou; tel. 31-30-02; fax 31-37-01; Man. Dir GILBERT HOUNKPAIN.

Crédit Promotion Bénin: 03 BP 1672, Cotonou; tel. 31-31-44; fax 31-31-66; wholly owned by private investors; cap. 150m., total assets 409m. (Dec. 1998); Pres. BERNARD ADIKPETO; Man. Dir DÉNIS OBA CHABI.

Equipbail Bénin: blvd Jean-Paul II, 08 BP 0690, Cotonou; tel. 31-11-45; fax 31-31-17; e-mail afg.sec@firstnet.bj; 49% owned by Bank of Africa—Bénin; cap. and res 527m., total assets 2,779m. (Dec. 1999); Pres. PAUL DERREUMAUX; Dir FAUSTIN AMOUSSOU.

Financial Institution

Caisse Autonome d'Amortissement du Bénin: BP 59, Cotonou; tel. 31-47-81; fax 31-53-56; manages state funds; Man. Dir IBRAHIM PEDRO-BONI.

STOCK EXCHANGE

Bourse Régionale des Valeurs Mobilières (BRVM): Antenne Nationale des Bourses du Bénin, Immeuble Chambre de Commerce et d'Industrie du Bénin, ave Charles de Gaulle, 01 BP 2985, Cotonou; tel. 31-21-26; fax 31-20-77; e-mail agnigla@brvm.org; internet www.brvm.org; f. 1998; national branch of BRVM (regional stock exchange based in Abidjan, Côte d'Ivoire, serving the member states of UEMOA); Man. in Benin YVETTE AISSI GNIGLA.

INSURANCE

A&C Benin: Cotonou; all branches; Dir. Gen. JUSTIN HERBERT AGBOTON.

ASA Benin: 01 BP 5508, Cotonou; tel. and fax 30-00-40; fmrly Société Nationale d'Assurance; Pres. EGOULETI MONTETCHO.

Assurances et Réassurance du Golfe de Guinée (ARGG): 04 BP 0851, Cotonou; tel. 30-56-43; fax 30-55-55; non-life insurance and re-insurance; Man. Dir COLETTE POSSET TAGNON.

Gras Savoye Benin: Immeuble Goussanou, rue Colineau, BP 294, Cotonou; tel. 31-24-34; fax 31-25-32; Man. YVES MEHOU-LOKO.

SOBAC: Carré 5, ave Delorme, 01 BP 544, Cotonou; tel. 31-67-35; fax 31-67-34; e-mail sobac@intnet.bj; affiliate of AGF (France).

Société Nationale d'Assurances et de Réassurances (SONAR): BP 2030, Cotonou; tel. 30-16-49; fax 30-09-84; parastatal co; Pres. S. ATTOLOU.

Union Béninoise d'Assurance-Vie: 08 BP 0322, Cotonou; tel. 30-06-90; fax 30-07-69; e-mail uba@firstnet.bj; f. 1994; cap. 400m; 51% owned by Union Africaine Vie (Côte d'Ivoire); Man. Dir VENANCE AMOUSSOUGA.

Trade and Industry

GOVERNMENT AGENCIES

Centre Béninois de la Recherche Scientifique et Technique (CBRST): 03 BP 1665, Cotonou; tel. 32-12-63; fax 32-36-71; e-mail cbrst@bow.intnet.bj; internet www.cbrst.org; f. 1986 to promote scientific and technical research and training; 10 specialized research units.

Centre Béninois du Commerce Extérieur: place du Souvenir, BP 1254, Cotonou; tel. 30-13-20; fax 30-04-36; e-mail cbce@bow.intnet.bj; f. 1988; provides information to export cos.

Centre de Promotion et de l'Artisanat: à côté du Hall des Arts et de la Culture, BP 2651, Cotonou; tel. 30-38-59; fax 30-34-91; e-mail cpa.info@netcourrier.com; f. 1987; Dir FRIEDA HOUESSOU.

Centre de Promotion et d'Encadrement des Petites et Moyennes Entreprises (CEPEPE): face à la Mairie de Xlacondji, BP 2093, Cotonou; tel. 31-44-47; e-mail cepepe@uva.org; f. 1989; promotes business and employment; offers credits and grants to small businesses; undertakes management training and recruitment; publishes bi-monthly journal, *Initiatives*; Dir-Gen. THÉOPHILE CAPO-CHICHI.

Cellule des Opérations de Dénationalisation (COD): 02 BP 8140, Cotonou; tel. 31-59-18; fax 31-23-15; Co-ordinator VICTORIN DOSSOU-SOGNON.

Institut National de Recherches Agricoles du Bénin (INRAB): BP 884, Cotonou; tel. 30-14-51; fax 30-37-70; e-mail inrabdg4@intnet.bj; internet www.bj.refer.org/benin_ct/rec/inrab/inrab.htm; f. 1992; undertakes research into agricultural improvements; publicizes advances in agriculture; Dirs JEAN DÉTONGNON, ANDRÉ KATARY.

Office Béninois de Recherches Géologiques et Minières (OBRGM): Ministère des mines, de l'énergie et de l'hydraulique, 01 BP 249, Cotonou; tel. 31-03-09; fax 31-41-20; e-mail obrgm@planben.intnet.bj; f. 1996 as govt agency responsible for mining policy, exploitation and research; Dir-Gen. ALIOU MORIBA DJIBRIL.

Office National d'Appui à la Sécurité Alimentaire (ONASA): 06 BP 2544, Cotonou; tel. 33-15-02; fax 33-02-93; e-mail onasamdr@intnet.bj; f. 1992; distribution of cereals; state-owned; Pres. IMAROU SALÉ; Dir-Gen. MOUSSA ASSOUMA.

Office National du Bois (ONAB): BP 1238, Cotonou; tel. 33-16-32; fax 33-39-83; e-mail onabdgle@intnet.bj; f. 1983; reorganized and partially privatized in 2002; forest development and management, manufacture and marketing of wood products; transfer of industrial activities to private ownership pending; Man. Dir PASCAL PATINVOH.

DEVELOPMENT ORGANIZATIONS

Agence Française de Développement (AFD): blvd de France, 01 BP 38, Cotonou; tel. 31-35-80; fax 31-20-18; e-mail adfcot@leland.bj; internet www.afd.fr; fmrly Caisse Française de Développement; Dir YVES TERRACOL.

Mission de Coopération et d'Action Culturelle (Mission Française d'Aide et de Coopération): BP 476, Cotonou; tel. 30-08-24; administers bilateral aid from France; Dir BERNARD HADJADJ.

CHAMBER OF COMMERCE

Chambre de Commerce et d'Industrie du Bénin (CCIB): ave du Général de Gaulle, 01 BP 31, Cotonou; tel. 31-20-81; fax 31-32-99; e-mail ccib@bow.intnet.bj; f. 1962; Sec.-Gen. CHAKIROU TIDJANI; brs at Parakou, Abomey and Porto-Novo.

EMPLOYERS' ORGANIZATIONS

Conseil National des Chargeurs du Bénin: 06 BP 2528, Cotonou; tel. 31-59-47; fax 31-59-07; e-mail cncb@intnet.bj; internet www.sdnpben.org.bj/slabtrad/CNCB.htm; f. 1983; represents interests of shippers; Dir IDRISSOU TCHENEGNON.

Conseil National du Patronat du Bénin (CNP–Bénin): 01 BP 1260, Cotonou; tel. 30-74-06; fax 30-83-22; e-mail lucien.glele@intnet.bj; f. 1984 as Organisation Nationale des Employeurs du Bénin; Pres. LUCIEN G. GLÈLÈ.

Fondation de l'Entrepreneurship du Bénin (FEB): place du Québec, 08 BP 1155, Cotonou; tel. 31-35-37; fax 31-37-26; e-mail fonda@intnet.bj; internet www.placequebec.org; non profit-making org. encourages the devt of the private sector and of small- and medium-sized businesses.

Syndicat des Commerçants Importateurs et Exportateurs du Bénin: Cotonou; Pres. M. BENCHIMOL.

Syndicat Interprofessionnel des Entreprises Industrielles du Bénin: Cotonou; Pres. M. DOUCET.

Syndicat National des Commerçants et Industriels Africains du Bénin (SYNACIB): BP 367, Cotonou; Pres. URBAIN DA SILVA.

UTILITIES

Communauté Electrique du Bénin (CEB): Vedoko, BP 537, Cotonou; tel. 30-06-75; f. 1968; as a jt venture between Benin and Togo to exploit energy resources in the two countries; Dir N'PO CYR KOUAGOU.

Société Béninoise d'Electricité et d'Eau (SBEE): 01 BP 123, Cotonou; tel. 31-21-45; fax 31-50-28; f. 1973; state-owned; production and distribution of electricity and water; separation and privatization of electricity and water sectors pending in 2003; Man. Dir ROGER KOUESSI.

TRADE UNIONS

Centrale des Organisations Syndicales Indépendantes (COSI): 04 BP 706, Cotonou; tel. 30-20-12; principally active in the health and education sectors; Sec.-Gen. JOSÉ DE SOUZA.

Centrale Syndicale des Travailleurs du Bénin (CSTB): 03 BP 0989, Cotonou; tel. 30-13-15; fax 33-26-01; actively opposes privatization and the influence of the international financial community; linked to the Parti Communiste du Bénin; Sec.-Gen. GASTON AZOUA.

Centrale des Syndicats Autonomes du Bénin (CSA—Bénin): 04 BP 1115, Cotonou; tel. 30-31-82; fax 30-04-48; principally active in private-sector enterprises; Sec.-Gen. GUILLAUME ATTIGBÉ.

Centrale des Syndicats du Secteur Privé et Informel du Bénin (CSPIB): 03 BP 2961, Cotonou; tel. 33-53-53.

Centrale des Syndicats Unis du Bénin (CSUB): Cotonou; tel. 33-10-27.

Confédération Générale des Travailleurs du Bénin (CGTB): 06 BP 2449, Cotonou; tel. and fax 33-50-07; principally active in public administration; Sec.-Gen. PASCAL TODJINOU; 33,275 mems (2002).

Union Nationale des Syndicats de Travailleurs du Bénin (UNSTB): 1 blvd Saint-Michel, BP 69, Cotonou; tel. and fax 30-36-13; principally active in public administration; sole officially recognized trade union 1974–90; Sec.-Gen. LAWANI AMINOU.

Transport

In 1996 the World Bank approved a credit of US $40m., to be issued through the International Development Association, in support of a major programme of investment in Benin's transport network. The integrated programme aimed to enhance Benin's status as an entrepôt for regional trade, and also to boost domestic employment and, by improving the infrastructure and reducing transport costs, agricultural and manufacturing output.

RAILWAYS

In 1997 the network handled 311,400 metric tons of goods. In January 1999 the line between Cotonou and Porto-Novo was re-opened after nine years of closure.

Organisation Commune Bénin-Niger des Chemins de Fer et des Transports (OCBN): BP 16, Cotonou; tel. 31-33-80; fax 31-41-50; e-mail ocbn@intnet.bj; f. 1959; 50% owned by Govt of Benin, 50% by Govt of Niger; total of 579 track-km; main line runs for 438 km from Cotonou to Parakou in the interior; br. line runs westward via Ouidah to Segboroué (34 km); also line of 107 km from Cotonou via Porto-Novo to Pobé (near the Nigerian border); Man. Dir JOSEPH KETCHION.

ROADS

In 1998 there were 7,704 km of roads, including 1,405 km of paved roads and 2,019 km of classified roads.

Agence Générale de Transit et de Consignation (AGETRAC): blvd Maritime, BP 1933, Cotonou; tel. 31-32-22; fax 31-29-69; e-mail agetrac@leland.bj; f. 1967; goods transportation and warehousing.

Compagnie de Transit et de Consignation du Bénin (CTCB Express): Cotonou; f. 1986; Pres. SOULÉMAN KOURA ZOUMAROU.

SHIPPING

The main port is at Cotonou. In 1999 the port handled some 2,596,600 metric tons of goods.

Port Autonome de Cotonou (PAC): BP 927, Cotonou; tel. 31-28-90; fax 31-28-91; e-mail pac@leland.bj; f. 1965; state-owned port authority; private-sector involvement planned in 2002; Dir-Gen. FERDINAND ASSOGBA-DOGNON.

Association pour la Défense des Intérêts du Port de Cotonou (AIPC) (Communauté Portuaire du Bénin): Port Autonome de Cotonou; tel. 31-17-26; fax 31-28-91; f. 1993; promotes, develops and co-ordinates port activities at Cotonou; Pres. ISSA BADAROU-SOULÉ; Sec.-Gen. CAMILLE MÉDÉGAN.

Compagnie Béninoise de Navigation Maritime (COBENAM): Place Ganhi, 01 BP 2032, Cotonou; tel. 31-27-96; fax 31-09-78; e-mail direction@cobenam.com; internet www.cobenam.com; f. 1974; 51% state-owned, 49% by Govt of Algeria; Pres. ABDEL KADER ALLAL; Man. Dir COCOU THÉOPHILE HOUNKPONOU.

Maersk Bénin: Centre Kodeih, ave Steinmetz, BP 2826, Cotonou; tel. 31-43-30; fax 31-15-83; e-mail coologmng@maersk-logistics.com; internet www.maersk-logistics.com/sw1059.asp; subsidiary of Maersk Sealand (Denmark); Dir AUGIS ROBERT.

SDV Bénin: route du Collège de l'Union, Akpakpa, 01 BP 433, Cotonou; tel. 31-21-19; fax 31-59-26; e-mail sdvbenin@bow.intnet.bj; f. 1986; affiliated to SDV Group (France); Pres. J. F. MIGNONNEAU; Dir-Gen. R. PH. RANJARD.

Société Béninoise d'Entreprises Maritimes (SBEM): BP 1733, Cotonou; tel. 31-23-57; fax 31-59-26; warehousing, storage and transportation; Dir RÉGIS TISSER.

Société Béninoise des Manutentions Portuaires (SOBEMAP): 35 blvd de la Marina, BP 35, Cotonou; tel. 31-41-45; fax 31-53-71; e-mail infos@sobemap.com; internet www.sobemap.com; f. 1969; state-owned; Dir-Gen. BERNARD AMOUSSOU-SOSSOU.

Société Béninoise Maritime (SOBEMAR): Carré 8, Cruintomé, 08 BP 0956, Cotonou; tel. 31-49-65; fax 31-67-72; e-mail sobemar@intnet.bj.

CIVIL AVIATION

The international airport at Cotonou (Cotonou-Cadjehoun) has a 2.4-km runway, and there are secondary airports at Parakou, Natitingou, Kandi and Abomey.

Aéro Bénin: Cotonou; f. 2002; regional flights.

Trans Air Bénin (TAB): Cotonou; f. 2000; regional flights; Dir BRICE KIKI.

Tourism

Benin's rich cultural diversity and its national parks and game reserves are the principal tourist attractions. About 152,000 tourists visited Benin in 1998, when receipts from tourism were estimated at US $33m.

Direction du Tourisme et de l'Hôtellerie du Bénin: BP 2037, Guincomey, Cotonou; tel. 31-52-58; fax 31-59-31; internet www.benintourisme.com.

BHUTAN

Introductory Survey

Location, Climate, Language, Religion, Flag, Capital

The Kingdom of Bhutan lies in the Himalaya range of mountains, with Tibet (the Xizang Autonomous Region), part of China, to the north and India to the south. Average monthly temperature ranges from 4.4°C (40°F) in January to 17°C (62°F) in July. Rainfall is heavy, ranging from 150 cm (60 ins) to 300 cm (120 ins) per year. The official language is Dzongkha, spoken mainly in western Bhutan. Written Dzongkha is based on the Tibetan script. The state religion is Mahayana Buddhism, primarily the Drukpa school of the Kagyupa sect, although Nepalese settlers, who comprise about one-quarter of the country's total population, practise Hinduism. The Nepali-speaking Hindus dominate southern Bhutan and are referred to as southern Bhutanese. The national flag (proportions 2 by 3) is divided diagonally from the lower hoist to the upper fly, so forming two triangles, one orange and the other maroon, with a white dragon superimposed in the centre. The capital is Thimphu.

Recent History

The first hereditary King of Bhutan was installed in December 1907. An Anglo-Bhutanese Treaty, signed in 1910, placed Bhutan's foreign relations under the supervision of the Government of British India. After India became independent, this treaty was replaced in August 1949 by the Indo-Bhutan Treaty of Friendship, whereby Bhutan agrees to seek the advice of the Government of India with regard to its foreign relations but remains free to decide whether or not to accept such advice. King Jigme Dorji Wangchuk, installed in 1952, established the National Assembly (Tshogdu Chenmo) in 1953 and a Royal Advisory Council (Lodoi Tsokde) in 1965. He formed the country's first Council of Ministers (Lhengye Zhungtshog) in 1968. He died in 1972 and was succeeded by the Western-educated 16-year-old Crown Prince, Jigme Singye Wangchuk. The new King stated his wish to preserve the Indo-Bhutan Treaty and further to strengthen friendship with India. In 1979, however, during the Non-aligned Conference and later at the UN General Assembly, Bhutan voted in opposition to India, in favour of Chinese policy. In 1983 India and Bhutan signed a new trade agreement concerning overland trade with Bangladesh and Nepal. India raised no objection to Bhutan's decision to negotiate directly with the People's Republic of China over the Bhutan–China border, and discussions between Bhutan and China were begun in 1984 (see below).

When Chinese authority was established in Tibet (Xizang) in 1959, Bhutan granted asylum to more than 6,000 Tibetan refugees. As a result of the discovery that many refugees were allegedly engaged in spying and subversive activities, the Bhutanese Government decided in 1976 to disperse them in small groups, introducing a number of Bhutanese families into each settlement. In June 1979 the National Assembly approved a directive establishing the end of the year as a time-limit for the refugees to decide whether to acquire Bhutanese citizenship or accept repatriation to Tibet. By September 1985 most of the Tibetans had chosen Bhutanese citizenship, and the remainder were to be accepted by India. A revised Citizenship Act, adopted by the National Assembly in 1985, confirmed residence in Bhutan in 1958 as a fundamental basis for automatic citizenship (as provided for by the 1958 Nationality Act), but this was to be interpreted flexibly. Provision was also made for citizenship by registration for Nepalese immigrants who had resided in the country for at least 20 years (15 years if employed by the Government) and who could meet linguistic and other tests of commitment to the Bhutanese community.

The violent ethnic Nepalese agitation in India for a 'Gurkha homeland' in the Darjeeling-Kalimpong region during the late 1980s and the populist movement in Nepal in 1988–90 (see the chapters on India and Nepal, respectively) spread into Bhutan in 1990. Ethnic unrest became apparent in that year when a campaign of intimidation and violence, directed by militant Nepalese against the authority of the Government in Thimphu, was initiated. In September thousands of southern Bhutanese villagers, and Nepalese who entered Bhutan from across the Indian border, organized demonstrations in border towns in southern Bhutan to protest against domination by the indigenous Buddhist Drukpa. The 'anti-nationals' ('ngolops'), as they were called by the Bhutanese authorities, demanded a greater role in the country's political and economic life and were bitterly opposed to official attempts to strengthen the Bhutanese sense of national identity through an increased emphasis on Tibetan-derived, rather than Nepalese, culture and religion (including a formal dress code, Dzongkha as the sole official language, etc.). Bhutanese officials, on the other hand, viewed the southerners as recent arrivals who abused the hospitality of their hosts through acts of violence and the destruction of development infrastructure.

Most southern villagers are relatively recent arrivals from Nepal, and many of them have made substantial contributions to the development of the southern hills. The provision of free education and health care by the Bhutanese Government for many years attracted Nepalese who had been struggling to survive in their own country and who came to settle illegally in Bhutan. This population movement was largely ignored by local administrative officials, many of whom accepted incentives to disregard the illegal nature of the influx. The Government's policy of encouraging a sense of national identity, together with rigorous new procedures (introduced in 1988) to check citizenship registration, revealed the presence of thousands of illegal residents in southern Bhutan—many of whom had lived there for a decade or more, married local inhabitants and raised families. During the ethnic unrest in September 1990 the majority of southern villagers were coerced into participating in the demonstrations by groups of armed and uniformed young men (including many of Nepalese origin who were born in Bhutan). Many of these dissidents, including a large number of students and former members of the Royal Bhutan Army and of the police force, had fled Bhutan in 1989 and early 1990. In 1988–90 a large number of the dissidents resided in the tea gardens and villages adjoining southern Bhutan. Following the demonstrations that took place in Bhutan in September–October 1990, other ethnic Nepalese left Bhutan. In January 1991 some 234 persons, claiming to be Bhutanese refugees, reportedly arrived in the Jhapa district of eastern Nepal. In September, at the request of the Nepalese Government, the office of the UN High Commissioner for Refugees (UNHCR) inaugurated a relief programme providing food and shelter for more than 300 people in the *ad hoc* camps. By December the number of people staying in the camps had risen to about 6,000. This number was substantially augmented by landless and unemployed Nepalese, who had been expelled from Assam and other eastern states of India. The small and faction-ridden ethnic Nepalese Bhutan People's Party (BPP) purported to lead the agitation for 'democracy' but presented no clear set of objectives and attracted little support from within Bhutan itself. Schools and bridges became principal targets for arson and looting during 1990–92. Most of the schools in southern Bhutan were closed indefinitely from the end of September 1990, in response to threats to the lives of teachers and students' families, but the majority of pupils affected by these closures were provided with temporary places in schools in northern Bhutan. By mid-1995, despite the continuing security problems, some 74 schools and 89 health facilities had been reopened in the five southern districts.

Between 1988 and the end of 1999 King Jigme personally authorized the release of more than 1,700 militants captured by the authorities. The King asserted that, while he had an open mind regarding the question of the pace and extent of political reform (including a willingness to hold discussions with any discontented minority group), his Government could not tolerate pressures for change if based on intimidation and violence. Although several important leaders of the dissident movement remained in custody, the King stated that they would be released upon a return to normal conditions of law and order. Some leaders of the BPP declared that they had no differences with the King, but with 'corrupt officials'; on the other hand, certain militants strongly condemned the King as their 'main enemy'.

A number of southern Bhutanese officials (including the Director-General of Power, Bhim Subba, and the Managing Director of the State Trading Corporation, R. B. Basnet) absconded in June 1991 (on the eve of the publication of departmental audits) and went directly to Nepal, where they reportedly sought political asylum on the grounds of repression and atrocities against southern Bhutanese. These accusations were refuted by the Government in Thimphu. The former Secretary-General of the BPP, D. K. Rai, was tried by the High Court in Thimphu in May 1992 and was sentenced to life imprisonment for terrorist acts; a further 35 defendants received lesser sentences. Teknath Rizal, who was alleged to be responsible for the ethnic unrest and who had been held in prison since November 1989, came to trial, and was sentenced to life imprisonment in November 1993, having been found guilty of offences against the Tsawa Sum ('the country, the King, and the people'). (Rizal, together with 40 other 'political prisoners', was pardoned by the King and released from prison in December 1999; he decided to remain in Thimphu.)

Violence continued in the disturbed areas of Samtse, Chhukha, Tsirang, Sarpang and Gelephu throughout the early 1990s, and companies of trained militia volunteers were posted to these areas to relieve the forces of the regular army. The state government of West Bengal in India, whose territory abuts much of southern Bhutan, reaffirmed in 1991 and 1992 that its land would not be used as a base for any agitation against Bhutan.

In late 1991 and throughout 1992 several thousand legally-settled villagers left southern Bhutan for the newly established refugee camps in eastern Nepal. The Bhutanese Government alleged that the villagers were being enticed or threatened to leave their homes by militants based outside Bhutan, in order to augment the population of the camps and gain international attention; the dissidents, on the other hand, claimed that the Bhutanese Government was forcing the villagers to leave. The formation of the Bhutan National Democratic Party (BNDP), including members drawn from supporters of the BPP and with R. B. Basnet as its President, was announced in Kathmandu in February 1992. Incidents of ethnic violence, almost all of which involved infiltration from across the border by ethnic Nepalese who had been trained and dispatched from the camps in Nepal, reportedly diminished substantially in the first half of 1993, as talks continued between Bhutanese and Nepalese officials regarding proposals to resolve the issues at stake. The Nepalese Government steadfastly refused to consider any solution that did not include the resettlement in Bhutan of all ethnic Nepalese 'refugees' living in the camps (by November 1993 the number of alleged ethnic Nepalese refugees from Bhutan totalled about 85,000). This proposal was rejected by the Bhutanese Government, which maintained that the majority of the camp population merely claimed to be from Bhutan, had absconded from Bhutan (and thus forfeited their citizenship, according to Bhutan's citizenship laws), or had departed voluntarily after selling their properties and surrendering their citizenship papers and rights. The apparent deadlock was broken, however, when a joint statement was signed by the two countries' Ministers of Home Affairs in July, which committed each side to establishing a 'high-level committee' to work towards a settlement and, in particular, to fulfilling the following mandate prior to undertaking any other related activity: to determine the different categories of people claiming to have come from Bhutan in the refugee camps in eastern Nepal (which now numbered eight); and to specify the positions of the two Governments on each of these categories, which would provide the basis for the resolution of the problem. The two countries held their first ministerial-level meeting regarding the issue in Kathmandu in October, at which it was agreed that four categories would be established among the people in the refugee camps: '(i) bona fide Bhutanese who have been evicted forcefully; (ii) Bhutanese who emigrated; (iii) non-Bhutanese; and (iv) Bhutanese who have committed criminal acts' (henceforth referred to as Category I, II, III and IV). Further meetings were held in 1994. Following the election of a new Government in Nepal in November of that year, however, little progress was made at joint ministerial meetings held in the first half of 1995. Nepal's communist Government demanded that all persons in the camps be accepted by Bhutan; the Bhutanese authorities, on the other hand, were prepared to accept only the unconditional return of any bona fide Bhutanese citizens who had left the country involuntarily. Nevertheless, diplomatic exchanges continued in the latter half of the year, despite serious political instability in Nepal.

In January 1996 the new Nepalese Prime Minister, Sher Bahadur Deuba, proposed a resumption of intergovernmental talks, this time at foreign minister level. King Jigme welcomed the proposal, but the seventh round of talks, which was held in April, resulted in demands by Nepal that exceeded the mandate drawn up by the joint ministerial committee in mid-1993. It was widely understood that the Nepalese Government had again reverted to a requisition that all persons in the camps be accepted by Bhutan, regardless of status. This demand remained unacceptable to the Bhutanese Government, which stated that the problem of the people in the camps would not have arisen if conditions (such as prospects of free food, shelter, health and education, and 'moral support' by the Nepalese authorities for all persons claiming to be Bhutanese refugees) had not been created when there were reportedly only 234 persons in Jhapa making such claims. In addition, the Bhutanese Government stated that even with such conditions attracting people to the refugee camps, a well-organized screening process would have prevented the sheer scale of ethnic Nepalese claiming to be Bhutanese refugees. (Until June 1993 no screening of claimants to refugee status had been enforced on the India–Nepal border.) In August 1996 a UNHCR delegation visited Bhutan at the invitation of the authorities, who provided detailed information pertaining to the camps. Talks at ministerial level were held in 1997, without any public communiqué. Following informal discussions during the summit meeting of the South Asian Association for Regional Co-operation (SAARC, see p. 310) in Colombo, Sri Lanka, in July 1998, the new Chairman of the Council of Ministers, Lyonpo Jigmi Y. Thinley, held talks with the Nepalese Prime Minister, G. P. Koirala; both leaders stated that their meeting had been 'very positive'. Thinley and Koirala agreed that bilateral negotiations would continue through their respective Ministers of Foreign Affairs on the issue of persons claiming refugee status in Nepal (who now numbered about 100,000). The 77th National Assembly session, which took place in June–August 1999, unanimously reiterated that the Bhutanese Government accepted full responsibility for any Bhutanese found to have been forcefully evicted (Category I—see above): such persons would be recognized and accepted as genuine refugees, while those responsible for their eviction would be punished. Category II persons who had voluntarily emigrated from the country would be dealt with according to the respective immigration and citizenship laws of Bhutan and Nepal; those classified as Category III 'must return to their own country'; and the repatriation of those in Category IV was to be conducted in accordance with the laws of the two countries. At the eighth round of joint ministerial negotiations between Bhutan and Nepal, which was held in Kathmandu in September, the Bhutanese Minister of Foreign Affairs agreed that some of those previously classified as voluntary emigrants (under Category II) might be reclassified as Category I (according to the Bhutanese Government, the number of people in this category totalled only about 3,000, while the Nepalese Government claimed that all of the camp dwellers had been compelled to leave Bhutan). In 1999 the Bhutanese Government was reported to have resettled people from the central and eastern hill regions of Bhutan in the southern areas of the country.

No real progress was reported to have been made with regard to the refugee crisis at the ninth round of joint ministerial talks held in Thimphu in March 2000. However, at the 10th round of joint ministerial negotiations, held in December, the Bhutanese and Nepalese Ministers of Foreign Affairs agreed that nationality would be verified on the basis of the head of the refugee family for those over 25 years of age, and that refugees under 25 years of age would be verified on an individual basis. This important advance in bilateral negotiations signified a major concession by Bhutan, which had hitherto insisted that verification be conducted on an individual basis. By the end of January 2001 a Joint Verification Team (JVT), consisting of five officials each from the Nepalese and Bhutanese Governments, had concluded the inspection of the refugee camps. Verification of the nationality of 98,897 people claiming refugee status (including 13,000 minors born in the camp) began at the end of March, commencing with the Khudanabari camp. Despite criticisms in the Nepalese press that the pace was too slow, the minister argued that it was essential for both parties to maintain a credible verification process. The Assembly endorsed the ongoing verification process, and decided that any ensuing problems should be resolved first at the secretary level of the two Governments, or if necessary, at the ministerial level. At a meeting in early November the Ministers of Foreign Affairs of Bhutan and Nepal were unable to harmonize the positions of their respective governments with regard to the four categories (established in October 1993—see above) for the people in the camps. The Nepalese Minister of Foreign Affairs requested a meeting at the ministerial level to be convened in early 2002. In late 2001 the verification of the Khudanabari camp was completed; however, with the recent disagreements over harmonization, the process reached a standstill. Discussions continued to take place between Bhutanese and Nepalese officials, although progress was very slow.

A diminution in guerrilla violence in Bhutan from late 1995 coincided with the adoption of the 'peace march' tactic by persons claiming to be Bhutanese and seeking to travel from Nepal into Bhutan. These marches continued throughout 1996; a small group of marchers actually reached Phuentsholing in August and again in December before being forced to return to India (which maintained a neutral stance with regard to the refugee issue). Bhutan's Minister of Home Affairs asserted that those participating in the marches were not Bhutanese, but were nonnationals and emigrants attempting to enter the country illegally. A number of isolated bombing incidents occurred in Bhutan during 1998–99, most notably in Thimphu's main stadium in November 1998, and were attributed by Bhutanese authorities to Nepalese militants. In June 1999 it was reported that Bhutanese police had arrested 80 alleged Bhutanese refugees who were conducting a peaceful demonstration (organized by the Bhutan Gurkha National Liberation Front) in Phuentsholing; the demonstrators claimed to be genuine Bhutanese citizens who were seeking to travel from the camps in Nepal back into Bhutan.

In 1991 'Rongthong' Kinley Dorji (also styled Kuenley or Kunley), a former Bhutanese businessman accused of unpaid loans and of acts against the State, had absconded to Nepal and joined the anti-Government movement. In 1992 he established and became President of the Druk National Congress, claiming human rights violations in Bhutan. The Bhutan Government's 74th Assembly held in July 1996 discussed Kinley Dorji's case at length, and unanimously demanded his extradition from Nepal in conjunction with the Bhutan-Nepal talks. Following the signing of an extradition treaty between India and Bhutan in December, Kinley was arrested by the Indian authorities during a visit to Delhi in April 1997; he remained in detention until June 1998, when he was released on bail while his case was being examined by the Indian courts. Meanwhile, the extradition treaty was read to the 75th Assembly in July 1997, when Kinley Dorji's case was again discussed and demands for his return to Bhutan for trial were unanimously supported (as they were also at the 76th Assembly in 1998 and the 77th Assembly in 1999). At the same time the Assembly resolved that all relatives of alleged 'anti-national militants' in government service should be compulsorily retired as soon as possible. The 75th Assembly also discussed the intrusions into Bhutan's south-eastern border forests by Bodo and Maoist extremists from the neighbouring Indian state of Assam.

During 1997 anti-Government activities (culminating in rallies in south-eastern Bhutan in October) were alleged to have been organized by several lay-preacher (Gomchen) students of Lam Dodrup in Sikkim, India; a number of arrests were subsequently made. Part of the famous historic retreat of Taktsang Monastery was badly damaged by fire under suspicious circumstances in April 1998. Reconstruction work, which had cost more than Nu 65m. by late 2002, was expected to be completed in 2003.

Important institutional changes were introduced in mid-1998, whereby King Jigme relinquished his role as Head of Government (while remaining Head of State) in favour of a smaller elected Council of Ministers, which was to enjoy full executive power under the leadership of a Chairman (elected by ministers, on a rotational basis, for a one-year term in office) who would be Head of Government. In June the King informed the members of the existing Council of Ministers that it was to be dissolved, and stated that he had issued a royal decree to the Speaker of the National Assembly, which was to be discussed at the forthcoming 76th session. In the decree the King stressed the necessity to promote greater popular participation in the decision-making process, to strengthen the Government's mandate, and to enhance the administration's transparency and efficiency with integral checks and balances. He stated that the Council of Ministers should now be restructured as an elected body 'vested with full executive powers', and he presented three key points: (i) all government ministers should henceforth be elected by the National Assembly, with the first election to take place during the 76th session; (ii) a decision should be taken on the exact role and responsibilities of the Council of Ministers; and (iii) the National Assembly should have a mechanism to move a vote of confidence in the King. King Jigme further advised that the Council of Ministers should henceforth consist of six elected ministers and all nine members of the Royal Advisory Council; ministers should be elected by secret ballot; candidates should be selected from those who had held senior government posts at the rank of Secretary or above; and a candidate must secure a majority of the votes cast to be considered elected. The portfolios for the elected ministers were to be awarded by the King. A minister's term in office was to be five years, after which he would undergo a vote of confidence in the National Assembly (previously there had been no limit on the tenure of ministerial posts). All decisions adopted by the Council of Ministers were to be based on consensus, and, while the Council was to govern Bhutan with full executive powers, it was also to be obliged to keep the King fully informed on all matters concerning the security and sovereignty of the country. The procedures of the Council of Ministers were to be supervised by a Cabinet Secretary appointed by the Council. The 76th session of the National Assembly voted by secret ballot on six new ministerial nominees; all were successful, but all received some negative votes.

An act to regulate the Council of Ministers, which was framed by a committee comprising members of the Government, clergy and people's representatives of the 20 districts, was presented to the 77th session of the National Assembly in mid-1999 and was subjected to extensive discussion and amendment. The rules as finally endorsed explicitly specified that the King had full power to dissolve the Council of Ministers. Procedures for a confidence vote with regard to the King were also drafted by the aforementioned committee and presented to the 77th session of the National Assembly, where members unanimously expressed regret over (and opposition to) the draft and repeatedly requested that King Jigme withdraw the proposal. Following a further earnest plea by the King, however, a key draft provision that a confidence vote regarding the monarch should only be placed on the agenda of an assembly session if a minimum of 50% of the districts requested it, was amended to allow the initiative if supported by at least one-third of the assembly members. The 77th session also agreed that ministers should serve a maximum of two consecutive five-year terms.

King Jigme informed the Council of Ministers at a special session in mid-August 1999 that it should streamline the Government and create mobility in the higher levels of the civil service when staffing ministries and other organizations, and that it must be responsive to the needs of the people. He also stressed that while governance was the responsibility of the Council of Ministers, the Royal Advisory Council was empowered to ensure that all the policies, laws and resolutions approved by the National Assembly were implemented by the Government. The outgoing Chairman of the Council, Lyonpo Jigmi Yozer Thinley, stated that all the elements were now in place for a democratic system of decision-making, while government was being institutionalized and made more accountable and transparent. At the ceremony held for the formal rotation of Chairman of the Council of Ministers in August 2001, King Jigme expressed satisfaction at the progress of political reform, and advised that changes in the fields of national security, the development of the Ninth Plan, and youth employment should be the Council's priorities. At the 11th SAARC summit, held in Kathmandu in January 2002, the incumbent Chairman of the Council, Lyonpo Khandu Wangchuk, was referred to as 'Prime Minister' of Bhutan, a title that subsequently became accepted usage. In accordance with a decree issued by King Jigme in September 2001, a committee to draft a written constitution for Bhutan was inaugurated in late November and began functioning at the end of the year. The 39-member committee was chaired by the Chief Justice and included the Chairman and members of the Royal Advisory Council, five government representatives, the Speaker of the National Assembly, representatives from each of the 20 local districts, and two lawyers from the High Court. It was agreed that, on completion, the draft would be subjected to extensive public comment and review before being presented to the Assembly for formal approval. In December 2002 the preliminary draft of the Constitution was presented by the committee to King Jigme; the King subsequently referred the draft to the Prime Minister for further scrutiny, envisaging widespread public debate. Further reform of the National Assembly and the Royal Advisory Council was expected to continue alongside constitutional discussions.

The activities of the militant 'anti-nationals' were unanimously condemned at the 76th session of the National Assembly in mid-1998, but the most pressing security issue was judged to be the perceived threat from the presence of Assamese tribal (Bodo) and Maoist (United Liberation Front of Assam—ULFA) militants, who had established military training bases in the jungle border regions of south-eastern Bhutan. Particular concern was expressed regarding the Indian military incursions into Bhutanese territory in an attempt to expel the militants. A serious incident that had taken place in May in Sarpang, reportedly involving 165 armed Indian soldiers, was discussed during the session, and was to be investigated by the Bhutanese and Indian authorities. The Indian authorities subsequently apologized for the incident. In mid-1999 the Minister of Home Affairs reported that talks with ULFA leaders (in November 1998 and May 1999) had elicited the response that members of the ULFA had been forced to enter Bhutanese territory in 1992, but that they were not ready to leave Bhutan for at least another 18 months. They asserted that they were determined to fight until independence for Assam was achieved, but offered to reduce their military presence in Bhutan. The Government of Bhutan reiterated to the ULFA leadership that its concern was at the very presence of any number of armed militants on Bhutanese soil. After detailed discussion, assembly members decided that all supplies of food and other essentials to the ULFA and National Democratic Front of Bodoland (NDFB) must be stopped, that any Bhutanese who assisted the militants should be punished according to the National Security Act, and that discussions should continue with the ULFA to seek a peaceful withdrawal of these forces from Bhutan. At the 78th session of the National Assembly in July 2000, members adopted a resolution stating that the problem should be solved through peaceful means, but that if negotiations failed military force should be used to evict the insurgents from Bhutanese territory. Supplies of rations had already been halted, and the police had taken action against Bhutanese citizens found to be helping the militants. Some groups of militants began to return to India. However, most ULFA and Bodo militants, who had hitherto refrained from carrying out violent activities in Bhutan, were angered by the decision. Bhutan's security forces were put on maximum alert in September, amid fears that King Jigme might be a target of the insurgents. In December some 13 people were killed when members of the Bodo Liberation Tigers attacked a convoy of Bhutanese vehicles on the Bhutan–India border. The act was perceived as a warning to the Bhutanese Government not to shelter ULFA and NDFB militants. The Indian Government subsequently agreed to escort Bhutanese vehicles travelling to Assam.

In mid-2001 the Minister of Home Affairs, addressing the 79th session of the National Assembly, reported that negotiations had been held with leaders of the NDFB in October 2000 and May 2001. During the talks NDFB leaders had responded to a demand for the removal of their camps by declaring their intention to leave Bhutan, but would not commit themselves to a deadline. Following three days of discussions in June, representatives of the ULFA agreed to seven points, including the removal of four of the nine military camps in Bhutan by December 2001 and the reduction in strength of the cadres in the remaining camps; further meetings were planned in order to find a solution to the issue of the remaining five camps. Members of the National Assembly were informed of the Government's preparations in the event of armed conflict with the militants: security had been strengthened, funds had been reserved for fuel supplies and medical support services, and contingency plans had been made to ensure the continued operation of the communications and transport systems. In addition, supplies of grains and other essential foods, sufficient to last for three to six months, were stored in towns throughout Bhutan. Disappointment and concern were expressed at the low level of volunteer recruitment; of the 880 men recruited to the army in 2000/01, 27 had deserted and 131 had requested special leave. Districts were asked to send lists of volunteers to army headquarters immediately after the Assembly session. Members were warned that military action could begin as early as December 2001 if the ULFA militants failed to honour their commitments. It was subsequently reported at the 80th session of the National Assembly in mid-2002 that of the 2,581 men who

had volunteered for militia training, only 1,410 had reported for training, and of those 380 were medically unfit and 198 sought to leave because of domestic problems. The remaining 808 volunteers wished to join the army permanently as soldiers. Only 24 volunteers from the 20 districts wished to join as militia. The training of volunteers for the militia, therefore, was rendered unviable.

On 31 December 2001 the army visited the four designated ULFA training camps and confirmed that these had been abandoned. Initially, however, the whereabouts of their militants was unknown. It was not possible immediately to ascertain whether the ULFA units had managed to leave Bhutan and, evading Indian military forces in Assam, reach their presumed goals of Bangladesh and Myanmar. At the same time there were concerns that the militants had repositioned their camps elsewhere in Bhutan. At the 80th session of the National Assembly in mid-2002 the Minister of Home Affairs confirmed that the ULFA had closed down a military training centre and three camps. The ULFA, however, had opened a new camp on a mountain ridge above the main Samdrup Jongkhar–Trashigang highway, raising the total number of camps remaining in Bhutan to six. In the mean time, the NDFB had three main camps and four mobile camps between Lhamoizingkha and Daifam. The Minister of Home Affairs also reported that the Government had only recently become aware that the Indian militant Kamtapur Liberation Organization (KLO) had established camps in Bhangtar dungkhag and near Piping in Lhamoizingkha dungkhag. The KLO armed militants were Rajbansi tribals of North Bengal, bordering Chhukha and Samtse dzongkhags, who were campaigning for separate statehood for the Kamtapuris.

The Minister for Home Affairs stressed that the presence of armed militants in Bhutan remained a grave threat. It appeared that no further negotiations could be held with the NDFB. The issue was further complicated by the presence of KLO militants. Following extensive discussions, the National Assembly endorsed three decisions proposed by the Council of Ministers: first, to hold negotiations with the Chairman and the military commander of the ULFA; second, the Government would not agree to participate in any more meetings on the reduction of ULFA camps but was prepared only to discuss the closure of the militants' main training camp and headquarters. Finally, if ULFA leaders refused to relocate their headquarters, there would be no option but to evict them physically. King Jigme informed the Assembly that it was important to hold talks with the ULFA and NDFB separately. Although the KLO was a new, relatively unknown group, the King warned that if the authorities had to resort to military action, they would have to deal with all three organizations.

Reflecting the increasing complexities of contemporary administration, the 77th Assembly also approved an unprecedented number of acts in mid-1999 to enhance the prevailing legal framework relating to telecommunications (providing for the creation of a state-owned public corporation, Bhutan Telecom, from the existing Telecommunications Division), the postal sector (enabling Bhutan Post to become an autonomous public-sector corporation), bankruptcy (giving a contemporary context for the rights and duties of borrowers and lenders), property (setting a legal framework for the management of loans, mortgages and related securities and financial services), legal deposit, municipalities (establishing legal authority for municipalities to enforce rules relating to urban development), and road safety. Further indications of the modernization of Bhutan were the inauguration of (limited) television and internet services in mid-1999, and the election of nine women to attend the 1999 session of the National Assembly (this number had increased to 11 and 16 by 2000 and 2001, respectively). Furthermore, the mid-2001 Assembly session for the first time elected a woman to the Royal Advisory Council. At the end of 1999 a government-endorsed report proposed the rationalization of government under 10 ministries, to be fully implemented by 2002. Also in late 1999 two new government agencies—the Office of Legal Affairs and the National Employment Board—were established, and a new Department of Aid and Debt Management was created. The 78th session of the National Assembly, in mid-2000, approved new legislation regarding the environment. The 79th session reviewed and adopted eight draft laws (six of which had been circulated at the previous session), notably a Copyright Act, a Personal Income Tax Act, and a revised Civil and Criminal Procedure Code. Rules for the establishment of a standing legislative committee to draft, review, amend and ratify national legislation were also submitted. At the end of 2001 revised rules for geog (village block) and district development committees to create a legal basis for local autonomy in development issues (a fundamental issue under the Ninth Plan) were under discussion. The revisions were approved by the National Assembly at its 80th session in mid-2002. In accordance with the 1999 Municipal Act, residents of Thimphu elected members of the municipal council in late December 2001. The response to elections in late 2002, however, was indifferent.

In mid-2001 the Council of Ministers decided to reduce the number of skilled expatriate workers from 50,000 to 25,000 with immediate effect, and aimed further to lower the number to 12,500 by the end of 2002. The decision was strongly criticized as unduly hasty by the Bhutan Chamber of Commerce and Industry, on the grounds that Bhutan's labour force was seasonal owing to rural harvesting and that the Bhutanese generally disparage manual labour. In October 2001 the Council of Ministers permitted the mining industry more time to reduce imported labour, but insisted that all firms and industries would have similar obligations from 2004.

Following the relaxation of many policies in the People's Republic of China from 1978, and anticipating improved relations between India and China, Bhutan moved cautiously to assert positions on regional and world affairs that took into account the views of India but were not necessarily identical to them. Discussions with China regarding the formal delineation and demarcation of Bhutan's northern border were begun in 1984, and substantive negotiations commenced in 1986. At the 12th round of talks, held in Beijing in December 1998, the Ministers of Foreign Affairs of Bhutan and China signed an official interim agreement (the first agreement ever to be signed between the two countries) to maintain peace and tranquillity in the Bhutan–China border area and to observe the status quo of the border as it was prior to May 1959, pending a formal agreement on the border alignment. The disputed area, which was 1,128 sq km during the early rounds of bilateral talks, was subsequently reduced to 269 sq km in three areas in the north-west of Bhutan. Meanwhile, demarcation of Bhutan's southern border was agreed with India, except for small sectors in the middle zone (between Sarpang and Gelephu) and in the eastern zone of Arunachal Pradesh and the *de facto* China–India border. Following bilateral discussions in Thimphu in September 1999, the 14th round of 'satisfactory' border discussions took place in Beijing in November 2000, at which Bhutan extended the area of its claim beyond the boundary offered by the Chinese Government. The three sections under discussion were in the Doglam, Sinchulumba and Dramana areas. The negotiations continued in November 2001, following which the Chinese Deputy Minister of Foreign Affairs stated that the boundary question generally had been resolved, although relatively minor issues remained outstanding. The 16th round of talks was held in Beijing in October 2002 and was described by the Bhutanese delegation as 'yet another step towards permanent solution'. Two delegations from Bhutan (a 'cultural' group and an 'officials' group) also visited China, in April and July 2001, respectively.

Bhutan became a member of the UN in 1971 and of the Non-aligned Movement in 1973.

Government

Bhutan's state system is a modified form of constitutional monarchy, hitherto without a formal, written constitutional document. In accordance with a decree by the King in September 2001, a 39-member special committee convened at the end of the year to draft a written constitution (see above). In December 2002 the King announced that the number of ministries would be expanded in 2003. The system of government is unusual in that power is shared by the monarchy (assisted by the Royal Advisory Council—Lodoi Tsokde), the Council of Ministers (Lhengye Zhungtshog), the National Assembly (Tshogdu Chenmo) and the Head Abbot (Je Khempo) of Bhutan's 3,000–4,000 Buddhist monks.

Important institutional changes were introduced at the 76th session of the National Assembly in July 1998. In accordance with a royal decree, King Jigme relinquished his role as Head of Government (while remaining Head of State) in favour of an elected Council of Ministers, which was to enjoy full executive powers (although the King was to retain authority with regard to strategic security issues) and was to be headed by a Chairman (elected by ministers, on a rotational basis, for a one-year period), who would be Head of Government. The new Council of Ministers was subsequently elected by the National Assembly by secret ballot and the portfolios of the elected ministers were

awarded by the King. The term in office of a minister was to be five years, after which he would be obliged to undergo a vote of confidence in the National Assembly. In 1999 the National Assembly agreed that ministers should serve a maximum of two consecutive five-year terms.

The National Assembly, which serves a three-year term, has 150 members, including 105 directly elected by adult suffrage; 10 seats in the Assembly are reserved for religious bodies, while the remainder are occupied by officials, ministers and members of the Royal Advisory Council.

There are 20 local districts (dzongkhags), each headed by a Dzongda (district officer, in charge of administration and law and order) and a Drangpon (magistrate, in charge of judicial matters, formerly known as a Thrimpon). Dzongdas are appointed by the Royal Civil Service Commission and are responsible to the commission and the Ministry of Home Affairs. Drangpons are responsible to the High Court. The principal officers under the Dzongda are the Dzongda Wongma and the Dzongrab, responsible for locally administered development projects and fiscal matters respectively. Seven of the districts are further sub-divided into sub-districts (dungkhags), and the lowest administrative unit in all districts is the block (geog) of several villages. There are Geog Yargye Tshogchungs (GYT—Geog Development Committees) in each of the geogs (of which there were 202 in January 2002). New rules governing GYTs and Dzongkhag Yargye Tshogchungs (DYTs—District Development Committees) were adopted by the National Assembly at its session in mid-2002, and in October secret ballots were held in all 202 geogs to re-elect gups (heads of geogs), who, under the new rules, were to chair the GYT meetings. Other GYT members number between eight and 31, depending on the size of the block, and include a mangmi (deputy gup) and tshogpas (village elders). Public meetings (zomdue) are held periodically, at the village level, to discuss local issues.

Defence

The strength of the Royal Bhutanese Army, which is under the direct command of the King, is officially said to number just over 6,000, and is based on voluntary recruitment. Army training facilities are provided by an Indian military training team. Although India is not directly responsible for the country's defence, the Indian Government has indicated that any act of aggression against Bhutan would be regarded as an act of aggression against India.

Economic Affairs

In 2001, according to estimates by the World Bank, Bhutan's gross national income (GNI), measured at average 1999–2001 prices, was US $529m., equivalent to $640 per head (or $1,530 per head on an international purchasing-power parity basis). During 1990–2001, it was estimated, the population increased at an average annual rate of 3.0%, while gross domestic product (GDP) per head increased, in real terms, by an average of 3.3%. Overall GDP increased, in real terms, at an average annual rate of 6.4% in 1990–2001. Real GDP growth was estimated at 7.0% in both 2000 and 2001.

Agriculture (including livestock and forestry) contributed an estimated 33.2% of GDP in 2000. About 94% of the economically active population were employed in the sector in that year. The principal sources of revenue in the agricultural sector are apples, oranges and cardamom. Timber production is also important; about 60% of the total land area is covered by forest. Agricultural GDP increased, in real terms, at an average annual rate of 2.9% in 1990–2000; it increased by an estimated 3.5% in both 1999 and 2000.

Industry (including mining, manufacturing, utilities and construction) employed only about 0.9% of the labour force in 1990, but contributed an estimated 37.3% of GDP in 2000. Industrial GDP increased at an average annual rate of 9.7% in 1990–2000; growth in the sector was estimated at 7.3% in 1999, and at 7.5% in 2000.

Mining and quarrying contributed an estimated 1.4% of GDP in 1999. Calcium carbide is the principal mineral export (contributing 13.1% of total export revenue in 1998). Gypsum, coal, limestone, slate and dolomite are also mined. Mining GDP increased by an average rate of an estimated 9.9% per year in 1990–99.

Manufacturing contributed an estimated 10.2% of GDP in 2000. The most important sector is cement production, and there is a calcium carbide plant and a ferro-alloy plant. Small-scale manufacturers produce, *inter alia*, textiles, soap, matches, candles and carpets. Manufacturing GDP increased at an average annual rate of an estimated 8.9% in 1990–2000; it increased by an estimated 12.0% in 1999, and by a similar level in 2000.

Energy is derived principally from hydroelectric power. The Chhukha hydroelectric power (HEP) project, with a generating capacity of about 338 MW, provides electricity for domestic consumption and also for export to India. The Indian-financed Tala HEP project, scheduled for completion in 2005, is to have an installed capacity of 1,020 MW. Expenditure on the project (including the cost of repairing damage by floods in 2000) was expected to reach some Nu 36,000m. The Kurichhu power project was nearing completion in early 2003. In 1997 exports of electricity provided 30.2% of total export revenue, while the cost of imports of diesel oil and petroleum was equivalent to 4.7% of total import costs.

The services sector, which employed only about 3.4% of the labour force in 1981/82, contributed an estimated 29.5% of GDP in 2000. The tourism sector has become increasingly significant. In 2000 the total number of foreign visitors was 7,553, although the number declined to 6,393 in 2001. In 2001 receipts from tourism totalled US $9.2m. The GDP of the services sector increased at an average annual rate of an estimated 6.3% in 1990–2000; growth was estimated at 7.5% in 1999 and at 7.3% in 2000.

In the financial year ending 30 June 2001, according to the Asian Development Bank (ADB), Bhutan recorded a visible trade deficit of US $101.3m., and there was a deficit of $123.3m. on the current account of the balance of payments. In 2000/01 the principal source of imports (an estimated 74.0%) was India, which was also the principal market for exports (an estimated 94.4%). The principal exports in 1999 were electricity, calcium carbide, cement and particle board. The principal imports in 1997 were telecommunications equipment, rice and diesel oil.

The 2002/03 budget envisaged a deficit of Nu 1,652.4m. (revenue Nu 9,532.2m., expenditure Nu 11,184.6m.). Bhutan's total external debt amounted to US $198.4m. at the end of 2000, of which $197.3m. was long-term public debt. In that year the cost of debt-servicing was equivalent to 4.2% of the value of exports of goods and services. The average annual rate of inflation was 8.7% in 1990–2001. Consumer prices increased by an annual average of 4.4% in 2000 and 3.3% in 2001. By 2000 the rising level of unemployment was beginning to cause concern; an estimated 50,000 school-leavers were expected to join the labour force over the next five years.

Bhutan is a member of the Asian Development Bank (ADB, see p. 143), of the Colombo Plan (see p. 339) and of the South Asian Association for Regional Co-operation (SAARC, see p. 310), all of which seek to improve regional co-operation, particularly in economic development.

The Seventh Plan (1992–97) asserted seven main objectives: self-reliance, with emphasis on internal resource mobilization; sustainability, with emphasis on environmental protection; private-sector development; decentralization and popular participation; human resources' development; balanced development in all districts; and national security. The Eighth Plan (1997–2002) further refined the seven objectives of the Seventh Plan and explicitly added another: 'the preservation and promotion of cultural and traditional values'. During these five years, GDP was forecast to expand at an average annual rate of 6.7%, while the annual rate of population growth was projected to decline to 2.56% by 2002. Revenue, which was forecast to reach Nu 15,912m. during the plan, was to cover 53% of the total plan outlay of Nu 30,000m. The agricultural sector was projected to expand over the plan period through productivity gains and horticultural development; exports to India and third countries were also expected to increase. The guiding goal was declared as the establishment of sustainability in development, while balancing achievements with the popular sense of contentment. Core areas were to be the further development of HEP, further industrialization, development of the infrastructure and social services, human resource development, and renewable natural resources. The mid-term review of the Eighth Plan, which was carried out in February 2000, indicated that the Government had made satisfactory progress in reaching its targets. Fund utilization had reached around 40% of the original outlay of Nu 30,000m.; total outlay was expected to increase by 10%, while domestic revenue was projected to increase to Nu 18,673m., largely owing to the power tariff increase. This review was to serve as the basis for the Ninth Plan (2002–07). The Ninth Plan, effective from July 2002, consisted, unlike previous plans, of separate programmes and budget allocations

for individual sectors and dzongkhags (local districts). The dzongkhag plans became geog-based through the devolution of powers to GYT members, under new rules approved by the National Assembly at its 80th session. Central Government, however, maintained financial control in order to ensure budgetary discipline. Expenditure during these five years was expected to reach Nu 70,000m. Domestic revenue, which was forecast to reach Nu 30,000m., and external resources, amounting to an estimated Nu 35,000m. (of which Nu 20,000m. was requested as assistance from India) were expected to cover the proposed outlay. GDP was forecast to grow at an average annual rate of 6%–7% in 2002–07.

The production of low-cost electricity by the Chhukha HEP project helped to stimulate growth in the industrial sector in the 1990s. It was hoped that, on completion, Bhutan's Kurichhu and Tala schemes would earn sufficient revenue for Bhutan to achieve economic self-reliance. In mid-2001 new legislation was enacted to reform the electricity supply industry and to develop and regulate the country's HEP resources; a Bhutan Electricity Authority was established. Multilateral investment in Bhutan's financial sector was agreed by the Government for the first time in September 1998, when the ADB and the US Citibank purchased shares in the Bhutan National Bank. Two important measures were implemented in 1999: a formal personal income tax (to be levied only on wealthier Bhutanese) was introduced, and the country was opened up to foreign investment (foreign investors were to be permitted up to 51% ownership in a joint venture), although the stock exchange remained closed to external investors.

Education

Education is not compulsory. Pre-primary education usually lasts for one year. Primary education begins at six years of age and lasts for five years. Secondary education, beginning at the age of 12, lasts for a further five years, comprising three cycles. Virtually free education is available (nominal fees are demanded), but there are insufficient facilities to accommodate all school-age children. In order to accommodate additional children, community schools (established in 1989 as 'extended classrooms', but renamed as above in 1991) were set up as essentially one-teacher schools for basic primary classes, whence children were to be 'streamed' to other schools. In 1988 the total enrolment at primary schools was equivalent to an estimated 26% of children in the relevant age-group (31% of boys; 20% of girls), while the comparable ratio for secondary schools was only 5% (boys 7%; girls 2%). All schools are co-educational. English is the language of instruction and Dzongkha is a compulsory subject. Bhutan has no mission schools. By 2002 some 14 private schools had been established (the majority in Thimphu); these schools are under the supervision of the Department of Education. Owing to a shortage of qualified staff (despite the existence of two teacher-training institutes with a combined enrolment of 1,014 students in 2002), many Indian teachers are employed. In July 2002 the total number of enrolled pupils was 133,997 (boys 70,034; girls 63,963), and the total number of teachers was 4,206. In 2002 there were more than 408 educational institutions under the supervision of the Department of Education, including 182 community schools, 97 primary schools, 65 lower secondary schools, 27 middle secondary schools, 12 higher secondary schools, one degree college and seven post-secondary institutions. A further four technical institutes are directly administered by the National Technical Training Authority. Some Bhutanese students were receiving higher education abroad. The 2001/02 budget allocated an estimated Nu 1,528.4m. (15.6% of total projected expenditure) to education.

Public Holidays

2003 and 2004: The usual Buddhist holidays are observed, as well as three days for Thimphu Tsechu (September/October, in Thimphu district only), the Winter Solstice, the Birthday of the late third King Jigme Dorji Wangchuck (2 May), Coronation Day of HM Jigme Singye Wangchuck (2 June), the Anniversary of the death of the late third King (7 August), the Birthday of HM Jigme Singye Wangchuck (11–13 November), the movable Hindu feast of Dussehra and the National Day of Bhutan (17 December).

Weights and Measures

The metric system is in operation.

Statistical Survey

Source (unless otherwise stated): Royal Government of Bhutan, Thimphu.

Area and Population

AREA, POPULATION AND DENSITY

Area (sq km)	46,500*
Population (official estimates)†	
2000	638,000
2001	654,269
2002	670,953
Density (per sq km) in 2002	14.4

* 17,954 sq miles.

† These figures are much lower than former estimates. The figures for 2001 and 2002 are based on the 2000 estimate and assume an annual population growth rate of 2.55%. It was previously reported that a census in 1969 enumerated a population of 931,514, and a 1980 census recorded a total of 1,165,000. On the basis of the latter figure, a mid-1988 population of 1,375,400 was projected. Other figures in this Survey are derived from the earlier, higher estimates of Bhutan's population.

POPULATION OF DISTRICTS*
(mid-1985 estimates, based on 1980 census)

Bumthang	23,842
Dagana	28,352
Gasa†	16,907
Gelephug	111,283
Ha	16,715
Lhuentse.	39,635
Mongar	73,239
Paro	46,615
Pemagatshel	37,141
Punakha†	16,700
Samdrup Jongkhar.	73,044
Samtse	172,109
Zhemgang	44,516
Thimphu.	58,660
Trashigang	177,718
Trongsa	26,017
Tsirang	108,807
Wangdue Phodrang	47,152
Total population	**1,286,275**
Rural	1,119,452
Urban	167,823

* The above figures are approximate, and predate the creation of a new district, Chhukha, in 1987. Chhukha has an estimated total population of about 13,372 (based on the figure of 3,343 households, with an estimated average of four persons per household), who were formerly included in Samtse, Paro or Thimphu districts. The above figures also predate the creation of a further two new districts, Gasa (previously within Punakha) and Trashi Yangtse (previously within Trashigang), in 1992.

† Gasa and Punakha were merged into a single district, which was to be known as Punakha, in 1987.

PRINCIPAL TOWNS
(1997 estimates)

Thimphu (capital) .	45,000	Geylephug . . .	12,500
Phuentsholing . .	45,000	Samdrup Jongkhar .	12,500

Source: Thomas Brinkhoff, *City Population* (internet www.citypopulation.de).

BIRTHS AND DEATHS
(UN estimates, annual averages)

	1985–90	1990–95	1995–2000
Birth rate (per 1,000) . . .	40.9	38.6	36.2
Death rate (per 1,000) . . .	14.4	11.4	9.8

Source: UN, *World Population Prospects: The 2000 Revision.*

Expectation of life (WHO estimates, years at birth): 61.6 (males 60.5; females 62.7) in 2001 (Source: WHO, *World Health Report*).

ECONOMICALLY ACTIVE POPULATION
(estimates, '000 persons, 1981/82)

Agriculture, etc..	613
Industry	6
Trade	9
Public services	22
Total	**650**

Mid-2001 (estimates in '000): Agriculture, etc. 968; Total labour force 1,033 (Source: FAO).

Health and Welfare

KEY INDICATORS

Total fertility rate (children per woman, 2001)	5.2
Under-5 mortality rate (per 1,000 live births, 2001) . .	95
HIV/AIDS (% of persons aged 15–49, 2001)	<0.10
Physicians (per 1,000 head, 1995)	0.16
Hospital beds (per 1,000 head, 1994)	1.61
Health expenditure (2000): US $ per head (PPP) . . .	64.0
Health expenditure (2000): % of GDP	4.1
Health expenditure (2000): public (% of total) . . .	90.6
Access to water (% of persons, 2000)	62
Access to sanitation (% of persons, 2000)	69
Human Development Index (2000): ranking	140
Human Development Index (2000): value	0.494

For sources and definitions, see explanatory note on p. vi.

Agriculture

PRINCIPAL CROPS
(FAO estimates, '000 metric tons)

	1999	2000	2001
Wheat*	20	20	20
Rice (paddy)	50	50	50
Barley	5*	5	5
Maize*	70	70	70
Millet	7	7	7
Other cereals	7.3	7.3	7.3
Potatoes	34.1	34.1	34.1
Other roots and tubers . . .	21.8	21.8	21.8
Sugar cane	12.8	12.8	12.8
Chillies and green peppers . .	8.5	8.5	8.5
Oranges	58	58	58
Other fruits (excl. melons) . .	7	7	7
Nutmeg, mace and cardamon . .	5.8	5.8	5.8
Other spices	8.1	8.1	8.1

* Unofficial figure(s).

Source: FAO.

LIVESTOCK
(FAO estimates, '000 head, year ending September)

	1999	2000	2001
Horses	30	30	30
Mules	10	10	10
Asses	18	18	18
Cattle	435	435	435
Buffaloes	4	4	4
Pigs	75	75	75
Sheep	59	59	59
Goats	42	42	42
Poultry.	310	310	310

Source: FAO.

Yaks ('000 head): 35 in 1993; 39 in 1994 (provisional); 40 in 1995 (estimate) (Source: IMF, *Bhutan—Selected Issues* (February 1997)).

LIVESTOCK PRODUCTS
(FAO estimates, '000 metric tons)

	1999	2000	2001
Beef and veal	5.8	5.8	5.8
Buffalo meat	0.1	0.1	0.1
Mutton and lamb	0.2	0.2	0.2
Goat meat	0.2	0.2	0.2
Pig meat	1.2	1.2	1.2
Poultry meat	0.3	0.3	0.3
Cows' milk	29.0	29.0	29.0
Buffaloes' milk	2.7	2.7	2.7
Goats' milk	0.2	0.2	0.2
Hen eggs	0.4	0.4	0.4
Cattle hides (fresh)	1.2	1.2	1.2
Sheepskins (fresh)	0.1	0.1	0.1

Source: FAO.

Forestry

ROUNDWOOD REMOVALS
('000 cubic metres, excl. bark)

	1999	2000	2001
Sawlogs, veneer logs and logs for sleepers*	67	64	64
Other industrial wood	72	70	70
Fuel wood	4,142	4,221	4,284
Total	4,281	4,355	4,418

* FAO estimates.
Source: FAO.

SAWNWOOD PRODUCTION
(FAO estimates, '000 cubic metres, incl. railway sleepers)

	1998	1999	2000
Coniferous (softwood)	12	15	21
Broadleaved (hardwood)	6	7	10
Total	18	22	31

2001: Annual production as in 2000 (FAO estimates).
Source: FAO.

Fishing

(FAO estimates, metric tons, live weight)

	1998	1999	2000
Capture			
Freshwater fishes	300	300	300
Aquaculture			
Freshwater fishes	30	30	30
Total catch	330	330	330

Source: FAO, *Yearbook of Fishery Statistics*.

Mining

(metric tons, unless otherwise indicated, year ending 30 June)

	1999	2000	2001
Dolomite	214,300	224,200	283,700
Limestone	301,500	415,900	434,900
Gypsum	74,000	100,500	87,000
Coal	67,500	68,200	65,800
Marble chips (sq ft)	32,100	42,800	33,500
Slate (sq m)*	9,000	9,000†	9,000†
Quartzite	73,000	29,900	48,700
Talc	10,300	11,500	8,900
Iron ore	1,100	3,100	3,100

* Twelve months ending 31 December of year stated.
† Estimate.

Sources: Geology and Mines Division, Ministry of Trade and Industry, Royal Government of Bhutan; US Geological Survey.

Industry

GROSS SALES AND OUTPUT OF SELECTED INDUSTRIES
(million ngultrum)

	1999	2000	2001
Penden Cement Authority	684.5	696.7	n.a.
Bhutan Ferro Alloys	534.7	428.4	579.0
Bhutan Fruit Products	124.9	108.5	111.6
Army Welfare Project*	234.9	255.0	283.8
Bhutan Carbide and Chemicals	569.3	474.6	675.9
Bhutan Board Products	257.1	228.6	294.1
Eastern Bhutan Coal Company	97.1	126.5	132.7
Druk Satair Corporation Ltd	77.4	94.0	98.3

* Manufacturer of alcoholic beverages.

Source: Royal Monetary Authority.

Electric energy (million kWh, year ending 30 June): 1,972.2 in 1995/96; 1,838.4 in 1996/97; 1,800.0 in 1997/98.

Revenue from the Chhukha Hydroelectric Project (million ngultrum): 2,141.7 (Internal consumption 122.5, Exports 2,019.1) in 1999; 2,307.4 (Internal consumption 117.8, Exports 2,189.6) in 2000; 2,175.1 (Internal consumption 140.2; Exports 2,034.9) in 2001.

Source: Department of Power, Royal Government of Bhutan.

Finance

CURRENCY AND EXCHANGE RATES

Monetary Units
100 chetrum (Ch) = 1 ngultrum (Nu)

Sterling, Dollar and Euro Equivalents (31 December 2002)
£1 sterling = 77.42 ngultrum
US $1 = 48.03 ngultrum
€1 = 50.37 ngultrum
1,000 ngultrum = £12.92 = $20.82 = €19.85

Average Exchange Rate (ngultrum per US $)
2000   44.942
2001   47.186
2002   48.610

Note: The ngultrum is at par with the Indian rupee, which also circulates freely within Bhutan. The foregoing figures relate to the official rate of exchange, which is applicable to government-related transactions alone. Since April 1992 there has also been a market rate of exchange, which values foreign currencies approximately 20% higher than the official rate of exchange.

BUDGET
(million ngultrum, year ending 30 June)

Revenue	1999/2000	2000/01	2001/02*
Taxation	1,977.1	1,916.9	2,196.5
Taxes on income, profit and capital gains	1,056.7	1,257.6	1,232.9
Income tax	223.5	338.1	293.7
Corporation tax	833.2	919.5	939.2
Domestic taxes on goods and services	842.5	564.1	860.6
General sales, turnover or value-added tax	299.9	342.7	330.4
Excises	470.3	130.3	458.8
Taxes on international trade	70.5	94.6	94.0
Import duties	57.9	78.3	78.3
Export duties	9.4	13.2	12.7
Other current revenue	2,537.0	2,982.7	2,906.4
Entrepreneurial and property income	1,692.5	2,285.7	1,976.0
Administrative fees and charges, non-industrial and incidental sales	71.5	80.7	64.1
Other	773.0	616.3	866.3
Capital revenue	71.3	76.1	37.7
Grants	3,274.1	3,711.0	2,918.4
Total revenue and grants	7,859.5	8,686.7	8,059.0

Expenditure	1999/2000	2000/01	2001/02*
General public services . . .	1,787.0	2,466.6	2,149.9
Public order and safety	453.6	474.6	486.1
Education	1,120.5	1,215.2	1,528.4
Health	768.3	804.0	1,000.2
Housing and community amenities	276.9	279.3	751.0
Recreational, cultural and religious affairs	69.5	113.9	172.2
Economic services	3,778.2	5,285.1	3,640.5
Fuel and energy	1,990.4	3,349.9	1,289.2
Agriculture, forestry, fishing and hunting	666.0	753.1	1,007.2
Mining and mineral resources, manufacturing and construction	42.7	24.2	28.9
Transportation and communication	1,029.9	1,084.0	1,216.8
Other purposes	80.2	77.8	85.4
Net lending	289.9	461.0	2.0
Total expenditure and net lending	**8,624.1**	**11,177.5**	**9,815.7**

* Provisional figures.

Source: IMF, *Government Finance Statistics Yearbook.*

2002/03 (million ngultrum, forecast): *Revenue:* Domestic revenue 5,100.2; Other receipts 18.3; Grants 4,413.7; Total 9,532.2. *Expenditure:* Current expenditure 4,597.3; Capital expenditure 6,318.8; Net lending 28.3; Repayments 240.3; Total 11,184.6.

Source: Royal Government of Bhutan.

FOREIGN EXCHANGE RESERVES
(at 30 June)

	2000	2001	2002
Indian rupee reserves (million Indian rupees)	3,165.0	3,617.3	3,730.6
Royal Monetary Authority . .	102.0	89.4	635.7
Bank of Bhutan	1,819.5	2,149.7	1,980.9
Bhutan National Bank . . .	1,191.9	1,328.3	1,064.1
Royal Insurance Corporation of Bhutan	51.5	50.0	50.0
Convertible currency reserves (US $ million)	221.8	217.3	240.7
Royal Monetary Authority* . .	197.7	186.1	202.6
Bank of Bhutan	11.4	16.3	18.5
Bhutan National Bank . . .	12.6	14.8	19.5
Royal Insurance Corporation of Bhutan	—	—	0.1

* Includes tranche position in the International Monetary Fund.

Source: Royal Monetary Authority of Bhutan.

MONEY SUPPLY
(million ngultrum at 31 December)

	1999	2000	2001
Currency outside banks* . . .	969.2	1,269.6	1,609.9
Demand deposits at the Bank of Bhutan	2,754.9	2,669.5	3,238.2
Total money†	**12,665.8**	**15,661.0**	**16,312.7**

* Including an estimate for Indian rupees.
† Including non-monetary deposits with the Royal Monetary Authority by financial institutions.

Source: Royal Monetary Authority of Bhutan.

COST OF LIVING
(Consumer Price Index at 31 December; base: 1979 = 100)

	1999	2000	2001
All items (excl. rent)	587.0	612.9	632.8

Source: Central Statistical Office of the Planning Commission, Royal Government of Bhutan.

NATIONAL ACCOUNTS
(million ngultrum at current prices)

Expenditure on the Gross Domestic Product

	1998	1999	2000
Government final consumption expenditure.	3,308	4,271	4,422
Private final consumption expenditure.	9,322	10,067	11,329
Increase in stocks	45	108	49
Gross fixed capital formation . .	6,200	8,127	9,447
Total domestic expenditure. .	**18,875**	**22,573**	**25,247**
Exports of goods and services . .	5,148	5,714	6,456
Less Imports of goods and services	7,686	9,164	10,004
GDP in purchasers' values . .	**16,337**	**19,122**	**21,698**

Source: IMF, *International Financial Statistics.*

Gross Domestic Product by Economic Activity

	1998*	1999*	2000†
Agriculture, forestry and livestock	6,057.5	6,640.8	7,769.1
Mining and quarrying	262.3	325.9	341.0
Manufacturing	1,621.8	1,761.8	1,734.7
Electricity	1,937.1	2,317.9	2,519.8
Construction	1,687.0	2,113.1	2,717.3
Trade, restaurants and hotels . .	1,159.7	1,281.6	1,465.3
Transport, storage and communications	1,369.5	1,636.7	1,863.2
Finance, insurance and real estate	1,004.0	1,042.0	1,324.1
Community, social and personal services	1,436.9	1,835.9	1,920.0
Sub-total	**16,535.8**	**18,955.7**	**21,654.5**
Less Imputed bank service charges	458.3	441.6	528.0
GDP at factor cost	**16,077.5**	**18,514.1**	**21,126.5**
GDP at constant 1980 factor cost	**3,514.3**	**3,773.4**	**3,989.5**

* Revised figures.
† Projected figures.

Source: Royal Monetary Authority of Bhutan.

BALANCE OF PAYMENTS
(US $ million, year ending 30 June)

	1998/99	1999/2000	2000/01
Merchandise exports f.o.b. . . .	103.6	111.0	110.3
Merchandise imports c.i.f. . . .	−160.6	−179.7	−211.6
Trade balance	**−57.0**	**−68.7**	**−101.3**
Services and transfers	−39.9	−57.4	−22.0
Current balance	**−96.9**	**−126.1**	**−123.3**
Grants and loans	145.2	167.9	155.1
Foreign direct investment . . .	1.1	—	—
Net errors and omissions . . .	−5.7	−6.4	−8.0
Overall balance	**43.7**	**35.4**	**23.8**

Source: Asian Development Bank, *Key Indicators of Developing Asian and Pacific Countries.*

OFFICIAL DEVELOPMENT ASSISTANCE
(US $ million)

	1998	1999	2000
Bilateral donors	39.8	52.1	33.3
Multilateral donors	16.0	14.7	20.0
Total	**55.8**	**66.8**	**53.3**
Grants	48.2	60.2	42.5
Loans	7.6	6.6	10.8
Per caput assistance (US $) . .	28.3	33.1	25.5

Source: UN, *Statistical Yearbook for Asia and the Pacific.*

SELECTED COMMODITIES
(million ngultrum, provisional)

Imports c.i.f.	1995	1996	1997
Wood charcoal	n.a.	122.3	139.6
Telecommunications equipment	n.a.	302.0	491.0
Beer	n.a.	66.0	86.3
Coal	n.a.	44.6	103.3
Diesel oil	136.1	138.8	163.2
Petroleum	64.0	67.4	73.0
Rice	217.3	209.1	215.3
Wheat	39.3	89.0	100.0
Vegetable fats and oils	134.7	134.4	121.1
Cotton fabric	41.9	38.2	n.a.
Industrial machinery	142.0	77.5	54.3
Tyres for buses and trucks	37.5	34.5	n.a.
Iron and steel	115.4	109.6	117.0
Electricity	10.7	7.6	n.a.
Total (incl. others)	3,802.3	4,250.0	4,980.0

Exports f.o.b.	1995	1996	1997
Electricity	721.9	747.6	1,290.0
Calcium carbide	497.9	533.0	546.3
Cement	278.4	253.0	371.4
Particle board	329.1	286.0	329.0
Non-coniferous plywood	32.8	2.2	n.a.
Sawn logs (hard)	71.8	79.1	78.1
Sawn timber (soft)	60.7	27.1	76.5
Cardamom	73.8	68.2	36.9
Wheat and flour	23.8	58.0	n.a.
Mixed fruit/vegetable juice	119.5	86.7	7.8
Coal (bituminous)	n.a.	19.9	25.6
Rum	n.a.	65.0	58.8
Total (incl. others)	3,349.1	3,553.8	4,270.0

1998 (million ngultrum): Electricity 1,338.7; Calcium carbide 583.6; Cement 547.3; Particle board 285.8.

1999 (million ngultrum): Electricity 2,019.1; Calcium carbide 546.8; Cement 433.7; Particle board 247.6.

2000 (estimate, million ngultrum): Calcium carbide 145.4 (Source: Asian Development Bank, *Key Indicators of Developing Asian and Pacific Countries*).

PRINCIPAL TRADING PARTNERS
(estimates, US $ million, year ending 30 June)

Imports c.i.f.	1998/99*	1999/2000	2000/01†
India	115.5	139.0	159.3
Other countries	46.8	46.0	56.0
Total	162.3	185.0	215.3

Exports f.o.b.	1998/99	1999/2000	2000/01†
India	98.2	108.0	106.0
Other countries	6.6	6.3	6.3
Total	104.8	114.3	112.3

* Revised figures.
† Preliminary estimates.

Source: Royal Monetary Authority of Bhutan.

Transport

ROAD TRAFFIC: In 2000 there were 19,463 registered, roadworthy vehicles—7,438 light four-wheeled vehicles, 7,793 two-wheeled vehicles (motorcycles and scooters), 2,062 heavy vehicles (trucks, buses, bulldozers, etc.) and 770 taxis (Source: Central Statistical Office, Ministry of Planning).

CIVIL AVIATION
(traffic on scheduled services)

	1997	1998	1999
Kilometres flown (million)	1	1	1
Passengers carried ('000)	36	36	31
Passenger-km (million)	49	49	49
Total ton-km (million)	4	4	4

Source: UN, *Statistical Yearbook*.

2000: Paying passengers 19,233; Revenue (million ngultrum, year ending 30 June) 157.3.

Source: Central Statistical Office, Ministry of Planning, Royal Government of Bhutan.

Tourism

FOREIGN VISITORS BY COUNTRY OF ORIGIN*

	1998	1999	2000
Australia	64	131	179
Austria	270	197	131
France	366	236	399
Germany	520	574	662
Italy	218	276	156
Japan	1,032	1,102	875
Netherlands	370	362	359
Switzerland	170	296	137
Taiwan	135	179	175
United Kingdom	686	646	595
USA	1,471	2,122	2,754
Total (incl. others)	6,203	7,158	7,559

* Figures relate to tourists paying in convertible currency.

Foreign visitor arrivals: 6,393 in 2001.

Receipts (US $ million): 8.65 in 1999; 9.87 in 2000; 9.20 in 2001.

Sources: Tourism Authority of Bhutan; World Tourism Organization, *Yearbook of Tourism Statistics*.

Government hotel rooms: 560 in 1996; 560 in 1997; 560 in 1998 (provisional) (Source: IMF, *Bhutan—Statistical Annex* (July 1999)).

Communications Media

	1998	1999	2000
Television receivers ('000 in use) .	12.5	13.0	13.5
Telephone ('000 main lines in use).	10.4	11.8	13.3
Facsimile machines ('000 in use) .	1.5	n.a.	n.a.
Personal computers ('000 in use) .	2.5	3.0	3.5
Internet users ('000)	—	0.5	1.5

Radio receivers ('000 in use): 37 in 1997.

Sources: International Telecommunications Union; UNESCO, *Statistical Yearbook*.

Education

(August 2002)

	Institu-tions	Teachers	Students Males	Females	Total
Community primary schools .	182	531	11,353	9,635	20,988
Primary schools	97	753	15,382	13,497	28,879
Lower secondary schools . .	65	1,154	21,798	20,277	42,075
Middle secondary schools. .	27	669	10,256	8,938	19,194
Higher secondary schools. .	12	346	4,962	3,502	8,464
Private schools.	14	215	2,002	1,811	3,813
Institutes	11	282	2,071	1,025	3,096
Non-formal education (NFE) centres	292	256	2,210	5,278	7,488

Source: Ministry of Health and Education, Thimphu.

Adult literacy rate (UNESCO estimates): 42.2% (males 56.3%; females 28.2%) in 1995 (Source: UNESCO, *Statistical Yearbook*).

Directory

The Constitution

The Kingdom of Bhutan has no formal constitution. However, the state system is a modified form of constitutional monarchy. Written rules, which are changed periodically, govern procedures for the election of members of the Council of Ministers, the Royal Advisory Council and the Legislature, and define the duties and powers of those bodies. A special committee was convened in late 2001 to prepare a draft written constitution. The first draft was formally presented to King Jigme Singye Wangchuck in December 2002, who then passed the draft to the Head of Government. The document was to be subjected to public review before being submitted to the National Assembly for formal approval.

The Government

Head of State: HM Druk Gyalpo ('Dragon King') JIGME SINGYE WANGCHUCK (succeeded to the throne in July 1972).

LODOI TSOKDE
(Royal Advisory Council)
(April 2003)

The Royal Advisory Council (Lodoi Tsokde), established in 1965, comprises nine members: two monks representing the Central Monk Body (Dratshang) and District Monastic Body (Rabdeys) respectively, six people's representatives, and a Chairman (Kalyon) nominated by the King. Each geog (group of villages, known also as a block) within a dzongkhag (district) selects one representative, from whom the respective Dzongkhag Yargye Tshogchungs (DYTs—District Development Committees) each agree on one nomination to be forwarded to the National Assembly (Tshogdu Chenmo). From these 20 nominees, the National Assembly, in turn, elects six persons to serve on the Royal Advisory Council as people's representatives for the whole country. The Council's principal task is to advise the Chairman of the Council of Ministers (Lhengye Zhungtshog), as head of government, and to supervise all aspects of administration. The Council is in permanent session, virtually as a government department, and acts, on a daily basis, as the *de facto* Standing Committee of the National Assembly. Representatives of the monastic bodies serve for one year, representatives of the people for three years, and the duration of the Chairman's term of office is at the discretion of the King. Representatives may be re-elected, but not for consecutive terms; they are all full members of the Council of Ministers.

Chairman: Dasho RINZIN GYELTSHEN.

Councillors: Dasho ADAP PASANG*, Dasho LEKI PEMA*, Dasho JAMYANG*, Dasho CHADOR WANGDI*, Dasho (Aum) SONAM WANGCHUK*, Dasho GYELTSHEN*, PHURPA TENZIN†, THUKTEN NORBU†.
* From November 2001 to November 2004.
† From November 2002 to November 2003.

LHENGYE ZHUNGTSHOG
(Council of Ministers)
(April 2003)

Prime Minister and Chairman (August 2002–July 2003) and Minister of Agriculture: Lyonpo KINZANG DORJI.

Minister of Trade and Industry: Lyonpo KHANDU WANGCHUK.

Minister of Finance: Lyonpo YESHEY ZIMBA.

Minister of Foreign Affairs: Lyonpo JIGMI YOZER THINLEY.

Minister of Health and Education: Lyonpo SANGYE NGEDUP DORJI.

Minister of Home Affairs: Lyonpo THINLEY GYAMTSHO.

Cabinet Secretary: Aum NETEN ZANGMO.

All members of the Royal Advisory Council are also members of the Council of Ministers.

MINISTRIES AND OTHER MAJOR GOVERNMENT BODIES

Ministry of Agriculture: POB 252, Thimphu; tel. 322129; fax 323153; internet www.moa.gov.bt.

Ministry of Communications: Division of Information Technology, Old Banquet Hall, Conference Centre, Thimphu; tel. 323215; fax 322184; e-mail dit@druknet.bt; internet www.dit.gov.bt.

Ministry of Finance: Tashichhodzong, POB 117, Thimphu; tel. 322223; fax 323154; internet www.mof.gov.bt.

Ministry of Foreign Affairs: Convention Centre, POB 103, Thimphu; tel. 323297; fax 323240; internet www.foa.gov.bt.

Ministry of Health and Education: Tashichhodzong, POB 726, Thimphu; tel. 322351; fax 324649; internet www.health.gov.bt (Health Services division); tel. 325146; fax 324823; internet www .education.gov.bt (Education Division).

Ministry of Home Affairs: Tashichhodzong, POB 133, Thimphu; tel. 322301; fax 322214.

Ministry of Trade and Industry: Tashichhodzong, POB 141, Thimphu; tel. 322211; fax 323617; internet www.mti.gov.bt.

National Commission for Cultural Affairs: Thimphu; tel. 322001; fax 323040; e-mail dorwang@druknet.bt; internet www.ctf .gov.bt (Cultural Trust Fund); internet www.library.gov.bt; fmrly Special Commission for Cultural Affairs; Chair. Lyonpo THINLEY GYAMTSHO; Sec. Dasho SANGAY WANGCHUG.

National Environment Commission: Thimphu, POB 466; tel. 323384; fax 323385; e-mail rnrec@druknet.bt; Hon. Dep. Minister Dasho NADO RINCHEN.

Office of the Royal Advisory Council: Tashichhodzong, POB 200, Thimphu; tel. 312339; fax 325343.

Royal Audit Authority: Thimphu; tel. 322111; internet www.raa .gov.bt; Auditor-Gen. Dasho KUNZANG WANGDI.

Cabinet Secretariat: Thimphu; tel. 321437; fax 321438.

Legislature

TSHOGDU CHENMO

A National Assembly (Tshogdu Chenmo) was established in 1953. The Assembly has a three-year term and meets (in recent years) at least once a year (usually in June–July). The size of the membership is based, in part, on the population of the districts; although the size is, in principle, subject to periodic revision, in practice the basis for popular representation has remained unchanged since 1953. In 2000 the Assembly had 152 members, including the Speaker and Deputy Speaker. Of this number, 99 were elected by direct popular consensus in the districts (formal voting is used, however, in the event of a deadlock); 10 of the 20 districts elected new public members (chimis) in November 2001, to replace those whose term of office had expired. (Not all of the chimis are elected simultaneously; there are, therefore, overlaps in tenure.) Six were members of the Royal Advisory Council (RAC), elected by secret ballot; the Chairman (Kalyon) of the RAC also sits in the Assembly. Ten seats were reserved for representatives of the Central and District Monk Bodies (of whom two sit as members of the RAC), one was reserved for a representative of industry (elected by the Bhutan Chamber of Commerce and Industry), and the remainder (35) were occupied by officials (including the 20 Dzongdas) selected by the King in conjunction with the National Assembly Secretariat. The Assembly elects its own Speaker from among its members, for a three-year (renewable) term. It enacts laws, advises on constitutional and political matters and debates all important issues. There is provision for a secret ballot on controversial issues, but, in practice, decisions are reached by consensus. Ministers and the six public members of the RAC are chosen by the entire Assembly in a secret ballot. Both the RAC and the Council of Ministers are responsible to the Assembly.

Speaker: Dasho UGYEN DORJI.

Political Organizations

Political parties are banned in Bhutan, in accordance with long-standing legislation. There are, however, a small number of anti-Government organizations, composed principally of Nepali-speaking former residents of Bhutan, which are based in Kathmandu, Nepal.

Bhutan Gurkha National Liberation Front (BGNLF): Nepal; f. 1994; Sec.-Gen. R. P. SUBBA.

Bhutan National Democratic Party (BNDP): POB 3334, Kathmandu, Nepal; tel. 525682; f. 1992; also has offices in Delhi and Varanasi, India, and in Thapa, Nepal; Pres. R. B. BASNET; Gen. Secs Dr HARI P. ADHIKARI (Organization), D. N. S. DHAKAL (Planning and External Affairs).

Bhutan People's Party (BPP): f. 1990 as a successor to the People's Forum on Democratic Rights (f. 1989); advocates unconditional release of all political prisoners, judicial reform, freedom of religious practices, linguistic freedom, freedom of press, speech and expression, and equal rights for all ethnic groups; Pres. (vacant); Gen. Sec. R. K. CHETTRI.

Druk National Congress (DNC): Maharagunj, Chakrapath, Kathmandu, Nepal; f. 1992; claims to represent 'all the oppressed people of Bhutan'; Pres. 'RONGTHONG' KINLEY DORJI.

Human Rights Organization of Bhutan (HUROB): POB 172, Patan Dhoka, Lalitpur, Kathmandu, Nepal; tel. 525046; fax 526038; f. 1991; documents alleged human rights violations in Bhutan and co-ordinates welfare activities in eight refugee camps in Nepal for ethnic Nepalese claiming to be from Bhutan; Chair. S. B. SUBBA; Gen. Sec. OM DHUNGEL.

United Liberation People's Front: f. 1990; Leader BALARAM POUDYAL.

Diplomatic Representation

EMBASSIES IN BHUTAN

Bangladesh: POB 178, Upper Choubachu, Thimphu; tel. 322362; fax 322629; e-mail bdoot@druknet.bt; Ambassador AHMED RAHIM.

India: India House, Lungtenzampa, Thimphu; tel. 322100; fax 323195; internet www.eoithimphu.org; Ambassador K. J. JASROTIA.

Judicial System

Bhutan has Civil and Criminal Codes, which are based on those laid down by the Shabdrung Ngawang Namgyal in the 17th century. An independent judicial authority was established in 1961, but law was mostly administered at the district level until 1968, when the High Court was set up. Existing laws were consolidated in 1982, although annual or biennial conferences of Drangpons (previously styled Thrimpons) are held to keep abreast of changing circumstances and to recommend (in the first instance, to the King) amendments to existing laws. Most legislation is sent by the Council of Ministers to the National Assembly for approval and enactment. A substantially-revised Civil and Criminal Procedure Code was endorsed by the 79th National Assembly session in July 2001. Further review and reform of the judicial system was under way in 2002–03.

Appeal Court: The Supreme Court of Appeal is the King.

High Court
(Thrimkhang Gongma)

Thimphu; tel. 322344; fax 322921.

Established 1968 to review appeals from Lower Courts, although some cases are heard at the first instance. The Full Bench is presided over by the Chief Justice. There are normally seven other judges, who are appointed by the King on the recommendation of the Chief Justice and who serve until their superannuation. Three judges form a quorum. The judges are assisted by senior rabjams/ramjans (judges in training). Assistance to defendants is available through jabmis (certificated pleaders). The operation of the legal system and proposed amendments are considered by regular meetings of all the judges and Thrimpons (usually annually, or at least once every two years). Under the mid-1998 grant of governance to an elected Council of Ministers and pending the adoption of detailed regulations, proposed amendments are expected to be submitted to the Council of Ministers for consideration. Major changes to structure, administration and personnel were implemented from mid-2001.

Chief Justice: Lyonpo SONAM TOBGYE.

Judges (Drangpons) of the High Court: Dasho THINLEY YOEZER, Dasho PASANG TOBGYE, Dasho KARMA D. SHERPA, Dasho PHUB DORJI.

Magistrates' Courts (Dzongkhag Thrimkhang): Each district has a court, headed by the drangpon (magistrate) and aided by a junior rabjam/ramjam, which tries most cases. Appeals are made to the High Court, and less serious civil disputes may be settled by a gup or mandal (village headman) through written undertakings by the parties concerned.

All citizens have the right to make informal appeal for redress of grievances directly to the King, through the office of the gyalpoi zimpon (court chamberlain).

Department of Legal Affairs: tel. 326889; fax 324606; f. 2000; consists of a prosecution division, with civil and criminal sections, to indict offenders on behalf of the Government; and a legal services division, to assist in the drafting of laws and acts, advance Bhutan's interest internationally in accordance with public international laws, develop the legal profession, and create public awareness of laws and acts; Dir Dasho KUENLAY TSHERING.

Religion

The state religion is Mahayana Buddhism, but the southern Bhutanese are predominantly followers of Hinduism. Buddhism was introduced into Bhutan in the eighth century ad by the Indian saint Padmasambhava, known in Bhutan as Guru Rimpoche. In the 13th century Phajo Drugom Shigpo made the Drukpa school of Kagyupa Buddhism pre-eminent in Bhutan, and this sect is still supported by the dominant ethnic group, the Drukpas. The main monastic group, the Central Monastic Body (comprising 1,160 monks), is led by an elected Head Abbot (Je Khenpo), is directly supported by the State and spends six months of the year at Tashichhodzong and at Punakha respectively. A further 2,120 monks, who are members of the District Monastic Bodies, are sustained by the lay population. The Council for Ecclesiastical Affairs oversees all religious bodies. Monasteries (Gompas) and shrines (Lhakhangs) are numerous. Religious proselytizing, in any form, is illegal.

Council for Ecclesiastical Affairs (Dratshang Lhentshog): POB 254, Thimphu; tel. 322754; fax 323867; e-mail dratsang@druknet.bt; f. 1984; replacing the Central Board for Monastic Studies, to oversee all Buddhist meditational centres and schools of Buddhist studies, as well as the Central and District Monastic Bodies; daily affairs of the Council are run by the Central Monastic Secretariat; Chair. His Holiness the 70th Je-Khenpo Trulku JIGME CHOEDRA; Sec. SANGAY WANGCHUG; Dep. Sec. NGAWANG PHUNTSHO.

The Press

The Bhutan Review: POB 172, Patan Dhoka, Lalitpur, Kathmandu, Nepal; tel. 525046; fax 523819; f. 1993; monthly organ of the Human Rights Organization of Bhutan (HUROB); opposed to existing government policies.

Kuensel Corporation: POB 204, Thimphu; tel. 322483; fax 322975; internet www.kuenselonline.com; f. 1965 as a weekly govt bulletin; reorg. as a national weekly newspaper in 1986; became autonomous corporation in 1992 (previously under Dept of Information), incorporating former Royal Government Press; in English, Dzongkha and Nepali; Man. Dir and Editor-in-Chief KINLEY DORJI; Editors (vacant) (Nepali), TENZIN RIGDEN (English), MINDU DORJI (Dzongkha); circ. 280 (Nepali), 12,875 (English), 4,280 (Dzongkha).

Broadcasting and Communications

TELECOMMUNICATIONS

Bhutan Telecom Corporation: POB 134, Thimphu; tel. 322678; fax 324312; e-mail info@telecom.bt; internet www.telecom.bt; f. 2000; state-owned public corpn; regulation authority; agency for satellite phones; Chair. Dasho LEKI DORJI; Exec. Dir Dasho SANGEY TENZING.

DrukNet: Bhutan Telecom, 2/28 Drophen Lam, POB 134, Thimphu; tel. 326998; fax 328160; e-mail info@druknet.bt; internet www.druknet.bt; f. 1999; internet service provider; Head GANGA SHARMA.

BROADCASTING

Radio

In 1994 there were 52 radio stations for administrative communications. Of these, 34 were for internal communications (to which the public had access), and three were external stations serving Bhutan House at Kalimpong and the Bhutanese diplomatic missions in India and Bangladesh.

BBS Corporation (Bhutan Broadcasting Service): POB 101, Thimphu; tel. 323071; fax 323073; e-mail bbs@bbs.com.bt; internet www.bbs.com.bt; f. 1973 as Radio National Youth Association of Bhutan (NYAB); became autonomous corporation in 1992 (previously under Dept of Information); short-wave radio station broadcasting daily in Dzongkha, Sharchopkha, Nepali (Lhotsamkha) and English; a daily FM programme (for Thimphu only) began in 1987; simultaneous broadcasting in FM for western Bhutan and parts of central and southern Bhutan began in 2000; a one-hour daily television service for Thimphu was introduced in mid-1999 and later increased to two hours daily; Chair. Dasho LEKI DORJI; Exec. Dir KINGA SINGYE.

Television

In June 1999 the BBS Corporation started operating a television service (in Dzongkha and English) in Thimphu; the service was gradually to be expanded throughout the country. Broadcasts were to be limited to a few hours a day and were to consist entirely of national news and documentaries about the Bhutanese. By March 2000, according to the Ministry of Communications, each of the two cable television operators was providing 25 channels.

Finance

(cap. = capital; auth. = authorized; p.u. = paid up; res = reserves; dep. = deposits; m. = million; brs = branches; amounts in ngultrum)

BANKING

Central Bank

Royal Monetary Authority (RMA): POB 154, Thimphu; tel. 323111; fax 322847; e-mail rma-rsd@druknet.bt; f. 1982; bank of issue; frames and implements official monetary policy, co-ordinates the activities of financial institutions and holds foreign-exchange deposits on behalf of the Govt; cap. 1.5m. Chair. Lyonpo YESHEY ZIMBA; Man. Dir SONAM WANGCHUK.

Commercial Banks

Bank of Bhutan: POB 75, Phuentsholing; tel. 252983; fax 252641; e-mail bobho1@druknet.bt; f. 1968; 20% owned by the State Bank of India and 80% by the Govt of Bhutan; wholly managed by Govt of Bhutan from 1997; cap. p.u. 100m., res 548.2m., dep. 6,979.7m. (Dec. 2001); Dirs nominated by the Bhutan Govt: Chair. Lyonpo YESHEY ZIMBA; Dirs KARMA DORJI, Dasho YESHI TSHERING; Dirs nominated by the State Bank of India C. RAMNATH, M. HANUMANTHA RAO; Man. Dir TSHERING DORJI; 27 brs and 2 extension counters.

Bhutan National Bank (BNB): POB 439, Thimphu; tel. 252198; fax 252647; e-mail bnbpling@druknet.bt; internet www.bnb.com.bt; Bhutan's second commercial bank, in 1996; partially privatized in 1998; 27% owned by Govt, 20.1% by Asian Development Bank and 19.9% by Citibank; auth. cap. 200m., cap. p.u. 59.5m., res 122.3m., dep. 2,489.9m. (1999); Chair. Lyonpo KHANDU WANGCHUK; Man. Dir KIPCHU TSHERING; 4 brs.

Development Bank

Bhutan Development Finance Corporation (BDFC): POB 256, Thimphu; tel. 322579; fax 323428; e-mail bdfc@druknet.bt; f. 1988; provides industrial loans and short- and medium-term agricultural loans; cap. p.u. 100m., loans 500m. (2000); Chair. Dasho WANGDI NORBU; Man. Dir KARMA RANGDOL.

STOCK EXCHANGE

Royal Securities Exchange of Bhutan Ltd (RSEB): POB 742, Thimphu; tel. 323995; fax 323849; e-mail rseb@druknet.bt; f. 1993; supervised by the Royal Monetary Authority; open to Bhutanese nationals only; 13 listed cos (1998); Chair. SONAM WANGCHUK; CEO TASHI YEZER.

INSURANCE

Royal Insurance Corporation of Bhutan: POB 77, Phuentsholing; tel. 252869; fax 252640; e-mail ricb@druknet.bt; f. 1975; provides general and life insurance and credit investment services; Chair. Lyonpo YESHEY ZIMBA; Man. Dir LAMKEY TSHERING; 10 brs and development centres.

Trade and Industry

GOVERNMENT AGENCIES

Food Corporation of Bhutan (FCB): POB 80, Phuentsholing; tel. 252241; fax 252289; e-mail drukfood@druknet.bt; f. 1974; activities include procurement and distribution of food grains and other essential commodities through appointed Fair Price Shop Agents; marketing of surplus agricultural and horticultural produce through FCB-regulated market outlets; logistics concerning World Food Programme food aid; maintenance of buffer stocks to offset any emergency food shortages; maintenance of SAARC Food Security Reserve Stock; exporting certain fruits; Man. Dir SHERUB GYALTSHEN; 18 outlets and 100 Fair Price Shops.

Forestry Development Corporation: tel. 323834; fax 325585; Man. Dir NAMGAY WANGCHUK.

Planning Commission: Gyalong Tshokhang, POB 127, Thimphu; tel. 326786; fax 322928; e-mail pcs@pcs.gov.bt; internet www.pcs.gov.bt; headed by the King until 1991, formally reconstituted 1999; consists of 21 officials; proposes socio-economic policy guidelines, issues directives for the formulation of development plans, ensures efficient and judicious allocation of resources, directs socio-economic research, studies and surveys, and appraises the Government on the progress of development plans and programmes; Chair. Lyonpo KINZANG DORJI; Sec. DAW TENZIN.

State Trading Corpn of Bhutan Ltd (STCB): POB 76, Phuentsholing; tel. 252286; fax 252619; e-mail stcbl@druknet.bt; manages imports and exports on behalf of the Govt; Chair. Dasho KARMA DORJEE; Man. Dir Dasho DORJI NAMGAY; brs in Thimphu (POB 272; tel. 322953; fax 323781; e-mail stcbthim@druknet.bt) and Kolkata (Calcutta), India.

CHAMBER OF COMMERCE

Bhutan Chamber of Commerce and Industry (BCCI): POB 147, Thimphu; tel. 322742; fax 323936; e-mail bcci@druknet.bt; f. 1980; reorg. 1988; promotion of trade and industry and privatization, information dissemination, private-sector human resource development; 434 registered mems; 12-mem. technical advisory committee; 21-mem. district executive committee; Pres. Dasho UGYEN DORJI; Sec.-Gen. Dasho TSHERING DORJI.

UTILITIES

Electricity

Department of Energy: c/o Ministry of Trade and Industry, Tashichhodzong, POB 141, Thimphu; tel. 22159; fax 223507.

Basochhu Power Authority: Basochhu; tel. 471021; fax 471020; co-ordinates construction of dam and hydroelectric power-generating facilities.

Bhutan Electricity Authority (BEA): Thimphu; f. 2001; regulates the electricity supply industry.

Bhutan Power Corporation: Thimphu; f. 2002; responsible for ensuring electricity supply for the whole country at an affordable cost by 2020 and for providing uninterrupted transmission access for export of surplus power; Man. Dir SONAM TSHERING.

Chhukha Hydropower Corporation: Phuentsholing; tel. 252575; fax 252582; f. 1991; state-owned; Chair. Lyonpo YESHEY ZIMBA; Man. Dir YESHEY WANGDI.

Kurichhu Hydropower Corporation: Gyelpozhing (Mongar); tel. 744113; fax 744130; e-mail kpa@druknet.bt; operates and maintains a 60 MW-hydroelectric power-generating facility at Gyelpozhing; Chair. Lyonpo KHANDU WANGCHUK; Man. Dir. CHHEWANG RINZIN.

Tala Hydroelectric Project Authority: POB 908, Tala; tel. 272001; fax 272010; e-mail mdthpa@druknet.bt; co-ordinates construction of dam and hydroelectric power-generating facilities; Man. Dir R. N. KHAZANCHI.

Water

Thimphu City Corporation (Water Supply Unit): POB 215, Thimphu; tel. 324710; fax 24315; f. 1982; responsible for water supply of Thimphu municipality (population 32,000); Head BHIMLAL DHUNGEL.

TRADE UNIONS

Under long-standing legislation, trade union activity is illegal in Bhutan.

Transport

ROADS AND TRACKS

In June 1999 there were 3,690.5 km of roads in Bhutan, of which 2,228.9 km were black-topped. Surfaced roads link the important border towns of Phuentsholing, Gelephu, Sarpang and Samdrup Jongkhar in southern Bhutan to towns in West Bengal and Assam in India. There is a shortage of road transport. Yaks, ponies and mules are still the chief means of transport on the rough mountain tracks. By 1990 most of the previously government-operated transport facilities (mainly buses and minibuses) on major and subsidiary routes had been transferred to private operators on the basis of seven-year contracts.

Road Safety and Transport Authority: Thimphu; tel. 321282; fax 322538; under Ministry of Communications; regulates condition of goods and passenger transport services; Dir YESHI TSHERING.

Transport Corpn of Bhutan: Phuentsholing; tel. 252476; f. 1982; subsidiary of Royal Insurance Corpn of Bhutan; operates direct coach service between Phuentsholing and Kolkata via Siliguri.

Other operators are Barma Travels (f. 1990), Dawa Transport (Propr Sherub Wangchuck), Dhendup Travel Service (Phuentsholing; tel 252437), Gyamtsho Transport, Gurung Transport Service, Namgay Transport, Nima Travels (Phuentsholing tel. 252384), and Rimpung Travels (Phuentsholing tel. 252354).

Lorries for transporting goods are operated by the private sector.

CIVIL AVIATION

There is an international airport at Paro. There are also some 30 helicopter landing pads, which are used, by arrangement with the Indian military and aviation authorities, solely by government officials. The Council of Ministers approved the operation of a domestic helicopter service to improve mobility and to promote tourism, to be operated by Bhutan Airways Pvt Ltd. An ambulance helicopter, donated by a Swiss company, was to become available at the end of 2002.

Department of Civil Aviation: c/o Ministry of Communications, Woochu, Paro; tel. 271347; fax 271909; e-mail aviation@druknet.bt; Dir PHALA DORJI.

Druk-Air Corpn Ltd (Royal Bhutan Airlines): Head Office, Nemizampa, PO Paro; tel. 271856; fax 271861; e-mail drukair@druknet.bt; internet www.drukair.com; national airline; f. 1981; became fully operational in 1983; services from Paro to Bangladesh, India, Myanmar (from October 2002), Nepal and Thailand; charter services also undertaken; Chair. Dasho Lyonpo JIGMI Y. THINLEY; Man. Dir SANGAY KHANDU.

Tourism

Bhutan was opened to tourism in 1975. In 2001 the total number of foreign visitors was 6,393. Receipts from tourism in 2001 totalled US $9.2m. Tourists travel in organized 'package', cultural or trekking tours, or individually, accompanied by trained guides. Hotels have been constructed at Phuentsholing, Paro, Bumthang, Wangduephodrang and Thimphu, with lodges at Trongsa, Trashigang and Mongar. In addition, there are many small privately operated hotels and guest-houses. Plans for three foreign-managed commercial hotels, in the style of resorts, were under way in early 2002. The Government exercises close control over the development of tourism. In 1987 the National Assembly resolved that all monasteries, mountains and other holy places should be inaccessible to tourists from 1988 (this resolution is flexibly interpreted, however—e.g. Japanese Buddhist tour groups are permitted to visit 'closed' monasteries). In 1991 the Government began transferring the tourism industry to the private sector and licences were issued to new private tourism operators. Rules were introduced in 1995, asserting more stringent controls over private operators, through the Tourism Authority of Bhutan (TAB). In 1998 the Government's tourism policy was liberalized further; by the end of 2001 94 private travel agencies were operating in Bhutan. In 2001 the TAB was reorganized as the Department of Tourism, under the Ministry of Trade and Industry. The Government had identified the industry's potential to grow and to provide significant employment opportunities.

Department of Tourism: POB 126, Thimphu; tel. 323252; fax 323695; e-mail tab@druknet.bt; internet www.tourism.gov.bt; f. 2001 to replace Tourism Authority of Bhutan; under regulatory authority of Ministry of Trade and Industry; exercises overall authority over tourism policy, pricing, hotel, restaurant and travel agency licensing, visa approvals, etc. Dir LHATU WANGCHUK.

Bhutan Tourism Corporation Ltd: POB 159, Thimphu; tel. 322854; fax 323392; e-mail btcl@druknet.bt; internet www.kingdomofbhutan.com.

Association of Bhutan Travel Operators: POB 938, Thimphu; tel. 322862; fax 325286; e-mail abto@net.druknet.bt; f. 1998 to provide forum for members' views and to unite, supervise and co-ordinate activities of members; Chair. Dasho UGEN TSECHUP DORJI.

BOLIVIA

Introductory Survey

Location, Climate, Language, Religion, Flag, Capital

The Republic of Bolivia is a land-locked state in South America, bordered by Chile and Peru to the west, by Brazil to the north and east, and by Paraguay and Argentina to the south. The climate varies, according to altitude, from humid tropical conditions in the northern and eastern lowlands, which are less than 500 m (1,640 ft) above sea-level, to the cool and cold zones at altitudes of more than 3,500 m (about 11,500 ft) in the Andes mountains. The official languages are Spanish, Quechua and Aymará. Almost all of the inhabitants profess Christianity, and the great majority are adherents of the Roman Catholic Church. The national civil flag (proportions 2 by 3) has three equal horizontal stripes, of red, yellow and green. The state flag has, in addition, the national coat of arms in the centre of the yellow stripe. The legal capital is Sucre. The administrative capital and seat of government is La Paz.

Recent History

The Incas of Bolivia were conquered by Spain in 1538 and, although there were many revolts against Spanish rule, independence was not achieved until 1825. Bolivian history has been characterized by recurrent internal strife, resulting in a lengthy succession of presidents, and frequent territorial disputes with its neighbours, including the 1879–83 War of the Pacific between Bolivia, Peru and Chile, and the Chaco Wars of 1928–30 and 1932–35 against Paraguay.

At a presidential election in May 1951 the largest share of the vote was won by Dr Víctor Paz Estenssoro, the candidate of the Movimiento Nacionalista Revolucionario (MNR), who had been living in Argentina since 1946. He was denied permission to return to Bolivia and contested the election *in absentia*. However, he failed to gain an absolute majority, and the incumbent President transferred power to a junta of army officers. This regime was itself overthrown in April 1952, when a popular uprising, supported by the MNR and a section of the armed forces, enabled Dr Paz Estenssoro to return from exile and assume the presidency. His Government, a coalition of the MNR and the Labour Party, committed itself to profound social revolution. The coalition nationalized the tin mines and introduced universal suffrage (the franchise had previously been limited to literate adults) and land reform. Dr Hernán Siles Zuazo, a leading figure in the 1952 revolution, was elected President for the 1956–60 term, and Dr Paz Estenssoro was again elected President in 1960. However, the powerful trade unions came into conflict with the Government, and in November 1964, following widespread strikes and disorder, President Paz Estenssoro was overthrown by the Vice-President, Gen. René Barrientos Ortuño, who was supported by the army. After serving with Gen. Alfredo Ovando Candía as Co-President under a military junta, Gen. Barrientos resigned in January 1966 to campaign for the presidency; he was elected in July 1966.

President Barrientos encountered strong opposition from left-wing groups, including mineworkers' unions. There was also a guerrilla uprising in south-eastern Bolivia, led by Dr Ernesto ('Che') Guevara, the Argentine-born revolutionary who had played a leading role in the Castro regime in Cuba. However, the insurgency was suppressed by government troops, with the help of US advisers, and guerrilla warfare ended in October 1967, when Guevara was captured and killed. (In July 1997 Guevara's remains, together with those of three of his comrades, were finally located and returned to Cuba.) In April 1969 President Barrientos was killed in an air crash and Dr Luis Adolfo Siles Salinas, the Vice-President, succeeded to the presidency. In September, however, President Siles Salinas was deposed by the armed forces, who reinstated Gen. Ovando. He was forced to resign in October 1970, when, after a power struggle between right-wing and left-wing army officers, Gen. Juan José Torres González, who had support from leftists, emerged as President, pledging support for agrarian reform and worker participation in management. A 'People's Assembly', formed by Marxist politicians, radical students and leaders of trade unions, was allowed to meet and demanded the introduction of extreme socialist measures, causing disquiet in right-wing circles. President Torres was deposed in August 1971 by Col (later Gen.) Hugo Bánzer Suárez, who drew support from the right-wing Falange Socialista Boliviana and a section of the MNR, as well as from the army. In June 1973 President Bánzer announced an imminent return to constitutional government, but elections were later postponed to June 1974. The MNR withdrew its support and entered into active opposition.

Following an attempted military coup in June 1974, all portfolios within the Cabinet were assigned to military personnel. After another failed coup attempt in November, President Bánzer declared that elections had been postponed indefinitely and that his military regime would retain power until at least 1980. All political and union activity was banned. Political and industrial unrest in 1976, however, led President Bánzer to announce that elections would be held in July 1978. Allegations of fraud rendered the elections void, but Gen. Juan Pereda Asbún, the armed forces candidate in the elections, staged a successful military coup. In November 1978 his right-wing Government was overthrown in another coup, led by Gen. David Padilla Aranciba, Commander-in-Chief of the Army, with the support of national left-wing elements.

Presidential and congressional elections were held in July 1979. The presidential poll resulted in almost equal support for two ex-Presidents, Dr Siles Zuazo (with 36.0% of the vote) and Dr Paz Estenssoro (with 35.9%), who were now leading rival factions of the MNR. The Congreso (Congress), which was convened in August to resolve the issue, failed to award a majority to either candidate. An interim Government was formed under Walter Guevara Arce, President of the Senado (the upper house of the Congreso), but this administration was overthrown on 1 November by a right-wing army officer, Col Alberto Natusch Busch. He withdrew 15 days later after failing to gain the support of the Congreso, which elected Dra Lidia Gueiler Tejada, President of the Cámara de Diputados (Chamber of Deputies, the lower congressional house), as interim Head of State pending presidential and congressional elections scheduled for June 1980.

The result of the 1980 presidential election was inconclusive, and in July, before the Congreso could meet to decide between the two main contenders (again Siles Zuazo and Paz Estenssoro), a military junta led by an army commander, Gen. Luis García Meza, staged a coup—the 189th in Bolivia's 154 years of independence. In August 1981 a military uprising forced Gen. García to resign. In September the junta transferred power to another army commander, Gen. Celso Torrelio Villa, who declared his intention to fight official corruption and to return the country to democracy within three years. Labour unrest, provoked by Bolivia's severe economic crisis, was appeased by restitution of trade-union and political rights, and a mainly civilian Cabinet was appointed in April 1982. Elections were scheduled for April 1983. The political liberalization disturbed the armed forces, who attempted to create a climate of violence, and President Torrelio resigned in July 1982, amid rumours of an impending coup. The junta installed the less moderate Gen. Guido Vildoso Calderón, the Army Chief of Staff, as President. Unable to resolve the worsening economic crisis or to control a general strike, in September the military regime announced that power would be handed over in October to the Congreso that had originally been elected in 1980. Dr Siles Zuazo, who had obtained most votes in both 1979 and 1980, was duly elected President by the Congreso, and was sworn in for a four-year term in October 1982.

President Siles Zuazo appointed a coalition Cabinet consisting of members of his own party, the Movimiento Nacionalista Revolucionario de Izquierda (MNRI), the Movimiento de la Izquierda Revolucionaria (MIR) and the Partido Comunista de Bolivia (PCB). Economic aid from the USA and Europe was resumed, but the Government found itself unable to fulfil the expectations that had been created by the return to democratic rule. The entire Cabinet resigned in August 1983, and the President appointed a Cabinet in which the number of portfolios that were held by the right-wing of the MNRI, the Partido

Demócrata Cristiano (PDC) and independents was increased. The MIR joined forces with the MNR and with business interests in rejecting the Government's policy of complying with IMF conditions for assistance, which involved harsh economic measures. The Government lost its majority in the Congreso and was confronted by strikes and mass labour demonstrations. In November the opposition-dominated Senate approved an increase of 100% in the minimum wage, in defiance of the Government's austerity measures. Following a 48-hour general strike, the whole Cabinet resigned once again in December, in anticipation of an opposition motion of censure; the ministers accused the Senate of planning a 'constitutional coup' and urged the formation of a government of 'national unity'. In January 1984 President Siles Zuazo appointed a new coalition Cabinet, including 13 members of the previous Government.

The new Cabinet's main priority was to reverse Bolivia's grave economic decline. However, constant industrial agitation by the trade-union confederation, the Central Obrera Boliviana (COB), coupled with rumours of an imminent coup, seriously undermined public confidence in the President. In June 1984 the country was again thrown into turmoil by the temporary abduction of President Siles Zuazo. Two former cabinet ministers and some 100 right-wing army officers were arrested in connection with the kidnapping, which was believed to have been supported by leading figures in the illicit drugs trade.

At elections in July 1985, amid reports of electoral malpractice and poor organization, the right-wing Acción Democrática Nacionalista (ADN), whose presidential candidate was Gen. Hugo Bánzer Suárez (the former dictator), received 28.6% of the votes cast, and the MNR obtained 26.4%, while the MIR was the leading left-wing party. At a further round of voting in the Congreso in August, an alliance between the MNR and the leading left-wing groups, including the MIR, enabled Dr Víctor Paz Estenssoro of the MNR to secure the presidency (which he had previously held in 1952–56 and 1960–64). The armed forces pledged their support for the new Government.

On taking office in August 1985, the new Government immediately introduced a very strict economic programme, designed to reduce inflation, which was estimated to have reached 14,173% in the year to August. The COB rejected the programme and called an indefinite general strike in September. The Government responded by declaring the strike illegal and by ordering a 90-day state of siege throughout Bolivia. Leading trade unionists were detained or banished, and thousands of strikers were arrested. The strike was called off in October, when union leaders agreed to hold talks with the Government. The conclusion of the strike was regarded as a considerable success for the new administration which, in spite of having achieved office with the assistance of left-wing parties, had subsequently found a greater ally in the right-wing ADN.

Throughout 1986 demonstrations and strikes were held by the COB in protest at the Government's austerity measures. Following a general strike in August, the Government imposed another 90-day state of siege. Social discontent persisted in 1987 and extensive unrest continued in 1988 (following a further increase in the price of petrol in February of that year), which culminated in April with a national hunger strike, called by the COB, to protest against the continuing austerity measures. These problems led to the resignation of the Cabinet in August, although all except four ministers were reappointed.

Presidential and congressional elections took place in May 1989. Of the votes cast in the presidential election, Gonzalo Sánchez de Lozada of the MNR obtained 23.1%, Gen. Hugo Bánzer Suárez of the ADN 22.7%, and Jaime Paz Zamora of the MIR 19.6%. As no candidate had gained the requisite absolute majority, responsibility for the choice of President passed to the newly-elected Congreso, which was to convene in August. Shortly before the second stage of the election, Bánzer withdrew his candidacy in order to support his former adversary, Paz Zamora. The 46 ADN and 41 MIR seats in the Congreso were sufficient to assure a majority vote for Paz Zamora, who assumed the presidency. A coalition Government of 'national unity', the Acuerdo Patriótico, was then formed. At the same time, a joint political council (with undefined powers), headed by Bánzer, was established.

From 1988 the Government increased its attempts to reduce the illegal production of coca. As a result, during 1989 clashes between the drugs-control troops, Unidad Móvil de Patrullaje Rural (UMOPAR), and drugs-traffickers intensified, particularly on the in coca-processing region of northern Beni. By the middle of the year, however, it became clear that the Govern-

ment had failed to attain the targets of its coca-eradication programme (begun in 1986 after the US Government had agreed to provide more than US $100m. in aid), having encountered staunch opposition from the powerful coca-growers' organizations. Paz Zamora was critical of the militaristic approach of the USA to coca eradication and emphasized the need for economic and social support. In May 1990, however, he accepted US $35m. in military aid from the USA. In late 1990 reaction to US involvement in Bolivia became increasingly violent. The left-wing Nestor Paz Zamora guerrilla group claimed responsibility for several bomb attacks, declaring that its actions were in response to the violation of Bolivia's political and territorial sovereignty by the USA.

In December 1989 a serious institutional conflict arose when the Government allowed a former Minister of the Interior, Migration and Justice, Col Luis Arce Gómez, to be taken to Miami, Florida (USA), to be tried on drugs-trafficking charges, despite the absence of a formal extradition treaty between Bolivia and the USA. Arce Gómez had been on trial in Bolivia since 1986, accused of violating human rights. His extradition, therefore, constituted a contravention of Bolivian law, which states that a Bolivian cannot be extradited while undergoing trial in Bolivia. Following an acrimonious conflict between the Government and the judiciary, the Congreso temporarily suspended eight of the 12 supreme court judges in late 1990. In retaliation, the court threatened to annul the 1989 elections. The conflict was resolved in early 1991 with the signing by the country's five main political parties of a pact affirming the independence of the Supreme Court. In January 1991 a federal jury in Miami found Arce Gómez guilty on two charges of drugs-trafficking, and he was sentenced to 30 years' imprisonment.

In March 1991 the reputation of the Government was seriously undermined when three of its senior officials were forced to resign amid allegations of corruption. Moreover, the appointment in February of Col. Faustino Rico Toro as the new head of Bolivia's anti-drugs-trafficking force, La Fuerza Especial de Lucha Contra el Narcotráfico (FELCN) had provoked widespread outrage. In addition to his alleged connections with illegal drugs-traffickers, Rico was accused of having committed human rights abuses during his tenure as chief of army intelligence under the regime of Gen. Luis García Meza (1980–81). After considerable pressure from the USA (including the suspension of all military and economic aid), Rico resigned from his new position in early March. Later that month, following accusations by the USA linking them with illegal drugs-traffickers, the Minister of the Interior, Migration and Justice and the Chief of Police resigned from their posts, although both maintained their innocence. In July the Government announced a decree granting a period of amnesty, lasting 120 days, for drugs-traffickers to surrender voluntarily. A condition of the amnesty was that those giving themselves up confess their crimes and contribute effectively to the apprehension of other such criminals. In return, they were offered minimum prison sentences and the guarantee that they would not risk extradition to the USA. As many as seven of the country's most powerful drugs-traffickers were reported to have taken advantage of the amnesty.

Government plans to privatize state-owned enterprises, including the state mining corporation, COMIBOL, resulted in a series of strikes, organized by the COB, in late 1991 and early 1992. In July the COB called a further general strike, and in October, in what was regarded as a major reversal for the Government and a considerable victory for the mining union, Federación Sindical de Trabajadores Mineros de Bolivia (FSTMB), the Government suspended its programme of joint ventures between COMIBOL and private companies. Continued social unrest led to violent confrontation between protesters and troops throughout the country in early 1993, and the military occupation of La Paz in March of that year.

In April 1993 the Supreme Court found the former military dictator Gen. Luis García Meza guilty on 49 charges of murder, human rights abuses, corruption and fraud, and sentenced him, *in absentia*, to 30 years' imprisonment. Similar sentences were imposed on 14 of his collaborators. García Meza was arrested in Brazil in March 1994 and, following his extradition to Bolivia in October of that year, began his prison sentence in March 1995.

Presidential and congressional elections were held in June 1993. Sánchez de Lozada was the MNR's presidential candidate, while Bánzer Suárez was supported by both the ADN and the MIR, as Paz Zamora was ineligible for re-election. Of the votes cast in the presidential election, Sánchez de Lozada received

33.8%, Bánzer secured 20.0% and Carlos Palenque Aviles, a popular television presenter and leader of Conciencia de Patria (Condepa), received 13.6%. Since no candidate had secured the requisite absolute majority, a congressional vote was scheduled to take place in August to decide between the two main contenders. However, Bánzer withdrew from the contest, thereby leaving Sánchez de Lozada's candidacy unopposed. At legislative elections, conducted simultaneously, the MNR secured 69 of the 157 seats in the bicameral Congreso, while the ruling Acuerdo Patriótico coalition won only 43. The MNR subsequently concluded a pact with the Unión Cívica Solidaridad (UCS) and the Movimiento Bolivia Libre (MBL), thus securing a congressional majority. Sánchez de Lozada was sworn in as President on 6 August.

Despite the new Government's stated intention to combat corruption in Bolivia's political and public life, evidence of fraudulent practice continued to feature widely in the country's affairs in 1994. In March former President Jaime Paz Zamora announced his retirement from political life following the presentation of a report by the FELCN to the Congreso alleging his co-operation with drugs-traffickers (However, his retirement proved short-lived: in January 1995 Paz Zamora announced his return to political life, while denying the allegations against him in the FELCN report.) In June the President of the Supreme Court and its third judge were found guilty of bribery by the Senate and were dismissed and banned from holding public office for 10 years. In the same month it was revealed that a large proportion of the US $20m. seized from drugs-traffickers between 1988 and 1993 had disappeared. Members of the FELCN, trustees from the Attorney-General's office and local government officials were implicated in the affair.

Meanwhile, the US-funded coca-eradication programme continued to cause serious unrest during 1994, particularly in the Chapare valley of Cochabamba, where UMOPAR forces were occupying the area. Large-scale demonstrations throughout the year culminated in August and September in protests across the country by teachers, students and COB members, as well as coca producers. The unrest subsided in late September, when the Government pledged to cease forcible eradication of coca and to withdraw its forces gradually from Chapare.

In early 1995 some 80,000 teachers across the country undertook a campaign of industrial action in opposition to a proposed programme of education reforms, which advocated the privatization of much of the education system and the restriction of teachers' rights to union membership. In response to a call by COB for an indefinite strike, and in an attempt to quell several weeks of civil unrest, the Government declared a state of siege for 90 days. Military units were deployed throughout the country, and 370 union leaders were arrested and banished to remote areas. However, protests continued nation-wide and the state of siege was extended by a further 90 days in July, owing to continued civil unrest, which had become particularly intense in the Chapare valley, where, despite the introduction of a voluntary coca-eradication programme, UMOPAR forces had begun to occupy villages and to destroy coca plantations. Violent clashes between peasant farmers and UMOPAR personnel between July and September resulted in the arrest of almost 1,000 coca growers. Human rights organizations expressed alarm at the force with which UMOPAR was conducting its operations and at the number of peasants killed and injured in the campaign. In October the state of siege was revoked, and negotiations between the Government and the coca growers were undertaken, although the talks soon broke down, and further violent clashes were reported. Despite sustained resistance by coca growers throughout 1995, a total of 5,520 ha of the crop were destroyed during the year (some 120 ha more than the target set by the US Government in its eradication programme).

Meanwhile, allegations implicating senior public officials in corruption and, particularly, the illegal drugs trade continued to emerge in 1995 and 1996. Four members of the FELCN, including the organization's second-in-command, Col Fernando Tarifa, were dismissed in September, following an investigation into their links with drugs-traffickers. A further 100 FELCN members were detained in November on drugs-related charges. Moreover, a serious political scandal erupted in October, following allegations that Guillermo Bedregal, the President of the Senate and a deputy leader of the MNR, had co-operated with leading drugs-traffickers. In early 1996 allegations concerning the abuse of the personal expenses system resulted in the resignation of 10 MNR members of the Congreso and the suspension of 12 others on criminal charges. Moreover, in March a

supreme court judge who had presided over numerous cases involving drugs-related offences was arrested by the FELCN, after having been filmed accepting money from a defendant's relative.

Continued opposition to the Government's capitalization programme led to further industrial unrest and a general strike in early 1996. In April more than 100,000 transport workers undertook a series of strikes and demonstrations in protest at the sale of the Eastern Railway to a Chilean company. Riots in La Paz resulted in damage to Chilean-owned railway property, which prompted threats from the Chilean Government to withdraw its investment from Bolivia. During violent clashes with the police several protesters were injured and one was killed. The dispute ended later in the month, when the COB signed an agreement with the Government which provided for modest public-sector wage increases, but did not include concessions in the Government's plans to continue implementation of its capitalization policies.

The proposed introduction of an agrarian reform law proved highly controversial and led to a series of protests in September and October 1996 by indigenous and peasant groups who feared that their land rights would be undermined by measures contained in the proposed legislation. In early October the leaders of several peasant farmers' groups began a hunger strike, while the COB called an indefinite general strike. Shortly afterwards Sánchez de Lozada agreed to hold discussions with representatives of some of the indigenous and peasant groups (although not with the COB) and subsequently secured their support for the law by making a number of significant concessions. The most important of these was the modification of the proposed role of the Agrarian Superintendency, such that it would not be authorized to rule on issues of land ownership. The law was approved by the Congreso later that month.

Dissatisfaction with the continued privatization of major industrial companies in Bolivia, particularly in the mining sector, resulted in further unrest in late 1996. In mid-December a group of miners occupied a pit at Amayapampa in northern Potosí to protest at the actions of the mine's Canadian operators, who, they alleged, had failed to pay local taxes and had caused damage to the environment. When troops arrived at the site to remove the miners 10 protesters were killed and 50 others injured in ensuing violent clashes. The incident provoked outrage throughout the country and was the subject of an investigation by the Organization of American States' Inter-American Human Rights Commission in 1997.

Presidential elections were held on 1 June 1997. The MNR's candidate was Juan Carlos Durán (owing to the fact that Sánchez de Lozada was ineligible for re-election), the MIR presented Paz Zamora, while Bánzer Suárez, in a fourth attempt to gain the presidency by democratic means, was the nominee of the ADN. In the event, Bánzer secured 22.3% of the total votes, Durán won 17.7% and Paz Zamora received 16.7%. At legislative elections held concurrently the ADN won a total of 46 congressional seats, the MIR won 31, the MNR secured 29 and the UCS and Condepa secured 23 and 20 seats, respectively. The ADN subsequently concluded a pact with the MIR, the UCS and Condepa to form a congressional majority. The inclusion of the MIR in the coalition prompted concern among some observers, as it was feared that previous allegations of corruption and of involvement in the illegal drugs trade against the party and, in particular, against Paz Zamora (see above) would jeopardize the country's ability to attract international aid and investment. However, the grouping remained, and on 5 August Bánzer was elected President for a newly-extended term of five years with 118 congressional votes. The new administration pledged to consolidate the free-market reforms introduced by the previous Government and sought to assure the USA that the alliance with the MIR would not compromise its commitment to combating the illegal drugs trade.

In August 1997 the newly-elected Government signed a financial co-operation agreement with the USA for continued action to combat the illegal drugs trade. The agreement, which provided finance for the implementation of eradication programmes, was criticized for its emphasis on the suppression of coca cultivation rather than on the development of alternative crops. The previous Government's commitment to destroy 7,000 ha of coca plantations during 1997 in order to keep Bolivia's 'certification' status led to concern that violence might erupt if the new Government felt under pressure to implement an aggressive eradication programme in order to meet this target. Moreover, many observers believed the policy to be ineffective, as, despite the provision of US finance worth US $500m. since 1990 to eradicate the crop, there had been no net reduction in coca production in Bolivia. There was also evidence that compensation payments given to coca growers for the destruction of their crops had been used to replant coca in more remote areas. Meanwhile, discontent with some of the new Government's economic policies, particularly an increase in petrol prices and taxes announced in November, prompted several COB-organized strikes in late 1997 and early 1998.

In February 1998 coca producers in the Cochabamba region announced their rejection of the Government's new anti-coca policy (the so-called 'Dignity Plan', which aimed to eradicate all illegal coca plantations by 2002), claiming that an agreement, signed in October 1997, to provide alternative development programmes had not been honoured. Violent clashes ensued when army and police personnel converged on the region in April to implement the eradication programme, and in the following month the Government agreed temporarily to suspend the measures.

More than 1,000 coca growers undertook a 800-km protest march from Chapare to La Paz in August 1998 to demand that the Government review its coca-eradication programme. The farmers denounced new measures, including the confiscation of land used for coca cultivation, the incarceration of new coca growers and the reduction, by more than 50%, of compensation rates paid to farmers who voluntarily ceased to grow coca. The Government rejected the demands of the coca producers, reiterating its intention to eradicate more than 9,000 ha of the crop by the end of the year. Demonstrations and roadblocks by protesters in La Paz and Cochabamba during September were disrupted by security forces, leading to violent confrontation in many cases. The announcement in late 1998 that the headquarters of the armed forces were to be moved from La Paz to Cochabamba in 1999 was interpreted by some observers as a further measure to suppress the activities of the coca-growing community. The Government, however, denied that a process of militarization of the Cochabamba region was being implemented. In late 1998 it was announced that the 'Dignity Plan' was progressing successfully, with more than 11,500 ha of coca having been destroyed during that year. The Bolivian Government stated that funding for the programme had been received from the USA and the European Union (EU), but that a further US $300m. was required to develop alternative resources to replace revenue lost from the illegal sale of coca. In 1999 the amount of eradicated coca crops increased to 14,000 ha.

During the first half of 1999 there were a number of high-profile resignations: in March the Minister of Labour, Leopoldo López, resigned following revelations, in a report published by the Ministry of Finance, that he had been involved in smuggling activities; in the subsequent month the commander of the national police force, Ivar Narváez, was forced to stand down from his post as a result of accusations of corruption and misuse of funds; and in June the resignation of the Minister of the Interior, Guido Nayor, prompted a major cabinet reorganization, including the appointment of eight new ministers. In mid-1999 a number of reforms of the judicial system were announced, including the appointment of a people's ombudsman, a constitutional tribunal and an independent judicial council. It was hoped that these measures, when implemented, would help to reduce levels of corruption, particularly with regard to the accountability of the police force. Bolivia's new penal code, which came into effect at the end of May 1999, was groundbreaking in that it formally incorporated into the country's legal system the customary law of indigenous Indian peoples.

In December 1999 a sharp increase in water charges in Cochabamba prompted violent demonstrations, which spread to other areas. Further violent protests in April 2000 led to the imposition of a state of emergency by the Government. In the same month a brief strike by the police, coinciding with a general strike in protest at the water charges, forced the Government to withdraw the measure, which had been intended to help the newly privatized water authority fund improvements in supply. The reverse in policy precipitated a cabinet reshuffle, which increased the representation of the ADN by one post at the expense of the MIR. The Government was put under further pressure in September when striking teachers demanding higher salaries were joined by peasants protesting against the Government's plan to tax water used for crop irrigation. As coca growers were already protesting against the Government's plans to restrict the cultivation of the coca leaf, the combination

of roadblocks and demonstrations brought the country to a standstill. Violence ensued between the protesters and riot police, resulting in at least 10 fatalities. A settlement was achieved in October, whereby the teachers received bonus payments and the Government signed a 50-point agreement with the peasant farmers' union, which included a pledge to draft new agrarian reform legislation and to review the controversial water privatization law. Later in the month the Government acceded to coca growers' demands for a halt to the construction of new military bases in the Chapare region; however, the process of coca eradication intensified. The civil unrest prompted a further government reshuffle in late October. In December President Bánzer announced that most of the coca leaf in the Chapare region had been eradicated, with only 1,500 acres remaining. However, in September 2001 the Minister of the Interior, Leopoldo Fernández Ferreira, admitted that the success of the eradication programme had been exaggerated and that about 6,000 ha of coca plantations were yet to be destroyed in the Chapare region.

In May 2001, following further protests against the Government's privatization and coca-eradication policies, a tentative agreement was reached in which seven commissions would be established, comprising representatives of government and civic opposition groups, to review government policy in areas such as agrarian reform, coca eradication and water privatization. Nevertheless, popular protests continued throughout the country. A new criminal code was introduced in June that allowed for trial by public jury and made provision for the creation of a prosecution service independent of the police force.

In early August 2001, after it was confirmed that he was undergoing chemotherapy for cancer of the lung and liver, President Bánzer resigned. (He died in May 2002.) The Vice-President, Jorge Quiroga Ramírez, assumed the presidency on 6 August and immediately replaced 12 of the 16 members of the Government; almost one-half of the new Cabinet was not affiliated to any political party. The new Government's main stated aims were to stabilize the economy, implement anti-corruption measures and continue the dialogue with aggrieved peasants and indigenous groups. In August the Government reached an agreement with the main peasant farmers' union to implement a US $70m. rural development programme.

Presidential and legislative elections were held on 30 June 2002. The main contenders in the presidential contest were former President Sánchez de Lozada, again representing the MNR, Manfred Reyes Villa of the centre-right Nueva Fuerza Republicana (NFR) and Evo Morales, a coca-grower leader, representing the left-wing Movimiento al Socialismo (MAS). In the event, Sánchez de Lozada won the largest share of the ballot (22.5%). Morales, who opposed the Government's free-market economic policy and its coca-eradication programme, performed unexpectedly well, coming second with 20.9% of the votes cast. As no candidate had achieved an absolute majority, however, responsibility for choosing the new President again passed to the Congreso. On 4 August it voted, by 84 votes to 43, to appoint Sánchez de Lozada to the presidency once more. In the concurrently-held legislative elections, the MNR won the largest number of seats (36) in the Cámara de Diputados, followed by the MAS with 27 seats, the MIR with 26 seats and the NFR with 25 seats. The MNR also secured the greatest representation in the Senado, winning 11 seats, compared with the eight won by the MAS and the five secured by the MIR (the NFR won two seats while the ADN secured the remaining seat).

Sánchez de Lozada was inaugurated as President on 6 August 2002. He formed a coalition Government comprising representatives of the MNR, the MIR, the UCS, the MBL and the ADN, although the new Cabinet was dominated by MNR and MIR members. The new President's priorities were to continue the coca-eradication policy of its predecessor and to bring about economic recovery, by implementing a public-works programme that would create jobs. Sánchez de Lozada also pledged to review the country's privatization programme. However, the ruling coalition was a fragile one; the MNR could not rely on the support of the other alliance parties in the Congreso. This, coupled with the strong performance of the opposition parties in the elections meant that the new administration was likely to encounter considerable resistance to its proposed agenda.

In light of renewed pressure from the US Administration to intensify eradication efforts, in September 2002 the Government held talks with coca-growers' representatives, led by Morales. The USA had threatened to suspend preferential access to certain US markets, agreed under the Andean Trade

Promotion and Drug Eradication Act, if Bolivia failed to meet the agreed eradication target of 9,000 ha of coca crops. The talks ended inconclusively, although the Government did agree to suspend eradication temporarily in the Chapare region; however, it remained committed to the programme in the long term. In October the USA published a report in which it was claimed that there were an estimated 24,400 ha of coca plantations in Bolivia in 2002, twice the agreed level, and that, contrary to government claims, new plantation rates exceeded eradication levels.

In response to the US study, the Government announced its intention to commission an independent survey of illegal coca plantations, as well as a review of legal cultivation levels (which stood at 12,000 ha in 2002). Peasant organizations insisted that eradication be suspended while the study was under way. In January 2003 coca growers staged roadblocks and demonstrations in protest at the Government's refusal to meet their demands. At the same time, about 5,000 pensioners marched from Patacamaya to La Paz in protest at legislation, approved in December 2002, which linked pensions to the consumer price index, rather than to the US dollar. Following two weeks of clashes with the police, in which 11 people were killed, in late January President Sánchez de Lozada and Evo Morales agreed to restart negotiations on coca eradication, as well as on trade issues and the privatization programme. However, a plan to increase the maximum area for the legal cultivation of coca prompted strong protests from the USA in March.

In February 2003 the Sánchez de Lozada administration's budget proposals increased popular dissatisfaction still further. Faced with a fiscal deficit of some 8.6% of GDP, and under IMF pressure to secure new sources of revenue to finance a planned US $3,900m. public-works programme, the Government proposed increasing income tax rates. The new measure —known as an *impuestazo*, or 'tax shock'— drew widespread condemnation from representatives of middle and lower-income groups, and civil unrest began to spread. On 12 February, following the Government's dismissal of their 40% wage demand, approximately 7,000 armed police officers joined civilian protests in central La Paz. During the ensuing confrontation with elements of the military, an estimated 32 people were killed, and President Sánchez de Lozada was forced to withdraw to safety. The riots prompted the resignation, on 19 February, of the entire Cabinet. A new Government was appointed the following day. Seven ministers were reappointed to their previous posts, and in a measure intended to restore public confidence and lower spending, President Sánchez de Lozada announced that the number of ministries would be reduced from 18 to 13. However, protests continued in March, despite the Government's effective abandonment of the budget measures and, as a consequence, its hopes of a more sympathetic hearing in negotiations with the IMF.

In March 2003 several sources, including the US Ambassador in La Paz, brought unsubstantiated allegations that members of MAS had been planning a *coup d'état*, scheduled to take place on 9 April. The reports claimed that Bolivian military officers had been approached by unidentified affiliates of MAS, with a view to the simultaneous overthrow of President Sánchez de Lozada and assassination of the MAS leader, Evo Morales. The reports were dismissed as erroneous by the major participants in the controversy; however, the affair led to the resignation of the leading MAS Senator, Filemón Escóbar, in late March.

In September 1990, following a protest march by indigenous Indians, the Government issued four decrees in an unprecedented act of recognition of Indian land rights. Besides acknowledging as Indian territory more than 1.6m. ha of tropical rainforest in northern Bolivia, a multi-party commission was to be established in order to draft a new Law for Indigenous Indians of the East and Amazonia. In October 2000 a new Ministry for Peasants', Indigenous Peoples' and Ethnic Affairs was created, headed by Wigberto Rivero Pintoremain; however, the ministry was abolished in February 2003 as part of the Government's cost-cutting programme. In September 2002 the new Government of Sánchez de Lozada announced a Land Reform Programme, under which some 500,000 ha of land and some 700,000 ha of forest concessions were to be bought by the Government and redistributed to some 11,000 landless families. The cost of the Programme was estimated at US $2,500m.

Bolivia's relations with Peru and Chile have been dominated by the long-standing issue of possible Bolivian access to the Pacific Ocean. An agreement with Peru, completed in 1993, granted Bolivia free access from the border town of Desagua-

dero, Bolivia, to the Pacific port of Ilo, Peru, until 2091. Bolivia's desire to regain sovereign access to the sea, however, continued to impair relations with Chile. In February 1997 Bolivia's Minister of Foreign Affairs directly accused Gen. Augusto Pinochet Ugarte, the Commander-in-Chief of the Chilean Army, of being the main obstacle in Bolivia's quest for access to the sea. Moreover, talks which aimed to improve trade arrangements between the two countries were suspended in March and again in May following failure to reach agreement. Relations deteriorated further in late 1997 when the Bolivian Government filed an official protest note to Chile regarding its failure to remove land-mines along the common border (planted during the 1970s). However, following a meeting between government representatives in August 1998 Bolivia announced that it was to abandon its policy of actively pursuing access to the sea in Chile and, after discussions with the Chilean Minister of Foreign Affairs in June 1999, President Bánzer announced that Bolivia was considering the resumption of diplomatic relations with Chile. However, subsequent talks between representatives of the two countries appeared to collapse later in the year, when the Chilean Government indicated that it would not be willing to resume negotiations over Bolivia's access to the Chilean coastline. The issue of poor relations remained pressing in 2003, particularly in view of Bolivia's continued reluctance to authorize the export of its natural gas reserves to the USA through Chilean territory.

In 1992 Bolivia signed an agreement with Brazil for the construction of a 3,150-km pipeline to carry natural gas from Bolivia to southern Brazil. The outlines of the project, which was expected to cost US $1,800m. and was the largest of its kind in South America, were finalized, following considerable delay, in mid-1996. The pipeline (the first 1,970 km of which were completed in early 1999) was expected to transport an initial 3.7m. cu m of natural gas per day to Brazil, increasing to 30m. cu m by 2004, when the pipeline was due to reach full capacity.

In November 1994 an agreement to provide a waterway linking Bolivia with the Atlantic coast in Uruguay was concluded. However, by 2003 the controversial project, which involved dredging a deep-water channel in the Paraguay and Paraná Rivers, still had not begun, owing to Brazilian fears that the scheme would devastate a large, undeveloped area of ecological importance in south-western Brazil, known as the Pantanal.

Government

Legislative power is held by the bicameral Congreso Nacional (Congress), comprising a Senate (27 members) and a Chamber of Deputies (130 members). Both houses are elected for a four-year term by universal adult suffrage. Executive power is vested in the President and the Cabinet, which is appointed by the President. The President is directly elected for five years (extended from four years in 1997). If no candidate gains an absolute majority of votes, the President is chosen by the Congreso. The country is divided, for administrative purposes, into nine departments, each of which is governed by a prefect, appointed by the President.

Defence

Military service, for one year, is selective. In August 2002 the armed forces numbered 31,500 men (there were plans to increase this to 35,000), of whom the army had 25,000 (including 18,000 conscripts), the air force 3,000, and the navy 3,500. Expenditure on defence by the central Government in 2001 was 917m. bolivianos.

Economic Affairs

In 2001, according to World Bank estimates, Bolivia's gross national income (GNI), measured at average 1999–2001 prices, totalled US $8,044m., equivalent to about $940 per head (or $2,380 per head on an international purchasing-power parity basis). During 1990–2001, it was estimated, the population increased at an average annual rate of 2.4%, while gross domestic product (GDP) per head increased, in real terms, by an average of 1.1% per year. Bolivia's overall GDP increased, in real terms, at an average annual rate of 3.5% in 1990–2001; GDP increased by an estimated 1.2% in 2001.

Agriculture (including forestry and fishing) contributed an estimated 14.9% of GDP in 2001. In 2000 an estimated 44.2% of the economically active population were employed in agriculture. Wood accounted for 1.9% of export earnings in 2000. The principal cash crops are soybeans (which accounted for 12.8% of export earnings in 2000), sugar, chestnuts and coffee. Beef and hides are also important exports. In the period 1992–2001 agricultural GDP increased at an average annual rate of 2.8%; it rose by an estimated 3.8% in 2000 and by an estimated 1.1% in 2000.

Industry (including mining, manufacturing, construction and power) provided some 27.2% of GDP in 2001. In 1997 18.4% of the working population were employed in industry. During the period 1992–2001 industrial GDP increased at an average annual rate of 3.5%; it increased by an estimated 1.9% in 2000 and by an estimated 5.5% in 2001.

Mining (including petroleum exploration) contributed an estimated 6.8% of GDP in 2001 and employed about 1% of the working population in 1997. Investment in mineral exploitation increased 10-fold between 1991 and 1996. Funding for gold-exploration projects, however, decreased from US $45m. in 1996 to $20m. in 1997, while investment in polymetallic projects increased from $8m. in 1996 to $15m. in the following year. Investment in petroleum exploration totalled US $129m. in 1997. Zinc, tin, silver, gold, lead and antimony are the major mineral exports. Tungsten and copper continue to be mined. Exports of zinc and tin earned an estimated $120.7m. and $56.2m., respectively, in 2001. In 1992–2001 the GDP of the mining sector increased at an average annual rate of 3.4%; mining GDP increased by an estimated 7.2% in 2000 and by an estimated 2.7% in 2001.

In 2001 manufacturing accounted for an estimated 14.5% of GDP, and in 1997 some 11.0% of the working population were employed in manufacturing. The GDP of this sector increased during 1992–2001 at an average annual rate of 3.5%; it rose by an estimated 1.7% in 2000 and by an estimated 1.1% in 2001. Measured by the value of output, the principal branches of manufacturing in 1998 were petroleum refining (36.4%), food products (34.2%—including beverages 12.6% and meat preparations 8.0%) and cement (5.0%).

Energy is derived principally from petroleum and natural gas, although hydroelectricity is also important. In 2000 production of crude petroleum decreased by an estimated 5.4%, to 10.1m. barrels. In 2000 imports of fuels comprised an estimated 5.0% of total merchandise imports, compared with 3.4% in the previous year. Earnings from exports of petroleum and petroleum products accounted for 3.5% of the total in 2000. Exports of natural gas accounted for 26.1% of total export earnings in 1991, but only 8.7% in 2000. Reserves of natural gas were estimated at 18,300,000m. cu ft at the end of 2000. During the late 1990s several major new natural gas deposits were discovered, which significantly increased the country's total known reserves. In 2002 the new Government of Gonzalo Sánchez de Lozada announced a plan to sell natural gas to the USA at a discounted price. In February 2003 it was announced that a gas export terminal was to be built in the Chilean port of Patillos.

The services sector accounted for some 57.9% of GDP in 2001 and engaged 38.5% of the employed population in 1997. During the period 1992–2001 the GDP of this sector increased at an average annual rate of 4.2%; services GDP increased by an estimated 1.7% in 2000 and by an estimated 0.9% in 2001.

In 2001 Bolivia recorded a visible trade deficit of US $209.0m., and there was a deficit of $292.5m. on the current account of the balance of payments. In 2000 the main sources of imports were the USA (21.8%), Argentina (15.3%), Brazil (14.1%) and Chile (8.3%). The USA, Colombia, the United Kingdom and Brazil were the major recipients of Bolivian exports in 2000 (24.2%, 13.4%, 11.6% and 11.4%, respectively). The principal imports in that year included industrial materials and machinery, transport equipment and consumer goods. The principal legal exports were metallic minerals, natural gas, soybeans and wood. In 1997 the UN claimed that more than 50% of Bolivia's export earnings came from the illegal trade in coca and its derivatives (mainly cocaine).

In 2000 Bolivia's overall budget deficit amounted to 2,064m. bolivianos (equivalent to 3.9% of GDP). Bolivia's total external debt at the end of 2000 was US $5,762m., of which $4,120m. was long-term public debt. The cost of debt-servicing in that year was equivalent to 39.1% of the total value of exports of goods and services. In 1990–2001 the average annual rate of inflation was 8.3%. Consumer prices increased by an average of 2.2% in 1999, 4.6% in 2000 and 1.6% in 2001. In October 2002 an estimated 12.9% of the labour force in urban areas were unemployed.

In May 1991 Bolivia was one of five Andean Pact countries to sign the Caracas Declaration providing the foundation for a common market. In October 1992 Bolivia officially joined the Andean free-trade area, removing tariff barriers to imports from Colombia, Ecuador and Venezuela. Bolivia also agreed to sign a free-trade accord with Mexico in September 1994. In January 1997 a free-trade agreement with Mercosur (see p. 316), equivalent to associate membership of the organization, came into effect. In mid-1999 an agreement on the rationalization of their respective customs systems (thus moving closer to the formation of a regional free-trade area) was reached between Mercosur and the Andean Community (see p. 133); the two-year accord came into effect in August. Bolivia is a member of the Andean Community, and in 1989 the Andean Social Development Fund was established. The country is also a member of the Organization of American States (OAS, see p. 288), and of the Latin American Integration Association (ALADI, see p. 259). Bolivia became the 97th contracting party to GATT (which was superseded by the World Trade Organization, WTO (see p. 323), in 1995) in 1989.

A public-sector capitalization programme, which aimed to attract more private-sector involvement in Bolivia's principal industries by selling a 50% controlling share in several state-owned companies to private investors, began in early 1995 under the first Government of Sánchez de Lozada. However, following the re-election of Sánchez de Lozada to the presidency in mid-2002, the new Government announced there would be an 'audited review' of all those companies privatized from the mid-1990s; however, it pledged that there would be no renationalization programme.

The continued success of exploratory missions in locating new sources of petroleum and natural gas, in particular, resulted in a series of projects in the late 1990s, which aimed to develop Bolivia's potential as one of the region's most important energy-producing countries. A major new gas deposit near Santa Cruz, with total reserves estimated at 1,700,000m. cu ft, was discovered in 1998. The development of the natural gas export sector was seen as crucial to economic growth at the beginning of the 21st century. Natural gas exports increased substantially to Brazil in 2001 and plans to export liquefied natural gas to Mexico and the USA were announced in July of that year. Official development assistance was equivalent to almost 10% of GNP annually in the late 1990s. The country's severe debt burden was widely acknowledged to be a major factor in inhibiting economic growth, and in recognition of this the World Bank and the IMF approved a debt-relief package worth US $760m. (under its Heavily Indebted Poor Countries' Initiative), which was released in October 1998. Also in late 1998 a three-year loan worth US $138m. was secured from the IMF. However, economic growth in the early 21st century (of 2.4% in 2000) was adversely affected by social unrest (which paralysed the country in April and September 2000 and persisted throughout 2001), low commodity prices and coca eradication policies, which reduced incomes in the informal sector. Despite demands for increased public spending to alleviate social ills, successive Governments committed themselves to the maintenance of IMF-sponsored fiscal economic policies. Upon taking office in August 2002, President Sánchez de Lozada announced a five-year economic recovery plan that aimed to reduce unemployment and increase internal demand. The plan was to receive US $1,800m. in funding from the Corporación Andina de Formento—CAF (Andean Development Corporation, see p. 136) and $1,000m. in funding from both the Inter-American Development Bank (IDB, see p. 239) and the World Bank. Further aid from the USA was likely to be dependent on the success of the coca-eradication programme. GDP growth of 2.6% was forecast for 2002.

Education

Primary education, beginning at six years of age and lasting for eight years, is officially compulsory and is available free of charge. Secondary education, which is not compulsory, begins at 14 years of age and lasts for up to four years. In 1990 the total enrolment at primary and secondary schools was equivalent to 77% of the school-age population (81% of boys; 73% of girls). In that year enrolment at primary schools included an estimated 91% of children in the relevant age-group (95% of boys; 87% of girls), while the comparable ratio for secondary enrolment was only 29% (32% of boys; 27% of girls). There are eight state universities and two private universities. Expenditure on education by the Central Government in 1998 was 2,023.4m. bolivianos, representing 19.6% of total spending.

Public Holidays

2003: 1 January (New Year), 10 February (Oruro only), 15 April (Tarija only), 18 April (Good Friday), 1 May (Labour Day), 25 May (Sucre only), 19 June (Corpus Christi), 16 July (La Paz only), 6 August (Independence), 14 September (Cochabamba only), 24 September (Santa Cruz and Pando only), 1 October (Pando only), 1 November (All Saints' Day and Potosí), 10 November (Oruro only), 18 November (Beni only), 25 December (Christmas).

2004: 1 January (New Year), 10 February (Oruro only), 9 April (Good Friday), 15 April (Tarija only), 1 May (Labour Day), 25 May (Sucre only), 10 June (Corpus Christi), 16 July (La Paz

only), 6 August (Independence), 14 September (Cochabamba only), 24 September (Santa Cruz and Pando only), 1 October (Pando only), 1 November (All Saints' Day and Potosí), 10 November (Oruro only), 18 November (Beni only), 25 December (Christmas).

Weights and Measures

The metric system is officially in force, but various old Spanish measures are also used.

Statistical Survey

Sources (unless otherwise indicated): Instituto Nacional de Estadística, Plaza Mario Guzmán Aspiazu No. 1, Casilla 6129, La Paz; tel. (2) 36-7443; internet www.ine.gov.bo ; Banco Central de Bolivia, Ayacucho esq. Mercado, Casilla 3118, La Paz; tel. (2) 37-4151; fax (2) 39-2398; internet www.bcb.gov.bo.

Area and Population

AREA, POPULATION AND DENSITY

Area (sq km)	
Land	1,084,391
Inland water	14,190
Total	1,098,581*
Population (census results)†	
3 June 1992	6,420,792
5 September 2001	
Males	4,123,850
Females	4,150,475
Total	8,274,325
Population (official estimates at mid-year)	
1998	7,949,933
1999	8,137,113
2000	8,328,700
Density (per sq km) at 2001 census	7.5

* 424,164 sq miles.

† Figures exclude adjustment for underenumeration. This was estimated at 6.92% in 1992.

DEPARTMENTS

(2001 census)

	Area (sq km)	Population	Density (per sq km)	Capital
Beni . . .	213,564	362,521	1.7	Trinidad
Chuquisaca . .	51,524	531,522	10.3	Sucre
Cochabamba . .	55,631	1,455,711	26.2	Cochabamba
La Paz . . .	133,985	2,350,466	17.5	La Paz
Oruro . . .	53,588	391,870	7.3	Oruro
Pando . . .	63,827	52,525	0.8	Cobija
Potosí . . .	118,218	709,013	6.0	Potosí
Santa Cruz . .	370,621	2,029,471	5.5	Santa Cruz de la Sierra
Tarija . . .	37,623	391,226	10.4	Tarija
Total . . .	1,098,581	8,274,325	7.5	

PRINCIPAL TOWNS

(2001 census)

Santa Cruz de la Sierra . . .	1,135,526	Oruro	215,660
La Paz (administrative capital) . . .	793,293	Tarija	153,457
El Alto . . .	649,958	Potosí	145,057
Cochabamba . .	517,024	Sacaba	117,100
Sucre (legal capital) .	215,778	Quillacollo . . .	104,206

BIRTHS AND DEATHS

(UN estimates, annual averages)

	1985–90	1990–95	1995–2000
Birth rate (per 1,000) . . .	36.6	35.7	33.2
Death rate (per 1,000) . . .	11.5	10.2	9.1

Source: UN, *World Population Prospects: The 2000 Revision*.

Expectation of life (WHO estimates, years at birth): 62.7 (males 61.1; females 64.3) in 2001 (Source: WHO, *World Health Report*).

ECONOMICALLY ACTIVE POPULATION

(labour force surveys, '000 persons aged 10 years and over, at November)

	1996	1997
Agriculture	1,620.7	1,518.7
Forestry and fishing	14.6	23.1
Mining and quarrying	53.7	63.9
Manufacturing	403.6	393.5
Electricity, gas and water supply	9.9	11.0
Construction	172.4	187.0
Wholesale and retail trade; repair of motor vehicles, motorcycles and personal and household goods	562.3	505.9
Hotels and restaurants	135.2	126.5
Transport, storage and communications . .	147.6	170.5
Financial intermediation	18.1	20.1
Real estate, renting and business activities . .	51.9	58.8
Public administration and defence; compulsory social security	91.8	78.8
Education.	137.9	158.8
Health and social work	59.9	62.9
Other community, social and personal service activities	67.5	70.4
Private households with employed persons . .	127.0	117.8
Extra-territorial organizations and bodies . .	1.6	2.1
Total employed	3,675.7	3,569.7
Unemployed	65.0	75.4
Total labour force.	3,740.7	3,645.2
Males	2,008.7	2,048.8
Females	1,731.9	1,596.4

Mid-2001 (estimates in '000): Agriculture, etc. 1,531; Total labour force 3,487 (Source: FAO).

Health and Welfare

KEY INDICATORS

Total fertility rate (children per woman, 2001)	4.1
Under-5 mortality rate (per 1,000 live births, 2001) . . .	77
HIV/AIDS (% of persons aged 15–49, 2001)	0.10
Physicians (per 1,000 head, 1997)	1.30
Hospital beds (per 1,000 head, 1996)	1.67
Health expenditure (2000): US $ per head (PPP) . . .	158
Health expenditure (2000): % of GDP	6.7
Health expenditure (2000): public (% of total) . . .	72.4
Access to water (% of persons, 2000)	79
Access to sanitation (% of persons, 2000) . . .	66
Human Development Index (2000): ranking . . .	114
Human Development Index (2000): value	0.653

For sources and definitions, see explanatory note on p. vi.

Agriculture

PRINCIPAL CROPS
('000 metric tons)

	1999	2000	2001
Wheat	141	104	117
Rice (paddy)	257	299	287
Barley	66	64	64
Maize	489	653	678
Sorghum	148	95	105
Potatoes	709	721	902
Cassava (Manioc)	328	342	517
Other roots and tubers*	123	114	114
Sugar cane	3,696	3,602	3,859
Pulses	33	33	33
Brazil nuts	30	36*	36*
Chestnuts	34	34	35*
Soybeans (Soya beans)	974	1,232	834
Sunflower seeds	95	111	149
Cottonseed*	38	38	40
Tomatoes	95	98	138
Pumpkins, squash and gourds	107	109	110*
Onions (dry)	49	49	49
Peas (green)	19	22	30
Broad beans (green)	45	49	66
Carrots	35	36	36
Green corn*	62	60	60
Other vegetables	75	75	97
Bananas	419†	695	688
Plantains	180†	187†	187*
Oranges	106	110	110
Tangerines, mandarins clementines and satsumas	60	62	62
Lemons and limes	63	64	64
Grapefruit and pomelos	29	29	29
Pineapples	53	59	60
Papayas	23	23	23
Peaches and nectarines	36	37	37*
Grapes	22	24	29
Watermelons	22	23	23
Other fruits and berries*	54	43	43
Coffee (green)	23	25	25
Cotton (lint)*	20	20	20

* FAO estimate(s).
† Unofficial figure.

Source: FAO.

LIVESTOCK
('000 head, year ending September)

	1999	2000	2001
Horses*	322	322	322
Mules*	81	81	81
Asses*	631	631	631
Cattle	6,556	6,725	6,865
Pigs	2,715	2,793	2,851
Sheep	8,575	8,752	8,902
Goats	1,500	1,500*	1,500*
Chickens	85,000	73,856†	74,000*
Ducks*	280	280	280
Turkeys*	150	150	150

* FAO estimate(s).
† Unofficial figure.

Source: FAO.

LIVESTOCK PRODUCTS
('000 metric tons)

	1999	2000	2001
Beef and veal	155.3	159.8	160.0*
Mutton and lamb	15.2	16.0	16.0*
Goat meat*	5.8	5.8	5.8
Pig meat*	74.1	76.4	76.4
Poultry meat	138.8	135.4	143.1
Cows' milk	230.7	231.5	232.0*
Sheep's milk	29.0	29.0*	29.1*
Goats' milk	11.2	11.2*	11.5*
Cheese*	6.8	6.8	6.8
Hen eggs	41.2	36.7	38.7
Wool: greasy	3.4	3.4	3.5
Cattle hides (fresh)*	18.2	18.6	18.6
Sheepskins (fresh)*	5.3	5.8	5.8

* FAO estimate(s).

Source: FAO.

Forestry

ROUNDWOOD REMOVALS
('000 cubic metres, excl. bark)

	1999	2000	2001
Sawlogs, veneer logs and logs for sleepers	502	468	468
Fuel wood*	2,116	2,142	2,163
Total	2,618	2,610	2,631

* FAO estimates.

Source: FAO.

SAWNWOOD PRODUCTION
('000 cubic metres, incl. railway sleepers)

	1998	1999	2000
Coniferous (softwood)*	15	15	15
Broadleaved (hardwood)	500	244	239
Total	515	259	254

* FAO estimates.
2001: Annual production as in 2000 (FAO estimates).
Source: FAO.

Fishing

(metric tons, live weight)

	1998	1999	2000
Capture	6,055	6,052	6,106
Freshwater fishes	4,865	4,860	4,911
Rainbow trout	340	342	345
Silversides (sand smelts)	850	850	850
Aquaculture	385	398	405
Rainbow trout	320	328	335
Total catch	6,440	6,450	6,511

Note: Figures exclude crocodiles and alligators, recorded by number rather than by weight. The number of spectacled caimans caught was: 1,757 in 1998 and 17,500 in 1999.

Source: FAO, *Yearbook of Fishery Statistics*.

Mining

(metric tons, unless otherwise indicated)

	1998	1999	2000*
Crude petroleum ('000 barrels). .	12,628	10,680	10,106
Natural gas (million cu feet) . .	109,673	92,232	127,044
Copper	48	250	110
Tin	11,308	12,417	12,503
Lead	13,848	10,153	9,523
Zinc	152,110	146,144	149,134
Tungsten (Wolfram) . .	627	421	495
Antimony	4,735	2,790	1,907
Silver	404	423	434
Gold (kg)	14,445	11,782	12,000

* Provisional figures.

Figures for metallic minerals refer to the metal content of ores.

Source: partly IMF, *Bolivia: Statistical Annex* (June 2001).

Industry

SELECTED PRODUCTS

('000 metric tons, unless otherwise indicated)

	1997	1998	1999*
Flour	465	549	576
Cement	970	1,095	1,163
Refined sugar.	332	285	294
Carbonated drinks ('000 hectolitres)	1,867	2,368	2,281
Beer ('000 hectolitres) . . .	1,702	1,922	1,840
Cigarettes (packets)	73,166	69,949	67,332
Alcohol ('000 litres)	27,678	31,154	26,412
Diesel oil ('000 barrels) . . .	2,866	3,034	3,063
Motor spirit (petrol) ('000 barrels)	3,941	4,003	4,176
Electric energy (million kWh) .	3,528	2,580	n.a.

* Provisional figures.

Finance

CURRENCY AND EXCHANGE RATES

Monetary Units

100 centavos = 1 boliviano (B).

Sterling, Dollar and Euro Equivalents (31 December 2002)

£1 sterling = 12.072 bolivianos
US $1 = 7.490 bolivianos
€1 = 7.855 bolivianos
1,000 bolivianos = £82.83 = $133.51 = €127.31.

Average Exchange Rate (bolivianos per US $)

2000   6.1835
2001   6.6069
2002   7.1700

BUDGET

(million bolivianos)*

Revenue†	1999	2000	2001
Taxation	6,749.2	7,276.1	7,302.6
Taxes on income, profits, etc. .	710.9	723.5	635.0
Social security contributions. .	951.3	872.9	964.7
Taxes on property	641.9	697.8	703.2
Domestic taxes on goods and services	3,561.9	4,450.1	4,388.0
Value-added tax.	2,206.8	2,315.0	2,331.2
Excises	1,345.7	2,123.5	2,045.4
Import duties	480.7	519.7	465.1
Other tax revenue	402.5	12.1	146.1
Other current revenue . . .	1,294.2	1,740.8	1,752.2
Capital revenue	594.9	261.8	113.2
Total	8,638.3	9,278.7	9,168.1

Expenditure‡	1999	2000	2001
General public services	800.2	799.3	1,076.8
Defence	857.7	864.5	1,047.3
Public order and safety	767.9	939.3	1,013.8
Education	2,280.3	2,442.8	2,796.9
Health	426.0	1,287.0	1,397.9
Social security and welfare . .	2,793.5	2,588.2	2,905.6
Housing and community amenities	173.2	278.1	269.0
Recreational, cultural, and religious affairs and services. .	38.3	42.5	42.5
Economic services	1,795.0	1,854.7	2,027.1
Fuel and energy	483.5	108.9	150.5
Agriculture, forestry, fishing and hunting	290.6	364.5	374.4
Transportation and communications	825.9	997.1	767.8
Other purposes	1,234.6	1,217.9	1,513.2
Total	11,166.9	12,314.4	14,089.9
Current§	9,395.7	10,184.5	12,117.3
Capital.	1,771.2	2,129.9	1,972.6

* Budget figures refer to the consolidated accounts of the central Government, including government agencies and social security institutions.

† Excluding grants received (million bolivianos): 950.6 in 1999; 908.8 in 2000; 1,350.5 in 2001.

‡ Excluding lending minus repayments (million bolivianos): −473.7 in 1999; −397.0 in 2000; −9.6 in 2001.

§ Including interest payments (million bolivianos): 627.6 in 1999; 890.5 in 2000; 1,103.0 in 2001.

Source: IMF, *Government Finance Statistics Yearbook*.

INTERNATIONAL RESERVES

(US $ million at 31 December)

	2000	2001	2002
Gold*	244.8	259.6	316.4
IMF special drawing rights . .	35.6	34.3	37.2
Reserve position in IMF. . .	11.6	11.2	12.1
Foreign exchange.	879.3	840.9	531.2
Total	1,170.8	1,146.0	896.9

* National valuation (US $ 250 per troy oz each year).

Source: IMF, *International Financial Statistics*.

MONEY SUPPLY

(million bolivianos at 31 December)

	1999	2000	2001
Currency outside banks . . .	2,173	2,189	2,422
Demand deposits at commercial banks	1,031	1,150	1,353
Total money (incl. others) . .	3,670	3,995	4,743

Source: IMF, *International Financial Statistics*.

COST OF LIVING

(Consumer Price Index for urban areas; base: 1990 = 100)

	1999	2000	2001
Food and beverages	220.5	225.2	226.6
Fuel and light	281.8	320.7	n.a.
Clothing and footwear	200.0	210.8	216.8
Rent	163.4	172.0	172.3
All items (incl. others)	227.3	237.8	241.6

Source: ILO.

NATIONAL ACCOUNTS

Expenditure on the Gross Domestic Product
(million bolivianos at current prices)

	1999	2000	2001*
Government final consumption expenditure	7,026	7,412	7,769
Private final consumption expenditure	37,002	40,009	41,292
Increase in stocks	−157	−219	−599
Gross fixed capital formation	9,197	9,112	7,427
Total domestic expenditure	53,168	56,314	55,889
Exports of goods and services	8,129	9,174	9,658
Less Imports of goods and services	13,141	13,820	12,895
GDP in purchasers' values	48,156	51,668	52,652
GDP at constant 1990 prices	21,809	22,325	22,599

* Preliminary figures.

Source: IMF, *International Financial Statistics*.

Gross Domestic Product by Economic Activity
(million bolivianos at current prices)

	1999	2000*	2001*
Agriculture, hunting, forestry and fishing	6,384.5	6,759.6	7,240.9
Mining and quarrying	2,613.5	3,469.0	3,292.8
Manufacturing	6,546.4	6,933.7	7,048.6
Electricity, gas and water	1,374.1	1,488.1	1,549.6
Construction	1,574.3	1,403.3	1,301.6
Trade	3,547.9	3,687.5	3,768.9
Hotels and restaurants	1,561.4	1,718.6	1,922.5
Transport, storage and communications	5,695.5	5,858.4	6,292.1
Finance, insurance, real estate and business services	7,030.9	7,176.3	6,740.7
Government services	5,778.8	6,090.3	6,268.0
Other community, social and personal services	2,495.9	2,833.6	3,103.2
Sub-total	44,603.2	47,418.4	48,528.9
Value-added tax	} 5,891.0	6,697.8	6,460.8
Import duties			
Less imputed bank charge	−2,338.1	−2,448.8	−2,337.6
GDP in purchasers' values†	48,156.2	51,667.6	52,652.3

* Preliminary figures.

† Totals may not be equal to the sum of component parts, owing to rounding.

BALANCE OF PAYMENTS
(US $ million)

	1999	2000	2001
Exports of goods f.o.b.	1,051.1	1,246.0	1,284.9
Imports of goods f.o.b.	−1,539.1	−1,610.1	−1,493.9
Trade balance	−487.8	−364.1	−209.0
Exports of services	259.4	224.1	235.8
Imports of services	−449.7	−468.1	−501.9
Balance on goods and services	−678.1	−608.1	−475.9
Other income received	157.3	139.7	121.2
Other income paid	−353.3	−365.3	−331.6
Balance on goods, services and income	−874.1	−833.7	−685.5
Current transfers received	414.7	419.9	428.4
Current transfers paid	−28.6	−33.2	−35.4
Current balance	−488.0	−447.0	−292.5
Capital account (net)	—	—	3.2
Direct investment abroad	−2.4	−2.4	−2.4
Direct investment from abroad	1,010.5	725.1	662.3
Portfolio investment assets	−44.4	55.4	−23.0
Portfolio investment liabilities	−16.9	—	—
Other investment assets	−47.7	−164.0	−202.0
Other investment liabilities	−30.5	−185.9	−104.1
Net errors and omissions	−353.6	−20.7	−78.8
Overall balance	27.0	−39.5	−37.3

Source: IMF, *International Financial Statistics*.

External Trade

PRINCIPAL COMMODITIES
(distribution by SITC, US $ million)

Imports c.i.f.	1998	1999	2000
Food and live animals	162.2	161.5	180.2
Cereals and cereal preparations	72.5	78.2	87.2
Mineral fuels, lubricants, etc.	110.9	66.0	90.6
Petroleum, petroleum products, etc.	110.8	66.0	90.5
Refined petroleum products	104.1	61.0	80.8
Gas oils (distillate fuels)	78.8	47.8	69.4
Chemicals and related products	253.3	237.6	258.6
Basic manufactures	421.7	333.4	350.4
Iron and steel	225.3	125.2	103.8
Tubes, pipes and fittings	163.5	71.1	48.2
'Seamless' tubes and pipes	149.6	27.2	25.6
Machinery and transport equipment	1,170.4	820.8	680.4
Power generating machinery and equipment	32.7	91.6	31.7
Rotating electric plant and parts	16.4	78.1	11.4
Motors and generators	2.0	69.4	6.7
Machinery specialized for particular industries	187.7	184.0	109.0
Civil engineering and contractors' plant and equipment	111.6	125.1	56.3
Construction and mining machinery	49.0	65.0	29.8
General industrial machinery equipment and parts	122.9	97.2	93.7
Telecommunications and sound equipment	117.4	89.0	90.9
Electrical line telephonic and telegraphic apparatus	55.4	29.0	36.7
Other electrical machinery apparatus, etc.	63.9	65.7	69.8
Road vehicles and parts*	524.9	254.7	141.6
Passenger motor cars (excl. buses)	238.8	110.6	63.2
Motor vehicles for the transport of goods, etc.	189.2	99.5	45.9
Goods vehicles	177.8	74.9	41.0
Other road motor vehicles	73.7	23.5	14.6
Other transport equipment and parts*	91.6	5.3	103.5
Aircraft, associated equipment and parts*	86.6	1.3	99.6
Miscellaneous manufactured articles	147.0	142.6	174.5
Total (incl. others)	2,350.2	1,835.4	1,848.7

* Excluding tyres, engines and electrical parts.

Exports f.o.b.	1998	1999	2000
Food and live animals . . .	216.8	217.0	246.1
Vegetables and fruit	48.9	44.9	43.3
Feeding-stuff for animals (excl. unmilled cereals)	106.0	114.5	147.8
Oil-cake and residues from soya beans	100.8	108.9	140.9
Crude materials (inedible) except fuels . . .	379.1	336.0	391.2
Oil seeds and oleaginous fruit . .	64.6	56.2	87.3
Soya beans	47.3	40.1	46.5
Cork and wood	50.5	26.8	28.0
Sawn non-coniferous wood . .	45.1	22.4	24.1
Metalliferous ores and metal scrap	238.1	224.3	255.1
Base metal ores and concentrates . .	178.7	166.7	188.5
Zinc ores and concentrates. .	157.8	154.3	170.6
Precious metal ores and concentrates . .	58.8	55.9	65.3
Mineral fuels, lubricants etc. .	96.4	73.9	177.6
Petroleum, petroleum products, etc.	40.1	35.3	50.4
Gas (natural and manufactured) .	56.3	38.5	127.2
Petroleum gases and other gaseous hydrocarbons . . .	55.5	34.9	120.5
Animal and vegetable oils, fats and waxes	72.6	61.0	76.3
Fixed vegetable oils and fats . .	72.5	60.9	76.3
Soya bean oil	68.7	53.5	68.2
Basic manufactures . . .	115.5	135.7	151.1
Non-ferrous metals	74.1	76.5	75.7
Unwrought tin and alloys . .	57.8	63.2	65.8
Machinery and transport equipment	189.0	351.0	194.0
Transport equipment and parts* .	156.1	282.3	145.3
Aircraft, associated equipment and parts*	148.7	281.3	144.2
Miscellaneous manufactured articles	115.6	113.7	113.7
Jewellery, goldsmiths' and silversmiths' wares, etc. . . .	61.6	52.0	51.5
Non-monetary gold (excl. ores and concentrates) . . .	112.7	89.1	87.8
Total (incl. others)	1,323.3	1,401.9	1,456.7

* Excluding tyres, engines and electrical parts.

Source: UN, *International Trade Statistics Yearbook*.

PRINCIPAL TRADING PARTNERS
(US $ million)*

Imports c.i.f.	1998	1999	2000
Argentina	232.4	243.8	302.7
Brazil	256.8	269.0	278.8
Canada	27.7	15.3	14.0
Chile	141.9	129.9	163.1
Colombia	46.2	40.2	47.0
Denmark	25.7	5.8	n.a.
Germany	57.9	48.9	39.5
Italy	37.8	31.1	42.7
Japan	463.0	155.5	103.2
Korea, Republic	29.0	34.0	n.a.
Mexico	38.8	43.2	45.7
Peru	94.9	87.4	98.8
Spain	36.9	50.9	n.a.
Sweden	108.0	37.4	22.7
United Kingdom	18.0	15.6	10.4
USA	550.7	438.0	430.6
Venezuela	23.5	19.8	14.3
Total (incl. others)	2,350.2	1,854.5	1,976.7

Exports f.o.b.	1998	1999	2000
Argentina	141.3	76.6	48.5
Belgium-Luxembourg . . .	64.0	71.3	41.6
Brazil	30.1	40.9	164.1
Chile	34.2	27.7	29.2
Colombia	86.5	126.9	192.7
Ecuador	80.2	71.4	5.2
Germany	21.4	14.9	13.3
Mexico	6.6	7.7	6.5
Peru	140.5	75.3	59.9
Switzerland-Liechtenstein . .	83.8	69.3	163.2
United Kingdom	198.9	180.0	167.6
USA	303.2	464.7	349.3
Uruguay	50.1	78.0	69.3
Total (incl. others) . . .	1,323.3	1,401.9	1,441.7

* Imports by country of provenance; exports by country of last consignment.

Source: partly UN, *International Trade Statistics Yearbook*.

Transport

RAILWAYS
(traffic)

	1997	1998	1999
Passenger-kilometres (million) . .	225	270	271
Freight ton-kilometres (million) .	839	908	832

Source: UN, *Statistical Yearbook*.

ROAD TRAFFIC
(motor vehicles in use at 31 December, estimates)

	1998	1999	2000
Passenger cars	163,051	168,611	181,409
Buses	18,910	19,581	21,183
Lorries and vans	204,134	213,455	234,746
Tractors	776	804	944
Motorcycles	25,506	25,917	27,897

Source: IRF, *World Road Statistics*.

CIVIL AVIATION
(traffic on scheduled services)

	1996	1997	1998
Kilometres flown (million) . . .	24	28	28
Passengers carried ('000) . . .	1,783	2,251	2,115
Passenger-km (million)	1,634	2,143	2,179
Freight ton-km (million) . . .	223	274	273

Source: UN, *Statistical Yearbook*.

Tourism

ARRIVALS AT HOTELS
(regional capitals only, '000)

Country of origin	1998	1999	2000
Argentina	53.7	48.1	43.8
Brazil	36.1	26.8	24.3
Canada	8.7	8.7	7.9
Chile	28.9	25.1	22.4
France	21.9	23.0	21.0
Germany	22.9	23.4	23.6
Israel	10.6	8.0	10.0
Italy	8.4	9.6	7.7
Japan	6.3	8.6	7.0
Netherlands	11.5	14.6	13.9
Peru	66.2	56.1	50.2
Spain	11.2	11.3	9.6
Switzerland	9.3	10.6	9.7
United Kingdom	13.2	17.3	18.0
USA	45.0	47.4	44.2
Total (incl. others)	420.5	409.1	381.1

Source: World Tourism Organization, *Yearbook of Tourism Statistics*.

Total tourism receipts (US $ million): 174 in 1998; 179 in 1999; 160 in 2000 (Source: World Tourism Organization).

Communications Media

	1999	2000	2001
Television receivers ('000 in use)*	960	990	n.a.
Telephones ('000 main lines in use)	502.5	504.2	514.8
Mobile cellular telephones ('000 subscribers).	420.3	579.8	744.0
Personal computers ('000 in use)* .	100	n.a.	170
Internet users ('000)*	80	120	n.a.

* Estimates.

Source: International Telecommunication Union.

Radio receivers ('000): 5,250 in use in 1997 (Source: UNESCO, *Statistical Yearbook*).

Daily newspapers: 18 in 1996 (average circulation 420,000 copies) (Source: UNESCO, *Statistical Yearbook*).

Education

(1999)

	Institutions	Teachers	Students
Pre-primary	2,294*	4,142	187,760
Primary	12,639†	63,258	1,578,090
Secondary	n.a.	15,346	341,240
Higher:			
Universities and equivalent	n.a.	4,261‡	184,169§
other	n.a.	1,302‖	34,889‖

* 1988.
† 1987.
‡ 1991.
§ 1997.
‖ 1989.

Source: partly UNESCO, *Statistical Yearbook*.

Adult literacy rate (UNESCO estimates): 85.5% (males 92.0%; females 79.3%) in 2000 (Source: UN Development Programme, *Human Development Report*).

Directory

The Constitution

Bolivia became an independent republic in 1825 and received its first Constitution in November 1826. Since that date a number of new Constitutions have been promulgated. Following the *coup d'état* of November 1964, the Constitution of 1947 was revived. Under its provisions, executive power is vested in the President, who chairs the Cabinet. According to the revised Constitution, the President is elected by direct suffrage for a five-year term (extended from four years in 1997) and is not eligible for immediate re-election. In the event of the President's death or failure to assume office, the Vice-President or, failing the Vice-President, the President of the Senate becomes interim Head of State.

The President has power to appoint members of the Cabinet and diplomatic representatives from a panel proposed by the Senate. The President is responsible for the conduct of foreign affairs and is also empowered to issue decrees, and initiate legislation by special messages to Congress.

Congress consists of a Senate (27 members) and a Chamber of Deputies (130 members). Congress meets annually and its ordinary sessions last only 90 working days, which may be extended to 120. Each of the nine departments (La Paz, Chuquisaca, Oruro, Beni, Santa Cruz, Potosí, Tarija, Cochabamba and Pando), into which the country is divided for administrative purposes, elects three senators. Members of both houses are elected for five years.

The supreme administrative, political and military authority in each department is vested in a prefect appointed by the President. The sub-divisions of each department, known as provinces, are administered by sub-prefects. The provinces are further divided into cantons. There are 94 provinces and some 1,000 cantons. The capital of each department has its autonomous municipal council and controls its own revenue and expenditure.

Public order, education and roads are under national control.

A decree issued in July 1952 conferred the franchise on all persons who had reached the age of 21 years, whether literate or illiterate. Previously the franchise had been restricted to literate persons. (The voting age for married persons was lowered to 18 years at the 1989 elections.)

The Government

HEAD OF STATE

President: Gonzalo ('Goni') Sánchez de Lozada ((MNR) took office 6 August 2002).

Vice-President: Carlos Mesa Gisbert.

THE CABINET
(April 2003)

Minister of Foreign Affairs: Carlos Saavedra Bruno (MIR).

Minister of the Interior: Yerko Kukoc del Carpio (MNR).

Minister of National Defence: Freddy Teodovic Ortiz (MNR).

Minister of Finance: Javier Comboni Salinas (MNR).

Minister of Sustainable Development and Planning: Moira Paz Cortex Estenssoro (MNR).

Minister of the Presidency: José Guillermo Justiniano Sandóval (MNR).

Minister of Health and Social Welfare: Javier Torres Goitía Caballero (MNR).

Minister of Labour and Small Enterprises: Juan Walter Subirana Suárez (UCS).

Minister of Education, Culture and Sport: HUGO CARVAJAL DONOSO (MIR).

Minister of Agriculture, Livestock and Rural Development: ARTURO LIEBERS BALDIVIESO (MIR).

Minister of Economic Development: JORGE TORRES OBLEAS (MIR).

Minister of Housing: CARLOS MORALES LANDÍVAR (MNR).

Minister without Portfolio responsible for Hydrocarbons and Energy: Ing. JORGE BERINDOAGUE ALCOCER.

MINISTRIES

Ministry of Agriculture, Livestock and Rural Development: Avda Camacho 1471, La Paz.

Ministry of Economic Development: Edif. Palacio de Comunicaciones, Avda Mariscal Santa Cruz, La Paz; tel. (2) 237-7234; fax (2) 235-9955; e-mail contactos@desarrollo.gov.bo; internet www.desarrollo.gov.bo.

Ministry of Education, Culture and Sport: Casilla 6500, La Paz.

Ministry of Finance: Edif. Palacio de Comunicaciones, Avda Mariscal Santa Cruz, La Paz; tel. (2) 237-7234; fax (2) 235-9955.

Ministry of Foreign Affairs: Calle Ingavi, esq. Junin, La Paz; tel. (2) 237-1150; fax (2) 237-1155; e-mail mreuno@rree.gov.bo; internet www.rree.gov.bo.

Ministry of Health and Social Welfare: Plaza del Estudiante, La Paz; tel. (2) 237-1373; fax (2) 239-1590; e-mail minsalud@ceibo.entelnet.bo; internet www.sns.gov.bo.

Ministry of Housing: Avda Edif. Ex-Conavi, 20 de Octubre 2230, La Paz; tel. (2) 236-0469; fax (2) 237-1335; e-mail minviv@ceibo.entelnet.bo.

Ministry of Hydrocarbons and Energy: La Paz.

Ministry of the Interior: Avda Arce 2409, esq. Belisario Salinas, La Paz; tel. (2) 237-0460; fax (2) 237-1334.

Ministry of Labour and Small Enterprises: Calle Yanacocha, esq. Mercado, La Paz; tel. (2) 236-4164; fax (2) 237-1387; e-mail mintrabajo@unete.com.

Ministry of National Defence: Plaza Avaroa, esq. Pedro Salazar y 20 de Octubre 2502, La Paz; tel. (2) 243-2525; fax (2) 243-3153; e-mail comunicaciones@mindef.gov.bo; internet www.mindef.gov.bo.

Ministry of the Presidency: Palacio de Gobierno, Plaza Murillo, La Paz; tel. (2) 237-1082; fax (2) 237-1388.

Ministry of Sustainable Development and Planning: Avda Mariscal Santa Cruz, Edif. De la Ex-Comibol, 8°, Casilla 12814, La Paz; tel. and fax (2) 231-0860; e-mail sdnp@coord.rds.org.bo; internet www.rds.org.bo.

President and Legislature

PRESIDENT

At the presidential election that took place on 30 June 2002 the majority of votes were spread between five of the 11 candidates. Gonzalo ('Goni') Sánchez de Lozada of the Movimiento Nacionalista Revolucionario (MNR) obtained 22.49% of the votes cast, Evo Morales of the Movimiento al Socialismo (MAS) won 20.94%, Manfred Reyes Villa of the Nueva Fuerza Republicana (NFR) won 20.91%, Jaime Paz Zamora of the Movimiento de la Izquierda Revolucionaria (MIR) secured 16.31% and Felipe Quispe Huanca of Movimiento Indígena Pachakuti (MIP) won 6.09%. As no candidate obtained the requisite absolute majority, responsibility for the selection of the President passed to the new Congreso Nacional (National Congress), which, on 4 August 2002, voted, by 84 votes to 43, to appoint Gonzalo ('Goni') Sánchez de Lozada to the presidency.

CONGRESO NACIONAL

President of the Senate: JUAN ENRIQUE TORO TEJADA.

President of the Chamber of Deputies: LUIS VÁSQUEZ VILLAMOR.

General Election, 30 June 2002

Party	Seats	
	Chamber of Deputies	Senate
Movimiento Nacionalista Revolucionario (Histórico) (MNR) . .	36	11
Movimiento al Socialismo (MAS) . . .	27	8
Movimiento de la Izquierda Revolucionaria (MIR)	26	5
Nueva Fuerza Republicana (NFR)	25	2
Movimiento Indígena Pachakuti (MIP)	6	—
Unión Cívica Solidaridad (UCS) . .	5	—
Acción Democrática Nacionalista (ADN)	4	1
Partido Socialista (PJ)	1	—
Total	**130**	**27**

Political Organizations

Acción Democrática Nacionalista (ADN): La Paz; internet www.bolivian.com/adn; f. 1979; right-wing; Leader JORGE QUIROGA; Nat. Exec. Sec. JORGE LANDÍVAR.

Alianza de Renovación Boliviana (ARBOL): La Paz; f. 1993; conservative; Leader CASIANO ACALLE CHOQUE.

Bolivia Insurgente: La Paz; f. 1996; populist party; Leader MÓNICA MEDINA.

Conciencia de Patria (Condepa): La Paz; f. 1988; populist party; Leader NICOLAS FELIPE VALDIVIA ALMANZA.

Frente Revolucionario de Izquierda (FRI): La Paz; left-wing; Leader OSCAR ZAMORA.

Movimiento Bolivariano: La Paz; f. 1999; Leader CRISTINA CORRALES.

Movimiento Bolivia Libre (MBL): Edif. Camiri, Of. 601, Calle Comercio 972 esq. Yanacocha, Casilla 10382, La Paz; tel. (2) 234-0257; fax (2) 239-2242; f. 1985; left-wing; breakaway faction of MIR; Leader FRANK BARRIOS.

Movimiento al Socialismo (MAS): La Paz; f. 1987; left-wing; Leader EVO MORALES.

Movimiento Indígena Pachakuti (MIP): indigenous movement; f. 2002; Leader FELIPE QUISPE HUANCA.

Movimiento de la Izquierda Revolucionaria (MIR): Avda América 119, 2°, La Paz; e-mail mir@ceibo.entelnet.bo; internet www.cibergallo.com; f. 1971; split into several factions in 1985; left-wing; Leader JAIME PAZ ZAMORA; Sec.-Gen. OSCAR EID FRANCO.

Movimiento sin Miedo: La Paz; f. 1999; left-wing; Leader JUAN DEL GRANADO.

Movimiento Nacionalista Revolucionario (Histórico) (MNR): Calle Nicolás Acosta 574, La Paz; tel. (2) 249-0748; fax (2) 249-0009; e-mail mnr2002@ceibo.entelnet.bo; formerly part of the Movimiento Nacionalista Revolucionario (MNR, f. 1942); centre-right; Leader GONZALO SÁNCHEZ DE LOZADA; Sec.-Gen. CARLOS SÁNCHEZ BERZAIN; 360,000 mems.

Movimiento Revolucionario Túpac Katarí de Liberación (MRTKL): Avda Baptista 939, Casilla 9133, La Paz; tel. (2) 235-4784; f. 1978; peasant party; Leader VÍCTOR HUGO CÁRDENAS CONDE; Sec.-Gen. NORBERTO PÉREZ HIDALGO; 80,000 mems.

Nueva Fuerza Republicana (NFR): Cochabamba; f. 1996; centre-right; Leader MANFRED REYES VILLA.

Partido Comunista de Bolivia (PCB): La Paz; f. 1950; Leader MARCOS DOMIC; First Sec. SIMÓN REYES RIVERA.

Partido Demócrata Cristiano (PDC): Casilla 4345, La Paz; f. 1954; Pres. BENJAMÍN MIGUEL HARB; Sec. ANTONIO CANELAS-GALATOIRE; 50,000 mems.

Partido Obrero Revolucionario (POR): Correo Central, La Paz; f. 1935; Trotskyist; Leader GUILLERMO LORA.

Partido Revolucionario de la Izquierda Nacionalista (PRIN): Calle Colón 693, La Paz; f. 1964; left-wing; Leader JUAN LECHIN OQUENDO.

Partido Socialista (PS): La Paz; f. 1987; Leader JORGE ROLANDO MORALES ANAYA.

Partido de Vanguardia Obrera: Plaza Venezuela 1452, La Paz; Leader FILEMÓN ESCOBAR.

Unión Cívica Solidaridad (UCS): Calle Mercado 1064, 6°, La Paz; tel. (2) 236-0297; fax (2) 237-2200; f. 1989; populist; Leader JOHNNY FERNÁNDEZ.

Vanguardia Revolucionaria 9 de Abril: Avda 6 de Agosto 2170, Casilla 5810, La Paz; tel. (2) 232-0311; fax (2) 239-1439; Leader Dr CARLOS SERRATE REICH.

Other parties include the Alianza Democrática Socialista and the Eje Patriótica.

Diplomatic Representation

EMBASSIES IN BOLIVIA

Argentina: Calle Aspiazu 497, POB 497, La Paz; tel. (2) 242-2912; fax (2) 242-2727; e-mail embarbol@caoba.entelnet.bo; Ambassador ARTURO E. OSSORIO ARANA.

Belgium: Calle 9 n 6, Achumani, Casilla 2433, La Paz; tel. (2) 278-1430; fax (2) 279-1219; e-mail amblapaz@entelnet.bo; Ambassador ALAIN KUNDYCKI.

Brazil: Edif. Metrobol, Calle Capitán Ravelo 2334, Casilla 429, La Paz; tel. (2) 244-0202; fax (2) 244-0043; internet www.embajadabrasil.org.bo; Ambassador STELIO MARCOS AMARANTE.

China, People's Republic: Calle 1, Los Pinos 8532, Casilla 10005, La Paz; tel. (2) 279-3851; fax (2) 279-7121; e-mail emb-china@kolla.net; Ambassador ZHANG TUO.

Colombia: Calle 20 de Octubre 2427, Casilla 1418, La Paz; tel. (2) 278-4491; fax (2) 278-6510; e-mail emcol@caoba.entelnet.bo; Ambassador LAURA OCHOA DE ARDILA.

Costa Rica: Calle 15, No 100, esq. Clemento Inofuentes Calacoto, La Paz; tel. and fax (2) 279-3201; e-mail embcrbo@kolla.net; Ambassador DIDIER CARRANZA RODRÍGUEZ.

Cuba: Avda Arequipa 8037, Calacoto, La Paz; tel. (2) 272-1157; fax (2) 272-3419; e-mail embacuba@ceibo.entelnet.bo; Ambassador LUIS FELIPE VÁSQUEZ.

Denmark: Edif. Fortaleza, Avda Arce 2799 esq. Cordero, 9°, Casilla 9860, La Paz; tel. (2) 243-2070; fax (2) 243-3150; e-mail ambdklp@ceibo.entelnet.bo; Ambassador MOGENS PEDERSEN.

Ecuador: Edif. Herrman, 14°, Plaza Venezuela, Casilla 406, La Paz; tel. (2) 233-1588; fax (2) 239-1932; e-mail mecuabol@caoba.entelnet.bo; Ambassador LUIS MORENO GUERRA.

Egypt: Avda Ballivián 599, Casilla 2956, La Paz; tel. (2) 278-6511; fax (2) 278-4325; Ambassador Dr MAHMOUD AMIN HASSANEIN.

France: Avda Hernando Silés 5390, esq. Calle 8, Obrajes, Casilla 717, La Paz; tel. (2) 278-6114; fax (2) 278-6746; e-mail amfrabo@ceibo.entelnet.bo; internet www.ambafrance-bo.org.bo; Ambassador FRANÇOISE LE BIHAN.

Germany: Avda Arce 2395, Casilla 5265, La Paz; tel. (2) 244-0066; fax (2) 244-1441; e-mail germany@ceibo.entelnet.bo; Ambassador Dr BERND SPROEDT.

Holy See: Avda Arce 2990, Casilla 136, La Paz; tel. (2) 243-1007; fax (2) 243-2120; e-mail nunzibol@caoba.entelnet.bo; Apostolic Nuncio Most Rev. IVO SCAPOLO (Titular Archbishop of Tagaste).

Israel: Edif. Esperanza, 10°, Avda Mariscal Santa Cruz, Casilla 1309, La Paz; tel. (2) 239-1126; fax (2) 239-1712; e-mail emisrabo@ceibo.entelnet.bo; Ambassador ISAAC LAVIE BACHMAN.

Italy: Avda 6 de Agosto 2575, Casilla 626, La Paz; tel. (2) 243-4929; fax (2) 243-4975; e-mail ambital@ceibo.entelnet.bo; internet www.ambital.org.bo; Ambassador Dr EUGENIO CAMPO.

Japan: Calle Rosendo Gutiérrez 497, Casilla 2725, La Paz; tel. (2) 237-3151; fax (2) 239-1052; Ambassador HIROYUKI KIMOTO.

Korea, Democratic People's Republic: La Paz; Ambassador KIM CHAN SIK.

Mexico: Sánchez Bustamante 509, Casilla 430, La Paz; tel. (2) 277-1824; fax (2) 277-1855; e-mail embamex@kolla.net; internet www.embamex-bolivia.org; Ambassador ELIEZER MORALES ARAGÓN.

Panama: Calle 10, No 7853 de Colacoto, Casilla 678, La Paz; tel. (2) 277-7334; fax (2) 279-7290; e-mail empanbol@ceibo.entelnet.bo; Ambassador MARCOS IVÁN ROLLA.

Paraguay: Edif. Illimani II, 1°, Avda 6 de Agosto y Pedro Salazar, Casilla 882, La Paz; tel. (2) 243-3176; fax (2) 243-2201; e-mail emparabo@ceibo.entelnet.bo; Ambassador EMILIO LORENZO GIMÉNEZ FRANCO.

Peru: Calle F. Guachalla 300, Casilla 668, La Paz; tel. (2) 244-1250; fax (2) 244-1240; e-mail embbol@caoba.entelnet.bo; Ambassador Dr HARRY BELEVAN-MCBRIDE.

Russia: Avda Walter Guevara Arce 8129, Casilla 5494, La Paz; tel. (2) 278-6419; fax (2) 278-6531; e-mail embrusia@ceibo.entelnet.bo; Ambassador GUENNADI VASILIEVICH SIZOV.

Spain: Avda 6 de Agosto 2860, Casilla 282, La Paz; tel. (2) 243-3518; fax (2) 243-2752; e-mail embespa@ceibo.entelnet.bo; Ambassador VÍCTOR LUIS FAGILDE GONZALES.

Switzerland: Edif. Petrolero, Avda 16 de Julio 1616, Casilla 657, La Paz; tel. (2) 231-5471; fax (2) 239-1462; e-mail swiembol@ceibo.entelnet.bo; Ambassador ERIC MARTIN.

United Kingdom: Avda Arce 2732–2754, Casilla 694, La Paz; tel. (2) 243-3424; fax (2) 243-1073; e-mail ppa@mail.megalink.com; Ambassador WILLIAM BALDIE SINTON.

USA: Avda Arce 2780, Casilla 425, La Paz; tel. (2) 243-0251; fax (2) 243-3900; internet www.megalink.com/usemblapaz; Ambassador DAVID N. GREENLEE.

Uruguay: Avda 6 de Agosto 2577, Casilla 441, La Paz; tel. (2) 243-0080; fax (2) 243-0087; e-mail urulivia@datacom-bo.net; Ambassador JUAN A. PACHECO RAMÍREZ.

Venezuela: Edif. Illimani, 4°, Avda Arce esq. Campos, Casilla 960, La Paz; tel. (2) 243-1365; fax (2) 243-2348; e-mail hecmaldo@ceibo.entelnet.bo; Chargé d'affaires MARÍA EUGENIA PÉREZ GODOY.

Judicial System

SUPREME COURT

Corte Suprema

Calle Pilinco 352, Sucre; tel. (4) 642-1883; fax (4) 643-2696.

Judicial power is vested in the Supreme Court. There are 12 members, appointed by Congress for a term of 10 years. The court is divided into four chambers of three justices each. Two chambers deal with civil cases, the third deals with criminal cases and the fourth deals with administrative, social and mining cases. The President of the Supreme Court presides over joint sessions of the courts and attends the joint sessions for cassation cases.

President of the Supreme Court: ARMANDO VILLAFUERTES CLAROS.

DISTRICT COURTS

There is a District Court sitting in each Department, and additional provincial and local courts to try minor cases.

ATTORNEY-GENERAL

In addition to the Attorney-General at Sucre (appointed by the President on the proposal of the Senate), there is a District Attorney in each Department as well as circuit judges.

Attorney-General: OSCAR CRESPO.

Religion

The majority of the population are Roman Catholics; there were an estimated 7.2m. adherents at 31 December 2000, equivalent to 85.0% of the population. Religious freedom is guaranteed. There is a small Jewish community, as well as various Protestant denominations, in Bolivia.

CHRISTIANITY

The Roman Catholic Church

Bolivia comprises four archdioceses, six dioceses, two Territorial Prelatures and five Apostolic Vicariates.

Bishops' Conference

Conferencia Episcopal Boliviana, Calle Potosí 814, Casilla 2309, La Paz; tel. (2) 240-6855; fax (2) 240-6941; e-mail asc@scbbs-bo.com.

f. 1972; Pres. Cardinal JULIO TERRAZAS SANDOVAL (Archbishop of Santa Cruz de la Sierra).

Archbishop of Cochabamba: Most Rev. TITO SOLARI, Avda Heroínas esq. Zenteno Anaya, Casilla 129, Cochabamba; tel. (4) 425-6562; fax (4) 425-0522; e-mail arz.cbba@supernet.com.bo.

Archbishop of La Paz: Most Rev. EDMUNDO LUIS FLAVIO ABASTOFLOR MONTERO, Calle Ballivián 1277, Casilla 259, La Paz; tel. (2) 234-1920; fax (2) 239-1244; e-mail arzonslp@ceibo.entelnet.bo.

Archbishop of Santa Cruz de la Sierra: Cardinal JULIO TERRAZAS SANDOVAL, Calle Ingavi 49, Casilla 25, Santa Cruz; tel. (3) 332-4286; fax (3) 333-0181; e-mail asc@scbbs-bo.com.

Archbishop of Sucre: Most Rev. JESÚS GERVASIO PÉREZ RODRÍGUEZ, Calle Bolívar 702, Casilla 205, Sucre; tel. (4) 645-1587; fax (4) 646-0336; e-mail arzsucre@mara.scr.entelnet.bo.

The Anglican Communion

Within the Iglesia Anglicana del Cono Sur de América (Anglican Church of the Southern Cone of America), Bolivia forms part of the diocese of Peru. The Bishop is resident in Lima, Peru.

Protestant Churches

Baptist Union of Bolivia: Casilla 2199, La Paz; tel. (2) 222-9538; Pres. Rev. AUGUSTO CHULJO.

Convención Bautista Boliviana (Baptist Convention of Bolivia): Casilla 3147, Santa Cruz; tel. (3) 334-0717; fax (3) 334-0717; f. 1947; Pres. EIRA SORUCO DE FLORES.

Iglesia Evangélica Metodista en Bolivia (Evangelical Methodist Church in Bolivia): Casillas 356 y 8347, La Paz; tel. (2) 234-2702; fax (2) 235-7046; autonomous since 1969; 10,000 mems; Bishop Rev. EFRAÍN YANAPA.

BAHÁ'Í FAITH

National Spiritual Assembly of the Bahá'ís of Bolivia: Casilla 1613, La Paz; tel. (2) 278-5058; fax (2) 278-2387; e-mail aebahais@caoba.entelnet.bo; mems resident in 6,262 localities.

The Press

DAILY NEWSPAPERS

Cochabamba

Opinión: General Acha 0252, Casilla 287, Cochabamba; tel. (4) 425-4402; fax (4) 421-5121; f. 1985; Dir EDWIN TAPIA FRONTANILLA; Man. Editor JAIME BUITRAGO.

Los Tiempos: Plaza Quintanilla-Norte, Casilla 525, Cochabamba; tel. (4) 425-4561; fax (4) 425-4577; e-mail lostiempos@lostiempos.bo.net; internet www.lostiempos.com; f. 1943; morning; independent; Dir FERNANDO CANELAS; Man. Editor MIGUEL LORA; circ. 19,000.

La Paz

El Diario: Calle Loayza 118, Casilla 5, La Paz; tel. (2) 239-0900; fax (2) 236-3846; e-mail contacto@eldiario.net; internet www.eldiario.net; f. 1904; morning; conservative; Dir JORGE CARRASCO JAHNSEN; Man. Editor MAURICIO CARRASCO; circ. 55,000.

Jornada: Edif. Almirante Grau 672, Casilla 1628, La Paz; tel. (2) 235-3844; fax (2) 235-6213; e-mail jornada@ceibo.entelnet.bo; f. 1964; evening; independent; Dir JAIME RÍOS CHACÓN; circ. 11,500.

La Razón: Colinas de Santa Rita, Auquisamaña, Casilla 13100, La Paz; tel. (2) 227-1415; fax (2) 277-0908; e-mail larazon@la-razon.com; internet www.la-razon.com; f. 1990; Pres. DIETER GARAFULIC LEHM; Dir JUAN CRISTÓBAL SORUCO; circ. 35,000.

Oruro

El Expreso: Potosí 4921 esq. Villarroel, Oruro; f. 1973; morning; independent; right-wing; Dir ALBERTO FRONTANILLA MORALES; circ. 1,000.

La Patria: Avda Camacho 1892, Casilla 48, Oruro; tel. (2) 525-0761; fax (2) 525-0781; f. 1919; morning; independent; Pres. MARCELO MIRRALLES BOVÁ; Dir ENRIQUE MIRALLES BONNECARRERE; circ. 6,000.

Potosí

El Siglo: Calle Linares 99, Casilla 389, Potosí; f. 1975; morning; Dir WILSON MENDIETA PACHECO; circ. 1,500.

Santa Cruz

El Deber: Avda El Trompillo 1144, Casilla 2144, Santa Cruz; tel. (3) 353-8000; fax (3) 353-9053; e-mail info.eldeber@eldeber.com; internet www.eldeber.com; f. 1955; morning; independent; Dir PEDRO RIVERO MERCADO; Man. Editor GUILLERMO RIVERO JORDÁN; circ. 35,000.

La Estrella del Oriente: Calle Sucre 558, Casilla 736, Santa Cruz; tel. (3) 337-0707; fax (3) 337-0557; e-mail estrella@mitai.nrs.bolnet.bo; internet www.laestrella.com; f. 1864; Pres. JORGE LANDÍVAR ROCA; Man. Editor TUFFI ARÉ.

El Mundo: Parque Industrial PI-7, Casilla 1984, Santa Cruz; tel. (3) 346-4646; fax (3) 346-5057; e-mail elmundo@mitai.nrs.bolnet.bo; f. 1979; morning; owned by Santa Cruz Industrialists' Association; Pres. WALTER PAREJAS MORENO; Dir JUAN JAVIER ZEBALLOS GUTIÉRREZ; circ. 15,000.

El Nuevo Día: Calle Independencia 470, Casilla 5344, Santa Cruz; tel. (3) 333-7474; fax (3) 336-0303; f. 1987; Dir NANCY EKLUND VDA DE GUTIÉRREZ; Man. Editor JORGE ORÍAS HERRERA.

Trinidad

La Razón: Avda Bolívar 295, Casilla 166, Trinidad; tel. (3) 462-1377; f. 1972; Dir CARLOS VÉLEZ.

PERIODICALS

Actualidad Boliviana Confidencial (ABC): Fernando Guachalla 969, Casilla 648, La Paz; f. 1966; weekly; Dir HUGO GONZÁLEZ RIOJA; circ. 6,000.

Aquí: Casilla 10937, La Paz; tel. (2) 234-3524; fax (2) 235-2455; f. 1979; weekly; circ. 10,000.

Bolivia Libre: Edif. Esperanza, 5°, Avda Mariscal Santa Cruz 2150, Casilla 6500, La Paz; fortnightly; govt organ.

Carta Cruceña de Integración: Casilla 3531, Santa Cruz de la Sierra; weekly; Dirs HERNÁN LLANOVARCED A, JOHNNY LAZARTE J.

Comentarios Económicos de Actualidad (CEA): Casilla 312097, La Paz; tel. (2) 242-4766; fax (2) 242-4772; e-mail veceba@caoba.entelnet.bo; f. 1983; fortnightly; articles and economic analyses; Editor GUIDO CESPEDES.

Información Política y Económica (IPE): Calle Comercio, Casilla 2484, La Paz; weekly; Dir GONZALO LÓPEZ MUÑOZ.

Informe R: La Paz; weekly; Editor SARA MONROY.

Notas: Casilla 5782, La Paz; tel. (2) 237-3773; fax (2) 236-5153; weekly; political and economic analysis; Editor JOSÉ GRAMUNT DE MORAGAS.

El Noticiero: Sucre; weekly; Dir DAVID CABEZAS; circ. 1,500.

Prensa Libre: Sucre; tel. (4) 646-2447; fax (4) 646-2768; e-mail prelibre@mara.scr.entelnet.bo; f. 1989; weekly; Dir JULIO PEMINTEL A.

Servicio de Información Confidencial (SIC): Elías Sagárnaga 274, Casilla 5035, La Paz; weekly; publ. by Asociación Nacional de Prensa; Dir JOSÉ CARRANZA.

Siglo XXI: La Paz; weekly.

Unión: Sucre; weekly; Dir JAIME MERILES.

Visión Boliviana: Calle Loayza 420, Casilla 2870, La Paz; 6 a year.

PRESS ASSOCIATIONS

Asociación Nacional de la Prensa: Avda 6 de Agosto 2170, Casilla 477, La Paz; tel. (2) 236-9916; Pres. Dr CARLOS SERRATE REICH.

Asociación de Periodistas de La Paz: Avda 6 de Agosto 2170, Casilla 477, La Paz; tel. (2) 236-9916; fax (2) 232-3701; f. 1929; Pres. MARIO MALDONADO VISCARRA; Vice-Pres. MARÍA EUGENIA VERASTEGUI A.

NEWS AGENCIES

Agencia de Noticias Fides (ANF): Edif. Mariscal de Ayacucho, 5°, Of. 501, Calle Loayza, Casilla 5782, La Paz; tel. (2) 236-5152; fax (2) 236-5153; owned by Roman Catholic Church; Dir JOSÉ GRAMUNT DE MORAGAS.

Foreign Bureaux

Agencia EFE (Spain): Edif. Anibal Mz 01, Avda Sánchez Lima 2520, Casilla 7403, La Paz; tel. (2) 241-9222; fax (2) 241-8388; e-mail efeadmon@entelnet.bo; Bureau Chief PATRICIA VÁZQUEZ ORBEGOZO.

Agenzia Nazionale Stampa Associata (ANSA) (Italy): La Paz; tel. (2) 235-5521; fax (2) 236-8221; Correspondent RAÚL PENARANDA UNDURRAGA.

Associated Press (AP) (USA): Edif. Mariscal de Ayacucho, Of. 1209, Calle Loayza 273, Casilla 9569, La Paz; tel. (2) 220-1557; fax (2) 220-1558; e-mail varrington@ap.org; Correspondent VANESSA ARRINGTON.

Deutsche Presse-Agentur (dpa) (Germany): Edif. Esperanza, 9°, Of. 3, Av. Mariscal Santa Cruz 2150, Casilla 13885, La Paz; tel. (2) 235-2684; fax (2) 239-2488; Correspondent ROBERT BROCKMANN.

Informatsionnoye Telegrafnoye Agentstvo Rossii—Telegrafnoye Agentstvo Suverennykh Stran (ITAR—TASS) (Russia): Casilla 6839, San Miguel, Bloque 0–33, Casa 958, La Paz; tel. (2) 279-2108; Correspondent ELDAR ABDULLAEV.

Inter Press Service (IPS) (Italy): Edif. Esperanza, 6°, Of. 6, Casilla 4313, La Paz; tel. (2) 236-1227; Correspondent RONALD GREBE LÓPEZ.

Prensa Latina (Cuba): La Paz; tel. (2) 232-3479; Correspondent MANUEL ROBLES SOSA.

Reuters (United Kingdom): Edif. Loayza, 3°, Of. 301, Calle Loayza 349, Casilla 4057, La Paz; tel. (2) 235-1106; fax (2) 239-1366; Correspondent RENÉ VILLEGAS MONJE.

Rossiyskoye Informatsionnoye Agentstvo—Novosti (RIA—Novosti) (Russia): La Paz; tel. (2) 237-3857; Correspondent VLADIMIR RAMÍREZ.

Agence France-Presse and Telam (Argentina) are also represented.

Publishers

Editora Khana Cruz SRL: Avda Camacho 1372, Casilla 5920, La Paz; tel. (2) 237-0263; Dir GLADIS ANDRADE.

Editora Lux: Edif. Esperanza, Avda Mariscal Santa Cruz, Casilla 1566, La Paz; tel. (2) 232-9102; fax (2) 234-3968; f. 1952; Dir FELICISIMO TARILONTE PÉREZ.

Editorial los Amigos del Libro: Avda Ayacucho 0-156, Casilla 450, Cochabamba; tel. (4) 450-4150; fax (4) 411-5128; e-mail amigol@amigol.bo.net; internet www.librosbolivia.com; f. 1945; general; Man. Dir WERNER GUTTENTAG; Gen. Man. INGRID GUTTENTAG.

Editorial Bruño: Loayza 167, Casilla 4809, La Paz; tel. (2) 233-1254; fax (2) 233-5043; f. 1964; Dir IGNACIO LOMAS.

Editorial Don Bosco: Avda 16 de Julio 1899, Casilla 4458, La Paz; tel. (2) 237-1757; fax (2) 236-2822; f. 1896; social sciences and literature; Dir GRAMAGLIA MAGLIANO.

Editorial Icthus: La Paz; tel. (2) 235-4007; f. 1967; general and textbooks; Man. Dir DANIEL AQUIZE.

Editorial Popular: Plaza Pérez Velasco 787, Casilla 4171, La Paz; tel. (2) 235-0701; f. 1935; textbooks, postcards, tourist guides, etc; Man. Dir GERMÁN VILLAMOR.

Editorial Puerta del Sol: Edif. Litoral Sub Suelo, Avda Mariscal Santa Cruz, La Paz; tel. (2) 236-0746; f. 1965; Man. Dir OSCAR CRESPO.

Empresa Editora Proinsa: Avda Saavedra 2055, Casilla 7181, La Paz; tel. (2) 222-7781; fax (2) 222-6671; f. 1974; school books; Dirs FLOREN SANABRIA G, CARLOS SANABRIA C.

Gisbert y Cía, SA: Calle Comercio 1270, Casilla 195, La Paz; tel. (2) 220-2626; fax (2) 220-2911; e-mail libgis@ceibo.entelnet.bo; f. 1907; textbooks, history, law and general; Pres. JAVIER GISBERT; Dirs MARÍA DEL CARMEN SCHULCZEWSKI, ANTONIO SCHULCZEWSKI.

Ivar American: Calle Potosí 1375, Casilla 6016, La Paz; tel. (2) 236-1519; Man. Dir HÉCTOR IBÁÑEZ.

Librería Editorial Juventud: Plaza Murillo 519, Casilla 1489, La Paz; tel. (2) 240-7033; f. 1946; textbooks and general; Dir GUSTAVO URQUIZO MENDOZA.

Librería El Ateneo SRL: Calle Ballivián 1275, Casilla 7917, La Paz; tel. (2) 236-9925; fax (2) 239-1513; Dirs JUAN CHIRVECHES D., MIRIAN C. DE CHIRVECHES.

Librería Dismo Ltda: Calle Comercio 806, Casilla 988, La Paz; tel. (2) 240-6411; fax (2) 31-6545; e-mail dismo@caoba.entelnet.bo; Dir TERESA GONZÁLEZ DE ALVAREZ.

Librería La Paz: Calle Campos y Villegas, Edif. Artemis, Casilla 539, La Paz; tel. (2) 243-4927; fax (2) 243-5004; e-mail liblapaz@ceibo.entelnet.bo; f. 1900; Dirs EDUARDO BURGOS R, CARLOS BURGOS M.

Librería La Universal SRL: Calle Genaro Sanjines 538, Casilla 2888, La Paz; tel. (2) 234-2961; f. 1958; Man. Dir ROLANDO CONDORI.

Librería San Pablo: Calle Colón 627, Casilla 3152, La Paz; tel. (2) 232-6084; f. 1967; Man. Dir MARÍA DE JESÚS VALERIANO.

PUBLISHERS' ASSOCIATION

Cámara Boliviana del Libro: Calle Capitán Ravelo 2116, Casilla 682, La Paz; tel. (2) 244-4239; fax (2) 244-1523; e-mail cabolib@ceibo.entelnet.bo; f. 1947; Pres. CARMEN TEJERINA DE TERRAZAS; Gen. Man. VERONICA FLORES BEDREGAL.

Broadcasting and Communications

TELECOMMUNICATIONS

Cámara Nacional de Medios de Comunicación: Casilla 2431, La Paz.

Empresa Nacional de Telecomunicaciones (ENTEL): Calle Federico Zuazo 1771, Casilla 4450, La Paz; tel. (2) 231-3030; fax (2) 239-1789; internet www.entel.com.bo; f. 1965; privatized under the Govt's capitalization programme in 1995; CEO FRANCO BERTONE.

Superintendencia de Telecomunicaciones: Edif. M. Cristina, Plaza España, Casilla 6692, La Paz; tel. (2) 241-6641; fax (2) 241-8183; e-mail supertel@ceibo.entelnet.bo; f. 1995; govt-controlled broadcasting authority; Superintendent Ing. GUIDO LOAYZA.

BROADCASTING

Radio

The majority of radio stations are commercial. Broadcasts are in Spanish, Aymará and Quechua. In 1999 there were 171 MW and LW radio stations and 73 FM stations, as well as 77 short-wave stations

Asociación Boliviana de Radiodifusoras (ASBORA): Edif. Jazmin, 10°, Avda 20 de Octubre 2019, Casilla 5324, La Paz; tel. (2) 236-5154; fax (2) 236-3069; broadcasting authority; Pres. TERESA SANJINÉS L; Vice-Pres. LUIS ANTONIO SERRANO.

Educación Radiofónica de Bolivia (ERBOL): Calle Ballivian 1323, 4°, Casilla 5946, La Paz; tel. (2) 235-4142; fax (2) 239-1985; asscn of 28 educational radio stations in Bolivia; Gen. Sec. RONALD GREBE LÓPEZ.

Television

There were 48 television stations in 1999.

Corporación Boliviana de Televisión Canal 30: Calle Obispo Cárdenas 1475, Casilla 8980, La Paz; tel. (2) 231-5031; fax (2) 231-9563; f. 1996; Pres. RICARDO CLAURE; Dir ALEX MEJÍA.

Empresa Nacional de Televisión Boliviana Canal 7: Edif. La Urbana, 6° y 7°, Avda Camacho 1486, Casilla 900, La Paz; tel. (2) 237-6356; fax (2) 235-9753; f. 1969; govt network operating stations in La Paz, Oruro, Cochabamba, Potosí, Chuquisaca, Pando, Beni, Tarija and Santa Cruz; Gen. Man. MIGUEL N. MONTERO VACA.

Televisión Boliviano Canal 2: Casilla 4837, La Paz.

Televisión Universitaria Canal 13: Edif. 'Hoy', 12°–13°, Avda 6 de Agosto 2170, Casilla 13383, La Paz; tel. (2) 235-9297; fax (2) 235-9298; f. 1980; educational programmes; stations in Oruro, Cochabamba, Potosí, Sucre, Tarija, Beni and Santa Cruz; Dir Lic. ROBERTO CUEVAS RAMÍREZ.

Finance

(cap. = capital; res = reserves; dep. = deposits; m. = million; brs = branches; amounts are in bolivianos, unless otherwise stated)

BANKING

Supervisory Authority

Superintendencia de Bancos y Entidades Financieras: Plaza Isabel la Católica 2507, Casilla 447, La Paz; tel. (2) 243-1919; fax (2) 243-0028; e-mail sbef@sbef.gov.bo; internet www.sbef.gov.bo; f. 1928; Supt Dr LUIS FERNANDO CALVO UNZUETA.

State Bank

Banco Central de Bolivia: Avda Ayacucho esq. Mercado, Casilla 3118, La Paz; tel. (2) 237-4151; fax (2) 239-2398; e-mail vmarquez@mail.bcb.gov.bo; internet www.bcb.gov.bo; f. 1911 as Banco de la Nación Boliviana, name changed as above 1928; bank of issue; cap. 515.8m., res 2,814.9m. (Oct. 2001); Pres. Dr JUAN ANTONIO MORALES ANAYA; Gen. Man. Lic. MARCELA NOGALES.

Commercial Banks

Banco Bisa SA: Avda 16 de Julio 1628, Casilla 1290, La Paz; tel. (2) 236-3394; fax (2) 231-6597; e-mail bancobisa@grupobisa.com; internet www.grupobisa.com; f. 1963; cap. 479.7m., res 73.2m., dep. 4,355.3m. (Dec. 2001); Pres. Ing. JULIÓ LEÓN PRADO; CEO JOSÉ LUIS ARANGUREN AGUIRRE.

Banco de Crédito de Bolivia, SA: Calle Colón esq. Mercado 1308, Casilla 907, La Paz; tel. (2) 220-1154; fax (2) 223-2203; e-mail bancnalp@acaoba.entelnet.bo; f. 1993 as Banco Popular, SA, name changed as above 1994; 61% owned by Banco de Crédito del Perú; cap. 255.4m., res 28.0m., dep. 3,568.1m. (Dec. 1999); Chair. DIONISIO ROMERO SEMINARIO; Gen. Man. DAVID SAETTONE WATMOUGH; 6 brs.

Banco Económico SA-SCZ: Calle Ayacucho 166, Casilla 5603, Santa Cruz; tel. (3) 336-1177; fax (3) 336-1184; e-mail bcneco@roble.scz.entelnet.bo; f. 1990; dep. US $290.4m., total assets US $328.1m. (Dec. 1998); Pres. LUIS PERROGÓN TOLEDO; Gen. Man. Ing. JUSTO YEPEZ KAKUDA; 14 brs.

Banco Ganadero SA-Santa Cruz: Calle 24 de Setiembre 110, Casilla 4492, Santa Cruz; tel. (3) 336-1616; fax (3) 333-2567; e-mail hkrutzfeldt@bancoganadero.co.bo; internet www.bancoganadero.com; f. 1994; cap. and res 108.1m., dep. 1,078.1m. (Dec. 2000); Pres. FERNANDO MONASTERIO NIEME; Gen. Man. HERMANN KRUTZFELDT.

Banco Mercantil, SA: Calle Ayacucho 277, Casilla 423, La Paz; tel. (2) 231-5131; fax (2) 231-1324; e-mail bercant@bancomercantil.com.bo; internet www.bancomercantil.com.bo; f. 1905; cap. and res

57.5m., dep. 456m. (Dec. 2001); Pres. EDUARDO QUINTANILLA; Gen. Man. MONICA ENRICO DE ESPINOZA; 39 brs.

Banco Nacional de Bolivia: Avda Camacho esq. Colón 1312, Casilla 360, La Paz; tel. (2) 235-4616; fax (2) 237-1279; e-mail info@bnb.com.bo; internet www.bnb.com.bo; f. 1871; cap. 189.3m., res 46.1m., dep. 3,108.9m. (Dec. 1998); Pres. RONALDO KEMPFF BACIGALUPO; Gen. Man. GONZALO ARGANDOÑA; 9 brs.

Banco Santa Cruz, SA: Calle Junín 154, Casilla 865, Santa Cruz; tel. (3) 336-9911; fax (3) 335-0114; e-mail bancruz@mailbsc.com; internet www.bsc.com.bo; f. 1965; 90% owned by Banco Central Hispanoamericano (Spain); cap. and res 44.2m., dep. 315.4m. (June 1990); Pres. ANTONIO ESCÁMEZ TORRES; Gen. Man. LUIS YAGÜE JIMENO; 44 brs.

Banco Unión, SA: Calle Libertad 156, Casilla 4057, Santa Cruz; tel. (3) 336-6869; fax (3) 334-0684; e-mail info@bancounion.com.bo; internet www.bancounion.com.bo; f. 1982; cap. 339.9m., res 56.0m., dep. 2,514.2m. (Dec. 2001); Pres. Ing. ANDRÉS PETRICEVIC; Gen. Man. JULIAN SECO; 2 brs.

Foreign Banks

Banco ABN AMRO Real, SA (USA): Avda 16 de Julio 1642, Casilla 10008, La Paz; tel. (2) 233-4477; fax (2) 233-5588; f. 1978 as Banco Real, name changed as above 2000; dep. US $8.3m., total assets US $17.5m. (Dec. 1997); Operations Man. JOSÉ PORFIRIO VASCONCELOS.

Banco do Brasil, SA: Avda Camacho 1468, Planta Baja, Casilla 1650, La Paz; tel. (2) 237-7272; fax (2) 239-1036; e-mail bblapaz@caoba.entelnet.bo; f. 1961; Gen. Man. LEO SCHNEIDERS; 1 br.

Banco de la Nación Argentina: Avda 16 de Julio 1486, Casilla 2745-4312, La Paz; tel. (2) 235-9218; fax (2) 239-1392; e-mail bancnalp@caoba.entelnet.bo; internet www.bna.com.ar; f. 1891; Man. EDUARDO CASADO; 2 brs.

Citibank NA (USA): Edif. Multicentro Torre B, Calle Rosendo Gutiérrez esq. Arce 146, La Paz; tel. (2) 243-0099; fax (2) 244-0433; e-mail juan.leyes@citicorp.com; f. 1966; Vice-Pres. MARIO BEDOYA GARLAND; Gen. Man. AGUSTÍN DÁVALOS; 2 brs.

Dresdner Bank Lateinamerika AG (Germany): Calle Rosendo Gutiérrez esq. Arce 136, Edif. Multicentro Torre B, La Paz; tel. (2) 243-4114; fax (2) 243-4115; fmrly Deutsch-Südamerikanische Bank AG and Dresdner Bank AG; Gen. Man. NILS HUPKA.

Banking Association

Asociación de Bancos Privados de Bolivia (ASOBAN): Edif. Cámara Nacional de Comercio, 15°, Avda Mariscal Santa Cruz esq. Colombia 1392, Casilla 5822, La Paz; tel. (2) 233-4839; fax (2) 239-1093; e-mail info@asoban.bo; internet www.asoban.bo; f. 1957; Pres. JOSÉ LUIS ARANGUREN; Exec. Sec. MARCELO MONTERO NUÑEZ DEL PRADO; 18 mems.

STOCK EXCHANGE

Supervisory Authorities

Superintendencia de Pensiones, Valores y Seguros: Calle Reyes Ortiz esq. Federico Zuazo, Torres Gundlach, 3°, Casilla 6118, La Paz; tel. (2) 233-1212; fax (2) 233-0001; e-mail spvs@caoba.entelnet.bo; Superintendent Dr PABLO GOTTRET VALDÉS; Intendent FRANCISCO GÓMEZ.

Bolsa Boliviana de Valores SA: Edif. Zambrana P.B., Calle Montevideo 142, Casilla 12521, La Paz; tel. (2) 244-3232; fax (2) 244-2308; e-mail info@bolsa-valores-bolivia.com; internet www.bolsa-valores-bolivia.com; f. 1989; Pres. Lic. LUIS FELIPE RIVERO MENDOZA; Gen. Man. Lic. ARMANDO ALVAREZ ARNAL.

INSURANCE

Supervisory Authority

Superintendencia de Pensiones, Valores y Seguros: see above.

National Companies

Adriatica Seguros y Reaseguros, SA: Avda Cristóbal de Mendoza 250, Santa Cruz; tel. (3) 336-6667; fax (3) 336-0600; e-mail adriatica@cotas.com.bo; Pres. ANTONIO OLEA BAUDOIN; Gen. Man. EDUARDO LANDÍVAR ROCA.

Alianza, Cía de Seguros y Reaseguros, SA: Avda 20 de Octubre 2680, esq. Campos Zona San Jorge, Casilla 11873, La Paz; tel. (2) 243-2121; fax (2) 243-2511; e-mail alianza@ceibo.entelnet.bo; Pres. JUAN MANUEL PEÑA ROCA; Gen. Man. CÉSAR EYZAGUIRRE ANGELES.

Alianza Vida Seguros y Reaseguros, SA: Avda Viedma 19, Casilla 1043, Santa Cruz; tel. (3) 337-5656; fax (3) 337-5666; e-mail alejandro@sc.alianzaseguros.com; Pres. RAÚL ADLER K; Gen. Man. ALEJANDRO YBARRA C.

Bisa Seguros y Reaseguros, SA: Edif. San Pablo, 13°, Avda 16 de Julio 1479, Casilla 3669, La Paz; tel. (2) 235-2123; fax (2) 239-2500; e-mail bisaseguros@grupobisa.com; Pres. JULIO LEÓN PRADO; Exec. Vice-Pres. ALEJANDRO MACLEAN C.

La Boliviana Ciacruz de Seguros y Reaseguros, SA: Calle Colón, esq. Mercado 288, Casilla 5959, La Paz; tel. (2) 220-3131; fax (2) 220-4087; e-mail bolseg@caoba.entelnet.bo; f. 1946; all classes; Pres. GONZALO BEDOYA HERRERA.

Compañía de Seguros y Reaseguros Cruceño, SA: Calle René Moreno esq. Lemoyne 607, Santa Cruz; tel. (3) 333-8985; fax (3) 333-8984; e-mail seg.crycena@mail.cotas.com.bo; Pres. Lic. GUIDO HINOJOSA; Gen. Man. NELSON HINOJOSA.

Credinform International SA de Seguros: Edif. Credinform, Calle Potosí esq. Ayacucho 1220, Casilla 1724, La Paz; tel. (2) 231-5566; fax (2) 239-1225; e-mail credinfo@caoba.entelnet.bo; f. 1954; all classes; Pres. Dr ROBÍN BARRAGÁN PELÁEZ; Gen. Man. MIGUEL ANGEL BARRAGÁN IBARGUEN.

Nacional de Seguros y Reaseguros, SA: Calle Libertad esq. Cañoto 879, Casilla 6794, Santa Cruz; tel. (3) 334-6969; fax (3) 334-2415; e-mail nalseg@bibosi.scz.entelnet.bo; f. 1977; fmrly known as Condor, SA de Seguros y Reaseguros; Pres. TONCHI ETEROVIC NIEGOVIC; Gen. Man. LUIS ALBERTO FLOR CORTEZ.

Seguros Illimani, SA: Edif. Mariscal de Ayacucho, 10°, Calle Loayza, Casilla 133, La Paz; tel. (2) 220-3040; fax (2) 239-1149; e-mail sisalp@ceibo.entelnet.bo; f. 1979; all classes; Pres. FERNANDO ARCE GRANDCHANT; Gen. Man. LUIS ARCE OSTRIA.

La Vitalicia Seguros y Reaseguros de Vida, SA: Avda 6 de Agosto 2860, Edif. Hoy Mezzanine, POB 8424, La Paz; tel. (2) 212-5355; fax (2) 211-3480; e-mail aibanez@grupobisa.com; Pres. JULIO C. LEON PRADO; CEO ALFONSO IBAÑEZ MONTES.

There are also four foreign-owned insurance companies operating in Bolivia: American Life Insurance Co, American Home Assurance Co, United States Fire Insurance Co and International Health Insurance Danmarck.

Insurance Association

Asociación Boliviana de Aseguradores: Edif. Castilla, 5°, Of. 506, Calle Loayza esq. Mercado 250, Casilla 4804, La Paz; tel. (2) 231-0056; fax (2) 220-1088; e-mail abasegu@ceibo.entelnet.bo; f. 1962; Pres. ALFONSO IBAÑEZ; Gen. Man. CARLOS BAUDOIN D.

Trade and Industry

GOVERNMENT AGENCIES

Cámara Nacional de Exportadores (CAMEX): Avda Arce 2017, esq. Goitia, Casilla 12145, La Paz; tel. (2) 234-1220; fax (2) 236-1491; e-mail camex@caoba.entelnet.bo; internet www.camex-lpb.com; f. 1970; Pres. LUIS NEMTALA YAMIN; Gen. Man. JORGE ADRIAZOLA REIMERS.

Centro de Promoción Bolivia (CEPROBOL): Calle Mercado 1328, 18°, Casilla 10871, La Paz; tel. (2) 233-6886; fax (2) 233-6996; e-mail ceprobol@ceprobol.gov.bo; internet www.ceprobol.gov.bo; f. 1998 as a successor to the Instituto Nacional de Promoción de Exportaciones (INPEX).

Instituto Nacional de Inversiones (INI): Edif. Cristal, 10°, Calle Yanacocha, Casilla 4393, La Paz; tel. (2) 237-5730; fax (2) 236-7297; e-mail abeseg@kolla.net.bo; f. 1971; state institution for the promotion of new investments and the application of the Investment Law; Exec. Dir Ing. JOSÉ MARIO FERNÁNDEZ IRAHOLA.

Sistema de Regulación Sectorial (SIRESE): Edif. Capitán Ravelo, 8°, Casilla 9647, La Paz; tel. (2) 244-4545; fax (2) 244-4017; e-mail sg@sirese.gov.bo; internet www.sirese.gov.bo; f. 1994; regulatory body for the formerly state-owned companies and utilities; oversees the general co-ordination and growth of the regulatory system and the work of its Superintendencies of Electricity, Hydrocarbons, Telecommunications, Transport and Water; Superintendent Gen. CLAUDE BESSE ARZE.

DEVELOPMENT ORGANIZATIONS

Consejo Nacional de Acreditación y Medición de la Calidad Educativa (CONAMED): La Paz; f. 1994; education quality board.

Consejo Nacional de Planificación (CONEPLAN): Edif. Banco Central de Bolivia, 26°, Calle Mercado esq. Ayacucho, Casilla 3118, La Paz; tel. (2) 237-4151; fax (2) 235-3840; e-mail claves@mail.bcb.gov.bo; internet www.bcb.gov.bo; f. 1985.

Corporación de las Fuerzas Armadas para el Desarrollo Nacional (COFADENA): Avda 6 de Agosto 2649, Casilla 1015, La Paz; tel. (2) 237-7305; fax (2) 236-0900; f. 1972; industrial, agricultural and mining holding company and development organization owned by the Bolivian armed forces; Gen. Man. Col JUAN MANUEL ROSALES.

Corporación Regional de Desarrollo de La Paz (CORDEPAZ): Avda Arce 2529, Edif. Santa Isabel, Casilla 6102, La Paz; tel. (2) 243-0313; fax (2) 243-2152; f. 1972; decentralized government institution to foster the development of the La Paz area; Pres. Lic. RICARDO PAZ BALLIVIÁN; Gen. Man. Ing. JUAN G. CARRASCO R.

Instituto para el Desarrollo de la Pequeña Unidad Productiva: La Paz.

CHAMBERS OF COMMERCE

Cámara Nacional de Comercio: Edif. Cámara Nacional de Comercio, Avda Mariscal Santa Cruz 1392, 1°, Casilla 7, La Paz; tel. (2) 235-0042; fax (2) 239-1004; e-mail cnc@boliviacomercio.org.bo; internet www.boliviacomercio.org.bo; f. 1890; 30 brs and special brs; Pres. GUILLERMO MORALES; Gen. Man. JOSÉ KUHN POPPE.

Cámara de Comercio de Oruro: Pasaje Guachalla s/n, Casilla 148, Oruro; tel. and fax (2) 525-0606; e-mail camacor@coteor.net.bo; f. 1895; Pres. ALVARO CORNEJO GAZCÓN; Gen. Man. LUIS CAMACHO VARGAS.

Cámara Departamental de Industria y Comercio de Santa Cruz: Calle Suárez de Figueroa 127, 3°, Casilla 180, Santa Cruz; tel. (3) 333-4555; fax (3) 334-2353; e-mail cainco@cainco.org.bo; internet www.cainco.org.bo; f. 1915; Pres. ZVONKO MATKOVIC FLEIG; Gen. Man. Lic. OSCAR ORTIZ ANTELO.

Cámara Departamental de Comercio de Cochabamba: Calle Sucre E-0336, Casilla 493, Cochabamba; tel. (4) 425-7715; fax (4) 425-7717; e-mail camcom@pino.cbb.entelnet.bo; internet www.camind.com/cadeco; f. 1922; Pres. Ing. CARLOS OLMEDO Z; Gen. Man. Lic. JUAN CARLOS AVILA S.

Cámara Departamental de Comercio e Industria de Potosí: Calle Matos 12, Casilla 149, Potosí; tel. (2) 622-2641; fax (2) 622-2641; Pres. JAVIER FLORES CASTRO; Gen. Man. WALTER ZABALA AYLLON.

Cámara Departamental de Industria y Comercio de Chuquisaca: Calle España 64, Casilla 33, Sucre; tel. (4) 645-1194; fax (4) 645-1850; e-mail cicch@camara.scr.entelnet.bo; f. 1923; Pres. MARCO MIHAIC; Gen. Man. Lic. ALFREDO YÁñEZ MERCADO.

Cámara Departamental de Comercio e Industria de Cobija—Pando: Plaza Germán Busch, Casilla 110, Cobija; tel. (3) 842-3139; fax (3) 842-2291; Pres. NEMESIO RAMÍREZ.

Cámara Departamental de Industria y Comercio de Tarija: Avda Bolívar 0413, 1°, Casilla 74, Tarija; tel. (4) 662-2737; fax (4) 662-4053; e-mail metfess@olivo.tja.entelnet.bo; Pres. RENE SILBERMANN U. Gen. Man. VÍCTOR ARAMAYO.

Cámara Departamental de Comercio de Trinidad—Beni: Casilla 96, Trinidad; tel. (3) 462-2365; fax (3) 462-1400; Pres. EDUARDO AVILA ALVERDI.

INDUSTRIAL AND TRADE ASSOCIATIONS

Asociación Nacional de Exportadores de Café (ANDEC): Calle Nicaragua 1638, Casilla 9770, La Paz; tel. (2) 224-4290; fax (2) 224-4561; e-mail andec@caoba.entelnet.bo; internet www.boliviancoffee.bo; controls the export, quality and marketing of coffee producers; Exec. Pres. CARMEN DONOSO DE ARAMAYO.

Cámara Agropecuaria del Oriente: 3 anillo interno zona Oeste, Casilla 116, Santa Cruz; tel. (3) 352-2200; fax (3) 352-2621; e-mail caosrz@bibosi.scz.entelnet.bo; f. 1964; agriculture and livestock association for eastern Bolivia; Pres. RICARDO FRERKING ORTIZ; Gen. Man. WALTER NÚñEZ RODRÍGUEZ.

Cámara Agropecuaria de La Paz: Avda 16 de Julio 1525, Casilla 12521, La Paz; tel. (2) 239-2911; fax (2) 235-2308; Pres. ALBERTO DE OLIVA MAYA; Gen. Man. JUAN CARLOS ZAMORANO.

Cámara Forestal de Bolivia: Prolongación Manuel Ignacio Salvatierra 1055, Casilla 346, Santa Cruz; tel. (3) 333-2699; fax (3) 333-1456; e-mail foresbol@cotas.com.bo; internet www.cadex.org/camaraforestal; f. 1969; represents the interests of the Bolivian timber industry; Pres. MARIO BARBERY SCIARONI; Gen. Man. Lic. ARTURO BOWLES OLHAGARAY.

Cámara Nacional de Industrias: Edif. Cámara Nacional de Comercio, 14°, Avda Mariscal Santa Cruz 1392, Casilla 611, La Paz; tel. (2) 237-4476; fax (2) 236-2766; e-mail cni@mail.megalink.com; internet www.bolivia-industry.com; f. 1931; Pres. ROBERTO MUSTAFÁ; Man. GERARDO VELASCO T.

Cámara Nacional de Minería: Pasaje Bernardo Trigo 429, Casilla 2022, La Paz; tel. (2) 235-0623; f. 1953; mining institute; Pres. Ing. LUIS PRADO BARRIENTOS; Sec.-Gen. GERMÁN GORDILLO S.

Comité Boliviano de Productores de Antimonio: Edif. El Condor, Batallon Colorados 1404, 14°, Casilla 14451, La Paz; tel. (2) 244-2140; fax (2) 244-1653; f. 1978; controls the marketing, pricing and promotion policies of the antimony industry; Pres. MARIO MARISCAL MORALES; Sec.-Gen. Dr ALCIDES RODRÍGUEZ J.

Comité Boliviano del Café (COBOLCA): Calle Nicaragua 1638, Casilla 9770, La Paz; tel. (2) 222-3883; fax (2) 224-4591; e-mail cobolca@ceibo.entelnet.bo; controls the export, quality, marketing and growing policies of the coffee industry; Gen. Man. MAURICIO VILLARROEL.

EMPLOYERS' ASSOCIATIONS

Asociación Nacional de Mineros Medianos: Calle Pedro Salazar 600 esq. Presbítero Medina, Casilla 6190, La Paz; tel. (2) 241-7522; fax (2) 241-4123; e-mail anmm@caoba.entelnet.bo; f. 1939; association of the 14 private medium-sized mining companies; Pres. Dr OSCAR BONIFAZ G. Sec.-Gen. Dr HUGO URIONA.

Confederación de Empresarios Privados de Bolivia (CEPB): Calle Méndez Arcos 117, Plaza España, Zona Sopacachi, Casilla 4239, La Paz; tel. (2) 242–0999; fax (2) 242-1272; e-mail cepbol@ceibo.entelnet.bo; internet www.cepb.org.bo; largest national employers' organization; Pres. Lic. CARLOS CALVO GALINDO; Exec. Sec. Lic. JOHNNY NOGALES VIRUEZ.

There are also employers' federations in Santa Cruz, Cochabamba, Oruro, Potosí, Beni and Tarija.

UTILITIES

Electricity

Superintendencia de Electricidad: Avda 16 de Julio 1571, La Paz; tel. (2) 231-2401; fax (2) 231-2393; e-mail superele@superele.gov.bo; internet www.superele.gov.bo; f. 1996; regulates the electricity sector; Superintendent ALEJANDRO NOWOTNY VERA; Gen. Sec. ROLANDO LÓPEZ.

Compañia Boliviana de Energía Eléctrica, SA (COBEE): Avda Hernando Siles 5635, Casilla 353, La Paz; tel. (2) 278-2474; fax (2) 278-5920; e-mail cobee@cobee.com; f. 1925; second largest private producer and distributor of electricity serving the areas of La Paz and Oruro; in 2002 the company generated 27.2% of all electricity produced in Bolivia; Gen. Man. JULIO LEMAITRE SOLARES.

Electropaz: Avda Illimani 1987, La Paz; tel. (2) 222-2200; fax (2) 222-3756; Gen. Man. Ing. ANGEL GÓMEZ.

Empresa Nacional de Electricidad, SA (ENDE): Avda Ballivián 503, esq. México, Casilla 565, Cochabamba; tel. (4) 452-0317; fax (4) 425-0318; f. 1962; former state electricity company; privatized under the Govt's capitalization programme in 1995 and divided into three arms concerned with generation, transmission and distribution, respectively; Gen. Man. RAMIRO RICO NEGRETE.

Gas

Numerous distributors of natural gas exist throughout the country, many of which are owned by the petroleum distributor, Yacimientos Petrolíferos Fiscales Bolivianos (YPFB).

CO-OPERATIVE

Instituto Nacional de Co-operativas (INALCO): Edif. Lotería Nacional, 4°, Avda Mariscal Santa Cruz y Cochabamba, La Paz; tel. (2) 237-4366; fax (2) 237-2104; e-mail inalcolp@ceibo.entelnet.bo; f. 1974; Pres. DAVID AYAVIRI.

TRADE UNIONS

Central Obrera Boliviana (COB): Edif. COB, Calle Pisagua 618, Casilla 6552, La Paz; tel. (2) 228-3220; fax (2) 228-0420; f. 1952; main union confederation; 800,000 mems; Exec. Sec. ALBERTO CAMACHO PARDO; Sec.-Gen. OSCAR SALAS MOYA.

Affiliated unions:

Central Obrera Departamental de La Paz: Estación Central 284, La Paz; tel. (2) 235-2898; Exec. Sec. GENARO TORRICO.

Confederación Sindical Unica de los Trabajadores Campesinos de Bolivia (CSUTCB): Calle Sucre, esq. Yanacocha, La Paz; tel. (2) 236-9433; f. 1979; peasant farmers' union; Exec. Sec. FELIPE QUISPE.

Federación de Empleados de Industria Fabril: Edif. Fabril, 5°, Plaza de San Francisco, La Paz; tel. (2) 240-6799; fax (2) 240-7044; Exec. Sec. ALEX GÁLVEZ.

Federación Sindical de Trabajadores Mineros de Bolivia (FSTMB): Plaza Venezuela 1470, Casilla 14565, La Paz; tel. (2) 235-9656; fax (2) 248-4948; f. 1944; mineworkers' union; Exec. Sec. MILTON GONZÁLEZ; Gen. Sec. EDGAR RAMÍREZ SANTIESTÉBAN; 27,000 mems.

Federación Sindical de Trabajadores Petroleros de Bolivia: Calle México 1504, La Paz; tel. (2) 235-1748; Exec. Sec. NEFTALYMENDOZA DURÁN.

Confederación General de Trabajadores Fabriles de Bolivia (CGTFB): Avda Armentia 452, Casilla 21590, La Paz; tel. (2) 237-1603; fax (2) 232-4302; e-mail dirabc@bo.net; f. 1951; manufacturing workers' union; Exec. Sec. ANGEL ASTURIZAGA; Gen. Sec. ROBERTO ENCINAS.

Transport

RAILWAYS

Empresa Nacional de Ferrocarriles (ENFE): Estación Central de Ferrocarriles, Plaza Zalles, Casilla 428, La Paz; tel. (2) 235-9935; fax (2) 239-2106; f. 1964; administers most of the railways in Bolivia; privatized under the Government's capitalization programme in 1995. Total networks: 3,608 km (1999); Andina network: 2,274 km; Eastern network: 1,424 km; Pres. J. L. LANDIVAR.

There are plans to construct a railway line with Brazilian assistance, to link Cochabamba and Santa Cruz. There were also plans for the construction of a rail link between Santa Cruz and Mutún on the border with Brazil.

ROADS

In 2000 Bolivia had some 53,790 km of roads, of which an estimated 6.5% (3,496 km) were paved. Almost the entire road network is concentrated in the altiplano region and the Andes valleys. A 560-km highway runs from Santa Cruz to Cochabamba, serving a colonization scheme on virgin lands around Santa Cruz. The Pan-American Highway, linking Argentina and Peru, crosses Bolivia from south to north-west. In 1997 the Government announced the construction of 1,844 km of new roads in the hope of improving Bolivia's connections with neighbouring countries.

INLAND WATERWAYS

By agreement with Paraguay in 1938 (confirmed in 1939), Bolivia has an outlet on the River Paraguay. This arrangement, together with navigation rights on the Paraná, gives Bolivia access to the River Plate and the sea. The River Paraguay is navigable for vessels of 12-ft draught for 288 km beyond Asunción, in Paraguay, and for smaller boats another 960 km to Corumbá in Brazil. In late 1994 plans were finalized to widen and deepen the River Paraguay, providing a waterway from Bolivia to the Atlantic coast in Uruguay. However, work on the project was delayed, owing largely to environmental concerns.

In 1974 Bolivia was granted free duty access to the Brazilian coastal ports of Belém and Santos and the inland ports of Corumbá and Port Velho. In 1976 Argentina granted Bolivia free port facilities at Rosario on the River Paraná. In 1992 an agreement was signed with Peru, granting Bolivia access to (and the use, without customs formalities, of) the Pacific port of Ilo. Most of Bolivia's foreign trade is handled through the ports of Matarani (Peru), Antofagasta and Arica (Chile), Rosario and Buenos Aires (Argentina) and Santos (Brazil). An agreement between Bolivia and Chile to reform Bolivia's access arrangements to the port of Arica came into effect in January 1996.

Bolivia has over 14,000 km of navigable rivers, which connect most of Bolivia with the Amazon basin.

Bolivian River Navigation Company: f. 1958; services from Puerto Suárez to Buenos Aires (Argentina).

OCEAN SHIPPING

Líneas Navieras Bolivianas (LINABOL): Edif. Hansa, 16°, Avda Mariscal Santa Cruz, Apdo 11160, La Paz; tel. (2) 237-9459; fax (2) 239-1079; Pres. Vice-Adm. LUIS AZURDUY ZAMBRANA; Vice-Pres. WOLF-GANG APT.

CIVIL AVIATION

Bolivia has 30 airports, including the two international airports at La Paz (El Alto) and Santa Cruz (Viru-Viru).

Dirección General de Aeronáutica Civil: Avda Mariscal Santa Cruz 1278, Casilla 9360; La Paz; tel. (2) 237-4142; e-mail dgacbol@ceibo-entelnet.bo; internet www.dgac.gov.bo; f. 1947; Dir-Gen. ORLANDO MONTOYA KOËSTER.

AeroSur: Calle Colón y Avda Irala, Casilla 3104, Santa Cruz; tel. (3) 336-4446; fax (3) 333-0666; e-mail javiedr.gonzalez@aerosur.com; f. 1992; by the merger of existing charter cos following deregulation; privately-owned; Pres. OSCAR ALCOCER; Gen. Man. FERNANDO PRUDENCIO.

Lloyd Aéreo Boliviano, SAM (LAB): Casilla 132, Aeropuerto 'Jorge Wilstermann', Cochabamba; tel. (4) 425-1270; fax (4) 425-0766; e-mail lider@labairlines.bo.net; internet www.labairlines.bo.net; f. 1925; privatized under the Government's capitalization programme in 1995; jtly-owned by Bolivian Govt (48%), and private interests (52%); operates a network of scheduled services to 12 cities within Bolivia and to 21 international destinations in South America, Central America and the USA; Pres. ULISSES CANHEDO AZEVEDO; Gen. Man. ANTONIO SANCHES.

Transportes Aéreos Bolivianos (TAB): Casilla 12237, La Paz; tel. (2) 237-8325; fax (2) 235-9660; f. 1977; regional scheduled and charter cargo services; Gen. Man. LUIS GUERECA PADILLA; Chair. CARLO APARICIO.

Transportes Aéreos Militares: Avda Montes 738, La Paz; tel. (2) 237-9286; internal passenger and cargo services; Dir-Gen. REMBERTO DURÁN.

Tourism

Bolivia's tourist attractions include Lake Titicaca, at 3,810 m (12,500 ft) above sea-level, pre-Incan ruins at Tiwanaku, Chacaltaya in the Andes mountains, which has the highest ski-run in the world, and the UNESCO World Cultural Heritage Sites of Potosí and Sucre. In 2000 381,077 foreign visitors arrived at hotels in Bolivian regional capitals. In that year receipts from tourism totalled US $160m. Tourists come mainly from South American countries, the USA and Europe.

Asociación Boliviana de Agencias de Viajes y Turismo: Edif. Litoral, Avda Mariscal Santa Cruz 1351, Casilla 3967, La Paz; f. 1984; Pres. EUGENIO MONROY VÉLEZ.

Viceministerio de Turismo: Avda Mariscal Santa Cruz, 16°, Casilla 1868, La Paz; tel. (2) 235-8312; fax (2) 237-4630; e-mail dkwacz@mcei-gov.bo; internet www.mcei.gov.bo; Vice-Minister of Tourism DANIEL KWACZ.

BOSNIA AND HERZEGOVINA

Introductory Survey

Location, Climate, Language, Religion, Flag, Capital

Bosnia and Herzegovina is situated in south-eastern Europe. It is bounded by Croatia to the north and west, by Serbia to the east and by Montenegro to the south-east, and has a short (20 km—12 miles) western coastline on the Adriatic Sea. It is a largely mountainous territory with a continental climate and steady rainfall throughout the year; in areas nearer the coast, however, the climate is more Mediterranean. The principal language is Serbo-Croat. Although it is a single spoken language, Serbo-Croat has two written forms: the Muslims (Bosniaks) and Croats use the Roman alphabet, while the Serbs use Cyrillic script. The Muslims (the majority of whom belong to the Sunni sect) are the largest religious grouping in Bosnia and Herzegovina, comprising 43.7% of the population in 1991. Religious affiliation is roughly equated with ethnicity, the Serbs (31.4% of the population) belonging to the Serbian Orthodox Church and the Croats (17.3%) being members of the Roman Catholic Church. The national flag (proportions 1 by 2) consists of two unequal vertical sections of blue, separated by a yellow triangle, which is bordered on the left by a diagonal line of nine white five-pointed stars. The capital is Sarajevo.

Recent History

The provinces of Bosnia and Herzegovina formed part of the Turkish (Ottoman) Empire for almost 400 years before annexation to the Habsburg Empire of Austria-Hungary in 1878. The population of the provinces was composed of an ethnic mixture of Orthodox Serbs, Roman Catholic Croats and Muslims (mainly Bosnian Slavs who had converted to Islam). Serbian expansionist aims caused tension from the beginning of the 20th century, and in 1914, following the assassination of the heir to the Habsburg throne in Sarajevo, Austria-Hungary declared war on Serbia, thereby precipitating the First World War. On 4 December 1918 the Kingdom of Serbs, Croats and Slovenes was proclaimed when the Serbs and Croats agreed with other ethnic groups to establish a common state under the Serbian monarchy. The provinces of Bosnia and Herzegovina formed part of the new kingdom. Bitter disputes ensued between Serbs and Croats (see chapter on Croatia), however, and in January 1929 King Alexander imposed a dictatorship, formally renaming the country Yugoslavia in October.

Although officially banned in 1921, the Communist Party of Yugoslavia (CPY) operated clandestinely, and in 1937 Josip Broz (alias Tito) became its General Secretary. During the Second World War (1939–45) Tito's communist-led Partisan movement, comprising members from a variety of ethnic groups, dominated most of Bosnia and Herzegovina. Following Tito's victory in 1945, Bosnia and Herzegovina became one of the six constituent republics of the Yugoslav federation (despite Serbian pressure to limit the region to provincial status, as with Kosovo and the Vojvodina). In the 1960s Tito established Muslim power in Bosnia and Herzegovina, in an effort to counter increasing tension between the Serbs and Croats of the republic. Slav Muslims were granted a distinct ethnic status, as a nation of Yugoslavia, for the 1971 census, and a collective state presidency was established in that year, with a regular rotation of posts.

Increasing ethnic tension in Bosnia and Herzegovina became evident in September 1990. Followers of the Party of Democratic Action (PDA), the principal Bosnian Muslim (Bosniak) party, demonstrated in the neighbouring Sandjak area of Serbia in support of Muslim rights in the Novi Pazar district, clashing with Serb nationalists. Ethnic affiliation proved to be a decisive factor in the republican elections in November and December. The ruling League of Communists of Bosnia and Herzegovina was ousted, and three main nationalist parties subsequently emerged: the PDA, with 86 seats; the Serbian Democratic Party (SDP), with 72 seats; and the Croatian Democratic Union of Bosnia and Herzegovina (CDU—BH), an affiliate of the ruling CDU party of Croatia, with 44 seats. The three nationalist parties also took all seven seats on the directly elected collective Presidency and formed a coalition administration for the republic. On 20 December they announced that Dr Alija Izetbe-

gović of the PDA was to be President of the Presidency, Jure Pelivan of the CDU—BH was to be President of the Executive Council (Prime Minister) and Momčilo Krajišnik of the SDP was to be President of the Assembly.

In 1991 the politics of Bosnia and Herzegovina were increasingly dominated by the Serb–Croat conflict. Following the declarations of independence by Slovenia and Croatia in June, Serb-dominated territories in Bosnia and Herzegovina declared their intent to remain within the Yugoslav federation (or in a 'Greater Serbia'). On 27 June the self-proclaimed Serb 'Municipal Community of Bosanska Krajina' announced its unification with the 'Serb Autonomous Region (SAR) of Krajina' in Croatia. An SAR of Bosanska Krajina was proclaimed on 16 September. The republican Government rejected these moves and declared the inviolability of the internal boundaries of Yugoslavia. Armed incidents contributed to the rising tension throughout mid-1991 and many Serb areas announced the formation of further 'Autonomous Regions'. Other ethnic groups accused the Serbs of planning a 'Greater Serbia', with the support of the Jugoslavenska Narodna Armija (JNA—Yugoslav People's Army). In October the JNA assumed effective control of Mostar, to the north-west of the Serb 'Old' Herzegovina, and began a siege of the Croatian city of Dubrovnik.

In October 1991 both the republican Presidency (with the dissenting votes of the Serb members) and the PDA proposed to the Assembly that the republic declare its independence. Later that month the Serb deputies rejected the resolution as a move towards secession. No compromise was reached, and the Serb representatives subsequently withdrew from the chamber. On 15 October, however, the remaining members of the Assembly, dominated by the PDA and the CDU—BH, approved a resolution declaring the sovereignty of Bosnia and Herzegovina.

The 'Autonomous Regions' of the Serbs rejected the republican Assembly's resolution and declared that only the federal laws and Constitution would apply on their territory. On 24 October 1991 the Serb deputies of the Bosnia and Herzegovina Assembly constituted an 'Assembly of the Serb Nation' (Serb Assembly). In early November another SAR was proclaimed, comprising the Serbs of Northern Bosnia, with an Assembly based in Doboj (an area without a Serb majority). On 9–10 November a referendum, organized by the Serb Assembly, indicated overwhelming support for remaining in a common Serb State. However, in another referendum on 29 February and 1 March 1992, which was boycotted by the Serbs, 99.4% of the 63% of the electorate who participated were in favour of full independence. President Izetbegović immediately declared the republic's independence and omitted the word 'socialist' from the new state's official title.

Following the declaration of independence, there was renewed Serb–Muslim tension, leading to clashes in Sarajevo, the republican capital, and elsewhere. On 18 March 1992, following mediation by the European Community (EC, now European Union—EU, see p. 199), the leaders of the Serb, Croat and Bosniak communities signed an agreement providing for the division of Bosnia and Herzegovina into three autonomous units. (The EC and the USA recognized Bosnia and Herzegovina's independence on 7 April.) On 27 March the Serbs announced the formation of a 'Serb Republic of Bosnia and Herzegovina', which comprised Serbian-held areas of the republic (about 65% of the total area), including the SARs, and which was to be headed by Dr Radovan Karadžić. The Bosnian Government immediately declared this secessionist republic, the headquarters of which were based in Banja Luka, to be illegal. In April fighting between the Serbian-dominated JNA in Bosnia and Herzegovina and Bosniak and Croatian forces intensified; several cities, including Sarajevo, were besieged by Serbian troops. In early May, however, the newly established Federal Republic of Yugoslavia (FRY—comprising solely the republics of Serbia and Montenegro), in an apparent attempt to disclaim any responsibility for Bosnia and Herzegovina's internal strife, ordered all of its citizens in the JNA to withdraw from the republic within 15 days. Early EC and UN efforts at mediation proved unsuccessful, and their respective peace monitors were withdrawn from Sarajevo in mid-May after a state of emergency had been declared and successive cease-fires had failed to take effect. Izetbegović requested foreign military intervention, but the UN, while deploying the United Nations Protection Force (UNPROFOR) in Croatia, decided against the deployment of a peace-keeping force in the republic under prevailing conditions. On 20 May the Government of Bosnia and Herzegovina declared the JNA to be an 'occupying force' and announced the formation of a republican army. Two days later Bosnia and Herzegovina was accepted as a member of the UN. On 30 May the UN imposed economic sanctions against the FRY for its continuing involvement in the Bosnian conflict. In early June, in an apparent effort to placate the UN, Serb leaders in Belgrade (the FRY capital) ordered the Bosnian Serbs to end the siege of Sarajevo and to surrender Sarajevo airport to UN control. In the same month the UN Security Council decided to redeploy 1,000 of the UNPROFOR troops in Croatia to protect Sarajevo airport.

On 7 July 1992 the declaration of a breakaway Croat state, the 'Croat Union of Herzeg-Bosna', represented a major development in the Bosnian conflict. The new state, which covered about 30% of the territory of Bosnia and Herzegovina and was headed by Mate Boban, was immediately declared to be illegal by Izetbegović's Government. Despite their political differences, Izetbegović and President Franjo Tudjman of Croatia (who supported the establishment of the Croat Union of Herzeg-Bosna) signed a co-operation agreement in late July. Under this accord, the Governments of Bosnia and Herzegovina and of Croatia formed a Joint Defence Committee in late September, and repeated demands that the UN end an armaments embargo (which had been imposed on the former Yugoslavia in September 1991). Within Bosnia and Herzegovina, however, hostilities erupted between Bosnian Croats and Muslims in mid-October, and the towns of Mostar, Novi Travnik and Vitez were captured by the Croats. Mostar was subsequently proclaimed the capital of the 'Croat Union of Herzeg-Bosna'. In early November Jure Pelivan (a Croat) resigned as Prime Minister of Bosnia and Herzegovina, and was replaced by Mile Akmadžić. In mid-November the Croatian Government admitted for the first time that Croatian regular army units had been deployed in Bosnia and Herzegovina, and accordingly became a signatory to the latest cease-fire agreement in Bosnia and Herzegovina. In early December, following allegations of 'ethnic cleansing' and organized rape, the UN Human Rights Commission declared that the Serbs were largely responsible for violations of human rights in Bosnia and Herzegovina. Later that month the UN Security Council unanimously adopted a resolution condemning the atrocities and demanding access to all Serb detention camps.

In early January 1993 the co-Chairmen of the Geneva Peace Conference (a permanent forum for talks on the conflict, established in 1992), Lord (David) Owen (a former British Secretary of State for Foreign and Commonwealth Affairs) and Cyrus Vance (the UN mediator and a former US Secretary of State), visited Belgrade for talks with the newly re-elected President of Serbia, Slobodan Milošević. Their aim was to persuade him to convince the Bosnian Serbs to agree to a division of Bosnia and Herzegovina into 10 provinces (with three provinces allocated to each faction and Sarajevo as a province with special status). The peace plan was approved by the leader of the Bosnian Croats, Mate Boban, and, in part, by Izetbegović, but was rejected by Karadžić, who insisted on the establishment of an autonomous Serbian state within the territory of Bosnia and Herzegovina.

In mid-January 1993 Milošević attended the peace talks in Geneva, Switzerland, for the first time. Karadžić, under pressure from Milošević and President Dobrica Cosić of the FRY, agreed to the constitutional proposals included in the plan and, subsequently, to the military arrangements. On 19–20 January the Bosnian Serb Assembly voted to accept the general principles of the Vance-Owen plan. However, hostilities between Croats and Muslims intensified in central Bosnia. In February the UN Security Council adopted a resolution providing for the establishment of an international court to try alleged war criminals for acts committed since 1991 in the former Yugoslav republics. In the following month the UN Security Council adopted a resolution permitting NATO aircraft to fire on any aircraft violating the 'no-fly zone' imposed on Bosnian airspace in October 1992.

During March 1993, at further peace talks, Izetbegović agreed to both the military arrangements and the proposed territorial divisions included in the Vance-Owen plan. In April, however, the Bosnian Serb Assembly rejected the territorial arrangements, incurring international disapproval (including that of

Serbia, which had endorsed the plan under pressure from UN and EC sanctions). In early May Karadžić signed the Vance-Owen plan in Geneva, but two days later it was decisively rejected by the Serb Assembly at Pale, since, under the terms of the plan, the Bosnian Serbs would be forced to surrender some territory that had been seized during the fighting. In late May the USA, France, Russia, Spain and the United Kingdom signed a communiqué declaring that the arms embargo on the former Yugoslavia would continue and that international armed forces would not intervene in the conflict on behalf of the Muslims; they proposed instead the creation of six UN 'safe areas' (Sarajevo, Bihać, Tuzla, Goražde, Srebreniča and Žepa) to protect the Muslim population from Serb attack (to take effect from 22 July). In early June a UN Security Council resolution permitted UNPROFOR to use force, including air power, in response to attacks against 'safe areas'. Later that month a joint Serb-Croat offensive began against the northern Muslim town of Maglaj, and in July Bosniaks and Croats engaged in hostilities for control of the city of Mostar. In mid-June new peace proposals were announced in Geneva by Lord Owen and Thorvald Stoltenberg (formerly Norwegian Minister of Foreign Affairs, who had replaced Vance as the UN mediator in May), under which Bosnia and Herzegovina would become a confederation of three states divided on ethnic grounds. Izetbegović refused to discuss the tripartite division of Bosnia and boycotted the remainder of the Geneva talks, although other members of the Presidency continued discussions.

On 30 July 1993 the three warring factions reached a constitutional agreement in Geneva on the reconstruction of Bosnia and Herzegovina into a confederation of three ethnically-based states, styled the 'Union of Republics of Bosnia and Herzegovina', under a central government with powers limited to foreign policy and foreign trade. Under this agreement, Sarajevo, except for the municipality of Pale, would be placed under UN administration during a two-year transitional period. Despite this agreement and numerous negotiated cease-fires, fighting continued, and in early August the three Croat members of the Bosnian State Presidency (including Mile Akmadžić, the Prime Minister of Bosnia and Herzegovina) left the Bosnian Geneva delegation, in protest at Bosniak attacks on Croat populations, and joined the Croatian negotiating team. On 27 August Akmadžić was dismissed from the premiership. On the following day the 'Croatian Republic of Herzeg-Bosna' was proclaimed by a Croat 'House of Representatives of the Assembly of the Croatian Republic of Herzeg-Bosna' (Croat Assembly) in Grude, which proceeded to accept the Owen-Stoltenberg plan on condition that the Serbs and Bosniaks also accepted it. On the same day the Serb Assembly in Pale also voted in favour of the plan. On 31 August, however, a session of the Assembly of Bosnia and Herzegovina rejected the Geneva plan in its existing form, while agreeing to use it as a basis for further peace negotiations.

On 10 September 1993 Fikret Abdić, a Muslim member of the Bosnian State Presidency and a rival of President Izetbegović, announced the creation of an 'Autonomous Province of Western Bosnia' in the Muslim region around Bihać, which was to form part of the 'Union of Republics of Bosnia and Herzegovina'. On 27 September the Province was formally established and Abdić was elected President by a 'Constituent Assembly' in Velika Kladusa. Abdić was subsequently dismissed from the Bosnian State Presidency, Izetbegović imposed martial law on the area and fighting erupted between Abdić's followers and government forces. In October the Muslim Democratic Party was established in Bihać, with Abdić as Chairman. Later that month two Croats and one Bosniak were elected to the three vacant positions in the Bosnian State Presidency, and Dr Haris Silajdžić, formerly the Minister of Foreign Affairs, was appointed Prime Minister of the Bosnian Government, replacing Akmadžić. Silajdžić's Government took office on 30 October.

In early February 1994 the shelling of a Sarajevo marketplace, causing many casualties, prompted the UN to threaten military intervention if Serb forces failed to cease their bombardment. Following a Russian diplomatic initiative, the Bosnian Serbs withdrew most of their heavy weaponry, and Russian peace-keeping troops were deployed in the 'exclusion zone' around Sarajevo. However, the city remained effectively blockaded. In late February NATO forces shot down four Serb aircraft near Banja Luka, which had violated the UN 'no-fly zone' over Bosnia and Herzegovina. The incident represented the first aggressive military action taken by NATO since its establishment. There was continuous Serb shelling of the

Maglaj area in northern Bosnia throughout March, while other UN-designated 'safe areas' were also bombarded.

Following a cease-fire, which was agreed by the Bosnian Government and the Bosnian Croats in late February 1994, Silajdžić and Kresimir Zubak (who had replaced Mate Boban as the leader of the Bosnian Croats) signed an agreement on 18 March, in Washington, DC, USA, providing for the creation of a Federation of Bosnia and Herzegovina, with power shared equally between Bosniaks and Croats. Under the federal Constitution (finalized earlier in the month), a federal government was to be responsible for defence, foreign affairs and the economy. Greater executive power was to be vested in the prime ministerial post than in the presidency; the offices were to rotate annually between the two ethnic groups. Until the full implementation of the Federation and the holding of elections, Izetbegović was to remain President of the collective Presidency of Bosnia and Herzegovina; the emerging federal institutions were to operate in parallel during the interim period. At the same ceremony a second 'preliminary' agreement was signed by Presidents Izetbegović and Tudjman, which provided for the eventual creation of a loose confederation of the Federation and Croatia. As well as the establishment of a 'Confederative Council', closer economic ties between the two states were to be introduced, with the eventual aim of establishing a common market and monetary union. In late March the accords were approved by the Bosnian Croat Assembly, and the new Constitution was ratified by the Bosnian Assembly. However, the Bosnian Serb Assembly in Pale vetoed Serb participation in the agreements.

In April 1994, in response to the continued shelling of the 'safe area' of Goražde by Bosnian Serb forces, UN-sanctioned air strikes were launched by NATO aircraft on Serb ground positions. However, Serb forces captured Goražde later that month, prompting strong criticism from the Russian Government, which hitherto had been perceived as sympathetic towards the Serbs, but which now indicated that it would not oppose the use of force against them. Bosnian Serb forces withdrew from Goražde in late April. On 26 April a new negotiating forum, the 'Contact Group', comprising representatives from Russia, the USA, France, Germany and the United Kingdom, was established.

In late May 1994 the Constituent Assembly of the Federation of Bosnia and Herzegovina held its inaugural meeting, at which it elected Kresimir Zubak to the largely ceremonial post of President of the Federation. Ejup Ganić, a Bosniak, was elected Vice-President of the Federation (he was concurrently Vice-President of the collective Presidency of Bosnia and Herzegovina) and Silajdžić was appointed Prime Minister of the Federation. A joint Government of the Republic of Bosnia and Herzegovina and the Federation, led by Silajdžić, was appointed in late June. (The existing Bosnian Assembly was to act, additionally, as the interim legislature of the Federation.)

Following peace negotiations in Geneva in early June 1994, a one-month cease-fire was declared throughout Bosnia and Herzegovina. Repeated violations were reported by the end of the month, however, by which time Bosnian government forces had captured Serb-held areas of central Bosnia. The Contact Group presented new peace proposals in early July, after its members had reached agreement on a territorial division of Bosnia and Herzegovina in late June. According to the new plan, the Federation of Bosnia and Herzegovina would be granted 51% of the territory of Bosnia and Herzegovina, while the Bosnian Serbs would yield approximately one-third of the territory they controlled. Key sensitive areas, including Sarajevo, Srebrenica, Goražde and Brčko, would be placed under UN and EU administration. In an indication of the international community's increasing impatience with the warring factions, the Contact Group warned of various measures that would be taken in the event of the parties' refusal of the plan.

On 17 July 1994 Izetbegović and Tudjman endorsed the Contact Group plan, which was also approved by the Bosnian Assembly. However, the proposed territorial division was rejected by the Bosnian Serb Assembly at Pale. The Serbs' refusal to accept the plan centred on the question of Serb access to the Adriatic Sea, the status of Sarajevo and the right of the Bosnian Serbs to enter a confederation with the FRY. President Milošević of Serbia subsequently criticized the Bosnian Serbs for rejecting the plan, and in early August the FRY announced the closure of its border with Serb-occupied Bosnia and Herzegovina. On 5 August NATO air strikes (the first since April) were launched against Bosnian Serb targets, following Serb attacks

against UN forces and the renewed shelling of Sarajevo. In late August the Bosnian Serbs held a referendum in which 96% of participants voted to reject the Contact Group plan; the result was unanimously approved by the Bosnian Serb Assembly on 1 September. Meanwhile, on 21 August the Bihać enclave, held by Abdić's forces, was captured by the Bosnian government army.

On 30 November 1994 an attempt by the UN Secretary-General to protect the Bihać 'safe area' from further Bosnian Serb attack and to salvage the UN peace-keeping operation in Bosnia and Herzegovina met with failure when Karadžić boycotted the proposed discussions, owing to the UN's refusal to recognize the 'Serbian Republic'. In early December the Contact Group issued proposals based on the July peace plan (dividing Bosnia between the Federation and the Bosnian Serbs), which indicated the possibility of confederal links between the Bosnian Serbs and the FRY. On 31 December the Bosnian Serbs and the Bosnian Government signed a four-month cease-fire agreement, to take effect on the following day. Both sides expressed their readiness to resume peace negotiations based on the revised Contact Group plan.

The cease-fire was generally observed throughout Bosnia and Herzegovina during January 1995. However, intense fighting continued in the Bihać enclave between government forces and troops loyal to Abdić, supported by troops from the self-proclaimed 'Republic of Serbian Krajina' (RSK) in Croatia (adjoining the Bihać enclave). Following renewed disagreements between Bosniaks and Croats over the implementation of the new Federation, in early February Zubak and Silajdžić signed an accord allowing grievances concerning the implementation of the Federation of Bosnia and Herzegovina to be submitted to some form of (then unspecified) international arbitration. In the same month the USA refused to continue negotiations with Karadžić until the Bosnian Serbs accepted the Contact Group plan.

In February 1995, with hostilities continuing in Bihać, the UN announced that Serb and rebel Bosniak attacks on humanitarian aid convoys into the enclave were resulting in the starvation of Muslim civilians within the 'safe area'. On 20 February representatives of the Bosnian Serbs and the Croatian Serbs signed a military pact, guaranteeing mutual assistance in the event of attack and providing for the establishment of a joint Supreme Defence Council, which was to be led by Karadžić and the Croatian Serb leader, Milan Martić. In early March, following talks in Zagreb, Croatia, a formal military alliance was announced between the armies of Croatia, the Bosnian Croats and the Bosnian Government. On 8 April President Zubak of the Federation and Ejup Ganić, the Vice-President of both the Federation and of Bosnia and Herzegovina, signed an agreement to accelerate the establishment of federal institutions. The inaugural session of the Federation's Constituent Assembly duly took place in Novi Travnik on 4 May, during which the Bonn Agreement on the implementation of federal principles was unanimously adopted. In mid-May heavy fighting was reported around the Serb-held corridor near Brčko and hostilities intensified around Sarajevo, with Bosnian government forces regaining territory to the south-east of the capital. On 25 May, following a UN request in response to the continued Serb bombardment of Sarajevo, NATO aircraft carried out strikes on Serb ammunition depots near Pale, prompting strong criticism from Russia. Within hours of the NATO air strikes, Serb forces responded by shelling five of the six UN 'safe areas' and, following further NATO air strikes against Serb positions on 26 May, retaliated with a massive bombardment of Tuzla, which resulted in at least 70 deaths. Serb troops subsequently disarmed and took hostage 222 UNPROFOR personnel in the Goražde 'safe area', thereby preventing the UN and NATO from taking retaliatory action against fighting in the region. However, the UN rejected the Serbs' offer of conditional negotiations on the release of the hostages. In early June defence ministers from NATO and other European states agreed on the creation of a 10,000-strong 'rapid reaction force', which was to operate in Bosnia and Herzegovina under UN command from mid-July, with a mandate to provide 'enhanced protection' to UNPROFOR. The ongoing hostage crisis, led, however, to a withdrawal of UNPROFOR troops from Bosnian Serb territory around Sarajevo in mid-June and the consequent collapse of the 20-km 'exclusion zone'. Although the UN denied that any deal had been reached with the Bosnian Serbs, the release of the remaining hostages coincided with the withdrawal of UNPROFOR from around the capital.

On 11 July 1995 the 'safe area' of Srebreniča in south-eastern Bosnia was captured by the Bosnian Serbs, after Dutch peace-keeping troops based in the town were taken hostage (despite NATO air strikes on Serb tanks approaching the town). Following the capture of Srebreniča, some 7,500 of the Muslim civilians who had taken refuge in the town were massacred by Serb forces. Bihać was attacked on 20 July, in a concerted effort by Bosnian Serbs, Croatian Serbs, and rebel Bosniaks, led by Abdić. The situation in Bihać prompted the signature of a military co-operation agreement between Izetbegović and Tudjman in Split, Croatia, on 22 July. Croatian and Bosnian Croat troops subsequently launched attacks on Serb positions around Bihać, thereby blocking Serb supply routes into the Krajina enclave. The nearby 'safe area' of Žepa was captured on 25 July.

Croatian government forces invaded Serb-held Krajina on 4 August 1995, and rapidly recaptured the entire enclave, prompting a massive exodus of Serb civilians from the region into Serb-held areas of Bosnia and Herzegovina and into Serbia itself. On 6–7 August the siege of Bihać was ended by Bosnian government and Croatian troops. On 9 August a further peace initiative (devised by Richard Holbrooke, the US Assistant Secretary of State for European and Canadian Affairs) was announced by the US Government; the proposals, which were based on the Contact Group plan of 1994, allowed the Bosnian Serbs to retain control of Srebreniča and Žepa.

On 28 August 1995 a Serb mortar attack near a market place in central Sarajevo resulted in some 40 deaths, prompting Silajdžić to demand clarification of the UN peace-keeping role in the 'safe area' of Sarajevo. NATO responded to the attack by commencing a series of air strikes (known as 'Operation Deliberate Force') on Serb positions across Bosnia and Herzegovina two days later.

On 8 September 1995 major progress in the peace process was achieved when, at a meeting in Geneva, chaired by the Contact Group, the Ministers of Foreign Affairs of Bosnia and Herzegovina, Croatia and the FRY (the latter acting on behalf of the Bosnian Serbs) signed an agreement determining basic principles for a peace accord. These principles incorporated the territorial division of Bosnia and Herzegovina as earlier proposed by the Contact Group, with 51% apportioned to the Federation and 49% to the Bosnian Serbs. They also included the continuing existence of Bosnia and Herzegovina within its present borders, but the country was to comprise two entities, namely the Federation of Bosnia and Herzegovina (as stated in the Washington Agreements of 1994) and a Serb Republic, with each entity retaining its existing Constitution. In mid-September 'Operation Deliberate Force' was suspended, following the withdrawal of Bosnian Serb weaponry from the 'exclusion zone' around Sarajevo. Agreement on further basic principles for a peace accord was reached by the foreign ministers of Bosnia and Herzegovina, Croatia and the FRY, meeting in New York, USA, on 26 September. These included a one-third share in the republican parliamentary seats for the Serb Republic, while the Federation was to control two-thirds of the seats (legislative decisions were only to be implemented, however, with the approval of at least one-third of the deputies of each entity). A collective presidency was also to be organized according to the one-third Serb to two-thirds Bosniak-Croat proportional division, with all decisions to be taken by majority vote. It was decided, furthermore, that free elections, under international auspices, would be held in Bosnia and Herzegovina at the earliest opportunity. A 60-day cease-fire came into effect on 12 October; the UN simultaneously announced its intention to reduce the number of peace-keeping troops in the area. In late October, at a summit meeting between President Bill Clinton of the USA and his Russian counterpart, Boris Yeltsin, it was agreed that Russian peace-implementation troops would co-operate with, but work independently of, the NATO Peace Implementation Force, which was to be deployed in the country following the signature of a formal peace accord.

On 1 November 1995 peace negotiations between the three warring parties in the Bosnian conflict began in Dayton, Ohio, USA, attended by Presidents Izetbegović, Tudjman and Milošević (the latter representing both the FRY and the Bosnian Serbs), and representatives of the Contact Group and the EU. On 10 November Izetbegović and Tudjman signed an accord reinforcing the 1994 federation agreement, which included a provision for the unification of the divided city of Mostar as the federal capital and seat of the federal presidency. The Croatian Government and the Croatian Serbs of Eastern Slavonia sub-sequently concluded an accord providing for the eventual reintegration of Serb-held Eastern Slavonia into Croatia. The most comprehensive peace agreement was achieved on 21 November, when Izetbegović, Tudjman and Milošević initialled a definitive accord, dividing Bosnia and Herzegovina between the Federation, with 51% of the territory, and the Serb Republic (Republika Srpska), which would control 49% of the area; it was stressed, however, that relations with neighbouring countries should honour the sovereignty and territorial integrity of Bosnia and Herzegovina. The Dayton agreement, which was based on the agreements that had been signed in Geneva and New York in September, included provisions for a central government with a democratically elected collective presidency and a parliament, based in Sarajevo, and provisions for a single monetary system, central bank and other institutions for the economic reconstruction of Bosnia and Herzegovina. It also stipulated the right of all refugees and displaced persons to return to their homes and either to have seized property returned to them or to receive fair compensation. Sarajevo was granted special status as a united city within the Federation and it was also envisaged that each of the warring factions would relinquish some of the territory under its control at the time of the October cease-fire. Serb-held suburbs of Sarajevo were to be transferred to the administration of the Federation, and Bosnian Serbs were to retain control of Srebreniča and Žepa; Goražde was to remain under the control of the Federation and was to be linked to Sarajevo via a Federation-administered land corridor. No agreement was reached, however, regarding the width of the strategically vital Posavina corridor, connecting the northern sector of the Serb Republic with the southern sector, and control of the town of Brčko, located at this point; the three sides agreed to place the issue under international arbitration. Under the Dayton agreement, UNPROFOR troops were to be replaced by an international, NATO-commanded, 60,000-strong 'Implementation Force' (IFOR). The agreement provided IFOR with a mandate to oversee the withdrawal of the warring parties from zones of separation and to monitor the agreed exchanges of territory.

Following the initialling of the Dayton peace agreement, the UN voted to suspend the remaining economic sanctions against the FRY and to remove gradually the arms embargo imposed on all of the former Yugoslav republics in September 1991. At the end of November 1995 the UN Security Council established the deadline of 31 January 1996 for the withdrawal of UNPROFOR troops from Bosnia and Herzegovina. At a conference on the implementation of the Dayton peace agreement, which took place in London, United Kingdom, in early December 1995, it was agreed that an Organization for Security and Co-operation in Europe (OSCE, see p. 283) mission would organize and monitor parliamentary elections in Bosnia and Herzegovina and that the Contact Group would be replaced by a Peace Implementation Council based in Brussels, Belgium. The former Swedish Prime Minister and EU envoy to the Bosnian peace talks, Carl Bildt, was appointed High Representative of the International Community in Bosnia and Herzegovina, with responsibility for the implementation of the civilian aspects of the Dayton agreement. On 14 December the Dayton peace agreement was formally signed by Izetbegović, Tudjman and Milošević and by President Clinton and a number of European political leaders in Paris, France. The formal transfer of power from UNPROFOR to IFOR took place on 20 December.

In mid-December 1995 the People's Assembly of the Serb Republic elected a new Government, headed by Rajko Kasagić. On 30 January 1996 Hasan Muratović was elected by the republican Assembly as Prime Minister of the Republic of Bosnia and Herzegovina, following the resignation from the premiership of Silajdžić, apparently in protest at the increasing Bosniak nationalism of the ruling PDA; a new central Government was appointed on the same day. On 31 January the Constituent Assembly of the Federation appointed a new federal Government, with Izudin Kapetanović as Prime Minister. In mid-February, in response to unrest in the city of Mostar and isolated attacks elsewhere, an emergency summit meeting took place in Rome, Italy, during which Izetbegović, Tudjman and Milošević reaffirmed their adherence to the Dayton agreement. A joint Croat-Bosniak security patrol, accompanied by officers from the UN International Police Task Force (IPTF) and Western European Union (WEU) subsequently began operating in Mostar.

By the end of April 1996 substantial progress had been made in the implementation of the military aspects of the Dayton agreement. The former warring parties completed staged withdrawals from the IFOR-controlled zone of separation; agreement was reached, under the auspices of the OSCE in Vienna, Austria, on the exchange of information on weaponry and the submission of arsenals to OSCE inspection; and the majority of prisoners of war were released, albeit with some delays. However, the exchange of territory between the two Bosnian 'entities' did not proceed as envisaged in the peace agreement. From mid-January there was a mass exodus from the Serb-held suburbs of Sarajevo that were passing to the control of the Bosnian Federation. The Serb authorities in Pale were criticized for using intimidation to coerce the Serb inhabitants of these districts into leaving to resettle in towns in the Serb Republic from which Muslims had been driven during the war. By late March only about 10% of the previous Serb population in the Sarajevo area remained.

In early April 1996 Muslim and Croat leaders agreed on a customs union linking the two parts of the Bosnian Federation, a single state budget and a unitary banking system. In mid-May further agreement was reached between the two sides, meeting in Washington, on the merger of their armed forces and the return of refugees. The agreement on a unified federation army was the principal precondition for the implementation of the controversial US programme to train and equip the Federation's army in order to give it equal military status with that of the Serb Republic. Also in mid-May Karadžić dismissed Kasagić as Serb Prime Minister and appointed Gojko Klicković, a former Serb Minister for Health, in his place; Klicković's appointment was endorsed by the Bosnian Serb People's Assembly. Kasagić, who was considered a moderate, had been co-operating to a large extent with the international community and high-level diplomatic efforts were undertaken both to effect Kasagić's reinstatement and to oust Karadžić from the presidency. Karadžić had been indicted by the International Criminal Tribunal for the former Yugoslavia (ICTY, see p. 15), based in The Hague, Netherlands, for war crimes, notably responsibility for the massacre at Srebrenica in July 1995. His continued position as President (as well as that of Gen. Ratko Mladić, also indicted for war crimes, as head of the armed forces) was in breach of the Dayton agreement, which prohibited indicted war criminals from holding public office. In response to international pressure, Karadžić announced the delegation of some of his powers to his deputy, Dr Biljana Plavšić. In early June 1996 the USA threatened Milošević with renewed sanctions against the FRY unless he effected the removal from office of Karadžić and Mladić and their extradition to the Netherlands to stand trial. At the Peace Implementation Conference on Bosnia and Herzegovina held in Florence, Italy, in mid-June, it was agreed that national elections would take place in September. The Chairman-in-Office of the OSCE, which was given responsibility under the Dayton accord for the organization and supervision of the Bosnian elections, subsequently announced that these would proceed on 14 September.

In mid-June 1996 Bosnian Croats in Mostar announced a new government of Herzeg-Bosna, in contravention of agreements that the separate Croat state would be dissolved; Pero Marković was appointed Prime Minister of the new Government. Municipal elections in Mostar were held on 30 June: the PDA-dominated List for a United Mostar obtained 21 of the council seats, while the CDU—BH secured 16 seats. At a summit meeting of the Presidents of Bosnia and Herzegovina, Croatia and Serbia, which was convened by the USA in Geneva in mid-August, Tudjman and Izetbegović agreed on the full establishment of the Bosnian Federation by the end of the month. The three Presidents signed a further declaration committing themselves to the Dayton agreement.

In late June 1996 western European countries issued an ultimatum to Karadžić to resign, on penalty of the reimposition of sanctions against the Serb Republic (suspended in April, following the Serb withdrawal behind IFOR's line of separation). In defiance of this, the SDP re-elected Karadžić as party leader. At the end of June Karadžić sent a letter to Bildt announcing his temporary resignation and the appointment of Plavšić as the acting Serb President. It was then confirmed that Karadžić would not contest the election to the Serb presidency in September, and Plavšić was nominated as the SDP candidate. None the less, it was deemed unacceptable that Karadžić should retain the powerful position of party leader, and the OSCE Bosnian mission declared that the SDP would be excluded from the elections if Karadžić retained any office in the party. In mid-July the ICTY issued arrest warrants for Karadžić and Mladić;

however, IFOR's mandate was not changed, and NATO remained cautious regarding their pursuit. A few days later the USA dispatched Holbrooke to the former Yugoslavia in an attempt to bring about Karadžić's removal. Following intensive negotiations with Milošević and Bosnian Serb leaders, Holbrooke secured Karadžić's resignation on 19 July both from the presidency and as head of the SDP. Plavšić remained acting President, while Aleksa Buha succeeded Karadžić as leader of the SDP.

During the electoral campaign there were increasing reports of harassment and violence perpetrated by the PDA and its supporters against members of the opposition. Opposition candidates in the Serb Republic were also subjected to intimidation, and many international observers, as well as opposition activists, protested that the conditions would prevent free and fair elections from being conducted. In late August 1996 the OSCE announced that the Bosnian municipal elections, which were to have been held concurrently with the other elections, were to be postponed, in response to evidence that the Serb authorities were forcibly registering displaced Serbs in formerly Muslim-dominated localities. This arose from the provision included in the Dayton agreement permitting refugees and displaced persons to vote either in their former homes or in the place where they chose to settle. National elections were held on 14 September for the republican Presidency and legislature, the presidency and legislature of the Serb Republic, and the legislature and cantonal authorities of the Bosnian Federation. The elections were monitored by about 1,200 OSCE observers, while IFOR and the IPTF forces maintained security.

At the elections for the republican Presidency, Izetbegović won 80% of the Bosniak votes cast; Kresimir Zubak (CDU—BH) 88% of the Croat votes; and Momčilo Krajišnik (SDP) 67% of the Serb votes. Having received the largest number of votes of the three winning presidential candidates, Izetbegović became Chairman of the Presidency. The Federation section of the republican House of Representatives and the Federation's own House of Representatives were dominated by the PDA and the CDU—BH. None the less, the Joint List of Bosnia and Herzegovina, comprising an alliance of social-democrat Bosniak and Croat parties, and the Party for Bosnia and Herzegovina (established earlier that year by the former Prime Minister, Haris Silajdžić) won a significant number of votes in the elections to both the republican and federation Houses. Although the SDP secured a majority of votes in both the Serb section of the House of Representatives and in the Serb National Assembly, the PDA won about one-sixth of the votes cast on the territory of the Serb Republic. The People's Alliance for Peace and Progress also obtained a significant proportion of the Serb votes cast in the elections to the House of Representatives and the Serb National Assembly. Plavšić was elected President of the Serb Republic and Dragolub Mirjanić the Vice-President, securing some 59% of the votes. The validity of the election results was questioned by the International Crisis Group, comprising senior western European politicians, which claimed that a large number of voting papers had been fraudulently added to the ballot boxes. The OSCE subsequently revised its estimate of the Bosnian electorate upwards and refused to order a recount of the ballot papers. Following the OSCE's endorsement of the election results, the UN Security Council decided on 1 October 1996 to remove the sanctions imposed against the FRY and the Serb Republic. A few days later Izetbegović and Milošević, meeting in Paris, agreed to establish full diplomatic relations; Milošević pledged to respect the territorial integrity of Bosnia and Herzegovina, and Izetbegović consented to recognize the FRY as the successor state to Yugoslavia. The inauguration of the Presidency took place on 5 October. The inaugural session of the republican Assembly was to have been held on the same day, but was boycotted by the Serb deputies.

In mid-October 1996 the OSCE changed the regulations regarding voting in the delayed municipal elections, ruling that people could only vote in their places of residence prior to 1992. The municipal elections, which were due to have taken place in November 1996, were rescheduled for early 1997 (when, however, they were again postponed). In early November 1996 Plavšić announced that she had dismissed Gen. Mladić as Commander of the Serb armed forces, replacing him with a little-known officer, Maj.-Gen. Pero Colić. A large number of the members of Mladić's general staff were also replaced, but Mladić and the other officers refused to accept their dismissal. After a power struggle, during which the Minister of Defence of the Serb

Republic was briefly held captive by Mladić's supporters, Mladić agreed to surrender his position at the end of November.

In mid-November 1996 clashes were reported between Muslims and Serbs along the inter-entity boundary near the Serb-held village of Gajevi, to which the Muslims were attempting to return. There were repeated incidents in which Muslims seeking to reclaim their homes on Serb-held territory were forcibly repulsed. In many parts of the country hostility between the ethnic groups continued, with minority elements being intimidated and often driven from their homes. At a conference on Bosnia and Herzegovina, hosted by the French Government in mid-November, it was agreed that the post of High Representative of the International Community would be maintained for a further two years, and that the High Representative would become the final arbiter in the interpretation of the civilian provisions of the Dayton agreement. A Bosnian Peace Implementation Conference was held in London in early December; the NATO Secretary-General announced the establishment of a successor contingent to IFOR, to be known as the Stabilization Force (SFOR), with a mandate of 18 months, subject to six-monthly reviews. SFOR officially replaced IFOR on 20 December. In mid-December, after some delay, the Presidency appointed the two Co-Prime Ministers of the republican Council of Ministers: Haris Silajdžić of the Party for Bosnia and Herzegovina and Boro Bosić of the SDP. One week later the federal House of Representatives elected Edhem Bičakčić as the federal Prime Minister, replacing Izudin Kapetanović. (On the previous day the Bosnian Croats had announced that 'Herzeg-Bosna' had ceased to exist.) The republican Council of Ministers was appointed by the Co-Prime Ministers and approved by the inaugural session of the Bosnian Assembly, which was finally held on 3 January 1997. The Council of Ministers comprised Ministers for Foreign Affairs, for Foreign Trade and Economic Relations, and for Communications and Civilian Affairs. Each post had two Deputy Ministers, with each of the Bosnian ethnic groups holding an equal number of offices. In February a ruling on the future status of the disputed town of Brčko was postponed by an international arbitration commission until March 1998 (when, however, the commission announced a further deferral of judgment). In March 1997 Robert Farrand, a US diplomat, was appointed to act as supervisor of the town in the interim period. In the same month Vladimir Soljić was elected to replace Kresimir Zubak as President of the Federation. (Soljić, in turn, was succeeded by the Vice-President, Dr Ejup Ganić, in December.)

On 28 February 1997 Krajišnik signed, on behalf of the Serb Republic, an agreement with the FRY to foster mutual economic co-operation and to collaborate on regional security. The accord was ratified by the National Assembly of the Serb Republic in March, despite opposition voiced by Plavšić and by a number of Bosnian Muslim and Bosnian Croat leaders. In June Bildt was replaced as High Representative by Carlos Westendorp. At the end of that month the National Assembly opposed the decision by Plavšić to suspend the Serb Republic's Minister of Internal Affairs, over his alleged failure to consult with her. In July Plavšić announced the dissolution of the National Assembly and scheduled parliamentary elections for the beginning of September. Although this action was supported by both the UN and the OSCE, it was sharply criticized by Gojko Klicković, the Prime Minister of the Serb Republic, and a number of resolutions designed to undermine Plavšić were approved by the National Assembly. In mid-August the Constitutional Court ruled that Plavšić's decision to dissolve the legislature had been illegal: the Assembly proceeded to vote to disregard future decrees by her. Plavšić's position was strengthened in August, following a decision by the Serb Republic's Vice-President, Dragolub Mirjanić, to abandon the Assembly in Pale and join the presidential team in Banja Luka. Municipal elections for both entities finally took place on 13–14 September; although some 91 parties contested the elections (in which the rate of voter participation was estimated at about 60%), the three main nationalist parties, the PDA, the CDU—BH and the SDP, received the vast majority of the votes cast. In late September a constitutional crisis in the Serb Republic was averted, following a meeting in Belgrade hosted by President Milošević and attended by Plavšić and Krajišnik. A joint statement was issued detailing an agreement, whereby elections to the National Assembly would take place in November, and presidential elections for both the Serb Republic and the Bosnian collective Presidency on 7 December.

Elections to the National Assembly of the Serb Republic were held on 22–23 November 1997, under the supervision of the OSCE. Participating parties included the Serb National Alliance (SNA), which had been established by Plavšić in September, following her expulsion from the SDP in July. The SDP secured 24 seats (compared with 45 in 1996), but remained the largest party in the Assembly. A newly formed electoral alliance, the Coalition for a Single and Democratic Bosnia and Herzegovina, which included the PDA and the Party for Bosnia and Herzegovina, secured 16 seats, while the SNA and the Serb Radical Party (SRP) each achieved 15 seats. At the inaugural session of the new Assembly on 27 December, Plavšić nominated as prime minister Mladen Ivanić, an economist with no political affiliation. The nomination was immediately challenged by the leadership of the SDP, which insisted that as the largest party in the new Assembly it should have the first opportunity to propose a new prime minister and government. Ivanić declared that he would continue negotiating with all the parties represented in the new Assembly in order to form an interim government of 'national unity'. On 18 January 1998, however, following the failure of Ivanić's inter-party talks, Milorad Dodik, who was considered to be a proponent of moderate policies, secured sufficient parliamentary support to form a new government. Following the announcement of the new administration, which contained a large number of Bosnian Muslims, Dodik assured the international community of his determination to govern according to the terms of the Dayton peace agreement. His appointment was condemned, however, by Krajišnik, who warned that it would result in the destabilization of the Serb Republic. At the end of January Dodik announced that government bodies were to be transferred from Pale to Banja Luka.

At a further Bosnian Peace Implementation Conference, held in Sintra, Portugal, in May 1997, NATO stipulated deadlines for the approval by the entities of a number of laws on property, passports and citizenship, and, in addition, demanded a new list of ambassadors, which would reflect the ethnic diversity of the country. In early July the EU announced the suspension of economic aid to the Serb Republic, owing to its failure to extradite suspected war criminals to the ICTY. Following the expiry on 1 August of the deadline for the submission of a new diplomatic list, the USA and the EU suspended recognition of Bosnia and Herzegovina's ambassadors. On 17 December the Bosnian Assembly approved the law on passports within the deadline established by the international community, but failed to ratify the law on citizenship; on the following day Westendorp announced that the citizenship law would be imposed on Bosnian territory from 1 January 1998. (An agreement had been signed earlier in the month by Krajišnik and the FRY Government, which accorded Bosnian Serbs citizenship of both Bosnia and Herzegovina and the FRY.) In late December 1997 it was announced that NATO had agreed to extend indefinitely the mandate of the peace-keeping forces; in November Westendorp had warned that renewed hostilities might ensue, following the scheduled withdrawal of SFOR troops at the expiry of their mandate in June 1998. In February 1998 NATO formally approved the establishment of a new peace-keeping force for Bosnia and Herzegovina, initially to comprise 33,000 troops, which was to be deployed following the expiry of SFOR's mandate.

In April 1998 the OSCE dissolved the Serb-dominated municipal assembly of Srebrenica, owing to its failure to assist in the resettlement of displaced Muslims in the town; a provisional executive council, headed by a senior OSCE official, was established to replace the assembly. In June the UN Security Council officially voted in favour of extending the mandate of SFOR to remain in the country indefinitely, with six-monthly reviews. In that month Krajišnik criticized a motion by the National Assembly of the Serb Republic expressing 'no confidence' in its Speaker, Dragan Kalinić, and Deputy Speaker. Buha subsequently resigned the chairmanship of the SDP, citing what he claimed to be interference in his leadership by Krajišnik; Kalinić was elected as the new Chairman of the SDP.

In September 1998 elections took place, as scheduled, for a new Bosnian collective Presidency and national legislature, for the presidency and National Assembly of the Serb Republic, and for the Federation House of Representatives. Izetbegović was re-elected as the Bosniak member of the collective Presidency. The Chairman of the Socialist Party of the Bosnian Serb Republic (Socijalistička partija za Republiku Srpsku—SPRS), which was a member of the SNA-led Accord Coalition, Zivko Radišić, replaced Krajišnik, and the Chairman of the CDU—BH, Ante Jelavić, was elected as the Croat member of the Presidency. In the election to the Serb presidency the Chairman of the SRP, Dr

Nikola Poplasen (who represented a coalition of the SRP and the SDP), defeated Plavšić. The SDP retained 19 of the 83 seats in the National Assembly of the Serb Republic, while the Coalition for a Single and Democratic Bosnia and Herzegovina won 15 seats; the latter also secured 14 of the 42 seats in the Bosnian House of Representatives and 68 of the 140 seats in the Federation House of Representatives.

On 13 October 1998 the newly elected Presidency of Bosnia and Herzegovina was inaugurated. Radišić became the first Serb to chair the Presidency (replacing Izetbegović) for an eight-month term, in accordance with the rotational schedule. Poplasen was inaugurated as President of the Serb Republic; he pledged to maintain good relations with western Governments and to comply with the Dayton agreement. The major parties represented in the Serb National Assembly subsequently conducted negotiations regarding the appointment of a new Council of Ministers in the Serb Republic. The Accord Coalition, which held 32 seats in the National Assembly, rejected Poplasen's nomination of Kalinić as Prime Minister, while supporting the reappointment of Dodik to the post.

In December 1998 the Federation Parliament re-elected Ganić as President, while Ivo Andrić-Luzanski (a member of the CDU —BH) became Federation Vice-President; a new Federation Council of Ministers, nominated by Bičakčić, was established. Following the continued failure of the National Assembly of the Serb Republic to agree on a new government, in early January 1999 Poplasen nominated Brane Miljus, a member of the Party of Independent Social Democrats (Stranko Nezavisnih Socijaldemokrata—SNSD) as Prime Minister. The Accord Coalition objected to Miljus' candidacy, and Dodik (the leader of the SNSD) announced his expulsion from the party. (Miljus subsequently formed a breakaway organization, which was entitled the Party of Independent Social Democrats of the Serb Republic.) Later in January the National Assembly rejected Miljus' nomination to the office of Prime Minister (while continuing to support Dodik).

In February 1999 the Council of Ministers of the Presidency was reorganized. Later that month Westendorp declared that supreme command of the armed forces of the Federation and the Serb Republic was to be transferred to the members of the collective Presidency. However, the Government of the Serb Republic contested the decision, and announced that Poplasen would remain Commander of the Serb armed forces, pending a ruling by the Constitutional Court of Bosnia and Herzegovina. In early March Poplasen proposed a motion in the Serb Republic National Assembly in an attempt to instigate Dodik's dismissal. Westendorp announced Poplasen's removal from office, on the grounds that he had exceeded his authority. In the same month international arbitrators, who had met in Vienna in February, ruled that Serb control of Brčko would end, and that the town would henceforth be governed jointly by the Serb Republic and the Federation, under international supervision. Dodik tendered his resignation (which he later withdrew) in protest at the announcement, and the National Assembly rejected both the ruling on Brčko and Westendorp's decision to remove Poplasen from office. (The National Assembly subsequently withdrew its opposition to Poplasen's dismissal, and Mirko Sarović, the incumbent Vice-President, provisionally assumed the presidential office.) In mid-April a new municipal government, comprising Serbs, Bosniaks and Croats, was elected in Brčko, with an SPRS candidate as mayor.

In May 1999 the ICTY sentenced a former Bosnian Croat detention camp commander to 30 months' imprisonment for war crimes, but acquitted him of charges brought under the 1949 Geneva Convention governing international warfare, on the grounds that the Muslim–Croat conflict had been internal. In June, in accordance with the Constitution, Jelavić became Chairman of the Bosnia and Herzegovina Presidency, replacing Radišić. In the same month the UN Security Council voted to extend the mandate of SFOR and the principally civilian security force, the UN Mission in Bosnia and Herzegovina (UNMIBH), for a further year; NATO announced that the strength of the SFOR contingent was to be reduced to about 16,500. In July SFOR members arrested Radislav Brdjanin, a former Bosnian Serb official (who had served as Deputy Prime Minister under Karadžić), following his indictment by the ICTY in connection with massacres of Muslims and Croats near Banja Luka by Serb forces in 1992.

In August 1999 Wolfgang Petritsch, hitherto the Austrian ambassador to the FRY, succeeded Westendorp as High Representative in Bosnia (following Westendorp's appointment to the European Parliament). In September Plavšić was re-elected leader of the SNA at a party congress. In October Petritsch prohibited Poplasen and a further two SRP officials from contesting forthcoming local elections, on the grounds that they had obstructed the implementation of the Dayton peace agreement. In December Andrić Luzanski assumed the Federation presidency, in accordance with the one-year rotational mandate stipulated in the Constitution. In February 2000 Izetbegović replaced Jelavić as Chairman of the collective Presidency. In the same month legislation allowing for a reconstituted state Presidency, comprising a Chairman (with a rotational mandate) and two other members, was agreed. Later in February the SPRS withdrew from the governing Accord Coalition of the Serb Republic, in protest at the dismissal in January of the SPRS Deputy Prime Minister, Tihomir Gligorić, by Dodik, who had accused him of provoking dissension within the Government. In March a senior Bosnian Croat commander, Gen. Tihomir Blaskić, was sentenced by the ICTY to 45 years' imprisonment (the most severe sentence issued by the Tribunal) for war crimes perpetrated against Muslims in 1992–93. In early April Krajišnik was arrested in Pale by SFOR troops and extradited to the ICTY.

At local government elections, which took place on 8 April 2000, the SDP won control of 49 of the country's 145 municipal councils (mainly in the Serb Republic), while the CDU—BH secured 25 and the PDA 23; the multi-ethnic Social Democratic Party of Bosnia and Herzegovina (Socijaldemokratska Partija BiH—SDP BiH) made significant electoral gains in the Federation. In the same month the national House of Representatives adopted legislation providing for the restructuring of the Bosnian Council of Ministers, which would henceforth comprise a Chairman (appointed by the collective Presidency for an eight-month term) and five ministers. In late May a motion, proposed by the SDP, expressing 'no confidence' in the Federation Government was defeated in the entity's House of Representatives. The Federation Vice-President, Ejup Ganić, was expelled from the PDA, after failing to comply with the party's decision that he resign from his government office. In early June a new Bosnian Council of Ministers was appointed, after the national House of Representatives confirmed the nomination of Spasoje Tusevljak (a non-party candidate) to the office of Prime Minister. In July Dodik announced his candidacy in the election to the Serb Republic presidency, which was scheduled for 11 November; elections to the national House of Representatives and to the legislatures of both entities were to take place concurrently.

In July 2000 the Minister of Information of the Serb Republic resigned, after the international community criticized his alleged interference in the appointment of television officials. In early August the Minister of Refugees and Displaced Persons of the Serb Republic also resigned, after international representatives expressed dissatisfaction concerning the Republic's implementation of the Dayton peace accord. In early September the National Assembly of the Serb Republic adopted a motion, proposed by the SDP, expressing 'no confidence' in Dodik's administration. However, the Government submitted a legal challenge to the entity's Constitutional Court and announced that it would remain in office pending the forthcoming legislative election. In October Izetbegović retired from the collective Presidency; Halid Genjac, a senior official of the PDA, replaced him as the Bosniak member of the Presidency, and the Serb representative, Zirko Radišić, became Chairman. A member of the CDU—BH, Martin Raguz, subsequently replaced Tusevljak as Prime Minister, owing to a constitutional stipulation that the Chairman of the collective Presidency and that of the Council of Ministers should not belong to the same ethnic group.

On 11 November 2000 concurrent elections to the national House of Representatives, the legislatures of both entities and the presidency of the Serb Republic took place. At the national legislative election the SDP BiH secured nine seats, the PDA eight seats, the SDP six seats and the CDU—BH five seats in the 42-member House of Representatives. At the federal election the PDA won 38 seats, the SDP BiH 37 seats, the CDU—BH 25 seats and the Party for Bosnia and Herzegovina 21 seats in the 140-member legislature. The SDP secured 31 of the 83 seats in the republican National Assembly, and the SPRS and the Party of Democratic Progress of the Serb Republic (PDP) each received 11 seats. Mirko Sarović, the SDP candidate who had reportedly been selected by Karadžić, was elected, with some 49.8% of votes cast, to the presidency of the Serb Republic, defeating Dodik. The SDP subsequently announced that it was to establish a parliamentary coalition with the PDP, the SPRS and the PDA, thereby securing a majority in the National Assembly.

In December 2000 Sarović designated Mladen Ivanić, a member of the PDP, as Prime Minister of the Serb Republic. In mid-January 2001 Ivanić formed the Republic's first multi-ethnic Council of Ministers. However, the inclusion in the Council of Ministers of several SDP representatives proved controversial, following warnings by the USA that it might suspend financial aid to the Serb Republic if the SDP entered the Government. Ivanić subsequently requested that government members suspend party activities, and replaced the newly appointed Minister of Trade and Tourism (a prominent SDP member), in an attempt to address international concerns over SDP representation. In the same month Raguz was redesignated as national Prime Minister by the Presidency. Meanwhile, the SDP BiH had established a parliamentary coalition with a further nine non-nationalist parties (known as the Alliance for Change), which held 17 seats in the national House of Representatives and 69 seats in the federal legislature. The CDU—BH and six other allied Croat parties subsequently threatened to withdraw from Federation government institutions, after members of the Alliance for Change were elected Speaker and Deputy Speaker of the federal House of Representatives.

In January 2001 Plavšić surrendered to the ICTY, following her indictment in April 2000, but subsequently denied charges that she, together with other Serb officials, had organized a campaign of genocide and deportation against the Muslim and Croat inhabitants of Bosnia and Herzegovina between July 1991 and December 1992. In February 2001 three Bosnian Serbs were sentenced to terms of imprisonment by the ICTY for crimes against humanity perpetrated against Muslim women in the town of Foca in 1992 (the first case at the Tribunal concerning systematic rape and sexual enslavement). In the same month a former Bosnian Croat commander and President of the CDU—BH received a custodial term of 25 years for authorizing crimes against humanity to be committed against Bosniaks in 1993–94.

In early February 2001 the national House of Representatives rejected the nomination of Raguz to the office of Prime Minister, as a result of the opposition of the Alliance for Change deputies. The Presidency's subsequent designation of a member of the SDP BiH, Bozidar Matić, to the post, with the support of the Alliance for Change, was endorsed in the legislature. On 22 February the House of Representatives approved a new Bosnian Council of Ministers, which had been nominated by Matić. On 28 February the Federation legislature elected a member of the SDP BiH, Karlo Filipović, as President of the entity. In early March the Federation legislature endorsed the nomination of Alija Behmen, a member of the SDP BiH, as Prime Minister of the entity, and a new Government, comprising members of the Alliance for Change, was approved. Meanwhile, in response to the rejection of Raguz's candidacy to the Bosnian premiership, a newly formed grouping of parties, led by the CDU—BH, the self-styled Croat People's Assembly, declared self-government in three Croat-majority cantons, and voted to establish autonomous power structures. Petritsch subsequently dismissed Jelavić of the CDU—BH from the collective Presidency. Many Croat members of the armed forces and local officials declared support for the Croat People's Assembly, which announced that it intended to secede from the Federation. On 28 March the House of Representatives voted in favour of appointing Jozo Križanović of the SDP BiH as the new Croat member of the collective Presidency. (Beriz Belkić, a member of the Party for Bosnia and Herzegovina, replaced Halid Genjac.) In early April 18 members of SFOR were injured, after attempting to seize control of a private bank in Mostar held by Croat separatists. Following negotiations with the federal authorities and international community officials, however, the Croat alliance agreed to end its boycott of government institutions in May.

In mid-June 2001 Križanović assumed the chairmanship of the collective Presidency for a period of eight months. Later in June Matić resigned from the office of Prime Minister, after new electoral legislation, regarded as essential for the country's admission to the Council of Europe, was rejected by the Parliamentary Assembly. On 7 July the national legislature accepted the nomination of Zlatko Lagumdzija, the leader of the SDP BiH and the incumbent Minister of Foreign Affairs, as Prime Minister. The controversial legislation, which stipulated the principles regulating elections at all levels, was finally approved by the Parliamentary Assembly in August.

In late July 2001 the Serb National Assembly provisionally approved legislation providing for the entity's co-operation with the ICTY, after the SDP withdrew its opposition to the proposals. (The new legislation, which required the Serb Republic security forces actively to pursue and extradite war crimes suspects, was finally adopted by the National Assembly in early October.) At the beginning of August a former officer in the Serb security forces was sentenced to 10 years' imprisonment by the ICTY, after pleading guilty to participation in the killing and torture of Muslims and Croats in 1992–93. On 2 August a former senior Serb army officer, Radislav Krstić, received a term of imprisonment of 46 years for his involvement in the massacre at Srebreniča in 1995. Although the Tribunal succeeded in gaining a conviction on charges of genocide for the first time, the sentence was criticized as inadequate by relatives of those killed. At the end of August the ICTY provisionally released Plavšić (who was then the only woman in detention at the Hague), pending her trial. In late September Gen. Sefer Halilović, a former Chief of Staff of the Bosnian army and the hitherto Federation Minister of Social Welfare and Refugees, surrendered to the ICTY. Halilović (who was the most senior Muslim official to be indicted by the Tribunal) pleaded not guilty to charges relating to the killing of 62 Croatian citizens by troops under his command in 1993.

Following the terrorist attacks on the USA on 11 September 2001, SFOR took measures to investigate suspected supporters of the Saudi Arabian-born Islamist leader held responsible, Osama bin Laden. In early October the Federation Minister of the Interior, Mohammed Besić, was forced to resign, after media ridicule of his statement that supporters of bin Laden's al-Qa'ida (Base) organization were planning to take refuge in Bosnia and Herzegovina. (He was replaced by Ramo Masleša in December.) A number of civilians were arrested on suspicion of involvement in terrorist activities, including six (five of Algerian and one of Yemeni origin) who remained under investigation by the Federation Supreme Court. (In January 2002 the Federation Supreme Court ordered the release from detention of the six suspected terrorists, on grounds of insufficient evidence; it was reported, however, that they had been transferred to the custody of US forces.) Also in October 2001 three Croats, who had been sentenced in 2000 for involvement in the massacre of more than 100 Muslims at Ahmici in 1993, succeeded in having their convictions overturned on appeal, and the custodial terms of a further two Croats were reduced. In early November 2001 five Serbs received terms of imprisonment at the ICTY for participating in the torture and killing of prisoners at a detention camp at Omarska, in the north of the country, in 1992. Later that month Milošević (who had been extradited to the ICTY in June 2001 and had been charged with crimes against humanity relating to Croatia in 1991–92 and Kosovo in 1999) was also indicted with perpetrating genocide against the Muslim and Croat populations of Bosnia in 1992–95. (In April 2002 the Dutch Government resigned, after a report by the Netherlands Institute for War Documentation emphasized the failure of Dutch peace-keeping troops to prevent the massacre at Srebreniča in 1995.) At the end of December 2001 NATO transferred partial control of Bosnian airspace to the local authorities. In January 2002 US proposals that the SFOR contingent deployed in the country (then numbering 18,000) be reduced by one-third were strongly opposed by Petritsch, on the grounds that the existing military presence was essential to maintain stability in the country.

In March 2002 Dragen Mikerević was appointed to the rotating chairmanship of the national Council of Ministers. Later in March the leading Bosnian political parties, under pressure from Petritsch, reached agreement on the adoption of constitutional reforms, which would guarantee equal rights to the three principal constituent peoples (Serb, Croat and Bosniak) throughout the country. The reforms, which ensured the representation of the three constituent peoples at all levels of government, were officially adopted in April. Petritsch amended the electoral law accordingly, and elections were scheduled for 5 October. In May Petritsch issued a ruling, providing for the adoption of judiciary reforms, which would ensure the independent appointment of judges and prosecutors. On 27 May he announced the appointment of eight judges to a new State Court, which was to become the country's highest judiciary organ. On the same day Sir Jeremy John Durham (Paddy) Ashdown, a British politician, officially replaced Petritsch as High Representative. In mid-June Ashdown dismissed the Federation Deputy Prime Minister and Minister of Finance, Nikola

Grabovac, and the Serb Republic Minister of Finance, Milenko Vracar, tendered his resignation, following pressure from the new High Representative (who had criticized official malpractice in both entities). At the end of that month the USA vetoed a further extension of the mandate of the UNMIBH, after failing to secure immunity from prosecution in the new International Criminal Court for US peace-keeping troops. The UN Security Council subsequently voted in favour of a provisional extension of the mandate to allow further time to resolve the US objections. In early July, after a compromise agreement was reached with the US Government, the UN Security Council extended the mandate of the UNMIBH until the end of 2002, when responsibility for peace-keeping was to be transferred to the EU. In August SFOR troops launched a surveillance operation near the border with Montenegro, in an effort to locate supporters of Radovan Karadžić.

In September 2002 an organ of the Serb Republic Government issued a report disputing the veracity of the Srebreniča massacre and claiming that only some 2,000 members of the Bosnian armed forces had been killed (mainly in military operations) in the region. The report was strongly condemned as a fabrication by the Bosnian Muslim community and by Ashdown. At the end of September the head of the Bosnian Serb security forces was shot and killed in Sokalac. In early October Plavšić agreed to plead guilty at the ICTY to one charge of crimes against humanity. The prosecution subsequently abandoned seven other charges, including one of genocide (although speculation that a compromise arrangement had been reached was officially denied). Later that month a Serbian former official, Milan Simić (who had surrendered to the Tribunal in February 1998), was sentenced to five years' imprisonment, after pleading guilty in May 2002 to two charges in connection with incidents of torture perpetrated in 1992.

On 5 October 2002 elections were conducted to the national presidency, the presidency of the Serb Republic, the national and entity legislatures, and cantonal assemblies throughout the country. OSCE monitors subsequently declared that electoral standards had been satisfactory, although the national rate of voter participation was estimated at only some 55%. In the three separate ballots to the collective Presidency, which took place on an ethnic basis in the two entities, the Chairman of the PDA, Sulejman Tihić, was elected the Bosniak member, with 37.3% of the votes cast, while Dragan Covič of the CDU—BH became the Croat member (with 61.5%) and Mirko Sarović of the SDP (35.5%) the Serb member. The SDP leader, Dragan Cavić, secured the presidency of the Serb Republic with 40.1% of the votes cast. The alliance led by the SDP—BH lost its majority in the elections to the 42-member national House of Representatives, and the PDA became the strongest single party, with 10 seats. The PDA also secured the highest number of seats (32) in the 98-member federal House of Representatives. In the elections to the 83-member National Assembly of the Serb Republic the SDP secured 26 seats and the SNSD 19 seats. At the end of October both the Minister of Defence and the army Chief of the General Staff of the Serb Republic resigned, after it emerged that a state-owned aviation company had exported military equipment to Iraq, in contravention of a UN armaments embargo (see chapter on Iraq). The central Government subsequently imposed an indefinite ban on the export of all armaments and military equipment. On 28 November Cavić was inaugurated as President of the Serb Republic.

At the end of November 2002 the former leader of a Serbian paramilitary group, Mitar Vasiljević, was sentenced to 20 years' imprisonment at the ICTY on two charges relating to atrocities perpetrated against Bosnian Muslims in 1992–94. On 7 December 2002 Cavić nominated Dragan Mikerević, hitherto the national Prime Minister and Minister of European Integration, and a member of the PDP, as Prime Minister of the Serb Republic. Later that month the Presidency of Bosnia and Herzegovina nominated Adnan Terzić of the PDA as Prime Minister. Also in December 2002 Ashdown introduced new legislation to strengthen the powers of the all-Bosnian Government: two new ministries, of security and justice, were to be established and the Prime Minister was henceforth to be appointed for a four-year term (replacing the system of rotation between the three ethnic representatives). The 14 Serbian delegates in the new House of Representatives boycotted its first session in protest at the amendments to the government system. At the end of 2002 the mandate of the UNMIBH officially expired, and the UN transferred responsibility for peace-keeping to an EU Police Mission,

which was to supervise the reorganization and training of the country's security forces.

On 13 January 2003 the national House of Representatives elected Terzić as Prime Minister and a new Council of Ministers was formed. Although the new all-Bosnian Government was dominated by the three main nationalist parties (the PDA, the CDU and the SDP), representatives of the moderate PDP and the Party for Bosnia and Herzegovina were also included to ensure a legislative majority. On 17 January the National Assembly approved Mikerević's nomination as Prime Minister, and a new Government for the entity, which (under constitutional amendments designed to ensure equal rights for the three Bosnian ethnic communities) comprised eight Serbian, five Muslim and three Croatian representatives. Later that month the Federation legislature elected a Croat, Niko Lozancić, to the presidency and, in an amendment to the entity's system of government, a Bosniak and a Serb to the office of joint Vice-President. The new President and Vice-Presidents were inaugurated on 27 January (the first occasion that a Serb had been elected to public office in the Federation). On the same day the newly established State Court of Bosnia and Herzegovina officially commenced operations; a state Prosecutor's Office was set up in the same month. At the end of January the two entities elected the 15-member, national House of Peoples (comprising 10 deputies elected by the Federation legislature and five by the Serb Republic legislature). The appointment of a new Federation Government, under Ahmet Hadžipašić, was approved in mid-February.

At the end of January 2003 the Dutch legislature released a report, which attributed principal responsibility for the Srebreniča massacre to the French former commander of UNPROFOR. In early February the office of the UN High Commissioner for Refugees announced that about one-half of those displaced during the Bosnian conflict (some 400,000 civilians) had returned to their homes since 1995. On 27 February 2003 the ICTY sentenced Plavšić to 11 years' imprisonment for the remaining charge of crimes against humanity. In March international investigators presented to Ashdown a report confirming that aircraft equipment had been exported to Iraq by a Serb Republic aviation company since 1997, in violation of UN sanctions (see chapter on Iraq). On 2 April Sarović resigned from the tripartite presidency, after being implicated in both the illicit exports to Iraq and alleged espionage activities by the Serb Republic military. Ashdown (who had been expected to dismiss Sarović) announced the abolition of the Serb Republic Supreme Defence Council; command of the armed forces was transferred provisionally to the entity's President. He also removed all references of statehood from the entity's Constitution, and amended legislation governing the Serb Republic military and state defence. On 10 April the national House of Peoples confirmed the nomination of Borislav Paravac, also a member of the SDP, to replace Sarović.

Government

In accordance with the General Framework Agreement for Peace in Bosnia and Herzegovina, signed in December 1995, Bosnia and Herzegovina is a single state, which consists of two independent political entities: the Federation of Bosnia and Herzegovina, comprising the Bosniak (Muslim)- and Croat-majority areas, and the Serb Republic (Republika Srpska), comprising the Serb-majority area. The central Government of Bosnia and Herzegovina has a three-member collective presidency of one Bosniak, one Croat and one Serb. Members of the Presidency are directly elected for a term of four years, and are eligible to serve for only two consecutive terms. Chairmanship of the Presidency is rotated between the members every eight months. The bicameral Parliamentary Assembly of Bosnia and Herzegovina comprises the House of Peoples and the House of Representatives. The House of Representatives has 42 deputies, of whom 28 are directly elected from the Federation and 14 directly elected from the Serb Republic for a four-year term. The House of Peoples has 15 deputies, of whom 10 are selected by the Federation legislature and five by the Serb Republic legislature for a four-year term. The Presidency appoints a Prime Minister (subject to the approval of the House of Representatives), who subsequently appoints the national Council of Ministers.

The Federation of Bosnia and Herzegovina and the Serb Republic each retain an executive presidency, government and legislature. The bicameral parliament of the Federation comprises a 98-member House of Representatives, which is directly elected for a four-year term, and a 58-member House of Peoples, comprising 17 Serb, 17 Bosniak, 17 Croat and seven other deputies, who are elected by the cantonal assemblies. The unicameral legislature of the Serb Republic, known as the National Assembly, has 83 deputies, who are directly elected for a four-year term. The Federation legislature elects a President and two Vice-Presidents, comprising one Bosniak, one Croat and one Serb, for a term of four years. The Serb National Assembly also elects a President and two Vice-Presidents, comprising one Bosniak, one Croat and one Serb, for a four-year term. The Federation is divided into 10 cantons, each headed by a župan or governor.

Defence

At August 2002 the two entities of Bosnia and Herzegovina maintained separate armed forces: at that time the Serb Republic had an army of about 6,600 and the Federation an army (comprising the former Croatian Defence Council—HVO —and Bosniak forces) of more than 13,200. Under the terms of the Dayton agreement of 1995, the size of the armed forces of the two entities was restricted.

On 20 December 1995 power was formally transferred to an international NATO-commanded 60,000-strong 'Implementation Force' (IFOR), which was granted authority to oversee the implementation of the peace accord. In December 1996 IFOR was superseded by a Stabilization Force (SFOR), which initially comprised about 32,000 troops. In early 1998 NATO agreed to extend SFOR's mandate to remain in the region indefinitely, with six-monthly reviews. Following restructuring, SFOR numbered about 12,900 personnel at the beginning of 2003. It was envisaged that SFOR would be replaced by a European Union operation in early 2004. At the end of 2002 the mandate of the UN Mission in Bosnia and Herzegovina (UNMIBH), established in 1995, was officially completed, and the UN transferred responsibility for peace-keeping to a European Union Police Mission (EUPM). The EUPM, which comprised 512 police officers, supported by 50 civilian monitors and 300 local staff, was to supervise the reorganization and training of the country's security forces. The central Government allocated US $130m. to defence in 2002.

Economic Affairs

In 2001, according to World Bank estimates, Bosnia and Herzegovina's gross national income (GNI), measured at average 1999–2001 prices, was US $5,037m., equivalent to $1,240 per head. During 1995–2001, it was estimated, the population of Bosnia and Herzegovina increased at an average annual rate of 2.9%, while gross domestic product (GDP) per head increased, in real terms, by an average of 19.4% per year. Overall GDP increased, in real terms, at an average annual rate of 22.9% in 1995–2001; real growth in 2001 was 6.0%.

Agriculture (including forestry and fishing) contributed an estimated 13.0% of GDP in Bosnia and Herzegovina in 2001. In that year about 4.8% of the labour force were employed in the agricultural sector. The major agricultural products were tobacco and fruit, and the livestock sector was also significant. Imports of foodstuffs comprised 4.1% of total imports in 1997. According to World Bank estimates, the GDP of the agricultural sector increased, in real terms, by an annual average of 5.0% in 1994–2000. Real agricultural GDP declined by 8.3% in 2000.

Industry (mining, manufacturing, utilities and construction) contributed an estimated 27.6% of GDP in Bosnia and Herzegovina in 2001. Some 47.5% of the labour force were employed in the industrial sector in 1990. According to World Bank estimates, industrial GDP increased, in real terms, by an annual average of 26.0% in 1994–2000. Real growth in industrial GDP was estimated at 5.7% in 2000.

The mining sector contributed 2.0% of GDP in 2001. Bosnia and Herzegovina possesses extensive mineral resources, including iron ore, lignite, copper, lead, zinc and gold. Mining output increased by about 10.4% in 2000 (compared with the previous year).

Manufacturing contributed 12.5% of GDP in 2001. The manufacturing sector is based largely on the processing of iron ore, non-ferrous metals, coal, and wood and paper products. Manufacturing GDP increased, in real terms, by an annual average of 17.2% in 1994–2000. Manufacturing GDP increased by 7.2% in 2000.

The civil conflict resulted in the destruction of much of the electric power system in Bosnia and Herzegovina. Prior to the conflict, the system comprised 13 hydroelectric installations and 12 coal- and lignite-fuelled thermal power installations. In 1999 61.2% of electricity production was derived from hydroelectric

power and 33.7% from coal. Electric power accounted for 3.2% of total imports in 1997.

The services sector contributed an estimated 59.4% of GDP in 2001. According to World Bank estimates, the GDP of the services sector increased, in real terms, by an annual average of 35.9% in 1994–2000. Growth in services GDP was estimated at 9.4% in 2000.

In 2001 Bosnia and Herzegovina recorded a visible trade deficit of US $2,751.5m., and there was a deficit of $1,364.6m. on the current account of the balance of payments. In 2001 the principal source of imports was Croatia (which accounted for 15.2% of total imports); other important suppliers were Italy, Slovenia, Germany, Yugoslavia (now Serbia and Montenegro), Hungary and Austria. In that year the main market for exports was Italy (which accounted for 21.7% of total exports); other significant purchasers were Yugoslavia, Germany, Croatia, Switzerland and Slovenia. The principal exports in 1997 were wood and paper products, iron and steel, electric power and fabricated metal products. The main imports in that year were foodstuffs and electric power.

Bosnia and Herzegovina's overall budget deficit for 2001 was estimated at 514.2m. konvertibilna marka (convertible marka). The country's total external debt was estimated at US $2,828m. at the end of 2000 (of which $2,569m. was public debt), and the cost of debt-servicing was equivalent to about 22.1% of the value of exports of goods and services. In 1999 consumer prices declined by 1.0% in the Federation, but increased by 14.0% in the Serb Republic. In 2000 the rate of inflation was 1.9% in the Federation and 14.6% in the Serb Republic. In 2001 the rate of consumer-price inflation was 1.5% in the Federation and 8.2% in the Serb Republic. According to official estimates, the unemployment rate in Bosnia and Herzegovina was 39.9% at the end of 2001.

Bosnia and Herzegovina became a member of the IMF in December 1995 and was admitted to the World Bank in April 1996. In July 1999 the first summit meeting of the Stability Pact for South-Eastern Europe took place in Bosnia and Herzegovina, with the aim of adopting a common strategy for regional stability.

The civil conflict in 1992–95 resulted in extensive damage to the economy of Bosnia and Herzegovina. Following the signing of the Dayton peace agreement in December 1995, the reconstruction of the economy commenced, and Bosnia and Herzegovina was admitted to the IMF. An early priority of the reconstruction programme was the resolution of the considerable foreign debt that Bosnia and Herzegovina had inherited from the former Yugoslavia. In May 1998 the IMF approved a stand-by credit to support the Bosnian Government's economic programme. The World Bank subsequently granted further assistance in economic reconstruction and development. The new national currency, fixed at par with the German Deutsche Mark, was officially introduced in June. In October agreement was reached with the so-called Paris Club of creditor governments on the reduction of external debt. Following large inflows of foreign assistance, the economy rapidly recovered from the effects of the civil war (with growth exceeding 80% in 1996–97). The country made further progress under an IMF-supported economic programme, although unemployment remained high, and corruption and poor customs controls contributed to a major loss of revenue (and consequently to the increasing current-account deficit and rising levels of public debt). In addition, performance continued to vary widely in each of the two entities, with a high level of inflation and declining industrial production recorded in the Serb Republic. A further stand-by arrangement was approved by the IMF in August 2002. However, legislative and presidential elections, which took place in both entities in October, resulted in the replacement of the ruling coalitions that had implemented most of the fiscal and structural reforms agreed with the IMF. During 2002 the Bosnian High Representative imposed a series of economic regulations, with the ultimate aim of unifying principal sectors, such as telecommunications, banking, and tax and customs administration, throughout the country. He also planned to introduce value-added tax at state level by 2004. Further large-scale privatization, with greater progress in enterprise restructuring in order to stimulate exports (to compensate for an anticipated decline in aid), remained a major priority for the authorities.

Education

Elementary education is free and compulsory for all children between the ages of seven and 15 years, when children attend the 'eight-year school'. Various types of secondary education are available to all who qualify, but the vocational and technical schools are the most popular. Alternatively, children may attend a general secondary school (gymnasium), where they follow a four-year course to prepare them for university entrance. At the secondary level there are also a number of art schools, apprentice schools and teacher-training schools. In 1996/97 some 260,407 pupils were enrolled in 955 primary schools, and in 1997/98 some 97,303 pupils attended 184 secondary schools. In 2001 an estimated 57,800 students attended the country's four universities, which were situated in Sarajevo, Banja Luka, Mostar and Tuzla. In the Federation, 256,169 pupils were enrolled in primary education, 111,444 pupils in secondary education, and 48,866 students in higher education institutions in 2001.

Public Holidays

2003: 1–2 January (New Year), 7 January (Orthodox Christmas), 14 January (Orthodox New Year), 12 February* (Great Bayram, Feast of the Sacrifice), 1 March (Independence Day), 18–21 April (Catholic Easter), 25–28 April (Orthodox Easter), 1 May (Labour Day), 15 August (Assumption), 1 November (All Saints' Day), 25 November (National Statehood Day), 26 November* (Small Bayram, end of Ramadan), 25 December (Christmas Day).

2004: 1–2 January (New Year), 7 January (Orthodox Christmas), 14 January (Orthodox New Year), 2 February* (Great Bayram, Feast of the Sacrifice), 1 March (Independence Day), 9–12 April (Catholic and Orthodox Easter), 1 May (Labour Day), 15 August (Assumption), 1 November (All Saints' Day), 14 November* (Small Bayram, end of Ramadan), 25 November (National Statehood Day), 25 December (Christmas Day).

* These holidays are dependent on the Islamic lunar calendar and may vary by one or two days from the dates given.

Weights and Measures

The metric system is in force.

Statistical Survey

Source (unless otherwise stated): Agencija za statistiku Bosne i Hercegovine, 71000 Sarajevo; tel. and fax (33) 2206222; e-mail bhas@bih.net.ba; internet www.bhas.ba.

Area and Population

AREA, POPULATION AND DENSITY

Area (sq km)	51,129*
Population (census results)	
31 March 1981	4,124,008
31 March 1991	
Males	2,183,795
Females.	2,193,238
Total	4,377,033
Population (UN estimates at mid-year)†	
1999	3,846,000
2000	3,977,000
2001	4,067,000
Density (per sq km) at mid-2001	79.5

* 19,741 sq miles.

† Source: UN, *World Population Prospects: The 2000 Revision.*

PRINCIPAL ETHNIC GROUPS

(1991 census, provisional)

	Number	% of total population
Muslims	1,905,829	43.7
Serbs	1,369,258	31.4
Croats	755,892	17.3
'Yugoslavs'	239,845	5.5
Total (incl. others)	4,364,574	100.0

PRINCIPAL TOWNS (population at 1991 census): Sarajevo (capital) 416,497; Banja Luka 143,079, Zenica 96,027, Tuzla 83,770, Mostar 75,865, Bihać 45,995, Brčko 41,405, Bijeljina 37,216, Prijedor 34,613 (Source: Thomas Brinkhoff, *City Population*—internet www.citypopulation.de).

BIRTHS, MARRIAGES AND DEATHS

1990: Registered live births 66,952; Registered marriages 29,990; Registered deaths 29,093.

1991: Registered live births 64,769; Registered deaths 31,411 (Source: UN, *Population and Vital Statistics Report*).

1995: Registered deaths 114,670 (death rate 13.6 per 1,000) (Source: UN, *Demographic Yearbook*).

1998: Registered live births 45,007 (birth rate 12.3 per 1,000); Registered deaths 28,679 (death rate 7.9 per 1,000) (Source: UN, *Population and Vital Statistics Report*).

1990–95 (UN estimates, annual averages): Birth rate 12.6 per 1,000; Death rate 7.1 per 1,000 (Source: UN, *World Population Prospects: The 1998 Revision*).

1995–2000 (UN estimates, annual averages): Birth rate 10.5 per 1,000; Death rate 7.4 per 1,000 (Source: UN, *World Population Prospects: The 2000 Revision*).

Expectation of life (WHO estimates, years at birth): 72.8 (males 69.3; females 76.4) in 2001 (Source: WHO, *World Health Report*).

EMPLOYMENT

(Federation of Bosnia and Herzegovina, average for December)

	1997	1998	1999
Activities of the material sphere . . .	173,857	204,117	217,000
Non-material services	113,723	131,945	127,345
Total	287,580	336,062	344,345

Source: IMF, *Bosnia and Herzegovina: Selected Issues and Statistical Appendix* (June 2000).

Total employed (at 31 December): 412,805 in 2000, 405,689 in 2001 (Federation of Bosnia and Herzegovina); 228,834 in 2000 (Republika Srpska).

Unemployed (persons registered at 31 December): 267,934 in 2000, 269,004 in 2001 (Federation of Bosnia and Herzegovina); 153,264 in 2000, 147,749 in 2001 (Republika Srpska) (Source: Central Bank of Bosnia and Herzegovina).

Health and Welfare

KEY INDICATORS

Total fertility rate (children per woman, 2001)	1.3
Under-5 mortality rate (per 1,000 live births, 2001) . . .	18
HIV/AIDS (% of persons aged 15–49, 1999)	0.10
Physicians (per 1,000 head, 1998)	1.43
Hospital beds (per 1,000 head, 1995)	1.84
Health expenditure (2000): US $ per head (PPP) . . .	319
Health expenditure (2000): % of GDP	4.5
Health expenditure (2000): public (% of total)	69.0

For sources and definitions, see explanatory note on p. vi.

Agriculture

PRINCIPAL CROPS
('000 metric tons)

	1999	2000	2001
Wheat	257.8*	338.5*	269.5
Barley	56.3*	53.1*	64.6
Maize	984.1*	474.9*	510.2
Rye	9.0*	11.7*	13.9
Oats	61.7*	56.9*	45.7
Potatoes	437.8*	282.8*	185.1
Dry beans	14.1*	5.8*	7.1
Soybeans (Soya beans) . .	8.7*	4.0*	3.6
Cabbages	111.6*	68.5*	68.4
Tomatoes	36.9*	29.6*	23.3
Chillies and green peppers . .	36.9*	37.0†	37.0†
Dry onions	36.6*	21.6*	23.4
Garlic	8.5*	4.0*	7.4
Carrots	14.5*	5.6*	10.2
Other vegetables† . . .	458.8	504.7	510.8
Grapes	12.7*	13.2*	13.3†
Apples	25.9*	14.4*	14.4
Pears	10.6*	9.0†	8.1
Plums	27.0*	26.8*	26.8
Tobacco (leaves)	4.1*	3.3*	3.4

* Unofficial figure.
† FAO estimate(s).
Source: FAO.

LIVESTOCK
('000 head, year ending September)

	1999	2000	2001
Horses	20*	18†	18*
Cattle	443†	462†	440*
Pigs*	350	355	330
Sheep	633†	662†	640*
Chickens	1,100*	1,000*	4,740†
Ducks*	120	120	120
Geese*	150	150	150
Turkeys*	120	120	120

* FAO estimate(s).
† Unofficial figure.
Source: FAO.

LIVESTOCK PRODUCTS
('000 metric tons)

	1999	2000	2001
Beef and veal	12.4*	12.5†	13.0†
Mutton and lamb	2.7*	2.7	2.7*
Pig meat*	11.7	5.0	6.0
Poultry meat	8.9*	8.4	8.4*
Cows' milk	569.4†	540.0*	460.0*
Sheep's milk	7.6†	7.1†	7.0*
Cheese	11.0*	8.7†	8.5*
Hen eggs*	15.0	15.2	15.1
Cattle and buffalo hides* . .	2.4	2.4	2.4

* FAO estimate(s).
† Unofficial figure.
Source: FAO.

Forestry

ROUNDWOOD REMOVALS
('000 cubic metres, excluding bark)

	1999*	2000	2001
Sawlogs, veneer logs and logs for sleepers	2,800	2,875	2,531
Pulpwood	130	158	141
Other industrial wood . . .	290	299	286
Fuel wood	910	950	860
Total	4,130	4,282	3,818

* Unofficial figures.
Source: FAO.

SAWNWOOD PRODUCTION
(FAO estimates, '000 cubic metres, including railway sleepers)

	1999	2000	2001
Coniferous (softwood) . . .	80	50	60
Broadleaved (hardwood) . . .	250	270	250
Total	330	320	310

Source: FAO.

Fishing

(FAO estimates, metric tons, live weight)

	1998	1999	2000
Total catch (capture, freshwater fish)	2,500	2,500	2,500

Source: FAO, *Yearbook of Fishery Statistics*.

Mining

('000 metric tons)

	1998	1999	2000
Lignite and brown coal . . .	1,764	1,800*	1,800*
Iron ore: gross weight* . . .	100	100	100
Iron ore: metal content* . . .	35	35	36
Bauxite*	75	75	75
Kaolin (crude)*	3	3	3
Ceramic clay (crude)* . . .	20	20	20
Barite (Barytes) concentrate* . .	2	2	2
Salt (unrefined)*	50	50	50
Gypsum (crude)*	30	30	30

* Estimated production.
Source: US Geological Survey.

Industry

SELECTED PRODUCTS
('000 metric tons, unless otherwise indicated)

	1990
Electric energy (million kWh)	14,632
Crude steel	1,421
Aluminium	89
Machines	16
Tractors (number)	34,000
Lorries (number)	16,000
Motor cars (number)	38,000
Cement	797
Paper and paperboard	281
Television receivers (number)	21,000

Electric energy (million kWh): 2,393 in 1996; 2,461 in 1997; 2,538 (estimate) in 1998 (Source: UN, *Industrial Commodity Statistics Yearbook*).

Mineral manufactures (estimates, '000 metric tons): Crude steel 115 in 1996, 110 per year in 1997–2000; Aluminium (primary and secondary) 15 per year in 1996–2000; Cement 150 in 1996, 200 in 1997, 300 per year in 1998–2000 (Source: US Geological Survey).

Finance

CURRENCY AND EXCHANGE RATES

Monetary Units

100 pfeninga = 1 konvertibilna marka (KM or convertible marka).

Sterling, Dollar and Euro Equivalents (31 December 2002)

£1 sterling = KM 3.3059
US $1 = KM 2.0511
€1 = KM 1.9558
KM 100 = £30.25 = $48.75 = €51.13.

Average Exchange Rate (KM per US $)

2000   2.1244
2001   2.1872
2002   2.0796

Note: The new Bosnia and Herzegovina dinar (BHD) was introduced in August 1994, with an official value fixed at 100 BHD = 1 Deutsche Mark (DM). The DM, the Croatian kuna and the Yugoslav dinar also circulated within Bosnia and Herzegovina. On 22 June 1998 the BHD was replaced by the KM, equivalent to 100 of the former units. The KM was thus at par with the DM. From the introduction of the euro, on 1 January 1999, the German currency had a fixed exchange rate of €1 = DM 1.95583.

BUDGET

(KM million*)

Revenue†	1999	2000	2001
Tax revenue	3,660.9	4,094.8	4,209.2
Indirect taxes	1,474.6	1,554.6	1,470.3
Trade taxes	491.6	599.0	840.0
Direct taxes	336.1	415.3	362.4
Social security contributions	1,358.7	1,526.0	1,536.5
Other revenue (incl. grants)	470.7	355.1	446.7
Total	4,131.6	4,449.9	4,655.9

Expenditure	1999	2000	2001
Interest payments	103.1	131.2	129.3
Subsidies and transfers to non-public agents‡	1,631.2	1,918.9	2,011.1
Other current expenditure	2,530.5	2,567.6	2,571.6
Investment expenditure	1,505.5	1,340.8	1,235.4
Total	5,770.3	5,958.5	5,947.4

* Figures represent a consolidation of the budgetary accounts of the central Government and the authorities in the Federation of Bosnia and Herzegovina and (except for local and district administration) the Serb Republic.

† Excluding grants (KM million): 1,143.4 in 1999; 939.8 in 2000; 777.3 in 2001.

‡ Excluding transfers by Federation Cantons.

Source: IMF, *Bosnia and Herzegovina: First Review Under the Stand-By Arrangement and Request for Waiver of Performance Criteria* (January 2003).

INTERNATIONAL RESERVES

(US $ million at 31 December)

	1999	2000	2001
IMF special drawing rights	7.7	10.7	6.1
Foreign exchange	444.7	485.9	1,215.1
Total	452.3	496.6	1,221.2

Source: IMF, *International Financial Statistics*.

MONEY SUPPLY

(KM million at 31 December)

	2000	2001	2002
Currency outside banks	651.7	1,674.1	1,737.2
Demand deposits at banks	730.3	957.3	1,181.0
Total money (incl. others)	1,470.6	2,790.1	3,131.1

Source: IMF, *International Financial Statisitics*.

COST OF LIVING

(Retail Price Index; base: December 1995 = 100)

Federation

	1999	2000	2001
All items	123.5	125.8	127.7

Republika Srpska

	1999	2000	2001
All items	84.0	96.3	104.2

Source: IMF, *Bosnia and Herzegovina: Statistical Appendix* (March 2002).

NATIONAL ACCOUNTS

Expenditure on the Gross Domestic Product

(US $ million at current prices)

	1996	1997	1998
Government final consumption expenditure			
	3,237	3,589	3,914
Private final consumption expenditure			
Increase in stocks			
Gross fixed capital formation	1,124	1,438	1,481
Total domestic expenditure	4,361	5,027	5,396
Exports of goods and services	658	1,002	1,367
Less Imports of goods and services	−2,278	−2,606	−2,864
GDP in purchasers' values	2,741	3,423	3,899

Source: IMF, *Bosnia and Herzegovina: Selected Issues and Statistical Appendix* (June 2000).

GDP (US $ million): 4,702 in 1999; 4,451 in 2000 (Source: Central Bank of Bosnia and Herzegovina, *Annual Report 2001*).

Gross Domestic Product by Economic Activity

(KM million at current prices)

	2000	2001
Agriculture, hunting and forestry	1,061.4	1,112.6
Fishing	2.6	1.6
Mining and quarrying	182.2	172.7
Manufacturing	1,014.0	1,073.5
Electricity, gas and water	630.1	691.7
Construction	463.8	439.3
Wholesale and retail trade	789.7	995.7
Hotels and restaurants	188.9	202.9
Transport and communications	804.3	947.7
Financial intermediation	323.6	329.6
Real estate and business services	197.2	199.9
Public administration and defence	1,147.3	1,265.3
Education	501.9	523.5
Health and social welfare	450.5	455.4
Other personal services	177.9	190.7
Sub-total	7,935.4	8,602.1
Less Imputed bank service charges	212.5	236.5
GDP at basic prices	7,723.0	8,365.5
Taxes, less subsidies, on products	1,888.2	2,114.4
GDP in purchasers' values	9,611.2	10,480.0

BALANCE OF PAYMENTS
(estimates, US $ million.)

	1999	2000	2001
Exports of goods f.o.b.	816.2	1,151.5	1,166.4
Imports of goods f.o.b.	-4,149.2	-3,811.3	-3,917.9
Trade balance	-3,333.1	-2,659.9	-2,751.5
Exports of services	284.9	261.2	288.1
Imports of services	-249.9	-224.1	-228.3
Balance on goods and services	-3,298.1	-2,622.8	-2,691.7
Other income received	454.7	391.8	401.4
Other income paid	-61.3	-68.4	-65.1
Balance on goods, services and income	-2,904.7	-2,299.4	-2,355.4
Current transfers received	1,361.5	1,020.9	994.3
Current transfers paid	-2.5	-2.8	-3.4
Current balance	-1,545.7	-1,281.3	-1,364.6
Capital account (net)	531.5	406.0	386.7
Direct investment from abroad	176.7	146.0	125.3
Other investment assets	350.3	548.5	1,363.6
Other investment liabilities	-40.2	38.3	19.7
Net errors and omissions	194.1	111.1	124.7
Overall balance	-333.3	-31.4	655.4

Source: IMF, *International Financial Statistics*.

External Trade

SELECTED COMMODITIES
(US $ million*)

Imports	1996	1997
Electric power	19.7	39.6
Fabricated metal products	33.9	22.9
Electrical machinery and equipment	5.1	28.7
Wood and paper products	11.5	29.9
Foodstuffs	39.9	50.2
Total (incl. others)	1,172.6	1,225.0

Exports	1996	1997
Electric power	0.3	5.7
Iron and steel	7.0	12.4
Fabricated metal products	4.5	5.3
Transport equipment	6.5	3.4
Electrical machinery and equipment	0.3	4.6
Wood and paper products	18.2	18.1
Textile products	2.1	0.8
Total (incl. others)	57.8	87.3

* Figures are provisional and refer only to the Federation of Bosnia and Herzegovina (the Bosniak- and Croat-majority areas, excluding the Serb Republic).

1999 (Federation and Serb Republic, KM million): Total imports 6,047; Total exports 1,375 (Source: Office of the High Representative).

PRINCIPAL TRADING PARTNERS
(KM '000)

Imports	2000	2001
Austria	316,310	397,479
Croatia	1,453,671	1,075,698
France	41,287	94,051
Germany	694,911	735,596
Hungary	234,898	405,272
Italy	1,103,200	929,991
Slovenia	846,399	917,001
Switzerland	156,258	206,462
Yugoslavia	27,144	521,050
Total (incl. others)	5,911,631	7,062,382

Exports	2000	2001
Austria	91,115	80,546
Croatia	161,771	234,006
Germany	188,870	326,918
Italy	480,865	515,136
Slovenia	110,018	170,476
Switzerland	284,336	228,650
Yugoslavia	444,282	456,833
Total (incl. others)	1,781,906	2,370,013

Source: Central Bank of Bosnia and Herzegovina, *Annual Report 2000 and 2001*.

Transport

RAILWAYS
(traffic)

	1998	1999	2000
Passenger-km ('000):			
Federation	5,118	9,386	9,320
Republika Srpska	52,000	41,000	38,000
Freight ton-km ('000):			
Federation	73,115	114,839	140,000
Republika Srpska	12,292	31,000	83,000

Source: IMF, *Bosnia and Herzegovina: Statistical Appendix* (March 2002).

Tourism

Foreign tourist arrivals: ('000): 90 in 1998; 89 in 1999; 110 (estimate) in 2000.

Tourism receipts (US $ million): 21 in 1998; 21 in 1999; 17 (estimate) in 2000 (Source: World Tourism Organization).

Communications Media

	1999	2000	2001
Telephones ('000 main lines in use)	367.9	407.6	450.1
Mobile cellular telephones ('000 subscribers)	52.6	219.7	233.3
Internet users ('000)	7.0	n.a.	45.0

Daily newspapers (government-controlled areas only): 2 (average circulation 520,000 copies) in 1995; 3 in 1996.

Non-daily newspapers (1992): 22 (average circulation 2,508,000 copies).

1997: Radio receivers ('000 in use) 940; Television receivers ('000 in use) 900.

Sources: UN, *Statistical Yearbook*; UNESCO, *Statistical Yearbook*, International Telecommunication Union.

Education

(1997/98)

	Institutions	Teachers	Students
Primary*	955	11,331	260,407
Secondary	184	6,065	97,303
Higher	55	2,833	34,477

* 1996/97 figures.

Source: US Information Service, Sarajevo.

Directory

The Constitution*

The Constitution of Bosnia and Herzegovina was Annexe 4 to the General Framework Agreement for Peace in Bosnia and Herzegovina, signed in Paris, France, on 14 December 1995. These peace accords were negotiated at Dayton, Ohio, the USA, in November and became the Elysées or Paris Treaty in December. Annexe 4 took effect as a constitutional act upon signature, superseding and amending the Constitution of the Republic of Bosnia and Herzegovina.

The previous organic law, an amended version of the 1974 Constitution of the then Socialist Republic of Bosnia and Herzegovina (part of the Socialist Federal Republic of Yugoslavia—the name was changed to the Republic of Bosnia and Herzegovina upon the declaration of independence following a referendum on 29 February–1 March 1992), provided for a collective State Presidency, a Government headed by a Prime Minister and a bicameral Assembly.

The institutions of the Republic continued to function until the firm establishment of the bodies provided for by the Federation of Bosnia and Herzegovina, which was formed on 31 March 1994. This was an association of the Muslim- or Bosniak-led Republic and the Croat Republic of Herzeg-Bosna. The federal Constitution provided for a balance of powers between Bosniak and Croat elements in a Federation divided into cantons. The federal Government was to be responsible for defence, foreign and economic affairs, and its head, the Prime Minister, was to have a greater executive role than the President. These two posts were to rotate between the two ethnic groups.

According to the General Framework Agreement, the Federation was one of the two constituent 'entities' of the new union of Bosnia and Herzegovina, together with the Serb Republic (Republika Srpska) of Bosnia and Herzegovina. The Serb Republic was proclaimed by the Serb deputies of the old Bosnian Assembly on 27 March 1992. Its Constitution provided for an executive President (with two Vice-Presidents), a Government headed by a Prime Minister and a unicameral National Assembly. Under the terms of the General Framework Agreement, known as the Dayton accords (after the US town where the treaty was negotiated in November 1995), the two Entities were to exist under their current Constitutions, which were to be amended to conform with the peace agreement.

The Dayton accords included 12 annexes on: the military aspects of the peace settlement (including the establishment of an international Implementation Force—IFOR, superseded by a Stabilization Force—SFOR in 1996); regional stabilization; inter-entity boundaries; elections; arbitration; human rights; refugees and displaced persons; a Commission to Preserve National Monuments; Bosnia and Herzegovina public corporations (specifically a Transportation Corporation); civilian implementation (including the office of a High Representative of the International Community); and an international police task force. One of the annexes was the Constitution of Bosnia and Herzegovina, summarized below, and it was signed by representatives of the Republic, the Federation and the Serb Republic.

CONSTITUTION OF BOSNIA AND HERZEGOVINA

The Preamble declares the basic, democratic principles of the country and its conformity with the principles of international law. The Bosniaks, Croats and Serbs are declared to be the constituent peoples (along with Others) of Bosnia and Herzegovina.

Article I affirms the continuation of Bosnia and Herzegovina with the Republic of Bosnia and Herzegovina, within its existing international boundaries, but with its internal structure modified. Bosnia and Herzegovina is a democratic state, consisting of two Entities, the Federation of Bosnia and Herzegovina and the Serb Republic. The capital of the country is Sarajevo and the symbols are to be determined by the legislature. Citizenship is to exist both for Bosnia and Herzegovina and for the Entities.

Article II guarantees human rights and fundamental freedoms, and makes specific mention of the Human Rights Commission to be established under Annexe 6 of the General Framework Agreement. The provisions of a number of international agreements are assured and co-operation and access for the international war-crimes tribunal specified. The provisions of this Article, according to Article X, are incapable of diminution or elimination by any amendment to the Constitution.

The responsibilities of and relations between the Entities and the institutions of Bosnia and Herzegovina are dealt with in Article III. The institutions of Bosnia and Herzegovina are responsible for foreign policy (including trade and customs), overall financial policy, immigration and refugee issues, international and inter-entity law enforcement, common and international communications facilities, inter-entity transportation and air-traffic control. Any governmental functions or powers not reserved to the institutions of Bosnia and Herzegovina by this Constitution are reserved to the Entities, unless additional responsibilities are agreed between the Entities or as provided for in the General Framework Agreement (Annexes 5–8). The Entities may establish special, parallel relations with neighbouring states, provided this is consistent with the sovereignty and territorial integrity of Bosnia and Herzegovina. The Constitution of Bosnia and Herzegovina has primacy over any inconsistent constitutional or legal provisions of the Entities.

The Parliamentary Assembly

Bosnia and Herzegovina has a bicameral legislature, known as the Parliamentary Assembly. It consists of a House of Peoples and a House of Representatives. The House of Peoples comprises 15 Members, five each from the Bosniaks, the Croats and the Serbs, who are elected for a term of four years. The Bosniak and Croat Delegates are selected by, respectively, the Bosniak and Croat Delegates to the House of Representatives of the Federation, and the Serb Delegates by the National Assembly of the Serb Republic.

The House of Representatives consists of 42 Members, of whom two-thirds are directly elected from the territory of the Federation and one-third from the territory of the Serb Republic. Deputies are elected for a term of four years.

The Parliamentary Assembly convenes in Sarajevo and each chamber rotates its chair between three members, one from each of the constituent peoples. The Parliamentary Assembly is responsible for: necessary legislation under the Constitution or to implement Presidency decisions; determining a budget for the institutions of Bosnia and Herzegovina; and deciding whether to ratify treaties.

The Presidency

Article V concerns the state Presidency of Bosnia and Herzegovina. The head of state consists of three Members: one Bosniak and one Croat, each directly elected from the Federation; and one Serb, directly elected from the Serb Republic. Members are elected for a term of four years and are restricted to two consecutive terms. Chairmanship of the Presidency is rotated between the Members every eight months. A Presidency decision, if declared to be destructive of a vital interest of an Entity, can be vetoed by a two-thirds' majority in the relevant body: the National Assembly of the Serb Republic if the declaration was made by the Serb Member; or by the Bosniak or Croat Delegates in the Federation House of Peoples if the declaration was made by, respectively, the Bosniak or Croat Members of the Presidency. The Presidency is responsible for the foreign policy and international relations of Bosnia and Herzegovina. It is required to execute the decisions of the Parliamentary Assembly and to propose an annual central budget to that body, upon the recommendation of the Council of Ministers.

The Chair of the Council of Ministers is nominated by the Presidency and confirmed in office by the House of Representatives. The post of Chair rotates between Bosniak, Croat and Serb representatives every eight months. Each appointed Chair of the Council of Ministers is to be from a different constituent people to the Chair of the Presidency. In addition, the Chair holds one of the six ministerial posts in the Council of Ministers. Other Ministers and Deputy Ministers are nominated by the Chair of the Council of Ministers, and also approved by the House of Representatives. The Council of Ministers is responsible for carrying out the policies and decisions of Bosnia and Herzegovina and reporting to the Parliamentary Assembly. There are also guarantees that no more than two-thirds of Ministers be from the territory of the Federation, and Deputy Ministers are to be from a different constituent people to their Minister.

Each Member of the Presidency has, *ex officio* , civilian command authority over armed forces. Each Member is a member of a Standing Committee on Military Matters, appointed by the Presidency and responsible for co-ordinating the activities of armed forces in the country. The inviolability of each Entity to any armed force of the other is assured.

Other Institutions and Provisions

Article VI is on the Constitutional Court, which is to have nine members, four selected by the House of Representatives of the Federation and two by the National Assembly of the Serb Republic. The three remaining judges, at least initially, are to be selected by the President of the European Court of Human Rights. The first judges will have a term of office of five years; thereafter judges will usually serve until they are 70 years of age (unless they retire or are removed by the consensus of the other judges). The Constitutional

Court of Bosnia and Herzegovina is to uphold the Constitution, to resolve the jurisdictions of the institutions of Bosnia and Herzegovina and the Entities, to ensure consistency with the Constitution and to guarantee the legal sovereignty and territorial integrity of the country. Its decisions are final and binding.

The Central Bank of Bosnia and Herzegovina is the sole authority for issuing currency and for monetary policy in Bosnia and Herzegovina. For the first six years of the Constitution, however, it is not authorized to extend credit by creating money; moreover, during this period the first Governing Body will consist of a Governor, appointed by the International Monetary Fund, and three members appointed by the Presidency (a Bosniak and a Croat, sharing one vote, from the Federation, and one from the Serb Republic). The Governor, who may not be a citizen of Bosnia and Herzegovina or any neighbouring state, will have a deciding vote. Thereafter, the Governing Body shall consist of five members, appointed by the Presidency for a term of six years, with a Governor selected by them from among their number.

Article VIII concerns the finances of Bosnia and Herzegovina and its institutions. Article IX concerns general provisions, notably forbidding anyone convicted or indicted by the International Criminal Tribunal for the former Yugoslavia from standing for or holding public office in Bosnia and Herzegovina. These provisions also guarantee the need for all public appointments to be generally representative of the peoples of Bosnia and Herzegovina. Amendments to the Constitution need a two-thirds majority of those present and voting in the House of Representatives. The penultimate Article XI is on transitional arrangements provided for in an annexe to the Constitution.

* At the instigation of the High Representative, constitutional reforms were agreed by the leading political parties, and were officially adopted in both entities on 19 April 2002, thereby amending the terms of the General Framework Agreement. Under the new reforms, the Serbian, Croat and Bosniak languages received equal status in both entities, and the three principal constituent peoples and other minorities were ensured representation in government institutions throughout the country. The electoral law was amended accordingly.

The Government
(April 2003)

HIGH REPRESENTATIVE OF THE INTERNATIONAL COMMUNITY IN BOSNIA AND HERZEGOVINA

Under the terms of the treaty and annexes of the General Framework Agreement for Peace in Bosnia and Herzegovina, signed in December 1995, the international community, as authorized by the UN Security Council, was to designate a civilian representative to oversee the implementation of the peace accords and the establishment of the institutions of the new order in Bosnia and Herzegovina.

High Representative: Sir JEREMY JOHN DURHAM (PADDY) ASHDOWN, 71000 Sarajevo, Emerika Bluma 1; tel. (33) 283500; fax (33) 283501; internet www.ohr.int.

BOSNIA AND HERZEGOVINA

Presidency

The Dayton accords, which were signed into treaty in December 1995, provide for a three-member Presidency for the state, comprising one Bosniak (Muslim), one Croat and one Serb. The Presidency has responsibility for governing Bosnia and Herzegovina at the state level. The Presidency was subsequently reconstituted to comprise a Chairman and a further two members, with the post of Chairman rotating every eight months between Bosniak, Croat and Serb representatives. The Presidency nominates a Prime Minister (subject to the approval of the legislature), who appoints a Council of Ministers.

Chairman of the Presidency: BORISLAV PARAVAC (Serbian Democratic Party of Bosnia and Herzegovina).

Member of the Presidency: SULEJMAN TIHIĆ (Party of Democratic Action).

Member of the Presidency: DRAGAN ČOVIĆ (Croatian Democratic Union of Bosnia and Herzegovina).

Council of Ministers
(April 2003)

A coalition of the Party of Democratic Action (PDA), the Party of Democratic Progress (PDP), the Croatian Democratic Union of Bosnia and Herzegovina (CDU), the Party for Bosnia and Herzegovina, and the Serbian Democratic Party (SDP).

Prime Minister and Minister of European Integration: ADNAN TERZIĆ (PDA).

Minister of Foreign Affairs: MLADEN IVANIĆ (PDP).

Minister of Security: BARISA COLAK (CDU).

Minister of Civil Affairs: SAFET HALILOVIĆ (Party for Bosnia and Herzegovina).

Minister of Foreign Trade and Economic Relations: MILA GADZIĆ (CDU).

Minister of Human Rights and Refugees: MIRSAD KEBO (PDA).

Minister of Finance and the Treasury of the Institutions of Bosnia and Herzegovina: LJERKA MARIČT (CDU).

Minister of Transportation and Communications: BRANKO DOKIĆ (PDP).

Ministries

Office of the Presidency: 71000 Sarajevo, Musala 5; tel. (33) 664941; fax (33) 472491.

Office of the Prime Minister: 71000 Sarajevo, Vojvode Putnika 3; tel. (33) 664941; fax (33) 443446.

Ministry of Civil Affairs: 71000 Sarajevo, Vojvode Putnika 3; tel. (33) 786822; fax (33) 786944.

Ministry of Finance and the Treasury of the Institutions of Bosnia and Herzegovina: 71000 Sarajevo.

Ministry of Foreign Affairs: 71000 Sarajevo, Musala 2; tel. (33) 663813; fax (33) 472188; e-mail info@mvp.gov.ba; internet www.mvp.gov.ba.

Ministry of Foreign Trade and Economic Relations: 71000 Sarajevo, trg Oktobra bb; tel. (33) 445750; fax (33) 655060.

Ministry of Human Rights and Refugees: Sarajevo.

Ministry of Security: Sarajevo.

Ministry of Transportation and Communications: Sarajevo.

THE FEDERATION OF BOSNIA AND HERZEGOVINA

Following an agreement reached in Washington, DC, the USA, by representatives of the Republic of Bosnia and Herzegovina and the 'Croat Republic of Herzeg-Bosna' (declared on 28 August 1993), the Federation of Bosnia and Herzegovina was formed on 31 March 1994. The President and Vice-President of the Federation were elected in May. The Federation was reorganized as one of the two constituent entities of Bosnia and Herzegovina in the peace agreements of 1995.

President: NIKO LOZANCIĆ (Croatian Democratic Community).

Vice-Presidents: SAHBAZ DZIKANOVIĆ (Party for Bosnia and Herzegovina), DEZNICA RADIVOJEVIĆ (Party of Democratic Action).

Government
(April 2003)

Prime Minister: Dr AHMET HADŽIPAŠIĆ.

Deputy Prime Minister and Minister of Finance: DRAGAN VRANKIĆ.

Deputy Prime Minister and Minister of Culture and Sports: GAVRILO GRAHOVAC.

Minister of Defence: MIROSLAV NIKOLIĆ.

Minister of Internal Affairs: MEVLUDIN HALILOVIĆ.

Minister of Justice: BORJANA KRIŠTO.

Minister of Energy, Mining and Industry: Dr IZET ŽIGIĆ.

Minister of Transport and Communications: NEDŽAC BRANKOVIĆ.

Minister of Labour and Social Policy: RADOVAN VIGNJEVIĆ.

Minister of Displaced Persons and Refugees: EDIN MUŠIĆ.

Minister of Issues of War Veterans and the Disabled: IBRAHIM NADAREVIĆ.

Minister of Health: TOMO LUČIĆ.

Minister of Education and Science: Dr ZIJAD PAŠIĆ.

Minister of Trade: MAID LJUBOVIĆ.

Minister of Urban Planning and the Environment: RAMIZ MEHMEDAGIĆ.

Minister of Agriculture, Water Management and Forestry: MARINKO BOŽIĆ.

Minister of Development, Entrepreneurship and Crafts: MLADEN ČABRILO.

Ministries

All ministries are based in Sarajevo.

Office of the President: 71000 Sarajevo; tel. and fax (33) 472618.

Office of the Prime Minister: 71000 Sarajevo, Alipašina 41; tel. (33) 663649; fax (33) 444718; e-mail ebicakcic@fbihvlada.gov.ba.

Ministry of Agriculture, Water Management and Forestry: 71000 Sarajevo, Titova 15; tel. (33) 443338; fax (33) 663659; e-mail fmpvs@bih.net.ba; internet www.fmpvs.gov.ba.

Ministry of Defence: 71000 Sarajevo, Hamdije Kresevljakovica 98; tel. (33) 664926; fax (33) 663785; e-mail cabmod@bih.net.ba.

Ministry of Displaced Persons and Refugees: 71000 Sarajevo, Alipašina 41/II; tel. (33) 663977; e-mail povratak@bih.net.ba.

Ministry of Education and Science: 71000 Sarajevo, Obala Maka Dizdara 2; tel. (33) 663691; fax (33) 664381; e-mail fmonks@bih.net.ba.

Ministry of Energy, Mining and Industry: 71000 Sarajevo, Alipašina 41; tel. (33) 663779; fax (33) 220619; e-mail fmeri-mo@bih.net.ba.

Ministry of Finance: 71000 Sarajevo, Mehmeda Spahe 5; tel. (33) 203147; fax (33) 203152; e-mail info@fmf.gov.ba; internet www.fmf.gov.ba.

Ministry of Health: 71000 Sarajevo, Titova 9; tel. and fax (33) 664245; e-mail moh@bih.net.ba.

Ministry of Internal Affairs: 71000 Sarajevo, Mehmeda Spahe 7; tel. (33) 667246; fax (33) 472976; internet www.fmup.ba.

Ministry of Issues of Veterans and the Disabled: 71000 Sarajevo, Alipašina 41; tel. (33) 212932; fax (33) 209333; e-mail fpurisevic@fbihvlada.gov.ba.

Ministry of Justice: 71000 Sarajevo, Valtera Perica 15; tel. and fax (33) 213151; e-mail zeljas@pris.gov.ba.

Ministry of Trade: Mostar, Kneza Domagoja 12; tel. (36) 310148; fax (36) 318684.

Ministry of Transport and Communications: 71000 Sarajevo, Alipašina 41; tel. (33) 668907; fax (33) 667866; internet www.fmpik.gov.ba.

Ministry of Urban Planning and the Environment: 71000 Sarajevo, Marsala Tita 9A; tel. and fax (33) 473124; e-mail fmpuio@fbihvlada.gov.ba.

SERB REPUBLIC (REPUBLIKA SRPSKA) OF BOSNIA AND HERZEGOVINA

On 27 March 1992 a 'Serb Republic of Bosnia and Herzegovina' was proclaimed. It was immediately declared illegal by the President of the State Presidency. The Republic comprised Serb-held areas of Bosnia and Herzegovina, including the 'Serb Autonomous Regions' of Eastern and Old Herzegovina, Bosanska Krajina, Romanija and Northern Bosnia. According to the peace treaty of December 1995, the Serb Republic constituted one of the two territorial entities comprising Bosnia and Herzegovina, with 49% of the country's area. It retained its own executive presidency, government and parliament (henceforth known as the National Assembly, see below).

President: DRAGAN CAVIĆ (Serbian Democratic Party).

Vice-President: ADIL OSMANOVIĆ (Party of Democratic Action).

Vice-President: IVAN TOMLJENOVIĆ (Serbian Democratic Party).

Government
(April 2003)

Prime Minister: DRAGAN MIKEREVIĆ.

Minister of the Interior: DZORAN DJERIĆ.

Minister of Justice: SAUD FILIPOVIĆ.

Minister of Education and Culture: Dr GOJKO SAVANOVIĆ.

Minister of Finance: SIMEUN VILENDECIĆ.

Minister of Defence: MILOVAN STANKOVIĆ.

Minister of Administration and Local Government: SLAVEN PEKIĆ.

Minister of Science and Technology: Dr DZEMAL KONOLIĆ.

Minister of Health and Social Welfare: Dr MARIN KVATERNIK.

Minister of the Economy, Energy and Development: MILAN BOGICEVIĆ.

Minister of Agriculture, Water Resources and Forestry: RODOLJUB TRKULJA.

Minister of Transport and Communications: DRAGAN SOLAJA.

Minister of Trade and Tourism: BORIS GASPAR.

Minister of Urban Planning, Housing and the Environment: MENSUR SEHAGIĆ.

Minister of War Veterans and Labour Affairs: MICO MICIĆ.

Minister of Foreign Economic Relations and Co-ordination: OMER BRANKOVIĆ.

Minister of Refugees and Displaced Persons: JASMIN SAMARDZIĆ.

Ministries

Office of the Prime Minister: 78000 Banja Luka; tel. (51) 331333; fax (51) 331332; e-mail kabinet@vladars.net.

Ministry of Administration and Local Government: 51000 Banja Luka, Vuka Karadžica 4; tel. (51) 331680; fax (51) 331681; e-mail muls@muls.vladars.net.

Ministry of Agriculture, Water Resources and Forestry: 76300 Bijelina, Milosa Obilica 51; tel. (55) 471412; fax (55) 472353; e-mail mps@mps.vladars.net.

Ministry of Defence: 51000 Banja Luka, Bana Lazarevica; tel. (51) 218823; fax (51) 300243; e-mail mo@mo.vladars.net.

Ministry of the Economy, Energy and Development: 51000 Banja Luka, Vuka Karadžica; tel. (51) 331710; fax (51) 331702; e-mail mer@mer.vladars.net.

Ministry of Education and Culture: 51000 Banja Luka, Vuka Karadžica 4; tel. (51) 331422; fax (51) 331423; e-mail mp@mp.vladars.net.

Ministry of Finance: 51000 Banja Luka, Vuka Karadžica 4; tel. (51) 331350; fax (51) 331351; e-mail mf@mf.vladars.net.

Ministry of Foreign Economic Relations and Co-ordination: 51000 Banja Luka, Vuka Karadžica 4; tel. (51) 331430; fax (51) 331436; e-mail meoi@meoi.vladars.net; internet www.vladars.net.

Ministry of Health and Social Welfare: 51000 Banja Luka, Zdrave Korde 8; tel. (51) 331600; fax (51) 331601; e-mail mzsz@mzsz.vladars.net.

Ministry of the Interior: 78000 Banja Luka, Jug Bogdana 108; tel. (51) 331100; e-mail mup@mup.vladars.net.

Ministry of Justice: 51000 Banja Luka, Vuka Karadžica 4; tel. (51) 331582; fax (51) 331593; e-mail mpr@mpr.vladars.net.

Ministry of Refugees and Displaced Persons: 51000 Banja Luka, Vuka Karadžica 4; tel. (51) 331470; fax (51) 331471; e-mail mirl@mirl.vladars.net.

Ministry of Science and Technology: 51000 Banja Luka, Vuka Karadžica 4; tel. (51) 331542; fax (51) 331548; e-mail mnk@mnk.vladars.net.

Ministry of Trade and Tourism: 51000 Banja Luka, Vuka Karadžica 4; tel. (51) 331523; fax (51) 331499; e-mail mtt@mtt.vladars.net.

Ministry of Transport and Communications: 51000 Banja Luka, Vuka Karadžica 4; tel. (51) 331611; fax (51) 331612; e-mail msv@msv.vladars.net.

Ministry of Urban Planning, Housing and the Environment: 51000 Banja Luka, trg Srpskih Junaka 4; tel. (51) 215511; fax (51) 215548; e-mail mgr@mgr.vladars.net.

Ministry of War Veterans and Labour Affairs: 51000 Banja Luka, Vuka Karadžica 4; tel. (51) 331651; fax (51) 331652; e-mail mpb@mpb.vladars.net.

Presidency and Legislature

PRESIDENCY OF BOSNIA AND HERZEGOVINA

Election, 5 October 2002

	Votes	% of votes
Bosniak Candidates		
Sulejman Tihić (Party of Democratic Action)	192,661	37.29
Haris Silajdžić (Party for Bosnia and Herzegovina)	179,726	34.79
Alija Behmen (Social Democratic Party of Bosnia and Herzegovina)	90,434	17.51
Fikret Abdić (Democratic People's Union)	21,164	4.10
Others	32,625	6.31
Croat Candidates		
Dragan Cović (Croatian Democratic Union of Bosnia and Herzegovina/Croatian Christian Democratic Union)	114,606	61.52

— *continued*

	Votes	% of votes
Mladen Ivanković-Lijanović (Economic Bloc HDU-For Progress)	32,411	17.40
Mijo Anić (New Croatian Initiative)	16,345	8.77
Stjepan Kljuić (Republican Party)	9,413	5.05
Others	13,516	7.26
Serb Candidates		
Mirko Sarović (Serbian Democratic Party of Bosnia and Herzegovina)	180,212	35.52
Nebojsa Radmanović (Party of Independent Social Democrats)	101,119	19.93
Ognjen Tadić (Serb Radical Party of the Serb Republic)	44,262	8.72
Desnica Radivojević (Party of Democratic Action)	41,667	8.21
Ranko Bakić (Party of the Social Democratic Centre)	41,228	8.13
Mirko Banjac (Alliance of National Renesans)	23,238	4.58
Grahovac Mladen (Social and Democratic Party of Bosnia and Herzegovina)	22,852	4.50
Dragutin Ilić (Socialist Party of the Serb Republic)	18,533	3.65
Milorad Djokić (Democratic National Alliance)	16,129	3.18
Others	18,174	3.58

PARLIAMENTARY ASSEMBLY

The General Framework Agreement, signed in December 1995, provided for a Parliamentary Assembly of Bosnia and Herzegovina, comprising two chambers, the House of Peoples and the House of Representatives. The House of Representatives has 42 deputies, of whom 28 are directly elected from the Federation and 14 from the Serb Republic for a two-year term.

Dom Naroda
(House of Peoples)

There are 15 deputies in the House of Peoples, of whom 10 are elected by the Federation legislature and five by the Serb Republic legislature.

Speaker: VELIMIR JUKIĆ.

Zastupnièki dom
(House of Representatives)

Speaker: SEFIĆ DZAFEROVIĆ.

General Election, 5 October 2002

Party	% of votes	Seats
Party of Democratic Action	21.9	10
Serbian Democratic Party of Bosnia and Herzegovina	14.0	5
Party for Bosnia and Herzegovina	10.5	6
Social Democratic Party of Bosnia and Herzegovina	10.4	4
Party of Independent Social Democrats	9.8	3
Croatian Democratic Community/Croatian Christian Democratic Union—Bosnia and Herzegovina	9.5	5
Party of Democratic Progress of the Serb Republic	4.6	2
Socialist Party of the Serb Republic	1.9	1
Bosnian Party	1.5	1
Others	15.9	5
Total	**100.0**	**42**

ZASTUPNIÈKI DOM FEDERACIJE
(House of Representatives of the Federation)

Speaker: SLAVKO MATIĆ.

General Election, 5 October 2002

Party	Votes	% of votes	Seats
Party of Democratic Action	234,923	32.7	32
Croatian Democratic Community/Croatian Christian Democratic Union—Bosnia and Herzegovina	113,197	15.8	16
Social Democratic Party of Bosnia and Herzegovina	111,668	15.6	15
Party for Bosnia and Herzegovina	109,843	15.3	15

Party — *continued*	Votes	% of votes	Seats
Bosnian Party	20,188	2.8	3
Pensioners' Party of Bosnia and Herzegovina	16,583	2.3	2
Democratic People's Union	16,363	2.3	2
Economic Bloc HDU-For Progress	14,130	2.0	2
New Croatian Initiative	13,967	2.0	2
Others	67,230	9.2	9
Total	**718,092**	**100.0**	**98**

PRESIDENCY OF THE SERB REPUBLIC (REPUBLIKA SRPSKA)

Election, 5 October 2002

Candidate	Votes	% of votes
Dragan Čavić (Serbian Democratic Party)	183,121	35.9
Milan Jelić (Party of Independent Social Democrats)	112,612	22.1
Dragan Mikerivić (Party of Democratic Progress of the Serb Republic)	39,978	7.8
Adil Osmanović (Party of Democratic Action)	34,129	6.7
Petar Cokić (Socialist Party of the Serb Republic)	27,137	5.3
Others	113,286	22.2
Total	**510,263**	**100.0**

NARODNA SKUPŠTINA REPUBLIKA SRPSKA
(National Assembly of the Serb Republic)

Speaker: DRAGAN KALINIĆ.

Election, 5 October 2002

Party	Votes	% of votes	Seats*
Serbian Democratic Party of Bosnia and Herzegovina	159,164	31.2	26
Party of Independent Social Democrats	111,226	21.8	19
Party of Democratic Progress of the Serb Republic	54,756	10.7	9
Party of Democratic Action	36,212	7.1	6
Serbian Radical Party of the Serb Republic	22,396	4.4	4
Socialist Party of the Serb Republic	21,502	4.2	3
Democratic People's League	29,375	4.0	3
Party for Bosnia and Herzegovina	18,624	3.7	4
Social Democratic Party of Bosnia and Herzegovina	17,227	3.4	3
Others	39,895	6.5	6
Total	**510,377**	**100.0**	**83**

*About three-quarters of deputies are elected in multi-seat constituencies, with the remainder selected through compensatory lists.

Political Organizations

Association of the Democratic Initiative of Sarajevo Serbs (Udruženje demokratske inicijative Srba iz Sarajeva): Sarajevo; f. 1996 to affirm and protect the rights of Serbs in Muslim-held Sarajevo; Chair. MAKSIM STANISIĆ.

Bosnia and Herzegovina Democratic Alternative: Sarajevo; f. 1990; Chair. MUHAMED CENGIĆ.

Bosnian Party (Bosanska Stranka): Tuzla, Stari Grad 9; tel. and fax (35) 251035; e-mail boss.bh@delta.com.ba; Chair. MIRNES AJANOVIĆ.

Bosnian Rights Party of Bosnia and Herzegovina (Bosanska Stranka Prava Bosne i Hercegovine—BSP BiH): Sarajevo.

Civic Democratic Party (Gradjanska Demokratska Stranka): Sarajevo, Maršala Tita 9A; tel. (33) 666621; fax (33) 213435; Chair. IBRAHIM SPAHIĆ.

Croatian Christian Democratic Union—Bosnia and Herzegovina (Hrvatska Kršćanska Demokratska Unija—Bosne i Hercegovine): 80240 Tomislavgrad; tel. and fax (80) 52051; e-mail bihdem@posluh.hr; internet www.posluh.hr; Pres. ANTE PASALIĆ.

Croatian Democratic Community: f. May 2002 by mems of the CDU—BH; Leader MIRO GRABOVAC-TITAN.

Croatian Democratic Union of Bosnia and Herzegovina (CDU —BH) (Hrvatska Demokratska Zajednica Bosne i Hercegovine— HDZ BiH): 71000 Sarajevo, Titova 16; tel. (33) 471213; internet www .hdzbih.org; f. 1990; affiliate of the CDU in Croatia; adopted new party statute July 2000; Croat nationalist party; Chair. ANTE JELAVIĆ; Gen.-Sec. MARKO TOKIĆ.

Croatian Peasants' Party (Hrvatska Seljacka Stranka): Sarajevo, Radićeva 4; tel. and fax (33) 441987; affiliated to Croatian Peasants' Party in Croatia; Chair. ILIJA SIMIĆ.

Croatian Rights Party (Hrvatska Stranka Prava): Ljubuški, Fra Petra Bakule 2; tel. and fax (36) 834917; contested 1996 elections; nationalist; Pres. ZDRAVKO HRSTIĆ.

Democratic National Alliance: Banja Luka; f. 2000, by fmr mems of the Serb National Alliance (q.v.); Chair. DRAGAN KOSTIĆ.

Democratic Party for Banja Luka and Krajina: Banja Luka; f. 1997, by fmr mems of Serb Radical Party of the Serb Republic (q.v.); Chair. NIKOLA SPIRIĆ.

Democratic Party of Pensioners of Bosnia and Herzegovina (Demokratska Stranka Penzionera BiH): Tuzla, 6 Basanske 51; tel. (61) 151390; e-mail dsp.bih@bih.net.ba; Pres. ALOJZ KNEZOVIĆ.

Democratic Party of the Serb Republic (Demokratska Stranka Republike Srpske): Banja Luka.

Democratic Patriotic Bloc of the Serb Republic (Demokratski Patriotski Blok Republike Srpske): contested 1996 elections; Chair. PREDRAG RADIĆ.

Democratic People's League (Demokratski Narodni Savez).

Democratic People's Union (Narodna Demokratska Zajednica— NDZ): Velika Kladuša, D. Pucara Starog 23; tel. and fax (77) 770407; e-mail dnzbih@bih.net.ba; f. 1996; Chair. FIKRET ABDIĆ.

Democratic Socialist Party: Bijeljina; f. 2000, by fmr mems of Socialist Party of the Bosnian Serb Republic (q.v.); member of the Accord Coalition; Pres. NEBOJSA RADMANOVIĆ.

Eastern Bosnian Muslim Party (Istočnobosanska Muslimanska Stranka): Sarajevo; f. 1997; Chair. IBRAN MUSTAFIĆ.

Homeland Party: Banja Luka; f. 1996 by fmr members of Serb Democratic Union—Homeland Front; nationalist; Chair. PREDRAG RASIĆ.

Liberal Democratic Party (LDP) (Liberalna Demokratska Stranka): Sarajevo, Maršala Tita 9A; tel. (33) 664540; e-mail liberali@bih.net.ba; f. 2000 by merger of Liberal Party of Bosnia and Herzegovina and the Liberal Bosniak Organization; Chair. RASIM KADIĆ.

Liberal Social Party of Bosnia and Herzegovina (Liberalna Socijalna Partija—LSP): Sarajevo; f. 1998; centre party; Chair. HIDAJET REPOVAĆ; Deputy Chair. JADRANKA MIKIĆ, NAMIK TERZIMEHEC, VINKO CURO.

Muslim Democratic Alliance (Muslimanski Demokratski Savez —MDS): Bihać; f. 1994; seeks to promote equality between the ethnic groups of Bosnia and Herzegovina.

New Croatian Initiative (Nova Hrvatska Inicijativa): Sarajevo, Sime Milutinovića 2/II; tel. (33) 214602; fax (33) 214603; e-mail nhi@ nhi.ba; f. 1998 by fmr mems of the Croatian Democratic Union of Bosnia and Herzegovina (q.v.); Chair. KREŠIMIR ZUBAK.

New Radical Party: member of the People's Alliance for Peace and Progress electoral coalition; Chair. GORAN ZMIJANAĆ.

Party for Bosnia and Herzegovina: Sarajevo, Maršala Tita 7A; tel. and fax (33) 214417; f. 1996; integrationist; member of the Coalition for a Single and Democratic Bosnia electoral alliance; Pres. SAFET HALILOVIĆ.

Party of Democratic Action (PDA) (Stranka Demokratske Akcije —SDA): 71000 Sarajevo, Mehmeda Spahe 14; tel. (33) 667274; fax (33) 650429; e-mail sda@bih.net.ba; internet www.sda.ba; f. 1990; leading Muslim nationalist party; has brs in Yugoslavia; member of the Coalition for a Unified and Democratic Bosnia electoral alliance; Chair. SULEJMAN TIHIĆ; Sec.-Gen. MIRSAD CEMAN.

Party of Democratic Development: Bijeljina; f. 2001; Chair. RADOVAN SIMIĆ.

Party of Democratic Progress (PDP): Banja Luka; Chair. MLADEN IVANIĆ.

Party of Economic Prosperity (Stranka Privednog Prosperita— SPP): Zenica; f. 1996; Chair. PANE SKRBIĆ; Sec.-Gen. SAFET RED-ZEPAGIĆ.

Party of Independent Social Democrats (Stranka Nezavisnih Socijaldemokrata—SNSD): Banja Luka; e-mail snsd@inecco.net; internet www.snsd.org; member of the Accord Coalition; Chair. MILORAD DODIK; Sec.-Gen. SLAVKO MITROVIĆ.

Party of Independent Social Democrats of the Serb Republic: f. 1999; breakaway faction of the Party of Independent Social Democrats; Leader BRANE MILJUS.

Party of Serb Unity (Stranka Srpskog Jedinstva): Bijeljina; extreme nationalist; Chair. (vacant).

Patriotic Party of Bosnia and Herzegovina (Patriotska Stranka BiH): Sarajevo, Hakije Kulenovića 9; tel. and fax (33) 216881; Pres. SEFER HALILOVIĆ.

Pensioners' Party of the Bosnia and Herzegovina Federation (Stranka Penzionera Federacije BiH).

Pensioners' Party of the Serb Republic (Penzionerska Stranka Republike Srpske).

People's Party of the Serb Republic (Narodna Stranka Republicka Srpska): Leader MILAN TRBOJEVIĆ.

Radical Party of the Serb Republic (Radikalna Stranka Republika Srpska).

Republican Party (Republikanska Stranka BiH): Sarajevo, Antuna Hangija 35; tel. and fax (33) 834917; e-mail republ94@bih .net.ba; integrationist; Chair. STJEPAN KLJUIĆ.

Serbian Civic Council: Sarajevo; anti-nationalist; org. of Serbs in the Federation of Bosnia and Herzegovina; Chair. Dr MIRKO PEJA-NOVIĆ.

Serbian Democratic Party of Bosnia and Herzegovina (SDP) (Srpska Demokratska Stranka Bosne i Hercegovine—SDS BiH): c/o Pale, National Assembly of the Serb Republic; f. 1990; allied to SDP of Croatia; Serb nationalist party; member of the Serb Coalition of the Serb Republic electoral alliance; Chair. DRAGAN KALINIĆ.

Serb Democratic Union—Homeland Front: nationalist; Pres. BOŽIDAR BOJANIĆ.

Serb National Alliance (SNA) (Srpski Narodni Savez—SNS): Banja Luka; f. 1997; member of the Accord Coalition; Chair. Dr BILJANA PLAVŠIĆ.

Serb Patriotic Party (Srpska Patriotska Stranka): contested 1996 elections; Chair. STOJAN ZUPLJANIN; Vice-Chair. PETAR DJAKOVIĆ.

Serb Party of Krajina (Srpska Stranka Krajina—SSK): Banja Luka; f. 1996; regional party in favour of the creation of clear borders between nations; Pres. PREDRAG LAZAREVIĆ; Chair. of Exec. Cttee DJORDJE UMICEVIĆ.

Serbian People's Party of the Serb Republic (Srpski Narodni Savez): moderate; Pres. BILJANA PLAVŠIĆ.

Serb Radical Party of the Serb Republic (Srpska Radikalna Stranka Srpske Republike—SRS SR): internet www.srpskastrars .org; br. of SRS in Serbia; member of the Serb Coalition of the Serb Republic; Chair. RADISLAV KANJERIĆ; Chair. of Exec. Bd MIRKO BLAGO-JEVIĆ; Gen. Sec. OGNJEN TADIĆ.

Social Alliance: c/o 71000 Sarajevo, trg Dure Pucara bb; fmr communist mass organization; allies of Social Democratic Party; left-wing.

Social Democratic Party of Bosnia and Herzegovina (Socijal-demokratska Partija BiH—SDP BiH): 71000 Sarajevo, Branislava Durdeva 8; tel. (33) 203667; fax (33) 210942; e-mail sdp@ sdpbih-centar.com; internet www.sdpbih-centar.com; f. 1908; merged with Social Democrats of Bosnia and Herzegovina; Chair. Dr ZLATKO LAGUMDŽIJA; Sec.-Gen. KARLO FILIPOVIĆ.

Social Liberal Party: Banja Luka; reintegrationist; member of the People's Alliance for Peace and Progress electoral coalition; merged with the Party of Independent Social Democrats in Dec. 1999; Chair. MIODRAG ZIVANOVIĆ; Gen. Sec. MILAN TUKIĆ.

Socialist Party of the Serb Republic (Socijalistička partija za Republiku Srpsku—SPRS): Kralja Petra 1 Karadorćevića 103/1; tel. and fax (51) 231643; e-mail sprs@inecco.net; f. 1993; br. of the Socialist Party of Serbia; member of the Accord Coalition until Feb. 2000; Chair. ŽIVKO RADIŠIĆ; Sec.-Gen. ŽELJKO MIRJANIĆ; 40,000 mems.

Yugoslav Left of the Serb Republic: Bijeljina; f. 1996; branch of pro-Communist party based in Belgrade (Yugoslavia); Pres. MILORAD IVOSEVIĆ.

Diplomatic Representation

EMBASSIES IN BOSNIA AND HERZEGOVINA

Austria: 71000 Sarajevo, Džidžikovac 7; tel. (33) 279400; fax (33) 668339; Ambassador GERHARD JANDL.

Belgium: Sarajevo, Abdesthana 4; tel. (33) 233772; fax (33) 233774; Ambassador ROBERT DEVRIESE.

Bulgaria: Sarajevo, Trampina 14/11; tel. (33) 668191; fax (33) 668182; Ambassador GEORGI DOJCEV JURUKOV.

Canada: Sarajevo, Logavina 7; tel. (33) 447900; fax (33) 447901; Ambassador SAM HANSON.

China, People's Republic: Sarajevo, Braće Begića 17; tel. (33) 215102; fax (33) 215108; Ambassador LI SHUYUAN.

Croatia: 71000 Sarajevo, Mehmeda Spahe 20; tel. (33) 444330; fax (33) 472434; Ambassador Dr JOSIP VRBOŠIĆ.

Czech Republic: 71000 Sarajevo, Potoklinica 6; tel. (33) 447525; fax (33) 447526; Ambassador JIŘÍ KUDĚLA.

Denmark: 71000 Sarajevo, Splitska 9; tel. (33) 665901; fax (33) 665902; e-mail danamb@bih.net.ba; Ambassador JOHANNES DAHL-HANSEN.

Egypt: Sarajevo, Nurudina Gackića 58; tel. (33) 666498; fax (33) 666499; e-mail eg.em.so@bih.net.ba; Ambassador Dr SALAH RIYAD EL ASHRY.

France: 71000 Sarajevo, Kapetanović Ljubušaka 18; tel. (33) 668149; fax (33) 668103; e-mail france-1@bih.net.ba; internet www.ambafrance.com.ba; Ambassador BERNARD BAJOLET.

Germany: 71000 Sarajevo, ul. Buka 11-13; tel. (33) 275000; fax (33) 652978; e-mail debosara@bih.net.ba; Ambassador HANS JOCHEN PETERS.

Greece: Sarajevo, Obala Maka Dizdara I; tel. (33) 203516; fax (33) 203512; e-mail greekemb@bih.net.ba; Ambassador MIHAIL KOUKAKIS.

Holy See: Pehlivanuša 9, 71000 Sarajevo, Nadbiskupa Josipa Stadlera 5; tel. (33) 207847; fax (33) 207863; e-mail nunbosnia@lsinter.net; Apostolic Nuncio Mgr GIUSEPPE LEANZA.

Hungary: 71000 Sarajevo, Satvetbega Basagicá 58/A; tel. (33) 238512; fax (33) 218685; e-mail hungcons@bih.net.ba; Ambassador ISTVÁN VÁRGA.

Iran: 71000 Sarajevo, Obala Maka Dizdara 6; tel. (33) 650210; fax (33) 663910; e-mail iries1@bih.net.ba; Ambassador SEYED HOMAYOUN AMIR KHALILI.

Italy: 71000 Sarajevo, Čekaluša 39; tel. (33) 218022; fax (33) 659368; e-mail ambsara@bih.net.ba; Ambassador SABA D'ELIA.

Japan: Sarajevo, Mula Mustafe Bašeskije 2; tel. (33) 209580; fax (33) 209583; Chargé d'affaires a.i. MITSUNORI NAMBA.

Libya: 71000 Sarajevo, Tahtali sokak 17; tel. (33) 657534; fax (33) 663620; Head of People's Bureau IBRAHIM ALI TAGIURI.

Macedonia, former Yugoslav republic: 71000 Sarajevo, Emerika Bluma 23; tel. and fax (33) 206004; Chargé d'affaires a.i. STOJAN RUMENOVSKI.

Malaysia: 71000 Sarajevo, Trnovska 6; tel. (33) 201578; fax (33) 667713; e-mail malsrjevo@bih.net.ba; Ambassador ZAKARIA BIN SULONG.

Malta: 71000 Sarajevo, Mula Mustafe Bašeskije 12; tel. and fax (33) 668632; e-mail lor.tac@tiscalinet.it; Ambassador Dr LORENZO TACCHELLA.

Netherlands: 71000 Sarajevo, Obala Kulina Bana 4/2; tel. (33) 668422; fax (33) 668423; e-mail nlgovsar@bih.net.ba; internet www.netherlandsembassy.ba; Ambassador ROBERT BOSSCHER.

Norway: 71000 Sarajevo, Ferhadija 20; tel. (33) 666373; fax (33) 666505; Ambassador HENRIK OFSTAD.

Pakistan: 71000 Sarajevo, Emerika Bluma 17; tel. (33) 211836; fax (33) 211837; e-mail parep@bih.net.ba; Ambassador TARIQ AZIZUDDIN.

Poland: 71000 Sarajevo, Emerika Bluma 27; tel. (33) 201142; fax (33) 233796; Ambassador Dr LESZEK HENSEL.

Romania: 71000 Sarajevo, Tahtali sokak 13–15; tel. (33) 207447; fax (33) 668940; e-mail rumunska@bih.net.ba; Ambassador PETRE CATRINCIUC.

Russia: 71000 Sarajevo, Urjan Dedina 93–95; tel. (33) 668147; fax (33) 668148; Ambassador ALEXANDER S. GRISHCHENKO.

Saudi Arabia: 71000 Sarajevo, Koševo 44; tel. (33) 211861; fax (33) 211744; Ambassador FAHD BIN ABDUL-MUHSIN AL-ZEIDA.

Serbia and Montenegro: 71000 Sarajevo, Obala Maka Dizdara 3A; tel. (33) 260080; fax (33) 221469; e-mail yugoamba@bih.net.ba; Ambassador STANIMIR VUKIĆEVIĆ.

Slovenia: 71000 Sarajevo, Bendbaša 7; tel. (33) 271260; fax (33) 271270; Chargé d'affaires a.i. VOJKO KUZMAN.

Spain: 71000 Sarajevo, Čekaluša 16; tel. (33) 278560; fax (33) 208758; Ambassador RAFAEL VALLE GARAGORRI.

Sweden: 71000 Sarajevo, Ferhadija 20; tel. (33) 276030; fax (33) 276060; e-mail ambassaden.sarajevo@foreign.ministry.se; Ambassador ANDREAS MÖLLANDER.

Switzerland: 71000 Sarajevo, Josipa Štadlera 15; tel. (33) 275850; fax (33) 665246; e-mail swissemb@bih.net.ba; Ambassador HEIDI TAGLIAVINI.

Turkey: 71000 Sarajevo, Hamdije Kreševljakovića 5; tel. and fax (33) 472437; e-mail turksa@bih.net.ba; Ambassador AHMET KAMIL EROZAN.

United Kingdom: 71000 Sarajevo, Tina Ujevića 8; tel. (33) 444429; fax (33) 666131; e-mail britemb@bih.net.ba; internet www.britishembassy.ba; Ambassador IAN CAMERON CLIFF.

USA: 71000 Sarajevo, Alipašina 43; tel. (33) 659969; fax (33) 445700; internet www.usis.com.ba; Ambassador CLIFFORD BOND.

Judicial System

The Constitutional Court of Bosnia and Herzegovina has three international judges (selected by the President of the European Court of Human Rights) and six national judges (of whom four are elected by the House of Representatives of the Federation and two by the National Assembly of the Serb Republic). The Constitutional Court has competence regarding constitutional matters in both entities, but there are separate judicial systems in the Bosnian Federation and the Serb Republic. The judicial system of each entity comprises a Constitutional Court, a Supreme Court and local district courts. The State Court of Bosnia and Herzegovina, which was officially inaugurated on 27 January 2003, represents the country's highest judicial organ. The eight judges of the Court were appointed by the Bosnian High Representative.

State Court of Bosnia and Herzegovina: Sarajevo; inaugurated 27 Jan. 2003; state-level court and highest judicial organ; comprises eight judges and four prosecutors; Pres. MARTIN RAGUZ.

Constitutional Court of the Republic of Bosnia and Herzegovina: 71000 Sarajevo, Reisa Dzemaludina Causevića 6/III; tel. (33) 251210; fax (33) 663784; e-mail info@ccbh.ba; internet www.ccbh.ba; nine mems; elected for a five-year term; Pres. DUSAN KALEMBER.

Constitutional Court of the Serb Republic: Banja Luka; internet www.ustavnisud.org; eight mems; Pres. RAJKO KUZMANOVIĆ; Sec. MIODRAG SIMOVIĆ.

Supreme Court of the Federation of Bosnia and Herzegovina: 71000 Sarajevo, Valtera Perića 15; tel. (33) 664754; Pres. VENCESLAV ILIĆ.

Supreme Court of the Serb Republic: Banja Luka; Pres. JOVO ROSIĆ.

Office of the Federal Prosecutor: 71000 Sarajevo, Valtera Perića 11; tel. (33) 214990; internet www.tuzilastvo-rs.org; Federal Prosecutor SULJO BABIĆ.

Religion

Bosnia and Herzegovina has a diversity of religious allegiances. Just over one-half of the inhabitants are nominally Christian, but these are divided between the Serbian Orthodox Church and the Roman Catholic Church. The dominant single religion is Islam. The Reis-ul-ulema, the head of the Muslims in the territory comprising the former Yugoslavia, is resident in Sarajevo. Most of the Muslims are ethnic Muslims or Bosniaks (Slavs who converted to Islam under the Ottomans). There are, however, some ethnic Albanian and Turkish Muslims. Virtually all are adherents of the Sunni persuasion. There is a small Jewish community; since 1966, however, there has been no rabbi in the community. In June 1997 an agreement to establish an inter-religious council was signed by the leaders of the Roman Catholic, Serbian Orthodox, Jewish and Islamic communities.

ISLAM

Islamic Community of the Sarajevo Region: 71000 Sarajevo; Pres. of Massahat SALIH EFENDIJA COLAKOVIĆ; Mufti of Bosnia and Herzegovina Hadži MUSTAFA TIRIĆ; Reis-ul-ulema MUSTAFA EFENDI CERIĆ.

CHRISTIANITY

The Serbian Orthodox Church

Metropolitan of Dabrobosna: NICOLAJ, c/o Serbian Patriarchate, 11001 Belgrade, Kralja Petra 5, POB 182, Yugoslavia.

The Roman Catholic Church

For ecclesiastical purposes, Bosnia and Herzegovina comprises one archdiocese and three dioceses. At 31 December 2000 adherents of the Roman Catholic Church represented about 16.1% of the total population.

Bishops' Conference

(Biskupska Konferencija Bosne i Hercegovine)
Nadbiskupski Ordinarijat, 71000 Sarajevo, Kaptol 7; tel. (33) 664784; fax (33) 472178.

f. 1995; Pres. Cardinal VINKO PULJIĆ (Archbishop of Vrhbosna-Sarajevo); Vice-Pres. Rt Rev. FRANJO KOMARICA (Bishop of Banja Luka).

Archbishop of Vrhbosna-Sarajevo: Cardinal VINKO PULJIĆ, Nadbiskupski Ordinarijat Vrhbosanski, 71000 Sarajevo, Kaptol 7; tel. (33) 664784; fax (33) 472178.

JUDAISM

Jewish Community of the Sarajevo Region: 71000 Sarajevo, Hamdije Kreševljekoviće 59; tel. (33) 663472; fax (33) 663473; e-mail la-bene@open.net.ba; internet www.soros.org.ba; Pres. JAKOB FINCI.

The Press

In 2000 five daily newspapers (with a total circulation of about 100,000 copies per day) and six principal weekly, or bi-weekly, newspapers were published.

PRINCIPAL DAILIES

Dnevni Avaz: 71000 Sarajevo; e-mail redakacija@avaz.ba; internet www.avaz.ba.

Glas Srpski: Banja Luka; Serb Republic government newspaper; Editor-in-Chief TOMO MARIĆ; Deputy Editor-in-Chief NIKOLA GUZIJAN.

Nezavisne novine (The Independent): 51000 Banja Luka, Krajiskih brigada 8; tel. (51) 213515; fax (51) 213341; e-mail nnovine@blic.net; f. 1995; Editor-in-Chief ŽELJKO KOPANJA.

Oslobodjenje (Liberation): 71000 Sarajevo, Džemala Bijedića 185; tel. (33) 454144; fax (33) 460982; e-mail info@obodjenje.net; internet www.oslobodjenje.com.ba; f. 1943; morning; Editor MEHMED HALILOVIĆ; circ. 56,000.

Večernje novine: 71000 Sarajevo, Pruščakova St 13; tel. (33) 664874; fax (33) 664875; f. 1964; special edition published daily in Serb Republic; privatized in May 2000; Editor-in-Chief AHMED BOSNIĆ; Dir IRFAN LJEVAKOVIĆ; circ. 15,000.

WEEKLY NEWSPAPERS

Glas Srpski: Banja Luka; Serb Republic government newspaper; Editor-in-Chief TOMO MARIĆ; Deputy Editor-in-Chief NIKOLA GUZIJAN.

Hrvatska Rijec: 71000 Sarajevo; e-mail h_rijec@bih.net.ba; internet www.hrvatska-rijec.com; Croat weekly.

Ljiljan: 71000 Sarajevo, Sime Milutinovica Sarajlije 12; tel. (33) 664895; fax (33) 664697; e-mail ljiljan@bih.net.ba; internet www.nippljiljan.com; official newspaper of the PDA; Chair. MENSUR BRDAR; Editor-in-Chief DŽEMALUDIN LATIĆ.

Slobodna Bosna: 71000 Sarajevo, Muhameda Kantardžića 3; tel. (33) 444041; fax (33) 444895; e-mail slobo-bosna@zamir-sa.ztn.atc.org; Editor SENAD AVDIĆ.

PERIODICALS

Alternativa: Doboj; f. 1996; every two weeks; Editor-in-Chief PAVLE STANISIĆ; Deputy Editor-in-Chief ŽIVKO SAVKOVIĆ; Dir SLOBODAN BABIĆ; circ. 5,000.

Dani: 71000 Sarajevo, Skenderija 31A; e-mail bhdani@bih.net.ba; internet www.bhdani.com; independent; political and cultural; 4 a week; Editor-in-Chief SENAD PECANIN.

Reporter: 78000 Banja Luka, Grčka 20; tel. (51) 221220; fax (51) 221228; e-mail rep@inecco.net; internet www.reportermagazin.com; f. 1996; independent; Editor PERICA VUCINIĆ.

Svijet: Sarajevo; illustrated; weekly; Editor-in-Chief JELA JEVREMOVIĆ; circ. 115,000.

Zadrugar: Sarajevo, Omladinska 1; f. 1945; weekly; journal for farmers; Editor-in-Chief FADIL ADEMOVIĆ; circ. 34,000.

NEWS AGENCIES

Alternativna Informativna Mreza (AIM) (Alternative Information Network): Sarajevo; exchange of information between independent media in the former Yugoslavia; non-commercial and dependent on financial support from abroad.

BH Press: 71000 Sarajevo, Branilaca grada 21/II; tel. (33) 663389; e-mail bhpress@bih.net.ba; internet www.bihpress.com; state news agency.

HABENA: 88000 Mostar, Kralja Tvrtka 9; tel. (36) 319222; fax (36) 319422; e-mail habena@habena.ba; f. 1993; Bosnian Croat news agency; Man. MARKO DRAGIĆ; Editor-in-Chief ZDRAVKO NIKIĆ.

Novinska Agencija Bosne i Hercegovine: 71000 Sarajevo, Branilaca grada 21; tel. (33) 445336; fax (33) 445312; e-mail bhpres@bih.net.ba; internet www.bihpress.ba.

ONASA (Oslobodjenje News Agency): Sarajevo, Hasana Kikića 3; tel. (33) 276580; fax (33) 276599; e-mail onasa@onasa.com.ba; internet www.onasa.com.ba; f. 1994; Gen. Man. MEHMED HUSIĆ.

SNRA: Banja Luka; Bosnian Serb news agency; Man. Dir DRAGAN DAVIDOVIĆ.

Publishers

Novi Glas: 78000 Banja Luka, Borisa Kidriča 1; tel. (51) 12766; fax (51) 12758; general literature; Dir MIODRAG ŽIVANOVIĆ.

Public Company for Newspaper Publication Organization, Official Gazette of Bosnia and Herzegovina: Sarajevo, Magribija 3; tel. (33) 663470; e-mail slist@bih.net.ba; internet www.sllist.ba; publishes legislation for official newspapers, and books and other material from the field of newspaper-publication activities.

Student's Printing House of the University of Sarajevo: Sarajevo, Obala Kulina Bana 7; tel. and fax (33) 526138; university textbooks; Dir EMIR KADRIĆ; Chief Editor DRAGAN S. MARKOVIĆ.

Svjetlost: 71000 Sarajevo, Petra Preradovića 3; tel. (33) 212144; fax (33) 272352; f. 1945; textbooks and literature; Dir SAVO ZIROJEVIĆ.

Veselin Masleša (Sarajevo Publishing): 71000 Sarajevo, Obala Kulina Bana 4; tel. (33) 521476; fax (33) 272369; f. 1950; school and university textbooks, general literature; Dir RADOSLAV MIJATOVIĆ.

PUBLISHERS' ASSOCIATION

Association of Publishers and Booksellers of Bosnia and Herzegovina: 71000 Sarajevo, M. Tita brigade 9A; tel. and fax (33) 207945; Pres. IBRAHIM SPAHIĆ; Gen. Sec. DRAGAN S. MARKOVIĆ.

Broadcasting and Communications

TELECOMMUNICATIONS

HPT Mostar: 88000 Mostar, Kneza Branimira; tel. and fax (36) 395555; internet www.hpt-mostar.ba; scheduled for privatization in 2002; Dir of Man. Bd FARUK KUCIĆ.

Bosnia-Herzegovina Post: 71000 Sarajevo, Obala Kulina bana 8; tel. (33) 252606; fax (33) 252711; internet www.bhp.ba; f. 1992; Gen. Dir KASIM DZAJIĆ.

Telekom Srpske: Banja Luka, Kralja Petra I, Karadjordjevica 61A; tel. (51) 211150; fax (51) 240101; e-mail ts.office@telekom-rs.com; Deputy Dir-Gen. MILE BAJALICA.

BROADCASTING

In the late 1990s broadcasting in Bosnia and Herzegovina was largely controlled by the three nationalist parties: the Party of Democratic Action (PDA); the Croatian Democratic Union of Bosnia and Herzegovina (CDU—BH); and the Serbian Democratic Party (SDP). There were, however, a number of locally based independent radio and television stations. In May 1996 two such organizations, NTV Zetel and ITV Hayat (both television companies), had created, with the Mostar and Tuzla branches of Radio-Televizija Bosne i Hercegovine, the TVIN-TV International Network. This was to be open to media and correspondents from the Bosniak–Croat Federation and the Serb Republic, in accordance with the aims of the Dayton accords.

Regulatory Authority

At the decision of the High Representative for Bosnia and Herzegovina, the Communication Regulatory Authority was established in 2001 through the merger of the former Independent Media Commission, which had regulated the broadcasting sector, and the Telecommunication Regulatory Agency, responsible for telecommunications. The new regulatory body was to have jurisdiction over both broadcasting and telecommunications as an independent state agency.

Communication Regulatory Agency (CRA): Sarajevo, Vilsonovo setaliste 10; tel. (33) 250600; fax (33) 713080; e-mail info@cra.ba; internet www.cra.ba; f. 2001.

Radio

Croat Radio Herzeg-Bosna: Mostar; Dir TOMISLAV MAZALO; Editor-in-Chief IVAN KRISTIĆ.

Pan Radio: Bijegina, Brace Subotića 3; tel. and fax (55) 402661; e-mail panorama@bn.rstel.net.

Radio Fern: 71000 Sarajevo, Mula Mustafe Baseskije 6; tel. (33) 668052; e-mail radio.fern@ekis.com.ba.

Radio Kameleon: 75000 Tuzla, Milana Jovanovića 6; tel. and fax (35) 250055; e-mail kameleon@kameleon.ba; internet www.kameleon.ba; f. 1992; independent radio station; Gen. Dir ZLATKO BERBIĆ.

Radio Q: 71300 Visoko, ul. Hazima Dedića 13; tel. and fax (32) 735280; e-mail radioq@radioq.co.ba; internet www.radioq.co.ba.

Radio-Televizija (RTV) Bosne i Hercegovine: 71000 Sarajevo, Bulevar Meše Selimovića 12; tel. (33) 455124; fax (33) 455104; f. 1945; 4 radio programmes; broadcasts in Serbo-Croat; Dir-Gen. JOHN SHEARER; Dir of Radio NADJA PAŠIĆ; Editor-in-Chief ESAD CEROVIĆ.

Radio-Televizija Republika Srpska (RTRS): Banja Luka; Editor-in-Chief DRAGOLJUB MILANOVIĆ.

Radio ZID: Sarajevo; f. Dec. 1992; commenced broadcasts March 1993; independent radio station; cultural and educative programmes; Chair. ZDRAVKO GREBO; Editor-in-Chief VLADO AZINOVIĆ.

Serb Radio Banja Luka: Banja Luka; f. 1997 as independent radio station following breakaway from Serb Radio and Television (q.v.); eight-mem. editorial council; Chair. RADOMIR NESKOVIĆ.

Studio 99: Sarajevo; f. 1991; independent radio station; broadcast political information during the civil conflict; Editor-in-Chief ADIL KULENOVIĆ; Editor of Programmes ZORAN ILIĆ.

Television

Alternativna Televizija Informisanje: 78000 Banja Luka, Karadjordjeva 2; tel. and fax (51) 311904; e-mail atv@inecco.net; Dir NATASA TESANOVIC.

Independent TV Tuzla: Tuzla; f. 1991 by a group of journalists; promotes the values of democratic society.

Independent TV Zetel: Stara carsija bb, 72000 Zenica; tel. (32) 410552; fax (32) 417317; e-mail zetel@bih.net.ba; f. 1992; transmits 13 hours per day to Zenica and surrounding area; cultural, political, educative and sports programmes; Dir ZELJKO LINCNER; Editor TAIB BAJARAMOVIĆ.

ITV Hayat: Sarajevo; e-mail itvhayat@bih.net.ba; internet www.ntvhayat.com; Muslim influences; broadcasts 18 hours daily; Dir and Editor-in-Chief ELVIR SVRAKIĆ.

Konjic Radio-TV: Konjic; fmrly a public-service station, sold in April 2000; Owners ERMIN MUSTAFIC, ENES RATKUSIĆ.

Open Broadcast Network: 71000 Sarajevo, Bulevar Mese Selimovića 18; tel. (33) 460550; fax (33) 460547.

Radio-Televizija (RTV) Bosne i Hercegovine: 71000 Sarajevo, Bulevar Meše Selimovića 12; tel. (33) 652333; fax (33) 461569; e-mail radio@rtvbih.ba; internet www.rtvbih.ba; f. 1969; 2 TV programmes; incorporated news channel (BHTV 1) in 2002; Dir-Gen. JOHN SHEARER; Dir of TV AMILA OMERSOFTIĆ; Editor-in-Chief ESAD CEROVIĆ.

Radio-Televizija Republika Srpska (RTRS): Banja Luka; Editor-in-Chief DRAGOLJUB MILANOVIĆ.

Finance

(d.d. = dioničko društvo (joint-stock company); cap. = capital; res = reserves; dep. = deposits; m. = million; amounts in konvertibilna marka (KM or convertible marka) unless otherwise stated; brs = branches)

BANKING

In 2001 there were some 69 banks operating in Bosnia and Herzegovina, of which 50 were in the Federation and 19 in the Serb Republic.

Central Bank

Central Bank of Bosnia and Herzegovina: 71000 Sarajevo, 25 Maršala Tita; tel. (33) 664548; fax (33) 201517; e-mail contact@cbbh.gov.ba; internet www.cbbh.gov.ba; replaced the National Bank of the Federation of Bosnia and Herzegovina, and the National Bank of the Republika Srpska, which ceased monetary operations in August 1997; cap. 25.0m., res 96.5m., dep. 785.6m. (2001); Gov. PETER NICHOLL.

Selected Banks

Balkan Investment Bank a.d.: 78000 Banja Luka, Krajških Brigada 2; tel. (51) 216285; fax (51) 211445; e-mail contact@balkaninvestment.com; internet www.balkaninvestment.com; f. 2000; cap. 5m., dep. 8.7m. (Dec. 2000); Chair. VALDAS VARANAVICIUS.

Bobar Banka a.d.: 76300 Bijeljina, Filipa Višnjica 211; tel. (55) 211153; fax (55) 401863; e-mail bobarbank@rstel.net; internet www.bobar.com; f. 1998; cap. 10.0m., res 0.1m., dep. 4.0m. (2001); Gen. Man. DRAGAN RADUMILO.

Central Profit Banka d.d. Sarajevo: Sarajeva, Zelenih Beretki 24; tel. (33) 663307; fax (33) 238340; e-mail international@cpb.ba; internet www.cpb.ba; f. 1919; cap. 10.7m., res 4.1m., dep. 261.6m. (2001); Gen. Man. FEHIM F. KAPIDŽIĆ; 13 brs.

Ekvator Banka a.d.: 78000 Banja Luka, POB 59, Marije Bursac 2; tel. and fax (51) 211885; e-mail ekvator@inecco.net; internet www.ekvator.com; f. 1996; cap. and res 6.3m., dep. 8.1m. (1999); Pres. DJORDJE DAVIDOVIĆ.

Federation Investment Bank: 71000 Sarajevo, Igmanska 1; tel. (33) 277900; fax (33) 668952; e-mail info@ibf-bih.com; internet www.ibf-bih.com; total assets 130.4m. (2000); Gen. Man. ASIM OMANIĆ.

Hercegovačka Banka d.d. Mostar: 88000 Mostar, Kneza Domagoja b.b. tel. (36) 320555; fax (36) 324771; e-mail herbank@hercegovacka-banka.com; internet www.hercegovacka-banka.com; f. 1997; cap. 15.6m., res 0.6m., dep. 103.9m. (1999); Chair. FRANKA EREŠ.

Investiciono-Komercijalna Banka d.d., Zenica: 72000 Zenica, POB 62, trg Samoupravljača 1; tel. (32) 401804; fax (32) 417022; e-mail ikbsejo@ikbze.com.ba; internet www.ikbze.com.ba; f. 1990; cap. 10.7m., res 7.0m., dep. 76.4m. (Dec. 2000); Gen. Man. UZEIR FETIĆ.

Nova Banka a.d., Bijeljina: Bijeljina, ul. Svetog Save br. 46; tel. (55) 401409; fax (55) 401410; e-mail office@novabanka.com; internet www.novabanka.com; f. 1992 as Export Banka a.d. Bijeljina; name changed 1999; cap. 10.9m., res 2.0m., dep. 42.9m. (2001); Pres. MIHAJLO VIDIĆ; Chair. DJURO STANOJEVIĆ.

Privredna Banka a.d. Doboj: 74000 Doboj, Svetog Save 1; tel. (53) 241657; fax (53) 241662; e-mail pbaddo@inecco.net; f. 1992; cap. 11.4m., res 2.6m., dep. 5.5m. (2001); Pres. RADMILA STOJNIĆ; Chair. MIODRAG KUDIĆ.

Privredna Banka Gradiška d.d.: Gradiška, Vidovdanska bb; tel. (51) 813333; fax (51) 813205; e-mail pbgrad@pbanka-gradiska.com; internet www.pbanka-gradisko.com; f. 1953, registered as independent bank since 1992; privatization commenced in early 2001; cap. 8.1m., res 2.1m., dep. 55.0m. (Dec. 1999); Pres. MIRA STRAZIVUK.

Privredna Banka Sarajevo a.d.: Pale, ul. Srpskih Ratnika br. 14; tel. (33) 664852; fax (33) 663807; f. 1970 by merger of five banks; Man. Dir MOMČILO MANDIĆ.

Privredna Banka Sarajevo d.d., Sarajevo: 71000 Sarajevo, Alipašina 6; tel. (33) 209804; fax (33) 210360; e-mail pbscba22@bih.net.ba; f. 1971; cap. 19.1m., res 9.1m., dep. 45.0m. (Dec. 1999); Chair. ALIJA ĆELIKOVI; 10 brs.

Raiffeisen Bank HPB Mostar: 88000 Mostar, Kneza Domagoja b.b. tel. (36) 398301; fax (36) 317010; e-mail hpb_hb@int.tel.hr; f. 1994 as Hrvatska Postanska Banka d.d. Mostar; name changed 2001; cap. 10.0m., res 0.3m., dep. 41.0m. (2000); Pres. MICHAEL MÜLLER.

Turkish Ziraat Bank Bosnia d.d.: 71000 Sarajevo, Ferhadija 295; tel. (33) 230619; fax (33) 441902; e-mail ziraat@bih.net.ba; internet www.ziraatbosnia.com; f. 1996; cap. 25.0m., res 7.8m., dep. 30.8m. (Dec. 2001); Chair. SUPHI KABADAYL.

Tuzlanska Banka d.d. Tuzla: 75000 Tuzla, Maršala Tita 34; tel. (35) 259259; fax (35) 250596; e-mail tuzbank@bih.net.ba; internet www.tuzbank.ba; f. 1990; cap. 12.0m., dep. 144.5m., res 12.5m. (2001); Pres. MUHAMED HAJDARBEGOVIĆ; Chair. NUSRET SOFTIĆ.

Union Banka d.d. Sarajevo: 71000 Sarajevo, Dubrovačka 6; tel. (33) 664470; fax (33) 219201; e-mail unionban@bih.net.ba; f. 1955; cap. 34.3m., res 16.4m., dep. 71.0m. (2001); Gen. Man. SULEJMAN HODŽIĆ.

VB Banka a.d. Banja Luka: 78000 Banja Luka, Milana Tepica 4; tel. (51) 221610; fax (51) 221623; e-mail info@vbbanka.com; internet www.vbbanka.com; f. 1998; cap. 13.0m., res 0.2m., dep. 32.0m. (2001); Gen. Man. RADOVAN BAJIĆ.

Volksbank BH d.d.: 71000 Sarajevo, Fra Andjela Zvizdovića 1; tel. (33) 483265; fax (33) 263832; e-mail info@volksbank.ba; internet www.volksbank.ba; cap. 10.0m., dep. 25.0m. (2000); Gen. Man. Dr PETER SETZER.

Zagrebačka Banka BH d.d.: 88000 Mostar, Kardinala Štepinca b.b. tel. (36) 312121; fax (36) 312129; e-mail zababh@zaba.hr; internet www.zaba.ba; f. 1992 as Hrvatska Banka d.d. Mostar; name changed 2000; cap. 34.2m., res 8.1m., dep. 499.1m. (Dec. 2001); Pres. DAMIR ODAK; Gen. Man. BERISLAV KUTLE.

Banking Agencies

Agency for Banking of the Federation of Bosnia and Herzegovina (Agencija za Bankarstvo Federacije Bosne i Hercegovine): 71000 Sarajevo; f. 1996; Dir ZLATKO BARŠ.

Banking Agency of Republika Srpska: Banja Luka, Marije Bursac 4; tel. (58) 218111; fax (58) 216675.

STOCK EXCHANGES

Banja Luka Stock Exchange: Banja Luka; f. March 2002.

Sarajevo Stock Exchange: Sarajevo; f. April 2002; Dir Akif Ser-darević.

Trade and Industry

GOVERNMENT AGENCIES

Foreign Investment Promotion Agency: 71000 Sarajevo, Branilaca Sarajeva 21; tel. (33) 278000; fax (33) 278081; e-mail fipa@fipa.gov.ba; internet www.fipa.gov.ba; f. July 1999; provides services to foreign investors.

Privatization Agency of the Federation of Bosnia and Herzegovina: Sarajevo, Alipašina 41; tel. (33) 212884; fax (33) 212883; e-mail apfbih@bih.net.ba; internet www.apf.com.ba; Dir Adnad Mujagić.

Republika Srpska Directorate for Privatization: 51000 Banja Luka, Mladena Stoganovića 4; tel. (51) 308311; fax (51) 311245; e-mail dip@inecco.net; internet www.rsprivatizacija.com; Dir Borislav Obradović.

Securities Commission of the Federation of Bosnia and Herzegovina: 71000 Sarajevo, Ćemaluša 9; tel. (33) 665897; fax (33) 211655; e-mail komvp@bih.net.ba; internet www.komvp.gov.ba; f. 1999; Pres. Edib Basić.

DEVELOPMENT ORGANIZATIONS

Bosnia and Herzegovina Local Economic Development Agency: Travnik, Zenjak 21B; tel. (32) 511877; fax (32) 818495; e-mail lebeda@bih.net.ba; internet www.ilsleda.com.

Directorate for the Reconstruction and Development of Sarajevo: Sarajevo, Hamdije Kresevljakovice 19; tel. (33) 650563; fax (33) 470887.

Federal Development Planning Institute: Sarajevo, Alipašina 41; tel. (33) 667272; fax (33) 212625; e-mail fzzprfbh@bih.net.ba; internet www.fzzpr.gov.ba; Dir Prof. Neset Muminagić.

CHAMBERS OF COMMERCE

Chamber of Economy of Bosnia and Herzegovina: 71000 Sarajevo, Branislava Durdeva 10; tel. (33) 663631; fax (33) 663632; e-mail cis@komorabih.com; internet www.komorabih.com; Pres. Mahir Hadžiahmetović.

Chamber of Economy of the Federation of Bosnia and Herzegovina: 71000 Sarajevo, Branislava Durdeva 10; tel. (33) 217782; fax (33) 217783; Pres. Avdo Rapa.

Chamber of Economy of Sarajevo Canton: 71000 Sarajevo, Hamdije Kreševljakovića 3; tel. and fax (33) 664597; e-mail webmaster@pksa.com.ba; internet www.pksa.com.ba; Pres. Kemal Grebo.

UTILITIES

Electricity

Elektroprivreda of Bosnia and Herzegovina Ltd: 88000 Mostar, ul. Mile Budaka 106a; tel. and fax (36) 310847; fax (36) 317157; e-mail ephzhb@tel.net.ba; internet www.ephzhb.com; generation, transmission and distribution of electric energy; Dir-Gen. Matan Žarić.

Gas

Bosnia and Herzegovina Gas (BH—Gas): 71000 Sarajevo, Hamdije Cemerlića 2; tel. (33) 279000; fax (33) 231621; e-mail development@bh-gas.ba; internet www.bh-gas.ba; f. 1997; Man. Dir Huso Hadžidedić.

TRADE UNIONS

Independent Union of Professional Journalists: Obala Kulina Bana, 2/III Sarajevo; tel. (33) 670813; fax (33) 534495; e-mail nupnbih@bih.net.ba; f. 1994; Pres. Mehmed Husić.

Trade Unions of Bosnia and Herzegovina: Sarajevo, Obala Kulina Bana 1; tel. (33) 664872.

Trade Unions of Republika Srpska: Banja Luka, Srpska 32; tel. (51) 310711; fax (51) 304241.

Transport

RAILWAYS

At the beginning of the 1990s the railway system consisted of some 1,030 km of track, of which 75% was electrified. Much of the system was damaged or destroyed during the civil war, but in July 1996 the Sarajevo–Mostar service was restored and in 1997 the Tuzla–Doboj service reopened. The Tuzla–Brčko service resumed in 2002. Following the outbreak of hostilities, the state railway company was divided into three regional state-owned companies: the Bosnia and Herzegovina Railway Company (ZBH), based in Sarajevo; the Herzeg-Bosnia Railway Company (ZHB), based in the Croat-majority part of the Federation; and the Serb Republic Railway and Transport Company (ZTP), based in Banja Luka. In 1998 an overarching organization, the Bosnia and Herzegovina Railways Public Corpn, was established. In March 2000 the Presidents of Bosnia and Herzegovina and Croatia signed an agreement to recommence railway traffic between the two countries. By the end of that year post-war reconstruction assistance had resulted in the restoration of about 85% of track; however, regular train services between the Federation and the Serb Republic remained suspended.

ROADS

The transport infrastructure in Bosnia and Herzegovina was badly damaged during the civil war of 1992–95. Some 35% of the country's roads and 40% of its bridges were affected by the conflict. A new Transportation Corporation was established (with its headquarters in Sarajevo), under the terms of the Dayton accords, in order to organize and operate roads, ports and railways on the territory of the two entities. The agreement also provided for the construction of a new road linking the Goražde enclave, in the east of Bosnia and Herzegovina, with the rest of the Federation. There were 21,846 km of roads in Bosnia and Herzegovina in 2001, of which 14,020 km were paved. In 1997 an internationally-funded project to rehabilitate and rebuild the road network in the Serb Republic commenced. In June 2000 the Governments of Bosnia and Herzegovina and Croatia signed an accord on the construction of the Ploče–Budapest corridor, linking the Croatian seaport with the Hungarian capital through Bosnian territory.

c/o Federation Ministry of Transport and Communications: 71000 Sarajevo, Alipašina 41; tel. (33) 668907; fax (33) 667866; internet www.fmpik.gov.ba.

Republic Directorate for Roads: Banja Luka, Vase Pelagica 10; tel. (51) 309061; fax (51) 308316; Dir Nemanja Vasić.

CIVIL AVIATION

The country has an international airport at Sarajevo, and three smaller civil airports, at Tuzla, Banja Luka and Mostar. Civil aviation was severely disrupted by the 1992–95 civil war. Commercial flights resumed to Sarajevo in August 1996, to Banja Luka in November 1997 and to Mostar in July 1998. In June 1997 it was announced that a new airport at Dubrave, near Tuzla, was to be built.

Department of Civil Aviation of Bosnia and Herzegovina: 33000 Sarajevo, Envera Sehovića 2; tel. (33) 653016; fax (33) 653008; e-mail bhdca@bhdca.gov.ba; internet www.bhdca.gov.ba.

Air Bosna: 71000 Sarajevo, Cemalasa 6; tel. (33) 667953; fax (33) 650974; e-mail marketing@airbosna.ba; internet www.airbosna.ba; f. 1994; 51% state-owned; regular services to Croatia, Germany, Slovenia, Sweden, Turkey and Serbia and Montenegro; Man. Dir Omer Kulić.

Air Srpska: 78000 Banja Luka, Veselina Maslese 28; tel. (51) 212806; fax (51) 211348; f. 1999; flights from Banja Luka airport to Yugoslavia and Switzerland.

Mast Air: 78000 Banja Luka; tel. (51) 304551; flights from Tuzla airport to Hungary, Italy, Slovenia and Turkey.

RS Airlines: Pale; f. 1997; flights from Banja Luka airport to Bulgaria, Greece, Hungary, Romania, Serbia and Montenegro and Russia; Dir Jovan Tintor.

Tourism

Following the adverse affects of the civil conflict of 1992–95, the tourism sector recovered rapidly. Tourist arrivals increased from 89,000 in 1999 to an estimated 110,000 in 2000, when receipts from tourism were estimated at US $17m.

BOTSWANA

Introductory Survey

Location, Climate, Language, Religion, Flag, Capital

The Republic of Botswana is a land-locked country in southern Africa, with South Africa to the south and east, Zimbabwe to the north-east and Namibia to the west and north. A short section of the northern frontier adjoins Zambia. The climate is generally sub-tropical, with hot summers. Annual rainfall averages about 457 mm (18 ins), varying from 635 mm (25 ins) in the north to 228 mm (9 ins) or less in the western Kalahari desert. The country is largely near-desert, and most of its inhabitants live along the eastern border, close to the main railway line. English is the official language, and Setswana the national language. Most of the population follow traditional animist beliefs, but several Christian churches are also represented. The national flag (proportions 2 by 3) consists of a central horizontal stripe of black, edged with white, between two blue stripes. The capital is Gaborone.

Recent History

Botswana was formerly Bechuanaland, which became a British protectorate, at the request of the local rulers, in 1885. It was administered as one of the High Commission Territories in southern Africa, the others being the colony of Basutoland (now Lesotho) and the protectorate of Swaziland. The British Act of Parliament that established the Union of South Africa in 1910 also allowed for the inclusion in South Africa of the three High Commission Territories, on condition that the local inhabitants were consulted. Until 1960 successive South African Governments asked for the transfer of the three territories, but the native chiefs always objected to such a scheme.

Within Bechuanaland, gradual progress was made towards self-government, mainly through nominated advisory bodies. A new Constitution was introduced in December 1960, and a Legislative Council (partly elected, partly appointed) first met in June 1961. Bechuanaland was made independent of High Commission rule in September 1963, and the office of High Commissioner was abolished in August 1964. The seat of government was transferred from Mafeking (now Mafikeng), in South Africa, to Gaberones (now Gaborone) in February 1965. On 1 March 1965 internal self-government was achieved, and the territory's first direct election, for a Legislative Assembly, was held on the basis of universal adult suffrage. Of the Assembly's 31 seats, 28 were won by the Bechuanaland Democratic Party (BDP or Domkrag), founded in 1962. The leader of the BDP, Seretse Khama, was sworn in as the territory's first Prime Minister. Bechuanaland became the independent Republic of Botswana, within the Commonwealth, on 30 September 1966, with Sir Seretse Khama (as he had become) taking office as the country's first President, while the Legislative Assembly was renamed the National Assembly. The BDP, restyled the Botswana Democratic Party at independence, won elections to the National Assembly, with little opposition, in 1969, 1974 and 1979.

Khama died in July 1980, and was succeeded as President by Dr Quett Masire (later Sir Ketumile Masire), hitherto Vice-President and Minister of Finance. Following elections to the National Assembly in September 1984, at which the BDP again achieved a decisive victory, Masire was re-elected President by the legislature. However, the BDP fared badly in local government elections, which were held simultaneously with the parliamentary elections, apparently reflecting discontent at the country's high level of unemployment. An unprecedented outbreak of rioting, in March 1987, was similarly attributed by observers to popular dissatisfaction with the Government as a result of increasing unemployment. The Government accused the principal opposition party, the Botswana National Front (BNF), of fomenting the unrest. At a referendum in September a large majority endorsed amendments to the electoral system, as defined by the Constitution, although the BNF boycotted the vote.

Despite widespread labour unrest during 1989, in October the BDP received 65% of the votes cast at a general election to the National Assembly, winning 27 of the 30 elective seats (the remaining three seats were won by the BNF), and the new legislature re-elected Masire for a third term as President. In November 1991 the Government dismissed some 12,000 members of public-service trade unions who had been campaigning for wage increases.

In March 1992 the Vice-President and Chairman of the BDP, Peter Mmusi, resigned as Vice-President and Minister of Local Government and Lands, while the party's Secretary-General, Daniel Kwelagobe, resigned as Minister of Agriculture, having been accused of corruption involving the illegal transfer of land. Festus Mogae, the Minister of Finance and Development Planning, was appointed as the new Vice-President. In June Mmusi and Kwelagobe were suspended from the Central Committee of the BDP; both were, however, re-elected to their former positions within the party in July 1993. In July 1995 the Minister of Presidential Affairs and Public Administration, Ponatshego Kedikilwe, was elected Chairman of the BDP—a post that had remained vacant since the death of Mmusi in October 1994.

For the general election of 15 October 1994 the number of directly elective seats in the National Assembly was increased to 40. The BDP, which received 53.1% of the votes cast, won 26 seats, while the BNF, which obtained 37.7% of the votes, increased its representation to 13 seats. More than 70% of registered voters participated in the election. In general, the BDP retained its dominance in rural areas, while the BNF received strong support in urban constituencies. The National Assembly re-elected Masire to the presidency on 17 October. Kwelagobe was included in the new Cabinet appointed one week later, having been acquitted by the High Court in connection with the allegations made in 1992.

In August 1997 the National Assembly formally adopted a constitutional amendment restricting the presidential mandate to two terms of office and providing for the automatic succession to the presidency of the Vice-President, in the event of the death or resignation of the President. In September a national referendum endorsed further revisions, lowering the age of eligibility to vote from 21 to 18 years and providing for the establishment of an independent electoral commission. In November Masire announced his intention to retire from politics in March 1998; in accordance with the amended Constitution, Vice-President Mogae was to assume the presidency pending the holding of elections in 1999. Mogae was inaugurated as President on 1 April 1998 and subsequently appointed a new Cabinet, in which the only new minister was Lt-Gen. Seretse Ian Khama, son of Botswana's first President (the late Sir Seretse Khama) and hitherto Commander of the Botswana Defence Force (BDF). Khama received the portfolio of presidential affairs and public administration, and was later designated as Mogae's Vice-President, subject to his election to the National Assembly. Kedikilwe, who had been favoured for the vice-presidency by certain prominent members of the BDP leadership, was appointed Minister of Finance and Development Planning. Khama was elected to the National Assembly in July, and was sworn in as Vice-President in the same month.

Meanwhile, hostility between Kenneth Koma, the leader of the BNF, and his deputy, Michael Dingake, had led to a split in the party. At the BNF's annual congress in April 1998 relations deteriorated over the issue of dissident members who had been expelled from the party. Koma, supported by the dissidents, ordered the expulsion from the party of central committee members. His actions were upheld by the party's constitution, and ultimately on appeal by the High Court. In June members of the dissolved central committee formed the Botswana Congress Party (BCP), under the leadership of Dingake. The BCP was declared the official opposition in mid-July, after 11 of the BNF's 13 deputies joined the new party.

In August 1999 President Mogae dissolved the National Assembly in preparation for the holding of a general election in mid-October. In early September, to the surprise and consternation of the opposition parties, Mogae declared a state of emergency, the purpose of which was to reconvene the legislature in order to amend the Electoral Act, thus permitting the Independent Electoral Commission (IEC) to complete its work and prevent the disenfranchisement of around 60,000 Batswana. The general election was held, as scheduled, on 16

October, despite opposition demands that it be postponed owing to the Government's apparent disregard for correct electoral procedure. The BDP, which received 57.2% of the votes, increased its representation in the National Assembly from 26 to 33 seats, while the number of seats held by the BNF (with 26.0% of the votes) fell significantly to only six seats, and the BCP (having received 11.9%) obtained just one seat. The IEC declared that the election had been conducted in a free and fair manner and recorded that 77.3% of the electorate had participated in the polls. Mogae was re-elected to the presidency by the new National Assembly on 20 October and announced the formation of a new Cabinet the following day.

In December 1999 Mogae provoked outrage among the opposition parties, and tension within the ruling party, when he granted Vice-President Khama an unprecedented one-year sabbatical leave, effective from 1 January 2000. In July Kedikilwe resigned as Minister of Education, a position he had held since October 1999. Khama resumed his duties as Vice-President in September 2000, and a minor cabinet reshuffle was effected.

The Government's attempts to relocate Basarwa (San/Bushmen) people from their homeland within the Central Kalahari Game Reserve to a new settlement outside the Reserve provoked international concern in 1996–2001. It was claimed that officials had forced many Bushmen to move by disconnecting water supplies and threatening military intervention; 2,160 Bushmen had been resettled by mid-2001, according to reports. At the end of January 2002 the Government withdrew services to the remaining Bushmen living in the Reserve (estimated to number 500–700), in accordance with a decision announced in August 2001. A legal appeal brought to halt the process of relocation and to return hunting rights to the Bushmen was rejected on a technicality in April 2002. Fewer than 100 Bushmen were estimated to be left in the Reserve at the end of that year. Meanwhile, in August a delegation from the European Union accused the Botswana Government of providing false information about the number of Bushmen remaining in the Reserve, and of failing to fulfil their human rights requirements, including the supply of fresh water. In October the Goverment awarded some US $0.3m in compensation to more than 3,000 Basarwa who had been removed from the Reserve. In late 2002 the Government was criticized for granting mining companies concessions to explore for diamonds in the Reserve.

Meanwhile, in November 2001 a number of changes to the structure and conditions of service of the judiciary were approved in a national referendum, although less than 5% of the electorate were reported to have participated in the vote. Ethnic tensions arose over a clause providing for an increase in the retirement age for judges. Pitso Ya Batswana, a Tswana nationalist group, claimed that this proposal was evidence of the over-representation in the judiciary and other professions of the Kalanga people, who constituted approximately 10% of the population, and that the referendum represented an attempt by the Kalanga community to advance its own interests. However, the Kalanga, together with numerous other ethnic groups, were not recognized in the Constitution as one of the eight tribes with the right to be represented in the House of Chiefs, Botswana's second legislative house. The Government had established a constitutional commission in July 2000 to investigate allegations of discrimination against minority groups, including the Kalanga, Wayeyi and Basarwa. On the basis of the recommendations of this commission, in December 2001 the Government presented a number of draft constitutional amendments. Under the proposals, the House of Chiefs would be renamed the Ntlo ya Dikgosi and its membership increased from 15 to 33, comprising 30 members elected by senior tribal authorities and three specially appointed members. Elections to the Ntlo ya Dikgosi would be held every five years. In April 2002 the draft amendments were revised to allow the eight paramount chiefs to retain their *ex-officio* status in the chamber.

In June 2002 the National Assembly approved legislation providing for an expansion in its directly elected membership from 40 to 57, with effect from the next general election (due in 2004), and a gradual increase in both the number of ministries, from 12 to 16, and in the number of assistant ministers, from four to eight. In September these reforms were partly implemented in a cabinet reshuffle, with the creation of two new ministries, the Ministry of Communications, Science and Technology, and the Ministry of Conservation, Wildlife and Tourism, and the appointment of two additional assistant ministers. In early 2003 the BNF, BCP and the Botswana Alliance Movement

initiated negotiations aimed at forming an alliance ahead of the 2004 general election. Meanwhile, dissidents from the BNF, led by Koma, who had been expelled from the party in 2002, formed a new party, the New Democratic Front.

Although, as one of the 'front-line' states, Botswana did not have diplomatic links with the apartheid regime in South Africa, it was (and remains) heavily dependent on its neighbour for trade and communications. Botswana is a member of the Southern African Development Community (SADC, see p. 311), which superseded the Southern African Development Co-ordination Conference (SADCC), in 1992. The SADC, of which South Africa became a member in 1994, has its headquarters in Gaborone.

From independence, it was the Botswana Government's stated policy not to permit any guerrilla groups to operate from its territory. Relations with South Africa deteriorated in May 1984, when Masire accused the South African Government of exerting pressure on Botswana to sign a non-aggression pact, aimed at preventing the alleged use of Botswana's territory by guerrilla forces of the (then outlawed) African National Congress of South Africa (ANC). In the second half of the 1980s South African forces launched a number of raids on alleged ANC bases in Botswana, causing several deaths. Owing to Botswana's vulnerable position, however, the Government did not commit itself to the imposition of economic sanctions against South Africa when this was recommended by the SADCC in August 1986. In 1988–89 Botswana took action against the extension onto its territory of hostilities between South African government and anti-apartheid forces. Two South African commandos, who had allegedly opened fire on Botswana security forces while engaged in a raid, were sentenced to 10 years' imprisonment, nine South Africans were expelled for 'security reasons', and five ANC members were convicted on firearms charges. It was reported in August 1989 that the South African army had erected an electrified fence along a 24-km section of the South Africa–Botswana border, in order to halt the reputed threat of guerrilla infiltration into South Africa via Botswana.

With the dismantling of apartheid in the first half of the 1990s, Botswana's relations with South Africa improved markedly, and full diplomatic relations were established in June 1994. In August it was announced that the 'front-line' states were to form a political and security wing within the SADC. In April 1999 Botswana and South Africa signed a bilateral agreement on the administrative merger of their adjacent national parks. The Kgalagadi Transfrontier Park was formally opened in May 2000 by President Mogae and President Thabo Mbeki of South Africa. In November the inaugural meeting of the Botswana-South Africa joint permanent commission on defence and security was held in Gaborone.

In August 1998 Botswana participated in attempts made by the SADC to resolve a political crisis in Lesotho, where opposition parties were demanding the annulment of elections held in May of that year. Following an increase in civil and military unrest and reports of an imminent coup attempt, on 22 September 200–300 members of the BDF and 600 South African troops entered Lesotho, in response to requests from the Prime Minister, Pakalitha Mosisili. The SADC-sponsored military intervention encountered strong resistance from dissident members of the Lesotho armed forces and civilians, but after three days of heavy fighting and looting, in which more than 70 people died, relative calm was restored to the devastated capital, Maseru. In early 1999 the role of the BDF troops in Lesotho was the subject of debate in Botswana itself, and in May all the remaining SADC forces were withdrawn. A group of instructors from Botswana and South Africa remained in Lesotho, in an advisory and training capacity, until May 2000.

In 1983, following allegations that armed dissidents from Zimbabwe were being harboured among Zimbabwean refugees encamped in Botswana, the Botswana Government agreed to impose stricter restrictions on the refugees. In May Botswana and Zimbabwe established full diplomatic relations. The first meeting of the Botswana-Zimbabwe joint commission for co-operation was held in October 1984. A new influx of refugees, following the Zimbabwe general election in July 1985, threatened to strain relations between the two countries. In April 1989 about 600 Zimbabwean refugees remained in Botswana, prompting the Botswana Government to announce that refugee status for Zimbabwean nationals was to be revoked; by September almost all former Zimbabwean refugees had reportedly left Botswana. In the mid-1990s, however, the Government expressed concern at the growing number of illegal immigrants in the country, the majority of whom were from Zimbabwe; of more than 40,000 illegal immigrants repatriated during 1995, more than 14,000 were Zimbabwean. Relations between the two countries were again strained in 2000, when Zimbabwe's construction of a railway line from Bulawayo (its second largest city) to Beitbridge (on the border with South Africa) severely reduced transit freight traffic on Botswana Railways. In late 2001 and early 2002 Mogae participated in SADC efforts to encourage the Zimbabwean President, Robert Mugabe, to conduct his Government's land reform programme within the rule of law. Following the controversial re-election of Mugabe to the Zimbabwean presidency in March 2002, the Botswana Government became more critical of government policy in Zimbabwe, as the economic crisis in that country prompted an influx of immigrants into Botswana, with many entering illegally.

Following Namibian independence, in July 1990 it was announced that a commission for bilateral co-operation was to be established by Botswana and Namibia. In 1992, however, a border dispute developed between the two countries regarding their rival territorial claims over a small island (Sedudu-Kasikili) in the Chobe river. In early 1995 the two states agreed to present the issue of the demarcation of their joint border for arbitration at the International Court of Justice (ICJ, in The Hague, Netherlands), and in February 1996 the two countries signed an agreement committing themselves in advance to the Court's eventual judgment. Meanwhile, Namibia appealed to Botswana to remove its troops—stated by the Botswana authorities to be anti-poaching patrols—and national flag from the island. In the following month the two countries agreed joint measures aimed at deterring smuggling and illegal border crossings. Namibia's decision to construct a pipeline to take water from the Okavango river caused some concern in Botswana in 1996–97. (The river feeds the Okavango delta, which is an important habitat for Botswana's varied wildlife, and therefore of great importance to the tourist industry.) In early 1997 it was reported that Namibia had been angered by Botswana's erection of a fence along Namibia's Caprivi Strip, which separates the two countries to the north; Botswana insisted, however, that the fence was simply a measure to control the spread of livestock diseases. In January 1998 an emergency meeting of the Botswana-Namibia joint commission on defence and security was held to discuss ownership of another island (Situngu) in the Chobe river, following allegations by Namibia that the BDF had occupied the island and was stealing crops planted by Namibian farmers resident there. In December 1999 the ICJ granted Botswana control over Sedudu-Kasikili. A joint technical commission was subsequently established to consider other demarcation disputes between Botswana and Namibia.

In late 1998 relations between the two countries were further strained by the arrival in Botswana of more than 300 refugees (a number of whom were reportedly leading political dissidents) from the Caprivi Strip in Namibia. President Mogae rejected Namibian demands for the extradition of the refugees, whose number had increased to more than 2,000 by early 1999. In May, however, a formal agreement was signed by the two Governments, according to which prominent dissidents among the refugees would be allowed to leave Botswana for another country and an amnesty would be extended to other refugees returning to Namibia. In response to a request from the Namibian Government, in September 2001 the Gaborone Magistrates' Court ruled in favour of the extradition of a group of 13 suspected Caprivi separatists who were wanted to stand trial for alleged high treason; however, this decision was reportedly reversed by Botswana's High Court in December 2002. Meanwhile, in April 2002 officials from Botswana and Namibia concluded a tripartite agreement with the office of the UN High Commissioner for Refugees on the voluntary repatriation of Namibian refugees in Botswana. Between August and October around 1,000 refugees were reported to have been repatriated, leaving some 1,300 in Botswana.

Government

Legislative power is vested in Parliament, consisting of the President and the National Assembly. The National Assembly is elected for a term of five years and comprises 40 members directly elected by universal adult suffrage, together with four members who are elected by the National Assembly from a list of candidates submitted by the President; the President and the Attorney-General are also *ex-officio* members of the Assembly. In June 2002 the National Assembly approved legislation providing for an expansion in its directly elected membership from 40 to 57, with effect from the next general election. Executive power is vested in the President, elected by the Assembly for its duration. The President is restricted to two terms of office. He appoints and leads a Cabinet, which is responsible to the Assembly. The President has powers to delay implementation of legislation for six months, and certain matters also have to be referred to the 15-member House of Chiefs for approval, although this advisory body has no power of veto. In December 2001 the Government presented a number of draft constitutional amendments relating to the House of Chiefs. Under the proposals, the House of Chiefs would be renamed the Ntlo ya Dikgosi and its membership increased from 15 to 33, comprising 30 members elected by senior tribal authorities and three specially appointed members; elections to the Ntlo ya Dikgosi would be held every five years; the measures remained under consideration in early 2003. Local government is effected through nine district councils and four town councils.

Defence

Military service is voluntary. In August 2002 the total strength of the Botswana Defence Force was some 9,000, comprising an army of 8,500 and an air force of 500. In addition, there was a paramilitary police force of 1,000. There are plans to enlarge the strength of the army to 10,000 men. Projected budgetary expenditure on defence for 2002 was P1,720m.

Economic Affairs

In 2001, according to estimates by the World Bank, Botswana's gross national income (GNI), measured at average 1999–2001 prices, was US $5,863m., equivalent to $3,630 per head (or $8,810 on an international purchasing-power parity basis). During 1990–2001, it was estimated, the population increased by an average of 2.2% per year, while gross domestic product (GDP) per head increased, in real terms, by an average of 3.1% per year. Overall GDP increased, in real terms, at an average annual rate of 5.3% in 1990–2001; growth in 2001 was 5.7%.

Agriculture (including hunting, forestry and fishing) contributed 2.6% of GDP in 2000/01, according to provisional figures, and engaged 15.6% of the employed labour force in 1996. The principal agricultural activity is cattle-raising (principally beef production), which supports about one-half of the population and contributes more than 80% of agricultural GDP. As a member of the African, Caribbean and Pacific (ACP) group of states and a signatory to successive Lomé Conventions, Botswana has traditionally enjoyed preferential trade relations with the European Union (EU), including a quota to supply 18,910 metric tons of beef per year; however, under the Cotonou Agreement, which was concluded in mid-2000, the quota was to be phased out by 2007, when Botswana and the other ACP states were to establish reciprocal trade arrangements with the EU in order to achieve compatibility with the rules of the World Trade Organization. The main subsistence crops are vegetables, pulses and roots and tubers, although Botswana is not self-sufficient in basic foods. Agricultural GDP increased at an average annual rate of 1.8% in 1990–2001; growth in 2001 was 6.0%.

Industry (including mining, manufacturing, construction and power) engaged 25.6% of the employed labour force in 1996 and, according to provisional figures, provided 50.0% of GDP in 2000/01. Industrial GDP increased at an average annual rate of 3.1% in 1990–2001; growth in 2001 was 6.0%.

Mining contributed 37.0% of GDP in 2000/01, according to provisional figures, although the sector engaged only 4.3% of the employed labour force in 1996. In terms of value, Botswana is the world's largest producer of diamonds (which accounted for 84.5% of export earnings in 2001, according to provisional figures); copper-nickel matte and soda ash are also exported. In addition, coal, gold, cobalt and salt are mined, and there are known reserves of plutonium, asbestos, chromite, fluorspar, iron, manganese, potash, silver, talc and uranium. In 1998 a new minerals code included measures to encourage non-diamond mining projects. According to provisional official figures, the GDP of the mining sector increased, in real terms, at an average annual rate of 5.1% in 1991/92–2000/01; growth in 2000/01 was 19.6%.

Manufacturing engaged 8.5% of the employed labour force in 1996 and provided 4.9% of GDP in 2000/01, according to provisional figures. The GDP of the manufacturing sector increased at an average annual rate of 4.5% in 1990–2001; growth in 2001 was 5.9%.

Energy is derived principally from fuel wood and coal; the use of solar power is currently being promoted as an alternative source of energy. According to provisional figures, imports of fuels accounted for 6.7% of the value of total imports in 2001.

The services sector contributed 47.4% of GDP in 2000/01, according to provisional figures, and engaged 58.7% of the employed labour force in 1996. Within the sector, tourism is of considerable importance, and the tourist industry is the third largest source of total foreign exchange. The GDP of the services sector increased at an average annual rate of 7.9% in 1990–2001; growth in 2001 was 5.5%.

In 1999 Botswana recorded a visible trade surplus of US $674.5m., and there was a surplus of $516.8m. on the current account of the balance of payments. In 2001 countries of the Southern African Customs Union (SACU—see below) provided 77.6% of imports. European countries (principally the United Kingdom) took 89.0% of exports in 2001; other important purchasers were the countries of SACU. The principal exports in that year were diamonds and copper-nickel matte. The principal imports were machinery and electrical equipment, food, beverages and tobacco, vehicles and transport equipment, and chemicals and rubber products.

In the financial year to 31 March 2002 the central Government recorded a budgetary deficit of an estimated P43.1m. Botswana's external debt totalled US $413.0m. at the end of 2000, of which $397.6m. was long-term public debt. In that year the cost of debt-servicing was equivalent to 1.8% of the value of exports of goods and services. The average annual rate of inflation was 10.1% in 1990–2001; consumer prices increased by an annual average of 6.6% in 2001. Some 15.8% of the labour force were unemployed in 2000.

Botswana is a member of the Southern African Development Community (SADC, see p. 311) and (with Lesotho, Namibia, South Africa and Swaziland) of SACU. In September 2000 the SADC implemented a free-trade agreement, whereby all trade tariffs between member countries were to be eliminated gradually over a 12-year period.

Botswana's high rate of growth during the 1980s was based predominantly on the successful exploitation of diamonds and other minerals. However, domestic factors, such as a vulnerability to drought, in conjunction with the world-wide economic recession of the early 1990s, depressed Botswana's economy and exemplified the need to reduce dependence on diamond-mining, to diversify agricultural production and to broaden the manufacturing base. The encouragement of private-sector growth was a key element of Botswana's eighth National Development Plan (1997/98–2002/03); privatizations were planned in the telecommunications and aviation sectors—Air Botswana was scheduled to be privatized fully by May 2003. The ninth National Development Plan (2003/04–2008/09) was presented in 2002; the Government's main priority was to effect economic diversification by embracing recent technological developments. Diamond exports declined in 1998, but recovered in 1999, and increased again in 2000, when the expansion of the Orapa diamond mine was completed. However, Botswana's persistent dependence on the diamond sector has remained a source of potential weakness, and in 2001 production and demand fell, as economic growth slowed, particularly in the USA; none the less, revenue increased, largely as a result of the pula losing value against the dollar. A new diamond mine began production in north-eastern Botswana in October 2002. In 2000, as part of efforts to diversify the economic base and create sustainable employment, the Government established an International Financial Services Centre (IFSC). Botswana's proximity to South Africa, substantial tax incentives, and the stability of a well-established democratic system of government were all expected to attract international financial companies to the country, and by November 2002 11 projects had been approved for operation under the IFSC. In 2001 the Government created an agency aimed at encouraging the development of domestic small- and medium-sized enterprises. Meanwhile, the HIV/AIDS pandemic represented a significant threat to continued economic growth, with expenditure on projects to counter the disease inevitably depleting government resources. With more than one-third of the population estimated to be infected with HIV, estimated average life expectancy had declined from around 60 years in the early 1990s to less than 45 years by 2000, and was expected to fall to about 36 years by 2005.

Education

Although education is not compulsory in Botswana, enrolment ratios are high. Primary education, which is provided free of charge, begins at seven years of age and lasts for up to seven years. Secondary education, beginning at the age of 13, lasts for a further five years, comprising a first cycle of three years and a second of two years. As a proportion of the school-age population, the total enrolment at primary and secondary schools increased from 52% in 1975 to the equivalent of 91% (boys 90%; girls 93%) in 1996. Enrolment at primary schools in 1999/2000 included 83.6% of children in the relevant age-group, while, according to UNESCO estimates, the comparable ratio for secondary enrolment was 58.8% (boys 54.5%; girls 63.1%). By the late 1990s the Government provided universal access to 10 years of basic education. Botswana has the highest teacher-pupil ratio in Africa, but continues to rely heavily on expatriate secondary school teachers. In 1999 tertiary education was provided by 47 technical and vocational training centres (including health institutes), four teacher-training colleges, two further education colleges, an agricultural college and a university (which was attended by 9,595 students in 1999). Expenditure on education by the central Government in 2002/03 was forecast at P4,053.3m. (representing 23.8% of total government spending).

Public Holidays

2003: 1–2 January (New Year), 18–21 April (Easter), 1 May (Labour Day), 29 May (Ascension Day), 1 July (Sir Seretse Khama Day), 21–22 July (for President's Day), 30 September (Botswana Day), 25–26 December (Christmas).

2004: 1–2 January (New Year), 9–12 April (Easter), 1 May (Labour Day), 20 May (Ascension Day), 1 July (Sir Seretse Khama Day), 19–20 July (for President's Day), 30 September (Botswana Day), 25–26 December (Christmas).

Weights and Measures

The metric system is in use.

Statistical Survey

Source (unless otherwise stated): Central Statistics Office, Private Bag 0024, Gaborone; tel. 352200; fax 352201; e-mail csobots@gov.bw; internet www.cso.gov.bw/cso.

Area and Population

AREA, POPULATION AND DENSITY

Area (sq km)	581,730*
Population (census results)	
21 August 1991	1,326,796
17 August 2001	1,678,891
Males	813,488
Females.	867,375
Total	1,680,863
Population (official estimates at 19 August)	
1998	1,571,728
1999	1,611,021
2000	1,651,296
Density (per sq km) at August 2001	2.9

* 224,607 sq miles.

POPULATION BY ADMINISTRATIVE DISTRICT
(August 2001 census)

			Kgatleng	73,507
Barolong . . .	47,477		Kweneng	230,535
Central . . .	501,381		Lobatse	29,689
Central Kalahari				
Game Reserve .	689		Ngamiland . . .	122,024
Chobe	18,258		Ngwaketse West . .	10,471
Delta	2,688		North-East . . .	49,399
Francistown . .	83,023		Orapa	9,151
Gaborone . . .	186,007		Selebi-Phikwe . .	49,849
Ghanzi . . .	32,481		South-East . . .	60,623
Jwaneng . . .	15,179		Southern . . .	113,704
Kgalagadi . . .	42,049		Sowa	2,879

PRINCIPAL TOWNS
(population at August 2001 census)

Gaborone (capital) .	186,007	Serowe . . .	42,444
Francistown . .	83,023	Kanye . . .	40,628
Molepolole . .	54,561	Mahalapye . .	39,719
Selebi-Phikwe .	49,849	Mochudi . . .	36,692
Maun . . .	43,776	Lobatse . . .	29,689

BIRTHS AND DEATHS
(UN estimates, annual averages)

	1985–90	1990–95	1995–2000
Birth rate (per 1,000) . . .	40.1	36.9	33.6
Death rate (per 1,000) . . .	7.7	8.6	17.0

Source: UN, *World Population Prospects: The 2000 Revision.*

Expectation of life (WHO estimates, years at birth): 39.1 (males 39.3; females 38.6) in 2001 (Source: WHO, *World Health Report*).

Health and Welfare

KEY INDICATORS

Total fertility rate (children per woman, 2001). . . .	4.1
Under-5 mortality rate (per 1,000 live births, 2001) . .	110
HIV/AIDS (% of persons aged 15–49, 2001)	38.80
Physicians (per 1,000 head, 1994)	0.24
Hospital beds (per 1,000 head, 1990)	1.58
Health expenditure (2000): US $ per head (PPP) . .	191
Health expenditure (2000): % of GDP	6.0
Health expenditure (2000): public (% of total) . .	63.1
Human Development Index (2000): ranking	126
Human Development Index (2000): value	0.572

For sources and definitions, see explanatory note on p. vi.

ECONOMICALLY ACTIVE POPULATION*
(sample survey, persons aged 12 years and over, year ending August 1996)

	Males	Females	Total
Agriculture, hunting, forestry and fishing	37,050	16,729	53,779
Mining and quarrying . . .	12,754	2,379	15,133
Manufacturing	14,157	15,373	29,530
Electricity, gas and water supply .	2,633	172	2,805
Construction	28,096	12,929	41,025
Wholesale and retail trade; repair of motor vehicles, motorcycles and personal and household goods	19,526	24,615	44,141
Hotels and restaurants . .	2,524	7,491	10,015
Transport, storage and communications . . .	5,778	1,937	7,715
Financial intermediation . .	1,781	2,315	4,096
Real estate, renting and business services	5,766	1,875	7,641
Public administration and defence; compulsory social security . .	37,928	22,029	59,957
Education	12,377	20,854	33,231
Health and social work . . .	2,096	7,280	9,376
Other community, social and personal service activities . .	4,330	2,977	7,307
Private households with employed persons	1,957	16,997	18,954
Extra-territorial organizations and bodies	197	27	224
Activities not adequately defined .	351	125	476
Total employed	189,301	156,104	345,405
Unemployed	45,461	49,067	94,528
Total labour force . . .	234,762	205,171	439,933

* Excluding members of the armed forces and those not actively seeking work.

Source: Labour Statistics Unit, Central Statistics Office.

Mid-2001 (estimates, '000 persons): Agriculture, etc. 301; Total labour force 680 (Source: FAO).

Agriculture

PRINCIPAL CROPS
('000 metric tons)

	1999	2000	2001*
Maize	5†	9	9
Sorghum	13†	11	11
Roots and tubers* . . .	12	13	13
Pulses*	16	17	17
Vegetables*	16	17	17
Fruit*	10	2	2

* FAO estimates.
† Unofficial figure.

Source: FAO.

LIVESTOCK
(FAO estimates, '000 head, year ending September)

	1999	2000	2001
Cattle	1,850	1,855	2,400
Horses	33	33	33
Asses	325	330	330
Sheep	320	350	370
Goats	2,150	2,200	2,250
Pigs	5	6	7
Poultry	3,000	3,500	4,000

Source: FAO.

LIVESTOCK PRODUCTS
(FAO estimates, '000 metric tons)

	1999	2000	2001
Beef and veal	37	39	39
Goat meat	6	6	6
Poultry meat	6	7	7
Other meat	14	15	15
Cows' milk	98	102	102
Goats' milk	4	4	4
Cheese	2	4	4
Butter	1	1	1
Hen eggs	3	3	3
Cattle hides	5	5	5

Source: FAO.

Forestry

ROUNDWOOD REMOVALS
('000 cubic metres, excl. bark)

	1998	1999	2000
Industrial wood	103	105	105
Fuel wood	631	635	640
Total	734	740	745

2001: Production as in 2000 (FAO estimates).

Source: FAO.

Fishing

(FAO estimates, metric tons, live weight)

	1998	1999	2000
Tilapias	88	93	92
Other freshwater fishes . .	103	64	74
Total catch . . .	191	157	166

Source: FAO, *Yearbook of Fishery Statistics.*

Mining

(metric tons, unless otherwise indicated)

	1998	1999	2000
Hard coal	928,100	945,316	950,000*
Copper ore†	25,043	37,604	38,420
Nickel ore†	21,700	33,733	34,465
Cobalt‡	335	331	319
Salt.	214,700	233,069	184,755
Diamonds ('000 carats) . .	19,772	22,898	24,218
Soda ash (natural)	189,700	233,643	191,043
Crushed stone (cu metres) .	997,244	1,466,100	1,050,700

* Estimate.

† Figures refer to the metal content of ores.

‡ Figures refer to the cobalt content of copper-nickel matte exported for refining.

Source: US Geological Survey.

Industry

SELECTED PRODUCTS

	1997	1998	1999
Beer ('000 hectolitres) . . .	1,005	1,019	1,591
Soft drinks ('000 hectolitres) .	348	411	410
Electric energy (million kWh) .	925	1,608	1,817

Source: UN, *Industrial Commodity Statistics Yearbook*.

Finance

CURRENCY AND EXCHANGE RATES

Monetary Units

100 thebe = 1 pula (P)

Sterling, Dollar and Euro Equivalents (31 December 2002)

£1 sterling = 8.812 pula

US $1 = 5.467 pula

€1 = 5.734 pula

100 pula = £11.35 = $18.29 = €17.44

Average Exchange Rate (pula per US $)

2000	5.1018
2001	5.8412
2002	6.3278

BUDGET

(million pula, year ending 31 March)

Revenue*	2000/01	2001/02†	2002/03‡
Taxation	12,077.6	11,333.2	13,017.2
Mineral revenues . . .	8,367.8	7,462.9	8,492.0
Customs pool revenues . .	2,188.4	1,735.0	1,541.0
Non-mineral income tax . .	925.3	1,454.3	1,902.5
General sales tax . . .	523.8	615.6	1,006.0
Other current revenue . . .	1,973.0	1,975.1	2,363.1
Interest	205.2	156.2	180.6
Other property income . .	1,194.7	1,117.2	1,185.7
Fees, charges, etc. . . .	508.1	641.7	936.2
Sales of fixed assets and land .	65.0	60.0	60.7
Total	**14,050.6**	**13,308.3**	**15,380.3**

* Excluding grants received (million pula): 64.5 in 2000/01; 39.0 in 2001/02; 31.0 in 2002/03.

† Estimates.

‡ Forecasts.

Expenditure*	2000/01	2001/02†	2002/03‡
General services (incl. defence). .	3,296.1	3,736.3	4,755.1
Education	2,865.6	3,075.0	4,053.3
Health	629.9	865.0	1,322.7
Housing, urban and regional development	732.1	1,020.2	1,328.2
Food and social welfare programme	423.9	165.6	124.3
Other community and social services	345.1	384.4	582.9
Economic services	2,042.5	2,818.0	3,103.9
Agriculture, forestry and fishing	451.7	575.4	642.8
Mining	74.5	405.8	186.0
Electricity and water supply .	678.1	575.3	947.0
Roads	580.2	691.3	853.3
Interest on public debt . . .	83.0	105.2	104.1
Deficit grants to local authorities .	998.4	1,163.1	1,502.1
Other grants	120.0	100.0	154.0
Total	**11,536.6**	**13,432.7**	**17,030.5**

* Figures refer to recurrent and development expenditure, excluding net lending (million pula): −101.2 in 2000/01; −42.3 in 2001/02; 47.1 in 2002/03.

† Estimates.

‡ Forecasts.

Source: Bank of Botswana, Gaborone.

INTERNATIONAL RESERVES

(US $ million at 31 December)

	2000	2001	2002
IMF special drawing rights . .	38.94	39.62	44.36
Reserve position in IMF. . .	23.11	28.00	32.36
Foreign exchange.	6,256.16	5,829.63	n.a.
Total	**6,318.21**	**5,897.25**	**n.a.**

Source: IMF, *International Financial Statistics*.

MONEY SUPPLY

(million pula at 31 December)

	1999	2000	2001
Currency outside banks . . .	403.7	427.0	481.4
Demand deposits at commercial banks	1,370.9	1,469.6	1,869.3
Total money	**1,774.6**	**1,896.6**	**2,350.7**

Source: IMF, *International Financial Statistics*.

COST OF LIVING

(Consumer Price Index; base: 1990 = 100)

	1999	2000	2001
Food (incl. beverages) . . .	259.0	271.2	278.3
Clothing (incl. footwear) . . .	262.1	269.4	279.5
All items (incl. others) . . .	249.5	270.7	288.6

Source: ILO, *Yearbook of Labour Statistics*.

NATIONAL ACCOUNTS
(million pula at current prices, year ending 30 June)

National Income and Product
(provisional)

	1996/97	1997/98	1998/99
Compensation of employees . .	4,580.0	5,432.4	6,618.6
Operating surplus	9,762.7	10,807.4	10,480.0
Domestic factor incomes . .	14,342.7	16,239.8	17,098.6
Consumption of fixed capital . .	2,210.7	2,421.3	2,647.4
Gross domestic product			
(GDP) at factor cost . . .	16,553.4	18,661.1	19,746.0
Indirect taxes	1,264.8	1,597.5	1,887.8
Less Subsidies	78.0	96.0	110.0
GDP in purchasers' values .	17,740.2	20,162.6	21,523.8
Factor income received from abroad. . . . . . }	−685.0	−11.7	−353.8
Less Factor income paid abroad .}			
Gross national product . .	17,055.2	20,150.9	21,170.0
Less Consumption of fixed capital	2,210.7	2,421.3	2,647.4
National income in market prices.	14,844.5	17,729.6	18,522.6
Other current transfers from abroad. . . . . . }	−61.0	−90.0	−30.1
Less Other current transfers paid abroad . . . . }			
National disposable income .	14,783.5	17,639.6	18,492.5

Expenditure on the Gross Domestic Product
(provisional figures)

	1998/99	1999/2000	2000/01
Government final consumption expenditure.	6,578.8	7,524.5	9,268.1
Private final consumption expenditure.	6,936.8	7,841.1	8,718.2
Increase in stocks	1,653.9	−2,063.2	−2,091.1
Gross fixed capital formation . .	6,263.3	6,744.5	6,701.6
Total domestic expenditure. .	21,432.8	20,046.9	22,596.6
Exports of goods and services .	10,051.6	15,318.5	16,510.7
Less Imports of goods and services	9,960.6	10,002.7	9,755.0
GDP in purchasers' values .	21,523.8	25,362.7	29,352.7
GDP at constant 1993/94 prices	14,295.6	15,451.1	16,865.8

Source: Bank of Botswana, Gaborone.

Gross Domestic Product by Economic Activity
(provisional figures)

	1998/99	1999/2000	2000/01
Agriculture, hunting, forestry and fishing	654.2	665.2	716.0
Mining and quarrying . . .	6,692.9	8,389.4	10,286.5
Manufacturing	1,127.7	1,239.9	1,367.7
Water and electricity . . .	458.1	567.5	691.5
Construction	1,360.2	1,423.6	1,562.7
Trade, restaurants and hotels .	2,338.7	2,734.9	3,197.7
Transport	813.6	935.4	1,089.1
Finance, insurance and business services	2,410.4	2,761.1	3,159.0
Government services. . . .	3,751.3	4,104.6	4,654.2
Social and personal services .	870.2	993.8	1,090.2
Sub-total	20,477.3	23,815.4	27,814.6
Less Imputed bank service charge .	731.2	879.3	960.9
GDP at basic prices . . .	19,746.1	22,936.0	26,853.7
Import duties	1,419.2	1,984.2	2,050.0
Taxes on products	468.6	542.4	606.8
Less Subsidies on products . .	110.0	100.0	158.0
GDP in purchasers' values . .	21,523.9	25,362.7	29,352.5

Source: Bank of Botswana, Gaborone.

BALANCE OF PAYMENTS
(US $ million)

	1997	1998	1999
Exports of goods f.o.b.	2,819.8	2,060.6	2,671.0
Imports of goods f.o.b.	−1,924.4	−1,983.1	−1,996.5
Trade balance	895.4	77.5	674.5
Exports of services	210.2	255.3	372.6
Imports of services	−440.7	−522.4	−515.9
Balance on goods and services	664.9	−189.6	531.2
Other income received . . .	622.1	622.7	429.8
Other income paid	−766.9	−503.1	−696.0
Balance on goods, services and income	520.1	−70.0	265.1
Current transfers received . .	456.8	460.9	474.4
Current transfers paid . . .	−255.5	−220.8	−222.6
Current balance	721.5	170.1	516.8
Capital account (net)	16.9	31.8	20.6
Direct investment abroad . .	−4.1	−3.5	−1.5
Direct investment from abroad. .	100.1	95.3	36.7
Portfolio investment assets . .	−28.5	−42.8	−22.8
Portfolio investment liabilities .	10.8	−14.1	−7.5
Financial derivatives assets .	−15.4	5.2	−4.6
Other investment assets . . .	−166.5	−310.8	−206.1
Other investment liabilities . .	109.3	68.2	30.7
Net errors and omissions . . .	−108.9	44.6	8.7
Overall balance	635.1	44.2	371.0

Source: IMF, *International Financial Statistics*.

External Trade

PRINCIPAL COMMODITIES
(million pula)

Imports c.i.f.	1999	2000*	2001*
Food, beverages and tobacco . .	1,411.7	1,494.2	1,475.7
Fuels	494.9	523.2	711.7
Chemicals and rubber products .	940.6	1,033.4	1,090.3
Wood and paper products . .	819.4	817.1	928.2
Textiles and footwear . . .	596.1	616.5	494.1
Metals and metal products . . .	877.2	769.0	813.8
Machinery and electrical equipment	2,142.3	2,356.4	2,078.4
Vehicles and transport equipment	1,373.7	1,314.8	1,285.0
Total (incl. others)	10,164.4	10,613.1	10,556.9

* Provisional figures.

Exports f.o.b.	1999	2000*	2001*
Meat and meat products . . .	223.4	263.5	365.9
Diamonds	9,706.4	11,383.6	12,085.9
Copper-nickel matte	557.9	830.3	597.4
Textiles	248.5	243.7	193.0
Vehicles and parts	666.8	270.4	298.7
Total (incl. others)	12,227.8	13,834.7	14,306.5

* Provisional figures.

PRINCIPAL TRADING PARTNERS
(million pula)

Imports c.i.f.	1999	2000*	2001*
SACU†	7,783.6	7,846.1	8,193.4
Zimbabwe	396.6	366.6	335.2
United Kingdom.	272.5	442.3	467.8
Other Europe	664.3	1,306.7	832.7
Korea, Repub.	264.0	21.5	22.2
USA	188.0	174.1	190.0
Total (incl. others)	10,164.4	10,613.1	10,556.9

Exports f.o.b.	1999	2000*	2001*
SACU†	1,270.9	927.1	924.1
Zimbabwe	291.0	540.6	373.8
Other Africa	137.2	125.8	107.7
United Kingdom	8,130.1	9,644.3	12,283.3
Other Europe	2,220.9	2,417.1	452.0
USA	86.5	81.6	35.3
Total (incl. others)	12,227.8	13,834.7	14,306.5

* Provisional figures.

† Southern African Customs Union, of which Botswana is a member; also including Lesotho, Namibia, South Africa and Swaziland.

Transport

RAILWAYS
(traffic)

	1998/99	1999/2000	2000/01
Number of passengers ('000)	360	310	637
Passenger-km (million)	89	75	106
Freight ('000 metric tons)	2,812	2,448	1,956
Freight net ton-km (million)	1,282	1,037	747

Source: Botswana Railways.

ROAD TRAFFIC
(registered vehicles)

	1999	2000	2001
Passenger cars	44,452	47,396	52,873
Lorries and vans	67,933	65,444	70,157
Buses	5,262	5,602	6,055
Tractors	3,648	2,421	2,900
Others	9,587	9,092	9,041
Total	131,796	129,955	141,026

Source: Department of National Transport and Road Safety.

CIVIL AVIATION
(traffic on scheduled services)

	1997	1998	1999
Kilometres flown (million)	2	2	2
Passengers carried ('000)	88	92	108
Passenger-km (million)	41	42	50
Total ton-km (million)	4	4	5

Source: UN, *Statistical Yearbook*.

Tourism

FOREIGN TOURIST ARRIVALS

Country of origin	1997	1998	1999
Namibia	17,433	35,508	39,952
South Africa	258,120	359,292	393,528
United Kingdom	15,329	14,426	15,519
Zambia	22,057	26,971	28,888
Zimbabwe	207,244	195,789	245,630
Total (incl. others)	606,790	749,535	843,314

Receipts from tourism (US $ million): 184 in 1997; 175 in 1998; 234 in 1999.

Source: World Tourism Organization, *Yearbook of Tourism Statistics*.

Communications Media

	1999	2000	2001
Television receivers ('000 in use)	33	40	n.a.
Telephones ('000 main lines in use)	123.8	150.3	150.3
Mobile cellular telephones ('000 subscribers)	120	200	278
Personal computers ('000 in use)	50	60	65
Internet users ('000)	12	15	25

Source: International Telecommunication Union.

Radio receivers ('000 in use): 237 in 1997 (Source: UNESCO, *Statistical Yearbook*).

Facsimile machines: 3,529 in use in 1997/98 (Source: UNESCO, *Statistical Yearbook*).

Book production (first editions only): 158 titles in 1991, including 61 pamphlets (Source: UNESCO, *Statistical Yearbook*).

Daily newspapers: 1 in 2000 (average circulation 50,000 copies) (Source: UNESCO, *Statistical Yearbook*).

Non-daily newspapers: 3 in 1996 (average circulation 51,000 copies) (Source: UNESCO, *Statistical Yearbook*).

Other periodicals: 14 titles in 1992 (average circulation 177,000 copies) (Source: UNESCO, *Statistical Yearbook*).

Education

(1999)

	Institutions	Teachers	Students
Primary	736	11,950	323,874
Secondary	265	8,470	148,195
Brigades* and Technical Education	47	1,003	9,609
Teacher training	4	184	1,137
Colleges of education	2‡	170‡	1,259
Agricultural college	1	87†	392†
University	1	697	9,595

* Semi-autonomous units providing craft and practical training.

† 1997 figure.

‡ 1998 figure.

Source: Ministry of Education, Gaborone.

Adult literacy rate (UNESCO estimates): 77.2% (males 74.5%; females 79.8%) in 2000 (Source: UN Development Programme, *Human Development Report*).

Directory

The Constitution

The Constitution of the Republic of Botswana took effect at independence on 30 September 1966; it was amended in August and September 1997.

EXECUTIVE

President

Executive power lies with the President of Botswana, who is also Commander-in-Chief of the armed forces. Election for the office of President is linked with the election of members of the National Assembly. The President is restricted to two terms of office. Presidential candidates must be over 30 years of age and receive at least 1,000 nominations. If there is more than one candidate for the Presidency, each candidate for office in the Assembly must declare support for a presidential candidate. The candidate for President who commands the votes of more than one-half of the elected members of the Assembly will be declared President. In the event of the death or resignation of the President, the Vice-President will automatically assume the Presidency. The President, who is an *ex-officio* member of the National Assembly, holds office for the duration of Parliament. The President chooses four members of the National Assembly.

Cabinet

There is also a Vice-President, whose office is ministerial. The Vice-President is appointed by the President and deputizes in the absence of the President. The Cabinet consists of the President, the Vice-President and other Ministers, including Assistant Ministers, appointed by the President. The Cabinet is responsible to the National Assembly.

LEGISLATURE

Legislative power is vested in Parliament, consisting of the President and the National Assembly, acting after consultation in certain cases with the House of Chiefs. The President may withhold assent to a Bill passed by the National Assembly. If the same Bill is again presented after six months, the President is required to assent to it or to dissolve Parliament within 21 days.

House of Chiefs

The House of Chiefs comprises the Chiefs of the eight principal tribes of Botswana as *ex-officio* members, four members elected by sub-chiefs from their own number, and three members elected by the other 12 members of the House. Bills and motions relating to chieftaincy matters and alterations of the Constitution must be referred to the House, which may also deliberate and make representations on any matter. Proposals to rename the House of Chiefs as the Ntlo ya Dikgosi and to increase its membership from 15 to 33 were under consideration in early 2003.

National Assembly

The National Assembly consists of 40 members directly elected by universal adult suffrage, together with four members who are elected by the National Assembly from a list of candidates submitted by the President; the President, the Speaker and the Attorney-General are also *ex-officio* members of the Assembly. The life of the Assembly is five years. In June 2002 the National Assembly voted to increase its membership from 40 directly elected members to 57, with effect from the following general election.

The Constitution contains a code of human rights, enforceable by the High Court.

The Government

HEAD OF STATE

President: Festus G. Mogae (took office 1 April 1998; sworn in 20 October 1999).

Vice-President: Lt-Gen. Seretse Ian Khama (sworn in 13 July 1998).

CABINET
(April 2003)

President: Festus G. Mogae.

Vice-President: Lt-Gen. Seretse Ian Khama.

Minister of Presidential Affairs and Public Administration: Daniel Kwelagobe.

Minister of Health: Joy Phumaphi.

Minister of Agriculture: Johnnie Swartz.

Minister of Foreign Affairs: Lt-Gen. Mompati Merafhe.

Minister of Minerals, Energy and Water Affairs: Boometswe Mokgothu.

Minister of Trade and Industry: Jacob Nkate.

Minister of Local Government: Michael Tshipinare.

Minister of Works and Transport: Tebelelo Seretse.

Minister of Communications, Science and Technology: Lephimotswe Boyce Sebetela.

Minister of Conservation, Wildlife and Tourism: Pelonomi Venson.

Minister of Finance and Development Planning: Baledzi Gaolathe.

Minister of Education: Ponatshego Kedikilwe.

Minister of Labour and Home Affairs: Thebe Mogami.

Minister of Lands and Housing: Margaret Nasha.

In addition, there are six Assistant Ministers.

MINISTRIES

Office of the President: Private Bag 001, Gaborone; tel. 3950800; fax 3912525.

Ministry of Agriculture: Private Bag 003, Gaborone; tel. 3950603; fax 3956027.

Ministry of Communications, Science and Technology: Gaborone.

Ministry of Conservation, Wildlife and Tourism: Gaborone.

Ministry of Education: Private Bag 005, Gaborone; tel. 3655400; fax 3655458.

Ministry of Finance and Development Planning: Private Bag 008, Gaborone; tel. 3950100; fax 3956086; e-mail kbaleseng@gov.bw.

Ministry of Foreign Affairs: Private Bag 00368, Gaborone; tel. 3600700; fax 3913366.

Ministry of Health: Private Bag 0038, Gaborone; tel. 3952000; fax 3953100; e-mail lmanthe@gov.bw.

Ministry of Labour and Home Affairs: Private Bag 002, Gaborone; tel. 3611100; fax 3913584.

Ministry of Lands and Housing: Private Bag 006, Gaborone; tel. 3954100; fax 3952382.

Ministry of Local Government: Private Bag 006, Gaborone; tel. 3954100; fax 3952091.

Ministry of Minerals, Energy and Water Affairs: Khama Crescent, Private Bag 0018, Gaborone; tel. 3656600; fax 3972738.

Ministry of Presidential Affairs and Public Administration: Private Bag 001, Gaborone; tel. 3950800.

Ministry of Trade and Industry: Private Bag 004, Gaborone; tel. 3601200; fax 3971538.

Ministry of Works and Transport: Private Bag 007, Gaborone; tel. 3958500; fax 3913303.

Legislature

HOUSE OF CHIEFS

The House has a total of 15 members. Proposals to rename the House of Chiefs as the Ntlo ya Dikgosi and to increase its membership from 15 to 33 were under consideration in early 2003.

Chairman: Chief Tawana II.

NATIONAL ASSEMBLY

Speaker: Ray Matlapeng Molomo.

General Election, 16 October 1999

Party	Votes	%	Seats
Botswana Democratic Party. .	192,598	57.2	33
Botswana National Front . .	87,457	26.0	6
Botswana Congress Party . .	40,096	11.9	1
Botswana Alliance Movement .	15,805	4.7	—
Others	1,026	0.3	—
Total	336,982	100.0	40*

*The President and the Attorney-General are also *ex-officio* members of the National Assembly.

Political Organizations

Botswana Alliance Movement (BAM): Private Bag BO 210, Gaborone; tel. 3913476; fax 3914634; f. 1998 as an alliance of three opposition parties to contest the 1999 general election; Botswana People's Party withdrew in July 2000; Pres. LEPETU SETSHWAELO; Chair. MOTSAMAI MPHO; Sec.-Gen. MATLHOMOLA MODISE.

Independence Freedom Party (IFP): POB 3, Maun; f. by merger of Botswana Freedom Party and Botswana Independence Party; Pres. MOTSAMAI K. MPHO.

United Action Party (UAP): Private Bag BO 210, Gaborone; f. 1998; Leader LEPETU SETSHWAELO.

Botswana Congress Party (BCP): POB 2918, Gaborone; tel. and fax 3181805; f. 1998 following a split in the Botswana National Front; Pres. OTLAADISA KOOSALETSE; Chair. PEBA SETHANTSHO; Sec.-Gen. MOKGWEETSI KGOSIPULA.

Botswana Democratic Party (BDP): POB 28, Tsholetsa House, Gaborone; tel. 3952564; fax 3913911; e-mail domkrag@info.bw; f. 1962; Pres. FESTUS G. MOGAE; Chair. PONATSHEGO KEDIKILWE; Sec.-Gen. DANIEL K. KWELAGOBE.

Botswana Labour Party: POB 140, Mahalapye; f. 1989; Pres. LENYELETSE KOMA.

Botswana National Front (BNF): POB 1720, Gaborone; tel. 3951789; fax 3184970; f. 1966; Pres. OTSWELETSE MOUPO; Chair. KLAAS MOTSHIDISI.

Botswana People's Party (BPP): POB 484, Francistown; f. 1960; Pres. MOTLATSI MOLAPISI; Chair. JOSEPH MOGOTLE; Sec.-Gen. KOPANO CHINGAPANE.

Botswana Progressive Union (BPU): POB 328, Nkange; f. 1982; Leader G. KAELO.

Botswana Workers' Front (BWF): POB 597, Jwaneng; tel. 5880420; f. 1993; Leader M. M. AKANYANG.

MELS Movement of Botswana: POB 501818, Gaborone; tel. and fax 3906005; f. 1993; Leader THEMBA JOINA.

New Democratic Front (NDF): Gaborone; f. 2003 following split in the BNF; Leader Dr KENNETH KOMA.

Social Democratic Party (SDP): POB 201818, Gaborone; tel. 3956516; f. 1994; Leader O. MARUMO.

United Socialist Party (USP): POB 233, Lobatse; f. 1994; Leader N. MODUBULE.

Diplomatic Representation

EMBASSIES AND HIGH COMMISSIONS IN BOTSWANA

Angola: 5131 Kopanyo House, Nelson Mandela Dr., Private Bag BR 111, Gaborone; tel. 3900204; fax 3975089; Ambassador EVARISTO DOMINGOS KIMBA.

China, People's Republic: 3096 North Ring Rd, POB 1031, Gaborone; tel. 3952209; fax 3900156; e-mail chnemb@info.bw; Ambassador BAO SHUSHENG.

Cuba: Plot 5158, Gaborone; tel. 3951750; fax 3911485; Ambassador ANA VILMA VALLEJERA.

France: POB 1424, Gaborone; tel. 3973863; fax 3971733; Ambassador PIERRE COULONT.

Germany: Professional House, Broadhurst, Segodithsane Way, POB 315, Gaborone; tel. 3953143; fax 3953038; e-mail germanembassy@info.bw; Ambassador HANS-DIETRICH VON BOTHMER.

India: 5375 President's Dr., Private Bag 249, Gaborone; tel. 3972676; fax 3974636; e-mail hicomind@global.bw; High Commissioner LAL T. MUANA.

Kenya: Plot 5373, President's Dr., Private Bag 0297, Gaborone; tel. 3951408; fax 3951409; e-mail kenya@info.bw; High Commissioner RICHARD OKWARO.

Libya: POB 180, Plot 8851 (Government Enclave), Gaborone; tel. 3952481; Ambassador JUMA MOHAMED JUBAIL.

Namibia: POB 987, Plot 186, Morara Close, Gaborone; tel. 3902181; fax 3902248; e-mail nhc.gabs@info.bw; High Commissioner JOSHUA HOEBEB.

Nigeria: POB 274, The Mall, Gaborone; tel. 3913561; fax 3913738; High Commissioner OGBONNAYA AJA-NWACHUKWU.

Russia: Plot 4711, Tawana Close, POB 81, Gaborone; tel. 3953389; fax 3952930; e-mail embrus@info.bw; Ambassador VALERII A. KALUGIN.

South Africa: Private Bag 00402, Kopanyo House, 3rd Floor, Plot 5131, Nelson Mandela Dr., Gaborone; tel. 3904800; fax 3905501; High Commissioner THANDI LUJABE-RANKOE.

Sweden: Development House, Private Bag 0017, Gaborone; tel. 3953912; fax 3953942; e-mail ambassaden.gaborone@foreign.ministry.se; Ambassador CHRISTINA REHLEN.

United Kingdom: Private Bag 0023, Gaborone; tel. 3952841; fax 3956105; e-mail british@bc.bw; internet www.british.global.bw; High Commissioner DAVID MERRY.

USA: POB 90, Gaborone; tel. 3953982; fax 3956947; e-mail uscomml@mega.bw; Ambassador Dr JOSEPH HUGGINS.

Zambia: POB 362, Gaborone; tel. 3951951; fax 3953952; High Commissioner J. PHIRI.

Zimbabwe: Plot 8850, POB 1232, Gaborone; tel. 3914495; fax 3905863; High Commissioner PHELEKEZELA MPHOKO.

Judicial System

There is a High Court at Lobatse and a branch at Francistown, and Magistrates' Courts in each district. Appeals lie to the Court of Appeal of Botswana. The Chief Justice and the President of the Court of Appeal are appointed by the President.

Chief Justice: JULIAN NGANUNU.

High Court

Private Bag 1, Lobatse; tel. 5330396; fax 5332317.

Judges of the High Court: I. R. ABOAGYE, J. B. GITTINGS, M. DIBOTELO, M. GAEFELE, J. Z. MASOJANE, I. K. B. LESETEDI (acting).

President of the Court of Appeal: A. N. E. AMISSAH.

Justices of Appeal: T. A. AGUDA, W. H. R. SCHREINER, J. STEYN, P. H. TEBBUTT, W. COWIE, G. G. HOEXTER, W. ALLANBRIDGE.

Registrar and Master: W. G. GRANTE.

Office of the Attorney-General

Private Bag 009, Gaborone; tel. 3954700; fax 3957089.

Attorney-General: PHANDU SKELEMANI.

Religion

The majority of the population hold animist beliefs; an estimated 30% are thought to be Christians. There are Islamic mosques in Gaborone and Lobatse. The Bahá'í Faith is also represented.

CHRISTIANITY

Lekgotla la Sekeresete la Botswana (Botswana Christian Council): POB 355, Gaborone; tel. and fax 3951981; e-mail bots.christ.c@info.bw; f. 1966; comprises 34 churches and organizations; Pres. Rev. RUPERT I. HAMBIRA; Gen. Sec. DAVID J. MODIEGA.

The Anglican Communion

Anglicans are adherents of the Church of the Province of Central Africa, comprising 12 dioceses and covering Botswana, Malawi, Zambia and Zimbabwe. The Province was established in 1955, and the diocese of Botswana was formed in 1972.

Archbishop of the Province of Central Africa and Bishop of Botswana: Most Rev. WALTER PAUL KHOTSO MAKHULU, POB 769, Gaborone; fax 3913015; e-mail acenter@info.bw.

Protestant Churches

African Methodist Episcopal Church: POB 141, Lobatse; Rev. L. M. MBULAWA.

Evangelical Lutheran Church in Botswana: POB 1976, Gaborone; tel. 3952227; fax 3913966; e-mail elcb@info.bw; Bishop Rev. Philip Robinson; 16,305 mems.

Evangelical Lutheran Church in Southern Africa (Botswana Diocese): POB 400, Gaborone; tel. 3953976; Bishop Rev. M. Ntuping.

Methodist Church in Botswana: POB 260, Gaborone; District Supt Rev. Z. S. M. Mosai.

United Congregational Church of Southern Africa (Synod of Botswana): POB 1263, Gaborone; tel. 3952491; synod status since 1980; Chair. Rev. D. T. Mapitse; Sec. Rev. M. P. P. Dibeela; 24,000 mems.

Other denominations active in Botswana include the Church of God in Christ, the Dutch Reformed Church, the United Methodist Church and the Seventh-day Adventists.

The Roman Catholic Church

Botswana comprises one diocese and an apostolic vicariate. The metropolitan see is Bloemfontein, South Africa. The church was established in Botswana in 1928, and had an estimated 78,187 adherents (some 5.5% of the total population) in the country at 31 December 2000. The Bishop participates in the Southern African Catholic Bishops' Conference, currently based in Pretoria, South Africa.

Bishop of Gaborone: Rt Rev. Boniface Tshosa Setlalekgosi, POB 218, Bishop's House, Gaborone; tel. 3912958; fax 3956970.

Vicar Apostolic of Francistown: Rt Rev. Franklyn Nubuasah.

The Press

DAILY NEWSPAPER

Dikgang tsa Gompieno (Daily News): Private Bag 0060, Gaborone; tel. 3952541; f. 1964; publ. by Dept of Information and Broadcasting; Setswana and English; Mon.–Fri. Editor Lamong Leshaga; circ. 40,000.

PERIODICALS

Agrinews: Private Bag 003, Gaborone; f. 1971; monthly; agriculture and rural development; circ. 6,000.

Botswana Advertiser: POB 130, 5647 Nakedi Rd, Broadhurst, Gaborone; tel. 3912844; weekly.

Botswana Business Month Magazine: POB 1605, Gaborone; fax 3912774; bimonthly; Editor Clara Olsen; circ. 500.

Botswana Business News: Private Bag 00367, Gaborone; fax 3905375; monthly; publ. by Ministry of Trade andIndustry; Editors Mukram Sheikh, Monty Letshwiti; circ. 3,000.

The Botswana Gazette: POB 1605, 83 Makaba Rd, Ext. 3, Gaborone; tel. 3912833; fax 3972283; e-mail gazette@info.bw; internet www.gazette.bw; f. 1985; weekly; Editor Abraham Motsokono; circ. 19,000.

Botswana Guardian: POB 1641, Gaborone; tel. 3908432; fax 3908457; e-mail guardsun@info.bw; f. 1952; weekly; Editor Outsa Mokone; circ. 20,683.

Business and Financial Times: POB 402396, Gaborone; tel. 3186397; fax 3161700; e-mail bftimes@info.bw.

Government Gazette: Private Bag 0081, Gaborone; tel. 3914441; fax 3912001; weekly.

Kutlwano: Private Bag 0060, Gaborone; tel. 3952541; fax 3952971; monthly; Setswana and English; publ. by Dept of Information and Broadcasting; Editor Russ Molosiwa; circ. 24,000.

The Midweek Sun: POB 00153, Gaborone; tel. 3908432; fax 3908457; e-mail guardsun@info.bw; f. 1989; weekly; Editor Mike Mothibi; circ. 18,000.

Mmegi/The Reporter: Private Bag BR50, Gaborone; tel. 3974784; fax 3905508; e-mail mmegi@info.bw; internet www.mmegi.bw; f. 1984; weekly; Setswana and English; publ. by Dikgang Publishing Co; Man. Editor Titus Mbuya; circ. 20,000.

Motswana Woman: 686 Botswana Rd, Gaborone; tel. 3975362; fax 3975378; monthly; women's interests; circ. 4,000.

Northern Advertiser: POB 402, Francistown; tel. 2412265; fax 2413769; e-mail rsfish@global.bw; f. 1985; weekly; advertisements, local interest, sport; Editor Grace Fish; circ. 6,000.

The Zebra's Voice: Private Bag 00114, National Museum, 331 Independence Ave, Gaborone; tel. 3974616; fax 3902797; e-mail national.museum@gov.bw; f. 1980; quarterly; cultural affairs; Editor Berlinah Motswakhumo; circ. 5,000.

NEWS AGENCIES

Botswana Press Agency (BOPA): Private Bag 0060, Gaborone; tel. 3913601; f. 1981.

Foreign Bureaux

Deutshe Presse-Agentur (Germany) and Reuters (UK) are also represented in Botswana.

Publishers

A. C. Braby (Botswana) (Pty) Ltd: POB 1549, Gaborone; tel. 3971444; fax 3973462; telephone directories.

The Botswana Society: POB 71, Gaborone; tel. 3951500; fax 3959321; f. 1968; archaeology, arts, history, law, sciences.

Department of Information and Broadcasting: Private Bag 0060, Gaborone; tel. 3952541; fax 3957138; Dir Andrew Sesinyi.

Heinemann Educational Botswana (Pty) Ltd: POB 10103, Gaborone; tel. 3972305; fax 3971832; e-mail hein@info.bw; Man. Dir Lesedi Seitei.

Longman Botswana (Pty) Ltd: POB 1083, Lobatse Rd, Gaborone; tel. 3922969; fax 3922682; e-mail lb@longman.info.bw; f. 1981; educational; Man. Dir J. K. Chalashika.

Macmillan Botswana Publishing Co (Pty) Ltd: POB 1155, Gaborone; tel. 3911770; fax 3911987; e-mail uiterwijkw@macmillan .bw; Gen. Man W. Uiterwijk.

Magnum Press (Pty) Ltd: Gaborone; tel. 3972852; fax 3974558.

Morula Press: Business School of Botswana, POB 402492, Gaborone; tel. 3953499; fax 3904809; f. 1994; business, law.

Printing and Publishing Co (Botswana) (Pty) Ltd: POB 130, 5647 Nakedi Rd, Broadhurst, Gaborone; tel. 3912844; e-mail ppcb@ info.bw.

Sygma Publishing: POB 753, Gaborone; tel. 3972532; fax 3972531; e-mail sygma@info.bw.

Government Publishing House

Department of Government Printing and Publishing Services: Private Bag 0081, Gaborone; tel. 3914441; fax 3912001.

Broadcasting and Communications

TELECOMMUNICATIONS

In early 1998 two companies were granted licences to operate mobile cellular telephone networks.

Botswana Telecommunications Authority (BTA): Private Bag 00495, Gaborone; tel. 3957755; fax 3957976; e-mail bta@bta.org.bw; internet www.bta.org.bw; f. 1996; Chair. C. M. Lekaukau.

Botswana Telecommunications Corporation: POB 700, Gaborone; tel. 3958411; fax 3952777; e-mail desiree@btc.bw; internet www.btc.bw; f. 1980; state-owned; Chair. Wilfred Mandlebe; CEO Noel Herrity.

BROADCASTING

Department of Information and Broadcasting: Private Bag 0060, Gaborone; tel. 3952541; fax 3957138; Dir Andrew Sesinyi.

Radio

Radio Botswana: Private Bag 0060, Gaborone; tel. 3952541; fax 3957138; e-mail rbeng@info.bw; broadcasts in Setswana and English; govt-owned; f. 1965; Dir Andrew Sesinyi; Chief Eng. Habuji Sosome.

Radio Botswana II: Private Bag 0060, Gaborone; tel. 3952541; fax 3971588; f. 1992; commercial service.

Yarona FM: Gaborone; f. 1999; independent; Gen. Man. Moraki Mokgasana.

Television

Botswana Television: Dept of Information & Broadcasting, Private Bag 0060, Gaborone; tel. 3900050; fax 3900051; e-mail simon .higman@btv.bw; govt-funded national TV service; broadcasts commenced in July 2000; Gen. Man. Simon Higman.

TV Association of Botswana: Gaborone; relays SABC-TV and BOP-TV programmes from South Africa.

Finance

(cap. = capital; res = reserves; dep. = deposits; m. = million; brs = branches; amounts in pula)

BANKING

Central Bank

Bank of Botswana: POB 712, Private Bag 154, Plot 1863, Khama Crescent, Gaborone; tel. 3960600; fax 3901100; e-mail rakhudue@ bob.bw; internet www.bankofbotswana.bw; f. 1975; bank of issue; cap. 25m., res 6,604.7m., dep. 33,480.5m. (Dec. 2001); Gov. LINAH MOHOHLO.

Commercial Banks

Bank of Baroda (Botswana) Ltd: POB 21559, Plot 50370, Ground Floor, Acumen Park, Gaborone; tel. 3188878; fax 3188879; e-mail botswana@barodabank.co.bw; internet www.bankofbaroda.com; f. 2001; subsidiary of the Bank of Baroda (India); Man. Dir K. M RAMASUBRAMONEY.

Barclays Bank of Botswana Ltd: POB 478, Barclays House, 6th Floor, Plot 8842, Khama Crescent, Gaborone; tel. 3952041; fax 3913672; f. 1975; 74.9% owned by Barclays Bank PLC (UK); cap. and res 225.9m., total assets 2,845.2m. (Dec. 1999); Chair. C. TIBONE; Man. Dir DUNCAN D. MLAZIE; 48 brs, etc.

First National Bank of Botswana Ltd: POB 1552, Finance House, 5th Floor, Plot 8843, Khama Crescent, Gaborone; tel. 3911669; fax 3906130; e-mail pbellos@fnbbotswana.co.bw; internet www.fnbbotswana.co.bw; f. 1991; 70% owned by First National Bank Holdings Botswana Ltd; cap. and res 249.8m., total assets 2,301.0m. (June 2001); Chair. H. C. L. HERMANS; Man. Dir J. K. MACASKILL; 12 brs.

Stanbic Bank Botswana Ltd: Private Bag 00168, Travaglini House, Plot 1271, Old Lobatse Rd, Gaborone; tel. 3901600; fax 3900171; e-mail stanbic@mega.bw; internet www.stanbic.co.bw; f. 1992; by merger; subsidiary of Standard Bank Investment Corpn Africa Holdings Ltd; cap. 23.1m., res 19.9m., dep 632.0m. (Dec. 2000); Chair. O. M. GABORONE; Man. Dir W. L. V. PRICE; 4 brs.

Standard Chartered Bank Botswana Ltd: POB 496, Standard House, 5th Floor, Plots 1124–1127, The Mall, Gaborone; tel. 3953111; fax 3972933; internet www.standardcharteredbank.com; f. 1975; 75% owned by Standard Chartered Holdings (Africa) BV, Amsterdam; cap. and res 196.5m., total assets 2,393.0m. (Dec. 2000); Chair. P. L. STEENKAMP; CEO D. N. T. KUWANA; 15 brs.

Other Banks

Botswana Savings Bank: POB 1150, Gaborone; tel. 3912555; fax 3952608; e-mail bsb@info.bw; cap. and res 48.4m., dep. 101.5m. (March 2000); Chair. F. MODISE; Man. Dir E. B. MATHE.

Investec Bank: Gaborone; f. 1998; merchant bank; Man. Dir KUMBULANI MUNAMTI.

National Development Bank: POB 225, Development House, Queens Rd, Gaborone; tel. 3952801; fax 3974446; f. 1964; cap. 77.7m., res 17.2m., total assets 247.6m. (March 1999); priority given to agricultural credit for Botswana farmers, and co-operative credit and loans for local business ventures; Chair. F. MODISE; Gen. Man. O. M. RAMASEDI; 5 brs.

STOCK EXCHANGE

Botswana Stock Exchange: Private Bag 00417, Finance House, 4th Floor, Khama Crescent, Gaborone; tel. 3974078; fax 3974079; e-mail stockex@ncs.com.gh; f. 1989; commenced formal functions of a stock exchange in 1995; Chair. LOUIS NCHINDO; CEO R. McCAMMON.

INSURANCE

Botswana Co-operative Insurance Co Ltd: POB 199, Gaborone; tel. and fax 313654; Man. Dir PHILIP MAKGALEMELE.

Botswana Eagle Insurance Co Ltd: POB 1221, 501 Botsalano House, Gaborone; tel. 3919910; fax 3919911; Gen. Man. JOHN MAIN.

Botswana Insurance Holdings: POB 336, Gaborone; tel. 3951791; fax 3906386; Chair. W. A. JACK; Man. Dir J. A. BURDIDGE.

Botswana Life: Private Bag 00296, Gaborone; tel. 3951791; fax 3905884; e-mail blil@lifeinsurance.bw.

Mutual and Federal Insurance Co of Botswana Ltd: Private Bag 00347, Gaborone; tel. 3903333; fax 3903400; Gen. Man. JEAN WALKIN.

Sedgwick James Insurance Brokers (Pty) Ltd: POB 103, Plot 730, The Mall, Botswana Rd, Gaborone; tel. 3914241; fax 3973120.

Tshireletso Insurance Brokers: POB 1967, Gaborone; tel. 3957064; fax 3971558.

Trade and Industry

GOVERNMENT AGENCIES

Botswana Housing Corporation: POB 412, Gaborone; tel. 39605102; fax 3914101; e-mail info@bhc.bw; internet www.bhc.bw; f. 1971; provides housing for central govt and local authority needs and assists with private-sector housing schemes; Gen. Man. E. M. MAPHANYANE; 950 employees.

Department of Food Resources: POB 96, Gaborone; tel. 3954124; f. 1982; procurement, storage and distribution of food commodities under the Drought Relief Programme; Admin. Officer M. S. SEHLULANE.

Department of Town and Regional Planning: Private Bag 0042, Gaborone; tel. 3951935; e-mail infoterra@info.bw; f. 1972; responsible for physical planning matters throughout the country, including formulation of national physical planning policy; prepares devt plans for settlements and regions and provides physical planning advice to govt and local authorities as well as private bodies.

DEVELOPMENT ORGANIZATIONS

Botswana Development Corporation Ltd: Private Bag 160, Moedi, Plot 50380, Gaborone International Showgrounds, off Machel Drive, Gaborone; tel. 3651300; fax 3904193; e-mail bdc@bdc.bw; internet www.bdc.bw; f. 1970; Chair. S. S. G. TUMELO; Man. Dir KENNETH O. MATAMBO.

Botswana Enterprise Development Unit (BEDU): POB 0014, Plot 1269, Lobatse Rd, Gaborone; f. 1974; promotes industrialization and rural devt; Dir J. LINDFORS.

Botswana Export Development and Investment Authority (BEDIA): POB 3122, Plot 28, Matsitama Rd, The Main Mall, Gaborone; tel. 3181931; fax 3181941; e-mail bedia@bedia.bw; internet www.bedia.co.bw; f. 1998; promotes and facilitates local and foreign investment; Chair. UTTUM COREA; CEO MMASEKEGOA MASIREMWAMBA.

Department of Trade and Investment Promotion (TIPA) Ministry of Trade and Industry: Private Bag 00367, Gaborone; tel. 3951790; fax 3905375; e-mail tipa@info.bw; internet www.tipa.bw; promotes industrial and commercial investment, diversification and expansion; offers consultancy, liaison and information services; participates in overseas trade fairs and trade and investment missions; Dir D. TSHEKO.

Financial Services Co of Botswana (Pty) Ltd: POB 1129, Finance House, Khama Crescent, Gaborone; tel. 3951363; fax 3957815; f. 1974; hire purchase, mortgages, industrial leasing and debt factoring; Chair. M. E. HOPKINS; Man. Dir R. A. PAWSON.

Integrated Field Services: Private Bag 004, Ministry of Trade and Industry, Gaborone; tel. 3953024; fax 3971539; promotes industrialization and rural development; Dir B. T. TIBONE.

International Financial Services Centre: Private Bag 160, Gaborone; tel. 3651385; fax 3913075; e-mail info@ifsc.co.bw; internet www.ifsc.co.bw; f. 2000; Resident Project Man. JOHN CURTIN.

CHAMBER OF COMMERCE

Botswana National Chamber of Commerce and Industry: POB 20344, Gaborone; tel. 3952677.

INDUSTRIAL AND TRADE ASSOCIATIONS

Botswana Agricultural Marketing Board (BAMB): Private Bag 0053, 1227 Haile Selassie Rd, Gaborone; tel. 3951341; fax 3952926; Chair. the Perm. Sec., Ministry of Agriculture; Gen. Man. S. B. TAUKOBONG.

Botswana Meat Commission (BMC): Private Bag 4, Lobatse; tel. 5331000; fax 5330504; e-mail mmannathoko@bmc.bw; f. 1966; slaughter of livestock, export of hides and skins, carcasses, frozen and chilled boneless beef; operates tannery and beef products cannery; Chair. and Exec. Chair. Dr M. MANNATHOKO.

EMPLOYERS' ORGANIZATION

Botswana Confederation of Commerce, Industry and Manpower (BOCCIM): POB 432, BOCCIM House, Gaborone; e-mail boccim@info.bw; f. 1971; Pres. MOGOLORI MODISI; Dir ELIAS DEWAH.

UTILITIES

Electricity

Botswana Power Corporation: POB 48, Motlakase House, Macheng Way, Gaborone; tel. 3603203; fax 3973563; f. 1971; operates power stations at Selebi-Phikwe (capacity 65 MW) and Morupule (132 MW); Chair. C. M. LEKAUKAU; CEO KETANE SITHOLE.

Water

Department of Water Affairs: Khama Crescent, Private Bag 0018, Gaborone; tel. 3656600; fax 3972738; provides public water supplies for rural areas.

Water Utilities Corporation: Private Bag 00276, Gaborone; tel. 3604400; fax 3973852; e-mail metsi@wuc.bw; f. 1970; 100% state-owned; supplies water to main urban centres; Chair. the Perm. Sec., Ministry of Minerals, Energy and Water Affairs; Chief Exec. F. MAUNGE.

CO-OPERATIVES

Department of Co-operative Development: POB 86, Gaborone; f. 1964; promotes marketing and supply, consumer, dairy, horticultural and fisheries co-operatives, thrift and loan societies, credit societies, a co-operative union and a co-operative bank.

Botswana Co-operative Union: Gaborone; f. 1970; Dir AARON RAMOSAKO.

TRADE UNIONS

Botswana Federation of Trade Unions: POB 440, Gaborone; tel. and fax 3952534; e-mail bot.ftu@info.bw; f. 1977; Gen. Sec. MARANYANE KEBITSANG.

Affiliated Unions

Air Botswana Employees' Union: POB 92, Gaborone; Gen. Sec. DANIEL MOTSUMI.

Barclays Management Staff Union: POB 478, Gaborone; Gen. Sec. TEFO LIONJANGA.

BCL Senior Staff Union: POB 383, Selebi-Phikwe; Gen. Sec. KABELO MATTHEWS.

Botswana Agricultural Marketing Board Workers' Union: Private Bag 0053, Gaborone; Gen. Sec. M. E. SEMATHANE.

Botswana Bank Employees' Union: POB 111, Gaborone; Gen. Sec. KEOLOPILE GABORONE.

Botswana Beverages and Allied Workers' Union: POB 41358, Gaborone; Gen. Sec. S. SENWELO.

Botswana Brigade Teachers' Union: Private Bag 007, Molepolole; Gen. Sec. SADIKE KGOKONG.

Botswana Commercial and General Workers' Union: Gaborone; Gen. Sec. KEDIRETSE MPETANG.

Botswana Construction Workers' Union: POB 1508, Gaborone; Gen. Sec. JOSHUA KESIILWE.

Botswana Diamond Sorters-Valuators' Union: POB 1186, Gaborone; Gen. Sec. FELIX T. LESETEDI.

Botswana Housing Corporation Staff Union: POB 412, Gaborone; Gen. Sec. GORATA DINGALO.

Botswana Meat Industry Workers' Union: POB 181, Lobatse; Gen. Sec. JOHNSON BOJOSI.

Botswana Mining Workers' Union: Gaborone; Gen. Sec. BALEKAMANG S. GANASIANE.

Botswana Postal Services Workers' Union: POB 87, Gaborone; Gen. Sec. AARON MOSWEU.

Botswana Power Corporation Workers' Union: Private Bag 0053, Gaborone; Gen. Sec. MOLEFE MODISE.

Botswana Railways and Artisan Employees' Union: POB 1486, Gaborone; Gen. Sec. PATRICK MAGOWE.

Botswana Railways Senior Staff Union: Mahalapye; Gen. Sec. LENTSWE LETSWELETSE.

Botswana Railways Workers' Union: POB 181, Gaborone; Gen. Sec. ERNEST T. G. MOHUTSIWA.

Botswana Telecommunications Employees' Union: Gaborone; Gen. Sec. BOITUMELO KAUTA.

Botswana Vaccine Institute Staff Union: Private Bag 0031, Gaborone; Gen. Sec. ELLIOT MODISE.

Central Bank Union: POB 712, Gaborone; Gen. Sec. GODFREY NGIDI.

National Amalgamated Local and Central Government, Parastatal, Statutory Body and Manual Workers' Union: POB 374, Gaborone; Gen. Sec. DICKSON KELATLHEGETSWE.

National Development Bank Employees' Union: POB 225, Gaborone; Sec.-Gen. MATSHEDISO FOLOGANG.

Non-Academic Staff Union: Private Bag 0022, Gaborone; Gen. Sec. ISAAC THOTHE.

Transport

RAILWAYS

The 960-km railway line from Mafikeng, South Africa, to Bulawayo, Zimbabwe, passes through Botswana and has been operated by Botswana Railways (BR) since 1987. In 1997 there were 888 km of 1,067-mm-gauge track within Botswana, including three branches serving the Selebi-Phikwe mining complex (56 km), the Morupule colliery (16 km) and the Sua Pan soda-ash deposits (175 km). BR derives 85%–90% of its earnings from freight traffic, although passenger services do operate between Gaborone and Francistown, and Lobatse and Bulawayo. Through its links with Spoornet, which operates the South African railways system and the National Railways of Zimbabwe, BR provides connections with Namibia and Swaziland to the south, and an unbroken rail link to Zambia, the Democratic Republic of the Congo, Angola, Mozambique, Tanzania and Malawi to the north. Freight traffic on BR has been severely reduced, however, since Zimbabwe's construction in 1999 of a rail link from Bulawayo to Beitbridge, on its border with South Africa.

Botswana Railways (BR): Private Bag 52, Mahalapye; tel. 4711375; fax 4711385; e-mail botrail@info.bw; f. 1987; Gen. Man. C. B. BOTANA.

ROADS

In 1999 there were 10,217 km of roads, including 3,360 km of main roads, and 2,210 km of secondary roads; some 55.0% of the road network was paved (including a main road from Gaborone, via Francistown, to Kazungula, where the borders of Botswana, Namibia, Zambia and Zimbabwe meet). The construction of a 340-km road between Nata and Maun was completed in the late 1990s. Construction of the 600-km Trans-Kalahari Highway, from Jwaneng to the port of Walvis Bay on the Namibian coast, commenced in 1990 and was completed in 1998. A car-ferry service operates from Kazungula across the Zambezi river into Zambia.

Department of Road Transport and Safety: Private Bag 0026, Gaborone; tel. 3905442; responsible for national road network; responsible to the Ministry of Works and Transport; Dir MOSES K. SEBOLAI.

CIVIL AVIATION

The main international airport is at Gaborone. Four other major airports are located at Kasane, Maun, Francistown and Ghanzi. In 2000 there were also 108 airfields throughout the country. Scheduled services of Air Botswana are supplemented by an active charter and business sector.

Air Botswana: POB 92, Sir Seretse Khama Airport, Gaborone; tel. 3951921; e-mail tmaswiki@airbotswana.co.bw; internet www .airbotswana.co.bw; f. 1972; govt-owned; transfer to private sector scheduled for mid-2003; domestic services and regional services to countries in eastern and southern Africa; Dir-Gen. WILLIE MOKGATLHE.

Tourism

There are five game reserves and three national parks, including Chobe, near Victoria Falls, on the Zambia–Zimbabwe border. Efforts to expand the tourism industry include plans for the construction of new hotels and the rehabilitation of existing hotel facilities. In 1999 foreign tourist arrivals totalled 843,314; receipts from tourism amounted to US $234m. in 1999.

Department of Tourism: Ministry of Conservation, Wildlife and Tourism; Private Bag 0047, Standard House, 2nd Floor, Main Mall, Gaborone; tel. 3953024; fax 3908675; e-mail botswanatourism@gov .bw; internet www.botswanatourism.org; f. 1994; Dir T. NDZINGE.

Department of Wildlife and National Parks: POB 131, Gaborone; tel. 3971405; fax 3912354; e-mail dwnp@gov.bw; Dir J. MATLHARE.

Hotel and Tourism Association of Botswana: Gaborone; tel. 3957144; Dir MODISE MOTHOAGAE.

BRAZIL

Introductory Survey

Location, Climate, Language, Religion, Flag, Capital

The Federative Republic of Brazil, the fifth largest country in the world, lies in central and north-eastern South America. To the north are Venezuela, Colombia, Guyana, Suriname and French Guiana, to the west Peru and Bolivia, and to the south Paraguay, Argentina and Uruguay. Brazil has a very long coastline on the Atlantic Ocean. Climatic conditions vary from hot and wet in the tropical rain forest of the Amazon basin to temperate in the savannah grasslands of the central and southern uplands, which have warm summers and mild winters. In Rio de Janeiro temperatures are generally between 17°C (63°F) and 29°C (85°F). The official language is Portuguese. Almost all of the inhabitants profess Christianity, and about 90% are adherents of the Roman Catholic Church. The national flag (proportions 7 by 10) is green, bearing, at the centre, a yellow diamond containing a blue celestial globe with 26 white five-pointed stars (one for each of Brazil's states), arranged in the pattern of the southern firmament, below an equatorial scroll with the motto 'Ordem e Progresso' ('Order and Progress'), and a single star above the scroll. The capital is Brasília.

Recent History

Formerly a Portuguese possession, Brazil became an independent monarchy in 1822, and a republic in 1889. A federal constitution for the United States of Brazil was adopted in 1891. Following social unrest in the 1920s, the economic crisis of 1930 resulted in a major revolt, led by Dr Getúlio Vargas, who was installed as President. He governed the country as a benevolent dictator until forced to resign by the armed forces in December 1945. During Vargas's populist rule, Brazil enjoyed internal stability and steady economic progress. He established a strongly authoritarian corporate state, similar to fascist regimes in Europe, but in 1942 Brazil entered the Second World War on the side of the Allies.

A succession of ineffectual presidential terms (including another by Vargas, who was re-elected in 1950) failed to establish stable government in the late 1940s and early 1950s. President Jânio Quadros, elected in 1960, resigned after only seven months in office, and in September 1961 the Vice-President, João Goulart, was sworn in as President. Military leaders suspected Goulart, the leader of the Partido Trabalhista Brasileiro (PTB), of communist sympathies, and they were reluctant to let him succeed to the presidency. As a compromise, the Constitution was amended to restrict the powers of the President and to provide for a Prime Minister. However, following the appointment of three successive premiers during a 16-month period of mounting political crisis, the system was rejected when a referendum, conducted in January 1963, approved a return to the presidential system of government, whereupon President Goulart formed his own Cabinet.

Following a period of economic crisis, exacerbated by allegations of official corruption, the left-wing regime of President Goulart was overthrown in April 1964 by a bloodless right-wing military coup led by Gen. (later Marshal) Humberto Castelo Branco, the Army Chief of Staff, who was promptly elected President by the National Congress (Congresso Nacional). In October 1965 President Castelo Branco assumed dictatorial powers, and all 13 existing political parties were banned. In December, however, two artificially-created parties, the pro-Government Aliança Renovadora Nacional (ARENA) and the opposition Movimento Democrático Brasileiro (MDB), were granted official recognition. President Castelo Branco nominated as his successor the Minister of War, Marshal Artur da Costa e Silva, who was elected in October 1966 and took office in March 1967 as President of the redesignated Federative Republic of Brazil (a new Constitution was introduced simultaneously). The ailing President da Costa e Silva was forced to resign in September 1969 and was replaced by a triumvirate of military leaders.

The military regime granted the President wide-ranging powers to rule by decree. In October 1969 the ruling junta introduced a revised Constitution, vesting executive authority in an indirectly-elected President. The Congress, suspended since December 1968, was recalled and elected Gen. Emílio Garrastazú Médici as President. Médici was succeeded as President by Gen. Ernesto Geisel and Gen. João Baptista de Figueiredo, respectively. Despite the attempts of both Presidents to pursue a policy of *abertura*, or opening to democratization (legislation to end the controlled two-party system was approved in 1979), opposition to military rule intensified throughout the 1970s and early 1980s. In November 1982 the government-sponsored Partido Democrático Social (PDS) suffered significant losses at elections to the Câmara dos Deputados (Chamber of Deputies), state governorships and municipal councils. However, the PDS secured a majority of seats in the Senado Federal (Federal Senate) and, owing to pre-election legislation, seemed likely to enjoy a guaranteed majority in the electoral college, scheduled to choose a successor to Gen. Figueiredo in 1985.

However, in July 1984 Vice-President Chaves de Mendonça and the influential Marco de Oliveira Maciel, a former Governor of Pernambuco State, announced the formation of an alliance of liberal PDS members with members of the Partido do Movimento Democrático Brasileiro (PMDB). This offered the opposition a genuine opportunity to defeat the PDS in the electoral college. In December the liberal alliance formed an official political party, the Partido Frente Liberal (PFL). At the presidential election, conducted in January 1985, the PFL candidate, Tancredo Neves (Prime Minister in 1961–62) was elected as Brazil's first civilian President for 21 years, winning 480 of the 686 votes in the electoral college. Prior to the inauguration ceremony in March, however, Neves was taken ill, and died the following month. The PFL vice-presidential candidate, José Sarney, who had assumed the role of Acting President in Neves' absence, took office as President in April. President Sarney made no alterations to the Cabinet selected by Neves, and he affirmed his commitment to fulfilling the objectives of the late President-designate. In May the Congress approved a constitutional amendment restoring direct elections by universal suffrage.

The introduction in February 1986 of an anti-inflation programme, the Cruzado Plan, proved, initially, to be successful and boosted the popularity of President Sarney. Support for the Government was further demonstrated in November 1986 at elections to the Congress, which was to operate as a Constitutional Assembly. The Constitutional Assembly was installed in February 1987, and the constitutional debate was dominated by the issue of the length of the presidential mandate. In June 1988 the Constitutional Assembly finally approved a presidential mandate of five years. The first round of voting for the presidential election was provisionally set for 15 November 1989, thereby enabling Sarney to remain in office until March 1990. This *de facto* victory for the President precipitated a series of resignations by some of the leading members of the PMDB, who subsequently formed a new centre-left party, the Partido da Social Democracia Brasileira (PSDB). The Constitution was approved by the Congress on 22 September 1988, and was promulgated on 5 October. Among its 245 articles were provisions transferring many hitherto presidential powers to the legislature. In addition, censorship was abolished as was the National Security Law, whereby many political dissidents had been detained; the minimum voting age was lowered to 16 years; and the principle of habeas corpus was recognized. However, the Constitution offered no guarantees of land reform, and was thought by many to be nationalistic and protectionist.

In April 1988 the Government revealed its commitment to drastic reductions in planned public-sector expenditure, primarily based on a 'freeze' on salary increases for state employees. The resulting combination of industrial unrest and social tension was thought to have been a decisive factor in the PMDB's poor results at municipal elections held on 15 November, when the centre-left Partido Democrático Trabalhista (PDT) and the left-wing Partido dos Trabalhadores (PT) made important gains at the expense of the ruling party.

Brazil's first presidential election by direct voting since 1960 took place on 15 November 1989. The main contenders were the conservative Fernando Collor de Mello, of the newly-formed

Partido de Reconstrução Nacional (PRN), Luiz Inácio (Lula) da Silva of the PT and Leonel Brizola of the PDT. A second round was held on 17 December, contested by the two leading candidates, Collor de Mello and da Silva, neither having achieved the required 50% of votes in November. Collor de Mello was declared the winner, with 53% of the votes cast. Following his inauguration as President on 15 March 1990, Collor de Mello announced an ambitious programme of economic reform, entitled 'New Brazil' (known as the 'Collor Plan'), with the principal aim of reducing inflation, which had reached a monthly rate of more than 80%. A new currency, the cruzeiro (to replace, at par, the novo cruzado) was also introduced. The results of congressional and state gubernatorial elections, conducted in October and November 1990, rejected extreme left- and right-wing parties in favour of familiar candidates from small, centre-right parties. Nevertheless, the President was confident of securing sufficient support to continue to pursue a programme of radical economic reform.

The Government's loss of popularity was largely attributed to the severity and apparent failure of its economic austerity programme. A second economic plan, presented as a simple intensification of the first Collor Plan, was implemented in February 1991 by Minister of the Economy, Zélia Cardoso de Mello. In March Collor de Mello announced a new Plan for National Reconstruction, which envisaged further deregulation and rationalization of many state-controlled areas, including the ports, and the communications and fuel sectors. By May 1991, despite a considerable decrease in the monthly rate of inflation, Cardoso de Mello's political popularity had been undermined by her confrontational style of negotiation, and she was forced to resign.

Collor de Mello's position became increasingly precarious towards the end of 1991, after allegations of mismanagement of federal funds were made against his wife and against several associates in the President's home state of Alagoas. During informal multi-party negotiations in September 1991, the President attempted to achieve greater congressional consensus and to reinforce his own mandate. Following a specially-convened meeting of the emergency Council of the Republic in the same month, Collor de Mello presented a comprehensive series of proposals for constitutional amendment before the Congress. Nevertheless, allegations of high-level corruption persisted into 1992 and, despite comprehensive cabinet changes in January and April, the President failed to dispel suspicions sufficiently to attract the wider political participation in government necessary to facilitate the passage of legislation through an increasingly ineffectual Congress. In May, moreover, the President became the focus of further allegations, following a series of disclosures made by Collor de Mello's younger brother, which appeared to implicate the President in a number of corrupt practices orchestrated by Paulo César Farias, Collor de Mello's 1989 election campaign treasurer. While the President dismissed the allegations as false, in May the Congress approved the creation of a special commission of inquiry to investigate the affair. In early September, acting upon the report of the special commission of inquiry, and bolstered by massive popular support, a 49-member congressional committee authorized the initiation of impeachment proceedings against the President, within the Câmara dos Deputados. On 29 September the Câmara voted to proceed with the impeachment of the President for abuses of authority and position, prompting the immediate resignation of the Cabinet. On 2 October Collor de Mello surrendered authority to Vice-President Itamar Franco for a six-month period, pending the final pronouncement regarding his future in office, to be decided by the Senado. Following lengthy negotiations, Franco announced the composition of a new Cabinet in October, representing a broad political base.

In December 1992 the Senado voted overwhelmingly to proceed with Collor de Mello's impeachment and to indict the President for 'crimes of responsibility'. Within minutes of the opening of the impeachment trial on 29 December, however, Collor de Mello announced his resignation from the presidency. Itamar Franco was immediately sworn in as President (to serve the remainder of Collor de Mello's term). On the following day the Senado, which had agreed to continue with proceedings against Collor de Mello, announced that the former President's political rights (including immunity from prosecution) were to be removed. In January 1993 Collor de Mello was notified by the Supreme Court that he was to stand trial, as an ordinary citizen, on charges of 'passive corruption and criminal association'. Proceedings against Collor de Mello were initiated in June, and

in December the Supreme Federal Tribunal endorsed the Senado's eight-year ban on his holding public office. In December 1994, however, the Tribunal voted to acquit Collor de Mello of the charges, owing to insufficient evidence. In January 1998 the former President was cleared of charges of illegal enrichment.

At a referendum conducted in April 1993 voters overwhelmingly rejected the introduction of a parliamentary system of government or the restoration of the monarchy, opting instead to retain the presidential system.

Following several unsuccessful attempts in late 1992 and early 1993 to address the problems of burgeoning inflation and massive budget deficit, in June 1993 the new Minister of the Economy, Fernando Henrique Cardoso, announced the terms of the Government's latest economic programme, the 'plano de verdade' (real plan). A new currency, the cruzeiro real, was introduced in August. A programme for economic stability, announced in December 1993, sought to regulate the flow of federal resources to states and municipalities. Congressional approval for the establishment of a Social Emergency Fund (providing for further centralization of control over the expenditures and revenue of states and government agencies) prompted the activation of a transitional index, the Unidade Real de Valor (URV), linked to the US dollar, on 1 March 1994. On 1 July the new currency, the real, was introduced, at par with the dollar.

In April 1993 the PDT leader, Leonel Brizola, announced the party's withdrawal from the ruling coalition, following Franco's decision to proceed with the privatization of the prestigious national steel company, the Companhia Siderúrgica Nacional (CSN). In August the Partido Socialista Brasileiro (PSB) also withdrew from the coalition, and in the following month the PMDB national council narrowly defeated a motion to end its association with the Government. The fragility of the Government was exacerbated by a new corruption scandal in October, in which numerous senior politicians were implicated in a fraudulent scheme in which political influence was allegedly exercised in order to secure state projects for individual construction companies, in exchange for bribes. A congressional committee of inquiry was established, which in January 1994 recommended the expulsion of 18 federal deputies, and the further investigation of a number of deputies, governors and one senator. In mid-April the Câmara dos Deputados voted to expel three of the named deputies and to continue investigations into four deputies who had recently resigned, in order to prevent their participation in the October elections. In the same month Congress concluded a review of the Constitution, having adopted just six amendments, including a reduction in the length of the presidential term from five to four years.

Allegations of corruption and misconduct preceding the elections in October 1994 forced the replacement of the vice-presidential running mates of both Cardoso and da Silva, the withdrawal from the contest of the presidential candidate of the PL and the resignation of the Ministers of Finance and Mines and Energy. Cardoso, whose candidacy was supported by the PFL, the PTB, the PL and the business community, won the presidential contest of 3 October in the first round, with an overall majority of 54.3% of the votes, following a campaign that had focused largely on the success of his economic initiatives. The discovery of large-scale, organized electoral fraud in the State of Rio de Janeiro forced the annulment of elections for state and federal deputies there, which were reorganized to coincide with the second-round gubernatorial elections of 15 November. PSDB candidates secured six of the 27 state governorships. Although the PMDB increased its number of state governorships from seven to nine, and continued to boast the largest single-party representation in the Congress, the party's presidential candidate, Orestes Quércia, had attracted only 4.4% of the votes cast.

Cardoso was inaugurated as President on 1 January 1995 and a new Cabinet was installed on the following day. The multi-party composition of the Cabinet (with portfolios allocated not only to those parties that had supported his candidacy, but also to the PT and the PMDB) demonstrated the new President's need to maintain a broad base of congressional support in order to secure prompt endorsement for proposed constitutional reform of the taxation and social security systems. Cardoso immediately made clear his intention to continue the programme of economic reform in order to control public expenditure and reduce inflation. However, opposition to the programme of economic stabilization and to renewed efforts by the Government to introduce constitutional amendments, including those that would end state monopolies in the telecommunications and petroleum sectors, resulted, in May 1995, in a general strike, organized by the Central Unica dos Trabalhadores (CUT) trade-union confederation. The President's decision to order military intervention in a number of crucial petroleum refineries was widely interpreted as evidence of the Government's intent to undermine the concerted action of the political opposition and the trade unions. However, on 20 June the Câmara dos Deputados approved the proposal to open the sector to private participation. (The amendment relating to the petroleum sector was subsequently approved by the Senado in November; constitutional amendments providing for an end to state control of telecommunications, natural gas distribution and a number of shipping routes, were formally promulgated by the Congress in August.)

In September 1995 three existing right-wing parties merged to create the Partido Progressista Brasileiro (PPB), which expressed cautious support for the Government. By December, however, Cardoso's integrity had been seriously compromised by the alleged involvement of a number of his political associates in irregular financial transactions organized by the Banco Econômico in support of recent electoral campaigns, and by an influence-peddling scandal arising from the award to a US company, Raytheon, of the contract for development of an Amazon Regional Surveillance System (Sivam), which resulted in the resignation, in November, of the Minister of the Air Force. A congressional inquiry into the Sivam affair was initiated in the same month. In February 1996 a special committee of the Senado made a recommendation, supported by Cardoso, that the Government should negotiate a substantial foreign loan to honour the Sivam contract with Raytheon, and in October 1996 the President was able to endorse the agreement.

Meanwhile, investigation of the so-called 'pink folder' of politicians continued during 1996, as the banking sector was plunged into further crisis. In March it was revealed that the Government had withheld details of a US $5,000m.-fraud perpetrated at the Banco Nacional a decade earlier. Moreover, it emerged that the Government had extended a recent credit facility of US $5,800m. to the bank in order to facilitate its merger with UNIBANCO in November 1995. Throughout the year renewed attempts by the Government to secure congressional approval for constitutional reforms relating to taxation, public administration and social security were repeatedly obstructed, delayed or defeated in the Congress, despite the adoption of a number of concessionary clauses and the successful negotiation of a compromise agreement on social security with trade-union organizations in January.

The results of municipal elections conducted on 3 October 1996 revealed a reduction in support for the PSDB and represented a disappointment for many veteran parties. The PPB, the PFL and the PSB, however, all made significant gains. None the less, Cardoso's own popularity benefited from the success of the Government's attempts to control inflation.

In mid-1996 the moderate Força Sindical trade union organization joined the CUT in urging workers to observe Brazil's first general strike in five years, on 21 June. Despite the Government's announcement, in April, of a job-creation programme to provide employment for 3m. Brazilians, the unions were dissatisfied with the Government's failure to halt rising levels of unemployment. However, the strike was only partially observed, and on the same day the Government announced details of the next phase of its massive divestment programme. Several companies in the power sector, 31 ports and the prestigious mining company, Companhia Vale do Rio Doce (CVRD) were among those state concerns to be offered for sale. In July the Government announced that the state telecommunications company, Telebrás, together with large sections of the rail and power networks, would be privatized by the end of 1998. Further reductions in public spending were announced in August and a new programme of economic measures designed to further reduce the fiscal deficit was introduced in October.

In February 1997 the Câmara dos Deputados confirmed its approval of a constitutional amendment to permit the President to stand for re-election in 1998, Cardoso's position having been strengthened by the election of two of his supporters to the presidencies of both chambers of the Congress. Following the Senado vote in favour of the legislation (despite allegations of bribery relating to its passage through the lower house), the constitutional amendment received the upper house's final approval in June and was swiftly ratified by President Cardoso.

In March 1997 legislation was approved ending the long-standing monopoly of PETROBRAS over the petroleum industry. In June the Senado's rejection of legislation to reform

the civil service, however, was a major set-back to the Government's programme of economic reform and in particular to its attempts to reduce the budget deficit. Nevertheless, a series of compromises enabled the Government to renew its plans for civil-service reform, and in July an opposition amendment to the proposed legislation was narrowly defeated in the legislature. In November the lower house gave its final approval to the legislation.

In June 1997 the PT ordered an inquiry into allegations of corruption on the part of its presidential candidate, Lula da Silva. Although da Silva was exonerated by the investigation (thus permitting him to renew his candidacy for the 1998 election), other financial irregularities were uncovered, leading to a sharp decline in the PT's popularity. As the 1998 presidential election approached, various potential candidates announced changes in their party affiliation. In August 1997 Ciro Gomes, a former Minister of Finance, defected from the PSDB to the smaller Partido Popular Socialista (PPS), thereby exacerbating the internal crisis within the PSDB. In July 1997 an investigation by the Senado into a financial scandal arising from fraudulent bond issues concluded that 20 prominent politicians and senior officials (including three state governors, the mayor of São Paulo, Celso Pitta, and his predecessor, Paulo Maluf) had been involved in a criminal operation. A total of 161 financial institutions, including Banco Bradesco, Brazil's largest private bank, were implicated in the scandal. In January 1998 Celso Pitta was found guilty of fraud, but remained in office pending an appeal.

Despite his declared commitment to further economic austerity measures, at the presidential election held on 4 October 1998 Cardoso, again the PSDB's candidate, became the first President to be re-elected for a second consecutive term, securing almost 53.1% of the valid votes cast. Lula da Silva of the PT won 31.7% of the votes, while Ciro Gomes of the PPS received 11.0%. At the concurrent legislative elections, the PSDB also performed well, securing 99 of the 513 seats in the lower chamber, while its electoral allies—the PFL, PMDB, PPB and PTB—won a total of 278 seats, bringing the coalition's total representation to 377. Opposition candidates defeated the incumbent governors of the populous states of Rio de Janeiro, Rio do Sul and Minas Gerais. Prior to formally resuming office on 1 January 1999, President Cardoso announced the composition of his Cabinet. Although most ministers retained their portfolios, changes included the creation of a new development ministry, headed by Celso Láfer, which, it was hoped, would improve relations with the business community.

In January 1999, Itamar Franco, the newly-elected Governor of Minas Gerais, declared that the state was defaulting on its debt to the federal Government, indirectly precipitating the devaluation of the Brazilian currency. In the same month, however, the Câmara dos Deputados endorsed long-proposed reforms to the country's munificent pension system. The passage of the controversial legislation through the Senado in late January considerably enhanced the prospects of President Cardoso's programme of fiscal austerity.

Following the withdrawal of the PTB from the ruling coalition in March 1999 as a result of the unexpected dismissal of the Minister of the Budget and Administration, Paulo Paiva, Cardoso's Government came under further pressure in May when the PFL announced its intention to present its own candidate at the next presidential election, scheduled for 2002. In July, in an attempt to promote unity within the administration and to give impetus to the programme of economic reform, President Cardoso announced a reorganization of the Cabinet. A new Ministry of National Integration was established. The administration's popularity continued to decline, however, and in August demonstrations against the Government's economic and social policies culminated in the arrival in Brasília of as many as 100,000 marchers, comprising political opponents led by the PT, trade unionists and landless individuals. In early September, Clovis Covilho, Minister of Development, Industry and Trade, was dismissed by the President, following a public disagreement over the policy of economic austerity. He was replaced by Alcides Tápias.

Meanwhile, in April 1999 a congressional commission commenced investigations into allegations of organized criminal activities. In September Hildebrando Pascoal became the second deputy that year to be expelled from the lower house as a result of accusations of murder. It was alleged that Pascoal had been the leader of a cocaine-trafficking gang involved in the torture and murder of numerous victims in the state of Acre. In October the congressional commission exposed a nation-wide criminal network that allegedly encompassed politicians, government officials, judges, police officers, business executives and banking officials. Embarrassed by the scale of the revelations (which extended to reports of drugs-trafficking within the National Congress building), in November President Cardoso announced the establishment of a new anti-corruption force to combat the growing problem of organized crime. In the following month, in an effort to improve accountability and to strengthen congressional powers of investigation, the Senado approved a constitutional amendment to restrict presidential use of provisional measures, to which successive Governments had frequently resorted as a means to circumvent the cumbersome legislative process.

In January 2000 the Minister of Defence, Elcio Alvares, was dismissed by President Cardoso and replaced by the former Attorney-General, Geraldo Magela da Cruz Quintão. In April, the Minister of Justice, José Carlos Dias, resigned following a disagreement over a joint drugs-control programme with Bolivia. He was replaced by the former National Secretary for Human Rights, José Gregori. In May the Minister of Sports and Tourism, Rafael Greca de Macedo, was dismissed and replaced by Carlos Melles, a PFL member. In mid-February the PSDB announced a new congressional alliance with the centrist PTB, thus becoming the largest legislative bloc in the Câmara dos Deputados and further bolstering support for the ruling executive.

In late March 2000 the Mayor of São Paulo, Celso Pitta, was accused of bribing members of the city council to reject a move for his dismissal in 1997 after being found guilty of fraud. It was later alleged that Pitta had received a substantial loan from a businessman in return for favourable treatment from his administration, and Pitta was dismissed as Mayor. However, he was again permitted to remain in office, pending a further appeal and, following a ruling in mid-June by the Federal Court of Appeal, he was reinstated. In August the announcement by the PTB that it was to dissolve the recently-formed alliance with the PSDB, owing to the Government's increasing unpopularity, re-established the PFL as the largest party in the Câmara dos Deputados.

At municipal elections in October 2000 the PT made significant gains, obtaining 14.1% of votes cast; the PSDB received 15.9% of votes and the PMDB 15.7%. A second round of voting was required in 16 cities, where no candidate secured more than 50% of the vote. In the same month Pedro Simon was selected as the PMDB's candidate in presidential elections scheduled to be held in October 2002.

In January 2001 Celso Láfer, hitherto Minister of Development, Industry and Trade, was appointed Minister of Foreign Affairs following the resignation, on personal grounds, of Luiz Felipe Lampréia. In mid-February Jader Barbalho, the PMDB leader, was elected Senate President and the PSDB's Aéceo Neves was elected leader of the lower house. However, the outgoing Senate President, António Carlos Margalhães of the PFL, alleged that Barbalho was involved in corrupt activities, leading to tension between members of the ruling coalition. In late February President Cardoso dismissed two PFL ministers from his Cabinet, on the grounds that they had failed to defend the Government against Margalhães' allegations. However, in July Barbalho relinquished his position as President of the Senado, for a period of two months, after it emerged that he had been involved in fraudulent and corrupt activities while Governor of the state of Pará in the 1980s. He was replaced, in an acting capacity, by Edison Lobão. In October Barbalho resigned from the Senado in an attempt to prevent his own impeachment, were he to be found guilty of corruption.

Accusations of corruption against senior members of government continued throughout 2001. In April the credibility of the ruling coalition was further undermined by the unauthorized release of telephone transcripts secretly recorded by police during investigations into the disappearance of some US $830m. from an Amazonian development company, Superintendência do Desenvolvimento da Amazônia (SUDAM), with which Barbalho was personally connected. In May the former leader of the PSDB, José Roberto Arruda, resigned his Senado seat after it was alleged that he had improperly disclosed confidential computerized voting records. Furthermore, a few days later, a congressional investigation revealed that Margalhães may also have been implicated in the scandal. Despite initially refuting the allegations, Margalhães subsequently resigned his seat in the Senado. Also in May, the Minister of National Integration,

Fernando Bezerra, resigned following allegations of corruption; it was believed that he had used his position to ensure that a company in which he was a major shareholder received funding from the Superintendência do Desenvolvimento do Nordeste (SUDENE), another state development agency (both SUDENE and SUDAM were dissolved in early May). Shortly after Bezerra's departure, the Minister of Labour and Employment, Francisco Oswaldo Neves Dornelles, also left the Government following a disagreement over the creation of a congressional committee to investigate public-sector corruption. In July the Minister of Development, Industry and Trade, Alcides Tápia, resigned for personal reasons, although it was thought that his decision was connected to Brazil's increasing current account deficit. He was succeeded by Sérgio Amaral. A minor cabinet reshuffle was effected in October in which Aloysio Nunes Ferreira was appointed Minister of Justice, and Ney Suassuna was given the post of Minister of National Integration, in succession to Ramez Tebet, who had become President of the Senado.

During 2002 investigations into corruption and organized crime continued. In April a federal intervention was requested in the state of Espírito Santo after a lawyer was murdered and four court buildings set on fire. On 16 July Paulo de Tarso Ramos Ribeiro was appointed Minister of Justice, replacing Miguel Reale, who had been in the office for only three months. Reale and several other key figures, including the general director of the federal police, had resigned, apparently in protest at President Cardoso's involvement in the reversal of a decision by Attorney-General, Geraldo Brindeiro, to request a federal judiciary investigation into organized crime in Espírito Santo, whose capital, Vitória, had the highest murder rate in Latin America. Cardoso suspended the investigation, which focused on the activities of a paramilitary group, Scuderie le Coq, and instead deployed a 90-day police task-force in the state.

Late 2001 and early 2002 were dominated by speculation surrounding the party candidacies for the forthcoming presidential elections, which were to take place in October 2002. The ruling PSDB-PFL-PMDB coalition suffered a set-back in August 2001 when the PFL proposed its own presidential candidate, Roseanna Sarney, the Governor of Maranhão. It had been widely predicted that the former President and current Governor of the state of Minas Gerais, Itamar Franco, would secure the PMDB's presidential nomination; however, following a dispute between Franco, who took an isolationist stance on the coalition, and Cardoso, in November 2001 the President made clear his support for the nomination of the Minister of Health, José Serra, as the PMDB candidate. In early 2002 Serra's main opposition came from Lula da Silva of the PT, who had announced his candidacy in the previous year and who was already leading opinion polls, and from Roseanna Sarney. However, in early March 2002 the offices of one of Sarney's businesses were raided by the federal police as part of an investigation into the misappropriation of funds from the regional development agency SUDAM. Sarney claimed that the raid had been engineered by her political rivals, including the PMDB, and the PFL withdrew from the governing coalition in protest one week later. Nevertheless, the accusations damaged her reputation enough to force her to withdraw from the presidential race in April. In the same month Anthony Garotinho, the Governor of Rio de Janeiro, declared his candidacy for the PSB. In mid-June Serra was officially endorsed as the PMDB candidate; however, his popularity fell in the months preceding the election, mainly owing to a growing dissatisfaction with the Cardoso Government. Lula da Silva's campaign manifesto, released in June, pledged economic reform, GDP growth of 5%, the implementation of a 'Zero Hunger' poverty-alleviation programme and the creation of 10m. new jobs. Such pledges won him popular approval but aroused corresponding concern among international investors, who feared that the election of a left-wing President, who promised large increases in government expenditure, would result in Brazil defaulting on its foreign debt (see Economic Affairs).

In the presidential election of 6 October 2002 Lula da Silva emerged as the leading candidate, securing 46.4% of the votes cast in the first round ballot. Serra, the government-backed candidate, was second-placed with 23.2% of the ballot, followed by PSB nominee Garotinho with 17.9% and Ciro Gomes, the candidate of the centre-left PPS, who secured 12.0% of the ballot. As no candidate had achieved the required 50%, a second ballot between the two leading candidates was held, on 27 October. Aided by the support of Garotinho, Gomes and Sarney, Lula secured 61.3% of the votes cast in the second round (the largest ever proportion of the vote since the system's introduction in 1945), while Serra attracted 38.7%. In congressional elections, also held on 6 October, Lula's party, the PT, took 91 of the 513 seats in the Câmara dos Deputados and increased its representation in the Senado to 14 seats (two-thirds of the Senado's 81 seats were contested). The PFL secured 84 lower-house seats, followed by the PMDB with 74 seats and the PSDB with 71 seats. The PFL's representation in the Senado remained unchanged, at 19 seats; however, the number of PMDB senators decreased, from 27 seats to 19, as did the PSDB's upper-house representation, from 16 to 11 seats. PT candidates performed less well in the provincial elections, winning only three state governorships, despite contesting eight, and the party also lost control of the socialist heartland of Rio Grande do Sul to Germano Rogotto of the PMDB. The PSDB won seven governorships, including those of São Paulo and Minas Gerais, and the PMDB secured five.

Owing to the fractured nature of the new Congress, Lula had to confirm support from the centrist parties in order to form a Government. The PT entered a coalition agreement with the PFL in October and, in early November, Lula also gained the support of the PMDB, who led the Câmara dos Deputados. This, in combination with the severity of the economic situation during 2002, resulted in a more cautious approach from Lula and his advisers following the elections; a left-wing alliance with the political centre ensured greater support for new legislation and greater confidence from international investors.

President da Silva took office on 2 January 2003. His new Cabinet was dominated by members of the PT, although it also included representatives from the PPS, PDT, PSB and the Partido Liberal. Antônio Palocci of the PT was appointed Minister of Finance, while Guido Mantega, Lula's economic adviser, became Minister of Planning, Budget and Administration. Several key posts were given to members of the business community, such as Roberto Rodrigues, head of the country's agri-business federation, who was given the agriculture portfolio. Furthermore, some PT traditionalists were disturbed by Lula's choice of the industrialist and friend of former President Cardoso, Luis Fernando Ferlán, as Minister for Development, Industry and Commerce. The 'Zero Hunger' campaign was headed by José Graciano. The exclusion of the PMDB from the Cabinet, as well as a delay in negotiations with the PMDB over the appointment of the President of the Senado, led to the loss of the PT's majority in both houses of Congress. However, in mid-January the situation was resolved when the PMDB united behind José Sarney as candidate for the presidency of the Senado. Sarney, a member of the PMDB and an ally of Lula, was elected to the post at the end of the month by an overwhelming majority. Another Lula ally, João Paulo Cunha, was elected President of the lower house.

Upon assuming the presidency, Lula affirmed his intention to proceed with a poverty-alleviation programme, and in early January 2003 he announced that agreement had been reached with the Armed Forces for their help in the reconstruction of roads and the transport of supplies to remote areas, despite an intended reduction of £177m. in military spending in 2003. In addition to the postponement of a large defence project, the new President announced immediate spending cuts in all areas of government, in order to fund the 'war on hunger' campaign.

In the mid-1990s the Government suffered from repeated criticism of its failure to address burgeoning urban crime (particularly in Rio de Janeiro) and the demands of the Landless Peasant Movement, the Movimento dos Sem-Terra (MST), which organized a number of illegal occupations of disputed land during 1995, in support of demands for an acceleration of the Government's programme of expropriation of uncultivated land for distribution to landless rural families. In January 1996 protests and land occupations were renewed following the enactment of a new law regulating the demarcation of Indian lands, which many indigenous groups interpreted as a serious erosion of the previously-existing land rights of the Indian population. Meanwhile, landless peasant groups challenged government claims that 100,000 itinerant families had been resettled during 1995 and 1996, and described the Government's reallocation programme as inadequate. (Official estimates of the number of landless families in Brazil were considerably lower than the figure of 4.8m. quoted by the MST.) Rapidly deteriorating relations between the authorities and the MST were further exacerbated in April 1996 by the violent intervention of the local military police in a demonstration at Eldorado de Carajás in the State of Pará, which resulted in the deaths of 19 demonstrators.

(It was subsequently alleged that a number of those killed had been summarily executed.) Widespread public outrage prompted Cardoso to request immediate congressional priority for legislation relating to land expropriation, and to afford full cabinet status to the former agriculture ministry department responsible for executing the agrarian reform programme. However, Cardoso's attempts to propel land reform legislation through the Congress were promptly obstructed, and the emergence of a number of reports detailing the creation of close associations between local military police units and powerful rural landowners seemed likely to undermine efforts to bring to justice those responsible for the Eldorado de Carajás atrocity. Despite the Minister of Agrarian Reform's stated intention to facilitate dialogue amongst opposing groups in the dispute through the creation of a discussion council, the MST-sponsored campaign of illegal land seizures and occupations of federal and state government buildings intensified during the rest of the year.

In April 1997, in response to the growing unrest and the arrival in Brasília of 1,500 MST members at the conclusion of a two-month march, the Government announced new measures to accelerate the process of land reform. In May, despite various legal challenges, the sale of assets in CVRD proceeded. In the following month José Rainha Júnior, an MST leader, was sentenced to more than 26 years' imprisonment for his involvement in the murder in 1989 of a landowner and of a police officer (he was acquitted of the charges in April 2000). In early 1998 the MST intensified its campaign for land reform and in March thousands of activists occupied government premises. In September the head of the agrarian reform institute in São Paulo was obliged to suspend the state's land-expropriation proceedings when the organization's offices were occupied by 500 MST members.

In May 2000 in one of the largest demonstrations in history by the movement, over 30,000 members of the MST occupied a number of public buildings, including the Ministry of Finance and the Ministry of Agrarian Reform, to demand land reform. The occupations were widely condemned and prompted the Government to introduce legislation preventing further land invasions. Following inconclusive negotiations with the Government, the MST scaled down its protest and ministers agreed to resume talks. However, following renewed occupations by the MST in September (the MST claimed that the Government had failed to honour a number of agreements reached in July), the Government suspended its negotiations on land reform. A constitutional crisis ensued, provoked by the request by the Governor of Minas Gerais, Itamar Franco, that federal troops, sent to protect the President's estate, withdraw. When his request was not met, Franco threatened to mobilize state military police to remove the troops; moreover, the Supreme Federal Tribunal ruled that the state Government had acted within the Constitution. However, it was reported later that month that, following the temporary withdrawal of MST activists, the Government had agreed to resume negotiations with the movement, and in early October the Government announced that loans of R $2,000 per family were to be made available for those already settled on their own land. Following a decision by the Government and the MST to resume negotiations, in October 2001 hundreds of MST activists occupied the Senado building in an attempt to oblige the Minister of Agrarian Reform, Raúl Belens Jungmann Pinto, to meet with them. Meanwhile, the Government initiated a 25,000 ha land-distribution scheme in the state of Mato Grosso do Sul. Following the election of Lula da Silva to the presidency in October 2002, the MST, traditional supporters of the PT, agreed to a temporary suspension of illegal land occupations. The MST soon declared its autonomy from the Government, however, amid concerns that Lula's policies were more conversative than expected.

The murder, in December 1988, of Francisco (Chico) Mendes, the leader of the rubber-tappers' union and a pioneering ecologist brought Brazil's environmental problems to international attention. Widespread concern was expressed that large-scale development projects, together with the 'slash-and-burn' farming techniques of cattle ranchers, peasant smallholders and loggers, and the release of large amounts of mercury into the environment by an estimated 60,000 gold prospectors (or *garimpeiros*) in the Amazon region, presented a serious threat to the survival of both the indigenous Indians and the rain forest. International criticism of the Government's poor response to the threat to the environment persisted throughout the 1990s and into the 2000s. Of particular concern to many international observers was the plight of the Yanomami Indian tribe in Roraima. It was estimated that, since the arrival of the *garimpeiros* in the region, some 10%–15% of the Yanomami's total population had been exterminated as a result of pollution and disease, introduced to the area by the gold prospectors. The Fundação Nacional do Indio (FUNAI—National Indian Foundation) was heavily criticized for its role in the affair and was accused of failing to provide effective protection and support for Brazil's Indian population. In August 1993 international attention was again focused on the region, following the slaughter of 73 members of the Yanomami tribe by *garimpeiros*, in the context of the ongoing territorial dispute prompted by the miners' attempts to exploit the rich mineral deposits of the Yanomami land. A new cabinet post of Minister with Special Responsibility for the Brazilian Amazon was subsequently created. In March 1996 a US $5,700m.-rain forest protection programme (to be funded by the Brazilian Government, the European Union and the G-7 group of industrialized countries over a five-year period) was concluded between President Cardoso and the UN Secretary-General. At a meeting in Manaus in October 1997, the G-7 group pledged an additional US $68m. In July 1997 Júlio Gaiger, the head of FUNAI, resigned, claiming that the Government had failed to honour its commitment to assist indigenous people. Legislation to provide greater protection for Brazil's natural resources, through the establishment of criminal penalties for illegal activities, was approved by the President in February 1998. In August 2002 Cardoso's Government created the world's biggest national park in the Tumucumaque Mountains, with funding promised by the World Bank and the UN's Global Environmental Facility.

In 1990 a series of bilateral trade agreements was signed with Argentina, representing the first stage in a process which led to the establishment of a Southern Cone Common Market (Mercado Comum do Sul—Mercosul, see p. 316), also to include Paraguay and Uruguay. In March 1991, in Paraguay, the four nations signed the Asunción treaty whereby they reaffirmed their commitment to the creation of such a market by the end of 1994. Mercosul duly came into effect on 1 January 1995, following the signing, by the Presidents of the four member nations, of the Ouro Prêto Protocol, in Brazil, in December 1994. While a complete common external tariff was not expected until 2006, customs barriers on 80%–85% of mutually exchanged goods were removed immediately. In 1999, however, Brazil's commercial relations with Argentina, in particular, were severely strained by the devaluation of the real, which prompted the latter country to impose curbs on certain Brazilian exports. Argentina's currency devaluation, in January 2002, led to a further decrease in the trade between the two countries.

In May 1994 Brazil declared its full adherence to the 1967 Tlatelolco Treaty for the non-proliferation of nuclear weapons in Latin America and the Caribbean. The Treaty was promulgated by presidential decree in September 1994. Brazil signed the international Treaty on the Non-Proliferation of Nuclear Weapons in June 1997. The President ratified this and also the Comprehensive Test Ban Treaty (see p. 82) in July 1998.

Government

Under the 1988 Constitution, the country is a federal republic comprising 26 States and a Federal District (Brasília). Legislative power is exercised by the bicameral Congresso Nacional (National Congress), comprising the Senado Federal (Federal Senate—members elected by a system of proportional representation for four years) and the Câmara dos Deputados (Chamber of Deputies—members elected by the majority principle in rotation for eight years). The number of deputies is based on the size of the population. Election is by universal adult suffrage. Executive power is exercised by the President, elected by direct ballot for four years. The President appoints and leads the Cabinet. Each State has a directly elected Governor and an elected legislature. For the purposes of local government, the States are divided into municipalities.

Defence

Military service, lasting 12 months, is compulsory for men between 18 and 45 years of age. In August 2002 the armed forces totalled 287,600 (including 48,200 conscripts): army 189,000 (40,000 conscripts), navy 48,600 (including 3,200 conscripts) and air force 50,000 (including 5,000 conscripts). Public security forces number about 385,600. Defence expenditure for 2002 was budgeted at R $26,000m.

Economic Affairs

In 2001, according to estimates by the World Bank, Brazil's gross national income (GNI), measured at average 1999–2001 prices, was US $528,503m., equivalent to US $3,060 per head (or $7,450 per head on an international purchasing-power parity basis). During 1990–2001, it was estimated, the population increased at an average annual rate of 1.4%, while gross domestic product (GDP) per head increased, in real terms, by an average of 1.2% per year. Overall GDP increased, in real terms, at an average annual rate of 2.6% in 1990–2001; growth in 2001 was 1.5%. GDP was forecast to grow by 2.5% in 2002.

Agriculture (including hunting, forestry and fishing) engaged 18.7% of the economically active population, according to census figures, in 2000, and contributed 8.0% of GDP in 2001. The principal cash crops are soya beans, coffee, tobacco, sugar cane and cocoa beans. Subsistence crops include wheat, maize, rice, potatoes, beans, cassava and sorghum. Beef and poultry production are also important, as is fishing (particularly tuna, crab and shrimp). During 1990–2000, according to the World Bank, agricultural GDP increased at an average annual rate of 3.5%. Agricultural GDP increased by an estimated 7.4% in 1999 and by 3.0% in 2000.

Industry (including mining, manufacturing, construction and power) employed 21.4% of the working population in 2000 and, according to the World Bank, provided 35.8% of GDP in 2001. During 1990–2000 industrial GDP increased at an average annual rate of 2.1%. Industrial GDP declined by 1.7% in 1999; however, growth of 5.0% was recorded in the sector in 2000.

Mining contributed 1.6% of GDP in 1999. The major mineral exports are iron ore (haematite—in terms of iron content, Brazil is the largest producer in the world), manganese, tin and aluminium (Brazil was the world's third largest producer of bauxite in 1997). Gold, phosphates, platinum, uranium, copper and coal are also mined. In 1990 deposits of niobium, thought to be the world's largest, were discovered in the state of Amazonas. Brazil's reserves of petroleum were estimated at 9m. 42-gallon barrels in 2000.

Manufacturing contributed 24.1% of GDP in 2000. In 2000 the sector engaged 13.5% of the total employed population. There is considerable state involvement in a broad range of manufacturing activity. While traditionally-dominant areas, including textiles and clothing, footwear and food- and beverage-processing, continue to contribute a large share to the sector, more recent developments in the sector have resulted in the emergence of machinery and transport equipment (including road vehicles and components, passenger jet aircraft and specialist machinery for the petroleum industry), construction materials (especially iron and steel), wood and sugar cane derivatives, and chemicals and petrochemicals as significant new manufacturing activities. According to the World Bank, manufacturing GDP increased at an average rate of 1.2% per year in 1990–2000. The sector's GDP decreased by 0.7% in 1999, but rose by 4.0% in 2000.

In 1999 88.1% of total electricity production was provided by hydroelectric power. Other energy sources, including petroleum, coal and nuclear power, accounted for the remaining 11.9%. Attempts to exploit further the country's vast hydroelectric potential (estimated at 213,000 MW) were encouraged by the completion of ambitious dam projects at Itaipú, on the border with Paraguay (expected to produce as much as 35% of Brazil's total electricity requirements when fully operational), and at Tucuruí, on the Tocantins river. In late 2000 it was announced that plans were under way to further expand the hydroelectric power-station at Itaipú, increasing its generating capacity to 14,000 MW. By 1999 electricity production by hydroelectric sources was more than 50 times that of 1989. However, in 2001 the Government introduced a six-month hydroelectricity rationing system , in an attempt to reduce consumption by some 20%, following a severe drought. None the less, the construction of 49 thermal power-stations was expected to be completed by 2003, and the Government was reported to be considering the development of windpower and of sugar-derived bagasse as alternative sources of energy. The Angra I nuclear power plant, inaugurated in 1985, has subsequently operated only intermittently, while financial constraints hindered the completion of the Angra II plant, which became operational in mid-2000, preventing further development of the country's nuclear programme. However, Cardoso's Government indicated in mid-2001 that because of the new US Government's favourable attitude towards nuclear energy, it was intending to invest in the construction of a further plant, Angra III. Fuel imports comprised 15.1% of the value of total merchandise imports in 2000.

The services sector contributed an estimated 56.2% of GDP in 2001 and engaged 59.9% of the employed labour force in 2000. According to the World Bank, the GDP of the services sector increased at an average rate of 2.1% per year in 1990–2000. The GDP of the services sector was estimated to have increased by 3.9% in 2000.

In 2001 Brazil recorded a trade surplus of US $2,645m. There was a deficit of US $23,211m. on the current account of the balance of payments. In 2002 the principal source of imports (21.8%) was the USA, which was also the principal market for exports (25.4%). Other major trading partners were Germany, Argentina, Japan, the Netherlands, Mexico and the People's Republic of China. The principal exports in 2000 were machinery and transport equipment, basic manufactures and food and food-processing products (notably coffee). The principal imports in the same year were machinery and transport equipment, chemical products and mineral fuels (notably petroleum).

The 2001 federal budget recorded expenditure of R $173,832m. and revenue of R $209,739m. Brazil's external debt was US $237,953m. at the end of 2000, of which US $92,590m. was long-term public debt. In that year the cost of debt-servicing was equivalent to 90.7% of revenue from exports of goods and services. The annual rate of inflation averaged 64.9% in 1993–2001. Consumer prices increased by an average of 7.1% in 2000 and by 6.8% in 2001. Official figures indicated an unemployment rate of 9.6% of the labour force in 1999. (Unemployment in São Paulo was estimated at a record 16.3% in September 1997.)

Brazil is a member of ALADI (see p. 259), Mercosul/Mercosur (see p. 316), the Association of Tin Producing Countries (ATPC) and the Cairns Group (see p. 389). Brazil also joined the Comunidade dos Países de Língua Portuguesa (CPLP, see p. 349), founded in 1996.

Upon his re-election in October 1998, President Cardoso immediately reiterated his pledge to reform the public sector and announced details of a three-year programme of fiscal adjustment, including drastic cuts in budgetary expenditure. In January 1999, however, the unexpected resignation of the President of the Central Bank and his successor's decision to devalue the Brazilian currency (thus abandoning the exchange-rate policy agreed with the IMF) precipitated a period of renewed capital flight, seriously depleting the country's reserves and leading to turmoil on international financial markets. Brazil and the IMF subsequently reached agreement on a revised programme for 1999–2001, thus permitting lending to resume. Requirements included an increase in Brazil's budgetary surplus, which was to be raised from 2.6% of GDP to 3.1%, a reduction of the country's public debt to a level below the original specification of 46.5% of GDP, the introduction of a new monetary policy and the acceleration of the Government's privatization programme. In 2000 the Government introduced measures aimed at reducing the country's significant trade deficit, incorporating means for reducing export costs and developing the production of goods destined for export. In the same year industrial production increased by some 6.2% and inflation levels remained within the 6% boundary established by the Government. However, by November the level of public debt had reached 48.5% of GDP, above the target set by the IMF. Moreover, the recovery that followed the 1999 crisis was adversely affected in 2001 by the effects of the terrorist attacks in the USA in September and by the financial crisis in Argentina, as well as by high petroleum prices and by the need to ration electricity. Inflationary pressure increased throughout the year, leading to high interest rates, which reached 19% in July 2001. In an attempt to increase confidence in the country's economy, and also partly because of Brazil's strong overall economic performance, in August a US $15,000m. loan was approved by the IMF. In exchange, Cardoso's Government was required to reduce expenditure by some US $4,120m. in 2001–02; however, public-sector workers expressed concern that this would lead to further wage reductions.

The success of the left-wing candidate Lula da Silva in polls in the months preceding the presidential elections of October 2002 resulted in anxiety in international financial circles about the possibility of increased government expenditure should he come to power. This, coupled with a first-quarter decrease in GDP, led President Cardoso, in June, to draw US $10,000m. of the previously-negotiated IMF loan, in order to replenish reserves and buy back foreign debt. Massive depreciation of the real in July contributed to an increase in public debt to 58.6% of GDP, of which almost one-half was linked to the US dollar. In mid-July the Central Bank unexpectedly cut interest rates by 0.5%, to 18%, in an attempt to stimulate growth before the elections, while one week later the Government further reduced budgetary expenditure. Nevertheless, the economy continued to flounder, with the greatest ever depreciation of the real in a single day occurring on 29 July. On 7 August, after negotiations with Cardoso's Government, the IMF announced a rescue package of US $30,400m., part of a 15-month stand-by agreement until December 2003. The loan was the largest ever disbursed by the Fund. The deal was dependent on the agreement of all presidential candidates to maintain current fiscal policy and commit to a primary budget surplus of 3.75% of GDP in 2003. Though the IMF loan settled financial markets temporarily, the real continued to depreciate, while the public debt/GDP ratio rose to 63.9% by September.

Moves towards a proposed Free Trade Area of the Americas (FTAA), first broached at the First Summit of the Americas held in Miami, USA, in 1994 and to be concluded by 2005, faltered in late 2002 with Brazil's resistance to open its markets further without receiving greater access to US markets in return; specifically targeted were agricultural products such as orange juice, sugar, cotton and soya, which enjoyed protection in the USA. Soya was a cause of specific complaint, with the Brazilian Government claiming that though farm subsidies were not open to renegotiation until 2004, they should be maintained at 1994 levels (soya was unsubsidized in the USA in 1994 and by 2002 receieved some US $4,000m. in support). The protected US steel industry was another source of contention. A meeting of foreign ministers in Quito, Ecuador, in November 2002 failed to resolve differences between South American countries and the USA. There had been fears that, upon taking office, President da Silva might adopt an isolationist stance towards the FTAA; however, in January 2003 Lula expressed his intention to participate in FTAA negotiations.

Following his election to the presidency in October 2002, Lula da Silva declared that many of the PT's electoral pledges would have to be postponed in favour of the primary issue of reducing public debt. The President-elect also promised to respect Brazil's existing debt obligations, thus allaying fears of an intention to default on foreign debt, a large amount of which would fall due in 2003. There were, however, concerns that, in order to meet the IMF's requirement of a 3.75% budget surplus, the new Government would be forced to renege on some of the PT's more expensive policies, such as a 20% increase in the minunum wage, an overhaul of the social security system and the implementation of the 'Zero Hunger' campaign against poverty. An IMF delegation's visit in November 2002, to discuss the terms of the first US $3,000m. loan disbursement, confirmed Lula's fiscal policy as 'prudent and appropriate', and approved the disbursement. This was quickly followed by the offer of a US $6,000m.–10,000m. loan from the World Bank for social projects, in addition to a previously pledged US $4,500m. In the same month the real began to recover and, by the end of November stood at just 18% below its January 2002 value. In January 2003 Lula announced spending cuts to help fund the anti-poverty campaign, while Henrique Meirelles, the President of the Central Bank, announced an intended 4% budget surplus in 2003. Interest rates were also increased to 25.5%, in an attempt to beat inflation.

Education

Education is free in official pre-primary schools and is compulsory between the ages of seven and 14 years. Primary education begins at seven years of age and lasts for eight years. Secondary education, beginning at 15 years of age, lasts for three years and is also free in official schools. In 1998 95.8% of children in the relevant age-group were enrolled at primary schools, but only 30.7% of those aged 15 to 17 were enrolled at secondary schools. The Federal Government is responsible for higher education, and in 1997 there were 150 universities, of which 77 were state-administered. Numerous private institutions exist at all levels of education. Expenditure on education by the central Government was forecast at R $5,100m. for 2000.

Public Holidays

2003: 1 January (New Year's Day—Universal Confraternization Day), 1–4 March (Carnival), 18 April (Good Friday), 21 April (Tiradentes Day—Discovery of Brazil), 1 May (Labour Day), 29 May (Ascension Day), 19 June (Corpus Christi), 7 September (Independence Day), 12 October (Our Lady Aparecida, Patron

Saint of Brazil), 2 November (All Souls' Day), 15 November (Proclamation of the Republic), 25 December (Christmas Day).
2004: 1 January (New Year's Day—Universal Confraternization Day), 21–24 February (Carnival), 9 April (Good Friday), 21 April (Tiradentes Day—Discovery of Brazil), 3 May (for Labour Day), 20 May (Ascension Day), 10 June (Corpus Christi), 7 September (Independence Day), 12 October (Our Lady Aparecida, Patron

Saint of Brazil), 2 November (All Souls' Day), 15 November (Proclamation of the Republic), 25 December (Christmas Day).
Other local holidays include 20 January (Foundation of Rio de Janeiro) and 25 January (Foundation of São Paulo).

Weights and Measures
The metric system is in force.

Statistical Survey

Sources (unless otherwise stated): Economic Research Department, Banco Central do Brasil, SBS, Q 03, Bloco B, Brasília, DF; tel. (61) 414-1074; fax (61) 414-2036; e-mail coace.depec.@bcb.gov.br; internet www.bcb.gov.br/ ; Instituto Brasileiro de Geografia e Estatística (IBGE), Centro de Documentação e Disseminação de Informações (CDDI), Rua Gen. Canabarro 706, 4°, 20271-201 Maracanã, Rio de Janeiro, RJ; tel. (21) 569-2901; fax (21) 284-1959; internet www.ibge.gov.br.

Area and Population

AREA, POPULATION AND DENSITY

Area (sq km)	8,547,403.5*
Population (census results)†	
1 August 1996	157,070,163
1 August 2000	
Males	83,576,015
Females.	86,223,155
Total	169,799,170
Population (official estimates at mid-year)†	
2000‡	167,724,000
2001‡	169,369,557
Density (per sq km) at 2000 census	19.9

* 3,300,170.9 sq miles.

† Excluding Indian jungle population, numbering 45,429 in 1950.

‡ Not adjusted to take account of results from the August 2000 census.

ADMINISTRATIVE DIVISIONS
(population at census of 1 August 2000)

State	Population	Capital
Acre (AC)	557,526	Rio Branco
Alagoas (AL)	2,822,621	Maceió
Amapá (AP)	477,032	Macapá
Amazonas (AM)	2,812,557	Manaus
Bahia (BA)	13,070,250	Salvador
Ceará (CE)	7,430,661	Fortaleza
Espírito Santo (ES)	3,097,232	Vitória
Goiás (GO)	5,033,228	Goiânia
Maranhão (MA)	5,651,475	São Luís
Mato Grosso (MT)	2,504,353	Cuiabá
Mato Grosso do Sul (MS) . .	2,078,001	Campo Grande
Minas Gerais (MG)	17,891,494	Belo Horizonte
Pará (PA)	6,192,307	Belém
Paraíba (PB)	3,443,825	João Pessoa
Paraná (PR)	9,563,458	Curitiba
Pernambuco (PE)	7,918,344	Recife
Piauí (PI)	2,843,278	Teresina
Rio de Janeiro (RJ)	14,391,282	Rio de Janeiro
Rio Grande do Norte (RN) . .	2,776,782	Natal
Rio Grande do Sul (RS) . .	10,187,798	Porto Alegre
Rondônia (RO)	1,379,787	Porto Velho
Roraima (RR)	324,397	Boa Vista
Santa Catarina (SC)	5,356,360	Florianópolis
São Paulo (SP)	37,032,403	São Paulo
Sergipe (SE)	1,784,475	Aracaju
Tocantins (TO)	1,157,098	Palmas
Distrito Federal (DF) . . .	2,051,146	Brasília
Total.	169,799,170	—

PRINCIPAL TOWNS
(population at census of 1 August 2000)*

São Paulo. . .	10,434,252	João Pessoa .	597,934
Rio de Janeiro .	5,857,904	Jaboatão . . .	581,556
Salvador . . .	2,443,107	São José dos	
Belo Horizonte .	2,238,526	Campos. . . .	539,313
Fortaleza . . .	2,141,402	Contagem . . .	538,017
Brasília (capital) .	2,051,146	Ribeirão Preto .	504,923
Curitiba . . .	1,587,315	Uberlândia . .	501,214
Recife	1,422,905	Sorocaba . . .	493,468
Manaus	1,405,835	Cuiabá. . . .	483,346
Porto Alegre . .	1,360,590	Feira de Santana .	480,949
Belém	1,280,614	Aracaju . . .	461,534
Goiânia . . .	1,093,607	Niterói. . . .	459,451
Guarulhos. . .	1,072,717	Juíz de Fora . .	456,796
Campinas . . .	969,396	São João de	
Nova Iguaçu . .	920,599	Meriti . . .	449,476
São Gonçalo . .	891,119	Londrina . . .	447,065
São Luís . . .	870,028	Joinville . . .	429,604
Maceió. . . .	797,759	Santos. . . .	417,983
Duque de Caxias.	775,456	Campos dos	
Teresina . . .	715,360	Goytacazes . .	406,989
Natal	712,317	Ananindeua . .	393,392
São Bernardo do		Olinda. . . .	367,902
Campo . . .	703,177	Mauá	363,392
Campo Grande . .	663,621	São José do	
Osasco. . . .	652,593	Rio Preto . .	358,523
Santo André . .	649,331	Diadema . . .	356,389

* Figures refer to *municípios*, which may contain rural districts.

2001 (UN estimate, including suburbs): Brasília 2,073,000 (Source: UN, *World Urbanization Prospects: The 2001 Revision*).

BIRTHS, MARRIAGES AND DEATHS
(official estimates)

	Birth rate (per 1,000)	Death rate (per 1,000)
1992	22.09	7.04
1993	21.37	6.98
1994	20.75	6.92
1995	20.14	6.87
1996	19.69	6.82
1997	19.25	6.78
1998	20.30	6.75
1999	20.10	6.72

Registered marriages: 724,738 in 1997; 698,614 in 1998; 788,744 in 1999; 732,721 in 2000.

Expectation of life (WHO estimates, years at birth): 68.7 (males 65.5; females 72.0) in 2001 (Source: WHO, *World Health Report*).

ECONOMICALLY ACTIVE POPULATION

(persons aged 10 years and over, census of 1 August 2000)

	Males	Females	Total
Agriculture, hunting and forestry	9,176,490	2,594,521	11,771,011
Fishing	319,400	28,979	348,378
Mining and quarrying . . .	218,003	16,866	234,869
Manufacturing	6,001,199	2,755,840	8,757,040
Electricity, gas and water . . .	275,081	53,837	328,918
Construction	4,397,397	170,998	4,568,396
Commerce, repair of automotive vehicles and household goods .	7,256,900	3,642,097	10,898,997
Accommodation and food . . .	1,627,910	1,443,904	3,071,814
Transport, storage and communications	2,918,456	400,358	3,318,814
Financial services	458,501	365,207	823,708
Real estate, rental and business services	2,546,652	1,217,150	3,763,802
Public administration, defence and social security	2,204,241	1,138,626	3,522,868
Education	845,937	2,976,451	3,822,388
Health and social services . .	598,538	1,533,368	2,151,906
Other community, social and personal services	1,104,286	1,287,766	2,392,052
Domestic services	376,268	4,640,001	5,016,269
International organizations and external institutions . . .	1,387	1,452	2,839
Activities not adequately defined .	533,449	302,374	835,823
Total employed	40,860,097	24,769,796	65,629,892
Unemployed	5,596,322	6,151,258	11,837,581
Total labour force . . .	46,546,419	30,921,054	77,467,473

Health and Welfare

KEY INDICATORS

Total fertility rate (children per woman, 2001) . . .	2.2
Under-5 mortality rate (per 1,000 live births, 2001) . . .	36
HIV/AIDS (% of persons aged 15–49, 2001) . . .	0.65
Physicians (per 1,000 head, 1996)	1.27
Hospital beds (per 1,000 head, 1996)	3.11
Health expenditure (2000): US $ per head (PPP) . . .	631
Health expenditure (2000): % of GDP	8.3
Health expenditure (2000): public (% of total)	40.8
Access to water (% of persons, 2000)	87
Access to sanitation (% of persons, 2000)	77
Human Development Index (2000): ranking	73
Human Development Index (2000): value	0.757

For sources and definitions, see explanatory note on p. vi.

Agriculture

PRINCIPAL CROPS

('000 metric tons)

	1999	2000	2001
Wheat	2,438	1,662	3,261
Rice (paddy)	11,783	11,090	10,195
Barley	315	275	287
Maize	32,038	31,879	41,439
Oats	288	193	333
Sorghum	574	780	905
Buckwheat*	50	50	50
Potatoes	2,843	2,561	2,787
Sweet potatoes*	480	500	485
Cassava (Manioc)	20,892	22,336	22,479
Yams*	230	230	235
Sugar cane	337,165	327,705	345,941
Dry beans	2,817	3,038	2,436
Brazil nuts	27	33	27
Cashew nuts	131	114	117
Soybeans (Soya beans) . . .	30,901	32,735	37,683
Groundnuts (in shell) . . .	173	184	198
Coconuts	1,723	1,880	1,999
Oil palm fruit*	360	360	388
Castor beans	31	101	80
Sunflower seed†	103	125	90
Cottonseed†	890	1,267	2,643
Tomatoes	3,251	2,983	3,042
Onions (dry)	990	1,142	1,031
Garlic	69	84	101
Other fresh vegetables* . . .	2,200	2,200	2,200
Bananas	5,528	6,079	5,959
Oranges	22,768	21,212	16,844
Tangerines, mandarins, clementines and satsumas . .	760†	770*	905*
Lemons and limes*	520	520	578
Grapefruit and pomelos* . .	65	65	66
Apples	945	1,160	723
Peaches and nectarines* . .	155	155	183
Grapes	895	999	1,013
Watermelons*	600	600	600
Cantaloupes and other melons* .	145	145	150
Mangoes*	500	500	540
Avocados*	85	85	88
Pineapples	1,175	1,293	1,350
Persimmons*	61	61	65
Cashewapple*	1,500	1,500	1,550
Papayas*	1,403	1,403	1,450
Coffee beans (green)† . . .	1,634	1,889	1,918
Cocoa beans	205	193	184
Mate*	450	430	530
Sisal	194	195	181
Cotton (lint)†	467	664	872
Other fibre crops	107	107*	99*
Tobacco (leaves)	626	578	565
Natural rubber	70†	72†	73*

* FAO estimate(s).
† Unofficial figure(s).
‡ Official figures, reported in terms of dry cherries, have been converted into green coffee beans at 50%.

Source: FAO.

LIVESTOCK

('000 head, year ending September)

	1999	2000	2001
Cattle	163,470	167,471	171,786
Buffaloes	1,068	1,100*	1,150*
Horses	5,831	5,900*	5,850*
Asses	1,236	1,250*	1,250*
Mules	1,336	1,400*	1,400*
Pigs	29,768	29,574	29,424
Sheep	14,400	15,000*	15,000*
Goats	8,623	8,700*	8,700*
Chickens	804,575	860,000*	1,006,000*
Ducks*	3,750	3,400	3,400
Turkeys*	8,700	9,000	9,300*

* FAO estimate(s).

Source: FAO.

LIVESTOCK PRODUCTS
('000 metric tons)

	1999	2000	2001
Beef and veal	6,413	6,540	6,671
Mutton and lamb*	71	71	72
Goat meat*	38	39	36
Pig meat	1,684	1,888	1,968
Horse meat*	15	15	18
Poultry meat	5,647	6,125	6,395
Cows' milk	19,661	22,134†	22,580†
Goats' milk	141	141	138*
Butter and ghee†	69	71	76
Cheese	39	39	39*
Hen eggs†	1,467	1,508	1,538
Other poultry eggs . . .	44*	44*	45
Honey	20	20*	20*
Wool: greasy	13	14*	15*
Wool: scoured*	8	9	n.a.
Cattle hides (fresh) . . .	667†	667*	670*
Goatskins (fresh)	5	5	5*
Sheepskins (fresh) . . .	15	15	15*

* FAO estimate(s).
† Unofficial figure(s).

Source: FAO.

Forestry

ROUNDWOOD REMOVALS
('000 cubic metres, excl. bark)

	1998	1999	2000
Sawlogs, veneer logs and logs for sleepers	46,779	48,300	49,290
Pulpwood	30,701*	44,734	45,861
Other industrial wood . . .	6,284	7,361	7,843
Fuel wood*	129,939	131,168	132,408
Total	213,703	231,563	235,402

* FAO estimate(s).

Source: FAO.

SAWNWOOD PRODUCTION
(FAO estimates, '000 cubic metres, incl. railway sleepers)

	1998	1999	2000
Coniferous (softwood) . . .	8,591	6,730	7,500
Broadleaved (hardwood) . .	10,000*	10,550	10,600
Total	18,591	17,280	18,100

* Unofficial figure.

Source: FAO.

Fishing

('000 metric tons, live weight)

	1998	1999	2000
Capture	706.8	703.9	693.7
Characins	61.0	65.1	64.3*
Freshwater siluroids . .	49.9	57.0	56.3*
Weakfishes	26.7	39.3	39.3*
Whitemouth croaker . .	27.9	2.9	22.0*
Brazilian sardinella . .	82.3	25.5	22.0*
Skipjack Tuna . . .	23.8	23.2	21.3
Aquaculture	103.9	140.7*	153.6*
Common carp	33.5	49.3*	52.3*
Tilapias	24.1	27.1*	28.8*
Total catch	810.7	844.6*	847.3*

* FAO estimate.
Note: Figures exclude aquatic mammals, recorded by number rather than by weight. The number of baleen whales caught was: 1 in 1997; 1 in 1998. The number of toothed whales caught was: 133 in 1998; 514 in 1999; 861 in 2000. Also excluded are crocodiles. The number of spectacled caimans caught was: 2,092 in 1998; 4,619 in 1999; 8,286 in 2000.

Source: FAO, *Yearbook of Fishery Statistics*.

Mining

('000 metric tons, unless otherwise indicated)

	1999	2000	2001
Hard coal	6,063	6,974	n.a.
Crude petroleum ('000 cu m) . .	65,451	71,844	n.a.
Natural gas (million cu m) . .	11,854	13,328	14,046
Iron ore:			
gross weight[1]	194,000	195,000	n.a.
metal content[1]	124,000	125,000	n.a.
Copper concentrates (metric tons)[2]	31,371	31,786	30,111
Nickel ore (metric tons)[2] . .	41,522	45,317	47,097
Bauxite	13,839	13,846	13,790
Lead concentrates (metric tons)[2] .	10,281	8,832	9,754
Zinc concentrates (metric tons)[2] .	98,590	100,254	111,432
Tin concentrates (metric tons)[2]. .	13,202	13,773	12,300
Manganese ore	1,656	1,925	1,863
Chromium ore (metric tons)[3] . .	190,473	253,248	174,042
Tungsten concentrates (metric tons)[2] .	13	14	31
Niobium concentrates (metric tons)[2] .	31,352	31,190	37,283
Ilmenite (metric tons) . . .	96,000	123,000	111,113
Rutile (metric tons)	4,300	3,162	1,791
Zirconium concentrates (metric tons)[4] .	27,160	29,805	20,553
Silver (kilograms)[5]	42,000	41,000	46,046
Gold (kilograms)[6].	51,422	52,420	51,867
Bentonite (beneficiated). . .	274.6	274.0	160.4
Kaolin (beneficiated) . . .	1,516.7	1,639.7	1,817.4
Magnesite (beneficiated) . .	259.8	279.9	265.7
Phosphate rock[7]	4,344	4,725	4,805
Potash salts[8]	348.2	351.7	357.0
Fluorspar (Fluorite) (metric tons)[9,10] .	44,926	42,962	43,734
Barite (Barytes) (beneficiated) (metric tons) .	44,906	55,462	63,882
Quartz (natural crystals) (metric tons)[11] .	1,470	3,651	4,350
Salt (unrefined):			
marine	4,528	4,626	4,370
rock	1,430	1,448	1,208
Gypsum and anhydrite (crude) .	1,456.3	1,498	1,507
Graphite (natural) (metric tons)[9]	53,503	71,208	70,091
Asbestos (fibre)[1,9,11]	170	170	n.a.
Mica (metric tons)	3,000	5,000	5,000[11]
Vermiculite (beneficiated) (metric tons).	23,400	27,074[11]	21,464[11]
Talc and pyrophyllite (crude) . .	358.8	473.7	470.0
Diamonds ('000 carats):			
gem[1,11]	300	300	n.a.
industrial[1,11]	600	600	n.a.

[1] Data from the US Geological Survey.
[2] Figures refer to the metal content of ores and concentrates.
[3] Figures refer to the chromic oxide (Cr_2O_3) content.
[4] Including production of baddeleyite-caldasite.
[5] Figures refer to primary production only. The production of secondary silver (in kilograms) was: 50,000 per year in 1999–2001.
[6] Including official production by independent miners (garimpeiros): 9,055 kg in 1999; 10,395 kg in 2000; 5,866 kg in 2001.
[7] Figures refer to the gross weight of concentrates. The phosphoric acid (P_2O_5) content (in '000 metric tons) was: 1,560 in 1998; 1,528 in 1999.
[8] Figures refer to the potassium oxide (K_2O) content.
[9] Figures refer to marketable products.
[10] Acid-grade and metallurgical-grade concentrates.
[11] Estimated production.

2001: Iron (beneficiated, '000 metric tons) 210,500; Diamonds (natural, '000 carats) 700.

Source (unless otherwise indicated): Departamento Nacional de Produção Mineral, Ministério de Minas e Energia.

Industry

SELECTED PRODUCTS
('000 metric tons, unless otherwise indicated)

	1997	1998	1999
Asphalt	1,572	2,060	n.a.
Electric power (million kWh)	330,358	341,880	n.a.
Pig-iron	25,013	25,111	25,549
Crude steel	26,153	25,760	24,996
Cement*	38,096	39,942	40,234
Passenger cars ('000 units)	2,070	1,586	1,351
Commercial vehicles (units)	390,800	331,614	248,367
Tractors (units)	24,494	25,167	22,157
Newsprint	265	273	242

* Portland cement only.

2000: Crude steel 27,865; Cement 39,559; Passenger cars ('000 units) 1,682.

2001: Crude steel 26,717; Cement 38,735; Passenger cars ('000 units) 1,787.

Source: partly UN, *Industrial Commodity Statistics Yearbook*.

Finance

CURRENCY AND EXCHANGE RATES

Monetary Units
100 centavos = 1 real (plural: reais).

Sterling, Dollar and Euro Equivalents (31 December 2002)
£1 sterling = 5.6950 reais
US $1 = 3.5333
€1 = 3.7054 reais
100 reais = £17.56 = $28.30 = €26.99.

Average Exchange Rates (reais per US $)
2000   1.830
2001   2.358
2002   2.921

Note: In March 1986 the cruzeiro (CR $) was replaced by a new currency unit, the cruzado (CZ $), equivalent to 1,000 cruzeiros. In January 1989 the cruzado was, in turn, replaced by the new cruzado (NCZ $), equivalent to CZ $1,000 and initially at par with the US dollar (US $). In March 1990 the new cruzado was replaced by the cruzeiro (CR $), at an exchange rate of one new cruzado for one cruzeiro. In August 1993 the cruzeiro was replaced by the cruzeiro real, equivalent to CR $1,000. On 1 March 1994, in preparation for the introduction of a new currency, a transitional accounting unit, the Unidade Real de Valor (at par with the US $), came into operation, alongside the cruzeiro real. On 1 July 1994 the cruzeiro real was replaced by the real (R $), also at par with the US $ and thus equivalent to 2,750 cruzeiros reais.

BUDGET
(R $ million)*

Revenue	1997	1998	1999
Tax revenue	108,731	130,681	147,366
Income tax	32,244	41,675	46,471
Value-added tax on industrial products	16,551	16,092	16,084
Tax on financial operations	3,769	3,514	4,843
Import duty	5,103	6,490	7,806
Tax on financial and share transactions	6,908	8,113	7,948
Social security contributions	18,405	17,732	30,935
Tax on profits of legal entities	7,241	7,183	9,477
Contributions to Social Integration Programme and Financial Reserve Fund for Public Employees	7,228	6,783	6,776
Repayment of loans	7,200	8,278	11,386
Transfer of profits from Banco do Brasil	103	127	29
Total	116,034	139,086	158,781

Expenditure	1997	1998	1999
Earmarked expenditures	32,193	38,468	40,062
Transfers to state and local governments†	25,042	29,166	33,432
Other expenditures	86,965	107,471	121,233
Wages and social contributions	42,848	47,296	50,169
Interest payments	17,975	27,706	35,439
Funding and investment	24,252	32,469	35,625
Lending	2,522	2,394	2,414
Total	121,680	148,333	163,709

* Figures refer to cash operations of the National Treasury, including the collection and transfer of earmarked revenues for social expenditure purposes. The data exclude the transactions of other funds and accounts controlled by the Federal Government.
† Constitutionally mandated participation funds.

2000 (R $ million): *Revenue:* Tax revenues 176,814; Total revenue 180,816; *Expenditure:* Transfers to states and local governments 40,283; Total expenditure 149,118.

2001 (R $ million): *Revenue:* Tax revenues 196,758; Total revenue 209,739; *Expenditures:* Transfers to states and local governments 46,024; Total expenditure 173,832.

CENTRAL BANK RESERVES
(US $ million at 31 December)

	2000	2001	2002
Gold*	523	127	153
IMF special drawing rights	—	11	275
Foreign exchange	32,488	35,729	37,409
Total	33,011	35,867	37,837

* Valued at market-related prices.

Source: IMF, *International Financial Statistics*.

MONEY SUPPLY
(R $ million at 31 December)

	1999	2000	2001
Currency outside banks	25,978	28,641	32,625
Demand deposits at deposit money banks	36,251	45,060	50,880
Total money (incl. others)	62,287	74,081	83,550

Source: IMF, *International Financial Statistics*.

COST OF LIVING
(Consumer Price Index; base: 1995 = 100)

	2000	2001	2002
All items	143.4	153.2	166.1

Source: IMF, *International Financial Statistics*.

NATIONAL ACCOUNTS
(R $ million at current prices)

National Income and Product

	1999	2000	2001
Compensation of employees	371,501	417,072	444,002
Net operating surplus	394,598	447,492	491,716
Net mixed income	55,358	58,616	60,469
Gross domestic product (GDP) at factor cost	821,457	923,180	996,187
Taxes on production and imports	155,644	181,897	208,578
Less Subsidies	3,256	3,822	4,704
GDP in market prices (purchasers' values)	973,846	1,101,255	1,200,060
Primary incomes received from abroad	6,696	6,176	7,002
Less Primary incomes paid abroad	41,059	39,131	53,689
Statistical discrepancy	256	145	219
Gross national income (GNI)	939,739	1,068,445	1,153,592
Current transfers from abroad	3,750	3,376	4,934
Less Current transfers paid abroad	723	577	1,004
Net national disposable income	942,238	1,071,244	1,157,522

Expenditure on the Gross Domestic Product

	1999	2000	2001
Government final consumption expenditure	185,828	209,953	230,741
Private final consumption expenditure	606,701	670,702	727,095
Gross fixed capital formation	184,098	212,384	233,376
Increase in stocks	12,238	24,871	20,750
Total domestic expenditure	988,865	1,117,910	1,211,962
Exports of goods and services	100,136	117,423	158,501
Less Imports of goods and services	115,154	134,079	170,403
GDP in purchasers' values (market prices)	973,846	1,101,255	1,200,060
GDP at constant 1990 prices	14.4	15.0	15.7

Gross Domestic Product by Economic Activity

(at factor cost)

	1997	1998	1999
Agriculture, hunting forestry and fishing	68,005.5	75,764.4	79,405.3
Mining and quarrying	7,777.0	5,758.8	15,950.2
Manufacturing	183,882.8	182,662.3	206,238.6
Electricity, gas and water	22,898.9	24,744.9	27,480.5
Construction	86,411.1	92,320.9	91,185.4
Trade, restaurants and hotels	66,363.7	65,236.5	73,793.9
Transport, storage and communications	43,724.0	50,389.6	52,366.8
Finance, insurance, real estate and business services	56,858.5	58,847.8	61,206.7
Government services	131,863.3	139,291.2	155,082.5
Rents	131,344.9	138,031.5	138,267.5
Other community, social and personal services	109,310.0	113,286.6	106,174.8
Sub-total	908,439.9	946,334.5	1,007,075.3
Less Imputed bank service charge	44,328.9	46,520.4	46,217.3
Total	864,111.0	899,814.1	960,858.0

BALANCE OF PAYMENTS

(US $ million)

	1999	2000	2001
Exports of goods f.o.b.	48,011	55,087	58,224
Imports of goods f.o.b.	−49,272	−55,783	−55,579
Trade balance	−1,261	−696	2,645
Exports of services	7,189	9,382	9,323
Imports of services	−14,172	−16,956	−17,070
Balance on goods and services	−8,244	−8,270	−5,102
Other income received	3,936	3,620	3,279
Other income paid	−22,780	−21,504	−23,024
Balance on goods, services and income	−27,088	−26,154	−24,847
Current transfers received	1,969	1,828	1,934
Current transfers paid	−281	−306	−295
Current balance	−25,400	−24,632	−23,208
Capital account (net)	339	272	−36
Direct investment abroad	−1,690	−2,280	2,259
Direct investment from abroad	28,576	32,779	22,636
Portfolio investment assets	258	−1,697	−796
Portfolio investment liabilities.	3,542	8,646	873
Financial derivatives assets	642	386	567
Financial derivatives liabilities	−729	−583	−1,038
Other investment assets	−4,399	−2,992	−6,284
Other investment liabilities	−18,144	−4,890	1,862
Net errors and omissions	240	2,971	−253
Overall balance	−16,765	7,980	−3,418

Source: IMF, *International Financial Statistics*.

External Trade

PRINCIPAL COMMODITIES

(distribution by SITC, US $ million)

Imports f.o.b.	1998	1999	2000
Food and live animals	5,096.8	3,560.3	3,443.1
Cereals and cereal preparations	2,247.3	1,611.0	1,662.0
Crude materials (inedible) except fuels	1,883.0	1,680.9	1,978.6
Mineral fuels, lubricants, etc.	5,660.8	5,887.4	8,912.4
Petroleum, petroleum products etc.	4,352.7	4,634.8	7,121.1
Crude petroleum and bituminous oils	2,141.7	2,277,9	3,304.9
Refined petroleum products	2,098.6	2,245.7	3,671.3
Gasoline and other light oils	1,041.8	1,203.9	1,963.2
Chemicals and related products	9,834.5	9,512.4	10,363.4
Organic chemicals	3,250.4	3,041.7	3,159.8
Medicinal and pharmaceutical products	1,606.3	1,950.5	1,804.3
Artificial resins and plastic materials	1,468.7	1,295.0	1,656.2
Basic manufactures	6,734.5	5,161.6	6,016.7
Machinery and transport equipment	26,632.3	22,197.2	24,211.7
Power-generating machinery and equipment	2,532.0	2,335.1	2,165.8
Machinery specialized for particular industries	2,934.5	2,383,6	2,196.4
General industrial machinery equipment and parts	3,805.8	2,888.7	2,944.7
Office machines and automatic data-processing machines	1,826.9	1,614.5	2,054.9
Telecommunications and sound equipment	2,866.7	2,673.0	3,206.4
Other electrical machinery apparatus, etc.	4,908.0	4,604.8	6,041.1
Thermionic, microcircuits, transistors and valves, etc.	1,513.6	1,634.8	2,638.6
Road vehicles and parts*	5,789.8	3,583.0	3,861.6
Other transport equipment*	1,682.1	1,581.7	1,741.2
Miscellaneous manufactured articles	4,273.5	3,295.3	3,533.3
Total (incl. others)	60,793.2	51,747.4	58,931.2

* Excluding tyres, engines and electrical parts.

Exports f.o.b.	1998	1999	2000
Food and live animals . . .	10,358.0	10,384.8	9,230.9
Meat and meat preparations . .	1,591.9	1,929.1	1,927.2
Vegetables and fruit	1,665.9	1,690.9	1,525.0
Sugar, sugar preparations and honey	2,027.2	2,010.1	1,295.2
Sugar and honey	1,953.3	1,925.1	1,203.9
Coffee, tea, cocoa and spices . .	2,937.1	2,760.7	2,066.8
Coffee and coffee substitutes .	2,604.7	2,463.9	1,784.6
Unroasted coffee, coffee husks and skins	2,330.9	2,330.8	1,559.6
Feeding-stuff for animals (excl. unmilled cereals)	1,800.7	1,587.1	1,716.0
Oilcake and other residues of soya beans	1,749.9	1,503.6	1,652.6
Beverages and tobacco . . .	1,624.5	1,017.8	911.6
Tobacco and tobacco manufactures	1,558.9	961.2	841.5
Crude materials (inedible) except fuels	7,931.1	7,153.2	8,650.9
Oil seeds and oleaginous fruit .	2,177.3	1,595.1	2,189.9
Soya beans	2,175.4	1,593.3	2,187.9
Pulp and waste paper	1,049.4	1,243.6	1,602.4
Metalliferous ores and metal scrap	3,659.7	3,168.2	3,536.1
Iron ore and concentrates . .	3,251.1	2,746.0	3,048.2
Iron ore and concentrates, not agglomerated	2,101.0	1,726.0	1,852.9
Chemicals and related products	3,145.8	2,980.4	3,502.5
Basic manufactures . . .	10,271.7	9,879.8	11,219.3
Iron and steel	3,697.7	3,139.3	3,685.0
Iron and steel in primary form .	1,549.0	1,295.0	1,635.0
Non-ferrous metals	1,276.0	1,499.3	1,772.0
Machinery and transport equipment	12,582.1	11,366.2	15,485.1
Power-generating machinery and equipment	1,550.2	1,384.3	1,514.5
General industrial machinery equipment and parts . . .	1,539.0	1,442.0	1,598.0
Telecommunications and sound equipment	595.2	724.7	1,648.5
Road vehicles and parts* . . .	4,827.4	3,499.6	4,367.8
Passenger motor cars (excl. buses)	1,618.7	1,138.5	1,768.5
Other transport equipment* . .	1,481.3	1,937.7	3,618.7
Miscellaneous manufactured articles	2,835.9	2,851.5	3,443.2
Total (incl. others)	51,119.9	48,011.4	55,282.5

* Excluding tyres, engines and electrical parts.
Source: UN, *International Trade Statistics Yearbook*.

Imports (US $ million, 2001): Crude petroleum 3,193.0; Motor vehicle parts 1,502.3; Motors, generators and electrical equipment 1,475.4; Electronic equipment 1,445.3; Passenger vehicles 1,404.5; Naphthas 1,327.3; Total (incl. others) 55,580.7.

Exports (US $ million, 2001): Metalliferous ores and concentrates 2,931.5; Soya beans 2,725.5; Oil-cake and other residues from soya beans 2,065.2; Airplanes 2,839.3; Passenger cars 1,951.1; Radio transmitters and receivers and parts thereof 1,761.9; Total (incl. others) 58,222.6.

PRINCIPAL TRADING PARTNERS
(US $ million)*

Imports f.o.b.	2000	2001	2002
Algeria	1,509	1,096	1,098
Argentina	6,841	6,207	4,747
Belgium-Luxembourg . . .	571	585	535
Canada	1,087	927	740
Chile	975	862	654
China, People's Republic . . .	1,222	1,328	1,554
France	1,887	2,083	1,747
Germany	4,427	4,812	4,398
India	271	542	573
Italy	2,172	2,185	1,762
Japan	2,961	3,064	2,347
Korea, Republic	1,430	1,574	1,067
Mexico	754	695	580
Netherlands	698	532	537
Nigeria	733	1,372	1,091
Saudi Arabia	779	816	677
Spain	1,119	1,226	975
Sweden	762	812	575
Switzerland	831	1,004	898
Taiwan.	825	735	687
United Kingdom	1,234	1,235	1,341
USA	12,894	12,894	10,285
Uruguay	602	503	485
Venezuela	1,328	748	627
Total (incl. others) . . .	55,834	55,581	47,232

Exports f.o.b.	2000	2001	2002
Argentina	6,232	5,002	2,342
Belgium-Luxembourg . . .	1,867	1,812	1,892
Canada	566	555	732
Chile	1,246	1,352	1,461
China, People's Republic . .	1,085	1,902	2,520
Colombia	515	606	637
France	1,732	1,648	1,525
Germany	2,526	2,502	2,537
India	217	285	654
Italy	2,146	1,809	1,817
Japan	2,472	1,986	2,098
Korea, Republic	581	736	852
Mexico	1,711	1,868	2,342
Netherlands	2,796	2,863	3,182
Paraguay	832	720	558
Russia	423	1,103	1,252
Spain	1,008	1,042	1,120
United Kingdom	1,498	1,705	1,769
USA	13,181	14,190	15,354
Uruguay	669	641	410
Venezuela	751	1,092	797
Total (incl. others) . . .	55,086	58,270	60,362

* Imports by country of purchase; exports by country of last consignment.

Source: Ministério do Desenvolvimento, Indústria e Comércio Exterior, Brasília, DF.

Transport

RAILWAYS*

	1998	1999	2000
Passengers (million)	1,255	n.a.	n.a.
Passenger-km (million) . . .	12,667	n.a.	n.a.
Freight ('000 metric tons) . .	271,829	273,649	302,441
Freight ton-km (million) . .	142,446	140,957	154,870

* Including suburban and metro services.

Source: Empresa Brasileira de Planejamento de Transportes (GEIPOT), Brasília, DF.

ROAD TRAFFIC
(motor vehicles in use at 31 December)

	1998	1999	2000
Passenger cars	21,313,351	22,347,423	23,241,966
Buses and coaches	430,062	400,048	427,213
Light goods vehicles	3,313,774	3,193,058	3,469,927
Heavy goods vehicles	1,755,877	1,778,084	1,836,203
Motorcycles and mopeds	3,854,646	4,222,705	4,732,331

Source: Empresa Brasileira de Planejamento de Transportes (GEIPOT).

SHIPPING

Merchant Fleet
(registered at 31 December)

	1999	2000	2001
Number of vessels	503	505	475
Total displacement ('000 grt)	3,933	3,809	3,687

Source: Lloyd's Register-Fairplay, *World Fleet Statistics*.

International Sea-borne Freight Traffic
('000 metric tons)

	1998	1999	2000
Goods loaded	269,935	269,863	279,734
Goods unloaded	173,070	165,847	179,755

Source: Empresa Brasileira de Planejamento de Transportes (GEIPOT).

CIVIL AVIATION
(embarked passengers, mail and cargo)

	1998	1999	2000
Number of passengers ('000)	32,175	30,541	33,933
Passenger-km (million)	49,291	44,161	40,867
Freight ton-km ('000)*	6,005,571	5,371,752	5,619,374

* Including mail.

Source: Empresa Brasileira de Planejamento de Transportes (GEIPOT), Brasília, DF.

Tourism

FOREIGN TOURIST ARRIVALS

Country of origin	1999	2000	2001
Argentina	1,548,570	1,744,004	1,374,584
Bolivia	145,072	134,640	107,673
Chile	170,564	172,807	154,093
France	131,978	165,117	185,033
Germany	282,846	290,335	320,602
Italy	177,589	202,903	216,517
Paraguay	501,425	371,873	285,752
Portugal	115,088	147,143	165,908
Spain	99,677	110,765	126,973
United Kingdom	125,607	127,903	143,823
USA	559,366	648,026	594,309
Uruguay	383,750	403,896	305,084
Total (incl. others)	5,107,169	5,313,463	4,772,575

Receipts from tourism (US $ million): 3,678 in 1998; 3,994 in 1999; 4,228 in 2000.

Source: Instituto Brasileiro de Turismo—EMBRATUR, Brasília, DF.

Communications Media

	1999	2000	2001
Personal computers ('000 in use)	6,100	7,500	10,800
Internet users ('000)	3,500	5,000	8,000
Telephones in use ('000 main lines)	24,985.0	30,926.3	37,430.8
Mobile cellular telephones ('000 subscribers)	15,032.7	23,188.2	28,745.8

Source: International Telecommunication Union (ITU).

Radio receivers ('000 in use): 71,000 in 1997 (Source: UNESCO, *Statistical Yearbook*).

Television receivers ('000 in use): 58,283 in 2000 (Source: International Telecommunication Union (ITU)).

Daily newspapers: 380 (average circulation, '000 copies: 6,472) in 1996 (Source: UNESCO, *Statistical Yearbook*).

Non-daily newspapers: 938 in 1996 (Source: UNESCO, *Statistical Yearbook*).

Facsimile machines: 500,000 in 1997 (Source: UN, *Statistical Yearbook*).

Education
(2001)

	Institutions	Teachers	Students
Pre-primary	90,682	248,632	4,818,803
Literacy classes (Classe de Alfabetização)	30,794	41,045	625,866
Primary	177,780	1,553,181	35,298,089
Secondary	20,220	448,569	8,398,008
Higher*	1,180	183,194	2,694,245

* 2000 figures (preliminary).

Adult literacy rate: 86.4% in 2000.

Source: Ministério da Educação, Brasília, DF.

Directory

The Constitution

A new Constitution was promulgated on 5 October 1988. The following is a summary of the main provisions:

The Federative Republic of Brazil, formed by the indissoluble union of the States, the Municipalities and the Federal District, is constituted as a democratic state. All power emanates from the people. The Federative Republic of Brazil seeks the economic, political, social and cultural integration of the peoples of Latin America.

All are equal before the law. The inviolability of the right to life, freedom, equality, security and property is guaranteed. No one shall be subjected to torture. Freedom of thought, conscience, religious belief and expression are guaranteed, as is privacy. The principles of habeas corpus and 'habeas data' (the latter giving citizens access to personal information held in government data banks) are granted. There is freedom of association, and the right to strike is guaranteed.

There is universal suffrage by direct secret ballot. Voting is compulsory for literate persons between 18 and 69 years of age, and optional for those who are illiterate, those over 70 years of age and those aged 16 and 17.

Brasília is the federal capital. The Union's competence includes maintaining relations with foreign states, and taking part in international organizations; declaring war and making peace; guaranteeing national defence; decreeing a state of siege; issuing currency; supervising credits, etc.; formulating and implementing plans for economic and social development; maintaining national services, including communications, energy, the judiciary and the police; legislating on civil, commercial, penal, procedural, electoral, agrarian, maritime, aeronautical, spatial and labour law, etc. The Union, States, Federal District and Municipalities must protect the Constitution, laws and democratic institutions, and preserve national heritage.

The States are responsible for electing their Governors by universal suffrage and direct secret ballot for a four-year term. The organization of the Municipalities, the Federal District and the Territories is regulated by law.

The Union may intervene in the States and in the Federal District only in certain circumstances, such as a threat to national security or public order, and then only after reference to the National Congress.

LEGISLATIVE POWER

The legislative power is exercised by the Congresso Nacional (National Congress), which is composed of the Câmara dos Deputados (Chamber of Deputies) and the Senado Federal (Federal Senate). Elections for deputies and senators take place simultaneously throughout the country; candidates for the Congresso must be Brazilian by birth and have full exercise of their political rights. They must be at least 21 years of age in the case of deputies and at least 35 years of age in the case of senators. The Congresso meets twice a year in ordinary sessions, and extraordinary sessions may be convened by the President of the Republic, the Presidents of the Câmara and the Senado, or at the request of the majority of the members of either house.

The Câmara is made up of representatives of the people, elected by a system of proportional representation in each State, Territory and the Federal District for a period of four years. The total number of deputies representing the States and the Federal District will be established in proportion to the population; each Territory will elect four deputies.

The Senado is composed of representatives of the States and the Federal District, elected according to the principle of majority. Each State and the Federal District will elect three senators with a mandate of eight years, with elections after four years for one-third of the members and after another four years for the remaining two-thirds. Each Senator is elected with two substitutes. The Senado approves, by secret ballot, the choice of Magistrates, when required by the Constitution; of the Attorney-General of the Republic, of the Ministers of the Accounts Tribunal, of the Territorial Governors, of the president and directors of the central bank and of the permanent heads of diplomatic missions.

The Congresso is responsible for deciding on all matters within the competence of the Union, especially fiscal and budgetary arrangements, national, regional and local plans and programmes, the strength of the armed forces and territorial limits. It is also responsible for making definitive resolutions on international treaties, and for authorizing the President to declare war.

The powers of the Câmara include authorizing the instigation of legal proceedings against the President and Vice-President of the Republic and Ministers of State. The Senado may indict and impose sentence on the President and Vice-President of the Republic and Ministers of State.

Constitutional amendments may be proposed by at least one-third of the members of either house, by the President or by more than one-half of the legislative assemblies of the units of the Federation. Amendments must be ratified by three-fifths of the members of each house. The Constitution may not be amended during times of national emergency, such as a state of siege.

EXECUTIVE POWER

Executive power is exercised by the President of the Republic, aided by the Ministers of State. Candidates for the Presidency and Vice-Presidency must be Brazilian-born, be in full exercise of their political rights and be over 35 years of age. The candidate who obtains an absolute majority of votes will be elected President. If no candidate attains an absolute majority, the two candidates who have received the most votes proceed to a second round of voting, at which the candidate obtaining the majority of valid votes will be elected President. The President holds office for a term of four years and (under an amendment adopted in 1997) is eligible for re-election.

The Ministers of State are chosen by the President and their duties include countersigning acts and decrees signed by the President, expediting instructions for the enactment of laws, decrees and regulations, and presentation to the President of an annual report of their activities.

The Council of the Republic is the higher consultative organ of the President of the Republic. It comprises the Vice-President of the Republic, the Presidents of the Câmara and Senado, the leaders of the majority and of the minority in each house, the Minister of Justice, two members appointed by the President of the Republic, two elected by the Senado and two elected by the Câmara, the latter six having a mandate of three years.

The National Defence Council advises the President on matters relating to national sovereignty and defence. It comprises the Vice-President of the Republic, the Presidents of the Câmara and Senado, the Minister of Justice, military Ministers and the Ministers of Foreign Affairs and of Planning.

JUDICIAL POWER

Judicial power in the Union is exercised by the Supreme Federal Tribunal; the Higher Tribunal of Justice; the Regional Federal Tribunals and federal judges; Labour Tribunals and judges; Electoral Tribunals and judges; Military Tribunals and judges; and the States' Tribunals and judges. Judges are appointed for life; they may not undertake any other employment. The Tribunals elect their own controlling organs and organize their own internal structure.

The Supreme Federal Tribunal, situated in the Union capital, has jurisdiction over the whole national territory and is composed of 11 ministers. The ministers are nominated by the President after approval by the Senado, from Brazilian-born citizens, between the ages of 35 and 65 years, of proved judicial knowledge and experience.

The Government

HEAD OF STATE

President: Luiz Inácio (Lula) da Silva (took office 2 January 2003).

Vice-President: José Alencar.

THE CABINET
(April 2003)

Minister of Foreign Affairs: Celso Amorim.

Minister of Justice: Márcio Thomaz Bastos.

Minister of Finance: Antônio Palocci.

Minister of Defence: José Viegas, Filho.

Minister of Agriculture, Fisheries and Food Supply: Roberto Rodrigues.

Minister of Agrarian Development: Miguel Rossetto.

Minister of Labour and Employment: Jacques Wagner.

Minister of Transport: Anderson Adouto.

Minister of Cities: Olivio Dutra.

Minister of Planning, Budget and Administration: Guido Mantega.

Minister of Mines and Energy: Dilma Rousseff.

Minister of Culture: Gilberto Gil.

Minister of the Environment: Marina Silva.

Minister of Development, Industry and Trade: Luiz Fernando Furlan.

Minister of Education: Cristovam Buarque.

Minister of Health: Humberto Costa.

Minister of National Integration: Ciro Gomes.

Minister of Social Security: Ricardo Berzoini.

Minister of Social Assistance and Promotion: Benedita da Silva.

Minister of Communications: Miro Teixeira.

Minister of Science and Technology: Roberto Mota Amaral.

Minister of Sport: Agnelo Quiroz.

Minister of Tourism: Walfrido Mares Guia.

Extraordinary Minister for Food Security and the Fight against Hunger: José Graziano da Silva.

Comptroller-General: Waldir Pires.

Cabinet Chief: José Dirceu de Oliveira e Silva.

MINISTRIES

Office of the President: Palácio do Planalto, 4° andar, 70150-900 Brasília, DF; tel. (61) 411-1573; fax (61) 323-1461; e-mail casacivil@planalto.gov.br; internet www.presidencia.gov.br.

Office of the Civilian Cabinet: Palácio do Planalto, 4° andar, Praça dos Três Poderes, 70150 Brasílila, DF; tel. (61) 211-1034; fax (61) 321-5804.

Ministry of Agrarian Development: Esplanda dos Ministérios, Bloco A, 8° andar, Brasília, DF; tel. (61) 223-8002; fax (61) 223-1630; internet www.mda.gov.br.

Ministry of Agriculture, Fisheries and Food Supply: Esplanada dos Ministérios, Bloco D, 8° andar, 70043–000 Brasília, DF; tel. (61) 226-5161; fax (61) 218-2586; e-mail cenagri@agricultura.gov.br; internet www.agricultura.gov.br.

Ministry of Cities: Brasília, DF.

Ministry of Communications: Esplanada dos Ministérios, Bloco R, 8° andar, 70044 Brasília, DF; tel. (61) 311-6000; fax (61) 226-3980; e-mail webmaster@mc.gov.br; internet www.mc.gov.br.

Ministry of Culture: Esplanada dos Ministérios, Bloco B, 3° andar, 70068-900 Brasília, DF; tel. (61) 316-2172; fax (61) 225-9162; e-mail info@minc.gov.br; internet www.minc.gov.br.

Ministry of Defence: Esplanada dos Ministérios, Bloco Q, 70049-900 Brasília, DF; tel. (61) 223-5356; fax (61) 321-2477; e-mail faleconosco@defesa.gov.br; internet www.defesa.gov.br.

Ministry of Development, Industry and Trade: Esplanada dos Ministérios, Bloco J, 7° andar, Sala 700, 70056-900 Brasília, DF; tel. (61) 325-2056; fax (61) 325-2063; e-mail webmaster@mdic.gov.br; internet www.mdic.gov.br.

Ministry of Education: Esplanada dos Ministérios, Bloco L, 8° andar, 70047-900 Brasília, DF; tel. (61) 225-6515; fax (61) 223-0564; e-mail acordabr@acb.mec.gov.br; internet www.mec.gov.br.

Ministry of the Environment: Esplanda dos Ministérios, Bloco B, 5°–9° andar,, Brasília, DF 70.068–900; tel. (61) 226-8221; fax (61) 322-1058; internet www.mma.gov.br.

Ministry of Finance: Esplanada dos Ministérios, Bloco P, 5° andar, 70048 Brasília, DF; tel. (61) 412-2548; fax (61) 226-9084; e-mail acs@fazenda.gov.br; internet www.fazenda.gov.br.

Extraordinary Ministry for Food Security and the Fight against Hunger: Brasília, DF; e-mail mesa@planalto.gov.br; internet www.presidencia.gov.br/mesa.

Ministry of Foreign Affairs: Palácio do Itamaraty, Esplanada dos Ministérios, Bloco H, 70170-900 Brasília, DF; tel. (61) 411-6161; fax (61) 225-1272; internet www.mre.gov.br.

Ministry of Health: Esplanada dos Ministérios, Bloco G, 5° andar, 70058 Brasília, DF; tel. (61) 223-3169; fax (61) 224-8747; internet www.saude.gov.br.

Ministry of Justice: Esplanada dos Ministérios, Bloco T, 4° andar, 70064-900 Brasília, DF; tel. (61) 226-4404; fax (61) 322-6817; e-mail acs@mj.gov.br; internet www.mj.gov.br.

Ministry of Labour and Employment: Esplanada dos Ministérios, Bloco F, 5° andar, 70059-900 Brasília, DF; tel. (61) 225-0041; fax (61) 226-3577; e-mail internacional@mtb.gov.br; internet www.mtb.gov.br.

Ministry of Mines and Energy: Esplanada dos Ministérios, Bloco U, 7° andar, 70000 Brasília, DF; tel. (61) 225-8106; fax (61) 225-5407; internet www.mme.gov.br.

Ministry of National Integration: Esplanada dos Ministérios, Bloco E, 70062-900 Brasília, DF; tel. (61) 414-5800; e-mail ascom@integracao.gov.br; internet www.integracao.gov.br.

Ministry of Planning, Budget and Administration: Esplanada dos Ministérios, Bloco K, 70040-602 Brasília, DF; tel. (61) 215-4100; fax (61) 321-5292; e-mail info@planejamento.gov.br; internet www.planejamento.gov.br.

Ministry of Science and Technology: Esplanada dos Ministérios, Bloco E, 4° andar, 70062-900 Brasília, DF; tel. (61) 224-4364; fax (61) 225-7496; e-mail webgab@mct.com.br; internet www.mct.gov.br.

Ministry of Social Assistance and Promotion: Esplanada dos Ministérios, Bloco A, 1° andar, 70054-900, Brasília, DF; tel. (61) 315-1729; fax (61) 224-0324; internet www.assistenciasocial.gov.br.

Ministry of Social Security: Esplanada dos Ministérios, Bloco A, 6° andar, 70054-900 Brasília, DF; tel. (61) 224-7300; fax (61) 226-3861; internet www.mpas.gov.br.

Ministry of Sport: Esplanada dos Ministérios, Bloco A, 70054-900 Brasília, DF; tel. (61) 217-1800; fax (61) 217-1707; internet www.met.gov.br.

Ministry of Tourism: Esplanada dos Ministérios, Brasília, DF; internet www.met.gov.br.

Ministry of Transport: Esplanada dos Ministérios, Bloco R, 70000 Brasília, DF; tel. (61) 218-6335; fax (61) 218-6315; internet www.transportes.gov.br.

President and Legislature

PRESIDENT

Election, First Round, 6 October 2002

Candidate	Valid votes cast	% valid votes cast
Luiz Inácio (Lula) da Silva (PT)	39,443,876	46.4
José Serra (PSDB)	19,700,470	23.2
Antônio Garotinho (PSB)	15,175,776	17.9
Ciro Gomes (PPS)	10,167,650	12.0
Others	440,646	0.5
Total	84,928,418	100.0

Election, Second Round, 27 October 2002

Candidate	Valid votes cast	% valid votes cast
Luiz Inácio (Lula) da Silva (PT)	52,793,364	61.3
José Serra (PSDB)	33,370,739	38.7
Total	86,164,103	100.0

CONGRESSO NACIONAL
(National Congress)

Câmara dos Deputados
(Chamber of Deputies)

President: EFRAIM MORAIS (PFL).

The Chamber has 513 members who hold office for a four-year term.

General Election, 6 October 2002

Party	Seats
Partido dos Trabalhadores (PT)	91
Partido da Frente Liberal (PFL)	84
Partido do Movimento Democrático Brasileiro (PMDB)	74
Partido da Social Democracia Brasileira (PSDB) . . .	71
Partido Progressista Brasileiro (PPB)	49
Partido Liberal (PL)	26
Partido Trabalhista Brasileiro (PTB).	26
Partido Socialista Brasileiro (PSB)	22
Partido Democrático Trabalhista (PDT)	21
Partido Popular Socialista (PPS)	15
Partido Comunista do Brasil (PC do B)	12
Partido de Reedificação da Ordem Nacional (PRONA) .	6
Partido Verde (PV)	5
Others	11
Total	513

Senado Federal
(Federal Senate)

President: JOSÉ SARNEY (PMDB).

The 81 members of the Senate are elected by the 26 States and the Federal District (three Senators for each) according to the principle of majority. The Senate's term of office is eight years, with elections after four years for one-third of the members and after another four years for the remaining two-thirds.

Following the elections of 6 October 2002, in which 54 seats were contested, the PMDB and the PFL were both represented by 19 senators each, the PT by 14, the PSDB by 11, and the PDT by 5. The PSB, the PL, the PTB, the PPS, the PSD and the PPB were also represented.

Governors

STATES

Acre: JORGE NEY VIANA (PT).

Alagoas: RONALDO AUGUSTO LESSA (PSB).

Amapá: ANTONIO WALDEZ GÓES (PDT).

Amazonas: EDUARDO BRAGA (PPS).

Bahia: PAULO SOTA (PFL).

Ceará: LÚCIO ALCÂNTARA (PSDB).

Espírito Santo: PAULO HARTUNG (PSB).

Goiás: MARCONI FERREIRA PERILLO (PSDB).

Maranhão: JOSÉ REINALDO (PFL).

Mato Grosso: BLAIRO MAGGI (PPS).

Mato Grosso do Sul: ANTÓNIO ZECA (PT).

Minas Gerais: AÉCIO NEVES (PSDB).

Pará: SIMÃO ROBISON OLIVEIRA JATENE (PSDB).

Paraíba: CASSIO CUNHA LIMA (PSDB).

Paraná: ROBERTO REQUIÃO (PMDB).

Pernambuco: JARBAS DE ANDRADE VASCONCELOS (PMDB).

Piauí: WELLINGTON DIAS (PT).

Rio de Janeiro: ROSINHA GAROTINHO (PSB).

Rio Grande do Norte: VILMA DE FARIA (PSB).

Rio Grande do Sul: GERMANO RIGOTTO (PMDB).

Rondônia: IVO CASSOL (PSDB).

Roraima: FLAMARION POTELA (PSL).

Santa Catarina: LUIZ ENRIQUE DA SILVEIRA (PMDB).

São Paulo: GERALDO ALCKMIN (PSDB).

Sergipe: JOÃO ALVES (PFL).

Tocantins: MARCELO MIRANDA (PFL).

FEDERAL DISTRICT

Brasília: JOAQUIM DOMINGOS RORIZ (PMDB).

Political Organizations

Partido Comunista do Brasil (PC do B): Rua Major Diogo 834, Bela Vista, 01324-000 São Paulo, SP; tel. (11) 3243-1622; fax (11) 3242-4245; e-mail pcdobccri@uol.com.br; internet www.pcdob.org .br; f. 1922; Pres. RENATO REBELO; Sec.-Gen. JOÃO AMAZONAS; 185,000 mems.

Partido Democrático Trabalhista (PDT): Rua Marechal Câmara 160, 4°, 20050 Rio de Janeiro, RJ; fax (21) 262-8834; e-mail pdtnac@domain.com.br; internet www.pdt.org.br; f. 1980; formerly the PTB (Partido Trabalhista Brasileiro), renamed 1980 when that name was awarded to a dissident group following controversial judicial proceedings; member of Socialist International; Pres. LEONEL BRIZOLA; Gen. Sec. MANOEL DIAS.

Partido da Frente Liberal (PFL): Câmara dos Deputados, 70160-900 Brasília, DF; internet www.pfl.org.br; f. 1984 by moderate members of the PDS and PMDB; Pres. JORGE BORNHAUSEN; Gen. Sec. JOSÉ CARLOS ALELUIA.

Partido Liberal (PL): Câmara dos Deputados, 70160-900 Brasília, DF; tel. (61) 318-5899; internet www.pl.org.br; Pres. VALDEMAR COSTA NETO.

Partido do Movimento Democrático Brasileiro (PMDB): Câmara dos Deputados, Edif. Principal, 70160-900 Brasília, DF; tel. (61) 318-5120; e-mail pmdb@tba.com.br; internet www.pmdb.org.br; f. 1980; moderate elements of former MDB; merged with Partido Popular February 1982; Pres. MICHEL TEMER; Sec.-Gen. SARANA FELIPE; factions include: the **Históricos** and the **Movimento da Unidade Progressiva (MUP)**.

Partido Popular Socialista (PPS): Rua Coronel Lisboa 260, Vila Mariana, 04020-040, São Paulo, SP; tel. (11) 570-2182; fax (11) 549-9841; internet www.pps.org.br; f. 1922; Pres. ROBERTO FREIRE; Sec.-Gen. RUBENS BUENO.

Partido Progressista Brasileiro (PPB): Senado Federal, Anexo 1, 17° andar, 70165-900 Brasília, DF; tel. (61) 311-3041; fax (61) 226-8192; internet www.ppb.org.br; f. 1995 by merger of Partido Progressista Reformador (PPR), Partido Progressista (PP) and the Partido Republicano Progressista (PRP); right-wing; Pres. PAULO SALIM MALUF; Sec.-Gen. BENEDITO DOMINGOS.

Partido de Reconstrução Nacional (PRN): Brasília, DF; f. 1988; right-wing; Leader FERNANDO COLLOR DE MELLO.

Partido da Social Democracia Brasileira (PSDB): SCN, Quadro 04, Bloco B, Torre C, Sala 303/B, Centro Empresarial Varig, 70710-500 Brasília, DF; tel. (61) 328-0045; fax (61) 328-2120; e-mail tucano@psdb.org.br; internet www.psdb.org.br; f. 1988; centre-left; formed by dissident members of the PMDB (incl. Históricos), PFL, PDS, PDT, PSB and PTB; Pres. JOSÉ ANIBAL PONTES; Sec.-Gen. MÁRCIO FORTES.

Partido Socialista Brasileiro (PSB): Brasília, DF; tel. (61) 318-6951; fax (61) 318-2104; e-mail psb@bauru.net; internet www.psb .org.br; f. 1947; Pres. MIGUEL ARRAES; Sec.-Gen. RENATO SOARES.

Partido dos Trabalhadores (PT): Congresso Nacional, 70160, Brasília, DF; tel. (61) 224-1699; internet www.pt.org.br; f. 1980; first independent labour party; associated with the *autêntico* branch of the trade union movement; 350,000 mems; Pres. JOSÉ DIRCEU DE OLIVEIRA E SILVA; Vice-Pres. JACÓ BITTAR.

Partido Trabalhista Brasileiro (PTB): SCLN 303, Bloco C, Sala 105, Asa Norte, 70735-530 Brasília, DF; tel. (61) 226-0477; fax (61) 225-4757; e-mail ptb@ptb.org.br; internet www.ptb.org.br; f. 1980; Pres. JOSÉ EDUARDO ANDRADE VIEIRA; Sec.-Gen. RODRIGUES PALMA.

Other political parties represented in the Congreso Nacional include the Partido de Reedificação da Ordem Nacional (PRONA), the Partido Verde (PV; internet www.pv.org.br), the Partido Social-Democrático (PSD), the Partido Social Trabalhista (PST), the Partido da Mobilização Nacional (PMN; internet www.pmn.org.br), the Partido Social Cristão (PSC; internet www.psc.org.br), the Partido Social Liberal (PSL) and the Partido Social Democrata Cristão (PSDC; internet www.psdc.org.br).

Diplomatic Representation

EMBASSIES IN BRAZIL

Algeria: SHIS, QI 09, Conj. 13, Casa 01, Lago Sul, 70472-900 Brasília, DF; tel. (61) 248-4039; fax (61) 248-4691; e-mail sanag277@ bsb.terra.com.br; Ambassador LAHCÈNE MOUSSAOUI.

Angola: SHIS, QI 07, Conj. 11, Casa 09, 71625-160 Brasília, DF; tel. (61) 248-4489; fax (61) 248-1567; e-mail emb.angola@tecnolink.com .br; internet www.angola.org.br; Ambassador ALBERTO CORREIA NETO.

Argentina: SHIS, QL 02, Conj. 01, Casa 19, Lago Sul, 70442-900 Brasília, DF; tel. (61) 364-7600; fax (61) 364-7666; e-mail embarg@ linkexpress.com.br; internet www.embarg.org.br; Ambassador JUAN JOSÉ URANGA.

Australia: SES, Av. Das Nações, Quadra 801, Conj. K, Lote 7, 70469-900 Brasília, DF; tel. (61) 226-3111; fax (61) 226-1112; e-mail embaustr@zaz.com.br; Ambassador JOHN WILLIAM SULLIVAN.

Austria: SES, Av. das Nações, Quadra 811, Lote 40, 70426-900 Brasília, DF; tel. (61) 443-3111; fax (61) 443-5233; e-mail emb .austria@zaz.com.br; Ambassador DANIEL KRUMHOLZ.

Belgium: SES, Av. das Nações, Lote 32, 70422-900 Brasília, DF; tel. (61) 443-1133; fax (61) 443-1219; e-mail brasilia@diplobel.org; Ambassador JEAN-MICHEL VERANNEMAN DE WATERVLIET.

Bolivia: SHIS, QI 19, Conj. 13, Casa 19, 71655-130 Brasília, DF; tel. (61) 366-3432; fax (61) 366-3136; e-mail embolivia-brasilia@zinet .com.br; internet www.embolivia.cjb.net; Ambassador GONZALO MONTENEGRO IRIGOYEN.

Bulgaria: SEN, Av. das Nações, Lote 08, 70432-900 Brasília, DF; tel. (61) 223-6193; fax (61) 323-3285; e-mail tchavo@tba.com.br; Ambassador VENTZISLAV ANGUELOV IVANOV.

Cameroon: SHIS, QI 09, Conj. 07, Casa 01, 71625-0170 Brasília, DF; tel. (61) 248-5403; fax (61) 248-0443; e-mail embcameroun@ embcameroun.org.br; internet www.embcameroon.org.br; Ambassador MARTIN NGUELE MBARGA.

Canada: SES, Av. das Nações, Quadra 803, Lote 16, 70410-900 Brasília, DF; CP 00961, 70359-970 Brasília, DF; tel. (61) 321-2171; fax (61) 321-4529; e-mail brsla@dfait.maeci.gc.ca; Ambassador JEAN-PIERRE JUNEAU.

Cape Verde: SHIS, QL 08, Conj. 08, Casa 07, 71620-285 Brasília, DF; tel. (61) 248-0543; fax (61) 364-4059; e-mail embcaboverde@ rudah.com.br; Ambassador LUÍS ANTÓNIO VALADARES DUPRET.

Chile: SES, Av. das Nações, Quadra 803, Lote 11, 70407-900 Brasília, DF; tel. (61) 322-5151; fax (61) 322-2966; e-mail embchile@ embchile.org.br; internet www.embchile.org.br; Ambassador CARLOS EDUARDO MENA KEYMER.

China, People's Republic: SES, Av. das Nações, Quadra 813, Lote 51, 70443-900 Brasília, DF; tel. (61) 346-4436; fax (61) 346-3299; internet www.embchina.org.br; Ambassador JIANG YUANDE.

Colombia: SES, Av. das Nações, Quadra 803, Lote 10, 70444-900 Brasília, DF; tel. (61) 226-8997; fax (61) 224-4732; e-mail embjcol@ terra.com.br; Ambassador JUAN MANUEL GONZÁLEZ AYERBE.

Congo, Democratic Republic: SQS 405, Bloco U, Apdo 307, Asa Sul, CP 07-041, Brasília, DF; tel. and fax (61) 552-0335; Chargé d'affaires a.i. DANIEL MUANDA LENDO.

Costa Rica: SRTVN 701, Conj. C, Ala A, Salas 308/310, Edif. Centro Empresarial Norte, 70710-200 Brasília, DF; tel. (61) 328-2219; fax (61) 328-2243; e-mail embrica@solar.com.br; Ambassador SARA FAIGENZICHT DE GLOOBE.

Côte d'Ivoire: SEN. Av. das Nações, Lote 09, 70473-900, Brasília, DF; tel. (61) 321-4656; fax (61) 321-1306; e-mail embacostamarfim@ sagres.com.br; Ambassador COLETTE GALLIE LAMBIN.

Croatia: SHIS QI 09, Conj. 11, Casa 03, 71625-110 Brasília, DF; tel. and fax (61) 248-0610; e-mail embaixada.croacia@zaz.com.br; Chargé d'affaires a.i. NANCY BUTIJER.

Cuba: SHIS, QI 05, Conj. 18, Casa 01, 70481-900 Brasília, DF; tel. (61) 248-4710; fax (61) 248-6778; Ambassador JORGE LEZCANO PÉREZ.

Czech Republic: Av. das Nações, Quadra 805, Lote 21, 70414-900, CP 970 Brasília, DF; tel. (61) 242-7785; fax (61) 242-7833; e-mail brasilia@embassy.mzv.cz; Chargé d'affaires a.i. PAVEL PROCHÁZKA.

Denmark: SES, Av. das Nações, Quadra 807, Lote 26, 70416-900 Brasília, DF; tel. (61) 443-8188; fax (61) 443-5232; e-mail dkembassy@denmark.org.br; internet www.denmark.org.br; Ambassador ANITA HUGAU.

Dominican Republic: SHIS, QL 08, Conj. 04, Casa 08B, 70460-900 Brasília, DF; tel. (61) 248-1405; fax (61) 364-3214; e-mail embajdargan@nutcnet.com.br; Ambassador IVÁN BÁEZ BRUGAL.

Ecuador: SHIS, QI 11, Conj. 09, Casa 24, 71625-290 Brasília, DF; tel. (61) 248-5560; fax (61) 248-1290; e-mail embeq@solar.com.br; Ambassador DIEGO RIBADENEIRA ESPINOSA.

Egypt: SEN, Av. das Nações, Lote 12, 70435-900 Brasília, DF; tel. (61) 323-8800; fax (61) 323-1039; e-mail embegito@opengate.com.br; internet www.opengate.com.br/embegito; Ambassador SHADIA HUSSEIN FAHMY FARRAG.

El Salvador: SHIS, QI 07, Conj. 06, Casa 14, 71615-260 Brasília, DF; tel. (61) 364-4141; fax (61) 364-2459; e-mail embelsalvador@aol.com.br; internet www.elsalvador.hpg.com.br; Ambassador JOSÉ ROBERTO ANDINO SALAZAR.

Finland: SES, Av. das Nações, Quadra 807, Lote 27, 70417-900 Brasília, DF; tel. (61) 443-7151; fax (61) 443-3315; e-mail finlandia@terra.com.br; internet www.finlandia.org.br; Ambassador HANNU UUSI-VIDENOJA.

France: SES, Av. das Nações, Lote 04, 70404-900 Brasília, DF; tel. (61) 312-9100; fax (61) 312-9108; e-mail france@ambafrance.org.br; internet www.ambafrance.org.br; Ambassador ALAIN ROUQUIÉ.

Gabon: SHIS QI 09, Conj. 11, Casa 24, 71625-900 Brasília, DF; tel. (61) 248-3536; fax (61) 248-2241; e-mail mgabao@terra.com.br; Ambassador MARCEL ODONGUI-BONNARD.

Germany: SES, Av. das Nações, Lote 25, 70415-900 Brasília, DF; tel. (61) 443-7330; fax (61) 443-7508; e-mail embaixadalemnha@cd-graf.com.br; Ambassador UWE KAESTNER.

Ghana: SHIS, QL 10, Conj. 08, Casa 2, CP 07-0456, 70466-900 Brasília, DF; tel. (61) 248-6047; fax (61) 248-7913; Ambassador DANIEL YAW ADJEI.

Greece: SES, Av. das Nações, Quadra 805, Lote 22, 70480-900 Brasília, DF; tel. (61) 443-6573; fax (61) 443-6902; e-mail emb-grecia@terra.com.br; internet www.emb-grecia.org.br; Ambassador STRATOS DOUKAS.

Guatemala: SHIS, QI 09, Conj. 02, Casa 08, 71625-020 Brasília, DF; tel. (61) 248-3318; fax (61) 248-4383; e-mail embaguatebra@zaz.com.br; Ambassador GLORIA VICTORIA PENSABENE DE TROCHE.

Guyana: SHIS, QI 05, Conj. 19, Casa 24, 71615-190 Brasília, DF; tel. (61) 248-0874; fax (61) 248-0886; e-mail embguyana@apis.com.br; Ambassador MARILYN CHERYL MILES.

Haiti: SHIS, QI 17, Conj. 04, Casa 19, 70465-900 Brasília, DF; tel. (61) 248-6860; fax (61) 248-7472; e-mail embhaiti@zaz.com.br; Chargé d'affaires a.i. MADSEN CHERUBIN.

Holy See: SES, Av. das Nações, Quadra 801, Lote 01, CP 153, 70359-970 Brasília, DF; tel. (61) 223-0794; fax (61) 224-9365; e-mail nunapost@solar.com.br; Apostolic Nuncio Most Rev. LORENZO BALDISSERI (Titular Archbishop of Diocleziana).

Honduras: SBN, Quadra 02, Edif. Engenheiro Paulo Maurício, Salas 712–716, 70040-905 Brasília, DF; tel. (61) 326-5557; fax (61) 326-9192; Ambassador VICTOR MANUEL LOZANO URBINA.

Hungary: SES, Av. das Nações, Quadra 805, Lote 19, 70413-900 Brasília, DF; tel. (61) 443-0836; fax (61) 443-3434; e-mail embhung@uninet.com.br; internet www.hungria.org.br; Ambassador TAMÁS RÓZSA.

India: SHIS, QL 08, Conj. 08, Casa 01, 71620-285 Brasília, DF; tel. (61) 248-4006; fax (61) 248-7849; e-mail ambassador.india@zaz.com.br; Ambassador AMITAVA TRIPATHI.

Indonesia: SES, Av. das Nações, Quadra 805, Lote 20, 70479-900 Brasília, DF; tel. (61) 443-8800; fax (61) 443-6732; e-mail inubriga@persocom.com.br; Ambassador PIETER TARUYU VAU.

Iran: SES, Av. das Nações, Quadra 809, Lote 31, 70421-900 Brasília, DF; tel. (61) 242-5733; fax (61) 224-9640; e-mail embiran@linkexpress.com.br; internet www.webiran.org.br; Ambassador MANSOUR MOAZAMI.

Iraq: SES, Av. das Nações, Quadra 815, Lote 64, 70430-900 Brasília, DF; tel. (61) 346-2822; fax (61) 346-7034; Ambassador HASHIM IBRAHIM HASHIM.

Ireland: SCES, Trecho 4, Academia de Tênis, Apdo 654, 70200-004 Brasília, DF; tel. (61) 316-6654; fax (61) 316-6264; e-mail irishembassybrasilia@eircom.net; Ambassador MARTIN GREENE.

Israel: SES, Av. das Nações, Lote 38, 70424-900 Brasília, DF; tel. (61) 244-7675; fax (61) 244-6129; e-mail emisrael@terra.com.br; Ambassador DANIEL GAZIT.

Italy: SES, Av. das Nações, Lote 30, 70420-900 Brasília, DF; tel. (61) 442-9900; fax (61)443-1231; e-mail embitalia@zaz.com.br; internet www.embitalia.org.br; Ambassador VINCENZO PETRONE.

Japan: SES, Av. das Nações, Quadra 811, Lote 39, 70425-900 Brasília, DF; tel. (61) 242-6866; fax (61) 242-0738; e-mail japao1@yawl.com.br; internet www.japao.org.br; Ambassador TADASHI IKEDA.

Jordan: SHIS, QI 09, Conj. 18, Casa 14, 70483-900 Brasília, DF; tel. (61) 248-5407; fax (61) 248-1698; e-mail emb.jordania@apis.com.br; Ambassador FARIS SHAWKAT MUFTI.

Korea, Republic: SEN, Av. das Nações, Lote 14, 70436-900 Brasília, DF; tel. (61) 321-2500; fax (61) 321-2508; e-mail embcoreia@terra.com.br; Ambassador KIM MYONG-BAI.

Kuwait: SHIS, QI 05, Chácara 30, 71600-750 Brasília, DF; tel. (61) 248-2323; fax (61) 248-0969; e-mail ekuwait@opendf.com.br; Ambassador NASSER SABEEH B. AS-SABEEH.

Lebanon: SES, Av. das Nações, Quadra 805, Lote 17, 70411-900 Brasília, DF; tel. (61) 443-9837; fax (61) 443-8574; e-mail emblibano@uol.com.br; Ambassador ISHAYA EL-KHOURY.

Libya: SHIS, QI 15, Chácara 26, 70462-900 Brasília, DF; tel. (61) 248-6710; fax (61) 248-0598; e-mail emblibia@terra.com.br; Ambassador MOHAMED HEIMEDA SAAD MATRI.

Malaysia: SHIS, QI 05, Chácara 62, 70477-900 Brasília, DF; tel. (61) 248-5008; fax (61) 248-6307; e-mail mwbrasilia@persocom.com.br; Ambassador TAI KAT MENG.

Mexico: SES, Av. das Nações, Quadra 805, Lote 18, 70412-900 Brasília, DF; tel. (61) 244-1011; fax (61) 244-1755; e-mail embamexbra@cabonet.com.br; Ambassador CECILIA SOTO GONZÁLEZ.

Morocco: SEN, Av. das Nações, Lote 02, 70432-900 Brasília, DF; tel. (61) 321-4487; fax (61) 321-0745; e-mail sifamarbr@onix.com.br; internet www.embmarrocos.org.br; Ambassador ABDELMALEK CHARKAOUI GHAZOUANI.

Mozambique: SHIS, QL 12, Conj. 07, Casa 09, 71630-275 Brasília, DF; tel. (61) 248-4222; fax (61) 248-3917; e-mail embamoc-bsb@uol.com; Ambassador AMADEU PAULO SAMUEL DE CONCEIÇÃO.

Myanmar: SHIS, QI 07, Conj. 14, Casa 05, 71615-340 Brasília, DF; tel. (61) 248-3747; fax (61) 364-2747; e-mail mebrsl@brnet.com.br; Ambassador (vacant).

Netherlands: SES, Av. das Nações, Quadra 801, Lote 05, 7045-900 Brasília, DF; tel. (61) 321-4769; fax (61) 321-1518; e-mail bra@minbuza.nl; internet www.embaixada-holanda.org.br; Ambassador ROBERT HANS MEYS.

New Zealand: SHIS, QI 09, Conj. 16, Casa 01, 71625-160 Brasília, DF; tel. (61) 248-9900; fax (61) 248-9916; e-mail zelandia@terra.com.br; Ambassador DENISE ALMÃO.

Nicaragua: SHIS, QI 11, Conj. 05, Casa 03, 71625-250 Brasília, DF; tel. (61) 248-1115; fax (61) 364-0825; e-mail embanibra@zaz.com.br; Ambassador GUILLERMO FILIPE PÉREZ-ARGUELLO.

Nigeria: SEN, Av. das Nações, Lote 05, 70459-900 Brasília, DF; tel. (61) 226-1717; fax (61) 226-5192; e-mail nigemb@persocom.com.br; Ambassador JOSEF SOOKORE EGBUSON.

Norway: SES, Av. das Nações, Quadra 807, Lote 28, CP 07-0670, 70418-900 Brasília, DF; tel. (61) 443-8720; fax (61) 443-2942; e-mail emb.brasilia@mfa.no; internet www.brasilia.mfa.no; Ambassador JAN GERHARD LASSEN.

Pakistan: SHIS, QL 12, Conj. 02, Casa 19, 71615-140 Brasília, DF; tel. (61) 364-1632; fax (61) 248-0246; e-mail parepbra@bruturbo.com; Ambassador KHALID KHATTAK.

Panama: SHIS, QL 06, Conj. 11, Casa 18, 71625-260 Brasília, DF; tel. (61) 248-7309; fax (61) 248-2834; e-mail empanama@nettur.com.br; Ambassador MARIO ANTONIO BOYD GALINDO.

Paraguay: SES, Av. das Nações, Quadra 811, Lote 42, 70427-900 Brasília, DF; tel. (61) 242-3742; fax (61) 242-4605; e-mail embapar@yawl.com.br; Ambassador LUIS GONZÁLEZ ARIAS.

Peru: SES, Av. das Nações, Quadra 811, Lote 43, 70428-900 Brasília, DF; tel. (61) 242-9933; fax (61) 244-9344; e-mail embperu@embperu.org.br; internet www.embperu.org.br; Ambassador CARLOS HIGUEROS RAMOS.

Philippines: SEN, Av. das Nações, Lote 01, 70431-900 Brasília, DF; tel. (61) 223-5143; fax (61) 226-7411; e-mail ambaphilbr@persocom .com.br; Ambassador OSCAR G. VALENZUELA.

Poland: SES, Av. das Nações, Lote 33, 70423-900 Brasília, DF; tel. (61) 443-3438; fax (61) 242-8543; Ambassador KRZYSZTOF JACEK HINZ.

Portugal: SES, Av. das Nações, Quadra 801, Lote 02, 70402-900 Brasília, DF; tel. (61) 321-3434; fax (61) 224-7347; e-mail portugalbr@uol.com.br; Ambassador ANTÓNIO MANUEL CANASTREIRO FRANCO.

Romania: SEN, Av. das Nações, Lote 06, 70456 Brasília, DF; tel. (61) 226-0746; fax (61) 226-6629; e-mail romenia@solar.com.br; Ambassador MONICA MARIANA GRIGORESCU.

Russia: SES, Av. das Nações, Quadra 801, Lote A, 70476-900 Brasília, DF; tel. (61) 223-3094; fax (61) 226-7319; e-mail embrus@ linkexpress.com.br; internet www.users.linkexpress.com.br/ embrus; Ambassador VASSILII PETROVICH GROMOV.

Saudi Arabia: SHIS, QL 10, Conj. 09, Casa 20, 70471-900 Brasília, DF; tel. (61) 248-3523; fax (61) 284-2905; Ambassador ANWAR ABD RABBUH.

Senegal: SEN, Av. das Nações, Lote 18, QL 12, Conj. 04, Casa 13, Lago Sul, Brasília, DF; tel. (61) 223-7822; fax (61) 322-7822; e-mail senebrasilia@bol.com.br; Ambassador CÉSAR COLY.

Serbia and Montenegro: SES, Av. das Nações, Quadra 803, Lote 15, 70409-900 Brasília, DF; tel. (61) 223-7272; fax (61) 223-8462; e-mail embiugos@nutecnet.com.br; Ambassador RADIVOJE LAZAREVIĆ.

Slovakia: Av. das Nações, Quadra 805, Lote 21, 70414-900 Brasília, DF; tel. (61) 443-1263; fax (61) 443-1267; e-mail eslovaca@loreno .net; Ambassador JOZEF ADAMEC.

South Africa: SES, Av. das Nações, Quadra 801, Lote 06, CP 11-1170, 70406–900 Brasília, DF; tel. (61) 312-9500; fax (61) 322-8491; e-mail saemb@solar.com.br; Ambassador MBULELO RAKWENA.

Spain: SES, Av. das Nações, Quadra 811, Lote 44, 70429-900 Brasília, DF; tel. (61) 244-2121; fax (61) 242-1781; e-mail embespbr@ correo.mae.es; Ambassador JOSÉ CODERCH PLANAS.

Sri Lanka: SHIS, QI 09, Conj. 09, Casa 07, 71625-090 Brasília DF; tel. (61) 248-2701; fax (61) 364-5430; e-mail lankaemb@yawl.com.br; Ambassador Gen. ROHAN DE SILVA DALUWATTE.

Suriname: SHIS, QI 09, Conj. 08, Casa 24, 70457-900 Brasília, DF; tel. (61) 248-6706; fax (61) 248-3791; e-mail sur.emb@persocom.com .br; Ambassador RADJENDRAKUMAR NIHALCHAND SONNY HIRA.

Sweden: SES, Av. das Nações, Quadra 807, Lote 29, 70419-900 Brasília, DF; tel. (61) 443-1444; fax (61) 443-1187; e-mail swebra@ opengate.com.br; Ambassador STAFFAN ÅBERG.

Switzerland: SES, Av. das Nações, Lote 41, 70448-900 Brasília, DF; CP 08671, 70312-970 Brasília, DF; tel. (61) 443-5500; fax (61) 443-5711; e-mail swissembra@brasilia.com.br; Ambassador JÜRG LEUTERT.

Syria: SEN, Av. das Nações, Lote 11, 70434-900 Brasília, DF; tel. (61) 226-0970; fax (61) 223-2595; Ambassador CHAHINE FARAH.

Thailand: SEN, Av. das Nações, Lote 10, 70433-900 Brasília, DF; tel. (61) 224-6943; fax (61) 223-7502; e-mail thaiemb@brnet.com.br; Ambassador SUPHAT CHITRAUKROH.

Trinidad and Tobago: SHIS, QL 02, Conj. 02, Casa 01, 71665-028 Brasília, DF; tel. (61) 365-1132; fax (61) 365-1733; e-mail trinbago@ terra.com.br; Ambassador WINSTON CLYDE MOORE.

Tunisia: SHIS, QI 09, Conj. 16, Casa 20, 71625-160 Brasília, DF; tel. (61) 248-3725; fax (61) 248-7355; e-mail at.brasilia@terra.com .br; Ambassador HASSINE BOUZID.

Turkey: SES, Av. das Nações, Quadra 805, Lote 23, 70452-900 Brasília, DF; tel. (61) 242-1850; fax (61) 242-1448; e-mail turquia@ conectanet.com.br; Ambassador SEVINÇ DALYANOĞLU.

Ukraine: SHIS, QL 06, Conj. 02, Casa 17, 71620-025 Brasília, DF; tel. (61) 365-3889; fax (61) 365-3898; e-mail brucremb@zaz.com.br; Chargé d'affaires a.i. YURII BOHAIEVSKYI.

United Arab Emirates: SHIS, QI 05, Conj. 10, Casa 01, 70486-901 Brasília, DF; tel. (61) 248-0717; fax (61) 248-7543; e-mail u.a.e.emb@ opengate.com.br; internet www.the-emirates.com; Ambassador SAEED HAMED AL-JUNAIBI.

United Kingdom: SES, Quadra 801, Conj. K, Lote 08, CP 07-0586, 70408-900 Brasília, DF; tel. (61) 225-2710; fax (61) 225-1777; e-mail britemb@nutecnet.com.br; internet www.uk.org.br; Ambassador Sir ROGER BONE.

USA: SES, Av. das Nações, Quadra 801, Lote 03, 70403-900 Brasília, DF; tel. (61) 321-7000; fax (61) 321-7241; internet www .embaixadaamericana.org.br; Ambassador DONNA JEAN HRINAK.

Uruguay: SES, Av. das Nações, Lote 14, 70450-900 Brasília, DF; tel. (61) 322-1200; fax (61) 322-6534; e-mail urubras@emburuguai .org.br; internet www.emburuguai.org.br; Ambassador AGUSTÍN ESPINOSA LLOVERAS.

Venezuela: SES, Av. das Nações, Quadra 803, Lote 13, 70451-900 Brasília, DF; tel. (61) 322-1011; fax (61) 226-5633; e-mail embven1@ rudah.com.br; Ambassador HELY VLADIMIR VILLEGAS POLJAK.

Viet Nam: SHIS, QI 05, Conj. 07, Casa 21, 71615-070 Brasília, DF; tel. (61) 364-5836; fax (61) 364-5876; e-mail tlsqvnsp@uol.com.br; Ambassador NGUYEN VAN HUYNH.

Judicial System

The judiciary powers of the State are held by the following: the Supreme Federal Tribunal, the Higher Tribunal of Justice, the five Regional Federal Tribunals and Federal Judges, the Higher Labour Tribunal, the 24 Regional Labour Tribunals, the Conciliation and Judgment Councils and Labour Judges, the Higher Electoral Tribunal, the 27 Regional Electoral Tribunals, the Electoral Judges and Electoral Councils, the Higher Military Tribunal, the Military Tribunals and Military Judges, the Tribunals of the States and Judges of the States, the Tribunal of the Federal District and of the Territories and Judges of the Federal District and of the Territories.

The Supreme Federal Tribunal comprises 11 ministers, nominated by the President and approved by the Senate. Its most important role is to rule on the final interpretation of the Constitution. The Supreme Federal Tribunal has the power to declare an act of Congress void if it is unconstitutional. It judges offences committed by persons such as the President, the Vice-President, members of the Congresso Nacional, Ministers of State, its own members, the Attorney General, judges of other higher courts, and heads of permanent diplomatic missions. It also judges cases of litigation between the Union and the States, between the States, or between foreign nations and the Union or the States; disputes as to jurisdiction between higher Tribunals, or between the latter and any other court, in cases involving the extradition of criminals, and others related to the writs of habeas corpus and habeas data, and in other cases.

The Higher Tribunal of Justice comprises at least 33 members, appointed by the President and approved by the Senado. Its jurisdiction includes the judgment of offences committed by State Governors. The Regional Federal Tribunals comprise at least seven judges, recruited when possible in the respective region and appointed by the President of the Republic. The Higher Labour Tribunal comprises 27 members, appointed by the President and approved by the Senado. The judges of the Regional Labour Tribunals are also appointed by the President. The Regional Electoral Tribunals are also composed of seven members. The Higher Military Tribunal comprises 15 life members, appointed by the President and approved by the Senate; three from the navy, four from the army, three from the air force and five civilian members. The States are responsible for the administration of their own justice, according to the principles established by the Constitution.

SUPREME FEDERAL TRIBUNAL

Supreme Federal Tribunal: Praça dos Três Poderes, 70175-900 Brasília, DF; tel. (61) 316-5000; fax (61) 316-5483; internet www.stf .gov.br.

President: MARCO AURÉLIO MENDES DE FARIAS MELLO.

Vice-President: ILMAR NASCIMENTO GALVÃO.

Justices: JOSÉ CARLOS MOREIRA ALVES, JOSÉ NÉRI DA SILVEIRA, SYDNEY SANCHES, JOSÉ PAULO SEPÚLVEDA PERTENCE, JOSÉ CELSO DE MELLO, MAURÍCIO JOSÉ CORRÊA, NELSON DE AZEVEDO JOBIM (Filho), CARLOS VELLOSO, ELLEN GRACIE, GILMAR MENDES.

Attorney-General: GERALDO BRINDEIRO.

Director-General (Secretariat): FRANCISCO SILVINO DE JESUS FERREIRA MATOS.

Religion

CHRISTIANITY

Conselho Nacional de Igrejas Cristãs do Brasil (CONIC) (National Council of Christian Churches in Brazil): SCS, Quadra 01, Bloco E, Edif. Ceará, Sala 713, 70303-900 Brasília, DF; tel. (61) 321-8341; fax (61) 321-3034; e-mail conic.brasil@zaz.com.br; internet www.conic.org.br; f. 1982; seven mem. churches; Pres. Bishop ADRIEL DE SOUZA MAIA; Exec. Sec. P. ERVINO SCHMIDT.

The Roman Catholic Church

Brazil comprises 41 archdioceses, 210 dioceses (including one each for Catholics of the Maronite, Melkite and Ukrainian Rites), 14 territorial prelatures and two territorial abbacies. The Archbishop of São Sebastião do Rio de Janeiro is also the Ordinary for Catholics of other Oriental Rites in Brazil (estimated at 10,000 in 1994). The great majority of Brazil's population are adherents of the Roman Catholic Church (around 106m. at the time of the 1980 census), although a report published by the Brazilian weekly *Veja* in July 1989 concluded that since 1950 the membership of non-Catholic Christian Churches had risen from 3% to 6% of the total population, while membership of the Roman Catholic Church had fallen from 93% to 89% of Brazilians.

Bishops' Conference: Conferência Nacional dos Bispos do Brasil, SE/Sul Quadra 801, Conj. B, CP 02067, 70259-970 Brasília, DF; tel. (61) 313-8300; fax (61) 313-8303; e-mail cnbb@cnbb.org.br; internet www.cnbb.org.br; f. 1980; statutes approved 1986; Pres. JAYME HENRIQUE CHEMELLO (Bishop of Pelotas, RS); Sec.-Gen. RAYMUNDO DAMASCENO ASSIS.

Latin Rite

Archbishop of São Salvador da Bahia, BA: Cardinal GERALDO MAJELLA AGNELO, Primate of Brazil, Cúria Metropolitana, Rua Martin Afonso de Souza 270, 40100-050 Salvador, BA; tel. and fax (71) 328-6699; e-mail gma@atarde.com.br.

Archbishop of Aparecida, SP: Cardinal ALOÍSIO LORSCHEIDER.

Archbishop of Aracaju, SE: JOSÉ PALMEIRA LESSA.

Archbishop of Belém do Pará, PA: VICENTE JOAQUIM ZICO.

Archbishop of Belo Horizonte, MG: Cardinal SERAFIM FERNANDES DE ARAÚJO.

Archbishop of Botucatu, SP: ALOYSIO JOSÉ LEAL PENNA.

Archbishop of Brasília, DF: Cardinal JOSÉ FREIRE FALCÃO.

Archbishop of Campinas, SP: GILBERTO PEREIRA LOPES.

Archbishop of Campo Grande, MS: VITÓRIO PAVANELLO.

Archbishop of Cascavel, PR: LÚCIO IGNÁCIO BAUMGAERTNER.

Archbishop of Cuiabá, MT: BONIFÁCIO PICCININI.

Archbishop of Curitiba, PR: PEDRO ANTÔNIO MARCHETTI FEDALTO.

Archbishop of Diamantina, MG: PAULO LOPES DE FARIA.

Archbishop of Feira de Santana, BA: ITAMAR VIAN.

Archbishop of Florianópolis, SC: MURILO SEBASTIÃO RAMOS KRIEGER.

Archbishop of Fortaleza, CE: JOSÉ ANTÔNIO APARECIDO TOSI MARQUES.

Archbishop of Goiânia, GO: WASHINGTON CRUZ.

Archbishop of Juiz de Fora, MG: EURICO DOS SANTOS VELOSO.

Archbishop of Londrina, PR: ALBANO BORTOLETTO CAVALLIN.

Archbishop of Maceió, AL: JOSÉ CARLOS MELO.

Archbishop of Manaus, AM: LUIZ SOARES VIEIRA.

Archbishop of Mariana, MG: LUCIANO PEDRO MENDES DE ALMEIDA.

Archbishop of Maringá, PR: JOÃO BRAZ DE AVIZ.

Archbishop of Montes Claros, MG: GERALDO MAJELA DE CASTRO.

Archbishop of Natal, RN: HEITOR DE ARAÚJO SALES.

Archbishop of Niterói, RJ: CARLOS ALBERTO ETCHANDY GIMENO NAVARRO.

Archbishop of Olinda e Recife, PE: JOSÉ CARDOSO SOBRINHO.

Archbishop of Palmas, PR: ALBERTO TAVEIRA CORRÊA.

Archbishop of Paraíba, PB: MARCELO PINTO CARVALHEIRA.

Archbishop of Porto Alegre, RS: DADEUS GRINGS.

Archbishop of Porto Velho, RO: MOACYR GRECHI.

Archbishop of Pouso Alegre, MG: RICARDO PEDRO CHAVES PINTO, FILHO.

Archbishop of Ribeirão Preto, SP: ARNALDO RIBEIRO.

Archbishop of São Luís do Maranhão, MA: PAULO EDUARDO DE ANDRADE PONTE.

Archbishop of São Paulo, SP: Cardinal CLÁUDIO HUMMES.

Archbishop of São Salvador da Bahia, BA: Cardinal GERALDO MAJELLA AGNELLO.

Archbishop of São Sebastião do Rio de Janeiro, RJ: Cardinal EUSÉBIO OSCAR SCHEID.

Archbishop of Sorocaba, SP: JOSÉ LAMBERT.

Archbishop of Teresina, PI: CELSO JOSÉ PINTO DA SILVA.

Archbishop of Uberaba, MG: ALOÍSIO ROQUE OPPERMANN.

Archbishop of Vitória, ES: SILVESTRE LUÍS SCANDIAN.

Archbishop of Vitória da Conquista, BA: GERALDO LYRIO ROCHA.

Maronite Rite

Bishop of Nossa Senhora do Líbano em São Paulo, SP: JOSEPH MAHFOUZ.

Melkite Rite

Bishop of Nossa Senhora do Paraíso em São Paulo, SP: FARES MAAKAROUN.

Ukrainian Rite

Bishop of São João Batista em Curitiba, PR: EFRAIM BASÍLIO KREVEY.

The Anglican Communion

Anglicans form the Episcopal Anglican Church of Brazil (Igreja Episcopal Anglicana do Brasil), comprising seven dioceses.

Igreja Episcopal Anglicana do Brasil: Rua Comendador Elias Zarzur, 1239, Sala 01, Santo Amaro, 04736-002, São Paulo, SP; tel. and fax (11) 246-0383; internet www.ieab.org.br; f. 1890; 103,021 mems (1997); Primate Most Rev. GLAUCO SOARES DE LIMA (Bishop of São Paulo-Brazil); Gen. Sec. Rev. MAURICIO J. A. DE ANDRADE; e-mail mandrade@ieab.org.br.

Protestant Churches

Igreja Cristã Reformada do Brasil: Rua Domingos Rodrigues, 306/Lapa, 05075-000, São Paulo, SP; tel. (11) 260-7514; e-mail icbcuritiba@hotmail.com; internet www.igrejadopaidejesus.hpg.ig.com.br; f. 1932; Pres. Rev. ANTÔNIO BONZOI.

Igreja Evangélica de Confissão Luterana no Brasil (IECLB): Rua Senhor dos Passos 202, 4° andar, CP 2876, 90020-180 Porto Alegre, RS; tel. (51) 3221-3433; fax (51) 3225-7244; e-mail secretariageral@ieclb.org.br; internet www.ieclb.org.br; f. 1949; 714,000 mems; Pres. Pastor HUBERTO KIRCHHEIM.

Igreja Evangélica Congregacional do Brasil: CP 414, 98700 Ijuí, RS; tel. (55) 332-4656; f. 1942; 41,000 mems, 310 congregations; Pres. Rev. H. HARTMUT W. HACHTMANN.

Igreja Evangélica Luterana do Brasil: Rua Cel. Lucas de Oliveira 894, 90440-010 Porto Alegre, RS; tel. (51) 3332-2111; fax (51) 3332-8145; e-mail ielb@ielb.org.br; internet www.ielb.org.br; f. 1904; 221,113 mems; Pres. Rev. CARLOS WALTER WINTERLE.

Igreja Maná do Brasil: Rua Marie Satzke, 47, Jardim Marajoara, 04664-150, São Paulo,, SP; tel. (11) 5521-7571; e-mail adm_brasil@igrejamana.com; internet www.igrejamana.com.

Igreja Metodista do Brasil: Rua Oswaldo Cruz, 182, 16200-000, Birigui, SP; tel. (18) 642-1198; e-mail informatica@metodista.org.br; internet www.metodista.org.br; Exec. Sec. Bishop JOÃO ALVES DE OLIVEIRA .

Igreja Presbiteriana Unida do Brasil (IPU): Rua Cândida Nogueira. 20/603, Grajaú, 30430-630, Belo Horizonte, MG; tel. (31) 3291-7513; internet www.ipu.org.br; f. 1978; Sec. Rev. ÉSER TÉRCIO PACHECO.

BAHÁ'Í FAITH

Bahá'í Community of Brazil: SHIS, QL 08, Conj. 02, Casa 15, 71620-285, Brasília, DF; CP 7035, 71620-225 Brasília, DF; tel. (61) 364-3594; fax (61) 364-3470; e-mail secext@bahai.org.br; f. 1921; Sec. IRADJ ROBERTO EGHRARI.

BUDDHISM

Federação das Seitas Budistas do Brasil: Av. Paulo Ferreira 1133, 02915-100, São Paulo, SP; tel. (11) 876-5771; fax (11) 877-8687.

Sociedade Budista do Brasil (Rio Buddhist Vihara): Dom Joaquim Mamede 45, Lagoinha, Santa Tereza, 20241-390 Rio de Janeiro, RJ; tel. (21) 205-4400; f. 1972; Principal Dr PUHULWELLE VIPASSI.

The Press

The most striking feature of the Brazilian press is the relatively small circulation of newspapers in comparison with the size of the population. The newspapers with the largest circulations are *O Dia* (250,000), *O Globo* (350,000), *Fôlha de São Paulo* (560,000), and *O Estado de São Paulo* (242,000). The low circulation is mainly owing to high costs resulting from distribution difficulties. In consequence there are no national newspapers. In 1996 a total of 380 daily newspaper titles were published in Brazil.

DAILY NEWSPAPERS

Belém, PA

O Liberal: Rua Gaspar Viana 253, 66020 Belém, PA; tel. (91) 222-3000; fax (91) 224-1906; internet www.oliberal.com.br; f. 1946; Pres. LUCIDEA MAIORANA; circ. 20,000.

Belo Horizonte, MG

Diário da Tarde: Rua Goiás 36, 30190 Belo Horizonte, MG; tel. (31) 273-2322; fax (31) 273-4400; f. 1931; evening; Dir-Gen. PAULO C. DE ARAÚJO; total circ. 150,000.

Diário de Minas: Rua Francisco Salles 540, 30150-220 Belo Horizonte, MG; tel. (31) 222-5622; f. 1949; Pres. MARCO AURÍLIO F. CARONE; circ. 50,000.

Diário do Comércio: Av. Américo Vespúcio 1660, 31230 Belo Horizonte, MG; tel. (31) 469-1011; fax (31) 469-1080; f. 1932; Pres. JOSÉ COSTA.

Estado de Minas: Rua Goiás 36, 30190 Belo Horizonte, MG; tel. (31) 273-2322; fax (31) 273-4400; internet www.estaminas.com.br; f. 1928; morning; independent; Pres. PAULO C. DE ARAÚJO; circ. 65,000.

Blumenau, SC

Jornal de Santa Catarina: Rua São Paulo 1120, 89010-000 Blumenau, SC; tel. (2147) 340-1400; e-mail redacao@santa.com.br; f. 1971; Dir ALVARO IAHNIG; circ. 25,000.

Brasília, DF

Correio Brasiliense: SIG, Q2, Lotes 300/340, 70610-901 Brasília, DF; tel. (61) 321-1314; fax (61) 321-2856; internet www.correioweb.com.br; f. 1960; Dir-Gen. PAULO C. DE ARAÚJO; circ. 30,000.

Jornal de Brasília: SIG, Trecho 1, Lotes 585/645, 70610-400 Brasília, DF; tel. (61) 225-2515; f. 1972; Dir-Gen. FERNANDO CÔMA; circ. 25,000.

Campinas, SP

Correio Popular: Rua Conceição 124, 13010-902 Campinas, SP; tel. (19) 3736-3050; fax (19) 3234-8984; e-mail sygon@rac.com.br; f. 1927; Pres. SYLVINO DE GODOY NETO; circ. 40,000.

Curitiba, PR

O Estado do Paraná: Rua João Tschannerl 800, 80820-000 Curitiba, PR; tel. (41) 335-8811; fax (41) 335-2838; f. 1951; Pres. PAULO CRUZ PIMENTEL; circ. 15,000.

Gazeta do Povo: Rua Pedro Ivo 459, Centro, 80010-020, Curitiba, PR; tel. (41) 224-0522; fax (41) 225-6848; internet tudoparana.globo.com/gazetadepovo; f. 1919; Pres. FRANCISCO CUNHA PEREIRA (Filho); circ. 40,000.

Tribuna do Paraná: Rua João Tschannerl 800, 80820-010 Curitiba PR; tel. (41) 335-8811; fax (41) 335-2838; f. 1956; Pres. PAULO CRUZ PIMENTEL; circ. 15,000.

Florianópolis, SC

O Estado: Rodovia SC-401, Km 3, 88030 Florianópolis, SC; tel. (482) 388-8888; fax (482) 380-0711; f. 1915; Pres. JOSÉ MATUSALÉM COMELLI; circ. 20,000.

Fortaleza, CE

Jornal O Povo: Av. Aguanambi 282, 60055 Fortaleza, CE; tel. (85) 211-9666; fax (85) 231-5792; internet www.noolhar.com/opovo; f. 1928; evening; Pres. DEMÓCRITO ROCHA DUMMAR; circ. 20,000.

Tribuna do Ceará: Av. Desemb. Moreira 2900, 60170 Fortaleza, CE; tel. (85) 247-3066; fax (85) 272-2799; f. 1957; Dir JOSÉ A. SANCHO; circ. 12,000.

Goiânia, GO

Diário da Manhã: Av. Anhanguera 2833, Setor Leste Universitário, 74000 Goiânia, GO; tel. (62) 261-7371; internet www.dm.com.br; f. 1980; Pres. JULIO NASSER CUSTÓDIO DOS SANTOS; circ. 16,000.

Jornal O Popular: Rua Thómas Edson Q7, Setor Serrinha, 74835-130 Goiânia, GO; tel. (62) 250-1000; fax (62) 241-1018; f. 1938; Pres. JAIME CÂMARA JÚNIOR; circ. 65,000.

João Pessoa, PB

Correio da Paraíba: Av. Pedro II, Centro, João Pessoa, PB; tel. (083) 216-5000; fax (083) 216-5009; e-mail jcorreio@zaz.com.br; internet www.correiodaparaiba.com.br.

Londrina, PR

Fôlha de Londrina: Rua Piauí 241, 86010 Londrina, PR; tel. (432) 24-2020; fax (432) 21-1051; f. 1948; Pres. JOÃO MILANEZ; circ. 40,000.

Manaus, AM

A Crítica: Av. André Araújo, Km 3, 69060 Manaus; tel. (92) 642-2000; fax (92) 642-1501; internet www.acritica.com.br; f. 1949; Dir UMBERTO CADERARO; circ. 19,000.

Natal, RN

Diario de Natal: Av. Deodoro 245, Petrópolis, 59012-600, Natal, RN; tel. (84) 220-0166; internet www.diariodenatal.com.br; Dir ALBIMAR FURTADO.

Niterói, RJ

O Fluminense: Rua Visconde de Itaboraí 184, 24030 Niterói, RJ; tel. (21) 719-3311; fax (21) 719-6344; f. 1978; Dir ALBERTO FRANCISCO TORRES; circ. 80,000.

A Tribuna: Rua Barão do Amazonas 31, 24030111 Niterói, RJ; tel. (21) 2719-1886; e-mail icarai@urbi.com.br; f. 1936; daily; Dir-Supt GUSTAVO SANTANO AMÓRO; circ. 10,000.

Palmas, TO

O Girassol: 104 N (ACNE 2), Conj. 03, Lote 22, Pousada Araguaia, Palmas, TO; tel. and fax (63) 225-5456; e-mail ogirassol@ogirassol.com; internet www.ogirassol.com.br; Pres. WILBERGSON ESTRELA GOMES.

Porto Alegre, RS

Zero Hora: Av. Ipiranga 1075, 90169-900 Porto Alegre, RS; tel. (51) 218-4101; fax (51) 218-4405; internet www.rbs.com.br; f. 1964; Pres. NELSON SIROTSKY; circ. 165,000 Monday, 170,000 weekdays, 240,000 Sunday.

Recife, PE

Diário de Pernambuco: Praça da Independência 12, 2° andar, 50010-300 Recife, PE; tel. (81) 424-3666; fax (81) 424-2527; internet www.pernambuco.com/diario; f. 1825; morning; independent; Pres. ANTÔNIO C. DA COSTA; circ. 31,000.

Ribeirão Preto, SP

Diário da Manhã: Rua Duque de Caxias 179, 14015 Ribeirão Preto, SP; tel. (16) 634-0909; f. 1898; Dir PAULO M. SANT'ANNA; circ. 17,000.

Rio de Janeiro, RJ

O Dia: Rua Riachuelo 359, 20235 Rio de Janeiro, RJ; tel. (21) 272-8000; fax (21) 507-1038; f. 1951; morning; centrist labour; Pres. ANTÔNIO ARY DE CARVALHO; circ. 250,000 weekdays, 500,000 Sundays.

O Globo: Rua Irineu Marinho 35, CP 1090, 20233-900 Rio de Janeiro, RJ; tel. (21) 534-5000; fax (21) 534-5510; internet oglobo.globo.com; f. 1925; morning; Dir FRANCISCO GRAELL; circ. 350,000 weekdays, 600,000 Sundays.

Jornal do Brasil: Av. Brasil 500, 6° andar, São Cristóvão, 20949-900 Rio de Janeiro, RJ; tel. (21) 585-4422; internet www.jb.com.br; f. 1891; morning; Catholic, liberal; Pres. M. F. DO NASCIMENTO BRITO; circ. 200,000 weekdays, 325,000 Sundays.

Jornal do Comércio: Rua do Livramento 189, 20221 Rio de Janeiro, RJ; tel. (21) 253-6675; f. 1827; morning; Pres. AUSTREGÉSILO DE ATHAYDE; circ. 31,000 weekdays.

Jornal dos Sports: Rua Tenente Possolo 15/25, 20230-160 Rio de Janeiro, RJ; tel. (21) 232-8010; e-mail esportes@vol.com.br; f. 1931; morning; sporting daily; Dir MILTON COELHO DA GRAÇA; circ. 39,000.

Ultima Hora: Rua Equador 702, 20220 Rio de Janeiro, RJ; tel. (21) 223-2444; fax (21) 223-2444; f. 1951; evening; Dir K. NUNES; circ. 56,000.

Salvador, BA

Jornal Correio da Bahia: Av. Luis Viana Filho s/n, 41100 Salvador, BA; tel. (71) 371-2811; fax (71) 231-3944; f. 1979; Pres. ARMANDO GONÇALVES.

Jornal da Tarde: Av. Tancredo Neves 1092, 41820-020 Salvador, BA; tel. (71) 231-9683; fax (71) 231-1064; f. 1912; evening; Pres. REGINA SIMÕES DE MELLO LEITÃO; circ. 54,000.

Santarém, PA

O Impacto—O Jornal da Amazônia: Av. Presidente Vargas, 3728, Caranazal 68040–060 Santarém, PA; tel. (93) 523-3330; fax (93) 523-9131; e-mail oimpacto@oimpacto.com.br; internet www.oimpacto.com.br; Pres. ADMILTON ALMEIDA.

Santo André, SP

Diário do Grande ABC: Rua Catequese 562, 09090-900 Santo André, SP; tel. (11) 715-8112; fax (11) 715-8257; e-mail MauryDotto@dgabc.com.br; internet www.dgabc.com.br; f. 1958; Pres. MAURY DE CAMPOS DOTTO; circ. 78,500.

Santos, SP

A Tribuna: Rua General Câmara 90/94, 11010-903 Santos, SP; tel. (13) 3211-7000; fax (13) 3219-6783; e-mail rmsantini@atribuna.com .br; internet www.atribuna.com.br; f. 1984; Dir ROBERTO M. SANTINI; circ. 40,000.

São Luís, MA

O Imparcial: Empresa Pacotilha Ltda, Rua Assis Chateaubriand s/n, Renascença 2, 65075-670 São Luís, MA; tel. (98) 212-2010; e-mail redacao@pacotilha.com.br; internet www.oimparcial.com.br; f. 1926; Dir-Gen. PEDRO BATISTA FREIRE.

São Paulo, SP

Diário Comércio e Indústria: Rua Alvaro de Carvalho 354, 01050-020 São Paulo, SP; tel. (11) 256-5011; fax (11) 258-1989; f. 1933; morning; Pres. HAMILTON LUCAS DE OLIVEIRA; circ. 50,000.

Diário Popular: Rua XV de Novembro, 718, Pelotas, RS; tel. (53) 284-7000; internet www.diariopopular.com.br; f. 1884; evening; independent; Dir RICARDO GURAL DE SABEYA; circ. 90,000.

O Estado de São Paulo: Av. Eng. Caetano Álvares 55, 02550 São Paulo, SP; tel. (11) 856-2122; fax (11) 266-2206; internet www.estado .com.br; f. 1875; morning; independent; Dir FRANCISCO MESQUITA NETO; circ. 242,000 weekdays, 460,000 Sundays.

Fôlha de São Paulo: Alameda Barão de Limeira 425, Campos Elíseos, 01202-900 São Paulo, SP; tel. (11) 224-3222; fax (11) 223-1644; internet www.folha.com.br; f. 1921; morning; Editorial Dir OCTAVIO FRIAS (Filho); circ. 557,650 weekdays, 1,401,178 Sundays.

Gazeta Mercantil: Av. Chucri Zaidan 80, Bloco C, 8 andar, CP 04583-110, Vila Cordeiro São Paulo, SP; tel. (11) 3443-8100; fax (11) 3443-8117; e-mail info@investnews.net; internet www.investnews .net; f. 1920; business paper; Pres. LUIZ FERREIRA LEVY; circ. 80,000.

Jornal da Tarde: Rua Peixoto Gomidi 671, 01409 São Paulo, SP; tel. (11) 284-1944; fax (11) 289-3548; internet www.jt.com.br; f. 1966; evening; independent; Dir R. MESQUITA; circ. 120,000, 180,000 Mondays.

Notícias Populares: Alameda Barão de Limeira 425, 01202 São Paulo, SP; tel. (11) 874-2222; fax (11) 223-1644; f. 1963; Dir RENATO CASTANHARI; circ. 150,000.

Vitória, ES

A Gazeta: Rua Charic Murad 902, 29050 Vitória, ES; tel. (27) 222-8333; fax (27) 223-1525; f. 1928; Pres. MARIO LINDENBERG; circ. 19,000.

PERIODICALS

Rio de Janeiro, RJ

Amiga: Rua do Russel 766/804, 22214 Rio de Janeiro, RJ; tel. (21) 285-0033; fax (21) 205-9998; weekly; women's interest; Pres. ADOLPHO BLOCH; circ. 83,000.

Antenna-Eletrônica Popular: Av. Marechal Floriano 151, 20080-005 Rio de Janeiro, RJ; tel. (21) 2223-2442; fax (21) 2263-8840; e-mail antenna@unisys.com.br; internet www.anep.com.br; f. 1926; monthly; telecommunications and electronics, radio, TV, hi-fi, amateur and CB radio; Dir GILBERTO AFFONSO PENNA (Filho); circ. 15,000.

Carinho: Rua do Russel 766/804, 22214 Rio de Janeiro, RJ; tel. (21) 285-0033; fax (21) 205-9998; monthly; women's interest; Pres. ADOLPHO BLOCH; circ. 65,000.

Conjuntura Econômica: Praia de Botafogo 190, Sala 923, 22253-900 Rio de Janeiro, RJ; tel. (21) 536-9267; fax (21) 551-2799; f. 1947; monthly; economics and finance; published by Fundação Getúlio Vargas; Pres. JORGE OSCAR DE MELLO FLÔRES; Editor LAURO VIEIRA DE FARIA; circ. 20,000.

Desfile: Rua do Russel 766/804, 22214 Rio de Janeiro, RJ; tel. (21) 285-0033; fax (21) 205-9998; f. 1969; monthly; women's interest; Dir ADOLPHO BLOCH; circ. 120,000.

ECO21: Av. Copacabana 2, Gr. 301, 28010-122, Rio de Janeiro,, RJ; tel. (21) 2275-1490; internet www.eco21.com.br; ecological issues; Dirs. LÚCIA CHAYB, RENÉ CAPRILES.

Ele Ela: Rua do Russel 766/804, 22214 Rio de Janeiro RJ; tel. (21) 285-0033; fax (21) 205-9998; f. 1969; monthly; men's interest; Dir ADOLPHO BLOCH; circ. 150,000.

Manchete: Rua do Russel 766/804, 20214 Rio de Janeiro, RJ; tel. (21) 285-0033; fax (21) 205-9998; f. 1952; weekly; general; Dir ADOLPHO BLOCH; circ. 110,000.

São Paulo, SP

Carícia: Av. das Nações Unidas 5777, 05479-900 São Paulo, SP; tel. (11) 211-7866; fax (11) 813-9115; monthly; women's interest; Dir ANGELO ROSSI; circ. 210,000.

Caros Amigos: Rua Fidalga 162, Vila Madalena, São Paulo, SP; tel. (11) 3819-0130; internet carosamigos.terra.com.br; f. 1997; monthly; general interest; Editor SÉRGIO DE SOUZA; circ. 57,000.

Casa e Jardim: São Paulo, SP; fax (11) 824-9079; internet www .casaejardim.globo.com; f. 1953; monthly; homes and gardens, illustrated; Pres. LUCIANA JALONETSKY; circ. 120,000.

Claudia: Editora Abril, Avda das Nações Unidas 7221, Pinheiros 05425-902, São Paulo, SP; tel. (11) 3037-2000; internet www.claudia .abril.uol.com.br; f. 1962; monthly; women's magazine; Dir ROBERTO CIVITA; circ. 460,000.

Criativa: São Paulo, SP; tel. (11) 874-6003; fax (11) 864-0271; internet www.criativa.globo.com; monthly; women's interest; Dir-Gen. RICARDO A. SÁNCHEZ; circ. 121,000.

Digesto Econômico: Associação Comercial de São Paulo, Rua Boa Vista 51, 01014-911 São Paulo, SP; tel. (11) 234-3322; fax (11) 239-0067; every 2 months; Pres. ELVIO ALIPRANDI; Chief Editor JOÃO DE SCANTIMBURGO.

Disney Especial: Av. das Nações Unidas 7221, 05477-000 São Paulo, SP; tel. (11) 3037-2000; fax (11) 3037-4124; every 2 months; children's magazine; Dir ROBERTO CIVITA; circ. 211,600.

Elle: Av. das Nações Unidas 7221, 05425-902 São Paulo, SP; tel. (11) 3037-5197; fax (11) 3037-5451; internet www.uol.com.br/elle; f. 1988; monthly; women's magazine; Editor CARLOS COSTA; circ. 100,000.

Exame: Av. Octaviano Alves de Lima, 4400, 02909-900 São Paulo, SP; tel. (11) 877-1421; fax (11) 877-1437; e-mail publicidade.exame@ email.abril.com.br; f. 1967; 2 a week; business; Dir JOSÉ ROBERTO GUZZO; circ. 168,300.

Manequim: São Paulo, SP; tel. (11) 534-5668; fax (11) 534-5632; monthly; fashion; Dir ROBERTO CIVITA; circ. 300,000.

Máquinas e Metais: Alameda Olga 315, 01155-900, São Paulo, SP; tel. (11) 3824-5300; fax (11) 3662-0103; e-mail info@arandanet.com .br; internet www.arandanet.com.br; f. 1964; monthly; machine and metal industries; Editor JOSÉ ROBERTO GONÇALVES; circ. 15,000.

Marie Claire: São Paulo, SP; tel. (11) 866-3373; internet www .marieclaire.globo.com; monthly; women's magazine; Publr REGINA LEMUS; circ. 273,000.

Mickey: Av. das Nações Unidas 7221, 05477-000 São Paulo, SP; tel. (11) 3037-2000; fax (11) 3037-4124; monthly; children's magazine; Dir ROBERTO CIVITA; circ. 76,000.

Micromundo-Computerworld do Brasil: Rua Caçapava 79, 01408 São Paulo, SP; tel. (11) 289-1767; monthly; computers; Gen. Dir ERIC HIPPEAU; circ. 38,000.

Pato Donald: Av. das Nações Unidas 7221, 05477-000 São Paulo, SP; tel. (11) 3037-2000; fax (11) 3037-4124; every 2 weeks; children's magazine; Dir ROBERTO CIVITA; circ. 120,000.

Placar: Av. das Nações Unidas 7221, 14° andar, 05477-000 São Paulo, SP; tel. (11) 3037-5816; fax (11) 3037-5597; e-mail placar .leitor@email.abril.com.br; f. 1970; monthly; soccer magazine; Dir MARCELO DURATE; circ. 127,000.

Quatro Rodas: São Paulo, SP; tel. (11) 534-5491; fax (11) 530-8549; internet www2.uol.com.br/quatrorodas; f. 1960; monthly; motoring; Pres. ROBERTO CIVITA; circ. 250,000.

Revista O Carreteiro: Rua Palacete das Aguias 239, 04035-021 São Paulo, SP; tel. (11) 542-9311; monthly; transport; Dirs JOÃO ALBERTO ANTUNES DE FIGUEIREDO, EDSON PEREIRA COELHO; circ. 80,000.

Saúde: Av. das Nações Unidas 5777, 05479-900 São Paulo, SP; tel. (11) 211-7675; fax (11) 813-9115; monthly; health; Dir ANGELO ROSSI; circ. 180,000.

Veja: Rua do Copturno 571, 6°, São Paulo, SP; tel. (11) 877-1322; fax (11) 877-1640; internet www.veja.com.br; f. 1968; news weekly; Dirs JOSÉ ROBERTO GUZZO, TALES ALVARENGA, MÁRIO SERGIO CONTI; circ. 800,000.

Visão: São Paulo, SP; tel. (11) 549-4344; f. 1952; weekly; news magazine; Editor HENRY MAKSOUD; circ. 148,822.

NEWS AGENCIES

Editora Abril, SA: Av. Otaviano Alves de Lima 4400, CP 2372, 02909-970 São Paulo, SP; tel. (11) 877-1322; fax (11) 877-1640; f. 1950; Pres. ROBERTO CIVITA.

Agência ANDA: Edif. Correio Brasiliense, Setor das Indústrias Gráficas 300/350, Brasília, DF; Dir EDILSON VARELA.

Agência o Estado de São Paulo: Av. Eng. Caetano Alvares 55, 02588-900 São Paulo, SP; tel. (11) 856-2122; Rep. SAMUEL DIRCEU F. BUENO.

Agência Fôlha de São Paulo: Alameda Barão de Limeira 425, 4° andar, 01290-900 São Paulo, SP; tel. (11) 224-3790; fax (11) 221-0675; Dir MARION STRECKER.

Agência Globo: Rua Irineu Marinho 35, 2° andar, Centro, 20233-900 Rio de Janeiro, RJ; tel. (21) 292-2000; fax (21) 292-2000; Dir CARLOS LEMOS.

Agência Jornal do Brasil: Av. Brasil 500, 6° andar, São Cristóvão, 20949-900 Rio de Janeiro, RJ; tel. (21) 585-4453; fax (21) 580-9944; f. 1966; Exec. Dir. EDGAR LISBOA.

Foreign Bureaux

Agence France-Presse (AFP) (France): SRTV/S Quadra 701, Edif. Centro Empresarial Brasilia, Bloco A, Sala 434, 70340-107 Brasília, DF; tel. (61) 224-3776; fax (61) 226-4068; Bureau Chief (Brazil) ALAIN BOEBION.

Agencia EFE (Spain): Praia de Botafogo 228, Bloco B, Gr. 1106, 22359-900 Rio de Janeiro, RJ; tel. (21) 553-6355; fax (21) 553-8823; e-mail redario@efebrasil.com.br; Bureau Chief FRANCISCO R. FIGUÉROA.

Agência Lusa de Informação (Portugal): São Paulo; Bureau Chief GONÇALO CÉSAR DE SÁ.

Agenzia Nazionale Stampa Associata (ANSA) (Italy): Av. São Luís 258, 20° andar, Conj. 2004, 01046-000 São Paulo, SP; tel. (11) 3258-7022; fax (11) 3129-5543; e-mail ansasp@uol.com.br; internet www.eurosul.com; Dir OLIVIERO PLUVIANO.

Associated Press (AP) (USA): Av. Brasil 500, Sala 847, CP 72-ZC-00, 20001 Rio de Janeiro, RJ; tel. (21) 580-4422; Bureau Chief BRUCE HANDLER; Correspondent STAN LEHMAN; Correspondent JORGE MEDEROS.

Deutsche Presse-Agentur (dpa) (Germany): Rua Abade Ramos 65, 22461-90 Rio de Janeiro, RJ; tel. (21) 266-5937; fax (21) 537-8273; Bureau Chief ESTEBAN ENGEL.

Inter Press Service (IPS) (Italy): Rua Vicente de Souza 29, 2° andar, 22251-070 Rio de Janeiro, RJ; tel. (21) 286-5605; fax (21) 286-5324; Correspondent MARIO CHIZUO OSAVA.

Jiji Tsushin-Sha (Jiji Press) (Japan): Av. Paulista 854, 13° andar, Conj. 133, Bela Vista, 01310-913 São Paulo, SP; tel. (11) 285-0025; fax (11) 285-3816; e-mail jijisp@nethall.com.br; f. 1958; Chief Correspondent MUTSUHIRO TAKABAYASHI.

Kyodo Tsushin (Japan): Praia do Flamengo 168-701, Flamengo, 22210 Rio de Janeiro, RJ; tel. (21) 285-2412; fax (21) 285-2270; Bureau Chief TAKAYOSHI MAKITA.

Prensa Latina (Cuba): Marechal Mascarenhas de Moraís 121, Apto 602, Copacabana, 22030-040 Rio de Janeiro, RJ; tel. and fax (21) 237-1766; Correspondent FRANCISCO FORTEZA.

Reuters (United Kingdom): Av. Nações Unidas 17891, 8° andar, 04795-100 São Paulo, SP; tel. (11) 232-4411; fax (11) 604-6538; Bureau Chief (News and Television) ADRIAN DICKSON.

Xinhua (New China) News Agency (People's Republic of China): SHIS QI 15, Conj. 16, Casa 14, CP 7089, 71.600 Brasília, DF; tel. (61) 248-5489; Chief Correspondent WANG ZHIGEN.

Central News Agency (Taiwan) and Rossiyskoye Informatsionnoye Agentstvo—Novosti (Russia) are also represented in Brazil.

PRESS ASSOCIATIONS

Associação Brasileira de Imprensa: Rua Araújo Porto Alegre 71, Castelo, 20030 Rio de Janeiro, RJ; f. 1908; 4,000 mems; Pres. (vacant); Sec. JOSUÉ ALMEIDA.

Associação Nacional de Editores de Revistas: SCS, Edif. Bandeirantes 201/204, 70300-910 Brasília, DF; tel. (61) 322-5511; fax (61) 321-8348; e-mail arkoadvice@arkoadvice.com.br; Pres. JOSÉ CARLOS SALLES NETO; Exec. Vice-Pres. Dr MURILLO DE ARAGÃO.

Federação Nacional dos Jornalistas (FENAJ): Higs 707, Bloco R, Casa 54, 70351-718 Brasília, DF; tel. (61) 244-0650; fax (61) 242-6616; e-mail fenaj@fenaj.org.br; internet www.fenaj.org.br; f. 1946; represents 30 regional unions; Pres. ELISABETH VILLELA DA COSTA.

Publishers

Rio de Janeiro, RJ

Ao Livro Técnico Indústria e Comércio Ltda: Rua Sá Freire 36/40, São Cristóvão, 20930-430 Rio de Janeiro, RJ; tel. (21) 2580-6230; fax (21) 2580-9955; internet www.editoraaolivrotécnico.com.br; f. 1993; textbooks, children's and teenagers' fiction and non-fiction, art books, dictionaries; Man. Dir REYNALDO MAX PAUL BLUHM.

Distribuidora Record de Serviços de Imprensa, SA: Rua Argentina 171, São Cristóvão, CP 884, 20921 Rio de Janeiro, RJ; tel. (21) 585-2000; fax (21) 580-4911; e-mail sacm@record.com.br; internet www.record.com.br; f. 1941; general fiction and non-fiction, education, textbooks, fine arts; Pres. SÉRGIO MACHADO.

Ediouro Publicações, SA: Rua Nova Jerusalém 345, CP 1880, Bonsucesso, 21042-230 Rio de Janeiro, RJ; tel. (21) 260-6122; fax (21) 280-2438; e-mail editoriallivros@ediouro.com.br; internet www.ediouro.com.br; f. 1939; general; Pres. JORGE CARNEIRO.

Editora Artenova, SA: Rua Pref. Olímpio de Mello 1774, Benfica, 20000 Rio de Janeiro, RJ; tel. (21) 264-9198; f. 1971; sociology, psychology, occultism, cinema, literature, politics and history; Man. Dir ALVARO PACHECO.

Editora Brasil-América (EBAL), SA: Rua Gen. Almério de Moura 302/320, São Cristóvão, 20921-060 Rio de Janeiro, RJ; tel. (21) 580-0303; fax (21) 580-1637; f. 1945; children's books; Dir PAULO ADOLFO AIZEN.

Editora Campus: Rua Sete de Setembro 111, 16° andar, 20050-002 Rio de Janeiro, RJ; tel. (21) 509-5340; fax (21) 507-1991; e-mail c.rothmuller@campus.com.br; internet www.campus.com.br; business, computing, non-fiction; Man. Dir CLAUDIO ROTHMULLER.

Editora Delta, SA: Av. Almirante Barroso 63, 26° andar, CP 2226, 20031 Rio de Janeiro, RJ; tel. (21) 240-0072; f. 1958; reference books.

Editora Expressão e Cultura—Exped Ltda: Estrada dos Bandeirantes 1700, Bloco E, 22710-113, Rio de Janeiro, RJ; tel. (21) 444-0676; fax (21) 444-0700; e-mail exped@ggh.com.br; f. 1967; textbooks, literature, reference; Gen. Man. RICARDO AUGUSTO PAMPLONA VAZ.

Editora e Gráfica Miguel Couto, SA: Rua da Passagem 78, Loja A, Botafogo, 22290-030 Rio de Janeiro, RJ; tel. (21) 541-5145; f. 1969; engineering; Dir PAULO KOBLER PINTO LOPES SAMPAIO.

Editora Nova Fronteira, SA: Rua Bambina 25, Botafogo, 22251-050 Rio de Janeiro, RJ; tel. (21) 537-8770; fax (21) 286-6755; e-mail nova2@embratel.net.br; f. 1965; fiction, psychology, history, politics, science fiction, poetry, leisure, reference; Pres. CARLOS AUGUSTO LACERDA.

Editora Vozes, Ltda: Rua Frei Luís 100, CP 90023, 25689-900 Petrópolis, RJ; tel. (242) 43-5112; fax (242) 31-4676; e-mail editorial@vozes.com.br; internet www.vozes.com.br; f. 1901; Catholic publishers; management, theology, anthropology, fine arts, history, linguistics, science, fiction, education, data processing, etc. Dir ANTONIO MOSER.

Livraria Francisco Alves Editora, SA: Rua Uruguaiana, 94, 13° andar, centro, Rio de Janeiro, RJ 20050–091; tel. (21) 221-3198; fax (21) 242-3438; f. 1854; textbooks, fiction, non-fiction; Pres. CARLOS LEAL.

Livraria José Olympio Editora, SA: Rua da Glória 344, 4° andar, Glória, 20241-180 Rio de Janeiro, RJ; tel. (21) 509-6939; fax (21) 242-0802; f. 1931; juvenile, science, history, philosophy, psychology, sociology, fiction; Dir MANOEL ROBERTO DOMINGUES.

São Paulo, SP

Atual Editora, Ltda: São Paulo, SP; tel. (11) 5071-2288; fax (11) 5071-3099; e-mail atendprof@atualeditora.com.br; internet www.atualeditora.com.br; f. 1973; school and children's books, literature; Dirs GELSON IEZZI, OSVALDO DOLCE.

Barsa Planeta Internacional: Rua Rego Freitas 192, Vila Buarque, CP 299, 01059-970 São Paulo, SP; tel. (11) 3225-1900; fax (11) 3225-1960; e-mail atnedimento@barsaplaneta.com.br; internet www.barsa.com; f. 1951; reference books.

Cia Editora Nacional: Rua Joli 294, Brás, CP 5312, 03016 São Paulo, SP; tel. (11) 291-2355; fax (11) 291-8614; f. 1925; textbooks, history, science, social sciences, philosophy, fiction, juvenile; Dirs JORGE YUNES, PAULO C. MARTI.

Ebid-Editora Páginas Amarelas Ltda: Av. Liberdade 956, 5° andar, 01502-001 São Paulo, SP; tel. (11) 278-6622; fax (11) 279-8723; e-mail mail@guiaspaginasamarelas.com.br; f. 1947; commercial directories.

Editora Abril, SA: Av. da Nações Unidas 7221, 05425-902 São Paulo, SP; tel. (11) 3037-2000; fax (11) 3037-5638; f. 1950; Pres. ROBERTO CIVITA.

Editora Atica, SA: Rua Barão de Iguape 110, 01507-900 São Paulo, SP; tel. (11) 3346-3000; fax (11) 3277-4146; e-mail editora@atica.com .br; f. 1965; textbooks, Brazilian and African literature; Pres. VICENTE PAZ FERNANDEZ.

Editora Atlas, SA: Rua Conselheiro Nébias 1384, Campos Elíseos, 01203-904 São Paulo, SP; tel. 221-9144; fax (11) 220-7830; e-mail edatlas@editora-atlas.com.br; f. 1944; business administration, data-processing, economics, accounting, law, education, social sciences; Pres. LUIZ HERRMANN.

Editora Brasiliense, SA: Rua Airi 22, Tatuapé, 03310-010 São Paulo, SP; tel. and fax (11) 6198-1488; e-mail brasilienseedit@uol .com.br; internet www.editorabrasiliense.com.br; f. 1943; education, racism, gender studies, human rights, ecology, history, literature, social sciences; Man. YOLANDA C. DA SILVA PRADO; Vice-Pres. MARIA TERESA B. DE LIMA.

Editora do Brasil, SA: Rua Conselheiro Nébias 887, Campos Elíseos, CP 4986, 01203-001 São Paulo, SP; tel. (11) 222-0211; fax (11) 222-9655; e-mail editora@editoradobrasil.com.be; internet www .editoradobrasil.com.br; f. 1943; education; Pres. Dr CARLOS COSTA.

Editora FTD, SA: Rua Manoel Dutra 225, 01328-010 São Paulo, SP; tel. (11) 253-5011; fax (11) 288-0132; e-mail ftd@dial&ta.com.br; f. 1897; textbooks; Pres. JOÃO TISSI.

Editora Globo, SA: Av. Jaguare 1485/1487, 05346-902 São Paulo, SP; tel. (11) 3767-7400; fax (11) 3767-7870; e-mail globolivros@ edglobo.com.br; internet globolivros.globo.com; f. 1957; fiction, engineering, agriculture, cookery, environmental studies; Gen. Man. JUAN OCERIN.

Editora Luzeiro Ltda: Rua Almirante Barroso 730, Brás, 03025-001 São Paulo, SP; tel. (11) 292-3188; f. 1973; folklore and literature.

Editora Melhoramentos Ltda: Rua Tito 479, 05051-000 São Paulo, SP; tel. (11) 3874-0854; fax (11) 3874-0855; e-mail blerner@ melhoramentos.com.br; internet www.melhoramentos.com.br; f. 1890; general non-fiction; childrens books, dictionaries; Dir BRENO LERNER.

Editora Michalany Ltda: Rua Pereira Stéfano 316, Saúde, 04144-070 São Paulo, SP; tel. (11) 585-2012; fax (11) 276-8775; e-mail editora@editoramichalany.com.br; internet www.editoramichalany .com.br; f. 1965; biographies, economics, textbooks, geography, history, religion, maps; Dir DOUGLAS MICHALANY.

Editora Moderna, Ltda: Rua Padre Adelino 758, Belenzinho, 03303-904, São Paulo, SP; tel. (11) 6090-1316; fax (11) 6090-1369; e-mail moderna@moderna.com.br; internet www.moderna.com.br; Pres. RICARDO ARISSA FELTRE.

Editora Revista dos Tribunais Ltda: Rua do Bosque 820, 01136-000 São Paulo, SP; tel. (11) 3613-8400; fax (11) 3613-8474; e-mail gmarketing@rt.com.br; internet www.rt.com.br; f. 1912; law and jurisprudence books and periodicals; Dir CARLOS HENRIQUE DE CARVALHO (Filho).

Editora Rideel Ltda: Alameda Afonso Schmidt 879, Santa Terezinha, 02450-001 São Paulo, SP; tel. (11) 6977-8344; fax (11) 6976-7415; e-mail sac@rideel.com.br; internet www.rideel.com.br; f. 1971; general; Dir ITALO AMADIO.

Editora Scipione Ltda: Praça Carlos Gomes 46, 01501-040 São Paulo, SP; tel. (11) 239-2255; fax (11) 239-1700; e-mail scipione@ scipione.com.br; internet www.scipione.com.br; f. 1983; school-books, literature, reference; Dir LUIZ ESTEVES SALLUM.

Instituto Brasileiro de Edições Pedagógicas, Ltda: Rua Joli 294, 03016-020 São Paulo, SP; tel. (11) 6099-7799; fax (11) 6694-5338; e-mail editoras@ibep-nacional.com.br; internet www .ibep-nacional.com.br; f. 1965; textbooks, foreign languages and reference books.

Lex Editora, SA: Frei Eusébio Soledade 94, Vila Mariana, 04106-030 São Paulo, SP; tel. (11) 5549-0122; fax (11) 5575-9138; e-mail adm@lexli.com.br; internet www.lexli.com.br; f. 1937; legislation and jurisprudence; Dir MILTON NICOLAU VITALE PATARA.

Saraiva SA Livreiros Editores: Av. Marquês de São Vicente 1697, CP 2362, 01139-904 São Paulo, SP; tel. (11) 861-3344; fax (11) 861-3308; f. 1914; education, textbooks, law, economics; Pres. JORGE EDUARDO SARAIVA.

Thomson Pioneira: Rua Traipu, 114, Perdizes, 01235-000 São Paulo, SP; tel. (11) 3665-9900; fax (11) 3665-9901; internet www .thomsonlearning.com.br; f. 1960 as Editora Pioneira; acquired by Thomson Learning in 2000; architecture, computers, political and social sciences, business studies, languages, children's books; Dirs ROBERTO GUAZZELLI, LILIANA GUAZZELLI.

Belo Horizonte, MG

Editora Lê, SA: Av. D. Pedro II, 4550 Jardin Montanhês, CP 2585, 30730 Belo Horizonte, MG; tel. (31) 34131720; f. 1967; textbooks.

Editora Lemi, SA: Av. Nossa Senhora de Fátima 1945, CP 1890, 30000 Belo Horizonte, MG; tel. (31) 201-8044; f. 1967; administration, accounting, law, ecology, economics, textbooks, children's books and reference books.

Editora Vigília, Ltda: Belo Horizonte, MG; e-mail lerg@ planetarium.com.br; tel. (31) 337-2744; fax (31) 337-2834; f. 1960; general.

Curitiba, PR

Editora Educacional Brasileira, SA: Rua XV de Novembro 178, Salas 101/04, CP 7498, 80000 Curitiba, PR; tel. (41) 223-5012; f. 1963; biology, textbooks and reference books.

PUBLISHERS' ASSOCIATIONS

Associação Brasileira do Livro: Av. 13 de Maio 23, 16°, 20031-000 Rio de Janeiro, RJ; tel. (21) 240-9115; fax (21) 532-6678; e-mail abralivro@uol.com.br; Pres. MARCOS DAVID GOMES.

Câmara Brasileira do Livro: Av. Ipiranga 1267, 10° andar, 01039-907 São Paulo, SP; tel. (11) 3315-8277; fax (11) 229-7463; e-mail cbl@cbl.org.br; internet www.cbl.org.br; f. 1946; Pres. RAUL WASSERMANN.

Sindicato Nacional dos Editores de Livros (SNEL): Av. Rio Branco 37, 1503/6 and 1510/12, 20090-003 Rio de Janeiro, RJ; tel. (21) 2233-6481; fax (21) 2253-8502; e-mail snel@snel.org.br; internet www.snel.org.br; 200 mems; Pres. PAULO ROBERTO ROCCO; Man. ANTÔNIO LASKOS.

There are also regional publishers' associations.

Broadcasting and Communications

TELECOMMUNICATIONS

BCP Telecomunicações: São Paulo, SP; internet www.bcp.com.br; f. 1997; mobile services in São Paulo area; Pres. ROBERTO PEÓN.

Brasil Telecom: SIA Sul, Área dos Servicos Públicos, Lote D, Bloco B, 71.215-000 Brasília, DF; tel. (61) 415-1128; fax (61) 415-1133; internet www.brasiltelecom.com.br; fixed line services in 10 states; Chair. MODESTO SOUZA BARROS CARVALHOSO; Pres. HENRIQUE SUTTON DE SOUSA NEVES.

Empresa Brasileira de Telecomunicações, SA (EMBRATEL): Av. Pres. Vargas 1012, CP 2586, 20179-900 Rio de Janeiro, RJ; tel. (21) 519-8182; e-mail cmsocial@embratel.net.br; internet www .embratel.com.br; f. 1965; operates national and international telecommunications system; controlled by MCI WorldCom of USA; Chair. DANIEL CRAWFORD.

Telecomunicações de São Paulo, SA (Telesp): Rua Martiniano de Carvalho 851, Bela Vista, 01321-000 São Paulo, SP; tel. (11) 3549-7200; fax (11) 3549-7202; e-mail webmaster@telesp.com.br; internet www.telesp.com.br; services operated by Telefónica, SA, of Spain; Pres. FERNANDO XAVIER FERREIRA; Chief Exec. SAMPAIO DORIA.

Telemar: Rua Lauro Muller 116, 22° andar, Botafogo, Rio de Janeiro, RJ; tel. (21) 2815-2921; fax (21) 2571-3050; internet www .telemar.com.br; fixed line services in 16 states; f. 1998 as Tele Norte Leste; Chair. CARLOS JEREISSATI; Pres. MANOEL DE SILVA.

Regulatory Authority

Agência Nacional de Telecomunicações (ANATEL): SAS Quadra 06, Bloco H, 3° andar, 70313-900 Brasília, DF; tel. (61) 312-2336; fax (61) 312-2211; e-mail biblioteca@anatel.gov.br; internet www.anatel.gov.br/default.htm; f. 1998; Pres. RENATO GUERREIRO.

RADIO

In April 1992 there were 2,917 radio stations in Brazil, including 20 in Brasília, 38 in Rio de Janeiro, 32 in São Paulo, 24 in Curitiba, 24 in Porto Alegre and 23 in Belo Horizonte.

The main broadcasting stations in Rio de Janeiro are: Rádio Nacional, Rádio Globo, Rádio Eldorado, Rádio Jornal do Brasil, Rádio Tupi and Rádio Mundial. In São Paulo the main stations are Rádio Bandeirantes, Rádio Mulher, Rádio Eldorado, Rádio Gazeta and Rádio Excelsior; and in Brasília: Rádio Nacional, Rádio Alvorada, Rádio Planalto and Rádio Capital.

Rádio Nacional do Brásil (RADIOBRÁSIL): CP 070747, 70359-970 Brasília, DF; tel. 321-3949; fax 321-7602; e-mail maurilio@ radiobras.gov.br; internet www.radiobras.gov.br; Pres. MAURÍLIO FERREIRA LIMA.

TELEVISION

In April 1992 there were 256 television stations in Brazil, of which 118 were in the state capitals and six in Brasília.

The main television networks are:

TV Bandeirantes—Canal 13: Rádio e Televisão Bandeirantes Ltda, Rua Radiantes 13, 05699 São Paulo, SP; tel. (11) 842-3011; fax (11) 842-3067; 65 TV stations and repeaters throughout Brazil; Pres. JOÃO JORGE SAAD.

RBS TV-TV Gaúcha, SA: Rua Rádio y TV Gaúcha 189, 90850-080 Porto Alegre, RS; tel. (51) 218-5002; fax (51) 218-5005; Vice-Pres WALMOR BERGESCH.

TV Globo—Canal 4: Rua Lopes Quintas 303, Jardim Botânico, 22460-010 Rio de Janeiro, RJ; tel. (21) 511-1711; fax (21) 511-4305; e-mail apm@domain.com.br; internet www.redeglobo.com.br; f. 1965; 8 stations; national network; Dir ADILSON PONTES MALTA.

TV Manchete—Canal 6: Rua do Russel 766, 20000 Rio de Janeiro, RJ; tel. (21) 265-2012; Dir-Gen. R. FURTADO.

TV Record—Rede Record de Televisão—Radio Record, SA: Rua de Várzea 240, Barra Funda, 01140-080 São Paulo, SP; tel. (11) 824-7000; Pres. JOÃO BATISTA R. SILVA; Exec. Vice-Pres. H. GONÇALVES.

TV SBT—Canal 4 de São Paulo, SA: São Paulo, SP; tel. (11) 292-9044; fax (11) 264-6004; internet www.sbt.com.br; Vice-Pres. GUILHERME STOLIAR.

BROADCASTING ASSOCIATIONS

Associação Brasileira de Emissoras de Rádio e Televisão (ABERT): Centro Empresarial Varig, SCN Quadra 04, Bloco B, Conj. 501, Pétala A, 70710-500 Brasília, DF; tel. (61) 327-4600; fax (61) 327-3660; e-mail abert@abert.org.br; internet www.abert.org.br; f. 1962; mems: 32 shortwave, 1,275 FM, 1,574 medium-wave and 80 tropical-wave radio stations and 258 television stations (1997); Pres. PAULO MACHADO DE CARVALHO NETO; Exec. Dir OSCAR PICONEZ.

There are regional associations for Bahia, Ceará, Goiás, Minas Gerais, Rio Grande do Sul, Santa Catarina, São Paulo, Amazonas, Distrito Federal, Mato Grosso and Mato Grosso do Sul (combined) and Sergipe.

Finance

(cap. = capital; dep. = deposits; res = reserves; m. = million; brs = branches; amounts in reais, unless otherwise stated)

BANKING

Conselho Monetário Nacional: SBS, Q.03, Bloco B, Edif. Sede do Banco do Brasil, 21° andar, 70074-900 Brasília, DF; tel. (61) 414-1945; fax (61) 414-2528; f. 1964 to formulate monetary policy and to supervise the banking system; Pres. Minister of Finance.

Central Bank

Banco Central do Brasil: SBS, Q 03, Bloco B, CP 04-0170, 70074-900 Brasília, DF; tel. (61) 414-1000; fax (61) 223-1033; e-mail secre .surel@bcb.gov.br; internet www.bcb.gov.br; f. 1965 to execute the decisions of the Conselho Monetário Nacional; bank of issue; cap. 2,576.4m., res 594.2m., dep. 213,519.7m. (Dec. 2000); Pres. HENRIQUE MEIRELLES; 10 brs.

State Commercial Banks

Banco do Brasil, SA: Setor Bancário Sul, SBS, Quadra 4, Bloco C, Lote 32, 70089-900 Brasília, DF; tel. (61) 310-3400; fax (61) 310-2563; internet www.bancobrasil.com.br; f. 1808; cap. 7,984.4m.m., res 823.1m.m., dep. 79,710.2m.m. (June 2002); Pres. PAOLO CÉSAR XIMENES ALVES FERREIRA; 3,096 brs.

Banco do Estado do Rio Grande do Sul, SA (BANRISUL): Rua Capitão Montanha 177, CP 505, 90010-040 Porto Alegre, RS; tel. (51) 215-2501; fax (51) 215-1715; e-mail banrisul@banrisul.com.br; internet www.banrisul.com.br; f. 1928; cap. 599.8m., res 55.3m., dep. 5,859.3m. (Dec. 2002); Pres. JOÃO ALCIR VERLE; 359 brs.

Banco do Estado de Santa Catarina SA: Centro Administrativo BESC, Rodovia SC 401, Km 5, 4600, Bairro Saco Grande, CP 210 88032-000, Florianpolis, SC; tel. (48) 239-9000; e-mail decam/dinte@besc.com.br; internet www.besc.com.br; f. 1962; cap. 158.1m., res 104.3m., dep. 1,329.6m. (Dec. 1997); Pres. JOÃO MAXIMO IURK.

Banco do Estado de São Paulo, SA (Banespa): Praça Antônio Prado 6, 01010-010 São Paulo, SP; tel. (11) 259-7722; fax (11) 239-2409; e-mail presidencia@banespa.com; internet www.banespa.com .br; f. 1926; cap. 5,975.7m., res 1,258.5m., dep. 17,163.4m. (June 2002); sold in Nov. 2000 to Banco Santander (Spain); Chair. GABRIEL JARAMILLO SANINT; 1,015 brs.

Banco do Nordeste do Brasil, SA: Av. Paranjana 5700, Passaré, 60740-000 Fortaleza, CE; tel. (85) 299-3022; fax (85) 299-3585; e-mail info@banconordeste.gov.br; internet www.banconordeste.gov .br; f. 1954; cap. 1,057.9m., res 25.5m., dep. 3,074.2m. (June 2002); Pres. and CEO BYRON COSTA DE QUEIROZ; 175 brs.

Banco Nossa Caixa, SA: São Paulo, SP; internet www.nossacaixa .com.br; f. 1917 as Caixa Econômica do Estado de São Paulo; cap. 1,27.4m., res. 171.2m., dep. 16,793.3m. (June 2002); Pres. GERALDO GARDENALI; 498 brs.

Private Banks

Banco ABN AMRO SA: Av. Paulista 1374, 3° andar, 01310-916 São Paulo, SP; tel. (11) 525-6000; fax (11) 525-6387; internet www .bancoreal.com.br; cap. 5,213,2m., res 392.4m., dep. 12,371.1m (June 2002); 847 brs.

Banco Alfa, SA: São Paulo, SP; internet www.alfanet.com.br; cap. 882.3m., res 45.2m., dep. 1,195.7m. (June 2002); 9 brs.

Banco da Amazônia, SA: Av. Presidente Vargas 800, 66017-000 Belém, PA; tel. (91) 216-3000; fax (91) 223-5403; internet www .bancoamazonia.com.br; f. 1942; cap. 124.2m., res 100.8m., dep. 897.3m. (Dec. 1999); Pres. ANIVALDO JUVENIL VALE; 109 brs.

Banco América do Sul, SA: Av. Brigadeiro Luís Antônio 2020, 01318-911 São Paulo, SP; tel. (11) 3170-9899; fax (11) 3170-9564; e-mail bas@bas.com.br; internet www.bas.com.br; f. 1940; cap. 214.6m., dep. 2,832.8m. (Dec. 1997); CEO YVES L. J. LEJEUNE; 139 brs.

Banco Barclays e Galicia, SA: Av. Paulista 1842, Edif. Cetenco Plaza, Torre Norte, 24°–25° andares, 01310-200 São Paulo, SP; tel. (11) 269-2700; fax (11) 283-3168; e-mail barclays@barclays.com.br; internet www.barclays.com; f. 1967 as Banco de Investimento; cap. 170.1m., res 22.9m., dep. 197.8m. (Dec. 1999); Pres. PETER ANDERSON.

Banco BBA-Creditanstalt, SA: Av. Paulista 37, 20°, 01311-902 São Paulo, SP; tel. (11) 281-8000; fax (11) 284-2158; e-mail bancobba@bba.com.br; internet www.bba.com.br; f. 1988; acquired by Banco Itaú 2002; cap. 1,454.4m., res 169.8m., dep. 4,321.6m. (June 2002); Pres. FERNÃO CARLOS BOTELHO BRACHER; 5 brs.

Banco BMC, SA: Av. das Nações Unidas 12.995, 24° andar, 04578-000 São Paulo, SP; tel. (11) 5503-7807; fax (11) 5503-7676; e-mail bancobmc@bmc.com.br; internet www.bmc.com.br; f. 1939; adopted current name in 1990; cap. 159.8m., res 13.5m., dep. 1,134.8m. (Dec. 1999); Chair. FRANCISCO JAIME NOGUEIRA PINHEIRO; 9 brs.

Banco BMG, SA: Av. Alvares Cabral 1707, Santo Agostinho, 30170-001 Belo Horizonte, MG; tel. (31) 290-3000; fax (31) 290-3315; f. 1988; cap. 89.8m., res 50.9m., dep. 305.0m. (Dec. 1996); Pres. FLÁVIO PENTAGNA GUIMARÃES; 4 brs.

Banco Bandeirantes, SA: Rua Boa Vista 162, 01014-902 São Paulo, SP; tel. (11) 233-7155; fax (11) 233-7329; e-mail band@bandeirantes.com.br; f. 1944; cap. 546.4m., res 225.8m., dep. 3,534.7m. (Dec. 1998); acquired by Unibanco in 2000; Pres. Dr CARLOS TRAGUELHO; 167 brs.

Banco Bemge, SA: Av. João Pinheiro 195, Mazanino, Bairro Funcionários, 30.130-180 Belo Horizante, MG; tel. (31) 3249-3585; fax (31) 3249-3570; f. 1967; fmrly Banco do Estado de Minas Gerais SA; acquired by Banco Itaú, SA, in Sept. 1998; cap. 250.8m., res -157.6m, dep. 2,450.3m. (Dec. 1997); Pres. ROBERTO EGYDIO SETÚBAL.

Banco Bilbao Vizcaya Brasil, SA: Av. Antônio Carlos Magalhães 2728, 41840-000 Salvador, BA; tel. (71) 354-7000; fax (71) 354-7106; internet www.bbvbrasil.com.br; f. 1996; as a result of merger of Excel Banco and Banco Econômico; acquired by Banco Bradesco in Jan. 2003; cap. 2,422.5m., res 56.4m., dep. 6,421.5m. (June 2002); Pres. EZEQUIEL NASSER; 442 brs.

Banco Boavista Interatlântico, SA: Praça Pio X 118, 20091-040 Rio de Janeiro, RJ; tel. (21) 849-1661; fax (21) 253-1579; e-mail boavista@ibm.net; internet www.boavista.com.br; f. 1997; cap. 627.9m., res 111.8m., dep. 4,050.6m. (Dec. 1998); acquired by Banco Bradesco in 2000; Pres. and Gen. Man. JOSÉ LUIZ SILVEIRA MIRANDA.

Banco Bozano, Simonsen, SA: Av. Rio Branco 138-Centro, 20057-900 Rio de Janeiro, RJ; tel. (21) 508-4711; fax (21) 508-4479; e-mail info@bozano.com.br; f. 1967; cap. 248.2m., res 266.4m., dep. 5,103.1m. (Dec. 1998); Pres. PAULO VEIGA FERRAZ PEREIRA; 4 brs.

Banco Bradesco, SA: Av. Ipiranga 282, 10° andar, CP 01046-920 São Paulo, SP; tel. (11) 3235-9566; fax (11) 3235-9161; internet www .bradesco.com.br; f. 1943; fmrly Banco Brasileiro de Descontos; cap. 10,500.1m., res 912.6m., dep. 51,133.1m. (June 2002); Chair. LÁZARO DE MELLO BRANDÃO; Vice-Chair. ANTÔNIO BORNIA; 2,936 brs.

Banco CCF Brasil SA: Av. Brigadeiro Faria Lima 3064, 1°–4° andares, Itaim Bibi, 01451-000 São Paulo, SP; tel. (11) 827-5000; fax (11) 827-5299; internet www.ccfbrasil.com.br; f. 1980; cap. 409.2m., res 189.4m., dep. 537.8m. (Dec. 1999); Pres. BERNARD MENCIER.

Banco Cidade, SA: Praça Dom José Gaspar 106, 01047-010 São Paulo, SP; tel. (11) 3150-5000; fax (11) 255-4176; e-mail cambio .comercial@bancocidade.com.br; internet www.bancocidade.com.br; f. 1965; cap. 75.0m., res 99.5m., dep. 1,278.1m. (Dec. 1998); Pres. EDMUNDO SAFDIÉ; 25 brs.

Banco de Crédito Nacional, SA (BCN): Av. das Nações Unidas 12901, CENU-Torre Oeste, 04578-000 Vila Cordeiro, SP; tel. (11) 5509-2801; fax (11) 5509-2802; internet www.bcn.com.br; f. 1924; acquired by Banco Bradesco in 1997; cap. 580.0m., res 327.3m., dep. 7,713.5m. (Dec. 1999); Pres. JOSÉ LUIZ ACAR PEDRO; 122 brs.

Banco Dibens, SA: Alameda Santos 200, Cerqueira Cesar, 01418-000 São Paulo, SP; tel. (11) 253-2177; fax (11) 284-3132; internet www.dibens.com.br; f. 1989; jt owned by Unibanco and Grupo Verdi; cap. 81.7m., res 84.0m., dep. 760.9m. (Dec. 1996); Pres. MAURO SADDI; 23 brs.

Banco do Estado do Paraná, SA (Banestado): Rua Máximo João Kopp 274, Santa Cândida, 82630-900 Curitiba, PR; tel. (41) 351-8745; fax (41) 351-7252; e-mail helphb@email.banestado.com.br; internet www.banestado.com.br; f. 1928; cap. 3,988.9m., res 3,555.3m., dep. 4,203.5m. (Dec. 1999); acquired by Banco Itaú in 2000; Pres. REINHOLD STÉPHANES; 389 brs.

Banco Fibra: Av. Brigadeiro Faria Lima 3064, 7° andar, Itaim Bibi, 01451-000, São Paulo, SP; tel. (11) 3827-6700; fax (11) 3827-6620; e-mail internacional@bancofibra.com.br; f. 1988; cap. 106.1m., res 111.4m., dep. 1,334.0m. (Dec. 1998); Pres. BENJAMIN STEINBRUCH; CEO JOÃO AYRES RABELLO (Filho).

Banco Francês e Brasileiro, SA: Av. Paulista 1294, 01310-915 São Paulo, SP; tel. (11) 238-8216; fax (11) 238-8622; e-mail bfb .international@itau.com.br; internet www.bfb.com.br; f. 1948; affiliated with Crédit Lyonnais; cap. 472.3m., res 29.5m., dep. 1,152.0m. (Dec. 1997); Pres. ROBERTO EGYDIO SETÚBAL; 32 brs.

Banco Industrial e Comercial, SA: Rua Boa Vista 192, 01014-030 São Paulo, SP; tel. (11) 237-6904; fax (11) 3107-5290; e-mail bicbanco .dinte@uol.com.br; internet www.bicbanco.com.br; f. 1938; cap. 191.7m., res 62.9m., dep. 725.6m. (June 2000); Pres. JOSÉ BEZERRA DE MENEZES; 38 brs.

Banco Itaú, SA: Rua Boa Vista 176, CP 30341, 01014-919 São Paulo, SP; tel. (11) 237-3000; fax (11) 277-1044; e-mail info@itau.com .br; internet www.itau.com.br; f. 1944; cap. 11,110.0m., res 1,003.2m., dep. 28,868.6m. (June 2002); Chair. OLAVO EGYDIO SETÚBAL; Pres. and CEO ROBERTO EGYDIO SETÚBAL; 2,203 brs.

Banco Mercantil do Brasil, SA: Rua Rio de Janerio 654, 10°, Centro, 30160–912 Belo Horizonte, MG; tel. (31) 3239-6163; fax (31) 3239-6444; e-mail sac@mercantil.br; internet www.mercantil .br; cap. 429.4m., res 12.9m., dep. 2,060.3m. (June 2002); Chair., Pres. and CEO MILTON DE ARAÚJO; 203 brs.

Banco Mercantil de São Paulo—Finasa: CP 4077, Av. Paulista 1450, 01310-917 São Paulo, SP; tel. (11) 252-2121; fax (11) 284-3312; e-mail finasa@finasa.com.br; internet mercantilsp.finasa.com.br; f. 1938; name changed 2000; owned by Banco Bradesco; cap. 817.4m., res 189.6m., dep. 3,832.6m. (Dec. 1999); Pres. Dr GASTÃO EDUARDO DE BUENO VIDIGAL.

Banco Pactual: Av. República do Chile 230, 28° e 29° andares, 20031-170 Rio de Janeiro, RJ; tel. (21) 272-1100; fax (21) 533-1661; e-mail webmaster@pactual.com.br; internet www.pactual.com.br; f. 1983; cap. 476.1., res 30.3m., dep. 433.3m. (June 2002); Pres. LUÍS CEZAR FERNANDES; 4 brs.

Banco Safra, SA: Av. Paulista 2100, 16° andar, 01310-930 São Paulo, SP; tel. (11) 3175-7575; fax (11) 3175-8605; e-mail safrapact@ uol.com.br; internet www.safra.com.br; f. 1940; cap. 2,065.8m., res 183.0m., dep. 7,875.8m. (June 2002); Pres. CARLOS ALBERTO VIEIRA; 77 brs.

Banco Santander Brasil, SA: Rua Funchal 160, 04551-903 São Paulo, SP; tel. (11) 828-7322; fax (11) 828-7208; internet www .santander.com.br; f. 1942; fmrly Banco Geral do Comercio; Pres. LUIZ ROBERTO ORTIZ NASCIMENTO; 41 brs.

Banco Santander Meridional, SA: Rua General Câmara 156, Centro, 90010-230 Porto Alegre, RS; tel. (51) 287-5700; fax (51) 508-5769; internet www.meridional.com.br; f. 1985; formerly Banco Sulbrasileiro, SA; taken over by the Government in Aug. 1985; acquired by Banco Bozano, Simonsen in 1997; name changed 2000; cap. 1,200.5m., res –121.1m., dep. 5,782.5m. (Dec. 1998); Pres. PAULO VEIGA FERRAZ PEREIRA; 227 brs.

Banco Sogeral, SA: Rua Verbo Divino 1207, 3° e 4° andares, CP 8785, 04719-002 São Paulo, SP; tel. (11) 5180-5052; fax (11) 5180-5258; internet www.sogeral.com.br; f. 1981; cap. 83.0m., res 18.7m., dep. 457.2m. (Dec. 1998); Pres. ERIC DHOSTE; 1 br.

Banco Sudameris Brasil, SA: Av. Paulista 1000, 2°, 10°–16° andares, 01310-100 São Paulo, SP; tel. (11) 3170-9899; fax (11) 289-1239; internet www.sudameris.com.br; f. 1910; cap. 1,385.9m., res

139.9m., dep. 5,832.0m. (June 2002); Exec. Dirs YVES L. J. LEJEUNE, SEBASTIÃO G. T. CUNHA; 297 brs.

Banco Votorantim, SA: Av. Roque Petroni, Jr 999, 16° andar, 04707-910 São Paulo, SP; tel. (11) 5185-1700; fax (11) 5185-1900; internet www.bancovotorantim.com.br; cap. 1,378.7m., res 110.8m., dep. 5,720,6m (June 2002); 4 brs.

BankBoston SA: Rua Líbero Badaró 487-3°, 01009-000 São Paulo, SP; tel. (11) 3118-5622; fax (11) 3118-4438; internet www .bankboston.com.br; cap. 1,932,8m., res 210.2m., dep. 3,015.1m. (June 2002); Pres. GERALDO JOSÉ CARBONE; 59 brs.

HSBC Bank Brasil, SA, Banco Multiplo: Travessa Oliveira Belo 34, Centro, 80020-030 Curitiba, PR; tel. (41) 321-6161; fax (41) 321-6081; internet www.hsbc.com.br; f. 1997; cap. 1,207.4m., res 126.0m., dep. 9,573.8m. (June 2002); Pres. M. F. GEOGHEGAN; 966 brs.

UNIBANCO (União de Bancos Brasileiros, SA): Av. Eusébio Matoso 891, 22° andar, CP 8185, 05423-901 São Paulo, SP; tel. (11) 867-4461; fax (11) 814-0528; e-mail investor.relations@unibanco.com.br; internet www.unibanco.com.br; f. 1924; cap. 6,372.2m., res 481.2m.m., dep. 21,836.4m. (June 2002); Chair. PEDRO MOREIRA SALLES; 913 brs.

Development Banks

Banco de Desenvolvimento de Minas Gerais, SA (BDMG): Rua da Bahia 1600, CP 1026, 30160-011 Belo Horizonte, MG; tel. (31) 226-3292; fax (31) 273-5084; f. 1962; long-term credit operations; cap. 250.5m., res –124.6m., dep. 3.3m. (Dec. 1997); Pres. MARCOS RAYMUNDO PESSÔA DUARTE.

Banco de Desenvolvimento do Espírito Santo, SA: Av. Princesa Isabel 54, Edif. Caparão, 12° andar, CP 1168, 29010-906 Vitória, ES; tel. (27) 223-8333; fax (27) 223-6307; total assets US \$12.5m. (Dec. 1993); Pres. SÉRGIO MANOEL NADER BORGES.

Banco Nacional de Crédito Cooperativo, SA: Brasília, DF; tel. (61) 224-5575; established in association with the Ministry of Agriculture and guaranteed by the Federal Government to provide co-operative credit; cap. 4.7m. (cruzeiros, July 1990); Pres. ESUPÉRIO S. DE CAMPOS AGUILAR (acting); 41 brs.

Banco Nacional do Desenvolvimento Econômico e Social (BNDES): Av. República do Chile 100, 20139-900 Rio de Janeiro, RJ; tel. (21) 277-7447; fax (21) 533-1665; internet www.bndes.gov.br; f. 1952 to act as main instrument for financing of development schemes sponsored by the Government and to support programmes for the development of the national economy; charged with supervision of privatization programme of the 1990s; cap. 12,500.1m., res 576.4m. dep. 8,617.0m. (June 2002); Pres. CARLOS LESSA; 1 br.

Banco Regional de Desenvolvimento do Extremo Sul (BRDE): Rua Uruguai 155, 3°–4° andares, CP 139, 90010-140 Porto Alegre, RS; tel. (51) 121-9200; f. 1961; cap. 15m. (Dec. 1993); development bank for the states of Paraná, Rio Grande do Sul and Santa Catarina; finances small- and medium-sized enterprises; Dir-Pres. NELSON WEDEKIN; 3 brs.

Investment Bank

Banco de Investimentos CSFB Garantia, SA: Av. Brigadeiro Faria Lima 3064, 13° andar, Itaim Bibi, 01451-020 São Paulo, SP; tel. (11) 821-6000; fax (11) 821-6900; f. 1971; fmrly Banco de Investimentos Gerais; cap. 956.6m., res 107.2m., dep. 1,794.7m. (Dec. 1996); Dir LUIS ALBERTO MENDES RODRIGUES; 1 br.

State-owned Savings Bank

Caixa Econômica Federal: Brasília, DF; tel. (61) 321-9209; fax (61) 225-0215; internet www.caixa.gov.br; f. 1860; cap. 4,301.1m., res 564.4m., dep. 73,611.2m.m. (June 2002); Pres. EMÍLIO CARRAZAI; 2,026 brs.

Foreign Banks

Banco de la Nación Argentina: Av. Paulista 2319, Sobreloja, 01310 São Paulo, SP; tel. (11) 883-1555; fax (11) 881-4630; e-mail bnaspbb@dialdata.com.br; f. 1891; Dir-Gen. GERARDO LUIS PONCE; 2 brs.

Banco Chase Manhattan, SA: Rua Verbo Divino, 04719-002 São Paulo, SP; tel. (11) 546-4433; fax (11) 546-4624; f. 1925; fmrly Banco Lar Brasileiro, SA; Chair. PETER ANDERSON.

Banco Unión (Venezuela): Av. Paulista 1708, 01310 São Paulo, SP; tel. (11) 283-3722; fax (11) 283-2434; f. 1892; Dir-Gen. DONALDISON MARQUES DA SILVA.

Dresdner Bank Lateinamerika AG (Germany): Rua Verbo Divino 1488, Centro Empresarial Transatlântico, CP 3641, 01064-970 São Paulo, SP; e-mail brazil.rep-office@dresdner-bank.com; tel. (11) 5188-6700; fax (11) 5188-6900; fmrly Deutsch-Sudamerikanische Bank; f. 1969; Chair. WALTER U. HAAGEN; 3 brs.

Lloyds TSB Bank PLC (United Kingdom): São Paulo, SP; tel. (11) 818-8311; fax (11) 818-8403; e-mail lloyds.dmkt@lloyds.com.br; internet www.lloyds.com.br; cap. 814.5m., res 162.4m., dep. 1,286.8m. (June 2002); Gen. Man. DAVID V. THOMAS; 4 brs.

Banking Associations

Federação Brasileira das Associações de Bancos: Rua Líbero Badaró 425, 17° andar, 01069-900 São Paulo, SP; tel. (11) 239-3000; fax (11) 607-8486; f. 1966; Pres. MAURÍCIO SCHULMAN; Vice-Pres ROBERTO EGYDIO SETÚBAL, JOSÉ AFONSO SANCHO.

Sindicato dos Bancos dos Estados do Rio de Janeiro e Espírito Santo: Av. Rio Branco 81, 19° andar, Rio de Janeiro, RJ; Pres. THEÓPHILO DE AZEREDO SANTOS; Vice-Pres. Dr NELSON MUFARREJ.

Sindicato dos Bancos dos Estados de São Paulo, Paraná, Mato Grosso e Mato Grosso do Sul: Rua Líbero Badaró 293, 13° andar, 01905 São Paulo, SP; f. 1924; Pres. PAULO DE QUEIROZ.

There are other banking associations in Maceió, Salvador, Fortaleza, Belo Horizonte, João Pessoa, Recife and Porto Alegre.

STOCK EXCHANGES

Comissão de Valores Mobiliários CVM: Rua Sete de Setembro 111, 32° andar, 20159-900 Rio de Janeiro, RJ; tel. (21) 212-0200; fax (21) 212-0524; e-mail pte@cvm.gov.br; f. 1977 to supervise the operations of the stock exchanges and develop the Brazilian securities market; Chair. JOSÉ LUIZ OSORIO DE ALMEIDA (Filho).

Bolsa de Valores do Rio de Janeiro: Praça XV de Novembro 20, 20010-010 Rio de Janeiro, RJ; tel. (21) 514-1010; fax (21) 242-8066; e-mail info@bvrj.com.br; internet www.bvrj.com.br; f. 1845; focuses on the trading of fixed income government bonds and foreign exchange; Chair. SERGIO LUIZ BERARDI.

Bolsa de Valores de São Paulo (BOVESPA): Rua XV de Novembro 275, 01013-001 São Paulo, SP; tel. (11) 233-2000; fax (11) 233-2099; e-mail bovespa@bovespa.com.br; internet www.bovespa.com.br; f. 1890; 550 companies listed in 1997; CEO GILBERTO MIFANO.

There are commodity exchanges at Porto Alegre, Vitória, Recife, Santos and São Paulo.

INSURANCE

Supervisory Authorities

Superintendência de Seguros Privados (SUSEP): Rua Buenos Aires 256, 4° andar, 20061-000 Rio de Janeiro, RJ; tel. (21) 297-4415; fax (21) 221-6664; f. 1966; within Ministry of Finance; Supt HELIO PORTOCARRERO.

Conselho Nacional de Seguros Privados (CNSP): Rua Buenos Aires 256, 20061-000 Rio de Janeiro, RJ; tel. (21) 297-4415; fax (21) 221-6664; f. 1966; Sec. THERESA CHRISTINA CUNHA MARTINS.

Federação Nacional dos Corretores de Seguros e de Capitalização (FENACOR): Av. Rio Branco 147, 6° andar, 20040-006 Rio de Janeiro, RJ; tel. (21) 507-0033; fax (21) 507-0041; e-mail leoncio@fenacor.com.br; Pres. LEÔNCIO DE ARRUDA.

Federação Nacional das Empresas de Seguros Privados e de Capitalização (FENASEG): Rua Senador Dantas 74, 20031-200 Rio de Janeiro, RJ; tel. (21) 524-1204; fax (21) 220-0046; e-mail fenaseg@fenaseg.org.br; Pres. JOÃO ELISIO FERRAZ DE CAMPOS.

IRBBrasil Resseguros: Av. Marechal Câmara 171, Castelo, 20020-900 Rio de Janeiro, RJ; tel. (21) 272-0200; fax (21) 240-6261; e-mail info@irb-brasilre.com.br; internet www.irb-brasilre.com.br; f. 1939; fmrly Instituto de Resseguros do Brasil; reinsurance; Pres. DEMÓSTHENES MADUREIRA DE PINHO (Filho).

Principal Companies

The following is a list of the principal national insurance companies, selected on the basis of assets.

AGF Brasil Seguros, SA: Rua Luís Coelho 26, 01309-000 São Paulo, SP; tel. (11) 281-5572; fax (11) 283-1401; internet www.agf.com.br; Dir EUGÊNIO DE OLIVEIRA MELLO.

Cia de Seguros Aliança da Bahia: Rua Pinto Martins 11, 2° andar, 40015-020 Salvador, BA; tel. (71) 242-1055; fax (71) 242-8998; f. 1870; general; Pres. PAULO SÉRGIO FREIRE DE CARVALHO GONÇALVES TOURINHO.

Cia de Seguros Aliança do Brasil: Rua Senador Dantas 105, 32° andar, 20031-201 Rio de Janeiro, RJ; tel. (21) 533-1080; fax (21) 220-2105; Pres. KHALID MOHAMMED RAOUF.

Allianz-Bradesco Seguros, SA: Rua Barão de Itapagipe 225, 20269-900 Rio de Janeiro, RJ; tel. (21) 563-1101; fax (21) 293-9489.

BCN Seguradora, SA: Alameda Santos 1940, 9° andar, 01418-100 São Paulo, SP; tel. (11) 283-2244; fax (11) 284-3415; internet www.bcn.com.br/seguro.htm; f. 1946; Pres. ANTÔNIO GRISI (Filho).

Bradesco Previdência e Seguros, SA: Av. Deputado Emílio Carlos 970, 06028-000 São Paulo, SP; tel. (11) 704-4466; fax (11) 703-3063; internet www.bradesco.com.br/prodserv/bradprev.html; f. 1989; Pres. ANTÔNIO LOPES CRISTÓVÃO.

Bradesco Seguros, SA: Rua Barão de Itapagipe 225, 20269-900 Rio de Janeiro, RJ; tel. (21) 563-1199; fax (21) 503-1466; internet www.bradesco.com.br/prodserv/bradseg.html; f. 1935; general; Pres. EDUARDO VIANNA.

CGU Cia de Seguros: Av. Almirante Barroso 52, 23° e 24° andares, 20031-000 Rio de Janeiro, RJ; tel. (21) 292-1125; fax (21) 262-0291; internet www.york.com.br/york0700.html; Pres. ROBERT CHARLES WHEELER.

Finasa Seguradora, SA: São Paulo, SP; tel. (11) 253-8181; fax (11) 285-1994; internet www.finasa.com.br/ficoli02.html; f. 1939; Pres. MARCELLO DE CAMARGO VIDIGAL.

Golden Cross Seguradora, SA: Rua Maestro Cardim 1164, 013200-301 Rio de Janeiro, RJ; tel. (21) 283-4922; fax (21) 289-4624; e-mail comunica@goldencross.com.br; internet www.golden.com.br; f. 1971; Pres. ALBERT BULLUS.

HSBC Seguros (Brasil), SA: Rua Ten. Francisco Ferreira de Souza 805, Bloco 1, Ala 4, Vila Hauer, 81.570-340, Curitiba, PR; tel. (41) 217-2000; fax (41) 321-8800; f. 1938; all classes; Supt Dir BRIAN J. GUEST.

Itaú Seguros, SA: Praça Alfredo Egydio de Souza Aranha 100, Bloco A, 04344-920 São Paulo, SP; tel. (11) 5019-3322; fax (11) 5019-3530; e-mail itauseguros@itauseguros.com.br; internet www.itauseguros.com.br; f. 1921; all classes; Pres. LUIZ DE CAMPOS SALLES.

Cia de Seguros Minas-Brasil: Rua dos Caetés 745, 5° andar, 30120-080 Belo Horizonte, MG; tel. (31) 219-3882; fax (31) 219-3820; f. 1938; life and risk; Pres. JOSÉ CARNEIRO DE ARAÚJO.

Cia Paulista de Seguros: Rua Dr Geraldo Campos Moreira 110, 04571-020 São Paulo, SP; tel. (11) 5505-2010; fax (11) 5505-2122; internet www.pauliseg.com.br; f. 1906; general; Pres. PHILLIP NORTON MOORE.

Porto Seguro Cia de Seguros Gerais: Rua Guaianazes 1238, 01204-001 São Paulo, SP; tel. (11) 224-6129; fax (11) 222-6213; internet www.porto-seguro.com.br; f. 1945; life and risk; Pres. ROSA GARFINKEL.

Sasse, Cia Nacional de Seguros Gerais: SCN Qd. 01, Bl. A, 15°–17° andares, 70710-500 Brasília, DF; tel. (61) 329-2400; fax (61) 321-0600; internet www.sasse.com.br; f. 1967; general; Pres. PEDRO PEREIRA DE FREITAS.

Sul América Aetna Seguros e Previdência, SA: Rua Anchieta 35, 9° andar, 01016-030 São Paulo, SP; tel. (11) 232-6131; fax (11) 606-8141; internet www.sulaamerica.com.br; f. 1996; Pres. RONY CASTRO DE OLIVEIRA LYRIO.

Sul América, Cia Nacional de Seguros: Rua da Quitanda 86, 20091-000 Rio de Janeiro, RJ; tel. (21) 276-8585; fax (21) 276-8317; f. 1895; life and risk; Pres. RONY CASTRO DE OLIVEIRA LYRIO.

Sul América Santa Cruz Seguros, SA: Tv. Franc. Leonardo Truda 98, 6° andar, 90010-050 Porto Alegre, RS; tel. (51) 211-5455; fax (51) 225-5894; f. 1943; Pres. RONY CASTRO DE OLIVEIRA LYRIO.

Unibanco Seguros, SA: Av. Eusébio Matoso 1375, 13° andar, 05423-180 São Paulo, SP; tel. (11) 819-8000; fax (11) 3039-4005; internet www.unibancoseguros.com.br; f. 1946; life and risk; Pres. JOSÉ CASTRO ARAÚJO RUDGE.

Vera Cruz Seguradora, SA: Av. Maria Coelho Aguiar 215, Bloco D, 3° andar, 05804-906 São Paulo, SP; tel. (11) 3741-3815; fax (11) 3741-3827; internet www.veracruz.com.br; f. 1955; general; Pres. ALFREDO FERNANDEZ DE L. ORTIZ DE ZARATE.

Trade and Industry

GOVERNMENT AGENCIES

Agência Nacional de Petróleo (ANP): Brasília, DF; internet www.anp.gov.br; f. 1998; regulatory body of the petroleum industry; Chair. DAVID ZYLBERSTAJN.

Comissão de Fusão e Incorporação de Empresa (COFIE): Ministério da Fazenda, Edif. Sede, Ala B, 1° andar, Esplanada dos Ministérios, Brasília, DF; tel. (61) 225-3405; mergers commission; Pres. SEBASTIÃO MARCOS VITAL; Exec. Sec. EDGAR BEZERRA LEITE (Filho).

Conselho de Desenvolvimento Comercial (CDC): Bloco R, Esplanada dos Ministérios, 70044 Brasília, DF; tel. (61) 223-0308; commercial development council; Exec. Sec. Dr RUY COUTINHO DO NASCIMENTO.

Conselho de Desenvolvimento Econômico (CDE): Bloco K, 7° andar, Esplanada dos Ministérios, 70063 Brasília, DF; tel. (61) 215-

4100; f. 1974; economic development council; Gen. Sec. João Batista de Abreu.

Conselho de Desenvolvimento Social (CDS): Bloco K, 3° andar, 382, Esplanada dos Ministérios, 70063 Brasília, DF; tel. (61) 215-4477; social development council; Exec. Sec. João A. Teles.

Conselho Nacional do Comércio Exterior (CONCEX): Fazenda, 5° andar, Gabinete do Ministro, Bloco 6, Esplanada dos Ministérios, 70048 Brasília, DF; tel. (61) 223-4856; f. 1966; responsible for foreign exchange and trade policies and for the control of export activities; Exec. Sec. Namir Salek.

Conselho Nacional de Desenvolvimento Científico e Tecnológico (CNPq): Brasília, DF; tel. (61) 348-9401; fax (61) 273-2955; f. 1951; scientific and technological development council; Pres. José Galizia Tundisi.

Conselho Nacional de Desenvolvimento Pecuário (CONDEPE): to promote livestock development.

Conselho de Não-Ferrosos e de Siderurgia (CONSIDER): Ministério da Indústria e Comércio, Esplanada dos Ministérios, Bloco 7, 7° andar, 70056-900 Brasília, DF; tel. (61) 224-6039; f. 1973; exercises a supervisory role over development policy in the non-ferrous and iron and steel industries; Exec. Sec. William Rocha Cantal.

Fundação Instituto Brasileiro de Geografia e Estatística (IBGE): Centro de Documentação e Disseminação de Informações (CDDI), Rua Gen. Canabarro 706, 2° andar, Maracanã, 20271-201 Rio de Janeiro, RJ; tel. (21) 569-5997; fax (21) 569-1103; e-mail webmaster@ibge.gov.br; internet www.ibge.gov.br; f. 1936; produces and analyses statistical, geographical, cartographic, geodetic, demographic and socio-economic information; Pres. (IBGE) Sérgio Besserman Vianna; Supt (CDDI) David Wu Tai.

Instituto Nacional de Metrologia, Normalização e Qualidade Industrial (INMETRO): Rua Santa Alexandrina 416, Rio Comprido, 20261-232 Rio de Janeiro, RJ; tel. (21) 273-9002; fax (21) 293-0954; e-mail pusi@inmetro.gov.br; in 1981 INMETRO absorbed the Instituto Nacional de Pesos e Medidas (INPM), the weights and measures institute; Pres. Dr Júlio Cesar Carmo Bueno.

Instituto de Pesquisa Econômica Aplicada (IPEA): CP 2672, Avda Presidente António Carlos 51, 16° andar, 20020-010 Rio de Janeiro, RS; tel. (21) 3804-8118; fax (21) 2220-5533; e-mail editrj@ipea.gov.br; internet www.ipea.gov.br; f. 1970; economics and planning institute; Editors. Octávio Augusto Fontes Tourinho, Marco António Cavalcanti.

Secretária Especial de Desenvolvimento Industrial: Brasília, DF; tel. (61) 225-7556; fax (61) 224-5629; f. 1969; industrial development council; offers fiscal incentives for selected industries and for producers of manufactured goods under the Special Export Programme; Exec. Sec. Dr Ernesto Carrara.

REGIONAL DEVELOPMENT ORGANIZATIONS

Agência de Desenvolvimento da Amazônia (ADA): Av. Almirante Barroso 426, Marco, 66090-900 Belém, PA; tel. (91) 210-5440; fax (91) 266-0366; e-mail gabinete@ada.gov.br; internet www.ada.gov.br; f. 2001 to coordinate the development of resources in Amazonia; Dir-Gen. Teresa Lusia Mártires Coelho Cativo Rosa.

Agência de Desenvolvimento do Nordeste (ADENE): internet www.adene.gov.br; f. 2001 to replace the defunct Superintendência de Desenvolvimento do Nordeste (SUDENE); Dir-Gen. Evandro José Moreira Avelar.

Companhia de Desenvolvimento dos Vales do São Francisco e do Parnaíba (CODEVASF): SGAN, Q 601, Lote 1, Edif. Manoel Novaes, 70830-901 Brasília, DF; tel. (61) 312-4758; fax (61) 226-8819; e-mail divulgacao@codevasf.gov.br; internet www.codevasf.gov.br/indice.html; f. 1974; promotes integrated development of resources of São Francisco and Parnaíba Valley; Pres. Aírson Bezerra Lócio.

Superintendência da Zona Franca de Manaus (SUFRAMA): Rua Ministro João Gonçalves de Souza s/n, Distrito Industrial, 69075-770 Manaus, AM; tel. (92) 237-1691; fax (92) 237-6549; e-mail super@suframa.gov.br; internet www.suframa.gov.br; to assist in the development of the Manaus Free Zone; Supt Dr Ozias Monteiro Rodrigues.

AGRICULTURAL, INDUSTRIAL AND TRADE ORGANIZATIONS

Associação do Comércio Exterior do Brasil (AEB): Av. General Justo 335, 4° andar, Rio de Janeiro, RJ; tel. (21) 240-5048; fax (21) 240-5463; e-mail aebbras@embratel.net.br; internet www.probrazil.com/aeb.html; exporters' association.

Associação Comercial do Rio de Janeiro: Rua da Calendária 9, 11°–12° andares, Centro, 20091-020 Rio de Janeiro, RJ; tel. (21) 2291-1229; fax (21) 2253-6236; e-mail acrj@acrj.org.br; internet www.acrj.org.br; f. 1820; Pres. Marcílio Marques Moreira.

Companhia de Pesquisa de Recursos Minerais (CPRM): Serviço Geológico do Brasil, Av. Pasteur 404, Urca, 22290-240 Rio de Janeiro, RJ; tel. (21) 2295-5337; fax (21) 2542-3647; e-mail cprm@cprm.gov.br; internet www.cprm.gov.br; mining research, attached to the Ministry of Mining and Energy; Pres. Umberto Raimundo Costa.

Confederação das Associações Comerciais do Brasil: Brasília, DF; confederation of chambers of commerce in each state; Pres. Amaury Tenporal.

Confederação Nacional da Agricultura (CNA): Brasília, DF; tel. (61) 225-3150; national agricultural confederation; Pres. Alysson Paulinelli.

Confederação Nacional do Comércio (CNC): SCS, Edif. Presidente Dutra, 4° andar, Quadra 11, 70327 Brasília, DF; tel. (61) 223-0578; national confederation comprising 35 affiliated federations of commerce; Pres. António José Domingues de Oliveira Santos.

Confederação Nacional da Indústria (CNI): Av. Nilo Peçanha 50, 34° andar, 20044 Rio de Janeiro, RJ; tel. (21) 292-7766; fax (21) 262-1495; f. 1938; national confederation of industry comprising 26 state industrial federations; Pres. Dr Albano do Prado Franco; Vice-Pres. Mário Amato.

Conselho dos Exportadores de Café Verde do Brasil (CECAFE): Av. Nove de Julho 4865, Torre A, Conj. 61, Chácara Itaim, 01407-200 São Paulo, SP; tel. (11) 3079-3755; fax (11) 3167-4060; internet www.cecafe.com; f. 1999; through merger of Federação Brasileira dos Exportadores de Café and Associação Brasileira dos Exportadores de Café; council of green coffee exporters.

Departamento Nacional da Produção Mineral (DNPM): SAN, Quadra 1, Bloco B, 3° andar, 70040-200 Brasília, DF; tel. (61) 224-7097; fax (61) 225-8274; e-mail webmaster@dnpm.gov.br; internet www.dnpm.gov.br; f. 1934; responsible for geological studies and control of exploration of mineral resources; Dir-Gen. João R. Pimentel.

Empresa Brasileira de Pesquisa Agropecuária (EMBRAPA): SAIN, Parque Rural, W/3 Norte, CP 040315, 70770-901 Brasília, DF; tel. (61) 348-4433; fax (61) 347-1041; f. 1973; attached to the Ministry of Agriculture; agricultural research; Pres. Alberto Duque Portugal.

Federação das Indústrias do Estado de São Paulo (FIESP): Av. Paulista 1313, 01311-923 São Paulo, SP; tel. (11) 252-4200; fax (11) 284-3611; regional manufacturers' association; Pres. Carlos Eduardo Moreira Ferreira.

Instituto Brasileiro do Meio Ambiente e Recursos Naturais Renováveis (IBAMA): Ed. Sede IBAMA, Av. SAIN, L4 Norte, Bloco C, Subsolo, 70800-200 Brasília, DF; tel. (61) 316-1205; fax (61) 226-5094; e-mail cnia@sede.ibama.gov.br; internet www.ibama.gov.br; f. 1967; responsible for the annual formulation of national environmental plans; merged with SEMA (National Environmental Agency) in 1988 and replaced the IBDF in 1989; Pres. Eduardo Mailius.

Instituto Brasileiro do Mineração (IBRAM): SCS, Quadra 2, Bloco D, Edif. Oscar Niemeyer, 11° andar, 70316-900, Brasília, DF; tel. (61) 226-9367; fax (61) 226-9580; e-mail ibram@ibram.org.br; internet ibram.org.br; f. 1976 to foster the development the mining industry; Pres. João Sérgio Marinho Nunes.

Instituto Nacional da Propriedade Industrial (INPI): Praça Mauá 7, 18° andar, 20081-240 Rio de Janeiro, RJ; tel. (21) 223-4182; fax (21) 263-2539; e-mail inpipres@inpi.gov.br; internet www.inpi.gov.br; f. 1970; intellectual property, etc. Pres. Jorge Machado.

Instituto Nacional de Tecnologia (INT): Av. Venezuela 82, 8° andar, 20081-310 Rio de Janeiro, RJ; tel. (21) 206-1100; fax (21) 263-6552; e-mail int@riosoft.softex.br; internet www.int.gov.br; f. 1921; co-operates in national industrial development; Dir João Luiz Hanriot Selasco.

UTILITIES

Electricity

Centrais Elétricas Brasileiras, SA (ELETROBRÁS): Edif. Petrobrás, Rua Dois, Setor de Autarquias Norte, 70040-903 Brasília, DF; tel. (61) 223-5050; fax (61) 225-5502; e-mail maryann@eletrobras.gov.br; internet www.eletrobras.gov.br; f. 1962; government holding company responsible for planning, financing and managing Brazil's electrical energy programme; scheduled for division into eight generating cos and privatization; Pres. Firmino Ferreira Sampaio Neto.

Centrais Elétricas do Norte do Brasil, SA (ELETRONORTE): SCN, Quadra 6, Conj. A, Blocos B/C, Sala 602, Super Center Venâncio 3000, 70718-500 Brasília, DF; tel. (61) 429-5151;

fax (61) 328-1566; e-mail elnweb@eln.gov.br; internet www.eln
.gov.br; f. 1973; Pres. Benedito Aparecido Carraro.

Centrais Elétricas do Sul do Brasil, SA (ELETROSUL): Rua
Deputado Antônio Edu Vieira 999, Pantanal, 88040-901 Florianópolis, SC; tel. (48) 231-7000; fax (48) 234-3434; Gerasul
responsible for generating capacity; f. 1968; Pres. Firmino Ferreira
Sampaio Neto.

Companhia Hidro Elétrica do São Francisco (CHESF): 333
Edif. André Falcão, Bloco A, Sala 313 Bongi, Rua Delmiro Golveia,
50761-901 Recife, PE; tel. (81) 229-2000; fax (81) 229-2390; e-mail
chesf@chesf.com.br; internet www.chesf.com.br; f. 1948; Pres.
Mozart de Siqueira Campos Araújo.

Furnas Centrais Elétricas, SA: Rua Real Grandeza 219, Bloco
A, 16° andar, Botafogo, 22281-031 Rio de Janeiro, RJ; tel. (21) 528-
3112; fax (21) 528-3438; internet www.furnas.com.br; f. 1957;
Pres. Luiz Carlos Santos.

Associated companies include:

Espírito Santo Centrais Elétricas, SA (ESCELSA): Rua Sete de
Setembro 362, Centro, CP 01-0452, 29015-000 Vitória, ES; tel. (27)
321-9000; fax (27) 322-0378; internet www.escelsa.com.br; f. 1968;
Pres. José Gustavo de Souza.

Centrais Elétricas de Santa Catarina, SA (CELESC): Rodovia
SC 404, Km 3, Itacorubi, 88034-900 Florianópolis, SC; tel. (48) 231-
5000; fax (48) 231-6530; e-mail celesc@celesc.com.br; internet www
.celesc.com.br; production and distribution of electricity throughout
state of Santa Catarina; Pres. Francisco de Assis Küster.

Comissão Nacional de Energia Nuclear (CNEN): Rua General
Severiano 90, Botafogo, 22294-900 Rio de Janeiro, RJ; tel. (21) 295-
2232; fax (21) 546-2442; e-mail corin@cnen.gov.br; internet www
.cnen.gov.br; f. 1956; state organization responsible for management
of nuclear power programme; Pres. Marcio Costa.

Companhia de Eletricidade do Estado da Bahia (COELBA):
Av. Edgard Santos 300, Cabula IV, 41186-900 Salvador, BA; tel. (71)
370-5130; fax (71) 370-5132; Pres. Eduardo López Aranguren
Marcos.

**Companhia de Eletricidade do Estado do Rio de Janeiro
(CERJ):** Rua Visconde do Rio Branco 429, Centro, 24020-003
Niterói, RJ; tel. (21) 613-7120; fax (21) 613-7196; internet www.cerj
.com.br; f. 1907; Pres. Alejandro Danús Chirighin.

Companhia Energética Ceará (COELCE): Av. Barão de Studart
2917, 60120-002 Fortaleza, CE; tel. (85) 247-1444; fax (85) 272-4711;
internet www.coelce.com.br; f. 1971; Pres. Carlos Eduardo Carvalho
Alves.

Companhia Energética de Minas Gerais (CEMIG): Av. Barbacena 1200, 30123-970 Belo Horizonte, MG; tel. (31) 349-2111; fax
(31) 299-3700; e-mail mail@cemig.com.br; internet www.cemig.com
.br; fmrly state-owned, sold to a Brazilian-US consortium in May
1997; Pres. José da Costa Carvalgo Neto.

Companhia Energética de Pernambuco (CELPE): Av. João de
Barros 111, Sala 301, 50050-902 Recife, PE; tel. (81) 3217-5168;
e-mail celpe@celpe.com.br; internet www.celpe.com.br; state distributor of electricity; CEO João Bosco de Almeida.

Companhia Energética de São Paulo (CESP): Al. Ministro
Rocha Azevedo 25, 01410-900 São Paulo, SP; tel. (11) 234-6015; fax
(11) 288-0338; e-mail presiden@cesp.com.br; internet www.cesp.com
.br; f. 1966; Pres. Guilherme Augusto Cirne de Toledo.

Companhia Força e Luz Cataguazes-Leopoldina: Praça Rui
Barbosa 80, 36770-000 Cataguases, MG; tel. (32) 429-6000; fax (32)
421-4240; internet www.cataguazes.com.br; f. 1905; Pres. Manoel
Otoni Neiva.

Companhia Paranaense de Energia (COPEL): Rua Coronel
Dulcídio 800, 80420-170 Curitiba, PR; tel. (41) 322-3535; fax (41)
331-4145; e-mail copel@mail.copel.com.br; internet www.copel.com
.br; f. 1954; state distributor of electricity and gas; Pres. Ney Aminthas de Barros Braga.

Companhia Paulista de Força e Luz: Rodovia Campinas Mogi-
Mirim Km 2.5, Campinas, SP; tel. (192) 253-8704; fax (192) 252-
7644; provides electricity through govt concessions.

Eletricidade de São Paulo, SA (ELETROPAULO): Av. Alfredo
Egidio de Souza Aranha 100, 04791-900 São Paulo, SP; tel. (11) 546-
1467; fax (11) 239-1387; e-mail administracao@eletropaulo.com.br;
internet www.eletropaulo.com.br; f. 1899; acquired by AES in 2001;
Pres. Marc André Perreira.

Indústrias Nucleares do Brasil, SA (INB): Rua Mena Barreto
161, Botofogo 22271-100, Rio de Janeiro, RJ; tel. (21) 2536-1600; fax
(21) 2537-9391; e-mail inbrio@inb.gov.br; internet www.inb.gov.br;
Pres. Roberto Nogueira da Franca.

Itaipú Binacional: Av. Tancredo Neves 6731, 85856-970 Foz de
Iguaçu, PR; tel. (45) 520-5252; e-mail itaipu@itaipu.gov.br; internet

www.itaipu.gov.br; f. 1974; 1,490 employees (Itaipú Brasil–1998);
Dir-Gen. (Brazil) Euclides Scalco.

LIGHT—Serviços de Eletricidade, SA: Av. Marechal Floriano
168, CP 0571, 20080-002 Rio de Janeiro, RJ; tel. (21) 211-7171; fax
(21) 233-1249; e-mail light@lightrio.com.br; internet www.lightrio
.com.br; f. 1905; electricity generation and distribution in Rio de
Janeiro; formerly state-owned, sold to a Brazilian-French-US consortium in 1996; Pres. Luiz David Travesso.

Regulatory Agency

Agência Nacional de Energia Elétrica (ANEEL): SGAN 603,
Módulo J, 70830-030 Brasília, DF; e-mail aneel@aneel.gov.br;
internet www.aneel.gov.br; Dir José Maria Abdo.

Gas

Companhia Distribuidora de Gás do Rio de Janeiro (CEG):
Av. Pedro II 68, São Cristovão, 20941-070 Rio de Janeiro, RJ; tel.
(21) 585-7067; internet www.ceg.com.br; f. 1969; gas distribution in
the Rio de Janeiro region; privatized in July 1997.

Companhia de Gás de Alagoas, SA (ALGÁS): Rua Comendador
Palmeria 129, Farol, 57051-150 Maceió, AL; tel. (82) 221-9407; fax
(82) 336-6447; e-mail algas@algas.com.br; internet www.algas.com
.br; 51% state-owned; Pres. Dr Cornitho Onélio Campelo de Paz.

Companhia de Gás de Bahia (BAHIAGÁS): Avda Tancredo
Neves 450, Sala 1801, Edif. Suarez Trade, 41820-020 Salvador, BA;
tel. (71) 340-9000; fax (71) 341-9001; e-mail bahiagas@bahiagas
.br; internet www.bahiagas.com.br; 51% state-owned; Pres. Dr Luiz
Fernando Mueller Koser.

Companhia de Gás do Ceará (CEGÁS): Av. Santos Dumont 7700,
5°-6° andares, 20941-070 Fortaleza, CE; tel. (85) 265-1144; fax (85)
265-2026; e-mail cegas@secrel.com.br; internet www.cegas.com.br;
51% owned by the state of Amazonas; Pres. Dr José Rego (Filho).

Companhia de Gás de Minas Gerais (GASMIG): Av. Álvares
Cabral 1740, 7° andar, 30170-001 Belo Horizonte, MG; tel. (31) 3291-
2001; e-mail gasmig@gasmig.com.br; internet www.gasmig.com.br;
Pres. Djalma Bastos de Morais.

Companhia de Gás de Pernambuco (COPERGÁS): Av. Eng.
Domingo Ferreira 4060, 15° andar, 51021-040 Recife, PE; tel. (81)
3463-2000; e-mail copergas@copergas.com.br; internet www
.copergas.com.br; 51% state-owned; Pres. Dr Romero de Oliveira e
Silva.

Companhia de Gás do Rio Grande do Sul (SULGÁS): Travessa
Francisco Leonardo Truda 40, 90010-050 Porto Alegre, RS; tel. (51)
227-4111; internet www.sulgas.rs.gov.br; 51% state-owned; Pres. Dr
Giles Carreconde Azevedo.

Companhia de Gás de Santa Catarina (SCGÁS): Rua Antônia
Luz 255, Centro Empresarial Hoepcke, 88010-410 Florianópolis, SC;
tel. (48) 229-1200; fax (48) 229-1230; e-mail scgasonline.com.br;
internet www.scgas.com.br; 51% state-owned; Pres. Dr Luiz Gomes.

Companhia de Gás de São Paulo (COMGÁS): Rua Augusta
1600, 9° andar, 01304-901 São Paulo, SP; tel. (11) 3177-5000; fax
(11) 3177-5042; e-mail gaspla@comgas.com.br; internet www
.comgas.com.br; f. 1978; distribution in São Paulo of gas; sold in
April 1999 to consortium including British Gas PLC and Royal
Dutch/Shell Group; Pres. Julio Cesar Lamounier Napa.

Companhia Paraibana de Gás (PBGÁS): Av. Epitácio Pessoa
4840, Sala 210, 1° andar, Tambaú, 58030-001 João Pessoa, PB; tel.
(83) 247-2244; e-mail cicero@pbgas.com.br; internet www.pbgas.com
.br; 51% state-owned; Pres. Dr Cícero Ernesto Leite de Souza.

Companhia Paranaense de Gás (COMPAGÁS): Rua Pasteur
463, 7° andar, Batel, 80250-080 Curitiba, PR; tel. (41) 312-1900; fax
(41) 222-6633; e-mail compagas@mail.copel.br; internet www
.compagas.com.br; Pres. Dr Antônio Fernando Krempel.

Companhia Potiguar de Gás (POTIGÁS): Rua Dão Silveira
3672, Candelária, 59066-180 Natal, RN; tel. (84) 217-3322; fax (84)
217-3309; e-mail ismael@potigas.com.br; internet www.potigas.com
.br; 17% state-owned; Pres. Dr Ismael Wanderley Gomes (Filho).

Companhia Rondoniense de Gás, SA (RONGÁS): Av. Carlos
Gomes 1223, Sala 403, Centro, 78903-000 Porto Velho, RO; tel. and
fax (69) 229-0333; e-mail rongas@enter-net.com.br; internet www
.rongas.com.br; f. 1998; 17% state-owned; Pres. Gerson Acursi.

Empresa Sergipana de Gás, SA (EMSERGÁS): Rua Dom Bosco
1223 B, Suíça, 49050-220 Aracaju, SE; tel. and fax (79) 211-5213;
e-mail emsergas@infonet.com.br; internet www.emsergas.com.br;
Pres. Dr Luiz Machado Mendonça.

Water

Agua e Esgostos do Piauí (AGESPISA): Av. Mal Castelo Branco
101, Cabral, 64000 Teresina, PI; tel. (862) 239-300; f. 1962; state-
owned; water and waste management; Pres. Olivão Gomes da Sousa.

Companhia de Agua e Esgosto de Ceará (CAGECE): Rua Lauro Vieira Chaves 1030, Fortaleza, CE; tel. (85) 247-2422; internet www.cagece.com.br; state-owned; water and sewerage services; Gen. Man. JOSÉ DE RIBAMAR DA SILVA.

Companhia Algoas Industrial (CINAL): Rodovia Divaldo Suruagy, Km 12, 57160-000 Marechal Deodoro, AL; tel. (82) 269-1100; fax (82) 269-1199; internet www.cinal.com.br; f. 1982; management of steam and treated water; Dir PAULO ALBERQUERQUE MARANHÃO.

Companhia Espírito Santense de Saneamento (CESAN): Av. Governador Bley, 186, Edif. BEMGE, 29010-150 Vitória ES; tel. (27) 322-8399; fax (27) 322-4551; internet www.cesan.com.br; f. 1968; state-owned; construction, maintenance and operation of water supply and sewerage systems; Pres. CLÁUDIO DE MORAES MACHADO.

Companhia Estadual de Aguas e Esgostos (CEDAE): Rua Sacadura Cabral 103, 9° andar, 20081-260 Rio de Janeiro, RJ; tel. (21) 296-0025; fax (21) 296-0416; state-owned; water supply and sewerage treatment; Pres. ALBERTO JOSÉ MENDES GOMES.

Companhia Pernambucana Saneamento (COMPESA): Av. Cruz Cabugá 1387, Bairro Santo Amaro, 50040-905 Recife, PE; tel. (81) 421-1711; fax (81) 421-2712; state-owned; management and operation of regional water supply in the state of Pernambuco; Pres. GUSTAVO DE MATTO PONTUAL SAMPAIO.

Companhia Riograndense de Saneamento (CORSAN): Rua Caldas Júnior 120, 18° andar, 90010-260 Porto Alegre, RS; tel. (51) 228-5622; fax (51) 215-5700; e-mail ascon@corsan.com.br; internet www.corsan.com.br; f. 1965; state-owned; management and operation of regional water supply and sanitation programmes; Dir. DIETER WARTCHOW.

Companhia de Saneamento Básico do Estado de São Paulo (SABESP): Rua Costa Carvalho 300, 05429-000 São Paulo, SP; tel. (11) 3030-4000; internet www.sabesp.com.br; f. 1973; state-owned; supplies basic sanitation services for the state of São Paulo, including water treatment and supply; Pres. ARIOVALDO CARMIGNANI.

TRADE UNIONS

Central Unica dos Trabalhadores (CUT): Rua Caetano Pinto 575, Brás, 03041-000 São Paulo, SP; tel. (11) 3272-9411; e-mail duvaier@cut.org.br; internet www.cut.org.br; f. 1983; central union confederation; left-wing; Pres. VINCENTE PAULO DA SILVA; Gen. Sec. GILMAR CARNEIRO.

Confederação Geral dos Trabalhadores (CGT): Rua Tomaz Gonzaga 50, 2° andar, Liberdade, 01506–020 São Paulo; tel. (11) 3209–6577; e-mail cgt@cgt.org.br; internet www.cgt.org.br; f. 1986; fmrly Coordenação Nacional das Classes Trabalhadoras; represents 1,012 labour organizations linked to PMDB, containing 6.3m workers; Pres. ANTÔNIO CARLOS DOS REIS MEDEIROS; Sec.-Gen. FRANCISCO CANÍNDE PEGADO DO NASCIMENTO.

Confederação Nacional dos Metalúrgicos (Metal Workers): e-mail imprensa@cnmcut.org.br; internet www.cnmcut.org.br; f. 1985; Pres. HEIGUIBERTO GUIBA DELLA BELLA NAVARRO; Gen. Sec. FERNANDO AUGUSTO MOREIRA LOPES.

Confederação Nacional das Profissões Liberais (CNPL) (Liberal Professions): SAU/SUL, Edif. Belvedere Gr. 202, 70070-000 Brasília, DF; tel. (61) 223-1683; fax (61) 223-1944; e-mail cnpl@cnpl.org.br; internet www.cnpl.org.br; f. 1953; Pres. LUÍS EDUARDO GAUTÉRIO GALLO; Exec. Sec. JOSÉ ANTÔNIO BRITO ANDRADE.

Confederação Nacional dos Trabalhadores na Indústria (CNTI) (Industrial Workers): Av. W/3 Norte, Quadra 505, Lote 01, 70730-517 Brasília, DF; tel. (61) 274-4150; fax (61) 274-7001; f. 1946; Pres. JOSÉ CALIXTO RAMOS.

Confederação Nacional dos Trabalhadores no Comércio (CNTC) (Commercial Workers): Av. W/5 Sul, SGAS Quadra 902, Bloco C, 70390–020 Brasília, DF; tel. (61) 217-7100; fax (61) 217-7122; e-mail secretaria@cntc.org.br; internet www.cntc.org.br; f. 1946; Pres. ANTÔNIO DE OLIVEIRA SANTOS.

Confederação Nacional dos Trabalhadores em Transportes Marítimos, Fluviais e Aéreos (CONTTMAF) (Maritime, River and Air Transport Workers): Av. Pres. Vargas 446, gr. 2205, 20071 Rio de Janeiro, RJ; tel. (21) 233-8329; f. 1957; Pres. MAURÍCIO MONTEIRO SANT'ANNA.

Confederação Nacional dos Trabalhadores em Comunicações e Publicidade (CONTCOP) (Communications and Advertising Workers): SCS, Edif. Serra Dourada, 7° andar, gr. 705/709, Q 11, 70315 Brasília, DF; tel. (61) 224-7926; fax (61) 224-5686; f. 1964; 350,000 mems; Pres. ANTÔNIO MARIA THAUMATURGO CORTIZO.

Confederação Nacional dos Trabalhadores nas Empresas de Crédito (CONTEC) (Workers in Credit Institutions): SEP-SUL, Av. W4, EQ 707/907 Lote E, 70351 Brasília, DF; tel. (61) 244-5833; e-mail contec@yawl.com.br; internet www.contec.org.br; f. 1958; 814,532 mems (1988); Pres. LOURENÇO FERREIRA DO PRADO.

Confederação Nacional dos Trabalhadores em Estabelecimentos de Educação e Cultura (CNTEEC) (Workers in Education and Culture): SAS, Quadra 4, Bloco B, 70070-908 Brasília, DF; tel. (61) 321-1140; fax (61) 321-2704; internet www.cnteec.org.br; f. 1966; Pres. MIGUEL ABRÃO NETO.

Confederação Nacional dos Trabalhadores na Agricultura (CONTAG) (Agricultural Workers): SDS, Ed Venâncio VI, 1° andar, 70393-900 Brasília, DF; tel. (61) 321-2288; fax (61) 321-3229; internet www.contag.org.br; f. 1964; represents 25 state federations and 3,630 syndicates; Pres. MANOEL JOSÉ DOS SANTOS.

Força Sindical (FS): São Paulo, SP; internet www.fsindical.org.br; f. 1991; 6m. mems (1991); Pres. PAULO PEREIRA DA SILVA.

Transport

Ministério dos Transportes: see section on the Government (Ministries).

RAILWAYS

Rede Ferroviária Federal, SA (RFFSA) (Federal Railway Corporation): Praça Procópio Ferreira 86, 20221-310 Rio de Janeiro, RJ; tel. (21) 516-1890; fax (21) 516-1390; internet www.rffsa.gov.br; f. 1957; holding company for 18 railways grouped into regional networks, with total track length of 20,500 km in 1998; privatization of federal railways was completed in 1997; freight services; Pres. ISAAC POPOUTCHI.

Companhia Brasileira de Trens Urbanos (CBTU): Estrada Velha da Tijuca 77, Usina, 20531-080 Rio de Janeiro, RJ; tel. (21) 575-3399; fax (21) 571-6149; fmrly responsible for surburban networks and metro systems throughout Brazil; 252 km in 1998; the transfer of each city network to its respective local government is currently under way; Pres. LUIZ OTAVIO MOTA VALADARES.

Belo Horizonte Metro (CBTU/STU/BH-Demetrô): Belo Horizonte, MG; tel. (31) 250-4002; fax (31) 250-4004; e-mail metrobh@gold.horizontes.com.br; f. 1986; 21.2 km open in 1997; Gen. Man. M. L. L. SIQUEIRA.

Trem Metropolitano de Recife: Rua José Natário 478, Areias, 50900-000 Recife, PE; tel. (81) 455-4655; fax (81) 455-4422; f. 1985; 53 km open in 1997; Supt FERNANDO ANTÔNIO C. DUEIRE.

There are also railways owned by state governments and several privately-owned railways:

Companhia Ferroviária do Nordeste: Av. Francisco de Sá 4829, Bairro Carlito Pamplona, 60310-002, Fortaleza, CE; tel. (85) 286-2525; fax (85) 286-6156; e-mail kerley@cfn.com.br; internet www.cfn.com.br; Dir MARTINIANO DIAS.

Companhia Fluminense de Trens Urbanos (Flumitrens): Praça Cristiano Otoni, Sala 445, 20221 Rio de Janeiro, RJ; tel. (21) 233-8594; fax (21) 253-3089; f. 1975 as operating division of RFFSA, current name adopted following takeover by state government in 1994; suburban services in Rio de Janeiro and its environs; 293 km open in 1998; Supt MURILO JUNQUEIRA.

Companhia do Metropolitano do Rio de Janeiro: Av. Nossa Senhora de Copacabana 493, 22021-031 Rio de Janeiro, RJ; tel. (21) 235-4041; fax (21) 235-4546; 2-line metro system, 42 km open in 1997; Pres. ALVARO J. M. SANTOS.

Companhia do Metropolitano de São Paulo: Rua Augusta 1626, 03310-200 São Paulo, SP; tel. (11) 283-7411; fax (11) 283-5228; f. 1974; 3-line metro system, 56 km open in 1998; Pres. PAULO CLARINDO GOLDSCHMIDT.

Companhia Paulista de Trens Metropolitanos (CPTM): Av. Paulista 402, 5° andar, 01310-000 São Paulo, SP; tel. (11) 3371-1530; fax (11) 3285-0323; e-mail ctpm@ctpm.sp.gov.br; internet www.ctpm.sp.gov.br; f. 1992 to incorporate suburban lines fmrly operated by the CBTU and FEPASA; 286 km; CEO Eng. OLIVER HOSSEPIAN SALLES DE LIMA.

Departamento Metropolitano de Transportes Urbanos: SES, Quadra 4, Lote 6, Brasília, DF; tel. (61) 317-4090; fax (61) 226-9546; internet www.dmtu.df.gov.br; the first section of the Brasília metro, linking the capital with the western suburb of Samambaia, was inaugurated in 1994; 38.5 km open in 1997; Dir LEONARDO DE FARIA E SILVA.

Empresa de Trens Urbanos de Porto Alegre, SA: Av. Ernesto Neugebauer 1985, 90250-140 Porto Alegre, RS; tel. (51) 371-5000; fax (51) 371-1219; e-mail secos@trensurb.com.br; internet www.trensurb.com.br; f. 1985; 31 km open in 1998; Pres. PEDRO BISCH NETO.

Estrada de Ferro do Amapá: Praia de Botafogo 300, 11° andar, ala A, 22250-050 Rio de Janeiro, RJ; tel. (21) 552-4422; f. 1957;

operated by Indústria e Comércio de Minérios, SA; 194 km open in 1998; Pres. Osvaldo Luiz Senra Pessoa.

Estrada de Ferro Campos do Jordão: Rua Martin Cabral 87, CP 11, 12400-000 Pindamonhangaba, SP; tel. (22) 242-4233; fax (22) 242-2499; operated by the Tourism Secretariat of the State of São Paulo; 47 km open in 1998; Dir Arthur Ferreira dos Santos.

Estrada de Ferro Carajás: Av. dos Portugueses s/n, 65085-580 São Luís, MA; tel. (98) 218-4000; fax (98) 218-4530; f. 1985 for movement of minerals from the Serra do Carajás to the new port at Ponta da Madeira; operated by the Companhia Vale do Rio Doce; 955 km open in 1998; Supt Juares Salibra.

Estrada de Ferro do Jari: Monte Dourado, 68230-000 Pará, PA; tel. (91) 735-1155; fax (91) 735-1475; transportation of timber and bauxite; 68 km open; Dir Armindo Luiz Baretta.

Estrada de Ferro Mineração Rio do Norte, SA: Praia do Flamengo 200, 5° e 6° andares, 22210-030 Rio de Janeiro, RJ; tel. (21) 205-9112; fax (21) 545-5717; 35 km open in 1998; Pres. Antônio João Torres.

Estrada de Ferro Paraná-Oeste, SA (Ferroeste): Av. Iguaçu 420-7°, 80230-902 Curitiba, PR; tel. (41) 322-1811; fax (41) 233-2147; f. 1988 to serve the grain-producing regions in Paraná and Mato Grosso do Sul; 248 km inaugurated in 1995; privatized in late 1996, Brazilian company, Ferropar, appointed as administrator; Pres. José Heraldo Carneiro Lobo.

Estrada de Ferro Vitória-Minas: Av. Dante Michelini 5.500, 29090-900 Vitória, ES; tel. (27) 335-3666; fax (27) 226-0093; f. 1942; operated by Companhia Vale de Rio Doce; transport of iron ore, general cargo and passengers; 898 km open in 1998; Dir Thier Barsotti Manzano.

Ferrovia Bandeirante, SA (Ferroban): São Paulo, SP; tel. (11) 222-3392; fax (11) 220-8852; e-mail ferroban@ferroban.com.br; internet www.ferroban.com.br; f. 1971 by merger of five railways operated by São Paulo State; transferred to private ownership, Nov. 1998; fmrly Ferrovia Paulista; 4,235 km open in 1998; Dir João Gouveia Ferrão Neto.

Ferrovia Centro Atlântica, SA: Rua Sapucaí 383, Floresta 30150-904, Belo Horizonte, MG; tel. (31) 3279-5520; fax (31) 3279-5709; e-mail thiers@centro-atlantica.com.br; internet www.fcasa.com.br; f. 1996 following the privatization of Rede Ferroviária Federal, SA; industrial freight; 7,080 km; Man. Dir Thiers Manzano Barsotti.

Ferrovia Norte-Sul: Avda Marechal Floriano 45, Centro, 20080-003 Rio de Janeiro, RJ; tel. (21) 2253-9659; fax (21) 2263-9119; e-mail valecascom@ferrovianortesul.com.br; internet www.ferrovianortesul.com.br; 2,066 km from Belém to Goiânia; Man. Dir Luiz Raimundo Carneiro de Azevedo.

Ferrovia Tereza Cristina, SA: Rua dos Ferroviários 100, Oficinas, 88702-230 Tubarão, SC; tel. (48) 621-7700; fax (48) 621-7747; e-mail ftc@ftc.com.br; internet www.ftc.com.br; Man. Dir Benony Schmidt (Filho).

Ferrovias Norte do Brasil, SA (FERRONORTE): Rua do Rócio 351, 3° andar, Vila Olímpia, 04552-905 São Paulo, SP; tel. (11) 3845-4966; fax (11) 3841-9252; e-mail jhomero@novoeste.com.br; internet www.ferronorte.com.br; Man. Dir Nelson de Sampaio Bastos.

ROADS

In 2000 there were an estimated 1,700,000 km of roads in Brazil, of which 161,500 km were paved. Brasília has been a focal point for inter-regional development, and paved roads link the capital with every region of Brazil. The building of completely new roads has taken place predominantly in the north. Roads are the principal mode of transport, accounting for 63% of freight and 96% of passenger traffic, including long-distance bus services, in 1998. Major projects include the 5,000-km Trans-Amazonian Highway, running from Recife and Cabedelo to the Peruvian border, the 4,138-km Cuibá–Santarém highway, which will run in a north–south direction, and the 3,555-km Trans-Brasiliana project, which will link Marabá, on the Trans-Amazonian highway, with Aceguá, on the Uruguayan frontier. A 20-year plan to construct a highway linking São Paulo with the Argentine and Chilean capitals was endorsed in 1992 within the context of the development of the Southern Cone Common Market (Mercosul).

Departamento Nacional de Estradas de Rodagem (DNER) (National Roads Development): SAN, Quadra 3, Blocos N/O, 4° andar, Edif. Núcleo dos Transportes, 70040-902 Brasília, DF; tel. (61) 315-4100; fax (61) 315-4050; e-mail diretoria.geral@dner.gov.br; internet www.dner.gov.br; f. 1945 to plan and execute federal road policy and to supervise state and municipal roads in order to integrate them into the national network; Exec. Dir Rogério Gonzales Alves.

INLAND WATERWAYS

River transport plays only a minor part in the movement of goods. There are three major river systems, the Amazon, Paraná and the São Francisco. The Amazon is navigable for 3,680 km, as far as Iquitos in Peru, and ocean-going ships can reach Manaus, 1,600 km upstream. Plans have been drawn up to improve the inland waterway system and one plan is to link the Amazon and Upper Paraná to provide a navigable waterway across the centre of the country. In 1993 the member governments of Mercosul, together with Bolivia, reaffirmed their commitment to a 10-year development programme (initiated in 1992) for the extension of the Tietê Paraná river network along the Paraguay and Paraná Rivers as far as Buenos Aires, improving access to Atlantic ports and creating a 3,442 km waterway system, navigable throughout the year.

Agência Nacional de Transportes Aquaviários: Ministério dos Transportes, SAN, Quadra 3, Blocos N/O, 70040-902 Brasília, DF; tel. (61) 315-8102; Sec. Wildjan da Fonseca Magno.

Administração da Hidrovia do Paraguai (AHIPAR): Rua Treze de Junho 960, Corumbá, MS; tel. (67) 231-2841; fax (67) 231-2661; Supt. Paulo César C. Gomes da Silva.

Administração da Hidrovia do Paraná (AHRANA): Rua Vinte e Quatro de Maio 55, 9° andar, Conj. B, 01041-001 São Paulo, SP; tel. (11) 221-3230; fax (11) 220-8689; Supt Luiz Eduardo Garcia.

Administração da Hidrovia do São Francisco (AHSFRA): Praça do Porto 70, Distrito Industrial, 39270-000 Pirapora, MG; tel. (38) 741-2555; fax (38) 741-2510; Supt José H. Borato Jabur Júnior.

Administração das Hidrovias do Sul (AHSUL): Praça Oswaldo Cruz 15, 3° andar, 90030-160 Porto Alegre, RS; tel. (51) 228-3677; fax (51) 226-9068; Supt José Luiz F. de Azambuja.

Empresa de Navegação da Amazônia, SA (ENASA): Belém, PA; tel. (91) 223-3878; fax (91) 224-0528; f. 1967; cargo and passenger services on the Amazon river and its principal tributaries, connecting the port of Belém with all major river ports; Pres. Antônio de Souza Mendonça; 48 vessels.

SHIPPING

There are more than 40 deep-water ports in Brazil, all but two of which (Luis Correia and Imbituba) are directly or indirectly administered by the Government. The majority of ports are operated by eight state-owned concerns (Cia Docas do Pará, Maranhão, Ceará, Rio Grande do Norte, Bahia, Espírito Santo, Rio de Janeiro and Estado de São Paulo), while a smaller number (including Suape, Cabedelo, Barra dos Coqueiros, São Sebastião, Paranaguá, Antonina, São Francisco do Sul, Porto Alegre, Pelotas and Rio Grande) are administered by state governments.

The ports of Santos, Rio de Janeiro and Rio Grande have specialized container terminals handling more than 1,200,000 TEUs (20-ft equivalent units of containerized cargo) per year. Santos is the major container port in Brazil, accounting for 800,000 TEUs annually. The ports of Paranaguá, Itajaí, São Francisco do Sul, Salvador, Vitória and Imbituba cater for containerized cargo to a lesser extent.

Total cargo handled by Brazilian ports in 1999 amounted to 436m. tons, compared with 443m. tons in 1998 (of which 250m. was bulk cargo, 148m. was liquid cargo and 45m. was general cargo). Some 43,000 vessels used Brazil's ports in 1998.

Brazil's merchant fleet comprised 475 vessels totalling 3,687,077 grt in December 2001.

Departamento de Marinha Mercante: Coordenação Geral de Transporte Maritimo, Av. Rio Branco 103, 6° e 8° andar, 20040-004 Rio de Janeiro, RJ; tel. (21) 221-4014; fax (21) 221-5929; Dir Paulo Octávio de Paiva Almeida.

Port Authorities

Departamento de Portos: SAN, Quadra 3, Blocos N/O, CEP 70040-902 Brasília, DF; Dir Paulo Roberto K. Tannenbaum.

Paranaguá: Administração dos Portos de Paranaguá e Antonina (APPA), BR-277, km 0, 83206-380 Paranaguá, PR; tel. (41) 420-1102; fax (41) 423-4252; Port Admin. Eng. Osiris Stenghel Guimarães.

Recife: Administração do Porto do Recife, Praça Artur Oscar, 50030-370 Recife, PE; tel. (81) 424-4044; fax (81) 224-2848; Port Dir Carlos do Rego Vilar.

Rio de Janeiro: Companhia Docas do Rio de Janeiro (CDRJ), Rua do Acre 21, 20081-000 Rio de Janeiro, RJ; tel. (21) 296-5151; fax (21) 253-0528; CDRJ also administers the ports of Forno, Niterói, Sepetiba and Angra dos Reis; Pres. Mauro Orofino Campos.

Rio Grande: Administração do Porto de Rio Grande, Av. Honório Bicalho, CP 198, 96201-020 Rio Grande do Sul, RS; tel. (532) 31-1996; fax (532) 31-1857; Port Dir Luiz Francisco Spotorno.

Santos: Companhia Docas do Estado de São Paulo (CODESP), Av. Conselheiro Rodrigues Alves s/n, 11015-900 Santos, SP; tel. (13) 222-5485; fax (13) 222-3068; e-mail codesp@carrier.com.br; internet www.portodesantos.com; CODESP also administers the ports of Charqueadas, Estrela, Cáceres, Corumbá/Ladário, and the waterways of Paraná (AHRANA), Paraguai (AHIPAR) and the South (AHSUL); Pres. WAGNER GONÇALVES ROSSI.

São Francisco do Sul: Administração do Porto de São Francisco do Sul, Av. Eng. Leite Ribeiro 782, CP 71, 89240-000 São Francisco do Sul, SC; tel. (474) 44-0200; fax (474) 44-0115; Dir-Gen. ARNALDO S. THIAGO.

Tubarão: Companhia Vale do Rio Doce, Porto de Tubarão, Vitória, ES; tel. (27) 335-5727; fax (27) 228-0612; Port Dir CANDIDO COTTA PACHECO.

Vitória: Companhia Docas do Espírito Santo (CODESA), Av. Getúlio Vargas 556, Centro, 29020-030 Vitória, ES; tel. (27) 321-1311; fax (27) 222-7360; e-mail assecs@codesa.com.br; internet www.codesa.com.br; f. 1983; Pres. FÁBIO NUNES FALCE.

Other ports are served by the following state-owned companies:

Companhia Docas do Estado de Bahia: Av. da França 1551, 40010-000 Salvador, BA; tel. (71) 243-5066; fax (71) 241-6712; administers the ports of Aracaju, Salvador, Aratu, Ilhéus and Pirapora, and the São Francisco waterway (AHSFRA); Pres. JORGE FRANCISCO MEDAUAR.

Companhia Docas do Estado de Ceará (CDC): Praça Amigos da Marinha s/n, 60182-640 Fortaleza, CE; tel. (85) 263-1551; fax (85) 263-2433; administers the port of Fortaleza; Dir MARCELO MOTA TEIXEIRA.

Companhia Docas de Maranhão (CODOMAR): Porto do Itaquí, Rua de Paz 561, 65085-370 São Luís, MA; tel. (98) 222-2412; fax (98) 221-1394; administers ports of Itaquí and Manaus, and waterways of the Western Amazon (AHIMOC) and the North-East (AHINOR); Dir WASHINGTON DE OLIVEIRA VIEGAS.

Companhia Docas do Pará (CDP): Av. Pres. Vargas 41, 2° andar, 66010-000 Belém, PA; tel. (91) 216-2011; fax (91) 241-1741; f. 1967; administers the ports of Belém, Macapá, Porto Velho, Santarém and Vila do Conde, and the waterways of the Eastern Amazon (AHIMOR) and Tocantins and Araguaia (AHITAR); Dir-Pres. CARLOS ACATAUSSÚ NUNES.

Companhia Docas do Estado do Rio Grande do Norte (CODERN): Av. Hildebrando de Góis 2220, Ribeira, 59010-700 Natal, RN; tel. (84) 211-5311; fax (84) 221-6072; administers the ports of Areia Branca, Natal, Recife and Maceió; Dir EMILSON MEDEIROS DOS SANTOS.

Other State-owned Companies

Companhia de Navegação do Estado de Rio de Janeiro: Praça 15 de Novembro 21, 20010-010 Rio de Janeiro, RJ; tel. (21) 533-6661; fax (21) 252-0524; Pres. MARCOS TEIXEIRA.

Frota Nacional de Petroleiros (Fronape): Rua Carlos Seidl 188, CP 51015, 20931 Rio de Janeiro, RJ; tel. (21) 585-3355; f. 1953; fleet of tankers operated by the state petroleum company, PETROBRÁS, and the Ministry of Transport; Chair. ALBANO DE SOUZA GONÇALVES.

Private Companies

Companhia Docas de Imbituba (CDI): Porto de Imbituba, Av. Presidente Vargas s/n, 88780-000 Imbituba, SC; tel. (482) 55-0080; fax (482) 55-0701; administers the port of Imbituba; Exec. Dir. MANUEL ALVES DO VALE.

Companhia de Navegação do Norte (CONAN): Av. Rio Branco 23, 25° andar, 20090-003 Rio de Janeiro, RJ; tel. (21) 223-4155; fax (21) 253-7128; f. 1965; services to Brazil, Argentina, Uruguay and inland waterways; Chair. J. R. RIBEIRO SALOMÃO.

Empresa de Navegação Aliança, SA: Av. Pasteur 110, Botafogo, 22290-240 Rio de Janeiro, RJ; tel. (21) 546-1112; fax (21) 546-1161; f. 1950; cargo services to Argentina, Uruguay, Europe, Baltic, Atlantic and North Sea ports; Pres. CARLOS G. E. FISCHER.

Companhia de Navegação do São Francisco: Av. São Francisco 1517, 39270-000 Pirapora, MG; tel. (38) 741-1444; fax (38) 741-1164; Pres. JOSÉ HUMBERTO BARATA JABUR.

Frota Oceânica Brasileira, SA: Av. Venezuela 110, CP 21-020, 20081-310 Rio de Janeiro, RJ; tel. (21) 291-5153; fax (21) 263-1439; f. 1947; Pres. JOSÉ CARLOS FRAGOSO PIRES; Vice-Pres. LUIZ J. C. ALHANATI.

Serviço de Navegação Bacia Prata: Av. 14 de Março 1700, 79370-000 Ladário, MS; tel. (67) 231-4354; Dir LUIZ CARLOS DA SILVA ALEXANDRE.

Vale do Rio Doce Navegação, SA (DOCENAVE): Av. Graça Aranha 26, 8°–9° andar, 20005-900, Rio de Janerio, RJ; fax (21) 814-4971; internet www.docenave.com.br; bulk carrier to Japan, Arabian Gulf, Europe, North America and Argentina; Pres. ALVARO DE OLIVEIRA (Filho).

CIVIL AVIATION

There are about 1,500 airports and airstrips. Of the 67 principal airports 22 are international, although most international traffic is handled by the two airports at Rio de Janeiro and two at São Paulo.

Empresa Brasileira de Infra-Estrutura Aeroportuária (INFRAERO): SCS, Q 04, NR 58, Edif. Infraero, 6° andar, 70304-902 Brasília, DF; tel. (61) 312-3170; fax (61) 312-3105; e-mail fernandalima@infraero.gov.br; internet www.infraero.gov.br; Pres. EDUARDO BOGALHO PETTENGILL.

Principal Airlines

Lider Taxi Aéreo, SA: Av. Santa Rosa 123, 31270-750 Belo Horizonte, MG; tel. (31) 490-4500; fax (31) 490-4600; internet www.lidertaxiaereo.com.br; f. 1958; Pres. JOSÉ AFONSO ASSUMPÇÃO.

Nordeste: Av. Tancredo Neves 1672, Edif. Catabas Empresarial, 1° andar, Pituba, 41820-020 Salvador, BA; tel. (71) 341-7533; fax (71) 341-0393; e-mail nordeste@provider.com.br; internet www.voenordeste.com.br; f. 1976; services to 26 destinations in north-east Brazil; Pres. PERCY LOURENÇO RODRIGUES.

Pantanal Linhas Aéreas Sul-Matogrossenses, SA: Av. das Nações Unidas 10989, 8° andar, São Paulo, SP; tel. (11) 3040-3900; fax (11) 866-3424; e-mail pantanal@uninet.com.br; internet www.pantanal-airlines.com.br; f. 1993; regional services; Pres. MARCOS FERREIRA SAMPAIO.

Rio Sul: Av. Rio Branco 85, 11° andar, 20040-004 Rio de Janeiro, RJ; tel. (21) 263-4282; fax (21) 253-2044; internet www.voeriosul.com.br; f. 1976; subsidiary of VARIG; domestic passenger services to cities in southern Brazil; Pres. PAULO ENRIQUE MORÃES COCO.

TAM (Transportes Aéreos Regionais—TAM): Av. Pedro Bueno 1400, 04342-001 São Paulo, SP; tel. (11) 5582-8811; fax (11) 578-5946; e-mail tamimprensa@tam.com.br; internet www.tam.com.br; f. 1976; scheduled passenger and cargo services from São Paulo to destinations throughout Brazil; Pres. DANIEL MANDELLI MARTIN.

Transportes Aéreos Regionais da Bacia Amazônica (TABA): Av. Governador José Malcher 883, 66055-260 Belém, PA; tel. (91) 223-6300; fax (91) 223-0471; f. 1976; domestic passenger services throughout north-west Brazil; Chair. MARCÍLIO JACQUES GIBSON.

VARIG, SA (Viação Aérea Rio Grandense): Rua 18 de Novembro 120, 90240-040 Porto Alegre, RS; tel. (51) 358-4233; fax (51) 358-7001; internet www.varig.com.br; f. 1927; international services throughout North, Central and South America, Africa, Western Europe and Japan; domestic services to major Brazilian cities; cargo services; Chair. and Pres. FERNANDO PINTO.

VASP, SA (Viação Aérea São Paulo): Praça Comte-Lineu Gomes s/n, Aeroporto Congonhas, 04626-910 São Paulo, SP; tel. (11) 532-3000; fax (11) 542-0880; internet www.vasp.com.br; f. 1933; privatized in Sept. 1990; domestic services throughout Brazil; international services to Argentina, Belgium, the Caribbean, South Korea and the USA; Pres. WAGNER CANHEDO.

Tourism

In 2001 some 4.8m. tourists visited Brazil. Receipts from tourism totalled US $4,228m. in 2000. Rio de Janeiro, with its famous beaches, is the centre of the tourist trade. Like Salvador, Recife and other towns, it has excellent examples of Portuguese colonial and modern architecture. The modern capital, Brasília, incorporates a new concept of city planning and is the nation's show-piece. Other attractions are the Iguaçu Falls, the seventh largest (by volume) in the world, the tropical forests of the Amazon basin and the wildlife of the Pantanal.

Instituto Brasileiro de Turismo (EMBRATUR): SCN, Q 02, Bloco G, 3° andar, 70710-500 Brasília, DF; tel. (61) 224-9100; fax (61) 223-9889; internet www.embratur.gov.br; f. 1966; Pres. CAIO LUIZ DE CARVALHO.

Seção de Feiras e Turismo/Departamento de Promoção Comercial: Ministério das Relações Exteriores, Esplanada dos Ministérios, 5° andar, Sala 523, 70170-900 Brasília, DF; tel. (61) 411-6394; fax (61) 322-0833; e-mail docstt@mre.gov.br; internet www.braziltradenet.gov.br; f. 1977; organizes Brazil's participation in trade fairs and commercial exhibitions abroad; Principal Officer ANTÓNIO J. M. DE SOUZA E SILVA.

BRUNEI

Introductory Survey

Location, Climate, Language, Religion, Flag, Capital

The Sultanate of Brunei (Negara Brunei Darussalam) lies in South-East Asia, on the north-west coast of the island of Borneo (most of which is comprised of the Indonesian territory of Kalimantan). It is surrounded and bisected on the landward side by Sarawak, one of the two eastern states of Malaysia. The country has a tropical climate, characterized by consistent temperature and humidity. Annual rainfall averages about 2,540 mm (100 ins) in coastal areas and about 3,300 mm (130 ins) in the interior. Temperatures are high, with average daily temperatures ranging from 24°C (75°F) to 32°C (90°F). The principal language is Malay, although Chinese is also spoken and English is widely used. The Malay population (an estimated 66.7% of the total at the 2001 census) are mainly Sunni Muslims. Most of the Chinese in Brunei (11.1% of the population) are Buddhists, and some are adherents of Confucianism and Daoism. Europeans and Eurasians are predominantly Christians, and the majority of indigenous tribespeople (Iban, Dayak and Kelabit—3.5% of the population) adhere to various animist beliefs. The flag (proportions 1 by 2) is yellow, with two diagonal stripes, of white and black, running from the upper hoist to the lower fly; superimposed in the centre is the state emblem (in red, with yellow Arabic inscriptions). The capital is Bandar Seri Begawan (formerly called Brunei Town).

Recent History

Brunei, a traditional Islamic monarchy, formerly included most of the coastal regions of North Borneo (now Sabah) and Sarawak, which later became states of Malaysia. During the 19th century the rulers of Brunei ceded large parts of their territory to the United Kingdom, reducing the sultanate to its present size. In 1888, when North Borneo became a British Protectorate, Brunei became a British Protected State. In accordance with an agreement made in 1906, a British Resident was appointed to the court of the ruling Sultan as an adviser on administration. Under this arrangement, a form of government that included an advisory body, the State Council, emerged.

Brunei was invaded by Japanese forces in December 1941, but reverted to its former status in 1945, when the Second World War ended. The British-appointed Governor of Sarawak was High Commissioner for Brunei from 1948 until the territory's first written Constitution was promulgated in September 1959, when a further agreement was made between the Sultan and the British Government. The United Kingdom continued to be responsible for Brunei's defence and external affairs until the Sultanate's declaration of independence in 1984.

In December 1962 a large-scale revolt broke out in Brunei and in parts of Sarawak and North Borneo. The rebellion was undertaken by the 'North Borneo Liberation Army', an organization linked with the Parti Rakyat Brunei (PRB—Brunei People's Party), led by Sheikh Ahmad Azahari, which was strongly opposed to the planned entry of Brunei into the Federation of Malaysia. The rebels proclaimed the 'revolutionary State of North Kalimantan', but the revolt was suppressed, after 10 days' fighting, with the aid of British forces from Singapore. A state of emergency was declared, the PRB was banned, and Azahari was given asylum in Malaya. In the event, the Sultan of Brunei, Sir Omar Ali Saifuddin III, decided in 1963 against joining the Federation. From 1962 he ruled by decree, and the state of emergency remained in force. In October 1967 Saifuddin, who had been Sultan since 1950, abdicated in favour of his son, Hassanal Bolkiah, who was then 21 years of age. Under an agreement signed in November 1971, Brunei was granted full internal self-government.

In December 1975 the UN General Assembly adopted a resolution advocating British withdrawal from Brunei, the return of political exiles and the holding of a general election. Negotiations in 1978, following assurances by Malaysia and Indonesia that they would respect Brunei's sovereignty, resulted in an agreement (signed in January 1979) that Brunei would become fully independent within five years. Independence was duly proclaimed on 1 January 1984, and the Sultan took office as Prime Minister and Minister of Finance and of Home Affairs,

presiding over a Cabinet of six other ministers (including two of the Sultan's brothers and his father, the former Sultan).

The future of the Chinese population, which controlled much of Brunei's private commercial sector but had become stateless since independence, appeared threatened in 1985, when the Sultan indicated that Brunei would become an Islamic state in which the indigenous, mainly Malay, inhabitants, known as *bumiputras* ('sons of the soil'), would receive preferential treatment. Several Hong Kong and Taiwan Chinese, who were not permanent Brunei residents, were repatriated.

In May 1985 a new political party, the Parti Kebangsaan Demokratik Brunei (PKDB—Brunei National Democratic Party), was formed. The new party, which comprised business executives loyal to the Sultan, based its policies on Islam and a form of liberal nationalism. However, the Sultan forbade employees of the Government (about 40% of the country's working population) to join the party. Persons belonging to the Chinese community were also excluded from membership. Divisions within the new party led to the formation of a second group, the Parti Perpaduan Kebangsaan Brunei (PPKB—Brunei National Solidarity Party), in February 1986. This party, which also received the Sultan's official approval, placed greater emphasis on co-operation with the Government, and was open to both Muslim and non-Muslim ethnic groups.

Although the Sultan was not expected to allow any relaxation of restrictions on radical political activities, it became clear during 1985 and 1986 that a more progressive style of government was being adopted. The death of Sir Omar Ali Saifuddin, the Sultan's father, in September 1986 was expected to accelerate modernization. In October the Cabinet was enlarged to 11 members, and commoners and aristocrats were assigned portfolios that had previously been given to members of the royal family. In February 1988, however, the PKDB was dissolved by the authorities after it had demanded the resignation of the Sultan as Head of Government (although not as Head of State), an end to the 26-year state of emergency and the holding of democratic elections. The official reason for the dissolution of the party was its connections with a foreign organization, the Pacific Democratic Union. The leaders of the PKDB, Abdul Latif Hamid and Abdul Latif Chuchu, were arrested, under the provisions of the Internal Security Act, and detained until March 1990. Abdul Latif Hamid died in May of that year. In January 1990 the Government ordered the release of six political prisoners, who had been detained soon after the revolt in 1962.

In 1990 the Government encouraged the population to embrace *Melayu Islam Beraja* (Malay Islamic Monarchy) as the state ideology. This affirmation of traditional Bruneian values for Malay Muslims was widely believed to be a response to an increase in social problems, including the abuse of alcohol and mild narcotics. Muslims were encouraged to adhere more closely to the tenets of Islam, greater emphasis was laid on Islamic holiday celebrations, and the distribution of alcohol was discouraged.

Extremely moderate progress towards reform was apparent in subsequent years. In 1994 a constitutional committee, appointed by the Government and chaired by the Minister of Foreign Affairs, Prince Mohamad Bolkiah, submitted a recommendation that the Constitution be amended to provide for an elected legislature. In February 1995 the PPKB was given permission to convene a general assembly, at which Abdul Latif Chuchu, the former Secretary-General of the PKDB, was elected President. Latif Chuchu was, however, compelled to resign shortly afterwards, owing to a condition of his release from detention in 1990. In May 1998 the PKDB was permitted to hold a further annual general meeting, at which Hatta Zainal Abidin, the son of a former opposition leader, was elected party President.

In February 1997 the Sultan replaced his brother, Prince Jefri Bolkiah, as Minister of Finance. It was rumoured that the Sultan's assumption of the finance portfolio was due to alleged financial disagreements rather than Prince Jefri's frequently criticized extravagant lifestyle. In March the Sultan and Prince Jefri denied accusations of misconduct made by a former winner of a US beauty contest, Shannon Marketic. A US court granted the Sultan immunity from legal action in August, owing to his status as a foreign head of state; this immunity was extended to Prince Jefri in March 1998. Similar allegations against Prince Jefri, submitted to a court in Hawaii, resulted in an undisclosed financial settlement, following the judge's rejection of Prince Jefri's claims to immunity. Marketic subsequently appealed against the granting of exemption from prosecution in her case. Further allegations concerning the extravagant lifestyle of Prince Jefri emerged in a court case in the United Kingdom in February, in which Jefri was being sued for £80m. by two former business associates, Watche (Bob) and Rafi Manoukian. The Manoukian brothers claimed that Prince Jefri had reneged on two property agreements; Prince Jefri was counter-suing them for £100m., alleging that they had exploited their relationship with him to amass considerable wealth. The case, which was unreported in Brunei, was also settled out of court for an undisclosed sum.

Following the dismissal in March 1998, after 14 years in office, of Dato' Dr Haji Johar bin Dato' Haji Noordin, reportedly owing to the inadequacy of his response to the haze over Brunei caused by forest fires in Indonesia and Malaysia, Abdul Aziz assumed responsibility for the health portfolio. The resignations of the Attorney-General, Pengiran Haji Bahrin bin Pengiran Haji Abbas (who was granted leave from his position as Minister of Law), and of the Solicitor-General were accepted by the Sultan in June. An acting Attorney-General and Solicitor-General were appointed, while the Sultan assumed temporary responsibility for the law portfolio. On 10 August the Sultan's son, Prince Al-Muhtadee Billah Bolkiah, was installed as the heir to the throne.

Prince Jefri, who had left Brunei in April 1998, was removed as Chairman of the Brunei Investment Agency (BIA), which controls the country's overseas investments, at the end of July, following the collapse earlier in the month of his business conglomerate, the Amedeo Development Corporation. (The Amedeo Development Corporation was formally liquidated by the High Court of Brunei in July 1999, with reported debts of at least US $3,500m.) Prince Jefri was also removed from the boards of seven communications companies. He claimed that he was the victim of a conspiracy of conservative Islamists, led by his estranged brother, Prince Mohamad Bolkiah (the Minister of Foreign Affairs), and the Minister of Education, Pehin Dato' Haji Abdul Aziz bin Pehin Haji Umar. Prince Jefri's removal from positions of authority took place amid a more rigorous enforcement of the ban on alcohol and the confiscation from retailers of non-Islamic religious artefacts. Abdul Aziz, who replaced Prince Jefri as Chairman of the BIA, also headed an investigation (which was initiated in June) into the finances of the BIA. In September Abdul Aziz announced that large amounts of government funds had been misappropriated during Prince Jefri's tenure as Chairman. In January 2000, following a long period during which the Government made no significant comment about the misappropriation of BIA funds or about the role of the Sultan's younger brother in the affair, Prince Jefri returned to Brunei after many months of self-imposed exile. Private negotiations ensued between Prince Jefri and the parties involved in the investigation. These negotiations failed, however, and in February the Government and the BIA began civil proceedings against Prince Jefri, alleging his improper withdrawal and use of substantial BIA funds during the period in which he had served as Minister of Finance and Chairman of the BIA; 71 other people were named in the action, including Prince Jefri's eldest son, Prince Muda Abdul Hakeem, and his private secretary. In May an out-of-court settlement was reached between Prince Jefri and the prosecuting parties, in accordance with which all of Prince Jefri's assets, both in Brunei and overseas, that had been acquired with funds derived from the BIA were to be returned to the State. These assets were sold for £5.5m. at a public auction in August 2001.

In October 2000 Haji Awang Kassim, Prince Jefri's former confidential secretary, who was also former deputy managing director of the BIA and a prominent figure in Amedeo management, was arrested, following his extradition from the Philippines. Civil proceedings were also instigated against another six of Prince Jefri's former colleagues. In the mean time, legal wrangling over responsibility for Amedeo's huge losses continued. In November 2000 a meeting of Amedeo creditors resulted in angry outbursts when they rejected initial compensatory terms offered by the BIA. In October 2001 the Sultan, dissatisfied with the unsuccessful and expensive attempts by

leading international accountancy and law companies, requested his newly created local company, Global Evergreen, to resolve the long-standing dispute with more than 300 creditors who were owed an estimated B $1,000m. Negotiations proceeded swiftly, and creditors were strongly recommended to accept a new, highly favourable offer whereby they would be repaid on a 'sliding scale' according to the magnitude of their claim. Larger claims would be dealt with on an individual basis. The settlement brought to an end much of the legal contention arising from the Government's closure of the company two years previously.

In May 2002 it was reported that 13 foreign Global Evergreen employees (of whom three were citizens of Australia, four of the United Kingdom, five of New Zealand and one of Malaysia), who had been investigating the whereabouts of the state funds that had disappeared as a result of the Amedeo scandal, had been refused permission to leave the country, ostensibly owing to visa irregularities. It was thought that, during the course of their investigation, they had angered both the Chairman of the company, Minister of Education Pehin Dato' Haji Abdul Aziz bin Pehin Haji Umar, and the Minister of Home Affairs, Pehin Dato' Haji Isa bin Pehin Haji Ibrahim. They were granted permission to leave Brunei shortly afterwards. In August the Sultan formally swore in Dato' Seri Paduka Dr Haji Ahmad bin Haji Jumat as the Minister of Development and Pehin Dato' Haji Abu Bakar bin Haji Apong as the Minister of Health.

In February 2000 the Brunei Darussalam Economic Council (BDEC), which had been established in September 1998 to explore ways of improving the Sultanate's economy, released a report in which it warned that Brunei's economy was becoming increasingly unsustainable. The report was endorsed by the Sultan, who appointed Prince Mohamad to oversee the implementation of the economic recovery plan recommended by the BDEC. In his address to mark Brunei's 16th National Day, also in February, the Sultan focused on the issue of the economy and the importance of the development of alternative sources of revenue, in an unprecedented acknowledgement of the country's fundamental economic problems. In November 2000 the Sultan launched the Islamic Development Bank of Brunei, as part of his efforts to create an international Islamic banking centre and transform Brunei into one of the region's most important financial centres.

Relations with the United Kingdom, meanwhile, had become strained during 1983, following the Brunei Government's decision, in August, to transfer the management of its investment portfolio from the British Crown Agents to the newly created BIA. However, normal relations were restored in September, when the British Government agreed that a battalion of Gurkha troops, stationed in Brunei since 1971, should remain in Brunei after independence, at the Sultanate's expense, specifically to guard the oil and gas fields.

Brunei has developed close relations with the members of the Association of South East Asian Nations (ASEAN, see p. 146), in particular Singapore, and became a full member of the organization immediately after independence. Brunei also joined the UN, the Commonwealth (see p. 164) and the Organization of the Islamic Conference (see p. 295) in 1984. In September 1992 Brunei was formally admitted to the Non-aligned Movement (see p. 350). In late 1991 Brunei established diplomatic relations with the People's Republic of China at ambassadorial level. As a member of ASEAN, Brunei's relations with Viet Nam improved during 1991 (following Viet Nam's withdrawal from Cambodia in September 1989). In February 1992 diplomatic relations were formally established with Viet Nam during a visit to Brunei of the Vietnamese Prime Minister. In October 1993 the Brunei Government announced the establishment of diplomatic relations at ambassadorial level with Myanmar.

In July 1990, in response to the uncertainty over the future of US bases in the Philippines (see the chapter on the Philippines), Brunei joined Singapore in offering the USA the option of operating its forces from Brunei. A bilateral memorandum of understanding was subsequently signed, providing for up to three visits a year to Brunei by US warships. Under the memorandum, Brunei forces were to train with US personnel.

Conflicting claims (from Brunei, Viet Nam, the People's Republic of China, the Philippines, Malaysia and Taiwan) to all, or some, of the uninhabited Spratly Islands, situated in the South China Sea, remained a source of tension in the region. Brunei is the only claimant not to have stationed troops on the islands, which are both strategically important and possess potentially large reserves of petroleum. During the 1990s attempts to resolve the dispute through a negotiated settlement resulted in little progress, and military activity in the area increased. Talks at the annual summit meeting of ASEAN ministers of foreign affairs held in Hanoi, Viet Nam, in July 2001 failed to make any further advances in ending the impasse. However, during the annual ASEAN summit meeting held in Phnom-Penh, Cambodia, in November 2002, the members of the grouping signed an agreement with China approving a 'code of conduct' for the islands, which was aimed at resolving the conflict.

In February 2000 Brunei hosted its first Asia-Pacific Economic Co-operation (APEC, see p. 139) Senior Officials' Meeting, attended by 3,000 delegates from 21 countries. In April an ASEAN Regional Forum (ARF) meeting to discuss security issues was held in Brunei. In November Brunei hosted the annual summit meeting of APEC leaders; attended by some 6,000 delegates, this was the largest international event ever held in the country.

In an attempt to promote tourism and enhance the nation's international standing, in January 2001 the Sultan launched 'Visit Brunei Year' and 'Visit ASEAN Year 2002', in association with the regional Asian Tourism Forum. In August 2001 Brunei was the venue for the first International Islamic Exposition, attended by representatives from 25 other countries. In November Brunei hosted the seventh summit meeting of ASEAN leaders, which was also attended by representatives from the People's Republic of China, Japan and South Korea. At the end of the meeting Brunei pledged its support for a programme proposed by Philippine President Gloria Macapagal Arroyo, which focused on encouraging close regional co-operation in countering international terrorism in the aftermath of the September suicide attacks on the USA. In late July and early August 2002 the 35th ASEAN Ministerial Meeting, the ninth ARF and the Post-Ministerial Meeting were held in Brunei; ASEAN leaders subsequently signed a Declaration on Counter-Terrorism with the USA. In September 2002 the 34th ASEAN Economic Ministers' Meeting was also convened in the country.

Government

The 1959 Constitution confers supreme executive authority on the Sultan. He is assisted and advised by four Constitutional Councils: the Religious Council, the Privy Council, the Council of Cabinet Ministers and the Council of Succession. Since the rebellion of 1962 certain provisions of the Constitution (including those pertaining to elections and to a fifth Council, the Legislative Council) have been suspended, and the Sultan has ruled by decree.

Defence

At 1 August 2002 the Royal Brunei Malay Regiment numbered 7,000 (including 700 women): army 4,900; navy 1,000; air force 1,100. Military service is voluntary, but only Malays are eligible for service. Paramilitary forces comprised 1,750 Royal Brunei Police. Defence expenditure in 2002 was budgeted at an estimated B $455m. One Gurkha battalion of the British army, comprising about 1,100 men, has been stationed in Brunei since 1971. There are also about 500 troops from Singapore, operating a training school in Brunei.

Economic Affairs

In 1998, according to estimates by the World Bank, Brunei's gross national income (GNI), measured at average 1996–98 prices, was US $7,754m., equivalent to US $24,100 per head (or US $24,910 on an international purchasing-power parity basis). In 1990–2001, it was estimated, the population increased by an annual average of 2.7%, while gross domestic product (GDP) per head decreased, in real terms, by an average of 0.7% per year during 1990–98. Brunei's overall GDP increased at an estimated average annual rate of 1.5% during 1990–2000. Real GDP grew by an estimated 2.8% in 2000 and by an estimated 1.5% in 2001.

Agriculture (including forestry and fishing) employed an estimated 0.8% of the working population in 2000 and provided 2.7% of GDP in 2001. In 2000 an estimated 1.3% of the total land area was cultivated; the principal crops include rice, cassava, bananas and pineapples. In the 1990s Brunei imported about 80% of its total food requirements. Owing to the increasing emphasis on Islamic values in Brunei, a severe shortage of meat was caused in 1999 following a decision to ensure that all food was *halal* (slaughtered in accordance with Islamic traditions) by either imposing supervisors in foreign abattoirs or by slaughtering imported livestock in Brunei. During 1990–98 agricultural GDP increased, in real terms, at an average annual rate of

2.7%. Agricultural GDP increased by an estimated 1.8% in 2000 and by an estimated 2.3% in 2001.

Industry (comprising mining, manufacturing, construction and utilities) employed 24.1% of the working population in 1991 and contributed an estimated 46.4% of GDP in 2001. Total industrial GDP increased at an average annual rate of 1.2% in 1990–98. Industrial GDP, including oil and gas services, increased by an average of 6.6% per year in 1993–97. Industrial GDP increased by an estimated 2.1% in 1997, and declined by 1.0% in 1998.

Brunei's economy depends almost entirely on its petroleum and natural gas resources. Mining and quarrying employed only 5.0% of the working population in 1991, but the petroleum sector provided an estimated 36.3% of GDP in 2001. Proven reserves of petroleum at the end of 2001 amounted to 1,400m. barrels, sufficient to sustain production at that year's levels (averaging 195,000 barrels per day) for less than 20 years. Output of natural gas in 2001 totalled 11,400m. cu m, from proven reserves at the end of that year of some 390,000m. cu m (sustainable for less than 35 years). Crude petroleum, natural gas and petroleum products together accounted for an estimated 89.7% of total export earnings in 2000. The GDP of the petroleum and gas sector declined by an annual average of 0.3% in 1990–97 and by an estimated 1.6% in 1998. However, in 2000 it recovered by an estimated 3.2%.

Manufacturing is dominated by petroleum refining. The sector employed 3.8% of the working population in 1991 (increasing to 5.4% in 1995) and, together with mining and quarrying, contributed an estimated 40.2% of GDP in 2001. Since the mid-1980s Brunei has attempted to expand its manufacturing base. In the mid-1990s the textile industry provided the largest non-oil and -gas revenue; other industries included cement, mineral water, canned food, dairy products, silica sands products, footwear and leather products, the design and manufacture of printed circuits, publishing and printing. Manufacturing GDP (including mining and quarrying) increased by an estimated 3.5% in 2000 and by an estimated 1.0% in 2001.

Services employed 73.7% of the working population in 1991 and provided 50.9% of GDP in 2001. In that year the sector comprising wholesale and retail trade, restaurants and hotels contributed 9.0% of GDP, and the finance sector also 9.0%. Plans are under way to develop Brunei as a regional centre for finance and banking. The GDP of the banking and finance sector increased by an annual average of 7.7% in 1993–97 and by an estimated 3.8% in 1998. The tourism sector is also being actively promoted as an important part of Brunei's policy of diversification away from its reliance on petroleum and natural gas; 2001 was designated 'Visit Brunei Year'. In 2000 1.3m. people visited Brunei, and in 1998 receipts from tourism totalled US $37m. During 1990–98 the combined GDP of the service sectors increased, in real terms, at an average rate of 3.5% per year. GDP of the services sector increased by an estimated 7.1% in 1997 and by 3.9% in 1998.

In 2001 Brunei recorded a visible trade surplus of B $4,553.6m. and, as a result of high investment income from abroad, in the same year there was a surplus of $6,789.1m. on the current account of the balance of payments. In 2001 the principal source of imports (23.4%) was Singapore; other major suppliers were Malaysia, the USA, the United Kingdom and Japan. The principal market for exports in that year was Japan, which accounted for 46.0% of total exports (mainly natural gas on a long-term contract); other significant purchasers were the Republic of Korea (also a purchaser of natural gas), Thailand and Singapore. Principal imports comprised basic manufactures, machinery and transport equipment, food and live animals and miscellaneous manufactured articles; principal exports were mineral fuels and lubricants.

In 1997 there was a budgetary deficit of B $27m. (equivalent to 0.3% of GDP). Brunei has no external public debt. International reserves were unofficially estimated at US $38,000m. in 1997 but were estimated to have declined to US $20,000m. in late 1998. Annual inflation averaged 1.9% in 1992–2001; consumer prices increased by 1.2% in 2000 and by 0.6% in 2001. Foreign workers, principally from Malaysia and the Philippines, have helped to ease the labour shortage resulting from the small size of the population, and comprised about 41% of the labour force in 2000, compared with 30% in 1998 (owing to an exodus of foreign workers in that year). However, the rate of unemployment was estimated at 4.7% in 2001, reflecting a shortage of non-manual jobs for the well-educated Bruneians.

Brunei is a member of the Association of South East Asian Nations (ASEAN, see p. 146). In October 1991 the member states formally announced the establishment of the ASEAN Free Trade Area (AFTA), which was to be implemented over 15 years (later reduced to 10), and, as a member of ASEAN, Brunei endorsed Malaysia's plan for an East Asia Economic Caucus. AFTA was formally established in 2002. Brunei was a founder member of the Asia-Pacific Economic Co-operation forum (APEC, see p. 139), initiated in November 1989, and is also a member of the UN Economic and Social Commission for Asia and the Pacific (ESCAP), which aims to accelerate economic progress in the region. In 1994 the East ASEAN Growth Area (EAGA) was established, encompassing Mindanao, in the Philippines, Sarawak and Sabah, in Malaysia, Kalimantan and Sulawesi, in Indonesia, and Brunei.

The eighth (2001–05) National Development Plan continued the emphasis of the sixth (1991–95) and seventh (1996–2000) Plans on diversification of the economy to reduce the country's dependence on income from petroleum and natural gas. In 1996 the Government announced proposals to develop Brunei as a Service Hub for Trade and Tourism (SHuTT) by 2003, following earlier plans for the development of the private sector and the conversion of Brunei into a regional centre for banking and finance. Various measures were taken to accelerate the broadening of Brunei's economic base, which had been impeded by high labour costs, a limited internal market and lack of a domestic entrepreneurial culture. However, the regional financial crisis, which began in 1997, resulted in the depreciation of the Brunei dollar, a decrease in income from the stock market and a sharp reduction in tourist arrivals, owing to the recession in other Asian countries. The situation was compounded by a significant decline in the international price of petroleum from mid-1997, by the huge financial losses arising from alleged mismanagement of the Brunei Investment Agency (BIA), and by the collapse of the Amedeo Development Corporation, which was responsible for many building projects in Brunei (see Recent History). In an attempt to address the economic situation, budgetary allocations were drastically reduced, halting much government investment (although complaints from the business community caused the Government to reverse some decisions). Service industries were then also adversely affected by the exodus of thousands of unemployed foreign workers. Concerns over the future of the Sultanate's economy increased; a report released by the Brunei Darussalam Economic Council (BDEC) in February 2000 warned of its unsustainable nature. In December 2000, however, the discovery of significant new oil and gas reserves by Brunei Shell Petroleum provided a stimulus for renewed activity in the petroleum sector, although a further downturn in world oil prices in the latter part of 2001 compounded losses in other sectors of the economy, which continued to suffer the effects of the regional economic deceleration. While the disputes arising from the collapse of the Amedeo Corporation were largely resolved by the Sultan's formation of Global Evergreen Sdn Bhd in 2001, foreign investors continued to be deterred by the repercussions of the scandal. In early 2003 the Brunei Economic Development Board announced plans to attract foreign investment in the country through the solicitation of proposals for the development of a gas pipeline, power plant and jetty at Sungai Liang, as well as the development of an

additional port facility; it was hoped that the projects would create an estimated 6,000 jobs and attract US $4,500m. of investment over the next five years.

Education

Education is free and is compulsory for 12 years from the age of five years. Islamic studies form an integral part of the school curriculum. Pupils who are Brunei citizens and reside more than 8 km (5 miles) from their schools are entitled to free accommodation in hostels, free transport or a subsistence allowance. Schools are classified according to the language of instruction, i.e. Malay, English or Chinese (Mandarin). In 1996 enrolment at pre-primary level was equivalent to 53% of children in the relevant age-group (males 53%; females 53%). Primary education lasts for six years from the age of six years. Secondary education, usually beginning at 12 years of age, lasts for seven years, comprising a first cycle of three years (lower secondary), a second of two years (upper secondary) and a third of two years (pre-tertiary). In 1996 enrolment at primary level was equivalent to 106% of children in the relevant age-group (males 109%; females 104%), while the comparable enrolment ratio at secondary level was 77% (males 72%; females 82%). In 2001 there were six vocational colleges, one teacher-training college, two institutes of higher education and one university. The University of Brunei Darussalam was formally established in 1985, but many students continue to attend universities abroad, at government expense. In 1994 enrolment at tertiary level was equivalent to 6.6% of the relevant age-group (males 5.3%; females 8.0%). Of total ordinary expenditure by the Government in 1997, B $347m. (13.5%) was for the Ministry of Education.

Public Holidays

2003: 1 January (New Year's Day), 1 February* (Chinese New Year), 12 February† (Hari Raya Aidiladha, Feast of the Sacrifice), 23 February (National Day), 5 March† (Hijrah, Islamic New Year), 14 May† (Hari Mouloud, Birth of the Prophet), 31 May (Royal Brunei Armed Forces Day), 15 July (Sultan's Birthday), 24 September† (Israk Mikraj, Ascension of the Prophet Muhammad), 27 October† (Beginning of Ramadan), 12 November† (Memperingati Nuzul Al-Quran, Anniversary of the Revelation of the Koran), 26 November† (Hari Raya Aidilfitri, end of Ramadan).

2004: 1 January (New Year's Day), 22 January* (Chinese New Year), 2 February† (Hari Raya Aidiladha, Feast of the Sacrifice), 22 February† (Hijrah, Islamic New Year), 23 February (National Day), 2 May† (Hari Mouloud, Birth of the Prophet), 31 May (Royal Brunei Armed Forces Day), 15 July (Sultan's Birthday), 12 September† (Israk Mikraj, Ascension of the Prophet Muhammad), 15 October† (Beginning of Ramadan), 31 October† (Memperingati Nuzul Al-Quran, Anniversary of the Revelation of the Koran), 14 November† (Hari Raya Aidilfitri, end of Ramadan).

* The first day of the first moon of the lunar calendar.

† These holidays are dependent on the Islamic lunar calendar and may vary by one or two days from the dates given.

Weights and Measures

The imperial system is in operation but local measures of weight and capacity are used. These include the gantang (1 gallon), the tahil (11/3 oz) and the kati (11/3 lb).

Statistical Survey

Source (unless otherwise stated): Department of Economic Planning and Development, Ministry of Finance, Bandar Seri Begawan 2012; tel. (2) 241991; fax (2) 226132; internet www.depd.gov.bn.

AREA AND POPULATION

Area: 5,765 sq km (2,226 sq miles); *By district:* Brunei/Muara 570 sq km (220 sq miles), Seria/Belait 2,725 sq km (1,052 sq miles), Tutong 1,165 sq km (450 sq miles), Temburong 1,305 sq km (504 sq miles).

Population (excluding transients afloat): 260,482 at census of 7 August 1991; 332,844 (males 168,925, females 163,919) at census of 21 August 2001. *By district* (2001 census): Brunei/Muara 230,030; Seria/Belait 55,602; Tutong 38,649; Temburong 8,563.

Density (2001 census): 57.7 per sq km.

Ethnic Groups (2001 census): Malay 222,145, Chinese 37,039, Other indigenous 11,658, Others 62,002, Total 332,844.

Principal Towns: Bandar Seri Begawan (capital): population 27,285 at 2001 census, 45,900 at 1991 census; Kuala Belait: population 21,200 at 1991 census; Seria: population 21,100 at 1991 census; Tutong: population 13,000 at 1991 census.

Births, Marriages and Deaths (registrations, 2000): Live births 7,481 (birth rate 22.1 per 1,000); Deaths 965 (death rate 2.9 per 1,000); Marriages (1999) 2,089 (marriage rate 6.3 per 1,000). *2001:* Birth rate 21.9 per 1,000; Death rate 2.9 per 1,000; Registered marriages 2,091.

Expectation of Life (WHO estimates, years at birth): 74.4 (males 73.2; females 75.9) in 2001. Source: WHO, *World Health Report.*

Economically Active Population (persons aged 15 years and over, 1991 census): Agriculture, hunting, forestry and fishing 2,162; Mining and quarrying 5,327; Manufacturing 4,070; Electricity, gas and water 2,223; Construction 14,145; Trade, restaurants and hotels 15,404; Transport, storage and communications 5,392; Financing, insurance, real estate and business services 5,807; Community, social and personal services 52,121; Activities not adequately defined 95; *Total employed* 106,746 (males 72,338; females 34,408); Unemployed 5,209 (males 2,745; females 2,464); *Total labour force* 111,955 (males 75,083; females 36,872). *Mid-2001 (estimate)* Total labour force 157,000.

HEALTH AND WELFARE

Key Indicators

Total Fertility Rate (children per woman, 2001): 2.6.

Under-5 Mortality Rate (per 1,000 live births, 2001): 6.

HIV/AIDS (% of persons aged 15–49, 1999): 0.2.

Physicians (per 1,000 head, 1995): 0.85.

Health Expenditure (2000): US $ per head (PPP): 618.

Health Expenditure (2000): % of GDP: 3.1.

Health Expenditure (2000): public (% of total): 80.0.

Human Development Index (2000): ranking: 32.

Human Development Index (2000): value: 0.856.
For sources and definitions, see explanatory note on p. vi.

AGRICULTURE, ETC.

Principal Crops (estimates, '000 metric tons, 2001): Rice (paddy) 0.4, Vegetables 8.8, Fruit and arable crops 4.1.

Livestock ('000 head, 2001): Cattle 1.6, Buffaloes 5.7, Goats 2.4, Poultry 10,540.

Livestock Products ('000 metric tons, 2001): Beef and veal 16.2; Poultry meat 5.3; Poultry eggs 4.3 (FAO estimate); Cattle hides (fresh) 2.7. Source: FAO.

Forestry ('000 cubic metres, 2001): Round timber 107.2; Sawn timber 39.7; Firewood 0.1; Poles ('000 pieces) 67.3.

Fishing (metric tons, live weight, 2001): Capture 3,500; Aquaculture 339; Total catch 3,839. Source: FAO, *Yearbook of Fishery Statistics*.

MINING

Production (2001, estimates): Crude petroleum ('000 barrels, incl. condensate) 71,000; Natural gas (million cu m, gross) 11,000. Source: US Geological Survey.

INDUSTRY

Production ('000 barrels, unless otherwise indicated, 2001, estimates): Motor spirit (petrol) 1,600; Distillate fuel oils 1,100; Residual fuel oil 500; Cement ('000 metric tons) 227; Electric energy (million kWh, 2000) 2,579. Source: mainly US Geological Survey.

FINANCE

Currency and Exchange Rates: 100 sen (cents) = 1 Brunei dollar (B $). *Sterling, US Dollar and Euro Equivalents* (31 December 2002): £1 sterling = B $2.7989; US $1 = B $1.7365; €1 = B $1.8211; B $100 = £35.73 = US $57.59 = €54.91. *Average Exchange Rate* (Brunei dollars per US $): 1.7240 in 2000; 1.7917 in 2001; 1.7906 in 2002. Note: The Brunei dollar is at par with the Singapore dollar.

Budget (B $ million, 1997): *Revenue:* Tax revenue 1,561 (Import duty 224, Corporate income tax 1,333); Non-tax revenue 1,282 (Commercial receipts 303, Property income 957); Transfers from Brunei Investment Agency 1,146; Total 3,989. *Expenditure:* Ordinary expenditure 2,564 (Prime Minister's Office 183, Defence 548, Foreign Affairs 116, Finance 502, Home Affairs 94, Education 347, Industry and Primary Resources 43, Religious Affairs 113, Development 286, Health 178); Other current expenditure 36; Capital expenditure 1,350; Investment in public enterprises by Brunei Investment Agency 67; Total 4,016. *1998 (B $ million, estimates):* Revenue 2,775 (excl. transfers from Brunei Investment Agency); Expenditure 4,295 (excl. investment by Brunei Investment Agency). Source: IMF, *Brunei Darussalam: Recent Economic Developments* (April 1999).

Money Supply (B $ million, 2001): Currency outside banks 648.3; Demand deposits at banks 1,724.7; Total money 2,373.0.

Cost of Living (Consumer Price Index; base: 1990 = 100): All items 120.2 in 1999; 121.7 in 2000 (Food 117.8; Clothing and footwear 135.7; Housing 107.2; Transport and communication 137.8; Miscellaneous 122.2); 122.4 in 2001 (Food 118.4; Clothing and footwear 134.5; Housing 107.4; Transport and communication 139.6; Miscellaneous 123.3).

Gross Domestic Product by Economic Activity (B $ million in current prices, 2001): Agriculture, hunting, forestry and fishing 210.0; Mining, quarrying and manufacturing 3,140.9; Electricity, gas and water 65.2; Construction 425.2; Trade, restaurants and hotels 705.0; Transport, storage and communications 434.4; Finance, insurance, real estate and business services 701.0; Community, social and personal services 2,138.7; *Sub-total* 7,820.4; *Less* Imputed bank service charge 201.2; *GDP in purchasers' values* 7,619.2.

Balance of Payments (B $ million, 2001): Exports of goods 6,521.8; Imports of goods −1,968.2; *Trade balance* 4,553.6; Exports of services 863.6; Imports of services −1,887.5; *Balance on goods and services* 3,529.7; Other income received 3,764.7; Other income paid −329.9; *Balance on goods, services and income* 6,964.5; Current transfers received 0; Current transfers paid −175.4; *Current balance* 6,789.1; Foreign investment (net) 448.6; Long-term capital (net) −3,605.9; Short-term capital (net) 330.

EXTERNAL TRADE

Principal Commodities (B $ million, 2001): *Imports c.i.f.:* Food and live animals 341.27; Chemicals 157.83; Basic manufactures 636.80; Machinery and transport equipment 630.17; Miscellaneous manufactured articles 228.95; Total (incl. others) 2,076.39. *Exports f.o.b.:* Mineral fuels, lubricants, etc. 5,826.72; Machinery and transport equipment 260.72; Miscellaneous manufactured articles 295.65; Total (incl. others) 6,521.76.

Principal Trading Partners (B $ million, 2001): *Imports:* Australia 72.2; People's Republic of China 67.6; France 35.1; Germany 70.8; Hong Kong 104.6; Indonesia 47.8; Italy 93.0; Japan 133.2; Republic of Korea 30.8; Malaysia 456.3; Netherlands 18.1; Singapore 486.9; United Kingdom 82.9; USA 190.0; Total (incl. others) 2,076.4. *Exports:* Japan 2,999.0; Republic of Korea 773.4; Malaysia 42.9; Singapore 549.6; Thailand 770.6; USA 491.7; Total (incl. others) 6,521.8.

TRANSPORT

Road Traffic (registered vehicles, 2001): Private cars 188,720, Goods vehicles 17,828, Motorcycles and scooters 7,162, Buses and taxis 2,267, Others 4,470.

Merchant Fleet (displacement, '000 grt at 31 December): 362.0 in 1999; 361.7 in 2000; 362.7 in 2001. Source: Lloyd's Register-Fairplay, *World Fleet Statistics*.

International Sea-borne Shipping (freight traffic, freight tons, 2001): Goods loaded 103,082; Goods unloaded 891,976. Note: One freight ton equals 40 cubic feet (1.133 cubic metres) of cargo.

Civil Aviation (2001): Passenger arrivals 530,552, passenger departures 522,576; freight loaded 9,699 metric tons, freight unloaded 14,610 metric tons; mail loaded 37 metric tons, mail unloaded 223 metric tons.

TOURISM

Visitor Arrivals by Nationality (incl. excursionists, 2000): Indonesia 68,527; Malaysia 974,132; Philippines 65,842; Singapore 27,995; United Kingdom 43,865; Total (incl. others) 1,306,764.

Tourism Receipts (US $ million): 38 in 1996; 39 in 1997; 37 in 1998. Source: World Bank.

COMMUNICATIONS MEDIA

Radio Receivers (2000, estimate): 362,712 in use.

Television Receivers (2000, estimate): 216,223 in use.

Telephones (2000): 82,600 direct exchange lines in use.

Facsimile Machines (1996, estimate): 2,000 in use. Source: UN, *Statistical Yearbook*.

Mobile Cellular Telephones (2001): 131,246 subscribers.

Personal Computers ('000 in use, 2001 estimate): 25. Source: International Telecommunication Union.

Internet Users ('000, 2001): 35.0. Source: International Telecommunication Union.

Book Production (1992): 45 titles. (1990): 25 titles; 56,000 copies. Source: UNESCO, *Statistical Yearbook*.

Newspapers (2001): Daily 4; Non-daily 3 (English 2, with circulation of 22,000 copies; Malay 3, with circulation of 39,500 copies; Malay and English 1, with circulation of 9,000 copies).

Other Periodicals (1998): 15 (estimated combined circulation 132,000 copies per issue).

EDUCATION

Pre-primary and Primary: 186 schools; 3,806 teachers; 59,369 pupils in 2001.

General Secondary: 40 schools; 2,891 teachers; 34,809 pupils in 2001.

Teacher Training: 1 college; 51 teachers; 247 pupils in 2001.

Vocational: 6 colleges; 505 teachers; 2,509 pupils in 2001.

Higher Education: 3 institutes (incl. 1 university); 403 teachers; 3,885 students in 2001.

Adult literacy rate (UNESCO estimates): 91.5% (males 94.6%; females 88.1%) in 2000. Source: UN Development Programme, *Human Development Report*.

Directory

The Constitution

Note: Certain sections of the Constitution relating to elections and the Legislative Council have been in abeyance since 1962

A new Constitution was promulgated on 29 September 1959 (and amended significantly in 1971 and 1984). Under its provisions, sovereign authority is vested in the Sultan and Yang Di-Pertuan, who is assisted and advised by five Councils: the Religious Council, the Privy Council, the Council of Cabinet Ministers, the (inactive) Legislative Council and the Council of Succession. Power of appointment to the Councils is exercised by the Sultan.

The 1959 Constitution established the Chief Minister as the most senior official, with the British High Commissioner as adviser to the Government on all matters except those relating to Muslim and Malay customs.

In 1971 amendments were introduced reducing the power of the British Government, which retained responsibility for foreign affairs, while defence became the joint responsibility of both countries.

In 1984 further amendments were adopted as Brunei acceded to full independence and assumed responsibility for defence and foreign affairs.

THE RELIGIOUS COUNCIL

In his capacity as head of the Islamic faith in Brunei, the Sultan and Yang Di-Pertuan is advised on all Islamic matters by the Religious Council, whose members are appointed by the Sultan and Yang Di-Pertuan.

THE PRIVY COUNCIL

This Council, presided over by the Sultan and Yang Di-Pertuan, is to advise the Sultan on matters concerning the Royal prerogative of mercy, the amendment of the Constitution and the conferment of ranks, titles and honours.

THE COUNCIL OF MINISTERS

Presided over by the Sultan and Yang Di-Pertuan, the Council of Cabinet Ministers considers all executive matters.

THE LEGISLATIVE COUNCIL

The role of the Legislative Council is to scrutinize legislation. However, following political unrest in 1962, provisions of the Constitution relating, *inter alia*, to the Legislative Council were amended, and the Legislative Council has not met since 1984. In the absence of the Legislative Council, legislation is enacted by royal proclamation.

THE COUNCIL OF SUCCESSION

Subject to the Constitution, this Council is to determine the succession to the throne, should the need arise.

The State is divided into four administrative districts, in each of which is a District Officer responsible to the Prime Minister and Minister of Home Affairs.

The Government

HEAD OF STATE

Sultan and Yang Di-Pertuan: HM Sultan Haji HASSANAL BOLKIAH (succeeded 4 October 1967; crowned 1 August 1968).

COUNCIL OF CABINET MINISTERS
(April 2003)

Prime Minister, Minister of Defence and of Finance: HM Sultan Haji HASSANAL BOLKIAH.

Minister of Foreign Affairs: HRH Prince MOHAMED BOLKIAH.

Minister of Home Affairs and Special Adviser to the Prime Minister: Pehin Dato' Haji ISA BIN Pehin Haji IBRAHIM.

Minister of Education: Pehin Dato' Haji ABDUL AZIZ BIN Pehin Haji UMAR.

Minister of Industry and Primary Resources: Dato' Haji ABDUL RAHMAN TAIB.

Minister of Religious Affairs: Pehin Dato' Dr Haji MOHAMAD ZAIN BIN Haji SERUDIN.

Minister of Development: Dato' Seri Paduka Dr Haji AHMAD BIN Haji JUMAT.

Minister of Health: Pehin Dato' Haji ABU BAKAR BIN Haji APONG.

Minister of Culture, Youth and Sports: Pehin Dato' Haji HUSSEIN BIN Pehin Haji MOHAMAD YOSOF.

Minister of Communications: Pehin Dato' Haji ZAKARIA BIN Haji SULEIMAN.

There are, in addition, eight deputy ministers.

MINISTRIES

Office of the Prime Minister (Jabatan Perdana Menteri): Istana Nurul Iman, Bandar Seri Begawan BA 1000; tel. (2) 229988; fax (2) 241717; e-mail PRO@jpm.gov.bn; internet www.pmo.gov.bn.

Ministry of Communications (Kementerian Perhubungan): Jalan Menteri Besar, Bandar Seri Begawan BB 3910; tel. (2) 383838; fax (2) 380127; e-mail info@mincom.gov.bn; internet www.mincom.gov.bn.

Ministry of Culture, Youth and Sports (Kementerian Kebudayaan, Belia dan Sukan): Simpang 336, Jalan Kebangsaan, Bandar Seri Begawan BC 4415; tel. (2) 380911; fax (2) 380653; e-mail info@kkbs.gov.bn; internet www.kkbs.gov.bn.

Ministry of Defence (Kementerian Pertahanan): Bolkiah Garrison, Bandar Seri Begawan BB 3510; tel. (2) 386000; fax (2) 331615; e-mail info@mindef.gov.bn; internet www.mindef.gov.bn.

Ministry of Development (Kementerian Pembangunan): Old Airport, Jalan Berakas, Bandar Seri Begawan BB 3510; tel. (2) 241911; e-mail info@mod.gov.bn; internet www.mod.gov.bn.

Ministry of Education (Kementerian Pendidikan): Old Airport, Jalan Berakas, Bandar Seri Begawan BB 3510; tel. (2) 382233; fax (2) 380050; e-mail sutmoe@brunet.bn; internet www.moe.gov.bn.

Ministry of Finance (Kementerian Kewangan): Bandar Seri Begawan 1130; tel. (2) 241991; fax (2) 226132; e-mail info@finance.gov.bn; internet www.finance.gov.bn.

Ministry of Foreign Affairs (Kementerian Hal Ehwal Luar Negeri): Jalan Subok, Bandar Seri Begawan BD 2710; tel. (2) 261177; fax (2) 262904; e-mail info@mfa.gov.bn; internet www.mfa.gov.bn.

Ministry of Health (Kementerian Kesihatan): Jalan Menteri Besar, Bandar Seri Begawan BB 3910; tel. (2) 226640; fax (2) 240980; e-mail moh2@brunet.bn; internet www.moh.gov.bn.

Ministry of Home Affairs (Kementerian Hal Ehwal Dalam Negeri): Jalan Menteri Besar, Bandar Seri Begawan BB 3910; tel. (2) 223225; e-mail info@home-affairs.gov.bn; internet www.home-affairs.gov.bn.

Ministry of Industry and Primary Resources (Kementerian Perindustrian dan Sumber-sumber Utama): Jalan Menteri Besar, Bandar Seri Begawan BB 3910; tel. (2) 382822; fax (2) 382807; e-mail MIPRS2@brunet.bn; internet www.industry.gov.bn.

Ministry of Religious Affairs (Kementerian Hal Ehwal Ugama): Jalan Menteri Besar, Jalan Berakas, Bandar Seri Begawan BB 3910; tel. (2) 382525; fax (2) 382330; e-mail info@religious-affairs.gov.bn; internet www.religious-affairs.gov.bn.

Political Organizations

Parti Perpaduan Kebangsaan Brunei (PPKB) (Brunei National Solidarity Party—BNSP): Bandar Seri Begawan; f. 1986; after split in PKDB (see below); ceased political activity in 1988, but re-emerged in 1995; Pres. HATTA ZAINAL ABIDIN.

Former political organizations included: **Parti Rakyat Brunei—PRB** (Brunei People's Party), banned in 1962, leaders are all in exile; **Barisan Kemerdeka'an Rakyat—BAKER** (People's Independence Front), f. 1966 but no longer active; **Parti Perpaduan Kebangsaan Rakyat Brunei—PERKARA** (Brunei People's National United Party), f. 1968 but no longer active; and **Parti Kebangsaan Demokratik Brunei—PKDB** (Brunei National Democratic Party—BNDP), f. 1985 and dissolved by government order in 1988.

Diplomatic Representation

EMBASSIES AND HIGH COMMISSIONS IN BRUNEI

Australia: Teck Guan Plaza, 4th Floor, Jalan Sultan, Bandar Seri Begawan BS 8811; tel. (2) 229435; fax (2) 221652; e-mail ozcombrn@pso.brunet.bn; High Commissioner ALLASTER COX.

Bangladesh: 125 Kampong Kiulap, Bandar Seri Begawan BE 1518; tel. (2) 238420; fax (2) 238421; High Commissioner Maj.-Gen. ABU ISHAQ IBRAHIM.

Cambodia: 8 Simpang 845, Kampong Tasek, Meradun, Jalan Tutong, Bandar Seri Begawan BF 1520; tel. (2) 654046; fax (2) 650646; Ambassador ITH DETTOLA.

Canada: 5th Floor, Jalan McArthur Bldg, 1 Jalan McArthur, Bandar Seri Begawan BS 8711; tel. (2) 220043; fax (2) 220040; e-mail hicomcda@brunet.bn; internet www.dfait-maeci.gc.ca/Brunei/; High Commissioner PAUL S. H. LAU.

China, People's Republic: 1, 3 & 5 Simpang 462, Kampong Sungai Hanching, Jalan Muara, Bandar Seri Begawan BC 2115; tel. (2) 334163; fax (2) 335710; e-mail embproc@brunet.bn; Ambassador WEI WEI.

France: Kompleks Jalan Sultan, Units 301–306, 3rd Floor, 51–55 Jalan Sultan, Bandar Seri Begawan BS 8811; tel. (2) 220960; fax (2) 243373; e-mail france@brunet.bn; internet www.france.org.bn; Ambassador THIERRY BORJA DE MOZOTA.

Germany: Kompleks Bangunan Yayasan Sultan Haji Hassanal Bolkiah, Unit 2.01, Block A, 2nd Floor, Jalan Pretty, Bandar Seri Begawan BS 8711; tel. (2) 225547; fax (2) 240634; e-mail prgerman@brunet.bn; Ambassador ADALBERT RITTMÜLLER.

India: 'Baitussyifaa', Simpang 40–22, Jalan Sungai Akar, Bandar Seri Begawan BC 3915; tel. (2) 339947; fax (2) 339783; e-mail hicomind@brunet.bn; internet www.brunet.bn/gov/emb/india; High Commissioner AJAI CHOUDHRY.

Indonesia: Simpang 528, Lot 4498, Kampong Sungai Hanching Baru, Jalan Muara, Bandar Seri Begawan BC 2115; tel. (2) 330180; fax (2) 330646; e-mail kbribsb@brunet.bn; internet www.indonesia.org.bn; Ambassador YUSBAR DJAMIL.

Iran: 19 Simpang 477, Kampong Sungai Hanching, Jalan Muara, Bandar Seri Begawan BC 2115; tel. (2) 330021; fax (2) 331744; Ambassador ABD AL-FAZL MUHAMMAD ALIKHANI.

Japan: 1 and 3 Jalan Jawatan Dalam, 33 Simpang 122, Kampong Kiulap, Bandar Seri Begawan BE 1518; tel. (2) 229265; fax (2) 229481; e-mail embassy@japan.com.bn; Ambassador SATOSHI HARA.

Korea, Republic: POB 2169, Bandar Seri Begawan BS 8674; tel. (2) 426038; fax (2) 426041; e-mail koreaemb@brunet.bn; Ambassador (vacant).

Laos: Lot 19824, 11 Simpang 480, Jalan Kebangsaan Lama, off Jalan Muara, Bandar Seri Begawan BC 4115; tel. (2) 345666; fax (2) 345888; e-mail LAOSEMBA@brunet.bn; Ambassador BOUNTHONG VONGSALY.

Malaysia: 27–29 Simpang 396–39, Lot 9075, Kampong Sungai Akar, Mukim Berakas B, Jalan Kebangsaan, POB 2826, Bandar Seri Begawan BC 4115; tel. (2) 345652; fax (2) 345654; e-mail mwbrunei@brunet.bn; High Commissioner SALMAN AHMAD.

Myanmar: 14 Lot 2185/46292, Simpang 212, Jalan Kampong Rimba, Gadong, Bandar Seri Begawan BE 3119; tel. (2) 450506; fax (2) 451008; e-mail myanmar@brunet.bn; Ambassador U THET WIN.

Oman: 35 Simpang 100, Kampong Pengkalan, Jalan Tungku Link, Gadong, Bandar Seri Begawan BE 3719; tel. (2) 446953; fax (2) 449646; e-mail omnembsb@brunet.bn; Ambassador Haji MOHAMMAD BIN 'OMAR AHMAD AIDID.

Pakistan: 6 Simpang 23, Kampong Serusop, Jalan Muara, POB 3026, Bandar Seri Begawan BB 2313; tel. (2) 339797; fax (2) 334990; e-mail hcpak@brunet.bn; internet www.brunet.bn/gov/emb/pakistan; High Commissioner BADR-UD-DEEN.

Philippines: 17 Simpang 126, Km 2, Jalan Tutong, Bandar Seri Begawan BA 2111; tel. (2) 241465; fax (2) 237707; e-mail bruneipe@brunet.bn; Ambassador VIRGINIA H. BENDAVIDEZ.

Saudi Arabia: 1 Simpang 570, Kampong Salar, Jalan Muara, Bandar Seri Begawan BT 2528; tel. (2) 792821; fax (2) 792826; e-mail bnemb@mofa.gov.sa; Ambassador USTAZ IBRAHIM MUHAMMAD M. USILI.

Singapore: 8 Simpang 74, Jalan Subok, Bandar Seri Begawan; tel. (2) 262741; fax (2) 262743; e-mail singa@brunet.bn; internet www.gov.sg/mfa/brunei/; High Commissioner V. P. HIRUBALAN.

Thailand: 2 Simpang 682, Jalan Tutong, Kampong Bunut, Bandar Seri Begawan BF 1320; tel. (2) 653108; fax (2) 653032; e-mail thaiemb@brunet.bn; Ambassador (vacant).

United Kingdom: POB 2197, Bandar Seri Begawan BS 8674; tel. (2) 222231; fax (2) 234315; e-mail brithc@brunet.bn; internet www.britain-brunei.org; High Commissioner ANDREW CAIE.

USA: Teck Guan Plaza, 3rd Floor, Jalan Sultan, Bandar Seri Begawan BS 8811; tel. (2) 220384; fax (2) 225293; e-mail ConsularBrunei@state.gov; internet bandar.usembassy.gov; Ambassador GENE B. CHRISTY.

Viet Nam: 7 Simpang 538-37-19, Jalan (Duong) Kebangsaan Lama, Bandar Seri Begawan BC 2115; tel. (2) 343167; fax (2) 343169; e-mail vnembassy@hotmail.com; Ambassador TRAN TIEN VINH.

Judicial System

SUPREME COURT

The Supreme Court consists of the Court of Appeal and the High Court. Syariah (*Shari'a*) courts coexist with the Supreme Court and deal with Islamic laws.

Supreme Court

Km 11/2, Jalan Tutong, Bandar Seri Begawan BA 1910; tel. (2) 225853; fax (2) 241984; e-mail judiciarybn@hotmail.com; internet www.judicial.gov.bn/supr_court.htm.

Chief Registrar: Haji HAIROLARNI ABD MAJID.

The Court of Appeal

Composed of the President and two Commissioners appointed by the Sultan. The Court of Appeal considers criminal and civil appeals against the decisions of the High Court and the Intermediate Court. The Court of Appeal is the highest appellate court for criminal cases. In civil cases an appeal may be referred to the Judicial Committee of Her Majesty's Privy Council in London if all parties agree to do so before the hearing of the appeal in the Brunei Court of Appeal.

President: Sir ALLAN ARMSTRONG HUGGINS.

The High Court

Composed of the Chief Justice and judges sworn in by the Sultan as Commissioners of the Supreme Court. In its appellate jurisdiction, the High Court considers appeals in criminal and civil matters against the decisions of the Subordinate Courts. The High Court has unlimited original jurisdiction in criminal and civil matters.

Chief Justice: Dato' Seri Paduka MOHAMMED SAIED.

OTHER COURTS

Intermediate Courts: have jurisdiction to try all offences other than those punishable by the death sentence and civil jurisdiction to try all actions and suits of a civil nature where the amount in dispute or value of the subject/matter does not exceed B $100,000.

The Subordinate Courts

Presided over by the Chief Magistrate and magistrates, with limited original jurisdiction in civil and criminal matters and civil jurisdiction to try all actions and suits of a civil nature where the amount in dispute does not exceed B $50,000 (for Chief Magistrate) and B $30,000 (for magistrates).

Chief Magistrate: ROSTAINA BINTI Pengiran Haji DURAMAN (acting).

The Courts of Kathis

Deal solely with questions concerning Islamic religion, marriage and divorce. Appeals lie from these courts to the Sultan in the Religious Council.

Chief Kathi: Dato' Seri SETIA Haji SALIM BIN Haji BESAR.

Attorney-General: Dato' Paduka Haji KIFRAWI BIN PEHIN DATO' HAJI KIFLI, Attorney-General's Chambers, The Law Bldg, Km 1, Jalan Tutong, Bandar Seri Begawan BA 1910; tel. (2) 244872; fax (2) 223100; e-mail info@agc.gov.bn; internet www.agc.gov.bn.

Solicitor-General: Datin MAGDELENE CHONG.

Religion

The official religion of Brunei is Islam, and the Sultan is head of the Islamic community. The majority of the Malay population are Muslims of the Shafi'is school of the Sunni sect; at the 1991 census Muslims accounted for 67.2% of the total population. The Chinese population is either Buddhist (accounting for 12.8% of the total population at the 1991 census), Confucianist, Daoist or Christian. Large numbers of the indigenous ethnic groups practise traditional animist forms of religion. The remainder of the population are mostly Christians, generally Roman Catholics, Anglicans or members of the American Methodist Church of Southern Asia. At the 1991 census Christians accounted for 10.0% of the total population.

ISLAM

Supreme Head of Islam: (vacant) (Sultan and Yang Di-Pertuan).

CHRISTIANITY

The Anglican Communion

Within the Church of the Province of South East Asia, Brunei forms part of the diocese of Kuching (Malaysia).

The Roman Catholic Church

Brunei comprises a single apostolic prefecture. At December 2000 an estimated 7.6% of the population were adherents.

Prefect Apostolic: Rev. CORNELIUS SIM, St John's Church, POB 53, Kuala Belait KA 1131; tel. (3) 334207; fax (3) 342817; e-mail frcsim@brunet.bn; internet www.catholicbrunei.org.

The Press

NEWSPAPERS

Borneo Bulletin: Locked Bag No. 2, MPC (Old Airport, Berakas), Bandar Seri Begawan 3799; tel. (2) 451468; fax (2) 451461; e-mail brupress@brunet.bn; internet www.brunet.bn/news/bb; f. 1953; daily; English; independent; owned by QAF Group; Editor CHARLES REX DE SILVA; circ. 25,000.

Brunei Darussalam Newsletter: Dept of Information, Prime Minister's Office, Istana Nurul Iman, Bandar Seri Begawan BA 1000; tel. (2) 229988; fortnightly; English; govt newspaper; distributed free; circ. 14,000.

Daily News Digest: Dept of Information, Prime Minister's Office, Istana Nurul Iman, Bandar Seri Begawan BA 1000; internet www .brunet.bn/news/dndbd/digest.htm; English; govt newspaper.

Media Permata: Locked Bag No. 2, MPC (Old Airport, Berakas), Bandar Seri Begawan BB 3510; tel. (2) 451468; fax (2) 451461; e-mail mediapermata@brunet.bn; internet www.brunei-online.com/mp; f. 1995; daily (not Sun.); Malay; owned by QAF Group; Editor ABDUL LATIF; circ. 10,000.

Pelita Brunei: Dept of Information, Prime Minister's Office, Old Airport, Berakas BB 3510; tel. (2) 383941; fax (2) 381004; e-mail pelita@brunet.bn; internet www.brunet.bn/news/pelita/pelita1.htm; f. 1956; weekly (Wed.); Malay; govt newspaper; distributed free; Editor TIMBANG BIN BAKAR; circ. 27,500.

Salam: c/o Brunei Shell Petroleum Co Sdn Bhd, Seria 7082; tel. (3) 4184; fax (3) 4189; internet www.shell.com.bn/salam; f. 1953; monthly; Malay and English; distributed free to employees of the Brunei Shell Petroleum Co Sdn Bhd; circ. 46,000.

Publishers

Avesta Printing & Trading Sdn Bhd: 31–35, Block D, Bangunan Pg Anak Siti Rafeah, Jalan Gadong, Bandar Seri Begawan 3180; tel. (2) 445220; fax (2) 441372; Man. PETER WONG.

Borneo Printers & Trading Sdn Bhd: POB 2211, Bandar Seri Begawan BS 8674; tel. (2) 651387; fax (2) 654342; e-mail bptl@brunet.bn.

Brunei Press Sdn Bhd: Lots 8 and 11, Perindustrian Beribi II, Jalan Gadong, Bandar Seri Begawan BE 1118; tel. (2) 451468; fax (2)

451462; e-mail brupress@brunet.bn; internet www.bruneipress.com.bn; f. 1953; Gen. Man. REGGIE SEE.

Capital Trading & Printing Pte Ltd: POB 1089, Bandar Seri Begawan; tel. (2) 244541.

Leong Bros: 52 Jalan Bunga Kuning, POB 164, Seria; tel. (3) 22381.

Offset Printing House: POB 1111, Bandar Seri Begawan; tel. (2) 224477.

The Star Press: Bandar Seri Begawan; f. 1963; Man. F. W. ZIMMERMAN.

Government Publishing House

Government Printer: Government Printing Department, Office of the Prime Minister, Bandar Seri Begawan BB 3510; tel. (2) 382541; fax (2) 381141; e-mail info@printing.gov.bn; internet www.printing.gov.bn; Dir Dato' Paduka WAHID Haji SALLEH.

Broadcasting and Communications

TELECOMMUNICATIONS

Authority for the Information Communication Technology Industry (AiTi): Bandar Seri Begawan; f. 2003; regulatory body for telecommunications industry; responsible for development of information communication technology industry; Chair. Dato' Paduka Awang Haji ABDULLAH BIN Haji BAKAR; CEO Awang BUNTAR BIN OSMAN.

DST Communications Sdn Bhd: Block D, Yayasan Sultan Haji Hassanal Bolkiah Kompleks, Bandar Seri Begawan; tel. (2) 232323; e-mail dst-group@simpur.net.bn; internet www.dst-group.com; mobile service provider.

Jabatan Telecom Brunei (Department of Telecommunications of Brunei): Ministry of Communications, Jalan Berakas, Bandar Seri Begawan BB 3510; tel. (2) 382382; fax (2) 382445; e-mail info@telecom.gov.bn; internet www.telecom.gov.bn; scheduled to become Telekom Brunei Bhd (govt-owned company) in April 2003; telecommunications services provider; Dir of Telecommunications Awang BUNTAR BIN OSMAN.

BROADCASTING

Radio

Radio Televisyen Brunei (RTB): Prime Minister's Office, Jalan Elizabeth II, Bandar Seri Begawan BS 8610; tel. (2) 243111; fax (2) 241882; e-mail rtbpits@brunet.bn; internet www.rtb.gov.bn; f. 1957; five radio networks: four broadcasting in Malay, the other in English, Chinese (Mandarin) and Gurkhali; Dir Pengiran Dato' Paduka Haji ISMAIL BIN Pengiran Haji MOHAMED.

The British Forces Broadcasting Service (Military) broadcasts a 24-hour radio service to a limited area.

Television

Radio Televisyen Brunei (RTB): Prime Minister's Office, Jalan Elizabeth II, Bandar Seri Begawan BS 8610; tel. (2) 243111; fax (2) 241882; e-mail rtbpits@brunet.bn; internet www.rtb.gov.bn; f. 1957; programmes in Malay and English; a satellite service relays RTB television programmes to the South-East Asian region for nine hours per day; Dir Pengiran Dato' Paduka Haji ISMAIL BIN Pengiran Haji MOHAMED.

Finance

(cap. = capital; res = reserves; dep. = deposits; brs = branches; amounts in Brunei dollars unless otherwise stated)

BANKING

The Department of Financial Services (Treasury), the Brunei Currency Board and the Brunei Investment Agency (see Government Agencies below), under the Ministry of Finance, perform most of the functions of a central bank.

Commercial Banks

Baiduri Bank Bhd: Block A, Units 1-4, Kiarong Complex, Lebuhraya Sultan Hassanal Bolkiah, Bandar Seri Begawan BE 1318; tel. (2) 455111; fax (2) 455599; e-mail bank@baiduri.com; internet www.baiduri.com; cap. 30m., res 20.1m., dep. 968.9m. (Aug. 2002); Gen. Man. PIERRE IMHOF; 9 brs.

Islamic Bank of Brunei Bhd: Lot 159, Bangunan IBB, Jalan Pemancha, POB 2725, Bandar Seri Begawan BS 8711; tel. (2)

235686; fax (2) 235722; e-mail ibb@brunet.bn; internet www.ibb.com
.bn; f. 1981 as Island Development Bank; name changed from
International Bank of Brunei Bhd to present name in January 1993;
practises Islamic banking principles; Chair. Haji ABDUL RAHMAN BIN
Haji ABDUL KARIM; Man. Dir Haji ZAINASALLEHEN BIN Haji MOHAMED
TAHIR; 13 brs.

Islamic Development Bank of Brunei Bhd: Ground–4th Floor,
Kompleks Setia Kenangan, Kampong Kiulap, Jalan Gadong,
Bandar Seri Begawan BE 1518; tel. (2) 232547; fax (2) 233540;
e-mail hrdadmin@dbb-bank.com; internet www.idbb-bank.com.bn;
f. 1995 as Development Bank of Brunei Bhd; name changed to
present in July 2000; practises Islamic banking principles; Man. Dir
Pengiran Datin Paduka Hajah URAI Pengiran ALI; 3 brs.

Foreign Banks

Citibank NA (USA): Darussalam Complex, 12–15 Jalan Sultan,
Bandar Seri Begawan BS 8811; tel. (2) 243983; fax (2) 237344; e-mail
glen.rase@citicorp.com; Vice-Pres. and Country Head PAGE STOCK-
WELL; 2 brs.

The Hongkong and Shanghai Banking Corpn Ltd (Hong Kong):
Jalan Sultan, cnr Jalan Pemancha, Bandar Seri Begawan BS 8811;
POB 59, Bandar Seri Begawan BS 8670; tel. (2) 242305; fax (2)
241316; e-mail hsbc@hsbc.com.bn; internet www.hsbc.com.bn; f.
1947; acquired assets of National Bank of Brunei in 1986; CEO
MARCUS HURRY; 10 brs.

Maybank (Malaysia): 1 Jalan McArthur, Bandar Seri Begawan BS
8711; tel. (2) 226462; fax (2) 226404; e-mail maybank@brunet.bn; f.
1960; Country Man. AZIZUL ABDUL RASHID; 3 brs.

RHB Bank Bhd (Malaysia): Unit G. 02, Block D, Bangunan
Yayasan Sultan Haji Hassanal Bolkiah, Ground Floor, Jalan Pretty,
Bandar Seri Begawan BS 8711; tel. (2) 222515; fax (2) 237487; e-mail
rhbbsb@brunet.bn; fmrly Sime Bank Bhd; Branch Man. SHAFIK
YUSSOF; 1 br.

Standard Chartered Bank (United Kingdom): 1st Floor, 51–55
Jalan Sultan, POB 186, Bandar Seri Begawan BS 8811; tel. (2)
242386; fax (2) 242390; internet www.standardchartered.com/bn; f.
1958; CEO SIMON MORRIS; 8 brs.

United Overseas Bank Ltd (Singapore): Unit G5, RBA Plaza,
Jalan Sultan, Bandar Seri Begawan BS 8811; POB 2218, Bandar
Seri Begawan BS 8674; tel. (2) 225477; fax (2) 240792; f. 1973; Gen.
Man. SIA KEE HENG; 2 brs.

'Offshore' Bank

Royal Bank of Canada: 1 Jalan McArthur, 4A, 4th Floor, Bandar
Seri Begawan BS 8711; tel. (2) 224366; fax (2) 224368; Gen. Man.
MATTHEW YONG.

STOCK EXCHANGE

In May 2002 the International Brunei Exchange Ltd (IBX) was
granted an exclusive licence to establish an international securities
exchange in Brunei.

International Brunei Exchange Ltd (IBX): The Empire, Muara-
Tutong Highway, Jerudong BG 3122; tel. (2) 611222; fax (2) 611020;
e-mail info@ibx.com.bn; internet www.ibx.com.bn; f. 2001; CEO
B. C. YONG.

INSURANCE

In 1998 there were 18 general, three life and two composite (takaful)
insurance companies operating in Brunei, including:

General Companies

AGF Insurance (Singapore) Pte Ltd: c/o A&S Associates Sdn
Bhd, Bangunan Gadong Properties, 03-01, Jalan Gadong, Bandar
Seri Begawan BE 4119; tel. (2) 420766; fax (2) 440279; Gen. Man.
JEAN NOEL ROUSSELLE.

The Asia Insurance Co Ltd: Unit A1 & A2, 1st Floor, Block A,
Bangunan Hau Man Yong Complex, Simpang 88, Kg. Kiulap BE
1518, POB 2226, Bandar Seri Begawan BS 8674; tel. (2) 236100; fax
(2) 236102; Man. DAVID WONG KOK MIN.

BALGI Insurance (B) Sdn Bhd: Unit 13, Kompleks Haji Tahir II,
2nd Floor, 3180 Jalan Gadong, Bandar Seri Begawan BE 4119; tel.
(2) 422726; fax (2) 445204; Man. Dir PATRICK SIM SONG JUAY.

Borneo Insurance Sdn Bhd: Unit 103, Bangunan Kambang
Pasang, Km 2, Jalan Gadong, Bandar Seri Begawan BE 4119; tel. (2)
420550; fax (2) 428550; Man. LIM TECK LEE.

CGU Insurance Bhd: Unit 311, 3rd Floor, Mohamad Yussof Complex, 1.5 Mile, Jalan Tutong, Bandar Seri Begawan BA 1712; tel. (2)
223632; fax (2) 220965; e-mail cgu@brunet.bn; Man. PETER SHACK.

Commercial Union Assurance (M) Sdn Bhd: c/o Jasra Harrisons
Sdn Bhd, Jalan McArthur, cnr Jalan Kianggeh, Bandar Seri
Begawan BS 8711; tel. (2) 242361; fax (2) 226203; Man. WHITTY LIM.

Cosmic Insurance Corpn Sdn Bhd: Block J, Unit 11, Abdul
Razak Complex, 1st Floor, Jalan Gadong, Bandar Seri Begawan BE
3919; tel. (2) 427112; fax (2) 427114; Man. RONNIE WONG.

GRE Insurance (B) Sdn Bhd: Unit 608, 6th Floor, Jalan Sultan
Complex, 51–55 Jalan Sultan, Bandar Seri Begawan BS 8811; tel.
(2) 226138; fax (2) 243474; Man. MOK HAI TONG.

ING General Insurance International NV: Shop Lot 86, 2nd
Floor, Jalan Bunga Raya, Kuala Belait KA 1131; tel. (3) 335338; fax
(3) 335338; Man. SHERRY SOON PECK ENG.

Liberty Citystate Insurance Pte Ltd: 1st Floor, Unit 25, Block C,
Bangunan Hau Man Yong Complex, Simpang 88, Kampong Kiulap
BE 1518, POB 1323, Bandar Seri Begawan BS 8672; tel. (2) 238282;
fax (2) 236848; Man. ROBERT LAI CHIN YIN.

Malaysia National Insurance Bhd: 9 Bangunan Haji Mohd
Salleh Simpang 103, 1st Floor, Jalan Gadong, Bandar Seri Begawan
BE 4119; tel. (2) 443393; fax (2) 427451; Man. ANDREW AK NYAGORN.

MBA Insurance Sdn Bhd: 7 Bangunan Hasbullah I, 1st Floor, Km
4, Jalan Gadong, Bandar Seri Begawan BE 3519; tel. (2) 441535; fax
(2) 441534; e-mail cheahmbabrunei@brunet.bn; Man. CHEAH LYE
CHONG.

Motor and General Insurance Sdn Bhd: 6 Bangunan Hasbullah
II, Km 4, Jalan Gadong, Bandar Seri Begawan BE 3919; tel. (2)
440797; fax (2) 445342; Man. Dir Haji ABDUL AZIZ BIN ABDUL LATIF.

National Insurance Co Bhd: 3rd Floor, Scouts' Headquarters
Bldg, Jalan Gadong, Bandar Seri Begawan BE 1118; tel. (2) 426888;
fax (2) 429888; e-mail insurance@brunet.bn; internet www.national
.com.bn; Gen. Man. CHAN LEK WEI.

Royal and Sun Alliance Insurance (Global) Ltd: Unit 7, 1st
Floor, Block B, Kiarong Complex, Lebuhraya Sultan Hassanal Bol-
kiah, Bandar Seri Begawan BE 1318; tel. (2) 423233; fax (2) 423325;
Gen. Man. TOMMY LEONG TONG KAW.

South East Asia Insurance (B) Sdn Bhd: Unit 2, Block A, Abdul
Razak Complex, 1st Floor, Jalan Gadong, Bandar Seri Begawan BE
3919; tel. (2) 443842; fax (2) 420860; Gen. Man. JOSEPH WONG SIONG
LION.

Standard Insurance (B) Sdn Bhd: 2 Bangunan Hasbullah I,
Ground Floor, Bandar Seri Begawan BE 3919; tel. (2) 450077; fax (2)
450076; e-mail feedback@standard-ins.com; internet www
.standard-ins.com; Man. PAUL KONG.

Winterthur Insurance (Far East) Pte Ltd: c/o Borneo Co (B) Sdn
Bhd, Lot 9771, Km 3½, Jalan Gadong, Bandar Seri Begawan BE
4119; tel. (2) 422561; fax (2) 424352; Gen. Man. ANNA CHONG.

Life Companies

American International Assurance Co Ltd: Unit 509A, Wisma
Jaya Building, 5th Floor, No 85/94, Jalan Pemancha, Bandar Seri
Begawan BS 8511; tel. (2) 239112; fax (2) 221667; Man. PHILIP TAN.

The Asia Life Assurance Society Ltd: Unit 2, 1st Floor, Block D,
Abdul Razak Complex, Jalan Gadong, Bandar Seri Begawan BE
4119; tel. (2) 423755; fax (2) 423754; e-mail asialife@simpur.net.bn;
Exec. Officer PATRICIA CHIN YUNG YIN.

The Great Eastern Life Assurance Co Ltd: Suite 1, Badi'ah
Complex, 2nd Floor, Jalan Tutong, Bandar Seri Begawan BA 2111;
tel. (2) 243792; fax (2) 225754; Man. HELEN YEO.

Takaful (Composite Insurance) Companies

Syarikat Insurans Islam TAIB Sdn Bhd: Bangunan Pusat
Komersil dan Perdagangan Bumiputera, Ground Floor, Jalan Cator,
Bandar Seri Begawan BS 8811; tel. (2) 237724; fax (2) 237729; e-mail
insuranstaib@brunet.bn; internet www.insuranstaib.com.bn; f.
1993; provides Islamic insurance products and services; Man. Dir
Haji MOHAMED ROSELAN BIN Haji MOHAMED DAUD.

Takaful IBB Bhd: Unit 5, Block A, Kiarong Complex, Lebuhraya
Sultan Hassanal Bolkiah, Bandar Seri Begawan BE 1318; tel. (2)
451804; fax (2) 451808; e-mail takaful@brunet.bn; f. 1993; Man. Dir
Awang Haji MOHAMED ROSELAN BIN Haji MOHAMED DAUD (acting).

Trade and Industry

GOVERNMENT AGENCIES

Brunei Currency Board: Ministry of Finance Complex, Simpang
295, Jalan Kebansaan, Bandar Seri Begawan BB 3910; tel. (2)
383999; fax (2) 382232; e-mail bcb@brunet.bn; internet www.finance
.gov.bn/bcb/bcb_index.htm; f. 1967; maintains control of currency

circulation; Sec. Haji MAHADI HAJI IBRAHIM; Chair. (vacant) (Minister of Finance).

Brunei Darussalam Economic Council (BDEC): Bandar Seri Begawan; internet www.brudirect.com/BruneiInfo/info/BD_EconomicCouncil.htm; f. 1998; convened to examine the economic situation in Brunei and to recommend short- and long-term measures designed to revitalize the economy; Chair. HRH Prince MOHAMED BOLKIAH.

Brunei Investment Agency: Ministry of Finance, Bandar Seri Begawan 1130; f. 1973; Chair. YAHYA BAKAR.

DEVELOPMENT ORGANIZATIONS

Brunei Economic Development Board (BEDB): Jalan Ong Sum Ping, Bandar Seri Begawan BA 1311; tel. (2) 230069; fax (2) 230053; f. 2001; promotes Brunei as an investment destination; facilitates and assists industrial development; Chair. Dato' Paduka Haji YUSOF; CEO JOHN A. PERRY.

Brunei Industrial Development Authority (BINA): Ministry of Industry and Primary Resources, Km 8, Jalan Gadong, Bandar Seri Begawan BE 1118; tel. (2) 444100; fax (2) 423300; e-mail bruneibina@brunet.bn; internet www.bina.gov.bn; f. 1996; Dir Haji MOHD ZAIN BIN Haji GAFFAR.

Brunei Islamic Trust Fund (Tabung Amanah Islam Brunei): Block A, Unit 2, Ground Floor, Kiarong Complex, Lebuhraya Sultan Hj Hassanal Bolkiah, Bandar Seri Begawan BE 1318; tel. (2) 452666; fax (2) 450877; f. 1991; promotes trade and industry; Chair. Haji Awang YAHYA BIN Haji IBRAHIM.

Industrial and Trade Development Council: Bandar Seri Begawan; facilitates the industrialization of Brunei; Chair. (vacant) (Minister of Industry and Primary Resources).

Semaun Holdings Sdn Bhd: Unit 2.02, Block D, 2nd Floor, Yayasan Sultan Haji Hassanal Bolkiah Complex, Jalan Pretty, Bandar Seri Begawan BS 8711; tel. (2) 232950; e-mail semaun@brunet.bn; internet www.semaun.gov.bn; promotes industrial and commercial development through direct investment in key industrial sectors; 100% govt-owned; the board of directors is composed of ministers and senior govt officials; Chair. (vacant) (Minister of Industry and Primary Resources); Man. Dir Pengiran Haji MARIANA P. D. N. Pengiran Haji ABDUL MOMIN.

CHAMBERS OF COMMERCE

Brunei Darussalam International Chamber of Commerce and Industry: Unit 402–403A, 4th Floor, Wisma Jaya, Jalan Pemancha, Bandar Seri Begawan 8811; tel. (2) 228382; fax (2) 228389; Chair. SULAIMAN Haji AHAI; Sec. Haji SHAZALI BIN Dato' Haji SULAIMAN; 108 mems.

Brunei Malay Chamber of Commerce and Industry: Unit 15, First Floor, Bangunan Halimadul Saadiah, Jalan Gadong, Bandar Seri Begawan BE 3519; POB 1099, Bandar Seri Begawan BS 8672; tel. (2) 422752; fax (2) 422753; f. 1964; Pres. Dato' A. A. HAPIDZ; 160 mems.

Chinese Chamber of Commerce: Chinese Chamber of Commerce Bldg, 72 Jalan Roberts, Bandar Seri Begawan; POB 281, Bandar Seri Begawan BS 8670; tel. (2) 235494; fax (2) 235492; Pres. ROBERT KOH HOE KIAT.

National Chamber of Commerce and Industry of Brunei Darussalam: 2nd Floor, 144 Jalan Pemancha, Bandar Seri Begawan BS 8711; tel. (2) 243321; fax (2) 228737; e-mail abas@nccibd.com; internet www.bruneichamber.com; Pres. Sheikh ABAS Sheikh MOHAMAD.

STATE HYDROCARBON COMPANIES

Brunei Gas Carriers Sdn Bhd (BGC): Bandar Seri Begawan; f. 1998; LNG shipping co; owned jointly by Brunei Govt, Shell International Gas and Mitsubishi Corpn.

Brunei LNG Sdn Bhd: Lumut KC 2935, Seria; tel. (3) 378125; fax (3) 236919; e-mail hamdillah.b.wahab@shell.com.bn; f. 1969; natural gas liquefaction; owned jointly by the Brunei Govt, Shell and Mitsubishi Corpn; operates LNG plant at Lumut, which has a capacity of 7.2m. tons per year; Man. Dir H. A. W. HAMDILLAH.

Brunei National Petroleum Co Sdn Bhd (PetroleumBrunei): 5th Floor, Bangunan Bahirah, Jalan Menteri Besar, Bandar Seri Begawan BB 3910; tel. (2) 383003; fax (2) 383004; e-mail brupet@brunet.bn; f. 2001; wholly govt-owned; CEO Dato' Paduka MOHD ALIMIN ABDUL WAHAB.

Brunei Shell Marketing Co Bhd: Maya Puri Bldg, 36/37 Jalan Sultan, POB 385, Bandar Seri Begawan; tel. (2) 25739; fax (2) 240470; internet www.bsm.com.bn; f. 1978; (from the Shell Marketing Co of Brunei Ltd), when the Govt became equal partner with

Shell; markets petroleum and chemical products throughout Brunei; Man. Dir MAT SUNY Haji MOHD HUSSEIN.

Brunei Shell Petroleum Co Sdn Bhd: Jalan Utara, Panagia, Seria KB 3534; tel. (3) 373999; fax (3) 372040; internet www.shell.com.bn; f. 1957; the largest industrial concern in the country; 50% state holding; Man. Dir JOHN J. C. DARLEY.

Jasra International Petroleum Sdn Bhd: RBA Plaza, 2nd Floor, Jalan Sultan, Bandar Seri Begawan; tel. (2) 228968; fax (2) 228929; petroleum exploration and production; Man. Dir ROBERT A. HARRISON.

TRADE UNIONS

Brunei Government Junior Officers' Union: Bandar Seri Begawan; tel. (2) 241911; Pres. Haji ALI BIN Haji NASAR; Gen. Sec. Haji OMARALI BIN Haji MOHIDDIN.

Brunei Government Medical and Health Workers' Union: Bandar Seri Begawan; Pres. Pengiran Haji MOHIDDIN BIN Pengiran TAJUDDIN; Gen. Sec. HANAFI BIN ANAI.

Brunei Oilfield Workers' Union: XDR/11, BSP Co Sdn Bhd, Seria KB 3534; f. 1964; 470 mems; Pres. SUHAINI HAJI OTHMAN; Sec.-Gen. ABU TALIB BIN Haji MOHAMAD.

Royal Brunei Custom Department Staff Union: Badan Sukan dan Kebajikan Kastam, Royal Brunei Customs and Excise, Kuala Belait KA 1131; tel. (3) 334248; fax (3) 334626; Chair. Haji MOHD DELI BAKAR; Sec. HAMZAH Haji ABD. HAMID.

Transport

RAILWAYS

There are no public railways in Brunei. The Brunei Shell Petroleum Co Sdn Bhd maintains a 19.3-km section of light railway between Seria and Badas.

ROADS

In 1999 there were 1,150 km of roads in Brunei, of which almost 400 km were paved. The main highway connects Bandar Seri Begawan, Tutong and Kuala Belait. A 59-km coastal road links Muara and Tutong. The Eighth National Development Plan (2001–05) prioritized the development of Brunei's roads and, in particular, the construction of a network of main roads that would connect Brunei Muara, Tutong, Kuala Belait and Temburong. In September 2002 construction of the 15-km Jalan Lumut Bypass was completed.

Land Transport Department: 451979 Km 6, Jalan Gadong, Beribi, Bandar Seri Begawan BE 1110; tel. (2) 451979; fax (2) 424775; e-mail latis@brunet.bn; internet www.land-transport.gov.bn; Dir Awang Haji OTHMAN BIN Haji MOMIN.

SHIPPING

Most sea traffic is handled by a deep-water port at Muara, 28 km from the capital, which has a 611-m wharf and a draught of 8 m. The port has a container terminal, warehousing, freezer facilities and cement silos. In October 2000 a plan to deepen the port to enable its accommodation of larger vessels was announced. The original, smaller port at Bandar Seri Begawan itself is mainly used for local river-going vessels, for vessels to Malaysian ports in Sabah and Sarawak and for vessels under 30 m in length. There is a port at Kuala Belait, which takes shallow-draught vessels and serves mainly the Shell petroleum field and Seria. Owing to the shallow waters at Seria, tankers are unable to come up to the shore to load, and crude petroleum from the oil terminal is pumped through an underwater loading line to a single buoy mooring, to which the tankers are moored. At Lumut there is a 4.5-km jetty for liquefied natural gas (LNG) carriers.

Four main rivers, with numerous tributaries, are an important means of communication in the interior, and boats or water taxis are the main form of transport for most residents of the water villages. Larger water taxis operate daily to the Temburong district.

Bee Seng Shipping Co: 7 Block D, Sufri Complex, Km 2, Jalan Tutong, POB 92, Bandar Seri Begawan; tel. (2) 220033; fax (2) 224495; e-mail beeseng@brunet.bn.

Belait Shipping Co (B) Sdn Bhd: B1, 2nd Floor, 94 Jalan McKerron, Kuala Belait 6081; POB 632, Kuala Belait; tel. (3) 335418; fax (3) 330239; f. 1977; Man. Dir Haji FATIMAH BINTE Haji ABDUL AZIZ.

Brunei Shell Tankers Sdn Bhd: Seria KB 3534; tel. (3) 373999; f. 1986; vessels operated by Shell International Trading and Shipping Co Ltd; Man. Dir CHRIS FINLAYSON.

Harper Wira Sdn Bhd: B2 Bangunan Haji Mohd Yussof, Jalan Gadong, Bandar Seri Begawan 3188; tel. (2) 448529; fax (2) 448529.

Inchcape Borneo: Bangunan Inchcape Borneo, Km 4, Jalan Gadong, Bandar Seri Begawan; tel. (2) 422561; fax (2) 424352; f. 1856; Gen. Man. LO FAN KEE.

New Island Shipping: POB 850, Bandar Seri Begawan 1908; tel. (2) 451800; fax (2) 451480; f. 1975; Chair. TAN KOK VOON; Man. JIMMY VOON.

Pansar Co Sdn Bhd: First Floor, 27 Kompleks Mubibbah 3, Jalan Gadong, Bandar Seri Begawan 3180; tel. (2) 445246; fax (2) 445247.

Seatrade Shipping Co: Muara Port; tel. (2) 421457; fax (2) 421453.

Silver Line (B) Sdn Bhd: Muara Port; tel. (2) 445069; fax (2) 430276.

Wei Tat Shipping and Trading Co: Mile 41, Jalan Tutong, POB 103, Bandar Seri Begawan; tel. (2) 65215.

CIVIL AVIATION

There is an international airport near Bandar Seri Begawan, which can handle up to 1.5m. passengers and 50,000 metric tons of cargo per year. In early 2003 expansion of the airport was ongoing. The Brunei Shell Petroleum Co Sdn Bhd operates a private airfield at Anduki for helicopter services.

Department of Civil Aviation: Brunei International Airport, Bandar Seri Begawan BB 2513; tel. (2) 330142; fax (2) 331706; e-mail dea@brunet.bn; internet www.civil-aviation.gov.bn; Dir Haji KASIM BIN Haji LATIP.

Royal Brunei Airlines Ltd: RBA Plaza, Jalan Sultan, POB 737, Bandar Seri Begawan BS 8671; tel. (2) 240500; fax (2) 244737; internet www.bruneiair.com; f. 1974; operates services within the Far East and to the Middle East, Australia and Europe; Chair. Pehin Dato' Haji YAHYA; CEO PETER WILLIAM FOSTER.

Tourism

Tourist attractions in Brunei include the flora and fauna of the rainforest and the national parks, as well as mosques and water villages. There were 964,080 foreign visitor arrivals (including same-day visitors) in 1998. Foreign visitor arrivals increased to 1,306,764 in 2000. In 1998 international tourist receipts totalled US $37m. The year 2001 was designated 'Visit Brunei Year'.

Brunei Tourism: c/o Ministry of Industry and Primary Resources, Jalan Menteri Besar, Bandar Seri Begawan BB 3910; tel. (2) 382822; fax (2) 382824; e-mail info@industry.gov.bn; internet www .tourismbrunei.com; Dir-Gen. Sheikh JAMALUDDIN BIN Sheikh MOHAMED.

BULGARIA

Introductory Survey

Location, Climate, Language, Religion, Flag, Capital

The Republic of Bulgaria lies in the eastern Balkans, in south-eastern Europe. It is bounded by Romania to the north, by Turkey and Greece to the south, by Serbia and Montenegro to the west and by the former Yugoslav republic of Macedonia to the south-west. The country has an eastern coastline on the Black Sea. The climate is one of fairly sharp contrasts between winter and summer. Temperatures in Sofia are generally between −5°C (23°F) and 28°C (82°F). The official language is Bulgarian, a member of the Slavonic group, written in the Cyrillic alphabet. Minority languages include Turkish and Macedonian. The majority of the population are Christian, most of whom adhere to the Bulgarian Orthodox Church, although there is a substantial minority of Muslims. The national flag (proportions 2 by 3) has three equal horizontal stripes, of white, green and red. The capital is Sofia.

Recent History

After almost 500 years of Ottoman rule, Bulgaria declared itself an independent kingdom in 1908. In both the First and Second World Wars Bulgaria allied itself with Germany, and in 1941 joined in the occupation of Yugoslavia. Soviet troops occupied Bulgaria in 1944. In September the Fatherland Front, a left-wing alliance formed in 1942, seized power, with help from the USSR, and installed a Government, led by Kimon Georgiev. In September 1946 the monarchy was abolished, following a popular referendum, and a republic was proclaimed. The first post-war election was held in October, when the Fatherland Front received 70.8% of the votes cast and won 364 seats, of which 277 were held by the Bulgarian Communist Party (BCP), in the 465-member National Assembly. In November Georgi Dimitrov, the First Secretary of the BCP and a veteran international revolutionary, became Chairman of the Council of Ministers (Prime Minister) in a Government that comprised members of the Fatherland Front. All opposition parties were abolished and a new Constitution, based on the Soviet model, was adopted in December 1947, when Bulgaria was designated a People's Republic. Dimitrov was replaced as Prime Minister by Vasil Kolarov in March 1949, but remained leader of the BCP until his death in July. His successor as party leader, Vulko Chervenkov, became Prime Minister in February 1950.

Todor Zhivkov succeeded Chervenkov as leader of the BCP in March 1954, although the latter remained Prime Minister until April 1956, when he was replaced by Anton Yugov. Following an ideological struggle within the BCP, Zhivkov was Prime Minister from November 1962 until July 1971, when, after the adoption of a new Constitution in May, Zhivkov became the first President of the newly formed State Council. He was re-elected in 1976, 1981 and 1986. At a BCP Congress held in March and April 1981 the party's leader was restyled General Secretary. In June, following elections to the National Assembly, a new Government was formed; Grisha Filipov, a member of the BCP's Political Bureau, succeeded Stanko Todorov, who had been Prime Minister since 1971. In March 1986 Filipov was replaced by Georgi Atanasov, a former Vice-President of the State Council.

In local elections in March 1988, the nomination of candidates other than those endorsed by the BCP was permitted for the first time. Candidates presented by independent public organizations and workers' collectives obtained about one-quarter of the total votes cast. At a plenum of the BCP, held in July, several prominent proponents of the Soviet-style programme of reform were dismissed.

On 10 November 1989 Zhivkov was unexpectedly removed from his post of General Secretary of the BCP and from the Political Bureau. He was replaced as General Secretary by Petur Mladenov, Minister of Foreign Affairs since 1971, and a member of the BCP's Political Bureau since 1977. Mladenov also replaced Zhivkov as President of the State Council. In mid-November 1989 the National Assembly voted to abolish part of the penal code prohibiting 'anti-State propaganda' and to grant an amnesty to persons who had been convicted under the code's provisions. Zhivkov was subsequently denounced by the BCP

and divested of his party membership, and an investigation into corruption during his tenure of power was initiated. In 1990 Zhivkov was arrested on charges of embezzlement of state funds.

In early December 1989 Angel Dimitrov became leader of the Bulgarian Agrarian People's Union (BAPU, the sole legal political party apart from the BCP, with which it was originally allied); the BAPU was subsequently reconstituted as an independent opposition party. In mid-December the BCP proposed amendments to the Constitution and the adoption of a new electoral law to permit free and democratic elections to be held in 1990. In January 1990 the National Assembly voted to remove from the Constitution the article guaranteeing the BCP's dominant role in society and approved legislation permitting citizens to form independent groups and to stage demonstrations. Discussions regarding political and economic reforms commenced in early January 1990 between the BCP, the BAPU and the Union of Democratic Forces (UDF), a co-ordinating organization (established in December 1989), which comprised several dissident and independent groups, including Ecoglasnost and the Podkrepa (Support) Trade Union Confederation. In early February the BCP adopted a new manifesto, pledging its commitment to extensive political and economic reforms, the separation of party and state, and the introduction of a multiparty system, while retaining its Marxist orientation. The party's Central Committee was replaced by a Supreme Council, chaired by Aleksandur Lilov, a former head of the BCP's ideology department, who had been expelled from the party in 1983 for criticism of Zhivkov. The Political Bureau and Secretariat of the Central Committee were replaced by the Presidium of the Supreme Council, also with Lilov as Chairman. The President of the State Council, Mladenov, proposed the formation of an interim coalition government, pending elections to the National Assembly. The UDF and the BAPU, however, rejected Mladenov's invitation to participate in such a coalition. Accordingly, the new Council of Ministers, appointed on 8 February 1990, was composed solely of BCP members, chaired by Andrei Lukanov, the former Minister of Foreign Economic Relations, who was regarded as an advocate of reform.

There was unrest in mid-February 1990, when an estimated 200,000 supporters of the UDF gathered in Sofia to demand the end of BCP rule. Following discussions in late March, with the participation of the BAPU and other political and public organizations, it was finally agreed that Mladenov was to be re-elected as President, pending elections to the National Assembly in June and the subsequent approval of a new constitution. The participants in the talks also decided to dissolve the State Council. In early April the National Assembly adopted an electoral law, together with legislation that provided for political pluralism and guaranteed the right to form political parties. Also in early April the BCP voted to rename itself the Bulgarian Socialist Party (BSP).

Following an electoral campaign marred by acts of intimidation and violence, elections to the 400-member Grand National Assembly were held in two rounds, on 10 and 17 June 1990. The BSP won 211 seats, but failed to secure the two-thirds' majority of seats in the legislature necessary to secure support for the approval of constitutional and economic reforms. The UDF, which won the majority of votes in urban areas, obtained 144 seats in the Assembly. The Movement for Rights and Freedoms (MRF), which had been established earlier in 1990 to represent the country's Muslim minority, won a large percentage of the votes in areas populated by ethnic Turks, and secured 23 seats. The BAPU won 16 seats in the legislature, considerably fewer than had been expected. The UDF, after initial protests against alleged electoral fraud, accepted the validity of the result, although it again rejected the BSP's invitation to join a coalition government.

In July 1990 Mladenov announced his resignation as President, following a campaign of protests and strikes, led by students. Zhelyu Zhelev, the Chairman of the UDF, was elected to replace him in early August. Zhelev was succeeded as Chairman of the UDF first by Petur Beron, hitherto the party's Secretary, and, from December, by Filip Dimitrov, a lawyer and the Vice-President of the Green Party.

The severe deterioration in the economy in 1990 resulted in widespread shortages of food and fuel. Increasing division between conservative and reformist elements within the BSP became manifest in early November 1990, when 16 BSP delegates to the Grand National Assembly announced their decision to form a separate parliamentary group, as a result of which the party no longer held an absolute majority in the legislature. Following a four-day general strike organized by Podkrepa, Lukanov's Government resigned at the end of the month. Subsequent discussions between representatives of all the political forces in the Grand National Assembly resulted in the formation of a new 'government of national consensus' in mid-December, comprising members of the BSP, the UDF, the BAPU and four independents. Dimitur Popov, a lawyer with no party affiliation, had been elected in early December to chair the new Council of Ministers.

In mid-November 1990 the Grand National Assembly voted to rename the country the Republic of Bulgaria and to remove from the national flag the state emblem, which included communist symbols. The Grand National Assembly adopted a new Constitution in mid-July 1991; it subsequently voted to dissolve itself, although it continued sessions in an interim capacity, pending a legislative election. The Constitution stipulated, *inter alia*, a five-year residency qualification for presidential candidates, effectively disqualifying the candidacy of Simeon Saxe-Coburg Gotha (Saxe-Coburgotski—Simeon II), the pretender to the Bulgarian throne, who had lived in exile since 1946. In the months preceding the parliamentary election, internal divisions arose in many of the major parties, including the UDF. Nevertheless, at the election to the new, 240-seat National Assembly, held on 13 October, the UDF obtained the largest share of the votes cast (34.4%), defeating the BSP (which contested the election in alliance with a number of smaller parties) by just over 1%. The UDF won a total of 110 seats in the legislature, while the BSP obtained 106. The ethnic Turkish MRF became the third strongest political force, securing 24 seats. The new Council of Ministers, composed of UDF members and six independents, was announced in early November. Filip Dimitrov, the leader of the UDF, was elected Chairman of the new Government. A direct presidential election was held in January 1992. Following an inconclusive first round, a second ballot, involving the two leading candidates (the incumbent President, Zhelev, and Velko Valkanov, an independent supported by the BSP), took place. Zhelev was re-elected for a five-year term, receiving 53% of the votes cast.

In March 1992 the Minister of Foreign Affairs, Stoyan Ganev, and President Zhelev agreed that the National Intelligence Service was eventually to be placed under the jurisdiction of the Government, rather than the Office of the Presidency. In early April, despite BSP opposition, the Government adopted legislation restoring ownership of land and property that had been transferred to the state during 1947–62; legislation approving the privatization of state-owned companies followed. In the same month a programme of price liberalization, which had been adopted in early 1991 in fulfilment of IMF conditions, caused trade-union disaffection.

In May 1992, in what was widely believed to be indicative of a broader struggle for control of the increasingly factional UDF, Dimitrov threatened to resign as Prime Minister, unless the Minister of Defence, Dimitur Ludzhev, relinquished his post. Ludzhev resigned later that month, and Dimitrov implemented an extensive reorganization of the Council of Ministers. In July the former BCP Prime Minister, Lukanov (by that time a BSP deputy), was arrested, prompting the remaining BSP deputies to withdraw from a meeting of the National Assembly in protest. Legal proceedings were initiated against Lukanov and a further 60 senior officials (including two other former Prime Ministers, Grisha Filipov and Georgi Atanasov) on charges of misappropriating state funds. (Atanasov was pardoned in August 1994.)

In mid-July 1992 there were strikes, supported by Podkrepa, by miners and other public-sector employees. In early August the Chairman of Podkrepa, Konstantin Trenchev, was arrested with 37 others, and charged with incitement to destroy public property in 1990. Meanwhile, relations between President Zhelev and the UDF became increasingly strained. At the end of October MRF and BSP deputies in the National Assembly defeated the Government in a motion of confidence proposed by Dimitrov; the Government subsequently resigned.

In November 1992 President Zhelev invited Dimitrov (as the nominee of the party with the largest representation in the National Assembly) to form a new government. The MRF, however, declined to form a coalition with the UDF, and Dimitrov's nomination was thus defeated in the National Assembly. President Zhelev then rejected the candidacy of a BSP nominee, who held dual nationality, in contravention of the terms of the Constitution. Following the failure of the UDF and the MRF to reach agreement for a coalition under the MRF mandate, in December the MRF nominated an academic, Prof. Lyuben Berov, hitherto an economic adviser to President Zhelev, to the office of Prime Minister. The UDF accused Berov of collaborating with the former communist regime and organized a large rally to protest against his candidacy, while threatening to expel members who voted in his favour in the National Assembly. In the event, the majority of UDF deputies abstained, but Berov was approved as Prime Minister on 30 December by 124 votes to 25, in a secret ballot. Berov's proposed Council of Ministers, principally composed of 'experts' without party political allegiances, was also accepted by the National Assembly. On the same day, the BSP and the MRF voted in the National Assembly to discharge Lukanov from custody. It was widely speculated that BSP support for Berov's Government had been, in part, conditional on Lukanov's release.

In March 1993 internal divisions within the UDF became more apparent when a breakaway faction of the party formed a new, pro-Berov organization, known as the New Union for Democracy (NUD); in response, the UDF intensified its campaign of opposition. Large-scale demonstrations were staged by the UDF in Sofia and several other cities in June, to accuse Zhelev of attempting to restore communism, and to demand immediate elections. On 29 June the Vice-President, Blaga Dimitrova, resigned. The crisis finally subsided when three votes expressing 'no confidence' in Berov's Government, which were proposed by the UDF in the National Assembly, proved unsuccessful; political unrest continued, however.

In January 1994 Zhivkov was sentenced to seven years in prison for embezzlement of government funds. (In February 1996, however, the Supreme Court upheld his appeal against the sentence.) By February 1994 the Berov Government had survived its fifth motion of 'no confidence'. In early April Zhelev announced that he could no longer give his support to Berov's administration, citing its failure to implement objectives such as an accelerated privatization programme. Following the controversial introduction of value-added tax (VAT), unpopular increases in fuel prices and the dramatic fall of the national currency, the lev, thousands of demonstrators protested in Sofia against government policies. In May Berov's Government survived two further votes of 'no confidence'; the UDF deputies subsequently boycotted National Assembly sessions throughout June.

In late June 1994 the Government finally launched the delayed privatization programme. Each citizen was offered a 500-leva voucher, which could be invested either directly into state enterprises or into private investment funds. In early September, however, Berov's Government submitted its resignation, following criticism of the poor organization of the programme. Both the BSP and the UDF refused presidential mandates to form a new Government. In October President Zhelev dissolved the National Assembly and announced that a general election would take place in December. Later in October Zhelev appointed an interim neutral Government, headed by Reneta Indzhova.

At the general election, which was held as scheduled on 18 December 1994, the BSP (in alliance, as the Democratic Left, with two small parties, the Aleksandur Stamboliyski Bulgarian Agrarian People's Union and the Ecoglasnost Political Club—the political wing of the Ecoglasnost National Movement)—obtained an outright majority in the National Assembly, with 125 seats (43.5% of the total votes cast); the UDF won 69 seats (24.2%). Other groups that obtained more than the 4% of votes required for representation in the legislature were: the People's Union (an alliance of the BAPU and the Democratic Party), the MRF and the Bulgarian Business Bloc (BBB). A new Government, headed by the Chairman of the BSP, Zhan Videnov, was appointed at the end of January 1995; the majority of the ministers were BSP members.

In February 1995 the National Assembly amended the 1992 property restitution law (see above), extending for a further three years the deadline by which certain properties had to be restored to their rightful owners. In March the National

Assembly abolished a law, adopted by the UDF Government in 1992, prohibiting former communists from holding senior academic positions. In the same month the Government drafted a programme for mass privatization in 1995, which envisaged payment through a combination of cash, debt bonds and investment vouchers (made available from January 1996). Demonstrations took place throughout March 1995, however, reflecting widespread dissatisfaction with government amendments to the Agricultural Land Tenure Act, that they feared would restrict landowners' rights to dispose of their property and would encourage the restoration of communist-style collective farms. In late April President Zhelev exercised his right of veto against the highly unpopular amendments.

In late June 1995 the dismissals of the heads of the state television and radio services and the Director-General of the national news agency led to opposition allegations that the BSP was attempting to control the state media. In late September the Government survived a motion of 'no confidence', which was introduced in protest at its failure to control the rapid increase in levels of crime. At municipal elections in late October and early November, the ruling coalition won 195 of a total of 255 mayoralties, although the UDF secured the mayoralties in the country's three main cities. In January 1996 a further motion of 'no confidence' in the Videnov administration, proposed in protest at a severe shortage of grain, which had resulted from the Government's repeal of a ban on grain exports in July 1995, was defeated, although the situation prompted the resignations of the Deputy Prime Minister and an additional two ministers. Meanwhile, a sharp devaluation of the lev resulted in further economic hardship. In June 1996 the UDF proposed a motion expressing 'no confidence' in the Government's management of the economy, which was, however, defeated by a large majority.

In primary elections for a UDF presidential candidate, which were conducted in early June 1996, Petar Stoyanov, a lawyer and senior member of the opposition alliance, secured 66% of the votes cast, defeating Zhelev. Zhelev subsequently announced his support for Stoyanov's candidature. In July the National Assembly scheduled the presidential election for 27 October. In the same month the Constitutional Court ruled that the candidacy of the Minister of Foreign Affairs, Georgi Pirinski, nominated on behalf of the BSP (and widely considered to be the most popular nominee), was ineligible, on the grounds that he was not a Bulgarian citizen by birth, as stipulated in the Constitution; Pirinski declared that political bias had influenced the decision. In September the BSP selected the Minister of Culture, Ivan Marazov, as its presidential candidate; Marazov was to represent a newly formed electoral alliance, known as Together for Bulgaria, which comprised the parties in the Democratic Left parliamentary coalition (the BSP, Aleksandur Stamboliyski and the Ecoglasnost Political Club).

In early October 1996 the former Prime Minister, Andrei Lukanov (who had remained an influential member of the BSP), was assassinated. Ensuing speculation regarding the motive for the killing focused, in particular, on Lukanov's critical stance towards the Videnov administration's slow implementation of economic reforms. Later that month the main trade-union federations, the Confederation of Independent Trade Unions in Bulgaria (CITUB) and Podkrepa, organized a demonstration in Sofia to demand the resignation of the Government. In the first round of the presidential election, which took place on 27 October (as scheduled), Stoyanov secured 44.1% of the votes cast; Marazov received only 27.0% of the votes, while the candidate of the BBB, Georgi Ganchev, won 21.9%. Only 61% of the electorate voted in the second round, which took place on 3 November, reflecting increasing public disaffection with the Government's management of the critical economic situation. Stoyanov was elected to the presidency, with 59.7% of the votes cast. He subsequently announced plans to establish a Council of National Salvation, which would devise measures to improve financial stability. Following Stoyanov's election, the political council of the UDF agreed to initiate a campaign to demand that a parliamentary election be conducted later that year (earlier than scheduled). The defeat of the BSP candidate in the presidential election aggravated existing divisions within the organization; in early November several senior members of the BSP accused Videnov of causing the party's unpopularity and demanded the resignation of the Government. Later in November Pirinski, who was a leading opponent of Videnov within the BSP, submitted his resignation.

In December 1996 the UDF staged a series of demonstrations to demand an early legislative election and the resignation of the Government. On 21 December, at an extraordinary congress of the BSP, Videnov tendered his resignation from the office of Prime Minister and the post of party leader. (The incumbent Council of Ministers was to remain in office, pending the formation of a new administration.) Georgi Purvanov, who was a supporter of Videnov, subsequently replaced him as Chairman of the BSP. At the end of December the National Assembly voted by a large majority to accept the resignation of Videnov's Government. The UDF, however, intensified its campaign of demonstrations; in early January an attempt by protesters to seize the parliamentary building was suppressed by security forces. On 19 January Stoyanov was inaugurated as President, and at the end of January the BSP accepted a proposal by Stoyanov that the party form a new government, pending a legislative election. In early February the BSP announced the appointment of a new Council of Ministers; following continued protests and strikes by supporters of the UDF, however, Nikolai Dobrev (the Minister of the Interior in the previous administration) agreed to relinquish the party's mandate to form a new government, owing to increasing concern that the disorder might escalate into civil conflict. The Consultative National Security Council adopted recommendations (which were approved by the National Assembly) that, in the absence of agreement between the political parties represented in the legislature on the formation of a government, the President should appoint an interim council of ministers, dissolve the National Assembly and schedule a legislative election. Stoyanov subsequently nominated the mayor of Sofia, Stefan Sofiyanski, to the office of Prime Minister, and formed an interim Council of Ministers, pending the election, which was scheduled to be held in mid-April; the National Assembly was dissolved on 19 February. Following the resumption of negotiations between the new Government and the IMF, agreement was reached in March regarding the establishment of a currency control board, as a prerequisite to economic and financial stability. Later in March the interim Government announced that Videnov was to be charged with criminal negligence as a result of government policies that had caused the severe shortage of grain in 1995–96; the Minister of Agriculture in the Videnov administration and three of his deputies were also prosecuted.

At the election to the National Assembly, which took place, as scheduled, on 19 April 1997, the UDF secured 137 seats, while the BSP (which again contested the elections in the Democratic Left alliance) obtained only 58 seats; the Alliance for National Salvation (a coalition comprising the MRF and other monarchist and centrist groups) won 19 seats, a newly established left-wing organization, known as Euro-Left, obtained 14 seats and the BBB 12 seats. Later in April the UDF formally nominated the party Chairman, Ivan Kostov, to the office of Prime Minister (subject to the approval of the National Assembly). At the first session of the new National Assembly, which was convened in early May, deputies adopted, despite some opposition, a seven-point declaration of national consensus, which had been proposed by the UDF; the stated policies included the implementation of economic reforms that had been agreed with the IMF, the acceleration of measures to restore agricultural land to rightful ownership and support for Bulgaria's accession to the European Union (EU, see p. 199) and NATO (see p. 271). Later in May the National Assembly elected Kostov to the office of Prime Minister; only deputies belonging to the Democratic Left alliance opposed his nomination. The new Council of Ministers, which had been formed by Kostov, included five members of the outgoing interim administration.

In June 1997 the National Assembly adopted legislation providing for the establishment of the currency control board, which was installed at the beginning of July. In a further effort to impose fiscal discipline, the Government replaced the senior officials of the Bulgarian National Bank; Svetoslav Gavriyski, who had served as Minister of Finance in the interim Council of Ministers, was appointed Governor. At the end of July the National Assembly voted in favour of declassifying security files on politicians and public officials, and adopted legislation to expedite the restoration of land to rightful ownership. In early September two parliamentary representatives of the BBB were expelled from the party after criticizing the leadership of Ganchev, who, they claimed, intended to establish links with the BSP; another deputy resigned in protest at their removal. The BBB was consequently obliged to dissolve its parliamentary group, which had been reduced to below the required minimum of 10 representatives. In October a government commission announced that 23 prominent public officials, including 14 members of the National Assembly, had been members of the security services of former communist governments. In early November, following protests from deputies belonging to the Democratic Left, the Constitutional Court ruled that the appointment of directors of the national radio and television stations by the National Assembly (rather than by an independent media council) was in contravention of the Constitution. In January 1998 the National Assembly rejected a motion expressing 'no confidence' in the Government, which had been proposed by Democratic Left deputies in protest at the Council of Ministers' policy on health care. In March, at an annual congress of the BSP, Purvanov was re-elected as Chairman of the party, obtaining 58% of the votes cast. In late September a Security Council, chaired by the Prime Minister, was established to advise on state security activities.

In April 1999 the Government, accused of nepotism and corruption, survived a second vote of 'no confidence' in the National Assembly. Local government elections took place on 16 and 23 October: the UDF won 31.3% of the votes cast, and the BSP secured 29.4%. In December Kostov reorganized the Council of Ministers, reducing the number of deputy premiers from three to one, and appointing Boiko Noev as Minister of Defence. In May 2000 Kostov's administration survived a third vote of 'no confidence', and in February 2001 the National Assembly rejected a further confidence motion, proposed in response to the worsening crime situation. Meanwhile, in January, in advance of presidential and legislative elections, the BSP attempted to consolidate support by forming an alliance, known as the Coalition for Bulgaria, with 14 other, smaller leftist and nationalist groups. Several parliamentary deputies subsequently defected from the UDF in order to form a new party, the Conservative Union. In April the former monarch, Simeon Saxe-Coburg Gotha, who returned to Bulgaria at the beginning of the month, failed to be permitted legally to register his new National Movement as a party. None the less, in May the Movement was permitted to form an alliance with two smaller, registered parties, the Party of Bulgarian Women and the Oborishte Party for National Revival, as the National Movement Simeon II (NMSII), under a nominal leader, Vesela Draganova, in order to participate in the legislative election. Saxe-Coburg Gotha asserted that he had no desire to restore the monarchy, and pledged to combat official corruption and reform the economy, in order to fulfil the criteria for EU membership.

In the general election, which was held on 17 June 2001, the NMSII received 42.7% of the votes cast (120 seats), while the incumbent UDF secured only 18.2% of the votes (51 seats), reflecting an emphatic rejection of the party's regime of economic austerity and its perceived links with corruption. Other parties to win seats in parliament were the Coalition for Bulgaria, which obtained 17.1% of the votes (48 seats), and the MRF, with 7.5% of the votes (21 seats). The NMSII held just one seat fewer than the 121 required to secure an absolute majority in the National Assembly; however, it had declared its intention to form a coalition government throughout its election campaign, and it approached the MRF and the UDF as potential partners. The MRF agreed to be represented (for the first time) in government, but the latter party refused to participate in a government that comprised members of the MRF; the BSP subsequently became an informal coalition partner. Saxe-Coburg Gotha was sworn in as Prime Minister on 24 July. The Council of Ministers, in which two ministerial portfolios were allocated to both the MRF and the BSP, was approved by the National Assembly on the same day, although members of the UDF voted against the new cabinet, in protest at the presence of the BSP. Kostov subsequently resigned his leadership of the UDF.

In the first round of voting in the presidential election, held on 11 November 2001, at which the rate of participation by the electorate was just 39.2%, Georgi Purvanov of the Coalition for Bulgaria won 36.4% of the votes cast, and the incumbent, Stoyanov, who stood as an independent candidate, secured 34.9% of the votes. Purvanov confirmed his victory in a second round of voting on 18 November, in which he obtained 54.1% of the votes cast, compared with the 45.9% of the votes received by Stoyanov; the rate of voter participation was some 54.6%. The result of the election, which was largely unanticipated, given the electorate's rejection of the BSP in the legislative election and the support of both Saxe-Coburg Gotha and the UDF for the incumbent, was widely interpreted as an expression of protest by a frustrated electorate. Purvanov was sworn in as President on 19 January 2002 and took office three days later.

A rally was held by the CITUB and Podkrepa in November 2001, in protest at the NMSII's failure to bring about the promised economic progress within its first 100 days in government (partly owing to fiscal constraints resulting from IMF recommendations). In early December the Government released a report, which accused the Kostov Government of unscrupulous actions with regard to the privatization process, and announced the establishment of an investigative commission. In mid-February 2002 the Government survived a vote of 'no confidence', which had been proposed by the UDF, by 134 votes to 50 (a number of BSP deputies abstained from voting). In the following month five members of the National Assembly left the NMSII, in protest at Saxe-Coburg Gotha's perceived failure to fulfil electoral pledges. In April the NMSII was finally legally registered as a political party, and Saxe-Coburg Gotha was elected as its Chairman. The new post of Minister of European Affairs was created in late May, and Meglena Kuneva was appointed to fill it. At the end of October Kostadin Paskalev of the BSP submitted his resignation as Deputy Prime Minister and Minister of Regional Development and Public Works, reportedly owing to frustration at the Ministry's increasingly restricted budget. In mid-December an NMSII member, Valentin Tserovski, was nominated to replace Paskalev as Minister of Regional Development and Public Works.

In early October 2002 the National Assembly voted in favour of closing the third and fourth reactors of the Kozluduy nuclear power plant (in compliance with EU demands) following Bulgaria's accession to the Union, which was not anticipated to take place before 2007. However, in mid-November 2002 the Government signed an agreement with the EU, according to which it undertook to decommission the reactors by 2006. Later in November 2002 the Government survived votes of 'no confidence' brought by the UDF and the Coalition for Bulgaria, which, respectively, regarded the agreement as a violation of the Constitution and accused the Government of failing to act in the country's interests. In early January 2003, following a legal challenge by the BSP, the Supreme Administrative Court ruled the government agreement to be invalid, announcing that only the National Assembly could decide on the closure of the two reactors. Meanwhile, in December 2002 the Government passed controversial draft legislation, which required all religious organizations, with the exception of the Bulgarian Orthodox Church, to be registered officially; the legislation was opposed by the NMSII's junior coalition partner, the MRF. In the same month the Supreme Judicial Council requested the resignation of the Prosecutor-General, Nikola Filchev, citing accusations that included abuse of office. However, the Council was not empowered to remove the Prosecutor-General's legal immunity and there was no legal obligation for Filchev to resign. In late December Nikolai Kolev, a senior prosecutor at the Supreme Administrative Prosecution Office (and an opponent of Filchev), was shot and killed.

Following efforts by the Supreme Administrative Court to suspend the sales of both Bulgartabac and the Bulgarian Telecommunications Company in late 2002 (see Economic Affairs), at the end of January 2003 the National Assembly approved controversial legislation removing the Court's power to block the privatization of key state enterprises; divestments were, instead, to be decided by the Government, with the approval of the National Assembly. In late February Purvanov exercised his right of veto, on the grounds that the legislation contravened the Constitution; later that month, however, the ruling majority in the National Assembly voted to override the presidential veto. A petition was subsequently lodged with the Constitutional Court by the President, the UDF and the BSP. Meanwhile, in mid-February five members of parliament had left the NMSII, alleging widespread corruption within the Government, and thereby reducing the governing coalition's majority in the National Assembly to just 10 seats. In early March Ilya Pavlov, a prominent *oligarch*, was shot and killed, one day after testifying in the trial of five people accused of the murder of former Prime Minister Andrei Lukanov.

Bulgaria's establishment of formal relations with the former Yugoslav republic of Macedonia (FYRM) in January 1992 prompted harsh criticism from the Greek Government, although relations with Greece appeared to improve thereafter. In November 1993 the FYRM expressed its desire to establish full diplomatic relations with Bulgaria, and in the following month Bulgaria announced that it was to open an embassy in the FYRM and relax border procedures between the two states. In February 1999 Prime Minister Kostov and the Prime Minister of the FYRM, Ljubčo Georgievski, signed a declaration pledging that neither country had a territorial claim on the other. In March the Ministers of Defence of Bulgaria and the FYRM signed a joint declaration providing for increased military co-operation, including joint exercises and the supply of military equipment to the FYRM, in connection with the aim of both countries to join NATO. Public opposition in Bulgaria to the NATO air bombardment of Yugoslavia in March–June 1999 (see chapter on Serbia and Montenegro), increased, after a mis-directed NATO missile damaged a private residence in the outskirts of Sofia in April. Nevertheless, the Bulgarian National Assembly approved a decision made by the Council of Ministers to allow NATO use of the country's airspace.

In June 2000, after eight years of discussions, relations with Romania were significantly improved by the signature of an agreement on the construction of a second bridge over the River Danube, from Vidin to Calafat, in Romania; the link was to improve road connections between the Balkans and western Europe. Ties with Romania were strengthened from 2000, owing to that country's concurrent negotiations for accession to the EU, and in August 2001 Bulgaria and Romania agreed to campaign jointly for membership of both the EU and NATO.

Relations between Bulgaria and Russia improved in 1992, following the signature of co-operation agreements, and the visit of the Russian President, Boris Yeltsin, to Sofia in August. In April 1998 the Bulgarian Government signed a significant agreement with the Russian national gas company, Gazprom, providing for the supply and transit of Russian gas (see Economic Affairs). In December 2000 Russia expressed its dis-appointment at Bulgaria's decision to terminate, in accordance with conditions for accession to the EU, a 1978 bilateral agree-ment on visa-free travel, with effect from June 2001. However, in March 2003 Russian President Vladimir Putin visited Bul-garia, resulting in strongly enhanced economic relations (already a significant trading partner, Russia sought to increase its influence with regard to Balkan power supplies), despite failing to persuade Bulgaria to withdraw its support for a US-led war in Iraq (see below).

Relations with neighbouring Turkey were intermittently strained from the mid-1980s, when the Zhivkov regime began a campaign of forced assimilation of Bulgaria's ethnic Turkish minority (which constitutes an estimated 10% of the total popu-lation). The ethnic Turks were forced to adopt Slavic names prior to the December 1985 census, and were banned from practising Islamic religious rites. In February 1988 Bulgaria and Turkey signed a protocol to further bilateral economic and social relations. However, in May 1989 Bulgarian militia units violently suppressed demonstrations by an estimated 30,000 ethnic Turks in eastern Bulgaria against the assimilation cam-paign. In June more than 80,000 ethnic Turks were expelled from Bulgaria, although the Bulgarian authorities claimed that the Turks had chosen to settle in Turkey, following a relaxation in passport regulations. By mid-August an estimated 310,000 Bulgarian Turks had crossed into Turkey, and in late August the Turkish Government, alarmed by the continued influx of refugees, closed the border. In the following month a substantial number of the Bulgarian Turks, disillusioned with conditions in Turkey, began to return to Bulgaria. The Turkish Government repeatedly proposed that discussions with the Bulgarian Gov-ernment be held, under the auspices of the UN High Commis-sioner for Refugees, to establish the rights of the Bulgarian Turks and to formulate a clear immigration policy. Finally, Bulgaria agreed to negotiations and friendly relations between Bulgaria and Turkey had apparently been restored by late 1991.

Meanwhile, in December 1989 some 6,000 Pomaks (ethnic Bulgarian Muslims) held demonstrations to demand religious and cultural freedoms, as well as an official inquiry into alleged atrocities against Pomaks during Zhivkov's tenure of office. In January 1990 anti-Turkish demonstrations were held in the Kurdzhali district of southern Bulgaria, in protest at the Gov-ernment's declared intention to restore civil and religious rights to the ethnic Turkish minority. Despite continuing demon-strations by Bulgarian nationalist protesters, in March the National Assembly approved legislation that permitted ethnic Turks and Pomaks to use their original Islamic names. This development was welcomed by the Turkish Government. Never-theless, inter-ethnic disturbances continued, particularly in the Kurdzhali region, during 1990. In May 1992 Prime Minister Dimitrov visited Turkey, and the two countries signed a treaty of friendship and co-operation. By 1993 ethnic tensions had generally been contained in Bulgaria, although there were

reports of some disturbances between ethnic Turks and ethnic Bulgarian Muslims in the south of the country. In July 1995 a visit by President Demirel of Turkey to Bulgaria indicated a significant improvement in Bulgarian-Turkish relations. In June 1998 the National Assembly ratified an agreement demar-cating the border between Bulgaria and Turkey (which had been signed during an official visit to Sofia by the Turkish Prime Minister, Mesut Yılmaz, in December 1997). In February 2001 Bulgaria and Turkey signed a joint protocol on combating ter-rorism and organized crime.

Bulgaria's relations with the USA became stronger during 2002, and in February 2003 the National Assembly voted to allow US forces to make use of Bulgarian airspace, as well as the air base at Sarafovo, on the Black Sea, for military operations during the impending US-led campaign to remove the regime of Saddam Hussein in Iraq (see chapters on Iraq and the USA); Bulgaria had previously offered its support to the USA during the military campaign in Afghanistan, initiated following the terrorist attacks on the US cities of New York and Washington, DC, on 11 September 2001 (see US chapter). Also in February 2003, during a visit by Prime Minister Saxe-Coburg Gotha to Washington, the US offered guarantees of the repayment of Iraq's foreign debt to Bulgaria (halted since 1990), in the event of a war. The conflict in Iraq (which commenced in March) was strongly opposed by a number of European countries, notably France, and in February 2003 French President Jacques Chirac condemned both Bulgaria and Romania as 'irresponsible' in offering the USA their support.

In mid-1992 Bulgaria became a member of the Council of Europe (see p. 181), and in May 1994 Bulgaria was granted associate partnership status by Western European Union (WEU, see p. 317). In June 1992 Bulgaria, together with 10 other countries (including six of the former Soviet republics), signed a pact to establish what became the Organization of the Black Sea Economic Co-operation (see p. 294), which envisaged the creation of a Black Sea economic zone that would comple-ment the European Community (now EU). In 1996 Bulgaria submitted an official application for membership of the EU. In October of that year Bulgaria joined the World Trade Organ-ization (see p. 322). Negotiations on Bulgaria's accession to the EU, which was conditional on the Government's fulfilment of certain criteria (see Economic Affairs), began in March 2000, and Bulgaria was expected to be admitted as a full member in 2007. In November 2002, at a NATO summit meeting held in Prague, Czech Republic, seven countries, including Bulgaria, were formally invited to accede to the Organization in 2004.

Government

Legislative power is held by the unicameral National Assembly, comprising 240 members, who are elected for four years by universal adult suffrage. The President of the Republic (Head of State) is directly elected for a period of five years, and is also Supreme Commander-in-Chief of the Armed Forces. The Council of Ministers, the highest organ of state administration, is elected by the National Assembly. For local administration purposes, Bulgaria comprises 28 regions (divided into a total of 259 municipalities).

Defence

Military service is compulsory and lasts for nine months. The total strength of the armed forces in August 2002 was estimated at 68,450 (including some 49,000 conscripts), comprising an army of 31,050, an air force of 17,780, a navy of an estimated 4,370, and 15,250 centrally controlled and Ministry of Defence staff. Paramilitary forces include an estimated 12,000 border guards, 18,000 railway and construction troops and 4,000 se-curity police. In late 1999 the Government announced plans to reduce the armed forces to number 45,000 by 2004. The defence budget for 2002 allocated some 828m. leva to defence. Bulgaria joined NATO's 'Partnership for Peace' programme of military co-operation in 1994. In November 2002 Bulgaria was invited to join NATO, and it was expected to accede to the Organization in 2004.

Economic Affairs

In 2001, according to estimates by the World Bank, Bulgaria's gross national income (GNI), measured at average 1999–2001 prices, was US $12,644m., equivalent to $1,560 per head (or $5,950 per head on an international purchasing-power parity basis). During 1990–2001, it was estimated, the population decreased at an average rate of 0.6% per year, while gross domestic product (GDP) per head decreased, in real terms, at an average annual rate of 0.8%. According to the World Bank, Bulgaria's overall GDP declined, in real terms, by an average of 1.4% annually during 1990–2001. However, real GDP increased by 5.8% in 2000 and by 4.5% in 2001.

Agriculture contributed some 13.7% of GDP in 2001, when the sector (including hunting, forestry and fishing) engaged 26.3% of the employed labour force. In 1990 private farming was legalized, and farmland was restituted, in its former physical boundaries, to former owners and their heirs; by the end of 1999 96% of land restitution had been completed. In 1996 privately owned farms supplied 75.4% of total agricultural production. The principal crops are wheat, maize, barley, sunflower seeds, potatoes, tomatoes and melons. Bulgaria is a major exporter of wine, although grape production declined in the late 1990s. There is a large exportable surplus of processed agricultural products. During 1990–2001, according to the World Bank, the average annual GDP of the agricultural sector decreased, in real terms, by 1.0%. Agricultural GDP declined by 10.1% in 2000 and by 0.1% in 2001.

Industry provided some 28.4% of GDP in 2001, and the sector (including mining, manufacturing, construction and utilities) engaged 27.6% of the employed labour force. According to the World Bank, industrial GDP declined, in real terms, at an average annual rate of 2.3% in 1990–2001. However, industrial GDP increased by 15.3% in 1999 and by 5.4% in 2001.

In 1999 mining accounted for some 1.7% of GDP, and in 2001 mining and quarrying engaged 1.2% of the employed labour force. Coal, iron ore, copper, manganese, lead and zinc are mined, and petroleum is extracted on the Black Sea coast.

The manufacturing sector accounted for 17.8% of GDP in 2001, when it engaged 20.1% of the employed labour force. Based on the value of output, the main branches of manufacturing in 1998 were food products, beverages and tobacco products, refined petroleum products, basic metals, and chemicals and chemical products. The GDP of the manufacturing sector increased by 6.5% in 1998, but declined by 5.9% in 1999.

Bulgaria's production of primary energy in 1998 was equivalent to 51.3% of gross consumption. Coal and nuclear power, produced by the country's sole nuclear power station, at Kozloduy, are the main domestic sources of energy. Coal accounted for 43.4% of electricity production in 1999, and nuclear power provided 41.6% of electric energy in that year. Bulgaria has established itself as a major regional electricity exporter, and in 2000 it more than doubled its electricity exports. Imports of mineral fuels and lubricants comprised 22.2% of the value of merchandise imports in 2001, according to provisional figures.

The services sector contributed some 57.9% of GDP in 2001, and engaged 46.0% of the employed labour force. According to preliminary figures, in 2002 tourism revenues increased significantly. The World Bank estimated that the real GDP of the services sector increased at an average rate of 0.5% per year in 1990–2001. The sector's GDP increased by 5.6% in 2000 and by 6.3% in 2001.

In 2001 Bulgaria recorded a visible trade deficit of US $1,576m., and there was a deficit of $889m. on the current account of the balance of payments. In that year the principal sources of imports were Russia, which provided 14.7% of the total and Germany, which provided 14.3%. Italy, Greece and France were also major suppliers. The main market for exports in 2002 was Italy (taking 15.3% of the total); Germany, Turkey and Greece were also significant purchasers. The principal exports in 2001 were base metals, mineral products, chemicals, and clothing and accessories. The principal imports in that year were mineral fuels and lubricants (particularly petroleum and petroleum products), chemicals and related products, nuclear machinery and mechanical appliances, vehicles and transport equipment, electrical equipment and machinery, and base metals.

In 2001 Bulgaria recorded a budgetary surplus of 555.9m. leva (equivalent to 1.1% of GDP). Bulgaria's total external debt at the end of 2000 was US $10,026m., of which $7,513m. was long-term public debt. In that year the cost of debt-servicing was equivalent to 16.2% of revenue from exports of goods and services. The annual rate of inflation averaged 82.6% in 1995–2001. Consumer prices increased by 1,058.4% in 1997, but by only 22.3% in 1998 and by 2.6% in 1999, before increasing by 10.3% in 2000, by 7.4% in 2001 and by 5.8% in 2002. Some 16.8% of the labour force were registered as unemployed at December 2002 .

Bulgaria is a member of the International Bank for Economic Co-operation (see p. 340), the UN Economic Commission for Europe (see p. 27), and the Organization of the Black Sea Economic Co-operation. In 1990 Bulgaria became a member of the IMF and the World Bank. Bulgaria made a formal application for membership of the European Union (EU) in 1996, and in 1999 was admitted to the Central European Free Trade Association (CEFTA). Bulgaria is a founding member of the European Bank for Reconstruction and Development (EBRD, see p. 193), established in 1990.

At the beginning of the 1990s, in an effort to prevent economic collapse, the Government introduced an extensive programme of privatization and restructuring of the banking system, and in 1991 adopted austerity measures in fulfilment of conditions stipulated by the IMF. In May 1996 there was a dramatic reduction in the value of the lev, and in September the IMF suspended the disbursement of funds. Following the resumption of negotiations between a new interim administration (see Recent History) and the IMF, agreement was reached in March 1997 on the adoption of structural reforms. In an effort to impose fiscal discipline, the Government established a currency control board in July, which fixed the exchange rate of the lev to that of the German Deutsche Mark. Bulgaria began accession talks with the EU in March 2000 and was expected to accede to the organization in 2007. In order to comply with conditions for EU membership, two of the Kozloduy nuclear power installation's six reactors were closed at the end of 2002; an agreement had been reached with the EU in November on the closure of two additional reactors by 2006, and the country was to be granted financial assistance to restructure the energy sector and upgrade the remaining two nuclear reactors, which accounted for much of the country's electricity production. However, in early 2003 the Supreme Administrative Court ruled the Government's decision on the early closure of the third and fourth reactors to be illegal, as it had been made without the approval of the National Assembly. Investor confidence was shaken in late 2002, when long-delayed progress towards the privatization of the state tobacco company, Bulgartabac, and the Bulgarian Telecommunications Company was halted, owing to claims that legislation on privatization had been violated; however, in early January 2003 the Supreme Administrative Court ruled that the privatization of the telecommunications company could proceed as planned. In the following month the Government introduced new legislation on privatization, overriding a presidential veto in order to rescind the right of the Supreme Court to suspend or cancel major privatization deals considered to be in the national interest. Meanwhile, in February the Government agreed to form a joint-stock company, the Trans-Balkan Oil Pipeline Bulgaria, which was to manage the country's 33% stake in a project to construct a petroleum pipeline to transport Russian petroleum from the port of Burgas to Alexandroupolis (Greece). An accord on the construction of the proposed pipeline had been signed by Greece and Bulgaria in the previous month, resolving a number of outstanding issues, which had delayed progress since the signature of an original agreement in January 1997. In 2002 progress was made in reducing the unemployment rate (which, none the less, remained high), maintaining a low rate of consumer-price inflation and increasing growth, and the budget for 2003 envisaged continued growth, of some 4.6%, and an annual rate of inflation of around 4.0%. However, the IMF expressed concern at government plans to use fiscal reserves to establish an emergency investment fund, and was critical of the delayed implementation of education and health reforms.

Education

Education is free and compulsory between the ages of seven and 16 years. Children between the ages of three and six years may attend kindergartens (in 1995 62% of pre-school age children attended). A 12-year system of schooling was introduced in 1998. Primary education, beginning at seven years of age, lasts for four years. Secondary education, from 11 years of age, lasts for up to eight years, comprising two cycles of four years each. Secondary education is undertaken at general schools, which provide a general academic course, or vocational and technical schools, and art schools, which offer specialized training. In 1998 primary enrolment included 93% of children in the relevant age-group, while enrolment at secondary schools included 81% of those in the relevant age-group. In the mid-1990s the system of higher education was reorganized extensively. In 1999/2000 there were a total of 41 higher educational institutions, with a total enrolment of 242,860 students, and an additional 47 colleges. Tuition fees for university students were introduced in mid-1999.

In 1997 enrolment in higher education courses was equivalent to 41.2% of those in the relevant age-group. The 2001 state budget allocated 456.1m. leva to education (representing 4.5% of total expenditure by the central Government).

Public Holidays

2003: 1 January (New Year), 3 March (National Day), 18–21 April (Easter), 1 May (Labour Day), 6 May (St George's Day), 24 May (Education Day), 6 September (Union of Eastern Rumelia and the Bulgarian Principality), 22 September (Independence Day), 1 November (Commemoration of the Leaders of the Bulgarian National Revival), 24–26 December (Christmas).

2004: 1 January (New Year), 3 March (National Day), 9–12 April (Easter), 1 May (Labour Day), 6 May (St George's Day), 24 May (Education Day), 6 September (Union of Eastern Rumelia and the Bulgarian Principality), 22 September (Independence Day), 1 November (Commemoration of the Leaders of the Bulgarian National Revival), 24–26 December (Christmas).

Weights and Measures

The metric system is in force.

Statistical Survey

Sources (unless otherwise indicated): National Statistical Institute, 10038 Sofia, P. Volov St 2; tel. (2) 985-77-00; fax (2) 985-76-40; e-mail info@nsi.bg; internet www.nsi.bg ; Bulgarian National Bank, 1000 Sofia, Blvd Aleksandur Battenberg 1; tel. (2) 914-51-203; fax (2) 980-24-25; e-mail press–office@ bnbank.org; internet www.bnb.bg; Center for Economic Development, 1408 Sofia, j. k. Ivan Vazov, Balsha 1, Bl. 9; tel. (2) 953-42-04; e-mail stat@ced.bg; internet www.stat.bg.

Area and Population

AREA, POPULATION AND DENSITY

Area (sq km)*	110,994†
Population (census results)	
4 December 1992.	8,487,317
1 March 2001	
Males	3,888,440
Females.	4,085,231
Total	7,973,671
Population (official estimates at 31 December)	
2001	7,891,095
2002	7,845,499
Density (per sq km) at 31 December 2002	70.7

* Including territorial waters of frontier rivers (261.4 sq km).

† 42,855 sq miles.

ETHNIC GROUPS

(2001 census)

	Number	%
Bulgarian.	6,660,682	83.53
Turkish	757,781	9.50
Gypsy	365,797	4.59
Others.	121,773	1.53
Unknown	67,640	0.85
Total	**7,973,673**	**100.00**

ADMINISTRATIVE REGIONS

(2001 census)

	Area (sq km)	Population	Density (per sq km)
Sofia (town)*	1,310.8	1,173,811	895.5
Burgas	14,724.3	802,932	54.5
Khaskovo	13,824.1	816,874	59.1
Lovech	15,150.0	924,505	61.0
Montana†	10,606.8	559,449	52.7
Plovdiv	13,585.4	1,175,628	86.5
Ruse	10,842.5	702,292	64.8
Sofia (region)*	19,021.1	930,958	48.9
Varna	11,928.6	887,222	74.4
Total	**110,993.6**	**7,973,671**	**71.8**

* The city of Sofia, the national capital, has separate regional status. The area and population of the capital region are not included in the neighbouring Sofia region.

† Formerly Mikhailovgrad.

PRINCIPAL TOWNS

(population at 2001 census)

Sofia (capital)	. .	1,096,389	Dobrich* . . .	100,379
Plovdiv	. . .	340,638	Shumen . . .	89,054
Varna	. . .	314,539	Pernik . . .	86,133
Burgas (Bourgas)	. .	193,316	Yambol . . .	82,924
Ruse (Roussé)	. .	162,128	Khaskovo . . .	80,870
Stara Zagora	. .	143,989	Pazardzhik . .	79,476
Pleven	. . .	122,149	Blagoevgrad . .	71,361
Sliven	. . .	100,695		

* Dobrich was renamed Tolbukhin in 1949, but its former name was restored in 1990.

BIRTHS, MARRIAGES AND DEATHS

	Registered live births		Registered marriages*		Registered deaths	
	Number	Rate (per 1,000)	Number	Rate (per 1,000)	Number	Rate (per 1,000)
1994 . .	79,442	9.4	37,910	4.5	111,787	13.2
1995 . .	71,967	8.6	36,795	4.4	114,670	13.6
1996 . .	72,188	8.6	n.a.	4.3	117,056	14.0
1997 . .	64,125	7.7	34,772	4.2	121,861	14.7
1998 . .	65,361	7.9	35,591	4.3	118,190	14.3
1999 . .	72,291	8.8	35,540	4.3	111,786	13.6
2000 . .	73,679	9.0	n.a.	4.3	115,087	14.1
2001 . .	68,180	8.7	n.a.	4.0	112,368	14.3

* Including marriages of Bulgarian nationals outside the country, but excluding those of aliens in Bulgaria.

Source: partly UN, *Population and Vital Statistics* and *Monthly Bulletin of Statistics*.

Expectation of life (WHO estimates, years at birth): 71.5 (males 68.4; females 74.8) in 2001 (Source: WHO, *World Health Report*).

EMPLOYMENT
(annual averages, excluding armed forces)

	1999	2000	2001
Agriculture, hunting, forestry and fishing	818,195	781,566	774,080
Mining and quarrying	47,941	40,684	35,520
Manufacturing	662,963	615,691	591,838
Electricity, gas and water supply	57,860	59,710	58,632
Construction	123,736	127,554	126,967
Wholesale and retail trade; repair of motor vehicles, motorcycles and personal and household goods	337,696	352,383	355,190
Hotels and restaurants	68,200	85,059	94,484
Transport and communications	232,857	219,453	214,194
Financial intermediation	35,799	32,791	34,344
Real estate, renting and business activities	95,188	121,035	131,824
Public administration; compulsory social security	91,744	91,700	96,869
Education	231,977	218,302	203,972
Health and social work	165,096	148,250	138,325
Other community, social and personal service activities	102,661	85,930	84,046
Total employees	3,071,913	2,980,108	2,940,285

Unemployment (persons registered at 31 December): 610,551 in 1999; 682,792 in 2000; 662,260 in 2001.

Health and Welfare

KEY INDICATORS

Total fertility rate (children per woman, 2001)	1.1
Under-5 mortality rate (per 1,000 live births, 2001)	16
HIV/AIDS (% of persons aged 15–49, 2001)	<0.10
Physicians (per 1,000 head, 1998)	3.45
Hospital beds (per 1,000 head, 1997)	8.6
Health expenditure (2000): US $ per head (PPP)	198
Health expenditure (2000): % of GDP	3.9
Health expenditure (2000): public (% of total)	77.6
Access to water (% of persons, 2000)	100
Access to sanitation (% of persons, 2000)	100
Human Development Index (2000): ranking	62
Human Development Index (2000): value	0.779

For sources and definitions, see explanatory note on p. vi.

Agriculture

PRINCIPAL CROPS
('000 metric tons)

	1998	1999	2000
Wheat	3,203.4	2,637.0	2,775.0
Rice (paddy)	10.3	7.0	10.0
Barley	717.1	652.0	676.0
Maize	1,303.4	1,719.0	818.0
Rye	26.6	30.0*	20.0*
Oats	63.7	52.0*	49.0*
Other cereals	20.3	34.8*	15.0*
Potatoes	478.3	566.0	398.0
Sugar beet	61.7	53.0	23.0
Dry beans	23.5	24.0	9.0
Groundnuts (in shell)	9.7	10.0	8.0
Sunflower seed	524.2	606.0	423.0
Cabbages	142.9	154.0	151.2*
Asparagus	12.5	12.7*	13.2*
Tomatoes	490.2	446.0	410.0
Pumpkins, squash and gourds	47.0	45.0†	45.0†
Cucumbers and gherkins	193.3	171.0	131.0
Aubergines (Eggplants)	32.8	33.0*	34.7*
Chillies and green peppers	242.3	202.0	190.0
Dry onions	107.1	104.0	68.0
Garlic	28.2	28.7*	29.8*
Green beans	17.2	17.5*	18.2*
Carrots	23.3	26.7*	24.6*
Other vegetables	122.2	121.9*	129.0†
Apples	129.1	92.0	89.0
Pears	20.2	18.6	20.0†
Apricots	9.1	10.9	13.0*
Cherries	33.5	32.0	28.0
Peaches and nectarines	42.0	39.0	42.0
Plums	61.8	66.0	62.0
Strawberries	7.8	10.0	9.0
Grapes	396.3	400.6	416.5
Watermelons	288.2	384.0	233.0
Other fruit	28.0	28.4	43.2*
Tobacco (leaves)	38.7	34.5	6.7*

* Unofficial figure.
† FAO estimate.

Source: FAO.

LIVESTOCK
('000 head at 1 January each year)

	1999	2000	2001
Horses	133	141	140
Asses	221	208	196
Cattle	671	682	640
Pigs	1,721	1,512	1,144
Sheep	2,774	2,549	2,286
Goats	1,048	1,046	970
Poultry	15,686†	14,963†	16,035*
Rabbits	466	431	550*

* FAO estimate.
† Unofficial figure.

Source: FAO.

LIVESTOCK PRODUCTS
('000 metric tons)

	1998	1999	2000
Beef and veal .	55.0*	63.4*	66.6†
Mutton and lamb.	45.7*	50.0*	45.8†
Goat meat .	7.3†	7.0*	7.3†
Pig meat .	248.1	267.1	243.0*
Poultry meat .	105.1	106.0	100.0*
Rabbit meat .	5	5	5†
Cows' milk .	1,327.0	1,388.8	1,389.8
Buffaloes' milk .	11.3	11.3	11.5*
Sheeps' milk .	109.3	106.2	105.0*
Goats' milk .	190.7	200.0	200.0*
Cheese.	71.6	56.1	48.3
Butter .	1.7	1.3	1.6
Hen eggs .	90.5	88.3	92.4
Other poultry eggs .	5.1	5.2	2.0†
Honey .	5.5	5.7	5.7†
Wool: greasy .	8	8	8†
Wool: scoured .	3.8*	3.8*	3.7†
Sheepskins† .	18	18	16
Goatskins† .	2.5	2.5	2.5
Cattle and buffalo hides† .	9.0	8.5	9.0

* Unofficial figure.
† FAO estimate(s).

Source: FAO.

Forestry

ROUNDWOOD REMOVALS
('000 cubic metres, excl. bark)

	1999	2000	2001
Sawlogs, veneer logs and logs for sleepers .	2,218	1,626	1,292
Pulpwood .	939	957*	971*
Other industrial wood* .	94	94	94
Fuel wood .	1,101	2,107	1,635
Total .	4,352	4,784	3,992

* FAO estimate(s).

Source: FAO.

SAWNWOOD PRODUCTION
('000 cubic metres, incl. sleepers)

	1998*	1999	2000
Coniferous (softwood) .	186	290	258
Broadleaved (hardwood).	67	35	54
Total .	253	325	312

* FAO estimates.

Source: FAO.

Fishing
('000 metric tons, live weight)

	1998	1999	2000
Capture .	10.8	10.6	7.0
Silver carp .	0.6	0.5	0.0
Other cyprinids .	1.3	1.5	0.5
Gobies .	0.4	0.4	0.1
European sprat .	3.3	3.6	1.7
Sea snails .	4.3	3.8	3.8
Aquaculture .	4.3	7.8	3.6
Common carp .	1.5	2.9	1.3
Grass carp .	0.2	0.9	0.7
Other cyprinids .	1.5	1.0	0.9
Wels (som) catfish .	0.2	1.4	0.1
Rainbow trout .	0.6	0.4	0.4
Total catch .	15.0	18.3	10.6

Source: FAO, *Yearbook of Fishery Statistics*.

Mining
('000 metric tons, unless otherwise indicated)

	1998	1999	2000
Anthracite.	16	17	18*
Other hard coal .	105	106	100*
Lignite.	27,435	22,696	23,765*
Other brown coal.	3,692	3,074	3,211*
Crude petroleum .	32	39	41*
Natural gas (million cu metres) .	33	27	15*
Iron ore: gross weight .	895	699	559
Iron ore: metal content .	250*	223	178
Copper concentrate† .	88	96	92*
Lead concentrate† .	24.2*	17.0*	10.5
Zinc concentrate* † .	17.0	10.2	9.4
Manganese ore† .	17*	—	—
Silver (metric tons)† .	68	59	60*
Gold (kilograms)‡ .	1,253	2,743	2,347
Bentonite .	176	232	296
Kaolin (washed)* .	150	140	150
Barite (Barytes)* .	100	120	120
Salt (unrefined) .	2,400	1,300	1,700
Gypsum and anhydrite (crude).	184	149	170

* Estimated production.
† Figures relate to the metal content of ores and concentrates.
‡ Figures relate to metal production.

Source: US Geological Survey.

Industry

SELECTED PRODUCTS
('000 metric tons, unless otherwise indicated)

	1997	1998	1999
Flour	757	473	760
Refined sugar.	114	121	250
Wine ('000 hectolitres) . .	2,096	2,333	1,715
Beer ('000 hectolitres) . .	3,031	3,796	4,045
Cigarettes and cigars (metric tons)	43,315	33,181	25,715
Cotton yarn (metric tons)[1] . .	28,200	26,900	19,800
Woven cotton fabrics ('000 metres)[2]	75,700	80,200	52,000
Flax and hemp yarn (metric tons)	500	400	300
Wool yarn (metric tons)[1] . .	11,600	7,300	7,800
Woven woollen fabrics ('000 metres)[2]	11,200	6,200	4,800
Woven fabrics of man-made fibres ('000 metres)[3] . .	16,500	16,400	n.a.
Leather footwear ('000 pairs) .	6,838	6,401	4,591
Rubber footwear ('000 pairs) . .	654	1,014	812
Chemical wood pulp	92.4	88.7	79
Paper and paperboard . . .	178.4	114.7	n.a.
Rubber tyres ('000)[4] . . .	391	124	n.a.
Sulphuric acid (100%) . . .	556.2	498.9	456
Nitrogenous fertilizers[5] . . .	677	629	529
Phosphate fertilizers[5] . . .	110.2	91.4	n.a.
Coke (gas and coke-oven) . .	1,239	n.a.	n.a.
Unworked glass—rectangles ('000 sq metres)	10,462	9,551	n.a.
Clay building bricks (million) .	412	361	259
Cement	1,654	1,742	2,060
Pig-iron and ferro-alloys . .	1,624	1,399	1,140
Crude steel	2,628	2,216	1,846
Refined copper—unwrought (metric tons)	34,530	32,100	21,900
Refined lead—unwrought (metric tons)	72,600	79,900	83,300
Zinc—unwrought (metric tons)	70,400	72,600	70,200
Metal-working lathes (number) .	2,315	1,761	1,611
Fork-lift trucks (number)[6] . .	3,313	2,366	1,448
Refrigerators—household (number)	21,100	58,000	47,000
Washing machines—household (number)	4,900	n.a.	n.a.
Radio receivers (number) . . .	30	n.a.	n.a.
Television receivers (number) .	5,900	2,800	n.a.
Construction: dwellings completed (number)[7]	7,452	4,942	9,824
Electric energy (million kWh) . .	42,803	41,712	n.a.

[1] Pure and mixed yarn. Figures for wool include yarn of man-made staple.
[2] Pure and mixed fabrics, after undergoing finishing processes.
[3] Finished fabrics, including fabrics of natural silk.
[4] Tyres for road motor vehicles (passenger cars and commercial vehicles).
[5] Figures for nitrogenous fertilizers are in terms of nitrogen, and for phosphate fertilizers in terms of phosphoric acid. Data for nitrogenous fertilizers include urea.
[6] Including hoisting gears.
[7] Including restorations and conversions.

Source: partly UN, *Industrial Commodity Statistics Yearbook*.

Finance

CURRENCY AND EXCHANGE RATES

Monetary Units
100 stotinki (singular: stotinka) = 1 new lev (plural: leva)

Sterling, Dollar and Euro Equivalents (31 December 2002)
£1 sterling = 3.0382 new leva
US $1 = 1.8850 new leva
€1 = 1.9768 new leva
100 new leva = £32.91= $53.05 = €50.59

Average Exchange Rate (new leva per US$)
2000   2.1233
2001   2.1847
2002   2.0770

Note: On 5 July 1999 a new lev, equivalent to 1,000 old leva, was introduced. In January 1999 the value of the old lev had been linked to the German currency, the Deutsche Mark (DM), when an official exchange rate of DM1 = 1,000 old leva was established. The new lev was thus at par with the DM. From the establishment of the euro, on 1 January 1999, the German currency had a fixed exchange rate of €1 = 1.95583.
Some of the figures in this Survey are still in terms of old leva.

STATE BUDGET
(million new leva)*

Revenue†	1999	2000	2001
Taxation	6,143.6	7,140.7	7,495.5
Taxes on income, profits, etc. .	1,029.0	1,044.6	1,277.0
Social security contributions .	1,883.2	2,241.8	2,310.3
From employers	1,506.9	1,427.7	1,439.5
Domestic taxes on goods and services	2,633.7	3,529.8	3,603.7
Sales, turnover or value-added taxes	1,926.9	2,359.0	2,454.4
Excises	691.2	1,131.3	1,106.7
Taxes on international trade and transactions	258.4	220.7	195.4
Import duties	258.3	220.6	195.4
Other current revenue . . .	1,738.0	1,872.2	2,310.3
Entrepreneurial and property income	271.5	480.1	973.0
Administrative fees and charges, non-industrial and incidental sales	689.1	730.6	836.7
Fines and forfeits	424.0	353.1	271.4
Contributions to government employee pension and welfare funds	248.5	227.1	187.6
Capital revenue	124.1	111.6	68.5
Total revenue	**8,005.7**	**9,124.5**	**9,874.3**

Expenditure‡	1999	2000	2001
General public services	729.3	731.8	673.0
Defence	681.3	644.3	622.2
Public order and safety	532.8	509.2	553.9
Education	347.9	425.7	456.1
Health	409.9	524.1	984.9
Social security and welfare . . .	2,689.1	3,461.4	3,622.1
Housing and community amenities	108.8	134.0	192.8
Recreational, cultural and religious affairs and services . .	141.6	153.5	143.3
Economic affairs and services . .	816.8	914.8	1,157.3
Fuel and energy	189.3	103.6	95.7
Agriculture, forestry, fishing and hunting	147.9	165.3	202.3
Transport and communications	327.4	515.9	489.9
Other purposes	1,665.3	1,945.9	1,806.9
Total expenditure	**8,122.7**	**9,444.8**	**10,212.6**
Current§	7,243.5	8,436.9	9,136.4
Capital.	879.2	1,007.9	1,076.2

* Figures refer to the consolidated accounts of the central Government (including social security funds and other extrabudgetary units).
† Excluding grants received (million new leva): 214.2 in 1999; 215.4 in 2000; 394.0 in 2001.
‡ Excluding lending minus repayments (million new leva): −251.5 in 1999; −259.6 in 2000; −500.2 in 2001.
§ Including interest payments (million new leva): 892.6 in 1999; 1,067.0 in 2000; 1,095.6 in 2001.

Source: IMF, *Government Finance Statistics Yearbook*.

INTERNATIONAL RESERVES
(US $ million at 31 December)

	2000	2001	2002
Gold*	305.3	289.6	340.0
IMF special drawing rights	84.6	2.3	0.7
Reserve position in IMF	42.7	41.2	44.6
Foreign exchange	3,027.6	3,247.3	4,361.8
Total	3,460.2	3,580.4	4,747.1

* Valued at market-related prices.

Source: IMF, *International Financial Statistics*.

MONEY SUPPLY
(million new leva at 31 December)

	2000	2001	2002
Currency outside banks	2,374.1	3,081.0	3,334.9
Demand deposits at deposit money banks	1,323.1	1,655.4	2,086.5
Total money	3,976.3	4,883.8	5,542.7

Source: IMF, *International Financial Statistics*.

COST OF LIVING
(Consumer Price Index; base: 1995 = 100)

	1998	1999	2000
Food	2,962.4	2,724.3	3,003.5
Fuel and light	4,494.2	5,415.4	6,411.8
Clothing	4,938.6	5,956.6	6,922.4
Rent	3,227.1	3,243.3	4,489.9
All items (incl. others)	3,046.4	3,124.8	3,447.1

Source: ILO.

All items (base: 1995=100): 3,700.8 in 2001; 3,915.9 in 2002 (Source: IMF, *International Financial Statistics*).

NATIONAL ACCOUNTS
(million new leva at current prices)

Expenditure on the Gross Domestic Product

	1999	2000	2001
Government final consumption expenditure		4,786	5,211
Private final consumption expenditure	20,901	18,506	20,614
Increase in stocks	662	688	775
Gross fixed capital formation	3,600	4,206	5,259
Statistical discrepancy	—	—	-24
Total domestic expenditure	25,163	28,185	31,836
Exports of goods and services	10,601	14,902	16,494
Less Imports of goods and services	11,974	16,334	18,712
GDP in purchasers' values	23,790	26,753	29,618

Gross Domestic Product by Economic Activity

	1997*	1998*	1999
Agriculture	4,008,331	3,980,383	3,363
Forestry	54,367	64,992	77
Mining	344,731	294,011	336
Manufacturing	2,857,613	3,664,261	3,303
Electricity, gas and water	689,325	832,850	950
Construction	424,637	717,629	737
Trade	1,304,910	1,470,290	1,486
Transport	814,387	1,025,663	959
Communications	340,634	551,610	778
Financial services	398,232	407,244	585
Other services	4,057,315	6,194,271	7,317
Sub-total	15,294,482	19,203,204	19,891
Excises and value-added tax	1,754,786	2,351,362	2,896
Import duties	368,131	389,903	299
Less Imputed bank service charge	362,194	367,449	310
GDP in purchasers' values	17,055,205	21,577,020	22,776

* In millions of old leva.

BALANCE OF PAYMENTS
(US $ million)

	1999	2000	2001
Exports of goods f.o.b.	4,006.4	4,824.6	5,106.8
Imports of goods f.o.b.	-5,087.4	-6,000.1	-6,682.4
Trade balance	-1,081.0	-1,175.5	-1,575.6
Exports of services	1,786.3	2,175.3	2,419.2
Imports of services	-1,471.1	-1,669.4	-1,879.2
Balance on goods and services	-765.8	-669.6	-1,035.6
Other income received	265.5	322.9	351.6
Other income paid	-484.2	-644.2	-693.4
Balances on goods, services and income	-984.5	-990.9	-1,377.4
Current transfers received	328.7	354.1	588.5
Current transfers paid	-28.9	-64.4	-100.1
Current balance	-684.7	-701.2	-889.0
Capital account (net)	-2.4	25.0	—
Direct investment abroad	-16.8	1.9	-9.8
Direct investment from abroad	806.1	1,001.5	691.9
Portfolio investment assets	-207.5	-62.0	-40.2
Portfolio investment liabilities	8.0	-114.9	105.1
Financial derivatives liabilities	—	-1.8	17.5
Other investment assets	16.6	-136.6	349.2
Other investment liabilities	171.0	195.2	-19.0
Net errors and omissions	6.1	-70.1	167.6
Overall balance	96.4	137.0	373.3

Source: IMF, *International Financial Statistics*.

External Trade

PRINCIPAL COMMODITIES
(US $ million)

Imports c.i.f.	1999	2000	2001*
Mineral products	1,454.6	2,044.5	1,926.8
Ores, slag and ash	168.0	216.0	247.7
Mineral fuels, mineral oils and products of their distillation	1,189.0	1,741.2	1,604.6
Products of chemical or allied industries; plastics, rubber and articles thereof	676.8	731.6	878.6
Plastics and articles thereof	159.3	195.6	230.5
Base metals and articles thereof	290.8	391.7	426.6
Nuclear reactors, boilers machinery and mechanical appliances; parts thereof	718.8	734.3	756.7
Electrical machinery, equipment and parts; sound and television apparatus, parts and accessories	375.1	365.9	568.7
Vehicles other than railway or tramway rolling-stock, and parts and accessories	457.3	454.5	580.7
Total (incl. others)	5,515.1	6,507.1	7,240.1

Exports f.o.b.	1999	2000	2001*
Mineral products	466.4	814.8	777.6
Mineral fuels, mineral oils and products of their distillation	358.3	711.0	690.2
Products of chemical or allied industries; plastics, rubber and articles thereof	496.5	628.6	629.5
Knitted or crocheted clothing and accessories	219.3	289.5	362.4
Non-knitted clothing and accessories	357.4	410.5	545.6
Footwear, gaiters, etc., and parts	111.9	118.0	159.9
Base metals and articles thereof	652.8	1,000.2	915.0
Iron and steel	263.8	387.7	352.4
Copper and articles thereof	170.5	354.3	299.7
Nuclear reactors, boilers machinery and mechanical appliances; parts thereof	264.6	274.2	319.3
Electrical machinery, equipment and parts; sound and television apparatus, parts and accessories	126.9	156.6	196.3
Total (incl. others)	4,006.4	4,824.6	5,106.5

* Figures are provisional.

PRINCIPAL TRADING PARTNERS
(US $ million*)

Imports c.i.f.	2000	2001	2002
Austria.	145.2	144.5	163.9
Belgium	85.7	107.3	109.9
Czech Republic	118.2	116.3	121.5
France.	316.4	437.9	441.1
Germany	902.6	1,109.4	1,117.5
Greece .	317.9	411.6	469.8
Italy .	549.6	695.9	883.4
Japan .	62.6	76.8	87.4
Netherlands	109.4	132.5	157.6
Poland .	89.5	106.8	98.7
Romania .	230.8	172.3	158.4
Russia .	1,582.4	1,452.7	1,145.8
Spain .	98.1	120.3	152.0
Switzerland	82.4	84.7	98.8
Turkey.	214.4	273.3	386.5
Ukraine	182.4	234.9	239.5
United Kingdom	138.6	180.6	204.3
USA	190.7	190.8	169.6
Total (incl. others)	6,507.1	7,260.8	7,806.1

Exports f.o.b.	2000	2001	2002
Austria.	68.3	85.1	95.3
Belgium	301.7	249.5	274.9
France.	231.2	286.4	299.0
Georgia	58.1	53.6	n.a.
Germany .	437.0	487.7	539.3
Greece .	377.0	448.6	515.6
Italy .	687.7	766.3	854.5
Macedonia, former Yugoslav republic .	110.3	112.5	124.7
Netherlands	86.1	80.0	100.5
Poland .	27.6	34.8	40.7
Romania .	86.7	129.1	158.0
Russia .	118.7	119.5	90.7
Slovenia .	27.3	19.4	24.4
Spain .	101.3	168.0	183.2
Switzerland	47.2	58.4	94.3
Turkey.	492.8	412.8	516.1
Ukraine	59.6	61.8	52.5
United Kingdom	114.4	134.9	161.7
USA	189.5	284.7	253.6
Yugoslavia, Federal Republic	374.7	212.8	171.3
Total (incl. others)	4,824.6	5,112.9	5,578.1

* Imports by country of purchase; exports by country of sale.

Transport

RAILWAYS
(traffic)

	1997	1998	1999
Passengers carried ('000)	82,656	64,260	53,112
Passenger-kilometres (million) .	5,886	4,740	3,819
Freight carried ('000 metric tons) .	29,220	24,461	21,090
Freight net ton-kilometres (million)	7,444	6,152	5,297

ROAD TRAFFIC
(motor vehicles in use at 31 December)

	1998	1999	2000
Passenger cars	1,809,350	1,908,392	1,908,392
Buses and coaches	41,487	41,971	41,971
Lorries and vans .	220,948	230,131	271,463
Motorcycles and mopeds	515,701	519,212	519,212

Source: International Road Federation, *World Road Statistics*.

INLAND WATERWAYS
(traffic)

	1997	1998	1999
Passengers carried ('000)	10	10	10
Passenger-kilometres (million) .	11	13	12
Freight carried ('000 metric tons) .	919	836	439
Freight ton-kilometres (million)	677	711	274

SHIPPING

Merchant Fleet
(registered at 31 December)

	1999	2000	2001
Number of vessels	173	164	172
Total displacement ('000 grt)	1,035.8	989.6	955.3

Source: Lloyd's Register-Fairplay, *World Fleet Statistics*.

Sea-borne Traffic
(international and coastal)

	1997	1998	1999
Passengers carried ('000)	21	7	n.a.
Freight ('000 metric tons)	19,623	16,446	16,822

CIVIL AVIATION
(traffic)

	1997	1998	1999*
Passengers carried ('000)	1,209	1,269	1,354
Passenger-kilometres (million) .	2,711	2,868	2,680
Freight carried ('000 metric tons) .	13	14	30
Freight ton-kilometres (million)	41	39	63

* Including the private sector.

Tourism

ARRIVALS OF FOREIGN VISITORS

Country of origin	2000	2001	2002
Austria.	8,382	27,253	24,358
Belgium	17,499	24,946	29,076
Czech Republic	28,992	36,986	48,485
Denmark	15,035	19,372	31,628
Finland	19,275	29,178	38,108
France .	21,416	27,305	30,983
Germany .	263,034	374,323	480,460
Greece .	321,651	344,677	391,386
Israel .	30,910	50,368	64,064
Macedonia, former Yugoslav republic*	658,395	643,106	621,875
Poland .	18,968	31,492	48,738
Romania *	203,974	227,286	92,826
Russia .	105,622	130,886	99,389
Slovakia .	18,739	30,999	42,452
Sweden .	39,998	48,070	54,898
Turkey.	95,567	44,243	29,645*
Ukraine	59,279	70,168	39,426
United Kingdom	51,973	69,202	110,902
USA	20,969	25,560	25,417
Yugoslavia, Federal Republic* .	218,394	359,467	534,816
Total (incl. others)	2,354,052	2,775,717	2,992,590

* Includes 'shuttle traders'.

Source: Ministry of the Economy, Sofia.

Receipts from tourism (US $ million): 496 in 1997; 966 in 1998; 932 in 1999; 1,074 in 2000 (Sources: World Bank and Bulgarian National Bank).

Communications Media

	1998	1999	2000
Television receivers ('000 in use)	3,400	3,550	3,692
Telephones ('000 main lines in use)	2,758.0	2,833.4	2,881.8
Mobile cellular telephones ('000 subscribers).	127	350	738
Personal computers ('000 in use)	200	220	361
Internet users ('000) .	150.0	234.6	430.0
Book production:*			
Titles .	4,863	4,850	n.a.
Copies ('000) .	11,900	10,800	n.a.
Newspapers:			
Titles .	644	622	545
Total circulation ('000 copies) .	428,400	411,500	n.a.
Magazines:†			
Titles .	639	631	n.a.
Total circulation ('000 copies) .	14,100	13,500	n.a.

* Including pamphlets.

† Including bulletins.

Facsimile machines (number in use): 15,000 in 1995 (estimate).

2001: Telephones ('000 main lines in use) 2,913.9; Mobile cellular telephones ('000 subscribers) 1,550; Internet users ('000) 605; Book production: titles 4,984, copies ('000) 6,567.1; Newspapers: titles 465 (dailies 60, non-dailies 405), average circulation ('000 copies) 3,376.6 (dailies 1,009.4, non-dailies 2,367.2).

Sources: partly UN, *Statistical Yearbook*, UNESCO, *Statistical Yearbook*, and International Telecommunication Union.

Education

(1999/2000)

	Institutions	Teachers	Students
Kindergartens	3,434	20,022	212,000
General schools	3,011	65,885	887,213
Special	146	2,597	15,984
Vocational technical . .	2	26	2,376
Secondary vocational . . .	150	3,206	50,727
Technical colleges and schools of arts.	369	14,264	132,240
Semi-higher institutes* . .	47	2,367	18,461
Higher educational . . .	41	24,368	242,860†

* Including technical, teacher-training, communications and librarians' institutes.

† Including post-graduate students.

Adult literacy rate (UNESCO estimates): 98.4% (males 97.9%; females 99.0%) in 2000 (Source: UN Development Programme, *Human Development Report*).

Directory

The Constitution

The Constitution of the Republic of Bulgaria, summarized below, took effect upon its promulgation, on 13 July 1991, following its enactment on the previous day.

FUNDAMENTAL PRINCIPLES

Chapter One declares that the Republic of Bulgaria is to have a parliamentary form of government, with all state power derived from the people. The rule of law and the life, dignity and freedom of the individual are guaranteed. The Constitution is the supreme law; the power of the State is shared between the legislature, the executive and the judiciary. The Constitution upholds principles such as political and religious freedom (although no party may be formed on separatist, ethnic or religious lines), free economic initiative and respect for international law.

FUNDAMENTAL RIGHTS AND OBLIGATIONS OF CITIZENS

Chapter Two establishes the basic provisions for Bulgarian citizenship and fundamental human rights, such as the rights of privacy and movement, the freedoms of expression, assembly and association, and the enfranchisement of Bulgarian citizens aged over 18 years. The Constitution commits the State to the provision of basic social welfare and education and to the encouragement of culture, science and the health of the population. The study and use of the Bulgarian language is required. Other obligations of the citizenry include military service and the payment of taxes.

THE NATIONAL ASSEMBLY

The National Assembly is the legislature of Bulgaria and exercises parliamentary control over the country. It consists of 240 members, elected for a four-year term. Only Bulgarian citizens aged over 21 years (who do not hold a state post or another citizenship and are not under judicial interdiction or in prison) are eligible for election to parliament. A member of the National Assembly ceases to serve as a deputy while holding ministerial office. The National Assembly is a permanently acting body, which is free to determine its own recesses and elects its own Chairman and Deputy Chairmen. The Chairman represents and convenes the National Assembly, organizes its proceedings, attests its enactments and promulgates its resolutions.

The National Assembly may function when more than one-half of its members are present, and may pass legislation and other acts by a majority of more than one-half of the members present, except where a qualified majority is required by the Constitution. Ministers are free to, and can be obliged to, attend parliamentary sessions. The most important functions of the legislature are: the enactment of laws; the approval of the state budget; the scheduling of presidential elections; the election and dismissal of the Chairman of the Council of Ministers (Prime Minister) and of other members of the Council of Ministers; the declaration of war or conclusion of peace; the foreign deployment of troops; and the ratification of any fundamental international instruments to which the Republic of Bulgaria has agreed. The laws and resolutions of the National Assembly are binding on all state bodies and citizens. All enactments must be promulgated in the official gazette, *Durzhaven Vestnik*, within 15 days of their passage through the legislature.

THE PRESIDENT OF THE REPUBLIC

Chapter Four concerns the Head of State, the President of the Republic of Bulgaria, who is assisted by a Vice-President. The President and Vice-President are elected jointly, directly by the voters, for a period of five years. A candidate must be eligible for election to the National Assembly, but also aged over 40 years and a resident of the country for the five years previous to the election. To be elected, a candidate must receive more than one-half of the valid votes cast, in an election in which more than one-half of the eligible electorate participate. If necessary, a second ballot must then be conducted, contested by the two candidates who received the most votes. The one who receives more votes becomes President. The President and Vice-President may hold the same office for only two terms and, during this time, may not engage in any unsuitable or potentially compromising activities. If the President resigns, is incapacitated, impeached or dies, the Vice-President carries out the presidential duties. If neither official can perform their duties, the Chairman of the National Assembly assumes the prerogatives of the Presidency, until new elections take place.

The President's main responsibilities include the scheduling of elections and referendums, the conclusion of international treaties and the promulgation of laws. The President is responsible for appointing a Prime Minister-designate (priority must be given to the leaders of the two largest parties represented in the National Assembly), who must then attempt to form a government.

The President is Supreme Commander-in-Chief of the Armed Forces of the Republic of Bulgaria and presides over the Consultative National Security Council. The President has certain emergency powers, usually subject to the later approval of the National Assembly. Many of the President's actions must be approved by the Chairman of the Council of Ministers. The President may return legislation to the National Assembly for further consideration, but can be overruled.

THE COUNCIL OF MINISTERS

The principal organ of executive government is the Council of Ministers, which supervises the implementation of state policy and the state budget, the administration of the country and the Armed Forces, and the maintenance of law and order. The Council of Ministers is headed and co-ordinated by the Chairman (Prime Minister), who is responsible for the overall policy of government. The Council of Ministers, which also includes Deputy Chairmen and Ministers, must resign upon the death of the Chairman or if the National Assembly votes in favour of a motion of no confidence in the Council or in the Chairman.

JUDICIAL POWER

The judicial branch of government is independent. All judicial power is exercised in the name of the people. Individuals and legal entities are guaranteed basic rights, such as the right to contest administrative acts and the right to legal counsel. One of the principal organs is the Supreme Court of Cassation, which exercises supreme judicial responsibility for the precise and equal application of the law by all courts. The Supreme Administrative Court rules on all challenges to the legality of acts of any organ of government. The Chief Prosecutor supervises all other prosecutors and ensures that the law is observed, by initiating court actions and ensuring the enforcement of penalties, etc.

The Supreme Judicial Council is responsible for appointments within the ranks of the justices, prosecutors and investigating magistrates, and recommends to the President of the Republic the appointment or dismissal of the Chairmen of the two Supreme Courts and of the Chief Prosecutor (they are each appointed for a single, seven-year term). These last three officials are, *ex officio*, members of the Supreme Judicial Council, together with 22 others, who must be practising lawyers of high integrity and at least 15 years of professional experience. These members are elected for a term of five years, 11 of them by the National Assembly and 11 by bodies of the judiciary. The Supreme Judicial Council is chaired by the Minister of Justice, who is not entitled to vote.

LOCAL SELF-GOVERNMENT AND LOCAL ADMINISTRATION

Chapter Seven provides for the division of Bulgaria into regions and municipalities. Municipalities are the basic administrative territorial unit at which local self-government is practised; their principal organ is the municipal council, which is elected directly by the population for a term of four years. The council elects the mayor, who is the principal organ of executive power. Bulgaria is also divided into regions. Regional government, which is entrusted to regional governors (appointed by the Council of Ministers) and administrations, is responsible for regional policy, the implementation of state policy at a local level and the harmonization of local and national interests.

THE CONSTITUTIONAL COURT

The Constitutional Court consists of 12 justices, four of whom are elected by the National Assembly, four appointed by the President of the Republic and four elected by the justices of the two Supreme Courts. Candidates must have the same eligibility as for membership of the Supreme Judicial Council. They serve a single term of nine years, but a part of the membership changes every three years. A chairman is elected by a secret ballot of the members.

The Constitutional Court provides binding interpretations of the Constitution. It rules on the constitutionality of: laws and decrees; competence suits between organs of government; international agreements; national and presidential elections; and impeachments. A ruling of the Court requires a majority of more than one-half of the votes of all the justices.

CONSTITUTIONAL AMENDMENTS AND THE ADOPTION OF A NEW CONSTITUTION

Chapter Nine provides for constitutional changes. Except for those provisions reserved to the competence of a Grand National Assembly (see p. 892) (see below), the National Assembly is empowered to amend the Constitution with a majority of three-quarters of all its Members, in three ballots on three different days. Amendments must be proposed by one-quarter of the parliamentary membership or by the President. In some cases, a majority of two-thirds of all the Members of the National Assembly will suffice.

Grand National Assembly

A Grand National Assembly consists of 400 members, elected by the generally established procedure. It alone is empowered to adopt a new constitution, to sanction territorial changes to the Republic of Bulgaria, to resolve on any changes in the form of state structure or form of government, and to enact amendments to certain parts of the existing Constitution (concerning the direct application of the Constitution, the domestic application of international agreements, the irrevocable nature of fundamental civil rights and of certain basic individual rights even in times of emergency or war, and amendments to Chapter Nine itself).

Any bill requiring the convening of a Grand National Assembly must be introduced by the President of the Republic or by one-third of the members of the National Assembly. A decision to hold elections for a Grand National Assembly must be supported by two-thirds of the members of the National Assembly. Enactments of the Grand National Assembly require a majority of two-thirds of the votes of all the members, in three ballots on three different days. A Grand National Assembly may resolve only on the proposals for which it was elected, whereupon its prerogatives normally expire.

The Government

HEAD OF STATE

President: GEORGI PURVANOV (elected 18 November 2001; inaugurated 19 January 2002).

COUNCIL OF MINISTERS
(April 2003)

A coalition of the National Movement Simeon II NMSII, the Movement for Rights and Freedoms MRF, and the Bulgarian Socialist Party (BSP).

Prime Minister: SIMEON SAXE-COBURG GOTHA (NMSII).

Deputy Prime Minister and Minister of the Economy: NIKOLAI VASSILEV VASSILEV (NMSII).

Deputy Prime Minister and Minister of Labour and Social Policy: LIDIYA SANTOVA SHULEVA (NMSII).

Minister of Defence: NIKOLAI AVRAMOV SVINAROV (NMSII).

Minister of Foreign Affairs: SOLOMON ISAK PASSI (NMSII).

Minister of Finance: MILEN EMILOV VELCHEV (NMSII).

Minister of the Interior: GEORGI PETROV PETKANOV (NMSII).

Minister of Justice: ANTON ILIEV STANKOV (NMSII).

Minister of Education and Science: VLADIMIR ATANASOV ATANASOV (NMSII).

Minister of European Affairs: MEGLENA KUNEVA (NMSII).

Minister of Agriculture and Forestry: MEKHMED MEKHMED DIKME (MRF).

Minister of Regional Development and Public Works: VALENTIN IVANOV TSEROVSKI (NMSII).

Minister of Transport and Communications: PLAMEN VASILEV PETROV (NMSII).

Minister of Health: BOZHIDAR TODOROV FINKOV (NMSII).

Minister of Culture: BOZHIDAR ZAFIROV ABRASHEV (NMSII).

Minister of the Environment and Water: DOLORES BORISOVA ARSENOVA (NMSII).

Minister of Energy and Energy Resources: MILKO KOVACHEV (NMSII).

Minister of State Administration: DIMITAR GEORGIEV KALCHEV (BSP).

Minister of Youth and Sport: VASSIL MINCHEV IVANOV (NMSII).

Minister without Portfolio: NEZHDET ISMAIL MOLLOV (MRF).

MINISTRIES

Office of the President: 1123 Sofia, Blvd Dondukov 2; tel. (2) 923-93-33; e-mail press@president.bg; internet www.president.bg.

Council of Ministers: 1000 Sofia, Blvd Dondukov 1; tel. (2) 940-27-70; fax (2) 980-20-56; e-mail iprd@government.bg; internet www.government.bg.

Ministry of Agriculture and Forestry: 1040 Sofia, Blvd Botev 55; tel. (2) 980-99-27; fax (2) 980-62-56; internet www.mzgar.government.bg.

Ministry of Culture: 1040 Sofia, Blvd A. Stamboliyski 17; tel. (2) 980-53-84; fax (2) 981-81-45; e-mail press.culture@bta.bg; internet www.culture.government.bg.

Ministry of Defence: 1000 Sofia, Aksakov St 1; tel. (2) 987-95-62; fax (2) 87-32-28; internet www.md.government.bg.

Ministry of the Economy: 1000 Sofia, Slavyanska St 8; tel. (2) 988-55-32; fax (2) 980-26-90; e-mail s.bozukova@mi.government.bg; internet www.mi.government.bg.

Ministry of Education and Science: 1540 Sofia, A. Stamboliyski 18; tel. (2) 84-87-44; fax (2) 988-26-93; e-mail press_mon@minedu.government.bg; internet www.minedu.government.bg.

Ministry of Energy and Energy Resources: 1040 Sofia, Triadica St 8; tel. and fax (2) 987-84-25; e-mail pressall@doe.bg; internet www.doe.bg/cgi-bin/i.pl.

Ministry of the Environment and Water: 1000 Sofia, William Gladstone St 67; tel. (2) 940-62-31; fax (2) 988-59-13; internet www.moew.govrn.bg.

Ministry of European Affairs: Sofia.

Ministry of Finance: 1000 Sofia, Rakovski St 102; tel. (2) 985-920-20; fax (2) 87-05-81; e-mail feedback@minfin.government.bg; internet www.minfin.government.bg.

Ministry of Foreign Affairs: 1113 Sofia, Al. Zhendov St 2; tel. (2) 73-79-97; fax (2) 70-30-41; internet www.mfa.government.bg.

Ministry of Health: 1000 Sofia, Blvd Sveta Nedelya 5; tel. (2) 930-011-07; fax (2) 981-26-39; e-mail press@mh.government.bg; internet www.mh.government.bg.

Ministry of the Interior: 1000 Sofia, Shesti Septemvri St 29; tel. (2) 982-20-14; fax (2) 982-20-47; e-mail spvo@mvr.bg; internet www.mvr.bg.

Ministry of Justice: 1040 Sofia, Slavyanska St 1; tel. (2) 988-48-23; fax (2) 981-91-57; e-mail pr@mjeli.government.bg; internet www.mjeli.government.bg.

Ministry of Labour and Social Policy: 1051 Sofia, Triaditza St 2; tel. (2) 87-33-94; fax (2) 986-13-18; e-mail mlsp@mlsp.government.bg; internet www.mlsp.government.bg.

Ministry of Regional Development and Public Works: Sofia, Kirili Metodi 17–19; tel. (2) 988-29-54; fax (2) 987-58-56; e-mail press@mrrb.government.bg; internet www.mrrb.government.bg.

Ministry of State Administration: 1594 Sofia, Blvd Dondukov 1; tel. (2) 940-27-17; fax (2) 940-21-70; e-mail k.zdravskovska@government.bg.

Ministry of Transport and Communications: 1000 Sofia, Levski St 9; tel. (2) 940-95-00; fax (2) 987-18-05; e-mail vluleva@mtc.government.bg; internet www.mtc.government.bg.

Ministry of Youth and Sport: Sofia.

President and Legislature

PRESIDENT

Presidential Election, First Ballot, 11 November 2001

Candidates	% of votes
Georgi Purvanov (Coalition for Bulgaria)	36.4
Petar Stoyanov (Independent)	34.9
Bogomil Bonev (Civic Party for Bulgaria)	19.3
Reneta Indzhova (Democratic Alliance)	4.9
Others	4.5
Total	100.0

Second Ballot, 18 November 2001

Candidates	% of votes
Georgi Purvanov	54.1
Petar Stoyanov	45.9
Total	100.0

NARODNO SOBRANIYE
(National Assembly)

National Assembly: 1000 Sofia, Blvd Narodno Sobraniye 3; tel. (2) 980-85-01; fax (2) 981-01-81; e-mail infocenter@nt52.parliament.bg; internet www.parliament.bg.

Chairman: OGNYAN GERDZHIKOV.

General Election, 17 June 2001

Parties	% of votes	Seats
National Movement Simeon II*	42.73	120
Union of Democratic Forces	18.17	51
Coalition for Bulgaria†	17.14	48
Movement for Rights and Freedoms	7.45	21
Gergyovden Movement—Inner Macedonian Revolutionary Organization	3.63	—
Others	10.88	—
Total	100.00	240

* The National Movement contested the election in alliance (as the National Movement Simeon II) with the Party of Bulgarian Women and Oborishte Party for National Revival, in order to be permitted legally to register.
† The Bulgarian Socialist Party contested the election in alliance, as part of the Coalition for Bulgaria, comprising 15 left and left-of-centre parties.

Political Organizations

There are over 80 registered political parties in Bulgaria, many of them incorporated into electoral alliances. The most significant political forces are listed below:

Aleksandur Stamboliyski Bulgarian Agrarian People's Union (Bulgarski Zemedelski Naroden Sayuz 'Aleksandur Stamboliyski'): Sofia.

Christian Republican Party: Sofia; f. 1989; Chair. KONSTANTIN ADZHAROV.

Civic Party for Bulgaria: Sofia; f. 2000; centre-right; also known as Citizens' Party for Bulgaria; Chair. BOGOMIL BONEV.

Coalition for Bulgaria: Sofia; f. by the Bulgarian Socialist Party to contest the legislative election of June 2001; alliance of 15 left and left-of-centre parties.

Confederation—Kingdom Bulgaria (Tsarstvo Bulgaria): 7000 Ruse, Vassil Kolarov 45; tel. (82) 299-64; f. 1990; monarchist; Chair. GEORGI BAKARDZHIEV.

Conservative Union—EKIP: Sofia; f. 2001 by members of the Union of Democratic Forces, who supported Simeon Saxe-Coburg Gotha; Chair. CHRISTO BISEROV.

Democratic Alliance/Democratic Alternative for the Republic (DAR): c/o National Assembly, 1000 Sofia, Blvd Narodno Sobraniye 3; left-of-centre coalition; Co-Chair. RENETA INDZHOVA, Dr KONSTANTIN TRENCHEV.

Democratic Party of Justice: Sofia; f. 1994; ethnic Turkish group; fmrly part of the Movement for Rights and Freedoms; Chair. NEDIM GENDZHEV.

Fatherland Party of Labour: 1000 Sofia, Slavyanska St 3, Hotel Slavyanska Beseda; tel. (2) 65-83-10; nationalist; Chair. RUMEN POPOV.

Fatherland Union: Sofia, Blvd Vitosha 18; tel. (2) 88-12-21; f. 1942 as the Fatherland Front (a mass organization unifying the BAPU, the BCP—now the BSP—and social organizations); named as above when restructured in 1990; a socio-political organization of independents and individuals belonging to different political parties; Chair. GINYO GANEV.

Free Radical Democratic Party: Sofia.

Georgi Ganchev Bloc: 1000 Sofia, Shipka 13; tel. (2) 44-61-28; f. 2000 as a successor to the Bulgarian Business Bloc; Leader GEORGI GANCHEV; Chair. DOBRI DOBREV.

Gergyovden Movement (St George's Day Political Movement): Sofia; contested the legislative election of June 2001 in alliance with the Inner Macedonian Revolutionary Organization.

Green Party: 1000 Sofia, Alabin St 3; tel. (2) 987-69-24; f. 1989; Chair. ALEKSANDUR KARAKACHANOV.

Inner Macedonian Revolutionary Organization (IMRO): 1301 Sofia, Pirotska St 5; tel. (2) 980-25-82; fax (2) 980-25-83; e-mail vmro@vmro.org; internet www.vmro.org; f. 1893; contested the legislative election of June 2001 in alliance with the Gergyovden Movement; Chair. KRASSIMIR KARAKACHANOV.

Liberal Congress Party: Sofia; f. 1989 as the Bulgarian Socialist Party, renamed Bulgarian Social Democratic Party (non-Marxist) in 1990 and as above in 1991; membership of the Union of Democratic Forces suspended 1993; c. 20,000 mems; Chair. YANKO N. YANKOV.

Liberal Democratic Alternative: 1000 Sofia, Triaditsa St 4; tel. (2) 986-37; e-mail lda@bulgarianspace.com; internet www .bulgarianspace.com/lda/; f. 1997; Leader ZHELYU ZHELEV.

Movement for Rights and Freedoms (MRF) (Dvizhenie za Prava i Svobodi—DPS): Sofia; tel. (2) 88-18-23; f. 1990; represents the Muslim minority in Bulgaria; 95,000 mems (1991); Pres. AHMED DOGAN.

National Movement for Rights and Freedoms: f. 1999; breakaway faction of the MRF; Leader GYUNER TAHIR.

New Choice Liberal Alliance: f. 1994 by a former faction of the Union of Democratic Forces; Co-Chair. DIMITUR LUDZHEV, IVAN PUSHKAROV.

New Union for Democracy (NUD): Sofia; f. 1993; fmrly section of the Union of Democratic Forces.

Party of Free Democrats (Centre): 6000 Stara Zagora; tel. (42) 2-70-42; f. 1989; Chair. Asst Prof. CHRISTO SANTULOV.

Union of Democratic Forces (UDF) (Sayuz na Demokratichnite Sili—SDS): 1000 Sofia, Blvd Rakovski 134; tel. (2) 93-06-132; fax (2) 981-05-22; e-mail pr@sds.bg; internet www.sds.bg; Pres. IVAN KOSTOV; Chair. NADEZHDA MIHAILOVA; f. 1989 as an alliance that included the following parties, organizations and movements; plans for its reconstitution as a single, centre-right Christian Democratic Party were announced in 2001.

Bulgarian Agrarian People's Union—'Nikola Petkov' (Bulgarski Zemedelski Naroden Sayuz—'Nikola Petkov'): 1000 Sofia, Vrabtcha St 1; tel. (2) 87-80-81; fax (2) 981-09-49; f. 1899; Leader GEORGI PINCHEV.

Bulgarian Democratic Forum: 1000 Sofia, Blvd Dondukov 9, 2nd Floor; tel. (2) 980-31-42; internet bdf.hit.bg; Chair. MURAVEI RADEV.

Bulgarian Social Democratic Party (United—BSDP): 1504 Sofia, Ekzarkh Yosif St 37; tel. (2) 80-15-84; fax (2) 39-00-86; e-mail biltd@vt.bia-bg.com; internet www.bsdp.dir.bg; f. 1891; re-established 1989; Chair. PETAR DERTLIEV.

Christian Democratic Union: Sofia; Chair. JULIUS PAVLOV.

Christian 'Salvation' Union: Sofia; Chair. Bishop CHRISTOFOR SAHEV.

Citizens' Initiative Movement: Sofia; tel. (2) 39-01-93; Chair. TODOR GAGALOV.

Democratic Party: 1000 Sofia, Blvd Dondukov 34; tel. (2) 80-01-87; re-formed 1990; Chair. ALEKSANDUR PRAMATARSKI.

Democratic Party 1896: f. 1994 by a former faction of the Democratic Party; Chair. STEFAN RAYCHEVSKI.

Federation of Democracy Clubs: Sofia; f. 1988 as Club for the Support of Glasnost and Perestroika; merged with other groups, as above in 1990; Chair. YORDAN VASSILEV.

Federation of Independent Student Committees: Sofia; Leader ANDREI NENOV.

New Social Democratic Party: 1504 Sofia, POB 14; tel. (2) 44-99-47; f. 1990; membership of UDF suspended 1991, resumed 1993; Chair. Dr VASSIL MIKHAILOV.

New United Labour Bloc: f. 1997; Chair. KRUSTYU PETKOV.

Radical Democratic Party: 1220 Sofia, Blvd Rogen 101; tel. (2) 936-04-76; fax (2) 936-02-06; e-mail kvelev@online.bg; Chair. KIRIL VELEV.

Republican Party: 1000 Sofia, POB 787, Christo Belchev St 1, 3rd Floor; tel. (2) 986-35-72; fax (2) 986-67-22; e-mail republican_party_bg@hotmail.com; f. 1990; Chair. LENKO RUSSANOV.

United Christian Democratic Centre: 1000 Sofia, Blvd Dondukov 34; tel. (2) 80-04-09.

Union of Free Democrats: Sofia; f. 2001 as a breakaway faction of the Union of Democratic Forces; Leader STEFAN SOFIYANSKI.

The Independent Association for Human Rights in Bulgaria (Leader STEFAN VALKOV), the Union of Victims of Repression (Leader IVAN NEVROKOPSKY) and the Union of Non-Party Members (Leader BOYAN VELKOV) all enjoyed observer status in the UDF.

Diplomatic Representation

EMBASSIES IN BULGARIA

Afghanistan: 1618 Sofia, Ovcha Kupel, Boryana St 61, Bl. 216A; tel. (2) 55-61-96; fax (2) 955-99-76.

Albania: Sofia, Krakra St 10; tel. (2) 946-12-22; fax (2) 943-30-69; Ambassador KOCO KOTE.

Algeria: Sofia, Slavyanska St 16; tel. (2) 980-22-50; Ambassador ZINE EL-ABIDINE HACHICHI.

Argentina: Sofia, Dragan Tsankov 36, 2nd Floor, POB 635; tel. (2) 971-25-39; fax (2) 71-61-30-28; Ambassador ARTURO HOTTON RISLER.

Armenia: 1606 Sofia, 20 April St 11, 11th Floor; tel. and fax (2) 52-60-46; e-mail armembsof@sof.omega.bg; Ambassador SEVDA SEVAN.

Austria: 1000 Sofia, Shipka St 4; tel. (2) 980-35-72; fax (2) 987-22-60; e-mail obsofia@online.bg; Ambassador Dr GEORG POTYKA.

Belarus: 1113 Sofia, Charles Darwin St 6; tel. and fax (2) 973-31-00; e-mail embassyblr@omega.bg; Ambassador ALYAKSANDR PETROV.

Belgium: 1164 Sofia, Velchova Zavera St 1; tel. (2) 988-72-90; fax (2) 963-36-38; e-mail ambabel@einet.bg; Ambassador EDMOND DE WILDE.

Brazil: 1113 Sofia, Frédéric Joliot Curie St 19, Bl. 156/1; tel. (2) 72-35-27; fax (2) 971-28-18; e-mail sofbrem@main.infotel.bg; Ambassador CARLOS ALBERTO PESSÔA PARDELLAS.

Cambodia: Sofia, Mladost 1, Blvd S. Allende, Res. 2; tel. (2) 75-71-35; fax (2) 75-40-09; Ambassador BO RASSI.

China, People's Republic: 1113 Sofia, Aleksandur von Humboldt St 7; tel. (2) 973-39-10; fax (2) 971–10–81; internet www .chinaembassy.bg; Ambassador XIE HANGSHENG.

Croatia: 1504 Sofia, Veliko Turnovo St 32; tel. (2) 943-32-55; fax (2) 946-13-55; e-mail dkp_rh@infotel.bg; internet www.infotel.bg/ croembassy.

Cuba: 1113 Sofia, Konstantin Shtarkelov St 1; tel. (2) 72-09-96; fax (2) 72-04-60; e-mail consulcuba@mbox.digsys.bg; Ambassador LUIS FELIPE VÁZQUEZ.

Cyprus: Sofia, G. Gagarin St, Bl. 154A, Flat 2; tel. (2) 971-22-41; fax (2) 971-37-70; e-mail cyembsof@fintech.bg; Chargé d'affaires PHILIPPOS KRITIOTIS.

Czech Republic: 1000 Sofia, Yanko Sakazov St 9; tel. (2) 946-11-10; fax (2) 946-18-00; e-mail sofia@embassy.mzv.cz; Ambassador PETR DOKLÁDAL.

Denmark: 1000 Sofia, Blvd Dondukov 54, POB 1393; tel. (2) 980-08-30; fax (2) 980-08-31; e-mail sofambu@um.dk; Ambassador CHRISTIAN FABER-ROD.

Egypt: 1000 Sofia, Shesti Septemvri St 5; tel. (2) 87-02-15; fax (2) 980-12-63; Ambassador MAY ABOUL-DAHAB.

Finland: 1504 Sofia, Krakra St 16, Flat 4; tel. (2) 942-49-10; fax (2) 942-49-11; e-mail finembassy@online.bg; Ambassador TAISTO TOLVANEN.

France: 1054 Sofia, Oborishte St 27–29; tel. (2) 965-11-00; fax (2) 965-11-20; internet www.ambafrance-bg.org; Ambassador JEAN-LOUP KUHN-DELFORGE.

Germany: 1113 Sofia, Frédéric Joliot Curie St 25, POB 869; tel. (2) 91-83-80; fax (2) 963-16-58; e-mail gemb@vilmat.com; internet www .german-embassy.bg; Ambassador URSULA SEILER-ALBRING.

Ghana: Sofia, POB 38; tel. (2) 70-65-09; Chargé d'affaires a.i. HENRY ANDREW ANUM AMAH.

Greece: Sofia, Blvd Klement Gottwald 68; tel. (2) 44-37-70; Ambassador PROKOPIOUS MANDZURANIS.

Holy See: 1000 Sofia, 11 August 6, POB 9; tel. (2) 981-17-43; fax (2) 981-61-95; e-mail nuntius@mbox.digsys.bg; Apostolic Nuncio (VACANT) (Titular Archbishop of Ferento).

Hungary: Sofia, Shesti Septemvri St 57; tel. (2) 963-04-60; fax (2) 963-21-10; Ambassador BÉLA KOLOZSI.

India: Sofia, Blvd Patriiarkh Evtimii 31; tel. (2) 981-17-02; fax (2) 981-41-24; e-mail india@inet.bg; Ambassador (VACANT).

Indonesia: 1700 Sofia, Blvd Simeonovsko Shosse 53; tel. (2) 962-52-40; fax (2) 962-58-42; e-mail indosof@geobiz.net; Ambassador ANAK AGUNG GDE RAKA.

Iran: Sofia, Blvd Vassil Levski 77; tel. (2) 44-10-13; Ambassador FEREIDUN HAKBIN.

Iraq: 1113 Sofia, Anton Chekhov St 21; tel. (2) 973-33-48; fax (2) 971-11-91; e-mail iraqiyah@asico.net.

Israel: Sofia, Blvd Bulgaria 1, NDK Administration Bldg, 7th Floor; tel. (2) 951-50-29; fax (2) 952-11-01; e-mail sofia@israel.net; Ambassador EMANUEL ZISMAN.

Italy: Sofia, Shipka St 2; tel. (2) 980-45-07; fax (2) 980-37-17; e-mail italdiplsofia@online.bg; Ambassador ALESSANDRO GRAFFINI.

Japan: Sofia, Lyulyakova Gradina St 14; tel. (2) 971-27-08; fax (2) 971-10-95; Ambassador YASUYOSHI ICHIHASHI.

Korea, Democratic People's Republic: Sofia, Mladost 1, Blvd S. Allende, Res. 4; tel. (2) 77-53-48; Ambassador KIM HA-DONG.

Korea, Republic: 1414 Sofia, Blvd Bulgaria 1, National Palace of Culture; tel. (2) 650-162; Ambassador PILL-JOO SUNG.

Kuwait: 1700 Sofia, Blvd Simeonovsko Shosse, Res. 15; tel. (2) 962-51-30; e-mail kwtemsf@omega.bg; Ambassador MUHAMMAD A. AL-AWADHI.

Lebanon: 1113 Sofia, Frédéric Joliot Curie St 19; tel. (2) 971-31-69; fax (2) 973-32-56; e-mail amliban@bgnet.bg; Ambassador HUSSEIN MOUSSAWI.

Libya: 1784 Sofia, Blvd Andrei Sakharov 1; tel. (2) 974-35-56; fax (2) 974-32-73; Secretary of People's Bureau FARAG GIBRIL.

Macedonia, former Yugoslav republic: 1113 Sofia, Frédéric Joliot Curie St 17, Bl. 2, Floor 1, Suite 1; Ambassador LJUBISA GEORGIEVSKI.

Moldova: 1000 Sofia, Blvd Patriiarkh Evtimii 17; tel. (2) 981-73-70; fax (2) 981-85-53; e-mail moldova@www1.infotel.bg; Ambassador VASILE STURZA.

Mongolia: 1113 Sofia, Frédéric Joliot Curie St 52; tel. (2) 65-84-03; fax (2) 963-07-45; e-mail mongemb@mbox.infotel.bg.

Morocco: Sofia, Blvd Evlogui Georgiev 129; tel. (2) 44-27-94; fax (2) 946-10-43; e-mail sifmasof@bulnet.bg; Ambassador ABDESSELAM ALEM.

Mozambique: Sofia; Ambassador GONÇALVES RAFAEL SENGO.

Netherlands: 1126 Sofia, Galichitsa St 38; tel. (2) 962-57-90; fax (2) 962-59-88; e-mail info@netherlandsembassy.bg; internet www.netherlandsembassy.bg; Ambassador H. J. C. M. VAN LYNDEN.

Nicaragua: Sofia, Mladost 1, Blvd Allende, Res. 1; tel. (2) 75-41-57; Ambassador UMBERTO CARIÓN.

Peru: 1113 Sofia, POB 514, Frédéric Joliot Curie St 17, Bl. 2, 2nd Floor; tel. (2) 971-37-08; fax (2) 973-33-46; e-mail peru@mail.bol.bg; Chargé d'affaires JULIO VEGA ERAUSQUÍN.

Poland: Sofia, Khan Krum St 46; tel. (2) 987-26-10; fax (2) 987-29-39; e-mail polamba@internet-bg.net; Ambassador JAROSŁAW LINDEN-BERG.

Portugal: 1124 Sofia, Ivatz Voivoda St 6; tel. (2) 943-36-67; fax (2) 943-30-89; e-mail embport@online.bg; Ambassador PAULO TIAGO GERÓNIMO DA SILVA.

Romania: Sofia, Sitniakovo St 4; tel. (2) 971-28-58; fax (2) 973-34-12; e-mail ambsofro@exco.net; Ambassador CONSTANTIN GRIGORIE.

Russia: Sofia, Blvd Dragan Tsankov 28; tel. (2) 963-44-58; fax (2) 963-41-03; e-mail consulate@datacom.bg; Ambassador VLADIMIR TITOV.

Serbia and Montenegro: Sofia, Veliko Turnovo St 3; tel. (2) 946-16-33; fax (2) 946-10-59; e-mail yembisof@tradenel.net; Ambassador CEDOMIR RADOJKOVIĆ.

Slovakia: 1504 Sofia, Blvd Janko Sakazov 9; tel. (2) 943-32-81; fax (2) 943-38-37; e-mail svkemba@tba.bg; Ambassador JÁN KOVÁČ.

Spain: Sofia, Sheinovo St 27, Ap. P. K. 381; tel. (2) 943-30-32; fax (2) 946-12-01; e-mail embespbg@mail.mae.es; Ambassador JOSÉ CORDERCH.

Sweden: Sofia, Alfred Nobel St 4; POB 620; tel. (2) 971-24-31; fax (2) 973-37-95; e-mail sweembg@einet.bg; Ambassador STEN ASK.

Switzerland: 1504 Sofia, Shipka St 33; tel. (2) 946-01-97; fax (2) 946-11-86; Ambassador GAUDENZ RUF.

Syria: Sofia, Christo Georgiev 10; tel. (2) 44-15-85; fax (2) 946-14-31; Chargé d'affaires SADDIK SADDIKNI.

Turkey: 1000 Sofia, Blvd Vassil Levski 80; tel. (2) 987-14-64; fax (2) 981-93-58; e-mail turkel@techno-link.com; Ambassador HAYDAR BERK.

Ukraine: 1618 Sofia, Ovcha Kupel, Boriana St 29; tel. (2) 955–94-78; e-mail puvrb@mail.bol.bg; internet www.ukramb.bol.bg; Ambassador VYACHESLAV POKHVALSKYI.

United Kingdom: 1000 Sofia, Moskovska St 9; tel. (2) 980-12-20; fax (2) 980-12-29; e-mail britembsof@mbox.cit.bg; internet www.british-embassy.bg; Ambassador IAN SOUTAR.

USA: 1000 Sofia, Suborna St 1; tel. (2) 980-52-41; fax (2) 981-89-77; e-mail irc@usembassy.bg; internet www.usembassy.bg; Ambassador JAMES W. PARDEW.

Uruguay: Sofia, Tsar Ivan Asen II St 91; POB 213; tel. (2) 943-45-45; fax (2) 943-40-40; e-mail urubulg@mbox.digsys.bg; Ambassador OLGA BARBAROV.

Venezuela: 1504 Sofia, Tulovo St 1, Flat 2; tel. (2) 943-30-61; fax (2) 943-30-10; e-mail embavenez@mbox.digsys.bg; internet www.embavenez-sofia.bgi; Ambassador GERARDO E. WILLS.

Viet Nam: 1113 Sofia, Jetvarka St 1; tel. (2) 963-26-09; fax (2) 963-36-58; e-mail dsqvietnam@sf.icn.bg; Ambassador NGUYEN VAN DAC.

Yemen: Sofia, Blvd S. Allende, Res. 3; tel. (2) 75-61-63; Ambassador ALI MUNASSAR MUHAMMAD.

Judicial System

The 1991 Constitution provided for justice to be administered by the Supreme Court of Cassation, the Supreme Administrative Court, courts of appeal, courts of assizes, military courts and district courts. The main legal officials are the justices, or judges, of the higher courts, the prosecutors and investigating magistrates. The judicial system is independent, most appointments being made or recommended by the Supreme Judicial Council. The Ministry of Justice coordinates the administration of the judicial system and the prisons. There is also the Constitutional Court, which is the final arbiter of constitutional issues. Under transitional arrangements attached to the 1991 Constitution, the existing Supreme Court of Bulgaria was to exercise the prerogatives of the two new Supreme Courts until the new judicial system was enacted and established.

Supreme Court of Cassation: 1000 Sofia, Blvd Vitosha 2, Sudebna Palata; tel. (2) 987-76-98; fax (2) 88-39-85; Pres. IVAN GRIGOROV.

Supreme Administrative Court: Sofia, Blvd A. Stamboliyski 18; tel. (2) 981-30-42; fax (2) 981-87-51; internet www.sac.government.bg; Pres. VLADISLAV SLAVOV.

Constitutional Court: 1594 Sofia, Blvd Dondukov 1; tel. (2) 987-50-08; fax (2) 987-19-86; e-mail s.petrova@constcourt.government.bg; internet www.constcourt.bg; Chair. LAZAR GRUEV; Sec.-Gen. KIRIL A. MANOV.

Supreme Judicial Council: Sofia; tel. (2) 981-79-74; Head ANTON ILIEV STANKOV (Minister of Justice).

Ministry of Justice: see The Government (Ministries, see p. 893).

Office of the Prosecutor-General: 1040 Sofia, Blvd Vitocha 2; tel. and fax (2) 988-52-13; Prosecutor-General NIKOLA FILTCHEV; Deputy Prosecutor-General CHRISTO MANCHEV.

Religion

Most of the population profess Christianity, the main denomination being the Bulgarian Orthodox Church, with a membership of more than 80% of the population. The 1991 Constitution guarantees freedom of religion, although Eastern Orthodox Christianity is declared to be the 'traditional religion in Bulgaria'. In accordance with the 1949 Bulgarian Law on Religious Faith, all new religious denominations must be registered by a governmental board before being allowed to operate freely. There is a significant Muslim minority (some 9% of the population), most of whom are ethnic Turks, although there are some ethnic Bulgarian Muslims, known as Pomaks. There is a small Jewish community.

Directorate of Religious Affairs: 1000 Sofia, Blvd Dondukov 1; tel. and fax (2) 988-04-88; a dept of the Council of Ministers; conducts relations between govt and religious organizations; Chair. Dr IVAN ZHELEV DIMITROV.

CHRISTIANITY

In 1992 a schism occurred in the Bulgarian Orthodox Church, although this was resolved in October 1998.

Bulgarian Orthodox Church: 1090 Sofia, Oborishte St 4, Synod Palace; tel. (2) 87-56-11; fax (2) 89-76-00; f. 865; autocephalous Exarchate 1870 (recognized 1945); administered by the Bulgarian Patriarchy; 11 dioceses in Bulgaria and two dioceses abroad (Diocese of North and South America and Australia, and Diocese of West Europe), each under a Metropolitan; Chair. of the Bulgarian Patriarchy His Holiness Patriarch MAKSIM.

Armenian Apostolic Orthodox Church: Sofia 1080, Nishka St 31; tel. (2) 88-02-08; 20,000 adherents (1996); Bishop DIRAYR MARDIKIYAN; administered by (resident in Bucharest, Romania); Chair. of the Diocesan Council in Bulgaria OWANES KIRAZIAN.

The Roman Catholic Church

Bulgarian Catholics may be adherents of either the Latin (Western) Rite, which is organized in two dioceses, or the Byzantine-Slav (Eastern) Rite (one diocese). All three dioceses are directly responsible to the Holy See.

Bishops' Conference (Mejduritualna Episcopska Konferenzia vâv Bâlgaria): 1606 Sofia, Lulin Planina 5; tel. (2) 953-04-06; fax (2) 952-61-86; e-mail proykov@techno-link.com; Pres. CHRISTO NIKOLOV PROYKOV (Titular Bishop of Briula).

Western Rite

Bishop of Nicopolis: PETKO CHRISTOV, 7000 Ruse, Ivan Vazov St 26A; tel. (82) 22-52-45; fax (82) 82-28-81; e-mail dio_nicop@elits.rousse.bg; 30,000 adherents (2000).

Diocese of Sofia and Plovdiv: GEORGI IVANOV JOVČEV (Apostolic Administrator), 4000 Plovdiv, Blvd Maria Luisa 3; tel. (32) 62-20-42; fax (32) 62-15-22; e-mail lubovenkov@hotmail.com; 35,000 adherents (2000).

Eastern Rite

Apostolic Exarch of Sofia: CHRISTO NIKOLOV PROYKOV (Titular Bishop of Briula), 1606 Sofia, Lulin Planina 5; tel. (2) 953-04-06; fax (2) 952-61-86; e-mail proykov@techno-link.com; 15,000 adherents (2000).

The Protestant Churches

Bulgarian Church of God: Sofia 1408, Petko Karavelov St 1; tel. (2) 65-75-52; fax (2) 51-91-31; 30,000 adherents (1992); Head Pastor PAVEL IGNATOV.

Bulgarian Evangelical Church of God: Plovdiv, Velbudge St 71; tel. (32) 43-72-92; 300 adherents (1992); Head Pastor BLAGOI ISEV.

Bulgarian Evangelical Methodist Episcopal Church: 1000 Sofia, Rakovski St 86; tel. (2) 981-37-83; fax (2) 980-94-83; e-mail umc-supint@mbox.digsys.bg; 2,000 adherents (2000); Gen. Superintendent Rev. BEDROS G. ALTUNIAN.

Church of Jesus Christ of Latter-day Saints in Bulgaria: Sofia, Drugba estate, Bl. 82/B/6, Flat 54; tel. (2) 74-08-06; f. 1991; 64 adherents (1992); Pres. VENTSESLAV LAZAROV.

Open Biblical Confraternity: 9300 Dobrich, General Kolev St 8; f. 1991; Head Pastor ANTONIA POPOVA.

Union of the Churches of the Seventh-day Adventists: Sofia, Solunska St 10; tel. (2) 88-12-18; fax (2) 980-17-09; e-mail sda.bg@sbline.net; 6,700 adherents (1997); Head Pastor AGOP TACHMISSJAN.

Union of Evangelical Baptist Churches: 1303 Sofia, Ossogovo St 63; tel. and fax (2) 931-06-82; 4,000 adherents (1999); Pres. Dr THEODOR ANGELOV.

Union of Evangelical Congregational Churches: Sofia, Solunska St 49; tel. (2) 980-56-85; fax (2) 980-69-02; e-mail sescbg@yahoo.com; f. 1888; 4,000 adherents (1998); Head Pastor Rev. Dr CHRISTO KULICHEV.

Union of Evangelical Pentecostal Churches: 1557 Sofia, Bacho Kiro St 21; tel. (2) 83-51-69; f. 1928; 30,000 adherents (1991); Head Pastor VIKTOR VIRCHEV.

Universal White Fraternity: 1612 Sofia, Balshik St 8B, Flat 27; tel. (2) 54-69-43; f. 1900; unifies the principles of Christianity with the arts and sciences; more than 6,000 adherents (1994); Chair. Dr ILIYAN STRATEV.

ISLAM

Supreme Muslim Theological Council: Sofia, Bratya Miladinovi St 27; tel. (2) 87-73-20; fax (2) 39-00-23; adherents estimated at 9% of the actively religious population, with an estimated 708 acting regional imams; Chair. Hadzhi NEDIM GENDZHEV; Chief Mufti of the Muslims in Bulgaria HADZHIBASRI HADZHISHARIF.

JUDAISM

Central Jewish Theological Council: 1000 Sofia, Ekzarkh Yosif St 16; tel. (2) 83-12-73; fax (2) 83-50-85; 5,000 adherents (1992); Head YOSSIF LEVI.

The Press

PRINCIPAL DAILIES

24 Chasa (24 Hours): 1504 Sofia, Blvd Tzarigradsko 47; tel. (2) 44-19-45; fax (2) 433-93-39; f. 1991; privately-owned; Editor-in-Chief VALERI NAIDENOV; circ. 330,000.

Bulgarska Armiya (Bulgarian Army): 1080 Sofia, Ivan Vasov St 12, POB 629; tel. (2) 87-47-93; fax (2) 987-91-26; f. 1944 as *Narodna Armiya*, name changed 1991; organ of the Ministry of Defence; Editor-in-Chief Col VLADI VLADKOV; circ. 30,000.

Chernomorsky Far (Black Sea Lighthouse): 8000 Burgas, Milin Kamak St 9; tel. (56) 422-48; fax (56) 401-78; f. 1958; independent regional from 1988; Editorial Dir GEORGI INGILISOV; circ. 37,000.

Duma (Word): Sofia, Positano St 20; Sofia, POB 382; tel. (2) 980-12-91; fax (2) 980-52-91; e-mail bsp@mail.bol.bg; internet www.bsp.bg/media-en/index.html; f. 1990 as an organ of the Bulgarian Socialist Party; resumed publication in Oct. 2001; Editor-in-Chief VYACHESLAV TUNEV.

Kontinent: 1000 Sofia, Blvd Tzarigradsko 47A; tel. (2) 943-44-46; fax (2) 44-19-04; e-mail kont@bgnet.bg; internet www.tetracom.com/

kontinent; f. 1992; independent; Editor-in-Chief BOIKO PANGELOV; circ. 12,000.

Maritza: 4000 Plovdiv, Blvd Christo Botev 27A; tel. (32) 60-34-50; fax (32) 60-34-22; e-mail mpolit@maritsa.com; internet www.digsys.bg/bgnews/maritsa; f. 1991; Editor-in-Chief ANTON BAYEV; circ. 30,000.

Narodno Delo (People's Cause): 9000 Varna, Blvd Christo Botev 3; tel. (52) 23-10-71; fax (52) 23-90-67; f. 1944; 6 a week; regional independent; business, politics and sport; Editor-in-Chief DIMITUR KRASIMIROV; circ. 56,000.

Noshten Trud (Night Labour): 1000 Sofia, Blvd Dondukov 52; tel. and fax (2) 87-70-63; f. 1992; 5 a week; Editor-in-Chief PLAMEN KAMENOV; circ. 332,000.

Nov Glas (New Voice): 5500 Lovech, G. Dimitrov St 24, 3rd Floor; tel. (68) 2-22-42; f. 1988; regional independent; Editor-in-Chief VENETSII GEORGIEV.

Novinar: 1505 Sofia, Oborishte 44; tel. (2) 43-55-22; fax (2) 943-45-32; e-mail novinar@novinar.net; internet www.novinar.org; f. 1992; Editor-in-Chief Dr STOYKO TONEV; circ. 45,000 (1997).

Otechestven Vestnik (Fatherland Newspaper): 1504 Sofia, Blvd Tzarigradsko 47; tel. (2) 43-431; fax (2) 46-31-08; f. 1942 as *Otechestven Front*; published by the journalists' co-operative 'Okchestvo'; Editor-in-Chief KONSTANCE ANSCHVA; total circ. 16,000.

Pari (Money): 1504 Sofia, Blvd Tzarigradsko 47A; POB 46; tel. (2) 943-36-46; fax (2) 943-31-88; e-mail office@pari.bg; internet www.pari.bg; f. 1991; 5 a week; financial and economic news online; in Bulgarian and English; Editor-in-Chief STEFAN NEDELCHEV; circ. 10,000.

Podkrepa (Support): 1000 Sofia, Ekzarkh Yosif St 37; tel. (2) 83-12-27; fax (2) 46-73-74; f. 1991; organ of the Podkrepa (Support) Trade Union Confederation; Editor-in-Chief (vacant); circ. 18,000.

Shipka: Khaskovo; tel. (38) 12-52-52; fax (38) 3-76-28; f. 1988; independent regional newspaper; Editor-in-Chief DIMITUR DOBREV; circ. 25,000.

Sport: 1000 Sofia, Vassil Levski Stadium, Sektor V; Sofia, POB 88; tel. (2) 88-03-43; fax (2) 88-36-28; f. 1927; Editor-in-Chief IVAN NANKOV; circ. 80,000.

Standart News Daily: 1784 Sofia, Blvd Tzarigradsko 113A; tel. (2) 975-36-88; fax (2) 76-28-77; e-mail root@standartnews.com; internet www.standartnews.com; f. 1992; Editor-in-Chief YULY MOSKOV; circ. 110,000.

Trud (Labour): 1000 Sofia, Blvd Dondukov 52; tel. (2) 987-98-05; fax (2) 80-11-40; f. 1923; organ of the Confederation of Independent Trade Unions in Bulgaria; Editor-in-Chief TOSHO TOSHEV; circ. 200,000.

Vecherni Novini (Evening News): Sofia; f. 1951; independent newspaper; centre-left; publ. by the Vest Publishing House; Dir GEORGI GANCHEV; Editor-in-Chief LYUBOMIR KOLAROV; circ. 35,000.

Vselena (Universe): Montana; tel. (96) 2-25-06; fmrly *Delo*; Editor-in-Chief BOYAN MLADENOV.

Zemedelsko Zname (Agrarian Banner): 1000 Sofia, Vrabcha St 23; tel. (2) 87-38-51; fax (2) 87-45-35; f. 1902; organ of the Aleksandur Stamboliyski Bulgarian Agrarian People's Union; Editor ILIYA DANOV.

Zemya (Earth): Sofia, 11 August St 18; tel. (2) 88-50-33; fax (2) 83-52-77; f. 1951 as *Kooperativno Selo*; renamed 1990; fmrly an organ of the Ministry of Agriculture; Editor-in-Chief KOSTA ANDREEV; circ. 53,000.

PRINCIPAL PERIODICALS

168 Chasa (168 Hours): 1504 Sofia, Blvd Tzarigradsko 47; tel. (2) 433-92-88; fax (2) 433-93-15; f. 1990; weekly; business, politics, entertainment; Editor-in-Chief VASELKA VALILEVA; circ. 93,000.

166 Politzeiski Vesti (166 Police News): 1680 Sofia, J. K. Belite Brezi, Solun St, Bl. 25 and 26, Ground Floor; tel. (2) 82-30-30; fax (2) 82-30-28; f. 1945; fmrly *Naroden Strazh*; weekly; criminology and public security; Editor-in-Chief PETAR VITANOV; circ. 22,000.

Anti: 1000 Sofia, Blvd Dondukov 9; tel. and fax (2) 80-43-03; f. 1991; weekly; Editor-in-Chief VASIL STANILOV; circ. 7,000.

Avto-moto Svyat (Automobile World): 1000 Sofia, Sveta Sofia St 6, POB 1348; tel. and fax (2) 88-08-08; f. 1957; monthly; illustrated publication on cars and motor sports; Editor-in-Chief ILJA SELIKTAR; circ. 33,600.

Az Buki (Alphabet): 1113 Sofia, Blvd Tzarigradsko 125; tel. (2) 71-65-73; f. 1991; weekly; education and culture; for schools; sponsored by the Ministry of Education and Science; Editor-in-Chief MILENA STRAKOVA; circ. 11,800.

Bulgarski Biznes (Bulgarian Business): 1505 Sofia, Oborishte St 44, POB 15; tel. (2) 46-70-23; fax (2) 44-63-61; weekly; organ of National Union of Employers; Editor-in-Chief DETELIN SERTOV; circ. 10,000–15,000.

Bulgarski Fermer (Bulgarian Farmer): 1797 Sofia, Blvd Dr G. M. Dimitrov 89; tel. (2) 71-04-48; fax (2) 73-10-08; f. 1990; weekly; Editor-in-Chief VASSIL ASPARUHOV; circ. 20,000.

Computer: 1504 Sofia, Panayot Volov St 11; tel. and fax (2) 943-41-28; e-mail office@newteck.bg; internet www.newteck.bg; f. 1991; monthly; information technology; Editor-in-Chief PETAR PETROV; circ. 7,000.

Computer World: 1421 Sofia, Blvd Hr. Smirnenski 1, Bl. B, Flat 1111; tel. (2) 963-20-17; fax (2) 963-28-41; internet www.eunet.bg/idg/; f. 1991; weekly; US-Bulgarian joint venture; information technology; Editor-in-Chief TATIANA HINOVA; circ. 7,000.

Domashen Maistor (Household Manager): 1000 Sofia, Blvd Tolbukhin 51A; tel. (2) 87-09-14; f. 1991; monthly; magazine for household repairs; Editor-in-Chief GEORGI BALANSKI; circ. 12,000.

Durzhaven Vestnik (State Gazette): 1169 Sofia, Blvd Aleksandur Battenberg 1; tel. (2) 986-10-76; e-mail dv@nt52.parliament.bg; f. 1879; 2 a week; official organ of the National Assembly; 2 bulletins of parliamentary proceedings and the publication in which all legislation is promulgated; Editor-in-Chief IVAN GAJDARSKI; circ. 42,000.

Ekho (Echo): 1000 Sofia, 'Vassil Levski' St 75; tel. (2) 87-54-41; f. 1957; weekly; organ of the Bulgarian Tourist Union; tourism publication; Editor-in-Chief LUBOMIR GLIGOROV; circ. 7,000.

Emigrant: Sofia; tel. (2) 87-23-08; fax (2) 87-46-17; f. 1991; (to replace *Kontakti*); weekly; magazine for Bulgarians living abroad; Editor-in-Chief MANOL MANOV; circ. 20,000.

Film: 1184 Sofia, Blvd Tzarigradsko 113A,Rodina Co; tel. (2) 76-15-02; fax (2) 77-02-27; e-mail film@online.bg; f. 1993; monthly; Editor DIMA DIMOVA; circ. 11,000.

Futbol (Football): 1000 Sofia, Blvd Bulgaria 1, Vassil Levski Stadium; tel. (2) 87-19-51; fax (2) 65-72-57; f. 1988; weekly; independent soccer publication; Editor-in-Chief IVAN CHOMAKOV; circ. 132,500.

Ikonomicheski Zhivot (Economic Life): 1000 Sofia, Alabin St 33; tel. (2) 87-95-06; fax (2) 87-65-60; e-mail ikonzhiv@dir.bg; f. 1970; weekly; independent; marketing and finance; Editor-in-Chief VASIL ALEKSIEV; circ. 21,000.

Kapital: 1000 Sofia, Ivan Vazov 9; tel. (2) 981-58-16; fax (2) 87-69-07; f. 1993; weekly; also online; Man. Editor FILIP HARMANDJIEV; circ. 30,000 (1999).

Komunistichesko Delo (Communist Cause): Sofia; tel. (2) 59-16-73; organ of the Bulgarian Communist Party; Editor-in-Chief VLADIMIR SPASSOV.

Krile (Wings): 1784 Sofia, POB 11; tel. (2) 974-51-26; fax (2) 974-51-25; e-mail kaloian_1999@yahoo.com; f. 1911; fmrly *Kam Nebeto*, renamed 1991; monthly; official organ; civil and military aviation; Pres. and Editor-in-Chief ROSSEN KALUDOV PANTCHELIEV; circ. 20,000.

Kultura (Culture): 1040 Sofia, Blvd Aleksandur Battenberg 4; tel. (2) 988-33-22; fax (2) 980-04-95; e-mail kultura@online.bg; internet www.online.bg/kultura; f. 1957; weekly; issue of the Culture Space Foundation; arts, publicity and cultural affairs; Editor-in-Chief KOPRINKA CHERVENKOVA; circ. 5,000.

Kurier 5 (Courier 5): 1000 Sofia, Blvd Tzarigradsko 47; tel. (2) 46-30-26; f. 1991; weekdays; advertising newspaper; Editor-in-Chief STEPAN ERAMIAN; circ. 30,000.

Liberalen Kongres (Liberal Congress): Sofia; tel. (2) 39-00-18; fax (2) 68-77-14; f. 1990; weekly; organ of the Liberal Congress Party; Editor-in-Chief ROSSEN ELEZOV; circ. 12,000.

LIK: Sofia, Blvd Tzarigradsko 49; weekly; publication of the Bulgarian Telegraph Agency; literature, art and culture; Editor-in-Chief SIRMA VELEVA; circ. 19,000.

Literaturen Forum (Literary Forum): 1000 Sofia, Blvd Aleksandur Battenberg 4; tel. (2) 88-10-69; fax (2) 88-10-69; f. 1990; weekly; independent; Editor-in-Chief ATANAS SVILENOV; circ. 5,300.

Makedonia (Macedonia): 1301 Sofia, Pirotska St 5; tel. (2) 80-05-32; fax 87-46-64; e-mail mpress@virbus.bg; f. 1990; weekly; organ of the Inner Macedonian Revolutionary Organization IMRO —Union of Macedonian Societies; Editor-in-Chief DINKO DRAGANOV; circ. 22,000.

Missul (Thought): 1000 Sofia, Pozitano St 20, POB 382; tel. (2) 85-141; f. 1990; weekly; organ of the Marxist Alternative Movement; politics, culture; Editor-in-Chief GEORGI SVEZHIN; circ. 15,000.

Napravi Sam (Do It Yourself): 1504 Sofia, Panayot Volov St 11; tel. and fax (2) 943-41-28; e-mail newteck@einet.bg; internet www .newteck.bg; f. 1981; monthly; Editor-in-Chief GEORGI BALANSKI; circ. 8,000.

Nie Zhenite (We the Women): Sofia; tel. (2) 52-31-98; f. 1990; weekly; organ of the Democratic Union of Women; Editor-in-Chief EVGINIA KIRANOVA; circ. 176,600.

Nov Den (New Day): 1000 Sofia, Lege St 5; tel. (2) 77-39-82; e-mail ivan_kalchev@yahoo.com; f. 1991; weekly; organ of the Union of Free Democrats; Editor-in-Chief IVAN KALCHEV; circ. 25,000.

Novo Vreme (New Time): Sofia, Positano St 20; Sofia, POB 382; tel. (2) 980-12-91; fax (2) 980-52-91; e-mail bsp@mail.bol.bg; internet www.bsp.bg/media-en/nv.html; monthly; organ of the Bulgarian Socialist Party.

Paraleli: 1040 Sofia, Blvd Tzarigradsko 49; tel. (2) 87-40-35; f. 1964; weekly; illustrated publication of the Bulgarian Telegraph Agency; Editor-in-Chief KRASSIMIR DRUMEV; circ. 50,000.

Pardon: 1504 Sofia, Blvd Tzarigradsko 47; tel. (2) 43-431; f. 1991; weekly; satirical publication; Editor-in-Chief CHAVDAR SHINOV; circ. 8,560.

PC Magazine Bulgaria: 1000 Sofia, Blvd Vassil Levski 3, Saga Technology; f. 1993; monthly; Chief Exec. ANNA BAKALOVA; circ. 12,000.

Pogled (Review): 1090 Sofia, Blvd Slaveikov 11; tel. (2) 87-70-97; fax (2) 65-80-23; f. 1930; weekly; organ of the Union of Bulgarian Journalists; Editor-in-Chief DAMYAN OBRECHKOV; circ. 47,300.

Prava i Svobodi (Rights and Freedoms): Sofia; tel. (2) 46-72-12; fax (2) 46-73-35; f. 1990; weekly; organ of the Movement for Rights and Freedoms; politics, culture; Editor-in-Chief (vacant); circ. 7,500.

Progres (Progress): 1000 Sofia, Gurko St 16; tel. (2) 89-06-24; fax (2) 89-59-98; f. 1894; fmrly *Tekhnichesko Delo*; weekly; organ of the Federation of Scientific and Technical Societies in Bulgaria; Editor-in-Chief PETKO TOMOV; circ. 35,000.

Starshel (Hornet): 1111 Sofia, Hemus St 59; tel. and fax (2) 70-85-54; f. 1946; weekly; humour and satire; Editor-in-Chief KRASTYN KRASTEV; circ. 45,200.

Start: 1000 Sofia, Vassil Levski Stadium, POB 797; tel. (2) 980-25-17; fax (2) 981-29-42; f. 1971; weekly; sports, illustrated; Editor-in-Chief NIKOLAY RANGELOV; circ. 21,300.

Televiziya i Radio (Television and Radio): 1756 Sofia, Bulgarska Natsionalna Televiziya, Blvd Tzarigradsko 111; tel. (2) 70-01-88; fax (2) 974-36-93; e-mail petmar@mail.techno-link.com; f. 1964; weekly; broadcast listings; Editor-in-Chief LUBOMIR YANKOV; circ. 30,000 (1999).

Tsarkoven Vestnik (Church Newspaper): 1000 Sofia, Oborishte St 4; tel. (2) 87-56-11; f. 1900; weekly; organ of the Bulgarian Orthodox Church; Editor-in-Chief DIMITUR KIROV; circ. 4,000.

Uchitelsko Delo (Teachers' Cause): 1113 Sofia, Blvd Tzarigradsko 125, Studentski Obshezhitiya, Bl. 5; tel. and fax (2) 70-00-12; f. 1905; weekly; organ of the Union of Bulgarian Teachers; Editor-in-Chief MARGARITA CHOLAKOVA; circ. 12,000.

Vek 21 (21st Century): 1000 Sofia, Kaloyan St 10; tel. (2) 46-54-23; fax (2) 46-61-23; f. 1990; weekly; organ of the Radical Democratic Party; liberal politics and culture; Editor-in-Chief ALEKSANDUR YORDANOV; circ. 5,900.

Zdrave (Health): 1421 Sofia, Blvd Chr Smirnenski 44; tel. (2) 44-30-26; fax (2) 65-68-35; f. 1955; monthly; published by Bulgarian Red Cross; Editor-in-Chief YAKOV YANAKIEV; circ. 55,000.

Zhenata Dnes (Women Today): 1000 Sofia, Blvd Narodno Sobraniye 12; tel. (2) 89-16-00; f. 1946; monthly; organ of Zhenata Dnes Ltd; Editor-in-Chief BOTIO ANGELOV; circ. 50,000.

Zname (Banner): 1184 Sofia, Blvd Kniyas Korsakov 34; tel. (2) 80-01-83; f. 1894; publ. until 1934 and 1945–49, resumed publication 1990; weekly; Editor-in-Chief BOGDAN MORFOV; circ. 20,000.

NEWS AGENCIES

Bulgarska Telegrafna Agentsia (BTA) (Bulgarian Telegraph Agency): 1024 Sofia, Blvd Tzarigradsko 49; tel. (2) 92-62-42; fax (2) 986-22-89; e-mail bta@bta.bg; internet www.bta.bg; f. 1898; official news agency; domestic, Balkan and international news in Bulgarian and English; also economic and sports news; publishes weekly surveys of science and technology, international affairs, literature and art; Gen. Dir MAKSIM MINCHEV.

Bulnet: 1000 Sofia, Rakovski St 127; tel. (2) 987-11-22; fax (2) 980-30-71; e-mail support@bulnet.bg; f. 1994; provides online access, internet services, communications software, hardware and consultancy; photo service; Exec. Dir INA STOIANOVA.

LEFF Information Service: 1000 Sofia, Rakovski St 127; tel. (2) 87-11-22; fax (2) 81-34-42; e-mail leffnews@bulnet.bg; private and independent news agency via internet; publishes daily economic and current affairs newsletters; Pres. BORIS BASMADJIYEV.

Sofia-Press Agency: 1040 Sofia, Slavyanska St 29; tel. (2) 88-58-31; fax (2) 88-34-55; internet sun.iecs.bas.bg/press; f. 1967 by the Union of Bulgarian Writers, the Union of Bulgarian Journalists, the Union of Bulgarian Artists and the Union of Bulgarian Composers; publishes socio-political and scientific literature, fiction, children's and tourist literature, publications on the arts, a newspaper, magazines and bulletins in foreign languages; also operates.

Sofia-Press Info: tel. (2) 87-66-80; Pres. ALEKSANDUR NIKOLOV; which provides up-to-date information on Bulgaria, in print and for broadcast; Dir-Gen. KOLIO GEORGIEV.

Foreign Bureaux

Agence France-Presse (AFP): 1504 Sofia, Blvd Yanko Sakazov 19; tel. (2) 944-10-78; fax (2) 46-34-63; e-mail afpsofia@afp.com.

Agencia EFE Spain: Sofia; tel. (2) 87-29-63; Correspondent SAMUEL FRANCÉS.

Ceska kancelar (CTK) (Czech Republic): Sofia; tel. (2) 70-91-36; Correspondent VĚRA IVANOVIĆOVÁ.

Deutsche Presse-Agentur (dpa) (Germany): Sofia; tel. (2) 72-02-02; Correspondent ELENA LALOVA.

Informatsionnoye Telegrafnoye Agentstvo Rossii—Telegrafnoye Agentstvo Suverennykh Stran (ITAR—TASS) (Russia): 1000 Sofia, A. Gendov St 1, Flat 29; tel. (2) 87-38-03; Correspondent ALEKSANDR STEPANENKO.

Magyar Távirati Iroda (MTI) (Hungary): Sofia, Frédéric Joliot Curie St 15, Bl. 156/3, Flat 28; tel. (2) 70-18-12; Correspondent TIVADAR KELLER.

Novinska Agencija Tanjug (Yugoslavia): 1000 Sofia, L. Koshut St 33; tel. (2) 71-90-57; Correspondent PERO RAKOSEVIĆ.

Polska Agencja Prasowa (PAP) (Poland): Sofia; tel. (2) 44-14-39; Correspondent BOGDAN KORNEJUCK.

Prensa Latina (Cuba): Sofia; tel. (2) 71-91-90; Correspondent SUSANA UGARTE SOLER.

Reuters (United Kingdom): 1000 Sofia, Ivan Vazov 16; tel. (2) 911-88; fax (2) 980-91-31; e-mail sofia.newsroom@reuters.com; Correspondent THALIA GRIFFITHS.

Rossiyskoye Informatsionnoye Agentstvo—Novosti (RIA—Novosti) (Russia): Sofia; Bureau Man. YEVGENII VOROBYOV.

United Press International (UPI) (USA): Sofia; tel. (2) 62-24-65; Correspondent GUILLERMO ANGELOV.

Xinhua (New China) News Agency (People's Republic of China): Sofia; tel. (2) 88-49-41; Correspondent U. SIZIUN.

The following agencies are also represented: SANA (Syria) and Associated Press (USA).

PRESS ASSOCIATIONS

Union of Bulgarian Journalists: 1000 Sofia, Ekzarkh Yosif St 37; tel. (2) 83-19-95; fax (2) 83-54-84; f. 1944; Pres. CHAVDAR TONCHEV; 5,500 mems.

Publishers

Darzhavno Izdatelstvo 'Christo G. Danov' ('Christo G. Danov' State Publishing House): 4005 Plovdiv, Stoyan Chalakov St 1; tel. (32) 23-12-01; fax (32) 26-05-60; f. 1855; fiction, poetry, literary criticism; Dir NACHO CHRISTOSKOV.

Darzhavno Izdatelstvo 'Tekhnika': 1000 Sofia, Blvd Slaveikov 1; tel. (2) 87-12-83; fax (2) 87-49-06; f. 1958; textbooks for technical and higher education and technical literature; Dir NINA DENEVA.

Darzhavno Izdatelstvo 'Zemizdat': 1504 Sofia, Blvd Tzarigradsko 47; tel. (2) 44-18-29; f. 1949; specializes in works on agriculture, shooting, fishing, forestry, livestock-breeding, environmental studies and popular scientific literature and textbooks; Dir PETAR ANGELOV.

Galaktika: 9000 Varna, Blvd Nezavissimost 6; tel. (52) 24-11-56; fax (52) 23-47-50; f. 1960; science fiction, economics, Bulgarian and foreign literature; Dir ASSYA KADREVA.

Izdatelstvo na Bulgarskata Akademiya na Naukite 'Marin Drinov': 1113 Sofia, Acad. Georgi Bonchev St, Bl. 6; tel. (2) 72-09-22; fax (2) 70-40-54; f. 1869; scientific works and periodicals of the Bulgarian Academy of Sciences; Dir TODOR RANGELOV.

Izdatelstvo 'Bulgarski Houdozhnik': 1504 Sofia, Shipka St 6; tel. (2) 46-72-85; fax (2) 946-02-12; e-mail filchev@mail.orbitel.bg; f. 1952; art books, children's books; Dir BOUYAN FILCHEV.

Izdatelstvo 'Bulgarsky Pisatel': Sofia, Shesti Septemvri St 35; tel. (2) 87-58-73; fax (2) 87-24-95; publishing house of the Union of Bulgarian Writers; Bulgarian fiction and poetry, criticism; Dir GERTCHO ATANASOV.

Izdatelstvo 'Christo Botev': 1504 Sofia, Blvd Tzarigradsko 47; tel. (2) 44-14-08; f. 1944; fmrly the Publishing House of the Bulgarian Communist Party, renamed as above 1990; Dir IVAN DINKOV.

Izdatelstvo 'Medizina i Fizkultura': 1080 Sofia, Blvd Slaveikov 11; tel. (2) 987-13-09; fax (2) 987-99-75; e-mail medpubl@netplus.bg; f. 1948; medicine, physical culture and tourism; Dir PETKO PETKOV.

Izdatelstvo na Ministerstvo na Otbranta (Ministry of Defence Publishing House): 1000 Sofia, Ivan Vazov St 12; tel. (2) 88-44-31; fax (2) 88-15-68; Head Maj. BOYAN SULTANOV.

Izdatelstvo Mladezh, (Youth Publishing House): Sofia; tel. (2) 88-21-37; fax (2) 87-61-35; f. 1945; art, history, original and translated fiction, political science and sociology; Gen. Dir STANIMIR ILCHEV.

Izdatelstvo 'Profizdat' (Publishing House of the Central Council of Bulgarian Trade Unions): Sofia; specialized literature and fiction; Dir STOYAN POPOV.

Izdatelstvo 'Prosveta' AS: 1184 Sofia, Blvd Tzarigradsko 117; tel. (2) 76-11-82; fax (2) 76-44-51; e-mail prosveta@intech.bg; internet www.mobilis.bg/prosveta; f. 1945; educational publishing house; Pres. JOANA TOMOVA; Dir YONKO YONCHEV.

Naouka i Izkoustvo Ltd: 1000 Sofia, Slaveikov Sq. 11; tel. (2) 987-47-90; fax (2) 987-24-96; e-mail nauk_izk@sigma-bg.com; f. 1948; general publishers; Man. LORETA PUSHKAROVA.

'Narodna Kultura' Publishers: 1000 Sofia, Angel Kanchev St 1; POB 421; tel. (2) 987-80-63; e-mail nauk-izk@sigma-bg.com; f. 1944; general; Dir PETAR MANOLOV.

Reporter Ltd Publishing Co: 1184 Sofia, Blvd Tzarigradsko 113; tel. (2) 76-90-28; fax (2) 71-83-77; e-mail reporter@techno-link.com; f. 1990; private publishers of fiction and documentary literature.

Sinodalno Izdatelstvo: Sofia, Oborishte St 4; tel. (2) 87-56-11; religious publishing house; Dir ANGEL VELITEHKOV.

STATE ORGANIZATION

Jusautor: Sofia; tel. (2) 87-28-71; fax (2) 87-37-40; state organization of the Council of Ministers; Bulgarian copyright agency; represents Bulgarian authors of literary, scientific, dramatic and musical works, and deals with the granting of options, authorization for translations, and drawing up of contracts for the use of works by foreign publishers and producers; Dir-Gen. YANA MARKOVA.

PUBLISHERS' ASSOCIATION

Bulgarian Book Publishers' Association: 1000 Sofia, Blvd Slaveikov 11; POB 1046; tel. and fax (2) 986-79-70; e-mail bba@otel.net; internet www.bba-bg.org; f. 1994; Exec. Dir MADLENA ROMANOVA; Chair. RAYMOND WAGENSTEIN.

WRITERS' UNION

Union of Bulgarian Writers: Sofia, Blvd Slaveikov 2; tel. (2) 88-06-85; fax (2) 87-47-57; f. 1913; Chair. NIKOLAI HAITOV; 495 mems.

Broadcasting and Communications

TELECOMMUNICATIONS

At 31 December 2000 12% of the telephone network was digitized. In 2000 there were 2.9m. main telephone lines in use, and a total of 0.7m. subscribers to mobile cellular telephone services.

Committee of Posts and Telecommunications: 1000 Sofia, Gourko St 6; POB 1352; tel. (2) 981-29-49; fax (2) 980-61-05; internet www.cpt.bg; supervises and regulates the post and telecommunications systems; Pres. ANTONI SLAVINSKI.

Bulgarian Telecommunications Company (BTC): 1606 Sofia, Blvd Totleben 8; tel. (2) 88-94-38; fax (2) 87-58-85; e-mail central.office@btc.bg; internet www.btc.bg; agreement on divestment of 65% stake to Viva Ventures (based in Austria) signed in March 2003; provides telecommunications and information services; Chair. NIKOLAI NIKOLOV; Exec. Dir IVAN SPASSOV; 23,000 employees.

MobilTel EAD: 1408 Sofia, Balsha St 3, Bl. 8; tel. (88) 50-00-31; fax (88) 50-00-32; e-mail pr@mobiltel.bg; internet www.mobiltel.bg; f. 1994 as a private joint-stock co; provides mobile telecommunications services.

BROADCASTING

National Radio and Television Council: 1504 Sofia, San Stefano St 29; tel. (2) 46-81; internet www.bild.net/nsrt; Dir IVAN BORISLAVOV.

Radio

Bulgarsko Nationalno Radio: 1040 Sofia, Blvd Dragan Tzankov 4; tel. (2) 963-43-30; fax (2) 963-44-98; e-mail bgintrel@nationalradio.bg; internet www.nationalradio.bg; f. 1929; two Home Service programmes; local stations at Blagoevgrad, Plovdiv, Shumen, Stara Zagora and Varna. The Foreign Service broadcasts in Bulgarian, Turkish, Greek, Serbo-Croat, French, German, English, Russian, Spanish and Albanian; Dir-Gen. POLYA STANCHEVA.

Radio Alma Mater: 1000 Sofia, Moskovska St 49; tel. (2) 986-16-07; fax (2) 930-84-80; f. 1993; cable radio service introduced by Sofia Univ. from July 1998 24-hour broadcasting at 87.7 MHz in Sofia; culture and science programmes; Editor-in-Chief DILIANA KIRKOVSKA.

Television

Balkan News Corporation: Sofia; daily news transmission of commercial news, family entertainment and locally-produced programmes, on bTV channel; Chief Exec. MARTY POMPADUR.

Bulgarska Natsionalna Televiziya: 1504 Sofia, San Stefano St 29; tel. (2) 44-63-29; fax (2) 946-12-10; internet www.bnt.bg; f. 1959; daily transmission of programmes on Channel 1 and Efir 2 and on the satellite channel—TV Bulgaria; Dir-Gen. KIRIL GOTSEV; 3,000 employees.

Nova Televiziya: 1000 Sofia, Blvd Sveta Nedelya 16; tel. (2) 80-50-25; fax (2) 87-02-98; f. 1994; first private television channel in Bulgaria; commercial news and entertainment.

Finance

(cap. = capital; dep. = deposits; res = reserves; m. = million; amounts in new leva, unless otherwise indicated)

BANKING

By late 1991 the transition to a two-tier banking sector had been achieved. In late 1992 21 commercial banks merged to form the United Bulgarian Bank, which opened in 1993. In early 1993 two new banks emerged, Commercial Bank Expressbank (formed from the merger of 12 banks) and Hebrosbank (a merger of eight banks). In 1996 14 banks, including five state-owned banks, collapsed. In May 1996 the total number of banks was 47, and in October 1997 state-owned banks accounted for 73% of the total. A currency board was established in July 1997. By early 2003 34 commercial bank were in operation in Bulgaria (of which six were branches of foreign banks). The country's remaining state-owned bank, DSK Bank plc, was scheduled for privatization in 2003.

Currency Board

Currency Board of the Republic of Bulgaria: Sofia; f. 1997; monetary supervision; Head MARTIN ZAIMOV.

Central Bank

Bulgarian National Bank (Bulgarska Narodna Banka): 1000 Sofia, Blvd Aleksandur Battenberg 1; tel. (2) 914-51-203; fax (2) 980-24-25; e-mail press_office@bnbank.org; internet www.bnb.bg; f. 1879; bank of issue; cap. 20m., res 1,353.6m., dep. 780.7m. (Dec. 2001); Gov. SVETOSLAV GAVRIYSKI; 6 brs; 1,000 employees.

State Savings Bank

DSK Bank plc: 1040 Sofia, Moskovska St 19; tel. (2) 985-57-220; fax (2) 980-64-77; e-mail office@dskbank.bg; internet www.dskbank.bg; f. 1951 as State Savings Bank; name changed as above in 1998; provides general retail banking services throughout the country; scheduled for privatization; cap. 70.0m., res 113.6m., dep. 1,316.5m. (Dec. 2001); Chair. KRASSIMIR ANGARSKI; 126 brs.

Commercial Banks

BNP-Paribas (Bulgaria) AD: 1000 Sofia, Blvd Tsar Osvoboditel 2; POB 11; tel. (2) 921-86-40; fax (2) 921-86-95; e-mail bulgaria_bnpparibas@bnpparibas.com; f. 1994; fmrly BNP-Dresdner Bank; name changed as above in 2001; 20% owned by the European Bank for Reconstruction and Development; cap. 36.0m., res 13.8m., dep. 220.2m. (Dec. 2001); Chief Exec. ULLRICH GUENTER SCHUBERT.

Bulbank AD: 1000 Sofia, Blvd Sveta Nedelya 7; tel. (2) 923-21-11; fax (2) 988-46-36; e-mail info@sof.bulbank.bg; internet www.bulbank.bg; f. 1964 as the Bulgarian Foreign Trade Bank; name changed in 1994; privatized in 2000; 85.2% owned by UniCredito Italiano SpA (Italy); cap. 166.4m., res 50.0m., dep. 2,114.9m. (Dec. 2001); Chair. and Chief Exec. LEVON HAMPARTZOUMIAN; 98 brs.

Bulgarian-American Credit Bank AD: 1504 Sofia, Shipka St 3; tel. (2) 965-83-45; fax (2) 944-50-10; e-mail bacb@baefinvest.com; f. 1996; cap. US $8.9m., dep. $6.6m. Chief Exec. FRANK BAUER.

Bulgarian Post Bank JSC: 1414 Sofia, Bulgaria Sq. 1; tel. (2) 963-20-96; fax (2) 963-04-82; e-mail intldiv@postbank.bg; internet www.postbank.bg; f. 1991; privatized in 1999; cap. 56,697m., res 15,219m., dep. 576,903m. (Dec. 2002); Chair. and Chief Exec. PANAIOTIS VARELAS; 112 brs and offices.

CB Unionbank Ltd: 1606 Sofia, Damyan Gruev St 10–12; tel. (2) 915-33-33; fax (2) 980-20-04; e-mail mainmail@unionbank.bg; internet www.unionbank.bg; f. 1992; cap. 15,412m., res 14,470m., dep. 83,004m. (Dec. 2002); Chair. and Exec. Dir DORCHO DIMITROV ILCHEV; 10 brs.

Central Co-operative Bank plc: 1000 Sofia, G. S. Rakovski St 103; tel. (2) 926-62-37; fax (2) 987-19-48; e-mail falev@ccbank.bg; internet www.ccbank.bg; f. 1991; cap. 16.2m., res 10.9m., dep. 170.7m. (Dec. 2001); Chair. ALEKSANDUR VODENICHAROV; 33 brs.

Commercial Bank Biochim: 1026 Sofia, Ivan Vazov St 1; tel. (2) 926-92-10; fax (2) 926-94-40; e-mail info@biochim.com; internet www.biochim.com; f. 1987; scheduled for privatization; cap. 28.8m., res 27.4m., dep. 534.7m. (2001); Chair. RUMEN BEREMSKI; Exec. Dirs NIKOLAI KAVARDJIKLIEV, EMILIA PALIBACHIYSKA; 40 brs.

Commercial Bank Bulgaria Invest AD: 1202 Sofia, Blvd Maria Louiza 65; tel. (2) 980-52-00; fax (2) 981-93-07; e-mail admin@bank.allianz.bg; internet www.allianz.bg; f. 1989 as Yambol Commercial Bank; cap. 27.8m., dep. 155.2m. (Dec. 2001); Chair. DIMITAR ZHELEV.

Corporate Commercial Bank AD: 1000 Sofia, Graf Ignatiev St 10; POB 632; tel. (2) 980-93-62; fax (2) 980-89-48; e-mail corpbank@corpbank.bg; internet www.corpbank.bg; f. 1989 as BSFK Bulgarso-vinvest; cap. 10.0m., res 1.3m., dep. 50.1m. (Dec. 2001); Chair. TZVETAN VASSILEV.

Demirbank (Bulgaria) AD: 1000 Sofia, Blvd Tsar Osvoboditel 8; tel. (2) 989-44-44; fax (2) 989-48-48; e-mail info@demirbank.bg; internet www.demirbank.bg; f. 1999; cap. 15.0m., dep. 55.0m. (Dec. 2002); Chief Exec. HALUK KURCER; Sr Man. SINAN KIRCALI ,MARIN SHOSHKOV.

EIBANK AD: 1000 Sofia, Saborna St 11A; tel. (2) 985-00-240; fax (2) 981-25-26; e-mail info@hq.eibank.bg; internet www.eibank.bg; f. 1994 as Bulgarian Russian Investment Bank; known as Bribank AD in 1999–2000; cap. 20.0m., res 8.0m., dep. 219.9m. (Dec. 2001); Chair. VASSIL SIMOV; 10 brs.

Eurobank plc: 1407 Sofia, Blvd Cherni Vrach 43; tel. (2) 62-33-66; fax (2) 68-10-86; e-mail eurobank@eurobank.bg; internet www.eurobank.bg; f. 1993 as Commercial Bank Mollov Ltd; cap. 39.6m., dep. 112.2m. (Dec. 2001); Chair. EMIL ANGELOV.

First East International Bank: 1504 Sofia, Blvd Vassil Levski 106, POB 256; tel. (2) 946-16-82; fax (2) 946-16-83; e-mail correbanking@feibbank.com; internet www.feibank.com; f. 1989 as Trade Bank Kremikovzi, name changed in 1991; cap. 20.1m., res 4.9m., dep. 54.0m. (Dec. 2001); Pres. ANNA SABEVA; 29 brs.

First Investment Bank Ltd: 1000 Sofia, St Karadja St 10; tel. (2) 910-01-00; fax (2) 980-50-33; e-mail fib@fibank.bg; internet www.fibank.bg; f. 1993; cap. 60.2m., dep. 342.2m. (2001); Exec. Dirs MAJA GEORGIEVA, MATTHEW MATTEEV; Chair. of Supervisory Bd GEORGI DIMITROV MUTAFCHIEV; 29 brs.

Hebrosbank: 4018 Plovdiv, Blvd Tsar Boris III Obedinitel 37; tel. (32) 90-26-68; fax (32) 62-39-64; e-mail hebros@hebros.bg; internet www.hebros.bg; f. 1993 following merger of eight banks; commercial, investment, corporate and retail banking; cap. and res 80.0m., dep. 320.8m. (Dec. 2001); Chair. and Chief Exec. GAUTAM VIR; 59 brs.

HVB Bank Bulgaria EAD: 1000 Sofia, Rakovsky St 90; tel. (2) 932–01-00; fax (2) 980-53-13; e-mail vladimir_babursky@bg.hypovereinsbank.com; f. 1987 as Bayerisch-Bulgarische Handelsbank GmbH; name changed to Hypovereinsbank Bulgaria GmbH in 1998, and as above in 2002; cap. 10.2m., res 0.3m., dep. 83.9m. (Dec. 2000); Gen. Man. LUDMIL GATCHEV.

Municipal Bank plc: 1000 Sofia, 6 Vrabcha St; tel. (2) 930-01-85; fax (2) 981-51-47; f. 1996 as Sofia Municipal Bank Plc; name changed Jan. 1998; cap. 25.0m., res 8.1m., dep. 227.7m. (Dec. 2001); Chief Exec. VANYA GEORGIEVA VASSILEVA; 15 brs.

Neftinvestbank plc: 1000 Sofia, 155 Rakovski St; POB 1138; tel. (2) 981-69-38; fax (2) 980-77-22; e-mail office@nib.bg; internet www.nib.bg; f. 1994 as International Orthodox Bank 'St Nikola'; cap. 84.8m., dep. 47.8m. (Dec. 2001); Chair. PETIA IVANOVA BARAKOVA-SLAVOVA; 9 brs.

Raiffeisenbank (Bulgaria) AD: 1504 Sofia, Gogol St 18–20; tel. (2) 919-85-101; fax (2) 943-45-28; e-mail ibgamts@rbb-sofia.raiffeisen.at; internet www.rbb.bg; f. 1994; cap. 16.7m., res 14.4m., dep. 390.1m. (Dec. 2001); Chair. JOHANN JONACH.

Roseximbank plc: 1000 Sofia, Blvd Dondukov 4–6; tel. (2) 930-71-36; fax (2) 980-26-23; e-mail info@roseximbank.bg; internet www.roseximbank.bg; f. 1994; cap. 51.1m., dep. 233.4m. (Dec. 2001); Chair. DIANA MLADENOVA; Chief Exec. Dir VLADIMIR VLADIMIROV.

SG Expressbank AD: 9000 Varna, Blvd Vl. Varnenchik 92; tel. (52) 66-04-80; fax (52) 60-13-24; e-mail office@expressbank.bg; internet www.expressbank.bg; f. 1987 as Transport Bank, name changed following merger of 12 banks in 1993; privatized in 1999; 97.95% owned by Société Générale (France); cap. 28.5m., res 37.4m., dep. 483.8m. (Dec. 2001); Chief Exec. SANDY GILLIO; 23 brs; 900 employees.

Teximbank: 1202 Sofia, Blvd Maria Louiz 107, Serdika Municipality; tel. (2) 31-40-38; fax (2) 931-12-07; e-mail texim@omega.bg; f. 1992; private entrepreneurial bank; cap. 10,000m. old leva, res 982,500m. old leva, dep. 2,869.1m. old leva (Dec. 1998); Pres. MARIA VIDOLOVA.

United Bulgarian Bank AD: 1040 Sofia, Sveta Sofia St 5; tel. (2) 98-54-00; fax (2) 988-08-22; e-mail info@sof.ubb.bg; internet www.ubb.bg; f. 1993 following a merger of 22 commercial banks; universal commercial bank; privatized in 1999; 89.9% owned by National Bank of Greece SA; cap. 76.0m., res 33.7m., dep. 1,266.0m. (Dec. 2001); Chief Exec. STILIAN VATEV; 57 brs.

STOCK EXCHANGE

Bulgarian Stock Exchange: 1040 Sofia, Blvd Makedonia 1; tel. (2) 986-59-15; fax (2) 986-58-63; e-mail bsemail@online; internet www.online.bg/bs; Chair. GEORGI PROHASKI; Chief Exec. APOSTOL APOSTOLOV.

INSURANCE

In 1947 all insurance firms were nationalized, and reorganized into a single state insurance company. In 1989 private insurance companies began to reappear.

General Insurance Plc (DZI): 1000 Sofia, Georgi Benkovski St 3; tel. (2) 981-57-99; fax (2) 987-45-33; e-mail general.ins@dzi.bg; internet www.dzi.bg; f. 1946; all areas of insurance; privatization approved in Aug. 2002; Chair. DANCHO DANCHEV; 27 agencies, 101 brs.

Bulstrad Insurance and Reinsurance: 1000 Sofia, Blvd Pozitano 5, POB 627; tel. (2) 985-66-100; fax (2) 985-66-103; f. 1961; all classes of insurance and reinsurance; Chief Exec. RUMEN YANCHEV.

Trade and Industry

GOVERNMENT AGENCIES

Privatization Agency: 1000 Sofia, Aksakov St 29; tel. (2) 897-75-79; fax (2) 981-62-01; e-mail bgpriv@priv.government.bg; internet www.priv.government.bg; f. 1992; organizes the privatization of state-owned enterprises; Exec. Dir APOSTOL APOSTOLOV.

INTERNATIONAL FREE-TRADE ZONES

Burgas Free-Trade Zone: 8000 Burgas, Trapezitza St 5, POB 154; tel. (56) 84-20-47; fax (56) 84-15-62; e-mail freezone@bse.bg; internet www.freetradezone-bourgas.com; f. 1989; Exec. Dirs ANGELIN POPOV, KRASIMIR GRUDOV.

Dobrotitza Free-Trade Zone: 4649 Kranevo, Dobrich District.

Dragoman Free-Trade Zone: 2210 Dragoman; tel. (9971) 72-20-14.

Plovdiv Free-Trade Zone: 4003 Plovdiv, Vassil Levski St 242A; POB 75; tel. (32) 90-62-33; fax (32) 96-08-33; e-mail frzone@plovdiv.techno-link.com; internet www.freezone-plovdiv.com; f. 1990; Exec. Dir ALEKSANDUR NIKOLOV.

Ruse International Free-Trade Zone: 7000 Ruse, Knyazheska St 5, POB 107; tel. (82) 27-22-47; fax (82) 27-00-84; e-mail trade@freezone-rousse.bg; internet www.freezone-rousse.bg; f. 1988; Gen. Man. YORDAN KAZAKOV.

Svilengrad Free-Trade Zone: 6500 Svilengrad; tel. (359) 379-74-45; fax (359) 379-75-41; e-mail sbz@svilengrad.com; internet www.svilengrad.com/sbz; f. 1990; Exec. Dir DIMO HARAKCHIEV.

Vidin Free-Trade Zone: 3700 Vidin; tel. (94) 228-37; fax (94) 309-47; f. 1988; Gen. Man. K. MARINOV.

CHAMBER OF COMMERCE

Bulgarian Chamber of Commerce and Industry (BCCI): 1058 Sofia, Parchevich St 42; tel. (2) 987-26-31; fax (2) 987-32-09; e-mail bcci@bcci.bg; internet www.bcci.bg; f. 1895; promotes economic relations and business contacts between Bulgarian and foreign cos and orgs; organizes participation in international fairs and exhibitions; publishes economic pubs in Bulgarian and foreign languages; organizes foreign trade advertising and publicity; provides legal and

economic consultations, etc. registers all Bulgarian cos trading internationally (more than 40,000 at the end of 2000); Pres. BOJIDAR BOJINOV; 28 regional chambers.

EMPLOYERS' ASSOCIATIONS

Bulgarian Industrial Association (BIA): 1000 Sofia, Alabin St 16–20; tel. (2) 932-09-11; fax (2) 987-26-04; e-mail office@bia-bg.com; internet www.bia-bg.com; f. 1980; assists Bulgarian economic enterprises with promotion and foreign contacts; economic analysis; legal and arbitration services; intellectual property protection; training and qualification; Chair. and Exec. Pres. BOJIDAR DANEV.

National Union of Employers: 1505 Sofia, Oborishte St 44, POB 15; f. 1989; federation of businessmen in Bulgaria.

Union of Private Owners in Bulgaria: Sofia; f. 1990; Chair. DIMITUR TODOROV.

Vuzrazhdane Union of Bulgarian Private Manufacturers: 1618 Sofia, Blvd Todor Kableshkov 2; tel. (2) 55-00-16; Chair. DRAGOMIR GUSHTEROV.

UTILITIES

Electricity

Central Laboratory of Solar Energy and New Energy Sources: 1784 Sofia, Blvd Tzarigradsko 72; tel. and fax (2) 75-40-16; e-mail solar@phys.bas.bg; research into alternative energy production; Dir Assoc. Prof. PETKO VITANOV.

National Electricity Company (Natsionalna Elektricheska Kompania): 1022 Sofia, Vestlets St 5; tel. (2) 549-09; fax (2) 980-12-43; e-mail nek@nek.bg; internet www.nek.bg; f. 1991; wholly state-owned, scheduled for privatization; national transmission company responsible for all thermal, nuclear and hydroelectric electricity production from 14 plants; Chair. of Bd ANGEL MINEV; Exec. Dir VASIL ANASTASOV.

State Agency on the Peaceful Use of Nuclear Energy: 1574 Sofia, Blvd Shipchenski Prokhod 69; tel. (2) 72-02-17; fax (2) 70-21-43; f. 1957; Chair. TINKO GANCHEV (acting).

Gas

Bulgargaz: Sofia; tel. (2) 25-90-74; Chair. KRASIMIR NIKOLOV; Dir KIRIL GEGOV.

Topenergy Joint-Stock Co: Sofia; f. 1995; owned by Gazprom of Russia; responsible for supply of Russian natural gas to Bulgaria; Chair. BOGDAN BUDZULIAK; Dir SERGEI PASHIN.

CO-OPERATIVE

Central Union of Workers' Productive Co-operatives: 1000 Sofia, Blvd Dondukov 11; POB 55; tel. (2) 80-39-38; fax (2) 87-03-20; f. 1988; over-arching organization of 164 workers' productive co-operatives; Pres. STILIAN BALASSOPOULOV; 60,000 mems.

TRADE UNIONS

Confederation of Independent Trade Unions in Bulgaria (CITUB): 1040 Sofia, Blvd Makedonia 1; tel. (2) 917-04-79; fax (2) 988-59-69; f. 1904; name changed from Bulgarian Professional Union and independence declared from all parties and state structures in 1990; in 1998 remained the main trade-union organization; approx. 75 mem. federations and four associate mems (principal mems listed below); Chair. Prof. Dr KRUSTYU PETKOV; Sec. MILADIN STOYNOV; some 3m. mems.

Edinstvo (Unity) People's Trade Union: 1000 Sofia, Moskovska St 5; tel. (2) 87-96-40; f. 1990; co-operative federation of Clubs, based on professional interests, grouped into 84 asscns, 2 prof. asscns and 14 regional groups; Chair. OGNYAN BONEV; 384,000 mems.

Podkrepa (Support) Trade Union Confederation: 1000 Sofia, Angel Kanchev St 2; tel. (2) 981-45-51; fax (2) 981-29-28; e-mail koseva@bulinfo.net; f. 1989 as the first opposition trade union (affiliated to the Union of Democratic Forces); 35 regional and 27 branch union orgs; Chair. DIMITAR MANOLOV; Gen. Sec. PETAR GANCHEV; 155,000 mems (2000).

Principal CITUB Trade Unions

Federation of Independent Agricultural Trade Unions: 1606 Sofia, Dimo Hadzhidimov St 29; tel. (2) 52-15-40; Pres. LYUBEN KHARALAMPIEV; 44,600 mems (mid-1994).

Federation of Independent Trade Unions of Construction Workers: Sofia; tel. (2) 80-16-003; Chair. NIKOLAI RASHKOV; 220,000 mems.

Federation of the Independent Trade Unions of Employees of the State and Social Organizations: 1000 Sofia; tel. (2) 87-98-52; Chair. PETAR SUCHKOV; 144,900 mems.

Federation of Independent Mining Trade Unions: 1233 Sofia, 32 Veania St; tel. (2) 931-07-00; fax (2) 931-00-50; f. 1992; Pres. PENCHO TOKMAKCHIEV; 20,000 mems.

Federation of Light Industry Trade Unions: 1040 Sofia, Blvd Makedonia 1; tel. (2) 88-15-70; fax (2) 88-15-20; Chair. IORDAN VASSILEV IVANOV; 64,320 mems (1997).

Federation of Metallurgical Trade Unions: Sofia; tel. (2) 88-48-21; fax (2) 88-27-10; f. 1992; Pres. VASSIL YANACHKOV; 20,000 mems.

Federation of Trade Unions in the Chemical Industry: 1040 Sofia, Blvd Makedonia 1; tel. (2) 87-39-07; Pres. LYUBEN MAKOV; 60,000 mems (mid-1993).

Federation of Trade Union Organizations in the Forestry and Woodworking Industries: 1606 Sofia, Vladayska St 29; tel. (2) 52-31-21; fax (2) 51-73-97; Pres. PETER IVANOV ABRACHEV; 16,570 mems (mid-1999).

Federation of Trade Unions of Health Services: 1202 Sofia, Blvd Maria Louiza 45; tel. (2) 988-20-97; fax (2) 83-18-14; e-mail fsz-citub@mail.orbitel.bg; f. 1990; Pres. Dr IVAN KOKALOV; 24,065 mems (2000).

Independent Trade Union Federation of the Co-operatives: 1000 Sofia, Rakovski St 99; tel. (2) 87-36-74; Chair. NIKOLAI NIKOLOV; 96,000 mems.

Independent Trade Union Federation for Trade, Co-operatives, Services and Tourism: 1000 Sofia, 6 Septemvri St 4; tel. (2) 88-02-51; Chair. PETAR TSEKOV; 212,221 mems.

Independent Trade Union of Food Industry Workers: 1606 Sofia, Dimo Hadzhidimov St 29; tel. (2) 52-30-72; fax (2) 52-16-70; Pres. SLAVCHO PETROV; 53,000 mems (mid-1994).

National Federation of Energy Workers: 1040 Sofia, Blvd Makedonia 1; tel. (2) 88-48-22; f. 1927; Pres. BOJIL PETROV; 15,000 mems.

National Trade Union Federation 'Metal-elektro': 1040 Sofia, Blvd Makedonia 1; POB 543; tel. (2) 987-48-06; fax (2) 987-75-38; e-mail nsf-me@netbg.com; Pres. ASSEN ASSENOV; 40,000 mems (1999).

Trade Union of Bulgarian Teachers: 1000 Sofia, Gen. Parensov St 11; tel. (2) 987-78-18; fax (2) 988-17-94; e-mail seb@internet-bg .net; internet sbu.internet-bg.net; f. 1905; Pres. IANKA TANEVA; 186,153 mems.

Union of Transport Workers: 1233 Sofia, Blvd Maria Louiza 106; tel. (2) 31-51-24; fax (2) 31-71-24; f. 1911; Pres. IORDANKA MILANOVA RADEVA; 18,000 mems (Dec. 2001).

Other Principal Trade Unions

Bulgarian Military Legion 'G. S. Rakovski': Sofia; tel. (2) 87-72-96; Chair. DOICHIN BOYADZHIEV.

Construction, Industry and Water Supply Federation 'Podkrepa': 1000 Sofia, Uzundjovska St 12; tel. (2) 987-96-70; fax (2) 98-87-38; e-mail fciw@mail.techno-link.com; Pres. IOANIS PARTENIOTIS; 15,000 mems (2000).

Podkrepa National Union of Petrochemical Workers: 8000 Burgas, Neftohim EAD; tel. (56) 80-09-01; fax (56) 80-12-89.

Podkrepa Professional Trade Union for Chemistry, Geology and Metallurgy Workers: 1000 Sofia, Angel Kanchev St 2; Chair. LACHEZAR MINKOV (acting); 15,000 mems.

Podkrepa Professional Trade Union for Doctors and Medical Personnel: 1000 Sofia, Angel Kanchev St 2; Chair. Dr K. KRASTEV; 20,000 mems.

Podkrepa Union of Journalists: 1000 Sofia, Angel Kanchev St 2; tel. (2) 87-21-98.

Union of Architects in Bulgaria: 1504 Sofia, Krakra St 11; tel. (2) 46-31-09; fax (2) 946-08-00; e-mail sab@bguet.bg; internet www .bulgarianarchitects.org; f. 1893; Chair. TANKO SERAFIMOV.

Union of Bulgarian Lawyers: 1000 Sofia, Treti April St 7; tel. (2) 87-58-59; Chair. PETAR KORNAZHEV.

Transport

Ministry of Transport and Communications: 1000 Sofia, Levski St 9; tel. and fax (2) 988-53-29; directs the state rail, road, water and air transport organizations.

Despred International Freight Forwarders JSC: 1202 Sofia, Vesletz St 284; tel. (2) 931-39-56; fax (2) 983-14-84; e-mail info@ despred.com; internet www.despred.com; f. 1947; Exec. Dir STOJAN INDJEV.

RAILWAYS

In 1996 there were 4,293 km of track in Bulgaria, of which 2,708 km were electrified. The international and domestic rail networks are centred on Sofia. Construction of a 52-km underground railway system for Sofia commenced in 1979; the first section, comprising 6.1 km, was opened in January 1998.

Bulgarian State Railways (BDZ): 1080 Sofia, Ivan Vazov St 3; tel. (2) 987-30-45; fax (2) 987-71-51; e-mail bdzboev@bg400.bg; internet www.bg400.bg/bdz; f. 1888; owns and controls all freight and passenger railway transport; manufactures railway coaches and equipment; Pres. KRASSIMIRA MARTINOVA; Exec. Dir VLADIMIR DUNCHEV; 18,554 employees.

ROADS

There were 37,286 km of roads in Bulgaria in 2000, of which 3,011 km were principal roads; 94% of the network was paved. Two important international motorways traverse the country and a major motorway runs from Sofia to the coast.

Road Executive Agency: 1606 Sofia, Blvd Makedonia 3; tel. (2) 952-17-68; fax (2) 951-54-22; e-mail pdikovsky@rea.bg; f. 1952; develops, manages and maintains the national road network; provides conditions for the realization of state road policy; Dir-Gen. PAVEL DIKOVSKY.

SHIPPING AND INLAND WATERWAYS

The Danube (Dunav) River is the main waterway, with Ruse and Lom the two main ports. There are external services from Black Sea ports (the largest being Varna and Burgas) to the former USSR, the Mediterranean and Western Europe. The port of Tsarevo was opened to international shipping in 1995. In September 1998 it was announced that the port of Burgas was to be modernized, with financial assistance from the Japanese Government. In 2001 the European Commission provided €22m. for the restoration of navigation along the Danube, which had been blocked for two years, following the aerial bombardment of the Federal Republic of Yugoslavia (now Serbia and Montenegro) by NATO forces in 1999.

Bulgarian River Shipping Company: 7000 Ruse, Blvd Otets Paisi 2; tel. (82) 82-20-81; fax (82) 82-21-30; e-mail main@brp.bg; internet www.brp.bg; f. 1935; shipment of cargo and passengers on the Danube; storage, handling and forwarding of cargo; scheduled for privatization; Chair. STEFAN ZAGOROV; Gen. Dir VRANGEL NIKIFOROV; 1,100 employees.

Bulgarski Morski Flot Co.: 9000 Varna, Panaguirishte St 17; tel. (52) 22-63-16; fax (52) 22-53-94; organization of sea and river transport; carriage of goods and passengers on waterways; controls all aspects of shipping and shipbuilding; research, design and personnel training; Dir-Gen. ATANAS YONKOV.

Burgas Port Authority: 8000 Burgas, Aleksandur Battenberg St 1; tel. (56) 84-04-93; fax (56) 84-01-56; e-mail ivanov@port-burgas .com; internet www.port-burgas.com; Chief Exec. GEORGE DERELIEV.

Lom Port Authority: 3600 Lom, Pristanishtna St 21; tel. (971) 422-08; fax (971) 269-31; e-mail port@lom-bg.com; internet port.lom-bg .com.

Navigation Maritime Bulgare Ltd: 9000 Varna, Blvd Primorski 1; tel. (52) 22-24-74; fax (52) 22-24-91; e-mail office@navbul.com; internet www.navbul.com; f. 1892; scheduled for privatization; major enterprise in Bulgaria employed in sea transport; owns 103 tankers, bulk carriers and container, ferry, cargo and passenger vessels with a capacity of 1,817,169 dwt (1995); Dir-Gen. Capt. IVAN BORISSOV; 7,100 employees.

Varna Port Authority: Varna; tel. (52) 69-25-08; fax (52) 63-29-53; e-mail tihomir@port-varna.bg; internet port-varna.bg; Dir DANAIL PAPAZOV.

CIVIL AVIATION

There are three international airports in Bulgaria; at Sofia, Varna and Burgas, and seven other airports for domestic services. Construction work to modernize Sofia Airport was initiated in the mid-1990s.

Air Sofia: 1000 Sofia, Blvd Patriiarkh Evtimii 64; tel. (2) 981-09-25; fax (2) 980-29-07; internet www.airsofia.com; f. 1992; international charter flights; Pres. LILIAN TODOROV; Man. Dir GEORGI IVANOV.

Air Via Bulgarian Airways (Via): Sofia, Blvd Dimitros 54; tel. (2) 971-28-69; fax (2) 973-34-54; f. 1990; began services in 1997; first private charter airline, internal charter services to Burgas, Plovdiv and Varna; Man. Dir MIKHAIL DONSKY.

Balkan Air Tour: 1540 Sofia, Sofia Airport; tel. (2) 98-44-89; fax (2) 79-12-06; e-mail balkan@balkanairlines.bg; f. 1991 as a tour operator owned by Sofia Airport; transformed into a state-owned national carrier in 2002, as the successor to the bankrupt co Balkan

Bulgarian Airlines (Balkanair); scheduled for privatization; passenger and cargo services.

Heli Air Services: 1540 Sofia, Sofia Airport North; tel. (2) 79-50-36; fax (2) 71-75-26; e-mail heliair@intech.bg; f. 1991; Exec. Dir GEORGI SPASSOV.

Hemus Airlines: 1540 Sofia, Sofia Airport; tel. (2) 70-20-76; fax (2) 79-63-80; internet www.geocities.com/CapeCanaveral/3514/hemus .html; f. 1991; 66% state-owned; Man. Dir DIMITAR PAVLOV.

Tourism

Bulgaria's tourist attractions include the resorts on the Black Sea coast, mountain scenery and historic centres. Under the communist regime most visitors to Bulgaria were from former Eastern bloc countries, or in transit to or from Turkey. Following the end of communist rule, fewer Eastern Europeans holidayed within Eastern Europe, and there was, overall, a severe reduction in the numbers of tourists staying at Black Sea resorts. The European Community (now the European Union) granted aid for developing tourism in 1993–95. In 1997 the tourism authorities promoted the creation of a national system of tourist offices, to be managed by local governments. In 2002 there were 2,992,590 foreign visitor arrivals. Tourism receipts totalled US $1,074m. in 2000 and an estimated $1,350m. in 2002, compared with $496m. in 1997.

Bulgarian Tourist Chamber: 1000 Sofia, Sveta Sofia St 8; tel. (2) 987-40-59; fax (2) 986-51-33; e-mail btk_tz@yahoo.com; internet www.btch.org; f. 1991; assists tourism enterprises, provides training, and co-ordinates non-governmental organizations; Chair. TSVETAN TONCHEV.

Balkantourist: 1040 Sofia, Blvd Vitosha 1; tel. (2) 980-23-24; fax (2) 981-01-14; e-mail sofia.agency@balkantourist.bg; internet www .balkantourist.bg; f. 1948; Bulgaria's first privatized travel company; leading tour operator and travel agent; Chair. and Man. Dir VLADIMIR ANGELOU.

BURKINA FASO

Introductory Survey

Location, Climate, Language, Religion, Flag, Capital

Burkina Faso (formerly the Republic of Upper Volta) is a land-locked state in West Africa, bordered by Mali to the west and north, by Niger to the east, and by Benin, Togo, Ghana and Côte d'Ivoire to the south. The climate is hot and mainly dry, with an average temperature of 27°C (81°F) in the dry season (December–May). A rainy season occurs between June and October. Levels of rainfall are generally higher in the south than in the north; average annual rainfall in Ouagadougou is 718 mm (28 ins). The official language is French, and there are numerous indigenous languages (principally Mossi), with many dialects. The majority of the population follow animist beliefs; about 30% are Muslims and some 10% Christians, mainly Roman Catholics. The national flag (proportions 2 by 3) has two equal horizontal stripes, of red and green, with a five-pointed gold star in the centre. The capital is Ouagadougou.

Recent History

Burkina Faso (Upper Volta until August 1984) was formerly a province of French West Africa. It became a self-governing republic within the French Community in December 1958 and achieved full independence on 5 August 1960, with Maurice Yaméogo as President. In January 1966 Yaméogo was deposed in a military coup, led by Lt-Col (later Gen.) Sangoulé Lamizana, the Chief of Staff of the army, who took office as President and Prime Minister. The new regime dissolved the legislature, suspended the Constitution and established a Conseil suprême des forces armées. Political activities were suspended between September 1966 and November 1969. A new Constitution, approved by referendum in June 1970, provided for a return to civilian rule after a four-year transitional period. Elections for an Assemblée nationale took place in December, at which the Union démocratique voltaïque (UDV) won 37 of the 57 seats. In early 1971 Lamizana appointed the UDV leader, Gérard Ouédraogo, as Prime Minister at the head of a mixed civilian and military Council of Ministers.

A series of conflicts between the Government and the legislature prompted Lamizana to announce that the army had again assumed power in February 1974. Ouédraogo was dismissed, the legislature was dissolved, and the Constitution and all political activity were suspended. The Assemblée was replaced in July by a Conseil national consultatif pour le renouveau, with 65 members nominated by the President. Political parties were allowed to resume their activities from October 1977. A referendum in November of that year approved a draft Constitution providing for a return to civilian rule. Seven parties contested elections for a new Assemblée nationale in April 1978. The UDV won 28 of the 57 seats, while the Union nationale pour la défense de la démocratie (UNDD), led by Hermann Yaméogo, the son of the former President, secured 13 seats. In May Lamizana was elected President, and in July the Assemblée elected Lamizana's nominee, Dr Joseph Conombo, as Prime Minister.

In November 1980 Lamizana was overthrown in a bloodless coup, led by Col Saye Zerbo. A 31-member Comité militaire de redressement pour le progrès national (CMRPN) was established, and a new Government, comprising both army officers and civilians, was formed. The Constitution was suspended, the legislature was dissolved, and political parties were banned. Opposition to the Zerbo regime soon emerged, and in November 1982 Zerbo was deposed by a group of non-commissioned army officers. Maj. Jean-Baptiste Ouédraogo, President of the Conseil de salut du peuple (CSP), emerged as leader of the new regime. The CMRPN was dissolved, and a predominantly civilian Government was formed. A power struggle within the CSP became apparent with the arrest, in May 1983, of radical left-wing elements within the Government, including the recently appointed Prime Minister, Capt. Thomas Sankara. Ouédraogo announced the withdrawal of the armed forces from political life and disbanded the CSP. Sankara and his supporters were released following a rebellion by pro-Sankara commandos at Pô, near the border with Ghana, under the leadership of Capt. Blaise Compaoré.

In August 1983 Sankara seized power in a violent coup. A Conseil national révolutionnaire (CNR) was established, and Jean-Baptiste Ouédraogo and other perceived opponents of the new administration were placed under house arrest. Compaoré, as Minister of State at the Presidency, became the regime's second-in-command. In September Zerbo was arrested after his supporters attempted to overthrow the new Government. Administrative, judicial and military reforms were announced, and Tribunaux populaires révolutionnaires (TPRs) were inaugurated to consider cases of alleged corruption. Several former politicians, including Zerbo, appeared before these tribunals and were subsequently imprisoned. Meanwhile, citizens were urged to join Comités pour la défense de la révolution (CDRs), which, by imposing government policies and organizing local affairs, played an important role in consolidating Sankara's position.

In June 1984 seven army officers were executed, convicted of plotting to overthrow the Government. Sankara accused an outlawed left-wing political group, the Front progressiste voltaïque, of complicity in the plot, alleging that it had been supported by France and other foreign powers; the French Government vigorously denied any involvement, and relations between the two countries were strained. In August the country was renamed Burkina Faso ('Land of the Incorruptible Men').

In December 1985 a long-standing border dispute with Mali erupted into a six-day war that left some 50 people dead. The conflict centred on a reputedly mineral-rich area known as the Agacher strip. Following a cease-fire, arranged by the regional defence grouping, Accord de non-agression et d'assistance en matière de défense, and as a result of an interim decision on the dispute delivered by the International Court of Justice (ICJ) in January 1986, troops were withdrawn from the Agacher area. Ambassadors were exchanged in June, and both countries accepted the ICJ's ruling, made in December, that the territory be divided equally between the two.

Amnesty measures for Sankara's political opponents were gradually effected. However, tensions between the Government and trade unions were exacerbated by policies aimed at developing the rural economy and by the introduction, from 1985, of austerity measures. There was, moreover, evidence of growing disharmony within the CNR (in part engendered by Sankara's suppression of the trade unions), and in August 1987 two members of a leading communist faction were dismissed from the Government. On 15 October a self-styled Front populaire (FP), led by Compaoré, overthrew the CNR in a violent coup, in which Sankara and 13 of his entourage were killed. A predominantly civilian Council of Ministers included seven members of the previous administration. Compaoré became Head of State, with the title of Chairman of the FP. Many of Sankara's close associates were detained without trial in the months following the coup, although most had been released by mid-1988.

Among institutional reforms instigated in the aftermath of the coup, the CDRs were disarmed and replaced by Comités révolutionnaires (which had only limited success in recruiting members), and the powers of the TPRs were curtailed. In April 1989 a new political grouping, the Organisation pour la démocratie populaire/Mouvement du travail (ODP/MT), was established, under the leadership of Clément Oumarou Ouédraogo. The swift dismissal of government members who had declined to join the new party was an indication that the ODP/MT was to assume a prominent role in Compaoré's regime.

In August 1989 an amnesty was proclaimed for all political prisoners. In the following month it was announced that the Commander-in-Chief of the Armed Forces and Minister of Popular Defence and Security, Maj. Jean-Baptiste Boukary Lingani, and the Minister of Economic Promotion, Capt. Henri Zongo (both of whom had been prominent at the time of the 1983 and 1987 coups), had been executed, together with two others, following the discovery of a plot to overthrow Compaoré. It was widely believed that Lingani and Zongo had been opposed to aspects of economic reform, notably the promotion of private enterprise and the principle of co-operation with the IMF and the World Bank (funding negotiations with which had begun in

1988). Compaoré subsequently assumed personal responsibility for defence. In December 1989 it was announced that a further attempt to overthrow the Government had been thwarted; in November 1990 19 people (including a former Minister of Justice under Sankara) were officially said to be awaiting trial in connection with the alleged plot.

The first congress of the FP, in March 1990, sanctioned the establishment of a commission to draft a new constitution that would define a process of 'democratization'. Hermann Yaméogo, widely regarded as a political moderate, was appointed to the Executive Committee of the FP. (Three months later, however, Yaméogo and his supporters were expelled from the organization.) In April Clément Oumarou Ouédraogo was dismissed from the Council of Ministers and replaced as Secretary for Political Affairs of the FP and as Secretary-General of the ODP/MT by Roch Marc-Christian Kaboré, hitherto Minister of Transport and Communications and, unlike Ouédraogo, a known supporter of Compaoré's ideals. In September Kaboré was appointed as a Minister of State.

The final draft of the Constitution, which was completed in late 1990, delineated the division of power between the executive, legislature and judiciary, in a 'revolutionary, democratic, unitary and secular state'. Multi-party elections, by universal suffrage, would take place for a President and legislative Assemblée des députés du peuple (ADP), while provision was made for the establishment of a second, appointed and consultative chamber of the legislature, the Chambre des représentants, to be composed of the 'active forces of the nation'.

In March 1991, at its first congress, the ODP/MT adopted Compaoré as the party's presidential candidate and renounced its Marxist-Leninist ideology. In April an amnesty was proclaimed for the alleged perpetrators of the coup attempt of late 1989. In May 1991 a congress was convened to restructure the FP and to provide for the separation, upon the adoption of the new Constitution, of the functions of the FP and the organs of state. Compaoré, redesignated Secretary-General of the FP, was confirmed as Head of State pending the presidential election. Delegates also approved the rehabilitation of Maurice Yaméogo, and an appeal was made to all political exiles to return to Burkina. In June plans were announced for the construction of a memorial honouring Sankara.

About 49% of the registered electorate voted in the constitutional referendum, which took place on 2 June 1991: of these, 93% were reported to have endorsed the Constitution of what was to be designated the Fourth Republic. The new document took effect on 11 June. A transitional Government was subsequently appointed, its most senior member being Kaboré (as Minister of State, responsibile for the Co-ordination of Government Action). The dominant role of the ODP/MT was widely criticized, and several nominated government members declined their posts. In July Hermann Yaméogo, now leader of the Alliance pour la démocratie et la fédération (ADF), and several other representatives of parties outside the FP were appointed to the Government. In August, however, Yaméogo (who had announced his intention to contest the presidency) was one of three government members who resigned in protest against proposed electoral procedures. Seven further opposition members resigned from the transitional administration in September, when Compaoré rejected demands for a national conference. Grouped in a Coordination des forces démocratiques (CFD), the opposition organized rallies and demonstrations in support of the campaign for a national conference. Attempts to achieve a compromise failed, and in October five CFD candidates withdrew from the presidential contest.

The presidential election proceeded on 1 December 1991, whereupon Compaoré (who had resigned from the army to contest the presidency as a civilian) was elected, unopposed, with the support of 90.4% of those who voted. The CFD claimed that an abstention rate of 74.7% reflected the success of its appeal for a boycott of the poll. Compaoré emphasized the need for national reconciliation, but shortly after the election Clément Oumarou Ouédraogo was assassinated; attacks on other opposition members were also reported. Although the Government condemned the violence, the CFD denounced Compaoré as personally responsible for the incidents, and further disturbances followed Ouédraogo's funeral. Apparently in response, the Government announced the indefinite postponement of the legislative elections, which had been scheduled for January 1992: the CFD had been advocating a boycott of the elections, and few political parties had registered their intention to contest the poll.

Compaoré was inaugurated as President of the Fourth Republic on 24 December 1991, and in January 1992 it was announced that some 4,000 people who had been convicted in connection with political or trade-union activities since the time of Sankara's accession to power were to be rehabilitated. By contrast, Compaoré imposed restrictions on the remit of a 'national reconciliation forum', which convened in February 1992 but was suspended by the Government within two weeks, following disagreements regarding the broadcasting of debates by the state-owned media. None the less, four opposition members were appointed to the Government later in the month, including Hermann Yaméogo as Minister of State.

The legislative elections finally took place on 24 May 1992, contested by 27 political parties. According to official results, the ODP/MT won 78 of the ADP's 107 seats. Nine other parties secured representation. The rate of participation by voters was reported to have been little more than 35%. In June Compaoré appointed Youssouf Ouédraogo, hitherto President of the Economic and Social Council, as Prime Minister. Although his Council of Ministers included representatives of seven political parties, the ODP/MT was allocated most strategic posts.

Following the 50% devaluation of the CFA franc, in January 1994, trade unions began a campaign for salary increases of 40%–50%. Negotiations between the Government and workers' representatives failed to reach a compromise, and in March Ouédraogo resigned. He was replaced as Prime Minister by Kaboré, hitherto Minister of State, responsible for Relations with the Organs of State.

In February 1996 Kadré Désiré Ouédraogo, hitherto Deputy Governor of the Banque centrale des états de l'Afrique de l'ouest, replaced Kaboré as Prime Minister. Kaboré was named Special Adviser to the Presidency, and also First Vice-President of a new, pro-Compaoré political party, the Congrès pour la démocratie et le progrès (CDP). The CDP, termed a social-democratic party, grouped the ODP/MT and some 10 other parties. Named as its President was a long-time ally of Compaoré, Arsène Bognessan Yè, the President of the legislature and the former head of the ODP/MT. Most of the members of the outgoing administration were reappointed to Ouédraogo's first Council of Ministers. The new premier subsequently joined the CDP.

Constitutional amendments and a new electoral code were approved by the ADP in January 1997. Restrictions were removed on the renewal of the Head of State's mandate (hitherto renewable only once); with effect from the forthcoming elections, the number of parliamentary seats was to be increased to 111, while the ADP was renamed the Assemblée nationale. In addition, the number of provinces was increased from 30 to 45.

Elections to the Assemblée nationale took place on 11 May 1997, contested by some 569 candidates from 13 parties. The CDP won a resounding victory, securing 101 seats. The results of voting for four seats, all of which had been won by the CDP, were annulled by the Supreme Court, but these were regained by the party at by-elections in June. The Parti pour la démocratie et le progrès (PDP), led by veteran politician Joseph Ki-Zerbo, secured six seats, and the ADF and Gérard Kango Ouédraogo's Rassemblement démocratique africain (RDA) each won two. Mélégué Maurice Traoré was elected President of the incoming legislature in June, and a new Government, under Kadré Désiré Ouédraogo, was appointed. Hermann Yaméogo left the Council of Ministers, while Bognessan Yè was named Minister of State at the Presidency of the Republic.

In April 1998, following consultations with pro-Government and opposition parties, the Council of Ministers adopted legislation providing for the establishment of an independent electoral commission: the 26-member Commission électorale nationale indépendante (CENI) was to be composed of six representatives of the parliamentary majority and an equal number of opposition delegates, together with civic representatives. However, when the CENI was inaugurated, in July, several opposition parties, including the PDP, refused to take up their seats and indicated their intention to boycott the forthcoming presidential election. The Groupe du 14 février (G-14f) opposition coalition protested about a lack of transparency in the electoral process, alleging corruption and unfair provisions for campaign funding and disputing the impartiality of the CENI, the judiciary and the media regulatory authority, the Conseil supérieur de l'information. The national human rights movement, the Mouvement burkinabè des droits de l'homme et des peuples (MBDHP), also declined representation on the electoral commission.

Several prominent opposition figures, among them Hermann Yaméogo, whose party had absorbed a faction of the RDA to form the Alliance pour la démocratie et la fédération—Rassemblement démocratique africain (ADF—RDA), and Joseph Ki-Zerbo, refused to participate in the presidential election. Compaoré was challenged by Ram Ouédraogo, of the ecologist Union des verts pour le développement du Burkina (UVDB), and Frédéric Guirma, representing the faction of the RDA that remained outside Yaméogo's party. Despite demands by the G-14f that the election be postponed, voting proceeded, as scheduled, on 15 November 1998. The opposition denounced the election as fraudulent, but international monitors and national observers pronounced themselves broadly satisfied with the conduct of the campaign and voting. The provisional results, issued by the CENI on 18 November 1998, confirmed a decisive victory for Compaoré, with 87.53% of the valid votes cast; Ram Ouédraogo took 6.61%, and Guirma 5.86%. Despite the appeal by the G-14f for a boycott, the rate of voter participation, at 56.08%, was considerably higher than in 1991. A new Government, again headed by Kadré Désiré Ouédraogo, was appointed in January 1999.

The political climate deteriorated rapidly after Norbert Zongo, the managing editor of the newspaper *L'Indépendant*, was found dead, together with three colleagues, in December 1998. Zongo, a frequent critic of the Compaoré regime, had been investigating the death of David Ouédraogo, a driver employed by François Compaoré, younger brother and special adviser of the President; Ouédraogo had allegedly been tortured to death by members of the presidential guard for having stolen money from his employer. Opposition parties and human rights organizations, grouped in a Collectif d'organisations démocratiques de masse et de partis politiques, demanded a full investigation of the case. The deaths provoked violent demonstrations, and it was subsequently reported that Hermann Yaméogo had been detained, accused of fomenting unrest. Meanwhile, opposition groups refused to participate in an independent commission of inquiry into Zongo's apparent murder, established by presidential decree in January 1999, stating that a similar commission had failed to bring to justice those responsible for the assassination of Clément Oumarou Ouédraogo in 1991. Furthermore, the MBDHP suspended participation in the commission, on the grounds that its preconditions for membership, including an end to legal proceedings against activists involved in recent protests, had not been met. Shortly afterwards a three-day general strike, organized by the opposition collective, was widely observed in the capital.

In its final report, submitted in May 1999, the commission of inquiry stated that it had been unable to prove the identity of the culprits, but indicated the likelihood that the members of the presidential guard implicated in the death of François Compaoré's driver were also responsible for the murders of the journalists. Shortly afterwards the only foreign member of the commission of inquiry, Robert Ménard, the head of an international press freedom group, Reporters sans frontières, was deported. The announcement of the commission's findings provoked renewed unrest. In mid-May three prominent members of the opposition, including Halidou Ouédraogo, the Chairman of the Collectif, and Hermann Yaméogo, were arrested by the security forces, accused of having repeated Ménard's denunciation of the presidential guard and of having plotted a *coup d'état*. Two were released after a brief detention, but Yaméogo remained in custody for three days. Shortly afterwards Compaoré stated that the examining magistrate responsible for the Zongo case would be given his full support. He further announced a reorganization of the presidential guard, an amnesty for all those arrested in the recent protests, the reopening of the educational establishments closed during the unrest, and compensation for the relatives of victims of the murders that had provoked the political crisis. The Collectif welcomed these measures, but criticized what they perceived as official pressure on the judiciary. Public discontent subsequently intensified, culminating in the organization, in late June and mid-August, of two-day general strikes by trade unions, to protest against low wages, labour reforms and the privatization of parastatal enterprises, as well as alleged human rights abuses by the state.

In June 1999 Compaoré established a Collège des sages, composed of Burkinabè state elders, and religious and ethnic leaders. The 16-member Collège was to promote national reconciliation and, most notably, to investigate unpunished political crimes since independence. In mid-June the Collège ordered the

arrest of the three members of the presidential guard accused of the murder of David Ouédraogo. The main recommendations of the Collège's report, published in August, were that a government of national unity should be formed, as well as a 'commission of truth and justice' to oversee the transition to a truly plural political system and to investigate unresolved political murders, including that of Sankara. The Collège also suggested that an amnesty should be granted to those implicated during the investigations of the commission, and that compensation should be paid to the families of victims. The Collège further recommended the creation of a commission to examine certain clauses of the Constitution and to formulate rules governing political parties; also that Compaoré should not seek re-election, and that fresh elections should be held for the Assemblée nationale. Although Compaoré praised the work of the Collège, opposition organizations rejected the proposed amnesty and criticized the need for the President to assent to any proposed reforms. Meanwhile, on the eve of the publication of the elders' report, Roch Marc-Christian Kaboré was appointed to the new post of Executive Secretary of the CDP.

In September 1999 the Prime Minister, Kadré Désiré Ouédraogo, began consultations with the leaders of the major political parties in order to identify the principal objectives of any government of national unity. Most opposition parties stipulated that participation in such a government would be conditional upon the expedition of legal action in the cases of David Ouédraogo and Norbert Zongo. Thus, the reshuffled Council of Ministers, announced in October, included just two representatives of the opposition: Noyabtigungu Congo Kaboré, of the Mouvement pour la tolérance et le progrès, and Ram Ouédraogo. Kadré Désiré Ouédraogo, who had retained his post as Prime Minister, subsequently reiterated the Government's willingness to maintain a dialogue with the G-14f.

In November 1999, in accordance with the recommendations of the Collège des sages, two advisory commissions were inaugurated: one to consider possible changes to the Constitution, and another to promote national reconciliation. Despite official assurances that the commissions' findings would be binding, the G-14f refused to participate, claiming that debate would be restricted and that any recommendations would carry little weight. Shortly afterwards the Collectif organized a series of mass demonstrations intended to commemorate the first anniversary of the murder of Zongo.

In January 2000 the ruling CDP organized a public demonstration in favour of the proposals of the advisory commission on political reform, which had recommended the modification of the electoral code and the reform of the judiciary and the Constitution. Most notably, the commission proposed the restriction of the presidential mandate to no more than two successive terms. The Assemblée nationale subsequently voted to revise the electoral code, to accord greater powers to the CENI, and to postpone the municipal elections scheduled for February in order to allow the implementation of the revisions. The opposition, however, criticized what they perceived to be the limited nature of the reforms and expressed their determination to boycott any elections until the Ouédraogo and Zongo cases had been fully resolved.

In February 2000 the advisory commission on national reconciliation published its report, which urged the prosecution of those suspected of involvement in the embezzlement of public funds and in so-called political killings. The report also recommended that victims of political violence or their relations receive an official apology, compensation and a guarantee regarding their future security. The commission also called for greater freedom of speech, of the press, and of assembly, the resolution of legal proceedings in the Ouédraogo and Zongo cases, the enactment of an amnesty law, and the construction of a monument to former President Sankara. The commission's final proposal was that a further commission be established to monitor the implementation of its recommendations.

In April 2000 a demonstration in Ouagadougou, held in support of demands for the resolution of the Zongo case, resulted in violent clashes between student demonstrators and the security forces. The opposition subsequently called for a three-day general strike and a series of protests against the intervention of the security forces. Halidou Ouédraogo, the Chairman of the Collectif, and 38 other activists were briefly detained on charges of endangering public order. Later that month the Government sought to defuse the tension with the announcement that it was to encourage the return to Burkina Faso of political exiles, and that a mausoleum for Sankara was to be constructed.

The Assemblée nationale approved revisions to the electoral code in April 2000; under the new regulations, which introduced a system of proportional representation, 90 deputies would be elected from regional lists, while 21 would be elected from a national list. The new legislation also reduced the presidential mandate from seven to five years, renewable only once. However, as the new limits were not to take effect until the next election, Compaoré would be able to stand again in 2005 and 2010. In addition, the Assemblée approved significant judicial reforms, which provided for the abolition of the Supreme Court and the replacement of its four permanent chambers with four new state institutions: a Constitutional Council, a Council of State, a Court of Appeal and a National Audit Court. (Pending the full implementation of these reforms, the Supreme Court continued to function.) In the same month Hermann Yaméogo was expelled from the G-14f for having criticized the group's refusal to co-operate with the Government.

In early May 2000 the Government announced that the postponed municipal elections would be held on 30 July. However, several opposition parties reiterated their demand for the Ouédraogo and Zongo cases to be resolved prior to the elections. In late May Compaoré held a meeting with Halidou Ouédraogo and other members of the Collectif in order to discuss the process of reform. However, the death of a police-officer who had been implicated in attempts to conceal the murder of David Ouédraogo was widely viewed as suspicious by the opposition. In July the Chairman of the CENI urged the postponement of the elections in order to allow the commission time to resolve logistical difficulties. The elections were postponed until 24 September, although the Collectif and the G-14f continued to call for a further delay. However, by mid-August several constituent parties of the Collectif and the G-14f had chosen to nominate candidates for the elections. As a result, the ADF—RDA, the Union des démocrates et patriotes indépendants and the Convention panafricaine sankariste were expelled from the Collectif and the G-14f. The increasingly fragmented nature of the opposition was also evident in the formation of several breakaway groups by former ADF—RDA members. The CDP held outright control of 40 of the 49 municipalities following the elections, which were contested by 25 parties, although the G-14f and the PDP boycotted the poll.

Meanwhile, the trial of the soldiers accused of murdering David Ouédraogo began in August 2000. Two of the defendants were acquitted by the military tribunal, but two members of Compaoré's presidential guard, including Marcel Kafando, head of the guard at the time of Ouédraogo's death, were sentenced to 20 years' imprisonment, with a third member sentenced to 10 years'. The G-14f expressed dissatisfaction at the resolution of the case, and at what it termed 'ongoing economic crimes'.

In November 2000, amid ongoing social unrest, Kadré Désiré Ouédraogo resigned as Prime Minister and was replaced by Paramanga Ernest Yonli, hitherto the Minister of the Civil Service and Institutional Development. President Compaoré subsequently formed a 36-member Council of Ministers, one-third of which was composed of members of the opposition. The new appointments resulted from an agreement reached by Yonli and representatives from several political parties, including the ruling CDP, the ADF—RDA and the Union des libéraux pour la démocratie, a pro-Compaoré grouping that had broken away from the ADF—RDA, but not the principal opposition party, the PDP, which refused to participate. The agreement specified the parties' conditions for joining the Government, notably the prompt and thorough completion of pending legal cases and the reopening of the University of Ouagadougou, which the Government had closed in October, following five months of protests and strikes by students demanding improved facilities and living conditions. The leaders of the participating parties were to meet with the Prime Minister every three months to evaluate the implementation of the accord.

Meanwhile, the protests continued, and in late November 2000 three days of demonstrations erupted into riots between secondary-school pupils and the police. In early December the Government issued a decree prohibiting all demonstrations, except those of a religious nature, in public places across Burkina Faso. Nevertheless, demonstrations to commemorate the second anniversary of Norbert Zongo's death were held later that month, precipitating clashes with the security forces. The University of Ouagadougou was finally reopened in mid-December.

In early February 2001 Marcel Kafando was charged with arson and the murder of Norbert Zongo and three others. In late March, at a rally attended by some 30,000 people, President Compaoré apologized for some 176 unpunished crimes allegedly committed by state representatives since independence in 1960. This act constituted the most significant element of a 'day of forgiveness' that had been proposed by the Collège des sages, but which was boycotted by protesters, including, notably, relations of Sankara and Zongo.

In mid-June 2001 the Supreme Court ruled that a civil court was not competent to hear a case filed by the widow of former President Sankara, in which she accused unknown persons of attempting to conceal the murder of her husband by claiming on his death certificate that he had died of natural causes; it was announced that an appeal for the case to be heard in a military court would be lodged. In late June several thousand people participated in a demonstration, led by the Collectif, in Ouagadougou, calling for those whom they believed to have ordered the killing of Zongo, including François Compaoré, to be brought to justice. Meanwhile, the PDP merged with the Parti socialiste burkinabè (PS), to form the PDP—PS, in a move that was expected to consolidate left-wing opposition movements.

In August 2001 workers from 13 state enterprises participated in a 24-hour strike to protest against the planned privatization of their companies, which had been approved by the Assemblée nationale in July. Also in August, following the appointment of two of their members to the CENI, the constituent parties of the G-14f announced their intention to contest the forthcoming legislative elections. Michel Tapsoba, a human rights activist, was elected as Chairman of the commission in the following month. In November it was announced that the judicial investigation into Kafando's alleged involvement in Zongo's death had been hampered by the poor health of the defendant; little progress was reported in the case throughout 2002, in spite of official assurances of advances in the investigation.

In February 2002 the Assemblée nationale adopted a constitutional amendment, providing for the abolition of the Chambre des représentants, following the failure to appoint replacement representatives for those whose terms had expired in December 2001. The Government announced proposals for the eventual replacement of the Chambre by a Conférence générale de la nation, the membership and responsibilities of which were to be determined in due course.

In early February 2002 the Government denied reports, issued by a human rights organization, that the security forces had been implicated in the extrajudicial killings of more than 100 suspected criminals in late 2001, during a campaign against armed criminals. In early March it was announced that the forthcoming legislative elections, initially scheduled for 28 April, would be postponed until 5 May, as a result of difficulties in the voter-registration programme. In late April workers, primarily in the telecommunications, banking, energy and education sectors, staged a two-day strike, demanding a pay increase of 25% and a reduction in income tax of 30%; further strikes were held in late May and mid-July.

Meanwhile, some 30 parties contested the elections to the Assemblée nationale on 5 May 2002. The polls were the first to be conducted in Burkina with the use of a single ballot paper, in accordance with the demands of opposition parties. The CDP remained the largest party, securing 57 of the 111 seats, with 49.52% of the votes cast, although its representation was much reduced. The ADF—RDA won 17 seats, with 12.61% of the votes cast, to become the largest opposition party, followed by the PDP—PS, with 10 seats. Ten other parties secured legislative representation. Kaboré was elected as President of the Assemblée nationale in early June, prior to the reappointment of Yonli as Prime Minister. Despite the slim majority held by the CDP in the Assemblée nationale and the precedent set by the inclusion of ministers from opposition parties in the outgoing administration, the new 31-member Government, appointed in mid-June, did not contain any representatives of the opposition.

In June 2002 the Council of Ministers announced the appointment of First Presidents to head the new judicial institutions that were to replace the Supreme Court; however, the formation of the institutions themselves remained in abeyance. In September a faction of the PDP—PS, headed by Emile Paré, announced its secession from the party and the formation of a new party, the Mouvement du peuple pour le socialisme—Parti fédéral. Also in September, Ram Ouédraogo resigned as leader of Les verts du Burkina (as the UVDB had been renamed) and announced that he had joined the PDP—PS. In October the membership of the Constitutional Council was approved by the

Council of Ministers. In late November a demonstration by students at the University of Ouagadougou, organized to protest against the doubling of academic registration fees, degenerated into violent unrest, precipitating the arrest of the leader of the national students' association.

Compaoré has, in recent years, gained wide recognition for his efforts as a regional mediator and as a proponent of inter-African conflict-resolution initiatives. In the early 1990s, however, relations with some members of the Economic Community of West African States (ECOWAS, see p. 187) suffered a reverse, owing to the Compaoré Government's support for Charles Taylor's rebel National Patriotic Front of Liberia (NPFL) and Burkina's refusal to participate in the military intervention by the ECOWAS cease-fire monitoring group (ECOMOG, see p. 189) in Liberia. In September 1991 Compaoré admitted that Burkinabè troops had been dispatched to Liberia to assist the NPFL in the overthrow of Samuel Doe's regime in mid-1990, but asserted that the country's involvement in Liberia had ended. In November 1992 the US Government recalled its ambassador to Burkina, and announced that the recently appointed Burkinabè ambassador to the USA would not be welcome in Washington, DC, owing to Burkina's alleged role in transporting arms from Libya to the NPFL. Allegations of Burkinabè support for the NPFL persisted, but in September 1995 the Compaoré administration, stating that it regarded the peace agreement that had been signed in Abuja, Nigeria, in the previous month as more 'credible' than earlier peace settlements for Liberia, announced that Burkina would contribute peace-keeping troops to ECOMOG. In February 1997 the Burkinabè legislature approved legislation authorizing the participation of Burkinabè military personnel in the cease-fire monitoring group, and members of the Burkinabè military subsequently remained in Liberia to assist in the training of new armed forces.

In early 1999 President Ahmed Tejan Kabbah of Sierra Leone and the Nigerian Government alleged that Burkina Faso and Liberia were co-operating to provide support and supply arms to the rebel fighters of the Revolutionary United Front (RUF) in Sierra Leone. (Sierra Leonean refugees, entering Guinea in early 1998, had made similar accusations.) The Burkinabè Government denied any involvement, although in early 2000 a report to the UN Security Council accused Burkina of having supplied weapons to the RUF in exchange for diamonds on several occasions. It was also alleged that Burkina had supplied weapons to Liberia and to Angolan rebel groups, despite international embargoes on the supply of weapons to those countries. The report, which further accused Compaoré of having conducted personal negotiations with the Angolan rebel leader Jonas Savimbi, was strenuously denied by the Burkinabè Government. Two missions from the UN Security Council visited Burkina Faso in mid-2000, at the invitation of the Burkinabè Government, to investigate the claims regarding the breaching of arms embargoes against Angola and Sierra Leone. Following the onset of heightened insurgency in southern regions of Guinea in September 2000, the President of Guinea, Lassana Conté, accused Burkina of aiding rebels, associated with the RUF in Sierra Leone and sympathetic to President Taylor of Liberia, in order to destabilize the Guinean Government. In December it was reported that Burkina Faso was to introduce measures aimed at controlling its weapons imports in an attempt to allay international concern. Although Compaoré, in May 2001, criticized a decision by the UN to impose travel restrictions on Liberian officials, subsequent relations with the Taylor Government have been more distant. Notably, in July 2002 the Burkinabè Government hosted a conference intended to promote a peaceful resolution of the political crisis in Liberia; Taylor's Government was not represented at the meeting.

In early November 1999 a dispute over land rights between Burkinabè settlers in the south-west of Côte d'Ivoire and the indigenous minority Krou population, which caused two deaths, led to the violent and systematic expulsion from the region of several hundred Burkinabè plantation workers by militant Krou. Several deaths were reported, and it was estimated that up to 20,000 expatriates subsequently returned to Burkina. Following the *coup d'état* in Côte d'Ivoire in December, the military authorities assured the Government of Burkina that the expulsions would cease and that measures would be taken in order to allow workers to return. None the less, tensions between the two countries intensified as the former Prime Minister of Côte d'Ivoire and leader of the Rassemblement des républicains, Alassane Ouattara, was excluded from participation in the Ivorian presidential election of October 2000

because of his Burkinabè origins. Following a coup attempt in Abidjan in early January 2001, which the Ivorian Government attributed to the influence of unnamed, neighbouring states, attacks on Burkinabè expatriates in Côte d'Ivoire reportedly increased; by late January it was reported that up to 10,000 Burkinabè were returning to Burkina each week. In June, following allegations that hundreds of Burkinabè children were working illegally on coffee and cocoa plantations in Côte d'Ivoire, the two countries announced that they would commence joint patrols of their common border. In early July a meeting between Compaoré and the Ivorian President, Laurent Gbagbo (who had himself been granted political asylum in Burkina Faso in the early 1990s), in Sirte, Libya, was reported to have defused tensions somewhat between the two countries.

Following the outbreak of unrest in Côte d'Ivoire in mid-September 2002, Gbagbo again alleged that an unnamed, neighbouring country was implicated in the rebellion; these allegations were widely believed to refer to Burkina, although the Burkinabè Government denied any involvement in the uprising. However, in late November, following an attack on the residence of the Burkinabè President in Abidjan, the Ivorian Minister of Agriculture and Rural Development, Sébastien Danon Djédjé, met Compaoré to express the Ivorian Government's regret for the attack. As a result of the upsurge in violence in Côte d'Ivoire, some 105,000 Burkinabè citizens were reported to have fled Côte d'Ivoire for Burkina by early February 2003. A statement by Compaoré in an interview with the French newspaper *Le Parisien*, in late January, to the effect that the restoration of peace in Côte d'Ivoire would necessitate the resignation of Gbagbo as President of that country, led to a further deterioration in relations between the two countries. In late January the Ivorian Government and rebel groups signed a peace agreement in France, known as the Marcoussis Accords, which provided for the creation of a government of national reconciliation in Côte d'Ivoire. Compaoré welcomed the provisions of the accord, which was, however, widely opposed in Côte d'Ivoire. At the end of the month the Burkinabè embassy in Abidjan was attacked and set on fire by opponents of the agreement.

The Assemblée nationale authorized the dispatch of a Burkinabè military contingent to the surveillance mission for the Central African Republic (CAR) in February 1997, and a Burkinabè force remained in the CAR as part of the UN peace-keeping operation that succeeded the regional mission between April 1998 and February 2000. A contingent of 165 Burkinabè troops was scheduled to arrive in the CAR in October 2002, under the auspices of the Libyan-sponsored Community of Sahel-Saharan States (see p. 339), of which Burkina Faso was a founder member in 1997.

Government

Under the terms of the Constitution of June 1991, as subsequently revised, executive power is vested in the President and in the Government, and is counterbalanced by a legislative Assemblée nationale, and by an independent judiciary. Presidential and legislative elections are conducted by universal adult suffrage, in the context of a multi-party political system. The President is elected for a seven-year term, and delegates to the Assemblée nationale are elected for a five-year term. In April 2000 the Assemblée nationale adopted legislation, effective from the next elections, which reduced the presidential mandate from seven to five years, renewable only once, and introduced a system of proportional representation for elections to the Assemblée nationale, according to which 90 deputies would be elected from a regional list, while 21 would be elected from a national list. The President is empowered to appoint a Prime Minister; however, the Assemblée nationale has the right to veto any such appointment.

Burkina is divided into 45 provinces, each of which is administered by a civilian governor.

Defence

National service is voluntary, and lasts for two years on a part-time basis. In August 2002 the active armed forces numbered 10,200 (army 5,800, air force 200, gendarmerie 4,200). Other units include a 'security company' of 250 and a part-time people's militia of 45,000. The defence budget for 2002 was estimated at 27,500m. francs CFA.

Economic Affairs

In 2001, according to estimates by the World Bank, Burkina Faso's gross national income (GNI), measured at average 1999–2001 prices, was US $2,349m., equivalent to $210 per head (or

$1,020 on an international purchasing-power parity basis). During 1990–2001, it was estimated, the population increased at an average annual rate of 2.4%, while gross domestic product (GDP) per head increased, in real terms, by an average of 2.6% per year. Overall GDP increased, in real terms, at an average annual rate of 5.1% in 1990–2001; growth in 2001 was 5.7%.

According to the Banque centrale des états de l'Afrique de l'ouest, agriculture (including livestock-rearing, forestry and fishing) contributed 35.0% of GDP in 2001. About 92.2% of the labour force were employed in agriculture in that year. The principal cash crop is cotton (exports of which accounted for 56.9% of the value of total exports in 2001). Smaller amounts of other crops, including karité nuts (sheanuts) and sesame seed, are also exported. The main subsistence crops are millet, sorghum, maize and rice. Burkina is almost self-sufficient in basic foodstuffs in non-drought years. Livestock-rearing is of considerable significance, contributing 11.5% of GDP in 2000 and an estimated 19.3% of export revenue in 2001. During 1990–2001 agricultural GDP increased at an average annual rate of 4.9%. Agricultural GDP declined by 3.8% in 2000, but increased by 8.5% in 2001.

Industry (including mining, manufacturing, construction and power) contributed 17.5% of GDP in 2001, but engaged only 2.0% of the employed labour force in 1996. During 1990–2001 industrial GDP increased at an average annual rate of 5.1%; growth in 2001 was 3.3%.

Although Burkina has considerable mineral resources, extractive activities accounted for 1.0% of GDP in 1997, and engaged only 0.1% of the employed labour force in 1996. However, the development of reserves of gold (exports of which contributed an estimated 2.1% of the value of total exports in 2001) has since brought about an increase in the sector's economic importance, while there is considerable potential, subject to the development of an adequate infrastructure, for the exploitation of manganese, zinc and limestone. The country's other known mineral reserves include phosphates, silver, lead and nickel.

The manufacturing sector engaged only 1.4% of the employed labour force in 1996, and (including mining) contributed 12.2% of GDP in 2000. The sector is dominated by the processing of primary products: major activities are cotton-ginning, the production of textiles, food-processing (including milling and sugar-refining), brewing and the processing of tobacco and of hides and skins. Motorcycles and bicycles are also assembled. According to the World Bank, manufacturing GDP increased at an average annual rate of 5.8% in 1990–2001; growth was 3.3% in 2001.

Two hydroelectric stations supplied about one-third of Burkina's electricity output in 1998; the remainder was derived from thermal power stations (using imported fuel). The country's hydropower capacity is being expanded, and in 2000 the interconnection of the south of Burkina Faso with the electricity network of Côte d'Ivoire was finalized; a link with Ghana's electricity grid is also planned. Imports of petroleum products comprised 18.2% of the value of total imports in 2001.

The services sector contributed 47.5% of GDP in 2001, and engaged 7.8% of the employed labour force in 1996. The GDP of the services sector increased at an average annual rate of 5.0% in 1990–2001; growth was 4.9% in 2001.

In 2001 Burkina recorded an estimated visible trade deficit of 211,700m. francs CFA, while there was a deficit of an estimated 216,600m. francs CFA on the current account of the balance of payments. In 2000 the principal sources of imports were Côte d'Ivoire (which provided 22.7% of the total) and France (22.4%); Japan and the People's Republic of China were also major suppliers. The principal markets for exports in that year were France (21.6%), Côte d'Ivoire and Belgium-Luxembourg. The principal exports in 2001 were cotton, and livestock and livestock products (including hides and skins). In the same year the principal imports were capital equipment, petroleum products, food products and raw materials.

In 2001 Burkina recorded an overall budget deficit of 42,300m. francs CFA, equivalent to an estimated 2.5% of GDP. Burkina's total external debt was US $1,332m. at the end of 2000, of which $1,135m. was long-term public debt. In that year the cost of debt-servicing was equivalent to 17.3% of the value of exports of goods and services. The annual rate of inflation, which was negligible prior to the 50% devaluation of the CFA franc in January 1994, increased to 25.1% in 1994, but slowed thereafter, to 7.4% in 1995 and an average of 2.2% per year in 1996–2001. Consumer prices decreased by by 0.3% in 2000, but increased by 4.9% in 2001. Some 71,280 people were unemployed in 1996, according to the national census, equivalent to only 1.4% of the total labour force.

Burkina is a member of numerous regional organizations, including the Economic Community of West African States (ECOWAS, see p. 187), the West African organs of the Franc Zone (see p. 238), the Conseil de l'Entente (see p. 339), the Liptako–Gourma Integrated Development Authority (see p. 341), and the Permanent Inter-State Committee on Drought Control in the Sahel (CILSS, see p. 341).

Burkina Faso has experienced strong growth since the devaluation of the CFA franc in 1994, as the competitiveness notably of cotton, livestock and gold have been enhanced. An Enhanced Structural Adjustment Facility (ESAF) was agreed with the IMF in 1996. In September 1999 the IMF approved funding under a further ESAF (later replaced by the Poverty Reduction and Growth Facility), equivalent to some US $49m., in support of the Government's economic programme for 1999–2002. During this period considerable success was achieved in enhancing efficiency in taxation collection, particularly with regard to the taxation of international trade. Meanwhile, in July 2000 the IMF and the World Bank announced that Burkina Faso was to receive some $400m. in debt-service relief under their original Heavily Indebted Poor Countries initiative and a further $300m. under an enhanced framework. In 2000 lower economic growth than forecast was attributed to a decrease in agricultural output, resulting from drought conditions, an increase in world petroleum prices and a decline in workers' remittances from Côte d'Ivoire. However, a record cotton crop in 2001 contributed to a recovery in that year, and in 2002 real GDP growth of 5.6% was forecast, although a decline in the international price of cotton and an increase in international petroleum prices were of concern. Meanwhile, the Government was to continue with its programme of structural reform, although the proposed privatizations of the telecommunications company, the Office National des Télécommunications, and of the electricity company, the Société Nationale Burkinabè d'Electricité, were delayed. None the less, by September 2002 some 26 enterprises had been transferred to the private sector, while a further 16 had been liquidated or were in the process of liquidation. The economy of Burkina Faso continued to be dependent on a narrow resource base, particularly on cotton, and therefore vulnerable to external exigencies, while poverty remained widespread, particularly in rural areas; in particular, the political crisis in Côte d'Ivoire from late 2002 was expected to have a negative impact on Burkina's economy.

Education

Education is provided free of charge, and is officially compulsory for six years between the ages of seven and 14. Primary education begins at seven years of age and lasts for six years. Secondary education, beginning at the age of 13, lasts for a further seven years, comprising a first cycle of four years and a second of three years. Enrolment levels are among the lowest in the region. In 1999/2000 primary enrolment included only 34.6% of children in the relevant age-group (males 40.9%; females 28.3%). According to UNESCO estimates, secondary education in that year included only 8.3% of children in the appropriate age-group (males 10.1%; females 6.6%). There is a university in Ouagadougou, a polytechnic university at Bobo-Dioulasso and an école normale supérieure at Koudougou. The number of students enrolled at tertiary-level institutions in 1996/97 was 8,911. A radio service has been established to further general and technical education in rural areas. Expenditure on education by the central Government in 1994 totalled 36,315m. francs CFA, representing 11.1% of total government spending in that year. In 2000 spending on education represented 11.0% of total budgetary expenditure.

Public Holidays

2003: 1 January (New Year's Day), 12 February* (Aid el Kebir—Tabaski, Feast of the Sacrifice), 8 March (International Women's Day), 21 April (Easter Monday), 1 May (Labour Day), 14 May* (Mouloud, Birth of the Prophet), 29 May (Ascension Day), 5 August (Independence Day), 15 August (Assumption), 1 November (All Saints' Day), 26 November* (Aid es Segheir, end of Ramadan), 11 December (Proclamation of the Republic), 25 December (Christmas).

2004: 1 January (New Year's Day), 2 February* (Aid el Kebir—Tabaski, Feast of the Sacrifice), 8 March (International Women's Day), 12 April (Easter Monday), 1 May (Labour Day), 2 May* (Mouloud, Birth of the Prophet), 20 May (Ascension Day), 5 August (Independence Day), 15 August (Assumption), 1

November (All Saints' Day), 14 November* (Aid es Segheir, end of Ramadan), 11 December (Proclamation of the Republic), 25 December (Christmas).

*These holidays are dependent on the Islamic lunar calendar and may vary by one or two days from the dates given.

Weights and Measures

The metric system is in force.

Statistical Survey

Source (except where otherwise stated): Institut National de la Statistique et de la Démographie, 555 blvd de la Révolution, 01 BP 374, Ouagadougou 01; tel. 32-49-76; fax 31-07-60.

Area and Population

AREA, POPULATION AND DENSITY

Area (sq km)	274,200*
Population (census results)	
10–20 December 1985	7,964,705
10 December 1996	
Males	4,970,882
Females.	5,341,727
Total	10,312,609
Population (official estimate at mid-year)	
1998	10,683,000
Density (per sq km) at mid-1998	38.9

* 105,870 sq miles.

ETHNIC GROUPS

1995 (percentages): Mossi 47.9; Peul 10.3; Bobo 6.9; Lobi 6.9; Mandé 6.7; Sénoufo 5.3; Gourounsi 5.0; Gourmantché 4.8; Tuareg 3.1; others 3.1 (Source: La Francophonie).

PROVINCES

(population at 1996 census)

Province	Population	Capital	Population of capital
Balé	168,170	Boromo. . . .	n.a.
Bam	211,551	Kongoussi . . .	17,893
Banwa . . .	215,297	Solenzo. . .	n.a.
Bazèga. . .	213,824	Kombissiri. . .	16,821
Bougouriba .	76,498	Diébougou . .	11,637
Boulgou . .	415,583	Tenkodogo . .	31,466
Boulkiemdé .	421,302	Koudougou . .	72,490
Comoé . . .	241,376	Banfora . . .	49,724
Ganzourgou .	256,921	Zorgo	17,466
Gnagna . . .	307,372	Bogandé . . .	8,960
Gourma . . .	220,116	Fada N'Gourma .	29,254
Houet . . .	672,114	Bobo-Dioulasso .	309,771
Ioba. . . .	161,484	Dano	n.a.
Kadiogo . .	941,894	Ouagadougou . .	709,736
Kénédougou .	198,541	Orodara . . .	16,581
Komandjari .	50,484	Gayéri . . .	n.a.
Kompienga .	40,766	Pama . . .	n.a.
Kossi . . .	230,693	Nouna . . .	19,105
Koulpélogo. .	187,399	Ouargaye . .	n.a.
Kouritenga .	250,117	Koupéla . . .	17,619
Kourwéogo. .	117,996	Boussé . . .	n.a.
Léraba . . .	92,927	Sindou . . .	n.a.
Lorom . . .	111,339	Titao . . .	n.a.
Mouhoun . .	235,391	Dédougou . .	33,815
Nahouri . .	119,739	Pô	17,146
Namentenga .	252,738	Boulsa . . .	12,280
Nayala . . .	136,393	Toma . . .	n.a.
Noumbiel . .	51,431	Batié . . .	n.a.
Oubritenga .	197,237	Ziniaré . . .	11,153
Oudalan . .	137,160	Gorom-Gorom . .	5,669
Passoré. . .	271,864	Yako	18,472
Poni . . .	195,900	Gaoua . . .	6,424
Sanguié . .	249,583	Réo	22,534
Sanmatenga .	464,032	Kaya	33,958
Séno . . .	201,760	Dori. . . .	23,768
Sissili . . .	153,434	Léo	18,988
Soum . . .	252,993	Djibo . . .	20,080

Province — *continued*	Population	Capital	Population of capital
Sourou . . .	188,512	Tougan. . .	15,218
Tapoa . . .	234,968	Diapaga . .	5,017
Tuy. . . .	160,722	Houndé . .	21,830
Yagha . . .	116,419	Sebba . . .	n.a.
Yatenga . . .	444,563	Ouahigouya . .	52,193
Ziro. . . .	119,219	Sapouy. . .	n.a.
Zondoma . .	127,654	Gourcy . . .	n.a.
Zoundwéogo .	197,133	Manga . . .	14,035
Total	**10,312,609**		

PRINCIPAL TOWNS

(population at 1996 census)

Ouagadougou (capital). . .	709,736	Ouahigouya . . .	52,193
Bobo-Dioulasso .	309,771	Banfora . . .	49,724
Koudougou . .	72,490	Kaya . . .	33,958

BIRTHS AND DEATHS

(UN estimates, annual averages)

	1985–90	1990–95	1995–2000
Birth rate (per 1,000)	48.2	47.0	46.7
Death rate (per 1,000)	17.8	17.9	17.9

Source: UN, *World Population Prospects: The 2000 Revision.*

Expectation of life (WHO estimates, years at birth, 2000): 42.9 (males 42.2; females 43.5 (Source: WHO, *World Health Report*).

ECONOMICALLY ACTIVE POPULATION

(1996 census, persons aged 10 years and over)

	Males	Females	Total
Agriculture, hunting, forestry and fishing	2,284,744	2,229,124	4,513,868
Mining and quarrying	2,946	1,033	3,979
Manufacturing	46,404	25,161	71,565
Electricity, gas and water . . .	2,279	534	2,813
Construction	20,678	398	21,076
Trade, restaurants and hotels . .	98,295	126,286	224,581
Transport, storage and communications	20,024	556	20,580
Finance, insurance, real estate and business services	10,466	2,665	13,131
Community, social and personal services	76,690	27,236	103,926
Activities not adequately defined .	15,104	13,712	28,816
Total employed.	**2,577,630**	**2,426,705**	**5,004,335**
Unemployed	51,523	19,757	71,280
Total labour force	**2,629,153**	**2,446,462**	**5,075,615**

Mid-2001 (estimates in '000): Agriculture, etc. 5,174; Total labour force 5,609 (Source: FAO).

Health and Welfare

KEY INDICATORS

Total fertility rate (children per woman, 2001) 6.8
Under-5 mortality rate (per 1,000 live births, 2001) . . . 197
HIV/AIDS (% of persons aged 15–49, 2001) 6.50
Physicians (per 1,000 head, 1995) 0.03
Hospital beds (per 1,000 head, 1996) 1.42
Health expenditure (2000): US $ per head (PPP) . . . 37
Health expenditure (2000): % of GDP 4
Health expenditure (2000): public (% of total) 70.7
Access to water (% of persons, 1990) 53
Access to sanitation (% of persons, 2000) 29
Human Development Index (2000): ranking 169
Human Development Index (2000): value 0.325

For sources and definitions, see explanatory note on p. vi.

Agriculture

PRINCIPAL CROPS
('000 metric tons)

	1999	2000	2001
Rice (paddy)	94.2	103.1	109.9
Maize	468.9	423.5	606.3
Millet	945.0	725.6	1,009.0
Sorghum	1,178,4	1,016.3	1,371.6
Sweet Potatoes	17.3	27.4	41.6
Yams	43.0	55.0	70.7
Sugar cane*	400	400	400
Bambara beans	39.4	22.0	37.7
Other pulses*	37	38	38
Groundnuts (in shell) . . .	282.8	169.1	301.1
Karité nuts (Sheanuts)* . .	70	70	70
Cottonseed*	136	102	215
Okra*	26	26	26
Other vegetables*	203.2	203.2	203.2
Fruit*	73.1	73.1	73.1
Cotton (lint)†	120	109	114

* FAO estimates.
† Unofficial figures.

LIVESTOCK
('000 head, year ending September)

	1999	2000	2001*
Cattle	4,704	4,798	4,800
Sheep	6,585	6,782	6,800
Goats	8,395	8,647	8,700
Pigs	610	622	630
Horses	24	26	27
Asses	491	501	502
Camels	14	15	15
Poultry	21,767	22,420	23,000

* FAO estimates.

Source: FAO.

LIVESTOCK PRODUCTS
('000 metric tons)

	1999	2000	2001
Beef and veal*	51.7	55.0	55.0
Mutton and lamb* . . .	13.4	13.6	13.6
Goat meat*	22.3	23.1	23.5
Pig meat*	8.5	8.8	8.9
Poultry meat*	25.6	26.4	27.0
Other meat*	8.1	8.2	8.2
Cows' milk	163.0	170.0*	170.0*
Goats' milk*	52.0	54.0	54.0
Ghee*	1.2	1.3	1.3
Hen eggs*	17.5	17.5	17.5
Cattle hides*	8.5	9.0	9.0
Sheepskins*	3.3	3.3	3.3
Goatskins*	5.8	6.0	6.1

* FAO estimate(s).

Source: FAO.

Forestry

ROUNDWOOD REMOVALS
('000 cubic metres, excluding bark)

	1999	2000	2001*
Sawlogs, veneer logs and logs for sleepers . . .	83	85	85
Other industrial wood* . . .	509	509	509
Fuel wood	7,228	7,402	11,242
Total	7,820	7,996	11,836

* FAO estimates.

Source: FAO, *Yearbook of Forest Products*.

SAWNWOOD PRODUCTION
('000 cubic metres)

	1997	1998	1999
Total (all broadleaved)	2	1	1

2000–2001: Annual production as in 1999 (FAO estimates).

Source: FAO, *Yearbook of Forest Products*.

Fishing

(metric tons, live weight)

	1998	1999	2000
Capture	8,335	7,600	8,500
Freshwater fishes	8,335	7,600	8,500
Aquaculture	40*	25*	5
Total catch	8,375*	8,360*	8,505

* FAO estimate.

Source: FAO, *Yearbook of Fishery Statistics*.

Mining

	1999	2000	2001
Gold (kg)	936	625	229

Source: Banque centrale des états de l'Afrique de l'ouest.

Industry

SELECTED PRODUCTS
(metric tons, unless otherwise indicated)

	1998	1999	2000
Edible oils	16,070	11,850	17,888
Shea (karité) butter	316	121	186
Flour	41,577	21,454	12,289
Pasta	257	496	211
Sugar	44,088	29,905	43,412
Beer ('000 hl)	501	387	494
Soft drinks ('000 hl)	195	155	169
Cigarettes (million packets) . . .	74	60	82
Printed fabric ('000 sq metres) . .	3,818	1,462	275
Soap	12,349	9,910	12,079
Matches (cartons)	8,814	8,056	9,358
Bicycles (units)	35,924	24,079	22,215
Mopeds (units)	20,875	17,364	16,531
Tyres ('000)	314	417	397
Inner tubes ('000)	1,755	2,540	2,655
Electric energy ('000 kWh) . . .	338,094	359,917	390,322

Finance

CURRENCY AND EXCHANGE RATES

Monetary Units
100 centimes = 1 franc de la Communauté financière africaine (CFA)

Sterling, Dollar and Euro Equivalents (31 December 2002)
£1 sterling = 1,008.17 francs CFA
US $1 = 625.50 francs CFA
€1 = 655.96 francs CFA
10,000 francs CFA = £9.992 = $15.987 = €15.245

Average Exchange Rate (francs CFA per US $)
2000   711.98
2001   733.04
2002   696.99

Note: An exchange rate of 1 French franc = 50 francs CFA, established in 1948, remained in force until January 1994, when the CFA franc was devalued by 50%, with the exchange rate adjusted to 1 French franc = 100 francs CFA. This relationship to French currency remained in effect with the introduction of the euro on 1 January 1999. From that date, accordingly, a fixed exchange rate of €1 = 655.957 francs CFA has been in operation.

BUDGET
('000 million francs CFA)

Revenue	1999	2000	2001
Current revenue	238.0	219.3	228.0
Tax revenue	222.2	202.9	213.2
Income and profits	53.7	61.4	56.1
Domestic goods and services	103.3	97.7	111.8
International trade	60.2	38.2	39.2
Non-tax revenue	15.8	16.4	14.7
Capital revenue	0.1	0.0	139.7
Total	238.1	219.3	367.7

Expenditure and net lending	1999	2000	2001
Domestic expenditure and net lending	246.9	244.9	282.0
Wages and salaries	82.6	88.7	98.2
Goods and services	37.6	40.0	40.7
Interest payments	13.7	16.6	17.6
Current transfers	45.4	49.0	62.7
Budgetary contribution to investment	67.3	47.5	64.7
Net lending*	0.3	3.1	-1.9
Foreign-financed government investment	185.3	176.2	168.5
Restructuring operations . . .	1.4	2.2	—
Total	433.7	423.3	450.5

* Including proceeds from privatization, which are excluded from revenue and are treated as a deduction from expenditure.

Source: IMF, *Burkina Faso: Selected Issues and Statistical Annex* (April 2002).

INTERNATIONAL RESERVES
(US $ million at 31 December)

	2000	2001	2002
IMF special drawing rights . . .	0.4	0.5	0.4
Reserve position in IMF	9.4	9.1	9.9
Foreign exchange	233.8	250.9	303.1

Source: IMF, *International Financial Statistics.*

MONEY SUPPLY
(million francs CFA at 31 December)

	2000	2001	2002
Currency outside banks	136,631	120,910	83,207
Demand deposits at deposit money banks*	126,010	135,679	152,877
Checking deposits at post office .	2,257	1,906	2,550
Total money (incl. others) . .	270,409	262,279	243,729

* Excluding the deposits of public establishments of an administrative or social nature.

Source: IMF, *International Financial Statistics.*

COST OF LIVING
(Consumer Price Index for African households in Ouagadougou; base: 1996 = 100)

	1999	2000	2001
Food, beverages and stimulants .	107.3	102.1	110.0
Clothing	107.2	107.0	107.1
Housing	103.7	104.7	103.5
All items (incl. others) . . .	106.8	106.5	111.7

NATIONAL ACCOUNTS
('000 million francs CFA at current prices)

Expenditure on the Gross Domestic Product

	1999	2000	2001
Government final consumption expenditure	215.7	236.0	252.0
Private final consumption expenditure	1,162.9	1,189.1	1,281.2
Gross fixed capital formation . .	411.6	430.3	454.2
Total domestic expenditure . .	1,790.2	1,823.6	1,987.4
Exports of goods and services . .	176.7	167.5	190.8
Less Imports of goods and services	448.7	430.4	471.3
GDP in purchasers' values . .	1,518.1	1,560.7	1,706.9
GDP at constant 1985 prices .	1,162.7	1,187.7	1,255.3

Sources: Banque centrale des états de l'Afrique de l'ouest; IMF, *International Financial Statistics.*

Gross Domestic Product by Economic Activity

	1999	2000	2001
Agriculture, livestock, forestry and fishing	532.5	530.7	586.3
Mining and manufacturing . .	194.8	187.7	230.9
Electricity, gas and water. . .	17.7	20.9	
Construction and public works .	55.1	55.2	61.8
Trade	247.4	272.7	290.7
Transport and communications .	70.1	77.3	82.4
Non-marketable services . . .	190.5	205.6	219.5
Other services	169.4	187.0	204.2
Sub-total	1,477.4	1,537.1	1,675.8
Import taxes and duties . . .	55.3	38.2	45.7
Less imputed bank service charge	14.6	14.6	14.6
GDP in purchasers' values .	1,518.1	1,560.6	1,706.9

Source: Banque centrale des états de l'Afrique de l'ouest.

BALANCE OF PAYMENTS
('000 million francs CFA)

	1999	2000	2001*
Exports of goods f.o.b.	156.2	146.2	161.6
Imports of goods f.o.b.	-357.4	-368.6	-373.3
Trade balance	-201.2	-222.4	-211.7
Services (net)	-70.8	-77.3	-76.0
Balance on goods and services	-272.0	-299.7	-287.7
Income (net)	-11.3	-14.3	-13.9
Balance on goods, services and income	-283.3	-314.0	-301.6
Private unrequited transfers (net) .	39.7	39.1	25.8
Official unrequited transfers (net) .	48.9	47.7	59.3
Current balance	-194.6	-227.1	-216.6
Capital transfers (net)	120.4	115.4	124.4
Official capital (net)	57.8	26.4	54.3
Private capital (net)	11.7	32.4	19.5
Net errors and omissions . . .	-8.6	5.3	-5.6
Overall balance	-13.3	-47.5	-24.1

* Estimates.

Source: IMF, *Burkina Faso: Sixth Review Under the Poverty Reduction and Growth Facility, and Requests for Waiver of Performance Criteria—Staff Report and News Brief on the Executive Board Discussion* (November 2002).

External Trade

PRINCIPAL COMMODITIES
('000 million francs CFA)

Imports f.o.b.	1999	2000	2001
Food products.	45.5	45.0	53.6
Petroleum products	62.4	65.0	67.9
Capital equipment	135.8	122.8	115.5
Raw materials	35.0	33.3	36.5
Total (incl. others)	368.7	368.7	373.4

Exports f.o.b.	1999	2000	2001
Livestock and livestock products	29.3	32.1	32.5
Live animals	15.8	16.5	19.2
Hides and skins	11.7	13.8	11.7
Cotton .	83.6	72.2	96.0
Gold	9.2	6.2	3.5
Total (incl. others)	156.2	146.2	168.8

Source: IMF, *Burkina Faso: Selected Issues and Statistical Annex* (April 2002).

PRINCIPAL TRADING PARTNERS
('000 million francs CFA)*

Imports c.i.f.	1998	1999	2000
Argentina .	4.1	0.4	0.7
Belgium-Luxembourg	8.9	8.7	10.5
China, People's Repub.	5.9	6.9	15.0
Côte d'Ivoire	67.0	66.8	83.8
France .	115.2	91.7	82.7
Germany .	11.1	12.2	13.3
Ghana .	3.5	3.0	4.8
India .	9.8	3.8	2.2
Italy .	12.8	7.9	11.5
Japan .	20.7	22.9	20.8
Netherlands .	11.4	8.4	7.8
Nigeria.	3.7	2.5	6.5
Pakistan .	5.0	3.8	0.9
Senegal .	4.2	4.4	5.7
Thailand .	5.1	3.8	2.6
Togo .	5.3	6.8	9.8
United Kingdom .	5.3	7.3	9.7
USA .	n.a.	11.9	10.1
Viet Nam .	6.4	—	—
Total (incl. others)	385.9	329.7	368.9

Exports f.o.b.	1998	1999	2000
Belgium-Luxembourg	15.2	6.9	10.5
Benin .	2.6	0.2	0.2
Colombia .	3.7	n.a.	n.a.
Côte d'Ivoire	13.7	32.8	14.4
France .	32.3	28.5	27.0
Ghana .	3.0	1.9	1.9
Italy .	0.3	2.4	9.7
Japan .	0.4	0.9	1.7
Mali .	2.4	3.5	6.3
Niger .	1.4	0.6	4.3
Nigeria.	1.1	1.2	0.1
Singapore .	7.8	3.5	7.0
Togo .	2.1	0.8	2.0
United Kingdom .	0.2	0.1	5.2
Total (incl. others)	140.0	123.4	125.0

* Figures refer to recorded trade only.

Source: IMF, *Burkina Faso: Selected Issues and Statistical Annex* (April 2002).

Transport

RAILWAYS
(international freight traffic, '000 metric tons)

	1999	2000	2001
To Côte d'Ivoire .	43.2	59.2	34.0
From Côte d'Ivoire .	377.7	356.0	279.2

Source: IMF, *Burkina Faso: Selected Issues and Statistical Annex* (April 2002).

Passenger-km (million, 1993): 403 (Source: UN Economic Commission for Africa, *African Statistical Yearbook*).

ROAD TRAFFIC
(motor vehicles in use)

	1994	1995	1996*
Passenger cars .	32,224	35,460	38,220
Buses and coaches .	1,939	2,237	2,460
Lorries and vans .	14,439	14,985	15,520
Road tractors .	2,087	2,251	2,400
Motorcycles and mopeds .	97,900	100,591	105,000

* Estimates.

Source: IRF, *World Road Statistics*.

CIVIL AVIATION
(traffic on scheduled services)*

	1997	1998	1999
Kilometres flown (million) .	3	3	4
Passengers carried ('000) .	97	102	147
Passenger-km (million) .	248	264	269
Total ton-km (million) .	39	39	39

* Including an apportionment of the traffic of Air Afrique.

Source: UN, *Statistical Yearbook*.

Tourism

FOREIGN VISITORS BY COUNTRY OF ORIGIN*

	1996	1997	1998
Côte d'Ivoire .	14,381	15,172	12,906
France .	29,972	31,621	45,136
Germany .	4,661	4,918	4,810
Mali .	8,143	8,591	5,774
Niger .	4,990	5,265	5,629
Senegal .	5,190	5,476	4,545
Togo .	4,329	4,567	4,223
USA .	3,854	4,066	5,310
Total (incl. others) .	131,113	138,364	160,284

* Arrivals at hotels and similar establishments.

Receipts from tourism ('000 million francs CFA): 13.2 in 1996; 17.6 in 1997; 25.1 in 1998 (Source: Direction du Tourisme et de l'Hôtellerie: *Statistiques du Tourisme (Année 1994–1998)*).

1999: Tourist arrivals 218,000 (Source: World Tourism Organization).

Communications Media

	1999	2000	2001
Television receivers ('000 in use)	130	140	n.a.
Telephones ('000 main lines in use)	47.3	53.8	57.6
Mobile cellular telephones ('000 subscribers)	5	25	75
Personal computers ('000 in use)	12	15	17
Internet users ('000)	7	10	21

Source: International Telecommunication Union.

Radio receivers ('000 in use, 1997): 370 (Source: UNESCO, *Statistical Yearbook*).

Daily newspapers (1996): 4 (average circulation 14,000 copies) (Source: UNESCO, *Statistical Yearbook*).

Non-daily newspapers (1995): 9 (average circulation 42,000 copies) (Source: UNESCO, *Statistical Yearbook*).

Book production (first editions, 1996): 12 titles (14,000 copies) (Source: UNESCO, *Statistical Yearbook*).

Education

(1995/96, unless otherwise indicated)

	Institu-tions	Tea-chers	Students		
			Males	Females	Total
Pre-primary* . .	147	441	8,921	9,124	18,045
Primary . . .	3,568	14,037	426,869	275,335	702,204
Secondary:					
general . .	252	4,162	89,609	47,648	137,257
vocational† . .	41	731	4,890	4,703	9,539
Tertiary . . .	9	632‡	7,245	2,286	9,531

* 1997/98.
† Including teacher training.
‡ Teachers at the Universities of Ouagadougou and Bobo-Dioulasso.

Tertiary (1996/97): Teachers 352; Students 8,911 (males 6,889; females 2,022)

1998/99: *Primary:* 816,393 students; *Secondary (including teacher training):* 173,200 students; *Higher:* 9,900 students.

Sources: Ministère de l'Enseignement de Base et de l'Alphabétisation, Ouagadougou; UNESCO, *Statistical Yearbook*.

Adult literacy rate (UNESCO estimates): 23.9% (males 33.9%; females 14.1%) in 2000 (Source: UN Development Programme, *Human Development Report*).

Directory

The Constitution

The present Constitution was approved in a national referendum on 2 June 1991, and was formally adopted on 11 June. The following are the main provisions of the Constitution, as amended in January 1997, April 2000 and February 2002:

The Constitution of the 'revolutionary, democratic, unitary and secular' Fourth Republic of Burkina Faso guarantees the collective and individual political and social rights of Burkinabè citizens, and delineates the powers of the executive, legislature and judiciary.

Executive power is vested in the President, who is Head of State, and in the Government, which is appointed by the President upon the recommendation of the Prime Minister. With effect from the election due in 2005, the President was to be elected, by universal suffrage, for a five-year term, renewable only once (previously a seven-year term had been served).

Legislative power is exercised by the multi-party Assemblée nationale. Deputies are elected, by universal suffrage, for a five-year term. The number of deputies and the mode of election is determined by law. The President appoints a Prime Minister and, at the suggestion of the Prime Minister, appoints the other ministers. The President may, having consulted the Prime Minister and the President of the Assemblée nationale, dissolve the Assemblée nationale. Both the Government and the Assemblée nationale may initiate legislation.

The judiciary is independent and, according to constitutional amendments approved in April 2000 (see Judicial System), was to consist of a Court of Cassation, a Constitutional Council, a Council of State, a National Audit Court, a High Court of Justice, and other courts and tribunals instituted by law. Judges are accountable to a Higher Council, under the chairmanship of the Head of State, who is responsible for guaranteeing the independence of the judiciary.

The Constitution also makes provision for an Economic and Social Council, for a Higher Council of Information, and for a national ombudsman.

The Constitution denies legitimacy to any regime that might take power as the result of a *coup d'état*.

The Government

HEAD OF STATE

President: BLAISE COMPAORÉ (assumed power as Chairman of the Front populaire 15 October 1987; elected President 1 December 1991; re-elected 15 November 1998).

COUNCIL OF MINISTERS
(April 2003)

President: BLAISE COMPAORÉ.

Prime Minister: PARAMANGA ERNEST YONLI.

Minister of State, Minister of Foreign Affairs and Regional Co-operation: YOUSSOUF OUÉDRAOGO.

Minister of State, Minister of Agriculture, Water Resources and Fisheries: SALIF DIALLO.

Minister of Health: BÉDOUMA ALAIN YODA.

Minister of Justice: BOUREIMA BADINI.

Minister of Defence: KOUAMÉ LOUGUÉ.

Minister of Territorial Administration and Decentralization: MOUMOUNI FABRÉ.

Minister of Security: DJIBRILL YIPÈNÈ BASSOLET.

Minister of Finance and the Budget: JEAN-BAPTISTE MARIE PASCAL COMPAORÉ.

Minister of the Economy and Development: SEYDOU BOUDA.

Minister of Labour, Employment and Youth: ALAIN LUDOVIC TOU.

Minister of Mines, Quarries and Energy: ABDUL KADER CISSÉ.

Minister of Trade, the Promotion of Business and Crafts: BENOÎT OUATTARA.

Minister of Infrastructure, Transport and Housing: HIPPOLYTE LINGANI.

Minister of Secondary and Higher Education and Scientific Research: LAYA SAWADOGO.

Minister of Basic Education and Literacy: MATHIEU R. OUÉDRAOGO.

Minister of the Civil Service and the Reform of the State: LASSANÉ SAWADOGO.

Minister of Culture, Arts and Tourism: MAHAMOUDOU OUÉDRAOGO.

Minister of Posts and Telecommunications: JUSTIN TIÈBA THIOMBIANO.

Minister of Animal Resources: ALPHONSE BONOU.

Minister of Social Action and National Solidarity: MARIAM LAMIZANA.

Minister of Information: RAYMOND EDOUARD OUÉDRAOGO.

Minister for the Promotion of Women: MARIE GISÈLE GUIGMA.

Minister of Relations with Parliament, Spokesperson for the Government: ADAMA FOFANA.

Minister for the Promotion of Human Rights: MONIQUE ILBOUDO.

Minister of the Environment and Quality of Life: DAKAR DJIRI.

Minister of Sport and Leisure: TIOUNDOUN SESSOUMA.

There are, in addition, four Ministers-delegate responsible for Regional Co-operation, Transport, Literacy and Informal Education, and Youth.

MINISTRIES

Office of the President: 03 BP 7030, Ouagadougou 03; tel. 30-66-30; fax 31-49-26; internet www.primature.gov.bf/republic/fpresident.htm.

Office of the Prime Minister: 03 BP 7027, Ouagadougou 03; tel. 32-48-89; fax 31-47-61; internet www.primature.gov.bf.

Ministry of Agriculture, Water Resources and Fisheries: 03 BP 7005, Ouagadougou 03; tel. 32-49-63.

Ministry of Animal Resources: 03 BP 7026, Ouagadougou 03; tel. 32-46-51; fax 31-84-75.

Ministry of Basic Education and Literacy: 03 BP 7032, Ouagadougou 03; tel. 32-48-70; fax 30-80-86.

Ministry of the Civil Service and the Reform of the State: 03 BP 7006, Ouagadougou 03; tel. 32-40-10.

Ministry of Culture, Arts and Tourism: 03 BP 7007, Ouagadougou 03; tel. 33-09-63; fax 33-09-64; e-mail mca@cenatrin.bf; internet www.culture.gov.bf.

Ministry of Defence: 01 BP 496, Ouagadougou 01; tel. 30-72-14; fax 31-36-10.

Ministry of the Economy and Development: Ouagadougou.

Ministry of the Environment and Quality of Life: 565 rue Neto, Koulouba, 03 BP 7044, Ouagadougou 03; tel. 32-40-74; fax 30-70-39.

Ministry of Finance and the Budget: 03 BP 7050, Ouagadougou 03; tel. 30-69-95; fax 31-27-15; e-mail finances@cenatrin.bf; internet www.finances.gov.bf.

Ministry of Foreign Affairs and Regional Co-operation: rue 988, blvd du Faso, 03 BP 7038, Ouagadougou 03; tel. 32-47-34; fax 30-87-92; e-mail webmaster.mae@mae.gov.bf; internet www.mae.gov.bf.

Ministry of Health: 03 BP 7009, Ouagadougou 03; tel. 32-41-71.

Ministry of Information: 03 BP 7045, Ouagadougou 03; tel. 31-45-72.

Ministry of Infrastructure, Transport and Housing: 03 BP 7011, Ouagadougou 03; tel. 32-49-54; fax 31-84-08.

Ministry of Justice: 01 BP 526, Ouagadougou 01; tel. 32-48-33.

Ministry of Labour, Employment and Youth: 03 BP 7016, Ouagadougou 03; tel. 30-09-60; fax 31-88-01; e-mail zephirin.kiendrebeog@delgi.gov.bf; internet www.metss.gov.bf.

Ministry of Mines, Quarries and Energy: 01 BP 644, Ouagadougou 01; tel. 31-84-29; fax 31-84-30.

Ministry of Posts and Telecommunications: 387 ave Georges Conseiga, 01 BP 5175, Ouagadougou 01; tel. 33-73-85; fax 33-73-87; e-mail mpt.secretariat@onatel.bf; internet www.mpt.bf.

Ministry for the Promotion of Human Rights: Ouagadougou.

Ministry for the Promotion of Women: Ouagadougou.

Ministry of Regional Integration: 01 BP 06, Ouagadougou 01; tel. 32-48-33; fax 31-41-90.

Ministry of Relations with Parliament: 03 BP 2079, Ouagadougou 03; tel. 32-40-70.

Ministry of Secondary and Higher Education and Scientific Research: 03 BP 7047, Ouagadougou 03; tel. 31-29-11; fax 32-61-16.

Ministry of Security: Ouagadougou.

Ministry of Social Action and National Solidarity: 01 BP 515, Ouagadougou 01; tel. 31-69-01; fax 37-02-12; e-mail webmaster@delgi.gov.bf; internet www.actionsocial.gov.bf.

Ministry of Sport and Leisure: 03 BP 7035, Ouagadougou; tel. 32-45-99.

Ministry of Territorial Administration and Decentralization: 03 BP 7034, Ouagadougou 03; tel. 32-47-83; fax 30-84-17.

Ministry of Trade, the Promotion of Business and Crafts: 01 BP 514, Ouagadougou 01; tel. 32-47-86; fax 32-48-28.

President and Legislature

PRESIDENT

Presidential Election, 15 November 1998

Candidate	Votes	% of votes
Blaise Compaoré	1,996,151	87.53
Ram Ouédraogo	150,793	6.61
Frédéric Guirma	133,552	5.86
Total	**2,280,496***	**100.00**

* There were, in addition, 89,458 blank votes.

ASSEMBLÉE NATIONALE

Assemblée nationale: BP 6482, Ouagadougou 01; tel. 31-46-84; fax 31-45-90.

President: ROCH MARC CHRISTIAN KABORÉ.

General Election, 5 May 2002

Parties	% of total votes*	National list seats	Total seats†
CDP	49.52	11	57
ADF—RDA	12.61	3	17
PDP—PS	7.01	2	10
CFD‡	4.38	1	5
PAI	3.62	1	5
PAREN	2.73	1	4
CPS	2.63	1	3
UNIR—MS	2.45	1	3
PDS	2.41	—	2
CNDP	2.02	—	2
UDPI	1.04	—	1
FPC	0.97	—	1
APL	0.67	—	1
Total (incl. others)	**100.00**	**21**	**111**

* Including votes from regional and national party lists.
† Including seats filled by voting from regional lists, totalling 90.
‡ The Coalition des forces démocratiques, an electoral alliance of six parties.

Advisory Council

Economic and Social Council: 01 BP 6162, Ouagadougou 01; tel. 32-40-91; fax 31-06-54; e-mail ces@ces.gov.bf; internet www.ces.gov.bf; f. 1985; present name adopted in 1992; 90 mems; Pres. JULIETTE BONKOUNGOU.

Political Organizations

Some 30 political parties contested the legislative elections held in May 2002. In early 2003 the most important political parties included the following:

Alliance pour la démocratie et la fédération—Rassemblement démocratique africain (ADF—RDA): 01 BP 1943, Ouagadougou 01; tel. 31-15-15; e-mail maclau.y@fasonet.bf; internet www.adf-rda.com; f. 1990 as Alliance pour la démocratie et la fédération, absorbed faction of Rassemblement démocratique africain in 1998; several factions broke away in mid-2000; Pres. Me HERMANN YAMÉOGO.

Alliance pour le progrès et la liberté (APL): Ouagadougou; Sec.-Gen. JOSÉPHINE TAMBOURA-SAMA.

Congrès pour la démocratie et le progrès (CDP): 01 BP 1605, Ouagadougou; tel. 31-50-18; e-mail cdp@cenatrin.bf; internet www.cdp.bf; f. 1996 by merger, to succeed the Organisation pour la démocratie populaire/Mouvement du travail as the prin. political org. supporting Pres. Compaoré; social democratic; Exec. Sec. ROCH MARC CHRISTIAN KABORÉ.

Convention nationale des démocrates progressistes (CNDP): Ouagadougou; tel. 36-39-73; f. 2000; Leader ALFRED KABORÉ.

Convention panafricaine sankariste (CPS): Ouagadougou; tel. 36-14-37; f. 1999 by merger of four parties, expanded in 2000 to include two other parties; promotes the policies of fmr Pres. Sankara; Pres. NONGMA ERNEST OUÉDRAOGO.

Convention pour la démocratie et la fédération (CDF): Ouagadougou; tel. 36-23-63; f. 1998; Leader AMADOU DIEMDIODA DICKO.

Convergence pour la démocratie sociale (CDS): Ouagadougou; f. 2002; socialist, opposed to Govt of Pres. Compaoré; Chair. VALERIE DIEUDONNÉ SOMÉ; Exec. Sec.-Gen. SESSOUMA SANOU.

Front des forces sociales (FFS): Ouagadougou; tel. 32-32-32; e-mail tino8@caramail.com; internet membres.lycos.fr/FFS; f. 1996; Sankarist; member of the Groupe du 14 février and opposition Collectif d'organisations démocratiques de masse et de partis politiques; Chair. NORBERT MICHEL TIENDRÉBÉOGO.

Front patriotique pour le changement (FPC): BP 8539, Ouagadougou; tel. 25-32-45; Pres. TAHIROU IBRAHIM ZON.

Mouvement du peuple pour le socialisme—Parti fédéral (MPS—PF): Ouagadougou; f. 2002 by split from PDP—PS; Leader Dr EMILE PARÉ.

Mouvement pour la tolérance et le progrès/Moog Teeb Panpaasgo (MTP): Ouagadougou; tel. 31-85-11; f. 2000; Sankarist; contested 2002 legislative elections as part of the Coalition des forces démocratiques (CFD); Leader EMMANUEL NAYABTIGUNGOU CONGO KABORÉ.

Parti africain de l'indépendance (PAI): Ouagadougou; tel. 25-15-05; f. 1999; Sec.-Gen. SOUMANE TOURÉ.

Parti pour la démocratie et le progrès—Parti socialiste (PDP —PS): BP 606, Ouagadougou; tel. 31-57-79; f. 2001 by merger of the Parti pour la démocratie et le progrès and the Parti socialiste burkinabè; Nat. Pres. JOSEPH KI-ZERBO.

Parti pour la démocratie et le socialisme (PDS): Ouagadougou; Pres. FÉLIX SOUBEIGA.

Parti de la renaissance nationale (PAREN): Ouagadougou; tel. 30-65-87; f. 2000; social-democratic; Pres. LAURENT BADO.

Parti socialiste unifié: Ouagadougou; f. 2001 by mems of fmr Parti socialiste burkinabè; Leader BENOÎT LOMPO.

Union des démocrates et progressistes indépendants (UDPI): BP 536, Ouagadougou; tel. 38-27-99; expelled from Groupe du 14 février in mid-2000; Leader LONGO DONGO.

Union pour la renaissance—Mouvement sankariste (UNIR—MS): Ouagadougou; tel. 36-30-45; f. 2000; Pres. BÉNÉWENDÉ STANISLAS SANKARA.

Diplomatic Representation

EMBASSIES IN BURKINA FASO

Algeria: place des Nations Unies, 01 BP 3893, Ouagadougou 01; tel. 30-64-01; fax 30-37-46; Ambassador HAMID DAOUDI BOUCHOUAREB.

Belgium: rue du Commerce, 01 BP 1264, Ouagadougou 01; tel. 31-21-64; fax 31-06-60; e-mail ouagadougou.coop@diplobel.org; Ambassador (vacant).

Canada: 01 BP 548, Ouagadougou 01; tel. 31-18-94; fax 31-19-00; e-mail ouaga@dfait-maeci.gc.ca; Ambassador DENIS BRIAND.

China (Taiwan): 01 BP 5563, Ouagadougou 01; tel. 31-61-95; fax 31-61-97; e-mail ambachine@fasonet.bf; Ambassador TAO WEN-LUNG.

Côte d'Ivoire: place des Nations Unies, 01 BP 20, Ouagadougou 01; tel. 31-82-28; fax 31-82-30; Ambassador RICHARD KODJO.

Cuba: Rotonde, prolongement de la rue 4/64 du feu rouge du MAET, 01 BP 3422, Ouagadougou 06; tel. 30-64-91; fax 31-73-24; Ambassador ISAAC ROBERTO TORRES-BARRIOS.

Denmark: rue Agostino Neto, 01 BP 1760, Ouagadougou 01; tel. 31-31-92; fax 31-31-89; e-mail ouaamb@um.dk; Ambasssador STIG BARLYNG.

Egypt: Zone du Conseil de L'Entente, 03 BP 3893, Ouagadougou 03; tel. 30-66-37; Ambassador ELSYED ADELKADER ELSYED EL TANTANWI.

France: 33 rue Yalgado Ouédraogo, 01 BP 504, Ouagadougou 01; tel. 30-67-74; fax 31-41-66; e-mail ambassade.france@cenatrin.bf; internet www.france-burkina.bf; Ambassador MAURICE ELIE PORTICHE.

Germany: 01 BP 600, Ouagadougou 01; tel. 30-67-31; fax 31-39-91; e-mail amb.allemagne@fasonet.bf; Ambassador Dr HELMUT RAU.

Ghana: 22 ave d'Oubritenga, 01 BP 212, Ouagadougou 01; tel. 30-76-35; Ambassador GEORGES MINYILA.

India: 167 rue Joseph Badoua, 01 BP 6648, Ouagadougou 01; tel. 31-43-67; fax 33-90-71; Ambassador MOHAN LAL.

Iran: rue Raoul Follereau, Koulouba, BP 1342, Ouagadougou; tel. 30-77-07; fax 31-16-26; Ambassador NOUROUF ALI RAOUFZADEH.

Libya: 01 BP 1601, Ouagadougou 01; tel. 30-67-53; fax 31-34-70; Ambassador ABDUL NASSER SALEH MOHAMED YOUNES.

Mali: 2569 ave Bassawarga, 01 BP 1911, Ouagadougou 01; tel. 38-19-22; Ambassador MOHAMED SALIA SOKONA.

Mauritania: Ouagadougou; Ambassador MOHAMED OULD SID AHMED LEKHAL.

Morocco: Ouagadougou; Ambassador ABDELMAJID BOUAB.

Netherlands: 415 ave Dr Kwamé N'Krumah, 01 BP 1302, Ouagadougou 01; tel. 30-61-34; fax 30-76-95; e-mail hmaouaga@fasonet.bf; internet www.ambassadepays-bas.bf; Ambassador HENRICUS MAURITUS STEPHANUS SCHAAQUELD.

Nigeria: rue de l'Hôpital Yalgado, 01 BP 132, Ouagadougou 01; tel. 36-30-15; Ambassador AHMED KASHIM.

Saudi Arabia: Ouagadougou; Ambassador AID BEN MOHAMED AL-THAKFI.

Senegal: Immeuble FADIMA, 01 BP 3226, Ouagadougou 01; tel. 31-14-18; Ambassador CHEIKH SYLLA.

USA: 602 ave Raoul Follereau, Koulouba, 01 BP 35, Ouagadougou 01; tel. 30-67-23; fax 31-23-68; e-mail amembouaga@state.gov; internet ouagadougou.usembassy.gov; Ambassador JOSEPH ANTHONY HOLMES.

Judicial System

Judges are accountable to a Higher Council, under the chairmanship of the President of the Republic, in which capacity he is officially responsible for ensuring the independence of the judiciary.

Constitutional Council: Ouagadougou; f. 2002 to replace fmr Constitutional Chamber of the Supreme Court (q.v.); Pres. IDRISSA TRAORÉ; Sec.-Gen. HONIBIPÈ MARIAM MARGUERITE OUÉDRAOGO.

Supreme Court: 01 BP 586, Ouagadougou 01; tel. 31-36-09; fax 31-02-71; internet www.primature.gov.bf/republic/acc_cs.htm; comprises three permanent chambers: the Administrative Chamber, the Judicial Chamber and the Audit Chamber; Pres. SAMBO ANTOINE KOMI.

Constitutional amendments approved by the Assemblée nationale in April 2000 provided for the abolition of the Supreme Court and the replacement of its four permanent chambers by a Constitutional Council, a Council of State, a Court of Cassation and a National Audit Court. In June 2002, in advance of the establishment of these new institutions, First Presidents were appointed to the Council of State (HARIDIATE DAKOURE SERE), the Court of Cassation (DIMKINSEDO CHEICK OUÉDRAOGO), and to the National Audit Court (BOUREIMA PIERRE NEBIE). The members of the Constitutional Council were appointed in October 2002, and the Council replaced the former Constitutional Chamber of the Supreme Court in December of that year. Pending the full implementation of the constitutional amendments, the three remaining chambers of the Supreme Court continued to function. The Constitution also provides for the existence of a High Court of Justice.

Religion

The Constitution provides for freedom of religion, and the Government respects this right in practice. The country is a secular state. Islam, Christianity and traditional religions operate freely without government interference. More than 50% of the population follow animist beliefs.

ISLAM

An estimated 30% of the population are Muslims.

Association Islamique Tidjania du Burkina Faso: Ouagadougou; Pres. Cheick ABOUBACAR MAÏGA II.

CHRISTIANITY

The Roman Catholic Church

Burkina Faso comprises three archdioceses and nine dioceses. At 31 December 2000 there were an estimated 1.3m. Roman Catholics in Burkina, comprising 11.4% of the total population.

Bishops' Conference

Conférence des Evêques de Burkina Faso et du Niger, 01 BP 1195, Ouagadougou 01; tel. 30-60-26; fax 31-64-81; e-mail ccbn@fasonet.bf. f. 1966; legally recognized 1978; Pres. Rt Rev. PHILIPPE OUÉDRAOGO (Bishop of Ouahigouya).

Archbishop of Bobo-Dioulasso: Most Rev. ANSELME TITIANMA SANON, Archevêché, Lafiaso, 01 BP 312, Bobo-Dioulasso; tel. 97-00-53; fax 97-19-50; e-mail ddec.bobo@fasonet.bf.

Archbishop of Koupéla: Most Rev. Séraphin F. Rouamba, Archevêché, BP 51, Koupéla; tel. and fax 70-01-80; e-mail archevkou@fasonet.bf.

Archbishop of Ouagadougou: Most Rev. Jean-Marie Untaani Compaoré, Archevêché, 01 BP 1472, Ouagadougou 01; tel. 30-67-04; fax 30-72-75; e-mail untaani@fasonet.bf.

Protestant Churches

Assemblées de Dieu du Burkina Faso: 01 BP 458, Ouagadougou; tel. 30-54-60; e-mail ad@adburkina.org; internet www.adburkina.org; f. 1921; Pres. Pastor Jean Pawentaoré Ouédraogo.

BAHÁ'Í FAITH

Assemblée spirituelle nationale: 01 BP 977, Ouagadougou 01; tel. 34-29-95; e-mail gnampa@fasonet.bf; Nat. Sec. Jean-Pierre Swedy.

The Press

Direction de la presse écrite: Ouagadougou; govt body responsible for press direction.

DAILIES

Bulletin de l'Agence d'Information du Burkina: 01 BP 1332, Ouagadougou; tel. 32-46-39; fax 32-46-40; e-mail aib.redaction@delgi.gov.bf; internet www.aib.bf; Dir James Dabire.

L'Express du Faso: Bobo-Dioulasso; tel. 97-93-26; fax 33-50-27; f. 2000; privately-owned.

L'Observateur Paalga (New Observer): 01 BP 584, Ouagadougou 01; tel. 33-27-05; fax 31-45-79; e-mail lobs@fasonet.bf; internet www.lobservateur.bf; f. 1991; privately-owned; also a Sunday edn, *L'Observateur Dimanche*; Dir Edouard Ouédraogo; circ. 8,000.

Le Pays: Koulouba, route de l'aéroport, 01 BP 4577, Ouagadougou 01; tel. 31-35-46; fax 31-45-40; e-mail ed.lepays@cenatrin.bf; internet www.lepays.bf; f. 1991; independent; Dir-Gen. Boureima Jérémie Sigue; Editor-in-Chief Mahorou Kanazoe; circ. 5,000.

Sidwaya Quotidien (Daily Truth): 5 rue du Marché, 01 BP 507, Ouagadougou 01; tel. 30-63-06; fax 31-03-62; e-mail sidwayas@mcc.gov.bf; internet www.sidwaya.bf; f. 1984; state-owned; Dir Issaka Sourwema; circ. 3,000.

24 Heures: 01 BP 3654, Ouagadougou 01; tel. 31-41-08; fax 30-57-39; f. 2000; privately-owned; Dir Boubakar Diallo.

PERIODICALS

L'Aurore: Immeuble abritant Lotte Photo, Ouagadougou; tel. 25-22-81.

Bendré (Drum): 16.38 ave du Yatenga, 01 BP 6020, Ouagadougou 01; tel. 33-27-11; fax 31-28-53; e-mail bendrekan@hotmail.com; internet www.bendre.africa-web.org; f. 1990; weekly; current affairs; Dir Sy Moumina Cheriff; circ. 7,000 (2002).

Les Echos: Ouagadougou; f. 2002; weekly; Editor David Sanhouidi.

Evasion: Koulouba, route de l'aéroport, 01 BP 4577, Ouagadougou 01; tel. 31-35-46; fax 31-45-40; f. 1996; publ. by Editions le Pays; weekly; current affairs; Dir-Gen. Boureima Jérémie Sigue.

L'Evènement: 01 BP 1860, Ouagadougou 01; tel. and fax and fax 31-69-34; f. 2001; monthly; Editor-in-Chief Newton Ahmed Barry.

L'Hebdomadaire: Ouagadougou; tel. 31-47-62; e-mail hebdcom@fasonet.bf; internet www.hebdo.bf/hebdo; f. 1999; Fridays; Dir Zéphirin Kpoda; Editor-in-Chief Djibril Touré.

L'Indépendant: 01 BP 5663, Ouagadougou 01; tel. 33-37-75; e-mail sebgo@fasonet.bf; internet www.independant.bf; f. 1993 by Norbert Zongo; weekly; Dir Liermé Dieudonné Somé; Editor-in-Chief Talato Siid Saya.

Le Journal du Jeudi (JJ): 01 BP 3654, Ouagadougou 01; tel. 31-41-08; fax 30-01-62; e-mail jj@liptinfor.bf; internet www.journaldujeudi.com; f. 1991; weekly; Dir Boubakar Diallo; Editor-in-Chief Damien Glez; circ. 10,000.

Laabaali: Association Tin-Tua, BP 167, Fada N'Gourma; e-mail tintua1@fasonet.bf; f. 1992; monthly; promotes literacy, cultural affairs, Gourmanché; Dir Aminata Ndounga; circ. 3,500.

Label Magazine: Seydoni Production, 01 BP 4912, Ouagadougou 01; tel. 35-80-11; fax 36-21-34; e-mail cdt.burkina@fasonet.bf; f. 2001; music, arts, youth activities.

Le Marabout: 01 BP 3564, Ouagadougou 01; tel. 31-41-08; e-mail info@marabout.net; internet www.marabout.net; f. 2001; monthly;

publ. by the Réseau africain pour la liberté d'informer; pan-African politics; satirical; Dirs Boubakar Diallo, Damien Glez.

Le Matin: 01 BP 6624, Ouagadougou 01; tel. 31-30-98; fax 31-30-99; f. 1992; weekly; Dir Dofinita Flaurent Bonzi.

L'Opinion: 01 BP 6459, Ouagadougou 01; tel. 30-89-48; fax 30-89-47; e-mail zedcom@fasonet.bf; internet www.zedcom.bf/actualite/actualite.htm; weekly; Editor Issaka Lingani.

Regard: 01 BP 4707, Ouagadougou 01; tel. 31-16-70; fax 31-57-47; weekly; Dir Chris Valéa; Editor Patrick Ilboudo; circ. 4,000.

San Finna: Immeuble Photo Luxe, 01 BP 2061, Ouagadougou 01; tel. and fax 33-09-09; e-mail maclau.y@fasonet.bf; internet www.sanfinna.com; f. 1999; Mondays; independent; current affairs, international politics; Editor-in-Chief Mathieu N'Do.

Sidwaya Hebdo (Weekly Truth): 5 rue du Marché, 01 BP 507, Ouagadougou 01; tel. 31-36-05; fax 31-03-62; e-mail sidwayas@mcc-gov.bf; internet www.sidwaya.bf; f. 1997; state-owned; weekly; Dir Issaka Sourwema.

Sidwaya Magazine (Truth): 5 rue du Marché, 01 BP 507, Ouagadougou 01; tel. 30-63-07; fax 31-03-62; e-mail sidwayas@mcc.gov.bf; internet www.sidwaya.bf; f. 1989; state-owned; monthly; Editor-in-Chief Boniface Coulibaly; circ. 2,500.

La Voix du Sahel: 01 BP 5505, Ouagadougou 01; tel. 33-20-75; e-mail voixdusahel@yahoo.fr; privately-owned.

Votre Santé: Koulouba, route de l'aéroport, 01 BP 4577, Ouagadougou 01; tel. 31-35-46; fax 31-45-40; internet www.lepays.bf/mensuel/laune.asp; f. 1996; publ. by Editions le Pays; monthly; Dir-Gen. Boureima Jérémie Sigue.

NEWS AGENCY

Agence d'Information du Burkina (AIB): 01 BP 1332, Ouagadougou 01; tel. 32-46-39; fax 32-46-40; e-mail aib.redaction@delgi.gov.bf; internet www.aib.bf; f. 1964; fmrly Agence Voltaïque de Presse; state-controlled; Dir James Dabiré.

PRESS ASSOCIATIONS

Association Rayimkudemdé—Association Nationale des Animateurs et Journalistes en Langues Nationales du Burkina Faso (ARK): Sigh-Noghin, Ouagadougou; f. 2001; Pres. Rigobert Ilboudo; Sec.-Gen. Pierre Ouédraogo.

Centre National de Presse—Norbert Zongo (CNP—NZ): 04 BP 8524, Ouagadougou 04; tel. and fax 34-37-45; e-mail cnpress@fasonet.bf; internet www.cnpress-zongo.net; f. 1998 as Centre National de Presse; centre of information and documentation, provides journalistic training, seeks to defend the liberty of the press as an element in a civil, democratic society; incorporates Association des Journalistes du Burkina (f. 1988); Dir Abdoulaye Diallo.

Publishers

Editions Contact: 04 BP 8462, Ouagadougou 04; tel. 61-28-72; e-mail contact.evang@cenatrin.bf; f. 1992; evangelical Christian and other books in French.

Découvertes du Burkina: 06 BP 9237, Ouagadougou 06; tel. 36-22-38; e-mail jacques@liptinfor.bf; human and social sciences, poetry; Dir Jacques Guégané.

Editions Firmament: 01 BP 3392, Ouagadougou 01; tel. 38-44-25; e-mail roger.kabore@uemoa.int; literary fiction; Dir Roger Kaboré.

Editions Flamme: 01 BP 458, Ouagadougou 01; tel. 21-10-28; e-mail ad-lagengo-bf@cenatrin.bf; internet www.adburkina.org/imprimerie/flamme.html; owned by the Assembleés de Dieu du Burkina Faso; literature of Christian interest in French and in Mooré; Dir Pastor Zacharie Delma.

Editions Gambidi: 01 BP 5743, Ouagadougou 01; tel. 36-59-42; e-mail jp.guigane@liptinfor.bf; politics, philosophy; Dir Jean-Pierre Guinane.

Graphic Technic International and Biomedical Publishers: 01 BP 3230, Ouagadougou 01; tel. and fax 31-67-69; e-mail hien.ignace@fasonet.bf; medicine, literary, popular and children's fiction, poetry; Dir Ansomwin Ignace Hien.

Presses Africaines SA: 01 BP 1471, Ouagadougou 01; tel. 30-71-75; fax 30-72-75; general fiction, religion, primary and secondary textbooks; Man. Dir A. Wininga.

Société Nationale d'Edition et de Presse (SONEPRESS): BP 810, Ouagadougou; f. 1972; general, periodicals; Pres. Martial Ouédraogo.

Broadcasting and Communications

TELECOMMUNICATIONS

The introduction of a regulatory framework for the telecommunications industry is ongoing and the increased liberalization of the sector is expected.

Office National des Télécommunications (ONATEL): ave Nelson Mandela, 01 BP 10000, Ouagadougou 01; tel. 33-40-01; fax 31-03-31; e-mail acotel.centre@onatel.bf; internet www.onatel.bf; privatization scheduled for completion in 2003; Dir-Gen. JACQUES LOUARI.

TELMOB: f. 2002; mobile cellular telecommunications in 19 cities.

Celtel Burkina Faso: Ouagadougou; tel. 34-44-55; fax 34-16-67; e-mail rjlaforce@cs.com; internet www.msi-cellular.com; f. 2001; mobile cellular telephone operator in Ouagadougou, Bobo-Dioulasso and other towns; subsidiary of MSI Cellular Investments Holding (Netherlands); Dir-Gen. RAYMOND LAFORCE; 30,000 subscribers (Nov. 2002).

Telecel-Faso: 08 BP 11059, Ouagadougou 08; tel. 33-35-56; fax 33-35-58; e-mail info@telecelfaso.bf; internet www.telecelfaso.bf; f. 2000; mobile cellular telephone operator in Ouagadougou, Bobo-Dioulasso and 14 other towns; 80% owned by Orascom Telecom (Egypt).

BROADCASTING

Regulatory Authority

Higher Council of Information: 290 ave Ho Chi Minh, 01 BP 6618, Ouagadougou 01; tel. 30-11-24; fax 30-11-33; internet www.primature.gov.bf/republic/acc_csi.htm; f. 1995; Pres. LUC ADOLPHE TIAO.

Radio

In November 1999 there were 53 officially registered radio stations in Burkina Faso: four international stations, 17 commercial and two state-owned stations chiefly broadcasting music, six community stations, 10 other independent stations and 14 religious stations. There were 47 licensed FM radio stations in Burkina Faso in December 2001.

Radio Télévision du Burkina: 01 BP 2530, Ouagadougou 01; tel. 31-83-53; fax 32-48-09; f. 2001; Dir-Gen. AZAD SEYDOU SAWADOGO.

Radio Nationale du Burkina (La RNB): 03 BP 7029, Ouagadougou 03; tel. 32-43-02; fax 31-04-41; f. 1959; state radio service; comprises national broadcaster of informative and discussion programmes, music stations *Canal Arc-En-Ciel* and *Canal Arc-en-Ciel Plus*, and two regional stations, broadcasting in local languages, in Bobo-Dialasso and Gaoua; Dir MAFARMA SANOGO.

Radio Evangile Développement (RED): 04 BP 8050, Ouagadougou 04; tel. 43-51-56; e-mail regd.burkina@cenatrin.bf; f. 1993; four stations, at Ouagadougou; Bobo-Dioulasso, Ouahigouya and Léo; three stations, at Houndé, Koudougou and Yako, to be established in 2002; evangelical Christian; Dir-Gen. JOANNA ILBOUDO.

Horizon FM: 01 BP 2714, Ouagadougou 01; tel. 33-23-23; fax 35-60-54; e-mail horizonfm@fasonet.bf; f. 1990; private commercial station; broadcasts in French, English and eight vernacular languages; operates 10 stations nationally; Dir MOUSTAPHA LAABLI THIOMBIANO.

Radio Locale-Radio Rurale: 03 BP 7029, Ouagadougou 03; tel. 31-27-81; fax 79-10-22; f. 1969; community broadcaster; local stations at Diapaga, Djibasso Gasson, Kongoussi, Orodara and Poura; Dir-Gen. BÉLIBIÉ SOUMAÏLA BASSOLE.

Radio Maria: Archevêché, 01 BP 90, Ouagadougou 01; tel. 31-70-70; fax 30-72-75; e-mail mcsburkina@yahoo.com; f. 1993; Roman Catholic; Dir Fr DOMINIQUE YANOGO.

Radio Salankoloto-Association Galian: 01 BP 1095, Ouagadougou 01; tel. 31-64-93; fax 31-64-71; f. 1996; community broadcaster; Dir ROGER NIKIÉMA.

Radio Vive le Paysan: 05 BP 6274, Ouagadougou 05; tel. 31-16-36; fax 38-52-90; e-mail aeugene@fasonet.bf.

Radio la Voix du Paysan: BP 100, Ouahigouya; tel. 55-04-11; fax 55-01-62; community broadcaster; f. 1996; Pres. BERNARD LÉDÉA OUÉDRAOGO.

Television

Radio Télévision du Burkina: (see above); Dir of Television INOUSSA KINDA.

Télévision Canal Viim Koéga: Ouagadougou; private broadcaster.

Multi Media Télévision (MMTV): 01 BP 5592, Ouagadougou 01; tel. 30-54-55; fax 31-44-58; commercial broadcaster.

TV5: 01 BP 5592, Ouagadougou 01; tel. 31-71-71; fax 31-23-19.

Finance

(cap. = capital; res = reserves; m. = million; brs = branches; amounts in francs CFA)

BANKING

Central Bank

Banque Centrale des Etats de l'Afrique de l'Ouest (BCEAO): ave Gamal-Abdel-Nasser, BP 356, Ouagadougou; tel. 30-60-15; fax 31-01-22; e-mail akangni@bceao.int; internet www.bceao.int; HQ in Dakar, Senegal; f. 1962; bank of issue for the mem. states of the Union économique et monétaire ouest-africaine (UEMOA, comprising Benin, Burkina Faso, Côte d'Ivoire, Guinea-Bissau, Mali, Niger, Senegal and Togo); cap. and res 850,500m., total assets 5,157,700m. (Dec. 2001); Dir in Burkina Faso CÉLESTIN KOUKA ZALLE; br. in Bobo-Dioulasso.

Other Banks

Bank of Africa—Burkina Faso (BOA—BF): 770 ave de la Résistance du 17 mai, 01 BP 1319, Ouagadougou 01; tel. 30-88-70; fax 30-88-74; e-mail boadg@fasonet.bf; internet www.bkofafrica.net; f. 1998; cap. 1,250m., res −409.5m., dep. 20,324.4m. (Dec. 2001); Pres. LASSINÉ DIAWARA; Dir-Gen. JOSÉ ESPEILLAC; 2 brs.

Banque Commerciale du Burkina (BCB): ave de la Nation, 01 BP 1336, Ouagadougou 01; tel. 30-78-78; fax 31-06-28; e-mail bcb@fasonet.bf; internet www.bcb.bf; f. 1988; 50% owned by Libyan Arab Foreign Bank, 25% state-owned, 25% owned by Caisse Nationale de Sécurité Sociale; cap. 5,000m., dep. 25,287m., total assets 40,207m. (Jan. 2002); Pres. IBRAHIMA OUATTARA; Man. Dir MAHAMUD HAMMUDA; 2 brs.

Banque Internationale du Burkina (BIB): ave Dimdolobsom, 01 BP 362, Ouagadougou 01; tel. 30-61-70; fax 31-00-94; e-mail bib.ouaga@fasonet.bf; f. 1974; cap. and res 10,676m., total assets 126,169m. (Dec. 1999); Pres. and Dir-Gen. GASPARD-JEAN OUÉDRAOGO; 21 brs.

Banque Internationale pour le Commerce, l'Industrie et l'Agriculture du Burkina (BICIA—B): 479 ave Dr Kwamé N'Krumah, 01 BP 08, Ouagadougou 01; tel. 30-62-26; fax 31-19-55; e-mail biciabdg@fasonet.bf; f. 1973; affiliated to BNP Paribas (France); 25% state-owned; cap. 5,000m., res 4,432m., dep. 116,487m. (Dec. 2000); Chair. AMADOU TRAORÉ; Dir-Gen. JEAN-PIERRE BAJON-ARNAL; 11 brs.

Caisse Nationale de Crédit Agricole du Burkina (CNCA—B): 2 ave Gamal-Abdel-Nasser, 01 BP 1644, Ouagadougou 01; tel. 33-33-33; fax 31-43-52; e-mail cncabf@cenatrin.bf; f. 1980; 25% state-owned; cap. and res 9,657m., total assets 35,774m. (Dec. 1999); Pres. ANGÈLE SOUDRE; Man. Dir LÉONCE KONE; 4 brs.

Ecobank—Burkina SA: 633 rue Maurice Bishop, 01 BP 145, Ouagadougou 01; tel. 31-89-75; fax 31-89-81; e-mail ecobankbf@ecobank.com; internet www.ecobank.com; f. 1997; 48% owned by Ecobank Transnational Inc, 12% by Ecobank Benin, 12% by Ecobank Togo; cap. 1,500m., total assets 37,474m. (Dec. 2000); Pres. PAUL BALKOUMA; Man. Dir Dr OLAYEMI ALAMU AKAPO.

Société Générale de Banques au Burkina (SGBB): 4 rue du Marché, 01 BP 585, Ouagadougou 01; tel. 30-60-34; fax 31-05-61; e-mail bhfm.mail@socgen.com; internet groupe.socgen.com/sgbb; f. 1998; affiliate of Société Générale (France); cap. 1,600m., total assets 48,516m. (Dec. 2000); Pres. and Dir-Gen. EMILE PARÉ.

Credit Institutions

Burkina Bail, SA: 01 BP 362, Ouagadougou 01; tel. 30-61-69; fax 30-07-02; e-mail burkina.bail@fasonet.bf; internet www.burkinabail.com; 52% owned by BIB; cap. 500m. Dir-Gen. ABDOULAYE K. SORY.

Réseau des Caisses Populaires du Burkina (RCPB): 01 BP 5282, Ouagadougou 01; tel. 30-48-41; Dir-Gen. DAOUDA SAWADOGA; 276,966 mems (June 2002), 104 co-operatives.

Société Burkinabè de Financement (SOBFI): Immeuble Nassa, 1242 ave Dr Kwamé N'Krumah, 10 BP 13876, Ouagadougou 10; tel. 31-80-04; fax 33-71-62; e-mail sobfi@fasonet.bf; f. 1997; cap. 500m., total assets 1,699m. (Dec. 1999); Pres. D. DIACK; Man. Dir J. OREGA.

Bankers' Association

Association Professionnelle des Banques et Etablissements Financiers (APBEF): Ouagadougou; tel. 30-60-37; e-mail apbef-bf@cenatrin.bf; Pres. HAMADÉ OUÉDRAOGO.

STOCK EXCHANGE

Bourse Régionale des Valeurs Mobilières (BRVM): s/c Chambre de Commerce, d'Industrie et d'Artisanat du Burkina, 01 BP 502, Ouagadougou 01; tel. 30-87-73; fax 30-87-19; e-mail louedraogo@brvm.org; internet www.brvm.org; f. 1998; national branch of BRVM (regional stock exchange based in Abidjan, Côte d'Ivoire, serving the member states of UEMOA); Man. Léopold Ouédraogo.

INSURANCE

FONCIAS—TIARD: 99 ave Léo Frobénius, 01 BP 398, Ouagadougou 01; tel. 30-62-04; tel. 31-01-53; e-mail groupe-foncias@foncias.bf; f. 1978; 51% owned by AGF (France), 20% state-owned; non-life insurance and reinsurance; cap. 400m. Dir-Gen. Bernard Girardin; also **Foncias-Vie**, life insurance; Dir-Gen. Joseph Baro.

Société Nationale d'Assurances et de Réassurances (SONAR): 284 ave de Loudun, 01 BP 406, Ouagadougou 01; tel. 30-62-43; fax 30-89-75; e-mail sonar@cenatrin.bf; f. 1974; 42% owned by Burkinabè interests, 33% by French, Ivorian and US cos, 22% state-owned; life and non-life; cap. 720m. (SONAR-IARD, non-life), 500m. (SONAR-Vie, life); Dir-Gen. André Bayala; 5 brs.

Union des Assurances du Burkina (UAB): 08 BP 11041, Ouagadougou 08; tel. 31-26-15; fax 31-26-20; e-mail uab@fasonet.bf; f. 1991; 42% owned by AXA Assurances Côte d'Ivoire; cap. 500m. Pres. Appolinaire Compaoré; Dir-Gen. Reynatou Bado.

Trade and Industry

GOVERNMENT AGENCIES

Bureau des Mines et de la Géologie du Burkina (BUMIGEB): 4186 route de Fada–N'Gourma, 01 BP 601, Ouagadougou 01; tel. 36-48-02; fax 36-48-88; e-mail bumigeb@burkinaonline.bf; internet www.bumigeb.bf; f. 1978; restructured 1997; research into geological and mineral resources; Dir-Gen. Jean-Léonard Compaoré.

Commission de Privatisation: 01 BP 6451, Ouagadougou 01; tel. 33-58-93; fax 30-77-41; e-mail privatisation@fasonet.bf; internet www.privatisation-bf.com.

Comptoir Burkinabè des Métaux Précieux (CBMP): Ouagadougou; tel. 30-75-48; fax 31-56-34; promotes gold sector, liaises with artisanal producers; Dir-Gen. Yacouba Barry.

Office National d'Aménagement des Terroirs (ONAT): 01 BP 3007, Ouagadougou 01; tel. 30-61-10; fax 30-61-12; f. 1974; fmrly Autorité des Aménagements des Vallées des Voltas; integrated rural development, including economic and social planning; Man. Dir Zacharie Ouédraogo.

Office National des Barrages et des Aménagements Hydro-agricoles (ONBAH): 03 BP 7056, Ouagadougou 03; tel. 30-89-82; fax 31-04-26; e-mail onbah@cenatrin.bf; f. 1976; control and development of water for agricultural use, construction of dams, water and soil conservation; state-owned; Dir-Gen. Aïzo Tindano.

Office National du Commerce Extérieur (ONAC): 30 ave Léo Frobénius, 01 BP 389, Ouagadougou 01; tel. 31-13-00; fax 31-14-69; e-mail info@tradepoint.bf; internet www.tradepoint.bf; f. 1974; promotes and supervises external trade; Man. Dir Sériba Ouattara (acting); br. at Bobo-Dioulasso.

DEVELOPMENT ORGANIZATIONS

Agence Française de Développement (AFD): 52 ave Nelson Mandela, 01 BP 529, Ouagadougou 01; tel. 30-60-92; fax 31-19-66; e-mail afdburkina@liptinfor.bf; internet www.afd.fr; fmrly Caisse Française de Développement; Dir Yves Jorlin.

Association Française des Volontaires du Progrès (AFVP): 01 BP 947, Ouagadougou 01; tel. 30-70-43; fax 31-44-91; e-mail afvp.bf@liptinfor.bf; internet www.afvp.org; f. 1973; supports small business; Nat. Delegate François Lecarpentier.

Bureau d'Appui aux Micro Entreprises (BAME): BP 610, Bobo-Dioulasso; tel. 97-16-28; fax 97-21-76; e-mail bame@fasonet.bf; f. 1991; supports small business; Dir Félix Sanon.

Cellule d'Appui à la Petite et Moyenne Entreprise d'Ouagadougou (CAPEO): 01 BP 6443, Ouagadougou 01; tel. 31-37-62; fax 31-37-64; e-mail capeod@fasonet.bf; internet www.spid.com/capeo; f. 1991; supports small- and medium-sized enterprises.

Fondation pour la Promotion de l'Entreprise et de l'Emploi (FEE): Ouagadougou; tel. 31-27-90; promotes private enterprise.

Promotion du Développement Industriel, Artisanal et Agricole (PRODIA): Secteur 8, Gounghin, 01 BP 2344, Ouagadougou 01; tel. 34-31-11; fax 34-71-47; e-mail prodia@cenatrin.bf; internet www.afraca.org/frprodia.html; f. 1981; supports small business; issued 1,266 loans amounting to 391.7m. francs CFA in 1998; Dir Mamadou Ouédraogo.

CHAMBER OF COMMERCE

Chambre de Commerce, d'Industrie et d'Artisanat du Burkina: 180/220 rue 3-119, 01 BP 502, Ouagadougou 01; tel. 30-61-14; fax 30-61-16; e-mail webmaster.ccia@ccia.bf; internet www.ccia.bf; f. 1948; Pres. El Hadj Oumarou Kanazoé; Dir-Gen. Hamadé Ouédraogo; brs in Bobo-Dioulasso, Koupéla and Ouahigouya.

EMPLOYERS' ORGANIZATIONS

Association Femmes Solidaritées (AFS): 01 BP 1749, Ouagadougou 01; tel. 30-01-50; association of female employers.

Club des Hommes d'Affaires Franco-Burkinabé: 01 BP 4382, Ouagadougou; tel. 30-67-70; fax 30-89-00; e-mail chafb@liptinfor.bf; internet www.chafb.bf; f. 1990; represents 65 major enterprises; Pres. Jean-Pierre Bajon-Arnal.

Conseil National du Patronat Burkinabè (CNPB): 01 BP 660, Ouagadougou 02; tel. 33-29-24; fax 30-25-21; e-mail belco@fasonet.bf; f. 1998; comprises 27 professional groupings; Pres. El Hadj Oumarou Kanazoé; Exec. Sec. Emile Kaboré.

Groupement Professionnel des Industriels: 01 BP 5381, Ouagadougou 01; tel. and fax 30-11-59; e-mail gpi@fasonet.bf; f. 1974; Pres. Martial Ouédraogo.

Fédération Nationale des Exportateurs du Burkina (FENEB): Ouagadougou; Permanent Sec. Seydou Fofana.

Syndicat des Commerçants Importateurs et Exportateurs du Burkina (SCIMPEX): 01 BP 552, Ouagadougou 01; tel. 31-18-70; fax 31-30-36; e-mail scimpex@cenatrin.bf; Pres. Lassiné Diawara.

UTILITIES

Electricity

Société Générale de Travaux et de Constructions Electriques (SOGETEL): Zone Industrielle, Gounghin, 01 BP 429, Ouagadougou 01; tel. 34-29-80; fax 34-25-70; e-mail sogetel@cenatrin.bf; internet www.cenatrin.bf/sogetel; transport and distribution of electricity.

Société Nationale Burkinabè d'Electricité (SONABEL): ave Nelson Mandela, 01 BP 54, Ouagadougou 01; tel. 30-61-00; fax 31-03-40; f. 1954; state-owned; partial privatization pending in 2003; production and distribution of electricity; Dir-Gen. Salif Kaboré.

Water

Office National de l'Eau et de l'Assainissement (ONEA): 01 BP 170, Ouagadougou 01; tel. 34-34-59; fax 34-33-97; e-mail onea@fasonet.bf; internet www.onea.bf; f. 1977; storage, purification and distribution of water; transferred to private management in 2001; Dir-Gen. Kouate Mamadou.

CO-OPERATIVES

Union des Coopératives Agricoles et Maraîchères du Burkina (UCOBAM): 01 BP 277, Ouagadougou 01; tel. 30-65-27; fax 30-65-28; e-mail ucobam@cenatrin.bf; f. 1968; comprises 8 regional co-operative unions (20,000 mems); production and marketing of fruit, vegetables, jams and conserves.

TRADE UNIONS

In 2001 there were more than 20 autonomous trade unions. The five trade-union syndicates were:

Confédération Générale du Travail Burkinabè (CGTB): Ouagadougou; f. 1988; confed. of several autonomous trade unions; Sec.-Gen. Tolé Sagnon.

Confédération Nationale des Travailleurs Burkinabè (CNTB): BP 445, Ouagadougou; f. 1972; Sec.-Gen. Laurent Ouédraogo; 10,000 mems.

Confédération Syndicale Burkinabè (CSB): Ouagadougou; f. 1974; mainly public service unions; Sec.-Gen. Roger Tapsoba.

Organisation Nationale des Syndicats Libres (ONSL): BP 99, Ouagadougou; f. 1960; 6,000 mems.

Union Syndicale des Travailleurs Burkinabè (USTB): BP 381, Ouagadougou; f. 1958; Sec.-Gen. Boniface Somdah; 35,000 mems in 45 affiliated orgs.

Transport

RAILWAY

At the end of 1991 there were some 622 km of track in Burkina Faso. A 105-km extension from Donsin to Ouagadougou was inaugurated in December of that year. Plans exist for the construction of an extension to the manganese deposits at Tambao.

SITARAIL—Transport Ferroviaire de Personnes et de Marchandises: rue Dioncolo, 01 BP 5699, Ouagadougou 01; tel. 31-07-35; fax 30-85-21; 67% owned by Groupe Bolloré, 15% state-owned, 15% owned by Govt of Côte d'Ivoire; national branch of SITARAIL (based in Abidjan, Côte d'Ivoire); responsible for operations on the railway line between Kaya, Ouagadougou and Abidjan (Côte d'Ivoire); Rep. in Burkina SOULEYMANE YAMÉOGO.

Société de Gestion du Patrimoine Ferroviaire du Burkina (SOPAFER—B): 01 BP 192, Ouagadougou 01; tel. 31-35-99; fax 31-35-94; railway network services; Dir-Gen. BRIGITTE-MARIE DAYAMBA.

ROADS

In 1999 there were an estimated 58,461 km of roads, including 10,469 km of classified roads; only around 3% of the total network, or 19% of the length of classified roads, was paved at that time. A major aim of current road projects is to improve transport links with other countries of the region. In 1999 a US $37m. project was begun to upgrade the road linking Ouagadougou with the Ghanaian border via the more isolated southern provinces.

Interafricaine de Transport et de Transit (IATT): 04 BP 8242, Ouagadougou 04; tel. 30-25-12; fax 30-37-04.

Société Africaine de Transit (SAT): 01 BP 4249, Ouagadougou 01; tel. 31-09-16.

Société Africaine de Transports Routiers (SATR): 01 BP 5298, Ouagadougou 01; tel. 34-08-62.

Société Nationale du Transit du Burkina (SNTB): 474 ave Bishop, 01 BP 1192, Ouagadougou 01; tel. 30-60-54; fax 30-85-21; f. 1977; 31% owned by Groupe SAGA (France); 12% state-owned; road haulage and warehousing; Dir-Gen. SEYDOU DIAKITÉ.

CIVIL AVIATION

There are international airports at Ouagadougou and Bobo-Dioulasso, 49 small airfields and 13 private airstrips. Ouagadougou airport handled an estimated 275,400 passengers and 5,880 metric tons of freight in 1999.

Air Burkina: ave Loudun, 01 BP 1459, Ouagadougou 01; tel. 30-76-76; fax 31-48-80; f. 1967 as Air Volta; privatized in Feb. 2001; 56% owned by Aga Khan Group; 14% state-owned; operates domestic and regional services; Dir MOHAMED GHELALA.

Tourism

Burkina Faso, which possesses some 2.8m. hectares of nature reserves, is considered to provide some of the best opportunities to observe wild animals in West Africa. Some big game hunting is also permitted. Several important cultural events are also held in Burkina Faso: the biennial pan-African film festival, FESPACO, is held in Ouagadougou, as is the biennial international exhibition of handicrafts, while Bobo-Dioulasso hosts the biennial week of national culture. In 1999 there were 218,000 foreign visitors. Receipts from tourism were estimated at 25,128m. francs CFA in 1998.

Office National du Tourisme Burkinabè (ONTB): ave Frobénius, BP 1318, Ouagadougou; tel. 31-19-59; fax 31-44-34; e-mail ontb@ontb.bf; internet www.ontb.bf; Dir-Gen. ISIDORE NABALOUM.

BURUNDI

Introductory Survey

Location, Climate, Language, Religion, Flag, Capital

The Republic of Burundi is a land-locked country lying on the eastern shore of Lake Tanganyika, in central Africa, a little south of the Equator. It is bordered by Rwanda to the north, by Tanzania to the south and east, and by the Democratic Republic of the Congo (formerly Zaire) to the west. The climate is tropical (hot and humid) in the lowlands, and cool in the highlands, with an irregular rainfall. The population is composed of three ethnic groups: the Hutu (85%), the Tutsi (14%) and the Twa (1%). The official languages are French and Kirundi, while Swahili is used, in addition to French, in commercial circles. More than 65% of the inhabitants profess Christianity, with the great majority of the Christians being Roman Catholics. A large minority still adhere to traditional animist beliefs. The national flag (proportions 3 by 5) consists of a white diagonal cross on a background of red (above and below) and green (hoist and fly), with a white circle, containing three green-edged red stars, in the centre. The capital is Bujumbura.

Recent History

Burundi (formerly Urundi) became part of German East Africa in 1899. In 1916, during the First World War, the territory was occupied by Belgian forces from the Congo (now the Democratic Republic of the Congo, DRC). Subsequently, as part of Ruanda-Urundi, it was administered by Belgium under a League of Nations mandate and later as a UN Trust Territory. Elections in September 1961, conducted under UN supervision, were won by the Union pour le progrès national (UPRONA), which had been formed in 1958 by Ganwa (Prince) Louis Rwagasore, the son of the reigning Mwami (King), Mwambutsa IV. As leader of UPRONA, Prince Rwagasore became Prime Minister later in the month, but was assassinated after only two weeks in office. He was succeeded by his brother-in-law, André Muhirwa. Internal self-government was granted in January 1962 and full independence on 1 July, when the two parts of the Trust Territory became separate states, as Burundi and Rwanda. Tensions between Burundi's two main ethnic groups, the Tutsi (traditionally the dominant tribe, despite representing a minority of the overall population) and the Hutu, escalated during 1965. Following an unsuccessful attempt by the Hutu to overthrow the Tutsi-dominated Government in October, nearly all the Hutu political élite were executed, eliminating any significant participation by the Hutu in Burundi's political life until the late 1980s (see below). In July 1966 the Mwami was deposed, after a reign of more than 50 years, by his son Charles, and the Constitution was suspended. In November Charles, now Mwami Ntare V, was himself deposed by his Prime Minister, Capt. (later Lt-Gen.) Michel Micombero, who declared Burundi a republic.

Several alleged plots against the Government in 1969 and 1971 were followed by an abortive coup in 1972, during which Ntare V was killed. Hutu activists were held responsible for the attempted coup, and this served as a pretext for the Tutsi to conduct a series of large-scale massacres of the rival tribe, in which, it was estimated, about 100,000 were killed; large numbers of the Hutu fled to neighbouring countries.

In 1972 Micombero began a prolonged restructuring of the executive, which resulted, in 1973, in the appointment of a seven-member Presidential Bureau, headed by himself. In July 1974 the Government introduced a new republican Constitution, which vested sovereignty in UPRONA, the sole legal political party. Micombero was elected Secretary-General of the party and re-elected for a seven-year presidential term.

On 1 November 1976 an army coup deposed Micombero, who died in exile in July 1983. The leader of the coup, Lt-Col (later Col) Jean-Baptiste Bagaza, was appointed President by the Supreme Revolutionary Council (composed of army officers), and a new Council of Ministers was formed. In October 1978 Bagaza abolished the post of Prime Minister. The first national congress of UPRONA was held in December 1979, and a party Central Committee, headed by Bagaza, was elected to take over the functions of the Supreme Revolutionary Council in January 1980. A new Constitution, adopted by national referendum in November 1981, provided for the establishment of a national assembly, to be elected by universal adult suffrage. The first legislative elections were held in October 1982. Having been re-elected President of UPRONA in July 1984, Bagaza, the sole candidate, was elected President of Burundi by direct suffrage in August, winning 99.63% of the votes cast.

On 3 September 1987 Bagaza was deposed in a military coup, led by Maj. Pierre Buyoya, who accused Bagaza of corruption. Buyoya immediately formed a Military Committee for National Salvation (CMSN) to administer the country, pending the appointment of a new President. The Constitution was suspended, and the National Assembly was dissolved. On 2 October Buyoya was inaugurated as President of the Third Republic.

In August 1988 tribal tensions erupted into violence in the north of the country when groups of Hutus, claiming Tutsi provocation, slaughtered hundreds of Tutsis in the towns of Ntega and Marangara. The Tutsi-dominated army was immediately dispatched to the region to restore order, and large-scale tribal massacres occurred. In October Buyoya announced changes to the Council of Ministers, including the appointment of a Hutu, Adrien Sibomana, to the newly restored post of Prime Minister. For the first time the Council included a majority of Hutu representatives. Buyoya subsequently established a Committee for National Unity (comprising an equal number of Tutsis and Hutus) to investigate the massacres and make recommendations for national reconciliation. Following the publication of the Committee's report, Buyoya announced plans to combat all forms of discrimination against the Hutu and to introduce new regulations to ensure equal opportunities in education, employment and in the armed forces. Nevertheless, political tension remained at a high level in 1989.

In May 1990, in response to a new draft charter on national unity, Buyoya announced plans to replace military rule with a 'democratic constitution under a one-party government'. A charter designed to reconcile the Tutsi and the Hutu was to be the subject of a referendum. In December, at an extraordinary national congress of UPRONA, the CMSN was abolished and its functions transferred to an 80-member Central Committee, with Buyoya as Chairman and with a Hutu, Nicolas Mayugi, as Secretary-General. At a referendum in February 1991 the draft charter on national unity was overwhelmingly approved, despite vociferous criticism from opposition groups. Later in the month a ministerial reorganization, whereby Hutus were appointed to 12 of the 23 government portfolios, was viewed with scepticism by political opponents. In March a commission was established to prepare a report on the democratization of political structures, in preparation for the drafting of a new constitution. The commission's report, presented in September, recommended the establishment of a multi-party parliamentary system, which was to operate in conjunction with a renewable five-year presidential mandate. The proposals received the support of more than 90% of the voters in a referendum held on 9 March 1992, and the new Constitution was promulgated on 13 March.

In an extensive ministerial reorganization in April 1992, seven ministers left the Government, while Buyoya relinquished the defence portfolio, and Hutus were appointed to 15 of the 25 portfolios. In the same month Buyoya approved legislation relating to the creation of new political parties in accordance with the provisions of the new Constitution. New political parties were to be obliged to demonstrate impartiality with regard to ethnic or regional origin, gender and religion, and were to refrain from militarization. In October Buyoya announced the creation of the National Electoral Preparatory Commission (NEPC), a 33-member body comprising representatives of the eight recognized political parties, together with administrative, judicial, religious and military officials. In early December Buyoya appointed a new 12-member technical commission, charged with drafting an electoral code and a communal law.

A presidential election, which took place on 1 June 1993, was won, with 64.8% of the votes cast, by Melchior Ndadaye, the candidate of the Front pour la démocratie au Burundi (FRODEBU), with the support of the Rassemblement du peuple burundien (RPB), the Parti du peuple and the Parti libéral;

Buyoya received 32.4% of the vote as the UPRONA candidate, with support from the Rassemblement pour la démocratie et le développement économique et social (RADDES) and the Parti social démocrate. Legislative elections for 81 seats in the National Assembly were conducted on 29 June. FRODEBU again emerged as the most successful party, with 71% of the votes and 65 of the seats in the new legislature. UPRONA, with 21.4% of the votes, secured the remaining 16 seats. Ndadaye, Burundi's first Hutu Head of State, assumed the presidency on 10 July. A Tutsi, Sylvie Kinigi, became Prime Minister, while the new Council of Ministers included a further six Tutsi representatives.

On 21 October 1993 more than 100 army paratroopers swiftly overwhelmed supporters of the Government and occupied the presidential palace and the headquarters of the national broadcasting company. Ndadaye and several other prominent Hutu politicians and officials were detained and subsequently killed by the insurgents, who later proclaimed François Ngeze, one of the few Hutu members of UPRONA and a minister in the Government of former President Buyoya, as head of a National Committee for Public Salvation (CPSN). While members of the Government sought refuge abroad and in the offices of foreign diplomatic missions in Bujumbura, the armed forces declared a state of emergency, closing national borders and the capital's airport. However, international condemnation of the coup, together with the scale and ferocity of renewed tribal violence (fuelled by reports of Tutsi-dominated army units seeking out and eliminating Hutu intellectuals), undermined support for the insurgents from within the armed forces, and precipitated the collapse of the CPSN, which was disbanded on 25 October. Kinigi ended the curfew, but remained in hiding and urged the deployment of an international force in Burundi to protect the civilian Government. On 28 October the UN confirmed that the Government had resumed control of the country. Ngeze and 10 coup leaders were arrested, while some 40 other insurgents were believed to have fled to Zaire (now the DRC). In December a commission of judicial inquiry was created to investigate the insurgency.

Meanwhile, in early November 1993 several members of the Government, including the Prime Minister, had left the French embassy (where they had remained throughout the uprising) with a small escort of French troops, and on 8 November Kinigi met with 15 of the 17 surviving ministers, in an attempt to address the humanitarian crisis arising from the massacre and displacement of hundreds of thousands of Burundians following the failed coup. On the same day the Constitutional Court officially recognized the presidential vacancy resulting from the murder of both Ndadaye and his constitutional successor, Giles Bimazubute, the Speaker of the National Assembly, and stated that presidential power should be exercised by the Council of Ministers, pending a presidential election, which was to be conducted within three months. However, the Minister of External Relations and Co-operation, Sylvestre Ntibantunganya (who succeeded Ndadaye as leader of FRODEBU), suggested that no electoral timetable should be considered before the resolution of internal security difficulties and the initiation of a comprehensive programme for the repatriation of refugees. In December Ntibantunganya was elected Speaker of the National Assembly. The foreign affairs portfolio was assumed by Jean-Marie Ngendahayo, previously Minister of Communications and Government Spokesman.

Meanwhile, in November 1993, following repeated requests by the Government for an international contribution to the protection of government ministers in Burundi, the Organization of African Unity (OAU)—now the African Union (AU, see p. 130)—agreed to the deployment of a 200-strong protection force (MIPROBU), to comprise civilian and military personnel, for a period of six months. In December opposition parties, including UPRONA and the RADDES, organized demonstrations in protest at the deployment of the 180-strong military contingent, scheduled for January 1994, claiming that it infringed Burundi's sovereignty. As a compromise, in March the Government secured a significant reduction in the size of the force. The mandate of the mission (comprising a military contingent of 47 and 20 civilian observers) was subsequently extended at three-monthly intervals.

In early January 1994 FRODEBU deputies in the National Assembly approved a draft amendment to the Constitution, allowing a President of the Republic to be elected by the National Assembly, in the event of the Constitutional Court's recognition of a presidential vacancy. UPRONA deputies, who had boycotted the vote, expressed concern that such a procedure represented election by indirect suffrage, in direct contravention of the terms of the Constitution. The continued boycott of the National Assembly by UPRONA deputies forced the postponement, on 10 January, of an attempt by FRODEBU deputies to elect their presidential candidate, the Minister of Agriculture and Livestock, Cyprien Ntaryamira. Three days later, none the less, following the successful negotiation of a political truce with opposition parties, Ntaryamira was elected President by the National Assembly. A Tutsi Prime Minister, Anatole Kanyenkiko, was appointed in early February, and the composition of a new multi-party Council of Ministers was subsequently agreed. During that month ethnic tension was renewed, as armed Hutu and Tutsi extremist factions attempted to establish territorial strongholds.

On 6 April 1994, returning from a regional summit meeting in Dar es Salaam, Tanzania, Ntaryamira was killed (together with the Ministers of Development, Planning and Reconstruction and of Communications) when the aircraft of the Rwandan President, Juvénal Habyarimana, in which he was travelling, was the target of a rocket attack above Kigali airport, Rwanda, and exploded on landing. Habyarimana, who was also killed, was widely acknowledged to have been the intended victim of the attack. In contrast to the violent political and tribal chaos that erupted in Rwanda (q.v.) in the aftermath of the death of Habyarimana, Burundians responded positively to appeals for calm issued by Ntibantunganya, the Speaker of the National Assembly, who, on 8 April, was confirmed (in accordance with the Constitution) as interim President for a three-month period. However, violent exchanges between Hutu extremist rebels and factions of the armed forces continued in April, claiming numerous victims. The failure of the warring militias to respond to an ultimatum, issued by Ntibantunganya in late April, to surrender all illegal arms by 1 May, resulted in the military bombardment of several rebel strongholds, forcing the withdrawal and surrender of a number of insurgents. Relations between the Government and the armed forces subsequently improved, and were further reinforced by the Prime Minister's announcement, in early May, that the Minister of State for the Interior and Public Security, Léonard Nyangoma, who had been accused of attempting to instigate civil unrest, had forfeited his position in the Council of Ministers, having failed to return from official business abroad.

Having discounted the possibility of organizing a general election, owing to security considerations, in June 1994 all major political parties joined lengthy negotiations to establish a procedure for the restoration of the presidency. The mandate of the interim President was extended for three months by the Constitutional Court in July, and by the end of August it had been decided that a new President would be elected by a broadly representative commission. A new power-sharing agreement, the Convention of Government, was announced on 10 September. Detailing the terms of government for a four-year transitional period (including the allocation of 45% of cabinet posts to opposition parties), it was incorporated into the Constitution on 22 September. The Convention also provided for the creation of a National Security Council (Conseil de sécurité nationale, CSN), which was formally inaugurated on 10 October. On 30 September the Convention elected Ntibantunganya to the presidency from a list of six candidates, including Charles Mukasi, the UPRONA leader. Ntibantunganya's appointment was endorsed by the National Assembly, and he was formally inaugurated on 1 October. Anatole Kanyenkiko was reappointed as Prime Minister, and a coalition Government was announced in accordance with the terms of the Convention. In December, however, UPRONA announced its intention to withdraw from the Government and from the legislature, following the election earlier that month of Jean Minani (a prominent FRODEBU member) to the post of Speaker of the National Assembly. UPRONA members accused Minani of having incited Hutu attacks against Tutsis in the aftermath of the October 1993 attempted coup. In January 1995 the political crisis was averted by agreement on a compromise FRODEBU candidate, Léonce Ngendakumana. Minani subsequently assumed the FRODEBU party leadership. UPRONA declared its willingness to rejoin the Government, but later in January Kanyenkiko resisted attempts by the UPRONA leadership to expel him from the party for having failed to comply with party demands for the withdrawal from the Government of all party members over the Minani affair. Two UPRONA ministers were subsequently dismissed from the Council of Ministers, in apparent retaliation, prompting Mukasi in mid-February to demand the resignation of the Prime Minister and to declare an indefinite general strike in support of this demand. Increased political opposition to Kanyenkiko forced the Prime Minister to acknowledge that he no longer commanded the necessary mandate to continue in office, and on 22 February Antoine Nduwayo, a UPRONA candidate selected in consultation with other opposition parties, was appointed Prime Minister by presidential decree. A new coalition Council of Ministers was announced on 1 March, but political stability was undermined immediately by the murder of the Hutu Minister of Energy and Mines, Ernest Kabushemeye.

Ethnic tension persisted in the second half of 1994, exacerbated by the scale and proximity of the violence in Rwanda and by the presence in Burundi of an estimated 200,000 Rwandan Hutu refugees. Ethnically-motivated atrocities became a daily occurrence in parts of the country (several prominent politicians and government officials were murdered), resulting in the imposition of a partial curfew in the capital in December. Fears that the security crisis in Burundi would develop into civil war were exacerbated in late 1994 by reports that the 30,000-strong Force pour la défense de la démocratie (FDD), the armed wing of Nyangoma's extremist Conseil national pour la défense de la démocratie (CNDD), was preparing for an armed struggle against the armed forces.

An escalation in the scale and frequency of incidents of politically- and ethnically-motivated violence during 1995 prompted renewed concern that the security crisis would precipitate a large-scale campaign of ethnic massacres similar to that in Rwanda during 1994. Government-sponsored military initiatives were concentrated in Hutu-dominated suburbs of Bujumbura and in the north-east, where an aggressive campaign was waged against the alleged insurgent activities of the Parti de libération du peuple hutu (PALIPEHUTU—a small, proscribed, Hutu opposition group based in Tanzania), resulting in the deaths of hundreds of Hutu civilians. The Government accused Hutu extremist militias of conducting an intimidating and violent programme of recruitment in the region. Anti-insurgency operations were intensified in June in several suburbs of the capital, where an estimated 2,000 troops sought to apprehend members of the FDD. It was reported that as many as 130 civilians were killed in the ensuing hostilities. Also in June a report published by the human rights organization Amnesty International claimed that national security forces in Burundi had collaborated with extremist Tutsi factions in the murder of thousands of Hutus since 1993. Increased security measures announced by Ntibantunganya in the same month included restrictions on a number of civil liberties. None the less, in late June the Minister of State in charge of External Relations and Co-operation, Jean-Marie Ngendahayo, resigned, expressing dissatisfaction at the Government's inability to guarantee the safety and basic rights of the population. Later that month a meeting of the OAU, convened in Addis Ababa, Ethiopia, concluded that some degree of military intervention in Burundi would be necessary should ethnic violence continue to escalate. (In April the Burundian Government had declined an OAU offer of military intervention in favour of increasing the number of MIPROBU personnel to 67.)

By early 1996 reports of atrocities perpetrated against both Hutu and Tutsi civilians by rogue elements of the Tutsi-led armed forces (including militias known as the *Sans Echecs*) and by extremist Hutu rebel groups had become almost commonplace in rural areas. It was believed that the capital had been effectively 'cleansed' of any significant Hutu presence by the end of 1995. In late December the UN Secretary-General petitioned the Security Council to sanction some form of international military intervention in Burundi to address the crisis. However, the Burundian Government remained vehemently opposed to a foreign military presence.

In early April 1996 representatives of the US Agency for International Development and the Humanitarian Office of the European Union (EU, see p. 199) visited Burundi. Their findings, which were severely critical of the administration's failure to reconcile the country's various ethnic and political interests within government, prompted the USA and the EU immediately to suspend aid to Burundi. Despite pledges by Ntibantunganya in late April 1996 to undertake comprehensive reforms of the security forces and the judiciary, violence continued to escalate, prompting the suspension of French military co-operation with Burundi at the end of May.

Representatives of some 13 political parties (including FRODEBU and UPRONA) participated in discussions conducted in

Mwanza, Tanzania, in April 1996, with mediation from the former President of Tanzania, Julius Nyerere. Talks resumed in Mwanza in early June; Mukasi, the UPRONA leader, with support from an informal coalition of seven smaller, predominantly Tutsi parties (the Rassemblement unitaire), accused FRODEBU deputies of seeking to abrogate the Convention of Government, a charge that was strenuously denied by FRODEBU following the talks. At a conference of regional powers in Arusha, Tanzania, in late June, it was reported that Ntibantunganya and Nduwayo had requested foreign intervention to protect government installations. By early July a regional technical commission to examine the request for 'security assistance' (comprising regional defence ministers, but not representatives of the Burundian armed forces) had convened in Arusha and had reached preliminary agreement, with UN support, for an intervention force, to comprise units of the Ugandan and Tanzanian armed forces and security officers from Kenya. Meanwhile, significant differences of interpretation with regard to the purpose and mandate of such a force had emerged between Ntibantunganya and Nduwayo (who suggested that the President was attempting to neutralize the country's military capability). At a mass rally in Bujumbura of Tutsi-dominated opposition parties, the Prime Minister joined Mukasi and other anti-Government figures in rejecting foreign military intervention. Some days later, however, full endorsement of the Arusha proposal for intervention was recorded by member nations of the OAU at a summit meeting convened in Yaoundé, Cameroon.

Political and ethnic enmities intensified still further when reports of a massacre of more than 300 Tutsi civilians at Bugendana, allegedly committed by Hutu extremists, including heavily armed Rwandan Hutu refugees, emerged shortly after the UN accused the Burundian authorities of collaborating with the Rwandan administration in a new initiative of (largely enforced) repatriation of Rwandan refugees in Burundi. While FRODEBU members made an urgent appeal for foreign military intervention to contain the increasingly violent civil and military reaction to these events, former President Bagaza urged civil resistance to foreign intervention; his appeal for a general strike in Bujumbura was partially observed. Meanwhile, students (with the support of the political opposition) began a second week of protests against regional military intervention, and demonstrated in support of demands for the removal of the country's leadership. On 23 July 1996 Ntibantunganya was forced to abandon an attempt to attend the funeral of the victims of the Bugendana massacre when mourners stoned the presidential helicopter. The following day, amid strong indications that UPRONA intended to join a number of smaller opposition parties that had already withdrawn from the Convention of Government, it was reported that Ntibantunganya had sought refuge in the US embassy building. Several government ministers and the Speaker of the National Assembly similarly sought refuge within the German embassy compound.

On 25 July 1996 the armed forces were extensively deployed in the capital in a military coup. A statement made by the Minister of National Defence, Lt-Col Firmin Sinzoyiheba, criticized the failure of the administration to safeguard national security, and announced the suspension of the National Assembly and all political activity, the imposition of a nationwide curfew and the closure of national borders and the airport at Bujumbura. Former President Buyoya was declared interim President of a transitional republic, and immediately sought to reassure former ministers and government officials that their safety would be guaranteed by the new regime. Ntibantunganya conveyed his refusal to relinquish office, but Nduwayo resigned, attributing his failure to effect national reconciliation principally to Ntibantunganya's ineffective leadership. In response to widespread external condemnation of the coup, Buyoya announced that a largely civilian government of national unity would be promptly installed, and that future negotiations with all Hutu groups would be considered. The forced repatriation of Rwandan Hutu refugees was halted with immediate effect.

Despite the appointment at the end of July 1996 of Pascal-Firmin Ndimira, a Hutu member of UPRONA, as Prime Minister, and an urgent attempt by Buyoya to obtain regional support, the leaders of Ethiopia, Kenya, Rwanda, Tanzania, Uganda and Zaire, meeting in Arusha, under OAU auspices, declared their intention to impose stringent economic sanctions against the new regime unless constitutional government was restored immediately. In early August the composition of a new 23-member, multi-ethnic Cabinet was announced. In mid-August Buyoya announced that an expanded transitional national assembly, incorporating existing elected deputies, would be inaugurated during September for a three-year period. A consultative council of elders was also to be established to oversee a period of broad political debate, during which time formal political activity would remain proscribed. Buyoya was formally inaugurated as President on 27 September.

Despite some evidence of violations, the regional sanctions that were imposed in early August 1996 resulted in the suspension of all significant trade and in Burundi's virtual economic isolation. However, the threat of a humanitarian crisis prompted the sanctions co-ordinating committee, meeting in Arusha in September, to authorize a relaxation of the embargo to facilitate the distribution of food and medical aid. An attempt by Buyoya later that month to secure the repeal of all sanctions by announcing an end to the ban on political parties and the restoration of the National Assembly was received with scepticism by opponents, in view of the continued suspension of the Constitution and Buyoya's refusal to address preconditions to the ending of sanctions that required the organization of unconditional peace negotiations. In October Buyoya agreed to enter into negotiations with the CNDD, but a subsequent meeting of regional leaders in Arusha decided that sanctions should be maintained until evidence emerged of constructive progress in the negotiations. This prompted the Burundian Government to withdraw the offer of unconditional dialogue with the CNDD as long as sanctions remained in place. Meanwhile, in early October some 37 deputies had attended the formal reopening of the National Assembly, which was boycotted by the majority of FRODEBU deputies. (It was reported that 22 of the Assembly's original 81 deputies had been murdered during the recent hostilities, while a large number remained in exile or in hiding.)

Reports emerged that the armed forces were targeting Hutus (thousands were estimated to have been killed since the coup), in an attempt to safeguard rural and border regions for Tutsi communities, to which the CNDD and other Hutu militia retaliated with attacks against military installations near Bujumbura, as well as against Tutsi civilians. A UN report on the causes of the 1993 coup, published in August, implicated two of Buyoya's military leaders, who were subsequently dismissed. By late 1996 the military action in eastern Zaire had led to the repatriation of 30,000 Burundians and had severely weakened FDD fighting capacity, although some activists continued the fight from Tanzania. A report issued by the office of the UN High Commissioner for Refugees (UNHCR) in December estimated that more than 1,100 individuals (predominantly Hutu refugees) had been killed by the armed forces during October and November alone. Also in December Amnesty International denounced what it termed a 'policy of systematic extermination of a section of population' on the part of the armed forces, alleging that the army had massacred as many as 500 Hutu civilians in Butaganza, in the north-west, earlier in the month. Such reports were denied by the Burundian Government. In January 1997 UNHCR reported that the army had massed more than 100,000 (mainly Hutu) civilians in camps, as part of a 'regroupment' scheme, which the authorities claimed to be an initiative to protect villagers in areas of rebel activity. By mid-1997, according to government figures, some 200,000 civilians had been 'regrouped' in about 50 camps, while non-governmental organizations variously estimated the number of civilians affected at 350,000–500,000.

The security situation was, meanwhile, further troubled by the return of CNDD fighters among large numbers of Hutu refugees effectively expelled by the Tutsi-led rebellion in eastern Zaire, as well as by the enforced repatriation of refugees from Tanzania. In January 1997 Buyoya condemned the killing of some 120 Hutu refugees who had apparently been expelled from Tanzania, accused of fomenting unrest in camps there. In May UNHCR appealed to bordering countries to cease repatriating Burundian refugees, owing to renewed massacres, notably in the 'regroupment' centres.

The trial began in May 1997 of some 79 military officers accused of involvement in the October 1993 coup attempt. In May 1999 five of those accused were sentenced to death and a number of others received prison terms; however, all of the senior officers, including Bikomagu, were acquitted. Meanwhile, at the end of July 1997 it was reported that six people convicted of involvement in acts of genocide perpetrated in 1993 had been executed. During July–August 1997 the Burundian courts issued 30 death sentences in relation to such crimes; 10 defendants were sentenced to life imprisonment, and 19 to 20 years' custody.

Six ministers were replaced in a reorganization of Ndimira's Government in May 1997, and in August Ambroise Niyonsaba was allocated the new post of Minister of the Peace Process. Civil unrest continued later that year, and on 1 January 1998 an attack on Bujumbura airport by more than 1,000 Hutu rebels resulted in at least 250 deaths. Similar attacks, although on a smaller scale, continued during early 1998. On 18 February the second stage of the inter-Burundian peace talks was held. The discussions, which had been delayed following the death of the Minister of Defence in a helicopter crash, were attended by representatives of the Government, the political parties and the National Assembly, and prominent civilians. The CNDD, however, suspended its participation in protest at human rights violations on the part of the Government. Following the announcement in late February that a regional summit, held in Kampala, Uganda, had voted to maintain the sanctions on Burundi, President Buyoya announced the impending repeal of travel restrictions that had been applied to former Presidents Bagaza and Ntibantunganya, and to the Speaker of the National Assembly, Ngendakumana. In mid-March the courts dismissed a case against Ngendakumana, on charges of genocide.

Following negotiations between the Government and the National Assembly concerning the expiry of FRODEBU's electoral mandate in June 1998, Buyoya and Ngendakumana publicly signed a political accord, and a new transitional Constitution was promulgated on 6 June, replacing the law (enabling him to rule by decree) enacted by Buyoya after he took power in July 1996. The new charter provided for institutional reforms, including the creation of two vice-presidencies to replace the office of Prime Minister, the enlargement of the National Assembly from 81 to 121 seats, and the creation of a seven-member Constitutional Court, which was sworn in on 24 June 1998. In accordance with the transitional Constitution, Buyoya was inaugurated as President on 11 June. On the following day the two Vice-Presidents were appointed: Frédérique Bavuginyumvira, a senior member of FRODEBU, who was allocated responsibility for political and administrative affairs, and Mathias Sinamenye (a Tutsi and hitherto the Governor of the Central Bank), with responsibility for economic and social issues. A new 22-member Council of Ministers, sworn in on 13 June, included 13 Hutus and eight Tutsis. The newly enlarged National Assembly, which was inaugurated on 18 July, incorporated nine representatives from smaller political parties (with four further seats remaining provisionally vacant), together with 27 civilian representatives and 21 new representatives of FRODEBU to replace those who had been killed or had fled into exile. On 22 July the inter-Burundian peace talks were adjourned at the request of the Government, as the parties were unable to reach agreement on the structure of the negotiations.

Meanwhile, little substantive progress was made in regional efforts to bring about direct peace talks between the Buyoya Government and its opponents. Consultations in Arusha in December 1996 were attended by representatives of the Buyoya administration, FRODEBU, the CNDD, PALIPEHUTU and other organizations. However, the Government's stipulation that fighting must be brought to a formal halt prior to any negotiations effectively precluded direct contacts. The first of a series of national discussions on the peace process began in January 1997, attended by academics, religious leaders, politicians and representatives of civil society. However, prominent political organizations, notably FRODEBU, refused to attend the talks. Buyoya attended the fourth Arusha summit meeting on the Burundi conflict in April. The leaders of the Great Lakes countries agreed to ease economic sanctions in the interest of alleviating conditions for the civilian population. The full revocation of sanctions was made dependent on the opening of direct, unconditional peace talks between the Burundian Government and opposition.

Initial optimism that inter-party discussions, commencing in Arusha in August 1997, would achieve progress in ending the political crisis diminished as the Buyoya Government became increasingly hostile to the mediation of Nyerere, claiming him to be biased in favour of the opposition. After it became evident that the sanctions would not be revoked immediately upon the opening of negotiations, the Buyoya Government announced that it would not be attending the Arusha talks, stating that it required more time to prepare, and the session was subsequently abandoned. Nyerere openly condemned the stance of the Buyoya regime, appealing for wider international assistance in resolving the crisis. A meeting of regional leaders, convened (in Buyoya's absence) in the Tanzanian capital in early September, reaffirmed its support for Nyerere's mediation, criticized the Burundian Government for its intransigence, and resolved to maintain all existing sanctions.

In May 1998 Nyerere conducted discussions with Burundian political leaders, in preparation for the peace negotiations, which commenced in mid-June in Arusha. At the talks, which were attended by 17 groupings involved in the conflict, it was agreed that the next round of discussions would take place on 20 July, and that all factions would suspend hostilities on that date. The Government, however, expressed reservations concerning the cease-fire, citing the need to maintain state security. The FDD, which had rejected the political leadership of the CNDD and subsequently became a separate rebel movement, also refused to accept the cease-fire. It was agreed that the negotiations were to continue for three months, and that commissions would be established to negotiate each of the main issues of contention. At the July discussions, however, little progress was made. Prior to the third round of negotiations, division emerged in UPRONA between those who supported Mukasi's opposition to the Arusha talks and those who were prepared to negotiate with the Hutu opposition. In October some moderate members of the UPRONA central committee elected a rival Chairman, Dr Luc Rukingama, the Minister of Information and a supporter of Buyoya. Mukasi was arrested in August, following outspoken criticism of the Government. The commissions were duly established during further discussions in October and January 1999.

At a regional summit meeting, which took place in Arusha in January 1999, following an appeal from the UN Security Council earlier in the month, regional Heads of State voted to suspend the economic sanctions, in recognition of the progress made in the peace negotiations, although they emphasized that the eventual lifting of the sanctions would be dependent on the progress made in the peace talks. In May Buyoya announced his proposals for reconciliation; these included a 10-year transitional period during which he would occupy the presidency for the first five years and a Hutu representative would assume the post for the second five years. The plan also envisaged the extension of the National Assembly to include Hutu rebel factions, the creation of a senate, the establishment of communal police forces, to resolve the issue of Tutsi-dominated defence and security forces, and the establishment of a national truth commission. Buyoya's opponents dismissed the proposals, citing his failure to honour his commitment to return the country swiftly to civilian rule in 1996 and the absence of any reference to elections in his plan. A round of discussions took place in Arusha in July; Nyerere criticized the lack of progress achieved at the negotiations, and the failure of the commissions to reach agreement. The absence from the negotiations of the two most significant rebel movements, the FDD and an armed wing of PALIPEHUTU, known as Forces nationales de libération (FNL), was also viewed as a major impediment to agreement on a peace plan. (The CNDD had rejoined the discussions.) Further talks at Arusha in September were impeded by the escalation of violence throughout the country, particularly around Bujumbura. Subsequent discussions were postponed owing to the death of Nyerere in mid-October. All the participating parties expressed their commitment to the process, and nine organizations, including FRODEBU and UPRONA, created a movement for peace and solidarity, the Convergence nationale pour la paix et réconciliation (CNPR), which proposed that negotiations continue on neutral territory, owing to the alleged role of Tanzania in sheltering Hutu rebels. In December regional Heads of State, meeting in Arusha, nominated the former President of South Africa, Nelson Mandela, as the new mediator of the peace negotiations.

Unrest continued throughout 1999 and increased in the second half of the year. The escalation of Hutu-led attacks around the capital led to the alleged rearming of Tutsi militias by the Tutsi-dominated security forces. A further response to increased Hutu rebel activity was the enforced relocation of more than 320,000 Hutus into 'regroupment' camps. The Government claimed that the camps provided protection for the civilian population and would prevent members from seeking shelter in the community. However, the UN, the USA and the EU all expressed concern at the Government's enforced 'regroupment' of Hutu civilians in these camps, which lacked basic supplies and medical assistance. In mid-October, following an ambush in which two UN aid workers were killed attempting to inspect a 'regroupment' camp, the UN announced that it was to restrict its operations and confine its staff to Bujumbura.

In June 1999 a new penal code was adopted by the National Assembly; the code, which entered into effect on 1 January 2000, protected civil rights and liberties, and introduced controls to prohibit torture and reduce the length of detention. In January 2000 a major cabinet reorganization was effected. Peace negotiations (the first to be attended by Mandela) resumed in Arusha in late February. Mandela criticized Tutsi domination of public office and urged equal representation of Hutu and Tutsi in the armed forces, while also denouncing Hutu rebel attacks on civilians. At a further round of discussions, which commenced in Arusha in late March, agreement was reached on draft proposals for a new ethnically-balanced armed force. (Nevertheless, government forces continued attacks against Hutu rebel positions, prompting fierce fighting south of Bujumbura.) In April Mandela visited Burundi for the first time, meeting government and militia leaders. Following a further meeting with Buyoya in Johannesburg, South Africa, in June, Mandela announced that the Burundian President had agreed to ensure equal representation of Hutu and Tutsi in the armed forces and the closure of 'regroupment' camps by the end of July.

In July 2000 the leader of the FDD, Jean-Bosco Ndayikengurukiye, for the first time accepted an invitation by Mandela to participate in the peace negotiations. In the same month the drafting of a peace accord was finalized; the agreement stipulated the terms for the establishment of a transitional government for a period of three years, the integration of former Hutu rebels into the armed forces, and the creation of an electoral system that would ensure power-sharing between the Tutsi and the Hutu. At a summit meeting, which was attended by several regional Heads of State in Arusha, negotiating groups were presented with the draft peace agreement, which included compromise proposals on unresolved issues. However, the FDD demanded the release by the authorities of political prisoners, the fulfilment of the pledge to dismantle the 'regroupment' camps, and bilateral negotiations with the armed forces, as a precondition to the cessation of hostilities. (The FNL had again failed to attend the discussions.) On 28 August the peace agreement was formally endorsed by representatives of the Government, the National Assembly, seven Hutu political associations and seven Tutsi parties. The remaining three Tutsi groups that had attended the previous negotiations subsequently signed the accord at cease-fire discussions, which took place in Nairobi, Kenya, in late September, following assurances by Mandela that measures would be taken to ensure that the Hutu rebels cease hostilities. At the same time an Implementation and Monitoring Committee, comprising representatives of the negotiating parties, and international and civil society representatives, was established. Following the conclusion of these discussions, a statement was issued demanding that the FDD and FNL suspend rebel activity and sign the peace agreement.

In late 2000 negotiations on the establishment of power-sharing structures continued. In January 2001 14 of the 19 signatories of the peace accord agreed on the composition of a new National Assembly, which would allocate Hutu parties 60% and Tutsi 40% representation in the legislature. Six candidates for the transitional presidency had emerged; however, the negotiating groups had failed to agree to return Buyoya to the office. Hostilities between government troops and Hutu rebels continued, and at the end of February the FNL launched an offensive on the northern outskirts of Bujumbura, which resulted in some 50,000 civilians fleeing to the centre of the capital. Government forces had regained control of Bujumbura by early March, but heavy fighting continued in regions outlying the capital. Later that month FDD forces launched a major attack against the principal town of Gitega, 100 km east of Bujumbura, which was repelled by government troops. On 18 April, while Buyoya was attending peace negotiations with the FDD leadership in Gabon, Tutsi army officers seized control of the state radio station in Bujumbura and announced that the Government had been overthrown. Troops loyal to Buyoya rapidly suppressed the coup attempt, and about 40 members of the armed forces were subsequently arrested in connection with the uprising.

At the end of June 2001 Mandela announced that a regional summit meeting was to be convened in Arusha on 23 July, in an effort to resolve the impasse in the peace process. On 22 July disaffected members of the armed forces staged an abortive coup attempt, kidnapping a senior military officer and endeavouring to seize the central prison in Bujumbura (where the instigators of the failed coup in April were in detention). Troops loyal to Buyoya counter-attacked the rebels, killing three and arresting many others. Nevertheless, the peace summit of regional Heads of State, chaired by Mandela, proceeded as scheduled, and the signatory groups to the Arusha accord finally reached agreement on the nature of the transitional leadership. A new multi-party transitional government, according the Hutu and Tutsi ethnic groups balanced representation, was to be installed on 1 November. The Secretary-General of FRODEBU, Domitien Ndayizeye, was nominated to the vice-presidency of the transitional administration. Buyoya was to continue in the office of President for 18 months (from 1 November), after which time he was to transfer the office to Ndayizeye. It was envisaged that legislative and presidential elections would take place in 2004. However, the FDD and the FNL persisted in rejecting the peace accord and announced that they would continue hostilities against the transitional authorities, while one of the principal Tutsi opposition parties, the Parti pour le redressement national (PARENA), refused to join the proposed new government.

Following further negotiations in Arusha and in Pretoria, South Africa, in early October 2001, agreement was reached on the composition of the new 26-member transitional Government. FRODEBU and UPRONA were the most dominant parties in the new power-sharing administration, while portfolios were allocated to a further 13 parties that had signed the Arusha agreement. (In total, Hutus received 14 of the 26 ministerial posts.) On 29 October a transitional Constitution, which was drafted by a technical law commission and included principles incorporated in the previous Constitution of 1992 and the Arusha peace accord, was formally adopted by the National Assembly. The new transitional Constitution provided for the establishment of an upper legislative chamber, the Senate, and four new commissions to assist in the peace and reconciliation process. Former combatants belonging to political movements were to be integrated into the armed and security forces during the transitional period. Also at the end of October the South African Government dispatched troops to Burundi as part of a proposed 700-member contingent, in an effort, initiated by Mandela, to enforce national security and support the transitional authorities. In a reversal to the peace efforts, however, the FDD had divided, with the emergence of a new faction, led by Jean-Pierre Nkurunziza, which commanded the support of most of the movement's combatants.

On 1 November 2001 the newly established transitional Government was officially installed, as scheduled. However, the FNL continued to launch attacks on the outskirts of Bujumbura, despite the deployment of the South African troops. In January 2002 the nomination to the National Assembly of a number of deputies, representing civil society and 14 of the political parties that had signed the peace agreement, was endorsed by the Constitutional Court. (FRODEBU and UPRONA retained their seats in the chamber.) Jean Minani, the Chairman of FRODEBU, was subsequently elected Speaker of the National Assembly. At the end of that month the Constitutional Court approved the establishment of a 51-member Senate.

Efforts to bring about a cease-fire in the civil conflict continued, with a series of meetings in Pretoria in February 2002, which were attended by representatives of the Government and armed forces, and both factions of the FDD (but not by the FNL). In March a further regional summit meeting was convened in Dar es Salaam, which the FNL and Nkurunziza's FDD faction again boycotted. In response to the continued lack of progress in peace efforts, FRODEBU issued a statement in April condemning the Government's failure to suppress the rebel militia. The South African Deputy Prime Minister, Jacob Zuma (who had replaced Mandela as the principal mediator), hosted a new series of consultations between the militia groups and the Burundi Government in Pretoria later that month. However, both the FNL and Nkurunziza's faction failed to participate, and Nkurunziza subsequently announced his opposition to Zuma's involvement in the cease-fire process. Further discussions between government and rebel delegations regarding the implementation of a cease-fire were scheduled to take place in Dar es Salaam in August. Early that month, following an attempt to remove the FNL 'hardline' leader, Agathon Rwasa, from his post, the movement divided: a new faction, led by Alain Mugabarabona, emerged, while Rwasa remained in control of most of the combatants. The peace negotiations, which commenced on 12 August, were attended for the first time by Mugabarabona's FNL faction and both FDD factions. At the end of that month, however, renewed fighting between FNL supporters and government troops was reported on the outskirts of Bujumbura. In early September it was reported that government forces had massacred a large number of civilians during an operation to suppress rebel activity in the central town of Gitega.

A summit meeting on Burundi (attended by regional Presidents), which was convened in Dar es Salaam on 7 October 2002, resulted in a cease-fire agreement between the Government and the smaller factions of the FDD and FNL. Negotiations with the main FDD faction continued, amid hostilities between government and rebel forces in central and northern Burundi. The authorities placed Bagaza (now the leader of PARENA) under house arrest, on suspicion of involvement with several attacks in Bujumbura. Also in November Maj.-Gen. Vincent Niyungeko, hitherto Chief of Staff of the armed forces, became the new Minister of Defence.

On 3 December 2002, following mediation from Uganda and South Africa, the Government finally reached a cease-fire agreement with the FDD, which was scheduled to enter into effect at the end of that month. Under the Arusha agreement of August 2000, the rebel factions were to be reconstituted as political parties, while Buyoya was to relinquish the presidency to Ndayizeye at the end of April 2003. However, the cease-fire agreement was not imposed at the end of December 2002, owing to delays in the arrival of observers from the AU. Hostilities between government and FDD forces continued, particularly in Gitega, and Nkurunziza, attributing responsibility for the failure to implement the accord to the Government, suspended further discussions. In early 2003 it was reported that some 60,000 civilians had fled the region in response to the heavy fighting. In late February the AU Cease-fire Observer Mission, comprising 35 monitors (from Burkina Faso, Mali, Togo and Tunisia), arrived in Bujumbura, with a mandate to monitor the peace agreement. In late April the first 100 members of an AU peace-keeping force arrived in Burundi; the contingent (which was expected to number about 3,000) was to assist in the enforcement of the cease-fire between the Government and the rebel factions. Despite the reported reluctance of Buyoya to relinquish the presidency, Ndayizeye was officially inaugurated as President on 30 April, thereby improving the prospects for sustained peace. On 5 May Ndayizeye appointed a representative of Mugabarabona's FNL faction and Ndayikengurukiye's FDD faction to the transitional Council of Ministers, as part of a government reorganization.

The cross-border movement of vast numbers of refugees, provoked by regional ethnic and political violence, has dominated recent relations with Rwanda, Tanzania and the DRC (formerly Zaire), and has long been a matter of considerable concern to the international aid community. In late 1993, following the abortive coup by factions of the Tutsi-dominated armed forces (see above), ethnic violence erupted on a massive scale throughout the country, resulting in the death of some 150,000 and the displacement of a further 800,000 civilians. Limited relief resources were overburdened in April 1994 by the exodus into Burundi of thousands of Rwandans, and by the repatriation of vast numbers of Burundians from refugee camps in Rwanda, as a result of the political violence and accompanying massacres following the death of President Habyarimana. At 31 December 1996, following a programme of forced repatriation in July of that year, the refugee population in Burundi finally declined to less than 1,000. (At that time some 882,900 internally displaced Burundians and 71,031 returnees from Tanzania were of concern to UNHCR.)

The uprising by Laurent-Désiré Kabila's Alliance des forces démocratiques pour la libération du Congo-Zaïre (AFDL) in eastern Zaire in January 1997 resulted in the return of large numbers of refugees to Burundi, reportedly undermining the operations from Zaire of large numbers of FDD combatants. Moreover, the seizure of power by the AFDL in May was welcomed by the Buyoya regime, which moved to forge close relations with Kabila's DRC. In April 1998 Burundi, the DRC and Uganda agreed to establish a combined police force to provide security along their common borders. Burundi initially denied any involvement in the civil war that commenced in the DRC in August, but by May 1999 some 3,000 Burundian troops were reported to be stationed in the east of the country, with the aim of destroying FDD camps. (The FDD has supported the DRC Government in the civil war and has used the conflict as an opportunity to regroup and rearm.) In June the DRC instituted proceedings against Burundi, together with Rwanda and Uganda, at the International Court of Justice (in The Hague, Netherlands), accusing them of acts of armed aggression in contravention of the terms of both the UN Charter and the Charter of the OAU. In early February 2001, however, the DRC abandoned proceedings against Burundi and Rwanda. In January 2002 the Burundian Government made a formal commitment to withdraw all troops (reported to number about 1,000) from the DRC, while the DRC authorities pledged to end their alliance with the FDD. At September the number of refugees in Burundi was estimated at 27,896, of whom 26,670 were from the DRC.

Meanwhile, the continued presence of large numbers of Burundian refugees in Tanzania, and increasingly strong accusations on the part of the Buyoya Government that Tanzania was supporting the Hutu rebellion, prompted tension between the two countries in mid-1997. These allegations were strenuously denied by the Tanzanian Government, which stated that it would never allow the use of refugee camps on its territory for military training. Mutual suspicion was exacerbated by Tanzania's refusal to allow a representative of the Buyoya regime to take the position of chargé d'affaires at the Burundian embassy in Dar es Salaam. In late August Tanzania announced that it had placed its armed forces on alert, stating that Burundian forces were mobilizing near the border in preparation for an invasion of the refugee camps. Meanwhile, the Buyoya Government's assertions that Nyerere was unduly biased in his role as mediator in the Burundian conflict further strained bilateral ties. In late 1997 Burundian allegations that the Tanzanian Government was involved in cross-border raids by Hutu militias, based in Tanzania, adversely affected relations, and in November there were reports of clashes between troops on the Tanzanian–Burundian border. In the same month Burundi's ambassador-designate to Tanzania was ordered to assume control of the Burundian embassy in Dar es Salaam, which was occupied by members of the CNDD and FRODEBU, but was arrested by the Tanzanian authorities and expelled. In 1998 bilateral relations improved slightly, and in July Tanzania agreed to the reopening of the Burundian embassy. Relations appeared to improve further in early 1999 and, following a meeting of the Burundian and Tanzanian ministers of foreign affairs, it was announced that a tripartite commission was to be established (with representatives from Burundi, Tanzania and UNHCR) to investigate allegations that armed militia groups had used Tanzania as a base from which to launch attacks on Burundi. Exchanges of fire between members of the Tanzanian armed forces and Burundian rebels on the border between the two countries were reported in September 2000. In late 2001 Tanzania denied further accusations by the Government of Burundi that Burundian rebels were operating from Tanzanian territory. Although some 26,000 refugees were repatriated to Burundi during the first nine months of 2002, with hostilities in Burundi continuing, about 512,000 remained in Tanzania at September.

Government

Following the coup of 25 July 1996, the Constitution of March 1992 was suspended. A peace agreement, which was signed by representatives of the incumbent Government, the National Assembly and 17 political groupings on 28 August 2000, provided for the installation of a transitional administration, in which power-sharing between the Hutu and Tutsi ethnic groups was guaranteed (see Recent History). A transitional Constitution, which was drafted by a technical law commission and included principles incorporated in the 1992 Constitution and the peace accord, was formally adopted on 29 October 2001. In accordance with the new Constitution, a transitional multiparty Government was installed on 1 November 2001. Executive power was vested in the President, who was empowered to appoint the Council of Ministers. The incumbent Tutsi President remained in office for the first 18 months of a three-year transitional period; under the peace agreement, he then transferred the office to the Hutu Vice-President on 30 April 2003. The transitional Constitution vested legislative power in the 121-member National Assembly (which included representatives of civil society and most of the political parties that had signed the peace agreement) and an upper chamber, the 51-member Senate.

For the purposes of local government, Burundi comprises 15 provinces (administered by civilian governors), each of which is divided into districts and further subdivided into communes.

Defence

The total strength of the armed forces in August 2002 was 45,500, comprising an army of an estimated 40,000 (including an air wing of 200), and a paramilitary force of an estimated 5,500 gendarmes (including a 50-strong marine police force). In

February 2003 some 35 observers from the African Union (AU, see p. 130) arrived in Burundi, with a mandate to monitor a cease-fire agreement (which had been scheduled to enter into effect at the end of December 2002, although hostilities continued). In April 2003 the first 100 members of an AU peace-keeping force arrived in Burundi; the contingent (which was expected to number about 3,000) was to assist in the enforcement of the cease-fire between the Government and the rebel factions. The power-sharing agreement of August 2000 provided for the establishment of a new army, comprising equal proportions of government forces and former rebel combatants. Military expenditure for 2001 was estimated at 44,200m. Burundian francs (equivalent to 29.9% of total expenditure).

Economic Affairs

In 2001, according to estimates by the World Bank, Burundi's gross national income (GNI), measured at average 1999–2001 prices, was US $692m., equivalent to $100 per head (or $590 per head on an international purchasing-power parity basis). During 1990–2001, it was estimated, the population increased at an average annual rate of 2.2% annually, while gross domestic product (GDP) per head declined, in real terms, at an average of 3.4% per year. Overall GDP declined, in real terms, at an average annual rate of 1.3% in 1990–2001; growth in 2001 was 3.2%.

Agriculture (including forestry and fishing) contributed an estimated 39.5% of GDP in 2001, according to the IMF. An estimated 90.2% of the labour force were employed in the sector at mid-2001. The principal cash crops are coffee (which accounted for an estimated 58.1% of export earnings in 2001) and tea. The main subsistence crops are cassava and sweet potatoes. Although Burundi is traditionally self-sufficient in food crops, population displacement as a result of the political crisis resulted in considerable disruption in the sector. The livestock-rearing sector was also severely affected by the civil war. During 1990–2001, according to the World Bank, agricultural GDP declined at an average annual rate of 0.4%; growth in 2001 was 3.7%.

Industry (comprising mining, manufacturing, construction and utilities) engaged 21.8% of the employed labour force in 1991 and contributed an estimated 19.0% of GDP in 2001. Industrial GDP decreased at an average annual rate of 1.7% in 1990–2001, although growth of 16.5% was recorded in 2001.

Mining and power engaged 0.1% of the employed labour force in 1990 and contributed an estimated 1.1% of GDP in 2001. Gold (alluvial), tin, tungsten and columbo-tantalite are mined in small quantities, although much activity has hitherto been outside the formal sector. Burundi has important deposits of nickel (estimated at 5% of world reserves), vanadium and uranium. In addition, petroleum deposits have been discovered. The GDP of the mining sector increased at an average annual rate of 3.4% in 1997–2001, according to IMF estimates; growth in 2001 was an estimated 14.3%.

Manufacturing engaged 1.2% of the employed labour force in 1990 and contributed an estimated 8.8% of GDP in 2001. The sector consists largely of the processing of agricultural products (coffee, cotton, tea and the extraction of vegetable oils). A number of small enterprises also produce beer, flour, cement, footwear and textiles. Manufacturing GDP increased at an average annual rate of 2.5% in 1997–2001, according to IMF estimates. Manufacturing GDP increased by 3.2% in 2000 and remained constant in 2001.

Energy is derived principally from hydroelectric power (an estimated 38.6% of electricity consumed in 2001 was imported). Peat is also exploited as an additional source of energy. Imports of refined petroleum products comprised 11.7% of the value of imports in 2000.

The services sector contributed an estimated 41.5% of GDP in 2001, but engaged only 4.4% of the employed labour force in 1990. According to the World Bank, the GDP of the services sector declined at an average annual rate of 0.5% in 1990–2001, but increased by 3.6% in 2001.

In 2001 Burundi recorded an estimated trade deficit of US $69.2m., and there was a deficit of $34.4m. on the current account of the balance of payments. In 2001 the principal source of imports (15.5%) was Belgium; other important suppliers in that year were Saudi Arabia, France and Kenya. The principal market for exports in 2001 (31.0%) was the United Kingdom; other important markets were Belgium, Germany, Kenya and Rwanda. The main imports in 2000 were machinery and transport equipment, basic manufactures, food and livestock, chemicals and mineral fuels (principally petroleum products). The principal exports in 2001 were coffee, tea, and hides and skins.

In 2001 the budget deficit was 28,400m. Burundian francs, equivalent to 5.2% of GDP. Burundi's external debt at the end of 2000 was US $1,100m., of which $1,028m. was long-term public debt. In that year the cost of debt-servicing was equivalent to 37.2% of revenue from the export of goods and services. Total outstanding debt at the end of 2001 was estimated at $1,046m. (including $116m. of arrears). The annual rate of inflation averaged 14.3% in 1990–2001. Consumer prices increased by an average of 9.2% in 2001, but declined by 1.2% in 2002.

Burundi, with its neighbours Rwanda and the Democratic Republic of the Congo, is a member of the Economic Community of the Great Lakes Countries (CEPGL, see p. 340). Burundi is also a member of the Common Market for Eastern and Southern Africa (COMESA, see p. 162), and of the International Coffee Organization (see p. 336).

Burundi's acute economic decline after 1993, owing to the severe political upheaval and accompanying population displacement, was further exacerbated by the regional economic sanctions imposed following the coup of July 1996. In addition, the decline in the international price of coffee (the principal export crop) resulted in substantial losses in the sector from 1997. By early 1999, when sanctions were revoked, a sustained decline in government revenue had resulted in the depletion of official reserves, and the Government was obliged to borrow heavily in order to meet its financing requirements. As a result, domestic and foreign debts had accumulated at an unsustainable level, and Burundi was defaulting on its debt-servicing obligations, while smuggling and tax evasion were largely unchecked. In May 2000 the IMF and the World Bank announced the resumption of international credit to Burundi. Following the signing of a peace agreement in August of that year (see Recent History), a transitional power-sharing Government was installed in November 2001. Economic activity began to recover in 2001, and inflation declined dramatically (reflecting an increase in basic foodstuffs). GDP grew in 2002, mainly as a result of favourable weather conditions, and was expected to increase in 2003. Although hostilities continued in part of the country, further agreements (including one signed with a major rebel group in December 2002) improved prospects for reaching a permanent peace settlement. In October the IMF approved further emergency post-conflict assistance for Burundi to support financial reforms. The Government's economic programme for 2002–03, which was designed to promote national reconciliation and private-sector development, laid emphasis on fiscal restraint, the continued policy of a flexible exchange rate, and the restoration of profitability in the coffee sector (principally through reduced producer prices). Although the country remained dependent on large-scale external assistance, prospects for economic development were expected to improve when relief on external debt was finally granted by bilateral creditors in 2003. The full restoration of national stability was essential for the resumption of private-sector investment.

Education

Education is provided free of charge. Kirundi is the language of instruction in primary schools, while French is used in secondary schools. Primary education, which is officially compulsory, begins at seven years of age and lasts for six years. Secondary education begins at the age of 13 and lasts for up to seven years, comprising a first cycle of four years and a second of three years. In 1999/2000, according to UNESCO estimates, 44.5% of children in the relevant age-group (49.4% of boys; 39.6% of girls) were enrolled at primary schools. Enrolment at secondary schools in 1998/99 was equivalent to only an estimated 7.1% of the population in the appropriate age-group (8.1% of boys; 6.1% of girls). There is one university, in Bujumbura; in 1998 5,037 students were enrolled in higher education. Expenditure on education by the central Government in 2001 was estimated at 20,000m. Burundian francs (equivalent to 13.5% of total government expenditure).

Public Holidays

2003: 1 January (New Year's Day), 5 February (Unity Day), 21 April (Easter Monday), 1 May (Labour Day), 29 May (Ascension Day), 1 July (Independence Day), 15 August (Assumption), 18 September (Victory of UPRONA Party), 13 October (Rwagasore Day), 21 October (Ndadaye Day), 1 November (All Saints' Day), 25 December (Christmas).

2004: 1 January (New Year's Day), 5 February (Unity Day), 12 April (Easter Monday), 1 May (Labour Day), 20 May (Ascension Day), 1 July (Independence Day), 15 August (Assumption), 18 September (Victory of UPRONA Party), 13 October (Rwagasore Day), 21 October (Ndadaye Day), 1 November (All Saints' Day), 25 December (Christmas).

Weights and Measures

The metric system is in force.

Statistical Survey

Area and Population

AREA, POPULATION AND DENSITY

Area (sq km)	27,834*
Population (census results)†	
15–16 August 1979	4,028,420
16–30 August 1990	
Males	2,473,599
Females.	2,665,474
Total	5,139,073
Population (UN estimates at mid-year)‡	
1999	6,255,000
2000	6,356,000
2001	6,502,000
Density (per sq km) at mid-2001	233.6

* 10,747 sq miles.

† Excluding adjustment for underenumeration.

‡ Source: UN, *World Population Prospects: The 2000 Revision*.

PRINCIPAL TOWNS: Bujumbura (capital), population 235,440 (census result, August 1990); Gitega 15,943 (1978) (Source: Banque de la République du Burundi).

BIRTHS AND DEATHS
(UN estimates, annual averages)

	1985–90	1990–95	1995–2000
Birth rate (per 1,000)	47.3	45.6	43.1
Death rate (per 1,000)	18.1	22.0	21.3

Source: UN, *World Population Prospects: The 2000 Revision*.

Expectation of life (WHO estimates, years at birth): 40.4 (males 38.4; females 42.3) in 2001 (Source: WHO, *World Health Report*).

ECONOMICALLY ACTIVE POPULATION*
(persons aged 10 years and over, 1990 census)

	Males	Females	Total
Agriculture, hunting, forestry and fishing	1,153,890	1,420,553	2,574,443
Mining and quarrying	1,146	39	1,185
Manufacturing	24,120	9,747	33,867
Electricity, gas and water	1,847	74	1,921
Construction	19,447	290	19,737
Trade, restaurants and hotels	19,667	6,155	25,822
Transport, storage and communications	8,193	311	8,504
Financing, insurance, real estate and business services	1,387	618	2,005
Community, social and personal services	68,905	16,286	85,191
Activities not adequately defined	8,653	4,617	13,270
Total labour force	1,307,255	1,458,690	2,765,945

* Figures exclude persons seeking work for the first time, totalling 13,832 (males 9,608; females 4,224), but include other unemployed persons.

Source: UN, *Demographic Yearbook.*

Mid-2001 (estimates in '000): Agriculture, etc. 3,097; Total 3,433 (Source: FAO).

Health and Welfare

KEY INDICATORS

Total fertility rate (children per woman, 2001)	6.8
Under-5 mortality rate (per 1,000 live births, 2000)	190
HIV/AIDS (% of persons aged 15–49, 2001)	8.30
Hospital beds (per 1,000 head, 1991)	0.66
Health expenditure (2000): US $ per head (PPP)	16
Health expenditure (2000): % of GDP	3.1
Health expenditure (2000): public (% of total)	53.1
Access to water (% of persons, 1990)	65
Access to sanitation (% of persons, 1990)	89
Human Development Index (2000): ranking	171
Human Development Index (2000): value	0.313

For sources and definitions, see explanatory note on p. vi.

Agriculture

PRINCIPAL CROPS
('000 metric tons)

	1999	2000	2001
Wheat	7.1	6.1	8.7
Rice (paddy)	58.6	51.7	60.9
Maize	128.7	117.8	124.4
Millet	10.1	8.7	8.7*
Sorghum	60.0	61.0	69.1
Potatoes	24.4	24.0	27.3
Sweet potatoes	734.2	687.4	780.9
Cassava (Manioc)	617.5	656.7	712.7
Taro (Coco yam)	90.1	80.7	84.7
Yams	12.8	9.6	9.9
Sugar cane	175.0	200.0*	200.0*
Dry beans	227.4	187.4	248.9
Dry peas	32.4	29.8	33.2†
Groundnuts (in shell)	9.9	8.8	8.8*
Oil palm fruit*	14.0	13.0	13.0
Vegetables and melons*	230	240	250
Bananas and plantains	1,511.4	1,514.0	1,548.9
Other fruits (excl. melons)*	84	84	84
Coffee (green)	30.0	18.5	13.0†
Tea (made)	6.9	8.2	8.8†

* FAO estimate(s).
† Unofficial figure.

Source: FAO.

LIVESTOCK
('000 head, year ending September)

	1999	2000*	2001*
Cattle	329	320	315
Pigs	61	50	70
Sheep*	200	220	230
Goats*	720	600	600
Poultry*	4,400	4,100	4,700

* FAO estimates.

Source: FAO.

LIVESTOCK PRODUCTS
('000 metric tons)

	1999	2000	2001*
Beef and veal	9.2	8.6	9.1
Mutton and lamb*	1.0	0.7	1.0
Goat meat	3.4	2.9	2.9
Pig meat*	4.3	4.9	4.9
Poultry meat	6.2	5.5*	5.5
Cows' milk	23.0	18.6	19.3
Sheep's milk	1.0	0.6	0.6
Goats' milk*	8.2	8.4	8.4
Poultry eggs	3.4	3.0	3.0
Cattle hides (fresh)*	1.8	1.8	1.8

* FAO estimate(s).

Source: FAO.

Forestry

ROUNDWOOD REMOVALS
('000 cubic metres, excl. bark)

	1999	2000	2001*
Sawlogs, veneer logs and logs for sleepers*	259	266	266
Other industrial wood*	67	67	67
Fuel wood	5,252	5,420	7,952
Total	5,578	5,753	8,285

* FAO estimates.

Source: FAO.

SAWNWOOD PRODUCTION
(FAO estimates, '000 cubic metres, incl. railway sleepers)

	1998	1999	2000
Coniferous (softwood)	7	17	18
Broadleaved (hardwood)	26	63	65
Total	33	80	83

Figures for 2001 assumed to be unchanged from 2000.

Source: FAO.

Fishing

(metric tons, live weight)

	1998	1999	2000*
Capture	13,426	9,199	10,000
Freshwater perches	3,925	1,523	1,550
Dagaas	8,646	7,030	7,800
Aquaculture*	55	55	55
Total catch (incl. others)	13,481	9,254	10,055

* FAO estimates.

Source: FAO, *Yearbook of Fishery Statistics.*

Mining

(metric tons, unless otherwise indicated)

	1998	1999	2000
Tin ore*†	23	10	10
Tantalum and niobium (columbium) concentrates*‡ . .	30	42	42
Gold (kilograms)*† . . .	1,500	1,500	1,500
Kaolin*	1,000	800	800
Peat ('000 metric tons) . .	10	17	15*

* Estimated production.
† Figures refer to the metal content of ores.
‡ The estimated tantalum content (in metric tons) was: 7 in 1998; 10 in 1999; 10 in 2000.

Source: US Geological Survey.

Industry

SELECTED PRODUCTS

('000 metric tons, unless otherwise indicated)

	1996	1997	1998*
Beer ('000 hectolitres) . .	1,227.9	1,161.2	1,036.3
Soft drinks ('000 hectolitres) . .	179.1	146.6	62.6
Cottonseed oil ('000 hectolitres) .	234.6	199.7	133.6
Sugar	17.8	19.6	21.7
Paint	0.4	0.4	0.5
Insecticides	2.4	2.4	1.8
Soap	3.4	2.8	3.7
Bottles	2.5	1.8	3.3
Blankets ('000)	116.2	217.3	174.4
Fibro-cement products . .	0.2	0.5	1.6
Batteries ('000 cartons)† . .	14.5	2.2	5.6
Electric energy (million kWh) .	103.1	85.8	107.1

* Estimates.
† Cartons of 240 batteries.

1999: Electric energy 99.1 million kWh (estimate).

Source: IMF, *Burundi: Statistical Annex* (April 2000).

Finance

CURRENCY AND EXCHANGE RATES

Monetary Units
100 centimes = 1 Burundian franc

Sterling, Dollar and Euro Equivalents (31 December 2002)
£1 sterling = 1,726.6 francs
US $1 = 1,071.2 francs
€1 = 1,123.4 francs
10,000 Burundian francs = £5.792 = $9.335 = €8.902

Average Exchange Rate (Burundian francs per US dollar)
2000   720.67
2001   830.35
2002   930.75

BUDGET

(million Burundian francs)*

Revenue†	1997	1998	1999
Tax revenue	42,880	61,554	66,627
Taxes on income and profits	10,322	13,139	15,122
Social security contributions . .	3,731	4,281	5,357
Domestic taxes on goods and services	20,744	25,305	31,640
Transaction tax	7,281	11,435	12,643
Excise tax	13,155	13,870	18,997
Taxes on international trade	7,229	18,829	14,508
Import duties	6,527	10,726	11,022
Export tax	702	4,562	28
Entrepreneurial and property income	1,920	3,106	3,071
Other current revenue . .	1,345	1,610	2,238
Capital revenue	108	64	111
Total	46,253	66,334	72,047

Expenditure‡	1997	1998	1999
General public services	18,154	20,513	25,122
Defence	21,100	23,325	24,564
Public order and safety	1,344	2,153	2,502
Education	11,204	14,080	15,990
Health	2,085	2,421	2,271
Social security and welfare . . .	4,718	6,510	2,401
Recreational, cultural and religious affairs and services . .	334	286	345
Economic affairs and services . .	n.a.	3,062	3,721
Fuel and energy	n.a.	232	543
Agriculture, forestry, fishing and hunting	n.a.	1,499	1,941
Mining, manufacturing and construction	n.a.	995	1,068
Transport and communications	n.a.	336	169
Other purposes	n.a.	25,711	28,265
Interest payments	6,071	6,844	9,507
Total	80,800	98,061	105,181
Current	58,207	74,082	80,966
Capital	12,322	23,979	24,215
Adjustment to total expenditure .	10,271	—	—

* Figures refer to the consolidated operations of the central Government, comprising the general budget, social security funds and extrabudgetary accounts (covering transactions undertaken through foreign borrowing arrangements and grants not recorded in treasury accounts). The data exclude the operations of other central government units with individual budgets.
† Excluding grants received.
‡ Excluding lending minus repayments.

2000 ('000 million Burundian francs): *Revenue:* Tax revenue 93.7 (Income tax 20.0, Taxes on goods and services 46.8, Taxes on international trade 22.8); Non-tax revenue 4.7; Total 98.3, excl. grants received, (15.9). *Expenditure:* Current 96.5 (Salaries 33.9, Goods and services 37.9, Transfers and subsidies 9.9, Interest payments 14.8); Capital 31.1 (Domestic resources 8.8, External resources 22.3); Total 127.7, excl. net lending (-3.6).

2001 ('000 million Burundian francs, estimates): *Revenue:* Tax revenue 103.1 (Income tax 28.5, Taxes on goods and services 48.7, Taxes on international trade 21.7); Non-tax revenue 7.0; Total 110.1, excl. grants received, (9.2). *Expenditure:* Current 118.6 (Salaries 40.1, Goods and services 44.2, Transfers and subsidies 15.9, Interest payments 18.5); Capital 33.0 (Domestic resources 18.5, External resources 10.7); Total 151.6, excl. net lending (-3.9).

Source: IMF, *Burundi: Statistical Annex* (November 2002).

INTERNATIONAL RESERVES

(US $ million at 31 December)

	2000	2001	2002
Gold*	4.74	0.27	0.34
IMF special drawing rights . .	0.04	0.06	0.16
Reserve position in IMF . . .	7.64	0.45	0.49
Foreign exchange	25.24	17.20	58.13
Total	37.66	17.98	59.12

* Valued at market-related prices.

Source: IMF, *International Financial Statistics.*

MONEY SUPPLY

(million Burundian francs at 31 December)

	2000	2001	2002
Currency outside banks . . .	31,300	34,058	42,990
Deposits at central bank . . .	1,044	347	449
Demand deposits at commercial banks	34,860	44,244	55,904
Demand deposits at other monetary institutions . . .	1,369	1,431	2,075
Total money	68,573	80,080	101,419

Source: IMF, *International Financial Statistics.*

COST OF LIVING
(Consumer Price Index for Bujumbura; base: January 1991 = 100)

	1996	1997	1998
Food	199.0	268.7	302.3
Clothing	199.3	308.7	342.2
Housing, heating and light	192.1	235.4	276.0
Transport	176.4	229.1	217.1
All items (incl. others)	193.4	253.6	285.3

Source: IMF, *Burundi: Statistical Annex* (April 2000).

All items (base: 1995 = 100): 239.7 in 2000; 261.9 in 2001; 258.6 in 2002 (Source: IMF, *International Financial Statistics*).

NATIONAL ACCOUNTS

Composition of the Gross National Product
(million Burundian francs at current prices)

	1999	2000	2001
Gross domestic product (GDP) in purchasers' values	455,488	511,789	548,656
Net factor income from abroad	−5,498	−8,698	−7,503
Gross national product (GNP)	449,990	503,091	541,153

Source: IMF, *International Financial Statistics*.

Expenditure on the Gross Domestic Product
(million Burundian francs at current prices)

	1999	2000	2001
Government final consumption expenditure	66,501	95,608	94,008
Private final consumption expenditure	386,157	474,498	473,594
Increase in stocks	6,739	−18,672	−142
Gross fixed capital formation	34,314	38,564	71,770
Total domestic expenditure	493,711	589,998	639,230
Exports of goods and services	34,452	30,341	37,454
Less Imports of goods and services	72,675	108,550	128,028
GDP in purchasers' values	455,488	511,789	548,656

Source: IMF, *International Financial Statistics*.

Gross Domestic Product by Economic Activity
('000 million Burundian francs at current prices)

	1999	2000	2001*
Agriculture, hunting, forestry and fishing	184.8	184.0	195.8
Mining and quarrying	} 4.7	5.1	5.6
Electricity, gas and water	}		
Manufacturing†	52.6	59.8	65.6
Construction	18.2	20.6	23.1
Trade, restaurants and hotels	32.1	36.8	41.0
Transport, storage and communications	33.8	38.7	43.1
Government services	23.8	27.2	30.4
Other services	73.0	83.2	91.0
GDP at factor cost	423.0	455.5	495.7
Indirect taxes, *less* subsidies	32.5	55.6	54.3
GDP in purchasers' values	455.5	511.1	550.0

* Estimates.
† Including handicrafts ('000 million Burundian francs): 17.9 in 1999; 20.3 in 2000; 22.1 in 2001 (estimate).

Source: IMF, *Burundi: Statistical Annex* (November 2002).

BALANCE OF PAYMENTS
(US $ million)

	1998	1999	2000
Exports of goods f.o.b.	64.0	55.0	49.1
Imports of goods f.o.b.	−123.5	−97.3	−107.9
Trade balance	−59.5	−42.3	−58.8
Exports of services	7.6	6.3	6.1
Imports of services	−49.5	−32.6	−43.4
Balance on goods and services	−101.3	−68.7	−96.1
Other income received	3.6	1.9	2.4
Other income paid	−11.9	−11.3	−14.5
Balance on goods, services and income	−109.6	−78.1	−108.2
Current transfers received	59.3	52.9	61.1
Current transfers paid	−3.3	−1.8	−1.8
Current balance	−53.6	−27.0	−48.8
Direct investment from abroad	—	0.2	11.7
Other investment assets	10.7	13.7	5.1
Other investment liabilities	18.1	3.1	42.2
Net errors and omissions	5.4	8.7	−6.2
Overall balance	−19.5	−1.2	3.9

Source: IMF, *International Financial Statistics*.

2001 (US $ million): Exports of goods (f.o.b.) 39.2; Imports of goods (f.o.b.) −108.4; *Trade balance* −69.2; Service and factor income (net) −44.3; *Balance on goods, services and income* −113.5; Current transfers (net) 79.2; *Current balance* −34.4; Capital and financial account (net) −9.2; Net errors and omissions 11.0; *Overall balance* −32.6 (Source: *Burundi: Statistical Annex* (November 2002).

External Trade

PRINCIPAL COMMODITIES
(distribution by SITC, US $ million)

Imports c.i.f.	1998	1999	2000
Food and live animals	29.3	12.9	20.4
Cereals and cereal preparations	19.1	9.6	14.4
Malt (incl. malt flour)	12.0	5.0	5.5
Crude materials (inedible) except fuels	5.6	5.6	5.6
Mineral fuels, lubricants, etc.	22.4	19.1	17.9
Refined petroleum products	22.0	18.9	17.5
Motor spirit (gasoline) and other light oils	10.1	9.0	8.2
Motor spirit (incl. aviation spirit)	9.3	8.5	7.6
Gas oils	9.6	8.5	7.5
Animal and vegetable oils, fats and waxes	2.1	0.4	13.4
Chemicals and related products	22.3	20.9	19.6
Medicinal and pharmaceutical products	9.7	8.5	10.1
Basic manufactures	35.2	24.3	28.6
Non-metallic mineral manufactures	7.1	6.1	7.1
Lime, cement, etc.	6.3	5.3	6.1
Cement	6.1	5.3	6.0
Machinery and transport equipment	37.7	40.0	34.4
Telecommunications and sound equipment	3.5	2.1	13.1
Road vehicles and parts (excl. tyres, engines and electrical parts)	12.7	22.1	8.8
Miscellaneous manufactured articles	6.9	6.9	8.7
Total (incl. others)	162.2	132.0	150.2

Source: UN, *International Trade Statistics Yearbook*.

Exports f.o.b.	1997	1998	1999
Food and live animals	86,094	62,933	53,761
Coffee, tea, cocoa and spices	85,583	62,015	52,836
Coffee (incl. husks and skins)	76,567	51,048	41,953
Tea	9,015	10,967	10,883
Total (incl. others)	87,320	63,950	54,956

Source: Banque de la République du Burundi.

PRINCIPAL TRADING PARTNERS

Imports c.i.f. (US $ '000)	1997	1998	1999
Belgium	22,358	30,254	19,851
China, People's Repub.	2,812	6,403	3,961
France	11,645	14,217	5,980
Germany	8,042	9,585	5,901
Italy	4,220	4,811	3,423
Japan	7,567	5,989	3,677
Kenya	5,305	8,784	6,199
Netherlands	5,234	4,656	2,246
Tanzania	3,057	3,113	5,118
United Arab Emirates	5,445	5,224	3,909
United Kingdom	2,041	2,314	2,511
USA	2,281	2,339	2,557
Zambia	6,761	12,530	6,734
Zimbabwe	2,806	1,562	2,208
Total (incl. others)	122,745	156,944	117,658

Exports (million Burundian Francs)	1997	1998	1999
Belgium-Luxembourg	4,929.3	2,624.8	995.5
France	37.3	17.8	358.1
Germany	6,579.5	2,968.8	1,520.9
United Kingdom	8,305.7	8,125.9	10,278.9
Total (incl. others)	30,767.2	28,634.8	30,970.8

Source: Banque de la République du Burundi.

Transport

ROAD TRAFFIC
(estimates, '000 motor vehicles in use)

	1992	1993	1994
Passenger cars	17.5	18.5	17.5
Commercial vehicles	11.8	12.3	10.2

Source: UN, *Statistical Yearbook*.

1996 (estimates, '000 motor vehicles in use): Passenger cars 19.2; Lorries and vans 18.2; Total 37.2 (Source: International Road Federation, *World Road Statistics*).

LAKE TRAFFIC
(Bujumbura, '000 metric tons)

	1997	1998	1999
Goods:			
arrivals	70.9	123.1	142.5
departures	28.1	28.1	28.2

Source: Banque de la République du Burundi.

CIVIL AVIATION
(traffic on scheduled services)

	1996	1997	1998
Passengers carried ('000)	9	12	12
Passenger-km (million)	2	8	8

Source: UN, *Statistical Yearbook*.

Tourism

TOURIST ARRIVALS BY REGION*

	1996	1997	1998
Africa	13,004	5,011	7,394
Americas	1,660	639	1,092
Asia	2,213	852	1,218
Europe	10,514	4,051	5,700
Total	27,391	10,553	15,404

* Including Burundian nationals residing abroad.

Tourist arrivals ('000): 26 in 1999; 30 (estimate) in 2000 (Source: World Tourism Organization, *Yearbook of Tourism Statistics*).

Tourism receipts (US $ million): 1 in 1998; 1 in 1999; 1 in 2000 (estimate) (Source: World Tourism Organization).

Communications Media

	1998	1999	2000
Television receivers ('000 in use)	80	100	200
Telephones ('000 main lines in use)	17.8	19.0	20.0
Mobile cellular telephones ('000 subscribers)	0.6	0.8	16.3
Internet users ('000)	1.0	2.5	3.0

2001: Telephones ('000 main lines in use) 20.0.

Radio receivers ('000 in use): 440 in 1997.

Facsimile machines (number in use): 4,000 in 1996.

Daily newspapers: 1 in 1996 (circulation 20,000 copies).

Sources: International Telecommunication Union; UNESCO, *Statistical Yearbook*.

Education
(1998, unless otherwise indicated)

	Institutions	Teachers	Students Males	Students Females	Students Total
Pre-primary	n.a.	49*	2,455	2,438	4,938
Primary†	1,512	12,107	307,079	250,265	557,344
Secondary†:					
general			30,604	26,268	56,872
technical and vocational	400	3,546			
			n.a.	n.a.	4,610
Higher	n.a.	379	3,549	1,488	5,037

* Figure refers to 1988/89.
† Figures refer to public education only.

Source: UNESCO Institute for Statistics.

Adult literacy rate (UNESCO estimates): 48.0% (males 56.2%; females 40.4%) in 2000 (Source: UN Development Programme, *Human Development Report*).

Directory

The Constitution

A transitional Constitution, which was drafted by a technical law commission and included principles incorporated in the previous Constitution of 1992 and the peace accord reached in August 2000, was formally adopted on 29 October 2001. Under the new Constitution, transitional organs of government, which were to be responsible for consolidating peace and national security in Burundi, were officially installed on 1 November 2001 and were to remain in place during a three-year period.

The transitional Constitution upholds the rights of the individual, guarantees press freedom and provides for a multi-party political system. Political parties are required to conform to the principles of national unity and are prohibited from organizing public demonstrations. The civic obligations of the individual are emphasized.

Executive power is vested in the President, who is the Head of State and Chief of Staff of the armed forces. The President appoints the Council of Ministers in consultation with the Vice-President. The transitional Government installed on 1 November 2001 was a multi-party administration, in which the Hutu and Tutsi ethnic groups were accorded equal representation. Under the transitional arrangements, the interim President transferred the office to the incumbent Vice-President after a period of 18 months.

The transitional Constitution provides for the establishment of a bicameral legislature. The lower chamber, the Assemblée nationale, numbers 121 deputies and includes representatives of civil society and of the principal political parties that signed the power-sharing agreement of August 2000. The nomination of new deputies by their respective political parties for a term of five years is subject to endorsement by the Constitutional Court. The upper house, the Sénat, comprises 51 members, of whom 48 are nominated from the country's provinces, with balanced representation between the ethnic groups.

The President guarantees the independence of the judiciary. The highest judicial power is vested in the Supreme Court. The Constitutional Court interprets the provisions of the transitional Constitution and ensures the conformity of new legislation. Judges are nominated to the Supreme Court and the Constitutional Court by the President. The Constitution provides for the establishment of an Office for the Ombudsman and a Supreme Court Council.

The transitional Constitution provides for the creation by the President of a consultative Council for National Unity and Reconciliation, an international inquiry commission, a truth and reconciliation commission, a commission for the rehabilitation of displaced civilians, and a commission for the implementation of the peace and reconciliation agreement.

The Government

HEAD OF STATE

President: Maj. DOMITIEN NDAYIZEYE (inaugurated 30 April 2003).

Vice-President: ALPHONSE-MARIE KADEGE.

COUNCIL OF MINISTERS
(May 2003)

A transitional Government, comprising representatives of the Union pour le progrès national (UPRONA), the Front pour la démocratie au Burundi (FRODEBU), the AV–Intware (Alliance of the Brave), the Parti de libération du peuple hutu (PALIPEHUTU), the Inkinzo y'Ijambo Ry'abarundi (Inkinzo), the Parti social démocrate (PSD), the Rassemblement pour la démocratie et le développement économique et social (RADDES), the Conseil national pour la défense de la démocratie (CNDD), the Alliance burundaise-africaine pour le salut (ABASA), the Rassemblement pour le peuple du Burundi (RPB), the Parti pour la réconciliation du peuple (PRP), the Parti du peuple (PP), the Alliance nationale pour les droits et le développement économique (ANADDE), the Parti indépendant des travailleurs (PIT), the Forces nationales de libération (FNL) and the Force pour la défense de la démocratie (FDD).

Minister of External Relations and Co-operation: TÉRENCE SINUNGURIIZA (UPRONA).

Minister of the Interior and Public Security: SALVATOR NTIHABOSE (FRODEBU).

Minister of Justice: FULGENCE DWIMA-BAKANA (FRODEBU).

Minister of National Defence: Maj.-Gen. VINCENT NIYUNGEKO (UPRONA).

Minister of Development, Planning and Reconstruction: SÉRAPHINE WAKANA (PRP).

Minister of Communal Development and Handicrafts: CASIMIR NGENDANGANYA (PALIPEHUTU).

Minister of Relocation and Resettlement of Displaced and Repatriated Persons: FRANÇOISE NGENDAHAYO (Inkinzo).

Minister of Mobilization for Peace and National Reconciliation: LUK RUKINGAMA (UPRONA).

Minister of Territorial Development, the Environment and Tourism: BARNABÉ MUTERAGIRANWA (RPB).

Minister of Agriculture and Livestock: PIERRE NDIKUMAGENGE (UPRONA).

Minister of Handicrafts, Vocational Training and Adult Literacy: GODEFROY HAKIZIMANA (PSD).

Minister of Labour and Social Security: DISMAS NDITABIRIYE (RADDES).

Minister of the Civil Service: CYRILLE HICINTUKA (CNDD).

Minister of Finance: ATHANASE GAHUNGU.

Minister of Good Governance and Privatization: DIDACE KIGANAHE (FRODEBU).

Minister of Commerce and Industry: CHARLES KARIKURUBU (FRODEBU).

Minister of National Education: PROSPER MPAWENAYO (FRODEBU).

Minister of Social Action and Women's Affairs: MARIE GORETH NDUWIMANA (PP).

Minister of Culture, Youth and Sport: RODOLPHE BARANYIZIGIYE (FNL).

Minister of Public Health: JEAN KAMANA (FRODEBU).

Minister of Information and Government Spokesman: ALBERT MBONERANE (CNDD).

Minister of Public Works and Equipment: GASPAR KOBAKO (FDD).

Minister of Transport, Posts and Telecommunications: SÉVERIN NDIKUMUGONGO (PP).

Minister of Energy and Mines: ANDRÉ NKUNDIKIJE (AV–Intware).

Minister of Human Rights, Institutional Reforms and Relations with the Assemblée nationale: ALPHONSE BARANCIRA (ANADDE).

Minister in the Office of the President, in charge of AIDS Control: GENEVIÈVE SINDABIZERA (PIT).

MINISTRIES

All ministries are based in Bujumbura

Office of the President: Bujumbura; tel. 226063.

Ministry of Agriculture and Livestock: Bujumbura; tel. 222087.

Ministry of Commerce and Industry: BP 492, Bujumbura; tel. 225330; fax 225595.

Ministry of Culture, Youth and Sport: Bujumbura; tel. 226822.

Ministry of Development, Planning and Reconstruction: BP 1830, Bujumbura; tel. 223988.

Ministry of Energy and Mines: BP 745, Bujumbura; tel. 225909; fax 223337; e-mail dgee@cbinf.com.

Ministry of External Relations and Co-operation: Bujumbura; tel. 222150.

Ministry of Finance: BP 1830, Bujumbura; tel. 225142; fax 223128.

Ministry of Information: BP 2870, Bujumbura.

Ministry of Justice: Bujumbura; tel. 222148.

Ministry of Labour and Social Security: BP 1480, Bujumbura; tel. 225645; fax 228715; e-mail mtpe@cbinf.com; internet www .burundi.gov.bi/appoffre.htm.

Ministry of Public Works and Equipment: BP 1860, Bujumbura; tel. 226841; fax 226840; e-mail mtpe@cbinf.com; internet www .burundi.gov.bi/appoffre.htm.

Ministry of Social Action and Women's Affairs: Bujumbura; tel. 225039.

Ministry of Transport, Posts and Telecommunications: BP 2000, Bujumbura; tel. 222923; fax 226900.

President and Legislature

PRESIDENT

In July 1996 the President elected by the Assemblée nationale, Cyprien Ntibantunganya, was deposed in a military coup and replaced by Maj. Pierre Buyoya. Under a power-sharing agreement, which was reached in August 2000, in Arusha, Tanzania, Buyoya was to remain in the office of the President for the first 18 months of a three-year transitional period (commencing on 1 November 2001). After this time he was to be replaced by the serving Vice-President, a Hutu leader, for the following 18 months. A new transitional Government was duly installed on 1 November 2001.

SÉNAT

The transitional Constitution, adopted on 29 October 2001, provided for the creation of an upper chamber, the Sénat. In January 2002 the Constitutional Court approved the nomination of 51 deputies (48 representing the country's provinces) to a transitional ethnically balanced Sénat.

President: LIBÈRE BARARUNYERETSE (UPRONA).

ASSEMBLÉE NATIONALE*

President: JEAN MINANI (FRODEBU).

Vice-President: FRÉDÉRIC NGENZEBUHORO (UPRONA).

Legislative Elections, 29 June 1993

Party	Votes cast	% of votes cast	Seats
FRODEBU	1,532,107	71.04	65
UPRONA	462,324	21.44	16
RPB	35,932	1.67	—
PRP	29,966	1.39	—
RADDES	26,631	1.23	—
PP	24,372	1.13	—
Independents	853	0.04	—
Invalid votes	44,474	2.06	—
Total	2,156,659	100.00	81

*The National Assembly was suspended following the July 1996 coup, but was reconvened in October. Under transitional constitutional arrangements promulgated in June 1998, the membership of the National Assembly was enlarged from 81 to 121 members in order to incorporate representatives of smaller parties and the civilian population. In January 2002 54 deputies representing 14 of the political parties signatory to the Arusha agreement of August 2000 were appointed to the expanded chamber.

Political Organizations

Political parties are required to demonstrate firm commitment to national unity, and impartiality with regard to ethnic or regional origin, gender and religion, in order to receive legal recognition. By late 2002 the number of registered political parties had increased to 18.

Alliance burundaise-africaine pour le salut (ABASA): Bujumbura; f. 1993; Tutsi; Leader SERGE MUKAMARAKIZA.

Alliance libérale pour le développement (Imboneza): f. Aug. 2002; Leader JOSEPH NTIDENDEREZA.

Alliance nationale pour les droits et le développement économique (ANADDE): Bujumbura; f. 1992; Tutsi; Leader PATRICE NSABABAGANWA.

Alliance nouvelle pour la démocratie et le développement au Burundi: f. Aug. 2002; Leader JEAN-PAUL BURAFUTA.

AV-Intware (Alliance of the Brave): Bujumbura; f. 1993; Tutsi; Leader ANDRÉ NKUNDIKIJE.

Conseil national pour la défense de la démocratie (CNDD): Bujumbura; e-mail cndd_bur@usa.net; internet www.club.euronet .be/pascal.karolero.cndd.burundi; f. 1994; Hutu; Leader LÉONARD NYANGOMA.

Convergence nationale pour la paix et la réconciliation (CNPR): Bujumbura; f. Oct. 1999; alliance comprising Union pour le progrès national, a faction of Front pour la démocratie au Burundi and several Tutsi parties; Pres. AUGUSTIN NZOJIBWAMI.

Force pour la défense de la démocratie (FDD): fmr armed wing of the Hutu CNDD; split into two factions in Oct. 2001, one led by JEAN-BOSCO NDAYIKENGURUKIYE and the other by JEAN-PIERRE NKURUNZIZA, both of which were in conflict with Govt, prior to peace agreement in Dec. 2002.

Forces nationales de libération (FNL): fmr armed wing of Hutu PALIPEHUTU; in conflict with Govt in 2003; split into two factions in Aug. 2002, one led by Dr ALAIN MUGABARABONA, and the other by AGATHON RWASA.

Forum démocratique (FODE): Bujumbura; f. Nov. 1999; Leader DEOGRATIAS BABURIFATO.

Front pour la démocratie au Burundi (FRODEBU): Bujumbura; f. 1992; split in June 1999; Hutu; Chair. JEAN MINANI; Sec.-Gen. DOMITIEN NDAYIZEYE.

Inkinzo y'Ijambo Ry'abarundi (Inkinzo) (Guarantor of Freedom of Speech in Burundi): Bujumbura; f. 1993; Tutsi; Pres. Dr ALPHONSE RUGAMBARARA.

Mouvement de la résistance pour la réhabilitation du citoyen (MRC—Rurenzangemero): Bujumbura; f. June 2001; regd Nov. 2002; Leader Lt-Col EPITACE BAYAGANAKANDI.

Parti indépendant des travailleurs (PIT): Bujumbura; f. 1993; Tutsi; Leader ETIENNE NYAHOZA.

Parti libéral (PL): BP 2167, Bujumbura; tel. 214848; fax 225981; e-mail liberalburundi@yahoo.fr; f. 1992; Hutu; Leader JOSEPH NTIDENDEREZA.

Parti de libération du peuple hutu (PALIPEHUTU): Bujumbura; f. 1980 in Tanzania, with the aim of advancing the interests of the Hutu ethnic group.

Parti du peuple (PP): Bujumbura; f. 1992; Hutu; Leader SHADRAIK NIYONKURU.

Parti pour le démocratie et la réconciliation: f. May 2002; Leader AUGUSTIN NZOJLBWAMI.

Parti pour la réconciliation du peuple (PRP): Bujumbura; f. 1992; Tutsi; Leader MATHIAS HITIMANA.

Parti pour le redressement national (PARENA): Bujumbura; f. 1994; Leader JEAN-BAPTISTE BAGAZA.

Parti social démocrate (PSD): Bujumbura; f. 1993; Tutsi; Leader GODEFROID HAKIZIMANA.

Rassemblement pour la démocratie et le développement économique et social (RADDES): Bujumbura; f. 1992; Tutsi; Chair. JOSEPH NZEYZIMANA.

Rassemblement pour le peuple du Burundi (RPB): Bujumbura; f. 1992; Hutu; Leader BALTHAZAR BIGIRIMANA.

Solidarité pour la défense des minorités (SOJEDEM): Bujumbura.

Sonovi-Ruremesha (Party for a Non-Violent Society): f. Aug. 2002; Tutsi; Chair. DEOGRATIAS NDAYISHIMIYE.

Union pour la paix et le développement (Zigamibanga): f. Aug. 2002; Leader FREDDY FERUVI.

Union pour le progrès national (UPRONA): BP 1810, Bujumbura; tel. 225028; f. 1958; following the 1961 elections, the numerous small parties which had been defeated merged with UPRONA, which became the sole legal political party in 1966; party activities were suspended following the coup of Sept. 1987, but resumed in 1989; Chair. CHARLES MUKASI; in Oct. 1999 moderate mems of the cen. cttee who opposed Mukasi's rejection of the Arusha talks elected Dr LUC RUKINGAMAas a rival Chair.

Diplomatic Representation

EMBASSIES IN BURUNDI

Belgium: 9 blvd de la Liberté, BP 1920, Bujumbura; tel. 223676; fax 223171; e-mail bujumbura@diplobel.org; Ambassador JAN F. MUTTON.

China, People's Republic: 675 sur la Parcelle, BP 2550, Bujumbura; tel. 224307; fax 213735; Ambassador SHI TONGNING.

Egypt: 31 ave de la Liberté, BP 1520, Bujumbura; tel. 223161; Ambassador MUHAMMAD MOUSA.

France: 60 blvd de l'Uprona, BP 1740, Bujumbura; tel. 226767; fax 221793; Ambassador CHRISTIAN DAZIANO.

Germany: 22 rue 18 septembre, BP 480, Bujumbura; tel. 226412; Ambassador Dr BERND MORAST.

Holy See: 46 chaussée Prince Louis-Rwagasore, BP 1068, Bujumbura (Apostolic Nunciature); tel. 222326; fax 223176; e-mail nonciat@cbinf.com; Apostolic Nuncio Most Rev. MICHAEL A. COURTNEY (Titular Archbishop of Eanach Duin).

Korea, Democratic People's Republic: BP 1620, Bujumbura; tel. 222881; Ambassador PAE SOK JUN.

Russia: 78 blvd de l'UPRONA, BP 1034, Bujumbura; tel. 226098; fax 222984; Ambassador IGOR S. LIAKIN-FROLOV.

Rwanda: 24 ave du Zaïre, BP 400, Bujumbura; tel. 223140; Ambassador SYLVESTRE UWIBAJIJE.

Tanzania: BP 1653, Bujumbura; Ambassador ANTHONY NYAKYI.

USA: ave des Etats-Unis, BP 1720, Bujumbura; tel. 223454; fax 222926; e-mail jyellin@bujumbura.us-state.gov; Ambassador JAMES YELLIN.

Judicial System

Constitutional Court: Bujumbura; comprises a minimum of five judges, who are nominated by the President for a four-year term.

Supreme Court: BP 1460, Bujumbura; tel. and fax 213544; Court of final instance; three divisions: ordinary, cassation and administrative.

Courts of Appeal: Bujumbura, Gitega and Ngozi.

Tribunals of First Instance: There are 17 provincial tribunals and 123 smaller resident tribunals in other areas.

Tribunal of Trade: Bujumbura.

Tribunals of Labour: Bujumbura and Gitega.

Administrative Courts: Bujumbura and Gitega.

Religion

More than 65% of the population are Christians, the majority of whom (an estimated 61%) are Roman Catholics. Anglicans number about 60,000. There are about 200,000 other Protestant adherents, of whom about 160,000 are Pentecostalists. Fewer than 40% of the population adhere to traditional beliefs, which include the worship of the God 'Imana'. About 1% of the population are Muslims. The Bahá'í Faith is also active in Burundi.

CHRISTIANITY

Conseil National des Eglises Protestantes du Burundi (CNEB): BP 17, Bujumbura; tel. 224216; fax 227941; e-mail cneb@cbninf.com; f. 1935; 10 mem. churches; Pres. Rt Rev. JEAN NDUWAYO (Anglican Bishop of Gitega); Gen. Sec. Rev. OSIAS HABINGABWA.

The Anglican Communion

The Church of the Province of Burundi, established in 1992, comprises five dioceses.

Archbishop of Burundi and Bishop of Buye: Most Rev. SAMUEL NDAYISENGA, BP 94, Ngozi; fax 302317.

Provincial Secretary: Rev. PASCAL BIGIRIMANA, BP 2098, Bujumbura; tel. 224389; fax 229129; e-mail eebprov@cbninf.com.

The Roman Catholic Church

Burundi comprises one archdiocese and six dioceses. At 31 December 2000 there were an estimated 3,990,845 adherents, equivalent to 63.4% of the total population.

Bishops' Conference

Conférence des Evêques Catholiques du Burundi, 5 blvd de l'UPRONA, BP 1390, Bujumbura; tel. 223263; fax 223270; e-mail cecab@cbninf.com.

f. 1980; Pres. Most Rev. SIMON NTAMWANA (Archbishop of Gitega).

Archbishop of Gitega: Most Rev. SIMON NTAMWANA, Archevêché, BP 118, Gitega; tel. 402160; fax 402620; e-mail archigi@bujumbura.ocicnet.net.

Other Christian Churches

Union of Baptist Churches of Burundi: Rubura, DS 117, Bujumbura 1; Pres. PAUL BARUHENAMWO.

Other denominations active in the country include the Evangelical Christian Brotherhood of Burundi, the Free Methodist Church of Burundi and the United Methodist Church of Burundi.

BAHÁ'Í FAITH

National Spiritual Assembly: BP 1578, Bujumbura.

The Press

National Communications Council: Bujumbura; f. by the President under the terms of the transitional Constitution; responsible for ensuring press freedom; Pres. JEAN-PIERRE MANDA.

NEWSPAPERS

L'Aube de la Démocratie: Bujumbura; opposition independent paper.

Le Renouveau du Burundi: Ministry of Information, BP 2573, Bujumbura; tel. 226232; f. 1978; publ. by UPRONA; 3 a week; French; circ. 20,000; Dir JEAN NZEYIMANA.

PERIODICALS

Au Coeur de l'Afrique: Association des conférences des ordinaires du Rwanda et Burundi, BP 1390, Bujumbura; fax 223027; e-mail cnid@cbninf.com; bimonthly; education; circ. 1,000.

Bulletin Économique et Financier: BP 482, Bujumbura; bimonthly.

Bulletin Mensuel: Banque de la République du Burundi, Service des études, BP 705, Bujumbura; tel. 225142; monthly.

In-Burundi: c/o Cyber Média, Bujumbura, BP 5270, ave du 18 septembre; tel. 244464; internet www.in-burundi.net; current affairs internet publication; Editor-in-Chief EDGAR C. MBANZA.

Ndongozi Y'uburundi: Catholic Mission, BP 690, Bujumbura; tel. 222762; fax 228907; fortnightly; Kirundi.

Revue Administration et Juridique: Association d'études administratives et juridiques du Burundi, BP 1613, Bujumbura; quarterly; French.

PRESS ASSOCIATION

Burundian Association of Journalists (BAJ): Bujumbura; Pres. FRANÇOIS SENDAZIRASA.

NEWS AGENCIES

Agence Burundaise de Presse (ABP): ave Nicolas Mayugi, BP 2870, Bujumbura; tel. 213083; fax (2) 22282; e-mail abp@cbinf.com; internet www.abp.info.bi; f. 1975; publ. daily bulletin.

Agence d'Information Net Press: Bujumbura; internet www.cbinf.com/netpress.bi; independent agency; operations suspended Jan. 2002; Dir JEAN-CLAUDE KAVUMBAGU.

Publishers

BURSTA: BP 1908, Bujumbura; tel. 231796; fax 232842; f. 1986; Dir RICHARD KASHIRAHAMWE.

Editions Intore: 14 ave Patrice Emery Lumumba, BP 2524, Bujumbura; tel. 223499; e-mail anbirabuza@yahoo.fr; f. 1992; philosophy, history, journalism, literature, social sciences; Dir Dr ANDRÉ BIRABUZA.

IMPARUDI: ave du 18 septembre 3, BP 3010, Bujumbura; tel. 223125; fax 222572; f. 1982; Dir THÉONESTE MUTAMBUKA.

Imprimerie la Licorne: 29 ave de la Mission, BP 2942, Bujumbura; tel. 223503; fax 227225; f. 1991.

Les Presses Lavigerie: 5 ave de l'UPRONA, BP 1640, Bujumbura; tel. 222368; fax 220318.

Régie de Productions Pédagogiques: BP 3118, Bujumbura II; tel. 226111; fax 222631; e-mail rpp@cbinf.com; f. 1984; school textbooks; Dir LÉONARD BIZONGWAKO.

Government Publishing House

Imprimerie Nationale du Burundi (INABU): BP 991, Bujumbura; tel. 224046; fax 225399; f. 1978; Dir NICOLAS NIJIMBERE.

Broadcasting and Communications

TELECOMMUNICATIONS

Direction Générale des Transports, Postes et Télécommunications: BP 2390, Bujumbura; tel. 225422; fax 226900; govt telecommunications authority; Dir-Gen. APOLLINAIRE NDAYIZEYE.

Office National des Télécommunications (ONATEL): BP 60, Bujumbura; tel. 223196; fax 226917; e-mail onatel@cbinf.com; f. 1979; service provider; privatization pending; Dir-Gen. AUGUSTIN NDABIHORE.

Téléphonie Cellulaire du Burundi (TELECEL): Bujumbura; 40% govt-owned; mobile telephone service provider.

BROADCASTING

Radio

Radio Umwizero/Radio Hope: BP 5314, Bujumbura; tel. 217068; e-mail umwizero@cbinf.com; f. 1996; EU-funded, private station promoting national reconciliation, peace and development projects; broadcasts nine hours daily in Kirundi, Swahili and French; Dir. HUBERT VIEILLE.

Studio Ijambo (Wise Words): Bujumbura; f. 1995.

Voix de la Révolution/La Radiodiffusion et Télévision Nationale du Burundi (RTNB): BP 1900, Bujumbura; tel. 223742; fax 226547; e-mail rtnb@cbinf.com; internet www.burundi-quotidien.com; f. 1960; govt-controlled; daily radio broadcasts in Kirundi, Swahili, French and English; Dir-Gen. INNOCENT MUHOZI; Dir (Radio) EMMANUEL NZEYIMANA.

Television

Voix de la Révolution/La Radiodiffusion et Télévision Nationale du Burundi (RTNB): BP 1900, Bujumbura; tel. 223742; fax 226547; e-mail rtnb@cbinf.com; internet www.burundi-quotidien.com; f. 1960; govt-controlled; television service in Kirundi, Swahili, French and English; Dir (Television) DAVID HICUBURUMAI.

Finance

(cap. = capital; res = reserves; dep. = deposits; m. = million; brs = branches; amounts in Burundian francs)

BANKING

Central Bank

Banque de la République du Burundi (BRB): BP 705, Bujumbura; tel. 225142; fax 223128; e-mail brb@cbinf.com; f. 1964 as Banque du Royaume du Burundi; state-owned; bank of issue; cap. and res 12,478.0m., dep. 11,233.4m. (Dec. 1999); Gov. GRÉGOIRE BANYIYEZAKO; Vice-Gov. CYPRIEN SINZOBAHAMVYA; 2 brs.

Commercial Banks

Banque Burundaise pour le Commerce et l'Investissement SARL (BBCI): blvd du Peuple Murundi, BP 2320, Bujumbura; tel. 223328; fax 223339; f. 1988; cap. and res 507.4m., total assets 3,451.0m. (Dec. 1998); Pres. ZACHARIE GASABANYA; Vice-Pres. CLÓTILDE NIZIGAMA.

Banque Commerciale du Burundi SARL (BANCOBU): 84 chaussée Prince Louis-Rwagasore, BP 990, Bujumbura; tel. 222317; fax 221018; e-mail bancobu@cbinf.com; f. 1988; by merger; cap. and res 4,652.5m., total assets 34,188.5m. (Dec. 2001); Pres. P. C. GAHUNGU; Dir-Gen. LIBÈRE NDABAKWAJE; 6 brs.

Banque de Commerce et de Développement (BCD): ave de Grèce, BP 2020, Bujumbura; tel. 210950; fax 210952; e-mail bcd@cbinf.com; f. 1999; cap. and res 1,016.0m., total assets 5,024.7m. (June 1999); Pres. FRANÇOIS BUTOKE; Man. Dir ANTOINE NDUWAYO.

Banque de Crédit de Bujumbura SMei: ave Patrice Emery Lumumba, BP 300, Bujumbura; tel. 222091; fax 223007; e-mail bcb@cbinf.com; f. 1964; cap. and res 3,282.4m., total assets 22,546.8m. (Dec. 1998); Pres. CHARLES NIHANGAZA; Man. ATHANASE GAHUNGU; 6 brs.

Banque de Gestion et de Financement: 1 blvd de la Liberté, BP 1035, Bujumbura; tel. 221352; fax 221351; e-mail bgf@cbinf.com; f. 1992; cap. and res 760.1m., total assets 3,847.8m. (Dec. 1998); Pres. DIDACE NZOHABONAYO; Dir-Gen. MATHIAS NDIKUMANA.

Banque Populaire du Burundi (BPB): 10 ave du 18 septembre, BP 1780, Bujumbura; tel. 221257; fax 221256; e-mail bpb@cbinf.com; internet www.cbinf.com; f. 1992; cap. and res 1,155.8m., dep. 6,756.8m. (Dec. 2000); Pres. THÉODORE KAMWENUBUSA; Dir-Gen. D. BUKOBERO.

Interbank Burundi SARL: 15 ave de l'Industrie, BP 2970, Bujumbura; tel. 220629; fax 220461; e-mail interb@cbinf.com; cap. and res 1,623.6m., total assets 14,545.7m. (Dec. 1997); Pres. GEORGES COUCOULIS.

Development Bank

Banque Nationale pour le Développement Economique SARL (BNDE): 3 ave du Marché, BP 1620, Bujumbura; tel. 222888; fax 223775; e-mail bnde@cbinf.com; f. 1966; cap. 740m., res 1,288.4m., dep. 8,572.1m. (Dec. 2000); Pres. and Dir-Gen. GASPARD SINDIYIGAYA; Gen. Sec. FRANÇOIS BARWENDERE.

Co-operative Bank

Banque Coopérative d'Epargne et de Crédit Mutuel (BCM): BP 1340, Bujumbura; operating licence granted in April 1995; Vice-Pres. JULIEN MUSARAGANY.

INSURANCE

Société d'Assurances du Burundi (SOCABU): 14–18 rue de l'Amitié, BP 2440, Bujumbura; tel. 226520; fax 226803; e-mail socabu@cbinf.com; f. 1977; partly state-owned; cap. 180m. Dir-Gen. (Admin.) SÉRAPHINE RUVAHAFI.

Société Générale d'Assurances et de Réassurance (SOGEAR): BP 2432, Bujumbura; tel. 222345; fax 229338; f. 1991; Pres. BENOÎT NDORIMANA; Dir-Gen. L. SAUSSEZ.

Union Commerciale d'Assurances et de Réassurance (UCAR): BP 3012, Bujumbura; tel. 223638; fax 223695; f. 1986; cap. 150m. Chair. Lt-Col EDOUARD NZAMBIMANA; Man. Dir HENRY TARMO.

Trade and Industry

GOVERNMENT AGENCIES

Agences de Promotion des Echanges Extérieurs (APEE): Bujumbura; promotes and supervises foreign exchanges.

Office du Café du Burundi (OCBU): BP 450, Bujumbura; tel. 224017; fax 225532; e-mail dgo@usan-bu.net; f. 1964; supervises coffee plantations and coffee exports; Dir-Gen. BARTHÉLÉMY NIYIKIZA.

Office du Thé du Burundi (OTB): 52 blvd de l'UPRONA, Bujumbura; tel. 224228; fax 224657; e-mail otb@cbinf.com; f. 1979; supervises production and marketing of tea; Man. Dir SALVATORE NIMUBONA.

Office National du Commerce (ONC): Bujumbura; f. 1973; supervises international commercial operations between the Govt of Burundi and other states or private orgs; also organizes the import of essential materials; subsidiary offices in each province.

Office National du Logement (ONL): BP 2480, Bujumbura; tel. 226074; f. 1974 to supervise housing construction.

DEVELOPMENT ORGANIZATIONS

Institut des Sciences Agronomiques du Burundi (ISABU): BP 795, Bujumbura; tel. 223390; fax 225798; e-mail isabu@cni.cbinf .com; f. 1962 for the scientific development of agriculture and livestock.

Office National de la Tourbe (ONATOUR): BP 2360, Bujumbura; tel. 226480; fax 226709; f. 1977 to promote the exploitation of peat deposits.

Société d'Exploitation du Quinquina du Burundi (SOKINABU): 16 blvd Mwezi Gisabo, BP 1783, Bujumbura; tel. 223469; f. 1975 to develop and exploit cinchona trees, the source of quinine; Dir RAPHAËL REMEZO.

Société de Financement et Développement de l'Habitat Urbain (SOFIDHAR): Bujumbura; urban development.

Société Régionale de Développement de l'IMBO (SRDI): Bujumbura; promotes development of IMBO region.

Société Régionale de Développement de Kayanza (SRD KAYANZA): Kayanza; promotes development of Kayanza region.

Société Régionale de Développement de Kirimiro (SRD KIRIMIRO): Bujumbura; promotes development of Kirimiro region.

Société Régionale de Développement de Kirundo (SRD KIRUNDO): Bujumbura; promotes development of Kirundo region.

Société Régionale de Développement de Mumirwa (SRD MUMIRWA): Bujumbura; promotes development of Mumirwa region.

Société Régionale de Développement de Rumonge (SRD RUMONGE): Bujumbura; promotes development of Rumonge region.

CHAMBER OF COMMERCE

Chambre de Commerce, d'Industrie, d'Agriculture et d'Artisanat du Burundi: BP 313, Bujumbura; tel. 222280; fax 227895; f. 1923; Pres. DIDACE NZOHABONAYO; Sec.-Gen. CYRILLE SINGEJEJE; 130 mems.

UTILITY

Régie de Distribution d'Eau et d'Electricité (REGIDESCO): Bujumbura; state-owned distributor of water and electricity services.

TRADE UNIONS

Confédération des Syndicats du Burundi (COSIBU): Bujumbura; Chair. Dr PIERRE-CLAVIER HAJAYANDI.

Union des Travailleurs du Burundi (UTB): BP 1340, Bujumbura; tel. 223884; f. 1967 by merger of all existing unions; closely allied with UPRONA; sole authorized trade union prior to 1994, with 18 affiliated nat. professional feds; Sec.-Gen. MARIUS RURAHENYE.

Transport

RAILWAYS

There are no railways in Burundi. Plans have been under consideration since 1987 for the construction of a line passing through Uganda, Rwanda and Burundi, to connect with the Kigoma–Dar es Salaam line in Tanzania. This rail link would relieve Burundi's isolated trade position.

ROADS

In 1996 Burundi had a total of 14,480 km of roads, of which 1,950 km were national highways and 2,530 km secondary roads. A new crossing of the Ruzizi River, the Bridge of Concord (Burundi's longest bridge), was opened in early 1992.

Office des Transports en Commun (OTRACO): Bujumbura; 100% govt-owned; operates public transport.

INLAND WATERWAYS

Bujumbura is the principal port for both passenger and freight traffic on Lake Tanganyika, and the greater part of Burundi's external trade is dependent on the shipping services between Bujumbura and lake ports in Tanzania, Zambia and the Democratic Republic of the Congo.

Exploitation du Port de Bujumbura (EPB): Bujumbura; 43% state-owned; controls Bujumbura port.

CIVIL AVIATION

The international airport at Bujumbura is equipped to take large jet-engined aircraft.

Air Burundi: 40 ave du Commerce, BP 2460, Bujumbura; tel. 224609; fax 223452; e-mail airbdi@cbinf.com; f. 1971 as Société de Transports Aériens du Burundi; state-owned; operates charter and scheduled passenger services to destinations throughout central Africa; CEO Col ANTOINE GATOTO; Dir C. KAGARI.

Tourism

Tourism is relatively undeveloped. The annual total of tourist arrivals declined from 125,000 in 1991 (with receipts amounting to US $4m.) to only 10,553 in 1997. Total arrivals increased gradually, to 15,404 in 1998, to 26,000 in 1999 and to an estimated 30,000 in 2000. However, continued failure to resolve conflict between the Government and rebel groups effectively prevented any significant revival of tourism.

Office National du Tourisme (ONT): 2 ave des Euphorbes, BP 902, Bujumbura; tel. 224208; fax 229390; f. 1972; responsible for the promotion and supervision of tourism; Dir HERMENEGILDE NIMBONA (acting).

CAMBODIA

Introductory Survey

Location, Climate, Language, Religion, Flag, Capital

The Kingdom of Cambodia occupies part of the Indo-Chinese peninsula in South-East Asia. It is bordered by Thailand and Laos to the north, by Viet Nam to the east and by the Gulf of Thailand to the south. The climate is tropical and humid. There is a rainy season from June to November, with the heaviest rainfall in September. The temperature is generally between 20°C and 36°C (68°F to 97°F), with March and April usually the hottest months; and the annual average temperature in Phnom-Penh is 27°C (81°F). The official language is Khmer, which is spoken by everybody except the Vietnamese and Chinese minorities. The state religion is Theravada Buddhism. The national flag (proportions 2 by 3) consists of three horizontal stripes, of dark blue, red (half the depth) and dark blue, with a stylized representation (in white) of the temple of Angkor Wat, showing three of its five towers, in the centre. The capital is Phnom-Penh.

Recent History

The Kingdom of Cambodia became a French protectorate in the 19th century and was incorporated into French Indo-China. In April 1941 Norodom Sihanouk, then aged 18, succeeded his grandfather as King. In May 1947 he promulgated a Constitution which provided for a bicameral Parliament, including an elected National Assembly. Cambodia became an Associate State of the French Union in November 1949 and attained independence on 9 November 1953. In order to become a political leader, King Sihanouk abdicated in March 1955 in favour of his father, Norodom Suramarit, and became known as Prince Sihanouk. He founded a mass movement, the Sangkum Reastr Niyum (Popular Socialist Community), which won all the seats in elections to the National Assembly in 1955, 1958, 1962 and 1966. King Suramarit died in April 1960, and in June Parliament elected Prince Sihanouk as Head of State. Prince Sihanouk's Government developed good relations with the People's Republic of China and with North Viet Nam, but it was highly critical of the USA's role in Asia. From 1964, however, the Government was confronted by an underground Marxist insurgency movement, the Khmers Rouges, while it also became increasingly difficult to isolate Cambodia from the war in Viet Nam.

In March 1970 Prince Sihanouk was deposed by a right-wing coup, led by the Prime Minister, Lt-Gen. (later Marshal) Lon Nol. The new Government pledged itself to the removal of foreign communist forces and appealed to the USA for military aid. Sihanouk went into exile and formed the Royal Government of National Union of Cambodia (GRUNC), supported by the Khmers Rouges. Sihanoukists and the Khmers Rouges formed the National United Front of Cambodia (FUNC). Their combined forces, aided by South Viet Nam's National Liberation Front and North Vietnamese troops, posed a serious threat to the new regime, but in October 1970 Marshal Lon Nol proclaimed the Khmer Republic. In June 1972 he was elected the first President. During 1973 several foreign states recognized GRUNC as the rightful government of Cambodia. In 1974 the republican regime's control was limited to a few urban enclaves, besieged by GRUNC forces, mainly Khmers Rouges, who gained control of Phnom-Penh on 17 April 1975. Prince Sihanouk became Head of State again but did not return from exile until September. The country was subjected to a pre-arranged programme of radical social deconstruction immediately after the Khmers Rouges' assumption of power; towns were largely evacuated, and their inhabitants forced to work in rural areas. During the following three years an estimated 1.7m. people died as a result of ill-treatment, hunger, disease and executions.

A new Constitution, promulgated in January 1976, renamed the country Democratic Kampuchea, and established a republican form of government; elections for a 250-member People's Representative Assembly were held in March 1976. In April Prince Sihanouk resigned as Head of State, and GRUNC was dissolved. The Assembly elected Khieu Samphan, formerly Deputy Prime Minister, to be President of the State Presidium (Head of State). The little-known Pol Pot (formerly Saloth Sar) became Prime Minister. In September 1977 it was officially disclosed that the ruling organization was the Communist Party of Kampuchea (CPK), with Pol Pot as the Secretary of its Central Committee.

After 1975 close links with the People's Republic of China developed, while relations with Viet Nam deteriorated. In 1978, following a two-year campaign of raids across the Vietnamese border by the Khmers Rouges, the Vietnamese army launched a series of offensives into Kampuchean territory. In December the establishment of the Kampuchean National United Front for National Salvation (KNUFNS, renamed Kampuchean United Front for National Construction and Defence—KUFNCD—in December 1981, and United Front for the Construction and Defence of the Kampuchean Fatherland—UFCDKF—in 1989), a communist-led movement opposed to Pol Pot and supported by Viet Nam, was announced. Later in the month, Viet Nam invaded Kampuchea, supported by the KNUFNS.

On 7 January 1979 Phnom-Penh was captured by Vietnamese forces, and three days later the People's Republic of Kampuchea was proclaimed. A People's Revolutionary Council was established, with Heng Samrin, leader of the KNUFNS, as President. It pledged to restore freedom of movement, freedom of association and of religion, and to restore the family unit. The CPK was replaced as the governing party by the Kampuchean People's Revolutionary Party (KPRP). The Khmer Rouge forces, however, remained active in the western provinces, near the border with Thailand, and conducted sporadic guerrilla activities elsewhere in the country. Several groups opposing both the Khmers Rouges and the Heng Samrin regime were established, including the Khmer People's National Liberation Front (KPNLF), headed by a former Prime Minister, Son Sann. In July, claiming that Pol Pot's regime had been responsible for 3m. deaths, the KPRP administration sentenced Pol Pot and his former Minister of Foreign Affairs, Ieng Sary, to death *in absentia*. In January 1980 Khieu Samphan assumed the premiership of the deposed Khmer Rouge regime, while Pol Pot became Commander-in-Chief of the armed forces. In 1981 the CPK was reportedly dissolved and was replaced by the Party of Democratic Kampuchea (PDK).

During the first few years of the KPRP regime Viet Nam launched regular offensives on the Thai-Kampuchean border against the united armed forces of Democratic Kampuchea, the coalition Government-in-exile of anti-Vietnamese resistance groups formed in June 1982. As a result of the fighting, and the prevalence of starvation and disease, thousands of Kampuchean refugees crossed the border into Thailand; in turn, a large number of Vietnamese citizens subsequently settled on Kampuchean territory. The coalition Government-in-exile, of which Prince Sihanouk became President, Khieu Samphan (PDK) Vice-President and Son Sann (KPLNF) Prime Minister, received the support of the People's Republic of China and of member states of the Association of South East Asian Nations (ASEAN, see p. 146), whilst retaining the Kampuchean seat in the UN General Assembly.

In the mid-1980s an increasingly conciliatory attitude between the USSR and the People's Republic of China led to a number of diplomatic exchanges, aimed at reconciling the coalition Government-in-exile with the Government in Phnom-Penh, led by the General Secretary of the KPRP, Heng Samrin. Largely, however, because of mistrust of the PDK (due to Pol Pot's continuing influence), the Heng Samrin Government rejected peace proposals from ASEAN and the coalition Government-in-exile in 1985 and 1986. In September 1987 the Government of the People's Republic of China stated that it would accept a Kampuchean 'government of national reconciliation' under Prince Sihanouk, but that the presence of Vietnamese troops in Kampuchea remained a major obstacle. In the same month the USSR also declared that it was 'prepared to facilitate a political settlement' in Kampuchea. In October, having announced its readiness to conduct negotiations with some PDK leaders (but not Pol Pot), the Heng Samrin Government offered Prince Sihanouk a government post and issued a set of peace proposals which included the complete withdrawal of Vietnamese troops, internationally observed elections and the formation of a coalition government. In December 1987 Prince Sihanouk and Hun Sen, the Chairman of the Council of Ministers in the Heng Samrin Government, met in France for private discussions for the first time since the invasion by Viet Nam. The meeting ended in a joint communiqué, stating that the conflict was to be settled politically by negotiations among all the Kampuchean parties, and that any resulting agreement should be guaranteed by an international conference.

Under increasing pressure from the USSR and the People's Republic of China, the four Kampuchean factions participated in a series of 'informal meetings', held in Indonesia, which were also attended by representatives of Viet Nam, Laos and the six ASEAN members. At the first of these meetings, in July 1988, Viet Nam advanced its deadline for a complete withdrawal of its troops from Kampuchea to late 1989. In April 1989 the National Assembly in Phnom-Penh ratified several constitutional amendments, whereby the name of the country was changed to the State of Cambodia, a new national flag, emblem and anthem were introduced, Buddhism was reinstated as the state religion, and the death penalty was abolished. In July 1989 the Paris International Conference on Cambodia (PICC) met for the first time. The PICC agreed to send a UN reconnaissance party to Cambodia to study the prospects for a cease-fire and the installation of a peace-keeping force.

The withdrawal of Vietnamese forces, completed on schedule in September 1989, was followed by renewed offensives into Cambodia by the resistance forces, particularly the PDK. In November, following substantial military gains by the PDK, the UN General Assembly adopted a resolution supporting the formation of an interim government in Cambodia which would include members of the PDK, but which retained a clause, introduced in 1988, relating to past atrocities committed by the organization. The resolution also cast doubt on the Vietnamese withdrawal (since it had not been monitored by the UN) and, in reference to the alleged presence of 1m. Vietnamese settlers in Cambodia, condemned 'demographic changes' imposed in the country. An Australian peace initiative was unanimously approved by the five permanent members of the UN Security Council in January 1990. In February Prince Sihanouk declared that the coalition Government-in-exile would henceforth be known as the National Government of Cambodia.

In July 1990 the USA withdrew its support for the National Government of Cambodia's occupation of Cambodia's seat at the UN. In August the UN Security Council endorsed the framework for a comprehensive settlement in Cambodia. The agreement provided for UN supervision of an interim government, military arrangements for the transitional period, free elections and guarantees for the future neutrality of Cambodia. A special representative of the Secretary-General of the UN was to control the proposed United Nations Transitional Authority in Cambodia (UNTAC). The UN would also assume control of the Ministries of Foreign Affairs, National Defence, Finance, the Interior and Information, Press and Culture. China and the USSR pledged to cease supplies of military equipment to their respective allies, the PDK and the Phnom-Penh Government.

At a fourth 'informal meeting' in Jakarta in September 1990 the four Cambodian factions accepted the UN proposals. They also agreed to the formation of the Supreme National Council (SNC), with six representatives from the Phnom-Penh Government and six from the National Government of Cambodia. SNC decisions were to be taken by consensus, effectively allowing each faction the power of veto, and the SNC was to occupy the Cambodian seat at the UN General Assembly. Prince Sihanouk was subsequently elected to the chairmanship of the SNC (a position in which he would have final arbitration if a consensus could not be reached), and resigned as leader of the resistance coalition and as President of the National Government of Cambodia (positions to which Son Sann was appointed). Agreement was also reached on the four factions reducing their armed forces by 70% and the remaining 30% being placed in cantonments under UN supervision; the introduction of a system of multi-party democracy; the Phnom-Penh Government abandoning its demand for references to genocide to be included in a draft plan; and the holding of elections to a constituent assembly, which would subsequently become a legislative assembly comprising 120 seats.

Following the release of political prisoners by the Phnom-Penh Government in October 1991, including former 'reformist' associates of Hun Sen (who had been arrested in 1990 and replaced by supporters of the more conservative chairman of the National Assembly, Chea Sim), a congress of the KPRP was

convened at which the party changed its name to the Cambodian People's Party (CPP). The communist insignia was removed from its emblem, Heng Samrin was replaced as Chairman of the Central Committee (formerly the Politburo) by Chea Sim and Hun Sen was elected as Vice-Chairman.

On 23 October 1991 the four factions signed the UN peace accord in Paris, under the auspices of the PICC. UNTAC was expected to be in place by August 1992. The mainly military UN Advance Mission in Cambodia (UNAMIC), comprising 300 men, was in place by the end of 1991. The peace-keeping operation was expected to be completed in 1993. The agreement also provided for the repatriation, under the supervision of the UN High Commissioner for Refugees, of the estimated 340,000 Cambodian refugees living in camps in Thailand. There were continuing fears that the PDK would, in an attempt to ensure electoral support, endeavour forcibly to repatriate refugees to areas of western Cambodia under their control.

In November 1991 Prince Sihanouk returned to Phnom-Penh, accompanied by Hun Sen. The CPP and the United National Front for an Independent, Neutral, Peaceful and Co-operative Cambodia (FUNCINPEC), led by Prince Sihanouk, subsequently formed an alliance and announced their intention to establish a coalition government. (The alliance was abandoned in December, in response to objections from the KPNLF and the PDK.) On 23 November the four factions endorsed the reinstatement of Prince Sihanouk as the Head of State of Cambodia, pending a presidential election in 1993. Political protest increased towards the end of 1991. An attack by demonstrators on Khieu Samphan on his return to Phnom-Penh in late November led senior PDK officials to flee to Bangkok where the SNC met and agreed that, henceforth, officials of the party would occupy the SNC headquarters in Phnom-Penh with members of UNAMIC. Further demonstrations took place in December and in January 1992 in protest against corruption and in support of human rights, during which the security forces killed several protesters. The authorities closed all schools and colleges in the capital, imposed a curfew and prohibited any unauthorized demonstrations. However, following an agreement with representatives of the UN Security Council, the Phnom-Penh Government released all remaining political prisoners between January and March 1992. The UN Security Council expanded UNAMIC's mandate to include mine-clearing operations, and in February authorized the dispatch of a 22,000-member peace-keeping force to Cambodia to establish UNTAC. In mid-March UNAMIC transferred responsibility for the implementation of the peace agreement to UNTAC.

The refugee repatriation programme, which began in March 1992, was threatened by continued cease-fire violations, which were concentrated in the central province of Kompong Thom. In June the continued obduracy of the PDK disrupted the implementation of the second phase of the peace-keeping operation, which comprised the cantonment and disarmament of the four factions' forces. Although by mid-July about 12,000 troops from three of the factions had reported to the designated areas, the PDK intensified its violations of the cease-fire agreement, continued to deny the UN access to its zones, and failed to attend meetings on the implementation of the peace agreement. At the Ministerial Conference on the Rehabilitation and Reconstruction of Cambodia, which was convened in Tokyo in late June, the application of economic sanctions against the PDK was considered. The PDK reiterated demands that power be transferred from the Phnom-Penh Government to the SNC and that both the SNC and UNTAC should co-operate in ensuring that all Vietnamese forces had withdrawn from Cambodia. During August Yasushi Akashi (who had been appointed UN Special Representative to Cambodia in charge of UNTAC in January 1992) affirmed that the elections would proceed without the participation of the PDK if it continued to refuse to co-operate. The UN set a deadline for compliance of 15 November. By the end of November, however, no consensus had been reached, and the Security Council adopted a resolution condemning PDK obduracy. The Security Council approved an embargo on the supplies of petroleum products to the PDK and endorsed a ban on the export of timber (a principal source of income for the party) from 31 December. On the day the sanctions were adopted, however, the PDK announced the formation of a subsidiary party to contest the forthcoming elections, the Cambodian National Unity Party, led by Khieu Samphan and Son Sen.

In December 1992 the seizure of six members of the UN peace-keeping forces in PDK-controlled areas reflected a growing distrust of UNTAC by the PDK, which had previously alleged

UN bias in favour of the Phnom-Penh Government. The slow progress of the peace initiative, coupled with the poor conduct of UN troops, resulted in widespread disaffection with UNTAC, and in the latter part of 1992 resentment towards ethnic Vietnamese intensified, largely as a result of PDK and, subsequently, KPLNF propaganda.

By the final deadline at the end of January 1993 20 parties, excluding the PDK, had registered to contest the elections. The Phnom-Penh Government subsequently launched an offensive against the PDK in northern and western Cambodia, recovering much of the territory gained by the PDK since the signing of the peace agreement in October 1991. In early February 1993 Prince Sihanouk returned to Phnom-Penh from Beijing amidst intensifying politically motivated violence. There were also continuing attacks by the PDK on ethnic Vietnamese, and, following several rural massacres, thousands of Vietnamese took refuge in Viet Nam. Despite the violence, UNTAC's voter registration campaign, which ended in February, had been extremely successful; 4.7m. Cambodians were registered, constituting about 97% of the estimated eligible electorate. The repatriation programme for refugees on the Thai border was also successfully concluded; 360,000 refugees had been returned to Cambodia on schedule by the end of April.

On 23–28 May 1993 about 90% of the electorate participated in the elections to the Constituent Assembly. The PDK offered support to the FUNCINPEC Party, in the hope of securing a role in government following the elections but, owing to the massive voter participation in the election, Prince Sihanouk abandoned his proposals for the inclusion of the PDK in a future Government. Early results from the election, indicating a FUNCINPEC victory, prompted CPP allegations of electoral irregularities. UNTAC, however, rejected CPP requests for fresh elections in at least four provinces. In early June, without prior consultation with the UN and disregarding the incomplete election results, Prince Sihanouk announced the formation of a new Government, with himself as Prime Minister and Prince Ranariddh and Hun Sen as joint Deputy Prime Ministers. The coalition was created and renounced within hours, owing to objections from Prince Ranariddh, who had not been consulted, and to suggestions by UN officials that it was tantamount to a coup. Two days later the official results of the election were released: the FUNCINPEC Party secured 58 seats with 46% of the votes cast, the CPP 51 seats with 38% of the votes, the Buddhist Liberal Democratic Party (BLDP, founded by the KPNLF) 10 seats (3%) and a breakaway faction from the FUNCINPEC Party, MOLINAKA (National Liberation Movement of Cambodia), one seat. Despite the UN's endorsement of the election as fair, the CPP refused to dissolve the State of Cambodia Government in Phnom-Penh and announced that certain eastern provinces were threatening to secede unless demands for an independent examination of the results were met. Prince Norodom Chakkrapong (a son of Prince Sihanouk who had been appointed to the Council of Ministers of the Phnom-Penh Government in December 1991) subsequently led a secessionist movement in seven provinces in the east and north-east of the country, which was reportedly sanctioned by the CPP leadership in an attempt to secure a power-sharing agreement with the FUNCINPEC Party.

On 14 June 1993, at the inaugural session of the Constituent Assembly, Prince Sihanouk was proclaimed Head of State, and 'full and special' powers were conferred on him. The Assembly adopted a resolution declaring null and void the overthrow of Prince Sihanouk 23 years previously and recognizing him retroactively as Head of State of Cambodia during that period. The secessionist movement in the eastern provinces collapsed, and on the following day an agreement was reached on the formation of an interim government, with Hun Sen and Prince Ranariddh as Co-Chairmen of the Provisional National Government of Cambodia, pending the drawing up of a new constitution. Prince Chakkrapong returned to Phnom-Penh, where he was reconciled with Prince Sihanouk. A few days later the CPP officially recognized the results of the election.

The PDK had immediately accepted the results of the election and supported the formation of a coalition government, but continued to engage in military action to support its demands for inclusion in a future government. In July 1993 the PDK offered to incorporate its forces into the newly formed Cambodian National Armed Forces (later restyled the Royal Cambodian Armed Forces), which had been created through the merger of the forces of the other three factions in June. PDK offensives escalated, however, after the party was denied a role in govern-

ment, largely owing to US threats to withhold economic aid from Cambodia if the PDK were included prior to a renunciation of violence. In late August Cambodia's united armed forces initiated a successful offensive against PDK positions in north-western Cambodia. The Government rejected an appeal for urgent discussions by the PDK after government forces had captured PDK bases, insisting that the party surrender unconditionally the estimated 20% of Cambodian territory under its control. The PDK suffered from defections as disillusioned troops were offered the same rank in the Cambodian National Armed Forces under a government amnesty, which ended in January 1995.

On 21 September 1993 the Constituent Assembly adopted a new Constitution, which provided for an hereditary monarchy. On 24 September Prince Sihanouk promulgated the Constitution, thus terminating the mandate of UNTAC (whose personnel left the country by mid-November). The Constituent Assembly became the National Assembly, and Prince Sihanouk acceded to the throne of the new Kingdom of Cambodia. Chea Sim was re-elected Chairman of the National Assembly. Government ministers were to be chosen from parties represented in the National Assembly, thus precluding the involvement of the PDK. In October talks scheduled between the Cambodian Government and the PDK were postponed indefinitely, owing to the ill health of King Sihanouk, who was undergoing medical treatment in Beijing (Chea Sim assumed the position of acting Head of State while the King was out of the country). At the end of October the National Assembly approved the new Royal Government of Cambodia (previously endorsed by King Sihanouk), in which Prince Ranariddh was named First Prime Minister and Hun Sen Second Prime Minister. Between November 1993 and January 1994 initiatives to incorporate the PDK into the new Government failed, owing to objections from various parties. In May 1994 King Sihanouk threatened to stop negotiating with the PDK and the Government to end the fighting in the north-west of the country, which had reached a severity not witnessed since 1989, and forced the postponement of proposed peace talks in Pyongyang, the Democratic People's Republic of Korea. Following the failure of peace talks held in May and June 1994, the Government ordered the PDK to leave Phnom-Penh and closed the party's mission in the capital.

In July 1994 the Government claimed to have suppressed a coup attempt led by Prince Chakkrapong and Gen. Sin Song, a former Minister of National Security under the State of Cambodia. Following a personal appeal from King Sihanouk, Prince Chakkrapong, who protested his innocence, was exiled from Cambodia, while Gen. Sin Song was placed under arrest. (Gen. Sin Song escaped from prison in September and was captured by Thai authorities in November.) Hun Sen also suspected his rival, Sar Kheng, a Deputy Prime Minister and Minister of the Interior, of involvement in the alleged revolt. Sar Kheng was, however, protected by his powerful brother-in-law, Chea Sim. The coup attempt was also used by the increasingly divided Government as a pretext to suppress criticism of the regime. Newspapers were closed, editors fined and imprisoned and in September an editor renowned as an outspoken critic of the Government was killed by unidentified assailants.

Despite King Sihanouk's continued advocacy of national reconciliation, in July 1994 legislation providing for the outlawing of the PDK was adopted by the National Assembly (whilst allowing for an immediate six-month amnesty for the lower ranks of the party). The proposed legislation was initially opposed by a group led by the Minister of Finance, Sam Rainsy and the Minister of Foreign Affairs, Prince Norodom Sirivudh but, following the inclusion of guarantees safeguarding civil liberties, the bill was approved. In response, the PDK announced the formation of a Provisional Government of National Unity and National Salvation of Cambodia (PGNUNSC), under the premiership of Khieu Samphan, which was to co-ordinate opposition to the Government in Phnom-Penh from its headquarters in Preah Vihear in the north of the country. In October Sam Rainsy, who was highly regarded by independent foreign observers, was dismissed as Minister of Finance, apparently owing to his efforts to combat high-level corruption. Prince Sirivudh subsequently resigned as Minister of Foreign Affairs in protest at Rainsy's removal, which also demonstrated the decline in King Sihanouk's political influence—Prince Ranariddh and Hun Sen had jointly proposed Rainsy's dismissal in March, but King Sihanouk had withheld his consent. Prince Sirivudh also criticized the FUNCINPEC Party, of which he was Secretary-General, for submitting too readily to CPP demands, as it became increasingly apparent that real power lay with the former communists.

In May 1995 Rainsy was expelled from the FUNCINPEC Party and in April he was expelled from the National Assembly. This caused international disquiet and provoked criticism from human rights groups. Rainsy formed a new party, the Khmer Nation Party (KNP), which was officially launched in November. The Government declared the KNP illegal but refrained from action to disband it. Rainsy's expulsion from the National Assembly coincided with the adoption of the revised draft of a draconian press law, which imposed substantial fines and prison sentences for reporting issues affecting 'national security' or 'political stability'.

Politically motivated violence, organized crime and drugs-trafficking all developed as serious problems in Cambodia. The situation was exacerbated by the inadequacies of law enforcement, the lack of any specific legislation to deter 'money-laundering' and endemic corruption among senior government officials and the armed forces. In October Prince Sirivudh was expelled from the National Assembly (and thus deprived of diplomatic immunity) and charged with conspiring to assassinate Hun Sen. Human rights groups declared that Prince Sirivudh, who protested his innocence, was a political prisoner. Under an agreement reached with King Sihanouk's intervention, Prince Sirivudh was allowed to go into exile in France in December on condition that he refrain from political activity. In January 1996 Prince Sirivudh was convicted and sentenced to 10 years' imprisonment *in absentia* on charges of criminal conspiracy and possession of unlicensed firearms. Also in January the Government began to adopt repressive measures against the KNP. In March Rainsy nominally merged the KNP with a defunct but still legally registered party, in an attempt to gain legal status. However, in April the Government ordered all parties without parliamentary representation to close their offices. Several KNP officials were assassinated during the year.

In August 1996 the prominent PDK leader, Ieng Sary, together with two military divisions that controlled the significant PDK strongholds of Pailin and Malai, defected from the movement and negotiated a peace agreement with the Government. Ieng Sary subsequently denied responsibility for the atrocities committed during Pol Pot's regime, and was granted a royal amnesty in September, at the request of both Hun Sen and Prince Ranariddh. Following his defection, Ieng Sary formed a new political organization, the Democratic National United Movement (DNUM), while his supporters retained control of Pailin and Malai, despite efforts by troops loyal to the PDK leadership to recapture the region (where lucrative mineral and timber resources were situated). Former PDK troops (numbering about 4,000) were integrated into the national army in November. An estimated 2,500 PDK troops transferred allegiance to the Government in October.

Throughout 1996 political instability increased. In September the partial dissolution of the PDK increased tensions within the ruling coalition, as both the CPP and the FUNCINPEC Party attempted to attract former PDK troops. However, as the FUNCINPEC Party appeared more successful than the CPP at recruiting former PDK commanders and cadres, Hun Sen became concerned that the alliance between the royalists and the PDK as former resistance forces would be re-established. In February 1997 Prince Ranariddh sent a helicopter mission to Anlong Veng to negotiate with the central PDK faction. However, PDK members opposed to peace talks ambushed the helicopter, killing the majority of the Prince's emissaries. Meanwhile, the two Prime Ministers were stockpiling weapons, violations of human and civil rights were becoming increasingly prevalent, corruption was rampant, and labour unrest was widespread. King Sihanouk announced his concern and raised the possibility of his abdication. The potential involvement of the popular monarch in the forthcoming polls provoked a threat from Hun Sen to cancel both the local and national elections and to amend the Constitution to prohibit all members of the royal family from participating in politics, to guarantee the neutrality of the constitutional monarchy. In March 1997 Rainsy, who had increased his attacks against Hun Sen and the CPP-controlled judicial system and police force, led a demonstration outside the National Assembly. The meeting was attacked by assailants who threw four grenades, killing 19 and injuring more than 100 protesters in a presumed attempt to assassinate Rainsy. Rainsy accused Hun Sen of orchestrating the attack and expressed no confidence in the commission established to investigate the incident.

In April 1997 Ung Phan, a former CPP member who had joined the FUNCINPEC Party in the early 1990s, led a rebellion against the party leadership of Prince Ranariddh, with the support of Hun Sen. The National Assembly, which was due to adopt legislation pertaining to local and national elections scheduled for 1998, was unable to convene, as the FUNCINPEC Party refused to attend until its dissident members were expelled from the Assembly, whereas the CPP insisted on their retention. In June the dissident FUNCINPEC members organized a party congress and formed a rival FUNCINPEC Party, with Toan Chhay, the Governor of Siem Reap, as its chairman. Also in June Prince Sirivudh was prevented from returning to Cambodia, as he was refused permission to board flights to Cambodia in Hong Kong, owing to threats by Hun Sen, who had earlier refused to support a royal pardon for the Prince.

In May 1997 Khieu Samphan announced the creation of a new political party, the National Solidarity Party, which would support the National United Front (an alliance founded in February by Prince Ranariddh) at the next election. Prince Ranariddh declared that, if the notorious former leadership of the PDK were excluded, he would welcome such an alliance. Hun Sen, however, deemed the potential alliance to be a threat to the CPP and, following the seizure of a shipment of weapons destined for Prince Ranariddh, accused the Prince of illegally importing weapons to arm PDK soldiers. The PDK was divided over the issue of peace negotiations. Pol Pot began a violent purge, ordering the death of Son Sen and also that of Ta Mok. Following the execution of Son Sen and his family, many PDK commanders rallied behind Ta Mok, and fighting erupted between the two factions. Pol Pot and his supporters fled into the jungle, with Khieu Samphan as a hostage, but were captured by Ta Mok's forces and returned to the PDK base at Anlong Veng, near the Thai border. In late July a US journalist, Nate Thayer, was invited by the PDK to Anlong Veng to witness the trial of Pol Pot. He was condemned by a 'people's court' for 'destroying national unity' and for the killing of Son Sen and his family. In October Thayer was permitted to interview the former leader, who denied that atrocities had occurred under his regime.

In June 1997 Prince Ranariddh claimed that Pol Pot was under arrest and that Khieu Samphan would surrender. Hun Sen, meanwhile, demanded that Ranariddh choose between himself and Khieu as a partner in government. Tensions between Prince Ranariddh and Hun Sen increased, as FUNCINPEC military forces were strengthened. Hun Sen continued to warn that PDK defectors were massing in Phnom-Penh. On 3 July, following several attempts by CPP troops to detect the presence of PDK soldiers in FUNCINPEC units, CPP forces disarmed a unit of Prince Ranariddh's bodyguards, on the grounds that they were allegedly PDK troops. On the following day Prince Ranariddh left the country. On 5 July serious fighting erupted in Phnom-Penh, and on 6 July, the day on which Khieu Samphan had been scheduled to broadcast the PDK's agreement with the FUNCINPEC Party to end its resistance and rejoin the political system, Hun Sen appeared on television to demand Prince Ranariddh's arrest (on charges of negotiating with the PDK, introducing proscribed PDK troops into Phnom-Penh and secretly importing weapons to arm those forces) and to urge FUNCINPEC officials to select another leader. More than 24 hours of pillage then ensued. The UN subsequently claimed that it had documentary evidence showing that at least 43 people, principally from the royalist army structure, had been murdered by forces loyal to Hun Sen after the events of 5–6 July. Many more FUNCINPEC and KNP officials, as well as many FUNCINPEC members of the legislature, fled the country.

King Sihanouk's appeals for both sides to travel to the People's Republic of China to negotiate a settlement were rejected by Hun Sen. Prince Ranariddh announced from Paris that a resistance movement was being organized in western Cambodia. Meanwhile, Hun Sen began negotiations with certain prominent members of the FUNCINPEC Party who remained in Phnom-Penh (the General Secretary, Loy Simchheang, the Co-Minister of the Interior, You Hockry, and the Minister of Defence, Tie Chamrat) in an effort to attain the two-thirds' majority of the National Assembly necessary for the investiture of a new government. By the end of July 1997 the National Assembly had reconvened, with 98 of the 120 deputies present, including 40 of the 58 FUNCINPEC deputies. Hun Sen protested to the international community that his actions did not constitute a *coup d'état*, as he had not abolished the Constitution or the monarchy and had not dissolved the Government or the National

Assembly. He also declared that he was in favour of free elections in 1998. Despite these assurances, aid was temporarily suspended by the USA, Japan, Germany and later Australia. However, the UN refused to condemn Hun Sen by name, although it expressed a 'grave preoccupation' with the situation in Cambodia. King Sihanouk, who had been in the People's Republic of China since February, also insisted on remaining neutral and accepted that Chea Sim should continue to sign royal decrees in his absence. In August the National Assembly voted to remove Ranariddh's legal immunity (a warrant subsequently being issued for his arrest) and elected Ung Huot, the FUNCINPEC Minister of Foreign Affairs, to the post of First Prime Minister. The USA opposed his election as undemocratic, but Japan resumed its aid programme, and China also accepted Prince Ranariddh's replacement.

In July 1997 troops loyal to Prince Ranariddh, led by Gen. Nhiek Bunchhay (the former military Deputy Chief of Staff and a principal negotiator with the PDK), were swiftly forced into the north-west of the country by CPP troops. They regrouped near the Thai border in an effective alliance with PDK troops under Ta Mok. Prolonged fighting took place for control of the town of O'Smach, about 70 km west of Anlong Veng, which was the last base for the resistance coalition led by Prince Ranariddh, the Union of Cambodian Democrats. At the end of August the King arrived in Siem Reap. Hun Sen rejected another proposal from the King to act as a mediator in peace talks, insisting that Ranariddh had to be tried for his alleged crimes.

In September 1997 Hun Sen announced a cabinet reorganization that effectively removed remaining supporters of Prince Ranariddh from the Government. However, in a secret ballot the National Assembly failed by 13 votes to approve the changes by the required two-thirds' majority. Hun Sen continued his efforts to encourage the return of all opposition representatives who had fled the country in July, except Ranariddh and Gen. Nhiek Bunchhay. In November Rainsy returned to Cambodia, whereupon he organized a peace march through Phnom-Penh, which was attended by several thousand supporters. In a conciliatory gesture in December, Hun Sen and Rainsy held a cordial meeting, at which they agreed to co-operate in the national interest.

In mid-December 1997 the National Assembly voted, for technical reasons, to postpone local and legislative elections from May until July 1998 and to increase the number of seats from 120 to 122, owing to Ieng Sary's decision in October 1997 to transfer nominal control of Pailin and Malai to the Government. At the beginning of February 1998 Rainsy withdrew the KNP from the electoral process in protest at the unlawful methods allegedly employed by Hun Sen, including the registration of a breakaway faction of the KNP bearing an identical title and logo and the fatal shooting in January of a KNP official and his daughter. Rainsy subsequently restyled the KNP the Sam Rainsy Party.

Hun Sen and Ranariddh agreed to the terms of a Japanese peace proposal in February 1998, which provided for the severance of Ranariddh's links with the PDK, the implementation of a cease-fire in the north-west (which came into effect on 27 February), a royal pardon for Ranariddh if he were convicted *in absentia* of the charges against him and his guaranteed safe return to participate in the general election. Ranariddh was convicted in March of illegally importing weapons and of conspiring with the proscribed PDK, and sentenced to 30 years' imprisonment and a fine of US $54m. for damage caused on 5–6 July 1997. At the formal request of Hun Sen, Sihanouk granted Ranariddh a royal pardon, but no amnesty was accorded to Nhiek Bunchhay or Serei Kosal, the commanders of Ranariddh's troops in the north-west, who were found guilty on the same day. Ranariddh returned to Phnom-Penh at the end of March 1998, but the FUNCINPEC Party had been severely weakened by the killing of many of its senior personnel, the closure of its offices across the country and the defection of some principal officials, including Loy Simchheang and You Hockry.

In March 1998 two divisions of PDK troops mutinied against their leader, Ta Mok; further divisions rebelled in the following week, surrendering control of the PDK headquarters, Anlong Veng, to government troops. During the ensuing clashes thousands of civilians were evacuated to Thailand. Pol Pot died on 15 April, shortly after his comrades had offered to surrender him for trial by an international tribunal. It was later reported that he had committed suicide. Ta Mok announced that he was prepared to reach agreement with the Government but demanded autonomy for Anlong Veng. Sporadic clashes between

the remnants of the PDK and government forces continued in late 1998. The grouping was practically defunct, however, by the end of the year, following further significant defections in October and December. In late December Nuon Chea (Pol Pot's former deputy) and Khieu Samphan defected to the Government, seeking sanctuary in Pailin, an area effectively controlled by Ieng Sary. In February 1999 a final 4,332 PDK troops surrendered to the Co-Ministers of National Defence in Anlong Veng. Ta Mok, however, remained in the border area.

The election campaign period was characterized by intimidation and violence. All demonstrations were banned, as was the dissemination of political information by private news media. Ranariddh and, more particularly, Rainsy (who did finally contest the election) sought to exploit traditional Cambodian hatred of the Vietnamese. Hun Sen refused to campaign, but the ruling CPP dominated the National Election Committee, the Constitutional Council, the armed forces and the judiciary, as well as central and local government. However, the general election, which took place on 26 July 1998, was characterized by the UN-co-ordinated Joint International Observer Group as free and fair. Voting took place relatively peacefully, except for an attack on a polling station by PDK remnants, in which 10 people were killed. Ninety per cent of the 5,395,024 registered voters (representing 98% of the population of voting age) participated in the election, which was contested by 39 parties. Under a newly introduced modified system of proportional representation that favoured larger parties, the CPP secured 64 seats (with 41.4% of the popular vote), the FUNCINPEC Party 43 seats (31.7%) and the Sam Rainsy Party 15 seats (14.3%). At an audience with the King at the end of July Hun Sen proposed a three-party coalition, but this was rejected by Ranariddh and Rainsy, who demanded a national recount, on the grounds of electoral fraud, and threatened to boycott the new National Assembly.

In August 1998 Rainsy was detained for questioning, following a grenade explosion at the Ministry of the Interior. Several thousand Cambodians took part in a demonstration in Phnom-Penh, organized by Sam Rainsy, to denounce electoral fraud and to demand the removal of Hun Sen. Despite a ruling by the Constitutional Court upholding the National Election Committee's decision to reject allegations of electoral fraud, the peaceful demonstration outside the National Assembly lasted for more than two weeks. Talks between the three principal parties failed to produce a resolution. In September, however, following a grenade attack on a disused residence of Hun Sen, the protesters were violently dispersed by security forces, and Hun Sen ordered the arrest of Rainsy on charges of murder. The opposition accused Hun Sen of staging the incident in order to justify his suppression of the peaceful protest. Rainsy took refuge under the protection of the UN, and both Rainsy and Ranariddh abandoned claims for a recount. Sporadic violence continued, and Hun Sen announced that the FUNCINPEC Party and the Sam Rainsy Party would be expelled from the National Assembly if they failed to attend its inauguration on 24 September. Prior to the inauguration Hun Sen, Rainsy and Ranariddh met, under the chairmanship of Sihanouk, in Siem Reap Province, but failed to resolve the crisis. Tension was further heightened by a rocket-propelled grenade attack on a convoy of vehicles en route to the convening ceremony of the National Assembly. Hun Sen, who claimed to be the intended victim of the attack, issued retaliatory threats prompting Ranariddh and Rainsy to flee to Thailand. Following the failure of further negotiations in early October, a declaration was issued, stating that the present Government, which was due to leave office, would continue to administer the country until a new government was formed. The situation continued to deteriorate in October 1998 with the arrest, torture and execution of many opposition supporters. Human rights' groups estimated that more than 200 people had disappeared during September.

Ranariddh agreed to return to Cambodia to attend a meeting with Hun Sen, under the auspices of King Sihanouk, from which Rainsy was excluded. In November 1998 agreement was reached on the formation of a coalition Government, which would be supported by 107 of the 122 deputies, with Hun Sen as Prime Minister and Ranariddh as the Chairman of the National Assembly. The accord also provided for the creation of a Senate (to be presided over by Chea Sim), the reintegration of resistance soldiers into the armed forces, royal pardons for Gen. Nhiek Bunchhay and Serei Kosal, as well as Prince Sirivudh and Prince Chakkrapong, and restitution for property damaged during fighting in July 1997. On Rainsy's return to Phnom-Penh in November 1998, a large crowd of his supporters was violently dispersed by security forces. On 25 November the National Assembly convened, and Ranariddh was duly elected Chairman of the Assembly, with two CPP deputies. The new Royal Government was approved on 30 November and included Co-Ministers for the influential Ministries of Defence and of the Interior, while the CPP controlled the foreign affairs and finance portfolios and the FUNCINPEC Party assumed responsibility for information and health. Rainsy became the official leader of the opposition. The Senate, which was empowered to scrutinize and amend bills passed by the National Assembly, held its inaugural session on 25 March 1999. Representation in the 61-member upper chamber was proportionate to elected strength in the National Assembly; the CPP was allocated 31 seats, the FUNCINPEC Party 21 and the Sam Rainsy Party seven, whilst a further two members were appointed by the King. Chea Sim was duly elected as Chairman, and Nhiek Bunchhay became one of the three Deputy Chairmen.

Reform of the Royal Cambodian Armed Forces began in January 1999 with Hun Sen's resignation as Commander-in-Chief, to demonstrate the neutrality of the armed forces. He was replaced by the former Chief of the General Staff, Gen. Ke Kimyan. By the end of September 15,551 'ghost' troops (soldiers who had been killed or had deserted, but whose pay continued to be collected by senior officers) had been removed from the army payroll. Plans announced in November 1999 provided for the demobilization of 11,500 troops in 2000, followed by a further 10,000 in both 2001 and 2002. The coalition Government also expressed its commitment to administrative and environmental reforms.

In March 1999 Ta Mok was captured near the Thai border and placed in detention. In May Kang Kek Ieu, known as Duch, the director of the Tuol Sleng detention centre where 16,000 detainees had been tortured and executed during the Democratic Kampuchean regime, was arrested and charged with belonging to a proscribed organization. These detentions intensified domestic and international pressure for the establishment of a tribunal to try former Khmer Rouge leaders for atrocities committed during 1975–79. Three jurists, commissioned by the UN to assess the evidence against the leaders of the PDK, recommended that 20–30 Khmer Rouge leaders be brought to trial and reparations be made to their victims. The Cambodian Government, however, in the interests of national reconciliation, was reluctant to indict former Khmer Rouge leaders who had surrendered to the Government, for fear that former PDK members might revert to armed insurrection. The Cambodian Government and the UN also differed as to the composition and structure of a tribunal. The UN doubted Cambodia's ability to conduct a trial in accordance with international standards and thus favoured an international tribunal, whereas Hun Sen claimed that this would constitute an infringement of Cambodian sovereignty and insisted that any trials take place within the existing Cambodian court structure. In April, however, Hun Sen conceded that UN-appointed foreign judges could take part in a trial in Cambodia, although he still favoured the nomination of a Cambodian prosecutor. Cambodia submitted draft legislation recommending a majority of Cambodian judges to the UN for approval in December. Hun Sen announced in January 2000 that the trials would begin on 17 April, the 25th anniversary of Pol Pot seizing control of Phnom-Penh, with or without UN support. The Government approved draft legislation establishing a court in January, but the UN finally issued its rejection of the draft in February, stating that the legislation did not conform to international standards. In December 1999 the office of the UN Secretary-General's special envoy to Cambodia was closed at the request of the Cambodian Government, despite UN pleas that it remain open for a further year. The Cambodian Government had, however, agreed in August to extend the mandate of the representative of the UN High Commissioner for Human Rights based in Cambodia, Thomas Hammarberg. Following the delays in establishing a tribunal, in August 1999 the National Assembly approved legislation extending pre-trial detention for those accused of genocide and crimes against humanity from six months to three years, effectively postponing the trials of Ta Mok and Duch. In September both Ta Mok and Duch were formally charged with genocide under a 1979 decree of the People's Republic of Kampuchea, and in the first half of 2002 both were also charged with having committed crimes against humanity; the pair remained in government custody, awaiting trial, in early 2003. In June 1999, following pressure from Australia and the United Kingdom, Gen. Nuon Paet, a senior Khmer Rouge commander, was convicted in connection with the abduction and murder of three foreign tourists (Australian, British and French nationals) in July 1994 and sentenced to life imprisonment. Gen. Nuon Paet's sentence was upheld by the appeals court in September 2000 and again in September 2002. In July Col Chhouk Rin, one of a number of other Khmer Rouge leaders charged in connection with the murder of the three tourists, was freed after it was announced that he was covered by the amnesty granted to Khmer Rouge cadres who surrendered to the Cambodian Government. However, in September 2002, following formal protests from the Australian, British and French Governments, his acquittal was reversed by the appeals court and Col Chhouk Rin was sentenced to life imprisonment; he refused to recognize the verdict. Meanwhile, in May 2002 Gen. Sam Bith was arrested and charged in connection with the murder of the three tourists. In December, following a trial during which former Khmer Rouge leader Nuon Chea testified on his behalf, Bith was convicted of the charges against him and also received a life sentence; he expressed his intention to appeal against his conviction.

In April 2000 US Senator John Kerry announced that, following extensive negotiations between the Cambodian Government and the UN, an agreement had been reached on a formula for the establishment of a tribunal to try former Khmer Rouge leaders for atrocities committed under the regime. The details of a draft accord on the establishment of the tribunal were finalized in July, whereupon the requisite legislation was submitted to the Cambodian National Assembly. In early August the Sam Rainsy Party presented a petition expressing unreserved support for the Government's agreement with the UN. Despite the opposition's support for the legislation, however, significant delays ensued; the National Assembly finally approved the draft legislation in January 2001. However, it specified that only those individuals deemed 'most responsible' for the atrocities would face the tribunal, thereby implicitly exempting significant numbers of middle- and lower-ranking former Khmer Rouge officials from prosecution. The legislation was approved by the Senate later the same month.

In July 2001 the final version of legislation providing for the trial of Khmer Rouge leaders was passed by the National Assembly, and, in the following month, after receiving the approval of the Constitutional Council, it was signed into law by King Sihanouk. The UN was left to determine whether or not the trial framework would ensure the adequate implementation of international standards of justice. In June, following the departure of the UN Secretary-General's Special Representative for Human Rights in Cambodia, Peter Leuprecht, who had voiced doubts as to the efficacy of the proposed legislation, Prime Minister Hun Sen accused the UN of interfering with Cambodian sovereignty. His views were reiterated by Prince Ranariddh. In October more than 5,000 weapons were burnt in the town of Pailin, initiating the country's first arms reduction effort in areas formerly controlled by the Khmers Rouges.

In February 2002 the UN unexpectedly announced that it had decided to abandon negotiations with the Cambodian Government over a UN role in the establishment of a joint tribunal to try former Khmer Rouge leaders. It claimed that the legal framework created by the Government did not conform to international standards of justice and that it would not ensure either the independence or impartiality of proceedings. Of particular concern, according to the UN, was a legal failure to clarify that the royal pardon previously granted to Ieng Sary would not prove to be an obstacle to his prosecution. In response, the Government stated that it intended to proceed with the trials and that it would make no further concessions to the UN in order to facilitate the establishment of a tribunal. The Sam Rainsy Party, however, filed a petition requesting that the Government explain why the UN had elected to withdraw from the negotiations. In June Peter Leuprecht visited the country again and intimated that attempts were under way to facilitate the restarting of talks, with the possibility that the trials could be conducted in a Cambodian court but with the inclusion of foreign judges. In the following month Prime Minister Hun Sen announced that Cambodia was prepared to compromise with the UN by amending the laws that would govern the establishment of any tribunal. In November the UN voted in favour of a draft resolution submitted by Japan and France requesting that it resume negotiations with the Cambodian Government without further delay. Hun Sen affirmed his Government's intention to co-operate with the UN in the renewal of efforts to establish a satisfactory judicial framework for the tribunal. In January 2003 the UN held one week of exploratory talks with the

Cambodian Government, during which the two sides were reported to have made some progress in reaching an agreement to restart negotiations.

In November 2000, meanwhile, dozens of armed men launched an attack on official buildings in Phnom-Penh. At least seven of the gunmen were killed in the raid, which government officials initially attributed to unspecified 'terrorists'; however, some of those involved alleged that they had been brought to Phnom-Penh under false pretences and forced to carry weapons. The leader of the US-based Cambodian Freedom Fighters organization, Chhun Yasith (a citizen of the USA), subsequently issued a statement claiming responsibility for the attack on behalf of his organization and alleging that its principal intention had been to disrupt the forthcoming visit of the President of Viet Nam, Tran Duc Luong (which had originally been scheduled for late November, but which was then postponed indefinitely). Forty-seven people, including two members of the Sam Rainsy Party, were subsequently reported to have been charged with terrorism in connection with the attack. The arrest of two of its members provoked an angry response from the opposition party, and some observers expressed concerns that the Government was attempting to discredit the political opposition by connecting it with the violence.

In late June and July 2001 the trial of 32 of those who had participated in the attempted coup took place, amid accusations that the Government had played a part in fomenting the violence in order to facilitate the intimidation of political opponents by local leaders. Three US citizens, among those arrested, were sentenced to life imprisonment *in absentia*; 27 Cambodians were also given sentences ranging in length from three years to life. In November a further 26 nationals were imprisoned for terms of up to 15 years, following a second mass trial which had begun in October. Two people were released owing to lack of evidence. In February 2002 a further 20 people were tried in connection with the attempted coup and sentenced to prison terms; those convicted included one US citizen.

In 2001 the Prime Minister continued to prevaricate on questions of democratic reform. The stagnation of democracy in the country was reflected by the violence that surrounded the registration period for Cambodia's first multi-party local elections (scheduled for February 2002), which ended in August 2001. At least 20 of the candidates planning to mount a challenge to Hun Sen and the ruling CPP were shot dead during the election campaign. Furthermore, during the campaign period the opposition was denied access to the state-controlled media, effectively preventing it from communicating with potential voters. In December 2001 the CPP continued to exert its authority over the country's legislature, expelling three senators from both the Senate and the party for challenging a bill intended to lengthen the amount of time that the authorities could detain a person without formal charge (the bill was approved by the National Assembly but subsequently defeated by the Senate).

In February 2002 polling for the 1,621 *khum* (communes) resulted in an overwhelming victory for the CPP, which secured control of 1,598 *khum*. The Sam Rainsy Party won control of 13 and the FUNCINPEC Party 10. Despite numerous allegations of intimidation and electoral irregularities, the opposition parties accepted the results; according to election monitors, however, the elections could be deemed neither free nor fair.

Meanwhile, in February 2001 the Sam Rainsy Party had begun to broadcast a one-hour opposition radio programme, entitled 'Voice of Justice', from an overseas location, as it continued its efforts to draw attention to governmental corruption. In response, the Cambodian Government warned its fellow ASEAN members not to allow the programme to be broadcast from within their borders. In September the security authorities announced the arrest of 10 suspected members of the Cambodian Freedom Fighters, following the discovery of plans for a large-scale attack on Phnom-Penh.

In 2002, following its disappointing performance in the local elections, a rift developed within the FUNCINPEC Party. As an indirect result, in May 2002 Prince Norodom Chakrapong, one of the sons of King Norodom Sihanouk, founded a new political party, the Prince Norodom Chakrapong Khmer Soul party; he claimed that he had already applied for permission to contest the general election that was scheduled for 2003 and that he intended to form an alliance with the Sam Rainsy Party. In the same month Co-Minister of the Interior You Hockry was forced to stand down by FUNCINPEC leader Prince Norodom Ranariddh following accusations of disloyalty from party members; he was criticized for failing to win substantial voter support and for involvement in corruption. However, in August, following a parliamentary vote (necessary if a minister was to be removed), Hockry retained his cabinet position; Ranariddh narrowly failed to secure the majority necessary to replace him with rival candidate Gen. Khan Saveoun. Meanwhile, in June the party was weakened further by the defection of one of its founding members, Hang Dara, who announced the formation of the Hang Dara Movement Democratic Party to contest the next general election.

International relations were severely affected by the events of 5–6 July 1997. The USA, Germany and Japan suspended all but humanitarian assistance, and in October 1998 the US House of Representatives adopted a resolution accusing Hun Sen of genocide. One of the most serious international consequences of the events of July 1997 was the decision by ASEAN to postpone indefinitely Cambodia's admission to the grouping. Cambodia had attended an ASEAN meeting in July 1995 with official observer status, had its application for membership accepted in July 1996 and had been due to join in late July 1997. Hun Sen was angered by ASEAN's decision and initially rejected the grouping's attempts to negotiate a diplomatic solution to the Cambodian crisis. However, at the end of July Hun Sen invited ASEAN to mediate in the dispute and held talks with the grouping in early August. At the end of August the Prime Minister of Singapore announced that Cambodia would not be considered for admission to ASEAN until after elections had been held. Prior to the ASEAN summit meeting in Hanoi in December 1998, despite the formation of a Cambodian coalition Government in November, Singapore, Thailand and the Philippines remained opposed to Cambodia's immediate accession to the organization. However, in the event, the host country, Viet Nam, announced that Cambodia had been accepted as the 10th member of ASEAN, although the formal admission was to take place at a later unspecified date. Cambodia duly acceded to ASEAN on 30 April 1999. A further significant consequence of the events of 5–6 July 1997 was the decision of the UN Accreditation Committee to leave Cambodia's seat at the UN vacant. However, following the formation of a coalition Government in November 1998, Cambodia regained its seat at the UN in December.

In August 2002, following a meeting of ASEAN in Brunei, Cambodia became a signatory to an anti-terrorism pact originally drawn up by Malaysia, Indonesia and the Philippines in May of that year; the pact was intended to increase regional co-operation on security issues. In November the country hosted the annual ASEAN summit meeting, which was also attended by the Republic of Korea, Japan and China, as well as India, which was present for the first time. During the meeting a framework agreement was signed to establish an ASEAN-China free trade area by 2010.

Relations between Cambodia and the People's Republic of China (which had formerly supported the PDK) had already improved during the mid-1990s. However, following the events of 5–6 July 1997, Hun Sen deliberately aligned himself with China, possibly as a reaction to the disapproval of ASEAN, which considered itself to be a counterbalance to the influence of China in the region. China continued to provide political and limited financial support, and in November 2000 President Jiang Zemin paid a two-day official visit to Cambodia, the first by a Chinese Head of State in more than 35 years. On the first day of Jiang's visit, China defended its support of the Khmers Rouges during the 1970s, claiming that its limited assistance had been intended to help maintain Cambodia's independence from foreign powers. In February 2001 the Chinese Minister of National Defence, Chi Haotian, arrived for a five-day goodwill visit. Subsequent visits from other senior Chinese officials further consolidated cordial relations between the two countries.

In January 1994 Chuan Leekpai undertook the first-ever official visit to Cambodia by a Thai Prime Minister. Relations between Cambodia and Thailand had been strained by the Thai armed forces' unauthorized links with the PDK (which controlled illicit trade in gems and timber along the Thai border) and by Cambodian allegations of Thai involvement in the July 1994 coup attempt, but improved in September 1995 when the two countries signed an agreement to establish a joint border commission. Thailand remained neutral following the events of 5–6 July 1997, but extended humanitarian assistance to the estimated 35,000 refugees who crossed into Thailand to avoid the fighting in the north-west of Cambodia. The Thai Deputy Minister of Foreign Affairs, Sukhumbhand Paribatra, was instrumental in securing the coalition agreement between the

CPP and the FUNCINPEC Party in November 1998. In June 2001 the Thai Prime Minister, Thaksin Shinawatra, visited Cambodia, emphasizing the improved state of relations between the two countries and, in October, King Sihanouk presented Thaksin Shinawatra with an honorary medal for his efforts to promote bilateral ties. However, in January 2003 relations became extremely strained when demonstrators attacked the Thai embassy and several Thai-owned businesses in Phnom-Penh, having been provoked by comments, wrongly attributed to a Thai actress, that implied that the temples at Angkor Wat had been stolen from Thailand. The violence escalated, resulting in the death of a Cambodian man and prompting the Thai Government to withdraw its ambassador, together with more than 500 Thai nationals resident in Cambodia, and downgrade diplomatic relations. Cambodians were forbidden from entering Thailand, and domestic flights between the two countries were suspended. In the aftermath of the riots Prime Minister Hun Sen issued a formal apology to the Thai Government and promised compensation; bilateral relations subsequently began to improve and the joint border was reopened.

In August 1994 the National Assembly adopted an immigration bill which prompted concern that it might be used to enforce the mass expulsion of ethnic Vietnamese from Cambodia, given that the legislation had no provision for the definition of Cambodian citizenship. In January 1995 Prince Ranariddh held talks in Viet Nam on improving bilateral relations, following an increase in tension over the issue of ethnic Vietnamese in Cambodia. The Vietnamese President made an official state visit to Cambodia in August. In early 1996 Cambodia accused Viet Nam of encroaching on disputed border territory, but in April discussions in Phnom-Penh resulted in an agreement providing for the settlement of all border issues through further negotiations.

In April 1995 Cambodia, Thailand, Viet Nam and Laos signed an agreement providing for the establishment of the Mekong River Commission (see p. 341), which was to co-ordinate the sustainable development of the resources of the Lower Mekong River Basin. In October 1999 the leaders of Cambodia, Laos and Viet Nam convened in the Laotian capital for their first 'unofficial' Indo-Chinese summit meeting. The opening of Cambodia's first bridge over the Mekong River in December 2001 was intended to promote the country's trade links with Viet Nam and Laos. The bridge connected East and West Cambodia by road for the first time.

Government

The Kingdom of Cambodia is a constitutional monarchy. The monarch is the Head of State and is selected by the Throne Council from among descendants of three royal lines. Legislative power is vested in the 122-member National Assembly, the lower chamber, which is elected for a term of five years by universal adult suffrage, and the 61-member Senate, the upper chamber, whose members are appointed by political parties in proportion to their representation in the National Assembly. Executive power is held by the Cabinet (the Royal Government of Cambodia), headed by the Prime Minister, who is appointed by the King at the recommendation of the Chairman of the National Assembly from among the representatives of the winning party.

For local administration the Kingdom of Cambodia is divided into provinces, municipalities, districts, *khan*, *khum* and *sangkat*.

Defence

In August 2002 the total strength of the Royal Cambodian Armed Forces was estimated to be 125,000, comprising an army of 75,000, a navy of 3,000, an air force of 2,000 and provincial forces of about 45,000. A system of conscription was in force, for those aged between 18 and 35, for five years. However, conscription has not been implemented since 1993. In 2002 government expenditure on defence was budgeted at an estimated 620,000m. riels.

Economic Affairs

In 2001, according to the World Bank, Cambodia's gross national income (GNI), measured at average 1999–2001 prices, was US \$3,329m., equivalent to \$270 per head (or \$1,520 per head on an international purchasing-power parity basis). During 1990–2001, it was estimated, the population increased at an average annual rate of 2.7% while gross domestic product (GDP) per head increased, in real terms, by an average of 2.2% per year. Cambodia's overall GDP increased, in real terms, at an

average annual rate of 5.0% during 1990–2001. According to the Asian Development Bank (ADB), GDP increased by 7.7% in 2000 and by 6.3% in 2001.

Agriculture (including hunting, forestry and fishing) contributed 39.2% of GDP in 2001. In 2000 the sector engaged 73.7% of the economically active population, but remained extremely vulnerable to adverse weather conditions, this problem being compounded by inadequate rural infrastructure and a lack of farm inputs such as fertilizers. In October 1999 Cambodia announced its intention to export rice for the first time since 1970, owing to an estimated rice surplus of 140,000 metric tons. In 2002 severe droughts followed by flooding resulted in approximately one-fifth of the land area normally used for rice production not being planted, leading to fears of future rice shortages. Other principal crops include cassava, maize, sugar cane and bananas. Timber and rubber are the two principal export commodities. The forestry sector accounted for only an estimated 2.5% of GDP in 2000, as reserves continued to be depleted and reafforestation remained inadequate. From 1999 it was hoped that, following agreements with the IMF and multilateral donors for conditional loans, Cambodia would take measures to enforce logging bans and forestry regulations imposed in conjunction with the aid donors. However, in late 2002 the Government terminated the contract of Global Witness, an independent international group monitoring efforts being made to combat illegal logging, prompting concerns that efforts to reform the forestry sector might be disrupted and that some aid might be withheld. The fishing sector was also adversely affected by deforestation, which caused reductions in freshwater fishing catches, owing to the silting up of lakes and rivers. According to estimates published by the IMF, however, the GDP of the fishing sector increased at an average annual rate of 4.7% in 1995–2000, following a period of decline in the early 1990s, and contributed an estimated 7.4% of GDP in 2000. According to the ADB, agricultural GDP increased, in real terms, at an average annual rate of 6.5% during 1993–2001. The GDP of the agricultural sector contracted by 0.3% in 2000, but expanded by 3.9% in 2001.

Industry (including mining, manufacturing, construction and power) contributed 23.3% of GDP in 2001, and employed 8.4% of the labour force in 2000. According to the ADB, in real terms, industrial GDP increased at an average annual rate of 15.8% during 1993–2001. Growth in industrial GDP was 34.6% in 2000 and 15.5% in 2001.

In 2001 mining and quarrying contributed less than 0.2% of GDP. Cambodia has limited mineral resources, including phosphates, gem stones, iron ore, bauxite, silicon and manganese ore, of which only phosphates and gem stones are, at present, being exploited. In the 1990s several agreements on petroleum exploration were signed with foreign enterprises. Cambodia's resources of natural gas were unofficially estimated to be 1,500,000m.–3,500,000m. cu m in 1992, and petroleum reserves were estimated to be between 50m. and 100m. barrels. According to the ADB, the GDP of the mining sector increased, in real terms, at an average annual rate of 3.9% during 1993–2001; growth in mining GDP was an estimated 9.6% in 2001.

The manufacturing sector contributed 16.7% of GDP in 2001 and employed 7.0% of the labour force in 2000. The sector is dominated by rice milling and the production of ready-made garments, household goods, textiles, tyres and pharmaceutical products. The manufacture of garments, mostly for export, grew rapidly during the 1990s; employment in the sector increased from 2,270 workers in 1994 to 36,717 in 1997. By the end of 2000 160,000 workers were engaged in garment manufacture. Exports of clothing rose in value by almost 50% in 2000, compared with the previous year, to reach US \$1,012m. The Government was also attempting to promote the establishment of agro-industrial enterprises (sugar and vegetable oil refineries and factories producing paper pulp) and to encourage the production of fertilizers, petroleum and heavy construction and mechanical equipment. According to the ADB, the GDP of the manufacturing sector increased, in real terms, at an average annual rate of 18.9% during 1993–2001. Growth in manufacturing GDP was 44.6% in 2000 and 17.3% in 2001.

Energy is derived principally from timber. All commercial energy used in Cambodia is imported. In the late 1990s the country had an installed capacity of 28.7 MW, of which 15 MW was accounted for by an oil-fired thermal power plant and the rest by diesel generating units. Owing to a lack of spare parts and a shortage of fuel, only a small percentage of the generating capacity can be utilized. Cambodia has considerable hydropower potential, and two hydropower plants were under construction in the late 1990s. In late 2002 Cambodia signed an agreement with the Governments of China, Thailand, Laos, Myanmar and Viet Nam to form a regional power distribution system, which would enable hydropower development in the Mekong River area.

The services sector contributed 37.5% of GDP in 2001 and engaged 17.9% of the economically active population in 2000. The tourism sector has become increasingly significant. In 2000 greater political stability led to an increase in tourist arrivals to 466,365. Receipts from tourism in that year were estimated at US $228m. In 2001, despite the effects of the terrorist attacks on the USA in September, arrivals increased to 604,919. However, it was feared that the bombing in Bali, Indonesia, in October 2002 would affect the growth of Cambodia's tourism sector by deterring visitors to the region. As part of a government campaign to encourage tourism, 2003 was designated 'Visit Cambodia Year'. In real terms, according to the ADB, the GDP of the services sector increased at an average annual rate of 2.7% during 1993–2001. Growth in the sector was 5.8% in 2000 and 2.9% in 2001.

In 2001 Cambodia recorded a visible trade deficit of US $347.5m., while there was a deficit of $104.6m. on the current account of the balance of payments. In 2001 the principal sources of imports were Thailand (23.5%) and Singapore (18.6%); other major sources were Hong Kong, the People's Republic of China and the Republic of Korea. In the same year the principal market for exports was the USA (57.9%); other important purchasers were Germany, the United Kingdom and Hong Kong. The principal exports in 2000 were garments (accounting for 72.3% of the total), sawn timber, logs and rubber. The principal imports were petroleum products (accounting for 9.3% of the total), cigarettes and motorcycles. Re-exports (which were a result of the differences in tariffs on goods imported by Cambodia and its neighbours) remained important, although they declined from 53% of total exports in 1993 to an estimated 21.2% in 2000.

Cambodia's overall budget deficit in 2001 was 439,860m. riels. Cambodia's external debt at the end of 2000 totalled US $2,357m., of which $2,180m. was long-term public debt. In that year the cost of debt-servicing was equivalent to 2.0% of revenue from exports of goods and services. The annual rate of inflation averaged 5.0% during 1995–2001; consumer prices declined by 0.8% in 2000, remained static in 2001 and increased by 3.2% in 2002.

Cambodia is a member of the Asian Development Bank (see p. 143), of the Mekong River Commission (see p. 341) and of the Colombo Plan (see p. 339). Cambodia was formally admitted to the Association of South East Asian Nations (ASEAN, see p. 146) in April 1999. Following the implementation of the ASEAN Free Trade Area (AFTA, see p. 147) in January 2002, Cambodia was granted until 2007 to comply with the 0%–5% tariff agreement.

Prospects for economic development in Cambodia were greatly enhanced by the formation of the coalition Government in November 1998, owing both to the resumption of lending by foreign donors (who had suspended aid in mid-1997) and to the possibility of the sustained implementation of reformist policies. In 1999 economic growth exceeded expectations, the rate of inflation decreased sharply and export growth was maintained. In February 2000 the Government announced a three-year US $1,400m. economic development programme intended to promote growth and to reduce poverty. At the annual meeting of bilateral and multilateral donors in Paris in May, $548m. of fresh aid was pledged to Cambodia in response to the Government's appeals. At the next annual meeting, held in Tokyo in June 2001, the country received a further $615m. and, in June

2002, at a meeting held in Phnom-Penh, it was awarded a further $635m. (Aid, however, was partly dependent upon the fulfilment of government pledges to reduce military spending, to address the problem of illegal logging and to decrease expenditure on the civil service payroll.) From 2000 there was considerable progress in the structural reform of several key areas, particularly the financial sector. Consistent expansion in agricultural output, a recovery in levels of tourism and the rapid increase in garment exports ensured that the nation continued to experience economic growth of an average annual rate of 5%–6%. In 2001 the Government initiated its second Socioeconomic Development Plan, to be implemented in 2001–05, as part of its ongoing effort to combat poverty. The Plan aimed to expand opportunities for the poor through the promotion of stable and sustained economic growth. In August a $42m. demobilization programme was endorsed by the World Bank and other bodies, enabling Cambodia to continue the reduction of its armed forces and permit higher levels of expenditure on the social sector. In 2002, however, the programme attracted controversy after the Government admitted that many of those allegedly demobilized had never undertaken military service and were thus receiving payments from the programme fraudulently. Severe droughts and flooding in the same year resulted in the loss of rice crops worth an estimated $30m., prompting fears of serious food shortages. In November the Chinese Government announced that it had cancelled Cambodia's foreign debt, significantly improving the country's situation. However, it was widely recognized that the Government needed to continue to implement key reforms, particularly in the public sector, if Cambodia was eventually to be able to compete with its regional neighbours. The forthcoming general election, due to be held in July, was perceived to be the primary cause of uncertainty with regard to the performance of the economy in 2003; it was feared that the possibility of violence, often endemic to Cambodian elections, would act as a deterrent to foreign investment and tourism. Economic growth in 2002 was between 5% and 5.5%, according to official estimates.

Education

Education is compulsory for six years between the ages of six and 12. Primary education begins at six and lasts for six years. In 1997 enrolment at primary level was equivalent to 113% of children in the relevant age-group (males 123%; females 104%). Secondary education comprises two cycles, each lasting three years. In 1997 enrolment at secondary level was equivalent to 24% of the relevant age-group (males 31%; females 17%). In the same year enrolment at tertiary level was equivalent to 1.0% of the relevant age-group (males 2.0%; females 0.5%). In 2000 the Ministry of Education, Youth and Sport was allocated 166,000m. riels (8.0% of total expenditure).

Public Holidays

2003: 1 January (International New Year's Day), 7 January (Remembrance Day), 13–15 April (Cambodian New Year), 1 May (Labour Day), 20 May (Day of Remembrance), 24 September (Constitution Day), 23 October (Anniversary of Paris Peace Agreement on Cambodia), 9 November (Independence Day).

2004: 1 January (International New Year's Day), 7 January (Remembrance Day), 13–15 April (Cambodian New Year), 1 May (Labour Day), 20 May (Day of Remembrance), 24 September (Constitution Day), 23 October (Anniversary of Paris Peace Agreement on Cambodia), 9 November (Independence Day).

Weights and Measures

The metric system is in force.

Statistical Survey

Source (unless otherwise stated): National Institute of Statistics, Ministry of Planning, Sangkat Boeung Keng Kong 2, blvd Preh Monivong, Phnom-Penh; tel. (23) 216538; fax (23) 213650; e-mail census@camnet.wm.kh; internet www.nis.gov.kh .

Note: Some of the statistics below represent only sectors of the economy controlled by the Government of the former Khmer Republic. During the years 1970–75 no figures were available for areas controlled by the Khmers Rouges.

Area and Population

AREA, POPULATION AND DENSITY

Area (sq km)	181,035*
Population (census results)†	
17 April 1962.	5,728,771
Prior to elections of 1 May 1981	6,682,000
3 March 1998	
Males	5,511,408
Females.	5,926,248
Total	11,437,656
Population (official estimates at mid-year)	
1999	12,660,000
2000	12,990,000
2001	13,311,000
Density (per sq km) at mid-2001	73.5

* 69,898 sq miles.
† Excluding adjustments for underenumeration.

PROVINCES
(1998 census)

	Area (sq km)*	Population	Density (per sq km)
Banteay Mean Chey	6,679	577,772	86.5
Bat Dambang.	11,702	793,129	67.8
Kampong Cham	9,799	1,608,914	164.2
Kampong Chhnang . . .	5,521	417,693	75.7
Kampong Spueu . . .	7,017	598,882	85.3
Kampong Thum	13,814	569,060	41.2
Kampot	4,873	528,405	108.4
Kandal.	3,568	1,075,125	301.3
Kaoh Kong	11,160	132,106	11.8
Kracheh	11,094	263,175	23.7
Mondol Kiri	14,288	32,407	2.3
Phnom Penh	290	999,804	3,447.6
Preah Vihear	13,788	119,261	8.6
Prey Veaeng	4,883	946,042	193.7
Pousat	12,692	360,445	28.4
Rotanak Kiri	10,782	94,243	8.7
Siem Reab.	10,299	696,164	67.6
Krong Preah Sihanouk . . .	868	155,690	179.4
Stueng Traeng	11,092	81,074	7.3
Svay Rieng	2,966	478,252	161.2
Takaev.	3,563	790,168	221.8
Otdar Mean Chey	6,158	68,279	11.1
Krong Kaeb	336	28,660	85.3
Krong Pailin	803	22,906	28.5
Total	178,035	11,437,656	64.2

* Excluding Tonlé Sap lake (3,000 sq km).

PRINCIPAL TOWNS
(population at 1998 census)

Phnom-Penh (capital). . .	999,804	Bat Dambang (Battambang)	139,964
Preah Sihanouk (Sihanoukville)*	155,690	Siem Reab (Siem Reap)	119,528

* Also known as Kampong Saom (Kompong Som).

BIRTHS AND DEATHS
(annual averages)

	1985–90	1990–95	1995–2000*
Birth rate (per 1,000)	44.2	38.2	38.1
Death rate (per 1,000)	16.5	14.1	10.8

* UN estimates. (Source: UN, *World Population Prospects: The 2000 Revision*).

Source (unless otherwise indicated): Ministry of Economy and Finance, Phnom-Penh.

1997: Death rate (per 1,000) 12.0 (Source: World Health Organization).

1998: Birth rate (per 1,000) 38.0 (Source: World Health Organization).

Expectation of life (WHO estimates, years at birth): 56.2 (males 53.3; females 59.0) in 2001 (Source: WHO, *World Health Report*).

EMPLOYMENT

	1998*	1999†	2000‡
Agriculture, forestry and fishing .	3,770,982	4,213,620	3,889,048
Mining and quarrying . . .	6,385	5,508	3,328
Manufacturing	158,969	258,876	367,286
Electricity, gas and water . .	3,278	5,508	3,799
Construction	47,716	82,620	69,773
Wholesale and retail trade . .	341,351	402,084	436,308
Restaurants and hotels . . .	15,281	27,540	18,794
Transport and communications .	118,001	121,176	119,596
Financial intermediation, real estate and renting	4,416	16,524	16,636
Public administration . . .	221,966	187,272	146,986
Education	81,073	88,128	87,385
Health and social work . . .	26,219	27,540	30,235
Other social services. . . .	68,311	38,556	40,098
Other services	45,270	44,064	45,905
Total employed	4,909,218	5,519,016	5,275,177

* Based on the results of the 1998 Population Census.
† Based on the results of the Socioeconomic Survey of Cambodia.
‡ Based on the results of the Labour Force Survey of Cambodia.

Source: IMF, *Cambodia: Statistical Appendix* (February 2002).

Health and Welfare

KEY INDICATORS

Total fertility rate (children per woman, 2001). . . .	4.9
Under-5 mortality rate (per 1,000 live births, 2001) . . .	138
HIV/AIDS (% of persons aged 15–49, 2001).	2.70
Physicians (per 1,000 head, 1998)	0.30
Hospital beds (per 1,000 head, 1990)	2.07
Health expenditure (2000): US $ per head (PPP) . . .	111
Health expenditure (2000): % of GDP	8.1
Health expenditure (2000): public (% of total) . . .	24.5
Access to water (% of persons, 2000).	30
Access to sanitation (% of persons, 2000)	18
Human Development Index (2000): ranking	130
Human Development Index (2000): value	0.543

For sources and definitions, see explanatory note on p. vi.

Agriculture

PRINCIPAL CROPS
('000 metric tons)

	1999	2000	2001
Rice (paddy)	4,029.6	4,049.9	4,026.1
Maize	95.3	157.0	173.7
Sweet potatoes	32.5	28.2	26.0
Cassava (Manioc)	228.5	147.8	131.1
Other roots and tubers*	18.5	19.0	19.0
Dry beans	15.9	15.1	17.3
Soybeans (Soya beans)	35.1	28.1	37.5
Groundnuts (in shell)	9.2	7.5	7.5
Sesame seed	7.4	9.9	8.9
Coconuts†	70.0	70.0	70.0
Sugar cane	159.9	164.2	167.1
Tobacco (leaves)	6.4	7.7	7.7
Natural rubber	45.2	42.4	35.9
Vegetables*	470.0	470.0	472.0
Oranges	63.0	63.0	63.0
Mangoes	35.0	35.0	35.0
Pineapples	16.0	16.0	16.0
Bananas	147.0	146.0	146.0
Other fruits and berries*	59.2	61.7	62.2

* FAO estimates.
† Unofficial figure(s).

Source: FAO.

LIVESTOCK
('000 head, year ending September)

	1999	2000	2001
Horses*	25	26	26
Cattle	2,826	2,993	2,869
Buffaloes	654	694	626
Pigs	2,189	1,934	2,115
Chickens	13,417	15,249	15,248
Ducks*	4,600	4,600	4,600

* FAO estimates.

Source: FAO.

LIVESTOCK PRODUCTS
('000 metric tons)

	1999	2000	2001
Beef and veal*	42.1	56.7	58.2
Buffalo meat*	13.1	13.1	13.1
Pig meat*	102.5	105.0	107.8
Poultry meat*	25.0	25.1	25.3
Cows' milk*	20.4	20.4	20.4
Hen eggs	11.7	11.7	11.7
Other poultry eggs*	3.3	3.3	3.3
Cattle hides (fresh)*	10.5	14.2	14.6
Buffalo hides (fresh)*	2.7	2.7	2.7

* FAO estimates.

Source: FAO.

Forestry

ROUNDWOOD REMOVALS
('000 cubic metres, excl. bark)

	1999	2000	2001
Sawlogs, veneer logs and logs for sleepers	291	143	100
Other industrial wood	630*	36	21
Fuel wood*	10,316	10,119	9,924
Total	11,237	10,298	10,045

* FAO estimate(s).
Source: FAO.

SAWNWOOD PRODUCTION
('000 cubic metres, incl. railway sleepers)

	1999	2000	2001
Total (all broadleaved)	26	20	5

Source: FAO.

Fishing
('000 metric tons, live weight)

	1998	1999	2000
Capture	107.9	269.1	284.4
Freshwater fishes	75.6	230.7	245.3
Marine fishes	23.7	28.1	26.6
Aquaculture	14.1	15.0	14.4
Total catch	122.0	284.1	298.8

Note: Figures exclude crocodiles, recorded by number rather than by weight. The total of estuarine crocodiles caught was: 40,700 in 1998; 25,380 in 1999; 26,300 in 2000.

Source: FAO, *Yearbook of Fishery Statistics*.

Mining
(estimates, '000 metric tons)

	1999	2000	2001
Salt (unrefined)	40	40	40

Source: US Geological Survey.

Industry

SELECTED PRODUCTS
('000 metric tons, unless otherwise indicated)

	1971	1972	1973
Distilled alcoholic beverages ('000 hectolitres)	45	55	36
Beer ('000 hectolitres)	26	23	18
Soft drinks ('000 hectolitres)	25	25*	25*
Cigarettes (million)	3,413	2,510	2,622
Cotton yarn—pure and mixed (metric tons)	1,068	1,094	415
Bicycle tyres and tubes ('000)	208	200*	200*
Rubber footwear ('000 pairs)	1,292	1,000*	1,000*
Soap (metric tons)	469	400*	400*
Motor spirit (petrol)	2	—	—
Distillate fuel oils	11	—	—
Residual fuel oils	14	—	—
Cement	44	53	78
Electric energy (million kWh)†	148	166	150

* Estimate.
† Production by public utilities only.

Cigarettes (million): 4,175 in 1987; 4,200 annually in 1988–92 (estimates by US Department of Agriculture).

Cement ('000 metric tons): 50 in 2001 (estimate by the US Geological Survey).

Electric energy (estimates, million kWh): 194 in 1995; 201 in 1996; 208 in 1997.

Plywood ('000 cu m): 15 in 1999; 18 in 2000; 14 in 2001 (Source: FAO).

Source: partly UN, *Industrial Commodity Statistics Yearbook*.

Finance

CURRENCY AND EXCHANGE RATES

Monetary Units
100 sen = 1 riel

Sterling, Dollar and Euro Equivalents (31 December 2002)
£1 sterling = 6,334.4 riels
US $1 = 3,930.0 riels
€1 = 4,121.4 riels
10,000 riels = £1.579 = $2.545 = €2.426

Average Exchange Rate (riels per US $)
2000   3,840.8
2001   3,916.3
2002   3,912.1

BUDGET
('000 million riels)

Revenue*	1998	1999	2000
Tax revenue	679.4	947.7	1,026.0
Direct taxes	55.5	82.7	135.6
Profit tax	42.1	63.8	100.9
Indirect taxes	247.5	431.6	500.0
Turnover tax	65.9	21.8	12.6
Value-added tax	90.1	314.9	371.6
Excise duties	76.1	91.8	112.6
Taxes on international trade	376.3	433.4	390.4
Import duties	372.5	415.3	372.8
Other current revenue	230.1	354.8	353.3
Forestry	22.8	36.3	41.0
Receipts from public enterprises	55.5	30.5	51.4
Posts and telecommunications	87.2	108.9	91.9
Public services	17.5	141.9	101.4
Capital revenue	33.2	13.7	29.3
Total	942.7	1,316.2	1,408.6

Expenditure†	1998	1999	2000
Council of Ministers	57	54	85
Ministry of Defence	312	336	309
Ministry of the Interior	173	147	142
Ministry of Economy and Finance	109	134	96
Ministry of Public Works and Transport	13	29	20
Ministry of Agriculture, Forestry, Hunting and Fisheries	18	21	23
Ministry of Education, Youth and Sport	102	156	166
Ministry of Industry, Mines and Energy	3	4	5
Ministry of Health	44	126	102
Ministry of Posts and Telecommunications	54	114	29
Ministry of Social Affairs, Labour, Professional Training and Youth Rehabilitation	48	19	26
Total (incl. others)	1,571	1,825	2,083
Current expenditure	941	1,097	1,189
Capital expenditure	630	728	896

* Excluding grants received.

† Figures for individual ministries exclude externally financed capital expenditure ('000 million riels): 510 in 1998; 504 in 1999; 593 in 2000.

Source: IMF, *Cambodia: Statistical Appendix* (February 2002).

INTERNATIONAL RESERVES
(US $ million at 31 December)

	2000	2001	2002
IMF special drawing rights	0.18	0.51	0.55
Foreign exchange	501.50	586.30	776.10
Total	501.68	586.81	776.65

Source: IMF, *International Financial Statistics* .

MONEY SUPPLY
(million riels at 31 December)

	2000	2001	2002
Currency outside banks	494,600	577,780	765,980
Demand deposits at deposit money banks	45,041	31,940	47,300
Total money	539,641	609,720	813,280

Sources: Ministry of Economy and Finance, Phnom-Penh, and IMF, *International Financial Statistics*.

COST OF LIVING
(Consumer Price Index for Phnom-Penh; base: 1995 = 100)

	1998	1999	2000
Food, beverages and tobacco	130.9	140.8	136.1
All items	132.8	138.1	137.0

Source: UN, *Monthly Bulletin of Statistics* .

All items (base: 1995 = 100): 133.7 in 2001; 138.0 in 2002 (Source: IMF, *International Financial Statistics*).

NATIONAL ACCOUNTS
('000 million riels at current prices)

Expenditure on the Gross Domestic Product

	1999	2000	2001
Government final consumption expenditure	661.2	736.9	803.9
Private final consumption expenditure	11,082.5	10,925.5	11,032.6
Increase in stocks	181.5	−213.9	265.4
Gross fixed capital formation	1,814.4	1,957.1	2,125.7
Statistical discrepancy	−138.9	−196.9	−482.6
Total domestic expenditure	13,600.7	13,208.7	13,745.0
Exports of goods and services	4,783.8	6,372.8	6,768.6
Less Imports of goods and services	5,797.4	6,649.9	7,148.6
GDP in purchasers' values	12,587.1	12,931.5	13,364.9
GDP at constant 1993 prices	8,889.1	9,569.7	10,176.2

Source: Asian Development Bank, *Key Indicators of Developing Asian and Pacific Countries* .

Gross Domestic Product by Economic Activity

	1999	2000	2001
Agriculture, hunting, forestry and fishing	5,384.8	4,935.3	4,930.0
Mining and quarrying	17.2	18.6	23.8
Manufacturing	1,485.0	1,996.3	2,100.6
Electricity, gas and water	43.5	43.3	56.8
Construction	606.2	631.4	742.9
Trade, restaurants and hotels	1,798.4	1,812.4	1,867.0
Transport, storage and communications	778.9	875.5	940.9
Financing, real estate and business services	893.0	1,000.9	990.5
Public administration	388.6	376.6	369.4
Other services	483.6	525.9	551.1
Sub-total	11,879.2	12,216.1	12,573.0
Less Imputed bank service charge	157.4	154.8	128.0
GDP at factor cost	11,721.8	12,061.3	12,445.0
Indirect taxes, *less* subsidies	865.3	870.2	920.0
GDP in purchasers' values	12,587.1	12,931.5	13,364.9

Source: Asian Development Bank, *Key Indicators of Developing Asian and Pacific Countries*.

BALANCE OF PAYMENTS
(US $ million)

	1999	2000	2001
Exports of goods f.o.b.	886.4	1,264.0	1,377.5
Imports of goods f.o.b.	−1,239.0	−1,628.2	−1,725.0
Trade balance	−352.6	−364.2	−347.5
Exports of services	198.7	244.2	256.9
Imports of services	−194.4	−240.4	−243.8
Balance on goods and services	−348.3	−360.4	−334.4
Other income received	20.6	32.0	21.0
Other income paid	−61.6	−82.3	−63.9
Balance on goods, services and income	−389.3	−410.7	−377.3
Current transfers received	235.9	305.3	273.1
Current transfers paid	−1.6	−0.4	−0.4
Current balance	−155.0	−105.8	−104.6
Capital account (net)	44.0	38.1	63.3
Direct investment from abroad	143.6	111.7	113.1
Other investment assets	−61.1	−80.3	−103.0
Other investment liabilities	43.7	67.9	64.7
Net errors and omissions	34.8	54.3	39.0
Overall balance	50.0	85.9	72.5

Source: IMF, *International Financial Statistics*.

External Trade

PRINCIPAL COMMODITIES
(US $ million)

Imports c.i.f.	1998	1999	2000*
Cigarettes	144	119	70
Petroleum products	111	131	175
Motorcycles	44	36	31
Total (incl. others)	1,189	1,337	1,885

Exports f.o.b.	1998	1999	2000*
Crude rubber†	27	28	30
Logs and sawn timber†	178	111	49
Clothing	392	564	1,012
Total (incl. others)‡	867	971	1,399

* Estimates.

† Including estimates for illegal exports.

‡ Including re-exports (US $ million): 263 in 1998; 261 in 1999; 296 (estimate) in 2000.

Source: IMF, *Cambodia: Statistical Appendix* (February 2002).

PRINCIPAL TRADING PARTNERS
(US $ million)

Imports c.i.f.	1999	2000	2001
China, People's Republic	85.9	112.9	169.7
France	41.9	39.3	52.5
Hong Kong	185.7	254.3	288.5
Indonesia	50.9	68.4	73.8
Japan	73.9	58.4	52.4
Korea, Republic	79.9	76.9	111.7
Malaysia	49.9	64.2	66.5
Singapore	99.1	106.0	406.9
Thailand	195.2	221.8	513.2
Viet Nam	85.6	91.5	100.7
Total (incl. others)	1,240.9	1,417.6	2,183.4

Exports f.o.b.	1999	2000	2001
China, People's Republic	8.9	23.8	33.5
France	20.7	27.7	38.5
Germany	40.4	66.0	121.1
Japan	9.3	10.7	55.9
Hong Kong	38.3	262.2	67.7
Singapore	181.7	18.0	49.6
Thailand	18.5	22.9	11.2
United Kingdom	53.4	81.6	105.4
USA	235.8	739.7	898.1
Viet Nam	391.8	19.5	21.5
Total (incl. others)	1,322.8	1,357.6	1,550.5

Source: Asian Development Bank, *Key Indicators of Developing Asian and Pacific Countries*.

Transport

RAILWAYS
(traffic)

	1997	1998	1999
Freight carried ('000 metric tons)	16	294	259
Freight ton-km ('000)	36,514	75,721	76,171
Passengers ('000)	553	438	431
Passenger-km ('000)	50,992	43,847	49,894

Source: Ministry of Economy and Finance, Phnom-Penh.

2000: Passenger-km ('000) 15; Freight ton-km ('000) 91 (Source: UN, *Statistical Yearbook*).

ROAD TRAFFIC
(motor vehicles in use at 31 December)

	1998	1999	2000
Passenger cars	208,452	257,711	312,303
Buses and coaches	10,335	14,241	18,918
Lorries and vans	17,494	36,768	49,036
Road tractors	52,021	64,080	77,139
Motorcycles and mopeds	1,138,705	1,361,874	1,609,839

Source: International Road Federation, *World Road Statistics*.

SHIPPING

Merchant Fleet
(registered at 31 December)

	1999	2000	2001
Number of vessels	300	405	564
Displacement ('000 grt)	998.7	1,447.5	1,996.7

Source: Lloyd's Register-Fairplay, *World Fleet Statistics*.

International Sea-borne Freight Traffic
(estimates, '000 metric tons)

	1988	1989	1990
Goods loaded	10	10	11
Goods unloaded	100	100	95

Source: UN, *Monthly Bulletin of Statistics*.

CIVIL AVIATION
(traffic on scheduled services)

	1975	1976	1977
Passenger-kilometres (million)	42	42	42
Freight ton-kilometres ('000)	400	400	400

Source: Statistisches Bundesamt, Wiesbaden, Germany.

Tourism

FOREIGN TOURIST ARRIVALS
(by air)*

Country of residence	1999	2000	2001
Australia	9,471	11,350	13,078
Canada	5,415	5,646	6,191
China, People's Repub.	26,805	30,586	32,002
France	23,754	24,883	23,328
Germany	6,490	7,298	6,861
Japan	17,885	19,906	17,952
Korea, Repub..	6,377	7,536	9,579
Malaysia	12,541	14,701	15,994
Singapore	10,634	10,734	10,982
Taiwan.	20,607	21,626	23,098
Thailand	15,272	16,550	17,496
United Kingdom	13,843	15,912	17,686
USA	30,301	35,814	37,033
Viet Nam	5,217	8,333	7,828
Total (incl. others†)	262,907	351,661	408,377

* Figures for individual countries refer to arrivals at Pochentong (Phnom-Penh) airport only.

† Including arrivals at Siem Reap airport (28,525 in 1999; 87,012 in 2000; 133,688 in 2001).

Total arrivals (incl. arrivals by land and sea): 367,743 in 1999; 466,365 in 2000; 604,919 in 2001.

Source: Ministry of Tourism, Phnom-Penh.

Tourism receipts (US $ million): 166 in 1998; 190 in 1999; 228 in 2000 (Source: World Bank).

Communications Media

	1999	2000	2001
Television receivers ('000 in use)	98	99	n.a.
Telephones ('000 main lines in use)	27.7	30.9	33.5
Mobile cellular telephones ('000 subscribers).	89.1	130.5	223.5
Personal computers ('000 in use)	13	15	20
Internet users ('000)	4.0	6.0	10.0

Facsimile machines (number in use): 884 in 1995; 1,470 in 1996; 2,995 in 1997.

Source: International Telecommunication Union.

Radio receivers ('000 in use): 1,120 in 1995; 1,300 in 1996; 1,340 in 1997 (Source: UNESCO, *Statistical Yearbook*).

Education

(2000/01*)

	Institutions	Teachers	Students
Primary	5,468	52,168	2,408,109
Secondary	662	23,952	388,664
Junior high school	511	18,952	283,578
Senior high school	151	5,000	105,086

* Excluding technical and vocational education and higher education.

Source: IMF, *Cambodia: Statistical Appendix* (February 2002).

Adult literacy rate (UNESCO estimates): 67.8% (males 79.8%; females 57.1%) in 2000 (Source: UN Development Programme, *Human Development Report*).

Directory

The Constitution

The Constitution was promulgated on 21 September 1993; a number of amendments were passed on 4 March 1999. The main provisions are summarized below:

GENERAL PROVISIONS

The Kingdom of Cambodia is a unitary state in which the King abides by the Constitution and multi-party liberal democracy. Cambodian citizens have full right of freedom of belief; Buddhism is the state religion. The Kingdom of Cambodia has a market economy system.

THE KING

The King is Head of State and the Supreme Commander of the Khmer Royal Armed Forces. The monarchist regime is based on a system of selection: within seven days of the King's death the Royal Council of the Throne (comprising the Chairman of the Senate, the Chairman of the National Assembly, the Prime Minister, the Supreme Patriarchs of the Mohanikay and Thoammayutikanikay sects, the First and Second Vice-Chairmen of the Senate and the First and Second Vice-Chairmen of the National Assembly) must select a King. The King must be at least 30 years of age and be a descendant of King Ang Duong, King Norodom or King Sisowath. The King appoints the Prime Minister and the Cabinet. In the absence of the King, the Chairman of the Senate assumes the duty of acting Head of State.

THE LEGISLATURE

Legislative power is vested in the National Assembly (the lower chamber) and the Senate (the upper chamber). The National Assembly has 122 members who are elected by universal adult suffrage. A member of the National Assembly must be a Cambodian citizen by birth over the age of 25 years and has a term of office of five years, the term of the National Assembly. The National Assembly may not be dissolved except in the case where the Royal Government (Cabinet) has been dismissed twice in 12 months. The National Assembly may dismiss cabinet members or remove the Royal Government from office by passing a censure motion through a two-thirds majority vote of all the representatives in the National Assembly. The Senate comprises nominated members, the number of which does not exceed one-half of all of the members of the National Assembly; two are nominated by the King, two are elected by the National Assembly and the remainder are elected by universal adult suffrage. A member of the Senate has a term of office of six years. The Senate reviews legislation passed by the National Assembly and acts as a co-ordinator between the National Assembly and the Royal Government. In special cases, the National Assembly and the Senate can assemble as the Congress to resolve issues of national importance.

CABINET

The Cabinet is the Royal Government of the Kingdom of Cambodia, which is led by a Prime Minister, assisted by Deputy Prime Ministers, with state ministers, ministers and state secretaries as members. The Prime Minister is designated by the King at the recommendation of the Chairman of the National Assembly from among the representatives of the winning party. The Prime Minister appoints the members of the Cabinet, who must be representatives in the National Assembly or members of parties represented in the National Assembly.

THE CONSTITUTIONAL COUNCIL

The Constitutional Council's competence is to interpret the Constitution and laws passed by the National Assembly and reviewed completely by the Senate. It has the right to examine and settle disputes relating to the election of members of the National Assembly and the Senate. The Constitutional Council consists of nine members with a nine-year mandate. One-third of the members are replaced every three years. Three members are appointed by the King, three elected by the National Assembly and three appointed by the Supreme Council of the Magistracy.

The Government

HEAD OF STATE

King: HM King NORODOM SIHANOUK acceded to the throne on 24 September 1993.

ROYAL GOVERNMENT OF CAMBODIA
(April 2003)

A coalition of the Cambodian People's Party (CPP) and the FUNCINPEC Party.

Prime Minister: HUN SEN (CPP).

Deputy Prime Minister and Co-Minister of the Interior: SAR KHENG (CPP).

Deputy Prime Minister and Minister of Education, Youth and Sport: TOL LAH (FUNCINPEC).

Senior Ministers: TEA BANH (CPP), KEAT CHHON (CPP), SOK AN (CPP), HOR NAM HONG (CPP), LU LAY SRENG (FUNCINPEC), CHHIM SEAK LENG (FUNCINPEC), HONG SUN HUOT (FUNCINPEC), YOU HOCKRY (FUNCINPEC).

Minister in charge of the Council of Ministers: SOK AN (CPP).

Co-Ministers of National Defence: TEA BANH (CPP), Prince SISOWATH SIREIRATH (FUNCINPEC).

Co-Minister of the Interior: YOU HOCKRY (FUNCINPEC).

Minister of Parliamentary Affairs and Inspection: KHUN HAING (FUNCINPEC).

Minister of Foreign Affairs and International Co-operation: HOR NAM HONG (CPP).

Minister of Economy and Finance: KEAT CHHON (CPP).

Minister of Information: LU LAY SRENG (FUNCINPEC).

Minister of Health: HONG SUN HUOT (FUNCINPEC).

Minister of Industry, Mines and Energy: SUY SEM (CPP).

Minister of Planning: CHHAY THAN (CPP).

Minister of Commerce: CHAM PRASIDH (CPP).

Minister of Agriculture, Forestry, Hunting and Fisheries: CHAN SARUN (CPP).

Minister of Culture and Fine Arts: Princess NORODOM BOPHA DEVI (FUNCINPEC).

Minister of Environment: Dr MOK MARETH (CPP).

Minister of Rural Development: LY THUCH (FUNCINPEC).

Minister of Social Affairs, Labour, Professional Training and Youth Rehabilitation: ITH SAM HENG (CPP).

Minister of Posts and Telecommunications: SO KHUN (CPP).

Minister of Cults and Religions: CHEA SAVOEURN (FUNCINPEC).

Minister of Women's Affairs and Veterans: MOU SOK HUOR (FUNCINPEC).

Minister of Public Works and Transport: KHY TAING LIM (FUNCINPEC).

Minister of Justice: NIEV SITHONG (FUNCINPEC).

Minister of Tourism: VENG SEREIVUTH (FUNCINPEC).

Minister of Territorial Organization, Urbanization and Construction: IM CHHUN LIM (CPP).

Minister of Water Resources and Meteorology: LIM KEAN HOR (CPP).

Secretary of State for Public Civil Servants: PICH BUN THIN (CPP).

Secretary of State for Civil Aviation: POK SAM EL (FUNCINPEC).

There are also 52 further Secretaries of State.

MINISTRIES

Ministry of Agriculture, Forestry and Fisheries: 200 blvd Norodom, Phnom-Penh; tel. (23) 211351; fax (23) 217320; e-mail ranyvireak@hotmail.com; internet www.fadinap.org/cambodia.

Ministry of Commerce: 20 blvd Norodom, Phnom-Penh; tel. (23) 723775; fax (23) 426396; e-mail sekimoto@bigpond.com.kh; internet www.moc.gov.kh.

Ministry of Cults and Religions: Preah Sisowath Quay, rue 240, Phnom-Penh; tel. (23) 723172; fax (23) 725699; e-mail sophearin@camnet.com.kh.

Ministry of Culture and Fine Arts: 227 blvd Monivong, cnr rue Red Cross, Phnom-Penh; tel. (23) 217645; fax (23) 725749.

Ministry of National Defence: blvd Pochentong, Phnom-Penh; tel. (23) 366170; fax (23) 366169.

Ministry of Economy and Finance: 60 rue 92, Phnom-Penh; tel. (23) 722863; fax (23) 427798; e-mail mefcg@hotmail.com.

Ministry of Education, Youth and Sport: 80 blvd Norodom, Phnom-Penh; tel. (23) 217253; fax (23) 217250; e-mail crsmeys@camnet.com.kh; internet www.moeys.gov.kh.

Ministry of Environment: 48 blvd Sihanouk Tonle Bassac, Chamkar Morn, Phnom-Penh; tel. (23) 724901; fax (23) 427844; e-mail minenvlb@forum.org.kh; internet www.camnet.com.kh/moe-library/.

Ministry of Foreign Affairs and International Co-operation: 161 Preah Sisowath Quay, Phnom-Penh; tel. (23) 216141; fax (23) 216144; e-mail mfaicasean@bigpond.com.kh; internet www.mfaic .gov.kh.

Ministry of Health: 128 blvd Kampuchea Krom, Phnom-Penh; tel. (23) 366553; fax (23) 426841.

Ministry of Industry, Mines and Energy: 45 blvd Preah Norodom, Phnom-Penh; tel. and fax (23) 428263.

Ministry of Information: Department of International Co-operation and ASEAN Affairs, 62 blvd Monivong, Phnom-Penh; tel. (16) 815237; fax (23) 722618; e-mail coci@camnet.com.kh; internet www .moi-coci.gov.kh.

Ministry of the Interior: 275 blvd Norodom, Phnom-Penh; tel. (23) 363653; fax (23) 212708.

Ministry of Justice: 240 blvd Sothearos, cnr rue 240, Phnom-Penh; tel. (23) 360320; fax (23) 360327.

Ministry of Parliamentary Affairs and Inspection: rue Jawaharlal Nehru, Phnom-Penh; tel. (23) 884261; fax (23) 884264.

Ministry of Planning: 386 blvd Monivong, Sangkat Boeung Keng Kong 2, Phnom-Penh; tel. (23) 212049; fax (23) 210698.

Ministry of Posts and Telecommunications: cnr rue Preah Ang Eng and rue Ang Non, Phnom-Penh; tel. (23) 426510; fax (23) 426011; e-mail koyks@camnet.com.kh; internet www.mptc.gov.kh.

Ministry of Public Works and Transport: 200 blvd Norodom, Phnom-Penh; tel. and fax (23) 427862; e-mail mpwt@mpwt.gov.kh; internet www.mpwt.gov.kh.

Ministry of Rural Development: blvd Czechoslovakia/blvd Pochentong, Phnom-Penh; tel. (23) 722425; fax (23) 722425.

Ministry of Social Affairs, Labour, Professional Training and Youth Rehabilitation: 68 blvd Norodom, Phnom-Penh; tel. (23) 725191; fax (23) 427322.

Ministry of Territorial Organization, Urbanization and Construction: 771–773 blvd Monivong, Phnom-Penh; tel. (23) 215660; fax (23) 217035.

Ministry of Tourism: 3 blvd Monivong, Phnom-Penh 12258; tel. (23) 212837; fax (23) 426877; e-mail info@mot.gov.kh; internet www .mot.gov.kh.

Ministry of Water Resources and Meteorology: 47 blvd Norodom, Phnom-Penh; tel. (23) 724289; fax (23) 426345; internet www.domc.com.kh.

Ministry of Women's Affairs and Veterans: Toultum Poung II, Khan Chamcarmon, Phnom-Penh; tel. (23) 366412; fax (23) 428084.

Legislature

NATIONAL ASSEMBLY

National Assembly, blvd Samdech Sothearos, cnr rue 240, Phnom-Penh; tel. (23) 214136; fax (23) 217769; e-mail kimhenglong@cambodian-parliament.org; internet www.cambodian-parliament .org.

Chairman: Prince NORODOM RANARIDDH (FUNCINPEC).

Election, 26 July 1998

	% of Votes	Seats
Cambodian People's Party	41.4	64
FUNCINPEC Party	31.7	43
Sam Rainsy Party	14.3	15
Others	12.6	—
Total	100.0	122

SENATE

Senate, Chamcarmon Palace, blvd Norodom, Phnom-Penh; tel. (23) 211446; fax (23) 211441; e-mail oum_sarith@camnet.com.kh; internet www.khmersenate.org.

Chairman: CHEA SIM (CPP).

First Vice-Chairman: CHIVAN MONIRAK (FUNCINPEC).

Second Vice-Chairman: NHIEK BUNCHHAY (FUNCINPEC).

Inauguration, 25 March 1999

	Seats
Cambodian People's Party	31
FUNCINPEC Party	21
Sam Rainsy Party	7
King's appointees	2
Total	61

Political Organizations

Buddhist Liberal Party (Kanakpak Serei Niyum Preah Put Sasna): Phnom-Penh; internet www.blp.org; f. 1998; Chair. IENG MULI; Gen. Sec. SIENG LAPRESSE.

Cambodian Freedom Fighters: 2728 E 10th Street, Long Beach, CA 90804, USA; tel. (562) 433-9930; fax (562) 7490; internet www .cffighters.org; f. 1998; in opposition to Hun Sen's leadership; Leader CHHUN YASITH; Sec.-Gen. RICHARD KIRI KIM.

Cambodian People's Party (CPP) (Kanakpak Pracheachon Kampuchea): Chamcarmon, 203 blvd Norodom, Phnom-Penh; tel. and fax (23) 2158801; e-mail cpp@thecpp.org; internet www.thecpp.org; known as the Kampuchean People's Revolutionary Party 1979–91; 21-mem. Standing Cttee of the Cen. Cttee; Cen. Cttee of 153 full mems; Hon. Chair. of Cen. Cttee HENG SAMRIN; Chair. of Cen. Cttee CHEA SIM; Vice-Chair. HUN SEN; Chair. of Permanent Cttee SAY CHHUM.

Democratic National United Movement (DNUM): Pailin; f. 1996 by Ieng Sary, following his defection from the PDK; not a national political party, did not contest 1998 election; DNUM members are also free to join other political parties.

FUNCINPEC Party (United National Front for an Independent, Neutral, Peaceful and Co-operative Cambodia Party): 11 blvd Monivong (93), Sangkat Sras Chak, Khan Daun Penh, Phnom Penh; tel. (23) 428864; fax (23) 426521; e-mail funcinpec@funcinpec.org; internet www.funcinpec.org; FUNCINPEC altered its title to the FUNCINPEC Party when it adopted political status in 1992; the party's military wing was the National Army of Independent Cambodia (fmrly the Armée Nationale Sihanoukiste—ANS); merged with the Son Sann Party in Jan. 1999; Pres. Prince NORODOM RANARIDDH; Sec.-Gen. Prince NORODOM SIRIVUDH.

Hang Dara Movement Democratic Party: c/o National Assembly, blvd Samdech Sotheáros, cnr rue 240, Phnom-Penh; f. 2002 by Hang Dara, to contest 2003 general election; breakaway faction of the FUNCINPEC Party.

Khmer Citizens' Party (Kanakpak Pulroat Khmer): Phnom-Penh; f. 1996; breakaway faction of Khmer Nation Party (now Sam Rainsy Party); Chair. NGUON SOEUR; Sec.-Gen. IEM RA.

Khmer Democracy Party (Kanakpak Pracheathippatei Khmer): Phnom-Penh; Pres. UK PHURI.

Khmer Neutral Party (Kanakpak Kampuchea Appyeakroet): 14A rue Keo Chea, Phnom-Penh; tel. (23) 62365; fax (23) 27340; e-mail Masavang@datagraphic.fr; internet www.datagraphic.fr/knp/; Pres. BUO HEL.

Khmer Republican Democratic Party (KRDP): Phnom-Penh; f. 1997; supports CPP; Chair. NHUNG SEAP.

Liberal Democratic Party: Phnom-Penh; f. 1993; receives support from members of the armed forces; pro-Government; Chair. Gen. CHHIM OM YON.

MOLINAKA (National Liberation Movement of Cambodia): c/o National Assembly, blvd Samdech Sotheáros, cnr rue 240, Phnom-Penh; a breakaway faction of FUNCINPEC; Pres. PRUM NEAKAREACH.

National Union Party (Kanakpak Ruop Ruom Cheat): Phnom-Penh; established by rebel mems of FUNCINPEC Party; Chair. TOAN CHHAY; Sec.-Gen. UNG PHAN.

New Society Party: see Sangkum Thmei Party.

Norodom Chakrapong Khmer Soul Party: c/o National Assembly, blvd Samdech Sotheáros, cnr rue 240, Phnom-Penh; f. 2002 by Prince Norodom Chakrapong; breakaway faction of FUNCINPEC Party.

Reastr Niyum (Nationalist Party): blvd Norodom, Phnom-Penh; tel. (23) 215659; fax (23) 215279; f. 1998; breakaway faction of the FUNCINPEC Party; Pres. UNG HUOT; Sec.-Gen. PU SOTHIRAK.

Sam Rainsy Party (SRP): 71 blvd Sotheáros, Phnom-Penh; tel. and fax (23) 217452; e-mail samrainsycabinet@forum.org.kh; internet www.samrainsyparty.org; f. 1995 as the Khmer Nation Party; name changed as above in 1998; 441,159 mems (Aug. 2001); Pres. SAM RAINSY; Sec.-Gen. MENG RITA (acting).

Sangkum Thmei Party (New Society Party): 4 rue 310, Phnom-Penh; f. 1997 by Loy Simchheang, formerly the Gen. Sec. of FUN-CINPEC.

United Front for the Construction and Defence of the Kampuchean Fatherland (UFCDKF): Phnom-Penh; f. 1978 as the Kampuchean National United Front for National Salvation (KNUFNS), renamed Kampuchean United Front for National Construction and Defence (KUFNCD) in 1981, present name adopted in 1989; mass organization supporting policies of the CPP; an 89-mem. Nat. Council and a seven-mem. hon. Presidium; Chair. of Nat. Council CHEA SIM; Sec.-Gen. ROS CHHUN.

Uphold the Cambodian Nation Party: Phnom-Penh; f. 1997 by Pen Sovan, fmr Sec.-Gen. of the Cen. Cttee of the CPP, to contest the 1998 legislative elections; Chair. PEN SOVAN.

Diplomatic Representation

EMBASSIES IN CAMBODIA

Australia: Villa 11, R. V. Senei Vinnavaut Oum (rue 254), Chartaumuk, Khan Daun Penh, Phnom-Penh; tel. (23) 213470; fax (23) 213413; e-mail australian.embassy.cambodia@dfat.gov.au; Ambassador LOUISE HAND.

Brunei: 237 rue Pasteur 51, Sangkat Boeung Keng Kang 1, Khan Chamcarmon, Phnom-Penh; tel. (23) 211457; fax (23) 211455; e-mail brunei@bigpond.com.kh; Ambassador ZAINIDI BIN Haji SIDUP.

Bulgaria: 227/229 blvd Norodom, Phnom-Penh; tel. (23) 217504; fax (23) 212792; e-mail bulgembpnp@camnet.com.kh; Chargé d'affaires a.i. ROUMEN DONTCHEV.

Canada: Villa 9, R.V. Senei Vinnavaut Oum, Sangkat Chaktaumuk, Khan Daun Penh, Phnom-Penh; tel. (23) 213470; fax (23) 211389; e-mail pnmpn@dfait-maeci.gc.ca; internet www.dfait-maeci .gc.ca/cambodia; Ambassador STEFANIE BECK.

China, People's Republic: 156 blvd Mao Tse Toung, Phnom-Penh; tel. (12) 810928; fax (23) 364738; Ambassador NING FUKUI.

Cuba: 96/98 rue 214, Sangkat Veal Vong, Khan 7 Makara, Phnom-Penh; tel. (23) 213212; fax (23) 217428; e-mail embacuba@camnet .com.kh; Ambassador NIVSIA CASTRO GUEVARA.

France: 1 blvd Monivong, Phnom-Penh; tel. (23) 430020; fax (23) 430041; e-mail ambafrance@bigpond.com.kh; internet www .ambafrance.gov.kh; Ambassador ANDRÉ-JEAN LIBOUREL.

Germany: 76–78 rue Yougoslavie, BP 60, Phnom-Penh; tel. (23) 216381; fax (23) 427746; e-mail germanembassy@everyday.com.kh; Ambassador Dr HELMUT OHLRAUN.

India: Villa 777, blvd Monivong, Phnom-Penh; tel. (23) 210912; fax (23) 213640; e-mail embindia@bigpond.com.kh; Ambassador PRADEEP KUMAR KAPUR.

Indonesia: 90 blvd Norodom, Phnom-Penh; tel. (23) 216148; fax (23) 216571; e-mail kukppenh@bigpond.com.kh; internet www .indonesia-phnompenh.org; Ambassador NAZARUDDIN NASUTION.

Japan: 194 blvd Norodom, Sangkat Tonle Bassac, Khan Chamkarmon, Phnom-Penh; tel. (23) 217161; fax (23) 216162; e-mail eojc@ bigpond.com.kh; internet www.kh.emb-japan.go.jp/index-e.htm; Ambassador GOTARO OGAWA.

Korea, Democratic People's Republic: 39 rue 268, Phnom-Penh; tel. (15) 912567; fax (23) 426230; Ambassador KIM JONG NAM.

Korea, Republic: 64 rue 214, Sangkat Beung Rain, Khan Daun Penh, Phnom-Penh; tel. (23) 211901; fax (23) 211903; e-mail koreanemb@bigpond.com.kh; internet www.koreanembcam.go.kr; Ambassador LEE WUN-HYUNG.

Laos: 15–17 blvd Mao Tse Toung, POB 19, Phnom-Penh; tel. (23) 982932; fax (23) 720907; Ambassador LY SOUTHAVILAY.

Malaysia: 5 rue 242, Sangkat Chaktomouk, Khan Daun Penh, Phnom-Penh; tel. (23) 216176; fax (23) 216004; e-mail mwppenh@ bigpond.com.kh; Ambassador Dato' AHMAD ANUAR ABDUL HAMID.

Myanmar: 181 blvd Norodom, Phnom-Penh; tel. (23) 213664; fax (23) 213665; e-mail M.E.PHNOMPENH@bigpond.com.kh; Ambassador U TINT LWIN.

Philippines: 33 rue 294, Khan Chamcarmon, Sangkat Tonle Bassac, Phnom-Penh; tel. (23) 215145; fax (23) 215143; e-mail phnompenhpe@bigpond.com.kh; Ambassador VOLTAIRE T. GAZMIN.

Poland: 767 blvd Monivong, POB 58, Phnom-Penh; tel. (23) 217782; fax (23) 217781; e-mail emb.pol.pp@bigpond.com.kh; Ambassador KAZIMIERZ A. DUCHOWSKI.

Russia: 213 blvd Sotheáros, Phnom-Penh; tel. (23) 210931; fax (23) 216776; e-mail russemba@bigpond.com.kh; Ambassador VICTOR V. SAMOILENKO.

Singapore: 92 blvd Norodom, Phnom-Penh; tel. (23) 360855; fax (23) 210862; e-mail singemb@bigpond.com.kh; internet www.mfa .gov.sg/phnompenh; Ambassador VERGHESE MATHEWS.

Thailand: 196 blvd Norodom, Sangkat Tonle Bassac, Khan Chamkarmon, Phnom-Penh; tel. (23) 363869; fax (18) 810860; e-mail thaipnp@mfa.go.th; Ambassador CHATCHAWED CHARTSUWAN.

United Kingdom: 27–29 Sras Chak, Khan Daun Penh, Phnom-Penh; tel. (23) 427124; fax (23) 427125; e-mail BRITEMB@bigpond .com.kh; Ambassador STEPHEN BRIDGES.

USA: 16 rue 228, Phnom-Penh; tel. (23) 216436; fax (23) 216437; internet www.phnompenh.usembassy.gov; Ambassador CHARLES AARON RAY.

Viet Nam: 436 blvd Monivong, Phnom-Penh; tel. (23) 362741; fax (23) 427385; e-mail embbvnpp@camnet.com.kh; Ambassador NGUYEN DU HONG.

Judicial System

An independent judiciary was established under the 1993 Constitution.

Supreme Court: rue 134, cnr rue 63, Phnom-Penh; tel. 17816663; Chair. DID MONTY.

Religion

BUDDHISM

The principal religion of Cambodia is Theravada Buddhism (Buddhism of the 'Tradition of the Elders'), the sacred language of which is Pali. A ban was imposed on all religious activity in 1975. By a constitutional amendment, which was adopted in April 1989, Buddhism was reinstated as the national religion and was retained as such under the 1993 Constitution. By 1992 2,800 monasteries (of a total of 3,369) had been restored and there were 21,800 Buddhist monks. In 1992 about 90% of the population were Buddhists.

Supreme Patriarchs: Ven. Patriarch TEP VONG, Ven. Patriarch BOU KRI.

Patriotic Kampuchean Buddhists' Association: Phnom-Penh; mem. of UFCDKF; Pres. LONG SIM.

CHRISTIANITY

The Roman Catholic Church

Cambodia comprises the Apostolic Vicariate of Phnom-Penh and the Apostolic Prefectures of Battambang and Kompong-Cham. At 31 December 2000 there were an estimated 19,959 adherents in the country, equivalent to about 0.2% of the population. An Episcopal Conference of Laos and Kampuchea was established in 1971. In 1975 the Government of Democratic Kampuchea banned all religious practice in Cambodia, and the right of Christians to meet to worship was not restored until 1990.

Vicar Apostolic of Phnom-Penh: Rt Rev. EMILE DESTOMBES (Titular Bishop of Altava), 787 blvd Monivong (rue 93), BP 123, Phnom-Penh; tel. and fax (23) 212462; e-mail evecam@camnet.com.kh.

ISLAM

Islam is practised by a minority in Cambodia. Islamic worship was also banned in 1975, but it was legalized in 1979, following the defeat of the Democratic Kampuchean regime.

The Press

NEWSPAPERS

Newspapers are not widely available outside Phnom-Penh.

Areyathor (Civilization): 52 rue Lyuk Lay, Sangkat Chey, Chummneah, Phnom-Penh; tel. (23) 913662; Editor CHIN CHAN MONTY.

Bayon Pearnik: 3 rue 174, POB 2279, Phnom-Penh; tel. (12) 803968; tel. (23) 211921; e-mail bp@forum.org.kh; internet www .bayonpearnik.com; f. 1995; English; monthly; Publr and Editor ADAM PARKER; circ. 10,000.

Cambodia Daily: 50B rue 240, Phnom-Penh; tel. (23) 426602; fax (23) 426573; e-mail aafc@forum.org.kh; internet www .cambodiadaily.com; f. 1993; in English and Khmer; Mon.–Sat. Editor CHRIS DECHERD; Publr BERNARD KRISHER; circ. 3,500.

Cambodia New Vision: POB 158, Phnom-Penh; tel. (23) 219898; fax (23) 360666; e-mail cabinet1b@camnet.com.kh; internet www .cnv.org.kh; f. 1998; official newsletter of the Cambodian Govt.

Cambodia Times: 236 blvd Mao Tse Toung, Phnom-Penh; tel. (23) 721274; fax (23) 426647; f. 1992 in Kuala Lumpur, Malaysia; English; weekly; Editor KAMARAI ZAMANTABY.

Chakraval: 3 rue 181, Sangkat Tumnop Teuk, Khan Chamkar Mon, Phnom-Penh; tel. (23) 913667; fax (23) 720141; Khmer; daily; Publr KEO SOPHORN; Editor SO SOVAN RITH.

Commercial News: 394 blvd Preah Sihanouk, Phnom-Penh; tel. (23) 721665; fax (23) 721709; e-mail tcnews@camnet.com.kh; f. 1993; Chinese; Chief Editor LIU XIAO GUANG; circ. 6,000.

Construction (Kasang): 126 rue 336, Sangkat Phsar Deum Kor, Khan Tuol Kok, Phnom-Penh; tel. 18818292; Khmer; Editor CHHEA VARY.

Equality Voice: 470 rue 163, Sangkat Boeung Keng Kang, Khan Chamkar Mon, Phnom-Penh; tel. 12842471; Khmer; Publr HUON MARA.

Kampuchea: 158 blvd Norodom, Phnom-Penh; tel. (23) 725559; f. 1979; weekly; Chief Editor KEO PRASAT; circ. 55,000.

Khmer Wisdom: 1588 Khan Russei Keo, Phnom-Penh; tel. 12841377; Khmer; Publr CHEA CHAN THON.

Khmer Youth Voice: 240 rue 374, Sangkat Toul Prey 2, Khan Chamkar Mon, Phnom-Penh; tel. (23) 211336; fax (23) 210137; e-mail sovann@camnet.com.kh; Khmer; twice weekly; Editor UO SOVANN.

Koh Santepheap (Island of Peace): 165 rue 199, East of Sport City, Phnom-Penh; tel. (23) 880052; fax (23) 364515; e-mail kohsantepheap@camnet.com.kh; Khmer; Publr THONG UY PANG.

Moneaksekar Khmer: 27 rue 318, Sangkat Toul Svay Prey 1, Khan Chamkar Mon, Phnom-Penh; tel. (23) 990777; Editor DAM SITHIK.

Neak Chea: 1 rue 158, Daun Penh, Phnom-Penh; tel. (23) 428653; fax (23) 427229; e-mail adhoc@forum.org.kh.

Phnom Penh Daily: 5 rue 84, Corner 61, Sangkat Srah Chak, Khan Daun Penh, Phnom-Penh; tel. 15917682; e-mail ppenhdaily@ camnet.com.kn; internet www.phnompenhdaily.com.kh; Khmer; available online in English; Editor VA DANE.

Phnom Penh Post: 10A rue 264, Phnom-Penh; tel. (23) 210309; fax (23) 426568; e-mail michael.pppost@bigpond.com.kh; internet www .phnompenhpost.com; f. 1992; English; fortnightly; Editor-in-Chief MICHAEL HAYES; Publrs MICHAEL HAYES, KATHLEEN HAYES.

Pracheachon (The People): 101 blvd Norodom, Phnom-Penh; tel. (23) 723665; f. 1985; 2 a week; organ of the CPP; Editor-in-Chief SOM KIMSUOR; circ. 50,000.

Rasmei Kampuchea: 476 blvd Monivong, Phnom-Penh; tel. (23) 362881; fax (23) 362472; e-mail rasmei_kampuchea@yahoo.com; daily; f. 1993; local newspaper in northern Cambodia; Editor PEN SAMITTHY.

Samleng Thmei (New Voice): 91 rue 139, Sangkat Veal Vong, Khan 7, Phnom-Penh; tel. 15920589; Khmer; Editor KHUN NGOR.

NEWS AGENCIES

Agence Kampuchia de Presse (AKP): 62 blvd Monivong, Phnom-Penh; tel. (23) 430564; e-mail akp@camnet.com.kh; internet www .camnet.com.kh/akp; f. 1978; Dir-Gen. KIT-KIM HUON.

Foreign Bureaux

Agence France-Presse (AFP) (France): 8 rue 214, POB 822, Phnom-Penh; tel. (23) 426227; fax (23) 426226; Correspondent STEFAN SMITH.

Associated Press (AP) (USA): 18C rue 19, BP 870, Phnom-Penh; tel. (23) 426607; e-mail ap@bigpond.com.kh; Correspondent CHRIS FONTAINE.

Deutsche Presse-Agentur (dpa): 5E rue 178, Phnom-Penh; tel. (23) 427846; fax (23) 427846; Correspondent JOE COCHRANE.

Reuters (UK): 201, 2nd Floor, Hong Kong Centre, 108–112 blvd Sothearos,, Phnom-Penh; tel. (23) 216977; fax (23) 216970; Bureau Chief ROBERT BIRSEL.

Xinhua (New China) News Agency (People's Republic of China): 19 rue 294, Phnom-Penh; tel. (23) 211608; fax (23) 426613; Correspondent LEI BOSONG.

ASSOCIATIONS

Cambodian Association for the Protection of Journalists (CAPJ): POB 816, Phnom-Penh; tel. (15) 997004; fax (23) 215834; e-mail umsarin@hotmail.com; Pres. UM SARIN.

Cambodian Club of Journalists: Phnom-Penh; Pres. PEN SAMITHY; Sec.-Gen. PRACH SIM.

Khmer Journalists' Association: 101 blvd Preah Norodom, Phnom-Penh; tel. (23) 725459; f. 1979; mem. of UFCDKF; Pres. PIN SAMKHON.

League of Cambodian Journalists (LCJ): 74 rue 205, Sangkat Toulsvayprey, Khan Chamkamon, Phnom-Penh; tel. and fax (23) 360612; Pres. OM CHANDARA.

Broadcasting and Communications

TELECOMMUNICATIONS

Cambodian Samart Communication: 2 rue 120, Phnom-Penh; tel. (16) 810001; fax (16) 810004; e-mail somchai.an@hello016-gsm.com; internet www.hello016-gsm.com; f. 1992; operates a national mobile telephone network; CEO SOMCHAI AN.

Camintel: 1 cnr Terak Vithei Sisowath and Vithei Phsar Dek, Phnom-Penh; tel. (23) 986789; fax (23) 986277; e-mail sales@camintel.com; internet www.camintel.com; a jt venture between the Ministry of Posts and Telecommunications and the Indonesian co, Indosat; operates domestic telephone network; Chair. NHEK KORSOL VYTHYEA.

Camshin Corporation: 26 rue Preah Monivong, Phnom-Penh; tel. (23) 60001; fax (23) 61234; a jt venture between the Ministry of Posts and Telecommunications and the Thai co, Shinawatra International Co Ltd; telephone communications co.

BROADCASTING

Radio

Apsara: 69 rue 57, Sangkat Boeung Keng Kang 1, Khan Chamkarmorn, Phnom-Penh; tel. (23) 303002; fax (23) 214302; internet www.apsaratv.com.kh; Head of Admin. KEO SOPHEAP; News Editor SIN SO CHEAT.

Bayon: c/o Bayon Media Group, 954 rue 2, Takhmau, Kandal Province; tel. (23) 363695; fax (23) 363795; e-mail bayontv@camnet.com.kh; internet www.bayontv.com.kh; Dir-Gen. KEM KUNNAVATH.

Bee Hive Radio: 41 rue 214, Phnom-Penh; tel. (23) 720401; Dir-Gen. MAM SONANDO.

FM 90 MHZ: 65 rue 178, Phnom-Penh; tel. (23) 363699; fax (23) 368623; Dir-Gen. NHIM BUN THON; Dep. Dir-Gen. TUM VANN DET.

FM 99 MHZ: 41 rue 360, Phnom-Penh; tel. (23) 426794; Gen. Man. SOM CHHAYA.

FM 107 MHZ: 81 rue 562, Phnom-Penh; tel. (23) 428047; fax (23) 368212; Dir-Gen. KHUN HANG.

Phnom-Penh Municipality Radio: 131–132 blvd Pochentong, Phnom-Penh; tel. (23) 725205; fax (23) 360800; Gen. Man. KHAMPUN KEOMONY.

Ta Prohm Radio: Phnom-Penh; f. 2003; launched by FUNCINPEC Party as opposition radio station; broadcasts news programmes in Khmer to Phnom-Penh and surrounding area.

RCAF Radio: c/o Borei Keila, rue 169, Phnom-Penh; tel. (23) 366061; fax (23) 366063; f. 1994; Royal Cambodian Armed Forces radio station; Dir THA TANA; News Editor SENG KATEKA.

Vithyu Cheat Kampuchea (National Radio of Cambodia): rue Preah Kossamak, Phnom-Penh; tel. (23) 368140; fax (23) 427319; f. 1978; fmrly Vithyu Samleng Pracheachon Kampuchea (Voice of the Cambodian People); controlled by the Ministry of Information and the Press; home service in Khmer; daily external services in English, French, Lao, Vietnamese and Thai; Dir-Gen. VANN SENG LY; Dep. Dir-Gen. TAN YAN.

Voice of Cambodia: Phnom Penh; e-mail vocri@vocri.org; internet www.vocri.org; Cambodia's first international internet radio station.

There are also eight private local radio stations based in Phnom-Penh, Battambang Province, Sihanoukville, and Stung Treng Province.

Television

Apsara Television (TV11): 69 rue 57, Sangkat Boeung Keng Kang 1, Khan Chamkamorn, Phnom-Penh; tel. (23) 303002; fax (23) 214302; internet www.apsaratv.com.kh; Dir-Gen. SOK EISAN.

Bayon Television (TV27): 954 rue 2, Takhmau, Kandal Province; tel. (23) 363695; fax (23) 363795; e-mail bayontv@camnet.com.kh; internet www.bayontv.com.kh; Dir-Gen. KEM KUNNAVATH.

National Television of Cambodia (Channel 7): 26 blvd Preah Monivong, Phnom-Penh 12201; tel. (23) 722943; fax (23) 426407; e-mail tvk@camnet.gov.kh; internet www.tvk.gov.kh; opened 1983;

broadcasts for 10 hours per day in Khmer; Dir-Gen. (Head of Television) MAO AYUTH.

Phnom-Penh Television (TV3): 2 blvd Russia, Phnom-Penh; tel. (12) 814323; fax (23) 360800; e-mail tv3@camnet.com.kh; internet www.tv3.com.kh; Dir-Gen. KHAMPHUN KEOMONY.

RCAF Television (TV5): 165 rue 169, Borei Keila, Phnom-Penh; tel. (23) 366061; fax (23) 366063; e-mail mica.t.v.5@bigpond.com.kh; Editor-in-Chief PRUM KIM.

TV Khmer (TV9): 81 rue 562, Phnom-Penh; tel. (23) 428047; fax (23) 368212; Dir-Gen. KHOUN ELYNA; News Editor PHAN TITH.

Finance

(cap. = capital; res = reserves; dep. = deposits; brs = branches)

BANKING

The National Bank of Cambodia, which was established as the sole authorized bank in 1980 (following the abolition of the monetary system by the Government of Democratic Kampuchea in 1975), is the central bank, and assumed its present name in February 1992. The adoption of a market economy led to the licensing of privately owned and joint-venture banks from July 1991. Following the implementation of the 1999 Financial Institutions Law 29 of the banks operative in Cambodia were considered for re-licensing. In 2001 11 banks were closed, having failed to meet new capital requirements. At November 2001 there were 21 banks (excluding the central bank) operating in Cambodia, including: one state-owned bank; three specialized banks; 12 locally-incorporated private banks; and five branches of foreign banks.

Central Bank

National Bank of Cambodia: 22–24 blvd Preah Norodom, BP 25, Phnom-Penh; tel. (23) 722563; fax (23) 426117; e-mail nbc@bigpond.com.kh; f. 1980; cap. 100,000m., res 652,837m., dep. 1,704,761m. riels (Dec. 2002); Gov. CHEA CHANTO; Dep. Gov. ENG THAYSAN.

State Bank

Foreign Trade Bank: 22–24 blvd Preah Norodom, Khan Daun Penh, Phnom-Penh; tel. (23) 724466; fax (23) 426108; e-mail ftb@camnet.com.kh; scheduled for privatization; Man. TIM BO PHOL.

Specialized Banks

ACLEDA Bank Ltd: 28 blvd Mao Tse Tung, Phnom-Penh; tel. (23) 364619; fax (23) 364914; e-mail acledabank@acledabank.com.kh; internet www.acledabank.com.kh; f. 1993; became full commercial bank in Oct. 2000; provides financial and investment aid to rural poor; Gen. Man. IN CHANNY; 75 brs.

Peng Heng SMI Bank: tel. (23) 219243; fax (23) 219185; f. 2001.

Rural Development Bank: 5 rue Preah Ang Eng and rue Preah Ang No, Sangkat Wat Phnom, Khan Daun Penh, Phnom-Penh; tel. (23) 982434; e-mail rdb@bigpond.com.kh.

Private Banks

Advanced Bank of Asia Ltd: 97–99 blvd Preah Norodom, Sangkat Boeung Raing, Khan Daun Penh, Phnom-Penh; tel. (23) 720434; fax (23) 720435; e-mail jeong@camnet.com.kh; Dir CHAE WAN CHO.

Cambodia Agriculture Industrial Specialized Bank: 87 blvd Preah Norodom, Sangkat Phsar Thmey III, Khan Daun Penh, Phnom-Penh; tel. (23) 218667; fax (23) 217751; e-mail kien@bigpond.com.kh; Man. CHHOR SANG.

Cambodia Asia Bank Ltd: 252 blvd Preah Monivong, Sangkat Phsar Thmey II, Khan Daun Penh, Phnom-Penh; tel. (23) 722105; fax (23) 426628; e-mail cab@camnet.com.kh; Man. WONG TOW FOCK.

Cambodia Mekong Bank: 1 rue Kramoun Sar, Sangkat Phsar Thmey I, Khan Daun Penh, Phnom-Penh; tel. (23) 217114; fax (23) 217122; e-mail ho.mailbox@mekongbank.com; cap. US $13m., dep. US $4.4m. (Dec. 2001); Chair. MICHAEL C. STEPHEN; Pres. and CEO KHOV BOUN CHHAY.

Cambodian Commercial Bank Ltd: 26 blvd Preah Monivong, Sangkat Phsar Thmey II, Khan Daun Penh, Phnom-Penh; tel. (23) 426145; fax (23) 426116; e-mail CCBPP@bigpond.com.kh; f. 1991; cap. US $10m., res US $0.2m., dep. US $44.7m. (Dec. 2000); Chair MALEERATNA PLUMCHITCHOM; Dir and Gen. Man. SAHASIN YUTTARAT; 4 brs.

Cambodian Public Bank (Campu Bank): Villa 23, rue Kramoun Sar, Sangkat Phsar Thmey II, Khan Daun Penh, Phnom-Penh; tel. (23) 214111; fax (23) 217655; e-mail campu@bigpond.com.kh; cap. US $15m., dep. US $40.6m. (Dec. 2001); Man. CHAN KOK CHOY.

Canadia Bank Ltd: 265–269 rue Preah Ang Duong, Sangkat Wat Phnom, Khan Daun Penh, Phnom-Penh; tel. (23) 215286; fax (23) 427064; e-mail canadia@camnet.com.kh; internet www .canadiabank.com; f. 1991; cap. 50.6m. riels; res 32.3m. riels; dep. 411.6m. riels (2001); Man. PUNG KHEAV SE; 8 brs.

Emperor International Bank Ltd: 230–232 blvd Preah Mon-ivong, Sangkat Phsar Thmey II, Khan Daun Penh, Phnom-Penh; tel. (23) 426254; fax (23) 428585; e-mail eib@bigpond.com.kh; Man. VAN SOU IENG.

Singapore Banking Corporation Ltd: 68 rue Samdech Pan, BP Sangkat Boeung Reang, Khan Daun Penh, Phnom-Penh; tel. (23) 217772; fax (23) 212121; e-mail info@sbc-bank.com; internet www .sbc-bank.com; f. 1993; cap. US $5.5m., dep. US $6.8m. (Dec. 2000); Pres. ANDY KUN; Chair. KAY HONG KUN.

Union Commercial Bank Ltd: UCB Building, 61 rue 130, Sangkat Phsar Chas, Khan Daun Penh, Phnom-Penh; tel. (23) 427995; fax (23) 427997; e-mail ucb@bigpond.com.kh; internet www.ucb.com.kh; f. 1994; cap. US $13m., res US $4m., dep. US $28m. (2001); CEO YUM SUI SANG; 3 brs.

Foreign Banks

First Commercial Bank (Taiwan): 263 rue Preah Ang Duong, Sangkat Wat Phnom, Khan Daun Penh, Phnom-Penh; tel. (23) 210027; fax (23) 210029; e-mail fcbpp@bigpond.com.kh.

Krung Thai Bank PLC (Thailand): 149 rue 215 Jawaharlal Nehru, Depot Market 1, Khan Tuolkok Division, Phnom-Penh; tel. (23) 366005; fax (23) 428737; e-mail ktbpmp@bigpond.com.kh; Man. NAKROB U-SETTHASAKDI.

Lippo Bank (Indonesia): 273 Preah Andoung, S.K. Wat Phnom, Khan Daun Penh, Phnom-Penh; Man. MARKUS PARMADI.

Maybank Bhd (Malaysia): 4 rue Kramoun Sar, Sangkat Boeung Raing, Khan Daun Penh, Phnom-Penh; tel. (23) 210123; fax (23) 210099; e-mail mbb@camnet.com.kh; internet www.maybank2u .com.my; Man. ABDUL MALEK MOHD KHAIR.

Standard Chartered Bank (UK): 89 blvd Preah Norodom, POB 46, Sangkat Boeung Raing, Khan Daun Penh, Phnom-Penh; tel. (23) 212732; fax (23) 216687; CEO ONG TENG HOON; 1 br.

INSURANCE

Commercial Union: 28 rue 47, Phnom-Penh; tel. (23) 426694; fax (23) 427171; general insurance; Gen. Man. PAUL CABLE.

Indochine Insurance Ltd: 55 rue 178, BP 808, Phnom-Penh; tel. (23) 210701; fax (23) 210501; e-mail insurance@indochine.com.kh; internet www.indochine.net; Dir PHILIPPE LENAIN.

Trade and Industry

DEVELOPMENT ORGANIZATIONS

Council for the Development of Cambodia (CDC): Government Palace, quai Sisowath, Wat Phnom, Phnom-Penh; tel. (23) 981156; fax (23) 428426; f. 1993; Chair. HUN SEN; Sec.-Gen. SOK CHENDA.

Cambodian Investment Board (CIB): Government Palace, quai Sisowath, Wat Phnom, Phnom-Penh; tel. (23) 981156; fax (23) 428426; e-mail CDC.CIB@bigpond.com.kh; internet www .cambodiainvestment.gov.kh; f. 1993; part of CDC; sole body responsible for approving foreign investment in Cambodia, also grants exemptions from customs duties and other taxes, and provides other facilities for investors; Chair. HUN SEN; Sec.-Gen. SOK CHENDA.

National Information Communications Technology Development Authority (NiDA): 3rd Floor, Satellite Bldg, Office of the Council of Ministers, blvd Confederation de la Russie, Phnom-Penh; tel. (23) 880635; fax (23) 880637; e-mail info@nida.gov.kh; internet www.nida.gov.kh; f. 2000; promotes information technology and formulates policy for its development; Chair. HUN SEN; Sec.-Gen. PHU LEEWOOD.

CHAMBER OF COMMERCE

Phnom-Penh Chamber of Commerce: 22 rue Kramuon Sar, Sangkat Phsar Thmei 2, Khan Daun Penh, Phnom-Penh; tel. (23) 212265; fax (23) 212270; f. 1995; Pres. SOK KONG.

INDUSTRIAL AND TRADE ASSOCIATIONS

Cambodian Garment Factory Association (CGFA): Phnom-Penh; tel. (12) 888222; fax (23) 427983; Pres. VAN SOU IENG; Sec. ROGER TAN.

Export Promotion Department: Ministry of Commerce, 57–59 rue 136, Sangkat Phsar Thmey Kandal II, Khan Daun Penh,

Phnom-Penh; tel. (23) 216948; fax (23) 217353; e-mail praknork@ everyday.com.kh; internet www.moc.gov.kh; f. 1997; Dir PRAK NORK.

UTILITIES

Electricity

Electricité du Cambodge: rue 19, Wat Phnom, Khan Daun Penh, Phnom-Penh; tel. (23) 724771; fax (23) 426938; e-mail yim_nolson@ bigpond.com.kh; state-owned; Man. Gen. TAN KIM VIN.

Water

Phnom-Penh Water Supply Authority: rue 108, 12201 Phnom-Penh; tel. (23) 724046; fax (23) 428969; e-mail eksonnchan@ppwsa .com.kh; f. 1996 as an autonomous public enterprise; Dir-Gen. EK SON CHAN.

TRADE UNIONS

Association of Independent Cambodian Teachers: 33 rue 432, Sangkat Boeng Trabaek, Khan Chamka Morn, Phnom Penh; Pres. RUNG CHHUN; Gen.-Sec. CHEA MUNI.

Cambodia Federation of Independent Trade Unions (CFITU): 45 rue 63, Boeng Keng Kang 1, Chamkarmon, Phnom-Penh; tel. (23) 213356; e-mail CFITU@bigpond.com.kh; f. 1979 as Cambodia Federation of Trade Unions; changed name as above in 1999; Chair. ROS SOK; Vice-Chair. TEP KIM VANNARY, KIENG THISOTHA.

Cambodia Labour Union Federation (CLUF): 78 rue 474, Sangkat Boeung Trabek, Khan Chamkarmon, Phnom-Penh; tel. (23) 866682; f. 1999; Pres. SOM AUN.

Cambodian Union Federation (CUF): 18 rue 112, Sangkat Phsar Depo III, Khan Toulkok , Phnom-Penh; tel. (23) 882453; fax (23) 427632; e-mail CUF@bigpond.com.kh; f. 1997; with the support of the CPP in response to the formation of the FTUWKC.

Cambodian Union Federation of Building and Wood Workers: 18A rue 112, Sangkat Phsar Depo III, Khan Tuol Kok, Phnom-Penh; tel. (23) 842382; fax (23) 882453; f. 2001; Pres. SAY SAM ON.

Coalition of Cambodia Apparel Workers' Democratic Union: 6C rue 476, Sangkat Tuol Tum Pong I, Khan Chamcarmon, Phnom-Penh; tel. (23) 210481; f. 2001; Pres. CHHORN SOKHA.

Free Trade Union of Workers of the Kingdom of Cambodia (FTUWKC): 28B rue 222, Sangkat Boeung Reang, Khan Daun Penh, , Phnom-Penh; tel. (23) 216870; fax (23) 216870; e-mail ftuwkc@yahoo.com; fmrly Free Trade Union of Khmer Workers; f. 1996 by Mary Ou with the assistance of Sam Rainsy; Leader CHEA VICHEA; Gen. Sec. SUM SAMNEANG.

National Independent Federation Textile Union of Cambodia (NIFTUC): 29B rue 432, Sangkat Toul Tompoung II, Khan Chamkarmon , Phnom-Penh; tel. and fax (23) 219239; e-mail niftuc@ forum.org.kh; f. 1999; Pres. MORM NHIM.

Transport

RAILWAYS

Royal Railway of Cambodia: Central Railway Station, Railway Square, Sangkat Srach Chak, Khan Daun Penh, Phnom-Penh; tel. 12994168; fax (23) 430815; e-mail RRCcambodia@mobitel.mibitel .com.kh; comprises two 1,000 mm-gauge single-track main lines with a total length of 650 km: the 385-km Phnom-Penh to Poipet line (of which the 48-km Sisophon to Poipet link is awaiting restoration), the 264-km Phnom-Penh to Sihanoukville line and branch lines and special purpose sidings 100 km; the condition of the lines is very poor, with many temporary repairs, owing to mine damage, and the service also suffers from other operational difficulties, such as a shortage of rolling stock; there are 14 'Gares' (main stations), 19 stations and 38 halts; Dir SOKHOM PHEAKAVANMONY.

ROADS

In 1997 the total road network was 35,769 km in length, of which 4,165 km were highways and 3,604 km were secondary roads. In the same year about 7.5% of the road network was paved, but this figure rose to an estimated 11.6% in 1999. West and East Cambodia were linked by road for the first time in December 2001, with the opening of a bridge across the Mekong River.

INLAND WATERWAYS

The major routes are along the Mekong river, and up the Tonlé Sap river into the Tonlé Sap (Great Lake), covering, in all, about 2,400 km. The inland ports of Neak Luong, Kompong Cham and

Prek Kdam have been supplied with motor ferries, and the ferry crossings have been improved.

SHIPPING

The main port is Sihanoukville, on the Gulf of Thailand, which has 11 berths and can accommodate vessels of 10,000–15,000 tons. Phnom-Penh port lies some distance inland. Steamers of up to 4,000 tons can be accommodated.

CIVIL AVIATION

There is an international airport at Pochentong, near Phnom-Penh. Prince Norodom Chakrapong established a new airline named Royal Phnom-Penh Airways in 1999.

State Secretariat of Civil Aviation (SSCA): 62 blvd Norodom, Phnom-Penh; tel. (16) 855373; fax (23) 426169; e-mail ksaphal-ssca@ camnet.com.kh; Dir-Gen. KEO SAPHAL.

Mekong Airlines: Phnom-Penh; f. 2002; joint venture between Hun Kim Leng Investment (51%) and Australian co Via Aviation (49%); domestic and international flights to eight destinations.

President Airlines: 50 blvd Norodom, Phnom-Penh; tel. (23) 427402; fax (23) 212992; f. 1998; domestic and, from August 2002, international passenger services.

Royal Khmer Airlines: 19 Unit 12, rue Preah Kossomak, Phnom-Penh; tel. (23) 216899; fax (23) 428279; f. 2000; domestic and international services.

Royal Phnom-Penh Airways: 209 rue 19, Zingkat Chey Chumneah, Khan Daun Penh, Phnom-Penh; tel. (23) 217419; fax (23) 217420; internet www.rippairways.com; f. 1999; scheduled and charter passenger flights to domestic and regional destinations; Chair. NORODOM CHAKRAPONG.

Siem Reap Airways International: 61A rue 214, Sangkat Beoung Rang, Khan Daun Penh, Phnom-Penh; tel. (23) 720022; fax (23) 720522; internet www.siemreapairways.com; f. 2000; scheduled international and domestic passenger services; CEO PRASERT PRASARTTONG-OSOTH.

Tourism

Tourist arrivals increased to 367,743 in 1999, owing to the improvement in the security situation, and rose to an estimated 466,365 in 2000, in which year tourist receipts reached US \$178m. In late 2001, however, Cambodia's tourism sector was badly affected by the repercussions of the terrorist attacks on the USA in September; an estimated 604,919 tourists visited in that year, an increase of 29.7% from the previous year. In 2002 tourist arrivals totalled approximately 800,000. In an attempt to encourage the development of the tourism sector, 2003 was designated 'Visit Cambodia Year'.

General Directorate for Tourism: 3 blvd Monivong, Phnom-Penh; tel. (23) 427130; fax (23) 426107; e-mail tourism@camnet.com .kh; f. 1988; Dir So MARA.

CAMEROON

Introductory Survey

Location, Climate, Language, Religion, Flag, Capital

The Republic of Cameroon lies on the west coast of Africa, with Nigeria to the west, Chad and the Central African Republic to the east, and the Republic of the Congo, Equatorial Guinea and Gabon to the south. The climate is hot and humid in the south and west, with average temperatures of 26°C (80°F). Annual rainfall in Yaoundé averages 4,030 mm (159 ins). The north is drier, with more extreme temperatures. The official languages are French and English; many local languages are also spoken, including Fang, Bamileke and Duala. Approximately 53% of Cameroonians profess Christianity, 25% adhere to traditional religious beliefs, and about 22%, mostly in the north, are Muslims. The national flag (proportions 2 by 3) has three equal vertical stripes, of green, red and yellow, with a five-pointed gold star in the centre of the red stripe. The capital is Yaoundé.

Recent History

In 1884 a German protectorate was established in Cameroon (Kamerun). In 1916, during the First World War, the German administration was overthrown by British and French forces. Under an agreement reached between the occupying powers in 1919, Cameroon was divided into two zones: a French-ruled area in the east and south, and a smaller British-administered area in the west. In 1922 both zones became subject to mandates of the League of Nations, with France and the United Kingdom as the administering powers. In 1946 the zones were transformed into UN Trust Territories, with British and French rule continuing in their respective areas.

French Cameroons became an autonomous state within the French Community in 1957. Under the leadership of Ahmadou Ahidjo, a northerner who became Prime Minister in 1958, the territory became independent, as the Republic of Cameroon, on 1 January 1960. The first election for the country's National Assembly, held in April 1960, was won by Ahidjo's party, the Union camerounaise. In May the new National Assembly elected Ahidjo to be the country's first President.

British Cameroons, comprising a northern and a southern region, was attached to neighbouring Nigeria, for administrative purposes, prior to Nigeria's independence in October 1960. Plebiscites were held, under UN auspices, in the two regions of British Cameroons in February 1961. The northern area voted to merge with Nigeria (becoming the province of Sardauna), while the south voted for union with the Republic of Cameroon, which took place on 1 October 1961.

The enlarged country was named the Federal Republic of Cameroon, with French and English as joint official languages. It comprised two states: the former French zone became East Cameroon, while the former British portion became West Cameroon. John Ngu Foncha, the Prime Minister of West Cameroon and leader of the Kamerun National Democratic Party, became Vice-President of the Federal Republic. Under the continuing leadership of Ahidjo, who (as the sole candidate) was re-elected President in May 1965, the two states became increasingly integrated. In September 1966 the two governing parties and several opposition groups combined to form a single party, the Union nationale camerounaise (UNC). The only significant opposition party, the extreme left-wing Union des populations camerounaises (UPC), was suppressed in 1971 (although it was allowed to operate again when multi-party politics was reintroduced in the early 1990s). Meanwhile, Ahidjo was re-elected as President in March 1970, and Solomon Muna (who had replaced Foncha as Prime Minister of West Cameroon in 1968) became Vice-President.

In June 1972, following the approval by referendum of a new Constitution, the federal system was ended, and the country was officially renamed the United Republic of Cameroon. The office of Vice-President was abolished. A centralized political and administrative system was rapidly introduced, and in May 1973 a new National Assembly was elected for a five-year term. After the re-election of Ahidjo as President in April 1975, the Constitution was revised, and a Prime Minister, Paul Biya (a bilingual Christian southerner), was appointed in June. In April 1980 Ahidjo was unanimously re-elected to the presidency for a fifth five-year term of office.

Ahidjo resigned as President in November 1982, and nominated Biya as his successor. In subsequent cabinet reorganizations Biya removed a number of supporters of the former President. In August 1983 Biya announced the discovery of a conspiracy to overthrow his Government, and simultaneously dismissed the Prime Minister and the Minister of the Armed Forces, both northern Muslims. Later in August Ahidjo resigned as President of the UNC, strongly criticizing Biya's regime. In September Biya was elected President of the ruling party, and in January 1984 he was re-elected as President of the Republic, reportedly obtaining 99.98% of the votes cast. The post of Prime Minister was subsequently abolished, and it was announced that the country's name was to revert to the Republic of Cameroon.

In February 1984 Ahidjo and two of his close military advisers were tried (Ahidjo *in absentia*) for their alleged complicity in the coup plot of August 1983, and received death sentences, which were, however, commuted to life imprisonment. On 6 April 1984 rebel elements in the presidential guard, led by Col Saleh Ibrahim (a northerner), attempted to overthrow the Biya Government. After three days of intense fighting, in which hundreds of people were reported to have been killed, the rebellion was suppressed by forces loyal to the President; a total of 51 defendants subsequently received death sentences. Following extensive changes within the military hierarchy, the UNC Central Committee and the leadership of state-controlled companies, Biya reorganized his Government in July and introduced more stringent press censorship.

In March 1985 the UNC was renamed the Rassemblement démocratique du peuple camerounais (RDPC). In January 1986 members of the exiled UPC movement claimed that 200–300 opponents of the Biya Government (most of whom were anglophones or members of clandestine opposition movements) had been arrested in the preceding months, and that some of those in detention were being subjected to torture. A number of detainees were subsequently released. In July 1987 the National Assembly approved a new electoral code providing for multiple candidacy in public elections, and in October voters had a choice of RDPC-approved candidates in local government elections.

Presidential and legislative elections were held in April 1988. Biya was re-elected unopposed to the presidency, securing 98.75% of the votes cast. In the elections to the National Assembly voters were presented with a choice of RDPC-approved candidates; 153 of the 180 deputies elected were new members.

In February 1990 11 people, including the former President of the Cameroonian Bar Association, Yondo Black, were arrested in connection with their alleged involvement in an unofficial opposition organization, the Social Democratic Front (SDF). In April Black was sentenced to three years' imprisonment on charges of 'subversion'. Later that month Biya announced that all the prisoners who had been detained in connection with the 1984 coup attempt were to be released. In May 1990 a demonstration organized by the SDF was violently suppressed by security forces, and six deaths were subsequently reported. In June the Vice-President of the RDPC, John Ngu Foncha, resigned, alleging corruption and human rights violations on the part of the Government, while the Congress of the RDPC re-elected Biya as President of the party. In response to continued civil unrest, Biya stated that he envisaged the future adoption of a multi-party system and announced a series of reforms, including the abolition of laws governing subversion, the revision of the law on political associations, and the reinforcement of press freedom. In the same month a committee was established to revise legislation on human rights. In August several political prisoners, including Black, were released. In September Biya announced an extensive cabinet reshuffle. In December the National Assembly adopted legislation whereby Cameroon officially became a multi-party state.

In January 1991 anti-Government demonstrators protested at Biya's failure (despite previous undertakings) to grant an amnesty to prisoners implicated in the 1984 coup attempt. Meanwhile, opposition leaders reiterated demands for Biya's resignation and the convening of a national conference to formulate a timetable for multi-party elections. Biya's continued opposition to the holding of a conference provoked a series of demonstrations, which were violently suppressed by the security forces. In April the principal anti-Government groups created an informal alliance, the National Co-ordination Committee of Opposition Parties (NCCOP), which organized a widely observed general strike. Later in April, in response to increasing pressure for political reform, the National Assembly approved legislation granting a general amnesty for political prisoners and reintroducing the post of Prime Minister. Biya subsequently appointed Sadou Hayatou, hitherto Secretary-General at the Presidency, to the position. Hayatou named a transitional Government, principally composed of members of the former Cabinet. The Government's refusal to comply with the NCCOP's demands for an unconditional amnesty for all political prisoners (the existing provisions for an amnesty excluded an estimated 400 political prisoners jailed for allegedly non-political crimes) and for the convening of a national conference prompted the alliance to organize a campaign of civil disobedience, culminating in a general strike in June. The Government placed seven of Cameroon's 10 provinces under military rule, prohibited opposition gatherings, and later in June, following continued civil disturbances, banned the NCCOP and several opposition parties, alleging that the opposition alliance was responsible for terrorist activities. Although opposition leaders announced that the campaign of civil disobedience would continue, the effect of the general strike declined in subsequent months.

In October 1991 Biya announced that legislative elections were to be held in February 1992, and that a Prime Minister would be appointed from the party that secured a majority in the National Assembly. Following tripartite negotiations between the Government, opposition parties and independent officials, in mid-November 2001 the Government and about 40 of the 47 registered opposition parties (including some parties belonging to the NCCOP) signed an agreement providing for the establishment of a committee to draft constitutional reforms. The opposition undertook to suspend the campaign of civil disobedience, while the Government agreed to end the ban on opposition meetings and to release all prisoners who had been arrested during anti-Government demonstrations. However, several principal opposition parties belonging to the NCCOP, including the SDF, subsequently declared the agreement to be invalid, and stated that the campaign of civil disobedience would continue. The Government revoked the ban on opposition gatherings later in November, and in December ended the military rule that had been imposed in seven provinces.

In January 1992 the Government postponed the legislative elections until March, in order to allow parties sufficient time for preparation. However, several opposition movements, including two of the principal parties, the SDF and the Union démocratique du Cameroun (UDC), refused to contest the elections, on the grounds that the scheduled date was still too early and benefited the RDPC. In February more than 100 people were killed in the northern town of Kousseri, following violent clashes between the Kokoto and Arab Choa ethnic groups during the registration of voters. In the same month those opposition parties that had not accepted the tripartite agreement in November 1991 formed the Alliance pour le redressement du Cameroun (ARC), and announced that they were to boycott the elections.

The legislative elections, which took place on 1 March 1992, were contested by 32 political parties; the RDPC won 88 of the National Assembly's 180 seats, while the Union nationale pour la démocratie et le progrès (UNDP) obtained 68, the UPC 18 and the Mouvement pour la défense de la République (MDR) six seats. The RDPC subsequently formed an alliance with the MDR, thereby securing an absolute majority in the National Assembly. In April Biya formed a 25-member Cabinet, principally comprising members of the previous Government and including five MDR members; Simon Achidi Achu, an anglophone member of the RDPC, was appointed Prime Minister.

In August 1992 Biya announced that the forthcoming presidential election, scheduled for May 1993, was to be brought forward to 11 October 1992. In September Biya promulgated legislation regulating the election of the President that prohibited the formation of electoral alliances. Shortly before the election two of the seven opposition candidates withdrew in favour of the Chairman of the SDF, John Fru Ndi, who received the support of the ARC. The presidential election, which took place as scheduled, immediately provoked opposition allegations of malpractice on the part of the Government. In mid-October Fru Ndi proclaimed himself President, following unconfirmed reports that he had won the election. Later that month, however, the Government announced that Biya had been re-elected by 39.9% of the votes cast, while Fru Ndi had secured 35.9%, prompting violent demonstrations by opposition supporters in many areas, particularly in the north-west and in Douala. The Supreme Court rejected a subsequent appeal by Fru Ndi that the results of the election be declared invalid. At the end of October, in response to the continued unrest, the Government placed Fru Ndi and several of his supporters under house arrest, and imposed a three-month state of emergency in North-West Province. Biya was inaugurated as President on 3 November and pledged to implement further constitutional reforms. Later that month international condemnation of the Government increased, following the death by torture of a detained opposition member; the USA and Germany suspended economic aid to Cameroon in protest at the continued enforcement of the state of emergency. At the end of November Biya appointed a new 30-member Cabinet, which, in addition to three members of the MDR, included representatives of the UPC, the UNDP and the Parti national du progrès. In late December the state of emergency was revoked in North-West Province.

In March 1993 an informal alliance of opposition parties (led by the SDF), the Union pour le changement, organized a series of demonstrations and a boycott of French consumer goods (in protest at the French Government's involvement with Biya) in support of demands for a new presidential election. The Government accused the alliance of incitement to civil disorder and continued efforts to suppress opposition activity. Later in March three people were killed in clashes between members of the armed forces and opposition supporters in Bamenda, in North-West Province, while a number of members of a prominent opposition movement, the Union des forces démocratiques du Cameroun, were arrested shortly before a demonstration was due to take place. In response to international pressure, however, the Government announced its intention to conduct a national debate on constitutional reform. In April a gathering organized by the Cameroon Anglophone Movement (CAM) in Buéa, in South-West Province, demanded the restoration of a federal system of government, in response to the traditional dominance of the French-speaking section of the population. In the following month the Government promulgated draft constitutional amendments that provided for the installation of a democratic political system, with the establishment of new organs of government, including an upper legislative chamber, to be known as the Senate, and restricted the power vested in the President (who was to serve a maximum of two five-year terms of office). The draft legislation retained a unitary state, but, in recognition of demands by supporters of federalism, envisaged a more decentralized system of local government.

During the second half of 1993 the opposition organized a series of anti-Government strikes and demonstrations, which led to the detention of many activists. In December public-sector workers initiated a general strike, with the support of the opposition, after the Government announced substantial salary reductions. In early 1994, however, strike action in protest at the devaluation of the CFA franc subsided, following the imposition of sanctions against striking civil servants. Meanwhile, in September 1993 a peace agreement was signed between the Kokoto and Arab Choa ethnic groups in Kousseri, although further clashes were reported later in the year. In February 1994 security forces killed some 50 members of the Arab Choa ethnic group at the village of Karena in northern Cameroon, apparently in retaliation for acts of armed banditry in the region, which were, however, widely attributed to former Chadian rebels. In March some 1,200 citizens took refuge in Chad, in response to continuing clashes between security forces and bandits in northern Cameroon.

In September 1994 an informal alliance of 16 opposition movements, the Front des alliés pour le changement (FAC), was established, effectively replacing the Union pour le changement; the FAC denounced alleged human rights violations on the part of the authorities, together with the indefinite postponement of municipal elections and the transfer of state-owned enterprises to the private sector. The UNDP and the UDC refused to join the alliance, however, on the grounds that it was dominated by the

SDF. In November Biya announced that discussions on the revision of the Constitution were to resume, following the establishment of a Consultative Constitutional Review Committee, and that municipal elections were to take place in 1995. Constitutional discussions commenced in December 1994, but were boycotted by the opposition, which cited limitations in the agenda of the debate. In early 1995, however, the Consultative Constitutional Review Committee submitted revised constitutional amendments to Biya for consideration.

In July 1995 members of a new anglophone organization, the Southern Cameroons National Council (SCNC, which demanded that the former portion of the British Cameroons that had amalgamated with the Republic of Cameroon in 1961 be granted autonomy), staged a demonstration in Bamenda. In the same month a number of independently-owned newspapers temporarily suspended publication in protest at alleged increasing press censorship and intimidation of journalists. In August representatives of anglophone movements, including the SCNC and the CAM, officially presented their demands for the establishment of an independent, English-speaking republic of Southern Cameroons at the UN; the organizations claimed that the plebiscite of 1961, whereby the former southern portion of British Cameroons had voted to merge with the Republic of Cameroon on terms of equal status, had been rendered invalid by subsequent francophone domination.

In October 1995 a special congress of the RDPC re-elected Biya as leader of the party for a further term of five years. Meanwhile, Cameroon's pending application for membership of the Commonwealth (which had been accepted, in principle, in 1993, subject to the Government's fulfilment of certain democratic conditions) prompted further controversy; opposition movements urged the Commonwealth to refuse admission to Cameroon on the grounds that no progress had been achieved with regard to human rights and the democratic process, while the SCNC submitted a rival application for membership on behalf of the proposed independent republic of Southern Cameroons. In November, however, Cameroon was formally admitted to the Commonwealth. In December the National Assembly adopted the revised constitutional amendments, submitted by Biya earlier that month, which increased the presidential mandate from five to seven years (while restricting the maximum tenure of office to two terms) and provided for the establishment of a Senate. Municipal elections, in which some 38 political parties participated, took place in January 1996; the RDPC won the majority of seats in 56% of local councils, and the SDF in 27%, while the UNDP received popular support in the north of the country. In March the SDF and the UNDP urged a campaign of civil disobedience in protest at the Government's appointment by decree of representatives to replace the elected mayors in principal towns (following the municipal elections, the opposition had gained control of 13 towns). In April the Government imposed a total ban on all media reports of the SDF/UNDP campaign of civil disobedience. In May–June the two parties organized general strikes, which were principally observed in western and northern regions. In September Simon Achidi Achu was replaced as Prime Minister by Peter Mafany Musonge, the General Manager of the Cameroon Development Corporation, and a new Cabinet was appointed.

In January 1997 the Government postponed the legislative elections (which had been scheduled to take place in March) owing to organizational difficulties. At the end of March some 10 people were killed when unidentified armed groups staged attacks against government and security buildings in Bamenda and other towns in North-West Province; the violence was generally attributed to members of the SCNC. In April the Government announced that the elections were to take place on 17 May. Pre-election violence, in which some five people were killed, prompted the imposition of increased security measures, including the closure of the country's borders. The elections, which were contested by 46 political parties, were monitored by a Commonwealth observer mission. The announcement of provisional results (which attributed a large majority of seats to the RDPC) prompted opposition claims of widespread electoral malpractice; the observer group also expressed general dissatisfaction with the election process. The Supreme Court, however, rejected opposition appeals against RDPC victories. Three people were killed in clashes between RDPC and SDF members in South-West Province, where the election result was disputed by the two parties. In early June the Supreme Court announced the official election results: the RDPC had secured 109 of the 180 seats in the legislature, while the SDF had obtained 43, the

UNDP 13 and the UDC five seats; the Mouvement pour la jeunesse du Cameroun, the UPC and the MDR obtained one seat each. The Cabinet remained virtually unchanged from the previous administration. In August further polls were conducted in seven constituencies where the results had been annulled, owing to alleged irregularities; the RDPC won all of the seats, thus increasing its representation in the National Assembly to 116 seats.

It was announced in September 1997 that the presidential election would be held on 12 October. Shortly afterwards the SDF, the UNDP and the UDC declared a boycott of all elections, in protest at the absence of an independent electoral commission; a fourth opposition party, the Union du peuple africain, later joined the boycott. In mid-September Biya was officially elected as the RDPC presidential candidate. At the election, which was contested by seven candidates, Biya was re-elected, winning 92.6% of the votes cast. The level of voter participation in the election was much disputed, with official sources asserting that a record 81.4% of the electorate took part, while opposition leaders claimed that the abstention rate was higher than 80%. Biya was formally inaugurated on 3 November, beginning, in accordance with the revised Constitution, a seven-year term in office. Following talks with various opposition groups, the RDPC reached an agreement with the UNDP on the creation of a coalition government; the SDF, however, refused to co-operate with the ruling party. In December, having reappointed Musonge as Prime Minister, Biya effected a major cabinet reshuffle. The new Government included representatives from four of the country's many political groups, although the RDPC retained 45 of the 50 ministerial posts.

In July 1998 10 of the 43 SDF deputies resigned from the party, in protest at the perceived tribalism and authoritarianism of its leadership. In October the SDF expelled its First National Vice-President, Soulaimane Mahamad, following the latter's criticism of Fru Ndi as authoritarian. In January 1999 Fru Ndi announced that he was prepared to initiate direct dialogue with President Biya. It was, however, alleged that the leader of the SDF had announced this radical change of policy in the hope of securing a favourable verdict in his imminent court appearance on charges of defamation. In April Fru Ndi was, none the less, found guilty and was fined and given a three-year suspended sentence. At the SDF party conference in the same month Fru Ndi was re-elected Chairman of the party by an overwhelming majority of delegates, despite accusations made by opponents that he had presided over the disintegration of the SDF as a political force. The conference voted not to enter into dialogue with the Government until an independent electoral commission had been established.

Meanwhile, in September 1998 it was reported that some 60 English-speaking Cameroonians, who were alleged to be secessionists campaigning for the independence of Southern Cameroons, were being detained and tortured in Yaoundé, following attacks on police premises. There were counter-accusations made by the opposition, however, that the raids had been staged by government agents as a pretext for further suppression of demands for increased decentralization. In January 1999 the opposition condemned the Government for the alleged marginalization of the anglophone minority in Cameroon, noting that only three of the 2,000 soldiers recently recruited by the armed forces were English-speaking. In June the trial of the alleged anglophone secessionists (the majority of whom had been arrested in 1997) began in Yaoundé. The trial was notable for frequent adjournments and complaints by defence lawyers relating to the competence of the military tribunal to hear the case. In July several of the defendants claimed that confessions that they were members of the separatist SCNC had been extracted under torture and threats of summary execution. In August the accused formally denied all charges against them, although several individuals admitted to being members of a cultural association linked to the SCNC. In October three of the defendants were sentenced to life imprisonment, others received lengthy prison sentences, while 29 were acquitted. The human rights organization Amnesty International criticized the verdicts, alluding to the alleged bias of the military court and the reported torture of detainees, and in November the UN Human Rights Committee criticized Cameroon for its alleged failure to protect and to respect fundamental human rights.

In September 1999 Mounchipou Seydou was dismissed from his post as Minister of Posts and Telecommunications and was subsequently arrested on charges of embezzlement of public funds. In October a report by a German non-governmental organization, Transparency International (see p. 351), rated Cameroon as the most corrupt country in the world. Although the Government strenuously denied the allegations of Transparency International, a meeting was held in November of the National Commission on Corruption, which had met infrequently since its creation in 1997, at which senior government officials outlined strategies to curb corruption in their areas of responsibility.

There was a cabinet reshuffle in March 2000, which was widely interpreted as a response to an escalation in urban crime (several foreign diplomats, including the ambassadors of the USA and the Netherlands, had been attacked). All ministers linked to security matters were involved in the reshuffle. Furthermore, some 70% of police-officers were reportedly replaced. In November deputies staged a sit-in outside the National Assembly after the security forces prevented a protest march, from the legislative building to the presidential palace, from proceeding. The march had been organized by the SDF in support of demands for the creation of an independent electoral commission. In the following month the National Assembly adopted legislation on the establishment of a National Elections Observatory and on the regulation of state funding for political parties and electoral campaigns. However, five opposition parties boycotted the vote on the elections observatory, claiming that it would be unconstitutional, as it would perform the same functions as the Constitutional Council, and criticizing the President's role in appointing its 11 members. President Biya subsequently postponed municipal elections, due on 21 January 2001, until January 2002, ostensibly on the grounds that the new electoral legislation had yet to become fully operational, and that the 21st Franco-African summit was to convene in Yaoundé a few days prior to the original date.

In early 2001 the disappearance and suspected extrajudicial killing of nine youths from Douala, who had been arrested in January on charges of robbery, led to widespread protests and marches, in which several demonstrators and opposition leaders were injured. (In July 2002 a military court convicted two police-officers on charges relating to the disappearances.) A cabinet reshuffle was effected in April 2001, following accusations of corruption against several ministers. At the beginning of October at least three people died in clashes with the security forces during a demonstration organized by the SCNC in Kumbo, in North-West Province, on the 40th anniversary of the reunification of Cameroon. Later that month the National Elections Observatory was inaugurated, amid opposition criticism that the 11 appointees were all supporters of the ruling RDPC. In December the municipal elections were postponed for a further six months.

Legislative and municipal elections were held concurrently on 30 June 2002, despite initial technical problems. Voting had been delayed by one week, owing to insufficient voting materials, leading to the dismissal of the Minister of Territorial Administration, Ferdinand Koungou Edima. Some 47 parties contested the elections to the National Assembly, at which the RDPC's majority increased to 133 seats, while its closest rival, the SDF, secured 21 seats, the UDC five, the UPC three and the UNDP only one seat. Electoral turn-out was reported to be less than 50%, and the elections were boycotted by the SCNC. Voting for the remaining 17 seats was cancelled by the Supreme Court, in response to complaints of various irregularities in the nine constituencies concerned. At the municipal elections, the RDPC also performed strongly, winning 286 of the 336 council seats contested. Opposition parties alleged widespread electoral fraud, however, and demanded that the elections be declared void. The SDF initially refused to participate in the newly elected legislature and municipal councils, although in mid-July Fru Ndi announced the end of the boycott, provoking internal conflict within his party. Several SDF senior officials subsequently resigned from the party and formed the Alliance des forces progressistes, claiming that Fru Ndi's unilateral decision to end the boycott had been inspired by covert plans to join the Government. In August there was an extensive cabinet reshuffle, in which 18 new members of government were appointed. On 15 September voting took place for the 17 legislative seats that had remained vacant since June; the RDPC secured a further 16 seats, increasing its majority to 149 of the 180 seats in the National Assembly, while the SDF won the remaining seat.

In 1991 the Nigerian Government claimed that Cameroon had annexed nine Nigerian fishing settlements, following a long-standing border dispute, based on a 1913 agreement between Germany and the United Kingdom that ceded the Bakassi peninsula in the Gulf of Guinea (a region of strategic significance) to Cameroon. Subsequent attempts by the Governments of Nigeria and Cameroon to resolve the dispute achieved little progress. In December 1993 some 500 Nigerian troops were dispatched to the region, in response to a number of incidents in which Nigerian nationals had been killed by Cameroonian security forces. Later that month the two nations agreed to establish a joint patrol in the disputed area, and to investigate the incidents. In February 1994, however, Cameroon announced that it was to submit the dispute for adjudication by the UN, the Organization of African Unity (OAU, now the African Union (see p. 130) and the International Court of Justice (ICJ), based in The Hague, Netherlands. Subsequent reports of clashes between Cameroonian and Nigerian forces in the region prompted fears of a full-scale conflict. In March Cameroon agreed to enter into negotiations with Nigeria (without the involvement of international mediators) to resolve the issue. In the same month the OAU issued a resolution urging the withdrawal of troops from the disputed region. In May negotiations between the two nations, with mediation by the Togolese Government, resumed in Yaoundé. In September the Cameroonian Government submitted additional claims to territory in north-eastern Nigeria to the ICJ.

In February 1996 renewed hostilities between Nigerian and Cameroonian forces in the Bakassi region resulted in several casualties. Later that month, however, Cameroon and Nigeria agreed to refrain from further military action, and delegations from the two countries resumed discussions, again with Togolese mediation. In March the ICJ ruled that Cameroon had failed to provide sufficient evidence to substantiate its contention that Nigeria had instigated the border dispute, and ordered both nations to cease military operations in the region, to withdraw troops to former positions, and to co-operate with a UN investigative mission, which was to be dispatched to the area. In April, however, clashes continued, with each Government accusing the other of initiating the attacks. Claims by Nigeria that the Cameroonian forces were supported by troops from France were denied by the French Government. Diplomatic efforts to avoid further conflict increased. Nevertheless, both nations continued to reinforce their contingents in the region (where some 5,000 Cameroonian and 3,000 Nigerian troops were deployed at the end of May). Further tension arose in July, when Nigeria accused Cameroon of substantially increasing troops and artillery on the Bakassi peninsula. In September both countries assured the UN investigative mission of their commitment to a peaceful settlement of the dispute. In December and again in May 1997, however, the Nigerian authorities claimed that Cameroonian troops had resumed attacks in the region. Further clashes were reported in late 1997 and early 1998.

In May and September 1998 Cameroon denied reports that it was massing troops on the peninsula. In October further contention arose when Nigeria alleged that Cameroon had awarded a Canadian company a concession to prospect for petroleum in the disputed area. Cameroon insisted that no such concession had been granted. From late 1998 relations between Cameroon and Nigeria began to improve, and in November the International Committee of the Red Cross organized an exchange of prisoners between the two sides. In April 1999 the President-elect of Nigeria, Gen. Olusegun Obasanjo, visited Cameroon, the first such visit since the beginning of the border conflict in 1994. The two countries reportedly agreed to resolve the dispute 'in a fraternal way'. It was, however, announced that ICJ proceedings would be continued, and in late May 1999 Nigeria filed its defence. Following the submission to the ICJ of various written counter-claims by Cameroon and Nigeria in 2000–01, both countries presented their evidence at public hearings in The Hague in February and March 2002.

In October 2002 the ICJ issued its final verdict on the demarcation of the land and maritime boundary between Cameroon and Nigeria, notably ruling in favour of Cameroon's sovereignty over the Bakassi peninsula, citing the 1913 Anglo-German partition agreement. Despite having no option to appeal, Nigeria refused to accept the Court's decision, and troop deployments began to increase on both sides of the border, prompting fears of armed conflict between the two countries. In mid-November, however, at a meeting in Geneva, Switzerland, mediated by the Secretary-General of the UN, Kofi Annan, the Presidents of Cameroon and Nigeria signed a joint communiqué announcing the creation of a bilateral 12-member Mixed Commission, to be headed by a UN Special Representative, with a mandate to achieve a peaceful solution to the Bakassi peninsula dispute. At its inaugural meeting in Yaoundé in early December, the Commission agreed on a 15-point peace agenda and decided to establish a sub-commission to undertake the demarcation of the boundary; a second meeting was held in Abuja, the Nigerian capital, in February 2003.

Government

Under the amended 1972 Constitution, the Republic of Cameroon is a multi-party state. Executive power is vested in the President, as Head of State, who is elected by universal adult suffrage for a term of seven years, and may serve a maximum of two terms. Legislative power is held by the National Assembly, which comprises 180 members and is elected for a term of five years. In December 1995 constitutional amendments provided for the establishment of an upper legislative chamber (to be known as the Senate). The Cabinet is appointed by the President. Local administration is based on 10 provinces, each with a governor who is appointed by the President.

Defence

In August 2002 Cameroon's armed forces were estimated to total 23,100 men, including 9,000 in paramilitary forces. The army numbered 12,500, the navy about 1,300 and the air force 300. Cameroon has a bilateral defence agreement with France. The defence budget for 2002 was estimated at US $132m.

Economic Affairs

In 2001, according to estimates by the World Bank, Cameroon's gross national income (GNI), measured at average 1999–2001 prices, was US $8,723m., equivalent to $570 per head (or $1,670 per head on an international purchasing-power parity basis). During 1990–2001, it was estimated, the population increased at an average annual rate of 2.5%, while gross domestic product (GDP) per head declined, in real terms, by an average of 0.7% per year. Overall GDP increased, in real terms, at an average annual rate of 1.7% in 1990–2001; growth in 2001 was 5.3%.

Agriculture (including hunting, forestry and fishing) contributed 43.9% of GDP in 2000/01. An estimated 58.2% of the labour force were employed in agriculture in 2001. The principal cash crops are cocoa beans (which accounted for 4.5% of export earnings in 2000/01), cotton and coffee. The principal subsistence crops are roots and tubers (mainly cassava), maize and sorghum; Cameroon is not, however, self-sufficient in cereals. In 1995 an estimated 42% of the country's land area was covered by forest, but an inadequate transport infrastructure has impeded the development of the forestry sector. However, environmental concerns were raised in June 2001, after it was reported that 80% of Cameroon's indigenous forests had been allocated for logging. Illegal logging and poaching in the country's forests remains a significant problem. Livestock-rearing makes an important contribution to the food supply. During 1990–2001, according to the World Bank, the real GDP of the agricultural sector increased at an average annual rate of 5.1%; growth in 2001 was 6.8%.

Industry (including mining, manufacturing, construction and power) employed 8.9% of the labour force in 1990, and contributed 20.2% of GDP in 2000/01. During 1990–2001, according to the World Bank, industrial GDP declined at an average annual rate of less than 0.1%; however, growth of 7.7% was recorded in 2001.

Mining contributed 4.0% of GDP in 2000/01, but employed only 0.05% of Cameroon's working population in 1985. Receipts from the exploitation of the country's petroleum reserves constitute a principal source of government revenue. Deposits of limestone are also quarried. Significant reserves of natural gas, bauxite, iron ore, uranium and tin remain largely undeveloped. According to the IMF, the GDP of the mining sector increased by 2.5% in 1995/96–2000/01; growth in 2000/01 was 0.6%.

Manufacturing contributed an estimated 10.9% of GDP in 2000/01, and employed an estimated 7% of the working population in 1995. The sector is based on the processing of both indigenous primary products (petroleum-refining, agro-industrial activities) and of imported raw materials (an aluminium smelter uses alumina imported from Guinea). According to the World Bank, manufacturing GDP increased at an average annual rate of 3.0% in 1990–2001; growth in 2001 was 10.8%.

In 1999 hydroelectric power installations supplied 98.8% of Cameroon's energy. In the same year imports of fuel products accounted for 15.8% of the value of total imports.

Services contributed 35.9% of GDP in 2000/01. During 1990–2001, according to the World Bank, the GDP of the services sector declined at an average annual rate of 0.1%; however, growth of 2.6% was recorded in 2001.

In 2000/01 Cameroon recorded a visible trade surplus of an estimated 380,500m. francs CFA, but there was a deficit of 109,900m. francs CFA on the current account of the balance of payments. In 2000/01 the principal source of imports (24.5%) was France; other major suppliers were Nigeria, Germany and the USA. The principal market for exports in that year (29.9%) was Italy; other significant purchasers were France, Spain, the Netherlands, the People's Republic of China and the Republic of China (Taiwan). The principal exports in 2000/01 were petroleum and petroleum products (accounting for 57.2% of the total), timber and timber products, aluminium, cocoa beans and raw cotton. The principal imports in that year were minerals and other raw materials (accounting for 20.8% of the total), semi-finished goods, enterprise consumption goods, industrial equipment, and food, beverages and tobacco.

In the financial year ending June 2001 there was a budget deficit of 34,000m. francs CFA (equivalent to 0.5% of GDP). Cameroon's total external debt at the end of 2000 was US $9,241m., of which $7,357m. was long-term public debt. In that year the cost of debt-servicing was equivalent to 20.5% of revenue from exports of goods and services. The annual rate of inflation averaged 4.8% in 1990–2001; consumer prices declined by an average of 2.0% in 2000, but increased by an average of 4.5% in 2001. An estimated 5.8% of the labour force were unemployed in mid-1985.

Cameroon is a member of the Central African organs of the Franc Zone, see p. 239), of the Communauté économique des états de l'Afrique centrale (CEEAC, see p. 339), of the International Cocoa Organization (see p. 336) and of the International Coffee Organization (see p. 336).

Increases in international prices for Cameroon's major export commodities contributed to an improvement in economic conditions in 1995–96. In 1997 the IMF approved a three-year loan for Cameroon, equivalent to about US $221m., under the Enhanced Structural Adjustment Facility. In October 2000 the IMF and the World Bank's International Development Association agreed to support a debt-reduction package for Cameroon, worth an estimated $2,000m., under the enhanced Heavily Indebted Poor Countries initiative, thus substantially reducing Cameroon's debt-service obligations and allowing increased expenditure on social and welfare services. In December the IMF approved another three-year loan, equivalent to about $144m., under the Poverty Reduction and Growth Facility, in support of efforts to improve social services, reduce poverty and maintain a stable macroeconomic environment. The construction of a 1,070-km pipeline to transport crude petroleum from southern Chad to the southern Cameroonian port of Kribi was expected to be completed by mid-2003. It was hoped that royalties from the pipeline would partially offset the decline in direct revenue from petroleum, daily production of which decreased from a peak of 164,000 barrels in the mid-1980s to some 85,000 barrels in 2002. In addition, in 2002 the Government was seeking to attract investment for the development of significant reserves of natural gas. Real GDP growth was estimated at 4.4% for 2001/02, as a result of the expanding non-petroleum sector and the implementation of structural reforms. None the less, fraud and corruption remained a hindrance to the economic development of Cameroon, as did the country's generally poor physical infrastructure.

Education

Since independence, Cameroon has achieved one of the highest rates of school attendance in Africa, but provision of educational facilities varies according to region. Education, which is bilingual, is provided by the Government, missionary societies and private concerns. Education in state schools is available free of charge, and the Government provides financial assistance for other schools. Primary education begins at six years of age. It lasts for six years in Eastern Cameroon (where it is officially compulsory), and for seven years in Western Cameroon. Secondary education, beginning at the age of 12 or 13, lasts for a further seven years, comprising two cycles of four years and three years in Eastern Cameroon and five years and two years in Western Cameroon. In 1999/2000 primary enrolment was equivalent to 91.1% of children in the appropriate age-group (males 98.2%; females 83.9%), while, according to UNESCO estimates, in 1998/99 enrolment at secondary schools was equivalent to only 19.6% (males 22.0%; females 17.2%). Expenditure on education by the central Government in 2000/01 was 307,000m. francs CFA (20.8% of total spending).

Public Holidays

2003: 1 January (New Year), 11 February (Youth Day), 12 February* (Festival of Sheep), 18 April (Good Friday), 21 April (Easter Monday), 1 May (Labour Day), 20 May (National Day), 29 May (Ascension Day), 15 August (Assumption), 26 November* (Djoulde Soumae, end of Ramadan), 25 December (Christmas).

2004: 1 January (New Year), 2 February* (Festival of Sheep), 11 February (Youth Day), 9 April (Good Friday), 12 April (Easter Monday), 1 May (Labour Day), 20 May (National Day and Ascension Day), 15 August (Assumption), 14 November* (Djoulde Soumae, end of Ramadan), 25 December (Christmas).

*These holidays are dependent on the Islamic lunar calendar and may vary by one or two days from the dates given.

Weights and Measures

The metric system is in force.

Statistical Survey

Source (unless otherwise stated): Direction de la Prévision, Ministère de l'Economie et des Finances, BP 18, Yaoundé; tel. 23-40-40; fax 23-21-50.

Area and Population

AREA, POPULATION AND DENSITY

Area (sq km)	475,442*
Population (census results)	
9 April 1976†	7,663,246
9 April 1987	
Males	5,162,878
Females.	5,330,777
Total	10,493,655
Population (official estimates at mid-year)	
1998	14,439,000
1999	14,859,000
2000	14,876,000
Density (per sq km) at mid-2000	31.3

* 183,569 sq miles.

† Including an adjustment for underenumeration, estimated at 7.4%. The enumerated total was 7,090,115.

PROVINCES

(population at 1987 census)

	Urban	Rural	Total
Centre	877,481	774,119	1,651,600
Littoral	1,093,323	259,510	1,352,833
West	431,337	908,454	1,339,791
South-West	258,940	579,102	838,042
North-West	271,114	966,234	1,237,348
North	234,572	597,593	832,165
East	152,787	364,411	517,198
South	104,023	269,775	373,798
Adamaoua.	178,644	316,541	495,185
Far North	366,698	1,488,997	1,855,695
Total	3,968,919	6,524,736	10,493,655

PRINCIPAL TOWNS

(population at 1987 census)

Douala.	810,000	Bamenda	110,000
Yaoundé (capital) .	649,000	Nkongsamba . . .	85,420
Garoua	142,000	Kumba	70,112
Maroua	123,000	Limbé	44,561
Bafoussam . . .	113,000		

2000 (estimated population, '000): Douala 1,642; Yaoundé 1,420 (Source: Ministry of Public Investments and Regional Planning, *Indicateurs démographiques sur le Cameroun*).

BIRTHS AND DEATHS

(official estimates, annual averages)

	1987–92	1993–97	1998–2000
Birth rate (per 1,000) . . .	41.7	39.7	38.2
Death rate (per 1,000) . . .	12.8	11.4	10.1

Expectation of life (WHO estimates, years at birth): 49.7 (males 48.9; females 50.5) in 2001 (Source: WHO, *World Health Report*).

ECONOMICALLY ACTIVE POPULATION

(official estimates, persons aged six years and over, mid-1985)

	Males	Females	Total
Agriculture, hunting, forestry and fishing	1,574,946	1,325,925	2,900,871
Mining and quarrying . . .	1,693	100	1,793
Manufacturing	137,671	36,827	174,498
Electricity, gas and water . .	3,373	149	3,522
Construction	65,666	1,018	66,684
Trade, restaurants and hotels .	115,269	38,745	154,014
Transport, storage and communications	50,664	1,024	51,688
Financing, insurance, real estate and business services . .	7,447	562	8,009
Community, social and personal services	255,076	37,846	292,922
Activities not adequately defined .	18,515	17,444	35,959
Total in employment . . .	2,230,320	1,459,640	3,689,960
Unemployed	180,016	47,659	227,675
Total labour force	2,410,336	1,507,299	3,917,635

Source: ILO, *Yearbook of Labour Statistics*.

Mid-2001 (estimates in '000): Agriculture, etc. 3,647; Total labour force 6,261 (Source: FAO).

Health and Welfare

KEY INDICATORS

Total fertility rate (children per woman, 2001).	4.89
Under-5 mortality rate (per 1,000 live births, 2001) . . .	155
HIV/AIDS (% of persons aged 15–49, 2001). . . .	11.83
Physicians (per 1,000 head, 1996)	0.07
Hospital beds (per 1,000 head, 1990)	2.55
Health expenditure (2000): US $ per head (PPP) . . .	24
Health expenditure (2000): % of GDP	4.3
Health expenditure (2000): public (% of total)	24.7
Access to water (% of persons, 2000).	62
Access to sanitation (% of persons, 2000)	92
Human Development Index (2000): ranking	135
Human Development Index (2000): value	0.512

For sources and definitions, see explanatory note on p. vi.

Agriculture

PRINCIPAL CROPS
('000 metric tons)

	1999	2000	2001
Rice (paddy)	67	70	70*
Maize	785	850	850*
Millet*	71	71	71
Sorghum	272	420	450*
Potatoes	55	55	55*
Sweet potatoes	179	180*	180*
Cassava (Manioc)	1,984	1,500	1,700*
Yams	262	260*	260
Other roots and tubers	838	541	600*
Sugar cane*	1,350	1,350	1,350
Dry beans	171	170*	170*
Groundnuts (in shell)	184	95†	100*
Oil palm fruit*	1,050	1,050	1,050
Melonseed*	55	56	56
Cottonseed*	75	90	80
Tomatoes	70	70*	70*
Pumpkins, squash and gourds	121	120*	120*
Dry onions	56	55*	55*
Other vegetables*	517	520	520
Bananas	750*	730	850*
Plantains	1,332	1,332	1,400*
Avocados*	49	50	50
Pineapples	42	42*	42*
Other fruit*	104	105	105
Coffee (green)	98	86	83†
Cocoa beans	116	123	115†
Cotton (lint)	80	95	102
Natural rubber	58	59	60*

* FAO estimate(s).
† Unofficial figure.

Source: FAO.

LIVESTOCK
('000 head, year ending September)

	1999	2000	2001*
Horses	17	17*	17
Asses*	37	38	38
Cattle	5,500	5,822	5,900
Pigs	1,000	1,346*	1,350
Sheep	3,650*	3,753	3,880
Goats	3,800*	4,410	4,400
Poultry*	30,400	22,000	30,000

* FAO estimate(s).

Source: FAO.

LIVESTOCK PRODUCTS
('000 metric tons)

	1999	2000	2001
Beef and veal*	91.2	93.0	94.8
Mutton and lamb†	15.8	16.2	16.4
Goat meat†	13.7	15.4	15.4
Pig meat†	12.0	16.2	16.2
Poultry meat†	30.4	22.4	30.4
Other meat	46.4	46.4	46.4
Cows' milk†	125.0	125.0	125.0
Sheep's milk†	17.0	17.0	17.0
Goats' milk†	42.0	42.0	42.0
Poultry eggs†	13.8	13.2	13.8
Honey†	3.0	3.0	3.0
Cattle hides (fresh)†	12.1	12.9	13.0
Sheepskins (fresh)†	2.6	2.7	2.7
Goatskins (fresh)†	1.4	1.5	1.5

* Unofficial figures.
† FAO estimates.

Source: FAO.

Forestry

ROUNDWOOD REMOVALS
('000 cubic metres, excl. bark)

	1999	2000	2001
Sawlogs, veneer logs and logs for sleepers	1,767	1,809	1,809
Other industrial wood	65	85	—
Fuel wood*	9,033	9,111	9,183
Total	10,865	11,005	10,992

* FAO estimates.

Source: FAO.

SAWNWOOD PRODUCTION
('000 cubic metres, incl. railway sleepers)

	1999	2000	2001
Total (all broadleaved)	600	900	1,150

Source: FAO.

Fishing

(FAO estimates, '000 metric tons, live weight)

	1998	1999	2000
Capture	106.8	110.0	112.1
Freshwater fishes	45.0	50.0	55.0
Cassava croaker	2.9	3.2	2.0
Bobo croaker	4.4	1.9	3.4
Other croakers and drums	3.5	3.5	3.3
Sardinellas	23.0	23.5	21.6
Bonga shad	23.0	23.5	21.6
Aquaculture	0.1	0.1	0.1
Total catch	106.9	110.1	112.2

Source: FAO, *Yearbook of Fishery Statistics*.

Mining*

	1999	2000	2001
Crude petroleum (million barrels)	43	41	40
Gold (kilograms)†	1,000	1,000	1,000
Pozzolan ('000 metric tons)	632	605	600
Limestone ('000 metric tons)	168	259	260

* Estimated production.
† Data refer to the metal content of ores.

Source: US Geological Survey.

Industry

SELECTED PRODUCTS
('000 metric tons, unless otherwise indicated)

	1996	1997	1998
Palm oil	161	135	136
Raw sugar.	53	54	52
Veneer sheets ('000 cu metres) .	31	61	59
Plywood ('000 cu metres) . .	43	90	89
Aviation gasoline. . . .	17	17	17
Jet fuels	10	10	10
Motor spirit (petrol)	301	303	304
Kerosene	245	42	42
Gas-diesel (distillate fuel) oil . .	290	291	295
Residual fuel oils	155	155	157
Lubricating oils	40	42	42
Petroleum bitumen (asphalt) . .	10	12	12
Liquefied petroleum gas. . .	22	22	22
Cement*	305	620	740
Aluminium (unwrought)* . . .	82	91	82
Electric energy (million kWh) . .	2,753	2,758	2,765

* Data from the US Geological Survey.

1999 ('000 metric tons): Palm oil 123; Raw sugar 54(unofficial figure); Veneer sheets ('000 cu metres) 92; Aluminium (unwrought, '000 cu metres) 92.

2000 ('000 metric tons): Palm oil 125; Raw sugar 82 (unofficial figure); Veneer sheets ('000 cu metres) 70; Aluminium (unwrought, '000 cu metres) 95.

2001 ('000 metric tons): Palm oil 145 (FAO estimate); Raw sugar 98 (unofficial figure); Veneer sheets ('000 cu metres) 80 (FAO estimate); Aluminium (unwrought, '000 cu metres) 81.

Sources: UN, *Industrial Commodity Statistics Yearbook*; FAO.

Finance

CURRENCY AND EXCHANGE RATES

Monetary Units
100 centimes = 1 franc de la Coopération financière en Afrique central (CFA)

Sterling, Dollar and Euro Equivalents (31 December 2002)
£1 sterling = 1,088.17 francs CFA
US $1 = 625..50 francs CFA
€1 = 655.96 francs CFA
10,000 francs CFA = £9.918 = $15.987 = €15.245

Average Exchange Rate (francs CFA per US $)
2000   711.98
2001   733.04
2002   696.99

Note: An exchange rate of 1 French franc = 50 francs CFA, established in 1948, remained in force until January 1994, when the CFA franc was devalued by 50%, with the exchange rate adjusted to 1 French franc = 100 francs CFA. This relationship to French currency remained in effect with the introduction of the euro on 1 January 1999. From that date, accordingly, a fixed exchange rate of €1 = 655.957 francs CFA has been in operation.

BUDGET
('000 million francs CFA, year ending 30 June)

Revenue*	1998/99	1999/2000	2000/01
Oil revenue	133	334	438
National oil company's			
contributions.	113	316	365
Profit taxes	21	18	74
Non-oil revenue	716	758	863
Tax revenue	652	699	804
Taxes on income and profits .	174	186	220
Individual income taxes . .	52	64	65
Wages and salaries . .	28	—	34
Progressive surcharge . .	25	—	31
Profit taxes	63	72	92
Taxes on goods and services .	340	372	436
Domestic taxes . . .	169	206	250
Turnover taxes . . .	128	156	195
Excise taxes. . . .	23	2	2
Taxes collected by customs .	99	58	63
Turnover taxes . . .	97	101	117
Excise taxes. . . .	2	2	2
Excise tax on petroleum			
products	65	58	63
Taxes on international trade .	138	141	138
Import duties	101	113	128
Export duties	26	14	5
Non-tax revenue	64	59	59
Privatization proceeds . .	11	79	0
Total	849	1,171	1,301

Expenditure†	1998/99	1999/2000	2000/01
General government services . .	65	80	88
Defence	83	89	56
Public order and justice . . .	55	48	71
Education	102	256	307
Health	31	58	72
Social security	4	5	6
Housing and community affairs .	9	11	12
Recreational and cultural affairs .	8	11	18
Economic affairs and services .	666	740	848
Energy and mining . . .	1	2	5
Agriculture, forestry and fishing	25	33	37
Public works, transport and			
communications . . .	37	54	60
Other economic services . .	603	651	746
Interest on public debt . .	282	147	161
Total	1,023	1,297	1,476

* Excluding grants received ('000 million francs CFA): 10 in 1998/99; 0 in 1999/2000; 26 in 2000/01, and privatization proceeds ('000 million francs CFA): 11 in 1998/99; 79 in 1999/2000; 0 in 2000/01.
† Excluding adjustment for changes in payments arrears, and including investment.

Source: IMF, *Cameroon: Statistical Appendix* (August 2002).

INTERNATIONAL RESERVES*
(US $ million at 31 December)

	1999	2000	2001
IMF special drawing rights. . .	2.61	7.73	0.02
Reserve position in IMF. . .	0.69	0.67	0.68
Foreign exchange.	1.13	203.60	331.14
Total	4.43	212.00	331.83

* Excluding reserves of gold (30,000 troy ounces each year). At 31 December 1998 the national valuation of these reserves (based on market-related prices) was US $8.61 million.

Source: IMF, *International Financial Statistics*.

MONEY SUPPLY
(million francs CFA at 31 December)

	1999	2000	2001
Currency outside banks . . .	237,396	264,960	296,136
Demand deposits at deposit money			
banks	294,485	361,991	410,937
Total money (incl. others). . .	537,734	631,064	711,984

Source: IMF, *International Financial Statistics*.

COST OF LIVING
(Consumer Price Index; base: 1995 = 100)

	1999	2000	2001
All items	114.4	111.7	116.8

Source: IMF, *International Financial Statistics*.

NATIONAL ACCOUNTS
('000 million francs CFA at current prices, year ending 30 June)

Expenditure on the Gross Domestic Product

	1998/99	1999/2000	2000/01
Government final consumption expenditure.	542	593	706
Private final consumption expenditure.	3,869	4,048	4,322
Gross capital formation . . .	1,010	959	1,125
Total domestic expenditure.	5,422	5,600	6,153
Exports of goods and services	1,319	1,791	2,010
Less Imports of goods and services	1,334	1,564	1,843
GDP in purchasers' values . .	5,406	5,827	6,320
GDP at constant 1989/90 prices	3,693	3,846	4,050

Source: IMF, *Cameroon: Statistical Appendix* (August 2002).

Gross Domestic Product by Economic Activity

	1998/99	1999/2000	2000/01
Agriculture, hunting, forestry and fishing	2,288	2,482	2,699
Mining and quarrying . . .	211	227	246
Manufacturing	572	617	669
Electricity, gas and water . .	81	87	95
Construction	200	215	229
Services	1,903	2,033	2,205
GDP at factor cost. . . .	5,255	5,661	6,143
Indirect taxes, *less* subsidies . .	152	164	177
GDP in purchasers' values . .	5,406	5,827	6,320

Source: IMF, *Cameroon: Statistical Appendix* (August 2002).

BALANCE OF PAYMENTS
(million francs CFA, year ending 30 June)

	1998/99	1999/2000	2000/01
Exports of goods f.o.b. . . .	989,700	1,399,000	1,582,600
Imports of goods f.o.b. . . .	−872,700	−1,012,300	−1,202,100
Trade balance	117,100	386,800	380,500
Services and other income (net) .	−407,800	−550,700	−578,800
Balance on goods, services and income	−290,700	−163,900	−198,300
Transfers (net)	59,000	63,500	88,400
Current balance	−231,800	−100,400	−109,900
Long-term capital (net) . .	−86,500	−218,400	−222,700
Short-term capital (net). . .	3,900	107,000	36,300
Net errors and omissions . . .	—	78,300	91,900
Overall balance	−314,500	−133,500	−204,400

Source: IMF, *Cameroon: Statistical Appendix* (August 2002).

External Trade

PRINCIPAL COMMODITIES
(million francs CFA, year ending 30 June)

Imports c.i.f.	1998/99	1999/2000	2000/01
Food, beverages and tobacco . .	99,500	106,600	130,300
Animal and vegetable raw materials	40,600	46,200	54,900
Mineral and other raw materials .	93,500	155,500	250,000
Semi-finished goods	140,300	144,300	189,700
Transportation equipment . .	90,600	90,700	120,800
Industrial equipment . . .	117,200	105,400	161,500
Household consumption . .	91,000	87,100	110,300
Enterprise consumption. . .	146,700	152,500	168,100
Total (incl. others)	827,700	906,000	1,204,500

Exports f.o.b.	1998/99	1999/2000	2000/01
Petroleum and petroleum products	314,300	651,800	779,000
Cocoa beans	74,000	62,900	61,300
Cocoa products	18,200	15,500	15,100
Coffee (robusta)	50,800	68,700	44,800
Coffee (arabica)	5,500	8,400	6,800
Raw cotton	47,100	55,500	58,400
Sawlogs, veneer logs, etc. . .	119,900	109,300	117,500
Aluminium	49,600	64,200	90,200
Total (incl. others)	864,800	1,222,600	1,362,800

Source: IMF, *Cameroon: Statistical Appendix* (August 2002).

PRINCIPAL TRADING PARTNERS
(estimates, '000 million francs CFA)*

Imports c.i.f.	1998/99	1999/2000	2000/01
Belgium-Luxembourg . . .	42	47	56
Canada	15	15	18
China, People's Repub. . . .	18	28	33
Côte d'Ivoire	14	16	1
Equatorial Guinea . . .	2	10	12
France	226	233	289
Germany	57	43	61
Guinea	19	23	29
India	9	5	6
Indonesia	3	4	13
Italy	38	33	38
Japan	44	49	56
Netherlands	23	26	23
Nigeria	65	141	235
Senegal	12	10	8
South Africa	9	9	18
Spain	14	11	17
Sweden	4	4	19
Turkey	11	11	6
United Kingdom	23	21	24
USA	50	40	59
Total (incl. others)	816	906	1,181

Exports f.o.b.	1998/99	1999/2000	2000/01
Angola	1	1	16
Belgium-Luxembourg . . .	18	27	29
Chad	21	13	14
China, People's Repub. . . .	20	42	112
Congo, Repub.	10	10	13
Equatorial Guinea . . .	13	4	5
France	168	173	150
Gabon	18	11	8
Germany	19	15	22
Hong Kong	11	3	2
Ireland	11	6	10
Italy	223	274	385
Korea, Repub.. . . .	13	17	0
Netherlands	93	82	116
Spain	125	100	143
Taiwan	10	154	109
Thailand	5	13	8
United Kingdom	21	19	23
USA	12	33	21
Total (incl. others)	929	1,092	1,288

* Data are compiled on the basis of reporting by Cameroon's trading partners.

Source: IMF, *Cameroon: Statistical Appendix* (August 2002).

Transport

RAILWAYS
(traffic, year ending 30 June)

	1996/97	1997/98	1998/99
Freight ton-km (million) . . .	850	888	916
Passenger-km (million) . . .	283	292	311

Source: UN, *Statistical Yearbook*.

ROAD TRAFFIC
(estimates, motor vehicles in use at 31 December)

	1994	1995	1996
Passenger cars	89,000	93,000	98,000
Goods vehicles	57,000	60,000	64,350

Source: International Road Federation, *World Road Statistics*.

SHIPPING
Merchant Fleet
(registered at 31 December)

	1999	2000	2001
Number of vessels	61	61	58
Total displacement ('000 grt) . .	13.6	13.6	13.6

Source: Lloyd's Register-Fairplay, *World Fleet Statistics*.

International Sea-borne Freight Traffic
(freight traffic at Douala, '000 metric tons)

	1995	1996	1997
Goods loaded	1,841	1,967	2,385
Goods unloaded	2,317	2,211	2,497

Source: Banque des états de l'Afrique centrale, *Etudes et Statistiques*.

CIVIL AVIATION
(traffic on scheduled services)

	1997	1998	1999
Kilometres flown (million) . . .	6	6	6
Passengers carried ('000) . . .	279	290	293
Passenger-km (million) . . .	547	568	597
Total ton-km (million) . . .	84	108	106

Source: UN, *Statistical Yearbook*.

Tourism
FOREIGN VISITORS BY COUNTRY OF ORIGIN*

	1995	1996	1997
Belgium	2,562	2,597	3,696
Canada	2,650	2,687	2,763
France	35,612	36,096	35,626
Germany	6,211	6,296	6,659
Italy	4,237	4,295	3,083
Switzerland	2,516	2,550	5,443
United Kingdom	3,798	3,849	4,106
USA	4,974	5,041	11,317
Total (incl. others)	99,749	101,106	132,839

* Arrivals at hotels and similar establishments.

Receipts from tourism (US $ million): 36 in 1995; 38 in 1996; 39 in 1997.

1998: Tourist arrivals 135,000; Tourism receipts US $40m. (Source: World Bank).

Source: World Tourism Organization, *Yearbook of Tourism Statistics*.

Communications Media

	1999	2000	2001
Television receivers ('000 in use) .	500	520	n.a.
Telephones ('000 main lines in use)	94.6	n.a.	101.4
Mobile cellular telephones ('000 subscribers)	6	148	310
Personal computers ('000 in use) .	40	50	60
Internet users ('000)	20	40	45

Radio receivers ('000 in use): 2,270 in 1997.

Daily newspapers: 2 in 1996 (average circ. 91,000).

Non-daily newspapers: 7 in 1996 (average circ. 152,000).

Sources: mainly UNESCO, *Statistical Yearbook*; International Telecommunication Union.

Education
(1998, unless otherwise indicated)

	Institu-tions	Teachers	Students
Pre-primary	1,371	4,438	103,908
Primary	9,459	41,142	2,133,707
Secondary:			
General	700*	19,515	341,439
Vocational	324*	7,245*	122,122
Universities	6†	2,645	66,902

* 1995/96 figure.
† 1996/97 figure.

Sources: UNESCO Institute for Statistics; *Annuaire statistique du Cameroun*.

Adult literacy rate (UNESCO estimates): 75.8% (males 82.4%; females 69.5%) in 2000 (Source: UN Development Programme, *Human Development Report*).

Directory

The Constitution*

The Republic of Cameroon is a multi-party state. The main provisions of the 1972 Constitution, as amended, are summarized below:

The Constitution declares that the human being, without distinction as to race, religion, sex or belief, possesses inalienable and sacred rights. It affirms its attachment to the fundamental freedoms embodied in the Universal Declaration of Human Rights and the UN Charter. The State guarantees to all citizens of either sex the rights and freedoms set out in the preamble of the Constitution.

SOVEREIGNTY

1. The Republic of Cameroon shall be one and indivisible, democratic, secular and dedicated to social service. It shall ensure the equality before the law of all its citizens. Provisions that the official languages be French and English, for the motto, flag, national anthem and seal, that the capital be Yaoundé.

2–3. Sovereignty shall be vested in the people who shall exercise it either through the President of the Republic and the members returned by it to the National Assembly or by means of referendum. Elections are by universal suffrage, direct or indirect, by every citizen aged 21 or over in a secret ballot. Political parties or groups may take part in elections subject to the law and the principles of democracy and of national sovereignty and unity.

4. State authority shall be exercised by the President of the Republic and the National Assembly.

THE PRESIDENT OF THE REPUBLIC

5. The President of the Republic, as Head of State and Head of Government, shall be responsible for the conduct of the affairs of the Republic. He shall define national policy and may charge the members of the Government with the implementation of this policy in certain spheres.

6–7. Candidates for the office of President must hold civic and political rights, be at least 35 years old and have resided in Cameroon for a minimum of 12 consecutive months, and may not hold any other elective office or professional activity. The President is elected for seven years, by a majority of votes cast by the people, and may serve a maximum of two terms. Provisions are made for the continuity of office in the case of the President's resignation.

8–9. The Ministers and Vice-Ministers are appointed by the President to whom they are responsible, and they may hold no other appointment. The President is also head of the armed forces, he negotiates and ratifies treaties, may exercise clemency after consultation with the Higher Judicial Council, promulgates and is responsible for the enforcement of laws, is responsible for internal and external security, makes civil and military appointments, provides for necessary administrative services.

10. The President, by reference to the Supreme Court, ensures that all laws passed are constitutional.

11. Provisions whereby the President may declare a state of emergency or state of siege.

THE NATIONAL ASSEMBLY

12. The National Assembly shall be renewed every five years, though it may at the instance of the President of the Republic legislate to extend or shorten its term of office. It shall be composed of 180 members elected by universal suffrage.

13–14. Laws shall normally be passed by a simple majority of those present, but if a bill is read a second time at the request of the President of the Republic a majority of the National Assembly as a whole is required.

15–16. The National Assembly shall meet twice a year, each session to last not more than 30 days; in one session it shall approve the budget. It may be recalled to an extraordinary session of not more than 15 days.

17–18. Elections and suitability of candidates and sitting members shall be governed by law.

RELATIONS BETWEEN THE EXECUTIVE AND THE LEGISLATURE

19. Bills may be introduced either by the President of the Republic or by any member of the National Assembly.

20. Reserved to the legislature are the fundamental rights and duties of the citizen; the law of persons and property; the political, administrative and judicial system in respect of elections to the National Assembly, general regulation of national defence, authorization of penalties and criminal and civil procedure etc., and the organization of the local authorities; currency, the budget, dues and taxes, legislation on public property; economic and social policy; the education system.

21. The National Assembly may empower the President of the Republic to legislate by way of ordinance for a limited period and for given purposes.

22–26. Other matters of procedure, including the right of the President of the Republic to address the Assembly and of the Ministers and Vice-Ministers to take part in debates.

27–29. The composition and conduct of the Assembly's programme of business. Provisions whereby the Assembly may inquire into governmental activity. The obligation of the President of the Republic to promulgate laws, which shall be published in both languages of the Republic.

30. Provisions whereby the President of the Republic, after consultation with the National Assembly, may submit to referendum certain reform bills liable to have profound repercussions on the future of the nation and national institutions.

THE JUDICIARY

31. Justice is administered in the name of the people. The President of the Republic shall ensure the independence of the judiciary and shall make appointments with the assistance of the Higher Judicial Council.

THE SUPREME COURT

32–33. The Supreme Court has powers to uphold the Constitution in such cases as the death or incapacity of the President and the admissibility of laws, to give final judgments on appeals on the Judgment of the Court of Appeal and to decide complaints against administrative acts. It may be assisted by experts appointed by the President of the Republic.

IMPEACHMENT

34. There shall be a Court of Impeachment with jurisdiction to try the President of the Republic for high treason and the Ministers and Vice-Ministers for conspiracy against the security of the State.

THE ECONOMIC AND SOCIAL COUNCIL

35. There shall be an Economic and Social Council, regulated by the law

AMENDMENT OF THE CONSTITUTION

36–37. Bills to amend the Constitution may be introduced either by the President of the Republic or the National Assembly. The President may decide to submit any amendment to the people by way of a referendum. No procedure to amend the Constitution may be accepted if it tends to impair the republican character, unity or territorial integrity of the State, or the democratic principles by which the Republic is governed.

*In December 1995 the National Assembly formally adopted constitutional amendments that provided for a democratic system of government, with the establishment of an upper legislative chamber (to be known as the Senate), a Council of Supreme Judiciary Affairs, a Council of State, and a Civil Service High Authority, and restricted the power vested in the President, who was to serve a maximum of two seven-year terms. The restoration of decentralized local government areas was also envisaged.

The Government

HEAD OF STATE

President: Paul Biya (took office 6 November 1982; elected 14 January 1984; re-elected 24 April 1988, 11 October 1992 and 12 October 1997).

CABINET
(April 2003)

A coalition of the Rassemblement démocratique du peuple camerounais (RDPC), the Union nationale pour la démocratie et le progrès (UNDP) and the Union des populations camerounaises (UPC).

Prime Minister: Peter Mafany Musonge (RDPC).

Ministers of State

Minister of State and Secretary-General of the Presidency: Jean-Marie Atangana Mebara (RDPC).

Minister of State in charge of Territorial Administration and Decentralization: Marafa Hamidou Yaya (RDPC).

Minister of State in charge of Justice: Amadou Ali (RDPC).

Minister of State in charge of External Relations: François Xavier Ngoubeyou (RDPC).

Minister of State in charge of Culture: Ferdinand Léopold Oyono (RDPC).

Minister of State in charge of Industrial and Commercial Development: Bello Bouba Maïgari (UNDP).

Minister of State in charge of Agriculture: Augustin Frédéric Kodock (UPC).

Ministers

Minister of Finance and the Budget: Michel Meva'a Meboutou (RDPC).

Minister of Economic Affairs, Planning and Regional Development: Martin Aristide Okouda (RDPC).

Minister of Scientific and Technical Research: Zacharie Perevet (RDPC).

Minister of Technical and Professional Training: Louis Bapes Bapes (RDPC).

Minister of the Environment and Forests: Tanyi Mbianyor Oben (RDPC).

Minister of Housing and Urban Affairs: Tadji Abdoulaye Haman (RDPC).

Minister of Town Planning: LEKENE DONFACK (RDPC).

Minister of Higher Education: MAURICE TCHUENTE (RDPC).

Minister of Social Affairs: CÉCILE BOMBA NKOLO (RDPC).

Minister of Public Works: DIEUDONNÉ AMBASSA ZANG (RDPC).

Minister of Transport: NDEH JOHN BEGHENI (RDPC).

Minister of Employment, Labour and Social Welfare: ROBERT NKILI (RDPC).

Minister of Mines, Water Resources and Energy: JOSEPH AOUDOU (RDPC).

Minister of Communication: JACQUES FAME NDONGO (RDPC).

Minister of Women's Affairs: CATHERINE BAKANG MBOCK (RDPC).

Minister of National Education: JOSEPH OWONA (RDPC).

Minister of Livestock, Fisheries and Animal Industries: Dr HAMADJOUDA ADJOUDJI (RDPC).

Minister of Public Service and Administrative Reform: RENÉ ZE NGUELE (RDPC).

Minister of Youth and Sports: PIERRE BIDOUNG MKPATT (RDPC).

Minister of Posts and Telecommunications: MAXIMIN PAUL NKOUÉ NKONGO (RDPC).

Minister of Public Health: URBAIN OLANGUENA AWONO (RDPC).

Minister of Tourism: PIERRE HELE (UNDP).

Ministers-delegate

Minister-delegate at the Ministry of Territorial Administration, in charge of Local Councils: ADRIEN KOUAMBO (RDPC).

Minister-delegate at the Ministry of Finance and the Budget, in charge of the Budget: ROGER MELINGUI (RDPC).

Minister-delegate at the Ministry of Economic Affairs, Planning and Regional Development, in charge of the Recovery Plan: JOSEPH DÉSIRÉ NGUENANG (RDPC).

Minister-delegate at the Presidency, in charge of Defence: LAURENT ESSO (RDPC).

Minister-delegate at the Ministry of External Relations, in charge of Relations with the Commonwealth: JOSEPH DION NGUTE (RDPC).

Minister-delegate at the Ministry of External Relations, in charge of Relations with the Islamic World: ADOUM GARGOUM (RDPC).

Minister-delegate at the Presidency, in charge of Relations with the National Assembly: GRÉGOIRE OWONA (RDPC).

Minister-delegate at the Presidency, in charge of the Supreme State Audit: NJIEMOUM MAMA (RDPC).

Ministers-delegate at the Presidency without Portfolio: JUSTIN NDIORO (RDPC), BABA HAMADOU (RDPC), ELVIS NGOLE NGOLE (RDPC), PHILIPPE MBARGA MBOUA (RDPC), KIBUH TUME HENRI (RDPC).

Secretaries of State

Secretary of State for Territorial Administration and Decentralization, in charge of Prisons Administration: OTEH EMMANUEL ANYIE (RDPC).

Secretary of State for Economic Affairs, Planning and Regional Development, in charge of Town Planning and Regional Development: SEYNI KATCHALLA (RDPC).

First Secretary of State for National Education: EMMANUEL NGAFEESON (RDPC).

Second Secretary of State for National Education: HAMAN ADAMA (RDPC).

Secretary of State for Industrial and Commercial Development: EDMOND MOUAMPÉA MBIO (RDPC).

Secretary of State for Public Health: ALIM HAYATOU (RDPC).

Secretary of State for Youth and Sports, in charge of Youth: DENIS OUMAROU (RDPC).

Secretary of State for Public Works: EMMANUEL BONDE (RDPC).

Secretary of State for Agriculture: ABOUBAKAR ABDOULAYE (RDPC).

Secretary of State for Housing and Urban Affairs, in charge of Lands: ANDRÉ TSALA MESSI (RDPC).

Secretary of State for Transport: Dr NANA ABOUBAKAR DJALLOH (RDPC).

Secretary of State for Defence, in charge of the National Gendarmerie: RÉMY ZE MEKA (RDPC).

Other Officials with the Rank of Minister

Assistant Secretary-General of the Presidency: EPHRAIM INONI (RDPC).

Assistant Secretary-General of the Presidency: RENÉ OWONA (RDPC).

Director of the Cabinet of the President of the Republic: NGO'O MEBE (RDPC).

MINISTRIES

Correspondence to ministries not holding post boxes should generally be addressed c/o the Central Post Office, Yaoundé.

Office of the President: Palais de l'Unité, Yaoundé; tel. 223-4025; internet www.camnet.cm/celcom/homepr.htm.

Office of the Prime Minister: Yaoundé; tel. 223-8005; fax 223-5735; e-mail spm@spm.gov.cm; internet www.spm.gov.cm.

Ministry of Agriculture: Quartier Administratif, Yaoundé; tel. 222-0553; fax 222-5091.

Ministry of Communication: Quartier Hippodrome, Yaoundé; tel. 223-3467; fax 223-3022; e-mail mincom@mincom.gov.cm; internet www.mincom.gov.cm.

Ministry of Culture: Quartier Hippodrome, Yaoundé; tel. 222-6579; fax 223-6579.

Ministry of Defence: Quartier Général, Yaoundé; tel. 223-4055.

Ministry of Economic Affairs, Planning and Regional Development: Yaoundé; tel. 223-3637; fax 222-1501; internet www.minpat.gov.cm.

Ministry of Employment, Labour and Social Welfare: Yaoundé; tel. 222-0186; fax 223-1820.

Ministry of the Environment and Forests: Yaoundé; BP 1341; tel. 220-4258; fax 222-9487; e-mail onadef@camnet.cm; internet www.camnet.cm/investir/envforet/index.htm.

Ministry of External Relations: Yaoundé; tel. 220-3850; fax 220-1133; internet www.diplocam.gov.cm.

Ministry of Finance and the Budget: Quartier Administratif, Yaoundé; tel. 223-2099; fax 223-3717; internet www.camnet.cm/investir/minfi/.

Ministry of Higher Education: 2 ave du 20 Mai, BP 1457, Yaoundé; tel. 222-1770; fax 222-9724; e-mail aowono@uycdc.uninet.cm; internet www.mineup.gov.cm.

Ministry of Housing and Urban Affairs: Quartier Administratif, Yaoundé; tel. 220-1558; fax 221-7212.

Ministry of Industrial and Commercial Development: Quartier Administratif, Yaoundé; tel. 223-2388; fax 222-2704; e-mail mindic@mindic.gov.cm; internet www.mindic.gov.cm.

Ministry of Justice: Quartier Administratif, Yaoundé; tel. 222-0189; fax 223-0005.

Ministry of Livestock, Fisheries and Animal Industries: Yaoundé; tel. 222-3311.

Ministry of Mines, Water Resources and Energy: Quartier Administratif, Yaoundé; tel. 223-3404; fax 222-6177; e-mail minmee@camnet.cm; internet www.camnet.cm/investir/minmee.

Ministry of National Education: Quartier Administratif, Yaoundé; tel. 223-4050; fax 223-1262.

Ministry of Posts and Telecommunications: Quartier Administratif, Yaoundé; tel. 223-0615; fax 223-3159; internet www.minpostel.gov.cm.

Ministry of Public Health: Quartier Administratif, Yaoundé; tel. 222-2901; fax 222-0233; internet www.camnet.cm/investir/hgy/index.htm.

Ministry of the Public Service and Administrative Reform: Yaoundé; tel. 222-0356; fax 223-0800.

Ministry of Public Works: Quartier Administratif, Yaoundé; tel. 222-1916; fax 222-0156.

Ministry of Scientific and Technical Research: Yaoundé; tel. 222-1331; fax 222-1333; internet www.minrest.gov.cm.

Ministry of Social Affairs: Quartier Administratif, Yaoundé; tel. 222-5867; fax 222-1121.

Ministry of Technical and Professional Training: Yaoundé.

Ministry of Territorial Administration and Decentralization: Quartier Administratif, Yaoundé; tel. 223-4090; fax 222-3735.

Ministry of Tourism: BP 266, Yaoundé; tel. 222-4411; fax 222-1295; e-mail mintour@camnet.cm; internet www.mintour.gov.cm.

Ministry of Town Planning: Yaoundé; tel. 223-2282.

Ministry of Transport: Quartier Administratif, Yaoundé; tel. 222-8709; fax 223-2238; e-mail mintrans@camnet.cm; internet www.camnet.cm/investir/transport.

Ministry of Women's Affairs: Quartier Administratif, Yaoundé; fax 223-3965.

Ministry of Youth and Sports: Quartier Administratif, Yaoundé; tel. 223-3257; e-mail minjes@minjes.gov.cm; internet www.minjes.gov.cm.

President and Legislature

PRESIDENT

Election, 12 October 1997

Candidate	Votes	% of votes
Paul Biya (RDPC)	3,167,820	92.57
Henri Hogbe Nlend (UPC)	85,693	2.50
Samuel Eboua (MDP)	83,506	2.44
Albert Dzongang (PPD)	40,814	1.19
Joachim Tabi Owono (AMEC)	15,817	0.46
Antoine Demannu (RDPF)	15,490	0.45
Gustave Essaka (DIC)	12,915	0.38
Total*	3,422,055	100.00

*Excluding invalid votes.

NATIONAL ASSEMBLY

President: Djibril Cavayé Yeguie.

General Election, 30 June 2002*

Party	Seats
Rassemblement démocratique du peuple camerounais (RDPC)	149
Social Democratic Front (SDF)	22
Union démocratique du Cameroun (UDC)	5
Union des populations camerounaises (UPC)	3
Union nationale pour la démocratie et le progrès (UNDP)	1
Total	180

*Includes the results of voting in nine constituencies (for 17 seats) where the elections were postponed until 15 September 2002, owing to irregularities.

Political Organizations

At the time of the June 2002 legislative elections there were 159 legal political parties, of which the most important are listed below:

Action for Meritocracy and Equal Opportunity Party (AMEC): Leader Joachim Tabi Owono.

Alliance des forces progressistes (AFP): f. 2002; Leader Maidadi Saidou Yaya.

Alliance pour la démocratie et le développement (ADD): Sec.-Gen. Garga Haman Adji.

Alliance démocratique pour le progrès du Cameroun (ADPC): Garoua; f. 1991.

Alliance pour le progrès et l'émancipation des dépossédés (APED): Yaoundé; f. 1991; Leader Bohin Bohin.

Alliance pour le redressement du Cameroun (ARC): f. 1992 by a number of opposition movements.

Association social-démocrate du Cameroun (ASDC): Maroua; f. 1991.

Cameroon Anglophone Movement (CAM): advocates a federal system of govt.

Congrès panafricain du Cameroun (CPC): BP 1248, Douala; f. 1991.

Convention libérale (CL): f. 1991; Leader Pierre-Flambeau Ngayap.

Démocratie intégrale au Cameroun (DIC): Douala; f. 1991; Leader Gustave Essaka.

Front des alliés pour le changement (FAC): Douala; f. 1994; alliance of 16 opposition movements; Leader Samuel Eboua.

Front démocratique et patriotique (FDP): f. 1994; alliance of six opposition parties.

Liberal Democratic Alliance (LDA): Buéa; Pres. Henri Fossung.

Mouvement africain pour la nouvelle indépendance et la démocratie (MANIDEM): fmrly a faction of the UPC; Leader Anicet Ekane.

Mouvement pour la défense de la République (MDR): f. 1991; Leader Dakole Daissala.

Mouvement pour la démocratie et le progrès (MDP): f. 1992; Leader Samuel Eboua.

Mouvement pour la jeunesse du Cameroun (MLJC): Leader Dieudonné Tina.

Mouvement pour la libération et le développement du Cameroun (MLDC): by a breakaway faction of the MLJC; Leader Marcel Yondo.

Mouvement social pour la nouvelle démocratie (MSND): Leader Yondo Black.

Nouvelle convention (NC): Yaoundé.

Parti des démocrates camerounais (PDC): BP 6909, Yaoundé; tel. 222-2842; f. 1991; Leader Louis-Tobie Mbida.

Parti libéral-democrate (PLD): f. 1991; Leader Njoh Litumbe.

Parti populaire pour le développement (PPD): f. 1997.

Parti républicain du peuple camerounais (PRPC): Bertoua; f. 1991; Leader Ateba Ngoua.

Parti socialiste camerounais (PSC): Leader Jean-Pierre Dembele.

Parti socialiste démocratique (PSD): BP 141, Douala; tel. 342-1995; f. 1991; Leader Nsame Mbongo Joseph.

Parti socialiste démocratique du Cameroun (PSDC): Leader Jean Michel Tekam.

Rassemblement démocratique du peuple camerounais (RDPC): BP 867, Yaoundé; tel. 23-27-40; f. 1966 as Union nationale camerounaise by merger of the Union camerounaise; the Kamerun National Democratic Party and four opposition parties; adopted present name in 1985; sole legal party 1972–90; Pres. Paul Biya; Sec.-Gen. Joseph-Charles Doumba.

Rassemblement démocratique du peuple sans frontières (RDPF): f. 1997.

Social Democratic Front (SDF): Bamenda; e-mail webmaster@sdfparty.org; internet www.sdfparty.org; f. 1990; Chair. John Fru Ndi; Sec.-Gen. Prof. Tazoacha Asonganyi.

Social Democratic Movement (SDM): f. 1995; breakaway faction of the Social Democratic Front; Leader Siga Asanga.

Southern Cameroons National Council (SCNC): f. 1995; supports the establishment of an independent republic in anglophone Cameroon; Chair. Sam Ekontang Elad; Leader Martin Luma.

Union démocratique du Cameroun (UDC): BP 1638, Yaoundé; f. 1991; Leader Adamou Ndam Njoya.

Union des forces démocratiques du Cameroun (UFDC): Yaoundé; f. 1991; Leader Victorin Hameni Bieleu.

Union nationale pour la démocratie et le progrès (UNDP): BP 656, Douala; tel. 220-6394; f. 1991; split in 1995; Chair. Bello Bouba Maigari.

Union des populations camerounaises (UPC): Douala; f. 1948; split into two main factions in 1996: UPC (N), led by Ndeh Ntumazah and UPC (K), led by Augustin Frédéric Kodock.

Diplomatic Representation

EMBASSIES AND HIGH COMMISSIONS IN CAMEROON

Algeria: BP 1619, Yaoundé; tel. 221-5351; fax 221-5354; Ambassador Mohamed Achache.

Belgium: BP 816, Yaoundé; tel. 220-6747; fax 220-0521; Ambassador Baudouin Vanderhulst.

Brazil: BP 348, Yaoundé; tel. 221-4567; fax 221-1957; Chargé d'affaires a.i. Sergio Couri Elias.

Canada: Immeuble Stamatiades, BP 572, Yaoundé; tel. 223-0203; fax 222-1090; e-mail Honore.Mondomobe@dfait-maeci.gc.ca; internet www.infoexport.gc.ca/cm; High Commissioner Michel Perrault.

Central African Republic: BP 396, Yaoundé; tel. and fax 220-5155; Ambassador Jean Poloko.

Chad: BP 506, Yaoundé; tel. and fax 221-0624; Ambassador Homsala Ouangmotching.

China, People's Republic: BP 1307, Yaoundé; tel. 221-0083; fax 221-4395; e-mail ambchine@camnet.cm; Ambassador Xu MENGSHUI.

Congo, Democratic Republic: BP 632, Yaoundé; tel. 222-5103; Ambassador (vacant).

Congo, Republic: BP 1422, Yaoundé; tel. 221-2458; Ambassador MARCEL MAKOME.

Côte d'Ivoire: Yaoundé; Ambassador LAURENT AYOMAN AMBOHALE.

Egypt: BP 809, Yaoundé; tel. 220-3922; fax 220-2647; Ambassador NOFAL IBRAHIM EL-SAYED.

Equatorial Guinea: BP 277, Yaoundé; tel. and fax 221-1404; Ambassador ANGUE ONDO PURIFICACIÓN.

France: Plateau Atémengué, BP 1631, Yaoundé; tel. 223-4013; fax 223-5043; e-mail ambafrancecam@camnet.cm; internet www .france-cam.cm; Ambassador JEAN-PAUL VÉZIANT.

Gabon: BP 4130, Yaoundé; tel. 221-0204; fax 221-4347; Ambassador FERDINAND MASSALA MALONGA.

Germany: rue Charles de Gaulle, BP 1160, Yaoundé; tel. 220-0566; fax 220-7313; Ambassador KLAUS-PETER BRANDES.

Greece: BP 82, Yaoundé; tel. and fax 220-3936; Ambassador IONNIS GEORGIADIS.

Holy See: rue du Vatican, BP 210, Yaoundé (Apostolic Nunciature); tel. 220-0475; fax 220-7513; Apostolic Pro-Nuncio Most Rev. FÉLIX DEL BLANCO PRIETO (Titular Archbishop of Vannida).

Israel: BP 5934, Yaoundé; tel. 220-1644; fax 221-0823; Ambassador YORAM ELRON.

Italy: Quartier Bastos, BP 827, Yaoundé; tel. 220-3376; fax 221-5250; e-mail ambyaounde@gcnet.com; Ambassador FRANCESCO LANATA.

Japan: Bastos-Ekoudou, Yaoundé; tel. 220-6202; fax 220-6203; Ambassador TAKERU SASAGUCHI.

Korea, Republic: BP 301, Yaoundé; tel. 221-3223; fax 220-1725; Ambassador DAE-TAEK LIM.

Liberia: Ekoudou, Quartier Bastos, BP 1185, Yaoundé; tel. 221-1296; fax 220-9781; Ambassador CARLTON ALEXWYN KARPEH.

Libya: Quartier Bastos, BP 1980, Yaoundé; tel. 222-4138.

Morocco: BP 1629, Yaoundé; tel. 220-5092; fax 220-3793; Ambassador OMAR EL-NASRI.

Nigeria: BP 448, Yaoundé; tel. 222-3455; High Commissioner EMMANUEL CHAME QUILTON TOMI NJWAH.

Romania: rue de Joseph Mballa Elounden, BP 6212, Yaoundé; tel. and fax 221-3986; Chargé d'affaires a.i. ION MOGOS.

Russia: BP 488, Yaoundé; tel. 220-1714; fax 220-7891; e-mail conrusse@camnet.cm; Ambassador POULATE ABDOULAYEV.

Saudi Arabia: BP 1602, Yaoundé; tel. 221-2675; fax 220-6689; Ambassador ABDULAZIZ FAHD AR-REBDI.

Spain: BP 877, Yaoundé; tel. 220-3543; fax 220-6491; Ambassador JOSÉ LUIS SOLANO.

Tunisia: rue de Rotary, BP 6074, Yaoundé; tel. 220-3368; fax 221-0507; Chargé d'affaires a.i. MOHAMED AMIRI.

United Kingdom: ave Winston Churchill, BP 547, Yaoundé; tel. 222-0545; fax 222-0148; e-mail BHC@yaounde.mail.fco.gov.uk; High Commissioner RICHARD WILDASH.

USA: rue Nachtigal, BP 817, Yaoundé; tel. 223-4014; fax 223-0753; internet www.usembassy.state.gov/yaounde/wwwhmain.html; Ambassador GEORGE STAPLES.

Judicial System

Supreme Court
Yaoundé; tel. 222-0164; fax 222-0576.
Consists of a president, nine titular and substitute judges, a procureur général, an avocat général, deputies to the procureur général, a registrar and clerks.

President: ALEXANDRE DIPANDA MOUELLE.

High Court of Justice
Yaoundé.
Consists of nine titular judges and six substitute judges, all elected by the National Assembly.

Attorney-General: RISSOUCK A. MOULLONG.

Religion

It is estimated that 53% of the population are Christians (mainly Roman Catholics), 25% adhere to traditional religious beliefs and 22% are Muslims.

CHRISTIANITY

Protestant Churches
There are about 1m. Protestants in Cameroon, with about 3,000 church and mission workers, and four theological schools.

Fédération des Eglises et missions évangéliques du Cameroun (FEMEC): BP 491, Yaoundé; tel. 222-3078; f. 1968; 10 mem. churches; Pres. Rev. Dr JEAN KOTTO (Evangelical Church of Cameroon); Admin. Sec. Rev. Dr GRÉGOIRE AMBADIANG DE MENDENG (Presbyterian Church of Cameroon).

Eglise évangélique du Cameroun (Evangelical Church of Cameroon): BP 89, Douala; tel. 342-3611; fax 342-4011; f. 1957; 500,000 mems (1992); Pres. Rev. CHARLES E. NJIKE; Sec. Rev. HANS EDJENGUELE.

Eglise presbytérienne camerounaise (Presbyterian Church of Cameroon): BP 519, Yaoundé; tel. 332-4236; independent since 1957; comprises four synods and 16 presbyteries; 220,000 mems (1985); Gen. Sec. Rev. GRÉGOIRE AMBADIANG DE MENDENG.

Eglise protestante africaine (African Protestant Church): BP 26, Lolodorf; f. 1934; 8,400 mems (1985); Dir-Gen. Rev. MARNIA WOUNGLY-MASSAGA.

Presbyterian Church in Cameroon: BP 19, Buéa; tel. 332-2336; 300,000 mems (1996); 302 ministers; Moderator Rev. NYANSAKO-NI-NKU.

Union des Eglises baptistes au Cameroun (Union of Baptist Churches of Cameroon): BP 6007, New Bell, Douala; tel. 342-4106; autonomous since 1957; 37,000 mems (1985); Gen. Sec. Rev. EMMANUEL MBENDA.

Other Protestant churches active in Cameroon include the Cameroon Baptist Church, the Cameroon Baptist Convention, the Church of the Lutheran Brethren of Cameroon, the Evangelical Lutheran Church of Cameroon, the Presbyterian Church in West Cameroon and the Union of Evangelical Churches of North Cameroon.

The Roman Catholic Church
Cameroon comprises five archdioceses and 18 dioceses. At 31 December 2000 adherents represented some 25.1% of the total population. There are several active missionary orders, and four major seminaries for African priests.

Bishops' Conference
Conférence Episcopale Nationale du Cameroun, BP 1963, Yaoundé; tel. 231-1592; fax 231-2977; e-mail basc@rctmail.net.
f. 1989; Pres. Rt Rev. CORNELIUS FONTEM ESUA (Bishop of Kumbo); Sec.-Gen. Fr PATRICK LAFON.

Archbishop of Bamenda: Most Rev. PAUL VERDZEKOV, Archbishop's House, BP 82, Bamenda; tel. 336-1241; fax 336-3487; e-mail abpbda@compuserve.com.

Archbishop of Bertoua: Most Rev. ROGER PIRENNE, Archevêché, BP 40, Bertoua; tel. 224-1748; fax 224-2585; e-mail r.pirenne@inmarsat .ocicnet.net.

Archbishop of Douala: Cardinal CHRISTIAN WIYGHAN TUMI, Archevêché, BP 179, Douala; tel. 342-3714; fax 342-1837; e-mail christiantumi@camnet.cm.

Archbishop of Garoua: Most Rev. ANTOINE NTALOU, Archevêché, BP 272, Garoua; tel. 227-1353; fax 227-2942.

Archbishop of Yaoundé: Most Rev. ANDRÉ WOUKING, Archevêché, BP 207, Yaoundé; tel. 220-2461; fax 221-9735; e-mail procure.yde@ rctmail.net.

BAHÁ'Í FAITH

National Spiritual Assembly: BP 145, Limbe; tel. 333-2146; mems in 1,744 localities.

The Press

DAILIES

Cameroon Tribune: BP 1218, Yaoundé; tel. 230-3109; fax 230-4362; e-mail cameroontribune@cameroontribune.com; internet www.cameroon-tribune.cm; f. 1974; govt-controlled; French and

English; Dir Jérôme Mvondo; Man. Editor Marie Claire Nnana; circ. 20,000.

Politiks Matinal: Yaoundé; f. 1999; independent; French; circ. 10,000.

Le Quotidien: BP 13088, Douala; tel. 339-1189; fax 339-1819; French.

PERIODICALS

Affaires Légales: BP 3681, Douala; tel. 342-5838; fax 343-2259; monthly; legal periodical.

Afrique en Dossiers: Yaoundé; f. 1970; French and English; Dir Ebongue Soelle.

Cameroon Outlook: BP 124, Limbe; f. 1969; 3 a week; independent; English; Editor Jerome F. Gwellem; circ. 20,000.

Cameroon Panorama: BP 46, Buéa; tel. 332-2240; f. 1962; monthly; English; Roman Catholic; Editor Sister Mercy Horgan; circ. 1,500.

Cameroon Post: Yaoundé; weekly; independent; English; Publr Paddy Mbawa; Editor Julius Wamey; circ. 50,000.

Cameroon Review: BP 408, Limbe; monthly; Editor-in-Chief Jerome F. Gwellem; circ. 70,000.

Cameroon Times: BP 408, Limbe; f. 1960; weekly; English; Editor-in-Chief Jerome F. Gwellem; circ. 12,000.

Challenge Hebdo: BP 1388, Douala; weekly; Editor Benjamin Zebaze.

Le Combattant: Yaoundé; weekly; independent; Editor Benyimbe Joseph; circ. 21,000.

Courrier Sportif du Bénin: BP 17, Douala; weekly; Dir Henri Jong.

Dikalo: BP 4320, Douala; tel. 337-0032; fax 337-1906; independent; 2 a week; French; Dir Emmanuel Noubissie Ngankam.

L'Effort Camerounais: BP 15231, Douala; tel. 343-2726; fax 343-1837; weekly; Catholic.

L'Expression: BP 15333, Douala; tel. 343-2227; fax 343-2669; e-mail expression@cybernum.com; 3 a week.

La Gazette: BP 5485, Douala; 2 a week; Editor Abodel Karimou; circ. 35,000.

The Herald: BP 3659, Yaoundé; tel. 231-5522; fax 231-8161; 3 a week; English; Dir Dr Boniface Forbin; circ. 8,000.

Al Houda: BP 1638, Yaoundé; quarterly; Islamic cultural review.

L'Indépendant Hebdo: Yaoundé; Chief Editor Evariste Menounga.

Le Jeune Observateur: Yaoundé; f. 1991; Editor Jules Koum.

Journal Officiel de la République du Cameroun: BP 1603, Yaoundé; tel. 223-1277; fortnightly; official govt notices; circ. 4,000.

Le Messager: 266 blvd de la Liberté, BP 5925, Douala; tel. 342-0439; fax 342-0214; e-mail lemessager@camnet.cm; internet wagne .net/messager; f. 1979; 3 a week; independent; Man. Editor Pius N. Njawe; circ. 39,000.

Le Messager Popoli: 266 blvd de la Liberté, BP 5925, Douala; tel. 342-0439; fax 342-0214; f. 1993; 2 a week; independent; Man. Editor Pius N. Njawe; circ. 24,000.

The Messenger: BP 15043, Douala; English edn of *Le Messager*; Editor Hilary Fokum.

Mutations: BP 12348, Yaoundé; tel. and fax 222-5104; e-mail mutations@cybernum.com; 3 a week; French; Man. Editor Haman Mana.

Nleb Ensemble: Imprimerie Saint-Paul, BP 763, Yaoundé; tel. 223-9773; fax 223-5058; f. 1935; fortnightly; Ewondo; Dir Most Rev. Jean Zoa; Editor Joseph Befe Ateba; circ. 6,000.

La Nouvelle Expression: BP 15333, Douala; independent; 3 a week; French; Man. Editor Séverin Tchounkou.

Presbyterian Newsletter: BP 19, Buéa; quarterly.

Que Savoir: Douala; monthly; industry, commerce and tourism.

Recherches et Études Camerounaises: BP 193, Yaoundé; monthly; publ. by Office National de Recherches Scientifiques du Cameroun.

La Révélation: Yaoundé; Dir Bosco Tchoubet.

Le Serment: Yaoundé; newspaper; Editor-in-Chief Anselme Mballa.

Le Serviteur: BP 1405, Yaoundé; monthly; Protestant; Dir Pastor Daniel Ako'o; circ. 3,000.

Le Travailleur/The Worker: BP 1610, Yaoundé; tel. 222-3315; f. 1972; monthly; French and English; journal of Organisation Syn-

dicale des Travailleurs du Cameroun/Cameroon Trade Union Congress; Sec.-Gen. Louis Sombes; circ. 10,000.

L'Unité: BP 867, Yaoundé; weekly; French and English.

Weekly Post: Obili, Yaoundé; Publr Chief Bisong Etahoben.

NEWS AGENCIES

CamNews: c/o SOPECAM, BP 1218, Yaoundé; tel. 230-3830; fax 230-4362; Dir Jean Ngandjeu.

Foreign Bureaux

Xinhua (New China) News Agency (People's Republic of China): ave Joseph Omgba, BP 1583, Yaoundé; tel. 220-2572; Chief Correspondent Sun Xingwen.

Agence France-Presse (France), **Reuters** (United Kingdom) and **ITAR—TASS** (Russia) are also represented.

Publishers

AES Presses Universitaires d'Afrique: BP 8106, Yaoundé; tel. 222-0030; fax 222-2325; e-mail aes@iccnet.cm; f. 1986; literature, social sciences and law; Dir-Gen. Serge Dontchueng Kouam.

Editions Buma Kor: BP 727, Yaoundé; tel. 222-4899; fax 223-2903; f. 1977; general, children's, educational and Christian; English and French; Man. Dir B. D. Buma Kor.

Editions Clé: BP 1501, Yaoundé; tel. 222-3554; fax 223-2709; e-mail cle@camnet.cm; f. 1963; African and Christian literature and studies; school textbooks; medicine and science; general non-fiction; Gen. Man. Tharcisse Gatwa.

Editions Le Flambeau: BP 113, Yaoundé; tel. 222-3672; f. 1977; general; Man. Dir Joseph Ndzie.

Editions Semences Africaines: BP 5329, Yaoundé-Nlongkak; tel. 222-4058; f. 1974; fiction, history, religion, textbooks; Man. Dir Philippe-Louis Ombede.

New Times Publishing House: Presbook Compound, BP 408, Limbe; tel. 333-3217; f. 1983; publishing and book trade reference; Dir and Editor-in-Chief J. F. Gwellem.

Government Publishing Houses

Centre d'Edition et de Production pour l'Enseignement et la Recherche (CEPER): BP 808, Yaoundé; tel. 222-1323; f. 1967; transfer pending to private ownership; general non-fiction, science and technology, tertiary, secondary and primary textbooks; Man. Dir Jean Claude Fouth.

Imprimerie Nationale: BP 1603, Yaoundé; tel. 223-1277; scheduled for transfer to private ownership; Dir Amadou Vamoulke.

Société de Presse et d'Editions du Cameroun (SOPECAM): BP 1218, Yaoundé; tel. 230-2640; fax 230-4362; f. 1977; under the supervision of the Ministry of Communication; Pres. Paul Tessa; Man. Editor Marie Claire Nnana.

Broadcasting and Communications

TELECOMMUNICATIONS

A Telecommunications Regulation Agency was established in early 1999.

Cameroon Telecommunications (CAMTEL): BP 1571, Yaoundé; tel. 223-4065; fax 223-0303; e-mail camtel@camnet.cm; internet www.camnet.cm; f. 1999; by merger of INTELCAM and the Dept of Telecommunications; 51% privatization pending; Pres. Nfon Victor Mukete; Dir-Gen. Emmanuel Nguiamba Nloutsiri.

Mobile Telephone Networks Cameroon (MTNC): Douala; f. 1999 as CAMTEL Mobile; mobile cellular telephone operator; 70% owned by MTN South Africa.

Société Camerounaise de Mobiles: Yaoundé; internet www.fcr .fr/fr/identite/pays/cameroun.htm; f. 1999; mobile cellular telephone operator; operates in Yaoundé, Douala and Bafoussam; 100% owned by France Câbles et Radio; Dir-Gen. Jean-Paul Gandet.

BROADCASTING

Radio

Office de Radiodiffusion-Télévision Camerounaise (CRTV): BP 1634, Yaoundé; tel. 221-4088; fax 220-4340; internet www.crtv .cm; f. 1987; by merger; broadcasts in French and English; satellite broadcasts commenced in Jan. 2001, reaching some 80% of the national territory; Pres. of Council of Administration Jacques Fame

NDONGO (Minister of Communication); Dir-Gen. Prof. GERVAIS MENDO ZÉ.

Radio Bertoua: BP 230, Bertoua; tel. 224-1363; Head of Station BAIVE NYONG PHILIP.

Radio Buéa: BP 86, Buéa; tel. 332-2615; programmes in English, French and 15 vernacular languages; Man. PETERSON CHIA YUH; Head of Station GIDEON MULU TAKA.

Radio Douala: BP 986, Douala; tel. 342-6060; programmes in French, English, Douala, Bassa, Ewondo, Bakoko and Bamiléké; Dir BRUNO DJEM; Head of Station LINUS ONANA MVONDO.

Radio Garoua: BP 103, Garoua; tel. 227-1167; programmes in French, Hausa, English, Foulfouldé, Arabic and Choa; Dir BELLO MALGANA; Head of Station MOUSSA EPOPA.

Radio Ngaoundéré: BP 135, Ngaoundéré; tel. 225-2148.

Radio Tam Tam: Yaoundé.

Radio Yaoundé FM 94: BP 1634, Yaoundé; tel. 220-2502; Head of Station LOUISE POM.

There are also provincial radio stations at Abong Mbang, Bafoussam, Bamenda, Ebolowa and Maroua.

Television

Television programmes from France were broadcast by the Office de Radiodiffusion-Télévision Camerounaise from early 1990.

Office de Radiodiffusion-Télévision Camerounaise (CRTV): see Radio.

Finance

(cap. = capital; res = reserves; dep. = deposits; m. = million; brs = branches; amounts in francs CFA)

BANKING

Central Bank

Banque des Etats de l'Afrique Centrale (BEAC): rue du Dr Jamot, BP 1917, Yaoundé; tel. 223-4030; fax 223-3329; internet www.beac.int; f. 1973; bank of issue for mem. states of the Communauté économique et monétaire de l'Afrique centrale (CEMAC, fmrly Union douanière et économique de l'Afrique centrale) Cameroon, the Central African Repub., Chad, the Repub. of the Congo, Equatorial Guinea and Gabon); res 177,417m., total assets 2,034,793m. (Dec. 2001); Gov. JEAN-FÉLIX MAMALEPOT; Dir in Cameroon SADOU HAYATOU; 5 brs in Cameroon.

Commercial Banks

Amity Bank Cameroon SA: BP 2705, Douala; tel. 343-2049; fax 343-2046; e-mail amibac@camnet.cm; internet www.afrika.com/amity-bank; f. 1990; cap. 1,000m., res 1,114m., total assets 21,365m. (June 2000); Pres. VICTOR ANOMAH NGU; Dir-Gen. OUMAROU SANDA; 4 brs.

Banque Internationale du Cameroun pour l'Epargne et le Crédit (BICEC): ave du Général de Gaulle, BP 1925, Douala; tel. 342-8431; fax 342-4116; e-mail bicec@bicec.com; f. 1962 as Banque Internationale pour le Commerce et l'Industrie du Cameroun; name changed as above in 1997, following restructuring; 52.5% owned by Groupe Banques Populaires (France); cap. 3,000m., dep. 172,282m., total assets 203,917m. (June 2000); Dir-Gen. JEAN PIERRE SCHIANO; 27 brs.

Citibank N.A. Cameroon: 96 rue Flatters, Bonanjo, BP 4571, Douala; tel. 342-4272; fax 342-4074; f. 1997; Dir-Gen. LOUIS ADANDE; Asst Dir-Gen. OSMAN EL TOUM.

Commercial Bank of Cameroon: BP 4004, Douala; tel. 342-0202; fax 342-3800; e-mail cbcbank@camnet.cm; f. 1997; cap. 4,500m., res 3,579m., total assets 64,385m. (June 2000); Pres. VICTOR FOTSO; Dir-Gen. JEAN LOUIS CHAPUIS.

Crédit Lyonnais Cameroun: 220 ave Monseigneur Vogt, BP 700, Yaoundé; tel. 222-8803; fax 222-8805; e-mail scb_cl_cameroun@creditlyonnais.fr; f. 1989 as Société Commerciale de Banque—Crédit Lyonnais Cameroun; name changed as above in 2002; 35% state-owned; cap. 6,000m., res 4,587m., dep. 204,937m. (June 2001); Pres. MARTIN ARISTIDE OKOUDA; Dir-Gen. ANDRÉ FERDINAND FROISSANT; 15 brs.

Ecobank Cameroun SA: BP 582, Douala; tel. 998-2670; fax 343-6247; e-mail ecobank@cyberkoki.net; internet www.ecobank.com; f. 2001; Pres. YVES QUAM-DESSOU; Dir-Gen. LOUIS VIEILLEDENT.

Highland Corporation Bank SA: Immeuble Hotel Hilton, blvd du 20 mai, BP 10039, Yaoundé; tel. 223-9287; fax 232-9291; e-mail

hicobk@camnet.cm; f. 1995; 100% privately owned; cap. 600m. (Dec. 1996); Exec. Pres. PAUL ATANGA NJI; Asst Dir-Gen. JOHANES MBATI.

Société Générale de Banques au Cameroun (SGBC): 78 rue Joss, BP 4042, Douala; tel. 342-7010; fax 343-0353; e-mail sgbcdla@camnet.cm; internet www.socgen.com/sgbc; f. 1963; 25.6% state-owned; cap. 6,250.0m., res 3,300.2m., dep. 195,225.8m. (June 1999); Pres. AHMADOU NJIFENDJOU MOULIOM; Dir-Gen. MICHEL SAUVAGNAC; 15 brs.

Standard Chartered Bank Cameroon SA: blvd de la Liberté, BP 1784, Douala; tel. 343-5200; fax 342-2789; internet www.standardchartered.com/cm/index.html; f. 1980 as Boston Bank Cameroon; 100% owned by Standard Chartered Bank (United Kingdom); cap. 3,500m., total assets 116,873m. (June 2000); Pres. EPHRAIM INONI; Man. Dir JOHN SPINK TAYLOR; 3 brs.

Development Banks

Banque de Développement des Etats de l'Afrique Centrale: see Franc Zone (see p. 239).

Crédit Foncier du Cameroun (CFC): 484 blvd du 20 mai 1972, BP 1531, Yaoundé; tel. 223-5215; fax 223-5221; f. 1977; 75% state-owned; res 2,355m., total assets 96,627m. (June 2001); provides assistance for low-cost housing; Pres. ANDRÉ BOOTO A. NGON; Dir-Gen. JOSEPH EDOU; 10 brs.

Société Nationale d'Investissement du Cameroun (SNI): place du 20 mai, BP 423, Yaoundé; tel. 222-4422; fax 223-1332; e-mail sni@sni.cm; internet www.sni.cm; f. 1964; state-owned investment and credit agency; cap. 19,000m., res 20,980m., total assets 33,426m. (June 2000); Dir-Gen. ESTHER BELIBI DANG.

Financial Institutions

Caisse Autonome d'Amortissement du Cameroun: BP 7167, Yaoundé; tel. 222-2226; fax 222-0129; e-mail camtis@camnet.cm; f. 1985; cap. 5,000m. (1998); Dir-Gen. DANIEL LAMERE NJANKOUO.

Caisse Commune d'Epargne et d'Investissement (CCEI): place de l'Indépendance, BP 11834, Yaoundé; tel. 223-3068; fax 222-1785; e-mail kengnea@hotmail.com; total assets 88,551m. (June 2000); Pres. Dr PAUL KANMOGNE FOKAM; Dir-Gen. DANIEL POTOUONJOU TAPONZIÉ.

Fonds d'Aide et de Garantie des Crédits aux Petites et Moyennes Entreprises (FOGAPE): BP 1591, Yaoundé; tel. 223-3859; fax 222-3274; f. 1984; cap. 1,000m. (Oct. 1997); Pres. JOSEPH HENGA; Vice-Pres. ARMAND FIRMIN MVONDO.

Société Camerounaise de Crédit Automobile (SOCCA): rue du Roi Albert, BP 554, Douala; tel. 342-7478; fax 342-1219; e-mail soccabail@camnet.cm; cap. 1,200m., res 2,705m., total assets 11,932m. (June 1999); Pres. VALENTIN MOUYOMBON; Dir-Gen. PHILIPPE DE LAPLAGNOLLE.

Société Camerounaise de Crédit-Bail (SOCABAIL): rue du Roi Albert, BP 554, Douala; tel. 342-7478; fax 342-1219; e-mail soccabail@camnet.cm; cap. 500m., res 1,343m., total assets 5,880m. (June 1999); Pres. ALAIN GUYON.

INSURANCE

Activa Assurances: BP 12970, Douala; tel. 343-4503; fax 343-4572; e-mail activa.assur@camnet.cm; f. 1999; all branches except life insurance; cap. 400m. 66% owned by Cameroonian investors, 33% by Ivorian investors; Chair. JEAN DIAGOU; Gen. Man. RICHARD LOWE.

Assurances Mutuelles Agricoles du Cameroun (AMACAM): BP 962, Yaoundé; tel. 222-4966; f. 1965; cap. 100m. state-owned; privatization pending; Pres. SAMUEL NGBWA NGUELE; Dir-Gen. LUC CLAUDE NANFA.

Compagnie Camerounaise d'Assurances et de Réassurances (CCAR): 11 rue Franqueville, BP 4068, Douala; tel. 342-3159; fax 342-6453; f. 1974; cap. 499.5m. Pres. YVETTE CHASSAGNE; Dir-Gen. CHRISTIAN LE GOFF.

Compagnie Nationale d'Assurances (CNA): BP 12125, Douala; tel. 342-4446; fax 342-4727; f. 1986; all classes of insurance; cap. 600m. Chair. THÉODORE EBOBO; Man. Dir PROTAIS AYANGMA AMANG.

General and Equitable Assurance Cameroon Ltd (GEACAM): 56 blvd de la Liberté, BP 426, Douala; tel. 342-5985; fax 342-7103; cap. 300m. Pres. V. A. NGU; Man. Dir J. CHEBAUT.

Société Camerounaise d'Assurances et de Réassurances (SOCAR): 1450 blvd de la Liberté, BP 280, Douala; tel. 342-5584; fax 342-1335; f. 1973; cap. 800m. state-owned; scheduled for transfer to private ownership in 2001; Chair. J. YONTA; Man. Dir R. BIOUELE.

Société Nouvelle d'Assurances du Cameroun (SNAC): rue Manga Bell, BP 105, Douala; tel. 342-9203; fax 343-0324; f. 1974; all classes of insurance; cap. 700m. Dir-Gen. JEAN CHEBAUT.

Trade and Industry

GOVERNMENT AGENCY

Economic and Social Council: BP 1058, Yaoundé; tel. 223-2474; advises the Govt on economic and social problems; comprises 150 mems and a perm. secr; mems serve a five-year term; Pres. Luc Ayang; Sec.-Gen. François Eyok.

DEVELOPMENT ORGANIZATIONS

Agence Française de Développement (AFD): BP 46, Yaoundé; tel. 222-2324; fax 223-5707; fmrly Caisse Française de Développement; Dir Dominique Dordain.

Cameroon Development Corporation (CAMDEV): Bota, Limbe; tel. 333-2251; fax 343-1740; f. 1947; reorg. 1982; cap. 15,626m. francs CFA; privatization pending; statutory corpn established to acquire and develop plantations of tropical crops for local and export markets; operates two oil mills, seven banana-packing stations, three tea and seven rubber factories; owned by Del Monte, USA; Chair. Nerius Namaso Mbile; Gen. Man. Njallu Quan.

Direction Générale des Grands Travaux du Cameroon (DGTC): BP 6604, Yaoundé; tel. 222-1803; fax 222-1300; f. 1988; commissioning, implementation and supervision of public works contracts; Chair. Jean Fouman Akame; Man. Dir Michel Kowalzick.

Hévéa-Cameroun (HEVECAM): BP 1298, Douala and BP 174, Kribi; tel. 342-7564; f. 1975; cap. 16,518m. francs CFA; state-owned; development of 15,000 ha rubber plantation; 4,500 employees; transferred to private ownership in 1997; Pres. Nyokwedi Malonga; Man. Dir Paul de Kippeleyr.

Mission d'Aménagement et d'Equipement des Terrains Urbains et Ruraux (MAETUR): BP 1248, Yaoundé; tel. 222-3113; f. 1977; Pres. Léopold Ferdinand Oyono; Dir-Gen. André Mama Fouda.

Mission de Développement de la Province du Nord-Ouest (MIDENO): BP 442, Bamenda; Dir Andrew Waindim Ndonyi.

Mission Française de Coopération et d'Action Culturelle: BP 1616, Yaoundé; tel. 223-0412; fax 222-5065; e-mail mission.coop@camnet.cm; administers bilateral aid from France; Dir Luc Hallade.

Office Céréalier dans la Province du Nord: BP 298, Garoua; tel. 227-1438; f. 1975 to combat effects of drought in northern Cameroon and stabilize cereal prices; Pres. Alhadji Mahamat; Dir-Gen. Gilbert Gourlemond.

Société de Développement du Cacao (SODECAO): BP 1651, Yaoundé; tel. 230-4544; fax 230-3395; f. 1974; reorg. 1980; cap. 425m. francs CFA; development of cocoa, coffee and food crop production in the Littoral, Centre, East and South provinces; Pres. Joseph-Charles Doumba; Dir-Gen. Joseph Ingwat II.

Société de Développement de l'Elevage (SODEVA): BP 50, Kousseri; cap. 50m. francs CFA; Dir Alhadji Oumarou Bakary.

Société de Développement et d'Exploitation des Productions Animales (SODEPA): BP 1410, Yaoundé; tel. 222-2428; f. 1974; cap. 375m. francs CFA; development of livestock and livestock products; Man. Dir Etienne Engueleguele.

Société de Développement de la Haute-Vallée du Noun (UNVDA): BP 25, N'Dop, North-West Province; f. 1970; cap. 1,380m. francs CFA; rice, maize and soya bean cultivation; Dir-Gen. Samuel Bawe Chi Wanki.

Société d'Expansion et de Modernisation de la Riziculture de Yagoua (SEMRY): BP 46, Yagoua; tel. 229-6213; f. 1971; cap. 4,580m. francs CFA; commercialization of rice products and expansion of rice-growing in areas where irrigation is possible; Pres. Albert Ekono; Dir-Gen. Limangana Tori.

Société Immobilière du Cameroun (SIC): BP 387, Yaoundé; tel. 223-3411; fax 222-5119; f. 1952; cap. 1,000m. francs CFA; housing construction and development; Pres. Enoch Kwayeb; Dir-Gen. Gilles-Roger Belinga.

CHAMBERS OF COMMERCE

Chambre d'Agriculture, d'Elevage et des Forêts du Cameroun: Parc Repiquet, BP 287, Yaoundé; tel. 223-1496; f. 1955; 120 mems; Pres. Philémon Adjibolo; Sec.-Gen. Solomon Nfor Gwei; other chambers at Yaoundé, Ebolowa, Bertoua, Douala, Ngaoundéré, Garoua, Maroua, Buéa, Bumenda and Bafoussam.

Chambre de Commerce, d'Industrie et des Mines du Cameroun (CCIM): rue de Chambre de Commerce, BP 4011, Douala; also at BP 36, Yaoundé; BP 211, Limbe; BP 59, Garoua; BP 944, Bafoussam; BP 551, Bamenda; tel. 342-6855; fax 342-5596; e-mail Cride-g77@camnet.cm; internet www.g77tin.org/ccimhp .html; f. 1921; 138 mems; Pres. Juimo Monthe Claude; Sec.-Gen. Saïdou Abdoulaye Bobboy.

EMPLOYERS' ORGANIZATIONS

Association Professionnelle des Établissements Financiers (APECAM): Yaoundé; tel. 223-5401; fax 223-5402.

Groupement des Femmes d'Affaires du Cameroun (GFAC): BP 1940, Douala; tel. 342-464; Pres. Françoise Foning.

Groupement Interpatronal du Cameroun (GICAM): ave Konrad Adenauer, BP 1134, Yaoundé; also at BP 829, Douala; tel. 220-2722; fax 220-9694; e-mail gicam-yde@camnet.cm; tel. and fax 342-3141; f. 1957; Pres. André Siaka; Sec.-Gen. Francis Sanzouango.

Syndicat des Commerçants Importateurs-Exportateurs du Cameroun (SCIEC): 16 rue Quillien, BP 562, Douala; tel. 342-0304; Sec.-Gen. G. Toscano.

Syndicat des Industriels du Cameroun (SYNDUSTRICAM): 17 blvd de Liberté, BP 673, Douala; tel. 342-3058; fax 342-5616; f. 1953; Pres. Samuel Kondo Ebellé.

Syndicat des Producteurs et Exportateurs de Bois du Cameroun: BP 570, Yaoundé; tel. 220-2722; fax 220-9694; Pres. Carlo Oriani.

Syndicat Professionnel des Entreprises du Bâtiment, des Travaux Publics et des Activités Annexes: BP 1134, Yaoundé; also at BP 660, Douala; tel. and fax 220-2722; Pres. (vacant).

Syndicats Professionnels Forestiers et Activités connexes du Cameroun: BP 100, Douala.

Union des Syndicats Professionnels du Cameroun (USPC): BP 829, Douala; Pres. Moukoko Kingue.

West Cameroon Employers' Association (WCEA): BP 97, Tiko.

UTILITIES

Electricity

Société Nationale d'Electricité du Cameroun (SONEL): BP 4077, 63 ave de Gaulle, Douala; tel. 342-5444; fax 342-2209; e-mail sonel@camnet.cm; internet www.camnet.cm/investir/minmee/sonelind.htm; f. 1974; 44% state-owned; 56% stake acquired by AES Sirocco in 2001; CEO Jean Fouman Akame; Dir-Gen. Marcel Niat Nji Fenji.

Water

Société Nationale des Eaux du Cameroun (SNEC): BP 157, Douala; tel. 342-8711; fax 342-2945; e-mail snec@camnet.cm; internet www.camnet.cm/investir/minmee/snec.htm; f. 1967; 73% state-owned; scheduled for transfer to the private sector; Pres. Amadou Ali; Dir-Gen. Clément Obouh Fegue.

PRINCIPAL CO-OPERATIVE ORGANIZATIONS

Centre National de Développement des Entreprises Coopératives (CENADEC): Yaoundé; f. 1970; promotes and organizes the co-operative movement; bureaux at BP 43, Kumba and BP 26, Bamenda; Dir Jacques Sangue.

Union Centrale des Coopératives Agricoles de l'Ouest (UCCAO): ave Samuel Wonko, BP 1002, Bafoussam; tel. 344-1439; fax 344-1101; f. 1957; marketing of cocoa and coffee; 110,000 mems; Pres. Victor Gnimpieba; Dir-Gen. Pierre Nzefa Tsachoua.

West Cameroon Co-operative Association Ltd: BP 135, Kumba; founded as cen. financing body of the co-operative movement; provides short-term credits and agricultural services to mem. socs; policy-making body for the co-operative movement in West Cameroon; 142 mem. unions and socs representing c. 45,000 mems; Pres. Chief T. E. Njea.

TRADE UNION FEDERATION

Confederation of Cameroon Trade Unions (CCTU): BP 1610, Yaoundé; tel. 222-3315; f. 1985; fmrly the Union National des Travailleurs du Cameroun (UNTC); Pres. Emmanuel Bakod; Sec.-Gen. Louis Sombes.

Transport

RAILWAYS

There are some 1,104 km of track—the West Line running from Douala to Nkongsamba (166 km), with a branch line leading southwest from Mbanga to Kumba (29 km), and the Transcameroon railway, which runs from Douala to Ngaoundéré (885 km), with a branch line from Ngoumou to Mbalmayo (30 km). In July 2002 the World Bank disbursed a loan of 15,600m. francs CFA to Cameroon to help rehabilitate the main line. In November the French Government approved a loan of US $12.5m. to Cameroon primarily to improve rolling stock.

Cameroon Railways (CAMRAIL): Gare Centrale de Bessengue, blvd de la Réunification, BP 766, Douala; tel. 340-6045; fax 340-8252; e-mail camrail@camnet.cm; internet www.camnet.cm/investir/transport/regie/regie.htm; f. 1999; Pres. ETIENNE GIROS; Dir-Gen. PATRICK CLAES.

Office du Chemin de Fer Transcamerounais: BP 625, Yaoundé; tel. 222-4433; supervises the laying of new railway lines and improvements to existing lines, and undertakes relevant research; Dir-Gen. LUC TOWA FOTSO.

ROADS

In 1999 there were an estimated 49,300 km of roads, of which about 4,100 km were paved.

SHIPPING

There are seaports at Kribi and Limbé-Tiko, a river port at Garoua, and an estuary port at Douala-Bonabéri, the principal port and main outlet, which has 2,510 m of quays and a minimum depth of 5.8 m in the channels and 8.5 m at the quays. In 1997 the port handled 4,882,000 metric tons of cargo. Total handling capacity is 7m. metric tons annually. Plans are under way to increase the annual capacity of the container terminal. There are also plans to modernize Limbé–Tiko and to promote it internationally.

Office National des Ports/National Ports Authority: Centre des Affaires Maritimes, 18 rue Joffre, BP 4002, Douala; tel. 342-0133; fax 342-6797; e-mail onpc@camnet.cm; internet www.camnet.cm/investir/transport/onpc; f. 1971; Chair. CHRISTOPHER NSALAI (Minister of Transport); Dir-Gen. ALPHONSE SIYAM SIEW.

Cameroon Shipping Lines SA (CAMSHIP): Centre des Affaires Maritimes, BP 4054, Douala; tel. 342-0038; fax 342-0114; f. 1975; scheduled for transfer to private-sector ownership; 6 vessels trading with Western Europe, USA, Far East and Africa; Chair. FRANÇOIS SENGAT KUO; Man. Dir RENÉ MBAYEN.

 Camafrica Liner Ltd: Centre des Affaires Maritimes, BP 4054, Douala; non-vessel owner container carrier co. trading between West Africa and Europe.

Compagnie Maritime Camerounaise SA (CMC): BP 3235, Douala; tel. 342-8540; fax 342-5842.

Conseil National des Chargeurs du Cameroun (CNCC): BP 1588, Douala; tel. 342-3206; fax 342-8901; f. 1986; promotion of the maritime sector; Gen. Man. EMMANUEL EDOU.

Delmas Cameroun: rue Kitchener, BP 263, Douala; tel. 342-4750; fax 342-8851; f. 1977; Pres. JEAN-GUY LE FLOCH; Dir-Gen. DANY CHUTAUX.

Société Africaine de Transit et d'Affrètement (SATA): Douala; tel. 342-8209; f. 1950; Man. Dir RAYMOND PARIZOT.

Société Agence Maritime de l'Ouest Africain Cameroun (SAMOA): 5 blvd de la Liberté, BP 1127, Douala; tel. 342-1680; f. 1953; shipping agents; Dir JEAN PERRIER.

Société Camerounaise de Manutention et d'Acconage (SOCAMAC): BP 284, Douala; tel. 342-4051; f. 1976; freight handling; Pres. MOHAMADOU TALBA; Dir-Gen. HARRY J. GHOOS.

Société Camerounaise de Transport et d'Affrètement (SCTA): BP 974, Douala; tel. 342-1724; f. 1951; Pres. JACQUES VIAULT; Dir-Gen. GONTRAN FRAUCIEL.

Société Ouest-Africaine d'Entreprises Maritimes—Cameroun (SOAEM—Cameroon): 5 blvd de la Liberté, BP 4057, Douala; tel. 342-5269; fax 342-0518; f. 1959; Pres. JACQUES COLOMBANI; Man. Dir JEAN-LOUIS GRECIET.

Société de Transports Urbains du Cameroun (SOTUC): BP 1697, Yaoundé; tel. 221-3807; fax 220-7784; f. 1973; 58% owned by Société Nationale d'Investissement du Cameroun; operates urban transport services in Yaoundé and Douala; Dir-Gen. MARCEL YONDO; Mans JEAN-VICTOR OUM (Yaoundé), GABRIEL VASSEUR (Douala).

SOCOPAO (Cameroon): BP 215, Douala; tel. 342-6464; f. 1951; shipping agents; Pres. VINCENT BOLLORE; Man. Dir E. DUPUY.

Transcap Cameroun: BP 4059, Douala; tel. 342-7214; f. 1960; Pres. RENÉ DUPRAZ; Man. Dir MICHEL BARDOU.

CIVIL AVIATION

There are international airports at Douala, Garoua and Yaoundé; there are, in addition, 11 domestic airports, as well as a number of secondary airfields.

Aéroports du Cameroun (ADC): Aéroport de Douala; tel. 342-3526; fax 342-3758; f. 1999; manages major airports; 35% owned by Aéroports de Paris, 29% state-owned.

Air Affaires Afrique: BP 1225, Douala; tel. 342-2977; fax 342-9903; f. 1978; regional and domestic charter passenger services; CEO BYRON BYRON-EXARCOS.

Cameroon Airlines (CAMAIR): 151 rue de l'Hôtel de Ville, BP 4092, Douala; tel. 342-2525; fax 342-3459; e-mail camair@camnet.cm; internet www.camnet.cm/investir/transpor/camair/index.htm; f. 1971; domestic flights and services to Africa and Europe; privatization pending; Pres. of Council of Administration ETIENNE NTSAMA; Dir-Gen. YVES-MICHEL FOTSO.

Tourism

Tourists are attracted by Cameroon's cultural diversity and by its national parks, game reserves and sandy beaches. In 1998 an estimated 135,000 tourists visited Cameroon. In that year receipts from tourism totalled some US $40m.

Ministère du Tourisme: BP 266, Yaoundé; tel. 222-4411; fax 222-1295; e-mail mintour@camnet.cm; internet www.mintour.gov.cm.

CANADA

Introductory Survey

Location, Climate, Language, Religion, Flag, Capital

Canada occupies the northern part of North America (excluding Alaska and Greenland) and is the second largest country in the world, after Russia. It extends from the Atlantic Ocean to the Pacific. Except for the boundary with Alaska in the north-west, Canada's frontier with the USA follows the upper St Lawrence Seaway and the Great Lakes, continuing west along latitude 49°N. The climate is an extreme one, particularly inland. Winter temperatures drop well below freezing but summers are generally hot. Rainfall varies from moderate to light and there are heavy falls of snow. The two official languages are English and French, the mother tongues of 59.3% and 23.2%, respectively, at the general census in 1996. Immigration during the 1990s made a profound impact on languages spoken in Canadian homes; at the 1996 census Chinese was the language most commonly spoken at home, after English and French. About 45% of the population are Roman Catholics. The main Protestant churches are the United Church of Canada and the Anglican Church of Canada. Numerous other religious denominations are represented. The national flag (proportions 1 by 2) consists of a red maple leaf on a white field, flanked by red panels. The capital is Ottawa.

Recent History

The Liberals, led by Pierre Trudeau, were returned to office at general elections in 1968, 1972, 1974, and again in 1980 after a short-lived minority Progressive Conservative Party (PC) administration. Popular support for the Liberals, however, was undermined by an economic recession, and the PC, led by Brian Mulroney, obtained a substantial legislative majority at general elections held in September 1984.

During 1986 the persistence of high rates of unemployment, together with the resignations in discordant circumstances of five cabinet ministers, led to a fall in the PC Government's popularity. Popular support for the Government further declined, in response to criticism by the Liberals and the New Democratic Party (NDP) of the Government's negotiation of a new US–Canadian trade treaty, which the Liberals and the NDP viewed as overly advantageous to US business interests and potentially damaging to Canada's national identity, and which was approved by the House of Commons in August 1988. Nevertheless, in general elections in November the PC was re-elected, although with a reduced majority, and full legislative ratification of the trade agreement followed in December. In February 1990 the federal Government opened negotiations with Mexico, to achieve a lowering of trade barriers. The US Government joined these discussions, and in December 1992 Canada, the USA and Mexico finalized terms for a tripartite North American Free Trade Agreement (NAFTA, see p. 270), with the aim of creating a free trade zone encompassing the whole of North America.

In the province of Québec, where four-fifths of the population speak French as a first language and which maintains its own cultural identity, the question of political self-determination has long been a sensitive issue. At provincial elections in 1976 the separatist Parti Québécois (PQ) came to power, and in 1977 made French the official language of education, business and government in Québec. In December 1985 the PQ was replaced by the Liberals as the province's governing party. The Liberals retained power at the next provincial elections, held in September 1989. However, political support for separatist aspirations was extended to the federal Parliament in May 1990, when seven PC members representing Québec constituencies, led by Lucien Bouchard (a former member of Mulroney's Cabinet), broke away from the party and formed the independent Bloc Québécois (BQ), with the object of acting in the interests of a 'sovereign Québec'. The BQ later expanded, with disaffected Liberal support, to nine members.

In 1982 the British Parliament transferred to Canada authority over all matters contained in British statutes relating to Canada, opening the way for institutional reform and the redistribution of legislative powers between Parliament and the provincial legislatures. All the provinces except Québec eventually accepted constitutional provisions that included a charter of rights and a formula for constitutional amendments, whereby such amendments would require the support of at least seven provinces representing more than 50% of the population. Québec, however, maintained that its legislature could exercise the right to veto constitutional provisions.

Following the return to office in 1985 of the Liberals in Québec, the federal Government adopted new initiatives to include Québec in the constitutional arrangements. In April 1987 Mulroney and the provincial premiers met at Meech Lake, Québec, to negotiate a constitutional accommodation for Québec. The resultant agreement, the Meech Lake Accord, recognized Québec as a 'distinct society' within the Canadian federation, and granted each of the provinces substantial new powers in the areas of federal parliamentary reform, judicial appointments and the creation of new provinces. The Accord was subject to ratification, not later than June 1990, by the federal Parliament and all provincial legislatures. By early 1990 the federal Parliament and each of the 10 provincial legislatures, except for New Brunswick and Manitoba, had approved the Accord.

Opposition to the Meech Lake arrangements, on the grounds that they afforded too much influence to Québec and failed to provide Inuit and Indian minorities with the same measure of protection as francophone groups, began to emerge in March 1990, when the Newfoundland legislature rescinded its earlier endorsement of the Accord. Following a meeting in June between Mulroney and the provincial premiers (at which a number of compromise amendments were adopted), the New Brunswick legislature agreed to accept the Accord, but the provinces of Manitoba and Newfoundland upheld their opposition. The Meech Lake Accord duly lapsed in late June, and the Québec Government, which had opposed any changes to the earlier terms of the Accord, responded by refusing to participate in future provincial conferences, and by appointing a commission to examine the province's political choices. In September 1991 the federal Government announced a new series of constitutional reform proposals, which, unlike the Meech Lake Accord, would require the assent of only seven provinces representing 50% of the total population. Under the new plan, Québec was to be recognized as a distinct society in terms of its language, culture and legal system, while each province would have full control of its cultural affairs. Native peoples were to receive full self-government within 10 years, inter-provincial trade barriers were to be abolished, and the federal Senate was to become an elected body with limited powers of legislative veto, except in matters involving natural resources, in which it would have full powers of veto. The reform proposals also included the creation of a Council of Federation to resolve disputes between the provinces and federal Government. A National Unity Committee, comprising an inter-party group of 30 federal legislators, was formed to ascertain public reaction to the plan, about which the Québec provincial government expressed initial reservations on economic grounds.

In March 1992 an all-party committee of the federal Parliament recommended new constitutional proposals providing for a system of 'co-operative federalism', which would grant Québec powers of veto over future constitutional changes, together with exclusive jurisdiction over the main areas of its provincial affairs. This plan was rejected by the Québec Government.

Further, inconclusive, discussions among the provincial premiers (in which Québec refused to participate) took place in mid-1992. Mulroney's proposal to revive the Meech Lake proposals was opposed by the western provinces, which sought increased representation in a reformed Senate and were unwilling to concede a constitutional veto to Québec until after these changes were carried out. In late August 1992, following resumed consultations between Mulroney and the provincial premiers, a new programme of constitutional reforms, known as the Charlottetown Agreement, was finalized for submission to a national referendum. The proposals, which were endorsed by all of the provincial premiers as well as the leaders of the three main political parties, provided for an equal and elected Senate, a guarantee in perpetuity to Québec of one-quarter of the seats in the federal House of Commons (regardless of future movements in population), as well as three of the nine seats on the Supreme Court of Canada. There was also to be recognition of provincial jurisdiction in cultural affairs, and increased provincial powers over certain economic affairs and immigration. The inherent right to self-government of the Indian and Inuit population was also to be recognized.

Despite the apparent political consensus, considerable opposition to the Charlottetown Agreement became evident prior to the referendum, which took place in October 1992. Disagreements emerged on a regional basis, as well as among NDP and Liberal supporters, and aspects of the proposed constitution were opposed by the PQ and the BQ, and by the Reform Party (RP), a conservative-populist movement which led opposition in the western provinces. Nationally, the proposals were defeated by a margin of 54.4% to 44.6%; only four of the provinces (Ontario, New Brunswick, Newfoundland and Prince Edward Island) and the Northwest Territories (NWT) endorsed the Agreement.

The defeat of the Charlottetown Agreement, together with the persistence of adverse economic conditions, led to a rapid erosion in the prestige of the Government, and in Mulroney's personal popularity. A reorganization of Cabinet posts in January 1993 failed to restore public confidence, and in the following month Mulroney announced that he was to relinquish office in June. He was succeeded by the former Minister of Defence and Veterans' Affairs, Kim Campbell, who became Canada's first female Prime Minister.

The Campbell Government proved unable to restore the PC's political standing, and, faced with the expiry in November 1993 of its five-year parliamentary mandate, general elections were scheduled for October. The outcome of the elections, which were contested primarily on domestic economic issues, resulted in a decisive victory for the Liberals, led by Jean Chrétien. A significant realignment of political forces was reflected in the new Parliament, in which PC representation was reduced to only two seats. The RP, which attracted support from disaffected PC voters, emerged with 52 seats, while the BQ, with 54 seats, became the official opposition party. The BQ, which had diverted support from the PC in Québec, declared that it would pursue the achievement of full sovereignty for Québec. Kim Campbell, who lost her seat in the federal Parliament, resigned as PC leader and was succeeded by Jean Charest.

The new Liberal Government set out to implement an economic recovery programme. Substantial reductions in defence expenditure were announced, as well as a C $6,000m. job-creation scheme, and in December 1993, following the renegotiation of certain treaty protocols with the US Government, NAFTA, which had received Canadian legislative ratification in June, was formally promulgated, to take effect from January 1994. The Liberals were re-elected at general elections held in June 1997, although with a reduced majority in the House of Commons. The RP replaced the BQ as the main opposition party.

The issue of separatism in Québec was reopened by provincial elections held in September 1994, in which the PQ, led by Jacques Parizeau, defeated the incumbent Liberal administration by a margin of 44.7% to 44.3%. Parizeau, whose campaign had included an undertaking that a new referendum on independence would be held during 1995, was supported at federal level by the BQ, although the federal Government asserted that considerable uncertainty was felt within Québec over the possible economic consequences of secession. In June 1995 the PQ and the BQ, together with a smaller provincial nationalist group, the Action Démocratique du Québec, agreed a framework for the province's proposed independence and in mid-September the referendum received provincial legislative approval.

On the eve of the referendum, held on 30 October 1995, Chrétien issued an appeal for national unity, and undertook to reinstate negotiations for a new constitutional accord. The sovereignty proposals were defeated by a margin of only 50,000 votes; in a turn-out of 93% of eligible voters, 49.4% were in favour of the sovereignty plan, and 50.6% opposed. Parizeau announced his intention to resign. In January 1996 Chrétien carried out an extensive reshuffle of his Cabinet and reaffirmed the federal Government's commitment to the maintenance of Canadian federation and national unity. In the following month Lucien Bouchard, having resigned from the federal House of Commons and relinquished the leadership of the BQ, succeeded Parizeau as Premier of Québec and leader of the PQ. Bouchard

indicated that his administration viewed the sovereignty issue as less urgent than the resolution of Québec's immediate economic problems. In September 1997 Bouchard refused to attend a conference of provincial premiers and territorial commissioners, at which a seven-point framework on Canadian unity was agreed. The conference, held in Calgary, recognized the 'unique character' of Québec, but asserted that any future change in the constitutional powers of one province should be applicable to all provinces. By June 1998 the resultant 'Calgary Declaration' had been endorsed by the legislatures of all provinces except Québec.

The Supreme Court, which had been requested in February 1998 to rule on the legality of a unilateral secession by Québec, declared in August that no province had the right, in constitutional or international law, to leave the federation without prior negotiations with the federal and provincial governments, and that secession would require the approval of the federal legislature, together with that of seven of the 10 provinces. It was further stated that an obligation would exist for negotiation with Québec if a clear majority of its voters expressed a wish to leave the federation.

In March 1998 Jean Charest resigned as leader of the PC, to accept the leadership of the Liberal Party of Québec, which had been perceived as losing popular support for its anti-separatist policy. The PQ Government, which was further encouraged by its success in addressing the province's economic problems, called a provincial legislative election in November, with the implication that a substantial victory for the PQ would open the way to a further referendum on independence. At the election, however, an unexpected rise in support for the Liberals awarded them 43.7% of the popular vote, against 42.7% for the PQ, which, none the less, obtained 76 seats in the 125-seat legislature, compared with 48 seats for the Liberals. Following the election, Bouchard conceded that the PQ had failed to attract sufficient support to merit an early referendum.

In November 1999 Chrétien proposed the introduction of legislation requiring the agreement of 60% of Québec voters in any future provincial referendum on independence as a precondition to federal–provincial negotiations of terms of separation. This plan, however, was postponed following objections from members of the Cabinet and from Liberal MPs representing Québec constituencies in the federal House of Commons.

In March 2000 members of the RP voted to form the Canadian Alliance (CA), an organization conceived at a convention held in September 1998 with the aim of uniting the major right-wing parties. The PC declined to join the CA, although a number of that party's prominent members chose to do so. Deborah Grey, formerly of the RP, became the temporary Leader of the Opposition, pending a formal contest for the leadership of the CA. In July Stockwell Day, a former PC member, was elected leader of the CA, defeating Preston Manning, the last leader of the RP. Day was elected to the House of Commons at a by-election in September.

In October 2000 Chrétien announced that a general election would be held on 27 November, despite his Government's mandate being valid until June 2002. At the election, Chrétien's Liberals received 40.8% of the votes cast and won 172 of the 301 seats in the House of Commons. The CA secured 25.5% of the votes cast and 66 parliamentary seats, compared with the 58 seats won by the RP at the election of June 1997. The BQ obtained 38 seats, compared with 44 at the previous election, the NDP 13 seats and the PC 12. The results demonstrated an increasing political polarization between the country's east and centre and its west—the CA won 50 of the 60 seats available in the two westernmost provinces, British Columbia and Alberta, but only two in Ontario (the Liberals being elected in 100 of the 103 constituencies in that province).

In January 2001 Bouchard announced his resignation as Premier of Québec, once a successor had been elected. He also resigned as a member of the provincial legislature and as leader of the PQ, stating that he had failed in his intention to achieve independence for the province and that he lacked both popular and party support. The BQ had lost several seats in Québec to the Liberals at the November 2000 federal general election and opinion polls continued to show a decline in support for the PQ's policy on independence. Also in January 2001 Lorne Calvert was elected Premier of Saskatchewan following the resignation of Roy Romanow. In early February Roger Grimes succeeded Brian Tobin as Premier of Newfoundland, following Tobin's appointment to the federal Government. (In December Newfoundland was officially renamed Newfoundland and Labrador.) In early

March Bernard Landry of the PQ, hitherto Minister of Finance in the province, was elected the new Premier of Québec.

In May 2001, at provincial elections in British Columbia, the NDP, which had been in government since 1991, retained just two seats in the 79-seat Legislative Assembly. The Liberal Party secured the remaining 77 seats. The provincial Liberal leader, Gordon Campbell, became Premier.

In mid-July 2001, following several months of internal dissent in the party owing to its poor performance in the 2000 legislative elections, 13 CA members resigned from the party in protest at Day's refusal to resign the leadership. Day had offered to step down temporarily if he could appoint his successor, an offer that had been rejected by CA members. The dissident MPs formed a new parliamentary party, the Democratic Representative Caucus, which, in September, formed a coalition in the House of Representatives with the PC. Day eventually resigned in December, and stood for re-election in March 2002, but was defeated by Stephen Harper. In the same month Ernie Eves succeeded Mike Harris as Premier of Ontario.

Throughout 2002 the Government was dogged by accusations of corruption. In May Chrétien dismissed the Minister of Defence, Art Eggleton, after it was revealed that Eggleton had awarded a C $36,000 contract in his ministry to a former girl-friend. At the same time, Don Boudria, who had been appointed Minister of Public Works and Services in January, was moved back to his former post as Leader of the Government in the House of Commons, a move widely regarded as a demotion, after he stayed in the holiday home of the head of a company that had been awarded lucrative government contracts. In June the Minister of Finance, Paul Martin, widely considered as a potential successor to Chrétien, was dismissed and replaced by Deputy Prime Minister John Manley. It was widely believed that Martin, a longtime rival of Chrétien, had been planning to launch a leadership challenge. In August Chrétien announced that he would stand down as Prime Minister in February 2004, and pass the premiership to another member of the Liberal Party. In October the Government faced further criticism when the Solicitor-General, Lawrence MacAulay, resigned following accusations that he had been involved in the awarding of federal grants to a community college headed by his brother. He was replaced as Solicitor-General by Wayne Easter.

In June 2002 the leader of the NDP, Alexa McDonough, announced her resignation; she was replaced by Jack Layton in January 2003. Legislative elections took place in the Yukon Territory in November 2002; Dennis Fentie of the Yukon Party replaced Pat Duncan of the Liberal Party as Premier. At provincial elections in April 2003, Charest became Premier of Québec when the Liberal Party secured 76 seats in the 125-member legislature, compared with 45 seats for the PQ.

The question of land treaty claims by Canada's indigenous peoples came to prominence during the early 1990s, when disputes over land rights arose in Ontario, Manitoba and, most notably, Québec, where armed confrontations took place in 1990 between the civil authorities and militant indigenous groups. During the 1980s debate began to intensify in the formulation of a new constitutional status for the NWT, in which a population of only 58,000 (of which Inuit and other indigenous peoples comprised about one-half) occupied an area comprising one-third of Canada's land mass. In November 1982 the federal Government agreed in principle to implement the decision of a territorial referendum held in April, in which 56% of the voters approved a division of the NWT. Proposals to replace the NWT with two self-governing units: Nunavut Territory (to the east of a proposed boundary running northwards from the Saskatchewan–Manitoba border), and a second newly-constituted territory to the west, were approved by the NWT legislature in January 1987 and were endorsed in May 1992 by a plebiscite among NWT residents. In December 1991 specific terms for the creation of a semi-autonomous Nunavut Territory, covering an area of 2.2m. sq km, were agreed by Inuit representatives and the federal Government. In September 1988, following 13 years of negotiations, the federal Government formally transferred to indigenous ownership an area covering 673,000 sq km in the NWT. In the Yukon Territory, an area of 41,000 sq km (representing 8.6% of the Territory's land) was transferred to indigenous control.

A formal agreement to settle all outstanding land treaty claims was finalized by the federal Government in May 1993, providing for Nunavut and a second territory, as yet unnamed, to come into official existence on 1 April 1999. Elections to a new, 17-seat Legislature for Nunavut, to be located at Iqaluit, were held in February 1999, and the new Territorial Government took office in April. In November 1996 an official inquiry into the social and economic condition of Canada's indigenous peoples recommended the creation of a new chamber of the federal Parliament to function as a permanent commission to review issues affecting the indigenous groups, and that these communities receive increased powers of self-government. In December 1997 the Supreme Court awarded legal title to 57,000 sq km of ancestral land to two native groups in British Columbia, and in the following month the federal Government offered a formal apology to all native groups for past mistreatment and injustices. The principle of 'aboriginal title', established by the Supreme Court ruling, was again exercised in April 1999 with the transfer, together with substantial powers of self-government, of a further 2,000 sq km of land to native ownership in British Columbia.

During his period in office, Mulroney sought to re-establish Canada's traditional 'special relationship' with the USA, which had operated until the Trudeau period. Subsequent administrations sought to emphasize Canada's independence from the USA in matters of foreign policy, while continuing the increased co-operation in areas such as trade and environmental protection. In the last two decades of the 20th century a number of bilateral environmental agreements were signed, including accords on gaseous emissions, both domestically and in the USA (which move northwards into Canada to produce environmentally destructive 'acid rain') and the elimination of industrial pollution from the Great Lakes, in conjunction with the implementation of a number of domestic environmental-improvement programmes. In 1991 Canada, with the USA and 23 European countries, signed an international treaty on cross-border pollution control, under which the signatories undertook to prevent, reduce and control environmental degradation caused by industrial activity. A further agreement with the USA on the reduction of industrial pollution was signed in April 1997. In December of that year, at the third Conference of the Parties to the Framework Convention on Climate Change (see World Meteorological Organization, p. 124), held in Kyoto, Japan, Canada undertook to implement reductions of its emissions of 'greenhouse gases' to 6% below 1990 levels by the year 2012. In July 2001, at the International Summit on Climate Change in Bonn, Germany, the Canadian Government pledged to ratify the Kyoto Protocol, although it had refused to do so the previous November at a summit in The Hague, Netherlands. The Minister of Natural Resources, Ralph Goodale, criticized the USA for refusing to commit to reductions. In December 2002 the Canadian Government ratified the Protocol, despite opposition from the gas and petroleum industries and the province of Alberta, which threatened to challenge the legality of ratification in the Supreme Court. Canada assumed a leading role in the establishment, with seven other circumpolar countries, of the Arctic Council (see p. 338), which commenced operation in September 1996. The aims of the Council include the protection of the environment of the polar region, the formation of co-ordinated policies governing its future, and the safeguarding of the interests of its indigenous population groups.

There have been recurrent disagreements between Canada and France concerning the boundary of disputed waters near the French-controlled islands of St Pierre and Miquelon, off the southern coast of Newfoundland and Labrador. In June 1992 an international arbitration tribunal presented its report, generally regarded as favourable to Canada, and in December 1994 the two countries agreed a 10-year accord on the allocation of fishing rights around the islands. In September 2001 France and Canada held talks on energy exploration in the waters off St Pierre and Miquelon; geologists believed there were large petroleum and natural gas deposits between the islands and Newfoundland and Labrador and Nova Scotia.

In December 1992 Canada and the EC (European Community, now European Union—EU) announced the resolution of a seven-year disagreement over the allocation of fishing rights to European commercial fleets in the north-west Atlantic Ocean. In 1994, however, the EU unilaterally awarded itself almost 70% of the internationally agreed quota of Greenland halibut (also known as turbot) caught in the north-west Atlantic fishing grounds. This action was not recognized by other members of the Northwest Atlantic Fishing Organization (NAFO), and was vigorously contested by the Canadian Government, which declared that it would act to prevent EU fishing trawlers (principally from Spain and Portugal) from overfishing the already seriously depleted stocks of Greenland halibut. It was also announced that Canada was extending its maritime jurisdiction beyond its Exclusive Economic Zone (EEZ), already extending 200 nautical miles (370 km) from the coastline. This action was rejected by the EU as contrary to international law.

In February 1995 the Canadian Government warned the EU that force would be used if necessary to ensure that total catches by EU vessels did not exceed 3,400 tons of the NAFO-agreed world Greenland halibut quota of 27,000 tons. On 6 March the Canadian Government declared a 60-day moratorium on all trawling for this fish in the north-west Atlantic, and three days later its enforcement vessels fired on and impounded a Spanish trawler fishing in international waters. The EU responded by suspending all official political contacts with Canada, pending the release of the trawler. The impasse was eased by the release of the trawler on 15 March, when it was agreed to initiate quota allocation negotiations. Divisions began to emerge within the EU when the British Government refused to endorse an EU protest against these interceptions, and declared its support of Canada's desire to conserve north-west Atlantic fishing stocks. A resolution was eventually reached in mid-April, under which Canada and EU countries each agreed to accept 41% of the 1996 Greenland halibut quota. It was agreed that independent observers would monitor the activities of trawlers in the north-west Atlantic fishing zone. However, during the negotiation of an accord in June 1996 governing bilateral relations between Canada and the EU, the Canadian Government rejected a Spanish request that it suspend the enforcement of its fishing regulations outside Canadian territorial waters. In early 2002 the Canadian Government imposed a ban on all vessels from Estonia and the Faeroe Islands from entering Canadian ports, accusing those fleets of violating NAFO-agreed shrimp quotas off the eastern coast of the country. In September the Government extended the ban to any foreign vessel which violated NAFO-agreed quotas. In December the ban on the Estonian fleet was lifted.

Canada, which maintains significant economic and commercial links with Cuba and operates a policy of 'constructive engagement' in its relations with that country, adopted a prominent role in international opposition to efforts, initiated by the US Government in March 1996, to penalize investors whose business in any way involves property in Cuba that was confiscated from US citizens following the 1959 revolution. The imposition of these measures, known as the Helms-Burton Act, led in July 1996 to the exclusion from the USA of nine Canadian businessmen involved in nickel-mining operations in Cuba. The Canadian Government responded by introducing legislation prohibiting Canadian companies from compliance with the Helms-Burton Act, and refused to recognize foreign court rulings arising from the Act. With Mexico, which also conducts significant trade with Cuba, Canada co-ordinated a joint challenge to the US Government through NAFTA dispute procedures. In November 1996 Canada actively promoted a resolution by the UN General Assembly condemning the US trade sanctions against Cuba, and in the same month joined the EU in a complaint against the embargo to the World Trade Organization (WTO, see p. 323). In April 1998, following an official visit to Cuba by Chrétien, the Canadian Government signed a series of co-operation agreements with Cuba. However, relations between the two countries subsequently experienced a sharp decline, owing to increasing official and public concern in Canada at the Cuban Government's human rights record, particularly in relation to the treatment of political prisoners. In July 1999 the Canadian Government stated that it would implement no further assistance programmes to Cuba that did not clearly further the protection of human rights, and it was indicated that Canada would not support, or encourage other countries to support, the admission of Cuba to the Organization of American States (see p. 288).

Relations with the USA improved in June 1999 following the resolution of a long-standing disagreement over the demarcation of salmon-fishing rights off the Pacific coast. However, in October the US Government criticized a Canadian petroleum company, Talisman Energy, Inc, for its presence in Sudan. The USA, which maintained sanctions against Sudan, claimed that Talisman's activities contributed to the continued conflict in that country. It also criticized the Canadian Government for allowing Talisman to operate there. The Canadian Government rejected such criticism and, in July 2000, re-established full diplomatic relations with Sudan. In mid-2001 the US House of Representatives voted to prevent non-US companies operating in Sudanese oilfields from selling their shares in the USA; under pressure from human rights organizations in Canada, Talisman announced in October 2002 that it was to cease operations in Sudan. In September 2000 a dispute arose over the USA's threat to impose export tariffs on Canadian timber which, the USA claimed, was subsidized by the Canadian Government, and which undercut the price of US timber. Canada requested a WTO investigation into US anti-subsidy policies, after the USA imposed duties of 32% on softwood lumber imports from Canada in response. In August 2001 Canada won a preliminary victory at the WTO, which adopted a report agreeing that the Government was not subsidizing exports. Canada hoped to remove US duties and replace an earlier quota agreement, which expired in March 2001, with a system based on free trade; however, the USA imposed tariffs of 27% on softwood lumber imports from Canada in May 2002 in order to protect its own timber industry.

Following the terrorist attacks on New York and Washington, DC, on 11 September 2001, Canada and the USA increased co-operation on intelligence and security matters: under the 'Smart Border Declaration' signed by the two countries in December, 400 US National Guards were to be deployed at 43 crossings along both sides of the 6,400-km (4,000-mile) Canadian–US border. In the same month, extensive anti-terrorist legislation was also introduced. Some 750 Canadian troops were deployed in Afghanistan in February 2002 as part of the US-led international forces present in that country. The Canadian contingent assisted in the continuing military campaign against the militant Islamist al-Qa'ida (Base) organization, suspected of orchestrating the attacks on the USA; in April four Canadian troops on a training exercise in Kandahar, Afghanistan were killed in a so-called 'friendly fire' incident when US forces mistook them for members of al-Qa'ida. All Canadian forces had returned home by November 2002.

Relations with Brazil were strained in 2000 when Canada requested, and was granted, permission from the WTO to impose sanctions in response to subsidies given by the Brazilian Government to Embraer, the world's fourth largest civilian aircraft manufacturer, and close rival to the Canadian firm Bombardier. Bilateral negotiations aimed at avoiding the imposition of sanctions failed, and in December Canada received final permission to impose tariffs to the value of C $344.2m. on goods imported from Brazil, the largest such award made by the WTO; the tariffs were never actually imposed, and in 2001 the federal Government approved subsidies to two national carriers worth over US $4,100m., claiming that Brazil was still in contravention of WTO rules, and that subsidies were preferable to the cost of imposing sanctions. In December 2002 the WTO ruled that Canada had subsidized the sale of Bombardier aircraft illegally, and awarded the Brazilian Government almost US $250m. in compensation.

In the mid-1990s Canada actively sought to obtain an international ban on the manufacture and use of land-mines. At a conference held in Ottawa in December 1997, Canada became the first signatory of the Ottawa Convention, a treaty agreed by 121 countries, undertaking to discontinue the use of these armaments and providing for the destruction of existing stockpiles. However, by early 2003 the USA, the Russian Federation and the People's Republic of China had not become parties to the agreement. Humanitarian concerns remained at the forefront of Canadian foreign policy: in 1999–2001 the Government contributed forces to humanitarian and peace-keeping operations in Kosovo, East Timor, Sierra Leone and the former Yugoslav republic of Macedonia; in October 1999 the Canadian Minister of Foreign Affairs led a Commonwealth delegation to Pakistan to seek the restoration of democratic government following a military coup. In September 2000 the Canadian Government strongly urged governments of creditor nations to accelerate programmes of debt relief for Heavily Indebted Poor Countries —in December the Government announced a moratorium on debt repayments due from 11 such countries, with effect from January 2001. In June 2002 Canada hosted the G-8 summit of industrialized countries, in Kananaskis, British Columbia.

Government

Canada is a federal parliamentary state. Under the Constitution Act 1982, executive power is vested in the British monarch, as Head of State, and exercisable by her representative, the Governor-General, whom she appoints on the advice of the Canadian Prime Minister. The Federal Parliament comprises the Head of State, a nominated Senate (a maximum of 112 members, appointed on a regional basis) and a House of Commons (301 members, elected by universal adult suffrage for single-member constituencies). A Parliament may last no longer than five years. The Governor-General appoints the Prime Minister and, on the latter's recommendation, other ministers to form the Cabinet. The Prime Minister should have the confidence of the House of Commons, to which the Cabinet is responsible. Canada comprises 10 provinces (each with a Lieutenant-Governor and a legislature, which may last no longer than five years, from which a Premier is chosen), and three territories constituted by Act of Parliament.

Defence

Canada co-operates with the USA in the defence of North America and is a member of NATO. Military service is voluntary. In August 2002 the armed forces numbered 52,300: army 19,300, navy 9,000, air force 13,500, and 10,500 not identified by service. There were 35,400 reserve troops. The Federal Government's defence budget for 2001 was C \$11,400m.

Economic Affairs

In 2001, according to estimates by the World Bank, Canada's gross national income (GNI), measured at average 1999–2001 prices, was US \$661,881m., equivalent to US \$21,340 per head (or \$27,870 on an international purchasing-power parity basis). The country's population increased at an average annual rate of 1.0% in 1990–2001, while gross domestic product (GDP) per head increased, in real terms, by an average of 1.6% per year. Overall GDP increased, in real terms, at an average rate of 2.6% per year in 1990–2001; GDP increased by 4.5% in 2000 and by 1.5% in 2001.

Agriculture (including forestry and fishing) contributed 2.2% of GDP (in constant 1997 prices) in 2001 and engaged 3.3% of the labour force in 2000. The agricultural sector (excluding forestry and fishing) employed 2.2% of the economically active population in 2001. The principal crops are wheat, barley and other cereals, which, together with livestock production (chiefly cattle and pigs) and timber, provide an important source of export earnings. Canada is a leading world exporter of forest products and of fish and seafood. The production of furs is also important. In real terms, the GDP of the agricultural sector increased at an average annual rate of 1.0% in 1990–1999. Agricultural GDP decreased by 1.0% in 2000 and by a further 7.3% in 2001.

Industry (including mining, manufacturing, construction and power) provided 29.1% of GDP (in constant 1997 prices), and employed 23.4% of the active labour force, in 2001. Industrial GDP increased, in real terms, at an average annual rate of 4.7% in 1997–2000. Industrial GDP increased by 5.4% in 2000, but decreased by 2.2% in 2001.

Mining provided 3.9% of GDP (in constant 1997 prices) in 2001, but employed only 1.1% of the labour force in 2000. Canada is a major world producer of zinc, asbestos, nickel, potash and uranium. Gold, silver, iron, copper, cobalt and lead are also exploited. There are considerable reserves of petroleum and natural gas in Alberta, off the Atlantic coast and in the Canadian Arctic islands. The GDP of the mining sector increased, in real terms, at an average rate of 2.1% in 1997–2000. Mining GDP rose by 7.6% in 2000 and by 1.6% in 2001.

Manufacturing contributed 17.0% of GDP (in constant 1997 prices), and employed 15.1% of the labour force, in 2001. The principal branches of manufacturing in 2002, measured by the value of shipments, were transport equipment (accounting for 23.1% of the total), food products (12.1%), chemical products (7.3%), paper and allied products (6.3%), primary metal industries (6.2%) and wood industries (5.7%). The GDP of the sector increased, in real terms, at an average rate of 6.0% per year in 1997–2000. Manufacturing GDP increased by 5.4% in 2000, but decreased by 4.7% in 2001.

Energy is derived principally from hydroelectric power (which provided 60% of the electricity supply in 1998) and from geothermal and nuclear power-stations. In 2000 Canada's total energy production (including nuclear energy) totalled an estimated 582,268 GWh. In 2001 energy products accounted for 13.2% of Canada's exports and 5.1% of imports.

Services engaged 74.4% of the labour force, and provided 68.5% of GDP (in constant 1997 prices), in 2001. The combined GDP of the service sectors increased, in real terms, at an average rate of 4.2% per year in 1997–2000. Services GDP increased by 4.6% in 2000 and by 3.0% in 2001.

In 2001 Canada recorded a visible trade surplus of US \$41,425m., and there was a surplus of US \$19,479m. on the current account of the balance of payments. In 2001 the USA accounted for 84.6% of Canada's total exports and 72.7% of total imports; the countries of the European Union (EU, see p. 199) and Japan were also important trading partners. The principal

exports in that year were machinery and equipment, motor vehicles and parts and industrial goods. The principal imports were machinery and equipment, motor vehicles and parts and industrial goods. In January 1989 a free-trade agreement with the USA entered into force, whereby virtually all remaining trade tariffs imposed between the two countries were to be eliminated over a 10-year period. Negotiations with the USA and Mexico, aimed at the eventual creation of a full North American free-trade area, concluded in December 1992 with the signing of an agreement. The North American Free Trade Agreement (NAFTA, see p. 270) entered into operation on 1 January 1994. Since the implementation of NAFTA, however, disagreements have persisted between Canada and the USA over alleged violations of the Agreement by the US Government in relation to bilateral trade in softwood lumber, wheat and other commodities. At a third Summit of the Americas, held in Québec in April 2001, a timetable for a proposed Free Trade Area of the Americas, to take effect by 2005, was agreed upon. Negotiations commenced in late 2002 and were to conclude by January 2005. Since the mid-1990s the Canadian Government has implemented measures aimed at expanding trade in the Far East, notably with the People's Republic of China, the Republic of Korea, Indonesia and Viet Nam. In November 1996 Canada finalized a trade agreement with Chile, which would, with effect from June 1997, phase out most customs duties by 2002. In October 1998 negotiations began with the members of the European Free Trade Association (EFTA, see p. 195) for the creation of a free-trade area, while Canada has also pursued efforts to develop similar arrangements with the EU.

For the financial year 2001/2002, there was a consolidated budget surplus of C \$2,599m. The annual rate of inflation averaged 2.0% in 1990–2001. Consumer prices increased by an average of 1.7% in 1999, by 2.7% in 2000 and by 2.6% in 2001. The rate of unemployment averaged 7.6% in 1999, 11.3% in 2000 and 7.2% in 2001.

Many sectors of Canadian industry rely heavily on foreign investment. Following the international recession of the mid-1970s, Canada's average annual rate of inflation remained above 4% throughout the 1980s. A series of budgetary deficits were attributable largely to high interest rates, which continued into the early 1990s, to the detriment of a sustained economic recovery. The persistence of substantial budgetary deficits both at federal and provincial level, together with political uncertainties surrounding the future of Québec, necessitated further rises in interest levels during 1994, despite the achievement at mid-year of a negative rate of inflation. Government spending and foreign borrowing were reduced in the mid-1990s, as part of a series of deflationary measures. This emphasis on fiscal stringency led, in part, in August 1996, to the country's first current-account surplus in the balance of payments since 1984. The recovery was further aided by low rates of domestic inflation and by the beneficial effects of NAFTA on Canadian export sales to the USA and continued strongly throughout the late 1990s and early 2000s. In 2001 Canada and Mexico agreed to eliminate tariffs on goods worth an annual US \$1,950m. Proposals for the 2003/2004 budget included provisions for increased expenditure on health care and for reductions in corporate and personal rates of taxation, while achieving a budgetary surplus for the third successive year. In late 2001 the rate of inflation fell below 1%, although by the end of 2002 it had risen to 2.8%. In 2001 the Bank of Canada cut interest rates to 2.75%, the lowest level in 40 years, in an effort to reverse a weakening trend in economic activity. GDP growth in 2002 was estimated at 3.3%, the highest of any G-7 member state. Growth of 3.2% was forecast for 2003. The Government projected a combined budgetary surplus of C \$95,000m. for the period 2000–05. Five of the 10 provinces reported a budgetary surplus in 2001/02. The predominance of trade with the USA (in which Canada, assisted by currency fluctuations favourable to its exports, maintained a substantial surplus in the late 1990s and early 2000s) compensated for deficits with other major trading partners, including the EU and Japan, and allowed Canada to record substantial trade surpluses in the early 2000s. However, in spite of its strong recovery, the Canadian economy remains vulnerable to adverse movements in world prices for its major exports of raw materials. The Canadian airline industry was particularly badly affected by the terrorist attacks on the USA in September 2001: in November of that year Canada 3000, the country's second largest airline, ceased operations, and the national carrier Air Canada reported heavy losses and made 9,000 staff redundant.

Education

Education policy is a provincial responsibility, and the period of compulsory school attendance varies. French-speaking students are entitled by law, in some provinces, to instruction in French. Primary education is from the age of five or six years to 13–14, followed by three to five years at secondary or high school. In 1998/99 some 5,370,000 pupils attended primary and secondary schools. In 2002 there were 58 universities in the country. Total government budgetary expenditure on education totalled C $64,136m. (14.9% of total spending) in 2001/02.

Public Holidays*

2003: 1 January (New Year's Day), 18 April (Good Friday), 21 April (Easter Monday), 19 May (Victoria Day), 1 July (Canada Day), 1 September (Labour Day), 13 October (Thanksgiving Day), 11 November (Remembrance Day), 25 December (Christmas Day), 26 December (Boxing Day).

2004: 1 January (New Year's Day), 9 April (Good Friday), 12 April (Easter Monday), 24 May (Victoria Day), 1 July (Canada Day), 6 September (Labour Day), 11 October (Thanksgiving Day), 11 November (Remembrance Day), 25 December (Christmas Day), 26 December (Boxing Day).

*Standard public holidays comprise the listed days, together with any other day so proclaimed by individual provinces.

Weights and Measures

The metric system is in force.

Statistical Survey

Source (unless otherwise stated): Statistics Canada, Ottawa, ON K1A 0T6; tel. (613) 951-8116; fax (613) 951-0581; internet www.statcan.ca.

Area and Population

AREA, POPULATION AND DENSITY

Area (sq km)
Land	9,093,507
Inland water	891,163
Total	9,984,670*

Population (census results)†
14 May 1996	28,846,761
15 May 2001	
Males‡	14,706,850
Females‡	15,300,245
Total	30,007,094

Population (official postcensal estimates at 1 July)
2000	30,769,700
2001	31,081,900
2002	31,414,000
Density (per sq km) at 1 July 2002	3.1

* 3,855,101 sq miles.

† Excluding census data for one or more incompletely enumerated Indian reserves or Indian settlements and excluding adjustment for under-enumeration.

‡ Figures are rounded to nearest 5.

PROVINCES AND TERRITORIES
(census results, 15 May 2001)

	Land area (sq km)	Population*	Capital
Provinces:			
Alberta . . .	638,233	2,974,807	Edmonton
British Columbia .	892,677	3,907,738	Victoria
Manitoba . .	547,704	1,119,583	Winnipeg
New Brunswick. .	71,569	729,498	Fredericton
Newfoundland†. .	371,635	512,930	St John's
Nova Scotia . . .	52,841	908,007	Halifax
Ontario . . .	916,734	11,410,046	Toronto
Prince Edward			
Island . . .	5,660	135,294	Charlottetown
Québec . . .	1,357,812	7,237,479	Québec
Saskatchewan . .	570,113	978,933	Regina
Territories:			
Northwest			
Territories .	1,004,471	37,360	Yellowknife
Nunavut Territory‡	2,241,919	26,745	Iqaluit
Yukon Territory	531,844	28,674	Whitehorse
Total	**9,203,210**	**30,007,094**	—

* Excluding census data for one or more incompletely enumerated Indian reserves or Indian settlements.

† Newfoundland and Labrador from December 2001.

‡ Formerly part of Northwest Territories. Constituted as a separate Territory with effect from 1 April 1999.

PRINCIPAL METROPOLITAN AREAS
(census results, 15 May 2001)

Toronto . . .	4,682,897	London	432,451
Montréal*. . .	3,426,350	Kitchener	414,284
Vancouver . .	1,986,965	St Catharines–	
		Niagara.	377,009
Ottawa–Hull			
(capital). . .	1,063,664	Halifax	359,183
Edmonton. . .	951,395	Victoria	311,902
Calgary . . .	937,845	Windsor	307,877
Québec . . .	682,757	Oshawa	296,298
Winnipeg . . .	671,274	Saskatoon. . . .	225,927
Hamilton . . .	662,401		

* Excluding census data for one or more incompletely enumerated Indian reserves or Indian settlements.

BIRTHS, MARRIAGES AND DEATHS

	Registered live births*		Registered marriages		Registered deaths*	
	Number	Rate (per 1,000)	Number	Rate (per 1,000)	Number	Rate (per 1,000)
1992 . .	398,642	14.0	164,573	5.8	196,535	6.9
1993 . .	388,394	13.5	159,316	5.6	204,912	7.1
1994 . .	385,112	13.3	159,959	5.5	207,077	7.1
1995 . .	378,011	12.9	160,251	5.5	210,733	7.2
1996 . .	366,200	12.3	156,692	5.3	212,859	7.2
1997 . .	348,598	11.6	153,306	5.1	215,669	7.2
1998 . .	342,418	11.3	153,190	5.1	219,834	7.3
1999 . .	335,627	11.0	153,380	5.0	225,123	7.4

* Including Canadian residents temporarily in the USA but excluding US residents temporarily in Canada.

Expectation of life (WHO estimates, years at birth): 79.3 (males 76.6; females 81.9) in 2001 (Source: WHO, *World Health Report*).

IMMIGRATION

Country of Origin	1999	2000	2001*
United Kingdom	4,626	4,829	5,549
USA	5,522	5,791	5,889
Other	179,817	216,380	238,617
Total	**189,965**	**227,000**	**250,055**

* Preliminary.

ECONOMICALLY ACTIVE POPULATION*
(annual averages, '000 persons aged 15 years and over)

	1999	2000	2001
Agriculture	410.3	372.6	328.6
Forestry, fishing, mining, petroleum and gas	267.5	283.0	293.1
Utilities	115.8	116.4	123.0
Construction	774.8	815.6	843.3
Manufacturing	2,217.4	2,280.2	2,274.5
Trade	2,248.3	2,318.1	2,383.6
Transportation and warehousing	744.5	779.8	773.2
Finance, insurance, real estate and leasing	862.9	867.0	874.5
Professional, scientific and technical services	905.0	945.9	987.0
Management, administrative and other support	507.2	546.2	555.3
Educational services	982.6	974.8	966.2
Health care and social assistance	1,444.4	1,526.4	1,542.1
Information, culture and recreation	630.0	665.5	707.2
Accommodation and food services	924.8	960.0	976.0
Public administration	774.2	761.7	766.4
Other services	721.6	695.8	682.7
Total employed	14,531.2	14,909.7	15,076.8
Unemployed	1,190.1	1,089.6	1,169.6
Total labour force	15,721.2	15,999.2	16,246.3
Males	8,534.0	8,649.2	8,769.2
Females	7,187.2	7,350.0	7,477.1

* Figures exclude military personnel, inmates of institutions, residents of the Yukon, Northwest and Nunavut Territories, and Indian Reserves.

Health and Welfare

KEY INDICATORS

Total fertility rate (children per woman, 2001)	1.6
Under-5 mortality rate (per 1,000 live births, 2001)	7
HIV/AIDS (% of persons aged 15–49, 2001)	0.3
Physicians (per 1,000 head, 1995)	2.29
Hospital beds (per 1,000 head, 1998)	4.1
Health expenditure (2000): US $ per head (PPP)	2,058
Health expenditure (2000): % of GDP	9.1
Health expenditure (2000): public (% of total)	72.0
Access to water (% of persons, 2000)	100
Access to sanitation (% of persons, 2000)	100
Human Development Index (2000): ranking	3
Human Development Index (2000): value	0.940

For sources and definitions, see explanatory note on p. vi.

Agriculture

PRINCIPAL CROPS
('000 metric tons)

	1999	2000	2001
Wheat	26,900.0	26,804.1	21,282.1
Barley	13,196.0	13,468.1	11,354.9
Corn for grain	9,161.3	6,826.7	8,170.8
Rye	386.6	260.3	193.9
Oats	3,641.3	3,389.4	2,769.2
Buckwheat	12.5	13.6	14.3
Mixed grain	446.8	382.1	370.6
Potatoes	4,253.0	4,568.5	n.a.
Beans (dry)	284.5	261.4	251.5
Peas (dry)	2,251.9	2,864.3	2,196.4
Soybeans	2,780.9	2,703.0	1,591.8
Sunflower seed	121.9	119.3	97.7
Rapeseed (Canola)	8,798.3	7,118.7	5,062.0
Linseed	1,022.4	693.4	702.3
Mustard seed	306.4	202.2	88.9
Sugar beets	743.9	821.0	544.3
Tame hay	26,739.2	23,145.1	19,103.6
Fodder corn	6,605.2	5,865.8	6,091.7

LIVESTOCK
('000 head at 1 July)

	2000	2001	2002
Milch cows	1,127	n.a.	1,072
Beef cattle	4,452	n.a.	4,752
Sheep	979	1,248	1,253
Pigs	12,301	14,050	14,594

LIVESTOCK PRODUCTS

	1998	1999	2000
Beef and veal (metric tons)	1,183,242	1,265,448	1,245,589
Mutton and lamb (metric tons)	9,819	10,510	10,788
Pig meat (metric tons)	1,391,962	1,566,414	1,638,218
Poultry meat (metric tons)	962,658	1,005,754	1,054,088
Milk (kilolitres)	7,456,000	7,589,501	7,496,212
Creamery butter (metric tons)	85,935	88,824	76,852
Cheddar cheese (metric tons)	127,446	128,251	134,829
Ice-cream mix (kilolitres)	154,802	151,948	137,857
Eggs ('000 dozen)	498,847	523,161	549,711

Forestry

ROUNDWOOD REMOVALS
(1999, '000 cubic metres)*

	Softwoods	Hardwoods	Total
Alberta†	12,008	7,387	19,395
British Columbia	74,324	2,606	76,933
Manitoba	1,560	611	2,171
New Brunswick	7,409	3,850	11,259
Newfoundland‡§	2,610	110	2,720
Nova Scotia	5,432	732	6,164
Ontario‡	18,399	6,415	24,814
Prince Edward Island	542	150	693
Québec	34,738	10,863	45,601
Saskatchewan	1,670	1,677	3,348
Total ‡	158,763	34,402	193,168

* Data for Northwest, Nunavut and Yukon Territories undisclosed.
† Preliminary.
‡ Estimates. The total includes undisclosed territorial data, except for Yukon.
§ Newfoundland and Labrador from December 2001 .

SAWNWOOD PRODUCTION
(million board feet)

	1998	1999	2000
Coniferous (softwood)	63,807.9	68,528.5	68,557.0
Broadleaved (hardwood)	1,002.2	1,051.0	1,082.6
Total	64,810.1	69,530.9	69,639.9

Fur Industry

NUMBER OF PELTS PRODUCED

	1998	1999	2000
Alberta	n.a.	n.a.	n.a.
British Columbia	231,332	270,671	267,020
Manitoba	138,940	125,542	158,406
New Brunswick	n.a.	n.a.	n.a
Newfoundland*	n.a.	n.a.	n.a
Northwest Territories†	14,952	37,124	13,092
Nova Scotia	383,107	426,219	448,354
Nunavut Territory	7,440	9,743	9,870
Ontario	599,018	613,764	468,359
Prince Edward Island	41,429	29,166	29,758
Québec	294,534	270,626	270,076
Saskatchewan	82,887	88,565	87,809
Yukon Territory	7,195	7,419	6,406
Total ‡	2,062,189	2,130,515	1,968,840

* Newfoundland and Labrador from December 2001.
† Includes Nunavut Territory.
‡ Includes undisclosed provincial and territorial data.

Fishing

('000 metric tons, live weight)

	1998	1999	2000
Capture	1,013.8	1,027.3	993.6
Atlantic cod	37.7	55.4	46.7
Capelin	38.2	23.5	21.5
Atlantic herring	190.9	202.0	201.7
Pacific herring	33.5	28.8	27.7
Queen crab	75.2	95.1	93.4
American lobster	41.0	43.4	43.6
Northern prawn	78.9	85.3	100.1
Other Pandalus shrimps	29.0	30.6	26.4
American sea scallop	56.4	54.8	83.8
Clams	29.3	30.5	27.1
Aquaculture	91.0	113.0	123.3
Atlantic salmon	49.5	62.0	68.4
Total catch	1,063.3	1,140.3	1,116.9

Note: Figures exclude aquatic plants ('000 metric tons, capture only): 27.5 in 1998; 30.7 in 1999; 14.8 in 2000. Also excluded are aquatic mammals, recorded by number rather than weight. The number of whales caught was: 1 in 1998; 0 in 1999; 1 in 2000. The number of seals caught was: 260,421 in 1998; 229,697 in 1999; 275,761 in 2000.

Sources: FAO, *Yearbook of Fishery Statistics*; Department of Fisheries and Oceans.

Mining

('000 metric tons, unless otherwise indicated)

	1999	2000	2001
Metallic			
Bismuth (metric tons)	217	202	258
Cadmium (metric tons)	1,115	934	1,058
Cobalt (metric tons)	2,014	2,022	2,048
Copper (metric tons)	581,582	621,888	611,159
Gold (kilograms)	157,617	153,715	157,853
Iron ore	33,789	35,247	26,981
Lead (metric tons)	155,369	143,303	149,429
Molybdenum (metric tons)	6,250	6,980	8,540
Nickel (metric tons)	176,749	181,138	183,643
Platinum group (kilograms)	13,872	15,304	18,154
Selenium (metric tons)	359	335	261
Silver (metric tons)	1,174	1,169	1,224
Uranium (metric tons)	10,157	9,921	12,982
Zinc (metric tons)	963,320	935,713	1,009,570
Non-metallic			
Asbestos	337	310	294
Gypsum	9,345	8,572	8,119
Nepheline syenite	676	717	734
Potash (K_2O)	8,475	9,033	8,184
Salt	12,686	12,164	13,548
Sulphur, in smelter gas	843	831	832
Sulphur, elemental	8,656	8,621	8,080
Fuels			
Coal	72,497	69,163	70,361
Natural gas (million cubic metres)	162,218	167,790	171,966
Natural gas by-products ('000 cubic metres)	28,805	30,543	29,789
Petroleum, crude ('000 cubic metres)	122,247	127,809	130,526
Structural materials:			
Cement	12,625	12,612	12,986
Stone	109,184	118,222	119,805

Source: Natural Resources Canada.

Industry

VALUE OF SHIPMENTS
(preliminary figures, C $ million)

	2000	2001	2002
Food industries	58,474.8	62,233.4	62,867.6
Beverage and tobacco products industries	12,264.0	12,826.7	13,309.0
Textile mills	3,760.6	3,331.4	3,200.1
Textile product mills	2,666.1	2,507.1	2,514.2
Clothing industries	7,379.9	6,991.9	6,799.2
Leather and allied products industries	896.8	862.1	777.5
Wood product industries	28,982.3	27,525.7	29,490.2
Paper industries	36,909.3	34,232.1	32,733.3
Printing, publishing and allied industries	10,577.3	10,492.0	10,067.9
Petroleum and coal products industries	32,491.9	32,000.2	32,363.4
Chemical and chemical products industries	35,207.3	36,315.2	37,779.3
Plastics and rubber products industries	21,075.8	21,555.0	23,026.2
Non-metallic mineral products industries	10,202.2	10,559.9	11,591.8
Primary metal industries	31,360.2	29,615.3	32,206.5
Fabricated metal products industries	27,225.1	26,767.1	27,543.5
Machinery industries (excl. electrical machinery)	24,948.2	23,793.4	24,304.6
Computer and electronic products industries	37,537.6	25,462.0	21,290.6
Electrical equipment, appliance and component industries	11,670.3	10,106.5	9,338.0
Transportation equipment industries	125,750.4	114,524.7	119,725.2
Furniture and fixture industries	12,326.0	12,009.0	12,290.8
Other manufacturing industries	5,299.2	5,093.0	5,552.5
Total	537,005.5	508,803.6	518,771.1

Electric energy (net production, million kWh): 575,150 in 1997; 543,100 in 1998; 541,900 in 1999.

Finance

CURRENCY AND EXCHANGE RATES

Monetary Units
100 cents = 1 Canadian dollar (C $)

Sterling, US Dollar and Euro Equivalents (31 December 2002)
£1 sterling = C $2.5460
US $1 = C $1.5796
€1 = C $1.6565
C $100 = £39.28 = US $63.31 = €60.37

Average Exchange Rate (C $ per US $)
2000   1.4851
2001   1.5488
2002   1.5693

BUDGET
(C $ million, year ending 31 March)*

Revenue	1999/00	2000/01	2001/02
Income taxes	177,830	189,993	185,085
Personal income taxes	138,194	142,475	141,798
Corporation income taxes	35,810	42,757	38,899
Property and related taxes	40,106	40,859	40,941
Consumption taxes	80,007	87,096	89,030
General sales taxes	51,386	55,517	56,644
Health insurance premiums	1,949	2,178	2,239
Contributions to social security plans	29,759	30,445	29,759
Other taxes	3,545	3,681	3,935
Sales of goods and services	32,759	36,302	34,410
Investment income	28,879	38,699	32,088
Other revenue from own sources	7,462	5,056	4,115
Total own source revenue	413,293	445,754	432,912

Expenditure	1999/00	2000/01	2001/02
General government services	13,640	16,595	14,571
Protection of persons and property	31,733	32,349	33,980
Transport and communications	18,464	16,965	17,877
Health	64,789	72,789	76,937
Social services	104,375	109,164	113,062
Education	59,104	61,306	64,136
Resource conservation and industrial development	13,976	15,219	15,536
Environment	8,690	9,064	9,223
Recreation and culture	9,699	10,322	10,686
Labour, employment and immigration	3,266	3,127	3,023
Housing	3,813	4,247	4,116
Foreign affairs and international assistance	4,256	4,452	4,257
Regional planning and development	1,772	1,662	1,796
Research establishments	2,071	1,482	2,058
Debt charges	60,173	62,433	56,654
Other expenditures	239	2,546	2,394
Total expenditure	400,069	423,730	430,313

*Figures refer to the consolidated accounts of federal, provincial and territorial governments.

INTERNATIONAL RESERVES
(US $ million at 31 December)

	2000	2001	2002
Gold*	323	291	205
IMF special drawing rights	574	614	719
Reserve position in IMF	2,509	2,863	3,580
Foreign exchange	28,841	30,484	32,685
Total	32,247	34,253	37,189

* National valuation.

Source: IMF, *International Financial Statistics*.

MONEY SUPPLY
(C $ million at 31 December)

	2000	2001	2002
Currency outside banks	36,344	38,657	41,130
Demand deposits at deposit money banks	188,579	214,888	227,083
Total money (incl. others)	224,923	253,545	268,213

Source: IMF, *International Financial Statistics*.

COST OF LIVING
(Consumer Price Index; base: 1992 = 100)

	1999	2000	2001
Food	110.7	112.2	117.2
Housing	105.1	108.8	112.8
Household expenses and furnishings	109.0	110.0	112.2
Clothing	105.3	105.5	106.0
Transport	124.5	130.7	130.8
Health and personal care	110.2	112.0	114.2
Recreation, education and reading	119.6	122.5	124.3
Tobacco and alcohol	94.5	97.6	105.1
All items	110.5	113.5	116.4

NATIONAL ACCOUNTS

National Income and Product
(C $ million at current prices)

	1999	2000	2001
Compensation of employees	502,726	545,110	568,864
Operating surplus	225,918	257,875	251,136
Domestic factor incomes	728,644	802,985	820,000
Consumption of fixed capital	128,625	135,781	144,315
Gross domestic product at factor cost	857,269	938,766	964,315
Indirect taxes, *less* subsidies	123,588	127,745	127,947
Statistical discrepancy	−333	−1,516	−16
GDP at market prices	980,524	1,064,995	1,092,246
Net factor income from abroad	−29,788	−22,368	−24,371
Gross national product	950,736	1,042,627	1,067,875
Less Consumption of fixed capital	128,625	135,781	144,315
Statistical discrepancy	333	1,516	15
National income at market prices	822,444	908,362	923,575
Other current transfers from abroad	5,643	6,098	7,024
Less Other current transfers paid abroad	4,636	4,624	5,074
National disposable income	823,451	909,836	925,525

Expenditure on the Gross Domestic Product
(C $ million at current prices)

	1999	2000	2001
Government final consumption expenditure	185,317	196,004	204,492
Private final consumption expenditure	560,954	594,089	620,777
Increase in stocks	4,984	8,052	−6,027
Gross fixed capital formation	195,297	209,937	216,487
Total domestic expenditure	946,552	1,008,082	1,035,729
Exports of goods and services	421,796	484,331	473,000
Less Imports of goods and services	388,157	428,934	416,498
Statistical discrepancy	333	1,516	15
GDP at market prices	980,524	1,064,995	1,092,246
GDP at constant 1997 prices	968,451	1,012,335	1,027,523

Gross Domestic Product by Economic Activity
(C $ million at constant 1997 prices)

	1999	2000	2001
Agriculture, hunting, forestry and fishing	23,112	22,880	21,210
Mining, petroleum and gas extraction	33,901	36,461	37,062
Manufacturing	160,150	168,825	160,935
Electricity, gas and water	26,705	27,960	27,288
Construction	46,529	48,498	50,346
Trade, restaurants and hotels	120,012	126,583	128,721
Transportation and warehousing	43,306	45,265	44,531
Finance, insurance, real estate and business services	174,227	180,834	186,989
Education	43,319	43,574	43,888
Health care and social assistance	53,199	53,921	54,989
Public administration	51,082	52,057	53,826
Other services	118,022	128,568	136,841
GDP at factor cost	893,564	935,426	948,108
Taxes, less subsidies, on products	74,887	76,909	79,415
GDP in purchasers' values	968,451	1,012,335	1,027,523

BALANCE OF PAYMENTS
(US $ million)

	1999	2000	2001
Exports of goods f.o.b.	247,240	286,476	267,915
Imports of goods f.o.b.	−220,159	−244,714	−226,490
Trade balance	27,080	41,763	41,425
Exports of services	35,715	38,496	36,576
Imports of services	−40,517	−43,493	−42,000
Balance on goods and services	22,278	36,766	36,001
Other income received	22,165	26,811	22,633
Other income paid	−43,759	−45,970	−40,411
Balance on goods, services and income	685	17,607	18,223
Current transfers received	3,796	4,109	4,535
Current transfers paid	−3,114	−3,120	−3,280
Current balance	1,367	18,596	19,479
Capital account (net)	3,400	3,552	3,673
Direct investment abroad	−15,623	−47,311	35,567
Direct investment from abroad	24,488	66,017	27,438
Portfolio investment assets	−15,556	−41,866	−24,468
Portfolio investment liabilities	2,315	9,875	19,750
Other investment assets	9,395	−2,759	−8,940
Other investment liabilities	−11,489	1,749	6,780
Net errors and omissions	7,637	−4,133	−5,972
Overall balance	5,933	3,720	2,172

Source: IMF, *International Financial Statistics*.

External Trade

PRINCIPAL COMMODITIES
(C $ million)

Imports f.o.b.	1999	2000	2001
Agricultural and fishing products	17,665.5	18,558.3	20,359.1
Energy products	10,707.9	17,860.1	17,752.7
Crude petroleum	7,160.3	13,436.6	12,814.5
Industrial goods and materials	62,173.3	70,476.3	68,456.6
Metals and metal ores	14,097.9	16,680.3	15,230.4
Chemicals and plastics	22,668.4	24,451.1	25,199.8
Machinery and equipment (excl. automotive products)	108,247.5	122,786.9	112,422.4
Industrial and agricultural machinery	27,813.3	29,805.5	28,194.4
Aircraft and other transportation equipment	13,240.6	14,583.6	16,233.0
Office machines and equipment	16,902.7	19,297.7	17,748.9
Automotive products	75,933.7	77,430.8	72,545.5
Passenger automobiles and chassis	19,589.8	21,723.3	22,216.2
Trucks and other motor vehicles	10,652.0	10,751.8	9,593.9
Motor vehicle parts	45,691.9	44,955.7	40,735.4
Other consumer goods	36,999.4	40,109.3	42,926.9
Total (incl. others)	326,961.2	363,431.8	350,622.7

Exports f.o.b.	1999	2000	2001
Agricultural and fishing products	25,572.2	27,501.4	30,883.4
Energy products	29,821.1	53,159.1	54,743.1
Crude petroleum	11,017.1	19,165.9	15,370.2
Natural gas	10,951.4	20,536.8	25,595.1
Forestry products	39,744.3	42,163.7	39,309.2
Lumber and sawmill products	19,996.9	18,682.1	17,762.6
Newsprint and other paper and paperboard products	13,043.6	14,560.7	14,835.6
Industrial goods and materials	59,412.5	67,245.2	66,797.4
Chemicals, plastics and fertilizers	19,492.0	22,804.8	23,428.5
Metals and alloys	18,355.9	20,649.4	20,220.9
Machinery and equipment (excl. automotive products)	87,920.7	107,798.7	99,732.1
Industrial and agricultural machinery	17,058.5	18,790.2	19,230.8
Aircraft and other transportation equipment	18,104.7	20,030.8	23,899.9
Automotive products	97,291.7	98,112.2	92,860.9
Passenger automobiles and chassis	51,059.2	51,501.8	48,525.3
Trucks and other motor vehicles	19,399.4	18,174.1	17,336.4
Motor vehicle parts	26,832.6	28,436.3	26,999.2
Other consumer goods	13,690.6	14,898.6	15,972.8
Total (incl. others)	367,170.9	425,587.2	414,638.2

PRINCIPAL TRADING PARTNERS
(C $ million, balance of payments basis)

Imports	1999	2000	2001
Japan	10,592.2	11,728.6	10,585.2
United Kingdom	7,685.4	12,287.0	11,863.4
USA	249,420.6	267,753.6	255,028.2
Other European Union countries	20,765.8	21,176.3	23,225.1
Other OECD countries	13,257.2	18,947.1	18,626.2
Other countries	25,240.1	31,539.3	31,294.7
Total	326,961.2	363,431.8	350,622.7

Exports	1999	2000	2001
Japan	9,855.3	10,701.3	9,481.5
United Kingdom	5,844.1	6,903.1	6,573.5
USA	309,075.1	359,671.6	350,908.1
Other European Union countries	14,068.0	15,982.0	15,726.7
Other OECD countries	9,514.4	10,899.3	10,925.4
Other countries	18,814.1	21,429.9	21,023.0
Total	367,170.9	425,587.2	414,638.2

Transport

RAILWAYS
(revenue traffic)*

	1998	1999	2000
Passengers carried ('000)	4,011	4,130	4,230
Passenger-km ('000)	11,832	11,628	11,645
Freight carried ('000 tons)	292,572	319,918	328,172
Freight ton-km ('000 tons)	292,572	319,918	328,172

* Intercity trains only.

ROAD TRAFFIC
('000 vehicles registered at 31 December)

	1999	2000	2001
Total vehicle registrations	23,637.1	23,627.4	23,427.2
Total road motor vehicle registrations	17,534.3	17,882.2	18,101.7
Passenger cars and light trucks	16,538	16,832.2	17,054.8
Heavy trucks	649	661.4	654.5
Buses	73	77.3	74.1
Motorcycles and mopeds	274	311.3	318.3
Trailers	4,145.3	3,988.9	4,023.2
Other (off-road, construction, farm vehicles, etc.)	1,957.5	1,756.3	1,302.3

INLAND WATER TRAFFIC
(St Lawrence Seaway, '000 metric tons)

	1998	1999	2000
Montréal—Lake Ontario . . .	39,264	36,400	35,406
Welland Canal	40,657	37,422	36,572

Source: St Lawrence Seaway Management Corporation.

SHIPPING

Merchant Fleet
(registered at 31 December)

	1999	2000	2001
Number of vessels	857	861	875
Total displacement ('000 grt) . .	2,495.9	2,657.6	2,727.0

Source: Lloyd's Register of Shipping, *World Fleet Statistics*.

International Sea-borne Freight Traffic

	1997	1998	1999
Goods ('000 metric tons):			
loaded	187,945	179,107	178,872
unloaded	94,704	100,377	101,555
Vessels (number):			
arrived	27,614	27,856	26,097
departed	27,549	27,959	25,889

CIVIL AVIATION
(Major Canadian airlines, '000)

	1999	2000	2001
Passengers	24,578	25,049	23,495
Passenger-km.	65,699,586	68,215,299	64,117,271
Goods ton-km.	2,013,821	1,930,970	1,631,127

Tourism

	1998	1999	2000
Travellers from the USA:			
number ('000)	14,893	15,180	15,225
expenditure (C $ million). . .	6,703	7,149	7,448
Travellers from other countries:			
number ('000)	3,935	4,187	4,393
expenditure (C $ million). . .	4,462	4,892	5,188

Communications Media

	1998	1999	2000
Total households ('000) . . .	11,385	11,553	11,699
Homes with television ('000) . .	11,235	11,418	11,575
Homes with telephone ('000) . .	11,165	11,343	11,433
Facsimile machines ('000 in use)* .	5,320	n.a.	n.a
Mobile cellular telephones ('000			
subscribers)*	5,365.5	6,911.0	8,751.3
Personal computers ('000 in use)* .	10,000	11,000	12,000
Internet users ('000)*	7,500	11,000	12,700

2001: Mobile cellular telephones ('000 subscribers)* 9,923.9; Internet users ('000)* 13,500; Daily newspapers 101; Non-daily newspapers 1,100.

* Source: International Telecommunication Union.

Book production (titles): 17,931 in 1995; 19,900 in 1996 (Source: UNESCO, *Statistical Yearbook*).

Education
(1998/99)

	Institutions	Teachers*	Pupils*
Primary and secondary . . .	15,637	300,261	5,370,000
Post-secondary colleges . . .	274	65,753	984,000
Universities.	75	33,665	580,000

* Full-time only.

Directory

The Constitution

Under the Constitution Act 1982, which entered into force on 17 April 1982, executive authority is vested in the Sovereign, and exercised in her name by a Governor-General and Privy Council. Legislative power is exercised by a Parliament of two Houses, the Senate and the House of Commons. The Constitution includes a Charter of Rights and Freedoms, and provisions which recognize the nation's multicultural heritage, affirm the existing rights of native peoples, confirm the principle of equalization of benefits among the provinces and strengthen provincial ownership of natural resources.

THE GOVERNMENT
The national government operates through three main agencies: Parliament (consisting of the Sovereign as represented by the Governor-General, the Senate and the House of Commons), which makes the laws; the Executive (the Cabinet or Ministry), which applies the laws; and the Judiciary, which interprets the laws.

The Prime Minister is appointed by the Governor-General and is habitually the leader of the political party commanding the confidence of the House of Commons. He chooses the members of his Cabinet from members of his party in Parliament, principally from those in the House of Commons. Each Minister or member of the Cabinet is usually responsible for the administration of a department, although there may be Ministers without portfolio whose experience and counsel are drawn upon to strengthen the Cabinet, but who are not at the head of departments. Each Minister of a department is responsible to Parliament for that department, and the Cabinet is collectively responsible before Parliament for government policy and administration generally.

Meetings of the Cabinet are presided over by the Prime Minister. From the Cabinet, signed orders and recommendations go to the Governor-General for his or her approval, and the Crown acts only on the advice of its responsible Ministers. The Cabinet takes the responsibility for its advice being in accordance with the support of Parliament and is held strictly accountable.

THE FEDERAL PARLIAMENT
Parliament must meet at least once a year, so that 12 months do not elapse between the last meeting in one session and the first meeting in the next. The duration of Parliament may not be longer than five years from the date of election of a House of Commons. Senators (normally a maximum of 104 in number) are appointed until age 75 by the Governor-General in Council. They must be at least 30 years of age, residents of the province they represent and in possession of C $4,000 of real property over and above their liabilities. Members of the House of Commons are elected by universal adult suffrage for the duration of a Parliament.

Under the Constitution, the federal Parliament has exclusive legislative authority in all matters relating to public debt and property; regulation of trade and commerce; raising of money by any mode of taxation; borrowing of money on the public credit; postal service, census and statistics; militia, military and naval service and defence; fixing and providing for salaries and allowances of the officers of the Government; beacons, buoys and lighthouses; navigation and shipping; quarantine and the establishment and maintenance of marine hospitals; sea-coast and inland fisheries; ferries on an international or interprovincial frontier; currency and coinage; banking, incorporation of banks, and issue of paper money; savings banks; weights and measures; bills of exchange and promissory notes; interest; legal tender; bankruptcy and insolvency; patents of invention and discovery; copyrights; Indians and lands reserved for Indians; naturalization and aliens; marriage and divorce; the criminal law, except the constitution of courts of criminal jurisdiction but including the procedure in criminal matters; the establishment, maintenance and management of penitentiaries; such classes of subjects as are expressly excepted in the enumeration of the classes of subjects exclusively assigned to the Legislatures of the provinces by the Act. Judicial interpretation and later amendment have, in certain cases, modified or clearly defined the respective powers of the federal Government and provincial governments.

Both the Parliament of Canada and the legislatures of the provinces may legislate with respect to agriculture and immigration, but provincial legislation shall have effect in and for the provinces as long and as far only as it is not repugnant to any Act of Parliament. Both Parliament and the provincial legislatures may legislate with respect to old age pensions and supplementary benefits, but no federal law shall affect the operation of any present or future law of a province in relation to these matters.

PROVINCIAL AND MUNICIPAL GOVERNMENT

In each of the 10 provinces the Sovereign is represented by a Lieutenant-Governor, appointed by the Governor-General in Council, and acting on the advice of the Ministry or Executive Council, which is responsible to the Legislature and resigns office when it ceases to enjoy the confidence of that body. The Legislatures are unicameral, consisting of an elected Legislative Assembly and the Lieutenant-Governor. The duration of a Legislature may not exceed five years from the date of the election of its members.

The Legislature in each province may exclusively make laws in relation to: amendment of the constitution of the province, except as regards the Lieutenant-Governor; direct taxation within the province; borrowing of money on the credit of the province; establishment and tenure of provincial offices and appointment and payment of provincial officers; the management and sale of public lands belonging to the province and of the timber and wood thereon; the establishment, maintenance and management of public and reformatory prisons in and for the province; the establishment, maintenance and management of hospitals, asylums, charities and charitable institutions in and for the province other than marine hospitals; municipal institutions in the province; shop, saloon, tavern, auctioneer and other licences issued for the raising of provincial or municipal revenue; local works and undertakings other than interprovincial or international lines of ships, railways, canals, telegraphs, etc., or works which, though wholly situated within the province are declared by the federal Parliament to be for the general advantage either of Canada or two or more provinces; the incorporation of companies with provincial objects; the solemnization of marriage in the province; property and civil rights in the province; the administration of justice in the province, including the constitution, maintenance and organization of provincial courts both in civil and criminal jurisdiction, and including procedure in civil matters in these courts; the imposition of punishment by fine, penalty or imprisonment for enforcing any law of the province relating to any of the aforesaid subjects; generally all matters of a merely local or private nature in the province. Further, provincial Legislatures may exclusively make laws in relation to education, subject to the protection of religious minorities; and to non-renewable natural resources, forestry resources and electrical energy, including their export from one province to another, and to the right to impose any mode or system of taxation thereon, subject in both cases to such laws not being discriminatory.

Under the Constitution Act, the municipalities are the creations of the provincial governments. Their bases of organization and the extent of their authority vary in different provinces, but almost everywhere they have very considerable powers of local self-government.

The Government

Head of State: HM Queen Elizabeth II (succeeded to the throne 6 February 1952).

Governor-General: Adrienne Clarkson (took office 7 October 1999).

FEDERAL MINISTRY
(April 2003)

Prime Minister: Jean Chrétien.

Deputy Prime Minister, Minister of Finance and Minister responsible for Border Issues: John Manley.

Minister of Transport, with responsibility for five Crown Corporations: David Collenette.

Minister of the Environment: David Anderson.

Minister of Natural Resources: Herb Dhaliwal.

Minister of Public Works and Government Services, Minister responsible for the Office of Indian Residential Schools Resolution, Minister responsible for the Canadian Wheat Board and Federal Interlocutor for Metis and Non-Status Indians: Ralph Goodale.

Minister of Industry, Minister responsible for Infrastructure and Minister responsible for the Atlantic Canada Opportunities Agency, for the Western Economic Diversification and Francophonie, for the Economic Development Agency of Canada for the Regions of Québec and for Rural Development: Allan Rock.

Minister of Canadian Heritage: Sheila Copps.

Minister of Foreign Affairs: Bill Graham.

Minister of National Defence: John McCallum.

Minister of Justice and Attorney-General: Martin Cauchon.

Minister of Health: Anne McLennan.

Solicitor-General: Wayne Easter.

Minister of State and Leader of the Government in the House of Commons: Don Boudria.

President of the Treasury Board and Minister responsible for Crown Corporation Policy: Lucienne Robillard.

Minister of National Revenue: Elinor Caplan.

Minister of Human Resources Development: Jane Stewart.

President of the Queen's Privy Council for Canada and Minister of Intergovernmental Affairs: Stéphane Dion.

Minister for International Trade: Pierre Pettigrew.

Minister of Agriculture and Agri-Food: Lyle Vanclief.

Minister of Fisheries and Oceans: Robert Thibault.

Minister of Veterans' Affairs and Secretary of State (Science, Research and Development): Dr Rey Pagtakhan.

Minister of Labour: Claudette Bradshaw.

Minister of Indian Affairs and Northern Development: Robert Nault.

Minister for International Co-operation: Susan Whelan.

Minister of Citizenship and Immigration: Denis Coderre.

Minister of State for the Atlantic Canada Opportunities Agency: Gerry Byrne.

Leader of the Government in the Senate: Sharon Carstairs.

Secretary of State (Children and Youth): Ethel Blondin-Andrew.

Secretary of State (Latin America and Africa and Francophonie): Denis Paradis.

Secretary of State (Central and Eastern Europe, Middle East): Gar Knutson.

Secretary of State (International Financial Institutions): Maurizio Bevilacqua.

Secretary of State (Parks, Rural Development and Federal Economic Development Initiative for Northern Ontario): Andrew Mitchell.

Secretary of State for Western Economic Diversification, Indian Affairs and Northern Development: Stephen Owen.

Secretary of State for the Economic Development Agency of Canada for the Regions of Québec: Claude Drouin.

Secretary of State (Amateur Sport) and Deputy Leader of the Government in the House of Commons: Paul DeVilliers.

Secretary of State (Asia–Pacific): David Kilgour.

MINISTRIES

Office of the Prime Minister: Langevin Block, 80 Wellington St, Ottawa, ON K1A 0A3; tel. (613) 992-4211; fax (613) 941-6900; e-mail pm@pm.gc.ca; internet www.pm.gc.ca.

Agriculture and Agri-Food Canada: Sir John Carling Bldg, 930 Carling Ave, Ottawa, ON K1A 0C5; tel. (613) 759-1000; fax (613) 759-6726; e-mail PIRS@em.agr.ca; internet www.agr.ca.

Canadian Heritage: Immeuble Jules Léger, 25 rue Eddy, Hull, QC K1A 0M5; tel. (819) 997-0055; fax (819) 953-5382; internet www.pch.gc.ca.

Citizenship and Immigration Canada: Jean Edmonds Towers, 365 ave Laurier ouest, Ottawa, ON K1A 1L1; tel. (613) 954-9019; fax (613) 954-2221; internet www.cic.gc.ca.

Department of Justice Canada: East Memorial Bldg, 284 Wellington St, Ottawa, ON K1A 0H8; tel. (613) 957-4222; fax (613) 954-0811; e-mail webadmin@justice.gc.ca; internet www.canada.justice.gc.ca.

Environment Canada: Ottawa, ON K1A 0H3; tel. (819) 997-2800; fax (819) 953-2225; e-mail enviroinfo@ec.gc.ca; internet www.ec.gc.ca.

Finance Canada: L'Esplanade Laurier, 140 O'Connor St, Ottawa, ON K1A 0G5; tel. (613) 992-1573; fax (613) 996-8404; e-mail consltcomm@fin.gc.ca; internet www.fin.gc.ca.

Fisheries and Oceans Canada: 200 Kent St, Ottawa, ON K1A 0E6; tel. (613) 993-0999; fax (613) 990-1866; e-mail info@www.ncr.dfo.ca; internet www.dfo-mpo.gc.ca.

Foreign Affairs and International Trade Canada: Lester B. Pearson Bldg, 125 Sussex Dr., Ottawa, ON K1A 0G2; tel. (613) 996-9134; fax (613) 952-3904; e-mail infotech@dfait-maeci.gc.ca; internet www.dfait-maeci.gc.ca.

Health Canada: Brooke Claxton Bldg, Tunney's Pasture, Ottawa, ON K1A 0K9; tel. (613) 957-2991; fax (613) 941-5366; e-mail info@hc-sc.gc.ca; internet www.hc-sc.gc.ca.

Human Resources Development Canada: 140 promenade du Portage, Hull, QC K1A 0J9; tel. (819) 994-6313; fax (819) 953-7260; internet www.hrdc-drhc.gc.ca.

Indian and Northern Affairs Canada: Les Terrasses de la Chaudière, Pièce 1415, 10 rue Wellington, Hull, QC K1A 0H4; tel. (819) 997-0380; fax (819) 953-3017; e-mail infopubs@inac.gc.ca; internet www.inac.gc.ca.

Industry Canada: C. D. Howe Bldg, 235 Queen St, Ottawa, ON K1A 0H5; tel. (613) 954-2788; fax (613) 954-2303; internet www.ic.gc.ca.

National Defence (Canada): National Defence Headquarters, Maj.-Gen. George R. Pearkes Bldg, 101 Colonel By Dr., Ottawa, ON K1A 0K2; tel. (613) 996-3100; fax (613) 995-8189; internet www.forces.gc.ca.

Natural Resources Canada: 580 Booth St, Ottawa, ON K1A 0E4; tel. (613) 995-0947; fax (613) 996-9094; internet www.nrcan-rncan.gc.ca/inter/index.html.

Public Works and Government Services Canada: Place du Portage, rue Laurier, Hull, QC K1A 0S5; tel. (819) 956-3115; e-mail NCREditor@pwgsc.gc.ca; internet www.pwgsc.gc.ca.

Revenue Canada: 871 Heron Rd, Ottawa, ON K1A 0L8; tel. (613) 952-0384; internet www.ccra-adrc.gc.ca/.

Solicitor-General Canada: Sir Wilfrid Laurier Bldg, 340 Laurier Ave West, Ottawa, ON K1A 0P8; tel. (613) 991-3283; fax (613) 993-7062; internet www.sgc.gc.ca.

Transport Canada: Place de Ville, Tower C, 29th Floor, 330 Sparks St, Ottawa, ON K1A 0N5; tel. (613) 991-0700; fax (613) 995-0327; e-mail mintc@tc.gc.ca; internet www.tc.gc.ca.

Treasury Board: East Tower, L'Esplanade Laurier, 140 O'Connor St, Ottawa, ON K1A 0R5; tel. (613) 957-2400; fax (613) 952-3658; e-mail tbs-sct@tbs-sct.gc.ca; internet www.tbs-sct.gc.ca.

Veterans Affairs Canada: 161 Grafton St, POB 7700, Charlottetown, PE C1A 8M9; tel. (902) 566-8888; fax (902) 566-8508; internet www.vac-acc.gc.ca.

Western Economic Diversification Canada: Canada Place, 9700 Jasper Ave, Suite 1500, Edmonton, AB T5J 4H7; tel. (780) 495-4164; fax (403) 495-6876; internet www.wd.gc.ca.

Federal Legislature

THE SENATE

Speaker: DANIEL HAYS.

Seats at April 2003

Liberal	63
Progressive Conservative	30
Independent	4
Canadian Alliance	1
Vacant	7
Total	105

HOUSE OF COMMONS

Speaker: PETER MILLIKEN.

General Election, 27 November 2000

	% of votes at election	Seats at election	Seats at April 2003
Liberal	40.8	172	169
Canadian Alliance	25.5	66	63
Bloc Québécois	10.7	38	34
New Democratic Party	8.5	13	14
Progressive Conservative	12.2	12	14
Independent	—	—	4
Vacant	—	—	3
Total (incl. others)	100.0	301	301

Provincial Legislatures

ALBERTA

Lieutenant-Governor: LOIS HOLE.

Premier: RALPH KLEIN.

Election, March 2001

	Seats at election	Seats at April 2003
Progressive Conservative	74	74
Liberal	7	7
New Democratic Party	2	2
Total	83	83

BRITISH COLUMBIA

Lieutenant-Governor: IONA CAMPAGNOLO.

Premier: GORDON CAMPBELL.

Election, May 2001

	Seats at election	Seats at April 2003
Liberal	76	75
New Democratic Party	3	2
Independent	—	2
Total	79	79

MANITOBA

Lieutenant-Governor: PETER M. LIBA.

Premier: GARY ALBERT DOER.

Election, September 1999

	Seats at election	Seats at April 2003
New Democratic Party	31	32
Progressive Conservative	25	24
Liberal	1	1
Total	57	57

NEW BRUNSWICK

Lieutenant-Governor: MARILYN TRENHOLME COUNSELL.

Premier: BERNARD LORD.

Election, June 1999

	Seats at election	Seats at April 2003
Progressive Conservative	44	46
Liberal	10	7
New Democratic Party	1	1
Vacant	—	1
Total	55	55

NEWFOUNDLAND AND LABRADOR

Lieutenant-Governor: EDWARD MOXON ROBERTS.

Premier: ROGER GRIMES.

Election, February 1999

	Seats at election	Seats at April 2003
Liberal	32	27
Progressive Conservative	14	19
New Democratic Party	2	2
Total	48	48

NOVA SCOTIA

Lieutenant-Governor: MYRA A. FREEMAN.

Premier: JOHN F. HAMM.

Election, July 1999

	Seats at election	Seats at April 2003
Progressive Conservative	30	31
New Democratic Party	11	11
Liberal	11	8
Independent	—	1
Vacant	—	1
Total	52	52

ONTARIO

Lieutenant-Governor: JAMES K. BARTLEMAN.

Premier: ERNIE EVES.

Election, June 1999

	Seats at election	Seats at April 2003
Progressive Conservative	59	57
Liberal	35	36
New Democratic Party	9	9
Independent	—	1
Total	103	103

PRINCE EDWARD ISLAND

Lieutenant-Governor: J. LÉONCE BERNARD.

Premier: PATRICK G. BINNS.

Election, April 2000

	Seats at election	Seats at April 2003
Progressive Conservative	26	26
Liberal	1	1
Total	27	27

QUÉBEC

Lieutenant-Governor: LISE THIBAULT.

Premier: JEAN CHAREST.

Election, April 2003

	Seats at election
Parti Québécois	76
Liberal	45
Action Démocratique du Québec	4
Total	125

SASKATCHEWAN

Lieutenant-Governor: LYNDA HAVERSTOCK.

Premier: LORNE CALVERT.

Election, September 1999

	Seats at election	Seats at April 2003
New Democratic Party	29	29
Saskatchewan Party	26	25
Independent	—	3
Vacant	—	1
Total	58	58

Territorial Legislatures

NORTHWEST TERRITORIES

Commissioner: GLENNA F. HANSEN.

Premier and Minister of the Executive Department: STEPHEN KAKFWI.

The Legislative Assembly, elected in December 1999, consists of 19 independent members without formal party affiliation.

NUNAVUT TERRITORY

Commissioner: PETER IRNIQ.

Premier: PAUL OKALIK.

The Legislative Assembly, elected in February 1999, consists of 19 independent members without formal party affiliation.

YUKON TERRITORY

Commissioner: JACK CABLE.

Government Leader and Minister of the Executive Council Office: DENNIS FENTIE.

Election, November 2002

	Seats at election	Seats at April 2003
Yukon Party	12	12
New Democratic Party	5	5
Liberal	1	1
Total	18	18

Political Organizations

Action Démocratique du Québec: 1050 rue de la Montagne, 3e étage, Montréal, QC H3G 1Y7; tel. (514) 932-5505; e-mail adq@dq.qc .ca; internet www.adq.qc.ca; f. 1994; provincial nationalist; Leader MARIO DUMONT; Pres. ISABELLE MARQUIS.

Bloc Québécois: 1200 ave Papineau, Montréal, QC H2K 4R5; tel. (514) 526-3000; fax (514) 526-2868; e-mail infobloc@bloc.org; internet www.blocquebecois.org; f. 1990 by group of seven Progressive Conservative MPs representing Québec constituencies in fed. parl. subsequently attracted Liberal support; main opposition party in Federal House of Commons during 1993–97; seeks negotiated sovereignty for Québec; Leader GILLES DUCEPPE; Dir-Gen. YVES DUFOUR.

Canadian Action Party: 99 Atlantic Ave, Suite 302, Toronto, ON M6K 3J8; tel. (416) 535-4144; fax (416) 535-6325; e-mail info@ canadianactionparty.ca; internet www.canadianactionparty.ca; Leader PAUL HELLYER.

Canadian Alliance: 833 Fourth Ave SW, Suite 600, Calgary, AB T2P 3T5; tel. (403) 269-1990; fax (403) 269-4077; internet www .canadianalliance.ca; f. 2000; incorporates the Reform Party; supports decentralization of fed. govt, with provincial jurisdiction over language and culture; advocates fiscal reform; main opposition party in Federal House of Commons since March 2000; Leader STEPHEN HARPER; Chair WERNER SCHMIDT.

Christian Heritage Party of Canada: POB 4958, Station E, Ottawa, ON K1S 5J1; tel. (819) 669-0673; fax (819) 669-6478; e-mail edchp@ottawa.com; internet www.chp.ca; f. 1986; Pres. THOMAS KROESBERGEN; Leader RONALD O. GRAY.

Communist Party of Canada (Marxist-Leninist): 396 Cooper St, Suite 405, Ottawa, ON K2P 2H7; tel. (613) 565-6446; fax (613) 565-8787; e-mail office@cpcml.ca; internet www.cpcml.ca; f. 1970; Nat. Leader SANDRA SMITH.

Confederation of Regions Party: 6155 99th St, Edmonton, AB T6E 3P1; tel. (780) 435-4185; fax (780) 437-2297; Nat. Leader ELMER S. KNUTSON.

COR (Confederation of Regions) Party of New Brunswick: POB 3322, Station B, Fredericton, NB E3A 5H1; tel. (506) 444-4040; fax (506) 444-4053; e-mail cor@nbnet.nb.ca; f. 1989 to promote populist democratic principles; opposes legislation and govt subsidies relating to linguistic and cultural matters; Leader JAMES A. WEBB (acting); Pres. DOLORES COOK.

Equality Party: Box 21, Station NDG, Montréal, QC H4A 3P4; tel. (514) 488-7586; fax (514) 488-7306; e-mail canadian@equality.qc.ca; internet www.equality.qc.ca; f. 1989; represents interests of federalists in Québec; Leader KEITH HENDERSON.

Green Party of Canada: POB 997, Station B, Ottawa, ON K1P 5RI; tel. (613) 235-7687; e-mail info@greenparty.ca; internet www.greenparty.ca; f. 1983; environmentalist; Leader JIM HARRIS.

Liberal Party of Canada: 81 Metcalfe St, Suite 400, Ottawa, ON K1P 6M8; tel. (613) 237-0740; fax (613) 235-7208; e-mail info@liberal.ca; internet www.liberal.ca; supports comprehensive social security, economic growth and a balanced economy; Leader JEAN CHRÉTIEN; Pres. STEPHEN LEDREW; Nat. Dir TERRY MERCER.

Libertarian Party of Canada: 2052 Ste Marie, Embrun, ON K0A 1W0; tel. (613) 443-5423; e-mail info@libertarian.ca; internet www.libertarian.ca; f. 1974; supports the extension of individual freedoms; Leader JEAN-SERGE BRISSON.

New Democratic Party of Canada: 85 Albert St, Suite 802, Ottawa, ON K1P 6A4; tel. (613) 236-3613; fax (613) 230-9950; e-mail ndpadmin@fed.ndp.ca; internet www.ndp.ca; f. 1961; social democratic; Leader JACK LAYTON; Pres. DAVE MACKINNON; Sec. JILL MARZETTI; 100,000 mems. (1996).

Parti Québécois: 1200 ave Papineau, Bureau 150, Montréal, QC H2K 4R5; tel. (514) 526-0020; fax (514) 526-0272; e-mail info@pq.org; internet www.pq.org; f. 1968; social democratic; seeks political sovereignty for Québec; governing party of Québec in 1976–85 and since Sept. 1994; Pres. BERNARD LANDRY; 200,000 mems (2001).

Progressive Conservative Party of Canada: 275 Slater St, Suite 501, Ottawa, ON K1P 5H9; tel. (613) 238-6111; fax (613) 238-7429; e-mail pcinfo@pcparty.ca; internet www.pcparty.ca; f. 1854; advocates individualism and free enterprise; Leader C. JOSEPH CLARK; Pres. BRUCK EASTON; Nat. Dir SUSAN ELLIOTT.

Saskatchewan Party: POB 546, Regina, SK SAP 3A2; tel. (306) 359-1638; fax (306) 359-9832; e-mail saskparty@sasktel.net; internet www.saskparty.ca; Leader ELWIN HERMANSON.

Socialist Party of Canada: POB 4280, Victoria, BC V8X 3X8; tel. (250) 478-5670; e-mail spc@iname.com; internet www.worldsocialism.org/canada/; f. 1931; Gen. Sec. DON POIRER.

Yukon Party: POB 31113, Whitehorse, YT Y1A 5P7; tel. (867) 668-6505; fax (867) 667-7660; e-mail yukonparty@mailcity.com; internet www.yukonparty.com; Leader DENNIS FENTIE.

Diplomatic Representation

EMBASSIES AND HIGH COMMISSIONS IN CANADA

Algeria: 435 Daly Ave, Ottawa, ON K1N 6H3; tel. (613) 789-8505; fax (613) 789-1406; e-mail ambalgott@sympatico.ca; internet www.ambalgott.com; Ambassador YOUCEF YOUSFI.

Angola: 75 Albert St, Suite 900, Ottawa, ON K1P 5E7; tel. (613) 234-1152; fax (613) 234-1179; e-mail info@ambangola-can.org; internet www.embangola-can.org; Ambassador MIGUEL MARIA N'ZAU PUNA.

Antigua and Barbuda, Dominica, Grenada, Montserrat, Saint Christopher and Nevis, Saint Lucia and Saint Vincent and the Grenadines: 130 Albert St, Suite 700, Ottawa, ON K1P 5G4; tel. (613) 236-8952; fax (613) 236-3042; e-mail echcc@travel-net.com; internet www.oecs-ottawa.com; High Commissioner GEORGE R. E. BULLEN.

Argentina: Royal Bank Centre, 90 Sparks St, Suite 910, Ottawa, ON K1P 5B4; tel. (613) 236-2351; fax (613) 235-2659; Ambassador CÉSAR F. MAYORAL.

Armenia: 130 Albert St, Suite 1006, Ottawa, ON K1P 5G4; tel. (613) 234-3710; fax (613) 234-3444; Ambassador LEVON BARKHUDARYAN.

Australia: 50 O'Connor St, Suite 710, Ottawa, ON K1P 6L2; tel. (613) 236-0841; fax (613) 236-4376; internet www.ahc-ottawa.org; High Commissioner ANTHONY JOHN HELY.

Austria: 445 Wilbrod St, Ottawa, ON K1N 6M7; tel. (613) 789-1444; fax (613) 789-3431; e-mail ottawa-ob@bmaa.gv.at; internet www.austro.org; Ambassador Dr WENDELIN ETTMAYER.

Bahamas: 360 Albert St, Suite 1020, Ottawa, ON K1R 7X7; tel. (613) 232-1724; fax (613) 232-0097; e-mail Ottawamission@bahighco.com; High Commissioner HARCOURT LOWELL TURNQUEST.

Bangladesh: 275 Bank St, Suite 302, Ottawa, ON K2P 2L6; tel. (613) 236-0138; fax (613) 567-3213; e-mail bdootcanda@iosphere.net; internet www.iosphere.net/~bhc; High Commissioner MOHSIN ALI KHAN.

Barbados: 130 Albert St, Suite 302, Ottawa, ON K1P 5G4; tel. (613) 236-9517; fax (613) 230-4362; e-mail ottawa@foreign.gov.bb; internet www.sunbeach.net/gov/foreign; High Commissioner VICTOR LEROY JOHNSON.

Belarus: 130 Albert St, Suite 600, Ottawa, K1P 5G4; tel. (613) 233-9994; fax (613) 233-8500; e-mail belamb@igs.net; Ambassador NINA MAZAI.

Belgium: 80 Elgin St, 4th Floor, Ottawa, ON K1P 1B7; tel. (613) 236-7267; fax (613) 236-7882; e-mail ambabel.Ottawa@diplobel.org; internet www.diplobel.org/canada/; Ambassador DANIEL LEROY.

Benin: 58 Glebe Ave, Ottawa, ON K1S 2C3; tel. (613) 233-4429; fax (613) 233-8952; Chargé d'affaires THOMAS D'AQUIN.

Bolivia: 130 Albert St, Suite 416, Ottawa, ON K1P 5G4; tel. (613) 236-5730; fax (613) 236-8237; e-mail bolcan@iosphere.net; internet www.iosphere.net/~bolcan/; Ambassador RENÉ A. SORIA GALVARRO HAENSEL.

Bosnia and Herzegovina: 130 Albert St, Suite 805, Ottawa, ON K1P 5G4; tel. (613) 236-0028; fax (613) 236-1139; e-mail embassyofbih@magma.ca; Ambassador KRUNOSLAV VASILJ.

Brazil: 450 Wilbrod St, Ottawa, ON K1N 6M8; tel. (613) 237-1090; fax (613) 237-6144; e-mail brasemb@ottawa.net; internet www.brasembottawa.org; Ambassador HENRIQUE RODRIGUES VALLE JÚNIOR.

Brunei: Hongkong Bank Bldg, 395 Laurier Ave East, Suite 400, Ottawa, ON K1N 6R4; tel. (603) 234-5656; fax (603) 234-4397; High Commissioner Dato' Paduka Haji ABDUL AZIZ MOHAMMAD.

Bulgaria: 325 Stewart St, Ottawa, ON K1N 6K5; tel. (613) 789-3215; fax (613) 789-3524; e-mail mailmn@storm.ca; Ambassador BRANIMIR STOYANOV ZAIMOV.

Burkina Faso: 48 Range Rd, Ottawa, ON K1N 8J4; tel. (613) 238-4796; fax (613) 238-3812; e-mail burkina.faso@sympatico.ca; internet www.amba.burkina-canada.org; Ambassador JULIETTE BONKOUNGOU.

Burundi: 325 Dalhousie St, Suite 815, Ottawa, ON K1N 8J4; tel. (613) 238-4796; fax (613) 238-3812; Ambassador EDONIAS NIYONGABO.

Cameroon: 170 Clemow Ave, Ottawa, ON K1S 2B4; tel. (613) 236-1522; fax (613) 238-3885; High Commissioner PHILÉMON YUNJI YANG.

Chile: 50 O'Connor St, Suite 1413, Ottawa, ON K1N 6L2; tel. (613) 235-4402; fax (613) 235-1176; e-mail echile@chile.ca; internet www.chile.ca; Ambassador ALVARO ZUÑIGA.

China, People's Republic: 515 St Patrick St, Ottawa, ON K1N 5H3; tel. (613) 789-3434; fax (613) 789-1911; e-mail cooffice@buildlink.com; internet www.chinaembassycanada.org; Ambassador PING MEI.

Colombia: 360 Albert St, Suite 1002, Ottawa, ON K1R 7X7; tel. (613) 230-3760; fax (613) 230-4416; e-mail embajada@embajadacolombia.ca; internet www.embajadacolombia.ca; Ambassador FANNY KERTZMANN YANKELEVITCH.

Congo, Democratic Republic: 18 Range Rd, Ottawa, ON K1N 8J3; tel. (613) 236-7103; fax (613) 567-1404; internet www.ambassadesrdcongo.org/ambass_canada.htm; Chargé d'affaires a.i. LEYAN' SIMBI M'FUMU KANUNU.

Costa Rica: 325 Dalhousie St, Suite 407, Ottawa, ON K1N 7G2; tel. (613) 562-2855; fax (613) 562-2582; e-mail embcrica@travel-net.com; Ambassador CARLOS MIRANDA ARRINDA.

Côte d'Ivoire: 9 Marlborough Ave, Ottawa, ON K1N 8E6; tel. (613) 236-9919; fax (613) 563-8287; e-mail ambaci@ican.net; Ambassador JEAN OBÉO-COULIBALY.

Croatia: 229 Chapel St, Ottawa, ON K1N 7Y6; tel. (613) 562-7820; fax (613) 562-7821; e-mail embcrott@sprint.ca; internet www.croatiaemb.net; Chargé d'affaires a.i. SMILIAN SIMAĆ.

Cuba: 388 Main St, Ottawa, ON K1S 1E3; tel. (613) 563-0141; fax (613) 563-0068; e-mail cuba@embacuba.ca; internet www.embacuba.ca; Ambassador CARLOS FERNÁNDEZ DE COSSIO DOMÍNGUEZ.

Czech Republic: 251 Cooper St, Ottawa, ON K2P 0G2; tel. (613) 562-3875; fax (613) 562-3878; e-mail ottawa@embassy.mzv.cz; internet www.czechembassy.org; Ambassador VLADIMÍR KOTZY.

Denmark: 47 Clarence St, Suite 450, Ottawa, ON K1N 9K1; tel. (613) 562-1811; fax (613) 562-1812; e-mail danemb@cyberus.ca; internet www.danish-embassy-canada.com; Ambassador SVEND ROED NIELSEN.

Dominican Republic: 130 Albert St, Suite 418, Ottawa, ON K1P 5G4; tel. (613) 569-9893; fax (613) 569-8673; e-mail info@drembassy.org; internet www.drembassy.org; Ambassador EDUARDO FERNANDEZ PICHARDO.

Ecuador: 50 O'Connor St, Suite 316, Ottawa, ON K1P 6L2; tel. (613) 563-8206; fax (613) 235-5776; e-mail mecucan@sprint.ca; internet www.ecua.net.ec; Ambassador ALEJANDRO SUÁREZ PASCUAL.

Egypt: 454 Laurier Ave East, Ottawa, ON K1N 6R3; tel. (613) 234-4931; fax (613) 234-9347; Ambassador SALLAMA MAHMOUD.

El Salvador: 209 Kent St, Ottawa, ON K2P 1Z8; tel. (613) 238-2939; fax (613) 238-6940; e-mail ambajada@elsalvador-ca.org; Ambassador Dr MAURICIO ROSALES RIVERA.

Estonia: 260 Dalhousie St, Suite 210, Ottawa, ON K1N 7E4; tel. (613) 789-4222; fax (613) 789-9555; e-mail estonianembassy@rogens .com; Ambassador (vacant).

Ethiopia: 151 Slater St, Suite 210, Ottawa, ON K1P 5H3; tel. (613) 235-6637; fax (613) 235-4638; e-mail infoethi@magi.com; internet www.ethiopia.ottawa.on.ca; Ambassador BERHANU DIBABA.

Finland: 55 Metcalfe St, Suite 850, Ottawa, ON K1P 6L5; tel. (613) 236-2389; fax (613) 238-1474; e-mail finembott@synapse.net; internet www.finemb.com; Ambassador ILKKA RISTIMÄKI.

France: 42 Sussex Dr., Ottawa, ON K1M 2C9; tel. (613) 789-1795; fax (613) 562-3735; e-mail politique@ambafrance-ca.org; internet www.ambafrance-ca.org; Ambassador PHILIPPE GUELLUY.

Gabon: 4 Range Rd, Ottawa, ON K1N 8J5; tel. (613) 232-5301; fax (613) 232-6916; e-mail ambgabon@sprint.ca; Ambassador ALPHONSE OYABI-GNALA.

Germany: 1 Waverley St, Ottawa, ON K2P 0T8; tel. (613) 232-1101; fax (613) 594-9330; e-mail germanembassyottawa@on.aibn.com; internet www.germanembassyottawa.org; Ambassador CHRISTIAN FRIEDEMANN PAULS.

Ghana: 1 Clemow Ave, Ottawa, ON K1S 2A9; tel. (613) 236-0871; fax (613) 236-0874; High Commissioner OLIVER K. K. LAWLUVI.

Greece: 76–80 MacLaren St, Ottawa, ON K2P 0K6; tel. (613) 238-6271; fax (613) 238-5676; e-mail greekembott@travel-net.com; internet www.greekembassy.ca; Ambassador LEONIDAS CHRYSANTHO-POULOS.

Guatemala: 130 Albert St, Suite 1010, Ottawa, ON K1P 5G4; tel. (613) 233-7237; fax (613) 233-0135; e-mail embguate@webruler.com; Ambassador CARLOS JIMÉNEZ LICONA.

Guinea: 483 Wilbrod St, Ottawa, ON K1N 6N1; tel. (613) 789-8444; fax (613) 789-7560; e-mail ambguineaott@sympatico.ca; Ambassador AMARA DJABAR SOUMAH.

Guyana: Burnside Bldg, 151 Slater St, Suite 309, Ottawa, ON K1P 5H3; tel. (613) 235-7249; fax (613) 235-1447; High Commissioner RAJNARINE SINGH.

Haiti: Place de Ville, Tower B, 112 Kent St, Suite 205, Ottawa, ON K1P 5P2; tel. (613) 238-1628; fax (613) 238-2986; e-mail bohio@ sympatico.ca; Ambassador RENAUD BERNARDIN.

Holy See: Apostolic Nunciature, 724 Manor Ave, Rockcliffe Park, Ottawa, ON K1M 0E3; tel. (613) 746-4914; fax (613) 746-4786; e-mail nuncioap@istar.ca; Nuncio Most Rev. LUIGI VENTURA (Titular Archbishop of Équilio).

Honduras: 151 Slater St, Suite 805, Ottawa, ON K1P 5H3; tel. (613) 233-8900; fax (613) 232-0193; e-mail embhonca@magma.ca; Ambassador ANA CAROLINA GALEANO.

Hungary: 299 Waverley St, Ottawa, ON K2P 0V9; tel. (613) 230-2717; fax (613) 230-7560; e-mail sysadmin@huembott.org; internet www.docuweb.ca/hungary/; Ambassador DÉNES TOMAJ.

Iceland: 360 Albert St, Suite 710, Ottawa, ON K1R 7X7; tel. (613) 482–1944; fax (613) 482–1945; e-mail icemb.ottawa@utn.stjr.is; Ambassador HJÁLMAR WAAG.

India: 10 Springfield Rd, Ottawa, ON K1M 1C9; tel. (613) 744-3751; fax (613) 744-0913; e-mail hicomind@sprint.ca; internet www .docuweb.ca/India; High Commissioner RAJANIKANTA VERMA.

Indonesia: 55 Parkdale Ave, Ottawa, ON K1Y 1E5; tel. (613) 724-1100; fax (613) 724-1105; e-mail info@prica.org; internet www .indonesia-ottawa.org; Ambassador EKI SYACHRUDIN.

Iran: 245 Metcalfe St, Ottawa, ON K2P 2K2; tel. (613) 235-4726; fax (613) 232-5712; e-mail iranemb@sonetis.com; internet www .salamiran.org; Ambassador SEYED MOHAMMAD ALI MOUSSAVI.

Iraq: 215 McLeod St, Ottawa, ON K2P 0Z8; tel. (613) 236-9177; fax (613) 567-1101; Chargé d'affaires a.i. MOHAMMAD H. RADHI AL-SAFAR.

Ireland: 130 Albert St, Suite 1105, Ottawa, ON K1P 5G4; tel. (613) 233-6281; fax (613) 233-5835; e-mail emb.ireland@sympatico.ca; Ambassador MARTIN BURKE.

Israel: 50 O'Connor St, Suite 1005, Ottawa, ON K1P 6L2; tel. (613) 567-6450; fax (613) 237-8865; e-mail ottawa@israel.org; internet www.israelca.org; Ambassador HAIM DIVON.

Italy: 275 Slater St, 21st Floor, Ottawa, ON K1P 5H9; tel. (613) 232-2401; fax (613) 233-1484; e-mail ambital@italyincanada.com; internet www.italyincanada.com; Ambassador MARCO COLOMBO.

Jamaica: 275 Slater St, Suite 800, Ottawa, ON K1P 5H9; tel. (613) 233-9311; fax (613) 233-0611; e-mail jhcott@comnet.ca; High Commissioner MAXINE ROBERTS.

Japan: 255 Sussex Dr., Ottawa, ON K1N 9E6; tel. (613) 241-8541; fax (613) 241-7415; e-mail infocul@embassyjapancanada.org; internet www.embassyjapancanada.org; Ambassador KENSAKU HOGEN.

Jordan: 100 Bronson Ave, Suite 701, Ottawa, ON K1R 6G8; tel. (613) 238-8090; fax (613) 232-3341; e-mail jordan@on.aibn.com; Ambassador FOUAD AYOUB.

Kenya: 415 Laurier Ave East, Ottawa, ON K1N 6R4; tel. (613) 563-1773; fax (613) 233-6599; e-mail kenrep@on.aibn.com; Ambassador GREEN H. O. JOSIAH.

Korea, Republic: 150 Boteler St, Ottawa, ON K1N 5A6; tel. (613) 244-5010; fax (613) 244-5043; internet www.emb-korea.ottawa.on .ca/; Ambassador CHANG KI-HO.

Kuwait: 80 Elgin St, Ottawa, ON K1P 1C6; tel. (613) 780-9999; fax (613) 780-9905; e-mail canada@embassyofkuwait.com; internet www.embassyofkuwait.com; Ambassador FAISIAL AL-MULAIFI.

Latvia: 280 Albert St, Suite 300, Ottawa, ON K1P 5G8; tel. (613) 238-6014; fax (613) 238-7044; e-mail embassy.canada@mfa.gov.lv; internet www.magma.ca/~latemb/; Ambassador ATIS SJANĪTS.

Lebanon: 640 Lyon St, Ottawa, ON K1S 3Z5; tel. (613) 236-5825; fax (613) 232-1609; e-mail emblebanon@synapse.net; internet www .synapse.net/~emblebanon/; Ambassador RAYMOND BAAKLINI.

Lithuania: 130 Albert St, Suite 204, Ottawa, ON K1P 5G4; tel. (613) 567-5458; fax (613) 567-5315; e-mail litemb@storm.ca; internet www.lithuanianembassy.ca; Ambassador Dr RIMANTAS SIDLAUSKAS.

Macedonia, former Yugoslav republic: 130 Albert St, Suite 1006, Ottawa, ON K1P 5G4; tel. (613) 234-3882; fax (613) 233-1852; e-mail emb.macedonia.ottawa@sympatico.ca; internet www3 .sympatico.ca/emb.macedonia.ottawa/; Chargé d'affaires a.i. ZVONKO MUCUNSKI.

Madagascar: 649 Blair Rd, Gloucester, ON K1J 7M4; tel. (613) 744-7995; fax (613) 744-2530; e-mail ambamadott@on.aibn.com; Ambassador RAKOTOARISOA FLORENT.

Malawi: 7 Clemow Ave, Ottawa, ON K1S 2A9; tel. (613) 236-8931; fax (613) 236-1054; e-mail malawi.highcommission@bellnet.ca; High Commissioner MACALPINE BYWELL MLOTHA.

Malaysia: 60 Boteler St, Ottawa, ON K1N 8Y7; tel. (613) 241-5182; fax (613) 241-5214; e-mail mwottawa@istar.ca; internet home.istar .ca/~mwottawa; High Commissioner Dato' DENNIS J. IGNATIUS.

Mali: 50 Goulburn Ave, Ottawa, ON K1N 8C8; tel. (613) 232-1501; fax (613) 232-7429; Ambassador MANASSA DANIOKO DIAKITÉ.

Mauritania: 121 Sherwood Dr., Ottawa, ON K1Y 3V1; tel. (613) 237-3283; fax (613) 237-3287; e-mail ambarimca@rogers.com; Ambassador TIJANI OULD MOHAMED EL KERIM.

Mexico: 45 O'Connor St, Suite 1500, Ottawa, ON K1P 1A4; tel. (613) 233-8988; fax (613) 235-9123; e-mail info@embamexcan.com; internet www.embamexcan.com; Ambassador MARÍA TERESA GARCÍA SEGOVIA DE MADERO.

Mongolia: 151 Slater St, Suite 503, Ottawa, ON K1P 5H3; tel. (613) 569–3830; fax (613) 569–3916; internet mail@mongolembassy.org; e-mail ; internet www.mongolembassy.org; Ambassador GALSAN BAT-SUKH.

Morocco: 38 Range Rd, Ottawa, ON K1N 8J4; tel. (613) 236-7391; fax (613) 236-6164; e-mail info@ambassade-maroc.ottawa.on.ca; internet www.ambassade-maroc.ottawa.on.ca; Ambassador ABDEL-KADER LECHEHEB.

Myanmar: 85 Range Rd, Suite 902/903, Ottawa, ON K1N 8J6; tel. (613) 232-6434; fax (613) 232-6435; e-mail meott@magma.ca; Ambassador U. NYUNT TIN.

Netherlands: 350 Albert St, Suite 2020, Ottawa, ON K1R 1A4; tel. (613) 237-5030; fax (613) 237-6471; e-mail nlgovott@ netherlandsembassy.ca; internet www.netherlandsembassy.ca; Ambassador JACQUES VAN HELLENBURG HUBAR.

New Zealand: Clarica Centre, 99 Bank St, Suite 727, Ottawa, ON K1P 6G3; tel. (613) 238-5991; fax (613) 238-5707; e-mail info@ nzhcottawa.org; internet www.nzhcottawa.org; High Commissioner GRAHAM KELLY.

Niger: 38 Blackburn Ave, Ottawa, ON K1N 8A3; tel. (613) 232-4291; fax (613) 230-9808; Ambassador RAKIATOU MAYAKI.

Nigeria: 295 Metcalfe St, Ottawa, ON K2P 1R9; tel. (613) 236-0522; fax (613) 236-0529; e-mail hc@nigeriahighcommottawa.com;

internet www.nigeriahighcommottawa; High Commissioner OLUWA-DERE PATRICK BEJIDE.

Norway: 90 Sparks St, Suite 532, Ottawa, ON K1P 5B4; tel. (613) 238-6571; fax (613) 238-2765; e-mail emb.ottawa@mfa.no; internet www.emb-norway.ca; Ambassador INGVARD HAVNEN.

Pakistan: Burnside Bldg, 151 Slater St, Suite 608, Ottawa, ON K1P 5H3; tel. (613) 238-7881; fax (613) 238-7296; e-mail parepottawa@sprint.ca; High Commissioner SAHID MALIK.

Panama: 130 Albert St, Suite 300, Ottawa, ON K1P 5G4; tel. (613) 236-7177; fax (613) 236-5775; e-mail pancanem@travel-net.com; Ambassador MARIANELA DÍAZ.

Papua New Guinea: 130 Albert St, Suite 300, Ottawa, ON K1A 5G4; fax (613) 236-5775; High Commissioner NAGORA Y. BOGAN.

Paraguay: 151 Slater St, Suite 501, Ottawa, ON K1P 5H3; tel. (613) 567-1283; fax (613) 567-1679; e-mail embapar@magmacom.com; internet www.magmacom.com/~embapar; Ambassador JUAN ESTEBAN O. AGUIRRE MARTÍNEZ.

Peru: 130 Albert St, Suite 1901, Ottawa, ON K1P 5G4; tel. (613) 238-1777; fax (613) 232-3062; e-mail emperuca@bellnet.ca; Ambassador JOSÉ E. ROMERO.

Philippines: 130 Albert St, Suite 606, Ottawa, ON K1P 5G4; tel. (613) 233-1121; fax (613) 233-4165; e-mail ottawape@istar.ca; internet www.philembassyca.org; Ambassador FRANCISCO L. BENEDICTO.

Poland: 443 Daly Ave, Ottawa, ON K1N 6H3; tel. (613) 789-0468; fax (613) 789-1218; e-mail polamb@alphainter.net; internet www.polonianet.com/pol/ambasada/; Ambassador PAWEL DOROWOLSKI.

Portugal: 645 Island Park Dr., Ottawa, ON K1Y 0B8; tel. (613) 729-0883; fax (613) 729-4236; e-mail embportugal@embportugal-ottawa.org; internet www.embportugal-ottawa.org; Ambassador JOSÉ PACHECO LUÍZ GOMES.

Romania: 655 Rideau St, Ottawa, ON K1N 6A3; tel. (613) 789-3709; fax (613) 789-4365; e-mail romania@cyberus.ca; internet www.cyberus.ca/~romania; Chargé d'affaires a.i. DRAGOS TIGAU.

Russia: 285 Charlotte St, Ottawa, ON K1N 8L5; tel. (613) 235-4341; fax (613) 236-6342; e-mail rusemb@magma.ca; internet www.magma.ca/~rusemb; Ambassador VITALII CHURKIN.

Rwanda: Ottawa; Ambassador LAURENT NKONGOLI.

Saudi Arabia: 99 Bank St, Suite 901, Ottawa, ON K1P 6B9; tel. (613) 237-4100; fax (613) 237-0567; Ambassador Dr MOHAMMED R. AL-HUSANI AL-SHARIF.

Senegal: 57 Marlborough Ave, Ottawa, ON K1N 8E8; tel. (613) 238-6392; fax (613) 238-2695; e-mail ambassn@simpatico.ca; internet www.ambassenecanada.org; Ambassador PIERRE DIOUF.

Serbia and Montenegro: 17 Blackburn Ave, Ottawa, ON K1N 8A2; tel. (613) 233-6289; fax (613) 233-7850; e-mail embotava@capitalnet.com; internet www.yuemb.ca; Ambassador MIODRAG PERISIC.

Slovakia: 50 Rideau Terrace, Ottawa, ON K1M 2A1; tel. (613) 749-4442; fax (613) 749-4989; e-mail slovakemb@sympatico.ca; internet www.slovakembassy.com; Chargé d'affaires a.i. Dr STEFAN ROZKOPÀL.

Slovenia: 150 Metcalfe St, Suite 2101, Ottawa, ON K2P 1P1; tel. (613) 565-5781; fax (613) 565-5783; e-mail vot@mzz-dkp.gov.si; Ambassador VERONIKA STABEJ.

South Africa: 15 Sussex Dr., Ottawa, ON K1M 1M8; tel. (613) 744-0330; fax (613) 741-1639; e-mail rsafrica@sympatico.ca; internet www.docuweb.ca/SouthAfrica; High Commissioner ANDRÉ JAQUET.

Spain: 74 Stanley Ave, Ottawa, ON K1M 1P4; tel. (613) 747-2252; fax (613) 744-1224; e-mail embespca@mail.mae.es; internet www.docuweb.ca/SpainInCanada/; Ambassador JOSÉ CUENCA ANAYA.

Sri Lanka: 333 Laurier Ave West, Suite 1204, Ottawa, ON K1P 1C1; tel. (613) 233-8449; fax (613) 238-8448; e-mail slhcgen@sprint.ca; internet infoweb.magi.com/~lankacom; High Commissioner M. N. GEETHANGANI DE SILVA.

Sudan: 85 Range Rd, Suite 507, Ottawa, ON K1N 8J6; tel. (613) 235-4000; fax (613) 235-6880; e-mail sudanembassy-canada@home-com; Chargé d'affaires a.i. ABD EL-HANI E. AWAD EL-KARIM.

Swaziland: 130 Albert St, Suite 1204, Ottawa, ON K1P 5G4; tel. (613) 567-1480; fax (613) 567-1058; High Commissioner BREMER M. NXUMALO.

Sweden: Mercury Court, 377 Dalhousie St, Ottawa, ON K1N 9N8; tel. (613) 241-8553; fax (613) 241-2277; e-mail ambassaden.ottawa@foreign.ministry.se; internet www.swedishembassy.ca; Ambassador LENNART ALVIN.

Switzerland: 5 Marlborough Ave, Ottawa, ON K1N 8E6; tel. (613) 235-1837; fax (613) 563-1394; e-mail vertretung@ott.rep.admin.ch; Ambassador URS ZISWILER.

Syria: 151 Slater St, Suite 1000, Ottawa, ON K1P 5H3; tel. (613) 569-5556; fax (613) 569-3800; Chargé d'affaires a.i. AHMAD FAROUK ARNOUS.

Tanzania: 50 Range Rd, Ottawa, ON K1N 8J4; tel. (613) 232-1500; fax (613) 232-5184; e-mail tzottawa@synapse.net; High Commissioner Dr BEN D. MOSES.

Thailand: 180 Island Park Dr., Ottawa, ON K1Y 0A2; tel. (613) 722-4444; fax (613) 722-6624; e-mail thaiott@magma.ca; internet www.magma.ca/~thaiott/index.html; Ambassador SUNAI BUNYASIRIPHANT.

Togo: 12 Range Rd, Ottawa, ON K1N 8J3; tel. (613) 238-5916; fax (613) 235-6425; Ambassador BAWOUMONDOM AMELETE.

Trinidad and Tobago: 200 First Ave, Ottawa, ON K1S 2G6; tel. (613) 232-2418; fax (613) 232-4349; e-mail ottawa@ttmissions.com; internet www.ttmissions.com; High Commissioner ROBERT M. SABGA.

Tunisia: 515 O'Connor St, Ottawa, ON K1S 3P8; tel. (613) 237-0330; fax (613) 237-7939; Ambassador MOHAMED SAAD.

Turkey: 197 Wurtemburg St, Ottawa, ON K1N 8L9; tel. (613) 789-4044; fax (613) 789-3442; e-mail turkishottawa@mfa.gov.tr; Ambassador AYDEMIR ERMAN.

Ukraine: 310 Somerset St West, Ottawa, ON K2P 0J9; tel. (613) 230-2961; fax (613) 230-2400; e-mail Ukrembassy@on.aibn.com; internet 209.82.14.226/ukremb; Ambassador YURII SCHERRAK.

United Arab Emirates: World Exchange Plaza, 45 O'Connor St, Suite 1800, Ottawa, ON K1P 1A4; tel. (613) 565-7272; fax (613) 565-8007; e-mail safara@uae-embassy.com; internet www.uae-embassy.com; Ambassador MOHAMMED OBAID AL-SUWAIDI.

United Kingdom: 80 Elgin St, Ottawa, ON K1P 5K7; tel. (613) 237-1530; fax (613) 237-7980; e-mail generalenquiries@britain-in-canada.org; internet www.britain-in-canada.org; High Commissioner Sir ANDREW BURNS.

USA: 490 Sussex Dr., POB 866, Station B, Ottawa, ON K1N 1G8; tel. (613) 238-5335; internet www.usembassycanada.gov; Ambassador ARGEO PAUL CELLUCCI.

Uruguay: 130 Albert St, Suite 1905, Ottawa, ON K1P 5G4; tel. (613) 234-2727; fax (613) 233-4670; e-mail urott@iosphere.net; internet www.iosphere.net/~uruott/; Ambassador GASTÓN LASARTE BURGHI.

Venezuela: 32 Range Rd, Ottawa, ON K1N 8J4; tel. (613) 235-5151; fax (613) 235-3205; e-mail embavene@travel-net.com; internet www.travel-net.com/~embavene/; Ambassador JORGE OSORIO GARCÍA.

Viet Nam: 470 Wilbrod St, Ottawa, ON K1M 6M8; tel. (613) 236-0772; fax (613) 236-2704; e-mail vietem@istar.ca; Ambassador NGUYEN THI HOI TRINH.

Yemen: 788 Island Park Dr., Ottawa, ON K1Y 0C2; tel. (613) 729-6627; fax (613) 729-8915; e-mail info@yemenembassy.ca; internet www.yemenembassy.ca; Ambassador MUSTAPHA AHMED NOMAN.

Zimbabwe: 332 Somerset St West, Ottawa, ON K2P 0J9; tel. (613) 237-4388; fax (613) 563-8269; e-mail zim.highcomm@sympatico.ca; internet www.docuweb.ca/zimbabwe; High Commissioner GABRIEL MHARADZE MACHINGA.

Judicial System

FEDERAL COURTS

The Supreme Court of Canada: Supreme Court Bldg, 301 Wellington St, Ottawa, ON K1A 0J1; tel. (613) 995-4330; fax (613) 996-3063; e-mail reception@scc-csc.gc.ca; internet www.scc-csc.gc.ca; ultimate court of appeal in both civil and criminal cases throughout Canada. The Supreme Court is also required to advise on questions referred to it by the Governor-General in Council. Important questions concerning the interpretation of the Constitution Act, the constitutionality or interpretation of any federal or provincial law, the powers of Parliament or of the provincial legislatures, among other matters, may be referred by the Government to the Supreme Court for consideration.

In most cases, appeals are heard by the Court only if leave to appeal is given from any final judgment of the highest court of last resort in a province or territory, or of the Federal Court of Appeal. Such leave, or permission, will be given by the Court when a case involves a question of public importance. There are cases, however, where leave is not required. In criminal cases, there is an automatic right of appeal where an acquittal has been set aside in the provincial court of appeal or where one judge in the provincial court of appeal dissents on a question of law.

Chief Justice of Canada: BEVERLEY McLACHLIN.

Puisne Judges: CHARLES DOHERTY GONTHIER, FRANK IACOBUCCI, JOHN C. MAJOR, MICHEL BASTARACHE, W. IAN BINNIE, LOUISE ARBOUR, LOUIS LEBEL, MARIE DESCHAMPS.

The Federal Court of Canada: 90 Elgin St, Ottawa, ON K1A 0H9; tel. (613) 992-4238; e-mail reception@fct-cf.gc.ca; internet www .fct-cf.gc.ca; has jurisdiction in claims against the Crown, claims by the Crown, miscellaneous cases involving the Crown, claims against or concerning crown officers and servants, relief against Federal Boards, Commissions, and other tribunals, interprovincial and fed-eral-provincial disputes, industrial or indus trial property matters, admiralty, income tax and estate tax appeals, citizenship appeals, aeronautics, interprovincial works and undertakings, residuary jurisdiction for relief if there is no other Canadian court that has such jurisdiction, jurisdiction in specific matters conferred by fed-eral statutes.

The Federal Court of Appeal

90 Elgin St, Ottawa, ON K1A 0H9; tel. (613) 996-6795; e-mail reception@fct-cf.gc.ca; internet www.fct-cf.gc.ca.

Has jurisdiction on appeals from the Trial Division, appeals from Federal Tribunals, review of decisions of Federal Boards and Com-missions, appeals from Tribunals and Reviews under Section 28 of the Federal Court Act, and references by Federal Boards and Com-missions. The Court has one central registry and consists of the principal office in Ottawa and local offices in major centres throughout Canada.

Chief Justice: JOHN D. RICHARD.

Associate Chief Justice: ALLAN LUTFY.

Trial Division Judges: PAUL ROULEAU, JAMES K. HUGESSEN, MAX TEITELBAUM, WILLIAM MACKAY, DONNA MCGILLIS, WILLIAM MCKEOWN, FREDERICK GIBSON, SANDRA SIMPSON, DANIÈLE TREMBLAY-LAMER, DOUGLAS CAMPBELL, PIERRE BLAIS, FRANÇOIS LEMIEUX, JOHN O'KEEFE, ELIZABETH HENEGHAN, DOLORES HANSEN, ELEANOR DAWSON, EDMOND BLANCHARD, MICHAEL A. KELEN, MICHAEL BEAUDRY, LUC MARTINEAU, CAROLYN LAYDEN-STEVENSON.

Court of Appeal Judges: ARTHUR STONE, BARRY STRAYER, ALICE DESJARDINS, ROBERT DÉCARY, ALLEN LINDEN, GILLES LÉTOURNEAU, MARC NOËL, J. EDGAR SEXTON, JOHN EVANS, KAREN SHARLOW, J. BRIAN MALONE, JULIUS A. ISAAC, MARSHALL E. ROTHSTEIN, MARC NADON.

PROVINCIAL COURTS

Alberta

Court of Appeal

Chief Justice of Alberta: CATHERINE A. FRASER.

Court of Queen's Bench

Chief Justice: ALLAN H. J. WACHOWICH.

Associate Chief Justice: A. B. SULATYCKY.

British Columbia

Court of Appeal

Chief Justice of British Columbia: LANCE SIDNEY GEORGE FINCH.

Supreme Court

Chief Justice: DONALD IAN BRENNER.

Associate Chief Justice: PATRICK DONALD DOHM.

Manitoba

Court of Appeal

Chief Justice of Manitoba: R. J. SCOTT.

Court of Queen's Bench

Chief Justice: B. HEWAK.

Associate Chief Justice: J. J. OLIPHANT.

Associate Chief Justice (Family Division): G. W. MERCIER.

New Brunswick

Court of Appeal

Chief Justice of New Brunswick: JOSEPH Z. DAIGLE.

Court of Queen's Bench

Chief Justice: DAVID D. SMITH.

Newfoundland and Labrador

Supreme Court—Court of Appeal

Chief Justice: CLYDE K. WELLS.

Trial Division

Chief Justice: J. D. GREEN.

Nova Scotia

Court of Appeal

Chief Justice of Nova Scotia: CONSTANCE R. GLUBE.

Supreme Court

Chief Justice: J. P. KENNEDY.

Associate Chief Justice: J. M. MACDONALD.

Supreme Court (Family Division)

Associate Chief Justice: R. F. FERGUSON.

Ontario

Court of Appeal

Chief Justice of Ontario: ROY R. MCMURTRY.

Associate Chief Justice of Ontario: DENNIS R. O'CONNER.

Court of Justice

Chief Justice: P. J. LESAGE.

Associate Chief Justice: MADAM H. J. SMITH.

Prince Edward Island

Supreme Court—Appeal Division

Chief Justice: GERARD E. MITCHELL.

Supreme Court—Trial Division

Chief Justice: J. ARMAND DESROCHES.

Québec

Court of Appeal

Chief Justice of Québec: J. J. MICHEL ROBERT.

Superior Court

Chief Justice: LYSE LEMIEUX.

Associate Chief Justice: ROBERT PIDGEON.

Saskatchewan

Court of Appeal

Chief Justice of Saskatchewan: E. D. BAYDA.

Court of Queen's Bench

Chief Justice: W. F. GEREIN.

Northwest Territories

Court of Appeal

Chief Justice: CATHERINE A. FRASER (Alberta).

Supreme Court

Judges of the Supreme Court: J. EDWARD RICHARD, J. Z. VERTES, J. P. FOISY, A.W. MALONEY, V. A. SCHULER.

Nunavut Territory

Court of Appeal

Chief Justice: CATHERINE A. FRASER (Alberta).

Court of Justice

Judges of the Court of Justice: B. A. BROWNE, R. G. KILPATRICK, E. D. JOHNSON.

Yukon Territory

Court of Appeal

Chief Justice: LANCE S. G. FINCH (British Columbia).

Supreme Court

Judges of the Supreme Court: RALPH E. HUDSON, R. S. VEALE.

Religion

CHRISTIANITY

About 75% of the population belong to the three main Christian churches: Roman Catholic, United and Anglican. Numerous other religious denominations are active in Canada.

Canadian Council of Churches/Conseil canadien des Eglises: 159 Roxborough Dr., Toronto, ON M4W; tel. (416) 972-9494; fax (416) 927-0405; e-mail council@ccc.cce.ca; internet www.ccc-cce.ca; f. 1944; 18 mem. churches, one assoc. mem; Pres. Most Rev. ANDRÉ VALLÉE (Roman Catholic Bishop of Hearst); Gen. Sec. JANET SOMERVILLE.

The Anglican Communion

The Anglican Church of Canada (L'Eglise anglicane du Canada) comprises 30 dioceses in four ecclesiastical provinces (each with a Metropolitan archbishop). The Church had 686,362 members in 1,793 parishes in 1999.

General Synod of the Anglican Church of Canada: Church House, 600 Jarvis St, Toronto, ON M4Y 2J6; tel. (416) 924-9192; fax (416) 968-7983; e-mail info@national.anglican.ca; internet www.anglican.ca; Gen. Sec. Archdeacon JAMES BOYLES.

Primate of the Anglican Church of Canada: Most Rev. MICHAEL G. PEERS.

Province of British Columbia and Yukon: Metropolitan Most Rev. DAVID P. CRAWLEY (Archbishop of Kootenay).

Province of Canada: Metropolitan Most Rev. ANDREW HUTCHISON (Archbishop of Montréal).

Province of Ontario: Metropolitan Most Rev. TERENCE FINLAY (Archbishop of Toronto).

Province of Rupert's Land: Acting Metropolitan Rt Rev. THOMAS O. MORGAN (Bishop of Saskatoon).

The Orthodox Churches

Greek Orthodox Metropolis of Toronto (Canada): 1 Patriarch Bartholomew Way, Toronto, ON M4H 1C6; tel. (416) 429-5757; fax (416) 429-4588; e-mail gocanada@total.net; internet www.gocanada.org; 350,000 mems (1997); Metropolitan Archbishop SOTIRIOS ATHANASSOULAS.

Ukrainian Orthodox Church of Canada: 9 St John's Ave, Winnipeg, MB R2W 1G8; tel. (204) 586-3093; fax (204) 582-5241; e-mail consistory@uocc.ca; internet www.uocc.ca; f. 1918; 281 parishes, 120,000 mems (1998); Metropolitan of Winnipeg and of all Canada His Beatitude WASYLY (Fedak); Chancellor Rt Rev WILLIAM MAKARENKO.

The Russian, Belarusian, Polish, Romanian, Serbian, Coptic, Antiochian and Armenian Churches are also represented in Canada.

The Roman Catholic Church

For Catholics of the Latin rite, Canada comprises 18 archdioceses (including one directly responsible to the Holy See), 46 dioceses and one territorial abbacy. There are also one archdiocese and four dioceses of the Ukrainian rite. In addition, the Maronite, Melkite and Slovak rites are each represented by one diocese (all directly responsible to the Holy See). In December 1999 the Roman Catholic Church had about 13.3m. adherents in Canada.

Canadian Conference of Catholic Bishops/Conférence des évêques catholiques du Canada: 2500 Don Reid Dr., Ottawa, ON K1H 2J2; tel. (613) 241-9461; fax (613) 241-9048; e-mail cecc@cccb.ca; internet www.cccb.ca; Pres. Most Rev. JACQUES BERTHELET (Bishop of St-Jean-Longueuil); Vice-Pres. Most Rev. BRENDAN O'BRIEN (Archbishop of St John's, NL).

Latin Rite

Archbishop of Edmonton: Most Rev. THOMAS COLLINS.

Archbishop of Gatineau-Hull: Most Rev. ROGER ÉBACHER.

Archbishop of Grouard-McLennan: Most Rev. ARTHÉ GUIMOND.

Archbishop of Halifax: Most Rev. TERRENCE PRENDERGAST.

Archbishop of Keewatin-Le Pas: Most Rev. PETER ALFRED SUTTON.

Archbishop of Kingston: Most Rev. FRANCIS J. SPENCE.

Archbishop of Moncton: Most Rev. ERNEST LÉGER.

Archbishop of Montréal: Most Rev. Cardinal JEAN-CLAUDE TURCOTTE.

Archbishop of Ottawa: Most Rev. MARCEL A. GERVAIS.

Archbishop of Québec: Most Rev. MAURICE COUTURE.

Archbishop of Regina: Most Rev. PETER J. MALLON.

Archbishop of Rimouski: Most Rev. BERTRAND BLANCHET.

Archbishop of St Boniface: Most Rev. EMILIUS GOULET.

Archbishop of St John's, NL: Most Rev. BRENDAN O'BRIEN.

Archbishop of Sherbrooke: Most Rev. ANDRÉ GAUMOND.

Archbishop of Toronto: Cardinal ALOYSIUS M. AMBROZIC.

Archbishop of Vancouver: Most Rev. ADAM J. EXNER.

Archbishop of Winnipeg: Most Rev. JAMES V. WEISGERBER.

Ukrainian Rite

Ukrainian Catholic Archeparchy of Winnipeg (Metropolitan See of Canada): 233 Scotia St, Winnipeg, MB R2V 1V7; tel. (204) 338-7801; fax (204) 339-4006; e-mail archepar@escape.ca; internet www.archeparchy.ca; 33,490 mems (1991 census); Archeparch-Metropolitan of Winnipeg Most Rev. MICHAEL BZDEL.

The United Church of Canada

The United Church of Canada (L'Eglise unie du Canada) was founded in 1925 with the union of Methodist, Congregational and Presbyterian churches in Canada. The Evangelical United Brethren of Canada joined in 1968. In 2001 there were 3,677 congregations and 637,941 mems.

Moderator: MARION PARDY.

General Secretary: K. VIRGINIA COLEMAN, 3250 Bloor St West, Suite 300, Toronto, ON M8X 2Y4; tel. (416) 231-5931; fax (416) 231-3103; e-mail info@uccan.org; internet www.uccan.org.

Other Christian Churches

Canadian Baptist Ministries: 7185 Millcreek Dr., Mississauga, ON L5N 5R4; tel. (905) 821-3533; fax (905) 826-3441; e-mail dphillips@cbmin.org; internet www.cbmin.org; 1,133 churches; 129,000 mems (1996); Pres. Dr BRUCE MILNE; Gen. Sec. Rev. DAVID PHILLIPS.

Christian Reformed Church in North America (Canadian Council): 3475 Mainway, POB 5070, Burlington, ON L7R 3Y8; tel. (905) 336-2920; fax (905) 336-8344; e-mail crcna@crcna.ca; internet www.crcna.org; f. 1857; 237 congregations; 82,474 mems (2001); Dir in Canada Rev. WILLIAM VEENSTRA.

Church of Jesus Christ of Latter-day Saints (Mormon): 1185 Eglinton Ave East, POB 116, Toronto, ON M3C 3C6; tel. (416) 424-2485; fax (416) 424-3326; 433 congregations; 157,000 mems in Canada (1999).

Evangelical Lutheran Church in Canada: 393 Portage Ave, Suite 302, Winnipeg, MB R3B 3H6; tel. (204) 984-9150; fax (204) 984-9185; e-mail rschultz@elcic.ca; internet www.elcic.ca/; f. 1967; 623 congregations, 186,624 mems (2002); Bishop Rev. RAYMOND L. SCHULTZ.

Lutheran Church–Canada: 3074 Portage Ave, Winnipeg, MB R3K 0Y2; tel. (204) 895-3433; fax (204) 897-4319; e-mail info@lutheranchurch.ca; internet www.lutheranchurch.ca; f. 1988; 332 congregations; 79,665 mems (2000); Pres. Rev. RALPH MAYAN.

Pentecostal Assemblies of Canada: 2450 Milltower Court, Mississauga, ON L5N 5Z6; tel. (905) 542-7400; fax (905) 542-7313; e-mail info@paoc.org; internet www.paoc.org; 1,108 congregations, 232,000 mems (2001); Gen. Supt Dr WILLIAM D. MORROW.

Presbyterian Church in Canada: 50 Wynford Dr., Toronto, ON M3C 1J7; tel. (416) 441-1111; fax (416) 441-2825; e-mail pccadmin@presbycan.ca; internet www.presbyterian.ca; f. 1875; 1,000 congregations; 134,683 mems (1999); Moderator Rev. MARK LEWIS; Prin. Clerk Rev. STEPHEN KENDALL.

Religious Society of Friends: 91A Fourth Ave, Ottawa, ON K1S 2L1; tel. (613) 235-8553; fax (613) 235-1753; e-mail cym-office@quaker.ca; internet www.quaker.ca; Clerk of Canadian Yearly Meeting JOHN CALDER.

Seventh-day Adventists: 1148 King St East, Oshawa, ON L1H 1H8; tel. (905) 433-0011; fax (905) 433-0982; e-mail namorim@sdacc.org; internet www.sdacc.org; 328 congregations; 50,756 mems (2002); Pres. DANIEL JACKSON; Sec. NILTON AMORIM.

BAHÁ'Í FAITH

Bahá'í Community of Canada: 7200 Leslie St, Thornhill, ON L3T 6L8; tel. (905) 889-8168; fax (905) 889-8184; e-mail secretariat@cdnbnc.org; internet www.ca.bahai.org; f. 1902; 29,000 mems (1998); Sec. JUDY FILSON.

BUDDHISM

Buddhist Churches of Canada: 11786 Fentiman Place, Richmond, BC V7E 6M6; tel. (604) 272-3330; fax (604) 272-6865; e-mail bcc@bcc.ca; internet www.bcc.ca; Jodo Shinshu Hongwanji-ha of Mahayana Buddhism; Bishop ORAI FUJIKAWA.

ISLAM

There are an estimated 260,000 Muslims in Canada.

Ahmadiyya Movement in Islam (Canada): 10610 Jane St, Maple, ON L6A 1S1; tel. (905) 832-2669; fax (905) 832-3220; e-mail info@islam.ahmadiyya.org; internet www.ahmadiyya.ca; f. 1965; Pres. and Missionary-in-Charge NASEEM MAHDI.

Canadian Islamic Congress: 420 Erb St West, Suite 424, Waterloo, ON N2L 6K6; tel. (519) 746–1242; fax (519) 746–2929; e-mail cic@canadianislamiccongress.com; internet www .canadianislamiccongress.com; Gen. Sec. MOHAMED ELMASRY.

Canadian Islamic Organization Inc: 2069 Kempton Park Dr., Mississauga, ON L5M 2Z4; tel. (905) 820-4655; fax (905) 820-0832; Gen. Sec. FAREED AHMAD KHAN.

Council of Muslim Communities of Canada: 1250 Ramsey View Court, Suite 504, Sudbury, ON P3E 2E7; co-ordinating agency; Dir MIR IQBAL ALI.

Federation of Islamic Associations: 73 Patricia Ave, North York, ON M2M 1J1; tel. (416) 222-2794; fax (416) 674-8168; internet www .islamerica.com; Pres. AYUBE ALLY.

Organization of North American Shi'a Itha-Asheri Muslim Communities (NASIMCO): 300 John St, POB 87629, Thornhill, ON L3T 5W0; tel. (905) 763-7512; fax (905) 763-7509.

JUDAISM

The are an estimated 350,000 Jews in Canada.

Canadian Council for Conservative Judaism: 1520 Steeles Ave, Suite 112, Concord, ON L4K 3B9; tel. (905) 738-1717; fax (905) 738-1331; e-mail 71263.302@compuserve.com; Pres. DAVID GREENBERG; Exec. Sec. RHONDA SCHILD.

Canadian Council for Reform Judaism: 36 Atkinson Ave, Thornhill, ON L4J 8C9; tel. (905) 709-2275; fax (905) 709-1895; e-mail ccrj@uahc.org; Pres. CHARLES ROTHSCHILD.

Canadian Jewish Congress: 100 Sparks St, Suite 650, Ottawa, ON K1P 5B7; tel. (613) 233-8703; fax (613) 233-8748; e-mail canadianjewishcongress@cjc.ca; internet www.cjc.ca; f. 1919; 10 regional offices; Exec. Vice-Pres. JACK SILVERSTONE.

SIKHISM

There are an estimated 250,000 Sikhs in Canada.

Federation of Sikh Societies of Canada: POB 91, Station B, Ottawa, ON K1P 6C3; tel. (613) 737-7296; fax (613) 739-7153; f. 1981; Pres. MOHINDER SINGH GOSAL.

The Press

The daily press in Canada is essentially local and regional in coverage, influence and distribution. Chain ownership has traditionally been predominant: at the beginning of 2000 63.4% of daily newspaper circulation was represented by two major groups: Hollinger Inc (42.0% of daily newspaper circulation) and Quebecor Inc (21.4%). However, in 2000 both Hollinger and the Thomson Corpn (10.5%) divested themselves of significant proportions of their newspaper interests—Thomson retaining only the Toronto *Globe and Mail*, control of which was subsequently transferred to Bell Globemedia, Inc, a joint venture between companies including Thomson and the telecommunications operator, BCE, Inc. In November 2000 CanWest Global Communications Corpn acquired 14 daily metropolitan newspapers, a number of community newspapers and a 50% interest in the National Post (Canada's first national daily newspaper, launched by Hollinger's Southam Inc division in October 1998). Torstar (which owns the *Toronto Star*) accounted for 13.8% of total circulation in 2000.

In 2002 there were 102 daily newspapers with a combined circulation of almost 5.1m., and, in 2000, about 1,100 weekly and twice-weekly community newspapers serving mainly the more remote areas of the country. A significant feature of the Canadian press is the number of newspapers catering for immigrant groups: there are over 80 of these daily and weekly publications appearing in over 20 languages.

There are numerous periodicals for business, trade, professional, recreational and special interest readership, although periodical publishing, particularly, encounters substantial competition from publications originating in the USA.

The following are among the principal newspaper publishing groups:

CanWest Global Communications Corpn: 3100 TD Center, 201 Portage Ave, Winnipeg, MB R3B 3L7; tel. (204) 956–2025; fax (204) 947–9841; e-mail inquiries@canwestinteractive.com; internet www .canwestglobal.com; Exec. Chair. I. H. ASPER; Pres. and CEO LEONARD ASPER.

Quebecor Inc: 612 rue St-Jacques, Montréal, QC H3C 1C8; tel. (514) 877-9777; fax (514) 877-9790; internet www.quebecor.com; f. 1965; Pres. and CEO PIERRE PELADIEU.

Thomson Corporation: POB 24, Toronto-Dominion Centre/Bank Tower, Toronto, ON M5K 1A1; e-mail paula.monaghan@thomson .com; internet www.thomson.com; tel. (416) 360-8700; fax (416) 360-8812; Chair. DAVID K. R. THOMSON; Pres. and CEO RICHARD HARRINGTON.

Torstar Corpn: 1 Yonge St, Toronto, ON M5E 1P9; tel. (416) 869-4010; fax (416) 869-4183; e-mail torstar@torstar.com; internet www .torstar.com; Chair. JOHN R. EVANS; Pres. CATHERINE ATKINSON MURRAY.

PRINCIPAL DAILY NEWSPAPERS

Alberta

Calgary Herald: 215 16th St, SE, POB 2400, Station M, Calgary, AB T2P 0W8; tel. (403) 235-7100; internet www.calgaryherald.com; f. 1883; Publr DAN GAYNOR; Editor-in-Chief PETER MENZIES; circ. 122,000 (Mon.-Sat.), 116,000 (Sun.).

Calgary Sun: 2615 12th St, NE, Calgary, AB T2E 7W9; tel. (403) 250-4200; fax (403) 250-4180; e-mail calpromo@sunpub.com; internet www.canoe.ca; f. 1980; Publr GUY HUNTINGFORD; Editor-in-Chief CHRIS NELSON; circ. 70,000 (Mon.-Sat.), 101,000 (Sun.).

Daily Herald–Tribune: 10604 100th St, Postal Bag 3000, Grande Prairie, AB T8V 6V4; tel. (403) 532-1110; fax (403) 532-2120; e-mail bowes@telusplanet.net; internet www.bowesnet.com/dht; f. 1913; evening; Publr PETER J. WOOLSEY; Man. Editor FRED RINNE; circ. 9,000.

Edmonton Journal: POB 2421, Edmonton, AB T5J 2S6; tel. (780) 429-5100; fax (780) 429-5536; e-mail bcox@the-journal.southam.ca; internet www.edmontonjournal.com; f. 1903; Publr LINDA HUGHES; Editor-in-Chief MURDOCH DAVIS; circ. 141,000 (Mon.-Sat.), 134,000 (Sun.).

Edmonton Sun: 4990 92nd Ave, Suite 250, Edmonton, AB T6B 3A1; tel. (780) 468-0100; fax (780) 468-0128; e-mail ed.sun@edm .sunpub.com; internet www.canoe.ca; f. 1978; Publr CRAIG MARTIN; Editor GRAHAM DALZIEL; circ. 73,000 (Mon.-Sat.), 110,000 (Sun.).

Fort McMurray Today: 8550 Franklin Ave, Fort McMurray, AB T9H 3G1; tel. (403) 743-8186; fax (403) 790-1006; e-mail today@ ccinet.ab.ca; evening; Publr TIM O'ROURKE; Editor DARRELL SKIDNUK; circ. 5,000.

Lethbridge Herald: 504 Seventh St South, POB 670, Lethbridge, AB T1J 3Z7; tel. (403) 328-4411; fax (403) 328-4536; internet www .lethbridgeherald.com; f. 1907; evening and Sun. Publr PETER SCOTT; Man. Editor MICHAEL J. HERTZ; circ. 22,000 (evening), 19,000 (Sun.).

Medicine Hat News: 3257 Dunmore Rd, SE, POB 10, Medicine Hat, AB T1A 7E6; tel. (403) 527-1101; fax (403) 527-6029; internet www.medicinehatnews.com; f. 1887; evening; Publr MICHAEL J. HERTZ; Man. Editor GORDON WRIGHT; circ. 14,000.

Red Deer Advocate: 2950 Bremner Ave, Bag 5200, Red Deer, AB T4N 5G3; tel. (403) 343-2400; fax (403) 341-4772; e-mail editorial@ advocate.red-deer.ab.ca; Editor JOE MCLAUGHLIN; circ. 19,000.

British Columbia

Alaska Highway News: 9916 89th St, Fort St John, BC V1J 3T8; tel. (250) 785-5631; fax (250) 785-3522; evening; Publr BRUCE LANTZ; Editor JOE PAVLIN; circ. 4,000.

Alberini Valley Times: 4918 Napier St, POB 400, Port Alberini, BC V9Y 7N1; tel. (250) 723-8171; fax (250) 723-0586; e-mail avtimes@arrowsmith.net; internet www.arrowsmith.net/~avtimes; Publr NIGEL E. HANNAFORD; circ. 7,000.

Daily Bulletin: 335 Spokane St, Kimberley, BC V1A 1Y9; tel. (250) 427-5333; fax (250) 427-5336; e-mail bulletin@cyberlink.bc.ca; f. 1932; evening; Publr STEEN JORGENSEN; Editor CHRIS DOUAN; circ. 2,000.

Daily Courier: 550 Doyle Ave, Kelowna, BC V1Y 7V1; tel. (250) 762-4445; fax (250) 763-0194; e-mail alison.yesilcimen@ok.bc.ca; internet www.TheOkangan.bc.ca; f. 1904; evening and Sun. Publr ALISON YESILCIMEN; Exec. Editor ROSS FREAKE; circ. 18,500 (evening); 33,250 (Sun.).

Daily News: 2575 McCullough Rd, Nanaimo, BC V9S 5W5; tel. (250) 758-4917; fax (250) 758-4513; f. 1874; evening; Publr NIGEL LARK; Man. Editor DOYLE MACKINNON; circ. 9,000.

Daily Townsman: 822 Cranbrook St North, Cranbrook, BC V1C 3R9; tel. (250) 426-5201; fax (250) 426-5003; e-mail townsman@ cyberlink.bc.ca; evening; Publr STEEN JORGENSEN; Editor DAVID SANDS; circ. 4,000.

Kamloops Daily News: 393 Seymour St, Kamloops, BC V2C 6P6; tel. (250) 372-2331; fax (250) 374-3884; e-mail kamnews@

wkpowerlink.com; internet www.southam.com/kamloopsdailynews/; f. 1930; evening; Publr DALE BRIN; Editor MEL ROTHENBURGER; circ. 14,000.

Nelson Daily News: 266 Baker St, Nelson, BC V1L 4H3; tel. (250) 352-3552; fax (250) 352-2418; e-mail adnews@netidea.com; internet www.nelsondailynews.com; f. 1902; evening; Publr JOHN A. SMITH; Editor DREW EDWARDS; circ. 4,000.

Peace River Block News: 901 100th Ave, Dawson Creek, BC V1G 1W2; tel. (250) 782-4888; fax (250) 782-6770; e-mail prbnews@pris .bc.ca; f. 1930; evening and Sun. Publr SUSAN RAND; Editor JOSE CORMIER; circ. 3,000 (evening), 11,000 (Sun.).

Penticton Herald: 186 Nanaimo Ave West, Suite 101, Penticton, BC V2A 1N4; tel. (250) 492-4002; fax (250) 492-2403; e-mail jhcoady@ok.bc.ca; internet www.ok.bc.ca/ph; evening; Publr ALISON YESILCIMEN; Man. Editor DAVID MARSDEN; circ. 9,000.

Prince George Citizen: 150 Brunswick St, POB 5700, Prince George, BC V2L 5K9; tel. (250) 562-2441; fax (250) 562-7453; e-mail pgcnews@prg.southam.ca; internet www.princegeorgecitizen.com; f. 1957; evening; Publr DEL LAVERDURE; Man. Editor JOHN HARDING; circ. 18,000.

The Province: 200 Granville St, Suite 1, Vancouver, BC V6C 3N3; tel. (604) 605-2222; fax (604) 605-2720; internet www .vancouverprovince.com; f. 1898; Publr DENNIS SKULSKY; Editor-in-Chief VIVIENNE SOSNOWSKI; circ. 160,000 (Mon.-Sat.), 196,000 (Sun.).

Sing Tao Daily News: 8874 Hudson St, Vancouver, BC V6A 2V1; tel. (604) 261-5066; fax (604) 261-7093; Chinese; Editor PAUL TSANG; circ. 15,000.

Times Colonist: 2621 Douglas St, POB 300, Victoria, BC V8T 4M2; tel. (250) 380-5211; fax (250) 380-5353; e-mail timesc@interlink.bc .ca; f. 1858; Publr PETER BAILLIE; Editor-in-Chief BOB POOLE; circ. 76,000 (Mon.-Sat.), 76,000 (Sun.).

Trail Daily Times: 1163 Cedar Ave, Trail, BC V1R 4B8; tel. (250) 368-8551; fax (250) 368-8550; e-mail konschuk@wkpowerlink.com; evening; Publr JON JARRETT; Editor TRACY KONSCHUK; circ. 7,000.

The Vancouver Sun: 200 Granville St, Suite 1, Vancouver, BC V6C 3N3; tel. (604) 732-2111; fax (604) 732-2323; internet www .vancouversun.com; f. 1886; Editor-in-Chief NEIL REYNOLDS; circ. 190,000 (Mon.-Fri.), 247,000 (Sat.).

World Journal (Vancouver): 2288 Clark Dr., Vancouver, BC V5N 3G8; tel. (604) 876-1338; fax (604) 876-9191; Chinese; Publr WILSON CHIEN; circ. 10,000.

Manitoba

Brandon Sun: 501 Rosser Ave, Brandon, MB R7A 0K4; tel. (204) 727-2451; fax (204) 727-0385; e-mail bmarshall@brandonsun.com; internet www.brandonsun.com; f. 1882; evening and Sun. Publr RUDY REDEKOP; Man. Editor BRIAN D. MARSHALL; circ. 18,000 (evening), 24,000 (Sun.).

Daily Graphic: 1941 Saskatchewan Ave West, POB 130, Portage La Prairie, MB R1N 3B4; tel. (204) 857-3427; fax (204) 239-1270; e-mail plpnews@mb.sympatico.ca; evening; Publr W. J. HAMILTON; Editor IAN R. WHITE; circ. 4,000.

Flin Flon Reminder: 10 North Ave, Flin Flon, MB R8A 0T2; tel. (204) 687-3454; fax (204) 687-4473; e-mail reminder@mb.sympatico .ca; f. 1946; evening; Publr RANDY DANELIUK; Editor RICH BILLY; circ. 4,000.

Winnipeg Free Press: 1355 Mountain Ave, Winnipeg, MB R2X 3B6; tel. (204) 697-7000; fax (204) 697-7375; internet www .winnipegfreepress.com; f. 1874; Publr H. R. REDEKOP; Editor NICHOLAS HIRST; circ. 131,000 (Mon.-Fri. evening), 187,000 (Sat.), 144,000 (Sun.).

Winnipeg Sun: 1700 Church Ave, Winnipeg, MB R2X 3A2; tel. (204) 694-2022; fax (204) 632-8709; e-mail editor@wpgsun.com; internet www.canoe.ca/winnipegsun/home.html; f. 1980; Publr GORDAN NORRIE; Man. Editor BILL DAVIDSON; circ. 45,000 (Mon.-Sat.), 58,000 (Sun.).

New Brunswick

L'Acadie Nouvelle: 476 blvd St-Pierre ouest, CP 5536, Caraquet, NB E1W 1B7; tel. (506) 727-4444; fax (506) 727-7620; e-mail infos@ acadienouvelle.com; internet www.capacadie.com/acadienouvelle/ index.cfm; f. 1984; Publr GILLES GAGNÉ; Editor LORIO ROY; circ. 17,000.

Daily Gleaner: POB 3370, Fredericton, NB E3B 5A2; tel. (506) 452-6671; fax (506) 452-7405; e-mail dgnews@nbnet.nb.ca; internet www .nbnews.com/dailygleaner; f. 1880; evening; Publr BRIAN BUTTERS; Editor-in-Chief HAL WOOD; circ. 30,000.

St John Times–Globe: 210 Crown St, POB 2350, Saint John, NB E2L 3V8; tel. (506) 632-8888; fax (506) 648-2654; e-mail tjetg@nbnet .nb.ca; internet www.nbnews.com; evening; Publr VICTOR MLODECKI; circ. 23,000.

Telegraph–Journal: 210 Crown St, POB 2350, Saint John, NB E2L 3V8; tel. (506) 632-8888; fax (506) 648-2654; e-mail tjetg@nbnet .nb.ca; internet www.nbnews.com; Publr JONATHAN FRANKIN; circ. 21,000.

Times–Transcript: 939 Main St, POB 1001, Moncton, NB E1C 8P3; tel. (506) 859-4900; fax (506) 859-4899; e-mail news@ timestranscript.com; internet www.nbnews.com/timestranscript; f. 1983; evening and Sat. Publr JONATHAN FRANKLIN; Man. Editor MIKE BEMBRIDGE; circ. 39,000 (Mon.-Fri.), 46,000 (Sat.).

Newfoundland and Labrador

Telegram: Columbus Dr., POB 5970, St John's, NL A1C 5X7; tel. (709) 364-6300; fax (709) 364-9333; e-mail telegram@thetelegram .com; internet www.thetelegram.com; f. 1879; evening and Sat. Publr MILLER H. AYRE; Man. Editor BRETTON LONEY; circ. 33,000 (Mon.-Fri.), 57,000 (Sat.).

Western Star: 106 West St, POB 460, Corner Brook, NL A2H 6E7; tel. (709) 634-4348; fax (709) 634-9824; e-mail star@thezone.net; internet www.canada.com/cornerbrook; f. 1900; Publr IAN BAIRD; Editor RICHARD WILLIAMS; circ. 9,000.

Nova Scotia

Amherst Daily News: POB 280, Amherst, NS B4H 3Z2; tel. (902) 667-5102; fax (902) 667-0419; e-mail cumbpub@istar.ca; f. 1893; Publr EARL J. GOUCHIE; Editor JOHN CONRAD; circ. 5,000.

Cape Breton Post: 255 George St, POB 1500, Sydney, NS B1P 6K6; tel. (902) 564-5451; fax (902) 562-7077; e-mail maned@cbpost.com; internet www.capebretonpost.com; f. 1900; Publr MILTON ELLIS; Man. Editor FRED JACKSON; circ. 28,000.

Chronicle–Herald: 1650 Argyle St, POB 610, Halifax, NS B3J 2T2; tel. (902) 426-2811; fax (902) 426-3014; e-mail ombud@herald.ns.ca; internet www.herald.ns.ca; Publr GRAHAM W. DENNIS; Man. Editor TERRY O'NEIL; circ. 90,000 (Mon.-Fri.), 54,000 (Sat.).

Daily News: POB 8330, Station A, Halifax, NS B3K 5M1; tel. (902) 468-1222; fax (902) 468-3609; e-mail citydesk@hfxnews.southam.ca; internet www.hfxnews.southam.ca/; f. 1974; Publr. MARK RICHARDSON; Editor-in-Chief BILL TURPIN; circ. 24,000 (Mon.-Sat.), 33,000 (Sun.).

Evening News: 352 East River Rd, POB 159, New Glasgow, NS B2H 5E2; tel. (902) 752-3000; fax (902) 752-1945; e-mail dmk@ newglasgownews.com; internet www.newglasgownews.com; f. 1910; evening; Publr RICHARD RUSSELL; Man. Editor DOUG MACNEIL; circ. 8,000.

Mail–Star: 1650 Argyle St, POB 610, Halifax, NS B3J 2T2; tel. (902) 426-2811; fax (902) 426-3014; e-mail ombud@herald.ns.ca; internet www.herald.ns.ca; evening; Publr GRAHAM W. DENNIS; Man. Editor TERRY O'NEIL; circ. 21,000.

Truro Daily News: 6 Louise St, POB 220, Truro, NS B2N 5C3; tel. (902) 893-9405; fax (902) 893-0518; e-mail editor.news@north.nsis .com; internet www.truro.canada.com; f. 1891; evening; Publr LEITH ORR; Man. Editor BILL MCGUIRE; circ. 8,000.

Ontario

Barrie Examiner: 16 Bayfield St, Barrie, ON L4M 4T6; tel. (705) 726-6537; fax (705) 726-7706; e-mail examiner@sympatico.ca; f. 1864; evening; Publr RON LAURIN; Man. Editor JOANNE KUSHNIER; circ. 9,000.

Beacon–Herald: 108 Ontario St, POB 430, Stratford, ON N5A 6T6; tel. (519) 271-2220; fax (519) 271-1026; e-mail beacan@cyg.net; f. 1854; evening; Publr CHARLES W. DINGMAN; Man. Editor JOHN KASTNER; circ. 12,000.

Brockville Recorder and Times: 23 King St West, POB 10, Brockville, ON K6V 5T8; tel. (613) 342-4441; fax (613) 342-4456; e-mail editor@recorder.ca; internet www.recorder.ca; f. 1821; evening; Publr BOB DOORNEBAL; Editor BARRY RAISON; circ. 13,000.

Cambridge Reporter: 26 Ainslie St South, POB 1510, Cambridge, ON N1R 5T2; tel. (519) 621-3810; fax (519) 621-8239; e-mail news@ cambridge-reporter.com; internet www.cambridge-reporter.com; f. 1846; evening; Publr L. R. (VERNE) SHAULL; Editor CLYDE WARRINGTON; circ. 7,000.

Chatham Daily News: 45 Fourth St, POB 2007, Chatham, ON N7M 5M6; tel. (519) 354-2000; fax (519) 436-0949; e-mail chathamnews@cha.southam.ca; f. 1862; evening; Publr JOHN CHEEK; Man. Editor JIM BLAKE; circ. 14,000.

Chronicle–Journal: 75 Cumberland St South, Thunder Bay, ON P7B 1A3; tel. (807) 343-6200; fax (807) 345-5991; e-mail cj-editorial@ cwconnect.ca; Publr COLIN BRUCE; Man. Editor PETER HAGGERT; circ. 32,000 (Mon.-Sat.), 38,000 (Sun.).

Cobourg Daily Star: 415 King St West, POB 400, Cobourg, ON K9A 4L1; tel. (905) 372-0131; fax (905) 372-4966; e-mail starletters@eagle.ca; internet www.eagle.ca/cobourgstar; evening; Publr MIKE WALSH; Editorial Dir JIM GROSSMITH; circ. 6,000.

Daily Observer: 186 Alexander St, Pembroke, ON K8A 4L9; tel. (613) 732-3691; fax (613) 732-2645; e-mail observer@webhart.net; f. 1855; evening; Publr STEVE GLOSTER; Man. Editor PETER LAPINSKIE; circ. 6,000.

Daily Press: 187 Cedar St South, POB 560, Timmins, ON P4N 2G9; tel. (705) 268-5050; fax (705) 268-7373; e-mail tdp@nt.net; internet www.timminspress.com; f. 1933; Publr SYL BÉLISLE; Man. Editor DAVE MCGEE; circ. 10,000.

Le Droit: 47 rue Clarence, Pièce 222, CP 8860, succursale Terminus, Ottawa, ON K1G 3J9; tel. (613) 562-0111; fax (613) 562-6280; e-mail publicite@ledroit.com; internet www.ledroit.com; f. 1913; Publr PIERRE BERGERON; Man. Editor FRANÇOIS ROY; circ. 35,000 (Mon.-Fri.), 42,000 (Sat.).

The Expositor: 53 Dalhousie St, POB 965, Brantford, ON N3T 5S8; tel. (519) 756-2020; fax (519) 756-4911; e-mail expnews@brtsoutham.ca; internet www.southam.com/brantfordexpositor/; f. 1852; Publr MICHAEL PEARCE; Editor DAVID SCHULTZ; circ. 23,000.

Financial Post: 333 King St East, Toronto, ON M5A 4N2; tel. (416) 350-6300; fax (416) 350-6301; e-mail letters@finpost.com; f. 1907; Publr and CEO WILLIAM NEILL; Editor ARTHUR JOHNSON; circ. 91,000.

The Globe and Mail: 444 Front St West, Toronto, ON M5V 2S9; tel. (416) 585-5000; fax (416) 585-5085; e-mail newsroom@globeandmail.ca; internet www.globeandmail.com; f. 1844; Publr PHILLIP CRAWLEY; Editor RICHARD ADDIS; circ. 363,779 (Mon.-Fri.), 436,795 (Sat.).

Guelph Mercury: 14 Macdonnell St, POB 3604, Guelph, ON N1H 6P7; tel. (519) 822-4310; fax (519) 767-1681; e-mail mercury@in.on.ca; f. 1854; evening; Publr STEPHEN RHODES; Editor ED CASSAVOY; circ. 13,000.

Hamilton Spectator: 44 Frid St, Hamilton, ON L8N 3G3; tel. (905) 526-3333; fax (905) 526-1139; internet www.hamiltonspectator.com; f. 1846; Publr JAGODA PIKE; Editor-in-Chief DANA ROBBINS; circ. 111,000.

Intelligencer: 45 Bridge St East, POB 5600, Belleville, ON K8N 5C7; tel. (613) 962-9171; fax (613) 962-9652; e-mail intel@intranet.on.ca; f. 1870; evening; Publr MICHAEL A. POWER; Man. Editor NICK PALMER; circ. 17,000.

Kingston Whig–Standard: 6 Cataraqui St, POB 2300, Kingston, ON K7L 1Z7; tel. (613) 544-5000; fax (613) 530-4119; e-mail kinwhig@thewhig.com; internet www.kingstonwhigstandard.com; f. 1834; Publr FRED LAFLAMME; Man. Editor STEVE LUKITS; circ. 28,000.

Lindsay Daily Post: 15 William St North, Lindsay, ON K9V 3Z8; tel. (705) 324-2114; fax (705) 324-0174; e-mail lindsaypost@sympatico.ca; evening; Publr MIKE WALKER; Editor TED MCFADDEN; circ. 9,000.

London Free Press: 369 York St, POB 2280, London, ON N6A 4G1; tel. (519) 679-1111; fax (519) 667-5520; e-mail letters@lfpress.com; internet www.lfpress.com; f. 1849; Publr LES PYETTE; Editor ROB PAYNTER; circ. 99,000 (Mon.-Fri.); 125,000 (Sat.).

Ming Pao Daily News: 1355 Huntingwood Dr., Scarborough, ON M1S 3J1; tel. (416) 321-0093; fax (416) 321-3499; Chinese; Editor-in-Chief K. M. LUI; circ. 33,000 (Mon.-Sat.), 51,000 (Sun.).

National Post: 1450 Don Mills Rd, Suite 300, Don Mills, ON M3B 2X7; tel. (416) 510-6748; fax (416) 510-6743; internet www.nationalpost.com; f. 1998; Publr DON BABICK; Editor-in-Chief KEN WHYTE; national newspaper with printing centres in nine cities; circ. 285,000 (Mon.-Fri.), 336,000 (Sat.).

Niagara Falls Review: 4801 Valley Way, POB 270, Niagara Falls, ON L2E 6T6; tel. (905) 358-5711; fax (905) 356-0785; e-mail review@nfreview.com; internet www.nfreview.com; f. 1879; evening; Publr DAVID A. BEATTIE; Man. Editor MICHAEL BROWN; circ. 18,000.

North Bay Nugget: 259 Worthington St, POB 570, North Bay, ON P1B 8J6; tel. (705) 472-3200; fax (705) 472-5128; e-mail nugnews@onlink.net; f. 1909; evening; Publr ROBERT HULL; Man. Editor BRUCE COWAN; circ. 18,000.

Northern Daily News: 8 Duncan Ave, POB 1030, Kirkland Lake, ON P2N 3L4; tel. (705) 567-5321; fax (705) 567-6162; f. 1922; evening; Publr SYL BÉLISLE; Editor TOM PERRY; circ. 6,000.

Ottawa Citizen: 1101 Baxter Rd, POB 5020, Ottawa, ON K2C 3M4; tel. (613) 829-9100; fax (613) 596-3755; internet www.ottawacitizen.com; f. 1845; Publr RUSSELL A. MILLS; Editor SCOTT ANDERSON; circ. 141,000 (Mon.-Fri.), 185,000 (Sat.).

Ottawa Sun: 380 Hunt Club Rd, POB 9729, Station T, Ottawa, ON K1G 5H7; tel. (613) 739-7000; fax (613) 739-9383; internet www.canoe.ca/OttawaSun/home.html; Publr JUDY BULLIS; Editor RICK GIBBONS; circ. 50,000 (Mon.-Sat.), 56,000 (Sun.).

The Packet and Times: 31 Colborne St East, Orillia, ON L3V 1T4; tel. (705) 325-1355; fax (705) 325-7691; e-mail packet@barint.on.ca; f. 1953; evening; Publr KEN KOYAMA; Man. Editor MARK BISSET; circ. 8,000.

Peterborough Examiner: 730 Kingsway, Peterborough, ON K9J 8L4; tel. (705) 745-4641; fax (705) 743-4581; e-mail news1@ptbo.igs.net; f. 1884; evening; Publr JIM AMBROSE; Man. Editor ED ARNOLD; circ. 22,000.

The Record: 225 Fairway Rd, Kitchener, ON N2G 4E5; tel. (519) 894-2231; fax (519) 894-3912; internet www.therecord.com; f. 1878; evening; Publr WAYNE MacDONALD; Editor LYNN HADDRALL; circ. 71,000.

St Catharines Standard: 17 Queen St, St Catharines, ON L2R 5G5; tel. (905) 684-7251; fax (905) 684-6670; e-mail akrulik@scs.southam.ca; internet www.scstandard.com; f. 1891; evening; Publr DAN GAYNOR; Man. Editor DOUG FIRBY; circ. 34,000.

St Thomas Times–Journal: 16 Hincks St, St Thomas, ON N5R 5Z2; tel. (519) 631-2790; fax (519) 631-5653; internet www.bowesnet.com/timesjournal; f. 1882; evening; Publr BRENT SPILAK; Man. Editor ROSS PORTER; circ. 9,000.

Sarnia Observer: 140 Front St South, POB 3009, Sarnia, ON N7T 7M8; tel. (519) 344-3641; fax (519) 332-2951; e-mail observer@xcelco.on.ca; f. 1917; evening; Publr DARYL C. SMITH; Man. Editor TERRY SHAW; circ. 22,000.

Sault Star: 145 Old Garden River Rd, POB 460, Sault Ste Marie, ON P6A 5M5; tel. (705) 759-3035; fax (705) 759-0102; e-mail ssmstar@ssmsoutham.ca; internet www.saultstar.comssm; f. 1912; evening; Publr ROBERT W. RICHARDSON; Man. Editor JOHN HALUCHA; circ. 22,000.

Sentinel–Review: 18 Brock St, POB 1000, Woodstock, ON N4S 8A5; tel. (519) 537-2341; fax (519) 537-3049; e-mail sentinel@annexweb.com; internet www.annexweb.com/sentinel; f. 1886; evening; Publr PAT LOGAN; Man. Editor ALISON DOWNIE; circ. 9,000.

Simcoe Reformer: 105 Donly Dr. South, POB 370, Simcoe, ON N3Y 4L2; tel. (519) 426-5710; fax (519) 426-9255; e-mail refedit@annexweb.com; internet www.annexweb.com/reformernet; f. 1858; evening; Publr MICHAEL FREDERICKS; Man. Editor KIM NOVAK; circ. 9,000.

Sing Tao Daily News: 417 Dundas St West, Toronto, ON M5T 1G6; tel. (416) 596-8168; fax (416) 861-8169; Chinese; Editor-in-Chief TONY KU; circ. 38,000.

Standard–Freeholder: 44 Pitt St, Cornwall, ON K6J 3P3; tel. (613) 933-3160; fax (613) 933-7168; e-mail publisher@standard-freeholder.southam.ca; Publr MILTON S. ELLIS; Editor ALF LAFAVE; circ. 15,000.

Sudbury Star: 33 MacKenzie St, Sudbury, ON P3C 4Y1; tel. (705) 674-5271; fax (705) 674-0624; e-mail editorial@sightseer.ca; f. 1909; evening; Publr KEN D. SEGUIN; Man. Editor ROGER CAZABON; circ. 22,000.

Sun Times: 290 Ninth St East, POB 200, Owen Sound, ON N4K 5P2; tel. (519) 376-2250; fax (519) 376-7190; e-mail owtimes@southam.ca; internet www.southam.com/owensoundsuntimes; f. 1853; evening; Publr CLYDE T. WICKS; Editor JIM MERRIAM; circ. 19,000.

Toronto Star: 1 Yonge St, Toronto, ON M5E 1E6; tel. (416) 367-2000; fax (416) 869-4328; e-mail newsroom@webramp.net; internet www.thestar.com; f. 1892; Publr JOHN A. HONDERICH; Man. Editor MARY DEANNE SHEARS; circ. 453,000 (Mon.-Fri.), 702,000 (Sat.), 501,000 (Sun.).

Toronto Sun: 333 King St East, Toronto, ON M5A 3X5; tel. (416) 947-2221; fax (416) 361-1205; internet www.canoe.ca; f. 1971; Publr and CEO LES PYETTE; Editor LAURIE GOLDSTEIN; circ. 231,000 (Mon.-Sat.), 400,000 (Sun.).

Welland-Port Colborne Tribune: 228 East Main St, POB 278, Welland, ON L3B 5P5; tel. (905) 732-2411; fax (905) 732-4883; e-mail tribune@iaw.on.ca; f. 1863; Publr L. R. (VERNE) SHAULL; Editor GARY MANNING; circ. 15,000.

Windsor Star: 167 Ferry St, Windsor, ON N9A 4M5; tel. (519) 256-5533; fax (519) 255-5515; e-mail letters@win.southam.ca; internet www.southam.com/windsorstar; f. 1918; Publr JIM McCORMACK; Editor WAYNE MORIARTY; circ. 77,000.

World Journal (Toronto): 415 Eastern Ave, Toronto, ON M4M 1B7; tel. (416) 778-0889; fax (416) 778-4889; Chinese; Editor-in-Chief LOUIS CHU; circ. 38,000.

Prince Edward Island

Guardian: 165 Prince St, POB 760, Charlottetown, PE C1A 4R7; tel. (902) 629-6000; fax (902) 566-3808; internet www.theguardian.pe.ca; e-mail newsroom@chg.southam.ca; f. 1887; Publr DON BRANDER; Editor GARY MacDOUGALL; circ. 22,000.

Journal–Pioneer: 4 Queen St, POB 2480, Summerside, PE C1N 4K5; tel. (902) 436-2121; fax (902) 436-0784; e-mail dshea@itas.net; f. 1865; evening; Publr SANDY RUNDLE; Editor DARLENE SHEA; circ. 11,000.

Québec

Le Devoir: 2050 rue de Bleury, 9e étage, Montréal, QC H3A 3M9; tel. (514) 985-3333; fax (514) 985-3360; e-mail redaction@ledevoir .com; internet www.ledevoir.com; Publr BERNARD DESCÔTEAUX; Editor-in-Chief JEAN ROBERT SANSFAÇON; circ. 27,000 (Mon.-Fri.), 34,000 (Sat.).

The Gazette: 250 rue St-Antoine ouest, Montréal, QC H2Y 3R7; tel. (514) 987-2222; fax (514) 987-2270; internet www.montrealgazette .com; e-mail library@thegazette.southam.ca; internet www.canada .com/Montreal/montrealgazette; f. 1778; Publr LARRY SMITH; Editor-in-Chief PETER STOCKLAND; circ. 140,000 (Mon.-Fri.), 188,000 (Sat.), 133,000 (Sun.).

Le Journal de Montréal: 4545 rue Frontenac, Montréal, QC H2H 2R7; tel. (514) 521-4545; fax (514) 525-542; e-mail transmission@ journalmtl.com; internet www.journalmtl.com; f. 1964; Publr and Editor PIERRE FRANCOEUR; circ. 267,000 (Mon.-Fri.), 334,000 (Sat.).

Le Journal de Québec: 450 ave Béchard, Vanier, QC G1M 2E9; tel. (418) 683-1573; fax (418) 683-1027; f. 1967; Publr JEAN-CLAUDE L'ABBÉE; Chief Editor SERGE CÔTÉ; circ. 98,000 (Mon.-Fri.), 126,000 (Sat.), 101,000 (Sun.).

Le Nouvelliste: 1920 rue Bellefeuille, CP 668, Trois Rivières, QC G9A 5J6; tel. (819) 376-2501; fax (819) 376-0946; e-mail information@lenouvelliste.qc.ca; internet www.lenouvelliste.qc.ca; f. 1920; Pres. and Publr JEAN SISTO; Editor-in-Chief ANDRÉ POITRAS; circ. 43,000.

La Presse: 7 rue St-Jacques, Montréal, QC H2Y 1K9; tel. (514) 285-7272; fax (514) 285-6808; f. 1884; Pres. and Editor ROGER D. LANDRY; circ. 187,000 (Mon.-Fri.), 286,000 (Sat.), 196,000 (Sun.).

Le Quotidien du Saguenay-Lac-St-Jean: 1051 blvd Talbot, Chicoutimi, QC G7H 5C1; tel. (418) 545-4474; fax (418) 690-8824; internet www.lequotidien.com; f. 1973; Pres. and Editor CLAUDE GAGNON; circ. 29,000.

The Record: CP 1200, Sherbrooke, QC J1H 5L6; tel. (819) 569-9525; fax (819) 569-3945; internet www.sherbrookerecord.com; f. 1837; Publr RANDY KINNEAR; Editor SHARON McCULLY; circ. 6,000.

Le Soleil: 925 chemin St-Louis, CP 1547, succursale Terminus, Québec, QC G1K 7J6; tel. (418) 686-3394; fax (418) 686-3374; internet www.cyberpresse.ca; f. 1896; Publr and Editor ALAN DUBUC; circ. 81,045 (Mon.-Fri.), 112,951 (Sat.), 90,304 (Sun.).

La Tribune: 1950 rue Roy, Sherbrooke, QC J1K 2X8; tel. (819) 564-5454; fax (819) 564-8098; e-mail redaction@latribune.qc.ca; internet www.latribune.qc.ca; f. 1910; Pres. and Publr RAYMOND TARDIF; Editor-in-Chief MAURICE CLOUTIER; circ. 31,000 (Mon.-Fri.), 39,000 (Sat.).

La Voix de L'Est: 76 rue Dufferin, Granby, QC J2G 9L4; tel. (450) 375-4555; fax (450) 777-4865; e-mail redaction@lavoixdelest.qc.ca; internet www.cyberpresse.ca; f. 1945; Pres. and Publr JACQUES PRONOVOST; circ. 16,000.

Saskatchewan

Daily Herald: 30 10th St East, Prince Albert, SK S6V 5R9; tel. (306) 764-4276; fax (306) 763-3331; e-mail editorial@paherald@sk.sk.ca; internet www.paherald.sk.ca; f. 1894; Publr BARB GUSTAFSON; Man. Editor DOUG DAHL; circ. 10,000.

Leader–Post: 1964 Park St, POB 2020, Regina, SK S4P 3G4; tel. (306) 565-8211; fax (306) 565-2588; internet www.leaderpost.com; f. 1883; Publr GREG McLEAN; Editor BOB HUGHES; circ. 58,000.

StarPhoenix: 204 Fifth Ave North, Saskatoon, SK S7K 2P1; tel. (306) 652-9200; fax (306) 664-0433; e-mail spnews@thesp.com; internet www.thestarphoenix.com; f. 1902; Publr LYLE SINKEWICZ; Editor STEVE GIBB; circ. 62,000.

Times–Herald: 44 Fairford St West, POB 3000, Moose Jaw, SK S6H 6E4; tel. (306) 692-6441; fax (306) 692-2101; e-mail editorial@ mjtimes.sk.ca; internet www.mjtimes.sk.ca; f. 1889; evening; Publr AB CALVERT; Editor LESLEY SHEPPARD; circ. 9,000.

Yukon Territory

Whitehorse Star: 2149 Second Ave, Whitehorse, Yukon, YT Y1A 1C5; tel. (867) 667-4481; fax (867) 668-7130; e-mail star@hypertech .yk.ca; internet www.whitehorsestar.com; f. 1985; evening; Publr ROBERT ERLAM; Editor JIM BUTLER; circ. 3,000.

SELECTED PERIODICALS

Alberta

Alberta FarmLIFE: 250 Shawville Blvd, SE, Calgary, AB T2Y 2Z7; tel. (403) 274-4002; fax (403) 274-4116; e-mail farmlife@cadvision .com; 24 a year; Man. BRUCE TUNNICLIFFE; circ. 65,000.

Ukrainski Visti (Ukrainian News): 12227 107th Ave, Suite 1, Edmonton, AB T5M 1Y9; tel. (780) 488-3693; fax (780) 488-3859; e-mail ukrnews@compusmart.ab.ca; f. 1929; fortnightly; Ukrainian and English; Editor MARCO LEVYTSKY; circ. 4,000.

British Columbia

BC Outdoors: 780 Beatty St, Suite 300, Vancouver, BC V6B 2M1; tel. (604) 687-1581; fax (604) 687-1925; e-mail oppubl@istar.ca; internet www.oppublishing.com; f. 1945; 8 a year; Editor GEORGE GRUENEFELD; circ. 37,000.

Pacific Yachting: 1080 Howe St, Suite 900, Vancouver, BC V6Z 2T1; tel. (604) 606-4644; fax (604) 687-1925; e-mail editorial@ pacificyachting.net; internet www.pacificyachting.com; f. 1968; monthly; Editor SIMON HILL; circ. 15,000.

Vancouver Magazine: 555 West 12th Ave, SE Tower, Suite 300, Vancouver, BC V5Z 4L4; tel. (604) 877-7732; fax (604) 877-4823; e-mail mail@vanmag.com; internet www.vanmag.com; f. 1957; 9 a year; Editor MATTHEW MALLON; circ. 60,000.

Western Living: 555 West 12th Ave, SE Tower, Suite 300, Vancouver, BC V5Z 4L4; tel. (604) 877-7732; fax (604) 877-4849; e-mail westernliving@ican.net; f. 1971; monthly; Publr LANCE NEIL; Editor JIM SUTHERLAND; circ. 253,000.

WestWorld BC: 4180 Lougheed Hwy, 4th Floor, Burnaby, BC V5C 6A7; tel. (604) 299-7311; fax (604) 299-9188; e-mail cwm@ canadawide.com; internet www.canadawide.com/westworldbc_ad .htm; f. 1974; quarterly; Editor PAT PRICE; circ. 495,000.

Manitoba

The Beaver: Exploring Canada's History: 167 Lombard Ave, Suite 478, Winnipeg, MB R3B 0T6; tel. (204) 988-9300; fax (204) 988-9309; e-mail beaver@historysociety.ca; internet www.beavermagazine.ca; f. 1920; 6 a year; Canadian history; Editor ANNALEE GREENBERG; circ. 50,000.

Cattlemen: 8th Floor, 220 Portage Ave, Winnipeg, MB R3C 0A5; tel. (204) 944-5750; fax (204) 942-8463; e-mail gwinslow@fbc .agricoreunited.com; internet www.agcanada.com; f. 1938; monthly; animal husbandry; Editor GREN WINSLOW; circ. 30,000.

Country Guide: 8th Floor, 220 Portage Ave, Winnipeg, MB R3C 0A5; tel. (204) 944-5750; fax (204) 942-8463; e-mail dwreford@fbc .agricoreunited.com; internet www.agcanada.com; f. 1882; 10 a year; agriculture; Editor DAVID WREFORD; circ. 55,000.

Grainews: 8th Floor, 220 Portage Ave, Winnipeg, MB R3C 0A5; tel. (204) 944-5587; fax (204) 944-5416; e-mail dbedard@fbc.unitedgrain .ca; internet www.agcanada.com; f. 1975; 17 a year; grain and cattle farming; Editor ANDY SIRSKI; circ. 47,000.

Kanada Kurier: 955 Alexander Ave, POB 1054, Winnipeg, MB R3C 2X8; tel. (204) 774-1883; fax (204) 783-5740; e-mail kanadakurier@ mb.simpatico.ca; f. 1889; weekly; German; Editor RENATE ACHENBACH; circ. 25,000.

The Manitoba Co-operator: 220 Portage Ave, POB 9800, Main Station, Winnipeg, MB R3C 3K7; tel. (204) 954-1400; fax (204) 954-1422; e-mail news@co-operator.mb.ca; f. 1925; weekly; farming; Man. Editor GORD GILMOUR; circ. 21,000.

New Brunswick

Atlantic Chamber Journal: 309 Amirault St, Dieppe, NB E1A 1G1; tel. (506) 858-8710; fax (506) 858-1707; e-mail eastpub@nbnet .nb.ca; f. 1984; 6 a year; Editor ELIE J. RICHARD.

Brunswick Business Journal: 599 Maint St, Suite 203, Moncton, NB E1E 1C8; tel. (506) 857-9696; fax (506) 859-7395; f. 1984; monthly; Editor SUZANNE McDONALD-BOYCE.

Newfoundland and Labrador

Atlantic Business Magazine: 197 Water St, POB 2356, St John's, NL A1C 6E7; tel. (709) 726-9300; fax (709) 726-3013; e-mail dchafe@ atlanticbusinessmagazine.com; internet www .atlanticbusinessmagazine.com; 6 a year; business; Editor DARREN CHAFE; circ. 30,000.

Northwest Territories

L'Aquilon: POB 1325, Yellowknife, NT X1A 2N9; tel. (403) 873-6603; fax (403) 873-2158; e-mail aquilon@internorth.com; f. 1985; weekly; Editor ALAIN BESSETTE; circ. 1,000.

The Hub: 3 Capital Dr., Suite 105, MacKenzie Hwy, Hay River, NT X0E 1Q2; tel. (867) 874-8577; fax (867) 874-2679; e-mail hub@cancom.net; f. 1973; weekly; Editor CHRIS BRODEUR; circ. 3,000.

Northern News Service: 5108 50th St, Yellowknife, NT X1A 2R1; tel. (403) 873-4031; fax (403) 873-8507; e-mail newsnorth@nnsl.yk.ca; internet www.nnsl.com; f. 1945 as News/North; weekly; Editor JACK SIGVALDASON; Man. Editor BRUCE VALPY; circ. 11,000.

Slave River Journal: 207 McDougal Rd, POB 990, Fort Smith, NT X0E 0P0; tel. (867) 872-2774; fax (867) 872-2754; e-mail srj@aurora.net.nt.ca; internet www.srji.com; f. 1978; weekly; Publr DON JAQUE; Man. Editor SANDRA JAQUE; circ. 2,000.

Yellowknifer: 5108 50th St, Yellowknife, NT X1A 2R1; tel. (403) 873-4031; fax (403) 873-8507; e-mail yellowknifer@nnsl.yk.com; weekly; Man. Editor BRUCE VALPY; circ. 5,000.

Nova Scotia

Atlantic Progress Magazine: 1660 Hollis St, Suite 603, Halifax, NS B3J 1V7; tel. (902) 494-0999; fax (902) 494-0997; e-mail app@app.ca; internet www.app.ca; f. 1993; 8 a year; regional business; Editor DAVID HOLT; circ. 22,000.

Canadian Forum: 5502 Atlantic St, Halifax, NS B3H 1G4; tel. (902) 421-7022; fax (902) 425-0166; f. 1920; 10 a year; political, literary and economic; Editor ROBERT CLUDOS; circ. 9,000.

Nunavut Territory

Kivalliq News: Rankin Inlet, NU; tel. (867) 645-3223; fax (867) 645-3225; e-mail editor@arctic.ca; f. 1994; owned by Northern News Services; English and Inuktitut; Publr JACK SIGVALDASON; Editor DARRELL GREER; circ. 1,400.

Nunatsiaq News: POB 8, Iqaluit, NU X0A 0H0; tel. (867) 979-5357; fax (867) 979-4763; e-mail nunat@nunanet.com; internet www.nunatsiaq.com; f. 1972; weekly; English and Inuktitut; Publr STEVEN ROBERTS; Editor JIM BELL; circ. 9,000.

Ontario

Anglican Journal: 600 Jarvis St, Toronto, ON M4Y 2J6; tel. (416) 924-9199; fax (416) 921-4452; e-mail editor@national.anglican.ca; internet www.anglicanjournal.com; f. 1871; 10 a year; official publ. of the Anglican Church of Canada; Editor VIANNEY CARRIERE; circ. 230,000.

Better Farming: RR2, Vanleek Hill, ON K0B 1R0; tel. (613) 687-2232; fax (613) 678-5993; e-mail admin@betterfarming.com; internet www.betterfarming.com; f. 1999; monthly; Man. Editor ROBERT LOWIN.

CAmagazine: The Canadian Institute of Chartered Accountants, 277 Wellington St West, Toronto, ON M5V 3H2; tel. (416) 977-3222; fax (416) 204-3409; e-mail christian.bellavance@cica.ca; internet www.camagazine.com; f. 1911; monthly; Editor-in-Chief CHRISTIAN BELLAVANCE; circ. 75,000 (60,000 in English; 15,000 in French).

Campus Canada: 5397 Eglington Ave West, Suite 101, Toronto, ON M9C 5K6; tel. (416) 928-2909; fax (416) 966-1181; e-mail turnbull@campus.ca; internet www.campus.ca; f. 1983; quarterly; 30 campus edns; Man. Editor LESLEY TURNBULL; circ. 145,000.

Canada Gazette: Canada Gazette Division, Communication Canada, 350 Albert St, Ottawa, ON K1A 1M4; tel. (613) 996-2495; fax (613) 991-3540; internet www.canada.gc.ca/gazette/gazette_e.html; f. 1867; weekly; official bulletin of the Govt of Canada.

Canadian Architect: 1450 Don Mills Rd, Don Mills, ON M3B 2X7; tel. (416) 442-3390; fax (416) 442-2213; e-mail cdnarchitect@southam.ca; internet www.cdnarchitect.com; f. 1955; monthly; Editor MARCO POLO; circ. 11,000.

Canadian Art: 56 The Esplanade, Suite 310, Toronto, ON M5E 1A7; tel. (416) 368-8854; fax (416) 368-6135; e-mail info@canadianart.ca; internet www.canadianart.ca; quarterly; Publr MELONY WARD; Man. Editor BRYNE MCLAUGHLIN; circ. 24,000.

Canadian Bar Review: Canadian Bar Foundation, 50 O'Connor St, Suite 902, Ottawa, ON K1P 6L2; tel. (613) 237-2925; fax (613) 237-0185; e-mail CBA:info@cba.org; internet www.cba.org; f. 1923; quarterly; Editor Prof. EDWARD VEITCH; circ. 36,000.

Canadian Business: 777 Bay St, 5th Floor, Toronto, ON M5W 1A7; tel. (416) 596-5100; fax (416) 596-5152; internet www.canbus.com; f. 1927; 21 a year; Editor JOE CHIDLEY; circ. 81,000.

Canadian Chemical News: 130 Slater St, Suite 550, Ottawa, ON K1P 6E2; tel. (613) 232-6252; fax (613) 232-5862; e-mail info@cheminst.ca; internet www.accn.ca; f. 1949; 10 a year; Editor DINAH LAPRARIE; circ. 5,000.

Canadian Defence Quarterly: 310 Dupont St, Toronto, ON M5R 1V9; tel. (416) 968-7252; fax (416) 968-2377; e-mail cdq@baxter.net; internet www.baxter.net/cdq/; f. 1970; quarterly; Publr W. H. BAXTER; Editor MICHAEL POITEVIN; circ. 6,000.

Canadian Dental Association Journal: 1815 Alta Vista Dr., Ottawa, ON K1G 3Y6; tel. (613) 523-1770; fax (613) 523-7736; e-mail reception@cda-adc.ca; internet www.cda-adc.ca; f. 1935; 11 a year; Editor Dr JOHN O'KEEFE.

Canadian Electronics: 135 Spy Court, Markham, ON L3R 5H6; tel. (905) 447-3222; fax (905) 477-4320; e-mail ce@actioncom.com; f. 1986; 6 a year; Editor TIM GOULDSON; circ. 22,000.

Canadian Geographic: 39 McArthur Ave, Ottawa, ON K1L 8L7; tel. (613) 745-4629; fax (613) 744-0947; e-mail editorial@cangeo.ca; internet www.canadiangeographic.ca; f. 1930; 7 a year; publ. of the Royal Canadian Geographical Soc. Editor RICK BOYCHUK; circ. 227,000.

Canadian Home Workshop: 340 Ferrier St, Suite 210, Markham, ON L3R 2Z5; tel. (905) 475-8440; fax (905) 475-9246; e-mail letters@canadianworkshop.ca; f. 1977; monthly; do-it-yourself; Editorial Dir DOUGLAS THOMPSON; circ. 104,000.

Canadian House & Home: 511 King St West, Suite 120, Toronto, ON M5V 2Z4; tel. (416) 593-0204; fax (416) 591-1630; e-mail exec@canhomepub.com; internet www.canadianhouseandhome.com; f. 1982; 9 a year; Editor COBI LADNER; circ. 142,000.

Canadian Jewish News: 1500 Don Mills Rd, Suite 205, North York, ON M3B 3KY; tel. (416) 391-1836; fax (416) 391-0829; e-mail torcjn1@aol.com; 50 a year; Editor MORDECHAI BEN-DAT; circ. 44,000.

Canadian Living: 25 Sheppard Ave West, Suite 100, North York, ON M2N 6S7; tel. (416) 733-7600; fax (416) 733-3398; internet www.canadianliving.com; f. 1975; 50 a year; Editor-in-Chief BONNIE COWAN; circ. 563,000.

Canadian Medical Association Journal: 1867 Alta Vista Dr., Ottawa, ON K1G 3Y6; tel. (613) 731-8610; fax (613) 565-5471; e-mail pubs@cma.ca; internet www.cma.ca; f. 1911; 25 a year; Editor Dr JOHN HOEY; circ. 59,000.

Canadian Musician: 23 Hannover Dr., Suite 7, St Catharines, ON L2W 1A3; tel. (905) 641-1512; fax (905) 641-1648; e-mail info@nor.com; internet www.canadianmusician.com; f. 1979; 6 a year; Man. Editor JEFF MACKAY; circ. 27,000.

Canadian Nurse/L'infirmière canadienne: 50 Driveway, Ottawa, ON K2P 1E2; tel. (613) 237-2133; fax (613) 237-3520; e-mail cnj@cna-nurses.ca; f. 1905; 10 a year; journal of the Canadian Nurses' Asscn; Editor-in-Chief JUDITH HAINES; circ. 111,000.

Canadian Pharmaceutical Journal: c/o C. K. Goodman, Inc, 1382 Hurontario St, Mississauga, ON L5G 3H4; tel. (905) 278-6700; fax (905) 278-4850; f. 1868; 10 a year; Editor ANDREW REINBOLDT; circ. 13,000.

Canadian Public Policy/Analyse de Politiques: School of Policy Studies, Rm 409, Queen's University, Kingston, ON K7L 3N6; tel. (613) 533-6644; fax (613) 533-6960; e-mail cpp@qsilver.queensu.ca; internet www.qsilver.queensu.ca/~cpp/; quarterly; Editor CHARLES M. BEACH; circ. 1,000.

Canadian Travel Press Weekly: 310 Dupont St, Toronto, ON M5R 1V9; tel. (416) 968-7252; fax (416) 968-2377; e-mail ctp@baxter.net; 46 a year; Editor-in-Chief EDITH BAXTER; circ. 13,000.

Chatelaine: 777 Bay St, Suite 405, Toronto, ON M5W 1A7; tel. (416) 596-5891; fax (416) 596-5158; e-mail chatcour@maclean.hunter-quebec.qc.ca; internet www.chatelaine.com; f. 1928; monthly; women's journal; Editor RONA MAYNARD; circ. 803,000.

ComputerWorld Canada: 55 Town Centre Court, Scarborough, ON M1P 4X4; tel. (416) 290-0240; fax (416) 290-0238; internet www.lti.on.ca; f. 1984; 25 a year; Editor-in-Chief NORMAN TOLLINSKY; circ. 47,000.

Elm Street: 665 Bay St, Suite 1100, Toronto, ON M5G 2K4; tel. (416) 595-9944; fax (416) 595-7217; e-mail elmstreet@m-v-p.com; f. 1996; 8 a year; women's interest; Editor-in-Chief GWEN SMITH; circ. 600,000.

Flare: 777 Bay St, Suite 405, Toronto, ON M5W 1A7; tel. (416) 596-5891; fax (416) 596-5158; e-mail editors@flare.com; internet www.flare.com; f. 1964; monthly; women's interest; Editor-in-Chief SUZANNE BOYD; circ. 174,000.

Hockey News: 777 Bay St, Suite 2700, Toronto, ON M5G 2N1; tel. (416) 340-8000; fax (416) 340-2786; internet www.thn.com; f. 1947; 42 a year; Editor-in-Chief STEVE DRYDEN; circ. 205,000.

Holstein Journal: 9120 Leslie St, Unit 105, Richmond Hill, ON L4B 3J9; tel. (905) 886-4222; fax (905) 886-0037; e-mail subs@holsteinjournal.com; internet www.holsteinjournal.com; f. 1938; monthly; Editor BONNIE COOPER; circ. 5,000.

Kanadai Magyarsag (Canadian Hungarians): 74 Advance Rd, Etobicoke, ON M8Z 2T7; tel. (416) 233-3131; fax (416) 233-5984; e-mail magyarsag@wellerpublishing.com; weekly; circ. 10,000.

Legion Magazine: 359 Kent St, Suite 407, Ottawa, ON K2P 0R6; tel. (613) 235-8741; fax (613) 233-7159; e-mail magazine@legion.ca;

internet www.legionmagazine.com; f. 1926; 6 a year; Editor MAC JOHNSTON; circ. 362,274.

Maclean's Canada's Weekly Newsmazagine: 777 Bay St, Toronto, ON M5W 1A7; tel. (416) 596-5386; fax (416) 596-7730; e-mail letters@macleans.ca; internet www.macleans.ca; f. 1905; Editor-in-Chief TONY WILSON-SMITH; circ. 500,000.

Northern Miner: 1450 Don Mills Rd, Don Mills, ON M3B 2X7; tel. (416) 510-6744; fax (416) 442-2181; e-mail tnm@southam.ca; internet www.northernminer.com; f. 1915; weekly; Editor JAMES B. WHYTE; circ. 23,000.

Now: 150 Danforth Ave, Toronto, ON M4K 1N1; tel. (416) 461-0871; fax (416) 461-2886; internet www.nowtoronto.com; f. 1981; weekly; young adult; Publr and Editor MICHAEL HOLLETT; circ. 100.000.

Ontario Medical Review: 525 University Ave, Suite 300, Toronto, ON M5G 2K7; tel. (416) 599-2580; fax (416) 340-2232; e-mail jeff_henry@oma.org; internet www.oma.org; f. 1922; monthly; Editor JEFF HENRY; circ. 25,100.

Oral Health: 1450 Don Mills Rd, Don Mills, ON M3B 2X7; tel. (416) 442-2193; fax (416) 442-2214; e-mail cwilson@oralhealthjournal .com; internet www.oralhealthjournal.com; f. 1911; monthly; dentistry; Man. Editor CATHERINE WILSON; circ. 17,000.

Photo Life: 1 Dundas St West, Suite 2500, POB 84, Toronto, ON M5G 1G3; tel. (800) 905-7468; fax (800) 664-2739; e-mail editor@ photolife.com; internet www.photolife.com; f. 1976; 6 a year; Editor-in-Chief MARK A. PRICE; circ. 74,000.

Quill & Quire: 70 The Esplanade, Suite 210, Toronto, ON M5E 1R2; tel. (416) 360-0044; fax (416) 955-0794; e-mail info@quillandquire .com; internet www.quillandquire.com; f. 1935; monthly; book-publishing industry; Editor SCOTT ANDERSON; circ. 6,000.

Style: 1448 Lawrence Ave East, Suite 302, Toronto, ON M4A 2V6; tel. (416) 755-5199; fax (416) 755-9123; e-mail style@style.ca; internet www.style.ca; f. 1888; monthly; Editor JILL MAYNARD; circ. 12,000.

Style at Home: 25 Sheppard Ave West, Suite 100, Toronto, ON M2N 6S7; tel. (416) 733-7600; fax (416) 218-3632; e-mail letters@ styleathome.com; f. 1997; 8 a year; Editor GAIL JOHNSTON HABS; circ. 204,000.

Sympatico Netlife: 25 Sheppard Ave West, Suite 100, North York, ON M2N 6S7; tel. (416) 733-7600; fax (416) 733-8272; e-mail giffen@ sympatico.ca; internet www.sympatico.ca/netlife; 6 a year; computer technology; Editor PETER GIFFEN; circ. 450,000.

Toronto Life Magazine: 59 Front St East, 3rd Floor, Toronto, ON M5E 1B3; tel. (416) 364-3333; fax (416) 861-1169; internet www .torontolife.com; f. 1966; monthly; Editor JOHN MACFARLANE; circ. 97,000.

Tribute Magazine: 71 Barber Greene Rd, Don Mills, ON M3C 2A2; tel. (416) 445-0544; fax (416) 445-2894; internet www.tribute.ca; f. 1984; 9 a year; entertainment; Publr and Editor SANDRA STEWART; circ. 500,000.

TV Guide: 25 Sheppard Ave West, Suite 100, North York, ON M2N 6S7; tel. (416) 733-7600; fax (416) 733-3632; e-mail tvguide@ telemedia.org; internet www.tvguide.ca; f. 1976; weekly; Editor CHRISTOPHER LOUDON; circ. 838,000.

TV Times: 1450 Don Mills Rd, Don Mills, ON M3B 2X7; tel. (416) 442-3444; fax (416) 442-2088; f. 1969; weekly; 14 regional edns; circ. 1,941,000.

Québec

L'actualité: 1001 blvd de Maisonneuve Ouest, Montréal, QC H3A 3E1; tel. (514) 845-2543; fax (514) 845-7503; e-mail redaction@ lactualite.com; f. 1976; monthly; current affairs; Editor CAROLE BEAULIEU; circ. 188,455.

Affaires Plus: 1100 blvd René-Lévesque ouest, 24e étage, Montréal, QC H3B 4X9; tel. (514) 392-9000; fax (514) 392-4726; e-mail aplus@ transcontinental.ca; internet www.transcontinental-gtc.com; f. 1978; monthly; Editor-in-Chief MARIE-AGNÈS THELLIER; circ. 96,000.

Le Bulletin des Agriculteurs: 1001 blvd de Maisonneuve ouest, Montréal, QC H3A 3E1; tel. (514) 845-5141; fax (514) 845-6261; e-mail info@lebulletin.com; internet www.lebulletin.com; f. 1918; monthly; Editor SIMON M. GUERTIN; circ. 24,000.

Châtelaine: 1001 blvd de Maisonneuve ouest, 11e étage, Montréal, QC H3A 3E1; tel. (514) 843-2504; fax (514) 845-4302; e-mail lettres@ chatelaine-quebec.com; internet www.chatelaine-quebec.com; f. 1960; monthly; Editor CATHERINE ELIE; circ. 207,000.

CIM Bulletin: 3400 blvd de Maisonneuve ouest, Bureau 1210, Montréal, QC H3Z 3B8; tel. (514) 939-2710; fax (514) 939-2714; internet www.cim.org; monthly; publ. by the Canadian Inst. of Mining, Metallurgy and Petroleum; Editor PERLA GANTZ; circ. 10,000.

Il Cittadino Canadese: 5960 Jean-Talon est, Bureau 209, Montréal, QC H1S 1M2; tel. (514) 253-2332; fax (514) 253-6574; f. 1941; weekly; Italian; Editor BASILIO GIORDANO; circ. 46,000.

Equinox: 11450 blvd Albert-Hudon, Montréal-Nord, QC H1G 3J9; tel. (514) 327-4464; fax (514) 327-7592; e-mail eqxmag@globetrotter .net; internet www.equinox.ca; f. 1982; 6 a year; Editor ALAN MORANTZ; circ. 130,000.

Harrowsmith Country Life: 11450 blvd Albert-Hudon, Montréal-Nord, QC H1G 3J9; tel. (514) 327-4464; fax (514) 327-0514; e-mail hclmag@globetrotter.net; f. 1986; 6 a year; Editor TOM CRUICKSHANK; circ. 190,000.

Le Lundi: 7 chemin Bates, Outremont, QC H2V 1A6; tel. (514) 270-1100; fax (514) 270-4810; f. 1976; weekly; Editor MICHAEL CHOINIÈRE; circ. 62,000.

Le Producteur de Lait Québécois: 555 blvd Roland-Thérrien, Longueuil, QC J4H 3Y9; tel. (514) 679-0530; fax (514) 670-4788; e-mail rioiseau@tcn.upa.qc.ca; f. 1980; monthly; dairy farming; Editor-in-Chief JEAN VIGNEAULT; circ. 12,000.

Progrès-Dimanche: 1051 blvd Talbot, Chicoutimi, QC G7H 5C1; tel. (418) 545-4474; fax (418) 690-8805; internet www.lequotidien .com; f. 1964; weekly; Pres. and Editor CLAUDE GAGNON; circ. 45,000.

Québec Science: 3430 rue St-Denis, Bureau 300, Montréal, QC H2X 3L3; tel. (514) 843-6888; fax (514) 843-4897; e-mail courrier@ QuebecScience.qc.ca; internet www.cybersciences.com; f. 1969; 10 a year; Editor-in-Chief RAYMOND LEMIEUX; circ. 32,000.

Reader's Digest/Sélection: 215 ave Redfern, Westmount, QC H3Z 2V9; tel. (514) 934-0751; fax (514) 935-4463; f. 1947; monthly; French and English edns; Editors ROBERT GOYETTE (French edn), MURRAY LEWIS (English edn); circ. 120,000.

Rénovation Bricolage: 7 chemin Bates, Outremont, QC H2V 4V7; tel. (514) 270-1100; fax (514) 270-9618; e-mail renobrico@publicor .ca; f. 1976; 9 a year; Editor CLAUDE LECLERC; circ. 40,000.

Revue Commerce: 1100 blvd René-Lévesque ouest, 24e étage, Montréal, QC H3B 4X9; tel. (514) 392-9000; fax (514) 3924726; e-mail commerce@transcontinental.ca; internet www .transcontinental-gtc.com; f. 1898; monthly; Editor-in-Chief PIERRE DUHAMEL; circ. 44,000.

Sélection du Reader's Digest: 1100 blvd Réne-Lévesque ouest, Montréal, QC H3B 5H5; tel. (514) 940-7328; fax (514) 940-7340; e-mail manon.sylvain@readersdigest.com; internet www .readersdigest.ca; f. 1947; monthly; Editor-in-Chief LISE VERSCHELDEN; circ. 321,000.

La Terre de Chez Nous: 555 blvd Roland-Thérrien, Longueuil, QC J4H 3Y9; tel. (514) 679-0530; fax (514) 679-5436; e-mail rioiseau@ tcn.upa.qc.ca; f. 1929; weekly; agriculture and forestry; Editor HUGUES BELZILLE; circ. 40,000.

TV Hebdo: 2020 rue Université, 20e étage, Montréal, QC H3A 2A5; tel. (514) 848-7000; fax (514) 848-7070; e-mail tv@trustar.com; f. 1960; weekly; Editor-in-Chief JEAN-LOUIS PODLESAK; circ. 223,000.

Saskatchewan

Farm Light & Power: 2352 Smith St, Regina, SK S4P 2P6; tel. (306) 525-3305; fax (306) 757-1810; f. 1959; monthly; Editor TOM BRADLEY; circ. 71,000.

Western Producer: 2310 Millar Ave, POB 2500, Saskatoon, SK S7K 2C4; tel. (306) 665-3500; fax (306) 934-2401; internet www .producer.com; f. 1923; weekly; agriculture; Editor ELAINE SHEIN; circ. 74,000.

Yukon Territory

Yukon News: 211 Wood St, Whitehorse, YT Y1A 2E4; tel. (867) 667-6285; fax (867) 668-3755; e-mail plesniak@yukon-news.com; internet www.yukon-news.com; f. 1960; Editor PETER LESNIAK; circ. 8,000; 3 a week.

NEWS AGENCIES

The Canadian Press: 36 King St East, Toronto, ON M5C 2L9; tel. (416) 364-0321; fax (416) 364-0207; internet www.cp.org; f. 1917; national news co-operative; 102 newspaper mems; Chair. MICHAEL G. SIFTON; Pres. ERIC MORRISON.

Foreign Bureaux

Agence France-Presse (AFP): 231 rue St-Jacques, Bureau 1201, Montréal, QC H2Y 1M6; tel. (514) 288-2777; fax (514) 288-3506; e-mail afpcanada@afp.com; internet www.afp.com; Bureau Chief CHRISTINE COURCOL; also office in Toronto.

Agenzia Nazionale Stampa Associata (ANSA) (Italy): 150 Wellington St, Press Gallery, Rm 703, Ottawa, ON K1P 5A4; tel. (613) 235-4248; fax (613) 235-4248; Rep. ELIO COPPOLA.

Associated Press (USA): 36 King St East, Toronto, ON M5C 2L9; tel. (416) 368-1388.

Deutsche Presse-Agentur (dpa) (Germany): 702 National Press Bldg, 150 Wellington St, Ottawa, ON K1P 5A4; tel. (613) 234-6024; Correspondent BARBARA HALSIG.

Informatsionnoye Telegrafnoye Agentstvo Rossii—Telegrafnoye Agentstvo Suverennykh Stran (ITAR—TASS) (Russia): 200 Rideau Terrace, Suite 1305, Ottawa, ON K1M OZ3; tel. (613) 745-4310; fax (613) 745-5581; e-mail tasscnd@simpatico.ca; Correspondent BORIS GROUSHIN.

Reuters (United Kingdom): 2020 rue Université, Bureau 1020, Montréal, QC H3A 2A5; tel. (514) 282-0744; fax (514) 844-2327; also office in Vancouver.

Agencia EFE (Spain), Jiji Tsushin (Japan), Prensa Latina (Cuba), United Press International (USA) and Xinhua (New China) News Agency (People's Republic of China) are also represented.

PRESS ASSOCIATIONS

Canadian Business Press: 40 Shields Court, Suite 201, Markham, ON L3R 0M5; tel. (905) 946-8889; fax (905) 479-1711; e-mail JJCBP@passport.ca; Chair. TERRY MALDEN; Pres. JUDY JOHNSON; 125 mems.

Canadian Community Newspapers Association: 90 Eglinton Ave East, Suite 206, Toronto, ON M4P 2Y3; tel. (416) 482-1090; fax (416) 482-1908; e-mail info@ccna.ca; internet www.ccna.ca; f. 1919; Exec. Dir SERGE LAVOIE; 692 mems.

Canadian Newspaper Association: 890 Yonge St, Suite 200, Toronto, ON M4W 3P4; tel. (416) 923-3567; fax (416) 923-7206; e-mail bcantley@cna-acj.ca; internet www.cna-acj.ca/; f. 1996; Chair. RUSS MILLS; 102 mems.

Canadian Magazine Publishers Association: 130 Spadina Ave, Suite 202, Toronto, ON M5V 2L4; tel. (416) 504-0274; fax (416) 504-0437; e-mail cminfo@cmpa.ca; internet www.cmpa.ca/; f. 1973; Chair. MICHAEL REA.

Magazines Canada: 777 Bay St, 4th Floor, Toronto, ON M5W 1A7; tel. (416) 596-5382; fax (416) 596-6043; e-mail info@magazinescanada.com; internet www.magazinescanada.com; Chair. PAUL JONES.

Publishers

Annick Press Ltd: 15 Patricia Ave, Willowdale, ON M2M 1H9; tel. (416) 221-4802; fax (416) 221-8400; e-mail annick@annickpress.com; internet www.annickpress.com; f. 1976; children's; Dir RICK WILKS.

Arsenal Pulp Press Book Publishers Ltd: 1014 Homer St, Suite 103, Vancouver, BC V6B 2W9; tel. (604) 687-4233; fax (604) 669-8250; e-mail contact@arsenalpulp.com; internet www.arsenalpulp.com; f. 1982; literary, native, cultural studies; Publr BRIAN LAM.

Black Rose Books: CP 1258, succursale place du Parc, Montréal, QC H2W 1Y5; tel. (514) 844-4076; fax (514) 849-1956; e-mail blackrose@web.net; internet www.web.net/blackrosebooks; f. 1969; social studies, humanities; Pres. JACQUES ROUX.

Blizzard Publishing: 73 Furby St, Winnipeg, MB R3C 2A2; tel. (204) 775-2923; fax (204) 775-2947; e-mail info@blizzard.mb.ca; internet www.blizzard.mb.ca/catalog; drama and criticism; Man. Editor PETER ATWOOD.

Borealis Press Ltd: 110 Bloomindale St, Ottawa, ON K2C 4A4; tel. (613) 798-9299; fax (613) 798-9747; e-mail borealis@istar.ca; internet www.borealispress.com; f. 1972; Canadian fiction and non-fiction, drama, juvenile, poetry; Pres. FRANK TIERNEY; Vice-Pres. W. GLENN CLEVER.

Breakwater Books/Softwares Ltd: 100 Water St, POB 2188, St John's, NL A1C 6E6; tel. (709) 722-6680; fax (709) 753-0708; e-mail info@breakwater.nf.net; internet www.breakwater.nf.net; f. 1973; fiction, non-fiction, children's, educational, folklore; Pres. CLYDE ROSE.

Canada Law Book Inc: 240 Edward St, Aurora, ON L4G 3S9; tel. (905) 841-6472; fax (905) 841-5085; internet www.canadalawbook.ca; f. 1855; law reports, law journals, legal textbooks, etc. Pres. STUART MORRISON.

Carswell-Thomson Professional Publishing Canada: 2075 Kennedy Rd, Toronto, ON M1T 3V4; tel. (416) 609-8000; fax (416) 298-5094; internet www.carswell.com/carswell.home; f. 1864; Pres. and CEO DON VAN MEER.

CDG Books Canada, Inc: 99 Yorkville Ave, Suite 400, Toronto, ON M5R 3K5; tel. (416) 963-8830; fax (416) 923-4821; e-mail info@cdgbooks.com; internet www.cdgbooks.com; f. 1998; trade, reference, publishing; Pres. TOM BEST.

Chenelière/McGraw-Hill: 7001 blvd St-Laurent, Montréal, QC H2S 3E3; tel. (514) 273-1066; fax (514) 276-0324; e-mail chene@dlcmcgrawhill.ca; textbooks; Pres. MICHEL DE LA CHENELIÈRE.

Coach House Books: 401 Huron St, Toronto, ON M5S 2G5; tel. (416) 979-2217; fax (416) 977-1158; internet www.chbooks.com; f. 1965; fiction, poetry, drama; Publr STAN BEVINGTON.

Crabtree Publishing Co Ltd: 612 Welland Ave, St Catharines, ON L2M 5V6; tel. (905) 682-5221; fax (905) 682-7166; e-mail letters@crabtreebooks.com; internet www.crabtreebooks.com; f. 1978; children's; Pres. PETER A. CRABTREE.

Doubleday Canada Ltd: 105 Bond St, Toronto, ON M5B 1Y3; tel. (416) 340-0777; fax (416) 977-8488; internet www.randomhouse.ca; f. 1944; general, trade, textbooks, mass market; Pres. JOHN NEALE.

Douglas & McIntyre Ltd: 2323 Québec St, Suite 201, Vancouver, BC V5T 4S7; tel. (604) 254-7191; fax (604) 254-9099; e-mail dm@douglas-mcintyre.com; internet www.douglas-mcintyre.com; f. 1964; fiction, general non-fiction, juvenile; Pres. SCOTT McINTYRE.

The Dundurn Group: 8 Market St, Suite 200, Toronto, ON M5E 1M6; tel. (416) 214-5544; fax (416) 214-5556; e-mail info@dundurn.com; internet www.dundurn.com; f. 1972; drama and performing arts, history, reference, fiction and non-fiction; Pres. KIRK HOWARD.

Editions d'Acadie: 236 rue St-Georges, Moncton, NB E1C 8N8; tel. (506) 857-8490; fax (506) 855-3130; e-mail edacadie@nbnet.nb.ca; f. 1972; Gen. Dir MARCEL OUELLETTE.

Editions Bellarmin: 165 rue Deslauriers, Ville St-Laurent, QC H4N 2S4; tel. (514) 745-4290; fax (514) 745-4299; e-mail editions@fides.qc.ca; internet www.fides.qc.ca; f. 1891; religious, educational, politics, sociology, ethnography, history, sport, leisure; Dir-Gen. ANTOINE DEL BUSSO.

Les Editions CEC Inc: 8101 blvd Métropolitain est, Anjou, Montréal, QC H1J 1J9; tel. (514) 351-6010; fax (514) 351-3534; e-mail infoped@ceceditions.com; f. 1956; textbooks; Pres. and Dir-Gen. JACQUES ROCHEFORT.

Editions Fides: 165 rue Deslauriers, Ville St-Laurent, PQ H4N 2S4; tel. (514) 745-4290; fax (514) 745-4299; e-mail editions@fides.qc.ca; internet www.editionsfides.com; f. 1937; juvenile, history, theology, textbooks and literature; Dir-Gen. ANTOINE DEL BUSSO.

Editions de l'Hexagone: 1010 rue de la Gauchetière est, Montréal, QC H2L 2N5; tel. (514) 523-1182; fax (514) 282-7530; internet www.edhexagone.com; f. 1953; literature; Editorial Dir PIERRE GRAVELINE.

Editions du Noroît Ltée: 6694 ave Papineau, Montréal, QC H2G 2X2; tel. (514) 727-0005; fax (514) 727-6660; e-mail lenoroit@ca.inter.net; f. 1971; poetry; Dir PAUL BÉLANGER.

Editions du Renouveau Pédagogique Inc: 5757 rue Cyphiot, St-Laurent, QC H4S 1R3; tel. (514) 334-2690; fax (514) 334-4720; e-mail info@erpi.com; internet www.erpi.com; f. 1965; textbooks; Pres. NORMAND CLÉROUX.

Editions du Septentrion: 1300 ave Maguire, Sillery, QC G1T 1Z3; tel. (418) 688-3556; fax (418) 527-4978; e-mail sept@septentrion.qc.ca; internet www.septentrion.qc.ca; f. 1988; history, essays, general; Man. DENIS VAUGEOIS.

Fenn Publishing Co Ltd: 34 Nixon Rd, Bolton, ON L7E 1W2; internet www.hbfenn.com; fiction and non-fiction; Publr C. JORDAN FENN.

Fifth House Publishers Ltd: 6125 11th St, SE, No. 9, Calgary, AB T2H 2L6; tel. (403) 571-5230; fax (403) 571-5235; f. 1982; native, literary and non-fiction; Publr FRASER SEELY.

Fitzhenry & Whiteside Ltd: 195 Allstate Pkwy, Markham, ON L3R 4T8; tel. (416) 477-9700; fax (416) 477-9179; e-mail godwit@fitzhenry.ca; internet www.fitzhenry.ca; f. 1966; textbooks, trade, educational; Pres. SHARON FITZHENRY.

Gage Educational Publishing Co: 164 Commander Blvd, Agincourt, ON M1S 3C7; tel. (416) 293-8141; fax (416) 293-9009; e-mail info@gage.canpub.ca; internet www.cornerstones.gagepub.ca; f. 1844; Pres. CHRIS R. BESSE.

General Publishing Co Ltd: 895 Don Mills Rd, Toronto, ON M3C 1W3; tel. (416) 445-3333; fax (416) 445-5991; e-mail sleeshew@genpub.com; internet www.genpub.com; fiction and non-fiction; Pres. NELSON DOUCET.

Grolier Ltd: 12 Banigan Dr., Toronto, ON M4H 1A6; tel. (416) 425-1924; fax (416) 425-4015; f. 1912; reference, children's; Gen. Man. ROB FURLONGER.

Harcourt Brace & Co Canada: 55 Horner Ave, Toronto, ON M8Z 4X6; tel. (416) 255-4491; fax (416) 255-4046; internet www.harcourtcanada.com; f. 1922; medical, educational, scholarly; Pres. JEAN-GUY BLANCHETTE.

Harlequin Books: 225 Duncan Mill Rd, Don Mills, ON M3B 3K9; tel. (416) 445-5860; fax (416) 445-8655; internet eharlequin.com; f. 1949; fiction, paperbacks; Chair. and CEO DONNA HAYES.

HarperCollins Canada Ltd: Hazleton Lanes, 55 Avenue Rd, Suite 2900, Toronto, ON M5R 3L2; tel. (416) 975-9334; fax (416) 975-9884; e-mail hccanada@harpercollins.com; internet www.harpercanada .com; f. 1932; trade, bibles, dictionaries, juvenile, paperbacks; Pres. and CEO DAVID KENT.

Hyperion Press Ltd: 300 Wales Ave, Winnipeg, MB R2M 2S9; tel. (204) 256-9204; fax (204) 255-7845; e-mail tamos@escape.ca; internet www.escape.ca/~tamos; children's illustrated; Pres. MARVIS TUTIAH.

Institut de Recherches psychologiques, inc/Institute of Psychological Research, Inc: 34 rue Fleury ouest, Montréal, QC H3L 1S9; tel. (514) 382-3000; fax (514) 382-3007; e-mail info@i-r-p.ca; internet www.i-r-p.ca; f. 1964; educational and psychological tests; Adviser ROBERT CHEVRIER.

Irwin Publishing Ltd: 325 Humber College Blvd, Toronto, ON M9W 7C3; tel. (416) 798-0424; fax (416) 798-1384; e-mail irwin@ irwin-pub.com; internet www.irwin-pub.com; f. 1945; educational; Pres. BRIAN O'DONNELL.

Jesperson Publishing: 39 James Lane, St John's, NL A1E 3H3; tel. (709) 753-0633; fax (709) 753-5507; f. 1974; educational and trade; Pres. and Publr JOHN SYMONDS.

Key Porter Books: 70 The Esplanade, 3rd Floor, Toronto, ON M5E 1R2; tel. (416) 862-7777; fax (416) 862-2304; e-mail iromain@ keyporter.com; internet www.keyporter.com; f. 1980; general trade; Pres. and CEO ANNA PORTER.

Leméac Editeur: 4609 d'Iberville, 3e étage, Montréal, QC H2H 2L9; tel. (514) 525-5558; fax (514) 524-3145; e-mail lemeac@lemeac .qc.ca; f. 1957; literary, academic, general; Gen. Dir LISE P. BERGEVIN.

Lidec Inc: 4350 ave de l'Hôtel-de-Ville, Montréal, QC H2W 2H5; tel. (514) 843-5991; fax (514) 843-5252; e-mail lidec@lidec.qc.ca; internet www.lidec.qc.ca; f. 1965; educational, textbooks; Pres. MARC-AIME GUÉRIN.

James Lorimer & Co Ltd: 35 Britain St, Toronto, ON M5A 1R7; tel. (416) 362-4762; fax (416) 362-3939; e-mail jlc@sympatico.ca; f. 1971; urban and labour studies, children's, general non-fiction; Pres. JAMES LORIMER.

McClelland and Stewart Ltd: 481 University Ave, Suite 900, Toronto, ON M5G 2E9; tel. (416) 598-1114; fax (416) 598-7764; internet www.mcclelland.com; f. 1906; trade, illustrated and educational; Pres. and Publr DOUGLAS M. GIBSON.

McGill-Queen's University Press: 3430 rue McTavish, Montréal, QC H3A 1X9; tel. (514) 398-3750; fax (514) 398-4333; e-mail mqup@ mqup.mcgill.ca; internet www.mqup.ca; f. 1960; scholarly and general interest; Exec. Dir PHILLIP J. CERCONE.

McGraw-Hill Ryerson Ltd: 300 Water St, Whitby, ON L1N 9B6; tel. (416) 430-5000; fax (416) 430-5020; e-mail johnd@mcgrawhill.ca; internet www.mcgrawhill.ca; f. 1944; educational and general; Pres. and CEO JOHN DILL.

Nelson–A Division of Thomson Learning: 1120 Birchmount Rd, Scarborough, ON M1K 5G4; tel. (416) 752-9100; fax (416) 752-9646; internet www.nelson.com; f. 1914; retailing, consumer affairs, textbooks; Pres. GEORGE W. BERGQUIST.

Oberon Press: 350 Sparks St, Suite 400, Ottawa, ON K1R 7S8; tel. and fax (613) 238-3275; e-mail oberon@sympatico.ca; internet www3 .sympatico.ca/oberon/; f. 1966; poetry, children's, fiction and general non-fiction; Pres. MICHAEL MACKLEM.

Oxford University Press Canada: 70 Wynford Dr., Don Mills, ON M3C 1J9; tel. (416) 441-2941; fax (416) 444-0427; e-mail custserv@ oupcan.com; internet www.oupcan.com; f. 1904; general, education, scholarly, Canadiana; Pres. JOANNA GERTLER.

Pearson Education Canada Inc: 26 Prince Andrew Pl., Toronto, ON M3C 2T8; tel. (416) 447-5101; fax (416) 443-0948; internet www .pearsoned.ca; educational; Pres. and CEO TONY VANDER WOUDE.

Penguin Books Canada Ltd: 10 Alcorn Ave, Suite 300, Toronto, ON M4V 3B2; tel. (416) 925-2249; fax (416) 925-0068; e-mail oper@ penguin.ca; internet www.penguin.ca; f. 1974; Pres. STEVEN PARR.

Pippin Publishing Corpn: 85 Ellesmere Rd, Suite 232, Toronto, ON M1R 4B9; tel. (416) 510-2918; fax (416) 510-3359; e-mail jld@ pippinpub.com; internet www.pippinpub.com; f. 1995; educational and trade publisher; Pres. JONATHAN LOVAT DICKSON.

Pontifical Institute of Mediaeval Studies: 59 Queen's Park Crescent East, Toronto, ON M5S 2C4; tel. (416) 926-7144; fax (416) 926-7258; e-mail pontifex@chass.utoronto.ca; internet www.pims .ca; f. 1939; scholarly publs concerning the Middle Ages; Dir of Publs RON B. THOMSON.

Prentice Hall Canada Inc: 1870 Birchmount Rd, Scarborough, ON M1P 2J7; tel. (416) 293-3621; fax (416) 299-2529; e-mail pub_canada@prenhall; internet www.prenhall.com/; f. 1960; trade, textbooks; Pres. BRIAN HEER.

Les Presses de l'Université Laval: Cité Universitaire, Ste-Foy, QC G1K 7P4; tel. (418) 656-2803; fax (418) 656-3305; e-mail presses@pul.ulaval.ca; internet www.ulaval.ca/pul; f. 1950; scholarly; Publr BENOIT BERNIER.

Les Presses de l'Université de Montréal: CP 6128, succursale Centre-Ville, Montréal, QC H3C 3J7; tel. (514) 343-6933; fax (514) 343-2232; e-mail pum@umontreal.ca; internet www.pum.umontreal .ca; f. 1962; scholarly and general; Gen. Man. ANTOINE DEL BUSSO.

Les Presses de l'Université du Québec: 2875 blvd Laurier, Suite 450, Ste-Foy, QC G1V 2M2; tel. (418) 657-4399; fax (418) 657-2096; e-mail puq@puq.uquebec.ca; internet www.puq.uquebec.ca; f. 1969; scholarly and general; Dir-Gen. ANGÈLE TREMBLAY.

Random House of Canada Ltd: 1265 Aerowood Dr., Mississauga, ON L4W 1B9; tel. (905) 624-0672; fax (905) 624-6217; internet www .randomhouse.ca; f. 1944; Pres. DAVID KENT.

Scholastic Canada Ltd: 175 Hillmount Rd, Markham, ON L6C 1Z7; tel. (905) 887-7323; fax (905) 887-1131; internet www.scholastic .ca; Pres. F. C. L. MULLER.

Sélection du Reader's Digest (Canada) Ltée/The Reader's Digest Association (Canada) Ltd: 1100 blvd René-Lévesque ouest, Montréal, QC H3B 5H5; tel. (514) 940-0751; fax (514) 940-3637; internet www.readersdigest.ca; Pres. and CEO PIERRE DION.

Sogides Ltée: 955 rue Amherst, Montréal, QC H2L 3K4; tel. (514) 523-1182; fax (514) 597-0370; e-mail franvin@sogides.com; internet www.sogides.com; f. 1958; general interest, fiction, psychology, biography; Pres. PIERRE LESPÉRANCE.

Stoddart Publishing Co Ltd: 895 Don Mills Rd, 400-2 Park Centre, Toronto ON M3C 1W3; tel. (416) 445-3333; fax (416) 445-5967; e-mail bhowson@stoddartpub.com; internet www.stoddartpub .com; f. 1984; general fiction and non-fiction, textbooks, children's; Pres. JACK STODDART.

Thistledown Press Ltd: 633 Main St, Saskatoon, SK S7H 0J8; tel. (306) 244-1722; fax (306) 244-1762; e-mail thistle@sk.sympatico.ca; internet www.thistledown.sk.ca; f. 1975; Canadian fiction, non-fiction and poetry; Pres. GLEN SORESTAD.

Thompson Educational Publishing Inc: 6 Ripley Ave, Suite 200, Toronto, ON M6S 3N9; tel. (416) 766-2763; fax (416) 766-0398; e-mail publisher@thompsonbooks.com; internet www .thompsonbooks.com; f. 1989; textbooks; Pres. KEITH THOMPSON.

University of Alberta Press: Ring House 2, Edmonton, AB T6G 2E1; tel. (780) 492-3662; fax (780) 492-0719; e-mail uap@ualberta.ca; internet www.uap.ualberta.ca; f. 1969; scholarly, general nonfiction; Dir LINDA D. CAMERON.

University of British Columbia Press: 2029 West Mall, Vancouver, BC V6T 1Z2; tel. (604) 822-5959; fax (604) 822-6083; e-mail info@ubcpress.ubc.ca; internet www.ubcpress.ubc.ca; f. 1971; humanities, forestry, social science; Dir PETER MILROY.

University of Manitoba Press: 423 University Cres., Winnipeg, MB R3T 2N2; tel. (204) 474-9495; fax (204) 474-7566; internet www .umanitoba.ca/uofmpress; f. 1967; regional history, Native, Icelandic and women's studies; Dir DAVID CARR.

University of Ottawa Press/Presses de l'Université d'Ottawa: 542 ave King Edward, Ottawa, ON K1N 6N5; tel. (613) 562-5246; fax (613) 562-5247; e-mail press@uottawa.ca; internet www.uopress .uottawa.ca; f. 1936; university texts, scholarly works in English and French; general; Editor-in-Chief VICKI BENNETT.

University of Toronto Press Inc: 10 St Mary's St, Suite 700, Toronto, ON M4Y 2W8; tel. (416) 978-2239; fax (416) 978-4738; e-mail publishing@utpress.utoronto.ca; internet www.utpress .utoronto.ca; f. 1901; scholarly books and journals; Pres. and Publr GEORGE MEADOWS.

John Wiley and Sons Canada Ltd: 22 Worcester Rd, Etobicoke, ON M9W 1L1; tel. (416) 236-4433; fax (416) 236-8743; e-mail canada@wiley.com; internet www.wiley.com; f. 1968; Pres. DIANE WOOD.

Government Publishing House

Canada Communications Group Publishing: 45 blvd Sacre-Coeur, D2200, Hull, QC K1A 0S9; tel. (819) 956-4800; fax (819) 994-1498; e-mail publishing@ccg.gcc.ca; internet www.ccg.gcc.ca; f. 1876; books and periodicals on numerous subjects, incl. agriculture, economics, environment, geology, history and sociology; Dir LESLIE-ANN SCOTT.

ORGANIZATIONS AND ASSOCIATIONS

Association of Canadian Publishers: 110 Eglinton Ave West, Suite 401, Toronto, ON M4R 1A3; tel. (416) 487-6116; fax (416) 487-8815; internet www.publishers.ca; f. 1976; trade asscn of Canadian-owned English-language book publrs; represents Canadian publishing internationally; 145 mems; Exec. Dir MONIQUE SMITH.

Association of Canadian University Presses: c/o University of Toronto Press, 10 Saint Mary St, Suite 700, Toronto, ON M4Y 2W8; tel. (416) 978-2239; Exec. Dir BRIAN HENDERSON.

Canadian Copyright Institute: 192 Spadina Ave, Suite 107, Toronto, ON M5T 2C2; tel. (416) 975-1756; fax (416) 975-1839; e-mail bkper@interlog.com; 83 mems; Chair. RON B. THOMSON.

Canadian Publishers' Council: 250 Merton St, Suite 203, Toronto, ON M4S 1B1; tel. (416) 322-7011; fax (416) 322-6999; e-mail pubadmin@pubcouncil.ca; internet www.pubcouncil.ca; f. 1910; trade asscn of Canadian-owned publrs and Canadian-incorp. subsidiaries of UK and USA publrs; 24 mems; Pres. JOHN DILL.

Broadcasting and Communications

The 1968 Broadcasting Act established the Canadian Broadcasting Corporation (CBC) as the national, publicly-owned, broadcasting service and created the Canadian Radio-Television and Telecommunications Commission (CRTC) as the agency regulating radio, television and cable television. The CRTC's telecommunications authority is currently derived from the 1985 Canadian Radio-Television and Telecommunications Act. Subsequent Broadcasting Acts, introduced in 1991 and 1993, reconfirmed the CRTC's regulatory powers.

Many privately-owned television and radio stations have affiliation agreements with the CBC and help to distribute the national services. A number of the major private television networks (see below) also have affiliates.

Canadian Broadcasting Corporation/Société Radio Canada (CBC/SRC): 250 Lanark Ave, POB 3220, Station C, Ottawa, ON K1Y 1E4; tel. (613) 724-1200; fax (613) 724-5707; internet www.cbc.radio-canada.ca; f. 1936; financed mainly by public funds, with supplementary revenue from commercial advertising on CBC television; 2 nation-wide television networks and 4 radio networks; services in French, English, Dene and Inuktitut languages; Pres. and CEO ROBERT RABINOVITCH.

Canadian Radio-Television and Telecommunications Commission (CRTC): Ottawa, ON K1A 0N2; tel. (819) 997-0313 (Information); fax (819) 994-0218; e-mail info@crtc.gc.ca; internet www.crtc.gc.ca; f. 1968; offices in Halifax, Winnipeg and Vancouver; Chair. CHARLES DALFEN; Vice-Chair. DAVID COLVILLE (Telecommunications), A. P. WYLIE (Broadcasting); Sec.-Gen. DIANE RHÉAUME.

TELECOMMUNICATIONS

Principal Telecommunications Networks

Aliant Telecom Inc: Station Central RPO, POB 880, Halifax, NS B3J 2W3; tel. (877) 225-4268; internet www.alianttelecom.ca; f. 1999 by merger of telecommunications providers in New Brunswick, Nova Scotia, Prince Edward Island and Newfoundland and Labrador; world-wide communications and information technology solutions; 39.2% owned by Bell Canada, 14.0% owned by BCE Inc; Pres. and CEO STEPHEN WETMORE.

Island Telephone Co Ltd: 69 Belevedere Ave, Charlottetown, PE C1A 7M1; tel. (902) 566-0131; fax (902) 566-4665; internet www.islandtel.pe.ca.

Island Tel Mobility: 69 Belvedere Ave, POB 820, Charlottetown, PE C1A 7M1.

Maritime Telegraph and Telephone Co Ltd (MTT): 1505 Barrington St, POB 880, Halifax, NS B3J 2W3; tel. (902) 487-4080; fax (902) 487-4161; internet www.mtt.ca; telecommunications for Nova Scotia.

MTT Mobility: Network Services, Park Place Centre, Tower 1, 238 Brownlow Ave, Suite 200, Dartmouth, NS B3B 1Y2.

New Brunswick Telephone Co Ltd (NBTel): 1 Brunswick Sq., POB 1430, Saint John, NB E2L 4K2; tel. (506) 658-7917; fax (506) 694-2722; internet www.nbtel.nb.ca; telecommunications for New Brunswick.

NBTel Mobility: 1 Brunswick Sq., POB 1430, Saint John, NB E2L 4K2.

Newfoundland Telephone Co Ltd (NewTel): Fort William Bldg, POB 2110, St John's, NL A1C 5H6; tel. (709) 739-2276; fax (709) 754-2500; internet www.newtel.com; telecommunications for Newfoundland and Labrador.

NewTel Mobility: POB 2110, St John's, NL A1C 5H6.

BCT.Telus Inc (Telus): 3777 Kingsway, Burnaby, BC V5H 3Z7; tel. (604) 432-2413; fax (604) 432-2949; internet www.telus.com; f. 1999; by merger of BC Telecom Inc and Telus Corporation; supplies services to residents of Alberta and British Columbia; Chair. BRIAN CANFIELD; Pres. and CEO GEORGE PETTY.

Bell Canada: 1800 ave Collège McGill, Montréal, QC H3B 4Y7; tel. (514) 870-6434; fax (514) 870-2630; internet www.bell.ca; Canada's largest regional telephone operating co; holds a monopoly in most of Québec and Ontario; also supplies services to the Northwest Territories and Nunavut Territory; 80% owned by BCE Inc; Chair. and CEO JEAN C. MONTY.

Bell Canada Enterprises Inc (BCE Inc): 1050 Beaver Hall Hill, Montréal, QC; tel. (514) 870-6434; fax (514) 870-2630; internet www.bell.ca; f. 1880; provides fixed-line and mobile telecommunications, satellite and internet services; Chair. and CEO JEAN C. MONTY.

Bell Mobility: 105 rue Hotel de Ville, 5e étage, Hull, QC J8X 4H7; internet www.bellmobility.ca; mobile telecommunications.

Manitoba Telecom Services: 333 Main St, POB 6666, Winnipeg, MB R3C 3V6; tel. (204) 941-7651; fax (204) 956-0836; telecommunications for Manitoba; provides fixed-line and mobile telecommunications services; partly owned by BCE.

Northwestel Inc: POB 2727, Whitehorse, YT Y1A 4Y4; provides fixed line and mobile telecommunications services.

Télébec Mobilité Inc: 600 Ave Centrale, Val-d'Or, QC J9P 1P8; mobile telecommunications.

Téléglobe Communications Corpn: 1000 rue de la Gauchetière West, Montréal, QC H3B 4X5; tel. (514) 868-7272; fax (514) 868-7234; internet www.teleglobe.ca; f. 1949; operates international telecommunications services.

Telesat Canada: 1601 Telesat Court, Gloucester, ON K1B 5P4; tel. (613) 748-0123; fax (613) 748-8712; e-mail info@telesat.ca; internet www.telesat.ca; f. 1969 by act of parliament; owns and operates Canada's commercial and domestic satellite system.

Call-Net Enterprises Inc: 2235 Sheppard Ave East, Suite 600, North York, ON M2J 5B5; tel. (416) 718-6400; fax (416) 718-6477; internet www.callnet.ca; wholly-owned subsidiary of Sprint Canada; Chair. LAWRENCE G. TAPP; Pres. and CEO BILL LINTON.

Globalstar Canada Co: 75 Watline Ave, Suite 140, Mississauga, ON L4Z 3E5; tel. (905) 890-1377; fax (905) 890-2175; e-mail info@globalstar.ca; internet www.globalstar.ca; mobile telecommunications.

Microcell Telecom: 1250 blvd René-Lévesque ouest, Suite 400, Montréal, QC H3B 4W8; internet www.microcell.ca; Pres. and CEO FRANÇOIS-CHARLES SIROIS.

Rogers Communications Inc: 333 Bloor St East, 9th Floor, Toronto, ON M4W 1G9; tel. (416) 935-8200; internet www.rogers.com; provides mobile, digital, cable and internet services.

Saskatchewan Telecommunications (SaskTel) International: 2121 Saskatchewan Dr., 12th Floor, Regina, SK S4P 3Y2; tel. (306) 777-4509; fax (306) 359-7475; internet www.sasktel.com; f. 1986; provides mobile, satellite and internet services for Saskatchewan.

SaskTel Mobility: 2550 Sandra Schmirler Way, Regina, SK S4P 3Y2; internet www.sasktelmobility.com.

TELUS: 4595 Canada Way, Burnaby, BC V5G 1J9; tel. (604) 482-2800; fax (604) 482-2700; internet www.telus.com; f. 2001 following merger of TELUS Communications and BC Telecom.

TELUS Mobility: 200 Consilium Pl., Suite 1600, Scarborough, ON M1H 3J3; mobile telecommunications; incorporates Clearnet, QuébecTel and TELUS Mobility West.

TELUS Québec: internet www.telusquebec.com; telecommunications for Québec; Pres. and CEO HUGUES ST-PIERRE.

RADIO

The CBC operates two AM and two FM networks, one each in English and French. The CBC's Northern Service provides both national network programming in English and French, and special local and short-wave programmes, some of which are broadcast in the eight principal languages of the Indian and Inuit peoples. In March 2002 there were 450 outlets for AM radio and 1,430 outlets for FM radio (including private affiliates and rebroadcasters). There were also 56 outlets for Digital Transitional Radio. The CBC radio service, which is virtually free of commercial advertising, is within reach of 99.5% of the population. Radio Canada International, the CBC's overseas short-wave service, broadcasts daily in 11 languages and distributes recorded programmes for use world-wide.

TELEVISION

The CBC operates two television networks, one in English and one in French. CBC's Northern Service provides both radio and television service to 98% of the 90,000 inhabitants of northern Québec, the Northwest Territories, Nunavut and the Yukon. Almost 41% of these inhabitants are native Canadians, and programming is provided in Dene and Inuktitut languages as well as English and French. As of March 2001, CBC television was carried on 1,303 outlets. CBC television is available to approximately 99% of the English- and French-speaking population.

Canadian Satellite Communication Inc (Cancom) of Toronto has been licensed since 1981 by the CRTC to conduct a multi-channel television and radio broadcasting operation via satellite for the distribution of CTV programme output, Réseau de Télévision (TVA) and independent television and radio programmes to remote and under-served communities. Cancom also distributes by satellite the programme output of five US television networks. A second satellite broadcaster, Star Choice, was licensed by the CRTC in June 1998.

In March 2002 there were 785 licensed cable operators. There are five educational services: TV-Ontario in Ontario and Radio-Québec in Québec operate their own television stations and networks; the Learning and Skills Television of Alberta provides educational programming in that province; the Saskatchewan Communications Network Corporation distributes educational programming in Saskatchewan; and the Open Learning Agency (OLA) provides child and adult education by television in British Columbia. Programmes obtainable by pay television services have been in operation since 1983.

Canadian Satellite Communications Inc (Cancom): 50 Burnhamthorpe Rd West, Suite 1000, Mississauga, ON L5B 3C2; tel. (905) 272-4960; fax (905) 272-3399; e-mail pdumas@cancom.ca; internet www.cancom.ca; a division of Shaw Communications Inc; Chair. Harold Roozen; Pres. and CEO Peter Classon.

CTV Television Network: 9 Channel Nine Court, POB 9, Station O, Toronto, ON M4A 2M9; tel. (416) 299-2000; fax (416) 299-2643; internet www.ctv.ca; 25 privately-owned affiliated stations from coast to coast, with 247 rebroadcasters; covers 99% of Canadian TV households; Pres. and CEO Trina McQueen.

Global Television Network: 81 Barber Greene Rd, Don Mills, ON M3C 2A2; tel. (416) 446-5311; fax (416) 446-5447; internet www.globaltv.com; 11 stations in eight provinces; a subsidiary of Can-West Global Communications Corpn; Pres. Kevin Shea.

Réseau de Télévision (TVA): 1600 blvd de Maisonneuve est, CP 368, succursale C, Montréal, QC H2L 4P2; tel. (514) 526-0476; fax (514) 526-4285; f. 1971; French-language network, with 10 stations in Québec and 19 rebroadcasters serving 98% of the province, together with francophone communities in Ontario and New Brunswick; Pres. and CEO Jean Gouepy.

Réseau TQS Inc: 612 rue St-Jacques, Bureau 100, Montréal, QC H3C 5R1; tel. (514) 390-6035; fax (514) 390-6067; e-mail tvpublic@tqs.qc.ca; internet www.tqs.qc.ca; f. 1986; French-language; 2 stations, 6 rebroadcasters and 2 retransmitters serving 95% of the province of Québec; Pres. René Guimond.

Telesat Canada: 1601 Telesat Court, Gloucester, ON K1B 5P4; tel. (613) 748-0123; fax (613) 748-8712; e-mail info@telesat.ca; internet www.telesat.ca; a subsidiary of BCE Inc; f. 1969; Chair. J. Monty; Pres. L. J. Boisvert.

ASSOCIATIONS

Canadian Association of Broadcasters: 350 Sparks St, Suite 306, Ottawa, ON K1R 7S2; tel. (613) 233-4035; fax (613) 233-6961; e-mail cab@cab-acr.ca; internet www.cab-acr.ca; f. 1926; Pres. and CEO Michael McCabe; 500 mem. broadcasting stations.

Canadian Cable Television Association: 360 Albert St, Suite 1010, Ottawa, ON K1R 7X7; tel. (613) 232-2631; fax (613) 232-2137; e-mail ccta@ccta.com; internet www.ccta.ca; Pres. Janet Yale; 846 mems.

Television Bureau of Canada, Inc: 160 Bloor St E, Suite 1005, Toronto, ON M4W 1B9; tel. (416) 923-8813; fax (416) 923-8739; e-mail tvb@tvb.ca; internet www.tvb.ca; f. 1962; Pres. Jim Patterson; 150 mems.

Finance

(cap. = capital; auth. = authorized; res = reserves; dep. = deposits; m. = million; brs = branches; amounts in Canadian dollars)

BANKING

Since Confederation in 1867, the Federal Government has exercised jurisdiction over banking operations throughout Canada. The Bank Act of 1980 created two categories of banking institution: Schedule 'I' banks, in which no one interest is allowed to own more than 10% of the shares; and Schedule 'II' banks, which are either subsidiaries of foreign financial institutions, or are banks controlled by Canadian non-bank financial institutions. In 2002 there were 10 Schedule 'I' banks and 50 Schedule 'II' banks. In that year there were more than 8,000 bank branches in Canada.

Major revisions to the Bank Act, the federal Trust and Loans Companies Act, the federal Insurance Companies Act and the Co-operative Credit Associations Act came into force in June 1992. This legislation permits federal financial institutions, with some restrictions, to diversify into each other's markets through subsidiaries. By 1 January 1995, following ratification of the North American Free Trade Agreement (NAFTA) and the enactment of the World Trade Organization Implementation Act, the domestic asset limitations on foreign-owned Schedule 'II' banks in the Canadian market were removed.

In the past, the Bank Act was generally reviewed once every 10 years. As a result of extensive revisions to the federal financial institutions legislation in 1992, a further review of the Bank Act was carried out in 1997. In addition, a Task Force on the Future of the Canadian Financial Services Sector was appointed by the Federal Government in 1996 to review the legislative framework of the financial services sector. The report of the Task Force, published in September 1998, recommended the abolition of existing barriers preventing financial institutions from providing unified services in banking, insurance and motor vehicle leasing. It was also proposed that commercial banks and trust companies (see below) be permitted to market all classes of insurance through their branch networks by 2002. The Task Force expressed support for the entry of foreign banks into the commercial loans market, and for the adoption of new regulations for consumer protection. No recommendations, however, were made concerning the proposed mergers between the Royal Bank of Canada and the Bank of Montréal (announced in January 1998) and between the Canadian Imperial Bank of Commerce and the Toronto-Dominion Bank (announced in April). The merger plans were subsequently considered by a committee of the Federal House of Commons, which in December recommended that they be allowed to proceed. In the following week, however, the Minister of Finance announced that the Government had rejected the merger plans on the grounds that they would create an unacceptably high concentration of economic power and market dominance by the merged groups. It was stated that the Government was to initiate a further review of the financial services industry, during which time no new bank merger proposals would be considered. The Government was also to introduce legislation to stimulate competition within the banking sector, and to ease the existing restraints on the operation of foreign banks in Canada.

Trust and loan companies, which were originally formed to provide mortgage finance and private customer loans, now occupy an important place in the financial system, offering current account facilities and providing access to money transfer services.

Central Bank

Bank of Canada: 234 Wellington St, Ottawa, ON K1A 0G9; tel. (613) 782-8111; fax (613) 782-8655; e-mail paffairs@bank-banque-canada.ca; internet www.bank-banque-canada.ca; f. 1934; bank of issue; cap. and res 30m., dep. 2,625.7m. (Dec. 2001); Gov. David Dodge.

Commercial Banks

Schedule 'I' Banks

Bank of Montréal: 129 rue St-Jacques ouest, Montréal, QC H2Y 1L6; tel. (514) 877-1285; fax (514) 877-6922; e-mail info@bmo.com; internet www.bmo.com; f. 1817; cap. 4,425m., dep. 154,290m. (Oct. 2001); Chair. and CEO Anthony F. Comper; 1,163 brs.

Bank of Nova Scotia (Scotiabank): Scotia Plaza, 44 King St West, Toronto, ON M5H 1H1; tel. (416) 866-6161; fax (416) 866-3750; e-mail email@scotiabank.ca; internet www.scotiabank.ca; f. 1832; cap. 4,695m., dep. 186,195m. (Oct. 2001); Chair. and CEO Peter C. Godsoe; 1,272 brs.

Canadian Imperial Bank of Commerce: Commerce Court, Toronto, ON M5L 1A2; tel. (416) 980-2211; internet www.cibc.com; f. 1867; cap. 5,126m., dep. 194,352m. (Oct. 2001); Chair. and CEO John S. Hunkin; 1,453 brs.

Canadian Western Bank: 10303 Jasper Ave, Suite 2300, Edmonton, AB T5J 3X6; tel. (780) 423-8888; fax (780) 423-8897; e-mail comments@cwb.com; internet www.cwbank.com; f. 1988; cap. 143.9m., dep. 3,042.3m. (Oct. 2001); Chair. Jack C. Donald; Pres. and CEO Larry M. Pollock; 27 brs.

Laurentian Bank of Canada: Laurentian Bank Tower, 1981 ave Collège McGill, Montréal, QC H3A 3K3; tel. (514) 284-4500; fax (514) 284-3396; e-mail laurentianbank@com; internet www.laurentianbank.com; f. 1846; cap. 394.6m., dep. 14,518.0m. (Oct. 2001); Pres. and CEO Raymond McManus; 230 brs.

National Bank of Canada: 600 rue de la Gauchetière ouest, Montréal, QC H3B 4L2; tel. (514) 394-5000; fax (514) 394-8434; internet www.nbc.ca; f. 1979; cap. 2,160m., dep. 51,436m. (Oct. 2001); Chair. André Bérard; Pres. and CEO Réal Raymond; 546 brs.

Royal Bank of Canada: 1 place Ville Marie, CP 6001, Montréal, QC H3C 3A9; tel. (514) 874-2110; e-mail banks@rbc.com; internet www.royalbank.com; f. 1869; cap. 8,949m., dep. 235,687m. (Oct. 2001); Chair GUY ST. PIERRE; CEO GORDON M. NIXON; 1,313 brs.

Toronto-Dominion Bank: Toronto-Dominion Centre, POB 1, Toronto, ON M5K 1A2; tel. (416) 982-8222; fax (416) 982-5671; internet www.td.com; f. 1855; cap. and res 3,751m., dep. 193,914m. (Oct. 2001); Chair. and CEO A. CHARLES BAILLIE; Pres. W. EDMUND CLARKE; 907 brs.

Principal Schedule 'II' Banks

Bank of Tokyo-Mitsubishi (Canada): Royal Bank Plaza, South Tower, Suite 2100, POB 42, Toronto, ON M5J 2J1; tel. (416) 865-0220; fax (416) 865-9511; internet www.btm.co.jp; f. 1981; subsidiary of Bank of Tokyo-Mitsubishi (Japan); total assets 2,565.8m. (October 2001); Chair., Pres. and CEO YOSHIO SAIHARA; 3 brs.

Citibank Canada: Citibank Place, 123 Front St West, Suite 1000, Toronto, ON M5J 2M3; tel. (416) 947-5500; fax (416) 947-5813; internet www.citibank.com/canada; f. 1981; subsidiary of Citibank NA (USA); total assets 8,635m. (2001); Chair. and CEO M. ROBERTS; 17 brs.

HSBC Bank Canada: 885 West Georgia St, Vancouver, BC V6C 3E9; tel. (604) 685-1000; fax (604) 641-1849; e-mail info@hsbc.ca; internet www.hsbc.ca; f. 1981; subsidiary of HSBC Holdings plc (United Kingdom); total assets 33,300m. (Dec. 2001); Pres. and CEO MARTIN GLYNN; 120 brs.

Société Générale (Canada): 1501 ave Collège McGill, Bureau 1800, Montréal, QC H3A 3M8; tel. (514) 841-6000; fax (514) 841-6250; internet www.socgen.com; f. 1981; subsidiary of Société Générale SA (France); total assets 3,239.4m. (October 2001); Pres. and CEO DIDIER COLIN; 3 brs.

Development Bank

Business Development Bank of Canada: 5 place Ville Marie, Plaza Level, Bureau 12525, Montréal, QC H3B 2G2; tel. (514) 496-7966; fax (514) 496-7974; internet www.bdc.ca; f. 1975; fed. govt corpn; auth. shareholders' equity 923m. (March 2001); Pres. and CEO MICHEL VENNAT; 80 brs.

Principal Trust and Loan Companies

Canada Trustco Mortgage Co: Canada Trust Tower, 275 Dundas St, London, ON N6A 4S4; tel. (519) 663-1500; fax (519) 663-5114; f. 1855; total assets 46,000m. (1997); Pres. and CEO W. EDMUND CLARK; 421 brs.

Montréal Trustco Inc: Scotia Plaza, 44 King St West, Toronto, ON M5H 1H1; tel. (416) 866-3675; fax (416) 866-5090; f. 1889; subsidiary of Scotiabank; total assets 18,044.3m. (1994); Chair. and CEO ROBERT W. CHISHOLM.

National Trust Co Ltd: 1 Adelaide St East, Toronto, ON M5C 2W8; tel. (416) 361-3611; fax (416) 361-4037; f. 1898; subsidiary of Scotiabank; cap. and res 253.7m., dep. 13,849.1m. (Oct. 1996); Chair. and CEO PAUL CANTOR.

Royal Trust Corporation of Canada: Royal Trust Tower, POB 7500, Station A, Toronto, ON M5W 1P9; tel. (416) 974-1400; fax (416) 861-9658; f. 1899; total assets 11,500m. (July 1997); Pres. HELEN AZEVEDO.

Savings Institutions with Provincial Charters

Alberta Treasury Branches: 9888 Jasper Ave, Edmonton, AB T5J 1P1; tel. (780) 493-7309; fax (780) 422-4178; internet www.atb.com; f. 1938; assets 11,464m. (Dec. 2000); Pres. and CEO PAUL G. HAGGIS; 144 brs.

Province of Ontario Savings Office: 40 King St West, 6th Floor, Oshawa, ON L1H 1A4; tel. (905) 433-5788; fax (905) 433-6519; e-mail poso@ofina.ca; internet www.ofina.on.ca/poso; f. 1921; assets 2,600m. (March 1996); Chair. BOB CHRISTIE; 23 brs.

Bankers' Organizations

Canadian Bankers Association: Commerce Court West, Suite 3000, Box 348, Toronto, ON M5L 1G2; tel. (416) 362-6092; fax (416) 362-7705; e-mail inform@cba.ca; internet www.cba.ca; f. 1891; 5 regional brs, 48 mems; Chair. GORDON FEENEY; Pres. RAYMOND J. PROTTI.

Trust Companies Association of Canada Inc: 1 Financial Pl., Suite 1002, 1 Adelaide St East, Toronto, ON M5C 2V9; tel. (416) 866-8842; fax (416) 364-2122; 20 mems; Chair. GERALD SOLOWAY; Exec. Dir GLENN GRAY.

STOCK EXCHANGES

Bourse de Montréal/Montreal Exchange: Tour de la Bourse, CP 61, 800 square Victoria, Montréal, QC H4Z 1A9; tel. (514) 871-2424; fax (514) 871-3553; e-mail info@me.org; internet www.me.org; f. 1874; 75 mems; Pres. and CEO LUC BERTRAND.

Canadian Venture Exchange (CDNX): 650 West Georgia St, Suite 2700, Vancouver, BC V6B 4N9; tel. (604) 689-3334; fax (604) 688-6051; e-mail information@cdnx.ca; internet www.cdnx.ca; f. 1999 by merger of Alberta and Vancouver Stock Exchanges, incorporated Winnipeg Stock Exchange 2000; 66 mems.

TSX Group (Toronto Stock Exchange): The Exchange Tower, 130 King St West, Toronto, ON M5X 1J2; tel. (416) 947-4700; fax (416) 947-4662; e-mail info@tsx.com; internet www.tsx.com; f. 1852; 101 mems; Pres. and CEO BARBARA STYMIEST.

INSURANCE

Principal Companies

Allianz Canada: 10 York Mills Rd, Suite 700, Toronto, ON M2P 2G5; tel. (416) 227-7800; fax (416) 227-9837; e-mail info@allianz.ca; internet www.allianz.ca; f. 1928; Pres. CHRISTIAN CASSEBAUM.

Blue Cross Life Insurance Co of Canada: POB 220, Moncton, NB E1C 8L3; tel. (506) 853-1811; fax (506) 853-4651; internet www.bluecross.ca; Pres. and CEO LEON R. FURLONG.

Canada Life Assurance Co: 330 University Ave, Toronto, ON M5G 1R8; tel. (416) 597-1456; fax (416) 597-1940; e-mail info@canadalife.com; internet www.canadalife.com; f. 1847; Pres. DAVID A. NIELD.

Canadian General Insurance Co: 2206 Eglinton Ave East, Suite 500, Scarborough, ON M1L 4S8; tel. (416) 288-1800; fax (416) 288-9756; f. 1907; Pres. and CEO R. LEWIS DUNN.

Clarica: 227 King St South, Waterloo, ON N2J 4C5; tel. (519) 888-2290; fax (519) 888-2990; e-mail service@clarica.com; internet www.clarica.com; f. 1999 following demutualization of The Mutual Group (f. 1870); Pres. and CEO ROBERT ASTLEY.

Crown Life Insurance Co: 1901 Scarth St, POB 827, Regina, SK S4P 3B1; tel. (306) 751-6000; fax (306) 751-6150; internet www.crownlife.ca; f. 1900; Pres. and CEO R. F. RICHARDSON.

Desjardins Financial Security Life Assurance Company: 200 ave des Commandeurs, Lévis, QC G6V 6R2; e-mail info@desjardinsfinancialsecurity.com; internet www.desjardinsfinancialsecurity.com; f. 2001; following merger of Assurance vie Desjardins–Laurentienne with Imperial Life Assurance Co of Canada; Pres. and CEO FRANÇOIS JOLY.

Dominion of Canada General Insurance Co: 165 University Ave, Toronto, ON M5H 3B9; tel. (416) 362-7231; fax (416) 362-9918; f. 1887; Pres. and CEO GEORGE L. COOKE.

Federation Insurance Co of Canada: 1000 rue de la Gauchetière ouest, Bureau 500, Montréal, QC H3B 4W5; tel. (514) 875-5790; fax (514) 875-9769; f. 1947; Pres. NOEL WALPOLE.

General Accident Group of Canada: 2206 Eglinton Ave East, Toronto, ON M1L 4S8; tel. (416) 288-1800; fax (416) 288-9756; internet www.genacc.ca; f. 1906; Pres. R. LEWIS DUNN.

Gerling Canada Insurance Co: 480 University Ave, Suite 1600, Toronto, ON M5G 1V6; tel. (416) 598-4651; fax (416) 598-5478; f. 1955; Pres. A. H. HENKE.

Gore Mutual Insurance Co: 262 Dundas St, Cambridge, ON N1R 5T3; tel. (519) 623-1910; fax (519) 623-8348; e-mail vision@goremutual.ca; internet www.goremutual.ca; f. 1839; Pres. and CEO KEVIN W. MCNEIL.

Guardian Insurance Co of Canada: 181 University Ave, Toronto, ON M5W 3M7; tel. (416) 941-5050; fax (416) 941-9791; f. 1911; Pres. and CEO HENRY J. CURTIS.

Halifax Insurance Co: 75 Eglinton Ave East, Toronto, ON M4P 3A4; tel. (416) 440-1000; fax (416) 440-0799; internet www.halifaxinsurance.com; f. 1809; Pres. and CEO DONALD K. LOUGH.

Industrial Alliance Pacific Life Insurance Co: 2165 Broadway West, POB 5900, Vancouver, BC V6B 5H6; tel. (604) 734-1667; fax (604) 734-8221; e-mail intouch@iapacificlife.com; internet www.iapacificlife.com; f. 2000 by merger; Pres. and CEO ROBERT SMITH.

ING Canada: 2450 rue Girouard ouest, St-Hyacinthe, QC J2S 3B3; tel. (514) 773-9701; fax (514) 773-3515; Pres. and CEO YVES BROUILLETTE.

Kings Mutual Insurance Co: POB 10, Berwick, NS B0P 1E0; tel. (902) 538-3187; fax (902) 538-7271; e-mail kings.mutual@ns.sympatico.com; f. 1904; Pres. J. J. UEFFING.

Manufacturers Life Insurance Co (Manulife Financial): 200 Bloor St East, Toronto, ON M4W 1E5; tel. (416) 926-0100; fax (416) 926-5454; e-mail webmaster@manulife.com; internet www.manulife.com; f. 1887; acquired Commercial Union Life Assurance Co of Canada in 2001; Pres. and CEO DOMINIC D'ALESSANDRO.

Metropolitan Life Insurance Co of Canada: 99 Bank St, Ottawa, ON K1P 5A3; tel. (613) 560-7446; fax (613) 560-7668; Pres. and CEO WILLIAM R. PRUETER.

The National Life Assurance Co of Canada: 522 University Ave, Toronto, ON M5G 1Y7; tel. (416) 598-2122; fax (416) 598-4948; internet www.nationallife.ca; f. 1897; Pres. VINCENT P. TONNA.

Portage La Prairie Mutual Insurance Co: 749 Saskatchewan Ave East, Portage La Prairie, MB R1N 3B8; tel. (204) 857-3415; fax (204) 239-6655; e-mail info@portagemutual.com; internet www .portagemutual.com; f. 1884; Pres. T. W. McCARTNEY.

Royal & Sun Alliance Insurance Co of Canada: 10 Wellington St East, Toronto, ON M5E 1L5; tel. (416) 366-7511; fax (416) 367-9869; internet www.royalsunalliance.ca; f. 1851; Pres. and CEO LARRY SIMMONS.

Société Nationale d'Assurance Inc: 425 blvd de Maisonneuve ouest, Bureau 1500, Montréal, QC H3A 3G5; tel. (514) 288-8711; fax (514) 288-8269; f. 1940; Pres. ANDRÉ NADON.

Sun Life Assurance Co of Canada: POB 4150, Station A, Toronto, ON M5W 2C9; tel. (416) 979-9966; fax (416) 585-9546; internet www .sunlife.ca; f. 1871; Chair. and CEO DONALD A. STEWART.

Toronto Mutual Life Insurance Co: 112 St Clair Ave West, Toronto, ON M4V 2Y3; tel. (416) 960-3463; fax (416) 960-0531; internet www.torontomutual.com; Pres. and CEO VAN M. CAMPBELL.

Wawanesa Mutual Insurance Co: 191 Broadway, Winnipeg, MB R3C 3P1; tel. (204) 985-3923; fax (204) 972-7724; internet www .wawanesa.com; f. 1896; Pres. and CEO G. J. HANSON.

Western Assurance Co: POB 3000, Stn Main, Ajax, ON L15 7L9; tel. (905) 686–8326; fax (416) 367-9869; f. 1851; Pres. and CEO LARRY SIMMONS.

Zurich Life of Canada: 2225 Sheppard Ave East, Willowdale, ON M2J 5C4; tel. (416) 502-3600; fax (416) 502-3488; Pres. and CEO MICHAEL P. STRAMAGLIA.

Insurance Organizations

Advocis (Financial Advisors' Association of Canada) (CAIFA): 350 Bloor Street East, 2nd Floor, Toronto, ON M4W 3W8; tel. (416) 444-5251; fax (416) 444-8031; e-mail info@advocis.ca; internet www.advocis.ca; f. 1906; Chair. BRIAN MALLARD; CEO STEVE HOWARD; 18,000 mems.

Canadian Association of Mutual Insurance Companies: 311 McArthur Ave, Suite 205, Ottawa, ON K1L 6P1; tel. (613) 789-6851; fax (613) 789-6854; e-mail nflafreniere@camic.ca; internet www .camic.ca; Pres. NORMAN LAFRENIÈRE; 103 mems.

Canadian Life and Health Insurance Association Inc: 1 Queen St East, Suite 1700, Toronto, ON M5C 2X9; tel. (416) 777-2221; fax (416) 777-1895; e-mail info@clhia.ca; internet www.clhia.ca; f. 1894; Pres. MARK DANIELS; 74 mems.

Insurance Brokers Association of Canada: 155 University Ave, Suite 1920, Toronto, ON M5H 3B7; tel. (416) 367-1831; fax (416) 367-3687; e-mail info@ibac.ca; internet www.ibac.ca; f. 1921; Exec. Dir (VACANT); 11 mem. asscns; need to put (vacant) in lower case.

Insurance Bureau of Canada: 151 Yonge St, Suite 1800, Toronto, ON M5C 2W7; tel. (416) 362-2031; fax (416) 361-5952; internet www .ibc.ca; f. 1964; Pres. and CEO GEORGE ANDERSON; 110 corporate mems.

Insurance Institute of Canada: 18 King St East, 6th Floor, Toronto, ON M5C 1C4; tel. (416) 362-8586; fax (416) 362-4239; e-mail genmail@iic-iac.org; internet www.iic-iac.org; f. 1952; Pres. PETER HOHMAN; 31,000 mems.

Life Insurance Institute of Canada: 1155 North Service Road West, Suite 11, Oakville, ON L6M 3E3; tel. (905) 847-8966; fax (905) 847-8897; e-mail cole-gauerd@loma.org; internet www.liic.ca; f. 1935; Exec. Dir DEBBIE COLE-GAUER; 57 mem. asscns.

Trade and Industry

CHAMBER OF COMMERCE

The Canadian Chamber of Commerce: 350 Sparks St, Suite 501, Ottawa, ON K1R 7S8; tel. (613) 238-4000; fax (613) 238-7643; e-mail info@chamber.ca; internet www.chamber.ca; f. 1925; mems: 500 community chambers of commerce and boards of trade, 80 nat. trade asscns and 2,500 business corpns; Nat. Pres. NANCY HUGHES ANTHONY.

INDUSTRIAL AND TRADE ASSOCIATIONS

Alliance of Manufacturers and Exporters Canada: 75 International Blvd, 4th Floor, Toronto, ON M9W 6L9; tel. (416) 798-8000; fax (416) 798-8050; e-mail national@the-alliance.com; internet www .palantir.ca/the-alliance/; f. 1871; the nat. org. of mfrs and exporters of Canada; Pres. STEPHEN VAN HOUTEN; 3,500 mems.

Agriculture and Horticulture

Canada Grains Council: 220 Portage Ave, Winnipeg, MB R3C 0A5; tel. (204) 925-2130; fax (204) 925-2132; e-mail office@ canadagrainscouncil.ca; internet www.canadagrainscouncil.ca; f. 1969; Chair. JIM WILSON; 27 mems.

Canadian Federation of Agriculture: 75 Albert St, Suite 1101, Ottawa, ON K1P 5E7; tel. (613) 236-3633; fax (613) 236-5749; e-mail info@cfafca.ca; internet www.cfa-fca.ca; f. 1935; Exec. Dir BRIGID RIVOIRE; 20 mems.

Canadian Horticultural Council: 1101 Prince of Wales Dr., Suite 310, Ottawa, ON K2C 3W7; tel. (613) 226-4187; fax (613) 226-2984; internet www.hortcouncil.ca; f. 1922; Exec. Vice-Pres. ANNE FOWLIE.

Canadian Nursery Landscape Association: 7856 Fifth Lane South, RR 4, Stn Main, Milton, ON L9T 2X8; tel. (905) 875-1399; fax (905) 875-1840; e-mail cnla@canadanursery.com; internet www .canadanursery.com; Exec. Dir CHRIS D. ANDREWS; 1,500 mems.

Canadian Seed Growers' Association: POB 8455, Ottawa, ON K1G 3T1; tel. (613) 236-0497; fax (613) 563-7855; e-mail seeds@ seedgrowers.ca; internet www.seedgrowers.ca; f. 1904; Exec. Dir DALE ADOLPHE; 4,600 mems.

National Dairy Council of Canada: 221 Laurier Ave East, Ottawa, ON K1N 6P1; tel. (613) 238-4116; fax (613) 238-6247; e-mail info@ndcc.ca; internet www.ndcc.ca; f. 1918; Pres. KEMPTON MATTE; 69 mem asscns, 250 individual mems.

National Farmers Union (NFU): 2717 Wentz Ave, Saskatoon, SK S7K 4B6; tel. (306) 652-9465; fax (306) 664-6226; e-mail nfu@nfu.ca; internet www.nfu.ca; f. 1969; Pres. STEWART WELLS; 10,000 mems.

L'Union des producteurs agricoles: 555 blvd Roland-Therrien, Longueuil, QC J4H 3Y9; tel. (514) 679-0530; fax (514) 679-4943; e-mail upa@upa.qc.ca; internet www.upa.qc.ca; f. 1924; Dir-Gen. JEAN LAROSE; 37 institutional mems, 45,000 individual mems.

Building and Construction

Canadian Construction Association: 75 Albert St, Suite 400, Ottawa, ON K1P 5E7; tel. (613) 236-9455; fax (613) 236-9526; e-mail cca@cca-acc.com; internet www.cca-acc.com; f. 1918; Pres. MICHAEL ATKINSON; over 20,000 mems.

Canadian Institute of Steel Construction: 201 Consumers Rd, Suite 300, Willowdale, ON M2J 4G8; tel. (416) 491-4552; fax (416) 491-6461; e-mail info@cisc-icca.ca; internet www.cisc-icca.ca; f. 1930; Pres. MIKE GILMOR; 245 mems.

Canadian Paint and Coatings Association: 9900 blvd Cavendish, Bureau 103, St-Laurent, QC H4M 2V2; tel. (514) 745-2611; fax (514) 745-2031; e-mail cpca@cdnpaint.org; internet www .cdnpaint.org; f. 1913; Pres. RICHARD MURRY; 132 mems.

Canadian Precast/Prestressed Concrete Institute: 196 Bronson Ave, Suite 100, Ottawa, ON K1R 6H4; tel. (613) 232-2619; fax (613) 232-5139; e-mail info@cpci.ca; internet www.cpci.ca; Pres. JOHN R. FOWLER; 300 mems.

Ontario Painting Contractors Association: 211 Consumers Rd, Suite 305, Willowdale, ON M2J 4G8; tel. (416) 498-1897; fax (416) 498-6757; e-mail mmarquardt@attglobal.net; internet www.ontpca .org; f. 1967; Exec. Dir MAUREEN MARQUARDT; 100 mems.

Clothing and Textiles

Canadian Apparel Federation: 504-124 O'Connor St, Ottawa, ON K1P 5M9; tel. (613) 231-3220; fax (613) 231-2305; e-mail info@ apparel.ca; internet www.apparel.ca; f. 1977; Exec. Dir BOB KIRKE.

Canadian Textiles Institute: 66 Slater St, Suite 1720, Ottawa, ON K1P 5H1; tel. (613) 232-7195; fax (613) 232-8722; e-mail cti@ textiles.ca; f. 1935; Pres. ELIZABETH SIWICKI; 60 mems.

Men's Clothing Manufacturers Association: 555 rue Chabanel ouest, Bureau 801, Montréal, QC H3N 2H8; tel. (514) 382-3846; fax (514) 382-3846; e-mail mcma@macten.net; f. 1961; Exec. Dir DAVID BALINSKY; 67 mems.

Textile Federation of Canada: c/o CTT, 3000 rue Boullé, St-Hyacinthe, QC J2S 1H9; tel. (450) 778-1870; fax (450) 778-9016; e-mail rleclerc@ctt.ca; Exec. Sec. ROGER LECLERC; 1,950 mems.

Electrical and Electronics

Canadian Electrical Contractors Assocation: 23 Lesmill Rd, Suite 207, North York, ON M3B 3P6; tel. (416) 391-3226; fax (416) 391-3926; Exec. Sec. ERYL M. ROBERTS.

Canadian Electricity Association: see Utilities—Electricity.

Electrical and Electronic Manufacturers Association of Canada: 10 Carlson Court, Suite 500, Rexdale, ON M9W 6L2; tel. (905) 674-7410; fax (905) 674-7412; f. 1976; Pres. NORMAN ASPIN; 175 mems.

Fisheries

Canadian Association of Fish Exporters: 1770 Woodward Dr., Suite 212, Ottawa, ON K2C 0P8; tel. (613) 228-9220; fax (613) 228-9223; e-mail jbarnett@seafood.ca; internet www.seafood.ca/index .htm; f. 1978; Pres. Dr JANE BARNETT.

Fisheries Council of Canada: 38 Antares Dr., Suite 110, Nepean, ON K2E 7V2; tel. (613) 727-7450; fax (613) 727-7453; e-mail ronbulmer@fisheriescouncil.org; f. 1945; Pres. R. W. BULMER; 200 mems.

Food and Beverages

Association of Sales and Marketing Companies International: 58 Meadowbrook Ave, Suite 100, Unionville, ON L3R 2N9; tel. (905) 477-4644; fax (905) 477-9580; e-mail asmc-i@rogers.com; internet www.asmc.org; f. 1942; Pres. KEITH BRAY; 70 mems, 60 assoc. mems in 20 countries.

Baking Association of Canada: 7895 Tranmere Dr., Mississauga, ON L5S 1V9; tel. (905) 405-0288; fax (905) 405-0993; e-mail info@ baking.ca; internet www.baking.ca; f. 1947; Pres. and CEO PAUL HETHERINGTON; 1,400 institutional mems, 200 assoc. mems.

Brewers Association of Canada: 155 Queen St, Suite 1200, Ottawa, ON K1P 6L1; tel. (613) 232-9601; fax (613) 232-2283; e-mail office@brewers.ca; internet www.brewers.ca; f. 1943; Pres. and CEO R. A. MORRISON; 29 mems.

Canadian Council of Grocery Distributors: CP 1082, succursale place-du-Parc, Montréal, QC H2W 2P4; tel. (514) 982-0267; fax (514) 849-3021; f. 1919; Pres. and CEO JOHN F. GECI; 69 institutional mems, 115 assoc. mems.

Canadian Food Brokers Association: 58 Meadowbrook Ave, Suite 100, Unionville, ON L3R 2N9; tel. (905) 477-4644; fax (905) 477-9580; e-mail kbray@idirect.com; f. 1942; Pres. KEITH BRAY; 70 mems, 60 assoc. mems.

Canadian Meat Council: 875 Carling Ave, Suite 410, Ottawa, ON K1S 5P1; tel. (613) 729-3911; fax (613) 729-4997; internet www .cmc-cvc.com; f. 1919; Gen. Man. ROBERT WEAVER; 65 mems.

Canadian National Millers' Association: 408 Queen St, Ottawa, ON K1R 5A7; tel. (613) 238-2293; fax (613) 235-5866; f. 1920; Pres. GORDON HARRISON; 15 mems.

Canadian Pork Council: 75 Albert St, Suite 1101, Ottawa, ON K1P 5E7; tel. (613) 236-9239; fax (613) 236-6658; e-mail info@cpc-ccp .com; Exec. Dir MARTIN RICE; 9 mems.

Confectionery Manufacturers Association of Canada: 885 Don Mills Rd, Suite 301, Don Mills, ON M3C 1V9; tel. (416) 510-8034; fax (416) 510-8044; e-mail carolh@fcpmc.com; f. 1919; Pres. CAROL L. HOCHU; 81 corporate mems.

Food and Consumer Products Manufacturers of Canada: 885 Don Mills Rd, Suite 301, Don Mills, ON M3C 1V9; tel. (416) 510-8024; fax (416) 510-8043; e-mail info@cpmc.com; internet www .fcpmc.com; Pres. GEORGE FLEISCHMANN; 180 corporate mems.

Food Institute of Canada: 1600 Scott St, Suite 415, Ottawa, ON K1Y 4N7; tel. (613) 722-1000; fax (613) 722-1404; e-mail fic@foodnet .fic.ca; internet www.fic.ca; f. 1989; Pres. JEAN GATTUSO; 200 mems.

Forestry, Lumber and Allied Industries

Canadian Lumbermen's Association: 27 Goulburn Ave, Ottawa, ON K1N 8C7; tel. (613) 233-6205; fax (613) 233-1929; e-mail info@ cla-ca.ca; internet www.cla-ca.ca; f. 1907; Pres. and Exec. Dir ROBERT RIVARD; 200 mems.

Canadian Pulp and Paper Association: Immeuble Sun Life, 1155 rue Metcalfe, 19e étage, Montréal, QC H3B 4T6; tel. (514) 866-6621; fax (514) 866-3035; e-mail cppacda@ibm.net; internet www .open.doors.cppa.ca/; f. 1913; Pres. LISE LACHAPELLE; 60 mems.

Canadian Wood Council: 1400 Blair Pl., Suite 210, Ottawa, ON K1J 9B8; tel. (613) 247-7077; fax (613) 247-7856; internet www.cwc .ca; f. 1959; Pres. CATHERINE LALONDE.

Council of Forest Industries: 1200-555 Burrard St, POB 276, Vancouver, BC V7X 1S7; tel. (604) 684-0211; fax (604) 687-4930; e-mail info@cofi.org; internet www.cofi.org; f. 1960; CEO RON MC-DONALD.

Ontario Forest Industries Association: 20 Toronto St West, Toronto, ON M5S 1W5; tel. (416) 368-6188; fax (416) 368-5445; e-mail info@ofia.com; internet www.ofia.com; f. 1943; CEO TIM MILLARD; 17 corporate mems.

Hotels and Catering

Canadian Restaurant and Foodservices Association: 316 Bloor St West, Toronto, ON M5S 1W5; tel. (416) 923-8416; fax (416) 923-1450; e-mail info@crfa.ca; internet www.crfa.ca; f. 1944; Pres. DOUGLAS NEEDHAM; 14,000 mems.

Hotel Association of Canada Inc: 130 Albert St, Suite 1206, Ottawa, ON K1P 5G4; tel. (613) 237-7149; fax (613) 237-8928; e-mail hac@hotels.ca; internet www.hotels.ca; f. 1929; Pres. ANTHONY POLLARD.

Hotel and Restaurant Suppliers' Association Inc: 2435 rue Guénette, St-Laurent, PQ H4R 2E9; tel. (514) 334-5161; fax (514) 334-1279; e-mail info@afhr.com; internet www.afhr.com; f. 1936; Pres. DENIS LAMOTHE; Gen. Man. GILBERT CREVIER.

Mining

Canadian Association of Petroleum Producers: 350 Seventh Ave, SW, Suite 2100, Calgary, AB T2P 3N9; tel. (403) 267-1100; fax (403) 261-4622; e-mail communication@capp.ca; internet www.capp .ca; f. 1952; Pres. PIERRE ALVAREZ; 150 institutional mems, 140 assoc. mems.

Canadian Gas Association: See Utilities—Gas.

Canadian Mining Contractors Association: 1088 Staghorn Court, Mississauga, ON L5C 3R2; tel. (905) 279-0104; fax (905) 279-1646; e-mail bcampbell@istar.ca; Pres. BRUCE CAMPBELL.

Mining Association of Canada: 350 Sparks St, Suite 1105, Ottawa, ON K1R 7S8; tel. (613) 233-9391; fax (613) 233-8897; e-mail gpeeling@mining.ca; internet www.mining.ca; f. 1935; Pres. GORDON R. PELLING; 60 mems.

Northwest Territories & Nunavut Chamber of Mines: POB 2818, Yellowknife, NT X1A 2R1; tel. (403) 873-5281; fax (403) 920-2145; e-mail nwtmines@ssimicro.com; internet www.miningnorth .com; f. 1967; Gen. Man. MIKE VAYDIK; 380 mems.

Ontario Mining Association: 110 Yonge St, 15th Floor, Toronto, ON M5C 1T4; tel. (416) 364-9301; fax (416) 364-5986; f. 1920; Pres. PATRICK REID; 47 mems.

Petroleum Services Association of Canada: 800 Sixth Ave SW, Suite 1150, Calgary, AB T2P 3G3; tel. (403) 264-4195; fax (403) 263-7174; e-mail infor@psac.ca; internet www.psac.ca; Pres. ROGER SOUCY.

Yukon Chamber of Mines: 3151BThird Ave, Whitehorse, YT Y1A 1G1; tel. (867) 667-2090; fax (867) 668-7127; e-mail info@ycmines.ca; internet www.ycmines.ca; f. 1956; Pres. MIKE POWER; 350 mems.

Pharmaceutical

Canada's Research-Based Pharmaceuticals (Rx & D): 1111 Prince of Wales Dr., Suite 302, Ottawa, ON K2C 3T2; tel. (613) 727-1380; fax (613) 727-1407; e-mail info@canadapharma.org; internet www.canadapharma.org; f. 1914 as Pharmaceutical Mfrs Asscn of Canada; Pres. MURRAY J. ELSTON; 65 mems.

Canadian Drug Manufacturers Association: 4120 Yonge St, Suite 409, Toronto, ON M2P 2B8; tel. (416) 223-2333; fax (416) 223-2425; e-mail info@cdma-acfpp.org; internet www.cdma-acfpp.org; Pres. JIM KEON; 18 mems.

Retailing

Retail Council of Canada: 121 Bloor St, Suite 1210, Toronto, ON M4W 3M5; tel. (416) 922-6678; fax (416) 922-8011; internet www .retailcouncil.org; f. 1963; Pres. and CEO DIANE J. BRISEBOIS; 8,500 mems.

Retail Merchants' Association of Canada Inc: 1780 Birchmount Rd, Scarborough, ON M1P 2H8; tel. (416) 291-7903; fax (416) 291-5635; f. 1896; Pres. SEAN MCMAHON; 3,000 mems.

Transport

Air Transport Association of Canada: see Transport—Civil Aviation.

Canadian Institute of Traffic and Transportation: 10 King St East, 4th Floor, Toronto, ON M5C 1C3; tel. (416) 363-5696; fax (416) 363-5698; e-mail citt@citt.ca; internet www.citt.ca; f. 1958; Chair. SUSAN COLLINS; 2,000 mems.

Canadian Shippers' Council: see Transport—Shipping.

Canadian Trucking Alliance: National Bldg, 130 Slater St, Suite 1025, Ottawa, ON K1P 6E2; tel. (613) 236-9426; fax (613) 563-2701; e-mail dugas@cantruck.com; internet www.cantruck.com; f. 1937; CEO DAVID BRADLEY.

Canadian Vehicle Manufacturers' Association: 170 Attwell Dr., Suite 400, Toronto, ON M9W 5Z5; tel. (416) 364-9333; fax (416) 367-3221; e-mail info@cvma.ca; internet www.cvma.ca; f. 1926; Pres. MARK A. NANTAIS; 5 mems.

Railway Association of Canada: see Transport—Railways.

Shipping Federation of Canada: see Transport—Shipping.

Miscellaneous

Canadian Association of Importers and Exporters, Inc: 438 University Ave, Suite 1618, Box 60, Toronto, ON M5G 2K8; tel. (416) 595-5333; fax (416) 595-8226; internet www.importers.ca; f. 1932; Pres. BOB ARMSTRONG; 550 mems.

Canadian Printing Industries Association: 75 Albert St, Suite 906, Ottawa, ON K1P 5E7; tel. (613) 236-7208; fax (613) 236-8169; e-mail pboucher@cpia-aci.ca; internet www.cpia-aci.ca; Pres. PIERRE BOUCHER; 789 mems.

Canadian Tobacco Manufacturers' Council: Ottawa, ON; tel. (613) 238-2799; fax (613) 238-4463; f. 1963; Pres. ROBERT PARKER.

Shipbuilding Association of Canada: 222 Queen St, Suite 1502, Ottawa, ON K1P 5V9; tel. (613) 232-7127; fax (613) 238-5519; e-mail pcairns@cfncon.com; internet www.shipbuilding.ca; f. 1995; Pres. PETER CAIRNS; 20 mems.

UTILITIES

Regulatory Authorities

Alberta Energy and Utilities Board: 640 Fifth Ave, SW, Calgary, AB T2P 3G4; tel. (403) 297-8311; fax (403) 297-8398; e-mail eub.info_services@eub.gov.ab.ca; internet www.eub.gov.ab.ca.

British Columbia Utilities Commission: 900 Howe St, 6th Floor, Box 250, Vancouver, BC V6Z 2N3; tel. (604) 660-4700; fax (604) 660-1102; e-mail commission.secretary@bcuc.com; internet www.bcuc.com; Chair. PETER OSTERGAARD.

Manitoba Public Utilities Board: 280 Smith St, 2nd Floor, Winnipeg, MB R3C 1K2; tel. (204) 945-2638; fax (204) 945-2643; Exec. Dir G. O. BARRON.

National Energy Board: 444 Seventh Ave, SW, Calgary, AB T2P 0X8; tel. (403) 292-4800; fax (403) 292-5503; internet www.neb.gc.ca; fed. regulatory agency; Chair. KENNETH W. VOLLMAN.

New Brunswick Board of Commissioners of Public Utilities: 110 Charlotte St, POB 5001, Saint John, NB E2L 4Y9; tel. (506) 658-2504; fax (506) 633-0163; e-mail dnichols@nbnet.nb.ca; Chair. DAVID C. NICHOLSON.

Newfoundland and Labrador Board of Commissioners of Public Utilities: POB 21040, St John's, NL A1A 5B2; tel. (709) 726-8600; fax (709) 726-9604; e-mail cheryl@pub.nf.ca; internet www.pub.nf.ca; Chair. and CEO ROBERT NOSEWORTHY.

Nova Scotia Utility and Review Board: POB 1692, Postal Unit M, Halifax, NS B3J 3S3; tel. (902) 424-4448; fax (902) 424-3919; e-mail uarb.board@gov.ns.ca; Chair. J. A. MORASH.

Ontario Energy Board: 2300 Yonge St, 26th Floor, Box 2319, Toronto, ON M4P 1E4; tel. (416) 481-1967; fax (416) 440-7656; e-mail boardsec@oeb.gov.on.ca; internet www.oeb.gov.on.ca; Chair. FLOYD LAUGHREN.

Prince Edward Island Regulatory and Appeals Commission: 134 Kent St, Suite 501, POB 577, Charlottetown PE C1A 7L1; tel. (902) 892-3501; fax (902) 566-4076; e-mail irac@irac.pe.ca; internet www.irac.pe.ca; Chair. and CEO STIRLING BREEDON.

Québec Electricity and Gas Board: 800 place Victoria, CP 001, succursale de la Bourse, Montréal, QC H4Z 1A2; tel. (514) 873-2070.

Saskatchewan Municipal Board: 2151 Scarth St, 4th Floor, Regina, SK S4P 3V7; internet www.gov.sk.ca/deptsorgs/overviews/?24; Chair. B. G. MCNAMEE.

Electricity

ATCO Electric: 10035 105th St, POB 2426, Edmonton, AB T5J 2V6; internet www.atcoelectric.com; formerly Alberta Power Ltd; generates and distributes electricity in Alberta.

BC Hydro: 6911 Southpoint Dr., Burnaby, BC V3N 4X8; tel. (604) 528-1600; fax (604) 623-3901; e-mail customer.service@bchydro.com; internet www.bchydro.com; generation, transmission and distribution of energy in British Columbia; Chair. and CEO LARRY I. BELL.

Canadian Electricity Association: 1155 rue Metcalfe, Bureau 1120, Montréal, QC H3Z 2P9; tel. (514) 866-6121; fax (514) 866-1880; e-mail info@canelect.ca; internet www.intertower.com/cea.html; mems include 36 corporate utility enterprises accounting for c. 95% of Canada's installed generating capacity; Pres. and CEO HANS R. KONOW.

Hydro-Québec: 75 blvd René-Lévesque ouest, Montréal, QC H2Z 1A4; tel. (514) 289-2211; fax (514) 843-3163; internet www.hydro.mb.ca; Pres. ANDRÉ CAILLÉ.

Manitoba Hydro: 820 Taylor Ave, POB 815, Winnipeg, MB R3C 2P4; tel. (204) 474-3311; fax (204) 475-9044; e-mail publicaffairs@hydro.mb.ca; internet www.hydro.mb.ca; Pres. and CEO ROBERT B. BRENNAN.

Newfoundland and Labrador Hydro: POB 12400, St John's, NL A1B 4K7; tel. (709) 737-1400; fax (709) 737-1231; internet www.nlh.nf.ca; Pres. and CEO WILLIAM E. WELLS.

Northwest Territories Power Corporation: 4 Capital Dr., Hay River, NT X0E 1G2; tel. (867) 874-5200; fax (867) 874-5251; e-mail info@ntpc.com; internet www.ntpc.com; f. 1988; Chair. GORDON STEWART; Pres. and CEO LEON COURNEYA.

Nova Scotia Power Inc: POB 910, Halifax, NS B3J 2W5; tel. (902) 428-6230; fax (902) 428-6110; internet www.nspower.ca; fmrly Crown Corporation of Nova Scotia; privatized 1992; distributes power to over 400,000 customers; CEO DAVID D. MCCANN.

Ontario Power Generation: 700 University Ave, Toronto, ON M5G 1X6; tel. (416) 592-5111; fax (416) 971-3691; internet www.ontariopowergeneration.com; f. 1907 as Ontario Hydro, renamed as above in 1999; Canada's largest public utility corpn; also the main producer of nuclear power; Chair. WILLIAM FARLINGER; Pres. and CEO RONALD OSBORNE.

Prince Edward Island Energy Corporation: Shaw Bldg, 105 Rochford St, 5th Floor, POB 2000, Charlottetown, PE C1A 7N8; tel. (902) 894-0288; fax (902) 368-4242; e-mail dwmacquarrie@gov.pe.ca; internet www.gov.pe.ca; CEO WAYNE MACQUARRIE.

SaskPower: 2025 Victoria Ave, Regina, SK S4P 0S1; tel. (306) 566-2121; fax (306) 566-2330; e-mail enquiries@saskpower.com; internet www.saskpower.com; f. 1930; f. 1930; Pres. and CEO JOHN WRIGHT.

Gas

Canadian Gas Association: 20 Eglinton Ave West, Suite 1305, POB 1305, Toronto, ON M4R 1K8; tel. (416) 481-1828; fax (416) 481-2625; e-mail info@cga.ca; internet www.cga.ca; f. 1907; Pres. and CEO MARIE C. ROUNDING; 220 corporate mems.

Ontario Natural Gas Association: 77 Bloor St, Suite 1104, Toronto, ON M5S 1M2; tel. (416) 961-2339; fax (416) 961-1173; e-mail onga@sympatico.ca; Chair. BERNARD JONES.

TransCanada Pipelines Ltd: 111 Fifth Ave, SW, POB 1000, Station M, Calgary, AB T2P 4K5; tel. (403) 267-6100; fax (403) 267-6444; internet www.transcanada.com; production, storage, transmission and sale of natural gas through six subsidiary cos; Pres. and CEO DOUGLAS D. BALDWIN.

Westcoast Energy Inc: 666 Burrard St, Suite 3400, Park Place, Vancouver, BC V6C 3M8; tel. (604) 488-8000; fax (604) 488-8500; internet www.westcoastenergy.com; production, storage, transmission and sale of natural gas through four operating cos in British Columbia, Alberta and Manitoba; Chair. and CEO MICHAEL E. J. PHELPS.

Water

Northwest Territories Water Board: POB 1500, Yellowknife, NT X1A 2R3; tel. (867) 669-2772; fax (867) 669-2719; internet canada.gc.ca/depts/agencies/ntwind_e.html.

Nunavut Water Board: Gjoa Haven, NU X0E 1J0; e-mail rbecker@polarnet.ca.

Resource Management and Environmental Protection Branch, Nova Scotia Department of Environment and Labour: 5151 Terminal Rd, 5th Floor, POB 2107, Halifax, NS B3J 3B7; tel. (902) 424-2554; fax (902) 424-0503; internet www.gov.ns.ca/enla/rmep.

SaskWater: Victoria Place, 111 Fairford St East, Moose Jaw, SK S6H 7X9; tel. (306) 694-3900; fax (306) 694-3944; e-mail comm@saskwater.com; internet www.saskwater.com; Pres. CLARE KIRKLAND.

Water Management Branch, British Columbia Ministry of Environment, Lands and Parks: 2975 Jutland Rd, POB 9340, Victoria, BC V8W 9M1; tel. (250) 952-6806; internet www.elp.gov.bc.ca/wat/; Dir JAMES S. MATTISON.

Water Resources Branch, Manitoba Natural Resources: 200 Saulteaux Cres., POB 80, Winnipeg, MB R3J 3W3; tel. (204) 945-7488; fax (204) 945-7419; Dir STEVEN TOPPING.

Water Resources Branch, Ontario, Ministry of Environment and Energy: 135 St Clair Ave West, 2nd Floor, Toronto, ON M4V 1P5; tel. (416) 323-4917; fax (416) 965-9807; Dir JIM ASHMAN.

Water Resources Division, Newfoundland Department of Environment and Labour: Confederation Bldg, POB 8700, St John's, NU A1B 4J6; tel. (709) 729-2563; fax (709) 729-0320; internet www.gov.nf.ca/env/env/water_resources.asp; Dir MARTIN GOEBEL.

Water Resources Division, Prince Edward Island Department of the Environment: Jones Bldg, 11 Kent St, POB 2000, Charlottetown, PE C1A 7N8; tel. (902) 368-5000; fax (902) 368-5830; e-mail jjyoung@gov.pe.ca; Dir JIM YOUNG.

Water Resources Planning Branch, New Brunswick Department of the Environment: Argyle Pl., POB 6000, Fredericton, NB

E3B 5H1; tel. (506) 457-4846; fax (506) 453-2390; Man. WILLIAM C. AYER.

TRADE UNIONS

At the beginning of 2000 there were 4,057,000 union members in Canada, representing 25.8% of the civilian labour force. Of these, 29.5% belonged to unions with headquarters in the USA.

In 2000 unions affiliated to the Canadian Labour Congress represented 69.4% of total union membership.

Canadian Labour Congress: 2841 Riverside Dr., Ottawa, ON K1V 8X7; tel. (613) 521-3400; fax (613) 521-4655; internet www .clc-ctc.ca; f. 1956; Pres. KEN GEORGETTI; Sec.-Treas. NANCY RICHE; 2,500,000 mems (2001).

Affiliated unions with more than 15,000 members:

Amalgamated Transit Union: 1450 Meyerside Dr., Suite 701, Mississauga, ON L5T 2N5; tel. (905) 670-4710; fax (905) 670-3659; e-mail atucc@on.aibn.com; internet www.atuccanada.com; Canadian Dir KEN FOSTER; 24,000 mems (2000).

American Federation of Musicians of the United States and Canada: 75 The Donway West, Suite 1010, Don Mills, ON M3C 2E9; tel. (416) 391-5161; fax (416) 391-5165; e-mail afmcan@afm .org; internet www.afm.org; Vice-Pres. in Canada DAVID J. JANDRISCH; 18,000 mems (2001).

British Columbia Nurses' Union: 4060 Regent St, Burnaby, BC V5C 6P5; tel. (604) 433-2268; fax (604) 433-7945; internet www .bcnu.org; Pres. CATHY FERGUSON; 25,000 mems (2000).

Canadian Union of Postal Workers: 337 Bank St, Ottawa, ON K2P 1Y3; tel. (613) 236-7238; fax (613) 563-7861; internet www .cupw.ca; f. 1965; Nat. Pres. DEBORAH BOURQUE; 54,000 mems (2000).

Canadian Union of Public Employees: 21 Florence St, Ottawa, ON K2P 0W6; tel. (613) 237-1590; fax (613) 237-5508; internet www.cupe.ca; Nat. Pres. JUDY DARCY; 500,000 mems (2001).

Communications, Energy and Paperworkers Union of Canada: 350 Albert St, 19th Floor, Ottawa, ON K1R 1A4; tel. (613) 230-5200; fax (613) 230-5801; internet www.cep.ca; Pres. BRIAN PAYNE; 140,000 mems (2000).

Hotel Employees and Restaurant Employees International Union: 1140 blvd de Maisonneuve ouest, Bureau 1150, Montréal, QC H3A 1M8; tel. (514) 844-4167; fax (514) 844-1536; e-mail jamesstamos@herecanadianoffice.com; Canadian Dir JAMES STAMOS; 31,000 mems (2001).

International Association of Fire Fighters: 350 Sparks St, Suite 403, Ottawa, ON K1R 7S8; tel. (613) 567-8988; fax (613) 567-8986; Assistant to the General President JIM LEE; 18,400 mems (2000).

International Association of Machinists and Aerospace Workers: 100 Metcalfe St, Suite 300, Ottawa, ON K1P 5M1; tel. (613) 236-9761; fax (613) 563-7830; Gen. Vice-Pres. in Canada DAVE L. RITCHIE; 45,000 mems (2000).

International Brotherhood of Electrical Workers: 1450 Meyerside Dr., Suite 300, Mississauga, ON L5T 2N5; tel. (905) 564-5441; fax (905) 564-8114; e-mail ivpd_oi@ibew.org; Int.Vice-Pres. DON E. LOUNDS; 59,000 mems (1999).

International Union of Operating Engineers: 28 Aberdeen St, Kentville, NS B4N 3X9; tel. (902) 678-9950; fax (902) 678-1838; e-mail iuoe@glinx.com; Canadian Dir EDGAR DOULL; 40,000 mems (2000).

IWA Canada (Industrial Wood and Allied Workers of Canada): 1285 Pender St, Suite 500, Vancouver, BC V6E 4B2; tel. (604) 683-1117; fax (604) 688-6416; internet www.iwa.ca; f. 1937; Pres. D. C. HAGGARD; 44,000 mems (2001).

Labourers' International Union of North America: 44 Hughson St South, Hamilton, ON L8N 2A7; tel. (905) 522-7177; fax (905) 522-9310; internet www.liuna.org; Canadian Dir and Vice-Pres. ENRICO H. MANCINELLI; 60,000 mems (2000).

National Automobile, Aerospace Transportation and General Workers Union of Canada (CAW–Canada): 205 Placer Court, North York, Willowdale, ON M2H 3H9; tel. (416) 497-4110; fax (416) 495-6552; e-mail caw@caw.ca; internet www.caw.ca; f. 1985; Nat. Pres. BASIL HARGROVE; 250,000 mems (2002).

National Union of Public and General Employees: 15 Auriga Dr., Nepean, ON K2E 1B7; tel. (613) 228-9800; fax (613) 228-9801; e-mail national@nupge.ca; internet www.nupge.ca; Nat. Pres. JAMES CLANCY; 325,000 mems (2000).

Office and Professional Employees' International Union: 1200 ave Papineau, Bureau 250, Montréal, QC H2K 4S6; tel. (514)

522-6511; fax (514) 522-9000; Canadian Dir MICHEL LAJEUNESSE; 33,000 mems (2000).

Ontario English Catholic Teachers' Association: 65 St Clair Ave East, Suite 400, Toronto, ON M4T 2Y8; tel. (416) 925-2493; fax (416) 925-7764; internet www.oecta.on.ca; Pres. JIM SMITH; 30,000 mems (2000).

Ontario Secondary School Teachers' Federation: 60 Mobile Dr., Toronto, ON M4A 2P3; tel. (416) 751-8300; fax (416) 751-3394; e-mail brennan@osstf.on.ca; internet www.osstf.on.ca; Pres. EARL MANNERS; 50,000 mems (2002).

Public Service Alliance of Canada: 233 Gilmour St, Ottawa, ON K2P 0P1; tel. (613) 560-4200; fax (613) 567-0385; internet www.psac-afpc.com; f. 1966; Nat. Pres. NYCOLE TURMEL; 150,000 mems (2000).

Service Employees International Union: 75 The Donway West, Suite 810, North York, ON M3C 2E9; tel. (416) 447-2311; fax (416) 447-2428; e-mail brownk@seiu.ca; internet www.seiu.org; Vice-Pres. in Canada SHARLEEN STEWART; 90,000 mems (2000).

Teamsters Canada: 2540 Daniel-Johnson, Bureau 804, Laval, QC H7T 2S3; tel. (514) 682-5521; fax (514) 681-2244; internet www.teamsters-canada.org; Canadian Pres. LOUIS LACROIX; 95,000 mems (2000).

Union of Needletrades, Industrial and Textile Employees-Canada: 15 Gervais Dr., Suite 700, Toronto, ON M3C 1Y8; tel. (416) 441-1806; fax (416) 441-9680; internet www.unite-svti.org; Canadian Dir JOHN ALLERUZZO; 25,000 mems (2000).

United Association of Journeymen and Apprentices of the Plumbing and Pipe Fitting Industry of the United States and Canada: 1959 152nd St, Suite 316, Surrey, BC V4A 9E3; tel. (604) 531-0516; fax (604) 531-0547; e-mail uacanada@direct.ca; internet www.ua.org; Vice-Pres. and Canadian Dir GEORGE MESERVIER; 37,000 mems (2000).

United Brotherhood of Carpenters and Joiners of America: 5799 Young St, Suite 807, Willowdale, ON M2M 3V3; tel. (416) 225-8885; fax (416) 225-5390; internet www.carpenters.org; Gen. Exec. Bd Mem. JAMES E. SMITH; 56,000 mems (2000).

United Food and Commercial Workers Canada: 61 International Blvd, Suite 300, Rexdale, ON M9W 6K4; tel. (416) 675-1104; fax (416) 675-6919; e-mail ufcw@.ufcw.ca; internet www.ufcw.ca; f. 1979; Canadian Dir MICHAEL J. FRASER; 220,000 mems (2000).

United Steelworkers of America: 234 Eglinton Ave East, 7th Floor, Toronto, ON M4P 1K7; tel. (416) 487-1571; fax (416) 482-5548; internet www.uswa.org; Nat. Dir in Canada LAWRENCE MCBREARTY; 190,000 mems (2000).

Other Central Congresses

Centrale des syndicats du Québec: 9405 rue Sherbrooke est, Montréal, QC H1L 6P3; tel. (514) 356-8888; fax (514) 356-9999; internet www.csq.qc.net; f. 1974; name changed as above 2000; Pres. MONIQUE RICHARD; 17 affiliated unions.

Affiliated union with over 15,000 members:

Fédération des syndicats de l'enseignment: 320 rue St-Joseph est, Bureau 100, Québec, QC G1K 9E7; tel. (418) 649-8888; fax (418) 649-1914; internet www.fse.qc.net; Pres. JOHANNE FORTIER; 80,000 mems (2000).

Centrale des syndicats démocratiques: 801 rue Québec, 4e étage, Québec, QC G1J 2T7; tel. (418) 529-2956; fax (418) 529-6323; f. 1972; Pres. FRANÇOIS VAUDREUIL; 2 federated and 382 affiliated unions (2000).

Confederation of Canadian Unions: 155 Skinner St, Suite 206, Nanaimo, BC V9R 5E8; tel. (250) 753-1060; fax (250) 753-1062; e-mail ccu@island.net; f. 1969; Pres. JOE ELWORTHY; 9 affiliated unions (1999).

Confédération des syndicats nationaux: 1601 ave de Lorimier, Montréal, QC H2K 4M5; tel. (514) 598-2121; fax (514) 598-2052; e-mail intcsn@total.net; internet www.csn.qc.ca; f. 1921; Pres. MARC LAVIOLETTE; 9 federated unions.

Federated unions with over 15,000 members:

Fédération des employées et employés de services publics inc: 1601 ave de Lorimier, Montréal, QC H2K 4M5; tel. (514) 598-2231; fax (514) 598-2398; Pres. GINETTE GUÉRIN; 36,000 mems (2000).

Fédération du commerce inc: 1601 ave de Lorimier, Montréal, QC H2K 4M5; tel. (514) 598-2181; fax (514) 598-2304; Pres. JEAN LORTIE; 34,000 mems (2000).

Fédération de la métallurgie: 2100 blvd de Maisonneuve est, Bureau 204, Montréal, QC H2K 4S1; tel. (514) 529-4937; fax (514) 529-4935; Pres. ALAIN LAMPRON; 20,000 mems (1998).

Fédération de la santé et des services sociaux: 1601 ave de Lorimier, Montréal, QC H2K 4M5; tel. (514) 598-2210; fax (514) 598-2223; Pres. Louis Roy; 97,000 mems (2000).

Fédération nationale des enseignantes et des enseignants du Québec (FNEEQ): 1601 ave de Lorimier, Montréal, QC H2K 4M5; tel. (514) 598-2241; fax (514) 598-2190; e-mail fneeq@videotron.net; internet www.fneeq.qc.ca; f. 1969; Pres. Pierre Patry; 20,000 mems (2000).

The American Federation of Labor and Congress of Industrial Organizations (AFL–CIO), with headquarters in Washington, DC, USA, represented 0.4% of the total union membership in Canada, at the beginning of 1997.

Affiliated union with over 15,000 members:

International Association of Bridge, Structural and Ornamental Iron Workers: 1350 L'Heritage Dr., Sarnia, ON N7S 6H8; tel. (519) 542-1413; fax (519) 542-3790; Gen. Vice-Pres. James Phair; 15,000 mems (2000).

Principal Unaffiliated Unions

Alberta Teachers' Association: 11010 142nd St, Edmonton, AB T5N 2R1; tel. (780) 447-9400; fax (780) 455-6481; e-mail postmaster@teachers.ab.ca; internet www.teachers.ab.ca; Pres. Larry Booi; 34,000 mems (2001).

British Columbia Teachers' Federation: 550 West Sixth Ave, Suite 100, Vancouver, BC V5Z 4P2; tel. (604) 871-2283; fax (604) 871-2294; internet www.bctf.bc.ca; Pres. David Chudnovsky; 44,000 mems (2000).

Canadian Telephone Employees' Association: place du Canada, Bureau 360; Montréal, QC H3B 2N2; tel. (514) 861-9963; Pres. Judith King; 16,000 mems (2000).

Christian Labour Association of Canada: 5920 Atlantic Dr., Mississauga, ON L4W 1N6; tel. (905) 670-7383; fax (905) 670-8416; e-mail headoffice@clac.ca; internet www.clac.ca; Pres. Stan Baker; 22,000 mems (2000).

Elementary Teachers' Federation of Ontario: 480 University Ave, Suite 1000, Toronto, ON M5G 1V2; tel. (416) 962-3836; fax (416) 642-2424; internet www.etfo.on.ca; f. 1998; Pres. Phyllis Benedict; 52,000 mems (2000).

Fédération des infirmières et d'infirmiers du Québec: 2050 rue de Bleury, 4e étage, Montréal, QC H3A 2J5; tel. (514) 987-1141; fax (514) 987-7273; internet www.fiiq.qc.ca/Default.htm; Pres. Jennie Skene; 48,000 mems (1998).

Ontario Nurses' Association: 85 Grenville St, Suite 400, Toronto, ON M5S 3A2; tel. (416) 964-8833; fax (416) 964-8864; e-mail onamail@mail.ona.on; internet www.ona.org; Pres. Barb Wahl; 45,000 mems (2001).

Professional Institute of the Public Service of Canada: 53 Auriga Dr., Nepean, ON K2E 8C3; tel. (613) 228-6310; fax (613) 228-9048; internet www.pipsc.ca; Pres. Steve Hindle; 45,000 mems (2002).

Syndicat de la fonction publique Québec: 5100 blvd des Gradins, Québec, QC G2J 1N4; tel. (418) 623-2424; fax (418) 623-6109; Gen. Pres. Serge Roy; 39,000 mems (2000).

United Nurses of Alberta: Park Plaza, 9th Floor, 10611 98th Ave, Edmonton, AB T5K 2P7; tel. (403) 425-1025; fax (403) 426-2093; Pres. Heather Smith; 17,000 mems (2000).

Transport

Owing to the size of the country, Canada's economy is particularly dependent upon its transport infrastructure. The St Lawrence Seaway allows ocean-going ships to reach the Great Lakes. In addition to an extensive railway network, the country's transport facilities are being increasingly augmented by new roads, air services and petroleum pipelines. The Trans-Canada Highway forms a main feature of a network of more than 900,000 km of roads and highways.

Canadian Transportation Agency (CTA): Ottawa, ON K1A 0N9; tel. (819) 997-0344; fax (819) 953-8353; internet www.cta-otc.gc.ca; f. 1996 to oversee the economic regulation of transport; Chair. Marian L. Robson.

RAILWAYS

BC Rail: POB 8770, Vancouver, BC V6B 4X6; tel. (604) 986-2012; fax (604) 984-5004; internet www.bcrail.com; f. 1912; publicly-owned; 2,314 km of track; Chair. J. Goldsmith; Pres. and CEO P. J. McElligott.

CN Rail: 935 rue de la Gauchetière ouest, CP 8100, succursale A, Montréal, QC H3C 3N4; tel. (514) 399-4937; fax (514) 399-6910; internet www.cn.ca; f. 1919; investor-owned; 32,500 km of track; Chair. David G. A. Smith; Pres. and CEO Paul Tellier.

CP Rail System (Canadian Pacific Railway): 401 Ninth Ave, SW, Calgary, AB T2P 4Z4; tel. (403) 319-7000; internet www.cpr.ca; f. 1881; 24,649 km of track; Pres. and CEO Robert Ritchie.

Ontario Northland Transportation Commission: 555 Oak St East, North Bay, ON P1B 8L3; tel. (705) 472-4500; fax (705) 476-5598; internet www.ontc.on.ca; an agency of the Govt of Ontario; operates rail services over 1,211 km of track; Chair. Royal Poulin; Pres. and CEO K. J. Wallace.

VIA Rail Canada Inc: 3 place Ville-Marie, CP 8116, succursale A, Montréal, QC H3C 3N3; tel. (514) 871-6000; fax (514) 871-6463; internet www.viarail.ca; f. 1977; fed. govt corpn; proposed transfer to private sector pending in 2000; operates passenger services over rail routes covering 13,822 km of track throughout Canada; Chair. Marc LeFrançois; Pres. and CEO Marc LeFrançois.

Association

Railway Association of Canada: 99 Bank St, Suite 1401, Ottawa, ON K1P 6B9; tel. (613) 567-8591; fax (613) 567-6726; e-mail rac@railcan.ca; internet www.railcan.ca; f. 1917; Pres. William Rowat; 54 mems.

ROADS

Provincial governments are responsible for roads within their boundaries. The federal Government is responsible for major roads in the Yukon, the Northwest Territories and Nunavut and in National Parks. In 2001 there were an estimated 1,427,000 km of roads (including 12,800 km of freeways and 192,700 km of highways). The Trans-Canada Highway extends from St John's, NL, to Victoria, BC.

INLAND WATERWAYS

The St Lawrence River and the Great Lakes provide Canada and the USA with a system of inland waterways extending from the Atlantic Ocean to the western end of Lake Superior, a distance of 3,769 km (2,342 miles). There is a 10.7-m (35-foot) navigation channel from Montréal to the sea and an 8.25-m (27-foot) channel from Montréal to Lake Erie. The St Lawrence Seaway (see below), which was opened in 1959, was initiated partly to provide a deep waterway and partly to satisfy the increasing demand for electric power. Power development has been undertaken by the provinces of Québec and Ontario, and by New York State. The navigation facilities and conditions are within the jurisdiction of the federal governments of the USA and Canada.

St Lawrence River and Great Lakes Shipping

St Lawrence Seaway Management Corporation: 202 Pitt St, Cornwall, ON K6J 3P7; tel. (613) 932-5170; fax (613) 932-7286; e-mail marketing@seaways.ca; internet www.seaway.ca; f. 1998; responsible for supervision of marine traffic through Canadian section of St Lawrence Seaway, which is operated jtly with the USA; Chair. Robert J. Swenor; Pres. and CEO Guy Véronneau.

Algoma Central Corpn: 62 Church St, Suite 600, St Catharines, ON L2R 3C4; tel. (905) 687-7888; fax (905) 687-7882; e-mail miatello@algonet.com; internet www.algonet.com; f. 1899; Pres. and CEO T. S. Dool; 24 bulk cargo vessels.

Canada Steamship Lines Inc (CSL Group): 759 square Victoria, Montréal, QC H2Y 2K3; tel. (514) 982-3800; fax (514) 982-3802; e-mail ships@csltml.com; internet www.csl.ca; f. 1913; Pres. Gerald Carter; 14 vessels.

Paterson, N. M., and Sons Ltd: 1918 Yonge St, Thunder Bay, ON P7C 4W6; tel. (807) 577-8421; fax (807) 475-3493; internet www.marmus.ca/marmus/PATSRN/; f. 1908; bulk carriers; Pres. and CEO Robert J. Paterson; 7 vessels; 95,536 grt.

SHIPPING

At 31 December 2001 the Canadian merchant fleet comprised 861 vessels, with a total displacement of 2,726,976 grt.

British Columbia Ferry Corporation: 1112 Fort St, Victoria, BC V8V 4V2; tel. (250) 386-3431; fax (250) 381-5452; internet www.bcferries.bc.ca; passenger and vehicle ferries; Pres. Frank Rhodes; 40 vessels.

Fednav Ltd: 1000 rue de la Gauchetière ouest, Bureau 3500, Montréal, QC H3B 4W5; tel. (514) 878-6500; fax (514) 878-6642; e-mail info@fednav.com; internet www.fednav.com; f. 1944; shipowners, operators, contractors, terminal operators; Pres. L. G. Pathy; owned and chartered fleet of 68 vessels.

Groupe Desagnés Inc: 21 rue du Marché-Champlain, Bureau 100, Québec, QC G1K 8Z8; tel. (418) 692-1000; fax (418) 692-6044; Chair. and CEO Louis-Marie Beaulieu; 10 vessels.

Marine Atlantic Inc: 355 Purves St, North Sydney, NS B2A 3V2; tel. (800) 341-7891; fax (902) 564-7480; internet www .marine-atlantic.ca; vehicle and passenger ferries serving Atlantic coast of Canada; Chair. SID HYNES.

Associations

Canadian Shipowners Association: 350 Sparks St, Suite 705, Ottawa, ON K1R 7S8; tel. (613) 232-3539; fax (613) 232-6211; e-mail csa@shipowners.ca; internet www.shipowners.ca; f. 1953; Pres. DONALD MORRISON; 8 mems.

Canadian Shippers' Council: 48 Balsam Dr., Baie d'Urfé, QC H9X 3K5; tel. (514) 457-7268; fax (514) 457-3175; e-mail wmueller@ qc.aibn.com; Sec. WALTER MUELLER; 12 institutional mems, 2 assoc. mems.

Shipping Federation of Canada: 300 rue St-Sacrement, Bureau 326, Montréal, QC H2Y 1X4; tel. (514) 849-2325; fax (514) 849-6992; f. 1903; Pres. GILLES J. BÉLANGER; 75 mems.

CIVIL AVIATION

Principal Company

Air Canada: CP 14000, succursale St-Laurent, Montréal, QC H4Y 1H4; tel. (514) 422-5000; fax (514) 422-5909; internet www .aircanada.ca; f. 1937; investor-owned; acquired Canadian Airlines International in Jan. 2000; Pres. and CEO ROBERT MILTON; operates scheduled and charter services throughout Canada and to the USA; also serves Europe, the Middle East and the Caribbean.

Association

Air Transport Association of Canada: 255 Albert St, Suite 1100, Ottawa, ON K1P 6A9; tel. (613) 233-7727; fax (613) 230-8648; e-mail atac@atac.ca; internet www.atac.ca; f. 1934; Pres. J. CLIFFORD MACKAY; 300 mems.

Tourism

Most tourist visitors (estimated at 15.2m. of a total 19.7m. in 2000) are from the USA. Expenditure by tourists in 2000 was estimated to total C $18,000m.

Canadian Tourism Commission: 235 Queen St, 8th Floor West, Ottawa, ON K1A 0H6; tel. (613) 946-1000; fax (613) 954-3964; e-mail ctc_feedback@businteractive.com; internet www.canadatourism .com; fed. govt org. Chair. J. BUDD BUCHANAN; Pres. and CEO JIM WATSON.

Tourism Industry Association of Canada: 130 Albert St, Suite 1608, Ottawa, ON K1P 5G4; tel. (613) 238-3883; fax (613) 238-3878; e-mail info@tiac-aitc.ca; internet www.tiac-aitc.ca; f. 1931; private-sector asscn; encourages travel to and within Canada; promotes devt of travel facilities and services; Pres. RANDY WILLIAMS.

CAPE VERDE

Introductory Survey

Location, Climate, Language, Religion, Flag, Capital

The Republic of Cape Verde is an archipelago of 10 islands and five islets in the North Atlantic Ocean, about 500 km (300 miles) west of Dakar, Senegal. The country lies in a semi-arid belt, with little rain and an average annual temperature of 24°C (76°F). The official language is Portuguese, of which the locally spoken form is Creole (Crioulo). Virtually all of the inhabitants profess Christianity, and more than 95% are Roman Catholics. The national flag, adopted in 1992 (proportions 3 by 5), comprises five horizontal stripes: blue (half the depth) at the top, white, red, white (each one-twelfth) and blue. Superimposed, to the left of centre, is a circle of 10 five-pointed gold stars (four on the white stripes and three each on the blue stripes above and below). The capital is Cidade de Praia.

Recent History

The Cape Verde Islands were colonized by the Portuguese in the 15th century. From the 1950s liberation movements in Portugal's African colonies were campaigning for independence, and, in this context, the archipelago was linked with the mainland territory of Portuguese Guinea (now Guinea-Bissau) under one nationalist movement, the Partido Africano da Independência do Guiné e Cabo Verde (PAIGC). The independence of Guinea-Bissau was recognized by Portugal in September 1974, but the PAIGC leadership in the Cape Verde Islands decided to pursue its independence claims separately, rather than enter into an immediate federation with Guinea-Bissau. In December 1974 a transitional Government, comprising representatives of the Portuguese Government and the PAIGC, was formed; members of other political parties were excluded. On 30 June 1975 elections for a legislative body, the Assembléia Nacional Popular (ANP—National People's Assembly) were held, in which only PAIGC candidates were allowed to participate. Independence was granted to the Republic of Cape Verde on 5 July 1975, with Aristides Pereira, Secretary-General of the PAIGC, becoming the country's first President. Cape Verde's first Constitution was approved in September 1980.

Although Cape Verde and Guinea-Bissau remained constitutionally separate, the PAIGC supervised the activities of both states. Progress towards the ultimate goal of unification was halted by the November 1980 coup in Guinea-Bissau (during which the President, Luiz Cabral, himself a Cape Verdean, was placed under house arrest). The Cape Verde Government condemned the coup, and in January 1981 the Cape Verde wing of the PAIGC was renamed the Partido Africano da Independência de Cabo Verde (PAICV). In February Pereira was re-elected as President by the ANP, and all articles concerning an eventual union with Guinea-Bissau were removed from the Constitution. Discussions concerning reconciliation were held in June 1982, however, after the release of Cabral, and diplomatic relations between the two countries were subsequently normalized. Cape Verde's relations with Guinea-Bissau improved further in 1988, when an agreement on bilateral co-operation was signed.

Meanwhile, elections to the ANP took place in December 1985. The candidates on the PAICV-approved list, not all of whom were members of the PAICV, obtained 94.5% of the votes cast. In January 1986 Pereira was re-elected for a further five-year term as President by the ANP. In 1989 two political commissions were established, to regulate legislative elections and to consider proposals for constitutional changes, and it was subsequently announced that, although elections to the ANP were to be held in 1990, local elections were to be deferred until 1991. In April 1990 a newly formed political organization, the Movimento para a Democracia (MPD), issued a manifesto in Paris, France, which advocated the immediate introduction of a multi-party system. Pereira subsequently announced that the next presidential election would be held, for the first time, on the basis of universal suffrage.

In July 1990, in an apparent response to increasing pressure from church and academic circles, a special congress of the PAICV reviewed proposals for new party statutes and the abolition of Article 4 of the Constitution, which guaranteed the supremacy of the PAICV. Pereira also resigned as Secretary-

General of the PAICV, and was later replaced by the Prime Minister, Gen. Pedro Verona Rodrigues Pires, hitherto Deputy Secretary-General of the party. In September the ANP approved a constitutional amendment abolishing the PAICV's monopoly of power and permitting a multi-party system. The legislative elections were rescheduled for January 1991. The MPD subsequently received official recognition as a political party. In November 1990 the MPD announced its support for an independent candidate, António Mascarenhas Monteiro, in the forthcoming presidential election. On 13 January 1991 the legislative elections, the first multi-party elections to take place in lusophone Africa, resulted in a decisive victory for the MPD, which secured 56 of the 79 seats in the ANP. In late January Dr Carlos Alberto Wahnon de Carvalho Veiga, the leader of the MPD, was sworn in as Prime Minister at the head of an interim Government, mostly comprising members of the MPD. The presidential election was duly held in mid-February, and resulted in victory for Mascarenhas, who secured 73.5% of the votes cast. The first multi-party local elections, held in December, resulted in another decisive victory for the MPD, which secured control of 10 of the 14 local councils.

On 25 September 1992 a new Constitution of the Republic of Cape Verde (also referred to as the 'Second Republic') came into force, enshrining the principles of multi-party democracy. In August 1993 the opposition PAICV elected Aristides Lima to the post of Secretary-General of the party, replacing Pires, who was appointed party Chairman. In December the Minister of Justice and Labour, Dr Eurico Correia Monteiro, was dismissed, following his announcement that he would be contesting the leadership of the MPD at an extraordinary national convention of the party, called by Veiga to take place in February 1994. At the convention Carlos Veiga was re-elected Chairman of the MPD. However, increasing conflict within the party resulted in some 30 party delegates, led by Monteiro and the former Minister of Foreign Affairs, Jorge Carlos Almeida Fonseca, boycotting the convention. That month Monteiro announced the establishment of a new political party, the Partido da Convergência Democrática (PCD).

At legislative elections conducted in December 1995 the MPD secured an outright majority, taking 50 of the 72 seats in the Assembléia Nacional (AN, as the ANP had become in 1992). The PAICV won 21 seats, while the remaining seat was obtained by the PCD. At a presidential election conducted in February 1996 Mascarenhas, the sole candidate, was re-elected. However, despite appeals for the electorate to demonstrate its support for Mascarenhas' second term of office, the turn-out was low, at only 45%. Veiga, meanwhile, expressed his intention to continue the policies of liberal economic and social reform that had been pursued in his previous term in office.

In May 1998, as part of a reorganization of the Council of Ministers, Veiga created several new ministries and appointed the Minister of Economic Co-ordination, António Gualberto do Rosário, to the newly created post of Deputy Prime Minister. In March 1999 Veiga confirmed speculation that he would not seek re-election as the Chairman of the MPD at the next party convention. Do Rosário and the Mayor of Praia, Jacinto Santos, subsequently announced their candidacies for the chairmanship of the MPD, and thus the premiership. However, in November 1999 Veiga dismissed several close associates of Santos. In municipal elections held in February 2000 the MPD sustained substantial losses, retaining only eight of 17 local councils and losing the capital, Praia, to the PAICV, which re-emerged as a credible political force. Following the resignation of Pedro Pires, who announced his candidacy for the presidential election, the PAICV elected José Maria Neves as its new President in June. In the following month do Rosário was elected Chairman of the MPD, and Santos subsequently formed a new political party, the Partido da Renovação Democratica.

In late July 2000 Veiga announced his resignation as Prime Minister and confirmed his candidacy for the presidential election scheduled to take place in early 2001; he was replaced by do Rosário. Veiga's decision to stand down was criticized by both President Mascarenhas and Neves, who argued that the unelected do Rosário had no mandate, and that his appointment was therefore unconstitutional. In October 2000 it was announced that the PCD, the União Caboverdiana Independente e Democrática and the Partido de Trabalho e Solidariedade were to form a coalition (the Aliança Democrática para a Mudança—ADM) to participate in the forthcoming legislative elections.

At the legislative elections, held on 14 January 2001, the opposition PAICV obtained 49.5% of the vote and 40 seats in the AN, compared with 40.5% (30 seats) for the MPD and 6.1% (two seats) for the ADM. A new Government, headed by Neves, was announced at the end of January; Prime Minister Neves indicated that his Government's priorities would include reducing unemployment levels and the rehabilitation of public finances. At the presidential election, conducted on 11 February, no candidate received an overall majority, necessitating a second round, held on 25 February, at which Pires narrowly defeated Veiga, receiving 50.01% of valid votes cast. Appeals against the result by Veiga, who cited voting irregularities, were rejected in March by the Supreme Court, which confirmed Pires as the new President. Aristides Raimundo Lima was elected Speaker of the AN in February.

In August 2001 Filomena Delgado became interim leader of the MPD, following do Rosário's resignation from the chairmanship; in December Delgado was replaced by Agostinho Lopes, who was elected unopposed as the new Chairman of the party. A government reshuffle was effected in late February 2002.

In June 2002, with famine threatening 30,000 inhabitants, the Government made its first appeal for emergency food aid in more than 20 years. The UN World Food Programme responded with an appeal to international donors for US $1.2m. in emergency aid. In October a cabinet reshuffle was effected; Maria de Fátima Lima Veiga was appointed as Minister of Foreign Affairs, Co-operation and Communities, replacing Manuel Inocência Sousa, who became Minister of State for Infrastructure and Transport, while the Ministry of Tourism, Industry, and Commerce, and the Ministry of State Reform, Public Administration and Local Affairs, were closed.

Cape Verde has traditionally professed a non-aligned stance in foreign affairs and maintains relations with virtually all the power blocs. On taking office in 1991, the MPD Government successfully sought to extend Cape Verde's range of international contacts, with special emphasis on potential new sources of development aid; substantial assistance has been received from both Israel and the Gulf states. The MPD Government enlarged the scope of Cape Verde's diplomatic contacts, establishing embassies in South Africa and Sweden, as well as diplomatic presences in Hong Kong, Macao, Singapore, Spain, the United Kingdom and the USA. In July 2001 Cape Verde established diplomatic relations at ambassadorial level with the People's Republic of China. The country has continued to maintain particularly close relations with Portugal and Brazil, and with other lusophone African former colonies—Angola, Guinea-Bissau, Mozambique and São Tomé and Príncipe, known collectively, with Cape Verde, as the Países Africanos da Língua Oficial Portuguesa (PALOP). In July 1996 a 'lusophone commonwealth', known as the Comunidade dos Países de Língua Portuguesa (CPLP), comprising the five PALOP countries together with Portugal and Brazil, was formed with the intention of benefiting each member state through joint co-operation on technical, cultural and social matters. In December 1996 Cape Verde became a full member of the Sommet francophone, a commonwealth comprising all the French-speaking nations of the world, and benefits in turn from membership of this body's Agence de coopération culturelle et technique, an agency which promotes cultural and technical co-operation among francophone countries. Although a lusophone nation, Cape Verde had been an observer at annual meetings of the Sommet francophone since 1977.

Government

Under the 1992 Constitution, Cape Verde is a multi-party state, although the formation of parties on a religious or geographical basis is prohibited. Legislative power is vested in the Assembléia Nacional (AN—National Assembly), which comprises 72 deputies, elected by universal adult suffrage for a five-year term. The Head of State is the President of the Republic, who is elected by universal suffrage for a five-year term. Executive power is vested in the Prime Minister, who is nominated by the deputies of the AN, appointed by the President and governs with the assistance of a Council of Ministers.

Defence

The armed forces, initially formed from ex-combatants in the liberation wars, totalled about 1,200 (army 1,000, air force less than 100, coastguard 100) in August 2002. There is also a police force, the Police for Public Order, which is organized by the local municipal councils. National service is by selective conscription. In October 2002 the Government announced a programme of reform, involving the coastguard, the military police and special forces dealing with drugs-trafficking and terrorism offences. Government defence expenditure in 2002 was budgeted at an estimated 600m. escudos (US $5m.).

Economic Affairs

In 2001, according to estimates from the World Bank, Cape Verde's gross national income (GNI), measured at average 1999–2001 prices, was US $596m., equivalent to $1,310 per head (or $4,870 per head on an international purchasing-power parity basis). During 1990–2001, it was estimated, the population increased at an average annual rate of 2.6%, while gross domestic product (GDP) per head increased, in real terms, by an average of 2.9% per year. Overall GDP increased, in real terms, at an average annual rate of 5.6% per year; growth in 2001 was 3.3%.

Agriculture (including forestry and fishing) contributed 11.0% of GDP in 2001, according to the World Bank, and employed an estimated 22.3% of the economically active population in that year. The staple crop is maize; potatoes, sweet potatoes, cassava, coconuts, sugar cane, mangoes, bananas and vegetables are also cultivated. Fish, crustaceans and molluscs provided almost one-half of total export earnings in 1994, although their contribution had declined to an estimated 7.1% in 2000. Lobster and tuna are among the most important exports. Moreover, the total fish catch declined from 14,730 metric tons in 1981 to 6,573 tons in 1992. In 1994 a five-year project was announced for the redevelopment of the fishing industry, with investment of US $28m. By 2000 the annual catch had recovered somewhat to 10,821 tons. During 1990–2001 the GDP of the agricultural sector increased, in real terms, at an average annual rate of 3.8%; growth in 2001 was 1.9%.

Industry (including construction and power) contributed 16.8% of GDP in 2001, and employed 30.6% of the labour force in 1990. During 1990–2001 industrial GDP increased, in real terms, at an average annual rate of 5.3%; growth in 2001 was 4.8%.

Mining employed 0.4% of the labour force in 1990 and contributed less than 1% of GDP in 1998. Salt and pozzolana, a volcanic ash used in cement manufacture, are the main non-fuel minerals produced.

Manufacturing contributed 8.1% of GDP in 2001 and employed about 6% of the labour force in 1995. The most important branches, other than fish-processing, are clothing, footwear, rum distilling and bottling. Legislation enacted in 1999 provided for the transformation of industrial parks at Mindelo and Praia into free-trade zones, and for the establishment of a further free-trade zone on Sal island. During 1990–2001 the GDP of the manufacturing sector increased, in real terms, at an average annual rate of 4.0%; an increase of 5.3% was recorded in 2001.

Energy is derived principally from hydroelectric power and gas. Imports of mineral fuels comprised 4.2% of the value of total estimated imports in 2000.

Services accounted for 72.2% of GDP in 2001. Tourism has been identified as the area with the most potential for economic development. Legislation introduced since 1991 has aimed to provide increased incentives and guarantees to investors. A new international airport at Praia, due to open in 2003, was expected to give considerable impetus to the development of the tourism sector. The airport on São Vicente island was upgraded to international capacity in 2000. Plans were also being prepared for the construction of an international airport on Boa Vista island, as well as a new airport on Santo Antão, in order to increase tourism. Tourist arrivals increased from 52,000 in 1998 to 145,000 in 2000. During 1990–2001 the combined GDP of the service sectors increased, in real terms, at an average annual rate of 6.0%; growth in 2001 was 3.2%.

In 2001 Cape Verde recorded a trade deficit of US $194.4m., and there was a deficit of $55.8m. on the current account of the balance of payments. In 2001 the principal source of imports was Portugal (52.1%); other major suppliers were the Netherlands and Belgium. Portugal was also the principal market for exports (90.7%) in that year. The principal exports in 2000 were footwear (51.8%) and clothing. The major imports in that year were machinery and electrical equipment, food and beverage products, mineral products, vegetable products and transportation material.

In 2000 there was an estimated budgetary deficit of 12,254m. escudos (equivalent to 18.9% of GDP). Cape Verde's total external debt at the end of 2000 was US $327.2m., of which $314.6m. was long-term public debt. In that year the cost of debt-servicing was equivalent to 7.5% of the value of exports of goods and services. The annual rate of inflation averaged 4.9% in 1990–2001. Consumer prices increased by an average of 3.8% in 2001 and by 1.8% in 2002. In 1999 unemployment was estimated to affect some 25.4% of the labour force.

Cape Verde is a member of the Economic Community of West African States (ECOWAS, see p. 187), which promotes trade and co-operation in West Africa, and is a signatory to the Lomé Convention and subsequent Cotonou Agreement (see p. 234).

Cape Verde's agricultural economy is highly vulnerable to severe periodic drought, making self-sufficiency in food production impossible; approximately 85% of the country's total food requirements are imported. The country benefits from considerable external assistance (which totalled 3,632m. escudos in 2000) and substantial remittances from emigrants. There are about 700,000 Cape Verdeans living outside the country, principally in the USA, the Netherlands, Portugal, Italy and Angola. In 2001 private remittances from emigrants provided an estimated 18,800m. escudos, equivalent to 27.2% of GDP. The Government has attempted to attract emigrants' capital into the light-industry and fishing sectors by offering favourable tax conditions to investors. In March 1998 Cape Verde and Portugal signed an agreement providing for their respective currencies to become linked through a fixed exchange rate, thus transforming the Cape Verde escudo into a convertible currency. In mid-2001 it was announced that a $28m. grant had been provided by the European Development Fund to improve sanitation and water. Furthermore, two financial co-operation agreements were signed by Portugal and Cape Verde, in an attempt to strengthen the Cape Verdean economy. In April 2002 the IMF approved a Poverty Reduction and Growth Facility of $11m. in support of Cape Verde's economic programme for 2002–05 (as outlined in a new National Development Plan). In an attempt to counter organized crime, legislation designed to preventing money-laundering was passed by the Assembléia Nacional in July 2002. In September the African Development Bank granted Cape Verde a $3.3m. loan to finance further economic reforms. In the same month the Government and the UN signed an assistance framework plan, valid until 2005, aimed at aiding Cape Verde's development and reducing poverty, which was estimated to affect some 30% of the population. The 2003 budget, approved in December 2002, provided for a reduction in income tax by 30%–35%. Also in December the IMF declared its satisfaction with the performance of the Cape Verde economy in 2002, welcoming a reduction in the fiscal deficit and increased foreign reserves; GDP growth of some 5% was forecast for 2003.

Education

Primary education, beginning at seven years of age and lasting for six years, comprises a first cycle of four years, which is compulsory, and a second cycle of two years. Secondary education, beginning at 13 years of age, is also divided into two cycles, the first comprising a three-year general course, the second a three-year pre-university course. There are three teacher-training units and two industrial and commercial schools of further education. In 1997 the total enrolment at primary and secondary schools was equivalent to 103% of all school-age children (males 104%; females 103%). In 1999/2000 91,636 pupils attended primary schools, and 40,214 attended secondary schools. Primary enrolment in 1998/99 included 98.9% of children in the relevant age-group (males 98.3%; females 99.5%). In that year, according to UNESCO estimates, secondary enrolment was equivalent to 68.6% of children in the relevant age-group. In 1996/97 there were 1,660 Cape Verdean students studying at overseas universities. In 2000 education received 43.2% of the central Government's total public expenditure.

Public Holidays

2003: 1 January (New Year), 20 January (National Heroes' Day), 1 May (Labour Day), 5 July (Independence Day), 15 August (Assumption), 1 November (All Saints' Day), 25 December (Christmas Day).

2004: 1 January (New Year), 20 January (National Heroes' Day), 1 May (Labour Day), 5 July (Independence Day), 15 August (Assumption), 1 November (All Saints' Day), 25 December (Christmas Day).

Weights and Measures

The metric system is in force.

Statistical Survey

Sources (unless otherwise stated): Instituto Nacional de Estatística, CP 116, Praia, Santiago; tel. 61-38-27; e-mail inecv@mail.cvtelecom.cv; internet www.ine.cv; Statistical Service, Banco de Cabo Verde, 117 Avda Amílcar Cabral, CP 101, Praia, Santiago; tel. 60-70-00; fax 61-19-14; internet www.bcv.cv.

AREA AND POPULATION

Area: 4,036 sq km (1,558 sq miles).

Population: 341,491 (males 161,494; females 179,997) at census of 23 June 1990; 434,812 (males 210,569; females 224,243) at census of 16 June 2000. *By island* (2000 census): Boa Vista 4,193; Brava 6,820; Fogo 37,409; Maio 6,742; Sal 14,792; Santo Antão 47,124; São Nicolau 13,536; Santiago 236,352; São Vicente 67,844.

Density (2000 census): 107.7 per sq km.

Principal Towns (population at 2000 census): Praia (capital) 94,757; Mindelo 62,970.

Births, Marriages and Deaths (annual averages, 1995–2000, unless otherwise indicated): Birth rate 29.3 per 1,000 (2000); Registered marriages (1994) 1,200 (marriage rate 3.2 per 1,000); Death rate 6.4 per 1,000 (UN estimate). Sources: partly UN, *Demographic Yearbook* and *World Population Prospects: The 2000 Revision*.

Expectation of Life (WHO estimates, years at birth): 69.5 (males 65.7; females 72.0) in 2001. Source: WHO, *World Health Report*.

Economically Active Population (persons aged 10 years and over, 1990 census): Agriculture, hunting, forestry and fishing 29,876; Mining and quarrying 410; Manufacturing 5,520; Electricity, gas and water 883; Construction 22,722; Trade, restaurants and hotels 12,747; Transport, storage and communications 6,138; Financing, insurance, real estate and business services 821; Community, social and personal services 17,358; Activities not adequately defined 24,090; Total labour force 120,565 (males 75,786; females 44,779), including 31,049 unemployed persons (males 19,712; females 11,337) (Source: International Labour Office, *Yearbook of Labour Statistics*). *2000 Census (persons aged 10 years and over):* Total employed 144,310; Unemployed 30,334; Total labour force 174,644.

HEALTH AND WELFARE

Key Indicators

Total Fertility Rate (children per woman, 2001): 3.3.

Under-5 Mortality Rate (per 1,000 live births, 2001): 38.

Physicians (per 1,000 head, 2000): 0.38.

Hospital Beds (per 1,000 head, 2000): 1.60.

Health Expenditure (2000): US $ per head (PPP): 92.

Health Expenditure (2000): % of GDP: 2.6.

Health Expenditure (2000): public (% of total): 68.5.

Access to Water (% of persons, 2000): 74.

Access to Sanitation (% of persons, 2000): 71.

Human Development Index (2000): ranking: 100.

Human Development Index (2000): 0.715.
For sources and definitions, see explanatory note on p. vi.

AGRICULTURE, ETC.

Principal Crops (FAO estimates, '000 metric tons, 2001): Maize 19.5*; Potatoes 3.4; Sweet potatoes 3.8; Cassava 3.0; Sugar cane 14.0; Pulses 3.0; Coconuts 5.5; Cabbages 4.5; Tomatoes 4.3; Dry onions 1.6; Green beans 2.0; Cucumbers and gherkins 1.0; Bananas 6.0; Mangoes 4.5; Other fruits 4.5; Pimento and allspice .0.9.
*Unofficial figure. Source: FAO.

Livestock (FAO estimates, '000 head, year ending September 2001): Cattle 21.5; Pigs 200; Sheep 8.5; Goats 110; Asses 13.5; Mules 1.8; Chickens 480. Source: FAO.

Livestock Products (FAO estimates, '000 metric tons, 2001): Pig meat 7.0; Other meat 1.4; Cows' milk 5.1; Goats' milk 4.6; Hen eggs 1.7. Source: FAO.

Fishing (metric tons, live weight, 2000): Total catch 10,821 (Wahoo 487, Little tunny 491, Skipjack tuna 789, Yellowfin tuna 1,851). Source: FAO, *Yearbook of Fishery Statistics*.

MINING

Production (estimates, '000 metric tons, 2000): Salt (unrefined) 2; Pozzolana 1. Source: US Geological Survey.

INDUSTRY

Production (metric tons, unless otherwise indicated, 1999): Biscuits 348 (1990 figure); Bread 5,628 (1995 figure); Canned fish 250 (1997 figure); Frozen fish 932 (1997 figure); Flour 15,901; Beer 4,104,546 litres; Soft drinks 922,714 litres (1996 figure); Cigarettes and tobacco 77 kg; Paint 628,243 kg (1997 figure); Footwear 670,676 pairs (1996 figure); Soap 1,371,045 kg; Electric energy 133.6m. kWh. Sources: mainly UN, *Industrial Commodity Statistics Yearbook*, and IMF, *Cape Verde: Statistical Appendix* (October 2001).

FINANCE

Currency and Exchange Rates: 100 centavos = 1 Cape Verde escudo; 1,000 escudos are known as a conto. *Sterling, Dollar and Euro Equivalents* (31 December 2002): £1 sterling = 175.36 escudos; US $1 = 108.80 escudos; €1 = 114.09 escudos; 1,000 Cape Verde escudos = £5.703 = $9.192 = €8.765. *Average Exchange Rate* (escudos per US dollar): 115.877 in 2000; 123.213 in 2001; 117.256 in 2002.

Budget (million escudos, 2000): *Revenue*: Taxation 11,761 (Taxes on income and profits 3,936, Taxes on international trade 6,996, Stamp and liquor tax 693); Other revenue 1,467 (Licences and miscellaneous fees 369, Transfers 587, Autonomous revenue 300); Total 13,228, excl. external grants (3,632). *Expenditure*: Recurrent 21,985 (Wages and salaries 6,412, Interest on public debt 1,741, Subsidies and transfers 6,837, Other current 6,221); Capital 7,128; Total 29,114. Source: IMF, *Cape Verde: Statistical Appendix* (October 2001).

International Reserves (US $ million at 31 December 2002): IMF special drawing rights 0.001; Foreign exchange 77.12; Total 77.13. Source: IMF, *International Financial Statistics*.

Money Supply (million escudos at 31 December 2002): Currency outside banks 6,459.3; Demand deposits at commercial banks 16,332.9; Total money (incl. others) 22,793.3. Source: IMF, *International Financial Statistics*.

Cost of Living (Consumer Price Index; base: 1989 = 100): 176.9 in 2000; 183.6 in 2001; 186.9 in 2002.

Expenditure on the Gross Domestic Product (million escudos at current prices, 2001): Government final consumption expenditure 18,324; Private final consumption expenditure 51,094; Increase in stocks 5,199; Gross fixed capital formation 18,148; *Total domestic expenditure* 92,765; Exports of goods and services 20,287; *Less* Imports of goods and services 43,940; *GDP in purchasers' values* 69,112.

Gross Domestic Product by Economic Activity (million escudos at current prices, 2000): Agriculture, forestry and livestock 6,402; Fishing 629; Industry and energy 5,907; Construction 5,448; Commerce 10,058; Hotels 4,253; Transport and communications 11,759; Banks and insurance 3,413; Housing 4,007; Public service 7,341; Other services 1,932; *Sub-total* 61,149; Import taxes 6,336; *Less* Imputed bank service charges 2,805; *GDP at market prices* 64,680. Source: IMF, *Cape Verde: Statistical Appendix* (October 2001).

Balance of Payments (estimates, US $ million, 2001): Exports of goods f.o.b. 37.2; Imports of goods f.o.b. –231.6; *Trade balance* –194.4; Exports of services 129.7; Imports of services –119.0; *Balance on goods and services* –183.7; Other income (net) –5.1; *Balance on goods, services and income* –188.9; Current transfers (net) 133.1; Current balance –55.89; Capital account (net) 24.4; Direct investment from abroad 9.1; Other capital (net) –34.2; Net errors and omissions –23.9; *Overall balance* –16.8. Source: IMF, *International Finance Statistics*.

EXTERNAL TRADE

Principal Commodities (estimates, million escudos, 2000): *Imports c.i.f.* : Live animals and animal products 1,255.8; Vegetable products 2,671.7; Edible oils and fats 1,154.0; Food and beverage products 3,962.1; Mineral products 2,731.2 (Cement 992.3); Chemical products 1,758.5; Plastics and rubber 858.9; Metal and metal products 1,795.3; Machines and electrical equipment 4,427.1; Transportation material 2,624.4; Total (incl. others) 27,584.6. *Exports f.o.b.* : Fish and crustaceans 90.1 (Frozen fish 42.8); Footwear (incl. parts) 658.7; Clothing 447.0; Total (incl. others) 1,272.0. Source: IMF, *Cape Verde: Statistical Appendix* (October 2001).

Principal Trading Partners (million escudos, 2001): *Imports c.i.f.*:Belgium 2,021.5; Brazil,672.3; France 922.0; Italy 922.8; Netherlands 4,279.8; Portugal 14,952.1; Spain 1,033.1; United Kingdom 460.5; USA 665.2; Total (incl. others) 28,694.4. *Exports f.o.b.*:Portugal 1,099.6; USA 76.0; Total (incl. others) 1,212.5.

TRANSPORT

Road Traffic (motor vehicles in use, 31 December 1999): Passenger cars 13,473; Commercial vehicles 3,085; Motorcycles 1,296.

Shipping: Merchant fleet (registered at 31 December 2001): Number of vessels 40, total displacement ('000 grt) 16.5 (Source: Lloyd's Register-Fairplay, *World Fleet Statistics*). International freight traffic (estimates, '000 metric tons, 1993): Goods loaded 144, goods unloaded 299 (Source: UN Economic Commission for Africa, *African Statistical Yearbook*.

Civil Aviation (traffic on scheduled services, 1998): Kilometres flown 5,000,000; passengers carried 236,000; passenger-km 269,000,000; total ton-km 26,000,000. Source: UN, *Statistical Yearbook*.

TOURISM

Tourist Arrivals by Country of Residence (2000): France 6,523, Italy 27,130, Netherlands 5,015; Portugal 25,078; Spain 2,924; Switzerland 2,237; Total (incl. others) 83,259. Source: World Tourism Organization, *Yearbook of Tourism Statistics*.

Tourism Receipts (US $ million): 20.2 in 1998; 28.8 in 1999; 40.8 (estimate) in 2000. Source: IMF, *Cape Verde: Statistical Appendix* (October 2001).

COMMUNICATIONS MEDIA

Radio Receivers* (1997): 73,000 in use.

Television Receivers† (2000): 2,000 in use.

Telephones† (2001): 62,300 main lines in use.

Mobile Cellular Telephones† (2001): 31,500 subscribers.

Facsimile Machines‡ (1996): 1,000 in use.

Internet Users† (2001): 12,000.

Non-daily Newspapers* (1996): 4 titles (average circulation 20,000 copies).

Book Production* (1989): 10 titles.
*Source: UNESCO, *Statistical Yearbook*.
† Source: International Telecommunication Union.
‡ Source: UN, *Statistical Yearbook*.

EDUCATION

Pre-primary (1986/87): 58 schools; 136 teachers; 4,523 pupils.

Primary (1999/2000): 370 schools (1990/91); 3,219 teachers (1997/98); 91,636 pupils.

Total Secondary (1999/2000): 1,372 teachers (1997/98); 40,214 pupils.

General Secondary (1993/94): 438 teachers; 11,808 pupils.

Teacher Training: 25 teachers (1987/88); 889 pupils (1993/94).

Vocational Schools (1993/94): 94 teachers; 1,400 pupils. Source: mainly UNESCO, *Statistical Yearbook*.

Adult Literacy Rate (UNESCO estimates): 73.8% (males 84.5%; females 65.7) in 2000 (Source: UN Development Programme, *Human Development Report*).

Directory

The Constitution

A new Constitution of the Republic of Cape Verde ('the Second Republic') came into force on 25 September 1992. The Constitution defines Cape Verde as a sovereign, unitary and democratic republic, guaranteeing respect for human dignity and recognizing the inviolable and inalienable rights of man as a fundament of humanity, peace and justice. It recognizes the equality of all citizens before the law, without distinction of social origin, social condition, economic status, race, sex, religion, political convictions or ideologies and promises transparency for all citizens in the practising of fundamental liberties. The Constitution gives assent to popular will, and has a fundamental objective in the realization of economic, political, social and cultural democracy and the construction of a society that is free, just and in solidarity.

The Head of State is the President of the Republic, who is elected by universal adult suffrage and must obtain two-thirds of the votes cast to win in the first round of the election. If no candidate secures the requisite majority, a new election is held within 21 days and contested by the two candidates who received the highest number of votes in the first round. Voting is conducted by secret ballot. Legislative power is vested in the Assembléia Nacional, which is also elected by universal adult suffrage. The Prime Minister is nominated by the Assembléia, to which he is responsible. On the recommendation of the Prime Minister, the President appoints the Council of Ministers, whose members must be elected deputies of the Assembléia. There are 17 local government councils, elected by universal suffrage for a period of five years.

A constitutional revision, adopted in July 1999, gave the President the right to dissolve the Assembléia Nacional, established a constitutional court (tribunal de constitução), created a new advisory chamber (conselho económico e social), and adopted *Crioulo* as the country's second official language.

The Government

HEAD OF STATE

President: PEDRO PIRES (elected 25 February 2001).

COUNCIL OF MINISTERS
(April 2003)

Prime Minister: JOSÉ MARIA PEREIRA NEVES.

Minister of State and of Infrastructure and Transport: MANUEL INOCÊNCIA SOUSA.

Minister of State and of Health: BASÍLIO MOSSO RAMOS.

Minister of Finance, Planning and Regional Development: CARLOS AUGUSTO DUARTE DE BURGO.

Minister of Foreign Affairs, Co-operation and Communities: MARIA DE FÁTIMA LIMA VEIGA.

Minister of Justice and Internal Administration: MARIA CRISTINA LOPES ALMEIDA FONTES LIMA.

Minister of Defence and Parliamentary Affairs: ARMINDO CIPRIANO MAURÍCIO.

Minister of the Presidency and of the Council of Minister: ARNALDO ANDRADE RAMOS.

Minister in Assistance to the Prime Minister's Office and Minster of Culture and Sports: JORGE HOMERO TOLENTINO ARAÚJO.

Minister of the Environment, Agriculture and Fisheries: MARIA MADALENA DE BRITO NEVES.

Minister of Education and Human Resources: VÍCTOR MANUEL BARBOSA BORGES.

Minister of Labour and Solidarity: JÚLIO LOPES CORREIA.

Minister of the Economy, Growth and Competitiveness: AVELINO BONIFÁCIO FERNANDES LOPES.

Secretary of State for Youth Affairs: MARIA DE JESUS VEIGA MIRANDA MASCARENHAS.

Secretary of State in Assistance to the Minister of Finance, Planning and Regional Development: MANUEL PINTO FREDERICO.

Secretary of State for State Reform and Public Administration: ILÍDIO ALEXANDRE DA CRUZ.

Secretary of State for Tourism: AMILCAR SOUSA LIMA.

MINISTRIES

All ministries are based in Praia, Santiago.

Office of the President: Presidência da República, CP 100, Plateau, Praia, Santiago; tel. 61-65-66; fax 61-43-56.

Office of the Prime Minister: Gabinete do Primeiro Ministro, Palácio do Governo, Várzea, CP 16, Praia, Santiago; tel. 61-05-13; fax 61-30-99.

Ministry of Defence and Parliamentary Affairs: Palácio do Governo, Várzea, Praia, Santiago; tel. 61-03-44; fax 61-20-81; e-mail armindo.mauricio@palgov.cv.

Ministry of Education and Human Resources: Palácio do Governo, Várzea, CP 111, Praia, Santiago; tel. 61-05-07; fax 61-27-64; internet www.gov.cv/minedu.

Ministry of the Environment, Agriculture and Fisheries: Ponta Belém, Praia, Santiago; tel. 61-57-13; fax 61-40-54.

Ministry of Finance, Planning and Regional Development: 107 Avda Amílcar Cabral, CP 30, Praia, Santiago; tel. 61-43-50; internet www.gov.cv/minfin.

Ministry of Foreign Affairs, Co-operation and Communities: Praça Dr Lorena, CP 60, Praia, Santiago; tel. 61-57-27; fax 61-39-52.

Ministry of Health: Palácio do Governo, Várzea, Praia, Santiago; tel. 61-05-01.

Ministry of Infrastructure and Transport: Ponta Belém, Praia, Santiago; tel. 61-56-99; fax 61-41-41; e-mail margarida.lobo@mih.gov.cv.

Ministry of Justice and Internal Administration: Rua Serpa Pinto, CP 205, Praia, Santiago; tel. 62-32-57; fax 62-32-61.

President and Legislature

PRESIDENT

Presidential Election, First ballot, 11 February 2001

Candidate	Votes	% of votes
Pedro Verona Rodrigues Pires (PAICV) . .	61,389	46.51
Carlos Alberto de Carvalho Veiga (MPD) .	60,472	45.82
Jorge Carlos de Almeida Fonseca (PCD) .	5,182	3.93
David Hopffer de Cordeiro Almada (Ind.) .	4,936	3.74
Total	131,979	100.00

Second ballot, 25 February 2001

Candidate	Votes	% of votes
Pedro Verona Rodrigues Pires (PAICV) . .	75,828	50.01
Carlos Alberto de Carvalho Veiga (MPD) .	75,811	49.99
Total	151,639	100.00

ASSEMBLÉIA NACIONAL

Speaker: ARISTIDES RAIMUNDO LIMA.

Legislative Elections, 14 January 2001

Party	Votes	% of votes	Seats
Partido Africano da Independência de Cabo Verde (PAICV)	67,862	49.5	40
Movimento para a Democracia (MPD)	55,581	40.5	30
Aliança Democrática para a Mudança (ADM)*	8,382	6.1	2
Partido da Renovação Democrática (PRD)	4,644	3.4	—
Partido Socialista Democrático (PSD)	622	0.5	—
Total	137,091	100.0	72

* An alliance of the Partido da Convêrgencia Democrática (PCD), the Partido de Trabalho e Solidariedade (PTS) and the União Caboverdiana Independente e Democrática—Partido Democrata Cristão (UCID—PDC), which disbanded following the elections.

Political Organizations

Movimento para a Democracia (MPD): Achada Santo António, CP 90A, Praia, Santiago; tel. 61-40-82; fax 61-41-22; f. 1990; advocates administrative decentralization; governing party since Jan. 1991; Chair. AGOSTINHO LOPES.

Partido Africano da Independência de Cabo Verde (PAICV): Avda Amílcar Cabral, CP 22, Praia, Santiago; tel. 61-27-20; fax 61-14-10; internet www.paicv.org; f. 1956 as the Partido Africano da Independência do Guiné e Cabo Verde (PAIGC); name changed in 1981, following the 1980 coup in Guinea-Bissau; sole authorized political party 1975–90; Pres. JOSÉ MARIA NEVES; Sec.-Gen. ARISTIDES LIMA.

Partido da Convergência Democrática (PCD): Praia, Santiago; f. 1994 by fmr mems of the MPD; Pres. Dr EURICO CORREIA MONTEIRO.

Partido da Renovação Democrática (PRD): Praia, Santiago; f. 2000 by fmr mems of the MPD; Pres. JACINTO SANTOS.

Partido Socialista Democrático (PSD): Praia, Santiago; f. 1992; Sec.-Gen. JOÃO ALÉM.

Partido de Trabalho e Solidariedade (PTS): Praia, Santiago; f. 1998; Leader (vacant).

União Caboverdiana Independente e Democrática—Partido Democrata Cristão (UCID—PDC): Praia, Santiago; f. 1974 by emigrants opposed to the PAICV; obtained legal recognition in 1991; name changed from UCID in 2001; Pres. MANUEL RODRIGUES.

Diplomatic Representation

EMBASSIES IN CAPE VERDE

Angola: Achada de Santo António, Praia, Santiago; tel. 62-32-35; Ambassador CÉSAR A. KILUANGE.

Brazil: Chã de Areia, CP 93, Praia, Santiago; tel. 61-56-07; fax 61-56-09; Ambassador ROMEO ZERO.

China, People's Republic: Achada de Santo António, CP 8, Praia, Santiago; tel. 62-30-29; fax 62-30-47; Ambassador HONG HONG.

Cuba: Prainha, Praia, Santiago; tel. 61-55-97; fax 61-55-90; Ambassador PABLO REIS DOMINGUES.

France: Achada de Santo António, CP 192, Praia, Santiago; tel. 61-55-89; fax 61-55-90; Ambassador ANDRÉ BARBE.

Portugal: Achada de Santo António, CP 160, Praia, Santiago; tel. 62-26-30; fax 61-40-58; Ambassador FRANCISCO RIBEIRO TELLES.

Russia: Achada de Santo António, CP 31, Praia, Santiago; tel. 62-27-39; fax 62-27-38; Ambassador VLADIMIR E. PETUKHOV.

Senegal: Achada de Santo António, Plateau, Santiago; tel. 61-52-21; e-mail silcarneyni@hotmail.com; Ambassador SILCARNEYNI GUEYE.

USA: Achada Orando, Praia, Santiago; tel. 61-56-16; fax 61-13-55; Ambassador MICHAEL METELITS.

Judicial System

Tribunal de Constitução: f. 1999; the supreme court.

Supremo Tribunal de Justiça

Gabinete do Juiz Presidente, Rua Cesário de Lacerda, CP 117, Praia, Santiago; tel. 61-58-10; fax 61-17-51.

f. 1975; the highest court; Pres. Dr OSCAR GOMES.

Attorney-General: Dr HENRIQUE MONTEIRO.

Religion

CHRISTIANITY

At 31 December 2000 there were an estimated 408,813 adherents of the Roman Catholic Church, representing 94.1% of the total population. Protestant churches, among which the Church of the Nazarene is the most prominent, represent about 1% of the population.

The Roman Catholic Church

Cape Verde comprises the single diocese of Santiago de Cabo Verde, directly responsible to the Holy See. The Bishop participates in the Episcopal Conference of Senegal, Mauritania, Cape Verde and Guinea-Bissau, currently based in Senegal.

Bishop of Santiago de Cabo Verde: Rt Rev. PAULINO DO LIVRAMENTO ÉVORA, Avda Amílcar Cabral, Largo 5 de Outubro, CP 46, Praia, Santiago; tel. 61-11-19; fax 61-21-26; e-mail pm.curia.pera@cvtelecom.cv.

The Anglican Communion

Cape Verde forms part of the diocese of The Gambia, within the Church of the Province of West Africa. The Bishop is resident in Banjul, The Gambia.

Other Christian Churches

Church of the Nazarene: District Office, Praia, Santiago; tel. 61-36-11.

Igreja Maná: Rua do Matadouro Velho 3, Mindelo, São Vicente; tel. 32-44-95; fax 32-76-69; internet www.igrejamana.com.

Jehovah's Witnesses: Vila Porto Novo, Santo Antão; tel. 22-12-14.

BAHÁ'Í FAITH

National Spiritual Assembly: Rua Madragoa, Plateau, Santiago; tel. 61-77-39.

The Press

Agaviva: Mindelo, São Vicente; tel. 31-21-21; f. 1991; monthly; Editor GERMANO ALMEIDA; circ. 4,000.

Boletim Oficial da República de Cabo Verde: Imprensa Nacional, CP 113, Praia, Santiago; tel. 61-41-50; weekly; official announcements.

O Cidadão: Praça Dr António Aurélio Gonçalves 2, CP 669, Mindelo, São Vicente; tel. 32-50-24; fax 32-50-22; e-mail ocidadao@mail.cvtelecom.cv; Editor JOSÉ MÁRIO CORREIA.

Contacto: CP 89c, Praia, Santiago; tel. 61-57-52; fax 61-14-42; f. 1993; quarterly; economic bulletin publ. by Centro de Promoção Turística, de Investimento Externo e das Exportações (PROMEX); Co-ordinator MANUELA GARCIA; circ. 1,500.

Expresso das Ilhas: Santiago; f. 2001 by the MPD; weekly.

Horizonte: Achada de Santo António, CP 40, Praia, Santiago; tel. 62-24-47; fax 62-33-30; e-mail infopress@cvtelecom.cv; f. 1999; weekly; pro-Government; Editor FERNANDO MONTEIRO; circ. 5,000.

Novo Jornal de Cabo Verde: Travessa do Mercado, CP 118, Praia, Santiago; tel. 61-64-96; fax 61-38-29.

Perspectiva: Achada de Santo António, CP 89c, Praia, Santiago; tel. 62-26-21; fax 62-26-57; e-mail promex@cvtelecom.cv; internet www.promex.cv; f. 1995; annual; economic bulletin publ. by Centro de Promoção Turística, de Investimento Externo e das Exportações (PROMEX); Dir of Marketing and Promotion MANUELA AZEVEDO GRAÇA; circ. 5,000.

Raízes: CP 98, Praia, Santiago; tel. 319; f. 1977; quarterly; cultural review; Editor ARNALDO FRANÇA; circ. 1,500.

A Semana: Rotunda Salmarego, CP 36c, Praia, Santiago; tel. 62-98-60; fax 62-86-61; e-mail jornalsemana@mail.cvtelecom.cv; weekly; independent; Editor FILOMENA SILVA; circ. 5,000.

Terra Nova: Rua Guiné-Bissau 1, CP 166, Mindelo, São Vicente; tel. 32-24-42; fax 32-14-75; e-mail terranova@cabonet.cv; f. 1975; monthly; Roman Catholic; Editor P. ANTÓNIO FIDALGO BARROS; circ. 3,000.

NEWS AGENCIES

Inforpress: Achada de Santo António, CP 40/A, Praia, Santiago; tel. 62-30-25; fax 62-30-23; internet www.inforpress.cv; f. 1988 as Cabopress.

Foreign Bureaux

Agência Lusa de Informação (Portugal): Prainha, Praia, Santiago; tel. 61-35-19; Bureau Chief FRANCISCO FONTES.

Inter Press Service (IPS) (Italy): CP 14, Mindelo, São Vicente; tel. 31-45-50; Rep. JUAN A. COLOMA.

Publisher

Government Publishing House

Imprensa Nacional: CP 113, Praia, Santiago; tel. 61-42-09; Admin. JOÃO DE PINA.

Broadcasting and Communications

TELECOMMUNICATIONS

Cabo Verde Telecom: CP 220, Varzea, Praia, Santiago; tel. 61-31-26; fax 61-42-26; e-mail cvtelecom@cvtelecom.cv; internet www.cvtelecom.cv; f. 1995; Chief Exec. ANTÓNIO PIRES CORREIA.

BROADCASTING

Rádio Televisão de Cabo Verde (RTC): Rua 13 de Janeiro, CP 1/A, Achada de Santo António; tel. 62-30-51; fax 62-30-54; e-mail rtc@mail.cvtelecom.cv; govt-controlled; five radio transmitters and five solar relay radio transmitters; FM transmission only; radio broadcasts in Portuguese and Creole for 18 hours daily; one television transmitter and seven relay television transmitters; television broadcasts in Portuguese and Creole for eight hours daily with co-operation of RTPI (Portugal); Pres. JACINTO ARAÚJO ESTRELA.

Praia FM: Rua Justino Lopes 1, CP 276-C, Praia, Santiago; tel. 61-63-56; fax 61-63-57; e-mail praiafm@cvtelecom.cv; internet www.praiafm.cv; Dir GIORDANO CUSTÓDIO.

Rádio Comercial: Achada Santo António, Prédio Gomes Irmãos 3° esq., CP 507, Santiago; tel. 62-31-56; fax 62-24-13; e-mail multimedia.rc@cvtelecom.cv; internet www.radiocomercial.net; f. 1997; Admin. HENRIQUE PIRES; Dir CARLOS FILIPE GONÇALVES.

Rádio Educativa de Cabo Verde: Achada de Santo António, Praia, Santiago; tel. 61-11-61.

Rádio Morabeza: Alto Matiota, CP 456, Mindelo, São Vicente; tel. 32-44-28; fax 30-00-11.

Rádio Nacional de Cabo Verde: CP 26, Praia; tel. 61-37-29.

Rádio Nova—Emissora Cristã de Cabo Verde: CP 166, Mindelo, São Vicente; tel. 32-20-82; fax 32-14-75; Dir ANTONIO FIDALGO BARROS.

Voz de São Vicente: CP 29, Mindelo, São Vicente; fax 31-10-06; f. 1974; govt-controlled; Dir JOSÉ FONSECA SOARES.

Finance

(cap. = capital; res = reserves; dep. = deposits; m. = million; brs = branches; amounts in Cape Verde escudos)

BANKING

Central Bank

Banco de Cabo Verde (BCV): 117 Avda Amílcar Cabral, CP 101, Praia, Santiago; tel. 60-70-80; fax 61-70-95; e-mail bcv@mail.cvtelecom.cv; internet www.bcv.cv; f. 1976; bank of issue; cap. and res 3,169m., dep. 5,143m. (Dec. 1998); Gov. OLAVO AVELINO GARCIA CORREIA.

Other Banks

Banco Comercial do Atlântico (BCA): Avda Amílcar Cabral, CP 474, Praia, Santiago; tel. 61-49-53; fax 61-32-35; e-mail bcadin@mail.cvtelecom.cv; f. 1993; privatized in 2000; main commercial bank; cap. 1,000m., res 148.9m., dep. 28,876.6m. (2000); Chair. JOÃO HENRIQUE REAL PEREIRA; 19 brs.

Banco Totta e Açores (BTA) (Portugal): Rua Justino Lopes 1, CP 593, Praia, Santiago; tel. 61-16-62; fax 61-40-06; e-mail bta@cvtelecom.cv; f. 1996; cap. 300m. (Dec. 1998); Gen. Man. RODRIGO NASCIMENTO; 3 brs.

Caixa Geral de Depósitos (Portugal): Achada da Praia, CP 131-A, Praia, Santiago; tel. 62-22-91; fax 62-20-79; e-mail cgdcv@mail.cvtelecom.cv; f. 1998; Pres. Dr ANTÓNIO MIGUEL ORNELAS AFONSO.

Caixa Económica de Cabo Verde (CECV): Avda Cidade de Lisboa, CP 199, Praia, Santiago; tel. 60-36-01; fax 61-55-60; e-mail cecv@caixaeconomica.cv; internet www.caixaeconomica.cv; f. 1928; privatized in 1999; commercial bank; cap. 348m., res 558.5m., dep. 8,161.2m. (Dec. 2000); Pres. ALBERTO JOSE DOS SANTOS RAMALHEIRA.

The **Fundo de Solidariedade Nacional** is the main savings institution; the **Fundo de Desenvolvimento Nacional** channels public investment resources; and the **Instituto Caboverdiano** administers international aid.

STOCK EXCHANGE

Bolsa de Valores de Cabo Verde: Achada de Santo António, CP 115-A, Praia, Santiago; tel. 60-30-30; fax 60-30-35; e-mail bcv@mail.cvtelecom.cv; f. 1998.

INSURANCE

Companhia Caboverdiana de Seguros (IMPAR): Avda Amílcar Cabral, CP 469, Praia, Santiago; tel. 61-14-05; fax 61-37-65; f. 1991; Pres. Dr CORSINO FORTES.

Garantia Companhia de Seguros: Rua Guerra Mendes, CP 138, Praia, Santiago; tel. 61-56-61; fax 61-25-55; e-mail garantia@cvtelecom.cv; f. 1991; privatized in 2000.

Trade and Industry

GOVERNMENT AGENCIES

Centro de Promoção Turística, de Investimento Externo e das Exportações (PROMEX): CP 89c, Achada de Santo António, Praia, Santiago; tel. 62-26-21; fax 62-26-57; e-mail promex@mail.cvtelecom.cv; internet www.promex.org; f. 1990; promotes foreign investment and exports; Pres. GEORGINA DE MELLO.

Gabinete de Apoio à Reestruturação do Sector Empresarial do Estado (GARSEE; Cabo Verde Privatization): Praia, Santiago; tel. 61-47-48; fax 61-23-34; e-mail cvprivatization@mail.cvtelecom.cv; internet http://cvprivatization.org; bureau in charge of planning and supervising restructuring and divestment of public enterprises; Project Dir Dr SÉRGIO CENTEIO.

DEVELOPMENT ORGANIZATION

Instituto Nacional de Investigação e Desenvolvimento Agrário: CP 84, Praia, Santiago; tel. 71-11-47; fax 71-11-33; e-mail inida@mail.cvtelecom.cv; f. 1979; under the supervision of the Ministry of Agriculture and Fisheries; research and training on agricultural issues.

CHAMBERS OF COMMERCE

Associação Comercial Industrial e Agrícola de Barlavento (ACIAB): CP 62, Mindelo, São Vicente; tel. 31-32-81; fax 32-36-58; e-mail aciab@mail.cvtelecom.cv; f. 1918; Chair. LUÍS VASCONCELOS LOPES.

Associação Comercial de Sotavento (ACAS): Rua Serpa Pinto 23, 1°, CP 78, Praia, Santiago; tel. 61-29-91; fax 61-29-64; e-mail acs@cvtelecom.cv.

STATE INDUSTRIAL ENTERPRISES

Empresa Nacional de Avicultura: CP 135, Praia; tel. 61-56-49; fax 61-12-92; poultry farming.

Empresa Nacional de Produtos Farmacêuticos (EMPROFAC): CP 59, Praia, Santiago; tel. 62-78-95; fax 62-78-99; f. 1979; state monopoly of pharmaceuticals and medical imports.

UTILITIES

Electricity and Water

Empresa de Electricidade e Água (ELECTRA): 10 Avda Baltazar Lopes Silva 10-1, CP 137, Mindelo, São Vicente; tel. 32-44-09; fax 32-44-46; e-mail electra@electra.cv; internet www.electra.cv; f. 1982; privatized in 1999; Pres. RUI MANUEL ALMEIDA PAISANA.

CO-OPERATIVES

Instituto Nacional das Cooperativas: Fazenda, CP 218, Praia, Santiago; tel. 61-41-12; fax 61-39-59; central co-operative org.

TRADE UNIONS

Confederação Caboverdiana dos Sindicatos Livres (CCSL): Rua Dr Júlio Abreu, Praia, Santiago; tel. 61-63-19; Sec.-Gen. JOSÉ MANUEL VAZ.

Sindicato dos Transportes, Comunicações e Turismo (STCT): Praia, Santiago; tel. 61-63-38.

União Nacional dos Trabalhadores de Cabo Verde—Central Sindical (UNTC—CS): Estrada do Aeroporto, Praia, CP 123, Santiago; tel. 60-08-20; fax 61-36-29; e-mail untc@mail.cvtelecom.cv; internet www.untc-cs.org; f. 1978; Chair. JÚLIO ASCENÇÃO SILVA.

Transport

ROADS

In 1999 there were an estimated 1,100 km of roads, of which 858 km were paved.

SHIPPING

Cargo-passenger ships call regularly at Porto Grande, Mindelo, on São Vicente, and Praia, on Santiago. In 1997 Porto Grande and the port at Praia were upgraded. There are small ports on the other inhabited islands.

Comissão de Gestão dos Transportes Marítimos de Cabo Verde: CP 153, São Vicente; tel. 31-49-79; fax 31-20-55.

Empresa Nacional de Administração dos Portos, SA (ENAPOR, SA): Avda Marginal, CP 82, Mindelo, São Vicente; tel. 32-44-14; fax 32-14-33; e-mail enapor@mail.cvtelecom.cv; f. 1982; Chair. and Man. Dir FRANKLIM DO ROSÁRIO SPENCER.

Companhia Caboverdiana de Navegação: Rua Cristiano Sena Barcelos 3–5, Mindelo, São Vicente; tel. 32-28-52.

Companhia Nacional de Navegação Arca Verde: Avda 5 de Julho 153, CP 41, Praia, Santiago; tel. 61-54-97; fax 61-54-96; f. 1975.

Companhia de Navegação Estrela Negra: Avda 5 de Julho 17, CP 91, Mindelo, São Vicente; tel. 32-35-44; fax 31-53-82.

Companhia Portuguesa de Transportes Marítimos: Agent in Santiago: João Benoliel de Carvalho, Lda, CP 56, Praia, Santiago.

Linhas Marítimas Caboverdianas (LINMAC): CP 357, Praia, Santiago; tel. 61-43-52; fax 61-37-15; Dir ESTHER SPENCER.

Seage Agência de Navegação de Cabo Verde: Avda Cidade de Lisboa, CP 232, Praia, Santiago; tel. 61-57-58; fax 61-25-24; f. 1986; Chair. CÉSAR MANUEL SEMEDO LOPES.

CIVIL AVIATION

The Amílcar Cabral international airport, at Espargos, on Sal island, can accommodate aircraft of up to 50 tons and 1m. passengers per year. The airport's facilities were expanded during the 1990s. A second international airport, under construction on Santiago, capable of accommodating long-range aircraft, was due for completion in 2003. There is also a small airport on each of the other inhabited islands. The airport on São Vicente was upgraded to international capacity in 2000. Plans were also under way for the construction of an international airport on Boa Vista, as well as a new airport on Santo Antão.

Empresa Nacional de Aeroportos e Segurança Aérea, EP (ASA): Aeroporto Amílcar Cabral, CP 58, Ilha do Sal; tel. 41-13-72; fax 41-15-70; e-mail asacv@mail.cvtelecom.cv; airports and aircraft security; Pres. MÁRIO LOPES.

Transportes Aéreos de Cabo Verde (TACV): Avda Amílcar Cabral, CP 1, Praia, Santiago; tel. 61-58-13; fax 61-35-85; e-mail cv.airline@milton.cvtelecom.cv; internet www.tacv.de; f. 1958; internal services connecting the nine inhabited islands; also operates regional services to Senegal, The Gambia and Guinea-Bissau, and long-distance services to Europe and the USA; Dir ALFREDO CARVALHO.

Tourism

The islands of Santiago, Santo Antão, Fogo and Brava offer attractive mountain scenery. There are extensive beaches on the islands of Santiago, Sal, Boa Vista and Maio. There are nine hotels on Sal, three on Boa Vista, three on São Vicente, and nine on Santiago. In 1999 there were some 1,825 hotel rooms in Cape Verde, with an estimated 2,000 beds in 2000. Some 83,259 tourists visited Cape Verde during 2000, when tourism receipts totalled an estimated US $40.8m. The sector is undergoing rapid expansion, with tourist arrivals projected to increase to about 400,000 annually by 2008.

THE CENTRAL AFRICAN REPUBLIC

Introductory Survey

Location, Climate, Language, Religion, Flag, Capital

The Central African Republic is a land-locked country in the heart of equatorial Africa. It is bordered by Chad to the north, by Sudan to the east, by the Democratic Republic of the Congo (formerly Zaire) and the Republic of the Congo to the south and by Cameroon to the west. The climate is tropical, with an average annual temperature of 26°C (79°F) and heavy rainfall in the south-western forest areas. The national language is Sango, but French is the official language and another 68 languages and dialects have been identified. It is estimated that about one-half of the population are Christian; another 15% are Muslims, while animist beliefs are held by an estimated 24%. The national flag (proportions 3 by 5) has four equal horizontal stripes, of blue, white, green and yellow, divided vertically by a central red stripe, with a five-pointed yellow star in the hoist corner of the blue stripe. The capital is Bangui.

Recent History

The former territory of Ubangi-Shari (Oubangui-Chari), within French Equatorial Africa, became the Central African Republic (CAR) on achieving self-government in December 1958. Barthélemy Boganda, the first Prime Minister, died in March 1959. He was succeeded by his nephew, David Dacko, who led the country to full independence, and became the first President, on 13 August 1960. In 1962 a one-party state was established, with the ruling Mouvement d'évolution sociale de l'Afrique noire (MESAN) as the sole authorized party. President Dacko was overthrown on 31 December 1965 by a military coup, which brought to power his cousin, Col (later Marshal) Jean-Bédel Bokassa, Commander-in-Chief of the armed forces.

In January 1966 Bokassa formed a new Government, rescinded the Constitution and dissolved the National Assembly. Bokassa, who became Life President in March 1972 and Marshal of the Republic in May 1974, forestalled several alleged coup attempts and employed increasingly repressive measures against dissidents. From January 1975 to April 1976 Elisabeth Domitien, the Vice-President of MESAN, was Prime Minister; she was the first woman to hold this position in any African country.

In September 1976 the Council of Ministers was replaced by the Council for the Central African Revolution, and the former President, Dacko, was appointed personal adviser to the President. In December the Republic was renamed the Central African Empire (CAE), and a new Constitution was instituted. Bokassa was proclaimed the first Emperor, and Dacko became his Personal Counsellor. The Imperial Constitution provided for the establishment of a national assembly, but no elections were held. In May 1978 Bokassa reorganized the army leadership and strengthened its powers. In July he appointed a new Council of Ministers, headed by a former Deputy Prime Minister, Henri Maidou. On 20 September 1979, while Bokassa was in Libya, Dacko deposed him in a bloodless coup, which received considerable support from France. The country was again designated a republic, with Dacko as its President and Maidou as Vice-President.

President Dacko's principal concern was to establish order and economic stability, but his Government encountered opposition, particularly from students who objected to the continuation in office of CAE ministers. In August 1980 Dacko accepted demands for the dismissal of both Maidou and the Prime Minister, Bernard Christian Ayandho. Bokassa, at that time in exile in Côte d'Ivoire (and subsequently in Paris), was sentenced to death in absentia in December. In February 1981 a new Constitution, providing for a multi-party system, was approved by referendum and promulgated by Dacko. He won a presidential election in March, amid allegations of electoral malpractice, and was sworn in for a six-year term in April. Political tension intensified in subsequent months, and on 1 September the Chief of Staff of the Armed Forces, Gen. André Kolingba, deposed Dacko in a bloodless coup. Kolingba was declared President, and a ruling Comité militaire pour le redressement national (CMRN) and an all-military Government were formed. All political activity was suspended.

In March 1982 the exiled leader of the banned Mouvement pour la libération du peuple centrafricain (MLPC), Ange-Félix Patassé, returned to Bangui and was implicated in an unsuccessful coup attempt. Patassé, who had been the Prime Minister under Bokassa in 1976–78 and who had contested the 1981 presidential election, sought asylum in the French embassy in Bangui, from where he was transported to exile in Togo. A visit by President Mitterrand of France to the CAR in October 1982 normalized bilateral relations, which had been strained by French support for Patassé. Domestic opposition to Kolingba's regime continued, and in August 1983 elements of the three main opposition parties formed a united front. In September 1984 Kolingba announced an amnesty for the leaders of banned political parties, who had been under house arrest since January.

In September 1985 the CMRN was dissolved and, for the first time since Kolingba's assumption of power, civilians were appointed to the Council of Ministers. In early 1986 a specially convened commission drafted a new Constitution, which provided for the creation of a sole legal political party, the Rassemblement démocratique centrafricain (RDC), and conferred extensive executive powers on the President, while defining a predominantly advisory role for the legislature. At a referendum in November some 91.17% of voters approved the draft Constitution and granted Kolingba a mandate to serve a further six-year term as President. The Council of Ministers was reorganized in December to include a majority of civilians. The RDC was officially established in February 1987, with Kolingba as founding President, and elections to the new Assemblée nationale took place in July, at which 142 candidates, all nominated by the RDC, contested the 52 seats.

In October 1986 Bokassa returned unexpectedly to the CAR and was immediately arrested. His new trial opened in November and continued until June 1987, when the former Emperor was sentenced to death, having been convicted on charges of murder, conspiracy to murder, the illegal detention of prisoners and embezzlement. In February 1988 Kolingba commuted the sentence to one of life imprisonment with hard labour.

The appointment during 1988 of former associates of Bokassa, Dacko and Patassé to prominent public offices appeared to represent an attempt by Kolingba to consolidate national unity. In August 1989, however, 12 opponents of his regime, including members of the Front patriotique oubanguien-Parti du travail and the leader of the Rassemblement populaire pour la reconstruction de la Centrafrique, Brig.-Gen. (later Gen.) François Bozizé, were arrested in Benin, where they had been living in exile, and extradited to the CAR. Bozizé was subsequently found guilty of complicity in the 1982 coup attempt.

In 1990 opposition movements exerted pressure on the Government to introduce a plural political system, and in October violent anti-Government demonstrations were suppressed by the security forces. In December the Executive Council of the RDC recommended a review of the Constitution and the re-establishment of the premiership. Accordingly, in March 1991 Edouard Franck, a former Minister of State at the Presidency, was appointed Prime Minister, and in July the Assemblée nationale approved a constitutional amendment providing for the establishment of a multi-party political system. Kolingba resigned from the presidency of the RDC in the following month, in order to remain 'above parties'. In October the Kolingba administration agreed to convene a national debate on the country's political future, with representatives of opposition movements invited to attend. In December Kolingba pardoned Brig.-Gen. Bozizé.

The Grand National Debate took place in August 1992, but was boycotted by the influential Concertation des forces démocratiques (CFD), an alliance of opposition groupings, which announced that it would only participate in a multi-party national conference with sovereign powers. At the end of August the Assemblée nationale approved legislation in accordance with decisions taken by the Grand National Debate: constitutional amendments provided for the strict separation of executive, legislative and judicial powers, and Kolingba was granted temporary powers to rule by decree until the election of a new multi-party legislature. Concurrent legislative and presidential elections commenced in October, but were suspended by presidential decree and subsequently annulled by the Supreme Court, owing to alleged sabotage of the electoral process. In December Franck resigned as Prime Minister and was replaced by Gen. Timothée Malendoma, the leader of the Forum civique.

In February 1993 Malendoma, who had accused Kolingba of curtailing his powers, was dismissed from the premiership and replaced by Enoch Derant Lakoué, the leader of the Parti social-démocrate. In June, in response to mounting pressure from both the opposition and the French Government, Kolingba announced that elections would commence in August. Accordingly, two rounds of concurrent legislative and presidential elections were held in late August and mid-September. At the legislative elections the MLPC won 34 of the 85 seats in the Assemblée nationale, while the RDC, in second place, secured 13 seats. Patassé, the MLPC leader and former Prime Minister, was elected President, winning 52.47% of the votes cast at a second round of voting. The seven other presidential candidates included Kolingba, Prof. Abel Goumba (the leader of the CFD) and former President Dacko. In late August Kolingba, who had been defeated at the first round of the presidential election, attempted to delay the publication of the election results by issuing two decrees that modified the electoral code and altered the composition of the Supreme Court; however, the decrees were revoked, after the French Government threatened to suspend all co-operation with the CAR in protest.

In September 1993 Bokassa was released from prison under a general amnesty for convicts; however, the former Emperor was banned for life from participating in elections and demoted from the military rank of marshal. He died in November 1996.

In October 1993 Patassé was inaugurated as President. Soon afterwards he appointed Jean-Luc Mandaba, the Vice-President of the MLPC, as Prime Minister; Mandaba formed a coalition Government, which had a working majority of 53 seats in the Assemblée nationale.

In December 1994 a draft Constitution was approved by 82% of voters in a national referendum. The new Constitution, which was adopted in January 1995, included provisions empowering the President to nominate senior military, civil service and judicial officials, and requiring the Prime Minister to implement policies decided by the President. In addition, provision was made for the creation of directly-elected regional assemblies and for the establishment of an advisory State Council, which was to deliberate on administrative issues. Several groups in the governing coalition (notably the Mouvement pour la démocratie et le développement—MDD, led by Dacko) expressed concern at the powers afforded to the President.

In April 1995 Mandaba resigned as Prime Minister, pre-empting a threatened vote of 'no confidence' in his administration (initiated by his own party), following accusations of corruption and incompetence. Patassé appointed Gabriel Koyambounou, formerly a civil servant, as the new Prime Minister. Koyambounou subsequently nominated a new Council of Ministers, with an enlarged membership. In August supporters of the RDC staged a peaceful demonstration in protest at perceived abuses of power by the Government, such as the imposition of a two-year term of imprisonment on the editor of the RDC newspaper, who had been found guilty of treason following the publication of an article critical of Patassé. In December several opposition movements (including the MDD, but not the RDC) united to form the Conseil démocratique des partis politiques de l'opposition (CODEPO), which aimed to campaign against alleged corruption and mismanagement by the Patassé regime.

In the mid-1990s the Government repeatedly failed to pay the salaries of public-sector employees and members of the security forces, prompting frequent strikes and mounting political unrest. In mid-April 1996 CODEPO staged an anti-Government rally in Bangui. Shortly afterwards part of the national army mutinied in the capital and demanded the immediate settlement of all salary arrears. Patassé promised that part of the overdue salaries would be paid and that the mutineers would not be subject to prosecution. The presence of French troops (the Eléments français d'assistance opérationelle—EFAO) in Bangui, with a mandate to secure the safety of foreign nationals and (in accordance with a bilateral military accord) to protect the presidential palace and other key installations, contributed to the swift collapse of the rebellion. About nine people, including civilians, were reported to have died in the uprising.

In late April Patassé appointed a new Chief of Staff of the Armed Forces, Col Maurice Regonessa, and banned all public demonstrations. In May, however, discontent resurfaced, and CODEPO organized another rally in Bangui, at which it demanded the resignation of the Government. Soon afterwards, in an attempt to tighten his hold on power, the President ordered that control of the national armoury should be transferred from the regular army to the presidential guard. However, adverse reaction to this move within the ranks of the armed forces rapidly escalated into a second, more determined insurrection. Once again EFAO troops were deployed to protect the Patassé administration; some 500 reinforcements were brought in from Chad and Gabon to consolidate the resident French military presence (numbering 1,400). Five hostages were taken by the mutineers, including Col Regonessa, a government minister and the President of the Assemblée nationale. After five days of fierce fighting between dissident and loyalist troops, the French forces intervened to suppress the rebellion. France's military action (which allegedly resulted in civilian deaths) prompted intense scrutiny of the role of the former colonial power, and precipitated large pro- and anti-French demonstrations in Bangui. In total, 11 soldiers and 32 civilians were reported to have been killed in the second army mutiny. Following extended negotiations between the mutineers and government representatives, the two sides eventually signed an accord, providing for an amnesty for the rebels (who were to return to barracks under EFAO guard), the immediate release of hostages, and the installation of a new government of national unity. The political opposition rejected the proposed government of national unity, however, demanding a transitional government followed by fresh legislative and presidential elections. The opposition also requested a revision of the Constitution to remove some executive powers from the President and enhance the role of the Prime Minister.

In June 1996 the Government and the opposition signed a protocol providing for the establishment of a government of national unity, led by a civilian Prime Minister with no official party ties. Although the Constitution was not to be amended to alter the balance of power between the President and the Prime Minister, Patassé agreed to permit 'some room for manoeuvre'. Following the publication of the protocol, Koyambounou's Government resigned. Jean-Paul Ngoupandé, hitherto Ambassador to France and with no official political affiliation (although he had been Secretary-General of the RDC in the late 1980s), was appointed as the new Prime Minister and immediately nominated a new Council of Ministers. National co-operation, however, remained elusive, as CODEPO, dissatisfied with the level of its ministerial representation, immediately withdrew from the Government of National Unity. Moreover, a growing animosity was reported between Patassé and Ngoupandé, with the former refusing to transfer any effective power to the latter.

At a conference on national defence held in August–September 1996, several resolutions were adopted regarding restructuring and improving conditions within the army. In October, however, it was reported that troops who had been involved in the insurrections of April and May were refusing to be transferred from their barracks in the capital to a more remote location; Patassé insisted that their departure would take place none the less. However, in mid-November a further mutiny erupted among these troops. A substantial part of Bangui was occupied by the rebels, and a number of hostages were taken. The latest uprising appeared to have a strong tribal and political motivation: the mutineers, who demanded the resignation of Patassé, belonged to the Yakoma ethnic group of Kolingba. EFAO troops were deployed once again, ostensibly to maintain order and protect foreign residents; however, by guarding key installations and government buildings, they also effectively prevented the overthrow of the Patassé administration. More than 100 people were killed in the unrest during late November and early December.

In December 1996 the Presidents of Burkina Faso, Chad, Gabon and Mali negotiated a 15-day truce, which was supervised by the former transitional President of Mali, Gen. Amadou Toumani Touré; a one-month extension to the cease-fire was subsequently agreed. In January 1997, following the killing of two French soldiers in Bangui (reportedly by mutineers), EFAO troops retaliated by killing at least 10 members of the rebel forces; French military involvement in the CAR was condemned by the opposition, which also sought (without success) to initiate impeachment proceedings against Patassé. Subsequent to the renewal of violence, Touré again came to Bangui as mediator and helped to create a cross-party Committee of Consultation and Dialogue. The 'Bangui Accords', drawn up by this committee, were signed towards the end of January; these, as well as offering an amnesty to the mutineers, provided for the formation of a new government of national unity and for the replacement of the EFAO troops by peace-keeping forces from African nations. The opposition at first threatened to boycott the new Government, largely owing to the appointment of Michel Gbezera-Bria (a close associate of Patassé and hitherto the Minister of Foreign Affairs) as Prime Minister. However, with the creation of new ministerial posts for opposition politicians, a 'Government of Action' (which did not include Ngoupandé) was formed on 18 February; soon afterwards Gen. Bozizé replaced Gen. Regonessa as Chief of Staff of the Armed Forces.

In February 1997 responsibility for peace-keeping operations was transferred from the EFAO to forces of the newly formed Mission interafricaine de surveillance des accords de Bangui (MISAB), comprising some 700 soldiers from Burkina Faso, Chad, Gabon, Mali, Senegal and Togo (with logistical support from 50 French military personnel). MISAB soldiers were also to assist in disarming the former mutineers; however, when in late March they attempted to do so, fighting broke out in which some 20 MISAB soldiers were killed. A spokesman for the rebels, Capt. Anicet Saulet, claimed that the lack of representation of the former mutineers in the new Government constituted a breach of the Bangui Accords. Following a meeting between Saulet and Patassé in early April, the Council of Ministers was expanded to include two military officers as representatives of the rebels. Later that month several hundred former mutineers attended a ceremony marking their reintegration into the regular armed forces.

In mid-April 1997 a curfew was imposed on Bangui, owing to a serious escalation in violent crime, much of which was allegedly perpetrated by groups of former mutineers. In May, following the deaths in police custody of three former rebels suspected of criminal activities, nine ministers representing the G11 (a grouping of 11 opposition parties, including the MDD—which had left CODEPO in November 1996—and the RDC), as well as the two representatives of the former mutineers, suspended participation in the Government. In June violent clashes erupted once again between MISAB forces and former mutineers. In response to several attacks on the French embassy by the rebels, several hundred EFAO troops were redeployed on the streets of Bangui, and MISAB forces launched a major offensive in the capital, capturing most of the rebel-controlled districts. This assault led to the arrest of more than 80 former mutineers, but also to some 100 deaths, both of soldiers and of civilians, while numerous homes and business premises were destroyed. Soon afterwards some 500 demonstrators gathered outside the French embassy to protest against alleged abuses of human rights by MISAB troops; MISAB officials claimed that criminals were impersonating their soldiers in order to perpetrate atrocities. On the same day Touré returned to Bangui in his capacity as Chairman of MISAB, and negotiated a four-day truce, which took effect at the end of June, followed by a 10-day cease-fire agreement, signed at the beginning of July; all of the former mutineers were to be reintegrated into the regular armed forces, and their safety and that of the people living in the districts under their control was guaranteed; the rebels, for their part, were to relinquish their weaponry. Towards the end of July many of the people who had been held in custody in relation to the previous month's violence were released by the authorities, and the curfew in Bangui was eased, while it was reported that almost all of the former mutineers had rejoined the regular armed forces. In September the nine representatives of opposition parties in the Council of Ministers resumed their vacant posts.

In July 1997, in accordance with a foreign policy decision to disengage forces from its former African colonies, France announced its intention to withdraw its troops from the CAR by April 1998; the first troops left the country in October 1997. France campaigned vigorously for the formation of a UN force, but encountered initial resistance from the USA. A National Reconciliation Conference, held in Bangui, in February 1998 led to the signing on 5 March of a National Reconciliation Pact by President Patassé and 40 representatives of all the country's political and social groups. The accord was countersigned by Gen. Touré and witnessed by many other African Heads of State. The Pact restated the main provisions of the Bangui Accords and of the political protocol of June 1996. It provided for military and political restructuring, to be implemented by a civilian Prime Minister, supported by all of the country's social and political groups. The powers and position of the President were, however, guaranteed, and a presidential election was scheduled for late 1999.

The signature of the Pact facilitated the authorization, later in March 1998, by the UN Security Council of the establishment of a peace-keeping mission, the UN Mission in the Central African Republic (MINURCA), to replace MISAB. MINURCA comprised 1,345 troops from Benin, Burkina Faso, Canada, Chad, Côte d'Ivoire, Egypt, France, Gabon, Mali, Portugal, Senegal and Togo, and was granted a mandate to remain in the country for an initial period of three months. MINURCA's initial mandate was to maintain security and stability around Bangui, to supervise the final disposition of weapons retrieved under the disarmament programme, to assist in efforts to train a national police force, and to provide advice and technical assistance for the legislative elections. The mission was subsequently extended until the end of February 1999 in order to support and verify the legislative elections.

There was substantial support for the new political solution, and, significantly, when in April 1998 the principal trade union, the Union Syndicale des Travailleurs de la Centrafrique, called for a 48-hour general strike to protest against outstanding pay arrears, their action received little support. However, preparations for the legislative elections were marked by disagreement between the Government and the G11 group of opposition parties over electoral procedure. When the authorities announced in August that the elections were to be postponed, owing to the difficulties of registering rural voters, the opposition claimed that there was little political will for the elections in government circles. Demonstrations took place outside the Assemblée nationale in September to protest against the indefinite postponement of the legislative elections and the subsequent extension of the term of office of deputies.

Elections to the newly reorganized Assemblée nationale finally took place on 22 November and 13 December 1998. A reportedly large number of the electorate participated in the polls, which were contested by 29 parties. The MPLC won 47 of the 109 seats in the legislature, but secured the co-operation of seven independent members. The opposition won 55 seats; however, the defection, amid allegations of bribery, of a newly elected deputy belonging to the Parti social-démocrate (PSD) gave the ruling MPLC a majority in the Assemblée. The opposition called for the defector to give up his seat, and the opening of the Assemblée nationale was delayed. Most of the opposition representatives boycotted the opening of the legislature, which was eventually held on 4 January 1999, and MINURCA troops were deployed to protect deputies from anti-Government protesters gathered outside. Patassé's decision to call on a close associate, the nominally independent erstwhile Minister of Finance, Anicet Georges Dologuélé, to form a new Government provoked public demonstrations and caused the opposition formally to withdraw from the legislature (the boycott lasted until March). Dologuélé announced the composition of a new coalition Council of Ministers in early January, but 10 opposition ministers immediately resigned in protest at the MPLC's alleged disregard for the results of the election. In mid-January Dologuélé announced the formation of another Council of Ministers, which included four members of the MDD, despite an earlier agreement made by the opposition not to accept posts in the new Government. The MDD leadership subsequently ordered its members to resign from their government positions; three of the four ministers did so, but Armand Sama, the nominated Minister of Town Planning, Housing and Public Buildings, defied his party's directives and retained his portfolio. In March two PSD deputies resigned from the party, announcing their intention to retain their seats in the Assemblée nationale as independents.

In February 1999 the UN Security Council extended MINURCA's mandate until mid-November in order that it might assist in preparations for, and the conduct of, the presidential election, which was scheduled to be held on 29 August. France was reported to have opposed an extension of the mandate, and in February the French contingent withdrew from MINURCA (as did the troops from Côte d'Ivoire in April). The UN Secretary-General, Kofi Annan, called on all factions in the CAR to co-operate in preparations for the presidential election. In particular, Annan criticized delays in the appointment of the independent electoral commission, the Commission électorale mixte indépendante (CEMI), the 27 members of which were finally approved in May. In July the Constitutional Court authorized 10 candidates to stand in the presidential election. President

Patassé was to seek re-election, while other candidates included two former Presidents, Gen. André Kolingba and David Dacko, two former Prime Ministers, Jean-Paul Ngoupandé and Enoch Derant Lakoué, as well as Prof. Abel Goumba, the opposition candidate in the 1993 presidential election. In the same month MINURCA supervised the destruction in Bangui of hundreds of weapons collected under the disarmament programme. In August, at the request of bilateral creditors and the UN, a 45-member body was established to supervise the activities of the CEMI, which comprised members of both opposition and pro-Patassé parties. In the event, the election was not held until 19 September, owing to organizational problems. The voting procedure was conducted in a peaceful manner, and international observers reported that, despite some attempts at fraud by a number of individuals, no widespread irregularities had been discovered. On 2 October the Constitutional Court announced that Patassé had been re-elected President, with 517,993 votes, equivalent to 51.6% of the total votes cast. Patassé's nearest rivals were Kolingba, who won 194,486 votes (19.4%), Dacko, who received 111,886 votes (11.2%), and Goumba, who obtained 60,778 votes (6.1%). The nine defeated candidates subsequently demanded the annulment of the election results, which they claimed had been manipulated. None the less, on 22 October Patassé was sworn in as President for a further six-year term. In early November recently reappointed Prime Minister Dologuélé announced the formation of a new Council of Ministers, which included members of parties loyal to Patassé as well as independents, three opposition representatives and two members of the armed forces. The Government stated that its main priorities were to improve human development in the CAR and to combat poverty; particular emphasis was also laid on the restructuring of the public sector and of the armed forces.

In October 1999 Kofi Annan requested that the UN Security Council authorize the gradual withdrawal of MINURCA from the CAR over a three-month period following the end of its mandate on 15 November. Annan highlighted the important role of MINURCA in guaranteeing stability in the post-electoral period, while he also noted that a delayed withdrawal would enable MINURCA units to complete a training course for local police recruits. In December the UN announced proposals to establish a Bureau de soutien à la consolidation de la paix en Centrafrique (BONUCA), in Bangui, the role of which would be to monitor developments in the CAR in the areas of politics, socio-economics, human rights and security issues, as well as to facilitate dialogue between political figures. BONUCA began its operation on the same day as the final withdrawal of MINURCA, 15 February 2000, with a mandate for a one-year period. In September 2000 BONUCA's mandate was extended until the end of 2001, and in September 2001, following continued unrest, it was extended for a further one-year period.

In April 2000 there was a ministerial reshuffle, which included the appointment of Antoine Grothe as the new Minister of Justice to replace Denis Wangao Kizmalé, who was transferred to the Ministry of the Civil Service and Employment. In the same month the Dologuélé Government survived a vote of 'no confidence', which was proposed by the opposition, in the Assemblée nationale. The Government was subject to further pressure in November, when thousands of civil servants staged a strike in support of their demands for the payment of at least 12 of the 30 months' salary arrears owed to them. The paralysis of public services exacerbated social tensions, and youths joined the protest movement, erecting barricades. Later that month 15 opposition parties united to demand the resignation of Patassé and to announce, in December, the formation of a co-ordination committee with the aim of organizing a peaceful transfer of power. In mid-December the security forces dispersed a mass demonstration, organized by trade unions and opposition political parties, arresting some 65 people, including four deputies of the Assemblée nationale. A subsequent sit-in planned by striking civil servants to protest against the arrests was banned by the Government. In April 2001 Patassé dismissed the Dologuélé administration. Martin Ziguélé was appointed as Prime Minister, and a new Government was formed.

On 28 May 2001 rebellious soldiers, thought to be supporters of Kolingba, attacked Patassé's official residence in an attempted coup. However, the insurgency was suppressed by troops loyal to Patassé, and at least 59 people were killed. Libya sent troops and helicopters, while a contingent of rebels from the Democratic Republic of the Congo (DRC) arrived to support the Patassé regime. Violence ensued throughout the country, with heavy fighting in Bangui resulting in some 300 deaths. Of an estimated 60,000–70,000 civilians who were reported to have fled the capital following the coup attempt, some 10,000 had returned by mid-July, according to aid agencies. In August 2002 Kolingba and 21 associates were sentenced to death *in absentia* for their alleged involvement in the coup; a further 500 defendants were reported to have received prison terms of 10–20 years.

In August 2001 the Council of Ministers was reshuffled; most notably, the Minister of National Defence, Jean-Jacques Démafouth, was replaced, following allegations regarding his involvement in the attempted coup in May (he was, however, acquitted of all charges at his trial in October 2002). In October 2001 Gen. Bozizé was dismissed from the post of Chief of Staff of the Armed Forces because of similar allegations. However, in early November violence erupted in Bangui between supporters of Bozizé and the presidential guard (supported by forces from Libya) after attempts were made to arrest Bozizé, at the request of a judicial commission of inquiry into the failed coup attempt. International and regional efforts to mediate between Bozizé and the CAR administration were unsuccessful, and later that month Bozizé fled to the southern town of Sarh in Chad, where he was granted refuge, with about 300 of his armed supporters. Tension reportedly increased between the CAR and Chad, as security forces pursued those loyal to Bozizé along the border between the two countries. At a meeting of the Communauté économique et monétaire de l'Afrique centrale (CEMAC) in Libreville, Gabon, on 6 December, a commission was created, chaired by President Omar Bongo of Gabon and also comprising Presidents Idriss Deby and Denis Sassou-Nguesso of Chad and the Republic of the Congo, respectively, to find a lasting solution to the crisis in the CAR. In late December the CAR judiciary abandoned legal proceedings against Bozizé, and in January 2002, during a meeting held in Chad, a government delegation invited Bozizé and his supporters to return to the CAR.

In April 2002, in consultation with political parties and development organizations, the Government announced a series of measures to reform public services and promote good governance. However, in July the Minister of State in charge of Finance and the Budget, Eric Sorongopé, was arrested on suspicion of embezzling government funds reportedly in excess of US $3m. More than 20 government officials were also detained on charges relating to the scandal. The subsequent withdrawal of IMF and World Bank representatives from Bangui also threatened to aggravate the ongoing budget crisis, and protests continued at the Government's failure to pay public-sector wages. In September BONUCA's mandate was extended until December 2003.

On 25 October 2002 the northern suburbs of Bangui were invaded by forces loyal to Bozizé (who had been granted asylum in France earlier in the month, in accordance with an agreement reached at a CEMAC summit aimed at defusing tension between the CAR and Chad—see below). After five days of heavy fighting, pro-Government forces, supported by Libyan troops and some 1,000 fighters from a DRC rebel grouping, the Mouvement pour la libération du Congo (MLC), succeeded in repelling Bozizé's insurgents. Initial reports indicated that some 28 people had been killed during the fighting. None the less, by December the Patassé Government had failed fully to suppress the forces allied to Bozizé, and the CAR was effectively divided between loyalist areas in the south and east and rebel-held northern regions between the Chadian border and Bangui. Throughout the conflict concerns were raised by the UN for the welfare of the approximately 150,000 refugees and displaced civilians positioned between Bozizé's forces and pursuing pro-Government troops. In November some 58 people were reported to have drowned while attempting to flee pro-Bozizé forces across a river.

In December 2002 the first contingent of a CEMAC peacekeeping force (eventually to number 350) arrived in Bangui, and in January 2003 Libyan forces were withdrawn. In December 2002 the CAR security forces dispersed residents of Bangui who had erected road-blocks in protest at the presence of rebel fighters from the DRC, accusing the MLC forces of mass rape and looting. Clashes were frequently claimed to have occurred between the regular CAR army and its allies, culminating in reports (denied by the CAR Government) of a massacre of MLC soldiers in December. In February 2003, however, MLC fighters began to withdraw from the CAR, in response to international pressure on the Patassé Government, which claimed that all 'misunderstandings' between fighters from the DRC and its own troops had been resolved.

Meanwhile, in November 2002 President Patassé pledged his support for a national dialogue in order to resolve the conflict in the CAR. However, co-ordination efforts undertaken by Bishop Paulin Pomodino were hampered by the refusal of both internal and exiled opposition leaders to agree on a date or location for the discussions. None the less, in late February 2003 President Patassé announced the establishment of a new commission to rehabilitate officials returning from exile, and in March the RDC and other opposition parties resumed their participation in the Assemblée nationale. A ministerial reshuffle was effected in January 2003.

On 15 March 2003 armed supporters of Bozizé entered Bangui, encountering little resistance from government troops. President Patassé, who had been attending a regional summit in Niger, was forced to withdraw to the Cameroonian capital, Yaoundé, after shots were fired at his aeroplane as it attempted to land at Bangui. Reports suggested that casualties during the coup had numbered no more than 15 people; following an outbreak of looting throughout Bangui, a curfew was imposed on 16 March. Following the surrender of the largely demoralized security forces in the capital, Bozizé declared himself Head of State, dissolved the Assemblée nationale and suspended the Constitution. Although the coup was condemned by the African Union, the UN, CEMAC, France and the USA, Bozizé insisted that his actions constituted only a 'temporary suspension of democracy' and that a new consensus government would be formed in consultation with the former opposition, human rights groups and development agencies. Following this announcement, Bozizé secured the approval of the Governments of Gabon and the Republic of the Congo at a meeting with the foreign ministers of those countries. France, meanwhile, deployed some 300 troops in Bangui in order to assist foreign nationals intending to leave the CAR. Bozizé also gained the support of opposition parties, which pledged to oppose any attempt by Patassé to return to power. In late March Abel Goumba, the leader of the Front patriotique pour le progrès, was appointed as Prime Minister, and a new, broad-based transitional Government was subsequently formed. Despite only receiving two positions in the new Council of Ministers, in mid-April the MLPC declared that it would adhere to the transitional arrangements decreed by Bozizé. Meanwhile, some 100,000 people were reported to have demonstrated in support of Bozizé in Bangui in late March. In early April Bozizé appointed a 63-member, advisory Conseil national de transition (including representatives of political parties, trade unions, religious organizations and human rights groups, among others) to assist him in exercising legislative power during the transitional period, which was to last 18–30 months.

In May 1997 the CAR recognized the administration of President Laurent Kabila in the DRC (formerly Zaire). In the same month the CAR and the DRC signed a mutual assistance pact, which provided for permanent consultation on internal security and defence. The pact also sought to guarantee border security; however, during mid-1997 armed soldiers of what had been the Zairean army were reported to be fleeing troops loyal to Kabila and crossing the Oubangui river into the CAR. In January 1999 there was a further influx of DRC civilians to the CAR. The refugees crossed the Oubangui river to escape the fighting between government and rebel soldiers, who were occupying the northern part of the DRC. In August the regional office of the UN High Commissioner for Refugees (UNHCR) estimated that the CAR was sheltering about 54,000 refugees from the DRC, Chad and Sudan. However, in December 2001 UNHCR announced plans to establish a new camp in the DRC for refugees who had fled the CAR. Following the attempted coup in the CAR in May 2001, UNHCR estimated that 23,000 people had escaped to the DRC; further movements were reported in the aftermath of the attempted coup of October 2002.

In late 1994 the CAR and Chad agreed to establish a bilateral security structure to ensure mutual border security. In 1994 the CAR also became the fifth member of the Lake Chad Basin Commission (see p. 340). Attacks on Chadian nationals resident in Bangui and on the Chadian contingent of the MISAB forces in late 1996 and early 1997 led the Chadian Government to issue a communiqué in March 1997 warning that further incidences of such aggression would not be tolerated. In June 1999 President Patassé issued an official apology to Chad following a disturbance at a market in Bangui in which five Chadian nationals were killed by members of the CAR security forces. In August the CAR Government agreed to pay compensation to the families of the victims. None the less, in December it was reported that some 1,500 Chadian refugees were preparing to leave the CAR, allegedly owing to fears for their security following the imminent departure of MINURCA forces. Relations between the CAR and Chad deteriorated when armed men, led by a Chadian rebel, raided southern Chad from the CAR on 29 and 31 December 2001; four people were killed during the raids. A further outbreak of violence in the border area was reported in April 2002, which resulted in at least one fatality. Despite pledges by both countries to increase co-operation, further clashes in August resulted in the deaths of 20 CAR soldiers. An emergency CEMAC summit took place later that month, chaired by the Gabonese President, Omar Bongo, and an observer mission was dispatched to examine the security situation along the common border. At the end of August the mission reported that, although tension remained high in the region, there was no concentration of troops on the border. The CAR's decision to appoint Col Martin Khoumtan-Madji (believed by the Chadian authorities to be an alias of Abdoulaye Miskine, a former senior Chadian rebel leader, who had been based in the CAR since 1998) as the head of a special unit in the CAR military, charged with securing the common border, further strained relations, as did Chad's reputed sponsorship of forces loyal to Bozizé. In early October a CEMAC summit in Libreville, Gabon, sought to defuse tensions between the two countries; in accordance with an accord reached at the summit, Bozizé and Khoumtan-Madji were subsequently granted asylum in France and Togo, respectively, and in December the first contingent of a CEMAC force was deployed in Bangui, initially to protect Patassé and later to monitor joint patrols of the border by Chadian and CAR troops. Meanwhile, at the end of October, following a coup attempt in the CAR (see above), Chad accused CAR security forces of the massacre of some 80–120 Chadian civilians in Bangui, a claim denied by the Patassé Government, which, in turn, accused Chad of planning the annexation of northern areas of the CAR. However, relations between the two countries subsequently began to improve somewhat, and in January 2003 the Governments of the CAR, Chad and Sudan announced their intention to establish a tripartite committee to oversee the security and stability of their joint borders. In February, following an official visit by President Deby to the CAR, many Chadian nationals were released from imprisonment in the CAR. Following Bozizé's assumption of power in the CAR in mid-March 2003, the Chadian Government dispatched some 400 troops to Bangui, apparently in order to reinforce CEMAC's peace-keeping force.

The CAR maintains amicable relations with Nigeria, and in June 1999 the two countries signed a bilateral trade agreement. The CAR is also a close ally of Libya, and in April 1999 joined the Libyan-sponsored Community of Sahel-Saharan States (see p. 339).

Government

Following the overthrow of President Ange-Félix Patassé in mid-March 2003, the Constitution of January 1995 was suspended, and the Assemblée nationale dissolved. The self-proclaimed Head of State, Gen. François Bozizé, appointed a 63-member Conseil national de transition, to assist him in exercising legislative power, and a transitional Government. The transitional period was to last 18–30 months.

For administrative purposes, the country is divided into 14 prefectures, two economic prefectures (Gribingui and Sangha), and one commune (Bangui). It is further divided into 67 sub-prefectures and two postes de contrôle administratif. At community level there are 65 communes urbaines, 102 communes rurales and seven communes d'élevage.

Defence

In August 2002 the armed forces numbered about 2,550 men (army 1,400, air force 150 and gendarmerie 1,000). Military service is selective and lasts for two years. The full withdrawal of the 1,345 troops of the United Nations Mission in the Central African Republic (MINURCA) was completed in mid-February 2000. In December 2002 the first contingent of a peace-keeping force (eventually to number some 350) from the Communauté économique et monétaire de l'Afrique centrale (CEMAC) arrived in Bangui; by early April 2003 272 CEMAC troops had been deployed in the CAR. Government expenditure on defence in 2001 was estimated at US $15m.

Economic Affairs

In 2001, according to estimates by the World Bank, the CAR's gross national income (GNI), measured at average 1999–2001 prices, was US $1,006m., equivalent to $270 per head (or $1,180 per head on an international purchasing-power parity basis). During 1990–2001, it was estimated, the population increased at an average annual rate of 2.3%, while gross domestic product (GDP) per head declined, in real terms, by an average of 0.6% per year. Overall GDP increased, in real terms, at an average annual rate of 1.6% in 1990–2001; growth in 2001 was 1.5%.

Agriculture (including hunting, forestry and fishing) contributed 54.7% of GDP in 2001. About 71.8% of the economically active population were employed in the sector in that year. The principal cash crops are coffee (which accounted for an estimated 10.2% of export earnings in 1999) and cotton (an estimated 10.4% of total exports in 1999). Livestock and tobacco are also exported. The major subsistence crops are cassava (manioc) and yams. The Government is encouraging the cultivation of horticultural produce for export. The exploitation of the country's large forest resources represents a significant source of export revenue (exports of wood accounted for an estimated 18.2% of the total in 1999); however, the full potential of this sector has yet to be realized, owing to the inadequacy of the transport infrastructure. Rare butterflies are also exported. Agricultural GDP increased at an average annual rate of 3.7% during 1990–2001; growth in 2001 was 4.0%.

Industry (including mining, manufacturing, construction and power) engaged 3.5% of the employed labour force in 1990 and provided 20.7% of GDP in 2001. Industrial GDP increased at an average annual rate of 1.3% in 1990–2001; growth in 2001 was 4.0%.

Mining and quarrying engaged a labour force estimated at between 40,000 and 80,000 in the late 1990s, and contributed 4.3% of GDP in 1999. The principal activity is the extraction of predominantly gem diamonds (exports of diamonds provided an estimated 45.9% of total export revenue in 1999). The introduction of gem-cutting facilities and the eradication of widespread 'black market' smuggling operations would substantially increase revenue from diamond mining. The reopening in 1997 of the Bangui diamond bourse, which had been established in 1996, was intended to increase revenue by levying a 10% sales tax on transactions. Deposits of gold are also exploited. The development of uranium resources may proceed. Reserves of iron ore, copper, tin and zinc have also been located. According to IMF estimates, the GDP of the mining sector increased at an average rate of 7.0% per year during 1992–94, but declined by an average of 4.6% per year in 1994–97, before increasing by 0.8% in 1998 and by 3.5% in 1999.

The manufacturing sector engaged 1.6% of the employed labour force in 1988. Manufacturing, which contributed 9.3% of GDP in 2000, is based upon the processing of primary products. In real terms, the GDP of the manufacturing sector increased at an average annual rate of 0.5% in 1990–2001; growth in 2001 was 3.9%.

In 1999, according to preliminary figures, 97.7% of electrical energy generated within the CAR was derived from the country's two hydroelectric power installations. Imports of petroleum products comprised an estimated 10.6% of the cost of merchandise imports in 1999.

Services engaged 15.5% of the employed labour force in 1988 and provided 24.6% of GDP in 2001. In real terms, the GDP of the services sector decreased at an average rate of 2.0% per year during 1990–2001; it declined by 5.2% in 2001.

In 1999 the CAR recorded a visible trade surplus of an estimated 13,000m. francs CFA, and there was a surplus of an estimated 18,300m. francs CFA on the current account of the balance of payments. In 1996 the principal source of imports was France (providing 39.5% of the total), while the principal markets for exports were Belgium-Luxembourg (accounting for 60.1% of the total) and France (30.9%). Other major trading partners in that year were Cameroon, Japan and the United Kingdom. The principal exports in 1999 were diamonds, wood products, cotton and coffee. The principal imports in 1996 were road vehicles, machinery, basic manufactures, cotton, mineral fuels and lubricants, chemical products and food.

In 1999 there was an estimated budget deficit of 58,900m. francs CFA (equivalent to 9.0% of GDP). At the end of 2000 the CAR's external debt was US $872.1m., of which $810.1m. was long-term public debt. In that year the cost of debt-servicing was equivalent to 9.0% of revenue from exports of goods and services. Consumer prices rose by 24.5% in 1994, following the devaluation of the currency, and by 19.2% in 1995. The annual rate of inflation averaged 3.8% in 1990–2000; consumer prices

decreased by an average of 2.3% in 1999, but increased by 3.0% in 2000. In 1995 7.6% of the labour force were unemployed.

The CAR is a member of the Central African organs of the Franc Zone (see p. 239) and of the Communauté economique des états de l'Afrique centrale (CEEAC, see p. 339).

The CAR's land-locked position, the inadequacy of the transport infrastructure and the country's vulnerability to adverse climatic conditions and to fluctuations in international prices for its main agricultural exports have impeded sustained economic growth. The January 1994 devaluation of the CFA franc improved export competitiveness, but also increased consumer prices. By late 1995 the Government was unable to control its mounting budget deficit and failed to pay the salaries of public-sector employees and the armed forces, thereby precipitating serious political instability during 1996–97, which, in turn, badly disrupted economic activity, destroying much of Bangui's industry. In mid-1998 the IMF approved a three-year Enhanced Structural Adjustment Facility (ESAF), valued at US $66m., to support the CAR's economic programme for 1998–2000. In order to normalize relations with external creditors, the CAR undertook to eliminate arrears on external payments in 1998 and to make regular payments on all external obligations. In September 1998 the 'Paris Club' of creditor nations rescheduled and reduced the CAR's external debt. Budget receipts improved significantly, and the IMF subsequently agreed to the early release of the second tranche of ESAF funding. However, economic growth in 2000 was lower than projected, partly owing to higher international petroleum prices and a doubling in petroleum transportation costs, following a temporary suspension of imports from the Democratic Republic of the Congo. The accumulation of external and domestic payments arrears aggravated social tensions and led to mass protests by public-sector workers from late 2000. In January 2001 the IMF approved an increase in the second annual allocation of funds to the CAR, thus allowing the Government to draw some $10m. to cover the shortfalls in state revenue. Value-added tax of 18% was introduced in the same month. Further unrest, following the attempted coups in May 2001 and October 2002, and the consequent disruption to road links with Cameroon, destabilized the domestic economy and adversely affected international trade. The corruption scandal of July 2002 (see above) also undermined creditor confidence in the CAR. The government was unable to complete its IMF-approved programme of structural and fiscal reforms, and the IMF and the World Bank suspended operations in the CAR. Despite forecasts of growth in 2002, government revenues continued to stagnate, and discussions with the IMF failed to reach agreement in March 2003, following the refusal of the USA to support further lending to the Patassé Government.

Education

Education is officially compulsory for eight years between six and 14 years of age. Primary education begins at the age of six and lasts for six years. Secondary education begins at the age of 12 and lasts for up to seven years, comprising a first cycle of four years and a second of three years. In 1998/99 an estimated 52.5% of children in the relevant age-group (62.7% of boys; 42.5% of girls) attended primary schools, while in 1991 secondary enrolment was equivalent to only 10% (boys 15%; girls 6%). Current expenditure by the Ministry of Education in 1995 totalled 8,820m. francs CFA, equivalent to 1.6% of gross national product. The provision of state-funded education was severely disrupted during the 1990s and early 2000s, owing to the inadequacy of the Government's resources.

Public Holidays

2003: 1 January (New Year), 29 March (Anniversary of death of Barthélemy Boganda), 21 April (Easter Monday), 1 May (May Day), 29 May (Ascension Day), 9 June (Whit Monday), 30 June (National Day of Prayer), 13 August (Independence Day), 15 August (Assumption), 1 November (All Saints' Day), 1 December (National Day), 25 December (Christmas).

2004: 1 January (New Year), 29 March (Anniversary of death of Barthélemy Boganda), 12 April (Easter Monday), 1 May (May Day), 20 May (Ascension Day), 31 May (Whit Monday), 30 June (National Day of Prayer), 13 August (Independence Day), 15 August (Assumption), 1 November (All Saints' Day), 1 December (National Day), 25 December (Christmas).

Weights and Measures

The metric system is officially in force.

Statistical Survey

Source (unless otherwise stated): Division des Statistiques et des Etudes Economiques, Ministère de l'Economie, du Plan et de la Coopération Internationale, Bangui.

Area and Population

AREA, POPULATION AND DENSITY

Area (sq km)	622,984*
Population (census results)	
8 December 1975.	2,054,610
8 December 1988	
Males	1,210,734
Females.	1,252,882
Total	2,463,616
Population (UN estimates at mid-year)†	
1999	3,649,000
2000	3,717,000
2001	3,782,000
Density (per sq km) at mid-2001	6.1

* 240,535 sq miles.

† Source: UN, *World Population Prospects: The 2000 Revision.*

PRINCIPAL TOWNS
(estimated population at mid-1994)

Bangui (capital) . .	524,000	Carnot. . . .	41,000
Berbérati	47,000	Bambari	41,000
Bouar	43,000	Bossangoa . . .	33,000

BIRTHS AND DEATHS
(UN estimates, annual averages)

	1985–90	1990–95	1995–2000
Birth rate (per 1,000)	42.0	41.1	39.6
Death rate (per 1,000)	18.1	17.9	19.1

Source: UN, *World Population Prospects: The 2000 Revision.*

1994: Registered live births 124,707 (birth rate 41.6 per 1,000); Registered deaths 50,063 (death rate 16.7 per 1,000) (Source: UN, *Population and Vital Statistics Report*).

Expectation of life (WHO estimates, years at birth): 42.7 (males 41.6; females 42.5) in 2001 (Source: WHO, *World Health Report*).

ECONOMICALLY ACTIVE POPULATION
(persons aged 6 years and over, 1988 census)

	Males	Females	Total
Agriculture, hunting, forestry and fishing	417,630	463,007	880,637
Mining and quarrying . . .	11,823	586	12,409
Manufacturing	16,096	1,250	17,346
Electricity, gas and water . . .	751	58	809
Construction	5,583	49	5,632
Trade, restaurants and hotels . .	37,435	54,563	91,998
Transport, storage and communications	6,601	150	6,751
Financing, insurance, real estate and business services . . .	505	147	652
Community, social and personal services	61,764	8,537	70,301
Activities not adequately defined .	7,042	4,627	11,669
Total employed.	565,230	532,974	1,098,204
Unemployed	66,624	22,144	88,768
Total labour force	631,854	555,118	1,186,972

Source: ILO.

Mid-2001 (estimates in '000): Agriculture, etc. 1,278; Total labour force 1,780 (Source: FAO).

Health and Welfare

KEY INDICATORS

Total fertility rate (children per woman, 2001)	5.0
Under-5 mortality rate (per 1,000 live births, 2001) . . .	180
HIV/AIDS (% of persons aged 15–49, 2001)	12.90
Physicians (per 1,000 head, 1995)	0.04
Hospital beds (per 1,000 head, 1991)	0.87
Health expenditure (2000): US $ per head (PPP) . . .	37
Health expenditure (2000): % of GDP . . .	2.9
Health expenditure (2000): public (% of total) . . .	48.4
Access to water (% of persons, 2000).	60
Access to sanitation (% of persons, 2000)	31
Human Development Index (2000): ranking	165
Human Development Index (2000): value	0.375

For sources and definitions, see explanatory note on p. vi.

Agriculture

PRINCIPAL CROPS
('000 metric tons)

	1999	2000	2001
Rice (paddy)	21.0	23.1	25.3
Maize	95	101	107
Millet*	12	12	12
Sorghum	45.0	47.6	50.3
Cassava (Manioc)	559.0	560.4	561.7
Taro (Coco yam)*	100	100	100
Yams*	360	360	360
Sugar cane	91.0	90*	90*
Pulses*	30	31	31
Groundnuts (in shell) . . .	110.0	115.9	121.9
Oil palm fruit*	40	40	40
Sesame seed	36.0	37.7	32.4
Melonseed	23	23*	23*
Cottonseed	21.4	11.7	14.2*
Pumpkins, squash and gourds† .	19.7	20.0	20.0
Other vegetables*	58	59	59
Bananas*	115	115	118
Plantains*	82	82	83
Oranges*	23	23	24
Pineapples*	13.8	14.0	14.0
Other fruits*	20.2	20.5	20.6
Coffee (green)	11.3	12.9	12.3†

* FAO estimate(s).

† Unofficial figure(s).

Source: FAO.

LIVESTOCK
('000 head, year ending September)

	1999	2000	2001*
Cattle	3,060	3,129	3,100
Goats	2,472	2,614	2,600
Sheep	211	222	220
Pigs	649	678	680
Chickens	4,040	4,211	4,200

* FAO estimates.

Source: FAO.

LIVESTOCK PRODUCTS
('000 metric tons)

	1998	1999	2000
Beef and veal*	51	51	60
Mutton and lamb.	1.2	1.2	1.3†
Goat meat	7.7†	7.8†	10.0*
Pig meat	11.9†	12.0†	12.0*
Poultry meat	2.7	2.6	3.0*
Other meat*	8.4	8.6	8.8
Cows' milk†	60	62	62
Cattle hides (fresh)	7.5	7.5	8.0†
Goatskins (fresh)	1	1	1†
Hen eggs	1.4	1.4	1.4
Honey†	12	13	13

* Unofficial figure(s).
† FAO estimate(s).

Source: FAO.

Forestry

ROUNDWOOD REMOVALS
('000 cubic metres, excluding bark)

	1999	2000	2001
Sawlogs, veneer logs and logs for sleepers	553	703	750
Other industrial wood*	308	308	308
Fuel wood	2,000	2,000	2,000*
Total	2,861	3,011	3,058

* FAO estimate(s).

Source: FAO.

SAWNWOOD PRODUCTION
('000 cubic metres, including railway sleepers)

	1999	2000	2001
Total (all broadleaved)	79	102	150

Source: FAO.

Fishing

('000 metric tons, live weight)

	1998	1999	2000
Capture*	14.5	15.0	15.0
Aquaculture	0.1	0.1	0.1
Total catch (freshwater fishes)	14.6	15.1	15.1

* FAO estimates.

Source: FAO, *Yearbook of Fishery Statistics*.

Mining

	1999	2000	2001
Gold (kg, metal content of ore)	41	12	20
Diamonds ('000 carats)	431.1*	461.0*	480.0

* Unofficial figure.

Source: US Geological Survey.

Industry

SELECTED PRODUCTS

	1996	1997	1998
Beer ('000 hectolitres)	156.4	208.6	218.8
Soft drinks and syrups ('000 hectolitres)	60.6	93.2	46.8
Cigarettes (million packets)	7.8	—	—
Palm oil ('000 metric tons)	n.a.	2.6	3.3
Groundnut oil ('000 metric tons)	n.a.	2.3	2.7
Plywood ('000 cubic metres)	1.5	1.4	1.0
Electric energy (million kWh)	98.7	100.7	114.7

Source: IMF, *Central African Republic: Statistical Annex* (August 2000).

Raw sugar ('000 metric tons): 10 in 1998 (unofficial figure); 10 in 1999; 13 in 2000; 13 in 2001 (FAO estimate) (Source: FAO).

Finance

CURRENCY AND EXCHANGE RATES

Monetary Units
100 centimes = 1 franc de la Coopération financière en Afrique centrale (CFA)

Sterling, Dollar and Euro Equivalents (31 December 2002)
£1 sterling = 1,088.17 francs CFA
US $1 = 625.50 francs CFA
€1 = 655.96 francs CFA
10,000 francs CFA = £9.918 = $15.987 = €15.245

Average Exchange Rate (francs CFA per US $)
2000   711.98
2001   733.04
2002   696.99

Note: The exchange rate of 1 French franc = 50 francs CFA, established in 1948, remained in force until January 1994, when the CFA franc was devalued by 50%, with the exchange rate adjusted to 1 French franc = 100 francs CFA. This relationship to French currency remained in effect with the introduction of the euro on 1 January 1999. From that date, accordingly, a fixed exchange rate of €1 = 655.957 francs CFA has been in operation.

BUDGET
(million francs CFA)

Revenue	1997*	1998*	1999*
Tax revenue	42,400	50,300	52,500
Taxes on income and profits	8,700	7,900	11,900
Domestic taxes on goods and services	16,500	17,200	18,000
Taxes on international trade	17,100	25,200	22,700
Import duties and taxes	15,400	18,000	15,400
Other receipts	2,600	6,100	7,200
Total	45,000	56,300	59,700

Expenditure	1997	1998	1999*
Current expenditure	51,200	50,200	56,900
Wages and salaries	26,600	26,500	27,000
Other goods and services	12,900	11,300	13,200
Transfers and subsidies	3,800	4,100	7,600
Interest payments	7,800	8,300	9,100
Capital expenditure	30,700	59,300	59,100
Sub-total	81,900	109,500	116,100
Adjustment for payments arrears†	−21,100	69,800	2,600
Total	60,800	179,300	118,700

* Estimates.
† Minus sign indicates an increase in arrears.

Source: IMF, *Central African Republic: Statistical Annex* (August 2000).

INTERNATIONAL RESERVES
(US $ million at 31 December)

	2000	2001	2002
Gold*	3.03	3.09	3.81
IMF special drawing rights	—	0.01	0.01
Reserve position in IMF	0.15	0.14	0.16
Foreign exchange	133.11	118.60	123.06
Total	136.29	121.84	127.04

* National valuation of reserves based on market-related prices.

Source: IMF, *International Financial Statistics*.

MONEY SUPPLY
(million francs CFA at 31 December)

	2000	2001	2002
Currency outside banks	88,624	82,566	77,431
Demand deposits at commercial and development banks	13,206	16,584	17,306
Total money (incl. others)	101,831	99,151	94,739

Source: IMF, *International Financial Statistics*.

COST OF LIVING
(Consumer Price Index for Bangui; base: 1990 = 100)

	1998	1999	2000
Food	144.2	139.8	145.2
Fuel and light	120.9	119.8	125.5
Clothing	148.1	155.3	150.3
All items (incl. others)*	145.0	141.6	145.9

* Excluding rent.

Source: ILO.

NATIONAL ACCOUNTS
(IMF estimates, million francs CFA at current prices)

Expenditure on the Gross Domestic Product*

	1997	1998	1999
Government final consumption expenditure	63,800	72,200	74,800
Private final consumption expenditure	494,800	521,600	529,800
Increase in stocks }	57,300	84,300	94,000
Gross fixed capital formation. }			
Total domestic expenditure	615,900	678,100	698,600
Exports of goods and services	114,000	100,400	109,500
Less Imports of goods and services	145,700	156,000	155,500
GDP in purchasers' values	584,300	622,600	652,500
GDP at constant 1985 prices	411,600	430,700	445,300

* Figures are rounded to the nearest 100 million francs CFA.

Source: IMF, *Central African Republic: Statistical Annex* (August 2000).

Gross Domestic Product by Economic Activity*

	1997	1998	1999
Agriculture, hunting, forestry and fishing	283,200	306,900	326,800
Mining and quarrying	33,300	23,500	26,200
Manufacturing	51,600	52,600	54,500
Electricity, gas and water	4,100	4,500	4,600
Construction	26,700	28,000	29,500
Trade, restaurants and hotels	75,500	75,600	78,800
Transport, storage and communications	14,800	14,800	15,400
Other private services	28,100	28,200	28,300
Government services	43,200	46,000	46,800
GDP at factor cost	550,600	580,200	611,900
Indirect taxes	33,600	42,400	40,700
GDP in purchasers' values	584,300	622,600	652,500

* Figures are rounded to the nearest 100 million francs CFA.

Source: IMF, *Central African Republic: Statistical Annex* (August 2000).

BALANCE OF PAYMENTS
('000 million francs CFA)

	1997	1998	1999*
Exports of goods	90.8	92.4	98.9
Imports of goods	−81.7	−93.9	−85.9
Trade balance	9.1	−1.5	13.0
Services and other income (net)	−31.0	−37.0	−53.7
Balance on goods, services and income	−21.9	−38.5	−40.7
Private unrequited transfers (net)	−5.7	−5.5	−5.2
Public unrequited transfers (net)	37.3	65.1	64.2
Current balance	9.7	21.1	18.3
Long-term capital (net)	−9.6	−6.7	−7.8
Short-term capital (net)	−29.4	−27.8	−16.7
Net errors and omissions	2.9	−19.9	−7.1
Overall balance	−26.4	−33.3	−13.3

* Estimates.

Source: La Zone Franc, *Rapport Annuel 1999*.

External Trade

PRINCIPAL COMMODITIES
(distribution by SITC, US $'000)

Imports c.i.f.	1994	1995	1996
Food and live animals	24,635	27,587	12,585
Cereals and cereal preparations	17,183	15,010	5,915
Flour of wheat or meslin	13,990	7,999	3,442
Beverages and tobacco	14,238	12,128	8,977
Tobacco and tobacco manufactures	12,216	9,244	6,709
Unmanufactured tobacco and tobacco refuse	4,417	8,510	3,632
Cigarettes	7,799	734	3,077
Crude materials (inedible) except fuels	10,353	27,184	25,177
Cork and wood	97	2,466	4,365
Coniferous sawlogs and veneer logs	90	1,921	3,901
Textile fibres (excl. wool tops) and waste	9,361	22,443	19,132
Cotton	7,951	20,547	17,501
Mineral fuels, lubricants, etc.	11,606	23,063	14,594
Petroleum, petroleum products, etc.	11,374	22,755	14,550
Refined petroleum products	11,223	22,715	14,447
Motor spirit (gasoline) and other light oils	3,223	8,364	4,756
Chemicals and related products	25,037	20,721	14,056
Medicinal and pharmaceutical products	16,759	9,522	6,416
Medicaments	15,912	8,300	5,960
Basic manufactures	21,404	29,201	19,118
Non-ferrous metals	4,685	3,548	1,812
Machinery and transport equipment	36,668	112,122	67,289
Machinery specialized for particular industries	2,809	26,240	7,912
Civil engineering and contractors' plant and equipment	876	23,753	4,939
Construction and mining machinery	460	20,437	3,685
Self-propelled bulldozers, angledozers and levellers	366	14,872	472
General industrial machinery, equipment and parts	5,969	9,441	5,042
Telecommunications and sound equipment	3,131	12,119	4,777
Television and radio transmitters, etc.	983	6,170	2,496
Road vehicles and parts*	16,456	49,770	33,043
Passenger motor cars (excl. buses)	2,948	8,935	5,473
Motor vehicles for goods transport and special purposes	4,847	17,160	13,314
Goods vehicles (lorries and trucks)	4,500	11,006	11,387
Parts and accessories for cars, buses, lorries, etc.*	4,204	9,836	7,056
Other transport equipment*	557	1,963	5,771
Aircraft, associated equipment and parts*	548	1,791	5,771
Miscellaneous manufactured articles	7,040	12,019	10,386
Armoured fighting vehicles, arms of war and ammunition	17	6	7,152
Tanks and other armoured fighting vehicles, motorized, and parts	—	—	6,830
Total (incl. others)	154,162	265,499	179,942

* Excluding tyres, engines and electrical parts.

Exports f.o.b.	1994	1995	1996
Food and live animals . . .	2,605	4,142	1,295
Crude materials (inedible)			
except fuels	42,858	59,829	57,334
Cork and wood	1,299	2,790	4,756
Coniferous sawlogs and veneer			
logs	142	1,736	3,883
Textile fibres (excl. wool tops) and			
waste	7,531	20,351	22,379
Cotton	7,528	20,309	22,379
Crude fertilizers and crude			
minerals (excl. coal, petroleum			
and precious stones) . .	33,545	35,998	29,437
Industrial diamonds (sorted). .	33,545	35,998	29,435
Basic manufactures	31,114	41,776	40,107
Non-metallic mineral			
manufactures	30,839	39,887	39,725
Diamonds (excl. sorted industrial			
diamonds), unmounted. . .	30,836	39,880	39,715
Sorted non-industrial			
diamonds, rough or simply			
worked	29,877	39,812	39,663
Machinery and transport			
equipment.	2,239	10,543	8,663
Road vehicles and parts* . .	2,008	9,259	7,119
Parts and accessories for cars,			
buses, lorries, etc.* . . .	1,237	3,351	4,141
Armoured fighting vehicles,			
arms of war and ammunition	692	—	6,992
Tanks and other armoured fighting			
vehicles, motorized, and parts .	—	—	6,829
Total (incl. others)	81,451	119,522	115,128

* Excluding tyres, engines and electrical parts.

Source: UN, *International Trade Statistics Yearbook*.

PRINCIPAL TRADING PARTNERS
(US $'000)*

Imports c.i.f.	1994	1995	1996
Belgium-Luxembourg	2,675	6,589	2,805
Cameroon	8,448	12,880	7,103
Congo, Dem. Repub.. . . .	1,386	1,841	1,938
Congo, Repub.	18,047	4,738	3,371
France (incl. Monaco) . . .	59,149	90,739	71,137
Germany	3,213	7,626	2,792
Italy	1,332	2,921	1,674
Japan	8,586	52,303	15,676
Netherlands	1,685	2,815	1,845
United Kingdom	1,437	1,563	3,148
USA	2,447	4,871	2,971
Total (incl. others)	154,162	265,499	179,942

Exports f.o.b.	1994	1995	1996
Belgium-Luxembourg . . .	64,906	75,487	69,192
Cameroon	226	1,825	1,184
Congo, Dem. Repub.. . .	437	1,917	1,904
Congo, Repub.	1,012	1,374	850
France (incl. Monaco) . .	9,862	30,207	35,556
Spain	1,154	4	—
United Kingdom	270	2,069	3,996
Total (incl. others)	81,451	119,522	115,128

* Imports by country of production; exports by country of consumption.

Source: UN, *International Trade Statistics Yearbook*.

Transport

ROAD TRAFFIC
(motor vehicles in use)

	1993	1994	1995
Passenger cars	10,400	11,900	8,900
Commercial vehicles	2,400	2,800	3,500

Source: UN, *Statistical Yearbook*.

INLAND WATERWAYS TRAFFIC—INTERNATIONAL SHIPPING
(metric tons)

	1996	1997	1998
Freight unloaded at Bangui . .	60,311	56,206	57,513
Freight loaded at Bangui . . .	5,348	5,907	12,524
Total	63,659	62,113	70,037

Source: Banque des états de l'Afrique centrale, *Etudes et Statistiques*.

CIVIL AVIATION
(traffic on scheduled services)*

	1996	1997	1998
Kilometres flown (million) . . .	3	3	3
Passengers carried ('000) . . .	75	86	91
Passenger-km (million) . . .	225	242	258
Total ton-km (million)	37	38	38

* Including an apportionment of the traffic of Air Afrique.

Source: UN, *Statistical Yearbook*.

Tourism

	1997	1998	1999
Tourist arrivals ('000)	21	7	10
Tourism receipts (US $ million) .	5	6	n.a.

Source: World Tourism Organization.

Communications Media

	1999	2000	2001
Television receivers ('000 in use) .	20	21	n.a.
Facsimile machines (subscribers) .	316	n.a.	n.a.
Telephones ('000 main lines in use)	9.9	9.5	10.0
Mobile cellular telephones ('000			
subscribers).	4.2	5.0	11.0
Personal computers ('000 in use) .	5	6	7
Internet users ('000)	1.0	1.5	2.0

Source: International Telecommunication Union.

Radio receivers: 283,000 in use in 1997 (Source: UNESCO, *Statistical Yearbook*).

Daily newspapers: 3 in 1996 (average circulation 6,000) (Source: UNESCO, *Statistical Yearbook*).

Non-daily newspapers: 1 in 1995 (average circulation 2,000) (Source: UNESCO, *Statistical Yearbook*).

Education

(1990/91, unless otherwise indicated)

	Schools	Teachers	Pupils
Pre-primary	162	572*	15,734
Primary	930	4,004	308,409
Secondary:			
general	46† }	1,005 {	46,989
vocational	n.a. }		1,862
Higher.	n.a.	136	2,823

* 1987/88 figure.
† State-funded general secondary schools.

1991/92: Primary pupils 277,961; General secondary pupils 42,263; Vocational secondary pupils 1,477; University teachers 139; University students 2,923.

1998: Primary teachers 3,125; Primary pupils 284,398; University teachers 300; University students 6,229 (Sources: UNESCO, *Statistical Yearbook*; UNESCO Institute for Statistics).

Adult literacy rate (UNESCO estimates): 46.7% (males 59.7%; females 34.9%) in 2000 (Source: UN Development Programme, *Human Development Report*).

Directory

The Constitution

Following the overthrow of President Ange-Félix Patassé in mid-March 2003, the Constitution of January 1995 was suspended. A 63-member Conseil national de transition and a transitional Government were to draft a new document and prepare for general elections. The transitional period was to last 18–30 months.

The Government

HEAD OF STATE

President of the Republic and Minister of National Defence, the Restructuring of the Armed Forces and Disarmament: Gen. FRANÇOIS BOZIZÉ (assumed power 16 March 2003).

COUNCIL OF MINISTERS
(April 2003)

Following a *coup d'état* in March 2003, a broad-based transitional Government was formed.

Prime Minister and Minister of the Economy, Finance, the Budget, Planning and International Co-operation: Prof. ABEL GOUMBA.

Minister of Foreign and Francophone Affairs, and Regional Integration: KARIM MECKASSOUA.

Minister of Justice, Human Rights and Good Governance: FAUSTIN NGBONDOU.

Minister of the Interior and Public Security: Lt-Col MICHEL PAULIN BONDÉBOLI.

Minister of Territorial Administration: MARCEL MALONGA.

Minister of Mines, Energy and Hydraulics: Lt SYLVAIN NDOUTINGÏ.

Minister of Trade, Industry and the Promotion of the Private Sector: YACINTHE WODOBODE.

Minister of National Education, Literacy, Higher Education and Research: HUBERT LALA-BEVARA.

Minister of Public Health and Population: Prof. NESTOR MAMADOU NALI.

Minister of the Civil Service, Labour and Social Security: JACQUES BOTI.

Minister of Posts and Telecommunications, in charge of New Technologies: IDRISS SALAO.

Minister of Communication, National Reconciliation and Democratic and Civic Culture: Capt. PARFAIT MBAYE.

Minister of Equipment and Transport: POCKOMANDJI SONY.

Minister of the Reconstruction of Public Buildings, Urban Planning and Housing: ABRAHAM NGOTO.

Minister of the Environment, Sustainable Development and Social Economy: JOSEPH KITICKI-KOUAMBA.

Minister of Development and Animal Husbandry: DENIS KOSSI-BELLA.

Minister of Water Resources, Forests, Hunting and Fishing: MAURICE YONDO.

Minister of Modernization and Agricultural Development: PIERRE GBIANZA.

Minister of Tourism Development and Artisanal Industries: BRUNO DACKO.

Minister of Youth, Sports, Culture and the Arts: LÉON SALAM.

Minister of Families, Social Affairs and National Solidarity: LÉA DOUMTA-KOYASSOUM.

Minister in charge of the Secretariat-General of the Government and Relations with the Conseil national de transition: ZARAMBAUD ASSINGAMBI.

Minister-delegate of Finance and the Budget: DANIEL N'DITIFEÏ.

Minister-delegate of Planning and International Co-operation: PHILIPPE WARADAGUE.

Secretary of State for Disarmament: Col JULES BERNARD OUANDE.

Secretary of State for Foreign and Francophone Affairs, and Regional Integration: CHARLES WENEZOUI.

Secretary of State for Education, in charge of Higher Education: LAZARE YAGAO-NGAMA.

MINISTRIES

All ministries are based in Bangui.

Office of the President: Palais de la Renaissance, Bangui; tel. 61-46-63; internet www.socatel.cf/patasse.htm.

Ministry of the Civil Service, Labour and Social Security: Bangui; tel. 61-01-44.

Ministry of Communication, National Reconciliation and Democratic and Civic Culture: BP 940, Bangui; tel. 61-27-66; fax 61-59-85.

Ministry of the Economy, Finance, the Budget, Planning and International Co-operation: BP 912, Bangui; tel. 61-70-55; fax 61-63-98.

Ministry of Equipment and Transport: BP 941, Bangui.

Ministry of Foreign and Francophone Affairs, and Regional Integration: Bangui; tel. 61-35-55; fax 61-20-76.

Ministry of Justice, Human Rights and Good Governance: Bangui; tel. 61-16-44.

Ministry of Mines, Energy and Hydraulics: Bangui; tel. 61-20-54; fax 61-60-76.

Ministry of National Defence, the Restructuring of the Armed Forces and Disarmament: Bangui; tel. 61-46-11.

Ministry of National Education, Literacy, Higher Education and Research: BP 791, Bangui.

Ministry of Public Health and Population: Bangui; tel. 61-29-01.

President and Legislature

Following the overthrow of President Ange-Félix Patassé in mid-March 2003, Gen. François Bozizé assumed power and dissolved the Assemblée nationale. A 63-member Conseil national de transition was to prepare for new general elections within 18–30 months.

Political Organizations

Alliance pour la démocratie et le progrès (ADP): Bangui; f. 1991; progressive; Leader FRANÇOIS PEHOUA; Nat. Sec. TCHAPKA BRÉDÉ.

Conseil démocratique des partis politiques de l'opposition (CODEPO): Bangui; f. 1995; political alliance led by AUGUSTE BOUKANGA; comprises the following parties.

> **Mouvement démocratique pour la renaissance et l'évolution de la République Centrafricaine (MDRERC):** Bangui; Chair. JOSEPH BENDOUNGA; Sec.-Gen. LÉON SEBOU.

> **Parti républicain centrafricain (PRC):** Bangui.

Convention nationale (CN): Bangui; f. 1991; Leader DAVID GALIAMBO.

Forum civique (FC): Bangui; Leader Gen. TIMOTHÉE MALENDOMA.

Forum démocratique pour la modernité (FODEM): Bangui; f. 1998; Pres. CHARLES MASSI.

Front patriotique pour le progrès (FPP): BP 259, Bangui; tel. 61-52-23; fax 61-10-93; f. 1972; aims to promote political education and debate; Leader Prof. ABEL GOUMBA.

G11: Bangui; f. 1997; alliance of 11 opposition parties led by Prof. ABEL GOUMBA; prin. mems: ADP, FPP, MDD and RDC.

Mouvement d'évolution sociale de l'Afrique noire (MESAN): Bangui; f. 1949; comprises two factions, led respectively by PROSPER LAVODRAMA and JOSEPH NGBANGADIBO.

Mouvement pour la démocratie et le développement (MDD): Bangui; f. 1993; aims to safeguard national unity and the equitable distribution of national wealth; Leader DAVID DACKO.

Mouvement pour la démocratie, l'indépendance et le progrès social (MDI-PS): BP 1404, Bangui; tel. 61-18-21; e-mail mdicentrafrique@chez.com; internet www.chez.com/mdicentrafrique; Sec.-Gen. DANIEL NDITIFEI BOYSEMBE.

Mouvement pour la libération du peuple centrafricain (MLPC): Bangui; f. 1979; leading party in govt since Oct. 1993; Pres. Ange-Félix Patassé.

Parti africain de développement (PAD): Bangui.

Parti libéral-démocrate (PLD): Bangui; Leader Nestor Kombo-Naguemon.

Parti social-démocrate (PSD): BP 543, Bangui; tel. 61-59-02; fax 61-58-44; Leader Enoch Derant Lakoué.

Parti pour l'union nationale (PUN): Bangui; Leader Jean-Paul Ngoupandé.

Rassemblement démocratique centrafricain (RDC): BP 503, Bangui; tel. 61-53-75; f. 1987; sole legal political party 1987–91; Leader Gen. André Kolingba.

Rassemblement populaire pour la reconstruction de la Centrafrique (RPRC): Bangui; Leader Gen. François Bozize.

Union démocratique pour le renouveau—Fini Kodro (UDR—FK): Bangui.

Union des forces acquises à la paix (UFAP): Bangui; f. 1998; opposition alliance, including political parties, trade unions and human rights orgs; weakened by withdrawals in Nov. 1999; Pres. Paul Bellét.

Union nationale démocratique du peuple centrafricain (UNDPC): Bangui; f. 1998; Islamic fundamentalist; based in southeast CAR; Leader Mahamat Saleh.

Union pour la république (UPR): Bangui.

Diplomatic Representation

EMBASSIES IN THE CENTRAL AFRICAN REPUBLIC

Cameroon: rue du Languedoc, BP 935, Bangui; tel. 61-18-57; fax 61-16-87; Chargé d'affaires a.i. Gilbert Noula.

Chad: ave Valérie Giscard d'Estaing, BP 461, Bangui; tel. 61-46-77; Ambassador Maintine Djoumbe.

China, People's Republic: Bangui; tel. 61-36-28; fax 61-37-41; Ambassador Wang Sifa.

Congo, Democratic Republic: BP 989, Bangui; tel. 61-33-44; Ambassador Embe Isea Mbambe.

Congo, Republic: BP 1414, Bangui; tel. 61-18-77; fax 61-03-09; Ambassador Eric Epény Obondzo.

Egypt: BP 1422, Bangui; tel. 61-46-88; fax 61-35-45; Ambassador Azmy Khalifah.

France: blvd du Général de Gaulle, BP 884, Bangui; tel. 61-30-00; fax 61-74-04; Ambassador Dominique Boché.

Holy See: ave Boganda, BP 1447, Bangui; tel. 61-26-54; fax 61-03-71; e-mail nonrca@intnet.cf; Apostolic Nuncio Most Rev. Joseph Chennoth (Titular Archbishop of Milevum).

Japan: ave Barthélemy Boganda, BP 1367, Bangui; tel. 61-16-10; fax 61-06-68; e-mail japonamb@intnet.cf; Ambassador Yoichi Hayashi.

Libya: Bangui; tel. 61-46-62; fax 61-12-79; Ambassador (vacant).

Nigeria: ave des Martyrs, BP 1010, Bangui; tel. 61-40-97; fax 61-12-79; Chargé d'affaires a.i. Ayodele J. Bakare.

Russia: rue Fourreau-lamy, BP 1405, Bangui; tel. 61-03-11; fax 61-56-45; e-mail ruscons@intent.cf; Ambassador Boris Krasnikov.

Sudan: ave de l'Indépendance, BP 1351, Bangui; tel. 61-38-21; Ambassador Tijani Salih Fadayl.

USA: ave David Dacko, BP 924, Bangui; tel. 61-02-00; fax 61-44-94; Ambassador Mattie R. Sharpless.

Judicial System

Supreme Court: BP 926, Bangui; tel. 61-41-33; highest judicial organ; acts as a Court of Cassation in civil and penal cases and as Court of Appeal in administrative cases; comprises four chambers: constitutional, judicial, administrative and financial; Pres. Edouard Franck.

There is also a Court of Appeal, a Criminal Court, 16 tribunaux de grande instance, 37 tribunaux d'instance, six labour tribunals and a permanent military tribunal. A High Court of Justice was established under the 1986 Constitution, with jurisdiction in all cases of crimes against state security, including high treason by the President of the Republic. The 1995 Constitution (which was suspended

by Gen. François Bozizé in mid-March 2003) established a Constitutional Court, the judges of which were to be appointed by the President.

Religion

It is estimated that 24% of the population hold animist beliefs, 50% are Christians (25% Roman Catholic, 25% Protestant) and 15% are Muslims. There is no official state religion.

CHRISTIANITY

The Roman Catholic Church

The Central African Republic comprises one archdiocese and seven dioceses. There were an estimated 718,196 adherents at 31 December 2000.

Bishops' Conference

Conférence Episcopale Centrafricaine, BP 1518, Bangui; tel. 50-24-84; fax 61-46-92.
f. 1982; Pres. Rt Rev Paulin Pomodimo (Bishop of Bossangoa).
Archbishop of Bangui: Most Rev. Joachim N'Dayen, Archevêché, BP 1518, Bangui; tel. 61-31-48; fax 61-46-92; e-mail cent_afr@intnet.cf.

Protestant Church

Eglise Protestante de Bangui: Bangui.

The Press

The independent press is highly regulated. Independent publications must hold a trading licence and prove their status as a commercial enterprise. They must also have proof that they fulfil taxation requirements. There is little press activity outside Bangui.

DAILIES

E le Songo: Bangui; f. 1986.

Le Citoyen: BP 974, Bangui; tel. 61-89-16; independent; Publr Maka Gbossokotto; circ. 3,000.

Le Novateur: BP 913, Bangui; tel. 61-48-84; fax 61-87-03; e-mail ccea_ln@intnet.cf; independent; Publr Marcel Mokwapi; circ. 750.

PERIODICALS

Bangui Match: Bangui; monthly.

Centrafrique-Presse: BP 1058, Bangui; tel. and fax 61-39-57; e-mail redaction@centrafrique-presse.com; internet www.centrafrique-presse.com; weekly; Publr Prosper N'Douba.

Le Courrier Rural: BP 850, Bangui; publ. by Chambre d'Agriculture.

Le Délit d'Opinion: Bangui; independent.

Demain le Monde: BP 650, Bangui; tel. 61-23-15; f. 1985; fortnightly; independent; Editor-in-Chief Nganam Nöel.

Journal Officiel de la République Centrafricaine: BP 739, Bangui; f. 1974; fortnightly; economic data; Dir-Gen. Gabriel Agba.

Nations Nouvelles: BP 965, Bangui; publ. by Organisation Commune Africaine et Mauricienne; politics and current affairs.

Le Peuple: BP 569, Bangui; tel. 61-76-34; f. 1995; weekly; Editor-in-Chief Vermond Tchendo.

Le Progrès: BP 154, Bangui; tel. 61-70-26; f. 1991; monthly; Editor-in-Chief Belibanga Clément; circ. 2,000.

Le Rassemblement: Bangui; organ of the RDC; Editor-in-Chief Mathias Gonevo Reapogo.

La Tortue Déchainée: Bangui; independent; satirical; Publr Maka Gbossokotto.

PRESS ASSOCIATION

Groupement des Editeurs de la Presse privée indépendante de Centrafrique (GEPAIC): Bangui; Pres. Maka Gbossokoto.

NEWS AGENCIES

Agence Centrafricaine de Presse (ACAP): BP 40, Bangui; tel. 61-10-88; f. 1974; Gen. Man. Victor Deto Teteya.

Informatsionnoye Telegrafnoye Agentstvo Rossii—Telegrafnoye Agentstvo Suverennykh Stran (ITAR—TASS) (Russia) and Agence France-Presse are represented in the CAR.

Publisher

Government Publishing House

Imprimerie Centrafricaine: BP 329, Bangui; tel. 61-00-33; f. 1974; Dir-Gen. PIERRE SALAMATE-KOILET.

Broadcasting and Communications

TELECOMMUNICATIONS

Société Centrafricaine de Télécommunications (SOCATEL): BP 939, Bangui; tel. 61-74-69; fax 61-44-49; e-mail postmaster@ intnet.cf; internet www.socatel.intnet.cf; f. 1990; 60% state-owned; 40% owned by France Cables et Radio; Dir-Gen. JOSEPH BOYKOTA-ZOUKETIA.

CARATEL Entreprises: BP 2439, Bangui; tel. 61-44-10; fax 61-44-49; e-mail telecomp@intnet.cf; internet www.socatel.intnet.cf/carat.html; mobile cellular telephone operator.

BROADCASTING

Radiodiffusion-Télévision Centrafricaine: BP 940, Bangui; tel. 61-25-88; f. 1958 as Radiodiffusion Nationale Centrafricaine; govt-controlled; broadcasts in French and Sango; Man. Dir PAUL SERVICE.

Radio Rurale: community stations operating in Bouar, Nola, Berbérati and Bambari.

Finance

(cap. = capital; res = reserves; dep. = deposits; m. = million; amounts in francs CFA)

BANKING

Central Bank

Banque des Etats de l'Afrique Centrale (BEAC): BP 851, Bangui; tel. 61-24-00; fax 61-19-95; HQ in Yaoundé, Cameroon; f. 1973; bank of issue for mem. states of the Communauté économique et monétaire de l'Afrique centrale (CEMAC, fmrly Union douanière et économique de l'Afrique centrale), comprising Cameroon, the Central African Repub., Chad, the Repub. of the Congo, Equatorial Guinea and Gabon; res 177,417m., total assets 2,034,793m. (Dec. 2001); Gov. JEAN-FÉLIX MAMALEPOT; Dir in CAR JONAS YOLOGAZA.

Commercial Banks

Banque Internationale pour le Centrafrique (BICA): place de la République, BP 910, Bangui; tel. 61-00-42; fax 61-61-36; e-mail bica@intnet.cf; internet www.socatel.intnet.cf/bica.html; f. 1946; present name adopted 1996; 35% owned by Banque Belgolaise SA, Brussels, 15% by group of African investors (COFIPA), 40.4% by private citizens, 9.6% by Govt; cap. 1,500m., res 1,670m., total assets 21,867m. (Dec. 1999); Pres. MARTIN BABA; Dir-Gen. JEAN-PAUL LE CALM; 1 br.

Banque Populaire Maroco-Centrafricaine (BPMC): rue Guerillot, BP 844, Bangui; tel. 61-12-90; fax 61-62-30; e-mail bpmc@ intnet.cf; f. 1991; 50% owned by Banque Centrale Populaire (Morocco), 12.5% owned by Banque Marocaine du Commerce Extérieur, 50% owned by Banque Centrale Populaire du Maroc and 37.5% state-owned; cap. 2,061m., res 2,292m., total assets 8,775m. (Dec. 1999); Dir-Gen. MOHAMED BENZIANI.

Commerciale Bank Centrafrique (CBCA): rue de Brazza, BP 839, Bangui; tel. 61-29-90; fax 61-34-54; e-mail cbca@intnet.cf; f. 1962; 41% owned by Groupe Fotso; 10% state-owned; cap. 1,000m., res 515.5m., total assets 19,259.8m. (Dec. 2000); Pres. SERGE PSIMHIS; Dir-Gen. THÉODORE DABANGA; 1 br.

Development Bank

Banque de Developpement des Etats de l'Afrique Centrale: see Franc Zone (see p. 239).

Investment Bank

Banque Centrafricaine d'Investissement (BCI): Bangui; tel. 61-00-64; f. 1976; 34.8% state-owned; cap. 1,000m. Pres. ALPHONSE KONGOLO; Man. Dir GÉRARD SAMBO.

Financial Institutions

Caisse Autonome d'Amortissement de la République Centrafricaine: Bangui; tel. 61-53-60; fax 61-21-82; management of state funds; Dir-Gen. JOSEPH PINGAMA.

Caisse Nationale d'Epargne (CNE): Office national des postes et de l'épargne, Bangui; tel. 61-22-96; fax 61-78-80; Pres. SIMONE BODEMO-MODOYANGBA; Dir-Gen. AMBROISE DAOUDA; Man. ANTOINE BEKOUANEBANDI.

Bankers' Association

Association Professionnelle des Banques: Bangui.

Development Agencies

Agence Française de Développement: rue de la Moyenne corniche, BP 817, Bangui; tel. 61-03-06; fax 61-22-40; e-mail afd@intnet.cf; internet www.afd.fr; administers economic aid and finances specific development projects; Man. FRANÇOIS GIOVALUCCHI.

Mission Française de Coopération et d'Action Culturelle: BP 934, Bangui; tel. 61-63-34; fax 61-28-24; administers bilateral aid from France; Dir HERVÉ CRONEL.

INSURANCE

Agence Centrafricaine d'Assurances (ACA): BP 512, Bangui; tel. 61-06-23; f. 1956; Dir Mme R. CERBELLAUD.

Assureurs Conseils Centrafricains Faugère et Jutheau: rue de la Kouanga, BP 743, Bangui; tel. 61-19-33; fax 61-44-70; f. 1968; Dir JEAN CLAUDE ROY.

Entreprise d'Etat d'Assurances et de Réassurances (SIRIRI): Bangui; tel. 61-36-55; f. 1972; Pres. EMMANUEL DOKOUNA; Dir-Gen. JEAN-MARIE YOLLOT.

Legendre, A. & Cie: rue de la Victoire, BP 896, Bangui; Pres. and Dir-Gen. ANDRÉ LEGENDRE.

Union Centrafricaine d'Assurances et de Réassurances: BP 343, Bangui; tel. 61-36-66; fax 61-33-40; e-mail ucardg@intnet.cf; Dir-Gen. ALAIN BLANCHARD.

Trade and Industry

DEVELOPMENT ORGANIZATION

Société Centrafricaine de Développement Agricole (SOCADA): ave David Dacko, BP 997, Bangui; tel. 61-30-33; f. 1964; reorg. 1980; 75% state-owned, 25% Cie Française pour le Développement des Fibres Textiles (France); purchasing, transport and marketing of cotton, cotton-ginning, production of cottonseed oil and groundnut oil; Pres. MAURICE METHOT.

INDUSTRIAL AND TRADE ASSOCIATIONS

Agence de Développement de la Zone Caféière (ADECAF): BP 1935, Bangui; tel. 61-47-30; coffee producers' asscn; assists coffee marketing co-operatives; Dir-Gen. J. J. NIMIZIAMBI.

Agence Nationale pour le Développement de l'Elevage (ANDE): BP 1509, Bangui; tel. 61-69-60; fax 61-50-83; assists with development of livestock.

Caisse de Stabilisation et de Péréquation des Produits Agricoles (CAISTAB): BP 76, Bangui; tel. 61-08-00; supervises marketing and pricing of agricultural produce; Dir-Gen. M. BOUNANDELE-KOUMBA.

Fédération Nationale des Eleveurs Centrafricains (FNEC): ave des Martyrs, BP 588, Bangui; tel. 61-23-97; fax 61-47-24.

Office National des Forêts (ONF): BP 915, Bangui; tel. 61-38-27; f. 1969; reafforestation, development of forest resources; Dir-Gen. C. D. SONGUET.

CHAMBERS OF COMMERCE

Chambre d'Agriculture, d'Elevage, des Eaux, Forêts, Chasses, Pêches et Tourisme: BP 850, Bangui; tel. 61-76-76; f. 1964; Sec.-Gen. MOÏSE DENISSIO.

Chambre de Commerce, d'Industrie, des Mines et de l'Artisanat (CCIMA): BP 813, Bangui; tel. 61-16-68; fax 61-35-70; internet www.admin.cf/ccima; Pres. RIGOBERT YOMBO; Sec. GERTRUDE ZOUTA-YAMANDJA.

EMPLOYERS' ORGANIZATION

Union Nationale du Patronat Centrafricain (UNPC): BP 2180, Bangui; tel. and fax 61-42-10; e-mail unpc-rca@intnet.cf; Pres. FAUSTIN ZAGUI.

UTILITIES

Electricity

Société Energie de Centrafrique (ENERCA): ave de l'Indépendance, BP 880, Bangui; tel. 61-20-22; fax 61-54-43; e-mail enerca@intnet.cf; f. 1967; state-owned; privatization pending; production and distribution of electric energy.

Water

Société Nationale des Eaux (SNE): BP 1838, Bangui; tel. 61-20-28; f. 1975; state-owned co responsible for supply, treatment and distribution of water; Dir-Gen. FRANÇOIS FARRA-FROND.

TRADE UNIONS

There are five officially recognized trade-union federations, including:

Organization of Free Public-Sector Unions: Bangui.

Union Syndicale des Travailleurs de la Centrafrique (USTC): Bangui; affiliated with the International Confed. of Free Trade Unions; Sec.-Gen. THÉOPHILE SONNY KOLLE.

Transport

RAILWAYS

There are no railways at present. There are long-term plans to connect Bangui to the Transcameroon railway. A line linking Sudan's Darfur region with the CAR's Vakaga province has also been proposed.

ROADS

In 1999 there were an estimated 23,810 km of roads. Only about 3% of the total network is paved. Eight main routes serve Bangui, and those that are surfaced are toll roads. Both the total road length and the condition of the roads are inadequate for current requirements. In 1997 the European Union provided 32,500m. francs CFA to improve infrastructure in the CAR. In September a vast road improvement scheme was launched, concentrating initially on roads to the south and north-west of Bangui. The CAR is linked with Cameroon by the Transafrican Lagos–Mombasa highway. Roads are frequently impassable in the rainy season (July–October).

Bureau d'Affrètement Routier Centrafricain (BARC): BP 523, Bangui; tel. 61-20-55; fax 61-37-44; Dir-Gen. J. M. LAGUEREMA-YA-DINGUIN.

Compagnie Nationale des Transports Routiers (CNTR): Bangui; tel. 61-46-44; state-owned; Dir-Gen. GEORGES YABADA.

INLAND WATERWAYS

There are some 2,800 km of navigable waterways along two main water courses. The first, formed by the Congo river and its tributary the Oubangui, can accommodate convoys of barges (of up to 800 metric tons load) between Bangui and Brazzaville and Pointe-Noire in the Republic of the Congo, except during the dry season, when the route is impassable. The second is the river Sangha, also a tributary of the Congo, on which traffic is again seasonal. There are two ports, at Bangui and Salo, on the rivers Oubangui and Sangha respectively. Bangui port has a handling capacity of 350,000 tons, with 350 m of wharfs and 24,000 sq m of warehousing. Efforts are being made to develop the Sangha upstream from Salo to increase the transportation of timber from this area, and to develop Nola as a timber port.

Agence Centrafricaine des Communications Fluviales (ACCF): BP 822, Bangui; tel. 61-31-10; f. 1969; state-owned; supervises development of inland waterways transport system; Man. Dir JUSTIN NDJAPOU.

Société Centrafricaine de Transports Fluviaux (SOCA-TRAF): BP 1445, Bangui; tel. and fax 61-43-15; e-mail socatraf@intnet.cf; f. 1980; 51% owned by ACCF; Man. Dir FRANÇOIS TOUSSAINT.

CIVIL AVIATION

The international airport is at Bangui-M'Poko. There are also 37 small airports for internal services.

Agence pour la sécurité de la navigation aérienne en Afrique et Madagascar (ASECNA): BP 828, Bangui; tel. 61-33-80; fax 61-49-18; internet www.asecna.com.

Centrafrican Airlines (CAL): Aéroport Bangui-M'Poko; f. 1999; privately-owned; internal flights.

Mondial Air Fret (MAF): BP 1883, Bangui; tel. 61-14-58; fax 61-62-62; f. 1998; Dir THÉOPHILE SONNY COLE.

Tourism

Although tourism remains relatively undeveloped, the Central African Republic possesses considerable scenic attractions in its waterfalls, forests and wildlife. Tourist arrivals were estimated at 10,000 in 1999, compared with only 1,599 in 1990. In 1998 receipts from tourism were estimated at US $6m.

Office National Centrafricain du Tourisme (OCATOUR): BP 655, Bangui; tel. 61-45-66.

CHAD

Introductory Survey

Location, Climate, Language, Religion, Flag, Capital

The Republic of Chad is a land-locked country in north central Africa, bordered to the north by Libya, to the south by the Central African Republic, to the west by Niger, Nigeria and Cameroon, and to the east by Sudan. The climate is hot and arid in the northern desert regions of the Sahara but very wet, with annual rainfall of 5,000 mm (197 ins) in the south. The official languages are French and Arabic, and various African languages are also widely spoken. Almost one-half of the population are Muslims, living in the north. About 30% of the population are Christians. Most of the remainder follow animist beliefs. The national flag (proportions 2 by 3) has three equal vertical stripes, of dark blue, yellow and red. The capital is N'Djamena.

Recent History

Formerly a province of French Equatorial Africa, Chad became an autonomous state within the French Community in November 1958, and achieved full independence on 11 August 1960. However, the sparsely populated northern territory of Borkou-Ennedi-Tibesti, accounting for some 47% of the area of Chad, remained under French military control until 1965. The first President of the independent republic was François (later Ngarta) Tombalbaye, a southerner and leader of the Parti progressiste tchadien (PPT). In 1962 the PPT was declared the sole political party. In 1965 a full-scale insurgency began, concentrated mainly in the north. The Muslims of northern Chad have historically been in conflict with their black southern compatriots, who are mainly Christians or animists. The banned Front de libération nationale du Tchad (FROLINAT, founded in Sudan in 1966) assumed leadership of the revolt. The rebellion was partially quelled in 1968, following French military intervention.

In 1973 several prominent figures in the regime, including Gen. Félix Malloum, the Army Chief of Staff, were imprisoned on charges of conspiracy. Also in that year Libyan troops occupied the so-called 'Aozou strip', an apparently mineral-rich region of some 114,000 sq km (44,000 sq miles) in northern Chad, over which Libya claimed sovereignty.

In April 1975 Tombalbaye was killed in a military coup. Malloum was released and appointed President, at the head of a Conseil militaire suprême, and the Mouvement national pour la révolution culturelle et sociale, which had succeeded the PPT in 1973, was dissolved. FROLINAT remained in opposition, receiving clandestine military assistance from Libya. In early 1978 FROLINAT seized control of a large area of the north before its advance was halted by French military intervention. In August, after negotiations with Malloum, Hissène Habré, a former leader of FROLINAT, was appointed Prime Minister. However, disagreements developed between Habré (a Muslim from the north) and Malloum over the status of Muslims in Chad.

In February 1979 armed conflict broke out between Habré's Forces armées du nord (FAN) and the government armed forces, the Forces armées tchadiennes (FAT). The FAN gained control of the capital, N'Djamena, and in March Malloum resigned and fled the country. In April a provisional Government was formed, comprising representatives of several groups, including FROLINAT, the FAN and the FAT, but sporadic fighting continued. In August 11 factions formed a Gouvernement d'union nationale de transition (GUNT), with Goukouni Oueddei, the leader of FROLINAT, as President and Lt-Col (later Gen.) Wadal Abdelkader Kamougué as Vice-President.

Goukouni's authority was undermined by continual disagreements with Habré, and in March 1980 fighting resumed. In October Libyan forces intervened directly in the hostilities, in support of Goukouni. By December Habré had been defeated, and a Libyan force of some 15,000 men was established in the country. In November 1981 Libyan troops were withdrawn, and a peace-keeping force was installed under the auspices of the Organization of African Unity (OAU—now the African Union, see p. 130). The conflict intensified, however, and in June 1982 Habré's forces captured N'Djamena. Habré was formally inaug-

urated as President in October, and Goukouni formed a rival administration in Bardai.

In January 1983 some members of the FAT joined Habré's FAN to form the Forces armées nationales tchadiennes (FANT). In August Goukouni's rebel forces, with Libyan support, captured the northern administrative centre of Faya-Largeau. France dispatched a further 3,000 troops to Chad and imposed an 'interdiction line' to separate the warring factions. In September it was announced that fighting had ceased.

In June 1984, in an attempt to consolidate his political support in the south, Habré replaced the FROLINAT-FAN movement with a new organization, the Union nationale pour l'indépendance et la révolution (UNIR). In July a more broadly-based Government was formed. In September Libya and France agreed to withdraw their troops from Chad. By mid-November all French troops had left the country; however, it was reported that some 3,000 Libyan troops remained in Chad.

By the end of 1985 hostilities in southern Chad had ceased. In February 1986, however, GUNT forces, with support from Libya, attacked government positions south of the 'interdiction line'. Habré appealed for French military assistance, and France agreed to establish a defensive air-strike force (designated Opération Epervier) in N'Djamena. The USA also provided additional military aid.

In March 1986 several former opponents of the Habré administration were given government posts. The GUNT, meanwhile, began to disintegrate. Kamougué resigned as Goukouni's Vice-President in June, and in February 1987 declared his support for Habré. In August 1986, meanwhile, Acheikh Ibn Oumar's Conseil démocratique révolutionnaire (CDR) also withdrew support from Goukouni. In October, following armed clashes between the Libyan-supported CDR and his own Forces armées populaires (FAP), Goukouni declared himself willing to seek a reconciliation with Habré.

In December 1986 clashes began in the Tibesti region between Libyan forces and the (now pro-Habré) FAP. FANT troops moved into northern Chad and, with increased logistical support from France and the USA, forced Libya to withdraw from Faya-Largeau. In May 1987 Libyan troops retreated to the 'Aozou strip'. In August FANT troops attacked and occupied the town of Aozou, which was, however, recaptured by Libyan forces three weeks later. In September the FANT made an incursion into southern Libya. An OAU-brokered cease-fire took effect, but sporadic fighting continued, and the Chadian Government claimed that Libyan aircraft were repeatedly violating Chadian airspace.

Following negotiations between the Ministers of Foreign Affairs of Chad and Libya in Gabon in July 1988, agreement was reached, in principle, to restore diplomatic relations. However, the issues of the sovereignty of the Aozou region, the fate of Libyan prisoners of war in Chad, and the security of common borders remained unresolved. In October 1988 diplomatic relations were resumed, and the September 1987 cease-fire agreement was reaffirmed, although Chad continued to accuse Libya of violating the conditions of the agreement.

The cohesion of the GUNT was undermined in 1988 by a dispute between Goukouni and Acheikh Ibn Oumar regarding its leadership. Several former opposition groups transferred their support to Habré, and in November, following negotiations with UNIR, Acheikh Ibn Oumar and his supporters returned to Chad. He was appointed Minister of Foreign Affairs in March 1989. In April Mahamat Itno, the Minister of the Interior and Territorial Administration, was arrested following the discovery of an alleged plot to overthrow Habré. Idriss Deby, a former Commander-in-Chief of the Armed Forces, who was also implicated in the attempted coup, fled to Sudan, where he established a new opposition group.

In June 1989 the Government accused Libya of planning a military offensive against Chad, with the complicity of Sudan. In July the Libyan leader, Col Muammar al-Qaddafi, and Habré met for the first time, in Mali, but their negotiations were inconclusive. On 31 August, however, Acheikh Ibn Oumar met his Libyan counterpart in Algiers, where they signed an outline peace accord. Under its terms, if a negotiated settlement to the dispute over sovereignty of the 'Aozou strip' was not achieved within one year, the issue was to be submitted to the International Court of Justice (ICJ) for adjudication. Provision was made for the withdrawal of all armed forces from the Aozou region and the release of all prisoners of war. Military engagements between FANT troops and pro-Libyan forces were, none the less, reported in late 1989. No agreement was reached at discussions between Habré and Qaddafi in Morocco in August 1990, and the territorial dispute was referred for adjudication by the ICJ.

In December 1989 a new Constitution, which granted greater powers to the President, was approved by a reported 99.94% of voters in a national referendum. In endorsing the document, the electorate also approved Habré in the office of President for a further seven-year term. The new Constitution confirmed UNIR as the sole legal party, and provided for the establishment of an elected legislature. Elections to this 123-seat Assemblée nationale followed in July 1990.

In March 1990 the Forces patriotiques du salut, led by Deby and subsequently styled the Mouvement patriotique du salut (MPS), invaded Chad from Sudan. Although government forces successfully countered this attack, the MPS launched a second invasion in November, during which a number of FANT troops transferred allegiance to Deby. France reiterated its policy of non-interference in Chad's internal affairs. The MPS subsequently advanced rapidly towards N'Djamena, and on 30 November Habré and his associates fled the country. Deby arrived in N'Djamena two days later. The Assemblée nationale was dissolved, and the Constitution suspended, pending the proposed introduction of a multi-party political system. A provisional Conseil d'Etat was installed, with Deby as interim Head of State. Several members of the former Habré regime, including Acheikh Ibn Oumar, were included in the new Government.

Following Deby's accession to power, many political organizations that had opposed Habré announced their support for the MPS. Deby announced that the FANT was to be restructured to form a smaller national army, the Armée nationale tchadienne (ANT). The French Government responded favourably to the new administration, and the Libyan and Sudanese Governments declared their support for the MPS, undertaking not to allow forces hostile to Deby to operate on their territory. Deby, however, reiterated Chad's claim to the Aozou region, which remained under consideration by the ICJ.

In March 1991 the Government promulgated a National Charter to operate for a 30-month transitional period, confirming Deby's appointment as President, Head of State and Chairman of the MPS, and replacing the provisional Conseil d'Etat with a Council of Ministers (headed by Jean Bawoyeu Alingué) and a 31-member legislative Conseil de la République. In May Deby announced that a national conference would be convened in May 1992 to prepare a new Constitution. Interim arrangements permitting the registration of political parties would enter into force in January 1992.

In September 1991 forces loyal to Habré apparently entered Chad from Niger and attacked military garrisons in northern Chad. In December some 3,000 pro-Habré rebels of the Libya-based Mouvement pour la démocratie et le développement (MDD) attacked towns in the Lake Chad region. Following expressions of concern by France (which had dispatched reinforcements for the Epervier contingent) at reported abuses of human rights, including the summary execution of a number of rebels, the Deby administration reiterated its commitment to the democratic process, and declared a general amnesty for political prisoners.

Meanwhile, in October 1991 disaffected troops attacked an arsenal at N'Djamena airport in an attempt to seize power; some 40 people were killed in the ensuing fighting. Several officials, including the Minister of the Interior, were arrested on charges connected with the incident, which some analysts believed had been provoked by discontent within the Hadjerai ethnic group at its perceived under-representation in government. France reaffirmed its support for the MPS and announced that an additional 300 troops would be dispatched to Chad. Following the coup attempt, Chad abrogated a recent co-operation agreement with Libya, on the grounds that the sovereignty of the Aozou region remained in dispute. In February 1992 a further *coup d'état* was attempted by members of the armed forces.

In April 1992 the MDD claimed that more than 40 of its activists, including its leader, Goukouni Guët, had been arrested in Nigeria, extradited to Chad, and subsequently imprisoned or executed. In May MDD rebels launched a new offensive in the Lake Chad region. In June an agreement between the Government and the Comité de sursaut national pour la paix et la démocratie (CSNPD), the dissident faction of the armed forces responsible for the abortive coup attempt in February, provided for the release of detained members of the CSNPD and their reintegration into the ANT. Later in June the Government announced that it had forestalled a further coup attempt. In June an agreement was signed in Libreville, Gabon, providing for a cessation of hostilities between government forces and the MDD.

In May 1992 a number of amendments to the National Charter were adopted, and Joseph Yodoyman, a member of an opposition movement, the Alliance nationale pour la démocratie et le développement (ANDD), was appointed Prime Minister. A new Council of Ministers included, for the first time, members of several opposition parties and human rights organizations.

In July 1992 Yodoyman was expelled from the ANDD, and another member of the ANDD subsequently left the Government. A reorganization of the Council of Ministers took place in August, after three representatives of human rights organizations resigned from the Government. In September an agreement was reached by the Government and an opposition group based in Sudan, the Front national du Tchad (FNT), which granted the FNT the status of a political party. Later that month the Government signed further peace agreements with the MDD, which had resumed activities in the Lake Chad region, and with the CSNPD, which had engaged in clashes with government forces in Doba, in the south, in August. In October, however, the MDD was reported to have begun a renewed offensive against government forces at Bagassola, near Lake Chad, and at the end of that month the MDD declared the peace agreement to be invalid, alleging that the Government was preparing to resume hostilities.

In October 1992 public-sector workers of the Union des syndicats du Tchad (UST) organized a one-month general strike in support of demands for higher salaries and the convening of the national conference on Chad's political future, which had been postponed. Two ministers resigned in protest at the Government's subsequent suspension of the activities of the UST. The general strike was extended for a further month, but concluded in January 1993, following the revocation of the ban on the UST.

The national conference was finally convened in January 1993. In April the conference, which had been accorded sovereign status, adopted a Transitional Charter, elected Dr Fidel Moungar, hitherto Minister of National and Higher Education, as Prime Minister, and established a 57-member interim legislature, the Conseil supérieur de la transition (CST). The leader of the Rassemblement pour la démocratie et le progrès (RDP), Lol Mahamat Choua—who had briefly served as President in 1979, was elected Chairman of the CST. Under the terms of the Transitional Charter, Deby was to remain Head of State and Commander-in-Chief of the Armed Forces for a period of one year (with provision for one extension), while a Transitional Government, under the supervision of the CST, was to implement economic, political and social programmes as drafted by the conference.

Meanwhile, in January 1993 troops loyal to Habré attempted a coup; several of the rebels were subsequently arrested. In February government troops, who were engaged in conflict with the MDD in the Lake Chad region, clashed with members of the Nigerien armed forces, after attacking rebel bases in Niger. Also in February, following renewed military engagements between ANT and CSNPD forces in southern Chad, opposition groups claimed that the Republican Guard (a special unit of the ANT, under Deby's direct supervision) had massacred civilians in the Goré region, in retaliation for local support for the CSNPD; by March some 15,000 people had fled to the Central African Republic (CAR). In May the Government confirmed the findings of a commission of inquiry that its forces had carried out massacres of civilians in southern Chad earlier that year. Moungar announced that members of the armed forces who were implicated in the violence had been arrested, that military units in the region were to be replaced, and that a judicial investigation was to be instituted.

In mid-1993 the Government announced that the ANT and other security forces were to be reorganized, in response to widespread public concern at increasing violence involving the armed and security forces. In August, however, armed men killed some 82 civilians in the southern prefecture of Ouaddaï. Shortly afterwards it was reported that some 41 people had been killed when a demonstration by residents of N'Djamena originating from Ouaddaï, in protest at the massacre, was suppressed by the Republican Guard. The CST subsequently accused the Government of exceeding its powers by deploying the Republican Guard to disperse the demonstration and by imposing a nation-wide curfew in response to the unrest.

In October 1993 the CST approved a motion expressing 'no confidence' in the Moungar administration, apparently initiated by supporters of Deby. Moungar resigned, and in November the CST elected Kassire Delwa Koumakoye, hitherto Minister of Justice, Keeper of the Seals, as Prime Minister. In December teachers and other government employees began strike action in protest at the Government's failure to pay salary arrears. The 50% devaluation of the CFA franc, in January 1994, precipitated further unrest.

Meanwhile, rebel activities by the so-called 'politico-military' movements continued. In January 1994 members of the FNT (who were to have been integrated into the ANT following the peace agreement with the Government) attacked a military garrison at Abéché, in the north-east. In February negotiations between the Chadian authorities and the CSNPD, with mediation by the CAR, failed to secure a lasting peace, and there further clashes were reported in southern Chad in late March.

In February 1994 the ICJ ruled in favour of Chad in the issue of the sovereignty of the Aozou region. In May 1994 the Governments of Chad and Libya issued a joint statement confirming that the withdrawal of Libyan troops from the region had been completed as scheduled. In June a co-operation agreement consolidated relations between the two countries

In March 1994 an Institutional Committee submitted constitutional recommendations, which included provisions for the introduction of a five-year presidential term, the installation of a bicameral legislature and a Constitutional Court, and the establishment of a decentralized administrative structure. In April the CST extended the transitional period by one year. A new electoral timetable was adopted, whereby the Government was obliged to provide funds for the organization of the elections, to reach an agreement with the UST in order to end industrial unrest, and, by June, to adopt an electoral code, to establish a national reconciliation council (to negotiate a peace settlement with the rebel movements), and to appoint electoral and human rights commissions. Government efforts to negotiate a settlement with the UST were impeded by strike action by public-sector workers in mid-1994, when agreement was reached on limited salary increases and the payment of arrears. In May Deby effected a comprehensive reorganization of the Government.

In August 1994 the Chadian authorities and the CSNPD signed a cease-fire agreement, providing for the recognition of the CSNPD as a legal political organization and the integration of its forces into the ANT. Later that month government troops were reported to have killed 26 civilians in the south, in reprisal for attacks by members of another rebel faction, the Forces armées pour la République fédérale (FARF). In October the Government and the FNT negotiated a peace agreement, which was, however, subsequently repudiated by the leader of the FNT. In November a number of former members of the CSNPD were integrated into the ANT.

In September 1994 it was reported that the Minister of Mines and Energy, Lt-Col Mahamat Garfa (who had recently been dismissed as Chief of Army Staff), had fled N'Djamena with substantial government funds, and, together with some 600 members of the ANT, had joined rebel forces of the Conseil national de redressement du Tchad in eastern Chad; Garfa subsequently established a co-ordination of eight rebel groups operative in eastern Chad from abroad, the Alliance nationale de la résistance (ANR), while remaining in exile himself. In October Choua was replaced as Chairman of the CST by a member of the MPS, Mahamat Bachar Ghadaia. Choua subsequently accused the Government of human rights violations, including the assassination of two prominent members of the RDP.

Deby officially announced in November 1994 that the process of democratic transition would conclude on 9 April 1995, following presidential and legislative elections. In December 1994 Deby declared a general amnesty for political prisoners and opposition members in exile, notably excluding Habré. In the same month an independent national electoral commission was established. In January 1995 the CST adopted a new electoral code and subsequently approved the draft Constitution, which had been amended in accordance with recommendations made by a national conference in August 1994.

In late March 1995 the CST extended the transitional period for a further year and amended the National Charter to debar the incumbent Prime Minister from contesting the forthcoming presidential election or from belonging to a political party. In April the Court of Appeal annulled the results of an electoral census conducted in February, citing procedural irregularities. In the same month the CST, which had criticized the Government's lack of progress in organizing democratic elections, voted to remove Koumakoye from the premiership and subsequently elected Djimasta Koibla, a prominent member of the Union pour la démocratie et la République (UDR), as Prime Minister.

In May 1995 human rights organizations claimed that members of the ANT had perpetrated violations of human rights against civilians in retaliation for rebel attacks. In June security forces raided the premises of an independent newspaper, *N'Djamena-Hebdo*, which had published an article criticizing the activities of the ANT.

In August 1995 the Chairman and other members of the Executive Bureau of the CST resigned, following accusations of the misappropriation of funds. In late August security forces raided the home of Saleh Kebzabo, the leader of the opposition Union nationale pour le développement et le renouveau (UNDR). In protest, an informal alliance of opposition parties, to which the UNDR belonged, announced that it was to suspend participation in the CST and demanded the resignation of the head of the security forces. In September Kebzabo was arrested and charged with endangering state security by associating with rebel groups; he was released on bail later that month.

In November 1995 the Government and the MDD agreed to a cease-fire, an exchange of prisoners and the integration of a number of MDD troops into the ANT. Reconciliation discussions between the Chadian Government and its opponents were convened in Franceville, Gabon, in January 1996. In March the Government and 13 opposition parties signed a cease-fire agreement. Although it appeared that the majority of the armed movements had rejected the agreement, the conclusion of the Franceville accord allowed the electoral programme to proceed. Although several opposition parties, particularly the southern-based organizations that favoured the adoption of a federal system of government, urged their supporters to reject the draft Constitution (which enshrined a unitary state), the new Constitution was endorsed by 63.5% of votes cast at a national referendum on 31 March 1996.

Deby was among 15 candidates authorized to contest the presidential election. Deby secured 43.9% of the votes cast in the first round of voting, which took place on 2 June, followed by Kamougué, who had contested the election on behalf of the Union pour le renouveau et la démocratie (URD), with 12.4%, and Kebzabo (8.5%). Deby and Kamougué proceeded to a second round of voting on 3 July. Although most of the unsuccessful first-round candidates urged a boycott of the vote, Kebzabo announced his support for Deby, who won a decisive victory, receiving 69.1% of votes cast. The rate of participation by voters exceeded 75% of the registered electorate. Deby was inaugurated as President on 8 August, and subsequently reappointed Koibla as Prime Minister. Koibla named an interim Council of Ministers, which included several former opposition members, notably Kebzabo as Minister of Foreign Affairs.

In September 1996 the Front national du Tchad renové (FNTR), led by Mahamat Moussa Abdelchaf and comprising former members of the FNT, threatened to abandon plans for peace negotiations with the Chadian authorities, after claiming that government forces had launched attacks against its positions in eastern Chad. The Government and the MDD signed a peace agreement in Niger in the same month.

Legislative elections, which had been postponed twice in late 1996, took place in two rounds on 5 January and 23 February 1997, contested by some 30 political organizations. Preliminary results were announced in early March, but were challenged by both the MPS and opposition parties. Later that month the Court of Appeal announced the final results, in which a further eight seats were allocated to the MPS. The MPS thus secured an absolute majority in the 125-member Assemblée nationale, with 65 seats, while the URD won 29 seats and the UNDR 15. The new Assemblée nationale was inaugurated on 4 April, and in May Kamougué was elected as its President, with the support of the MPS and the UNDR, as well as his own URD. Koibla's transitional Government resigned in the same month. Nassour

Guélengdouksia Ouaïdou, hitherto Secretary-General at the Presidency, was named as the new Prime Minister. His Government retained Kebzabo, as Minister of State for Public Works, Transport, Housing and Town Planning, although most strategic portfolios remained under the control of the MPS.

In April 1997 the Government and the FARF signed a conclusive peace agreement, providing for the cessation of all hostilities, a general amnesty for FARF members, the integration of its civilian and armed members into the state apparatus, and the legalization of the movement as a political party, the Front patriotique pour la démocratie. In August the Government was reported to have negotiated a peace agreement with the FAP, the military wing of Goukouni's FROLINAT. Agreement was reached on a general amnesty for the FNT, the FNTR and the Mouvement pour la justice sociale et la démocratie at reconciliation talks with the Government in October. However, later that month fighting erupted in Logone Occidental prefecture between FARF rebels and government troops; according to official figures, 42 FARF fighters, 52 civilians and four members of the ANT were killed. The FARF accused the Government of reneging on its commitment to integrate FARF fighters into the regular armed forces.

Insecurity persisted. Responsibility for the kidnap, in February 1998, of four French nationals in Moyen Chari prefecture was claimed by the Union des forces démocratiques (UFD). It was subsequently reported that 11 rebels had been killed, and 19 arrested, in an operation to liberate the hostages. French troops were mobilized in support of the Chadian security forces, although the military attaché at the French embassy in N'Djamena, said to be an associate of the UFD leader, Dr Mahamout Nahour, was declared *persona non grata* by the Chadian authorities after Nahour demanded only to negotiate with him.

In March 1998 it was revealed that discreet talks had been taking place since January between Kamougué and the FARF leader, Laokein Barde. Despite renewed violence in the south, and the issuing, in March, of a warrant for the arrest of Barde, negotiations between the President of the Assemblée nationale and the FARF continued. In May a presidential envoy and the FARF Chief of General Staff signed an agreement envisaging an immediate end to rebel activity; the Government undertook to withdraw élite elements of the National Nomadic Guard from the south, and there was to be a general amnesty for FARF militants. The terms of the April 1997 peace accord, whereby the FARF was to be legalized as a political party, were also to be renewed. (Reports later in 1998 stated that Barde had been presumed dead since that April.)

In an extensive government reshuffle in January 1998 Kebzabo was redesignated Minister of State, Minister of Mines, Energy and Petroleum (a new post, apparently emphasizing the importance attached by the Deby regime to the development of the petroleum and industrial mining sectors). In May, however, Kebzabo was removed from the Government, as were two UNDR secretaries of state.

In July 1998 Ngarledjy Yorongar, the sole parliamentary representative of the Front d'action pour le renouveau, was sentenced to three years' imprisonment (although Deby announced his release in January 1999). Yorongar, who had been an outspoken critic of provisions for the exploitation of petroleum in southern Chad, had claimed that Kamougué had received 1,500m. francs CFA from a French petroleum company, and had also alleged that Deby and his family were mismanaging the country's petroleum resources.

Reports emerged from late 1998 of a rebellion in the Tibesti region of northern Chad by the Mouvement pour la démocratie et la justice au Tchad (MDJT), led by Youssouf Togoimi—a former government member who had been dismissed as Minister of the Armed Forces in 1997. Despite MDJT claims of significant military and territorial successes, the Government did not acknowledge the existence of any rebellion in Tibesti until March 1999; even then, the authorities asserted that Togoimi was leading a group of only some 30 Toubou rebels. It was confirmed that military reinforcements, including a 3,000-strong élite force, had been deployed to prevent infiltration by Toubou sympathizers from neighbouring countries, and the authorities admitted that the ANT had suffered some losses in operations against the MDJT. However, claims by Togoimi that his movement was in control of much of the north of the country were categorically denied. In June 1999 FROLINAT announced that it was giving political and logistical support to the Tibesti rebellion. In November the MDJT announced that it had defeated ANT forces in Aozou, killing 80 and capturing 47 (a

further 42 ANT troops were said to have defected to the rebellion).

Ouaïdou resigned as Prime Minister in December 1999. He was replaced by Nagoum Yamassoum, whose new Government included five UNDR members, among them Kebzabo as Minister of State and Minister of Agriculture. A minor government reshuffle was effected in March 2000. Meanwhile, in December 1999 it was announced that 13 'politico-military' groups, including FROLINAT and the FNTR, had formed a new anti-Government alliance led by Antoine Bangui, the Coordination des mouvements armés et partis politiques de l'opposition (CMAP). In the same month another four 'politico-military' groups, led by Acheikh Ibn Oumar of the CDR, formed the Comité politique d'action et de liaison (CPAL). In February 2000 the Government admitted that its mediation mission to the north, led by former Prime Minister Koibla, had proved fruitless. In the same month it was reported that the former armed wing of the MDD had renamed itself the Mouvement pour l'unité et la République and allied itself with the MDJT and the CDR. No significant progress was achieved at talks held in Libya in April 2000 between Deby and Goukouni Oueddei, the leader of FROLINAT-Conseil provisoire de la révolution (FROLINAT-CPR), as the organization had been renamed.

In July 2000 the MDJT attacked a garrison in Bardaï and proclaimed its control of four towns in Tibesti. Official sources stated that 57 rebels and 13 government troops were killed during the fighting. The Prime Minister visited the region and invited MDJT negotiators to take part in peace discussions. In September it was reported that Moïse Ketté Nodji, the leader of the CSNPD, had been killed during clashes with ANT forces; it was subsequently reported that the CSNPD had been dissolved. In September Togoimi met with Deby for the first time, in Sirte, Libya. Togoimi's proposal for multilateral peace discussions, incorporating all opposition groups and Deby's administration, was followed later that month by a conference at which Deby met with representatives of some 30 opposition organizations (including trade unions and civil society groups, in addition to political parties), styling themselves the Forces vives, who were reportedly united, under the leadership of Abderaman Djasnabaille, in their disapproval of a new electoral code (see below). However, renewed fighting broke out in October between members of the MDJT and government forces in the far north and subsequently intensified, with the MDJT reportedly launching attacks from Libyan territory. In November the Government provoked international condemnation for reportedly spending some US $3m. of a bonus paid by petroleum companies on armaments.

Meanwhile, in July 2000 the Assemblée nationale approved proposals for the creation of an independent electoral body, the Commission électorale nationale indépendante (CENI), which was to plan a reorganization of constituencies in advance of elections due to be held in 2001. Several opposition parties were concerned by their apparent exclusion from the CENI and threatened to boycott the forthcoming elections in protest against the new arrangements, while fears were expressed that certain northern regions would be over-represented in comparison with those in the south. An extensive reshuffle of the Government at the end of August 2000 followed the dismissal of ministers belonging to the URD, owing to their party's rejection of the new electoral code. Furthermore, a number of members of the ruling MPS resigned from the party, in protest against violent acts reportedly committed by government forces.

In February 2001 it was announced that a presidential election would take place on 20 May and that legislative elections, initially scheduled for April, would be postponed until March 2002 for financial reasons. Following a minor ministerial reshuffle in February 2001, a further reorganization of the Government took place in April; on this occasion Deby dismissed all UNDR ministers, apparently in response to Kebzabo's announcement that he was to contest the presidential election. The Secretary-General of the Parti pour la liberté et le développement (PLD), Ibn Oumar Mahamat Saleh, who was also a presidential candidate, subsequently ordered his party's three ministers to withdraw from the Government.

In March 2001 opposition leaders and the CENI called for the election to be postponed, alleging that large-scale fraud had been committed in the compilation of the electoral register, although a subsequent legal challenge to have the electoral census annulled failed. In early May the six opposition presidential candidates, including Kamougué, Yorongar and former Prime Minister Alingué, signed an electoral pact, pledging to unite behind a single candidate in the event of a second round of voting. Meanwhile, in addition to the MDS, 27 political organizations, including the RDP, rallied behind Deby.

The presidential election took place, as scheduled, on 20 May 2001. Although international and national observers pronounced themselves largely satisfied with its conduct, the six opposition candidates alleged widespread fraud and malpractice. In late May, prior to the announcement of the results, eight members of the CENI resigned, in response to apparent irregularities in the vote counting. Following the CENI's announcement of preliminary results crediting Deby with 67.35% of the votes cast, all six opposition candidates were briefly arrested at Kebzabo's home, reportedly for breaching a temporary ban on political meetings. An opposition activist caught up in the affray subsequently died. The unsuccessful candidates were subsequently rearrested on charges of inciting violence and civil disobedience, as they attempted to organize a protest march to coincide with the funeral of the dead activist. Although the arrests were promptly rescinded, the Forces vives condemned the election result as fraudulent and called a general strike. Moreover, the opposition presented a petition to the Constitutional Council, requesting that the election be annulled. On 13 June the Constitutional Council issued the final results of the election, according to which Deby had won 63.17% of the valid votes cast, followed by Yorongar, with 16.35%. (Yorangar's supporters claimed that he had won more than one-half of the votes cast.) A turn-out of 61.4% was declared, compared with the 80.9% initially announced, while the total number of voters recorded by the Council was nearly 1m. lower than that previously reported by the CENI.

During June and July 2001 protests by opposition movements at the conduct of the election met with varying degrees of public support; notably, the defeated candidates announced a campaign of civil disobedience to coincide with Deby's inauguration as President on 8 August. Meanwhile, in mid-July the insurgency in the north escalated, as MDJT forces claimed to have captured the town of Fada, killing 86 government troops; however, although the Government acknowledged that an attack had taken place, it denied the losses and any involvement of the MDJT in the incident.

Yamassoum was reappointed as Prime Minister in mid-August 2001 and named a 35-member Government, which comprised 20 representatives from the MPS, five from the RDP and the remainder from other groups that had supported Deby in the presidential election. The CDR condemned the appointments and, despite a promise by Deby to review the voters' register, opposition parties continued to urge a boycott of the legislative elections scheduled for early 2002.

Disagreements between the CMAP and the CPAL became apparent in late 2001, following a declaration by Deby in August that he was willing to engage in dialogue with the two groups, although the CPAL continued to oppose any negotiations. In September FROLINAT-CPR was expelled from the CMAP, which accused Goukouni's party of engaging in separate discussions with the Government and with unnamed foreign politicians. In late October, however, the CMAP expressed a willingness to enter into discussions with Deby and offered to send a delegation to N'Djamena if its security could be assured.

A number of opposition leaders were critical of a meeting held between Deby and representatives of opposition parties at the end of October 2001, which was intended to prepare for legislative elections in April 2002. Yorongar claimed that the meeting had been deliberately scheduled for a period during which four of the defeated presidential candidates were overseas, lobbying officials of the European Union (see p. 199) about an alleged lack of electoral transparency in Chad.

In December 2001 the CMAP presented the Government with proposals for a peace plan, which were positively received by the Deby administration. In January 2002 the Minister of Foreign Affairs, Mahamat Saleh Annadif, held discussions with CMAP members in France and with other exiled opposition members in Benin and Nigeria. Meanwhile, during December 2001 and January 2002 negotiations took place in N'Djamena between the Government and principal opposition leaders (with the notable exception of Yorongar); although some progress was reported, opposition parties continued to demand a full reorganization of the voter registration exercise.

In late January 2002 Deby announced that the elections would be held on 21 April; according to the revised electoral code, the new Assemblée nationale was to be enlarged to 155 members. In early February Djasnabaille was indicted on

charges of fraud. Also in that month the FAR, the UNDR and the URD announced their intention to participate in the legislative elections.

Meanwhile, reports emerged in December 2001 that the Libyan Government, which was mediating between MDJT rebels and the Chadian Government, had assured the rebels of its support. The involvement of Libya in the peace process was regarded as a major factor in the beneficial terms offered to the MDJT in a peace agreement, signed by the group's deputy leader, Adoum Togoi (a former Chadian ambassador to Libya), and the Chadian Government in early January 2002. According to the agreement, both sides would institute an immediate cease-fire and a general amnesty for prisoners. Moreover, the MDJT was to participate in the Chadian Government and other state institutions, while the rebel forces were to be regularized. Notably, the Libyan Government was to be responsible for monitoring the implementation of the agreement. However, Togoimi did not give his approval to the arrangements, and, as a split in the rebel group became evident, in early April the MDJT issued a statement accusing the Government of inhibiting the peace process by its refusal to postpone legislative elections in order to allow the appointment of MDJT representatives to the Government. (It was, however, subsequently reported that Togoimi had demanded to be appointed as Prime Minister of Chad.) In late April the CMAP also announced the suspension of peace negotiations with the Government, accusing the latter of 'bad faith'.

Elections to the Assemblée nationale, which were held on 21 April 2002, were contested by 472 candidates, representing some 40 parties, although the UDR and PLD boycotted the polls. On the day of the elections Gueti Mahamat, the leader of the Parti africain démocratique, a faction within the Forces vives, was killed, when his car hit a landmine near Faya-Largeau. Although many unexploded artillery items were known to be in the region, the Government attributed Mahamat's death to an unspecified terrorist organization, stating that the intended target of the landmine had been soldiers at a nearby military camp. Several people, including at least two members of the MDJT, were arrested in connection with the killing, although the MDJT denied any involvement in the incident. According to the final election results, which were issued on 19 May, the MPS won 110 seats in the Assemblée nationale, significantly increasing its representation. (It was reported that MPS candidates were unopposed in some 50 constituencies.) The RDP became the second largest party, with 12 seats, while the FAR became the largest opposition party, with nine seats. Koumakoye's VIVA—Rassemblement national pour la démocratie et le progrès and the UNDR each won five seats, and the URD's representation was significantly reduced, to only three seats. The Constitutional Council annulled the results of voting in two constituencies. In mid-June Ouaïdou was elected as President of the Assemblée nationale, and Deby appointed his special counsellor, Haroun Kabadi, a senior official in the MPS, as Prime Minister, to head a 28-member Council of Ministers, in which several important ministers retained their portfolios. Notably, a new Ministry of Petroleum was created, distinct from the Ministry of Mines and Energy.

Meanwhile, in mid-May 2002 it was reported that Togoi was being held in detention by forces loyal to Togoimi, who had confirmed his rejection of the peace agreement signed in January; MDJT commanders denied that Togoi had been killed. None the less, in early July some 200 former MDJT fighters were reported to have joined government forces. In early June the FNTR announced the cessation of its armed struggle.

An attack, in mid-September 2002, on the eastern village of Tissi was attributed by the Chadian Government to troops supported by the CAR, although the ANR, which had been dormant for several years, claimed responsibility for the raid and, amid heightened tension with the CAR (see below), emphasized that the perpetrators of the attack were resident in Chad.

The death of Togoimi, in Libya, in late September 2002, while being treated for injuries sustained in a landmine explosion in northern Chad in August, raised hopes that peace talks between the Government and the MDJT would be reconvened, and Deby visited the north in order to encourage a resumption of negotiations. However, in early October renewed fighting broke out in the north; following an attack by the MDJT on an airport at Faya N'Gourma, in which some 20 ANT soldiers reportedly died, further clashes were reported near Fada, in which, according to official figures, 50 MDJT rebels were killed. Later in the month the Government announced that the ANT had mounted an offensive against the MDJT near Ennedi, killing 123 MDJT fighters and capturing a futher 63, as well as releasing 20 Sudanese and four Libyan civilians held hostage by the rebels. (These figures were disputed by the MDJT, however, which also continued to deny allegations that Togoi, whose whereabouts remained unknown, had been killed.) In mid-November rebels of the Forces des organisations nationales pour l'alternance et les libertés au Tchad (FONALT), one of the constituent groups of the ANR, claimed to have killed 116 ANT soldiers in clashes near Adré, close to the borders with Sudan and the CAR, although the Chadian Government made no official confirmation or denial of these reports.

A minor ministerial reshuffle was effected in mid-November 2002; notably, the Secretary-General of the MPS, Mahamat Saleh Ahmat, hitherto Minster of State, responsible for Land Management, Town Planning and Housing, left the Government, while a new Minister of Mines and Energy, Mahamat Madadou Adji, was among those appointed.

In early January 2003, following negotiations in Libreville, Gabon, hosted by the Gabonese President, Omar Bongo, the Government and the ANR signed a peace memorandum, in which rebels of the organization were granted a general amnesty prior to their reintegration into the civilian sector. Moreover, Garfa, the leader of the ANR, returned to Chad for the first time since 1994. However, the FONALT rejected the terms of the accord.

In early 1998 it was reported that Chad was to seek the extradition from Senegal of former President Habré, with a view to his prosecution in relation to human-rights abuses and in connection with the embezzlement of state funds. A committee of inquiry, established by the Deby administration, held Habré's 'political police' responsible for the deaths of some 40,000 people and the torture of 200,000 others; Habré was also alleged to have embezzled 7,000m. francs CFA in state funds when he fled Chad in 1990. In February 2000, following a ruling by a Senegalese court that he could be tried in that country, Habré was charged with complicity in acts of torture committed in Chad under his leadership, and placed under house arrest. The charges were dismissed in July, however, on the grounds that Senegal lacked the appropriate penal procedure to process such a case. In March 2001 Senegal's highest court of appeal, the Cour de cassation, upheld the previous ruling that Senegalese courts lacked the jurisdiction to try Habré. In September, in response to pressure from Amnesty International, Wade expressed his willingness to extradite Habré to stand trial in a third country, should a suitable country be identified. Habré remained in Senegal in early 2003, although his alleged victims were seeking his extradition to stand trial in Belgium.

Relations with France appeared uneasy in the late 1990s, particularly following the expulsion of a French military attaché in early 1998 (see above). Further tension arose in March 2000, when the Chadian Government demanded the recall of the French ambassador in N'Djamena, Alain du Boispéan. However, relations subsequently improved, and in September 2002 President Jacques Chirac became the first French Head of State to visit Chad for more than 30 years.

During the late 1990s Chad developed closer relations with its neighbours, particularly Libya. Chad was a founder member of the Community of Sahel-Saharan States (CEN-SAD, see p. 339), established in Tripoli in 1997, and Deby and members of his administration made several visits to Libya from 1997, including some by air prior to the ending of the UN embargo on air links with Libya in April 1999. Following the conclusion of a peace agreement between the Chadian Government and the rebel MDJT in Tripoli in January 2002 (see above), Libya pledged aid for the development of the Tibesti region.

Chad dispatched troops to the CAR in early 1997, as part of a regional surveillance mission, and Chadian forces remained in the CAR as part of a UN peace-keeping mission until its withdrawal in February 2000. In response to an attempted coup in the CAR in May 2001, Chad reportedly dispatched troops to defend the Government of President Ange-Félix Patassé. In early November heightened unrest broke out in the CAR, following an attempt to arrest the recently dismissed Chief of Staff of the Armed Forces, Gen. François Bozizé, in connection with the May coup attempt. Bozizé crossed into Chad, with an estimated 300 armed supporters, and was granted refuge in Sarh. Chad was subsequently involved in efforts by both CEN-SAD and the Communauté économique et monétaire de l'Afrique centrale (CEMAC) to find a lasting solution to the crisis in the CAR. In late December the CAR judiciary abandoned legal proceedings against Bozizé, and in January 2002, during a meeting held in Chad, a CAR government delegation invited Bozizé and his supporters to return. Meanwhile, repeated clashes were reported at the Chad–CAR border, and in mid-January CEMAC leaders decided to send a mission of experts to the area. Relations between the two countries were further strained in March, when the killing of 11 Chadians in the border regions of the CAR prompted a retaliatory attack against a village in the CAR. In mid-April a meeting of the Presidents of the two countries in N'Djamena resulted in the reopening of the border, which had been closed during the unrest. However, an additional source of tension was the appointment of Col Martin Khoumtan-Madji (believed by the Chadian authorities to be an alias of Abdoulaye Miskine, a former senior member of the CSNPD based in the CAR since 1998) as the head of a special unit in the CAR military, comprising some 300 soldiers, including many former Chadian rebels, and answerable directly to the presidency, charged with securing the common border of the two countries.

In early August 2002 the CAR Prime Minister, Martin Ziguélé, accused Chadian troops of launching cross-border attacks in the CAR, precipitating an emergency CEMAC summit later that month, chaired by President Bongo of Gabon, and the dispatch of a further observer mission to the affected region. (Chadian sources stated that the troops that had launched the attacks in the CAR were loyal to Bozizé, and not affiliated to the ANT.) The report issued by the mission, at the end of August, stated that, although tension remained high in the border region, there was no concentration of troops on the border, or of foreign troops in either country. An attack by the ANR in eastern Chad (see above), in early September, was attributed by the Chadian Government to troops supported by the CAR. In early October a CEMAC summit in Libreville, Gabon, sought to defuse tensions between the two countries; in accordance with an accord reached at the summit, Bozizé and Khoumtan-Madji weres subsequently granted asylum in France and Togo, respectively, and in December a CEMAC force was deployed in the CAR capital, Bangui, initially to protect Patassé and later to monitor joint patrols of the border by Chadian and CAR troops. However, bilateral relations remained strained in late 2002. In late October it was reported that some 120 Chadians had been killed by CAR troops in Bangui during disturbances that followed a further coup attempt, prompting the Chadian Government to call for an official inquiry into the events, and in November Patassé accused Chad of seeking to annex regions in the north of the CAR. Tensions subsequently abated somewhat, and in late January 2003 the Governments of Chad, the CAR and Sudan announced their intention to establish a tripartite committee to oversee the security and stability of their joint borders. In mid-February the Presidents of Chad and the CAR met in Bangui in an attempt to normalize relations between the two countries. Later that month some 20,000 refugees (many of whom were Chadian nationals who had been resident in the CAR for many years) entered southern Chad, fleeing renewed fighting in the CAR. Following Bozizé's assumption of power in mid-March, some 400 Chadian troops were reportedly dispatched to the CAR to reinforce the CEMAC force deployed in December 2002.

Government

A new Constitution was adopted by national referendum on 31 March 1996. Under the terms of the Constitution, the Republic of Chad is a unitary state with a multi-party political system. Executive power is vested in the President, who is the Head of State and Commander-in-Chief of the Armed Forces. The President is elected by direct universal suffrage for a maximum of two five-year terms of office. The President appoints the Prime Minister, who nominates the Council of Ministers. Legislative power is vested in a bicameral legislature, comprising the 155-member Assemblée nationale, which is elected by direct universal suffrage for a four-year term, and a Sénat, which has a six-year mandate (with one-third of the membership renewable every two years). However, by early 2003 the Sénat had not yet been established.

Chad is divided into 28 administrative departments.

Defence

In August 2002 the Armée nationale tchadienne (ANT) was estimated to number 30,350 (army approximately 25,000, air force 350, Republican Guard 5,000). In addition, there was a 4,500-strong gendarmerie. The army has been undergoing restructuring since 1996. Military service is by conscription.

Under defence agreements with France, the army receives technical and other aid: in August 2002 the number of troops deployed in Chad by France numbered 950. Direct aid from France to the Chadian army in 1999 was an estimated 6,160m. francs CFA. Defence expenditure for 2002 was budgeted at an estimated 10,000m. francs CFA.

Economic Affairs

In 2001, according to estimates by the World Bank, Chad's gross national income (GNI), measured at average 1999–2001 prices, was US $1,597m., equivalent to $200 per head (or $930 on an international purchasing-power parity basis). During 1990–2001, it was estimated, the population increased at an average annual rate of 2.9%, while gross domestic product (GDP) per head increased, in real terms, by an average of 0.1% per year. Overall GDP increased, in real terms, at an average annual rate of 3.1% in 1990–2001, according to the World Bank; growth in 2001 was 8.9%.

Agriculture contributed 38.6% of GDP in 2001, according to the World Bank; some 74.3% of the labour force were employed in the sector in that year. The principal cash crop is cotton (exports of which contributed an estimated 40.1% of total export revenue in 1999). The principal subsistence crops are sorghum, millet and groundnuts. Livestock-rearing, which contributed 12.5% of GDP in 2000, makes an important contribution both to the domestic food supply and to export earnings, although illicit trade accounts for a significant proportion of the output. During 1990–2001 agricultural GDP increased at an average annual rate of 5.2%; agricultural GDP declined by 3.4% in 2000, but increased by 4.1% in 2001.

Industry contributed 13.7% of GDP in 2001. About 4.2% of the population were employed in the sector in 1990. During 1990–2001 industrial GDP increased at an average annual rate of 1.6%; the sector's GDP increased by 0.4% in 2000 and by 12.5% in 2001.

The mining sector (including fishing) contributed 3.2% of GDP in 2000, according to the IMF. For many years the only minerals exploited were natron (sodium carbonate), salt, alluvial gold and materials for the construction industry. However, long-delayed plans to develop sizeable petroleum reserves in the Doba Basin and at Sedigi, in the south of the country, were being pursued in the early 2000s (see below). There is believed to be considerable potential for the further exploitation of gold, bauxite and uranium. During 1994–2000 the GDP of the mining sector (including fishing) declined at an average annual rate of 0.2%, according to the IMF; growth of 0.8% was recorded in 2000.

The manufacturing sector, which contributed 10.2% of GDP in 2001, operates mainly in the south of the country, and is dominated by agro-industrial activities, notably the processing of the cotton crop by the state-controlled Société Cotonnière du Tchad (COTONTCHAD). During 1994–2000 manufacturing GDP increased at an average annual rate of 14.0%, according to the IMF; however, the GDP of the sector declined by 1.9% in 2000.

Chad is heavily dependent on imports of mineral fuels (principally from Cameroon and Nigeria) for the generation of electricity. Imports of mineral fuels comprised an estimated 17.9% of the total value of merchandise imports in 1995. The use of wood-based fuel products by most households has contributed to the severe depletion of Chad's forest resources. In November 2000 the Cameroonian Prime Minister announced the creation of a technical committee to instigate the export of electricity to Chad. None the less, by 2002 only 2% of households in Chad had access to electricity.

Services contributed 47.7% of GDP in 2001. The GDP of the sector increased at an average annual rate of 2.7% in 1990–2001; growth in 2001 was 11.0%.

In 2000 Chad recorded a visible trade deficit of 44,000m. francs CFA, and there was a deficit of 137,800m. francs CFA on the current account of the balance of payments. In 1995 Chad's principal source of imports (41.3%) was France; other major suppliers were Cameroon, Nigeria and the USA. The principal markets for exports include Cameroon and France. The principal exports in 1999 were cotton and livestock. The principal imports in 1995 were petroleum products, road vehicles and parts, sugar and cereals.

In 2001 Chad recorded an overall budgetary surplus of 3,653m. francs CFA (equivalent to 0.3% of GDP). Chad's external debt at the end of 2000 totalled US $1,116m., of which $1,009m. was long-term public debt. In that year the cost of debt-servicing was equivalent to 9.3% of earnings from exports of goods and services. Consumer prices declined by an annual average of 2.1% in 1990–93. There was a sharp increase in the rate of inflation in 1994, to an average of 40.4%, following the 50% devaluation of the currency. Thereafter, the rate of inflation slowed to an average of 5.2% in 1995–2000; however, consumer prices increased by 12.4% in 2001.

Chad is a member of the Central African organs of the Franc Zone (see p. 239) and of the Communauté économique des états de l'Afrique centrale (CEEAC, see p. 339); the Lake Chad Basin Commission (see p. 340) is based in N'Djamena.

Economic growth in Chad has been inhibited by a number of factors: conflict has deterred investment in the development of considerable mineral wealth and other resources, leaving the economy over-dependent on cotton, while the country's landlocked position has been compounded by infrastructural deficiencies. Chad thus remains among the world's least developed countries. An energy crisis and intensified rebel fighting in northern regions were instrumental in generating only modest real GDP growth in 2000, although economic performance improved in 2001–02, as food production normalized, despite low cotton prices internationally. The signing of peace agreements with rebel groups active in the north and east of Chad in 2002–03 (see above), although subject to full implementation, has also been a factor in generating greater stability. The IMF has sought efforts to enhance government revenue and improve the efficiency of the agricultural sector, as well as banking reforms and measures to foster private investment. In January 2000 the IMF approved funding under its Poverty Reduction and Growth Facility (PRGF) in support of the Government's economic programme for 1999–2002. Furthermore, in May 2001 the Bretton Woods institutions declared Chad eligible for debt-service relief under the enhanced Heavily Indebted Poor Countries initiative. The IMF increased Chad's PRGF by some US $6.8m. in January 2002, in order to alleviate the adverse effects of declining world prices for cotton, and in October the IMF agreed to a request by the Chadian authorities to extend the facility to December 2003. Meanwhile, in late 2000 a consortium led by the US ExxonMobil Corporation, and supported by Petronas of Malaysia and the US ChevronTexaco Corporation, began work to develop the substantial petroleum resources in the Doba Basin, with peak output of 225,000 barrels per day anticipated by the mid-2000s; the first exports were expected in the second half of 2003, and production was forecast to continue for 25–30 years. The construction of a 1,070-km pipeline to transport petroleum to the port of Kribi in Cameroon commenced in October 2000, and was expected to be completed in the first half of 2003. The successful completion of the project was expected to double Chad's GDP, compared with that recorded in the early 2000s, in addition to alleviating the country's dependence on fuel imports. The Assemblée nationale adopted legislation whereby 80% of Chad's earnings from petroleum would be dedicated to the development of health, education, agriculture and infrastructure. However, concerns expressed by environmental and human rights organizations about the project were exacerbated in late 2000, when the Government was criticized for reportedly spending some US $3m of a bonus paid by the petroleum companies on armaments. In February 2001 the World Bank appointed an international advisory group to monitor the implementation of the project, and in September 2002, following the publication of a report by the group, which was critical of several aspects of the management of the project, the World Bank announced that it would intensify its monitoring of the development. Moreover, an independent committee was to give consent to all proposals for government expenditure from funds generated by the export of petroleum. Meanwhile, work commenced in mid-2000 on the construction of a pipeline from petroleum reserves at Sedigi to supply a new refinery in N'Djamena. The refinery would supply a new 16-MW power station in the capital, and provide fuel for local transportation requirements. The successful pursuit of this and other efforts to develop the Chadian economy will largely depend on the Government's ability to maintain domestic peace and to satisfy the international community of its commitment to transparent governance and respect for human rights.

Education

Education is officially compulsory for six years between six and 12 years of age. Primary education begins at the age of six and lasts for six years. Secondary education, from the age of 12, lasts for seven years, comprising a first cycle of four years and a second of three years. In 1999/2000 primary enrolment included 56.6% of children in the relevant age-group (males 68.7%; females 44.6%), while secondary enrolment included only 7.7%

of children in the appropriate age-group (males 11.8%; females 3.7%). The Université du Tchad was opened at N'Djamena in 1971. In addition, there are several technical colleges. Some 5,901 students were enrolled at higher education institutions in 1999. Total expenditure on education by the central Government (including foreign-financed investment) in 1996 was 32,196m. francs CFA (21.2% of total government expenditure).

Public Holidays

2003: 1 January (New Year), 12 February* (Id al-Adha, Feast of the Sacrifice), 21 April (Easter Monday), 1 May (Labour Day), 14 May* (Maloud, Birth of the Prophet), 25 May ('Liberation of Africa', anniversary of the OAU's foundation), 9 June (Whit Monday), 11 August (Independence Day), 15 August (Assumption), 1 November (All Saints' Day), 26 November* (Id al-Fitr, end of Ramadan), 28 November (Proclamation of the Republic),

1 December (Liberation and Democracy Day, anniversary of the 1990 coup d'état), 25 December (Christmas).

2004: 1 January (New Year), 2 February* (Id al-Adha, Feast of the Sacrifice), 12 April (Easter Monday), 1 May (Labour Day), 2 May* (Maloud, Birth of the Prophet), 25 May ('Liberation of Africa', anniversary of the OAU's foundation), 31 May (Whit Monday), 11 August (Independence Day), 15 August (Assumption), 1 November (All Saints' Day), 14 November* (Id al-Fitr, end of Ramadan), 28 November (Proclamation of the Republic), 1 December (Liberation and Democracy Day, anniversary of the 1990 coup d'état), 25 December (Christmas).

*These holidays are dependent on the Islamic lunar calendar and may vary by one or two days from the dates given.

Weights and Measures

The metric system is officially in force.

Statistical Survey

Source (unless otherwise stated): Direction de la Statistique, des Etudes Economiques et Démographiques, BP 453, N'Djamena; tel. 52-31-64.

Area and Population

AREA, POPULATION AND DENSITY

Area (sq km)	
Land	1,259,200
Inland waters	24,800
Total	1,284,000*
Population (sample survey)	
December 1963–August 1964 . . .	3,254,000†
Population (census result)	
8 April 1993‡	
Males	2,950,415
Females.	3,208,577
Total	6,158,992
Population (official estimate at mid-year)	
1999	7,557,000
Density (per sq km) at mid-1999	5.9

* 495,800 sq miles.

† Including areas not covered by the survey.

‡ Figures are provisional. The revised total, including an adjustment for underenumeration (estimated at 1.4%), is 6,279,931.

ETHNIC GROUPS

1995 (percentages): Sara, Bongo and Baguirmi 20.1; Chadic 17.7; Arab 14.3; M'Bourn 6.3; Masalit, Maba and Mimi 6.1; Tama 6.1; Adamawa 6.0; Sudanese 6.0; Mubi 4.1; Hausa 2.1; Kanori 2.1; Massa 2.1; Kotoko 2.0; Peul 0.5; Others 4.5 (Source: La Francophonie).

PREFECTURES

(1993 census)

	Area (sq km)	Population*	Density (per sq km)	Principal city
Batha	88,800	288,458	3.2	Ati
Biltine	46,850	184,807	3.9	Biltine
Borkou-Ennedi-Tibesti (BET) .	600,350	73,185	0.1	Faya-Largeau
Chari-Baguirmi† .	82,910	1,251,906	15.1	N'Djamena
Guéra	58,950	306,253	5.2	Mongo
Kanem	114,520	279,927	2.4	Mao
Lac	22,320	252,932	11.3	Bol
Logone Occidental .	8,695	455,489	52.4	Moundou
Logone Oriental .	28,035	441,064	15.7	Doba
Mayo-Kebbi . .	30,105	825,158	27.4	Bongor
Moyen Chari . .	45,180	738,595	16.3	Sarh
Ouaddaï . . .	76,240	543,900	7.1	Abéché
Salamat . . .	63,000	184,403	2.9	Am-Timan
Tandjile . . .	18,045	453,854	25.2	Lai
Total	1,284,000	6,279,931	4.9	

* Including adjustment for underenumeration.

† Including the capital district, N'Djamena (population 530,965).

Note: As a result of administrative reform, Chad's former prefectures have been replaced by the following departments: Assongha (principal city Adré), Baguirmi (Massenya), Bahr el Gazal (Moussoro), Bahr Kôh (Sarh), Batha Est (Oum-Hadjer), Batha Ouest (Ati), Biltine (Biltine), Borkou (Faya-Largeau), Dababa (Bokoro), Ennedi (Fada), Guera (Mongo), Hadjer Lamis (Massaguet), Kabia (Gounou Gaya), Kanem (Mao), Lac (Bol), Lac Iro (Kyabe), Logone Occidental (Moundou), Logone Oriental (Doba), Mandoul (Koumra), Mayo Boneye (Bongor), Mayo Dallah (Pala), Monts de Lam (Baïbokoum), Ouaddaï (Abéché), Salamat (Am-Timan), Sila (Goz-Beïda), Tandjile Est (Lai), Tandjile Ouest (Kelo), Tibesti (Bardaï). The capital city, N'Djamena, constitutes a separate administrative unit.

PRINCIPAL TOWNS

(population at 1993 census)

N'Djamena (capital).	530,965	Koumra	26,702
Moundou . . .	99,530	Pala	26,115
Sarh	75,496	Am Timan . . .	21,269
Abéché	54,628	Bongor. . . .	20,448
Kelo	31,319	Mongo	20,443

BIRTHS AND DEATHS

(UN estimates, annual averages)

	1985–90	1990–95	1995–2000
Birth rate (per 1,000)	48.3	48.6	48.4
Death rate (per 1,000)	20.7	20.3	19.6

Source: UN, *World Population Prospects: The 2000 Revision.*

Expectation of life (WHO estimates, years at birth): 48.6 (males 47.0; females 50.2) in 2001 (Source: WHO, *World Health Report*).

ECONOMICALLY ACTIVE POPULATION
(ILO estimates, '000 persons at mid-1990)

	Males	Females	Total
Agriculture, hunting, forestry and fishing.	1,179	1,102	2,281
Industry	105	9	115
Manufacturing.	50	6	56
Services	245	100	344
Total labour force	1,529	1,211	2,740

Source: ILO.

1993 census (persons aged six years and over): Total labour force 2,719,443 (males 1,416,449; females 1,302,994) (Source: ILO, *Yearbook of Labour Statistics*).

Mid-2001 (estimates in '000): Agriculture, etc. 2,765; Total 3,722 (Source: FAO).

Health and Welfare

KEY INDICATORS

Total fertility rate (children per woman, 2001).	6.7
Under-5 mortality rate (per 1,000 live births, 2001)	200
HIV/AIDS (% of persons aged 15–49, 2001).	3.61
Physicians (per 1,000 head, 1994)	0.03
Hospital beds (per 1,000 head, 1996)	0.72
Health expenditure (2000): US $ per head (PPP)	19
Health expenditure (2000): % of GDP	3.1
Health expenditure (2000): public (% of total)	79.8
Access to water (% of persons, 2000).	27
Access to sanitation (% of persons, 2000)	29
Human Development Index (2000): ranking	166
Human Development Index (2000): value	0.365

For sources and definitions, see explanatory note on p. vi.

Agriculture

PRINCIPAL CROPS
('000 metric tons)

	1999	2000	2001
Wheat	3.6	2.7	2.8
Rice (paddy)	138.3	92.6	112.2
Maize	94.2	64.0	105.3
Millet	361.1	258.8	397.6
Sorghum	456.6	391.7	497.2
Other cereals	177.1	120.2	206.2
Potatoes	27.0	25.0*	33.0*
Sweet potatoes*	62	62	64
Cassava (Manioc)	323.2	256.3	306.0
Taro (Coco yam)*	38	38	38
Yams*	230	230	230
Sugar cane	277.0	330.0	350.0
Dry beans	17.8	71.6	83.3
Other pulses	38.0*	22.4	42.5
Groundnuts (in shell)	371.9	358.8	448.1
Sesame seed	21.2	33.0	43.4
Cottonseed*	99	100	110
Dry onions*	14	14	14
Other vegetables*	81	81	81
Dates*	18	18	18
Mangoes*	32	32	32
Other fruit*	63	63	63
Cotton (lint)†	74	58	70

* FAO estimate(s).
† Unofficial figures.

Source: FAO.

LIVESTOCK
('000 head, year ending September)

	1999	2000	2001
Cattle	5,712	5,872	5,992
Goats	5,058	5,179	5,304
Sheep	2,318	2,374	2,431
Pigs	21*	22*	22†
Horses	198	202	205†
Asses	350	357	364
Camels†	715	720	725
Poultry†	4,900	4,900	5,000

* Unofficial figure.
† FAO estimate(s).

Source: FAO.

LIVESTOCK PRODUCTS
(FAO estimates, '000 metric tons)

	1999	2000	2001
Beef and veal	78.4	73.7	77.0
Mutton and lamb	11.5	11.8	12.1
Goat meat	17.7	18.7	19.8
Poultry meat	4.7	4.7	4.7
Other meat	4.9	5.1	5.1
Cows' milk	154.2	158.0	161.7
Sheep's milk	8.8	9.0	9.0
Goats' milk	30.7	31.1	31.8
Poultry eggs	4.4	4.4	4.5
Cattle hides (fresh)	13.3	13.5	14.1
Sheepskins (fresh)	1.9	2.0	2.0
Goatskins (fresh)	3.4	3.7	4.0

Source: FAO.

Forestry

ROUNDWOOD REMOVALS
(FAO estimates, '000 cubic metres, excl. bark)

	1999	2000	2001
Sawlogs, veneer logs and logs for sleepers*	14	14	14
Other industrial wood	747	747	747
Fuel wood	5,738	5,885	6,601
Total	6,499	6,646	6,762

* Output assumed to be unchanged since 1993.

Source: FAO.

SAWNWOOD PRODUCTION
('000 cubic metres, incl. railway sleepers)

	1994	1995	1996
Total (all broadleaved)	2*	2	2

* FAO estimate.

1997–2001: Annual production as in 1996 (FAO estimates).

Source: FAO.

Fishing

('000 metric tons, live weight)

	1998	1999	2000
Total catch (freshwater fishes)	84.0	84.0*	84.0*

* FAO estimate.

Source: FAO, *Yearbook of Fishery Statistics*.

Industry

SELECTED PRODUCTS

	1998	1999	2000
Edible oil (million litres)	12	9	10
Sugar ('000 metric tons)	29	30	27
Beer ('000 hectolitres)	99	79	78
Cigarettes (million packs)	36	38	30
Electric energy (million kWh)	75.0	83.0	86.4

Source: IMF, *Chad: Statistical Appendix* (February 2002).

Beer of millet (metric tons): 10,109 in 1998; 13,347 in 1999; 10,673 in 2000 (Source: FAO).

Finance

CURRENCY AND EXCHANGE RATES

Monetary Units

100 centimes = 1 franc de la Coopération financière en Afrique centrale (CFA)

Sterling, Dollar and Euro Equivalents (31 December 2002)
£1 sterling = 1,008.17 francs CFA
US $1 = 625.50 francs CFA
€1 = 655.96 francs CFA
10,000 francs CFA = £9.992 = $15.987 = €15.245

Average Exchange Rate (francs CFA per US $)
2000   711.98
2001   733.04
2002   696.99

Note: An exchange rate of 1 French franc = 50 francs CFA, established in 1948, remained in force until January 1994, when the CFA franc was devalued by 50%, with the exchange rate adjusted to 1 French franc = 100 francs CFA. This relationship to French currency remained in effect with the introduction of the euro on 1 January 1999. From that date, accordingly, a fixed exchange rate of €1 = 655.957 francs CFA has been in operation.

BUDGET
('000 million francs CFA)

Revenue*	1998	1999	2000
Tax revenue	69.8	68.0	68.3
Taxes on income and profits	22.6	23.8	24.3
Companies	10.7	12.4	11.3
Individuals	10.6	10.0	10.0
Employers' payroll tax	1.4	1.4	1.5
Property tax	0.7	1.3	1.5
Taxes on goods and services	14.4	15.8	18.8
Turnover tax	8.5	8.8	11.7
Tax on petroleum products	3.5	4.1	6.0
Taxes on international trade	27.4	23.0	21.8
Import taxes	25.7	19.9	18.5
Export taxes	1.3	2.1	2.2
Other tax revenues	4.7	4.1	1.9
Other revenue	6.5	9.7	11.9
Property income	1.3	0.9	1.9
Administrative fees	0.4	2.2	2.6
Non-industrial sales	1.3	1.8	1.7
Total	76.2	77.7	80.2

Expenditure†	1998	1999	2000
Current expenditure	75.4	87.9	99.9
Primary current expenditure	65.7	79.1	88.0
Wages and salaries	31.5	34.0	40.0
Materials and supplies	16.1	18.5	20.8
Health	2.7	3.1	4.2
Education	2.5	3.0	4.0
Transfers	8.6	6.6	11.3
Subsidies	2.5	2.7	7.1
Defence	9.5	12.9	15.2
Salaries	8.3	11.2	10.2
Materials and supplies	1.2	1.7	5.0
Interest	8.9	8.7	10.3
External	7.5	7.6	8.9
Investment expenditure	78.4	90.9	103.3
Domestically-financed	5.0	8.8	10.7
Foreign-financed	73.3	82.1	92.6
Total	153.8	178.8	203.2

* Excluding grants received ('000 million francs CFA): 38.1 in 1998; 42.9 in 1999; 48.0 in 2000.
† Excluding adjustment for payments arrears.

Source: IMF, *Chad: Statistical Appendix* (February 2002).

INTERNATIONAL RESERVES
(US $ million at 31 December)

	2000	2001	2002
Gold*	3.03	3.09	3.81
IMF special drawing rights	0.00	0.00	0.00
Reserve position in IMF	0.37	0.35	0.38
Foreign exchange	110.33	122.02	218.31
Total	113.73	125.46	222.51

* Valued at market-related prices.

Source: IMF, *International Financial Statistics*.

MONEY SUPPLY
(million francs CFA at 31 December)

	2000	2001	2002
Currency outside banks	81,272	94,765	116,799
Demand deposits at commercial and development banks	31,601	43,425	59,788
Total money (incl. others)	113,824	138,690	176,587

Source: IMF, *International Financial Statistics*.

COST OF LIVING
(Consumer Price Index for African households in N'Djamena; base: 1995 = 100)

	1999	2000	2001
All items	124.1	128.8	144.8

Source: IMF, *International Financial Statistics*.

NATIONAL ACCOUNTS
('000 million francs CFA at current prices)

Expenditure on the Gross Domestic Product

	1999	2000	2001
Government final consumption expenditure	63.1	74.5	90.8
Private final consumption expenditure	829.1	849.1	875.3
Increase in stocks	7.0	−15.0	−2.0
Gross fixed capital formation	168.6	210.1	546.8
Total domestic expenditure	1,067.8	1,118.7	1,510.9
Exports of goods and services	173.1	166.6	164.1
Less Imports of goods and services	304.2	335.6	584.6
GDP in purchasers' values	936.7	949.7	1,090.3
GDP at constant 1995 prices	813.7	806.1	871.2

Gross Domestic Product by Economic Activity

	1998	1999	2000
Agriculture*	354.2	324.9	348.9
Mining and quarrying† . . .	29.5	29.9	31.2
Electricity, gas and water. . .	5.5	6.0	5.9
Manufacturing	123.1	111.2	108.4
Construction	15.4	16.8	19.7
Wholesale and retail trade, restaurants and hotels . . ⎫ Transport and communications . ⎭	249.2	237.3	244.6
Public adminstration . . .	100.6	110.3	114.7
Other services	95.4	97.3	96.4
GDP at factor cost . . .	972.8	933.8	969.9
Indirect taxes, *less* subsidies .	25.9	29.1	32.5
GDP in purchasers' values .	998.7	962.9	1,002.4

* Excluding fishing.
† Including fishing.

Source: IMF, *Chad: Statistical Appendix* (February 2002).

BALANCE OF PAYMENTS
('000 million francs CFA)

	1998	1999	2000
Exports of goods f.o.b. . . .	151.5	115.7	129.4
Imports of goods f.o.b. . . .	−160.5	−149.9	−173.3
Trade balance	−9.0	−34.3	−44.0
Exports of services . . .	36.0	32.9	36.8
Imports of services . . .	−160.4	−141.4	−147.7
Balance on goods and services	−133.4	−142.8	−154.9
Other income (net) . . .	−8.3	−8.6	−6.7
Balance on goods, services and income .	−141.7	−151.4	−161.6
Current transfers (net) . . .	33.5	17.0	23.8
Current balance . . .	−108.2	−134.4	−137.8
Capital account	41.5	30.0	48.0
Direct investment (net) . . .	26.9	26.2	51.3
Other investment (net) . . .	22.1	49.9	28.0
Net errors and omissions . .	4.4	7.8	1.1
Overall balance	−13.2	−20.5	−9.4

Source: IMF, *Chad: Statistical Appendix* (February 2002).

External Trade

PRINCIPAL COMMODITIES

Imports c.i.f. (US $'000)	1995
Food and live animals	41,182
Cereals and cereal preparations	16,028
Wheat and meslin (unmilled). . . .	8,945
Sugar, sugar preparations and honey	17,078
Refined sugars, etc.	16,825
Beverages and tobacco	7,175
Mineral fuels, lubricants, etc.	38,592
Refined petroleum products	38,551
Motor spirit (gasoline) and other light oils . .	6,490
Kerosene and other medium oils. . . .	8,456
Gas oils	23,318
Chemicals and related products	15,507
Medicinal and pharmaceutical products . . .	7,789
Basic manufactures	26,190
Non-metallic mineral manufactures	7,654
Metal manufactures	8,804
Machinery and transport equipment . . .	51,246
General industrial machinery, equipment and parts .	8,175
Road vehicles (incl. air-cushion vehicles) and parts* . .	17,873
Parts and accessories for cars, lorries, buses, etc.* . .	8,253
Miscellaneous manufactured articles. . . .	27,335
Printed matter	13,565
Postage stamps, banknotes, etc.. . . .	11,622
Total (incl. others)	215,171

* Excluding tyres, engines and electrical parts.

Source: UN, *International Trade Statistics Yearbook*.

Exports ('000 million francs CFA)	1997	1998	1999*
Cotton	72.0	85.1	47.9
Livestock	31.2	28.2	32.7
Gum arabic	3.5	6.8	6.4
Total (incl. others)	133.8	147.7	119.5

* Estimates.

Source: La Zone Franc, *Rapport Annuel 1999*.

Total imports c.i.f. (million francs CFA): 169,733 in 1996; 194,732 in 1997; 210,207 in 1998; 194,523 in 1999; 225,700 in 2000; 464,600 in 2001 (Source: IMF, *International Financial Statistics*).

Total exports (million francs CFA): 132,200 in 2000; 121,200 in 2001 (Source: IMF, *International Financial Statistics*).

PRINCIPAL TRADING PARTNERS

Imports c.i.f. (US $'000)	1995
Belgium-Luxembourg	4,771
Cameroon	33,911
Central African Repub.	3,010
China, People's Repub.	6,251
France	88,887
Germany	2,988
Italy	6,452
Japan	5,121
Malaysia	2,234
Netherlands	2,843
Nigeria	25,269
Spain	3,402
USA	13,966
Total (incl. others)	215,171

Source: UN, *International Trade Statistics Yearbook*.

Transport

ROAD TRAFFIC
(motor vehicles in use at 31 December)

	1994	1995*	1996*
Passenger cars	8,720	9,700	10,560
Buses and coaches . . .	708	760	820
Lorries and vans	12,650	13,720	14,550
Tractors	1,413	1,500	1,580
Motorcycles and mopeds . .	1,855	2,730	3,640

* Estimates.

Source: International Road Federation, *World Road Statistics*.

CIVIL AVIATION
(traffic on scheduled services*)

	1997	1998	1999
Kilometres flown (million) . .	3	3	3
Passengers carried ('000) . .	93	98	84
Passengers-km (million). . .	247	263	235
Total ton-km (million) . . .	39	38	36

* Including an apportionment of the traffic of Air Afrique.

Source: UN, *Statistical Yearbook*.

Tourism

FOREIGN VISITORS BY COUNTRY OF ORIGIN*

	1998	1999	2000
Canada	762	877	2,470
France	19,464	22,277	13,707
Germany	241	270	1,361
Italy	489	567	1,254
USA	3,101	3,539	5,320
Total (incl. others)	41,244	46,603	43,034

* Arrivals at hotels and similar establishments.

Source: World Tourism Organization, *Yearbook of Tourism Statistics.*

Tourism receipts (US $ million): 10 in 1996; 9 in 1997; 10 in 1998 (Source: World Bank).

Communications Media

	1999	2000	2001
Television receivers ('000 in use)	10.6	10.9	n.a.
Telephones ('000 main lines in use)	9.7	n.a.	11.0
Mobile cellular telephones ('000 subscribers).	n.a.	5.5	22.0
Personal computers ('000 in use) .	10	n.a.	12
Internet users ('000)	1.0	n.a.	4.0

Radio receivers ('000 in use): 1,670 in 1997.

Facsimile machines (number in use): 182 in 1999.

Daily newspapers: 1 in 1996 (average circulation 2,000 copies); 2 in 1997; 2 in 1998.

Non-daily newspapers: 2 in 1995 (average circulation 10,000 copies); n.a. in 1996; 14 in 1997; 10 in 1998.

Periodicals: 51 in 1997; 53 in 1998.

Sources: International Telecommunication Union; UNESCO, *Statistical Yearbook*; UN, *Statistical Yearbook.*

Education

(1996/97, unless otherwise indicated)

	Institu-tions	Teachers	Students Males	Students Females	Students Total
Pre-primary* . . .	24	67	938	735	1,673
Primary	2,660†	10,151	447,685	233,224	680,909
Secondary:					
general . . .	153†	2,598	77,622	19,389	97,011
teacher training . .	6†	46	360	265	625
vocational . . .	12†	148	1,506	647	2,153
University-level† . .	n.a.	288	2,868‡	406‡	3,274‡

* 1994/95 figures; public education only.
† 1995/96 figures.
‡ Provisional figure.

Source: mainly UNESCO, *Statistical Yearbook.*

1997/98: *Primary:* 786,537 students, *Secondary:* 112,268 students, *Higher:* 4,799 students.

1998/99: *Primary:* 839,932 students.

Adult literacy rate (UNESCO estimates): 42.6% (males 51.6%; females 34.0%) in 2000 (Source: UN Development Programme, *Human Development Report*).

Directory

The Constitution

The Constitution of the Republic of Chad, which was adopted by national referendum on 31 March 1996, enshrines a unitary state. The President is elected for a term of five years by direct universal adult suffrage, and is restricted to a maximum of two terms in office. The Prime Minister, who is appointed by the President, nominates the Council of Ministers. The bicameral legislature includes a 155-member Assemblée nationale, which is elected by direct universal adult suffrage for a term of four years. Provision is also made for an upper legislative chamber, the Sénat, with one-third of members renewed every two years. The Constitution provides for an independent judicial system, with a High Court of Justice, and the establishment of a Constitutional Court and a High Council for Communication.

The Government

HEAD OF STATE

President: IDRISS DEBY (assumed office 4 December 1990; elected President 3 July 1996; re-elected 20 May 2001).

COUNCIL OF MINISTERS
(April 2003)

Prime Minister: HAROUN KABADI.

Minister of Land Management, Town Planning and Housing: BRAHIM SEID.

Minister of Planning, Development and Co-operation: DJIMRANGAR DADNADJI.

Minister of Foreign Affairs and African Integration: MAHAMAT SALEH ANNADIF.

Ministry of Territorial Administration: ABDERAHMANE MOUSSA.

Minister of National Defence, Veterans and Victims of War: MAHAMAT NOURI.

Ministry of Public Security and Immigration: MAHAMAT ALI ABDALLAH.

Minister of Agriculture: DAVID HOUDEINGAR NGARIMADEN.

Minister of Justice, Keeper of the Seals: DJIMNAYE GAOU.

Minister of Public Works and Transport: HASSAN TCHONAI.

Minister of the Economy and Finance: IDRISS AHMED IDRISS.

Minister of National Education: YOKABDJIM MANDIGUI.

Minister of Public Health: MAINA TOUKA SAHANAYE.

Minister of the Civil Service, Labour and Employment: Alhaji ABAKAKA MOUSTAPHA LOPA.

Minister of Posts and Telecommunications: ROUTOUANG YOMA GOLOM.

Minister of Higher Education, Scientific Research and Professional Training: ADOUM GUEMESSOU.

Minister of Social Welfare and the Family: AGNÈS ALAFI MAÏMOUNA.

Minister of Trade, Industry and Crafts: MAHAMAT ABDOULAYE.

Minister of Livestock: MAHAMAT ALLAHOU TAHER.

Minister of Communication, Government Spokesman: MOCTAR WAWA DABAB.

Minister of Petroleum: OUSMANE MOHAMED NOUR ELIMI.

Minister of the Environment and Water: OUMAR KADJALAMI BOUKAR.

Minister of Mines and Energy: MAHAMAT MADADOU ADJI.

Minister of Culture, Youth and Sports: MAHAMAT ZENE BADA.

Minister of the Development of Tourism: AKIA ABOUNA.

Minister, Secretary-General of the Government in charge of Relations with Parliament: ABDERAHIME BIREME HAMID.

Minister-delegate to the Prime Minister, in charge of Decentralization: DJIMTEBAYE LAPIA NELDJITA.

Minister-delegate to the Minister of the Economy and Finance, in charge of the Budget: YOUSSOUF ABSALA.

Assistant Secretary-General to the Government: MAHAMAT TAHER NAHAR.

MINISTRIES

Office of the President: BP 74, N'Djamena; tel. 51-44-37; fax 51-45-01; internet rapidrecettes.com/sodt.

Office of the Prime Minister: N'Djamena.

Ministry of Agriculture: BP 441, N'Djamena; tel. 52-21-48; fax 52-51-19.

Ministry of the Civil Service, Labour and Employment: BP 437, N'Djamena; tel. and fax 52-21-98.

Ministry of Communication: BP 154, N'Djamena; tel. 51-41-64; fax 51-60-94.

Ministry of Culture, Youth and Sports: BP 2056, N'Djamena.

Ministry of the Development of Tourism: BP 86, N'Djamena; tel. 52-44-20.

Ministry of the Economy and Finance: BP 144, N'Djamena; tel. 52-21-61; fax 52-49-08.

Ministry of the Environment and Water: BP 905, N'Djamena; tel. 52-44-70; fax 52-38-39; e-mail facdrem@intnet.td.

Ministry of Foreign Affairs and African Integration: BP 746, N'Djamena; tel. 51-50-82; fax 51-91-22.

Ministry of Higher Education, Scientific Research and Professional Training: BP 731, N'Djamena; tel. 51-44-76.

Ministry of Justice: BP 426, N'Djamena; tel. 52-21-72; fax 52-21-39; e-mail justice@intnet.td.

Ministry of Land Management, Town Planning and Housing: N'Djamena.

Ministry of Livestock: N'Djamena; tel. 51-59-07.

Ministry of Mines and Energy: BP 94, N'Djamena; tel. 52-38-50; fax 52-25-65.

Ministry of National Defence, Veterans and Victims of War: N'Djamena; tel. 51-58-89; fax 52-45-06.

Ministry of National Education: N'Djamena.

Ministry of Petroleum: N'Djamena.

Ministry of Planning, Development and Co-operation: BP 286, N'Djamena; tel. 51-46-37.

Ministry of Posts and Telecommunications: BP 154, N'Djamena; tel. 52-15-55; fax 52-15-30; e-mail dabye@intnet.td.

Ministry of Public Health: BP 440, N'Djamena; tel. 51-42-42.

Ministry of Public Security and Immigration: N'Djamena.

Ministry of Public Works and Transport: BP 984, N'Djamena; tel. 52-37-67.

Ministry of Social Welfare and the Family: N'Djamena.

Ministry of Territorial Administration: BP 742, N'Djamena; tel. 52-25-68; fax 52-59-06.

Ministry of Trade, Industry and Crafts: BP 458, N'Djamena; tel. 52-30-49; fax 52-27-33.

President and Legislature

PRESIDENT

Election, 20 May 2001

Candidate	Votes	% of vote
Idriss Deby (MPS*)	1,533,509	63.17
Ngarledjy Yorongar (FAR)	396,864	16.35
Saleh Kebzaboh (UNDR)	169,917	7.00
Gen. Wadal Abdelkader Kamougué (URD)	146,125	6.02
Ibn Oumar Mahamat Saleh (PLD)	70,248	2.89
Kassire Delwa Koumakoye (VIVA—RNDP)	57,382	2.36
Dr Jean Bawoyeu Alingué (UDR)	53,513	2.20
Total	2,427,558	100.00

* In coalition with 27 other parties.

ASSEMBLÉE NATIONALE

Assemblée nationale: Palais du 15 janvier, BP 01, N'Djamena; tel. 53-08-25; fax 53-00-95.

President: NASSOUR GUÉLENDOUKSIA OUAÏDOU.

General Election, 21 April 2002

Party	Seats
Mouvement patriotique du salut (MPS)	110
Rassemblement pour la démocratie et le progrès (RDP)	12
Fédération d'action pour la République (FAR)	9
VIVA—Rassemblement national pour la démocratie et le progrès (VIVA—RNDP)	5
Union nationale pour le développement et le renouveau (UNDR)	5
Union pour le renouveau et la démocratie (URD)	3
Others*	9
Vacant†	2
Total	155

* There were nine other parties.
† The Constitutional Council annulled the results of voting in two constituencies, in which by-elections were subsequently to be held.
Note: The Constitution also makes provision for an upper house of the legislature, the Sénat.

Political Organizations

Legislation permitting the operation of political associations, subject to official registration, took effect in October 1991. In early 2003 there were about 60 active political organizations, of which the following were among the most important:

Alliance nationale pour la démocratie et le développement (AND): BP 4066, N'Djamena; tel. 51-46-72; f. 1992; Leader SALIBOU GARBA.

Alliance tchadienne pour la démocratie et le développement (ATD): N'Djamena; e-mail info@atd-tchad.com; internet www.atd-tchad.com; Leader ABDERAMAN DJASNABAILLE.

Action tchadienne pour l'unité et le socialisme (ACTUS): N'Djamena; e-mail actus@club-internet.fr; Leader FIDEL MOUNGAR.

Convention pour la démocratie et le fédéralisme: N'Djamena; f. 2002; socialist; supports the establishment of a federal state; Leader ALI GOLHOR.

Convention nationale démocratique et sociale (CNDS): N'Djamena; Leader ADOUM DAYE ZERE.

Fédération d'action pour la République (FAR): BP 4197, N'Djamena; tel. and fax 51-45-59; e-mail yorongar@intnet.td; supports the establishment of a federal republic; Leader NGARLEDJY YORONGAR.

Mouvement patriotique du salut (MPS): N'Djamena; e-mail animation@patriotique.com; internet www.patriotique.com; f. 1990 as a coalition of several opposition movements; other opposition groups joined during the Nov. 1990 offensive against the regime of Hissène Habré, and following the movement's accession to power in Dec. 1990; Hon. Pres. MALDOM BADA ABBAS; Sec.-Gen. MAHAMAT SALEH AHMAT.

Parti pour la liberté et le développement (PLD): N'Djamena; f. 1993; boycotted legislative elections in 2002; Sec.-Gen. IBN OUMAR MAHAMAT SALEH.

Rassemblement pour la démocratie et le progrès (RDP): N'Djamena; f. 1992; pro-Govt; seeks to create a secure political environment by the establishment of a reformed national army; Leader Lol Mahamat Choua.

Union pour la démocratie et la République (UDR): N'Djamena; f. 1992; supports liberal economic policies and a secular, decentralized republic; boycotted legislative elections in 2002; Leader Dr Jean Bawoyeu Alingué.

Union nationale pour le développement et le renouveau (UNDR): N'Djamena; supports greater decentralization and increased limitations on the power of the state; Leader Saleh Kebzaboh.

Union pour le renouveau et la démocratie (URD): BP 92, N'Djamena; tel. 51-44-23; fax 51-41-87; f. 1992; Leader Gen. Wadal Abdelkader Kamougué.

VIVA—Rassemblement national pour la démocratie et le progrès (VIVA—RNDP): N'Djamena; f. 1992; supports a unitary, democratic republic; Pres. Kassiré Delwa Koumakoye.

Les forces vives du Tchad: is an opposition alliance of some 35 political parties, seven human rights organizations, one trade union federation, and five other civic society organizations, formed in late 2000, and headed by Abderaman Djasnabaille of the ATD.

A number of unregistered dissident groups (some based abroad) are also active. These 'politico-military' organizations incl. the following:

Alliance nationale de la résistance (ANR): f. 1995 as alliance of five movements; in early 2003 comprised eight rebel groups based in eastern Chad; signed peace agreement with Govt in Jan. 2003, although FONALT rejected this accord; Leader Col Mahamat Garfa.

> **Forces des organisations nationales pour l'alternance et les libertés au Tchad (FONALT):** rejected cease-fire signed by ANR with Govt in Jan. 2003; Leader Col Abdoulaye Issaka Sarwa.

Comité politique d'action et de liaison (CPAL): f. 1999; Leader Acheikh Ibn Oumar.

Conseil démocratique révolutionnaire (CDR): Leader Acheikh Ibn Oumar.

Front national du Tchad (FNT): based in Sudan; Leader Dr Faris Bachar.

Mouvement pour la démocratie et la justice au Tchad (MDJT): deputy leader, Adoum Togoi, signed a peace agreement with Govt in Jan. 2002, although this was subsequently rejected by elements close to fmr leader, Youssouf Togoimi (who died in Sept. 2002); Leader (vacant).

Mouvement pour l'unité et la République (MUR): f. 2000 by faction of the MDD; Leader Gaileth Gatoul Bourkoumandah.

Conseil national pour le redressement (CNR): Leader Hissène Koty Yacoub.

Convention populaire de la résistance (CPR): e-mail cpr60@voila.fr; internet www.maxpages.com/tchad/cpr; Leader Abdel-Aziz Abdallah Kodok.

Coordination des mouvements armés et partis politiques de l'opposition (CMAP): internet www.maxpages.com/tchad/cmap2; f. 1999 by 13 'politico-military' organizations; Leader Antoine Bangui; mems incl. the following:

> **Front extérieur pour la rénovation:** Leader Antoine Bangui.

> **Front de libération nationale du Tchad-Conseil provisoire de la révolution (FROLINAT-CPR):** f. 1968 in Sudan; based in Algeria; Leader Goukouni Oueddei.

Mouvement pour la démocratie et le développement (MDD): e-mail mdd@mdd-tchad.com; internet membres.lycos.fr/mddtchad; comprises two factions, led by Mahamat Issa Faki and Brahim Mallah.

Union des forces démocratiques (UFD): Leader Dr Mahamat Nahour.

Diplomatic Representation

EMBASSIES IN CHAD

Algeria: BP 178, N'Djamena; tel. 52-38-15; fax 52-37-92; Ambassador Boubakeur Ogab.

Cameroon: rue des Poids Lourds, BP 58, N'Djamena; tel. 52-28-94.

Central African Republic: rue 1036, près du Rond-Point de la Garde, BP 115, N'Djamena; tel. 52-25-75; Ambassador David Nguindo.

China (Taiwan): BP 1150, N'Djamena; tel. 52-44-05; fax 52-44-02; e-mail ambchine@intnet.td; Ambassador Shin Cheng.

Congo, Democratic Republic: ave du 20 août, BP 910, N'Djamena; tel. 52-29-35; Ambassador (vacant).

Egypt: BP 1094, N'Djamena; tel. 51-09-72; fax 51-09-73; Ambassador Aziz M. Nour el-Din.

France: rue du Lt Franjoux, BP 431, N'Djamena; tel. 52-25-75; fax 52-28-55; e-mail amba.france@intnet.td; internet www.ambafrance-td.org; Ambassador Jacques Courbin.

Holy See: BP 490, N'Djamena; tel. 52-31-15; fax 52-38-27; Apostolic Nuncio Most Rev. Joseph Chennoth (Titular Archbishop of Milevum).

Libya: BP 1096, N'Djamena; tel. 52-39-79; Ambassador Ghayth Salim.

Nigeria: 35 ave Charles de Gaulle, BP 752, N'Djamena; tel. 52-24-98; fax 52-30-92; Chargé d'affaires a.i. A. M. Aliyu Biu.

Russia: 2 rue Collin, BP 891, N'Djamena; tel. 52-31-72; fax 51-31-72; e-mail amrus@intnet.td.

Saudi Arabia: quartier Aéroport, rue Jander Miry, BP 974, N'Djamena; tel. 52-36-95; fax 52-33-28; e-mail tdemb@mofa.gov.sa.

Sudan: rue de la Gendarmerie, BP 45, N'Djamena; tel. 52-43-59; e-mail amb.soudan@intnet.td; Ambassador Hassan Beshir Abdelwahab.

USA: ave Félix Eboué, BP 413, N'Djamena; tel. 51-70-09; fax 51-56-54; e-mail gso_procurement@hotmail.com; internet usembassy.state.gov/ndjamena; Ambassador Christopher E. Goldthwait.

Judicial System

The highest judicial authority is the Supreme Court, which comprises a Judicial Chamber, an Administrative Chamber and a Chamber of Accounts. There is also a Constitutional Council, with final jurisdiction in matters of state. The legal structure also comprises the Court of Appeal, and magistrate and criminal courts. Under the terms of the Constitution adopted in 1996, a High Court of Justice was to be established.

Supreme Court: rue 0221, Quartier Résidentiel, 1er arrondissement, N'Djamena; tel. 52-00-00; fax 53-00-00; e-mail ccsrp@intnet.td; internet www.coursupreme.td; Pres. Ahmed Bartchiret; Pres. of the Judicial Chamber Belkoulaye Ben Coumareaux; Pres. of the Administrative Chamber (vacant); Pres. of the Chamber of Accounts Dolotan Noudjalbaye.

President of the Constitutional Council: Nagoum Yamassoum.

Court of Appeal: N'Djamena; tel. 51-24-26; Pres. Maki Adam Issaka.

Religion

It is estimated that some 50% of the population are Muslims and about 30% Christians. Most of the remainder follow animist beliefs.

ISLAM

Conseil Suprême des Affaires Islamiques
POB 1101, N'Djamena; tel. 51-81-80; fax 52-58-84.

Head of the Islamic Community: Imam Moussa Ibrahim.

CHRISTIANITY

The Roman Catholic Church

Chad comprises one archdiocese, six dioceses and one apostolic prefecture. At 31 December 2000 Roman Catholics numbered 560,512 (about 8.5% of the total population), most of whom resided in the south-west of the country.

Bishops' Conference
Conférence Episcopale du Tchad, BP 456, N'Djamena; tel. 51-44-43; fax 51-28-60.
f. 1991; Pres. Most Rev. Charles Vandame (Archbishop of N'Djamena).

Archbishop of N'Djamena: Most Rev. Charles Vandame, Archevêché, BP 456, N'Djamena; tel. 51-74-44; fax 52-50-51; e-mail diocndja@intnet.td.

Protestant Churches

Entente des Eglises et Missions Evangéliques au Tchad (EEMET): BP 2006, N'Djamena; tel. 51-53-93; fax 51-87-20; e-mail eemet@intnet.td; asscn of churches and missions working in Chad; includes Assemblées Chrétiennes au Tchad (ACT), Eglise Evangélique des Frères au Tchad (EEFT), Eglise Evangélique au Tchad

(EET), Eglise Fraternelle Luthérienne au Tchad (EFLT), Eglise Evangélique en Afrique Centrale au Tchad (EEACT); also five assoc. mems.

BAHÁ'Í FAITH

National Spiritual Assembly: BP 181, N'Djamena; tel. 51-47-05; e-mail ntirandaz@aol.com.

The Press

Al-Watan: N'Djamena; tel. 51-57-96; weekly; Editor-in-Chief MOUSSA NDORKOÏ.

Audy Magazine: BP 780, N'Djamena; tel. 51-49-59; f. 2000; 2 a month; women's interest; Dir TONGRONGOU AGOUNA GRÂCE.

Bulletin Mensuel de Statistiques du Tchad: BP 453, N'Djamena; monthly.

Carrefour: Centre al-Mouna, BP 456, N'Djamena; tel. 51-42-54; e-mail almouna@intnet.td; f. 2000; every 2 months; Dir Sister NADIA KARAKI; circ. 1,000 (2001).

Chronique: Association pour la Promotion des Libertés Fondamentales Tchad (APLFT), BP 4037, N'Djamena; tel. 51-91-14; monthly; promotes civic information and popular understanding of civic law; Dir MAOUNDONODJI GILBERT.

Comnat: BP 731, N'Djamena; tel. 51-46-75; fax 51-46-71; quarterly; publ. by Commission Nationale Tchadienne for UNESCO.

Grenier: BP 1128, N'Djamena; tel. 53-30-14; e-mail cedesep@intnet .td; monthly; economics; finance; Dir KOHOM NGAR-ONE DAVID.

Info-Tchad: BP 670, N'Djamena; tel. 51-58-67; news bulletin issued by Agence-Info Tchad; daily; French.

Informations Economiques: BP 458, N'Djamena; publ. by the Chambre de Commerce, d'Agriculture et d'Industrie; weekly.

La Lettre: BP 2037, N'Djamena; tel. and fax 51-91-09; e-mail ltdh@ intnet.td; f. 1993; monthly; publ. by the Ligue Tchadienne des droits de l'Homme; Dir DOBIAN ASSINGAR.

N'Djamena Hebdo: BP 4498, N'Djamena; tel. 51-53-14; fax 52-14-98; e-mail ndjh@intnet.td; 2 a week; Arabic and French; f. 1989; Dir YALDET BÉGOTO OULATAR; Editor-in-Chief DIEUDONNÉ DJONABAYE; circ. 3,500 (2001).

Notre Temps: BP 4352, N'Djamena; tel. and fax 51-46-50; e-mail ntemps.presse@yahoo.fr; f. 2000; weekly; opposed to the Govt of Pres. Deby; publication suspended in Feb. 2003; Editorial Dir NADJI KIMO; circ. 3,000 (2001).

L'Observateur: BP 2031, N'Djamena; tel. and fax 51-80-05; e-mail observer.presse@intnet.td; f. 1997; weekly; Dir SY KOUMBO SINGA GALI; circ. 4,000 (2001).

Le Progrès: 1976 ave Charles de Gaulle, BP 3055, N'Djamena; tel. 51-55-86; fax 51-02-56; e-mail progres@intnet.td; f. 1993; daily; Dir MAHAMAT HISSÈNE; circ. 3,000 (2001).

Tchad et Culture: BP 907, N'Djamena; tel. 51-54-32; fax 51-91-50; e-mail cefod@intnet.td; internet www.cefod.org; f. 1961; monthly; Dir RONEINGUÉ TORIAÏRA; Editor-in-Chief NAYGOTIMTI BAMBÉ; circ. 4,500 (2002).

Le Temps: face Ecole Belle-vue, Moursal, BP 1333, N'Djamena; tel. 51-70-28; fax 51-99-24; e-mail temps.presse@intnet.td; f. 1995; weekly; Dir MICHAËL N. DIDAMA; circ. 6,000 (2001).

Victoire Al Nassr: BP 1331, N'Djamena; tel. 51-64-17; weekly; Dir ABOUBAKAR MAHAMAT BORGHO.

La Voix du Paysan: BP 1671, N'Djamena; tel. 51-82-66; monthly; Dir DJALDI TABDI GASSISSOU NASSER.

NEWS AGENCIES

Agence-Info Tchad: BP 670, N'Djamena; tel. 52-58-67; f. 1966; Dir ABAKAR HASSAN ACHEICK.

Foreign Bureau

Agence France-Presse (AFP): N'Djamena; tel. 51-54-71; Correspondent ALDOM NADJI TITO.

Publisher

Imprimerie du Tchad (IDT): BP 453, N'Djamena; tel. 52-44-40; fax 52-28-60.

Broadcasting and Communications

TELECOMMUNICATIONS

Société des Télécommunications du Tchad (SOTEL TCHAD): BP 1132, N'Djamena; tel. 52-14-41; fax 52-14-14; f. 2000 by merger of telecommunications services of fmr Office Nationale des Postes et des Télécommunications and the Société des Télécommunications Internationales du Tchad; privatization proposed; Dir-Gen. ABAKAR SOUGUI.

Celtel-Tchad: N'Djamena; tel. 52-04-11; fax 52-02-33; e-mail j .mgalleron@celtel.td; internet www.mti-cellular.com; f. 2000; affiliated to MSI-Cellular (United Kingdom); provides mobile cellular telecommunications in N'Djamena and Moundou; Man. Dir JEAN-MICHEL GALLERON.

Tchad Mobile-Libertis: ave Charles de Gaulle, BP 5742, N'Djamena; tel. 52-02-00; fax 52-01-39; e-mail mobichad@intnet.td; f. 2000; provides mobile cellular telecommunications in N'Djamena, Abéché, Doba, Moundou and Sarh; jointly owned by Orascom Telecom (Egypt) and SOTEL TCHAD; Dir-Gen. SAMEH MANGOURY.

BROADCASTING

Regulatory Authority

High Council of Communication (HCC): N'Djamena; f. 1994; responsible for registration and regulation of radio and television stations, in addition to the printed press; funds independent radio stations; Pres. EMMANUEL TOUADÉ.

Radio

Private radio stations have been permitted to operate in Chad since 1994, although private broadcasts did not begin until 1997. By mid-2002 15 private and community stations had received licences, of which nine had commenced broadcasts. There was, additionally, a state-owned broadcaster, with four regional stations.

Radio Nationale Tchadienne (RNT): BP 4589, N'Djamena; tel. 53-32-00; f. 1955; state-controlled; programmes in French, Arabic and 11 vernacular languages; four regional stations; Dir N'GUÉR-ÉBAYE ADOUM SALEH.

Radio Abéché: BP 36, Abéché, Ouaddaï; tel. 69-81-49; Dir DIMA-NANGAR DJAINTA.

Radio Faya-Largeau: Faya-Largeau, Borkou.

Radio Moundou: BP 122, Moundou, Logone Occidental; tel. 69-13-22; programmes in French, Sara and Arabic; Dir DIMANANGAR DJAÏNTA.

Radio Sarh: BP 270, Sarh, Bahr Kôh; tel. 68-13-61; programmes in French, Sara and Arabic; Dir BIANA FOUDA NACTOUANDI.

Union des radios privées du Tchad (URPT): N'Djamena; f. 2002 as a federation of nine private and community radio stations, including the following.

DJA FM: BP 1312, N'Djamena; tel. 51-64-90; fax 52-14-52; e-mail myzara@intnet.td; f. 1999; music, cultural and informative programmes in French, Arabic and Sara; Dir ZARA YACOUB.

Radio Brakoss (Radio de l'Agriculture): Moïssala, Mandoul; f. 2000; community radio station; Dir TCHANGUIZ VATANKHAH.

Radio Duji Lohar: BP 155, Moundou, Logone Occidental; tel. 69-17-14; fax 69-12-11; e-mail cdave@intnet.td; f. 2001.

Radio FM Liberté: BP 892, N'Djamena; tel. 51-42-53; f. 2000; financed by nine civil-society organizations; broadcasts in French, Arabic and Sara; Dir DOBIAN ASSINGAR.

La Voix du Paysan: BP 22, Doba, Logone Oriental; f. 1996; Roman Catholic; Dir DJALDI TABDI GASSISSOU NASSER.

Television

TVT Télévision tchadienne: BP 274, N'Djamena; tel. 52-26-79; fax 52-29-23; state-controlled; broadcasts c. 12 hours per week in French and Arabic; Dir OUROUMADJI MOUSSA.

Broadcasts from Canal France International, TV5, CNN and seven Arabic television stations are also received in Chad.

Finance

(cap. = capital; res = reserves; dep. = deposits; m. = million; br. = branch; amounts in francs CFA)

BANKING

Central Bank

Banque des Etats de l'Afrique Centrale (BEAC): ave Charles de Gaulle, BP 50, N'Djamena; tel. 52-41-76; fax 51-44-87; internet www.beac.int; HQ in Yaoundé, Cameroon; f. 1973; bank of issue for mem. states of the Communauté économique et monétaire de l'Afrique centrale (CEMAC, fmrly Union douanière et économique de l'Afrique centrale), comprising Cameroon, the Central African Repub., Chad, the Repub. of the Congo, Equatorial Guinea and Gabon; res 177,417m., total assets 2,034,793m. (Dec. 2001); Gov. JEAN-FÉLIX MAMALEPOT; Dir in Chad MAHAMAD AMINE BEN BARKA; 2 brs.

Other Banks

Banque Agricole du Soudan au Tchad (BAST): ave el-Niméry, BP 1727, N'Djamena; tel. 51-90-41; fax 51-90-40; e-mail bast@intnet.td; cap. 1,200m. (2002), total assets 1,845m. (Dec. 1999); Pres. MOUHAMED OUSMAN AWAD; Dir-Gen. ABDELKADER OUSMAN HASSAN; 1 br.

Banque Commerciale du Chari (BCC): ave Charles de Gaulle, BP 757, N'Djamena; tel. 51-89-58; fax 51-62-49; e-mail bcc@intnet.td; 50% state-owned, 50% owned by Libya Arab Foreign Bank (Libya); cap. 1,000.0m., res 171.6m., dep. 12,248.4m. (Dec. 2000); Pres. BIDJERE BINDJAKI; Dir-Gen. HAMED EL MISTIRI.

Banque Internationale d'Afrique au Tchad (BIAT): ave Charles de Gaulle, BP 87, N'Djamena; tel. 52-43-14; fax 52-23-45; e-mail biat@intnet.td; f. 1980; cap. 3,000m., total assets 26,387m. (Dec. 2000); Pres. BABER TOUNKARA; Dir-Gen. GUY MALLETT.

Commerical Bank Tchad (CBT): rue Capitaine Ohrel, BP 19, N'Djamena; tel. 52-28-29; fax 52-33-18; e-mail expbdt@intnet.td; f. 1962; 50.7% owned by Groupe FOTSO (Cameroon), 17.5% state-owned; fmrly Banque de Développement du Tchad; cap. 2,010m. (2002), total assets 10,208m. (Dec. 1999); Pres. MAHAMAT AHMAT SALEH; Dir-Gen. ISSA OROZO BATIL.

Financial Bank Tchad (FBT): BP 804, N'Djamena; tel. 52-33-89; fax 52-29-05; e-mail fbt@intnet.td; f. 1992; 97.9% owned by Financial BC (Switzerland); cap. and res 884m., total assets 10,891m. (Dec. 1999); Pres. RÉMY BAYSSET; Dir-Gen. PIERRE LECLAIRE.

Société Générale Tchadienne de Banque (SGTB): 2–6 rue Robert Lévy, BP 461, N'Djamena; tel. 52-28-01; fax 52-37-13; e-mail bhfm.mail@socgen.com; internet groupe.socgen.com/sgtb; f. 1963; 30% owned by Société Générale (France), 15% by Sociéte Générale de Banque au Cameroun; cap. 1,100m., total assets 38.8m. (Dec. 2000); Pres. and Dir-Gen. CHEMI KOGRIMI; br. at Moundou.

Bankers' Organizations

Association Professionnelle des Banques au Tchad: 2–6 rue Robert Lévy, BP 461, N'Djamena; tel. 52-41-90; fax 52-17-13; Pres. CHEMI KOGRIMI.

Conseil National de Crédit: N'Djamena; f. 1965 to formulate a national credit policy and to organize the banking profession.

INSURANCE

Assureurs Conseils Tchadiens Cecar et Jutheau: rue du Havre, BP 139, N'Djamena; tel. 52-21-15; fax 52-35-39; e-mail biliou.alikeke@intnet.td; f. 1966; Dir BILIOU ALIKEKE.

Société Mutuelle d'Assurances des Cadres des Professions Libérales et des Indépendants (SMAC): BP 644, N'Djamena; tel. 51-70-19; fax 51-70-61.

Société de Représentation d'Assurances et de Réassurances Africaines (SORARAF): N'Djamena; Dir Mme FOURNIER.

Société Tchadienne d'Assurances et de Réassurances (STAR Nationale): ave Charles de Gaulle, Champs de Course, BP 914, N'Djamena; tel. 52-56-77; fax 52-51-89; Dir-Gen. PHILIPPE SABIT.

Trade and Industry

DEVELOPMENT ORGANIZATIONS

Agence Française de Développement (AFD): BP 478, route de Farcha, N'Djamena; tel. 52-70-71; fax 52-78-31; e-mail afdndjdi@intnet.td; internet www.afd.fr; fmrly Caisse Française de Développement; Dir LOUIS L'AOT.

Association Française des Volontaires du Progrès (AFVP): BP 448, N'Djamena; tel. 52-20-53; fax 52-26-56; e-mail afvptchd@intnet.td; internet www.afvp.org; f. 1965; Nat. Rep. CAROLE SAMBA.

Association Tchadienne pour le Développement: BP 470, Quartier Sabangali, N'Djamena; tel. 51-43-69; fax 51-89-23; e-mail darna.dnla@intnet.td; Dir DIGALI ZEUHINBA.

Mission Française de Coopération et d'Action Culturelle: BP 898, N'Djamena; tel. 52-42-87; fax 52-44-38; administers bilateral aid from France; Dir EDOUARD LAPORTE.

Office National de Développement Rural (ONDR): BP 896, N'Djamena; tel. 51-48-64; f. 1968; Dir MICKAEL DJIBRAEL.

Société pour le Développement du Lac (SODELAC): BP 782, N'Djamena; tel. 51-35-03; f. 1967 to develop the area of Lake Chad; cap. 180m. francs CFA; Pres. CHERIF ABDELWAHAB; Dir-Gen. MAHAMAT MOCTAR ALI.

CHAMBER OF COMMERCE

Chambre de Commerce, d'Industrie, d'Agriculture, des Mines et d'Artisanat: 13 rue du Col Moll, BP 458, N'Djamena; tel. 52-52-64; fax 52-14-52; f. 1935; Dir. YOUSSOUF ABASSALLAH; brs at Sarh, Moundou, Bol and Abéché.

TRADE ASSOCIATIONS

Office National des Céréales (ONC): BP 21, N'Djamena; tel. 51-37-31; fax 52-20-18; e-mail onc1@intnet.td; f. 1978; production and marketing of cereals; Dir-Gen. MAHAMAT ALI HASSABALLAH; 11 regional offices.

Société Nationale de Commercialisation du Tchad (SONACOT): N'Djamena; f. 1965; cap. 150m. francs CFA; 76% state-owned; nat. marketing, distribution and import-export co; Man. Dir MARBROUCK NATROUD.

EMPLOYERS' ORGANIZATIONS

Conseil National du Patronat Tchadien (CNPT): 17 ave Charles de Gaulle, BP 34, N'Djamena; tel. 52-25-71; fax 51-60-65; Pres. RAJHIS MANNANY; Sec.-Gen. MARC MADENGAR BEREMADJI; 67 mem. enterprises with total work-force of 8,000 (2002).

Union des Transporteurs Tchadiens: BP 529, N'Djamena; tel. 51-45-27.

UTILITIES

Electricity and Water

Société Tchadienne d'Eau et d'Electricité (STEE): 11 rue du Col Largeau, BP 44, N'Djamena; tel. 51-28-81; fax 51-21-34; f. 1968; state-owned; transferred to private management by Vivendi (France) in 2000; production and distribution of electricity and water; Pres. GOMON MAWATA WAKAG; Dir-Gen. ISMAEL MAHAMAT ADOUM.

TRADE UNIONS

Confédération Libre des Travailleurs du Tchad (CLTT): ave Charles de Gaulle, BP 553, N'Djamena; tel. 51-76-11; fax 52-44-56; Sec.-Gen. BRAHIM BAKAS; 22,500 mems (2001).

Union des Syndicats du Tchad (UST): BP 1143, N'Djamena; tel. 51-42-75; fax 51-48-08; f. 1988; federation of trade unions; Pres. DOMBAL DJIMBAGUE; Sec.-Gen. DJIBRINE ASSALI HAMDALLAH.

Transport

RAILWAYS

There are no railways in Chad. In 1962 the Governments of Chad and Cameroon signed an agreement to extend the Transcameroon railway from Ngaoundéré to Sarh, a distance of 500 km. Although the Transcameroon reached Ngaoundéré in 1974, its proposed extension into Chad remains indefinitely postponed.

ROADS

The total length of the road network in 1999 was an estimated 40,000 km, of which 3,100 km were principal roads and 1,400 km were secondary roads; only 412 km of the network was paved. There are also some 20,000 km of tracks suitable for motor traffic during the October–July dry season. The European Union is contributing to the construction of a highway connecting N'Djamena with Sarh and Léré, on the Cameroon border, and of a 400-km highway linking Moundou and Ngaoundéré.

Coopérative des Transportateurs Tchadiens (CTT): BP 336, N'Djamena; tel. 51-43-55; road haulage; Pres. SALEH KHALIFA; brs at

Sarh, Moundou, Bangui (CAR), Douala and Ngaoundéré (Cameroon).

Société Générale d'Entreprise Routière (SGER): BP 175, N'Djamena; tel. and fax 51-55-12; e-mail itralu@intnet.td; devt and maintenance of roads; 95% owned by Arcory International (Sudan); Pres. PATRICK MORIN.

Société Tchadienne d'Affrètement et de Transit (STAT): 21 ave Félix Eboué, BP 100, N'Djamena; tel. 51-88-72; fax 51-74-24; e-mail stat.tchad@intnet.td; affiliated to Groupe Saga (France); road haulage.

INLAND WATERWAYS

The Chari and Logone rivers, which converge to the south of N'Djamena, are navigable. These waterways connect Sarh with N'Djamena on the Chari and Bongor and Moundou with N'Djamena on the Logone.

CIVIL AVIATION

The international airport is at N'Djamena. There are also more than 40 smaller airfields.

Air Affaires Tchad: BP 256, N'Djamena; tel. 51-06-20; e-mail airaffaires@yahoo.st; passenger and freight internal and charter flights.

Air Tchad: BP 168, N'Djamena; tel. 52-45-64; fax 52-35-82; internal flights.

Minair Tchad: ave Charles de Gaulle, BP 1239, N'Djamena; tel. 51-31-51; fax 51-07-80; passenger and freight air transport.

Tourism

Chad's potential attractions for tourists include a variety of scenery from the dense forests of the south to the deserts of the north. Receipts from tourism in 1998 totalled an estimated US $10m. A total of 43,034 tourists visited Chad in 2000, compared with 26,980 in 1997.

Direction du Tourisme: BP 86, N'Djamena; tel. 52-23-03; fax 52-22-61.

CHILE

Introductory Survey

Location, Climate, Language, Religion, Flag, Capital

The Republic of Chile is a long, narrow country lying along the Pacific coast of South America, extending from Peru and Bolivia in the north to Cape Horn in the far south. Isla de Pascua (Rapa Nui or Easter Island), about 3,780 km (2,350 miles) off shore, and several other small islands form part of Chile. To the east, Chile is separated from Argentina by the high Andes mountains. Both the mountains and the cold Humboldt Current influence the climate; between Arica in the north and Punta Arenas in the extreme south, a distance of about 4,000 km (2,500 miles), the average maximum temperature varies by no more than 13°C. Rainfall varies widely between the arid desert in the north and the rainy south. The language is Spanish. There is no state religion but the great majority of the inhabitants profess Christianity, and some 79% are adherents of the Roman Catholic Church. The national flag (proportions 2 by 3) is divided horizontally: the lower half is red, while the upper half has a five-pointed white star on a blue square, at the hoist, with the remainder white. The capital is Santiago.

Recent History

Chile was ruled by Spain from the 16th century until its independence in 1818. For most of the 19th century it was governed by a small oligarchy of landowners. Chile won the War of the Pacific (1879–83) against Peru and Bolivia. The greater part of the 20th century was characterized by the struggle for power between right- and left-wing forces.

In September 1970 Dr Salvador Allende Gossens, the Marxist candidate of Unidad Popular (a coalition of five left-wing parties, including the Partido Comunista de Chile—PCCh), was elected to succeed Eduardo Frei Montalva, a Christian Democrat who was President between 1964 and 1970. Allende promised to transform Chilean society by constitutional means, and imposed an extensive programme of nationalization. The Government failed to obtain a congressional majority in the elections of March 1973 and encountered a deteriorating economic situation as well as an intensification of violent opposition to its policies. Accelerated inflation led to food shortages and there were repeated clashes between pro- and anti-Government activists. The armed forces finally intervened in September 1973. President Allende died during the coup. The Congreso (Congress) was subsequently dissolved, all political activity banned and strict censorship introduced. The military Junta dedicated itself to the eradication of Marxism and the reconstruction of Chile, and its leader, Gen. Augusto Pinochet Ugarte, became Supreme Chief of State in June 1974 and President in December. The Junta was widely criticized abroad for its repressive policies and violations of human rights. Critics of the regime were tortured and imprisoned, and several thousand were abducted or 'disappeared'. Some of those who had been imprisoned were released, as a result of international pressure, and sent into exile.

In September 1976 three constitutional acts were promulgated with the aim of creating an 'authoritarian democracy'. All political parties were banned in March 1977, when the state of siege was extended. Following a UN General Assembly resolution, adopted in December 1977, which condemned the Government for violating human rights, President Pinochet organized a referendum in January 1978 to seek endorsement of the regime's policies. Since more than 75% of the voters supported the President in his defence of Chile 'in the face of international aggression', the state of siege (in force since 1973) was ended and was replaced by a state of emergency.

At a plebiscite held in September 1980, 67% of voters endorsed a new Constitution, drafted by the Government, although dubious electoral practices were allegedly employed. Although the new Constitution was described as providing a 'transition to democracy' and President Pinochet ceased to be head of the armed forces, additional clauses allowed him to maintain his firm hold on power until 1989. The new Constitution became effective from March 1981. Political parties, which were still officially outlawed, began to re-emerge, and in mid-1983 five moderate parties formed a coalition, the Alianza Democrática,

which advocated a return to democratic rule within 18 months. A left-wing coalition was also created.

In February 1984 the Council of State, a government-appointed consultative body, began drafting a law to legalize political parties and to prepare for elections in 1989. Despite the Government's strenuous attempts to eradicate internal opposition through the introduction of anti-terrorist legislation and extensive security measures, a campaign of explosions and public protests continued throughout 1984 and 1985. A number of protesters were killed in violent clashes with security forces, and many opposition leaders and trade unionists were detained and sent into internal exile.

Throughout 1986 President Pinochet's regime came under increasing attack from the Roman Catholic Church, guerrilla organizations (principally the Frente Patriótico Manuel Rodríguez—FPMR) and international critics, including the US administration, which had previously refrained from condemning the regime's notorious record of violations of human rights. In September the FPMR made an unsuccessful attempt to assassinate Pinochet. The regime's immediate response was to impose a state of siege throughout Chile, under which leading members of the opposition were detained and strict censorship was introduced. One consequence of the state of siege was the reappearance of right-wing 'death squads', which were implicated in a series of murders following the assassination attempt.

President Pinochet clearly indicated his intention to remain in office beyond 1989 by securing, in mid-1987, the presidential candidacy to be rejected or approved by the same plebiscite which would decide the future electoral timetable. By mid-1988 several political parties and opposition groups had established the Comando por el No to co-ordinate the campaign for the anti-Government vote at the forthcoming referendum, on 5 October. Despite reports of electoral malpractice, the plebiscite took place without major incident. The official result recorded 54.7% of the votes cast for the anti-Pinochet campaign, and 43.1% for the President. Following the plebiscite, the opposition made repeated demands for changes to the Constitution, in order to accelerate the democratic process, and sought to initiate discussions with the armed forces. However, Pinochet rejected the opposition's proposals, and affirmed his intention to remain in office until March 1990.

In mid-1989 Patricio Aylwin Azócar, a lawyer and former senator who had been a vociferous supporter of the 'no' vote in the October 1988 plebiscite, emerged as the sole presidential candidate for the centre-left Concertación de los Partidos de la Democracia (CPD, formerly the Comando por el No), an alliance of 17 parties, including the Partido Demócrata Cristiano (PDC), of which Aylwin had hitherto been President. Throughout 1989 the election campaign was dominated by demands from both the CPD and right-wing parties for constitutional reform. A document detailing 54 amendments (including the legalization of Marxist political parties) ratified by the Junta was finally accepted by the opposition, with some reservations, and the constitutional reforms were approved by 85.7% of voters in a national referendum in July 1989.

The electoral campaign was conducted amid intermittent outbursts of political violence and government intervention. Uncertainty regarding President Pinochet's own intentions concerning the forthcoming elections was finally dispelled in mid-1989, when he dismissed the possibility of his candidacy as unconstitutional, but reiterated his intention to continue as Commander-in-Chief of the Army for at least four years. Opposition leaders interpreted subsequent actions by the Government (including the implementation of a law providing for the autonomy of the Banco Central de Chile, the appointment of directors to state-owned companies with mandates of up to 10 years and curbs on the Government's power to remove state officials from their posts) as an attempt by the President to retain a degree of influence beyond his term of office.

The presidential and congressional elections were conducted on 14 December 1989. Patricio Aylwin Azócar of the centre-left CPD secured 55.2% of the valid votes cast in the presidential election, thus achieving a clear victory over the former Minister of Finance, Hernán Büchi Buc, who was supported by the Government and won 29.4%. The transfer of power took place on 11 March. Two members of the outgoing Junta remained as commanders of the air force and police.

Having failed to obtain the support of the two-thirds' majority in the Congreso necessary to amend the 1981 Constitution significantly, Aylwin's new CPD administration was forced to reconcile attempts to fulfil campaign promises as quickly as possible with the need to adopt a conciliatory approach towards more right-wing parties in the Congreso. Agreement was reached almost immediately on a series of modifications to the tax laws, but attempts to amend existing legislation considered repressive by the new administration, including the death penalty and provisions for the censorship of the press, were less successful. (The death penalty was finally abolished in April 2001 and a press freedom law was approved in the following month.)

In April 1990 the Government created the National Commission for Truth and Reconciliation (Comisión Nacional de Verdad y Reconciliación—CNVR) to document and investigate alleged violations of human rights during the previous administration. Although Pinochet, before leaving office, had provided for the impunity of the former military Junta with regard to abuses of human rights, it was suggested by human rights organizations that such safeguards might be circumvented by indicting known perpetrators of atrocities on charges of 'crimes against humanity', a provision which gained considerable public support following the discovery, during 1990, of a number of mass graves containing the remains of political opponents of the 1973–90 military regime. The army High Command condemned the Commission for undermining the prestige of the armed forces and attempting to contravene the terms of a comprehensive amnesty declared in 1978. Although a new accord between military leaders and the Government-Elect had been negotiated in January 1990 (whereby the role of the armed forces was redefined as essentially subservient to the Ministry of Defence), relations between the new Government and the army High Command remained tense. Pinochet became the focus for widespread disaffection with the military élite, but resisted demands for his resignation, reiterating his intention to continue as Commander-in-Chief of the Army until 1997.

Escalating public and political antagonism towards the former military leadership was fuelled throughout 1990 and 1991 by further revelations of abuses of human rights and financial corruption, and erupted into widespread popular outrage and renewed political violence following the publication, in March 1991, of the findings of the CNVR. The report documented the deaths of 2,279 alleged political opponents of the former regime who were executed, died as a result of torture or disappeared (and were presumed to be dead) in 1973–90. In accordance with President Aylwin's recommendation that the report should foster national reconciliation and fulfil an expositionary rather than judicial function, those responsible for the deaths were identified only by the institutions to which they belonged. However, Aylwin pledged full government co-operation for families wishing to pursue private prosecutions. The report concluded that the military Government had embarked upon a 'systematic policy of extermination' of its opponents through the illegal activities of the covert military intelligence agency, Dirección de Inteligencia Nacional (Dina), and was also highly critical of the Chilean judiciary for failing to protect the rights of individuals by refusing thousands of petitions for habeas corpus submitted by human rights lawyers. Pinochet publicly denounced the document and declared his opposition to government plans to make material reparation to the families of the victims named in the report. Left-wing extremists meanwhile embarked on a series of attacks against right-wing opponents; however, fears of an escalation in extremist violence were partially dispelled by the announcement, in May 1991, of the FPMR's intention to renounce its armed struggle and join the political mainstream as the Movimiento Patriótico Manuel Rodríguez.

In November 1993, following a prolonged investigation and a controversial trial, former Dina officials Gen. Manuel Contreras and Col. Pedro Espinoza were convicted of the murder of Orlando Letelier, a former cabinet minister (and Chile's ambassador to the USA during the Government of Salvador Allende in the early 1970s), who was assassinated in 1976, together with a US associate, in Washington, DC. In February 2003 Contreras, along with four other former members of the security forces, appeared in court on charges relating to the murder of Gen.

Carlos Prats in 1974 (see below). In April Contreras was sentenced to 15 years' imprisonment for the kidnapping of Miguel Sandoval. Sandoval, a left-wing activist, had disappeared in 1975. Throughout the 1990s, hopes that an end to the apparent impunity of the former military regime was close had been somewhat frustrated; in late 1993, the Supreme Court ruled to withdraw charges recently brought against former police chief and Junta member, César Mendoza Durán, of complicity in the kidnap and murder of three members of the PCCh in 1985. Furthermore, in December 2000 the Supreme Court rejected an Italian request for the extradition of Contreras.

In November 1991, as part of the new Government's commitment to political decentralization, the Congreso approved constitutional amendments to local government statutes, which provided for the replacement of centrally-appointed local officials with directly-elected representatives. Elections to the 326 municipalities in June 1992 demonstrated clear public endorsement of the ruling coalition, which received some 53% of the votes, compared with 29% for the right-wing opposition. However, the considerable right-wing opposition in the Congreso continued to frustrate President Aylwin's attempts to enact legislation. Proposals to accelerate the prosecution of military personnel accused of human rights abuses, while safeguarding their anonymity, put forward by the President in August 1993, were rejected by the right as ill-considered and precipitate, while left-wing groups challenged the concessionary nature of the legislation, with regard to the military. In September Aylwin was forced to withdraw the proposals from the Congreso, following a declaration of opposition to the legislation, made by two member parties of the ruling coalition, in response to the petitions of human rights organizations.

A presidential election, held on 11 December 1993, was won by the CPD candidate Eduardo Frei Ruiz-Tagle, a PDC senator, with 58% of the votes cast, ahead of Arturo Alessandri Besa, the candidate of the right-wing coalition, the Unión para el Progreso de Chile (UPC), who received 24% of the votes. However, the ruling coalition failed to make significant gains at concurrently conducted congressional elections, attributing the disappointing results to the binomial electoral system, which requires each party to secure two-thirds of the votes in each district for the successful election of its two candidates to the legislature. In February 1994 formal congressional endorsement was secured for constitutional reform whereby henceforth the length of the non-renewable presidential term would be fixed at six years.

On 11 March 1994 Frei assumed the presidency. Some days later he identified the immediate aims of his Government as the alleviation of poverty, the elimination of corrupt government, and the fostering of significant economic growth. However, the President's affirmation of Pinochet's right to remain in office until 1997 appeared to compromise his pre-election demands for greater powers for the executive to nominate and remove the military High Command. In August Frei presented several constitutional reform proposals to the Congreso, including the abolition of the nine seats for appointed senators (installed by the former military regime) and the introduction of an electoral system based on proportional representation (to replace the unrepresentative binomial system). However, Frei encountered the same level of opposition to constitutional reform (particularly from the right and from the upper house), that had undermined most attempts at constitutional amendment made by the previous administration.

In November 1995 the Government secured the support of the opposition Partido Renovación Nacional (RN) for revised proposals for new legislation relating to human rights and constitutional reform. However, the compromised nature of the agreement provoked considerable disaffection within the RN, and within the opposition UPC alliance in general, which was effectively dissolved following the departure of the Partido Unión Demócrata Independiente (UDI) and the Unión de Centro-Centro (UCC) in protest at the actions of the RN. Concern was also expressed by members of the Partido Socialista (PS—within the ruling coalition) that the human rights legislation had been severely compromised.

During 1997 efforts by the Government to abolish the designated seats in the Senado were intensified, in response to Pinochet's stated intention to assume one of the seats assigned to former Presidents on retirement as Commander-in-Chief of the Army in March 1998, and by speculation that Pinochet would seek to exert considerable influence over future legislation by installing close military associates in other designated seats. In July 1997 the Senado rejected the Government's latest petition for reform to the system of appointments.

In October 1997 it was announced that Maj.-Gen. Ricardo Izurieta, previously chief of defence staff, was to succeed Pinochet as Commander-in-Chief of the Army. The announcement was made amid a number of changes in the military High Command, which appeared to confirm earlier predictions that military influence was henceforth to be concentrated in the Senado, where it would bolster the political right wing.

Legislative elections to renew all 120 seats in the Cámara de Diputados and 20 of the elective seats in the Senado were conducted on 11 December 1997. The Government expressed satisfaction with the performance of parties within the governing Concertación, which secured 50.5% of the votes for deputies and retained (with 70 seats) a comfortable majority in the lower house. However, political analysts noted an erosion of support for the centre-left alliance (which had attracted 55.4% of votes for the lower house at the 1993 elections) and observed that the group's disappointing showing at elections to the Senado (where one seat was lost to the UDI) would make future attempts to effect constitutional reform as problematic as those undertaken in the past, particularly given the predominance of right-wing sympathizers among the nine designated senators (three nominated by the Supreme Court, four by the National Security Council—from a list of former chiefs of the armed forces —and two by the President), named later in December, who were scheduled to take their seats, together with the newly elected senators, in March 1998. The elections revealed a shifting balance of power within the two major political groupings (support for the UDI, in particular, appeared to have superseded that for the RN within the Unión por Chile), and prompted renewed criticism of the country's binomial system of voting, the PCCh having failed to secure congressional representation despite attracting 8.4% and 6.9% of the votes to the upper and lower houses, respectively.

In December 1997 Pinochet reiterated his intention to assert his constitutional right, on retirement, to assume an *ex-officio* seat (for life) in the Senado (in addition to the nine designated senators). Expressing the opinion that to extend such an opportunity to Pinochet, who had headed an administration that had suspended all legislative processes for many years, would be wholly inappropriate, a number of centre-left politicians pledged to obstruct Pinochet's accession to the Senado. During January 1998 separate attempts were made by junior members of the Concertación (despite the declarations of senior members of the Government—anxious to ensure a peaceful exchange of offices in March—that such action was untimely and politically inconvenient) and by the leadership of the PCCh to begin judicial proceedings against Pinochet on charges related to gross abuses of human rights. Pinochet responded by announcing that he would not retire as Commander-in-Chief of the Army on 26 January, as previously suggested, but would continue in office until 10 March, thereby preserving the immunity from prosecution provided by the position for as long as possible. Pinochet's announcement and a perceived entrenchment of the divergent interests of the Government and the armed forces prompted the resignation of the Minister of National Defence, Edmundo Pérez Yoma.

On 6 March 1998 the military High Command announced that Pinochet had been named an honorary commander-in-chief—a position with no historical precedent. On 11 March Pinochet assumed his seat in the Senado. A largely symbolic, and unsuccessful, attempt by 11 Concertación deputies to instigate a formal impeachment action against Pinochet was initiated in the Cámara de Diputados in March. The motion's defeat prompted a crisis within the Concertación—the majority of PDC deputies having voted against it.

Preparations for the December presidential poll dominated domestic affairs during 1999. In January the RN and the UDI announced that they would present a joint presidential candidate to represent a new political alliance, the Alianza por Chile. In April Joaquín Lavín of the UDI was chosen as its candidate. In May a primary election to select the presidential candidate of the ruling Concertación was won by the former Minister of Public Works, Ricardo Lagos Escobar of the PS, with 71.3% of the estimated 1.4m. votes. The poor showing of the PDC candidate, Andrés Zaldívar, resulted in that party's adoption of a reformist manifesto and the selection of a new national executive in July. Meanwhile, in June a minor cabinet reshuffle had been implemented, in which the recall to government of Eduardo Pérez Yoma as Minister of National Defence was interpreted as an attempt to foster improved relations with the armed forces.

Although it was widely expected that a clear margin favouring Lagos would emerge in the presidential poll held on 12 December 1999, he received 47.96% of the total votes cast, with Lavín obtaining 47.52%. Four minor candidates, among whom only Gladys Marín (representing the PCCh) received more than 3.0% of the poll, were eliminated. At the second round of voting, which took place on 16 January 2000, Lagos emerged victorious with 51.3% of the total votes, while Lavín received 48.7%. (Lavín was subsequently elected Mayor of Santiago in local elections held in October.) Lagos was sworn in as President on 11 March. He set out a reduction in unemployment and an increase in economic growth to be the main priorities for his new Government.

The treatment of the Mapuche indigenous peoples was another problem that faced the incoming administration. Mining, dam and forestry projects prompted violent protests by the Mapuche indigenous peoples who were campaigning for the restitution of their ancestral lands. In May 2000 a Historical Truth and New Deal Commission was created to consider the demands and needs of the Mapuche communities. However, in October the Cámara de Diputados rejected legislation, drafted over a period of nine years, which would have granted constitutional recognition to the Mapuche peoples.

As the controversy surrounding the detention of former President Pinochet in the United Kingdom continued (see below), domestic attention was once again focused on the actions of the security forces during the post-1973 military regime. In June 1999 the arrest of five retired army officers (former commanders of a notorious élite army unit popularly referred to as the 'caravan of death') was ordered by an appeal court judge following renewed investigation into the disappearance of 72 political prisoners in the immediate aftermath of the 1973 military coup. The decision to arrest and prosecute the five men on charges of aggravated kidnapping was considered a breakthrough in Chilean judicial practice, since the absence of physical or documented evidence of the deaths of the prisoners meant that the crimes were technically in continuance, and that the accused men were not protected by the 1978 amnesty which guaranteed the impunity of military personnel for crimes committed before that year. In July 1999 the legality of the arrests was confirmed by the Supreme Court, and the indictment (and extradition from the USA) of a sixth former army officer was sought in connection with the case in August. Attempts by the Government to stem the resurgence of popular resentment of the past actions of the armed forces included, in August, the first direct discussions of the fate of the 'disappeared' between representatives of the armed forces and human rights organizations. However, tensions were exacerbated by the US National Security Council's declassification, in June, of some 5,800 CIA documents which recorded abuses of human rights during 1973–78, and appeared to support claims that the Chilean armed forces had falsified evidence purporting to demonstrate the threat posed by the Allende administration in order to justify the 1973 coup. In September 1999 the Supreme Court had ruled in favour of criminal proceedings brought against two retired generals, Humberto Gordon Rubio and Roberto Schmied, earlier in the month for their alleged involvement in the murder of trade union leader Tucapel Jiménez in 1982. (Gordon Rubio, a former head of covert national intelligence operations, was the most senior military officer to date to face prosecution in Chile for crimes committed during the period of military rule.) In the following month an arrest warrant was issued against Gen. (retd) Hugo Salas Wendel, a former Director of Dina, on charges of complicity in the killings in 1987 of 12 alleged members of a left-wing guerrilla group. (In August 2002 12 former military officers, including four generals, were sentenced to terms of imprisonment for their involvement in the murder of Tucapel Jiménez; it was considered likely that these would be among the last sentences passed for human rights abuses during the military regime.)

On 16 October 1998 former President Pinochet was arrested during a visit to London, United Kingdom, in response to a preliminary request, made to the British authorities by a Spanish judge, that Pinochet should be extradited to Spain to answer charges of 'genocide and terrorism' committed against some 4,000 individuals, including Spanish nationals, by his administration during 1973–90. A second Spanish request for Pinochet's extradition, received on 23 October 1998, cited his alleged involvement in institutionalized torture, conspiracy and the taking of hostages. In early November a formal request for extradition was made, although the Spanish Government (like the British Government) was anxious to emphasize its neutrality in what it considered to be a purely judicial affair.

In Chile the Frei Government protested that Pinochet's diplomatic immunity had been infringed by the British authorities, while the British Government denied Pinochet's status as an accredited diplomat. Meanwhile, supporters and opponents of Pinochet clashed during demonstrations in Santiago, and there were concerns that Pinochet's detention was threatening to undermine the country's delicate political and military balance.

The House of Lords' hearing of the extradition appeal concluded on 25 November 1998 with a 3–2 majority judgment by the panel of five senior law lords overturning a high court ruling in October that Pinochet was entitled to 'sovereign immunity' as a former head of state. Despite the remonstrances of the Chilean Minister of Foreign Affairs, José Miguel Insulza, and pressure from the US Secretary of State, Madeleine Albright, to allow Pinochet to return to Chile, on 9 December the British Secretary of State for the Home Department, Jack Straw, authorized the start of formal extradition proceedings.

President Frei reacted angrily to Straw's decision, recalling the Chilean ambassador in London for consultations. Pinochet appeared in a British court in person for the first time in December 1998, where initially he refused to recognize the competence of any court outside of Chile to try him with the 'lies of Spain'. Prior to the announcement of Straw's decision, meanwhile, it had emerged that one of the three law lords who rejected Pinochet's immunity in the November ruling had failed to declare potentially compromising personal links to the international human rights campaign group Amnesty International. In December a new panel of five senior judges unanimously suspended the November pronouncement and ordered the case to be re-submitted to a new appellate committee of seven law lords. Meanwhile, Pinochet remained under effective house arrest in the United Kingdom.

The new House of Lords' hearing began in January 1999. The ruling of the appellate committee, announced in March, supported the November 1998 pronouncement overturning Pinochet's claims to immunity, by a majority of six to one. However, the committee also found that only charges relating to events subsequent to December 1988 (at which time the 1984 UN Convention against Torture and Other Cruel, Inhuman or Degrading Treatment or Punishment had entered into British law) should be considered relevant, thus reducing the number of draft charges brought by Spain from 33 to three. In April Straw confirmed his decision to allow the petition to proceed, contending that the serious nature of the three remaining charges from the original draft petition was sufficient to justify the extradition. Formal extradition proceedings were initiated in a London magistrates' court in late September; in October the court found that Pinochet could be lawfully extradited to Spain to answer some 35 charges. Pinochet's lawyers made a formal appeal against the decision.

Attempts by the Chilean Government to persuade Spain to allow international arbitration in the case against Pinochet had been dismissed by the Spanish judiciary in September 1999, prompting the Chilean Minister of Foreign Affairs, Juan Gabriel Valdés, to announce that Chile would ask the International Court of Justice in The Hague, Netherlands, to examine Spain's claims to jurisdiction in the matter. In January 2000, having considered an independent doctors' report that Pinochet was medically unfit to undergo further legal proceedings, Straw indicated that he was inclined to order Pinochet's release, although he agreed to defer his final decision pending further representations from those seeking Pinochet's extradition. Such representations swiftly followed from legal authorities in Belgium, France, Spain and Switzerland, and from six human rights organizations. However, on 2 March Straw announced that Pinochet was to be released, and on the following day the former President returned to Chile.

The return of Pinochet to Chile was interpreted as a triumph for the former dictator and included a public welcome by the heads of the armed forces but no representation from the civilian Government. Both the outgoing and incoming Governments were reported to be embarrassed by Pinochet's robust appearance on landing in Chile and by the jubilant welcome given to him by the armed forces. Initially, expectations that Pinochet would ever stand trial in Chile were very low; however, these were raised in June 2000 following the Santiago Appeal Court's ruling to lift the former dictator's political immunity. In August,

in an historical judgment, the Supreme Court confirmed the decision, by 14 votes to six. The judgment was made possible by changes to Chile's judiciary, several members of which had retired and had been replaced by more independent-minded judges. Foremost among these was Juan Guzmán Tapia, who vigorously took up the legal case against Pinochet and others accused of human rights infringements. Over 200 lawsuits were filed against Pinochet. The former President's lawyers, meanwhile, argued that it would be too undignified for their client to submit to a medical examination to determine whether he was mentally fit to stand trial (compulsory in Chile for all citizens over the age of 70). In October an Argentine judge requested the extradition of Pinochet to stand trial for the 1974 killing, in Buenos Aires, of former Chilean army chief Carlos Prats and his wife. However, in November the Supreme Court ruled that Pinochet must not leave the country and placed him under court supervision. On 1 December Judge Guzmán indicted Pinochet on charges of aggravated kidnapping and murder in the 'caravan of death' case (see above) and placed him under house arrest. Although President Lagos promised not to interfere in the due process of law, he did accede to a request by the military to convene the National Security Council in order to discuss human rights issues. Before the meeting could take place, however, the Santiago Appeal Court overturned the house arrest order on the grounds that his case had been improperly handled (he was not questioned before being charged), a decision subsequently confirmed by the Supreme Court. The Supreme Court also ruled that Pinochet must face interrogation by Judge Guzmán within 20 days, though not before undergoing the medical tests required by law. In early January 2001, after failing to appear for previously scheduled tests, Pinochet finally consented to the medical examination and was subsequently questioned. On 31 January Judge Guzmán issued an order for the former General's arrest on charges of kidnap and murder. However, following an appeal by Pinochet, in March the Santiago Appeal Court ruled by a margin of 2–1 that the charges against Pinochet should be reduced to conspiracy to cover up the events, as opposed to responsibility for the 'caravan of death', and in July the Court ruled that the former dictator was mentally unfit to stand trial. In July 2002 the Supreme Court voted (by 4–1) to permanently close the case against Pinochet, as he was suffering from 'incurable' and 'irreversible' dementia. Within days Pinochet relinquished his position as senator for life.

Meanwhile, in June 2000 the Mesa de Diálogo, a round-table discussion between human rights lawyers and the military, agreed to guarantee the anonymity of any military person offering information on the whereabouts of any 'disappeared' person. The first official report as a result of the agreement was issued by President Lagos in January 2001 and disclosed information on the fate of 200 people—151 were allegedly thrown into the sea, 20 were buried in a mass grave and 29 were scattered in graves around central Chile.

During 2001 one of the main priorities of the Government was constitutional reform. Proposed reforms included the abolition of seats for non-elected senators and a revision of the binominal electoral system, which reformers believed entrenched the interests of the former authoritarian regime against social change. However, the results of legislative elections, held on 16 December, threatened progress on constitutional issues, as the right-wing UDI, a member of the Alianza por Chile, made significant gains in the Senado and the Cámara de Diputados. In the Senado, where 18 of the 38 elective seats were contested, the CPD won 51.3% of the votes cast and an overall 20 seats, but lost its one-seat majority, while the Alianza por Chile won 44.0% and increased its representation to 16 seats (the UDI's total increased to nine seats). The remaining two seats were won by Independents. In the Cámara de Diputados the CPD won 47.9% of the votes and 62 seats, a substantially reduced majority, while the Alianza por Chile secured 44.3% of the ballot and 57 seats (the UDI's representation increased to 35 deputies, replacing the PDC as Chile's largest party). In January 2002 President Lagos implemented a cabinet reshuffle in which, most notably, Michelle Bachelet Jeria was appointed the first ever female Chilean Minister of National Defence.

In October 2002 the mandate of President Lagos appeared to be compromised when he was prevented by the terms of the Constitution, as amended in 1989, from dismissing a commander of one of the armed forces. The Commander-in-Chief of the Air Force, Gen. Patricio Ríos, had been accused of obstructing a commission's investigations into human rights abuses that occurred during the military dictatorship; his resignation later that month was widely regarded as a triumph for Lagos, who strengthened his resolve to pursue constitutional reform. Shortly afterwards the President encountered serious political difficulties when the Government became embroiled in a corruption scandal. A number of government officials were accused of accepting bribes from a consultancy company, Gate, during 1999–2000, and it was alleged that some of the money had been used to finance CPD election campaigns. Lagos was quick to announce plans to increase government accountability and improve the transparency of party funding, but allegations of corruption within the ruling CPD continued. In November Patricio Tombolini, a former Deputy Secretary of Transport and trusted ally of the President, was dismissed on suspicion of accepting bribes and arrested by the police. Another close associate of Lagos, Carlos Cruz (a former Minister of Public Works), was later arrested in connection with the affair, and in January 2003 the Supreme Court stripped five CPD congressmen of their parliamentary immunity in order that they face corruption charges. As a result, the representation of Lagos's Concertación alliance was reduced to 58 seats in the Cámara de Diputados, compared with 57 for the opposition Alianza por Chile. In February there were reports of a further manipulation of public office, this time in connection with the alleged theft and transferral of some US $100m. of deposits belonging to CORFO (Corporación de Fomento de la Producción), a government development agency. Investigations centred on a private investment company, Inverlink, which appeared to have used the alleged stolen assets as collateral in speculative trading with a number of local pension funds. A former personal secretary to the Central Bank President was also sought in connection with the alleged leaking of confidential market data to the company. On 28 February President Lagos carried out a cabinet reshuffle in which seven of the 17 ministers were replaced. Most notably, Luis Bates Hidalgo—a former leading member of the anti-corruption campaign group Transparency International—was appointed Minister of Justice.

In August 1991 Argentina and Chile reached a settlement regarding disputed territory in the Antarctic region. Responsibility for the contentious Laguna del Desierto region, however, was to be decided by international arbitration. In October 1994 Argentina's claim to the territory was upheld by a five-member international arbitration panel. In July 1997 it was announced unexpectedly that the two countries were to conduct joint military exercises in 1998, and in September it was agreed to proceed with the creation of a conciliation commission, originally envisaged within the terms of a peace and friendship treaty concluded in 1984. Joint naval exercises began in August 1998. In December agreement on border demarcation of the still disputed 'continental glaciers' territory in the Antarctic region was reached by the Presidents of the two countries. In September 2000 both countries ratified the Mining and Co-operation Integration Treaty, signed in 1997, which allows joint exploitation of mineral deposits along their shared border.

Prospects for renewed diplomatic relations with Bolivia (which severed relations with Chile in 1978 over the issue of Bolivian access to the Pacific Ocean) were encouraged during 1993 by the successful conclusion of a comprehensive trade agreement and by a series of bilateral co-operation treaties. By 1997, however, relations had deteriorated again. The Bolivian Government made repeated requests during the year for the renewal of discussions on Bolivian access to the sea, and sought Peru's assistance in the dispute. Furthermore, later in the year the Bolivian Government made an official protest to Chile regarding its failure to remove land-mines (planted during the 1970s) from the two countries' border. Subsequent ministerial discussions failed to produce an effective formula for the restoration of diplomatic relations. In November 1999, following an Iberio-American summit meeting in Havana, Cuba, at which Bolivia sought to initiate a regional discussion of the dispute, Chile stated that the issue was a matter for bilateral, rather than international, negotiation. In the same month it was announced that Chile was to take immediate action to remove land-mines on all its borders.

A free-trade agreement with Colombia, the Acuerdo de Complementación Económica (ACE), took effect from 1 January 1994, and was expected to have eliminated tariffs on most goods by the time of its full implementation on 1 January 1999. A free-trade agreement with Ecuador came into effect on 1 January 1995. In December 1994 the signatory nations to the North American Free Trade Agreement (NAFTA) issued a formal

invitation to Chile to join the group. Discussions on Chile's accession to the Agreement by late 1996, began in June 1995. However, despite the removal of contentious clauses relating to labour and the environment, US President Bill Clinton failed to secure US congressional support for 'fast track' authorization for Chile's accession to the Agreement. In November 2000 President Clinton announced that the USA would negotiate a bilateral trade deal with Chile, as opposed to it formally becoming a full member of NAFTA. In the context of this delay, Chile intensified attempts to negotiate a bilateral free-trade agreement with Canada and a formal trade agreement with the Mercado Común del Sur (Mercosur, see p. 316). In November 1996 agreement was reached with Canada on the imminent removal of tariffs on three-quarters of bilateral trade, with the gradual removal of remaining duties over a five-year period. The agreement received congressional approval in mid-1997 and came into effect in July of that year; the terms of the agreement were modified and expanded in early 1998. Meanwhile, in June 1996, at a summit meeting of Mercosur member nations in San Luis, Argentina, Chile had secured associate membership of the group, following negotiations which established the immediate reduction of tariffs on 90% of Chilean goods, and the subsequent elimination of tariffs on 'sensitive' goods including meat, sugar, edible oils and wheat, over an 18-year period. Chile's associate membership became effective from 1 October. However, Chile's decision to negotiate a bilateral free-trade accord with the USA caused tension with Brazil at the Mercosur summit in Florianópolis, Brazil, in December 2000 and effectively stalled further negotiations on full membership.

In April 1998 Chile and Mexico signed a free-trade agreement, expanding the terms of an ACE in force since 1992. In June 1998 Chile signed an ACE agreement with Peru, whereby customs duties were to be abolished on 2,500 products from 1 July. The agreement also envisaged the free passage of 50% of all products by 2003 and the creation of a free-trade area within 18 years. With the exception of Bolivia, Chile has now negotiated free-trade agreements throughout the South American continent. During 1998 agreements to facilitate and increase trade between Chile and the countries of Central America were also signed. A second 'Summit of the Americas' was convened in Santiago in April 1998, and was attended by representatives of all nations in the region (with the exception of Cuba), who reiterated commitments to establishing a Free Trade Area of the Americas (FTAA) by 2005. At a third Summit of the Americas, held in Québec, Canada, in April 2001, a timetable for the FTAA, to take effect by 2005, was agreed upon. Negotiations were to commence in May 2002 and conclude by January 2005. In November 2002 Chile and the European Union signed an association agreement for political and economic co-operation, effective from January 2003. In December, moreover, Chile and the USA finally agreed on a free-trade pact that would eliminate immediately all barriers on 85% of trade between the two countries, with the remaining trade restrictions being phased out within 12 years. The agreement was scheduled to be signed in early 2003 and, if approved by both countries' legislatures, would come into effect from 2004. In February 2003 a new free-trade agreement was signed with the Republic of Korea. Discussions on a new trade arrangement between Chile and Japan were also scheduled for later in the year. In March the European Free Trade Association (EFTA, see p. 195) initialled a free trade accord with Chile. The agreement was due to be signed in June and was to come into effect from January 2004.

Government

Chile is a republic, divided into 12 regions and a metropolitan area. Under the terms of the Constitution, executive power is vested in the President, who is directly elected for a six-year term. The President is assisted by a Cabinet. Legislative power is vested in the bicameral Congreso Nacional (National Congress), comprising the 49-member Senado (Senate) and the 120-member Cámara de Diputados (Chamber of Deputies).

Defence

Military service is for one year (army) or 22 months (navy and air force) and is compulsory for men at 19 years of age. In August 2002 the army had a strength of 45,000, the navy 23,000 and the air force 12,500. Paramilitary security forces numbered about 36,800 carabineros. Defence expenditure for 2002 was budgeted at 810,000m. pesos.

Economic Affairs

In 2001, according to estimates by the World Bank, Chile's gross national product (GNI), measured at average 1999–2001 prices, was US $66,915m., equivalent to $4,350 per head (or $9,420 per head on an international purchasing-power parity basis). During 1990–2001, it was estimated, the population increased by an average of 1.5% per year, while gross domestic product (GDP) per head increased, in real terms, at an average annual rate of 4.7%. Overall GDP increased, in real terms, at an average annual rate of 6.3% in 1990–2001; real GDP increased by 4.4% in 2000, but growth slowed to 2.8% in 2001.

Agriculture (including forestry and fishing) contributed an estimated 6.0% of GDP, at constant prices, in 2001. About 13.5% of the employed labour force were engaged in this sector in 2002. Important subsistence crops include wheat, oats, barley, rice, beans, lentils, maize and chick-peas. Industrial crops include sugar beet, sunflower seed and rapeseed. Fruit and vegetables are also important export commodities (together contributing 8.4% of total export revenues in 2000), particularly, beans, asparagus, onions, garlic, grapes, citrus fruits, avocados, pears, peaches, plums and nuts. The production and export of wine has increased significantly in recent years. Forestry and fishing, and derivatives from both activities, also make important contributions to the sector. During 1990–2000 agricultural GDP increased, in real terms, by an average of 1.9% per year; agricultural GDP increased by 6.7% in 2000 and by 6.5% in 2001.

Industry (including mining, manufacturing, construction and power) contributed an estimated 37.8% of GDP, at constant prices, in 2001 and accounted for 23.9% of the employed labour force in 2002. During 1990–2000 industrial GDP increased by an average of 5.9% per year. GDP growth in all industrial sectors was 4.2% in 2000 and 2.2% in 2001.

Mining contributed an estimated 8.9% of GDP, at constant prices, in 2001 and engaged 1.3% of the employed labour force in 2002. Chile, with some 28% of the world's known reserves, is the world's largest producer and exporter of copper. Copper accounted for 87.5% of Chile's total export earnings in 1970, but the proportion had decreased to 40.9% by 2000. Gold, silver, iron ore, nitrates, molybdenum, manganese, lead and coal are also mined, and the whole sector contributed 44.1% of total export earnings in 2000. In real terms, the sector's GDP increased by an estimated 5.2% in 2000 and by 3.6% in 2001. Petroleum and natural gas deposits have been located in the south, and plans to exploit significant reserves of lithium are under consideration.

Manufacturing contributed an estimated 16.7% of GDP, at constant prices, in 2001, and engaged 14.1% of the employed labour force in 2002. The most important branches of manufacturing, measured by gross value of output, are food (22.3% of the total) and non-ferrous metals (15.4%). Manufacturing GDP increased by an average of 4.6% per year in 1990–2000. The sector's GDP increased by 4.0% in 2000, but declined by 0.3% in 2001.

In 1999 electric energy was derived mainly from hydroelectric power (37.0%), coal (36.0%) and natural gas (15.3%). Chile produces some 40% of its national energy requirements. Plans are under consideration to develop Chile's vast hydroelectric potential (estimated at 18,700 MW—the largest in the world). Meanwhile, Chile imported fuel and energy products equivalent to some 18.2% of the value of total merchandise imports in 2000.

The services sector contributed an estimated 56.1% of GDP, in constant prices, in 2001 and engaged some 62.6% of the employed labour force in 2002. The financial sector continued to expand in the 1990s, fuelled, in part, by the success of private pension funds. During 1990–2000 services GDP increased by an average of 5.6% per year. The sector's GDP increased, in real terms, by 3.8% in 2000 and by 24.0% in 2001.

In 2001 Chile recorded a visible trade surplus of US $2,094m., but there was a deficit of $1,241m. on the current account of the balance of payments. In 2001 Argentina was the principal source of imports (17.8%), while the USA was the principal market for exports (19.4%). Other major trading partners were Japan, the United Kingdom, Brazil and the People's Republic of China. In 2000 the principal exports were copper and copper manufactures (40.9% of total export revenue), fruit (6.5%), fish (6.5%) and wood pulp (6.1%). The principal imports in that year were machinery and transport equipment, and chemical and mineral products.

In 2001 there was a budgetary deficit of some 101,580m. pesos (equivalent to 0.2% of GDP). Chile's external debt totalled some US $36,978m. at the end of 2000, of which $5,210m. was long-term public debt. Debt-servicing costs in that year were equivalent to some 26.0% of the value of exports of goods and services. The annual rate of inflation averaged 8.9% in 1990–2001, and stood at 3.5% in 2001. An estimated 7.8% of the labour force were unemployed in 2002.

Chile is a member of the Latin American Integration Association (ALADI, see p. 259) and was admitted to the Rio Group (see p. 351) in 1990 and to the Asia-Pacific Economic Co-operation group (APEC, see p. 139) in 1994. Chile is also among the founding members of the World Trade Organization (WTO, see p. 323).

Owing to the relaxation of import duties in the early 1980s, Chile's potential in the agricultural and manufacturing sectors was stifled by cheaper imported goods. Exports of fruit, seafoods and wines, however, have expanded considerably, yet Chile remains heavily dependent on exports of copper and on the stability of the world copper market. Chile entered a period of recession during 1999, largely as a result of depressed world prices for copper; the economy contracted by 1.1% in that year. In September, in an attempt to stimulate exports, the Central Bank abandoned its strict regulation of the peso, allowing the currency to float against the US dollar. Confidence returned to the economy in 2000 with GDP growth at 4.4%. In an attempt to stimulate recovery, the new Government of President Lagos initiated a public works programme, designed to increase the incomes of skilled and semi-skilled workers, and introduced tax rebates of up to US $400 for about 1m. people. Other government initiatives included encouraging foreign investment in growth areas such as tourism and new technology and promoting investment in Chile's disparate regions. Tax and financial sector reforms were introduced to encourage inward investment and improve tax collection in 2001, but high unemployment and low investment levels continued to stifle consumer demand. Although high imported petroleum prices and declining prices for copper contributed to lower growth rates in 2001 and 2002 (2.8% and an estimated 2.0%, respectively), Chile's trade balance was, none the less, expected to remain stable, with a significant reduction in pressure on the peso owing to increased market confidence and the continued weakness of the US dollar.

Education

Pre-primary education is widely available for all children from five years of age. Primary education is officially compulsory, and is provided free of charge, for eight years, beginning at six or seven years of age. It is divided into two cycles: the first lasts for four years and provides a general education; the second cycle offers more specialized schooling. Secondary education, beginning at 13 or 14 years of age, is divided into the humanities-science programme (lasting for four years), with the emphasis on general education and possible entrance to university, and the technical-professional programme (lasting for between four and six years), designed to fulfil the requirements of specialist training. In 1996 the total enrolment at primary schools included an estimated 88% of children in the relevant age-group, while the comparable ratio for secondary enrolment was 58%. Higher education is provided by three kinds of institution: universities, professional institutes and centres of technical information. The provision for education in the 2001 central government budget was 1,774,410m. pesos (18.2% of total spending).

Public Holidays

2003: 1 January (New Year's Day), 18–19 April (Good Friday and Easter Saturday), 1 May (Labour Day), 21 May (Battle of Iquique), 15 August (Assumption), 4 September (National Unity Day), 18 September (Independence Day), 12 October (Day of the Race, anniversary of the discovery of America), 1 November (All Saints' Day), 8 December (Immaculate Conception), 25 December (Christmas Day).

2004: 1 January (New Year's Day), 9–10 April (Good Friday and Easter Saturday), 3 May (for Labour Day), 21 May (Battle of Iquique), 15 August (Assumption), 4 September (National Unity Day), 18 September (Independence Day), 12 October (Day of the Race, anniversary of the discovery of America), 1 November (All Saints' Day), 8 December (Immaculate Conception), 25 December (Christmas Day).

Weights and Measures

The metric system is officially in force.

Statistical Survey

Sources (unless otherwise stated): Instituto Nacional de Estadísticas, Avda Bulnes 418, Casilla 498-3, Correo 3, Santiago; tel. (2) 366-7777; fax (2) 671-2169; e-mail inesdadm@reuna.cl; internet www.ine.cl ; Banco Central de Chile, Agustinas 1180, Santiago; tel. (2) 696-2281; fax (2) 698-4847; e-mail bcch@bcentral.cl; internet www.bcentral.cl.

Area and Population

AREA, POPULATION AND DENSITY*

Area (sq km)	756,096†
Population (census results)‡	
22 April 1992	13,348,401
24 April 2002 (provisional results)	
Males	7,403,485
Females	7,646,856
Total	15,050,341
Population (official estimates at mid-year)	
1999	15,017,760
2000	15,211,308
2001	15,401,952
Density (per sq km) at 2002 census	19.9

* Excluding Chilean Antarctic Territory (approximately 1,250,000 sq km).
† 291,930 sq miles.
‡ Excluding adjustment for underenumeration.

REGIONS
(2002 census, provisional results)

	Area (sq km)	Population ('000)	Density (per sqkm)	Capital
I De Tarapacá . . .	59,099.1	426.4	7.2	Iquique
II De Antofagasta .	126,049.1	492.8	3.9	Antofagasta
III De Atacama . .	75,176.2	252.4	3.4	Copiapó
IV De Coquimbo. .	40,579.9	600.4	14.8	La Serena
V De Valparaíso . .	16,396.1	1,542.5	94.1	Valparaíso
VI Del Libertador Gen. Bernardo O'Higgins . . .	16,387.0	774.0	47.2	Rancagua
VII Del Maule . . .	30,296.1	904.1	29.8	Talca
VIII Del Bíobío . . .	37,062.6	1,853.7	50.0	Concepción
IX De la Araucanía .	31,842.3	864.9	27.2	Temuco
X De Los Lagos. . .	67,013.1	1,061.7	15.8	Puerto Montt
XI Aisén del Gen. Carlos Ibáñez del Campo . . .	108,494.4	86.7	0.8	Coihaique
XII De Magallanes y Antártica Chilena	132,297.2	151.9	1.1	Punta Arenas
Metropolitan Region (Santiago) . . .	15,403.2	6,039.0	392.1	—
Total	756,096.3	15,050.3	19.9	—

PRINCIPAL TOWNS
(2002 census, provisional results)

Gran Santiago (capital). . .	4,647,444	Rancagua . . .	.212,222
Puente Alto . . .	501,042	Talca	.203,231
Viña del Mar . . .	298,828	Arica	.184,134
Antofagasta . . .	298,153	Puerto Montt . .	.174,952
Valparaíso . . .	270,242	Los Angeles . .	.164,531
Talcahuano . . .	249,274	Coquimbo . . .	.163,201
Temuco . . .	243,731	Chillán . . .	.162,933
San Bernardo . . .	244,354	La Serena . . .	.159,361
Concepción . . .	214,505	Osorno . . .	.142,554
Iquique . . .	215,233	Valdivia . . .	.136,787
		Calama . . .	.136,739

BIRTHS, MARRIAGES AND DEATHS

	Registered live births		Registered marriages		Registered deaths	
	Number	Rate (per 1,000)	Number	Rate (per 1,000)	Number	Rate (per 1,000)
1992 . .	293,787	21.7	89,370	6.6	74,090	5.5
1993 . .	290,438	21.1	92,821	6.7	76,261	5.5
1994 . .	288,175	20.6	91,555	6.5	75,445	5.4
1995 . .	279,928	19.7	87,205	6.1	78,531	5.5
1996 . .	264,793	18.4	83,547	5.8	79,123	5.5
1997 . .	259,959	17.8	78,077	5.3	78,472	5.4
1998 . .	257,105	17.3	73,456	5.0	80,257	5.4
1999 . .	250,674	16.7	n.a.	n.a.	81,977	5.5

Source: partly UN, *Demographic Yearbook*.

Expectation of life (WHO estimates, years at birth): 76.3 (males 73.2; females 79.5) in 2001 (Source: WHO, *World Health Report*).

ECONOMICALLY ACTIVE POPULATION*
('000 persons aged 15 years and over, October–December)

	2000	2001	2002
Agriculture, hunting, forestry and fishing	770.0	745.4	746.6
Mining and quarrying	70.3	71.7	69.8
Manufacturing	754.2	781.8	780.4
Electricity, gas and water . . .	28.4	33.2	29.5
Construction	406.1	424.2	439.9
Trade, restaurants and hotels . .	995.5	1,028.9	1,073.1
Transport, storage and communications	430.2	439.0	444.8
Financing, insurance, real estate and business services	425.8	414.2	430.1
Community, social and personal services	1,494.2	1,541.0	1,516.2
Total employed	5,381.5	5,479.4	5,531.2
Unemployed	489.4	469.4	468.7
Total labour force	5,870.9	5,948.8	5,999.9
Males	3,913.0	3,966.2	3,995.5
Females	1,957.9	1,982.6	2,004.5

* Figures are based on sample surveys, covering 36,000 households, and exclude members of the armed forces. Estimates are made independently, therefore totals are not always the sum of the component parts.

Health and Welfare

KEY INDICATORS

Total fertility rate (children per woman, 2001)	2.4
Under-5 mortality rate (per 1,000 live births, 2001) . . .	12
HIV/AIDS (% of persons aged 15–49, 2001)	0.30
Physicians (per 1,000 head, 1994)	1.10
Hospital beds (per 1,000 head, 1996)	2.67
Health expenditure (2000): US $ per head (PPP)	697
Health expenditure (2000): % of GDP	7.2
Health expenditure (2000): public (% of total)	42.6
Access to water (% of persons, 2000).	94
Access to sanitation (% of persons, 2000)	97
Human Development Index (2000): ranking	38
Human Development Index (2000): value	0.831

For sources and definitions, see explanatory note on p. vi.

Agriculture

PRINCIPAL CROPS
('000 metric tons)

	1999	2000	2001
Wheat	1,197	1,493	1,780
Rice (paddy)	61	135	143
Barley	81	60	65
Maize	624	652	778
Oats	201	248	345
Potatoes	995	988	1,210
Sugar beet	3,047	3,092	3,232
Dry beans	31	44	60
Rapeseed	72	44	59
Cabbages *	60	60	68
Lettuce *	83	84	85
Tomatoes†	1,243	1,217	1,157
Pumpkins, etc. *	100	99	105
Chillies and green peppers *	72	55	60
Dry onions	263†	282†	285*
Carrots *	97	97	98
Green corn *	225	233	240
Other vegetables†	324	331	339
Oranges	85	88	92
Lemons and limes	110	117	120
Apples	1,165	805	1,135
Pears	350	333	340
Peaches and nectarines . .	310	250	250
Plums	198	164	205
Grapes	1,575	1,895	1,570
Watermelons *	65	75	80
Cantaloupes and other melons*	60	62	63
Avocados	82	98	120
Kiwi fruit	105	116	120

* FAO estimate(s).
† Unofficial figure(s).

Source: FAO.

LIVESTOCK
('000 head, year ending September)

	1999	2000	2001
Horses*	600	620	650
Cattle	4,134	4,068	4,150*
Pigs	2,221	2,465	2,500*
Sheep	4,116	4,144	4,200*
Goats*	740	745	800
Chickens*	70,000	75,000	78,000

* FAO estimate(s).

Source: FAO.

LIVESTOCK PRODUCTS
('000 metric tons)

	1999	2000	2001
Beef and veal	226.4	226.4	217.6
Mutton and lamb	12.8	11.1	10.9
Pig meat	243.7	261.5	303.0
Horse meat	11.2*	9.5	10.6*
Poultry meat	344.0	378.1	407.8
Cows' milk	2,050	1,990	2,200
Goats' milk*	10.1	10.2	10.4
Butter	11.0	9.9	11.8
Cheese	51.5	51.5	57.2
Hen eggs*	95	98	110
Wool: greasy*	16.7	17.0	17.2
Cattle hides*	34.0	33.9	31.3

* FAO estimate(s).

Source: FAO.

Forestry

ROUNDWOOD REMOVALS
('000 cubic metres, excluding bark)

	1999	2000	2001
Sawlogs, veneer logs and logs for sleepers	11,783	12,424	13,351
Pulpwood	11,147	11,802	12,142
Other industrial wood . . .	249	211	189
Fuel wood	10,794	12,131	12,108
Total	33,973	36,568	37,790

Source: FAO.

SAWNWOOD PRODUCTION
('000 cubic metres, including railway sleepers)

	1999	2000	2001
Coniferous (softwood) . . .	4,933	5,351	5,581
Broadleaved (hardwood) . .	321	347	291
Total	5,254	5,698	5,872

Source: FAO.

Fishing
('000 metric tons, live weight)

	1998	1999	2000
Capture	3,265.3	5,050.5	4,300.2
Patagonian grenadier . . .	354.2	309.9	91.3
Chilean jack mackerel . . .	1,612.9	1,219.7	1,234.3
South American pilchard . .	28.0	246.0	60.2
Araucanian herring . . .	317.6	782.1	722.5
Anchoveta (Peruvian anchovy) .	522.7	1,983.0	1,700.6
Chub mackerel	71.8	120.1	95.8
Aquaculture	293.0	274.2	391.6
Atlantic salmon	107.1	103.2	166.9
Total catch	3,558.4	5,324.7	4,691.7

Note: Figures exclude aquatic plants ('000 metric tons): 265.9 (capture 197.5, aquaculture 68.4) in 1998; 261.5 (capture 230.2, aquaculture 31.3) in 1999; 280.8 (capture 247.4, aquaculture 33.5) in 2000. Also excluded are aquatic mammals, recorded by number rather than by weight. The number of toothed whales caught was: 1 in 1998 and 1 in 1999. The number of sperm whales caught was: 1 in 1999.

Source: FAO, *Yearbook of Fishery Statistics*.

Mining
('000 metric tons, unless otherwise indicated)

	1999	2000	2001
Copper (metal content)	4,421.8	4,646.3	4,766.1
Coal	507.4	503.4	568.1
Iron ore*	8,345.0	8,728.9	5,437.1
Calcium carbonate	5,617.6	5,395.2	5,563.2
Sodium sulphate (metric tons) .	58,026	56,501	67,760
Zinc—metal content (metric tons) .	32,263	31,403	32,762
Molybdenum—metal content (metric tons)	27,270	33,639	33,492
Manganese (metric tons)† . .	40,505	41,716	31,320
Gold (kilograms)	48,069	54,143	42,673
Silver (kilograms)	1,380.7	1,242.2	1,348.7
Petroleum ('000 cubic metres) . .	367.8	325.8	309.8

* Gross weight. The estimated iron content is 61%.

† Gross weight. The estimated metal content is 32%.

Source: Servicio Nacional de Geología y Minería.

Industry

SELECTED PRODUCTS
('000 metric tons, unless otherwise indicated)

	1997	1998	1999
Refined sugar	470	470	434
Beer (million litres)	364	367	333
Soft drinks (million litres)	1,195	1,197	1,154
Cigarettes (million)	12,522	12,904	13,174
Non-rubber footwear ('000 pairs)	7,638	6,777	5,940
Particle board ('000 cu metres)	315	242	257
Mattresses ('000)	1,131	1,100	1,082
Sulphuric acid	1,864	1,983	2,436
Motor spirit (petrol)	1,972	2,078	2,153
Kerosene and jet fuel	814	753	831
Distillate fuel oils	2,937	3,544	3,840
Residual fuel oils	1,663	n.a.	n.a.
Cement	3,191	3,280	2,508
Tyres ('000)	2,509	2,350	2,551
Glass sheets ('000 sq metres)	21,075	21,313	21,523
Blister copper	181	165	177
Refined fire copper	125	129	163
Electrolytic copper	1,261	1,437	1,463
Electric energy (million kWh)	32,549	34,886	38,019

Finance

CURRENCY AND EXCHANGE RATES

Monetary Units
100 centavos = 1 Chilean peso.

Sterling, Dollar and Euro Equivalents (31 December 2002)
£1 sterling = 1,148.2 pesos
US $1 = 712.4 pesos
€1 = 747.1 pesos
10,000 Chilean pesos = £8.709 = $14.037 = €13.386.

Average Exchange Rate (pesos per US $)
2000   535.47
2001   634.94
2002   688.94

BUDGET
('000 million pesos)

Revenue	1999	2000	2001
Current revenue	7,730.61	8,960.05	9,620.25
Taxation	6,332.83	7,192.81	7,895.02
Taxes on income, profits and capital gains	1,312.20	1,647.14	1,952.69
Social security contributions	527.04	576.76	628.04
Domestic taxes on goods and services	3,629.35	4,113.61	4,421.93
Sales or turnover taxes	2,811.58	3,205.86	3,423.84
Excises	817.77	907.75	998.09
Taxes on international trade and transactions	535.49	548.56	510.25
Other taxes	328.75	306.74	382.11
Non-tax revenue	1,397.78	1,767.24	1,725.23
Entrepreneurial and property income	250.72	279.13	334.09
Administrative fees and charges, non-industrial and incidental sales	650.31	911.90	652.87
Other non-tax revenue	496.75	576.21	738.27
Capital revenue	7.14	3.29	11.98
Total revenue	7,737.75	8,963.34	9,632.23

Expenditure*	1999	2000	2001
General public services	340.90	347.68	355.24
Defence	679.39	709.07	746.25
Public order and safety	477.13	508.08	569.80
Education	1,400.44	1,577.03	1,774.41
Health	976.66	1,099.11	1,232.84
Social security and welfare	2,942.07	3,224.29	3,527.76
Housing	363.37	360.30	392.01
Economic services	1,111.72	1,052.20	1,107.09
Interest payments	120.71	180.33	202.76
Sub-total	8,412.39	9,058.09	9,908.16
Less Lending included in expenditure	176.99	204.76	174.35
Total expenditure	8,235.40	8,853.33	9,733.81
Current	6,882.15	7,555.88	8,269.76
Capital	1,353.25	1,297.45	1,464.05

* Excluding net lending.

INTERNATIONAL RESERVES
(US $ million at 31 December)

	2000	2001	2002
Gold*	318.3	18.6	2.3
IMF special drawing rights	24.6	28.9	36.5
Reserve position in IMF	324.2	308.7	490.7
Foreign exchange	14,686.1	14,041.3	14,813.9
Total	15,353.2	14,397.5	15,343.4

* National valuation.

Source: IMF, *International Financial Statistics*.

MONEY SUPPLY
('000 million pesos at 31 December)

	1999	2000	2001
Currency outside banks	1,185.6	1,128.3	1,232.7
Demand deposits at commercial banks	2,533.0	2,776.6	2,873.7
Total money (incl. others)	3,718.9	3,905.4	4,106.6

Source: IMF, *International Financial Statistics*.

COST OF LIVING
(Consumer Price Index for Santiago; base: 1990 = 100)

	1999	2000	2001
Food (incl. beverages)	231.2	234.5	236.3
Rent, fuel and light	229.6	243.7	258.5
Clothing (incl. footwear)	126.8	118.2	111.5
All items (incl. others)	236.5	245.7	254.4

Source: ILO.

NATIONAL ACCOUNTS

Expenditure on the Gross Domestic Product
('000 million pesos at current prices)

	1999	2000	2001
Government final consumption expenditure	4,587.0	4,981.7	5,379.2
Private final consumption expenditure	23,948.6	25,785.2	27,232.5
Increase in stocks	99.4	593.8	−313.5
Gross fixed capital formation	7,832.1	8,500.0	9,041.3
Total domestic expenditure	36,467.1	39,860.7	41,339.5
Exports of goods and services	10,897.2	12,837.8	14,630.6
Less Imports of goods and services	10,199.9	12,262.3	13,778.4
GDP in purchasers' values	37,164.4	40,436.2	42,191.8
GDP at constant 1996 prices	34,040.6	35,533.4	36,533.0

Source: IMF, *International Financial Statistics*.

Gross Domestic Product by Economic Activity
('000 million pesos at constant 1996 prices*)

	1999	2000	2001
Agriculture and forestry . . .	1,387.2	1,456.3	1,524.4
Fishing	418.7	471.2	528.5
Mining and quarrying . . .	2,798.1	2,944.4	3,050.7
Manufacturing	5,521.4	5,740.3	5,722.1
Electricity, gas and water . .	988.3	1,132.0	1,214.8
Construction	2,838.2	2,844.8	2,952.5
Trade, restaurants and hotels .	3,679.7	3,790.4	3,904.1
Transport, storage and communications	2,384.9	2,576.5	2,727.9
Financial services	4,269.2	4,440.0	4,557.2
Real estate, renting and business activities†	2,602.9	2,664.1	2,716.1
Personal services	3,688.9	3,824.8	3,936.3
Public administration . . .	1,314.8	1,334.5	1,354.4
Sub-total	31,892.2	33,219.3	34,189.0
Value-added tax	2,571.2	2,678.5	2,744.3
Import duties	726.4	838.7	830.2
Less Imputed bank service charge .	1,149.2	1,203.1	1,230.5
GDP in purchasers' values . .	34,040.6	35,533.4	36,533.0

* Figures are provisional.

† Including imputed rents of owner-occupied dwellings.

BALANCE OF PAYMENTS
(US $ million)

	1999	2000	2001
Exports of goods f.o.b. . . .	17,192	19,246	18,505
Imports of goods f.o.b. . . .	−14,737	−17,093	−16,411
Trade balance	2,455	2,153	2,094
Exports of services	3,595	3,725	3,810
Imports of services	−4,552	−4,609	−4,809
Balance on goods and services .	1,498	1,269	1,094
Other income received . . .	1,143	1,581	1,268
Other income paid	−3,372	−4,381	−4,025
Balance on goods, services and income	−731	−1,531	−1,663
Current transfers received . . .	769	821	794
Current transfers paid . . .	−339	−368	−372
Current balance	−301	−1,078	−1,241
Direct investment abroad . .	−2,785	−3,985	−1,432
Direct investment from abroad .	8,988	3,639	4,477
Portfolio investment assets .	−5,795	767	−1,386
Portfolio investment liabilities .	2,579	−127	1,433
Other investment assets . .	−3,371	−2,066	−737
Other investment liabilities .	626	2,598	−507
Net errors and omissions . .	−588	566	−1,118
Overall balance	−653	317	−599

Source: IMF, *International Financial Statistics*.

External Trade

PRINCIPAL COMMODITIES
(distribution by SITC, US $ million)

Imports c.i.f.	1998	1999	2000
Food and live animals . . .	995.9	999.8	1,080.7
Mineral fuels, lubricants, etc. .	1,506.3	1,869.3	3,022.8
Petroleum, petroleum products, etc.	1,140.4	1,387.4	2,428.8
Crude petroleum oils, etc. .	845.2	1,099.9	1,982.6
Chemicals and related products	1,934.4	1,865.4	2,044.4
Basic manufactures . . .	2,739.8	1,969.5	2,342.9
Iron and steel	605.9	284.2	384.0
Machinery and transport equipment	7,362.5	5,081.4	5,791.0
Machinery specialized for particular industries . . .	1,152.1	550.4	681.4
General industrial machinery equipment and parts . . .	1,297.5	909.0	981.6
Office machines and automatic data-processing equipment . .	595.5	614.2	654.4
Automatic data-processing equipment	407.8	435.3	469.2
Telecommunications and sound equipment	1,023.0	891.3	960.4
Other electrical machinery apparatus, etc. . . .	801.8	621.4	656.1
Road vehicles and parts* . .	1,794.8	982.6	1,529.1
Passenger motor cars (excl. buses)	689.3	415.2	629.4
Lorries and trucks	617.6	270.3	548.1
Miscellaneous manufactured articles	1,875.6	1,598.5	1,808.2
Total (incl. others)	17,082.5	13,891.5	16,619.7

* Data on parts exclude tyres, engines and electrical parts.

Exports f.o.b.	1998	1999	2000
Food and live animals . . .	3,564.4	3,684.0	3,788.2
Fish, crustaceans and molluscs and preparations thereof . . .	1,244.7	1,404.3	1,546.2
Fish, fresh (live or dead), chilled or frozen	920.7	1,060.4	1,190.1
Frozen fish	397.5	509.8	537.2
Vegetables and fruit	1,434.8	1,533.4	1,536.7
Fruit and nuts (excl. oil nuts) fresh or dried	1,066.0	1,109.8	1,191.7
Feeding-stuff for animals (excl. unmilled cereals)	371.8	303.6	255.0
Beverages and tobacco . . .	567.2	569.3	607.2
Beverages	553.9	556.3	593.8
Wine of fresh grapes . . .	510.4	523.7	576.8
Crude materials (inedible) except fuels	3,367.8	3,877.3	4,929.3
Cork and wood	525.6	649.4	643.4
Pulp and waste paper . . .	693.8	768.3	1,113.8
Chemical wood pulp	692.3	766.7	1,110.4
Chemical wood pulp, bleached or semi-bleached . .	586.1	641.3	955.6
Metalliferous ores and metal scrap	1,859.4	2,164.9	2,877.7
Copper ores and concentrates (excl. matte)	1,399.5	1,735.1	2,393.7
Chemicals and related products	765.1	750.6	1,015.3
Basic manufactures . . .	5,085.3	5,290.7	6,162.8
Non-ferrous metals	4,307.1	4,383.2	5,164.6
Copper	4,162.8	4,249.8	5,063.8
Copper and copper alloys refined or not, unwrought .	4,068.1	4,154.5	4,954.5
Refined copper (incl. copper alloys other than master alloys), unwrought . .	3,803.4	3,909.6	4,661.5
Machinery and transport equipment	492.0	495.0	494.6
Total (incl. others)	14,841.7	15,619.2	18,214.5

Source: UN, *International Trade Statistics Yearbook*.

2001 (US $ million): Imports c.i.f.: 17,181; Exports f.o.b.: 17,621 (Source: IMF, *International Financial Statistics*).

PRINCIPAL TRADING PARTNERS
(US $ million*)

Imports c.i.f.	1999	2000	2001
Argentina	2,023.2	2,876.9	3,063.9
Brazil	968.7	1,335.3	1,495.3
Canada	411.4	512.1	427.3
China, People's Republic	709.7	999.8	1,052.9
Colombia	166.1	206.3	189.3
Ecuador	228.1	254.3	123.5
France	417.6	447.8	575.3
Germany	627.2	622.2	692.2
Italy	514.8	419.0	436.5
Japan	635.9	710.1	560.6
Korea, Republic	405.4	535.3	540.0
Mexico	579.3	615.6	532.8
Nigeria	131.4	313.0	122.6
Peru	169.2	265.8	285.6
Spain	410.8	428.1	466.1
Sweden	270.8	284.4	182.3
Switzerland	154.2	124.2	109.6
Taiwan	164.2	190.5	173.7
United Kingdom	182.2	177.8	194.9
USA	3,024.4	3,338.5	2,888.6
Venezuela	210.2	236.8	185.0
Total (incl. others)	15,147.8	18,089.9	17,180.8

Exports f.o.b.	1999	2000	2001
Argentina	726.7	636.5	555.6
Belgium	303.3	364.8	231.7
Bolivia	192.3	166.0	144.0
Brazil	699.7	952.7	841.7
Canada	196.6	243.2	258.8
China, People's Republic	567.1	965.9	1,066.1
Colombia	205.7	237.0	243.0
Ecuador	109.6	158.2	230.5
France	507.2	630.9	600.3
Germany	579.2	453.4	517.7
Italy	655.4	815.9	800.2
Japan	2,358.9	2,546.2	2,127.0
Korea, Republic	702.3	795.1	554.4
Mexico	634.2	818.7	828.0
Netherlands	519.9	455.9	535.5
Peru	358.8	439.1	477.7
Spain	335.5	390.7	344.2
Taiwan	521.1	605.3	351.2
United Kingdom	1,095.9	1,072.8	1,225.2
USA	3,133.1	3,246.9	3,413.7
Venezuela	196.0	228.7	285.7
Total (incl. others)	16,255.7	18,425.8	17,620.6

* Imports by country of purchase; exports by country of sale.

Transport

PRINCIPAL RAILWAYS

	1999	2000	2001
Passenger journeys ('000)	10,012	13,197	16,095
Passenger-kilometres ('000)	637,954	736,696	870,836
Freight ('000 metric tons)	21,250	21,982	22,514
Freight ton-kilometres (million)	2,896	3,135	3,318

ROAD TRAFFIC
(motor vehicles in use)

	1998	1999	2000
Passenger cars (excl. taxis)	1,121,262	1,206,986	1,209,968
Buses and coaches (incl. taxis)	168,695	173,228	166,429
Lorries and vans	619,086	652,059	645,461
Specialized vehicles (incl. tractors)	14,310	13,714	14,377
Motorcycles and mopeds	30,893	31,419	27,284

2001: Passenger cars (excluding taxis) 1,247,985; Motorcycles and mopeds 26,318.

SHIPPING

Merchant Fleet
(registered at 31 December)

	1999	2000	2001
Number of vessels	472	471	480
Total displacement ('000 grt)	820.0	842.3	880.3

Source: Lloyd's Register-Fairplay, *World Fleet Statistics*.

International Sea-borne Shipping
(freight traffic, '000 metric tons)

	1998	1999	2000
Goods loaded	28,178	31,287	34,074
Goods unloaded	19,193	19,456	19,888

CIVIL AVIATION
(traffic on scheduled services)

	1997	1998	1999
Kilometres flown (million)	109	139	107
Passengers ('000)	4,693	5,102	5,188
Passenger-km (million)	8,597	9,698	10,650
Freight (million ton-km)	1,030	1,248	1,139

Source: Dirección de Aeronáutica Civil.

Tourism

ARRIVALS BY NATIONALITY

	1998	1999	2000
Argentina	815,601	801,660	858,709
Bolivia	150,895	118,676	110,427
Brazil	83,132	67,751	72,840
Germany	40,073	42,233	43,936
Peru	180,684	122,929	151,863
Spain	35,902	32,831	36,290
USA	127,652	124,044	134,117
Total (incl. others)	1,759,279	1,622,252	1,742,407

Tourism receipts (US $ million): 1,019 in 1997; 1,062 in 1998; 894 in 1999; 827 in 2000.

Sources: World Tourism Organization, *Yearbook of Tourism Statistics*; Servicio Nacional de Turismo.

Communications Media

	1999	2000	2001
Television receivers ('000 in use)	3,600	3,700	n.a.
Telephones ('000 main lines in use)	3,108.8	3,365.0	3,703.3
Mobile cellular telephones ('000 subscribers)	2,260.7	3,401.5	5,271.6
Personal computers ('000 in use)	1,083	1,260	1,300
Internet users ('000)	625	2,537	3,102

Radio receivers ('000 in use): 5,180 in 1997.

Facsimile machines: 40,000 in use in 1997.

Daily newspapers: 52 in 1996.

Sources: UNESCO, *Statistical Yearbook*; UN, *Statistical Yearbook*; International Telecommunication Union.

Education

(provisional figures, 1999)

	Males	Females	Total
		Students	
Pre-primary	139,767	134,820	274,587
Primary	1,200,259	1,127,433	2,327,692
Special primary	28,282	17,767	46,049
Secondary	442,481	443,514	885,995
Higher (incl. universities)	224,977	199,695	424,672

Adult literacy rate (UNESCO estimates): 95.8% (males 96.0%; females 95.6%) in 2000 (Source: UN Development Programme, *Human Development Report*).

Directory

The Constitution

The 1981 Constitution, described as a 'transition to democracy', separated the presidency from the Junta and provided for presidential elections and for the re-establishment of the bicameral legislature, consisting of an upper chamber (Senado) of both elected and appointed senators, who are to serve an eight-year term, and a lower chamber (Cámara de Diputados) of 120 deputies elected for a four-year term. All former Presidents are to be senators for life. There is a National Security Council consisting of the President of the Republic, the heads of the armed forces and the police, and the Presidents of the Supreme Court and the Senado.

In July 1989 a national referendum approved 54 reforms to the Constitution, including 47 proposed by the Government and seven by the Military Junta. Among provisions made within the articles were an increase in the number of directly elected senators from 26 to 38, the abolition of the need for the approval of two successive Congresos for constitutional amendments (the support of two-thirds of the Cámara de Diputados and the Senado being sufficient), the reduction in term of office for the President to be elected in 1989 from eight to four years, with no immediate re-election possible, and the redrafting of the provision that outlawed Marxist groups so as to ensure 'true and responsible political pluralism'. The President's right to dismiss the Congreso and sentence to internal exile were eliminated.

In November 1991 the Congreso approved constitutional changes to local government. The amendments provided for the replacement of centrally appointed local officials with directly elected representatives.

In February 1994 an amendment to the Constitution was approved whereby the length of the presidential term was reduced from eight to six years.

The Government

HEAD OF STATE

President: RICARDO LAGOS ESCOBAR (took office 10 March 2000).

THE CABINET
(April 2003)

A coalition of parties represented in the Concertación de los Partidos de la Democracia (CPD) (including the Partido Demócrata Cristiano—PDC, the Partido Socialista de Chile—PS, the Partido Por la Democracia—PPD, and the Partido Radical Socialdemócrata—PRSD) and four Independents (Ind.).

Minister of the Interior: JOSÉ MIGUEL INSULZA SALINAS (PS).

Minister of Foreign Affairs: MARÍA SOLEDAD ALVEAR VALENZUELA (PDC).

Minister of National Defence: MICHELLE BACHELET JERIA (PS).

Minister of Finance: NICOLÁS EYZAGUIRRE GUZMÁN (PPD).

Minister, Secretary-General of the Presidency: FRANCISCO HUENCHUMILLA JARAMILLO (PDC).

Minister, Secretary-General to the Government: FRANCISCO VIDAL SALINAS (PPD).

Minister of the Economy and Energy: JORGE RODRÍGUEZ GROSSI (PDC).

Minister of Mining: ALFONSO DULANTO RENCORET (Ind.).

Minister of Planning and Co-operation: ANDRÉS PALMA IRARRÁZAVAL (PDC).

Minister of Education: SERGIO BITAR CHACRA (PPD).

Minister of Justice: LUIS BATES HIDALGO (Ind.).

Minister of Labour and Social Security: RICARDO SOLARI SAAVEDRA (PS).

Minister of Public Works, Transport and Telecommunications: JAVIER ETCHEBERRY CELHAY (PPD).

Minister of Health: PEDRO GARCÍA ASPILLAGA (Ind.).

Minister of Housing and Urban Planning: JAIME RAVINET DE LA FUENTE (PDC).

Minister of Agriculture: JAIME CAMPOS QUIROGA (PRSD).

Minister of the National Women's Service (Sernam): CECILIA PÉREZ DÍAZ (Ind.).

MINISTRIES

Ministry of Agriculture: Teatinos 40, Santiago; tel. (2) 696-5698; fax (2) 696-4496; e-mail contacto@minagri.gob.cl; internet www.minagri.gob.cl.

Ministry of Economy and Energy: Teatinos 120, 10°, Santiago; tel. (2) 672-5522; fax (2) 672-6040; internet www.economia.cl.

Ministry of Education: Alameda 1371, 7°, Santiago; tel. (2) 698-3351; fax (2) 688-2300; internet www.mineduc.cl.

Ministry of Finance: Teatinos 120, 12°, Santiago; tel. (2) 675-5800; fax (2) 671-6479; e-mail webmaster@minhda.cl; internet www.minhda.cl.

Ministry of Foreign Affairs: Catedral 1158, Santiago; tel. (2) 679-4200; fax (2) 696-8796; e-mail info@minrel.cl; internet www.minrel.cl.

Ministry of Health: Enrique MacIver 541, 3°, Santiago; tel. (2) 639-4001; fax (2) 633-2405; e-mail consulta@minsal.cl; internet www.minsal.cl.

Ministry of Housing and Urban Development: Alameda 924, Santiago; tel. (2) 638-3366; fax (2) 633-3892; e-mail contactenos@minvu.cl; internet www.minvu.cl.

Ministry of the Interior: Palacio de la Moneda, Santiago; tel. (2) 690-4000; fax (2) 699-2165; internet www.interior.cl.

Ministry of Justice: Morandé 107, Santiago; tel. (2) 674-3100; fax (2) 695-4558; internet www.minjusticia.cl.

Ministry of Labour and Social Security: Huérfanos 1273, 6°, Santiago; tel. (2) 695-5133; fax (2) 698-8473; e-mail mintrab@mintrab.gob.cl; internet www.mintrab.gob.cl.

Ministry of Mining: Santiago; internet www.minmineria.cl.

Ministry of National Defence: Villavicencio 364, 22°, Edif. Diego Portales, Santiago; tel. (2) 222-1202; fax (2) 634-5339.

Ministry of the National Women's Service (Sernam): Teatinos 950, 5°, Santiago; tel. (2) 549-6100; fax (2) 549-6248; e-mail clopez@sernam.cl; internet www.mujereschile.cl.

Ministry of Planning and Co-operation (MIDEPLAN): Ahumada 48, 7°, Santiago; tel. (2) 675-1400; fax (2) 672-1879; internet www.mideplan.cl.

Ministry of Public Works: Santiago; tel. (2) 361-3000; fax (2) 672-5281; internet www.mop.cl.

Ministry of Transport and Telecommunications: Amunátegui 139, 3°, Santiago; tel. (2) 421-3000; fax (2) 672-2785; e-mail mtt@mtt.cl; internet www.mtt.cl.

Office of the Minister Secretary-General of Government: Palacio de la Moneda, Santiago; tel. (2) 690-4160; fax (2) 697-1756; e-mail cmladini@segegob.cl; internet www.segegob.cl.

Office of the Minister Secretary-General of the Presidency: Palacio de la Moneda, Santiago; tel. (2) 690-4218; fax (2) 690-4329.

President and Legislature

PRESIDENT

Election, 12 December 1999 and 16 January 2000

	% of votes cast, 12 Dec. 1999	% of votes cast, 16 Jan. 2000
Ricardo Lagos Escobar (CPD) . .	48.0	51.3
Joaquín Lavín Infante (Alianza por Chile)	47.5	48.7
Gladys Marín Millie (PCCh) . .	3.2	—
Tomás Hirsch Goldschmidt (PH) .	0.5	—
Sara Larraín Ruiz-Tagle . . .	0.4	—
Arturo Frei Bolívar (UCCP) . .	0.4	—
Total	**100.0**	**100.0**

CONGRESO NACIONAL

Senado*
(Senate)

President: ANDRÉS ZALDÍVAR LARRAÍN (PDC).

General Election, 16 December 2001*

	% of valid votes	Seats
Concertación de Partidos por la Democracia (CPD)†	51.3	20
Alianza por Chile‡	44.0	16
Partido Comunista de Chile (PCCh) .	2.6	—
Independents	1.6	2
Partido Humanista (PH) . . .	0.4	—
Partido Liberal (PL)	0.1	—
Total	**100.0**	**38**

1,716,942 valid votes were cast. In addition, there were 71,522 blank and 68,802 spoiled votes.

* Results of elections to renew 18 of the 38 elective seats in the Senado. In addition, there are nine designated senators, and a constitutional provision for former Presidents to assume a seat for life, in an ex-officio capacity. In July 2002 former President Pinochet resigned his senatorial seat, bringing the total number of senators to 48.

† Including the Partido Demócrata Cristiano (PDC), which won 12 seats, the Partido Socialista de Chile (PS), with five seats, and the Partido por la Democracia (PPD), with three seats.

‡ Including the Partido Unión Demócrata Independiente (UDI), which won nine seats, and the Partido Renovación Nacional (RN), which won seven seats.

Cámara de Diputados
(Chamber of Deputies)

President: ADRIANA MUÑOZ D'ALBORA (PPD).

General Election, 16 December 2001

	Valid votes	% of valid votes	Seats
Concertación de Partidos por la Democracia (CPD)* . . .	2,925,800	47.9	62
Alianza por Chile†	2,703,701	44.3	57
Partido Comunista de Chile (PCCh)	318,638	5.2	—
Independents	86,283	1.4	1
Partido Humanista (PH) . . .	69,265	1.1	—
Partido Liberal	3,453	0.1	—
Total	**6,107,140**	**100.0**	**120**

In addition, there were 236,132 blank and 648,232 spoiled votes.

* Including the Partido Demócrata Cristiano (PDC), which won 24 seats, the Partido por la Democracia (PPD), which won 21 seats, the Partido Socialista de Chile (PS), with 11 seats, and the Partido Radical Socialdemócrata (PRSD), with six seats.

† Including the Partido Unión Demócrata Independiente (UDI), which won 35 seats, and the Partido Renovación Nacional (RN), which won 22 seats.

Political Organizations

The most prominent political organizations are:

†**Alianza por Chile:** Santiago; f. 1996 as the Unión por Chile; name changed to above in 1999; right-wing alliance; Leader JOAQUÍN LAVÍN.

***Concertación de Partidos por la Democracia (CPD):** Londres 57, Santiago; tel. and fax (2) 633-1691; e-mail concert@ctcreuna.cl; f. 1988 as the Comando por el No, an opposition front to campaign against the military regime in the plebiscite of 5 October 1988; name changed to above following plebiscite; Leader RICARDO LAGOS ESCOBAR.

Partido Comunista de Chile (PCCh): Avda Vicuña Mackenna 31, Santiago; tel. and fax (2) 665-1654; achieved legal status in October 1990; Pres. GLADYS MARÍN MILLIE.

Partido Democracia Social: San Antonio 220, Of. 604, Santiago; tel. (2) 39-4244; democratic socialist party; Pres. LUIS ANGEL SANTI-BÁÑEZ; Sec.-Gen. JAIME CARMONA DONOSO.

***Partido Demócrata Cristiano (PDC):** Alameda B. O'Higgins 1460, 2°, Santiago; tel. (2) 252-6200; fax (2) 252-6254; f. 1957; member of CPD; Pres. ADOLFO ZALDÍVAR; Sec.-Gen. FRANCISCO HUENCHUMILLA JARAMILLO.

***Partido Democrático de Izquierda (PDI):** Santiago; tel. and fax (2) 632-144; Pres. LUIS GODOY GÓMEZ.

Partido Humanista (PH): Amunategui 86, Of. 801, Santiago; tel. (2) 632-5233; fax (2) 223-9016; internet www.partidohumanista.cl; Pres. JOSÉ G. FERES NAZARALA; Sec.-Gen. WILFREDO ALFSEN.

Partido Izquierda Cristiana (PIC): Compañia 2404, Santiago; tel. (2) 671-8410; fax (2) 671-7837; e-mail naitun@entelchile.net; Pres. CARLOS DONOSO PACHECO; Sec.-Gen. PATRICIO VÉJAR MERCADO.

***Partido Liberal:** Eduardo de la Barra 1384, Of. 404, Santiago; tel. (2) 688-3303; fax (2) 688-3294; internet www.partidoliberal.cl; liberal party; f. 1998 by dissident centrist politicians; Pres. ARMANDO JARAMILLO LYON; Sec.-Gen. JOSÉ DUCCI CLARO.

***Partido Mapu Obrero Campesino:** Eleuterio Ramírez 1463, Santiago; tel. and fax (2) 696-6342; Pres. SAMUEL BELLO SEPÚLVEDA; Sec.-Gen. HUMBERTO SOLAR DÁVILA.

***Partido por la Democracia (PPD):** Erasmo Escala 2154, Santiago; tel. and fax (2) 671-2320; internet www.ppd.cl; Pres. GUIDO GIRARDI LAVIN; Sec.-Gen. ESTEBAN VALENZUELA VAN TREEK.

***Partido Radical Socialdemócrata (PRSD):** Miraflores 495, Santiago; tel. (2) 639-4769; fax (2) 639-1053; centre-left; allied to CPD; Pres. ANSELMO SULE CANDIA; Sec.-Gen. ISIDRO SOLIS PALMA.

†**Partido Renovación Nacional (RN):** Antonio Varas 454, Providencia, Santiago; tel. (2) 373-8749; fax (2) 244-3966; e-mail rn@carn.cl; internet www.rn.cl; f. 1987; right-wing; Pres. SEBASTIÁN PIÑERA ECHENIQUE; Sec.-Gen. RENATO SEPÚLVEDA.

Partido Social Demócrata (PSD): París 815, Casilla 50.220, Correo Central, Santiago; tel. (2) 39-9064; f. 1973; Pres. ARTURO VENEGAS GUTIÉRREZ; Sec.-Gen. LEVIÁN MUÑOZ PELLICER.

***Partido Socialista de Chile (PS):** Concha y Toro 36, Santiago; tel. (2) 696-1638; fax (2) 697-0507; e-mail pschile@reuna.cl; internet www.pschile.cl; f. 1933; left-wing; member of Socialist International; Pres. CAMILO ESCALONA MEDINA; Sec.-Gen. PAMELA PEREIRA FERNANDEZ.

†**Partido Unión Demócrata Independiente (UDI):** Suecia 286, Santiago; tel. (2) 244-2331; fax (2) 233-6189; e-mail udi@caudi.cl;

internet www.udi.cl; f. 1989; right-wing; Pres. PABLO LONGUEIRA MONTES; Sec.-Gen. JUAN ANTONIO COLOMA CORREA.
* Members of the Concertación de Partidos por la Democracia.
† Members of the Alianza por Chile.

Diplomatic Representation

EMBASSIES IN CHILE

Argentina: Miraflores 285, Santiago; tel. (2) 633-1076; fax (2) 639-3321; e-mail embajada.dearg001@chilnet.cl; Ambassador CARLOS LEONARDO DE LA ROSA.

Australia: Gertrudis Echeñique 420, Casilla 33, Correo 10, Las Condes, Santiago; tel. (2) 228-5065; fax (2) 208-1707; e-mail cancilau@bellsouth.cl; Ambassador ELIZABETH SCHICK.

Austria: Barros Errázuríz 1968, 3°, Santiago; tel. (2) 233-4281; fax (2) 204-9382; e-mail santiagodechile@bmaa.gv.at; Ambassador WALTER HOWADT.

Belgium: Providencia 2653, 11°, Of. 1104, Santiago; tel. (2) 232-1070; fax (2) 232-1073; e-mail santiago@diplobel.org; Ambassador JOHAN BALLEGEER.

Brazil: Alonso Ovalle 1665, Santiago; tel. (2) 672-5000; fax (2) 698-1021; e-mail embrasil@brasembsantiago.cl; Ambassador GUILHERME LEITE-RIBEIRO.

Bulgaria: Rodolfo Bentjerodt 4895, Santiago; tel. (2) 228-3110; fax (2) 208-0404; e-mail embajada.debul0001@chilnet.cl.

Canada: Nueva Tajamar 481, 12°, Santiago; tel. (2) 362-9660; fax (2) 362-9665; e-mail stago@dfait-maeci.gc.ca; internet www.dfaitmaeci.gc.ca/santiago; Ambassador PATRICK PARISOT.

China, People's Republic: Pedro de Valdivia 550, Santiago; tel. (2) 233-9880; fax (2) 234-1129; e-mail embajadachina@entelchile.net; Ambassador REN JINGYU.

Colombia: Presidente Errázuriz 3943, Santiago; tel. (2) 206-1314; fax (2) 208-0712; e-mail emcolchi@entelchile.net; Ambassador RAFAEL PÉREZ MARTÍNEZ.

Costa Rica: Calle Zurich 255, Las Condes, Santiago; tel. (2) 334-9486; fax (2) 334-9490; e-mail embacostarica@adsl.tie.cr; Ambassador XIMENA SOLER LEGARRETA.

Croatia: Ezequias Alliende 2370, Providencia, Santiago; tel. (2) 269-6141; fax (2) 269-6092; e-mail embajada@croacia.cl; Ambassador IVE LIVLJANIĆ.

Cuba: Avda Los Leones 1346, Providencia, Santiago; tel. (2) 274-5021; fax (2) 274-5708; e-mail emcuchil@ctcinternet.cl; Ambassador ALFONSO FRAGA PÉREZ.

Czech Republic: Avda El Golf 254, Santiago; tel. (2) 231-1910; fax (2) 232-0707; e-mail santiago@embassy.mzv.cz; internet www.mfa.cz/santiago; Ambassador LUBOMIR HLADIK.

Denmark: Jacques Cazotte 5531, Casilla 13430, Vitacura, Santiago; tel. (2) 218-5949; fax (2) 218-1736; e-mail santiago@danish-embassy.cl; Ambassador BENT KIILERICH.

Dominican Republic: Augusto Leguia Norte 79, Santiago; tel. (2) 245-0667; fax (2) 245-1648; e-mail emrepdom@ctcinternet.cl; Ambassador AMABLE PADILLA GUERRERO.

Ecuador: Santiago; tel. (2) 231-5073; fax (2) 232-5833; e-mail eecuador@ctcinternet.cl; Ambassador JAIME MARCHANT.

Egypt: Roberto del Río 1871, Providencia, Santiago; tel. (2) 274-8881; fax (2) 274-6334; e-mail egipto@ctcinternet.cl; Ambassador SAMIR SHOMAN.

El Salvador: Coronel 2330, Of. 51, Santiago; tel. (2) 233-8324; fax (2) 231-0960; e-mail embajada.deels001@chilnet.cl; Ambassador MARIO JOSÉ IGNACIO AVILA ROMERO.

Finland: Alcántara 200, Of. 201, Las Condes, Santiago; tel. (2) 263-4917; fax (2) 263-4701; e-mail embajada@finlandia.co.cl; Ambassador PEKKA J. KORVENHEIMO.

France: Condell 65, Casilla 38D, Providencia, Santiago; tel. (2) 470-8000; fax (2) 274-1353; e-mail ambassade@ambafrance-cl.org; internet www.france.cl; Ambassador ALAIN LE GOURRIEREC.

Germany: Las Hualtatas 5677, Vitacura, Santiago; tel. (2) 463-2500; fax (2) 463-2525; e-mail central@embajadadealemania.cl; internet www.embajadadealemania.cl; Ambassador GEORG CLEMENS DICK.

Greece: Isidora Goyenechea 3356, Of. 21, Las Condes, Santiago; tel. (2) 231-1244; fax (2) 231-1246; e-mail embgrel@chilesat.net; Ambassador DIMITRIOS MANOLÓPOULOS.

Guatemala: Nuncio Sótero Sonz 55, 8°, Santiago; tel. (2) 335-1565; fax (2) 335-1285; e-mail embajada.degua001@chilnet.cl; Ambassador JULIO GÁNDARA VALENZUELA.

Haiti: Zurich 255, Of. 21, Las Condes, Santiago; tel. (2) 231-0767; fax (2) 231-0967; e-mail embhai@terra.cl; Ambassador GUY G. LAMOTHE.

Holy See: Calle Nuncio Sótero Sanz 200, Casilla 16.836, Correo 9, Santiago (Apostolic Nunciature); tel. (2) 231-2020; fax (2) 231-0868; e-mail nunciatu@entelchile.net; Nuncio Most Rev. ALDO CAVALLI (Titular Archbishop of Vibo Valentia).

Honduras: Zurich 255, Dpto 51, Las Condes, Santiago; tel. (2) 334-7946; fax (2) 334-4069; e-mail honduras@entelchile.net; Ambassador EDUARDO KAWAS GATTAS.

Hungary: Avda Los Leones 2279, Providencia, Santiago; tel. (2) 204-7977; fax (2) 234-1277; e-mail huembstg@entelchile-net; internet www.chilenet.net/huembstg; Ambassador TAMÁS TÓTH.

India: Triana 871, Casilla 10433, Santiago; tel. (2) 235-2005; fax (2) 235-9607; e-mail embindia@entelchile.net; Ambassador K. P. ERNEST.

Indonesia: Nueva Costanera 3318, Santiago; tel. (2) 207-6266; fax (2) 207-9901; e-mail kbristgo@mi-mail.cl; Ambassador SUWARNO ATMOPAWIRO.

Israel: San Sebastián 2812, 5°, Casilla 1224, Santiago; tel. (2) 750-0500; fax (2) 750-0555; e-mail eisraelp@rdc.cl; Ambassador ORI NOY.

Italy: Clemente Fabres 1050, Santiago; tel. (2) 225-9439; fax (2) 223-2467; e-mail italcom@entelchile.net; internet www.embitalia.cl; Ambassador GIOVANNI FERRERO.

Japan: Avda Ricardo Lyon 520, Santiago; tel. (2) 232-1807; fax (2) 232-1812; e-mail embajada.dejap001@chilnet.cl; Ambassador HAJIME OGAWA.

Jordan: San Pascual 446, Santiago; tel. (2) 228-8989; fax (2) 228-8783; e-mail embajada.dejor001@chilnet.cl; Ambassador ATEF HALASA.

Korea, Republic: Alcántara 74, Casilla 1301, Santiago; tel. (2) 228-4214; fax (2) 206-2355; e-mail embajada.decor001@chilnet.cl; Ambassador CHO YOUNG-HA.

Lebanon: Alianza 1728, Santiago; tel. (2) 232-5027; fax (2) 219-3502; e-mail líbano@netline.cl; Ambassador MASSOUD MALUF.

Malaysia: Tajamar 183, 10° y 11°, Of. 1002, Santiago; tel. (2) 233-6698; fax (2) 234-3853; e-mail mwstg@terra.cl; Ambassador A. GANAPATHY.

Mexico: Félix de Amesti 128, Santiago; tel. (2) 206-6133; fax (2) 206-6147; e-mail embamex@ia.cl; Ambassador OSCAR R. VALERO RECIO BECERRA.

Morocco: Avda Luis Pasteur 5850, Of. 203, Vitacura, Santiago; tel. (2) 218-0311; fax (2) 218-0266; e-mail ambmarch@entelchile.net; internet www.marruecos.cl; Ambassador ABDELLATIF EL ALOUI.

Netherlands: Las Violetas 2368, Casilla 56-D, Santiago; tel. (2) 756-9200; fax (2) 756-9226; e-mail sto@hinbuza.nl; internet www.holandapaisesbajas.cl; Ambassador H. NIJENHUIS.

New Zealand: El Golf 99, Of. 703, Casilla 112, Las Condes, Santiago; tel. (2) 290-9802; fax (2) 207-2333; e-mail nzembassychile@adsl.tie.cl; Ambassador RICHARD MANN.

Nicaragua: Zurich 255, Of. 111, Las Condes, Santiago; tel. (2) 234-1808; fax (2) 234-5071; e-mail embanic@embajadadenicaragua.tie.cl; Ambassador SILVIO ALIVEZ GALLO.

Norway: San Sebastián 2839, Of. 509, Casilla 2431, Santiago; tel. (2) 234-2888; fax (2) 234-2201; e-mail ambassade-santiago@ud.dep.telemax.no; Ambassador MARTIN TORE BJØRNDAL.

Panama: La Reconquista 640, Las Condes, Santiago; tel. (2) 229-7937; fax (2) 202-5439; e-mail panaembchhile@entelchole.net; Ambassador ALEJANDRO YOUNG DOWNEY.

Paraguay: Huérfanos 886, 5°, Ofs 514-515, Santiago; tel. (2) 639-4640; fax (2) 633-4426; e-mail embajada.delpa001@chilnet.cl; Ambassador ESTEBAN OJEDA SALDÍVAR.

Peru: Avda Andrés Bello 1751, Casilla 16277, Providencia, Santiago; tel. (2) 235-2356; fax (2) 235-8139; e-mail embstgo@entelchile.net; Ambassador JORGE COLUNGE VILLACORTA.

Philippines: Félix de Amesti 367, Santiago; tel. (2) 208-1313; fax (2) 208-1400; e-mail embajada.defil001@chilnet.cl; Ambassador HERMENEGILDO C. CRUZ.

Poland: Mar del Plata 2055, Santiago; tel. (2) 204-1213; fax (2) 204-9332; e-mail embchile@entelchile.net; Ambassador JAROSŁAW SPYRA.

Portugal: Coyancura 2241, 11°, Santiago; tel. (2) 232-3034; fax (2) 231-8809; e-mail embajada.depor001@chilnet.cl; Ambassador ANTÓNIO MACHADO DE FARIA E MAYA.

Romania: Benjamín 2955, Santiago; tel. (2) 231-1893; fax (2) 231-2325; e-mail embajada@rumania.tie.cl; internet www.embajadaderumania.cl; Ambassador ION VALCU.

Russia: Cristobal Colón 4152, Las Condes, Santiago; tel. (2) 208-3413; fax (2) 206-1386; e-mail embrusia@mcl.cl; internet www.rucl.virtualave.net; Ambassador ALEKSEI G. KVASVOV.

South Africa: Avda 11 de Septiembre 2353, 16°, Torre San Ramón, Santiago; tel. (2) 231-2860; fax (2) 231-3185; e-mail embsachi@interaccess.cl; internet www.embajadasudafrica.cl; Ambassador T. K. MASEKO.

Spain: Avda Andrés Bello 1895, Casilla 16456, Providencia, Santiago; tel. (2) 235-2755; fax (2) 235-1049; e-mail embespcl@correo.mae.es; Ambassador JUAN ALFONSO ORTIZ RAMOS.

Sweden: Avda 11 de Septiembre 2353, 4°, Torre San Ramón, Santiago; tel. (2) 940-1700; fax (2) 940-1730; e-mail santiago-de-chile@foreign.ministry.se; internet www.embajadasuecia.cl; Ambassador ARNE RODIN.

Switzerland: Avda Américo Vespucio Sur 100, 14°, Santiago; tel. (2) 263-4211; fax (2) 263-4094; e-mail vertretung@san.rep.admin.ch; internet www.eda.admin.ch/santiago_emb/s/home.html; Ambassador CHARLES-EDOUARD HELD.

Syria: Carmencita 111, Casilla 12, Correo 10, Santiago; tel. (2) 232-7471; Ambassador HISHAM HALLAJ.

Thailand: Avda Américo Vespucio 100, 15°, Las Condes, Santiago; tel. (2) 263-0710; fax (2) 263-0803; e-mail thaichil@ctcreuna.cl; internet www.rte-chile.thaiembdc.org; Ambassador PITHAYA POOKAMAN.

Turkey: Edif. Montolin, Of. 71, Monseñor Sotero Sanz 55, Providencia, Santiago; tel. (2) 231-8952; fax (2) 231-7762; e-mail turkemb@ctcreuna.cl; Ambassador SADI CALISLAR.

United Kingdom: Avda el Bosque Norte 0125, Casilla 72 D, Santiago; tel. (2) 370-4100; fax (2) 370-2140; e-mail chancery@Santiago.mail.fco.gov.uk; internet www.britemb.cl; Ambassador RICHARD WILKINSON.

USA: Avda Andrés Bello 2800, Las Condes, Santiago; tel. (2) 232-2600; fax (2) 330-3710; internet www.usembassy.cl; Ambassador WILLIAM R. BROWNFIELD.

Uruguay: Avda Pedro de Valdivia 711, Casilla 2636, Santiago; tel. (2) 204-7988; fax (2) 204-7772; e-mail urusgo@mailnet.rdl.cl; Ambassador ALFREDO BIANCHI PALAZZO.

Venezuela: Bustos 20–21, Casilla 16577, Santiago; tel. (2) 225-0021; fax (2) 209-9117; e-mail embajada@embavenez.cl; internet www.embavenez.cl; Ambassador DOMINGO MILIANI.

Judicial System

The Supreme Courts consist of 21 members.

There are Courts of Appeal (in the cities or departments of Arica, Iquique, Antofagasta, Copiapó, La Serena, Valparaíso, Santiago, San Miguel, Rancagua, Talca, Chillán, Concepción, Temuco, Valdivia, Puerto Montt, Coyhaique and Punta Arenas) whose members are appointed from a list submitted to the President of the Republic by the Supreme Court. The number of members of each court varies. Judges of the lower courts are appointed in a similar manner from lists submitted by the Court of Appeal of the district in which the vacancy arises. Judges and Ministers of the Supreme Court do not continue in office beyond the age of 75 years.

In March 1998 a major reform of the judiciary was implemented, including an increase, from 17 to 21, in the number of Ministers of the Supreme Court.

Corte Suprema

Plaza Montt Varas, Santiago; tel. (2) 698-0561; fax (2) 695-2144; internet www.poderjudicial.cl.

President of the Supreme Court: MARIO GARRIDO MONTT.

Ministers of the Supreme Court: HERNÁN ALVAREZ GARCÍA, MARCOS LIBEDINSKY TSCHORNE, ELEODORO ORTIZ SEPÚLVEDA, JOSÉ BENQUIS CAMHI, ENRIQUE TAPIA WITTING, RICARDO GÁLVEZ BLANCO, ALBERTO CHAIGNEAU DEL CAMPO, JORGE RODRÍGUEZ ARIZTÍA, ENRIQUE CURY URZÚA, JOSÉ LUIS PÉREZ ZAÑARTU, ORLANDO ALVAREZ HERNÁNDEZ, URBANO MARÍN VALLEJO, DOMINGO YURAC SOTO, HUMBERTO ESPEJO ZÚÑIGA, JORGE MEDINA CUEVAS, DOMINGO ALFONSO MOURGUES, MILTON IVAN ARANCIBIA, NIBALDO SEGURA PEÑA, MARIA MORALES VILLAGRAN, ADALIS OYARZUN MIRANDA.

Attorney-General: MONICA MALDONADO CROQUEVIELLE.

Secretary of the Court: CARLOS A. MENESES PIZARRO.

Corporación Nacional de Reparación y Reconciliación: f. 1992 in order to co-ordinate and implement the recommendations of the Comisión Nacional de Verdad y Reconciliación, which was established in 1990 to investigate violations of human rights committed during the military dictatorship, and which delivered its report in 1991; Pres. ALEJANDRO GONZÁLEZ POBLETE; Exec. Sec. ANDRÉS DOMÍNGUEZ VIAL.

Religion

Some 77% of the population are Roman Catholics; there were an estimated 10.9m. adherents at 31 December 2000.

CHRISTIANITY

The Roman Catholic Church

Chile comprises five archdioceses, 18 dioceses, two territorial prelatures and one apostolic vicariates.

Bishops' Conference

Conferencia Episcopal de Chile, Echaurren 4, 6°, Casilla 517-V, Correo 21, Santiago; tel. (2) 671-7733; fax (2) 698-1416; e-mail secretariageneral@episcopado.cl; internet www.episcopado.cl.

f. 1955 (statutes approved 2000); Pres. Cardinal FRANCISCO JAVIER ERRÁZURIZ OSSA (Archbishop of Santiago de Chile).

Archbishop of Antofagasta: PATRICIO INFANTE ALFONSO, San Martín 2628, Casilla E, Antofagasta; tel. (55) 26-8856; fax (55) 22-3021; e-mail arzoanto@cechnet.cl.

Archbishop of Concepción: ANTONIO MORENO CASAMITJANA, Calle Barros Arana 544, Casilla 65-C, Concepción; tel. (41) 22-8173; fax (41) 23-2844; e-mail arconcep@cechnet.cl.

Archbishop of La Serena: MANUEL DONOSO DONOSO, Los Carrera 450, Casilla 613, La Serena; tel. (51) 21-2325; fax (51) 22-5886; e-mail laserena@episcopado.cl.

Archbishop of Puerto Montt: CRISTIÁN CARO CORDERO, Calle Benavente 385, Casilla 17, Puerto Montt; tel. (65) 25-2215; fax (65) 27-1861; e-mail puertomontt@episcopado.cl.

Archbishop of Santiago de Chile: Cardinal FRANCISCO JAVIER ERRÁZURIZ OSSA, Erasmo Escala 1884, Casilla 30-D, Santiago; tel. (2) 696-3275; fax (2) 671-2042.

The Anglican Communion

Anglicans in Chile come within the Diocese of Chile, which forms part of the Anglican Church of the Southern Cone of America, covering Argentina, Bolivia, Chile, Paraguay, Peru and Uruguay.

Bishop of Chile: Rt Rev. H. F. ZAVALA M, Iglesia Anglicana, Casilla 50675, Santiago; tel. (2) 639-1509; fax (2) 639-4581; e-mail fzavala@evangel.cl.

Other Christian Churches

Baptist Evangelical Convention: Casilla 41-22, Santiago; tel. (2) 222-4085; fax (2) 635-4104; f. 1908; Pres. MOISÉS PINTO; Gen. Sec. VÍCTOR OLIVARES.

Evangelical Lutheran Church: Pedro de Valdivia 3420-H, Dpto 33, Nuñoa, Casilla 15167, Santiago; tel. (2) 223-3195; fax (2) 205-2193; e-mail ielch@entelchile.net; f. 1937 as German Evangelical Church in Chile; present name adopted in 1959; Pres. GLORIA ROJAS; 3,000 mems.

Jehovah's Witnesses: Avda Concha y Toro 3456, Puente Alto; tel. (2) 288-1264; fax (2) 288-1257; Dir PEDRO J. LOVATO GROSSO.

Methodist Church: Sargento Aldea 1041, Casilla 67, Santiago; tel. (2) 556-6074; fax (2) 554-1763; autonomous since 1969; 7,317 mems; Bishop NEFTALÍ ARAVENA BRAVO.

Orthodox Church of the Patriarch of Antioch: Santiago; tel. and fax (2) 737-4697; Archbishop Mons. SERGIO ABAD.

Pentecostal Church: Calle Pena 1103, Casilla de Correo 2, Curicó; tel. (75) 1035; f. 1945; 90,000 mems; Bishop ENRIQUE CHÁVEZ CAMPOS.

Pentecostal Church Mission: Santiago; tel. (2) 634-6785; fax (2) 634-6786; f. 1952; Sec. Rev. DANIEL GODOY FERNÁNDEZ; Pres. Rev. ERASMO FARFÁN FIGUEROA; 12,000 mems.

JUDAISM

Comité Representativo de las Entidades Judías en Chile (CREJ): Avda Ricardo Lyon 812, Providencia, Santiago; tel. (2) 274-7101; fax (2) 269-7005; Pres. ELIMAT Y. JASON.

Comunidad Israelita Sefardi de Chile: Avda Ricardo Lyon 812, Providencia, Santiago; tel. (2) 209-8086; fax (2) 204-7382; Pres. SALOMON CAMHI AVAYU, Rabbi IOSEF GABAY.

ISLAM

Sociedad Unión Musulmana: Mezquita As-Salam, Campoamor 2975, esq. Chile-España, Ñuñoa, Santiago; tel. (2) 343-1376; fax (2) 343-11378; Pres. OUSAMA ABUGHAZALÉ.

BAHÁ'Í FAITH

National Spiritual Assembly: Manuel de Salas 356, Casilla 3731, Ñuñoa, Santiago; tel. (2) 269-2002; fax (2) 225-8276; e-mail secretaria@aenchile.tie.cl; internet www.bahai.cl; Co-ordinator REED CHANDLER REED; Sec. JORGE ORÓSTICA MADRID.

The Press

Most newspapers of nation-wide circulation in Chile are published in Santiago.

DAILIES

Circulation figures listed below are supplied mainly by the Asociación Nacional de la Prensa. Other sources give much lower figures.

Santiago

La Cuarta: Diagonal Vicuña Mackenna 2004, Santiago; tel. (2) 555-0034; fax (2) 556-8727; morning; Gen. Man. JUAN CARLOS LARRAÍN WORMALD.

El Diario: San Crescente 81, 3°, Las Condes, Santiago; tel. (2) 339-1000; fax (2) 231-3340; e-mail buzon@eldiario; internet www.eldiario.cl; f. 1988; morning; Gen. Man. JOSÉ MIGUEL RESPALDIZA CHICHARNO; circ. 20,000.

Diario Oficial de la República de Chile: Agustinas 1269, Santiago; tel. (2) 695-5500; fax (2) 698-2222; internet www.diarioficial.cl; f. 1877; Dir FLORENCIO CEBALLOS B; circ. 10,000.

Estrategia: Santiago; tel. (2) 252-4000; fax (2) 236-1114; e-mail estrategia@reuna.cl; internet www.reuna.estrategia.cl; f. 1978; morning; Dir VÍCTOR MANUEL O. MÉNDEZ.

El Mercurio: Avda Santa María 5542, Casilla 13-D, Santiago; tel. (2) 330-1111; fax (2) 228-9042; e-mail mercurio@mercurio.cl; internet www.emol.com; f. 1827; morning; conservative; Gen. Man. FERNANDO CISTERNAS BRAVO; circ. 120,000 (weekdays), 280,000 (Sun.).

La Nación: Agustinas 1269, Casilla 81-D, Santiago; tel. (2) 787-0100; fax (2) 698-1059; f. 1917 to replace govt-subsidized *El Cronista*; morning; financial; Propr Soc. Periodística La Nación; Dir GUILLERMO HORMAZÁBAL SALGADO; circ. 45,000.

La Segunda: Avda Santa María 5542, Casilla 13-D, Santiago; tel. (2) 330-1111; fax (2) 228-9289; internet www.lasegunda.com; f. 1931; evening; Dir CRISTIÁN ZEGERS ARIZTÍA; circ. 40,000.

La Tercera: Avda Vicuña Mackenna 1870, Santiago; tel. (2) 551-7067; fax (2) 550-7999; e-mail latercera@copesa.cl; internet www.latercera.cl; f. 1950; morning; Dir FERNANDO PAULSEN; circ. 200,000.

Las Ultimas Noticias: Bellavista 0112, Providencia, Santiago; tel. (2) 730-3000; fax (2) 730-3331; f. 1902; morning; Gen. Man. JUAN ENRIQUE CANALES BESA; owned by the Proprs of *El Mercurio*; circ. 150,000 (except Sat. and Sun.).

Antofagasta

La Estrella del Norte: Manuel Antonio Matta 2112, Antofagasta; tel. (55) 26-4835; f. 1966; evening; Dir CAUPOLICÁN MÁRQUEZ VERGARA; circ. 5,000.

El Mercurio: Manuel Antonio Matta 2112, Antofagasta; tel. (55) 26-4815; fax (55) 25-1710; f. 1906; morning; conservative independent; Proprs Soc. Chilena de Publicaciones; Dir ROBERTO RETAMAL PACHECO; circ. 9,000.

Arica

La Estrella de Arica: San Marcos 580, Arica; tel. (58) 22-5024; fax (58) 25-2890; f. 1976; Dir REINALDO NEIRA RUIZ; circ. 10,000.

Atacama

Chañarcillo: Los Carrera 801, Chañaral, Atacama; tel. (52) 21-9044; f. 1992; morning; Dir LUIS CERPA HIDALGO.

Calama

El Mercurio: Sotomayor 2025, Calama; tel. (56) 25-1090; f. 1968; Propr Soc. Chilena de Publicaciones; Dir ROBERTO RETAMAL PACHECO; circ. 4,500 (weekdays), 7,000 (Sun.).

Chillán

La Discusión de Chillán, SA: Calle 18 de Septiembre 721, Casilla 479, Chillán; tel. (42) 21-2650; fax (42) 21-3578; e-mail ladiscu@ctcreuna.cl; f. 1870; morning; independent; Dir TITO CASTILLO PERALTA; circ. 5,000.

Concepción

El Sur: Calle Freire 799, Casilla 8-C, Concepción; tel. (41) 23-5825; f. 1882; morning; independent; Dir RAFAEL MAIRA LAMAS; circ. 28,000 (weekdays), 45,000 (Sun.).

Copiapó

Atacama: Manuel Rodríguez 740, Copiapó; tel. (52) 2255; morning; independent; Dir SAMUEL SALGADO; circ. 6,500.

Coyhaique

El Diario de Aisén: 21 de Mayo 410, Coyhaique; tel. (67) 234-850; fax (67) 232-318; Dir ALDO MARCHESSE COMPODÓNICO.

Curicó

La Prensa: Merced 373, Casilla 6-D, Curicó; tel. (75) 31-0453; fax (75) 31-1924; e-mail laprensa@entelchile.net; internet diariolaprensa.cl; f. 1898; morning; right-wing; Man. Dir MANUEL MASSA MAUTINO; circ. 4,000.

Iquique

La Estrella de Iquique: Luis Uribe 452, Iquique; tel. (57) 42-2805; fax (57) 42-7975; f. 1966; evening; Dir ARCADIO CASTILLO ORTIZ; circ. 10,000.

El Nortino: Baquedano 1470, Iquique; tel. (57) 41-6666; fax (57) 41-2997; e-mail nortino@entelchile.net; f. 1992; morning; Dir-Gen. REYNALDO BERRÍOS GONZÁLEZ.

La Serena

El Día: Brasil 431, La Serena; tel. (51) 22-2863; fax (51) 22-2844; f. 1944; morning; Dir ANTONIO PUGA RODRÍGUEZ; circ. 10,800.

Los Angeles

La Tribuna: Calle Colo Colo 464, Casilla 15-D, Los Angeles; tel. (43) 31-3315; fax (43) 31-1040; independent; Dir CIRILO GUZMÁN DE LA FUENTE; circ. 4,500.

Osorno

El Diario Austral: Avda B. O'Higgins 870, Osorno; tel. (64) 23-5191; fax (64) 23-5192; internet www.australvaldivia.cl; f. 1982; Dir CARLOS NOLI A; circ. 6,500 (weekdays), 7,300 (Sun.).

Ovalle

El Ovallino: Victoria 323-B, Ovalle; tel. and fax (53) 627-557; Dir JORGE CONTADOR ARAYA.

Puerto Montt

El Llanquíhue: Antonio Varas 167, Puerto Montt; tel. (65) 25-5115; fax (65) 432-401; e-mail ellanquihue@123click.cl; f. 1885; Dir ERNESTO MONTALBA; circ. 4,800 (weekdays), 5,700 (Sun.).

Punta Arenas

La Prensa Austral: Waldo Seguel 636, Casilla 9-D, Punta Arenas; tel. (61) 20-4000; fax (61) 24-7406; e-mail direccion@laprensaaustral.cl; internet www.laprensaaustral.cl; f. 1941; morning; independent; Dir MANUEL GONZÁLEZ ARAYA; circ. 10,000, Sunday (*El Magallanes*; f. 1894) 12,000.

Quillota

El Observador: La Concepción 277, Casilla 1-D, Quillota; tel. (33) 312-096; fax (33) 311-417; e-mail elobser@entelchile.net; Dir ROBERTO SILVA BIJIT.

Rancagua

El Rancagüino: O'Carroll 518, Casilla 50, Rancagua; tel. (72) 23-0358; fax (72) 22-1483; e-mail prensaelrancaguino@adsl.tie.cl; internet www.elrancaguino.cl; f. 1915; independent; Dir ALEJANDRO GONZÁLEZ; Gen. Man. FERNANDO REYES; circ. 10,000.

Talca

El Centro: Tres Oriente 798, Talca; tel. (71) 22-0946; fax (71) 22-0924; f. 1989; Gen. Man. HUGO SAAVEDRA OTEIZA.

Temuco

El Diario Austral: Antonio Varas 945, Casilla 1-D, Temuco; tel. (45) 21-2575; fax (45) 23-9189; f. 1916; morning; commercial, industrial and agricultural interests; Dir MARCO ANTONIO PINTO ZEPEDA; Propr Soc. Periodística Araucanía, SA; circ. 15,100 (weekdays), 23,500 (Sun.).

Tocopilla

La Prensa de Tocopilla: Bolívar 1244, Tocopilla; tel. (83) 81-3036; f. 1924; morning; independent; Gen. Man. Jorge Leiva Concha; circ. 3,000.

Valdivia

El Diario Austral: Yungay 499, Valdivia; tel. (63) 24-2200; fax (63) 24-2217; internet www.australvaldivia.cl; f. 1982; Dir Gustavo Serrano Cotapos; circ. 5,600.

Valparaíso

La Estrella: Esmeralda 1002, Casilla 57-V, Valparaíso; tel. (32) 26-4230; fax (32) 26-4241; e-mail estrell@entelchile.net; f. 1921; evening; independent; Dir Alfonso Castagneto; owned by the Proprs of *El Mercurio*; circ. 28,000 (weekdays), 35,000 (Sat.).

El Mercurio: Esmeralda 1002, Casilla 57-V, Valparaíso; tel. (32) 26-4264; fax (32) 26-4138; internet www.elmercuriovalpo.cl; f. 1827; morning; Dir Marco Antonio Pinto Zepada; owned by the Proprs of *El Mercurio* in Santiago; circ. 65,000.

Viña del Mar

El Expreso: 3 Poniente 61, Casilla 617, Viña del Mar; tel. (32) 972-020; fax (32) 972-217; e-mail editor@entelchile.net; internet www.imaginativa.cl/expreso; Man. Dir Enrique Alvarado Aguilera.

PERIODICALS

Santiago

Apsi: Santiago; tel. (2) 77-5450; f. 1976; fortnightly; Dir Marcelo Contreras Nieto; circ. 30,000.

La Bicicleta: José Fagnano 614, Santiago; tel. (2) 222-3969; satirical; Dir Antonio de la Fuente.

CA (Ciudad/Arquitectura) Revista Oficial del Colegio de Arquitectos de Chile AG: Manuel Montt 515, Santiago; tel. (2) 235-3368; fax (2) 235-8403; f. 1964; 4 a year; architects' magazine; Editor Arq. Jaime Márquez Rojas; circ. 3,500.

Carola: San Francisco 116, Casilla 1858, Santiago; tel. (2) 33-6433; fortnightly; women's magazine; published by Editorial Antártica, SA; Dir Isabel Margarita Aguirre de Maino.

Cauce: Huérfanos 713, Of. 604–60, Santiago; tel. (2) 38-2304; fortnightly; political, economic and cultural affairs; Dir Angel Flisfich; circ. 10,000.

Chile Agrícola: Teresa Vial 1170, Casilla 2, Correo 13, Santiago; tel. and fax (2) 522-2627; e-mail chileagricola@hotmail.com; f. 1975; 6 per year; farming; Dir Ing. Agr. Raúl González Valenzuela; circ. 10,000.

Chile Forestal: Avda Bulnes 285, Of. 601, Santiago; tel. (2) 671-1850; fax (2) 696-6724; f. 1974; monthly; technical information and features on forestry sector; Dir Ernesto Lagos Tapia; circ. 4,000.

Cosas: Almirante Pastene 329, Providencia, Santiago; tel. (2) 364-5100; fax (2) 235-8331; f. 1976; fortnightly; international affairs; Dir Mónica Comandari Kaiser; circ. 40,000.

Creces: Santiago; tel. (2) 223-4337; monthly; science and technology; Dir Sergio Prenafeta; circ. 12,000.

Deporte Total: Santiago; tel. (2) 251-6236; fax (2) 204-7420; f. 1981; weekly; sport, illustrated; Dir Juan Ignacio Oto Larios; circ. 25,000.

Ercilla: Avda Holanda 309, Providencia, Santiago; tel. (2) 251-6236; e-mail ercill@terra.cl; internet www.ercilla.com; f. 1936; weekly; general interest; Dir Joaquín González; circ. 28,000.

Gestión: Luis Carrera 1289, Vitacura, Santiago; tel. (2) 655-6100; fax (2) 655-6408; internet www.estrategia.cl/gestion.htm; f. 1975; monthly; business matters; Dir Víctor Manuel Ojeda Méndez; circ. 38,000.

Hoy: María Luisa Santander 0436, Clasificador 654, Correo Central, Santiago; tel. (2) 225-6926; fax (2) 225-4669; e-mail hoy@mailnet.rdc.cl; internet www.reuna.cl/hoy; f. 1977; weekly; general interest; Dir Ascanio Cavallo Castro; circ. 30,000.

Internet: Avda Carlos Valdovinos 251; tel. (2) 552-5599; e-mail director@interra.cl; monthly; internet and new technology; Dir Florencio Uteras.

Mensaje: Almirante Barroso 24, Casilla 10445, Santiago; tel. (2) 696-0653; fax (2) 671-7030; e-mail mensaje@ia.cl; internet www.mensaje.cl; f. 1951; monthly; national, church and international affairs; Dir Antonio Delfau; circ. 6,000.

Microbyte: Avda Condell 1879, Nuñoa, Santiago; tel. (2) 341-7507; fax (2) 341-7504; f. 1984; monthly; computer science; Dir José Kaffman; circ. 6,000.

News Review: Casilla 151/9, Santiago; tel. (2) 236-9511; fax (2) 236-0887; e-mail newsrevi@netline.cl; f. 1991; weekly; English language news; Dir Graham A. Wigg.

Paula: Avda Santa María 0120, Providencia,, Santiago; tel. (2) 200-0585; fax (2) 200-0490; e-mail revpaula@paula.cl; f. 1967; monthly; women's interest; Dir Paula Recart; circ. 85,000.

Punto Final: San Diego 31, Of. 606, Casilla 13954, Correo 21, Santiago; tel. (2) 697-0615; e-mail punto@interaccess.cl; internet www.puntofinal.cl; f. 1965; fortnightly; politics; left-wing; Dir Manuel Cabieses; circ. 15,000.

¿Qué Pasa?: Vicuña Mackenna 1870, Ñuñoa, Santiago; tel. (2) 551-7067; fax (2) 550-7529; f. 1971; weekly; general interest; Dir Bernadita del Solar Vera; circ. 30,000.

El Siglo: Diagonal Paraguay 458, Casilla 13479, Santiago; tel. and fax (2) 633-0074; f. 1989; fortnightly; published by the Communist Party of Chile (PCCh); Dir Claudio Denegri Quintana.

The Clinic: Santiago; tel. (2) 343-5850; fax (2) 343-4088; e-mail theclinic@bigfoot.com; fortnightly; political and social satire; Dir Patricio Fernández.

Vea: Avda Holanda 279, Providencia, Santiago; tel. (2) 422-8500; fax (2) 422-8571; internet www.vea.cl; f. 1939; weekly; general interest, illustrated; Dir Darío Rojas Morales; circ. 150,000.

PRESS ASSOCIATION

Asociación Nacional de la Prensa: Carlos Antúnez 2048, Santiago; tel. 232-1004; fax 232-1006; e-mail info@anp.cl; internet www.anp.cl; Pres. Carlos Schaerer Jiménez; Sec. Fernando Silva Vargas.

NEWS AGENCIES

Agencia Chile Noticias (ACN): Huérfanos 714, Of. 117, Santiago; tel. (2) 638-5568; fax (2) 638-3188; e-mail prensa@chilenoticias.cl; internet www.chilenoticias.cl; f. 1993; Dir Norberto Parra Hidalgo.

Chile Information Project (CHIP): Avda Santa María 227, Recoleta, Santiago; tel. (2) 777-5376; e-mail anderson@chip.mic.cl; internet www.santiagotimes.cl; English language; Dir Stephen J. Anderson.

Europa Press: Biarritz 1913, Providencia, Santiago; tel. and fax (2) 274-3552; e-mail europapress@rdc.cl; Dir José Ríos Vial.

Orbe Servicios Informativos, SA: Phillips 56, 6°, Of. 66, Santiago; tel. (2) 39-4774; Dir Sebastiano Bertolone Galletti.

Foreign Bureaux

Agence France-Presse (France): Avda B. O'Higgins 1316, 9°, Apt. 92, Santiago; tel. (2) 696-0559; Correspondent Humberto Zumarán Araya.

Agencia EFE (Spain): Coronel Santiago Bueras 188, Santiago; tel. (2) 638-0179; fax (2) 633-6130; e-mail direccion@agenciaefe.tie.cl; internet www.efe.es; f. 1966; Bureau Chief Man. Manuel Fuentes García.

Agenzia Nazionale Stampa Associata (ANSA) (Italy): Moneda 1040, Of. 702, Santiago; tel. (2) 698-5811; fax (2) 698-3447; f. 1945; Bureau Chief Giorgio Bagoni Bettollini.

Associated Press (AP) (USA): Tenderini 85, 10°, Of. 100, Casilla 2653, Santiago; tel. (2) 33-5015; Bureau Chief Kevin Noblet.

Bloomberg News (USA): Miraflores 222, Santiago; tel. (2) 638-6820; fax (2) 698-3447; Dir Mike Smith.

Deutsche Presse-Agentur (dpa) (Germany): San Antonio 427, Of. 306, Santiago; tel. (2) 639-3633; Correspondent Carlos Dorat.

Inter Press Service (IPS) (Italy): Santiago; tel. (2) 39-7091; Dir and Correspondent Gustavo González Rodríguez.

Prensa Latina (Cuba): Bombero Ossa 1010, Of. 1104, Santiago; tel. (2) 671-8222; fax (2) 695-8605; Correspondent Lidia Señaris Cejas.

Reuters (United Kingdom): Neuva York 33, 11°, Casilla 4248, Santiago; tel. (2) 672-8800; fax (2) 696-0161; Correspondent Roger Atwood.

Xinhua (New China) News Agency (People's Republic of China): Biarritz 1981, Providencia, Santiago; tel. (2) 25-5033; Correspondent Sun Kuoguowein.

Association

Asociación de Corresponsales de la Prensa Extranjera en Chile: Coronel Santiago Bueras 188, Santiago; tel. (2) 632-1890; fax (2) 633-6130; Pres. Omar Ruz.

Publishers

Distribuidora Molino, SA: Abtao 574, Santiago; tel. (2) 776-2295; fax (2) 776-6425; e-mail distribuidoramolino@chilnet.cl; Admin. Man. JORGE VARGAS ARAYA.

Ediciones y Comunicaciones Ltda: Luis Thayer Ojeda 0115, Santiago; tel. (2) 232-1241; fax (2) 234-9467; e-mail edicom@chilnet .cl; internet www.chilnet.cl/edicom/; publs include *Anuario Farmacológico*; Gen. Man. MARIO SILVA MARTÍNEZ.

Ediciones San Pablo: Vicuña Mackenna 10777, Casilla 3746, Santiago; tel. (2) 288-2025; fax (2) 288-2026; e-mail dgraledi@cnet .net; Catholic texts; Dir-Gen. P. LUIS NEIRA RAMÍREZ.

Ediciones Técnicas Ltda: Matilde Salamanca 736, 6°, Santiago; tel. (2) 209-8100; fax (2) 209-8101; e-mail editec@editec.cl; internet www.editec.cl; Pres. RICARDO CORTES DONOSO; Gen. Man. ROLY SOLIS SEPÚLVEDA.

Ediciones Universidad Católica de Valparaíso: Universidad Católica de Valparaíso, 12 de Febrero 187, Casilla 1415, Valparaíso; tel. (32) 27-3086; fax (32) 27-3429; e-mail euvsa@ucv.cl; internet www.ucv.cl/web/euv; f. 1970; general literature, social sciences, engineering, education, music, arts, textbooks; Gen. Man. ALEJANDRO DAMIÁN V.

Editora Nacional Gabriel Mistral Ltda: Santiago; tel. (2) 77-9522; literature, history, philosophy, religion, art, education; government-owned; Man. Dir JOSÉ HARRISON DE LA BARRA.

Editorial Andrés Bello/Jurídica de Chile: Avda Ricardo Lyon 946, Casilla 4256, Providencia, Santiago; tel. (2) 204-9900; fax (2) 225-3600; e-mail mmallea@entelchile.net; internet www .juridicadechile.com; f. 1947; history, arts, literature, politics, economics, textbooks, law and social science; Gen. Man. JULIO SERRANO LAMAS.

Editorial Antártica, SA: San Francisco 116, Santiago; tel. (2) 639-4650; fax (2) 633-4475; f. 1978; Gen. Man. HERNÁN AGUIRRE MACKAY.

Editorial Cuatro Vientos Ltda: Santiago; tel. (2) 225-8381; fax (2) 341-3107; e-mail 4vientos@netline.cl; internet www.cuatrovientos .net; Man. Editor JUAN FRANCISCO HUNEEUS COX.

Editorial El Sembrador: Sargento Aldea 1041, Casilla 2037, Santiago; tel. (2) 556-9454; Dir ISAÍAS GUTIÉRREZ.

Editorial Evolución, SA: General del Canto 105, Of. 707, Santiago; tel. (2) 236-4789; fax (2) 236-4796; e-mail evoluc@entelchile .net; internet www.evolucion.cl.

Editorial Nascimento, SA: Chiloé 1433, Casilla 2298, Santiago; tel. (2) 555-0254; f. 1898; general; Man. Dir CARLOS GEORGE NASCIMENTO MÁRQUEZ.

Editorial Renacimiento: Huérfanos 623, Santiago; tel. (2) 639-6621; fax (2) 633-9374; internet www.feriachilenodellibro.cl; Gen. Man. ALBERTO ALDEA.

Editorial Terra Chile: Santiago; tel. (2) 737-4455; fax (2) 738-0445; Gen. Man. ORLANDO MILESI.

Editorial Texido: Manuel Antonio Tocornal 1487, Santiago; tel. (2) 555-5534; fax (2) 555-5466; Gen. Man. ELSA ZLATER.

Editorial Tiempo Presente Ltda: Almirante Pastene 329, Providencia, Santiago; tel. (2) 364-5100; fax (2) 235-8331; e-mail cosas@ mailnet.rdc.cl; internet www.cosas.com; Gen. Man. JUAN LUIS SOMMERS.

Editorial Trineo, SA: Los Olmos 3685, Macul, Santiago; tel. (2) 272-5945; fax (2) 272-0212; e-mail triven@crnet.net; internet www .cmet.net/trineo/; Gen. Man. CARLOS JÉREZ HERNÁNDEZ.

Editorial Universitaria, SA: María Luisa Santander 0447, Casilla 10220, Providencia, Santiago; tel. (2) 223-4555; fax (2) 209-9455; e-mail edituniv@reuna.cl; f. 1947; general literature, social science, technical, textbooks; Man. Dir EDUARDO CASTRO.

Empresa Editora Zig-Zag SA: Los Conquistadores 1700, 17-B, Providencia, Santiago; tel. (2) 335-7477; fax (2) 335-7445; e-mail zigzag@zigzag.cl; f. 1934; general publishers of literary works, reference books and magazines; Pres. GONZALO VIAL C; Gen. Man. FRANCISCO PÉREZ FRUGONE.

McGraw-Hill/Interamericana de Chile Ltda: Avda Seminario 541, Santiago; tel. (2) 222-9405; fax (2) 635-4467; e-mail mcgrawhill .int001@chilnet.cl; internet www.bookshop.co.uk.

Publicaciones Técnicas, SA (PUBLITECSA): Serrano 172, Santiago; tel. (2) 365-8000; fax (2) 365-8010; e-mail acliente@publitecsa .cl; internet www.publitecsa.cl; Commercial Man. CARLOS MUNIZAGA.

Red Internacional del Libro Ltda: Avda Eliodoro Yáñez 1934, Dept 14, Providencia, Santiago; tel. (2) 223-4269; fax (2) 223-8100; e-mail ril@rileditores.com; internet www.rileditores.com; f. 1991; Commercial Man. ELEONORA FINKELSTEIN.

PUBLISHERS' ASSOCIATION

Cámara Chilena del Libro AG: Avda B. O'Higgins 1370, Of. 502, Casilla 13526, Santiago; tel. (2) 672-0348; fax (2) 687-4271; e-mail camlibro@terra.cl; internet www.camilbro.cl; Pres. EDUARDO CASTILLO GARCÍA; Exec. Sec. RAQUEL TORNERO GÓMEZ.

Broadcasting and Communications

TELECOMMUNICATIONS

Regulatory Authority

Subsecretaría de Telecomunicaciones (Department of Telecommunications, Ministry of Public Works, Transport and Telecommunications): Amunátegui 139, 5°, Casilla 120, Correo 21, Santiago; tel. (2) 672-6502; fax (2) 421-3553; e-mail subtel@ subtel.cl; Under-Sec. CHRISTIAN NICOLAI ORELLANA.

Major Operators

Alcatel de Chile: Monseñor Sótero Sanz 55, 3°, Providencia, Santiago; tel. (2) 230-3000; fax (2) 231-1862; internet www.alcatel.com; Pres. SERGE TCHURUK; Gen. Man. MARCEL MAFILLE.

AT&T Chile: Vitacura 2939, 8° y 9°, Vitacura, Santiago; tel. (2) 380-0171; fax (2) 382-5142; e-mail info@firstcom.cl; internet www.attla .cl; Pres. PATRICIO NORTHLAND; Gen. Man. CARLOS FERNÁNDEZ.

Chilesat: Rinconada El Salto 202, Huechuraba, Santiago; tel. (2) 380-0171; fax (2) 382-5142; e-mail tlchile@chilesat.net; internet www.chilesat.net; Pres. JUAN EDUARDO IBÁÑEZ; Gen. Man. RAMÓN VALDIVIESO.

CMET Compañía de Telefónos: Avda Los Leones 1412, Providencia, Santiago; tel. (2) 251-333; fax (2) 274-9573; Pres. JULIO YUBERO; Gen. Man. AGUSTIN CASTELLON.

Empresa Nacional de Telecomunicaciones, SA—ENTEL Chile, SA: Andrés Bello 2687, 14°, Casilla 4254, Santiago; tel. (2) 360-0123; fax (2) 661-7299; internet www.entel.cl; f. 1964; operates the Chilean land satellite stations of Longovilo, Punta Arenas and Coihaique, linked to INTELSAT system; 52% owned by Telecom Italia; Pres. JUAN HURTADO.

PTT Comunicaciones: Santiago; tel. (2) 665-1000; fax (2) 665-1004; e-mail pttsa@ctinternet.cl; internet www.pttsa.com; Gen. Man. JAVIER MOLINOS.

Telefónica Chile: Apoquindo 4499, 10°, Casilla 16-D, Santiago; tel. (2) 691-2020; fax (2) 691-2009; formerly Compañía de Telecomunicaciones de Chile, SA; Gen. Man. JACINTO DÍAZ SÁNCHEZ.

TELEX-CHILE, SA: Rinconada El Salto 202, Santiago; tel. (2) 380-0171; fax (2) 382-5142; internet www.telex.cl; Pres. JUAN EDUARDO IBÁÑEZ; Gen. Man. RAMÓN VALDIVIESO.

VTR Gobal Com: Reyes Lavalle 3340, 9°, Las Condes, Santiago; tel. (2) 310-1000; fax (2) 310-1560; internet www.aldea.com; Pres. BLAS TOMIC.

BROADCASTING

Regulatory Authority

Asociación de Radiodifusores de Chile (ARCHI): Pasaje Matte 956, Of. 801, Casilla 10476, Santiago; tel. (2) 639-8755; fax (2) 639-4205; e-mail archi@archiradios.cl; internet www.archiradios.cl; f. 1936; 455 broadcasting stations; Pres. CÉSAR MOLFINO MENDOZA.

Radio

In December 2000 there were 1,153 radio stations (981 FM and 172 AM) transmitting in Chile.

Agricultura (AM y FM): Avda Manuel Rodríguez 15, Santiago; tel. (2) 695-3088; fax (2) 672-2749; owned by Sociedad Nacional de Agricultura; Pres. MANUEL VALDÉS VALDÉS; Gen. Man. GUIDO ERRÁZURIZ MORENO.

Aurora FM (Iberoamerican Radio Chile): Phillips 40, 2°, Of. 26, Santiago; tel. (2) 632-4104; fax (2) 639-8868; f. 1982; Pres. ERNESTO CORONA BOZZO; Gen. Man. JUAN CARRASCO HERNÁNDEZ.

Beethoven FM: Garibaldi 1620, Ñuñoa, Santiago; tel. (2) 274-7951; fax (2) 274-3323; internet www.beethovenfm.cl; f. 1981; affiliate stations in Viña del Mar and Temuco; Dir ADOLFO FLORES SAYLER.

Belén AM: Benavente 385, 3°, Casilla 17, Puerto Montt; tel. (65) 25-8048; e-mail radiobel.en001@chilnet.cl; f. 1990; owned by Archbishopric of Puerto Montt; Dir NELSON GONZÁLEZ ANDRADE; Gen. Man. CARLOS WAGNER CATALÁN.

Bío Bío La Radio: Santiago; tel. (2) 231-2757; fax (2) 233-7997; affiliate stations in Concepción, Los Angeles, Temuco, Ancud, Castro, Osorno, Puerto Montt and Valdivia.

Compañía Radio Chilena: Phillips 40, 2°, Casilla 10277; tel. (2) 463-5000; fax (2) 463-5100; e-mail achia@radiochilena.cl; internet www.radiochilena.com; f. 1922; Exec. Dir JAIME MORENO LAVAL.

Radio El Conquistador FM: El Conquistador del Monte 4644, Huechuraba, Santiago; tel. (2) 740-9090; fax (2) 740-4992; e-mail rconquis@entelchile.net; internet www.openbox.com/conquistador; f. 1962; affiliate stations in Santiago, Iquique, Antofagasta, La Serena, Viña del Mar, Rancagua, Talca, Chillán, Concepción, Talcahuano, Pucón, Temuco, Villarrica, Lago Llanquihue, Osorno, Puerto Montt, Puerto Varas, Valdivia and Punta Arenas; Gen. Man. URSULA BURKERT FALK.

Radio Cooperativa (AM y FM): Antonio Bellet 223, Casilla 16367, Correo 9, Santiago; tel. (2) 364-8000; fax (2) 364-8010; e-mail info@cooperativa.cl; internet www.cooperativa.cl; f. 1936; affiliate stations in Copiapó, Arica, Coquimbo, La Serena, Valparaíso, Concepción, Calama, Temuco and Castro; Pres. LUIS AJENJO ISASI; Gen. Man. SERGIO PARRA GODOY.

La Clave FM: Monjitas 454, Of. 406, Santiago; tel. (2) 633-1621; fax (2) 639-2914; f. 1980; Pres. MIGUEL NASUR ALLEL; Gen. Man. VÍCTOR IBARRA NEGRETE.

Duna FM: Dr Torres Boonen 136, Santiago; tel. (2) 224-5494; fax (2) 225-6901; e-mail dunafm@entelchile.net; internet www.duna.cl; affiliate stations in Viña del Mar and Concepción; Pres. FELIPE LAMARCA CLARO; Gen. Man. ANA HOLUIGUE BARROS.

Estrella del Mar AM: Ramírez 207, Ancud-Isla de Chiloé; tel. (65) 62-2095; fax (65) 62-2722; e-mail estrella@telsur.cl; f. 1982; affiliate stations in Castro and Quellón; Dir MIGUEL ANGEL MILLAR SILVA.

Festival AM: Paseo Cousiño 8, Casilla 337, Viña del Mar; tel. (32) 88-1229; fax (32) 68-0266; e-mail administracion@festival.cl; internet www.festival.cl; f. 1976; Pres. LUIS MUÑOZ AHUMADA; Dir Gen. SANTIAGO CHIESA HOWARD.

Finísima FM: Santiago; tel. (2) 233-5771; fax (2) 231-0611; affiliate stations in Santiago, Arica, Iquique, Calama, Copiapó, La Serena, Ovalle, Isla de Pascua, Quilpe, San Antonio, San Felipe, Villa Alemana, Viña del Mar, Rancagua, Talca, Chillán, Concepción, Los Angeles, Temuco, Puerto Montt, Coihayque, Puerto Aysen and Punto Arenas; Gen. Man. CRISTIÁN WAGNER MUÑOZ.

FM-Hit: Eliodoro Yáñez 1783, Providencia, Santiago; tel. (2) 274-6737; fax (2) 274-8928; internet www.concierto.cl; affiliate stations in Santiago, Iquique, Antofagasta, San Antonio, La Serena, Viña del Mar, Concepción, Temuco, Osorno and Puerto Montt; Gen. Man. JAIME VEGA DE KUYPER.

Horizonte: Avda Los Leones 1625, Providencia, Santiago; tel. (2) 274-6737; fax (2) 274-8900; internet www.concierto.cl/horizon.htm; f. 1985; affiliate stations in Iquique, La Serena, Viña del Mar, Concepción, Temuco and Osorno.

Infinita FM: Avda Los Leones 1285, Casilla Los Leones 1285, Providencia, Santiago; tel. (2) 204-2813; fax (2) 341-6737; f. 1977; affiliate stations in Santiago, Viña del Mar, Concepción and Valdivia; Gen. Man. CARLOS ALBERTO PEÑAFIEL GUARACHI.

Radio Nacional de Chile: Argomedo 369, Santiago; tel. (2) 638-1348; fax (2) 632-1065; affiliate stations in Arica and Punta Arenas; Gen. Man. SANTIAGO AGLIATI.

Para Ti FM: El Conquistador del Monte 4644, Huechuraba, Santiago; tel. (2) 740-9393; fax (2) 740-9051; internet www.openbox.com/manquehue; affiliate stations in La Serena and Viña del Mar; Gen. Man. FELIPE MOLFINO BURKERT.

Radio Polar: Bories 871, 2°, Punta Arenas; tel. (61) 24-1417; fax (61) 22-8344; f. 1940; Pres. RENÉ VENEGAS OLMEDO.

Pudahuel FM: Eliodoro Yáñez 1783, Providencia, Santiago; tel. (2) 223-0704; fax (2) 223-7589; e-mail radio@pudahuel.cl; internet www.pudahuel.cl; f. 1966; affiliate stations in Arica, Iquique, Antofagasta, Calama, Copiapó, Coquimbo, La Serena, Ovalle, San Felipe, Valparaíso, Viña del Mar, Rancagua, Curico, Linares, Talca, Chillán, Concepción, Los Angeles, Talcahuano, Pucón, Temuco, Villarrica, Ancud-Castro, Osorno, Puerto Montt, Valdivia and Punta Arenas; Pres. SUSANA MUTINELLI ANCHUBIDART; Gen. Man. JOAQUÍN BLAYA BARRIOS.

Santa María de Guadalupe: Miguel Claro 161, Casilla 2626, Santiago; tel. (2) 235-7996; fax (2) 235-8527; affiliate stations in Arica, Iquique, Antofagasta, La Serena, Viña del Mar, Temuco, Puerto Varas, Coihayque and Punta Arenas; Dir ALFONSO CHADWICK.

Superandina FM: Santa Rosa 441, Of. 34, Casilla 401, Los Andes; tel. (34) 42-2515; fax (34) 42-4095; f. 1987; Dir JOSÉ ANDRÉS GÁLVEZ.

Universo FM: Félix de Amesti 124, 8°, Santiago; tel. (2) 206-6065; fax (2) 206-6049; affiliate stations in Iquique, Copiapó, La Serena, Ovalle, Concepción, Temuco, Puerto Montt, Coihayque and Punta Arenas; Pres. ALVARO LARRAÍN.

Television

Canal 2° Rock & Pop: Chucre Manzur 15, Providencia, Santiago; tel. (2) 73-7880; fax (2) 73-5845; Exec. Dir LUIS AJENJO ISAS.

Corporación de Televisión de la Universidad Católica de Chile—Canal 13: Inés Matte Urrejola 0848, Casilla 14600, Providencia, Santiago; tel. (2) 251-4000; fax (2) 630-2040; e-mail dasein@reuna.cl; internet www.reuna.cl/teletrece/corpora.html; f. 1959; noncommercial; Exec. Dir ELEODORO RODRÍGUEZ MATTE; Gen. Man. MANUEL VEGA RODRÍGUEZ.

La Red Televisión, S.A./TV Azteca Chile, S.A.: Manquehue Sur 1201, Las Condes, Santiago; tel. (2) 212-1111; fax (2) 246-5881; e-mail administracion@lared.cl; f. 1991; Pres. JUAN CARLOS LATORRE; Gen. Man. MARCELO PAMDOLFO.

Megavisión, S.A.—Canal 9: Avda Vicuña Mackenna 1348, Santiago; tel. (2) 555-5400; fax (2) 551-8916; e-mail mega@mcl.cl; internet www.mcl.cl./megavision; f. 1990; Pres. RICARDO CLARO VALDÉS; Gen. Man. JOSÉ DÍAZ DEL RÍO.

Red de Televisión SA/Chilevisión—Canal 11: Inés Matte Urrejola 0825, Casilla 16547, Correo 9, Providencia, Santiago; tel. (2) 737-2227; fax (2) 737-7923; e-mail chu@cmet.net; internet www.chilevision.emet.net; News Dir FELIPE POZO.

Televisión Nacional de Chile—Canal 7: Bellavista 0990, Casilla 16104, Providencia, Santiago; tel. (2) 707-7777; fax (2) 707-7766; e-mail rrpp@tvn.cl; internet www.tvn.cl; government network of 145 stations and an international satellite signal; Chair. LUIS ORTIZ QUIROGA; Gen. Man. MARIO CONCA ROSENDE.

Corporación de Televisión de la Universidad Católica de Valparaíso: Agua Santa Alta 2455, Casilla 247, Viña del Mar; tel. (32) 616-000; fax (32) 610-505; e-mail tv@ucv.cl; f. 1957; Dir JORGE A. BORNSCHEUER.

Finance

(cap. = capital; dep. = deposits; res = reserves; m. = million; amounts in pesos unless otherwise specified)

BANKING

Supervisory Authority

Superintendencia de Bancos e Instituciones Financieras: Moneda 1123, 6°, Casilla 15-D, Santiago; tel. (2) 442-6200; fax (2) 441-0914; e-mail superintendente@sbif.cl; internet www.sbif.cl; f. 1925; affiliated to Ministry of Finance; Superintendent ENRIQUE MARSHALL RIVERA.

Central Bank

Banco Central de Chile: Agustinas 1180, Santiago; tel. (2) 670-2000; fax (2) 698-4647; e-mail bcch@bcentral.cl; internet www.bcentral.cl; f. 1926; under Ministry of Finance until Dec. 1989, when autonomy was granted; bank of issue; cap. 250,101.6m., total assets 18,568,388.4m. (Dec. 2001); Pres. VITTORO CORBO; Gen. Man. CAMILO CARRASCO.

State Bank

Banco del Estado de Chile: Avda B. O'Higgins 1111, Santiago; tel. (2) 670-7000; fax (2) 670-5094; e-mail mforno@bech.cl; internet www.bancoestado.cl; f. 1953; state bank; cap. and res 328,551m., dep. 3,492,359m. (May 2002); Pres. JAIME ESTÉVEZ; Gen. Man. JOSÉ MANUEL MENA; 294 brs.

Commercial Banks

Banco de A. Edwards: Huérfanos 740, Santiago; tel. (2) 388-3000; fax (2) 388-4428; internet www.banedwards.cl; f. 1851; cap. 132,512.3m., res 85,030.5m., dep. 1,984,054.4m. (Dec. 1999); Pres. ANDRONICO LUKSIC; CEO GUSTAVO FAVRE DOMÍNGUEZ; 61 brs.

Banco BICE: Teatinos 220, Santiago; tel. (2) 692-2000; fax (2) 696-5324; e-mail webmaster@bice.cl; internet www.bice.cl; f. 1979 as Banco Industrial y de Comercio Exterior; name changed as above in 1988; cap. and res 83,989m., dep. 600,701m. (May 2002); Pres. and Chair. BERNARDO MATTE; Gen. Man. CRISTIAN EYZAGUIRRE; 13 brs.

Banco de Chile: Ahumada 251, Casilla 151-D, Santiago; tel. (2) 637-1111; fax (2) 637-3434; internet www.bancochile.cl; f. 1894; 55% owned by the Luksic group; cap. and res 538,126m., dep. 4,392,061m. (May 2002); Chair. SEGISMUNDO SCHULIN-ZEUTHEN SERRANO; CEO PABLO GRANIFO LAVÍN; 102 brs.

Banco de Crédito e Inversiones: Huérfanos 1134, Casilla 136-D, Santiago; tel. (2) 692-7000; fax (2) 695-3777; e-mail webmaster@bci .cl; internet www.bci.cl; f. 1937; cap. and res 248,029m., dep. 2,273,925m. (May 2002); Pres. LUIS ENRIQUE YARUR REY; Gen. Man. LIONEL OLAVARRÍA; 112 brs.

Banco del Desarrollo: Avda B. O'Higgins 949, 3°, Casilla 320-V, Correo 21, Santiago; tel. (2) 674-5000; fax (2) 671-5547; e-mail bdd@ bandes.cl; internet www.bancodeldesarrollo.cl; f. 1983; cap. and res 87,681m., dep. 645,028m. (May 2002); Chair. VICENTE CARUZ MIDDLETON; Gen. Man. HUGO TRIVELLI; 82 brs.

Banco Internacional: Moneda 818, Casilla 135-D, Santiago; tel. (2) 369-7000; fax (2) 369-7367; e-mail infor@binter.cl; f. 1944; cap. and res 14,128m., dep. 106,418m. (May 2002); Pres. ALEJANDRO L. FURMAN SIHMAN; Gen. Man. ALVARO ACHONDO GONZÁLEZ; 11 brs.

Banco Santander-Chile: Bandera 140, Casilla 57-D, Santiago; tel. (2) 320-2000; fax (2) 330-8877; internet www.bsantander.cl; f. 1926; cap. and res 362,433m., dep. 2,943,484m. (May 2002); subsidiary of Banco de Santander (Spain); incorporated Banco Osorno y La Unión in 1996; Pres. EMILIO BOTÍN SANZ DE SAUTUOLA Y GARCÍA DE LOS RÍOS; Gen. Man. OSCAR VON CHRISMAR; 72 brs.

Banco Santiago: Bandera 201, 3°, Casilla 14437, Santiago; tel. (2) 647-4000; fax (2) 671-7152; e-mail comelec@bancosantiago.cl; internet www.bancosantiago.cl; f. 1997 by merger of Banco O'Higgins and Banco de Santiago; cap. and res 424,652m., dep. 3,239,788m. (May 2002); Chair. CARLOS OLIVOS MARCHANT; Gen. Man. FERNANDO CAÑAS; 163 brs.

Banco Security: Agustinas 621, Santiago; tel. (2) 270-4000; fax (2) 270-4001; e-mail banco@security.cl; internet www.security.cl; f. 1981; fmrly Banco Urquijo de Chile; cap. and res 76,104m., dep. 630,622m. (May 2002); Pres. FRANCISCO SILVA S; Gen. Man. RAMÓN ELUCHANS O; 11 brs.

BBVA Banco BHIF: Huérfanos 1234, Casilla 517, Santiago; tel. (2) 679-1000; fax (2) 698-5640; internet www.bhif.cl; f. 1883; was merged with Banco Nacional in 1989; acquired Banesto Chile Bank in Feb. 1995; controlling interest acquired by Banco Bilbao Vizcaya (Spain) in Sept. 1998; name changed as above in 1999; cap. and res 228,163m., dep. 1,349,303m. (May 2002); Pres. JOSÉ SAID SAFFIE; CEO CARLOS SENENT-SALES; 78 brs.

Corpbanca: Huérfanos 1072, Casilla 80-D, Santiago; tel. (2) 687-8000; fax (2) 696-5763; e-mail fburgos@corpbanca.cl; internet www .corpbanca.cl; f. 1871 as Banco de Concepción, current name adopted in March 1997; cap. and res 156,349m., dep. 1,1925,583m. (May 2002); Chair. CARLOS ABUMOHOR; CEO MARIO CHAMARRO; 92 brs.

Dresdner Banque Nationale de Paris: Huérfanos 1219, Casilla 10492, Santiago; tel. (2) 731-4444; fax (2) 460-8177; e-mail info@ dresbnp.cl; internet www.dresbnp.cl; f. 1958 as Banco Continental; bought by Crédit Lyonnais in Sept. 1987; current name adopted in 1996; cap. and res 25,337m., dep. 174,477m. (May 2002); Pres. WALTER SIEBEL; Gen. Man. EWALD DOERNER; 1 br.

Scotiabank Sud Americano: Morandé 226, Casilla 90-D, Santiago; tel. (2) 692-6000; fax (2) 698-6008; e-mail bsa@bsa.cl; internet www.bsa.cl; f. 1944; cap. and res 94,197m., dep. 776,862m. (May 2002); Chair. RICHARD E. WAUGH; CEO LUIS FERNANDO TOBÓN; 49 brs.

Foreign Banks

Foreign banks with branches in Chile include the following:

ABN AMRO Bank (Netherlands), American Express Bank Ltd (USA), Banco do Brasil, Banco do Estado de São Paulo (Brazil), Banco de la Nación Argentina, Banco Real (Brazil), Banco Sudameris (France and Italy), Bank of America NT & SA (USA), Bank of Boston (USA), Bank of Tokyo-Mitsubishi Ltd (Japan), Chase Manhattan Bank NA, Citibank NA (USA), HSBC Bank (United Kingdom), Republic National Bank of New York (USA)

Finance Corporations

Financiera Atlas, SA: Nueva de Lyon 72, 7°, Santiago; tel. (2) 233-3151; fax (2) 233-3152; Gen. Man. NEIL A. DENTON FEILMANN.

Financiera Conosur: Avda B. O'Higgins 1980, 7°, Santiago; tel. (2) 697-1491; fax (2) 696-3133; internet www.financieraconosur.cl; Pres. JOSÉ LUIS DEL RÍO; Gen. Man. EDMUNDO HERMOSILLA.

Banking Association

Asociación de Bancos e Instituciones Financieras de Chile AG: Ahumada 179, 12°, Santiago; tel. (2) 699-3977; fax (2) 698-8945; e-mail general@abif.cl; internet www.abif.cl; f. 1945; Pres. HERNÁN SOMERVILLE SENN; Gen. Man. ALEJANDRO ALARCÓN PÉREZ.

Other Financial Supervisory Bodies

Superintendencia de Administradoras de Fondos de Pensiones (AFPs) (Superintendency of Pensions Fund Administrators): Huérfanos 1273, 9°, Casilla 3955, Santiago; tel. (2) 753-0120;

fax (2) 753-0122; e-mail aferreir@safp.cl; internet www.safp.cl; f. 1981; CEO ALEJANDRO FERREIRO YAZIGI.

Superintendencia de Previsión Social (Superintendency of Social Security): Huérfanos 1376, 5°, Santiago; tel. (2) 696-8092; fax (2) 696-4672; CEO LUIS ORLANDINI MOLINA.

STOCK EXCHANGES

Bolsa de Comercio de Santiago: La Bolsa 64, Casilla 123-D, Santiago; tel. (2) 399–3000; fax (2) 318–1961; e-mail flederman@ bolsadesantiago.com; internet www.bolsadesantiago.com; f. 1893; 35 mems; Pres. PABLO YRARRÁZAVAL VALDÉS; Gen. Man. JOSÉ ANTONIO MARTÍNEZ Z.

Bolsa de Corredores—Valores de Valparaíso: Prat 798, Casilla 218-V, Valparaíso; tel. (32) 25-0677; fax (32) 21-2764; e-mail bolsadec.orred001@chilnet.cl; f. 1905; Pres. CARLOS F. MARÍN ORREGO; Man. ARIE JOEL GELFENSTEIN FREUNDLICH.

Bolsa Electrónica de Chile: Huérfanos 770, 14°, Santiago; tel. (2) 639-4699; fax (2) 639-9015; e-mail info@bolchile.cl; internet www .bolchile.cl; Gen. Man. JUAN CARLOS SPENCER OSSA.

INSURANCE

In 1999 there were 60 general, life and reinsurance companies operating in Chile.

Supervisory Authority

Superintendencia de Valores y Seguros: Teatinos 120, 6°, Santiago; tel. (2) 549-5900; fax (2) 549-5965; e-mail svalseg@ibm.net; internet www.svs.cl; f. 1931; under Ministry of Finance; Supt ALVARO CLARK DE LA CERDA.

Principal Companies

Aetna Chile Seguros de Vida, SA: Suecia 211, 7°, Santiago; tel. (2) 364-2000; fax (2) 364-2010; e-mail jdupre@aetna.cl; internet www .aetna.cl; f. 1981; life; Pres. SERGIO BAEZA VALDÉS; Gen. Man. FERNANDO HASENBERG NATOLI.

Aseguradora Magallanes, SA: Agustinas 1022, Of. 722; tel. (2) 365-4800; fax (2) 365-4860; e-mail fvarela@magallanes.cl; internet www.magallanes.cl; f. 1957; general; Pres. SERGIO LARRAÍN; Gen. Man. FERNANDO VARELA.

Axa Seguros Generales, SA: Huérfanos 1189, 2°, 3° y 4°, Casilla 429-V, Santiago; tel. (2) 679-9200; fax (2) 679-9300; internet www .axa.cl; f. 1936; general; Gen. Man. BARNARDO SERRANO LÓPEZ.

Chilena Consolidada Seguros Generales, SA: Pedro de Valdivia 195, Casilla 16587, Correo 9, Providencia, Santiago; tel. (2) 200-7000; fax (2) 274-9933; internet www.chilena.cl; f. 1853; general; Gen. Man. IGNACIO BARRIGA UGARTE.

Chubb de Chile, SA: Gertrudis Echeñique 30, 4°, Santiago; tel. (2) 206-2191; fax (2) 206-2735; internet www.chubb.com/chile; f. 1992; general; Gen. Man. CLAUDIO M. ROSSI.

Cía de Seguros de Crédito Continental, SA: Avda Isidora Goyenechea 3162, 6°, Edif. Parque 1 Golf, Santiago; tel. (2) 636-4000; fax (2) 636-4001; e-mail comer@continental.cl; f. 1990; general; Gen. Man. FRANCISCO ARTIGAS CELIS.

Cía de Seguros Generales Aetna Chile, SA: Suecia 211, Santiago; tel. (2) 364-2000; fax (2) 364-2060; internet www.aetna.cl; f. 1899; general; Pres. SERGIO BAEZA VALDÉS; Gen. Man. MAXIMO ERRÁZURIZ DE SOLMINIHAC.

Cía de Seguros Generales Consorcio Nacional de Seguros, SA: Apoquindo 3039, Casilla 28, Correo 10, Santiago; tel. (2) 250-2500; fax (2) 364-2525; f. 1992; general; Gen. Man. ARMANDO BRICEÑO NEFF.

Cía de Seguros Generales Cruz del Sur, SA: Paseo Puente 574, 7°, Casilla 2682, Santiago; tel. (2) 690-6000; fax (2) 698-9126; f. 1974; general; Pres. ROBERTO ANGELINI; Gen. Man. MIKEL URIARTE.

Cía de Seguros Generales Euroamérica, SA: Agustinas 1127, 2°, Casilla 180-D, Santiago; tel. (2) 672-7242; fax (2) 696-4086; internet www.euroamerica.cl; f. 1986; general; Gen. Man. JUAN ENRIQUE BUDINICH SANTANDER.

Cía de Seguros de Vida Consorcio Nacional de Seguros, SA: Avda El Bosque Sur 180, 3°, Casilla 232, Correo 35, Providencia, Santiago; tel. (2) 230-4000; fax (2) 230-4050; f. 1916; life; Pres. JUAN BILBAO HORMAECHE; Gen. Man. MARCOS BÜCHI BUC.

Cía de Seguros de Vida La Construcción, SA: Avda Providencia 1806, 11°—18°, Providencia, Santiago; tel. (2) 340-3000; fax (2) 340-3024; e-mail seguros@laconstruccion.sa.cl; f. 1985; life; Pres. VÍCTOR MANUEL JARPA RIVEROS; Gen. Man. MANUEL ZEGERS IRARRÁZAVAL.

Cía de Seguros de Vida Cruz del Sur, SA: Paseo Puente 574, 4°, Casilla 2682, Santiago; tel. (2) 690-6000; fax (2) 698-9126; internet www.cruzdelsur.cl; f. 1992; life; Pres. ROBERTO ANGELINI; Gen. Man. MIKEL URIARTE.

Cía de Seguros de Vida Euroamérica, SA: Agustinas 1127, 3°, Casilla 21-D, Santiago; tel. (2) 782-7000; fax (2) 699-0732; e-mail deptoservicio@eurovida.cl; internet www.eurovida.cl; f. 1962; life; Pres. BENJAMIN DAVIS CLARKE; Gen. Man. PATRICIA JAIME VÉLIZ.

Cía de Seguros de Vida Santander, SA: Bandera 150, Santiago; tel. (2) 640-1177; fax (2) 640-1377; e-mail servicio@santanderseg.cl; internet www.netra.santanderseg.cl/index; f. 1989; life; Pres. FRANCISCO MARTÍN LÓPEZ-QUESADA.

ING, Seguros de Vida, SA: Nueva Tajamar 555, 18°, Casilla 70, Correo 10, Santiago; tel. (2) 252-1500; fax (2) 252-1504; internet www.INGgrupo.com; f. 1989; life; Gen. Man. ANDRÉS TAGLE DOMINGUEZ.

La Interamericana Compañía de Seguros de Vida: Agustinas 640, 9°, Casilla 163, Correo Central, Santiago; tel. (2) 630-3000; fax (2) 633-3222; internet www.intervida.cl/interamerica; f. 1980; life; Pres. RICARDO PERALTA VALENZUELA; Gen. Man. ANDRÉS SAAVEDRA ECHEVERRÍA.

Le Mans—ISE Compañia Seguros Generales, SA: Encomenderos 113, Casilla 185-D, Centro 192, Las Condes, Santiago; tel. (2) 230-9000; fax (2) 232-8209; e-mail lemans@lemans.cl; internet www.lemans.cl; f. 1888; general; Pres. IGNACIO WALKER CONCHA; Gen. Man. MARC GARÇON.

Mapfre Garantías y Crédito, SA: Teatinos 280, 5°, Santiago; tel. (2) 870-1500; fax (2) 870-1501; e-mail mapfreg@entelchile.net; f. 1991; general; Gen. Man. RODRIGO CAMPERO PETERS.

Renta Nacional Compañía de Seguros de Vida, SA: Amunátegui 178, 1° y 2°, Santiago; tel. (2) 670-0200; fax (2) 670-0399; e-mail renta@rentanac.cl; f. 1982; life; Pres. JORGE SIMS SAN ROMÁN; Gen. Man. ROBERTO MORA.

Seguros Previsión Vida, SA: Hendaya 60, 7°, Casilla 134, Correo 34, Santiago; tel. (2) 750-2400; fax (2) 750-2440; e-mail seguro@prevision.cl; internet www.prevision.cl; f. 1981; life; Pres. FRANCISCO SILVA; Gen. Man. CARLOS FERNÁNDEZ.

Reinsurance

American Re-Insurance Company (Chile), SA: Avda Nueva Tajamar 481, Torre Norte, Of. 505, Santiago; tel. (2) 339-7171; fax (2) 339-7117; f. 1981; general; Pres. MAHMOUD ABDALLAH; Gen. Man. MAURICIO RIESCO VALDÉS.

Caja Reaseguradora de Chile, SA (Generales): Apoquindo 4449, 8°, Casilla 2753, Santiago; tel. (2) 338-1200; fax (2) 206-4063; f. 1927; general; Pres. ANDRÉS JIMÉNES; Gen. Man. ANDRÉS CHAPARRO KAUFMAN.

Caja Reaseguradora de Chile, SA: Apoquindo 4449, 8°, Santiago; tel. (2) 228-6106; fax (2) 698-9730; f. 1980; life; Pres. ANDRÉS JIMÉNES.

Cía de Reaseguros de Vida Soince, SA: Bandera 150, Santiago; tel. (2) 640-1177; internet www.santanderseg.cl; f. 1990; life; Pres. FRANCISCO MARTÍN LÓPEZ-QUESADA.

Insurance Association

Asociación de Aseguradores de Chile, AG: La Concepción 322, Of. 501, Providencia, Santiago; tel. (2) 236-2596; fax (2) 235-1502; e-mail seguros@aach.cl; internet www.aach.cl; f. 1931; Pres. MARCOS BÜCHI BUC; Gen. Man. JORGE CLAUDE BOURDEL.

Trade and Industry

GOVERNMENT AGENCIES

Corporación de Fomento de la Producción (CORFO): Moneda 921, Casilla 3886, Santiago; tel. (2) 638-0521; fax (2) 671-1058; e-mail ftroncoso@corfo.cl; internet www.corfo.cl; f. 1939; holding group of principal state enterprises; grants loans and guarantees to private sector; responsible for sale of non-strategic state enterprises; promotes entrepreneurship; CEO and Exec. Vice-Pres GONZALO RIVAS; Gen. Man. BERNARDO ESPINOZA; 13 brs.

PROCHILE (Dirección General de Relaciones Económicas Internacionales): Avda B. O'Higgins 1315, 2°, Casilla 14087, Correo 21, Santiago; tel. (2) 565-9000; fax (2) 696-0639; e-mail info@prochile.cl; internet www.prochile.cl; f. 1974; bureau of international economic affairs; Dir MARÍA GABRIELA R. BARRENECHEA.

Servicio Nacional de Capacitación y Empleo (National Training and Employment Service): Huérfanos 1273, 11°, Santiago; tel. (2) 696-8213; fax (2) 696-5039; internet www.sence.cl; attached to Ministry of Labour and Social Security; Dir IGNACIO LARRAECHEA LOESSER.

STATE CORPORATION

Corporación Nacional del Cobre de Chile (CODELCO—Chile): Huérfanos 1270, Casilla 150-D, Santiago; tel. (2) 690-3000; fax (2) 690-3059; internet www.codelcochile.com; f. 1976 as a state-owned enterprise with five copper-producing operational divisions at Chuquicamata, Radomiro Tomić, Salvador, Andina and El Teniente; attached to Ministry of Mines; Exec. Pres. JUAN VILLARZÚ RHODE; 17,403 employees.

DEVELOPMENT ORGANIZATIONS

Comisión Chilena de Energía Nuclear: Amunátegui 95, Casilla 188-D, Santiago; tel. (2) 699-0070; fax (2) 699-1618; e-mail gtorres@gopher.cchen.cl; internet www.cchen.cl; f. 1965; government body to develop peaceful uses of atomic energy; concentrates, regulates and controls all matters related to nuclear energy; Exec. Dir GONZALO TORRES OVIEDO.

Corporación Nacional de Desarrollo Indígena (Conadi): Manuel Mott 1070, Temuco; tel. (45) 324-111; fax (2) 234-323; internet www.conadi.cl; promote the economic and social development of indigenous communities.

Corporación Nacional Forestal (CONAF): Avda Bulnes 285, Of. 501, Santiago; tel. (2) 672-2724; fax (2) 671-5881; f. 1970 to promote forestry activities, to enforce forestry law, to promote afforestation, to administer subsidies for afforestation projects and to increase and preserve forest resources; manages 13.97m. ha designated as National Parks, Natural Monuments and National Reserves; under Ministry of Agriculture; Exec. Dir Ing. CARLOS WEBER BONTE.

Empresa Nacional de Minería (ENAMI): MacIver 459, 2°, Casilla 100-D, Santiago; tel. (2) 637-5000; fax (2) 637-5436; promotes the development of the small and medium-sized mines; attached to Ministry of Mines; partially privatized; Exec. Vice-Pres. PATRICIO ARTIAGOITIA ALTI.

CHAMBERS OF COMMERCE

Cámara de Comercio de Santiago de Chile, AG: Edif. Del Comercio, Monjitas 392, Santiago; tel. (2) 360-7000; fax (2) 633-3595; f. 1919; 1,300 mems; Pres. ESTEBAN ALBANO; Man. CLAUDIO ORTIZ TELLO.

Cámara de la Producción y del Comercio de Concepción: Cauplicán 567, 2°, Concepción; tel. (41) 241-440; fax (41) 227-903; e-mail bseguel@cpcc.cl; internet www.cpcc.cl; Pres. HERNÁN ASCUI; Gen. Man. LEONCIO TÍO.

Cámara Nacional de Comercio, Servicios y Turismo de Chile: Merced 230, Santiago; tel. (2) 365-4000; fax (2) 365-4001; internet www.cnc.cl; f. 1858; Pres. FERNANDO LIHN CONCHA; Gen. Sec. JOSÉ MANUEL MELERO ABAROA; 120 mems.

There are chambers of commerce in all major towns.

INDUSTRIAL AND TRADE ASSOCIATIONS

Servicio Agrícola y Ganadero (SAG): Avda Bulnes 140, Santiago; tel. (2) 698-2244; fax (2) 672-1812; e-mail sag@sag.minagri.gob.cl; internet www.sag.gob.cl; under Ministry of Agriculture; responsible for the protection and development of safe practice in the sector; Exec. Dir ANTONIO YAKSIC SOULÉ.

Sociedad Agrícola y Servicios Isla de Pascua: Alfredo Lecannelier 1940, Providencia, Santiago; tel. (2) 232-7497; fax (2) 232-7497; administers agriculture and public services on Easter Island; Gen. Man. GERARDO VELASCO.

Subsecretaría de Pesca: Bellavista 168, 16-18°, Valparaíso; tel. (32) 21-2187; fax (32) 21-2790; f. 1976; controls and promotes fishing industry; Sub-Sec. PATRICIO BERNAL PONCE.

EMPLOYERS' ORGANIZATIONS

Confederación de la Producción y del Comercio: Monseñor Sótero Sanz 182, Providencia, Santiago; tel. (2) 231-9764; fax (2) 231-9808; f. 1936; Pres. WALTER RIESCO SALVO; Gen. Man. CRISTIÁN PIZARRO ALLARD.

Affiliated organizations:

Asociación de Bancos e Instituciones Financieras de Chile: q.v.

Cámara Chilena de la Construcción: Marchant Pereira 10, 3°, Providencia, Casilla Clasificador 679, Santiago; tel. (2) 376-3300; fax (2) 371-3430; internet www.camaraconstruccion.cl; f. 1951; Pres. JUAN IGNACIO SILVA; Gen. Man. ARTURO DEL RÍO; 3,000 mems.

Sociedad de Fomento Fabril, FG: Avda Andrés Bello 2777, 3°, Casilla 37, Correo 35, Tobalaba, Santiago; tel. (2) 203-3100; fax (2) 203-3101; f. 1883; largest employers' organization; Pres. PEDRO LIZANA GREVE; Man. FREDERICO MONTES LIRA; 2,000 mems.

Sociedad Nacional de Agricultura—Federación Gremial (SNA): Tenderini 187, 2°, Casilla 40-D, Santiago; tel. (2) 639-6710; fax (2) 633-7771; f. 1838; landowners' association; controls Radio Stations CB 57 and XQB8 (FM) in Santiago, CB-97 in Valparaíso, CD-120 in Los Angeles, CA-144 in La Serena, CD-127 in Temuco; Pres. RICARDO ARIZTÍA DE CASTRO; Gen. Sec. LUIS QUIROZA ARRAU.

Sociedad Nacional de Minería (SONAMI): Teatinos 20, 3°, Of. 33, Casilla 1807, Santiago; tel. (2) 695-5626; fax (2) 697-1778; f. 1883; Pres. WALTER RIESCO SALVO; Man. MANUEL CERECEDA VIDAL.

Confederación de Asociaciones Gremiales y Federaciones de Agricultores de Chile: Lautaro 218, Los Angeles; registered with Ministry of Economic Affairs in 1981; Pres. DOMINGO DURÁN NEUMANN; Gen. Sec. ADOLFO LARRAÍN V.

Confederación del Comercio Detallista de Chile, AG: Merced 380, 8°, Of. 74, Santiago; tel. (2) 39-5719; fax (2) 38-0338; f. 1938; retail trade; registered with Ministry of Economic Affairs in 1980; Nat. Pres. RAFAEL CUMSILLE ZAPAPA; Sec.-Gen. JAIME PÉREZ RODRÍGUEZ.

Confederación Gremial Nacional Unida de la Mediana y Pequeña Industria, Servicios y Artesanado (CONUPIA): Santiago; registered with Ministry of Economic Affairs in 1980; small and medium-sized industries and crafts; Pres. FÉLIX LUQUE PORTILLA.

There are many federations of private industrialists, organized by industry and region.

UTILITIES

Comisión Nacional de Energía: Teatinos 120, 7°, Santiago; tel. (2) 365-6842; fax (2) 365-6834; Pres. OSCAR LANDERRETCHE GACITÚA.

General

COLBUN: Avda 11 de Septiembre 2353, 9°, Santiago; tel. (2) 231-3414; fax (2) 231-6609; state power utility; scheduled for privatization once anti-monopoly legislation was in place.

Electricity

Arauco Generación: Vitacura 2771, 9°, Las Condes, Santiago; tel. (2) 560-6700; fax (2) 236-5090; e-mail gic@arauco.cl; Pres. ARMANDO LOLAS; Gen. Man. HERNÁN ARRIAGADA.

BMV Industrias Eléctricas: Avda Vicuña Mackenna 1540, Ñuñoa, Santiago; tel. (2) 555-8806; fax (2) 555-8807; Gen. Man. ANGÉLICA PADOVANI.

Chilectra, SA: Santo Domingo 789, Casilla 1557, Santiago; tel. (2) 632-2000; fax (2) 639-3280; e-mail rrpp@chilectra.cl; internet www.chilectra.cl; f. 1921; transmission and distribution of electrical energy; supplies distribution companies including the Empresa Eléctrica Municipal de Lo Barnechea, Empresa Municipal de Til-Til, Empresa Eléctrica de Colina, SA and the Cía Eléctrica del Río Maipo, SA; holds overseas distribution concessions in Argentina, Peru and Brazil; Pres. JORGE ROSENBLUT; Gen. Man. JULIO VALENZUELA.

Chilquinta Energía, SA: General Cruz 222, Valparaíso; tel. (32) 502-000; fax (32) 210-723; f. 1995; Pres. HÉCTOR MADARIAGA; Gen. Man. CRISTIÁN ARNOLDS.

Compañía Eléctrica del Litoral, SA: San Sebastián 2952, Of. 202, Las Condes, Santiago; tel. (2) 362-1436; fax (2) 362-1437; e-mail litoral@litoral.cl.

Compañía General de Electricidad, SA (CGE): Teatinos 280, Santiago; tel. (2) 624-3243; fax (2) 680-7104; e-mail cge@cge.cl; internet www.cge.cl; Pres. GABRIEL DEL REAL; Gen. Man. GUILLERMO MATTA FUENZALIDA.

EMELAT (Empresa Eléctrica Atacama, SA): Circunvalación Ignacio Carrera, Copiapó; tel. (52) 21-3551; fax (52) 21-3393; f. 1981; distribution company; Pres. DAURÓPEDIS GARCÍA DE LA PASTORA; Gen. Man. JUAN JAIME DÍAZ CARRASCO.

EMELSA (Empresa Eléctrica de Melpilla, Colchagua y Maule, SA): Alameda 886, 5° y 6°, Santiago; tel. (2) 633-3852; fax (2) 633-6944; Gen. Man. EDUARDO VALENZUELA.

Empresa Eléctrica de Antofagasta, SAELECDA: Orella 643, Antofagasta; tel. (55) 541-9209; Dir L. BITRAN.

Empresa Eléctrica de Arica, SA: Baquedano 731, Arica; tel. (58) 23-1880; fax (58) 23-1105; Dir DAURÓPEDIS GARCÍA DE LA PASTORA.

Empresa Eléctrica de Aysen, SA: Francisco Bilbao 412, Casilla 280, Coyhaique; tel. (67) 23-1293; fax (67) 23-1293; f. 1983; Gen. Man. JORGE BARRIENTOS TECA.

Empresa Eléctrica Emec, SA: Los Talleres 1831, Barrio Industrial, Coquimbo; tel. (51) 20-1000; fax (51) 24-0200; e-mail emecsa@entelchile.net; f. 1980; Pres. RAMÓN ABOITIZ M; Gen. Man. PABLO GUARDA B.

Empresa Eléctrica de Iquique, SA: Zegeres 469, Iquique; tel. (57) 42-3053; fax (57) 42-7181; CEO ALEJANDRO BLANCO SCHULER.

Empresa Eléctrica del Norte Grande (EDELNOR): Avda Grecia 750, Antofagasta; tel. (55) 24-8500; fax (55) 28-8094; f. 1981; Dir J. W. HOLDEN, III.

Empresa Eléctrica Pehuenche, SA (EEP): Santiago; fax (2) 696-5568; f. 1986; Gen. Man. ERNESTO SILVA BAFALLUY.

Empresa Eléctrica Pilmaiquen, SA: Providencia, Santiago; tel. (2) 233-4072; fax (2) 231-9780; Dir A. C. RODRÍGUEZ.

Empresa Nacional de Electricidad, SA (ENDESA): Santa Rosa 76, Casilla 1392, Santiago; tel. (2) 630-9000; fax (2) 635-3938; e-mail comunicacion@endesa.cl; internet www.endesa.cl; f. 1943; installed capacity 4,035 MW (Feb. 2002); ENERSIS (see below) obtained majority control of ENDESA in April 1999; Gen. Man. HECTOR LÓPEZ.

ENERSIS, SA: Santo Domingo 789, Casilla 1557, Correo Central, Santiago; tel. (2) 638-0840; fax (2) 633-4661; e-mail enersis@chilnet.cl; internet www.enersis.com; f. 1981; holding company generating and distributing electricity through its subsidiaries throughout South America, including ENDESA of Chile (see above); 32% interest acquired by ENDESA of Spain in 1997, a further 31.78% acquired in 1999; Gen. Man. PABLO IHNEN DE LA FUENTE.

Gener, SA: Miraflores 222, 4°, Casilla 3514, Santiago; tel. (2) 632-3909; fax (2) 633-4499; f. 1981 as Chilectra Generación, SA following the restructuring of Compañía Chilena de Electricidad, SA; privatized in 1988 and Chilgener, SA adopted in 1989; current name adopted in 1998; owned by AES Corpn (USA); responsible for operation of power plants Renca, Ventanas, Laguna Verde, El Indio, Altalfal, Maitenes, Queltehues and Volcán; total generating capacity 1,746.2 MW (Dec. 1997); Pres. NAVEED ISMAIL; Gen. Man. ANDRÉS GLUSKI.

Empresa Eléctrica Guacolda, SA: Santiago; tel. (2) 697-3212; fax (2) 671-5343; operates a thermoelectric power-station in Huasco; installed capacity of 304 MW.

Empresa Eléctrica Santiago: Miraflores 222, 4°, Santiago; tel. (2) 686-8664; fax (2) 686-8447; operates the Nueva Renca thermoelectric plant in Santiago; installed capacity of 370 MW.

Energía Verde: O'Higgins 940, Of. 90, Concepción; tel. (41) 25-3228; fax (41) 25-3227; operates two co-generation power-stations at Constitución and Laja and a steam plant at Nacimiento; supplies the Cabrero industrial plant.

Norgener: Miraflores 222, 5°, Santiago; tel. (2) 632-6291; fax (2) 696-8810; northern subsidiary supplying the mining industry; operates power plants with installed capacity of 274.4 MW.

SAESA (Sociedad Austral de Electricidad, SA): Manuel Bulnes 441, Osorno; tel. (64) 23-3531; fax (64) 23-6256; CEO FELIPE LAMARCA CLARO.

Gas

Abastecedora de Combustible: Avda Vicuña Mackenna 55, Providencia, Santiago; tel. (2) 639-9251; fax (2) 693-9249; internet www.abastible.cl; Pres. FELIPE LAMARCA; Gen. Man. JOSÉ ODONE.

AGA Chili, SA: Juan Bautista Pistene 2344, Santiago; tel. (2) 232-8711; natural gas utility.

Compañía de Consumidores de Gas de Santiago (GASCO, SA): Rosas 1062, Casilla 8-D, Santiago; tel. (2) 698-2121; fax (2) 695-2685; e-mail gasco@chilnet.cl; internet www.gasco.cl; natural gas utility; supplies Santiago and Punta Arenas regions; Pres. GABRIEL DEL REAL; Gen. Man. CARLOS ROCCA.

Compañía de Gas de Concepción, SA: En Continuidad De Giro, Avda Arturo Prat 175, Concepción; tel. (41) 235-133; natural gas utility.

Electrogas: Santiago; tel. (2) 232-1839; fax (2) 233-4931; Gen. Man. CARLOS ANDREANI.

Gas Valpo: Valparaíso; tel. (32) 27-7000; fax (32) 21-3092; e-mail info@gasvalpo.cl.

GasAndes: Santiago; distributes gas transported from the Argentine province of Mendoza via a 463-km pipeline.

Industrias Codigas: Camino a Melipilla 11000, Maipú, Santiago; tel. (2) 557-8870; fax (92) 538-6647; Pres. EDUARDO CABELLO; Gen. Man. CHRISTIAN CORNEJO.

Lipigas: Avda Libertad 51, Viña del Mar; tel. (32) 689-668; fax (32) 656-595; e-mail info@lipigas.cl; internet www.lipigas.cl; Pres. JAIME SANTA CRUZ; Gen. Man. MARIO FERNÁNDEZ.

Metrogas: El Bosque Norte 0177, 11°, Las Condes, Santiago; tel. (2) 337-8000; fax (2) 332-0348; internet www.metrogas.cl; natural gas utility; Pres. JUAN CLARO; Gen. Man. EDUARDO MORANDÉ.

Water

Aguas Andinas, SA: Avda Presidente Balmaceda 1398, Santiago; tel. (2) 688-1000; fax (2) 694-2777; e-mail info@aguasandinas.cl; internet www.aguasandinas.cl; water supply and sanitation services to Santiago and the surrounding area; sold to a French-Spanish consortium in June 1999; Gen. Man. ANGEL SIMON.

Desalari Ltda: Arturo Prat 391, Of. 73, Arica; tel. (58) 25-0179; fax (58) 25-6652; e-mail desalari.ltda001@chilnet.cl.

Sigsig Ltda (Tecnagent): Presidente Errázuriz 3262, Santiago; tel. (2) 335-2001; fax (2) 334-8466; e-mail tecnagent@tecnagent.cl; internet www.tecnagent.cl; Pres. RAÚL SIGREN BINDHOFF; Gen. Man. RAÚL A. SIGREN O.

TRADE UNIONS

There are more than 50 national labour federations and unions.

Central Unions

Central Autónoma de Trabajadores (CAT): Sazié 1761, Casilla 6510480, Santiago; tel. and fax (2) 695-3388; e-mail catchile@ entelchile.net; Pres. OSVALSO ERBACH ALVAREZ; Sec. Gen. PEDRO SAA-VEDRA.

Central Unitaria de Trabajadores de Chile (CUT): Avda B. O'Higgins 1346, Santiago; tel. (2) 361-9452; fax (2) 361-9452; e-mail presidencia.cut@entelchile.net; internet www.cutchile.cl; f. 1988; 12 associations, 32 confederations, 49 federations; 36 regional head-quarters, 16 trade unions; Pres. ARTURO MARTÍNEZ MOLINA; 411,000 mems.

Movimiento Unitario Campesino y Etnias de Chile (MUCECH): Portugal 623, Of. 1-A, Santiago; tel. (2) 222-6572; fax (2) 635-1518; e-mail mucech@ia.cl; Pres. EUGENIO LEÓN GAJARDO; Nat. Sec. RIGOBERTO TURRA PAREDES.

Union Confederations

There are 37 union confederations, of which the following are among the most important:

Agrupación Nacional de Empleados Fiscales (ANEF): Avda B. O'Higgins 1603, Santiago; tel. (2) 696-2957; fax 699-3806; affiliated to CUT; Pres. RAÚL DE LA PUENTE PEÑA; Sec.-Gen. FRESIA AROCS ALBARRACÍN.

Confederación Bancaria: Santiago; tel. (2) 699-5597; affiliated to CUT; Pres. DIEGO OLIVARES ARAVENA; Sec.-Gen. RAÚL REQUENA MAR-TÍNEZ.

Confederación de Empleados Particulares de Chile (CEPCH): Santiago; tel. (2) 72-2093; trade union for workers in private sector; affiliated to CUT; Pres. ANGÉLICA CARVALLO PRENAFETA; Sec.-Gen. ANDRÉS BUSTOS GONZÁLEZ.

Confederación de Personal en Retiro y Montepío de las Fuerzas Armadas (CAPREDENA): Nataniel Cox 265, Casilla 14988, Santiago; tel. (2) 698-4657; fax (2) 671-5980; Pres. OSCAR HEILCALEO CHEUQUE; Sec. Gen. OSCAR SÁEZ TRONCOSO.

Confederación General de Trabajadores del Transporte Ter-restre (CGTT): Almirante Latorre 355, 2°, Of. 3, Santiago; tel. and fax 695-9551; affiliated to CUT; Pres. ULISES MARTÍNEZ SEPÚLVEDA; Sec.-Gen. RODOLFO DOSSETTO UGALDE.

Confederación Nacional Campesina: Gorbea 1769, Santiago; tel. and fax (2) 695-2017; affiliated to CUT; Pres. EUGENIO LEÓN GAJARDO; Sec.-Gen. REÑE ASTUDILLO R.

Confederación Nacional de Federaciones y Sindicatos de Empresas e Interempresas de Trabajadores del Transporte Terrestre y Afines (CONATRACH): Concha y Toro 2-A, 2°, San-tiago; tel. (2) 698-0810; fax (2) 698-0810; Pres. PEDRO MONSALVE FUENTES; Sec. Gen. PEDRO JARA ESPINOZA.

Confederación Nacional de Federaciones y Sindicatos de Trabajadores Textiles y Ramos Similares (CONTEXTIL): Nataniel Cox 152 B, 1°, Santiago; tel. and fax (2) 696-8098; affiliated to CUT; Pres. PATRICIA C. CARRILLO; Sec.-Gen. MARIA FELISA GARAY ASTUDILLO.

Confederación Nacional de Gente de Mar, Marítimos, Por-tuarios y Pesqueros (CONGEMAR): Tomás Ramos 158-172, Val-paraíso; tel. (32) 255-430; fax (32) 257-580; affiliated to CUT; Pres. WALTER ASTORGA LOBOS; Sec.-Gen. JUAN GUZMÁN CARRASCO.

Confederación Nacional de Sindicatos Agrícolas—Unidad Obrera Campesina (UOC): Eleuterio Ramírez 1463, Santiago; tel. and fax (2) 696-6342; affiliated to CUT; Pres. OSCAR VALLADARES GONZÁLEZ; Sec.-Gen. DANIEL SAN MARTÍN VALLEJOS.

Confederación Nacional de Sindicatos de Trabajadores de la Construcción, Maderas, Materiales de Edificación y Activi-dades Conexas: Almirante Hurtado 2069, Santiago; tel. (2) 695-3908; fax (2) 696-4536; affiliated to CUT; Pres. MIGUEL ANGEL SOLÍS VIERA; Sec.-Gen. ADRIAN FUENTES HERMOSILLA.

Confederación Nacional de Sindicatos y Federaciones de Trabajadores Metalúrgicos (CONSTRAMET): Avda Francia 1317, Independencia, Santiago; tel. (2) 737-6875; fax (2) 443-0039;

e-mail contrame@mailnet.rdc.cl; affiliated to CUT; Pres. MIGUEL SOTO ROA; Sec.-Gen. MIGUEL CHÁVEZ SOAZO.

Confederación Nacional de Suplementeros de Chile (CON-ASUCH): Tucapel Jiménez 26, Santiago; tel. (2) 695-7639; fax (2) 699–1646; f. 1942; Pres. IVAN ENCINA CARO; Sec. JOSÉ CANALES ORTIZ.

Confederación Nacional de Trabajadores de la Alimentación y Afines (CONTALCH): Lizt 3082, San Joaquín, Santiago; tel. and fax (2) 553-2193; affiliated to CUT; Pres. CIJIFREDO VERA VERA.

Confederación Nacional de Trabajadores de la Industria del Pan (CONAPAN): Tucapel Jiménez 32, 2°, Santiago; tel. and fax (2) 672-1622; affiliated to CUT; Pres. LUIS ALEGRÍA ALEGRÍA; Sec. LUIS PALACIOS CAMPOS.

Confederación Nacional de Trabajadores de la Industria Textil (CONTEVECH): Agustinas 2349, Santiago; tel. (2) 699-3442; fax (2) 687-3269; affiliated to CUT; Pres. MIGUEL VEGA FUENTES; Sec.-Gen. OSCAR CÁCERES YÁNEZ.

Confederación Nacional de Trabajadores del Comercio (CONATRADECO): Santiago; tel. and fax (2) 638-6718; Pres. EDMUNDO LILLO ARAVENA; Sec.-Gen. FEDERICO MUJICA CANALES.

Confederación Nacional de Trabajadores del Comercio (CONSFECOVE): Monjitas 454, Of. 606, Santiago; tel. (2) 632-2950; fax (2) 632-2884; affiliated to CUT; Pres. CLAUDIO ARAVENA ALVAREZ; Sec.-Gen. SUSANA ROSAS VALDEBENITO.

Confederación Nacional de Trabajadores del Cuero y Cal-zado (FONACC): Arturo Prat 1490, Santiago; tel. (2) 556-9602; affiliated to CUT; Pres. MANUEL JIMÉNEZ TORRES; Sec.-Gen. VÍCTOR LABBÉ SILVA.

Confederación Nacional de Trabajadores Electrometalúr-gicos, Mineros, Automotrices (CONSFETEMA): Vicuña Mac-kenna 3101, Casilla 1803, Correo Central, San Joaquín, Santiago; tel. (2) 238-1732; fax 553-6494; Pres. LUIS SEPÚLVEDA DEL RÍO.

Confederación Nacional de Trabajadores Forestales (CTF): Rengo 884, Casilla 2717, Concepción; tel. and fax (41) 220-0407; Pres. JORGE GONZÁLEZ CASTILLO; Sec.-Gen. GUSTAVO CARRASO SALAZAR.

Confederación Nacional de Trabajadores Molineros: Bas-cuñan Guerrero 1739, Casilla 703, Correo 21, Santiago; tel. and fax (2) 683-8882; Pres. JOSÉ VÁSQUEZ ALIAGA.

Confederación Nacional Minera: Príncipe de Gales 88, Casilla 10361, Correo Central, Santiago; tel. (2) 696-6945; fax (2) 696-6945; Pres. MOISÉS LABRAÑA MENA; Sec.-Gen. JOSÉ CARRILLO BERMEDO.

Confederación Nacional Sindical Campesina y del Agro 'El Surco': Chacabuco 625, Santiago; tel. and fax (2) 681-1032; e-mail asurco@entelchile.net; affiliated to CUT; Pres. FERNANDO VALÁSQUEZ SERRANO; Sec.-Gen. SERGIO DÍAZ TAPIA.

There are also 45 union federations and over 100 individual unions.

Transport

RAILWAYS

State Railways

Empresa de los Ferrocarriles del Estado: Avda B. O'Higgins 3170, Santiago; tel. (2) 779-0707; fax (2) 689-8434; internet www.efe .cl; f. 1851; 3,977 km of track (2000); the State Railways are divided between the Ferrocarril Arica–La Paz, La Calera Puerto Montt, and Metro Regional de Valparaíso (passenger service only); several lines scheduled for privatization; Pres. NICOLÁS FLAÑO CALDERÓN; Gen. Man. JAIME MONDACA GÓMEZ.

Parastatal Railways

Ferrocarriles del Pacífico (FEPASA): Alfredo Barros Errázuriz 1960, 6°, Providencia, Santiago; tel. (2) 330-4900; fax (2) 330-4905; e-mail fepasa@chilnet.cl; f. 1993; privatized freight services; Gen. Man. F. LANGER.

Metro de Santiago: Empresa de Transporte de Pasajeros Metro, SA, Avda B. O'Higgins 1414, Santiago; tel. (2) 698-8218; fax (2) 252-6364; e-mail gerencia.marketing@metro-chile.cl; internet www .metro-chile.cl; started operations 1975; 40.4 km (2000); 3 lines; Pres. FERNANDO BUSTAMENTE HUENTA; Gen. Man. R. AZÓCAR HIDALGO.

Private Railways

Antofagasta (Chile) and Bolivia Railway PLC: Bolívar 255, Casillas ST, Antofagasta; tel. (55) 20-6700; fax (55) 20-6220; e-mail webmaster@fcab.cl; internet www.fcab.com; f. 1888; British-owned; operates an internat. railway to Bolivia and Argentina; cargo for-warding services; total track length 934 km; Chair. ANDRÓNICO LUKSIC ABAROA; Gen. Man. M. V. SEPÚLVEDA.

Empresa de Transporte Ferroviario, SA (Ferronor): Avda Alessandri 042, Coquimbo; tel. (51) 31-2442; fax (51) 31-3460; 2,200 km of track (1995); established as a public/private concern, following the transfer of the Ferrocarril Regional del Norte de Chile to the Ministry of Production Development (CORFO) as a *Sociedad Anónima* in 1989; controlling interest purchased by RailAmerica of the USA in 1997; operates cargo services only; Pres. G. MARINO; Gen. Man. P. ESPY.

Ferrocarril Codelco-Chile: Barquito, Region III, Atacama; tel. (52) 48-8521; fax (52) 48-8522; Gen. Man. B. BEHN THEUNE.

Diego de Almagro a Potrerillos: transport of forest products, minerals and manufactures; 99 km.

Ferrocarril Rancagua–Teniente: transport of forest products, livestock, minerals and manufactures; 68 km.

Ferrocarril Tocopilla–Toco: Calle Arturo Prat 1060, Casilla 2098, Tocopilla; tel. (55) 81-2139; fax (55) 81-2650; owned by Sociedad Química y Minera de Chile, SA; 117 km (1995); Gen. Man. SEGISFREDO HURTADO GUERRERO.

Association

Asociación Chilena de Conservación de Patrimonio Ferroviario (ACCPF—Chilean Railway Society): Casilla 179-D, Santiago; tel. (2) 210-2280; fax (2) 280-0252; Pres. H. VENEGAS.

ROADS

The total length of roads in Chile in 2000 was an estimated 79,814 km, of which some 15,508 km were highways and some 34,159 km were secondary roads. The road system includes the completely paved Pan American Highway extending 3,455 km from north to south. Toll gates exist on major motorways. The 1,200 km-Carretera Austral (Southern Highway), linking Puerto Montt and Puerto Yungay, was completed in 1996, at an estimated total cost of US $200m.

SHIPPING

As a consequence of Chile's difficult topography, maritime transport is of particular importance. In 1997 90% of the country's foreign trade was carried by sea (51m. metric tons). The principal ports are Valparaíso, Talcahuano, Antofagasta, San Antonio, Arica, Iquique, Coquimbo, San Vicente, Puerto Montt and Punta Arenas. Most port operations were privatized in the late 1990s.

Chile's merchant fleet amounted to 880,252 grt (comprising 480 vessels) at December 2001.

Supervisory Authorities

Asociación Nacional de Armadores: Blanco 869, 3°, Valparaíso; tel. (32) 21-2057; fax (32) 21-2017; e-mail armadore@entelchile.net; f. 1931; shipowners' association; Pres. ERICH STRELOW CASTILLO; Gen. Man. ARTURO SIERRA MERINO.

Cámara Marítima y Portuaria de Chile, AG: Blanco 869, 3°, Valparaíso; tel. (32) 25-3443; fax (32) 25-0231; e-mail camport@entelchile.net; Pres. BELTRÁN SAÉZ M. Vice-Pres. RODOLFO GARCÍA SÁNCHEZ.

Dirección General de Territorio Marítimo y Marina Mercante: Errázuriz 537, 4°, Valparaíso; tel. (32) 25-8061; fax (32) 25-2539; maritime admin. of the coast and national waters, control of the merchant navy; Dir Rear Adm. FERNANDO LAZCANO.

Empresa Portuaria Antofagasta: Grecia s/n, Antofagasta; tel. (55) 25-1737; fax (55) 22-3171; e-mail epa@puertoantofagasta.cl; Pres. BLAS ENRIQUE ESPINOZA SEPÚLVEDA; Dir EDUARDO SALVADOR ABEDRAPO BUSTOS.

Empresa Portuaria Arica: Máximo Lira 389, Arica; tel. (58) 25-5078; fax (58) 23-2284; e-mail puertoarica@entelchile.net; Pres. CARLOS EDUARDO MENA KEYMER; Dir RAÚL RICARDO BALBONTÍN FERNÁNDEZ.

Empresa Portuaria Austral: B. O'Higgins 1385, Punta Arenas; tel. (61) 24-1760; fax (61) 24-1822; e-mail portspug@ctc-mundo.net; Pres. LAUTARO HERNÁN POBLETE KNUDTZON-TRAMPE; Dir FERNANDO ARTURO JOFRÉ WEISS.

Empresa Portuaria Chacabuco: B. O'Higgins s/n, Puerto Chacabuco; tel. (67) 35-1198; fax (67) 35-1174; e-mail ptochb@entelchile.net; Pres. LUIS MUSALEM MUSALEM; Dir RAIMUNDO CRISTI SAAVEDRA.

Empresa Portuaria Coquimbo: Melgareja 676, Coquimbo; tel. (51) 31-3606; fax (51) 32-6146; e-mail ptoqq@entelchile.net; Pres. ARMANDO ARANCIBIA CALDERÓN; Gen. Man. MIGUEL ZUVIC MUJICA.

Empresa Portuaria Iquique: Jorge Barrera 62, Iquique; tel. (57) 40-0100; fax (57) 41-3176; e-mail epi@port-iquique.cl; internet www.port-iquique.cl; f. 1998; Pres. PATRICIO ARRAU PONS; Gen. Man. PEDRO DÁVILA PINO.

Empresa Portuaria Puerto Montt: Angelmó 1673, Puerto Montt; tel. (65) 25-2247; e-mail info@empormontt.cl; internet www.empormontt.cl; Pres. JOSÉ DANIEL BARRETA SÁEZ; Gen. Man. LUÍS RIVAS APABLAZA.

Empresa Portuaria San Antonio: Alan Macowan 0245, San Antonio; tel. (35) 21-2159; fax (35) 21-2114; e-mail correo@saiport.cl; internet www.saiport.cl; f. 1960; Pres. JOSÉ MANUEL MORALES TALLAR; Gen. Man. FERNANDO CRISÓSTOMO BURGOS.

Empresa Portuaria Talcahuano-San Vicente: Latorre 1590, Talcahuano; tel. (41) 54-1419; fax (41) 54-1807; e-mail eportuaria@ptotalsve.co.cl; Pres. JUAN ENRIQUE COEYMANS AVARIA; Gen. Man. PATRICIO CAMPAÑA CUELLO.

Empresa Portuaria Valparaíso: Errázuriz 25, 4°, Of. 1, Valparaíso; tel. (32) 44-8800; fax (32) 22-4190; e-mail gcomercial@portvalparaiso.cl; internet www.portvalparaiso.cl; Pres. GABRIEL ALDONEY V. Gen. Man. HARALD JAEGER KARL.

Principal Shipping Companies

Santiago

Cía Chilena de Navegación Interoceánica, SA: Avda Andrés Bello 2687, 17°, Las Condes, Santiago; tel. (2) 339-1300; fax (2) 203-9060; e-mail info@ccni.cl; internet www.ccni.cl; f. 1930; regular sailings to Japan, Republic of Korea, Taiwan, Hong Kong, USA, Mexico, South Pacific, South Africa and Europe; bulk and dry cargo services; Chair. BELTRAN F. URENDA; CEO EUGENIO VALENZUELA.

Marítima Antares, SA: Santiago; tel. (2) 38-3036; Pres. ALFONSO GARCÍA-MINAUR G; Gen. Man. LUIS BEDRIÑANA RODRÍGUEZ.

Naviera Magallanes, SA (NAVIMAG): Avda El Bosque, Norte 0440, 11°, Of. 1103/1104, Las Condes, Santiago; tel. (2) 442—3150; fax (2) 442–3156; f. 1979; Chair. PEDRO LECAROS MENÉNDEZ; Gen. Man. HÉCTOR HENRÍQUEZ NEGRÓN.

Nisa Navegación, SA: Avda El Bosque Norte 0440, 11°, Casilla 2829, Santiago; tel. (2) 203-5180; fax (2) 203-5190; Chair. PEDRO LECAROS MENÉNDEZ; Gen. Man. SERGIO VIAL.

Sociedad Anónima de Navegación Petrolera (SONAP): Moneda 970, 20°, Casilla 13D, Santiago; tel. (2) 630-1009; fax (2) 630-1041; e-mail valsonap@sonap.cl; f. 1954; tanker services; Chair. FELIPE VIAL C; Gen. Man. JOSÉ THOMSEN Q.

Valparaíso

A. J. Broom y Cía, SAC: Blanco 951, Casilla 910, Valparaíso and MacIver 225, 10°, Casilla 448, Santiago; e-mail genmanager@ajbroom.cl; f. 1920; Pres. GASTÓN ANRÍQUEZ; Man. Dir JAMES C. WELLS M.

Agencias Universales, SA (AGUNSA): Urriola 87, 3°, Valparaíso; tel. (32) 21-7333; fax (32) 25-4261; maritime transportation and shipping, port and docking services; Dir JOSÉ URENDA; Gen. Man. FRANCO MONTALBETTI.

Cía Sud-Americana de Vapores: Plaza Sotomayor 50, Casilla 49-V, Valparaíso; also Hendaya 60, 12°, Santiago; tel. (32) 20-3000; tel. (2) 330-7000; fax (32) 20-3333; fax (2) 330-7700; f. 1872; regular service between South America and US/Canadian ports, US Gulf ports, North European, Mediterranean, Scandinavian and Far East ports; bulk carriers, tramp and reefer services; Pres. RICARDO CLARO VALDÉS; Gen. Man. FRANCISCO SILVA DONOSO.

Empresa Marítima, SA (Empremar Chile): Almirante Gómez Carreño 49, Casilla 105-V, Valparaíso; tel. (32) 25-0563; fax (32) 21-3904; f. 1953; international and coastal services; Chair. LORENZO CAGLEVIC.

Naviera Chilena del Pacífico, SA: Almirante Señoret 70, 6°, Casilla 370, Valparaíso; also Serrano 14, Of. 502, Casilla 2290, Santiago; tel. (32) 25-0563; tel. (2) 633-3063; fax (32) 25-3869; fax (2) 639-2069; e-mail nachipav@entelchile.net; e-mail nachipa@entelchile.net; cargo; Pres. ARTURO FERNÁNDEZ ZEGERS; Gen. Man. PABLO SIMIAN ZAMORANO.

Transmares Naviera Chilena Ltda: Moneda 970, 20°, Edif. Eurocentro, Casilla 193-D, Santiago; also Cochrane 813, 8°, Casilla 52-V, Valparaíso; tel. (2) 630-1000; tel. (32) 20-2000; fax (2) 698-9205; fax (32) 25-6607; e-mail transmares@transmares.cl; f. 1969; dry cargo service Chile–Uruguay–Brazil; Chair. WOLF VON APPEN; CEO RICARDO SCHLECHTER.

Several foreign shipping companies operate services to Valparaíso.

Punta Arenas

Cía Marítima de Punta Arenas, SA: Avda Independencia 830, Casilla 337, Punta Arenas; also Casilla 2829, Santiago; tel. (61) 24-1702; tel. (2) 203-5180; fax (61) 24-7514; fax (2) 203-5191; f. 1949; shipping agents and owners operating in the Magellan Straits; Pres. PEDRO LECAROS MENÉNDEZ; Gen. Man. ARTURO STORAKER MOLINA.

Puerto Montt

Transporte Marítimo Chiloé-Aysén, SA: Angelmo 2187, Puerto Montt; tel. (65) 27-0419; Deputy Man. PEDRO HERNÁNDEZ LEHMAN.

San Antonio

Naviera Aysén Ltda: San Antonio; also Huérfanos 1147, Of. 542, Santiago; tel. (35) 32578; tel. (2) 698-8680; Man. RAÚL QUINTANA A.

CIVIL AVIATION

There are 325 airfields in the country, of which eight have long runways. Arturo Merino Benítez, 20 km north-east of Santiago, and Chacalluta, 14 km north-east of Arica, are the principal international airports.

Aero Continente: Marchant Pereira 357; tel. (2) 204-2424; fax (2) 209-2358; internet www.aerocontinente.com; Pres. LUPE ZEVALLOS.

Aerocardal: Aeropuerto CAMB, Pudahuel, Casilla 64, Santiago; tel. (2) 377-7400; fax (2) 377-7405; e-mail aerocard@aerocardal.cl; f. 1989; charter services; Chair. ALEX CASASEMPERE.

Aerovías DAP: Casilla 633, Punta Arenas; tel. (61) 22-3340; fax (61) 22-1693; f. 1980; domestic services; CEO ALEX PISCEVIC.

Línea Aérea Nacional de Chile (LAN-Chile): Américo Vespucio 901, Renca, Santiago; tel. (2) 565-2525; fax (2) 565-1729; internet www.lanchile.com; f. 1929; operates scheduled domestic passenger and cargo services, also Santiago–Easter Island; international services to French Polynesia, Spain, and throughout North and South America; under the Govt's privatization programme, 99% of LAN-Chile shares have been sold to private interests since 1989; Pres. JORGE AWAD MEHECH; CEO ENRIQUE CUETO.

Línea Aérea del Cobre SA (LADECO): Américo Vespucio 901, Renca, Santiago; tel. (2) 565-3131; fax (2) 639-9115; internet www.ladeco.cl; f. 1945; affiliated to LAN-Chile in 1996; internal passenger and cargo services; international passenger and cargo services to the USA and throughout South America; Chair. JOSÉ LUIZ IBÁÑEZ; CEO GASTÓN CUMMINS.

Tourism

Chile has a wide variety of attractions for the tourist, including fine beaches, ski resorts in the Andes, lakes, rivers and desert scenery. There are many opportunities for hunting and fishing in the southern archipelago, where there are plans to make an integrated tourist area with Argentina, requiring investment of US $120m. Isla de Pascua (Easter Island) may also be visited by tourists. In 2000 there were an estimated 1,742m. tourist arrivals, and receipts from tourism totalled US $827m.

Servicio Nacional de Turismo (SERNATUR): Avda Providencia 1550, Casilla 14082, Santiago; tel. (2) 731-8300; fax (2) 251-8469; e-mail info@sernatur.cl; internet www.senatur.cl; f. 1975; Dir OSCAR SANTELICES ALTAMIRANO.

Asociación Chilena de Empresas de Turismo (ACHET): Moneda 973, Of. 647, Santiago; tel. (2) 696-5677; fax (2) 699-4245; f. 1945; 240 mems; Pres. JOSÉ MARTÍNEZ URTUBIA; Man. EVA SAN MARTÍN ORELLANA.

THE PEOPLE'S REPUBLIC OF CHINA

Introductory Survey

Location, Climate, Language, Religion, Flag, Capital

The People's Republic of China covers a vast area of eastern Asia, with Mongolia and Russia to the north, Tajikistan, Kyrgyzstan and Kazakhstan to the north-west, Afghanistan and Pakistan to the west, and India, Nepal, Bhutan, Myanmar (formerly Burma), Laos and Viet Nam to the south. The country borders the Democratic People's Republic of Korea in the north-east, and has a long coastline on the Pacific Ocean. The climate ranges from subtropical in the far south to an annual average temperature of below 10°C (50°F) in the north, and from the monsoon climate of eastern China to the aridity of the north-west. The principal language is Northern Chinese (Mandarin); in the south and south-east local dialects are spoken. The Xizangzu (Tibetans), Wei Wuer (Uygurs), Menggus (Mongols) and other groups have their own languages. The traditional religions and philosophies of life are Confucianism, Buddhism and Daoism. There are also Muslim and Christian minorities. The national flag (proportions 2 by 3) is plain red, with one large five-pointed gold star and four similar but smaller stars, arranged in an arc, in the upper hoist. The capital is Beijing (Peking).

Recent History

The People's Republic of China was proclaimed on 1 October 1949, following the victory of Communist forces over the Kuomintang (KMT) Government, which fled to the island province of Taiwan. The new Communist regime received widespread international recognition, but it was not until 1971 that the People's Republic was admitted to the United Nations, in place of the KMT regime, as the representative of China. Most countries now recognize the People's Republic.

With the establishment of the People's Republic, the leading political figure was Mao Zedong, who was Chairman of the Chinese Communist Party (CCP) from 1935 until his death in 1976. Chairman Mao, as he was known, also became Head of State in October 1949, but he relinquished this post in December 1958. His successor was Liu Shaoqi, First Vice-Chairman of the CCP, who was elected Head of State in April 1959. Liu was dismissed in October 1968, during the Cultural Revolution (see below), and died in prison in 1969. The post of Head of State was left vacant, and was formally abolished in January 1975, when a new Constitution was adopted. The first Premier (Head of Government) of the People's Republic was Zhou Enlai, who held this office from October 1949 until his death in 1976. Zhou was also Minister of Foreign Affairs from 1949 to 1958.

The economic progress of the early years of Communist rule enabled China to withstand the effects of the industrialization programmes of the late 1950s (called the 'Great Leap Forward'), the drought of 1960–62 and the withdrawal of Soviet aid in 1960. To prevent the establishment of a ruling class, Chairman Mao launched the Great Proletarian Cultural Revolution in 1966. The ensuing excesses of the Red Guards caused the army to intervene; Liu Shaoqi and Deng Xiaoping, General Secretary of the CCP, were disgraced. In 1971 an attempted coup by the Defence Minister, Marshal Lin Biao, was unsuccessful, and by 1973 it was apparent that Chairman Mao and Premier Zhou Enlai had retained power. In 1975 Deng Xiaoping re-emerged as first Vice-Premier and Chief of the General Staff. Zhou Enlai died in January 1976. Hua Guofeng, hitherto Minister of Public Security, was appointed Premier, and Deng was dismissed. Mao died in September 1976. His widow, Jiang Qing, tried unsuccessfully to seize power, with the help of three radical members of the CCP's Politburo. The 'gang of four' and six associates of Lin Biao were tried in November 1980. All were found guilty and were given lengthy terms of imprisonment. (Jiang Qing committed suicide in May 1991.) The 10th anniversary of Mao's death was marked in September 1986 by an official reassessment of his life; while his accomplishments were praised, it was now acknowledged that he had made mistakes, although most of the criticism was directed at the 'gang of four'.

In October 1976 Hua Guofeng succeeded Mao as Chairman of the CCP and Commander-in-Chief of the People's Liberation Army (PLA). The 11th National Congress of the CCP, held in August 1977, restored Deng Xiaoping to his former posts. In September 1980 Hua Guofeng resigned as Premier, but retained his chairmanship of the CCP. The appointment of Zhao Ziyang, a Vice-Premier since April 1980, to succeed Hua as Premier confirmed the dominance of the moderate faction of Deng Xiaoping. In June 1981 Hua Guofeng was replaced as Chairman of the CCP by Hu Yaobang, former Secretary-General of the Politburo, and as Chairman of the party's Central Military Commission by Deng Xiaoping. A sustained campaign by Deng to purge the Politburo of leftist elements led to Hua's demotion to a Vice-Chairman of the CCP and, in September 1982, to his exclusion from the Politburo.

In September 1982 the CCP was reorganized and the post of Party Chairman abolished. Hu Yaobang became, instead, General Secretary of the CCP. A year later a 'rectification' (purge) of the CCP was launched, aimed at expelling 'Maoists', who had risen to power during the Cultural Revolution, and those opposed to the pragmatic policies of Deng. China's new Constitution, adopted in December 1982, restored the office of Head of State, and in June 1983 Li Xiannian, a former Minister of Finance, became President of China. In September 1986 the sixth plenary session of the 12th CCP Central Committee adopted a detailed resolution on the 'guiding principles for building a socialist society', which redefined the general ideology of the CCP, to provide a theoretical basis for the programme of modernization and the 'open door' policy of economic reform.

In January 1986 a high-level 'anti-corruption' campaign was launched, to investigate reports that many officials had exploited the programme of economic reform for their own gain. The field of culture and the arts underwent significant liberalization in 1986, with a revival of the 'Hundred Flowers' movement of 1956–57, which had encouraged the development of intellectual debate. However, a series of student demonstrations in major cities in late 1986 was regarded by China's leaders as an indication of excessive 'bourgeois liberalization'. In January 1987 Hu Yaobang unexpectedly resigned as CCP General Secretary, being accused of 'mistakes on major issues of political principles'. Zhao Ziyang became acting General Secretary. At the 13th National Congress of the CCP, which opened in October, Deng Xiaoping retired from the Central Committee, but amendments to the Constitution of the CCP permitted him to retain the influential positions of Chairman of the State and of the CCP Central Military Commissions. A new Politburo was appointed by the Central Committee in November. The majority of its 18 members were relatively young officials, who supported Deng Xiaoping's policies. The membership of the new Politburo also indicated a decline in military influence in Chinese politics. The newly-appointed Standing Committee of the Politburo was regarded, on balance, as being 'pro-reform'. In late November Li Peng was appointed Acting Premier of the State Council, in place of Zhao Ziyang. At the first session of the Seventh National People's Congress (NPC), held in March–April 1988, Li Peng was confirmed as Premier, and Yang Shangkun (a member of the CCP Politburo) was elected President.

The death of Hu Yaobang in April 1989 led to the most serious student demonstrations ever seen in the People's Republic. The students criticized the alleged prevalence of corruption and nepotism within the Government, and sought a limited degree of Soviet-style *glasnost* in public life. When negotiations between government officials and the students' leaders had failed to satisfy the protesters' demands, workers from various professions joined the demonstrations in Tiananmen Square, Beijing, which had now become the focal point of the protests. At one stage more than 1m. people congregated in the Square, as demonstrations spread to more than 20 other Chinese cities. In mid-May some 3,000 students began a hunger strike in Tiananmen Square, while protesters demanded the resignation of both Deng Xiaoping and Li Peng, and invited President Gorbachev of the USSR, who was visiting Beijing, to address them. The students ended their hunger strike at the request of Zhao Ziyang, who was generally regarded as being sympathetic to the students' demands. On 20 May a state of martial law was declared in Beijing. Within days, some 300,000 troops had assembled. At the end of May the students erected a 30 m-high replica of the US Statue of Liberty in the Square.

On 3 June 1989 a further unsuccessful attempt was made to dislodge the demonstrators, but on the following day troops of the PLA attacked protesters on and around Tiananmen Square, killing an unspecified number of people. Television evidence and eye-witness accounts estimated the total dead at between 1,000 and 5,000. The Government immediately rejected these figures and claimed, furthermore, that the larger part of the casualties had been soldiers and that a counter-revolutionary rebellion had been taking place. Arrests and executions ensued, although some student leaders eluded capture and fled to Hong Kong. Zhao Ziyang was dismissed from all his party posts and replaced as General Secretary of the CCP by Jiang Zemin, hitherto the secretary of the Shanghai municipal party committee. Zhao was accused of participating in a conspiracy to overthrow the CCP and placed under house arrest. In November Deng resigned as Chairman of the CCP Central Military Commission, his sole remaining party position, and was succeeded by Jiang Zemin, who was hailed as the first of China's 'third generation' of communist leaders (Mao being representative of the first, and Deng of the second). In January 1990 martial law was lifted in Beijing, and it was announced that a total of 573 prisoners, detained following the pro-democracy demonstrations, had been freed. Further groups of detainees were released subsequently. In March Deng Xiaoping resigned from his last official post, that of Chairman of the State Central Military Commission, and was succeeded by Jiang Zemin. An extensive military reshuffle ensued. At the CCP's 14th National Congress, held in October 1992, a new 319-member Central Committee was elected. The Politburo was expanded and a new Secretariat was chosen by the incoming Central Committee. Many opponents of Deng Xiaoping's support for a 'socialist market economy' were replaced.

At the first session of the Eighth NPC, convened in March 1993, Jiang Zemin was elected as the country's President, remaining CCP General Secretary. Li Peng was reappointed as Premier, and an extensive reorganization of the State Council was announced. The Congress also approved amendments to the 1982 Constitution. Changes included confirmation of the State's practice of a 'socialist market economy'. During 1993, however, the Government became concerned at the growing disparity between urban and rural incomes (exacerbated by the heavy taxes imposed on farmers) and the resultant problem of rural migration, and at the decline in support for the CCP in the countryside. In June thousands of peasants took part in demonstrations in Sichuan Province to protest against excessive official levies. In response to the ensuing riots, the central Government banned the imposition of additional local taxes.

In March 1995, at the third session of the Eighth NPC, the appointment of Wu Bangguo and of Jiang Chunyun as Vice-Premiers of the State Council was approved. In an unprecedented display of opposition, however, neither nominee received the NPC's full endorsement. Nevertheless, the position of Jiang Zemin, now regarded by many as the eventual successor to the 'paramount' leadership of the ailing Deng Xiaoping, appeared to have been strengthened. Personnel changes in the military hierarchy later in the year were also viewed as favourable to Jiang Zemin.

The death of Deng Xiaoping, on 19 February 1997, precipitated a period of uncertainty regarding China's future direction. President Jiang Zemin, however, declared that the economic reforms would continue, and this was reiterated in Premier Li Peng's address to the fifth session of the Eighth NPC in March 1997, which included a commitment to restructure state-owned enterprises (SOEs). Delegates at the Congress approved legislation reinforcing the CCP's control over the PLA, and revisions to the criminal code were also promulgated, whereby statutes concerning 'counter-revolutionary' acts (under which many of the pro-democracy demonstrators had been charged in 1989) were removed from the code, but were replaced by 11 crimes of 'endangering state security'. Financial offences, such as money laundering, were also included for the first time.

At the 15th National Congress of the CCP, convened in September 1997, emphasis was placed on radical reform of the 370,000 SOEs. No substantial commitment to political reform, however, was made. Delegates approved amendments to the party Constitution, enshrining the 'Deng Xiaoping Theory' of socialism with Chinese characteristics alongside 'Mao Zedong Thought' as the guiding ideology of the CCP. The Congress elected a new 344-member Central Committee, which re-elected

Jiang Zemin as General Secretary of the CCP, and appointed a 22-member Politburo. The composition of the new Politburo appeared to confirm Jiang Zemin's enhanced authority: Qiao Shi, a reformist and Jiang's most influential rival, who was ranked third in the party hierarchy, was excluded, reportedly because of his age, as was Gen. Liu Huaqing, China's most senior military figure. Zhu Rongji, a former mayor of Shanghai, replaced Qiao Shi, and was also widely regarded as the likely successor to Li Peng, on Li's retirement as Premier of the State Council in March 1998. Gen. Liu was replaced by a civilian, Wei Jinxiang, who was responsible for combating corruption within the CCP. The absence of the military from the Politburo, and the composition of the new Central Military Commission, confirmed Jiang's increased authority over the PLA.

At the first session of the Ninth NPC, which commenced in early March 1998, the number of ministry-level bodies was reduced from 40 to 29, mainly through mergers. On 16 March Jiang Zemin was re-elected President, and Hu Jintao was elected Vice-President. Li Peng resigned as Premier and was replaced by Zhu Rongji, who received overwhelming support from the NPC delegates. Li Peng replaced Qiao Shi as Chairman of the NPC, despite a lack of support from a number of delegates. Zhu's appointments to a new 39-member State Council included a number of associates of Jiang Zemin. Zhu also promoted a number of technocrats who were supportive of his own policies, most notably Xiang Huaicheng, hitherto a Vice-Minister of Finance, who was allocated the finance portfolio.

At the second session of the Ninth NPC, held in March 1999, a number of constitutional amendments were ratified, including the elevation in status of private-sector and other non-state enterprises to 'important components of the socialist market economy', a recommendation for adherence to the rule of law, and the incorporation of Deng Xiaoping's ideology into the Constitution alongside Marxism-Leninism and 'Mao Zedong thought'. In October Hu Jintao was appointed a Vice-Chairman of the Central Military Commission, and in December Zeng Qinghong became a full member of the Politburo, replacing Xie Fei, who had died in September.

Meanwhile, public disquiet over corruption within the CCP, the state bureaucracy and economic enterprises was acknowledged in August 1993, when the Party initiated an anti-corruption campaign. Hundreds of executions of officials were subsequently reported, and in April 1995, following allegations of corruption, Wang Baosen, a deputy mayor of Beijing, committed suicide. In the same month Chen Xitong, Secretary of the Beijing Municipality Committee, was arrested. An extensive inquiry concluded that Wang Baosen, a protégé of Chen Xitong, had been responsible for serious irregularities, including the embezzlement of the equivalent of millions of US dollars. In September, having been similarly disgraced, Chen Xitong was expelled from the Politburo and from the Central Committee of the CCP, later being expelled from the CCP itself. Owing to his implication in the scandal, the mayor of Beijing, Li Qiyan, finally resigned in October 1996. The campaign against corruption intensified in 1997 with the sentencing in August of Chen Xiaotong, son of Chen Xitong, to 12 years' imprisonment for the misappropriation of public funds. Lengthy prison terms were also conferred on two former senior officials in the Beijing administration for accepting bribes. In August 1998 Chen Xitong was sentenced to 16 years' imprisonment for corruption and dereliction of duty; a subsequent appeal was rejected by the Supreme People's Court. It was reported that between October 1992 and June 1997 121,000 people had been expelled from the CCP for corruption, while 37,500 others had faced criminal charges. In an attempt to eradicate illicit trade, in July 1998 President Jiang Zemin ordered the closure of all the business interests of the PLA, comprising some 15,000 companies across all sections of the economy. The divestment of all the PLA's enterprises to a state body, styled the Takeover Office for Military, Armed Police, Government and Judiciary Businesses, was completed by mid-December.

An extensive operation to counter the sharp increase in crimes such as drugs-trafficking, prostitution and the distribution of pornography continued, resulting in hundreds of executions. In April 1996 the Government initiated 'Strike Hard', a new campaign against crime, executing hundreds of people. In September 1998 Amnesty International, the human rights organization, released a report stating that China had executed 1,876 people in 1997, more than the rest of the world combined. This represented, however, a considerable reduction compared with the 4,367 executions documented in 1996.

China's treatment of political dissidents attracted international attention in November 1997, with the release on medical grounds into exile in the USA of Wei Jingsheng. Wei had been imprisoned in 1979, but was released on parole in September 1993. He was rearrested, however, in April 1994, and detained incommunicado until December 1995, when he was convicted of conspiring to overthrow the Government. His sentencing to 14 years' imprisonment provoked an international outcry, and he was released shortly after Jiang Zemin's visit to the USA in October 1997 (see below). Bao Ge, a prominent Shanghai dissident and campaigner for compensation for Chinese victims of Japanese war aggression, was released from three years' imprisonment without trial in June. He left for the USA in November.

In January 1991, meanwhile, the trials of many of those arrested during the pro-democracy protests of 1989 commenced. Most activists received relatively short prison sentences. In July 1992 Bao Tong, a senior aide of Zhao Ziyang, the former General Secretary of the CCP, was found guilty of involvement in the pro-democracy unrest of mid-1989. At the end of his seven-year prison sentence, Bao Tong was released in May 1996 and placed under house arrest. He was freed from house arrest in May 1997, but remained under constant police surveillance.

In February 1994 Asia Watch, an independent New York-based human rights organization, issued a highly critical report of the situation in China, which detailed the cases of more than 1,700 detainees, imprisoned for their political, ethnic or religious views. In April, shortly before the USA was due to decide upon a renewal of China's favourable trading status, Wang Juntao, imprisoned for his part in the 1989 protests, was unexpectedly released and permitted to travel to the USA for medical treatment. Other releases followed. In July, however, the trial on charges of counter-revolutionary activity of 14 members of a dissident group, in detention since 1992, commenced. In December 1994 nine of the defendants received heavy prison sentences.

In February 1993 Wang Dan and Guo Haifeng, leading student activists in the 1989 demonstrations, were freed. In late 1994, however, complaining of police harassment, Wang Dan filed a lawsuit against the authorities. He was rearrested in May 1995. The imposition of an 11-year sentence on Wang Dan at the conclusion of his cursory trial on charges of conspiracy, in October 1996, received international condemnation. Appeals for his release on medical grounds in 1997 were rejected, but in April 1998 he was released on medical parole and was sent into exile in the USA on the following day. In May 1993, having served 12 years of a 15-year sentence, Xu Wenli was released from prison. He was rearrested in April 1994, but released shortly afterwards. In August 1993 the arrest and expulsion from China of Han Dongfang, a trade union activist who had attempted to return to his homeland after a year in the USA, attracted much international attention.

In June 1995 Liu Gang, a leader of the 1989 uprising, was released from prison, and in May 1996 he was granted temporary asylum in the USA. Two further dissidents, Ren Wanding and Zhang Xianliang, were freed upon completion of their prison terms in June 1996. Having been released in the same month, Wang Xizhe escaped from Guangzhou and was permitted to enter the USA in October. His fellow activist, Liu Xiaobo, was arrested in Beijing, however, and ordered to serve three years in a labour camp. In November Chen Zeming, another alleged leader of the 1989 pro-democracy demonstrations, was released on medical parole.

In 1997 there was increasing pressure on the CCP to reconsider its assessment of the 1989 Tiananmen Square pro-democracy demonstrations as a 'counter-revolutionary rebellion'. In June 1997, in an unprecedented decision, a court in Liaoning Province overturned convictions of 'counter-revolution' against four dissidents imprisoned for their role in the 1989 pro-democracy movement. However, an appeal to the CCP National Congress by Zhao Ziyang (who remained under house arrest) to reassess the official verdict was dismissed. During President Jiang's visit to the USA, in October 1997, having first described the brutal treatment of the 1989 demonstrators as a 'necessary measure', a subsequent acknowledgement that mistakes might have been made was not, according to the Chinese authorities, to be regarded as an apology. In mid-1997 Beijing refuted Amnesty International reports that several pro-democracy activists remained among the numerous political prisoners in China, classifying as criminals the estimated 2,000 people imprisoned on charges of 'counter-revolution'.

The UN High Commissioner for Human Rights, Mary Robinson, made an unprecedented official visit to China, including Tibet, and Hong Kong in September 1998. Following the visit, in October China signed the International Covenant on Civil and Political Rights in New York, guaranteeing freedom of expression, a fair trial and protection against arbitrary arrest. Although the Government's signing of the Covenant was hailed as a great advance in its attitude towards human rights, the treaty would only come into force once ratified by the NPC. No date was set for ratification. Following a further visit by Robinson to Beijing in March 2000 (during which China refuted her right to criticize its conduct of internal affairs), in November a human rights training agreement was signed which, it was hoped, would be a precursor to ratification.

In 1998 attempts by dissidents in Beijing and the provinces to create and register an opposition party, the Chinese Democratic Party (CDP), with the principal aim of democratic elections, were suppressed by the Government. The exiled dissident, Wang Bingzhang, was deported to the USA in February after entering the country to meet fellow opposition activists. In November the Government published a judicial interpretation of the crimes of political subversion (thereby expanding existing punishable offences), specifying that 'incitement to subvert state power' would result in imprisonment for between three years and life for any publisher, musician, author, artist or film-maker found guilty of the charge. In December at least 30 members of the CDP were detained, and three veteran activists, Xu Wenli, Qin Yongmin and Wang Youcai, were sentenced to 13, 12 and 11 years' imprisonment, respectively, provoking strong international condemnation. Human rights groups declared the release on medical parole and subsequent exile to the USA of the prominent dissident, Liu Nianchun, shortly before the conviction of the CDP activists, to be an attempt to deflect criticism of their trials. A speech by President Jiang Zemin in December appeared to confirm the end of a period of relative tolerance of political dissent. By November 1999 a further 18 CDP leaders had been convicted of subverting state power and sentenced to lengthy terms of imprisonment.

At the first Sino-US discussions on human rights for four years in Washington, DC, in January 1999 members of the US delegation urged their Chinese counterparts to halt the harsh treatment of dissidents. In February of that year two dissidents, Gao Yu (a journalist) and Sun Weibang, who had received substantial sentences, were released ahead of schedule, prompting speculation that Beijing was attempting to counter criticism before the imminent visit to the People's Republic by the US Secretary of State and the forthcoming meeting of the UN Commission on Human Rights in Geneva. None the less, China continued its suppression of dissent. In late April, however, a US-sponsored resolution at the aforementioned UN Commission meeting, condemning China's human rights record, was defeated. The resolution was again defeated in April 2000. A number of activists were detained in June 1999 in advance of the 10th anniversary of the killings in Tiananmen Square; despite official fears, the day passed without major incident in Beijing. (In Hong Kong, however, thousands attended a commemorative rally.) The Square had been closed for some time, ostensibly for repairs before the 50th anniversary of the founding of the People's Republic in October, and did not reopen until late June. In August 2000 a group of Chinese dissidents filed a lawsuit in the USA accusing Li Peng of crimes against humanity for sanctioning the events of June 1989 in Tiananmen Square. China made a request to the USA that the case be abandoned, describing it as 'political farce'.

The killings in Tiananmen Square attracted renewed attention in early January 2001 following the 'leak' of papers and transcripts of government meetings at the time, which had been smuggled out of China by a reformist civil servant and subsequently published abroad as 'The Tiananmen Papers'. The papers, which were immediately denounced by the Government as forgeries, appeared to show a split in the leadership over how to deal with the protesters, with Zhao Ziyang having favoured a conciliatory approach, while Li Peng supported decisive action against the students, regarding them as part of a 'counter-revolutionary rebellion'. Deng Xiaoping had taken the decision to suppress the protesters, with the support of a group of semi-retired elders. The papers also indicated that Jiang Zemin had been appointed to his positions directly by Deng, thus circumventing the Party's rules of selection. The release of the papers was widely seen as part of an ongoing power struggle within the CCP, aimed at discrediting Li, and potentially Jiang, in advance of the Party Congress scheduled for late 2002. In June 2001, on the 12th anniversary of the Tiananmen Square massacre, some 111 mothers of the victims appealed for an investigation to determine responsibility for the killings and a reassessment of the violence used. In June 2002 the authorities reportedly detained at least 23 people in connection with the publication of 'The Tiananmen Papers' following a lengthy investigation into the matter, which also allegedly included the dispatch of agents overseas.

In early 2002 a report by Amnesty International claimed that there had been a total of 2,468 executions in China during 2001, mainly owing to the most recent campaign against crime. In August 2002 the US-based group Human Rights Watch reported that growing numbers of political dissidents were being detained in mental institutions, estimating that at least 3,000 people had been subjected to psychiatric detention for political activity in the preceding two decades. Those detained included members of Falun Gong (see below), independent labour organizers and other organized anti-Government activists.

In late December 2002 the authorities acknowledged that they had again arrested the US-based activist, Wang Bingzhang. Wang had disappeared in mid-2002 in Viet Nam, where he had travelled with two other Chinese dissidents, Yue Wu and Zhang Qi, in order to hold meetings with other activists. Wang was charged with espionage on behalf of Taiwan, and with terrorism—charges condemned by the China Democratic Party—and he went on trial in late January 2003. In early February he was sentenced to life imprisonment, and at the end of that month he lost his appeal. Also in late December 2002 the authorities released, on the basis of 'medical parole', Xu Wenli, who immediately returned to the USA. Xu's release was widely seen as a goodwill gesture towards the USA, Xu himself describing his release as 'political'. In mid-January 2003 the authorities charged an internet dissident, Ouyang Yi, with trying to overthrow the Government. Later that month the authorities expelled another prominent dissident, Fang Jue, to exile in the USA. Fang had, a few years previously, called for direct elections at all levels of government and for press freedom. He had been released from prison in July 2002, but had subsequently been detained during the CCP Congress in November. In early March 2003 the authorities released Zhang Qi, who immediately returned to the USA, where she was based.

The emergence of Falun Gong in the late 1990s posed new challenges to the supremacy of the CCP, which banned the popular religious cult in July 1999, on the grounds that it constituted a threat to society. The group, which was also known as Falun Dafa, had been established in 1992 by Li Hongzhi, who was based in the USA, and from 1999 it attracted increasing attention in China and abroad, claiming tens of millions of adherents, mainly in China. Beijing feared that Falun Gong would spread across the country and cause mass civil strife, as other mystical revolutionary groups had done in the 19th century. The ban imposed in 1999 was prompted by demonstrations, attended by tens of thousands of supporters in numerous towns and cities, in protest at the arrest of more than 100 adherents of the sect. The authorities embarked on a campaign of harsh persecution of those who refused to renounce their faith, and by the end of the month more than 6,000 arrests had been made. The authorities had initially been alarmed by a peaceful protest in central Beijing, attended by some 10,000 practitioners in April. Four members of the sect were imprisoned in December, with sentences ranging from seven to 18 years, for their part in organizing the demonstration. This followed the conviction and imprisonment of four of Falun Gong's provincial leaders in November. The authorities were also concerned by the high level of Falun Gong membership among CCP and PLA officials. The CCP took the opportunity to demonstrate its continuing power on 1 October 1999, with lavish but strictly-controlled, celebrations of the 50th anniversary of the foundation of the People's Republic of China. In a highly symbolic gesture, a picture of Jiang Zemin was paraded alongside portraits of Mao Zedong and Deng Xiaoping: the first time that the current President had been publicly placed on a par with his predecessors. Despite condemnation and prosecution by the full force of the law, and the lack of public appearances by Li Hongzhi, Falun Gong members continued to make quiet protests on a regular basis during 2000. The CCP's fear of losing its authority in the face of this increasing religious adherence became evident in October 2000, when Falun Gong was declared to be a political rival to the CCP and an enemy of the nation. The suppression of Falun Gong continued throughout 2001, with

dispersals of rallies, arrests and detentions in 're-education camps'. In July an anti-cult exhibition was held, and in late August the authorities sentenced 45 'die-hard' members to long prison sentences for organizing resistance. The group claimed in September that some 278 members had died in custody since 1999, while the Government blamed the group for the deaths of 1,600 people, including suicides. In November 2001 and February 2002 the authorities expelled on both occasions 30–40 Western followers of Falun Gong who had demonstrated in Tiananmen Square.

In early 2002 Falun Gong showed renewed signs of activity by infiltrating Chinese television broadcasts in several different cities and transmitting messages from Li Hongzhi, as well as short programmes contradicting the official government position on the sect. These activities reached new heights in late June with the heavy 'jamming' of *Sinosat* transmitters, prompting an admission by the Government that such interference had taken place, and emphasizing the technological sophistication and resourcefulness of Falun Gong. The ease of the interference, furthermore, led to concerns about the security of satellites, which were also used to transmit financial data. The authorities responded by denouncing the interference and attributing it to overseas-based followers of the sect. In late September 15 Falun Gong members were sentenced to between four and 20 years' imprisonment for violating anti-cult laws and damaging broadcasting equipment. At the same time the Government stated that Falun Gong had used Taiwan as a base from which to 'hijack' Chinese satellite transmissions and, while refraining from blaming the Taiwanese Government, urged it to curb the activities of the sect. Taiwan had generally been tolerant of the group, and Beijing particularly feared any collaboration between its two principal rivals.

In January 2000, meanwhile, five Catholic bishops were ordained in a display of strength by the state-controlled Chinese Catholic Church, impeding any improvement in relations with the Vatican, which opposed the ordination. In August 1999 Beijing had refused to grant permission for the Pope to visit Hong Kong, owing to the Vatican's links with Taiwan. According to a US-based Catholic organization, the arrest of an archbishop belonging to the clandestine Roman Catholic Church in February 2000 was part of an attempt by China to undermine allegiance to the Vatican. During the year there was substantial evidence of the CCP's intensification of repression of all non-official religious movements, many of which were classified as 'evil cults', with widespread arrests and church closures. In October the situation was exacerbated when, on China's National Day, the Pope canonized 120 missionary and Chinese Roman Catholic martyrs. Beijing responded with allegations of serious crimes perpetrated by several of the new saints. Despite a subsequent apology by the Pope for any errors committed by missionaries in China, relations between the two sides were severely damaged. By October 2001, however, there were signs that Beijing and the Vatican were moving towards a *rapprochement*, which would potentially allow the restoration of full diplomatic relations, thereby not only impelling the Vatican (and possibly several Catholic Latin American nations) to sever links with Taiwan but also diminishing the problems arising from the existence of an 'underground' Catholic church in China. In mid-October Catholic scholars from around the world gathered in Beijing to commemorate the 400th anniversary of the start of Italian Jesuit Matteo Ricci's mission to China in 1601. The event was downgraded somewhat, but Pope John Paul II expressed regret for past Vatican actions and appealed for the establishment of diplomatic relations. Meanwhile, it was estimated that 70% of Chinese bishops received mutual recognition from the Chinese Bishops' Conference and the Vatican.

In December 2001 a senior-level conference on religion was held in Beijing, attended by all seven members of the Politburo Standing Committee. The conference acknowledged the increasing importance of religion in China, in contrast to the anti-religious ideology of the past, and aimed to bring independent churches under state control, thereby obviating the need for clandestine churches. It was thought that Protestant churches were to be the main beneficiaries of the conference; Falun Gong remained illegal. Despite this conference, however, a Hong Kong businessman, Li Guangqiang, was arrested for delivering bibles to an evangelical group in south-eastern China, and in January 2002 he was sentenced to two years in prison, apparently receiving a light sentence in order to deflect criticism from the USA.

In February 2002 documents smuggled out of the country by Chinese Christians revealed that the authorities were working hard to suppress unauthorized religious faiths, such as Christian sects, as well as Falun Gong (see above). In May the authorities arrested more than 100 South Korean missionaries for assisting North Korean refugees fleeing to China. In mid-2002, however, the Government began co-operating with underground Christians in combating an extremist Christian fringe sect known as 'Eastern Lightning', which had kidnapped and attempted forcibly to convert 34 Christians in April. The group was known to target underground Christian movements with a view to forcible conversion. 'Eastern Lightning' had emerged in 1990 under Zhao Weishan, and its belief in the reincarnation of Jesus as a woman bore a resemblance to that of a group that had started an anti-Government rebellion in the 19th century. 'Eastern Lightning' had, like Falun Gong, been designated an 'evil cult' and an enemy of the State. Despite such co-operation, however, in late July the authorities sentenced three underground Roman Catholic priests to three years' labour for 'cult' activities, and in September they arrested the underground bishop of Qiqihar, Heilongjiang Province. In October 2002 the US State Department's annual report on religious freedom continued to designate China as a country engaged in widespread repression of religion.

By early 2003 China and the Vatican had held several rounds of informal discussions on improving bilateral relations. However, Beijing was in confrontation with Bishop Joseph Zen Zekiun, the head of the Catholic Church in the Hong Kong SAR, who had become increasingly critical of Beijing's administration in Hong Kong and its religious policies in China (see the chapter on Hong Kong). Observers noted that the division between the officially-endorsed 'patriotic' Catholic Church and the unofficial church was gradually being reduced, with 'patriotic' bishops privately seeking the Vatican's endorsement and guidance.

In February 2000, in an attempt definitively to refute the growing belief that China must eventually abandon one-party rule, Jiang Zemin had launched a new political theory entitled 'The Three Represents', which declared that the CCP would 'always represent the development needs of China's advanced social productive forces, always represent the onward direction of China's advanced culture and always represent the fundamental interests of the largest number of Chinese people'. It appeared, however, that with the advent of significant social change the CCP was finding it increasingly difficult to maintain control over its members.

Attempts were made by the Government in February and in November 2000 to regulate the publication of material on the internet, with the issuing of new rules first granting the regime the right to 'reorganize' or close down offending websites, and then requiring government approval prior to the posting of news bulletins. It was feared that the only permitted information would be that already published in the official media, particularly after the earlier fining and temporary suspension of a financial news website for publishing material that might damage the Government's image. In February 2001 the trial began of the first webmaster to have been prosecuted for publishing subversive material on the internet, and between April and November 2001, some 17,000 internet cafés were shut down in a nation-wide campaign against pornographic and subversive websites. In April 2000 it was reported that four academics had been dismissed from a Chinese academy, accused of being 'a branch of opposition within the Party', following the publication of an essay by one of them advocating political reform. In the following months there was harsh repression of provincial labour unrest. In April 2000 it was also reported that labour disputes had totalled more than 120,000 in 1999. Workers had become increasingly restless since 1998, when SOE restructuring began to result in widespread redundancies.

The firmest repressive action, however, proved to be necessary in regional and central government circles. The third session of the Ninth NPC, which convened in Beijing in March 2000, focused mainly on economic issues but also made a commitment to ending official corruption and smuggling. Earlier that month a former provincial deputy governor had been executed for bribery and possession of property acquired from unidentified sources. Corruption appeared to be rife throughout 2000 in many areas of government, including customs, finance, the military and the Three Gorges dam project. Among the most notable cases was that of former Vice-Chairman of the Standing Committee of the NPC, Cheng Kejie, who was executed in September for accepting huge bribes. Also in September, Maj.-

Gen. Ji Shengde, the former head of military intelligence of the PLA, was formally charged with taking massive bribes while in office. His trial formed part of the biggest corruption and smuggling case in the history of the People's Republic, with several senior officials in various Chinese cities facing prosecution. Fourteen were executed, while other defendants received sentences of life imprisonment. The leader of the smuggling ring, Lai Changxing, evaded capture and escaped to Canada, from where China was attempting to extradite him in late 2000. Meanwhile, at its Plenary Session in October, the CCP announced a new five-year plan, under which China was to concentrate on rural development, the creation of employment, economic modernization and combating corruption. Later that month, following a two-year investigation, government auditors reported the embezzlement or serious misuse of the equivalent of more than US $11,000m. of public funds by government officials. Further revelations of corruption emerged in January 2001 when the official media reported that Liu Yong, a municipal party official in Shenyang, had operated a criminal gang and used the proceeds to support his business activities. In June more than 100 officials from Shenyang, including the city's mayor, Mu Suixin, were detained in connection with their association to Liu. In February, meanwhile, it was reported that a massive investigation into tax fraud was under way, with a special emphasis on the city of Guangdong.

During the fourth session of the Ninth NPC, held in March 2001, Premier Zhu Rongji outlined plans for economic restructuring in preparation for China's membership of the World Trade Organization (WTO), and also called for scientific and technological advancement, the improvement of living standards, the reduction of rural poverty, development of the western regions, opening to the outside world and strengthening of the military. A 17.7% increase in the defence budget was also announced in March. In the mean time, from April 2001 the authorities renewed their action against dissent, as part of the latest nation-wide 'Strike Hard' campaign, which was believed to reflect political manoeuvring in advance of the CCP Congress in 2002. The campaign was co-ordinated by Luo Gan, a protégé of Li Peng, with the approval of Jiang Zemin. The victims of the suppression reportedly included ethnic separatists, 'underground' churches, unregistered internet cafés, tax-evading peasants, and also Chinese scholars returning from overseas, five of whom were US citizens. Human rights groups claimed that the rate of executions had also risen during this time. In April Jin Ruchao was sentenced to death for his alleged role in setting off a series of bombs in Hebei in March, which killed a total of 108 people. By early July Amnesty International claimed that at least 1,751 executions, out of 2,960 death sentences issued, had been carried out between April and June. The Government's campaign also resulted in the removal in June of two editors from *Southern Weekend* for criticizing the penal system. Other newspapers also faced punishment for their investigations into growing social dissatisfaction and injustices.

In mid-May 2001 a prominent intellectual who also served as a deputy director of economic reform, Pan Yue, presented to President Jiang a plan to transform the CCP into a more broadly representative body; the plan was subsequently discussed at the Politburo Standing Committee and reportedly contained a right-wing nationalist leaning combined with strong, centralized rule. Pan's plan was believed to reflect the views of an increasing number of party cadres, as a means to prolong CCP rule without effecting democratization. In early June the CCP released the *China Investigation Report 2000–2001: Studies of Contradictions Within the People under New Conditions*, which publicly acknowledged that its rule could be undermined by social discontent arising from the country's free-market reforms. It warned that growing inequality and corruption were important sources of discontent, ranging from angry farmers to dismissed workers. The report was chaired by Zeng Qinghong, a senior aide of Jiang, who was vying for a senior position at the 2002 CCP Congress.

On 1 July 2001, in a speech to mark the 80th anniversary of the foundation of the CCP, President Jiang urged the modernization of the Party and for the first time stated that business people would be welcome as party members, a formal reversal of decades of hostility to the entrepreneurial class. Jiang also spoke of the need to eliminate corruption, and warned that the alternative to CCP rule was chaos and the disintegration of the country. Jiang's rightward shift was not universally welcomed, however, and in mid-August he shut down a leading left-wing magazine, *Zhenli de Zhuiqiu (Search for the Truth)*, in a move that reflected increasing discord between the Party's leftist and rightist factions. The left-wing forces, which included orthodox Communists, supporters of moderate socialism, the agricultural lobby and liberals, all opposed the transformation of the CCP into a more business-orientated party. In mid-July, meanwhile, despite the growing campaign against dissent, the International Olympic Committee (IOC) awarded the 2008 Olympic Games to Beijing, resulting in mass celebrations across the country.

The end of 2001 and most of 2002 was dominated by preparations for the 16th CCP Congress. The 25th anniversary of the death of Mao Zedong passed without commemoration in early September 2001, a silence attributed to the debate within the CCP over future policy and to President Jiang's attempt to secure his own legacy—he was reportedly seeking to retain influence as an elder statesman by keeping the post of Chairman of the Central Military Commission. Other senior officials, including Premier Zhu Rongji and NPC Chairman Li Peng, were also expected to be replaced in March 2003, when the 10th NPC was scheduled to be convened. Jiang's designated successor was Vice-President Hu Jintao, who had slowly gained prominence and had made a tour of European countries in late 2001 to introduce himself to world leaders (see below). In November Jiang appointed the Deputy Party Secretary for Shanxi Province, Li Jingtian, to his personal staff, which also included policy aide Wang Huning, Jia Tingan and speechwriter Tang Wensheng. In December the mayor of Shanghai, Xu Kuangdi unexpectedly resigned to assume an academic post, reportedly owing to his differences with the Shanghai Party Secretary, Huang Ju.

Meanwhile, in March 2002 tens of thousands of workers who had been made redundant staged demonstrations in the northeastern industrial cities of Daqing and Liaoyang, protesting against job losses and the lack of adequate social security measures. (Since 1998 some 25m. workers had been laid off from State enterprises, according to official sources.) The principal organizer, Yao Fuxin, was arrested, prompting further demonstrations for his release. The events emphasized the potentially destabilizing effects of economic restructuring following China's admission to the WTO (see below), and were subsequently dispersed by military police. In April hundreds staged similar protests in Lanzhou. Several more such disturbances occurred during subsequent months, albeit on a smaller scale. In response the Ministry of Labour urged enterprises to re-employ some workers and ensure the timely payment of allowances and pensions. Additionally, bureaucrats and civil servants received pay rises in July, in an attempt to raise consumer spending and to reduce corruption. In an effort to maintain social stability, poorer urban dwellers were also allocated new allowances in July, under a new registration system that would allow the Government accurately to count the numbers within that group.

Attempts by the authorities to maintain order prior to the Party Congress resulted in renewed measures to curb access to the internet during 2002. In June, at the beginning of a three-month offensive, three leading internet providers were punished for disseminating harmful content and were forced to suspend a number of services. This was accompanied by a campaign to close down illegal internet cafés, after a fire at one such facility killed 24 people. By August 2002 it was announced that 14,000 'cybercafés' had been closed, 3,100 of which were permanent closures. The official reasons for the closures were to improve workplace safety practices, but critics stated that the closures were aimed at controlling internet access. In early September the authorities temporarily blocked access to the US-based 'Google' internet search engine, in order to limit access to potentially subversive material, but subsequently imposed new selective mechanisms to limit what could be accessed via 'Google'. Despite this, China was, by 2002, the world's third largest user of the internet, usage having risen by 72% in 2001–02 to reach 45m. users. At the same time, the authorities arrested 23 people in connection with the 'leak' and publication of official documents concerning the Tiananmen massacres (see above).

In July 2002 senior CCP officials gathered at the coastal resort of Beidaihe to determine the new positions to be allocated at the Congress, amid strong indications that Jiang Zemin would remain CCP General Secretary for another term. In late October Huang Ju and Jia Qinglin, the CCP secretaries in charge of Shanghai and Beijing respectively, and close allies of Jiang Zemin, were transferred to new central government posts.

The 16th CCP Congress was finally held in early November 2002, having been delayed from September, and resulted in the long-awaited transfer of power to the 'fourth generation' leadership headed by the new General Secretary, Hu Jintao. A new 356-member Central Committee was elected, as well as a 24-member Politburo, the Standing Committee (the highest decision-making body) of which was expanded from seven to nine members, of whom Hu was the only incumbent to be retained. The new members of the Standing Committee were Wu Bangguo, Wen Jiabao, Jia Qinglin, Zeng Qinghong, Huang Ju, Wu Guanzheng, Li Changchun and Luo Gan. Of these, Jia, Zeng, Huang, and Li were all known to be close allies of Jiang, who had successfully prevented rival Li Ruihuan from being re-elected to the Standing Committee. Luo Gan, however, was a protégé of NPC Chairman Li Peng. As expected, Jiang retained the chairmanship of the CCP Central Military Commission, which also contained three important military allies of his, Generals Cao Gangchuan, Guo Boxiong, and Xu Caihou, of whom Cao and Guo were also appointed to the Politburo. Another Jiang ally, Gen. Liang Guanglie, hitherto Commander of the Nanjing Military Region, was appointed Chief of the PLA's General Staff. Jiang thus retained full control of the powerful PLA.

The Congress stressed continuity in policy, but introduced some economic reforms designed to please the business community and foreign investors. Although state ownership would retain a dominant role, private businesses would be able to compete on a more equal basis, and there would be a greater emphasis on private capital. Discriminatory regulations on investment, financing, taxation, land use and foreign trade would be revised, and private property would be granted greater legal protection. However, there were no major political reforms, and foreign policy was to remain unchanged. In early December 2002 Zhou Yongkang, hitherto the party secretary for Sichuan Province, was appointed Minister of Public Security, replacing Jia Chunwang. In mid-January 2003 two men, including Yao Fuxin, went on trial accused of organizing the massive labour unrest of early 2002.

The final stage of the transfer of power to the 'fourth generation' of Chinese leadership took place during the 10th NPC, in mid-March 2003. As expected, Hu Jintao was appointed President, succeeding Jiang Zemin, while Zeng Qinghong became Vice-President. Wen Jiabao succeeded Zhu Rongji as premier, and appointed Huang Ju, Wu Yi, Zeng Peiyan, and Hui Liangyu as Vice-Premiers. The new State Council also included Ma Kai as Minister of State Development and Reform Commission, Jin Renqing as Minister of Finance, and Lu Fuyuan as Minister of Commerce. Both Ma and Jin were known to have economics backgrounds. Li Zhaoxing, a former ambassador to the USA and the UN and hitherto a Vice-Minister of Foreign Affairs, was appointed Minister of Foreign Affairs, replacing Tang Jiaxuan, who became one of five state councillors. Gen. Cao Gangchuan was appointed Minister of National Defence. Hua Jianmin, an ally of Jiang, was appointed Secretary-General of the State Council. The new Chairman of the NPC was Wu Bangguo, replacing Li Peng. Despite the change of personnel, the new leadership was widely expected to maintain continuity with the policies of recent years.

The incoming leadership immediately faced a new challenge with the outbreak of a previously unknown virus, Severe Acute Respiratory Syndrome (SARS), which by the end of April 2003 had affected almost 3,500 people and resulted in more than 150 deaths in the People's Republic alone. As the pneumonia-like virus spread across Asia and also to Canada, the Chinese authorities' initial lack of openness attracted much international criticism. Thousands of people were placed in quarantine in Beijing, and many public facilities and schools were closed. The Minister of Public Health, Zhang Wenkang, and the mayor of Beijing, Meng Xuenong, were accused of having concealed the extent of the disease and were relieved of their party and state positions. Wang Qishan, hitherto vice-mayor, was appointed mayor of Beijing.

Meanwhile, corruption remained an ongoing problem for the CCP and the financial system. In January 2002 Wang Xuebing, the president of China Construction Bank and an ally of Zhu Rongji, was placed under investigation for alleged financial mismanagement, and in November he was expelled from the CCP on bribe-taking charges. In February Huang Jin, an official at Minsheng Bank, was charged with illegally procuring and expropriating loans, and in March a 'money-laundering' and illegal loans scandal emerged at the Bank of China, the perpetrators having fled overseas. In August another former banking official, Zhu Xiaohua, the former president of Everbright Bank, was expelled from the CCP and subsequently sentenced to 15 years' imprisonment on corruption charges. In September three officials from CITIC Industrial Bank were arrested on suspicion of massive fraud. In June, meanwhile, Yang Rong, one of China's richest men and a former chairman of China Brilliance Automotive Holdings, fled the country owing to corruption allegations. Also in June, the authorities reported that companies in Jiangsu Province had paid bribes to local officials. In August Zhao Keming, a former deputy mayor of Xiamen, was sentenced to death, with a two-year reprieve, for accepting bribes. In December the former customs chief in Shenzhen, Zhao Yucun, was sentenced to life imprisonment, also for receiving bribes. In an unrelated scandal, the former chairman of Shenzhen Urban Construction Group, Li Yuguo, received a suspended death sentence for similar offences.

From the late 1990s there was increasing concern about the spread of HIV/AIDS in China. During 2001 the authorities took greater steps to acknowledge the seriousness of the problem, and in January new legislation was introduced in Chengdu that forbade infected people from marrying; compulsory tests were to be carried out on high-risk groups such as prostitutes, drug addicts and those who had spent extended time abroad. In early June it was reported that as many as 500,000 people in Henan Province had been infected with HIV after selling their blood plasma to companies that had employed unhygienic practices; these donations of blood had been encouraged by the local health authorities. At the UNAIDS summit meeting in late June, the Minister of Public Health, Zhang Wenkang, stated that there were 600,000 people infected with HIV in China; however, UN estimates placed the number at 1.5m. In late August the Vice-Minister of Health formally acknowledged the gravity of the AIDS crisis. The authorities announced an increase in funds to US $12m. annually to counter the spread of the virus, and an allocation of $117m. in 2001–02 to improve the safety of blood banks. In November 2001 China held its first national HIV/AIDS conference. In April 2002 the authorities reported a 17% increase in HIV cases to 850,000, a figure still well below UN estimates, and in June a UN report warned that China was on the brink of an AIDS catastrophe, estimating that the total number of cases could rise to 10m. by 2010. The fear was that, if unrestrained, the virus would spread from rural areas (the worst-affected regions) to the general urban population. In late August China's most prominent AIDS activist, Wan Yanhai, who had exposed the Henan epidemic, was detained by the Bureau of State Security. In September the authorities admitted that as many as 1m. might be infected with HIV, and initially announced that they would start mass-manufacturing anti-AIDS drugs, possibly in violation of international patents—although the latter was later denied. However, the authorities also for the first time requested international assistance in combating the virus, and released Wan Yanhai in late September. In late November it was reported that the health authorities in Guangdong Province were planning to issue, on a trial basis, sterile needles to drug users, in an attempt to limit the spread of HIV, and on 1 December—World AIDS Day—the Government announced a renewed effort to promote AIDS awareness. However, in early 2003 a draft UN report warned that China would be unlikely to meet its target of halting or reversing the increase in HIV/AIDS by 2010.

In November and early December 2001, meanwhile, the authorities announced plans to accelerate the development of China's space programme, including the launching of more satellites, space probes and a manned space flight by 2005, to be followed by a manned mission to the moon. In March 2002 China successfully launched and returned to earth an unmanned space capsule, *Shenzhou III*, and in January 2003 achieved the same results with *Shenzhou IV*, both of which could be used to carry astronauts into orbit. Also in January 2003 China announced plans to launch its first manned space flight later in that year, thereby becoming the third nation after the former USSR and the USA, to launch such missions. The long-term goal was to develop a space station and moon base.

Tibet (Xizang), a semi-independent region of western China, was occupied in October 1950 by Chinese Communist forces. In March 1959 there was an unsuccessful armed uprising by Tibetans opposed to Chinese rule. The Dalai Lama, the head of Tibet's Buddhist clergy and thus the region's spiritual leader, fled with some 100,000 supporters to Dharamsala, northern India, where a government-in-exile was established. The Chinese ended the former dominance of the lamas (Buddhist monks) and destroyed many monasteries. Tibet became an 'Autonomous Region' of China in September 1965, but the majority of Tibetans have continued to regard the Dalai Lama as

their 'god-king', and to resent the Chinese presence. In October 1987 violent clashes occurred in Lhasa (the regional capital) between the Chinese authorities and Tibetans seeking independence. Further demonstrations during a religious festival in March 1988 resulted in a riot and several deaths, and a number of Tibetan separatists were arrested and detained without trial. The Dalai Lama, however, renounced demands for complete independence, and in 1988 proposed that Tibet become a self-governing Chinese territory, in all respects except foreign affairs. In December 1988 an offer from the Dalai Lama to meet Chinese representatives in Geneva was rejected, and later that month two more demonstrators were killed by security forces during a march to commemorate the 40th anniversary of the UN General Assembly's adoption of the Universal Declaration of Human Rights.

On 7 March 1989 martial law was imposed in Lhasa for the first time since 1959, after further violent clashes between separatists and the Chinese police, which resulted in the deaths of 16 protesters. In October the Chinese Government condemned as an interference in its internal affairs the award of the Nobel Peace Prize to the Dalai Lama. In November several Tibetan Buddhist nuns claimed to have been severely tortured for their part in the demonstrations in March 1989. In May 1990 martial law was lifted in Lhasa. Human rights groups claimed that during the last six months of the period of martial law as many as 2,000 persons had been executed. Furthermore, political and religious repression and torture were reported to be continuing throughout 1990. Renewed anti-Chinese protests were reported in October 1991 and in March 1992. In May a report issued by Amnesty International was critical of the Chinese authorities' violations of the human rights of the monks and nuns of Tibet. A document entitled *Tibet—Its Ownership and Human Rights Situation* was published by the Chinese Government in September, attempting to prove that historically the region is part of China. In May 1993 several thousand Tibetans were reported to have demonstrated in Lhasa against Chinese rule. A number of protesters were believed to have been killed by the security forces. In January 1994 two prominent Tibetan activists were released from detention. In July, however, five secessionists were found guilty of counter-revolutionary acts and received prison sentences of up to 15 years.

In April 1994 China condemned the Dalai Lama's meeting with President Clinton during the former's lecture tour of the USA. In September the Dalai Lama warned China that Tibet might resort to armed uprising if oppression continued to worsen. In late 1994 the construction of new monasteries and temples in Tibet was banned. In March 1995 regulations restricting the number of Buddhist monks were announced, and in the same month the Dalai Lama's proposal that a referendum be held on the future of Tibet was dismissed by China. In May the Dalai Lama's nomination of the 11th incarnation of the Panchen Lama (the second position in the spiritual hierarchy, the 10th incumbent having died in 1989) was condemned by the Chinese authorities, which banned the six-year old boy, Gedhun Choekyi Nyima, from travelling to Dharamsala. In September 1995, as the 30th anniversary of the imposition of Chinese rule approached, it was reported that independence activists had carried out two bombings in Lhasa.

In September 1995, during the UN World Conference on Women and the Non-Governmental Organizations' Forum held concurrently in China, a silent protest by a group of female Tibetan exiles attracted much attention. Following an informal meeting between the Dalai Lama and US President Clinton in Washington in mid-September, China lodged a strong protest. In November the Chinese Government announced Gyaltsen (Gyaincain) Norbu as its own nomination of a new Panchen Lama. The boy was enthroned at a ceremony in Lhasa in December, the whereabouts of the Dalai Lama's choice remaining unknown until mid-1996, when China's ambassador to the UN in Geneva admitted that the boy was in detention in Beijing. There were violent confrontations in Tibet in May 1996, following the banning of any public display of images of the Dalai Lama. During the latter part of 1996 visits by the Dalai Lama to the United Kingdom and Australia aroused further protests from the Chinese Government. A series of minor explosions during 1996 culminated in late December with the detonation of a powerful bomb outside a government office in Lhasa, which injured several people. The attack was denounced by the Dalai Lama. In an unprecedented admission, the Chinese Government acknowledged the existence of a terrorist problem in Tibet.

The Chinese leadership condemned the Dalai Lama's visit to Taiwan in March 1997, despite assurances that he was visiting in his capacity as a spiritual leader. In May it was reported that Chadrel Rinpoche, an official in the Tibetan administration and one of Tibet's most senior monks, had been sentenced to six years' imprisonment for allegedly revealing information to the Dalai Lama about Beijing's search for the new Panchen Lama. The USA's decision in mid-1997 to appoint a special co-ordinator for Tibet was criticized by the Chinese authorities. In October the Dalai Lama appealed to the Chinese Government to reopen negotiations over the status of Tibet, confirming that he did not seek full independence for the region. In December the Geneva-based International Commission of Jurists (see p. 355) published a report accusing China of suppressing nationalist dissent in Tibet and attempting to extinguish Tibetan culture, and appealed for a referendum, under the auspices of the UN, to decide the territory's future status.

In April 1998 China agreed to allow envoys of the European Union (EU) to make a one-week investigatory visit to Tibet. Later that month in New Delhi, India, Thupten Ngodup, one of six Tibetan exiles who had been engaged in a hunger strike for 49 days, died after setting himself alight as security forces attempted forcibly to transport the protesters to hospital to end their hunger strike. The hunger strikers had declared their intention of starving themselves to death unless the UN agreed to debate the issue of Tibet in the General Assembly, to appoint a special rapporteur to investigate human rights violations and to oversee a referendum on independence. The protest was arranged by the Tibetan Youth Congress (TYC), a movement advocating independence for Tibet. In May 1998 the EU adopted two resolutions relating to China, condemning the sale of organs of executed prisoners and calling for a UN committee to investigate the transactions and, furthermore, urging the UN to appoint a rapporteur for Tibet issues.

During his visit to China and Hong Kong in late June 1998 (see below), the US President, Bill Clinton, discussed Tibet with Chinese leaders, with the Dalai Lama's support. Beijing proclaimed its readiness to open negotiations if the Dalai Lama first declared both Tibet and Taiwan to be inalienable parts of China. This statement was repeated regularly during 1998. In October the Dalai Lama admitted that since the 1960s he had received US $1.7m. annually from the Central Intelligence Agency (CIA) to support the Tibetan separatist movement. Whilst visiting the USA in early November, the Dalai Lama had an unofficial meeting with Bill Clinton, thereby angering the Chinese authorities. Later that month the Dalai Lama requested informal talks with the Chinese leadership before he would make any unilateral statement. In December, in Paris, he was presented with a human rights prize by the French Prime Minister.

In January 1999 a new US special co-ordinator for Tibetan affairs was appointed, amid opposition from China. Earlier in the month TYC activists had attempted to storm the Chinese embassy in New Delhi and had burnt Chinese flags outside the building to protest against China's occupation of Tibet. In May the Dalai Lama visited the United Kingdom and met the British Prime Minister, Tony Blair. In order to avoid criticism from Beijing, it was reported that Blair had received the religious leader in a spiritual capacity. The World Bank provoked US anger in the following month, when it approved a loan to settle 58,000 Chinese farmers on land in western China considered by Tibetans to be their own. Tibetan support groups feared that the project would aid China's policy of diminishing the minority Tibetan population living in the region. It was agreed that no funds would be disbursed until an independent panel had ensured that the plan conformed to World Bank rules. In August Sino-US relations deteriorated further following the injury in police custody of a US academic and human rights activist who had been detained whilst conducting an unofficial investigation into the project; he was reportedly released and repatriated in September. The project was abandoned in July 2000, owing to the perceived excessively demanding nature of the World Bank's conditions.

In January 2000 the Chinese Government was embarrassed by the flight of Tibet's second most important Lama, the Karmapa, from Tibet to Dharamsala. Frequent requests by him to be permitted to visit his guru in India had been ignored. The Karmapa, who had, unusually, been recognized both by the Dalai Lama and by Beijing, had previously been rewarded by the latter for his perceived loyalty to the Chinese regime. Reports that the Karmapa's parents had been detained by the Tibetan authorities, following anti-China remarks by their son, were

denied. The Karmapa's request for political asylum placed the Indian authorities in a difficult position; India maintained close contact with both the Dalai Lama and with Beijing, but by the end of 2000 no decision had been reached. Meanwhile, there was some discord between followers of the Karmapa and other Tibetans, the former proclaiming their leader to be the Dalai Lama's equal. Furthermore, three other people staked their claim to be the real Karmapa. In January 2000 in Lhasa, Soinam Puncog, a two-year-old boy selected by the Chinese authorities but rejected by followers of the Dalai Lama, was ordained as the new Reting Lama.

China continued to exert great influence over the Dalai Lama's movements in 2000. Following the UN's decision to exclude him from a summit meeting of world religious leaders in August, in October the Republic of Korea refused to grant a visa to the Dalai Lama, on the grounds that it would be 'inappropriate'. Reports confirmed that Beijing had expressed strong opposition to a trip planned by the Dalai Lama for the following month. In April, however, despite warnings from Beijing, Japan had granted the Dalai Lama a visa to lecture at a Buddhist college. He also made his first-ever visit to Northern Ireland, to promote peace, in October 2000. Also in October, the newly appointed Party Secretary for Tibet, Guo Jinlong, announced that he would continue to oppose separatism, but would open up the region's economy. In November the head of a visiting EU delegation urged Beijing to appoint the Dalai Lama as governor of Tibet, a suggestion that was immediately rebuffed. In December contact was resumed between the Dalai Lama and the Chinese authorities, following a visit to Beijing by the former's brother. Meanwhile, in October in Lhasa, following a bomb explosion attributed to the continuing campaign of resistance to Chinese rule, security was increased, and foreign tourists were confined to their hotels.

In February 2001 Beijing announced plans for the first railway link between Tibet and the rest of China. The new railway, linking Lhasa with Golmud, Qinghai Province, was to be 1,118 km long and take more than 10 years to build, at a cost of US $2,500m. Construction began at the end of June. The project was one of several planned for the region, aimed at raising the level of development, including a massive expansion of Lhasa through public building projects, and five new airports. Also in February, the Australian Minister of Health, Michael Wooldridge, visited Tibet while touring China, the first visit to the region by an Australian minister in 13 years. In early April the Dalai Lama paid a 10-day visit to Taiwan, which was largely religious in nature, but he none the less met President Chen Shui-bian and addressed the legislature, thus antagonizing Beijing, which opposed any co-operation between its two principal 'renegade provinces'. Later in the month, the Karmapa spoke for the first time about his escape from China in the previous year. In late May the CCP organized commemorative ceremonies in Tibet to mark the 50th anniversary of the 'peaceful liberation' (the signing of the 1951 treaty) of the region, with official media praising the 'great social progress' made since China's assumption of power. On the anniversary the Dalai Lama had a meeting with US President George W. Bush in Washington, DC, greatly angering Beijing.

In early July 2001 Beijing's chosen Panchen Lama visited Shanghai and Zhejiang Province at the invitation of Beijing, the trip being regarded as a move to promote him as an alternative Tibetan leader to the Dalai Lama. Later in the month, Beijing announced that it would build a monument to commemorate Chinese rule over Tibet in the grounds of the Potala Palace, the former winter residence of the Dalai Lama. The monument was completed in early 2002. In early August 2001 the Chinese Government declared that, upon the death of the current incumbent, it would appoint its own Dalai Lama, thus disregarding traditional Tibetan procedures for selecting the spiritual leader; the plan was condemned by the Tibetan government-in-exile. Later in August Chinese troops seized the largest Tibetan monastery, Serthar, and forced thousands of monks and nuns to denounce the Dalai Lama. Many of the buildings there were reportedly destroyed. At the same time, Beijing refused to free Chadrel Rinpoche, imprisoned since 1997 (see above). Also in late August, Chinese geologists announced the discovery of massive new petroleum and gas deposits in a 100-km belt in Tibet's Qiangtang basin. The discovery was expected to encourage foreign oil companies to help build a pipeline from Xinjiang to Shanghai, as well as assist the Government's 'go west' scheme of opening up the western, inner parts of China. Many Tibetans feared, however, that the massive development schemes, and the considerable influx of Han Chinese from neighbouring provinces (who dominated the new economy), were irreversibly transforming the character and culture of the region.

In November 2001 the Chinese Government announced the creation of a new enterprise zone in Lhasa, and issued a document outlining its main achievements during its 50 years of rule in Tibet. The issue of the document coincided with a visit to China by the UN High Commissioner for Human Rights, Mary Robinson, who urged Chinese leaders not to use the USA's 'war on terrorism' as a pretext for suppressing ethnic minorities.

In January 2002 Beijing released Ngawang Choephel, a Tibetan music scholar serving an 18-year sentence on spying charges, and in April the authorities released, on medical grounds, Tanag Jigme Sangpo, who had first been imprisoned in 1965, and again since 1983, for campaigning against Chinese rule. He was believed to be the country's longest-serving political prisoner, having endured a total of 32 years in detention. Both releases constituted apparent goodwill gestures to the USA. Tanag Jigme Sangpo subsequently sought medical treatment in the USA in mid-July 2002. In February, meanwhile, Beijing reiterated its request to the Dalai Lama for him to return from exile. In June the Party Secretary for Tibet, Guo Jinlong, visited Australia and met the Minister of Foreign Affairs, Alexander Downer, amid criticism of the latter for his refusal to meet the Dalai Lama. Also in June, CCP officials in Tibet formally welcomed Gyaltsen Norbu as the new Panchen Lama. In July the Dalai Lama announced the privatization of the Government-in-exile's businesses in India and Nepal, owing to their poor performance. However, in August the Russian authorities refused him a visa to visit three traditionally Buddhist Republics of the Russian Federation—Buryatiya, Tyva, and Kalmykiya—as Moscow sought to avoid displeasing Beijing.

In September 2002 exiled Tibetan officials travelled to China (including Tibet—the first such visit there since 1985) in a 16-day tour arranged by the elder brother of the Dalai Lama, Gyalo Thondup, who had visited Beijing in August. During the tour, the Dalai Lama's envoy to the USA, Lodi Gyaltsen Gyari, and the envoy to Europe, Kelsang Gyaltsen, held the first meetings with government officials since 1993, amid hopes of a more conciliatory attitude by Beijing. After returning to India, Gyari spoke favourably of the exchange. In late October the authorities freed Ngawang Sangdrol, a Tibetan nun whose three-year sentence in 1992 had been extended until 2011. In early November the Dalai Lama finally visited Mongolia, although the Chinese Government denounced the visit. Meanwhile, in the middle of that month, Beijing revealed that the Dalai Lama's chosen Panchen Lama, in detention since 1995, was 'very happy' and living with his family in Tibet. In December 2002, however, the authorities sentenced to death two Tibetans for their alleged role in a series of bombings in Sichuan Province during 1998–2002. The two men were from Ganzi, a region of Sichuan which had a Tibetan majority and had once been part of the territory. In late January 2003 10 more people were arrested in connection with the bombings, and one of the two men sentenced earlier was executed.

Anti-Chinese sentiment in the Xinjiang Uygur Autonomous Region intensified in the 1990s, resulting in the initiation of a new, often brutal, campaign by the authorities to repress the Islamist separatist movement, whose goal was to establish an independent 'East Turkestan'. The region had been conquered by the Chinese Manchus in the mid-18th century, and it had subsequently enjoyed brief periods of independence. However, Han Chinese had, for decades after 1949, been encouraged or forced to move to the region by Beijing, thereby reducing the proportion of the indigenous Uygur population and compounding resentment. The Han Chinese and the Uygur communities often had little contact with one another, with the Han occupying the higher-status jobs, and forming majorities in the cities. Separatist movements such as the Xinjiang Liberation Front and the Uygur Liberation Organization (ULO) often had support of the Uygur diaspora in Kyrgyzstan and Uzbekistan. Suppression of separatism increased in 1996, following a number of violent incidents. Hundreds of people were detained for their part in rioting and bomb attacks, and many were subsequently executed or imprisoned. Reports in late 1997 indicated that there had been a renewal of armed separatist activity, in which more than 300 people had been killed. In January 1998 13 people were executed in Xinjiang, allegedly for robbery and murder, although unofficial reports suggested that those executed were Muslim separatist demonstrators. Muslim

separatists were believed to be responsible for an incendiary device on a bus in Wuhan in February, which killed 16 people. Two leading activists, Yibulayin Simayi and Abudureyimu Aisha, were executed in January 1999. Detentions continued during the year, and a further 10 separatists were reportedly executed at the end of May. Three Muslims were sentenced to death in September for participating in the separatist campaign, whilst six others received long prison sentences. In October 2000 Abduhelil Abdulmejit, a leading organizer of resistance to Chinese rule in Xinjiang who had been imprisoned three years previously, was reported to have died of pneumonia while in custody; international groups alleged that he had been tortured and murdered.

Meanwhile, the NATO attacks on Yugoslavia in March–June 1999 greatly alarmed military planners in Beijing, who feared that the USA might carry out a similar operation in Xinjiang, on the grounds of humanitarian intervention on behalf of the Uygur separatists. The region was strategically important to China owing to its petroleum and gas reserves and its proximity to the increasingly important Caspian Sea-Central Asian region. China planned to build a 4,200-km pipeline from Xinjiang to Shanghai, thereby diversifying its sources of petroleum. A number of Western oil companies had shown interest in the project in 2000–01, and construction was due to begin in late 2001. Stability in Xinjiang was crucial to China's 'go west' programme of developing the country's remote inner regions.

During 2001 the authorities continued the 'strike hard' campaign against separatists, with multiple executions reported. In early August the PLA conducted large-scale military exercises involving 50,000 troops in the region. China's fears of Islamist separatism were heightened after the terrorist attacks on New York and Washington, DC, USA, on 11 September 2001, and Beijing stated that as many as 1,000 Uygur Islamist fighters had been trained in terrorist camps in Afghanistan operated by the al-Qa'ida network of the Saudi-born dissident, Osama bin Laden. In late September Chinese troops began anti-guerrilla operations in the Afghan border region of Xinjiang, aimed at preventing Islamist infiltration. International human rights groups, however, feared that Beijing would use the pretext of fighting terrorism to increase repression, and in November the Minister of Foreign Affairs, Tang Jiaxuan, likened China's anti-separatist campaign to the USA's 'war on terrorism'. In December, following the collapse of Afghanistan's ruling Taliban, China urged the USA to surrender captured Uygur Islamist fighters; the USA refused to comply, stating that it did not view the separatists as terrorists. At the same time, Jiang warned that religion should not be used to challenge the CCP or to undermine China's unity. In January 2002 Beijing released a new report alleging links between the separatists and Osama bin Laden, in an apparent bid to win international approval for its anti-separatist activities.

In March 2002 Amnesty International reported that thousands of Muslim Uygurs had been detained since 11 September 2001, and that up to 8,000 had been given 'political education' courses. In June 2002 the authorities announced that from September Xinjiang University would no longer teach courses in the Uygur language (for 50 years students had had a choice of studying in Uygur or Mandarin). The authorities claimed that this would raise the standards of education for Uygurs, but the latter viewed the changes as an attack on their culture and identity. In late August the USA designated the East Turkestan Islamic Movement a terrorist group and 'froze' the organization's assets, in a conciliatory gesture towards Beijing. The UN also added the organization to its list of terrorist organizations in September.

In September 1984, following protracted negotiations, China reached agreement with the British Government over the terms of the future administration of Hong Kong upon the territory's return to Chinese sovereignty, scheduled for 1 July 1997. In 1985 a Basic Law Drafting Committee (BLDC), including 25 representatives from Hong Kong, was established in Beijing to prepare a new Basic Law (Constitution) for Hong Kong, which was duly approved by the NPC in April 1990. In September 1991, during a visit to China by the British Prime Minister, a Memorandum of Understanding on the construction of a new airport in Hong Kong was signed. Relations between China and the United Kingdom were strained in 1992 by the announcement of ambitious plans for democratic reform in Hong Kong prior to 1997. In December 1993 China declared that it would regard as null and void any laws enacted by the territory's Legislative Council (which, it was subsequently confirmed, would be disbanded in 1997). In July 1995 the Chief Secretary of Hong Kong, Anson Chan, confirmed that she had had clandestine meetings with Chinese officials during a three-day visit to Beijing. In October Qian Qichen, the Chinese Vice-Premier and Minister of Foreign Affairs, visited London for discussions with the British Prime Minister and his Foreign Secretary. In January 1996 the 150-member Preparatory Committee of the Hong Kong Special Administrative Region (SAR) was formally established in Beijing, in succession to the Preliminary Working Committee (PWC), which had been formed in July 1993 to study issues relating to the transfer of sovereignty. The new body duly appointed a 400-member Selection Committee, responsible for the choice of Hong Kong's future Chief Executive. In December 1996 the Selection Committee chose Tung Chee-hwa as the SAR's first Chief Executive and elected the 60 members of the Provisional Legislative Council (PLC), which held its first meeting in January 1997. Objections from the United Kingdom and the USA to Chinese proposals to abolish the Legislative Council, and to repeal human rights legislation, were dismissed by China.

The transfer of Hong Kong from British to Chinese sovereignty was effected at midnight on 30 June 1997, whereupon some 4,000 PLA troops were deployed in the territory. In December 1997 36 deputies from Hong Kong were directly elected to the Ninth NPC in Beijing. Elections for the SAR's new Legislative Council took place in May 1998. The question of the right of abode in the territory for mainland-born children and the ultimate referral of the matter to the Standing Committee of the NPC caused tensions during 1999. Meanwhile, following the NATO bombing of the Chinese embassy in Yugoslavia in May 1999 (see below), US military aircraft and ships were temporarily denied access to Hong Kong. In April 2000 there were fears for the freedom of the Hong Kong media following a warning by Beijing against reporting any remarks advocating Taiwanese independence. In March 2001 the Hong Kong Government introduced the Chief Executive Election Bill, interpreting the powers of the central Government in Beijing to remove the Chief Executive and providing detailed arrangements for the next election for the latter. The Bill was passed in July 2001, and was widely seen as a set-back for Hong Kong's democratic process. Tung was re-elected unopposed on 24 March 2002, and in June appointed a new, cabinet-style expanded Executive Council, under new powers accorded to him. In June 2001, meanwhile, Tung declared Falun Gong to be an 'evil cult'. The sect had staged a number of protests in the SAR, which had displeased the Beijing authorities. Meanwhile, in late 2002 plans were under way for the introduction of new anti-subversion laws, which critics feared would undermine the 'one country, two systems' model and give Beijing greater control over Hong Kong's affairs. (See the chapter on Hong Kong for further information.)

In June 1986 China and Portugal opened formal negotiations for the return of the Portuguese overseas territory of Macao to full Chinese sovereignty. In January 1987 it was agreed that this would take place in December 1999. The agreement was based upon the 'one country, two systems' principle, which had formed the basis of China's negotiated settlement regarding the return of Hong Kong. In March 1993 the final draft of the Basic Law for Macao was approved by the NPC. In May 1995 China proposed the swift establishment of a preparatory working committee to facilitate the transfer of sovereignty. Cordial relations were maintained, and the Portuguese Minister of Foreign Affairs visited Beijing in February 1996. The two sides agreed to accelerate the pace of work of the Sino-Portuguese Joint Liaison Group (JLG). In January 1997 the Chinese Vice-Premier and Minister of Foreign Affairs, Qian Qichen, travelled to Portugal for discussions. Confidence in the future of Macao was reiterated. Following a series of murders, bombings and arson attacks in Macao, Qian Qichen announced that China would station an 'appropriate' number of troops in the territory to help combat organized crime and ensure public security upon its resumption of sovereignty in December 1999.

In April 1999 the 200-member Selection Committee, which was comprised entirely of residents of the territory and which was to be responsible for the appointment of members of Macao's post-1999 government, was established in Beijing. In the following month Edmund Ho, a banker and a member of the legislature since 1988, was elected the first Chief Executive of Macao. China resumed sovereignty of the territory at midnight on 19 December 1999, whereupon Ho was duly inaugurated and the PLA garrison was established. In general, local reaction was

favourable, as it was hoped that China would succeed, where Portugal had failed, in restoring public security. President Jiang Zemin visited Macao in December 2000 to mark the first anniversary of the territory's reversion to Chinese sovereignty, and praised the local administration. Ho visited Beijing in March 2001 to attend the fourth session of the Ninth NPC. During 2001 and 2002 Beijing, Hong Kong, and Macao increased co-operation in combating cross-border crime. In March 2002 a new representative office of the Macao SAR was opened in Beijing, and in July Beijing dispatched a new representative to the territory. Macao continued to develop economic relations with several provinces on the mainland. (See the chapter on Macao for further information.)

Taiwan has repeatedly rejected China's proposals for reunification, whereby the island would become a 'special administrative region' along the lines of Hong Kong and Macao, and has sought reunification under its own terms. China has never relinquished sovereignty over the island, however, and has repeatedly threatened to use military force against Taiwan should it formally declare itself independent of the mainland. During the early 1990s relations improved as both sides held meetings of their respective cross-Straits organizations, the mainland's Association for Relations Across the Taiwan Straits (ARATS, established in 1991) and Taiwan's Straits Exchange Foundation (SEF, established in 1990). However, in early 1996 China conducted massive military exercises near Taiwan, coinciding with the island's first-ever presidential elections. Taiwan refused to be intimidated, and tensions later eased. Beijing became increasingly angry, however, at Taiwan's insistence on state-to-state negotiations, and the island's possible inclusion in a US-led Theater Missile Defense (TMD) system. China responded by increasing its missile build-up in coastal regions facing Taiwan. In early 2000 China warned that it would invade Taiwan if it indefinitely postponed reunification talks, and reacted negatively to the election of Chen Shui-bian as President, amid fears that a new, Taiwanese identity was developing. By 2000 the island's politics had increasingly become polarized between 'native Taiwanese' (approximately 65% of the population) and mainlanders and their offspring (approximately 35% of the population). A PLA military document in late 2000 added two additional possible pretexts for invasion, namely a declaration of independence or occupation by a third country. Nevertheless, despite frequent political disputes, cross-Straits business ties flourished as Taiwanese investment continued to flow into the mainland. In late 2001 President Chen removed long-standing investment restrictions with the mainland, marking a new 'aggressive opening' policy. His critics feared that this would divert jobs from Taiwan and make the island too economically dependent on a hostile country. Beijing, however, remained unenthusiastic on the issue of full direct transport links unless Taiwan recognized the 'One China' principle, but by 2002 was showing greater flexibility towards the island. Relations were often volatile, however, with official Beijing media referring to Chen as a 'troublemaker' in May, while Chen referred to the mainland's threats as a form of 'terrorism' in September. Chen had, in August 2002, supported the notion of a referendum to determine the island's future. In January 2003 China permitted several Taiwanese airliners on charter flights to land in China for the first time in over 50 years. However, the operation of full cross-Straits transport links remained unlikely in the immediate future. (See the chapter on Taiwan for further information.)

In the early years of the People's Republic, China was dependent on the USSR for economic and military aid, and Chinese planning was based on the Soviet model, with highly centralized control. From 1955, however, Mao Zedong set out to develop a distinctively Chinese form of socialism. As a result, the USSR withdrew all technical aid to China in August 1960. Chinese hostility to the USSR increased, in what became known as the 'Sino-Soviet Split', and was aggravated by territorial disputes, and by the Soviet invasion of Afghanistan and the Soviet-supported Vietnamese invasion of Cambodia in the late 1970s. Sino-Soviet relations remained strained until 1987, when representatives of the two countries signed a partial agreement concerning the exact demarcation of the disputed common border at the Amur River. The withdrawal of Soviet troops from Afghanistan (completed in February 1989) and Viet Nam's assurance that it would end its military presence in Cambodia by September 1989 resulted in a further *rapprochement*. In May 1989 a full summit meeting was held in Beijing, at which normal state and party relations between China and the USSR were formally restored. During the next two years senior Chinese officials visited the USSR. In December 1991, upon the dissolution of the USSR, China recognized the newly independent states of the former union. The President of Russia, Boris Yeltsin, visited China in December 1992. In May 1994, in Beijing, Premier Li Peng and his Russian counterpart signed various co-operation agreements. In September President Jiang Zemin travelled to Moscow, the first visit to Russia by a Chinese Head of State since 1957. The two sides reached agreement on the formal demarcation of the western section of the border (the eastern section having been delimited in May 1991), and each pledged not to aim nuclear missiles at the other. In June 1995 the Chinese Premier paid an official visit to Russia, where several bilateral agreements were signed.

Sino-Russian relations continued to improve, and in April 1996 in Beijing Presidents Jiang and Yeltsin signed a series of agreements, envisaging the development of closer co-operation in areas such as energy, space research, environmental protection, and the combating of organized crime. Together with their counterparts from Kazakhstan, Kyrgyzstan and Tajikistan, the two Presidents also signed a treaty aimed at reducing tension along their respective borders. Progress on the Sino-Russian border question, and also on matters such as trade, was made during the Chinese Premier's visit to Moscow in December 1996. A further treaty on military co-operation and border demilitarization was signed by the Presidents of China, Russia, Kazakhstan, Kyrgyzstan and Tajikistan in April 1997, during a visit by President Jiang Zemin to Russia. Presidents Jiang and Yeltsin affirmed their commitment to building a strategic, co-operative partnership, and a Sino-Russian committee on friendship, peace and development was established. Progress on the Sino-Russian border issue culminated in the signing of an agreement, during President Yeltsin's visit to Beijing in November, which formally ended the territorial dispute.

In May 1998 a direct telephone link was established between Jiang Zemin and President Yeltsin of Russia. In November, in Moscow, representatives from Russia, China and the Democratic People's Republic of Korea signed an inter-governmental agreement on the delimitation of their borders along the Tumannaya River. Relations continued to improve between China and Russia in 1999. In February 11 agreements on bilateral economic and trade co-operation were signed during a visit to Russia by Zhu Rongji. In June, following a visit to China by the Russian Minister of Foreign Affairs, it was announced that a final accord on the demarcation of a common border between the two countries had been agreed after seven years of negotiations. The relevant legal documents were signed in December. During a summit meeting of China, Russia, Kazakhstan, Kyrgyzstan and Tajikistan (collectively known as the 'Shanghai Five'—see below) in the Kyrgyz capital, Bishkek, agreements were signed on the China–Kazakhstan–Kyrgyzstan and the Chinese–Kyrgyz borders. In November it was announced that all Chinese–Kazakh border issues had been completely resolved.

Following the resignation of Boris Yeltsin as Russian President in December 1999, his successor, Vladimir Putin, confirmed his commitment to maintaining and improving links with China. A 'significant upgrading' in Sino-Russian relations occurred during Putin's visit to Beijing in July 2000, when the two countries issued a joint statement condemning US plans for the deployment of a missile defence system (see above). Presidents Jiang and Putin expressed fears of a new nuclear arms race, should installation of the system be implemented. A number of bilateral agreements were also signed during the summit meeting. NPC Chairman Li Peng visited Russia in September 2000, mainly to discuss economic co-operation, particularly in energy issues. In November the Russian Prime Minister, Mikhail Kasyanov, visited China and concluded the sale of five A-50 early warning aircraft and two advanced naval destroyers to the Chinese armed forces.

In July 2001 Presidents Jiang and Putin signed a new 20-year Sino-Russian 'Good-neighbourly Treaty of Friendship and Co-operation' in Moscow and reaffirmed their opposition to the USA's plans for a National Missile Defence (NMD) system. The new treaty was a 'strategic partnership' rather than a military alliance, however, and was not officially aimed at any third countries. The treaty also agreed to further cultural, economic and scientific co-operation, and stated that neither country had any territorial claims on the other—the latter had become an important issue in the 1990s as an increasing number of illegal Chinese labourers had settled in the Russian Far East, raising fears in Russia that China would seek to reclaim territories

ceded to Russia in the 19th century. Following the summit meeting, it was announced that China would purchase as many as 38 advanced Su-30 fighter aircraft from Russia, valued at US $2,000m. Since the 1990s Russia had sold between 70 and 100 advanced fighter aircraft, many of which were jointly produced by the two countries in Shenyang. In August the Russian gas monopoly, Gazprom, indicated that it would help build new pipelines connecting Siberia with northern China. At the same time, a partially-completed former Soviet aircraft carrier, *Varyag* (the third to have been purchased from Russia), sailed from the Black Sea to China via the Bosporus waterway. Although officially to be used as a floating casino, China was believed to be interested in using the *Varyag* design to build its own aircraft carrier. In September Prime Minister Zhu Rongji visited Russia and signed several trade agreements, and in late October Vice-President Hu Jintao visited Moscow, where he met Putin.

In January 2002 Russia announced that it would build two new advanced warships for the Chinese navy by 2006, and in April the Russian state arms export agency, Rosoboroneksport, agreed to sell China hundreds of millions of dollars' worth of air defence missiles and related equipment. In May China and Russia reached agreement on the former's purchase of eight submarines costing US $1,500m., and at the end of that month the Russian Minister of Defence, Sergei Ivanov, visited Beijing and reiterated Moscow's commitment to their strategic partnership, which China feared was being undermined by Russia's increasingly pro-US and pro-NATO posture after the terrorist attacks on the USA in the previous September. However, despite these sales, observers noted that Russia was still withholding certain offensive weapons and technology, in order to keep China dependent on Russian goodwill. None the less, it was estimated that China was purchasing 40% of Russia's annual arms exports, accounting for 20% of total bilateral trade. It was acknowledged, furthermore, that Chinese weapons purchases were keeping key sectors of the Russian military-industrial complex in production, and in some cases new weapons were acquired by the PLA before entering service in Russia. In June both countries submitted a joint proposal to the UN Conference on Disarmament for a new international treaty to ban space weapons—a move aimed at preventing the USA from militarizing outer space. Russian Prime Minister Mikhail Kasyanov visited Beijing in late August to discuss strategic issues, and Putin himself visited China at the beginning of December to meet Jiang Zemin and Hu Jintao. The two countries issued a joint declaration on a number of global strategic issues, particularly urging a peaceful resolution to the USA's diplomatic crisis with Iraq, and for the USA and North Korea to normalize relations, with the latter abandoning its nuclear weapons programme. The two countries also sought to increase bilateral trade and economic co-operation, although there were disagreements regarding plans for a pipeline that would export Russian oil to Daqing, in north-eastern China, the route length and costs being the inhibiting factors.

During the 1990s China steadily consolidated its relations with the former Soviet republics of Central Asia. China shared with these republics a fear of the spread of Islamist terrorism, along with a common interest in developing and transporting the petroleum and gas deposits of the Caspian Sea-Central Asia region. In the late 1990s China, along with Russia, Kazakhstan, Kyrgyzstan, and Tajikistan, established the 'Shanghai Five' group (renamed the Shanghai Co-operation Organization—SCO at their annual meeting in June 2001, when Uzbekistan became the sixth member). The grouping aimed to stabilize the region in order to promote development. Both China and Russia hoped that the SCO would help counter US influence in Central Asia, but at a meeting of SCO ministers of foreign affairs in January 2002, it had become clear that following the US attack on Afghanistan in late 2001, the organization lacked cohesiveness and influence. During 2000–01 China also gradually began improving relations with the Taliban regime in Afghanistan, signing several economic and technical agreements in the expectation that the Taliban would cease supporting Islamist Uygur fighters in Xinjiang. Following the collapse of the Taliban regime in late 2001, the new Afghan Prime Minister, Hamid Karzai, visited Beijing in January 2002 to discuss Chinese aid towards the reconstruction of his country. Meanwhile, China strengthened its relations with Kyrgyzstan during 2002. In May of that year Kyrgyzstan ratified a 1999 border treaty which ceded nearly 95,000 ha of disputed territory to China, and in October 2002 the two countries staged their first-ever joint military exercises, under the auspices of the SCO. In December 2002 the President of Kazakhstan, Nursultan Nazarbayev, visited Beijing, where he reached an agreement to construct a pipeline from Kazakhstan to western China.

During the 1970s there was an improvement in China's relations with the West and Japan. Almost all Western countries had recognized the Government of the People's Republic as the sole legitimate government of China, and had consequently withdrawn recognition from the 'Republic of China', which had been confined to Taiwan since 1949. For many years, however, the USA refused to recognize the People's Republic, regarding the Taiwan administration as the legitimate Chinese government. In February 1972 President Richard Nixon of the USA visited the People's Republic and acknowledged that 'Taiwan is a part of China'. In January 1979 the USA recognized the People's Republic and severed diplomatic relations with Taiwan.

China's relations with the USA improved steadily throughout the 1980s. Following the suppression of the pro-democracy movement in 1989, however, all high-level government exchanges were suspended, and the export of weapons to China was prohibited. In November 1990 President George Bush received the Chinese Minister of Foreign Affairs in Washington, thereby resuming contact at the most senior level. In August 1993 the USA imposed sanctions on China, in response to the latter's sales of technology for nuclear-capable missiles to Pakistan, in alleged violation of international non-proliferation guidelines. The sanctions remained in force until October 1994. In October 1995 Sino-US relations appeared to improve when, at a meeting in New York, Presidents Jiang Zemin and Bill Clinton agreed to resume dialogue on various issues, the USA reaffirming its commitment to the 'one China' policy. In November the two countries reached agreement on the resumption of bilateral military contacts. During 1996 there were several causes of renewed Sino-US tension, mainly related to various trade issues, including China's prospective membership of the WTO.

Another obstacle to good relations between China and the USA is the question of Taiwan, and, in particular, the continued sale of US armaments to Taiwan. Sino-US relations deteriorated in September 1992, upon President Bush's announcement of the sale of fighter aircraft to Taiwan. China condemned the USA's decision, in September 1994, to expand its official links with Taiwan. In June 1995, following President Clinton's highly controversial decision to grant him a visa, President Lee of Taiwan embarked upon an unofficial visit to the USA, where he met members of the US Congress. The visit so outraged Beijing that the Chinese ambassador to Washington was withdrawn. In March 1996, as China began a new series of missile tests, the USA stationed two naval convoys east of Taiwan, its largest deployment in Asia since 1975. President Clinton's decision to sell anti-aircraft missiles and other defensive weapons to Taiwan was condemned by China.

In October 1999 the Taiwan Security Enhancement Act (TSEA), establishing direct military ties between the USA and Taiwan, was adopted, albeit in modified form, by the International Relations Committee of the US House of Representatives, despite opposition from the Clinton Administration. Reaction from the People's Republic was unfavourable, and its displeasure increased in February 2000 when the House of Representatives overwhelmingly approved the Act, the consideration of which was postponed by the US Senate in April 2000 at the behest of Taiwanese President-elect Chen Shui-bian (in order not to antagonize Beijing during the sensitive period preceding his inauguration). In the same month the US Government announced that it had decided to defer the sale of four naval destroyers to Taiwan, although it was prepared to supply long-range radar and medium-range air-to-air missiles.

Negotiations on the issue of human rights, the USA's growing trade deficit with China, and China's proposed entry into the WTO were the focus of Sino-US relations in 1997. President Jiang Zemin visited the USA in October 1997, the first such visit by a Chinese Head of State since 1985. Vocal public criticism of China's failure to observe human rights, particularly with regard to Tibet, was widespread in the USA, but the Clinton Administration defended its policy of engagement with China, warning of the dangers of isolation. Measures to reduce the trade deficit with China and to accelerate China's entry into the WTO were negotiated. In addition, the Chinese Government agreed to control the export of nuclear-related materials, in return for the removal of sanctions on the sale of nuclear-reactor technology to the People's Republic. Increased military co-oper-

ation and the holding of annual summit meetings were also agreed.

In April 1998 the US Secretary of State, Madeleine Albright, visited China to prepare for an official visit by President Clinton in late June and early July. Prior to his visit it was announced that China's most favoured nation (subsequently restyled normal trading relations) status would be renewed for a further year. Clinton continued to be criticized for his constructive engagement policy, and it was also alleged that the PLA had illegally funded Clinton's re-election campaign in 1996. The visit was a diplomatic success, notable for an unprecedented live broadcast in which Clinton and Jiang debated such issues as human rights, freedom of speech and the 1989 events in Tiananmen Square. In response to China's pledge in March 1998 to sign the International Covenant on Civil and Political Rights, the USA announced that it would abandon its sponsorship of an annual resolution of the UN Commission on Human Rights condemning China for human rights abuses. The decision, which followed a similar commitment by the EU in February, was deplored by human rights organizations.

Sino-US relations deteriorated significantly during 1999, owing to continued differences over China's human rights record, Tibet, trade relations, espionage and US plans for a missile defence system for Asia. During an official visit by Albright to the People's Republic at the end of February, she reiterated US disapproval at the suppression of organized dissent in China and urged the release of a number of political prisoners (although emphasizing that the USA would continue its policy of separating human rights issues from trade relations). Further acrimonious exchanges took place concerning demands from the US Congress that the proposed US TMD system, which was principally designed to protect Japan and the Republic of Korea, be extended to include Taiwan. During a visit to the USA by Zhu Rongji in April, despite the Chinese Premier's offer of a number of economic concessions in return for a bilateral trade agreement to facilitate WTO entry, no agreement was reached. At a final press conference, however, the two sides affirmed their commitment to signing an agreement by the end of 1999. Although China suspended bilateral negotiations in May, following the NATO bombing of the Chinese embassy in Yugoslavia (see below), China's normal trade relations status was renewed in July. China agreed to resume talks in September, and in November (following 13 years of negotiations) a bilateral trade agreement was concluded, which would allow for China's eventual accession to the WTO. The agreement with the USA facilitated the conclusion of bilateral trade agreements with the EU and other WTO members during 2000.

It was widely believed that the failure to reach a trade agreement in April 1999 was, in part, due to popular US anti-Chinese sentiment, which had been exacerbated by US claims in March that a Chinese spy had stolen important nuclear data during the 1980s. A further disclosure of Chinese espionage (which had allegedly taken place in 1995), involving information relevant to the construction of a 'neutron' bomb emerged during Zhu's visit to the USA. Beijing dismissed the reports as unfounded. The findings of a select committee of the US House of Representatives, which were released in May, confirmed that Chinese spies had systematically stolen US nuclear technology from the late 1970s until the mid-1990s. China denounced the document as a plot to encourage anti-Chinese sentiment and to deflect attention from the bombing of the Chinese embassy in Yugoslavia, which had occurred earlier that month. China had vigorously opposed the NATO bombing of Yugoslavia, during which the Chinese embassy had been severely damaged, leading to the deaths of three people and injuring 20 others. US apologies and explanations were rejected, and violent popular attacks on the US and British diplomatic missions in Beijing, allegedly encouraged by the Government, ensued. Bilateral relations improved slightly in July, when the USA agreed to pay US $4.5m. in compensation to the families of those killed and injured by the bombing, leading to the lifting of a ban on US military access to Hong Kong. In December compensation of US $28m. was agreed for damage caused to the Chinese embassy building, and in April 2000 the CIA dismissed one intelligence officer and reprimanded six managers for errors that had led to the bombing.

In June 2000 the US Secretary of State, Madeleine Albright, visited China, the most senior US official to do so since the events of May 1999. She criticized the People's Republic's human rights record and urged Beijing to increase its efforts for peace with Taiwan. In retaliation, the Chinese Government insisted that US military aid to Taiwan be immediately suspended. In October the situation improved upon the signature of a law granting China the status of Permanent Normal Trading Relations. In the following month Bill Clinton announced the waiving of penalties against China for supplying missile parts to Iran and Pakistan. Despite an agreement to resume discussions on human rights, tensions relating to China's treatment of dissidents persisted in late 2000.

There were initial fears that the election of George W. Bush to the presidency of the USA would lead to the termination of that country's policy of engagement of recent years. Bush, and his Republican Party in particular, had been critical of Clinton's policy on China, and the incoming President had indicated a harder line towards China during his election campaign, describing it as a 'strategic competitor'. Jiang Zemin, however, pronounced himself optimistic that relations would continue to develop positively. In late February 2001 the US State Department's annual report on human rights stated that China's situation had deteriorated for the third consecutive year, particularly owing to the campaign against Falun Gong practitioners. Beijing responded by releasing, for the second year, its own report on human rights abuses in the USA. The USA at the same time announced that it would sponsor a resolution condemning China's human rights record at a UN meeting in March. Vice-Premier Qian Qichen visited the USA in late March 2001, when he met several senior officials to discuss bilateral ties and urged against the sale of advanced weapons to Taiwan. Relations quickly became strained following the revelation that Senior Colonel Xu Junping of the PLA had defected while visiting the USA in December 2000, becoming the highest-level defector in over a decade. A US-based Chinese scholar, Gao Zhan, was also detained in China along with her husband and son, the latter a US citizen. Gao was accused of spying, although her husband and son were released. Gao was one of several US residents or citizens of Chinese origin who had been detained in China in late 2000 and early 2001.

A major test for Sino-US relations came at the beginning of April 2001, when a US surveillance plane was forced to make an emergency landing at a Chinese airbase on Hainan Island, China, following its collision with a Chinese fighter aircraft over the South China Sea. The Chinese pilot was killed in the incident, while the spy plane's crew of 24 was detained by the Chinese authorities. Intense negotiations followed, and the crew was released on 12 April, after a partial apology from the US ambassador. The aircraft remained on Hainan, however, while the Chinese military studied its technology, and was returned to the USA in components in early July. In the immediate aftermath of the incident, the USA announced that it would sell Taiwan a US $4,000m. armaments 'package', consisting of navy destroyers, anti-submarine aircraft, diesel submarines, amphibious assault vehicles, and surface-to-air missiles and torpedoes. Bush also announced that the USA would do whatever was necessary to defend Taiwan from China. However, the transaction stopped short of selling an advanced combat-radar system, which had been requested by Taiwan. In early May the USA resumed reconnaissance flights near the Chinese coast, and stated that military exchanges with China would be downgraded. At the same time, Beijing reiterated its warnings against the USA's planned NMD system, fearing that it would also protect Taiwan. Despite growing bilateral tensions, business links remained strong between the two countries, and former US President Bill Clinton held a meeting with President Jiang at a business forum in Hong Kong.

Relations between China and the USA were further strained by a meeting between President Bush and the Dalai Lama in Washington, DC, in late May 2001, and by a stopover by Taiwanese President Chen Shui-bian in New York during the same week. However, in early June the USA and China reached new trade accords, facilitating China's entry into the WTO. The USA reacted negatively, however, to the conviction of two US-based Chinese academics, Gao Zhan and Qin Guangguang, for espionage in late July. Gao, Qin and another academic, Li Shaomin, were freed prior to a visit by the US Secretary of State, Colin Powell, who sought to improve bilateral relations after recent tensions. In late August a US aircraft carrier made a visit to Hong Kong; however, two US Navy aircraft carrier battle groups staged a one-day exercise in the South China Sea, coinciding with Chinese military exercises in the Taiwan Straits.

In early September 2001 the USA sought to reduce China's fears over its NMD programme by promising to keep China informed of its development and by abandoning its objections to China's build-up of its nuclear forces, in return for China's acceptance of NMD. The USA also urged China not to transfer ballistic missile technology to countries it considered 'rogue states'. The terrorist attacks against the USA on 11 September 2001 were strongly condemned by China, which pledged co-operation in the US-led 'war on terrorism'. In late October Bush made his first official visit to China to attend the summit meeting of Asia-Pacific Economic Co-operation (APEC), which was dominated by the issue of terrorism. However, the USA did not share Beijing's view that Uygur and Tibetan separatists in Xinjiang and Tibet respectively were terrorists. Although Sino-US relations improved after September, Beijing was increasingly concerned that a long-term US military presence in Central Asia and Pakistan, combined with US troop deployments in the Philippines, would lead to encirclement. Disagreements also remained over the USA's successful NMD interceptor test in December. At the end of 2001, President Bush signed proclamations granting China 'permanent normal trading relations' commencing 1 January 2002, and also ended the Jackson-Vanik regulation preventing communist states from having normal trading relations with the USA if they restricted emigration. In January 2002 it became known that a US-built airliner intended for use by President Jiang Zemin contained numerous listening devices; however, Jiang attempted to diminish the significance of the incident.

US President Bush visited Beijing in late February 2002, and held discussions with Jiang. The talks were candid, but the two sides disagreed on the issues of human rights, China's close ties with Iran, Iraq and North Korea (countries the US President had described as forming an 'axis of evil'), the USA's planned missile defence system, China's export of nuclear technology to Pakistan and US support for Taiwan.

Relations deteriorated somewhat during March 2002, however, as Beijing released for the third consecutive year a report on human rights abuses in the USA, in response to the latter's annual report on the human rights situation in China. More significantly, the Taiwanese Minister of National Defense made the first non-transit visit to the USA since 1979 to attend a private security conference, and it was revealed that the USA maintained contingency plans for a nuclear attack on seven states, including China—a position described by Beijing as 'nuclear blackmail'. China indicated its displeasure by cancelling a planned visit by a US warship to Hong Kong later that month.

In late April 2002 Hu Jintao made his first official visit to the USA, where he held discussions with President Bush, and was introduced to senior governmental and business leaders in preparation for his accession to power as President Jiang's successor. Hu emphasized the importance of Taiwan as a major determinant of bilateral relations. Meanwhile, the former US President, Bill Clinton, made a private visit to China in May. In late June military officials from both countries began discussions to restore bilateral military relations, and in July the US Department of Defense sent a team to China to discover the remains of several US servicemen who had disappeared during Cold War espionage missions. Despite this progress, the release of two new reports in the USA in mid-July highlighted remaining concerns about China. The first report, issued by the US Department of Defense, warned that China was increasing its defence spending in order to intimidate Taiwan. The second, issued by the Congressional US-China Security Review Commission, warned that China had become a leading proliferator of missile technology to countries opposed to the USA, and that US corporations and their investments in China were assisting its emergence as a major economic power, to the detriment of the US trade balance. In late August China introduced the 'Regulations on Export Control of Missiles and Missile-related Items and Technologies' to curb the export of missiles and related technology, in an apparent goodwill gesture to the visiting US Deputy Secretary of State, Richard Armitage. In return, the USA designated the East Turkestan Islamic Movement a terrorist group (see above), in line with Beijing's view.

In late October 2002 Jiang Zemin visited the USA and was hosted by President George W. Bush at his ranch in Texas, a gesture of hospitality conferred on few other world leaders. The major issues discussed were the emerging diplomatic crises over Iraq and North Korea; China opposed any US attack on Iraq without UN authorization, while the USA urged China to put pressure on North Korea to end its nuclear weapons programme. Also on the agenda were the fight against global terrorism and the issue of Taiwan. However, Jiang was keen to avoid confrontation with the USA, regarding the improvement in bilateral relations as a major accomplishment of his presidency. The two leaders also attended the APEC summit meeting in Mexico at the end of October. In late November a US warship arrived in Qingdao, the first such visit since the Hainan aircraft incident of April 2001. In early December 2002, in Washington, DC, China and the USA held their first formal senior-level military talks since Bush assumed office, and days later the commander of US forces in the Pacific, Adm. Thomas Fargo, visited Beijing.

In January 2003 two major US aerospace companies, Hughes Electronics and Boeing Satellite Systems, were charged with illegally providing China with technology that could be used for intercontinental missiles. Both were fined millions of dollars as a punitive measure.

China's relations with Japan began to deteriorate in 1982, after China complained that passages in Japanese school textbooks sought to justify the Japanese invasion of China in 1937. In June 1989 the Japanese Government criticized the Chinese Government's suppression of the pro-democracy movement and suspended (until late 1990) a five-year aid programme to China. In April 1992 Jiang Zemin travelled to Japan, the first visit by the General Secretary of the CCP for nine years. In October Emperor Akihito made the first ever imperial visit to the People's Republic. Japan was one of many countries to criticize China's resumption of underground nuclear testing, at Lop Nor in Xinjiang Province, in October 1993. Relations were seriously strained in May 1994, when the Japanese Minister of Justice referred to the 1937 Nanjing massacre (in which more than 300,000 Chinese citizens were killed by Japanese soldiers) as a 'fabrication', and again in August, when a second Japanese minister was obliged to resign, following further controversial remarks about his country's war record. In May 1995, during a visit to Beijing, the Japanese Prime Minister expressed his deep remorse for the wartime atrocities, but offered no formal apology.

China's continuation of its nuclear-testing programme, in defiance of international opinion, prompted Japan to announce a reduction in financial aid to China. In August 1995 Japan suspended most of its grant aid to China. Following China's conduct of its 'final' nuclear test in July 1996, and its declaration of a moratorium, Japan resumed grant aid in March 1997. (China signed the Comprehensive Nuclear Test Ban Treaty in September 1996.) In July 1996, however, Sino-Japanese relations were affected by a territorial dispute relating to the Diaoyu (or Senkaku) Islands, a group of uninhabited islets in the East China Sea, which China had claimed as its own since ancient times, and Japan since 1895, and to which Taiwan also laid claim. The construction of a lighthouse on one of the islands by a group of Japanese nationalists led to strong protests from the Governments of both the People's Republic and Taiwan. The Japanese Government sought to defuse the tension by withholding recognition of the lighthouse, but did not condemn the right-wing activists responsible.

At a meeting with President Jiang Zemin during the APEC conference in November 1996, the Japanese Prime Minister apologized for Japanese aggression during the Second World War, and emphasized his desire to resolve the dispute over the Diaoyu Islands. In May 1997, following the landing on one of the Islands by a member of the Japanese Diet, the Japanese Government distanced itself from the incident. The US-Japanese agreement on expanded military co-operation caused further tension in Sino-Japanese relations. Nevertheless, Japan's support for China's entry into the WTO remained firm, while China backed Japanese proposals for a permanent seat on the UN Security Council.

Following the normalization of ties between the Japanese Communist Party (JCP) and its Chinese equivalent after a period of more than 30 years, the Chairman of the JCP, Tetsuzo Fuwa, paid an official visit to China in July 1998. During a visit by Jiang Zemin to Japan in November, the first of its kind by a Chinese Head of State, relations were strained when Japan failed to issue an unequivocal apology for its invasion and occupation of China during 1937–45. The summit meeting between Jiang and the Japanese Prime Minister, Keizo Obuchi, was, nevertheless, deemed to have been successful. Keizo Obuchi paid a reciprocal visit to the People's Republic, intended to repair ties, in July 1999, during which he held summit talks with Zhu Rongji and Jiang Zemin. Tensions remained, but a number of co-operation agreements were reached, including a bilateral accord on terms for China's WTO entry. The People's

Republic, however, opposed the new US-Japan defence co-operation guide-lines, as it suspected that they could be invoked to defend Taiwan. Obuchi refused to guarantee that Taiwan be excluded from the security arrangements.

In August 2000 China withdrew permission for the Japanese Minister of Transport, Hajime Morita, to visit the People's Republic in September, owing to scheduling difficulties with Chinese officials. The Japanese media, however, attributed the Chinese change of attitude to a recent visit by Morita to a shrine honouring Japan's war dead, including those convicted of war crimes. Zhu Rongji visited Japan in October, and admitted that his failure to demand an apology for the host country's wartime conduct had attracted criticism in China.

In April 2001 NPC Chairman Li Peng cancelled a visit to Japan, apparently in response to Tokyo's decision to permit former Taiwanese President Lee Teng-hui to visit Japan, and the publication of a new history textbook that attenuated Japan's wartime atrocities in China and South-East Asia. By mid-2001 China and Japan had become embroiled in trade disputes involving tariffs on imported goods. China was further angered by the visit of the Japanese Prime Minister, Junichiro Koizumi, to a controversial war memorial in Tokyo that glorified Japan's war dead, including several prominent war criminals. China claimed that the visit demonstrated that Japan did not regret its conquest of large parts of China in the 1930s.

China reacted cautiously to Japan's announcement in October 2001 that it would send warships to the Indian Ocean in support of the USA's 'war on terrorism'. However, some Chinese leaders feared that the USA was seeking to increase Japan's military power in order to contain China. Prime Minister Koizumi made a brief visit to China in early October to improve relations, and issued an apology for Japan's wartime atrocities in China. In early November China, Japan and South Korea agreed to hold regular meetings of their economy, finance and foreign ministers to foster closer co-operation.

Li Peng finally visited Japan in early April 2002, where he met Koizumi and toured Japan's regions. At the same time, a Japanese opposition leader, Ichiro Ozawa, publicly stated that Japan could rapidly become a major nuclear power, if challenged by China, drawing a muted response from Beijing. Later that month, Koizumi visited China to attend the Boao Forum, where he met Zhu Rongji. Relations were strained in May, however, when Chinese security forces forcibly removed North Korean refugees seeking asylum at a number of foreign diplomatic missions, including the Japanese consulate in Shenyang, thus violating international protocol. A diplomatic impasse was resolved in June when Beijing agreed to release the asylum-seekers to a third country. In August, meanwhile, a Tokyo court finally admitted that Japan had conducted biological warfare in China during the Second World War, but rejected the demands by 180 Chinese plaintiffs for individual compensation. Despite China's bitterness over Japanese wartime occupation, economic relations between the two remained strong, with increasing bilateral trade, and rising Japanese investment in China. In January 2003, however, the Diaoyu/Senkaku Islands dispute re-emerged when Japan announced plans to lease the islands to a private owner, prompting protests from Beijing.

The long-standing border dispute with India, which gave rise to a short military conflict in 1962, remained unresolved (see chapter on India). Discussions on the issue were held in 1988 and in 1991, and in September 1993 the two countries signed an agreement to reduce their troops along the frontier and to resolve the dispute by peaceful means. Discussions continued in 1994. In December China and India agreed to hold joint military exercises in mid-1995. In August 1995 it was confirmed that the two countries were to disengage their troops from four border posts in Arunachal Pradesh. Further progress was made at the ninth round of Sino-Indian border discussions, held in October 1996, and during the visit of President Jiang Zemin to India (the first by a Chinese Head of State) in November. Negotiations continued in August 1997. In May 1998, immediately prior to India's nuclear tests, the Indian Minister of Defence, George Fernandes, stated that China constituted India's main long-term security threat, citing its aid to Pakistan's nuclear programme and its military facilities in the Andaman Sea. However, the Indian Minister of External Affairs, Jaswant Singh, denied that India viewed China as a threat, when he visited Beijing in June 1999. The two countries subsequently improved relations following a series of bilateral meetings. Nevertheless, during the late 1990s both China and India were increasingly vying for influence in Myanmar, Nepal and the Indian Ocean, and Beijing feared that the USA was seeking to use India as a means of curtailing China's ambitions. Li Peng visited India in January 2001, and discussions were held with a view to the restoration of normal relations. Outstanding Indian concerns included the increasing levels of imports of cheap Chinese goods and the question of China's nuclear co-operation with Pakistan, while China resented India's decades-long hosting of Tibetan separatist organizations. The increase in fighting in Nepal in late 2001 threatened to lead China and India to support opposing sides. However, in early January 2002 Prime Minister Zhu Rongji led a business delegation to India, seeking greater commercial links and improved relations. In April officials from the two countries held discussions in New Delhi, aimed at establishing joint counter-terrorism measures.

In late April 2003 the Indian Minister of Defence, George Fernandes, began a week-long visit to Beijing, to discuss outstanding bilateral issues, including China's support for Pakistan and Chinese observation posts in the Bay of Bengal.

In late December 2001 China hosted Pakistani President Pervez Musharraf, who arrived to mark the 50th anniversary of relations between the two countries. China and Pakistan had long been close allies, and co-operated in economic and military issues. In early January 2002 it was reported that China had supplied several dozen fighter aircraft and air defence missiles to Pakistan. The two countries were also co-operating to develop a new fighter aircraft by 2005. Musharraf visited Beijing again in August 2002 and reaffirmed the close relations between the two countries. China had been increasingly concerned that Pakistan's closer relations with the USA since the terrorist attacks of 11 September 2001, would be at its own risk.

The question of the sovereignty of the Spratly (Nansha) Islands, situated in the South China Sea and claimed by six countries (Brunei, China, Malaysia, the Philippines, Taiwan and Viet Nam), remained unresolved in the early 21st century. The strategic importance of the sea was due to the major international shipping routes passing through the area, and China's claim to the islands and the sea raised concerns about its possible expansionist ambitions. By 1994 both China and Viet Nam had awarded petroleum exploration concessions to US companies, leading to increased tension among the claimants. In February 1995 it emerged that Chinese forces had occupied a reef to which the Philippines laid claim, resulting in a formal diplomatic protest from Manila. More than 60 Chinese fishermen and several vessels were subsequently detained by the Philippine authorities. Following consultations in August, China and the Philippines declared their intention to resolve peacefully their claims to the Spratly Islands. In January 1996 the Chinese Government denied any involvement in a naval skirmish in Philippine waters, during which a ship flying the Chinese flag and a Philippine patrol boat exchanged gunfire. In March China and the Philippines agreed to co-operate in combating piracy in the region. In November 1998 China angered the Philippine Government by building permanent structures on the disputed Mischief Reef. In late November 20 Chinese fishermen were arrested near Mischief Reef by the Philippine navy. Following Chinese protests, the men were released. In December China reiterated both its claim to sovereignty over the Spratly Islands and surrounding waters and its commitment to pursuing a peaceful solution through negotiation. Discussions between the two countries in April 1999 were unsuccessful, and relations deteriorated further in May when a Chinese fishing vessel sank following a collision with a Philippine navy boat, which was claimed to be accidental by the Philippines but deliberate by the People's Republic. A further Chinese fishing vessel sank in a collision with a Philippine navy vessel in July. A similar territorial dispute relating to the Paracel (Xisha) Islands, which had been seized by China from South Vietnamese forces in 1974, also remained unresolved. In May 1996, despite having agreed to abide by the UN Convention on the Law of the Sea, China declared an extension of its maritime boundaries in the South China Sea. Other claimants to the Paracel Islands, in particular Indonesia, the Philippines and Viet Nam, expressed grave concern at China's apparent expansionism. In November 2002, in Phnom-Penh, Cambodia, Prime Minister Zhu Rongji signed a landmark 'declaration on the conduct of parties in the South China Sea' with members of the Association of South East Asian Nations (ASEAN, see p. 146), which aimed to avoid conflict in the area. Under this agreement, which was similar to one drafted in late 1999 but not implemented, claimants would practise self-restraint in the event of potentially hostile action (such as inhabiting the islands), effect confidence-building

measures and give advance notice of military exercises in the region. However, the agreement did not include the Paracel Islands, and disagreements continued among the signatories on what the accord should encompass. Additionally, China introduced a provision requiring consensus to resolve outstanding issues, thereby allowing for future indecision among ASEAN members.

In August and October 1990 diplomatic relations were established with Indonesia and Singapore respectively. In late 1991, following many years of mutual hostility resulting from a border dispute and from the Vietnamese intervention in Kampuchea (now Cambodia) in 1978, the restoration of normal relations between China and Viet Nam was announced. Bilateral relations continued to improve throughout the 1990s; in late February 2002 President Jiang Zemin began his second official visit to Viet Nam. In November 2000 meanwhile, President Jiang Zemin toured Laos, Cambodia and Brunei, the tour culminating in his attendance at the APEC conference in Brunei. His visit to Cambodia was the first by a Chinese Head of State for more than 30 years. Local security forces suppressed protests at China's support for the Khmer Rouge regime in the late 1970s. In December 2001 Jiang visited Myanmar, seeking to increase its influence there vis-à-vis India and promising US $100m. in finance towards investment projects. China hoped to develop a new transport corridor from its land-locked south-western provinces to Myanmar's Indian Ocean ports, allowing the easier export of goods. During 2000–01 China also increased links with a number of South Pacific island nations, providing aid and investment. Furthermore, China played a leading role in organizing the private Boao Forum of regional business and political leaders, held on China's Hainan Island in April 2002. In September 2002 China and Indonesia signed an agreement to export liquefied natural gas from the Indonesian province of Papua (formerly West Papua), valued at US $8,000m., as bilateral relations improved. At the ASEAN summit meeting in Phnom-Penh, Cambodia, in November 2002, China and 10 South-East Asian nations signed an agreement to establish the world's largest free-trade area by 2010. In January 2003 the head of Myanmar's ruling State Peace and Development Council, Gen. Than Shwe, visited Beijing, where he was promised US $200m. in development loans.

During 1992 China established diplomatic relations with the Republic of Korea. China remained committed to the achievement of peace on the Korean peninsula, and in June 1996 it was reported that secret discussions between representatives of the Republic and of the Democratic People's Republic of Korea had been held in Beijing. In late 1997 China participated in quadripartite negotiations, together with the USA, the Democratic People's Republic of Korea and the Republic of Korea, to resolve the Korean issue. The Republic of Korea remained a major trading partner, and was one of the largest investors in China. Further quadripartite negotiations took place throughout 1999. In May 2000 the North Korean leader, Kim Jong Il, visited China, on his first trip abroad for 17 years. China was pleased in the following month by the holding of the first ever-inter-Korean presidential summit meeting in the Democratic People's Republic of Korea. Regular inter-Korean meetings followed. Kim Jong Il visited China again in January 2001, and President Jiang visited North Korea in September. During 2001, however, China increased measures to counter the growing number of North Korean refugees entering the country. Premier Zhu Rongji made his first trip to the Republic of Korea in October 2000. During 2002 China continued to play an important role on the Korean peninsula, its main interest being a reduction of tensions and the reconnection of the inter-Korean railway lines and their subsequent connection with China's own railway system. However, there were tensions with South Korea over the introduction of a bill that would grant special rights to ethnic Koreans in China and China's forcible removal of North Korean refugees from South Korean embassies in the People's Republic. In late June Beijing allowed 24 northern refugees who had been concealed in the embassy of South Korea to leave for that country. After that incident, Beijing began an operation against South Korean activists and missionaries who had been helping northerners to flee via China. In October North Korea appointed a Chinese tycoon of Dutch citizenship, Yang Bin, as the new governor of its recently created Sinuiju Special Administrative Region; however, the Beijing authorities arrested him on charges of bribery and fraud, thereby preventing him from assuming the post. By early 2003, China was becoming increasingly concerned about the growing diplomatic crisis between

North Korea and the USA over the former's decision formally to restart its nuclear programme. In January 2003 the vice-ministers of foreign affairs of China and South Korea met to discuss the crisis.

Following the reversion of Hong Kong to Chinese sovereignty, relations between China and the United Kingdom improved significantly in 1998. The British Secretary of State for Foreign and Commonwealth Affairs, Robin Cook, paid a visit to China and Hong Kong in January. The first China-EU summit meeting, which was scheduled to become an annual event, took place in London in April, prior to the Asia-Europe Meeting (ASEM). China and the EU, presided over at the time by the United Kingdom, committed themselves to greater mutual co-operation in the area of trade and economic relations. The Chinese Premier also had talks with his British counterpart, Tony Blair. Blair visited China and Hong Kong in October 1998. He declared his intention to broach the issue of human rights through 'persuasion and dialogue' rather than 'confrontation and empty rhetoric'. Following the visit, the two sides pledged to increase co-operation in a number of areas, and in October 1999 Jiang Zemin became the first Chinese Head of State to visit the United Kingdom. This visit was part of a six-nation tour, which also included France, Portugal, Morocco, Algeria and Saudi Arabia. In the United Kingdom and France, however, Jiang's visit prompted protests by supporters of human rights, resulting in complaints from the Chinese authorities. In December, during a China-EU summit meeting in Beijing, the Chinese Government rejected criticism of its human rights record, reiterating its previous position that economic development would precede an improvement in human rights and defending its use of the death penalty, citing social stability. In November 2000 further criticism, by a British parliamentary committee, was dismissed by the People's Republic. Meanwhile, in October China concluded bilateral trade agreements with the EU necessary for WTO accession. In May 2001 Beijing hosted an EU delegation, seeking a new comprehensive partnership with China, particularly in the area of commerce. The fourth annual China-EU summit took place in Brussels in early September, and discussed access by EU companies to China's insurance market, the last obstacle to China's admission to the WTO (which took place in December 2001). In late October–early November Vice-President Hu Jintao made his first official trip to the EU, visiting the United Kingdom, France, Germany and Spain. Jiang Zemin visited Germany in April 2002, the latter being the biggest European investor in China.

China established diplomatic relations with Israel in 1992, and during the 1990s co-operated in several military technology projects, including China's indigenous fighter aircraft programme. However, the USA, fearing that this would strengthen China's position against Taiwan, exerted pressure on Israel to cancel a lucrative contract to supply airborne warning and control (AWACS) aircraft to China in early 2000. Initially, Israel refused to comply, particularly after Jiang Zemin had made the first official trip to the country by a Chinese Head of State, in April. In July, however, Israel was obliged to yield to pressure, as it could not risk losing the USA as a major ally. In late 2001 China pressed Israel for US $1,000m. in compensation for the aborted sale, but in early 2002 accepted a payment of US $350m. In January 2003 Israel, responding to US pressure, ceased exports of weapons to China. In October 2000, meanwhile, China improved its relations with African nations when, during a Sino-African forum in Beijing, the People's Republic announced its decision to reduce or exempt outstanding debt totalling US $1,200m. China also maintained friendly relations with a number of Middle Eastern nations, including Iran and Iraq, and in June 2000 hosted Iranian President Muhammad Khatami, who was seeking closer economic ties. President Hosni Mubarak of Egypt visited Beijing in January 2002. In April 2001 President Jiang visited several Latin American nations, including Argentina, Brazil, Chile, Cuba, Uruguay and Venezuela, attempting to foster economic links. In August the Minister of National Defence, Gen. Chi Haotian, also visited Venezuela, and discussed energy and security issues with President Hugo Chávez. The pattern of cultivating relations with countries in the developing world continued during 2002: in April Zhu Rongji visited Turkey and Egypt, and Jiang made a tour of Libya, Nigeria, Tunisia and Iran. The issues discussed included business and energy, defence co-operation, and the war against global terrorism. In late February 2003 China hosted the visiting Cuban President, Fidel Castro.

Government

China is a unitary state. Directly under the Central Government there are 22 provinces, five autonomous regions, including Xizang (Tibet), and four municipalities (Beijing, Chongqing, Shanghai and Tianjin). The highest organ of state power is the National People's Congress (NPC). In March 2003 the first session of the 10th NPC was attended by 2,916 deputies, indirectly elected for five years by the people's congresses of the provinces, autonomous regions, municipalities directly under the Central Government, and the People's Liberation Army. The NPC elects a Standing Committee to be its permanent organ. The current Constitution, adopted by the NPC in December 1982 and amended in 1993, was China's fourth since 1949. It restored the office of Head of State (President of the Republic). Executive power is exercised by the State Council (Cabinet), comprising the Premier, Vice-Premiers and other ministers heading ministries and commissions. The State Council is appointed by, and accountable to, the NPC.

Political power is held by the Chinese Communist Party (CCP). The CCP's highest authority is the Party Congress, convened every five years. In November 2002 the CCP's 16th National Congress elected a Central Committee of 198 full members and 158 alternate members. To direct policy, the Central Committee elected a 24-member Politburo. The incoming Standing Committee of the Politburo comprised nine members.

Provincial people's congresses are the local organs of state power. Local revolutionary committees, created during the Cultural Revolution, were abolished in January 1980 and replaced by provincial people's governments.

Defence

China is divided into seven major military units. All armed services are grouped in the People's Liberation Army (PLA). In August 2002, according to Western estimates, the regular forces totalled 2,270,000, of whom 1,000,000 were conscripts: the army numbered 1,600,000, the navy 250,000 (including a naval air force of 26,000), and the air force 420,000 (including 220,000 air defence personnel). Reserves number some 500,000–600,000, and the People's Armed Police comprises an estimated 1.5m. Military service is by selective conscription, and lasts for two years in all services. A reduction in the number of forces in the PLA commenced in the late 1990s and remained in progress in 2002. Defence expenditure for 2002 was budgeted at 166,000m. yuan.

Economic Affairs

In 2001, according to estimates by the World Bank, China's gross national income (GNI), measured at average 1999–2001 prices, was US $1,130,984m., equivalent to some $890 per head (or $4,260 on an international purchasing-power parity basis). During 1990–2001, it was estimated, the population increased at an average annual rate of 1.0%, while gross domestic product (GDP) per head increased, in real terms, by an average annual rate of 8.7%, one of the highest growth rates in the world. Overall GDP increased, in real terms, at an average annual rate of 9.9% in 1990–2001; growth in 2001 was 7.3%.

Agriculture (including forestry and fishing) contributed 15.0% of GDP in 2001, and employed 45.2% of the working population in that year. China's principal crops are rice (production of which accounted for about 32% of the total world harvest in 2000), sweet potatoes, wheat, maize, soybeans, sugar cane, tobacco, cotton and jute. According to the World Bank, agricultural GDP increased at an average annual rate of 3.7%, in real terms, in 1990–2001. Growth in agricultural GDP was an estimated 2.3% in 2001.

Industry (including mining, manufacturing, construction and power) contributed 52.2% of GDP in 2001 and engaged 17.3% of the employed labour force in that year. According to the World Bank, industrial GDP increased at an average annual rate of 13.1%, in real terms, in 1990–2001. Growth in industrial GDP was an estimated 8.7% in 2001.

The mining sector accounted for less than 0.8% of total employment in 2001. Output in the sector accounted for some 6% of total industrial production in 1996. China has enormous mineral reserves and is the world's largest producer of natural graphite, antimony, tungsten and zinc. Other important minerals include coal, iron ore, molybdenum, tin, lead, mercury, bauxite, phosphate rock, diamonds, gold, manganese, crude petroleum and natural gas. A move to increase competitiveness, and to reduce air pollution caused by the burning of coal, resulted in the closure of some 14 major coal mines in 1999, with the loss of 400,000 jobs. The discovery of significant copper deposits in Xinjiang in September 2000 would, it was hoped, alleviate China's reliance on imports of that metal.

The manufacturing sector contributed an estimated 35.4% of GDP in 2001, and the sector accounted for 11.1% of total employment in that year. China is the world's leading producer of chemical fertilizers and cement, with output in 2000 totalling an estimated 31.9m. and 597.0m. metric tons, respectively. With output of more than 101m. metric tons in 1996, China also became the world's largest producer of steel; production increased to more than 128m. metric tons in 2000. The GDP of the manufacturing sector increased at an average annual rate of 12.9%, in real terms, during 1990–2001, according to the World Bank.

Energy is derived principally from coal (67.0% in 2001); other sources are petroleum (23.6%), hydroelectric power (6.9%) and natural gas (2.5%). China became a net importer of crude petroleum in 1993. By December 1999 the People's Republic's largest hydroelectric power station, at Ertan, was fully functioning. The 18,200-MW Three Gorges hydropower scheme on the Changjiang (River Yangtze), the world's largest civil engineering project, is scheduled for completion in 2009 and will have a potential annual output of 84,700m. kWh. China's national grid was also scheduled for completion in that year. Imports of mineral fuels comprised 7.2% of the cost of total imports in 2001. In the late 1990s China was increasingly seeking to develop and transport petroleum and gas reserves from Central Asia, and work on a 4,200-km pipeline from Xinjiang to Shanghai was under way in late 2002, with a view to completion in 2004.

Services contributed 32.8% of GDP in 2001 and engaged 23.8% of the employed labour force in that year. Tourism and retail and wholesale trade are expanding rapidly. During 1990–2001, according to the World Bank, the GDP of the services sector increased at an average annual rate of 8.9% in real terms. Growth in the GDP of the services sector was an estimated 7.2% in 2001.

In 2001 China recorded a trade surplus of US $34,017m., and there was a surplus of $17,401m. on the current account of the balance of payments. In 2001 the principal source of imports was Japan (which provided 17.6% of total imports). Other important suppliers were Taiwan (11.2%), the USA (10.8%), and the Republic of Korea (9.6%). The principal markets for exports in 2001 were the USA (20.4% of total exports), Hong Kong (17.5%) and Japan (16.9%). Most of the goods exported to Hong Kong are subsequently re-exported. The principal imports in 2000 were machinery and transport equipment, chemicals and related products, and basic manufactures such as textiles. The principal exports in that year were machinery and transport equipment, textiles and clothing, and footwear.

In 2001 China's overall budget deficit was 251,654m. yuan, equivalent to 2.6% of GDP. China's total external debt at the end of 2001 was officially estimated to be US $170,110m., of which $119,530m. was medium and long-term public debt. In 2000 the cost of debt-servicing was equivalent to 7.4% of the value of exports of goods and services. The annual rate of inflation averaged 7.2% in 1990–2000. Consumer prices declined by 1.4% in 1999, before rising by 0.3% in 2000 and again by 0.3% in 2001. According to official figures, the number of unemployed persons in 2001 was estimated at 17.5m. (5.1% of the total labour force). In the same year, according to the Asian Development Bank, the total number of registered unemployed in urban areas was some 6,810,000 (3.6% of the urban labour force). Meanwhile, the number of rural unemployed was unofficially estimated at 150m.

China joined the Asian Development Bank (ADB, see p. 143) in 1986 and the Asia-Pacific Economic Co-operation forum (APEC, see p. 139) in 1991. In 1994 China became a member of the Association of Tin Producing Countries (ATPC). In July 1995 China was granted observer status at the World Trade Organization (WTO, see p. 323), which had succeeded the General Agreement on Tariffs and Trade (GATT) in January of that year. Negotiations on full membership continued, and China was finally admitted as a full member in December 2001. China joined the Bank for International Settlements (BIS, see p. 154) in 1996. In the same year the secretariat of the Tumen River Economic Development Area (TREDA) was established in Beijing by the Governments of China, North and South Korea, Mongolia and Russia.

In 1978 Deng Xiaoping introduced the 'open door' reform policy, which aimed to decentralize the economic system and to attract overseas investment to China. The state monopoly on foreign trade was gradually relinquished, commercial links with foreign countries were diversified and several Special Economic Zones were established. China subsequently experienced many years of rapid economic expansion, becoming one of the fastest-growing economies in the world. However, critics warned that much of this growth was uneven, being concentrated mainly in the southern and eastern urban coastal regions, while leaving the rural interior of the country relatively underdeveloped. In response, the Government initiated a number of massive infrastructural projects to open up the western parts of the country in an attempt to balance national development. By the late 1990s the revitalization of the state-owned enterprises (SOEs) and the reform of the weak banking sector had become an increasingly urgent issue. The performance of the SOEs had suffered a significant decline in the 1990s, and failing SOEs were often supported by credit from the banking sector. SOE reform, however, was constrained by the necessity to minimize the number of workers being made redundant, amid concerns about possible social unrest. The serious labour unrest in the north-eastern industrial regions in early 2002 highlighted the sensitivity of the issue (see above). It was hoped that the restructuring of the SOEs would lead them away from traditional heavy industries in favour of more knowledge-based and consumer-orientated industries, with the assistance of private entrepreneurship. The CCP's decision in 2001 to admit private business people to its ranks for the first time indicated a new emphasis on private enterprise as the impetus for economic growth. In October 2001, in an effort to curb the pace of redundancies, the legislation regulating SOE bankruptcies was suspended. The creation of new employment opportunities and the improvement of social welfare provision were identified as official priorities. The 1997–98 Asian financial crisis resulted in a deceleration of growth, but did not affect China as adversely as other countries in the region. The objectives of the Tenth Five-Year Plan, for the period 2001–06, included a growth rate of 7% per annum, greater scientific and technological advancement, the intensification of infrastructure projects and improved environmental protection, as well as the completion of the transition to a socialist market economy. A survey of 20 economic forecasters in mid-2002 predicted GDP growth of 7%–8% in 2002 and 2003. Actual GDP growth accelerated to 8.1% year-on-year during the third quarter of 2002, and in January 2003 official figures indicated that GDP had increased by 8.0% in 2002. However, there were concerns about the validity of official figures: in 2001 officials from the National Bureau of Statistics admitted to widespread inaccuracies in reporting such figures. In August 2001, meanwhile, in preparation for WTO membership, the Government removed price controls on 128 items, but retained controls of prices of some strategic commodities, such as natural gas, electricity supplies and basic telecommunication services. It was anticipated that China's accession to the WTO, which took place in December 2001, would help to overcome the political obstacles to the restructuring of the SOEs and banks, as these institutions would henceforth be obliged to become competitive in external markets. In the short term, accession to the WTO was likely to cause a consolidation of domestic industries, which would exert negative pressures on the economy. Some analysts predicted that as many as 40m. jobs in the state sector would be lost in the five years following China's accession to the WTO. In the longer term, however, WTO entry was expected to generate increased investment in China. Foreign direct investment reached a record US $52,700m. in 2002, a 12.6% increase on the previous year. The deceleration in the economy of the USA, one the People's Republic's major trading partners, adversely affected China's trade balance in 2001, but this improved substantially in 2002. In February 2002, in an attempt to counter the effects of the global deceleration, the People's Bank of China reduced interest rates for the first time since June 1999. Despite strong growth overall in 2002, China's economy faced several serious problems in the medium term. Much of the impressive economic growth had been state-generated, in the form of expensive major public-works projects, and this had resulted in an increasing budget deficit. There were fears that the growing public debt would eventually lead to a major failure of state banks. In order to avoid this, the Government therefore needed to reduce public spending, at a time when social security provisions were coming under increasing pressure from newly redundant workers. Private consumption growth was weaker in 2002 than in 2001, as uncertainty and the rising costs of social services compelled people to save money. None the less, GDP growth for 2003 was forecast by the ADB and IMF at 7.3%. In April 2003, however,

China admitted that the repercussions of the recent outbreak of Severe Acute Respiratory Syndrome (SARS) were likely to affect economic growth (which, according to an official estimate, had reached 9.9% in the first quarter compared with the first three months of 2002). A major challenge for the Chinese Government in the early 21st century, meanwhile, remained the of balancing economic reform and political stability.

Education

The education system expanded rapidly after 1949. Fees are charged at all levels. Much importance is attached to kindergartens. Primary education begins for most children at seven years of age and lasts for five years. Secondary education usually begins at 12 years of age and lasts for a further five years, comprising a first cycle of three years and a second cycle of two years. Free higher education was abolished in 1985; instead, college students have to compete for scholarships, which are awarded according to academic ability. As a result of the student disturbances in 1989, college students were required to complete one year's political education, prior to entering college. In November 1989 it was announced that postgraduate students were to be selected on the basis of assessments of moral and physical fitness, as well as academic ability. Since 1979 education has been included as one of the main priorities for modernization. The whole educational system was being reformed in the late 1990s and early 2000s, with the aim of introducing nine-year compulsory education in 85% of the country. The establishment of private schools has been per-mitted since the early 1980s. As a proportion of the total school-age population, enrolment at primary and secondary schools in 1997 was equivalent to 98% (boys 99%; girls 96%). In that year 100% of both boys and girls in the relevant age-group were enrolled at primary schools. Total enrolment at secondary schools in 1997 was equivalent to 70% of the total school-age population (males 74%; females 66%). In 1996 enrolment at tertiary level schools was equivalent to 5.7% of the relevant age-group (males 7.3%; females 3.9%). In 1999, according to UNESCO, the rate had declined to 16.5% (males 8.8%, females 24.5%). Budgetary expenditure on education by all levels of government was 203,572m. yuan in 2001.

Public Holidays

2003: 1 January (Solar New Year), 1–4 February* (Lunar New Year), 8 March (International Women's Day, women only), 1 May (Labour Day), 1 August (Army Day), 9 September (Teachers' Day), 1–2 October (National Days).

2004: 1 January (Solar New Year), 22–25 January* (Lunar New Year), 8 March (International Women's Day, women only), 1 May (Labour Day), 1 August (Army Day), 9 September (Teachers' Day), 1–2 October (National Days).

*From the first to the fourth day of the first moon of the lunar calendar.

Weights and Measures

The metric system is officially in force, but some traditional Chinese units are still used.

Statistical Survey

Source (unless otherwise stated): State Statistical Bureau, 38 Yuetan Nan Jie, Sanlihe, Beijing 100826; tel. (10) 68515074; fax (10) 68515078; e-mail service@stats.gov.cn; internet www.stats.gov.cn.

Note: Wherever possible, figures in this Survey exclude Taiwan. In the case of unofficial estimates for China, it is not always clear if Taiwan is included or excluded. Where a Taiwan component is known, either it has been deducted from the all-China figure or its inclusion is noted. Figures for the Hong Kong Special Administrative Region (SAR — incorporated into the People's Republic of China on 1 July 1997) and for the Macao SAR (incorporated on 20 December 1999) are listed separately (pp. 1131–35 and pp. 1152–53 respectively). Transactions between the SARs and the rest of the People's Republic continue to be treated as external transactions.

Area and Population

AREA, POPULATION AND DENSITY

Area (sq km)	9,572,900*
Population (census results)	
1 July 1990	1,130,510,638
1 November 2000	
Males	640,275,969
Females	602,336,257
Total	1,242,612,226
Population (official estimates at 31 December)	
1999	1,257,860,000
2000	1,267,430,000
2001	1,276,270,000
Density (per sq km) at 31 December 2001	133.3

* 3,696,100 sq miles.

PRINCIPAL ETHNIC GROUPS

(at census of 1 November 2000)

	Number	%
Han (Chinese)	1,137,386,112	91.53
Zhuang	16,178,811	1.30
Manchu	10,682,262	0.86
Hui	9,816,805	0.79
Miao	8,940,116	0.72
Uygur (Uigur)	8,399,393	0.68
Tujia	8,028,133	0.65
Yi	7,762,272	0.63
Mongolian	5,813,947	0.47
Tibetan	5,416,021	0.44
Bouyei	2,971,460	0.24
Dong	2,960,293	0.24
Yao	2,637,421	0.21
Korean	1,923,842	0.16
Bai	1,858,063	0.09
Hani	1,439,673	0.12
Kazakh	1,250,458	0.10
Li	1,247,814	0.10
Dai	1,158,989	0.09
She	709,592	0.06
Lisu	634,912	0.05
Gelao	579,357	0.05
Dongxiang	513,805	0.04
Others	3,568,237	0.29
Unknown	734,438	0.06
Total	**1,242,612,226**	**100.00**

BIRTHS AND DEATHS
(sample surveys)

	1999	2000	2001
Birth rate (per 1,000) . . .	14.64	14.03	13.38
Death rate (per 1,000) . . .	6.46	6.45	6.43

Marriages (number registered): 8,799,079 in 1999; 8,420,044 in 2000; 7,971,144 in 2001.

Expectation of life (WHO estimates, years at birth): 71.2 (males 69.8; females 72.7) in 2001 (Source: WHO, *World Health Report*).

ADMINISTRATIVE DIVISIONS
(previous or other spelling given in brackets)

	Area ('000 sq km)	Population at 1 November 2000 Total	Density (per sq km)	Capital of province or region	Estimated population ('000) at mid-2000*
Provinces					
Sichuan (Szechwan)	487.0	82,348,296	169	Chengdu (Chengtu)	3,294
Henan (Honan). . . .	167.0	91,236,854	546	Zhengzhou (Chengchow)	2,070
Shandong (Shantung). . .	153.3	89,971,789	587	Jinan (Tsinan)	2,568
Jiangsu (Kiangsu)	102.6	73,043,577	712	Nanjing (Nanking)	2,740
Guangdong (Kwangtung) . .	197.1	85,225,007	432	Guangzhou (Canton)	3,893
Hebei (Hopei)	202.7	66,684,419	329	Shijiazhuang (Shihkiachwang)	1,603
Hunan (Hunan)	210.5	63,274,173	301	Changsha (Changsha)	1,775
Anhui (Anhwei)	139.9	58,999,948	422	Hefei (Hofei)	1,242
Hubei (Hupeh)	187.5	59,508,870	317	Wuhan (Wuhan)	5,169
Zhejiang (Chekiang) . . .	101.8	45,930,651	451	Hangzhou (Hangchow)	1,780
Liaoning (Liaoning) . . .	151.0	41,824,412	277	Shenyang (Shenyang)	4,828
Jiangxi (Kiangsi)	164.8	40,397,598	245	Nanchang (Nanchang)	1,722
Yunnan (Yunnan)	436.2	42,360,089	97	Kunming (Kunming)	1,701
Heilongjiang (Heilungkiang) . .	463.6	36,237,576	78	Harbin (Harbin)	2,928
Guizhou (Kweichow) . . .	174.0	35,247,695	203	Guiyang (Kweiyang)	2,533
Shaanxi (Shensi)	195.8	35,365,072	171	Xian (Sian)	3,123
Fujian (Fukien)	123.1	34,097,947†	277	Fuzhou (Foochow)	1,397
Shanxi (Shansi)	157.1	32,471,242	207	Taiyuan (Taiyuan)	2,415
Jilin (Kirin).	187.0	26,802,191	143	Changchun (Changchun)	3,093
Gansu (Kansu)	366.5	25,124,282	69	Lanzhou (Lanchow)	1,730
Hainan	34.3	7,559,035	220	Haikou	438‡
Qinghai (Tsinghai). . . .	721.0	4,822,963	7	Xining (Hsining)	691‡
Autonomous regions					
Guangxi Zhuang (Kwangsi Chuang)	220.4	43,854,538	199	Nanning (Nanning)	1,311
Nei Mongol (Inner Mongolia). .	1,177.5	23,323,347	20	Hohhot (Huhehot)	978
Xinjiang Uygur (Sinkiang Uighur)	1,646.9	18,459,511	11	Urumuqi (Urumchi)	1,415
Ningxia Hui (Ninghsia Hui) . .	66.4	5,486,393	83	Yinchuan (Yinchuen)	530‡
Tibet (Xizang)	1,221.6	2,616,329	2	Lhasa (Lhasa)	105§
Municipalities					
Shanghai	6.2	16,407,734	2,646	—	12,887
Beijing (Peking)	16.8	13,569,194	808	—	10,839
Tianjin (Tientsin)	11.3	9,848,731	872	—	9,156
Chongqing (Chungking) . .	82.0	30,512,763	372	—	4,900
Total	9,572.9	1,242,612,226‖	130		

* UN estimates, excluding population in counties under cities' administration.
† Excluding islands administered by Taiwan, mainly Jinmen (Quemoy) and Mazu (Matsu), with 49,050 inhabitants according to figures released by the Taiwan authorities at the end of March 1990.
‡ December 1998 figure.
§ 1982 figure.
‖ Excluding 2,500,000 military personnel and 1,050,000 persons with unregistered households.

PRINCIPAL TOWNS
(Wade-Giles or other spellings in brackets)

Population at mid-2000
(UN estimates, incl. suburbs, in '000)

Shanghai (Shang-hai)	12,887	Liupanshui	2,023
Beijing (Pei-ching or Peking, the capital)	10,839	Handan	1,996
Tianjin (T'ien-chin or Tientsin)	9,156	Jinxi	1,821
Wuhan (Wu-han or Hankow)	5,169	Liuan	1,818
Chongqing (Ch'ung-ch'ing or Chungking)	4,900	Hangzhou (Hang-chou or Hangchow)	1,780
Shenyang (Shen-yang or Mukden)	4,828	Tianmen	1,779
Guangzhou (Kuang-chou or Canton)	3,893	Changsha (Chang-sha)	1,775
Chengdu (Ch'eng-tu)	3,294	Wanxian	1,759
Xian (Hsi-an or Sian)	3,123	Lanzhou (Lan-chou or Lanchow)	1,730
Changchun (Ch'ang-ch'un)	3,093	Nanchang (Nan-ch'ang)	1,722
Harbin (Ha-erh-pin)	2,928	Kunming (K'un-ming)	1,701
Nanjing (Nan-ching or Nanking)	2,740	Yantai	1,681
Zibo	2,675	Xuzhou	1,636
Dalian (Ta-lien or Dairen)	2,628	Xiantao	1,614
Jinan (Chi-nan or Tsinan)	2,568	Shijiazhuang (Shih-chia-chuang or Shihkiachwang)	1,603
Guiyang	2,533	Heze	1,600
Linyi	2,498	Yancheng	1,562
Taiyuan (T'ai-yüan)	2,415	Yulin	1,558
Qingdao (Ch'ing-tao or Tsingtao)	2,316	Xinghua	1,556
Zhengzhou (Cheng-chou or Chengchow)	2,070	Taian	1,503
Zaozhuang	2,048	Pingxiang	1,502

Source: UN, *World Urbanization Prospects: The 2001 Revision.*

EMPLOYMENT*
(official estimates, '000 persons at 31 December)

	1999	2000	2001
Agriculture, forestry and fishing	334,930	333,550	329,740
Mining	6,670	5,970	5,610
Manufacturing	81,090	80,430	80,830
Electricity, gas and water	2,850	2,840	2,880
Construction	34,120	35,520	36,690
Transport, storage and communications	20,220	20,290	20,370
Wholesale and retail trade and catering	47,510	46,860	47,370
Banking and insurance	3,280	3,270	3,360
Social services	9,230	9,210	9,760
Health care, sports and social welfare	4,820	4,880	4,930
Education, culture, art, radio, film and television broadcasting	15,680	15,650	15,680
Government agencies, etc.	11,020	11,040	11,010
Others	53,490	56,430	58,520
Total	**624,910**	**625,940**	**626,750**

* In addition to employment statistics, sample surveys of the economically active population are conducted. On the basis of these surveys, the total labour force ('000 persons at 31 December) was: 727,910 in 1999; 739,920 in 2000; 744,320 in 2001. Of these totals, the number of employed persons ('000 at 31 December) was: 713,940 (agriculture, etc. 357,680; industry 164,210; services 192,050) in 1999; 720,850 (agriculture, etc. 360,430; industry 162,190; services 198,230) in 2000; 730,250 (agriculture, etc. 365,130; industry 162,840; services 202,280) in 2001.

Health and Welfare

KEY INDICATORS

Total fertility rate (children per woman, 2001)	1.8
Under-5 mortality rate (per 1,000 live births, 2001)	39
HIV/AIDS (% of persons aged 15–49, 2001)	0.11
Physicians (per 1,000 head, 1998)	1.62
Hospital beds (per 1,000 head, 2000)	2.38
Health expenditure (2000): US $ per head (PPP)	75
Health expenditure (2000): % of GDP	5.3
Health expenditure (2000): public (% of total)	36.6
Access to water (% of persons, 2000)	75
Access to sanitation (% of persons, 2000)	38
Human Development Index (2000): ranking	96
Human Development Index (2000): value	0.726

For sources and definitions, see explanatory note on p. vi.

Agriculture

PRINCIPAL CROPS
('000 metric tons)

	1999	2000	2001
Wheat	113,880	99,636	93,873
Rice (paddy)	198,487	187,908	177,580
Barley	3,300†	3,346*	2,893*
Maize	128,086	106,002	114,088
Rye†	628	650	600
Oats†	600	650	600
Millet	2,318	2,125	1,966*
Sorghum	3,241	2,582	2,696*
Buckwheat†	1,250	1,317	1,250
Triticale (wheat-rye hybrid)†	1,200	1,000	935
Potatoes	56,105	66,282	64,000*
Sweet potatoes	125,925	117,978	114,150*
Cassava (Manioc)†	3,750	3,800	3,850
Taro (Coco yam)†	1,450	1,500	1,500
Sugar cane	74,703	66,280	75,663
Sugar beet	8,639	8,073	10,889
Dry beans	1,670*	1,650*	1,540†
Dry broad beans*	1,780	1,788	1,700
Dry peas*	1,040	1,020	1,100
Other pulses	245*	230*	240†
Soybeans (Soya beans)	14,245	15,411	15,450*
Groundnuts (in shell)	12,639	14,437	14,416
Oil palm fruit†	630	640	650
Castor beans*	260	513	300
Sunflower seed	1,765	1,954	1,750*
Rapeseed	10,132	11,381	11,331
Tung nuts	448	453	475†
Sesame seed	743	811	804
Tallowtree seeds†	800	820	835
Linseed	404	344	560*
Cottonseed	11,487	13,251	15,972
Other oilseeds	793	823	905†
Cabbages†	18,700	22,500	24,650
Asparagus†	3,250	3,900	4,200
Lettuce†	6,000	7,250	7,600
Spinach†	5,800	6,950	7,400
Tomatoes†	18,500	22,200	24,000
Cauliflower†	4,700	5,700	6,100
Pumpkins, squash and gourds†	3,250	3,500	3,700
Cucumbers and gherkins†	16,500	19,800	21,600
Aubergines (Eggplants)†	13,600	13,750	14,000
Green chillies and peppers†	7,800	9,400	9,850
Green onions and shallots†	230	280	300
Dry onions†	11,700	14,070	15,000
Garlic†	6,100	7,380	7,800
Green beans†	1,400	1,680	1,800
Green peas†	1,400	1,450	1,530
Carrots†	4,680	5,600	6,000
Mushrooms†	675	800	960
Other vegetables†	100,505	120,613	128,126
Watermelons	46,165†	51,466†	54,600
Cantaloupes and other melons	5,831†	7,244†	8,000
Grapes	2,708	3,282	3,680
Apples	20,802	20,431	20,015
Pears	7,742	8,412	8,796
Peaches and nectarines*	3,960	3,950	4,150

— *continued*	1999	2000	2001
Plums*	3,880	3,900	4,141
Oranges*	3,090	2,638	3,480
Tangerines, mandarins, clementines and satsumas* . .	6,720	5,200	6,850
Lemons and limes*	242	260	348
Grapefruit and pomelos* . .	195	185	233
Other citrus fruit*	540	500	696
Mangoes*	2,920	3,000	3,000
Pineapples	883	857	919*
Persimmons	1,481	1,592	1,635*
Bananas	4,194	4,941	5,272
Other fruits and berries† . .	3,893	3,957	4,028
Walnuts	274	310	252
Other treenuts†	632	682	702
Tea (made)	676	683	702
Pimento and allspice† . .	215	212	212
Other spices†	309	339	354
Tobacco (leaves)	2,469	2,552	2,350
Jute and jute-like fibres* . .	165	126	136
Other fibre crops† . . .	339	426	447

* Unofficial figure(s).
† FAO estimate(s).

Source: mainly FAO.

LIVESTOCK

('000 head at 31 December)

	1999	2000	2001
Horses	8,981	8,914	8,766
Mules	4,739	4,673	4,530
Asses	9,558	9,348	9,227
Cattle	101,689	104,396	105,905
Buffaloes	22,665	22,587	22,758
Camels.	335	330	326
Pigs	422,563	430,198	446,815
Sheep	127,352	131,095	133,160
Goats	141,683	148,163	157,159
Rabbits*	175,000	185,000	190,000
Chickens*	3,300,000	3,500,000	3,650,000
Ducks*	550,000	600,000	625,000
Geese*	185,000	200,000	205,000

* FAO estimates.

Source: partly FAO.

LIVESTOCK PRODUCTS

('000 metric tons)

	1999	2000	2001
Beef and veal*	4,688	4,968	5,110
Buffalo meat*	366	360	378
Mutton and lamb* . . .	1,335	1,440	1,540
Goat meat*	1,178	1,300	1,387
Pig meat	40,056	40,314	41,845
Horse meat	163	166	156
Rabbit meat	310	360†	329†
Poultry meat*	11,155	12,075	12,424
Other meat	357	363	374
Cows' milk	7,176	8,274	10,255
Buffaloes' milk† . . .	2,600	2,650	2,650
Sheep's milk	893	847	974
Goats' milk†	190	200	225
Butter	80	82	84
Cheese	186	206	217
Hen eggs	18,145	19,068	19,862*
Other poultry eggs . . .	3,202	3,365	3,506*
Honey	230	246	252
Raw silk (incl. waste) . .	70	57*	62†
Wool: greasy	283	293	298
Wool: scoured	144	146	149
Cattle hides (fresh)† . .	1,156	1,226	1,272
Buffalo hides (fresh)† . .	110	108	113
Sheepskins (fresh)† . . .	257	281	297
Goatskins (fresh)† . . .	261	282	297

* Unofficial figure(s).
† FAO estimate(s).

Source: FAO.

Forestry

ROUNDWOOD REMOVALS

(FAO estimates, '000 cubic metres, excl. bark)

	1999	2000	2001
Sawlogs, veneer logs and logs for sleepers	55,160	53,200	51,500
Pulpwood	5,910	5,640	5,500
Other industrial wood . .	37,430	35,720	35,000
Fuel wood	190,883	190,833	190,833
Total	**289,383**	**285,423**	**282,833**

Source: FAO.

Timber production (official figures, '000 cubic metres): 52,368 in 1999; 47,240 in 2000; 45,520 in 2001.

SAWNWOOD PRODUCTION

(FAO estimates, '000 cubic metres, incl. railway sleepers)

	1999	2000	2001
Coniferous (softwood) . .	9,515	3,860	4,583
Broadleaved (hardwood). .	6,344	2,574	3,056
Total	**15,859**	**6,434**	**7,639**

Source: FAO.

Fishing

('000 metric tons, live weight)

	1998	1999	2000
Capture	17,229.9	17,240.0	16,987.3
Freshwater fishes . . .	1,218.2	1,394.6	1,223.0
Japanese anchovy . .	1,373.3	1,096.9	1,142.9
Largehead hairtail . .	1,223.4	1,222.5	1,285.5
Aquaculture	20,795.4	22,789.9	24,580.7
Common carp . . .	1,928.0	2,050.8	2,119.8
Crucian carp . . .	1,032.0	1,235.7	1,375.4
Bighead carp . . .	1,566.5	1,590.1	1,614.0
Grass carp (White amur) . .	2,807.5	3,062.4	3,162.6
Silver carp	3,133.0	3,180.2	3,227.9
Pacific cupped oyster . .	2,833.2	2,988.6	3,291.9
Japanese carpet shell . .	1,404.4	1,797.2	1,616.4
Total catch	**38,025.3**	**40,029.9**	**41,568.0**

Note: Figures exclude aquatic plants ('000 metric tons, wet weight): 6,447.1 (Capture 170.5, Aquaculture 6,276.6) in 1998; 7,469.9 (Capture 215.6, Aquaculture 7,254.3) in 1999; 8,067.8 (Capture 204.3, Aquaculture 7,863.5) in 2000.

Source: FAO, *Yearbook of Fishery Statistics*.

Aquatic products (official figures, '000 metric tons): 39,065.1 (marine 23,567.2, freshwater 15,497.9) in 1998; 41,224.1 (marine 24,719.2, freshwater 16,504.9) in 1999; 42,784.8 (marine 25,387.4, freshwater 17,397.5) in 2000; 43,813.4 (marine 25,717.0, freshwater 18,096.4) in 2001. The totals include artificially cultured products ('000 metric tons): 21,814.7 (marine 8,600.4, freshwater 13,214.3) in 1998; 23,970.1 (marine 9,743.0, freshwater 14,227.1) in 1999; 25,746.7 (marine 10,612.9, freshwater 15,133.8) in 2000; 27,261.3 (marine 11,310.8, freshwater 15,950.5) in 2001. Figures include aquatic plants on a dry-weight basis ('000 metric tons): 1,041.2 in 1998; 1,194.4 in 1999; 1,222.0 in 2000; 1,249.5 in 2001. Freshwater plants are not included.

Mining

(estimates, '000 metric tons, unless otherwise indicated)

	1998	1999	2000
Coal*	1,250,000	1,045,000	998,000
Crude petroleum*	161,000	160,000	163,000
Natural gas (million cu m)* . .	23,279	25,198	27,200
Iron ore: gross weight . . .	246,900	237,000	224,000
Iron ore: metal content . . .	74,500	71,000	67,200
Copper ore†	486	520	590
Nickel ore (metric tons)† . . .	48,700	49,500	51,100
Bauxite	8,200	8,500	9,000
Lead ore†	581	549	570
Zinc ore†	1,273	1,476	1,710
Tin concentrates (metric tons)† .	70,100	80,100	97,000
Manganese ore: gross weight . .	5,300	3,190	4,000
Manganese ore: metal content . .	1,060	630	800
Tungsten concentrates (metric tons)†	30,000	31,100	37,000
Ilmenite	175	180	185
Molybdenum ore (metric tons)† .	30,000	29,700	28,900
Vanadium (metric tons)† . .	15,500	26,000	30,000
Zirconium concentrates (metric tons).	15,000	15,000	15,000
Antimony ore (metric tons)† . .	97,400	89,600	98,700
Cobalt ore (metric tons)† . .	40	250	200
Mercury (metric tons)† . . .	230	200	200
Silver (metric tons)† . . .	1,300	1,320	1,600
Uranium (metric tons)†‡ . .	500	500	500
Gold (metric tons)† . . .	178	173	180
Magnesite.	2,400	2,450	2,500
Phosphate rock and apatite§ . .	25,000	20,000	19,400
Potash‖	120	150	250
Native sulphur	210	250	250
Fluorspar	2,350	2,400	2,450
Barite (Barytes)	3,300	2,800	3,500
Arsenic trioxide (metric tons) . .	15,500	16,000	16,000
Salt (unrefined)*	22,425	28,124	31,280
Gypsum (crude)	6,800	6,700	6,800
Graphite (natural) . . .	224	300	400
Asbestos	314	247	370
Talc and related materials . .	3,800	3,900	3,500
Diamonds ('000 carats):			
gem	230	230	230
industrial	900	920	920

* Official figures. Figures for coal include brown coal and waste. Figures for petroleum include oil from shale and coal. Figures for natural gas refer to gross volume of output.

† Figures refer to the metal content of ores, concentrates or (in the case of vanadium) slag.

‡ Data from the World Nuclear Association (London, United Kingdom).

§ Figures refer to gross weight. The estimated phosphoric acid content was 30%.

‖ Potassium oxide (K₂O) content of potash salts mined.

Source: mainly US Geological Survey.

Industry

SELECTED PRODUCTS

Unofficial Figures

('000 metric tons, unless otherwise indicated)

	1997	1998	1999
Rayon and acetate continuous filaments*	72.0	n.a.	n.a.
Rayon and acetate discontinuous fibres*	378.0	n.a.	n.a.
Non-cellulosic continuous filaments*	1,446.7	n.a.	n.a.
Plywood ('000 cu m)†‡ . . .	8,098	4,979†	7,790
Mechanical wood pulp†‡ . .	440	450	450
Chemical wood pulp†‡ . . .	1,755	1,775	2,140
Other fibre pulp†‡	15,986	15,986	16,432
Sulphur§‖¶(a). . . .	1,400	1,450	1,580
Sulphur§‖¶(b).	6,040	4,490	3,860
Kerosene	6,129	6,161¶	n.a.
Residual fuel oil	23,112	21,004¶	n.a.
Lubricating oils¶	4,100	4,200	n.a.
Paraffin wax¶.	850	900	n.a.
Petroleum coke	1,470	1,500	n.a.
Petroleum bitumen (asphalt) . .	2,900	3,000	n.a.
Liquefied petroleum gas. . .	6,679	7,474¶	n.a.
Aluminium (unwrought) . .	2,180.1	2,361.6	2,808.9
Refined copper (unwrought) . .	1,152.9	1,109.4	1,210.0§¶
Lead (unwrought)	707.5	758.5	945.1
Tin (unwrought)	67.7	79.3	90.5
Zinc (unwrought). . . .	1,434.4	1,491.9	1,669.8

* Data from the Fiber Economics Bureau, Inc, USA.

† Data from the FAO.

‡ Including Taiwan.

§ Data from the US Geological Survey.

‖ Figures refer to (a) sulphur recovered as a by-product in the purification of coal-gas, in petroleum refineries, gas plants and from copper, lead and zinc sulphide ores; and (b) the sulphur content of iron and copper pyrites, including pyrite concentrates obtained from copper, lead and zinc ores.

¶ Provisional or estimated figure(s).

Source: UN, *Industrial Commodity Statistics Yearbook*.

Official Figures

('000 metric tons, unless otherwise indicated)

	1999	2000	2001
Edible vegetable oils	7,337.9	8,353.2	13,831.7
Raw sugar	8,610	7,000	6,531
Beer	20,987.7	22,313.2	22,889.3
Cigarettes ('000 cases) . . .	33,400	33,970	34,021
Cotton yarn (pure and mixed) . .	5,670	6,570	7,607
Woven cotton fabrics—pure and mixed (million metres) . .	25,000	27,700	29,000
Woollen fabrics ('000 metres) . .	273,173.9	278,323.7	343,033.9
Silk fabrics (metric tons) . . .	70,200	73,300	87,300
Chemical fibres	6,000	6,940	8,414
Paper and paperboard . . .	21,593.0	24,869.4	37,770.7
Rubber tyres ('000)	109,698.4	121,578.7	135,730.0
Sulphuric acid	23,560	24,270	26,963.2
Caustic soda (Sodium hydroxide) . .	5,801.4	6,678.8	7,879.6
Soda ash (Sodium carbonate) . .	7,660	8,340	9,143.7
Insecticides	625	607	787
Nitrogenous fertilizers (a)* . . .	24,719.6	23,981.1	25,273.7
Phosphate fertilizers (b)* . . .	6,360.7	6,630.3	7,525.6
Potash fertilizers (c)* . . .	1,429.7	1,248.6	1,030.8
Synthetic rubber	732.8	865.2	1,219.8
Plastics	8,711.0	10,875.1	12,887.1
Motor spirit (gasoline) . . .	37,412.7	41,346.7	41,546.6
Distillate fuel oil (diesel oil) . .	63,026.8	70,796.2	74,856.6
Coke	120,737.4	121,840.2	131,307.7
Cement	573,000	597,000	661,040
Pig-iron	125,392.4	131,014.8	155,542.5
Crude steel	124,260	128,500	151,634
Internal combustion engines ('000 horse-power)†	178,016.2	188,573.0	205,311.7
Tractors—over 20 horse-power (number)	65,400	41,000	38,200
Railway freight wagons (number) .	18,600	27,300	30,700
Road motor vehicles ('000) . .	1,832	2,070	2,342
Bicycles ('000)	23,975.7	29,067.9	29,022.6
Electric fans ('000)	61,581.4	76,616.1	96,161.0
Mobile communication equipment ('000 units)	7,266	15,050	24,739
Floppy disks ('000)	460,000	473,000	488,000
Microcomputers ('000) . . .	4,050	6,720	8,777
Large semiconductor integrated circuits ('000)	1,400,000	2,392,000	2,226,000
Colour television receivers ('000) .	42,620	39,360	40,937
Cameras ('000)	48,322.9	55,145.2	59,620.9
Electric energy (million kWh) . .	1,239,300	1,355,600	1,480,802

* Production in terms of (a) nitrogen; (b) phosphoric acid; or (c) potassium oxide.

† Sales.

Finance

CURRENCY AND EXCHANGE RATES

Monetary Units

100 fen (cents) = 10 jiao (chiao) = 1 renminbiao (People's Bank Dollar), usually called a yuan

Sterling, Dollar and Euro Equivalents (31 December 2002)

£1 sterling = 13.341 yuan
US $1 = 8.277 yuan
€1 = 8.680 yuan
1,000 yuan = £74.95 = $120.81 = €115.20

Average Exchange Rate (yuan per US $)

2000	8.2785
2001	8.2771
2002	8.2770

Note: Since 1 January 1994 the official rate has been based on the prevailing rate in the interbank market for foreign exchange.

STATE BUDGET

(million yuan)*

Revenue	1999	2000	2001
Taxes	1,068,258	1,258,151	1,530,138
Industrial and commercial taxes	888,544	1,036,609	n.a.
Tariffs	56,223	75,048	84,052
Agricultural and animal husbandry taxes	42,350	46,531	48,170
Taxes on income of state-owned enterprises	63,900	82,741	n.a.
Taxes on income of collectively-owned enterprises	17,241	17,222	n.a.
Other receipts	105,153	109,250	138,470
Sub-total	1,173,411	1,367,401	n.a.
Less Subsidies for losses by enterprises	29,003	27,878	30,004
Total	1,144,408	1,339,523	1,638,604
Central Government	584,921	698,917	858,274
Local authorities	559,487	640,606	780,330

Expenditure †	1999	2000	2001
Capital construction	211,657	209,489	251,064
Agriculture, forestry and water conservancy	67,746	76,689	91,796
Culture, education, science and health care‡	240,806	273,688	336,102
National defence	107,640	120,754	144,204
Administration	152,568	178,758	219,752
Pensions and social welfare . .	17,988	21,303	26,668
Subsidies to compensate price increases	69,764	104,228	74,151
Development of enterprises . .	76,605	86,524	99,156
Other purposes	373,993	517,217	647,365
Total	1,318,767	1,588,650	1,890,258
Central Government	415,233	551,985	576,802
Local authorities	903,534	1,036,665	1,313,456

* Figures represent a consolidation of the regular (current) and construction (capital) budgets of the central Government and local administrative organs. The data exclude extrabudgetary transactions, totalling (in million yuan): Revenue 338,517 (central 23,045, local 315,472) in 1999; 382,643 (central 24,763, local 357,879) in 2000; Expenditure 313,914 (central 16,482, local 297,432) in 1999; 352,901 (central 21,074, local 331,828) in 2000.

† Excluding payments of debt interest.

‡ Current expenditure only.

INTERNATIONAL RESERVES

(US $ million at 31 December)

	1999	2000	2001
Gold*	608	578	3,093
IMF special drawing rights . . .	741	798	851
Reserve position in IMF . . .	2,312	1,905	2,590
Foreign exchange†	154,675	165,574	212,165
Total†	158,336	168,856	218,698

* Valued at SDR 35 per troy ounce.

† Excluding the Bank of China's holdings of foreign exchange.

Source: IMF, *International Financial Statistics*.

MONEY SUPPLY

(million yuan at 31 December)*

	2000	2001	2002
Currency outside banking institutions	1,464,990	1,568,730	1,727,800
Demand deposits at banking institutions	3,846,880	4,414,010	5,356,210
Total money (incl. others) . .	5,454,100	6,168,850	7,262,370

* Figures are rounded to the nearest 10 million yuan.

Source: IMF, *International Financial Statistics*.

COST OF LIVING
(General Consumer Price Index; base: previous year = 100)

	1999	2000	2001
Food	95.8	97.4	100.0
Clothing	97.3	99.1	98.1
Housing*	101.7	104.8	101.2
All items (incl. others)	98.6	100.4	100.7

* Including water, electricity and fuels.

NATIONAL ACCOUNTS
(million yuan at current prices)

Expenditure on the Gross Domestic Product*

	1999	2000	2001
Government final consumption expenditure	1,038,830	1,170,530	1,302,930
Private final consumption expenditure	3,933,440	4,291,140	4,592,330
Increase in stocks	122,610	−12,400	64,750
Gross fixed capital formation	2,947,550	3,262,380	3,681,330
Total domestic expenditure	8,042,430	8,711,650	9,641,340
Exports of goods and services			
Less Imports of goods and services	224,880	224,020	220,470
Sub-total	8,267,310	8,935,670	9,861,810
Statistical discrepancy†	−60,560	8,550	−268,480
GDP in purchasers' values	8,206,750	8,944,220	9,593,330

* Figures are rounded to the nearest 10 million yuan.
† Referring to the difference between the sum of the expenditure components and official estimates of GDP, compiled from the production approach.

Gross Domestic Product by Economic Activity*

	1999	2000	2001
Agriculture, forestry and fishing	1,447,200	1,462,820	1,460,990
Industry†	3,508,720	3,904,730	4,260,710
Construction	547,060	588,800	646,200
Transport, storage and communications	446,030	540,860	522,210
Wholesale and retail trade and catering	691,030	731,600	782,350
Other services	1,566,710	1,715,410	1,920,870
Total	8,206,750	8,944,220	9,593,330

* Figures are rounded to the nearest 10 million yuan.
† Includes mining, manufacturing, electricity, gas and water.

BALANCE OF PAYMENTS
(US $ million)

	1999	2000	2001
Exports of goods f.o.b.	194,716	249,131	266,075
Imports of goods f.o.b.	−158,734	−214,657	−232,058
Trade balance	35,982	34,474	34,017
Exports of services	26,248	30,430	33,334
Imports of services	−31,589	−36,031	−39,267
Balance on goods and services	30,641	28,874	28,084
Other income received	8,330	12,550	9,338
Other income paid	−22,800	−27,216	−28,563
Balance on goods, services and income	16,171	14,207	8,909
Current transfers received	5,368	6,861	9,125
Current transfers paid	−424	−550	−633
Current balance	21,115	20,518	17,401
Capital account (net)	−26	−35	−54
Direct investment abroad	−1,775	−916	−6,884
Direct investment from abroad	38,753	38,399	44,241
Portfolio investment assets	−10,535	−11,307	−20,654
Portfolio investment liabilities	−699	7,317	1,249
Other investment assets	−24,394	−43,864	20,813
Other investment liabilities	3,854	12,329	−3,933
Net errors and omissions	−17,641	−11,748	−4,732
Overall balance	8,652	10,693	47,447

Source: IMF, *International Financial Statistics*.

External Trade

PRINCIPAL COMMODITIES
(distribution by SITC, US $ million)

Imports c.i.f.	1998	1999	2000
Food and live animals	3,763.2	3,590.4	4,742.3
Crude materials (inedible) except fuels	10,536.1	12,526.9	19,685.8
Mineral fuels, lubricants, etc.	6,834.6	8,994.7	20,756.6
Petroleum, petroleum products, etc.	5,941.4	7,713.7	3,776.8
Crude petroleum oils, etc.	3,274.5	4,641.2	14,860.7
Chemicals and related products	19,907.2	23,693.3	29,768.7
Organic chemicals	3,512.3	5,418.4	8,301.5
Artificial resins, plastic materials, etc.	9,504.2	10,442.3	13,012.0
Products of polymerization, etc.	7,798.8	8,315.9	10,273.4
Basic manufactures	31,616.2	34,876.5	42,493.0
Textile yarn, fabrics, etc.	11,248.6	11,261.3	13,108.4
Iron and steel	6,563.1	7,586.8	9,795.2
Machinery and transport equipment	56,774.7	69,404.1	91,866.0
Machinery specialized for particular industries	8,152.4	8,146.1	10,556.8
General industrial machinery, equipment and parts	6,062.6	7,271.4	7,995.0
Office machines and automatic data-processing equipment	5,892.5	7,734.5	10,858.4
Telecommunications and sound equipment	7,817.9	9,363.7	12,412.8
Other electrical machinery, apparatus, etc.	16,670.9	23,866.0	35,641.7
Thermionic valves, tubes, etc.	8,331.6	13,391.0	21,155.6
Electronic microcircuits	4,602.7	7,533.0	13,300.0
Transport equipment and parts*	5,566.1	5,949.3	n.a.
Miscellaneous manufactured articles	8,348.6	9,632.8	12,699.8
Total (incl. others)	140,236.8	165,699.1	225,093.7

Source: Asian Development Bank, *Key Indicators of Developing Asian and Pacific Countries*.

Exports f.o.b.	1998	1999	2000
Food and live animals	10,599.5	10,447.0	12,270.8
Mineral fuels, lubricants, etc.	5,178.7	4,662.4	7,862.3
Chemicals and related products	10,205.9	10,230.0	11,917.5
Basic manufactures	33,067.6	33,858.9	43,305.0
Textile yarn, fabrics, etc.	12,967.7	13,193.0	16,316.4
Machinery and transport equipment	50,143.0	58,748.6	82,443.7
Office machines and automatic data-processing equipment	11,846.3	13,368.5	18,637.9
Automatic data-processing machines and units	7,066.6	7,922.0	10,994.1
Telecommunications and sound equipment	11,111.0	13,060.9	19,508.3
Other electrical machinery, apparatus, etc.	14,599.2	18,490.0	24,655.4
Transport equipment and parts*	5,566.1	6,259.8	n.a.
Miscellaneous manufactured articles	69,585.8	72,000.7	85,582.8
Clothing and accessories (excl. footwear)	30,121.2	30,146.4	36,147.3
Footwear	8,054.9	8,355.8	9,466.6
Baby carriages, toys, games and sporting goods	8,412.5	8,511.0	10,112.4
Children's toys, indoor games, etc.	7,258.4	7,324.1	8,555.3
Total (incl. others)	183,809.1	194,930.9	249,202.6

* Data on parts exclude tyres, engines and electrical parts.

Source: UN, *International Trade Statistics Yearbook*.

Imports (US $ million, 2001): Food and live animals 4,976; Crude materials (inedible) except fuels 22,128; Mineral fuels, lubricants, etc. 17,495; Chemicals and related products 32,106; Basic manufactures 41,939; Machinery and transport equipment 107,042; Miscellaneous manufactured articles 15,076; Total (incl. others) 243,610 (Source: Asian Development Bank, *Key Indicators of Developing Asian and Pacific Countries*).

Exports (US $ million, 2001): Food and live animals 12,778; Mineral fuels, lubricants, etc. 8,416; Chemicals and related products 13,354; Basic manufactures 43,823; Machinery and transport equipment 94,918; Miscellaneous manufactured articles 87,123; Total (incl. others) 266,160 (Source: Asian Development Bank, *Key Indicators of Developing Asian and Pacific Countries*).

PRINCIPAL TRADING PARTNERS
(US $ million)*

Imports c.i.f.	1999	2000	2001
Australia	3,607.2	5,024.0	5,426.4
Brazil	968.6	1,621.4	2,347.3
Canada	2,433.0	3,751.1	4,028.5
Finland	1,831.9	2,353.1	2,376.3
France	3,784.8	3,949.8	4,104.8
Germany	8,335.4	10,408.7	13,772.1
Hong Kong	6,891.9	9,429.0	9,423.0
Indonesia	3,050.9	4,402.0	3,888.1
Italy	2,679.9	3,078.4	3,789.2
Japan	33,763.4	41,509.7	42,796.9
Korea, Republic	17,226.2	23,207.4	23,389.2
Malaysia	3,605.6	5,480.0	6,205.2
Oman	635.4	3,261.8	1,609.6
Russia	4,222.6	5,769.9	7,959.4
Singapore	4,061.1	5,059.6	5,142.5
Sweden	2,151.8	2,674.7	2,173.2
Taiwan	19,526.8	25,493.6	27,339.5
Thailand	2,780.4	4,380.8	4,712.9
United Kingdom	2,994.8	3,592.5	3,527.1
USA	19,478.3	22,363.2	26,202.2
Total (incl. others)	165,699.1	225,093.7	243,613.5

Exports f.o.b.	1999	2000	2001
Australia	2,704.4	3,428.9	3,570.4
Canada	2,433.0	3,157.8	3,346.1
France	2,921.1	3,705.2	3,685.7
Germany	7,779.6	9,277.8	9,754.1
Hong Kong†	36,862.8	44,518.3	46,546.6
Indonesia	1,779.1	3,061.8	2,836.5
Italy	2,929.5	3,802.0	3,992.6
Japan	32,410.6	41,654.3	44,957.6
Korea, Republic	7,807.6	11,292.4	12,520.7
Malaysia	1,673.8	2,564.9	3,220.3
Netherlands	5,413.0	6,687.2	7,282.0
Russia	1,497.3	2,233.4	2,711.2
Singapore	4,502.2	5,761.0	5,791.9
Taiwan	3,949.9	5,039.0	5,000.2
United Kingdom	4,880.0	6,310.1	6,780.5
USA	41,946.9	52,099.2	54,282.7
Total (incl. others)	194,930.9	249,202.6	266,154.6

* Imports by country of origin; exports by country of consumption.
† The majority of China's exports to Hong Kong are re-exported.

Transport

	1999	2000	2001
Freight (million ton-km):			
Railways	1,283,840	1,366,260	1,457,510
Roads	572,430	612,940	633,040
Waterways	2,126,300	2,373,420	2,598,890
Air	4,230	5,027	4,372
Passenger-km (million):			
Railways	413,600	453,260	476,680
Roads	619,920	665,740	720,710
Waterways	10,730	10,050	8,990
Air	85,730	97,050	109,140

ROAD TRAFFIC
('000 motor vehicles in use)*

	1999	2000	2001
Passenger cars and buses	7,402.3	8,537.3	9,939.6
Goods vehicles	6,769.5	7,163.2	7,652.4
Total (incl. others)	14,529.4	16,089.1	18,020.4

* Excluding military vehicles.

SHIPPING

Merchant Fleet
(registered at 31 December)

	1999	2000	2001
Number of vessels	3,285	3,319	3,280
Total displacement ('000 grt)	16,314.5	16,498.8	16,646.1

Source: Lloyd's Register-Fairplay, *World Fleet Statistics*.

Sea-borne Shipping
(freight traffic, '000 metric tons)

	1999	2000	2001
Goods loaded and unloaded	1,051,620	1,256,030	1,426,340

Tourism

FOREIGN VISITORS
(arrivals, '000)

Country of origin	1999	2000	2001
Hong Kong and Macao	61,670.6	70,099.4	74,344.5
Taiwan.	2,584.6	3,108.6	3,442.0
Australia	203.5	234.1	255.1
Canada	213.7	236.6	253.9
France	155.6	185.0	199.5
Germany	217.6	239.1	253.4
Indonesia	182.9	220.6	224.2
Japan	1,855.2	2,201.5	2,385.7
Korea, Republic	992.0	1,344.7	1,678.8
Malaysia	372.9	441.0	468.6
Mongolia	354.5	399.1	387.1
Philippines	298.3	363.9	408.0
Russia	833.0	1,080.2	1,196.2
Singapore	352.5	399.4	415.0
Thailand	206.4	241.1	298.4
United Kingdom	258.9	283.9	302.5
USA	736.4	896.2	949.2
Total (incl. others)	72,795.6	83,443.8	89,012.9

Total tourism receipts (US $ million): 14,099 in 1999; 16,224 in 2000; 17,792 in 2001.

Communications Media

	1999	2000	2001
Television receivers ('000 in use)*	370,000	380,000	n.a.
Telephones ('000 main lines in use)	108,715.8	144,829*	179,034
Mobile cellular telephones ('000 subscribers)*	43,296	85,260	144,812
Personal computers ('000 in use)*	15,500	20,600	25,000
Internet users ('000)*	8,900	22,500	33,700
Book production:			
titles	141,831	143,376	154,526
copies (million)	7,316.3	6,270.0	6,310.0
Newspapers:			
number	2,038	2,007	2,111
average circulation ('000 copies)	186,320	179,140	181,300
Magazines:			
number	8,187	8,725	8,889
average circulation ('000 copies)	218,450	215,440	206,970

* Source: International Telecommunication Union.

1997 ('000 in use): Radio receivers 417,000; Facsimile machines 2,000 (Sources: UNESCO, *Statistical Yearbook*, and UN, *Statistical Yearbook*).

Education

(2001)

	Institutions	Full-time teachers ('000)	Students ('000)
Kindergartens	111,706	546	20,218
Primary schools	491,273	5,798	125,435
General secondary schools . .	80,432	4,188	78,360
Secondary technical schools .	2,690	184	3,917
Teacher-training schools . .	570	46	662
Agricultural and vocational schools	7,802	306	4,664
Special schools	1,531	28	386
Higher education	1,225	532	7,191

Adult literacy rate (UNESCO estimates): 84.1% (males 91.7%; females 76.3%) in 2000 (Source: UN Development Programme, *Human Development Report*).

Directory

The Constitution

A new Constitution was adopted on 4 December 1982 by the Fifth Session of the Fifth National People's Congress. Its principal provisions, including amendments made in 1993 and 1999, are detailed below. The Preamble, which is not included here, states that 'Taiwan is part of the sacred territory of the People's Republic of China'.

GENERAL PRINCIPLES

Article 1: The People's Republic of China is a socialist state under the people's democratic dictatorship led by the working class and based on the alliance of workers and peasants.

The socialist system is the basic system of the People's Republic of China. Sabotage of the socialist system by any organization or individual is prohibited.

Article 2: All power in the People's Republic of China belongs to the people.

The organs through which the people exercise state power are the National People's Congress and the local people's congresses at different levels.

The people administer state affairs and manage economic, cultural and social affairs through various channels and in various ways in accordance with the law.

Article 3: The state organs of the People's Republic of China apply the principle of democratic centralism.

The National People's Congress and the local people's congresses at different levels are instituted through democratic election. They are responsible to the people and subject to their supervision.

All administrative, judicial and procuratorial organs of the State are created by the people's congresses to which they are responsible and under whose supervision they operate.

The division of functions and powers between the central and local state organs is guided by the principle of giving full play to the initiative and enthusiasm of the local authorities under the unified leadership of the central authorities.

Article 4: All nationalities in the People's Republic of China are equal. The State protects the lawful rights and interests of the minority nationalities and upholds and develops the relationship of equality, unity and mutual assistance among all of China's nationalities. Discrimination against and oppression of any nationality are prohibited; any acts that undermine the unity of the nationalities or instigate their secession are prohibited.

The State helps the areas inhabited by minority nationalities speed up their economic and cultural development in accordance with the peculiarities and needs of the different minority nationalities.

Regional autonomy is practised in areas where people of minority nationalities live in compact communities; in these areas organs of self-government are established for the exercise of the right of autonomy. All the national autonomous areas are inalienable parts of the People's Republic of China.

The people of all nationalities have the freedom to use and develop their own spoken and written languages, and to preserve or reform their own ways and customs.

Article 5: The People's Republic of China shall be governed according to law and shall be built into a socialist country based on the rule of law.

The State upholds the uniformity and dignity of the socialist legal system.

No law or administrative or local rules and regulations shall contravene the Constitution.

All state organs, the armed forces, all political parties and public organizations and all enterprises and undertakings must abide by the Constitution and the law. All acts in violation of the Constitution and the law must be looked into.

No organization or individual may enjoy the privilege of being above the Constitution and the law.

Article 6: The basis of the socialist economic system of the People's Republic of China is socialist public ownership of the means of production, namely, ownership by the whole people and collective ownership by the working people.

The system of socialist public ownership supersedes the system of exploitation of man by man; it applies the principle of 'from each according to his ability, to each according to his work.'

In the initial stage of socialism, the country shall uphold the basic economic system in which the public ownership is dominant and diverse forms of ownership develop side by side, and it shall uphold the distribution system with distribution according to work remaining dominant and a variety of modes of distribution coexisting.

Article 7: The state-owned economy, namely the socialist economy under the ownership of the whole people, is the leading force in the national economy. The State ensures the consolidation and growth of the state-owned economy.

Article 8: The rural collective economic organizations shall implement a two-tier operations system that combines unified operations with independent operations on the basis of household contract operations and different co-operative economic forms in the rural areas—the producers', supply and marketing, credit, and consumers' co-operatives—are part of the socialist economy collectively owned by the working people. Working people who are all members of rural economic collectives have the right, within the limits prescribed by law, to farm plots of cropland and hilly land allotted for their private use, engage in household sideline production and raise privately-owned livestock.

The various forms of co-operative economy in the cities and towns, such as those in the handicraft, industrial, building, transport, commercial and service trades, all belong to the sector of socialist economy under collective ownership by the working people.

The State protects the lawful rights and interests of the urban and rural economic collectives and encourages, guides and helps the growth of the collective economy.

Article 9: Mineral resources, waters, forests, mountains, grassland, unreclaimed land, beaches and other natural resources are owned by the State, that is, by the whole people, with the exception of the forests, mountains, grassland, unreclaimed land and beaches that are owned by collectives in accordance with the law.

The State ensures the rational use of natural resources and protects rare animals and plants. The appropriation or damage of natural resources by any organization or individual by whatever means is prohibited.

Article 10: Land in the cities is owned by the State.

Land in the rural and suburban areas is owned by collectives except for those portions which belong to the State in accordance with the law; house sites and private plots of cropland and hilly land are also owned by collectives.

The State may in the public interest take over land for its use in accordance with the law.

No organization or individual may appropriate, buy, sell or lease land, or unlawfully transfer land in other ways.

All organizations and individuals who use land must make rational use of the land.

Article 11: The non-public sector of the economy comprising the individual and private sectors, operating within the limits prescribed by law, is an important component of the socialist market economy.

The State protects the lawful rights and interests of the non-public sector comprising the individual and private sectors. The State exercises guidance, supervision, and control over the individual and private sectors of the economy.

Article 12: Socialist public property is sacred and inviolable.

The State protects socialist public property. Appropriation or damage of state or collective property by any organization or individual by whatever means is prohibited.

Article 13: The State protects the right of citizens to own lawfully earned income, savings, houses and other lawful property.

The State protects by law the right of citizens to inherit private property.

Article 14: The State continuously raises labour productivity, improves economic results and develops the productive forces by enhancing the enthusiasm of the working people, raising the level of their technical skill, disseminating advanced science and technology, improving the systems of economic administration and enterprise operation and management, instituting the socialist system of responsibility in various forms and improving organization of work.

The State practises strict economy and combats waste.

The State properly apportions accumulation and consumption, pays attention to the interests of the collective and the individual as well as of the State and, on the basis of expanded production, gradually improves the material and cultural life of the people.

Article 15: The State practises a socialist market economy. The State strengthens economic legislation and perfects macro-control. The State prohibits, according to the law, disturbance of society's economic order by any organization or individual.

Article 16: State-owned enterprises have decision-making power in operations within the limits prescribed by law.

State-owned enterprises practise democratic management through congresses of workers and staff and in other ways in accordance with the law.

Article 17: Collective economic organizations have decision-making power in conducting economic activities on the condition that they abide by the relevant laws. Collective economic organizations practise democratic management, elect and remove managerial personnel, and decide on major issues in accordance with the law.

Article 18: The People's Republic of China permits foreign enterprises, other foreign economic organizations and individual foreigners to invest in China and to enter into various forms of economic co-operation with Chinese enterprises and other economic organizations in accordance with the law of the People's Republic of China.

All foreign enterprises and other foreign economic organizations in China, as well as joint ventures with Chinese and foreign investment located in China, shall abide by the law of the People's Republic of China. Their lawful rights and interests are protected by the law of the People's Republic of China.

Article 19: The State develops socialist educational undertakings and works to raise the scientific and cultural level of the whole nation.

The State runs schools of various types, makes primary education compulsory and universal, develops secondary, vocational and higher education and promotes pre-school education.

The State develops educational facilities of various types in order to wipe out illiteracy and provide political, cultural, scientific, technical and professional education for workers, peasants, state functionaries and other working people. It encourages people to become educated through self-study.

The State encourages the collective economic organizations, state enterprises and undertakings and other social forces to set up educational institutions of various types in accordance with the law.

The State promotes the nation-wide use of Putonghua (common speech based on Beijing pronunciation).

Article 20: The State promotes the development of the natural and social sciences, disseminates scientific and technical knowledge, and commends and rewards achievements in scientific research as well as technological discoveries and inventions.

Article 21: The State develops medical and health services, promotes modern medicine and traditional Chinese medicine, encourages and supports the setting up of various medical and health facilities by the rural economic collectives, state enterprises and undertakings and neighbourhood organizations, and promotes sanitation activities of a mass character, all to protect the people's health.

The State develops physical culture and promotes mass sports activities to build up the people's physique.

Article 22: The State promotes the development of literature and art, the press, broadcasting and television undertakings, publishing and distribution services, libraries, museums, cultural centres and other cultural undertakings, that serve the people and socialism, and sponsors mass cultural activities.

The State protects places of scenic and historical interest, valuable cultural monuments and relics and other important items of China's historical and cultural heritage.

Article 23: The State trains specialized personnel in all fields who serve socialism, increases the number of intellectuals and creates conditions to give full scope to their role in socialist modernization.

Article 24: The State strengthens the building of socialist spiritual civilization through spreading education in high ideals and morality, general education and education in discipline and the legal system, and through promoting the formulation and observance of rules of conduct and common pledges by different sections of the people in urban and rural areas.

The State advocates the civic virtues of love for the motherland, for the people, for labour, for science and for socialism; it educates the people in patriotism, collectivism, internationalism and communism and in dialectical and historical materialism; it combats capitalist, feudalist and other decadent ideas.

Article 25: The State promotes family planning so that population growth may fit the plans for economic and social development.

Article 26: The State protects and improves the living environment and the ecological environment, and prevents and remedies pollution and other public hazards.

The State organizes and encourages afforestation and the protection of forests.

Article 27: All state organs carry out the principle of simple and efficient administration, the system of responsibility for work and the system of training functionaries and appraising their work in order constantly to improve quality of work and efficiency and combat bureaucratism.

All state organs and functionaries must rely on the support of the people, keep in close touch with them, heed their opinions and suggestions, accept their supervision and work hard to serve them.

Article 28: The State maintains public order and suppresses treasonable and other criminal activities that endanger national security; it penalizes activities that endanger public security and disrupt the socialist economy as well as other criminal activities; and it punishes and reforms criminals.

Article 29: The armed forces of the People's Republic of China belong to the people. Their tasks are to strengthen national defence, resist aggression, defend the motherland, safeguard the people's peaceful labour, participate in national reconstruction, and work hard to serve the people.

The State strengthens the revolutionization, modernization and regularization of the armed forces in order to increase the national defence capability.

Article 30: The administrative division of the People's Republic of China is as follows:

(1) The country is divided into provinces, autonomous regions and municipalities directly under the central government;

(2) Provinces and autonomous regions are divided into autonomous prefectures, counties, autonomous counties and cities;

(3) Counties and autonomous counties are divided into townships, nationality townships and towns.

Municipalities directly under the central government and other large cities are divided into districts and counties. Autonomous prefectures are divided into counties, autonomous counties, and cities.

All autonomous regions, autonomous prefectures and autonomous counties are national autonomous areas.

Article 31: The State may establish special administrative regions when necessary. The systems to be instituted in special administrative regions shall be prescribed by law enacted by the National People's Congress in the light of the specific conditions.

Article 32: The People's Republic of China protects the lawful rights and interests of foreigners within Chinese territory, and while on Chinese territory foreigners must abide by the law of the People's Republic of China.

The People's Republic of China may grant asylum to foreigners who request it for political reasons.

FUNDAMENTAL RIGHTS AND DUTIES OF CITIZENS

Article 33: All persons holding the nationality of the People's Republic of China are citizens of the People's Republic of China.

All citizens of the People's Republic of China are equal before the law.

Every citizen enjoys the rights and at the same time must perform the duties prescribed by the Constitution and the law.

Article 34: All citizens of the People's Republic of China who have reached the age of 18 have the right to vote and stand for election, regardless of nationality, race, sex, occupation, family background, religious belief, education, property status, or length of residence, except persons deprived of political rights according to law.

Article 35: Citizens of the People's Republic of China enjoy freedom of speech, of the press, of assembly, of association, of procession and of demonstration.

Article 36: Citizens of the People's Republic of China enjoy freedom of religious belief.

No state organ, public organization or individual may compel citizens to believe in, or not to believe in, any religion; nor may they discriminate against citizens who believe in, or do not believe in, any religion.

The State protects normal religious activities. No one may make use of religion to engage in activities that disrupt public order, impair the health of citizens or interfere with the educational system of the state.

Religious bodies and religious affairs are not subject to any foreign domination.

Article 37: The freedom of person of citizens of the People's Republic of China is inviolable.

No citizen may be arrested except with the approval or by decision of a people's procuratorate or by decision of a people's court, and arrests must be made by a public security organ.

Unlawful deprivation or restriction of citizens' freedom of person by detention or other means is prohibited; and unlawful search of the person of citizens is prohibited.

Article 38: The personal dignity of citizens of the People's Republic of China is inviolable. Insult, libel, false charge or frame-up directed against citizens by any means is prohibited.

Article 39: The home of citizens of the People's Republic of China is inviolable. Unlawful search of, or intrusion into, a citizen's home is prohibited.

Article 40: The freedom and privacy of correspondence of citizens of the People's Republic of China are protected by law. No organization or individual may, on any ground, infringe upon the freedom and privacy of citizens' correspondence except in cases where, to meet the needs of state security or of investigation into criminal offences, public security or procuratorial organs are permitted to censor correspondence in accordance with procedures prescribed by law.

Article 41: Citizens of the People's Republic of China have the right to criticize and make suggestions to any state organ or functionary. Citizens have the right to make to relevant state organs complaints and charges against, or exposures of, violation of the law or dereliction of duty by any state organ or functionary; but fabrication or distortion of facts with the intention of libel or frame-up is prohibited.

In case of complaints, charges or exposures made by citizens, the state organ concerned must deal with them in a responsible manner after ascertaining the facts. No one may suppress such complaints, charges and exposures, or retaliate against the citizen making them.

Citizens who have suffered losses through infringement of their civic rights by any state organ or functionary have the right to compensation in accordance with the law.

Article 42: Citizens of the People's Republic of China have the right as well as the duty to work.

Using various channels, the State creates conditions for employment, strengthens labour protection, improves working conditions and, on the basis of expanded production, increases remuneration for work and social benefits.

Work is the glorious duty of every able-bodied citizen. All working people in state-owned enterprises and in urban and rural economic collectives should perform their tasks with an attitude consonant with their status as masters of the country. The State promotes socialist labour emulation, and commends and rewards model and advanced workers. The State encourages citizens to take part in voluntary labour.

The State provides necessary vocational training to citizens before they are employed.

Article 43: Working people in the People's Republic of China have the right to rest.

The State expands facilities for rest and recuperation of working people, and prescribes working hours and vacations for workers and staff.

Article 44: The State prescribes by law the system of retirement for workers and staff in enterprises and undertakings and for functionaries of organs of state. The livelihood of retired personnel is ensured by the State and society.

Article 45: Citizens of the People's Republic of China have the right to material assistance from the State and society when they are old, ill or disabled. The State develops the social insurance, social relief and medical and health services that are required to enable citizens to enjoy this right.

The State and society ensure the livelihood of disabled members of the armed forces, provide pensions to the families of martyrs and give preferential treatment to the families of military personnel.

The State and society help make arrangements for the work, livelihood and education of the blind, deaf-mute and other handicapped citizens.

Article 46: Citizens of the People's Republic of China have the duty as well as the right to receive education.

The State promotes the all-round moral, intellectual and physical development of children and young people.

Article 47: Citizens of the People's Republic of China have the freedom to engage in scientific research, literary and artistic creation and other cultural pursuits. The State encourages and assists creative endeavours conducive to the interests of the people that are made by citizens engaged in education, science, technology, literature, art and other cultural work.

Article 48: Women in the People's Republic of China enjoy equal rights with men in all spheres of life, political, economic, cultural and social, including family life.

The State protects the rights and interests of women, applies the principle of equal pay for equal work for men and women alike and trains and selects cadres from among women.

Article 49: Marriage, the family and mother and child are protected by the State.

Both husband and wife have the duty to practise family planning.

Parents have the duty to rear and educate their minor children, and children who have come of age have the duty to support and assist their parents.

Violation of the freedom of marriage is prohibited. Maltreatment of old people, women and children is prohibited.

Article 50: The People's Republic of China protects the legitimate rights and interests of Chinese nationals residing abroad and protects the lawful rights and interests of returned overseas Chinese and of the family members of Chinese nationals residing abroad.

Article 51: The exercise by citizens of the People's Republic of China of their freedoms and rights may not infringe upon the interests of the State, of society and of the collective, or upon the lawful freedoms and rights of other citizens.

Article 52: It is the duty of citizens of the People's Republic of China to safeguard the unity of the country and the unity of all its nationalities.

Article 53: Citizens of the People's Republic of China must abide by the Constitution and the law, keep state secrets, protect public property and observe labour discipline and public order and respect social ethics.

Article 54: It is the duty of citizens of the People's Republic of China to safeguard the security, honour and interests of the motherland; they must not commit acts detrimental to the security, honour and interests of the motherland.

Article 55: It is the sacred obligation of every citizen of the People's Republic of China to defend the motherland and resist aggression.

It is the honourable duty of citizens of the People's Republic of China to perform military service and join the militia in accordance with the law.

Article 56: It is the duty of citizens of the People's Republic of China to pay taxes in accordance with the law.

STRUCTURE OF THE STATE

The National People's Congress

Article 57: The National People's Congress of the People's Republic of China is the highest organ of state power. Its permanent body is the Standing Committee of the National People's Congress.

Article 58: The National People's Congress and its Standing Committee exercise the legislative power of the State.

Article 59: The National People's Congress is composed of deputies elected by the provinces, autonomous regions and municipalities directly under the Central Government, and by the armed forces. All the minority nationalities are entitled to appropriate representation.

Election of deputies to the National People's Congress is conducted by the Standing Committee of the National People's Congress.

The number of deputies to the National People's Congress and the manner of their election are prescribed by law.

Article 60: The National People's Congress is elected for a term of five years.

Two months before the expiration of the term of office of a National People's Congress, its Standing Committee must ensure that the election of deputies to the succeeding National People's Congress is completed. Should exceptional circumstances prevent such an election, it may be postponed by decision of a majority vote of more than two-thirds of all those on the Standing Committee of the incumbent National People's Congress, and the term of office of the incumbent National People's Congress may be extended. The election of deputies to the succeeding National People's Congress must be completed within one year after the termination of such exceptional circumstances.

Article 61: The National People's Congress meets in session once a year and is convened by its Standing Committee. A session of the National People's Congress may be convened at any time the Standing Committee deems this necessary, or when more than one-fifth of the deputies to the National People's Congress so propose.

When the National People's Congress meets, it elects a presidium to conduct its session.

Article 62: The National People's Congress exercises the following functions and powers:

(1) to amend the Constitution;

(2) to supervise the enforcement of the Constitution;

(3) to enact and amend basic statutes concerning criminal offences, civil affairs, the state organs and other matters;

(4) to elect the President and the Vice-President of the People's Republic of China;

(5) to decide on the choice of the Premier of the State Council upon nomination by the President of the People's Republic of China, and to decide on the choice of the Vice-Premiers, State Councillors, Ministers in charge of Ministries or Commissions and the Auditor-General and the Secretary-General of the State Council upon nomination by the Premier;

(6) to elect the Chairman of the Central Military Commission and, upon his nomination, to decide on the choice of all the others on the Central Military Commission;

(7) to elect the President of the Supreme People's Court;

(8) to elect the Procurator-General of the Supreme People's Procuratorate;

(9) to examine and approve the plan for national economic and social development and the reports on its implementation;

(10) to examine and approve the state budget and the report on its implementation;

(11) to alter or annul inappropriate decisions of the Standing Committee of the National People's Congress;

(12) to approve the establishment of provinces, autonomous regions, and municipalities directly under the Central Government;

(13) to decide on the establishment of special administrative regions and the systems to be instituted there;

(14) to decide on questions of war and peace; and

(15) to exercise such other functions and powers as the highest organ of state power should exercise.

Article 63: The National People's Congress has the power to recall or remove from office the following persons:

(1) the President and the Vice-President of the People's Republic of China;

(2) the Premier, Vice-Premiers, State Councillors, Ministers in charge of Ministries or Commissions and the Auditor-General and the Secretary-General of the State Council;

(3) the Chairman of the Central Military Commission and others on the Commission;

(4) the President of the Supreme People's Court; and

(5) the Procurator-General of the Supreme People's Procuratorate.

Article 64: Amendments to the Constitution are to be proposed by the Standing Committee of the National People's Congress or by more than one-fifth of the deputies to the National People's Congress and adopted by a majority vote of more than two-thirds of all the deputies to the Congress.

Statutes and resolutions are adopted by a majority vote of more than one-half of all the deputies to the National People's Congress.

Article 65: The Standing Committee of the National People's Congress is composed of the following:

the Chairman;
the Vice-Chairmen;
the Secretary-General; and
members.

Minority nationalities are entitled to appropriate representation on the Standing Committee of the National People's Congress.

The National People's Congress elects, and has the power to recall, all those on its Standing Committee.

No one on the Standing Committee of the National People's Congress shall hold any post in any of the administrative, judicial or procuratorial organs of the State.

Article 66: The Standing Committee of the National People's Congress is elected for the same term as the National People's Congress; it exercises its functions and powers until a new Standing Committee is elected by the succeeding National People's Congress.

The Chairman and Vice-Chairmen of the Standing Committee shall serve no more than two consecutive terms.

Article 67: The Standing Committee of the National People's Congress exercises the following functions and powers:

(1) to interpret the Constitution and supervise its enforcement;

(2) to enact and amend statutes with the exception of those which should be enacted by the National People's Congress;

(3) to enact, when the National People's Congress is not in session, partial supplements and amendments to statutes enacted by the National People's Congress provided that they do not contravene the basic principles of these statutes;

(4) to interpret statutes;

(5) to examine and approve, when the National People's Congress is not in session, partial adjustments to the plan for national economic and social development and to the state budget that prove necessary in the course of their implementation;

(6) to supervise the work of the State Council, the Central Military Commission, the Supreme People's Court and the Supreme People's Procuratorate;

(7) to annul those administrative rules and regulations, decisions or orders of the State Council that contravene the Constitution or the statutes;

(8) to annul those local regulations or decisions of the organs of state power of provinces, autonomous regions and municipalities directly under the Central Government that contravene the Constitution, the statutes or the administrative rules and regulations;

(9) to decide, when the National People's Congress is not in session, on the choice of Ministers in charge of Ministries or Commissions or the Auditor-General and the Secretary-General of

the State Council upon nomination by the Premier of the State Council;

(10) to decide, upon nomination by the Chairman of the Central Military Commission, on the choice of others on the Commission, when the National People's Congress is not in session.

(11) to appoint and remove the Vice-Presidents and judges of the Supreme People's Court, members of its Judicial Committee and the President of the Military Court at the suggestion of the President of the Supreme People's Court;

(12) to appoint and remove the Deputy Procurators-General and Procurators of the Supreme People's Procuratorate, members of its Procuratorial Committee and the Chief Procurator of the Military Procuratorate at the request of the Procurator-General of the Supreme People's Procuratorate, and to approve the appointment and removal of the Chief Procurators of the People's Procuratorates of provinces, autonomous regions and municipalities directly under the Central Government;

(13) to decide on the appointment and recall of plenipotentiary representatives abroad;

(14) to decide on the ratification and abrogation of treaties and important agreements concluded with foreign states;

(15) to institute systems of titles and ranks for military and diplomatic personnel and of other specific titles and ranks;

(16) to institute state medals and titles of honour and decide on their conferment;

(17) to decide on the granting of special pardons;

(18) to decide, when the National People's Congress is not in session, on the proclamation of a state of war in the event of an armed attack on the country or in fulfilment of international treaty obligations concerning common defence against aggression;

(19) to decide on general mobilization or partial mobilization;

(20) to decide on the enforcement of martial law throughout the country or in particular provinces, autonomous regions or municipalities directly under the Central Government; and

(21) to exercise such other functions and powers as the National People's Congress may assign to it.

Article 68: The Chairman of the Standing Committee of the National People's Congress presides over the work of the Standing Committee and convenes its meetings. The Vice-Chairmen and the Secretary-General assist the Chairman in his work.

Chairmanship meetings with the participation of the Chairman, Vice-Chairmen and Secretary-General handle the important day-to-day work of the Standing Committee of the National People's Congress.

Article 69: The Standing Committee of the National People's Congress is responsible to the National People's Congress and reports on its work to the Congress.

Article 70: The National People's Congress establishes a Nationalities Committee, a Law Committee, a Finance and Economic Committee, an Education, Science, Culture and Public Health Committee, a Foreign Affairs Committee, an Overseas Chinese Committee and such other special committees as are necessary. These special committees work under the direction of the Standing Committee of the National People's Congress when the Congress is not in session.

The special committees examine, discuss and draw up relevant bills and draft resolutions under the direction of the National People's Congress and its Standing Committee.

Article 71: The National People's Congress and its Standing Committee may, when they deem it necessary, appoint committees of inquiry into specific questions and adopt relevant resolutions in the light of their reports.

All organs of State, public organizations and citizens concerned are obliged to supply the necessary information to those committees of inquiry when they conduct investigations.

Article 72: Deputies to the National People's Congress and all those on its Standing Committee have the right, in accordance with procedures prescribed by law, to submit bills and proposals within the scope of the respective functions and powers of the National People's Congress and its Standing Committee.

Article 73: Deputies to the National People's Congress during its sessions, and all those on its Standing Committee during its meetings, have the right to address questions, in accordance with procedures prescribed by law, to the State Council or the Ministries and Commissions under the State Council, which must answer the questions in a responsible manner.

Article 74: No deputy to the National People's Congress may be arrested or placed on criminal trial without the consent of the presidium of the current session of the National People's Congress or, when the National People's Congress is not in session, without the consent of its Standing Committee.

Article 75: Deputies to the National People's Congress may not be called to legal account for their speeches or votes at its meetings.

Article 76: Deputies to the National People's Congress must play an exemplary role in abiding by the Constitution and the law and keeping state secrets and, in production and other work and their public activities, assist in the enforcement of the Constitution and the law.

Deputies to the National People's Congress should maintain close contact with the units which elected them and with the people, listen to and convey the opinions and demands of the people and work hard to serve them.

Article 77: Deputies to the National People's Congress are subject to the supervision of the units which elected them. The electoral units have the power, through procedures prescribed by law, to recall the deputies whom they elected.

Article 78: The organization and working procedures of the National People's Congress and its Standing Committee are prescribed by law.

The President of the People's Republic of China

Article 79: The President and Vice-President of the People's Republic of China are elected by the National People's Congress.

Citizens of the People's Republic of China who have the right to vote and to stand for election and who have reached the age of 45 are eligible for election as President or Vice-President of the People's Republic of China.

The term of office of the President and Vice-President of the People's Republic of China is the same as that of the National People's Congress, and they shall serve no more than two consecutive terms.

Article 80: The President of the People's Republic of China, in pursuance of decisions of the National People's Congress and its Standing Committee, promulgates statutes; appoints and removes the Premier, Vice-Premiers, State Councillors, Ministers in charge of Ministries or Commissions, and the Auditor-General and the Secretary-General of the State Council; confers state medals and titles of honour; issues orders of special pardons; proclaims martial law; proclaims a state of war; and issues mobilization orders.

Article 81: The President of the People's Republic of China receives foreign diplomatic representatives on behalf of the People's Republic of China and, in pursuance of decisions of the Standing Committee of the National People's Congress, appoints and recalls plenipotentiary representatives abroad, and ratifies and abrogates treaties and important agreements concluded with foreign states.

Article 82: The Vice-President of the People's Republic of China assists the President in his work.

The Vice-President of the People's Republic of China may exercise such parts of the functions and powers of the President as the President may entrust to him.

Article 83: The President and Vice-President of the People's Republic of China exercise their functions and powers until the new President and Vice-President elected by the succeeding National People's Congress assume office.

Article 84: In case the office of the President of the People's Republic of China falls vacant, the Vice-President succeeds to the office of President.

In case the office of the Vice-President of the People's Republic of China falls vacant, the National People's Congress shall elect a new Vice-President to fill the vacancy.

In the event that the offices of both the President and the Vice-President of the People's Republic of China fall vacant, the National People's Congress shall elect a new President and a new Vice-President. Prior to such election, the Chairman of the Standing Committee of the National People's Congress shall temporarily act as the President of the People's Republic of China.

The State Council

Article 85: The State Council, that is, the Central People's Government, of the People's Republic of China is the executive body of the highest organ of state power; it is the highest organ of state administration.

Article 86: The State Council is composed of the following: the Premier; the Vice-Premiers; the State Councillors; the Ministers in charge of ministries; the Ministers in charge of commissions; the Auditor-General; and the Secretary-General.

The Premier has overall responsibility for the State Council. The Ministers have overall responsibility for the respective ministries or commissions under their charge.

The organization of the State Council is prescribed by law.

Article 87: The term of office of the State Council is the same as that of the National People's Congress.

The Premier, Vice-Premiers and State Councillors shall serve no more than two consecutive terms.

Article 88: The Premier directs the work of the State Council. The Vice-Premiers and State Councillors assist the Premier in his work.

Executive meetings of the State Council are composed of the Premier, the Vice-Premiers, the State Councillors and the Secretary-General of the State Council.

The Premier convenes and presides over the executive meetings and plenary meetings of the State Council.

Article 89: The State Council exercises the following functions and powers:

(1) to adopt administrative measures, enact administrative rules and regulations and issue decisions and orders in accordance with the Constitution and the statutes;

(2) to submit proposals to the National People's Congress or its Standing Committee;

(3) to lay down the tasks and responsibilities of the ministries and commissions of the State Council, to exercise unified leadership over the work of the ministries and commissions and to direct all other administrative work of a national character that does not fall within the jurisdiction of the ministries and commissions;

(4) to exercise unified leadership over the work of local organs of state administration at different levels throughout the country, and to lay down the detailed division of functions and powers between the Central Government and the organs of state administration of provinces, autonomous regions and municipalities directly under the Central Government;

(5) to draw up and implement the plan for national economic and social development and the state budget;

(6) to direct and administer economic work and urban and rural development;

(7) to direct and administer the work concerning education, science, culture, public health, physical culture and family planning;

(8) to direct and administer the work concerning civil affairs, public security, judicial administration, supervision and other related matters;

(9) to conduct foreign affairs and conclude treaties and agreements with foreign states;

(10) to direct and administer the building of national defence;

(11) to direct and administer affairs concerning the nationalities, and to safeguard the equal rights of minority nationalities and the right of autonomy of the national autonomous areas;

(12) to protect the legitimate rights and interests of Chinese nationals residing abroad and protect the lawful rights and interests of returned overseas Chinese and of the family members of Chinese nationals residing abroad;

(13) to alter or annul inappropriate orders, directives and regulations issued by the ministries or commissions;

(14) to alter or annul inappropriate decisions and orders issued by local organs of state administration at different levels;

(15) to approve the geographic division of provinces, autonomous regions and municipalities directly under the Central Government, and to approve the establishment and geographic division of autonomous prefectures, counties, autonomous counties and cities;

(16) to decide on the enforcement of martial law in parts of provinces, autonomous regions and municipalities directly under the Central Government;

(17) to examine and decide on the size of administrative organs and, in accordance with the law, to appoint, remove and train administrative officers, appraise their work and reward or punish them; and

(18) to exercise such other functions and powers as the National People's Congress or its Standing Committee may assign it.

Article 90: The Ministers in charge of ministries or commissions of the State Council are responsible for the work of their respective departments and convene and preside over their ministerial meetings or commission meetings that discuss and decide on major issues in the work of their respective departments.

The ministries and commissions issue orders, directives and regulations within the jurisdiction of their respective departments and in accordance with the statutes and the administrative rules and regulations, decisions and orders issued by the State Council.

Article 91: The State Council establishes an auditing body to supervise through auditing the revenue and expenditure of all departments under the State Council and of the local government at different levels, and those of the state financial and monetary organizations and of enterprises and undertakings.

Under the direction of the Premier of the State Council, the auditing body independently exercises its power to supervise through auditing in accordance with the law, subject to no interference by any other administrative organ or any public organization or individual.

Article 92: The State Council is responsible, and reports on its work, to the National People's Congress or, when the National People's Congress is not in session, to its Standing Committee.

The Central Military Commission

Article 93: The Central Military Commission of the People's Republic of China directs the armed forces of the country.

The Central Military Commission is composed of the following: the Chairman; the Vice-Chairmen; and members.

The Chairman of the Central Military Commission has overall responsibility for the Commission.

The term of office of the Central Military Commission is the same as that of the National People's Congress.

Article 94: The Chairman of the Central Military Commission is responsible to the National People's Congress and its Standing Committee.

Two further sections, not included here, deal with the Local People's Congresses and Government and with the Organs of Self-Government of National Autonomous Areas, respectively.

The People's Courts and the People's Procuratorates

Article 123: The people's courts in the People's Republic of China are the judicial organs of the State.

Article 124: The People's Republic of China establishes the Supreme People's Court and the local people's courts at different levels, military courts and other special people's courts.

The term of office of the President of the Supreme People's Court is the same as that of the National People's Congress; he shall serve no more than two consecutive terms.

The organization of people's courts is prescribed by law.

Article 125: All cases handled by the people's courts, except for those involving special circumstances as specified by law, shall be heard in public. The accused has the right of defence.

Article 126: The people's courts shall, in accordance with the law, exercise judicial power independently and are not subject to interference by administrative organs, public organizations or individuals.

Article 127: The Supreme People's Court is the highest judicial organ.

The Supreme People's Court supervises the administration of justice by the local people's courts at different levels and by the special people's courts; people's courts at higher levels supervise the administration of justice by those at lower levels.

Article 128: The Supreme People's Court is responsible to the National People's Congress and its Standing Committee. Local people's courts at different levels are responsible to the organs of state power which created them.

Article 129: The people's procuratorates of the People's Republic of China are state organs for legal supervision.

Article 130: The People's Republic of China establishes the Supreme People's Procuratorate and the local people's procuratorates at different levels, military procuratorates and other special people's procuratorates.

The term of office of the Procurator-General of the Supreme People's Procuratorate is the same as that of the National People's Congress; he shall serve no more than two consecutive terms.

The organization of people's procuratorates is prescribed by law.

Article 131: People's procuratorates shall, in accordance with the law, exercise procuratorial power independently and are not subject to interference by administrative organs, public organizations or individuals.

Article 132: The Supreme People's Procuratorate is the highest procuratorial organ.

The Supreme People's Procuratorate directs the work of the local people's procuratorates at different levels and of the special people's procuratorates; people's procuratorates at higher levels direct the work of those at lower levels.

Article 133: The Supreme People's Procuratorate is responsible to the National People's Congress and its Standing Committee. Local people's procuratorates at different levels are responsible to the organs of state power at the corresponding levels which created them and to the people's procuratorates at the higher level.

Article 134: Citizens of all nationalities have the right to use the spoken and written languages of their own nationalities in court proceedings. The people's courts and people's procuratorates should provide translation for any party to the court proceedings who is not familiar with the spoken or written languages in common use in the locality.

In an area where people of a minority nationality live in a compact community or where a number of nationalities live together, hearings should be conducted in the language or languages in common use in the locality; indictments, judgments, notices and other documents should be written, according to actual needs, in the language or languages in common use in the locality.

Article 135: The people's courts, people's procuratorates and public security organs shall, in handling criminal cases, divide their functions, each taking responsibility for its own work, and they shall co-ordinate their efforts and check each other to ensure correct and effective enforcement of law.

THE NATIONAL FLAG, THE NATIONAL EMBLEM AND THE CAPITAL

Article 136: The national flag of the People's Republic of China is a red flag with five stars.

Article 137: The national emblem of the People's Republic of China is the Tiananmen (Gate of Heavenly Peace) in the centre, illuminated by five stars and encircled by ears of grain and a cogwheel.

Article 138: The capital of the People's Republic of China is Beijing (Peking).

The Government

HEAD OF STATE

President: Hu Jintao (elected by the 10th National People's Congress on 15 March 2003).

Vice-President: Zeng Qinghong.

STATE COUNCIL
(April 2003)

Premier: Wen Jiabao.

Vice-Premiers: Huang Ju, Wu Yi, Zeng Peiyan, Hui Liangyu.

State Councillors: Zhou Yongkang, Gen. Cao Gangchuan, Tang Jiaxuan, Hua Jianmin, Chen Zhili.

Secretary-General: Hua Jianmin.

Minister of Foreign Affairs: Li Zhaoxing.

Minister of National Defence: Gen. Cao Gangchuan.

Minister of State Development and Reform Commission: Ma Kai.

Minister of Education: Zhou Ji.

Minister of Science and Technology: Xu Guanhua.

Minister of State Commission of Science, Technology and Industry for National Defence: Zhang Yunchuan.

Minister of State Nationalities Affairs Commission: Li Dezhu.

Minister of Public Security: Zhou Yongkang.

Minister of State Security: Xu Yongyue.

Minister of Supervision: Li Zhilun.

Minister of Civil Affairs: Li Xueju.

Minister of Justice: Zhang Fusen.

Minister of Finance: Jin Renqing.

Minister of Personnel: Zhang Bolin.

Minister of Labour and Social Security: Zheng Silin.

Minister of Land and Natural Resources: Tian Fengshan.

Minister of Construction: Wang Guangtao.

Minister of Railways: Liu Zhijun.

Minister of Communications: Zhang Chunxian.

Minister of Information Industry: Wang Xudong.

Minister of Water Resources: Wang Shucheng.

Minister of Agriculture: Du Qinglin.

Minister of Commerce: Lu Fuyuan.

Minister of Culture: Sun Jiazheng.

Minister of Public Health: Wu Yi.

Minister of State Family Planning Commission: Zhang Weiqing.

Governor of the People's Bank of China: Zhou Xiaochuan.

Auditor-General of the National Audit Office: Li Jinhua.

MINISTRIES

Ministry of Agriculture: 11 Nongzhanguan Nanli, Chao Yang Qu, Beijing 100026; tel. (10) 64192293; fax (10) 64192468; e-mail webmaster@agri.gov.cn; internet www.agri.gov.cn.

Ministry of Civil Affairs: 147 Beiheyan Dajie, Dongcheng Qu, Beijing 100721; tel. (10) 65135333; fax (10) 65135332.

Ministry of Communications: 11 Jianguomennei Dajie, Dongcheng Qu. Beijing 100736; tel. (10) 65292114; fax (10) 65292345; internet www.moc.gov.cn.

Ministry of Construction: 9 Sanlihe Dajie, Xicheng Qu, Beijing 100835; tel. (10) 68394215; fax (10) 68393333; e-mail webmaster@ mail.cin.gov.cn; internet www.cin.gov.cn.

Ministry of Culture: 10 Chaoyangmen Bei Jie, Dongcheng Qu, Beijing 100020; tel. (10) 65551432; fax (10) 65551433; e-mail webmaster@whb1.ccnt.com.cn; internet www.ccnt.com.cn.

Ministry of Education: 37 Damucang Hutong, Xicheng Qu, Beijing 100816; tel. (10) 66096114; fax (10) 66011049; e-mail webmaster@moe.edu.cn; internet www.moe.edu.cn.

Ministry of Finance: 3 Nansanxiang, Sanlihe, Xicheng Qu, Beijing 100820; tel. (10) 68551888; fax (10) 68533635; e-mail webmaster@ mof.gov.cn; internet www.mof.gov.cn.

Ministry of Foreign Affairs: 225 Chaoyangmennei Dajie, Dongsi, Beijing 100701; tel. (10) 65961114; fax (10) 65962146; e-mail webmaster@fmprc.gov.cn; internet www.fmprc.gov.cn.

Ministry of Foreign Trade and Economic Co-operation: 2 Dongchangan Jie, Dongcheng Qu, Beijing 100731; tel. (10) 67081526; fax (10) 67081513; e-mail webmaster@moftec.gov.cn; internet www.moftec.gov.cn.

Ministry of Information Industry: 13 Xichangan Jie, Beijing 100804; tel. (10) 66014249; fax (10) 66034248; e-mail webmaster@ mii.gov.cn; internet www.mii.gov.cn.

Ministry of Justice: 10 Chaoyangmennan Dajie, Chao Yang Qu, Beijing 100020; tel. (10) 65205114; fax (10) 65205316.

Ministry of Labour and Social Security: 12 Hepinglizhong Jie, Dongcheng Qu, Beijing 100716; tel. (10) 84201235; fax (10) 64218350.

Ministry of Land and Natural Resources: 3 Guanyingyuanxiqu, Xicheng Qu, Beijing 100035; tel. (10) 66127001; fax (10) 66175348; internet www.mlr.gov.cn.

Ministry of National Defence: 20 Jingshanqian Jie, Beijing 100009; tel. (10) 66730000; fax (10) 65962146.

Ministry of Personnel: 12 Hepinglizhong Jie, Dongcheng Qu, Beijing 100716; tel. (10) 84223240; fax (10) 64211417.

Ministry of Public Health: 1 Xizhinenwai Bei Lu, Xicheng Qu, Beijing 100044; tel. (10) 68792114; fax (10) 64012369; e-mail zhou@ chsi.moh.gov.cn; internet www.moh.gov.cn.

Ministry of Public Security: 14 Dongchangan Jie, Dongcheng Qu, Beijing 100741; tel. (10) 65122831; fax (10) 65136577.

Ministry of Railways: 10 Fuxing Lu, Haidian Qu, Beijing 100844; tel. (10) 63244150; fax (10) 63242150; e-mail webmaster@ns .chinamor.cn.net; internet www.chinamor.cn.net.

Ministry of Science and Technology: 15B Fuxing Lu, Haidian Qu, Beijing 100862; tel. (10) 68515050; fax (10) 68515006; e-mail officemail@mail.most.gov.cn; internet www.most.gov.cn.

Ministry of State Security: 14 Dongchangan Jie, Dongcheng Qu, Beijing 100741; tel. (10) 65244702.

Ministry of Supervision: 4 Zaojunmiao, Haidian Qu, Beijing 100081; tel. (10) 62256677; fax (10) 62254181.

Ministry of Water Resources: 2 Baiguang Lu, Ertiao, Xuanwu Qu, Beijing 100053; tel. (10) 63203069; fax (10) 63202650.

STATE COMMISSIONS

State Commission of Science, Technology and Industry for National Defence: 2A Guang'anmennan Jie, Xuanwu Qu, Beijing 100053; tel. (10) 63571397; fax (10) 63571398; internet www.costind .gov.cn.

State Development and Planning Commission: 38 Yuetannan Jie, Xicheng Qu, Beijing 100824; tel. (10) 68504409; fax (10) 68512929; e-mail news@sdpc.gov.cn; internet www.sdpc.gov.cn.

State Economic and Trade Commission: 26 Xuanwumenxi Dajie, Xuanwumen Qu, Beijing 100053; tel. (10) 63192334; fax (10) 63192348; e-mail webmaster@setc.gov.cn; internet www.setc.gov.cn.

State Population and Family Planning Commission: 14 Zhichun Lu, Haidian Qu, Beijing 100088; tel. (10) 62046622; fax (10) 62051865; e-mail sfpcdfa@public.bta.net.cn; internet www.sfpc.gov .cn.

State Nationalities Affairs Commission: 252 Taipingqiao Dajie, Xicheng Qu, Beijing 100800; tel. and fax (10) 66017375.

Legislature

QUANGUO RENMIN DAIBIAO DAHUI
(National People's Congress)

The National People's Congress (NPC) is the highest organ of state power, and is indirectly elected for a five-year term. The first plenary session of the 10th NPC was convened in Beijing in March 2003, and was attended by 2,916 deputies. The first session of the 10th National Committee of the Chinese People's Political Consultative

Conference (CPPCC, Chair. Jia Qinglin), a revolutionary united front organization led by the Communist Party, took place simultaneously. The CPPCC holds discussions and consultations on the important affairs in the nation's political life. Members of the CPPCC National Committee or of its Standing Committee may be invited to attend the NPC or its Standing Committee as observers.

Standing Committee

In March 2003 158 members were elected to the Standing Committee, in addition to the following:

Chairman: WU BANGGUO.

Vice-Chairmen: WANG ZHAOGUO, LI TIEYING, ISMAIL AMAT, HE LULI, DING SHISUN, CHENG SIWEI, XU JIALU, JIANG ZHENGHUA, GU XIULIAN, RAIDI, SHENG HUAREN, LU YONGXIANG, UYUNQIMG, HAN QIDE, FU TIESHAN.

Secretary-General: SHENG HUAREN.

Provincial People's Congresses

Chairmen of Standing Committees of People's Congresses:

Provinces: WANG TAIHUA (Anhui), SONG DEFU (Fujian), LU KEJIAN (Gansu), LU ZHONGHE (Guangdong), QIAN YUNLU (Guizhou), WANG QISHAN (Hainan), BAI KEMING (Hebei), XU YOUFANG (Heilongjiang), LI KEQIANG (Henan), YANG YONGLIANG (Hubei), YANG ZHENGWU (Hunan), LI YUANCHAO (Jiangsu), MENG JIANZHU (Jiangxi), WANG YUNKUN (Jilin), WEN SHIZHEN (Liaoning), SU RONG (Qinghai), LI JIANGUO (Shaanxi), ZHAO ZHIHAO (Shandong), TIAN CHENGPING (Shanxi), ZHANG XUEZHONG (Sichuan), BAI ENPEI (Yunnan), XI JINPING (Zhejiang).

Special Municipalities: YU JUNBO (Beijing), HUANG ZHENDONG (Chongqing), GONG XUEPING (Shanghai), FANG FENGYOU (Tianjin).

Autonomous Regions: CAO BOCHUN (Guangxi Zhuang), CHU BO (Nei Monggol), CHEN JIANGUO (Ningxia Hui), RAIDI (Tibet—Xizang), ABULAHAT ABDURIXIT (Xinjiang Uygur).

People's Governments

Provinces

Governors: WANG JINSHAN (Anhui), LU ZHANGONG (Fujian), LU HAO (Gansu), HUANG HUAHUA (Guangdong), SHI XIUSHI (Guizhou), WANG XIAOFENG (Hainan), JI YUNSHI (Hebei), SONG FATANG (Heilongjiang), LI CHENGYU (Henan), LUO QINGQUAN (Hubei), ZHANG YUNCHUAN (Hunan), LIANG BAOHUA (Jiangsu), HUANG ZHIQUAN (Jiangxi), HONG HU (Jilin), BO XILAI (Liaoning), ZHAO LEJI (Qinghai), JIA ZHIBANG (Shaanxi), ZHANG GAOLI (Shandong), LIU ZHENUA (Shanxi), ZHANG ZHONGWEI (Sichuan), XU RONGKAI (Yunnan), LU ZUSHAN (Zhejiang).

Special Municipalities

Mayors: WANG QISHAN (acting—Beijing), WANG HONGJU (Chongqing), HAN ZHENG (Shanghai), DAI XIANGLONG (Tianjin).

Autonomous Regions

Chairmen: LI ZHAOZHUO (Guangxi Zhuang), UYUNQIMG (Nei Monggol), MA QIZHI (Ningxia Hui), LEGQOG (Tibet—Xizang), SIMAYI TIELI-WAERDI (Xinjiang Uygur).

Political Organizations

COMMUNIST PARTY

Zhongguo Gongchan Dang (Chinese Communist Party—CCP): Beijing; f. 1921; 61m. mems in Dec. 1998; at the 16th Nat. Congress of the CCP in Nov. 2002, a new Cen. Cttee of 198 full mems and 158 alternate mems was elected; at its first plenary session the 16th Cen. Cttee appointed a new Politburo.

Sixteenth Central Committee

General Secretary: HU JINTAO.

Politburo

Members of the Standing Committee: HU JINTAO, WU BANGGUO, WEN JIABAO, JIA QINGLIN, ZENG QINGHONG, HUANG JU, WU GUANZHENG, LI CHANGCHUN, LUO GAN.

Other Full Members: WANG LEQUAN, WANG ZHAOGUO, HUI LIANGYU, LIU QI, LIU YUNSHAN, LI CHANGCHUN, WU YI, WU BANGGUO, WU GUANZHENG, ZHANG LICHANG, ZHANG DEJIANG, CHEN LIANGYU, LUO GAN, ZHOU YONGKANG, HU JINTAO, YU ZHENGSHENG, HE GUOQIANG, JIA QINGLIN, Gen. GUO BOXIONG, HUANG JU, Gen. CAO GANGCHUAN, ZENG QINGHONG, ZENG PEIYAN, WEN JIABAO.

Alternate Member: WANG GANG.

Secretariat: ZENG QINGHONG, LIU YUNSHAN, ZHOU YONGKANG, HE GUOQIANG, WANG GANG, Gen. XU CAIHOU, HE YONG.

OTHER POLITICAL ORGANIZATIONS

China Association for Promoting Democracy: 98 Xinanli Guloufangzhuangchang, Beijing 100009; tel. (10) 64033452; f. 1945; mems drawn mainly from literary, cultural and educational circles; Chair. XU JIALU; Sec.-Gen. CHEN YIQUN.

China Democratic League: 1 Beixing Dongchang Hutong, Beijing 100006; tel. (10) 65137983; fax (10) 65125090; f. 1941; formed from reorganization of League of Democratic Parties and Organizations of China; 131,300 mems, mainly intellectuals active in education, science and culture; Chair. DING SHISUN; Sec.-Gen. ZHANG BAOWEN.

China National Democratic Construction Association: 208 Jixiangli, Chaowai Lu, Beijing 100020; tel. (10) 65523229; fax (10) 65523518; internet www.cndca.org.cn; f. 1945; 85,105 mems, mainly industrialists and business executives; Chair. CHENG SIWEI; Sec.-Gen. CHEN MINGDE.

China Zhi Gong Dang (Party for Public Interests): Beijing; e-mail zhigong@public2.east.net.cn; f. 1925; reorg. 1947; mems are mainly returned overseas Chinese and scholars; Chair. LUO HAOCAI; Sec.-Gen. QIU GUOYI.

Chinese Communist Youth League: 10 Qianmen Dongdajie, Beijing 100051; tel. (10) 67018132; fax (10) 67018131; e-mail guoji3acyt@yahoo.com; f. 1922; 68.5m. mems; First Sec. of Cen. Cttee ZHOU QIANG.

Chinese Peasants' and Workers' Democratic Party: f. 1930 as the Provisional Action Cttee of the Kuomintang; took present name in 1947; more than 65,000 mems, active mainly in public health and medicine; Chair. JIANG ZHENGHUA; Sec.-Gen. JIAO PINGSHENG (acting).

Jiu San (3 September) Society: f. 1946; fmrly Democratic and Science Soc. 68,400 mems, mainly scientists and technologists; Chair. WU JIEPING; Sec.-Gen. LIU RONGHAN.

Revolutionary Committee of the Chinese Kuomintang: tel. (10) 6550388; f. 1948; mainly fmr Kuomintang mems, and those in cultural, educational, health and financial fields; Chair. HE LULI; Sec.-Gen. LIU MINFU.

Taiwan Democratic Self-Government League: f. 1947; recruits Taiwanese living on the mainland; Chair. ZHANG KEHUI; Sec.-Gen. ZHANG HUAJUN.

During 1998 there were repeated failed attempts by pro-democracy activists to register an opposition party, the Chinese Democratic Party. The leaders of the party (Wang Youcai, Xu Wenli and Qin Yongmin) were sentenced to lengthy terms of imprisonment, and many other members of the party were detained.

Diplomatic Representation

EMBASSIES IN THE PEOPLE'S REPUBLIC OF CHINA

Afghanistan: 8 Dong Zhi Men Wai Dajie, Chao Yang Qu, Beijing 100600; tel. (10) 65321582; fax (10) 65321710; Chargé d'affaires QIAMUDDIN RAI BARLAS.

Albania: 28 Guang Hua Lu, Jian Guo Men Wai, Beijing 100600; tel. (10) 65321120; fax (10) 65325451; Ambassador KUJTIM XHANI.

Algeria: 2 Dong Zhi Men Wai Dajie, Chao Yang Qu, Beijing 100600; tel. (10) 65321231; fax (10) 65321648; Ambassador MADJID BOUGUERRA.

Angola: 1-13-1 Tayuan Diplomatic Office Bldg, Beijing 100600; tel. (10) 65326968; Ambassador JOÃO MANUEL BERNARDO.

Antigua and Barbuda: Guomen Bldg, Rm 1N, 1 Zuo Jia Zhuang, Chao Yang Qu, Beijing; tel. (10) 65326518; fax (10) 65326520; Ambassador JAMES THOMAS.

Argentina: Bldg 11, 5 Dong Wu Jie, San Li Tun, Beijing 100600; tel. (10) 65322090; fax (10) 65322319; e-mail echin@public.bta.net.cn; Ambassador JUAN CARLOS MORELLI.

Armenia: 9-2-62 Tayuan Diplomatic Office Bldg, Beijing 100600; tel. (10) 65325677; fax (10) 65325654; Ambassador VASILI GHAZARYAN.

Australia: 21 Dong Zhi Men Wai Dajie, San Li Tun, Beijing 100600; tel. (10) 65322331; fax (10) 65326718; e-mail webmaster@austemb.org.cn; Ambassador DAVID IRVINE.

Austria: 5 Xiu Shui Nan Jie, Jian Guo Men Wai, Beijing 100600; tel. (10) 65322726; fax (10) 65321505; e-mail oebpekin@public.bta.net.cn; Ambassador ERICH BUTTENHAUSER.

Azerbaijan: 3-2-31 San Li Tun Diplomatic Compound, Beijing 100600; tel. (10) 65324614; fax (10) 65324615; e-mail safirprc@public.fhnet.cn.net; Ambassador YASHAR TOFIGI ALIYEV.

Bahrain: 2-9-1 Tayuan Diplomatic Office Bldg, Beijing 100600; tel. (10) 65325025; fax (10) 65325016; Ambassador KARIM EBRAHIM AL-SHAKAR.

Bangladesh: 42 Guang Hua Lu, Beijing 100600; tel. (10) 65321819; fax (10) 65324346; e-mail embbd@public.intercom.com.cn; Ambassador IFTIKHARUL KARIM.

Belarus: 2-10-1 Tayuan Diplomatic Office Bldg, Xin Dong Lu, Chao Yang Qu, Beijing 100600; tel. (10) 65326426; fax (10) 65326417; Ambassador ULADZIMIR RUSAKEVICH.

Belgium: 6 San Li Tun Lu, Beijing 100600; tel. (10) 65321736; fax (10) 65325097; e-mail Beijing@diplobel.org; Ambassador GASTON VAN DUYSE-ADAM.

Benin: 38 Guang Hua Lu, Jian Guo Men Wai, Beijing 100600; tel. (10) 65323054; fax (10) 65325103; Ambassador PIERRE AGO DOSSOU.

Bolivia: 2-3-2 Tayuan Diplomatic Office Bldg, Beijing 100600; tel. (10) 65323074; fax (10) 65324686; e-mail embolch@public3.bta.net.cn; Ambassador OSCAR D. Z. MEDINACELI.

Bosnia and Herzegovina: 1-5-1 Tayuan Diplomatic Office Bldg; tel. (10) 65326587; fax (10) 65326418; Ambassador BORISLAV MARIĆ.

Botswana: 1-8-1/2 Tayuan Diplomatic Office Bldg, Beijing 100600; tel. (10) 65325751; fax (10) 65325713; Ambassador KGOSI SEEPAPITSO IV.

Brazil: 27 Guang Hua Lu, Jian Guo Men Wai, Beijing 100600; tel. (10) 65322881; fax (10) 65322751; e-mail empequim@public.bta.net.cn; Ambassador AFFONSO CELSO DE OURO-PRETO.

Brunei: Villa No. 3, Qijiayuan Diplomatic Compound, Jian Guo Men Wai Dajie, Chao Yang Qu, Beijing 100600; tel. (10) 65324094; fax (10) 65324097; Ambassador Haji ABD. HAMID ABD. HALID.

Bulgaria: 4 Xiu Shui Bei Jie, Jian Guo Men Wai, Beijing 100600; tel. (10) 65321946; fax (10) 65324502; Ambassador DIMITAR TSVETANOV TZANEV.

Burundi: 25 Guang Hua Lu, Jian Guo Men Wai, Beijing 100600; tel. (10) 65321801; fax (10) 65322381; e-mail ambbubei@yahoo.fr; Ambassador ALFRED NKURUNZIZA.

Cambodia: 9 Dong Zhi Men Wai Dajie, Beijing 100600; tel. (10) 65321889; fax (10) 65323507; Ambassador KHEK LERANG.

Cameroon: 7 San Li Tun, Dong Wu Jie, Beijing 100600; tel. (10) 65321771; fax (10) 65321761; Ambassador ELEIH-ELLE ETIAN.

Canada: 19 Dong Zhi Men Wai Dajie, Chao Yang Qu, Beijing 100600; tel. (10) 65323536; fax (10) 65324311; internet www.canada.org.cn/beijing; Ambassador JOSEPH CARON.

Cape Verde: 6-2-121, Tayuan Diplomatic Office Bldg, Beijing; tel. (10) 65327547; fax (10) 65327546.

Chile: 1 Dong Si Jie, San Li Tun, Beijing 100600; tel. (10) 65321591; fax (10) 65323170; e-mail echilecn@public3.bta.net.cn; Ambassador BENNY POLLACK ESKENAZI.

Colombia: 34 Guang Hua Lu, Jian Guo Men Wai, Beijing 100600; tel. (10) 65321713; fax (10) 65321969; Ambassador ALFONSO DE JESÚS CAMPO SOTO.

Congo, Democratic Republic: 6 Dong Wu Jie, San Li Tun, Beijing 100600; tel. (10) 65321995; fax (10) 65321360; Ambassador JOHNSON BACLONGANDI WA BINANA.

Congo, Republic: 7 Dong Si Jie, San Li Tun, Beijing 100600; tel. (10) 65321658; Ambassador PIERRE PASSI.

Côte d'Ivoire: 9 San Li Tun, Bei Xiao Jie, Beijing 100600; tel. (10) 65321223; fax (10) 65322407; Ambassador KONAN KRAMO.

Croatia: 2-72 San Li Tun Diplomatic Office Bldg, Beijing 100600; tel. (10) 65326241; fax (10) 65326257; e-mail vrhpek@public.bta.net.cn; Ambassador ZELJKO KIRINČIĆ.

Cuba: 1 Xiu Shui Nan Jie, Jian Guo Men Wai, Beijing 100600; tel. (10) 65321714; fax (10) 65322870; Ambassador ALBERTO RODRÍGUEZ ARUFE.

Cyprus: 2-13-2 Tayuan Diplomatic Office Bldg, Liang Ma He Nan Lu, Chao Yang Qu, Beijing 100600; tel. (10) 65325057; fax (10) 65324244; e-mail cyembpek@mail.sparkice.com.cn; Ambassador PETROS KESTORAS.

Czech Republic: Ri Tan Lu, Jian Guo Men Wai, Beijing 100600; tel. (10) 65326902; fax (10) 65325653; Ambassador TOMAS SMETANKA.

Denmark: 1 Dong Wu Jie, San Li Tun, Beijing 100600; tel. (10) 65322431; fax (10) 65322439; e-mail bjsamb@um.dk; internet www.dk-embassy-cn.org/; Ambassador OLE LOENSMANN POULSEN.

Djibouti: 2-2-102 Tayuan Diplomatic Office Bldg, Beijing; tel. (10) 65327857; fax (10) 65327858; Ambassador MOUSSA BOUH ODOWA.

Ecuador: 11-2-1 Diplomatic Apartments, Jian Guo Men Wai, Beijing 100600; tel. (10) 65322264; fax (10) 65323158; Ambassador JOSÉ RAFAEL SERRANO HERRERA.

Egypt: 2 Ri Tan Dong Lu, Jian Guo Men Wai, Beijing 100600; tel. (10) 65321825; fax (10) 65325365; Ambassador ALI HOUSSAM EL DIN MAHMOUD ELHEFNY.

Equatorial Guinea: 2 Dong Si Jie, San Li Tun, Beijing; tel. (10) 65323709; fax (10) 65323805; Ambassador MANUEL MOTO TOMO.

Eritrea: Tayuan Diplomatic Office Bldg, Beijing 100600; tel. (10) 56326534; fax (10) 65326532; Ambassador MOHAMMED NUR AHMED.

Ethiopia: 3 Xiu Shui Nan Jie, Jian Guo Men Wai, Beijing 100600; tel. (10) 65325258; fax (10) 65325591; e-mail ethembcn@public.bta.net.cn; Ambassador MAIT MARTINSON.

Fiji: 1-15-2 Tayuan Diplomatic Office Bldg, Beijing 100600; tel. (10) 65327305; fax (10) 6532 7253; e-mail lvratuvuki@hotmail.com; Ambassador LUKE VIDIRI RATUVUKI.

Finland: Beijing Kerry Centre, 26/F South Tower, 1 Guanghua Lu, Beijing 100020; tel. (10) 85298541; fax (10) 85298547; e-mail sanomat.pek@formin.fi; internet www.finland-in-china.com; Ambassador BENJAMIN BASIN.

France: 3 Dong San Jie, San Li Tun, Chao Yang Qu, Beijing 100600; tel. (10) 65321331; fax (10) 65324841; e-mail ambafra@public3.bta.net.cn; internet www.lotus.ia.ac.cn/ambafra; Ambassador JEAN-PIERRE LAFON.

Gabon: 36 Guang Hua Lu, Jian Guo Men Wai, Beijing 100600; tel. (10) 65322810; fax (10) 65322621; Ambassador M. OBIANG-NDOUDUM.

Germany: 17 Dong Zhi Men Wai Dajie, San Li Tun, Beijing 100600; tel. (10) 65322161; fax (10) 65325336; Ambassador JOACHIM BROUDRÉ-GRÖGER.

Ghana: 8 San Li Tun Lu, Beijing 100600; tel. (10) 65321319; fax (10) 65323602; Ambassador AFARE APEADU DONKOR.

Greece: 19 Guang Hua Lu, Jian Guo Men Wai, Beijing 100600; tel. (10) 65321588; fax (10) 65321277; Ambassador CHARALAMBOS ROCANAS.

Guinea: 2 Xi Liu Jie, San Li Tun, Beijing 100600; tel. (10) 65323649; fax (10) 65324957; Ambassador EL HADJI DJIGUI CAMARA.

Guinea-Bissau: Diplomatic relations re-established April 1998; Ambassador NICOLAU, DOS SANTOS.

Guyana: 1 Xiu Shui Dong Jie, Jian Guo Men Wai, Beijing 100600; tel. (10) 65321601; fax (10) 65325741; Ambassador RONALD MORTIMER AUSTIN.

Hungary: 10 Dong Zhi Men Wai Dajie, San Li Tun, Beijing 100600; tel. (10) 65321431; fax (10) 65325053; Ambassador OTTO JUHASZ.

Iceland: Landmark Tower 1, 802, 8 North Dongsanhuan Lu, Beijing 100004; tel. (10) 65907795; fax (10) 65907801; e-mail icemb.beijing@utn.stjr.is; internet www.iceland.org/cn; Ambassador OLAFUR EGILSSON.

India: 1 Ri Tan Dong Lu, Jian Guo Men Wai, Beijing 100600; tel. (10) 65321927; fax (10) 65324684; Ambassador SHIVSHANKAR MENON.

Indonesia: Diplomatic Office Bldg B, San Li Tun, Beijing 100600; tel. (10) 65325486; fax (10) 65325368; e-mail kombei@public3.bta.net.cn; Ambassador AA KUSTIA.

Iran: 13 Dong Liu Jie, San Li Tun, Beijing 100600; tel. (10) 65322040; fax (10) 65321403; Ambassador FEREYDOUN VERDINEJAD.

Iraq: 25 Xiu Shui Bei Jie, Jian Guo Men Wai, Beijing 100600; tel. (10) 65321950; fax (10) 65321596; Ambassador OSAMA B. MAHMOUD.

Ireland: 3 Ri Tan Dong Lu, Jian Guo Men Wai, Beijing 100600; tel. (10) 65322691; fax (10) 65326857; Ambassador DECLAN CONNOLLY.

Israel: Room 405, West Wing Office, 1 Jian Guo Men Wai Dajie, Beijing 100004; tel. (10) 65052970; fax (10) 65050328; e-mail israemb@public.bta.net.cn; Ambassador YEHOYADA HAIM.

Italy: 2 Dong Er Jie, San Li Tun, Beijing 100600; tel. (10) 65322131; fax (10) 65324676; e-mail ambpech@ambpech.org.cn; internet www.italianembassy.org.cn; Ambassador PAOLO BRUNI.

Japan: 7 Ri Tan Lu, Jian Guo Men Wai, Beijing 100600; tel. (10) 65322361; fax (10) 65324625; Ambassador KORESHIGE ANAMI.

Jordan: 5 Dong Liu Jie, San Li Tun, Beijing 100600; tel. (10) 65323906; fax (10) 65323283; Ambassador SAMIR I. AL-NAOURI.

Kazakhstan: 9 Dong Liu Jie, San Li Tun, Beijing 100600; tel. (10) 65326182; fax (10) 65326183; e-mail kazconscan@on.aibn.com; Ambassador ZHANYBEK SALIMOVICH KARIBZHANOV.

Kenya: 4 Xi Liu Jie, San Li Tun, Beijing 100600; tel. (10) 65323381; fax (10) 65321770; Ambassador MATTHEW KATHURIMA M'ITHIRI.

Korea, Democratic People's Republic: Ri Tan Bei Lu, Jian Guo Men Wai, Beijing 100600; tel. (10) 65321186; fax (10) 65326056; Ambassador CHOE JIN SU.

Korea, Republic: 3rd–4th Floors, China World Trade Centre, 1 Jian Guo Men Wai Dajie, Beijing 100600; tel. (10) 65053171; fax (10) 65053458; Ambassador KIM HA-JOONG.

Kuwait: 23 Guang Hua Lu, Jian Guo Men Wai, Beijing 100600; tel. (10) 65322216; fax (10) 65321607; Ambassador ABDUL-MUHSEN NASIR A. GEAN.

Kyrgyzstan: 2-4-1 Tayuan Diplomatic Office Bldg, Beijing 100600; tel. (10) 65326458; fax (10) 65326459; e-mail kyrgyzch@public2.east .net.cn; Ambassador ERLAN ABDYLDAEV.

Laos: 11 Dong Si Jie, San Li Tun, Chao Yang Qu, Beijing 100600; tel. (10) 65321224; fax (10) 65326748; e-mail laoemcn@public.east.cn .net; Ambassador THONGSAY BODHISANE.

Latvia: Unit 71, Green Land Garden, No. 1A Green Land Road, Chao Yang Qu, Beijing 100016; tel. (10) 64333863; fax (10) 64333810; e-mail kinas@163bj.com; Ambassador Dr EINARS SEMANIS.

Lebanon: 51 Dong Liu Jie, San Li Tun, Beijing; tel. (10) 65322197; fax (10) 65322770; Ambassador ZEIDAN AL-SAGHIR.

Lesotho: 2-3-13 San Li Tun Diplomatic Apartment, Beijing 100600; tel. (10) 65326842; fax (10) 65326845; e-mail doemli@public.bta.net .cn; Ambassador LEBOHANG K. MOLEKO.

Libya: 3 Dong Liu Jie, San Li Tun, Beijing 100600; tel. (10) 65323666; fax (10) 65323391; Secretary of the People's Bureau MUFTAH OTMAN MADI.

Lithuania: 8-2-12 Tayuan Diplomatic Office Bldg, Beijing 100600; tel. (10) 65324421; fax (10) 65324451; Ambassador ARTURAS ZUR-AUSKAS.

Luxembourg: 21 Nei Wu Bu Jie, Beijing 100600; tel. (10) 65135937; fax (10) 65137268; e-mail ambluxcn@public.bta.net.cn; Ambassador MARC UNGEHEUER.

Macedonia, former Yugoslav republic: 3-2-21 San Li Tun Diplomatic Office Bldg, Beijing; tel. (10) 65327846; fax (10) 65327847; e-mail macdebas@public3.bta.net.cn; Ambassador GEORGI EFREMOV.

Madagascar: 3 Dong Jie, San Li Tun, Beijing 100600; tel. (10) 65321353; fax (10) 65322102; e-mail ambpek@public2.bta.net.cn; Ambassador ROYAL MICHELSSON RAOELFILS.

Malaysia: 13 Dong Zhi Men Wai Dajie, San Li Tun, Beijing; tel. (10) 65322531; fax (10) 65325032; Ambassador Dato' ABDUL MAJID.

Mali: 8 Dong Si Jie, San Li Tun, Beijing 100600; tel. (10) 65321704; fax (10) 65321618; Ambassador MODIBO TIEMOKO TRAORE.

Malta: 1-52 San Li Tun Diplomatic Compound, Beijing 100600; tel. (10) 65323114; fax (10) 65326125; e-mail savfborg@public3.bta.net .cn; Ambassador SAVIOUR F. BORG.

Mauritania: 9 Dong San Jie, San Li Tun, Beijing 100600; tel. (10) 65321346; fax (10) 65321685; Ambassador ABDELLAHI OULD ABDI.

Mauritius: 202 Dong Wai Diplomatic Office Bldg, 23 Dong Zhi Men Wai Dajie, Chao Yang Qu, Beijing; tel. (10) 65325695; fax (10) 65325706; Ambassador L. K. C. LAM PO TANG.

Mexico: 5 Dong Wu Jie, San Li Tun, Beijing 100600; tel. (10) 65321717; fax (10) 65323744; e-mail embmxchn@public.bta.net.cn; Ambassador SERGIO LEY-LÓPEZ.

Moldova: 3-1-152 Tayuan Diplomatic Office Bldg, Beijing 100600; tel. (10) 65325379; Ambassador VICTOR BORSEVICI.

Mongolia: 2 Xiu Shui Bei Jie, Jian Guo Men Wai, Beijing 100600; tel. (10) 65321203; fax (10) 65325045; e-mail monembbj@public3.bta .net.cn; Ambassador L. AMARSANAA.

Morocco: 16 San Li Tun Lu, Beijing 100600; tel. (10) 65321489; fax (10) 65321453; e-mail embmor@public.bta.net.cn; Ambassador MIMOUN MEHDI.

Mozambique: 1-7-2 Tayuan Diplomatic Office Bldg, Beijing 100600; tel. (10) 65323664; fax (10) 65325189; e-mail embamoc@ public.bta.net.cn; Ambassador JOSÉ MARIA DA SILVA DE MORAIS.

Myanmar: 6 Dong Zhi Men Wai Dajie, Chao Yang Qu, Beijing 100600; tel. (10) 65321584; fax (10) 65321344; Ambassador U SEIN WIN AUNG.

Namibia: 2-9-2 Tayuan Diplomatic Office Bldg, Beijing 100600; tel. (10) 65324810; fax (10) 65324549; e-mail namemb@eastnet.com.cn; Ambassador H. U. IPINGE.

Nepal: 1 Xi Liu Jie, San Li Tun Lu, Beijing 100600; tel. (10) 65322739; fax (10) 65323251; Ambassador RAJESHWAR ACHARYA.

Netherlands: 4 Liang Ma He Nan Lu, Beijing 100600; tel. (10) 65321131; fax (10) 65324689; Ambassador PHILIP DE HEER.

New Zealand: 1 Ri Tan, Dong Er Jie, Chao Yang Qu, Beijing 100600; tel. (10) 65322731; fax (10) 65324317; e-mail nzemb@ eastnet.com.cn; Ambassador JOHN MCKINNON.

Niger: 3-2-12 San Li Tun, Beijing 100600; tel. (10) 65324279; e-mail nigerbj@public.bta.net.cn; Ambassador BOZARI SEYDOU.

Nigeria: 2 Dong Wu Jie, San Li Tun, Beijing; tel. (10) 65323631; fax (10) 65321650; Ambassador OLAGUNJU ADESAKIN.

Norway: 1 Dong Yi Jie, San Li Tun, Beijing 100600; tel. (10) 65322261; fax (10) 65322392; e-mail emb.beijing@mfa.no; Ambassador HAAKON B. HJELDE.

Oman: 6 Liang Ma He Nan Lu, San Li Tun, Beijing 100600; tel. (10) 65323956; fax (10) 65325030; Ambassador ABDULLAH HOSNY.

Pakistan: 1 Dong Zhi Men Wai Dajie, San Li Tun, Beijing 100600; tel. (10) 65322504; fax (10) 65322715; e-mail pak@public.bta.net.cn; Ambassador RIAZ MOHAMMAD KHAN.

Papua New Guinea: 2-11-2 Tayuan Diplomatic Office Bldg, Beijing 100600; tel. (10) 65324312; fax (10) 65325483; Ambassador BARNEY RONGAP.

Peru: 1-91 San Li Tun, Bangonglou, Beijing 100600; tel. (10) 65323477; fax (10) 65322178; e-mail embperu@public.bta.net.cn; internet www.embperu.cn.net; Ambassador MARTHA TOLEDO-OCAMPO UREÑA.

Philippines: 23 Xiu Shui Bei Jie, Jian Guo Men Wai, Beijing 100600; tel. (10) 65321872; fax (10) 65323761; e-mail beijingpe@ cinet.com.cn; internet www.philembassy-china.org; Ambassador JOSUE L. VILLA.

Poland: 1 Ri Tan Lu, Jian Guo Men Wai, Beijing 100600; tel. (10) 65321235; fax (10) 65321745; Ambassador KSAWERY BURSKI.

Portugal: 8 San Li Tun Dong Wu Jie, Beijing 100600; tel. (10) 65323497; fax (10) 65324637; Ambassador ANTONIO NUNES DE CAR-VALHO SANTANA.

Qatar: 2-9-2 Tayuan Diplomatic Office Bldg, 14 Liang Ma He Nan Lu, Beijing 100600; tel. (10) 65322231; fax (10) 65325274; Ambassador SALEH ABDULLA AL-BOUANIN.

Romania: Ri Tan Lu, Dong Er Jie, Beijing 100600; tel. (10) 65323442; fax (10) 65325728; e-mail roamb@ht.rol.cn.net; Ambassador VIOREL ISTICIOAIA.

Russia: 4 Dong Zhi Men Nei, Bei Zhong Jie, Beijing 100600; tel. (10) 65321291; fax (10) 65324853; e-mail rusemb@public3.bta.net.cn; Ambassador IGOR ROGACHEV.

Rwanda: 30 Xiu Shui Bei Jie, Jian Guo Men Wai, Beijing 100600; tel. (10) 65322193; fax (10) 65322006; e-mail ambarwda@public3.bta .net.cn; internet www.embarwanda-china.com; Ambassador JOSEPH BONESHA.

Saudi Arabia: 1 Bei Xiao Jie, San Li Tun, Beijing 100600; tel. (10) 65324825; fax (10) 65325324; Ambassador MOHAMMED A. AL-BESHIR.

Serbia and Montenegro: 1 Dong Liu Jie, San Li Tun, Beijing 100600; tel. (10) 65323516; fax (10) 65321207; e-mail ambyug@ netchina.com.cn; Ambassador ILIJA DJUKIĆ.

Sierra Leone: 7 Dong Zhi Men Wai Dajie, Beijing 100600; tel. (10) 65321222; fax (10) 65323752; Ambassador ALHUSIN DEEN.

Singapore: 1 Xiu Shui Bei Jie, Jian Guo Men Wai, Beijing 100600; tel. (10) 65323926; fax (10) 65322215; Ambassador CHIN SIAT-YOON.

Slovakia: Ri Tan Lu, Jian Guo Men Wai, Beijing 100600; tel. (10) 65321531; fax (10) 65324814; Ambassador PETER PAULEN.

Slovenia: Block F, 57 Ya Qu Yuan, King's Garden Villas, 18 Xiao Yun Lu, Chao Yang Qu, Beijing 100016; tel. (10) 64681030; fax (10) 64681040; Ambassador VLADIMIR GASPARIĆ.

Somalia: 2 San Li Tun Lu, Beijing 100600; tel. (10) 65321752; Ambassador MOHAMED HASSAN SAID.

South Africa: 5 Dongzhimen Wai Dajie, Chao Yang Qu, Beijing 100016; tel. (10) 65320171; fax (10) 65327319; e-mail safrican@163bj .com; Ambassador THEMBA M. N. KUBHEKA.

Spain: 9 San Li Tun Lu, Beijing 100600; tel. (10) 65321986; fax (10) 65323401; Ambassador EUGENIO BREGOLATY OBIOLS.

Sri Lanka: 3 Jian Hua Lu, Jian Guo Men Wai, Beijing 100600; tel. (10) 65321861; fax (10) 65325426; e-mail lkembj@public.east.cn.net; Ambassador B. A. B. GOONETILLEKE.

Sudan: Bldg 27, San Li Tun, Beijing 100600; tel. (10) 65323715; fax (10) 65321280; e-mail mission.sudan@itu.cn; Ambassador ABDEL-HAMEED ABDEEN MOHAMMED.

Sweden: 3 Dong Zhi Men Wai Dajie, San Li Tun, Beijing 100600; tel. (10) 65323331; fax (10) 65325008; e-mail ambassaden.peking@ foreign.ministry.se; internet www.swedemb-cn.org.cn; Ambassador BORJE LJUNGGREN.

Switzerland: 3 Dong Wu Jie, San Li Tun, Beijing 100600; tel. (10) 65322736; fax (10) 65324353; Ambassador DOMINIQUE DREYER.

Syria: 6 Dong Si Jie, San Li Tun, Beijing 100600; tel. (10) 65321563; fax (10) 65321575; Ambassador MOHAMMED KHEIR AL-WADI.

Tajikistan: 5-1-41 Tayuan Diplomatic Office Bldg, Beijing 100600; tel. (10) 65322598; internet (10) 65323039; Ambassador BOKHADYR NAJMIDINOVICH ABDOULLAYEV.

Tanzania: 8 Liang Ma He Nan Lu, San Li Tun, Beijing 100600; tel. (10) 65321408; fax (10) 65324985; Ambassador CHARLES ASILIA SANGA.

Thailand: 40 Guang Hua Lu, Jian Guo Men Wai, Beijing 100600; tel. (10) 65321903; fax (10) 65321748; Ambassador DON PRAMUDWINAI.

Togo: 11 Dong Zhi Men Wai Dajie, Beijing 100600; tel. (10) 65322202; fax (10) 65325884; Ambassador NOLANA TA-AMA.

Tunisia: 1 Dong Jie, San Li Tun, Beijing 100600; tel. (10) 65322435; fax (10) 65325818; e-mail ambtun@public.netchina.com.cn; Ambassador SALAH HAMDI.

Turkey: 9 Dong Wu Jie, San Li Tun, Beijing 100600; tel. (10) 65322490; fax (10) 65325480; e-mail trkelcn@public.bta.net.cn; Ambassador RAFET AKGUNAY.

Turkmenistan: King's Garden, Villa D-26, 18 Xiao Yuan Rd, Beijing; tel. (10) 65326975; fax (10) 65326976; e-mail China@a-1.net.cn; Ambassador GURBANMUKHAMMET KASYMOV.

Uganda: 5 Dong Jie, San Li Tun, Beijing 100600; tel. (10) 65322370; fax (10) 65322242; e-mail ugembssy@public.bta.net.cn; internet www.uganda.cn777.com.cn; Ambassador PHILIP IDRO.

Ukraine: 11 Dong Liu Jie, San Li Tun, Beijing 100600; tel. (10) 65324013; fax (10) 65326359; e-mail ukrembcn@public3.bta.net.cn; internet www.ukrembcn.org; Ambassador MYKHAYLO REZNYK.

United Arab Emirates: C801 Lufthansa Center, Office Building 50, Liangmaqiao Lu, Chao Yang Qu, Beijing 100016; tel. (10) 84514416; fax (10) 84514451; Ambassador JUMA RASHED JASSIM.

United Kingdom: 11 Guang Hua Lu, Jian Guo Men Wai, Beijing 100600; tel. (10) 65321961; fax (10) 65321937; internet www.britishembassy.org.cn; Ambassador Sir CHRISTOPHER HUM.

USA: 3 Xiu Shui Bei Jie, Beijing 100600; tel. (10) 65323831; fax (10) 65323178; internet www.usembassy-china.org.cn; Ambassador CLARK T. RANDT.

Uruguay: 1-11-2 Tayuan Diplomatic Office Bldg, Beijing 100600; tel. (10) 65324445; fax (10) 65327375; e-mail urubei@public.bta.net.cn; Ambassador PELAYO JOAQUÍN DÍAZ MUGUERZA.

Uzbekistan: 11 Bei Xiao Jie, San Li Tun, Beijing 100600; tel. (10) 65326305; fax (10) 65326304; Ambassador IZMATILLA R. IRGASHEV.

Venezuela: 14 San Li Tun Lu, Beijing 100600; tel. (10) 65321295; fax (10) 65323817; e-mail embvenez@public.bta.net.cn; Ambassador JUAN DE JESÚS MONTILLA SALDIVIA.

Viet Nam: 32 Guang Hua Lu, Jian Guo Men Wai, Beijing 100600; tel. (10) 65321155; fax (10) 65325720; Ambassador BUI HONG PHUC.

Yemen: 5 Dong San Jie, San Li Tun, Beijing 100600; tel. (10) 65321558; fax (10) 65324305; Ambassador ABDULWAHAB MOHAMED AL-SHAWKANI.

Zambia: 5 Dong Si Jie, San Li Tun, Beijing 100600; tel. (10) 65321554; fax (10) 65321891; Ambassador MWENYA LWATULA.

Zimbabwe: 7 Dong San Jie, San Li Tun, Beijing 100600; tel. (10) 65323795; fax (10) 65325383; Ambassador LUCAS PANDE TAVAYA.

Judicial System

The general principles of the Chinese judicial system are laid down in Articles 123–135 of the December 1982 Constitution (q.v.).

PEOPLE'S COURTS

Supreme People's Court: 27 Dongjiaomin Xiang, Beijing 100745; tel. (10) 65136195; f. 1949; the highest judicial organ of the State; handles first instance cases of national importance; handles cases of appeals and protests lodged against judgments and orders of higher people's courts and special people's courts, and cases of protests lodged by the Supreme People's Procuratorate in accordance with the procedures of judicial supervision; reviews death sentences meted out by local courts, supervises the administration of justice by local people's courts; interprets issues concerning specific applications of laws in judicial proceedings; its judgments and rulings are final; Pres. XIAO YANG (five-year term of office coincides with that of National People's Congress, by which the President is elected).

Local People's Courts: comprise higher courts, intermediate courts and basic courts.

Special People's Courts: include military courts, maritime courts and railway transport courts.

PEOPLE'S PROCURATORATES

Supreme People's Procuratorate: 147 Beiheyan Dajie, Beijing 100726; tel. (10) 65126655; acts for the National People's Congress in examining govt depts, civil servants and citizens, to ensure observance of the law; prosecutes in criminal cases; Procurator-Gen. JIA CHUNWANG (elected by the National People's Congress for five years).

Local People's Procuratorates: undertake the same duties at the local level. Ensure that the judicial activities of the people's courts, the execution of sentences in criminal cases and the activities of departments in charge of reform through labour conform to the law; institute, or intervene in, important civil cases that affect the interest of the State and the people.

Religion

During the 'Cultural Revolution' places of worship were closed. After 1977 the Government adopted a policy of religious tolerance, and the 1982 Constitution states that citizens enjoy freedom of religious belief and that legitimate religious activities are protected. Many temples, churches and mosques subsequently reopened. Since 1994 all religious organizations have been required to register with the Bureau of Religious Affairs. In the late 1990s a new religious sect, the Falun Gong (also known as Falun Dafa), emerged and quickly gained new adherents. However, the authorities banned the group, describing it as an 'evil cult'.

Bureau of Religious Affairs: Beijing; tel. (10) 652625; Dir YE XIAOWEN.

ANCESTOR WORSHIP

Ancestor worship is believed to have originated with the deification and worship of all important natural phenomena. The divine and human were not clearly defined; all the dead became gods and were worshipped by their descendants. The practice has no code or dogma and the ritual is limited to sacrifices made during festivals and on birth and death anniversaries.

BUDDHISM

Buddhism was introduced into China from India in AD 67, and flourished during the Sui and Tang dynasties (6th–8th century), when eight sects were established. The Chan and Pure Land sects are the most popular. According to official sources, in 1998 there were 9,500 Buddhist temples in China. There were 100m. believers in 1997.

Buddhist Association of China (BAC): f. 1953; Pres. YICHENG; Sec.-Gen. DAO SHUREN.

Tibetan Institute of Lamaism

Pres. BUMI JANGBALUOZHU; Vice-Pres. CEMOLIN DANZENGCHILIE.

14th Dalai Lama: His Holiness the Dalai Lama TENZIN GYATSO, Thekchen Choeling, McLeod Ganj, Dharamsala 176 219, Himachal Pradesh, India; tel. (91) 1892-21343; fax (91) 1892-21813; e-mail ohhdl@cta.unv.ernet.ind.

Spiritual and temporal leader of Tibet; fled to India after failure of Tibetan national uprising in 1959.

CHRISTIANITY

During the 19th century and the first half of the 20th century large numbers of foreign Christian missionaries worked in China. According to official sources, there were 10m. Protestants and more than 4m. Catholics in China in 2000, although unofficial sources estimate that the Christian total could be as high as 90m. The Catholic Church in China operates independently of the Vatican. In addition, there is an increasing number of Christian sects in China.

Three-Self Patriotic Movement Committee of Protestant Churches of China: Pres. JI JIANHONG; Sec.-Gen. DENG FUCUN.

China Christian Council: 169 Yuan Ming Yuan Lu, Shanghai 200002; tel. (21) 63210806; fax (21) 63232605; e-mail tspmccc@online.sh.cn; f. 1980; comprises provincial Christian councils; Pres. and acting Sec.-Gen. Rev. CAO SHENGJIE.

The Roman Catholic Church: Catholic Mission, Si-She-Ku, Beijing; Bishop of Beijing MICHAEL FU TIESHAN (not recognized by the Vatican).

Chinese Patriotic Catholic Association: Pres. MICHAEL FU TIESHAN; Sec.-Gen. LIU BAINIAN; c. 3m. mems (1988).

CONFUCIANISM

Confucianism is a philosophy and a system of ethics, without ritual or priesthood. The respects that adherents accord to Confucius are not bestowed on a prophet or god, but on a great sage whose teachings promote peace and good order in society and whose philosophy encourages moral living.

DAOISM

Daoism was founded by Zhang Daoling during the Eastern Han dynasty (AD 125–144). Lao Zi, a philosopher of the Zhou dynasty (born 604 BC), is its principal inspiration, and is honoured as Lord the Most High by Daoists. According to official sources, there were 600 Daoist temples in China in 1998.

China Daoist Association: Temple of the White Cloud, Xi Bian Men, Beijing 100045; tel. (10) 6367179; f. 1957; Pres. MIN ZHITING; Sec.-Gen. YUAN BINGDONG.

ISLAM

According to Muslim history, Islam was introduced into China in AD 651. There were some 18m. adherents in China in 1997, chiefly among the Wei Wuer (Uygur) and Hui people, although unofficial sources estimate that the total is far higher, in the tens of millions.

Beijing Islamic Association: Dongsi Mosque, Beijing; f. 1979; Chair. Imam Al-Hadji SALAH AN SHIWEI.

China Islamic Association: Beijing 100053; tel. (10) 63546384; fax (10) 63529483; f. 1953; Chair. Imam Al-Hadji SALAH AN SHIWEI; Sec.-Gen. YU ZHENGUI.

The Press

In December 2000 China had 2,007 newspaper titles (including those below provincial level) and 8,187 periodicals. Each province publishes its own daily. Only the major newspapers and periodicals are listed below. In late 1999 the Government announced its intention to merge or close down a number of newspapers, leaving a single publication in each province.

PRINCIPAL NEWSPAPERS

Anhui Ribao (Anhui Daily): 206 Jinzhai Lu, Hefei, Anhui 230061; tel. (551) 2827842; fax (551) 2847302; Editor-in-Chief ZHANG YUXUAN.

Beijing Ribao (Beijing Daily): 34 Xi Biaobei Hutong, Dongdan, Beijing 100743; tel. (10) 65131071; fax (10) 65136522; f. 1952; organ of the Beijing municipal cttee of the CCP; Dir WAN YUNLAI; Editor-in-Chief LIU ZONGMING; circ. 700,000.

Beijing Wanbao (Beijing Evening News): 34 Xi Biaobei Hutong, Dongdan, Beijing 100743; tel. (10) 65132233; fax (10) 65126581; f. 1958; Editor XIAO PEI; circ. 800,000.

Beijing Youth Daily: Beijing; national and local news; promotes ethics and social service; circ. 3m.–4m.

Changsha Wanbao (Changsha Evening News): 161 Caie Zhong Lu, Changsha, Hunan 410005; tel. (731) 4424457; fax (731) 4445167.

Chengdu Wanbao (Chengdu Evening News): Qingyun Nan Jie, Chengdu 610017; tel. (28) 664501; fax (28) 666597; circ. 700,000.

China Business Times: Beijing; f. 1989; Editor HUANG WENFU; circ. 500,000.

Chongqing Ribao (Chongqing Daily): Chongqing; Dir and Editor-in-Chief LI HUANIAN.

Chungcheng Wanbao (Chungcheng Evening News): 51 Xinwen Lu, Kunming, Yunnan 650032; tel. (871) 4144642; fax (871) 4154192.

Dazhong Ribao (Dazhong Daily): 46 Jinshi Lu, Jinan, Shandong 250014; tel. (531) 2968989; fax (531) 2962450; internet www.dzdaily.com.cn; f. 1939; Dir XU XIYU; Editor-in-Chief LIU GUANGDONG; circ. 2,100,000.

Economic News: Editor-in-Chief DU ZULIANG.

Fujian Ribao (Fujian Daily): Hualin Lu, Fuzhou, Fujian; tel. (591) 57756; daily; Dir HUANG SHIYUN; Editor-in-Chief HUANG ZHONGSHENG.

Gongren Ribao (Workers' Daily): Liupukang, Andingmen Wai, Beijing 100718; tel. (10) 64211561; fax (10) 64214890; f. 1949; trade union activities and workers' lives; also major home and overseas news; Dir LIU YUMING; Editor-in-Chief SHENG MINGFU; circ. 2.5m.

Guangming Ribao (Guangming Daily): 106 Yongan Lu, Beijing 100050; tel. (10) 63017788; fax (10) 63039387; f. 1949; literature, art, science, education, history, economics, philosophy; Editor-in-Chief YUAN ZHIFA; circ. 920,000.

Guangxi Ribao (Guangxi Daily): Guangxi Region; Dir and Editor-in-Chief CHENG ZHENSHENG.

Guangzhou Ribao (Canton Daily): 10 Dongle Lu, Renmin Zhonglu, Guangzhou, Guangdong; tel. (20) 81887294; fax (20) 81862022; f. 1952; daily; social, economic and current affairs; Editor-in-Chief LI YUANJIANG; circ. 600,000.

Guizhou Ribao (Guizhou Daily): Guiyang, Guizhou; tel. (851) 627779; f. 1949; Dir GAO ZONGWEN; Editor-in-Chief GAN ZHENGSHU; circ. 300,000.

Hainan Ribao (Hainan Daily): 7 Xinhua Nan Lu, Haikou, Hainan 570001; tel. (898) 6222021; Dir ZHOU WENZHANG; Editor-in-Chief CHANG FUTANG.

Hebei Ribao (Hebei Daily): 210 Yuhuazhong Lu, Shijiazhuang, Hebei 050013; tel. (311) 6048901; fax (311) 6046969; f. 1949; Dir GUO ZENGPEI; Editor-in-Chief PAN GUILIANG; circ. 500,000.

Heilongjiang Ribao (Heilongjiang Daily): Heilongjiang Province; Dir JIA HONGTU; Editor-in-Chief AI HE.

Henan Ribao (Henan Daily): 1 Weiyi Lu, Zhengzhou, Henan; tel. (371) 5958319; fax (371) 5955636; f. 1949; Dir YANG YONGDE; Editor-in-Chief GUO ZHENGLING; circ. 390,000.

Huadong Xinwen (Eastern China News): f. 1995; published by Renmin Ribao.

Huanan Xinwen (South China News): Guangzhou; f. 1997; published by Renmin Ribao.

Hubei Ribao (Hubei Daily): 65 Huangli Lu, Wuhan, Hubei 430077; tel. (27) 6833522; fax (27) 6813989; f. 1949; Dir ZHOU NIANFENG; Editor-in-Chief SONG HANYAN; circ. 800,000.

Hunan Ribao (Hunan Daily): 18 Furong Zhong Lu, Changsha, Hunan 410071; tel. (731) 4312999; fax (731) 4314029; Dir JIANG XIANLI; Editor-in-Chief WAN MAOHUA.

Jiangxi Ribao (Jiangxi Daily): 175 Yangming Jie, Nanchang, Jiangxi; tel. (791) 6849888; fax (791) 6772590; f. 1949; Dir ZHOU JINGUANG; circ. 300,000.

Jiefang Ribao (Liberation Daily): 300 Han Kou Lu, Shanghai 200001; tel. (21) 63521111; fax (21) 63516517; f. 1949; Editor-in-Chief JIA SHUMEI; circ. 1m.

Jiefangjun Bao (Liberation Army Daily): Beijing; f. 1956; official organ of the Central Military Comm. Editor-in-Chief Maj.-Gen. ZHANG SHIGANG; circ. 800,000.

Jilin Ribao (Jilin Daily): Jilin Province; Dir and Editor-in-Chief YI HONGBIN.

Jingji Ribao (Economic Daily): 2 Bai Zhi Fang Dong Jie, Beijing 100054; tel. (10) 63559988; fax (10) 63539408; f. 1983; financial affairs, domestic and foreign trade; administered by the State Council; Editor-in-Chief WU CHUNHE; circ. 1.2m.

Jinrong Shibao (Financial News): 44 Taipingqiao Fengtaiqu, Beijing 100073; tel. (10) 63269233; fax (10) 68424931.

Liaoning Ribao (Liaoning Daily): Liaoning Province; Dir XIE ZHENGQIAN.

Nanfang Ribao (Nanfang Daily): 289 Guangzhou Da Lu, Guangzhou, Guangdong 510601; tel. (20) 87373998; fax (20) 87375203; f. 1949; Dir LI MENGYU; Editor-in-Chief FAN YIJIN; circ. 1m.

Nanjing Ribao (Nanjing Daily): 53 Jiefang Lu, Nanjing, Jiangsu 210016; tel. (25) 4496564; fax (25) 4496544.

Nongmin Ribao (Peasants' Daily): Shilipu Beili, Chao Yang Qu, Beijing 100025; tel. (10) 65005522; fax (10) 65071154; f. 1980; 6 a week; circulates in rural areas nation-wide; Dir and Editor-in-Chief ZHANG DEXIU; circ. 1m.

Renmin Ribao (People's Daily): 2 Jin Tai Xi Lu, Chao Yang Men Wai, Beijing 100733; tel. (10) 65092121; fax (10) 65091982; f. 1948; organ of the CCP; also publishes overseas edn; Dir and Editor-in-Chief WANG CHEN; circ. 2.15m.

Shaanxi Ribao (Shaanxi Daily): Shaanxi Province; Dir LI DONG-SHENG; Editor-in-Chief DU YAOFENG.

Shanxi Ribao (Shanxi Daily): 24 Shuangtasi Jie, Taiyuan, Shanxi; tel. (351) 446561; fax (351) 441771; Dir ZHAO WENBIN; Editor-in-Chief LI DONGXI; circ. 300,000.

Shenzhen Commercial Press: Shenzhen; Editor-in-Chief GAO XINGLIE.

Shenzhen Tequ Bao (Shenzhen Special Economic Zone Daily): 4 Shennan Zhonglu, Shenzhen 518009; tel. (755) 3902688; fax (755) 3906900; f. 1982; reports on special economic zones, as well as mainland, Hong Kong and Macao; Dir CHEN XITIAN.

Sichuan Ribao (Sichuan Daily): Sichuan Daily Press Group, 70 Hongxing Zhong Lu, Erduan, Chengdu, Sichuan 610012; tel. and fax (28) 86968000; internet www.sconline.com.cn; f. 1952; Chair. of Bd LI ZHIXIA; Editor-in-Chief TANG XIAOQIANG; circ. 8m.

Tianjin Ribao (Tianjin Daily): 873 Dagu Nan Lu, Heri Qu, Tianjin 300211; tel. (22) 7301024; fax (22) 7305803; f. 1949; Dir and Editor-in-Chief ZHANG JIANXING; circ. 600,000.

Wenhui Bao (Wenhui Daily): 50 Huqiu Lu, Shanghai 200002; tel. (21) 63211410; fax (21) 63230198; f. 1938; Editor-in-Chief WU ZHEN-BIAO; circ. 500,000.

Xin Min Wan Bao (Xin Min Evening News): 839 Yan An Zhong Lu, Shanghai 200040; tel. (21) 62791234; fax (21) 62473220; f. 1929; specializes in public policy, education and social affairs; Editor-in-Chief JIN FUAN; circ. 1.8m.

Xinhua Ribao (New China Daily): 55 Zhongshan Lu, Nanjing, Jiangsu 210005; tel. (21) 741757; fax (21) 741023; Editor-in-Chief ZHOU ZHENGRONG; circ. 900,000.

Xinjiang Ribao (Xinjiang Daily): Xinjiang Region; Editor-in-Chief HUANG YANCAI.

Xizang Ribao (Tibet Daily): Tibet; Editor-in-Chief LI ERLIANG.

Yangcheng Wanbao (Yangcheng Evening News): 733 Dongfeng Dong Lu, Guangzhou, Guangdong 510085; tel. (20) 87776211; fax (20) 87765103; e-mail ycwbic@ycwb.com.cn; internet www.ycwb.com.cn; f. 1957; Editor-in-Chief PAN WEIWEN; circ. 1.3m.

Yunnan Ribao (Yunnan Daily): Yunnan Province; Editor-in-Chief SUN GUANSHENG.

Zhejiang Ribao (Zhejiang Daily): Zhejiang Province; Dir CHEN MINER; Editor-in-Chief YANG DAJIN.

Zhongguo Qingnian Bao (China Youth News): 2 Haiyuncang, Dong Zhi Men Nei, Beijing 100702; tel. (10) 64032233; fax (10) 64033792; f. 1951; daily; aimed at 14–40 age-group; Dir XU ZHUQING; Editor-in-Chief LI XUEQIAN; circ. 1.0m.

Zhongguo Ribao (China Daily): 15 Huixin Dongjie, Chao Yang Qu, Beijing 100029; tel. (10) 64918633; fax (10) 64918377; internet www.chinadaily.com.cn; f. 1981; English; China's political, economic and cultural developments; world, financial and sports news; also publishes *Business Weekly*(f. 1985), *Beijing Weekend*(f. 1991), *Shanghai Star*(f. 1992), *Reports from China*(f. 1992), *21st Century*(f. 1993); Editor-in-Chief ZHU YINGHUANG; circ. 300,000.

Zhongguo Xinwen (China News): 12 Baiwanzhuang Nanjie, Beijing; tel. (10) 68315012; f. 1952; daily; Editor-in-Chief WANG XIJIN; current affairs.

SELECTED PERIODICALS

Ban Yue Tan (China Comment): Beijing; tel. (10) 6668521; f. 1980; in Chinese and Wei Wuer (Uygur); Editor-in-Chief WANG QIXING; circ. 6m.

Beijing Review: 24 Baiwanzhuang Lu, Beijing 100037; tel. (10) 68326085; fax (10) 68326628; e-mail bjreview@public3.bta.net.cn; internet www.bjreview.com.cn; f. 1958; weekly; edns in English, French, Spanish, Japanese and German; also **Chinafrica** (monthly in English and French); Publr WANG GANGYI; Editor-in-Chief LII HAIBO.

BJ TV Weekly: 2 Fu Xing Men Wai Zhenwumiao Jie, Beijing 100045; tel. (10) 6366036; fax (10) 63262388; circ. 1m.

China TV Weekly: 15 Huixin Dong Jie, Chao Yang Qu, Beijing 100013; tel. (10) 64214197; circ. 1.7m.

Chinese Literature Press: 24 Baiwanzhuang Lu, Beijing 100037; tel. (10) 68326010; fax (10) 68326678; e-mail chinalit@public.east.cn.net; f. 1951; monthly (bilingual in English); quarterly (bilingual in French); contemporary and classical writing, poetry, literary criticism and arts; Exec. Editor LING YUAN.

Dianying Xinzuo (New Films): 796 Huaihai Zhong Lu, Shanghai; tel. (21) 64379710; f. 1979; bi-monthly; introduces new films.

Dianzi yu Diannao (Electronics and Computers): Beijing; f. 1985; popularized information on computers and microcomputers.

Elle (China): 14 Lane 955, Yan'an Zhong Lu, Shanghai; tel. (21) 62790974; fax (21) 62479056; f. 1988; monthly; fashion; Pres. YANG XINCI; Chief Editor WU YING; circ. 300,000.

Family Magazine: 14 Siheng Lu, Xinhepu, Dongshan Qu, Guangzhou 510080; tel. (20) 7777718; fax (20) 7185670; monthly; circ. 2.5m.

Feitian (Fly Skywards): 50 Donggan Xilu, Lanzhou, Gansu; tel. (931) 25803; f. 1961; monthly.

Guoji Xin Jishu (New International Technology): Zhanwang Publishing House, Beijing; f. 1984; also publ. in Hong Kong; international technology, scientific and technical information.

Guowai Keji Dongtai (Recent Developments in Science and Technology Abroad): Institute of Scientific and Technical Information of China, 54 San Li He Lu, Beijing 100045; tel. (10) 68570713; fax (10) 68511839; e-mail baiyr@istic.ac.cn; internet www.wanfang.com.cn;

f. 1962; monthly; scientific journal; Editor-in-Chief GUO YUEHUA; circ. 40,000.

Hai Xia (The Strait): 27 De Gui Xiang, Fuzhou, Fujian; tel. (10) 33656; f. 1981; quarterly; literary journal; CEOs YANG YU, JWO JONG LIN.

Huasheng Monthly (Voice for Overseas Chinese): 12 Bai Wan Zhuang Nan Jie, Beijing 100037; tel. (10) 68311578; fax (10) 68315039; f. 1995; monthly; intended mainly for overseas Chinese and Chinese nationals resident abroad; Editor-in-Chief FAN DONG-SHENG.

Jianzhu (Construction): Baiwanzhuang, Beijing; tel. (10) 68992849; f. 1956; monthly; Editor FANG YUEGUANG; circ. 500,000.

Jinri Zhongguo (China Today): 24 Baiwanzhuang Lu, Beijing 100037; tel. (10) 68326037; fax (10) 68328338; internet www.chinatoday.com.cn; f. 1952; fmrly *China Reconstructs*; monthly; edns in English, Spanish, French, Arabic, German, and Chinese; economic, social and cultural affairs; illustrated; Pres. and Editor-in-Chief HUANG ZU'AN.

Liaowang (Outlook): 57 Xuanwumen Xijie, Beijing; tel. (10) 63073049; f. 1981; weekly; current affairs; Gen. Man. ZHOU YICHANG; Editor-in-Chief JI BIN; circ. 500,000.

Luxingjia (Traveller): Beijing; tel. (10) 6552631; f. 1955; monthly; Chinese scenery, customs, culture.

Meishu Zhi You (Chinese Art Digest): 32 Beizongbu Hutong, East City Region, Beijing; tel. (10) 65591404; f. 1982; every 2 months; art review journal, also providing information on fine arts publs in China and abroad; Editors ZONGYUAN GAO, PEI CHENG.

Nianqingren (Young People): 169 Mayuanlin, Changsha, Hunan; tel. (731) 23610; f. 1981; monthly; general interest for young people.

Nongye Zhishi (Agricultural Knowledge): 21 Ming Zi Qian Lu, Jinan, Shandong 250100; tel. (531) 8932238; e-mail sdnyzs@jn-public.sd.cninfo.net; internet www.sdny.com.cn; f. 1950; fortnightly; popular agricultural science; Dir YANG LIJIAN; circ. 410,000.

Qiushi (Seeking Truth): 2 Shatan Beijie, Beijing 100727; tel. (10) 64037005; fax (10) 64018174; f. 1988 to succeed *Hong Qi*(Red Flag); 2 a month; theoretical journal of the CCP; Editor-in-Chief WANG TIANXI; circ. 1.83m.

Renmin Huabao (China Pictorial): Huayuancun, West Suburbs, Beijing 100044; tel. (10) 68411144; fax (10) 68413023; f. 1950; monthly; edns: two in Chinese, one in Tibetan and 12 in foreign languages; Dir and Editor-in-Chief ZHANG JIAHUA.

Shichang Zhoubao (Market Weekly): 2 Duan, Sanhao Jie, Heping Qu, Shenyang, Liaoning; tel. (24) 482983; f. 1979; weekly in Chinese; trade, commodities, and financial and economic affairs; circ. 1m.

Shufa (Calligraphy): 81 Qingzhou Nan Lu, Shanghai 200233; tel. (21) 64519008; fax (21) 64519015; f. 1977; every 2 months; journal on ancient and modern calligraphy; Chief Editor LU FUSHENG.

Tiyu Kexue (Sports Science): 8 Tiyuguan Lu, Beijing 100763; tel. (10) 67112233; f. 1981; sponsored by the China Sports Science Soc. every 2 months; summary in English; Chief Officer YUAN WEIMIN; in Chinese; circ. 20,000.

Wenxue Qingnian (Youth Literature Journal): 27 Mu Tse Fang, Wenzhou, Zhejiang; tel. (577) 3578; f. 1981; monthly; Editor-in-Chief CHEN YUSHEN; circ. 80,000.

Women of China English Monthly: 15 Jian Guo Men Dajie, Beijing 100730; tel. (10) 65134616; fax (10) 65225380; e-mail geo@womenofchina.com.cn; internet www.womenofchina.com.cn; f. 1956; monthly; in English; administered by All-China Women's Federation; women's rights and status, views and lifestyle, education and arts, etc. Editor-in-Chief YUN PENGJU.

Xian Dai Faxue (Modern Law Science): Southwest University of Political Science and Law, Chongqing, Sichuan 400031; tel. (23) 65382527; e-mail MLS@swupl.edu.cn; f. 1979; bi-monthly; with summaries in English; Dirs CAO MINGDE, LI YUPING.

Yinyue Aihaozhe (Music Lovers): 74 Shaoxing Lu, Shanghai 200020; tel. (21) 64372608; fax (21) 64332019; f. 1979; every two months; music knowledge; illustrated; Editor-in-Chief CHEN XUEYA; circ. 50,000.

Zhongguo Duiwai Maoyi Ming Lu (Directory of China's Foreign Trade): CCPIT Bldg, 1 Fuxingmen Wai Da Jie, Beijing 100860; tel. (10) 68022948; fax (10) 68510201; e-mail inform@press-media.com; f. 1974; monthly; edns in Chinese and English; information on Chinese imports and exports, foreign trade and economic policies; Editor-in-Chief YANG HAIQING.

Zhongguo Ertong (Chinese Children): 21 Xiang 12, Dongsi, Beijing; tel. (10) 6444761; f. 1980; monthly; illustrated journal for elementary school pupils.

Zhongguo Guangbo Dianshi (China Radio and Television): 12 Fucheng Lu, Beijing; tel. (10) 6896217; f. 1982; monthly; reports and comments.

Zhongguo Jin Rong Xin Xi: Beijing; f. 1991; monthly; economic news.

Zhongguo Sheying (Chinese Photography): 61 Hongxing Hutong, Dongdan, Beijing 100005; tel. (10) 65252277; fax (10) 65253197; e-mail cphoto@public.bta.net.cn; internet www.cphoto.com.cn; f. 1957; monthly; photographs and comments; Editor LIU BANG.

Zhongguo Zhenjiu (Chinese Acupuncture and Moxibustion): China Academy of Traditional Chinese Medicine, Dongzhimen Nei, Beijing 100700; tel. (10) 84014607; fax (10) 64013968; e-mail weihongliu@263.net; f. 1981; monthly; publ. by Chinese Soc. of Acupuncture and Moxibustion; abstract in English; Editor-in-Chief Prof. DENG LIANGYUE.

Zijing (Bauhinia): Pres. and Editor-in-Chief CHEN HONG.

Other popular magazines include **Gongchandang Yuan** (Communists, circ. 1.63m.) and **Nongmin Wenzhai** (Peasants' Digest, circ. 3.54m.).

NEWS AGENCIES

Xinhua (New China) News Agency: 57 Xuanwumen Xidajie, Beijing 100803; tel. (10) 63071114; fax (10) 63071210; internet www .xinhuanet.com; f. 1931; offices in all Chinese provincial capitals, and about 100 overseas bureaux; news service in Chinese, English, French, Spanish, Portuguese, Arabic and Russian, feature and photographic services; Pres. TIAN CONGMING; Editor-in-Chief NAN ZHENZHONG.

Zhongguo Xinwen She (China News Agency): POB 1114, Beijing; f. 1952; office in Hong Kong; supplies news features, special articles and photographs for newspapers and magazines in Chinese printed overseas; services in Chinese; Dir WANG SHIGU.

Foreign Bureaux

Agence France-Presse (AFP) (France): 11-11 Jian Guo Men Wai, Diplomatic Apts, Beijing 100600; tel. (10) 65321409; fax (10) 65322371; e-mail afppek@afp.com; Bureau Chief ELIZABETH ZINGO.

Agencia EFE (Spain): 2-2-132 Jian Guo Men Wai, Beijing 100600; tel. (10) 65323449; fax (10) 65323688; Rep. CARLOS REDONDO.

Agenzia Nazionale Stampa Associata (ANSA) (Italy): 1-11 Ban Gong Lu, San Li Tun, Beijing 100600; tel. (10) 65323651; fax (10) 65321954; e-mail barbara@public3.bta.net.cn; Bureau Chief BARBARA ALIGHIERO.

Allgemeiner Deutscher Nachrichtendienst (ADN) (Germany): 7-2-61, Jian Guo Men Wai, Qi Jia Yuan Gong Yu, Beijing 100600; tel. and fax (10) 65321115; Correspondent Dr LUTZ POHLE.

Associated Press (AP) (USA): 6-2-22 Jian Guo Men Wai, Diplomatic Quarters, Beijing 100600; tel. (10) 65326650; fax (10) 65323419; Bureau Chief ELAINE KURTENBACH.

Deutsche Presse-Agentur (dpa) (Germany): Ban Gong Lou, Apt 1-31, San Li Tun, Beijing 100600; tel. (10) 65321473; fax (10) 65321615; e-mail dpa@public3.bta.net.cn; Bureau Chief ANDREAS LANDWEHR.

Informatsionnoye Telegrafnoye Agentstvo Rossii (ITAR—TASS) (Russia): 6-1-41 Tayuan Diplomatic Office Bldg, Beijing 100600; tel. (10) 65324821; fax (10) 65324820; e-mail tassbj@public .bta.net.cn; Bureau Chief ANDREY KIRILLOV.

Inter Press Service (TIPS) (Italy): 15 Fuxing Lu, POB 3811, Beijing 100038; tel. (10) 68514046; fax (10) 68518210; e-mail tipscn@ istic.ac.cn; internet www.tips.org.cn; Dir WANG XIAOYING.

Jiji Tsushin (Japan): 9-1-13 Jian Guo Men Wai, Waijiao, Beijing; tel. (10) 65322924; fax (10) 65323413; Correspondents YOSHIHISA MURAYAMA, TETSUYA NISHIMURA.

Korean Central News Agency (Democratic People's Republic of Korea): Beijing; Bureau Chief SONG YONG SONG.

Kyodo News Service (Japan): 3-91 Jian Guo Men Wai, Beijing; tel. (10) 6532680; fax (10) 65322273; e-mail kyodob@ccnet.cn.net; Bureau Chief YASUHIRO MORI.

Magyar Távirati Iroda (MTI) (Hungary): 1-42 Ban Gong Lu, San Li Tun, Beijing 100600; tel. (10) 65321744; Correspondent GYÖRGY BARTA.

Prensa Latina (Cuba): 4-1-23 Jianguomenwai, Beijing 100600; tel. and fax (10) 65321914; e-mail prelatin@public.bta.net.cn; Correspondent ILSA RODRÍGUEZ SANTANA.

Press Trust of India: 5-131 Diplomatic Apts, Jian Guo Men Wai, Beijing 100600; tel. and fax (10) 65322221.

Reuters (UK): Hilton Beijing, 1 Dong Fang Lu/Bei Dong Sanhuan Lu, Chao Yang Qu, Beijing; tel. (10) 64662288; fax (10) 64653052;

e-mail hilton@hiltonbeijing.com.cn; internet www.hilton.com; Bureau Man. RICHARD PASCOE.

Tanjug News Agency (Serbia and Montenegro): Qijayuan Diplomatic Apt, Beijing 100600; tel. (10) 65324821.

United Press International (UPI) (USA): 7-1-11 Qi Jia Yuan, Beijing; tel. (10) 65323271; Bureau Chief CHRISTIAAN VIRANT.

The following are also represented: Rompres (Romania) and VNA (Viet Nam).

PRESS ORGANIZATIONS

All China Journalists' Association: Xijiaominxiang, Beijing 100031; tel. (10) 66023981; fax (10) 66014658; Chair. SHAO HUAZE.

China Newspapers Association: Beijing; Chair. XU ZHONGTIAN.

The Press and Publication Administration of the People's Republic of China: 85 Dongsi Nan Dajie, East District, Beijing 100703; tel. (10) 65124433; fax (10) 65127875; Dir YU YOUXIAN.

Publishers

In 2000 there were 565 publishing houses in China. A total of 143,376 titles (and 6,270m. copies) were published in that year.

Beijing Chubanshe Chuban Jituan (Beijing Publishing House Group): 6 Bei Sanhuan Zhong Lu, Beijing 100011; tel. (10) 62016699; fax (10) 62012339; e-mail geo@bph.com.cn; internet www.bph.com .cn; f. 1956; politics, history, law, economics, geography, science, literature, art, etc. Dir ZHU SHUXIN; Editor-in-Chief TAO XINCHENG.

Beijing Daxue Chubanshe (Beijing University Press): 205 Chengfu Lu, Zhongguancun, Haidian Qu, Beijing 100871; tel. (10) 62752024; fax (10) 62556201; f. 1979; academic and general.

China International Book Trading Corpn: POB 399, 35 Chegongzhuang Xilu, Beijing 100044; tel. (10) 68433113; fax (10) 68420340; e-mail bk@mail.cibtc.co.cn; internet www.cibtc.com.cn; f. 1949; foreign trade org. specializing in publs, including books, periodicals, art and crafts, microfilms, etc. import and export distributors; Pres. LIU ZHIBIN.

China Publishing Group: Beijing; f. 2002; aims to restructure and consolidate publishing sector; comprises 12 major publishing houses; Pres. of the Bd YANG MUZHI.

CITIC Publishing House: Ta Yuan Diplomatic Office Bldg, 14 Liangmahe Lu, Chao Yang Qu, Beijing 100600; tel. (10) 85323366; fax (10) 85322505; e-mail liyinghong@citicpub.com; internet www .publish.citic.com; f. 1988; finance, investment, economics and business; Pres. WANG BIN.

Dianzi Gongye Chubanshe (Publishing House of the Electronics Industry—PHEI): POB 173, Wan Shou Lu, Beijing 100036; tel. (10) 68159028; fax (10) 68159025; f. 1982; electronic sciences and technology; Pres. LIANG XIANGFENG; Vice-Pres. WANG MINGJUN.

Dolphin Books: 24 Baiwanzhuang Lu, Beijing 100037; tel. (10) 68326332; fax (10) 68326642; f. 1986; children's books in Chinese and foreign languages; Dir WANG YANRONG.

Falü Chubanshe (Law Publishing House): POB 111, Beijing 100036; tel. (10) 6815325; f. 1980; current laws and decrees, legal textbooks, translations of important foreign legal works; Dir LAN MINGLIANG.

Foreign Languages Press: 19 Chegongzhuang Xi Lu, Fu Xing Men Wai, Beijing 100044; tel. (10) 68413344; fax (10) 68424931; e-mail info@flp.com.cn; internet www.flp.com.cn; f. 1952; books in 20 foreign languages reflecting political and economic developments in People's Republic of China and features of Chinese culture; Dir GUO JIEXIN; Editor-in-Chief XU MINGQIANG.

Gaodeng Jiaoyu Chubanshe (Higher Education Press): 55 Shatan Houjie, Beijing 100009; tel. (10) 64014043; fax (10) 64054602; e-mail linm@public.bta.net.cn; internet www.hep.edu.cn; f. 1954; academic, textbooks; Pres. LIU ZHIPENG; Editor-in-Chief ZHANG ZENGSHUN.

Gongren Chubanshe (Workers' Publishing House): Liupukeng, Andingmen Wai, Beijing; tel. (10) 64215278; f. 1949; labour movement, trade unions, science and technology related to industrial production.

Guangdong Keji Chubanshe (Guangdong Science and Technology Press): 11 Shuiyin Lu, Huanshidong Lu, Guangzhou, Guangdong 510075; tel. (20) 87618770; fax (20) 87769412; e-mail gdkjzbb@ zlcn.com; internet www.gdstp.com.cn; f. 1978; natural sciences, technology, agriculture, medicine, computing, English language teaching; Dir HUANG DAQUAN.

Heilongjiang Kexue Jishu Chubanshe (Heilongjiang Science and Technology Press): 41 Jianshe Jie, Nangang Qu, Harbin 150001, Heilongjiang; tel. and fax (451) 3642127; f. 1979; industrial and agricultural technology, natural sciences, economics and management, popular science, children's and general.

Huashan Wenyi Chubanshe (Huashan Literature and Art Publishing House): 45 Bei Malu, Shijiazhuang, Hebei; tel. 22501; f. 1982; novels, poetry, drama, etc.

Kexue Chubanshe (Science Press): 16 Donghuangchenggen Beijie, Beijing 100717; tel. (10) 64034313; fax (10) 64020094; e-mail icd@cspg.net; f. 1954; books and journals on science and technology.

Lingnan Meishu Chubanshe (Lingnan Art Publishing House): 11 Shuiyin Lu, Guangzhou, Guangdong 510075; tel. (20) 87771044; fax (20) 87771049; f. 1981; works on classical and modern painting, picture albums, photographic, painting techniques; Pres. CAO LIXIANG.

Minzu Chubanshe (The Ethnic Publishing House): 14 Hepingli Beijie, Beijing 100013; tel. (10) 64211126; e-mail nova126@sina.com; f. 1953; books and periodicals in minority languages, e.g. Mongolian, Tibetan, Uygur, Korean, Kazakh, etc. Editor-in-Chief HUANG ZHONGCAI.

Qunzhong Chubanshe (Masses Publishing House): Bldg 15, Part 3, Fangxingyuan, Fangzhuan Lu, Beijing 100078; tel. (10) 67633344; f. 1956; politics, law, judicial affairs, criminology, public security, etc.

Renmin Chubanshe (People's Publishing House): 8 Hepinglidongjie, Andingmenwai, Beijing; tel. (10) 4213713; managed by the Ministry of Communications; science and technology, textbooks, laws and specifications of communications; Dir and Editor-in-Chief XUE DEZHEN.

Renmin Jiaoyu Chubanshe (People's Education Press): 55 Sha Tan Hou Jie, Beijing 100009; tel. (10) 64035745; fax (10) 64010370; f. 1950; school textbooks, guidebooks, teaching materials, etc.

Renmin Meishu Chubanshe (People's Fine Arts Publishing House): Beijing; tel. (10) 65122371; fax (10) 65122370; f. 1951; works by Chinese and foreign painters, sculptors and other artists, picture albums, photographic, painting techniques; Dir GAO ZONGYUAN; Editor-in-Chief CHENG DALI.

Renmin Weisheng Chubanshe (People's Medical Publishing House): Beijing; tel. (10) 67617283; fax (10) 645143; f. 1953; medicine (Western and traditional Chinese), pharmacology, dentistry, public health; Pres. LIU YIQING.

Renmin Wenxue Chubanshe (People's Literature Publishing House): 166 Chaoyangmen Nei Dajie, Beijing 100705; tel. and fax (10) 65138394; e-mail rwzbs@sina.com; internet www.rw-cn.com; f. 1951; largest publr of literary works and translations into Chinese; Dir and Editor-in-Chief NIE ZHENNING.

Shanghai Guji Chubanshe (Shanghai Classics Publishing House): 272 Ruijin Erlu, Shanghai 200020; tel. (21) 64370011; fax (21) 64339287; f. 1956; classical Chinese literature, history, philosophy, geography, linguistics, science and technology.

Shanghai Jiaoyu Chubanshe (Shanghai Educational Publishing House): 123 Yongfu Lu, Shanghai 200031; tel. (21) 64377165; fax (21) 64339995; f. 1958; academic; Dir and Editor-in-Chief CHEN HE.

Shanghai Yiwen Chubanshe (Shanghai Translation Publishing House): 14 Xiang 955, Yanan Zhonglu, Shanghai 200040; tel. (21) 62472890; fax (21) 62475100; e-mail cpbq@bj.cal.com.cn; internet www.cp.com.cn; f. 1978; translations of foreign classic and modern literature; philosophy, social sciences, dictionaries, etc.

Shangwu Yinshuguan (The Commercial Press): 36 Wangfujing Dajie, Beijing; tel. (10) 65252026; fax (10) 65135899; e-mail comprs@public.gb.com.cn; internet www.cp.com.cn; f. 1897; dictionaries and reference books in Chinese and foreign languages, translations of foreign works on social sciences; Pres. YANG DEYAN.

Shaonian Ertong Chubanshe (Juvenile and Children's Publishing House): 1538 Yan An Xi Lu, Shanghai 200052; tel. (21) 62823025; fax (21) 62821726; e-mail forwardz@public4.sta.net.cn; f. 1952; children's educational and literary works, teaching aids and periodicals; Gen. Man. ZHOU SHUNPEI.

Shijie Wenhua Chubanshe (World Culture Publishing House): Dir ZHU LIE.

Wenwu Chubanshe (Cultural Relics Publishing House): 29 Wusi Dajie, Beijing 100009; tel. (10) 64048057; fax (10) 64010698; e-mail web@wenwu.com; internet www.wenwu.com; f. 1956; books and catalogues of Chinese relics in museums and those recently discovered; Dir SU SHISHU.

Wuhan Daxue Chubanshe (Wuhan University Press): Suojia Hill, Wuhan, Hubei; tel. (27) 7820651; fax (27) 7812661; f. 1981; reference books, academic works, etc. Pres. and Editor-in-Chief Prof. NIU TAICHEN.

Xiandai Chubanshe (Modern Press): 504 Anhua Li, Andingmenwai, Beijing 100011; tel. (10) 64263515; fax (10) 64214540; f. 1981; directories, reference books, etc. Dir ZHOU HONGLI.

Xinhua Chubanshe (Xinhua Publishing House): 57 Xuanwumen Xidajie, Beijing 100803; tel. (10) 63074022; fax (10) 63073880; e-mail xhpub@xinhua.org; f. 1979; social sciences, economy, politics, history, geography, directories, dictionaries, etc. Dir WANG CHUNRONG; Editor-in-Chief ZHANG SHOUDI.

Xuelin Chubanshe (Scholar Books Publishing House): 120 Wenmiao Lu, Shanghai 200010; tel. and fax (21) 63768540; f. 1981; academic, including personal academic works at authors' own expense; Dir LEI QUNMING.

Zhongguo Caizheng Jingji Chubanshe (China Financial and Economic Publishing House): 8 Dafosi Dongjie, Dongcheng Qu, Beijing; tel. (10) 64011805; f. 1961; finance, economics, commerce and accounting.

Zhongguo Dabaike Quanshu Chubanshe (Encyclopaedia of China Publishing House): 17 Fu Cheng Men Bei Dajie, Beijing 100037; tel. (10) 68315610; fax (10) 68316510; e-mail ygh@bj.col.com.cn; f. 1978; specializes in encyclopaedias; Dir SHAN JIFU.

Zhongguo Ditu Chubanshe (China Cartographic Publishing House): 3 Baizhifang Xijie, Beijing 100054; tel. (10) 63530808; fax (10) 63531961; e-mail infa@chinamap.com; internet www.chinamap.com; f. 1954; cartographic publr; Dir WANG JIXIAN.

Zhongguo Funü Chubanshe (China Women Publishing House): 24A Shijia Hutong, 100010 Beijing; tel. (10) 65126986; f. 1981; women's movement, marriage and family, child-care, etc. Dir LI ZHONGXIU.

Zhongguo Qingnian Chubanshe (China Youth Press): 21 Dongsi Shiertiao, Beijing 100708; tel. (10) 84015396; fax (10) 64031803; e-mail cyph@eastnet.com.cn; internet www.cyp.com.cn; f. 1950; literature, social and natural sciences, youth work, autobiography; also periodicals; Dir HU SHOUWEN; Editor-in-Chief XU WENXIN.

Zhongguo Shehui Kexue Chubanshe (China Social Sciences Publishing House): 158A Gulou Xidajie, Beijing 100720; tel. (10) 64073837; fax (10) 64074509; f. 1978; Dir ZHENG WENLIN.

Zhongguo Xiju Chubanshe (China Theatrical Publishing House): 52 Dongsi Batiao Hutong, Beijing; tel. (10) 64015815; f. 1957; traditional and modern Chinese drama.

Zhongguo Youyi Chuban Gongsi (China Friendship Publishing Corpn): e-mail tmdoxu@public.east.cn.net; Dir YANG WEI.

Zhonghua Shuju (Zhonghua Book Co): 38 Taipingqiao Xili, Fenglai Qu, Beijing; tel. (10) 63458226; f. 1912; general; Pres. SONG YIFU.

PUBLISHERS' ASSOCIATION

Publishers' Association of China: Beijing; f. 1979; arranges academic exchanges with foreign publrs; Hon. Chair. SONG MUWEN; Chair. YU YOUXIAN.

Broadcasting and Communications

TELECOMMUNICATIONS

Ministry of Information Industry: 13 Xichangan Jie, Beijing 100804; tel. (10) 66014249; fax (10) 66034248; e-mail webmaster@mii.gov.cn; internet www.mii.gov.cn; regulates all issues concerning the telecommunications sector.

China Mobile (Hong Kong) Ltd: 60th Floor, The Center, 99 Queen's Rd, Central, Hong Kong; tel. (852) 31218888; fax (852) 25119092; e-mail ca@chinamobilehk.com; internet www.chinamobilehk.com; f. 1997; provides mobile telecommunications services in 13 provinces, municipalities, and autonomous regions of China; world's biggest cellular carrier (2002); Chair. and CEO WANG XIAOCHU.

China Netcom Corpn: Beijing 100032; 9–15/F, Building A, 15/F, Building C, Corporate Square, No.35 Financial St, Xicheng District; tel. (10) 8809-3588; fax (10) 8809-1446; e-mail cnc@china-netcom.com; internet www.cnc.net.cn; f. 1999; internet telephone service-provider; merged with China Telecom northern operations (10 provinces) in May 2002; CEO EDWARD TIAN.

China Telecom: 5th Floor, North Wing, Xibianmennei Jie, Xuanwu Qu, Beijing 100053; e-mail info@chinatelecom.com.cn; internet www.chinatelecom.com.cn; f. 1997 as a vehicle for foreign investment in telecommunications sector; operates 'Xiao Ling Tong' mobile phone services; restructured in May 2002 with responsibility for fixed-line network in 21 southern and western provinces; Pres. ZHOU DEQIANG.

China Telecommunications Satellite Group Corpn: Beijing; f. 2001 to provide internet, telephone and related services; Gen. Man. ZHOU ZEHE.

China United Telecommunications Corpn (UNICOM): 1/F, Hongji Centre Office Bldg, 18 Jianguomenei Dajie, Beijing; tel. (10) 65181800; fax (10) 65183405; e-mail webmaster@chinaunicom.com.cn; internet www.chinaunicom.com.cn; f. 1994; cellular telecommunications; Chair. and Pres. YANG XIANZU.

BROADCASTING

In 2000 there were 304 radio broadcasting stations, 737 radio transmitting and relay stations (covering 92.47% of the population), 354 television stations and 51,436 television transmitting and relay stations (covering 93.65% of the population).

Regulatory Authorities

State Administration of Radio, Film and Television (SARFT): 2 Fu Xing Men Wai Dajie, POB 4501, Beijing 100866; tel. (10) 68513409; fax (10) 68512174; internet www.dns.incmrft.gov.cn; controls the Central People's Broadcasting Station, the Central TV Station, Radio Beijing, China Record Co, Beijing Broadcasting Institute, Broadcasting Research Institute, the China Broadcasting Art Troupe, etc. Chair. TIAN CONGMING.

State Radio Regulatory Authority: Beijing; operates under the State Council; Chair. ZOU JIAHUA.

Radio

China National Radio (CNR): 2 Fu Xing Men Wai Dajie, Beijing 100866; tel. (10) 68045630; fax (10) 68045631; internet www.cnradio .com; f. 1945; domestic service in Chinese, Zang Wen (Tibetan), Min Nan Hua (Amoy), Ke Jia (Hakka), Hasaka (Kazakh), Wei Wuer (Uygur), Menggu Hua (Mongolian) and Chaoxian (Korean); Dir-Gen. YANG BO.

Zhongguo Guoji Guangbo Diantai (China Radio International): 16A Shijingshan Lu, Beijing 100039; tel. (10) 68891001; fax (10) 68891582; e-mail crieng@public.bta.net.cn; internet www.cri.com .cn; f. 1941; fmrly Radio Beijing; foreign service in 38 languages incl. Arabic, Burmese, Czech, English, Esperanto, French, German, Indonesian, Italian, Japanese, Lao, Polish, Portuguese, Russian, Spanish, Turkish and Vietnamese; Dir ZHANG ZHENHUA.

Television

China Central Television (CCTV): 11 Fuxing Lu, Haidian, Beijing 100859; tel. (10) 8500000; fax (10) 8513025; internet www.wtdb .com/CCTV/about.htm; operates under Bureau of Broadcasting Affairs of the State Council, Beijing; f. 1958; operates eight networks; 24-hour global satellite service commenced in 1996; Pres. YANG WEIGWANG.

In April 1994 foreign companies were prohibited from establishing or operating cable TV stations in China. By mid-1996 there were more than 3,000 cable television stations in operation, with networks covering 45m. households. The largest subscriber service is Beijing Cable TV (Dir Guo Junjin). Satellite services are available in some areas: millions of satellite receivers are in use. In October 1993 the Government approved new regulations, attempting to restrict access to foreign satellite broadcasts. In September 2001, the Government signed a deal that would allow News Corpn and AOL Time Warner to become the first foreign broadcasters to have direct access to China's markets, although broadcasts would be restricted to Guangdong Province.

Finance

(cap. = capital; auth. = authorized; p.u. = paid up; res = reserves; dep. = deposits; m. = million; amounts in yuan unless otherwise stated)

BANKING

Radical economic reforms, introduced in 1994, included the strengthening of the role of the central bank and the establishment of new commercial banks. The Commercial Bank Law took effect in July 1995. The establishment of private banks was to be permitted.

Regulatory Authority

China Bank Regulatory Commission: Beijing; plans were finalized in early 2003 to establish a supervisory and regulatory commission, headed by LIU MINGKANG.

Central Bank

People's Bank of China: 32 Chengfang Jie, Xicheng Qu, Beijing 100800; tel. (10) 66194114; fax (10) 66015346; e-mail master@pbc .gov.cn; internet www.pbc.gov.cn; f. 1948; bank of issue; decides and implements China's monetary policies; Gov. ZHOU XIAOCHUAN; 2,204 brs.

Other Banks

Agricultural Bank of China: 23A Fuxing Lu, Haidian Qu, Beijing 100036; tel. (10) 68424388; fax (10) 68424437; e-mail webmaster@ intl.abocn.com; internet www.abchina.com; f. 1951; serves mainly China's rural financial operations, providing services for agriculture, industry, commerce, transport, etc. in rural areas; cap. 132,011m., res 3,175m., dep. 1,898,957m. (Dec. 2000); Pres. SHANG FULIN; 2,100 brs.

Agricultural Development Bank of China: 2A Yuetanbei Jie, Xicheng Qu, Beijing 100045; tel. (10) 68081557; fax (10) 68081773; f. 1994; cap. 20,000m. Pres. HE LINXIANG.

Bank of China: 1 Fu Xing Men Nei Dajie, Beijing 100818; tel. (10) 66016688; fax (10) 66016886; e-mail webmaster@bank-of-china.com; internet www.bank-of-china.com; f. 1912; handles foreign exchange and international settlements; operates Orient AMC (asset management corporation) since 1999; cap. 142,100m., res 73,806m., dep. 2,309,746m. (Dec. 2001); Chair. and Pres. XIAO GANG; 121 brs.

Bank of Communications Ltd: 18 Xian Xia Lu, Shanghai 200335; tel. (21) 62751234; fax (21) 62752191; internet www.bankcomm.com; f. 1908; commercial bank; cap. 15,302.6m., res 13,267.0m., dep. 391,933.4m. (Dec. 2000); Chair. YIN JIEYAN; Pres. FANG CHENGGUO; 90 brs.

Bank of Shanghai Co Ltd: 585 Zhongshan Lu (E2), Shanghai 200010; tel. (21) 63370888; fax (21) 63370777; e-mail shenjie@ bankofshanghai.com.cn; internet www.bankofshanghai.com; f. 1995 as Shanghai City United Bank, assumed present name in 1998; cap. 2,600m., dep 140,000m. (Dec. 2002); Chair. JIN ZENGDE; Pres. FU JIANHUA.

Beijing City Commercial Bank Corpn Ltd: 2nd Floor, Tower B, Beijing International Financial Bldg, 156 Fu Xing Men Nei Jie, Beijing 100031; tel. (10) 66426928; fax (10) 66426691; e-mail bccbibd@sina.com; internet www.bccb.com.cn; f. 1996 as Beijing City United Bank Corpn, assumed present name in 1998; cap 1,504m., res 1,692m., dep 70,327m. (Dec. 2000); Chair. YAN BINGZHU.

Beijing City Co-op Bank: 65 You An Men Nei Lu, Xuanwu Qu, Beijing 100054; tel. and fax (10) 63520159; f. 1996; cap. 1,000m., res 3,466m., dep. 26,660m. (Dec. 1996); 90 brs.

Bengbu House Saving Bank: 85 Zhong Rong Jie, Bengbu 233000; tel. (552) 2042069.

Changsha City Commercial Bank: 1 Furong Mid-Rd, Changsha, Hunan; tel. (73) 14305570; fax (73) 14305560; internet www.hncccb .com.cn; f. 1997; cap. 232.0m., res 31.5m., dep. 10,885.1m. (Dec. 2001); Chair. YE ZHANG; Pres XIANG LILI.

China and South Sea Bank Ltd: 410 Fu Cheng Men Nei Dajie, Beijing; internet www.cssb.com; f. 1921; cap. 1,200.0m., res 3,735.1m., dep. 38,850.2m. (Dec. 1999); Chair. HUA QINGSHAN.

China Construction Bank (CCB): 25 Jinrong Jie, Beijing 100032; tel. (10) 67598628; fax (10) 67598544; e-mail ccb@bj.china.com; internet www.ccb.com.cn; f. 1954; fmrly People's Construction Bank of China; makes payments for capital construction projects in accordance with state plans and budgets; issues medium- and long-term loans to enterprises and short-term loans to construction enterprises and others; also handles foreign-exchange business; housing loans; operates Cinda AMC (asset management corporation) since 1998 and China Great Wall AMC since 1999; cap. 85,115m., res 20,687m., dep. 2,514,192m. (Dec. 2001); 49 brs; Pres ZHANG ENZHAO.

China Everbright Bank: Everbright Tower, 6 Fu Xing Men Wai Lu, Beijing 100045; tel. (10) 68565577; fax (10) 68561260; e-mail eb@ cebbank.com; internet www.cebbank.com; f. 1992 as Everbright Bank of China; acquired China Investment Bank and assumed present name in 1999; cap. 7,469.9m., res 4,810.7m., dep. 224,424.5m. (Dec. 2001); Pres. WANG CHUAN; Chair. WANG MINGQUAN; 10 brs.

China International Capital Corporation (CICC): 23rd Floor, Everbright Bldg, 6 Fu Xing Men Wai Dajie, Beijing 100045; tel. (10) 68561166; fax (10) 68561145; f. 1995; international investment bank; 42.5% owned by China Construction Bank; registered cap. US $100m. CEO EDWIN LIM.

China International Trust and Investment Corporation (CITIC): Capital Mansion, 6 Xianyuannan Lu, Chao Yang Qu, Beijing 100004; tel. (10) 64661105; fax (10) 64662137; f. 1979; economic and technological co-operation; finance, banking, investment and trade; registered cap. 3,000m. sales US $3,462.7m. (1999/2000); Chair. WANG JUN; Pres. KONG DAN.

China Merchants Bank: China Merchants Bank Tower, 7088 Shennan Blvd, Shenzhen 518040; tel. (755) 83198888; fax (755) 83195061; e-mail 00430@oa.cmbchina.com; internet www.cmbchina .com; f. 1987; cap. 4,207m., res 35.5m., dep. 252,948m. (Dec. 2001); Pres.and CEO MA WEIHUA; 19 brs.

China Minsheng Banking Corporation: 4 Zhengyi Lu, Dongcheng Qu, Beijing 100006; tel. (10) 65269578; fax (10) 65269593; e-mail cmbc@public.bta.net.cn; internet www.cmbc.com.cn; first non-state national commercial bank, opened Jan. 1996; cap. 2,249.3m., res 2,675.9m., dep. 127,851.7m. (Dec. 2001); Chair. JING SHUPING; Pres. DONG WENBIAO; 5 brs.

Chinese Mercantile Bank: Ground and 23rd Floors, Dongfeng Bldg, 2 Yannan Lu, Futian Qu, Shenzhen 518031; tel. (755) 3257880; fax (755) 3257801; e-mail szcmbank@public.szptt.net.cn; f. 1993; cap. US $85.3m., res US $3.3m., dep. US $183.8m. (Dec. 1999); Pres. HUANG MINGXIANG.

CITIC Industrial Bank: Block C, Fuhua Bldg, 8 Chao Yang Men Bei Dajie, Dongcheng Qu, Beijing 100027; tel. (10) 65541658; fax (10) 65541671; e-mail webmaster@citicb.com.cn; internet www.citicib .com.cn; f.1987; cap. 6,809.3m., res 829.5m., dep. 254,851.8m. (Dec. 2001); Chair. WANG JUN; Pres. DOU JIANZHONG; 26 brs.

Export and Import Bank of China: 1 Dingandongli, Yongdingmenwai, Beijing; tel. (10) 67626688; fax (10) 67638940; f. 1994; provides trade credits for export of large machinery, electronics, ships, etc. Chair. and Pres. YANG ZILIN.

Fujian Asia Bank Ltd: 2nd Floor, Yuan Hong Bldg, 32 Wuyi Lu, Fuzhou, Fujian 350005; tel. (591) 3330788; fax (591) 3330843; f. 1993; cap. US $27.0m., res US $2.1m., dep. US $0.3m. (Dec. 2001); Chair. MA HONG; Gen. Man. SONG JIANXIN.

Fujian Industrial Bank: Zhong Shang Bldg, 154 Hudong Lu, Hualin, Fuzhou, Fujian 350003; tel. (591) 7839338; fax (591) 7841932; internet www.fib.com.cn; f. 1982; cap. 3,000m., res 2,867.8m., dep. 117,935.2m. (Dec. 2001); Pres. GAO JIANPING; 19 brs.

Guangdong Development Bank: 83 Nonglinxia Lu, Dongshan Qu, Guangzhou, Guangdong 510080; tel. (20) 87310888; fax (20) 87310779; internet www.gdb.com.cn; f. 1988; cap. 3,585.7m., res 1,388.7m., dep. 166,079.3m. (Dec. 2001); Chair. LI RUOHONG; Pres. WANG XIN; 24 brs.

Hua Xia Bank: 9th–12th Floors, Xidan International Mansion, 111 Xidan Bei Dajie, Beijing 100032; tel. (10) 66151199; fax (10) 66188484; e-mail hxbk@public.bta.net.cn; internet www.hxb.cc; f. 1992 as part of Shougang Corpn; cap. 2,500m., res 482.6m., dep. 118,282.4m. (Dec. 2001); Chair. LU YUCHENG; Pres. WU JIAN.

Industrial and Commercial Bank of China: 55 Fuxingmennai Dajie, Xicheng Qu, Beijing 100031; tel. (10) 66106071; fax (10) 66106053; e-mail webmaster@icbc.com.cn; internet www.icbc.com .cn; f. 1984; handles industrial and commercial credits and international business; operates Huarong AMC (asset management corporation) since 1999; cap. 167,417m., res 15,908m., dep. 3,873,732m. (Dec. 2001); Chair. and Pres. JIANG JIANQING.

International Bank of Paris and Shanghai: 13th Floor, North Tower, Shanghai Stock Exchange Bldg, 528 Pudong Nan Lu, Shanghai 200120; tel. (21) 58405500; fax (21) 58889232; f. 1992; cap. US $33.6m., res US $1,337,000, dep. US $124.9m. (Dec. 2000); Chair. and Dir JI XIAOHUI.

Kincheng Banking Corporation: 410 Fu Cheng Men Nei Dajie, Beijing; internet kincheng.bocgroup.com; f. 1917; cap. 2,200.0m., res 6,768.8m., dep. 51,873.2m. (Dec. 2000); Chair. SUNG HUNGKAY.

Kwangtung (Gwangdong) Provincial Bank: 410 Fu Cheng Men Nei Dajie, Beijing 100818; internet www.kpb-hk.com; f. 1924; cap. 1,500.0m., res 6,240.0m., dep. 71,535.2m. (Dec. 2000).

National Commercial Bank Ltd: 410 Fu Cheng Men Nei Dajie, Beijing; e-mail hkbrmain@natcombank.bocgroup.com; internet www.natcombank.bocgroup.com; f. 1907; cap. 1,200.0m., res 4,927.6m., dep. 45,291.5m. (Dec. 2000); 26 brs.

Nantong City Commercial Bank Co Ltd: 300 Nanda Lu, Nantong, Jiangsu 226006; tel. (513) 5123040; fax (513) 5123039; e-mail ntccb.id@pub.nt.jsinfo.net; internet www.ntccb.com; f. 1997 as Nantong City United Bank; assumed present name in 1998; cap. 186.7m., res 18.4m., dep. 4,229.1m., (Dec. 2001); Chair. and Pres. LIU CHANGJI.

Qingdao International Bank: Full Hope Mansion C, 12 Hong Kong Middle Rd, Qingdao, Shandong 266071; tel. (532) 5026230; fax (532) 5026222; e-mail qibankc@public.qd.sd.cn; f. 1996; joint venture between Industrial and Commercial Bank of China and Korea First Bank; cap. 165.5m., res 8.5m., dep. 87.3m. (Dec. 2001); Pres. CHOI HYOUNG-JIB.

Shanghai Pudong Development Bank: 12 Zhongshan Lu, Shanghai 200002; tel. (21) 63296188; fax (21) 63232036; internet www.spdb.com.cn; f. 1993; cap. 2,410.0m., res 4,352.4m., dep. 162,073.1m. (Dec. 2001); Chair. ZHANG GUANGSHENG; Pres. JIN YUN.

Shenzhen Commercial Bank: Shenzhen Commercial Bank Building, 1099 Shennan Lu, Central, Shenzhen 518031; tel. (755) 25878092; fax (755) 25878212; e-mail ibd@bankofshenzhen.com; internet www.18ebank.com; cap. US $193m., res US $15m., dep.

US $4,044m. (Dec 2002); f. 1995; Chair. CHEN ZEMING; President WANG JI; 45 brs.

Shenzhen Development Bank Co Ltd: 5047 Shennan Dong Lu, Shenzhen 518001; tel. (755) 2088888; fax (755) 2081018; e-mail shudi@sdb.com.cn; internet www.sdb.com.cn; f. 1987; cap. 1,945.8m., res 1,632.1m., dep. 113,992.1m. (Dec. 2001); Chair. CHEN ZHAOMIN; Pres. ZHOU LIN.

Sin Hua Bank Ltd: 17 Xi Jiao Min Xiang, Beijing 100031; subsidiary of Bank of China; cap. 2,200.0m., res 7,723.2m., dep. 90,021.3m. (Dec. 1998); Chair. JIANG ZUQI.

State Development Bank (SDB): 29 Fuchengmenwai Lu, Xicheng Qu, Beijing 100037; tel. (10) 68306557; fax (10) 68306541; f. 1994; merged with China Investment Bank 1998; handles low-interest loans for infrastructural projects and basic industries; Gov. CHEN YUAN.

Xiamen International Bank: 10 Hu Bin Bei Lu, Xiamen, Fujian 361012; tel. (592) 5310686; fax (592) 5310685; e-mail xib@public.xm .fj.cn; internet www.xib.com.cn; f. 1985; cap. HK $800m., res HK $335.3m., dep. HK $7,184.4m. (Dec. 2001); Chair. LI LIHUI; 3 brs.

Yantai House Saving Bank: 248 Nan Da Jie, Yantai 264001; tel. (535) 6207047.

Yien Yieh Commercial Bank Ltd: 17 Xi Jiao Min Xiang, Beijing 100031; f. 1915; cap. 800m., res 4,425m., dep. 39,218m. (Dec. 2000); Chair. ZHAO ANGE; Gen. Man. WU GUORUI; 27 brs.

Zhejiang Commercial Bank Ltd: 88 Xi Zhongshan Lu, Ningbo 315010; tel. (574) 87252668; fax (574) 87245409; e-mail zcbho@mail .nbptt.zj.cn; f. 1993; cap. US $40m., dep. US $86m. (Dec. 1997); Pres. and Chair. DUAN YONGKUAN.

Zhongxin Shiye Bank is a nation-wide commercial bank. Other commercial banks include the Fujian Commercial Bank and Zhaoshang Bank.

Foreign Banks

Before mid-1995 foreign banks were permitted only to open representative offices in China. The first foreign bank established a full branch in Beijing in mid-1995, and by March 1998 there were 51 foreign banks in China. In March 1997 foreign banks were allowed for the first time to conduct business in yuan. However, they are only entitled to accept yuan deposits from joint-venture companies. Representative offices totalled 519 in December 1996. In March 1999 the Government announced that foreign banks, hitherto restricted to 23 cities and Hainan Province, were to be permitted to open branches in all major cities.

STOCK EXCHANGES

Several stock exchanges were in the process of development in the mid-1990s, and by early 1995 the number of shareholders had reached 38m. By 1995 a total of 15 futures exchanges were in operation, dealing in various commodities, building materials and currencies. By the end of 1997 the number of companies listed on the Shanghai and Shenzhen Stock Exchanges had reached 745. In August 1997, in response to unruly conditions, the Government ordered the China Securities Regulatory Commission (see below) to assume direct control of the Shanghai and Shenzhen exchanges.

Stock Exchange Executive Council (SEEC): Beijing; tel. (10) 64935210; f. 1989 to oversee the development of financial markets in China; mems comprise leading non-bank financial institutions authorized to handle securities; Vice-Pres. WANG BOMING.

Securities Association of China (SAC): Olympic Hotel, 52 Baishiqiao Lu, Beijing 100081; tel. (10) 68316688; fax (10) 68318390; f. 1991; non-governmental organization comprising 122 mems (stock exchanges and securities cos) and 35 individual mems; Pres. GUO ZHENQIAN.

Beijing Securities Exchange: 5 Anding Lu, Chao Yang Qu, Beijing 100029; tel. (10) 64939366; fax (10) 64936233.

Shanghai Stock Exchange: 528 Pudong Nan Lu, Shanghai 200120; tel. (21) 68808888; fax (21) 68807813; e-mail webmaster@ sse.com.cn; internet www.sse.com.cn; f. 1990; Chair. GENG LIANG; Pres. ZHU CONGJIU.

Shenzhen Stock Exchange: 5045 Shennan Dong Lu, Shenzhen, Guangdong 518010; tel. (755) 20833333; fax (755) 2083117; internet www.sse.org.cn; f. 1991; Chair. ZHENG KELIN; Pres. GUI MINJIE.

Regulatory Authorities

Operations are regulated by the State Council Securities Policy Committee and by the following:

China Securities Regulatory Commission (CSRC): Bldg 3, Area 3, Fangqunyuan, Fangzhuang, Beijing 100078; tel. (10) 67617343; fax (10) 67653117; e-mail csrcweb@publicf.bta.net.cn; internet www.csrc.gov.cn; f. 1993; Chair. SHANG FULIN; Sec.-Gen. WANG YI.

INSURANCE

A new Insurance Law, formulated to standardize activities and to strengthen the supervision and administration of the industry, took effect in October 1995. Changes included the separation of life insurance and property insurance businesses. By late 1998 the number of insurance companies totalled 25. Total premiums rose from 44,000m. yuan in 1994 to some 159,600m. yuan in December 2000. Of the latter figure, property insurance accounted for 58,000m. yuan, life insurance for 85,100m. yuan and health and accident insurance for 14,600m. yuan.

AXA-Minmetals Assurance Co: f. 1999; joint venture by Groupe AXA (France) and China Minmetals Group; Gen. Man. JOSEPH SIN.

China Insurance Co Ltd: 22 Xi Jiao Min Xiang, POB 20, Beijing 100032; tel. (10) 6654231; fax (10) 66011869; f. 1931; cargo, hull, freight, fire, life, personal accident, industrial injury, motor insurance, reinsurance, etc. Chair. YANG CHAO; Pres. WANG XIANGZHANG.

China Insurance Group: 410 Fu Cheng Men Nei Dajie, Beijing; tel. (10) 66016688; fax (10) 66011869; f. 1996; fmrly People's Insurance Co of China (PICC), f. 1949; hull, marine cargo, aviation, motor, life, fire, accident, liability and reinsurance, etc. in process of division into three subsidiaries (life insurance (China Life Insurance Co —CLIC), property-casualty insurance and reinsurance) by mid-1996, in preparation for transformation into joint-stock cos; 300m. policy-holders (1996); Chair. and Pres. MA YONGWEI.

China Pacific Insurance Co Ltd (CPIC): 12 Zhongshan Lu (Dong 1), Shanghai 200001; tel. (21) 63232488; fax (21) 63218398; internet www.cpic.com.cn; f. 1991; joint-stock co; Chair. WANG MINGQUAN; Pres. HUO LIANHONG.

China Ping An Insurance Co: Ping An Bldg, Bagua San Lu, Bagualing, Shenzhen 518029; tel. (755) 82262888; fax (755) 82431019; internet www.pa18.com; f. 1988; Chair. and CEO MA MINGZHE.

Hua Tai Insurance Co of China Ltd: Beijing; tel. (10) 68565588; fax (10) 68561750; f. 1996 by 63 industrial cos.

Pacific-Aetna Life Insurance Co: Shanghai; f. 1998 by CPIC and Aetna Life Insurance Co. China's first Sino-US insurance co.

Tai Ping Insurance Co Ltd: 410 Fu Cheng Men Nei Dajie, Beijing 100034; tel. (10) 66016688; fax (10) 66011869; marine freight, hull, cargo, fire, personal accident, industrial injury, motor insurance, reinsurance, etc. Pres. SUN XIYUE.

Taikang Life Insurance Co Ltd: Beijing; f. 1996; Chair. CHEN DONGSHENG.

Joint-stock companies include the Xinhua (New China) Life Insurance Co Ltd (Gen. Man. Sun Bing). By April 1998 a total of 84 foreign insurance companies had established some 150 offices in China, being permitted to operate in Shanghai and Guangzhou only.

Regulatory Authority

China Insurance Regulatory Commission (CIRC): 410 Fu Cheng Men Nei Dajie, Beijing 100034; tel. (10) 66016688; fax (10) 66018871; internet www.circ.gov.cn; f. 1998; under direct authority of the State Council; Chair. WU DINGFU.

Trade and Industry

GOVERNMENT AGENCIES

China Council for the Promotion of International Trade (CCPIT): 1 Fuxingmenwai Dajie, Beijing 100860; tel. (10) 68013344; fax (10) 68011370; e-mail ccpitweb@public.bta.net.cn; internet www.ccpit.org; f. 1952; encourages foreign trade and economic co-operation; sponsors and arranges Chinese exhbns abroad and foreign exhbns in China; helps foreigners to apply for patent rights and trade-mark registration in China; promotes foreign investment and organizes tech. exchanges with other countries; provides legal services; publishes trade periodicals; Chair. YU XIAO-SONG; Sec.-Gen. ZHONG MIN.

Chinese General Association of Light Industry: 22B Fuwai Dajie, Beijing 100833; tel. (10) 68396114; under supervision of State Council; Chair. YU CHEN.

Chinese General Association of Textile Industry: 12 Dong Chang An Jie, Beijing 100742; tel. (10) 65129545; under supervision of State Council; Chair. SHI WANPENG.

Ministry of Foreign Trade and Economic Co-operation: see under Ministries.

National Administration of State Property: Dir ZHANG YOUCAI.

State Administration for Industry and Commerce: 8 San Li He Dong Lu, Xicheng Qu, Beijing 100820; tel. (10) 68010463; fax (10) 68020848; responsible for market supervision and administrative execution of industrial and commercial laws; functions under the direct supervision of the State Council; Dir WANG ZHONGFU.

Takeover Office for Military, Armed Police, Government and Judiciary Businesses: Beijing; f. 1998 to assume control of enterprises formerly operated by the People's Liberation Army.

CHAMBERS OF COMMERCE

All-China Federation of Industry and Commerce: 93 Beiheyan Dajie, Beijing 100006; tel. (10) 65136677; fax (10) 65122631; f. 1953; promotes overseas trade relations; Chair. JING SHUPING; Sec.-Gen. CHENG LU.

China Chamber of International Commerce—Shanghai: Jinling Mansions, 28 Jinling Lu, Shanghai 200021; tel. (21) 53060228; fax (21) 63869915; e-mail ccpitllb@online.sh.cn; Chair. YANG ZHIHUA.

China Chamber of International Commerce (CCOIC)—Zhuhai Chamber of Commerce: Fa Zhan Bldg, Rm 1702, 131 Shui Wan Rd, Gong Bei, Zhuhai, Guangdong 519020; tel. (756) 8890808; fax (756) 8280888; e-mail zhh@ccpit.org.

TRADE AND INDUSTRIAL ORGANIZATIONS

Anshan Iron and Steel Co: Huangang Lu, Tiexi Qu, Anshan 114021; tel. and fax (412) 6723090; Pres. LIU JIE.

Baotou Iron and Steel Co: Gangtie Dajie, Kundulun Qu, Baotou 014010, Inner Mongolia; tel. (472) 2125619; fax (472) 2183708; Pres. ZENG GUOAN.

Beijing Urban Construction Group Co Ltd: 62 Xueyuannan Lu, Haidian, Beijing 100081; tel. (10) 62255511; fax (10) 62256027; e-mail cjp@mail.bucg.com; internet www.bucg.com; construction of civil and industrial buildings and infrastructure.

China Aviation Industry Corporation II: 67 Jiao Nan Street, Beijing 100712; tel. (10) 64094013; fax (10) 64032109; e-mail avic@public3.bta.net.cn; Pres. ZHANG YANZHONG.

China Aviation Supplies Corpn: 155 Xi Dongsi Jie, Beijing 100013; tel. (10) 64012233; fax (10) 64016392; f. 1980; Pres. LIU YUANFAN.

China Civil Engineering Construction Corpn (CCECC): 4 Beifeng Wo, Haidian Qu, Beijing 100038; tel. (10) 63263392; fax (10) 63263864; e-mail zongban@ccecc.com.cn; f. 1953; general contracting, provision of technical and labour services, consulting and design, etc. Pres. QIAN WUYUN.

China Construction International Inc: 9 Sanlihe Lu, Haidian Qu, Beijing; tel. (10) 68394086; fax (10) 68394097; Pres. FU RENZHANG.

China Electronics Corpn: 27 Wanshou Lu, Haidian Qu, Beijing 100846; tel. (10) 68218529; fax (10) 68213745; e-mail cec@public.gb .com.cn; internet www.cec.com.cn; Pres. WANG JINCHENG.

China Garment Industry Corpn: 9A Taiyanggong Beisanhuandong Lu, Chao Yang Qu, Beijing 100028; tel. (10) 64216660; fax (10) 64239134; Pres. DONG BINGGEN.

China General Technology (Group) Holding Ltd: f. 1998; through merger of China National Technical Import and Export Corpn, China National Machinery Import and Export Corpn, China National Instruments Import and Export Corpn and China National Corpn for Overseas Economic Co-operation; total assets 16,000m. yuan; Chair. and Pres. TONG CHANGYIN.

China Gold Co: 1 Bei Jie, Qingnianhu, Andingmenwai, Beijing; tel. (10) 64214831; Pres. CUI LAN.

China Great Wall Computer Group: 38A Xueyuan Lu, Haidian Qu, Beijing 100083; tel. (10) 68342714; fax (10) 62011240; internet www.gwssi.com.cn; f. 1988; Chair. ZHANG ZHIKAI; Gen. Man. GAO KEQIN.

China Great Wall Industry Corpn: Hangtian Changcheng Bldg, 30 Haidian Nanlu, Haidian Qu, Beijing 100080; tel. (10) 68748737; fax (10) 68748865; e-mail cgwic@cgwic.com; internet www.cgwic .com.cn; registered cap. 200m. yuan; Pres. ZHANG XINXIA.

China International Book Trading Corpn: see under Publishers.

China International Contractors Association: 28 Donghouxiang, Andingmenwai, Beijing 100710; tel. (10) 64211159; fax (10) 64213959; Chair. LI RONGMIN.

China International Futures Trading Corpn: 24th Floor, Capital Mansion, 6 Xinyuan Nan Lu, Chao Yang Qu, Beijing 100004; tel. (10) 64665388; fax (10) 64665140; Chair. TIAN YUAN; Pres. LU JIAN.

China International Telecommunications Construction Corpn (CITCC): 22 Yuyou Lane, Xicheng Qu, Beijing 100035; tel. (10) 66012244; fax (10) 66024103; Pres. QI FUSHENG.

China International Water and Electric Corpn: 3 Liupukang Yiqu Zhongjie, Xicheng Qu, Beijing 100011; tel. (10) 64015511; fax

(10) 64014075; e-mail cwe@mx.cei.go.cn; f. 1956 as China Water and Electric International Corpn, name changed 1983; imports and exports equipment for projects in the field of water and electrical engineering; undertakes such projects; provides technical and labour services; Pres. WANG SHUOHAO.

China Iron and Steel Industry and Trade Group Corpn: 17B Xichangan Jie, Beijing 100031; tel. (10) 66067733; fax (10) 66078450; e-mail support@sinosteel.com.cn; internet www.sinosteel .com; f. 1999; by merger of China National Metallurgical Import and Export Corpn, China Metallurgical Raw Materials Corpn and China Metallurgical Steel Products Processing Corpn; Pres. BAI BAOHUA.

China National Aerotechnology Import and Export Corpn: 5 Liangguochang, Dongcheng Qu, Beijing 100010; tel. (10) 64017722; fax (10) 64015381; f. 1952; exports signal flares, electric detonators, tachometers, parachutes, general purpose aircraft, etc. Pres. YANG CHUNSHU; Gen. Man. LIU GUOMIN.

China National Animal Breeding Stock Import and Export Corpn (CABS): 10 Yangyi Hutong Jia, Dongdan, Beijing 100005; tel. (10) 65131107; fax (10) 65128694; sole agency for import and export of stud animals including cattle, sheep, goats, swine, horses, donkeys, camels, rabbits, poultry, etc., as well as pasture and turf grass seeds, feed additives, medicines, etc. Pres. YANG CHENGSHAN.

China National Arts and Crafts Import and Export Corpn: Arts and Crafts Bldg, 103 Jixiangli, Chao Yang Men Wai, Chao Yang Qu, Beijing 100020; tel. (10) 65931075; fax (10) 65931036; e-mail po@mbox.cnart.com.cn; internet www.cnart-group.com; deals in jewellery, ceramics, handicrafts, embroidery, pottery, wicker, bamboo, etc. Pres. CHEN KUN.

China National Automotive Industry Corpn (CNAIC): 46 Fucheng Lu, Haidian Qu, Beijing 100036; tel. (10) 88123968; fax (10) 68125556; Pres. GU YAOTIAN.

China National Automotive Industry Import and Export Corpn (CAIEC): 5 Beisihuan Xi Lu, Beijing 100083; tel. (10) 62310650; fax (10) 62310688; e-mail info@chinacaiec.com; internet www.chinacaiec.com; sales US $540m. (1995); Pres. ZHANG FUSHENG; 1,100 employees.

China National Cereals, Oils and Foodstuffs Import and Export Corpn (COFCO): 7th–13th Floors, Tower A, COFCO Plaza, Jian Guo Men Nei Dajie, Beijing 100005; tel. (10) 65268888; fax (10) 65278612; e-mail minnie@cofco.com.cn; internet www.cofco .com.cn; f. 1952; imports, exports and processes grains, oils, food-stuffs, etc. also hotel management and property development; sales US $12,099.2m. (1999/2000); Chair. ZHOU MINGCHEN.

China National Chartering Corpn (SINOCHART): Rm 1601/1602, 1607/1608, Jiu Ling Bldg, 21 Xisanhuan Bei Lu, Beijing 100081; tel. (10) 68405601; fax (10) 68405628; e-mail sinochrt@ public.intercom.co.cn; f. 1950; functions under Ministry of Foreign Trade and Economic Co-operation; subsidiary of SINOTRANS (see below); arranges chartering of ships, reservation of space, managing and operating chartered vessels; Pres. LIU SHUNLONG; Gen. Man. ZHANG JIANWEI.

China National Chemical Construction Corpn: Bldg No. 15, Songu, Anzhenxili, Chao Yang Qu, Beijing 100029; tel. (10) 64429966; fax (10) 64419698; e-mail cnccc@cnccc.com.cn; internet www.cnccc.com.cn; registered cap. 50m. Pres. CHEN LIHUA.

China National Chemicals Import and Export Corporation (SINOCHEM): SINOCHEM Tower, A2 Fuxingmenwai Dajie, Beijing 100045; tel. (10) 68568888; fax (10) 68568890; internet www .sinochem.com; f. 1950; import and export, domestic trade and entrepôt trade of oil, fertilizer, rubber, plastics and chemicals; it has made notable development in other areas like industry, finance, insurance, transportation and warehousing; sales US $15,066.2m. (1999/2000); Pres. LIU DESHU.

China National Coal Industry Import and Export Corpn (CNCIEC): 88B Andingmenwai, Dongcheng Qu, Beijing 100011; tel. (10) 64287188; fax (10) 64287166; e-mail cnciec@chinacoal.com; internet www.chinacoal.com; f. 1982; sales US $800m. (1992); imports and exports coal and tech. equipment for coal industry, joint coal development and compensation trade; Chair. and Pres. WANG CHANGCHUN.

China National Coal Mine Corpn: 21 Bei Jie, Heipingli, Beijing 100013; tel. (10) 64217766; Pres. WANG SENHAO.

China National Complete Plant Import and Export Corpn (Group): 9 Xi Bin He Lu, An Ding Men, Beijing; tel. (10) 64253388; fax (10) 64211382; Chair. HU ZHAOQING; Pres. LI ZHIMIN.

China National Electronics Import and Export Corpn: 8th Floor, Electronics Bldg, 23A Fuxing Lu, Beijing 100036; tel. (10) 68219550; fax (10) 68212352; e-mail ceiec@ceiec.com.cn; internet www.ceiec.com.cn; imports and exports electronics equipment, light industrial products, ferrous and non-ferrous metals; advertising; consultancy; Chair. and Pres. QIAN BENYUAN.

China National Export Bases Development Corpn: Bldg 16–17, District 3, Fang Xing Yuan, Fang Zhuang Xiaoqu, Fengtai Qu, Beijing 100078; tel. (10) 67628899; fax (10) 67628803; Pres. XUE ZHAO.

China National Foreign Trade Transportation Corpn (Group) (SINOTRANS): Sinotrans Plaza, A43, Xizhimen Beidajie, Beijing 100044; tel. (10) 62295900; fax (10) 62295901; e-mail office@ sinotrans.com; internet www.sinotrans.com; f. 1950; agents for Ministry's import and export corpns; arranges customs clearance, deliveries, forwarding and insurance for sea, land and air transportation; registered cap. 150m. yuan; Chair. and Pres. LUO KAIFU.

China National Import and Export Commodities Inspection Corpn: 15 Fanghuadi Xi Jie, Chao Yang Qu, Beijing 100020; tel. (10) 65013951; fax (10) 65004625; internet www.ccic.com; inspects, tests and surveys import and export commodities for overseas trade, transport, insurance and manufacturing firms; Pres. ZHOU WENHUI.

China National Instruments Import and Export Corpn (Instrimpex): Instrimpex Bldg, 6 Xizhimenwai Jie, Beijing 100044; tel. (10) 68330618; fax (10) 68330528; e-mail zcb@instrimpex.com .cn; internet www.instrimpex.com.cn; f. 1955; imports and exports; technical service, real estate, manufacturing, information service, etc. Pres. ZHANG RUEN.

China National Light Industrial Products Import and Export Corpn: 910, 9th Section, Jin Song, Chao Yang Qu, Beijing 100021; tel. (10) 67766688; fax (10) 67747246; e-mail info@chinalight.com.cn; internet www.chinalight.com.cn; imports and exports household electrical appliances, audio equipment, photographic equipment, films, paper goods, building materials, bicycles, sewing machines, enamelware, glassware, stainless steel goods, footwear, leather goods, watches and clocks, cosmetics, stationery, sporting goods, etc. Pres. XU LIEJUN.

China National Machine Tool Corpn: 19 Fang Jia Xiaoxiang, An Nei, Beijing 100007; tel. (10) 64033767; fax (10) 64015657; f. 1979; imports and exports machine tools and tool products, components and equipment; supplies apparatus for machine-building industry; Pres. QUAN YILU.

China National Machinery and Equipment Import and Export Corpn (Group): 6 Xisanhuannan Lu, Liuliqiao, Beijing 100073; tel. (10) 63271392; fax (10) 63261865; f. 1978; imports and exports machine tools, all kinds of machinery, automobiles, hoisting and transport equipment, electric motors, photographic equipment, etc. Pres. HU GUIXIANG.

China National Machinery Import and Export Corpn: Sichuan Mansion, West Wing, 1 Fu Xing Men Wai Jie, Xicheng Qu, Beijing 100037; tel. (10) 68991188; fax (10) 68991000; e-mail cmc@cmc.com .cn; internet www.cmc.com.cn; f. 1950; imports and exports machine tools, diesel engines and boilers and all kinds of machinery; imports aeroplanes, ships, etc. Chair. and Pres. CHEN WEIGUN.

China National Medicine and Health Products Import and Export Corpn: Meheco Plaza, 18 Guangming Zhong Jie, Chongwen Qu, Beijing 100061; tel. (10) 67116688; fax (10) 67021579; e-mail webmaster@meheco.com.cn; internet www.meheco.com.cn; Pres. LIU GUOSHENG.

China National Metals and Minerals Import and Export Corpn: Bldg 15, Block 4, Anhuili, Chao Yang Qu, Beijing 100101; tel. (10) 64916666; fax (10) 64916421; e-mail support@minmetals .com.cn; internet www.minmetals.com.cn; f. 1950; principal imports and exports include steel, antimony, tungsten concentrates and ferrotungsten, zinc ingots, tin, mercury, pig-iron, cement, etc. Pres. MIAO GENGSHU.

China National Native Produce and Animal By-Products Import and Export Corpn (TUHSU): Sanli Bldg, 208 Anding-menwai Jie, Beijing 100011; tel. (10) 64248899; fax (10) 64204099; e-mail info@china-tuhsu.com; internet www.china-tuhsu.com; f. 1949; imports and exports include tea, coffee, cocoa, fibres, etc. 23 subsidiary enterprises; 9 tea brs; 23 overseas subsidiaries; Pres. ZHANG ZHENMING.

China National Non-Ferrous Metals Import and Export Corpn (CNIEC): 12B Fuxing Lu, Beijing 100814; tel. (10) 63975588; fax (10) 63964424; Chair. WU JIANCHANG; Pres. XIAO JUNQING.

China National Nuclear Corpn: 1 Nansanxiang, Sanlihe, Beijing; tel. (10) 68512211; fax (10) 68533989; internet www.cnnc.com.cn; Pres. LI DINGFAN.

China National Offshore Oil Corpn (CNOOC): PO Box 4705, No. 6 Dongzhimenwai, Xiaojie, Beijing 100027; tel. (10) 84521010; fax (10) 84521044; e-mail webmaster@cnooc.com.cn; internet www .cnooc.com.cn; f. 1982; operates offshore exploration and production of petroleum; sales US $1,341.5m. (1999/2000); Pres. WEN LIUCHENG.

China National Oil Development Corpn: Liupukang, Beijing 100006; tel. (10) 6444313; Pres. CHENG SHOULI.

China National Packaging Import and Export Corpn: Xinfu Bldg B, 3 Dong San Huan Bei Lu, Chao Yang Qu, Beijing 100027; tel. (10) 64611166; fax (10) 64616437; e-mail info@chinapack.net; internet www.chinapack.net; handles import and export of packaging materials, containers, machines and tools; contracts for the processing and converting of packaging machines and materials supplied by foreign customers; registered cap. US $30m. Pres. ZHENG CHONGXIANG.

China National Petroleum Corpn (CNPC): 6 Liupukang Jie, Xicheng Qu, Beijing 100724; tel. (10) 62094538; fax (10) 62094806; e-mail admin@hq.cnpc.com.cn; internet www.cnpc.com.cn; restructured mid-1998; responsible for petroleum extraction and refining in northern and western China, and for setting retail prices of petroleum products; Pres. MA FUCAI.

China National Publications Import and Export Corpn: 16 Gongrentiyuguandong Lu, Chao Yang Qu, Beijing; tel. (10) 65066688; fax (10) 65063101; e-mail cnpiec@cnpiec.com.cn; internet www.cnpiec.com.cn; imports and exports books, newspapers and periodicals, records, CD-ROMs, etc. Pres. SONG XIAOHONG.

China National Publishing Industry Trading Corpn: POB 782, 504 An Hua Li, Andingmenwai, Beijing 100011; tel. (10) 64215031; fax (10) 64214540; f. 1981; imports and exports publications, printing equipment technology; holds book fairs abroad; undertakes joint publication; Pres. ZHOU HONGLI.

China National Seed Group Corpn: 16A Xibahe, Chao Yang Qu, Beijing 100028; tel. (10) 64201817; fax (10) 64201820; imports and exports crop seeds, including cereals, cotton, oil-bearing crops, teas, flowers and vegetables; seed production for foreign seed companies etc. Pres. HE ZHONGHUA.

China National Silk Import and Export Corpn: 105 Bei He Yan Jie, Dongcheng Qu, Beijing 100006; tel. (10) 65123338; fax (10) 65125125; e-mail cnsiec@public.bta.net.cn; internet www.chinasilk .com; Pres. XU HONGXIN.

China National Star Petroleum Corpn: 1 Bei Si Huan Xi Lu, Beijing; e-mail jf@mail.cnspc.com.cn; internet www.cnspc.com.cn; f. 1997; petroleum and gas exploration, development and production; Pres. ZHU JIAZHEN.

China National Technical Import and Export Corpn: Jiuling Bldg, 21 Xisanhuan Beilu, Beijing 100081; tel. (10) 68404000; fax (10) 68414877; e-mail info@cntic.com.cn; internet www.cntic.com.cn; f. 1952; imports all kinds of complete plant and equipment, acquires modern technology and expertise from abroad, undertakes co-production and jt ventures, and technical consultation and updating of existing enterprises; registered cap. 200m. Pres. WANG HUIHENG.

China National Textiles Import and Export Corpn: 82 Donganmen Jie, Beijing 100747; tel. (10) 65123844; fax (10) 65124711; e-mail webmaster@chinatex.com; internet www.chinatex-group .com; imports synthetic fibres, raw cotton, wool, garment accessories, etc. exports cotton yarn, cotton fabric, knitwear, woven garments, etc. Pres. ZHAO BOYA.

China National Tobacco Import and Export Corpn: 11 Hufang Lu, Xuanwu Qu, Beijing 100052; tel. (10) 63533399; fax (10) 63015331; Pres. XUN XINGHUA.

China National United Oil Corpn: 57 Wangfujing Jie, Dongcheng Qu, Beijing 100006; tel. (10) 65223828; fax (10) 65223817; Chair. ZHANG JIAREN; Pres. ZHU YAOBIN.

China No. 1 Automobile Group: 63 Dongfeng Jie, Chao Yang Qu, Changchun, Jilin; tel. (431) 5003030; fax (431) 5001309; f. 1953; mfr of passenger cars; Gen. Man. GENG ZHAOJIE.

China North Industries Group: 46 Sanlihe Lu, Beijing 100821; tel. (10) 68594210; fax (10) 68594232; internet www.corincogroup .com.cn; exports vehicles and mechanical products, light industrial products, chemical products, opto-electronic products, building materials, military products, etc. Pres. MA ZHIGENG.

China Nuclear Energy Industry Corpn (CNEIC): 1A Yuetan Bei Jie, Xicheng Qu, Beijing 100037; tel. (10) 68013395; fax (10) 68512393; internet www.cnnc.com.cn; exports air filters, vacuum valves, dosimeters, radioactive detection elements and optical instruments; Pres. ZHANG ZHIFENG.

China Road and Bridge Corpn: Zhonglu Bldg, 88C, An Ding Men Wai Dajie, Beijing 100011; tel. (10) 64285616; fax (10) 64285686; e-mail crbc@crbc.com; internet www.crbc.com; overseas and domestic building of highways, urban roads, bridges, tunnels, industrial and residential buildings, airport runways and parking areas; contracts to do surveying, designing, pipe-laying, water supply and sewerage, building, etc., and/or to provide technical or labour services; Chair. ZHOU JICHANG.

China Shipbuilding Trading Corpn Ltd: 10 Yue Tan Bei Xiao Jie, Beijing 100861; tel. (10) 68032560; fax (10) 68033380; e-mail webmaster@cstc.com.cn; internet www.ctsc.com.cn; Pres. LI ZHUSHI.

China State Construction Engineering Corpn: Baiwanzhuang, Xicheng Qu, Beijing 100835; tel. (10) 68347766; fax (10) 68314326; e-mail cscec-us@worldnet.att.net; internet www.cscec.com; sales US $4,726.8m. (1999/2000); Pres. MA TINGGUI.

China State Shipbuilding Corpn: 5 Yuetan Beijie, Beijing; tel. (10) 68030208; fax (10) 68031579; Pres. CHEN XIAOJIN; Gen. Man. XU PENGHANG.

China Tea Import and Export Corpn: Zhongtuchu Bldg, 208 Andingmenwai Jie, Beijing 100011; tel. (10) 64204123; fax (10) 64204101; e-mail info@teachina.com; internet www.chinatea.com .cn; Pres. LI JIAZHI.

China Xinshidai (New Era) Corpn: 40 Xie Zuo Hu Tong, Dongcheng Qu, Beijing 100007; tel. (10) 64017384; fax (10) 64032935; Pres. QIN ZHONGXING.

China Xinxing Corpn (Group): 17 Xisanhuan Zhong Lu, Beijing 100036; tel. (10) 685166688; fax (10) 68514669; e-mail black-lily@ nihao.com; internet www.black-lily.com; Pres. FAN YINGJUN.

Chinese General Co of Astronautics Industry (State Aerospace Bureau): 8 Fucheng Lu, Haidian Qu, Beijing 100712; tel. (10) 68586047; fax (10) 68370080; Pres. LIU JIYUAN.

Daqing Petroleum Administration Bureau: Sartu Qu, Daqing, Heilongjiang; tel. (459) 814649; fax (459) 322845; Gen. Man. WANG ZHIWU.

Ma'anshan Iron and Steel Co: 8 Hongqibei Lu, Maanshan 243003, Anhui; tel. (555) 2883492; fax (555) 2324350; Chair. HANG YONGYI; Pres. LI ZONGBI.

Shanghai Automotive Industry Sales Corpn: 548 Caoyang Lu, Shanghai 200063; tel. and fax (21) 62443223; Gen. Man. XU JIANYU.

Shanghai Baosteel Group Corpn: Baosteel Tower, 370 Pudian Lu, Pudong New District, Shanghai; tel. (21) 58358888; fax (21) 68404832; e-mail webman@baosteel.com; internet www.bstl.sh.cn; f. 1998; incorporating Baoshan Iron and Steel Corpn, and absorption of Shanghai Metallurgical Holding Group Corpn, and Shanghai Meishan Group Corpn Ltd; produces steel and steel products; sales US $8,266.0m. (1999/2000); Pres. XIE QIHUA; Chair. of Bd XU DAQUA.

Shanghai Foreign Trade Corpn: 27 Zhongshan Dong Yi Lu, Shanghai 200002; tel. (21) 63217350; fax (21) 63290044; f. 1988; handles import-export trade, foreign trade transportation, chartering, export commodity packaging, storage and advertising for Shanghai municipality; Gen. Man. WANG MEIJUN.

Shanghai International Trust Trading Corpn: 201 Zhaojiabang Lu, Shanghai 200032; tel. (21) 64033866; fax (21) 64034722; f. 1979; present name adopted 1988; handles import and export business, international mail orders, processing, assembling, compensation trade etc.

Shougang Group: Shijingshan, Beijing 100041; tel. (10) 88294166; fax (10) 88295578; e-mail sgjtglb01@shougang.com.cn; internet www.shougang.com.cn; f. 1919; produces iron and steel; sales US $4,396.8m. (1999/2000); Chair. BI QUN; Gen. Man. LUO BINGSHENG.

State Bureau of Non-Ferrous Metals Industry: 12B Fuxing Lu, Beijing 100814; tel. (10) 68514477; fax (10) 68515360; under supervision of State Economic and Trade Commission; Dir ZHANG WULE.

Wuhan Iron and Steel (Group) Co: Qingshan Qu, Wuhan, Hubei Province; tel. (27) 6892004; fax (27) 6862325; proposals for merger with two other steel producers in Hubei announced late 1997; Pres. LIU BENREN.

Xinxing Oil Co (XOC): Beijing; f. 1997; exploration, development and production of domestic and overseas petroleum and gas resources; Gen. Man. ZHU JIAZHEN.

Yuxi Cigarette Factory: Yujiang Lu, Yuxi, Yunnan Province; tel. and fax (877) 2052343; Gen. Man. CHU SHIJIAN.

Zhongjiang Group: Nanjing, Jiansu; f. 1998; multi-national operation mainly in imports and exports, contract projects and real estate; group consists of 126 subsidiaries incl. 25 foreign ventures.

UTILITIES

Electricity

Beijing Power Supply Co: Qianmen Xidajie, Beijing 100031; tel. (10) 63129201.

Beijing Datang Power Generation: 33 Nanbinhe Lu, Xuanwu Qu, Beijing; one of China's largest independent power producers; Chair. JIAO YIAN.

Central China Electric Power Group Co: 47 Xudong Lu, Wuchang, Wuhan 430077; tel. (27) 6813398.

Changsha Electric Power Bureau: 162 Jiefang Sicun, Changsha 410002; tel. (731) 5912121; fax (731) 5523240.

China Atomic Energy Authority: Chair. ZHANG HUAZHU.

China Northwest Electric Power Group Co: 57 Shangde Lu, Xian 710004; tel. (29) 7275061; fax (29) 7212451; Chair. LIU HONG.

China Power Grid Development (CPG): f. to manage transmission and transformation lines for the Three Gorges hydroelectric scheme; Pres. ZHOU XIAOQIAN.

China Yangtze Three Gorges Project Development Corpn: 1 Jianshe Dajie, Yichang, Hubei Province; tel. (717) 6762212; fax (717) 6731787; Pres. LU YOUMEI.

Dalian Power Supply Co: 102 Zhongshan Lu, Dalian 116001; tel. (411) 2637560; fax (411) 2634430; Chief Gen. Man. LIU ZONGXIANG.

Fujian Electric Industry Bureau: 4 Xingang Dao, Taijrang Qu, Fuzhou 350009; tel. and fax (591) 3268514; Dir WANG CHAOXU.

Gansu Bureau of Electric Power: 306 Xijin Dong Lu, Qilihe Qu, Lanzhou 730050; tel. (931) 2334311; fax (93) 2331042; Dir ZHANG MINGXI.

Guangdong Electric Power Bureau: 757 Dongfeng Dong Lu, Guangzhou 510600; tel. (20) 87767888; fax (20) 87770307.

Guangdong Shantou Electric Power Bureau: Jinsha Zhong Lu, Shantou 515041; tel. (754) 8257606.

Guangxi Electric Power Bureau: 6 Minzhu Lu, Nanning 530023; tel. (771) 2801123; fax (771) 2803414.

Guangzhou Electric Power Co: 9th Floor, Huale Bldg, 53 Huale Lu, Guangzhou 510060; tel. (20) 83821111; fax (20) 83808559.

Hainan Electric Power Industry Bureau: 34 Haifu Dadao, Haikou 570203; tel. (898) 5334777; fax (898) 5333230.

Heilongjiang Electric Power Co: B12Fl High Tech Development Zone, Harbin 150001; tel. (451) 2308810; fax (451) 2525878; Chair. XUE YANG.

Huadong Electric Power Group Corpn: 201 Nanjing Dong Lu, Shanghai; tel. (21) 63290000; fax (21) 63290727; power supply.

Huaneng Power International: West Wing, Building C, Tianyin Mansion, 2C Fuxingmennan Lu, Xicheng, Beijing; tel. (10) 66491999; fax (10) 66491888; e-mail ir@hpi.com.cn; internet www.hpi.com.cn; f. 1998; Chair. and Pres. LI XIAOPENG.

Huazhong Electric Power Group Corpn: Liyuan, Donghu, Wuhan, Hubei Province; tel. (27) 6813398; fax (27) 6813143; electrical engineering; Gen. Man. LIN KONGXING.

Inner Mongolia Electric Power Co: 28 Xilin Nan Lu, Huhehaose 010021; tel. (471) 6942222; fax (471) 6924863.

Jiangmen Electric Power Supply Bureau: 87 Gangkou Lu, Jiangmen 529030; tel. and fax (750) 3360133.

Jiangxi Electric Power Bureau: 13 Yongwai Zheng Jie, Nanchang 330006; tel. (791) 6224701; fax (791) 6224830.

National Grid Construction Co: established to oversee completion of the National Grid by 2009.

North China Electric Power Group Corpn: 32 Zulinqianjie, Xuanwu Qu, Beijing 100053; tel. and fax (10) 63263377; Pres. JIAO YIAN.

Northeast China Electric Power Group: 11 Shiyiwei Lu, Heping Qu, Shenyang 110003; tel. (24) 3114382; fax (24) 3872665.

Shandong Electric Power Group Corpn: 150 Jinger Lu, Jinan 250001; tel. (531) 6911919.

Shandong International Power Development Co Ltd: 14 Jingsan Lu, Jinan, Shandong 250001; tel. (531) 6929898; fax (531) 6035469; e-mail sipd@sipd.com; internet www.sipd.com.cn; f. 1994; Chair. DA HONGXING.

Shandong Rizhao Power Co Ltd: 1st Floor, Bldg 29, 30 Northern Section, Shunyu Xiaoqu, Jinan 250002; tel. (531) 2952462; fax (531) 2942561.

Shanghai Electric Power Co: 181 Nanjing Dong Lu, Huangpu Qu, Shanghai 200002; tel. (21) 63291010; fax (21) 63248586; Dir GU YINZHANG.

Shenzhen Power Supply Co: 2 Yanhe Xi Lu, Luohu Qu, Shenzhen 518000; tel. (755) 5561920.

Sichuan Electric Power Co: Room 1, Waishi Bldg, Dongfeng Lu, Chengdu 610061; tel. (28) 444321; fax (28) 6661888.

State Power Corpn of China: No. 1 Lane 2, Baiguang Lu, Beijing 100761; tel. (10) 63416475; fax (10) 63548152; e-mail webmaster@sp .com.cn; internet www.cep.gov.cn; f. 1997; from holdings of Ministry of Electric Power; plans to split into three or four regional generating companies and two regional (North and South) grid companies announced in April 2002; Pres. GAO YAN.

Tianjin Electric Power Industry Bureau: 29 Jinbu Dao, Hebei Qu, Tianjin 300010; tel. (22) 24406326; fax (22) 22346965.

Wenergy Co Ltd: 81 Wuhu Lu, Hefei 230001; tel. (551) 2626906; fax (551) 2648061.

Wuhan Power Supply Bureau: 981 Jiefang Dadao, Hankou, Wuhan 430013; tel. (27) 2426455; fax (27) 2415605.

Wuxi Power Supply Bureau: 8 Houxixi, Wuxi 214001; tel. (510) 2717678; fax (510) 2719182.

Xiamen Power Transformation and Transmission Engineering Co: 67 Wenyuan Lu, Xiamen 361004; tel. (592) 2046763.

Xian Power Supply Bureau: Huancheng Dong Lu, Xian 710032; tel. (29) 7271483.

Gas

Beijing Gas Co: 30 Dongsanhuan Zhong Lu, Beijing 100020; tel. (10) 65024131; fax (10) 65023815; Dir LIU BINGIUN.

Beijing Natural Gas Co: Bldg 5, Dixingju, An Ding Men Wai, Beijing 100011; tel. (10) 64262244.

Changchun Gas Co: 30 Tongzhi Jie, Changchun 130021; tel. (431) 8926479.

Changsha Gas Co: 18 Shoshan Lu, Changsha 410011; tel. (731) 4427246.

Qingdao Gas Co: 399A Renmin Lu, Qingdao 266032; tel. (532) 4851461; fax (532) 4858653.

Shanghai Gas Supply Co: 656 Xizang Zhong Lu, Shanghai 200003; tel. (21) 63222333; fax (21) 63528600; Gen. Man. LI LONGLING.

Wuhan Gas Co: Qingnian Lu, Hankou, Wuhan 430015; tel. (27) 5866223.

Xiamen Gas Corpn: Ming Gong Bldg, Douxi Lukou, Hubin Nan Lu, Xiamen 361004; tel. (592) 2025937; fax (592) 2033290.

Water

Beijing District Heating Co: 1 Xidawang Lu, Hongmiao, Chao Yang Qu, Beijing 100026; tel. (10) 65060066; fax (10) 65678891.

Beijing Municipal Water Works Co: 19 Yangrou Hutong, Xicheng Qu, Beijing 100034; tel. (10) 66167744; fax (10) 66168028.

Changchun Water Co: 53 Dajing Lu, Changchun 130000; tel. (431) 8968366.

Chengdu Water Co: 16 Shierqiao Jie, Shudu Dadao, Chengdu 610072; tel. (28) 77663122; fax (28) 7776876.

The China Water Company: f. to develop investment opportunities for water projects.

Guangzhou Water Supply Co: 5 Huanshi Xi Lu, Guangzhou 510010; tel. (20) 81816951.

Haikou Water Co: 31 Datong Lu, Haikou 570001; tel. (898) 6774412.

Harbin Water Co: 49 Xi Shidao Jie, Daoli Qu, Harbin 150010; tel. (451) 4610522; fax (451) 4611726.

Jiangmen Water Co: 44 Jianshe Lu, Jiangmen 529000; tel. (750) 3300138; fax (750) 3353704.

Qinhuangdao Pacific Water Co: Hebei; Sino-US water supply project; f. 1998.

Shanghai Municipal Waterworks Co: 484 Jiangxi Zhong Lu, Shanghai 200002; tel. (21) 63215577; fax (21) 63231346; service provider for municipality of Shanghai.

Shenzhen Water Supply Group Co: Water Bldg, 1019 Shennan Zhong Lu, Shenzhen 518031; tel. (755) 2137836; fax (755) 2137888; e-mail webmaster@waterchina.com; internet www.waterchina.com.

Tianjin Waterworks Group: 54 Jianshe Lu, Heping Qu, Tianjin 300040; tel. (22) 3393887; fax (22) 3306720.

Xian Water Co: Huancheng Xi Lu, Xian 710082; tel. (29) 4244881.

Zhanjiang Water Co: 20 Renmin Dadaonan, Zhanjiang 524001; tel. (759) 2286394.

Zhongshan Water Supply Co: 23 Yinzhu Jie, Zhuyuan Lu, Zhongshan 528403; tel. (760) 8312969; fax (760) 6326429.

Zhuhai Water Supply General Corpn: Yuehai Zhong Lu, Gongbei, Zhuhai 519020; tel. (756) 8881160; fax (756) 8884405.

TRADE UNIONS

All-China Federation of Trade Unions (ACFTU): 10 Fu Xing Men Wai Jie, Beijing 100865; tel. (10) 68592114; fax (10) 68562030; f. 1925; organized on an industrial basis; 15 affiliated national industrial unions, 30 affiliated local trade union councils; membership is voluntary; trade unionists enjoy extensive benefits; 103,996,000 mems (1995); Chair. WEI JIANXING; First Sec. ZHANG JUNJIU.

Principal affiliated unions:

All-China Federation of Railway Workers' Unions: Chair. HUANG SICHUAN.

Architectural Workers' Trade Union: Sec. SONG ANRU.

China Self-Employed Workers' Association: Pres. REN ZHONG-LIN.

Educational Workers' Trade Union: Chair. JIANG WENLIANG.

Light Industrial Workers' Trade Union: Chair. LI SHUYING.

Machinery Metallurgical Workers' Union: Chair. ZHANG CUNEN.

National Defence Workers' Union: Chair. GUAN HENGCAI.

Postal and Telecommunications Workers' Trade Union of China: Chair. LUO SHUZHEN.

Seamen's Trade Union of China: Chair. ZHANG SHIHUI.

Water Resources and Electric Power Workers' Trade Union: Chair. DONG YUNQI.

Workers' Autonomous Federation (WAF): f. 1989; aims to create new trade union movement in China, independent of the All-China Federation of Trade Unions.

Transport

RAILWAYS

Ministry of Railways: 10 Fuxing Lu, Haidian Qu, Beijing 100844; tel. (10) 63244150; fax (10) 63242150; e-mail webmaster@ns .chinamor.cn.net; internet www.chinamor.cn.net; controls all railways through regional divisions. The railway network has been extended to all provinces and regions except Tibet (Xizang), where construction is in progress. Total length in operation in December 2000 was 58,656 km, of which 14,864 km were electrified. The major routes include Beijing–Guangzhou, Tianjin–Shanghai, Manzhouli–Vladivostok, Jiaozuo–Zhicheng and Lanzhou–Badou. In addition, special railways serve factories and mines. A new 2,536-km line from Beijing to Kowloon (Hong Kong) was completed in late 1995. Plans for a 1,450-km high-speed link between Beijing and Shanghai were announced in 1994, and construction was scheduled to begin by 2005. A high-speed link between Beijing and Guangzhou was also planned. China's first high-speed service, linking Guangzhou and Shenzhen, commenced in December 1994. A direct service between Shanghai and Hong Kong commenced in 1997. A new magnetic-levitation ('maglev') railway linking Shanghai to Pudong International airport was being built in co-operation with a German consortium in 2002.

An extensive programme to develop the rail network was announced in early 1998, which aimed to increase the total network to 68,000 km by the year 2000, and to more than 75,000 km by 2005. Railways were to be constructed along the Changjiang valley, starting at Sichuan, and along China's east coast, originating at Harbin. In December 1999 plans were announced for a railway to Kazakhstan. In June 2001 construction began on a new 1,118-km railway linking Tibet with the rest of China, to be completed after 10 years.

City Underground Railways

Beijing Metro Corpn: 2 Beiheyan Lu, Xicheng, Beijing 100044; tel. (10) 68024566; f. 1969; total length 54 km, with 98 km of further lines to be built by the year 2010; Gen. Man. FENG SHUANGSHENG.

Guangzhou Metro: 204 Huanshi Lu, Guangzhou 510010; tel. (20) 6665287; fax (20) 6678232; opened June 1997; total length of 18.5 km, with a further 133 km planned; Gen. Man. CHEN QINGQUAN.

Shanghai Metro Corpn: 12 Heng Shan Lu, Shanghai 200031; tel. (21) 64312460; fax (21) 64339598; f. 1995; 65.8 km open, with at least a further 181.5 km under construction or planned; Pres. SHI LIAN.

Tianjin Metro: 97 Jiefangbei Lu, Heping, Tianjin 300041; tel. (22) 23395410; fax (22) 23396194; f. 1984; total planned network 154 km; Gen. Man. WANG YUJI.

Underground systems were under construction in Chongqing, Nanjing, and Shenzhen, and planned for Chengdu and Qingdao.

ROADS

At the end of 2000 China had 1,402,698 km of highways (of which at least 90% were paved). Four major highways link Lhasa (Tibet) with Sichuan, Xinjiang, Qinghai Hu and Kathmandu (Nepal). A programme of expressway construction began in the mid-1980s. By 2000 there were 16,314 km of expressways (1,313 km of which were constructed in 1997), routes including the following: Shenyang–Dalian, Beijing–Tanggu, Shanghai–Jiading, Guangzhou–Foshan and Xian–Lintong. Expressway construction was to continue,

linking all main cities and totalling 55,000 km by 2020. A new 123-km highway linking Shenzhen (near the border with Hong Kong) to Guangzhou opened in 1994. A 58-km road between Guangzhou and Zhongshan connects with Zhuhai, near the border with Macao. Construction of a bridge, linking Zhuhai with Macao, began in June 1998 and was completed in late 1999. A bridge connecting the mainland with Hong Kong was to be built, with completion scheduled for the year 2004. In 1997 some 20% of villages in China were not connected to the road infrastructure.

INLAND WATERWAYS

At the end of 2000 there were some 119,325 km of navigable inland waterways in China. The main navigable rivers are the Changjiang (Yangtze River), the Zhujiang (Pearl River), the Heilongjiang, the Grand Canal and the Xiangjiang. The Changjiang is navigable by vessels of 10,000 tons as far as Wuhan, more than 1,000 km from the coast. Vessels of 1,000 tons can continue to Chongqing upstream.

There were 5,142 river ports at the end of 1996. In 1997 there were some 5,100 companies involved in inland waterway shipping.

SHIPPING

China has a network of more than 2,000 ports, of which more than 130 are open to foreign vessels. In May 2001 plans were announced for the biggest container port in the world to be built on the Yangshan Islands, off shore from Shanghai. The main ports include Dalian, Qinhuangdao, Tianjin, Yantai, Qingdao, Rizhao, Lianyungang, Shanghai, Ningbo, Guangzhou and Zhanjiang. In 2000 the main coastal ports handled 1,219m. metric tons of cargo. In December 2001 China's merchant fleet comprised 3,280 ships, totalling 16.6m. grt.

Bureau of Water Transportation: Beijing; controls rivers and coastal traffic.

China International Marine Containers Group Co Ltd: 5/F, Finance Centre, Shekou, Shenzhen 518067; tel. (755) 26691130; fax (755) 26692707; internet www.cimc.com; f. 1980; container-manufacturing, supply and storage; revenue US $1,081.6m. (2000); Chair. and Dir. LI JIANHONG.

China National Chartering Corpn (SINOCHART): see Trade and Industrial Organizations.

China Ocean Shipping (Group) Co (COSCO): 11th and 12th Floors, Ocean Plaza, 158 Fu Xing Men Nei, Xi Cheng Qu Chao Yang Qu, Beijing 100031; tel. (10) 66493388; fax (10) 66492288; internet www.cosco.com.cn; reorg. 1993, re-established 1997; head office transferred to Tianjin late 1997; br. offices: Shanghai, Guangzhou, Tianjin, Qingdao, Dalian; 200 subsidiaries (incl. China Ocean Shipping Agency—PENAVIC) and joint ventures in China and abroad, engaged in ship-repair, container-manufacturing, warehousing, insurance, etc. merchant fleet of 600 vessels; 47 routes; Pres. WEI JIAFU.

China Shipping (Group) Co: Shanghai; f. 1997; Pres. LI KELIN.

China Shipping Container Lines Co Ltd: 5th Floor, Shipping Tower, 700 Dong Da Ming Lu, Shanghai 200080; tel. (21) 65966978; fax (21) 65966498; Chair. LI SHAODE.

China Shipping Development Co Ltd Tanker Co: 168 Yuanshen Lu, Pudong New Area, Shanghai 200120; tel. (21) 68757170; fax (21) 68757929.

Fujian Shipping Co: 151 Zhong Ping Lu, Fuzhou 350009; tel. (591) 3259900; fax (591) 3259716; e-mail fusco@pub2.fz.fj.cn; internet www.fusco-cn.com; f. 1950; transport of bulk cargo, crude petroleum products, container and related services; Gen. Man. LIU QIMIN.

Guangzhou Maritime Transport (Group) Co: 22 Shamian Nan Jie, Guangzhou; tel. (20) 84104673; fax (20) 84103074.

CIVIL AVIATION

Air travel is expanding very rapidly. In 2000 a total of 139 civil airports were in operation. Chinese airlines carried a total of 67.2m. passengers in 2000. In 1998 there were 34 airlines, including numerous private companies, operating in China. During 2001–02 a number of regional airlines were in the process of forming alliances and mergers. The Government planned to merge the 10 CAAC (see below) airlines into three large groups, based in Guangzhou, Shanghai and Beijing. Air China was to incorporate China National Aviation Corpn and China Southwest Airlines; China Eastern Airlines was to incorporate China Northwest Airlines, Great Wall and Yunnan Airlines; and China Southern Airlines was to incorporate Air Xinjiang and China Northern Airlines.

General Administration of Civil Aviation of China (CAAC): POB 644, 155 Dongsixi Jie, Beijing 100710; tel. (10) 64014104; fax (10) 64016918; f. 1949 as Civil Aviation Administration of China; restructured in 1988 as a purely supervisory agency, its operational functions being transferred to new, semi-autonomous airlines (see below; also China United Airlines (division of the Air Force) and

China Capital Helicopter Service); domestic flights throughout China; external services are mostly operated by **Air China, China Eastern** and **China Southern Airlines**; Dir LIU JIANFENG.

Air China: Beijing International Airport, POB 644, Beijing 100621; tel. (10) 64599068; fax (10) 64599064; e-mail webmaster@ mail.airchina.com.cn; internet www.airchina.com.cn; international and domestic scheduled passenger and cargo services; Pres. WANG KAIYUAN.

China Eastern Airlines: 2550 Hongqiao Rd, Hongqiao Airport, Shanghai 200335; tel. (21) 62686268; fax (21) 62686116; e-mail webmaster@cea.online.sh.cn; internet www.cea.online.sh.cn; f. 1987; domestic services; overseas destinations include USA, Europe, Japan, Sydney, Singapore, Seoul and Bangkok; Pres. LIU SHAOYONG.

China Northern Airlines: 3-1 Xiaoheyan Lu, Dadong Qu, Shenyang, Liaoning 110043; tel. (24) 88294432; fax (24) 88294037; e-mail northern_air@163.net; internet www.cna.com.cn; f. 1990; scheduled flights to the Republic of Korea, Russia, Hong Kong, Macao and Japan; Pres. JIANG LIANYING.

China Northwest Airlines: Laodong Nan Lu, Xian, Shaanxi 710082; tel. (29) 7298000; fax (29) 8624068; e-mail cnwadzz@pub .xa-online.sn.cn; internet www.cnwa.com; f. 1992; domestic services and flights to Macao, Singapore and Japan; Pres. GAO JUNQUI.

China Southwest Airlines: Shuangliu Airport, Chengdu, Sichuan 610202; tel. (28) 5814466; fax (28) 5582630; e-mail szmaster@cswa.com; internet www.cswa.com; f. 1987; 70 domestic routes; international services to Singapore, Bangkok, Japan, the Republic of Korea and Kathmandu (Nepal); Pres. ZHOU ZHENGQUAN.

Changan Airlines: 16/F, Jierui Bldg, 5 South Er Huan Rd, Xian, Shaanxi 710068; tel. (29) 8707412; fax (29) 8707911; e-mail liulei@ hnair.com; internet www.changanair.com; f. 1992; local passenger and cargo services; Pres. SHE YINING.

China General Aviation Corpn: Wusu Airport, Taiyuan, Shanxi 030031; tel. (351) 7040600; fax (351) 7040094; f. 1989; 34 domestic routes; Pres. ZHANG CHANGJING.

China Southern Airlines: Baiyuan International Airport, Guangzhou, Guangdong 510406; tel. (20) 86128473; fax (20) 86658989; e-mail webmaster@cs-air.com; internet www.cs-air.com; f. 1991; merged with Zhong Yuan Airlines, 2000; domestic services; overseas destinations include Bangkok, Fukuoka, Hanoi, Ho Chi Minh City, Kuala Lumpur, Penang, Singapore, Manila, Vientiane, Jakarta and Surabaya; Chair. LIANG HUANFU; Pres. WANG CHANGSHUN.

China Xinhua Airlines: 1 Jinsong Nan Lu, Chao Yang Qu, Beijing 100021; tel. (10) 67740116; fax (10) 67740126; e-mail infocxh@ homeway.com.cn; internet www.chinaxinhuaair.com; f. 1992; Pres. ZHAO ZHONGYING.

China Xinjiang Airlines: Diwopu International Airport, Urumqi 830016; tel. (991) 3801703; fax (991) 3711084; f. 1985; 30 domestic routes; international services to Kazakhstan, Russia, Pakistan, and Uzbekistan; Pres. ZHANG RUIFU.

Hainan Airlines: Haihang Devt Bldg, 29 Haixiu Lu, Haikou, Hainan 570206; tel. (898) 6711524; fax (898) 6798976; e-mail webmaster@hnair.com; internet www.hnair.com; f. 1989; undergoing major expansion in 2001–02; 300 domestic services; international services to Korea; Chair. FENG CHEN.

Shandong Airlines: Jinan International Airport, Jinan, Shandong 250107; tel. (531) 8734625; fax (531) 8734616; e-mail webmaster@ shandongair.com.cn; internet www.shandongair.comf. 1994; domestic services; Pres. SUN DEHAN.

Shanghai Air Lines: 212 Jiangming Lu, Shanghai 200040; tel. (21) 62558888; fax (21) 62558885; e-mail liw@shanghai-air.com; internet www.shanghai-air.com; f. 1985; domestic services; also serves Phnom-Penh (Cambodia); Pres. ZHOU CHI.

Shenzhen Airlines: Lingtian Tian, Lingxiao Garden, Shenzhen Airport, Shenzhen, Guangdong 518128; tel. (755) 7771999; fax (755) 7777242; internet www.shenzhenair.com; f. 1993; domestic services; Pres. DUAN DAYANG.

Sichuan Airlines: Chengdu Shuangliu International Airport, Chengdu, Sichuan 610202; tel. (28) 5393001; fax (28) 5393888; e-mail scaloi@public.cd.sc.cn; internet www.hpis.com/sichuan/ sichuan.htm; f. 1986; domestic services; Pres. LAN XINGGUO.

Wuhan Air Lines: 435 Jianshe Dajie, Wuhan 430030; tel. (87) 63603888; fax (87) 83625693; e-mail wuhanair@public.wh.hb.cn; f. 1986; domestic services; Pres. CHENG YAOKUN.

Xiamen Airlines: Gaoqi International Airport, Xiamen, Fujian 361009; tel. (592) 5739888; fax (592) 5739777; internet www .xiamenair.com.cn; f. 1992; domestic services; also serves Bangkok (Thailand); Pres. WU RONGNAN.

Yunnan Airlines: Wujaba Airport, Kunming 650200; tel. (871) 7112999; fax (871) 7151509; internet www.chinayunnanair.com; f. 1992; 49 domestic services; also serves Bangkok, Singapore, and Vientiane (Laos); Pres. XUE XIAOMING.

Zhejiang Airlines: Jian Qiao Airport, 78 Shiqiao Lu, Hangzhou, Zhejiang 310021; tel. (571) 8082490; fax (571) 5173015; e-mail zjair@ public.hz.zj.cn; internet www.zjair.com; f. 1990; domestic services; Pres. LUO QIANG.

Tourism

China has enormous potential for tourism, and the sector is developing rapidly. Attractions include dramatic scenery and places of historical interest such as the Temple of Heaven and the Forbidden City in Beijing, the Great Wall, the Ming Tombs, and also the terracotta warriors at Xian. Tibet (Xizang), with its monasteries and temples, has also been opened to tourists. Tours of China are organized for groups of visitors, and Western-style hotels have been built as joint ventures in many areas. In 2001 7,358 tourist hotels were in operation. A total of 89.01m. tourists visited China in 2001. In that year receipts from tourism totalled US $17,792m.

China International Travel Service (CITS): 103 Fu Xing Men Nei Dajie, Beijing 100800; tel. (10) 66011122; fax (10) 66039331; e-mail mktng@cits.com.; internet www.cits.net; f. 1954; makes travel arrangements for foreign tourists; subsidiary overseas companies in 10 countries and regions; Pres. LI LUAN.

China National Tourism Administration (CNTA): 9A Jian Guo Men Nei Dajie, Beijing 100740; tel. (10) 65138866; fax (10) 65122096; Dir HE GUANGWEI.

Chinese People's Association for Friendship with Foreign Countries: 1 Tai Ji Chang Dajie, Beijing 100740; tel. (10) 65122474; fax (10) 65128354; f. 1954; Pres. QI HUAIYUAN; Sec.-Gen. BIAN QINGZU.

State Bureau of Tourism: Jie 3, Jian Guo Men Nei Dajie, Beijing 100740; tel. (10) 65122847; fax (10) 65122095; Dir LIU YI.

CHINESE SPECIAL ADMINISTRATIVE REGIONS

HONG KONG

Introductory Survey

Location, Climate, Language, Religion, Flag, Capital

The Special Administrative Region (SAR) of Hong Kong, as the territory became on 1 July 1997, lies in eastern Asia, off the south coast of the People's Republic of China. The SAR consists of the island of Hong Kong, Stonecutters Island, the Kowloon Peninsula and the New Territories, which are partly on the mainland. The climate is sunny and dry in winter, and hot and humid in summer. The average annual rainfall is 2,214 mm (87 ins), of which about 80% falls between May and September. The official languages are Chinese and English. Cantonese is spoken by the majority of the Chinese community, while Putonghua (Mandarin) is widely understood and of increasing significance. The main religion is Buddhism. Confucianism, Islam, Hinduism and Daoism are also practised, and there are about 500,000 Christians. The flag of the Hong Kong SAR (proportions 2 by 3), flown subordinate to the flag of the People's Republic of China, displays a bauhinia flower consisting of five white petals, each bearing a red line and a red five-pointed star, at the centre of a red field. The capital is Victoria.

Recent History

Hong Kong Island was ceded to the United Kingdom under the terms of the Treaty of Nanking (Nanjing) in 1842. The Kowloon Peninsula was acquired by the Convention of Peking (Beijing) in 1860. The New Territories were leased from China in 1898 for a period of 99 years. From the establishment of the People's Republic in 1949, the Chinese Government asserted that the 'unequal' treaties giving Britain control over Hong Kong were no longer valid.

Japanese forces invaded Hong Kong in December 1941, forcing the British administration to surrender. In August 1945, at the end of the Second World War, the territory was recaptured by British forces. Colonial rule was restored, with a British military administration until May 1946. Upon the restoration of civilian rule, the territory was again administered in accordance with the 1917 Constitution, which vested full powers in the British-appointed Governor. In 1946 the returning Governor promised a greater measure of self-government but, after the communist revolution in China in 1949, plans for constitutional reform were abandoned. Thus, unlike most other British colonies, Hong Kong did not proceed, through stages, to democratic rule. The essential features of the colonial regime remained unaltered until 1985, when, following the Sino-British Joint Declaration (see below), the first changes were introduced into the administrative system. Prior to 1985 the Executive and Legislative Councils consisted entirely of nominated members, including many civil servants in the colonial administration. There were, however, direct elections for one-half of the seats on the Urban Council, responsible for public health and other amenities, but participation was low.

Between 1949 and 1964 an estimated 1m. refugees crossed from the People's Republic to Hong Kong, imposing serious strains on Hong Kong's housing and other social services. More than 460,000 Chinese immigrants arrived, many of them illegally, between 1975 and 1980. Strict measures, introduced in October 1980, reduced the continuous flow of refugees from China, but the number of legal immigrants remained at a high level.

During the 1980s the influx of large numbers of refugees from Viet Nam, most of whom lived for substantial periods in detention camps, was problematic. The Hong Kong authorities, meanwhile, exerted pressure on the British Government to end its policy of granting first asylum to these refugees. In response, legislation was introduced in June 1988 to distinguish between political refugees and 'economic migrants'. The latter were to be denied refugee status, and in October the British and Viet-namese Governments agreed terms for their voluntary repatriation. In March 1989 the first group of co-operative 'economic migrants' flew back to Viet Nam. The number of Vietnamese arrivals increased sharply in the late 1980s, despite the unpleasant conditions in the camps where they were confined on arrival, and the restricting of the definition of refugee status. The relative paucity of those who agreed to return to Viet Nam (totalling 1,225 by February 1990) prompted the British Government to attempt, unsuccessfully, to gain general international endorsement for a policy of compulsory repatriation (which, it was claimed, would discourage further large-scale immigration). The Vietnamese Government announced in December 1989 that an agreement had been concluded between the United Kingdom and Viet Nam on a programme of 'involuntary' repatriation, whereby 'economic migrants' could be returned to Viet Nam against their will, on condition that no physical force were used. Reports of forcible repatriation caused violent disturbances in many of the camps. The programme was subsequently halted. At a meeting in January 1990, the UN steering committee for the Comprehensive Plan of Action on Indo-Chinese refugees failed to agree upon a policy. By May 1990 no further cases of the involuntary repatriation of Vietnamese had been reported. At an international conference held in that month, Hong Kong and the member countries of the Association of South East Asian Nations (ASEAN) threatened to refuse asylum to Vietnamese refugees altogether, unless the USA and Viet Nam gave approval to the policy of involuntary repatriation. In September Hong Kong, Viet Nam and the United Kingdom reached an agreement, supported by the UN High Commissioner for Refugees (UNHCR), to allow the repatriation of a new category of refugees—those who were not volunteering to return but who had indicated that they would not actively resist repatriation. This policy had little success, and the number of refugees increased. In October 1991, following protracted negotiations, it was announced that Viet Nam had agreed to the mandatory repatriation of refugees from Hong Kong. The first forcible deportation (mainly of recent arrivals) under the agreement was carried out in November. Tension and violence in the camps continued. In May 1992 an agreement between the United Kingdom and Viet Nam provided for the forcible repatriation of all economic migrants. By the end of 1995 the detention camp population had been greatly reduced, with only 1,479 being classified as refugees. Unrest in the camps continued intermittently. The People's Republic of China, meanwhile, continued to insist that all camps be cleared prior to the transfer of sovereignty in mid-1997. The Whitehead Detention Centre was closed in January 1997, and the refugees were transferred to other camps. Despite an acceleration in the repatriation programme, some 1,200 Vietnamese migrants remained in Hong Kong in December 1997. In January 1998 the SAR administration (see below) announced that it was abolishing the 'port of asylum' policy which had been applied to Vietnamese refugees. Those arriving illegally would no longer be given time to apply for asylum. At the end of May 2000 the last Vietnamese refugee camp, at Pillar Point, was closed. Most of the refugees were granted residency in the SAR.

Meanwhile, following a visit to Hong Kong by the British Prime Minister in September 1982, discussions between the United Kingdom and China were held regarding the territory's future status. In 1984 the United Kingdom conceded that in mid-1997, upon the expiry of the lease on the New Territories, China would regain sovereignty over the whole of Hong Kong. In September 1984 British and Chinese representatives met in Beijing and initialled a legally-binding agreement, the Sino-British Joint Declaration, containing detailed assurances on the future of Hong Kong. China guaranteed the continuation of the territory's capitalist economy and life-style for 50 years after 1997. The territory, as a Special Administrative Region of the People's Republic, would be designated 'Hong Kong, China', and would continue to enjoy a high degree of autonomy, except in matters of defence and foreign affairs. It was agreed that Hong Kong would retain its identity as a free port and separate customs territory, and its citizens would be guaranteed freedom of speech, of assembly, of association, of travel and of religious belief. In December 1984, after being approved by the National People's Congress (NPC—the Chinese legislature) and the British Parliament, the agreement was signed in Beijing by the British and Chinese Prime Ministers, and in May 1985 the two Governments exchanged documents ratifying the agreement. A Joint Liaison Group (JLG), comprising British and Chinese representatives, was established to monitor the provisions of the agreement, and this group held its first meeting in July 1985. A 58-member Basic Law Drafting Committee (BLDC), including 23 representatives from Hong Kong, was formed in Beijing in June, with the aim of drawing up a new Basic Law (Constitution) for Hong Kong, in accordance with Article 31 of the Chinese Constitution, which provides for special administrative regions within the People's Republic.

The majority of the population reportedly accepted the terms of the Joint Declaration, but the sensitive issue of the future nationality of Hong Kong residents proved controversial. The 1981 British Nationality Act had already caused alarm in the territory, where the reclassification of 2.3m. citizens was perceived as a downgrading of their status. As holders of Hong Kong residents' permits, they had no citizenship status under British laws. Following the approval of the Hong Kong agreement, the British Government announced a new form of nationality, to be effective from 1997, designated 'British National (Overseas)', which would not be transferable to descendants and would confer no right of abode in the United Kingdom.

In September 1985 indirect elections were held for 24 new members of an expanded Legislative Council, to replace the former appointees and government officials. The participation rate among the very small proportion of the population eligible to vote in the elections was low. In March 1986 municipal elections were held for the urban and regional councils, which were thus, for the first time, wholly directly-elected. A new Governor, Sir David Wilson (who had played a prominent part in the Sino-British negotiations on the territory's future), formally assumed office in April 1987, following the death of his predecessor, Sir Edward Youde, in December 1986. In May 1987 the Hong Kong Government published proposals regarding the development of representative government during the final decade of British rule. Among the options that it proposed was the introduction, in 1988, of direct elections to the Legislative Council, based upon universal adult suffrage. In spite of the disapproval of the Chinese Government, in February 1988 the Hong Kong Government published, with the support of the majority of the population, a policy document on the development of representative government; the principal proposal was the introduction, in 1991, of 10 (subsequently increased) directly-elected members of the Legislative Council.

In April 1988 the first draft of the Basic Law for Hong Kong was published, and a Basic Law Consultative Committee (BLCC) was established in Hong Kong, initially with 176 members, to collect public comments on its provisions, over a five-month period; the draft was to be debated by the Legislative Council and by the Parliament of the United Kingdom, but no referendum was to be held in Hong Kong, and final approval of the Basic Law rested with the NPC of China. The draft offered five options for the election of a chief executive and four regarding the composition of the future Legislative Council, none of which, however, proposed that the Council should be elected entirely by universal suffrage. Although the legislature would be empowered to impeach the chief executive for wrongdoing, the Chinese Government would have final responsibility for his removal. Critics of the draft Basic Law complained that it failed to offer democratic representation or to guarantee basic human rights; they argued that Hong Kong's autonomy was not clearly defined, and would be threatened by the fact that power to interpret those parts of the Basic Law relating to defence, foreign affairs and China's 'executive acts' would be granted to the NPC in Beijing and not to the Hong Kong judiciary.

In November 1988 the UN Commission on Human Rights criticized the British attitude to the transfer of Hong Kong, with particular reference to the lack of direct elections. A second draft of the Basic Law was approved by the Chinese NPC in February 1989, which ignored all five options previously proposed for the election of a chief executive. In May there were massive demonstrations in Hong Kong in support of the anti-Government

protests taking place in China. In June, following the killing of thousands of protesters by the Chinese armed forces in Tiananmen Square in Beijing, further demonstrations and a general strike took place in Hong Kong, expressing the inhabitants' revulsion at the massacres and their doubts as to whether the Basic Law would, in practice, be honoured by the Chinese Government after 1997. The British Government refused to consider renegotiating the Sino-British Joint Declaration but, in response to demands that the British nationality laws should be changed to allow Hong Kong residents the right to settle in the United Kingdom after 1997, it announced in December 1989 that the British Parliament would be asked to enact legislation enabling as many as 50,000 Hong Kong residents (chosen on a 'points system', which was expected to favour leading civil servants, business executives and professional workers), and an estimated 175,000 dependants, to be given the right of abode in the United Kingdom. The measure was intended to 'maintain confidence' in the colony during the transition to Chinese sovereignty, by curbing the emigration of skilled personnel. The Hong Kong authorities cautiously welcomed the announcement, but China warned prospective applicants that it would not recognize their British nationality after 1997. Widespread popular protests took place in Hong Kong itself over the unfairness of a scheme which was perceived as elitist. The bill containing the measures was approved in the United Kingdom's House of Commons in April 1990.

Among other recommendations made by the parliamentary select committee were the introduction of a Bill of Rights for Hong Kong and an increase in the number of seats subject to direct election in the Hong Kong Legislative Council, to one-half of the total in 1991, leading to full direct elections in 1995. A draft Bill of Rights, based on the UN International Covenant on Civil and Political Rights, was published by the Hong Kong Government in March 1990. The draft was criticized in principle because its provisions would have been subordinate, in the case of conflict, to the provisions of the Basic Law. Nevertheless, the Bill of Rights entered into law in June 1991, its enactment immediately being deemed unnecessary by the Government of China.

China's NPC approved a final draft of the Basic Law for Hong Kong in April 1990. In this version, 24 of the 60 seats in the Legislative Council would be subject to direct election from 1999, and 30 seats from 2003; a referendum, to be held after 2007, would consult public opinion on the future composition of the Council, although the ultimate authority to make any changes would rest with the NPC. The British Government had agreed to co-operate with these measures by offering 18 seats for direct election in 1991 and 20 seats in 1995. Under the Basic Law, the Chief Executive of the Hong Kong Special Administrative Region (SAR), as the territory was to be designated in 1997, would initially be elected for a five-year term by a special 800-member election committee; a referendum was to be held during the third term of office in order to help to determine whether the post should be subject to a general election. However, no person with the right of residence in another country would be permitted to hold an important government post. Particular concern was expressed over a clause in the Law that would 'prohibit political organizations and groups in the Hong Kong SAR from establishing contacts with foreign political organizations or groups'. The British Government and the Hong Kong authorities expressed disappointment that the Basic Law did not allow the development of democratic government at a more rapid pace.

In April 1990 liberal groups founded Hong Kong's first formal political party, the United Democrats of Hong Kong (UDHK), with Martin Lee as its Chairman. The party subsequently became the main opposition to the conservatives, and achieved considerable success in local elections in March and May 1991, and in the territory's first direct legislative elections in September. Of the 18 seats in the Legislative Council subject to election by universal suffrage, 17 were won by members of the UDHK and like-minded liberal and independent candidates. Only 39% of registered electors, however, reportedly voted. Despite the party's electoral success, the Governor nominated only one of the UDHK's 20 suggested candidates when selecting his direct appointees to the Legislative Council. Changes in the membership of the Executive Council were announced in October, liberal citizens again being excluded by the Governor.

In April 1992 Christopher Patten, hitherto Chairman of the Conservative Party in the United Kingdom, was appointed Governor to replace Sir David Wilson upon his retirement.

Patten took office in July. Plans for democratic reform in the territory, announced by the Governor in October, included the separation of the Executive Council from the Legislative Council. The former was reorganized to include prominent lawyers and academics. At the 1995 elections to the latter, the number of directly-elected members was to be increased to the maximum permissible of 20; the franchise for the existing 21 'functional constituencies', representing occupational and professional groups, was to be widened and nine additional constituencies were to be established, in order to encompass all categories of workers. Various social and economic reforms were also announced. In the same month Patten paid his first visit to China.

The proposed electoral changes were denounced by China as a contravention of the Basic Law and of the 1984 Joint Declaration. Although Patten's programme received the general support of the Legislative Council, many conservative business leaders were opposed to the proposals. In November 1992, following Hong Kong's announcement that it was to proceed with the next stage of preparations for the disputed construction of a new airport (without, as yet, the Chinese Government's agreement to the revised financing of the project), China threatened to cancel, in 1997, all commercial contracts, leases and agreements between the Hong Kong Government and the private sector that had been signed without its full approval. The dispute continued in early 1993, China's criticism of the territory's Governor becoming increasingly acrimonious. In February China announced plans to establish a 'second stove', or alternative administration for Hong Kong, if the Governor's proposed reforms were implemented. In April, however, the impasse was broken when the United Kingdom and China agreed to resume negotiations. In July the 57-member Preliminary Working Committee (PWC), established to study issues relating to the forthcoming transfer of sovereignty and chaired by the Chinese Minister of Foreign Affairs, held its inaugural meeting in Beijing. Negotiations between the United Kingdom and China continued intermittently throughout 1993. In December, however, no progress having been made, proposed electoral reforms were submitted to the Legislative Council. The Governor's decision to proceed unilaterally was denounced by China, which declared that it would regard as null and void any laws enacted in Hong Kong.

In February 1994 the Legislative Council approved the first stage of the reform programme, which included the lowering of the voting age from 21 to 18 years. China confirmed that all recently-elected bodies would be disbanded in 1997. The second stage was presented to the Legislative Council in March. Relations with China deteriorated further in April, upon the publication of a British parliamentary report endorsing Patten's democratic reforms. In the same month the UDHK and Meeting Point, a smaller party, merged and formed the Democratic Party of Hong Kong. In April the trial in camera of a Beijing journalist (who worked for a respected Hong Kong newspaper) on imprecise charges of 'stealing state secrets' and his subsequent severe prison sentence aroused widespread concern in the territory over future press freedom. Hundreds of journalists took part in a protest march through the streets of Hong Kong.

In June 1994, in an unprecedented development that reflected growing unease with Patten's style of government, the Legislative Council passed a motion of censure formally rebuking the Governor for refusing to permit a debate on an amendment to the budget. Nevertheless, at the end of the month the Legislative Council approved further constitutional reforms, entailing an increase in the number of its directly-elected members and an extension of the franchise. Despite China's strong opposition to these reforms, shortly afterwards the People's Republic and the United Kingdom concluded an agreement on the transfer of defence sites, some of which were to be retained for military purposes and upgraded prior to 1997, while others were to be released for redevelopment. At the end of August, following the issuing of a report by the PWC in the previous month, the Standing Committee of the NPC in Beijing approved a decision on the abolition, in 1997, of the current political structure of Hong Kong.

In September 1994, at elections to the 18 District Boards (the first to be held on a fully democratic basis), 75 of the 346 seats were won by the Democratic Party. The pro-Beijing Democratic Alliance for the Betterment of Hong Kong (DAB) won 37 seats, the progressive Association for Democracy and People's Livelihood (ADPL) 29 seats, and the pro-Beijing Liberal Party and Liberal Democratic Foundation 18 seats and 11 seats, respec-

tively. Independent candidates secured 167 seats. The level of voter participation was a record 33.1%. In December 1994 the director of the State Council's Hong Kong and Macao Affairs Office and secretary-general of the PWC, Lu Ping, formally confirmed that the Legislative Council would be disbanded in 1997.

Elections for the 32 seats on the Urban Council and the 27 seats on the Regional Council took place in March 1995. The Democratic Party took 23 seats, the DAB eight seats and the ADPL also eight seats. Fewer than 26% of those eligible voted in the polls. In the same month Donald Tsang was nominated as Financial Secretary; his predecessor, along with other expatriate senior officials, had been requested to take early retirement to allow for the appointment of a local civil servant. Tsang took office in September.

Following a redrafting of the legislation, in June 1995 the United Kingdom and China reached agreement on the establishment of the Court of Final Appeal. Contrary to the Governor's original wishes, this new body would not now be constituted until after the transfer of sovereignty in mid-1997. The agreement was approved by the Legislative Council in July 1995. In the same month an unprecedented motion of 'no confidence' in the Governor was defeated at a session of the Legislative Council. Also in July the territory's Chief Secretary, Anson Chan, confirmed that she had had clandestine meetings with senior Chinese officials during a three-day visit to Beijing.

At elections to the Legislative Council in September 1995, for the first time all 60 seats were determined by election. The Democratic Party won 19 seats in total, including 12 of the 20 seats open to direct election on the basis of geographical constituencies and two of the 10 chosen by an electoral committee. The Liberal Party took nine of the 60 seats, the pro-Beijing DAB six, and the ADPL four. Independent candidates won 17 seats.

The Governor aroused much controversy in September 1995, when he urged the United Kingdom to grant the right of abode to more than 3m. citizens of Hong Kong. The proposals were rebuffed by the British Home Secretary. In October, however, an improvement in Sino-British relations was confirmed by the visit of the Chinese Minister of Foreign Affairs to London. The two sides reached agreement on the establishment of a liaison office to improve bilateral contacts between civil servants. China's disclosure of a plan to establish a parallel administration six months prior to the transfer of sovereignty provoked outrage in Hong Kong.

In January 1996 the 150-member Preparatory Committee of the Hong Kong SAR was formally established in Beijing to succeed the PWC. The 94 Hong Kong delegates included representatives of the territory's business and academic communities. The Democratic Party was excluded from the new body, which was to appoint a 400-member Selection Committee responsible for the choice of the territory's future Chief Executive.

In March 1996, during a visit to the territory, the British Prime Minister announced that more than 2m. holders of the forthcoming Hong Kong SAR passports would be granted visa-free access to (but not residency in) the United Kingdom. He also declared that China had a legal obligation to maintain the Legislative Council and to uphold basic rights in the territory. The Preparatory Committee in Beijing, however, approved a resolution to appoint a provisional body to replace the Legislative Council. Towards the end of March, as the final deadline approached, thousands of Hong Kong residents rushed to submit applications for British Dependent Territories Citizenship (BDTC) which, although conferring no right of abode in the United Kingdom, would provide an alternative travel document to the new SAR passports. As tension continued to rise, in April Anson Chan travelled to Beijing for discussions with Lu Ping. A visit to Hong Kong by Lu Ping earlier in the month had been disrupted by pro-democracy demonstrators. In early July eight pro-democracy politicians from Hong Kong, including five members of the Legislative Council, were refused entry to China to deliver a petition of 60,000 signatures against the proposed establishment of a provisional legislative body for Hong Kong. In mid-August nominations opened for candidacy for the 400-member Selection Committee. In the same month a new pro-democracy movement, The Frontier, comprising teachers, students and trade unionists, was established. In October 1996 the Chinese Minister of Foreign Affairs declared that from mid-1997 the annual protests against the Tiananmen Square massacre of 1989 (and similar demonstrations) would not be tolerated in

Hong Kong; furthermore, criticism of the Chinese leadership by the territory's press would not be permitted.

In December 1996 the second ballot for the selection of Hong Kong's Chief Executive (the first having been held in November) resulted in the choice of Tung Chee-hwa, a shipping magnate and former member of the territory's Executive Council, who obtained 320 of the 400 votes. Later in the month the Selection Committee chose the 60 members of the SAR's controversial Provisional Legislative Council (PLC). More than 30 of the new appointees were members of the existing Legislative Council, belonging mainly to the DAB and to the Liberal Party. Despite much criticism of the PLC's establishment, the new body held its inaugural meeting in Shenzhen in January 1997, and elected Rita Fan as its President.

In early 1997 the Chief Executive-designate announced the composition of the Executive Council, which was to comprise three ex-officio members (as previously) and initially 11 non-official members. Anson Chan was to remain as Chief Secretary, while Donald Tsang was to continue as Financial Secretary; Elsie Leung was to become Justice Secretary, replacing the incumbent Attorney General. China's approval of Tung Chee-hwa's recommendations that senior civil servants be retained did much to enhance confidence in the territory's future. In February, however, relations with the outgoing administration deteriorated when the Preparatory Committee voted over-whelmingly in favour of proposals to repeal or amend 25 laws, thereby reducing the territory's civil liberties.

Meanwhile, Lawrence Leung had abruptly resigned as Director of Immigration in July 1996 for 'personal reasons'. In January 1997 he cast doubt on the integrity of the Hong Kong Government when he appeared before a hearing of the Legislative Council and claimed that he had in fact been dismissed, thus denying the official version of his departure from office. The scandal deepened with the revelation that Leung had been found to possess undisclosed business interests. Newspaper reports alleged that Leung had been involved in espionage activities on behalf of China. The Government finally admitted that Leung had indeed been dismissed, but denied the reports of espionage.

In May 1997 the PLC approved its first legislation (a bill on public holidays), despite protests from the British Government and pro-democracy groups in Hong Kong that the PLC was not entitled to pass laws during the transition period. The PLC declared, however, that the legislation would come into effect only on 1 July. Following the circulation in April of a public consultation document on proposed legislation governing civil liberties and social order, a series of amendments, relating to the holding of public demonstrations and the funding of political organizations, was announced in May. Pro-democracy groups and the outgoing administration remained dissatisfied with the legislation.

Shortly after the transfer of Hong Kong from British to Chinese sovereignty at midnight on 30 June 1997, the inauguration of the SAR Executive Council, the PLC and members of the judiciary was held. Some 4,000 dignitaries attended the ceremonies, although the British Prime Minister and Foreign Secretary, and the US Secretary of State, did not attend the inauguration of the PLC, to register their disapproval at the undemocratic nature of its formation. Pro-democracy groups and members of the former legislature staged peaceful demonstrations in protest at the abolition of the Legislative Council. More than 4,000 Chinese troops of the People's Liberation Army entered Hong Kong shortly after the handover ceremony, joining the small number of Chinese military personnel that had been deployed in the territory in April, following protracted negotiations with the British Government; a further 500 had entered the territory on 30 June, immediately prior to the handover.

Details of the procedure for elections to a new Legislative Council, which would replace the PLC, were announced by the SAR Government in early July 1997. The elections were scheduled to take place in May 1998, and were to be conducted under a new system of voting. Of the 60 seats in the legislature, 20 were to be directly elected by means of a revised system of proportional representation, 30 were to be elected by 'functional constituencies' (comprising professional and special interest groups) and 10 by an 800-member electoral college. Legislative amendments governing the electoral arrangements were approved by the PLC in late September 1997. The significant reduction of the franchise, by comparison with the 1995 legislative elections, was condemned by the Democratic Party. The appointment by indirect election of 36 Hong Kong delegates to

the Chinese NPC, in December 1997, also attracted criticism from pro-democracy activists. Nevertheless, the Government maintained that democracy and the rule of law were being upheld in Hong Kong.

Following the transfer of sovereignty to China, concerns continued about freedom of expression in the SAR. In March 1998 a prominent publisher and a member of the Chinese People's Political Consultative Conference (CPPCC), Xu Simin, challenged the right of the public broadcaster, Radio Television Hong Kong, to criticize government policy, while Tung stated on the same day that government policies should be positively presented by the media. Following expressions of popular discontent, Tung issued a denial that Xu's position reflected government policy. In the same month the Secretary of Justice, Elsie Leung, was criticized following the Government's decision not to prosecute another prominent publisher, CPPCC member and a friend of Tung's, Sally Aw Sian, for corruption, despite a ruling against her by the Independent Commission Against Corruption. Pro-democracy groups expressed fears regarding the independence of the Justice Department. This occurred two weeks after Leung had declined to prosecute the official Chinese news agency, Xinhua, for an alleged breach of privacy laws, after it took 10 months (despite a legal 40-day limit) to issue a denial that it possessed information pertaining to Emily Lau, the leader of The Frontier. (In March 1999 a motion of 'no confidence' in Elsie Leung, prompted by these controversial legal decisions, was defeated in the Legislative Council.) In May 1998 two pro-democracy activists were found guilty of defacing flags of China and the Hong Kong SAR at a rally in January, the first such conviction since Hong Kong's transfer to Chinese sovereignty. In March 1999 the Court of Final Appeal ruled that the law prohibiting the defacing of the SAR flag was an unconstitutional restriction of freedom of expression. In December, however, under pressure from Beijing, the Court rescinded its own decision, and the conviction was confirmed, provoking protests from civil rights organizations. In January 1998 a demonstration was staged to coincide with the visit of the former Chinese President, Yang Shangkun, who was regarded as one of those responsible for the Tiananmen Square massacre in 1989. Similar protests were conducted during a visit by Qiao Shi, the Chairman of the Standing Committee of the Eighth Chinese NPC, in February 1998, and in June a commemoration of the 1989 massacre took place without incident. In the following year, the 10th anniversary of the massacre was marked by a peaceful demonstration, attended by 70,000 protesters. On the second anniversary of the resumption of Chinese sovereignty, on 1 July 1999, more than 2,000 pro-democracy demonstrators protested against Chinese control. Tung Chee-hwa's unpopular policies were the subject of similar demonstrations on 1 July 2000.

In October 1999 the SAR administration announced the sudden transfer of Cheung Man-yee, Director of Broadcasting of the government-owned Radio Television Hong Kong, to a post as senior economic and trade representative in Tokyo, Japan. It was suspected that Cheung's defence of the broadcaster's editorial independence had made her unpopular with the pro-China establishment, resulting in her removal for political reasons. Shortly afterwards Emily Lau announced that she would report the transfer to the UN Committee on Human Rights, citing it as an example of the erosion of freedom of expression in Hong Kong.

In April 2000 there were renewed fears for the freedom of the Hong Kong media after a warning by Beijing against the reporting of any remarks advocating Taiwanese independence. The statement was issued following the broadcast in Hong Kong of an interview with Taiwanese Vice-President-elect Annette Lu, during which she made 'separatist' remarks. China's interference was widely condemned, prompting an assurance by Tung Chee-hwa that freedom of the press and freedom of speech continued to be guaranteed under the provisions of the Basic Law. In October, in Beijing, relations between the Hong Kong media and the People's Republic were further damaged when Hong Kong reporters were accused by Jiang Zemin of being 'naïve' for implying that Beijing's support for the Chief Executive would lead to Tung Chee-hwa's reappointment without election. A number of unprecedented personal attacks on the Chinese President subsequently appeared in the Hong Kong media, and in the following month journalists from the SAR were banned from attending celebrations in China to mark the 20th anniversary of the establishment of the Shenzhen Special Economic Zone. Those who attempted to contravene the ban were detained until after the ceremony. Concerns over press freedom had increased earlier in November when Willy Wo-Lap Lam, a prominent journalist and critic of mainland policy, resigned from the *South China Morning Post*. His work had been subject to 'pre-screening' for any material likely to anger the People's Republic.

Also in November 2000, students held the latest in a series of protests against the Public Order Ordinance (POO), which stipulated that permission for demonstrations had to be obtained from the security forces at least seven days in advance. Earlier in the month the Government had postponed until December a debate on POO in the Legislative Council, after opposition politicians protested that the administration was trying to enact the law by forcible means.

Fears concerning the SAR's autonomy were exacerbated by the rapid adoption by the PLC in April 1998 of the Adaptation of Laws Bill. The Bill was ostensibly simply to replace references to the British crown in existing legislation but in practice it exempted Xinhua, the office of the Chinese Ministry of Foreign Affairs and the garrison of the People's Liberation Army from all laws unless otherwise stated. Concerns about the territory's legal autonomy were also raised by the conviction and execution, in November and December respectively, of five criminals from Hong Kong in the People's Republic.

At the elections to the first Legislative Council (Legco) of the SAR on 24 May 1998, participation (53.3% of registered voters) was the highest since the introduction of direct elections in Hong Kong. The Democratic Party and other pro-democracy parties suffered a reduction in their overall political strength in the legislature, despite the fact that they won 14 of the 20 directly elective seats. A total of 19 seats were secured by pro-democracy candidates, including 13 by the Democratic Party (nine directly-elected), led by Martin Lee, which became the largest party in the Legislative Council. Lee advocated direct elections by universal suffrage for all 60 seats in the next poll, to be held in 2000. Pro-Beijing supporters dominated the functional constituencies and the election committee ballot. The pro-business Liberal Party, led by Allen Lee, failed to win a single seat in the direct elections but obtained nine in the other constituencies. The DAB also won nine seats, five of which were directly elective.

The powers of the new legislature were curbed by the Basic Law. Legislative Councillors were not permitted to introduce bills related to political expenditure, the political structure or the operation of the government. The passage of private members' bills or motions also required a majority of votes of both groups of councillors—those elected directly and those returned through functional constituencies and the election committee. At its first session in July 1998 the Legislative Council elected Rita Fan as its President. The division between the Chief Executive, who rarely consulted the legislature, and the Legislative Council became more apparent after Tung Chee-hwa's second annual policy address in October. He announced the abolition of urban and regional councils, a move opposed by many members of the legislature, who also criticized the Executive Council for failing to stimulate the territory's ailing economy.

In March 1999 Anson Chan agreed to continue serving as Chief Secretary for two years beyond her normal retirement age, until 2002, when Tung Chee-hwa's term of office was to end. In April 1999 the administration decided to abolish the municipal and regional councils, while existing district boards were to be replaced by district councils. Although the public had been dissatisfied with the performance of the municipal councils, there was resentment at the restructuring of local democracy, which was perceived as a regressive step. In November the Democratic Party threatened legal action if the plan was not abandoned, as it contravened the Basic Law. The first district elections in the Hong Kong SAR took place on 28 November. The Democratic Party won the largest number of elected seats (86), but the pro-Beijing DAB substantially increased its representation, from 37 seats to 83.

Popular support for the SAR Government declined substantially throughout 2000, and public unrest increased. In February Tung Chee-hwa effected a reshuffle of senior officials following the retirement of three officials from the civil service. In May Elsie Leung was reappointed Secretary of Justice for an additional two years. The reappointment was contentious as Leung was regarded as unpopular, having been responsible for some controversial decisions (see above). In June Tung Chee-hwa's administration was embarrassed by the resignation of Rosanna Wong as Secretary for Housing. Three days later the

Legislative Council passed a vote of 'no confidence' in Wong and one of her senior officials, holding them responsible for a series of scandals relating to sub-standard construction works. Wong, however, remained a member of the Executive Council. This affair appeared to justify the resignation in April of the prominent opposition politician, Christine Loh, from the Legislative Council. Loh had cited her frustration with the Government's reluctance to share power with the legislature. According to a public opinion poll conducted in July, only 20% of those surveyed were satisfied with the Government's performance. This was the lowest level of approval recorded in these surveys, which had been conducted regularly since the transfer of sovereignty to China. In September one of Tung Chee-hwa's aides and two officials of Hong Kong University resigned after an independent inquiry found them guilty of attempting to suppress the results of public opinion polls conducted by a university researcher.

The second elections to the Legislative Council took place on 10 September 2000. Twenty-four (increased from 20 in the previous legislature) of the seats were directly elective, with 30 seats elected by 'functional constituencies' and six (reduced from 10) by an 800-member electoral college. The level of voter participation was 43.6%. The Democratic Party won the highest number of seats, with 12 (of which nine were directly elected), just ahead of the DAB, which obtained 11 seats. The Democratic Party's share of the votes cast, however, was inferior to that obtained in the 1998 elections. Public apathy was attributed to dissatisfaction with the Government and to the main political parties' failure to publicize coherent manifestos. Nine days later the DAB legislator-elect, Gary Cheng, resigned from the Legislative Council following a scandal over his failure to declare business interests. (A by-election held in December was won by an independent candidate.) At the first session of the new Legislative Council, Rita Fan was re-elected President.

The Government suffered a reverse in January 2001, when Anson Chan unexpectedly announced that she was to resign in April, for 'personal reasons'. While visiting Beijing in September 2000, she had been publicly reprimanded by China for her perceived lack of support for the Chief Executive. Chan was widely respected by the international community, and there were fears that Hong Kong might lose some credibility as a result of her resignation. Chan was succeeded on 28 April 2001 by Donald Tsang, and the latter was replaced as Financial Secretary by Antony Leung, a former banker and member of the Executive Council, who was known to be close to Tung Chee-hwa.

In March 2001 the Hong Kong Government presented the new Chief Executive Election Bill, proposing the recognition of the powers of the central Government in Beijing to remove the Chief Executive and providing details of the procedure for the next election for that post, scheduled for 24 March 2002 (but see below). The new incumbent was to serve a five-year term commencing on 30 June 2002. The Bill was approved by the Legislative Council by 36 votes to 18 in July 2001 after minor amendments, but critics of the Bill regarded it as a set-back for the democratic process.

In early 2001 the Chinese Government warned that it would not allow Hong Kong to become a centre for the activities of Falun Gong, a religious sect banned on the mainland since mid-1999, and in May 2001 the Hong Kong Government increased its efforts to prevent the movement's followers from congregating in the territory in advance of a business forum. The conference was to be attended by President Jiang Zemin, former US President Bill Clinton, Thai Prime Minister Thaksin Shinawatra and hundreds of business leaders. Prior to Jiang's visit, scores of Falun Gong followers were prevented from entering Hong Kong; however, a small demonstration by followers was permitted to take place some 300 m from the forum venue. At the conference itself, President Jiang promised to guarantee Hong Kong's autonomy, and praised Tung Chee-hwa's work. At the same time, however, more than 100 Hong Kong academics urged Beijing to release Chinese scholars detained on the mainland in previous months (some of whom were citizens or residents of the USA, or residents of Hong Kong), including Li Shaomin and Gao Zhan, who had both been convicted for espionage. The two were freed in late July, and Li was allowed to resume his academic duties. Li's case was an apparent triumph of the autonomy of Hong Kong; however it was feared that his case would deter Hong Kong's academics from writing about 'sensitive' topics relating to democracy and making trips to the mainland, thereby stifling intellectual debate. By late July, meanwhile, a Falun Gong spokesman claimed that its membership in Hong

Kong had fallen by 50% during the past two years to 500 people. However, Tung Chee-hwa, who had previously reiterated Beijing's view that the group was an 'evil cult', stated that there were no plans to introduce anti-cult legislation.

In August 2001 a minor controversy emerged when Yeung Kwong, a former trade union leader (who in 1967—during the Cultural Revolution—had led riots in Hong Kong, leaving 51 dead), received the territory's highest honour. The case highlighted the debate over Hong Kong's post-1997 identity, with Yeung being symbolic of the pro-Beijing forces.

In October 2001 the Hong Kong Government proposed to Beijing draft legislation that would allow mainland citizens to invest legally in Hong Kong's stock market, as part of a plan to develop closer financial links with the mainland. The proposal threatened to increase the rivalry between Hong Kong and Shanghai for the position of China's foremost financial centre, however, with the Chinese Government thought to favour the latter. At the same time, Tung Chee-hwa delivered his fifth annual policy address to the Legislative Council, in which he announced major new infrastructure projects and warned of economic hardship ahead. However, his speech was criticized for lacking bold initiatives needed to improve the economy.

In November 2001 opposition groups and trade unions, led by Emily Lau, announced the formation of a coalition aimed at preventing the re-election of Tung Chee-hwa as Chief Executive. In early December Lau strongly criticized the procedures for the election of the Chief Executive as undemocratic, and accused Tung of cronyism and of being an unsuitable leader, adding that greater checks and balances were needed. Despite his growing unpopularity, in mid-December Tung announced his intention to stand for a second five-year term as Chief Executive, and was quickly endorsed by President Jiang Zemin, thus making his re-election certain. Tung was also endorsed by the convenor of the Executive Council, Leung Chun-ying, Liberal Party leader James Tien and the director of the Beijing Liaison Office, Jiang Enzhu. Martin Lee and his Democratic Party, however, boycotted the reception at which Tung formally announced his re-election bid. In late December the Chief Executive visited Beijing where he discussed the establishment of a free-trade arrangement between Hong Kong and the mainland. On 28 February 2002 Tung was nominated for re-election by 714 members of the 800-member Election Committee, thereby securing him a second term in office without challenge. He was formally sworn in for a second term on 1 July.

In mid-March 2002, meanwhile, police charged 16 Falun Gong members (11 locals, one New Zealander and four Swiss nationals) with obstruction following demonstrations outside the Beijing Liaison Office—the first time that legal action had been taken against the group in the SAR. The 16 went on trial in mid-June and were convicted in mid-August. Their HK $4,000 fines, however, were paid by an anonymous benefactor. Members of the group also demonstrated on 13 May 2002 to mark the 10th anniversary of the creation of the sect, and the birthday of its founder, Li Hongzhi.

In mid-April 2002 Harry Wu Hongda, a prominent US-based human rights activist, was prevented from entering Hong Kong. His detention on arrival at Chek Lap Kok airport, and deportation the following day, prompted concerns that Hong Kong's freedoms were increasingly under threat, particularly since Wu did not require a visa to enter the SAR, and had visited unimpeded on numerous occasions. Wu was again denied permission to enter the SAR in late June. In late April, the dismissal of the China correspondent of the *South China Morning Post*, Jasper Becker, led to fears that critical coverage of mainland issues would be suppressed.

Plans for a major reorganization of government structures were announced in mid-April 2002. Under the new system, the Executive Council would be expanded into a cabinet-style body consisting of 14 ministers, all appointed by the Chief Executive, and which would administer the 184,000-member civil service. Critics of the proposals warned that the new system would strengthen Tung's (and therefore Beijing's) control over the territory and compromise the independence of the professional civil service. The Legislative Council none the less adopted the changes, and a new cabinet was appointed in late June. However, Beijing's influence was highlighted by the fact that Tung's appointments were delayed by a few days while Beijing subjected them to scrutiny. When finally announced on 24 June 2002, the new Executive Council notably included five appointees from the private sector. These were Henry Tang Ying-yen, the new Secretary for Commerce, Industry and Tech-

nology; Arthur Li, the Secretary for Education and Manpower; Patrick Ho, the Secretary for Home Affairs; Sarah Liao, the Secretary for Environment, Transport and Works; and Frederick Ma, the Secretary for Financial Services and the Treasury. The portfolios of several leading officials, such as Donald Tsang, the Chief Secretary for Administration, Antony Leung, the Financial Secretary, and Elsie Leung, the Secretary for Justice, remained unchanged.

Hong Kong marked the fifth anniversary of its reversion to the People's Republic on 1 July 2002, amid calls from Jiang Zemin for Hong Kong's citizens to identify more closely with the mainland. Jiang, who was visiting the SAR, also issued a rare note of criticism of the territory's Government, urging it to improve its performance; Tung himself had acknowledged that the previous five years had been difficult. At the same time, Vice-Premier Qian Qichen seemingly ruled out democratic reforms in 2007, as promised by the Basic Law, instead emphasizing the need for stability. Tung had described the priority of economic recovery as his greatest challenge during his second term. However, by July there were also increasing tensions between Tung and the civil service following new legislation that allowed the Government to reduce civil service pay by 4.42%, owing to the growing budget deficit. Some 30,000 public servants marched in protest at the cuts, in the largest demonstrations in Hong Kong since 1989. By late August, Tung's approval rating had fallen to 16% —its lowest level since he assumed office—amid increasing concerns about the economy, record levels of unemployment and the new governmental structures.

In late September 2002 the Government revealed proposals for new anti-subversion laws, which it was required to introduce under Article 23 of the Basic Law, but which had thus far remained unimplemented. Chinese Vice-Premier Qian Qichen had, in June, specifically urged the SAR Government to introduce these laws, giving the impression that Beijing was seeking to extend its laws into the SAR. Critics immediately feared that the new laws would undermine civil liberties and freedom of speech. Suspicions were increased by the fact that a draft of the laws was not made available to the public. The proposals specifically sought to criminalize treason, secession, sedition and subversion, and would also give police the powers to conduct emergency 'search and entry' acts without a warrant. 'Secession' referred to attempts to break away from China, while 'subversion' was defined as threatening or using force to intimidate or overthrow the Government. The Government would also be able to ban any groups affiliated with a mainland organization that had been proscribed in the mainland by the central authorities on national security grounds. Furthermore, the laws could also ban any 'seditious publications' that incited treason, secession or subversion, or disclosed state secrets. A maximum penalty of life imprisonment would be imposed on violators of the new laws. The Secretary for Security, Regina Ip, stated that the laws would not be used to target specific groups such as Falun Gong, or specific individuals, and that existing freedoms would not be affected. In November 10 human rights groups, including the local branches of Amnesty International and Human Rights Watch, urged the Government to abandon the proposed laws, and the US Government expressed its own concerns. Hong Kong's financial community also feared that the laws would hinder the free flow of information, which had long constituted a competitive advantage for the SAR. At the end of that month a Hong Kong court convicted three democracy activists of organizing an unauthorized protest, the first such convictions since the territory's return to Chinese rule. The three offenders were released on bail with a warning.

In September 2002 the head of the Catholic Church in Hong Kong, Cardinal John Baptist Wu, died after a long illness and was succeeded by his deputy, Bishop Joseph Zen Ze-kiun. The latter was a strong critic of the Chinese and Hong Kong Governments, and in 1998 had been banned from visiting the mainland. In early December he publicly criticized the proposed anti-subversion laws, stating that they jeopardized the Falun Gong sect.

On 1 December 2002 Martin Lee retired from the leadership of the Democratic Party, after completing four two-year terms (the maximum allowed), and was succeeded by a former party vice-chairman, Yeung Sum. Lee remained a member of the Legislative Council, however, and was expected to continue pressing for greater democratization of the SAR. In early December the Hong Kong Bar Association condemned the anti-subversion laws, describing them as unacceptable and harmful to the territory's freedoms. In mid-December between 20,000 and 60,000 people from a broad section of society demonstrated against the planned anti-subversion laws, and demonstrations in late December by those in favour of the laws attracted 10,000 people. By late January 2003 the Government indicated that, following the end of a three-month public consultation period, some aspects of the laws would be scaled down, namely provisions dealing with the possession of seditious publications, and a ban on access to state secrets. The laws were none the less expected to be passed by the Legislative Council in mid-2003.

Legislation approved by the PLC in July 1997, meanwhile, included the introduction of measures to restrict the immigration into the territory of mainland-born children of Hong Kong residents. However, in January 1998 a judge ruled that this new legislation contravened the Basic Law. The Court of Final Appeal ruled against the SAR Government in January 1999, upholding the judgment that the legislation was unconstitutional, prompting condemnation of the Court by the People's Republic of China. Fearing that the ruling on the right of abode by the Court of Final Appeal would result in an influx of more than 1.6m. mainland Chinese, the SAR administration asked the Court in February to clarify its judgment, which apparently asserted the Court's right to overrule decisions relating to the Basic Law made by the NPC in Beijing. The Court of Final Appeal declared that it recognized the authority of the Standing Committee of the Chinese NPC. In May the Legislative Council voted to request the Standing Committee of the NPC to interpret the relevant articles of the Basic Law, to the dissatisfaction of lawyers and democrats, who protested that the SAR's autonomy was being undermined. The NPC published its interpretation, which was not retroactive, in June, stating that the Court of Final Appeal had failed to adhere to the Basic Law in not requesting an interpretation before delivering its judgment. The NPC stipulated that mainlanders were to be granted the right of abode in Hong Kong only if at least one parent had been permanently resident in the territory at the time of their birth and that mainland children of Hong Kong parents who wished to settle in the territory had to apply for mainland approval before entering the SAR. These changes to the interpretation of the Basic Law were estimated to reduce the number of successful applicants to 200,000. In December 17 immigrants with parents resident in Hong Kong were denied the right of abode by the Court of Final Appeal, which recognized China's unrestricted powers to interpret the Basic Law (three subsequently obtained permission to reside in the territory). Violent clashes between demonstrators and the security forces followed the ruling.

In August 2000 disaffected mainland Chinese immigrants seeking the right of abode in Hong Kong firebombed the Immigration Department building. Two people were killed, including one immigration officer; 22 people were subsequently arrested and charged with murder. In July 2001 Hong Kong's Court of Final Appeal ruled that a three-year-old boy born in Hong Kong while his mother was visiting the territory had the right to reside there, in a move praised as a triumph of rule of law. However, in early August the same court ordered the deportation of a 14-year-old girl to the mainland owing to the fact that she had been born there and subsequently adopted by Hong Kong parents. In June 2001 the Government planned to deport 5,000 migrants to the mainland, pending the outcome of a court case. The Court of Final Appeal in January 2002 announced that all except about 200 of these 5,000 people would be returned to the mainland by the end of March. Although some 400 people returned to the mainland before the 31 March deadline, approximately 4,300 refused to do so, and in April the authorities began forcibly deporting the remaining abode-seekers. The actions were particularly criticized because they resulted in children being separated from their parents and families being split up. Scores began legal proceedings against the deportations, amid strong protests by those concerned, and Bishop Joseph Zen personally intervened on behalf of several mentally ill or sick abode-seekers who were facing expulsion. It was reported that by January 2003 some 2,302 abode-seekers had been deported to the mainland during 2002.

In August 1999 the People's Republic banned the Pope from visiting Hong Kong later in the year, citing the Vatican's diplomatic relations with Taiwan. The decision was widely criticized as an infringement of the territory's autonomy. Later that month a former adviser to the Taiwanese President was denied a visa to enter Hong Kong to attend an academic conference, a decision widely regarded as indicative of deteriorating relations between China and Taiwan.

In September 1998 the Sino-British JLG met in Hong Kong, for the first time since Hong Kong's transfer to China, to resolve outstanding issues. The most significant problem was that of the 1,100 Vietnamese refugees remaining in Hong Kong; China requested funds from the United Kingdom to facilitate their repatriation. At the final meeting of the JLG before its dissolution (on 1 January 2000), in December 1999 there was a disagreement over the treatment of a Hong Kong resident who had reportedly been arrested in Thailand and deported to the People's Republic of China without any formal extradition proceedings. The man, who had a British National Overseas passport, was entitled to British consular protection. The Chinese authorities, however, maintained that, as he was a Chinese national suspected of perpetrating crimes in the mainland, their jurisdiction applied.

Despite the tensions surrounding the transfer of sovereignty, many citizens of Hong Kong supported the Government of the People's Republic of China in its territorial dispute with Japan regarding the Diaoyu (or Senkaku) Islands. In September 1996 a Hong Kong activist, David Chan, was accidentally drowned during a protest against Japan's claim to the islands. As issues of patriotism assumed greater significance in Hong Kong, more than 10,000 people attended a demonstration to mourn the death of David Chan and to denounce Japan. In October protesters from Hong Kong joined a flotilla of small boats from Taiwan and Macao, which successfully evaded Japanese patrol vessels and raised the flags of China and Taiwan on the disputed islands.

The European Union (EU, see p. 199) agreed in principle in December 2000 to grant residents of Hong Kong and Macao visa-free access to member states, subject to final approval by the European Parliament.

In July 2001 Tung Chee-hwa visited Washington, DC, and held a meeting with US President George W. Bush, at which Hong Kong's handling of Falun Gong and other issues of freedom were discussed. In late August a US aircraft carrier made a visit to Hong Kong, in a sign of improving Sino-US ties. However, in late March 2002 Beijing refused permission for a US warship to make a routine visit to Hong Kong, mainly in protest at the increasing links between the USA and Taiwan. In mid-April, however, the ban was removed. In mid-November, following an undercover operation by the US Federal Bureau of Investigation (FBI), three men were arrested for allegedly seeking to sells drugs in exchange for anti-aircraft missiles for the Islamist al-Qa'ida group. They agreed in January 2003 to be extradited to the USA, a move that was expected to be approved by the Hong Kong authorities.

Government

Since 1 July 1997 the Hong Kong SAR has been administered by a Chief Executive, who is accountable to the State Council of the People's Republic of China and serves a five-year term, there being a limit of two consecutive terms. The first incumbent was chosen by a 400-member Selection Committee in December 1996. Upon the expiry of his first term in 2002, the Chief Executive was chosen by an 800-member Election Committee. In early 2002 the Executive Council comprised the Chief Executive, three ex-officio members and nine non-official members. However, on 1 July of that year a new government structure was introduced, which expanded the Executive Council into a cabinet-style body comprising 14 ex-officio members (each with an individual portfolio) and five non-official members, all accountable to the Chief Executive. Elections to the second four-year term of the 60-member Legislative Council took place on 10 September 2000; 24 (compared with 20 in the previous legislature) of the seats were directly elective (under a system of proportional representation), with 30 seats elected by 'functional constituencies' (comprising professional and special interest groups) and six (reduced from 10) by an 800-member electoral college. At the 2004 elections the number of directly-elective seats on the Legislative Council was to be increased to from 24 to 30.

Defence

In December 1996 the Standing Committee of the National People's Congress in Beijing adopted the Hong Kong Garrison Law, which provided for the stationing in Hong Kong of troops of the People's Liberation Army (PLA). The Garrison Law defined the duties and obligations of the troops, jurisdiction over them and also the relationship between the troops and the Government of the Hong Kong SAR. The legislation took effect on 1 July 1997. Almost 200 unarmed members of the PLA were permitted to enter Hong Kong (in three stages) prior to the transfer of sovereignty. In July 1997 a garrison of 4,800 PLA troops was established in Hong Kong. The garrison can intervene in local matters only at the request of the Hong Kong Government, which remains responsible for internal security. In August 2002 a total of 7,000 Chinese troops were deployed in Hong Kong.

Economic Affairs

In 2000, according to estimates by the World Bank, Hong Kong's gross national income (GNI), measured at average 1998–2000 prices, was US $176,157m., equivalent to US $25,920 per head (or US $25,590 on an international purchasing-power parity basis). During 1990–2001, it was estimated, the population increased by an average of 1.7% per year, while gross domestic product (GDP) per head increased, in real terms, at an average annual rate of 2.3% per year. Overall GDP increased, in real terms, at an average rate of 4.1% in 1990–2001; growth in 2001 was 1.0%.

Agriculture and fishing together employed only 0.2% of the working population in 2001, and contributed an estimated 0.1% of GDP in 2000. Crop production is largely restricted to flowers, vegetables and some fruit and nuts, while pigs and poultry are the principal livestock. An outbreak of avian influenza led to the slaughter of some 1.25m. poultry in May 2001. Hong Kong relies heavily on imports for its food supplies.

Industry (including mining, manufacturing, construction and power) provided an estimated 14.3% of GDP in 2000 and employed 19.5% of the working population in that year.

Manufacturing employed 10.0% of the working population in 2001, and contributed an estimated 5.9% of GDP in 2000. Measured by the value of output, the principal branches of manufacturing are textiles and clothing, plastic products, metal products and electrical machinery (particularly radio and television sets).

The services sector plays the most important role in the economy, accounting for an estimated 85.6% of GDP in 2000 and employing 80.3% of the working population in 2001. The value of Hong Kong's invisible exports (financial services, tourism, shipping, etc.) was US $41,428m. in 2001. Revenue from tourism (including expenditure by visitors from mainland China) was HK $64,282m. in 2001, when 13.7m. people visited the territory. This represented an increase of 0.6m. compared with 2000. A new Disney theme park, to be opened in 2006, was expected further to increase the number of visitors to Hong Kong. The repercussions of the terrorist attacks on the USA in September 2001, however, adversely affected the tourism industry, as did the outbreak of Severe Acute Respiratory Syndrome (SARS) in April 2003 (see below). The territory's banking and mercantile houses have branches throughout the region, and Hong Kong is regarded as a major financial centre, owing partly to the existence of an excellent international telecommunications network and to the absence of restrictions on capital inflows.

In 2001 Hong Kong recorded a visible trade deficit of US $8,331m. and there was a surplus of US $11,736m. on the current account of the balance of payments. Re-exports constituted 89.6% of total exports in 2001. The principal sources of Hong Kong's imports in 2001 were the People's Republic of China (43.5%) and Japan (11.3%); the principal markets for exports (including re-exports) were the People's Republic of China (36.9%) and the USA (22.3%). Other major trading partners included Taiwan, Germany and the United Kingdom. In 2001 the principal domestic exports were clothing, textiles, electrical machinery, data-processing equipment, and photographic apparatus. The principal imports in that year were foodstuffs, chemicals, textiles, machinery, transport equipment, and other manufactured articles.

The budget deficit for 2002/03 was estimated at HK $70,00m, its highest ever level (equivalent to more than 5% of GDP), with only a minimal reduction in the deficit being anticipated for 2003/04. The annual rate of inflation averaged 5.2% in 1990–2000. The composite consumer price index declined by 3.7% in 2000 and by 1.6% in 2001. Consumer prices continued to decrease in 2002, at a level similar to that recorded in 2001, and were expected to decline for the fifth consecutive year in 2003. According to the census of 2001, almost 5.4% of the labour force were unemployed in that year. However, the rate of unemployment increased dramatically in 2002, to reach 7.2%. None the less, the shortage of skilled labour continued.

Hong Kong is a member of the Asian Development Bank (ADB, see p. 143) and an associate member of the UN's Economic and Social Commission for Asia and the Pacific (ESCAP). The territory became a member of Asia-Pacific Economic Co-operation (APEC, see p. 139) in 1991. Hong Kong joined the Bank for International Settlements (BIS, see p. 154) in 1996, and in early 1997 announced its participation in the IMF's New Arrangements to Borrow (NAB) scheme. After mid-1997 Hong Kong remained a separate customs territory, within the World Trade Organization (WTO, see p. 323).

Under the terms of the Basic Law, Hong Kong's financial system remained unchanged following the transfer to Chinese sovereignty in mid-1997. The territory continued as a free port, and the Hong Kong dollar was retained, remaining freely convertible and linked to the US currency. Hong Kong's economy declined into recession in 1998, owing to the regional financial crisis of 1997. Real GDP contracted, domestic demand declined and unemployment increased sharply. Recovery began slowly in 1999 and accelerated in 2000. As the regional economies continued to revive, Hong Kong benefited from a growth in its re-exports to Asian countries. Renewed external demand led to strong GDP growth of 10.5% in 2000. The high growth rate was unsustainable, however, given that private consumption (which accounted for 60% of Hong Kong's economic activity) had not increased substantially and investment remained relatively weak. In 2001 GDP grew by only 1.0%, highlighting the fragility of the recovery, and early estimates indicated that GDP growth improved only slightly in 2002, increasing by 1.4%. Although GDP was 3.3% higher during the third quarter of 2002 compared with the corresponding period of 2001, this was mainly on the strength of exports to and from China, and increased tourism from the latter. Domestic retail sales declined by 1.2% in 2001 and by 2.7% in 2002. The Hong Kong stock market, as measured by the Hang Seng Index, remained subdued during 2002, closing at 9,300 points at the end of December, compared with a level of 11,397 points at the end of December 2001. Furthermore, in 2001 the deceleration in the economy of the USA (one of Hong Kong's major export markets) caused concern, which was compounded by the events of 11 September of that year. Despite Hong Kong's recovery in other areas, consumer prices continued to fall, albeit at a slower pace. The property market remained depressed in 2002. The Government had, in September 2001, declared a moratorium on the sale of subsidized public housing, which was removed in July 2002. In November 2002, however, the Government imposed a moratorium on property sales and land auctions until the end of 2003, in an attempt to halt the decline in property prices, which had decreased by 65% since 1997. The Hong Kong Monetary Authority stated in June 2002 that some 150,000 middle-class homeowners were experiencing negative equity. Meanwhile, unemployment increased sharply, reaching a record 7.7% in mid-2002, as companies downsized operations and new graduates entered the labour market. During the first half of 2002 alone, there were 10,173 bankruptcies—more than the total for 2001. The rising budget deficit placed further pressure on the Government to reduce spending. By late 2002 there was increasing debate about delinking (and therefore devaluing) the Hong Kong dollar from its US counterpart, in order to allow Hong Kong prices to adjust more easily to those of mainland China, and granting Hong Kong more flexibility in monetary policy. The Hong Kong business community also feared that the planned anti-subversion laws (see above) would stifle the free flow of information essential to a free-market economy. In the longer term, Hong Kong faced increasing competition from Shanghai as China's leading financial centre. An increasing number of foreign investors were conducting business directly with the mainland and transferring regional offices there, where in the past Hong Kong had acted as an intermediary. Furthermore, Shanghai was expected to overtake Hong Kong as the world's largest container port by 2015. In April 2003, following the outbreak of SARS, the World Health Organization issued a warning against travel to Hong Kong. The new pneumonia-like disease, which by the end of April had killed more than 150 in Hong Kong alone, was expected to have a serious impact on the territory's economy, with the tourism industry and the aviation sector being particularly badly affected.

Education

In 2001/02 an estimated 156,202 children attended kindergarten. Full-time education is compulsory between the ages of six and 15. Primary education has been free in all government schools and in nearly all aided schools since 1971 and junior secondary education since 1978. There are three main types of secondary school: grammar, technical and pre-vocational. The four government-run teacher-training colleges merged to form the Hong Kong Institute of Education in 1994. The Hong Kong

Institute of Vocational Education (IVE), which was founded in 1999, incorporates seven government-funded technical institutes and two colleges. In 1995 total enrolment at primary and secondary schools was equivalent to 82% of the school-age population (males 80%, females 84%). Primary enrolment in that year included 91% of children in the relevant age-group (males 90%, females 92%), while the comparable ratio for secondary enrolment was 71% (males 69%, females 73%). In 2001/02 the seven universities, (including Lingnan University, formerly Lingnan College, renamed in July 1999) and the Hong Kong Institute of Education had an estimated combined enrolment of 83,657 full-time and part-time students. The Open Learning Institute of Hong Kong, founded in 1989, had 26,923 students in 2001/02. Budgetary expenditure (capital and recurrent) on education was an estimated HK $52,597m. for the financial year 2001/02.

Public Holidays

2003: 1 January (first weekday in January), 1–4 February (Chinese New Year), 5 April (Ching Ming), 18–21 April (Easter), 8 May (the Buddha's birthday), 4 June (Tuen Ng, Dragon Boat Festival), 1 July (SAR Establishment Day), 11 September (Chinese Mid-Autumn Festival), 1 October (National Day), 4 October (Chung Yeung Festival), 25–26 December (Christmas).

2004: 1 January (first weekday in January), 22–25 January (Chinese New Year), 5 April (Ching Ming), 9–12 April (Easter), 26 May (the Buddha's birthday), 22 June (Tuen Ng, Dragon Boat Festival), 1 July (SAR Establishment Day), 28 September (Chinese Mid-Autumn Festival), 1 October (National Day), 22 October (Chung Yeung Festival), 25–26 December (Christmas).

Weights and Measures

The metric system is in force. Chinese units include: tsün (37.147 mm), chek or ch'ih (37.147 cm); kan or catty (604.8 grams), tam or picul (60.479 kg).

Statistical Survey

Source (unless otherwise stated): Census and Statistics Department, 19/F Wanchai Tower, 12 Harbour Rd, Hong Kong; tel. 25825073; fax 28271708; e-mail genenq@censtatd.gcn.gov.hk; internet www.info.gov.hk/censtatd/eng/hkstat/index2.html/.

Area and Population

AREA, POPULATION AND DENSITY

Land area (sq km)	1,098*
Population (census results)†	
15 March 1996	6,412,937
15 March 2001	
Males	3,285,344
Females	3,423,045
Total	6,708,389
Population (official estimates at mid-year)‡	
2000	6,665,000
2001	6,724,900
2002	6,787,000
Density (per sq km) at mid-2002	6,181.2

* 424 sq miles.
† All residents (including mobile residents) on the census date, including those who were temporarily absent from Hong Kong.
‡ Revised figures, referring to resident population, including mobile residents.

DISTRICTS

(2001 census)

	Area (sq km)	Population*	Density (per sq km)
Hong Kong Island . . .	80.28	1,335,469	16,635
Kowloon	46.85	2,023,979	43,201
New Territories . . .	970.91	3,343,046	3,443
Total	1,098.04	6,702,494	6,104

* Excluding marine population (5,895).

PRINCIPAL TOWNS

(population at 1996 census)

Kowloon* . . .	1,988,515		Tai Po	271,661
Victoria (capital) . .	1,011,433		Tseun Wan . .	268,659
Tuen Mun . .	445,771		Sheung Shui . .	192,321
Sha Tin . . .	445,383		Tsing Yu . . .	185,495
Kwai Chung . .	285,231		Aberdeen . . .	164,439

* Including New Kowloon.

BIRTHS, MARRIAGES AND DEATHS*

	Known live births		Registered marriages		Known deaths	
	Number	Rate (per '000)	Number	Rate (per '000)	Number	Rate (per '000)
1995 . .	68,836	11.2	38,786	6.3	31,183	5.1
1996 . .	64,559†	10.2	37,045	5.9	32,049†	5.1
1997‡ .	60,379†	9.3	37,593	5.8	32,079†	4.9
1998‡ .	53,356†	7.9	31,673	4.7	32,680†	4.8
1999‡ .	50,513	7.5	31,287	4.6	33,387	4.8
2000‡ .	53,720	8.1	30,879	4.6	33,993	5.1
2001‡ .	49,144	7.3	32,825	4.9	33,305	5.0
2002‡ .	48,500	7.1	n.a.	n.a.	33,800	5.0

* Excluding Vietnamese migrants.
† Figure calculated by year of registration.
‡ Provisional. Figures prior to 2000 have not been revised to take account of the results of the 2001 population census.

Expectation of life (years at birth, 2001, provisional): Males 77.0; Females 82.2.

ECONOMICALLY ACTIVE POPULATION

('000 persons aged 15 years and over, excl. armed forces)

	1999	2000	2001
Agriculture and fishing	9.2	9.3	7.2
Mining and quarrying	0.3	0.3	0.2
Manufacturing	353.9	333.7	326.1
Electricity, gas and water . . .	17.0	16.6	15.7
Construction	286.8	301.7	291.1
Wholesale, retail and import/export trades, restaurants and hotels .	935.1	981.7	980.1
Transport, storage and communications	339.4	356.6	353.1
Financing, insurance, real estate and business services . . .	437.7	452.7	477.6
Community, social and personal services	732.9	754.7	798.0
Total employed	3,112.1	3,207.3	3,249.1
Unemployed	207.5	166.9	174.4
Total labour force	3,319.6	3,374.2	3,423.5
Males	1,957.1	1,964.1	1,963.3
Females	1,362.5	1,410.1	1,460.2

Source: mainly ILO.

Health and Welfare

KEY INDICATORS

Total fertility rate (children per woman, 1995–2000) . . .	1.2
Under-5 mortality rate (per 1,000 live births, provisional, 2001)	2.7
HIV/AIDS (% of persons aged 15–49, 2001)	0.08
Physicians (per 1,000 head, provisional, 2001)	1.5
Hospital beds (per 1,000 head, provisional, 2001)	5.2
Human Development Index (2000): ranking	23
Human Development Index (2000): value	0.888

For sources and definitions, see explanatory note on p. vi.

Agriculture

PRINCIPAL CROPS
(FAO estimates, '000 metric tons)

	1999	2000	2001
Lettuce.	5	5	5
Spinach	12	11	11
Onions and shallots (green).	4	4	4
Other vegetables .	34	24	24
Fruit	4	4	4

Source: FAO.

LIVESTOCK
(FAO estimates, '000 head, year ending September)

	1999	2000	2001
Cattle	32	30	28
Pigs	100	100	100
Chickens	3,000	3,000	3,000
Ducks	250	250	250

Source: FAO.

LIVESTOCK PRODUCTS
('000 metric tons)

	1999	2000	2001
Beef and veal*	18	18	15
Pig meat*	161	161	165
Poultry meat .	65	67	62
Game meat†	6	6	6
Cattle hides (fresh)	3	3†	3

* Unofficial figures.
† FAO estimate(s).

Source: FAO.

Fishing

('000 metric tons, live weight)

	1998	1999	2000
Capture	180.0	127.8	157.0
Lizardfishes	6.6	4.7	5.8
Threadfin breams .	19.4	14.0	17.0
Shrimps and prawns .	5.3	3.8	4.6
Squids	8.3	6.0	7.3
Aquaculture	6.4	6.0	5.0
Total catch	186.4	133.8	162.0

Source: FAO, *Yearbook of Fishery Statistics.*

Industry

SELECTED PRODUCTS
('000 metric tons, unless otherwise indicated)

	1997	1998	1999
Crude groundnut oil .	50	n.a.	18
Uncooked macaroni and noodle products.	93	99	127
Cigarettes (million)	20,929	13,470	n.a.
Cotton yarn (pure and mixed) .	163.3	101.1	n.a.
Cotton woven fabrics (million sq m)	506	n.a.	n.a.
Knitted sweaters ('000)	176,766	146,438	117,738
Men's and boys' jackets ('000) .	7,419	10,117	6,414
Men's and boys' trousers ('000).	44,086	41,953	32,937
Women's and girls' blouses ('000) .	94,453	74,571	63,596
Women's and girls' dresses ('000) .	6,457	6,612	5,668
Women's and girls' skirts, slacks and shorts ('000) .	61,336	70,136	77,344
Men's and boys' shirts ('000)	85,198	49,139	41,040
Telephones ('000).	91	n.a.	n.a.
Watches ('000) .	81,452	75,402	31,926
Electric energy (million kWh) .	28,943	31,414	n.a.

Source: UN, *Industrial Commodity Statistics Yearbook.*

Finance

CURRENCY AND EXCHANGE RATES

Monetary Units
100 cents = 1 Hong Kong dollar (HK $)

Sterling, US Dollar and Euro Equivalents (31 December 2002)
£1 sterling = HK $12.569
US $1 = HK $7.798
€1 = HK $8.178
HK $1,000 = £79.56 = US $128.24 = €122.28

Average Exchange Rate (HK $ per US $)
2000   7.7912
2001   7.7988
2002   7.7990

BUDGET
(HK $ million, year ending 31 March)

Revenue	1999/2000	2000/01	2001/02*
Direct taxes:			
Earnings and profits tax .	66,914	73,870	77,900
Estate duty.	1,272	1,503	1,400
Indirect taxes:			
Duties on petroleum products, beverages, tobacco and cosmetics .	7,377	7,293	6,781
General rates (property tax) .	7,132	14,428	12,470
Motor vehicle taxes	2,613	3,025	2,744
Royalties and concessions .	1,577	1,767	1,903
Others .	24,832	24,301	21,088
Fines, forfeitures and penalties .	1,093	1,061	966
Receipts from properties and investments	6,986	7,579	8,269
Reimbursements and contributions	5,672	4,210	4,143
Operating revenue from utilities:			
Water	2,434	2,412	2,505
Others	892	885	913
Fees and charges.	10,896	10,973	10,981
Interest receipts (operating revenue).	15,390	6,835	180
Land Fund (investment income) .	21,388	12,681	—
Capital Works Reserve Fund (land sales and interest).	39,111	32,183	10,078
Capital Investment Fund	2,665	2,949	2,819
Loan funds	11,515	3,612	5,466
Other capital revenue	3,236	13,493	3,441
Total government revenue .	232,995	225,060	174,047

Expenditure†	1999/2000	2000/01	2001/02*
Economic affairs and services . .	12,272	12,486	14,102
Internal security	20,171	20,937	21,941
Immigration	2,143	2,108	2,347
Other security services . . .	3,568	3,698	3,775
Social welfare	27,616	28,165	30,731
Health services	31,894	32,753	34,016
Education	50,307	51,408	52,597
Environmental services . . .	12,496	11,337	11,329
Recreation, culture and amenities .	7,409	6,443	6,522
Other community and external affairs	1,721	1,819	1,953
Transport	6,559	6,395	6,333
Land and buildings	8,099	8,513	10,843
Water supply	8,275	7,912	7,765
Support	31,082	30,927	35,710
Housing	45,872	42,606	33,187
Total	269,484	267,507	273,151
Recurrent	195,272	198,619	213,220
Capital	74,212	68,888	59,931

* Revised estimates.

† Figures refer to consolidated expenditure by the public sector. Of the total, government expenditure, after deducting grants, debt repayments and equity injections, was (in HK $ million): 214,533 in 1999/2000; 224,791 in 2000/01; 239,345 (estimate) in 2001/02. Expenditure by other public-sector bodies (in HK $ million) was: 54,951 in 1999/2000; 42,716 in 2000/01; 33,806 (estimate) in 2001/02.

INTERNATIONAL RESERVES

(US $ million at 31 December)

	2000	2001	2002
Gold*	18	19	23
Reserve position in the IMF . .	—	—	—
Foreign exchange†	107,542	111,155	111,898
Total	107,560	111,174	111,921

* National valuation.

† Including the foreign exchange reserves of the Hong Kong Special Administrative Region Government's Land Fund.

Source: IMF, *International Financial Statistics*.

MONEY SUPPLY

(HK $ million at 31 December)

	1999	2000	2001
Currency outside banks	99,267	91,509	101,375
Demand deposits at banking institutions	85,348	93,052	109,509
Total money	184,615	184,561	210,884

Source: IMF, *International Financial Statistics*.

COST OF LIVING

(Consumer price index; base: October 1999–September 2000 = 100)

	1999	2000	2001
Foodstuffs	101.9	99.7	98.9
Housing	107.3	98.5	95.5
Fuel and light	97.3	100.7	98.7
Alcoholic drinks and tobacco . .	101.1	100.1	103.4
Clothing and footwear . . .	109.2	97.9	93.4
Durable goods	103.7	98.7	91.7
Miscellaneous goods	99.6	100.5	101.8
Transport	99.4	100.3	100.7
Miscellaneous services . . .	100.2	99.9	100.4
All items	103.2	99.4	97.8

NATIONAL ACCOUNTS

(HK $ million at current market prices)

Expenditure on the Gross Domestic Product

	1999	2000	2001*
Government final consumption expenditure	121,540	121,834	130,659
Private final consumption expenditure	732,821	735,072	739,037
Change in stocks	−10,612	16,194	−207
Gross domestic fixed capital formation	316,960	333,003	326,040
Total domestic expenditure .	1,160,709	1,206,103	1,195,529
Exports of goods and services .	1,637,609	1,901,314	1,816,744
Less Imports of goods and services	1,571,335	1,840,764	1,749,688
GDP in purchasers' values .	1,226,983	1,266,653	1,262,585
GDP at constant 1990 prices .	808,656	893,263	894,587

* Figures are provisional.

Gross Domestic Product by Economic Activity

	1998	1999	2000*
Agriculture and fishing . . .	1,530	1,171	920
Mining and quarrying . . .	301	307	241
Manufacturing	70,849	65,767	69,753
Electricity, gas and water . . .	33,546	34,358	35,852
Construction	69,937	66,111	63,164
Wholesale, retail and import/export trades, restaurants and hotels .	288,081	282,194	308,410
Transport, storage and communications	107,958	108,957	121,104
Financing, insurance, real estate and business services . . .	282,686	267,017	273,897
Community, social and personal services	232,963	245,722	250,555
Ownership of premises . . .	170,660	162,488	152,737
Sub-total	1,258,510	1,234,091	1,276,633
Less Imputed bank service charges	89,446	94,580	95,945
GDP at factor cost	1,169,064	1,139,511	1,180,688
Indirect taxes, *less* subsidies . .	62,538	55,846	60,510
GDP in purchasers' values . .	1,231,602	1,195,357	1,241,198

* Figures are provisional.

BALANCE OF PAYMENTS

(US $ million)

	1999	2000	2001
Exports of goods f.o.b.	174,719	202,698	190,926
Imports of goods f.o.b.	−177,878	−210,891	−199,257
Trade balance	−3,159	−8,193	−8,331
Exports of services	35,983	40,759	41,428
Imports of services	−23,725	−24,584	−24,314
Balance on goods and services	9,098	7,981	8,783
Other income received . . .	47,031	53,494	48,010
Other income paid	−42,548	−50,699	−43,377
Balance on goods, services and income	13,581	10,777	13,417
Current transfers received . .	570	538	813
Current transfers paid . . .	−2,109	−2,208	−2,495
Current balance	12,041	9,107	11,736
Capital account (net)	−1,780	−1,546	−1,162
Direct investment abroad . .	−19,369	−59,352	−8,977
Direct investment from abroad .	24,578	61,924	22,834
Portfolio investment assets . .	−25,440	−22,022	−39,131
Portfolio investment liabilities . .	58,525	46,508	−531
Financial derivatives assets . .	21,224	8,445	17,506
Financial derivatives liabilities . .	−11,011	−8,240	−12,492
Other investment assets . . .	42,963	18,279	58,243
Other investment liabilities . .	−90,410	−41,375	−42,599
Net errors and omissions . . .	−1,295	−1,683	−744
Overall balance	10,028	10,044	4,684

Source: IMF, *International Financial Statistics*.

External Trade

PRINCIPAL COMMODITIES
(HK $ million, excl. gold)

Imports	1998	1999	2000
Food and live animals	57,483	55,746	57,438
Chemicals and related products	91,219	89,941	104,559
Basic manufactures	264,148	249,758	282,506
Textile yarn, fabrics, made-up articles, etc.	104,439	97,455	106,875
Machinery and transport equipment	562,814	540,679	707,766
Office machines and automatic data-processing equipment	103,145	108,295	142,920
Telecommunications and sound recording and reproducing apparatus and equipment	130,886	119,257	161,627
Electrical machinery, apparatus and appliances n.e.s., and electrical parts thereof	195,561	212,589	288,955
Miscellaneous manufactured articles	378,286	388,999	432,398
Clothing (excl. footwear)	110,744	114,485	124,735
Footwear	44,982	41,304	44,149
Photographic apparatus, equipment and supplies, optical goods, watches and clocks	54,627	54,145	59,871
Total (incl. others)	1,429,092	1,392,718	1,657,962

Domestic exports	1998	1999	2000
Chemicals and related products	6,753	5,655	6,300
Basic manufactures	18,164	15,623	15,877
Textile yarn, fabrics, made-up articles, etc.	10,767	9,488	9,164
Machinery and transport equipment	46,471	39,731	44,846
Office machines and automatic data-processing equipment	8,922	8,254	7,303
Telecommunications and sound recording and reproducing apparatus and equipment	6,304	3,796	4,206
Electrical machinery, apparatus and appliances n.e.s., and electrical parts thereof	26,688	23,790	28,533
Miscellaneous manufactured articles	108,770	103,114	107,773
Clothing (excl. footwear)	74,874	74,251	77,415
Photographic apparatus, equipment and supplies, optical goods, watches and clocks	12,535	8,353	5,715
Total (incl. others)	188,454	170,600	180,967

Re-exports	1998	1999	2000
Chemicals and related products	66,565	66,951	74,983
Basic manufactures	197,442	189,740	216,264
Textile yarn, fabrics, made-up articles, etc.	90,234	85,710	95,573
Machinery and transport equipment	407,400	431,673	560,832
Office machines and automatic data-processing equipment	92,902	98,136	120,509
Telecommunications and sound recording and reproducing apparatus and equipment	114,348	114,325	148,663
Electrical machinery, apparatus and appliances n.e.s., and electrical parts thereof	132,040	156,479	220,611
Miscellaneous manufactured articles	426,262	440,260	492,212
Clothing (excl. footwear)	96,799	99,308	111,268
Footwear	51,913	47,840	50,534
Photographic apparatus, equipment and supplies, optical goods, watches and clocks	58,379	59,790	69,583
Total (incl. others)	1,159,195	1,178,400	1,391,722

2001 (HK $ million): Total imports 1,568,194; Domestic exports 153,520; Re-exports 1,327,467.

PRINCIPAL TRADING PARTNERS
(HK $ million, excl. gold)

Imports	2000	2001	2002
China, People's Repub.	714,987	681,980	717,074
Germany	32,215	33,309	32,997
Japan	198,976	176,599	182,569
Korea, Repub.	80,600	70,791	75,955
Malaysia	37,906	39,200	39,729
Singapore	74,998	72,898	75,740
Taiwan	124,172	107,929	115,906
Thailand	28,001	27,370	29,556
United Kingdom	30,797	28,877	26,082
USA	112,801	104,941	91,478
Total (incl. others)	1,657,962	1,568,194	1,619,419

Domestic exports	2000	2001	2002
Canada	3,210	3,093	2,411
China, People's Repub.	54,158	49,547	41,374
France	2,730	n.a.	n.a.
Germany	9,294	5,818	4,273
Japan	5,084	4,060	2,969
Netherlands	3,910	4,619	3,470
Singapore	4,716	2,650	2,161
Taiwan	6,104	5,346	4,388
United Kingdom	10,681	8,578	7,588
USA	54,438	47,589	41,908
Total (incl. others)	180,967	153,520	130,926

Re-exports	2000	2001	2002
China, People's Repub.	488,823	496,574	571,870
France	25,205	21,516	n.a.
Germany	50,599	45,774	44,567
Japan	82,050	83,551	80,743
Korea, Repub.	26,978	24,640	29,264
Netherlands	20,373	20,693	22,775
Singapore	32,028	26,929	29,424
Taiwan	33,696	30,021	30,193
United Kingdom	52,356	46,764	46,644
USA	311,047	282,189	291,043
Total (incl. others)	1,391,722	1,327,467	1,429,590

Transport

RAILWAYS
(traffic)

	1999	2000	2001
Passenger trains:			
Arrivals	2,595	2,925	3,001
Departures	2,596	2,925	3,001
Freight (in metric tons):			
Loaded	173,415	132,911	97,139
Unloaded	293,061	318,323	273,051

ROAD TRAFFIC
(registered motor vehicles at 31 December)

	1999	2000	2001
Private cars	365,533	374,013	381,757
Private buses	447	451	485
Public buses	12,173	12,498	12,812
Private light buses	2,228	2,158	2,098
Public light buses	4,350	4,350	4,350
Taxis	18,138	18,138	18,138
Goods vehicles	130,374	128,656	126,233
Motorcycles	33,079	34,085	36,191
Government vehicles (excl. military vehicles)	7,368	7,242	7,127
Total (incl. others)	574,193	582,141	589,808

Note: Figures do not include tramcars.

SHIPPING

Merchant Fleet

(registered at 31 December)

	1999	2000	2001
Number of vessels	479	560	646
Total displacement ('000 grt) . .	7,972.6	10,242.2	13,709.7

Source: Lloyd's Register-Fairplay, *World Fleet Statistics.*

Traffic

(2001)

	Ocean-going vessels	River vessels
Vessels entered (number) . . .	37,350	177,390
Passengers landed ('000) . . .	9,779*	—
Passengers embarked ('000) . . .	10,238*	—
Cargo landed ('000 metric tons)† .	87,900	21,600
Cargo loaded ('000 metric tons)† .	42,400	27,400

* Includes helicopter passengers to/from Macao.
† Provisional.

CIVIL AVIATION

	1999	2000	2001
Passengers:			
Arrivals	10,699,000	11,566,000	11,533,000
Departures	10,623,000	11,458,000	11,488,000
Freight (in metric tons):			
Landed	841,161	952,514	895,000*
Loaded	1,133,130	1,288,071	1,181,000*

* Provisional.

Tourism

VISITOR ARRIVALS BY COUNTRY OF RESIDENCE

	1999	2000	2001
Australia	304,407	352,409	324,156
Canada	226,185	253,095	249,707
China, People's Repub.	3,206,452	3,785,845	4,448,583
Germany	189,292	193,837	173,359
Indonesia	196,221	236,275	212,260
Japan	1,174,071	1,382,417	1,336,538
Korea, Repub..	291,015	372,639	425,732
Macao	416,839	449,947	532,391
Malaysia	277,355	314,857	286,338
Philippines	274,587	278,460	293,105
Singapore	370,156	450,569	421,513
Taiwan.	2,063,027	2,385,739	2,418,827
Thailand	195,587	228,774	241,480
United Kingdom . . .	333,973	367,938	360,581
USA and Guam . . .	858,925	966,008	935,717
Total (incl. others)	11,328,272	13,059,477	13,725,332

Receipts from tourism: HK $52,986m. in 1999; HK $58,392m. in 2000; HK $64,282m. in 2001.

Source: Hong Kong Tourist Association, Hong Kong.

Communications Media

	1999	2000	2001
Television receivers ('000 in use) .	2,884	3,105	n.a.
Telephones ('000 in use). . . .	3,868.8	3,925.8	3,925.8
Facsimile machines (number in use)	384,000	404,000	411,000
Mobile cellular telephones ('000 subscribers).	4,275.0	5,447.3	5,701.7
Personal computers ('000 in use) .	2,000	2,360	2,600
Internet users ('000)	1,734	2,283	3,100

1997 ('000 in use): Radio receivers 4,450.

1998: Daily newspapers 45; Periodicals 684.

Sources: partly UNESCO, *Statistical Yearbook; UN, Statistical Yearbook;* International Telecommunication Union.

Education

(2001/02)*

	Institutions	Full-time teachers§	Students
Kindergartens	784	9,159	156,202
Primary schools	815	22,845	493,075
Secondary schools	537	25,093	465,503
Special schools	74	1,671	9,511
Institute of Vocational Education† .	1	1,033	54,825
Approved post-secondary college .	2	117	4,180
Other post-secondary colleges . .	10	—	3,263
UGC-funded institutions‡ . . .	8	5,620	83,657
Open University Institute . . .	1	105	26,923
Adult education institutions . .	1,415	—	184,288

* Provisional figures.
† Formed by merger of two technical colleges and seven technical institutes in 1999.
‡ Funded by the University Grants Committee.
§ As of 2000–01.

Adult literacy rate (UNESCO estimates): 93.5% (males 96.5%; females 90.2%) in 2000 (Source: UN Development Programme, *Human Development Report*).

Directory

The Constitution

Under the terms of the Basic Law of the Hong Kong Special Administrative Region, the Government comprises the Chief Executive, the Executive Council and the Legislative Council. The Chief Executive must be a Chinese citizen of at least 40 years of age; he is appointed for a five-year term, with a limit of two consecutive terms; in 2002 he was to be chosen by an 800-member Election Committee; he is accountable to the State Council of the People's Republic of China, and has no military authority; he appoints the Executive Council, judges and the principal government officials; he makes laws with the advice and consent of the legislature; he has a veto over legislation, but can be overruled by a two-thirds' majority; he may dissolve the legislature once in a term, but must resign if the legislative impasse continues with the new body. The Legislative Council has 60 members; 24 seats are directly elected under a system of proportional representation, 30 seats are elected by 'functional constituencies' (comprising professional and special interest groups) and six by an 800-member electoral college. The Legislative Council is responsible for enacting, revising and abrogating laws, for approving the budget, taxation and public expenditure, for debating the policy address of the Chief Executive and for approving the appointment of the judges of the Court of Final Appeal and of the Chief Justice of the High Court.

The Government

Chief Executive: TUNG CHEE-HWA (assumed office 1 July 1997; re-elected unopposed 28 February 2002).

EXECUTIVE COUNCIL
(April 2003)

Chairman: The Chief Executive.

Ex-Officio Members:

Chief Secretary for Administration: DONALD TSANG YAM-KUEN.

Financial Secretary: ANTONY LEUNG KAM-CHUNG.

Secretary for Justice: ELSIE LEUNG OI-SIE.

Secretary for Commerce, Industry and Technology: HENRY TANG YING-YEN.

Secretary for Housing, Planning and Lands: MICHAEL SUEN MING-YEUNG.

Secretary for Education and Manpower: ARTHUR LI KWOK-CHEUNG.

Secretary for Health, Welfare and Food: YEOH ENG-KIONG.

Secretary for the Civil Service: JOSEPH WONG WING-PING.

Secretary for Home Affairs: PATRICK HO CHI-PING.

Secretary for Security: REGINA IP LAU SUK-YEE.

Secretary for Economic Development and Labour: STEPHEN IP SHU-KWAN.

Secretary for the Environment, Transport and Works: SARAH LIAO SAU-TUNG.

Secretary for Financial Services and the Treasury: FREDERICK MA SI-HANG.

Secretary for Constitutional Affairs: STEPHEN LAM SUI-LUNG.

Non-Official Members: LEUNG CHUN-YING, JAMES TIEN PEI-CHUN, JASPER TSANG YOK-SING, CHENG YIU-TONG, ANDREW LIAO CHEUNG-SING.

LEGISLATIVE COUNCIL

The second Legislative Council to follow Hong Kong's transfer to Chinese sovereignty was elected on 10 September 2000. The Legislative Council comprises 60 members—30 chosen by functional constituencies, 24 (increased from 20 in the previous legislature) by direct election in five geographical constituencies and six (reduced from 10) by an 800-member Election Committee. The term of office of the Legislative Council commenced on 1 October 2000 and was to last for four years.

President: RITA FAN HSU LAI-TAI.

Election, 10 September 2000

Party	Directly-elective seats	Functional Constituency seats	Election Committee seats	Total seats
Democratic Party of Hong Kong . . .	9	3	—	12
Democratic Alliance for the Betterment of Hong Kong . . .	8	3	—	11
Liberal Party . . .	—	8	—	8
Hong Kong Progressive Alliance	—	1	3	4
The Frontier . . .	3	—	—	3
Association for Democracy and People's Livelihood .	1	—	—	1
New Century Forum. .	—	1	1	2
Independents and others	3	14	2	19
Total	**24**	**30**	**6**	**60**

GOVERNMENT OFFICES

Executive Council: Central Government Offices, Lower Albert Rd, Central; tel. 28102545; fax 28450176.

Office of the Chief Executive: 5/F Main Wing, Central Government Offices, Lower Albert Rd, Central; tel. 28783300; fax 25090577.

Government Secretariat: Central Government Offices, Lower Albert Rd, Central; tel. 28102900; fax 28457895.

Government Information Services: Murray Bldg, Garden Rd, Central; tel. 28428777; fax 28459078; internet www.info.gov.hk.

Political Organizations

Association for Democracy and People's Livelihood (ADPL): Sun Beam Commercial Bldg, Room 1104, 469–471 Nathan Rd, Kowloon; tel. 27822699; fax 27823137; e-mail info@adpl.org.hk;

internet www.adpl.org.hk; advocates democracy; Chair. FREDERICK FUNG KIN-KEE; Gen. Sec. TAM KWOK-KIU.

Citizens' Party: 1203 Dominion Centre, 43 Queen's Rd East, Wanchai; tel. 28930029; fax 21475796; e-mail enquiry@citizensparty.org; internet www.citizensparty.org; f. 1997; urges mass participation in politics; Leader CHRISTINE LOH.

Democratic Alliance for the Betterment of Hong Kong (DAB): SUP Tower, 12/F, 83 King's Rd, North Point; tel. 25280136; fax 25284339; e-mail info@dab.org.hk; internet www.dab.org.hk; f. 1992; pro-Beijing; supported return of Hong Kong to the motherland and implementation of the Basic Law; Chair. TSANG YOK-SING; Sec.-Gen. MA LIK.

Democratic Party: Hanley Commercial Bldg, 4/F, 776–778 Nathan Rd, Kowloon; tel. 23977033; fax 23978998; e-mail dphk@hknet.com; internet www.dphk.org; f. 1994 by merger of United Democrats of Hong Kong (UDHK—declared a formal political party in 1990) and Meeting Point; liberal grouping; advocates democracy; Chair. YEUNG SUM; Sec.-Gen. LAW CHI-KWONG.

The Frontier: Hong Kong House, Room 301, 11–19 Wellington St, Central; tel. 25372482; fax 28456203; f. 1996; pro-democracy movement, comprising teachers, students and trade unionists; Spokesperson EMILY LAU.

Hong Kong Democratic Foundation: Hong Kong House, Room 301, 17–19 Wellington St, Central; GPOB 12287; tel. 28696443; fax 28696318; advocates democracy; Chair. ALAN LUNG.

Hong Kong Progressive Alliance: c/o The Legislative Council, Hong Kong; tel. 25262316; fax 28450127; f. 1994; advocates close relationship with mainland China; 52-mem. organizing cttee drawn from business and professional community; Spokesman AMBROSE LAU.

Hong Kong Voice of Democracy: 7/F, 57 Peking Rd, Tsimshatsui; tel. 92676489; fax 27915801; internet www.democracy.org.hk; pro-democracy movement; Dir LAU SAN-CHING.

Liberal Democratic Foundation (LDF): Hong Kong; pro-Beijing.

Liberal Party: Shun Ho Tower, 2/F, 24–30 Ice House St, Central; tel. 28696833; fax 28453671; f. 1993 by mems of Co-operative Resources Centre (CRC); business-orientated; pro-Beijing; Leader ALLEN LEE PENG-FEI; Chair. JAMES TIEN.

New Hong Kong Alliance: 4/F, 14–15 Wo On Lane, Central; fax 28691110; pro-China.

The **Chinese Communist Party** (based in the People's Republic) and the **Kuomintang** (Nationalist Party of China, based in Taiwan) also maintain organizations.

Judicial System

The Court of Final Appeal was established on 1 July 1997 upon the commencement of the Hong Kong Court of Final Appeal Ordinance. It replaced the Privy Council in London as the highest appellate court in Hong Kong to safeguard the rule of law. The Court comprises five judges—the Chief Justice, three permanent judges and one non-permanent Hong Kong judge or one judge from another common-law jurisdiction.

The High Court consists of a Court of Appeal and a Court of First Instance. The Court of First Instance has unlimited jurisdiction in civil and criminal cases, while the District Court has limited jurisdiction. Appeals from these courts lie to the Court of Appeal, presided over by the Chief Judge or a Vice-President of the Court of Appeal with one or two Justices of Appeal. Appeals from Magistrates' Courts are heard by a Court of First Instance judge.

HIGH COURT

38 Queensway; tel. 28690869; fax 28690640; internet www.info.gov.hk/jud.

Chief Justice of the Court of Final Appeal: ANDREW K. N. LI.

Permanent Judges of the Court of Final Appeal: R. A. V. RIBEIRO, PATRICK S. O. CHAN, K. BOKHARY.

Chief Judge of the High Court: ARTHUR S. C. LEONG.

Justices of Appeal: K. H. WOO, M. STUART-MOORE, F. STOCK, Mrs D. LE PICHON, S. H. MAYO, A. G. ROGERS, M. K. C. WONG, B. R. KEITH, P. C. Y. CHEUNG.

Judges of the Court of First Instance: C. G. JACKSON, G. J. LUGAR-MAWSON, A. O. T. CHUNG, T. M. GALL, D. Y. K. YAM, W. S. Y. WAUNG, C. SEAGROATT, M. P. BURRELL, MS C. CHU, Mrs V. S. BOKHARY, K. K. PANG, W. D. STONE, MS C. M. BEESON, P. V. T. NGUYEN, M. J. HARTMANN, A. R. SUFFIAD, A. H. SAKHRANI, L. P. S. TONG, Miss S. S. H. KWAN, Mr Justice YEUNG, Mr Justice MA, Ms Justice YUEN.

OTHER COURTS

District Courts: There are 34 District Judges.

Magistrates' Courts: There are 59 Magistrates and 11 Special Magistrates, sitting in 9 magistracies.

Religion

The Chinese population is predominantly Buddhist. In 1994 the number of active Buddhists was estimated at between 650,000 and 700,000. Confucianism and Daoism are widely practised. The three religions are frequently found in the same temple. In 1999 there were some 527,000 Christians, approximately 80,000 Muslims, 12,000 Hindus, 1,000 Jews and 1,200 Sikhs. The Bahá'í faith and Zoroastrianism are also represented.

BUDDHISM

Hong Kong Buddhist Association: 1/F, 338 Lockhart Rd; tel. 25749371; fax 28340789; internet www.hkbuddhist.org; Pres. Ven. Kok Kwong.

CHRISTIANITY

Hong Kong Christian Council: 9/F, 33 Granville Rd, Kowloon; tel. 23687123; fax 27242131; e-mail hkcc@hkcc.org.hk; internet www.hkcc.org.hk; f. 1954; 22 mem. orgs; Chair. Rev. Li Ping-kwong; Gen. Sec. Rev. Eric So Shing-yit.

The Anglican Communion

Primate of Hong Kong Sheng Kung Hui and Bishop of Hong Kong Island and Macao: Most Rev. Peter K. K. Kwong, Bishop's House, 1 Lower Albert Rd, Central; tel. 25265355; fax 25212199; e-mail office1@hkskh.org.

Bishop of Eastern Kowloon: Rt Rev. Louis Tsui, Holy Trinity Bradbury Centre, 4/F, 139 Ma Tau Chung Rd, Kowloon; tel. 27139983; fax 27111609; e-mail ekoffice@ekhkskh.org.hk.

Bishop of Western Kowloon: Rt Rev. Thomas Soo, Ultra Grace Commercial Bldg, 15/F, 5 Jordan Rd, Kowloon; tel. 27830811; fax 27830799; e-mail hkskhdwk@netvigator.com.

The Lutheran Church

Evangelical Lutheran Church of Hong Kong: 50a Waterloo Rd, Kowloon; tel. 23885847; fax 23887539; e-mail info@elchk.org.hk; internet www.elchk.org.hk; 13,000 mems; Pres. Rev. Tso Shui-wan.

The Roman Catholic Church

For ecclesiastical purposes, Hong Kong forms a single diocese, nominally suffragan to the archdiocese of Canton (Guangzhou), China. According to Vatican sources, in 2000 there were an estimated 371,327 adherents in the territory, representing more than 5% of the total population.

Bishop of Hong Kong: Cardinal Joseph Zen Ze-kiun, Catholic Diocese Centre, 12/F, 16 Caine Rd; tel. 25241633; fax 25218737; e-mail bishophk@hk.super.net.

The Press

Hong Kong has a thriving press. At the end of 2000, according to government figures, there were 59 daily newspapers, including 32 Chinese-language and seven English-language dailies, and 717 periodicals.

PRINCIPAL DAILY NEWSPAPERS

English Language

Asian Wall Street Journal: GPOB 9825; tel. 25737121; fax 28345291; f. 1976; business; Editor Reginald Chua; circ. 85,000.

China Daily: Hong Kong edition of China's official English-language newspaper; launched 1997; Editor Liu Dizhong; circ. 11,000.

Hong Kong iMail: Sing Tao Bldg, 4/F, 1 Wang Kwong Rd, Kowloon Bay, Kowloon; tel. 27982798; fax 27953009; e-mail imail@hk-imail.com; internet www.hk-imail.com; f. 1949; Editor Andrew Lynch; circ. 45,000.

International Herald Tribune: 1201 K Wah Centre, 191 Java Rd, North Point; tel. 29221188; fax 29221190; internet www.iht.com; Correspondent Kevin Murphy.

South China Morning Post: Morning Post Centre, Dai Fat St, Tai Po Industrial Centre, Tai Po, New Territories; tel. 26808888; fax 26616984; internet www.scmp.com; f. 1903; CEO Owen Jonathan; Editor Robert Keatley; circ. 118,000.

Target Intelligent Report: Suite 2901, Bank of America Tower, 12 Harcourd Rd, Central; tel. 25730379; fax 28381597; e-mail info@targetnewspapers.com; internet www.targetnewspapers.com; f. 1972; financial news, commentary, politics, property, litigations, etc.

Chinese Language

Ching Pao: 3/F, 141 Queen's Rd East; tel. 25273836; f. 1956; Editor Mok Kong; circ. 120,000.

Hong Kong Commercial Daily: 1/F, 499 King's Rd, North Point; tel. 25905322; fax 25658947.

Hong Kong Daily News: All Flats, Hong Kong Industrial Bldg, 17/F, 444–452 Des Voeux Rd West; tel. 28555111; fax 28198717; internet www.hkdailynews.net; f. 1958; morning; CEO Roddy Yu; Chief Editor K. K. Yeung; circ. 120,000.

Hong Kong Economic Journal: North Point Industrial Bldg, 22/F, 499 King's Rd; tel. 28567567; fax 28111070; e-mail info@hkej.com; Editor-in-Chief H. C. Chiu; circ. 70,000.

Hong Kong Economic Times: Kodak House, Block 2, Room 808, 321 Java Rd, North Point; tel. 28802888; fax 28111926; f. 1988; Publr Perry Mak; Chief Editor Eric Chan; circ. 64,565.

Hong Kong Sheung Po (Hong Kong Commercial Daily): 499 King's Rd, North Point; tel. 25640788; f. 1952; morning; Editor-in-Chief H. Cheung; circ. 110,000.

Hsin Wan Pao (New Evening Post): 342 Hennessy Rd, Wanchai; tel. 28911604; fax 28382307; f. 1950; Editor-in-Chief Chao Tse-lung; circ. 90,000.

Ming Pao Daily News: Block A, Ming Pao Industrial Centre, 15/F, 18 Ka Yip St, Chai Wan; tel. 25953111; fax 28982534; e-mail mingpao@mingpao.com; internet www.mingpao.com; f. 1959; morning; Chief Editor Paul Cheung; circ. 84,217.

Oriental Daily News: Oriental Press Centre, Wang Tai Rd, Kowloon Bay, Kowloon; tel. 27951111; fax 27955599; Chair. C. F. Ma; Editor-in-Chief Ma Kai Lun; circ. 650,000.

Ping Kuo Jih Pao (Apple Daily): Hong Kong; tel. 29908685; fax 23708908; f. 1995; Propr Jimmy Lai; Publr Loh Chan; circ. 400,000.

Seng Weng Evening News: f. 1957; Editor Wong Long-chau; circ. 60,000.

Sing Pao Daily News: Sing Pao Bldg, 101 King's Rd, North Point; tel. 25702201; fax 28870348; f. 1939; morning; Chief Editor Hon Chung-suen; circ. 229,250.

Sing Tao Daily: Sing Tao Bldg, 3/F, 1 Wang Kwong Rd, Kowloon Bay, Kowloon; tel. 27982575; fax 27953022; f. 1938; morning; Editor-in-Chief Luk Kam Wing; circ. 60,000.

Ta Kung Pao: 342 Hennessy Rd, Wanchai; tel. 25757181; fax 28345104; e-mail tkp@takungpao.com; internet www.takungpao.com; f. 1902; morning; supports People's Republic of China; Editor T. S. Tsang; circ. 150,000.

Tin Tin Yat Pao: Culturecom Centre, 10/F, 47 Hung To Rd, Kwun Tong, Kowloon; tel. 29507300; fax 23452285; f. 1960; Chief Editor Ip Kai-wing; circ. 199,258.

Wen Wei Po: Hing Wai Centre, 2–4/F, 7 Tin Wan Praya Rd, Aberdeen; tel. 28738288; fax 28730657; internet www.wenweipo.com; f. 1948; morning; communist; Dir Zhang Guo-liang; First Editor-in-Chief Cheung Ching-wan; circ. 200,000.

SELECTED PERIODICALS

English Language

Asian Business: c/o TPL Corporation (HK) Ltd, Block C, 10/F, Seaview Estate, 2–8 Watson Rd, North Point; tel. 25668381; fax 25080197; e-mail absales@asianbusiness.com.hk; internet www.asianbusinessnet.com; monthly; Publr and Executive Editor James Leung; circ. 75,000.

Asian Medical News: Pacific Plaza, 8/F, 410 Des Voeux Rd West; tel. 25595888; fax 25596910; e-mail amn@medimedia.com.hk; internet www.amn.com; f. 1979; monthly; Man. Editor Ross Garbett; circ. 28,300.

Asian Profile: Asian Research Service, GPOB 2232; tel. 25707227; fax 25128050; f. 1973; 6 a year; multi-disciplinary study of Asian affairs.

Business Traveller Asia/Pacific: Unit 404, Printing Hse, 6 Duddell St, Central; tel. 25119317; fax 25196846; e-mail enquiry@businesstravellerasia.com; f. 1982; consumer business travel; 12 a year; Publr Peggy Teo; Editor Jonathan Wall; circ. 23,320.

Far Eastern Economic Review: Central Plaza, 25/F, 18 Harbour Rd, Wanchai, GPOB 160; tel. 25084338; fax 25031549; e-mail review@feer.com; internet www.feer.com; f. 1946; weekly; Editor Michael Vatikiotis; circ. 95,570.

Hong Kong Electronics: Office Tower, Convention Plaza, 38/F, 1 Harbour Rd; tel. 25844333; fax 28240249; e-mail hktdc@tdc.org.hk; internet www.tdctrade.com; f. 1985; bi-monthly; publ. by the Hong Kong Trade Development Council; Editor Geoff Picker; circ. 90,000.

Hong Kong Enterprise: Office Tower, Convention Plaza, 38/F, 1 Harbour Rd; tel. 25844333; fax 28240249; e-mail hktdc@tdc.org.hk; internet www.tdctrade.com; f. 1967; monthly; publ. by the Hong Kong Trade Development Council; Editor Tess Lugos; circ. 150,000.

Hong Kong Government Gazette: Govt Printing Dept, Cornwall House, Taikoo Trading Estate, 28 Tong Chong St, Quarry Bay; tel. 25649500; weekly.

Hong Kong Household: Office Tower, Convention Plaza, 38/F, 1 Harbour Rd, Wanchai; tel. 25844333; fax 28240249; e-mail hktdc@tdc.org.hk; internet www.tdctrade.com; f. 1983; publ. by the Hong Kong Trade Development Council; household and hardware products; 2 a year; Editor Geoff Picker; circ. 90,000.

Hong Kong Industrialist: Federation of Hong Kong Industries, Hankow Centre, 4/F, 5–15 Hankow Rd, Tsimshatsui, Kowloon; tel. 27323188; fax 27213494; e-mail fhki@fhki.org.hk; monthly; publ. by the Federation of Hong Kong Industries; Editor James Manning; circ. 6,000.

Hong Kong Trader: Office Tower, Convention Plaza, 38/F, 1 Harbour Rd, Wanchai; tel. 25844333; fax 28243485; e-mail trader@tdc.org.hk; internet www.tdc.org.hk/hktrader; f. 1983; publ. by the Hong Kong Trade Development Council; trade, economics, financial and general business news; monthly; Man. Editor Sophy Fisher; circ. 70,000.

Official Hong Kong Guide: Wilson House, 3/F, 19–27 Wyndham St, Central; tel. 25215392; fax 25218638; f. 1982; monthly; information on sightseeing, shopping, dining, etc. for overseas visitors; Editor-in-Chief Derek Davies; circ. 9,300.

Orientations: 17/F, 200 Lockhart Rd; tel. 25111368; fax 25074620; e-mail omag@netvigator.com; internet www.orientations.com.hk; f. 1970; 10 a year; arts of East Asia, the Indian subcontinent and South-East Asia; Publr and Editorial Dir Elizabeth Knight.

Reader's Digest (Asia Edn): 3 Ah Kung Ngam Village Rd, Shaukiwan; tel. 96906381; fax 96906389; e-mail friends@rdasia.com.hk; f. 1963; general topics; monthly; Editor Peter Dockrill; circ. 332,000.

Sunday Examiner: Catholic Diocese Centre, 11/F, 16 Caine Rd; tel. 25220487; fax 25369939; e-mail sundayex@catholic.org.hk; f. 1946; religious; weekly; Deputy Editor-in-Chief Fr Jim Mulroney; circ. 6,500.

Textile Asia: c/o Business Press Ltd, California Tower, 11/F, 30–32 D'Aguilar St, GPOB 185, Central; tel. 25233744; fax 28106966; e-mail texasia@netvigator.com; f. 1970; monthly; textile and clothing industry; Publr and Editor-in-Chief Kayser W. Sung; circ. 17,000.

Tradefinance Asia: Hong Kong monthly; Editor Richard Tourret.

Travel Business Analyst: GPO Box 12761; tel. 25072310; e-mail TBAoffice@aol.com; internet www.travelbusinessanalyst.com; f. 1982; travel trade; monthly; Editor Murray Bailey.

Chinese Language

Affairs Weekly: Hong Kong; tel. 28950801; fax 25767842; f. 1980; general interest; Editor Wong Wai Man; circ. 130,000.

Cheng Ming Monthly: Hennessy Rd, POB 20370; tel. 25740664; Chief Editor Wan Fai.

City Magazine: Hang Seng Bldg, 7/F, 200 Hennessy Rd, Wanchai; tel. 28931393; fax 28388761; f. 1976; monthly; fashion, wine, cars, society, etc. Publr John K. C. Chan; Chief Editor Peter Wong; circ. 30,000.

Contemporary Monthly: Unit 705, Westlands Centre, 20 Westlands Rd, Quarry Bay; tel. 25638122; fax 25632984; f. 1989; monthly; current affairs; 'China-watch'; Editor-in-Chief Ching Cheong; circ. 50,000.

Disc Jockey: Fuk Keung Ind. Bldg, B2, 14/F, 66–68 Tong Mei Rd, Taikoktsui, Kowloon; tel. 23905461; fax 27893869; e-mail vinpres@netvigator.com; f. 1990; monthly; music; Publr Vincent Leung; Editor Alge Cheung; circ. 32,000.

Elegance HK: Aik San Bldg, 14/F, 14 Westlands Rd, Quarry Bay; tel. 2963011; fax 25658217; f. 1977; monthly; for thinking women; Chief Editor Winnie Yuen; circ. 75,000.

Kung Kao Po (Catholic Chinese Weekly): 16 Caine Rd; tel. 25220487; fax 25213095; e-mail kkp@catholic.org.hk; internet kkp.catholic.org.hk; f. 1928; religious; weekly; Editor-in-Chief Fr Louis Ha.

Lisa's Kitchen Bi-Weekly: Fuk Keung Ind. Bldg, B2, 14/F, 66–68 Tong Mei Rd, Taikoktsui, Kowloon; tel. 23910668; fax 27893869; f. 1984; recipes; Publr Vincent Leung; circ. 50,000.

Metropolitan Weekly: f. 1983; weekly; entertainment, social news; Chief Editor Charles You; circ. 130,000.

Ming Pao Monthly: Ming Pao Industrial Centre, 15/F, Block A, 18 Ka Yip St, Chai Wan; tel. 25155107; fax 28982566; Chief Editor Koo Siu-sun.

Motor Magazine: Prospect Mansion, Flat D, 1/F, 66–72 Paterson St, Causeway Bay; tel. 28822230; fax 28823949; f. 1990; Publr and Editor-in-Chief Kenneth Li; circ. 32,000. (Publication suspended, 2001.).

Next Magazine: 8 Chun Ying St, T. K. O. Industrial Estate West, Tseung Kwan O, Hong Kong; tel. 27442733; fax 29907210; internet www.nextmedia.com; f. 1989; weekly; news, business, lifestyle, entertainment; Editor-in-Chief Cheung Kim Hung; circ. 172,708.

Open Magazine: Causeway Bay, POB 31429; tel. 28939197; fax 28915591; e-mail open@open.com.hk; internet www.open.com.hk; f. 1990; monthly; Chief Editor Jin Chong; circ. 15,000.

Oriental Sunday: Oriental Press Centre, Wang Tai Rd, Kowloon Bay, Kowloon; tel. 27951111; fax 27952299; f. 1991; weekly; leisure magazine; Chair. C. F. Ma; circ. 120,000.

Reader's Digest (Chinese Edn): Reader's Digest Association Far East Ltd, 3 Ah Kung Ngam Village Rd, Shaukiwan; tel. 28845590; fax 25671479; e-mail chrd@netvigator.com; f. 1965; monthly; Editor-in-Chief Victor Fung Keung; circ. 295,000.

Today's Living: Prospect Mansion, Flat D, 1/F, 66–72 Paterson St, Causeway Bay; tel. 28822230; fax 28823949; e-mail magazine@todayliving.com; f. 1987; monthly; interior design; Publr and Editor-in-Chief Kenneth Li; circ. 35,000.

TV Week: 1 Leighton Rd, Causeway Bay; tel. 28366147; fax 28346717; f. 1967; weekly; Publr Peter Chow; circ. 59,082.

Yazhou Zhoukan: Block A, Ming Pao Industrial Centre, 15/F, 18 Ka Yip St, Chai Wan; tel. 25155358; fax 25059662; e-mail loppoon@mingpao.com; internet www.yzzk.com; f. 1987; international Chinese news weekly; Chief Editor Yau Lop-poon; circ. 110,000.

Young Girl Magazine: Fuk Keung Ind. Bldg, B2, 14/F, 66–68 Tong Mei Rd, Taikoktsui, Kowloon; tel. 23910668; fax 27893869; f. 1987; biweekly; Publr Vincent Leung; circ. 65,000.

Yuk Long TV Weekly: Hong Kong; tel. 25657883; fax 25659958; f. 1977; entertainment, fashion, etc. Publr Tony Wong; circ. 82,508.

NEWS AGENCIES

International News Service: 2e Cheong Shing Mansion, 33–39 Wing Hing St, Causeway Bay; tel. 25665668; Rep. Au Kit Ming.

Xinhua (New China) News Agency, Hong Kong SAR Bureau: 387 Queen's Rd East, Wanchai; tel. 28314126; f. 2000; from fmr news dept of branch office of Xinhua (responsibility for other activities being assumed by Liaison Office of the Central People's Government in the Hong Kong SAR); Dir Zhang Guoliang.

Foreign Bureaux

Agence France-Presse (AFP): Telecom House, Room 1840, 18/F, 3 Gloucester Rd, Wanchai, GPOB 5613; tel. 28020224; fax 28027292; Regional Dir Yvan Chemla.

Agencia EFE (Spain): 10a Benny View House, 63–65 Wong Nai Chung Rd, Happy Valley; tel. 28080199; fax 28823101; Correspondent Miren Gutierrez.

Associated Press (AP) (USA): 1282 New Mercury House, Waterfront Rd; tel. 25274324; Bureau Chief Robert Liu.

Central News Agency (CNA) Inc (Taiwan): Hong Kong Bureau Chief Conrad Lu.

Jiji Tsushin-Sha (Japan): 3503 Far East Finance Centre, 16 Harcourt Rd; tel. 25237112; fax 28459013; Bureau Man. Katsuhiko Kabasawa.

Kyodo News Service (Japan): Unit 1303, 13/F, 9 Queen's Rd, Central; tel. 25249750; fax 28105591; e-mail tyoko@po.iijnet.or.jp; Correspondent Tsukasa Yokoyama.

Reuters Asia Ltd (United Kingdom): Hong Kong; tel. 258436363; Bureau Man. Geoff Weetman.

United Press International (UPI) (USA): 1287 Telecom House, 3 Gloucester Rd, POB 5692; tel. 28020221; fax 28024972; Vice-Pres. (Asia) Arnold Zeitlin; Editor (Asia) Paul H. Anderson.

PRESS ASSOCIATIONS

Chinese Language Press Institute: Tower A, Sing Tao Bldg, 1 Wang Kwong Rd, Kowloon Bay, Kowloon; tel. 27982501; fax 27953017; Pres. Aw Sian.

Hong Kong Chinese Press Association: Rm 2208, 22/F, 33 Queen's Rd Central; tel. 28613622; fax 28661933; 13 mems; Chair. HUE PUE-YING.

Hong Kong Journalists Association: GPOB 11726, Henfa Commercial Bldg, Flat 15A, 348–350 Lockhart Rd, Waichai; tel. 25910692; fax 25727329; e-mail hkja@hk.super.net; internet www .hkja.org.hk; f. 1968; 537 mems; Chair. MAK YIN-TING.

Newspaper Society of Hong Kong: Rm 904, 75–83 King's Rd, North Point; tel. 25713102; fax 25712627; f. 1954; Chair. LEE CHO JAT.

Publishers

Art House of Collectors HK Ltd: 37 Lyndhurst Terrace, Ground Floor, Central; tel. 28818026; fax 28904304; Dir. LI LAP FONG.

Asia 2000 Ltd: 15B The Parkside, 263 Hollywood Rd, Sheung Wan; tel. 25301409; fax 25261107; e-mail info@asia2000.com.hk; internet www.asia2000.com.hk; Asian studies, politics, photography, fiction; Man. Dir MICHAEL MORROW.

Asian Research Service: GPOB 2232; tel. 25707227; fax 25128050; f. 1972; maps, atlases, monographs on Asian studies and journals; Dir NELSON LEUNG.

Chinese University Press: Chinese University of Hong Kong, Sha Tin, New Territories; tel. 26096508; fax 26036692; e-mail cup@cuhk .edu.hk; internet www.cuhk.edu.hk/cupress; f. 1977; studies on China and Hong Kong and other academic works; Dir Dr STEVEN K. LUK.

Commercial Press (Hong Kong) Ltd: Eastern Central Plaza, 8/F, 3 Yiu Hing Rd, Shau Kei Wan; tel. 25651371; fax 25645277; e-mail webmaster@commercialpress.com.hk; internet www.commercial press.com.hk; f. 1897; trade books, dictionaries, textbooks, Chinese classics, art, etc. Man. Dir and Chief Editor CHAN MAN HUNG.

Excerpta Medica Asia Ltd: 8/F, 67 Wyndham St; tel. 25243118; fax 28100687; f. 1980; sponsored medical publications, abstracts, journals etc.

Hoi Fung Publisher Co: 125 Lockhart Rd, 2/F, Wanchai; tel. 25286246; fax 25286249; Dir. K. K. TSE.

Hong Kong University Press: Hing Wai Centre, 14/F, 7 Tin Wan Praya Rd, Aberdeen; tel. 25502703; fax 28750734; e-mail hkupress@ hkucc.hku.hk; internet www.hkupress.org; f. 1956; Publr COLIN DAY.

International Publishing Co: Rm 213–215, HK Industrial Technology Centre, 72 Tat Chee Ave, Kowloon Tong, Kowloon; tel. 23148882; fax 23192208; Admin. Man. KAREN CHOW.

Ismay Publications Ltd: C. C. Wu Building; tel. 25752270; Man. Dir MINNIE YEUNG.

Ling Kee Publishing Co Ltd: Zung Fu Industrial Bldg, 1067 King's Rd, Quarry Bay; tel. 25616151; fax 28111980; f. 1956; educational and reference; Chair. B. L. AU; Man. Dir K. W. AU.

Oxford University Press (China) Ltd: Warwick House, 18/F, 979 King's Rd, Taikoo Place, Quarry Bay; tel. 25163222; fax 25658491; e-mail oupchina@oupchina.com.hk; internet www.oupchina.com.hk; f. 1961; school textbooks, reference, academic and general works relating to Hong Kong, Taiwan and China; Regional Dir SIMON LI.

Taosheng Publishing House: Lutheran Bldg, 3/F, 50A Waterloo Rd, Yau Ma Tei, Kowloon; tel. 23887061; fax 27810413; e-mail taosheng@elchk.org.hk; Dir CHAN PUI TAK.

Textile Asia/Business Press Ltd: California Tower, 11/F, 30–32 D'Aguilar St, GPOB 185, Central; tel. 25233744; fax 28106966; e-mail texasia@netvigator.com; internet www.textileasia -businesspress.com; f. 1970; textile magazine; Man. Dir KAYSER W. SUNG.

The Woods Publishing Co: Li Yuen Building, 2/F, 7 Li Yuen St West, Central; tel. 25233002; fax 28453296; e-mail tybook@ netvigator.com; Production Man. TONG SZE HUNG.

Times Publishing (Hong Kong) Ltd: Seaview Estate, Block C, 10/F, 2–8 Watson Rd, North Point; tel. 25668381; fax 25080255; e-mail abeditor@asianbusiness.com.hk; internet www .asianbusinessnet.com; trade magazines and directories; CEO COLIN YAM; Executive Editor JAMES LEUNG.

Government Publishing House

Government Information Services: see Government Offices.

PUBLISHERS' ASSOCIATIONS

Hong Kong Publishers' and Distributors' Association: National Bldg, 4/F, 240–246 Nathan Rd, Kowloon; tel. 23674412; 45 mems; Chair. HO KAM-LING; Sec. HO NAI-CHI.

Society of Publishers in Asia: c/o Worldcom Hong Kong, 502–503 Admiralty Centre, Tower I, 18 Harcourt Rd, Admiralty; tel. 28654007; fax 28652559; e-mail worldcom@hkstar.com.

Broadcasting and Communications

TELECOMMUNICATIONS

Asia Satellite Telecommunications Co Ltd (AsiaSat): East Exchange Tower, 23/F, 38–40 Leighton Rd; tel. 28056666; fax 25043875; e-mail wpang@asiasat.com; internet www.asiasat.com; CEO PETER JACKSON.

Cable and Wireless HKT Ltd: Hongkong Telecom Tower, 39/F, Taikoo Place, 979 King's Rd, Quarry Bay; tel. 28882888; fax 28778877; e-mail info@cwhkt.com; internet www.cwhkt.com; fmrly Hong Kong Telecommunications; in 1998 acquired Pacific Link Communications to become largest mobile telephone operator in Hong Kong; monopoly on provision of international lines expired March 1998; full competition began Jan. 1999; CEO LINUS CHEUNG.

Regulatory Authority

Telecommunications Authority: statutory regulator, responsible for implementation of the Govt's pro-competition and pro-consumer policies; Dir.Gen. ANTHONY S. K. WONG.

Hutchison Telecom, New T and T Hong Kong Ltd, and New World Telecom also operate local services. In 2000 six companies were licensed to provide mobile telecommunications services, serving over 5.2m. customers.

BROADCASTING

Regulatory Authority

Broadcasting Authority: regulatory body;. administers and issues broadcasting licences.

Radio

Hong Kong Commercial Broadcasting Co Ltd: 3 Broadcast Drive, KCPOB 73000; tel. 23365111; fax 23380021; e-mail comradio@crhk.com.hk; internet www.crhk.com.hk; f. 1959; broadcasts in English and Chinese on three radio frequencies; Chair. G. J. HO; Dir and CEO WINNIE YU.

Metro Broadcast Corpn Ltd (Metro Broadcast): Hong Kong; tel. 23649333; fax 23646577; e-mail tech@metroradio.com.hk; internet www.metroradio.com.hk; f. 1991; broadcasts on three channels in English, Cantonese and Mandarin; Gen. Man. CRAIG B. QUICK.

Radio Television Hong Kong: Broadcasting House, 30 Broadcast Drive, POB 70200, Kowloon Central PO; tel. 23396300; fax 23380279; e-mail rthk@hk.super.net; internet www.rthk.org.hk; f. 1928; govt-funded; 24-hour service in English and Chinese on seven radio channels; service in Putonghua inaugurated in 1997; Dir CHU PUI-HING.

Star Radio: Hutchison House, 12/F, 10 Harcourt Rd, Central; f. 1995; satellite broadcasts in Mandarin and English; Gen. Man. MIKE MACKAY.

Television

Asia Television Ltd (ATV): Television House, 81 Broadcast Drive, Kowloon; tel. 29928888; fax 23380438; e-mail atv@hkatv.com; internet www.hkatv.com; f. 1973; operates two commercial television services (English and Chinese) and produces television programmes; Dir and CEO FENG XIAO PING.

STAR Group Ltd: One Harbourfront, 8/F, 18 Tak Fung St, Hunghom, Kowloon; tel. 26218888; fax 26213050; e-mail corp_aff@startv .com; internet www.startv.com; f. 1990; subsidiary of the News Corpn Ltd; broadcasts programming services via satellite to 300m. viewers in 53 countries across Asia, the Indian subcontinent and the Middle East; music, news, sport and entertainment broadcasts in English, Mandarin, Hindi, Japanese, Tagalog, Arabic, and Thai; subscription and free-to-air services on several channels; also owns Total TV (Taiwan) interactive digital cable services and radio stations in India; Chair. and CEO JAMES MURDOCH; Pres. BRUCE CHURCHILL.

Radio Television Hong Kong: see Radio; produces drama, documentary and public affairs programmes; also operates an educational service for transmission by two local commercial stations; Dir CHU PUI-HING (acting).

Television Broadcasts Ltd (TVB): TV City, Clearwater Bay Rd, Kowloon; tel. 23352288; fax 23581300; e-mail external.affairs@tvb .com.hk; internet www.tvb.com; f. 1967; operates Chinese and English language services; two colour networks; Exec. Chair. Sir RUN RUN SHAW; Man. Dir LOUIS PAGE.

Wharf Cable Ltd: Wharf Cable Tower, 4/F, 9 Hoi Shing Rd, Tsuen Wan; tel. 26115533; fax 24171511; f. 1993; 24-hour subscription service of news, sport and entertainment on 35 channels; carries BBC World Service Television; Chair. PETER WOO; Man. Dir STEPHEN NG.

Finance

(cap. = capital; res = reserves; dep. = deposits; m. = million; brs = branches; amounts in Hong Kong dollars unless otherwise stated)

BANKING

In December 2003 there were 133 licensed banks, of which 26 were locally incorporated, operating in Hong Kong. There were also 46 restricted licence banks (formerly known as licensed deposit-taking companies), 45 deposit-taking companies, and 94 foreign banks' representative offices.

Hong Kong Monetary Authority (HKMA): 30/F, 3 Garden Rd, Central; tel. 28788196; fax 28788197; e-mail hkma@hkma.gov.hk; internet www.hkma.gov.hk; f. 1993; by merger of Office of the Commissioner of Banking and Office of the Exchange Fund; carries out central banking functions; maintains Hong Kong dollar stability within the framework of the linked exchange rate system; supervises licensed banks, restricted licence banks and deposit-taking cos, their overseas brs and representative offices; manages foreign currency reserves; Chief Exec. JOSEPH YAM; Deputy Chief Execs DAVID CARSE, TONY LATTER, NORMAN CHAN.

Banks of Issue

Bank of China (Hong Kong) Ltd (People's Repub. of China): Bank of China Tower, 1 Garden Rd, Central; tel. 28266888; fax 28105963; internet www.bochk.com; f. 1917; became third bank of issue in May 1994; merged in Oct. 2001 with the local branches of 11 mainland banks (incl. Kwangtung Provincial Bank, Sin Hua Bank Ltd, China and the South Sea Bank Ltd, Kincheng Banking Corpn, China State Bank, National Commercial Bank Ltd, Yien Yieh Commercial Bank Ltd, Hua Chiao Commercial Bank Ltd and Po Sang Bank Ltd, to form the Bank of China (Hong Kong); cap. 43,043m., res 9,127m., dep. 692,233m. (Dec. 2001); Chair. LIU MINGKANG; Vice-Chair. and CEO LIU JINBAO; 369 brs.

The Hongkong and Shanghai Banking Corporation Ltd: 1 Queen's Rd, Central; tel. 28221111; fax 28101112; internet www.asiapacific.hsbc.com; f. 1865; personal and commercial banking; cap. 44,937m., res 38,192m., dep. 1,493,180m. (Dec. 2001); Chair. DAVID ELDON; more than 600 offices world-wide.

Standard Chartered Bank: Standard Chartered Bank Bldg, 4–4A Des Voeux Rd, Central; tel. 28203333; fax 28569129; internet www.standardchartered.com.hk; f. 1859; Group Exec. Dir (vacant).

Other Commercial Banks

Asia Commercial Bank Ltd: Asia Financial Centre, 120–122 Des Voeux Rd, Central; tel. 25419222; fax 25410009; internet www.asia-commercial.com; f. 1934; fmrly Commercial Bank of Hong Kong; cap. 800.0m., res 422.6m., dep. 11,797.7m. (Dec. 2001); Chair. and CEO ROBIN Y. H. CHAN; Gen. Man. and Exec. Dir STEPHEN TAN; 13 domestic, 1 overseas br.

Bank of East Asia Ltd: Bank of East Asia Bldg, 16/F, 10 Des Voeux Rd, Central; tel. 28423200; fax 28459333; internet www.hkbea.com; inc in Hong Kong in 1918, absorbed United Chinese Bank Ltd in Aug. 2001, and First Pacific Bank (FPB) in Apr. 2002; cap. 3,583.7m., res 13,211.6m., dep. etc. 154,887.5m. (Dec. 2001); Chair. and Chief Exec. DAVID K. P. LI; 105 brs in Hong Kong and 35 overseas brs.

Chekiang First Bank Ltd: Chekiang First Bank Centre, 1 Duddell St, Central; tel. 29221222; fax 28100531; e-mail contact@cfb.com.hk; internet www.cfb.com.hk; f. 1950; cap. 2,500m., res 1,105m., dep. 21,575.8m. (Dec. 2001); Chair. JAMES Z. M. KUNG; 18 brs.

Chiyu Banking Corpn Ltd: 78 Des Voeux Rd, Central; tel. 28430111; fax 25267420; f. 1947; cap. 300m., res 2,785.1m., dep. 24,248.4m. (Dec. 2001); Chair. TAN KONG PIAT; 15 brs.

CITIC Ka Wah Bank Ltd: 232 Des Voeux Rd, Central; tel. 25457131; fax 25417029; e-mail info@citickawahbank.com; internet www.citickawahbank.com; f. 1922; cap. 2,595.5m., res 3,658.2m., dep. 49,715.5m. (Dec. 2001); Chair. KONG DAN; Pres. and CEO CHANG ZHENMING; 26 domestic brs, 2 overseas brs.

Dah Sing Bank Ltd: Dah Sing Financial Centre, 36/F, 108 Gloucester Rd, Central; tel. 25078866; fax 25985052; e-mail ops@dahsing.com.hk; internet www.dahsing.com; f. 1947; cap. 800.0m., res 3,718.5m., dep. 38,506.4m. (Dec. 2001); Chair. DAVID S. Y. WONG; Man. Dir DEREK H. H. WONG; 38 domestic brs.

Dao Heng Bank Ltd: The Centre, 11/F, 99 Queen's Rd, Central; tel. 22188822; fax 22853822; e-mail webmaster@daoheng.com; internet www.daoheng.com; f. 1921; cap. 5,200m., res 8,221.3m., dep. 100,818.6m. (Dec. 2001); Chair. FRANK WONG; CEO RANDOLPH SULLIVAN; 44 domestic brs, 4 overseas brs.

DBS Kwong On Bank Ltd: 139 Queen's Rd, Central; tel. 28153636; fax 21678222; e-mail hkcs@dbs.com; internet www.dbs.com.hk; f. 1938; inc 1954 as Kwong On Bank, name changed 2000; subsidiary of the Development Bank of Singapore; cap. 750.0m., res 3,480.0m., dep. 29,595.7m. (Dec. 2001); Chair. RONALD LEUNG DING-BONG; Sr Man. Dir KENNETH T. M. LEUNG; 32 brs.

Hang Seng Bank Ltd: 83 Des Voeux Rd, Central; tel. 21981111; fax 28684047; e-mail ccd@hangseng.com; internet www.hangseng.com; f. 1933; cap. 9,559m., res 30,711m., dep. 408,295m. (Jun. 2002); Chair. DAVID ELDON; Vice-Chair. and CEO VINCENT CHENG; 155 domestic brs, 5 overseas brs.

Hongkong Chinese Bank Ltd: Lippo Centre, Floor Mezz. 1, 89 Queensway, Central; tel. 28676833; fax 28459221; internet www.hkcb.com.hk; f. 1954; cap. 2,393.3m., res 845.0m., dep. 16,398.1m. (Dec. 2001); Chair. MOCHTAR RIADY; Man. Dir and Chief Exec. RAYMOND LEE WING-HUNG; 21 domestic, 2 overseas brs.

Industrial and Commercial Bank of China (Asia): ICBC Tower, 122–126 Queen's Rd, Central; tel. 25343333; fax 28051166; internet www.icbcasia.com; f. 1964; fmrly Union Bank of Hong Kong; cap. 2,073.7m., res 2,501.0m., dep. 36,759.3m. (Dec. 2001); Chair. JIANG JIANQING; 20 brs.

International Bank of Asia Ltd: International Bank of Asia Bldg, 38 Des Voeux Rd, Central; tel. 28426222; fax 28101483; e-mail iba-info@iba.com.hk; internet www.iba.com.hk; f. 1982 as Sun Hung Kai Bank Ltd, name changed 1986; subsidiary of Arab Banking Corpn; cap. 1,172.2m., res 1,103.6m., dep. 24,027.9m. (Dec. 2001); Man. Dir and CEO MIKE M. MURAD; 26 brs.

Jian Sing Bank Ltd: 99–105 Des Voeux Rd, Central; tel. 25410088; fax 25447145; e-mail admin@jsb.com.hk; f. 1964 as Hongkong Industrial and Commercial Bank Ltd, acquired by Dah Sing Bank Ltd in 1987, 40% interest acquired by China Construction Bank in 1994, resulting in name change; cap. 300.0m., res 48.1m., dep. 2,175.2m. (Dec. 2001); Chair. ZHEFU LUO; CEO and Gen. Man. PATRICK P. T. HO.

Liu Chong Hing Bank Ltd: POB 2535, 24 Des Voeux Rd, Central; tel. 28417417; fax 28459134; e-mail intlcorrbankhk@lchbhk.com; internet www.lchbank.com; f. 1948; cap. 217.5m., res 5,578.5m., dep. 33,229.9m. (Dec. 2001); Chair. and Man. Dir LIU LIT-MAN; 36 domestic brs, 3 overseas brs.

Nanyang Commercial Bank Ltd: Nanyang Commercial Bank Bldg, 151 Des Voeux Rd, Central; tel. 28520888; fax 28153333; e-mail webmaster_nyc@bocgroup.com; internet www.nanyang-bank.com; f. 1949; cap. p.u. 600m., res 10,016.3m., dep. 72,204.4m. (Dec. 2000); Chair. LIU JINBAO; 41 brs, 6 mainland brs, 1 overseas br.

Overseas Trust Bank Ltd: The Centre, 11/F, 99 Queen's Rd, Central; tel. 22188822; fax 22853822; e-mail corpcomm@daoheng.com; internet www.daoheng.com; f. 1955; under govt control 1985–93; cap. 2,000m., res 2,569.9m., dep. 26,351.7m. (Dec. 2000); CEO R. G. SULLIVAN; 15 domestic brs, 1 overseas br.

Shanghai Commercial Bank Ltd: 12 Queen's Rd, Central; tel. 28415415; fax 28104623; e-mail contact@shacombank.com.hk; internet www.shacombank.com.hk; f. 1950; cap. 2,000m., res 6,845.6m., dep. 61,008.1m. (Dec. 2001); CEO, Man. Dir and Gen. Man. JOHN KAM-PAK YAN; 40 domestic brs, 4 overseas brs.

Standard Bank Asia Ltd (Standard Jardine Fleming Bank): 36/F, Two Pacific Place, 88 Queensway; tel. 28227888; fax 28227999; e-mail ashbanking@standardbank.com.hk; internet www.standardbank.com; f. 1970 as Jardine Fleming & Company Ltd, renamed Jardine Fleming Bank Ltd in 1993, absorbed by Standard Bank Investment Corpn Ltd and name changed as present in July 2001; cap. 66m., res 52.3m., dep. 1,571.4m. (Dec. 2001); Chair. PIETER PRINSLOO.

Tai Yau Bank Ltd: 130–32 Des Voeux Rd, Central; tel. 25229002; fax 28685334; f. 1947; cap. 150.0m., res 176.5m., dep 1,469.9m. (Dec. 2000); Chair. KO FOOK KAU.

Wayfoong Finance Ltd: 10/F, Tower 1, HSBC Centre, 1 Sham Mong Rd, Kowloon; tel. 22888777; fax 22888722; f. 1960; owned by HSBC Holdings plc; cap. 300.0m., res 882.2m., dep. 1,747.9m. (Dec. 1999).

Wing Hang Bank Ltd: POB 514, 161 Queen's Rd, Central; tel. 28525111; fax 25410036; e-mail whbpsd@whbhk.com; internet www.whbhk.com; f. 1937; cap. 293.4m., res 5,751.9m., dep. 48,597.2m. (Dec. 2001); Chair. and Chief Exec. PATRICK Y. B. FUNG; 27 domestic brs, 12 overseas brs.

Wing Lung Bank Ltd: 45 Des Voeux Rd, Central; tel. 28268333; fax 28100592; e-mail wlb@winglungbank.com.hk; internet www.winglungbank.com; f. 1933; cap. 1,161.0m., res 6,250.0m., dep.

51,970.0m. (Dec. 2001); Chair. MICHAEL PO-KO WU; Exec. Dir and Gen. Man. CHE-SHUM CHUNG; 34 domestic brs, 2 overseas brs.

Principal Mainland Chinese and Foreign Banks

ABN AMRO Bank NV (Netherlands): Edinburgh Tower, 3–4/F, Landmark, 15 Queen's Rd, Central; tel. 28429211; fax 28459049; CEO (China) SERGIO RIAL; 3 brs.

American Express Bank Ltd (USA): One Pacific Place, 36/F, 88 Queensway, Central; tel. 28440688; fax 28453637; Senior Country Exec. DOUGLAS H. SHORT III; 3 brs.

Australia and New Zealand Banking Group Ltd: 27/F, One Exchange Square, 8 Connaught Place, Central; tel. 28437111; fax 28680089; Gen. Man. PETER RICHARDSON.

BA Asia Ltd: GPOB 799, 2/F, Bank of America Tower, 12 Harcourt Rd; tel. 28476666; fax 28100821; Chair. COLM MCCARTHY; Man. Dir and CEO FREDERICK CHIN.

Bangkok Bank Public Co Ltd (Thailand): Bangkok Bank Bldg, 28 Des Voeux Rd, Central; tel. 28016688; fax 28451805; Gen. Man. CHEN MAN YING; 2 brs.

Bank of America (Asia) Ltd (USA): Devon House, 17/F, 979 King's Rd, Quarry Bay; tel. 25973333; fax 25972500; internet www .bankofamerica.com.hk; Pres. and CEO SAMUEL TSIEN; 13 brs.

Bank of Communications, Hong Kong Branch: 20 Pedder St, Central; tel. 28419611; fax 28106993; f. 1934; Gen. Man. FANG LIANKUI; 41 brs.

Bank of India: Ruttonjee House, 2/F, 11 Duddell St, Central; tel. 25240186; fax 28106149; e-mail boihk@netvigator.com; Chief Exec. O. P. GUPTA.

Bank of Scotland: Jardine House, 11/F, 1 Connaught Place, Central; tel. 25212155; fax 28459007; Sr Man. I. A. MCKINNEY; 1 br.

Barclays Capital Asia Ltd: Citibank Tower, 42/F, 3 Garden Rd, Central; tel. 29032000; fax 29032999; internet www.barclayscapital .com; f. 1972; Chair. and CEO ROBERT A. MORRICE.

BNP Paribas (France): Central Tower, 4–14/F, 28 Queen's Rd, Central; tel. 29098888; fax 25302707; e-mail didier.balme@ bnpgroup.com; internet www.bnpparibas.com.hk; f. 1958; Man. DIDIER BALME; 2 brs.

Citibank, NA (USA): Citibank Tower, 39–40/F and 44–50/F, Citibank Plaza, 3 Garden Rd, Central; tel. 28688888; fax 23068111; 20 brs.

Commerzbank AG (Germany): Hong Kong Club Bldg, 21/F, 3A Chater Rd, Central; tel. 28429666; fax 28681414; 1 br.

Crédit Agricole Indosuez (France): One Exchange Square, 42–45/F, 8 Connaught Rd, Central; tel. 28489000; fax 28681406; Sr Country Officer CHARLES REYBET-DEGAT; 1 br.

Deutsche Bank AG (Germany): 51–56/F, Cheung Kong Center, 2 Queen's Rd, Central; tel. 22038888; fax 28459056; Gen. Mans Dr MICHAEL THOMAS, REINER RUSCH; 1 br.

Equitable PCI Bank (Philippines): 7/F, No. 1, Silver Fortune Plaza, Wellington St; tel. 28680323; fax 28100050; Vice-Pres. PAUL LANG; 1 br.

Fortis Bank (Belgium): Fortis Bank Tower, 27/F, 77–79 Gloucester Rd, Wanchai; tel. 28230456; fax 25276851; e-mail info@fortisbank .com.hk; internet www.fortisbank.com.hk; Gen. Man. DAVID YU; 28 brs.

Indian Overseas Bank: POB 182, Ruttonjee House, 3/F, 11 Duddell St, Central; tel. 25227249; fax 28450159; 2 brs.

JP Morgan Chase Bank (USA): 39/F, One Exchange Square, Connaught Place, Central; tel. 28431234; fax 28414396.

Malayan Banking Berhad (Malaysia): Entertainment Bldg, 18–19/F, 30 Queen's Rd, Central; tel. 25227141; fax 28106013; trades in Hong Kong as Maybank; Man. HWAN WOON HAN; 2 brs.

Mevas Bank: 36/F, Dah Sing Financial Centre, 108 Gloucester Rd; tel. 31013286; fax 31013298; e-mail contactus@mevas.com; internet www.mevas.com; Chair. DAVID S. Y. WONG.

Mizuho Corporate Asia (HK) Ltd (Japan): 17/F, 2 Pacific Place, 88 Queensway, Admiralty; tel. 21033040; fax 28101326; Man. Dir and CEO NOBORU AKATSUKA; 1 br.

National Bank of Pakistan: 18/F, ING Tower, 308–320 Des Voeux Rd, Central; tel. 25217321; fax 28451703; Gen. Man. USMAN AZIZ; 2 brs.

Oversea-Chinese Banking Corpn Ltd (Singapore): 9/F, 9 Queen's Rd, Central; tel. 28682086; fax 28453439; Gen. Man. BENJAMIN YEUNG; 3 brs.

Philippine National Bank: Regent Centre Bldg, 7/F, 88 Queen's Rd, Central; tel. 25253638; fax 25253107; e-mail itdept@pnbhk.com; Sr Vice-Pres. and Gen. Man. ARTICER O. QUEBAL; 1 br.

N. M. Rothschild and Sons (Hong Kong) Ltd: 16/F, Alexandra House, 16–20 Chater Rd, Central; tel. 25255333; fax 28681773; Chair. PHILIP BRASS.

Société Générale Asia Ltd (France): 40/F, Edinburgh Tower, The Landmark, 15 Queen's Rd; tel. 25838600; fax 28400738; CEO JACKSON CHEUNG.

Sumitomo Mitsui Banking Corpn (SMBC) (Japan): 7–8F/, One International Finance Centre, 1 Harbour View St, Central; tel. 22062000; fax 22062888; Gen. Man. TOSHIO MORIKAWA; 1 br.

Tokyo-Mitsubishi International (HK) Ltd (Japan): 16/F, Tower 1, Admiralty Centre, 18 Harcourt Rd; tel. 25202460; fax 25291550; Man. Dir and CEO YOSHIAKI WATANABE.

UBAF (Hong Kong) Ltd (France): Far East Finance Centre, 18/F, 16 Harcourt Rd, Central; tel. 25201361; fax 25274256; Chair. ALY MOHAMED NEGM.

UFJ International Finance Asia Ltd (Japan): 6/F, Hong Kong Club Bldg, 3A Chater Rd, Central; tel. 25334300; fax 28453518; internet www.ufjifal.com; CEO and Man. Dir AKIHIKO KOBAYASHI.

United Overseas Bank Ltd (Singapore): United Overseas Bank Bldg, 54–58 Des Voeux Rd, Central; tel. 28425666; fax 28105773; Sr Vice-Pres. and CEO ROBERT CHAN TZE LEUNG; 5 brs.

Banking Associations

The Chinese Banks' Association Ltd: South China Bldg, 5/F, 1–3 Wyndham St, Central; tel. 25224789; fax 28775102; 1,666 mems; Chair. Bank of East Asia (vacant) (represented by David K. P. Li).

The DTC Association (The Hong Kong Association of Restricted Licence Banks and Deposit-Taking Companies): Suite 3738, 37/F, Sun Hung Kai Centre, 30 Harbour Rd; tel. 25264079; fax 25230180.

The Hong Kong Association of Banks: GPOB 11391; tel. 25211169; fax 28685035; e-mail hkab@pacific.net.hk; internet www .hkab.org.hk; f. 1981 to succeed The Exchange Banks' Asscn of Hong Kong; all licensed banks in Hong Kong are required by law to be mems of this statutory body, whose function is to represent and further the interests of the banking sector; 133 mems; Chair. Hongkong and Shanghai Banking Corpn Ltd (represented by RAYMOND OR); Sec. RONA MORGAN.

STOCK EXCHANGE

Honk Kong Exchanges and Clearing Ltd: 1 International Finance Centre, 12/F, 1 Harbour View St, Central; tel. 25221122; fax 22953106; e-mail info@hkex.com.hk; internet www.hkex.com.hk; f. 2000 by unification of the Stock Exchange of Hong Kong, the Hong Kong Futures Exchange and the Hong Kong Securities Clearing Co; 572 mems; Chair. LEE YEH KWONG; CEO KWONG KI CHI.

In 1998 Exchange Fund Investment Ltd: was established by the Government to manage its stock portfolio acquired during the intervention of August (Chair. YANG TI-LIANG).

SUPERVISORY BODY

Securities and Futures Commission (SFC): Edinburgh Tower, 12/F, The Landmark, 15 Queen's Rd, Central; tel. 28409222; fax 28459553; e-mail enquiry@hksfc.org.hk; internet www.hksfc.org.hk; f. 1989 to supervise the stock and futures markets; Chair. ANDREW SHENG; Dep. Chair. LAURA CHA.

INSURANCE

In December 2001 there were 204 authorized insurance companies, including 105 overseas companies. The following are among the principal companies:

Asia Insurance Co Ltd: World-Wide House, 16/F, 19 Des Voeux Rd, Central; tel. 28677988; fax 28100218; e-mail kclau@ asiainsurance.com.hk; internet www.asiainsurance.com.hk; Chair. SEBASTIAN KI CHIT LAU.

CGU International Insurance plc: Cityplaza One, 9/F, Taikoo Shing; tel. 28940555; fax 28905741; e-mail cguasia.com; Gen. Man. ANDREW LO.

Hong Kong Export Credit Insurance Corpn: South Seas Centre, Tower I, 2/F, 75 Mody Rd, Tsim Sha Tsui East, Kowloon; fax 27226277; Commr D. K. DOWDING.

Mercantile and General Reinsurance Co PLC: 13C On Hing Bldg, 1 On Hing Terrace, Central; tel. 28106160; fax 25217353; Man. T. W. Ho.

Ming An Insurance Co (HK) Ltd: Ming An Plaza, 19/F, 8 Sunning Rd, Causeway Bay; tel. 28151551; fax 25416567; e-mail mai@ mingan.com.hk; internet www.mingan.com; Dir and Gen. Man. K. P. CHENG.

National Mutual Insurance Co (Bermuda) Ltd: 151 Gloucester Rd, Wanchai; tel. 25191111; fax 25987204; life and general insurance; Chair. Sir DAVID AKERS-JONES; CEO TERRY SMITH.

Prudential Assurance Co Ltd: Cityplaza 4, 10/F, 12 Taikoo Wan Rd, Taikoo Shing; tel. 29773888; fax 28776994; life and general; CEO JAMES C. K. WONG.

Royal and Sun Alliance (Hong Kong) Ltd: Dorset House, 32/F, Taikoo Place, 979 King's Road, Quarry Bay; tel. 29683000; fax 29685111; Man. Dir KEITH LAND.

Summit Insurance (Asia) Ltd: Sunshine Plaza, 25/F, 253 Lockhart Rd, Wanchai; tel. 21059000; fax 25166992; e-mail psi@hcg.com.hk; internet www.hsinchong.com/summit; CEO IU PO SING.

Willis China (Hong Kong) Ltd: 3502, The Lee Gardens, 33 Hysan Ave, Causeway Bay; tel. 28270111; fax 28270966; internet www.willis.com; Man. Dir KIRK AUSTIN.

Winterthur Swiss Insurance (Asia) Ltd: Dah Sing Financial Centre, 19/F, 108 Gloucester Rd, Wanchai; tel. 25986282; fax 25985838; Man. Dir ALLAN YU.

Insurance Associations

Hong Kong Federation of Insurers (HKFI): First Pacific Bank Centre, Room 902, 9/F, 56 Gloucester Rd, Wanchai; tel. 25201868; fax 25201967; e-mail hkfi@hkfi.org.hk; internet www.hkfi.org.hk; f. 1988; 117 general insurance and 42 life insurance mems; Chair. CHOY CHUNG FOO; Exec. Dir LOUISA FONG.

Insurance Institute of Hong Kong: GPO Box 6747; tel. 25825601; fax 28276033; internet www.iihk.org.hk; f. 1967; Pres. STEPHEN LAW.

Trade and Industry

Hong Kong Trade Development Council: Office Tower, 38/F, Convention Plaza, 1 Harbour Rd, Wanchai; tel. 1830668; fax 28240249; e-mail hktdc@tdc.org.hk; internet www.tdctrade.com; f. 1966; Chair. PETER WOO KWONG-CHING; Exec. Dir MICHAEL SZE.

Trade and Industry Department: Trade and Industry Department Tower, 700 Nathan Rd, Kowloon; tel. 23985333; fax 27892491; e-mail enqtid@tid.gcn.gov.hk; internet www.info.gov.hk/tid; Dir-Gen. JOSHUA LAW.

DEVELOPMENT ORGANIZATIONS

Hong Kong Housing Authority: 33 Fat Kwong St, Homantin, Kowloon; tel. 27615002; fax 27621110; f. 1973; plans, builds and manages public housing; Chair. DOMINIC WONG; Dir of Housing J. A. MILLER.

Hong Kong Productivity Council: HKPC Bldg, 78 Tat Chee Ave, Yau Yat Chuen, Kowloon Tong, Kowloon; tel. 27885678; fax 27885900; e-mail bettylee@hkpc.org; internet www.hkpc.org; f. 1967 to promote increased productivity of industry and to encourage optimum utilization of resources; council of 23 mems appointed by the Government, representing management, labour, academic and professional interests, and govt depts associated with productivity matters; Chair. KENNETH FANG; Exec. Dir THOMAS TANG.

Kadoorie Agricultural Aid Loan Fund: c/o Director of Agriculture, Fisheries and Conservation, Cheung Sha Wan Govt Offices, 5/F, 303 Cheung Sha Wan Rd, Kowloon; tel. 21506666; fax 23113731; e-mail afcdenq@afcd.gcn.gov.hk; f. 1954; provides low-interest loans to farmers; HK \$9,035,000 was loaned in 2001/02.

J. E. Joseph Trust Fund: c/o Director of Agriculture, Fisheries and Conservation, Cheung Sha Wan Govt Offices, 5/F, 303 Cheung Sha Wan Rd, Kowloon; tel. 21506666; fax 23113731; e-mail afcdenq@afcd.gcn.gov.hk; f. 1954; grants low-interest credit facilities to farmers and farmers' co-operative socs; HK \$5,050,000 was loaned in 2001/02.

CHAMBERS OF COMMERCE

Chinese Chamber of Commerce, Kowloon: 2/F, 8–10 Nga Tsin Long Rd, Kowloon; tel. 23822309; f. 1936; 234 mems; Chair. and Exec. Dir YEUNG CHOR-HANG.

The Chinese General Chamber of Commerce: 4/F, 24–25 Connaught Rd, Central; tel. 25256385; fax 28452610; e-mail cgcc@cgcc.org.hk; internet www.cgcc.org.hk; f. 1900; 6,000 mems; Chair. Dr TSANG HIN-CHI.

Hong Kong General Chamber of Commerce: United Centre, 22/F, 95 Queensway, POB 852; tel. 25299229; fax 25279843; e-mail chamber@chamber.org.hk; internet www.chamber.org.hk; f. 1861; 4,000 mems; Chair. CHRISTOPHER CHENG; CEO EDEN WOON.

Kowloon Chamber of Commerce: KCC Bldg, 3/F, 2 Liberty Ave, Homantin, Kowloon; tel. 27600393; fax 27610166; e-mail kcc02@hkkcc.biz.com.hk; internet www.hkkcc.org.hk; f. 1938; 1,640 mems; Chair. TONG KWOK-WAH; Sec. of Gen. Affairs CHENG PO-WO.

FOREIGN TRADE ORGANIZATIONS

Hong Kong Chinese Importers' and Exporters' Association: Champion Bldg, 7–8/F, 287–291 Des Voeux Rd, Central; tel. 25448474; fax 25444677; e-mail info@hkciea.org.hk; internet www.hkciea.org.hk; f. 1954; 3,000 mems; Pres. HUI CHEUNG-CHING.

Hong Kong Exporters' Association: Room 824–825, Star House, 3 Salisbury Rd, Tsimshatsui, Kowloon; tel. 27309851; fax 27301869; e-mail exporter@exporters.org.hk; internet www.exporters.org.hk; f. 1955; 630 mems comprising leading merchants and manufacturing exporters; Pres. CLIFF K. SUN; Exec. Dir SHIRLEY SO.

INDUSTRIAL AND TRADE ASSOCIATIONS

Chinese Manufacturers' Association of Hong Kong: CMA Bldg, 64 Connaught Rd, Central; tel. 25456166; fax 25414541; e-mail info@cma.org.hk; internet www.cma.org.hk; f. 1934 to promote and protect industrial and trading interests; operates testing and certification laboratories; 3,700 mems; Pres. CHAN WING KEE; Exec. Dir FRANCIS T. M. LAU.

Federation of Hong Kong Garment Manufacturers: Cheung Lee Commercial Bldg, Room 401–3, 25 Kimberley Rd, Tsimshatsui, Kowloon; tel. 27211383; fax 23111062; e-mail info@garment.org.hk; f. 1964; 200 mems; Pres. NORMAN TAM; Sec.-Gen. MICHAEL LEUNG.

Federation of Hong Kong Industries (FKHI): Hankow Centre, 4/F, 5–15 Hankow Rd, Tsimshatsui, Kowloon; tel. 27323188; fax 27213494; e-mail fhki@fhki.org.hk; internet www.fhki.org.hk; f. 1960; 3,000 mems; Chair. VICTOR LO.

Federation of Hong Kong Watch Trades and Industries Ltd: Peter Bldg, Room 604, 58–62 Queen's Rd, Central; tel. 25233232; fax 28684485; e-mail hkwatch@netvigator.com; internet www.hkwatch.org; f. 1947; 700 mems; Chair. YIU KA CHEUNG.

Hong Kong Association for the Advancement of Science and Technology Ltd: 2A, Tak Lee Commercial Bldg, 113–17 Wanchai Rd, Wanchai; tel. 28913388; fax 28381823; e-mail info@hkaast.org.hk; internet www.hkaast.org.hk; Pres. LUI SUN WING.

Hong Kong Biotechnology Association Ltd: Rm 789, HITEC, 1 Trademart Drive, Kowloon Bay, Kowloon; tel. 26209955; fax 26201238; e-mail etang@hkbta.org.hk; internet www.hkbta.org.hk; Chair. LO YUK LAM.

Hong Kong Chinese Enterprises Association: Harbour Center, Room 2104–6, Harbour Centre, 25 Harbour Rd, Wanchai; tel. 28272831; fax 28272606; e-mail info@hkcea.com; internet www.hkcea.com; f. 1991; 1,000 mems; Chair. LIU JINBAO; Exec. Dir ZHOU JIE.

Hong Kong Chinese Textile Mills Association: 11/F, 38–40 Tai Po Rd, Sham Shiu Po, Kowloon; tel. 27778236; fax 27881836; f. 1931; 150 mems; Pres. LEE CHUNG-CHIU.

Hong Kong Construction Association Ltd: 3/F, 180–182 Hennessy Rd, Wanchai; tel. 25724414; fax 25727104; e-mail admin@hkca.com.hk; internet www.hkca.com.hk; f. 1920; 372 mems; Pres. BILLY WONG; Sec.-Gen. PATRICK CHAN.

Hong Kong Electronic Industries Association Ltd: Rm 1201, 12/F, Harbour Crystal Centre, 100 Granville Rd, Tsimshatsui, Kowloon; tel. 27788328; fax 27882200; e-mail hkeia@hkeia.org; internet www.hkeia.org; 370 mems; Chair. SAMSON TAM.

Hong Kong Garment Manufacturers Association: 401-3, Cheung Lee Commercial Bldg, 25 Kimberley Rd, Tsimshatsui, Kowloon; tel. 23052893; fax 23052493; e-mail mleung@textilecouncil.com; f. 1987; 40 mems; Chair. PETER WANG.

Hong Kong Information Technology Federation Ltd: The Center, 21/F, 99 Queen's Rd, Central; tel. 22878017; fax 22878038; e-mail info@hkitf.com; internet www.hkitf.org.hk; 250 mems; f. 1980; Pres. CHARLES MOK.

Hong Kong Jewellery and Jade Manufacturers Association: Flat A, 12/F, Kaiser Estate Phase 1, 41 Man Yue St, Hunghom, Kowloon; tel. 25430543; fax 28150164; e-mail hkjja@hkstar.com; internet www.jewellery-hk.org; f. 1965; 227 mems; Chair. CHARLES CHAN; Gen. Man. CATHERINE CHAN.

Hong Kong Jewelry Manufacturers' Association: Unit G, 2/F, Kaiser Estate Phase 2, 51 Man Yue St, Hunghom, Kowloon; tel. 27663002; fax 23623647; e-mail hkjma@jewelry.org.hk; internet www.jewelry.org.hk; f. 1988; 260 mems; Chair. PATRICK LUK NG.

Hong Kong Knitwear Exporters and Manufacturers Association: Cheung Lee Commercial Bldg, Rm 401–03, Tsimshatsui, Kowloon; tel. 27552621; fax 27565672; f. 1966; 108 mems; Chair. WILLY LIN; Exec. Sec. SHIRLEY LIU.

Hong Kong and Kowloon Footwear Manufacturers' Association: Kam Fung Bldg, 3/F, Flat D, 8 Cleverly St, Sheung Wan; tel. and fax 25414499; 88 mems; Pres. LOK WAI-TO; Sec. LEE SUM-HUNG.

Hong Kong Optical Manufacturers' Association Ltd: 2/F, 11 Fa Yuen St, Mongkok, Kowloon; tel. 23326505; fax 27705786; e-mail hkoma@netvigator.com; internet www.hkoptical.org.hk; f. 1982; 114 mems; Pres. Hui Leung-wah.

Hong Kong Plastics Manufacturers Association Ltd: Fu Yuen Bldg, 1/F, Flat B, 39–49 Wanchai Rd; tel. 25742230; fax 25742843; f. 1957; 200 mems; Chair. Jeffrey Lam; Pres. Dennis H. S. Ting.

Hong Kong Printers Association: 1/F, 48–50 Johnston Rd, Wanchai; tel. 25275050; fax 28610463; e-mail printers@hkprinters.org; internet www.hkprinters.org; f. 1939; 437 mems; Chair. Ho Ka-hun.

Hong Kong Rubber and Footwear Manufacturers' Association: Kar Tseuk Bldg, Block A, 2/F, 185 Prince Edward Rd, Kowloon; tel. 23812297; fax 23976927; f. 1948; 180 mems; Chair. Cheung Kam; Gen. Sec. Lai Yuen-man.

Hong Kong Sze Yap Commercial and Industrial Association: Cosco Tower, Unit 1205–6, 183 Queen's Rd, Central; tel. 25438095; fax 25449495; f. 1909; 1,082 mems; Chair. Louie Chick-nan; Sec. Wong Ka Chun.

Hong Kong Toys Council: Hankow Centre, 4/F, 5–15 Hankow Rd, Tsimshatsui, Kowloon; tel. 27323188; fax 27213494; e-mail fhki@fhki.org.hk; internet www.toyshk.org; f. 1986; 200 mems; Chair. Samson Chan.

Hong Kong Watch Manufacturers' Association: Yu Wing Bldg, 3/F and 11/F, Unit A, 64–66 Wellington St, Central; tel. 25225238; fax 28106614; e-mail hkwma@netvigator.com; internet www .hkwma.org; 658 mems; Pres. Stanley C. H. Lau; Sec.-Gen. Tommy Y. Leung.

Information and Software Industry Association Ltd: Suite 2, 8/F, Tower 6, China Hong Kong City, 33 Canton Rd, Tsimshatsui; tel. 26222867; fax 26222731; e-mail info@isia.org.hk; internet www .isia.org.hk; Chair. Satti Wong.

Internet and Telecom Association of Hong Kong: GPOB 13461; tel. 25042732; fax 25042752; e-mail info@itahk.org.hk; internet www.itahk.org.hk; 130 mems; Chair. Tony Hau.

New Territories Commercial and Industrial General Association Ltd: Cheong Hay Bldg, 2/F, 107 Hoi Pa St, Tsuen Wan; tel. 24145316; fax 24934130; f. 1973; 4,000 mems; Chair. Hok Lim Wan; Sec.-Gen. Kam Chuen Ngan.

Real Estate Developers Association of Hong Kong: Worldwide House, Room 1403, 19 Des Voeux Rd, Central; tel. 28260111; fax 28452521; f. 1965; 750 mems; Pres. Dr Stanley Ho; Sec.-Gen. Keith Kerr.

Textile Council of Hong Kong Ltd: 401-3, Cheung Lee Commercial Bldg, 25 Kimberley Rd, Tsimshatsui , Kowloon; tel. 23052893; fax 23052493; e-mail mleung@textilecouncil.com; internet www .textilecouncil.com; f. 1989; 10 mems; Chair. Andrew Leung; Exec. Dir Michael Leung.

Toys Manufacturers' Association of Hong Kong Ltd: Room 1302, Metroplaza, Tower 2, 223 Hing Fong Rd, Kwai Chung, New Territories; tel. 24221209; fax 24221639; e-mail tm_hk@hotmail .com; internet www.tmhk.net; 250 mems; Pres. Arthur Chan; Sec. Y. M. Ko.

EMPLOYERS' ORGANIZATIONS

Employers' Federation of Hong Kong: Suite 2004, Sino Plaza, 255–257 Gloucester Rd, Causeway Bay; tel. 25280536; fax 28655285; e-mail efhk@efhk.org.hk; internet www.efhk.org.hk; f. 1947; 446 mems; Chair. James C. Ng; Exec. Dir Jackie Ma.

Hong Kong Factory Owners' Association Ltd: Wing Wong Bldg, 11/F, 557–559 Nathan Rd, Kowloon; tel. 23882372; fax 23857129; f. 1982; 1,179 mems; Pres. Hwang Jen; Sec. Tsang Chun Wah.

UTILITIES

Electricity

CLP Power Ltd: 147 Argyle St, Kowloon; tel. 26788111; fax 27604448; internet www.clpgroup.com; f. 1918; fmrly China Light and Power Co Ltd; generation and supply of electricity to Kowloon and the New Territories; Chair. Michael D. Kadoorie; Man. Dir Ross Sayers.

The Hongkong Electric Co Ltd: 44 Kennedy Rd; tel. 28433111; fax 28100506; e-mail mail@hec.com.hk; internet www.hec.com.hk; generation and supply of electricity to Hong Kong Island, and the islands of Ap Lei Chau and Lamma; Chair. George C. Magnus; Man. Dir K. S. Tso.

Gas

Gas Authority: all gas supply cos, gas installers and contractors are required to be registered with the Gas Authority. At the end of 2000 there were seven registered gas supply cos.

Hong Kong and China Gas Co Ltd: 23/F, 363 Java Rd, North Point; tel. 29633388; fax 25632233; internet www.towngas.com; production, distribution and marketing of town gas and gas appliances; operates two plants; Chair. Lee Shau-kee; Man. Dir Alfred W. K. Chan.

Water

Drainage Services Department: responsible for planning, designing, constructing, operating and maintaining the sewerage, sewage treatment and stormwater drainage infrastructures.

Water Supplies Department: tel. 28294709; fax 25881594; e-mail wsdinfo@wsd.gov.hk; internet www.info.gov.hk/wsd/; responsible for water supplies; approx. 2.4m. customers (2001).

TRADE UNIONS

In December 2000 there were 638 trade unions in Hong Kong, comprising 594 employees' unions, 25 employers' associations and 19 mixed organizations.

Hong Kong and Kowloon Trades Union Council (TUC): Labour Bldg, 11 Chang Sha St, Kowloon; tel. 23845150; f. 1949; 66 affiliated unions, mostly covering the catering and building trades; 28,200 mems; supports Taiwan; affiliated to ICFTU; Officer-in-Charge Wong Yiu Kam.

Hong Kong Confederation of Trade Unions: Wing Wong Commercial Bldg, 19/F, 557–559 Nathan Rd, Kowloon; tel. 27708668; fax 27707388; e-mail hkctu@hkctu.org.hk; internet www.hkctu.org.hk; registered Feb. 1990; 63 affiliated independent unions and federations; 160,000 mems; Chair. Lau Chin-shek.

Hong Kong Federation of Trade Unions (FTU): 7/F, 50 Ma Tau Chung Rd, Tokwawan, Kowloon; tel. 27120231; fax 27608477; f. 1948; 171 member unions, mostly concentrated in shipyards, public transport, textile mills, construction, department stores, printing and public utilities; supports the People's Republic of China; 310,000 mems; Pres. Cheng Yiu-tong; Gen. Sec. Chan Jik-kwei.

Also active are the **Federation of Hong Kong and Kowloon Labour Unions** (31 affiliated unions with 21,700 mems) and the **Federation of Civil Service Unions** (29 affiliated unions with 12,000 mems).

Transport

Transport Department: Immigration Tower, 41/F, 7 Gloucester Rd, Wanchai; tel. 28042600; fax 28240433; internet www.info.gov .hk/td.

RAILWAYS

Kowloon–Canton Railway Corpn: KCRC House, 9 Lok King St, Fo Tan, Sha Tin, New Territories; tel. 26881333; fax 26880983; internet www.kcrc.com; operated by the Kowloon–Canton Railway Corpn, a public statutory body; f. 1983; operates both heavy and light rail systems; the 34-km East Rail runs from the terminus at Hung Hom to the frontier at Lo Wu; through passenger services to Guangzhou (Canton), suspended in 1949, were resumed in 1979; the electrification and double-tracking of the entire length and redevelopment of all stations has been completed, and full electric train service came into operation in 1983; in 1988 a light railway network serving Tuen Mun, Yuen Long and Tin Shui Wai in the northwestern New Territories was opened; passenger service extended to Foshan in 1993, Dongguan in 1994, Zhaoqing in 1995 and Shanghai in 1997; direct Kowloon–Beijing service commenced in May 1997; also freight services to several destinations in China; West Rail, a domestic passenger line linking Tuen Mun and Yuen Long with Kowloon, was scheduled to begin services in late 2003; three East Rail extensions due for completion in 2004–07; a Kowloon Southern Link connecting West Rail and East Rail was due for completion in 2008; a new 17–km railway linking Sha Tin and Central via a new cross-harbour tunnel was to be completed between 2008–11, providing the first direct rail route from the Chinese border to Hong Kong Island; Chair. and CEO Yueng Kai-yin.

MTR Corporation: MTR Tower, Telford Plaza, Kowloon Bay; tel. 29932111; fax 27988822; internet www.mtr.com.hk; f. 1975; privatized in 2000, shares commenced trading on Hong Kong Stock Exchange in Oct. 2000; network of 77 km of railway lines and 44 stations; the first section of the underground mass transit railway (MTR) system opened in 1979; a 15.6-km line from Kwun Tong to Central opened in 1980; a 10.5-km Tsuen Wan extension opened in 1982; the 12.5-km Island Line opened in 1985–86; in 1989 a second harbour crossing between Cha Kwo Ling and Quarry Bay, known as the Eastern Harbour Crossing, commenced operation, adding 4.6 km to the railway system; 34-km link to new airport at Chek Lap Kok and to Tung Chung New Town opened in mid-1998; an additional line, the Tseung Kwan O Extension, was completed in August 2002; additional lines were also planned for 2006; Chair. and Chief Exec. JACK C. K. SO.

TRAMWAYS

Hong Kong Tramways Ltd: Whitty Street Tram Depot, Connaught Rd West, Western District; tel. 21186338; fax 21186038; f. 1904; operates six routes and 161 double-deck trams between Kennedy Town and Shaukeiwan; Dir and Gen. Man. MICKY LEUNG.

ROADS

At the end of 2000 there were 1,904 km of roads and 1,023 highway structures. Almost all of them are concrete or asphalt surfaced. Owing to the hilly terrain, and the density of building development, the scope for substantial increase in the road network is limited. A new 29-km steel bridge linking Hong Kong's Lantau Island with Macao and Zhuhai City, in the Chinese province of Guangdong, was being planned in 2001, with studies being carried out to determine the project's financial and technological feasibility.

Highways Department: Ho Man Tin Government Offices, 5/F, 88 Chung Hau St, Ho Man Tin, Kowloon; tel. 27623304; fax 27145216; e-mail hyd@hyd.gov.hk; internet www.hyd.gov.hk; f. 1986; planning, design, construction and maintenance of the public road system; co-ordination of major highway and railway projects; Dir MAK CHAI-KWONG.

FERRIES

Conventional ferries, hoverferries and catamarans operate between Hong Kong, China and Macao. There is also an extensive network of ferry services to outlying districts.

Hongkong and Yaumati Ferry Co Ltd: 98 Tam Kon Shan Rd, Ngau Kok Wan, North Tsing Yi, New Territories; tel. 23944294; fax 27869001; e-mail hkferry@hkf.com; internet www.hkf.com; licensed routes on ferry services, incl. cross-harbour, to outlying islands, excursion, vehicular and dangerous goods; fleet of 50 vessels (passenger ferries, vehicular ferries, hoverferries, catamarans, oil barges and floating pontoons); also operates hoverferry services between Hong Kong and Shekou and catamaran service to Macao; Gen. Man. DAVID C. S. HO.

Hongkong Macao Hydrofoil Co Ltd: Turbojet Ferry Services (Guangzhou) Ltd, 83 Hing Wah St West, Lai Chi Kok, Kowloon; operates services to Macao, Fu Yong (Shenzhen airport) and East River Guangzhou.

'Star' Ferry Co Ltd: Kowloon Point Pier, Tsimshatsui, Kowloon; tel. 21186223; fax 21186028; e-mail sf@starferry.com.hk; f. 1898; operates 13 passenger ferries between the Kowloon Peninsula and Central, the main business district of Hong Kong; between Central and Hung Hom; between Tsimshatsui and Wanchai; between Tsimshatsui and Central; and between Wanchai and Hung Hom; Man. JOHNNY LEUNG.

SHIPPING

Hong Kong is one of the world's largest shipping centres and is a major container port. Hong Kong was a British port of registry until the inauguration of a new and independent shipping register in December 1990. Following Hong Kong's reunification with the People's Republic of China, Hong Kong maintains full autonomy in its maritime policy. At the end of 2001 the register comprised a fleet of 646 vessels, totalling 13.7m. grt. The eight container terminals at Kwai Chung, which are privately-owned and operated, comprised 18 berths in 1998. The construction of a ninth terminal (CT9) commenced in 1998 and was expected to be operational by 2003. Lantau Island has been designated as the site for any future expansion.

Marine Department, Hong Kong Special Administrative Region Government: Harbour Bldg, 22/F, 38 Pier Rd, Central, GPOB 4155; tel. 28523001; fax 25449241; e-mail mdenquiry@mardep.gcn.gov.hk; internet www.info.gov.hk/mardep; Dir of Marine S. Y. TSUI.

Shipping Companies

Anglo-Eastern Ship Management Ltd: Universal Trade Centre, 14/F, 3 Arbuthnot Rd, Central, POB 11400; tel. 28636111; fax 28612419; e-mail allhx470@ancomtext.com; internet www.webhk .com/angloeastern/; Chair. PETER CREMERS; Man. Dir MARCEL LIEDTS.

Chung Gai Ship Management Co Ltd: Admiralty Centre Tower 1, 31/F, 18 Harcourt Rd; tel. 25295541; fax 28656206; Chair. S. KODA; Man. Dir K. ICHIHARA.

Fairmont Shipping (HK) Ltd: Fairmont House, 21/F, 8 Cotton Tree Drive; tel. 25218338; fax 28104560; Man. CHARLES LEUNG.

Far East Enterprising Co (HK) Ltd: China Resources Bldg, 18–19/F, 26 Harbour Rd, Wanchai; tel. 28283668; fax 28275584; f. 1949; shipping, chartering, brokering; Gen. Man. WEI KUAN.

Gulfeast Shipmanagement Ltd: Great Eagle Centre, 9/F, 23 Harbour Rd, Wanchai; tel. 28313344; Finance Dir A. T. MIRMO-HAMMADI.

Hong Kong Borneo Shipping Co Ltd: 815 International Bldg, 141 Des Voeux Rd, Central; tel. 25413797; fax 28153473; Pres. Datuk LAI FOOK KIM.

Hong Kong Ming Wah Shipping Co: Unit 3701, China Merchants Tower, 37/F, Shun Tak Centre, 168–200 Connaught Rd, Central; tel. 25172128; fax 25473482; e-mail mwins@cmhk.com; Chair. CHEUNG KING WA; Man. Dir and Vice-Chair. Capt. MAO SHI JIAN.

Island Navigation Corpn International Ltd: Harbour Centre, 28–29/F, 25 Harbour Rd, Wanchai; tel. 28333222; fax 28270001; Man. Dir F. S. SHIH.

Jardine Ship Management Ltd: Jardine Engineering House, 11/F, 260 King's Rd, North Point; tel. 28074101; fax 28073351; e-mail jsmhk@ibm.net; Man. Dir Capt. PAUL UNDERHILL.

Oak Maritime (HK) Inc Ltd: 2301 China Resources Bldg, 26 Harbour Rd, Wanchai; tel. 25063866; fax 25063563; Chair. STEVE G. K. HSU; Pres. FRED C. P. TSAI.

Ocean Tramping Co Ltd: Hong Kong; tel. 25892645; fax 25461041; Chair. Z. M. GAO.

Orient Overseas Container Line Ltd: Harbour Centre, 31/F, 25 Harbour Rd, Wanchai; tel. 28333888; fax 25318122; internet www .oocl.com; member of the Grand Alliance of shipping cos (five partners); Chair. C. C. TUNG.

Teh-Hu Cargocean Management Co Ltd: Unit B, Fortis Bank Tower, 15/F, 77–79 Gloucester Rd, Wanchai; tel. 25988688; fax 28249339; e-mail tehhuhk@on-nets.com; f. 1974; Man. Dir KENNETH K. W. LO.

Wah Kwong Shipping Agency Co Ltd: Shanghai Industrial Investment Bldg, 26/F, 48–62 Hennessy Rd, POB 283; tel. 25279227; fax 28656544; e-mail wk@wahkwong.com.hk; Chair. GEORGE S. K. CHAO.

Wah Tung Shipping Agency Co Ltd: China Resources Bldg, Rooms 2101–5, 21/F, 26 Harbour Rd, Wanchai; tel. 28272818; fax 28275361; e-mail mgr@watunship.com.hk; f. 1981; Dir and Gen. Man. B. L. LIU.

Wallem Shipmanagement Ltd: Hopewell Centre, 46/F, 183 Queen's Rd East; tel. 28768200; fax 28761234; e-mail rgb@wallem .com; Man. Dir R. G. BUCHANAN.

Worldwide Shipping Agency Ltd: Wheelock House, 6–7/F, 20 Pedder St; tel. 28423888; fax 28100617; Man. J. WONG.

Associations

Hong Kong Cargo-Vessel Traders' Association: 21–23 Man Wai Bldg, 2/F, Ferry Point, Kowloon; tel. 23847102; fax 27820342; 978 mems; Chair. CHOW YAT-TAK; Sec. CHAN BAK.

Hong Kong Shipowners' Association: Queen's Centre, 12/F, 58–64 Queen's Rd East, Wanchai; tel. 25200206; fax 25298246; e-mail hksoa@hksoa.org.hk; internet www.hksoa.org.hk; 220 mems; Chair. K.H. KOO; Dir ARTHUR BOWRING.

Hong Kong Shippers' Council: Rm 2407, Hopewell Centre, 183 Queen's Rd East; tel. 28340010; fax 28919787; e-mail shippers@hkshippers.org.hk; internet www.hkshippers.org.hk; 63 mems; Chair. WILLY LIN; Exec. Dir SUNNY HO.

CIVIL AVIATION

By the end of 2000 Hong Kong was served by 64 foreign airlines. A new international airport, on the island of Chek Lap Kok, near Lantau Island, to replace that at Kai Tak, opened in July 1998, following delays in the construction of a connecting high-speed rail-link. The airport has two runways, with the capacity to handle 35m. passengers and 3m. metric tons of cargo per year. The second runway commenced operations in May 1999. A helicopter link with Macao was established in 1990.

Airport Authority of Hong Kong: Cheong Yip Rd, Hong Kong International Airport, Lantau; tel. 21887111; fax 28240717; f. 1995; Chair. Dr VICTOR FUNG KWOK-KING; CEO Dr DAVID J. PANG.

Civil Aviation Department: Queensway Government Offices, 46/F, 66 Queensway; tel. 28674332; fax 28690093; e-mail enquiry@cad.gov.hk; internet www.info.gov.hk/cad/; Dir-Gen. ALBERT K. Y. LAM.

AHK Air Hong Kong Ltd: Units 3601–8, 36/F, Tower 1, Millennium City, 388 Kwun Tong Rd, Kowloon; tel. 27618588; fax 27618586; e-mail ahk.hq@airhongkong.com.hk; f. 1986; international cargo carrier; Chief Operating Officer HUNTER CRAWFORD.

Cathay Pacific Airways Ltd: South Tower, 5/F, Cathay Pacific City, 8 Scenic Rd, Hong Kong International Airport, Lantau; tel. 27475000; fax 28106563; internet www.cathaypacific.com/hk; f. 1946; services to more than 40 major cities in the Far East, Middle East, North America, Europe, South Africa, Australia and New Zealand; Chair. and CEO DAVID TURNBULL.

Hong Kong Dragon Airlines Ltd (Dragonair): Dragonair House, 11 Tung Fai Rd, Hong Kong International Airport, Lantau; tel. 31933193; fax 31933194; internet www.dragonair.com; f. 1985; scheduled and charter flights to 25 destinations in Asia, 16 of which are in mainland China; scheduled regional services include Phuket (Thailand), Hiroshima and Sendai (Japan), Kaohsiung (Taiwan), Phnom-Penh (Cambodia), Dhaka (Bangladesh), Bandar Seri Begawan (Brunei), and Kota Kinabalu (Malaysia); five additional international routes, Seoul (Republic of Korea), Tokyo (Japan), Manila (Philippines), Bangkok (Thailand), and Sydney (Australia) to commence in 2003; Dir and CEO STANLEY HUI.

Tourism

Tourism is a major source of foreign exchange, tourist receipts reaching HK $64,282m. (including receipts from visitors from mainland China) in 2001. Some 13.7m. people visited Hong Kong in 2001. In December 2001 there were some 90 hotels, and the number of rooms available totalled 35,853. In November 1999 it was agreed that a new Disneyland theme park would be constructed in Hong Kong, to be opened in 2005. The Government expected the park to create a huge influx of tourists to the territory.

Hong Kong Tourist Association: Citicorp Centre, 9–11/F, 18 Whitfield Rd, North Point; tel. 28076543; fax 28076595; e-mail dm@hktourismboard.com; internet www.DiscoverHongKong.com; f. 1957; reconstituted as Hong Kong Tourism Board 1 April 2001; coordinates and promotes the tourist industry; has govt support and financial assistance; up to 20 mems of the Board represent the Govt, the private sector and the tourism industry; Chair. SELINA CHOW; Exec. Dir CLARA CHONG.

MACAO

Introductory Survey

Location, Climate, Language, Religion, Flag, Capital

The Special Administrative Region (SAR) of Macao comprises the peninsula of Macao, an enclave on the mainland of southern China, and two nearby islands, Taipa, which is linked to the mainland by two bridges (with a third bridge being under construction in 2003) , and Coloane. The latter island is connected to Taipa by a causeway and by an area of reclaimed land. The territory lies opposite Hong Kong on the western side of the mouth of the Xijiang (Sikiang) River. The climate is subtropical, with temperatures averaging 15°C in January and 29°C in July. There are two official languages, Chinese (Cantonese being the principal dialect) and Portuguese. English is also widely spoken. The predominant religions are Roman Catholicism, Chinese Buddhism, Daoism and Confucianism. The flag of the Macao SAR (proportions 2 by 3), introduced upon the territory's reversion to Chinese sovereignty in December 1999 and flown subordinate to the flag of the People's Republic of China, displays a stylized white flower below an arc of one large and four small yellow stars, above five white lines, on a green background. The capital, the city of Macao, is situated on the peninsula.

Recent History

Established by Portugal in 1557 as a permanent trading post with China, Macao became a Portuguese Overseas Province in 1951. After the military coup in Portugal in April 1974, Col José Garcia Leandro was appointed Governor of the province. A new statute, promulgated in February 1976, redefined Macao as a 'Special Territory' under Portuguese jurisdiction, but with a great measure of administrative and economic independence. Proposals to enlarge the Legislative Assembly from 17 to 21 members, thus giving the Chinese population an increased role in the administration of Macao, were abandoned when they did not receive the approval of the Government of the People's Republic of China in March 1980. China and Portugal established diplomatic relations in February 1979. In the same month Col Leandro was replaced as Governor by Gen. Nuno de Melo Egídio, deputy chief of staff of Portugal's armed forces. In June 1981 Gen. Egídio was, in turn, replaced by Cdre (later Rear-Adm.) Vasco Almeida e Costa, a Portuguese former minister and naval commander. Following a constitutional dispute in March 1984 over the Governor's plans for electoral reform (extending the franchise to the ethnic Chinese majority), the Legislative Assembly was dissolved. Elections for a new Assembly were held in August, at which the Chinese majority were allowed to vote for the first time, regardless of their length of residence in the territory. Following the elections, the Assembly was for the first time dominated by ethnic Chinese deputies.

In January 1986 Governor Almeida e Costa resigned. In May he was replaced by Joaquim Pinto Machado, whose appointment represented a break in the tradition of military governors for Macao. His political inexperience, however, placed him at a disadvantage. In May 1987 he resigned, citing 'reasons of institutional dignity' (apparently referring to the problem of corruption in the Macao administration). He was replaced in August by Carlos Melancia, a former Socialist deputy in the Portuguese legislature, who had held ministerial posts in several Portuguese governments.

The first round of negotiations between the Portuguese and Chinese Governments on the future of Macao took place in June 1986 in Beijing. Portugal's acceptance of China's sovereignty greatly simplified the issue. On 13 April 1987, following the conclusion of the fourth round of negotiations, a joint declaration was formally signed in Beijing by the Portuguese and Chinese Governments, during an official visit to China by the Prime Minister of Portugal. According to the agreement (which was formally ratified in January 1988), Macao was to become a 'special administrative region' (SAR) of the People's Republic (to be known as Macao, China) on 20 December 1999. Macao was thus to have the same status as that agreed (with effect from 1997) for Hong Kong, and was to enjoy autonomy in most matters except defence and foreign policy. A Sino-Portuguese Joint Liaison Group (JLG), established to oversee the transfer of power, held its inaugural meeting in Lisbon in April 1988. In 1999 a Chief Executive for Macao was to be appointed by the Chinese Government, following 'elections or consultations to be held in Macao', and the territory's legislature was to contain 'a majority of elected members'. The inhabitants of Macao were to become citizens of the People's Republic of China. The Chinese Government refused to allow the possibility of dual Sino-Portuguese citizenship, although Macao residents in possession of Portuguese passports were apparently to be permitted to retain them for travel purposes. The agreement guaranteed a 50-year period during which Macao would be permitted to retain its free capitalist economy, and to be financially independent of China.

In August 1988 a Macao Basic Law Drafting Committee was formed. Comprising 30 Chinese members and 19 representatives from Macao, the Committee was to draft a law determining the territory's future constitutional status within the People's Republic of China. Elections to the Legislative Assembly were held in October 1988. Low participation (fewer than 30% of the electorate) was recorded, and a 'liberal' grouping secured three of the seats reserved for directly-elected candidates, while a coalition of pro-Beijing and conservative Macanese (lusophone Eurasian) groups, won the other three.

In January 1989 it was announced that Portuguese passports were to be issued to about 100,000 ethnic Chinese inhabitants, born in Macao before October 1981, and it was anticipated that as many as a further 100,000 would be granted before 1999. Unlike their counterparts in the neighbouring British dependent territory of Hong Kong, therefore, these Macao residents (but not all) were to be granted the full rights of a citizen of the European Community (EC, now European Union—EU, see p. 199). In February 1989 President Mário Soares of Portugal visited Macao, in order to discuss the transfer of the territory's administration to China.

Following the violent suppression of the pro-democracy movement in China in June 1989, as many as 100,000 residents of Macao participated in demonstrations in the enclave to protest against the Chinese Government's action. The events in the People's Republic caused great concern in Macao. In August, however, China assured Portugal that it would honour the agreement to maintain the capitalist system of the territory after 1999.

In March 1990 the implementation of a programme to grant permanent registration to parents of 4,200 Chinese residents, the latter having already secured the right of abode in Macao, developed into chaos when other illegal immigrants demanded a similar concession. The authorities decided to declare a general amnesty, but were unprepared for the numbers of illegal residents, some 50,000 in total, who rushed to take advantage of the scheme, thereby revealing the true extent of previous immigration from China. Border security was subsequently increased, in an effort to prevent any further illegal immigration.

In late March 1990 the Legislative Assembly approved the final draft of the territory's revised Organic Law. The Law was approved by the Portuguese Assembly of the Republic in mid-April, and granted Macao greater administrative, economic, financial and legislative autonomy, in advance of 1999. The powers of the Governor and of the Legislative Assembly, where six additional seats were to be created, were therefore increased. The post of military commander of the security forces was abolished, responsibility for the territory's security being assumed by a civilian Under-Secretary.

Meanwhile, in February 1990, it was alleged that Carlos Melancia had accepted a substantial bribe from a foreign company in connection with a contract for the construction of the new airport in Macao. In September Melancia was served with a summons relating to the alleged bribery. Although he denied any involvement in the affair, the Governor resigned, and was replaced on an acting basis by the Under-Secretary for Economic Affairs, Dr Francisco Murteira Nabo. In September 1991 it was announced that Melancia and five others were to stand trial on charges of corruption. Melancia's trial opened in April 1993. In August the former Governor was acquitted on the grounds of insufficient evidence. In February 1994, however, it was announced that Melancia was to be retried, owing to irregularities in his defence case.

Meanwhile, many observers believed that the enclave was being adversely affected by the political situation in Lisbon, as differences between the socialist President and centre-right Prime Minister were being reflected in rivalries between officials in Macao. In an attempt to restore confidence, therefore, President Soares visited the territory in November 1990. In January 1991, upon his re-election as Head of State, the President appointed Gen. Vasco Rocha Vieira (who had previously served as the territory's Chief of Staff and as Under-Secretary for Public Works and Transport) Governor of Macao. In March 1991 the Legislative Assembly was expanded from 17 to 23 members. All seven Under-Secretaries were replaced in May.

Following his arrival in Macao, Gen. Rocha Vieira announced that China would be consulted on all future developments in the territory. The 10th meeting of the Sino-Portuguese JLG took place in Beijing in April 1991. Topics under regular discussion included the participation of Macao in international organizations, progress towards an increase in the number of local officials employed in the civil service (hitherto dominated by Portuguese and Macanese personnel) and the status of the Chinese language. The progress of the working group on the translation of local laws from Portuguese into Chinese was also examined, a particular problem being the lack of suitably-qualified bilingual legal personnel. It was agreed that Portuguese was to remain an official language after 1999. The two sides also reached agreement on the exchange of identity cards for those Macao residents who would require them in 1999. Regular meetings of the JLG continued.

In July 1991 the Macao Draft Basic Law was published by the People's Republic of China. Confidence in the territory's future was enhanced by China's apparent flexibility on a number of issues. Unlike the Hong Kong Basic Law, that of Macao did not impose restrictions on holders of foreign passports assuming senior posts in the territory's administration after 1999, the only exception being the future Chief Executive. Furthermore, the draft contained no provision for the stationing of troops from China in Macao after the territory's return to Chinese administration.

In November 1991 the Governor of Macao visited the People's Republic of China, where it was confirmed that the 'one country, two systems' policy would operate in Macao from 1999. In March 1993 the final draft of the Basic Law of the Macao SAR was ratified by the National People's Congress (NPC) in Beijing, which also approved the design of the future SAR's flag. The adoption of the legislation was welcomed by the Governor of Macao, who reiterated his desire for a smooth transfer of power in 1999. The Chief Executive of the SAR was to be selected by local representatives. The SAR's first Legislative Council was to comprise 23 members, of whom eight would be directly elected. Its term of office would expire in October 2001, when it would be expanded to 27 members, of whom 10 would be directly elected.

Meanwhile, elections to the Legislative Assembly were held in September 1992. The level of participation was higher than on previous occasions, with 59% of the registered electorate (albeit only 13.5% of the population) attending the polls. Fifty candidates contested the eight directly-elective seats, four of which were won by members of the main pro-Beijing parties, the União Promotora para o Progresso (UPP) and the União para o Desenvolvimento (UPD).

Relations between Portugal and China remained cordial. In June 1993 the two countries reached agreement on all outstanding issues regarding the construction of the territory's airport and the future use of Chinese air space. Furthermore, Macao was to be permitted to negotiate air traffic agreements with other countries. Later in the year visits by President Soares of Portugal to Macao and by the Chinese President, Jiang Zemin, to Lisbon took place. In February 1994 the Chinese Minister of Communications visited Macao to discuss with the Governor the progress of the airport project.

In April 1994, during a visit to China, the Portuguese Prime Minister received an assurance that Chinese nationality would not be imposed on Macanese people of Portuguese descent, who would be able to retain their Portuguese passports. Speaking in Macao itself, the Prime Minister expressed confidence in the territory's future. Regarding the issue as increasingly one of foreign policy, he stated his desire to transfer jurisdiction over Macao from the Presidency of the Republic to the Government, despite the necessity for a constitutional amendment.

In July 1994 a group of local journalists dispatched a letter, alleging intimidation and persecution in Macao, to President Soares, urging him to intervene to defend the territory's press freedom. The journalists' appeal followed an incident involving the director of the daily *Gazeta Macaense*, who had been fined for reproducing an article from a Lisbon weekly newspaper, and now faced trial. The territory's press had been critical of the Macao Supreme Court's decision to extradite ethnic Chinese to the mainland (despite the absence of any extradition treaty) to face criminal charges and a possible death sentence.

The draft of the new penal code for Macao did not incorporate the death penalty. In January 1995, during a visit to Portugal, Vice-Premier Zhu Rongji of China confirmed that the People's Republic would not impose the death penalty in Macao after 1999, regarding the question as a matter for the authorities of the future SAR. The new penal code, prohibiting capital punishment, took effect in January 1996.

On another visit to the territory in April 1995, President Soares emphasized the need for Macao to assert its identity, and stressed the importance of three issues: the modification of the territory's legislation; the rights of the individual; and the preservation of the Portuguese language. Travelling on to Beijing, accompanied by Gen. Rocha Vieira, the Portuguese President had successful discussions with his Chinese counterpart on various matters relating to the transition.

In May 1995, during a four-day visit to the territory, Lu Ping, the director of the mainland Hong Kong and Macao Affairs Office, proposed the swift establishment of a preparatory working committee (PWC) to facilitate the transfer of sovereignty. He urged that faster progress be made on the issues of the localization of civil servants and of the law, and on the use of Chinese as the official language. Lu Ping also expressed his desire that the reorganized legislative and municipal bodies to be elected in 1996–97 conform with the Basic Law.

In December 1995, while attending the celebrations to mark the inauguration of the territory's new airport, President Soares had discussions with the Chinese Vice-President, Rong Yiren. During a four-day visit to Beijing in February 1996, the Portuguese Minister of Foreign Affairs, Jaime Gama (who urged that the rights and aspirations of the people of Macao be protected), met President Jiang Zemin and other senior officials, describing the discussions as positive. While acknowledging the sound progress of recent years, Gama and the Chinese Minister of Foreign Affairs agreed on an acceleration in the pace of work of the Sino-Portuguese JLG. In the same month Gen. Rocha Vieira was reappointed Governor of Macao by the newly-elected President of Portugal, Jorge Sampaio. António Guterres, the new Portuguese Prime Minister, confirmed his desire for constitutional consensus regarding the transition of Macao.

At elections to the Legislative Assembly in September 1996 the pro-Beijing UPP received 15.2% of the votes and won two of the eight directly-elective seats, while the UPD won 14.5% and retained one of its two seats. The business-orientated groups were more successful: the Associação Promotora para a Economia de Macau took 16.6% of the votes and secured two seats; the Convergência para o Desenvolvimento (CODEM) and the União Geral para o Desenvolvimento de Macau each won one seat. The pro-democracy Associação de Novo Macau Democrático (ANMD) also won one seat. The level of voter participation was 64%. The 23-member legislature was to remain in place beyond the transfer of sovereignty in 1999.

In October 1996 Portugal and China announced the establishment of a mechanism for regular consultation on matters pertaining to international relations. In the same month citizens of Macao joined a flotilla of small boats carrying activists from Taiwan and Hong Kong to protest against a right-wing Japanese group's construction of a lighthouse on the disputed Diaoyu (or Senkaku) Islands, situated in the East China Sea (see the chapter on the People's Republic of China). Having successfully evaded Japanese patrol vessels, the protesters raised the flags of China and Taiwan on the disputed islands. In November activists from around the world attended a three-day conference in Macao, in order to discuss their strategy for the protection of the islands.

Meanwhile, the rising level of violent criminal activity had become a cause of increasing concern. During 1996 there were numerous bomb attacks and brutal assaults, including several serious attacks on local casino staff. Violent incidents continued in 1997, giving rise to fears for the future of the territory's vital tourism industry. Many attributed the alarming increase in organized crime to the opening of the airport in Macao, which was believed to have facilitated the entry of rival gangsters from mainland China, Taiwan and Hong Kong. In May, following the murder of three men believed to have associations with one such group of gangsters, the Chinese Government expressed its concern at the deterioration of public order in Macao and urged Portugal to observe its responsibility, as undertaken in the Sino-Portuguese joint declaration of 1987, to maintain the enclave's social stability during the transitional period, whilst pledging the enhanced co-operation of the Chinese security forces in the effort to curb organized crime in Macao.

The freedom of Macao's press was jeopardized in June 1997, when several Chinese-language newspapers, along with a television station, received threats instructing them to cease reporting on the activities of the notorious 14K triad, a 10,000-member secret society to which much of the violence had been attributed. In July an explosive device was detonated in the grounds of the Governor's palace, although it caused no serious damage. In the following month China deployed 500 armed police-officers to reinforce the border with Macao in order to intensify its efforts to combat illegal immigration, contraband and the smuggling of arms into the enclave. Despite the approval in July of a law further to restrict activities such as extortion and 'protection rackets', organized crime continued unabated. In early October the police forces of Macao and China initiated a joint campaign against illegal immigration.

Meanwhile, the slow progress of the 'three localizations' (civil service, laws and the implementation of Chinese as an official language) continued to concern the Government of China. In mid-1996 almost 50% of senior government posts were still held by Portuguese expatriates. In January 1997 the Governor pledged to accelerate the process with regard to local legislation, the priority being the training of the requisite personnel. In February President Sampaio travelled to both Macao and China, where he urged respect for Macao's identity and for the Luso-Chinese declaration regarding the transfer of sovereignty. In December 1997 details of the establishment in Macao of the office of the Chinese Ministry of Foreign Affairs, which was to commence operations in December 1999, were announced. In January 1998 the Macao Government declared that the vast

majority of senior civil service posts were now held by local officials.

In March 1998 the Chinese authorities reiterated their concern at the deteriorating situation in Macao. In April, by which month none of the 34 triad-related murders committed since January 1997 had been solved, the Portuguese and Chinese Governments agreed to co-operate in the exchange of information about organized criminal activities. Also in April 1998 the trial, on charges of breaching the gaming laws, of the head of the 14K triad, Wan Kuok-koi ('Broken Tooth'), was adjourned for two months, owing to the apparent reluctance of witnesses to appear in court. In early May Wan Kuok-koi was rearrested and charged with the attempted murder of Macao's chief of police, António Marques Baptista in a car-bomb attack. The case was dismissed by a judge three days later on the grounds of insufficient evidence. Wan Kuok-koi remained in prison, charged with other serious offences. His renewed detention led to a spate of arson attacks. The Portuguese Government was reported to have dispatched intelligence officers to the enclave to reinforce the local security forces. In June Marques Baptista travelled to Beijing and Guangzhou for discussions on the problems of cross-border criminal activity and drugs-trafficking.

The Preparatory Committee for the Establishment of the Macao SAR, which was to oversee the territory's transfer to Chinese sovereignty and was to comprise representatives from both the People's Republic and Macao, was inaugurated in Beijing in May 1998. Four subordinate working groups (supervising administrative, legal, economic, and social and cultural affairs) were subsequently established. The second plenary session of the Preparatory Committee was convened in July 1998, discussions encompassing issues such as the 'localization' of civil servants, public security and the drafting of the territory's fiscal budget for 2000. In July 1998, during a meeting with the Chinese Premier, the Governor of Macao requested an increase in the mainland's investment in the territory prior to the 1999 transfer of sovereignty.

In July 1998, as abductions continued and as it was revealed, furthermore, that the victims had included two serving members of the Legislative Assembly, President Jiang Zemin of China urged the triads of Macao to cease their campaign of intimidation. The police forces of Macao, Hong Kong and Guangdong Province launched 'S Plan', an operation aiming to curb the activities of rival criminal gangs. In August, in an apparent attempt to intimidate the judiciary, the territory's Attorney-General and his wife were shot and slightly wounded. In the following month five police-officers and 10 journalists who were investigating a bomb attack were injured when a second bomb exploded.

In August 1998 representatives of the JLG agreed to intensify Luso-Chinese consultations on matters relating to the transitional period. In September, in response to the increasing security problems, China unexpectedly announced that, upon the transfer of sovereignty, it was to station troops in the territory. This abandonment of a previous assurance to the contrary caused much disquiet in Portugal, where the proposed deployment was deemed unnecessary. Although the Basic Law made no specific provision for the stationing of a mainland garrison, China asserted that it was to be ultimately responsible for the enclave's defence. By October, furthermore, about 4,000 soldiers of the People's Liberation Army (PLA) were on duty at various Chinese border posts adjacent to Macao. During a one-week visit to Beijing, the territory's Under-Secretary for Public Security had discussions with senior officials, including the Chinese Minister of Public Security. In mid-October four alleged members of the 14K triad were detained without bail in connection with the May car-bombing and other incidents.

In November 1998 procedures for the election of the 200 members of the Selection Committee were established by the Preparatory Committee. Responsible for the appointment of the members of Macao's post-1999 Government, the delegates of the Selection Committee were required to be permanent residents of the territory: 60 members were to be drawn from the business and financial communities, 50 from cultural, educational and professional spheres, 50 from labour, social service and religious circles and the remaining 40 were to be former political personages.

In November 1998 raids on casinos believed to be engaged in illegal activities, conducted by the authorities, resulted in several arrests. Further violence took place in December. At the end of that month it was confirmed that Macao residents of wholly Chinese origin would be entitled to full mainland citizenship, while those of mixed Chinese and Portuguese descent would be obliged to decide between the two nationalities. In January 1999 several protesters were arrested during demonstrations to draw attention to the plight of numerous immigrant children, who had been brought illegally from China to Macao to join their legitimately-resident parents. The problem had first emerged in 1996 when, owing to inadequate conditions, the authorities had closed down an unofficial school attended by 200 children, who because of their irregular status were not entitled to the territory's education, health and social services.

In January 1999 details of the composition of the future PLA garrison were disclosed. The troops were to comprise solely ground forces, totalling fewer than 1,000 soldiers and directly responsible to the Commander of the Guangzhou Military Unit. They would be permitted to intervene to maintain social order in the enclave only if the local police were unable to control major triad-related violence or if street demonstrations posed a threat of serious unrest. In March, during a trip to Macao (where he had discussions with the visiting Portuguese President), Qian Qichen, a Chinese Vice-Premier, indicated that an advance contingent of PLA soldiers would be deployed in Macao prior to the transfer of sovereignty. Other sources of contention between China and Portugal remained the unresolved question of the post-1999 status of those Macao residents who had been granted Portuguese nationality and also the issue of the court of final appeal.

In April 1999, at the first plenary meeting of the Selection Committee, candidates for the post of the SAR's Chief Executive were elected. Edmund Ho received 125 of the 200 votes, while Stanley Au garnered 65 votes. Three other candidates failed to secure the requisite minimum of 20 votes. Edmund Ho and Stanley Au, both bankers and regarded as moderate pro-business candidates, thus proceeded to the second round of voting by secret ballot, held in May. Edmund Ho received 163 of the 199 votes cast, and confirmed his intention to address the problems of law and order, security and the economy. The Chief Executive-designate also fully endorsed China's decision to deploy troops in Macao.

During 1999, in co-operation with the Macao authorities, the police forces of Guangdong Province, and of Zhuhai in particular, initiated a new offensive against the criminal activities of the triads, which had been in regular evidence with further murders throughout the year. China's desire to deploy an advance contingent of troops prior to December 1999, however, reportedly continued to be obstructed by Portugal. Furthermore, the announcement that, subject to certain conditions, the future garrison was to be granted law-enforcement powers raised various constitutional issues. Some observers feared the imposition of martial law, if organized crime were to continue unabated. Many Macao residents, however, appeared to welcome the mainland's decision to station troops in the enclave. In a further effort to address the deteriorating security situation, from December 1999 Macao's 5,800-member police force was to be restructured.

In July 1999 the penultimate meeting of the JLG took place in Lisbon. In August, in accordance with the nominations of the Chief Executive-designate, the composition of the Government of the future SAR was announced by the State Council in Beijing. Appointments included that of Florinda da Rosa Silva Chan as Secretary for Administration and Justice. Also in August an outspoken pro-Chinese member of the Legislative Assembly was attacked and injured by a group of unidentified assailants. This apparently random assault on a serving politician again focused attention on the decline in law and order in the enclave. In September the Governor urged improved co-operation with the authorities of Guangdong Province in order to combat organized crime, revealing that the majority of the inmates of Macao's prisons were not residents of the territory. In the same month it was reported that 90 former Gurkhas of the British army were being drafted in as prison warders, following the intimidation of local officers. In September the Chief Executive-designate announced the appointment of seven new members of the Legislative Council, which was to succeed the Legislative Assembly in December 1999. While the seven nominees of the Governor in the existing Legislative Assembly were thus to be replaced, 15 of the 16 elected members (one having resigned) were to remain in office as members of the successor Legislative Council. The composition of the 10-member Executive Council was also announced.

In October 1999 President Jiang Zemin paid a two-day visit to Portugal, following which it was declared that the outstanding question of the deployment of an advance contingent of Chinese troops in Macao had been resolved. The advance party was to be restricted to a technical mission, which entered the territory in early December. In November the 37th and last session of the JLG took place in Beijing, where in the same month the Governor of Macao held final discussions with President Jiang Zemin.

Meanwhile, in April 1999 Wan Kuok-koi had been acquitted of charges of coercing croupiers. In November his trial on other serious charges concluded: he was found guilty of criminal association and other illegal gambling-related activities and sentenced to 15 years' imprisonment. Eight co-defendants received lesser sentences. In a separate trial Artur Chiang Calderon, a former police officer alleged to be Wan Kuok-koi's military adviser, received a prison sentence of 10 years and six months for involvement in organized crime. While two other defendants were also imprisoned, 19 were released on the grounds of insufficient evidence. As the transfer of the territory's sovereignty approached, by mid-December almost 40 people had been murdered in triad-related violence in Macao since January 1999.

In late November 1999 representatives of the JLG reached agreement on details regarding the deployment of Chinese troops in Macao and on the retention of Portuguese as an official language. At midnight on 19 December 1999, therefore, in a ceremony attended by the Presidents and heads of government of Portugal and China, the sovereignty of Macao was duly transferred; 12 hours later (only after the departure from the newly-inaugurated SAR of the Portuguese delegation), 500 soldiers of the 1,000-strong force of the PLA, in a convoy of armoured vehicles, crossed the border into Macao, where they were installed in a makeshift barracks. Prior to the ceremony, however, it was reported that the authorities of Guangdong Province had detained almost 3,000 persons, including 15 residents of Macao, suspected of association with criminal gangs. The celebrations in Macao were also marred by the authorities' handling of demonstrations by members of Falun Gong, a religious movement recently outlawed in China. The expulsion from Macao of several members of the sect in the days preceding the territory's transfer and the arrest of 30 adherents on the final day of Portuguese sovereignty prompted strong criticism from President Jorge Sampaio of Portugal. Nevertheless, in an effort to consolidate relations with the EU, in May 2000 the first official overseas visit of the SAR's Chief Executive was to Europe, his itinerary including Portugal. The EU agreed in principle in December 2000 to grant residents of Hong Kong and Macao visa-free access to member states, subject to final approval by the European Parliament.

Meanwhile, a spate of arson attacks on vehicles in February 2000 was followed by the fatal shooting, in a residential district of Macao, of a Hong Kong citizen believed to have triad connections. In March, in an important change to the immigration rules, it was announced that children of Chinese nationality whose parents were permanent residents of Macao would shortly be allowed to apply for residency permits. A monthly quota of 420 successful applicants was established, while the youngest children were to receive priority.

In May 2000 hundreds of demonstrators participated in a march to protest against Macao's high level of unemployment. This shortage of jobs was attributed to the territory's use of immigrant workers, mainly from mainland China and South-East Asia, who were estimated to total 28,000. During the ensuing clashes several police officers and one demonstrator were reportedly injured. Trade unions continued to organize protests, and in July (for the first time since the unrest arising from the Chinese Cultural Revolution of 1966) tear gas and water cannon were used to disperse about 200 demonstrators who were demanding that the immigration of foreign workers be halted by the Government. In the same month it was announced that, in early 2001, an office of the Macao SAR was to be established in Beijing, in order to promote links between the two Governments. In Guangzhou in August 2000, as cross-border crime continued to increase, senior officials of Macao's criminal investigation unit met with their counterparts from China and Hong Kong for discussions on methods of improving co-operation. It was agreed that further meetings were henceforth to be held twice a year, alternately in Beijing and Macao.

Celebrations to mark the first anniversary of the reversion to Chinese sovereignty were attended by Jiang Zemin, who made a speech praising Macao's local administration, but warning strongly against those seeking to use either of the SARs as a base for subversion. A number of Falun Gong adherents from

Hong Kong who had attempted to enter Macao for the celebrations were expelled. The same fate befell two Hong Kong human rights activists who had hoped to petition Jiang Zemin during his stay in Macao about the human rights situation in the People's Republic. A group of Falun Gong members in Macao, who held a protest the day before the Chinese President's arrival, were detained in custody and subsequently alleged that they had suffered police brutality.

In January 2001 China urged the USA to cease interfering in its internal affairs, following the signature by President Bill Clinton of the US Macao Policy Act, which related to the control of Macao's exports and the monitoring of its autonomy. In the same month voter registration began in Macao, in preparation for the expiry of the first Legislative Council's term of office in October and the election of a new assembly. In his Chinese Lunar New Year address on 23 January, Edmund Ho called for new efforts to revitalize the economy and achieve social progress.

The Governor of Guangdong Province, Lu Ruihua, made an official visit to Macao in early February 2001 to improve links between the two regions. At the same time, the Legislative Council announced plans to strengthen ties with legislative bodies in the mainland, and the President of the Legislative Council, Susana Chou, visited Beijing where she held discussions with Vice-Premier Qian Qichen. Also in February, a Macao resident was charged with publishing on-line articles about Falun Gong.

Edmund Ho visited Beijing in early March 2001 to attend the fourth session of the Ninth NPC, and held talks with President Jiang Zemin, who praised the former's achievements since the reversion of Macao to Chinese rule. On returning to Macao, Ho received the President of Estonia, Lennart Meri, who was touring the mainland and who thus became the first head of state to visit the SAR since its reversion to China. The two leaders discussed co-operation in the fields of tourism, trade, information technology and telecommunications, with Ho apparently seeking to learn from Estonia's experience in opening the telecommunications market. The EU announced in mid-March that SAR passport holders would, from May 2001, no longer require visas to enter EU countries. In the same month Jorge Neto Valente, a prominent lawyer and reputedly the wealthiest Portuguese person in Macao, was kidnapped by a gang, but freed in a dramatic police operation. The incident was the highest-profile kidnapping case in Macao since the return to Chinese rule.

The Macao, Hong Kong and mainland police forces established a working group in mid-March 2001 to combat cross-border crime, with a special emphasis on narcotics, and in late March the Macao, Hong Kong and Guangdong police forces conducted a joint anti-drugs operation, 'Spring Thunder', resulting in the arrest of 1,243 suspected traffickers and producers, and the seizure of large quantities of heroin, ecstasy, and marijuana. As part of the growing campaign against crime, a Shanghai court sentenced to death a Macao-based gangster, Zeng Jijun, on charges of running a debt-recovery group, members of which had committed murder. Three of Zeng's associates were given long prison sentences.

In May 2001 Macao and Portugal signed an agreement to strengthen co-operation in the fields of economy, culture, public security and justice during the visit of the Portuguese Minister of Foreign Affairs, Jaime Gama, the highest-ranking Portuguese official to visit Macao since its reversion to Chinese rule.

In early June 2001 Macao's Secretary for Security, Cheong Kuoc Va, visited Beijing and signed new crime-fighting accords aimed at reducing the trafficking of drugs, guns and people. In mid-June Chief Executive Edmund Ho made his first official visit to the headquarters of the EU in Brussels, where he sought to promote contacts and exchanges between the SAR and the EU.

China's most senior representative in Macao, Wang Qiren, died of cancer at the beginning of July 2001. Later in the month, another major campaign against illegal activities related to the triads was conducted by the Macao, Hong Kong and Guangdong police forces, and formed part of ongoing attempts to eradicate organized crime. At the end of the month, the Secretary for Security reported that cases of violent crime had declined by 37.3% year-on-year in the first half of 2001, and murders, robberies, arson, drug-trafficking and kidnapping had all decreased significantly over the same period. In a further sign of co-operation between Macao and the mainland against crime,

the two sides signed an agreement on mutual judicial co-operation and assistance in late August, the first of its kind.

In September 2001 José Proença Branco and Choi Lai Hang were appointed police commander and customs chief respectively. Following the terrorist attacks in New York and Washington, DC, on 11 September, several Pakistanis were detained in Macao; however, it was quickly announced that the detentions were not connected to the world-wide terrorist searches that had been initiated. In the mean time, the Macao, Hong Kong and Guangdong police departments began examining measures and directing activities aimed at fighting terrorism.

Elections to the Legislative Assembly (Council) were held on 23 September 2001, the first since Macao's reversion to Chinese rule. The number of seats was increased from 23 to 27: seven members were appointed by the Chief Executive, 10 elected directly and 10 indirectly. Of the 10 directly-elective seats, two seats each were won by the business-orientated CODEM, the pro-Beijing factions UPP and UPD and the pro-democracy ANMD. Two other factions won one seat each. Of the 10 indirectly-elective seats, four were won by the OMKC (a group representing business interests), and two seats each were one by the DCAR (a group representing welfare, cultural, educational, and sports interests), the CCCAE (a group representing labour), and the OMCY (a group representing professionals).

In mid-October 2001 China appointed Bai Zhijian as director of its liaison office in Macao, and later in the month Cui Shiping was selected as Macao's representative in the NPC, replacing the late Wang Qiren. At the same time, Edmund Ho attended the summit meeting of Asia-Pacific Economic Co-operation (APEC) in Shanghai, and the EU-Macao Joint Committee held a meeting in the SAR, aimed at improving trade, tourism and legal co-operation between the two entities. During late 2001, meanwhile, Macao increased co-operation with Hong Kong and the mainland in fighting crime and combating terrorism, amid reports that Russian mafias were becoming increasingly active in the SARs, and in mid-November the three police departments held an anti-drugs forum in Hong Kong. Later in the month, Edmund Ho announced that personal income tax would be waived and industrial and commercial taxes reduced for 2002, in order to alleviate the impact of the economic downturn. Ho also pledged to create 6,000 new jobs and invest more in infrastructure, and urged employers to avoid staff reductions.

In December 2001 the Government moved finally to break the 40-year monopoly on casinos and gambling held by Stanley Ho and his long-established company, the Sociedade de Turismo e Diversões de Macau (SDTM). Under the new arrangements, some 21 companies, none of which was Chinese-owned, were to be permitted to bid for three new operating licences for casinos in the SAR. The intention was to improve the image of the gambling industry, ridding the territory of its reputation for vice and making it more business- and family-orientated. Meanwhile, Stanley Ho's daughter Pansy was playing an increasingly prominent role in managing the family businesses (which included the shipping, property and hotel conglomerate, Shun Tak holdings); in December the group opened a new convention and entertainment centre.

Also in December 2001 Edmund Ho paid a visit to Beijing, where he and President Jiang Zemin discussed the situation in Macao. In early January 2002 Ho visited the mainland city of Chongqing, seeking to reinforce economic ties between the two places, and stating that Macao would play a more active role in developing the region. Also in January, the Government granted permission to the Taipei Trade and Cultural Office (TTCO) to issue visas for Taiwan-bound visitors from Macao and the mainland. In February Li Peng, Chairman of the Standing Committee of the NPC, paid an official visit to Macao, where he held discussions with the Chief Executive of the SAR. During Li's visit, a leading Macao political activist, along with several activists from the Hong Kong-based 'April 5th Action Group', were arrested for planning to stage protests against Li for his role in the Tiananmen Square suppression of 1989 and in favour of the release of mainland political dissidents. The Hong Kong activists were immediately deported. At the same time the Hong Kong media reported that a Hong Kong-based cameraman had been beaten and had his camera destroyed by a Macao policeman when he attempted to film the interception of the activists. Other journalists also claimed to have been treated aggressively, their allegations being disputed by the Macao police.

In early March 2002 a new representative office of the Macao SAR was established in Beijing, with the aim of enhancing ties between the SAR and the central Government and mainland. Wu Beiming was named as its director. At its inaugural ceremony, Edmund Ho and Chinese Vice-Premier Qian Qichen praised the 'one country, two systems' model, and the director of the central government liaison office in Macao, Bai Zhijian, suggested that Macao might become a model for Taiwan's eventual reunification with the mainland.

On 1 April 2002 Stanley Ho's STDM formally relinquished its 40-year monopoly on casinos. However, Ho retained influence in the gambling sector after his Macao Gaming Holding Company (SJM) won an 18-year licence to operate casinos (see Economy, below). Also in early April, Edmund Ho attended the first annual conference of the Boao Forum for Asia (BFA—a non-profit NGO), held on Hainan Island, China, where he met Hong Kong Chief Executive Tung Chee-hwa and Chinese Premier Zhu Rongji, as well as business leaders from both places.

The US Government in early April 2002 issued its second annual 'United States-Macao Policy Act Report'. This stated that the SAR continued to develop in a positive direction, citing its support for the USA's anti-terrorism campaign, the opening of the economy, the reorganization of its customs services, efforts to counter organized crime and the preservation of its own identity, including maintaining basic civil and human rights. As a result, Macao would continue to be accorded a special status distinct from mainland China under US law and policy. In the middle of the month the United Kingdom announced that it was granting visa-free access to holders of Macao SAR passports, and in late May the visiting Portuguese Minister of Foreign Affairs, António Martins da Cruz, also expressed confidence in Macao's future. In early June Macao hosted the Euro-China Business meeting, aimed at promoting small- and medium-sized enterprises in China to European investors. Also at this time, the Taiwanese Government eased restrictions on residents of Hong Kong and Macao applying for landing visas, essentially allowing those persons to obtain such visas on their first visit to Taiwan. However, in late July a Macao official criticized Taiwanese President Chen Shui-bian and accused him of seeking independence from the mainland.

In mid-June 2002 the Procurator-General, Ho Chio Meng, visited Portugal to promote judicial co-operation between the two territories, the first such visit by a Macao delegation since the territory's return to Chinese rule. Later in the month José Chu was appointed director of the Public Administration and Civil Services Bureau of the SAR.

Meanwhile, the Macao police force continued to maintain co-operation with Hong Kong and the mainland. In late June it was announced that almost 1,000 people had been arrested in Hong Kong during a one-month operation with the Macao police aimed at reducing cross-border and organized crime. At the end of July the Secretary for Security, Cheong Kuoc Va, stated that although overall crime had increased by 1.8% during the first half of the year, serious crimes had registered significant decreases.

In early July 2002 Beijing appointed Wan Yongxiang as the special commissioner of the Office of Special Commissioner of the Chinese Ministry of Foreign Affairs in the Macao SAR, succeeding Yuan Tao, who had held that post since 1999, when the office was established. At the end of July the Government announced the introduction of new identity cards, to be introduced in December 2002 over a period of four years. The cards were expected to function additionally as driving licences, border and medical access passes, and electronic payment methods.

The Russian Minister of Foreign Affairs, Igor Ivanov, visited Macao in late July 2002, mainly seeking to consolidate bilateral economic and trading relations, and to encourage Macao businesses to invest in Russia. In early August Edmund Ho visited the Chinese Autonomous Region of Nei Mongol (Inner Mongolia) to examine the possibility of developing links with the Sino-Russian border region, and later in the month he visited Guangzhou, in southern China, to discuss further economic co-operation and the joint development of Hengqin island (which is under the jurisdiction of Zhuhai City but located very close to Macao). In late September Ho visited Mozambique, where he and President Joaquim Alberto Chissano agreed to strengthen bilateral economic relations. At the same time, Secretary for Security Cheong Kuoc Va visited Portugal and signed security co-operation agreements aimed at combating transnational crime. In mid-October Edmund Ho visited the Republic of Korea (South Korea) and met President Kim Dae-Jung. While there, Ho sought increased investment and to promote tourism from

South Korea. The two leaders also agreed to extend reciprocal visa-free visits from a maximum of 30 days to 90 days, effective from January 2003.

In early December 2002 Macao selected its 12 candidates for the 10th National People's Congress, to be held in Beijing in March 2003. At the same time, Edmund Ho paid a routine visit to Beijing, where he held discussions with Jiang Zemin and Vice-President Hu Jintao. The Macao SAR and the EU signed a four-year legal co-operation programme in early December, aimed at consolidating Macao's legal system. In early January 2003 the Chairman of the National Committee of the Chinese People's Political Consultative Conference (CPPCC), Li Ruihuan, visited Macao and praised the way in which the territory had been administered. Observers noted that Beijing was more satisfied with the governance of the Macao SAR than that of Hong Kong.

Government

The Macao Special Administrative Region (SAR) is governed by a Chief Executive, who was chosen by a 200-member Selection Committee in May 1999. The Chief Executive is assisted by a number of Secretaries and is accountable to the State Council of China, the term of office being five years, with a limit of two consecutive terms. Upon the territory's transfer to Chinese sovereignty in December 1999, a 10-member Executive Council, appointed by the Chief Executive to assist in policy-making, assumed office. In 2001 the Legislative Council (commonly referred to as the Legislative Assembly) was expanded from 23 to 27 members, of whom 10 were directly elected, 10 indirectly elected and seven appointed by the Chief Executive, all with a mandate of four years. In 2005 the membership of the Legislative Council was to be increased to 29, to incorporate two additional deputies to be chosen by direct election. For the purposes of local government, the islands of Taipa and Coloane are administered separately.

Defence

The 1998 budget allocated 1,200m. patacas to Macao's security. Upon the territory's transfer of sovereignty in December 1999, troops of the People's Liberation Army (PLA) were stationed in Macao. The force comprises around 1,000 troops: a maximum of 500 soldiers are stationed in Macao, the remainder being positioned in China, on the border with the SAR. The unit is directly responsible to the Commander of the Guangzhou Military Region and to the Central Military Commission. The Macao garrison is composed mainly of ground troops. Naval and air defence tasks are performed by the naval vessel unit of the PLA garrison in Hong Kong and by the airforce unit in Huizhou. Subject to certain conditions, the garrison was granted law-enforcement powers, to assist the maintenance of public security.

Economic Affairs

In 2000, according to estimates by the World Bank, Macao's gross national income (GNI), measured at average 1998–2000 prices, was US $6,385m., equivalent to $14,580 per head (or $18,190 per head on an international purchasing-power parity basis). During 1990–2000, it was estimated, the population increased at an average annual rate of 1.7%, while gross domestic product (GDP) per head increased, in real terms, at an average annual rate of 0.8%. Overall GDP increased, in real terms, at an average annual rate of 2.6% in 1990–2000. In 2000 GDP increased by 4.6%. GDP growth subsequently decelerated to 2.1% in 2001, reflecting the global economic slowdown. Preliminary figures indicated that GDP had increased by 5%–6% in 2002.

Agriculture is of minor importance. The main crops are rice and vegetables. Cattle, pigs and chickens are reared.

Industry (including mining, manufacturing, construction and public utilities) accounted for 14.2% of total GDP in 2000 and employed 30.6% of the economically active population in 2001. The mining sector is negligible.

The manufacturing sector contributed 9.2% of total GDP in 2000 and engaged 21.7% of the economically active population in 2001. The most important manufacturing industry is the production of textiles and garments, which accounted for 61.0% of the value of total output in 2000. Exports of textiles and garments increased from 14,611.8m. patacas in 2000 to 15,325.2m. patacas in 2001. Other industries include toys, footwear, furniture and electronics.

Macao possesses few natural resources. Energy is derived principally from imported petroleum. Imports of fuels and lubricants accounted for 7.9% of total import costs in 2001. The territory receives some electricity and water supplies from the People's Republic of China.

The services sector accounted for 85.8% of GDP in 2000 and employed 69.4% of the economically active population in 2001. Tourism makes a substantial contribution to the territory's economy. Receipts from gambling taxes accounted for 60% of the Government's recurrent revenue in 2000. In that year, according to official figures, the tourism and gambling industries contributed an estimated 38% of GDP, while the 10 licensed casinos employed 6% of the labour force. The number of tourist arrivals increased steadily during the 1990s, with visitors from the People's Republic of China rising particularly rapidly. The number of tourist arrivals totalled 9.2m. in 2000, 10.3m. in 2001, and 11.5m. in 2002. Visitors from China and those from Hong Kong accounted for 36.8% and 44.2% respectively of the total of 11.5m. arrivals in 2002. Legislation regulating 'offshore' banking was introduced in 1987. It was hoped that the territory would develop as an international financial centre. The Financial System Act, which took effect in September 1993, aimed to improve the reputation of Macao's banks by curbing the unauthorized acceptance of deposits. A law enacted in April 1995 aimed to attract overseas investment by offering the right of abode in Macao to entrepreneurs with substantial funds (at least US $250,000) at their disposal. From December 1999, upon the territory's reversion to Chinese sovereignty, Macao administered its own finances and was exempt from taxes imposed by central government. The pataca was retained, remaining freely convertible.

In 2001 Macao recorded a trade deficit of 697.4m. patacas, compared with a surplus of 2,282.8m. patacas in 2000. The principal sources of imports in 2001 were the People's Republic of China (which supplied 42.6% of the total), Hong Kong (13.9%) and Taiwan (6.7%), followed by Japan. The principal market for exports was the USA (which purchased 48.2%), followed by the People's Republic of China (11.7%) and Hong Kong (6.4%). The main exports were textiles and garments (which accounted for 83.0% of the total), machines and apparatus, and footwear. The principal imports were raw materials for industry, fuels, foodstuffs and other consumer goods. In December 1999 Macao retained its status as a free port and remained a separate customs territory.

In 2001 a budgetary surplus of 420.8m. patacas was projected. The average annual rate of inflation (excluding rents) between 1990 and 1998 was 5.9%. The rate of inflation declined to only 0.2% in 1998. Deflation rates of 3.2% in 1999, 1.6% in 2000 and 3.3% in 2001 were recorded. The level of unemployment decreased from a peak of 7.1% of the labour force in early 2000 to 6.6% in the final quarter of 2000, according to official figures, and to 6.5% in the final quarter of 2001. The unemployment rate was estimated at 6.4% in late 2002. There is a shortage of skilled labour in Macao.

In 1991 Macao became a party to the General Agreement on Tariffs and Trade (GATT, now superseded by the World Trade Organization—WTO, see p. 322) and an associate member of the Economic and Social Commission for Asia and the Pacific (ESCAP). In June 1992 Macao and the European Community (now the European Union) signed a five-year trade and economic co-operation agreement, granting mutual preferential treatment on tariffs and other commercial matters. The agreement was extended in December 1997. Macao remained a 'privileged partner' of the EU after December 1999. Macao also retained its membership of WTO after December 1999.

After recording trade surpluses between 1998 and 2000, Macao's trade balance reverted to deficits in 2001 and 2002, as had been the case for most of the 1990s. Macao's trading position had been considerably weakened by the relative appreciation of the pataca against the currencies of its South-East Asian competitors. Attempts to diversify the economy in order to reduce dependence on tourism and the textile industry were made, although during the 1990s many non-textile operations were relocated to China and to South-East Asia, where labour costs were lower. Notably, Macao faced increasing competition from the nearby Zhuhai Special Economic Zone on the Chinese mainland. In 1993 the Macao Government announced a major land-reclamation programme, the 470,000-sq m Nam Van Lakes project, initially scheduled for completion in 2001, which was planned to enlarge the territory's peninsular area by 20%. The development was to incorporate residential and business accommodation for 60,000 people. The project was subsequently jeopardized by a sharp decline in the property market, which

remained depressed in 1999 and 2000. In 2002, however, the property market showed signs of recovery, with transactions increasing by 56.1% on an annual basis during the first three quarters of that year. The Nam Van Lakes scheme was just one of several large projects being developed in the SAR. Others included the 338m-high Macao Tower Convention and Entertainment Centre, which opened in December 2001, and the 140,000–sq m Fisherman's Wharf amusement park, a joint project between the STDM syndicate and the entertainment magnate, David Chow, to be completed in 2003. In August 2002 construction began on a new Macao Science Centre, and in late 2002 the authorities announced plans to build a light railway connecting the port areas with tourist zones. In October 2002 construction work began on a third bridge (22 km) linking Macao and Taipa Island, due for completion in 2004. The Government hoped that such public-works projects would create the new jobs necessary to reduce the relatively high level of unemployment. In December 2001 STDM lost its long-standing monopoly of the gambling industry (see Recent History). In its place the Government awarded casino-operating licences to three companies—Wynn Resorts (Macao) Ltd of the USA, the Galaxy Casino Co Ltd (a Hong Kong-Macao joint venture), and the Macao Gaming Holding Co (SJM—Sociedade de Jogos de Macau), a subsidiary of STDM. Gambling continued to be an important source of income for the SAR—the Government estimated that taxes from casinos would amount to 6,930m. patacas in 2003, or nearly half the Government's fiscal budget of 14,120m. patacas for that year. Tourism continued to be the best performing sector, with a record number of visitor arrivals in 2002. Further development of the hotel and tourism sector was envisaged, with a particular view to dispelling the territory's unsavoury reputation. The Chinese authorities also planned greater integration of Macao within the Zhujiang (Pearl River) Delta region, particularly with regard to infrastructural development. Among new schemes being considered in 2002 was a 29-km steel bridge linking Macao with Hong Kong's Lantau Island, and Zhuhai City, in Guangdong Province on the mainland. In early 2003 the authorities of the Macao SAR and the mainland Zhuhai Special Economic Zone planned jointly to develop a new industrial zone later that year. It was hoped that the new zone, located between Macao and Zhuhai, would bring benefits to both cities. Foreign investment rose sharply during the first half of 2002, totalling 1,000m. patacas, an increase of 20% year-on-year. In late 2002 the Government announced a series of tax reduction initiatives aimed at assisting the development of small- and medium-sized enterprises, to promote future growth. Preliminary figures showed that the economy had grown by between 5% and 6% in 2002, considerably more than in 2001. Prospects for 2003 also appeared favourable, with economic growth being forecast by the Government at 4%.

Education

The education system in Macao comprises: pre-school education (lasting two years); primary preparatory year (one year); primary education (six years); secondary education (five–six years, divided into junior secondary of three years and senior secondary of two–three years). Schooling normally lasts from the ages of three to 17. In 2001/02 schools enrolled a total of 99,990 pupils (including kindergarten 13,620; primary 43,886; secondary 41,840). From 1995/96 free education was extended from government schools to private schools. Private schools provide education for more than 90% of children. The majority of these schools have joined the free education system, and together with the government schools they form the public school system, in which all pupils from primary preparatory year up to the junior secondary level (10 years) receive free tuition. Based on the four years of free education, compulsory education was implemented from 1999/2000. In 2001/02 the enrolment rate was as follows: pre-school education and primary preparatory year 86.9% (some families leave their children in China); primary education 104.2%; secondary education (including vocational and technical) 82.0%; and higher education (24.4%). In higher learning, there are 12 public and private universities, polytechnic institutes and research centres. Some 12,749 students attended courses offered by those institutions in the academic year 2000/01, ranging from the bacharelato (three-year courses) to doctorate programmes. The University of Macao was inaugurated, as the University of East Asia, in 1981 (passing from private to government control in 1988), and had 3,314 students, with 231 teachers, in 1999/2000. The languages of instruction are primarily English, Cantonese and Portuguese. The 2001 budget allocated 565m. patacas to education and training (3.7% of total government expenditure).

Public Holidays

2003: 1 January (New Year), 1–4 February (Chinese Lunar New Year), 5 April (Ching Ming), 18–21 April (Easter), 1 May (Labour Day), 8 May (Feast of Buddha), 4 June (Dragon Boat Festival), 12 September (day following Chinese Mid-Autumn Festival), 1–2 October (National Day of the People's Republic of China and day following), 4 October (Festival of Ancestors— Chung Yeung), 2 November (All Souls' Day), 8 December (Immaculate Conception), 20 December (SAR Establishment Day), 22 December (Winter Solstice), 24–25 December (Christmas).

2004: 1 January (New Year), 22–25 January (Chinese Lunar New Year), 5 April (Ching Ming), 9–12 April (Easter), 1 May (Labour Day), 26 May (Feast of Buddha), 22 June (Dragon Boat Festival), 29 September (day following Chinese Mid-Autumn Festival), 1–2 October (National Day of the People's Republic of China and day following), 22 October (Festival of Ancestors— Chung Yeung), 2 November (All Souls' Day), 8 December (Immaculate Conception), 20 December (SAR Establishment Day), 22 December (Winter Solstice), 24–25 December (Christmas).

Weights and Measures

The metric system is in force.

Statistical Survey

Source (unless otherwise indicated): Direcção dos Serviços de Estatística e Censos, Alameda Dr Carlos d'Assumpção 411–417, Dynasty Plaza, 17° andar, Macao; tel. 728188; fax 561884; e-mail info@dsec.gov.mo; internet www.dsec.gov.mo.

AREA AND POPULATION

Area (2001): 25.80 sq km (9.96 sq miles).

Population: 435,235 (males 208,865, females 226,370) at census of 23 August 2001 (414,200 inhabitants were of Chinese nationality and 8,793 inhabitants were of Portuguese nationality); 436,686 (official estimate) at 31 December 2001.

Density (31 December 2001): 16,926 per sq km.

Births, Marriages and Deaths (2001): Registered live births 3,241 (birth rate 7.5 per 1,000); Registered marriages 1,222 (marriage rate 2.8 per 1,000); Registered deaths 1,327 (death rate 3.1 per 1,000).

Expectation of Life (years at birth, 1996–99): 77.7 (males 76.2; females 80.2).

Economically Active Population (2001): Manufacturing 44,055; Production and distribution of electricity, gas and water 1,020; Construction 16,897; Wholesale and retail trade; repair of motor vehicles, motorcycles and personal and household goods 30,196; Hotels, restaurants and similar activities 22,437; Transport, storage and communications 14,524; Financial activities 6,078; Real estate, renting and services to companies 10,733; Public administration, defence and compulsory social security 15,971; Education 8,117; Health and social work 5,069; Other community, social and personal service activities 22,143; Private households with employed persons 4,839; Others 728; Total employed 202,807.

HEALTH AND WELFARE

Key Indicators

Under-5 Mortality Rate (per 1,000 live births, 2001): 5.25.

HIV/AIDS (% persons aged 15–49, 2001): 0.004.

Physicians (per 1,000 head, 2001): 2.04.

Hospital Beds (per 1,000 head, 2001): 2.24.

Human Development Index (1999): value 0.867.
For definitions, see explanatory note on p. vi.

AGRICULTURE, ETC.

Livestock ('000 head, year ending September 2001): Poultry 600 (FAO estimate). Source: FAO.

Livestock Products ('000 metric tons, 2001): Beef and veal 1.0; Pig meat 7.7*; Poultry meat 4.8; Hen eggs 1.0*.
* FAO estimate.
Source: FAO.

Fishing (FAO estimates, metric tons, live weight, 2000): Marine fishes 1,020; Shrimps and prawns 230; Other marine crustaceans 210; Total catch (incl. others) 1,500. Source: FAO, *Yearbook of Fishery Statistics*.

INDUSTRY

Production (2000): Wine 414,492 litres; Knitwear 37.92m. units; Footwear 13.26m. pairs; Clothing 222.35m. units; Furniture 48,457 units; Electric energy (2001) 1,510.4 million kWh.

FINANCE

Currency and Exchange Rates: 100 avos = 1 pataca. *Sterling, Dollar and Euro Equivalents* (31 December 2002): £1 sterling = 12.947 patacas; US $1 = 8.033 patacas; €1 = 8.424 patacas; 1,000 patacas = £77.24 = $124.49 = €118.71. *Average Exchange Rate* (patacas per US dollar): 8.026 in 2000; 8.034 in 2001; 8.033 in 2002. Note: The pataca has a fixed link with the value of the Hong Kong dollar (HK $1 = 1.030 patacas).

Budget (million patacas, 2001, provisional): *Total revenue:* 15,641.6 (direct taxes 7,547.4; indirect taxes 840.8; others 7,253.4). *Total expenditure:* 15,220.8.

International Reserves (US $ million at 31 December 2001): Foreign exchange 3,508.4; Total 3,508.4. Source: IMF, *International Financial Statistics*.

Money Supply (million patacas at 31 December 2001): Currency outside banks 1,977.4; Demand deposits at commercial banks 4,020.8; Total money 5,998.2. Source: IMF, *International Financial Statistics*.

Cost of Living (Consumer Price Index; base: Oct. 1999–Sept. 2000 = 100): All items 99.49 in 2000; 97.52 in 2001; 94.94 in 2002.

Gross Domestic Product (million patacas at current prices): 49,071 in 1999; 49,742 in 2000; 49,802 in 2001.

Expenditure on the Gross Domestic Product (million patacas at current prices, 2001): Government final consumption expenditure 6,062.7; Private final consumption expenditure 20,625.4; Increase in stocks 71.9; Gross fixed capital formation 5,194.6; *Total domestic expenditure* 31,954.6; Exports of goods and services 48,678.5; Less Imports of goods and services 30,831.0; *GDP in purchasers' values* 49,802.1.

Gross Domestic Product by Economic Activity (provisional, million patacas at current prices, 2000): Mining and quarrying 3.3; Manufacturing 4,137.9; Electricity, gas and water supply 1,216.6; Construction 1,056.2; Trade, restaurants and hotels 4,581.5; Transport, storage and communications 3,240.2; Financial intermediation, real estate, renting and business activities 10,345.4; Public administration, other community, social and personal services (incl. gambling) 20,582.8; *Sub-total* 45,164.0; *Less* Financial intermediation services indirectly measured 2,427.4; *GDP at basic prices* 42,736.6; Taxes on products (net) 6,603.1; *GDP in purchasers' values* 49,339.6.

EXTERNAL TRADE

Principal Commodities (million patacas, 2001): *Imports c.i.f.:* (distribution by SITC): Food and live animals 1,098.7; Beverages and tobacco 1,448.9 (Beverages 1,055.9); Mineral fuels, lubricants, etc. 1,516.0 (Petroleum, petroleum products, etc. 1,204.4); Chemicals and related products 682.4; Basic manufactures 7,465.0 (Textile yarn, fabrics, etc. 6,750.4); Machinery and transport equipment 3,446.3 (Electrical machinery, apparatus, etc. 1,720.8, Transport equipment and parts 813.8); Miscellaneous manufactured articles 3,259.0 (Clothing and accessories 1,955.1); Total (incl. others) 19,170.4. *Exports f.o.b.:* Textile yarn and thread 856.7; Textile fabrics 1,266.5; Machinery and mechanical appliances 555.6; Clothing 13,202.0; Footwear 645.9; Total (incl. others) 18,473.0.

Principal Trading Partners (million patacas, 2001): *Imports c.i.f.:* Australia 226.9; China, People's Republic 8,164.7; France 805.7; Germany 457.4; Hong Kong 2,660.2; Italy 200.7; Japan 1,041.2; Korea, Republic 1,139.1; Singapore 510.3; Taiwan 1,278.2; United Kingdom 512.6; USA 796.8; Total (incl. others) 19,170.4. *Exports f.o.b.:* Canada 349.9; China, People's Republic 2,155.0; France 786.3; Germany 1,418.1; Hong Kong 1,177.6; Netherlands 596.5; United Kingdom 1,180.2; USA 8,907.1; Total (incl. others) 18,473.0.

TRANSPORT

Road Traffic (motor vehicles in use, Dec. 2001): Light vehicles 52,379; Heavy vehicles 4,136; Motorcycles 58,250.

Shipping (international sea-borne freight traffic*, '000 metric tons, 2001): Goods loaded 146.2; Goods unloaded 72.8.
* Containerized cargo only.

TOURISM

Visitor Arrivals by Country of Residence (2002): China, People's Republic 4,240,446; Hong Kong 5,101,437; Taiwan 1,532,929; Total (incl. others) 11,530,841.

COMMUNICATIONS MEDIA

Radio Receivers (1997): 160,000 in use.

Television Receivers (2000): 125,115 in use.

Daily Newspapers (2001): 11.

Telephones (Dec. 2002): 176,106 main lines in use.

Facsimile Machines (1999): 6,290 in use.

Mobile Cellular Telephones (2002): 276,138 subscribers.

Personal Computers (2001): 60,390 households.

Internet Users (2002): 41,517.

Sources: partly International Telecommunication Union and UNESCO, *Statistical Yearbook*.

EDUCATION

(2000/01)

Kindergarten: 60 schools; 551 teachers; 14,978 pupils.

Primary: 81 schools; 1,747 teachers; 45,474 pupils.

Secondary (incl. technical colleges): 48 schools; 1,753 teachers; 35,850 pupils.

Higher: 11 institutes; 923 teachers; 8,358 students.

Adult Literacy Rate: 93.7% in 1996.

Notes: Figures for schools and teachers refer to all those for which the category is applicable. Some schools and teachers provide education at more than one level. Institutions of higher education refer to those recognized by the Government of Macao Special Administrative Region.

Directory

The Constitution

Under the terms of the Basic Law of the Macao Special Administrative Region (SAR), which took effect on 20 December 1999, the Macao SAR is an inalienable part of the People's Republic of China. The Macao SAR, which comprises the Macao peninsula and the islands of Taipa and Coloane, exercises a high degree of autonomy and enjoys executive, legislative and independent judicial power, including that of final adjudication. The executive authorities and legislature are composed of permanent residents of Macao. The socialist system and policies shall not be practised in the Macao SAR, and the existing capitalist system and way of life shall not be changed for 50 years. In addition to the Chinese language, the Portuguese language may also be used by the executive, legislative and judicial organs.

The central people's Government is responsible for foreign affairs and for defence. The Government of Macao is responsible for maintaining social order in the SAR. The central people's Government appoints and dismisses the Chief Executive, principal executive officials and Procurator-General.

The Chief Executive of the Macao SAR is accountable to the central people's Government. The Chief Executive shall be a Chinese national of no less than 40 years of age, who is a permanent resident of the region and who has resided in Macao for a continuous period of 20 years. He or she is elected locally by a broadly-representative Selection Committee and appointed by the central people's Government.

The Basic Law provides for a 300-member Election Committee, which serves a five-year term. The Election Committee shall be composed of 300 members from the following sectors; 100 members from industrial, commercial and financial sectors; 80 from cultural, educational, and professional sectors; 80 from labour, social welfare and religious sectors; and 40 from the Legislative Council, municipal organs, Macao deputies to the National People's Congress (NPC), and representatives of Macao members of the National Committee of the Chinese People's Political Consultative Conference (NCCPPCC). The Selection Committee responsible for the choice of the Chief Executive in 1999 comprised 200 members; 60 representatives of business and financial circles; 50 from cultural, educational and professional circles; 50 from labour, social welfare and religious circles; and 40 former politicians and Macao deputies to the NPC and representatives of Macao members of the NCCPPCC. The term of office of the Chief Executive of the Macao SAR is five years; he or she may serve two consecutive terms. The Chief Executive's functions

include the appointment of a portion of the legislative councillors and the appointment or removal of members of the Executive Council.

With the exception of the first term (which was to expire on 15 October 2001), the term of office of members of the Legislative Council (commonly known as the Legislative Assembly) shall be four years. The second Legislative Council shall be composed of 27 members, of whom 10 shall be returned by direct election, 10 by indirect election and seven by appointment. The third and subsequent Legislative Councils shall comprise 29 members, of whom 12 shall be returned by direct election, 10 by indirect election and seven by appointment.

The Macao SAR shall maintain independent finances. The central people's Government shall not levy taxes in the SAR, which shall practise an independent taxation system. The Macao pataca will remain the legal currency. The Macao SAR shall retain its status as a free port and as a separate customs territory.

The Government

(April 2003)

Chief Executive: EDMUND H. W. HO.

Secretary for Administration and Justice: FLORINDA DA ROSA SILVA CHAN.

Secretary for Economy and Finance: FRANCIS TAM PAK YUEN.

Secretary for Security: CHEONG KUOC VA.

Secretary for Social and Cultural Affairs: FERNANDO CHUI SAI ON.

Secretary for Transport and Public Works: AO MAN LONG.

GOVERNMENT OFFICES

Office of the Chief Executive: Headquarters of the Government of the Macao Special Administrative Region, Av. da Praia Grande; tel. 726886; fax 726128; internet www.macau.gov.mo.

Office of the Secretary for Administration and Justice: Rua de S. Lourenço 28, Edif. dos Secretários; tel. 9895178; fax 726880; internet www.macau.gov.mo.

Office of the Secretary for Economy and Finance: Rua de S. Lourenço 28, Edif. dos Secretários; tel. 7978160; fax 726665.

Office of the Secretary for Security: Calçada dos Quarteis, Quartel de S. Francisco; tel. 7997510; fax 580702.

Office of the Secretary for Social and Cultural Affairs: Rua de S. Lourenço 28, Edif. dos Secretários; tel. 7978197; fax 725778.

Office of the Secretary for Transport and Public Works: Rua de S. Lourenço 28, Edif. dos Secretários, 1° andar; tel. 9895108; fax 727566.

Macao Government Information Bureau: Gabinete de Comunicação Social do Governo de Macau, Rua de S. Domingos 1, POB 706; tel. 332886; fax 336372; e-mail info@macau.gov.mo; internet www.macau.gov.mo; Dir VICTOR CHAN CHI PING.

Economic Services: Direcção dos Serviços de Economia, Rua Dr Pedro José Lobo 1–3, Edif. Luso Internacional, 25/F; tel. 386937; fax 590310; e-mail info@economia.gov.mo; internet www.economia.gov.mo.

EXECUTIVE COUNCIL

Members: FLORINDA DA ROSA SILVA CHAN, FRANCIS TAM PAK YUEN, CHEONG KUOC VA, FERNANDO CHUI SAI ON, AO MAN LONG, TONG CHI KIN (Spokesman), LEONG HENG TENG, VICTOR NG, LIU CHAK WAN, MA IAO LAI.

Legislature

LEGISLATIVE COUNCIL (LEGISLATIVE ASSEMBLY)

Following the election of 23 September 2001, the Legislative Assembly comprised 27 members: seven appointed by the Chief Executive, 10 elected directly and 10 indirectly. Members serve for four years. The Assembly chooses its President from among its members, by secret vote. At the election of September 2001, the business-orientated Convergência para o Desenvolvimento and União Geral para o Desenvolvimento de Macau (CODEM) each won two of the 10 directly-elective seats. The pro-Beijing candidates of the União Promotora para o Progresso (UPP) and of the União para o Desenvolvimento (UPD) won two seats each. The pro-democracy Associação de Novo Macau Democrático (ANMD) also took two seats. Four of the 10 directly-elective seats were taken by the OMKC, a group representing business interests. Groups representing various other interests occupied the remaining six seats. The Legislative Assembly was superseded, under the terms of the Basic Law, by the

Legislative Council. In practice, however, the legislature continues to be referred to as the Legislative Assembly.

Legislative Council (Legislative Assembly): Edif. da Assembléia Legislativa, Praça da Assembléia Legislativa, Aterros da Baía da Praia Grande; tel. 728377; fax 727857.

President: Susana Chou.

Political Organizations

There are no formal political parties, but a number of registered civic associations exist and may participate in elections for the Legislative Assembly by presenting a list of candidates. These include the União Promotora para o Progresso (UNIPRO), Associação Promotora para a Economia de Macau (APPEM), União para o Desenvolvimento (UPD), Associação de Novo Macau Democrático (ANMD), Convergência para o Desenvolvimento (CODEM), União Geral para o Desenvolvimento de Macau (UDM), Associação de Amizade (AMI), Aliança para o Desenvolvimento da Economia (ADE), Associação dos Empregados e Assalariados (AEA) and Associação pela Democracia e Bem-Estar Social de Macau (ADBSM). Civic associations that are considerably active in civic, educational, and charity activities and services are: Associação Geral dos Operários de Macau (General Workers' Association of Macao), União Geral das Associações dos Moradores de Macau (Union of Neighbourhood Associations), Instituto do Novo Macau (New Macao Institute), Santa Casa Misericórdia (Charity Organization), Tong Sin Tong (Charity Organization), and Associação dos Trabalhadores da Função Pública de Macau (Macao Civil Servants Association).

Judicial System

Formal autonomy was granted to the territory's judiciary in 1993. A new penal code took effect in January 1996. Macao operates its own five major codes, namely the Penal Code, the Code of Criminal Procedure, the Civil Code, the Code of Civil Procedure and the Commercial Code. In March 1999 the authority of final appeal was granted to the supreme court of Macao, effective from June. The judicial system operates independently of the mainland Chinese system.

Court of Final Appeal

Praçeta 25 de Abril, Edif. dos Tribunais de Segunda Instância e Ultima Instância; tel. 3984107; fax 326744.

Pres. Sam Hou Fai.

Procurator-General: Ho Chio Meng.

Religion

The majority of the Chinese residents profess Buddhism, and there are numerous Chinese places of worship, Daoism and Confucianism also being widely practised. The Protestant community numbers about 2,500. There are small Muslim and Hindu communities.

CHRISTIANITY

The Roman Catholic Church

Macao forms a single diocese, directly responsible to the Holy See. At 31 December 2000 there were 29,850 adherents in the territory.

Bishop of Macao: Rt Rev. Domingos Lam Ka Tseung, Paço Episcopal, Largo da Sé s/n, POB 324; tel. 309954; fax 309861; e-mail mdiocese@macau.ctm.net.

The Anglican Communion

Macao forms part of the Anglican diocese of Hong Kong (see p. 1137).

The Press

A new Press Law, prescribing journalists' rights and obligations, was enacted in August 1990.

PORTUGUESE LANGUAGE

Boletim Oficial: Rua da Imprensa Nacional, POB 33; tel. 573822; fax 596802; e-mail info@imprensa.macau.gov.mo; internet www.imprensa.macau.gov.mo; f. 1838; weekly govt gazette; Dir Dr António Gomes Martins.

O Clarim: Rua Central 26-A; tel. 573860; fax 307867; e-mail clarim@macau.ctm.net; f. 1948; weekly; Editor Albino Bento Pais; circ. 1,500.

Hoje Macau: Rua Francisco H. Fernandes 23, Edif. Walorly 13/AF; tel. 752401; fax 752405; e-mail hoje@macau.ctm.net; internet www.hojemacau.com; daily; Dir Carlos Morais José; circ. 1,000.

Jornal Tribuna de Macau: Av. Almeida Ribeiro 99, Edif. Comercial Nam Wah, 6 andar, Salas 603–05; tel. 378057; fax 337305; internet www.jtm.com.mo; f. 1998; through merger of Jornal de Macau (f. 1982) and Tribuna de Macau (f. 1982); daily; Dir José Firmino da Rocha Dinis; circ. 1,000.

MacaU: Livros do Oriente, Av. Amizade 876, Edif. Marina Gardens, 15E; tel. 700320; fax 700423; e-mail rclilau@macau.ctm.net; internet www.booksmacau.com; f. 1992; monthly magazine.

Ponto Final: Rua de Roma Kin Heng Long, Edif. Heng Hoi Kok, 10/F; tel. 339566; fax 339563; e-mail pontofin@macau.ctm.net; internet www.pontofinal.com.mo; Dir Ricardo Pinto; circ. 1,500.

CHINESE LANGUAGE

Boletim Oficial: see above.

Cheng Pou: Rua da Praia Grande 57–63, Edif. Hang Cheong, E–F; tel. 965972; fax 965741; daily; Dir Kung Su Kan; Editor-in-Chief Leong Chi Chun; circ. 5,000.

Jornal Informação: Rua de Fran António 22, 1° C, Edif. Mei Fun; tel. 561557; fax 566575; weekly; Dir Chao Chong Peng; circ. 8,000.

Jornal San Wa Ou: Av. Venseslau de Morais 221, Edif. Ind. Nam Fong, 2a Fase, 15°, Bloco E; tel. 717569; fax 717572; e-mail correiro@macau.ctm.net; daily; Dir Lam Chong; circ. 1,500.

Jornal 'Si-Si': Rua de Brás da Rosa 58, 2/F; tel. 974354; weekly; Dir and Editor-in-Chief Cheang Veng Peng; circ. 3,000.

Jornal Va Kio: Rua da Alfândega 7–9; tel. 345888; fax 580638; f. 1937; daily; Dir Chiang Sao Meng; Editor-in-Chief Tang Chou Kei; circ. 21,000.

O Pulso de Macau: Rua Oito do Bairro Iao Hon S/N; Edif. Hong Tai, Apt F0588 R/C; fax 400284; weekly; Dir Ho Si Vo.

Ou Mun Iat Pou (Macao Daily News): Rua Pedro Nolasco da Silva 37; tel. 371688; fax 331998; f. 1958; daily; Dir Lei Seng Chun; Editor-in-Chief Lei Pang Chu; circ. 100,000.

Semanário Desportivo de Macau: Estrada D. Maria II, Edif. Kin Chit Garden, 2 G–H; tel. 718259; fax 718285; weekly; sport; Dir Fong Sio Lon; Editor-in-Chief Fong Nim Lam; circ. 2,000.

Semenário Recreativo de Macau: Av. Sidónio Pais 31 D, 3/F A; tel. 553216; fax 516792; weekly; Dir. Ieong Cheok Kong; Editor-in-Chief Tong Iok Wa.

Seng Pou (Star): Travessa da Caldeira 9; tel. 938387; fax 388192; f. 1963; daily; Dir Kuok Kam Seng; Deputy Editor-in-Chief Tou Man Kum; circ. 6,000.

Sin Man Pou (Jornal do Cidadão): Rua dos Pescadores, Edif. Ind. Oceano, Bl. 11, 2/F–B; tel. 722111; fax 722133; f. 1944; daily; Dir and Editor-in-Chief Kung Man; circ. 8,000.

Tai Chung Pou: Rua Dr Lourenço; P. Marques 7A, 2/F; tel. 939888; fax 934114; f. 1933; daily; Dir Vong U. Kong; Editor-in-Chief Sou Kim Keong; circ. 8,000.

Today Macau Journal: Pátio da Barca 20, R/C; tel. 215050; fax 210478; daily; Dir Lam Vo I; Editor-in-Chief Iu Veng Ion; circ. 6,000.

NEWS AGENCIES

Associated Press (AP) (USA): POB 221; tel. 361204; fax 343220; Correspondent Adam Lee.

China News Service: Av. Gov. Jaime Silveiro Marques, Edif. Zhu Kuan, 14/F, Y/Z; tel. 594585; fax 594585.

LUSA (Agência de Noticias de Portugal): Av. Conselheiro Ferreira de Almeida 95-A; tel. 967601; fax 967605; e-mail lusa2@macau.ctm.net; internet www.lusamacau.com; Dir João Roque.

Reuters (United Kingdom): Rua da Alfândega 69; tel. 345888; fax 930076; Correspondent Harald Bruning.

Xinhua (New China) News Agency Macao SAR Bureau: Av. Gov. Jaime Silvério Marques, Edif. Zhu Kuan, 13 andar-V; tel. 727710; fax 700548; Dir Chen Boliang.

PRESS ASSOCIATIONS

Associação dos Jornalistas de Macau (Macao Journalists' Association): Rua Tomás Vieira, 70A R/C; tel. 921395; fax 921315; e-mail macauja@macau.ctm.net; internet home.macau.ctm.net/~macauja; f. 1999; Pres. Cheang Ut Meng.

Associação dos Trabalhadores da Imprensa de Macau: Travessa do Auto Novo 301–303, Edif. Cheng Peng; tel. 375245; Pres. Tang Chou Kei.

Clube de Jornalistas de Macau: Travessa dos Alfaiates 8–10; tel. 921395; fax 921315; e-mail cjm@macau.ctm.net; Pres. DAVID CHAN CHI WA.

Macao Chinese Media Workers Association: Travessa do Matadouro, Edif. 3, 3B; tel. 939486; Pres. LEE PANG CHU.

Publishers

Associação Beneficência Leitores Jornal Ou Mun: Nova-Guia 339; tel. 711631; fax 711630.

Fundação Macau: Av. República 6; tel. 966777; fax 968658; internet www.fmac.org.mo.

Instituto Cultural de Macau: see under Tourism; publishes literature, social sciences and history.

Livros do Oriente: Av. Amizade 876, Edif. Marina Gardens, 15 E; tel. 700320; fax 700423; e-mail rclilau@macau.ctm.net; internet www.loriente.com; f. 1990; publishes in Portuguese, English and Chinese on regional history, culture, etc; Gen. Man. ROGÉRIO BELTRÃO COELHO; Exec. Man. CECÍLIA JORGE.

Universidade de Macau—Centro de Publicações: POB 3001; tel. 3974506; fax 831694; e-mail PUB_GRP@umac.mo; internet www .umac.mo.pc; f. 1993; art, economics, education, political science, history, literature, management, social sciences, etc; Head Dr ZHENG DEHUA.

GOVERNMENT PUBLISHER

Imprensa Oficial: Rua da Imprensa Nacional s/n; tel. 573822; fax 596802; e-mail helpdesk@imprensa.macau.gov.mo.

Broadcasting and Communications

TELECOMMUNICATIONS

Companhia de Telecomunicações de Macau, SARL (CTM): Rua de Lagos, Edif. Telecentro, Taipa; tel. 833833; fax 8913031; e-mail mktg@macau.ctm.net; internet www.ctm.com.mo; holds local telecommunications monopoly; shareholders include Cable and Wireless (51%) and Portugal Telecom (28%); Chair. LINUS CHEUNG; CEO DAVID KAY; 1,000 employees.

Regulatory Authority

Office for the Development of Telecommunications and Information Technology (GDTTI): Av. da Praia Grande 789, 3/F; tel. 3969161; fax 356328; e-mail ifx@gdtti.gov.mo; internet www .gdtti.gov.mo.

BROADCASTING

Radio

Rádio Vila Verde: Macao Jockey Club, Taipa; tel. 822163; private radio station; programmes in Chinese; Man. KOK HOI.

Television

Teledifusão de Macau, SARL (TDM): Rua Francisco Xavier Pereira 157-A, POB 446; tel. 335888 (Radio), 519188 (TV); fax 520208; privately owned; two radio channels: **Rádio Macau** (Av. Dr Rodrigo Rodrigues, Edif. Nam Kwong, 7/F; fax 343220) in Portuguese, broadcasting 24 hours per day in Portuguese on **TDM Canal 1** (incl. broadcasts from RTP International in Portugal) and 17 hours per day in Chinese on **TDM Channel 2**; Chair. STANLEY HO; Exec. Vice-Chair. Dr MANUEL GONÇALVES.

Macao Satellite Television: Rua de Madrid S/N, Edif. Zhu Kuan, R/C, 'P'; tel. 786540; fax 752134; commenced transmissions in 2000; domestic and international broadcasts in Chinese aimed at Chinese-speaking audiences world-wide.

Macao is within transmission range of the Hong Kong television stations.

Cosmos Televisão por Satélite, SARL: Av. Infante D. Henrique 29, Edif. Va Iong, 4/F A; tel. 785731; fax 788234; commenced trial satellite transmissions in 1999, initially for three hours per day; by the year 2003 the company planned to provide up to six channels; Chair. NG FOK.

Finance

(cap. = capital; res = reserves; dep. = deposits; m. = million; brs = branches; amounts in patacas unless otherwise indicated)

BANKING

Macao has no foreign-exchange controls, its external payments system being fully liberalized on current and capital transactions. The Financial System Act, aiming to improve the reputation of the territory's banks and to comply with international standards, took effect in September 1993.

Issuing Authority

Autoridade Monetária de Macau (AMCM) (Monetary Authority of Macao): Calçada do Gaio 24–26, POB 3017; tel. 568288; fax 325432; e-mail amcm@macau.ctm.net; internet www.amcm.macau .gov.mo; f. 1989 as Autoridade Monetária e Cambial de Macau (AMCM), to replace the Instituto Emissor de Macau; govt-owned; Pres. ANSELMO L. S. TENG.

Banks of Issue

Banco Nacional Ultramarino (BNU), SA: Av. Almeida Ribeiro 22, POB 465; tel. 355111; fax 355653; e-mail markt@bnu.com.mo; internet www.bnu.com.mo; f. 1864; est. in Macao 1902; Head Office in Lisbon; agent of Macao Government; Gen. Man. Dr HERCULANO J. SOUSA; 10 brs.

Bank of China: Bank of China Bldg, Av. Dr Mário Soares; tel. 781828; fax 781833; e-mail bocmacau@macau.ctm.net; f. 1950 as Nan Tung Bank, name changed 1987; authorized to issue banknotes from Oct. 1995; Gen. Man. ZHANG HONGYI; 24 brs.

Other Commercial Banks

Banco da América (Macau), SA: Av. Almeida Ribeiro 70–76, POB 165; tel. 568821; fax 570386; f. 1937; fmrly Security Pacific Asian Bank (Banco de Cantão); cap. 100m., res 49.9m., dep. 1,061.3m. (Dec. 2001); Chair. SAMUEL NG TSIEN; Man. Dir KIN HONG CHEONG.

Banco Comercial de Macau, SA: Av. da Praia Grande 572, POB 545; tel. 7910000; fax 595817; e-mail bcmbank@bcm.com.mo; f. 1995; cap. 225m., res 316m., dep. 6,082m. (Dec. 2001); Chair. JORGE JARDIM GONÇALVES; CEO Dr MANUEL MARECOS DUARTE; 17 brs.

Banco Delta Asia, SARL: Av. Conselheiro Ferreira de Almeida 79; tel. 559898; fax 570068; e-mail contact@bdam.com; internet www .delta-asia.com; f. 1935; fmrly Banco Hang Sang; cap. 190.0m., res 50.6m., dep. 3,012.3m. (Dec. 2001); Chair. STANLEY AU; Exec. Dir PHILIP NG; 10 brs.

Banco Seng Heng, SARL: Seng Heng Bank Tower, Macao Landmark, Av. da Amizade 555; tel. 555222; fax 570758; e-mail sengheng@macau.ctm.net; internet www.senghengbank.com; f. 1972; cap. 150.0m., res 755.8m., dep. 11.9m. (Dec. 2001); Chair. STANLEY HO; Gen. Man. ALEX LI; 6 brs.

Banco Tai Fung, SARL: Tai Fung Bank Bldg, Av. Alameda Dr Carlos d'Assumpção 418; tel. 322323; fax 570737; e-mail tfbsecr@ taifungbank.com; internet www.taifungbank.com; f. 1971; cap. 1,000m., dep. 20,509m. (Dec. 2002); Chair. FUNG KA YORK; Gen. Man. LONG RONGSHEN; 20 brs.

Banco Weng Hang, SA: Av. Almeida Ribeiro 241; tel. 335678; fax 576527; e-mail wenghang@macau.ctm.net; internet www.whbmac .com; f. 1973; subsidiary of Wing Hang Bank Ltd, Hong Kong; cap. 120m., res 466m., dep. 7,452m. (Dec. 2001); Chair. PATRICK FUNG YUK-BUN; Gen. Man. and Dir LEE TAK LIM; 10 brs.

Guangdong Development Bank: Av. da Praia Grande 269; tel. 323628; fax 323668; Gen. Man. GUO ZHI-HANG.

Luso International Banking Ltd: Av. Dr Mário Soares 47; tel. 378977; fax 578517; e-mail lusobank@lusobank.com.mo; internet www.lusobank.com.mo; f. 1974; cap. 151.5m., res 184m., dep. 6,245.8m. (Dec. 2000); Chair. WONG XI CHAO; Gen. Man. IP KAI MING; 10 brs.

Foreign Banks

Banco Comercial Português (Portugal): Av. da Praia Grande 594, BCM Bldg, 12/F; tel. 786769; fax 786772; Gen. Man. MANUEL D'ALMEIDA MARECO DUARTE.

Banco Espírito Santo do Oriente (Portugal): Av. Dr Mário Soares 323, Bank of China Bldg, 28/F, E–F; tel. 785222; fax 785228; e-mail besor@macau.ctm.net; f. 1996; subsidiary of Banco Espírito Santo, SA (Portugal); Exec. Dir JOÃO MANUEL AMBRÓSIO; Man. Dir Dr LUÍS MORAIS SARMENTO.

Bank of East Asia Ltd (Hong Kong): Av. da Praia Grande 697, Edif. Tai Wah R/C; tel. 335511; fax 337557; Gen. Man. LAI TZE HIM.

BNP Paribas (France): Av. Central Plaza, 10/F, Almeida Ribeiro 61; tel. 562777; fax 560626; f. 1979; Man. SANCO SZE.

Citibank NA (USA): Rua da Praia Grande 251–53; tel. 378188; fax 578451; Pres. DANIEL CHOW SHIU LUN.

Finibanco (Macau) SA (Portugal): Av. Sa Praia Grande 811; tel. 322678; fax 322680.

The Hongkong and Shanghai Banking Corporation Ltd (Hong Kong): Av. da Praia Grande 639; tel. 553669; fax 315421; e-mail hsbc@macau.ctm.net; f. 1972; CEO THOMAS YAM.

International Bank of Taipei (Taiwan): Av. Infante D. Henrique 52–58; tel. 715175; fax 715035; e-mail tppmonx@macau.ctm.net; f. 1996; fmrly Taipei Business Bank; Gen. Man. KEVIN CHIOU.

Liu Chong Hing Bank Ltd (Hong Kong): Av. da Praia Grande 693, Edif. Tai Wah, R/C; tel. 339982; fax 339990; Gen. Man. LAM MAN KING.

Overseas Trust Bank Limited (Hong Kong): Rua de Santa Clara 5–7E, Edif. Ribeiro, Loja C e D; tel. 329338; fax 323711; e-mail otbmacau@macau.ctm.net; Senior Man. LAU CHI KEUNG.

Standard Chartered Bank (UK): 8/F Office Tower, Macao Landmark, Av. de Amizade; tel. 786111; fax 786222; f. 1982; Man. KIN YIP CHAN.

Banking Association

Associação de Bancos de Macau (ABM) (The Macao Association of Banks): Av. da Praia Grande 575, Edif. 'Finanças', 15/F; tel. 511921; fax 346049; Chair. ZHANG HONGYI.

INSURANCE

ACE Seguradora, SA: Rua Dr. Pedro José Lobo 1–3, Luso Bank Bldg, 17/F, Apt 1701–02; tel. 557191; fax 570188; Rep. ANDY AU.

AIA Co (Bermuda) Ltd: Central Plaza, 13/F, Av. Almeida Ribeiro 61; tel. 9881888; fax 315900; Rep. ALEXANDRA FOO.

American Home Assurance Co: Av. Almeida Ribeiro 61, Central Plaza, 15/F, 'G'.

American International Assurance Co: Av. Almeida Ribeiro 61, Central Plaza, 13/F; tel. 9881888; fax 315900; life insurance; Rep. ALEXANDRA FOO CHEUK LING.

Asia Insurance Co Ltd: Rua do Dr Pedro José Lobo 1–3, Luso International Bank Bldg, 11/F, Units 1103–04; tel. 570439; fax 570438; non-life insurance; Rep. S. T. CHAN.

AXA China Region Insurance Company: Rua de Xangai 175, Edif. da Associação Comercial de Macau, 17/F; tel. 781188; fax 780022; life insurance; Rep. KANE CHOW.

CGU International Insurance plc: Av. da Praia Grande 693, Edif. Tai Wah A & B, 13/F; tel. 923329; fax 923349; non-life insurance; Man. VICTOR WU.

China Insurance Co Ltd: Av. Dr. Rodrigo Rodrigues, Edif. Seguros da China, 19/F; non-life insurance.

China Life Insurance Co Ltd: Av. Dr Rodrigo Rodrigues Quarteirão 11, Lote A, Zape, China Insurance Bldg, 15/F; tel. 558918; fax 787287; e-mail cic@macau.ctm.net; Rep. CHENG MINGJIN.

Companhia de Seguros Fidelidade: Av. Almeida Ribeiro 22–38 (BNU); tel. 374072; fax 511085; life and non-life insurance; Man. LEONEL ALBERTO RANGE RODRIGUES.

Companhia de Seguros de Macau, SARL: Av. da Praia Grande 57, Centro Comercial Praia Grande, 18/F; tel. 555078; fax 551074; Gen. Man. IVAN CHEUNG.

Companhia de Seguros Delta SA: Av. da Praia Grande 369–71, Edif. Keng Ou, 13/F, D; tel. 337036; fax 337037; Rep. JOHNNY CHENG.

Crown Life Insurance Co: Av. da Praia Grande 287, Nam Yuet Commercial Centre, Bl. B, 8/F; tel. 570828; fax 570844; Rep. STEVEN SIU.

HSBC Insurance (Asia) Ltd: Av. da Praia Grande 619, Edif. Comercial Si Toi, 1/F, ; tel. 212323; fax 217162; non-life insurance; Rep. NORA CHIO.

Ing Life Insurance Co (Macao) Ltd: Av. Almeida Ribeiro 61, 11/F, Unit C and D; tel. 9886060; fax 9886100; Man. STEVEN CHIK YIU KAI.

Insurance Co of North America: Av. Almeida Ribeiro 32, Tai Fung Bank Bldg, Rm 806–7; tel. 557191; fax 570188; Rep. JOSEPH LO.

Luen Fung Hang Insurance Co Ltd: Rua de Pequim 202A–246, Macao Finance Centre, 6/F–A; tel. 700033; fax 700088; e-mail lfhins@macau.ctm.net; internet www.lfhins.com; non-life insurance; Rep. SI CHI HOK.

Macao Insurance Co: Av. da Praia Grande 429, Centro Comercial da Praia Grande, 18/F; non-life insurance.

Macao Life Insurance Co: Av. da Praia Grande 429, Centro Comercial da Praia Grande, 18/F; tel. 555078; fax 551074; Rep. MANUEL BALCÃO REIS.

Manulife (International) Ltd: Av. da Praia Grande 517, Edif. Comercial Nam Tung, 8/F, Unit B & C; tel. 3980388; fax 323312; internet www.manulife.com.hk; Rep. DANIEL TANG.

MassMutual Asia Ltd: Av. da Praia Grande 517, Edif. Nam Tung 16, 6/F; life insurance.

Min Xin Insurance Co Ltd: Rua do Dr Pedro José Lobo 1–3, Luso International Bank Bldg, 27/F, Rm 2704; tel. 305684; fax 305600; non-life insurance; Rep. PETER CHAN.

Mitsui Sumitomo Insurance Co Ltd: Rua Dr Pedro José Lobo 1–3, Edif. Banco Luso, 12/F, Apartment 1202; tel. 385917; fax 596667; non-life insurance; Rep. TAKAO YASUKOCHI.

QBE Insurance (International) Ltd: Av. da Praia Grande 369–71, Edif. Keng On 'B', 9/F; tel. 323909; fax 323911; non-life insurance; Rep. SALLY SIU.

The Wing On Fire & Marine Insurance Co Ltd: Av. Almeida Ribeiro 61, Central Plaza, 7/F, Block E; tel. 356688; fax 333710; non-life insurance; Rep. CHIANG AO LAI LAI.

Winterthur Swiss Insurance (Macao) Ltd: Av. da Praia Grande 599, Edif. Comercial Rodrigues, 10/F, C; tel. 356618; fax 356800; non-life insurance; Man. ALLAN YU KIN NAM.

Insurers' Association

Federation of Macao Professional Insurance Intermediaries: Rua de Pequim 244–46, Macao Finance Centre, 6/F, G; tel. 703268; fax 703266; Rep. DAVID KONG.

Macao Insurance Agents and Brokers Association: Av. da Praia Grande 309, Nam Yuet Commercial Centre, 8/F, D; tel. 378901; fax 570848; Rep. JACK LI KWOK TAI.

Macao Insurers' Association: Av. da Praia Grande 575, Edif. 'Finanças', 15/F; tel. 511923; fax 337531; e-mail minsa@macau.ctm.net; Pres. VICTOR WU.

Trade and Industry

CHAMBER OF COMMERCE

Associação Comercial de Macau: Rua de Xangai 175, Edif. ACM, 5/F; tel. 576833; fax 594513; Pres. MA MAN KEI.

INDUSTRIAL AND TRADE ASSOCIATIONS

Associação dos Construtores Civis (Association of Building Development Cos): Rua do Campo 9–11; tel. 323854; fax 345710; Pres. CHUI TAK KEI.

Associação dos Exportadores e Importadores de Macau: Av. Infante D. Henrique 60–62, Centro Comercial 'Central', 3/F; tel. 375859; fax 512174; e-mail aeim@macau.ctm.net; exporters' and importers' asscn; Pres. VITOR NG.

Associação dos Industriais de Tecelagem e Fiação de Lã de Macau (Macao Weaving and Spinning of Wool Manufacturers' Asscn): Av. da Amizade 271, Edif. Kam Wa Kok, 6/F–A; tel. 553378; fax 511105; Pres. WONG SHOO KEE.

Associação Industrial de Macau: Rua Dr Pedro José Lobo 34–36, Edif. AIM, 17/F, POB 70; tel. 574125; fax 578305; e-mail aim@macau.ctm.net; internet www.madeinmacau.net; f. 1959; Pres. PETER PAN.

Centro de Produtividade e Transferência de Tecnologia de Macau (Macao Productivity and Technology Transfer Centre): Rua de Xangai 175, Edif. ACM, 6/F; tel. 781313; fax 788233; e-mail cpttm@cpttm.org.mo; internet www.cpttm.org.mo; vocational or professional training; Dir Dr ERIC YEUNG.

Euro-Info Centre Macao: Av. Sidónio Pais 1-A, Edif. Tung Hei Kok, R/C; tel. 713338; fax 713339; e-mail eic@macau.ctm.net; internet www.ieem.org.mo/eic/eicmacau.html; promotes trade with EU; Man. SAM LEI.

Instituto de Promoção do Comércio e do Investimento de Macau (IPIM) (Macao Trade and Investment Promotion Institute): Av. da Amizade 918, World Trade Center Bldg, 3/F–4/F; tel. 710300; fax 590309; e-mail ipim@ipim.gov.mo; internet www.ipim.gov.mo; Pres. LEE PENG HONG.

SPIC (Concordia Industrial Park Ltd): Av. da Amizade 918, World Trade Center Bldg, 13/F A & B; tel. 786636; fax 785374; e-mail spic@macau.ctm.net; internet www.concordia-park.com; f. 1993; industrial park, promotion of investment and industrial diversification; Pres. of the Bd PAULINA Y. ALVES DOS SANTOS.

World Trade Center Macao, SARL: Av. da Amizade 918, Edif. World Trade Center, 16/F–19/F; tel. 727666; fax 727633; e-mail wtcmc@macau.ctm.net; internet www.wtc-macau.com; f. 1995; trade information and business services, office rentals, exhibition and conference facilities; Man. Dir Dr ANTÓNIO LEÇA DA VEIGA PAZ.

UTILITIES

Electricity

Companhia de Electricidade de Macau, SARL (CEM): Estrada D. Maria II 32–36, Edif. CEM; tel. 339933; fax 719760; f. 1972; sole distributor; Pres. Eng. CUSTÓDIO MIGUENS.

Water

Sociedade de Abastecimento de Aguas de Macau, SARL (SAAM): Av. do Conselheiro Borja 718; tel. 233332; fax 234660; e-mail info@saam.com.mo; internet www.saam.com.mo; f. 1984 as jt venture with Suez Lyonnaise des Eaux; Dir-Gen. JIM CONLON.

TRADE UNIONS

Macao Federation of Trade Unions: Rua Ribeira do Patane 2; tel. 576231; fax 553110; Pres. TONG SENG CHUN.

Transport

RAILWAYS

There are no railways in Macao. A plan to connect Macao with Zhuhai and Guangzhou (People's Republic of China) is under consideration. Construction of the Zhuhai–Guangzhou section was under way in 2001. In late 2002 the authorities announced plans to build a light railway connecting the port areas with tourism areas; however, these were suspended in early 2003.

ROADS

In 2000 the public road network extended to 324.2 km. The peninsula of Macao is linked to the islands of Taipa and Coloane by two bridges and by a 2.2-km causeway respectively. The first bridge (2.6 km) opened in 1974. In conjunction with the construction of an airport on Taipa (see below), a new 4.4-km four-lane bridge to the mainland was opened in April 1994. A second connection to the mainland, the 1.5-km six-lane road bridge (the Lotus Bridge) linking Macao with Hengqin Island (in Zhuhai, Guangdong Province), opened to traffic in December 1999. A new 29-km steel bridge linking Macao with Hong Kong's Lantau Island and Zhuhai City, Guangdong Province, was being planned in 2001, with studies being carried out to determine the project's financial and technological feasibility.

SHIPPING

There are representatives of shipping agencies for international lines in Macao. There are passenger and cargo services to the People's Republic of China. Regular services between Macao and Hong Kong are run by the Hong Kong-based **New World First Ferry** and **Shun Tak–China Travel Ship Management Ltd** companies. The principal services carried 7.4m. passengers in 1997. A new terminal opened in late 1993. The new port of Kao-ho (on the island of Coloane), which handles cargo and operates container services, entered into service in 1991.

CTS Parkview Holdings Ltd: Av. Amizade, Porto Exterior, Terminal Marítimo de Macau, Sala 2006B; tel. 726789; fax 727112; purchased by STDM in 1998.

STDM Shipping Dept: Av. da Amizade Terminal Marítimo do Porto Exterior; tel. 726111; fax 726234; affiliated to Sociedade de Turismo e Diversões de Macau; Gen. Man. ALAN HO; Exec. Man. Capt. AUGUSTO LIZARDO.

Association

Associação de Agências de Navegação e Congêneres de Macau: Av. Horta e Costa 7D–E, POB 6133; tel. 528207; fax 302667; Pres. VONG KOK SENG.

Port Authority

Capitania dos Portos de Macau: Rampa da Barra, Quartel dos Mouros, POB 47; tel. 559922; fax 511986; e-mail webmaster@marine .gov.mo; internet www.marine.gov.mo.

CIVIL AVIATION

In August 1987 plans were approved for the construction of an international airport, on reclaimed land near the island of Taipa, and work began in 1989. The final cost of the project was 8,900m. patacas. Macao International Airport was officially opened in December 1995. In 2001 the airport handled a total of 3,805,306 passengers. The terminal has the capacity to handle 6m. passengers a year. Between January and December 2001 76,076 tons of cargo were processed. By 2001 a total of 11 airlines operated 507 scheduled flights weekly to 22 destinations, mostly in China, but also to the Democratic People's Republic of Korea, the Philippines, Singapore, Taiwan, and Thailand. A helicopter service between Hong Kong and Macao commenced in 1990: East Asia Airlines transported a total of 72,579 helicopter passengers in 1999.

AACM (Civil Aviation Authority Macao): Rua Dr Pedro José Lobo 1–3, Luso International Bldg, 26/F; tel. 511213; fax 338089; e-mail aacm@macau.ctm.net; internet www.macau-airport.gov.mo; f. 1991; Pres. RUI ALFREDO BALACÓ MOREIRA.

Administração de Aeroportos, Lda (ADA): Av. de João IV, Centro Comercial Iat Teng Hou, 5/F; tel. 711808; fax 711803; e-mail adamkt@macau.ctm.net; internet www.ada.com.mo; airport administration; Chair. DUNG JUN; Dir CARLOS SERUCA SALGADO.

CAM (Sociedade do Aeroporto Internacional de Macau, SARL): Av. Dr Mário Soares, Bank of China Bldg, 29/F; tel. 785448; fax 785465; e-mail cam@macau.ctm.net; internet www.macau-airport.gov.mo; f. 1989; airport owner, responsible for design, construction, development and international marketing of Macao International Airport; Chair. Eng. JOÃO MANUEL DE SOUZA MOREIRA.

Air Macau: Av. da Praia Grande 693, Edif. Tai Wah, 9/F–12/F, POB 1910; tel. 3966888; fax 3966866; e-mail airmacau@airmacau.com .mo; internet www.airmacau.com.mo; f. 1994; controlled by China National Aviation Corporation (Group) Macao Co Ltd; services to several cities in the People's Republic of China, the Republic of Korea, the Philippines, Taiwan and Thailand; other destinations planned; Chair. GU TIEFEI; Pres. SUN BO.

Tourism

Tourism is now a major industry, a substantial portion of the Government's revenue being derived from the territory's casinos. The other attractions are the cultural heritage and museums, dog-racing, horse-racing, and annual events such as Chinese New Year (January/February), the Macao Arts Festival (February/March), Dragon Boat Festival (May/June), the Macao International Fireworks Festival (September/October), the International Music Festival, (October) the Macao Grand Prix for racing cars and motorcycles (November) and the Macao International Marathon (December). At the end of 2001 there were 25 hotels of two-stars and above. A total of 9,030 hotel rooms were available in 2001. Average per caput visitor spending in that year was 1,389 patacas. Total visitor arrivals rose from 10.3m. in 2001 to 11.5m. in 2002. Of the latter figure, 5.1m. were arrivals from Hong Kong and 4.2m. from the People's Republic of China.

Macao Government Tourist Office (MGTO): Direcção dos Serviços de Turismo, Largo do Senado 9, Edif. Ritz, POB 3006; tel. 315566; fax 510104; e-mail mgto@macautourism.gov.mo; internet www.macautourism.gov.mo; Dir Eng. JOÃO MANUEL COSTA ANTUNES.

Instituto Cultural de Macau: Praçeta de Miramar 87U, Edif. San On; tel. 700391; fax 700405; e-mail postoffice@icm.gov.mo; internet www.icm.gov.mo; f. 1982; organizes performances, concerts, exhibitions, festivals, etc; library facilities; Pres. HEIDI HO.

Macao Hotels Association: Rua Luís Gonzaga Gomes s/n, Bl. IV, r/c, Centro de Actividades Turísticas, Cabinet A; tel. 703416; fax 703415.

Sociedade de Turismo e Diversões de Macau (STDM), SARL: Hotel Lisboa, 9F, Old Wing, POB 3036; tel. 566065; fax 371981; e-mail stdmmdof@macau.ctm.net; operates 10 casinos, five hotels, tour companies, helicopter and jetfoil services from Hong Kong, etc. Man. Dir Dr STANLEY HO.

CHINA (TAIWAN)

Introductory Survey

Location, Climate, Language, Religion, Flag, Capital

The Republic of China has, since 1949, been confined mainly to the province of Taiwan (comprising one large island and several much smaller ones), which lies off the south-east coast of the Chinese mainland. The territory under the Republic's effective jurisdiction consists of the island of Taiwan (also known as Formosa) and nearby islands, including the P'enghu (Pescadores) group, together with a few other islands which lie just off the mainland and form part of the province of Fujian (Fukien), west of Taiwan. The largest of these is Kinmen (Jinmen), also known as Quemoy, which (with three smaller islands) is about 10 km from the port of Xiamen (Amoy), while five other islands under Taiwan's control, mainly Matsu (Mazu), lie further north, near Fuzhou. Taiwan itself is separated from the mainland by the Taiwan (Formosa) Strait, which is about 130 km (80 miles) wide at its narrowest point. The island's climate is one of rainy summers and mild winters. Average temperatures are about 15°C (59°F) in the winter and 26°C (79°F) in the summer. The average annual rainfall is 2,580 mm (102 in). The official language is Northern Chinese (Mandarin), but Taiwanese, a dialect based on the language of Fujian Province, is widely spoken. The predominant religions are Buddhism and Daoism (Taoism), but there are also adherents of I-kuan Tao, Christianity (mainly Roman Catholics and Protestants) and Islam. The philosophy of Confucianism has a large following. The national flag (proportions 2 by 3) is red, with a dark blue rectangular canton, containing a white sun, in the upper hoist. The capital is Taipei.

Recent History

China ceded Taiwan to Japan in 1895. The island remained under Japanese rule until the end of the Second World War in 1945, when it was returned to Chinese control, becoming a province of the Republic of China, then ruled by the Kuomintang (KMT, Nationalist Party). The leader of the KMT was Gen. Chiang Kai-shek, President of the Republic since 1928. The KMT Government's forces were defeated in 1949 by the Communist revolution in China. President Chiang and many of his supporters withdrew from the Chinese mainland to Taiwan, where they established a KMT regime in succession to their previous all-China administration. This regime continued to assert that it was the rightful Chinese Government, in opposition to the People's Republic of China, proclaimed by the victorious Communists in 1949. The Nationalists successfully resisted attacks by their Communist rivals, and declared that they intended to recover control of mainland China.

Although its effective control was limited to Taiwan, the KMT regime continued to be dominated by politicians who had formerly been in power on the mainland. Unable to replenish their mainland representation, the National Assembly (last elected fully in 1947) and other legislative organs extended their terms of office indefinitely, although fewer than half of the original members were alive on Taiwan by the 1980s. The political domination of the island by immigrants from the mainland caused some resentment among native Taiwanese, and led to demands for increased democratization and for the recognition of Taiwan as a state independent of China. The KMT, however, consistently rejected demands for independence, restating the party's long-standing policy of seeking political reunification, although under KMT terms, with the mainland.

The KMT regime continued to represent China at the United Nations (and as a permanent member of the UN Security Council) until October 1971, when it was replaced by the People's Republic. Nationalist China was subsequently expelled from several other international organizations. In November 1991, however, as 'Chinese Taipei', Taiwan joined the Asia-Pacific Economic Co-operation forum (APEC). In September 1992, under the name of the 'Separate Customs Territory of Taiwan, P'enghu, Kinmen and Matsu', Taiwan was granted observer status at the General Agreement on Tariffs and Trade (GATT), and in 2001 the island's application for full membership of the successor World Trade Organization (WTO) was well approved. In June 1995 Taiwan offered to make a donation of US $1,000m., to be used for the establishment of an interna-tional development fund, if the island were permitted to rejoin the UN. In September 2002, for the 10th consecutive year, the General Committee of the UN General Assembly rejected a proposal urging Taiwan's participation in the UN. However, Taiwan's leaders pledged to continue the island's campaign to gain re-entry. After 1971 a number of countries broke off diplomatic relations with Taiwan and recognized the People's Republic, and in early 2003, the Taiwan Government was recognized by some 27 countries.

In 1973 the Government of Taiwan rejected an offer from the People's Republic to hold secret discussions on the reunification of China. In October 1981 Taiwan rejected China's suggested terms for reunification, whereby Taiwan would become a 'special administrative region' and would have a substantial degree of autonomy, including the retention of its own armed forces. In 1983 China renewed its offer, including a guarantee to maintain the status quo in Taiwan for 100 years if the province agreed to reunification. In 1984, following the agreement between the People's Republic of China and the United Kingdom that China would regain sovereignty over the British colony of Hong Kong in 1997, mainland Chinese leaders urged Taiwan to accept similar proposals for reunification on the basis of 'one country—two systems'. The Taipei Government insisted that Taiwan would never negotiate with Beijing until the mainland regime renounced communism. In May 1986, however, the Government was forced to make direct contact with the Beijing Government for the first time, over the issue of a Taiwanese pilot who had defected to the mainland. In October 1987 the Government announced the repeal of the 38-year ban on visits to the mainland by Taiwanese citizens, with the exception of civil servants and military personnel. These regulations were relaxed in November 1998.

In April 1989 the Government announced that it was considering a 'One China, two governments' formula, whereby China would be a single country under two administrations, one in Beijing and one in Taipei. In May a delegation led by the Minister of Finance attended a meeting of the Asian Development Bank (ADB) in Beijing, as representatives of 'Taipei, China', demonstrating a considerable relaxation in Taiwan's stance. Reconciliation initiatives were abruptly halted, however, by the violent suppression of the pro-democracy movement in Beijing in June. In May 1990 a proposal by the President of Taiwan to open direct dialogue on a government-to-government basis with the People's Republic was rejected by Beijing, which continued to maintain that it would negotiate only on a party-to-party basis with the KMT. In December Taiwan announced that the state of war with the People's Republic would be formally ended by May 1991 (see below).

In February 1991 the recently-formed National Unification Council, under the chairmanship of the President of Taiwan, put forward radical new proposals, whereby Taiwan and the People's Republic of China might recognize each other as separate political entities. In March a national unification programme, which incorporated the demand that Taiwan be acknowledged as an independent and equal entity, was approved by the Central Standing Committee of the KMT. The programme also included a proposal for direct postal, commercial and shipping links with the mainland.

In April 1991 a delegation from the Straits Exchange Foundation (SEF), established in late 1990 to deal with bilateral issues, travelled to Beijing for discussions, the first such delegation ever to visit the People's Republic. In August 1991 a Beijing magazine published an informal 10-point plan for the eventual reunification of China, whereby Taiwan would become a special administrative region and retain its own legislative, administrative and judicial authority. Two senior envoys of the mainland Chinese Red Cross were allowed to enter Taiwan in August on a humanitarian mission.

As the Beijing Government continued to warn against independence for Taiwan, in September 1991 the island's President asserted that conditions were not appropriate for reunification with the mainland and that Taiwan was a *de facto* sovereign and autonomous country. The President of the People's Republic indicated that force might be used to prevent the separation of Taiwan. In December the non-governmental Association for Relations across the Taiwan Straits (ARATS) was established in Beijing. In January 1992 the SEF protested to the People's Republic over the detention of a former pilot of the mainland air force who had defected to Taiwan in 1965 and, upon returning to his homeland for a family reunion in December 1991, had been arrested. He subsequently received a 15-year prison sentence. In May 1992 the National Unification Council's proposal for a non-aggression pact between Taiwan and the People's Republic was rejected.

In July 1992 the Taiwanese Government reiterated that it would not consider party-to-party talks with Beijing. In the same month President Lee urged the establishment of 'one country, one good system'. In mid-July statutes to permit the further expansion of economic and political links with the People's Republic were adopted by the Legislative Yuan. In August the vice-president of the mainland Red Cross travelled to the island, thus becoming the most senior representative of the People's Republic to visit Taiwan since 1949. Delegates from the SEF and ARATS met in Hong Kong in October 1992 for discussions. The Chairman of the Mainland Affairs Council, however, insisted upon the People's Republic's renunciation of the use of military force prior to any dialogue on the reunification question. Upon taking office in February 1993, the new Premier of Taiwan confirmed the continuation of the 'One China' policy.

In 1993 divisions between Taiwan's business sector and political groupings (the former advocating much closer links with the People's Republic, the latter urging greater caution) became evident. In January, and again later in the year, the Secretary-General of the SEF resigned, following disagreement with the Mainland Affairs Council. Historic talks between the Chairmen of the SEF and of the ARATS were held in Singapore in April. Engaging in the highest level of contact since 1949, Taiwan and the People's Republic agreed on the establishment of a formal structure for future negotiations on economic and social issues.

In August 1993 the People's Republic issued a document entitled *The Taiwan Question and the Reunification of China*, reiterating its claim to sovereignty over the island. Relations were further strained by a series of aircraft hijackings to Taiwan from the mainland. An SEF-ARATS meeting, held in Taiwan in December, attempted to address the issue of the repatriation of hijackers. Incidents of air piracy continued in 1994, substantial prison sentences being imposed on the hijackers by the Taiwanese authorities.

Further meetings between delegates of the SEF and ARATS were held in early 1994. Relations between Taiwan and the mainland deteriorated sharply in April, however, when 24 Taiwanese tourists were among those robbed and killed on board a pleasure boat plying Qiandao Lake, in the People's Republic. Taiwan suspended all commercial and cultural exchanges with the People's Republic. In June three men were convicted of the murders and promptly executed. In February 1995 compensation totalling 1.2m. yuan was awarded to the victims' families by the People's Republic.

In July 1994 the Taiwanese Government released a White Paper on mainland affairs, urging that the division be acknowledged and the island accepted as a separate political entity. In August the SEF-ARATS talks were resumed when Tang Shubei, Vice-Chairman and Secretary-General of the ARATS, flew to Taipei for discussions with his Taiwanese counterpart, Chiao Jen-ho. Tang thus became the most senior Communist Chinese official ever to visit the island. Although the visit was marred by opposition protesters, the two sides reached tentative agreement on several issues, including the repatriation of hijackers and illegal immigrants from Taiwan to the mainland. Procedures for the settlement of cross-Straits fishing disputes were also established. In mid-November relations were strained once again when, in an apparent accident during a training exercise, Taiwanese anti-aircraft shells landed on a mainland village, injuring several people. Nevertheless, in late November a further round of SEF-ARATS talks took place in Nanjing, at which agreement in principle on the procedure for the repatriation of hijackers and illegal immigrants was confirmed. Further progress was made at meetings in Beijing in January 1995, although no accord was signed. It was announced in March that the functions of the SEF were to be enhanced. To improve co-ordination, the SEF board of directors would henceforth include government officials, while meetings of the Mainland Affairs Council would be attended by officials of the SEF. In the same month the Mainland Affairs Council approved a resolution

providing for the relaxation of restrictions on visits by mainland officials and civilians.

In 1995 President Jiang Zemin's Lunar New Year address, incorporating the mainland's 'eight-point' policy on Taiwan, was regarded as more conciliatory than hitherto. In April, in response, President Lee proposed a 'six-point' programme for cross-Straits relations: unification according to the reality of separate rules; increased exchanges on the basis of Chinese culture; increased economic and trade relations; admission to international organizations on an equal footing; the renunciation of the use of force against each other; and joint participation in Hong Kong and Macao affairs. In late April, however, the eighth round of working-level SEF-ARATS discussions was postponed, owing to disagreement over the agenda.

In May 1995 the SEF Chairman, Koo Chen-fu, and his mainland counterpart, Wang Daohan, formally agreed to meet in Beijing in July. In June, however, this proposed second session of senior-level negotiations was postponed by the ARATS, in protest at President Lee's recent visit to the USA. Tension between the two sides increased in July, when the People's Republic unexpectedly announced that it was about to conduct an eight-day programme of guided missile and artillery-firing tests off the northern coast of Taiwan. A second series of exercises took place in August, again arousing much anxiety on the island. In mid-August President Jiang Zemin confirmed that the People's Republic would not renounce the use of force against Taiwan. Nevertheless, at the end of that month President Lee reaffirmed the KMT's commitment to reunification. In October President Jiang Zemin's offer to visit Taiwan in person was cautiously received on the island. President Lee confirmed his Government's anti-independence stance in November.

In January 1996 the Taiwanese Premier again urged the early resumption of cross-Straits dialogue. In February there were unconfirmed reports of the extensive mobilization of mainland troops. In the same month, upon his appointment as Chairman of the Mainland Affairs Council, Chang King-yuh pledged to attempt to improve relations with the mainland. In March the People's Republic began a new series of missile tests, including the firing of surface-to-surface missiles into coastal areas around Taiwan. Live artillery exercises continued in the Taiwan Strait until after the island's presidential election, arousing international concern. The USA deployed two naval task forces in the area (see below).

In April 1996, as tension eased, the Mainland Affairs Council removed the ban on visits to Taiwan by officials of the People's Republic. The Ministry of Transportation and Communications announced that mainland container traffic was to be permitted direct entry to Taiwanese ports. At the end of April the SEF, which had lodged a strong protest with the ARATS during the missile tests of March, urged the resumption of bilateral discussions. In July President Lee re-affirmed his commitment to peaceful reunification. In the same month a number of business delegations from the mainland made visits to Taiwan.

In November 1996 the Mainland Affairs Council announced that the permanent stationing of mainland media representatives in Taiwan was to be permitted. President Lee's renewed offer to travel to the People's Republic was rejected and, despite repeated SEF requests, Tang Shubei of the ARATS continued to assert that Taiwan's pursuit of its 'two Chinas' policy (a reference to President Lee's attempts to raise the diplomatic profile of the island) prevented the resumption of cross-Straits discussions. In January 1997, however, as the reversion of the entrepôt of Hong Kong to Chinese sovereignty approached, shipping representatives of Taiwan and of the People's Republic reached a preliminary consensus on the establishment of direct sea links. Limited services resumed in April, thus ending a ban of 48 years. In March 1998 it was reported that Taiwan had agreed to allow a mainland Chinese shipping company to operate a direct shipping link between Shanghai and the northern Taiwanese port of Keelung.

In July 1997, upon the reversion to Chinese sovereignty of the British colony of Hong Kong, President Lee firmly rejected the concept of 'one country, two systems' and any parallel with Taiwan, and strenuously refuted a suggestion by President Jiang Zemin that Taiwan would eventually follow the example of Hong Kong. In September the Taiwanese Minister of Finance and the Governor of the central bank were obliged to cancel a visit to Hong Kong, where they had planned to have informal discussions with delegates to the forthcoming IMF/World Bank meeting, owing to Hong Kong's failure to issue them with visas.

The affair compounded fears that Taiwan's business dealings with Hong Kong might be jeopardized.

A call for the opening of political negotiations, made by the Minister of Foreign Affairs of the People's Republic in September 1997, was welcomed by the Mainland Affairs Council. However, the Taiwanese authorities continued to insist that Beijing remove all preconditions before the opening of dialogue. In November the Secretary-General of the SEF was invited by the ARATS to attend a seminar on the mainland in the following month. The SEF proposed instead that its Chairman head a delegation to the People's Republic.

The declaration by an ARATS official in January 1998 that Taiwan did not need to recognize the Government of the People's Republic as the central Government as a precondition for dialogue was regarded as a significant concession on the part of the mainland authorities. However, Taiwan continued to insist that China abandon its demand that talks be conducted under its 'One China' principle. In February the ARATS sent a letter to the SEF requesting the resumption of political and economic dialogue between the two sides, and inviting a senior SEF official to visit the mainland. The SEF responded positively to the invitation in March, and proposed that a delegation be sent to the People's Republic to discuss procedural details, prior to a visit to the mainland by the SEF Chairman.

In April 1998 a delegation of the SEF visited the People's Republic. Following negotiations with the ARATS, it was announced that the Chairman of the SEF would visit the People's Republic later in 1998 formally to resume the dialogue, which had been suspended since 1995. The arrest on the mainland in May 1998 of four Taiwanese business executives on charges of espionage, and their subsequent conviction, and the visit to Malaysia by the Taiwanese Premier, in April, threatened to reverse the recent improvement in relations. However, in July the Chinese Minister of Science and Technology visited Taiwan, the first such visit by a mainland Minister since the civil war. This was followed later in the month by a formal visit to Taiwan by the Deputy Secretary-General of the ARATS. The kidnap and murder in August in the People's Republic of a Taiwanese local government official caused serious concern for the Taiwanese authorities. In October Koo Chen-fu, the SEF Chairman, duly travelled to the People's Republic, where he held several meetings with his ARATS counterpart, Wang Daohan, and met with President Jiang Zemin (the highest level of bilateral contact since 1949) and had discussions with other senior officials. A four-point agreement was reached, allowing for increased communications between the two sides, but little was achieved in terms of a substantive breakthrough. However, the talks were considered to mark an important improvement in cross-Straits relations, and Wang Daohan accepted an invitation to visit Taiwan in March 1999.

In January 1999 the ARATS invited the SEF Deputy Secretary-General to visit the People's Republic for talks in order to prepare for Wang Daohan's visit. The SEF made a counter-proposal that ARATS officials visit Taiwan to discuss preparations. In March the Government announced that it was to establish a supra-ministerial task force to examine the suitability of trips by certain former government officials to the People's Republic of China, owing to security concerns. In the same month an ARATS delegation visited Taiwan. In April President Lee reaffirmed that Beijing should recognize Taiwan as being of equal status, that cross-Straits negotiations should concentrate on practical issues and that reunification could take place only if the mainland were to become a democracy. An SEF group went to Beijing in March, and preliminary agreement was reached that the ARATS Chairman would visit Taiwan in either mid-September or mid-October. In August, however, the ARATS suspended contacts with the SEF, following President Lee's insistence on the 'two-state theory' (see below), and it was confirmed in October that Wang Daohan would not visit Taiwan while the island continued to adhere to the theory.

Meanwhile, China was becoming increasingly demonstrative in its opposition to Taiwan's inclusion in the US-led Theater Missile Defence (TMD) anti-missile system. Ballistic missiles were deployed in mainland coastal regions facing Taiwan, and fears were heightened within the international community in July 1999, when the People's Republic announced that it had developed a neutron bomb, after declaring itself ready for war should Taiwan attempt to gain independence. This declaration was prompted by a radio interview given by President Lee, during which he asserted that relations with the People's Republic were 'state-to-state'. Chinese military exercises took

place in the Taiwan Strait later that month, allegedly to intimidate Taiwan. Faced with this aggression and a lack of US support, Taiwan promised that it would not amend its Constitution to enshrine its claim to statehood in law. In August the USA reaffirmed its readiness to defend Taiwan against Chinese military action. Shortly afterwards the Taiwanese Government refused a request by Beijing that it retract the 'state-to-state' theory with regard to cross-Straits relations, and tension increased in late August when the KMT incorporated the 'two-state theory' into the party resolution, claiming that this would henceforth become the administrative guide-line and priority of the Taiwanese authorities. Later that month the Mainland Affairs Council announced that former Taiwan government officials involved in affairs related to national intelligence or secrets were not to be permitted to travel to China within three years of leaving their posts. In September, following a severe earthquake in Taiwan that killed or injured several thousand people, China was among the many countries to offer emergency assistance to the island. Taiwan, however, accused the People's Republic of contravening humanitarian principles by trying to force other countries to seek its approval before offering help. Relations became increasingly strained following the reversion of Macao to Chinese sovereignty in December 1999. The People's Republic announced that reunification of the two sides of the Taiwan Strait would also be on the basis of 'one country, two systems'. Taiwan, however, insisted that its stance on the issue remained unchanged, and that the system was inapplicable in this case. By early 2000 it was clear that reunification was a mainland priority, by military means if necessary.

In February 2000 the People's Republic threatened to attack Taiwan if it indefinitely postponed reunification talks. The approval in the Legislative Yuan in March of a law providing for the first direct transport links between Taiwan's outlying islands and mainland China for 50 years did not substantially improve matters, and in April the Vice President-elect, Annette Lu, was denounced by the Chinese media after she made 'separatist' remarks, televised in Hong Kong, declaring that Taiwan was only a 'remote relative and close neighbour' of China. A Taiwanese opposition group subsequently endorsed a motion to dismiss Lu for putting the island at risk by provoking China. In an attempt to improve relations with the People's Republic, President Chen offered to compromise and to reopen negotiations on the basis that each side was free to interpret the 'One China' formula as it saw fit. Chinese Premier Zhu Rongji rejected the suggestion, and questioned Taiwan's motives, effectively dispelling all hopes of restarting negotiations in the near future. In July 2000 the Chinese authorities responded angrily when the United Kingdom issued a visa to former President Lee Teng-hui, who continued to be perceived as a dissident by the People's Republic. Despite the fact that Lee's visa was for the purpose of a private visit by an individual, and specified as a condition that no public statements would be made during the trip, China took action against British governmental and trade interests to register its displeasure.

In October 2000 Beijing published a policy document on its national defence, which confirmed that the People's Republic would use force to prevent Taiwanese secession, to stop occupation of the island, and also in the event of Taiwan indefinitely postponing reunification with the mainland. In November, however, there were signs of an improvement in relations when Wu Po-hsiung, the Vice-Chairman of the KMT, travelled to Beijing and met unofficially with Chinese Vice-Premier Qian Qichen. Wu was the most senior KMT official to visit mainland China for more than 50 years, and it was thought that Beijing was attempting to isolate Chen Shui-bian by consorting with his political rivals. During the meeting both sides agreed to hold important academic forums to discuss cross-Straits relations and to attempt to devise common positions. Qian stressed, however, the importance of Taiwan's recognition of the 'One China' principle before official negotiations could resume.

Also in November 2000, Taiwan announced that journalists from the People's Republic were to be granted permission to stay in Taiwan for periods of up to one month, during which time they would be invited to attend any press conferences called by the President's office and the Executive Yuan, in order to enhance cross-Straits exchanges and understanding. In the following month plans were announced for 'mini three links' with China, providing for direct trade, transport and postal links between Kinmen and Matsu islands and the mainland. The Taiwanese Government stressed, however, that any future direct links with Taiwan itself would be subject to rigorous security checks. In early January 2001 groups sailed from Kinmen and Matsu to Xiamen and Fuzhou, respectively, in the People's Republic. Beijing's response toward the initiative was guarded.

In March 2001, in Beijing, the press spokesman for the Fourth Session of the Ninth National People's Congress reiterated that China did not favour the confederal system of reunification, but rather the 'one country, two systems' model. Also in that month, exiled pro-democracy activist Wei Jingsheng visited Taiwan and had discussions with Vice-President Lu. By April cross-Straits relations had become strained, following the visit of the Dalai Lama to Taiwan, and the forthcoming sale of weapons by the USA to Taiwan (see above).

In May 2001 President Chen announced that he aspired to become the first Taiwanese leader to visit the mainland since 1949 by attending the APEC forum to be held there in October; however, Beijing rejected Chen's proposal. Although official cross-Straits relations were often hostile, links continued to develop between Taiwan and the mainland, particularly in the business sphere. Many Taiwanese companies continued to invest in the mainland, and it was hoped that the growing economic interdependence between the two entities would reduce the risk of war. President Chen in late August endorsed a plan by a special advisory committee to expand economic and commercial links with the mainland, a reversal of the previous Government's 'no haste, be patient' policy of limiting trade with the mainland for fear of becoming over-dependent on its main political enemy. The new policy of 'aggressive opening' included the removal of a US $50m. limit on individual investments in the mainland. Beijing responded cautiously to Chen's initiative, declaring that direct full transport links between the mainland and Taiwan would have to wait until Chen respected the 'One China' reunification formula, but a senior Chinese trade official stated that China would not block further Taiwanese investment. At the same time, state-owned oil companies from Taiwan and China announced plans to resume co-operative exploration of the Taiwan Straits. Chen's critics warned that his new policy would make Taiwan too economically dependent on the mainland. In September 2001 the Taiwanese Government approved a proposal allowing Chinese investment in Taiwan's land and property market, as part of the new opening to the mainland. The limit on individual investments in the mainland was formally removed on 7 November; restrictions on direct remits to and from the mainland via Taiwanese banks were also abolished.

In late October 2001, meanwhile, Taiwan boycotted the APEC summit meeting in Shanghai, following Beijing's refusal to allow Taiwan's chosen delegate, former Vice-President Li Yuan-tsu, to attend, on the grounds that he was not an 'economic' official. Despite this, the DPP deleted from its charter a vow to achieve the island's formal independence, since it was already a *de facto* separate entity. The change indicated a growing acceptance of the status quo by the DPP. It was hoped that the acceptance of China and Taiwan into the WTO in mid-November would improve cross-Straits relations, by enhancing communications in the field of trade.

The heavy defeat of the pro-mainland KMT by the pro-independence DPP at the legislative elections of December 2001 (see below) was initially seen as a reverse to cross-Straits relations; however, Beijing reacted with moderation to the event, in contrast to past bellicosity during elections, but insisted that Taiwan accept the 'One China' principle as a precondition for bilateral dialogue. Meanwhile, the Control Yuan reported that some 200 recently-retired Taiwanese military and intelligence officials had visited Hong Kong and the mainland in violation of laws stipulating that they wait three years before doing so. There were fears that a number of these officials had divulged military secrets to mainland military officials, thereby jeopardizing the island's security.

In January 2002 the Government announced a new passport design incorporating the words 'issued in Taiwan' on the cover, ostensibly to differentiate clearly Taiwanese passports from mainland ones. The initiative was regarded disapprovingly by Beijing, as a sign of symbolic statehood. In mid-January the Government announced a list of more than 2,000 items that would thenceforth be legally importable from the mainland, mostly consumer but also agricultural goods, and at the same time facilitated direct transport links with the mainland. Later in the month, Chinese Vice-Premier Qian Qichen invited members of the DPP to visit the mainland, stating that most DPP members were not independence activists. President Chen welcomed Qian's remarks, and Premier Yu said he was planning to

send a delegation to the mainland, but ruled out negotiations on the so-called '1992 consensus'. In February 2002 an unnamed senior Chinese official reportedly suggested, privately, that China was prepared to abandon its insistence that Taipei accept the 'One China' principle before commercial links could be realized.

In a sign of improving financial links, in early March 2002 Beijing announced that, for the first time, two Taiwanese banks would be allowed to open offices on the mainland. Taiwan would also allow mainland banks to establish offices on the island. At the end of the month, Taiwan eased restrictions on the island's companies investing in computer-chip manufacturing on the mainland; however, restrictions would remain on the number of plants established and type of chips produced. Underlying these restrictions was a fear that Taiwan's valuable electronics industry might become dependent on the mainland, and that the mainland might gain access to advanced semiconductor technology used to guide missiles. It was thought that Taiwan's efforts to open up to the mainland were being hampered by former President Lee Teng-hui's new political party, upon which the DPP depended to maintain a majority in the legislature and which generally favoured a slower approach to improving bilateral commercial relations.

At the beginning of May 2002 an official Chinese newspaper published Beijing's strongest criticism to date of President Chen, describing him as a 'troublemaker' who sought to damage bilateral relations, and criticizing his efforts to promote a separate 'Taiwanese' identity. The comments were thought to be a response to the strengthening of relations between Taiwan and the USA (see below). None the less, Taiwan at the same time reluctantly allowed China to ship more than 2,300 tons of water to its outlying islands in order to help relieve the worst drought in many years, an arrangement that would have been unthinkable a few years previously. Meanwhile, Chen in early May announced that he planned to send a DPP delegation to the mainland later in the year, in response to Qian Qichen's conciliatory speech in January. At the end of May the Mainland Affairs Council planned to introduce changes that would allow non-governmental organizations a greater role in promoting cross-Straits dialogue. Two state-owned oil companies from both sides at this time agreed upon a joint venture to explore petroleum and gas deposits in the straits. Taiwan's arrest in mid-June of one of its own military officers for passing military secrets to China failed to damage these improving commercial links, but offered a reminder that the intelligence 'war' between the two sides was far from over. Earlier, in mid-April, Taiwan had dispatched several navy vessels to monitor a Chinese research vessel operating just outside Taiwanese waters, and had tested an indigenously developed air-defence missile in May. Despite mutual suspicions, several Taiwanese legislators and retired generals secretly travelled to Beijing in June and discussed defence issues with their mainland counterparts.

In late June 2002 Beijing urged business groups to play the major role in establishing direct transport links between the two territories. However, in early July the mainland's Bank of China demanded that Taiwanese banks sign an acknowledgement of the 'One China' principle before cross-Straits banking services could begin. Taipei immediately rejected such demands, accusing Beijing of seeking to introduce a political element into the financial links between them, and questioning the sincerity of China's goodwill.

Bilateral relations again deteriorated in late July 2002, however, when the Pacific island nation of Nauru transferred its recognition from Taiwan to the People's Republic of China, thereby undermining Taipei diplomatically and prompting Chen to warn that Taiwan might have to chart its own future path. At the same time Taiwan's Ministry of National Defense warned in a biannual report that China's military spending was accelerating rapidly and that it would possess 600 short-range missiles targeting the island by 2005. Chen further incensed Beijing in early August by supporting demands for a referendum to determine the island's future, and referring to China and Taiwan as two countries. Although China warned against any such moves, Chen's rhetoric was believed to have reflected his frustration at the lack of a political breakthrough in cross-Straits relations, and was probably aimed at raising the DPP's popularity ahead of forthcoming mayoral elections. However, DPP officials stated that there had been no change in policy, and Chen subsequently softened his rhetoric. Taiwan then cancelled planned military exercises as a gesture of good faith, but Chen's comments delayed the introduction of direct transport links. At the end of July the Government announced that Chinese products could be advertised on the island and that Chinese employees of Taiwanese or foreign companies would be allowed to work in Taiwan. A Taiwanese semiconductor manufacturer, the world's largest, also announced plans to build a new factory on the Chinese mainland, in Shanghai.

The political atmosphere between China and Taiwan remained volatile, however, and in early September 2002 Chen described the mainland's threats against the island as a form of 'terrorism'. Later that month Beijing accused Taiwan of allowing the banned Falun Gong sect to use the island as a base for disrupting Chinese television and satellite broadcasts, although did not accuse Taipei of directly supporting the group. A Chinese official stated that the source of the sect's propaganda transmissions had been traced to the island, but a Taiwanese investigation revealed nothing, and the unofficial leader of Falun Gong in Taiwan, Chang Ching-hsi, emphasized that the sect had no desire to exacerbate the tensions in cross-Straits relations. At the same time, a retired Taiwanese air force officer, his wife and their son were charged with spying for China in the late 1980s. In mid-October 2002 a Taiwanese army officer fled to China via Thailand with his wife and family.

Attempts to restore direct transport links between China and Taiwan gained momentum in mid-October 2002 when Beijing abandoned the 'One China' principle as a condition for such links and agreed that these could be described as 'cross-Straits' rather than 'domestic'. However, two weeks later President Chen seemingly retreated from the proposal. A report by the Control Yuan in September 2002 had stated that only 2% of the money invested by Taiwanese firms in China was repatriated, and it was believed that Chen was reassessing the economic benefits of cross-Straits links. Elements in the DPP had long argued that these links with China were to Taiwan's economic disadvantage.

Meanwhile, the 16th CCP Congress held in Beijing in November 2002 stressed continuity in cross-Straits relations. However, the 'arms race' between China and Taiwan continued during 2002, with the two sides acquiring advanced weaponry from Russia and the USA respectively. In mid-October two Chinese ships and a submarine sailed around the east coast of Taiwan *en route* to the South China Sea, where the Chinese navy was staging military exercises. The voyage served to warn Taiwan that Beijing could encircle the island if necessary, prompting the Minister of National Defense, Tang Yao-ming, to urge a strengthening of Taiwan's navy. Analysts noted, however, that Taiwan's defence spending had been reduced in recent years, owing to the economic downturn.

Tension between Taipei and Beijing intensified in January 2003, however, when President Chen stated that Taiwan was a sovereign state, and would never accept a Hong Kong-style solution nor federate with the mainland. At the same time, Vice-President Lu described China as being of a 'terrorist nature', referring to its missile build-up across the Taiwan Straits and to its coercive diplomacy. In late January 2003 none the less, following discussions earlier in that month, the first Taiwanese airliner in more than 50 years flew to mainland China, via Hong Kong, landing in Shanghai. The flight was one of 16 charter operations organized by the Taiwanese carrier, China Airlines (CAL), to transport Taiwanese visitors in China home for Chinese new year celebrations. The flights were a special arrangement, however, and the instigation of direct cross-Straits flights on a regular basis appeared unlikely to be unrealized in the near future. Also in late January a member of the DPP made a private visit to the mainland, ostensibly to promote exchanges of views with.

In late February 2003 Tang Yao-ming stated that Taiwan would not reduce weapons purchases from the USA in return for the dismantling of Chinese missiles targeting the island. His remarks came in response to Chinese President Jiang Zemin's offer of such an arrangement, made to President Bush in October 2002.

In December 1972, meanwhile, legislative elections were held, for the first time in 24 years, to fill 53 seats in the National Assembly. The new members, elected for a fixed term of six years, joined 1,376 surviving 'life-term' members of the Assembly. President Chiang Kai-shek remained in office until his death in April 1975. He was succeeded as leader of the ruling KMT by his son, Gen. Chiang Ching-kuo, who had hitherto been Premier. Dr Yen Chia-kan, Vice-President since 1966, became the new President. In 1978 President Yen retired and was succeeded by Gen. Chiang. At elections for 71 seats in the Legislative Yuan in December 1983, the KMT won an overwhelming victory, confirming its dominance over the independent 'Tangwai' (non-party) candidates. In March 1984 President Chiang was re-elected for a second six-year term, and Lee Teng-hui, a former Mayor of Taipei and a native Taiwanese, became Vice-President. President Chiang died in January 1988 and was succeeded by Lee Teng-hui.

In September 1986 135 leading opposition politicians formed the Democratic Progressive Party (DPP), in defiance of the KMT's ban on the formation of new political parties. Partial elections to the National Assembly and the Legislative Yuan were held in December. The KMT achieved a decisive victory, but the DPP received about one-quarter of the total votes, and more than doubled the non-KMT representation. In February 1987 the KMT began to implement a programme of political reform. Martial law (in force since 1949) was replaced by the National Security Law in July and, under the terms of the new legislation, political parties other than the KMT were permitted, and civilians were removed from the jurisdiction of military courts. In April seven major posts in a reorganization of the Executive Yuan were allocated to reformist members of the KMT. In November 1987 the second annual Congress of the DPP approved a resolution declaring that Taiwanese citizens had the right to advocate independence. In January 1988, however, two opposition activists were imprisoned, on charges of sedition, for voicing such demands.

In February 1988 a plan to restructure the legislative bodies was approved by the Central Standing Committee of the KMT. Voluntary resignations were to be sought from 'life-term' members of the Legislative Yuan and National Assembly, and seats were no longer to be reserved for representatives of mainland constituencies. The 13th national Congress of the KMT was held in July. Following a decision to hold free elections for two-thirds of the members of the KMT's Central Committee, numerous new members were elected, and the proportion of native Taiwanese increased sharply. In January 1989 three legislative measures were enacted: a revision of regulations concerning the registration of political parties; a retirement plan for those members of the three legislative assemblies who had been elected by mainland constituencies in 1947; and a new law aiming to give greater autonomy to the Taiwan Provincial Government and its assembly, and in the following month the KMT became the first political party to register under the new legislation. Despite objections to the new laws, regarding the size of the retirement pensions being offered and the terms of the Civic Organizations Law (under which political parties were obliged to reject communism and any notion of official political independence for Taiwan), the DPP applied for official registration in April.

Partial elections to the Legislative Yuan and the Taiwan Provincial Assembly were held on 2 December 1989. A total of 101 seats in the Legislative Yuan were contested, with the KMT obtaining 72 seats and the DPP winning 21, thus securing the prerogative to propose legislation in the Legislative Yuan. In February 1990 the opening of the National Assembly's 35-day plenary session, convened every six years to elect the country's President, was disrupted by DPP members' violent action in a protest against the continuing domination of the Assembly by elderly KMT politicians, who had been elected on the Chinese mainland prior to 1949 and who had never been obliged to seek re-election. Many injuries resulted from clashes between riot police and demonstrators. In March 1990 DPP members were barred from the National Assembly for refusing to swear allegiance to 'The Republic of China', attempting instead to substitute 'Taiwan' upon taking the oath. Various amendments to the Temporary Provisions, which for more than 40 years had permitted the effective suspension of the Constitution, were approved by the National Assembly in mid-March. Revisions included measures to strengthen the position of the mainland-elected KMT members, who were granted new powers to initiate and veto legislation, and also an amendment to permit the National Assembly to meet annually. The revisions were opposed not only by the DPP but also by more moderate members of the KMT, and led to a large protest rally in Taipei, demanding the abolition of the National Assembly and the holding of direct presidential elections. Nevertheless, President Lee was duly re-elected, unopposed, by the National Assembly for a six-year term, two rival KMT candidates having withdrawn from the contest.

The National Affairs Conference (NAC) convened in June 1990 to discuss proposals for reform. A Constitutional Reform Planning Group was subsequently established. The NAC reached consensus on the issue of direct presidential elections, which would permit the citizens of Taiwan, rather than the members of the National Assembly, to select the Head of State. Meanwhile, the Council of Grand Justices had ruled that elderly members of the National Assembly and of the Legislative Yuan should step down by the end of 1991.

In October 1990 the National Unification Council, chaired by President Lee, was formed. In the same month the Mainland Affairs Council, comprising heads of government departments and led by the Vice-Premier of the Executive Yuan, was founded. In December President Lee announced that Taiwan would formally end the state of war with the mainland; the declaration of emergency was to be rescinded by May 1991. Plans were announced for gradual constitutional reform, to be implemented in 1991–93. Meanwhile, in early December 1990 Huang Hwa, the leader of a faction of the DPP and independence activist, had received a 10-year prison sentence upon being found guilty of 'preparing to commit sedition'.

In April 1991 the National Assembly was convened, the session again being marred by violent clashes between KMT and DPP members. The DPP subsequently boycotted the session, arguing that a completely new constitution should be introduced and that elderly KMT delegates, who did not represent Taiwan constituencies, should not have the right to make amendments to the existing Constitution. Some 20,000 demonstrators attended a DPP-organized protest march. Nevertheless, the National Assembly duly approved the constitutional amendments, and at midnight on 30 April the 'period of mobilization for the suppression of the Communist rebellion' and the Temporary Provisions were formally terminated. The existence, but not the legitimacy, of the Government of the People's Republic was officially acknowledged by President Lee. Furthermore, Taiwan remained committed to its 'One China' policy. In May 1991 widespread protests following the arrest of four advocates of independence for Taiwan led to the abolition of the Statute of Punishment for Sedition. The law had been adopted in 1949 and had been frequently employed by the KMT to suppress political dissent.

A senior UN official visited the island in August 1991, the first trip by such a representative since Taiwan's withdrawal from the organization in 1971. Large-scale rallies calling for a referendum to be held on the issue of Taiwan's readmission to the UN as an independent state, resulting in clashes between demonstrators and the security forces, took place in September and October.

In August 1991 the opposition DPP officially announced its alternative draft constitution for 'Taiwan', rather than for 'the Republic of China', thus acknowledging the *de facto* position regarding sovereignty. In September, after being reinstated in the Legislative Yuan, Huang Hsin-chieh, the Chairman of the DPP, relinquished his seat in the legislature and urged other senior deputies to do likewise. Huang had been deprived of his seat and imprisoned in 1980, following his conviction on charges of sedition. At the party congress in October 1991, Huang was replaced as DPP Chairman by Hsu Hsin-liang. Risking prosecution by the authorities, the DPP congress adopted a resolution henceforth to advocate the establishment of 'the Republic of Taiwan', and urged the Government to declare the island's independence.

Elections to the new 405-member National Assembly, which was to be responsible for amending the Constitution, were held in December 1991. The 225 seats open to direct election were widely contested. The campaign was dominated by the issue of Taiwan's possible independence. The opposition's independence proposal was overwhelmingly rejected by the electorate, the DPP suffering a humiliating defeat. The KMT secured a total of 318 seats (179 of which were won by direct election), while the DPP won 75 seats (41 by direct election). All elderly mainland-elected delegates were obliged to relinquish their seats. In February 1992 20,000 demonstrators protested against the sedition laws and demanded a referendum on the issue of independence.

In March 1992, at a plenary session of the KMT Central Committee, it was agreed to reduce the President's term of office from six to four years. The principal question of arrangements for future presidential elections, however, remained unresolved. In April street demonstrations were organized by the DPP to support demands for direct presidential elections. In May the National Assembly adopted eight amendments to the Constitution, one of which empowered the President to appoint members of the Control Yuan.

Meanwhile, the radical dissident, (Stella) Chen Wan-chen, who had established the pro-independence Organization for Taiwan Nation-Building upon her return from the USA in 1991, was sentenced to 46 months' imprisonment in March 1992, having been found guilty of 'preparing to commit sedition'. In May, however, Taiwan's severe sedition law was amended, non-violent acts ceasing to be a criminal offence. Several independence activists were released from prison and other dissidents were able to return from overseas exile. Nevertheless, in June (George) Chang Tsang-hung, the chairman of the banned, US-based World United Formosans for Independence (WUFI), who had returned from exile in the USA in December 1991, received a prison sentence of five (commuted from 10) years upon conviction on charges of sedition and attempted murder, involving the dispatch of letter-bombs to government officials in 1976. Chang was released for medical treatment in October 1992. In March 1993 he was acquitted of the sedition charges, on the grounds of insufficient evidence.

Taiwan's first full elections since the establishment of Nationalist rule in 1949 were held in December 1992. The KMT retained 102 of the 161 seats in the Legislative Yuan. The DPP, however, garnered 31% of the votes and more than doubled its representation in the legislature, winning 50 seats. Following this set-back, the Premier and the KMT Secretary-General resigned. In February 1993 Lien Chan, hitherto Governor of Taiwan Province, became the island's first Premier of Taiwanese descent.

In May 1993 about 30 conservative rebels resigned from the KMT, and formed the New Alliance Nationalist Party. Furthermore, in June the Government was defeated in the Legislative Yuan, when a group of KMT deputies voted with the opposition to approve legislation on financial disclosure requirements for elected and appointed public officials. The unity of the KMT was further undermined in August, when six dissident legislators belonging to the New Kuomintang Alliance, which had registered as a political group in March, announced their decision to leave the ruling party in order to establish the New Party. Nevertheless, in August 1993, at the 14th KMT Congress, Lee Teng-hui was re-elected Chairman of the party. A new 31-member Central Standing Committee and 210-member Central Committee, comprising mainly Lee's supporters, were selected. In a conciliatory gesture by the KMT Chairman, four vice-chairmanships were created, the new positions being filled by representatives of different factions of the party.

In September 1993, following a series of bribery scandals, the Executive Yuan approved measures to combat corruption. The administrative reform plan included stricter supervision of public officials and harsher penalties for those found guilty of misconduct. In the same month a KMT member of the Legislative Yuan was sentenced to 14 years' imprisonment for bribery of voters during the 1992 election campaign; similar convictions followed. At local government elections held in November 1993, although its share of the votes declined, the KMT secured 15 of the 23 posts at stake. The DPP, which accused the KMT of malpractice, won only six posts, despite receiving a substantial proportion of the votes; it retained control of Taipei County. Following allegations of extensive bribery at further local polls in early 1994 (at which the DPP and independent candidates made strong gains), the Ministry of Justice intensified its campaign against corruption. Proposals for constitutional amendments to permit the direct election in 1996 of the Taiwanese President by popular vote (rather than by electoral college) and to limit the powers of the Premier were approved by the National Assembly in July 1994.

At gubernatorial and mayoral elections in December 1994 the DPP took control of the Taipei mayoralty, in the first such direct polls for 30 years, while the KMT succeeded in retaining the provincial governorship of Taiwan, in the first ever popular election for the post, and the mayoralty of Kaohsiung. The New Party established itself as a major political force, its candidate for the mayoralty of Taipei receiving more votes than the KMT incumbent.

In March 1995, following the President's formal apology at a ceremony of commemoration in February, the Legislative Yuan approved a law granting compensation to the relatives of the victims of a massacre by Nationalist troops in 1947 (the 'February 28 Incident'), in which an estimated 18,000 native Taiwanese had been killed.

Elections to the Legislative Yuan were held on 2 December 1995. A major campaign issue was that of corruption, allegations of malpractice and indictments having reached alarming levels. The KMT's strength declined to 84 of the 164 seats, faring particularly badly in Taipei. The DPP increased its representation to 53 seats. The New Party, which favoured reconciliation with the mainland, secured 21 seats. The first direct presidential election was scheduled for March 1996, to coincide with the National Assembly polls. President Lee had declared his intention to stand for re-election in August 1995. There were a number of other candidates for the presidency. The campaign was dominated by the issue of reunification with the mainland. In mid-March a DPP demonstration on the streets of Taipei, in support of demands for Taiwan's independence, was attended by 50,000 protesters. At the presidential election, held on 23 March 1996, the incumbent President Lee received 54.0% of the votes cast, thus securing his re-election for a four-year term. At the concurrent elections for the National Assembly, the KMT took 183 of the 334 seats. The DPP won 99 seats and the New Party 46 seats. The Chairman of the DPP, Shih Ming-teh, resigned and Hsu Hsin-liang, who had resigned in November 1993, subsequently returned to the post.

In June 1996 the President's announcement of the composition of the new Executive Yuan aroused much controversy. Although several members retained their previous portfolios, the President (apparently under pressure from within the KMT and disregarding public concern at the rising levels of corruption and organized crime) demoted the popular Ministers of Justice, and of Transportation and Communications, who had exposed malpractice and initiated campaigns against corruption. Other changes included the replacement of the Minister of Foreign Affairs by John Chang, the grandson of Chiang Kai-shek. The most controversial nomination, however, was the reappointment as Premier of Lien Chan, despite his recent election as the island's Vice-President. As fears of a constitutional crisis grew, opposition members of the Legislative Yuan, along with a number of KMT delegates, demanded that the President submit the membership of the Executive Yuan to the legislature for approval, and threatened to boycott the chamber.

In December 1996 the multi-party National Development Conference (NDC), established to review the island's political system, held its inaugural meeting. The convention approved KMT proposals to abolish the Legislative Yuan's right to confirm the President's choice of Premier, to permit the legislature to introduce motions of no confidence in the Premier and to empower the President to dismiss the legislature. The Provincial Governor, (James) Soong Chu-yu, subsequently tendered his resignation in protest at the NDC's recommendations that elections for the provincial governorship and assembly be abolished, as the first stage of the dissolution of the provincial apparatus. The Provincial Government was responsible for the entire island, with the exception of the cities of Taipei and Kaohsiung. In January 1997 President Lee refused to accept the Governor's resignation, but the affair drew attention to the uneasy relationship between the island's President and its Governor, and brought to the fore the question of reunification with the mainland. In July the National Assembly approved a series of constitutional reforms, implementing the NDC's recommendations.

In early May 1997 more than 50,000 demonstrators, protesting against the problem of increasing crime (particularly crimes of violence), demanded the resignation of President Lee. Three members of the Executive Yuan subsequently resigned. The appointment of Yeh Chin-feng as Minister of the Interior (the first woman to oversee Taiwan's police force) did little to appease the public, which remained highly suspicious of the alleged connections between senior politicians and the perpetrators of organized crime. In mid-May thousands of protesters, despairing of the rapid deterioration in social order, again took to the streets of Taipei, renewing their challenge to President Lee's leadership and demanding the immediate resignation of Premier Lien Chan. In late June a 'Say No to China' rally attracted as many as 70,000 supporters.

In August 1997 Vincent Siew, former Chairman of the Council for Economic Planning and Development and also of the Mainland Affairs Council, replaced Lien Chan as Premier (Lien Chan retained the post of Vice-President), and John Chang was appointed Vice-Premier. In the same month President Lee was re-elected unopposed as Chairman of the ruling KMT. The KMT experienced a serious set-back in elections at mayoral and magistrate levels, held in November 1997. The DPP, which had campaigned on a platform of more open government, won 12 of the 23 constituency posts contested, while the KMT achieved only eight posts. Consequently, more than 70% of Taiwan's population was to come under DPP administration. Following the KMT's poor performance in the ballot, the Secretary-General of the party resigned, and was replaced by John Chang. A major reorganization of the party followed.

At local elections, held in January 1998, the KMT won an overwhelming majority of the seats contested, while the DPP, in a reversal of fortune, performed badly. In April the Minister of Justice tendered, and then subsequently withdrew, his resignation, claiming that lawmakers with connections to organized crime were exerting pressure on the Government to dismiss him. However, in July he was forced to resign, following his mishandling of an alleged scandal concerning the acting head of the Investigation Bureau.

In June 1998 the first-ever direct election for the leadership of the DPP was held. Lin Yi-hsiung won a convincing victory, assuming the chairmanship of the party in August. Meanwhile, in local elections in June, the KMT suffered a set-back, winning fewer than 50% of the seats contested. Independent candidates performed well. In August 17 new members were elected to the KMT Central Standing Committee, the 16 others being appointed by President Lee.

Elections to the newly-expanded 225-member Legislative Yuan took place on 5 December 1998. The KMT won 46.4% of the votes cast, securing 125 seats, the DPP received 29.6% of the votes and won 72 seats, while the pro-unification New Party secured only 7.1% of the votes and 11 seats. The New Nation Alliance, a breakaway group from the DPP (formed in September), won only one seat (with 1.6% of the votes cast). The KMT's victory was widely attributed to its management of the economy, in view of the Asian financial crisis, the developments in cross-Straits dialogue and a decline in factionalism within the party in 1998. In the election (held simultaneously) to select the mayor of Taipei, the KMT candidate, Ma Ying-jeou, a popular former Minister of Justice, defeated the DPP incumbent, Chen Shui-bian. However, Frank Hsieh, the DPP candidate, won the office of mayor of Kaohsiung. The KMT retained control of both city councils.

Chiou I-jen resigned as Secretary-General of the DPP in December 1998 and was replaced by Yu Shyi-kun. Later that month Chao Shu-po, a Minister without Portfolio, was appointed Governor of Taiwan Province, replacing the elected incumbent, James Soong, as part of the plans to dismantle the provincial government, agreed in 1997. In March 1999 an unprecedented vote of 'no confidence' in the leadership of Premier Vincent Siew was defeated in the Legislative Yuan. The motion was presented by the opposition following Siew's reversal of his earlier position and his decision to reduce the tax on share transactions, apparently as a result of pressure from President Lee. The National Assembly passed a controversial constitutional amendment on 4 September, which, *inter alia*, extended the terms of the deputies from May 2000 to June 2002. Election to the Assembly was henceforth to be on the basis of party proportional representation. Several politicians and critical citizens condemned the move as being 'against the public will'. Shortly afterwards, the KMT leadership expelled the Speaker of the National Assembly, Su Nan-cheng, from the party on the grounds that he had violated its policy on the tenure extension, thereby also removing him from his parliamentary seat and the post of Speaker. There was widespread dissatisfaction regarding the National Assembly's action, and in March 2000 the Council of Grand Justices of the Judicial Yuan ruled it to be unconstitutional. Later that month the DPP and the KMT reached an agreement on the abolition of the body and the cancellation of elections scheduled for early May. In April the National Assembly convened, and approved a series of constitutional amendments, which effectively deprived the body of most of its powers, and reduced it to an *ad hoc* institution. The powers to initiate constitutional amendments, to impeach the President or Vice-President and to approve the appointment of senior officials were transferred to the Legislative Yuan. The National Assembly was to retain the functions of ratifying constitutional amendments and impeachment proceedings, in which case 300 delegates, appointed by political parties according to a system of proportional representation, would convene for a session of a maximum duration of one month.

Meanwhile, in September 1999, following the earthquake (see above), the Legislative Yuan approved an emergency decree, which was to remain in effect for six months, permitting the use of police and troops to maintain order in stricken areas, the punishment of those engaging in 'black market' activities and the raising of relief bonds.

In November 1999 it was announced that a presidential election was to be held in March 2000. Five candidates registered: Lien Chan (with Vincent Siew as candidate for Vice-President) was the KMT nominee, while Chen Shui-bian, a former mayor of Taipei, was to stand for the DPP (with the feminist Annette Lu as vice-presidential candidate), and Li Ao was to represent the New Party; the former DPP Chairman, Hsu Hsin-liang, qualified as an independent candidate, as did James Soong, who was consequently expelled from the KMT, along with a number of his supporters. It became evident in December 1999, when Soong was publicly accused of embezzlement, that the election would be bitterly contested. Although Soong denied the charges, his popularity was affected. In January 2000 Lien Chan, in an attempt to regain the support of disillusioned voters, proposed that the KMT's extensive business holdings be placed in trust and that the party terminate its direct role in the management of the numerous companies in which it owned shares. The KMT adopted the proposal shortly afterwards. In a reflection of the tense political situation between Taiwan and China, Chen Shui-bian of the DPP modified the party's stance and pledged not to declare formal independence for the island unless Beijing attacked.

The presidential election, held on 18 March 2000, was won by Chen Shui-bian, who obtained 39.3% of the votes cast. James Soong, his closest rival, received 36.8% of the votes. (On the day after the election he founded the People First Party (PFP), in an attempt to take advantage of his popularity.) Lien Chan of the KMT secured only 23.1% of the votes. The remaining candidates obtained less than 1%. The poll attracted a high level of participation, 82.7% of the electorate taking part. (Upon his inauguration in May, Chen would thus become Taiwan's first non-KMT President since 1945.) Violence erupted as disappointed KMT supporters besieged the party's headquarters, attributing the KMT's defeat to the leadership's expulsion of James Soong and the resultant division of the party. Lee Teng-hui subsequently accepted responsibility for the defeat and resigned from the chairmanship of the Party. Lien Chan assumed the leadership. As the KMT continued to dominate the Legislative Yuan, however, the party did not entirely relinquish its influence, and in early April gave permission for Tang Fei, a KMT member and hitherto Minister of National Defense, to serve as Premier, although he was to be suspended from party activities while in the post. Following protracted negotiations, the membership of the new Executive Yuan, which incorporated 11 DPP members and 13 KMT members, was approved in early May. The incoming Government largely lacked ministerial experience. Furthermore, the DPP's lack of a legislative majority impeded the passage of favourable legislation. The size of the budget deficit also made it difficult for the DPP to fulfil specific electoral pledges on health, housing and education. In July Frank Hsieh replaced Lin Yi-hsiung as Chairman of the DPP.

In July 2000 the Government was heavily criticized after a river accident in which four workers, stranded by a flash flood, drowned as a result of the authorities' failure to provide a rescue helicopter. While the various government departments deliberated over the allocation of responsibility, the victims' final hours were broadcast live on national television. The Vice-Premier and Chairman of the Consumer Protection Commission, Yu Shyi-kun, subsequently resigned, as did senior officials of the emergency services. The Premier's offer of resignation was refused by President Chen Shui-bian. In October, however, Tang Fei resigned as Premier, ostensibly owing to ill-health. It was suggested his departure from the post was due to the Government's failure to agree upon the fate of Taiwan's fourth nuclear power plant, the DPP being opposed to the project. Vice-Premier Chang Chun-hsiung was appointed Premier, and a minor cabinet reorganization was effected. Changes included the appointment of Yen Ching-chang as Minister of Finance, his predecessor having resigned following a sharp decline in the stock market.

Political disputes over the construction of Taiwan's fourth nuclear power plant intensified later in October 2000. The Minister of Economic Affairs, Lin Hsin-yi, was expelled from the KMT for 'seriously opposing KMT policies and impairing the people's interests' after he had demonstrated his support for the cancellation of the project. At the end of the month Chang Chun-hsiung announced that the Executive Yuan had decided to halt construction of the plant for financial and economic reasons. Although environmentalists were pleased, citing Taiwan's inability to process nuclear waste and to cope with accidents, the KMT reacted furiously, rejecting the Government's right to

cancel a project approved by the legislature, and, together with the New Party and the People First Party, immediately began collecting legislators' signatures for the recall (dismissal) of Chen Shui-bian. The opposition was not mollified by a subsequent apology from Chen, and shortly afterwards the Legislative Yuan passed revised legislation on the process for presidential impeachment. Owing to the controversy, KMT member Vincent Siew refused to act as the President's representative to the annual APEC forum in Brunei in November and was replaced by Perng Fai-nan, the Governor of the Central Bank. The dispute became so serious that the business community issued an unprecedented public message that economic recovery should take priority over political differences, but in December some 10,000 protesters in Taipei demanded that Chen resign. In November the Government requested a constitutional interpretation on the issue from the Council of Grand Justices, which it agreed to be bound by. The Council ruled in mid-January 2001 that the Government should have sought the legislature's approval before halting construction of the plant, and in mid-February the Government decided immediately to resume construction of the plant. In March a minor government reorganization was effected. The most notable change was the appointment of Hu Ching-piao, hitherto a Minister without Portfolio, as Chairman of the Atomic Energy Council, replacing Hsia Der-yu. It was rumoured that Hsia had disagreed with Chang Chun-hsiung over the future of the nuclear plant.

Meanwhile, in September 2000 four retired naval officers and one still serving were arrested in connection with the suspected murder in 1993 of a naval captain, Yin Ching-feng, to prevent him from revealing a scandal surrounding Taiwan's 1991 purchase of French-built frigates. It was alleged that bribery had influenced the award of the contract, which had been abruptly withdrawn from a South Korean firm. In October the Control Yuan impeached three former naval admirals, including the former Commander-in-Chief of the Navy, Adm. (retd) Yeh Chang-tung, for their involvement in the affair. In December the Taiwanese authorities appealed to the French Government for information to assist their investigations. The report of a two-year investigation by the Control Yuan, released in March 2002, strongly criticized the Ministry of National Defense and the navy command for failing to investigate fully Capt. Yin's murder, and recommended the court-martial of Adm. (retd) Yeh and former Prime Minister and Minister of National Defense, Hau Pei-tsun. The report also revealed that France had divulged to China confidential information regarding the deal. Several retired admirals went on trial for corruption in late April 2002.

By March 2001 President Chen had lost popularity within his DPP for softening his stance on two of its key policies—independence for Taiwan and commitment to a nuclear power-free island. Fears emerged that the DPP might lose seats in legislative elections due in December, although opinion polls showed that some 60% of the public supported construction of the nuclear plant. However, polls also showed Chen's popularity to be in decline, with much of the optimism that had greeted his inauguration being replaced with concerns about his inexperience and lack of authority, his handling of the economy and the political gridlock in domestic affairs, as well as the impasse in cross-Straits relations.

Concerns about the economy were heightened in May 2001 when 20,000 demonstrators from 18 trade unions marched in Taipei to protest against the Government's inability to reduce the unemployment rate, which at nearly 4% was at a 16-year high; furthermore, economic growth had declined to its lowest rate in 26 years. Later in the month Chen announced that he was planning to form the island's first coalition government after the December elections, in order to end the political infighting. In late June Chen received a major political boost when former President Lee Teng-hui offered his public support and suggested that he would back Chen in the December elections. Lee had disagreed with KMT leader Lien Chan, and his possible defection to Chen's support base threatened significantly to weaken the KMT. The emerging alliance between the two pro-independence leaders signalled a potential realignment in Taiwanese politics into pro-mainland and pro-independence forces, and seemed to end Beijing's goals of developing a strong pro-mainland political bloc on the island. There were also concerns that the realignment could further polarize society in this regard.

Moves toward such a political environment gained momentum in early July 2001, when the KMT issued a policy paper arguing that Taiwan's best option in terms of its relations with China was to form a 'confederation' with the mainland—the furthest that any political party had moved in calling for a union with China. The architect of the new KMT policy, Su Chi, described this as being 'somewhere in the middle ground between independence and unification', although the party had adopted a noticeably more pro-reunification stance under Lien Chan. However, the KMT's Central Standing Committee in late July refrained from adopting the proposal, reflecting the party's uncertainty over mainland policy. In August 2001 a new political party, the Taiwan Solidarity Union (TSU), was formally launched with the support of former President Lee, and consisting of breakaway members of the KMT and DPP, led by the former Minister of the Interior, Huang Chu-wen. The party was formed in an attempt to secure for President Chen a majority in December's elections, an important goal given that the KMT had used its majority to block many of Chen's reforms during the previous one-year period. However, there were fears that the new party would drain support from Chen's DPP. Lee himself was expelled from the KMT in late September for supporting the TSU.

Meanwhile, in July 2001 President Chen urged major governmental reforms, including reorganization, streamlining measures, anti-corruption action and improved inter-departmental co-operation. At the end of August Chen also accepted proposals by a special advisory committee on closer economic relations with the mainland (see above).

The last months of 2001 were dominated by campaigning for legislative elections. As support for the KMT waned, politics increasingly became an ethnic issue, with the KMT and PFP drawing their support from those who had fled the mainland in 1949 and their descendants (approximately 15% of the population), while native Taiwanese (who comprised 65% of the population) supported the DPP and the TSU. Despite the economic recession, Chen's popularity rose in the period prior to the elections, amid rumours that the DPP would form a coalition to secure a majority. The DPP hoped that a coalition would enable reforms to the legislature, notably the abolition of the multi-member constituencies in favour of a single-seat, 'first-past-the-post' system, thereby ending the need for candidates from the same party to compete against each other.

At the elections held on 1 December 2001 the DPP emerged as the biggest single party in the new legislature, having won 36.6% of the votes cast and 87 seats, but failed to win a majority. The KMT won 31.3% of votes and 68 seats, thereby losing its dominance of the Legislative Yuan for the first time in its history. The PFP came third, winning 20.3% of the votes and 46 seats, while the newly formed TSU came fourth, with 8.5% of the votes and 13 seats. The New Party won only 2.9% of the votes and one seat, while independents took nine seats. The level of voter participation was registered as 66.2%.

In the immediate aftermath of the elections, political manoeuvring to establish a coalition began, as the DPP and KMT sought to have their candidate elected as Vice-President of the Legislative Yuan. On 21 January 2002 President Chen reorganized the Executive Yuan, appointing his hitherto Secretary-General, Yu Shyi-kun, as Premier. The move was seen as a consolidation of the President's power, aimed at improving his prospects for re-election in 2004; the new Premier was also thought to be a more efficient administrator than his predecessor. Other notable appointments included Chen Shih-meng, hitherto deputy governor of the Central Bank, as the Secretary-General to the President, replacing Yu. Lin Hsin-i, hitherto Minister of Economic Affairs, was appointed Vice-Premier and Chairman of the Council for Economic Planning and Development, Eugene Chien, hitherto Deputy Secretary-General to the President, as Minister of Foreign Affairs, and Gen. Tang Yao-ming, hitherto Chief of the General Staff, as the new Minister of National Defense. Tang was the first native-born Taiwanese to hold the newly-augmented defence post in a mainlander-dominated military, and he was to oversee military reforms in early 2002. Lee Yung-san, Chairman of the International Commercial Bank of China, was appointed Minister of Finance, while Lee Ying-yuan, hitherto deputy representative in Washington, DC, was appointed Secretary-General to the Executive Yuan; however, the ministers in charge of mainland and overseas Chinese affairs were retained, suggesting a desire for continuity in relations with China.

In late January 2002 elections were held for provincial city and township councillors. Although the KMT won the largest number of seats in these elections, it failed to expand its popularity on a national level, with the results reflecting the KMT's

competent organizational mobilization methods. At the beginning of February an alliance of the KMT and PFP ('pan-blue camp') successfully blocked the DPP-TSU ('pan-green camp') candidate for the post of Vice-President of the Legislative Yuan, electing Chiang Ping-kun of the KMT to that position. At the same time, the incumbent President of the legislature, Wang Jin-pyng of the KMT, was re-elected to his post. Following their success, officials from the KMT and PFP stated that they would consider presenting joint candidates for the mayorships of Taipei and Kaohsiung in late 2002, and possibly the presidency itself in 2004, with Wang as their candidate for the latter post.

In February 2002 the KMT-PFP alliance immediately challenged the new Government by attempting to force it to accept revisions to legislation concerning local budget allocations, which had been approved by the outgoing Legislative Yuan in December 2001. However, in the decisive vote in the new Legislative Yuan, the KMT and PFP failed to secure the majority necessary to accomplish this, thereby giving the Government a minor victory. The narrowness of this victory, however, indicated that the KMT continued to pose a formidable obstacle to the new administration. An early set-back for the Government came in late March 2002 when the Minister of Economic Affairs, Christine Tsung, resigned, citing a hostile political environment, particularly in the Legislative Yuan. She was replaced by her deputy, Lin Yi-fu.

A major political scandal erupted in late March 2002 when one daily and one weekly newspaper reported that the Government of former President Lee Teng-hui had, in co-operation with the island's intelligence service (National Security Bureau—NSB), clandestinely established an unauthorized fund worth US $100m. to finance covert operations on the mainland and to further Taiwanese interests among influential lobby groups abroad, including the USA. Prosecutors immediately raided the offices of the two newspapers and seized the offending copies, accusing the editors of revealing state secrets, amid fears that freedom of the press would come under threat. The scandal threatened to damage Lee's position, as well as jeopardize intelligence-gathering missions on the mainland and Taiwan's reputation for maintaining confidentiality; it was widely believed that the source of the 'leaks' was a former NSB colonel who had embezzled US $5.5m. and then fled the island. Following the revelations, President Chen reiterated his commitment to press freedom and proposed new oversights for the NSB.

In early April 2002 the Executive Yuan approved plans to abolish the posts of Speaker and Deputy Speaker of the National Assembly, and replace them with that of a chairman of the session. In early May the Government revealed proposals to reform the electoral system, which would reduce the number of seats in the Legislative Yuan from 225 to 150 and extend the term of legislators from three to four years. Some 90 seats would be filled from single-seat constituencies (thereby eliminating the need for candidates from the same party to compete against each other, as in the existing multi-seat constituencies), with the remaining seats divided proportionally among parties that received more than 5% of the total vote. It was hoped that such reforms would make government more efficient and less dependent upon the availability of finance. A disadvantage of the system of multi-seat constituencies was that it required the participation of larger numbers of candidates and thus greater funding, thereby encouraging corruption.

Also in early May 2002, KMT Chairman Lien Chan announced that his party would form an official alliance with the PFP in order to strengthen opposition to the ruling DPP. However, plans for a joint candidacy in the 2004 presidential elections were hampered by regulations stipulating that the presidential and vice-presidential candidates should belong to the same party. Meanwhile, in mid-May thousands of people demonstrated in favour of changing Taiwan's official name from the 'Republic of China' to 'Taiwan'—an initiative that was supported by 70% of respondents in an opinion poll conducted by the Ministry of Foreign Affairs in 2001, but strongly opposed by China.

In mid-June 2002 Premier Yu Shyi-kun appointed Liu Shyh-fang as the first female Secretary-General of the Executive Yuan, replacing Lee Ying-yuan, who was standing as the DPP's candidate in elections for the mayoralty of Taipei, in December. In late July President Chen Shui-bian formally assumed the chairmanship of the DPP, in a move designed to bring party policy into line with the Government. However, critics suggested that the dual leadership style was reminiscent of the excessively strong executive characterized by the decades of KMT rule. In mid-September 2002 the Executive Yuan approved drafts of the new Political Party Law, which would ban political parties from operating or investing in profit-making enterprises, and allow the Government to investigate and confiscate assets unlawfully obtained by political parties. Although ostensibly aimed at creating greater political fairness and financial openness, the draft legislation was viewed as being directed at the KMT which, during the decades of its rule, had amassed a vast commercial fortune worth an estimated NT $53,750m. (US $1,600m.) in 2001. As a result, the KMT would be obliged to sell many of its assets.

A new political dispute emerged in late September 2002 over planned reforms of the debt-ridden agricultural and fishermen's credit co-operatives. The Government sought to reduce the activities of these local financial bodies, which had traditionally been used as a source of funds and influence for local KMT politicians. However, opposition to the reforms from farmers, KMT politicians and also Lee Teng-hui and the TSU was so intense that by late November President Chen was forced to suspend the plans. At the same time, more than 120,000 farmers and fishermen marched through Taipei to protest against the reforms, in what was the largest demonstration on the island since Chen took office. The protesters also demanded the establishment of a new agricultural development fund to alleviate the difficulties caused by Taiwan's entry into the WTO. Supporters of the reforms warned that Chen's failure to deliver them raised doubts about his Government's commitment to broader financial reforms needed to promote growth. Premier Yu Shyi-kun offered to resign, but was retained by Chen, who instead accepted the resignations of the Minister of Finance, Lee Yung-san, and the Chairman of the Council of Agriculture, Fan Chen-tsung. They were replaced by Lin Chuan and Lee Chin-lung, respectively. The departure of the respected Lee Yung-san, and the appointment of the third finance minister in as many years, raised concerns about political uncertainty.

Meanwhile, Taiwan's political forces were also increasingly focused on elections for the mayoralties of Taipei and Kaohsiung, which took place in early December 2002, and were widely regarded as a preparation for the 2004 presidential elections. In Taipei the incumbent mayor, Ma Ying-jeou of the KMT, defeated his DPP rival, Lee Ying-yuan, winning 64.1% of the votes cast. Thus, he immediately emerged as a potential presidential candidate. His popularity complicated efforts by the KMT and PFP ('pan-blue camp') to select one of respective party chairmen Lien Chan and James Soong as their joint presidential candidate. In mid-December the two formally committed themselves to this goal. In Kaohsiung the incumbent mayor, Frank Hsieh of the DPP, narrowly beat his KMT rival Huang Chun-ying, by 50.0% to 46.8% of the votes cast.

In late December 2002–early January 2003 a political scandal in the Kaohsiung City Council embarrassed both the DPP and KMT, when it was alleged that Chu An-hsiung, a businessman and politician, had bribed councillors from both parties in order to secure his election as speaker of the city council. This was the second scandal in Kaohsiung in recent months. In late 2002 it was alleged that a local businesswoman, Su Hui-chen, had bribed officials in the DPP and KMT in order to win favourable treatment for her property company, Zanadau Development. The incidents led to renewed demands for the reform of campaign finance laws, to limit the use of irregular funding in Taiwan's politics.

In January 2003 the release from death row of three men accused of a double-murder in 1991 prompted fresh calls for a substantial reform of the judicial system. The men were released on the grounds of insufficient evidence, and human rights activists and lawyers hoped that the case would set a precedent for establishing a clearer burden of proof in future capital cases. New legislation was to take effect from September 2003, which would give a greater role for defence counsels in courts. Also on the agenda were reforms aimed at divesting political parties of their media interests, namely in radio and television stations. During the decades of KMT rule, the party had amassed control or ownership of various media outlets, which the DPP now sought to dismantle.

In early February 2003 President Chen appointed Chiou I-jen, hitherto Secretary-General of the National Security Council, as Secretary-General to the President, while Kang Ning-hsiang, hitherto Vice-Minister of National Defense, succeeded Chiou in his former position. Later that month the leaders of the KMT and PFP again pledged to field a joint candidate for the presidency of Taiwan in 2004, with Lien Chan ostensibly the presidential candidate, and Soong as his running mate. However, the rivalry between the two appeared to place the alliance in jeopardy.

In foreign relations, meanwhile, in January 1979 Taiwan suffered a serious set-back when the USA established full diplomatic relations with the People's Republic of China and severed relations with Taiwan. The USA also terminated the 1954 mutual security treaty with Taiwan. Commercial links are still maintained, however, and Taiwan's purchase of armaments from the USA has remained a controversial issue. In August 1982 a joint Sino-US communiqué was published, in which the USA pledged to reduce gradually its sale of armaments to Taiwan. In September 1992 President Bush announced the sale of up to 150 F-16 fighter aircraft to Taiwan. The announcement was condemned by the People's Republic. In December the US trade representative became the first senior US government official to visit the island since 1979. In September 1994 the USA announced a modification of its policy towards Taiwan, henceforth permitting senior-level bilateral meetings to be held in US government offices. In December the US Secretary of Transportation visited the Ministry of Foreign Affairs in Taipei, the first US official of cabinet rank to visit Taiwan for more than 15 years. In June 1995 President Lee was permitted to make a four-day unofficial visit to the USA, where he gave a speech at Cornell University, and met members of the US Congress. This visit provoked outrage in Beijing, and the Chinese ambassador to Washington was recalled. During 1996 the Taiwanese Vice-President was granted transit visas permitting him to disembark in the USA on a number of occasions.

In March 1996, as the mainland began a new series of missile tests off the Taiwanese coast (see above), the USA stationed two naval convoys in waters east of the island, representing the largest US deployment in Asia since 1975. The sale of defensive weapons to Taiwan was agreed. In September 1996 President Lee and the US Deputy Treasury Secretary met in Taipei for discussions, the most senior-level contact between the two sides since 1994. In late 1996, however, Taiwanese donors were implicated in reported irregularities in the financing of President Clinton's re-election campaign, and in a large illicit contribution to the US Democratic Party. In early 1997 the first of the Patriot anti-missile air defence systems, purchased from the USA under an arrangement made in 1993, were reported to have been deployed on the island. The first of the F-16s were delivered to Taiwan in April 1997. The Taiwanese Government expressed satisfaction at the USA's continued commitment to Taiwan's security, confirmed following the visit to the USA of the President of the People's Republic, Jiang Zemin, in October and again in June 1998, during President Clinton's visit to the People's Republic. However, a statement by Clinton affirming that the USA would not support Taiwan's membership of the UN was sharply criticized in Taiwan. In late October 1998 the Taiwanese Chief of Staff, Gen. Tang Fei, made a secret two-week visit to the USA. This was regarded as an extremely sensitive matter, in view of the fact that the SEF Chairman had recently met with Jiang Zemin. In the following month the People's Republic complained to the USA following the US Energy Secretary's visit to Taiwan.

In January 1999 the People's Republic was angered by Taiwan's proposed inclusion in the US-led TMD system (see above). Tensions continued throughout the year, and in August the USA reaffirmed its commitment to defend Taiwan against Chinese military action. In the following month, however, the USA again refused to support Taiwan's application for UN membership. In October of that year the island welcomed the adoption, albeit in modified form, of the Taiwan Security Enhancement Act (TSEA), establishing direct military ties, by the International Relations Committee of the US House of Representatives, despite opposition from the Clinton Administration. Reaction from the People's Republic was unfavourable, and its displeasure increased in early February 2000 when the House of Representatives overwhelmingly approved the Act. In April of that year the US Senate postponed consideration of the Act at the behest of the Taiwanese President-elect, Chen Shui-bian, in order not to antagonize Beijing during the sensitive period preceding his inauguration. In the same month the US Government announced that it had decided to defer the sale of four naval destroyers to Taiwan, although it was prepared to supply long-range radar and medium-range air-to-air missiles. In September the USA granted a transit visa to Taiwanese Vice-President Annette Lu to stay in New York *en route* to Central America. Lu subsequently declared that the stopover had marked a breakthrough in talks between the USA and Taiwan. In October China was angered by a resolution passed by the US Congress supporting Taiwan's participation in the UN and other international organizations.

The election of George W. Bush to the US Presidency in late 2000 was widely expected to boost US-Taiwan relations at the expense of the USA's relations with the mainland, since Bush had used uncompromising rhetoric against the latter in his election campaign. This became more apparent after the crisis over the detention of a US reconnaissance plane and its crew following its collision with a Chinese fighter aircraft on 1 April 2001 (see the chapter on the People's Republic of China). Following that incident, in late April the USA agreed to sell Taiwan armaments worth a total of US $4,000m., consisting of navy destroyers, anti-submarine aircraft, diesel submarines, amphibious assault vehicles, and surface-to-air missiles and torpedoes, all of which would substantially bolster the island's defences. However, the USA stopped short of selling Taiwan an advanced combat-radar system, for fear of provoking Beijing. At the same time President Bush declared that the USA would do whatever was necessary to defend Taiwan, in the event of an invasion by mainland forces. Beijing was further angered by the visit of President Chen Shui-bian to the USA in late May 2001, when he met business leaders and members of the US Congress. Chen's visit was followed by that of his predecessor, Lee Teng-hui, in late June, as well as by a group of Taiwanese military and intelligence officials on an exchange programme, the first such exchange since 1979. Also in June, Taiwan successfully tested its US-made 'Patriot' air defence missiles for the first time. Plans by the USA to sell diesel submarines to Taiwan encountered difficulties in May, however, when Germany and the Netherlands, the main owners of the submarine design technology, refused to raise tensions with Beijing by approving such a sale. In September an Australian company emerged as the most likely supplier of the submarines when it was rumoured that a US defence company would take a 40% stake in the former.

In late August 2001 two US Navy aircraft carrier battle groups staged a one-day exercise in the South China Sea coinciding with Chinese military exercises in the Taiwan Straits, a further reminder that the USA was committed to protecting Taiwan. In October the Minister of National Defense, Wu Shih-wen, began finalizing the purchase of the naval destroyers offered earlier in the year, and the USA also offered Taiwan anti-tank missiles. In December the US House of Representatives approved the 2002 Defense Authorization Act, which included weapons sales to Taiwan and the promise of US help in acquiring submarines.

In January 2002 the Bush Administration rejected demands by a former US State Department official, Richard Holbrooke, that a fourth communiqué on US-Taiwan relations was needed, stating that the existing 1982 communiqué was satisfactory. At the same time, a delegation from a US 'think tank', consisting of retired generals and officials, visited the mainland, and subsequently Taiwan, where they met President Chen and other senior officials and discussed the island's security. Also in January, Vice-President Annette Lu made a brief stopover in New York, en route to South America, and former President Lee Teng-hui announced that he planned to visit the USA in May to raise Taiwan's profile. During his visit to Beijing in late February 2002, President Bush pledged to adhere to the 1979 Taiwan Relations Act—the first time a US President had stated this in China itself.

There were indications that the USA's long-standing 'strategic ambiguity' regarding Taiwan was gradually coming to an end in early 2002. In mid-March the Minister of National Defense, Gen. (retd) Tang Yao-ming visited the USA to attend a private three-day defence and security conference in Florida, where he met the US Deputy Secretary of Defense, Paul Wolfowitz, and Assistant Secretary of State James Kelly. During the conference, Wolfowitz reportedly stated that the USA would assist in training Taiwan's military in areas of command and doctrine. Several days later the Asia-Pacific Center for Security Studies, an institute operating under the US Navy's Pacific Command, issued invitations for Taiwanese military personnel to attend a 12-week course on security issues—another indication of the greater access being given to the Taiwanese military by the USA. Tang was the first incumbent to make a non-transit visit to the USA since 1979, and the event emphasized the increasingly important security links between the two sides. China condemned Tang's visit as interference in its affairs and

responded by denying permission for a US warship to visit Hong Kong in April. Meanwhile, the scandal in late March concerning former President Lee Teng-hui's co-operation with the island's intelligence services in secretly establishing an unauthorized fund (see below) embarrassed Taiwan and several US lobbying groups, which had received sums of this money. Lee subsequently postponed his planned visit to the USA. In mid-April, however, the US Under-Secretary of Commerce for International Trade, Grant Aldonas, became the highest-ranking official of George W. Bush's Administration to visit Taiwan, where he met Chen Shui-bian. The latter proposed the establishment of a free-trade pact with the USA and Japan.

In June 2002 it became known that a US defence contractor would probably build eight new diesel-electric submarines for Taiwan's navy, having purchased a share of a German company that produced the relevant designs; a senior-level US delegation visited Taiwan in late July to discuss these arrangements. Also in July, the USA considered accelerating the transfer of advanced air-to-air missiles, purchased by Taiwan but undelivered, and a US Department of Defense report warned that preparations for a conflict with Taiwan was the main factor behind Beijing's military build-up. However, the USA refrained from commenting on Chen's reference in early August to a possible referendum to determine the island's future. Premier Yu Shyi-kun and the Chairwoman of the Mainland Affairs Council, Tsai Ing-wen, made a brief stopover in New York, USA, at the same time, their visits being denounced by Beijing.

In early September 2002 the Vice-Minister of National Defense, Kang Ning-hsiang, and the Vice-Commander of the Navy both visited Washington, DC, to discuss the planned acquisition of four new Kidd-class destroyers. However, the high costs of the vessels jeopardized their purchase, at a time when Taiwan's defence budget was being reduced. Later in the month Wu Shu-chen, the wife of President Chen, began a private 10-day visit to the USA, seeking to raise the island's profile.

Meanwhile, reflecting the occasional political aspects of commercial relations with the USA, the Taiwanese Government in September 2002 urged the state-owned airline, CAL, to place a US $2,000m. order for 12 aircraft for its fleet, with Boeing (of the USA) rather than the rival European-manufactured Airbus. However, in October CAL awarded the contract to Airbus, while also purchasing 10 Boeing aircraft for cargo and long-haul routes.

In September 2002 the US Congress also approved the Foreign Relations Authorization Act, Fiscal Year 2003, which for the first time allowed US State Department and other government agencies staff to work at the American Institute in Taiwan, the unofficial US mission to the island. Previously, US officials were required to embark upon sabbatical leave before serving at the institute. US military officers would also be allowed to work there, albeit not in uniform. The bill also recognized Taiwan as a major non-NATO ally of the USA, and served to strengthen US-Taiwanese relations.

President Chen in early January 2003 noted that only nine members of the US Congress had visited Taiwan during 2002, the lowest number in 20 years, and far fewer than the number visiting mainland China. Also in January 2003, the USA was considering participating in Taiwan's annual military exercises. In mid-February the Vice-Minister of National Defense, Chen Chao-min (who had succeeded Kang), attended a defence industry meeting in San Antonio, Texas, which was also attended by several US defence officials.

In January 1993 the official confirmation of Taiwan's purchase of 60 fighter aircraft from France again provoked strong protest from Beijing. In January 1994 Taiwan suffered a reverse when (following pressure from the People's Republic) France recognized Taiwan as an integral part of Chinese territory, and the French Prime Minister agreed not to sell weapons to the island. In March 1995, however, it was reported that Taiwan was to purchase anti-aircraft missiles from a French company. The sale of these missiles, as well as the delivery of the aircraft and six frigates, was confirmed in 1996. The aircraft and frigates were delivered in May 1997 and March 1998, respectively. Plans by the USA to sell diesel submarines to Taiwan were blocked by Germany and the Netherlands in May 2001, however; the two countries, being the main owners of the design technology, were unwilling to raise tensions with Beijing by approving such a sale. In September an Australian firm emerged as the most likely supplier of the submarines when it was rumoured that a US defence company would take a 40% stake in the former. The impasse appeared to have been resolved in mid-2002 when a US defence contractor took a stake in a German submarine manufacturer (see above).

Taiwan severed diplomatic relations with Japan in 1972, following Tokyo's *rapprochement* with Beijing. Mainland displeasure was compounded in February 1993, however, when, for the first time in two decades, the Taiwanese Minister of Foreign Affairs paid a visit to Japan. In September 1994 pressure from Beijing resulted in the withdrawal of President Lee's invitation to attend the forthcoming Asian Games in Hiroshima. Instead, however, the Taiwanese Vice-Premier was permitted to visit Japan. Similarly, in July 1995 Japan announced that the Taiwanese Vice-Premier would not be permitted to attend a meeting of APEC members to be held in Osaka in November. Instead, President Lee was represented by Koo Chen-fu, the SEF Chairman. The latter also attended the APEC meeting in the Philippines in November 1996. At the Kuala Lumpur APEC summit in November 1998 President Lee was represented by a Minister without Portfolio, Chiang Ping-kun, who also attended the 1999 APEC conference, held in September in Auckland, New Zealand. Perng Fai-nan, the Governor of the Central Bank, represented President Chen Shui-bian at the APEC meeting in Brunei in November 2000.

In 1996 Taiwan's relations with Japan continued to be strained by the issue of adequate compensation for the thousands of Asian (mostly Korean) women used by Japanese troops for sexual purposes during the Second World War. In October Taiwan rejected a Japanese offer of nominal compensation for Taiwanese women. Relations deteriorated further in 1996 on account of a dispute relating to a group of uninhabited islets in the East China Sea: known as the Tiaoyutai (Diaoyu Dao) in Chinese, or Senkaku in Japanese, the islands were claimed by Taiwan, China and Japan. In July, following the construction of a lighthouse on one of the islands by a Japanese right-wing group, the Taiwanese Ministry of Foreign Affairs lodged a strong protest over Japan's decision to incorporate the islands within its 200-mile (370-km) exclusive economic zone. In early October further discussions with Japan on the question of Taiwanese fishing rights within the disputed waters ended without agreement. In the same month a flotilla of small boats, operated by activists from Taiwan, Hong Kong and Macao, succeeded in evading Japanese patrol vessels. Having reached the disputed islands, protesters raised the flags of Taiwan and of China. In May 1997 the Taiwanese Minister of Foreign Affairs expressed grave concern, following the landing and planting of their national flag on one of the disputed islands by a Japanese politician. A number of protesters and journalists from Taiwan and Hong Kong set sail from the port of Shenao, ostensibly to participate in an international fishing contest. They were intercepted by Japanese coastguard vessels and failed to gain access to the islands. Reports in October that Japanese patrol boats were forcibly intercepting Taiwanese fishing vessels were a further cause for concern for the Taiwanese authorities. There was a significant development in relations between the two countries in November 1999, when the Governor of Tokyo paid an official visit to Taiwan, the most senior Japanese official to do so since the severing of diplomatic relations. The People's Republic condemned the visit, claiming that it undermined Sino-Japanese relations. The former President of Taiwan, Lee Teng-hui, made a private visit to Japan in late April 2001, ostensibly for medical treatment. In order to minimize tensions with Beijing, the Japanese authorities forbade Lee from making political statements while in Japan. In March 2002 it was revealed that Japanese politicians, including former Prime Minister Ryutaro Hashimoto, had received money from an unauthorized fund established by Lee in order to procure influence in Japan. However, the incident failed to damage bilateral relations, and in late 2001–early 2002 officials from both sides were investigating the possibility of establishing a free-trade agreement. In November 2002 the Japanese Government refused Lee a visa to visit Keio University, which subsequently withdrew its invitation for him to deliver a speech there. In January 2003 Taiwan, along with China, condemned Japan's moves to assert sovereignty over the Diaoyu Dao/Senkaku islands in the East China Sea by renting them out to private companies.

In March 1989, meanwhile, President Lee paid a state visit to Singapore, the first official visit overseas by a President of Taiwan for 12 years. In February 1994 President Lee embarked upon an eight-day tour of South-East Asia. Although the tour was described as informal, President Lee had meetings with the Heads of State of the Philippines, Indonesia and Thailand, leading to protests from Beijing. In May the Taiwanese President visited Central American and Southern African states. In 1995 President Lee made a number of what were described as private visits (Taiwan having no diplomatic relations with the countries visited). The visits provoked strong protest from China. In August 1996 Beijing continued to urge Pretoria to sever its diplomatic links with Taipei. In September the Taiwanese Minister of Foreign Affairs was obliged to curtail an ostensibly private visit to Jakarta, following protests from the People's Republic of China. In January 1997 the Vice-President was received by the Pope during a visit to the Holy See, the only European state that continued to recognize Taiwan. In the same month the Minister of Foreign Affairs embarked upon a tour of seven African nations, in order to consolidate relations. His itinerary included South Africa, despite that country's recent announcement of its intention to sever diplomatic relations with Taiwan (a major set-back to the island's campaign to gain wider international recognition). In March a visit to Taiwan by the Dalai Lama, during which he met with President Lee, was strongly condemned by the People's Republic of China. A second visit by the Dalai Lama, scheduled for July 1998, was indefinitely postponed, following mainland China's criticism of the opening of a representative office of the Dalai Lama's religious foundation in Taiwan. However, the Dalai Lama visited Taiwan in March–April 2001 and held talks with President Chen, much to the anger of Beijing.

In July 1997 the Taiwanese Minister of Foreign Affairs undertook an extensive tour of the countries of Central America and the Caribbean, in an effort to maintain their support. In September, during a tour of Central America, President Lee attended an international conference on the development of the Panama Canal. The USA granted a transit visa to the Taiwanese President. A visit to Europe in October by Vice-President Lien Chan was curtailed when pressure from Beijing forced the Spanish Government to withdraw an invitation. The Malaysian and Singaporean Prime Ministers met their Taiwanese counterpart in Taiwan in November, on their return from the APEC forum in Canada. The People's Republic expressed concern at the meetings.

In January 1998 the Taiwanese Premier, Vincent Siew, met senior officials during a visit to the Philippines and Singapore. It was believed that discussions had focused on the possibility of Taiwan extending economic assistance to those countries. Moreover, the Taiwanese Government expressed its intention to pursue the creation of a multilateral Asian fund, under the auspices of APEC, to support the ailing Asian economies. Relations with Taiwan's Asian neighbours were further strengthened in February, when a leading member of the KMT visited the Republic of Korea, again, it was understood, to discuss financial assistance in the wake of the Asian economic crisis. Negotiations between the Malaysian Deputy Prime Minister and Finance Minster and the Taiwanese Premier, held in Taiwan in February, also concentrated on economic and financial issues. Vincent Siew made a return visit to Malaysia in April. China was highly critical of these visits, accusing Taiwan of seeking to gain political advantage from the regional economic crisis. In August 1999 the Taiwanese Government threatened to refuse entry to the island to Philippine labourers in retaliation for Manila's unilateral termination of its aviation agreement with Taipei. In October the Philippine authorities decided to close the country to Taiwanese aircraft. Access was, however, temporarily granted in November during talks on the renewal of the agreement. Negotiations faltered in December, but reached a successful conclusion in early 2000, thus permitting flights to the Philippines to resume. In March, however, the agreement collapsed, and flights were suspended again. In June the Taiwanese Government imposed a three-month ban on new work permits for Philippine nationals, citing interference by the Philippines' representative office in Taiwan concerning labour disputes. Any connection with the aviation dispute was denied. In September a new aviation agreement, enabling flights between Manila and Taipei to restart, was signed.

Taiwanese officials made extensive efforts to maintain relations with Taiwan's diplomatic allies in Africa and Central America in 1998. The Minister of Foreign Affairs visited eight African countries in February, and in April it was announced that Taiwan's overseas aid budget was to be substantially increased in an attempt to retain diplomatic support. In May the Vice-President, Lien Chan, visited Taiwan's Central American and Caribbean allies. China expressed serious concern in November at New Zealand's decision to grant Taiwanese officials in Wellington privileges accorded to accredited diplomats.

In January 1999 diplomatic relations were established with the former Yugoslav republic of Macedonia, which received substantial financial aid from Taiwan throughout the year. In December Taiwan denied offering financial inducements to Albania in return for recognition.

Amid allegations of 'cash diplomacy', the Prime Minister of Papua New Guinea initiated diplomatic relations with Taiwan in July 1999. Following his resignation later that month, recognition was withdrawn from Taiwan, allegedly because of a failure to adhere to correct procedures for the establishment of relations. Full diplomatic relations were established with Palau in December of that year, and Taiwan opened an embassy in the capital of the Pacific nation in March 2000. In August 2000 the new Taiwanese President, Chen Shui-bian, embarked upon a tour of diplomatic allies in Central America and West Africa. In October Taiwan was concerned that it might lose a diplomatic ally when the Minister of Foreign Affairs of Solomon Islands unexpectedly cancelled a visit to Taipei and travelled instead to Hong Kong. The Premier of Solomon Islands, however, did not attend a Pacific regional forum, instead visiting Taipei to make amends and to reiterate his commitment to maintaining relations. There was speculation that this commitment arose from a need for substantial financial assistance from Taiwan.

In November 2000, after eight years' suspension, the 25th Joint Conference of Korea-Taiwan Business Councils took place in Seoul. It was agreed that henceforth conferences would be held annually alternately in Taipei and Seoul, and Taiwan ultimately hoped for a resumption of ministerial-level discussions on the establishment of bilateral air links. In the same month the European Parliament passed a resolution on strengthening relations with Taiwan, and in December Taiwan and Egypt agreed to exchange representative offices. Also in December, France refused to grant a visa to the Taiwanese Minister of Justice.

Throughout 2001 Taiwan continued to seek a higher diplomatic profile. President Chen in late May began a tour of five Latin American nations—El Salvador, Guatemala, Panama, Paraguay and Honduras—as part of Taiwan's 'dollar diplomacy' —a practice of giving aid and bringing investment in return for diplomatic recognition. Whilst in El Salvador, Chen met eight regional leaders, who pledged support for Taiwan. Both Taiwan and the People's Republic of China were increasingly bidding for support in this region to enhance their overall global standing. Taiwan was also in competition with China for support from Pacific island nations, five of which (the Marshall Islands, Nauru, Palau, Solomon Islands and Tuvalu) recognized Taiwan. Two of these nations, Solomon Islands and the Marshall Islands, were thought to be wavering in their support of Taiwan. In June the former Yugoslav republic of Macedonia announced that it would recognize the People's Republic of China, thus leading to a break in relations with Taiwan. In November Wu Shu-chen, wife of President Chen, travelled to Strasbourg, France, to accept the 'Prize for Freedom' awarded to her husband by Liberal International, a world grouping of liberal parties. Chen himself had been refused a visa by the European Union (EU).

On 1 January 2002 Taiwan formally became a member of the WTO. At the same time, it was reported that Taiwan had secretly been developing military and intelligence links with India, through mutual co-operation including bilateral visits of military personnel and the exchange of intelligence data. Also in January, Vice-President Lu visited Nicaragua and Paraguay, having visited The Gambia in December 2001. Vice-President Lu also visited Indonesia in mid-August 2002 and met several ministers, but not President Megawati Sukarnoputri, owing to pressure on the latter by Beijing. While in Indonesia, Lu discussed possible liquefied natural gas projects, investment and migrant labour. Taiwanese companies had in previous years invested US $17,000m. in Indonesia, the home of some 100,000 of Taiwan's migrant workers. President Chen completed a four-nation tour of Africa in early July 2002, having visited Senegal, São Tomé and Príncipe, Malawi and Swaziland. While en route to Swaziland, he was refused permission to land in South Africa, Pretoria being concerned not to offend Beijing.

In late July 2002 Taiwan broke off diplomatic relations with Nauru after the Pacific nation established relations with the People's Republic of China. In September Taiwan announced the opening of a trade and economic affairs representative office in Mongolia. In late 2002 Taiwan and the Democratic People's Republic of Korea (North Korea) were planning to open economic liaison offices in their respective capitals, the latter keen to attract new sources of investment. President Chen was forced to cancel a trip to Indonesia in December after the latter came under heavy pressure from Beijing.

The question of the sovereignty of the Spratly Islands, situated in the South China Sea and believed to possess petroleum resources, to which Taiwan and five other countries laid claim, remained unresolved in 2002. A contingent of Taiwanese marines is maintained on Taiping Island, the largest of the disputed islands, located some 1,574 km south-west of Taiwan. A satellite telecommunications link between Taiping and Kaohsiung was inaugurated in October 1995. In August 1993 Taiwan announced its intention to construct an airbase on Taiping Island, but in January 1996 the scheme was postponed. In late December 1998 the Legislative Yuan approved the first legal definition of Taiwan's sea borders. The Spratly Islands were claimed, as were the disputed Tiaoyutai Islands, within the 12- and 24-nautical mile zones. In November 2002, in Phnom-Penh, Cambodia, members of the Association of South East Asian Nations (ASEAN, see p. 146) signed a landmark 'declaration on the conduct of parties in the South China Sea', which aimed to avoid conflict in the area. Under this agreement, which was similar to one drafted in late 1999 but not implemented, claimants would practise self-restraint in the event of potentially hostile action (such as inhabiting the islands), effect confidence-building measures and give advance notice of military exercises in the region. However, the agreement did not include the Paracel Islands, and disagreements continued among the signatories on what the accord should encompass. Additionally, China introduced a provision requiring consensus to resolve outstanding issues, thereby allowing for future indecision among ASEAN members. It was unclear how the declaration affected Taiwan, since it was not a member of ASEAN.

Government

Under the provisions of the amended 1947 Constitution, the Head of State is the President, who is elected by popular vote for a four-year term. There are five Yuans (governing bodies), the highest legislative organ being the Legislative Yuan, to which the Executive Yuan (the Council of Ministers) is responsible. Following elections in December 2001, the Legislative Yuan comprised 225 members; 168 chosen by direct election, most of the remainder being appointed from separate lists of candidates on the basis of proportional representation. The Legislative Yuan serves a three-year term. There are also Control, Judicial and Examination Yuans. Their respective functions are: to investigate the work of the executive; to interpret the Constitution and national laws; and to supervise examinations for entry into public offices. In April 2000 the role of the National Assembly was revised. The powers to initiate constitutional amendments, to impeach the President or Vice-President, and to approve the appointment of senior officials were transferred to the Legislative Yuan. The National Assembly retained the functions of ratifying constitutional amendments and responsibility for impeachment proceedings, in which case 300 delegates appointed by political parties according to a system of proportional representation were to convene for a session of a maximum duration of one month. The Taiwan Provincial Government handles the general administrative affairs of the island (excluding the cities of Taipei and Kaohsiung). Its policy-making body is the Taiwan Provincial Government Council. In July 1997 the National Assembly approved a series of constitutional amendments, including the suspension of elections at local government level, as the first stage of the dissolution of the provincial apparatus. Accordingly, the elected Governor of Taiwan was replaced by an appointed Governor in December 1998. The Taiwan Provincial Assembly exercises the province's legislative power. The Fukien (Fujian) Provincial Government is responsible for the administration of Quemoy and Matsu.

Defence

In August 2002 the armed forces totalled an estimated 370,000: army 240,000 (with deployments of 15,000–20,000 and 8,000–10,000, respectively, on the islands of Quemoy and Matsu), air force 68,000 and navy 62,000 (including 30,000 marines). Paramilitary forces numbered 26,650. Reserves totalled 1,657,500. The total number of military personnel was gradually being reduced during 2002. Military service lasts for two years. Projected budgetary defence expenditure for 2002 was estimated at NT $227,581m. (equivalent to 15.0% of total projected expenditure).

Economic Affairs

In 2001, according to official figures, Taiwan's gross national income (GNI), at current prices, totalled US $286,840m., equivalent to US $12,876 per head. During 1990–2001, it was estimated, the population increased at an average annual rate of 0.9%, while gross domestic product (GDP) per head increased, in real terms, by an average of 4.7% per year. Overall GDP increased, in real terms, at an average annual rate of 5.6% in 1990–2001; GDP contracted by 2.2%, however, in 2001.

Agriculture (including hunting, forestry and fishing) contributed 1.9% of GDP, and employed 7.5% of the working population, in 2001. The principal crops are rice, sugar cane, maize, sweet potatoes and pineapples. Agricultural GDP declined by 0.4%, in real terms, during 1990–2001. Compared with the previous year, agricultural GDP decreased by 2.1% in 2001.

Industry (comprising mining, manufacturing, construction and utilities) employed 36.0% of the working population, and provided 29.7% of GDP, in 2001. Industrial GDP increased, in real terms, at an average rate of 4.1% per year between 1990 and 2001. Compared with the previous year, industrial GDP declined by 6.0% in 2001.

Mining contributed 0.4% of GDP, and employed 0.1% of the working population, in 2001. Coal, marble and dolomite are the principal minerals extracted. Taiwan also has substantial reserves of natural gas. The GDP of the mining sector decreased at an average rate of 1.2% per year between 1990 and 2001. Mining GDP decreased by 8.0% in 2001.

Manufacturing contributed 24.5% of GDP, and employed 27.6% of the working population, in 2001. The most important branches, measured by gross value of output, are electronics (particularly personal computers), plastic goods, synthetic yarns and the motor vehicle industry. The sector's GDP grew at an average annual rate of 4.3%, in real terms, in 1990–2001. Manufacturing GDP decreased by 5.7% in 2001, compared with the previous year.

In 2001 50.3% of Taiwan's energy supply was derived from imported petroleum. Imports of crude petroleum accounted for 6.3% of total import expenditure in 2001. In that year nuclear power supplied 8.1% of Taiwan's energy requirements.

The services sector contributed 68.3% of GDP in 2001, while engaging 56.5% of the employed labour force. In 1990–2001 the GDP of this sector increased at an average annual rate of 6.9%. In 2001 services GDP decreased by 0.1%, compared with the previous year.

In 2001 Taiwan recorded a visible trade surplus of US $20,181m., and there was a surplus of US $18,861m. on the current account of the balance of payments. In 2001 the principal sources of imports were Japan (accounting for 24.1%) and the USA (17.0%). The principal markets for exports in that year were the USA (22.5%), Hong Kong (21.9%) and Japan (10.4%). Trade with the People's Republic of China (mainly via Hong Kong) is of increasing significance. Taiwan's principal imports in 2001 were electronic products, machinery, mineral products and chemical and related products. The principal exports in that year were electronic products, machinery and electrical and mechanical appliances, textiles, and base metals.

The 2002 budget proposals envisaged revenue of NT $1,260,162m. and expenditure of NT $1,518,725m., the deficit thus being projected at NT $258,563m. At 30 June 2002 Taiwan's long-term external public debt was US $13.0m. The cost of debt-servicing remained equivalent to a negligible percentage of the value of exports of goods and services. The annual rate of inflation averaged 2.3% during the period 1990–2001. Consumer prices rose by an estimated 1.3% in 2000, but remained unchanged in 2001, with a similar trend being observed in 2002. Some 5.3% of the labour force were unemployed in October 2001, compared with 3.2% a year earlier. However, unemployment stabilized somewhat at 5.2% in 2002. There is a shortage of labour in certain sectors.

Taiwan became a member of the Asian Development Bank (ADB, see p. 143) in 1966, and of the Asia-Pacific Economic Co-operation forum (APEC, see p. 139) in late 1991. In September 1992 Taiwan was granted observer status at the General Agreement on Tariffs and Trade (GATT), and was finally granted membership of the successor World Trade Organization (WTO, see p. 323) in November 2001, effective from 1 January 2002.

Taiwan's economic growth since 1949 has been substantial, with its economy usually proving to be very resilient to world recession, owing to the versatility of its manufacturing base and its large reserves of foreign exchange (estimated at US $161,700m. in December 2002). Taiwan's GDP continued to expand rapidly during the 1990s, but in 2001 the economic deceleration in the USA (Taiwan's major export market) adversely affected the island's growth. Exports, normally accounting for approximately 50% of GDP, decreased sharply, with the electronics industry being particularly badly affected. By late 2001 Taiwan was experiencing its worst recession in 40 years. Furthermore, it was feared that Taiwan's membership of the WTO might result in the loss of up to 100,000 jobs over five years, as a consequence of increased foreign competition and the continued migration of industries to the mainland, where labour costs were far lower. Despite an extensive government-initiated employment-creation programme, the level of unemployment rose steadily during 2001. In February 2001, in an effort to improve domestic investment conditions, the Premier announced an eight-point programme of measures to stimulate the Taiwanese economy. Proposals included improvements in the island's electricity and water supplies and a relaxation of restrictions on the employment of foreign professional workers. In early 2002 Taiwan's economy began to show signs of recovery, as industrial output started to rise again, and it was estimated that real GDP increased by 3.0%–3.5% for that year as a whole. In May 2002 the Government announced a new national development plan, Challenge 2008, consisting of US $75,000m. of spending on infrastructure and public construction projects, as well as US $1,440m. in low-interest loans for research and development, and enhanced English-language education to take into account the growth of 'e-commerce' and the internet. One of the largest infrastructure projects in recent years, a US $12,800m. high-speed railway linking Taipei and Kaohsiung, when completed in 2005, was expected to integrate the island's western seaboard into a single commercial zone, as well as provide technology transfers from its Japanese developers. The national development plan also aimed to create 700,000 new jobs, with a view to keeping average unemployment below 4%, and maintaining GDP growth in 2002–07 at above 5%. The Government also hoped that the plan would double the number of tourist visits. Despite such plans, foreign investment decreased by 43.3% year-on-year during January–September 2002, partly owing to competition from China. The Government feared that the increasing cross-Straits links it had been promoting was causing excessive funds to flow to China. Also during 2002 moves toward a consolidation of the banking and financial sector gathered momentum, as regulatory barriers separating banks, insurance companies and securities firms were removed, following the introduction of a new law in late 2001. In May 2002 the Government also announced plans to privatize several state-owned banks by 2006, and sell all its stakes in commercial banks by 2010. Meanwhile, Taiwan's privatization programme (first introduced in 1989) continued, with Chinese Petroleum, China Shipbuilding, and Chunghwa Telecom scheduled for sale by the end of 2003, Taiwan Tobacco and Liquor, and Tang Eng Iron Works by the end of 2004 and Taiwan Power by the end of 2005. The privatization process had been delayed in recent years by opposition from labour unions and vested interest groups. Overall GDP was expected to increase by about 3.5% in 2003.

Education

Education at primary schools and junior high schools is free and compulsory between the ages of six and 15 years. Secondary schools consist of junior and senior middle schools, normal schools for teacher-training and vocational schools. There are also a number of private schools. Higher education is provided in universities, colleges, junior colleges and graduate schools. Total projected budgetary expenditure on education, science and culture in 2002 was estimated at NT $275,196m. (equivalent to 18.1% of total projected expenditure). In that year there were over 1.9m. pupils enrolled in state primary schools. There were 1.7m. children in secondary schools. There were over 150 universities and other institutes of higher education. The adult literacy rate in 2000 was 95.55%.

Public Holidays

2003: 1–2 January (Founding of the Republic/New Year), 1–4 February (Chinese New Year), 5 April (Ching Ming/Tomb-Sweeping Day and Death of President Chiang Kai-shek), 4 June (Dragon Boat Festival), 11 September (Mid-Autumn Moon Festival), 28 September (Teachers' Day/Birthday of Confucius), 10 October (Double Tenth Day, anniversary of 1911 revolution), 25 October (Retrocession Day, anniversary of end of Japanese occupation), 12 November (Birthday of Sun Yat-sen), 25 December (Constitution Day).

2004: 1–2 January (Founding of the Republic/New Year), 22–25 January (Chinese New Year), 5 April (Ching Ming/Tomb-Sweeping Day and Death of President Chiang Kai-shek), 22 June (Dragon Boat Festival), 28 September (Mid-Autumn Moon Festival), 28 September (Teachers' Day/Birthday of Confucius), 10 October (Double Tenth Day, anniversary of 1911 revolution), 25 October (Retrocession Day, anniversary of end of Japanese occupation), 12 November (Birthday of Sun Yat-sen), 25 December (Constitution Day).

Weights and Measures

The metric system is officially in force, but some traditional Chinese units are still used.

Statistical Survey

Source (unless otherwise stated): Bureau of Statistics, Directorate-General of Budget, Accounting and Statistics (DGBAS), Executive Yuan, 2 Kwang Chow St, Taipei 10729; tel. (2) 23710208; fax (2) 23319925; e-mail sicbs@emc.dgbas.gov.tw; internet www.dgbasey.gov.tw.

Area and Population

AREA, POPULATION AND DENSITY

Area (sq km)	36,006*
Population (census results)	
16 December 1990	20,393,628
16 December 2000	
Males	11,348,803
Females.	10,818,356
Total	22,167,159
Population (official figures at 31 December)	
1999	22,034,096
2000	22,216,107
2001	22,405,568
Density (per sq km) at 31 December 2001	619.1

* 13,902 sq miles.

PRINCIPAL TOWNS
(population at 31 December 2001)

Taipei (capital) . .	2,633,802		Hsinchu	373,296
Kaohsiung . . .	1,494,457		Taoyuan	338,361
Taichung . . .	983,694		Chungli	329,913
Tainan	740,846		Fengshan . . .	322,678
Panchiao . . .	532,694		Hsintien . . .	272,500
Chungho	401,619		Chiayi	267,993
Keelung	390,966		Changhwa . . .	231,129
Shanchung . . .	384,051		Yungho	229,383
Hsinchuang . . .	376,584		Pingtung . . .	215,245

BIRTHS, MARRIAGES AND DEATHS
(registered)

	Live births		Marriages		Deaths	
	Number	Rate (per 1,000)	Number	Rate (per 1,000)	Number	Rate (per 1,000)
1994 . .	322,938	15.31	170,864	8.10	113,866	5.40
1995 . .	329,581	15.50	160,249	7.53	119,112	5.60
1996 . .	325,545	15.18	169,424	7.90	122,489	5.71
1997 . .	326,002	15.07	166,216	7.68	121,000	5.59
1998 . .	271,450	12.43	145,976	6.69	123,180	5.64
1999 . .	283,661	12.89	173,209	7.87	126,113	5.73
2000 . .	305,312	13.76	181,642	8.19	125,958	5.68
2001 . .	260,354	11.65	170,515	7.63	127,647	5.71

Expectation of life (years at birth, 2001): Males 72.8; Females 78.5.

ECONOMICALLY ACTIVE POPULATION
(annual averages, '000 persons aged 15 years and over)*

	1999	2000	2001
Agriculture, forestry and fishing .	776	740	708
Mining and quarrying . . .	11	11	10
Manufacturing	2,603	2,655	2,587
Construction	843	832	746
Electricity, gas and water . . .	35	36	35
Commerce	2,130	2,163	2,165
Transport, storage and communications	476	481	486
Finance, insurance and real estate	406	412	410
Business services. . . .	284	313	339
Social, personal and related community services . . .	1,502	1,534	1,570
Public administration . . .	318	315	327
Total employed	9,385	9,491	9,383
Unemployed	283	293	450
Total labour force	9,668	9,784	9,832
Males	5,812	5,867	5,855
Females	3,856	3,917	3,977

* Excluding members of the armed forces and persons in institutional households.

Health and Welfare

KEY INDICATORS

Total fertility rate (children per woman, 2001).	1.40
Under-5 mortality rate (per 1,000 live births, 2001) . . .	1.43
HIV/AIDS (% of persons aged 15–49, 2001).	0.02
Physicians (per 1,000 head, 2001)	1.54
Hospital beds (per 1,000 head, 2001)	5.70
Health expenditure (2000): US $ per head (PPP) . . .	758
Health expenditure (2000): % of GDP	5.4
Health expenditure (2000): public (% of total)	64.6
Human Development Index (1999): value	0.886

For definitions, see explanatory note on p. vi.

Agriculture

PRINCIPAL CROPS
('000 metric tons)

	1999	2000	2001
Potatoes	36.1	43.2	32.1
Rice*	1,558.6	1,540.1	1,396.3
Sweet potatoes	218.6	197.8	188.7
Sorghum	33.6	26.5	21.7
Maize	201.2	178.3	166.0
Tea	21.1	20.3	19.8
Tobacco	9.3	11.5	9.2
Groundnuts	67.2	79.1	56.1
Sugar cane	3,255.8	2,893.8	2,180.3
Bananas	212.5	198.5	204.7
Pineapples	348.5	357.5	388.7
Citrus fruit	486.5	440.4	463.5
Vegetables.	3,513.8	3,262.2	3,046.2

* Figures are in terms of brown rice. The equivalent in paddy rice (in '000 metric tons) was: 1,916.3 in 1999; 1,906.1 in 2000; 1,723.9 in 2001.

LIVESTOCK
('000 head at 31 December)

	1999	2000	2001
Cattle	156.1	153.9	146.0
Buffaloes	9.2	7.8	6.5
Pigs	7,243.2	7,495.0	7,164.6
Sheep and goats	237.3	202.5	184.7
Chickens	121,512	117,885	117,310
Ducks	11,649	10,624	10,104
Geese	3,006	2,821	2,613
Turkeys	262	251	235

LIVESTOCK PRODUCTS

	1999	2000	2001
Beef (metric tons) . . .	5,168	4,901	5,057
Pig meat (metric tons) . .	996,780	1,115,883	1,165,998
Goat meat (metric tons). .	8,916	8,213	7,219
Chickens ('000 head)* . .	385,563	389,770	376,196
Ducks ('000 head)* . . .	35,208	34,099	32,142
Geese ('000 head)* . . .	7,464	6,503	6,330
Turkeys ('000 head)*. . .	488	500	458
Milk (metric tons) . . .	338,005	358,049	346,079
Duck eggs ('000) . . .	485,629	478,452	481,789
Hen eggs ('000)	7,274,451	7,270,033	7,325,125

* Figures refer to numbers slaughtered.

Forestry

ROUNDWOOD REMOVALS
('000 cubic metres)

	1999	2000	2001
Industrial wood	23.3	21.1	26.4
Fuel wood	4.3	4.8	6.0
Total	27.6	25.9	32.4

Fishing*

('000 metric tons, live weight, incl. aquaculture)

	1999	2000	2001
Tilapias	57.3	49.3	82.9
Other freshwater fishes . .	23.4	22.5	19.2
Japanese eel	16.5	30.5	34.2
Milkfish	50.8	39.7	59.4
Pacific saury	12.5	27.9	39.8
Skipjack tuna	163.9	198.9	186.7
Albacore	64.3	66.1	64.1
Yellowfin tuna	95.0	94.3	109.6
Bigeye tuna	76.8	73.1	81.2
Chub mackerel	45.3	28.6	24.3
Sharks, rays, skates, etc. .	42.7	48.1	44.2
Other fishes (incl. unspecified) .	292.9	282.5	286.5
Total fish.	941.4	961.5	1,032.1
Marine shrimps and prawns .	35.9	35.4	29.2
Other crustaceans . . .	6.7	9.2	9.8
Pacific cupped oyster . .	18.6	20.0	16.6
Common squids	15.9	13.1	13.7
Argentine shortfin squid . .	277.0	254.7	147.6
Flying squids	5.0	3.9	4.5
Other molluscs	0.5	0.3	0.3
Other aquatic animals . . .	47.3	46.6	47.4
Total catch	1,348.8	1,344.7	1,301.2

* Figures exclude aquatic plants, totalling (in '000 metric tons) 15.5 in 1999; 12.7 in 2000; 15.7 in 2001.

Mining
(metric tons, unless otherwise indicated)

	1999	2000	2001
Coal	91,673	83,380	—
Crude petroleum ('000 litres)	47,105	37,172	44,380
Natural gas ('000 cu m) . .	855,623	746,824	849,158
Salt	76,916	69,523	66,150
Sulphur	194,811	205,588	223,659
Marble (raw material) . .	17,771,530	17,831,591	20,475,479
Dolomite	200,595	119,257	70,698

Industry

SELECTED PRODUCTS
('000 metric tons, unless otherwise indicated)

	1999	2000	2001
Wheat flour	738.2	785.5	784.3
Granulated sugar	286.0	230.2	201.8
Carbonated beverages ('000 litres)	461,032	436,897	442,241
Alcoholic beverages—excl. beer ('000 hectolitres) .	2,482.0	2,507.4	2,482.4
Cigarettes (million)	22,735	21,064	22,226
Cotton yarn	353.6	337.6	313.6
Man-made fibres	3,227.9	n.a.	n.a.
Paper	1,246.2	1,259.9	1,114.6
Paperboard	3,073.5	3,233.9	2,590.5
Sulphuric acid	848.2	1,020.9	955.8
Spun yarn	485.9	439.6	360.3
Cement	18,283.2	17,572.3	18,127.6
Steel ingots	16,026.7	17,302.4	17,336.2
Sewing machines ('000 units) .	2,778.2	2,947.2	2,630.0
Electric fans ('000 units) . .	23,800.3	22,278.5	21,602.4
Personal computers ('000 units) .	12,959.1	16,431.7	16,650.6
Monitors ('000 units). . .	10,941.8	8,193.8	7,896.4
Radio cassette recorders ('000 units) . .	4,620.6	4,600.9	4,901.4
Radio receivers ('000 units) . .	2,156.6	2,038.1	1,985.8
Television receivers ('000 units) . .	1,021.5	1,154.6	927.6
Picture tubes ('000 units) . .	23,344.0	20,538.0	9,739
Integrated circuits (million units) .	3,985.2	5,068.6	4,799.3
Electronic condensers (million units) . .	80,670.6	111,071.2	118,127.0
Telephone sets ('000 units) . .	6,629.5	4,722.4	1,911.0
Passenger motor cars (units) . .	341,133	367,725	266,237
Trucks and buses (units) . .	4,227	3,358	2,326
Bicycles ('000 units) . . .	7,228.3	7,193.2	4,746.5
Ships ('000 dwt)*. . . .	665.5	868.0	1,014.3
Electric energy (million kWh) .	160,570	175,165	178,358
Liquefied petroleum gas. . .	746.3	943.2	975.2

* Excluding motor yachts.

Finance

CURRENCY AND EXCHANGE RATES

Monetary Units
100 cents = 1 New Taiwan dollar (NT $)

Sterling, US Dollar and Euro Equivalents (31 December 2002)
£1 sterling = NT $56.03
US $1 = NT $34.76
€1 = NT $36.45
NT $1,000 = £17.85 = US $28.77 = €27.43

Average Exchange Rate (NT $ per US $)
2000   31.235
2001   33.813
2002   34.579

BUDGET
(NT $ million, year ending 31 December)

Revenue	1999/2000	2001	2002*
Taxes	1,280,657	841,480	878,447
Monopoly profits	77,316	58,718	—
Non-tax revenue from other sources	672,872	517,491	381,715
Total	2,030,845	1,417,689	1,260,162

* Estimates.

Expenditure	1999/2000	2001	2002*
General administration	234,929	167,013	167,571
National defence	343,282	237,752	227,581
Education, science and culture . .	367,635	257,442	275,196
Economic development	356,418	277,094	267,952
Social welfare	411,023	293,421	266,413
Community development and environmental protection . . .	39,627	22,341	23,845
Pensions and survivors' benefits .	195,395	121,967	131,872
Obligations	249,584	151,242	103,258
Subsidies to provincial and municipal governments . . .	25,980	27,672	39,955
Other expenditure	6,273	4,234	15,082
Total	2,230,145	1,560,178	1,518,725

* Estimates.

Note: Figures refer to central government accounts, including Taiwan Province from 1999/2000. Owing to the modification of Budget Law, the financial year 1999/2000 was extended by six months to December 2000. Beginning in 2001, the financial year corresponds to the calendar year.

INTERNATIONAL RESERVES
(US $ million at 31 December)

	1999	2000	2001
Gold*	4,861	4,628	4,361
Foreign exchange	106,200	106,742	122,211
Total	111,061	111,370	126,572

* National valuation.

MONEY SUPPLY
(NT $ million at 31 December)

	1999	2000	2001
Currency outside banks	611,167	527,748	525,659
Demand deposits at deposit money banks	3,896,013	3,964,324	4,500,201
Total money	4,507,180	4,492,072	5,025,860

COST OF LIVING
(Consumer Price Index; base: 1996 = 100)

	1999	2000	2001
Food	102.97	103.13	102.12
Clothing	94.28	94.58	93.00
Housing	102.54	103.08	102.73
Transport and communications .	99.33	102.70	103.87
Medicines and medical care . .	106.91	110.93	112.41
Education and entertainment . .	108.60	111.71	113.96
All items (incl. others)	102.78	104.07	104.06

NATIONAL ACCOUNTS
(NT $ million in current prices)

National Income and Product

	1999	2000	2001
Compensation of employees . . .	4,687,235	4,939,685	4,809,210
Operating surplus	3,106,004	3,163,763	3,141,257
Domestic factor incomes . . .	7,793,239	8,103,448	7,950,467
Consumption of fixed capital . .	804,144	878,482	932,853
Gross domestic product (GDP) at factor cost	8,597,383	8,981,930	8,883,320
Indirect taxes	726,810	727,193	683,302
Less Subsidies	34,264	45,735	59,998
GDP in purchasers' values . .	9,289,929	9,663,388	9,506,624
Factor income from abroad . .	224,468	286,688	314,956
Less Factor income paid abroad .	138,556	146,728	123,533
Gross national product (GNP) .	9,375,841	9,803,348	9,698,047
Less Consumption of fixed capital .	804,144	878,482	932,853
National income in market prices	8,571,697	8,924,866	8,765,194
Other current transfers from abroad	100,750	99,990	88,131
Less Other current transfers paid abroad	171,150	181,477	180,353
National disposable income . .	8,501,297	8,843,379	8,672,972

Expenditure on the Gross Domestic Product

	1999	2000	2001
Government final consumption expenditure	1,221,717	1,246,983	1,240,437
Private final consumption expenditure	5,641,313	5,981,274	6,042,628
Increase in stocks	46,628	−54,978	−99,598
Gross fixed capital formation . .	2,124,744	2,267,328	1,781,752
Total domestic expenditure . .	9,034,402	9,440,607	8,965,219
Exports of goods and services . .	4,486,094	5,260,994	4,839,820
Less Imports of goods and services .	4,230,567	5,038,213	4,298,415
GDP in purchasers' values . .	9,289,929	9,663,388	9,506,624
GDP at constant 1996 prices . .	9,029,704	9,558,698	9,349,923

Gross Domestic Product by Economic Activity

	1999	2000	2001
Agriculture, hunting, forestry and fishing	237,531	201,810	185,182
Mining and quarrying	46,391	40,427	37,986
Manufacturing	2,470,012	2,550,380	2,431,213
Construction	358,300	329,567	277,651
Electricity, gas and water . . .	207,749	208,325	208,871
Transport, storage and communications	625,637	648,571	656,292
Trade, restaurants and hotels . .	1,717,692	1,865,320	1,833,533
Finance, insurance and real estate*	1,890,388	1,937,655	1,948,157
Business services	237,144	261,783	269,092
Community, social and personal services	835,631	907,084	962,939
Government services	946,549	984,982	1,011,122
Other services	96,514	107,436	114,981
Sub-total	9,669,538	10,043,340	9,937,019
Value-added tax	173,642	178,160	167,247
Import duties	139,348	146,443	119,100
Less Imputed bank service charge .	692,599	704,555	716,742
GDP in purchasers' values . .	9,289,929	9,663,388	9,506,624

* Including imputed rents of owner-occupied dwellings.

BALANCE OF PAYMENTS
(US $ million)

	1999	2000	2001
Exports of goods f.o.b.	121,119	147,548	122,079
Imports of goods f.o.b.	−106,077	−133,529	−101,898
Trade balance	15,042	14,019	20,181
Exports of services	17,259	19,952	20,435
Imports of services	−24,405	−26,930	−24,700
Balance on goods and services	7,896	7,041	15,916
Other income received	6,965	9,166	9,327
Other income paid	−4,160	−4,698	−3,648
Balance on goods, services and income	10,701	11,509	21,595
Current transfers received	3,126	3,202	2,607
Current transfers paid	−5,443	−5,806	−5,341
Current balance	8,384	8,905	18,861
Capital account (net)	−173	−287	−163
Direct investment abroad	−4,420	−6,701	−5,480
Direct investment from abroad	2,926	4,928	4,109
Portfolio investment assets	−4,835	−10,087	−12,427
Portfolio investment liabilities	13,914	9,559	11,136
Other investment assets	2,334	−8,368	−1,837
Other investment liabilities	−699	2,650	3,776
Net errors and omissions	1,162	1,878	−622
Overall balance	18,593	2,477	17,353

External Trade

PRINCIPAL COMMODITIES
(US $ million)

Imports c.i.f.	1999	2000	2001
Mineral products	9,145.6	14,094.0	12,763.7
Crude petroleum	4,596.3	8,088.2	6,808.6
Products of chemical or allied industries	10,596.4	13,085.4	10,231.0
Organic chemicals	4,448.4	5,638.6	3,901.2
Base metals and articles thereof	9,511.2	11,044.9	7,783.8
Iron and steel products	4,941.5	5,621.2	3,788.3
Metal products (excl. iron and steel)	4,569.7	5,423.7	3,995.5
Machinery and mechanical appliances; electrical equipment; sound and television apparatus	50,598.4	66,034.2	47,549.5
Electronic products	19,818.1	27,282.8	21,027.9
Machineries	13,517.5	17,064.7	10,488.2
Electrical machinery products	4,146.0	5,354.7	4,282.8
Information and communication products	8,524.2	11,282.5	8,119.6
Vehicles, aircraft, vessels and associated transport equipment	4,022.0	4,705.7	4,241.4
Optical, photographic, cinematographic, measuring, precision and medical apparatus; clocks and watches; musical instruments	6,186.2	9,116.4	6,214.8
Total (incl. others)	110,689.9	140,013.6	107,242.9

Exports f.o.b.	1999	2000	2001
Chemicals	3,266.9	4,049.7	4,138.7
Plastics, rubber and articles thereof	7,524.3	9,057.9	7,994.7
Textiles and textile articles	14,172.7	15,219.5	12,636.0
Fibre and yarn	10,121.7	10,849.3	8,983.7
Base metals and articles thereof	11,606.9	13,523.1	11,333.5
Iron and steel	6,886.5	8,320.5	6,890.5
Metal products (excl. iron and steel)	4,720.4	5,202.6	4,443.0
Machinery and mechanical appliances; electrical equipment; sound and television apparatus	64,161.9	82,601.8	66,876.1
Electronic products	21,832.5	31,699.4	23,610.2
Machineries	7,921.1	9,676.2	8,345.4
Electrical machinery products	4,601.1	5,394.3	4,667.1
Information and communication products	15,141.7	19,556.0	15,670.3
Vehicles, aircraft, vessels and associated transport equipment	5,151.9	5,755.9	4,441.6
Total (incl. others)	121,591.0	148,375.9	122,901.5

PRINCIPAL TRADING PARTNERS
(US $ million)

Imports c.i.f.	1999	2000	2001
Australia	2,957.1	3,501.5	3,084.9
Canada	1,124.6	1,276.3	996.1
China, People's Republic	4,526.3	6,223.3	5,901.9
France	1,887.3	1,830.1	2,130.5
Germany	5,312.6	5,542.2	4,246.0
Hong Kong	2,092.9	2,186.6	1,848.9
Indonesia	2,291.4	3,015.1	2,523.4
Italy	1,308.5	1,391.5	1,084.1
Japan	30,591.0	38,557.9	25,848.4
Korea, Republic	7,192.8	8,988.1	6,705.1
Malaysia	3,882.0	5,325.4	4,213.7
Netherlands	1,705.7	2,087.4	1,524.2
Philippines	2,172.5	3,593.9	3,250.5
Russia	1,183.2	1,379.6	603.5
Saudi Arabia	1,383.6	2,690.5	2,745.4
Singapore	3,312.2	5,013.8	3,367.2
Switzerland	1,105.5	1,058.6	865.8
Thailand	2,383.4	2,768.0	2,181.0
United Kingdom	1,720.5	1,937.4	1,442.8
USA	19,693.1	25,126.2	18,229.2
Total (incl. others)	110,689.9	140,010.6	107,237.4

Exports f.o.b.	1999	2000	2001
Australia	1,847.4	1,828.0	1,362.7
Canada	1,750.5	1,882.2	1,564.3
China, People's Republic	2,536.9	4,217.5	4,745.4
France	1,584.1	1,637.6	1,166.0
Germany	4,076.6	4,891.4	4,480.4
Hong Kong*	26,012.1	31,336.3	26,961.4
Indonesia	1,298.6	1,733.7	1,474.6
Italy	1,326.5	1,484.5	1,254.5
Japan	11,900.3	16,599.4	12,759.0
Korea, Republic	2,604.9	3,907.8	3,275.6
Malaysia	2,848.1	3,611.7	3,061.4
Netherlands	4,214.3	4,933.8	4,229.2
Philippines	2,611.4	3,035.7	2,148.7
Singapore	3,818.3	5,455.8	4,051.5
Thailand	2,104.5	2,562.3	2,125.7
United Kingdom	3,830.3	4,508.5	3,329.3
USA	30,901.5	34,814.7	27,654.5
Viet Nam	1,341.6	1,663.5	1,726.9
Total (incl. others)	121,590.9	148,320.6	122,866.4

* The majority of Taiwan's exports to Hong Kong are re-exported.

Revised totals (US $ million): *Imports c.i.f.*:140,013.6 in 2000; 107,242.9 in 2001. *Exports f.o.b.*: 148,375.9 in 2000; 122,901.5 in 2001.

Transport

RAILWAYS
(traffic)

	1999	2000	2001
Passengers ('000)	309,815	460,311	476,214
Passenger-km ('000)	11,020,369	12,623,814	12,268,691
Freight ('000 metric tons)	25,993	22,261	19,287
Freight ton-km ('000)	1,314,912	1,179,056	1,009,863

ROAD TRAFFIC
(motor vehicles in use at 31 December)

	1999	2000	2001
Passenger cars	4,509,430	4,716,217	4,825,581
Buses and coaches	23,798	23,923	24,053
Goods vehicles	779,912	808,586	830,673
Motorcycles and scooters	10,958,469	11,423,172	11,733,202

SHIPPING

Merchant Fleet
(at 31 December)

	1999	2000	2001
Number of vessels	684	680	656
Total displacement ('000 grt) . .	5,371.4	5,086.2	4,617.9

Source: Lloyd's Register-Fairplay, *World Fleet Statistics*.

Sea-borne freight traffic
('000 metric tons)

	1999	2000	2001
Goods loaded	209,518	223,728	221,154
Goods unloaded	324,567	343,222	331,719

CIVIL AVIATION
(traffic on scheduled services)

	1999	2000	2001
Passengers carried ('000) . .	50,342.2	46,430.5	44,114.7
Passenger-km (million) . . .	41,698.8	45,755.8	n.a.
Freight carried ('000 metric tons) .	1,447.5	1,620.0	1,310.2
Freight ton-km (million) . .	5,449.9	6,226.3	n.a.

Tourism

TOURIST ARRIVALS BY COUNTRY OF ORIGIN

	1999	2000	2001
Hong Kong	63,323	73,708	80,752
Indonesia	76,424	106,787	89,027
Japan	826,222	916,301	971,190
Korea, Republic	76,142	83,729	82,684
Malaysia	52,678	58,017	56,834
Philippines	123,000	84,088	69,118
Singapore	85,844	94,897	96,777
Thailand	137,972	133,185	116,420
USA	317,801	359,533	339,390
Overseas Chinese*	295,595	313,367	325,266
Total (incl. others)	2,411,248	2,624,037	2,617,137

* i.e. those bearing Taiwan passports.

Tourism receipts (US $ million): 3,571 in 1999; 3,738 in 2000; 3,990 in 2001.

Communications Media

	1999	2000	2001
Book production (titles)	30,871	34,533	36,546
Newspapers	384	445	454
Magazines.	6,463	6,641	7,236
Television receivers ('000 in use)* .	9,200	9,660	n.a.
Telephone subscribers ('000) . .	12,044	12,642	12,847
Mobile telephones ('000 in use). .	11,541	17,874	21,633
Personal computers ('000 in use)* .	4,353	4,964	5,000
Internet users ('000)*	4,540	6,260	7,550

Radio receivers (1994): more than 16 million in use.

* Source: International Telecommunication Union.

Education

(2001/02)

	Schools	Full-time teachers	Students
Pre-school	3,234	19,799	246,303
Primary	2,611	103,501	1,925,491
Secondary (incl. vocational). . .	1,181	98,609	1,684,449
Higher	154	44,769	1,187,225
Special	24	1,639	5,860
Supplementary	954	3,293	304,763
Total (incl. others)	8,158	271,610	5,354,091

Directory

The Constitution

On 1 January 1947 a new Constitution was promulgated for the Republic of China (confined to Taiwan since 1949). The form of government that was incorporated in the Constitution is based on a five-power system and has the major features of both cabinet and presidential government. A process of constitutional reform, initiated in 1991, continued in 2000. The following is a summary of the Constitution, as subsequently amended:

PRESIDENT

The President shall be directly elected by popular vote for a term of four years. Both the President and Vice-President are eligible for re-election to a second term. The President represents the country at all state functions, including foreign relations; commands land, sea and air forces, promulgates laws, issues mandates, concludes treaties, declares war, makes peace, declares martial law, grants amnesties, appoints and removes civil and military officers, and confers honours and decorations. The President convenes the National Assembly and, subject to certain limitations, may issue emergency orders to deal with national calamities and ensure national security; may dissolve the Legislative Yuan; also nominates the Premier (who may be appointed without the Legislative Yuan's confirmation), and the officials of the Judicial Yuan, the Examination Yuan and the Control Yuan.

NATIONAL ASSEMBLY

Three hundred delegates shall be elected by proportional representation to the National Assembly within three months of the expiration of a six-month period following the public announcement of a proposal by the Legislative Yuan to amend the Constitution or alter the national territory, or within three months of a petition initiated by the Legislative Yuan for the impeachment of the President or the Vice-President. Delegates to the National Assembly shall convene of their own accord within 10 days after the election results have been confirmed and shall remain in session for no more than one month. The term of office of the delegates to the National Assembly shall terminate on the last day of the convention. The powers of the National Assembly are: to vote on the Legislative Yuan's proposals to amend the Contitution or alter the National territory; to deliberate a petition for the impeachment of the President or the Vice-President initiated by the Legislative Yuan.

EXECUTIVE YUAN

The Executive Yuan is the highest administrative organ of the nation and is responsible to the Legislative Yuan; has three categories of subordinate organization:

Executive Yuan Council (policy-making organization);

Ministries and Commissions (executive organization);

Subordinate organization (19 bodies, including the Secretariat, Government Information Office, Directorate-General of Budget,

Accounting and Statistics, Council for Economic Planning and Development, and Environmental Protection Administration).

LEGISLATIVE YUAN

The Legislative Yuan is the highest legislative organ of the State, empowered to hear administrative reports of the Executive Yuan, and to change government policy. It may hold a binding vote of 'no confidence' in the Executive Yuan. It comprises 225 members, 168 chosen by direct election from two special municipalities and other cities and counties, eight members are elected from and by aborigines, and eight from and by overseas Chinese. The remaining 41 members are elected from a nationwide constituency on the basis of proportional representation. Members serve for three years and are eligible for re-election.

JUDICIAL YUAN

The Judicial Yuan is the highest judicial organ of state and has charge of civil, criminal and administrative cases, and of cases concerning disciplinary measures against public functionaries (see Judicial System).

EXAMINATION YUAN

The Examination Yuan supervises examinations for entry into public offices, and deals with personnel questions of the civil service.

CONTROL YUAN

The Control Yuan is the highest control organ of the State, exercising powers of impeachment, censure and audit. Comprising 29 members serving a six-year term, nominated and (with the consent of the National Assembly) appointed by the President, the Control Yuan may impeach or censure a public functionary at central or local level, who is deemed guilty of violation of law or dereliction of duty, and shall refer the matter to the law courts for action in cases involving a criminal offence; may propose corrective measures to the Executive Yuan or to its subordinate organs.

The Government

HEAD OF STATE

President: CHEN SHUI-BIAN (inaugurated 20 May 2000).

Vice-President: HSU-LIEN ANNETTE LU.

Secretary-General: CHIOU I-JEN.

THE EXECUTIVE YUAN
(April 2003)

Premier: YU SHYI-KUN.

Vice-Premier and Chairman of the Council for Economic Planning and Development: LIN HSIN-I.

Secretary-General: LIU SHYH-FANG.

Ministers without Portfolio: TSAY CHING-YEN, HU SHENG-CHENG, CHEN CHI-NAN, HUANG HWEI-CHEN, LIN SHENG-FENG, KUO YAO-CHI (Chairwoman of the Public Construction Commission), YEH JIUNN-RONG.

Minister of the Interior: YU CHENG-HSIEN.

Minister of Foreign Affairs: EUGENE Y. H. CHIEN.

Minister of National Defense: Gen. (retd) TANG YAO-MING.

Minister of Finance: LIN CHUAN.

Minister of Education: HUANG JONG-TSUN.

Minister of Justice: CHEN DING-NAN.

Minister of Economic Affairs: LIN YI-FU.

Minister of Transportation and Communications: LIN LING-SAN.

Minister of the Mongolian and Tibetan Affairs Commission: HSU CHIH-HSIUNG.

Minister of the Overseas Chinese Affairs Commission: CHANG FU-MEI.

Governor of the Central Bank of China: PERNG FAI-NAN.

Director-General of Directorate-General of Budget, Accounting and Statistics: HALE S. C. LIU.

Director-General of Central Personnel Administration: LEE YI-YIANG.

Director-General of the Government Information Office: ARTHUR IAP.

Minister of Health: TWU SHIING-JER.

Administrator of the Environmental Protection Administration: HAU LUNG-BIN.

Director-General of the Coast Guard Administration: WANG CHUN.

Director of the National Palace Museum: TU CHENG-SHENG.

Chairwoman of the Mainland Affairs Council: TSAI ING-WEN.

Chairman of Veterans' Affairs Commission: TENG TZU-LIN.

Chairwoman of the National Youth Commission: LIN FANG-MEI.

Chairman of the Atomic Energy Council: OUYANG MIN-SHEN.

Chairman of the National Science Council: WEI CHE-HO.

Chairman of the Research, Development and Evaluation Commission: LIN CHIA-CHENG.

Chairman of the Council of Agriculture: LEE CHING-LUNG.

Chairwoman of the Council for Cultural Affairs: TCHEN YU-CHIOU.

Chairwoman of the Council of Labor Affairs: CHEN CHU.

Chairman of the Fair Trade Commission: HWANG TZONG-LEH.

Chairman of the Council of Aboriginal Affairs: CHEN CHIEN-NIEN.

Chairman of the National Council on Physical Fitness and Sports: LIN TE-FU.

Chairwoman of the Council for Hakka Affairs: YEH CHU-LAN.

MINISTRIES, COMMISSIONS, ETC.

Office of the President: Chiehshou Hall, 122 Chungking South Rd, Sec. 1, Taipei 100; tel. (2) 23718889; fax (2) 23611604; e-mail public@mail.oop.gov.tw; internet www.oop.gov.tw.

Ministry of Economic Affairs: 15 Foo Chou St, Taipei; tel. (2) 23212200; fax (2) 23919398; e-mail service@moea.gov.tw; internet www.moea.gov.tw.

Ministry of Education: 5 Chung Shan South Rd, Taipei 10040; tel. (2) 23566051; fax (2) 23976978; internet www.moe.gov.tw.

Ministry of Finance: 2 Ai Kuo West Rd, Taipei; tel. (2) 23228000; fax (2) 23965829; e-mail root@www.mof.gov.tw; internet www.mof.gov.tw.

Ministry of Foreign Affairs: 2 Chiehshou Rd, Taipei 10016; tel. (2) 23119292; fax (2) 23144972; internet www.mofa.gov.tw.

Ministry of the Interior: 5–9/F, 5 Hsu Chou Rd, Taipei; tel. (2) 23565005; fax (2) 23566201; e-mail gethics@mail.moi.gov.tw; internet www.moi.gov.tw.

Ministry of Justice: 130 Chungking South Rd, Sec. 1, Taipei 100 10036; tel. (2) 23146871; fax (2) 23896759; internet www.moj.gov.tw.

Ministry of National Defense: 2/F, 164 Po Ai Rd, Taipei; tel. (2) 23116117; fax (2) 23144221; internet www.ndmc.edu.tw.

Ministry of Transportation and Communications: 2 Chang Sha St, Sec. 1, Taipei; tel. (2) 23492900; fax (2) 23118587; e-mail motceyes@motc.gov.tw; internet www.motc.gov.tw.

Mongolian and Tibetan Affairs Commission: 4/F, 5 Hsu Chou Rd, Sec. 1, Taipei; tel. (2) 23566166; fax (2) 23566432; internet www.mtac.gov.tw.

Overseas Chinese Affairs Commission: 4/F, 5 Hsu Chou Rd, Taipei; tel. (2) 23566166; fax (2) 23566323; e-mail ocacinfo@mail.ocac.gov.tw; internet www.ocac.gov.tw.

Directorate-General of Budget, Accounting and Statistics: 2 Kwang Chow St, Taipei 100; tel. (2) 23710208; fax (2) 23319925; e-mail sicbs@emc.dgbasey.gov.tw; internet www.dgbas.gov.tw.

Government Information Office: 2 Tientsin St, Taipei; tel. (2) 33568888; fax (2) 23568733; e-mail service@mail.gio.gov.tw; internet www.gio.gov.tw.

Council of Aboriginal Affairs: 16–17/F, 4 Chung Hsiao West Rd, Sec. 1, Taipei; tel. (2) 23882122; fax (2) 23891967.

Council of Agriculture: see under Trade and Industry—Government Agencies.

Atomic Energy Council (AEC): 80 Cheng Kung Rd, Sec. 1, Taipei 234; tel. (2) 82317919; fax (2) 82317864; internet www.aec.gov.tw.

Central Personnel Administration: 109 Huai Ning St, Taipei; tel. (2) 23111720; fax (2) 23715252; internet www.cpa.gov.tw.

Consumer Protection Commission: 1 Chung Hsiao East Rd, Sec. 1, Taipei; tel. (2) 23566600; fax (2) 23214538; e-mail tcpc@ms1.hinet.net; internet www.cpc.gov.tw.

Council for Cultural Affairs: 102 Ai Kuo East Rd, Taipei; tel. (2) 25225300; fax (2) 25519011; e-mail wwwadm@ccpdunx.ccpd.gov.tw; internet expo96.org.tw/cca/welcome_c.html.

Council for Economic Planning and Development: 9/F, 87 Nanking East Rd, Sec. 2, Taipei; tel. (2) 25225300; fax (2) 25519011; internet www.cepd.gov.tw.

Environmental Protection Administration: 41 Chung Hua Rd, Sec. 1, Taipei; tel. (2) 23117722; fax (2) 23116071; e-mail www@sun .epa.gov.tw; internet www.epa.gov.tw.

Fair Trade Commission: 12–14/F, 2-2 Chi Nan Rd, Sec. 2, Taipei; tel. (2) 23517588; fax (2) 23974997; e-mail ftcse@ftc.gov.tw; internet www.ftc.gov.tw.

Department of Health: 100 Ai Kuo East Rd, Taipei; tel. (2) 23210151; fax (2) 23122907; internet www.doh.gov.tw.

Council of Labor Affairs: 5–15/F, 132 Min Sheng East Rd, Sec. 3, Taipei; tel. (2) 27182512; fax (2) 25149240; internet www.cla.gov.tw.

Mainland Affairs Council: 5–13/F, 2-2 Chi Nan Rd, Sec. 1, Taipei; tel. (2) 23975589; fax (2) 23975700; e-mail macst@mac.gov.tw; internet www.mac.gov.tw.

National Science Council: 17–22/F, 106 Ho Ping East Rd, Sec. 2, Taipei; tel. (2) 27377501; fax (2) 27377668; e-mail nsc@nsc.gov.tw; internet www.nsc.gov.tw.

National Youth Commission: 14/F, 5 Hsu Chou Rd, Taipei; tel. (2) 23566271; fax (2) 23566290; internet www.nyc.gov.tw.

Research, Development and Evaluation Commission: 7/F, 2-2 Chi Nan Rd, Sec. 1, Taipei; tel. (2) 23419066; fax (2) 23928133; e-mail service@rdec.gov.tw; internet rdec.gov.tw.

Veterans' Affairs Commission: 222 Chung Hsiao East Rd, Sec. 5, Taipei; tel. (2) 27255700; fax (2) 27253578; e-mail hsc@www.vac.gov .tw; internet vac.gov.tw.

President and Legislature

PRESIDENT

Election, 18 March 2000

Candidate	Votes	% of votes
Chen Shui-bian (Democratic Progressive Party—DPP)	4,977,737	39.3
James C. Y. Soong (Independent)	4,664,932	36.8
Lien Chan (Kuomintang—KMT)	2,925,513	23.1
Hsu Hsin-lian (Independent)	79,429	0.6
Li Ao (New Party—NP)	16,782	0.1
Total	**12,664,393***	**100.0**

*Not including invalid or spoiled ballot papers, which numbered 122,278.

LI-FA YUAN
(Legislative Yuan)

The Legislative Yuan is the highest legislative organ of the State. It comprises 225 seats. The 168 directly elected members come from two special municipalities and other cities and counties. Eight members are elected from and by aboriginies, and eight from and by overseas Chinese. The remaining 41 members are elected from a nationwide constituency on the basis of proportional representation. Members serve for three years and are eligible for re-election.

President: WANG JIN-PYNG.

General Election, 1 December 2001

Party	% of votes	Seats
Democratic Progressive Party (DPP)	36.6	87
Kuomintang (KMT)	31.3	68
People First Party	20.3	46
Taiwan Solidarity Union (TSU)	8.5	13
New Party (NP)	2.9	1
Other	0.5	1
Independents	—	9
Total	**100.0**	**225**

Political Organizations

Legislation adopted in 1989 permitted political parties other than the KMT to function. By mid-2002 a total of 99 parties had registered with the Ministry of the Interior.

China Democratic Socialist Party (CDSP): 6/F, 7, Ho Ping East Rd, Sec. 3, Taipei; tel. (2) 27072883; f. 1932 by merger of National Socialists and Democratic Constitutionalists; aims to promote democracy, to protect fundamental freedoms, and to improve public welfare and social security; Chair. I BUH-LUEN; Sec.-Gen. KAO SHAO-CHUNG.

China Young Party: 12/F, 2 Shin Sheng South Rd, Sec. 3, Taipei; tel. (2) 23626715; f. 1923; aims to recover sovereignty over mainland China, to safeguard the Constitution and democracy, and to foster understanding between Taiwan and the non-communist world.

Chinese Republican Party (CRP): 3/F, 26 Lane 90, Jong Shuenn St, Sec. 2, Taipei; tel. (2) 29366572; f. 1988; advocates peaceful struggle for the salvation of China and the promotion of world peace; Chair. WANG YING-CHYUN.

Democratic Liberal Party (DLP): 4/F, 20 Lane 5, Ching Tyan, Taipei; tel. (2) 23121595; f. 1989; aims to promote political democracy and economic liberty for the people of Taiwan; Chair. HER WEI-KANG.

Democratic Progressive Party (DPP): 10/F, 30 Pei Ping East Rd, Taipei; tel. and fax (2) 23929989; e-mail foreign@dpp.org.tw; internet www.dpp.org.tw; f. 1986; advocates 'self-determination' for the people of Taiwan and UN membership; supports establishment of independent Taiwan following plebiscite; 140,000 mems; Chair. CHEN SHUI-BIAN; Sec.-Gen. CHANG CHUN-HSIUNG.

Democratic Union of Taiwan (DUT): 16/F, 15-1 Harng Joe South Rd, Sec. 1, Taipei; tel. (2) 23211531; f. 1998; Chair. HSU CHERNG-KUEN.

Green Party: 11/F-1, 273 Roosevelt Rd, Sec. 3, Taipei; tel. (2) 23621362; f. 1996 by breakaway faction of the DPP; Chair. CHEN GUANG-YEU.

Jiann Gwo Party (Taiwan Independence Party—TAIP): 2/F, 406 Guang Hwa 2 Rd, Kaohsiung; tel. (7) 7218127; internet www.taip .org.tw; f. 1996 by dissident mems of DPP; Chair. HER WEN-CHII; Sec.-Gen. LI SHENG-HSIUNG.

Kungtang (KT) (Labour Party): 2/F, 22 Kai Feng St, Sec. 2, Taipei; tel. (2) 23121472; fax (2) 23719687; e-mail no1hsieh@eagle.seed.net .tw; f. 1987; aims to become the main political movement of Taiwan's industrial work-force; 10,000 mems; Chair. JENG JAU-MING; Sec.-Gen. HSIEH CHENG-YI.

Kuomintang (KMT) (Nationalist Party of China): 11 Chung Shan South Rd, Taipei 100; tel. (2) 23121472; fax (2) 23434524; internet www.kmt.org.tw; f. 1894; fmr ruling party; aims to supplant communist rule in mainland China; supports democratic, constitutional government, and advocates the unification of China under the 'Three Principles of the People'; aims to promote market economy and equitable distribution of wealth; 2,523,984 mems; Chair. LIEN CHAN; Sec.-Gen. LIN FONG-CHENG.

Nationwide Democratic Non-Partisan Union (NDNU): c/o The Legislative Yuan, Taipei.

New Nation Alliance: 14/F, 9 Song Jiang Rd, Taipei; tel. (2) 23585643; f. 1998; promotes independence for Taiwan and the establishment of a 'new nation, new society and new culture'; Chair. PERNG BAE-SHEAN.

New Party (NP): 4/F, 65 Guang Fuh South Rd, Taipei; tel. (2) 27562222; fax (2) 27565750; e-mail webmaster@ mail.np.org.tw; internet www.np.org.tw; f. 1993 by dissident KMT legislators (hitherto mems of New Kuomintang Alliance faction); merged with China Social Democratic Party in late 1993; advocates co-operation with the KMT and DPP in negotiations with the People's Republic, the maintenance of security in the Taiwan Straits, the modernization of the island's defence systems, measures to combat government corruption, the support of small and medium businesses and the establishment of a universal social security system; 80,000 mems; Chair. YOK MU-MING; Sec.-Gen. PETER CHIN CHANG.

People First Party (PFP): c/o The Legislative Yuan, Taipei; internet www.pfp.org.tw; f. 2000; Chair. JAMES C. Y. SOONG; Sec.-Gen. TSAI CHUNG-HSIUNG.

Taiwan Solidarity Union (TSU): 5/F, 180 Hoping East Rd, Taipei; tel. (2) 23678990; fax (2) 23678408; f. 2001 by a breakaway faction of the Kuomintang (KMT); Chair. HUANG CHU-WEN; Sec.-Gen. SHU CHIN-CHIANG.

Workers' Party: 2/F, 181 Fu-hsing South Rd, Taipei; tel. (2) 27555868; f. 1989 by breakaway faction of the Kungtang; radical; Leader LOU MEIWEN.

Various pro-independence groups (some based overseas and, until 1992, banned in Taiwan) are in operation. These include the **World United Formosans for Independence** (WUFI—4,000 mems world-wide; Chair. George Chang) and the **Organization for Taiwan Nation-Building.**

Diplomatic Representation

EMBASSIES IN THE REPUBLIC OF CHINA

Belize: 11/F, 9 Lane 62, Tien Mou West Rd, Taipei 111; tel. (2) 28760894; fax (2) 28760896; e-mail embelroc@ms41.hinet.net; internet www.embassyofbelize.org.tw; Ambassador WILLIAM QUINTO.

Burkina Faso: 6/F, 9-1, Lane 62, Tien Mou West Rd, Taipei 111; tel. (2) 28733096; fax (2) 28733071; e-mail abftap94@ms17.hinet.net; Ambassador JACQUES Y. SAWADOGO.

Chad: 8/F, 9 Lane 62, Tien Mou West Rd, Taipei; tel. (2) 28742943; fax (2) 28742971; e-mail amchadtp@ms23.hinet.net; Ambassador HISSEIN BRAHIM TAHA.

Costa Rica: 5/F, 9-1, Lane 62, Tien Mou West Rd, Taipei 111; tel. (2) 28752964; fax (2) 28753151; e-mail oscaralv@ficnet.net; Ambassador OSCAR ALVAREZ.

Dominican Republic: 6/F, 9 Lane 62, Tien Mou West Rd, Taipei 111; tel. (2) 28751357; fax (2) 28752661; Ambassador MIGUEL HERNÁNDEZ.

El Salvador: 2/F, 9 Lane 62, Tien Mou West Rd, Shih Lin, Taipei 111; tel. (2) 28763509; fax (2) 28763514; e-mail embasal.taipei@msa.hinet.net; Ambassador FRANCISCO RICARDO SANTANA BERRÍOS.

The Gambia: 9/F, 9-1 Lane 62, Tien Mou West Rd, Taipei 111; tel. (2) 28753911; fax (2) 28752775; Ambassador JOHN-PAUL BOJANG.

Guatemala: 3/F, 9-1 Lane 62, Tien Mou West Rd, Taipei 111; tel. (2) 28756952; fax (2) 28740699; e-mail embchina@minex.gob.gt; Ambassador MANUEL ERNESTO GALVEZ CORONADO.

Haiti: 8/F, 9-1 Lane 62, Tien Mou West Rd, Taipei 111; tel. (2) 28766718; fax (2) 28766719; Ambassador LAFONTAINE SAINT-LOUIS.

Holy See: 87 Ai Kuo East Rd, Taipei 106 (Apostolic Nunciature); tel. (2) 23216847; fax (2) 23911926; e-mail aposnunc@tptsl.seed.net.tw; Chargé d'affaires Mgr AMBROSE MADTHA.

Honduras: 9/F, 9 Lane 62, Tien Mou West Rd, Taipei 111; tel. (2) 28755507; fax (2) 28755726; e-mail honduras@ms9.hinet.net; internet www.hondurasinfo.hn; Ambassador MARLENE VILLELA DE TALBOTT.

Liberia: 11/F, 9-1 Lane 62, Tien Mou West Rd, Taipei 111; tel. (2) 28751212; fax (2) 28751313; e-mail libemb@tpts5.seed.net.tw; Ambassador JOHN CUMMINGS.

Malawi: 2/F, 9 Lane 62, Tien Mou West Rd, Taipei 111; tel. (2) 28762284; fax (2) 28763545; Ambassador EUNICE KAZEMBE.

Marshall Islands: 4/F, 9-1 Lane 62, Tien Mou West Rd, Taipei 111; tel. (2) 28734884; fax (2) 28734904; internet www.rmiembassy.org.tw; Ambassador ALEX CARTER BING.

Nicaragua: 3/F, 9 Lane 62, Tien Mou West Rd, Taipei 111; tel. (2) 28749034; fax (2) 28749080; e-mail embni629@ms39.hinet.net; Ambassador LUIS A WONG.

Palau: 8/F, 128 Min Sheng East Rd, Sec. 3, Taipei; tel. (2) 27197761; fax (2) 27197774; Ambassador JOHNSON TORIBIONG.

Panama: 6/F, 111 Sung Kiang Rd, Taipei 104; tel. (2) 25099189; fax (2) 25099801; Ambassador JOSÉ ANTONIO DOMÍNGUEZ.

Paraguay: 7/F, 9-1 Lane 62, Tien Mou West Rd, Taipei 111; tel. (2) 28736310; fax (2) 28736312; e-mail eptaipei@seed.net.tw; Ambassador CEFERINO ADRIAN VALDEZ PERALTA.

São Tomé and Príncipe: 3/F, 18 Chi-lin Rd, Taipei 104; tel. (2) 25114111; fax (2) 25116255; e-mail stptw@ms69.hinet.net; Ambassador OVIDIO M. PEQUENO.

Senegal: 10/F, 9-1 Lane 62, Tien Mou West Rd, Taipei 111; tel. (2) 28766519; fax (2) 28734909; e-mail sngol@ms2.seeder.net; Ambassador YOUSSOU DIAGNE.

Solomon Islands: 7/F, 9-1 Lane 62, Tien Mou West Rd, Taipei 111; tel. (2) 28731168; fax (2) 28766442; Ambassador SETH GUKUNA.

Swaziland: 10/F, 9 Lane 62, Tien Mou West Rd, Taipei 111; tel. (2) 28725934; fax (2) 28726511; Ambassador MOSES MATHENDELE DLAMINI.

Judicial System

The power of judicial review is exercised by the Judicial Yuan's 16 Grand Justices nominated and appointed for nine years by the President of Taiwan with the consent of the National Assembly. The Grand Justices hold meetings to interpret the Constitution and unify the interpretation of laws and orders. From 2003 the Judicial Yuan shall have 15 Grand Justices, one of whom shall serve as its President and another as Vice-President, nominated and appointed by the President of Taiwan with the consent of the Legislative Yuan. The President of the Judicial Yuan is also the *ex-officio* chairman for the Plenary Session of the Grand Justices. The Ministry of Justice is under the jurisdiction of the Executive Yuan.

Judicial Yuan: 124 Chungking South Rd, Sec. 1, Taipei; tel. (2) 23141936; fax (2) 23898923; e-mail judicial@mail.judicial.gov.tw; internet www.judicial.gov.tw; Pres. WENG YUEH-SHENG; Vice-Pres. CHENG CHUNG-MO; Sec.-Gen. YANG JEN-SHOU; the highest judicial organ, and the interpreter of the constitution and national laws and ordinances; supervises the following:

Supreme Court: 6 Chang Sha St, Sec. 1, Taipei; tel. (2) 23141160; fax (2) 23114246; Court of third and final instance for civil and criminal cases; Pres. WU CHII-PIN.

High Courts: Courts of second instance for appeals of civil and criminal cases.

District Courts: Courts of first instance in civil, criminal and non-contentious cases.

Supreme Administrative Court: 1 Lane 126, Chungking South Rd, Sec. 1, Taipei; tel. (2) 23113691; fax (2) 23111791; e-mail jessie@judicial.gov.tw; Court of final resort in cases brought against govt agencies; Pres. JONG YAW-TANG.

High Administrative Courts: Courts of first instance in cases brought against government agencies.

Commission on Disciplinary Sanctions Against Functionaries: 124 Chungking South Rd, 3/F, Sec. 1, Taipei 10036; tel. (2) 23619375; fax (2) 23311934; decides on disciplinary measures against public functionaries impeached by the Control Yuan; Chief Commissioner LIN KUO-HSIEN.

Religion

According to the Ministry of the Interior, in 1999 34% of the population were adherents of Buddhism, 42% of Daoism (Taoism), 7.8% of I-kuan Tao and 3.6% of Christianity.

BUDDHISM

Buddhist Association of Taiwan: Mahayana and Theravada schools; 1,613 group mems and more than 9.61m. adherents; Leader Ven. CHIN-HSIN.

CHRISTIANITY

The Roman Catholic Church

Taiwan comprises one archdiocese, six dioceses and one apostolic administrative area. In December 2000 there were 310,218 adherents.

Bishops' Conference

Chinese Regional Bishops' Conference, 34, Lane 32, Kuangfu South Rd, Taipei 10552; tel. (2) 25782355; fax (2) 25773874; e-mail bishconf@ms1.hinet.net; internet www.catholic.org.tw.

f. 1967; Pres. Cardinal PAUL SHAN KUO-HSI (Bishop of Kaohsiung).

Archbishop of Taipei: Most Rev. JOSEPH TI-KANG, Archbishop's House, 94 Loli Rd, Taipei 10668; tel. (2) 27371311; fax (2) 27373710.

The Anglican Communion

Anglicans in Taiwan are adherents of the Protestant Episcopal Church. In 1999 the Church had 2,000 members.

Bishop of Taiwan: Rt Rev. DAVID JUNG-HSIN LAI, 7 Lane 105, Hangchow South Rd, Sec. 1, Taipei 100; tel. (2) 23411265; fax (2) 23962014; e-mail skhtpe@ms12.hinet.net; internet www.dfms.org/taiwan.

Presbyterian Church

Tai-oan Ki-tok Tiu-Lo Kau-Hoe (Presbyterian Church in Taiwan): No. 3, Lane 269, Roosevelt Rd, Sec. 3, Taipei 106; tel. (2) 23625282; fax (2) 23628096; f. 1865; Gen. Sec. Rev. L. K. LO; 224,679 mems (2000).

DAOISM (TAOISM)

In 1999 there were about 4.54m. adherents. Temples numbered 8,604, and clergy totalled 33,850.

I-KUAN TAO

Introduced to Taiwan in the 1950s, this 'Religion of One Unity' is a modern, syncretic religion, drawn mainly from Confucian, Buddhist and Daoist principles and incorporating ancestor worship. In 1998 there were 93 temples and 18,000 family shrines. Adherents totalled 845,000.

ISLAM

Leader MOHAMMED MA CHA-JENG; 53,000 adherents in 1999.

The Press

In 1999 the number of registered newspapers stood at 367. The majority of newspapers are privately owned.

PRINCIPAL DAILIES

Taipei

Central Daily News: 260 Pa Teh Rd, Sec. 2, Taipei; tel. (2) 27765368; fax (2) 27775835; internet www.cdn.com.tw; f. 1928; morning; Chinese; official Kuomintang organ; Publr and CEO SHAW YU-MING; circ. 600,000.

The China Post: 8 Fu Shun St, Taipei 104; tel. (2) 25969971; fax (2) 25957962; e-mail cpost@msl.hinet.net; internet www.chinapost.com.tw; f. 1952; morning; English; Publr and Editor JACK HUANG; readership 250,000.

China Times: 132 Da Li St, Taipei; tel. (2) 23087111; fax (2) 23063312; f. 1950; morning; Chinese; Chair. YU CHI-CHUNG; Publr YU ALBERT CHIEN-HSIN; circ. 1.2m.

China Times Express: 132 Da Li St, Taipei; tel. (2) 23087111; fax (2) 23082221; e-mail chinaexpress@mail.chinatimes.com.tw; f. 1988; evening; Chinese; Publr S. F. LIN; Editor C. L. HUANG; circ. 400,000.

Commercial Times: 132 Da Li St, Taipei; tel. (2) 23087111; fax (2) 23069456; e-mail commercialtimes@mail.chinatimes.com.tw; f. 1978; morning; Chinese; Publr PENG CHWEI-MING; Editor-in-Chief PHILLIP CHEN; circ. 300,000.

Economic Daily News: 555 Chung Hsiao East Rd, Sec. 4, Taipei; tel. (2) 27681234; fax (2) 27600129; f. 1967; morning; Chinese; Publr WANG PI-CHEN.

The Great News: 216 Chen Teh Rd, Sec. 3, Taipei; tel. (2) 25973111; f. 1988; morning; also *The Great News Daily-Entertainment* (circ. 460,000).

Liberty Times: 11/F, 137 Nanking East Rd, Sec. 2, Taipei; tel. (2) 25042828; fax (2) 25042212; f. 1988; Publr WU A-MING; Editor-in-Chief ROGER CHEN.

Mandarin Daily News: 2 Foo Chou St, Taipei; tel. (2) 23921133; fax (2) 23410203; f. 1948; morning; Publr LIN LIANG.

Min Sheng Daily: 555 Chung Hsiao East Rd, Sec. 4, Taipei; tel. (2) 27681234; fax (2) 27560955; f. 1978; sport and leisure; Publr WANG SHAW-LAN.

Taiwan Hsin Sheng Pao: 260 Pa Teh Rd, Sec. 2, Taipei; tel. (2) 87723058; fax (2) 87723026; f. 1945; morning; Chinese; Publr LIU CHZ-SHIEN.

Taiwan News: 7/F, 88 Hsin Yi Rd, Sec. 2, Taipei 106; tel. (2) 23517666; fax (2) 23518389; e-mail editor@etaiwannews.com; internet www.etaiwannews.com; f. 1949; morning; English; Chair. T. C. KAO; Publr LUIS KO.

United Daily News: 555 Chung Hsiao East Rd, Sec. 4, Taipei; tel. (2) 27681234; fax (2) 27632303; e-mail secretariat@udngroup.com.tw; f. 1951; morning; Publr WANG SHAW-LAN; Editor-in-Chief HUANG SHU-CHUAN; circ. 1.2m.

Provincial

China Daily News (Southern Edn): 57 Hsi Hwa St, Tainan; tel. (6) 2202691; fax (6) 2201804; f. 1946; morning; Publr LIU CHZ-SHIEN; circ. 670,000.

Keng Sheng Daily News: 36 Wuchuan St, Hualien; tel. (38) 340131; fax (38) 329664; f. 1947; morning; Publr HSIEH YING-YIN; circ. 50,000.

The Commons Daily: 180 Min Chuan 2 Rd, Kaohsiung; tel. (7) 3363131; fax (7) 3363604; f. 1950; frmrly Min Chung Daily News; morning; Executive-in-Chief WANG CHIN-HSIUNG; circ. 148,000.

Taiwan Daily News: 361 Wen Shin Rd, Sec. 3, Taichung; tel. (4) 22958111; fax (4) 2958950; f. 1964; morning; Publr ANTONIO CHIANG; Editor-in-Chief LIU CHIH TSUNG; circ. 250,000.

Taiwan Hsin Wen Daily News: 3 Woo Fu I Rd, Kaohsiung; tel. (7) 2226666; f. 1949; morning; Publr CHANG REI-TE.

Taiwan Times: 32 Kaonan Rd, Jen Wu Shan, Kaohsiung; tel. (7) 3428666; fax (7) 3102828; f. 1978; Publr WANG YUH-FA.

SELECTED PERIODICALS

Artist Magazine: 6/F, 147 Chung Ching South Rd, Sec. 1, Taipei; tel. (2) 23886715; fax (2) 23317096; e-mail artvenue@seed.net.tw; f. 1975; monthly; Publr HO CHENG KUANG; circ. 28,000.

Better Life Monthly: 11 Lane 199, Hsin-yih Rd, Sec. 4, Taipei; tel. (2) 27549588; fax (2) 27016068; e-mail bettlife@ms14.hinet.net; f. 1987; Publr JACK S. LIN.

Brain: 9/F, 47 Nanking East Rd, Sec. 4, Taipei; tel. (2) 27132644; fax (2) 27137318; f. 1977; monthly; Publr JOHNSON WU.

Business Weekly: 21/F, 62 Tun Hua South Rd, Sec. 2, Taipei; tel. (2) 27736611; fax (2) 27364620; f. 1987; Publr JIN WEI-TSUN.

Car Magazine: 1/F, 3 Lane 3, Tung-Shan St, Taipei; tel. (2) 23218128; fax (2) 23935614; e-mail carguide@ms13.hinet.net; f. 1982; monthly; Publr H. K. LIN; Editor-in-Chief TA-WEI LIN; circ. 85,000.

Central Monthly: 7/F, 11 Chung Shan South Rd, Taipei; tel. (2) 23433140; fax (2) 23435417; f. 1950; Publr HUANG HUI-TSEN.

China Times Weekly: 5/F, 25 Min Chuan East Rd, Sec. 6, Taipei; tel. (2) 27936000; fax (2) 27912238; f. 1978; weekly; Chinese; Editor CHANG KUO-LI; Publr CHUANG SHU-MING; circ. 180,000.

Commonwealth Monthly: 4/F, 87 Sung Chiang Rd, Taipei; tel. (2) 25078627; fax (2) 25079011; f. 1981; monthly; business; Pres. CHARLES H. C. KAO; Publr and Editor DIANE YING; circ. 83,000.

Cosmopolitan: 5/F, 8 Lane 181, Jiou-Tzung Rd, Nei Hu Area, Taipei; tel. (2) 287978900; fax (2) 287978990; e-mail hwaker@ms13.hinet.net; f. 1992; monthly; Publr MINCHUN CHANG.

Country Road: 14 Wenchow St, Taipei; tel. (2) 23628148; fax (2) 23636724; e-mail h3628148@ms15.hinet.net; internet www.coa.gov.tw/magazine/fst/road.htm; f. 1975; monthly; Editor CHRISTINE S. L. YU; Publr KAO YU-HSIN.

Crown Magazine: 50, Alley 120, Tun Hua North Rd, Sec. 4, Taipei; tel. (2) 27168888; fax (2) 25148285; f. 1954; monthly; literature and arts; Publr PING HSIN TAO; Editor CHEN LIH-HWA; circ. 76,000.

Defense Technology Monthly: 6/F, 6 Nanking East Rd, Sec. 5, Taipei; tel. (2) 27669628; fax (2) 27666092; f. 1894; Publr J. D. BIH.

Earth Geographic Monthly: 4/F, 16 Lane 130 Min Chuan Rd, Hsin-Tien, Taipei; tel. (2) 22182218; fax (2) 22185418; f. 1988; Publr HSU CHUNG-JUNG.

Elle-Taipei: 9/F, 5 Lane 30, Sec. 3, Min Sheng East Rd, Taipei; tel. (2) 87706168; fax (2) 87706178; e-mail jdewitt@hft.com.tw; f. 1991; monthly; women's magazine; Publr JEAN DE WITT; Editor-in-Chief LENA YANG; circ. 50,000.

Evergreen Monthly: 11/F, 2 Pa Teh Rd, Sec. 3, Taipei; tel. (2) 25782321; fax (2) 25786838; f. 1983; health care knowledge; Publr LIANG GUANG-MING; circ. 50,000.

Excellence Magazine: 3/F, 15 Lane 2, Sec. 2, Chien Kuo North Rd, Taipei; tel. (2) 25093578; fax (2) 25173607; f. 1984; monthly; business; Man. LIN HSIN-JYH; Editor-in-Chief LIU JEN; circ. 70,000.

Families Monthly: 11/F, 2 Pa Teh Rd, Sec. 3, Taipei; tel. (2) 25785078; fax (2) 25786838; f. 1976; family life; Editor-in-Chief THELMA KU; circ. 155,000.

Foresight Investment Weekly: 7/F, 52 Nanking East Rd, Sec. 1, Taipei; tel. (2) 25512561; fax (2) 25119596; f. 1980; weekly; Dir and Publr SUN WUN HSIUNG; Editor-in-Chief WU WEN SHIN; circ. 55,000.

Global Views Monthly: 2/F, 1 Lane 93, Taipei; tel. (2) 25173688; fax (2) 25078644; f. 1986; Pres. CHARLES H. C. KAO; Publr and Editor-in-Chief WANG LI-HSING.

Gourmet World: 4/F, 52 Hang Chou South Rd, Sec. 2, Taipei; tel. (2) 23972215; fax (2) 23412184; f. 1990; Publr HSU TANG-JEN.

Harvest Farm Magazine: 14 Wenchow St, Taipei; tel. (2) 23628148; fax (2) 23636724; e-mail h3628148@ms15.hinet.net; f. 1951; every 2 weeks; Publr KAO YU-HSIN; Editor KAO MING-TANG.

Information and Computer: 10/F, 116 Nang King East Rd, Taipei; tel. (2) 25422540; fax (2) 25310760; f. 1980; monthly; Chinese; Publr LIN FERNG-CHIN; Editor JENNIFER CHIU; circ. 28,000.

Issues and Studies: Institute of International Relations, 64 Wan Shou Rd, Wenshan, Taipei 116; tel. (2) 29386763; fax (2) 29397352; e-mail scchang@nccu.edu.tw; internet www.iir.nccu.edu.tw; f. 1965; quarterly; English; Chinese studies and international affairs; Publr and Editor HO SZU-YIN.

Jade Biweekly Magazine: 7/F, 222 Sung Chiang Rd, Taipei; tel. (2) 25811665; fax (2) 25210586; f. 1982; economics, social affairs, leisure; Publr HSU CHIA-CHUNG; circ. 98,000.

The Journalist: 16/F, 218 Tun Hua South Rd, Sec. 2, Taipei; tel. (2) 23779977; fax (2) 23775850; f. 1987; weekly; Publr WANG SHIN-CHING.

Ladies Magazine: 11/F, 3, 187 Shin Yi Rd, Sec. 4, Taipei; tel. (2) 27026908; fax (2) 27014090; f. 1978; monthly; Publr CHENG CHIN-SHAN; Editor-in-Chief THERESA LEE; circ. 60,000.

Living: 6/F, 100 Ai Kuo East Rd, Hsin Tien, Taipei; tel. (2) 23222266; fax (2) 33225050; f. 1997; monthly; Publr LISA WU.

Madame Figaro Taiwan: 5/F, 25 Min Chuan East Rd, Sec. 6, Taipei; tel. (2) 27936000; fax (2) 27928838; e-mail daisywang@mail .chinatimes.com.tw; f. 2001; Dir and Editor-in-Chief LAUREN HOMEI CHEN.

Management Magazine: 5/F, 220 Ta Tung Rd, Sec. 3, Hsichih, Taipei; tel. (2) 86471828; fax (2) 86471466; e-mail frankhung@mail .chinamgt.com; internet www.harment.com; f. 1973; monthly; Chinese; Publr and Editor FRANK L. HUNG; Pres. KATHY T. KUO; circ. 65,000.

Money Monthly: 10/F, 289 Chung Hsiao East Rd, Taipei; tel. (2) 25149822; fax (2) 27154657; f. 1986; monthly; personal financial management; Publr PATRICK SUN; Man. Editor JENNIE SHUE; circ. 55,000.

Music and Audiophile: 2/F, 2 Kingshan South Rd, Sec. 1, Taipei; tel. (2) 25684607; fax (2) 23958654; f. 1973; Publr CHANG KUO-CHING; Editor-in-Chief CHARLES HUANG.

National Palace Museum Bulletin: 211 Chih-shan Rd, Wai Shuang Hsi, Sec. 2, Taipei 11102; tel. (2) 28812021; fax (2) 28821440; e-mail service01@npm.gov.tw; internet www.npm.gov.tw; f. 1965; every 3 months; Chinese art history research in English; Publr and Dir TU CHENG-SHENG; Editor-in-Chief WANG YAO-T'ING; circ. 1,000.

National Palace Museum Monthly of Chinese Art: Wai Shuang Hsi, Shih Lin, Taipei 11102; tel. (2) 28821230; fax (2) 28821440; f. 1983; monthly in Chinese; Publr TU CHENG-SHENG; circ. 10,000.

Nong Nong Magazine: 7/F, 531-1 Chung Cheng Rd, Hsin Tien, Taipei; tel. (2) 22181828; fax (2) 22181081; e-mail group@nongnong .com.tw; f. 1984; monthly; women's interest; Publr ANTHONY TSAI; Editor VIVIAN LIN; circ. 70,000.

PC Home: 4/F, 100 Ai Kuo East Rd, Sec. 2, Taipei; tel. (2) 23965698; fax (2) 23926069; f. 1996; monthly; Publr HUNG-TZE JANG.

PC Office: 11/F, 8 Tun Hua North Rd, Taipei; tel. (2) 27815390; fax (2) 27780899; f. 1997; monthly; Publr HUNG-TZE JANG.

Reader's Digest (Chinese Edn): 3/F, 2 Ming Sheng East Rd, Sec. 5, Taipei; tel. (2) 27607262; fax (2) 27461588; monthly; Editor-in-Chief ANNIE CHENG.

Sinorama: 5/F, 54, Chunghsiao East Rd, Sec. 1, Taipei 100; tel. (2) 23922256; fax (2) 23970655; f. 1976; monthly; cultural; bilingual magazine with edns in Chinese with Japanese, Spanish and English; Publr SU TZA-PING; Editor-in-Chief ANNA Y. WANG; circ. 110,000.

Studio Classroom: 10 Lane 62, Ta-Chih St, Taipei; tel. (2) 25338082; fax (2) 25331009; internet www.studioclassroom.com; f. 1962; monthly; Publr DORIS BROUGHAM.

Taipei Journal: 2 Tientsin St, Taipei 10041; tel. (2) 23970180; fax (2) 23568233; e-mail tj@mail.gio.gov.tw; internet taipeijournal.nat .gov.tw; f. 1964; fmrly Free China Journal; weekly; English; news review; Publr ARTHUR IAP; Exec. Editor-in-Chief MICHAEL CHEN; circ. 30,000.

Taipei Review: 2 Tientsin St, Taipei 100; tel. (2) 23516419; e-mail tr@gio.gov.tw; f. 1951; monthly; English; illustrated; Publr ARTHUR IAP; Editor-in-Chief ANDREW T. H. CHENG.

Taipei Times: 5/F, 137 Nanking East Rd, Sec. 2, Taipei; tel. (2) 25182728; fax (2) 25189154; internet www.taipeitimes.com; f. 1999; Publr ANTONIO CHIANG.

Time Express: 7/F, 2, 76 Tun Hua South Rd, Sec. 2, Taipei; tel. (2) 27084410; fax (2) 27084420; f. 1973; monthly; Publr RICHARD C. C. HUANG.

Unitas: 10/F, 180 Keelung Rd, Sec. 1, Taipei; tel. (2) 27666759; fax (2) 27567914; e-mail unitas@udngroup.com.tw; monthly; Chinese; literary journal; Publr CHANG PAO-CHING; Editor-in-Chief HSU HUI-CHIH.

Vi Vi Magazine: 7/F, 550 Chung Hsiao East Rd, Sec. 5, Taipei; tel. (2) 27275336; fax (2) 27592031; f. 1984; monthly; women's interest; Pres. TSENG CHING-TANG; circ. 60,000.

Vogue: 5/F, 232 Tun Hua North Rd, Taipei; tel. (2) 27172000; fax (2) 27172004; f. 1996; monthly; Publr BENTHAM LIU.

Wealth Magazine: 7/F, 52 Nanking East Rd, Sec. 1, Taipei; tel. (2) 25816196; fax (2) 25119596; f. 1974; monthly; finance; Pres. TSHAI YEN-KUEN; Editor ANDY LIAN; circ. 75,000.

Win Win Weekly: 7/F, 52 Nanking East Rd, Taipei; tel. (2) 25816196; fax (2) 25119596; f. 1996; Publr GIN-HO HSHIE.

Youth Juvenile Monthly: 3/F, 66-1 Chung Cheng South Rd, Sec. 1, Taipei; tel. (2) 23112832; fax (2) 23612239; e-mail youth@ms2.hinet .net; internet www.youth.com.tw; f. 1965; Publr LEE CHUNG-GUAI.

NEWS AGENCIES

Central News Agency (CNA): 209 Sung Chiang Rd, Taipei; tel. (2) 25051180; fax (2) 25078839; e-mail cnamark@ms9.hinet.net; internet www.cna.com.tw; f. 1924; news service in Chinese, English and Spanish; feature and photographic services; 12 domestic and 30 overseas bureaux; Pres. HUI YUAN-HUI.

Foreign Bureaux

Agence France-Presse (AFP): Room 617, 6/F, 209 Sung Chiang Rd, Taipei; tel. (2) 25016395; fax (2) 25011881; e-mail AFPTPE@ ms11.hitnet.tw; Bureau Chief YANG HSIN-HSIN.

Associated Press (AP) (USA): Room 630, 6/F, 209 Sung Chiang Rd, Taipei; tel. (2) 25036651; fax (2) 25007133; Bureau Chief WILLIAM FOREMAN.

Reuters (UK): 8/F, 196 Chien Kuo North Rd, Sec. 2, Taipei; tel. (2) 25080815; fax (2) 25080204; Bureau Chief BENJAMIN KANG LIM.

Publishers

There are 7,810 publishing houses. In 2001 a total of 40,235 titles were published.

Art Book Co: 1/F, 18 Lane 283, Roosevelt Rd, Sec. 3, Taipei; tel. (2) 23620578; fax (2) 23623594; Publr HO KUNG SHANG.

Cheng Wen Publishing Co: 3/F, 277 Roosevelt Rd, Sec. 3, Taipei; tel. (2) 23628032; fax (2) 23660806; e-mail ccicncwp@ms17.hinet.net; Publr LARRY C. HUANG.

China Economic News Service (CENS): 555 Chung Hsiao East Rd, Sec. 4, Taipei 110; tel. (2) 26422629; fax (2) 26496311; e-mail webmaster@www.cens.com; internet www.cens.com; f. 1974; trade magazines.

China Times Publishing Co: 5/F, 240 Hoping West Rd, Sec. 3, Taipei; tel. (2) 23087111; fax (2) 23027844; e-mail ctpc@mse.hinet .net; internet www.publish.chinatimes.com.tw; f. 1975; Pres. MO CHAO-PING.

Chinese Culture University Press: 55 Hua Kang Rd, Yangming-shan, Taipei; tel. (2) 28611861; fax (2) 28617164; e-mail ccup@ccuo16 .pccu.edu.tw; Publr LEE FU-CHEN.

The Commercial Press Ltd: 37 Chungking South Rd, Sec. 1, Taipei; tel. (2) 23614739; fax (2) 23752201; e-mail cptw@ms12.hinet .net; Editor NANCY YI-YING CHIANG.

Crown Publishing Co: 50 Lane 120, Tun Hua North Rd, Taipei; tel. (2) 27168888; fax (2) 27161793; e-mail magazine@crown.com.tw; internet www.crown.com.tw; Publr PHILIP PING.

The Eastern Publishing Co Ltd: 121 Chungking South Rd, Sec. 1, Taipei; tel. (2) 23114514; fax (2) 23814132; Publr CHENG LI-TSU.

Elite Publishing Co: 1/F, 33-1 Lane 113, Hsiamen St, Taipei 100; tel. (2) 23671021; fax (2) 23657047; e-mail elite113@ms12.hinet.net; f. 1975; Publr KO CHING-HWA.

Far East Book Co: 10/F, 66-1 Chungking South Rd, Sec. 1, Taipei; tel. (2) 23118740; fax (2) 23114184; e-mail service@mail.fareast.com .tw; internet www.fareast.com.tw; art, education, history, physics, mathematics, law, literature, dictionaries, textbooks, language tapes, Chinese-English dictionary; Publr GEORGE C. L. PU.

International Cultural Enterprises: Rm 612, 6/F, 25 Po Ai Rd, Taipei 100; tel. (2) 23318080; fax (2) 23318090; e-mail itsits@ms69 .hinet.net; internet www.itsits.com.tw; Publr LAKE HU.

Kwang Fu Book Enterprises Co Ltd: 6/F, 38 Fushing North Rd, Taipei; tel. (2) 27410415; fax (2) 2718230; e-mail loatiao@kf.net.tw; internet www.kf.net; Publr C. H. LIN.

Kwang Hwa Publishing Co: 5/F, 54 Chung Hsiao East Rd, Sec. 1, Taipei; tel. (2) 23516419; fax (2) 23510821; e-mail service@sinorama .com.tw; internet www.sinorama.com.tw; Publr ARTHUR IAP.

Li-Ming Cultural Enterprise Co: 3/F, 49 Chungking South Rd, Sec. 1, Taipei 100; tel. (2) 23821233; fax (2) 23821244; e-mail liming2f@ms15.hinet.net; internet www.limingco.com.tw; Pres. SHEN FANG-SHIN.

Linking Publishing Co Ltd: 561 Chung Hsiao East Rd, Sec. 4, Taipei; tel. (2) 27683708; fax (2) 27634590; e-mail linking@udngroup .com.tw; internet www.udngroup.com.tw/linkingp; Publr LIU KUO-JUEI.

San Min Book Co Ltd: 386 Fushing North Rd, Taipei; tel. (2) 25006600; fax (2) 25064000; e-mail sanmin@ms2.hinet.net; internet www.sanmin.com.tw; f. 1953; literature, history, philosophy, social sciences, dictionaries, art, politics, law; Publr LIU CHEN-CHIANG.

Senseio Business Group: 259 Tun Hua South Rd, Sec. 1, Taipei; tel. (2) 27037777; fax (2) 27049948; f. 1966; Publr LIAW SUSHI-IGU.

Sitak Publishing Group: 10/F, 15 Lane 174, Hsin Ming Rd, Neihu Dist., Taipei; tel. (2) 27911197; fax (2) 27955824; e-mail rights@sitak .com.tw; Publr CHU PAO-LOUNG; Dir KELLY CHU.

Taiwan Kaiming Book Co: 77 Chung Shan North Rd, Sec. 1, Taipei; tel. (2) 25510820; fax (2) 25212894; Publr LUCY CHOH LIU.

Tung Hua Book Co Ltd: 105 Ermei St, Taipei; tel. (2) 23114027; fax (2) 23116615; Publr CHARLES CHOH.

The World Book Co: 6/F, 99 Chungking South Rd, Sec. 1, Taipei; tel. (2) 23311616; fax (2) 23317963; e-mail wbc@ms2.hinet.net; internet www.worldbook.com.tw; f. 1921; literature, textbooks; Chair. YEN FENG-CHANG; Publr YEN ANGELA CHU.

Youth Cultural Enterprise Co Ltd: 3/F, 66-1 Chungking South Rd, Sec. 1, Taipei; tel. (2) 23112837; fax (2) 23113309; e-mail youth@ ms2.hinet.net; internet www.youth.com.tw; Publr LEE CHUNG-KUEI.

Yuan Liou Publishing Co Ltd: 7F/5, 184 Ding Chou Rd, Sec. 3, Taipei 100; tel. (2) 23651212; fax (2) 23657979; e-mail ylib@.ylib .com; internet www.ylib.com; f. 1975; fiction, non-fiction, children's; Publr WANG JUNG-WEN.

Broadcasting and Communications

TELECOMMUNICATIONS

Directorate-General of Telecommunications: Ministry of Transportation and Communications, 16 Chinan Rd, Section 2, Taipei; tel. (2) 23433969; internet www.dgt.gov.tw; regulatory authority.

Chunghwa Telecommunications Co Ltd: 21 Hsinyi Rd, Sec. 1, Taipei; tel. (2) 23445385; fax (2) 23919166; internet www.cht.com .tw; f. 1996; state-controlled company, privatization commenced 2000; Chair. HO-CHEN TAN.

Far EasTone Telecom: 334 Sze Chuan Rd, Sec. 1, Taipei; tel. (2) 29505478; internet www.fareastone.com.tw; mobile telephone services.

KG Telecom: 43 Kuan Chien Rd, Taipei; tel. (2) 23888800; e-mail kgtweb@kgt.com.tw; internet www.kgt.com.tw; mobile telephone services.

Taiwan Cellular Corpn: internet www.twngsm.com.tw; f. 1998 as Pacific Cellular Corpn; mobile telephone and internet services; Pres. JOSEPH FAN.

BROADCASTING

Broadcasting stations are mostly commercial. The Ministry of Transportation and Communications determines power and frequencies, and the Government Information Office supervises the operation of all stations, whether private or governmental.

Radio

In July 2002 there were 143 radio broadcasting corporations in operation, and permission for the establishment of a further 30 radio stations was to be given by the end of 2002.

Broadcasting Corpn of China (BCC): 375 Sung Chiang Rd, Taipei 104; tel. (2) 25005555; fax (2) 25018793; internet www.bcc .com.tw; f. 1928; domestic (6 networks and 1 channel) services; 9 local stations, 131 transmitters; Pres. LEE CHING-PING; Chair. CHAO SHOU-PO.

Central Broadcasting System (CBS): 55 Pei An Rd, Tachih, Taipei 104; tel. (2) 28856168; fax (2) 28852315; e-mail rtm@cbs.org .tw; internet www.cbs.org.tw; domestic and international service; Dir CHOU TEN-RAY.

Cheng Sheng Broadcasting Corpn Ltd: 7/F, 66-1 Chungking South Rd, Sec. 1, Taipei; tel. (2) 23617231; fax (2) 23715665; internet www.csbc.com.tw; f. 1950; 6 stations, 3 relay stations; Chair. WENG YEN-CHING; Pres. PANG WEI-NANG.

International Community Radio Taipei (ICRT): 2/F, 373 Sung Chiang Rd, Taipei; tel. (2) 25184899; fax (2) 25183666; internet www .icrt.com.tw; predominantly English-language broadcaster; Gen. Man. DOC CASEY.

Kiss Radio: 34/F, 6 Min Chuan 2 Rd, Kaohsiung; tel. (7) 3365888; fax (7) 3364931; Pres. HELENA YUAN.

M-radio Broadcasting Corpn: 8/F, 1-18 Taichung Kang Rd, Sec. 2, Taichung City; tel. (4) 23235656; fax (4) 23231199; e-mail jason@ mradio.com.tw; internet www.mradio.com.tw; Pres. SHEN CHIN-HWEI; Gen. Man. JASON C. LIN.

UFO Broadcasting Co Ltd: 25/F, 102 Roosevelt Rd, Sec. 2, Taipei; tel. (2) 23636600; fax (2) 23673083; Pres. JAW SHAU-KONG.

Voice of Taipei Broadcasting Co Ltd: 10/F, B Rm, 15-1 Han Chou South Rd, Sec. 1, Taipei; tel. (2) 23957255; fax (2) 23941855; Pres. NITA ING.

Television

Legislation to place cable broadcasting on a legal basis was adopted in mid-1993, and by June 2002 63 cable television companies were in operation. A non-commercial station, Public Television (PTV), went on air in July 1998. Legislation to place satellite broadcasting on a legal basis was adopted in February 1999, and by June 2002 122 satellite broadcasting channels (provided by 59 domestic and 16 international companies) and 3 domestic and 3 international Digital Broadcasting System (DBS) channels were in operation.

China Television Co (CTV): 120 Chung Yang Rd, Nan Kang District, Taipei; tel. (2) 27838308; fax (2) 27826007; e-mail pubr@ mail.chinatv.com.tw; internet www.chinatv.com.tw; f. 1969; Pres. JIANG FENG-CHYI; Chair. SUMING CHENG.

Chinese Television System (CTS): 100 Kuang Fu South Rd, Taipei 10658; tel. (2) 27510321; fax (2) 27775414; e-mail public@mail .cts.com.tw; internet www.cts.com.tw; f. 1971; cultural and educational; Chair. JOU RUNG-SHENG; Pres. SHI LU.

Formosa Television Co (FTV): 14/F, 30 Pa Teh Rd, Sec. 3, Taipei; tel. (2) 25702570; fax (2) 25773170; internet www.ftv.com.tw; f. 1997; Chair. TSAI TUNG-RONG; Pres. CHEN KANG-HSING.

Public Television Service Foundation (PTS): 90, Lane 95, Sec. 9, Kang Ning Rd, Neihu, Taipei; tel. (2) 26329533; fax (2) 26338124; e-mail pts@mail.pts.org.tw; internet www.pts.org.tw; Chair. FRANK WU; Pres. YUNG-PE LEE.

Taiwan Television Enterprise (TTV): 10 Pa Teh Rd, Sec. 3, Taipei 10560; tel. (2) 25781515; fax (2) 25799626; internet www.ttv .com.tw; f. 1962; Chair. LAI KUO-CHOU; Pres. JENG IOU.

Finance

(cap. = capital; dep. = deposits; m. = million; brs = branches; amounts in New Taiwan dollars unless otherwise stated)

BANKING

In June 1991 the Ministry of Finance granted 15 new banking licences to private banks. A 16th bank was authorized in May 1992; further authorizations followed. Restrictions on the establishment of offshore banking units were relaxed in 1994. The banking sector was undergoing consolidation during 2002–03, and in September 2002 the Ministry of Finance announced plans to privatize government banks by 2006, and sell its stake in commercial banks by 2010.

Central Bank

Central Bank of China: 2 Roosevelt Rd, Sec. 1, Taipei 100; tel. (2) 23936161; fax (2) 23571974; e-mail adminrol@mail.cbc.gov.tw; internet www.cbc.gov.tw; f. 1928; bank of issue; cap. 80,000m., dep. 4,829,374m. (Jul. 2002); Gov. PERNG FAI-NAN.

Domestic Banks

Bank of Taiwan: 120 Chungking South Rd, Sec. 1, Taipei 10036; tel. (2) 23493456; fax (2) 23315840; e-mail bot076@mail.bot.com.tw; internet www.bot.com.tw; f. 1899; plans to merge with Central Trust of China and Land Bank of Taiwan in 2002 suspended; to be privatized by 2006; cap. 32,000m., dep. 1,916,188m. (Dec. 2001); Chair. M. T. CHEN; Pres. SHENG-YANN LII; 129 brs, incl. 6 overseas.

Chiao Tung Bank: 91 Heng Yang Rd, Taipei 100; tel. (2) 23613000; fax (2) 23310398; e-mail dp092@ctnbank.com.tw; internet www .ctnbank.com.tw; f. 1907; fmrly Bank of Communications; cap. 24,400m., dep. 360,787m. (Dec. 2000); Chair. SHEN-CHIH CHENG; Pres. KUO HSIUNG-CHUANG; 34 brs, incl. 2 overseas.

Export-Import Bank of the Republic of China (Eximbank): 8/F, 3 Nan Hai Rd, Taipei 100; tel. (2) 23210511; fax (2) 23940630; e-mail eximbank@eximbank.com.tw; internet www.eximbank.com .tw; f. 1979; cap. 10,000m., dep. 14,075m. (Dec. 2000); Chair. PAULINE FU; Pres. HERBERT S. S. CHUNG; 3 brs.

Farmers Bank of China: 85 Nanking East Rd, Sec. 2, Taipei 104; tel. (2) 21003456; fax (2) 25515425; internet www.farmerbank.com .tw; f. 1933; cap. 12,474m., dep. 448,723m. (Dec. 2000); Chair. CHIEH-CHIEN CHAO; Pres. C. C. HUANG; 76 brs.

International Commercial Bank of China (ICBC): 100 Chi Lin Rd, Taipei 10424; tel. (2) 25633156; fax (2) 25611216; e-mail service@icbc.com.tw; internet www.icbc.com.tw/; f. 1912; cap. 33,157m., dep. 756,910m. (Dec. 2000); Chair. TZONG-YEONG LIN; Pres. Y. T. (MCKINNEY) TSAI; 82 brs, incl. 18 overseas.

Land Bank of Taiwan: 46 Kuan Chien Rd, Taipei 10038; tel. (2) 23483456; fax (2) 23757023; e-mail lbot@imail.landbank.com.tw;

internet www.landbank.com.tw; f. 1946; plans to merge with bank of Taiwan and Central Trust of China in 2002 suspended; to be privatized by 2006; cap. 25,000m., res 55,151m., dep. 1,424,968m. (Dec. 2001); Chair. CHI-LIN WEA; 110 brs.

Taiwan Co-operative Bank: POB 33, 77 Kuan Chien Rd, Taipei 10038; tel. (2) 23118811; fax (2) 23890704; e-mail tacbid01@14.hinet .net; internet www.tcb-bank.com.tw; f. 1946; acts as central bank for co-operatives, and as major agricultural credit institution; to be privatized by Dec. 2003; cap. 20,835m., dep. 1,705,354m. (Dec. 2001); Chair. PATRICK C. J. LIANG; Pres. WILLIAM MING-CHUNG TSENG; 144 brs.

Commercial Banks

Asia Pacific Bank: 66 Minchuan Rd, Taichung; tel. (4) 22271799; fax (4) 22265110; e-mail service@apacbank.com.tw; internet www .apacbank.com.tw; f. 1992; cap. 12,115m., dep. 148,837m. (Dec. 2000); Chair. CHIOU JIA-SHYONG; Pres. WU WEN KE; 35 brs.

Bank of Kaohsiung: 168 Po Ai 2nd Rd, Kaohsiung; tel. (7) 5570535; fax (7) 5580529; e-mail service@mail.bok.com.tw; internet www.bok .com.tw; f. 1982; cap. 4,487m., dep. 172,442m. (Dec. 2000); Chair. FLANDY SUN; Pres. S. H. CHUANG; 31 brs.

Bank of Overseas Chinese: 8 Hsiang Yang Rd, Taipei 10014; tel. (2) 23715181; fax (2) 23814056; e-mail plan@mail.booc.com.tw; internet www.booc.com.tw; f. 1961; cap. 16,752m., dep. 238,008m. (Jun. 2001); Chair. CHUEN CHANG; Pres. WEN-LONG LIN; 56 brs.

Bank of Panhsin: 18 Cheng Tu St, Pan Chiao City, Taipei; tel. (2) 29629170; fax (2) 29572011; f. 1997; cap. 6,000m., dep. 77,602m. (Dec. 1999); Chair. L. P. HUI; Pres. JAMES J. C. CHEN; 28 brs.

Bank SinoPac: 9-1, Chien Kuo North Rd, Sec. 2, Taipei; tel. (2) 25082288; fax (2) 25083456; internet www.banksinopac.com.tw; f. 1992; cap. 17,577m., dep. 204,688m. (Dec. 2000); Chair. L. S. LIN; Pres. PAUL C. Y. LO; 35 brs.

Central Trust of China: 49 Wu Chang St, Sec. 1, Taipei 10006; tel. (2) 23111511; fax (2) 23611544; e-mail ctc17001@ctc.com.tw; internet www.ctoc.com.tw; f. 1935; cap. 10,000m., dep. 204,808m. (Dec. 2000); Chair. WANG RONG-JOU; Pres. JACK. H. HUANG; 19 brs; plans to merge with Bank of Taiwan and Land Bank of Taiwan in 2002 suspended.

Chang Hwa Commercial Bank Ltd: 38 Tsuyu Rd, Sec. 2, Taichung 40010; tel. (4) 2222001; fax (4) 2231170; e-mail customem@ ms1.chb.com.tw; internet www.chb.com.tw; f. 1905; cap. 35,356m., dep. 1,072,837m. (Dec. 2001); Chair. PO-SHIN CHANG; Pres. MIKE S. E. CHANG; 153 brs, 7 overseas.

Chinatrust Commercial Bank: 3 Sung Shou Rd, Taipei; tel. (2) 27222002; fax (2) 27239775; internet www.chinatrust.com.tw; f. 1966; cap. 73,925m., dep. 610,252m. (Dec. 2001); Chair. JEFFREY L. S. KOO; 57 brs, 11 overseas.

The Chinese Bank: 6 Chung Hsiao West Rd, Sec. 1, Taipei; tel. (2) 23880506; fax (2) 23880334; internet www.chinesebank.com.tw; f. 1992; cap. 15,171m., dep. 190,400m. (Dec. 2000); Chair. WANG YOU-THENG; Pres. CHEN FEN; 30 brs.

Chinfon Commercial Bank: 1 Nanyang St, Taipei 100; tel. (2) 23114881; fax (2) 23141068; e-mail ibd@chinfonbank.com.tw; internet www.chinfonbank.com.tw; f. 1971; cap 11,128m., dep. 150,201m. (Dec. 2000); Chair. HUANG SHI-HUI; Pres GREGORY C. P. CHANG; 34 brs, 2 overseas.

Chung Shing Bank: 228–230 Sung Chiang Rd, Taipei; tel. (2) 25616601; fax (2) 25114389; internet www.csbank.com.tw; f. 1992; cap. 15,076m., dep. 186,529m. (Dec. 1999); Chair. PAN LUNG-CHEN; Pres. WAN-SAN S. CHIEN; 25 brs.

Cosmos Bank: 39 Tun Hua South Rd, Taipei; tel. (2) 27011777; fax (2) 27541742; e-mail ibd@cosmosbank.com.tw; internet www.cosmosbank.com.tw; f. 1992; cap. 14,009m., dep. 174,374m. (Mar. 2002); Chair. HSUI SHENG-FA; Pres. C. C. HU; 35 brs.

COTA Commercial Bank: 32-1 Kung Yuan Rd, Taichung; tel. (4) 22245161; fax (4) 22275237; f. 1995; cap. 3,184m., dep. 53,906m. (Dec. 2001); Chair. LIAO CHUN-TSE; Pres CHANG YING-CHE; 18 brs.

E. Sun Commercial Bank: 77 Wuchang St, Sec. 1, Taipei; tel. (2) 23891313; fax (2) 23891115; e-mail esbintl@email.esunbank.com.tw; internet www.esunbank.com.tw; f. 1992; cap. 16,933m., dep. 215,066m. (Dec. 2000); Chair. HUANG YUNG-JEN; Pres. HOU YUNG-HSUNG; 36 brs.

EnTie Commercial Bank: 2/F, 158 Ming Sheng East Rd, Sec. 3, Taipei; tel. (2) 27189999; fax (2) 27187843; internet www.entiebank .com.tw; f. 1993; cap. 14,093m., dep. 174,572m. (Dec. 2001); Chair. YU-LING LIN; Pres. KEN-TENG CHANG; 39 brs.

Far Eastern International Bank: 27/F, 207 Tun Hua South Rd, Sec. 2, Taipei; tel. (2) 23786868; fax (2) 23779000; e-mail 800@mail .feib.com.tw; internet www.feib.com.tw; f. 1992; cap. 15,248m., dep. 156,861m. (Jun. 2001); Chair. DOUGLAS T. HSU; Pres. ELI HONG; 30 brs.

First Commercial Bank: POB 395, 30 Chungking South Rd, Sec. 1, Taipei; tel. (2) 23481111; fax (2) 23610036; e-mail fcb@mail .firstbank.com.tw; internet www.firstbank.com.tw; f. 1899; cap. 38,216m., dep. 1,179,017m. (Dec. 2001); Chair. JEROME J. CHEN; Pres. TSENG CHIEN-CHUNG; 159 brs, 11 overseas.

Fubon Commercial Bank: 2/F, 169 Jen Ai Rd, Sec. 4, Taipei 106; tel. (2) 27716699; fax (2) 87716939; e-mail fubon@fubonbank.com .tw; internet www.fubonbank.com.tw; f. 1992; cap. 21,857m., res 2,613m., dep. 218,674m. (2002); Chair. CHEN S. YU; Pres. WANG CHUAN-HSI; 39 brs.

Grand Commercial Bank: 17 Chengteh Rd, Sec. 1, Taipei; tel. (2) 25562088; fax (2) 25561579; e-mail service@grandbank.com.tw; internet www.grandbank.com.tw; f. 1991; cap. 16,043m. (Dec. 2000), dep. 171,090m. (Dec. 2001); Chair. KAO CHIH-YEN; Pres. ALEXANDER T. Y. DEAN; 43 brs.

Hsinchu International Bank: 106 Chung Yang Rd, Hsinchu 300; tel. (3) 5245131; fax (3) 5250977; f. 1948; cap. 12,665m., dep. 245,378m. (Dec. 1999); Chair. S. Y. CHAN; Pres C. W. WU; 73 brs.

Hua Nan Commercial Bank Ltd: POB 989, 38 Chungking South Rd, Sec. 1, Taipei; tel. (2) 23713111; fax (2) 23821060; e-mail service@ms.hncb.com.tw; internet www.hncb.com.tw; f. 1919; cap. 35,198m., dep. 1,085,254m. (Dec. 2000); Chair. LIN MING-CHEN; Pres. HSU TEH-NAN; 138 brs, 5 overseas.

Hwa Tai Commercial Bank: 246 Chang An E. Rd, Sec. 2, Taipei; tel. (2) 27525252; fax (2) 27711495; f. 1999; cap. 3,300m., dep. 50,111m. (Dec. 1999); Chair. M. H. LIN; Pres. S. Y. WU; 18 brs.

International Bank of Taipei: 36 Nanking East Rd, Sec. 3, Taipei; tel. (2) 25063333; fax (2) 25062462; e-mail b630@ibtpe.com.tw; internet www.ibtpe.com.tw; f. 1948; cap. 18,038m., dep. 285,131m. (Dec. 2001); Chair. S. C. HO; Pres. K. C. YU; 88 brs.

Jih Sun International Bank: 6/F, 68 Sungchiang Rd, Taipei; tel. (2) 25615888; fax (2) 25218878; internet www.jihsunbank.com.tw; f. 1992 as Baodao Commercial Bank, assumed present name in December 2001; cap. 10,815m., dep. 148,405m. (May 2000); Chair. CHUN-KUAN CHEN; Pres. TA HAO CHUNG; 24 brs.

Kao Shin Commercial Bank: 75 Lih Wen Rd, Kaohsiung; tel. (7) 3460711; fax (7) 3502980; f. 1997; cap. 2,300m., dep. 48,244m. (Dec. 1999); Chair. C. N. HUANG; Pres. F. T. CHAO; 27 brs.

Lucky Bank: 35 Chung Hua Rd, Sec. 1, Taichung 403; tel. (4) 2259111; fax (4) 22258624; f. 1997; cap. 3,146m., dep. 74,753m. (Dec. 1999); Chair. C. C. CHANG; Pres. T. Y. SU; 27 brs.

Macoto Bank: 134 Hsi Chang St, Taipei; tel. (2) 23812160; fax (2) 23752538; e-mail master@makoto.com.tw; internet www .makotobank.com.tw; f. 1997; cap. 7,090m., dep. 157,472m. (Dec. 2001); Chair. C. I. LIN; Pres. SHERMAN CHUANG; 49 brs.

Pan Asia Bank: 3–4/F, 60-8 Chungkang Rd, Taichung; tel. (02) 23279998; fax (02) 23271565; e-mail pabkdbu@ms4.hinet.net; internet www.pab.com.tw; f. 1992; cap. 14,700m., dep. 153,431m. (Dec. 2000); Chair. KOH FEI-LO; Pres. YIN YI-NA; 35 brs.

Shanghai Commercial and Savings Bank Ltd: 2 Min Chuan East Rd, Sec. 1, Taipei 104; tel. (2) 25817111; fax (2) 25638539; internet www.scsb.com.tw; f. 1915; cap. 13,260m., dep. 282,726m. (Dec. 2000); Chair. H. C. YUNG; Pres. Y. P. CHEN; 58 brs.

Sunny Bank: 88 Shih Pai Rd, Sec. 1, Taipei 112; tel. (2) 28208166; fax (2) 28233414; f. 1997; cap. 3,800m., dep. 82,129m. (Dec. 1999); Chair. S. H. CHEN; Pres. C. W. CHEN; 22 brs.

Ta Chong Bank: 58 Chungcheng 2nd Rd, Kaohsiung; tel. (7) 2242220; fax (7) 2245251; e-mail service@tcbank.com.tw; internet www.tcbank.com.tw; f. 1992; cap. 13,563m., dep. 144,953m. (Dec. 1999); Chair. and Pres. CHEN TIEN-MAO; 38 brs.

Taichung Commercial Bank: 87 Min Chuan Rd, Taichung 403; tel. (4) 22236021; fax (4) 22240748; e-mail webmaster@ms1.tcbbank .com.tw; internet www.tcbbank.com.tw; f. 1953; cap. 15,380m., dep. 181,772m. (Dec. 2000); Chair. Y. F. TSAI; Pres. Y. C. TSAI; 80 brs.

Taipeibank: 50 Chung Shan North Rd, Sec. 2, Taipei 10419; tel. (2) 25425656; fax (2) 25428870; e-mail br180@ms1.taipeibank.com.tw; internet www.taipeibank.com.tw; f. 1969; fmrly City Bank of Taipei; acquired by Fubon Financial Holding in August 2002; cap. 22,307m., res 20,283m., dep. 582,370m. (Dec. 2001); Chair. CHI YUAN LIN; Pres. JESSE Y. DING; 81 brs, 1 overseas.

Taishin International Bank: 44 Chung Shan North Rd, Sec. 2, Taipei; tel. (2) 25683988; fax (2) 25234551; e-mail pr@taishinbank .com.tw; internet www.taishinbank.com.tw; f. 1992; absorbed Dah An Commercial Bank in February 2002; cap. 23,874m., dep. 247,254m. (Dec. 2000); Chair. THOMAS T. L. WU; Pres. JULIUS H. C. CHEN; 39 brs.

Taitung Business Bank: 354 Chung Hwa Rd, Sec. 1, Taitung 950; tel. (89) 331191; fax (89) 331194; e-mail secretpb@ttbb.com.tw; internet www.ttbb.com.tw; f. 1955; Chair. KUWAN-MIN CHANG; Pres. H. I. YIN.

Taiwan Business Bank: 30 Tacheng St, Taipei; tel. (2) 25597171; fax (2) 25509245; e-mail tbb3688@hotmail.com; internet www.tbb .com.tw; f. 1915; reassumed present name 1994; cap. 35,878m., dep. 811,675m. (Dec. 2000); Chair. HSIAO CHIEH-JEN; Pres. LU HO-YI.

Union Bank of Taiwan: 109 Ming Sheng East Rd, Sec. 3, Taipei; tel. (2) 27180001; fax (2) 27137515; e-mail 014_0199@email.ubot .com.tw; internet www.ubot.com.tw; f. 1992; cap. US $426m., res US $69.7m., dep. US $4,201m. (Sept. 2002); Chair. C. C. HUANG; Pres. S. C. LEE; 40 brs.

United World Chinese Commercial Bank: 65 Kuan Chien Rd, POB 1670, Taipei 10038; tel. (2) 23125555; fax (2) 23311093; e-mail yinglin@uwccb.com.tw; internet www.uwccb.com.tw; f. 1975; acquired by Cathay Financial Holding in August 2002; cap. 37,717m., res 22,180m., dep. 637,940m. (Dec. 2001); Chair. GREGORY K. H. WANG; Pres. C. C. TUNG; 74 brs, incl. 6 overseas.

There are also a number of Medium Business Banks throughout the country.

Community Financial System

The community financial institutions include both credit co-operatives and credit departments of farmers' and fishermen's associations. These local financial institutions focus upon providing savings and loan services for the community. At the end of 1999 there were 50 credit co-operatives, 287 credit departments of farmers' associations and 27 credit departments of fishermen's associations, with a combined total deposit balance of NT $2,339,000m., while outstanding loans amounted to NT $1,340,200m.

Foreign Banks

In December 2001 a total of 36 foreign banks were in operation in Taiwan.

STOCK EXCHANGE

In January 1991 the stock exchange was opened to direct investment by foreign institutions, and in March 1996 it was also opened to direct investment by foreign individuals. By the end of June 2000 463 foreign institutional investors had been approved to invest in the local securities market. Various liberalization measures have been introduced since 1994. In March 1999 the limits on both single and aggregate foreign investment in domestic shares were raised to 50% of the outstanding shares of a listed company. In November of that year the 'ceiling' of investment amount for each qualified foreign institutional investor in domestic securities markets was increased from US $600m. to US $1,200m.

Taiwan Stock Exchange Corpn: 13/F, 17 Po Ai Rd, Taipei 100; tel. (2) 23485678; fax (2) 23485324; f. 1962; Chair. C. Y. LEE.

Supervisory Body

Securities and Futures Commission: 85 Hsin Sheng South Rd, Sec. 1, Taipei; tel. (2) 87734202; fax (2) 8734134; Chair. CHU JAW-CHYUAN; Sec.-Gen. CHEN WEI-LUNG.

INSURANCE

In 1993 the Ministry of Finance issued eight new insurance licences, the first for more than 30 years. Two more were issued in 1994.

Allianz President General Insurance Co Ltd: 11/F, 69 Ming Sheng East Rd, Sec. 3, Taipei; tel. (2) 25157177; fax (2) 25077506; e-mail azpl@ms2.seeder.net; internet www.allianz.com.tw; f. 1995; Chair. NAN-TEN CHUNG; Gen. Man. NICHOLAS CHANG.

Cathay Life Insurance Co Ltd: 296 Jen Ai Rd, Sec. 4, Taipei 10650; tel. (2) 27551399; fax (2) 27551322; e-mail master@cathlife .com.tw; internet www.cathlife.com.tw; f. 1962; Chair. TSAI HONG-TU; Gen. Man. LIU CHIU-TE.

Central Insurance Co Ltd: 6 Chung Hsiao West Rd, Sec. 1, Taipei; tel. (2) 23819910; fax (2) 23116901; internet www.cins.com.tw; f. 1962; Chair. H. K. SHE; Gen. Man. C. C. HUANG.

Central Reinsurance Corpn: 53 Nanking East Rd, Sec. 2, Taipei; tel. (2) 25115211; fax (2) 25235350; e-mail chlin@crc.com.tw; internet www.crc.com.tw; f. 1968; Chair. CHING-HSIEN LIN; Pres. C. T. YANG.

Central Trust of China, Life Insurance Dept: 3–8/F, 69 Tun Hua South Rd, Sec. 2, Taipei; tel. (2) 27849151; fax (2) 27052214; e-mail sectrl@ctclife.com.tw; internet www.ctclife.com.tw; f. 1941; life insurance; Pres. EDWARD LO; Gen. Man. MAN-HSIUNG TSAI.

China Life Insurance Co Ltd: 122 Tun Hua North Rd, Taipei; tel. (2) 27196678; fax (2) 27125966; e-mail services@mail.chinalife.com .tw; internet www.chinalife.com.tw; f. 1963; Chair. C. F. KOO; Gen. Man. CHESTER C. Y. KOO.

China Mariners' Assurance Corpn Ltd: 11/F, 2 Kuan Chien Rd, Taipei; tel. (2) 23757676; fax (2) 23756363; internet www.cmac.com .tw; f. 1948; Chair. VINCENT M. S. FAN; Pres. W. H. HUNG.

Chung Kuo Insurance Co Ltd: 10–12/F, ICBC Bldg, 100 Chilin Rd, Taipei 10424; tel. (2) 25513345; fax (2) 25414046; f. 1931; fmrly China Insurance Co Ltd; Chair. S. Y. LIU; Pres. C. Y. LIU.

Chung Shing Life Insurance Co Ltd: 18/F, 200 Keelung Rd, Sec. 1, Taipei 110; tel. (2) 27583099; fax (2) 23451635; f. 1993; Chair. T. S. CHAO; Gen. Man. DAH-WEI CHEN.

The First Insurance Co Ltd: 54 Chung Hsiao East Rd, Sec. 1, Taipei; tel. (2) 23913271; fax (2) 23930685; f. 1962; Chair. C. H. LEE; Gen. Man. M. C. CHEN.

Fubon Insurance Co Ltd: 237 Chien Kuo South Rd, Sec. 1, Taipei; tel. (2) 27067890; fax (2) 27042915; internet www.fubon-ins.com.tw; f. 1961; Chair. TSAI MING-CHUNG; Gen. Man. T. M. SHIH.

Fubon Life Assurance Co Ltd: 14/F, 108 Tun Hua South Rd, Sec. 1, Taipei; tel. (2) 87716699; fax (2) 87715919; f. 1993; Chair. RICHARD M. TSAI; Gen. Man. PEN-YUAN CHENG.

Global Life Insurance Co Ltd: 18 Chung Yang South Rd, Sec. 2, Peitou, Taipei 11235; tel. (2) 28967899; fax (2) 28958312; f. 1993; Chair. JOHN TSENG; Gen. Man. ROBERT KUO.

Hontai Life Insurance Co Ltd: 7/F, 70 Cheng Teh Rd, Sec. 1, Taipei; tel. (2) 25595151; fax (2) 25562840; internet www.hontai.com .tw; f. 1994; fmrly Hung Fu Life Insurance Co; Chair. TONY SHE; Gen. Man. YU-CHIEH YANG.

Kuo Hua Insurance Co Ltd: 166 Chang An East Rd, Sec. 2, Taipei; tel. (2) 27514225; fax (2) 27819388; e-mail kh11601@kuohua.com.tw; internet www.kuohua.com.tw; f. 1962; Chair. and Gen. Man. J. B. WANG.

Kuo Hua Life Insurance Co Ltd: 42 Chung Shan North Rd, Sec. 2, Taipei; tel. (2) 25621101; fax (2) 25423832; internet www.khl.com .tw; f. 1963; Chair. JASON CHANG; Pres. WEN-PO WANG.

Mercuries Life Insurance Co Ltd: 6/F, 2 Lane 150, Hsin-Yi North Rd, Sec. 5, Taipei; tel. (2) 23455511; fax (2) 23456616; internet www .mli.com.tw; f. 1993; Chair. HARVEY TANG; Gen. Man. CHUNG-SHIN LU.

Mingtai Fire and Marine Insurance Co Ltd: 1 Jen Ai Rd, Sec. 4, Taipei; tel. (2) 27725678; fax (2) 27729932; internet www.mingtai .com.tw; f. 1961; Chair. LARRY P. C. LIN; Gen. Man. H. T. CHEN.

Nan Shan Life Insurance Co Ltd: 144 Min Chuan East Rd, Sec. 2, Taipei 104; tel. (2) 25013333; fax (2) 25012555; internet www .nanshanlife.com.tw; f. 1963; Chair. EDMUND TSE; Pres. SUNNY LIN.

Prudential Life Assurance Co Ltd: 12/F, 550 Chung Hsiao East Rd, Sec. 4, Taipei; tel. (2) 27582727; fax (2) 27086758; internet www .prudential-uk.com.tw; f. 1999; Chair. DOMINIC LEUNG KA KUI; CEO DAN L. TING.

Shin Fu Life Insurance Co Ltd: 8/F, 6 Chung Hsiao West Rd, Sec. 1, Taipei; tel. (2) 23817172; fax (2) 23817162; f. 1993; Chair. and Gen. Man. SONG CHI CHIENG.

Shin Kong Insurance Co Ltd: 15 Chien Kuo North Rd, Sec. 2, Taipei; tel. (2) 25075335; fax (2) 25074580; internet www.shinkong .com.tw; f. 1963; Chair. ANTHONY T. S. WU; Pres. YIH HSIUNG LEE.

Shin Kong Life Insurance Co Ltd: 66 Chung Hsiao West Rd, Sec. 1, Taipei; tel. (2) 23895858; fax (2) 23758688; internet www.skl.com .tw; f. 1963; Chair. EUGENE T. C. WU; Gen. Man. HONG-CHI CHENG.

Sinon Life Insurance Co Ltd: 11-2F, 155 Tsu Chih St, Taichung; tel. (4) 3721653; fax (4) 3722008; e-mail sinonlife@mail.sinonlife.com .tw; internet www.sinonlife.com.tw; f. 1993; Chair. PO-YEN HORNG; Gen. Man. P. T. LAI.

South China Insurance Co Ltd: 5/F, 560 Chung Hsiao East Rd, Sec. 4, Taipei; tel. and fax (2) 27298022; internet www.south-china .com.tw; f. 1963; Chair. C. F. LIAO; Pres. ALLAN I. R. HUANG.

Tai Ping Insurance Co Ltd: 3–5/F, 550 Chung Hsiao East Rd, Sec. 4, Taipei; tel. (2) 27582700; fax (2) 27295681; f. 1929; Chair. C. C. HUANG; Gen. Man. JAMES SUN.

Taian Insurance Co Ltd: 59 Kwantsien Rd, Taipei; tel. (2) 23819678; fax (2) 23315332; e-mail taian@mail.taian.com.tw; f. 1961; Chair. C. H. CHEN; Gen. Man. PATRICK S. LEE.

Taiwan Fire and Marine Insurance Co Ltd: 8–9/F, 49 Kuan Chien Rd, Jungjeng Chiu, Taipei; tel. (2) 23821666; fax (2) 23882555; e-mail tfmi@mail.tfmi.com.tw; internet www.tfmi.com.tw; f. 1948; Chair. W. Y. LEE; Gen. Man. JOSEPH N. S. CHANG.

Taiwan Life Insurance Co Ltd: 16–19/F, 17 Hsu Chang St, Taipei; tel. (2) 23116411; fax (2) 23759714; e-mail service1@twlife .com.tw; internet www.twlife.com.tw; f. 1947; Chair. PING-YU CHU; Pres. CHENG-TAO LIN.

Union Insurance Co Ltd: 12/F, 219 Chung Hsiao East Rd, Sec. 4, Taipei; tel. (2) 27765567; fax (2) 27737199; internet www.unionins .com.tw; f. 1963; Chair. S. H. CHIN; Gen. Man. FRANK S. WANG.

Zurich Insurance Taiwan Ltd: 56 Tun Hua North Rd, Taipei; tel. (2) 27752888; fax (2) 27416004; internet www.zurich.com.tw; f. 1961; Chair. DEAN T. CHIANG; Gen. Man. YUNG H. CHEN.

Trade and Industry

GOVERNMENT AGENCIES

Board of Foreign Trade (Ministry of Economic Affairs): 1 Houkow St, Taipei; tel. (2) 23510271; fax (2) 23513603; internet www.trade.gov.tw; Dir-Gen. WU WEN-YEA.

Council of Agriculture (COA): 37 Nan Hai Rd, Taipei 100; tel. (2) 23812991; fax (2) 23310341; e-mail webmaster@www.coa.gov.tw; f. 1984; govt agency directly under the Executive Yuan, with ministerial status; a policy-making body in charge of national agriculture, forestry, fisheries, the animal industry and food administration; promotes technology and provides external assistance; Chair. Dr CHING-LUNG LEE; Chief Sec. CHIH-CHING CHEN.

Industrial Development Bureau (Ministry of Economic Affairs): 41-3 Hsin Yi Rd, Sec. 3, Taipei; tel. (2) 27541255; fax (2) 27030160; internet www.moeaidb.gov.tw; Dir-Gen. CHEN CHAO-YIN.

Industrial Development and Investment Center (Ministry of Economic Affairs): 8/F, 71 Kuan Chien Rd, Taipei; tel. (2) 23892111; fax (2) 23820497; e-mail njlin@mail.idic.gov.tw; internet www.idic.gov.tw; f. 1959 to assist investment and planning; Dir-Gen. ANGELA T. CHU (acting).

CHAMBER OF COMMERCE

General Chamber of Commerce of the Republic of China: 6/F, 390 Fu Hsing South Rd, Sec. 1, Taipei; tel. (2) 27012671; fax (2) 27542107; f. 1946; 65 mems, incl. 40 nat. feds of trade asscns, 22 district export asscns and 3 district chambers of commerce; Chair. Dr GARY WANG; Sec.-Gen. CHIU JAW-SHIN.

INDUSTRIAL AND TRADE ASSOCIATIONS

China External Trade Development Council: 4/F, CETRA Tower, 333 Keelung Rd, Sec. 1, Taipei 110; tel. (2) 27255200; fax (2) 27576653; internet www.cetra.org.tw; trade promotion body; Sec.-Gen. HUANG CHIH-PENG.

China Productivity Center: 2/F, 79 Hsin Tai 5 Rd, Sec. 1, Hsichih, Taipei County; tel. (2) 26982989; fax (2) 26982976; f. 1956; management, technology, training, etc; Pres. CHEN MING-CHANG.

Chinese National Association of Industry and Commerce: 13/F, 390 Fu Hsing South Rd, Sec. 1, Taipei; tel. (2) 27070111; fax (2) 27017601; Chair. JEFFREY L. S. KOO.

Chinese National Federation of Industries (CNFI): 12/F, 390 Fu Hsing South Rd, Sec. 1, Taipei; tel. (2) 27033500; fax (2) 27033982; e-mail cnfi@mail.industry.net.tw; internet www.cnfi.org.tw; f. 1948; 142 mem. asscns; Chair. LIN KUNG-CHUNG; Sec.-Gen. Y. H. KUO.

Taiwan Handicraft Promotion Centre: 1 Hsu Chou Rd, Taipei; tel. (2) 23933655; fax (2) 23937330; f. 1956; Pres. Y. C. WANG.

Trading Department of Central Trust of China: 49 Wuchang St, Sec. 1, Taipei 10006; tel. (2) 23111511; fax (2) 23821047; f. 1935; export and import agent for private and govt-owned enterprises.

UTILITIES

Electricity

Taiwan Power Co (Taipower): 242 Roosevelt Rd, Sec. 3, Taipei 100; tel. (2) 23651234; fax (2) 23678593; e-mail service@taipower.com.tw; internet www.taipower.com.tw; f. 1946; electricity generation; in process of privatization from 2001; Chair. LI NENG-BAI; Pres. LIN CHING-CHI.

Gas

The Great Taipei Gas Corpn: 5/F, 35 Kwang Fu North Rd, Taipei; tel. (2) 27684999; fax (2) 27630480; supply of gas and gas equipment.

Water

Taipei Water Dept: 131 Changxing St, Taipei; tel. (2) 7352141; fax (2) 7353185; f. 1907; responsible for water supply in Taipei and suburban areas; Commr LIN WEN-YUAN.

CO-OPERATIVES

In December 1999 there were 5,375 co-operatives, with a total membership of 5,679,976 and total capital of NT $46,000m. Of the specialized co-operatives the most important was the consumers' co-operative (4,440 co-ops).

The Co-operative League (f. 1940) is a national organization responsible for co-ordination, education and training and the movement's national and international interests (Chair. K. L. CHEN).

TRADE UNIONS

Chinese Federation of Labour: 11/F, Back Bldg, 201–18 Tun Hua North Rd, Taipei; tel. (2) 27135111; fax (2) 27135116; e-mail cfllabor@ms10.hinet.net; f. 1954; mems: 48 federations of unions representing 2,985,955 workers; Pres. LIN HUI-KUAN.

National Federations

Chinese Federation of Postal Workers: 9/F, 45 Chungking South Rd, Sec. 2, Taipei 100; tel. (2) 23921380; fax (2) 23414510; e-mail cfpw@ms16.hinet.net; f. 1930; 27,957 mems; Pres. CHEN SHIAN-JUH.

National Chinese Seamen's Union: 8/F, 25 Nanking East Rd, Sec. 3, Taipei; tel. (2) 25150265; fax (2) 25078211; f. 1913; 21,705 mems; Pres. FANG FU-LIANG.

Taiwan Railway Labor Union: Rm 6044, 6/F, 3 Peiping West Rd, Taipei; tel. (2) 23896615; fax (2) 23896134; f. 1947; 15,579 mems; Pres. CHANG WEN-CHENG.

Regional Federations

Taiwan Federation of Textile and Dyeing Industry Workers' Unions (TFTDWU): 2 Lane 64, Chung Hsiao East Rd, Sec. 2, Taipei; tel. (2) 23415627; f. 1958; 11,906 mems; Chair. CHANG MING-KEN.

Taiwan Provincial Federation of Labour: 11/F, 44 Roosevelt Rd, Sec. 2, Taipei; tel. and fax (2) 23938080; f. 1948; 81 mem. unions and 1,571,826 mems; Pres. SHIH YUAN-LIN; Sec.-Gen. HUANG YAO-TUNG.

Transport

RAILWAYS

Taiwan Railway Administration (TRA): 3 Peiping West Rd, Taipei 10026; tel. (2) 23815226; fax (2) 23831367; f. 1891; a public utility under the Ministry of Communications and Transportation; operates both the west line and east line systems, with a route length of 1,097.2 km, of which 592.2 km are electrified; the west line is the main trunk line from Keelung, in the north, to Fangliao, in the south, with several branches; electrification of the main trunk line was completed in 1979; the east line runs along the east coast, linking Hualien with Taitung; the north link line, with a length of 79.2 km from Suao Sing to Hualien, was opened in 1980; the south link line, with a length of 98.2 km from Taitung Shin to Fangliao, opened in late 1991, completing the round-the-island system; a Japanese consortium was building a high-speed link between Taipei and Kaohsiung (345 km), scheduled for completion in late 2005; Man. Dir T. P. CHEN.

There are also 1,440 km of private narrow-gauge track, operated by the Taiwan Sugar Corpn in conjunction with the Taiwan Forestry Bureau and other organizations. These railroads are mostly used for freight.

Construction of a five-line (including one elevated light rail line), 86.8-km, mass rapid-transit system (MRTS) in Taipei, incorporating links to the airport, began in 1987. The first 10.9-km section of the Mucha (light rail) line opened in March 1996 and the Tamshui line (22.8 km) opened in December 1997. The Chungho and Hsintien lines, and part of the Nankang line, were in operation by 1999. The remainder of the network was scheduled for completion after 2006. A 42.7-km system is planned for Kaohsiung, scheduled for completion in the year 2007. MRT systems are also projected for Taoyuan, Hsinchu, Taichung and Tainan.

Taipei Rapid Transit Corporation: 7, Lane 48, Chung Shan North Rd, Sec. 2, Taipei; tel. (2) 0800033068; fax (2) 25115003; internet www.trtc.com.tw; f. 1994; 66.7 km (incl. 10.5 km light rail) open, with further lines under construction; Chair. LEE PO-WEN; Pres. RICHARD C. L. CHEN.

ROADS

There were 20,635 km of highways in 2001, most of them asphalt-paved. The Sun Yat-sen (North–South) Freeway was completed in 1978. Construction of a 505-km Second Freeway, which is to extend to Pingtung, in southern Taiwan, began in July 1987 and was scheduled to be completed by the end of 2003. Work on the Taipei–Ilan freeway began in 1991.

Taiwan Area National Expressway Engineering Bureau: 1 Lane 1, Hoping East Rd, Sec. 3, Taipei; tel. (2) 27078808; fax (2) 27017818; e-mail neebeyes@taneeb.gov.tw; internet www.taneeb.gov.tw; f. 1990; responsible for planning, design, construction and maintenance of provincial and county highways; Dir-Gen. CHENG WEN-LON.

Taiwan Area National Freeway Bureau: POB 75, Hsinchuang, Taipei 242; tel. (2) 29096141; fax (2) 29093218; internet www .freeway.gov.tw; f. 1970; Dir-Gen. HO NUAN-HSUAN.

Taiwan Motor Transport Co Ltd: 5/F, 17 Hsu Chang St, Taipei; tel. (2) 23715364; fax (2) 23820634; f. 1980; operates national bus service; Gen. Man. CHEN WU-SHIUNG.

SHIPPING

Taiwan has five international ports: Kaohsiung, Keelung, Taichung, Hualien and Suao. In 2001 the merchant fleet comprised 656 vessels, with a total displacement of 4,617,900 grt.

Evergreen Marine Corpn: 166 Ming Sheng East Rd, Sec. 2, Taipei 104; tel. (2) 25057766; fax (2) 25055256; e-mail prd@ evergreen-marine.com; internet www.evergreen-marine.com; f. 1968; world-wide container liner services; Chair. KUO SHIUAN-YU; Pres. ARNOLD WONG.

Taiwan Navigation Co Ltd: 29, Chi Nan Rd, Sec. 2, Taipei 104; tel. (2) 23941769; Chair. FRANK LU; Pres. I. Y. CHANG.

U-Ming Marine Transport Corpn: 29/F, Taipei Metro Tower, 207 Tun Hua South Rd, Sec. 2, Taipei; tel. (2) 27338000; fax (2) 27359900; world-wide tramp services; Chair. DOUGLAS HSU; Pres. C. K. ONG.

Uniglory Marine Corpn: 6/F, 172 Ming Sheng East Rd, Sec. 2, Taipei; tel. (2) 25019001; fax (2) 25086024; Chair. LOH YAO-FON; Pres. LEE MUN-CHI.

Wan Hai Lines Ltd: 10/F, 136 Sung Chiang Rd, Taipei; tel. (2) 25677961; fax (2) 25216000; f. 1965; regional container liner services; Chair. CHEN CHAO HON; Pres. CHEN PO TING.

Yang Ming Marine Transport Corpn (Yang Ming Line): 271 Ming de 1st Rd, Chidu, Keelung 206; tel. (2) 24559988; fax (2) 24559958; e-mail winsor@imail.yml.com.tw; internet www.yml.com .tw; f. 1972; world-wide container liner services, bulk carrier and supertanker services; Chair. T. H. CHEN; Pres. HUANG WANG-HSIU.

CIVIL AVIATION

There are two international airports, Chiang Kai-shek at Taoyuan, near Taipei, which opened in 1979 (a second passenger terminal and expansion of freight facilities being completed in 2000), and Hsiao-kang, in Kaohsiung (where an international terminal building was inaugurated in 1997). In 2003 plans were unveiled to build a new 2000–ha international airport in Tainan. There are also 14 domestic airports.

Civil Aeronautics Administration: 340 Tun Hua North Rd, Taipei; tel. (2) 23496000; fax (2) 23496277; e-mail gencaa@mail.caa .gov.tw; internet www.caa.gov.tw; Dir-Gen. BILLY K. C. CHANG.

China Air Lines Ltd (CAL): 131 Nanking East Rd, Sec. 3, Taipei; tel. (2) 25062345; fax (2) 25145786; internet www.china-airlines .com; f. 1959; international services to destinations in the Far East, Europe, the Middle East and the USA; Chair. Capt. Y. L. LEE; Pres. WEI HSING-HSIUNG.

EVA Airways: Eva Air Bldg, 376 Hsin-nan Rd, Sec. 1, Luchu, Taoyuan Hsien; tel. (3) 3515151; fax (3) 3510005; internet www .evaair.com.tw; f. 1989; subsidiary of Evergreen Group; commenced flights in 1991; services to destinations in Asia (incl. Hong Kong and Macao), the Middle East, Europe, North America, Australia and New Zealand; Chair. CHANG KUO-CHENG; Pres. KITTY YEN.

Far Eastern Air Transport Corpn (FAT): 5, Alley 123, Lane 405, Tun Hua North Rd, Taipei 10592; tel. (2) 7121555; fax (2) 7122428; internet www.fat.com.tw; f. 1957; domestic services and regional international services; Chair. and Pres. M. W. CHENG.

Mandarin Airlines (AE): 13/F, 134 Ming Sheng East Rd, Sec. 3, Taipei; tel. (2) 7171188; fax (2) 7170716; e-mail mandarin@ mandarin-airlines.com; internet www.mandarin-airlines.com; f. 1991; subsidiary of CAL; merged with Formosa Airlines 1999; domestic and regional international services; Chair. Y. L. LEE; Pres. MICHAEL LO.

TransAsia Airways: 9/F, 139 Chengchou Rd, Taipei; tel. (2) 25575767; fax (2) 25570643; internet www.tna.com.tw; f. 1951; fmrly Foshing Airlines; domestic flights and international services; Chair. FAN CHIEH-CHIANG; Pres. SUN HUANG-HSIANG.

UNI Airways Corpn: 9/F, 260 Pah-Teh Rd, Sec. 2, Taipei; tel. (2) 27768576; fax (2) 87722029; internet www.uniair.com.tw; f. 1989; fmrly Makung Airlines; merged with Great China Airlines and Taiwan Airlines 1998; domestic flights and international services (to Kota Kinabalu, Malaysia; Bali, Indonesia; Phuket, Thailand); Chair and Pres. JENG KUNG-YEUN.

Tourism

The principal tourist attractions are the cuisine, the cultural artefacts and the island scenery. In 2001 there were 2,617,137 visitor arrivals (including 325,266 overseas Chinese) in Taiwan. Receipts from tourism in 2001 totalled US $3,991m.

Tourism Bureau, Ministry of Transportation and Communications: 9/F, 290 Chung Hsiao East Rd, Sec. 4, Taipei 106; tel. (2) 23491635; fax (2) 27735487; e-mail tbroc@tbroc.gov.tw; internet www.tbroc.gov.tw; f. 1972; Dir-Gen. CHANG SHUO-LAO.

Taiwan Visitors Association: 5/F, 9 Min Chuan East Rd, Sec. 2, Taipei; tel. (2) 25943261; fax (2) 25943265; internet www.tva.org.tw; f. 1956; promotes domestic and international tourism; Chair. STANLEY C. YEN.

COLOMBIA

Introductory Survey

Location, Climate, Language, Religion, Flag, Capital

The Republic of Colombia lies in the north-west of South America, with the Caribbean Sea to the north and the Pacific Ocean to the west. Its continental neighbours are Venezuela and Brazil to the east, and Peru and Ecuador to the south, while Panama connects it with Central America. The coastal areas have a tropical rain forest climate, the plateaux are temperate, and in the Andes mountains there are areas of permanent snow. The language is Spanish. Almost all of the inhabitants profess Christianity, and about 95% are Roman Catholics. There are small Protestant and Jewish minorities. The national flag (proportions 2 by 3) has three horizontal stripes, of yellow (one-half of the depth) over dark blue over red. The capital is Santafé de Bogotá (formerly Bogotá).

Recent History

Colombia was under Spanish rule from the 16th century until 1819, when it achieved independence as part of Gran Colombia, which included Ecuador, Panama and Venezuela. Ecuador and Venezuela seceded in 1830, when Colombia (then including Panama) became a separate republic. In 1903 the province of Panama successfully rebelled and became an independent country. For more than a century, ruling power in Colombia has been shared between two political parties, the Conservatives (Partido Conservador Colombiano, PCC) and the Liberals (Partido Liberal Colombiano, PL), whose rivalry has often led to violence. President Laureano Gómez of the PCC, who was elected 'unopposed' in November 1949, ruled as a dictator until his overthrow by Gen. Gustavo Rojas Pinilla in a coup in June 1953. President Rojas established a right-wing dictatorship but, following widespread rioting, he was deposed in May 1957, when a five-man military junta took power. According to official estimates, lawlessness during 1949–58, known as 'La Violencia', caused the deaths of about 280,000 people.

In an attempt to restore peace and stability, the PCC and the PL agreed to co-operate in a National Front. Under this arrangement, the presidency was to be held by the PCC and the PL in rotation, while cabinet portfolios would be divided equally between the two parties and both would have an equal number of seats in each house of the bicameral Congreso (Congress). In December 1957, in Colombia's first vote on the basis of universal adult suffrage, this agreement was overwhelmingly approved by a referendum and was subsequently incorporated in Colombia's Constitution, dating from 1886.

In May 1958 the first presidential election under the amended Constitution was won by the National Front candidate, Dr Alberto Lleras Camargo, a PL member who had been President in 1945–46. He took office in August 1958, when the ruling junta relinquished power. As provided by the 1957 agreement, he was succeeded by a member of the PCC, Dr Guillermo León Valencia, who was, in turn, succeeded by a PL candidate, Dr Carlos Lleras Restrepo, in 1966.

At the presidential election in April 1970, the National Front candidate, Dr Misael Pastrana Borrero (PCC) narrowly defeated Gen. Rojas, the former dictator, who campaigned as leader of the Alianza Nacional Popular (ANAPO), with policies that had considerable appeal for the poorer sections of the population. At elections to the Congreso, held simultaneously, the National Front lost its majority in each of the two houses, while ANAPO became the main opposition group in each. The result of the presidential election was challenged by supporters of ANAPO, and an armed wing of the party, the Movimiento 19 de Abril (M-19), began to organize guerrilla activity against the Government. It was joined by dissident members of a pro-Soviet guerrilla group, the Fuerzas Armadas Revolucionarias de Colombia (FARC), established in 1966.

The bipartisan form of government ended formally with the presidential and legislative elections of April 1974, although the 1974–78 Cabinet remained subject to the parity agreement. The PCC and the PL together won an overwhelming majority of seats in the Congreso, and support for ANAPO was greatly reduced. The presidential election was won by the PL candidate, Dr Alfonso López Michelsen.

At elections to the Congreso in February 1978, the PL won a clear majority in both houses, and in June the PL candidate, Dr Julio César Turbay Ayala, won the presidential election. President Turbay continued to observe the National Front agreement, and attempted to address the problems of urban terrorism and drugs-trafficking. In 1982 the guerrillas suffered heavy losses after successful counter-insurgency operations, combined with the activities of a new anti-guerrilla group associated with drugs-smuggling enterprises, the Muerte a Secuestradores (MAS, Death to Kidnappers), whose targets later became trade union leaders, academics and human rights activists.

At congressional elections in March 1982, the PL maintained its majority in both houses. In May the PCC candidate, Dr Belisario Betancur Cuartas, won the presidential election, benefiting from a division within the PL. President Betancur, who took office in August, declared a broad amnesty for guerrillas in November, reconvened the Peace Commission (first established in 1981) and ordered an investigation into the MAS. An internal pacification campaign, which was begun in November, met with only moderate success. Despite the Peace Commission's successful negotiation of cease-fire agreements with the FARC, the M-19 (now operating as a left-wing guerrilla movement) and the Ejército Popular de Liberación (EPL) during 1984, factions of all three groups which were opposed to the truce continued to conduct guerrilla warfare against the authorities. In May 1984 the Government's campaign for internal peace was severely hampered by the assassination of the Minister of Justice. His murder was regarded as a consequence of his energetic attempts to eradicate the flourishing drugs industry, and Colombia's leading drugs dealers were implicated in the killing. The Government declared a nation-wide state of siege and announced its intention to enforce its hitherto unobserved extradition treaty with the USA.

Relations between the M-19 and the armed forces deteriorated during 1985, and in June the M-19 formally withdrew from the cease-fire agreement. In November a dramatic siege by the M-19 at the Palace of Justice in the capital, during which more than 100 people were killed, resulted in severe public criticism of the Government and the armed forces for their handling of events. Negotiations with the M-19 were suspended indefinitely.

At congressional elections in March 1986, the traditional wing of the PL secured a clear victory over the PCC and obtained 49% of the votes cast. The Unión Patriótica (UP), formed by the FARC in 1985, won seats in both houses. At the presidential election in May, Dr Virgilio Barco Vargas of the PL was elected President, with 58% of the votes cast. The large majority secured by the PL at both elections obliged the PCC to form the first formal opposition to a government for 30 years.

Attempts by the new administration to address the problems of political violence and the cultivation and trafficking of illicit drugs enjoyed little success during 1986–87. Hopes that an indefinite cease-fire agreement, concluded between the FARC and the Government in March 1986, would facilitate the full participation of the UP in the political process were largely frustrated by the Government's failure to respond effectively to a campaign of assassinations of UP members, conducted by paramilitary 'death squads' during 1985–87, which resulted in an estimated 450 deaths. The crisis was compounded in October 1987 by the decision of six guerrilla groups, including the FARC, the Ejército de Liberación Nacional (ELN) and the M-19, to form a joint front, the Coordinadora Guerrillera Simón Bolívar (CGSB). Although in 1987 the Government extended police powers against drugs dealers, its efforts were severely hampered by the Supreme Court's ruling that Colombia's extradition treaty with the USA was unconstitutional.

In 1988 the Comisión de Convivencia Democrática (Commission of Democratic Cohabitation) was established, with the aim of holding further meetings between all sides in Colombia's internal conflict. Moreover, in September President Barco announced a peace initiative, composed of three phases: pacification; transition; and definitive reintegration into the democratic system. Under the plan, the Government was committed to entering into a dialogue with those guerrilla groups that renounced violence and intended to resume civilian life. However, violence continued to escalate, and in December it was estimated that some 18,000 murders had occurred in Colombia in 1988, of which at least 3,600 were attributed to political motives or related to drugs-trafficking.

In January 1989 the Government and the M-19 concluded an agreement to initiate direct dialogue between the Government, all political parties in the Congreso and the CGSB. In March the M-19 and the Government signed a document providing for the reintegration of the guerrillas into society. In the same month, the ELN, the EPL and the FARC publicly confirmed their willingness to participate in peace talks with the Government; in July the leading guerrilla groups (including the M-19) held a summit meeting, at which they agreed to the formation of a commission, which was to draft proposals for a peace dialogue with the Government. In September the M-19 announced that it had reached agreement with the Government on a peace treaty, under which its members were to demobilize and disarm in exchange for a full pardon. In addition, the movement was to enter the political mainstream; in October the M-19 was formally constituted as a political party. By March 1990 all M-19 guerrilla forces had surrendered their weapons. In exchange for firm commitments from the Barco administration that a referendum would be held to decide the question of constitutional reform and that proposals for comprehensive changes to the electoral law would be introduced in the Congreso, members of the M-19 were guaranteed a general amnesty, reintegration into civilian life and full political participation in forthcoming elections.

The increasingly destabilizing influence of the drugs cartels, meanwhile, continued to undermine government initiatives. The murder, in August 1989, of a popular PL politician and outspoken critic of the drugs-traffickers, was the latest in a series of assassinations of prominent citizens ascribed to the drugs cartels of Cali and Medellín, and prompted President Barco to introduce emergency measures, including the reactivation of Colombia's extradition treaty with the USA. The US administration requested the arrest by the Colombian authorities of 12 leading drugs-traffickers, popularly known as the 'Extraditables', who responded to the USA's request by issuing a declaration of 'total war' against the Government and all journalists, judges and trade unionists opposed to their activities.

At the congressional and municipal elections in March 1990 the PL won 72 of the 114 seats in the Senado (Senate) and an estimated 60% of the 199 contested seats in the Cámara de Representantes (House of Representatives).

Bernardo Jaramillo, the presidential candidate of the UP (who had secured the only left-wing seat in the Senado), was assassinated later in March 1990, and in April Carlos Pizarro of the M-19 became the third presidential candidate to be killed by hired assassins since August 1989. Pizarro was replaced by Antonio Navarro Wolff as M-19 presidential candidate, in conjunction with the recently established Convergencia Democrática (later Alianza Democrática—AD), an alliance of 13 (mainly left-wing) groups and factions.

At the presidential election held in May 1990 César Gaviria Trujillo of the PL was proclaimed the winner, with 47% of the votes cast. Some 90% of voters indicated their approval of proposals for the creation of a National Constituent Assembly in a *de facto* referendum held simultaneously.

Gaviria's Cabinet was described as a cabinet of 'national unity' and comprised seven members of the PL, four of the PCC and, most surprisingly, Navarro Wolff, the AD—M-19 presidential nominee. President Gaviria emphasized, however, that the diversity in composition of the Cabinet did not represent the installation of a coalition government. Gaviria confirmed his commitment to continuing the strenuous efforts to combat drugs-trafficking, having previously made comprehensive changes to police and military personnel in an apparent attempt to strengthen the Government's resistance to infiltration by the cartels. In October the Government proposed an initiative by which some articles of law would be relaxed and others not invoked (including the extradition treaty) for suspected drugs-traffickers who were prepared to surrender to the authorities. By early 1991 Jorge Luis Ochoa and two brothers, members of one of Medellín's most notorious cartels and all sought by US courts for drugs-related offences, had surrendered.

In October 1990 the creation of the National Constituent Assembly was declared constitutionally acceptable by the Supreme Court. Candidates for the AD—M-19 secured 19 of the 70 contested Assembly seats, forcing the ruling PL and the Conservatives to seek support from them and seven elected independents for the successful enactment of reform proposals.

In February 1991 the five-month session of the National Constituent Assembly was inaugurated. The composition of the Assembly had been expanded from 70 to 73 members in order to incorporate three invited members of former guerrilla groupings (two from the EPL and one from the Partido Revolucionario de Trabajadores—PRT) and was later expanded further to accommodate a representative of the Comando Quintín Lame. By June a political pact had been negotiated between President Gaviria and representatives of the PL, the AD—M-19 and the conservative Movimiento de Salvación Nacional (MSN), and an agreement was reached that, in order to facilitate the process of political and constitutional renovation, the Congreso should be dissolved prematurely. The Assembly subsequently voted to dismiss the Congreso, pending new congressional and gubernatorial elections, to be conducted in October (although congressional elections had not been scheduled to take place until 1994).

The new Constitution became effective on 6 July 1991. At the same time, the state of siege, imposed in 1984 in response to the escalation in political and drugs-related violence, was ended. The Constitution placed considerable emphasis upon provisions to encourage greater political participation and to restrict electoral corruption and misrepresentation. It also identified and sought to protect a comprehensive list of civil liberties, among which, controversially, was the prohibition of the extradition of Colombian nationals (see below). While the Constitution was welcomed enthusiastically by the majority of the population, reservations were expressed that clauses relating to the armed forces remained largely unchanged and that provisions which recognized the democratic rights of indigenous groups did not extend to their territorial claims.

Relations with the Medellín cartel improved considerably following the release, in May 1991, of two remaining hostages, and in June, following the decision to prohibit constitutionally the practice of extradition, the Government's efforts were rewarded with the surrender of Pablo Escobar, the supposed head of the Medellín cartel. Charges later brought against Escobar included several of murder, kidnapping and terrorism. In July spokesmen for the Medellín drugs cartel announced that its military operations were to be suspended and that the 'Extraditables' were to be disbanded. Hopes that Escobar's surrender might precipitate a decline in drugs-related violence were frustrated by reports that Escobar was continuing to direct the operations of the Medellín cocaine cartels from his purpose-built prison at Envigado, and by the emergence of the powerful Cali drugs cartel, which was expected to compensate for any shortfall in the supply of illicit drugs resulting from the demise of the Medellín cartel.

The Liberals were most successful in the congressional elections of October 1991, with a clear majority of seats in both chambers. The traditional Conservative opposition suffered from a division in their support between the PCC, the MSN and the Nueva Fuerza Democrática, securing around one-quarter of the seats in both houses between them. The AD—M-19 received only 10% of the votes cast, equivalent to nine seats in the Senado and 15 seats in the Cámara de Representantes.

Meanwhile, in February 1990 the Government had established the National Council for Normalization, in an attempt to repeat the success of recent peace initiatives with the M-19 in negotiations with other revolutionary groups. The EPL announced the end of its armed struggle in August and joined the political mainstream (retaining the Spanish acronym EPL as the Partido de Esperanza, Paz y Libertad), along with the Comando Quintín Lame and the PRT, in 1991. Attempts to negotiate with the FARC and the ELN, however, proved fruitless, and violent clashes between the remaining guerrilla groups (now co-ordinating actions as the Coordinadora Nacional Guerrillera Simón Bolívar—CNGSB) and security forces persisted.

An escalation in guerrilla activity in 1992 prompted the Government to intensify anti-insurgency measures. In October the Congreso approved government proposals for an increased counterinsurgency budget and for the creation of new armed units to combat terrorism. The Government's rejection of any agenda for renewed negotiations provoked an intensification of the conflict, and this, together with a resurgence of drugs-related violent incidents following the death of the supposed military commander of the Medellín cartel, prompted Gaviria, in November, to declare a 90-day state of internal disturbance, thereby extending wide-ranging powers to the security forces and imposing restrictions on media coverage. As a result, the M-19 announced that it was to withdraw from the Government and resume an active opposition role.

The security situation continued to deteriorate in 1993, leading the Government to announce, in February, a significant increase in its budget allocation for security, and in April, to double the length of prison terms for terrorist acts. The state of internal disturbance was also extended twice. Attempts by the Government and the ELN to negotiate a truce were frustrated by a perceived lack of commitment to compromise on both sides, and the prospects for future successful discussions were undermined by the insistence of security forces that ELN members were responsible for the murder of the Vice-President of the Senado in November. In December negotiations with the Corriente de Renovación Socialista (CRS), a dissident faction of the ELN more disposed to political assimilation, produced a tentative agreement for the guerrillas' reincorporation into civilian life and transformation into a legitimate political force. In April 1994, under the supervision of international observers, the CRS duly surrendered its weapons, and was subsequently awarded two seats in the newly elected Cámara de Representantes (see below).

An intensification of drugs-related violence in the capital during early 1993 was attributed to an attempt by Pablo Escobar (who had escaped from prison in mid-1992) to force the Government to negotiate more favourable conditions for his surrender, and prompted the formation of a vigilante group, Pepe (Perseguidos por Pablo Escobar—those Persecuted by Pablo Escobar), which launched a campaign of retaliatory violence against Escobar's family, associates and property. Pepe was thought to number among its members several of Escobar's disgruntled rivals from the Medellín cartel. A simultaneous and sustained assault by Pepe and by the security forces against the remnants of the Medellín cartel resulted in the death and surrender of many notable cartel members, culminating in the death of Escobar himself, in December, during an exchange of fire with security forces attempting to effect his arrest.

The dispatch of a contingent of US troops to the Valle del Cauca region in December 1993, described as a humanitarian mission to improve communications and health and education facilities, aroused widespread political outrage from the Government's opponents, who interpreted the accommodation of the troops as capitulation to US demands for military participation in the region, in order to ensure the destruction of the Cali cartel. By late February 1994, however, the troops had been withdrawn, the Council of State having ruled earlier in the month that President Gaviria had abused his authority by endorsing their deployment prior to consultation with the Senado. Relations with the USA deteriorated further in March following US criticism of the lenient terms of surrender being offered to leaders of the Cali cartel.

The results of congressional and local elections conducted in March 1994 represented a serious reversal for the political left in Colombia, and re-established the traditional two-party dominance of the PL and the PCC. The elections were particularly disappointing for the AD—M-19, whose representation was reduced from 13 seats to two in the Cámara de Representantes and from nine seats to just one in the Senado. The PL retained a comfortable congressional majority. Following a second round of voting in the presidential election on 19 June between the two leading candidates, Ernesto Samper Pizano (PL) and Andrés Pastrana Arango (PCC), Samper was declared the winner, with 50.9% of the valid votes cast. He was inaugurated on 7 August and a new Cabinet was installed.

Shortly after President Samper took office, allegations emerged that his election campaign had been partly funded by contributions from the Cali cartel. Tape-recordings of conversations which appeared to provide evidence that contact had at least been made with the cartels were subsequently dismissed by the Prosecutor-General as insufficient proof of such contributions actually having been made. In July 1994 a similar recording, which appeared to implicate the Colombian Chief of National Police in the payment of a bribe by the Cali cartel, prompted the US Senate to vote to make the disbursement of future aid to Colombia dependent on an assessment of the level of its co-operation in anti-drugs programmes. The existence of the tape-recordings was widely attributed to the US Drugs Enforcement Agency (DEA), which the Colombian media accused of fomenting mistrust in an attempt to ensure that the new administration would pursue an uncompromising anti-drugs policy. Restrictions were subsequently imposed on DEA

operations and access to information in Colombia. However, it was hoped that bilateral relations would improve following the appointment of a new Prosecutor-General and a new Chief of the National Police in late 1994, and the Cámara de Representantes' rejection, in December, of the 'narco bill', which sought to limit the powers of the authorities to confiscate funds and assets proceeding from illicit activities.

CNGSB offensives during 1994 were launched to coincide with campaigning for the March legislative elections, and to disrupt the weeks preceding the transfer of power from Gaviria to Samper in August. Fighting between guerrillas and the security forces resulted in numerous deaths on both sides and considerable damage was inflicted on power installations and the transport infrastructure. Prospects for the swift negotiation of a peace agreement between the new administration and the CNGSB were immediately undermined by the murder of the UP's Manuel Cepeda Vargas (the only left-wing member of the Senado) and deteriorated as guerrilla activities intensified. However, in November Samper complied with a guerrilla request that imprisoned rebel leaders should be moved from military installations to civilian prisons, and also declared the Government's willingness to enter into unconditional dialogue with the guerrillas.

During 1994 the Government was subject to intense international pressure to formalize a greater commitment to respect for human rights, following a series of revelations in which the security forces were implicated in abuses of human rights, and the publication of a report by Amnesty International which claimed that the vast majority of infringements of human rights in Colombia were perpetrated by the armed forces and associated paramilitary groups. In September the Minister of the Interior, Horacio Serpa Uribe, announced an initiative to address the human rights crisis, including plans to reform the National Police and to disband all paramilitary units. In September 1995 Brig.-Gen. Alvaro Velandia Hurtado was removed from active duty by the Government, after a report by the office of the Prosecutor for Human Rights had pronounced him responsible for the detention and murder of a prominent M-19 member in 1987. Velandia's dismissal marked the first such action undertaken by the Government against senior army personnel in response to abuses of human rights.

In February 1995, in the context of the US Government's persistence in attaching preconditions to the disbursement of financial aid to Colombia, President Samper reiterated his commitment to the eradication of all illegal drugs-related activities in the country. A number of initiatives to address the problem were launched in Cali, resulting in the capture of the head of the Cali drugs cartel, Gilberto Rodríguez Orejuela, and four other cartel leaders in mid-1995. Meanwhile, in April nine prominent PL politicians were suspended from the party pending their investigation by the office of the Prosecutor-General, following allegations of their maintaining links with the Cali cartel. In the following months it was confirmed that the Comptroller-General and the Attorney-General were also to be the subject of investigation as a result of similar allegations, while Samper's former election campaign treasurer, Santiago Medina, was arrested on charges related to the processing of drugs cartel contributions through Samper's election fund. In August the Minister of National Defence, Fernando Botero Zea, resigned, having been implicated in the affair by evidence submitted to the authorities by Medina. Medina also insisted that Samper had been fully aware of the origin of the funds. The President's former campaign manager was arrested in September, in which month Samper protested his own innocence before a congressional accusations committee.

In May 1995 the Government extended an offer of participation in legislative and consultative processes to the FARC, in the hope of securing their commitment to surrender arms. While the FARC responded positively to the initial proposal, further progress was to be dependent on the Government's successful execution of its stated intention to demilitarize the sensitive north-eastern region of La Uribe. A Government proposal for the exchange of armed struggle for a political agenda, issued to the ELN and dissident groups of the EPL and the M-19 at the same time, received a more cautious response from the guerrillas. However, all negotiations were hampered by renewed FARC and ELN offensives in late May. An escalation in the number of acts of violence perpetrated by guerrilla forces and by paramilitary defence groups in the north-western Urabá region prompted Samper to declare a state of internal disturbance for a 90-day period. In October, however, the Constitutional Court rejected the terms of the state of emergency, forcing the President to seek immediate congressional approval for alternative powers to extend the period of detention of some 3,500 suspected insurgents. Following the assassination, in November, of a prominent Conservative politician, the President declared a new 90-day state of internal disturbance. However, negotiations between the President and Andrés Pastrana of the PCC, for a 'national agreement against violence', were frustrated by the latter's insistence on the establishment of an independent commission of inquiry into the allegations of Samper's campaign funding by the Cali cartel as a precondition to political negotiation.

In December 1995 the congressional accusations committee voted against the initiation of a full-scale inquiry into allegations of Samper's impropriety in the use of funds proceeding from drugs cartels, on the grounds of insufficient evidence at that time. The repercussions of the scandal, however, were considered to have severely undermined the political integrity of the Government, both at home and abroad. Relations between the US Government and the Samper administration deteriorated dramatically during 1995, culminating in allegations—made by official sources in Colombia—that the US Government was attempting to destabilize the administration through the covert actions of the DEA.

In January 1996 Botero reiterated Medina's claim that Samper had been in full possession of the facts regarding the cartel's funding of his election campaign, prompting the PCC to announce an immediate suspension of co-operation with the Government and the resignation of two of the four incumbent PCC members of the Cabinet. Samper subsequently urged the Congreso to reopen investigations into his involvement in the affair, seeking to demonstrate his innocence. Evidence collected by the Prosecutor-General was submitted to the accusations committee in February, together with four formal charges to be brought against the President, including that of illegal enrichment. Later in the month congressional commissions of both parliamentary chambers decided to launch a new and public investigation into the funding of Samper's election campaign. In March Samper testified before the accusations committee and denied allegations that he had contrived the plan to solicit funding from the Cali cartel; however, he did concede that the cartel had part-financed the campaign, albeit without his knowledge.

In April 1996 the Supreme Court took the unprecedented step of requesting that the Senado suspend the Attorney-General, Orlando Vásquez Velásquez, in order that he face charges of obstructing the course of justice (he had allegedly fabricated evidence to discredit the Prosecutor-General). In October Vásquez Velásquez was found guilty of the charges; he was dismissed as Attorney-General and banned from holding public office for a five-year period. Moreover, in December 1997 he was sentenced to eight years' imprisonment on drugs charges. During 1996 Botero, Medina and María Izquierdo, a former PL senator, were all sentenced to terms of imprisonment for their involvement in the Samper affair.

In June 1996 the Congreso voted to acquit Samper of charges of having been aware of the part-financing of his election campaign by drugs-traffickers. The US Administration condemned the result and threatened to impose trade sanctions against Colombia. (In March the US Congress had refused to 'certify' Colombia as a co-operating nation with regard to US anti-drugs activities after a leading Cali cartel member escaped from prison.) In July, following the release of a prominent Medellín cartel member after only five-and-a-half years in prison, the US Government accused Samper of failing to take appropriate measures to deter drugs-trafficking and revoked his visa to travel to the USA.

Civil unrest and guerrilla activity continued during 1996. The state of internal disturbance was extended for a further 90 days in January, and then again in April following a CNGSB-organized nation-wide 'armed industrial strike', which had resulted in as many as 40 deaths. In March a FARC attack on a drugs-control police unit had renewed speculation of links between guerrilla groups and the drugs cartels. Moreover, it was suggested that a major offensive launched in August by FARC and ELN rebels (resulting in as many as 100 fatalities) had been deliberately timed to coincide with large-scale protests by coca growers demanding a review of the coca eradication programme, particularly the use of aerial spraying. Although 26 members of the FARC and some 250 dissident EPL rebels surrendered to the authorities during September and October, violent skirmishes

continued unabated, and disaffected members of the ELN were reported to have regrouped as the Ejército Revolucionario del Pueblo.

In September 1996 Samper's credibility was undermined by the resignation of the Vice-President, Humberto de la Calle, who appealed to the President to renounce his office in order to prevent the country from descending into 'total chaos'. Later in the same month Samper was again humiliated by the discovery of 3.7 kg of heroin aboard the aircraft in which he had been scheduled to fly to the USA (using a diplomat visa) to attend a meeting of the UN General Assembly. (A subsequent investigation into the drugs seizure did not implicate the President in any way.) In an apparent attempt to appease the US administration, Samper announced that Colombia's Congreso would debate whether to amend the Constitution in order to permit the extradition of Colombian nationals. Moreover, in December the Congreso approved controversial legislation to allow for the confiscation of drugs-traffickers' assets. (Many members of the congressional constitutional committees had been reluctant to adopt or even debate the law for fear of reprisals from drugs cartels.)

In early 1997 the Samper administration encountered increasing pressure from the USA to address the issues of drugs-trafficking and corruption. The appointment of Guillermo Alberto González as Colombia's Minister of National Defence was condemned by the USA, which alleged that he had maintained links with drugs-traffickers; González resigned as a result of the allegations in March. In February, meanwhile, the USA again refused to 'certify' Colombia, claiming that there had been a substantial increase in the production of illicit drugs in that country during 1996. In response, Samper announced the temporary suspension of Colombia's drugs-crop eradication programme. The programme was resumed shortly afterwards, but relations with the USA remained strained. Although legislation permitting the extradition of Colombian nationals sought for criminal offences abroad was approved in November, it was strongly criticized by the US administration as it would not have retroactive effect. Nevertheless, in February 1998 the USA waived sanctions on Colombia, although it did not fully 'certify' the country.

The activities of guerrilla and paramilitary groups in Colombia intensified during 1997. In May the Government agreed to the temporary demilitarization of part of the Caquetá department in order to secure the release of 70 members of the armed forces captured by the FARC. Notably, President Samper acknowledged that paramilitary groups had increasingly instigated violent attacks (sometimes with the tacit support of the security forces) and agreed that they should be included in peace negotiations. In July, after a series of assaults on the security forces by FARC and ELN rebels, Samper reorganized the military and police command, replacing the Commander-in-Chief of the Armed Forces, Gen. Harold Bedoya Pizzaro, who had vehemently opposed negotiating with the guerrillas. In addition, Samper presented legislation to the Congreso that would lead to the establishment of a national peace commission.

In mid-1997 there was a marked increase in violent attacks by guerrilla and paramilitary groups, apparently intent on sabotaging departmental and municipal elections, scheduled to be held in October. In the months preceding the elections more than 40 candidates were killed, some 200 were kidnapped and as many as 1,900 withdrew after receiving death threats. Voting was cancelled in numerous municipalities, while in August the vulnerability of the Government to rebel attacks was emphasized by the assassination of a PL senator who was a close ally of Samper. Meanwhile, reports of secret preliminary peace negotiations between government representatives and the FARC were undermined by a major military offensive in September, in which 652 FARC guerrillas were killed and a further 1,600 were captured. The Government's subsequent conciliatory gestures to the guerrillas, including a promise by the President to submit legislation to the Congreso granting an amnesty in return for the signing of a peace accord, were met with little enthusiasm by the FARC and the ELN. In November 1997 the ELN secured significant concessions from the Government in return for the release of two OAS election observers abducted in October. In the same month there was a sharp increase in attacks by paramilitary groups.

Horacio Serpa Uribe, a close ally of President Samper, resigned as Minister of the Interior in May 1997 and was selected as the official PL presidential candidate in January 1998. His candidature was strongly opposed by the US administration as he was alleged to have links with drugs-traffickers and was implicated in the affair regarding the illegal funding of Samper's 1994 election campaign. (In December 1997 Serpa was cleared of criminal charges relating to the affair.) Also in May 1997, Alfonso Valdivieso, whose vigorous investigations into corruption and drugs-trafficking had bolstered his popularity, resigned as Prosecutor-General in order to contest the presidency. In March 1998, however, Valdivieso withdrew his candidacy and pledged support for Pastrana, who had been selected again as the PCC nominee.

At congressional elections, conducted in March 1998, the PL retained a narrow overall majority in the legislature, obtaining 53 of the 102 seats in the Senado, and 84 of the 161 seats in the Cámara de Representantes. The PCC secured 27 and 28 seats in each chamber, respectively. An estimated 54% of the electorate participated in the elections, which were preceded by a period of violent attacks on the security forces by guerrilla groups; in one incident 80 counter-insurgency troops were killed by the FARC, and a further 43 were taken prisoner. In May tens of thousands of Colombians staged a demonstration to protest at the escalation of violence by guerrillas and paramilitary groups.

In the first round of the presidential election, held in May 1998, Serpa secured 34.6% of the valid votes cast, followed by Pastrana (34.3%), Noemí Sanín Posada—an independent candidate who performed particularly well in Medellín, Cali and the capital—(26.9%), and Gen. (retd) Bedoya (1.8%). Nine other candidates contested the election. A second ballot was held in June, at which Pastrana defeated Serpa, winning 50.4% of the valid votes cast. Pastrana was inaugurated as President on 7 August. Shortly afterwards the military leadership was re-organized and Gen. Fernando Tapias Stahelín, a moderate, was appointed Commander-in-Chief of the Armed Forces. Pastrana's immediate declared priorities included reaching a peace settlement with the guerrillas, eliminating corruption and strengthening the ailing economy.

In July 1998 President-elect Pastrana announced that he had held secret talks with Manuel Marulanda Vélez (alias 'Tirofijo'), the FARC leader, and that he had agreed to demilitarize five southern municipalities for a 90-day period (commencing in November) in order to facilitate negotiations with the guerrillas. Pastrana subsequently recognized the political status of the FARC, thereby allowing the Government to negotiate with an outlawed group. Notwithstanding, FARC attacks on the security forces continued, increasing significantly in August, before Pastrana's inauguration, and also in November, prior to the completion of the demilitarization of the five districts in the departments of Caquetá and Meta. Shortly before the negotiations between the Government and the FARC began in January 1999, it was revealed that in December the FARC had held informal talks in Costa Rica with government officials from the USA and Colombia. The FARC was reported to have invited the US officials to visit illegal crop plantations in Colombia and to consider possible substitution programmes. (Relations between Colombia and the USA had improved notably under the Pastrana administration: in October Pastrana made an official visit to the USA—the first by a Colombian Head of State in 23 years—and in December the two countries agreed on measures to improve military co-operation in the fight against the drugs trade.) In mid-January 1999 the FARC suspended talks with the Government until the authorities provided evidence that they were taking action against paramilitary groups, which claimed responsibility for the massacre of more than 130 civilians earlier in the month. In February Pastrana announced the extension of the period of demilitarization by three months, in order to facilitate negotiations.

The ELN, meanwhile, made tentative moves to negotiate a peace settlement during 1998. In February the group signed an accord with government peace negotiators in Madrid, Spain, on the holding of preliminary peace talks. In April the ELN disclosed that its leader, Gregorio Manuel Pérez Martínez, had died shortly afterwards; a collective leadership was appointed subsequently. In July, at a meeting in Mainz, Germany, between the ELN and representatives of Colombian 'civil society' (grouped in the National Peace Council—Consejo Nacional de Paz—CNP), the ELN made concessions on the 'humanization' of the war and agreed to facilitate talks between its members and the Government. The guerrillas subsequently postponed a meeting with the CNP in protest at its signing of an agreement with the Autodefensas Unidas de Colombia (AUC), an organization representing most of Colombia's paramilitary groups, to hold parallel peace talks. Nevertheless, in October representa-

tives of the ELN, the CNP and the Government agreed on a timetable for preliminary peace talks, beginning in February 1999, which would culminate in the assembling of a national convention. The Government recognized the political status of the ELN, but the group did not cease hostilities. Later in October 1998 an ELN attack on an oil pipeline in the department of Antioquia resulted in the deaths of at least 66 civilians. The planned peace negotiations failed to begin in February 1999, not least because of the Government's refusal to agree to the ELN's request that four districts in the department of Bolívar be demilitarized. The ELN intensified its operations, in an apparent attempt to increase pressure on the Government to accede to its demands. The guerrillas hijacked an AVIANCA domestic flight in April, kidnapping all 46 people on board, and abducted some 140 members of the congregation of a church in Cali in May. In June Pastrana withdrew political recognition of the ELN and made the release of hostages a precondition for future peace talks. A civilian commission was subsequently appointed by the Government to negotiate towards this end. The ELN freed the last hostage in November 2000.

Little progress was achieved in negotiations with the FARC until April 1999, as the guerrillas continued to insist that the Government demonstrate some success in its actions against paramilitary groups prior to a resumption of talks. The enforced resignation in that month of two senior army officers, alleged to have collaborated with paramilitary groups, appeared to appease the FARC, however, and in early May talks between Marulanda and President Pastrana resulted in an agreement on a comprehensive agenda for future peace negotiations; the period of demilitarization was again extended. Shortly afterwards a police offensive against a cocaine-production complex operated by paramilitaries in the central department of Magdalena was perceived as further evidence of a change in the attitude of the authorities towards paramilitary groups. However, Pastrana's strategy was not entirely supported by his administration, and at the end of May Rodrigo Lloreda, the Minister of National Defence, resigned in protest at concessions granted to the FARC. Meanwhile, the AUC sought to acquire political status and be included in the peace negotiations. Pastrana's position was further undermined by the Congreso's rejection of legislation aimed at increasing the President's power concerning the peace process, as independent deputies voted with the opposition PL for the first time. Furthermore, the FARC continued to pursue its military campaign. The postponement of talks in July, owing to a failure to agree on the role of international observers, was followed by a nation-wide guerrilla offensive that resulted in more than 200 deaths. The talks were subsequently postponed indefinitely, with the Government insisting that international monitors be allowed to investigate abuses allegedly committed by the FARC in the demilitarized zone. As negotiations resumed in October in La Uribe, after Pastrana had apparently withdrawn his demand for international observers, demonstrations for peace were attended by some 10m. people throughout the country. At further talks in November it was agreed that public hearings on the peace process would be held from late December. However, the FARC's commitment to the process was questioned by the military when, prior to the second round of November talks, the guerrillas launched attacks on 13 towns in several departments, amid renewed claims that they were using the demilitarized zone as a recruitment and training base from which to mount offensives. Guerrilla violence continued until, on 19 December, the FARC declared a 22-day unilateral cease-fire.

Relations between the US Government and the Colombian administration continued to improve under President Pastrana, notably regarding anti-drugs activities. In March 1999 the USA decided to 'certify' Colombia's efforts to combat drugs-trafficking and in September Pastrana announced the establishment of a new anti-narcotics battalion, to be trained and financed by the USA. Collaboration between the Colombian and US authorities led to the arrest of more than 60 suspected drugs-traffickers in two major operations conducted in October and December. However, the most important progress in Colombian–US relations came in 2000 with the development of Pastrana's so-called 'Plan Colombia'. This was an ambitious, US $7,500m. project intended to strengthen the Colombian state by increasing the efficiency of the security forces and the judicial system, eliminating drugs production through both eradication and crop substitution, and reducing unemployment. In July 2000 the US Congress approved a contribution to the Plan of $1,300m., which included a military component of $1,000m., but also significant sums for judicial reform and human-rights education. Human rights organizations warned of an escalation of human rights abuses following the Plan's implementation, as the main aid component was allocated to strengthening the security forces, whose links to paramilitary groups were, allegedly, yet to be severed. At the same time, Colombia's Andean neighbours feared that an escalation in violence would force thousands of refugees on to their territory, and subsequently reinforced their borders. During US President Bill Clinton's visit to Colombia in August, some 2,000 students and trade-union members demonstrated outside the US embassy in protest at his country's involvement in Colombia. Earlier that month President Clinton had waived the human rights conditions on which the disbursement of US aid to Colombia was dependent, in the interests of national security.

In May 2000 a so-called 'necklace' bomb killed a woman and four others in an abortive extortion scheme. The FARC was initially assumed to be responsible for the atrocity and peace talks were suspended. Negotiations were resumed in September. However, the FARC threatened to halt the peace process if plans for the US military component of Plan Colombia, to be directed against coca-growing areas of Putumayo, were implemented. The FARC effectively blockaded Putumayo from the end of September to retain control of the province, and it succeeded in delaying the aerial spraying of coca plantations, which was scheduled to begin in November. (The military offensive against the plantations began in December, although in February the aerial spraying of crops was suspended in the Putumayo region after local authorities warned of the adverse effects the herbicides used could have on people and licit crops.) In October the Government dismissed 388 members of the armed forces in a move designed to improve military efficiency as well as to allay accusations of corruption and violations of human rights. However, the dismissals did not prevent the FARC from withdrawing from peace talks in November in order to demand greater government action in combating the AUC. The Government's ombudsman reported that, in the first six months of 2000, 512 unarmed civilians were killed by the AUC, compared with 120 killed by guerrilla groups. The FARC was particularly angered by the decision of Minister of the Interior, Humberto de la Calle, to meet the AUC leader, Carlos Castaño. By the end of the year President Pastrana was under increasing pressure to take back by force control of the demilitarized zone; a report released in December estimated a 30% increase in FARC military capacity since the zone was created. The murder in late December of Diego Turbay Cote, President of the congressional peace commission, allegedly by members of the FARC, further heightened tensions. (The Vice-President of the peace commission was killed in September 2001.) However, following threats by the FARC that failure to prolong the demilitarized zone would lead to 'total war', Pastrana extended the deadline until the end of January 2001. A further extension was granted in February, after which the FARC leadership met the President in the demilitarized zone and signed a 13-point 'Pact of Los Pozos', including an agreement to revive the stalled negotiations, to expedite an exchange of sick prisoners, and to begin discussions on a cease-fire. In the same month Jaime Uscategui became the first army general to be convicted for failing to prevent a mass killing (in the department of Meta, in 1997) by right-wing paramilitaries. In March 2001 diplomats representing governments from Latin America, Europe, Japan and Canada met with FARC leaders to monitor the peace process. The new US Administration of George W. Bush refused an invitation to join the peace process, preferring instead to focus on drug eradication policies. In July the US House of Representatives approved a US $670m. aid package, known as the Andean Regional Initiative, to support Plan Colombia and to promote stability in the rest of the Andean region.

Violence escalated during 2001. In the first four months of the year an estimated 760 people were killed, and in the first seven months 1,700 were kidnapped, a significant increase on the previous year. However, in June progress was made in peace negotiations when the FARC signed a prisoner exchange agreement with the Government; about 300 prisoners were released by the FARC at the end of the month. Nevertheless, in August President Pastrana signed legislation giving new powers to the military to combat guerrilla forces. The legislation was controversial as it allowed for less scrutiny from government investigators, and was opposed by human rights organizations. In the same month three Irish nationals, suspected to have links to the Provisional Irish Republican Army (IRA), were arrested in the demilitarized zone on suspicion of collaborating with the FARC on training methods. The arrests, together with the murder of former culture minister Consuelo Araújo in late September, threatened to derail the fragile peace process. (The trial of the three Irishmen commenced in October 2002; following several delays, it resumed in March 2003.) None the less, in October the Government extended the existence of the demilitarized zone until January 2002, after the FARC agreed to reduce the number of kidnappings and to begin cease-fire negotiations. However, the Government refused demands by the FARC to remove military controls (including restrictions on entry for foreigners imposed after the arrest of the three Irish nationals) around the demilitarized zone. This impasse effectively prevented any progress on substantive issues such as cease-fire negotiations during the rest of the year. Finally, in a move that signalled the end of the peace process, on 9 January 2002 Pastrana announced that the FARC had 48 hours to leave the demilitarized zone. Hours before the expiry of the deadline the FARC rescinded demands for relaxed security around the demilitarized zone and agreed to recommence negotiations; as a result the guerrillas were able to continue their occupation of the zone. On 20 January, with the help of representatives from 10 facilitating countries and UN envoy James LeMoyne, agreement was reached on an extension, to 7 April, to the deadline for a cease-fire agreement. The existence of the demilitarized zone was extended until 10 April. However, on 20 February, following the hijacking of an aeroplane and the kidnapping of a prominent senator by the FARC, Pastrana terminated peace talks with the guerrilla organization and ordered the armed forces to regain control of the demilitarized zone. In May the FARC was held responsible for the deaths of at least 117 civilians sheltering in a church in Bojayá, in the department of Chocó. The church was hit by a FARC mortar bomb during a battle to regain control of the town from the AUC.

In April 2000 an agreement was reached with the ELN on the establishment of a demilitarized zone, similar to that granted to the FARC, in southern Bolívar. However, the Government faced much local opposition to the proposed zone, including roadblocks and demonstrations. In July informal discussions on a national convention, as demanded by the guerrilla movement as a precursor to peace talks, were held with the ELN in Geneva, Switzerland, with envoys from Cuba, France, Norway, Spain and Switzerland present, but ended without agreement. In response, the ELN continued to sabotage Colombia's oil industry by attacking pipeline transport. Tentative moves towards peace recommenced in December after the ELN released 42 hostages. Negotiations in Havana, Cuba, at the end of the year resulted in a preliminary agreement on the terms and conditions of the demilitarized zone in Bolívar, though it was conditional on the acceptance by the ELN of the presence of an international verification committee in the region, as well as representatives from local and judicial institutions and one civilian police agency. The agreement was strongly opposed by the AUC and by residents of the proposed region, and in February 2001 more than 10,000 people in Bolívar participated in a demonstration against the establishment of the zone. The prospects for a demilitarized zone were reduced after the ELN suspended negotiations with the Government in March in protest at the aerial spraying of coca in the Bolívar region. At the same time, the AUC began an offensive in the area in order to prevent the establishment of the demilitarized zone. The ELN resumed peace negotiations in April but later that month members of the guerrilla organization allegedly kidnapped 92 workers from the US oil firm Occidental. They were subsequently released. Peace negotiations faltered again in August when President Pastrana suspended unofficial talks, which had been taking place in Venezuela, accusing the ELN of inflexibility. Bomb attacks in Medellín and other parts of the country later that month were widely assumed to be the response of the ELN to the suspension of the talks. Although contact between the two sides resumed in December in Cuba, and in January 2002, following a Christmas truce, negotiations on a permanent cease-fire were initiated, the ELN withdrew from talks with the Pastrana administration in May.

In July 2000 the Congreso approved legislation that codified forced disappearances and displacements as crimes and increased the punishment for torture. In local elections, held in October, independent candidates won mayoral races in four of Colombia's five largest cities (including Santafé de Bogotá). The election campaign was overshadowed by an unprecedented number of kidnappings and murders of candidates. The results were interpreted as a sign of voters' frustration with the Government.

In legislative elections, held on 10 March 2002, the most significant gains were made by independents and parties allied to Alvaro Uribe Vélez, the former Governor of Antioquia and a candidate in the forthcoming presidential elections. The PL remained the largest single party in the Senado and the Cámara de Representantes, with 29 and 54 seats, respectively. However, its representation was substantially reduced, while the representation of the PCC diminished to 13 seats in the Senado and 21 lower-house seats. The rate of voter participation was 42.3%.

A presidential election was held on 26 May 2002, amid a climate of increased intimidation by both guerrilla and paramilitary groups. (Voter participation was estimated at only 46% of the electorate.) Alvaro Uribe, a dissident member of the PL, was elected President with 54.0% of the votes cast, compared with 32.3% secured by his nearest rival, Horacio Serpa (PL). Luis Eduardo Garzón (the leader of the main trade-union federation, the Central Unitaria de Trabajadores) and Noemí Sanín (again standing as an independent) won 6.3% and 5.9% of the votes, respectively. The PCC had withdrawn its candidate following the party's disappointing results in the legislative elections. Uribe outlined his plans as, *inter alia*, increasing military expenditure (creating a professional army and recruiting civilians as informants), continuing with Plan Colombia, reducing the Congreso to a single 150-seat chamber and reforming social security legislation. The PL, the PCC and a number of independents pledged their support to the President-elect, thus giving him an overwhelming majority in both parliamentary chambers.

In mid-2002 the leaders of the AUC announced that their federation would disband, as some of its members had become involved in drugs-trafficking and hostage-taking. The federation was subsequently re-established, but there was scepticism as to whether it had been 'purged' effectively. The FARC, meanwhile, pursued a campaign of intimidation against local officials (hundreds of whom were reported to have resigned from office under threat of execution), and on 7 August, the day of Uribe's inauguration as President, launched attacks on the presidential palace and other public buildings in Santafé de Bogotá. In response, in mid-August Uribe announced a 90-day state of internal disturbance (renewed for 90 days in November), including an emergency war tax (aimed to raise more than US $750m.) to be levied from September. Two 'Rehabilitation and Consolidation Zones' were established in the north-eastern departments of Sucre, Bolívar and Arauca, where the security forces were granted extensive powers. Further measures were introduced by decree in September. The authorities could thus embark on a range of activities, including the imposition of curfews, restricting the media and detaining civilians without a warrant. Military offensives were launched against the FARC in Antioquia, Tolima and Meta, and the aerial spraying of coca plantations was resumed in the department of Putumayo. The USA, meanwhile, certified that Colombia's armed forces had met their human rights requirements, allowing for the release of military aid of more than $40m. (in addition to $60m. given earlier in the year) for counter-insurgency operations.

The popularity of President Uribe soared, despite concerns regarding the infringement of human rights and the Constitutional Court's ruling, in November 2002, that some of the measures introduced in the 'internal disturbance decree' violated constitutional guarantees (the Court questioned the legality of establishing military-controlled areas, restricting journalists' access to such zones and using the military to conduct police functions). In December Uribe requested the renewal of the 'state of internal disturbance' for a third 90-day period. Meanwhile, the AUC, which had been conducting secret talks with the Government, declared an indefinite truce from 1 December, hoping to commence formal peace negotiations under the auspices of the Roman Catholic church. Not all paramilitary groups adhered to the truce. In January 2003 the President announced that official talks would begin with the AUC later in the month; Uribe stated his intention to negotiate the release of all hostages and demobilize paramilitary forces by the end of the year. Exploratory discussions between the Government and the ELN (resumed after Uribe's appointment) continued in Cuba, but negotiations with the FARC remained stalled, as the guerrilla group rejected proposals to hold talks in Venezuela, under French mediation.

In December 2002 President Uribe succeeded in gaining congressional approval for key political reforms regarding taxation, the pension system and labour legislation. Moreover, agreement was reached on 18 proposals, primarily concerning fiscal austerity measures, to be included in a national referendum, scheduled to be held in by mid-2003.

Colombia has a long-standing border dispute with Venezuela. However, relations between the countries improved following the signing, in October 1989, of a border integration agreement, which included a provision on joint co-operation in the campaign to eradicate drugs-trafficking. (A permanent reconciliation commission to investigate the border dispute had been established in March 1989.) In March 1990 the San Pedro Alejandrino agreement, signed by the two countries, sought to initiate the implementation of recommendations made by existing bilateral border commissions and to establish a number of new commissions, including one to examine the territorial claims of both sides. Colombia's efforts to improve relations with Venezuela were hampered by the activities of FARC guerrillas in the border region, leading the two countries to sign an agreement to improve border co-operation in February 1997; however, in April Venezuela deployed 5,000 troops along its frontier with Colombia in an attempt to halt repeated incursions by Colombian guerrillas. Agreements were subsequently signed by the two countries to strengthen military co-operation and intelligence sharing. In 2000 relations deteriorated, owing to Venezuelan President Hugo Chávez's opposition to Plan Colombia and accusations by Colombia that Venezuela was covertly aiding the guerrilla forces. In November Colombia temporarily recalled its ambassador to Venezuela after a FARC representative was allowed to speak in the Venezuelan National Assembly. Relations deteriorated further in 2001, after Venezuela refused to allow the extradition to Colombia of a suspect in the April 1999 hijack of an AVIANCA flight (see above). Following the appointment of President Uribe, bilateral relations improved: in November 2002 Chávez and Uribe held a meeting at which they agreed on measures to promote bilateral trade and, notably, to establish a system to deal with problems on their common border.

In June 1997 Panama announced its intention to station 1,200 soldiers along its border with Colombia to counter an increase in the activities of Colombian guerrilla and paramilitary groups in the country, and, following the death of a member of Panama's security forces during an attack by the FARC in November, the Heads of State of the two countries agreed to improve border co-operation. Increasing concern regarding the threat posed to regional stability by Colombia's internal conflict prompted neighbouring countries to boost security measures on the common border, particularly after concern that the implementation of Plan Colombia might lead to an escalation in violence.

In 1980 Nicaragua laid claim to the Colombian-controlled islands of Providencia and San Andrés. Colombia has a territorial dispute with Honduras over cays in the San Andrés and Providencia archipelago. In October 1986 the Colombian Senado approved a delimitation treaty of marine and submarine waters in the Caribbean Sea, which had been signed by the Governments of Colombia and Honduras in August. In late 1999 the Honduran National Assembly finally ratified the treaty, strengthening Colombia's claim to the islands of Providencia and San Andrés, and thus angering Nicaragua, which filed a complaint with the International Court of Justice.

On 1 January 1994 a 10-year trade liberalization programme came into effect between Colombia, Mexico and Venezuela. A free trade agreement with Chile, the Acuerdo de Complementación Económica (ACE), also took effect on the same day, and was expected to have eliminated tariffs on most goods by the time of its full implementation on 1 January 1999.

Government

Executive power is exercised by the President (assisted by a Cabinet), who is elected for a four-year term by universal adult suffrage. Legislative power is vested in the bicameral Congress, consisting of the Senate (102 members elected for four years) and the House of Representatives (161 members elected for four years). The country is divided into 32 Departments and one Capital District.

Defence

At 18 years of age, every male (with the exception of students) must present himself as a candidate for military service of between one and two years. In August 2002 the strength of the army was 136,000 (including 63,800 conscripts), the navy 15,000 (including 10,000 marines) and the air force 7,000. The paramilitary police force numbers about 104,600 men. Some

5,000,000m. pesos were allocated to defence expenditure as part of the state budget for 2001.

Economic Affairs

In 2001, according to estimates by the World Bank, Colombia's gross national income (GNI), measured at average 1999–2001 prices, was US $82,017m., equivalent to $2,281 per head (or $5,984 per head on an international purchasing-power parity basis). During 1990–2001, it was estimated, the population increased at an average annual rate of 1.9%, while gross domestic product (GDP) per head increased, in real terms, by an average of 0.7% per year. Colombia's overall GDP increased, in real terms, by an average of 2.6% per year in 1990–2001; growth in 2001 was 1.6%.

Agriculture (including hunting, forestry and fishing) contributed an estimated 12.8% of GDP in 2000, and employed some 22.2% of the labour force in 2001. The principal cash crops are coffee (which accounted for 6.2% of official export earnings in 2001), cocoa, sugar cane, bananas, tobacco, cotton and cut flowers. Rice, cassava, plantains and potatoes are the principal food crops. Timber and beef production are also important. During 1990–2000 agricultural GDP decreased at an average annual rate of 1.1%. Growth in agricultural GDP was 0.2% in 1999, but 5.2% in 2000.

Industry (including mining, manufacturing, construction and power) employed 18.4% of the labour force in 2001, and contributed an estimated 28.8% of GDP in the same year. During 1990–2000 real industrial GDP increased at an average annual rate of 1.5%. Industrial GDP declined, in real terms, by 9.0% in 1999, but increased by 3.8% in 2000.

Mining contributed an estimated 6.0% of GDP in 2000, and employed 1.1% of the labour force in 2000. Petroleum, natural gas, coal, nickel, emeralds and gold are the principal minerals exploited. Silver, platinum, iron, lead, zinc, copper, mercury, limestone and phosphates are also mined. According to the UN, growth in mining GDP was 7.4% in 1998 and 16.2% in 1999.

Manufacturing contributed an estimated 15.2% of GDP in 2000, and employed 12.8% of the labour force in 2001. During 1990–2000 manufacturing GDP declined at an average annual rate of 1.4%. Manufacturing GDP fell 10.2% in 1999, but increased by 9.3% in 2000. Based on the value of output, the most important branches of manufacturing in 1999 were food products (accounting for 29.3% of the total), beverages (7.2%), chemical products, textiles and transport equipment.

Hydroelectricity provided 76.4% of Colombia's electricity requirements in 1999. In the early 1990s a rapid expansion programme of thermal power-stations was undertaken in order to increase electricity output in line with demand, which increased by 4.5% per year in the 1990s, and to reduce reliance on hydroelectric power. Natural gas provided some 14.2% of electricity requirements in 1999. The country is self-sufficient in petroleum and coal, and these minerals accounted for 34.5% of export revenues in 2000.

The services sector contributed an estimated 58.4% of GDP in 2000, and engaged 59.4% of the labour force in 2001. During 1990–2000 the combined GDP of the service sectors increased, in real terms, at an estimated average rate of 3.8% per year. Growth in services GDP declined by 1.1% in 1999 and increased by 1.9% in 2000.

In 2001 Colombia recorded a visible trade surplus of US $508m. and there was a deficit of $1,789m. on the current account of the balance of payments. The country's principal trading partner in 2000 was the USA, which provided 33.7% of imports and took 50.0% of exports. Other important trading partners in that year were Venezuela and Ecuador. The principal exports in 2000 were minerals (particularly petroleum and its derivatives and coal), chemicals, vegetables and vegetable products, textiles and leather products, and foodstuffs, beverages and tobacco. The principal imports in 2000 were machinery and transport equipment, chemicals, foodstuffs, beverages and tobacco, textiles and leather products, and vegetables and vegetable products. A significant amount of foreign exchange is believed to be obtained from illegal trade in gold, emeralds and, particularly, the drug cocaine: in 1995 it was estimated that some $3,500m. (equivalent to around 4% of GDP) was entering Colombia each year as the proceeds of drugs-trafficking activities.

In 1998 there was a budgetary deficit of 6,940,600m. pesos in central government spending, equivalent to 5.3% of GDP. Colombia's external debt amounted to US $34,081m. at the end of 2000, of which $20,951m. was long-term public debt. Debt-servicing was equivalent to 28.6% of the value of exports of goods and services. In 1990–2001 the average annual rate of inflation was 19.2%; consumer prices increased by an annual average of 9.5% in 2000 and by 8.6% in 2001. Some 13.5% of the labour force were unemployed in December 2001.

Colombia is a member of ALADI (see p. 259) and of the Andean Community (see p. 133). Both organizations attempt to increase trade and economic co-operation within the region.

A programme of structural reform was adopted in 1990–94, resulting in the liberalization of trade and the reorganization of the public sector. Strong economic growth was recorded during this period, not least because of the discovery of significant petroleum reserves. However, during 1994–98 GDP slowed, unemployment soared and the fiscal deficit widened. In the late 1990s economic problems in Colombia were compounded by a fall in the international price of the country's principal export commodities, petroleum and coffee, and by high interest rates, which had led to a rise in the cost of debt-servicing. In September 1999 the central bank allowed the flotation of the peso, the value of which had depreciated by 23% since the beginning of the year. In the same month, the Government secured some US $6,900m. in financial assistance from international donors, including an IMF credit worth some $2,700m. (which was approved in December) in support of its economic programme for 1999–2002, which emphasized further fiscal reform, the restructuring of the financial sector and a reduction in public spending, as well as the introduction of new social welfare programmes to alleviate the effects of austerity measures. The privatization programme planned for 2000 failed to get underway, with the sale of electrical companies delayed as a result of guerrilla attacks on power installations and low investor interest in the public banks. Furthermore, Colombia was unable to take full advantage of the high price of petroleum during the year because of guerrilla attacks on pipelines. These attacks continued throughout 2001 and were a contributing factor to a further decline in petroleum export revenue. In February 2002 the US Administration announced plans to donate $98m. to the Colombian Government in order to establish a military unit to protect the Caño Limón pipeline. One of the Uribe Government's priorities, on assuming office in August 2002, was the reform of the tax, pensions and labour sectors. In support of these proposed reforms, in January 2003 the IMF and the World Bank announced new loans to Colombia of $1,500m. and $3,300m., respectively. The proposals received congressional approval in March 2003, prompting the disbursement of the first tranche of the funding. Further, more wide-ranging proposals were to be put to a public referendum by mid-2003. However, despite some progress, in 2003 Colombia faced continued risks from the weakness of the US economy and economic uncertainty in neighbouring Venezuela, in addition to the problems of high unemployment, low investment and increasing political violence. The extension of the USA's Andean Trade Preferences Act (ATPA) to Colombia and the country's scheduled inclusion within the Free Trade Area of the Americas (FTAA) in 2005 allowed for limited optimism, although much was dependent on the electorate's approval of the Government's proposals for further, comprehensive economic reform. GDP was forecast to increase by some 2.5% in 2003.

Education

Primary education is free and compulsory for five years, to be undertaken by children between six and 12 years of age. No child may be admitted to secondary school unless these five years have been successfully completed. Secondary education, beginning at the age of 11, lasts for up to six years. Following completion of a first cycle of four years, pupils may pursue a further two years of vocational study, leading to the Bachiller examination. In 1996 the total enrolment at primary schools included 89% of pupils in the relevant age-group, while the comparable ratio for secondary education in 1995 was 50%. In 2001 there were 24 public universities in Colombia. Government expenditure on education in the 1998 budget was 4,706,900m. pesos, representing 23.6% of total spending.

Public Holidays

2003: 1 January (New Year's Day), 6 January (Epiphany), 19 March (St Joseph's Day), 17 April (Maundy Thursday), 18 April (Good Friday), 1 May (Labour Day), 29 May (Ascension Day), 19 June (Corpus Christi), 27 June (Sacred Heart of Jesus), 30 June (for SS Peter and Paul), 20 July (Independence), 7 August (Battle of Boyacá), 15 August (Assumption), 13 October (for Discovery of America), 3 November (for All Saints' Day), 11

November (Independence of Cartagena), 8 December (Immaculate Conception), 25 December (Christmas Day).

2004: 1 January (New Year's Day), 6 January (Epiphany), 19 March (St Joseph's Day), 8 April (Maundy Thursday), 9 April (Good Friday), 1 May (Labour Day), 20 May (Ascension Day), 10 June (Corpus Christi), 28 June (for Sacred Heart of Jesus), 29 June (SS Peter and Paul), 20 July (Independence), 7 August (Battle of Boyacá), 16 August (for Assumption), 12 October (Discovery of America), 1 November (All Saints' Day), 11 November (Independence of Cartagena), 8 December (Immaculate Conception), 25 December (Christmas Day).

Weights and Measures

The metric system is in force.

Statistical Survey

Sources (unless otherwise stated): Departamento Administrativo Nacional de Estadística (DANE), Centro Administrativo Nacional (CAN), Avda El Dorado, Apdo Aéreo 80043, Santafé de Bogotá, DC; tel. (1) 222-1100; fax (1) 222-2107; internet www.dane.gov.co; Banco de la República, Carrera 7, No 14-78, Apdo Aéreo 3531, Santafé de Bogotá, DC; tel. (1) 343-1090; fax (1) 286-1731; internet www.banrep.gov.co.

Area and Population

AREA, POPULATION AND DENSITY

Area (sq km)	1,141,748*
Population (census results)†	
15 October 1985	
Males	14,642,835
Females.	14,838,160
Total	29,480,995
24 October 1993	37,664,711
Population (official estimates at mid-year)	
1999	41,589,018
2000	42,321,386
2001	43,070,703
Density (per sq km) at mid-2001	37.7

* 440,831 sq miles.

† Revised figures, including adjustment for underenumeration. The enumerated total was 27,853,436 (males 13,785,523; females 14,067,913) in 1985 and 33,109,840 (males 16,296,539; females 16,813,301) in 1993.

DEPARTMENTS
(census of 24 October 1993)*

Department	Area (sq km)	Population	Capital (with population)
Amazonas . . .	109,665	56,399	Leticia (30,045)
Antioquia . . .	63,612	4,919,619	Medellín (1,834,881)
Arauca . . .	23,818	185,882	Arauca (59,805)
Atlántico . . .	3,388	1,837,468	Barranquilla (1,090,618)
Bolívar . . .	25,978	1,702,188	Cartagena (747,390)
Boyacá . . .	23,189	1,315,579	Tunja (112,807)
Caldas . . .	7,888	1,055,577	Manizales (345,539)
Caquetá . . .	88,965	367,898	Florencia (107,620)
Casanare . . .	44,640	211,329	Yopal (57,279)
Cauca . . .	29,308	1,127,678	Popayán (207,700)
César . . .	22,905	827,219	Valledupar (278,216)
Chocó . . .	46,530	406,199	Quibdó (122,371)
Córdoba . . .	25,020	1,275,623	Montería (308,506)
Cundinamarca . . .	22,623	1,875,337	Santafé de Bogotá†
Guainía. . . .	72,238	28,478	Puerto Inírida (18,270)
La Guajira . . .	20,848	433,361	Riohacha (109,474)
Guaviare . . .	42,327	97,602	San José del Guaviare (48,237)
Huila	19,890	843,798	Neiva (278,350)
Magdalena. . . .	23,188	1,127,691	Santa Marta (313,072)
Meta	85,635	618,427	Villavicencio (272,118)
Nariño	33,268	1,443,671	Pasto (331,866)
Norte de Santander .	21,658	1,162,474	Cúcuta (538,126)
Putumayo . . .	24,885	264,291	Mocoa (25,910)
Quindío. . . .	1,845	495,212	Armenia (258,990)
Risaralda . . .	4,140	844,184	Pereira (401,909)
San Andrés y Providencia Islands	44	61,040	San Andrés (56,361)
Santander del Sur .	30,537	1,811,740	Bucaramanga (472,461)
Sucre	10,917	701,105	Sincelejo (194,962)
Tolima	23,562	1,286,078	Ibagué (399,838)
Valle del Cauca .	22,140	3,736,090	Cali (1,847,176)
Vaupés	65,268	24,671	Mitú (13,177)
Vichada	100,242	62,073	Puerto Carreño (11,452)
Capital District			
Santafé de Bogotá, DC	1,587	5,484,244	Bogotá†
Total	1,141,748	37,664,711	—

* Adjusted for underenumeration.

† The capital city, Santafé de Bogotá, exists as the capital of a department as well as the Capital District. The city's population is included only in Santafé de Bogotá, DC.

PRINCIPAL TOWNS
(estimated population at mid-1999)

Santafé de Bogotá, DC (capital)	6,260,862	Neiva	300,052
Cali	2,077,386	Soledad	295,058
Medellín	1,861,265	Armenia	281,422
Barranquilla	1,223,260	Villavicencio	273,140
Cartagena	805,757	Soacha	272,058
Cúcuta	606,932	Valledupar	263,247
Bucaramanga	515,555	Montería	248,245
Ibagué	393,664	Itagüí	228,985
Pereira	381,725	Palmira	226,509
Santa Marta	359,147	Buenaventura	224,336
Manizales	337,580	Floridablanca	221,913
Bello	333,470	Sincelejo	220,704
Pasto	332,396	Popayán	200,719

BIRTHS, MARRIAGES AND DEATHS*

	Registered live births	Registered deaths
1983	829,348	140,292
1984	825,842	137,189
1985	835,922	153,947
1986	931,956	146,346
1987	937,426	151,957

Registered live births: 989,071 in 1998; 989,117 in 1999.

Registered deaths: 167,172 in 1997; 171,210 in 1998; 235,112 in 1999.

Registered marriages: 102,448 in 1980; 95,845 in 1981; 70,350 in 1986.

* Data are tabulated by year of registration rather than by year of occurrence, although registration is incomplete. According to UN estimates, the average annual rates in 1990–95 were: births 27.0 per 1,000; deaths 6.4 per 1,000; and in 1995–2000: births 24.5 per 1,000; deaths 5.8 per 1,000. (Source: UN, *World Population Prospects: The 2000 Revision*).

Expectation of life (WHO estimates, years at birth): 70.7 (males 67.2; females 75.1) in 2001 (Source: WHO, *World Health Report*).

ECONOMICALLY ACTIVE POPULATION
(household survey, '000 persons, September)

	1999	2000	2001*
Agriculture, hunting, forestry and fishing	3,622	3,707	3,661
Mining, electricity, gas and water	171	184	279
Manufacturing	1,894	2,198	2,119
Construction	667	674	643
Trade, restaurants and hotels	3,410	3,588	4,235
Transport, storage and communications	869	852	1,069
Finance, insurance, real estate and business services	737	702	843
Community, social and personal services	3,932	4,403	3,645
Activities not adequately described	16	13	5
Total labour force	15,319	16,321	16,498

* Source: ILO.

Health and Welfare

KEY INDICATORS

Total fertility rate (children per woman, 2001)	2.7
Under-5 mortality rate (per 1,000 live births, 2001)	23
HIV/AIDS (% of persons aged 15–49, 2001)	0.40
Physicians (per 1,000 head, 1997)	1.16
Hospital beds (per 1,000 head, 1996)	1.46
Health expenditure (2000): US $ per head (PPP)	616
Health expenditure (2000): % of GDP	9.6
Health expenditure (2000): public (% of total)	55.8
Access to water (% of persons, 2000)	91
Access to sanitation (% of persons, 2000)	85
Human Development Index (2000): ranking	68
Human Development Index (2000): value	0.772

For sources and definitions, see explanatory note on p. vi.

Agriculture

PRINCIPAL CROPS
('000 metric tons)

	1999	2000	2001
Rice (paddy)	2,190	2,286	2,314
Maize	960	1,183	1,239
Sorghum	199	218	212
Potatoes	2,775	2,883	2,874
Cassava (Manioc)	1,762	1,792	1,980
Yams	206	255	255
Other roots and tubers	63	64*	60*
Sugar cane*	36,900	32,750	33,400
Dry beans	122	125	124
Soybeans (Soya beans)	44	38	56
Coconuts	60	101	99
Oil palm fruit	2,400†	2,470†	2,550
Cottonseed†	65	111	123
Cabbages*	250	290	300
Tomatoes	144	375	400
Dry onions	248	751	413
Carrots*	210	185	191
Other vegetables*	162	227	210
Bananas	1,650	1,651*	1,375
Plantains	2,526	2,682	2,827
Oranges	509	353	238
Watermelons*	55	57	64
Mangoes*	99	135	134
Avocados*	75	132	137
Pineapples	389	338	314
Papayas*	65	113	111
Other fruit*	1,327	1,331	1,373
Coffee (green)	546	636	656

* FAO estimate(s).

† Unofficial figure(s).

Source: FAO.

LIVESTOCK
('000 head, year ending September)

	1999	2000	2001
Horses*	2,500	2,550	2,600
Mules*	595	595	595
Asses*	715	718	720
Cattle	25,614	25,206	26,252
Pigs	2,765	2,172	2,700*
Sheep	2,196	2,288	2,256
Goats	1,115	1,185	1,136
Poultry*	98,000	105,000	110,000

* FAO estimate(s).

Source: FAO.

LIVESTOCK PRODUCTS
('000 metric tons)

	1999	2000	2001
Beef and veal	716	745	746*
Mutton and lamb	4.7*	6.9*	7.0†
Goat meat	6.3	8.6†	8.6†
Pig meat	107.0	72.5	79.6
Horse meat	5.4	5.4†	5.5†
Poultry meat	496	504	531
Cows' milk	5,734	5,629†	5,742
Cheese	51	51†	53†
Butter and ghee	18.4	18.4†	18.8†
Hen eggs	338.7	322.0	354.9
Cattle hides	86.2	83.6†	83.7†

* Unofficial figure.

† FAO estimate.

Source: FAO.

Forestry

ROUNDWOOD REMOVALS
('000 cu metres, excl. bark)

	1999	2000	2001
Sawlogs, veneer logs and logs for sleepers	1,461	1,296	1,190
Pulpwood	745	813	500
Other industrial wood	190	55	51
Fuel wood	8,194	10,893	10,760
Total	10,590	13,057	12,501

Source: FAO.

SAWNWOOD PRODUCTION
('000 cu metres, incl. railway sleepers)

	1999	2000	2001
Coniferous (softwood)	31	20	18
Broadleaved (hardwood)	699	567	521
Total	730	587	539

Source: FAO.

Fishing

('000 metric tons, live weight)

	1998	1999	2000
Capture*	132.9	117.9	129.6
Characins	6.4	8.7	6.6†
Other freshwater fishes	15.2	20.1	18.3†
Pacific anchoveta	28.5	15.8	22.5†
Skipjack tuna	3.5	27.9	6.3
Yellowfin tuna	14.5	29.3	16.5
Other tuna-like fishes	50.9	3.9	3.2†
Aquaculture	45.9	52.9	61.8
Tilapias and other cichlids	17.7	19.8	22.8
Cachama blanca	11.8	13.0	15.0
Rainbow trout	6.2	7.8	9.0
Whiteleg shrimp	7.5	9.2	11.4
Total catch	178.8	170.8	191.4

* Data refer to landings.

† FAO estimate.

Note: Figures exclude crocodiles, recorded by number rather than by weight. The number of spectacled caimans caught was: 670,389 in 1998; 771,456 in 1999; 646,712 in 2000.

Source: FAO, *Yearbook of Fishery Statistics*.

Mining

('000 metric tons, unless otherwise indicated)

	1999	2000	2001
Gold (kilograms)	34,847	37,018	21,813
Silver (kilograms)	7,593	7,970	7,242
Salt	496	461	395
Hard coal	32,754	38,142	43,910
Iron ore*	576	660	637
Crude petroleum ('000 barrels)	297,840	250,755	220,460

* Figures refer to the gross weight of ore. The estimated iron content is 46%.

Source: US Geological Survey.

Industry

SELECTED PRODUCTS
('000 metric tons, unless otherwise indicated)

	1996	1997	1998
Sugar	2,149.2	2,136.2	2,125.6
Cement	8,590.1	8,870.4	8,464.0
Steel ingots	298.4	344.9	264.5
Diesel oil ('000 barrels)	24,552	24,266	23,210
Fuel oil ('000 barrels)	19,453	19,700	18,758
Motor fuel ('000 barrels)	41,160	34,445	38,354

Finance

CURRENCY AND EXCHANGE RATES

Monetary Units
  100 centavos = 1 Colombian peso

Sterling, Dollar and Euro Equivalents (31 December 2002)
  £1 sterling = 4,617.5 pesos
  US $1 = 2,864.8 pesos
  €1 = 3,004.3 pesos
  10,000 Colombian pesos = £2.166 = $3.491 = €3.329

Average Exchange Rate (pesos per US $)
  2000   2,087.90
  2001   2,299.63
  2002   2,504.24

CENTRAL GOVERNMENT BUDGET
('000 million pesos)

Revenue	1996	1997	1998
Direct taxation	4,804.9	5,038.7	7,280.7
Indirect taxation	7,720.1	8,247.9	8,285.5
Rates and fines	102.7	399.7	104.6
Revenue under contracts	290.8	30.3	—
Credit resources	5,380.2	8,721.9	10,527.9
Other	2,387.4	4,386.4	2,047.6
Total	20,686.1	26,824.9	28,246.3

Expenditure*	1996	1997	1998
Congress and comptrollership	186.4	238.9	281.0
General administration	879.7	856.0	742.0
Home office and foreign affairs	123.2	127.7	147.8
Finance and public credit	3,184.6	3,509.1	3,263.7
Public works and transportation	1,370.6	1,519.6	1,207.4
Defence	2,039.5	2,466.6	2,605.4
Police	973.0	1,237.4	1,471.4
Agriculture	811.8	622.3	425.0
Health	1,309.4	1,597.9	1,862.7
Education	2,950.3	3,656.9	4,706.9
Development, labour, mines and communications	1,411.4	1,674.5	1,765.3
Justice and legal affairs	947.7	1,118.2	1,234.8
Trade	31.1	26.2	21.2
Environment	139.0	167.5	138.7
Culture	—	12.4	64.3
Total	16,357.7	18,831.1	19,937.4

* Excluding public debt.

INTERNATIONAL RESERVES
(US $ million at 31 December)

	2000	2001	2002
Gold*	89	91	112
IMF special drawing rights	135	135	154
Reserve position in IMF	372	359	389
Foreign exchange	8,409	9,659	10,190
Total	9,005	10,244	10,844

* Valued at market-related prices.

Source: IMF, *International Financial Statistics*.

MONEY SUPPLY

('000 million pesos at 31 December)

	2000	2001	2002
Currency outside banks . . .	7,676.6	8,653.6	10,188.5
Demand deposits at commercial banks	8,825.6	9,622.9	11,256.3
Total money (incl. others) . . .	16,837.0	18,450.6	21,576.4

Source: IMF, *International Financial Statistics*.

COST OF LIVING

(Consumer price index for low-income families; base: 1990 = 100)

	1998	1999	2000
Food and beverages	465.5	491.1	535.5
Clothing and footwear . . .	320.2	336.6	347.6
Rent, fuel and light*	617.3	680.7	686.9
All items (incl. others)	520.2	578.5	633.6

* Including certain household equipment.

Source: ILO, *Yearbook of Labour Statistics*.

NATIONAL ACCOUNTS

('000 million pesos at current prices)

Composition of the Gross National Product

	1997	1998	1999
Compensation of employees . .	45,299.5	52,104.3	56,482.1
Operating surplus . . . . . } Consumption of fixed capital . .}	64,472.3	75,843.2	81,671.2
Gross domestic product (GDP) at factor cost . .	109,771.8	127,947.5	138,153.3
Indirect taxes	12,598.9	13,263.0	14,242.5
Less Subsidies	663.2	727.4	830.8
GDP in purchasers' values .	121,707.5	140,483.3	151,565.0
Net factor income from abroad .	−2,705.7	−2,510.2	−2,807.7
Gross national product (GNP)	119,001.8	137,973.1	148,757.3

Expenditure on the Gross Domestic Product

	1998	1999	2000
Government final consumption expenditure	28,547.9	33,587.7	37,791.3
Private final consumption expenditure	92,501.2	97,631.2	112,180.0
Increase in stocks	941.1	−724.5	746.5
Gross fixed capital formation . .	26,602.6	20,079.1	22,129.0
Total domestic expenditure . .	148,592.8	150,573.5	172,846.8
Exports of goods and services .	21,082.8	27,807.0	34,593.9
Less Imports of goods and services	29,363.2	26,982.7	34,029.7
GDP in purchasers' values *	140,483.3	151,565.0	173,729.8

* Including adjustment.

Source: IMF, *International Financial Statistics*.

Gross Domestic Product by Economic Activity

	1998	1999	2000*
Agriculture, hunting and forestry	17,950.7	18,955.8	20,720.7
Fishing	643.4	748.8	844.5
Mining and quarrying . . .	4,495.7	7,989.8	10,108.9
Manufacturing	19,739.8	21,034.3	25,723.1
Electricity, gas and water . . .	4,734.9	5,168.2	6,544.1
Construction	8,106.4	6,350.6	6,176.0
Wholesale and retail trade; repair of motor vehicles motorcycles and personal and household goods	13,141.6	13,231.7	15,665.5
Hotels and restaurants . . .	3,173.8	3,423.9	3,370.8
Transport, storage and communications	10,396.7	11,047.6	12,696.9
Financial intermediation . . .	8,683.4	7,609.2	8,530.8
Real estate, renting and business activities	17,158.7	17,592.2	18,721.8
Public administration and defence; compulsory social security	12,946.2	15,387.0	17,375.0
Education	8,449.4	9,798.0	10,807.7
Health and social work . . .	5,716.6	6,747.5	7,416.5
Other community, social and personal service activities . .	2,416.9	2,638.1	3,056.3
Private households with employed persons	682.4	725.7	768.5
Sub-total	138,438.6	148,448.4	168,527.2
Less Imputed bank service charge	8,071.1	7,304.7	7,841.3
GDP in basic prices . . .	130,367.5	141,143.7	160,685.9
Taxes on products	10,291.4	10,694.8	13,373.4
Less Subsidies on products . .	175.6	273.6	329.5
GDP in purchasers' values .	140,483.3	151,565.0	173,729.8

* Provisional figures.

BALANCE OF PAYMENTS

(US $ million)

	1999	2000	2001
Exports of goods f.o.b.	12,037	13,620	12,775
Imports of goods f.o.b.	−10,262	−11,090	−12,267
Trade balance	1,775	2,531	508
Exports of services	1,882	2,004	2,157
Imports of services	−3,143	−3,311	−3,573
Balance on goods and services .	514	1,224	−908
Other income received	792	858	739
Other income paid	−2,388	−3,388	−3,714
Balance on goods, services and income	−1,082	−1,306	−3,882
Current transfers received . .	1,683	1,900	2,395
Current transfers paid . . .	−248	−238	−302
Current balance	353	356	−1,789
Direct investment abroad . .	−116	−250	−42
Direct investment from abroad .	1,468	2,281	2,328
Portfolio investment assets . .	−1,735	−1,014	−3,480
Portfolio investment liabilities .	689	1,436	3,452
Other investment assets . .	−438	−551	129
Financial derivatives liabilities .	101	−103	−112
Other investment liabilities . .	−562	−1,310	202
Net errors and omissions . .	−72	17	537
Overall balance	−312	862	1,226

Source: IMF, *International Financial Statistics*.

External Trade

PRINCIPAL COMMODITIES
(US $ million)

Imports c.i.f.	1999	2000	2001
Vegetables and vegetable products	652.3	717.0	724.3
Prepared foodstuffs, beverages and tobacco	788.3	765.9	852.1
Textiles and leather products . .	580.8	748.0	744.5
Paper and paper products . .	422.9	463.4	435.0
Chemical products	2,352.5	2,697.7	2,724.8
Petroleum and its derivatives .	302.6	267.9	218.5
Metals	379.8	585.7	573.9
Mechanical, electrical and transport equipment . . .	4,488.0	4,353.1	5,557.7
Total (incl. others)	10,659.1	11,538.5	12,820.6

Exports f.o.b.	1999	2000	2001
Vegetables and vegetable products	1,187.8	1,146.4	1,089.7
Coffee	1,323.7	1,068.7	764.2
Coal	847.9	861.2	1,178.8
Petroleum and its derivatives . .	3,757.0	4,569.3	3,054.7
Prepared foodstuffs, beverages and tobacco	799.5	869.6	972.0
Textiles and leather products . .	872.9	951.9	1,010.9
Paper and publishing . . .	259.3	316.3	397.2
Chemicals	1,103.0	1,691.6	1,770.6
Mechanical, electrical and transport equipment . . .	477.6	765.1	1,080.9
Total (incl. others)	11,568.7	13,115.0	12,282.3

Source: Dirección de Impuestos y Aduanas Nacionales.

PRINCIPAL TRADING PARTNERS
(US $ million)

Imports c.i.f.	1998	1999	2000
Argentina	243.1	122.9	146.0
Bolivia	n.a.	208.7	204.8
Brazil	520.0	422.3	506.4
Canada	406.4	259.0	294.3
Chile	238.8	224.0	254.8
Ecuador	318.5	252.8	318.2
France	376.9	405.4	367.6
Germany	749.3	494.5	496.3
Italy	357.9	246.6	261.7
Japan	844.7	527.5	528.6
Korea, Republic	273.9	184.4	224.4
Mexico	620.0	466.2	546.6
Peru	155.7	108.7	143.4
Spain	416.6	205.9	239.2
Switzerland	n.a.	136.5	165.2
Taiwan	n.a.	97.1	141.3
United Kingdom	301.7	184.7	184.2
USA	5,092.3	3,952.4	3,892.9
Venezuela	1,399.4	868.6	946.7
Total (incl. others)	14,634.7	10,659.2	11,538.5

Exports f.o.b.	1998	1999	2000
Belgium-Luxembourg . . .	318.1	261.0	220.6
Brazil	101.6	166.2	283.1
Canada	136.9	120.1	143.1
Chile	159.3	152.2	188.0
Costa Rica	102.1	115.8	121.1
Ecuador	581.5	323.8	461.6
France	231.0	140.5	135.2
Germany	684.5	485.5	412.8
Italy	214.6	198.8	203.0
Japan	268.5	245.0	229.9
Mexico	128.5	201.6	230.0
Netherlands	288.7	169.5	111.9
Panama	106.1	144.0	175.3
Peru	370.1	357.3	371.5
Puerto Rico	101.7	167.3	100.3
Spain	151.0	149.3	172.3
United Kingdom	236.6	212.5	229.0
USA	4,048.5	5,615.4	6,512.3
Venezuela	1,154.6	915.6	1,292.5
Total (incl. others)	10,865.6	11,568.7	13,037.4

Source: Dirección de Impuestos y Aduanas Nacionales.

Transport

RAILWAYS
(traffic)

	1996	1997	1998
Freight ('000 metric tons) . .	321	348	281
Freight ton-km ('000) . . .	746,544	736,427	657,585

Source: Sociedad de Transporte Ferroviario, SA.

ROAD TRAFFIC
(motor vehicles in use)

	1997	1998	1999
Passenger cars	1,694,323	1,776,100	1,803,201
Buses	126,362	131,987	134,799
Goods vehicles	179,530	183,335	184,495
Motorcycles	385,378	450,283	479,073

Source: IRF, *World Road Statistics*.

SHIPPING

Merchant Fleet
(registered at 31 December)

	1999	2000	2001
Number of vessels	113	111	105
Total displacement ('000 grt) .	96.9	81.4	65.6

Source: Lloyd's Register-Fairplay, *World Fleet Statistics*.

Domestic Sea-borne Freight Traffic
('000 metric tons)

	1987	1988	1989
Goods loaded and unloaded . .	772.1	944.8	464.6

International Sea-borne Freight Traffic
('000 metric tons)

	1996	1997	1998
Goods loaded	38,053	47,567	40,965
Goods unloaded	13,257	27,097	19,732

CIVIL AVIATION
(traffic)

	1997	1998	1999
Domestic			
Passengers carried ('000) . . .	8,027	7,947	7,545
Freight carried (metric tons) . .	135,154	113,790	129,806
International			
Passengers ('000):			
arrivals	1,311	1,373	1,337
departures	1,355	1,407	1,480
Freight (metric tons):			
loaded	198,572	205,866	145,596
unloaded	226,875	232,979	233,015

Source: Departamento Administrativo de Aeronáutica Civil.

Tourism

TOURIST ARRIVALS
('000)

Country of origin	1998	1999	2000
Argentina	25.8	23.2	18.1
Brazil	15.7	15.9	14.2
Canada	9.7	9.2	13.4
Costa Rica.	13.9	21.6	24.2
Ecuador	67.7	59.9	69.7
France	18.8	17.7	17.3
Germany	n.a.	13.8	16.1
Mexico	21.3	12.3	11.1
Panama	63.2	51.1	49.0
Peru	28.7	26.7	22.5
Spain	31.3	24.8	21.7
United Kingdom	15.7	14.3	11.8
USA	193.9	162.4	164.4
Venezuela	94.3	75.4	75.2
Total (incl. others)	674.4	546.0	557.3

Source: World Tourism Organization, *Yearbook of Tourism Statistics*.

Tourism receipts (US $ million): 929 in 1998; 928 in 1999; 1,028 in 2000 (World Tourism Organization).

Communications Media

	1999	2000	2001
Television receivers ('000 in use)	11,613	11,936	n.a.
Telephones ('000 main lines in use)	6,665.4	7,158.6	7,300.0
Mobile cellular telephones ('000			
subscribers)	1,966.5	2,256.8	3,160.0
Personal computers ('000 in use) .	1,400	1,500	1,800
Internet users ('000)	664	878	1,154

1996: 37 daily newspapers.

1997 ('000 in use): 21,000 radio receivers; 173 facsimile machines.

Book production: 1,481 titles in 1991.

Sources: UN, *Statistical Yearbook*; UNESCO, *Statistical Yearbook*; International Telecommunication Union.

Education

(2000)

	Institutions	Teachers	Pupils
Nursery	31,340	53,357	1,070,482
Primary	59,013	197,247	5,217,942
Secondary	13,047	182,449	3,506,741
Higher (incl. universities)* . . .	266	75,568	673,353

* 1996 figures.

Source: partly Ministerio de Educación Nacional.

Adult literacy rate (UNESCO estimates): 91.7% (males 91.7%; females 91.7%) in 2000 (Source: UN Development Programme, *Human Development Report*).

Directory

The Constitution

A new, 380-article Constitution, drafted by a 74-member National Constituent Assembly, took effect from 6 July 1991. The new Constitution retained the institutional framework of a directly-elected President with a non-renewable four-year term of office, together with a bicameral legislature composed of an upper house or Senate (with 102 directly-elected members) and a lower house or House of Representatives (with 161 members, to include at least two representatives of each national department). A Vice-President is elected at the same time as the President, and also holds office for a term of four years.

The new Constitution also contained comprehensive provisions for the recognition and protection of civil rights, and for the reform of the structures and procedures of political participation and of the judiciary.

The fundamental principles upon which the new Constitution is based are embodied in articles 1–10.

Article 1: Colombia is a lawful state, organized as a single Republic, decentralized, with autonomous territorial entities, democratic, participatory and pluralist, founded on respect for human dignity, on the labour and solidarity of its people and on the prevalence of the general interest.

Article 2: The essential aims of the State are: to serve the community, to promote general prosperity and to guarantee the effectiveness of the principles, rights and obligations embodied in the Constitution, to facilitate the participation of all in the decisions which affect them and in the economic, political, administrative and cultural life of the nation; to defend national independence, to maintain territorial integrity and to ensure peaceful coexistence and the validity of the law.

The authorities of the Republic are instituted to protect the residents of Colombia, in regard to their life, honour, goods, beliefs and other rights and liberties, and to ensure the fulfilment of the obligations of the State and of the individual.

Article 3: Sovereignty rests exclusively with the people, from whom public power emanates. The people exercise power directly or through their representatives in the manner established by the Constitution.

Article 4: The Constitution is the highest authority. In all cases of incompatability between the Constitution and the law or other juridical rules, constitutional dispositions will apply.

It is the duty of nationals and foreigners in Colombia to observe the Constitution and the law, and to respect and obey the authorities.

Article 5: The State recognizes, without discrimination, the primacy of the inalienable rights of the individual and protects the family as the basic institution of society.

Article 6: Individuals are solely responsible to the authorities for infringements of the Constitution and of the law. Public servants are equally accountable and are responsible to the authorities for failure to fulfil their function or abuse of their position.

Article 7: The State recognizes and protects the ethnic diversity of the Colombian nation.

Article 8: It is an obligation of the State and of the people to protect the cultural and natural riches of the nation.

Article 9: The foreign relations of the State are based on national sovereignty, with respect for self-determination of people and with recognition of the principles of international law accepted by Colombia.

Similarly, Colombia's external politics will be directed towards Caribbean and Latin American integration.

Article 10: Spanish (Castellano) is the official language of Colombia. The languages and dialects of ethnic groups are officially recognized within their territories. Education in communities with their own linguistic traditions will be bilingual.

The Government

HEAD OF STATE

President: ALVARO URIBE VÉLEZ (took office 7 August 2002).

Vice-President: FRANCISCO SANTOS CALDERÓN (took office 7 August 2002).

CABINET
(April 2003)

A coalition of the Partido Conservador Colombiano (PCC), the Partido Liberal Colombiano (PL) and independents (Ind.).

Minister of the Interior and Justice: FERNANDO LONDOÑO HOYOS.

Minister of Foreign Affairs: CAROLINA BARCO ISAKSON.

Minister of Finance and Public Credit: ROBERTO JUNGUITO BONNET.

Minister of National Defence: MARTHA LUCÍA RAMÍREZ DE RINCÓN.

Minister of Agriculture: CARLOS GUSTAVO CANO SANZ.

Minister of Labour, Social Security and Health: (vacant).

Minister of Mines and Energy: LUIS ERNESTO MEJÍA CASTRO.

Minister of Trade: JORGE HUMBERTO BOTERO.

Minister of National Education: CECILIA MARÍA VÉLEZ WHITE.

Minister of the Environment: CECILIA RODRÍGUEZ.

Minister of Communications: MARTHA ELENA PINTO DE HART.

Minister of Transport: ANDRÉS URIEL GALLEGO.

Minister of Culture: MARÍA CONSUELO ARAÚJO CASTRO.

MINISTRIES

Office of the President: Palacio de Nariño, Carrera 8A, No 7-26, Santafé de Bogotá, DC; tel. (1) 562-9300; fax (1) 286-8063.

Ministry of Agriculture: Avda Jiménez, No 7-65, Santafé de Bogotá, DC; tel. (1) 334-1199; fax (1) 284-1775; e-mail minagric@colomsat.net.co; internet www.minagricultura.gov.co.

Ministry of Communications: Edif. Murillo Toro, Carrera 7 y 8, Calle 12 y 13, Apdo Aéreo 14515, Santafé de Bogotá, DC; tel. (1) 286-6911; fax (1) 344-3434; internet www.mincomunicaciones.gov.co.

Ministry of Culture: Calle 8, No 6-97, Santafé de Bogotá, DC; tel. (1) 342-4100; fax (1) 342-1721; e-mail fvasquez@mincultura.gov.co; internet www.mincultura.gov.co.

Ministry of the Environment: Calle 37, No 8-40, Santafé de Bogotá, DC; tel. (1) 288-6877; fax (1) 288-9788; internet www.minambiente.gov.co.

Ministry of Finance and Public Credit: Carrera 8A, No 6-64, Of. 308, Santafé de Bogotá, DC; tel. (1) 284-5400; fax (1) 286-3858; internet www.minhacienda.gov.co.

Ministry of Foreign Affairs: Palacio de San Carlos, Calle 10A, No 5-51, Santafé de Bogotá, DC; tel. (1) 282-7811; fax (1) 341-6777; internet www.minrelext.gov.co.

Ministry of the Interior and Justice: Palacio Echeverry, Carrera 8A, No 8-09, Santafé de Bogotá, DC; tel. (1) 334-0630; fax (1) 341-9583; internet www.presidencia.gov.co/ministerios.

Ministry of Labour, Social Security and Health: Carrera 7A, No 34-50, Santafé de Bogotá, DC; tel. (1) 287-3434; fax (1) 285-7091; e-mail oaai@tutopia.com.

Ministry of Mines and Energy: Centro Administrativo Nacional (CAN), Avda El Dorado, Santafé de Bogotá, DC; tel. (1) 222-4555; fax (1) 222-3651; internet www.minminas.gov.co.

Ministry of National Defence: Centro Administrativo Nacional (CAN), 2°, Avda El Dorado, Santafé de Bogotá, DC; tel. (1) 220-4999; fax (1) 222-1874; internet www.mindefensa.gov.co.

Ministry of National Education: Centro Administrativo Nacional (CAN), Of. 501, Avda El Dorado, Santafé de Bogotá, DC; tel. (1) 222-2800; fax (1) 222-4578; e-mail oci@mineducacion.gov.co; internet www.mineducacion.gov.co.

Ministry of Transport: Centro Administrativo Nacional (CAN), Of. 409, Avda El Dorado, Santafé de Bogotá, DC; tel. (1) 222-4411; fax (1) 222-1647; internet www.mintransporte.gov.co.

President and Legislature

PRESIDENT
Presidential Election, 26 May 2002

	Votes	% of votes cast
Alvaro Uribe Vélez	5,862,655	54.0
Horacio Serpa Uribe	3,514,779	32.3
Luis Eduardo Garzón	680,245	6.3
Noemí Sanín Posada	641,884	5.9
Others	155,966	1.5
Total*	10,855,529	100.0

* Excluding 196,116 blank ballots.

CONGRESO

Senado
(Senate)

President: LUIS ALFREDO RAMOS.

General Election, 10 March 2002

	Seats	% of votes cast
Independent groups	52	51.5
Partido Liberal Colombiano (PL)	29	30.6
Partido Conservador Colombiano (PCC)	13	9.9
Coalitions	6	6.3
Indigenous groups*	2	1.7
Total	102	100.0

* Under the reforms of the Constitution in 1991, at least two Senate seats are reserved for indigenous groups.

Cámara de Representantes
(House of Representatives)

President: WILLIAM VÉLEZ.

General Election, 10 March 2002

	Seats	% of votes cast
Independent groups	69	52.6
Partido Liberal Colombiano (PL)	54	32.0
Partido Conservador Colombiano (PCC)	21	7.3
Coalitions	17	8.1
Total	161	100.0

Political Organizations

Alianza Democrática—M-19 (AD—M-19): Transversal 28, No 37-78, Santafé de Bogotá, DC; tel. (1) 368-9436; f. 1990; alliance of centre-left groups (including factions of Unión Patriótica, Colombia Unida, Frente Popular and Socialismo Democrático) which supported the M-19 campaign for elections to the National Constituent Assembly in December 1990; Leader DIEGO MONTAÑA CUÉLLAR.

Alianza Nacional Popular (ANAPO): Carrera 18, No 33-95, Santafé de Bogotá, DC; tel. (1) 287-7050; fax (1) 245-3138; f. 1971 by supporters of Gen. Gustavo Rojas Pinilla; populist party; Leader MARÍA EUGENIA ROJAS DE MORENO DÍAZ.

Democracia Cristiana: Avda 42, No 18-08, Apdo 25867, Santafé de Bogotá, DC; tel. (1) 285-6639; f. 1964; Christian Democrat party; 10,000 mems; Pres. JUAN A. POLO FIGUEROA; Sec.-Gen. DIEGO ARANGO OSORIO.

Frente Social y Político: f. 2001; left-wing; Presidential Candidate LUIS EDUARDO GARZÓN.

Frente por la Unidad del Pueblo (FUP): Santafé de Bogotá, DC; extreme left-wing front comprising socialists and Maoists.

Movimiento 19 de Abril (M-19): Calle 26, No 13B-09, Of. 1401, Santafé de Bogotá, DC; tel. (1) 282-7891; fax (1) 282-8129; f. 1970 by followers of Gen. Gustavo Rojas Pinilla and dissident factions from the FARC (see below); left-wing urban guerrilla group, until formally constituted as a political party in Oct. 1989; Leaders ANTONIO NAVARRO WOLFF, OTTY PATIÑO.

Movimiento Colombia Unida (CU): Santafé de Bogotá, DC; left-wing group allied to the UP; Leader ADALBERTO CARVAJAL.

Movimiento Nacional Conservador (MNC): Carrera 16, No 33-24, Santafé de Bogotá, DC; tel. (1) 245-4418; fax (1) 284-8529; Sec.-Gen. JUAN PABLO CEPERA MÁRQUEZ.

Movimiento Nacional Progresista (MNP): Carrera 10, No 19-45, Of. 708, Santafé de Bogotá, DC; tel. (1) 286-7517; fax (1) 341-9368; Sec.-Gen. EDUARDO AISAMAK LEÓN BELTRÁN.

Movimiento Obrero Independiente Revolucionario (MOIR): Calle 52A, No 20-09, Santafé de Bogotá, DC; tel. (1) 249-4312; e-mail moir@moir.org.co; internet www.moir.org.co; left-wing workers' movement; Maoist; Leader HÉCTOR VALENGA.

Movimiento de Salvación Nacional (MSN): Carrera 7A, No 58-00, Santafé de Bogotá, DC; tel. (1) 249-0209; fax (1) 310-1991; f. 1990; split from the Partido Conservador Colombiano.

Movimiento Unitario Metapolítico (MUM): Calle 13, No 68D-40, Santafé de Bogotá, DC; tel. (1) 292-1330; fax (1) 292-5502; internet www.metafisica.net; f. 1985; populist-occultist party; Leader REGINA BETANCOURT DE LISKA.

Mujeres para la Democracia: Santafé de Bogotá, DC; f. 1991; women's party; Leader ANGELA CUEVAS DE DOLMETSCH.

Partido Conservador Colombiano (PCC): Avda 22, No 37-09, Santafé de Bogotá, DC; tel. (1) 369-0011; fax (1) 369-0187; f. 1849; 2.9m. mems; Sec.-Gen. HUMBERTO ZULUAGA MONEDERO.

Partido Liberal Colombiano (PL): Avda Caracas, No 36-01, Santafé de Bogotá, DC; tel. (1) 287-9311; fax (1) 287-9540; f. 1815; divided into two factions the official group (Hernando Durán Lussán, Miguel Pinedo) and the independent group, Nuevo Liberalismo (New Liberalism led by Dr Alberto Santofimio Botero, Ernesto Samper Pizano, Eduardo Mestre); Pres. LUIS FERNANDO JARAMILLO.

Partido Nacional Cristiano (PNC): Calle 22C, No 31-01, Santafé de Bogotá, DC; tel. (1) 337-9211; fax (1) 269-3621; e-mail mision2@latino.net.co; Pres. LIÑO LEAL COLLAZOS.

Unidad Democrática de la Izquierda (Democratic Unity of the Left): Santafé de Bogotá, DC; f. 1982; left-wing coalition incorporating the following parties:

Firmes: Santafé de Bogotá, DC; democratic party.

Partido Comunista Colombiano (PC): Calle 18A, No 14-56, Apdo Aéreo 2523, Santafé de Bogotá, DC; tel. (1) 334-1947; fax (1) 281-8259; f. 1930; Marxist-Leninist party; Sec.-Gen. ALVARO VÁSQUEZ DEL REAL.

Partido Socialista de los Trabajadores (PST): Santafé de Bogotá, DC; workers' socialist party; Leader María SOCORRO RAMÍREZ.

Unión Patriótica (UP): Carrera 13A, No 38-32, Of. 204, Santafé de Bogota, DC; fax (1) 570-4400; f. 1985; Marxist party formed by the FARC (see below); obtained legal status in 1986; Pres. ERNÁN PASTRANA; Exec. Sec. OVIDIO SALINAS.

The following guerrilla groups and illegal organizations were active:

Autodefensas Campesinas de Córdoba y Urabá (ACCU): right-wing paramilitary org; Leaders CARLOS CASTAÑO, SALVATORE MANCUSO.

Autodefensas Unidas de Colombia (AUC): internet www.colombialibre.org; right-wing paramilitary org. 10,000 mems; disbanded in 2002.

Ejército de Liberación Nacional (ELN): Castroite guerrilla movement; f. 1965; 3,500 mems; political status recognized by the Govt in 1998; Leaders NICOLÁS ROGRÍGUEZ BAUTISTA, ANTONIO GARCÍA; factions include:

Corriente de Renovación Socialista (CRS): ceased hostilities in December 1993.

Frente Simón Bolívar: ceased hostilities in December 1985.

Frente Antonio Nariño: ceased hostilities in December 1985.

Frente Domingo Laín: formed splinter group in October 1993. armed wing.

Ejército Popular de Liberación (EPL): Maoist guerrilla movement; f. 1969; splinter group from Communist Party; abandoned armed struggle in March 1991; joined the political mainstream as the **Partido de Esperanza, Paz y Libertad (EPL)**; Leader FRANCISCO CARABALLO.

Frente Popular de Liberación Nacional (FPLN): f. 1994 by dissident members of the ELN and the EPL.

Fuerzas Armadas Revolucionarias de Colombia (FARC): internet www.farc-ep.org; fmrly military wing of the Communist Party; composed of 39 armed fronts and about 17,000 mems; political status recognized by the Govt in 1998; Leader MANUEL MARULANDA VÉLEZ (alias Tirofijo).

Movimiento de Autodefensa Obrera (MAO): workers' self-defence movement; Trotskyite; Leader ADELAIDA ABADIA REY.

Movimiento de Restauración Nacional (MORENA): right-wing; Leader ARMANDO VALENZUELA RUIZ.

Muerte a Secuestradores (MAS) (Death to Kidnappers): right-wing paramilitary org. funded by drugs dealers.

Nuevo Frente Revolucionario del Pueblo: f. 1986; faction of M-19; active in Cundinamarca region.

Partido Revolucionario de Trabajadores (PRT): left-wing; abandoned its armed struggle in 1991 and announced its intention to join the political mainstream as part of the Alianza Democrática.

Patria Libre: f. 1985; left-wing guerrilla movement.

In late 1985 the M-19, the Comando Ricardo Franco-Frente Sur and the **Comando Quintín Lame** (an indigenous organization active in the department of Cauca) announced the formation of a united front, the **Coordinadora Guerrillera Nacional (CGN)**. In 1986 the CGN participated in joint campaigns with the Movimiento Revolucionario Tupac Amarú (Peru) and the Alfaro Vive ¡Carajo! (Ecuador). The alliance operated under the name of **Batallón América**. In late 1987 six guerrilla groups, including the ELN, the FARC and the M-19, formed a joint front, to be known as the **Coordinadora Guerrillera Simón Bolívar (CGSB)** and subsequently as the **Coordinadora Nacional Guerrillera Simón Bolívar (CNGSB)**.

Diplomatic Representation

EMBASSIES IN COLOMBIA

Algeria: Carrera 11 No. 93-53, 302°, Santafé de Bogotá, DC; tel. (1) 635-0520; fax (1) 635-0531; e-mail ambalgbg@cable.net.co; Ambassador OMAR BENCHEHIDA.

Argentina: Avda 40A, No 13-09, 16°, Santafé de Bogotá, DC; tel. (1) 288-0900; fax (1) 288-8868; e-mail e_argentinaenbogota@cable.net.co; Ambassador CARLOS ALFREDO CARRASCO.

Austria: Carrera 11, No 75-29, Santafé de Bogotá, DC; tel. (1) 235-6628; e-mail eaustria@cable.net.co; Ambassador MARIANNE DA COSTA DE MORAES.

Belgium: Calle 26, No 4A-45, 7°, Santafé de Bogotá, DC; tel. (1) 380-0380; fax (1) 380-0340; e-mail bogota@diplobel.org; Ambassador FRANCOIS RONSE.

Bolivia: Transversal 14A, No 118A-26, Santa Barbara, Santafé de Bogotá, DC; tel. (1) 629-8237; fax (1) 612-9325; e-mail embolivia-bogota@rree.gov.bo; Ambassador RIGOBERTO PAREDES CANDIA.

Brazil: Calle 93, No 14-20, 8°, Santafé de Bogotá, DC; tel. (1) 218-0800; e-mail scomunic@colomsat.net.co; Ambassador MARCOS CAMACHO DE VINCENZI.

Canada: Calle 7, No 115-33, 14°, Apdo Aéreo 110067, Santafé de Bogotá, DC; tel. (1) 657-9800; fax (1) 657-9912; e-mail bgota@dfait-maeci.gc.ca; internet www.dfait-maeci.gc.ca/bogota; Ambassador JEAN-MARC DUVAL.

Chile: Calle 100, No 11B-44, Santafé de Bogotá, DC; tel. (1) 214-7926; e-mail echileco@colomsat.net.co; Ambassador OSCAR PIZARRO ROMERO.

China, People's Republic: Carrera 16, No 98-30, Santafé de Bogotá, DC; tel. (1) 622-3215; fax (1) 622-3114; e-mail embchina@andinet.com; Ambassador JU YIJIE.

Costa Rica: Carrera 8, No 95-48, Santafé de Bogotá, DC; tel. (1) 256-1105; fax (1) 691-8558; e-mail embacosta@andinet.com; Chargé d'affaires a.i. FRANCISCO VILLALOBOS GONZÁLEZ.

Cuba: Carrera 9, No 92-54, Santafé de Bogotá, DC; tel. (1) 257-3353; fax (1) 611-4382; e-mail embacuba@andinet.com; Ambassador LUIS HERNÁNDEZ OJEDA.

Czech Republic: Carrera 7, No 113-33, 6°, Santafé de Bogotá, DC; tel. (1) 640-0600; fax (1) 640-0599; e-mail bogota@embassy.msv.cz; Ambassador JOSEF RYCHTAR.

Dominican Republic: Carrera 7, No 115-33, 4°, Santafé de Bogotá, DC; tel. (1) 640-0560; fax (1) 522-0102; e-mail embajado@cable.net.co; Ambassador JUAN JORGE GARCÍA.

Ecuador: Calle 89, No 13-07, Santafé de Bogotá, DC; tel. (1) 257-0066; fax (1) 257-9799; e-mail mecucol@express.net.co; Ambassador Dr FERNANDO RIBADENEIRA.

Egypt: Tiasu 19A y 101–10, Santafé de Bogotá, DC; tel. (1) 256-2940; fax (1) 256-9255; e-mail embegyptbta@unete.com; Ambassador ATER ANWAR.

El Salvador: Carrera 9A, No 80-15, Of. 503, Edif. El Nogal, Santafé de Bogotá, DC; tel. (1) 349-6775; fax (1) 349-8492; e-mail elsalvadorcolombia@cable.net.co; Ambassador GUILLERMO RUBIO FUNES.

France: Carrera 11, No 93-12, Santafé de Bogotá, DC; tel. (1) 638-1400; fax (1) 638-1555; internet www.ambafrance-co.org; Ambassador DANIEL PARFAIT.

Germany: Edif. World Business Port, Carrera 69, No 43B-44, 7°, Santafé de Bogotá, DC; tel. (1) 423-2600; fax (1) 429-3145; e-mail embajalemana@andinet.com; Ambassador MATEI ION HOFFMANN.

Guatemala: Transversal 29A, No 139A-41, Santafé de Bogotá, DC; tel. (1) 259-1496; fax (1) 274-1196; e-mail embcolombia@minex.gob .gt; Ambassador MELVIN ARMINDO VALDEZ GONZÁLEZ.

Haiti: Carrera 11A, No 96-63, Santafé de Bogotá, DC; tel. (1) 256-6236; fax (1) 218-0326; Chargé d'affaires a.i. FRANTZ ROMULUS.

Holy See: Carrera 15, No 36-33, Apdo Aéreo 3740, Santafé de Bogotá, DC (Apostolic Nunciature); tel. (1) 320-0289; fax (1) 285-1817; e-mail nunciocol@col1.telecom.com.co; Apostolic Nuncio Most Rev. BENIAMINO STELLA (Titular Archbishop of Midila).

Honduras: Carrera 16, No 85-15, Of. 302, Santafé de Bogotá, DC; tel. (1) 236-0357; fax (1) 616-0774; e-mail emhoncol@andinet.com; Chargé d'affaires a.i. CARMEN LASTENIA FLORES SANTOS.

Hungary: Carrera 6A, No 77-46, Santafé de Bogotá, DC; tel. (1) 347-1467; fax (1) 347-1469; e-mail huemcol@cable.net.co; Ambassador JÓZSEF NAGY.

India: Edif. Bancafe, Torre B, Carrera 7, No 71-21, Of. 1001, Santafé de Bogotá, DC; tel. (1) 317-4865; fax (1) 317-4976; e-mail indembog@ cable.net.co; Ambassador HEMANT KRISHAN SINGH.

Indonesia: Carrera 9, No 76-27, Santafé de Bogotá, DC; tel. (1) 217-6738; fax (1) 210-3507; e-mail eindones@colsat.net.co; Ambassador M. WASAL FALAH.

Iran: Calle 96, No 11A-16/20, Santafé de Bogotá, DC; tel. (1) 218-6205; fax (1) 610-2556; Ambassador ABDOLAZIM HASHEMI NIK.

Israel: Calle 35, No 7-25, 14°, Santafé de Bogotá, DC; tel. (1) 287-7808; fax (1) 287-7783; e-mail embisrae@latino.net.co; Ambassador RAPHAEL YAACOV SCHUTZ.

Italy: Calle 93B, No 9-92, Apdo Aéreo 50901, Santafé de Bogotá, DC; tel. (1) 218-6680; fax (1) 610-5886; e-mail ambitbog@internet.co; internet www.ambitaliabogota.org; Ambassador FRANCESCO CAMILLO PEANO.

Japan: Carrera 9A, No 99-02, 6°, Edif. Latinoamericano de Seguros, Santafé de Bogotá, DC; tel. (1) 618-2800; fax (1) 618-2828; e-mail embajapol@colsat.net.co; Ambassador GUNKATSU KANO.

Korea, Republic: Calle 94, No 9-39, Santafé de Bogotá, DC; tel. (1) 616-7200; fax (1) 610-0338; e-mail embcorea@cable.net.co; Ambassador JONG CHAN WON.

Lebanon: Calle 74, No 12-44, Santafé de Bogotá, DC; tel. (1) 212-8360; fax (1) 347-9106; Ambassador MOUNIR KHREICH.

Mexico: Calle 114, No 9-01, Santafé de Bogotá, DC; tel. (1) 629-5314; fax (1) 629-5159; e-mail emcolmex@cable.net.co; internet www .sre.gob.mx/colombia; Ambassador LUIS ORTÍZ MONASTERIO CASTELLANOS.

Morocco: Carrera 13ANo 98-33, Santafé de Bogotá, DC; tel. (1) 218-7147; fax (1) 218-8068; e-mail sifamabogot@aldato.com.co; internet www.embamarruecos.org.co; Ambassador MOHAMED MAOULAININE.

Netherlands: Carrera 13, No 93-40, 5°, Apdo Aéreo 43585, Santafé de Bogotá, DC; tel. (1) 638-4200; fax (1) 623-3020; e-mail nlgovbog@ colmsat.net.co; internet www.embajadadeholanda.org.co; Ambassador TEUNIS KAMPER.

Nicaragua: Transversal 19A, No 108-77, Santafé de Bogotá, DC; tel. (1) 619-8934; fax (1) 612-0201; Ambassador DOMINGO SALINAS ALVARADO.

Norway: Carrera 13, No 50-78, 5°, Santafé de Bogotá, DC; tel. (1) 235-5419; fax (1) 249-0338; Chargé d'affaires a.i. TOM TYRIHJELL.

Panama: Calle 92, No 7-70, Santafé de Bogotá, DC; tel. (1) 257-5068; e-mail empanama@hotmail.com; Ambassador ALFREDO ANTONIO MONTANER.

Paraguay: Calle 57, No 7-11, Of. 702, Apdo Aéreo 20085, Santafé de Bogotá, DC; tel. (1) 255-4160; Ambassador NELSON ALCIDES MORA RODAS.

Peru: Carrera 10, No 93-48, Santafé de Bogotá, DC; tel. (1) 257-6292; fax (1) 623-5102; e-mail lbogota@reymoreno.net.co; Ambassador ALEJANDRO GORDILLO FERNÁNDEZ.

Poland: Calle 104A, No 23-48, Santafé de Bogotá, DC; tel. (1) 214-0143; fax (1) 218-0854; e-mail epolonia@col1.telecom.com.co; Ambassador PAWEL KULKA KULPIOWSKI.

Portugal: Calle 12, No 93-37, Of. 302, Santafé de Bogotá, DC; tel. (1) 622-1334; e-mail emporbo@coll.telecom.com; Ambassador AUGUSTO MARTINS GONÇALVES P.

Romania: Carrera 7, No 92-58, Santafé de Bogotá, DC; tel. (1) 256-6438; fax (1) 256-6158; e-mail emrubog@colomsat.net.co; Chargé d'affaires a.i. OCTAVIAN IONUT.

Russia: Carrera 4, No 75-00, Apdo Aéreo 90600, Santafé de Bogotá, DC; tel. (1) 212-1881; fax (1) 210-4694; e-mail embrusia@impsat.net .co; Ambassador VITALI MAKAROV.

Spain: Calle 92, No 12-68, Santafé de Bogotá, DC; tel. (1) 635-0218; fax (1) 621-0809; e-mail embespco@correo.mae.es; Ambassador YAGO PICO DE COAÑA.

Sweden: Calle 72, No 5-83, 9°, Santafé de Bogotá, DC; tel. (1) 325-2165; fax (1) 325-2166; e-mail ambassaden.bogota@foreign.ministry .se; internet www.embajadasuecia.org.co; Ambassador OLOF SKOOG.

Switzerland: Carrera 9, No 74-08/1101, 11°, Santafé de Bogotá, DC; tel. (1) 349-7230; fax (1) 349-7195; e-mail vertretung@bog.rep .admin.ch; Ambassador VIKTOR CHRISTEN.

United Kingdom: Carrera 9, No 76-49, 9°, Santafé de Bogotá, DC; tel. (1) 317-6690; fax (1) 317-6265; e-mail britain@cable.net.co; internet www.britain.gov.co; Ambassador TOM DUGGIN.

USA: Calle 22D-bis, No 47-51, Apdo Aéreo 3831, Santafé de Bogotá, DC; tel. (1) 315-0811; fax (1) 315-2197; internet usembassy.state .gov/posts/co1/wwwhmane.html; Ambassador ANNE W. PATTERSON.

Uruguay: Carrera 9A, No 80-15, 11°, Apdo Aéreo 101466, Santafé de Bogotá, DC; tel. (1) 235-2748; fax (1) 248-3734; e-mail urucolom@ impsat.com.co; Ambassador EDUARDO AÑÓN NOCETI.

Venezuela: Carrera 11, No 87-51, 5°, Santafé de Bogotá, DC; tel. (1) 640-1213; fax (1) 640-1242; e-mail embajada@embaven.org.co; internet www.embaven.org.co; Ambassador SANTIAGO RAMIREZ CARLOS RODOLFO.

Judicial System

The constitutional integrity of the State is ensured by the Constitutional Court. The Constitutional Court is composed of nine judges who are elected by the Senate for eight years. Judges of the Constitutional Court are not eligible for re-election.

President of the Constitutional Court: FABIO MORÓN DÍAZ.

Judges of the Constitutional Court: ALEJANDRO MARTÍNEZ CABALLERO, VLADIMIRO NARANJO MESA, ANTONIO BARRERO CARBONELL, CARLOS GAVIRIA DÍAZ, ALVARO TAFUR GALVIS, JOSÉ GREGORIO HERNÁNDEZ, EDUARDO CIFUENTES MUÑOZ, ALFREDO BELTRAN SIERRA.

The ordinary judicial integrity of the State is ensured by the Supreme Court of Justice. The Supreme Court of Justice is composed of the Courts of Civil and Agrarian, Penal and Laboral Cassation. Judges of the Supreme Court of Justice are selected from the nominees of the Higher Council of Justice and serve an eight-year term of office which is not renewable.

Prosecutor-General: ALFONSO GÓMEZ MÉNDEZ.

Attorney-General: CARLOS HOLGUIN SARDI.

SUPREME COURT OF JUSTICE

Supreme Court of Justice
Carrera 7A, No 27-18, Santafé de Bogotá, DC; fax (1) 334-8745; internet www.fij.edu.co.

President: GERMÁN VALDÉS SÁNCHEZ.

Vice-President: FERNANDO ARBOLEDA RIPOLL.

Court of Civil and Agrarian Cassation (seven judges): President JORGE ANTONIO CASTILLO RUGELES.

Court of Penal Cassation (nine judges): President JORGE ANIBAL GÓMEZ GALLEGO.

Court of Laboral Cassation (seven judges): President JOSÉ ROBERTO HERRERA VERGARA.

Religion

Roman Catholicism is the religion of 95% of the population.

CHRISTIANITY

The Roman Catholic Church
Colombia comprises 12 archdioceses, 48 dioceses and 10 Apostolic Vicariates.

Bishops' Conference
Conferencia Episcopal de Colombia, Carrera 47, No 84-85, Apdo Aéreo 7448, Santafé de Bogotá, DC; tel. (1) 437–5540; fax (1) 311-5575; e-mail colcec@cable.net.co.

f. 1978; statutes approved 1996; Pres. Cardinal PEDRO RUBIANO SÁENZ (Archbishop of Santafé de Bogotá).

Archbishop of Barranquilla: RUBÉN SALAZAR GÓMEZ, Carrera 45, No 53-122, Apdo Aéreo 1160, Barranquilla 4, Atlántico; tel. (5) 340-1648; fax (5) 340-6239; e-mail arquidio@arquidiocesibaq.org.co.

Archbishop of Bucaramanga: VÍCTOR MANUEL LÓPEZ FORERO, Calle 33, No 21-18, Bucaramanga, Santander; tel. (7) 642-4387; fax (7) 642-1361; e-mail prensacuria@latinmail.com.

Archbishop of Cali: (vacant), Carrera 4, No 7-17, Apdo Aéreo 8924, Cali, Valle del Cauca; tel. (2) 889-0562; fax (2) 83-7980.

Archbishop of Cartagena: CARLOS JOSÉ RUISECO VIEIRA, Apdo Aéreo 400, Cartagena; tel. (5) 664-5308; fax (5) 664-4974; e-mail arzoctg@telecartagena.com.

Archbishop of Ibagué: JUAN FRANCISCO SARASTI JARAMILLO, Calle 10, No 2-58, Ibagué, Tolima; tel. (82) 61-1680; fax (82) 63-2681.

Archbishop of Manizales: FABIO BETANCUR TIRADO, Carrera 23, No 19-22, Manizales, Caldas; tel. (68) 84-0114; fax (68) 82-1853.

Archbishop of Medellín: ALBERTO GIRALDO JARAMILLO, Calle 57, No 49-44, 3°, Medellín; tel. (4) 251-7700; fax (4) 251-9395; e-mail arquidiomed@epm.net.co.

Archbishop of Nueva Pamplona: GUSTAVO MARTÍNEZ FRÍAS, Carrera 5, No 4-87, Nueva Pamplona; tel. (4) 68-2886; fax (4) 68-4540.

Archbishop of Popayán: IVÁN MARÍN-LÓPEZ, Calle 5, No 6-71, Apdo Aéreo 593, Popayán; tel. (928) 24-1710; fax (928) 24-0101; e-mail ivanarzo@emtel.net.co.

Archbishop of Santa Fe de Antioquia: IGNACIO GÓMEZ ARISTIZÁBAL, Plazuela Martínez Pardo, No 12-11, Santa Fe de Antioquia; tel. (94) 853-1155; fax (94) 853-1596; e-mail arquistafe@edatel.net.co.

Archbishop of Santafé de Bogotá: Cardinal PEDRO RUBIANO SÁENZ, Carrera 7A, No 10-20, Santafé de Bogotá, DC; tel. (1) 350-5511; fax (1) 350-7290; e-mail cancilleria@arquidiocesisbogota.org.co.

Archbishop of Tunja: LUIS AUGUSTO CASTRO QUIROGA, Calle 17, No 9-85, Apdo Aéreo 1019, Tunja, Boyacá; tel. (987) 42-2094; fax (987) 42-2096; e-mail arquidio@telecom.com.co.

The Anglican Communion

Anglicans in Colombia are members of the Episcopal Church in the USA.

Bishop of Colombia: Rt Rev. BERNARDO MERINO BOTERO, Carrera 6, No 49-85, Apdo Aéreo 52964, Santafé de Bogotá, DC; tel. (1) 288-3167; fax (1) 288-3248; there are 3,500 baptized mems, 2,000 communicant mems, 29 parishes, missions and preaching stations; 5 schools and 1 orphanage; 8 clergy.

Protestant Churches

The Baptist Convention: Medellín; tel. (4) 38-9623; Pres. RAMÓN MEDINA IBÁÑEZ; Exec. Sec. Rev. RAMIRO PÉREZ HOYOS.

Iglesia Evangélica Luterana de Colombia: Calle 75, No 20-54, Apdo Aéreo 51538, Santafé de Bogotá, DC; tel. (1) 212-5735; fax (1) 212-5714; e-mail ofcentral@ielco.or; 3,000 mems; Pres. Bishop NEHEMÍAS PARADA.

BAHÁ'Í FAITH

National Spiritual Assembly: Apdo Aéreo 51387, Santafé de Bogotá, DC; tel. (1) 268-1658; fax (1) 268-1665; e-mail bahaicol@colombianet.net; adherents in 1,013 localities.

JUDAISM

There is a community of about 25,000 with 66 synagogues.

The Press

DAILIES

Santafé de Bogotá, DC

El Espacio: Carrera 61, No 45-35, Apdo Aéreo 80111, Avda El Dorado, Santafé de Bogotá, DC; tel. (1) 425-1570; fax (1) 410-4595; f. 1965; evening; Dir JAIME ARDILA CASAMITJANA; circ. 159,000.

El Nuevo Siglo: Calle 45A, No 102-02, Apdo Aéreo 5452, Santafé de Bogotá, DC; tel. (1) 413-9200; fax (1) 413-8547; f. 1925; Conservative; Dirs JUAN PABLO URIBE, JUAN GABRIEL URIBE; circ. 68,000.

La República: Calle 46, No 103-59, Santafé de Bogotá, DC; tel. (1) 413-5077; fax (1) 413-3725; f. 1953; morning; economics; Dir RODRIGO OSPINA HERNÁNDEZ; Editor JORGE EMILIO SIERRA M; circ. 55,000.

El Tiempo: Avda El Dorado, No 59-70, Apdo Aéreo 3633, Santafé de Bogotá, DC; tel. (1) 294-0100; fax (1) 410-5088; internet www.eltiempo.com; f. 1911; morning; Liberal; Dir ENRIQUE SANTOS CALDERÓN; Editor FRANCISCO SANTOS; circ. 265,118 (weekdays), 536,377 (Sundays).

Barranquilla, Atlántico

El Heraldo: Calle 53B, No 46-25, Barranquilla, Atlántico; tel. (5) 41-1090; fax (5) 41-6918; e-mail elheraldo@metrotel.net.co; internet www.elheraldo.com.co; f. 1933; morning; Liberal; Dir JUAN B. FERNÁNDEZ; circ. 70,000.

La Libertad: Carrera 53, No 55-166, Barranquilla, Atlántico; tel. (5) 31-1517; Liberal; Dir ROBERTO ESPER REBAJE; circ. 25,000.

El Tiempo Caribe: Carrera 50BNo 41-18, Barranquilla, Atlántico; tel. (5) 379-1510; fax (5) 341-7715; e-mail orlgam@eltiempo.com.co; internet www.eltiempo.com; f. 1956; daily; Liberal; Dir ORLANDA GAMBOA; circ. 45,000.

Bucaramanga, Santander del Sur

El Frente: Calle 35, No 12-22, Apdo Aéreo 665, Bucaramanga, Santander del Sur; tel. (7) 42-5369; fax (7) 33-4541; f. 1942; morning; Conservative; Dir RAFAEL SERRANO PRADA; circ. 10,000.

Vanguardia Liberal: Calle 34, No 13-42, Bucaramanga, Santander del Sur; tel. (7) 33-4000; fax (7) 30-2443; e-mail vanglibe@colomsat.net.co; f. 1919; morning; Liberal; Sunday illustrated literary supplement and women's supplement; Dir and Man. ALEJANDRO GALVIS RAMÍREZ; circ. 48,000.

Cali, Valle del Cauca

Occidente: Calle 12, No 5-22, Cali, Valle del Cauca; tel. (2) 895-9756; fax (2) 884-6572; e-mail occidente@cali.cercol.net.co; f. 1961; morning; Conservative; Dir ALVARO H. CAICEDO GONZÁLEZ; circ. 25,000.

El País: Carrera 2A, No 24-46, Apdo Aéreo 4766, Cali, Valle del Cauca; tel. (2) 883-5011; fax (2) 883-5014; e-mail diario@elpais-cali.com; internet www.elpais-cali.com; f. 1950; Conservative; Dir FRANCISCO JOSÉ LLOREDA MERA; circ. 60,000 (weekdays), 120,000 (Saturdays), 108,304 (Sundays).

El Pueblo: Avda 3A, Norte 35-N-10, Cali, Valle del Cauca; tel. (2) 68-8110; morning; Liberal; Dir LUIS FERNANDO LONDOÑO CAPURRO; circ. 50,000.

Cartagena, Bolívar

El Universal: Calle 30, No 17-36, Cartagena, Bolívar; fax (5) 666-1964; e-mail director@eluniversal.com.co; internet www.eluniversal.com.co; f. 1948; daily; Liberal; Dir PEDRO LUIS MOGOLLÓN; Man. GERARDO ARAÚJO; circ. 30,000.

Cúcuta, Norte de Santander

La Opinión: Avda 4, No 16-12, Cúcuta, Norte de Santander; tel. (75) 71-9999; fax (75) 71-7869; e-mail laopinion@coll.telecom.com.co; f. 1960; morning; Liberal; Dir Dr JOSÉ EUSTORGIO COLMENARES OSSA; circ. 26,000.

Manizales, Caldas

La Patria: Carrera 20, No 21-51, Apdo Aéreo 70, Manizales, Caldas; tel. (68) 84-2460; fax (68) 84-7158; e-mail lapatria@lapatria.com; f. 1921; morning; Independent; Dir Dr LUIS JOSÉ RESTREPO RESTREPO; circ. 22,000.

Medellín, Antioquia

El Colombiano: Carrera 48, No 30 sur-119, Apdo Aéreo 80636, Medellín, Antioquia; tel. (4) 331-5252; fax (4) 331-4858; e-mail elcolombiano@elcolombiano.com.co; internet www.elcolombiano.com; f. 1912; morning; Conservative; Dir ANA MERCEDES GÓMEZ MARTÍNEZ; circ. 90,000.

El Mundo: Calle 53, No 74-50, Apdo Aéreo 53874, Medellín, Antioquia; tel. (4) 264-2800; fax (4) 264-3729; e-mail elmundo@elmundo.com; internet www.elmundo.com; f. 1979; Dir GUILLERMO GAVIRIA; Man. ANÍBAL GAVIRIA CORREA; circ. 20,000.

Montería, Córdoba

El Meridiano de Córdoba: Avda Circunvalar, No 38-30, Montería, Córdoba; tel. (47) 82-6888; fax (47) 82-1981; e-mail meridiano@monteria.cetcol.net.co; internet www.elmeridianodecordoba.com; f. 1995; morning; Dir WILLIAM ENRIQUE SALLEG TABOADA; circ. 17,000.

Neiva

Diario del Huila: Calle 8A, No 6-30, Neiva; tel. (88) 71-2458; fax (88) 71-2446; f. 1966; Dir MARÍA M. RENGIFO DE D; circ. 12,000.

Pasto, Nariño

El Derecho: Calle 20, No 26-20, Pasto, Nariño; tel. (277) 2170; f. 1928; Conservative; Pres. Dr José Elías del Hierro; Dir Eduardo F. Mazuera; circ. 12,000.

Pereira, Risaralda

Diario del Otún: Carrera 8A, No 22-75, Apdo Aéreo 2533, Pereira, Risaralda; tel. (63) 51313; fax (1) 324-1900; e-mail eldiario@interco .net.co; internet www.eldiario.com.co; f. 1982; Financial Dir Javier Ignacio Ramírez Múnera; circ. 30,000.

El Imparcial: km 11 vía Pereira-Armenia, El Jordán, Pereira, Risaralda; tel. (63) 25-9935; fax (63) 25-9934; f. 1948; morning; Dir Zahur Klemath Zapata; circ. 15,000.

La Tarde: Carrera 9A, No 20-54, Pereira, Risaralda; tel. (63) 35-7976; fax (63) 35-5187; f. 1975; evening; Man. Luis Fernando Baena Mejía; circ. 15,000.

Popayán, Cauca

El Liberal: Carrera 3, No 2-60, Apdo Aéreo 538, Popayán, Cauca; tel. (28) 24-2418; fax (28) 23-3888; f. 1938; Man. Carlos Alberto Cabal Jiménez; circ. 6,500.

Santa Marta, Magdalena

El Informador: Calle 21, No 5-06, Santa Marta, Magdalena; f. 1921; Liberal; Dir José B. Vives; circ. 9,000.

Villavicencio, Meta

Clarín del Llano: Villavicencio, Meta; tel. (866) 23207; Conservative; Dir Elías Matus Torres; circ. 5,000.

PERIODICALS

Santafé de Bogotá, DC

Antena: Santafé de Bogotá, DC; television, cinema and show business; circ. 10,000.

Arco: Carrera 6, No 35-39, Apdo Aéreo 8624, Santafé de Bogotá, DC; tel. (1) 285-1500; f. 1959; monthly; history, philosophy, literature and humanities; Dir Alvaro Valencia Tovar; circ. 10,000.

ART NEXUS/Arte en Colombia: Carrera 5, No 67-19, Apdo Aéreo 90193, Santafé de Bogotá, DC; tel. (1) 312-9332; fax (1) 312-9252; e-mail artnexus@artnexus.com; f. 1976; quarterly; Latin American art, photography, visual arts; editions in English and Spanish; Dir Celia Sredni de Birbragher; Exec. Editor Ivonne Pini; circ. 26,000.

El Campesino: Carrera 39A, No 15-11, Santafé de Bogotá, DC; f. 1958; weekly; cultural; Dir Joaquín Gutiérrez Macías; circ. 70,000.

Consigna: Diagonal 34, No 5-11, Santafé de Bogotá, DC; tel. (1) 287-1157; fortnightly; Turbayista; Dir (vacant); circ. 10,000.

Coyuntura Económica: Calle 78, No 9-91, Apdo Aéreo 75074, Santafé de Bogotá, DC; tel. (1) 312-5300; fax (1) 212-6073; e-mail bibliote@fedesarrollo.org.co; f. 1970; quarterly; economics; published by Fundación para Educación Superior y el Desarrollo (FEDESARROLLO); Editor María Angélica Arbelaez; circ. 1,500.

Cromos Magazine: Calle 70A, No 7-81, Apdo Aéreo 59317, Santafé de Bogotá, DC; f. 1916; weekly; illustrated; general news; Dir Alberto Zalamea; circ. 102,000.

As Deportes: Calle 20, No 4-55, Santafé de Bogotá, DC; f. 1978; sports; circ. 25,000.

Economía Colombiana: Dirección Economía y Finanzas, San Agustín 6-45, Of. 126A, Santafé de Bogotá, DC; tel. (1) 282-4597; fax (1) 282-3737; f. 1984; published by Contraloría General de la República; 6 a year; economics.

El Espectador: Carrera 68, No 23-71, Apdo Aéreo 3441, Santafé de Bogotá, DC; tel. (1) 294-5555; fax (1) 260-2323; e-mail redactor@ elespectador.com; internet www.elespectador.com; f. 1887 as a daily paper, published weekly from 2001; Editor Carlos Lleras de la Fuente; circ. 200,000.

Estrategia: Carrera 4A, 25A–12B, Santafé de Bogotá, DC; monthly; economics; Dir Rodrigo Otero.

Guión: Carrera 16, No 36-89, Apdo Aéreo 19857; Santafé de Bogotá, DC; tel. (1) 232-2660; f. 1977; weekly; general; Conservative; Dir Juan Carlos Pastrana; circ. 35,000.

Hit: Calle 20, No 4-55, Santafé de Bogotá, DC; cinema and show business; circ. 20,000.

Informe Financiero: Dirección Economía y Finanzas, San Agustín 6-45, Of. 126A, Santafé de Bogotá, DC; tel. (1) 282-4597; fax (1) 282-3737; published by Contraloría General de la República; monthly; economics.

Menorah: Apdo Aéreo 9081, Santafé de Bogotá, DC; tel. (1) 611-2014; f. 1950; independent monthly review for the Jewish community; Dir Eliécer Celnik; circ. 10,000.

Nueva Frontera: Carrera 7A, No 17-01, 5°, Santafé de Bogotá, DC; tel. (1) 334-3763; f. 1974; weekly; politics, society, arts and culture; Liberal; Dir Carlos Lleras Restrepo; circ. 23,000.

Pluma: Apdo Aéreo 12190, Santafé de Bogotá, DC; monthly; art and literature; Dir (vacant); circ. 70,000.

Que Hubo: Santafé de Bogotá, DC; weekly; general; Editor Consuelo Montejo; circ. 15,000.

Revista Escala: Calle 30, No 17-70, Santafé de Bogotá, DC; tel. (1) 287-8200; fax (1) 285-9882; e-mail escala@col-online.com; f. 1962; fortnightly; architecture; Dir David Serna Cárdenas; circ. 14,000.

Revista Diners: Calle 85, No 18-32, 6°, Santafé de Bogotá, DC; tel. (1) 636-0508; fax (1) 623-1762; e-mail diners@cable.net.co; f. 1963; monthly; Dir Germán Santamaría; circ. 110,000.

Semana: Calle 93B, No 13-47, Santafé de Bogotá, DC; tel. (1) 622-2277; fax (1) 621-0475; general; Pres. Felipe López Caballero.

Síntesis Económica: Calle 70A, No 10-52, Santafé de Bogotá, DC; tel. (1) 212-5121; fax (1) 212-8365; f. 1975; weekly; economics; Dir Félix Lafaurie Rivera; circ. 16,000.

Tribuna Médica: Calle 8B, No 68A-41 y Calle 123, No 8-20, Santafé de Bogotá, DC; tel. (1) 262-6085; fax (1) 262-4459; f. 1961; monthly; medical and scientific; Editor Jack Alberto Grimberg; circ. 50,000.

Tribuna Roja: Santafé de Bogotá, DC; tel. (1) 243-0371; e-mail tribojar@moir.org.co; internet www.moir.org.co/tribuna/tribuna .htm; f. 1971; quarterly; organ of the MOIR (pro-Maoist Communist party); Dir Carlos Naranjo; circ. 300,000.

Vea: Calle 20, No 4-55, Santafé de Bogotá, DC; weekly; popular; circ. 90,000.

Voz La Verdad del Pueblo: Carrera 8, No 19-34, Of. 310–311, Santafé de Bogotá, DC; tel. (1) 284-5209; fax (1) 342-5041; weekly; left-wing; Dir Carlos A. Lozano G; circ. 45,000.

NEWS AGENCIES

Ciep—El País: Carrera 16, No 36-35, Santafé de Bogotá, DC; tel. (1) 232-6816; fax (1) 288-0236; Dir Jorge Téllez.

Colprensa: Diagonal 34, No 5-63, Apdo Aéreo 20333, Santafé de Bogotá, DC; tel. (1) 287-2200; fax (1) 285-5915; e-mail colpre@elsitio .net.co; f. 1980; Dir Roberto Vargas Galvis.

Foreign Bureaux

Agence France-Presse (AFP): Carrera 5, No 16-14, Of. 807, Apdo Aéreo 4654, Santafé de Bogotá, DC; tel. (1) 281-8613; Dir Marie Sanz.

Agencia EFE (Spain): Carrera 16, No 39A-69, Apdo Aéreo 16038, Santafé de Bogotá, DC; tel. (1) 285-1576; fax (1) 285-1598; Bureau Chief Antonio Martínez Martín.

Agenzia Nazionale Stampa Associata (ANSA) (Italy): Carrera 4, No 67-30, Apdo Aéreo 16077, Santafé de Bogotá, DC; tel. (1) 211-9617; fax (1) 212-5409; Bureau Chief Alberto Rojas Morales.

Associated Press (AP) (USA): Transversal 14, No 122-36, Apdo Aéreo 093643, Santafé de Bogotá, DC; tel. (1) 619-3487; fax (1) 213-8467; e-mail apbogota@bigfoot.com; Bureau Chief Frank Bajak.

Central News Agency Inc. (Taiwan): Carrera 13A, No 98-34, Santafé de Bogotá, DC; tel. (1) 25-6342; Correspondent Christina Chow.

Deutsche Presse-Agentur (dpa) (Germany): Carrera 15, No 76-60, Of. 302, Santafé de Bogotá, DC; tel. (1) 618-3788; fax (1) 635-2516; e-mail presse@hbg.dpa.de; internet www.dpa.de; Correspondent Rodrigo Ruiz Tovar.

Informatsionnoye Telegrafnoye Agentstvo Rossii—Telegrafnoye Agentstvo Suverennykh Stran (ITAR—TASS) (Russia): Calle 20, No 7-17, Of. 901, Santafé de Bogotá, DC; tel. (1) 243-6720; Correspondent Gennadii Kochuk.

Inter Press Service (IPS) (Italy): Calle 19, No 3-50, Of. 602, Apdo Aéreo 7739, Santafé de Bogotá, DC; tel. (1) 341-8841; fax (1) 334-2249; Correspondent María Isabel García Navarrete.

Prensa Latina: Carrera 3, No 21-46, Apdo Aéreo 30372, Santafé de Bogotá, DC; tel. (1) 282-4527; fax (1) 281-7286; Bureau Chief Fausto Triana.

Reuters (United Kingdom): Calle 94A, No 13-34, 4°, Apdo Aéreo 29848, Santafé de Bogotá, DC; tel. (1) 634-4090; fax (1) 610-7733; e-mail bogota.newsroom@reuters.com; Bureau Chief Jason Webb.

Xinhua (New China) News Agency (People's Republic of China): Calle 74, No 4-26, Apdo Aéreo 501, Santafé de Bogotá, DC; tel. (1) 211-5347; Dir Hou Yaoqi.

PRESS ASSOCIATIONS

Asociación Colombiana de Periodistas: Avda Jiménez, No 8-74, Of. 510, Santafé de Bogotá, DC; tel. (1) 243-6056.

Asociación Nacional de Diarios Colombianos (ANDIARIOS): Calle 61, No 5-20, Apdo Aéreo 13663, Santafé de Bogotá, DC; tel. (1) 212-8694; fax (1) 212-7894; f. 1962; 30 affiliated newspapers; Pres. LUIS MIGUEL DE BEDOUT; Vice-Pres. LUIS FERNANDO BAENA.

Asociación de la Prensa Extranjera: Pedro Meléndez, No 87-93, Santafé de Bogotá, DC; tel. (1) 288-3011.

Círculo de Periodistas de Santafé de Bogotá, DC (CPB): Calle 26, No 13A-23, 23°, Santafé de Bogotá, DC; tel. (1) 282-4217; Pres. MARÍA TERESA HERRÁN.

Publishers

Santafé de Bogotá, DC

Comunicadores Técnicos Ltda: Carrera 18, No 46-58, Apdo Aéreo 28797, Santafé de Bogotá, DC; technical; Dir PEDRO P. MORCILLO.

Ediciones Cultural Colombiana Ltda: Calle 72, No 16-15 y 16-21, Apdo Aéreo 6307, Santafé de Bogotá, DC; tel. (1) 217-6529; fax (1) 217-6570; f. 1951; textbooks; Dir JOSÉ PORTO VÁSQUEZ.

Ediciones Lerner Ltda: Calle 8A, No 68A-41, Apdo Aéreo 8304, Santafé de Bogotá, DC; tel. (1) 420-0650; fax (1) 262-4459; f. 1959; general; Commercial Man. FABIO CAICEDO GÓMEZ.

Editora Cinco, SA: Calle 61, No 13-23, 7°, Apdo Aéreo 15188, Santafé de Bogotá, DC; tel. (1) 285-6200; recreation, culture, textbooks, general; Man. PEDRO VARGAS G.

Editorial El Globo, SA: Calle 16, No 4-96, Apdo Aéreo 6806, Santafé de Bogotá, DC.

Editorial Presencia, Ltda: Calle 23, No 24-20, Apdo Aéreo 41500, Santafé de Bogotá, DC; tel. (1) 269-2188; fax (1) 269-6830; textbooks, tradebooks; Gen. Man. MARÍA UMAÑA DE TANCO.

Editorial San Pablo: Carrera 46, No 22A–90, Quintaparedes, Apdo Aéreo 080152, Santafé de Bogotá, DC; tel. (1) 368-2099; fax (1) 244-4383; e-mail spdiredit@andinet.com; f. 1951; religion, culture, humanism; Editorial Dir P. VICENTE MIOTTO.

Editorial Temis SA: Calle 13, No 6-45, Apdo Aéreo 5941, Santafé de Bogotá, DC; tel. (1) 269-0713; fax (1) 292-5801; f. 1951; law, sociology, politics; Man. Dir JORGE GUERRERO.

Editorial Voluntad, SA: Carrera 7A, No 24-89, 24°, Santafé de Bogotá, DC; tel. (1) 286-0666; fax (1) 286-5540; e-mail voluntad@ colomsat.net.co; f. 1930; school books; Pres. GASTÓN DE BEDOUT.

Fundación Centro de Investigación y Educación Popular (CINEP): Carrera 5A, No 33A-08, Apdo Aéreo 25916, Santafé de Bogotá, DC; tel. (1) 285-8977; fax (1) 287-9089; f. 1977; education and social sciences; Man. Dir FRANCISCO DE ROUX.

Instituto Caro y Cuervo: Carrera 11, No 64-37, Casilla 3456004, Santafé de Bogotá, DC; tel. (1) 255-8289; fax (1) 217-0243; e-mail direcciongeneral@caroycuervo.gov.co; internet www.caroycuervo .gov.co; f. 1942; philology, general linguistics and reference; Man. Dir IGNACIO CHAVES CUEVAS; Gen. Sec. CARLOS JULIO LUQUE CAGUA.

Inversiones Cromos SA: Calle 70A, No 7-81, Apdo Aéreo 59317, Santafé de Bogotá, DC; tel. (1) 217-1754; fax (1) 211-2642; f. 1916; Dir ALBERTO ZALAMEA; Gen. Man. JORGE EDUARDO CORREA ROBLEDO.

Legis, SA: Avda El Dorado, No 81-10, Apdo Aéreo 98888, Santafé de Bogotá, DC; tel. (1) 263-4100; fax (1) 295-2650; e-mail jcastrof@legis .com.co; internet www.legis.com.co; f. 1952; economics, law, general; Man. JUAN ALBERTO CASTRO.

McGraw Hill Interamericana, SA: Avda Américas, No 46-41, Apdo Aéreo 81078, Santafé de Bogotá, DC; tel. (1) 337-7800; fax (1) 245-4786; e-mail cmarquez@mcgraw-hill.com; university textbooks; Dir-Gen. CARLOS G. MÁRQUEZ.

Publicar, SA: Avda 68, No 75A-50, 4°, Centro Comercial Metrópolis, Apdo Aéreo 8010, Santafé de Bogotá, DC; tel. (1) 225-5555; fax (1) 225-4015; e-mail m-navia@publicar.com; internet www.publicar .com; f. 1954; directories; CEO MARÍA SOL NAVIA.

Siglo del Hombre Editores Ltda: Carrera 32, No 25-46, Santafé de Bogotá, DC; tel. (1) 337-7700; fax (1) 337-7665; e-mail siglodelhombre@sky.net.co; f. 1992; arts, politics, anthropology, history, fiction, etc. Gen. Man. EMILIA FRANCO DE ARCILA.

Tercer Mundo Editores SA: Transversal 2A, No 67-27, Apdo Aéreo 4817, Santafé de Bogotá, DC; tel. (1) 255-1539; fax (1) 212-5976; e-mail tmundoed@polcola.com.co; f. 1963; social sciences; Pres. SANTIAGO POMBO VEJARANO.

ASSOCIATIONS

Cámara Colombiana del Libro: Carrera 17A, No 37-27, Apdo Aéreo 8998, Santafé de Bogotá, DC; tel. (1) 288-6188; fax (1) 287-3320; e-mail camlibro@camlibro.com.co; internet www.camlibro.com .co; f. 1951; Pres. GONZALO ARBOLEDA; Exec. Dir RICHARD URIBE SCHROEDER; 120 mems.

Colcultura: Biblioteca Nacional de Colombia, Calle 24, No 5-60, Apdo Aéreo 27600, Santafé de Bogotá, DC; tel. (1) 282-8656; fax (1) 341-4028; e-mail mgiraldo@mincultura.go.co; Dir ISADORA DE NORDEN.

Fundalectura: Avda 40, No 16-46, Santafé de Bogotá, DC; tel. (1) 320-1511; fax (1) 287-7071; e-mail contactenos@fundalectura.org.co; internet www.fundalectura.org.co; Exec. Dir CARMEN BARVO.

Broadcasting and Communications

Ministerio de Comunicaciones, Dirección de Telecomunicaciones: Edif. Murillo Toro, Carreras 7AY 8A, Calle 12AY 13, Apdo Aéreo 14515, Santafé de Bogotá, DC; tel. (1) 286-6911; fax (1) 286-1185; broadcasting authority; Dir (vacant) (Minister of Communications).

Instituto Nacional de Radio y Televisión (INRAVISION): Centro Administrativo Nacional (CAN), Avda El Dorado, Santafé de Bogotá, DC; tel. (1) 222-0700; fax (1) 222-0080; e-mail inras@col1 .telecom.com.co; f. 1954; govt-run TV and radio broadcasting network; educational and commercial broadcasting; Dir GUSTAVO SAMPER RODRÍGUEZ.

TELECOMMUNICATIONS

Celumóvil SA: Calle 71A, No 6-30, 18°, Santafé de Bogotá, DC; tel. (1) 346-1666; fax (1) 211-2031; Sec.-Gen. CARLOS BERNARDO CARREÑO R.

Empresa Nacional de Telecomunicaciones (TELECOM): Calle 23, No 13-49, Santafé de Bogotá, DC; tel. (1) 286-0077; fax (1) 282-8768; e-mail jblackbu@bogota.telecom.net.co; internet www.telecom .com.co; f. 1947; national telecommunications enterprise; Pres. JULIO MOLANO GONZÁLEZ.

Empresa de Telecomunicaciones de Santafé de Bogotá (ETB): Carrera 7A, No 20–37, Santafé de Bogotá, DC; tel. (1) 341-4233; fax (1) 342-3550; e-mail sugeetb@axesnet.com; internet www .etb.com.co; Bogotá telephone co; scheduled for privatization; Pres. SERGIO REGUEROS.

BROADCASTING

Radio

The principal radio networks are as follows:

Cadena Melodía de Colombia: Calle 45, No 13-70, Santafé de Bogotá, DC; tel. (1) 323-1500; fax (1) 288-4020; Pres. EFRAÍN PÁEZ ESPITIA.

Cadena Radial Auténtica: Calle 32, No 16-12, Apdo Aéreo 18350, Santafé de Bogotá, DC; tel. (1) 285-3360; fax (1) 285-2505; f. 1983; stations include Radio Auténtica and Radio Mundial; Pres. JORGE ENRIQUE GÓMEZ MONTEALEGRE.

Cadena Radial La Libertad Ltda: Carrera 53, No 55-166, Apdo Aéreo 3143, Barranquilla; tel. (5) 31-1517; fax (5) 32-1279; news and music programmes for Barranquilla, Cartagena and Santa Marta; stations include Emisora Ondas del Caribe (youth programmes), Radio Libertad (classical music programmes) and Emisora Fuentes.

Cadena Super: Calle 16A, No 86A-78, Santafé de Bogotá, DC; tel. (1) 618-1371; fax (1) 618-1360; internet www.889.com.co; f. 1971; stations include Radio Super and Super Stereo FM; Pres. JAIME PAVA NAVARRO.

CARACOL, SA (Primera Cadena Radial Colombiana, SA): Carretera 39A, No 15-81, Apdo Aéreo 9291, Santafé de Bogotá, DC; tel. (1) 337-8866; fax (1) 337-7126; internet www.caracol.com.co; f. 1948; 107 stations; Pres. JOSÉ MANUEL RESTREPO FERNÁNDEZ DE SOTO.

Circuito Todelar de Colombia: Avda 13, No 84-42, Apdo Aéreo 27344, Santafé de Bogotá, DC; tel. (1) 616-1011; fax (1) 616-0056; f. 1953; 74 stations; Pres. BERNARDO TOBÓN DE LA ROCHE.

Colmundo Radio, SA ('La Cadena de la Paz'): Diagonal 58, 26A-29, Apdo Aéreo 36750, Santafé de Bogotá, DC; tel. (1) 217-8911; fax (1) 217-9358; f. 1989; Pres. Dr NÉSTOR CHAMORRO P.

Organización Radial Olímpica, SA (ORO, SA): Calle 72, No 48-37, 2°, Apdo Aéreo 51266, Barranquilla; tel. (5) 358-0500; fax (5) 345-9080; programmes for the Antioquia and Atlantic coast regions.

Radio Cadena Nacional, SA (RCN Radio): Carrera 13A, No 37-32, Santafé de Bogotá, DC; tel. (1) 288-2288; fax (1) 288-6130; e-mail rcn@impsat.net.co; internet www.rcn.com.co; 116 stations; official network; Pres. RICARDO LONDOÑO LONDOÑO.

Radiodifusora Nacional de Colombia: Centro Administrativo Nacional (CAN), Avda El Dorado, Santafé de Bogotá, DC; tel. (1) 222-0415; fax (1) 222-0409; e-mail radiodifusora@hotmail.com; f. 1940; national public radio; Dir ATHALA MORRIS.

Radiodifusores Unidos, SA (RAU): Carrera 13, No 85-51, Of. 705, Santafé de Bogotá, DC; tel. (1) 617-0584; commercial network of independent local and regional stations throughout the country.

Television

Television services began in 1954, and the NTSC colour television system was adopted in 1979. The government-run broadcasting network, INRAVISION, controls three national stations. Two national, privately-run stations began broadcasts in mid-1988. There are also two regional stations and one local, non-profit station. Broadcasting time is distributed among competing programmers through a public tender.

Cadena Uno: Centro Administrativo Nacional (CAN), Avda El Dorado, Santafé de Bogotá, DC; tel. (1) 342-3777; fax (1) 341-6198; e-mail cadena1@latino.net.co; internet www.cadena1.com.co; f. 1992; Dir FERNANDO BARRERO CHÁVEZ.

Canal 3: Centro Administrativo Nacional (CAN), Avda El Dorado, Santafé de Bogotá, DC; tel. (1) 222-1640; fax (1) 222-1514; f. 1970; Exec. Dir RODRIGO ANTONIO DURÁN BUSTOS.

Canal A: Calle 35, No 7-51, CENPRO, Santafé de Bogotá, DC; tel. (1) 232-3196; fax (1) 245-7526; f. 1966; Gen. Man. ROCÍO FERNÁNDEZ DEL CASTILLO.

Caracol Televisión, SA: Calle 76, No 11-35, Apdo Aéreo 26484, Santafé de Bogotá, DC; tel. (1) 319-0860; fax (1) 321-1720; f. 1969; Pres. RICARDO ALARCÓN GAVIRIA.

Teleantioquia: Carrera 41, No 52-28, Edif. EDA, 3°, Apdo Aéreo 8183, Medellín, Antioquia; tel. (4) 262-0311; fax (4) 262-0832; f. 1985; Pres. ALVARO URIBE VÉLEZ.

Telecafé: Carrera 24, No 19-51, Apdo Aéreo 770, Manizales, Caldas; tel. (68) 84-5678; fax (68) 84-4623; e-mail telecafe@col2.telecom.com .co; f. 1986; Gen. Man. JUAN MANUEL LENIS LARA.

Telecaribe: Carrera 54, No 72-142, 11°, Barranquilla, Atlántico; tel. (5) 358-2297; fax (5) 356-0924; e-mail ealviz@canal.telecaribe .com.co; internet www.telecaribe.com.co; f. 1986; Gen. Man. IVÁN OVALLE POVEDA.

Telepacífico: Calle 5A, No 38A-14, 3°, esq. Centro Comercial Imbanaco, Cali, Valle del Cauca; tel. (2) 589-933; fax (2) 588-281; Gen. Man. LUIS GUILLERMO RESTREPO.

TV Cúcuta: tel. (75) 74-7874; fax (75) 75-2922; f. 1992; Pres. JOSÉ A. ARMELLA.

ASSOCIATIONS

Asociación Nacional de Medios de Comunicación (ASOMEDIOS): Carrera 22, No 85-72, Santafé de Bogotá, DC; tel. (1) 611-1300; fax (1) 621-6292; e-mail informacion@asomedios.com; internet www.asomedios.com; f. 1978; and merged with ANRADIO (Asociación Nacional de Radio, Televisión y Cine de Colombia) in 1980; Pres. Dr SERGIO ARBOLEDA CASAS.

Finance

(cap. = capital; res = reserves; dep. = deposits; m. = million; amounts in pesos, unless otherwise indicated)

Contraloría General de la República: Carrera 10, No 17-18, Torre Colseguros, 27°, Santafé de Bogotá, DC; tel. (1) 282-7905; fax (1) 282-3549; Controller-General Dr MANUEL FRANCISCO BECERRA.

BANKING

Supervisory Authority

Superintendencia Bancaria: Carrera 7A, No 4-49, 11°, Apdo Aéreo 3460, Santafé de Bogotá, DC; tel. (1) 350-8166; fax (1) 350-7999; e-mail superban@superbancaria.gov.co; internet www .superbancaria.gov.co; Banking Supt PATRICIA CORREA BONILLA.

Central Bank

Banco de la República: Carrera 7A, No 14-78, 5°, Apdo Aéreo 3531, Santafé de Bogotá, DC; tel. (1) 343-1111; fax (1) 286-1686; e-mail wbanco@banrep.gov.co; internet www.banrep.gov.co; f. 1923; sole bank of issue; cap. 12.7m. res 311,599.7m. dep. 2,557.6m. (Dec. 2002); Gov. MIGUEL URRUTIA MONTOYA; 28 brs.

Commercial Banks

Santafé de Bogotá, DC

ABN AMRO Bank (Colombia), SA (fmrly Banco Real de Colombia): Carrera 7A, No 33-80, Apdo Aéreo 34262, Santafé de Bogotá, DC; tel. (1) 285-0763; fax (1) 285-5671; f. 1975; cap. 8,110.5m., res 6,217.7m., dep. 56,787.7m. (Dec. 1993); Pres. CARLOS EDUARDO ARRUDA PENTEADO; 17 brs.

Banco Agrario de Colombia: Carrera 6, No 14-98, Santafé de Bogotá, DC; tel. (1) 212-3404; fax (1) 345-2279; f. 1999; Pres. JUAN BAUTISTA PÉREZ RUBIANO.

Banco America Colombia (fmrly Banco Colombo-Americano): Carrera 7, No 71-52, Torre B, 4°, Apdo Aéreo 12327, Santafé de Bogotá, DC; tel. (1) 312-2020; fax (1) 312-1645; cap. 3,268m., res 6,205m., dep. 14,475m. (Dec. 1993); wholly-owned subsidiary of Bank of America; Pres. EDUARDO ROMERO JARAMILLO; 1 br.

Banco Andino Colombia, SA (fmrly Banco de Crédito y Comercio): Carrera 7A, No 71-52, Torre B, 1°, 18° y 19°, Apdo Aéreo 6826, Santafé de Bogotá, DC; tel. (1) 312-3666; fax (1) 312-3273; e-mail geraldo@latino.net.co; f. 1954; cap. 7,206.5m., res 10,705.9m., dep. 121,367.4m. (Dec. 1993); Pres. CARLOS CUEVAS; 21 brs.

Banco de Bogotá: Calle 36, No 7-47, 15°, Apdo Aéreo 3436, Santafé de Bogotá, DC; tel. (1) 332-0032; fax (1) 338-3375; internet www .bancodebogota.com.co; f. 1870; acquired Banco del Comercio in 1992; cap. 876.6m. res 572.4m. dep. 3,103.0m. (June 2000); Pres. Dr ALEJANDRO FIGUEROA JARAMILLO; 274 brs.

Banco Cafetero (Bancafe): Calle 28, No 13A-15, Apdo Aéreo 240332, Santafé de Bogotá, DC; tel. (1) 341-1511; fax (1) 284-6516; e-mail c.gaona@bancafe.com.co; internet www.bancafe.com; f. 1953; cap. 45,288.4m., res 598,622.2m., dep. 3,330,281.8m. (Dec. 1999); Pres. PEDRO SANTA MARÍA; 283 brs.

Banco Caja Social: Carrera 7, No 77-65, 11°, Santafé de Bogotá, DC; tel. (1) 310-0099; fax (1) 313-0809; e-mail bancaj_vjuridica@ fundacion-social; f. 1911; savings bank; cap. 93,077m., res 13,543m., dep. 559,729m. (Dec. 1996); Pres. EULALIA ARBOLEDA DE MONTES; 135 brs.

Banco Central Hipotecario: Carrera 6, No 15-32, 11°, Apdo Aéreo 3637, Santafé de Bogotá, DC; tel. (1) 336-0055; fax (1) 282-2802; f. 1932; Pres. MARÍA JOSÉ GARCÍA JARAMILLO; 132 brs.

Banco Colpatria, SA: Carrera 7A, No 24-89, 12°, Apdo Aéreo 30241, Santafé de Bogotá, DC; tel. (1) 286-8277; fax (1) 334-0867; internet www.banco.colpatria.com; f. 1955; cap. 1,002m., res 15,575m., dep. 197,390m. (Dec. 1994); Pres. SANTIAGO PERDOMO MALDONADO; 26 brs.

Banco de Comercio Exterior de Colombia, SA (BANCOLDEX): Calle 28, No 13A-15, 38°, Apdo Aéreo 240092, Santafé de Bogotá, DC; tel. (1) 341-0677; fax (1) 284-5087; internet www .bancoldex.com; f. 1992; provides financing alternatives for Colombian exporters; affiliate trust company FIDUCOLDEX, SA manages PROEXPORT (Export Promotion Trust); Pres. MIGUEL GÓMEZ MARTÍNEZ.

Banco de Crédito: Carrera 7, No 27-18, Santafé de Bogotá, DC; tel. (1) 286-8400; fax (1) 286-7236; e-mail loginter@impsat.net.co; internet www.bancodecredito.com; f. 1963; cap. 36,952.8m., res 73,409.6m., dep. 944,129.3m. (Dec. 1999); Pres. JAMES P. FENTON; 24 brs.

Banco Mercantil de Colombia, SA (fmrly Banco de los Trabajadores): Avda 82, No 12-18, 8°, Santafé de Bogotá, DC; tel. (1) 635-0035; fax (1) 623-7669; e-mail bmjuridi@impsat.net.co; internet www.bancomercantil.com; f. 1974; wholly-owned subsidiary of Banco Mercantil (Venezuela); cap. 19,409.9m., res 24,459.5m., dep. 98,699.7m. (Dec. 1997); Pres. GUSTAVO SINTES ULLOA; 10 brs.

Banco del Pacífico, SA: Calle 100, 19-05, Santafé de Bogotá, DC; tel. (1) 416-5945; fax (1) 611-2339; e-mail jcbernal@banpacifico.com .co; f. 1994; wholly-owned by Banco del Pacífico, SA, Guayaquil (Ecuador); cap. 12,000.0m., res 6,120.2m., dep. 196,873.3m. (Dec. 1996); Pres. JUAN CARLOS BERNAL; 3 brs.

Banco Popular, SA: Calle 17, No 7-43, 3°, Apdo Aéreo 6796, Santafé de Bogotá, DC; tel. (571) 339-5449; fax (1) 281-9448; e-mail vpinternacional@bancopopular.com.co; internet www.bancopopular .com.co; f. 1951; cap. 77,253m., res 104,814m., dep. 2,357,133m. (June 2002); Pres. HERNÁN RINCÓN GÓMEZ; 157 brs.

Banco Santander: Carrera 46, No 52-36, Edif. Bavaria, 16°, Santafé de Bogotá, DC; tel. (1) 284-3100; fax (1) 281-0311; internet www .bancosantander.com.co; f. 1961; Pres. MONICA IÑES MARÍA APARICIO; 30 brs.

Banco Standard Chartered: Calle 74, No 6-65, Santafé de Bogotá, DC; tel. (1) 217-7200; fax (1) 212-5786; f. 1982; cap. 10,312m., res 5,574m., dep. 84,200m. (Dec. 1996); Pres. HANS JUERGUEN HEILKUHL OCHOA; 11 brs.

Banco Sudameris Colombia (fmrly Banco Francés e Italiano): Carrera 11, No 94A-03, 5°, Apdo Aéreo 3440, Santafé de Bogotá, DC; tel. (1) 636-8729; fax (1) 636-7702; internet www.sudameris.com.co; cap. 14,113.6m., res 60,949.3m., dep. 528,588.2m. (Dec. 1997); Pres. JORGE RAMÍREZ OCAMPO; 6 brs.

Banco Tequendama, SA: Diagonal 27, No 6-70, 2°, Santafé de Bogotá, DC; tel. (1) 320-2100; fax (1) 287-7020; f. 1976; wholly-owned subsidiary of Banco Construcción (Venezuela); cap. 12,049m., dep. 53,522m. (Dec. 1992); Pres. HÉCTOR MUÑOZ ARJUELA; 11 brs.

Banco Unión Colombiano (fmrly Banco Royal Colombiano): Torre Banco Unión Colombiano, Carrera 7A, No 71-52, 2°, Apdo Aéreo 3438, Santafé de Bogotá, DC; tel. (1) 312-0411; fax (1) 312-0843; e-mail bancounioncolombiano@bancounion.com.co; internet www.bancounion.com.co; f. 1925; cap. 12,350.3m. res 27,667.2m., dep. 131,063.0m. (Dec. 1995); Pres. JUAN POSADA CORPAS; 20 brs.

BBV-Banco Ganadero: Carrera 9A, No 72-21, 11°, Apdo Aéreo 53859, Santafé de Bogotá, DC; tel. (1) 347-1600; fax (1) 235-1248; f. 1956 as Banco Ganadero; name changed as above 1998; cap. 879,467.8m., dep. 2,989,659.8m. (Dec. 1998); Exec. Pres. JOSÉ MARÍA AYALA VARGAS; 286 brs.

Citibank Colombia, SA: Carrera 9A, No 99-02, 3°, Santafé de Bogotá, DC; tel. (1) 618-4455; fax (1) 621-0259; internet www.citibank.com/colombia; wholly-owned subsidiary of Citibank (USA); cap. 483m., res 9,399m., dep. 152,139m. (Dec. 1992); Pres. ANTONIO URIBE; 23 brs.

Lloyds TSB Bank, SA (frmly Banco Anglo Colombiano): Carrera 7, No 71-21, 16°, Apdo Aéreo 3532, Santafé de Bogotá, DC; tel. (1) 334-5088; fax (1) 341-9433; e-mail contactenos@lloydstsbbank.com.co; internet www.lloydstsbcol.com.co; f. 1976; cap. 14,990.7m., res 24,983.8m., dep. 229,629.3m. (Dec. 1996); Pres. JAMES SCOTT DONALD; 52 brs.

Cali

Banco de Occidente: Carrera 4, No 7-61, 12°, Apdo Aéreo 7607, Cali, Valle del Cauca; tel. (2) 886-1117; fax (2) 886-1297; e-mail banoccdi@col2.telecom.com.co; internet www.bancooccidente.com.co; cap. 3,562.2m. res 459,052.2m., dep. 2,426,881.9m. (Dec. 2000); Pres. EFRAIN OTERO ÁLVAREZ; 122 brs.

Medellín

Bancolombia, SA (fmrly Banco Industrial de Colombia): Carrera 52, No 50-20, Medellín, Antioquia; tel. (4) 251-5474; fax (4) 513-4827; e-mail mfranco@bancolombia.com.co; internet www.bancolombia.com.co; f. 1945; renamed 1998; following merger with Banco de Colombia; cap. 169,524m., res 768,382m., dep. 4,386,515m. (Dec. 1999); Pres. JORGE LONDOÑO SALDARRIAGA; 321 brs.

Banking Associations

Asociación Bancaria y de Entidades Financieras de Colombia: Carrera 9A, No 74-08, 9°, Santafé de Bogotá, DC; tel. (1) 249-6411; fax (1) 211-9915; e-mail info@asobancaria.com; internet www.asobancaria.com; f. 1936; 56 mem. banks; Pres. PATRICIA CÁRDENAS SANTA MARÍA.

Asociación Nacional de Instituciones Financieras (ANIF): Calle 70A, No 7-86, Santafé de Bogotá, DC; tel. (1) 310-1500; fax (1) 235-5947; Pres. ARMANDO MONTENEGRO TRUJILLO.

STOCK EXCHANGES

Superintendencia de Valores: Avda El Dorado, Calle 26, No 68-85, Torre Suramericana, 2° y 3°, Santafé de Bogotá, DC; tel. (1) 427-0222; fax (1) 427-0870; f. 1979 to regulate the securities market; Supt JORGE GABRIEL TABOADA HOYOS.

Bolsa de Bogotá: Carrera 8A, No 13-82, 4°-8°, Apdo Aéreo 3584, Santafé de Bogotá, DC; tel. (1) 243-6501; fax (1) 281-3170; f. 1928; Pres. AUGUSTO ACOSTA TORRES; Sec.-Gen. MARÍA FERNANDA TORRES.

Bolsa de Medellín, SA: Carrera 50, No 50-48, 2°, Apdo Aéreo 3535, Medellín, Antioquia; tel. (4) 260-3000; fax (4) 251-1981; e-mail info@medellin.impsat.net.co; f. 1961; Pres. CRISTIÁN TORO LUDEKE.

Bolsa de Occidente, SA: Calle 10, No 4-40, 13°, Apdo Aéreo 11718, Santiago de Cali; tel. (2) 889-8400; fax (2) 889-9435; e-mail bolsaocc@cali.cetcol.net.co; internet www.bolsadeoccidente.com.co; f. 1983; Pres. JOSÉ RICARDO CAICEDO PEÑA.

INSURANCE

Principal National Companies

ACE Seguros, SA: Calle 72, No 10-51, 6°, 7° y 8°, Apdo Aéreo 29782, Santafé de Bogotá, DC; tel. (1) 319-0300; fax (1) 319-0304; internet www.ace-ina.com; fmrly Cigna Seguros de Colombia, SA; Pres. ALVARO A. ROZO PALOU.

Aseguradora Colseguros, SA: Carrera 13A, No 29-24, Parque Central Bavaria, Apdo Aéreo 3537, Santafé de Bogotá, DC; tel. (1) 561-6392; fax (1) 561-6427; e-mail thiermoo@colseguros.com; internet www.colseguros.com; f. 1874; Pres. MAX THIERMANN.

Aseguradora El Libertador, SA: Carrera 13, No 26-45, 9°, Apdo Aéreo 10285, Santafé de Bogotá, DC; tel. (1) 281-2427; fax (1) 286-0662; e-mail aselib@impsat.net.co; Pres. FERNANDO ROJAS CÁRDENAS.

Aseguradora Solidaria de Colombia: Carrera 12, No 93-30, Apdo Aéreo 252030, Santafé de Bogotá, DC; tel. (1) 621-4330; fax (1) 621-4321; e-mail eguzman@solidaria.com.co; Pres. CARLOS GUZMÁN.

Chubb de Colombia Cía de Seguros, SA: Carrera 7A, No 71-52, Torre B, 10°, Apdo Aéreo 26931, Santafé de Bogotá, DC; tel. (1) 312-3700; fax (1) 312-2401; e-mail jvelandia@chubb.com.co; Pres. LUIS FERNANDO MATHIEU.

Cía Agrícola de Seguros, SA: Carrera 11, No 93-46, Apdo Aéreo 7212, Santafé de Bogotá, DC; tel. (1) 635-5827; fax (1) 635-5876; e-mail agricola@impsat.net.co; f. 1952; Pres. Dr JOSÉ F. JARAMILLO HOYOS.

Cía Aseguradora de Fianzas, SA (Confianza): Calle 82, No 11-37, 7°, Apdo Aéreo 056965, Santafé de Bogotá, DC; tel. (1) 617-0899; fax (1) 610-8866; e-mail ccorreos@confianza.com.co; internet www.confianza.com.co; Pres. RODRIGO JARAMILLO ARANGO.

Cía Central de Seguros, SA: Carrera 7A, No 76-07, 9°, Apdo Aéreo 5764, Santafé de Bogotá, DC; tel. (1) 319-0700; fax (1) 640-5553; e-mail recursos@centralseguros.com.co; internet www.centralseguros.com.co; f. 1956; Pres. SYLVIA LUZ RINCÓN LEMA.

Cía de Seguros Atlas, SA: Calle 21, No 23-22, 3°-11°, Apdo Aéreo 413, Manizales, Caldas; tel. (68) 84-1500; fax (168) 84-1447; e-mail satlas@andi.org.co; internet www.andi.org.co/seguros_atlas.htm; Pres. JORGE HOYOS MAYA.

Cía de Seguros Bolívar, SA: Carrera 10A, No 16-39, Apdo Aéreo 4421, Santafé de Bogotá, DC; tel. (1) 341-0077; fax (1) 281-8262; e-mail maria.cristina.zuluga@bolnet.com.co; f. 1939; Pres. JORGE E. URIBE MONTAÑO.

Cía de Seguros Colmena, SA: Calle 72, No 10-07, 7° y 8°, Apdo Aéreo 6774, Santafé de Bogotá, DC; tel. (1) 211-9111; fax (1) 211-4952; e-mail juand@colmena-seguros.com.co; Pres. JUAN MANUEL DÍAZ-GRANADOS.

Cía de Seguros Generales Aurora, SA: Edif. Seguros Aurora, 1°, 2° y 3°, Carrera 7, No 74-21, Apdo Aéreo 8006, Santafé de Bogotá, DC; tel. (1) 212-2800; fax (1) 212-2138; e-mail aurosis@colmsat.net.co; Pres. GERMÁN ESPINOSA.

Cía Mundial de Seguros, SA: Calle 33, No 6-94, 2° y 3°, Santafé de Bogotá, DC; tel. (1) 285-5600; fax (1) 285-1220; e-mail mundial@impsat.net.co; Dir-Gen. CAMILO FERNÁNDEZ ESCOVAR.

Cía Suramericana de Seguros, SA: Centro Suramericana, Carrera 64B, No 49A-30, Apdo Aéreo 780, Medellín, Antioquia; tel. (4) 260-2100; fax (4) 260-3194; e-mail contactenos@suramericana.com.co; internet www.suramericana.com.co; f. 1944; Pres. Dr NICANOR RESTREPO SANTAMARÍA.

Condor SA, Cía de Seguros Generales: Calle 119, No 16-59, Apdo Aéreo 57018, Santafé de Bogotá, DC; tel. (1) 612-0666; fax (1) 215-6121; Pres. EUDORO CARVAJAL IBÁÑEZ.

Generali Colombia—Seguros Generales, SA: Carrera 7A, No 72-13, 1°, 7° y 8°, Apdo Aéreo 076478, Santafé de Bogotá, DC; tel. (1) 217-8411; fax (1) 255-1164; Pres. MARCO PAPINI.

La Ganadera Cía de Seguros, SA: Carrera 7, No 71-52, Torre B, 11°, Apdo Aéreo 052347, Santafé de Bogotá, DC; tel. (1) 312-2630; fax (1) 312-2599; e-mail ganadera@impsat.net.co; internet www.laganadera.com.co; Pres. CARLOS VERGARA GÓMEZ.

La Interamericana Cía de Seguros Generales, SA: Calle 78, No 9-57, 4° y 5°, Apdo Aéreo 92381, Santafé de Bogotá, DC; tel. (1) 210-2200; fax (1) 210-2021; e-mail interb1@ibm.net; Pres. DIDIER SERRANO.

La Previsora, SA, Cía de Seguros: Calle 57, No 8-93, Apdo Aéreo 52946, Santafé de Bogotá, DC; tel. (1) 211-2880; fax (1) 211-8717; e-mail previpr@andinet.com; Pres. ALVARO ESCALLÓN EMILIANI.

Liberty Seguros, SA: Calle 71A, No 6-30, 2°, 3°, 4° y 14°, Apdo Aéreo 100327, Santafé de Bogotá, DC; tel. (1) 212-4900; fax (1) 212-7706; e-mail lhernandez@impsat.net.co; f. 1954; fmrly Latinoamericana de Seguros, SA; Pres. MAURICIO GARCÍA ORTIZ.

Mapfre Seguros Generales de Colombia, SA: Carrera 7A, No 74-36, 2°, Apdo Aéreo 28525, Santafé de Bogotá, DC; tel. (1) 346-8702; fax (1) 346-8793; e-mail jmincha@mapfre.com.co; Pres. JOSÉ MANUEL INCHAUSTI.

Pan American de Colombia Cía de Seguros de Vida, SA: Carrera 7A, No 75-09, Apdo Aéreo 76000, Santafé de Bogotá, DC; tel. (1) 212-1300; fax (1) 217-8799; e-mail aponton@reymoreno.net.co; Pres. ALFONSO PONTÓN.

Real Seguros, SA: Carrera 7A, No 115-33, 10°, Apdo Aéreo 7412, Santafé de Bogotá, DC; tel. (1) 523-1400; fax (1) 523-4010; e-mail realseg@colomsat.net.co; Gen. Man. José Luiz Tomazini.

Royal and Sun Alliance Seguros (Colombia), SA: Carrera 7A, No 32-33, 6°, 7°, 11° y 12°, Santafé de Bogotá, DC; tel. (1) 561-0380; fax (1) 320-3726; e-mail meradeo@royal-sunalliance-col.com; internet www.royal-sunalliance-col.com; fmrly Seguros Fénix, SA; Pres. Dinand Blom.

Segurexpo de Colombia, SA: Calle 72, No 6-44, 12°, Apdo Aéreo 75140, Santafé de Bogotá, DC; tel. (1) 217-0900; fax (1) 211-0218; e-mail segurexp@col1.telecom.co; Pres. Juan Pablo Luque Luque.

Seguros Alfa, SA: Carrera 13, No 27-47, 22° y 23°, Apdo Aéreo 27718, Santafé de Bogotá, DC; tel. (1) 344-4720; fax (1) 344-6770; e-mail sistemas@andinet.lat.net; Pres. Jesús Hernando Gómez.

Seguros Colpatria, SA: Carrera 7A, No 24-89, 9°, Apdo Aéreo 7762, Santafé de Bogotá, DC; tel. (1) 616-6655; fax (1) 281-5053; e-mail capicolc@openway.com.co; Pres. Dr Fernando Quintero.

Seguros La Equidad, OC: Calle 19, No 6-68, 10°, 11° y 12°, Apdo Aéreo 30261, Santafé de Bogotá, DC; tel. (1) 284-1910; fax (1) 286-5124; e-mail equidad@colomsat.net.co; Pres. Dr Julio Enrique Medrano León.

Seguros del Estado, SA: Carrera 11, No 90-20, Apdo Aéreo 6810, Santafé de Bogotá, DC; tel. (1) 218-6977; fax (1) 218-0971; e-mail seguros2@latino.net.co; Pres. Dr Jorge Mora Sánchez.

Skandia Seguros de Vida, SA: Avda 19, No 113-30, Apdo Aéreo 100327, Santafé de Bogotá, DC; tel. (1) 214-1200; fax (1) 214-0038; Pres. Rafael Jaramillo Samper.

Insurance Association

Federación de Aseguradores Colombianos (FASECOLDA): Carrera 7A, No 26-20, 11° y 12°, Apdo Aéreo 5233, Santafé de Bogotá, DC; tel. (1) 210-8080; fax (1) 210-7090; e-mail fasecolda@fasecolda .com; internet www.fasecolda.com; f. 1976; 33 mems; Pres. Dr William R. Fadul Vergara.

Trade and Industry

GOVERNMENT AGENCIES

Departamento Nacional de Planeación: Calle 26, No 13-19, 14°, Santafé de Bogotá, DC; tel. (1) 336-1600; fax (1) 281-3348; f. 1958; supervises and administers devt projects; approves foreign investments; Dir José Antonio Ocampo Gaviria.

Instituto Colombiano de Comercio Exterior (INCOMEX): Calle 28, No 13A-15, 5°, Apdo Aéreo 240193, Santafé de Bogotá, DC; tel. (1) 283-3284; fax (1) 281-2560; sets and executes foreign trade policy; Dir. María Uriza Pardo.

Instituto Colombiano de la Reforma Agraria (INCORA): Centro Administrativo Nacional (CAN), Avda El Dorado, Apdo Aéreo 151046, Santafé de Bogotá, DC; tel. (1) 222-0963; f. 1962; a public institution which, on behalf of the govt, administers public lands and those it acquires; reclaims land by irrigation and drainage facilities, roads, etc. to increase productivity in agriculture and stock-breeding; provides technical assistance and loans; supervises the distribution of land throughout the country; Dir Germán Bula E.

Superintendencia de Industria y Comercio (SUPERINDUSTRIA): Carrera 13, No 27-00, 5°, Santafé de Bogotá, DC; tel. (1) 234-2035; fax (1) 281-3125; supervises chambers of commerce; controls standards and prices; Supt Marco Aurelio Zuluaga Giraldo.

Superintendencia de Sociedades (SUPERSOCIEDADES): Avda El Dorado, No 46-80, Apdo Aéreo 4188, Santafé de Bogotá, DC; tel. (1) 222-0566; fax (1) 221-1027; e-mail supersoc1@sinpro.gov.co; f. 1931; oversees activities of local and foreign corpns; Supt Darío Laguado Monsalve.

DEVELOPMENT ORGANIZATIONS

Fondo Nacional de Proyectos de Desarrollo (FONADE): Calle 26, No 13-19, 19°-22°, Apdo Aéreo 24110, Santafé de Bogotá, DC; tel. (1) 594-0407; fax (1) 282-6018; e-mail fonade@colomsat.net.co; f. 1968; responsible for channelling loans towards economic devt projects; administered by a committee under the head of the Departamento Nacional de Planeación; FONADE works in close association with other official planning orgs; Gen. Man. Dr Agustín Mejía Jaramillo.

Fundación para el Desarrollo Integral del Valle del Cauca (FDI): Calle 8, No 3-14, 17°, Apdo Aéreo 7482, Cali, Valle del Cauca; tel. (2) 80-6660; fax (2) 82-4627; f. 1969; industrial devt org. Pres. Gunnar Lindahl Hellberg; Exec. Pres. Fabio Rodríguez González.

CHAMBERS OF COMMERCE

Confederación Colombiana de Cámaras de Comercio (CONFECAMARAS): Carrera 13, No 27-47, Of. 502, Apdo Aéreo 29750, Santafé de Bogotá, DC; tel. (1) 288-1200; fax (1) 288-4228; e-mail confecamaras@inter.net.co; internet www.confecamaras.org.co; f. 1969; 56 mem. orgs; Exec. Pres. Eugenio Marulanda Gómez.

Cámara de Comercio de Bogotá: Carrera 9A, No 16-21, Santafé de Bogotá, DC; tel. (1) 334-7900; fax (1) 284-8506; internet www.ccb .org.co; f. 1878; 3,650 mem. orgs; Dir Ariel Jaramillo Jaramillo; Exec.-Pres. Guillermo Fernández de Soto.

There are also local Chambers of Commerce in the capital towns of all the Departments and in many of the other trading centres.

INDUSTRIAL AND TRADE ASSOCIATIONS

Colombiana de Minería (COLMINAS): Santafé de Bogotá, DC; state mining concern; Man. Alfonso Rodríguez Kilber.

Corporación de la Industria Aeronáutica Colombiana, SA (CIAC SA): Aeropuerto Internacional El Dorado, Entrada 1 y 2, Apdo Aéreo 14446, Santafé de Bogotá, DC; tel. (1) 413-9735; fax (1) 413-8673; Gen. Man. Alberto Meléndez.

Empresa Colombia de Niquel (ECONIQUEL): Santafé de Bogotá, DC; tel. (1) 232-3839; administers state nickel resources; Dir Javier Restrepo Toro.

Empresa Colombiana de Uranio (COLURANIO): Centro Administrativo Nacional (CAN), 4°, Ministerio de Minas y Energía, Santafé de Bogotá, DC; tel. (1) 244-5440; f. 1977 to further the exploration, processing and marketing of radio-active minerals; initial cap. US $750,000; Dir Jaime García.

Empresa de Comercialización de Productos Perecederos (EMCOPER): Santafé de Bogotá, DC; tel. (1) 235-5507; attached to Ministry of Agriculture; Dir Luis Fernando Londoño Ruiz.

Industria Militar (INDUMIL): Diagonal 40, No 47-75, Apdo Aéreo 7272, Santafé de Bogotá, DC; tel. (1) 222-3001; fax (1) 222-4889; attached to Ministry of National Defence; Man. Adm. (retd) Manuel F. Avendaño.

Instituto Colombiano Agropecuario (ICA): Calle 37, No 8-43, 4° y 5°, Santafé de Bogotá, DC; tel. (1) 285-5520; fax (1) 232-4689; e-mail comunicaciones@ica.gov.co; internet www.ica.gov.co; f. 1962; institute for promotion, co-ordination and implementation of research into and teaching and devt of agriculture and animal husbandry; Dir Dr Alvaro Abisambra Abisambra.

Instituto de Fomento Industrial (IFI): Calle 16, No 6-66, Edif. Avianca, 7°-15°, Apdo Aéreo 4222, Santafé de Bogotá, DC; tel. (1) 336-0377; fax (1) 286-4166; f. 1940; state finance corpn for enterprise devt; cap. 469,808m. pesos, total assets 2,246,480m. pesos (Dec. 1998); Pres. Enrique Camacho Matamoros.

Instituto de Hidrología, Meteorología y Estudios Ambientales (IDEAM): Diagonal 97, No 17-60, 1°, 2°, 3° y 7°, Santafé de Bogotá, DC; tel. (1) 283-6927; fax (1) 635-6218; f. 1995; responsible for irrigation, flood control, drainage, hydrology and meteorology; Dir Pablo Leyva.

Instituto de Investigaciones en Geociencias, Minería y Química (INGEOMINAS): Diagonal 53, No 34-53, Apdo Aéreo 4865, Santafé de Bogotá, DC; tel. (1) 222-1811; fax (1) 222-3597; f. 1968; responsible for mineral research, geological mapping and research including hydrogeology, remote sensing, geochemistry and geophysics; Dir Dr Adolfo Alarcón Guzmán.

Instituto de Mercadeo Agropecuario (IDEMA): Carrera 10A, No 16-82, Of. 1006, Santafé de Bogotá, DC; tel. (1) 342-2596; fax (1) 283-1838; state enterprise for the marketing of agricultural products; Dir-Gen. Enrique Carlos Ruiz Raad.

Instituto Nacional de Fomento Municipal (INSFOPAL): Centro Administrativo Nacional (CAN), Avda El Dorado, Santafé de Bogotá, DC; tel. (1) 222-3177; Gen. Man. Jaime Mario Salazar Velásquez.

Instituto Nacional de los Recursos Naturales Renovables y del Ambiente (INDERENA): Diagonal 34, No 5-18, 3°, Santafé de Bogotá, DC; tel. (1) 285-4417; f. 1968; govt agency regulating the devt of natural resources.

Minerales de Colombia, SA (MINERALCO): Calle 32, No 13-07, Apdo Aéreo 17878, Santafé de Bogotá, DC; tel. (1) 287-7136; fax (1) 87-4606; administers state resources of emerald, copper, gold, sulphur, gypsum, phosphate rock and other minerals except coal, petroleum and uranium; Gen. Man. Orlando Alvarez Pérez.

Sociedad Minera del Guainía (SMG): Santafé de Bogotá, DC; f. 1987; state enterprise for exploration, mining and marketing of gold; Pres. Dr Jorge Bendeck Olivella.

There are several other agricultural and regional development organizations.

EMPLOYERS' AND PRODUCERS' ORGANIZATIONS

Asociación Colombiana Popular de Industriales (ACOPI): Carrera 23, No 41-94, Apdo Aéreo 16451, Santafé de Bogotá, DC; tel. (1) 244-2741; fax (1) 268-8965; f. 1951; asscn of small industrialists; Pres. JUAN A. PINTO SAAVEDRA; Man. MIGUEL CARRILLO M.

Asociación de Cultivadores de Caña de Azúcar de Colombia (ASOCAÑA): Calle 58N, No 3N-15, Apdo Aéreo 4448, Cali, Valle del Cauca; tel. (2) 64-7902; fax (2) 64-5888; f. 1959; sugar planters' asscn; Pres. Dr RICARDO VILLAVECES PARDO.

Asociación Nacional de Exportadores (ANALDEX): Carrera 10, No 27, Int. 137, Of. 902, Apdo Aéreo 29812, Santafé de Bogotá, DC; tel. (1) 342-0788; fax (1) 284-6911; exporters' asscn; Pres. JORGE RAMÍREZ OCAMPO.

Asociación Nacional de Exportadores de Café de Colombia: Calle 72, No 10-07, Of. 1101, Santafé de Bogotá, DC; tel. (1) 347-8419; fax (1) 347-9523; e-mail asoexp@cable.net.co; internet www.asoexport.org; f. 1938; private asscn of coffee exporters; Pres. JORGE E. LOZANO MANCERA.

Asociación Nacional de Industriales (ANDI) (National Asscn of Manufacturers): Calle 52, No 47-48, Apdo Aéreo 997, Medellín, Antioquia; tel. (4) 511-1177; fax (4) 511-7575; e-mail comercial@andi.com.co; internet www.andi.com.co; f. 1944; Pres. LUIS CARLOS VILLEGAS ECHEVERRI; 9 brs; 756 mems.

Expocafé Ltda: Edif. Seguros Caribe, Carrera 7A, No 74-36, 3°, Apdo Aéreo 41244, Santafé de Bogotá, DC; tel. (1) 217-8900; fax (1) 217-3554; f. 1985; coffee exporting org. Gen. Man. LUIS JOSÉ ALVAREZ L.

Federación Colombiana de Ganaderos (FEDEGAN): Carrera 14, No 36-65, Apdo Aéreo 9709, Santafé de Bogotá, DC; tel. (1) 245-3041; fax (1) 232-7153; e-mail fedegan@fedegan.org.co; internet www.fedegan.org.co; f. 1963; cattle raisers' asscn; about 350,000 affiliates; Pres. JORGE VISBAL MARTELO.

Federación Nacional de Cacaoteros: Carrera 17, No 30-39, Apdo Aéreo 17736, Santafé de Bogotá, DC; tel. (1) 288-7188; fax (1) 288-4424; e-mail f_cacaoteros@hotmail.com; fed. of cocoa growers; Gen. Man. Dr JOSÉ OMAR PINZÓN USECHE.

Federación Nacional de Cafeteros de Colombia (National Federation of Coffee Growers): Calle 73, No 8-13, Apdo Aéreo 57534, Santafé de Bogotá, DC; tel. (1) 345-6600; fax (1) 217-1021; f. 1927; totally responsible for fostering and regulating the coffee economy; Gen. Man. JORGE CÁRDENAS GUTIÉRREZ; 203,000 mems.

Federación Nacional de Cultivadores de Cereales y Leguminosas (FENALCE): Carrera 14, No 97-62, Apdo Aéreo 8694, Santafé de Bogotá, DC; tel. (1) 218-2114; fax (1) 218-9463; e-mail fenalce@cable.net.co; f. 1960; fed. of grain growers; Gen. Man. JOSÉ ADEL CANCELADO PERRY; 30,000 mems.

Federación Nacional de Comerciantes (FENALCO): Carrera 4, No 19-85, 7°, Santafé de Bogotá, DC; tel. (1) 350-0600; fax (1) 350-9424; fed. of businessmen; Pres. SABAS PRETELT DE LA VEGA.

Sociedad de Agricultores de Colombia (SAC) (Colombian Farmers' Society): Carrera 7A, No 24-89, 44°, Apdo Aéreo 3638, Santafé de Bogotá, DC; tel. (1) 281-0263; fax (1) 284-4572; e-mail socdeagr@impsat.net.co; f. 1871; Pres. JUAN MANUEL OSPINA RESTREPO; Sec.-Gen. Dr GABRIEL MARTÍNEZ TELÁEZ.

There are several other organizations, including those for rice growers, engineers and financiers.

UTILITIES

Electricity

Corporación Eléctrica de la Costa Atlántica (Corelca): Calle 55, No 72-109, 9°, Barranquilla, Atlántico; tel. (5) 356-0200; fax (5) 356-2370; responsible for supplying electricity to the Atlantic departments; generates more than 2,000m. kWh annually from thermal power-stations; Man. Dir HERNÁN CORREA NOGUERA.

Empresa de Energía Eléctrica de Bogotá, SA (EEB): Avda El Dorado, No 55-51, Santafé de Bogotá, DC; tel. (1) 221-1665; fax (1) 221-6858; internet www.eeb.com.co; provides electricity for Bogotá area by generating capacity of 680 MW, mainly hydroelectric; Man. Dir PAULO OROZCO DÍAS.

Instituto Colombiano de Energía Eléctrica (ICEL): Carrera 13, No 27-00, 3°, Apdo Aéreo 16243, Santafé de Bogotá, DC; tel. (1) 342-0181; fax (1) 286-2934; formulates policy for the devt of electrical energy; constructs systems for the generation, transmission and distribution of electrical energy; Man. DOUGLAS VELÁSQUEZ JACOME; Sec.-Gen. PATRICIA OLIVEROS LAVERDE.

Interconexión Eléctrica, SA (ISA): Calle 12 Sur, No 18-168, Apdo Aéreo 8915, Medellín, Antioquia; tel. (4) 317-1331; fax (4) 823-970; e-mail isa@isa.com.co; internet www.isa.com.co; f. 1967; created by Colombia's principal electricity production and distribution cos to

form a national network; installed capacity of 2,641m. kWh; operates major power-stations at Chivor and San Carlos; scheduled for privatization; Man. Dir JAVIER GUTIÉRREZ.

Isagen: Medellín, Antioquia; e-mail isagen@isagen.com.co; internet www.isagen.com.co; state-owned, scheduled for privatization; generates electricity from three hydraulic and two thermal power plants.

Gas

Gas Natural ESP: Avda 40A, No 13-09, 9°, Santafé de Bogotá, DC; tel. (1) 338-1199; fax (1) 288-0807; f. 1987; private gas corpn; Pres. ANTONI PERIS MINGOT.

Gasoriente: distributes gas to 8 municipalities in north-eastern Colombia.

TRADE UNIONS

According to official figures, an estimated 900 of Colombia's 2,000 trade unions are independent.

Central Unitaria de Trabajadores (CUT): Calle 35, No 7-25, 9°, Apdo Aéreo 221, Santafé de Bogotá, DC; tel. (1) 323-7550; fax (1) 323-7550; f. 1986; comprises 50 feds and 80% of all trade union members; Pres. CARLOS RODRÍGUEZ DÍAZ; Sec.-Gen. BORIS MONTES DE OCA.

Frente Sindical Democrática (FSD): f. 1984; centre-right trade union alliance; comprises:

Confederación de Trabajadores de Colombia (CTC) (Colombian Confederation of Workers): Calle 39, No 26A-23, 5°, Apdo Aéreo 4780, Santafé de Bogotá, DC; tel. (1) 269-7119; f. 1934; mainly Liberal; 600 affiliates, including 6 national orgs and 20 regional feds; admitted to ICFTU; Pres. ALVIS FERNÁNDEZ; 400,000 mems.

Confederación de Trabajadores Democráticos de Colombia (CTDC): Carrera 13, No 59-52, Of. 303, Santafé de Bogotá, DC; tel. (1) 255-3146; fax (1) 484-581; f. 1988; comprises 23 industrial feds and 22 national unions; Pres. MARIO DE J. VALDERRAMA.

Confederación General de Trabajadores Democráticos (CGTD): Calle 39A, No 14-48, Apdo Aéreo 5415, Santafé de Bogotá, DC; tel. (1) 288-1560; fax (1) 288-1504; Christian Democrat; Sec.-Gen. JULIO ROBERTO GÓMEZ ESGUERRA.

Transport

Land transport in Colombia is rendered difficult by high mountains, so the principal means of long-distance transport is by air. As a result of the development of the El Cerrejón coal field, Colombia's first deep-water port was constructed at Bahía de Portete and a 150 km rail link between El Cerrejón and the port became operational in 1989.

Instituto Nacional del Transporte (INTRA): Edif. Minobras (CAN), 6°, Apdo Aéreo 24990, Santafé de Bogotá, DC; tel. (1) 222-4100; govt body; Dir Dr GUILLERMO ANZOLA LIZARAZO.

RAILWAYS

In 2000 there were 3,304 km of track.

Dirección General de Transporte Férreo y Masivo: Ministerio de Transporte, Centro Administrativo Nacional (CAN), Avda El Dorado, Santafé de Bogotá, DC; e-mail dgtuf@mintransporte.gov.co; internet www.mintransporte.gov.co/Ministerio/DGTFM/dgtferreo/html; part of the Ministry of Transport; formulates railway transport policies; Dir JUAN GONZALO JARAMILLO.

Empresa Colombiana de Vías Férreas (Ferrovías): Calle 16, No 96-64, 8°, Santafé de Bogotá, DC; tel. (1) 287-9888; fax (1) 287-2515; responsible for the maintenance and devt of the national rail network; Dir JUAN GONZALO JARAMILLO.

Ferroviario Atlántico, SA: Calle 72, No 13-23, 2°, Santafé de Bogotá, DC; tel. (1) 255-8684; fax (1) 255-8704; links port of Santa Marta with Santafé de Bogotá, DC; operated on a 30-year concession, awarded in 1998 to Asociación Futura Ferrocarriles de la Paz (Fepaz); 1,490 km (1993).

Fondo de Pasivo Social de Ferrocarriles Nacionales de Colombia: Santafé de Bogotá, DC; administers welfare services for existing and former employees of the FNC.

El Cerrejón Mine Railway: International Colombia Resources Corpn, Carrera 54, No 72-80, Apdo Aéreo 52499, Barranquilla, Atlántico; tel. (5) 350-5389; fax (5) 350-2249; f. 1989 to link the mine and the port at Bahía de Portete; 150 km (1996); Supt M. MENDOZA.

Metro de Medellín Ltda: Calle 44, No 46-001, Apdo Aéreo 9128, Medellín, Antioquia; tel. (4) 452-6000; fax (4) 452-4450; e-mail emetro@col3.telecom.com.co; two-line metro with 25 stations opened in stages in 1995–96; 29 km; Gen. Man. Luis Guillermo Gómez A.

Sociedad de Transporte Férreo de Occidente, SA: Avda Vásquez Cobo, Estación Ferrocarril, 2°, Cali; tel. (2) 660-3314; fax (2) 660-3320; runs freight services between Cali and the port of Buenaventura; Gen. Man. R. A. Guzman.

ROADS

In 1999 there were 112,988 km of roads, of which 16,575 km were highways and main roads and 70,483 km were secondary roads. About 14% of the total road network was paved in the same year. The country's main highways are the Caribbean Trunk Highway, the Eastern and Western Trunk Highways, the Central Trunk Highway and there are also roads into the interior. There are plans to construct a Jungle Edge highway to give access to the interior, a link road between Turbo, Bahía Solano and Medellín, a highway between Bogotá and Villavicencio and to complete the short section of the Pan-American highway between Panama and Colombia.

There are a number of national bus companies and road haulage companies.

Dirección General de Carreteras: Ministerio de Transporte, Centro Administrativo Nacional (CAN), Of. 508, Avda El Dorado, Santafé de Bogotá, DC; tel. (1) 222-7308; fax (2) 428-6749; e-mail dcarreteras@mintransporte.gov.co; internet www.mintransporte .gov.co/Ministerio/DGTCarreteras/; part of the Ministry of Transport; formulates road transport policies; Dir Manuel Arias Molano.

Instituto Nacional de Vías: Transversal 45, Entrada 2, Santafé de Bogotá, DC; tel. (1) 428-0400; fax (1) 315-6713; e-mail director@ latino.net.co; f. 1966; reorganized 1994; wholly state-owned; responsible to the Ministry of Transport; maintenance and construction of national road network; Gen. Man. Luis E. Tobon Cardona.

INLAND WATERWAYS

The Magdalena–Cauca river system is the centre of river traffic and is navigable for 1,500 km, while the Atrato is navigable for 687 km. The Orinoco system has more than five navigable rivers, which total more than 4,000 km of potential navigation (mainly through Venezuela); the Amazonas system has four main rivers, which total 3,000 navigable km (mainly through Brazil). There are plans to connect the Arauca with the Meta, and the Putumayo with the Amazon, and also to construct an Atrato–Truandó inter-oceanic canal.

Dirección General de Transporte Fluvial: Ministerio de Transporte, Centro Administrativo Nacional (CAN), Avda El Dorado, Santafé de Bogotá, DC; tel. (1) 428-7332; fax (2) 428-6233; e-mail omedina@mintransporte.gov.co; internet www.mintransporte.gov .co/Ministerio/DGTFLUVIAL/dgtfluvial.html; part of the Ministry of Transport; formulates river transport policies; Dir Luis Alejandro Espinosa Fierro.

Dirección de Navegación y Puertos: Edif. Minobras (CAN), Of. 562, Santafé de Bogotá, DC; tel. (1) 222-1248; responsible for river works and transport; the waterways system is divided into four sectors: Magdalena, Atrato, Orinoquia, and Amazonia; Dir Alberto Rodríguez Rojas.

SHIPPING

The four most important ocean terminals are Buenaventura on the Pacific coast and Santa Marta, Barranquilla and Cartagena on the Atlantic coast. The port of Tumaco on the Pacific coast is gaining in importance and there are plans for construction of a deep-water port at Bahía Solano.

In 2001 Colombia's merchant fleet totalled 65,645 grt.

Dirección General de Transporte Marítimo y Puertos: Ministerio de Transporte, Centro Administrativo Nacional (CAN), Avda El Dorado, Santafé de Bogotá, DC; tel. (1) 428-7332; fax (2) 428-6233; e-mail omedina@mintransporte.gov.co; internet www .mintransporte.gov.co/Ministerio/DGTMARITIMO/dgtmar.html; part of the Ministry of Transport; formulates shipping policies; Dir Oscar Humberto Medina Mora.

Port Authorities

Port of Barranquilla: Sociedad Portuaria Regional de Barranquilla, Carrera 38, Calle 1A, Barranquilla, Atlántico; tel. (5) 379-9555; fax (5) 379-9557; e-mail sprbbaq@latino.net.co; internet www .sprb.com.co; privatized in 1993; Port Man. Aníbal Dau.

Port of Buenaventura: Empresa Puertos de Colombia, Edif. El Café, Of. 1, Buenaventura; tel. (224) 22543; fax (224) 34447; Port Man. Víctor González.

Port of Cartagena: Sociedad Portuaria Regional de Cartagena, SA, Manga, Terminal Marítimo, Cartagena, Bolívar; tel. (5) 660-7781; fax (5) 650-2239; e-mail comercial@sprc.com.co; internet www.sprc

.com.co; f. 1959; Port Man. Alfonso Salas Trujillo; Harbour Master Capt. Gonzalo Parra.

Port of Santa Marta: Empresa Puertos de Colombia, Calle 15, No 3-25, 11°, Santa Marta, Magdalena; tel. (54) 210739; fax (54) 210711; e-mail spsm@spsm.com.co; internet www.spsm.com.co; Port Man. Julián Palacios.

Principal Shipping Companies

Colombiana Internacional de Vapores, Ltda (Colvapores): Avda Caracas, No 35-02, Apdo Aéreo 17227, Santafé de Bogotá, DC; cargo services mainly to the USA.

Flota Mercante Grancolombiana, SA: Edif. Grancolombiana, Carrera 13, No 27-75, Apdo Aéreo 4482, Santafé de Bogotá, DC; tel. (1) 286-0200; fax (1) 286-9028; f. 1946; owned by the Colombian Coffee Growers' Federation (80%) and Ecuador Development Bank (20%); f. 1946 one of Latin America's leading cargo carriers serving 45 countries world-wide; Pres. Luis Fernando Alarcón Mantilla.

Líneas Agromar, Ltda: Calle 73, Vía 40-350, Apdo Aéreo 3256, Barranquilla, Atlántico; tel. (5) 345-1874; fax (5) 345-9634; Pres. Manuel del Dago Fernández.

Petromar Ltda: Bosque, Diagonal 23, No 56-152, Apdo Aéreo 505, Cartagena, Bolívar; tel. (5) 662-7208; fax (5) 662-7592; Chair. Saverio Minervini S.

Transportadora Colombiana de Graneles, SA (NAVESCO, SA): Avda 19, No 118-95, Of. 214-301, Santafé de Bogotá, DC; tel. (1) 620-9035; fax (1) 620-8801; e-mail navesco@colomsat.net.co; Gen. Man. Guillermo Solano Varela.

Several foreign shipping lines call at Colombian ports.

CIVIL AVIATION

Colombia has more than 100 airports, including 11 international airports: Santafé de Bogotá, DC (El Dorado International Airport), Medellín, Cali, Barranquilla, Bucaramanga, Cartagena, Cúcuta, Leticia, Pereira, San Andrés and Santa Marta.

Dirección General de Transporte Aéreo: Ministerio de Transporte, Centro Administrativo Nacional (CAN), Of. 304, Avda El Dorado, Santafé de Bogotá, DC; tel. (1) 428-7397; fax (2) 428-7034; e-mail aereo@mintransporte.gov.co; internet www.mintransporte .gov.co/Ministerio/DGTAEREO/dgtaereo.html; part of the Ministry of Transport; formulates air transport policies; Dir Juan Carlos Salazar Gómez.

Airports Authority

Unidad Administrativa Especial de Aeronáutica Civil: Aeropuerto Internacional El Dorado, 4°, Santafé de Bogotá, DC; tel. (1) 413-9500; fax (1) 413-9878; f. 1967 as Departamento Administrativo de Aeronáutica Civil, reorganized 1993; wholly state-owned; Dir Ernesto Huertas Escacallón.

National Airlines

Aerolíneas Centrales de Colombia, SA (ACES): Calle 10, No 50C-75, Medellín; tel. (4) 360-5001; fax (4) 255-0630; e-mail gusuga@ acescolombia.com.co; internet www.acescolombia.com; f. 1971; operates scheduled domestic passenger services throughout Colombia, and charter and scheduled flights to the USA, the Andean region and the Caribbean; scheduled to merge with AVIANCA in 2002; Pres. Juan E. Posada.

Aerotaca, SA (Aerotransportes Casanare): Avda El Dorado, Entrada 1, Interior 20, Santafé de Bogotá, DC; tel. (1) 413-9884; fax (1) 413-5256; f. 1965; scheduled regional and domestic passenger services; Gen. Man. Rafael Urdaneta.

AVIANCA (Aerovías Nacionales de Colombia, SA): Avda El Dorado, No 93-30, 5°, Santafé de Bogotá, DC; tel. (1) 413-9511; fax (1) 413-8716; internet www.avianca.com; f. 1919; operates domestic services to all cities in Colombia and international services to the USA, France, Spain and throughout Central and Southern America; scheduled to merge with ACES in 2002; Chair. Andrés Obregón Santo Domingo; Pres. Vitys Didziulis.

Intercontinental de Aviación: Avda El Dorado, Entrada 2, Interior 6, Santafé de Bogotá, DC; tel. (1) 413-9700; fax (1) 413-8458; internet www.insite-network.com/inter; f. 1965 as Aeropesca Colombia (Aerovías de Pesca y Colonización del Suroeste Colombiano); operates scheduled domestic, regional and international passenger and cargo services; Pres. Capt. Luis Hernández Zia.

Servicio de Aeronavegación a Territorios Nacionales (Satena): Avda El Dorado, Entrada 1, Interior 11, Apdo Aéreo 11163, Santafé de Bogotá, DC; tel. (1) 413-7100; fax (1) 413-8178; internet www.satena.com; f. 1962; commercial enterprise attached to the Ministry of National Defence; internal services; CEO and Gen. Man. Maj.-Gen. Hector Campo.

Sociedad Aeronáutica de Medellín Consolidada, SA (SAM): Edif. SAM, Calle 53, No 45-211, 21°, Apdo Aéreo 1085, Medellín, Antioquia; tel. (4) 251-5544; fax (4) 251-0711; f. 1945; subsidiary of AVIANCA; internal services; and international cargo services to Central America and the Caribbean; Pres JULIO MARIO SANTO DOMINGO, GUSTAVO LENIS.

Transportes Aéreos Mercantiles Panamericanos (Tampa): Carrera 76, No 34A-61, Apdo Aéreo 494, Medellín, Antioquia; tel. (4) 439-7977; fax (4) 409-9211; e-mail Amartinez@tampacargo.com; internet www.tampacargo.com.co; f. 1973; operates international cargo services to destinations throughout South America, also to Puerto Rico and the USA; Pres. FREDERICK JACOBSEN.

In addition, the following airlines operate international and domestic charter cargo services: Aerosucre Colombia, Aero Transcolombiana de Carga (ATC), Aires Colombia, and Líneas Aéreas Suramericanas (LAS).

Tourism

The principal tourist attractions are the Caribbean coast (including the island of San Andrés), the 16th-century walled city of Cartagena, the Amazonian town of Leticia, the Andes mountains rising to 5,700 m above sea-level, the extensive forests and jungles, pre-Columbian relics and monuments of colonial art. In 2000 there were 557,300 visitors (compared with 546,000 in 1999), most of whom came from Venezuela, Ecuador and the USA. Tourism receipts in 2000 were estimated to be US $1,028m.

Viceministerio de Turismo: Calle 28, No 13A-15, 17°, Edif. Centro de Comercio Internacional, Santafé de Bogotá, DC; tel. (1) 283-9558; fax (1) 286-4492; Vice-Minister of Tourism MARÍA PAULINA ESPINOSA DE LÓPEZ.

Asociación Colombiana de Agencias de Viajes y Turismo—ANATO: Carrera 21, No 83-63/71, Santafé de Bogotá, DC; tel. (1) 610-7099; fax (1) 218-7103; e-mail presidencia@anato.com.co; internet www.anato.com.co; f. 1949; Pres. Dr OSCAR RUEDA GARCÍA.

THE COMOROS*

Introductory Survey

Location, Climate, Language, Religion, Flag, Capital

The Union of the Comoros (formerly the Federal Islamic Republic of the Comoros) is an archipelago in the Mozambique Channel, between the island of Madagascar and the east coast of the African mainland. The group comprises four main islands (Ngazidja, Nzwani and Mwali, formerly Grande-Comore, Anjouan and Mohéli respectively, and Mayotte) and numerous islets and coral reefs. The climate is tropical, with average temperatures ranging from 23°C (73.4°F) to 28°C (82.4°F). Average annual rainfall is between 1,500 mm (59 ins) and 5,000 mm (197 ins). The official languages are Comorian (a blend of Swahili and Arabic), French and Arabic. Islam is the state religion. The flag (proportions 2 by 3) has four equal horizontal stripes, of yellow, white, red and blue, with a green triangle at the hoist depicting a white crescent moon and a vertical row of four five-pointed white stars. The capital, which is situated on Ngazidja, is Moroni.

Recent History

Formerly attached to Madagascar, the Comoros became a separate French Overseas Territory in 1947. The islands achieved internal self-government in December 1961, with a Chamber of Deputies and a Government Council responsible for local administration.

Elections in December 1972 resulted in a large majority for parties advocating independence, and Ahmed Abdallah became President of the Government Council. In June 1973 he was restyled President of the Government. At a referendum in December 1974 96% of the voters expressed support for independence, despite the opposition of the Mayotte Party, which sought the status of a French Department for the island of Mayotte. On 6 July 1975, despite French insistence that any constitutional settlement should be ratified by all the islands voting separately, the Chamber of Deputies voted for immediate independence, elected Abdallah to be first President of the Comoros and reconstituted itself as the National Assembly. Although France made no attempt to intervene, it maintained control of Mayotte. Abdallah was deposed in August, and the National Assembly was abolished. A National Executive Council was established, with Prince Saïd Mohammed Jaffar, leader of the opposition party, the Front national uni, as its head, and Ali Soilih, leader of the coup, among its members. In November the Comoros was admitted to the UN, as a unified state comprising the whole archipelago. In December France officially recognized the independence of Ngazidja, Nzwani and Mwali, but all relations between France and the Comoros were effectively suspended. In February 1976 Mayotte voted overwhelmingly to retain its links with France.

In January 1976 Ali Soilih was elected Head of State, and adopted extended powers under the terms of a new Constitution. In May 1978 Soilih was killed, following a coup by a group of European mercenaries, led by a Frenchman, Bob Denard, on behalf of the exiled former President, Ahmed Abdallah, and the Comoros was proclaimed a Federal Islamic Republic. Shortly afterwards diplomatic relations with France were restored. In July the Comoran delegation was expelled from the Organization of African Unity (OAU, now the African Union, see p. 130) as a result of the continued presence of the mercenaries (but was readmitted in February 1979).

In October 1978 a new Constitution was approved in a referendum, on the three islands excluding Mayotte, by 99.3% of the votes cast. Abdallah was elected President in the same month, and in December elections for a new legislature, the Federal Assembly, took place. In January 1979 the Federal Assembly approved the formation of a one-party state (unofficial opposition groups, however, continued to exist). Ali Mroudjae, hith-

erto Minister of Foreign Affairs and Co-operation, was appointed Prime Minister in February 1982, and legislative elections took place in March. Constitutional amendments adopted in October vested additional powers in the President. In September 1984 Abdallah was re-elected President by 99.4% of the votes cast. Despite opposition appeals for a boycott of the election, 98% of the electorate participated. In January 1985, following further amendments to the Constitution, the position of Prime Minister was abolished, and Abdallah assumed the office of Head of Government.

In March 1985 an attempt by members of the presidential guard to overthrow Abdallah failed; in November 17 people, including Moustoifa Saïd Cheikh, the Secretary-General of the Front démocratique (FD), a banned opposition movement, were sentenced to forced labour for life for their involvement. In February 1987 Abdallah indicated that independent opposition candidates would be permitted to contest legislative elections scheduled for March. In the event, however, opposition candidates were only allowed to contest 20 seats on Ngazidja, where they received 35% of the total votes, and pro-Government candidates retained full control of the 42-seat Federal Assembly. There were allegations of widespread fraud and intimidation of opposition candidates. In November a further coup attempt by a left-wing group was suppressed.

In November 1989 a constitutional amendment permitting Abdallah to remain in office for a third six-year term was approved by 92.5% of votes cast in a popular referendum. The result of the referendum, however, was disputed by the President's opponents. Violent demonstrations followed, and opposition leaders were detained. On the night of 26–27 November Abdallah was assassinated by members of the presidential guard, under the command of Denard. The President of the Supreme Court, Saïd Mohamed Djohar, was appointed interim Head of State, pending a presidential election. However, Denard and his supporters defeated the regular army in a coup, in which 27 members of the security forces were reportedly killed. The mercenaries' action provoked international condemnation, despite denials by Denard of complicity in Abdallah's death. (In May 1999 Denard stood trial in Paris, France, in connection with the assassination. Both Denard and his co-defendant, Dominique Malacrino, were acquitted of the murder charge.) In mid-December Denard agreed to relinquish power and, following the arrival of French paratroops in Moroni, was transported to South Africa, together with the remaining mercenaries. Djohar subsequently announced that the French troops were to remain in the Comoros for up to two years in order to train local security forces.

At the end of December 1989 the main political groups formed a provisional Government of National Unity. An amnesty for all political prisoners was proclaimed, and an inquiry into the death of Abdallah was instigated. It was announced that a multi-candidate presidential election, which was to end the system of single-party rule, was to take place in January 1990. Following delays caused by alleged widespread irregularities and after an inconclusive first round held on 4 March, Djohar, the official candidate for the Union comorienne pour le progrès (Udzima), was elected President on 11 March, with 55.3% of the votes cast, defeating Mohamed Taki Abdulkarim, the leader of the Union nationale pour la démocratie aux Comores (UNDC). Djohar appointed a new Government, in which the eight political parties that had supported his presidential candidacy were represented. In April Djohar announced plans for the formal constitutional restoration of a multi-party political system.

In August 1990 an attempted coup was staged by armed rebels, who attacked various French installations on Ngazidja. The revolt was allegedly organized by a small group of European mercenaries, who intended to provoke Djohar's resignation through the enforced removal of French forces from the islands; supporters of Taki were also implicated in the conspiracy. In September the Minister of the Interior and Administrative Reforms was dismissed for his alleged involvement in the attempted coup. In October it was reported that the leader of the conspirators had been killed by Comoran security forces.

---

* Some of the information contained in this chapter refers to the whole Comoros archipelago, which the independent Comoran state claims as its national territory. However, the island of Mayotte (Mahoré) is, in fact, administered by France. Separate information on Mayotte may be found in the chapter on French Overseas Possessions.

In August 1991 the President of the Supreme Court, Ibrahim Ahmed Halidi, announced the dismissal of Djohar, on the grounds of negligence, and proclaimed himself interim President with the support of the Supreme Court. Opposition leaders declared the seizure of power to be legitimate under the terms of the Constitution. However, the Government condemned the coup attempt, and Halidi and several other members of the Supreme Court were arrested. A state of emergency was imposed, and remained in force until early September. A number of demonstrations in favour of Djohar took place in early August, although members of Udzima did not express support for the Government. Later that month the Government banned all public demonstrations.

In August 1991 Djohar established a new coalition Government, which included two members of the FD and, in an attempt to appease increasing discontent on Mwali, two members of the Mwalian opposition. However, the two leading political associations represented in the coalition Government, Udzima and the Parti comorien pour la démocratie et le progrès (PCDP), objected to the reshuffle, and shortly afterwards the ministers belonging to the two parties resigned. In November Udzima (which had been officially renamed Parti Udzima—Udzima) withdrew its support for Djohar and joined the opposition. Opposition leaders demanded the dissolution of the Federal Assembly, which was declared to be invalid on the grounds that it had been elected under the former one-party system. In the same month Mwali announced plans to conduct a referendum on self-determination for the island. Later in November agreement was reached between Djohar and the principal opposition leaders to initiate a process of national reconciliation, which would include the formation of a government of national unity and the convening of a constitutional conference. The accord also guaranteed the legitimacy of Djohar's election as President. In January 1992 a new transitional Government of National Unity was formed, under the leadership of Taki as its Co-ordinator, pending legislative elections.

In May 1992 opposition parties demanded the resignation of Djohar's son-in-law, Mohamed Saïd Abdallah M'Changama, as Minister of Finance, Commerce and Planning, following allegations of irregularities in the negotiation of government contracts. Djohar subsequently formed a new interim Council of Ministers, in which, however, M'Changama retained his portfolio. At a constitutional referendum, held on 7 June, reform proposals, which had been submitted in April, were approved by 74.3% of the votes cast, despite opposition from eight parties, notably Udzima and the FD. The new Constitution limited the presidential tenure to a maximum of two five-year terms of office and provided for a bicameral legislature, comprising a Federal Assembly, elected for a term of four years, and a 15-member Senate, selected for a six-year term by the regional Councils. In early July Djohar dismissed Taki, following the latter's appointment of a former mercenary to a financial advisory post in the Government. Later that month Djohar formed a new Government, although the post of Co-ordinator remained vacant.

In mid-1992 social and economic conditions on the Comoros deteriorated, following renewed strikes in a number of sectors. In September Djohar announced that legislative elections were to commence in the following month. Also in September an abortive coup attempt was staged by disaffected members of the armed forces, who seized the radio station at Moroni and announced that the Government had been overthrown. Six opposition leaders and six members of the armed forces, including two sons of the former President, Ahmed Abdallah, were subsequently charged with involvement in the attempted coup. In October some 100 rebel troops, led by a former member of Abdallah's presidential guard, attacked the military garrison of Kandani, in an attempt to release the detainees. Government forces attacked the rebels at Mbeni, to the north-east of Moroni; fighting was also reported on Nzwani. Later in October a demonstration was staged in protest at the French Government's support of Djohar. By the end of that month some 25 people had been killed in clashes between rebels and government forces in Moroni.

In October 1992 Djohar agreed to reschedule the legislative elections for late November, although opposition parties demanded a further postponement, and Udzima and the UNDC advocated a boycott. The first round of the legislative elections, which took place on 22 November, was contested by some 320 candidates representing 21 political parties. Numerous electoral irregularities and violent incidents were reported, however, and several opposition parties demanded that the results be declared invalid and joined the boycott. Election results in six constituencies were subsequently annulled, while the second round of voting on 29 November took place in only 34 of the 42 constituencies. Following partial elections on 13 and 30 December, reports indicated that candidates supporting Djohar —including seven members of the Union des démocrates pour la démocratie (UDD), a pro-Government organization based on Nzwani—had secured a narrow majority in the Federal Assembly. The leader of the UDD, Ibrahim Abdérémane Halidi, was appointed Prime Minister on 1 January 1993 and formed a new Council of Ministers. Later in January a Mwalian, Amir Attoumane, was elected as Speaker of the Federal Assembly, in response to demands by Mwalian deputies. Shortly after the new Government took office, however, disagreement between Djohar and Halidi was reported, while the presidential majority in the Federal Assembly fragmented into three dissenting factions.

In April 1993 nine people, including Abdallah's sons and two prominent members of Udzima, were convicted on charges of involvement in the coup attempt of September 1992 and sentenced to death. Following considerable domestic and international pressure, however, Djohar commuted the sentences to terms of imprisonment. In May 1993 eight supporters of M'Changama, allied with a number of opposition deputies, proposed a motion of 'no confidence' in the Government (apparently with the tacit support of Djohar), which was approved by 23 of the 42 deputies. Shortly afterwards, Djohar appointed an associate of M'Changama, Saïd Ali Mohamed, as Prime Minister, and a new Council of Ministers was formed. In June an alliance of pro-Halidi deputies proposed a motion of censure against the new Government, on the grounds that the Prime Minister had not been appointed from a party that commanded a majority in the Federal Assembly. Djohar, however, declared the motion to be unconstitutional and, in view of the continued absence of a viable parliamentary majority, dissolved the Federal Assembly and announced legislative elections. He subsequently dismissed Mohamed and appointed a former presidential adviser, Ahmed Ben Cheikh Attoumane, as Prime Minister. Shortly afterwards an interim Council of Ministers was formed (although two of the newly appointed ministers immediately resigned).

Following the dissolution of the Federal Assembly, opposition parties declared Djohar unfit to hold office, in view of the increasing political confusion, and demanded that legislative elections take place within the period of 40 days stipulated in the Constitution. In July 1993, however, Djohar announced that the legislative elections (which were to take place concurrently with local elections) were to be postponed until October. In response, opposition parties organized a one-day strike, in support of demands that Djohar bring forward the date of the legislative elections or resign. In September a number of opposition movements, notably Udzima and the UNDC, established an informal electoral alliance, known as the Union pour la République et le progrès, while the FD, the PCDP, CHUMA (Islands' Fraternity and Unity Party) and the Mouvement pour la démocratie et le progrès (MDP) agreed to present joint candidates. Later in September Djohar postponed the legislative elections until November, officially on financial grounds. In October Djohar (who had failed to induce the political parties that supported him to form an electoral alliance, owing to their hostility towards M'Changama) established a political organization, the Rassemblement pour la démocratie et le renouveau (RDR), principally comprising supporters of M'Changama and several prominent members of the Government. In November the legislative elections were rescheduled for December, while the local elections were postponed indefinitely. Later in November Djohar reorganized the Council of Ministers and established a new National Electoral Commission (NEC), in response to opposition demands.

At the first round of the legislative elections, which took place on 12 December 1993, four opposition candidates secured seats in the Federal Assembly, apparently prompting concern in the Government. Following a second round of voting on 20 December, it was reported that three people had been killed in violent incidents in Nzwani, where the authorities had assumed control of the electoral process. The NEC subsequently declared the results in several constituencies to be invalid. Opposition candidates refused to participate in further elections in these constituencies, on the grounds that voting was again to be conducted under the supervision of the authorities, rather than that of the NEC; RDR candidates consequently won all 10 contested seats, and 22 seats overall, thereby securing a narrow majority in the Federal Assembly. In January 1994 Djohar appointed the Secretary-General of the RDR, Mohamed Abdou Madi, as Prime Minister. The new Council of Ministers included several supporters of M'Changama, who was elected Speaker of the Federal Assembly. Later in January 12 principal opposition parties, which claimed that the RDR had assumed power illegally, formed a new alliance, the Forum pour le redressement national (FRN).

In May 1994 teachers (and later health workers) initiated strike action in support of demands for an increase in salaries and the reorganization of the public sector. In mid-June it was reported that five people had been killed on Mwali, after an opposition demonstration in support of the public-sector strike was violently suppressed by security forces. In September public-sector workers initiated further strike action; union officials refused to enter into negotiations with the authorities while Abdou Madi's Government remained in power. In October Djohar dismissed Abdou Madi from the office of Prime Minister and appointed Halifa Houmadi to the post. A new Council of Ministers included only two members of the former administration.

In December 1994 Djohar failed to accede to a request by the Federal Assembly that political prisoners who had been implicated in the abortive coup attempt in September 1992 be granted amnesty. In January 1995 public-sector workers suspended strike action, after the Government agreed to a number of union demands. In the same month Djohar condemned a decision by the French Government to reimpose visa requirements for Comoran nationals entering Mayotte (which further undermined the Comoros' claim of sovereignty over the territory). A demonstration at the French embassy in Moroni, which was staged in protest at the measure, was suppressed by security forces, after degenerating into violence. Later in January division emerged within the RDR, after both the party's Chairman and its Secretary-General (Abdou Madi) criticized the Government's failure to contain subsequent hostility towards French citizens. At a congress of the RDR in February the two officials were removed from the party, and Houmadi became Chairman. In the same month the Government announced that elections to the regional councils were to take place in April (later postponed until July) and were to be followed by the establishment of a Senate and a Constitutional Council. The opposition, however, accused Djohar of acting unconstitutionally in the preparation for elections and claimed that he planned to assume control of the electoral process.

In April 1995 reports emerged of a widening rift between Djohar and Houmadi, after the Prime Minister apparently claimed that Djohar and M'Changama had engaged in financial malpractice. At the end of that month Djohar dismissed Houmadi from the premiership and appointed a former Minister of Finance, Mohamed Caabi El Yachroutu, as his successor. A 13-member Council of Ministers, which included only five members of the previous administration, was established. In May three former Prime Ministers (Mohamed, Abdou Madi and Houmadi) conducted a series of political meetings urging public support for the removal of M'Changama (who, they claimed, exerted undue influence over Djohar) and demanded the dissolution of the Federal Assembly. In July further tension developed within the Government over an agreement whereby Air Comores was to be transferred to the joint management of an airline based in the United Arab Emirates; M'Changama and the Minister of Transport and Tourism, Ahmed Saïd Issilame, claimed that the agreement was technically invalid on the grounds that it had been signed by Djohar before legislation providing for the privatization of Air Comores had been approved in the Federal Assembly. Meanwhile, it was feared that the further postponement of elections to the regional councils would delay the presidential election. In an effort to facilitate the organization of the presidential election, the Government introduced minor constitutional amendments, including the relaxation of regulations governing the registration of political candidates and a provision empowering the Prime Minister to act as interim Head of State. At the end of July Djohar removed Issilame and a further three associates of M'Changama from the Council of Ministers.

In September 1995 about 30 European mercenaries, led by Denard, staged a military coup, seizing control of the garrison at Kandani and capturing Djohar. The mercenaries, who were joined by some 300 members of the Comoran armed forces, released a number of prisoners (including those detained for involvement in the failed coup attempt in September 1992) and

installed a former associate of Denard, Capt. Ayouba Combo, as leader of a Transitional Military Committee. The French Government denounced the coup and suspended economic aid to the Comoros, but initially refused to take military action, despite requests for assistance from El Yachroutu, who had taken refuge in the French embassy. In October Combo announced that he had transferred authority to Mohamed Taki Abdulkarim and the leader of CHUMA, Saïd Ali Kemal, (who had both welcomed the coup) as joint civilian Presidents, apparently in an attempt to avert military repercussions by the French Government. The FRN, however, rejected the new leadership and entered into negotiations with El Yachroutu. Following a further appeal for intervention from El Yachroutu, who invoked a defence co-operation agreement that had been established between the two countries in 1978, some 900 French military personnel landed on the Comoros and surrounded the mercenaries at Kandani. Shortly afterwards Denard and his associates, together with the disaffected members of the Comoran armed forces, surrendered to the French troops. (In October 1996, following his release from imprisonment in France in July, Denard claimed that the coup attempt had been planned at the request of several Comoran officials, including Taki.)

Following the French military intervention, El Yachroutu declared himself interim President, in accordance with the Constitution, and formed a Government of National Unity, which included members of the constituent parties of the FRN. Djohar (who had been transported to Réunion by the French in order to receive medical treatment) rejected El Yachroutu's assumption of power and announced the reappointment of Saïd Ali Mohamed as Prime Minister. Later in October 1995 a National Reconciliation Conference decided that El Yachroutu would remain interim President, pending the forthcoming election, which was provisionally scheduled for early 1996. The incumbent administration opposed Djohar's stated intention to return to the Comoros and announced that measures would be taken to prevent him from entering the country. At the end of October El Yachroutu granted an amnesty to all Comorans involved in the coup attempt and appointed representatives of the UNDC and Udzima (which had supported the coup) to the new Council of Ministers. In November Djohar announced the formation of a rival Government, headed by Mohamed. El Yachroutu, who was supported by the Comoran armed forces, refused to recognize the legitimacy of Djohar's appointments, while opposition parties equally opposed his return to power; only elements of the RDR continued to support Djohar's authority. It was reported that representatives of the OAU, who visited the Comoros and Réunion in November in an effort to resolve the situation, had unofficially concluded that only El Yachroutu's administration was capable of governing. There was also widespread speculation that the French Government had believed Djohar's authority to be untenable and had tacitly supported his removal from power. Later that month, however, supporters of Djohar, including M'Changama, organized a political gathering to demand the resignation of El Yachroutu's administration. Meanwhile, political leaders on Mwali rejected the authority of both rival Governments, urged a campaign of civil disobedience and established a 'citizens' committee' to govern the island; discontent with the central administration also emerged on Nzwani.

In January 1995 Djohar returned to the Comoros, after apparently signing an agreement stipulating that he would retain only symbolic presidential powers. A presidential election took place, in two rounds, on 6 and 16 March. At the first round, which was contested by some 15 candidates, Taki obtained the highest number of votes, with 21%, while the leader of the FRN, Abbas Djoussouf, secured about 15% of the votes. Taki was elected to the presidency on 16 March, obtaining 64% of the vote. International observers were satisfied with the electoral process; officials reported that 62% of the electorate had participated in the second round. The new Head of State was sworn in on 25 March. Taki appointed a new Council of Ministers, which included five of the presidential candidates who had supported him in the second round of the election.

In April 1996 Taki dissolved the Federal Assembly and announced that legislative elections would take place in October, despite the constitutional requirement that elections be held within a period of 40 days following the dissolution of the legislature. New Governors, all belonging to the UNDC, were appointed to each of the three islands. In August Taki issued a decree awarding himself absolute powers. This measure was widely criticized in the media and by opposition groups as being in violation of the Constitution. In a government reorganization later in the month, two ministers were dismissed, following their parties' refusal to disband in order to join the single pro-presidential party that Taki intended to establish.

In September 1996 Taki established a constitutional consultative committee, comprising 42 representatives of political parties and other organizations, which was to provide advice concerning the drafting of a new constitution; the FRN refused to participate in the committee. Also in that month the legislative elections were postponed until November. At the beginning of October a national referendum to endorse a new draft Constitution was scheduled for 20 October. In order to comply with a constitutional proposal, which effectively restricted the number of political parties to a maximum of three, 24 pro-Taki political organizations merged to form one presidential party, the Rassemblement national pour le développement (RND). The opposition condemned the extensive powers that the draft Constitution vested in the President, and the rapidity with which it was to be installed, and urged a boycott of the referendum. On 20 October, however, the new Constitution was approved by 85% of votes cast. The new Constitution vested legislative power in a unicameral parliament, the Federal Assembly, (thereby abolishing the Senate) and extended the presidential term to six years, with an unrestricted number of consecutive mandates. Political parties were required to have two parliamentary deputies from each island (following legislative elections) to be considered legal; organizations that did not fulfil these stipulations were to be dissolved. Extensive executive powers were vested in the President, who was to appoint the Governors of the islands and gained the right to initiate constitutional amendments. The official result of the referendum was disputed by the opposition parties.

Following unsuccessful negotiations with the Government, which rejected demands for the creation of an independent electoral commission and the revision of electoral lists, the opposition parties (having formed a new alliance) refused to participate in the electoral process. Consequently, the legislative elections, which took place after a further delay, in two rounds, in December 1996, were only contested by the RND and the Front national pour la justice (FNJ), a fundamentalist Islamic organization, together with 23 independent candidates (in apparent contravention of a stipulation in the new Constitution that only legally created political parties were entitled to participate in national elections). The RND secured 36 of the 43 seats in the Federal Assembly, while the FNJ won three, with four seats taken by independent candidates. Taki nominated Ahmed Abdou, who had served in the administration of former President Ahmed Abdallah, as Prime Minister to head a new Council of Ministers.

In December 1996 industrial action in the public sector in support of demands by civil servants for the payment of salary arrears resulted in severe disruption in government services. Civil unrest, exacerbated by severe shortages of water and electricity, culminated in February in a one-day general strike. Meanwhile, discontent with the Government intensified on Nzwani; in March a general strike escalated into riots, when some 3,000 demonstrators (reported to be secessionists) clashed with the security forces in Mutsamudu, the main town. Taki replaced the Governor of Nzwani and other senior island officials and carried out a government reshuffle. However, sympathy for the separatist movements on both Nzwani and Mwali continued to increase, amid claims that the Government had consistently ignored their political and economic interests. Separatist leaders declared their intention to seek the restoration of French rule and established a 'political directorate' on Nzwani, chaired by Abdallah Ibrahim, the leader of the Mouvement populaire anjouanais, a grouping of separatist movements on Nzwani. (The relative prosperity of neighbouring Mayotte appeared to have prompted the demand for a return to French rule; it was reported that up to 200 illegal migrants a day attempted to enter Mayotte from Nzwani.) Military reinforcements were sent to Nzwani and the Governor of the island was replaced once again.

On 3 August 1997 the 'political directorate' unilaterally declared Nzwani's secession from the Comoros. The separatists subsequently elected Ibrahim as president of a 13-member 'politico-administrative co-ordination', which included Abdou Madi, a former Prime Minister during Djohar's presidency, as spokesperson. The declaration of independence was condemned by Djoussouf, who appealed for French mediation in the crisis. However, France, while denouncing the secession, declared

itself in favour of the intervention of the OAU. The OAU responded by sending a special envoy, Pierre Yéré, to the Comoros. Meanwhile, separatist agitation intensified on Mwali, culminating on 11 August, when secessionists declared Mwali's independence from the Comoros, appointed a president and a prime minister to head a 12-member government, and called for reattachment to France.

As OAU mediation efforts continued, it was announced in mid-August 1997 that secessionist leaders on Mwali and Nzwani had agreed to negotiate with the authorities in Moroni, although those on Nzwani had insisted on the immediate withdrawal of the military reinforcements that had been sent to the island in July. By late August the Government had complied with this demand, and the OAU announced its intention to hold a reconciliation conference in September in Addis Ababa, Ethiopia, while maintaining that secession was unacceptable. Nzwani's Governor resigned and was not replaced. In early September, despite OAU and French opposition to military intervention, Taki despatched some 300 troops to Nzwani in an attempt forcibly to suppress the separatist insurrection. After two days of heavy fighting between secessionist and government forces, the OAU declared that the government troops had failed to quash the rebellion. The Government claimed that the separatists had been aided by foreign elements and expressed regret at France's refusal to support the military operation. As it emerged that some 40 Comoran soldiers and 16 Nzwani residents had been killed in the fighting, with many more injured, demonstrators demanding Taki's resignation clashed violently with the security forces in Moroni. The separatists on Nzwani reaffirmed their independence and empowered Ibrahim to rule by decree. Taki subsequently declared a state of emergency, assumed absolute power and dismissed the Government of Ahmed Abdou and his military and civilian advisers. (Abdou, from Mutsamudu, had reportedly resigned his position in late August, although this had not been announced publicly.) Shortly afterwards, Taki established a State Transition Commission, which included representatives from Nzwani and Mwali. The reconciliation conference was postponed indefinitely by the OAU. The League of Arab States (Arab League) agreed to a request from Taki for assistance, and following talks with the OAU regarding the co-ordination of the mediation effort, all three islands hosted discussions in late September, which were convened by envoys from both organizations. The opposition continued to call for Taki's resignation, the decentralization of power through constitutional reform and the organization of new elections.

In September 1997, despite the misgivings of some members of the 'politico-administrative co-ordination', notably Abdou Madi, Ibrahim announced his decision to hold a referendum on self-determination for Nzwani on 26 October, prior to a reconciliation conference sponsored by both the OAU and the Arab League, which all parties had agreed to attend. Despite international opposition, the referendum was conducted as scheduled; according to separatist officials, 99.9% of the electorate voted in favour of independence for Nzwani. The following day Ibrahim dissolved the 'politico-administrative co-ordination' and appointed a temporary government, which was charged with preparing a constitution and organizing a presidential election, although it did not receive international recognition. Taki responded by severing Nzwani's telephone lines, suspending air and maritime links and establishing a commission to liaise with opposition leaders prior to the appointment of a government of national unity. However, the opposition refused to participate in such a government before the reconciliation conference had taken place. The conference had been postponed several times, largely owing to disagreements regarding the composition and strength of the delegations. In November the OAU announced plans to deploy a force of military observers in the Comoros, despite the separatists' insistence that the force would not be allowed to land on Nzwani; an initial eight-member contingent, which arrived that month, was subsequently to be increased to 25 and was to receive logistical support from France. Meanwhile, amid reports of dissension within the separatist government, it was reported that Abdou Madi (believed to hold more moderate views than Ibrahim) was in Moroni, having fled Nzwani.

In early December 1997 Taki formed a new Council of Ministers, appointing Nourdine Bourhane as Prime Minister. The inter-Comoran reconciliation conference was held later that month; some agreement was reached on proposals for the establishment of an international commission of inquiry to investigate September's military intervention and on the holding of a Comoran inter-island conference to discuss institutional reform. In January 1998, following the first meeting in Fomboni, Mwali, of a committee charged with pursuing negotiations on the crisis, the OAU announced that both the Comoran Government and the Nzwani separatists had agreed to a number of conciliatory measures, including the restoration of air and maritime links and the release of federal soldiers still detained on Nzwani. However, Ibrahim subsequently rejected all the agreements that his delegation had signed in Fomboni, with the exception of the release of detainees.

In February 1998 tension increased further on Nzwani, where several rival separatist factions had emerged; fighting broke out between Ibrahim's supporters and followers of Abdou Madi, who had returned to the island, with the apparent support of both Taki and the OAU, in an abortive attempt to mount resistance to the secessionists. Later in February a separatist constitution was approved by a reported 99.5% of voters in a referendum on Nzwani. Ibrahim subsequently appointed a new separatist government. OAU mediation efforts effectively broke down in March, following an unsuccessful visit to Nzwani by a ministerial delegation.

In Moroni public discontent intensified in May 1998, when at least three people were reported to have been killed in violent anti-Government protests. Later that month Taki, who appeared to be moderating his stance, acted to break the political deadlock, forming a committee to re-establish dialogue with the opposition, appointing a new Council of Ministers, and releasing a prominent separatist from detention in Moroni. Abdou Madi returned to federal government, and, seemingly as a conciliatory gesture to the secessionists, the premiership (a position traditionally held by a Nzwanian) was left vacant. In June Taki held discussions with a number of opposition leaders, although the FRN refused to participate.

In July 1998, as social unrest on Nzwani escalated, a dispute over the future aims of the secessionist movement led to the dismissal of the island's government, provoking violent clashes between islanders loyal to Ibrahim, who favoured independence within the framework of an association of the Comoran islands, and supporters of the outgoing prime minister of the island, Chamassi Saïd Omar, who continued to advocate reattachment to France.

Meanwhile, as social and economic conditions deteriorated further, with salaries still unpaid and strike action ongoing, Taki sought overseas assistance in resolving the crisis. In August 1998 the Government provisionally suspended transport links with both Nzwani and Mayotte. France later refused the Government's request for a suspension of links between Mayotte and Nzwani, thus worsening the already fragile relations between the two countries. As industrial action continued into September, it was reported that the Government had banned news broadcasts by privately-owned radio and television stations. At meetings with Djoussouf and the leadership of his own party in October, Taki proposed the establishment of a government of public salvation, an idea opposed by many members of the RND and several government ministers.

On 6 November 1998 President Taki died unexpectedly, reportedly having suffered a heart attack, although several senior officials expressed serious doubts about the cause of death. Tadjidine Ben Saïd Massoundi, the President of the High Council of the Republic and a former Prime Minister, was designated acting President, in accordance with the Constitution, pending an election, which would be held after 30–90 days. Massoundi immediately revoked the ban on the movement of people and goods to Nzwani and, despite the continued opposition of several government ministers, proceeded with Taki's project for the formation of a government of public salvation. Djoussouf, the main opposition leader, was subsequently appointed Prime Minister, to head a Council of Ministers composed of members of the FRN and the RND. Divisions within the RND over its participation in the new Government led to a split in the party. In January 1999 Massoundi extended his presidential mandate, which was soon to expire, pending a resolution of the crisis dividing the islands.

Meanwhile, renewed tension within the separatist administration on Nzwani escalated in December 1998, provoking eight days of armed clashes between rival militias, which reportedly resulted in at least 60 deaths before a cease-fire agreement was signed. In January 1999 Ibrahim agreed to relinquish some of his powers to a five-member 'politico-administrative directorate', as meetings commenced between the rival separatist fac-

tions. No consensus was reached in the following months, however, and when Ibrahim replaced the directorate with a 'committee of national security' in March, the new administration was immediately rejected by rival leaders. In Moroni there were further protests against the ruling federal administration.

At an OAU-sponsored inter-island conference, held in Antananarivo, Madagascar, on 19–23 April 1999, an agreement was reached that envisaged substantial autonomy for Nzwani and Mwali, the changing of the country's name to the Union of the Comoran Islands and the rotation of the presidency among the three islands. However, the delegates from Nzwani refused to sign the agreement, insisting on the need to consult the Nzwani population prior to a full endorsement. Several days of rioting followed in Moroni, as demonstrators protested against Nzwani's failure to ratify the accord. On 30 April the Chief of Staff of the Comoran armed forces, Col Assoumani Azali, seized power in a bloodless coup, deposing Massoundi and dissolving the Government, the Federal Assembly and all other constitutional institutions. Azali promulgated a new constitutional charter, in which he proclaimed himself head of state and of government and Commander-in-Chief of the armed forces, and sought to justify the coup by claiming that the authorities had not taken the political measures necessary to control the security situation in the Comoros. Full legislative functions were also vested in Azali, who announced his intention to stay in power for one year only, during which time he pledged to oversee the creation of the new institutions envisaged in the Antananarivo accord. The appointment of a State Committee (composed of six members from Ngazidja, four from Mwali and two from Nzwani) was followed by that of a State Council, which was to supervise the activities of the State Committee and comprised eight civilians and 11 army officers. The coup was condemned by the OAU, which withdrew its military observers from the Comoros and urged the international community not to recognize the new regime; the UN, however, sent representatives to Azali's inauguration.

In June 1999 Azali created five technical commissions, which were charged with directing the implementation of the Antananarivo accord, including the drafting of new constitutions for the proposed union and its component parts. However, amid increasing discontent with the new administration, the main political parties boycotted a meeting at which they were to have nominated representatives to serve on the new commissions. Lt-Col Saïd Abeid Abdérémane, who had previously held the role of 'national mediator' on Nzwani, formed a government of national unity on the island and assumed the role of 'national co-ordinator'. In July delegates from the three islands, including Azali and Abeid, met on Mwali for talks aimed at resolving the political crisis. The negotiations represented the most senior-level contact between the islands since the secessions of August 1997.

In August 1999 elections to establish a 25-member national assembly on Nzwani were held. No official results were released, but reports indicated that the most staunch separatists won the majority of seats. In August and October the OAU Secretary-General's newly appointed special envoy for the Comoros, Francisco Caetano José Madeira, visited the islands in unsuccessful attempts to persuade the separatists on Nzwani to sign the Antananarivo accord. In December the OAU adopted a tougher stance towards the Nzwani separatists by threatening the imposition of sanctions on the island should its leaders not have signed the peace accord by 1 February 2000. In response, Abeid announced that a referendum would be held on Nzwani on 23 January 2000 regarding the signing of the Antananarivo accord. According to the separatist authorities of Nzwani, the results of the referendum revealed an overwhelming majority (94.47%) in favour of full independence for the island; the OAU, however, announced that it did not recognize the outcome of the ballot, following allegations of intimidation and repression of those in favour of reconciliation.

Meanwhile, following a series of meetings between Azali and a number of political parties from all three islands regarding the establishment of a more representative and decentralized government in Moroni, the State Committee underwent an extensive reorganization in December 1999, including the appointment of a Prime Minister, Bianrifi Tarmidi (from Mwali). Although Mwali was well represented in the new executive, only one Nzwanian minister was appointed.

On 1 February 2000, as threatened, the OAU imposed economic sanctions on Nzwani; the overseas assets of the separatist leaders were 'frozen' and they themselves were confined to the island. Furthermore, as part of the OAU sanctions, the federal Government suspended sea and air transport links, as well as telephone communications with Nzwani.

In March 2000 army units, led by Capt. Abdérémane Ahmed Abdallah (the son of former President Ahmed Abdallah), reportedly attempted, unsuccessfully, to overthrow Azali; Abdallah was subsequently arrested. In the following month demonstrations were organized by a number of political parties in protest at Azali's failure to transfer the country to civilian rule by 14 April, as he had promised following the April 1999 coup (see above). Azali later claimed that the conditions set for the holding of elections, namely the signing of the Antananarivo accord by the Nzwanian separatists, had not been met.

In May 2000 the OAU announced that the lifting of sanctions against Nzwanian separatists was dependent on a return to constitutional order on the Comoros; it advocated the restoration of the October 1996 Constitution, the reinstatement of Tajidine Ben Saïd Massoundi as Head of State, as well as the appointment of an interim government and Prime Minister. The following month an OAU delegation, led by Madeira, arrived in Moroni in an attempt to revive peace talks. However, Abeid reiterated his rejection of the Antananarivo accord. The possibility of armed intervention on Nzwani was rejected at an OAU summit, held in July, although it was agreed to establish a total maritime blockade of Nzwani.

On 26 August 2000 an agreement, known as the Fomboni Accord, was reached by Azali and Abeid, following negotiations on Mwali. The agreement provided for the establishment of a new Comoran entity and granted the three islands considerable control over internal matters. A new constitution was to be drafted and approved, by referendum, within 12 months. Moreover, Abeid and Azali called for the sanctions imposed on Nzwani to be lifted. The declaration was rejected by the OAU, however, on the grounds that it contravened the Antananarivo accord and threatened the integrity of the Comoros. Demonstrations, organized by opposition members displeased with the new settlement, took place on Nzwani following the signing of the declaration. Nevertheless, a tripartite commission, comprising delegates from Ngazidja, Nzwani and Mwali, was established in November to define the terms of the new constitution. In November Bianrifi Tarmidi was replaced as Prime Minister by Hamada Madi 'Boléro', who subsequently formed a new Government. Despite attempts to include them in the new Government and the tripartite commission, opposition members refused to participate, instead presenting to international mediators their own proposals for a resolution to the crisis.

With the mediation of the OAU and the Organisation internationale de la francophonie (OIF), negotiations between opposition and government members continued throughout late 2000 and early 2001. On 17 February the Framework Agreement for Reconciliation in the Comoros was signed in Fomboni by representatives of the Comoran Government, the Nzwani administration, opposition parties and civil society. The OAU, the OIF and the European Union (EU) were to be guarantors of the peace accord, which provided for the establishment of a new Comoran entity. Under the provisions of the agreement, an independent tripartite commission (comprising equal numbers of delegates from each of the islands, representing all the signatory groups) was to draft a new constitution, which would be subject to approval in a national referendum scheduled for June 2001. The new constitution was to define the areas of jurisdiction of the new entity and the individual islands, although the central administration would retain control over religion, nationality, currency, foreign affairs and defence. An independent national electoral commission was also to be created. Following the constitutional referendum, a transitional government of national union was to be formed and charged with creating the new institutions by 31 December. However, in mid-March, following disagreements over the composition of a follow-up committee intended to monitor the implementation of the Fomboni accord, the opposition withdrew from the reconciliation process. Nevertheless, the OAU suspended sanctions against Nzwani in May. In July the referendum was postponed until September, principally owing to the lack of available funds for its administration; it was subsequently delayed further.

On 8–9 August 2001 a bloodless military coup on Nzwani ended in the removal from power of Saïd Abeid Abdérémane. Abeid was replaced by a collective presidency, comprising Maj. Mohamed Bacar, Maj. Hassane Ali Toihili and Maj. Charif Halidi; a government of eight civilian commissioners (none of whom had been members of the previous government) was

appointed. The new leadership stated its commitment to the Fomboni agreement. However, on 24 September a further bloodless military coup was instigated by the deputy head of the Comoran army and close ally of Col Azali, Maj. Ayouba Combo. Although Combo was initially declared leader of the army, and Ahmed Aboubakar Foundi was installed as leader of Nzwani, they were captured the following day, before subsequently escaping the island. In November Abeid attempted unsuccessfully to regain control of Nzwani in a military coup; he was defeated by forces loyal to Bacar and was obliged to flee the island; the attempted coup was strongly condemned by the Government, which reaffirmed its support for the island's authorities. Abeid, however, denied his involvement in the events, maintaining that the instigator had in fact been Allaoui Ahmed, who had reportedly allied himself with the Organisation pour l'indépendance d'Anjouan, a political alliance that opposed the proposed constitutional changes.

In late October 2001 Yahaya Mohamed Iliasse resigned as Minister of Justice and Islamic Affairs at the request of his party, the FNJ, which had announced its opposition to the Government's decision to remove the word 'Islamic' from the country's official name. The FNJ also disagreed with proposed changes to the national flag and had previously stated its wish that Islam be proclaimed the national religion. In December some 100 people, claiming to belong to the US army, landed on Mwali and occupied a number of public buildings, as part of what they claimed was an attempt to liberate the Comoros from terrorism. However, the Comoran army regained control of the island, and two mercenaries were later arrested.

At the constitutional referendum of 23 December 2001, 76.37% of the electorate voted in favour of the proposed new constitution. The country, which was to change its name to the Union of the Comoros, was to be led by the President of the Union, at the head of a Council of the Union, and governed by a legislative assembly, the Assembly of the Union. The position of President was to rotate between the islands, while the Vice-Presidents, who were also members of the Council of the Union, were to be inhabitants of the two remaining islands; the first President was to come from Ngazidja. Each of the three islands was to become financially autonomous and was to be ruled by its own local government and institutions. The Union was to be responsible for matters of religion, nationality, currency, foreign affairs and external defence, while shared responsibilities between the Union and the islands were to be determined at a later date. A transitional government was to be installed to monitor the implementation of the new institutions. While the results of the referendum were welcomed by political leaders on Nzwani, some concerns were expressed by opponents of the new Constitution over the availability of funds required to implement the stipulated changes.

In early January 2002 Prime Minister Hamadi Madi 'Boléro' tendered his resignation. A transitional Government of National Unity was installed on 20 January, with 'Boléro' reappointed as Prime Minister, and included members of the former Government, opposition representatives and two of Nzwani's separatist leaders. However, on the following day the Government collapsed, following the withdrawal of the opposition representatives, as a result of a disagreement over the allocation of ministerial portfolios. The opposition ministers had expressed their disappointment at not having been offered the position of Prime Minister, nor the portfolios of foreign affairs or finance, the budget and privatization, which they claimed had been part of the agreement on national reconciliation of February 2001. Meanwhile, Col Azali resigned as Head of State and announced his intention to stand as an independent candidate in the forthcoming presidential election; 'Boléro' was to serve as President *ad interim*. In mid-February 2002 the Government of National Unity was re-established; notably, Soilihi Ali Mohammed, a member of the opposition, became Minister of Finance, the Budget and Privatization, replacing Assoumany Aboudou, who was appointed as Minister of the Interior and Decentralization, the position that Mohammed had been allocated in January.

On 10 March 2002 voters on Nzwani and Mwali approved new local Constitutions; this was followed on 7 April by the approval of a new Constitution on Ngazidja (an earlier draft had been rejected). In a first round of voting in the federal presidential election on 17 March, contested by nine candidates, Col Azali secured 39.8% of the vote. Mahamoud Mradabi won 15.7% and Saïd Ali Kemal 10.7%; however, both Mradabi and Kemal boycotted the second round. Consequently, on 14 April Col Azali was elected unopposed as Federal President of the Union of the Comoros, reportedly securing more than 75% of the votes cast. However, the result was declared invalid by the NEC, on the grounds that the election had not been free and fair. Nevertheless, following the dissolution of the NEC, and the appointment of an independent electoral body, Col Azali was declared Federal President. Meanwhile, in late March and early April, Maj. Mohamed Bacar and Mohamed Said Fazul were elected as regional Presidents of Nzwani and Mwali, respectively; on 19 May Abdou Soule Elbak was elected regional President of Ngazidja, defeating Azali's preferred candidate, Bakari Abdallah Boina. The regional Presidents subsequently formed local Governments. Col Azali appointed a new federal Government in early June.

However, the process of local devolution was complicated by uncertainty about the boundaries of jurisdiction on Ngazidja, as Moroni was to be the seat of government for both Azali and Elbak. According to a report issued by the World Bank in July 2002, this confusion had hindered the ability of international organizations to implement aid programmes. In mid-June disagreement over the new political structure prompted the occupation of a number of government buildings by troops. In response, the Government of Ngazidja boycotted the inauguration of the new head of the armed forces, Col Soilihi Ali Mohammed, and warned the OAU that it suspected a coup was being planned, to be led by Soilihi. President Elbak also dismissed a number of local government figures loyal to Azali. On 6 July Presidents Elbak and Bacar boycotted Independence Day celebrations.

In mid-July 2002 Col Azali declared his intention to bring forward the process of national reconciliation, holding legislative elections in September instead of December. As a result of a meeting in mid-August, Ngazidja was also granted its own internal security forces by Azali. Nevertheless, at the end of August street barricades were erected in Moroni, in protest at incomplete devolution on Ngazidja, which left Elbak with less authority than the other islands' Presidents. Soldiers dispersed the protests, injuring five (a subsequent inquiry revealed that real bullets had been used). In September Col Azali announced that the legislative elections would be delayed until October, and they were later postponed further, to March–April 2003, despite assertions from international representatives that the absence of institutions for dialogue was a threat to the national reconciliation process. Also in September supporters of Azali formed a new political party, the Convention pour le renouveau des Comores. Later that month Elbak accused Azali of tapping his telephone lines, while Mohamed Sasani, Elbak's cabinet director, circulated a letter to international bodies, including the EU, alleging an assassination plot by Azali against Elbak. The accusations were wholly rejected by the Azali administration. In October President Bacar of Nzwani effected a cabinet reshuffle, allocating five of the 10 portfolios to new ministers.

In late January 2003 the follow-up committee on the implementation of the reconciliation agreement proposed that elections to the islands' local assemblies be held on 13 and 20 April and elections to the Assembly of the Union on 11 and 19 May. In February two ministers in the local Government of Ngazidja and 12 police officers were arrested for involvement in an apparent coup plot against Col Azali. Elbak denied any involvement, and one of the ministers and 10 of the police-officers were later released without charge. In early March Elbak and Bacar denounced Azali's failure to implement measures to resolve the institutional crisis and accused the federal President of repeated constitutional violations, requesting that the EU temporarily delay payment for fishing rights to the federal Government. In mid-March the federal Government announced the indefinite postponement of the legislative elections.

Diplomatic relations between the Comoros and France, suspended in December 1975, were restored in July 1978; in November of that year the two countries signed agreements on military and economic co-operation, apparently deferring any decision on the future of Mayotte. In subsequent years, however, member countries of the UN General Assembly repeatedly voted in favour of a resolution affirming the Comoros' sovereignty over Mayotte, with only France dissenting. Following Djohar's accession to power, diplomatic relations were established with the USA in June 1990. In September 1993 the Arab League (see p. 260) accepted an application for membership from the Comoros. In mid-1999, following the military coup headed by Col Azali, France and the USA suspended all military co-operation with the Comoros; France resumed military co-operation in September 2002.

The Government of Madagascar suspended cattle exports to the Comoros in September 2002, accusing the archipelago of hosting members of the former Malagasy regime of Didier Ratsiraka. In late November Lt-Col Hubert Balbine, a pro-Ratsiraka army officer from Madagascar, was extradited from Moroni, charged with terrorism offences allegedly committed during the political crisis that followed the disputed presidential election held on Madagascar in December 2001.

Government

Under the Constitution of 23 December 2001, each of the islands in the Union of the Comoros is headed by a local government and is partially autonomous. The Head of State of the Union of the Comoros is the President, who appoints the members of the Government and heads the Council of the Union, which also comprises the two Vice-Presidents. The members of the Council are elected for a four-year term, and the position of President rotates between the islands, while the Vice-Presidents are inhabitants of the two remaining islands. Both the President and the Vice-Presidents are elected by absolute majority by the members of the legislature, the Assembly of the Union. The Assembly is composed of 30 deputies, elected for a five-year term.

Defence

In mid-1997 the national army, the Force Comorienne de Défense (FCD), numbered about 1,500 men. Government expenditure on defence in 1994 was an estimated US $3m. In December 1996 an agreement was ratified with France, which provided for the permanent presence of a French military contingent in the Comoros, which was to be renewed by rotation. In July 1997, however, it was reported that the rotations had ceased several months previously. French military co-operation with the Comoros was suspended after the coup of April 1999, but resumed in September 2002.

Economic Affairs

In 2001, according to estimates from the World Bank, the gross national income (GNI) of the Comoros (excluding Mayotte), measured at average 1999–2001 prices, was US $217m., equivalent to $380 per head (or $1,610 per head on an international purchasing-power parity basis). During 1990–2001, it was estimated, the population increased at an average annual rate of 2.6%, while gross domestic product (GDP) per head declined, in real terms, by an average of 2.3% per year. Overall GDP increased, in real terms, at an average annual rate of 0.3% in 1990–2001; real GDP decreased by 1.1% in 2000, but increased by 1.9% in 2001.

Agriculture (including hunting, forestry and fishing) contributed 38.5% of GDP in 2001. Approximately 73.3% of the labour force were employed in the agricultural sector in that year. In 2000 the sector accounted for some 88.4% of total export earnings. The principal cash crops are vanilla, cloves and ylang-ylang. Cassava, taro, rice, maize, pulses, coconuts and bananas are also cultivated. According to the World Bank, the real GDP of the agricultural sector increased at an average annual rate of 1.0% in 1990–2001; growth in 2001 was 0.9%.

Industry (including manufacturing, construction and power) contributed 11.2% of GDP in 2001. Some 9.4% of the labour force were employed in the industrial sector in 1990. According to the World Bank, the Comoros' industrial GDP increased at an average annual rate of 2.4% in 1990–2001; industrial GDP declined by 7.4% in 2000, but increased by 4.0% in 2001.

The manufacturing sector contributed 3.9% of GDP in 2001. The sector consists primarily of the processing of agricultural produce, particularly of vanilla and essential oils. According to the World Bank, manufacturing GDP declined at an average annual rate of 2.0% in 1990–2001; manufacturing GDP decreased by 11.1% in 2000, but remained constant in 2001.

Electrical energy is derived from wood (78%), and from thermal installations. Imports of fuel and energy comprised an estimated 4.0% of the total cost of imports in 2000.

The services sector contributed 50.3% of GDP in 2001. Strong growth in tourism from 1991 led to a significant expansion in trade, restaurant and hotel activities, although political instability inhibited subsequent growth. According to the World Bank, the GDP of the services sector decreased at an average rate of 0.8% per year in 1990–2001; it declined by 1.8% in 2000, but increased by 2.7% in 2001.

In 2000 the Comoros recorded a visible trade deficit of US $26.0m., and there was a deficit of $0.9m. on the current account of the balance of payments. In that year the principal source of imports was South Africa (accounting for some 54.2% of the total); other major sources were France, Pakistan and Kenya. France was the principal market for exports (43.5%); other important purchasers were Singapore, the USA and the UK. The leading exports in 2000 were vanilla (providing 66.7% of the total), cloves and ylang-ylang. The principal imports in that year were furniture for medical, surgical, dental or veterinary practice (50.6%), machinery and transport equipment, food and live animals (notably rice) and basic manufactures.

The Comoran budget deficit, excluding Nzwani, was estimated at 2,057m. Comoros francs in 2000 (equivalent to 1.9% of GDP). The Comoros' external public debt at the end of 2000 totalled US $231.7m., of which $201.9m. was long-term public debt. In that year the cost of debt-servicing was equivalent to 5.0% of the value of exports of goods and services. According to the IMF the annual rate of inflation averaged 1.5% during 1995–99. The rate rose to 25.3% in 1994, following a 33.3% devaluation of the Comoros franc in January 1994, but slowed thereafter, reaching 1.1% in 1999. An estimated 20% of the labour force were unemployed in 2000.

In 1985 the Comoros joined the Indian Ocean Commission (IOC, see p. 340). The country is also a member of the Common Market for Eastern and Southern Africa (COMESA, see p. 162) and of the Franc Zone (see p. 237).

The Comoros has a relatively undeveloped economy, with high unemployment, a limited transport system, a severe shortage of natural resources and heavy dependence on foreign aid, particularly from France. An intensification of political instability on the islands, following the seizure of power by the army in April 1999, had a particularly adverse effect on maritime trade and tourism. Following the conclusion of an agreement on national reconciliation in February 2001 (see above), in July a group of 'Friends of the Comoros', co-ordinated by the World Bank (and also including the European Union, the Organisation internationale de la francophonie, France, Mauritius and Morocco), pledged some US $11.5m. in aid to assist with constitutional developments towards the establishment of a new Comoran entity, as well as to alleviate poverty and improve the economy. Furthermore, it was hoped that a number of agreements reached later that year, worth an estimated €5.9m., would encourage the further development of the production of vanilla, ylang-ylang and cloves, and increase international demand for those crops. After partial devolution in 2002, conflicts over the distribution of political power led to the prolonged closure of ports on Ngazidja, which adversely affected local government finances on the island. Following a mission to the Comoros in July, the IMF rejected the possibility of granting a loan to the Comoros, owing to ongoing political instability, despite recent improvements in the economy, which were partly attributed to the suspension of sanctions against Nzwani by the Organization of African Unity (now the African Union) in May 2001. The IMF warned that the islands had experienced a significant decline in income, with a concurrent increase in consumer prices. In November 2002 the federal Government and the European Union signed a National Indicator Programme on co-operation during 2002–07; the Comoros was to receive €27.3m. under the Programme, mostly for education.

Education

Education is officially compulsory for 10 years between six and 16 years of age. Primary education begins at the age of six and lasts for six years. Secondary education, beginning at 12 years of age, lasts for seven years, comprising a first cycle of four years and a second of three years. Enrolment at primary schools in 1999/2000 included 54.8% of children in the relevant age-group (males 59.6%; females 49.9%), according to UNESCO estimates. Children may also receive a basic education through traditional Koranic schools, which are staffed by Comoran teachers. Enrolment at secondary schools in 1999/2000 was equivalent to 20.6% of children in the relevant age-group (males 22.6%; females 18.5%), according to UNESCO estimates. Current expenditure by the Ministry of Education in 1995 was 3,381m. Comoros francs, representing 21.1% of total current government expenditure.

Public Holidays

2003: 12 February* (Id al-Adha, Feast of the Sacrifice), 5 March* (Muharram, Islamic New Year), 14 March* (Ashoura), 14 May* (Mouloud, Birth of the Prophet), 6 July (Independence Day), 24 September* (Leilat al-Meiraj, Ascension of the Prophet), 27 October* (Ramadan begins), 26 November* (Id al-Fitr, end of Ramadan), 27 November (Anniversary of President Abdallah's assassination).

2004: 2 February* (Id al-Adha, Feast of the Sacrifice), 22 February* (Muharram, Islamic New Year), 2 March* (Ashoura), 2 May* (Mouloud, Birth of the Prophet), 6 July (Independence Day), 12 September* (Leilat al-Meiraj, Ascension of the Prophet), 15 October* (Ramadan begins), 14 November* (Id al-Fitr, end of Ramadan), 27 November (Anniversary of President Abdallah's assassination).

*Religious holidays, which are dependent on the Islamic lunar calendar, may differ by one or two days from the dates given.

Weights and Measures

The metric system is in force.

Statistical Survey

Source (unless otherwise stated): Ministry of Finance, the Budget and Privatization, BP 324, Moroni; tel. (74) 4145; fax (74) 4140.
Note: Unless otherwise indicated, figures in this Statistical Survey exclude data for Mayotte.

AREA AND POPULATION

Area: 1,862 sq km (719 sq miles). *By island*: Ngazidja (Grande-Comore) 1,146 sq km, Nzwani (Anjouan) 424 sq km, Mwali (Mohéli) 290 sq km.

Population: 335,150 (males 167,089 females 168,061), excluding Mayotte (estimated population 50,740), at census of 15 September 1980; 446,817 (males 221,152; females 225,665), excluding Mayotte, at census of 15 September 1991; 527,900 in 1998. *By island* (1991 census): Ngazidja (Grande-Comore) 233,533, Nzwani (Anjouan) 188,953, Mwali (Mohéli) 24,331.

Density (per sq km, 1998): 283.5.

Principal Towns (population at 1 January 2003): Moroni (capital) 60,200; Mutsamudu 30,900; Mitsamiouli 21,400; Domoni 19,100; Fomboni 13,300. Source: Stefan Helders, *World Gazetteer* (internet www.world-gazetteer.com).

Births and Deaths (including figures for Mayotte, UN estimates, 1995–2000): Average annual birth rate 38.9 per 1,000; average annual death rate 9.5 per 1,000. Source: UN, *World Population Prospects: The 2000 Revision*.

Expectation of Life (WHO estimates, years at birth, including Mayotte): 61.8 (males 59.8; females 63.8) in 2001. Source: WHO, *World Health Report*.

Economically Active Population (ILO estimates, '000 persons at mid-1980, including figures for Mayotte): Agriculture, forestry and fishing 150; Industry 10; Services 20; Total 181 (males 104, females 77). Source: ILO, *Economically Active Population Estimates and Projections, 1950–2025. 1991 Census (persons aged 12 years and over, excluding Mayotte):* Total labour force 126,510 (males 88,034; females 38,476). Source: UN, *Demographic Yearbook. Mid-2001 (estimates in '000):* Agriculture, etc. 250; Total labour force 341 Source: FAO.

HEALTH AND WELFARE
Key Indicators

Total Fertility Rate (children per woman, 2001): 5.1.

Under-5 Mortality Rate (per 1,000 live births, 2001): 79.

HIV/AIDS (% of persons aged 15–49, 1999): 0.12.

Physicians (per 1,000 head, 1997): 0.07.

Hospital Beds (per 1,000 head, 1990): 2.76.

Health Expenditure (2000): US $ per head (PPP): 35.

Health Expenditure (2000): % of GDP: 4.4.

Health Expenditure (2000): public (% of total): 71.6.

Access to Water (% of persons, 2000): 96.

Access to Sanitation (% of persons, 2000): 98.

Human Development Index (2000): ranking: 137.

Human Development Index (2000): value: 0.511.
For sources and definitions, see explanatory note on p. vi.

AGRICULTURE, ETC.

Principal Crops ('000 metric tons, unless otherwise indicated, 2001): Rice (paddy) 17.0*; Maize 3.8; Potatoes 1.0*; Sweet potatoes 6.0*; Cassava (Manioc) 54.1; Taro 9.0; Yams 3.8*; Pulses 13.5*; Groundnuts (in shell) 0.8; Coconuts 75.5; Oil crops 10.1; Tomatoes 0.6; Other vegetables 5.7*; Bananas 60.0; Other fruits 3.5*; Vanilla (dried, metric tons) 134; Cloves 1.0*.
* FAO estimate. Source: FAO.

Livestock (FAO estimates, unless otherwise indicated, '000 head, year ending September 2001): Asses 5.0; Cattle 52.0; Sheep 21.0; Goats 113.2 (unofficial figure); Chickens 490. Source: FAO.

Livestock Products (FAO estimates, metric tons, 2001): Beef and veal 1,012; Sheep and goat meat 435; Chicken meat 500; Cow milk 4,450; Hen eggs 820. Source: FAO.

Fishing (FAO estimates, '000 metric tons, live weight, 2000): Total catch 13.2 (Carangids 0.5, Sardinellas 1.1, Anchovies, etc. 1.0, Skipjack tuna 2.2, Yellowfin tuna 5.6). Source: FAO, *Yearbook of Fishery Statistics*.

INDUSTRY

Electric Energy (million kWh): 28.5 in 1998; 34.4 in 1999; 35.0 in 2000. Source: mainly Banque Centrale des Comores, *Rapport Annuel*.

FINANCE

Currency and Exchange Rates: 100 centimes = 1 Comoros franc. *Sterling, Dollar and Euro Equivalents* (31 December 2002): £1 sterling = 756.13 Comoros francs; US $1 = 469.12 Comoros francs; €1 = 491.97 Comoros francs; 1,000 Comoros francs = £1.323 = $2,132 = €2.033. *Average Exchange Rate* (Comoros francs per US $): 533.98 in 2000; 549.78 in 2001; 522.74 in 2002. Note: The Comoros franc was introduced in 1981, replacing (at par) the CFA franc. The fixed link to French currency was retained, with the exchange rate set at 1 French franc = 50 Comoros francs. This remained in effect until January 1994, when the Comoros franc was devalued by 33.3%, with the exchange rate adjusted to 1 French franc = 75 Comoros francs. This relationship to French currency remained in effect with the introduction of the euro on 1 January 1999. From that date, accordingly, a fixed exchange rate of €1 = 491.968 Comoros francs has been in operation.

Budget (estimates, million Comoros francs, excluding Nzwani 2000): *Revenue*: Tax revenue 9,724 (Taxes on income and profits 1,895; Taxes on goods and services 1,205; Taxes on international trade 6,367); Other revenue 1,294; Total 11,018, excluding grants received (4,539). *Expenditure*: Budgetary current expenditure 12,066 (Wages and salaries 6,093; Goods and services 4,169; Transfers 844; Interest payments 960); Current expenditure under technical assistance programmes 1,427; Budgetary capital expenditure 130; Capital expenditure financed with external resources 4,027; Total 17,649, excluding net lending (−35). Source: IMF, *Comoros: Recent Economic Developments* (July 2001).

International Reserves (US $ million at 31 December 2001): Gold n.a.; IMF special drawing rights 0.02; Reserve position in IMF 0.68; Foreign exchange 61.62; Total (excl. gold) 62.32. Source: IMF, *International Financial Statistics*.

Money Supply (million Comoros francs at 31 December 2001): Currency outside deposit money banks 12,355; Demand deposits at deposit money banks 8,955; Total money (incl. others) 22,937. Source: IMF, *International Financial Statistics*.

Cost of Living (Consumer Price Index; base: 1993 = 100): All items 137.4 in 1997; 139.0 in 1998; 140.5 in 1999. Source: IMF, *Comoros: Recent Economic Developments* (July 2001).

Expenditure on the Gross Domestic Product (million Comoros francs at current prices, 2000, estimates): Government final consumption expenditure 14,547; Private final consumption expenditure 85,726; Increase in stocks 3,000; Gross fixed capital formation 11,257; *Total domestic expenditure* 114,530; Exports of goods and services 27,638; *Less* Imports of goods and services 34,367; *GDP in purchasers' values* 107,801. Source: IMF, *Comoros: Recent Economic Developments* (July 2001).

Gross Domestic Product by Economic Activity (million Comoros francs at current prices, 2000): Agriculture, hunting, forestry and fishing 44,082; Manufacturing 4,488; Electricity, gas and water 1,654; Construction and public works 6,733; Trade, restaurants and hotels 27,155; Transport and communications 5,715; Finance, insurance, real estate and business services 4,648; Government services 15,420; Other services 595; *Sub-total* 110,490; *Less* Imputed bank service charge 2,688; *GDP in purchasers' values* 107,801. Source: IMF, *Comoros: Recent Economic Developments* (July 2001).

Balance of Payments (US $ million, 2000): Exports of goods f.o.b. 12.1; Imports of goods f.o.b. −38.1; *Trade balance* −26.0; Services and other income (net) 13.8; *Balance on goods, services and income* −12.2; Private transfers (net) 2.9; Official transfers (net) 8.5; *Current balance* −0.9; Direct investment from abroad (net) 0.1; Other long-term capital (net) −5.3; Short-term capital (incl. net errors and omissions) 8.2; *Overall balance* 2.1. Source: IMF, *Comoros: Recent Economic Developments* (July 2001).

EXTERNAL TRADE

Principal Commodities (US $ million, 2000): *Imports c.i.f.*: Food and live animals 13.5 (Meat and preparations 3.1; Rice 5.3); Mineral fuels, lubricants, etc. 2.9; Basic manufactures 5.5 (Cement 2.8); Machinery and transport equipment 7.2; Miscellaneous manufactured articles 37.9 (Furniture for medical, surgical, dental or veterinary practice 36.4); Total (incl. others) 71.9. *Exports f.o.b.*: Food and live animals 6.1 (Vanilla 4.6; Cloves 1.4); Essential oils 0.4; Total (incl. others) 6.9. Source: UN, *International Trade Statistics Yearbook*.

Principal Trading Partners (US $ million, 2000): *Imports*: Belgium 1.3; France-Monaco 14.0; Indonesia 1.5; Kenya 3.9; Pakistan 4.9; South Africa 39.0; United Arab Emirates 1.9; Total (incl. others) 71.9. *Exports*: Canada 0.3; France-Monaco 3.0; Germany 0.5; Israel 0.2; Singapore 1.1; United Kingdom 0.6; USA 1.1; Total (incl. others) 6.9. Source: UN, *International Trade Statistics Yearbook*.

TRANSPORT

Road Traffic (estimates, motor vehicles in use, 1996): Passenger cars 9,100; Lorries and vans 4,950. Source: International Road Federation, *World Road Statistics*.

International Shipping (estimated sea-borne freight traffic, '000 metric tons, 1991): Goods loaded 12; Goods unloaded 107. Source: UN Economic Commission for Africa, *African Statistical Yearbook*.

Civil Aviation (traffic on scheduled services, 1996): Passengers carried ('000) 27; Passenger-km (million) 3. Source: UN, *Statistical Yearbook*.

TOURISM

Tourist Arrivals: 27,474 in 1998; 24,479 in 1999; 23,893 in 2000.

Tourist Arrivals by Country (2000): France 5,836, Madagascar 779, Réunion 1,403, South Africa 9,146, United Kingdom 712; Zimbabwe 494; Total (incl. others) 23,893. Source: World Tourism Organization: *Yearbook of Tourism Statistics*.

Receipts from Tourism (US $ million): 26 in 1997; 16 in 1998; 17 in 1999. Source: World Bank.

COMMUNICATIONS MEDIA

Radio Receivers (1997): 90,000 in use. Source: UNESCO, *Statistical Yearbook*.

Television Receivers (1997): 1,000 in use. Source: UNESCO, *Statistical Yearbook*.

Telephones (2001): 8,900 main lines in use. Source: International Telecommunication Union.

Facsimile Machines (1998): 173 in use. Source: UN, *Statistical Yearbook*.

Personal Computers (2001): 4,000 in use. Source: International Telecommunication Union.

Internet Users (2001): 2,500. Source: International Telecommunication Union.

EDUCATION

Pre-primary (1980/81): 600 teachers; 17,778 pupils.

Primary (1998): 348 schools; 2,381 teachers; 82,789 pupils.

Secondary (1998): Teachers: general education 591 (1995/96, public education only); teacher training 11 (1991/92); vocational 31 (1986/87). Pupils: general education 28,559; vocational 159.

Higher (1998): 67 teachers; 649 pupils.

Adult Literacy Rate: 55.9% (males 63.2%; females 48.7%) in 2000. (Source: UN Development Programme, *Human Development Report*).

Source: mostly UNESCO Institute for Statistics.

Directory

The Constitution

In accordance with an agreement on national reconciliation, signed on 17 February 2001 by representatives of the Government, the separatist administration on Nzwani, opposition parties and civil society, a new Constitution was presented in August and approved by referendum on 23 December. Under the terms of the new Constitution, the country was renamed the Union of the Comoros, and each of the three islands, Ngazidja, Nzwani and Mwali, were to be granted partial autonomy and were to be headed by a local government. The Union, governed by a central government, was to be headed by the President. The main provisions of the Constitution are summarized below

PREAMBLE

The preamble affirms the will of the Comoran people to derive from the state religion, Islam, inspiration for the principles and laws that the State and its institutions govern; to guarantee the pursuit of a common future; to establish new institutions based on the rule of law, democracy and good governance, which guarantee an equal division of power between the Union and those islands that compose it; to adhere to the principles laid down by the Charters of the UN, the Organization of African Unity and the Organization of the Islamic Conference and by the Treaty of the League of Arab States; and to guarantee the rights of all citizens, without discrimination, in accordance with the UN Declaration of Human Rights and the African Charter of Human Rights.

The preamble guarantees solidarity between the Union and the islands, as well as between the islands themselves; equality amongst the islands and their inhabitants, regardless of race, origin, or religion; the right to freedom of expression, education, health and justice; the freedom and security of individuals; the inviolability of an individual's home or property; and the right of children to be protected against abandonment, exploitation and violence.

THE UNION OF THE COMOROS

The Comoros archipelago constitutes a republic. Sovereignty belongs to the people, and is exercised through their elected representatives or by the process of referendum. There is universal secret suffrage, which can be direct or indirect, for all citizens who are over the age of 18 and in full possession of their civil and political rights. Political parties and groups operate freely, respecting national sovereignty, democracy and territorial integrity.

COMPETENCIES OF THE UNION AND THE ISLANDS

Each island freely administers its own affairs, while respecting the unity of the Union and its territorial integrity. Each island establishes its own fundamental laws, which must respect the Constitution. All Comorans within the Union have equal rights, freedoms and duties. All the islands are headed by an elected Executive and Assembly. The Union has ultimate authority over the individual islands and legislates on matters of religion, nationality, currency, foreign affairs, external defence and national identity. As regards those competencies shared by both the Union and the islands, the Union has ultimate jurisdiction only if the issue concerned affects more than one island, if the matter cannot be resolved by one island alone, or if the judicial, economic and social integrity of the Union may be compromised. The islands are responsible for those matters not covered by the Union, or by shared responsibility. The islands are financially autonomous.

THE UNION'S INSTITUTIONS

Executive Power

The President of the Union is the symbol of national unity. He is the guarantor of national independence, the unity of the Republic, the autonomy of the islands, territorial integrity and adherence to international agreements. He is the Head of State and is responsible for external defence and security, foreign affairs and negotiating and ratifying treaties.

The Council of the Union is composed of the President and two Vice-Presidents, selected from each island. The members of the Council are elected for a four-year term, and the position of President rotates between the islands, while the Vice-Presidents are inhabitants of the two remaining islands. Both the President and the Vice-Presidents are elected by absolute majority by the members of the Assembly of the Union. The President appoints the members of the Government (ministers of the Union) and determines their respective portfolios. The composition of the Government must represent all of the islands equally.

Legislative Power

Legislative power is vested in the Assembly of the Union, which is composed of 30 deputies, elected for a period of five years. One-half of the deputies are selected by the islands' local assemblies (five deputies per island) and the other half are directly elected by universal suffrage. The Assembly sits for two sessions each year and, if necessary, for extraordinary sessions.

Judicial Power

Judicial power is independent of executive and legislative power. The President of the Union is the guarantor of the independence of the judicial system and is assisted by the Higher Council of the Magistracy (Conseil Supérieur de la Magistrature). The Supreme Court (Cour Suprême) is the highest ruling authority in judicial, administrative and fiscal matters, and its rulings are final and binding.

THE HIGH COUNCIL

The High Council considers constitutional matters, oversees the results of elections and referendums and guarantees basic human rights and civil liberties. Moreover, the High Council is responsible for ruling on any conflicts regarding the separate competencies of the Union and the islands. The President of the Union, the Vice-Presidents, the President of the Assembly of the Union, and each President of the local island executives appoint one member to the High Council. Members are elected for a six-year mandate, renewable once; the President of the High Council is appointed by the members for a six-year term.

REVISION OF THE CONSTITUTION

The power to initiate constitutional revision is jointly vested in the President of the Union and the members of the Assembly of the Union. Constitutional revision must be approved by a majority of two-thirds of the deputies in the Assembly and by two-thirds of the members of the islands' local assemblies. However, the organizational structure of the Union cannot be revised, and any revision that may affect the unity and territorial boundaries of the Union is not permitted.

PROVISIONAL ARRANGEMENTS

The Union's institutions, as defined in the Constitution, are to be established in accordance with the terms laid out in the agreement on national reconciliation of 17 February 2001. Institutions on the island of Mayotte will be established within a maximum period of six months following the island's decision to rejoin the Union of the Comoros.

The Government

HEAD OF STATE

Federal President: Col ASSOUMANI AZALI (elected 14 April 2002).

REGIONAL PRESIDENTS

Mwali: MOHAMED SAID FAZUL.

Ngazidja: ABDOU SOULE ELBAK.

Nzwani: Maj. MOHAMED BACAR.

GOVERNMENT OF OF THE UNION OF THE COMOROS
(April 2003)

Each island also has its own local Government.

Vice-President, with responsibility for Finance, the Budget, the Economy, Foreign Trade, Investments and Privatizations: MOHAMED CAABI EL YACHROUTU (Nzwani).

Vice-President, with responsibility for Justice, Territorial Security, Information, Religious Affairs, Human Rights and Relations with the Assemblies: RACHIDI BEN MASSOUNDI (Mwali).

Minister of State, with responsibility for Foreign Affairs, Co-operation, Francophony, the Environment and Comorans Abroad: MOHAMED ELAMINE SOEFOU.

Minister of State, with responsibility for Social Affairs, Solidarity, Decentralization, Posts and Telecommunications, and International Transport: SOLIHI ALI MOHAMMED.

Minister of Defence and Security: HAMADA MADI 'BOLÉRO'.

Minister-delegate for Transport and Francophony: HOUMED MSAIDIÉ.

Minister-delegate for Relations with the Assemblies: NOURDINE MIDILADJI.

Minister-delegate for Co-operation: ABDOU MOUSTRADOINE.

Minister-delegate for the Budget: CHARIF MAOULANA.

MINISTRIES

Office of the Head of State: BP 521, Moroni; tel. (74) 4814; fax (74) 4829; internet www.presidence-rfic.com.

Ministry of Comorans Abroad: Moroni.

Ministry of Decentralization: BP 520, Moroni; tel. (74) 4666.

Ministry of the Economy, Foreign Trade and Investments: Moroni; tel. (74) 4235.

Ministry of the Environment: Moroni.

Ministry of Finance, the Budget and Privatization: BP 324, Moroni; tel. (74) 4145; fax (74) 4140.

Ministry of Foreign Affairs, Co-operation and Francophony: BP 482, Moroni; tel. (74) 4100; fax (74) 4111.

Ministry of Human Rights: BP 73, Moroni; tel. (74) 4185; fax (74) 4180.

Ministry of Information: BP 421, Moroni.

Ministry of Posts and Telecommunications, and International Transport: Moroni; tel. (73) 2098.

Ministry of Justice and Religious Affairs: Moroni; tel. (74) 4200.

Ministry of Relations with Assemblies: Moroni.

Ministry of Solidarity and Social Affairs: Moroni.

Ministry of Territorial Security: Moroni; tel. (74) 4862.

President and Legislature

PRESIDENT

Presidential Election, First ballot, 17 March 2002

Candidate	% of votes
Col Assoumani Azali	39.8
Mahamoud Mradabi	15.7
Saïd Ali Kemal	10.7
Mtara Maécha	7.9
Abbas Djoussouf	7.8
Youssouf Saïd	6.1
Abdallah Halifa	4.5
Ali Mroudjaé	4.2
Moustoifa S. Cheick	3.4
Total	**100.0**

At the second ballot, held on 14 April 2002, Col ASSOUMANI AZALI was elected unopposed as Federal President of the Union of the Comoros after the withdrawal of his two qualifying opponents. Regional Presidents were elected on Mwali, Ngazidja and Nzwani in March–May 2002.

ASSEMBLY OF THE UNION

The Assembly of the Union was to be established following elections to the islands' local assemblies, which were postponed indefinitely in mid-March 2003.

Political Organizations

CHUMA (Islands' Fraternity and Unity Party): Moroni; e-mail chuma@pourlescomores.com; internet www.pourlescomores.com; f. 1985; Leader SAÏD ALI KEMAL.

Convention pour le renouveau des Comores (CRC): presidential party; f. 2002; Leader Col ASSOUMANI AZALI; Sec.-Gen. ABDOU SOEFOU.

Djawabu: Leader YOUSSOUF SAÏD SOILIHI.

Forces pour l'action républicaine (FAR): Leader Col ABDOURAZAK ABDULHAMID.

Forum pour le redressement national (FRN): f. 1994; alliance of 12 parties.

Front démocratique (FD): BP 758, Moroni; tel. (73) 3603; e-mail idriss@snpt.km; f. 1982; Leader MOUSTOIFA SAÏD CHEIKH.

Front national pour la justice (FNJ): Islamic fundamentalist orientation; Leader AHMED RACHID.

Mouvement des citoyens pour la République (MCR): f. 1998; Leader MAHAMOUD MRADABI.

Mouvement populaire anjouanais (MPA): f. 1997 by merger of Organisation pour l'indépendance d'Anjouan and Mouvement séparatiste anjouanais; principal separatist movement on Nzwani (Anjouan).

Mouvement pour la démocratie et le progrès (MDP—NGDC): Moroni; founder-mem. of the FRN (see above), from which it withdrew in May 1999; Leader ABBAS DJOUSSOUF.

Mouvement pour le socialisme et la démocratie (MSD): Moroni; f. 2000 by splinter group of the FD; Leader ABDOU SOEFOU.

Parti comorien pour la démocratie et le progrès (PCDP): Route Djivani, BP 179, Moroni; tel. (73) 1733; fax (73) 0650; Leader ALI MROUDJAE.

Parti républicain des Comores (PRC): BP 665, Moroni; tel. (73) 3489; fax (73) 3329; e-mail prc@online.fr; internet www.chez.com/prc; f. 1998; Leader MOHAMED SAÏD ABDALLAH M'CHANGAMA.

Parti socialiste des Comores (Pasoco): tel. (73) 1328; Leader AHMED AFFANDI ALI.

Rassemblement national pour le développement (RND): f. 1996; Chair. OMAR TAMOU; Sec. Gen. ABDOULHAMID AFFRAITANE.

Diplomatic Representation

EMBASSIES IN THE COMOROS

China, People's Republic: Coulée de Lave, C109, BP 442, Moroni; tel. (73) 2721; fax (73) 2866; e-mail ambassadechine@snpt.km; Ambassador ZHAO SHUNSHENG.

France: blvd de Strasbourg, BP 465, Moroni; tel. (73) 0753; fax (73) 1727; Ambassador JEAN PIERRE LAJAUNIE.

Korea, Democratic People's Republic: Moroni; Ambassador KIM RYONG YONG.

Libya: Moroni; tel. (73) 2819.

Judicial System

Under the terms of the Constitution, the President is the guarantor of the independence of the judicial system, and is assisted by the Higher Council of the Magistracy (Conseil Supérieur de la Magistrature). The highest ruling authority in judicial, administrative and fiscal matters is the Supreme Court (Cour Suprême). The High Council considers constitutional matters. Following the establishment of a Government of the Union of the Comoros, in June 2002, a Constitutional Court, comprising seven members, appointed by the President of the Union of the Comoros, the two Vice-Presidents and the three regional Presidents, was to be established.

Religion

The majority of the population are Muslims. At 31 December 2000 there were an estimated 2,000 adherents of the Roman Catholic Church, equivalent to 0.3% of the total population.

CHRISTIANITY

The Roman Catholic Church

Office of Apostolic Administrator of the Comoros: Mission Catholique, BP 46, Moroni; tel. (73) 0570; fax (73) 0503; e-mail mcatholique@snpt.km; Apostolic Pro-Admin. Fr JAN SZPILKA.

The Press

Al Watwan: Nagoudjou, BP 984, Moroni-Coulée; tel. and fax (74) 4047; e-mail alwatwan@snpt.km; internet www.comores-online .com/al-watwan; f. 1985; weekly; state-owned; Dir-Gen. AMAD MDAHOMA; Editor-in-Chief AHMED ALIAMIR; circ. 1,500.

L'Archipel: BP 1327, Moroni; f. 1988; monthly; independent; Publrs ABOUBACAR MCHANGAMA, SAINDOU KAMAL; circ. 300.

La Gazette des Comores: BP 2216, Moroni; tel. (73) 5234; e-mail la_gazette@snpt.km; internet site.voila.fr/la_gazette; weekly; Publication Dir ALLAOUI SAÏD OMAR.

Le Matin des Comores: BP 1040, Moroni; tel. (73) 2995; fax (73) 2939; e-mail lematin@snpt.km; internet www.lematindescomores .com; daily; Dir ALILOIAFA MOHAMED SAÏD.

NEWS AGENCY

Agence Comores Presse (ACP): Moroni.

Broadcasting and Communications

TELECOMMUNICATIONS

Société Nationale des Postes et des Télécommunications: BP 5000, Moroni; tel. (73) 0610; fax (73) 1079; e-mail snpt@snpt.km; internet www.snpt.km; operates post and telecommunications services; Dir-Gen. MGOMRI OUMARA.

BROADCASTING

Transmissions to the Comoros from Radio France Internationale commenced in early 1994. By 2002 a number of privately owned radio and TV stations were broadcasting in the Comoros.

Direction Générale Radio et TV Comores: Voidjou, Moroni; tel. (73) 2149.

Djabal TV: Iconi, BP 675, Moroni; tel. (73) 6767.

Mtsangani Television (MTV): Mtsangani, BP 845; tel. (73) 3316.

Radio-Comoro: BP 452, Moroni; tel. (73) 2531; fax (73) 0303; govt-controlled; domestic programmes in Comoran and French; international broadcasts in Swahili, Arabic and French; Dir-Gen. ISMAIL IBOUROI; Tech. Dir ABDULLAH RADJAB.

Radio KAZ: Mkazi, BP 1933; tel. (73) 5201.

TV—SHA: Shashagnogo; tel. (73) 3636.

Finance

BANKING

(cap. = capital; res = reserves; dep. = deposits; m. = million; brs = branches; amounts in Comoros francs)

Central Bank

Banque Centrale des Comores: Place de France, BP 405, Moroni; tel. (73) 1002; fax (73) 0349; e-mail bancecom@snpt.km; f. 1981; bank of issue; cap. 1,100m., res 7,260m., dep. 5,640m. (Dec. 1999); Gov. IBRAHIM BEN ALI.

Commercial Bank

Banque pour l'Industrie et le Commerce—Comores (BIC): place de France, BP 175, Moroni; tel. (73) 0243; fax (73) 1229; e-mail bic@snpt.km; f. 1990; 51% owned by Banque Nationale de Paris Intercontinentale; 34% state-owned; total assets 22,364m. (Dec. 1999); Pres. IDI NADHOIM; Dir-Gen. GUY CAZENAVE; 6 brs.

Development Bank

Banque de Développement des Comores: place de France, BP 298, Moroni; tel. (73) 0818; fax (73) 0397; e-mail bdc.moroni@snpt .km; f. 1982; provides loans, guarantees and equity participation for small- and medium-scale projects; 50% state-owned; cap. and res 1,242.0m., total assets 3,470.5m. (Dec. 2002); Pres. MZE CHEI OUBEIDI; Gen. Man. SAÏD ABDILLAHI.

Trade and Industry

GOVERNMENT AGENCIES

Office National du Commerce: Moroni; state-operated agency for the promotion and development of domestic and external trade.

Office National d'Importation et de Commercialisation du Riz (ONICOR): BP 748, Itsambouni, Moroni; tel. (73) 0370; fax (73) 0144; e-mail onicor_moroni@snpt.km.

Société de Développement de la Pêche Artisanale des Comores (SODEPAC): Moroni; state-operated agency overseeing fisheries development programme.

DEVELOPMENT ORGANIZATIONS

CEFADER: a rural design, co-ordination and support centre, with brs on each island.

CHAMBERS OF COMMERCE

Chambre de Commerce, d'Industrie et d'Agriculture: BP 763, Moroni; privatized in 1995.

Union des Chambres de Commerce des Comores: Moroni; Pres. MOINSALIMA MAHAMOUD SOIDIKI.

TRADE ASSOCIATION

Organisation Comorienne de la Vanille (OCOVA): BP 472, Moroni; tel. (73) 2709; fax (73) 2719.

EMPLOYERS' ORGANIZATIONS

Club d'Actions des Promoteurs Economiques: Moroni; f. 1999; Head SAID HASSANE DINI.

Organisation du Patronat Comorien (OPACO): Pres. SAÏD HASSANE NOURDINE.

UTILITIES

MA-MWE—Gestion de l'Eau et de l'Electricité aux Comores: BP 1762, Moroni; tel. (73) 3130; fax (73) 2359; e-mail cee@snpt.km; f. as Electricité et Eau des Comores; transferred to private management and renamed Comorienne de l'Eau et de l'Electricité in 1997; renationalized and renamed Service Public de l'Eau et de l'Electricité in 2001; reprivatized in Jan. 2002 and renamed as above; responsible for the production and distribution of electricity and water; Dir-Gen. MRADABI FAKRIDDINE.

TRADE UNION

Union des Syndicats Autonomes des Travailleurs des Comores: BP 1199, Moroni; tel. and fax (73) 5143; f. 1996; Sec.-Gen. IBOUROI ALI TABIBOU.

Transport

ROADS

In 1999 there were an estimated 880 km of classified roads. About 76.5% of the network was paved in that year.

SHIPPING

The port of Mutsamudu, on Ngazidja, can accommodate vessels of up to 11 m draught. Goods from Europe are routed via Madagascar, and coastal vessels connect the Comoros with the east coast of Africa.

Société Comorienne de Navigation: Moroni; services to Madagascar.

CIVIL AVIATION

The international airport is at Moroni-Hahaya on Nzwani. Each of the three other islands has a small airfield. At the end of 1995 it was announced that Air Comores, the national airline, was to be liquidated. In October 1999 Yemen Airways (Yemenia), following negotiations with the Comoran Government, was granted the status of the national airline of the Comoros and the use of the Comoran air traffic rights between Moroni and Paris, France. In September 2000 it was announced that an agreement had been signed with Air Gulf Falcon (based in the United Arab Emirates) to create a new Comoran airline, Comores Air International (CAI), which would service the Moroni–Paris route.

Comores Aviation: Moroni; f. 1999; twice weekly; charter flights between Moroni and Mayotte; Dir JEAN MARC HEINTZ.

Tourism

The principal tourist attractions are the beaches, underwater fishing and mountain scenery. In 1999 hotel capacity amounted to an estimated 780 beds. Receipts from tourism totalled US $26m. in 1997, but decreased to $16m. in 1998, before recovering very slightly to $17m. in 1999. Tourist arrivals increased to 27,474 in 1998, but had decreased to 23,893 by 2000, mainly as a result of the unstable political situation.

Société Comorienne de Tourisme et d'Hôtellerie (COMOTEL): Itsandra Hotel, BP 1027, Moroni; tel. (73) 2365; national tourist agency; Dir-Gen. SITTI ATTOMANE.

THE DEMOCRATIC REPUBLIC OF THE CONGO

Introductory Survey

Location, Climate, Language, Religion, Flag, Capital

The Democratic Republic of the Congo (formerly Zaire) lies in central Africa, bordered by the Republic of the Congo to the north-west, by the Central African Republic and Sudan to the north, by Uganda, Rwanda, Burundi and Tanzania to the east and by Zambia and Angola to the south. There is a short coastline at the outlet of the River Congo. The climate is tropical, with an average temperature of 27°C (80°F) and an annual rainfall of 150 cm–200 cm (59 ins–97 ins). French is the official language. More than 400 Sudanese and Bantu dialects are spoken; Kiswahili, Kiluba, Kikongo and Lingala being the most widespread. An estimated 50% of the population is Roman Catholic, and there is a smaller Protestant community. Many inhabitants follow traditional (mostly animist) beliefs. The national flag (proportions 2 by 3) is blue, with a large central yellow star and six smaller yellow stars arranged vertically at the hoist. The capital is Kinshasa.

Recent History

The Democratic Republic of the Congo, formerly the Belgian Congo, became independent from Belgium as the Republic of the Congo on 30 June 1960. Five days later the armed forces mutinied, and the UN subsequently dispatched troops to the region to maintain order. In September the Head of State, Joseph Kasavubu, dismissed the Prime Minister, Patrice Lumumba. Later in that month government was assumed temporarily by Col (subsequently Marshal) Joseph-Désiré Mobutu. Mobutu returned power to President Kasavubu in February 1961. A few days later Lumumba was murdered. In August a new Government was formed, with Cyrille Adoula as Prime Minister. In July 1964 Kasavubu appointed Moïse Tshombe, the former leader of a group supporting the secession of the Katangan region, as interim Prime Minister, pending elections, and in August the country was renamed the Democratic Republic of the Congo. Following elections in March and April 1965, a power struggle developed between Tshombe and Kasavubu; in November Mobutu intervened, seizing power and proclaiming himself head of the 'Second Republic'. In late 1970 Mobutu, as sole candidate, was elected President. (From January 1972, as part of a national policy of 'authenticity', he became known as Mobutu Sese Seko.) In November 1970 elections to a new National Assembly (subsequently renamed the National Legislative Council, NLC) took place. In October 1971 the Democratic Republic of the Congo was redesignated the Republic of Zaire, and one year later the Government of Zaire and the Executive Committee of the Mouvement populaire de la révolution (MPR), the sole legal political party, merged into the National Executive Council (NEC).

In March 1977, and again in May 1978, Katangan separatists invaded Zaire from Angola, taking much of Shaba (formerly Katanga) region; however, the separatists were repulsed on both occasions by the Zairean army, with armed support from a number of Western Governments. The invasion of 1977 prompted Mobutu to introduce a number of political reforms, including the introduction of a new electoral code. Legislative elections took place in October, and, at a presidential election in December, Mobutu (again the sole candidate) was re-elected for a further seven-year term. In August 1980 he assumed the new post of Chairman of the MPR. In early 1982 opponents of Zaire's one-party system of government formed the Union pour la démocratie et le progrès social (UDPS). This was followed by the formation of the Front congolais pour le rétablissement de la démocratie (FCD), a coalition of opposition parties, for which Nguza Karl-I-Bond, the First State Commissioner (Prime Minister) from August 1980 until April 1981, was the spokesman. Léon Kengo Wa Dondo was appointed First State Commissioner in a ministerial reshuffle in November 1982. Mobutu was re-elected President in July 1984. Elections to the NLC were held in September 1987. In November 1988 Mobutu replaced about one-third of the members of the NEC and reappointed Kengo Wa Dondo to the post of First State Commissioner, from which he had been removed in October 1986.

The organization of opposition demonstrations (violently suppressed by the security forces) during 1989 and early 1990, prompted Mobutu's announcement, in April 1990, that a plural political system, initially to comprise three parties, would be introduced after a transitional period of one year; the UDPS was immediately legalized. At the same time Mobutu declared the inauguration of the 'Third Republic' and relinquished the posts of Chairman of the MPR and State Commissioner for National Defence in the NEC, although remaining Head of State. N'Singa Udjuu Ongwakebi Untube, who had been First State Commissioner in 1981–82, was subsequently appointed the new Chairman of the MPR. The NEC was dissolved and Kengo Wa Dondo was replaced as First State Commissioner by Prof. Lunda Bululu, a distinguished international civil servant. In May 1990 a new, smaller, transitional NEC was formed, and Mobutu announced the imminent 'depoliticization' of the security forces and of the administration in general. In June Mobutu relinquished presidential control of the NEC and of foreign policy, and authorized the formation of independent trade unions. In October it was announced that a full multi-party political system would be established, and in November the necessary legislation was introduced. In the same month the USA announced that it was to suspend military and economic aid to Zaire, following renewed allegations of human rights abuses by the Mobutu regime (and continued speculation that Mobutu had personally misappropriated funds).

By February 1991 a large number of new parties had emerged. Prominent among them was the Union des fédéralistes et républicains indépendants (UFERI), led by Nguza Karl-I-Bond. An enlarged transitional Government, appointed in March and reshuffled in April, included members of minor opposition groups. None of the major opposition parties, including the UDPS and the UFERI, agreed to join the new Government. Prof. Mulumba Lukoji, an economist who had served in previous administrations, was appointed First State Commissioner.

In early April 1991 Mobutu announced that a national conference would be convened at the end of that month, at which government and opposition representatives would draft a new constitution. However, the Conference was postponed, owing to widespread disturbances and anti-Government demonstrations in several parts of the country. In late April Mobutu resumed the chairmanship of the MPR. In July some 130 opposition movements formed a united front, the Union sacrée. Later in July Mulumba Lukoji resigned as First State Commissioner. Etienne Tshisekedi Wa Mulumba, the leader of the UDPS, was appointed in his place, but refused the post following threats to his life, and Mulumba Lukoji was subsequently reappointed. The National Conference was convened at the beginning of August, but was repeatedly suspended, initially owing to the dissatisfaction of the Union sacrée with the composition of its participants, and eventually by the Government, prompting renewed civil unrest and the dispatch of French and Belgian troops to Zaire to evacuate nationals of those countries. Although Tshisekedi finally accepted the post of First State Commissioner in September, he later refused to swear allegiance to the President and the Constitution; shortly afterwards he was replaced as First State Commissioner by Bernardin Mungul Diaka, also a member of the opposition. In November Mobutu dismissed Mungul and appointed Nguza Karl-I-Bond to the premiership. The Union sacrée denounced the appointment and expelled UFERI members from its ranks. Despite the expiry of his mandate as President in early December, Mobutu remained in office. In mid-December the Roman Catholic Archbishop of Kisangani, Laurent Monsengwo Pasinya, was elected President of the National Conference.

In April 1992 the National Conference reopened and declared its status to be sovereign and its decisions to be binding. Mobutu reacted with cautious opposition to the erosion of his powers. In mid-August the National Conference elected Tshisekedi as First State Commissioner, following the resignation of Nguza Karl-I-Bond. A 'transition act', adopted by the Conference in early August, afforded Tshisekedi a mandate to govern for 24 months, pending the promulgation of a new constitution that would curtail the powers of the President. On 30 August Tshisekedi appointed a transitional 'Government of National Union', which included opponents of Mobutu.

The political interests of Tshisekedi and Mobutu clashed almost immediately when the President declared his intention to promote the adoption of a 'semi-presidential constitution', in opposition to the parliamentary system favoured by the Conference. On 14 November 1992 the National Conference (without the participation of Mobutu's supporters) adopted a draft Constitution, providing for the establishment of a 'Federal Republic of the Congo', the introduction of a bicameral legislature and the election of a President (who would fulfil a largely ceremonial function) by universal suffrage. (Executive and military power was to be exercised by the Prime Minister.) The draft document was vigorously opposed by Mobutu, who unsuccessfully attempted in early December to remove the Tshisekedi Government. On 6 December the National Conference dissolved itself and was succeeded by a 453-member High Council of the Republic (HCR), headed by Archbishop Monsengwo, which, as the supreme interim executive and legislative authority, was empowered to amend and adopt the new Constitution and to organize legislative and presidential elections. At the same time Monsengwo declared that the report of a special commission, established by the Conference in order to examine allegations of corruption brought against Mobutu and his associates, would be considered by the HCR. Mobutu responded by ordering the suspension of the HCR and the Government. Attempts by the presidential guard to obstruct the convening of the HCR ended, following the organization of a public rally in Kinshasa by Monsengwo and other members of the HCR. With support from the USA, Belgium and France, Monsengwo reiterated the HCR's recognition of Tshisekedi as head of Zaire's Government.

In mid-January 1993 the HCR declared Mobutu to be guilty of treason, on account of his mismanagement of state affairs, and threatened impeachment proceedings unless he recognized the legitimacy of the 'Government of National Union'. At the end of the month an attempt by the President to pay army units with discredited banknotes provoked a mutiny that resulted in 65 deaths (including that of the French ambassador to Zaire) and necessitated the intervention of French troops. In early March, in an attempt to reassert his political authority, Mobutu convened a special 'conclave' of political forces to debate the country's future. The HCR and the Union sacrée refused to attend. In mid-March the 'conclave' appointed Faustin Birindwa, a former UDPS member and adviser to Tshisekedi, as Prime Minister, charged with the formation of a 'Government of National Salvation'. The NLC was also revived to rival the HCR, and was reconvened to operate within the terms of reference of the old Mobutu-inspired Constitution. Birindwa's Cabinet, appointed in April, included Nguza Karl-I-Bond (as First Deputy Prime Minister in charge of Defence) and three members of the Union sacrée, who were immediately expelled from that organization. While the Birindwa administration was denied widespread official international recognition, Tshisekedi became increasingly frustrated at the impotence of his own Government (the armed forces recommenced blocking access to the HCR) and the deteriorating stability of the country. During April the army embarked upon a campaign of intimidation of opposition members, while tribal warfare re-emerged in Shaba and also erupted in the north-eastern region of Kivu. Tshisekedi urged the intervention of the UN to address these problems, and in July the Secretary-General of the UN appointed a Special Envoy to Zaire.

At the end of September 1993 an agreement was concluded between representatives of President Mobutu and of the principal opposition groups, providing for the adoption of a single constitutional text for the transitional period, which would be subject to approval by a national referendum. Under the provisions of the agreement, national transitional institutions would include the President of the Republic, a reorganized parliament, a government and national judiciary. During October, however, attempts to finalize the terms of the agreement were complicated by the insistence of Tshisekedi's supporters that he should continue in the office of Prime Minister, despite the objections of

Mobutu's representatives that Tshisekedi's mandate had been superseded by the September agreement. The opposing positions of the principal political parties (largely polarized as the pro-Tshisekedi Union sacrée de l'opposition radicale—USOR and the pro-Mobutu Forces politiques du conclave—FPC) became more firmly entrenched during November and December.

An ultimatum, issued to all political parties by President Mobutu in early January 1994, in an attempt to end the political impasse, resulted in the conclusion of an agreement to form a government of national reconciliation, signed by all major constituent parties of the FPC and the USOR (with the notable exception of Tshisekedi's own UDPS). Encouraged by the unexpected level of political support for the initiative, on 14 January Mobutu announced the dissolution of the HCR and the NLC, the dismissal of the Government of National Salvation, headed by Birindwa, and the candidacy for the premiership of two contestants, Tshisekedi and Mulumba Lukoji, to be decided by the transitional legislature (to be known as the Haut Conseil de la République—Parlement de Transition, HCR—PT). Despite widespread condemnation of Mobutu's procedural circumvention of the HCR's authority, the HCR—PT was convened for the first time on 23 January. The HCR—PT promptly rejected Mobutu's procedure for the selection of a new Prime Minister. Subsequent attempts by the legislature to formulate a new procedure were frustrated by the increasingly divergent interests of the member parties of the USOR, and by Tshisekedi's insistence of his legitimate claim to the office.

On 8 April 1994 the HCR—PT endorsed a new Transitional Constitution Act, reiterating the provisions of previous accords for the organization of a constitutional referendum and presidential and legislative elections, and defining the functions of transitional institutions during a 15-month period. The Government, to be accountable to the HCR—PT, was to assume some former powers of the President, including the control of the Central Bank and the security forces. A new Prime Minister was to be appointed from opposition candidates, to be nominated within 10 days of the President's promulgation of the Act (on 9 April). Widening divisions within the USOR frustrated attempts to unite the opposition behind Tshisekedi as sole candidate, prompting the expulsion, in May, of 10 dissident parties from the USOR.

In June 1994 the HCR—PT ratified the candidature of seven opposition representatives for the premiership, rejecting that of Tshisekedi on a technicality. On 14 June it was reported that Léon Kengo Wa Dondo had been elected Prime Minister by 322 votes to 133 in the HCR—PT. However, Kengo Wa Dondo's election was immediately denounced as illegitimate, under the terms of the April Constitution Act, by the opposition and by the Speaker of the HCR—PT, Monsengwo Pasinya (who refused to endorse the actions of the legislature). A new transitional Government, announced on 6 July, was similarly rejected by the radical opposition, despite the offer of two cabinet posts to the UDPS. On 11 July, during a motion of confidence, the Government received overwhelming support from the HCR—PT. In October an expanded radical opposition grouping (the Union sacrée de l'opposition radicale et ses alliés, USORAL) resumed its participation in the HCR—PT, having boycotted proceedings since the election of Kengo Wa Dondo in June. A reallocation of portfolios, carried out in November, included the appointment of two ministers and two deputy ministers who were (or had previously been) members of the UDPS.

In late June 1995 political consensus between the FPC and the USORAL resulted in the HCR—PT's adoption of a constitutional amendment (approved by Mobutu) whereby the period of national transition (due to end on 9 July) was to be extended by two years, owing to a shortage of government resources. On 1 July deputies from both groups voted to remove Monsengwo Pasinya from the post of President of the transitional legislature. Meanwhile, opposition frustration at the Government's failure to publish an electoral timetable intensified. In late July an anti-Government demonstration in the capital, organized by the Parti lumumbiste unifié (a group supporting the aims of the murdered former Prime Minister, Patrice Lumumba), led to violent clashes that resulted in 10 fatalities. A subsequent anti-Government protest in Kinshasa, organized by the USORAL in August, denounced international endorsement of Prime Minister Kengo Wa Dondo and urged his removal. In December opposition groups unanimously rejected a government offer to participate in a national coalition government and reiterated their demands for the prompt announcement of a timetable for multi-party elections. A National Electoral Commission, comprising 44 members (22 from both of the major political groupings) and headed by Bayona Bameya (a close political associate of President Mobutu), was formally installed in April 1996.

In mid-April 1996 it was announced that multi-party presidential and legislative elections would be conducted in May 1997, and would be preceded by a referendum on a new constitution in December 1996. President Mobutu announced that he was to contest the presidential poll. (However, neither the elections nor the referendum took place, as the security situation in the country worsened—see below.) A draft of the new Constitution, which provided for a federal state with a parliamentary system of government and a president with limited powers, was approved by the Government in late May.

In the mid-1990s existing ethnic tensions in eastern Zaire were heightened by the inflow of an estimated 1m. Hutu refugees from Rwanda (see below). The plight of the region's Zairean Tutsis (Banyamulenge) aroused international concern in late 1996, following reports of the organized persecution of Banyamulenge communities by elements of the Zairean security forces and by extremist Hutu refugees. In October the Sud-Kivu regional administration ordered all Banyamulenge to leave the area within one week or risk internment or forced expulsion. Although the order was subsequently rescinded, this threat provoked the mobilization of armed Banyamulenge rebels, who launched a violent counter-offensive, allegedly supported by the Tutsi-dominated authorities in Rwanda and Burundi. Support for the rebels from dissidents of diverse ethnic origin (including Shaba and Kasaï secessionists, and local Mai-Mai warriors) increased during the month, and later in October the rebels announced the formation of the Alliance des forces démocratiques pour la libération du Congo-Zaïre (AFDL), under the leadership of Laurent-Désiré Kabila (hitherto leader of the Parti de la révolution populaire, and a known opponent of the Mobutu regime since the 1960s). AFDL forces made rapid territorial gains, and the movement soon gathered momentum, emerging as a national rebellion aimed at overthrowing Mobutu. Counter-attacks by Zairean troops from January 1997 failed to recapture any significant area of territory. In March the AFDL entered the strategically important northern town of Kisangani (which had served as the centre of military operations for the Government), and in early April Mbuji-Mayi fell to the rebels. Nguza Karl-I-Bond, now leader of the pro-Mobutu FPC, urged his followers (for the most part Shaba secessionists) to support the AFDL. AFDL troops, entering Lubumbashi on 9 April, were welcomed as liberators, while government troops withdrew from the city. The Zairean Government continued to make allegations that the AFDL offensive was being supported by government troops from Rwanda, Uganda, Burundi and Angola, while the AFDL, in turn, claimed that the Zairean army was being augmented by white mercenary soldiers and by forces of the União Nacional para a Independência Total de Angola (UNITA).

Meanwhile, in August 1996 Mobutu had travelled to Switzerland to receive treatment for cancer. His absence, and uncertainties as to the state of his health, contributed to the poor co-ordination of the Zairean Government's response to the AFDL, which by the end of November was in control of most of Kivu. In that month the HCR—PT urged the expulsion of all Tutsis from Zairean territory; following attacks on Tutsis and their property, many Tutsi residents of Kinshasa fled to Brazzaville (Republic of the Congo). In the same month repeated public demonstrations demanded the resignation of Kengo Wa Dondo (himself part-Tutsi in origin) for having failed to respond effectively to the insurrection. In December Mobutu returned to Zaire, appointed Gen. Mahele Bokungu as Chief of General Staff and reorganized the Government, retaining Kengo Wa Dondo as Prime Minister.

The continued exclusion of Tshisekedi from the Government prompted his supporters to mount a campaign of civil disobedience, and in January 1997 his faction of the UDPS announced its support for the AFDL. In February, following a highly effective general strike in Kinshasa, Mobutu banned all demonstrations and industrial action. In March, following the capture of Kisangani, the HCR—PT voted to dismiss Kengo Wa Dondo, who tendered his resignation as Prime Minister towards the end of the month. He was replaced at the beginning of April by Tshisekedi, who, having offered government posts to members of the AFDL (which they refused), announced that he was dissolving the HCR—PT. Parliament, in turn, voted to dismiss Tshisekedi, whose supporters organized a demonstration of support in Kinshasa, only to come under attack from the security forces. On 8 April Mobutu declared a national state of emergency, dissolving the Government and ordering the deployment of security forces throughout Kinshasa. Gen. Likulia Bolongo was appointed Prime Minister at the head of a new 28-member 'Government of National Salvation', in which the USORAL refused to participate. An arrest warrant was subsequently issued for Kengo Wa Dondo, who was alleged to have fled to Switzerland with funds from the national treasury.

After peace talks between Mobutu and Kabila, mediated by the South African President, Nelson Mandela, ended in failure in early May 1997, Kabila reiterated his intention to take the capital by force. On 16 May Mobutu left Kinshasa (travelling to Togo, and then to Morocco, where he died in September), while many of his supporters and family fled across the border to Brazzaville. On 17 May AFDL troops entered Kinshasa (encountering no resistance), and Kabila, speaking from Lubumbashi, declared himself President of the Democratic Republic of the Congo (DRC, the name in use during 1964–71), which swiftly gained international recognition. He immediately announced plans to form a provisional government within 72 hours and a commission to draft a new constitution within 60 days; presidential and parliamentary elections were to be held in April 1999. On 20 May 1997 Kabila arrived in Kinshasa, and by 22 May the AFDL was in control of most of the country. On 23 May Kabila formed a transitional Government, which, while dominated by members of the AFDL, also included members of the UDPS and of the Front patriotique and avoided a potentially unpopular preponderance of ethnic Tutsis. No Prime Minister was appointed, and Tshisekedi was not offered a cabinet post; he refused to recognize the new Government and advocated public protest against the administration, but failed to raise the mass support that he had previously enjoyed. On 26 May, following a number of protest demonstrations, Kabila issued a decree indefinitely banning all political parties and public demonstrations. On 28 May Kabila issued a constitutional decree (which was to remain in force pending the adoption of a new constitution), investing the President with virtually absolute legislative and executive power, as well as control over the armed forces and the treasury. Of the previously existing state institutions, only the judiciary was not dissolved.

On 29 May 1997 Kabila was sworn in as President of the DRC, assuming full executive, legislative and military powers. Despite concern regarding the new administration's treatment of refugees, Kabila's assumption of power was well received internationally. In early June it was announced that a number of high-ranking officials from the Mobutu period, including the Secretary-General of the MPR and the Governor of the Central Bank, had been arrested, and that the directors of all parastatal companies had been suspended, pending further investigations. In late July it was reported that the Minister of Finance had been arrested on charges of fraud. Although any wrongdoing on the part of the minister (who was obliged to relinquish his post) was swiftly denied by the Government, it aroused fears of high-level corruption. Instability persisted for the remainder of 1997; in July a protest against the ban on political activity was reported to have resulted in three civilian deaths, following clashes between troops and demonstrators.

In August 1997 a military Court of Justice was established by decree, and at the end of October two statutory orders were signed by Kabila; one redesignated the administrative areas and local authorities of the DRC (the nine former regions were reorganized into 11 provinces), while the other created a para-military force (the Service national), which, under the control of the President, was to monitor and facilitate national reconstruction. In late October Kabila appointed a 42-member Constitutional Commission (originally due to be appointed in June), which was to draft a new constitution by March 1998. In the following month Kabila reaffirmed that the activities of political parties were suspended, pending presidential and legislative elections, scheduled to take place in 1999. At the end of November 1997 Kabila's Special Adviser for Security and the acting Army Chief of Staff, Gen. Masasu Nindanga, was arrested, and charged with maintaining a private militia and fraternizing with state enemies; he was later sentenced to 20 years' imprisonment. It was subsequently reported that up to 20 people had been killed in clashes between rival army factions, while ethnic violence continued between the Tutsi and Bantu groups in Eastern Province.

On 3 January 1998 Kabila reorganized the Cabinet, creating two new ministerial posts. On 20 January Joseph Olenghankoy, the Chairman of the opposition Forces novatrices pour l'union et la solidarité (FONUS), was arrested for reasons believed to be related to a complaint he had made against two government ministers. He was later sentenced by a military court to 15 years' imprisonment for violating the ban on political activity, although he was released from prison in June 1999. In February 1998 Tshisekedi was banished to his native village and placed under house arrest for his continued political activity on behalf of the UDPS. In March the new draft Constitution was presented to Kabila. In April UNESCO suspended co-operation with the DRC Government in protest at the detention of Arthur Z'Ahidi Ngoma, a UNESCO official and political activist who had been arrested in November 1997. Ngoma received a 12-month suspended sentence for breaking the ban on political activity in May 1998 and was released in June. In July Tshisekedi was returned to Kinshasa and announced that he was willing to co-operate with Kabila.

During 1998 there were problems with security on many of the DRC's borders, and agreements to increase border security were negotiated with Uganda, Burundi and the Central African Republic; talks were also held with Rwanda. In May a summit meeting of Great Lakes countries, which was to take place in the DRC on the first anniversary of Kabila's accession to power, was cancelled after only three of the 16 invited countries sent delegates to Kinshasa. This was widely interpreted as an indication of worsening relations between the DRC and its neighbours. On 1 June, following continued fighting in the east of the DRC, the military authorities announced the capture of 500 Mai-Mai insurgents in Kivu. Human rights organizations accused the Government of killing more than 1,000 civilians during its operation to suppress the Mai-Mai.

Following accusations of financial impropriety against several members of the Cabinet and the subsequent arrest of the Minister of Information and the Minister without Portfolio, on 6 June 1998 Kabila announced a cabinet reorganization, in which five ministers suspected of fraud or corruption were dismissed. Eight new posts were created, increasing the number of ministers from 29 to 37. In July a UN investigative team, which, despite continued obstruction by the Government, had conducted enquiries in the DRC between November 1997 and early 1998, published its report, concluding that the AFDL had massacred a large number of Rwandan Hutu refugees in 1996 and 1997; these findings were rejected by the Government on the grounds that they were based on an incomplete investigation.

On 27 July 1998 Kabila issued a decree expelling Rwandan troops from the country. He had earlier replaced the DRC Chief of Staff, James Kabereke, a Rwandan national, with Célestin Kifwa, a DRC citizen. In early August a rebellion was launched in Nord-Kivu province, in the east of the DRC, which was reported to have Rwandan and French support. The Minister of State for the Presidency, Deogratias Bugera, and the Minister of Foreign Affairs, Bizima Karaha, defected from the Government and joined the rebellion. Karaha was subsequently replaced by Jean-Charles Okoto, formerly deputy Governor of Kasaï Oriental province. Western Governments advised their citizens to leave the country, and several diplomatic missions were closed. The rebels advanced quickly in the east of the country and were soon reported to have captured Bukavu and Goma. Shortly afterwards a second front was opened from Kitona, in the west of the country, where further advances placed the rebels in control of Boma, Banana and Matadi. The Inga Dam, which supplies both electricity and water to Kinshasa and the Katanga mining region, was also captured, enabling the rebels to interrupt power supplies. At that time the rebel forces announced that they had formed a political organization, the Rassemblement congolais démocratique (RCD), with the aim of introducing political democracy in the DRC. The RCD leadership included Arthur Z'Ahidi Ngoma, together with a former Prime Minister, Lunda Bululu, and Ernest Wamba dia Wamba. In mid-August Kabila was reported to have left Kinshasa for Lubumbashi, the former base of the AFDL insurgency. Kabila returned to Kinshasa at the end of the month, by which time he had installed his son, Joseph, as Chief of Staff. In late August a number of human rights organizations expressed their concern over alleged incitement to violence by the DRC Government and the media, following reports that government troops were detaining and killing Tutsis and Rwandans and that rebels, retreating from the west, were victims of mob attacks.

Other countries in the region were, meanwhile, becoming involved in the conflict. While Rwanda had initially denied accusations that it was supporting the rebels, it quickly became evident that the anti-Kabila insurgents had the support of both

Rwanda and Uganda, and that Kabila was receiving support from Angola, Namibia and Zimbabwe. Angolan troops, in particular, were instrumental in recapturing rebel-held towns in the western DRC, and in early September 1998 had expelled the rebels from that part of the country. Regional divisions were clearly evident at a meeting of Ministers of Defence of the Southern African Development Community (SADC, see p. 311), convened by President Mugabe of Zimbabwe on 18–19 August, to mobilize support for Kabila; only one-half of the participating delegates favoured intervention in the conflict. Regional efforts to reach a political solution to the civil conflict continued in September. The Government refused to negotiate with the RCD and a newly formed rebel grouping, the Mouvement pour la libération du Congo (MLC), however, on the grounds that their activities were supported by Rwanda and Uganda, respectively.

In September 1998 an Institutional Reform Commission (IRC), headed by the Minister of Justice, was established by Kabila to examine the draft Constitution. Kabila still maintained that elections would be held in April 1999, and, as part of the electoral preparations, a census was to be conducted in October 1998. At the end of that month the IRC presented the revised draft Constitution to Kabila.

Although their advance had been halted in the west, the rebels continued to make progress in the east, capturing towns in Kasaï Oriental and Katanga. Despite their continued military successes, however, the rebels lacked popular support, and the movement was widely perceived as a Rwandan-backed Tutsi invasion. In mid-October the rebels shot down a passenger plane, which, they claimed, was transporting troops to the front; the Government denied this and stated that a number of civilians had been on board. In late October the Minister of Finance and the Budget, Ferdinand Tala Ngai, was arrested; his duties were assumed by the Minister of Agriculture. (In August 1999 Tala Ngai was found guilty of embezzlement and sentenced to seven months' hard labour.)

In January 1999 the ongoing civil war led to the declaration of a state of siege in six of the 11 provinces of the DRC. On 29 January Kabila issued a decree ending the ban on political parties. However, the new system was widely criticized for continuing restrictions, which effectively prevented many existing parties from registering. Kabila also announced that the AFDL was to be transformed into People's Power Committees to encourage involvement in the political process at a local level. Following Kabila's dissolution of the Cabinet on 20 February, a new Government was formed in March and was subsequently enlarged to comprise 37 members.

In May 1999 the RCD announced changes to its executive committee; Wamba dia Wamba was replaced as President by Dr Emile Ilunga. (Ngoma had resigned in February.) However, a number of the RCD's founding members opposed this move, and Wamba dia Wamba denounced it as a coup. Following clashes in Kisangani between supporters of Wamba dia Wamba and those of Ilunga, two factions emerged; one led by Ilunga, based in Goma with the support of Rwanda, the other led by Wamba dia Wamba, based in Kisangani and supported by Uganda. In June the DRC began proceedings at the International Court of Justice against Burundi, Rwanda and Uganda for acts of armed aggression, which it claimed to have been in contravention of both the charters of the Organization of African Unity (OAU, now the African Union, see p. 130) and the UN. (In February 2001 the DRC abandoned the proceedings against Burundi and Rwanda.)

Despite a number of regional initiatives to end the civil war in late 1998 and early 1999, no lasting cease-fire agreement was negotiated, largely owing to Kabila's continued insistence that the rebels were supported by Rwanda and Uganda, and that they, therefore, be excluded from any talks. Although Col Muammar al-Qaddafi, the Libyan leader, hosted two rounds of regional talks in Sirte (Libya), it was in Lusaka, Zambia, under the mediation of Zambia's President Chiluba, that the rebels were first accorded a place at the negotiations, during a summit held in late June. Following this meeting, a cease-fire agreement was signed by the Heads of State of the DRC, Angola, Namibia, Zimbabwe, Rwanda and Uganda on 10 July (witnessed by the OAU, the SADC, the UN and Zambia), by the leader of the MLC, Jean-Pierre Bemba, on 1 August and, following the resolution of a dispute (owing to the divisions within the RCD), by all 50 founding members of the RCD on 31 August. The agreement provided for an immediate cease-fire, the establishment of a Joint Military Commission (JMC), which was to investigate cease-fire violations, disarm militia groups and monitor the withdrawal of foreign troops, the deployment of a UN peace-keeping force and the organization of a national debate within the DRC. However, the UN stressed that authorization for a full peace-keeping force would have to be preceded by a 90-member military liaison mission and a subsequent 500-strong military observer mission. In July a general amnesty for rebels within the DRC was announced, and in that month the JMC was formed, comprising representatives of the rebel groups and the six Lusaka signatory states (the DRC, Angola, Namibia, Rwanda, Uganda and Zimbabwe). In mid-August the UN military liaison mission received official approval.

In August 1999 further fighting erupted in Kisangani between forces from Rwanda and Uganda and their respective factions of the RCD. A cease-fire was negotiated in late August, and at the end of the month the Ilunga faction of the RCD announced a new executive committee. An investigation into the causes of the fighting recommended that all fighting forces be removed from Kisangani; as a result, the MLC transferred its headquarters to Gbadolite, while the Wamba dia Wamba faction of the RCD, which had become known as the RCD—Mouvement de libération (RCD—ML), withdrew from Bunia. In early September the rebels raised objections to the composition of the cease-fire commission and voiced doubts over the neutrality of the mediators. At the end of the month, however, the rebels and the Government agreed that the national debate would be facilitated by the Italian Sant'Egidio Roman Catholic Community, although differences remained over the location for the conference and over OAU involvement. In October the rebels denied that they had violated the cease-fire in Katanga province, and at the end of the month the discovery of evidence of mass graves in rebel-held territory was reported. During the civil war both the rebels and the Government were accused of perpetrating large-scale massacres of civilians.

Unrest became increasingly evident in late 1999. In November both factions of the RCD announced that they no longer respected the cease-fire, and the Ilunga faction of the movement accused the Government of openly violating the agreement. On 5 November the UN Security Council voted to extend the mandate of the military liaison mission until 15 January 2000, owing to the difficulties experienced in obtaining security assurances and permission to deploy throughout the DRC. At the end of the month the Council approved the establishment of the Mission de l'organisation des nations unies en République démocratique du Congo (MONUC, see p. 66), with an initial mandate until 1 March 2000. It was principally to comprise liaison and technical assessment officers, although the Council requested that up to 500 military observers be equipped ready for deployment pending further recommendations on the security situation. Their deployment, together with a protective force of up to 5,037 troops, was approved on 24 February; at the same time the mandate of the mission was extended until 31 August.

At a meeting of the UN Security Council concerning the conflict in the DRC, which took place in New York, USA, in January 2000, regional Heads of State expressed support for the rapid deployment of MONUC forces to support the Lusaka peace accord. In February the UN Security Council adopted a proposal extending the mandate of MONUC to the end of August and expanding the force to number 5,537. In late February the national debate was convened in Kinshasa, but was boycotted by opposition politicians, as well as by representatives of the rebel groups. Participants in the discussions subsequently submitted a final report, urging the establishment of a new national assembly and the revision of the Lusaka accord. The rebel groups rejected an offer by Kabila of a general amnesty in return for the cessation of hostilities, and fierce fighting between government and rebel forces continued in the east of the country, particularly in Kasaï Occidental. In early April participants at a meeting of the JMC signed a new cease-fire agreement, whereby all the forces involved in the conflict were to suspend hostilities and remain in position for a period of three months, pending the deployment of MONUC personnel to form a neutral zone between them. In early May, however, Ugandan and Rwandan forces again clashed in Kisangani, in violation of the cease-fire. After meeting a UN Security Council delegation, the Rwandan and Ugandan contingents agreed to the demilitarization of the town, and its transfer to the control of MONUC. Later that month RCD, Rwandan and Ugandan forces commenced withdrawal to a certain distance from the town. In June, however, it was reported that some 400 civilians had been killed in further hostilities between Rwandan and Ugandan troops in Kisangani. At the end of the month UN military personnel confirmed that Rwandan and Ugandan forces had withdrawn from the town, although some RCD members remained.

In June 2000 three ministers, responsible, respectively, for the portfolios of energy, the economy, commerce and industry, and mines, were arrested in connection with fraudulent activities and subsequently removed from office. In early July the Government withdrew the DRC ambassador in Belgium, in protest at an international arrest warrant issued by a Belgian magistrate against the Minister of State for Foreign Affairs and International Co-operation, Abdoulaye Yérodia Ndombasi, for crimes against humanity. (DRC refugees in Belgium had submitted a legal appeal accusing Ndombasi of inciting violence against the Tutsi ethnic group.) In the same month 240 deputies of a new 300-member transitional Parliament were elected by a commission under the supervision of the Ministry of Internal Affairs, while the remaining 60 were nominated by Kabila. A presidential decree, adopted in that month, provided for the decentralization of the Government, with the transferral of the legislature to Lubumbashi and the Supreme Court to Kisangani. On 22 August the new transitional Parliament was inaugurated in Lubumbashi, despite criticism from the international community, which accused Kabila of acting in contravention of the Lusaka accord.

In August 2000 the UN Security Council adopted a resolution extending the mandate of MONUC until mid-October to allow further time for the implementation of the cease-fire agreement. Kabila subsequently informed the UN that he had authorized the immediate deployment of MONUC troops throughout the DRC. In early September the Cabinet was extensively reorganized, following the dismissal of the ministers in June. (A further government reshuffle was effected in November.) Later in September it was reported that, after the resumption of hostilities between government and MLC forces, the MLC had recaptured the north-western town of Dongo. In October Ilunga was replaced in a reorganization of the leadership of the main RCD faction. In the same month an attempt to oust Wamba dia Wamba from the leadership of the RCD—ML was reported to have been suppressed. In early December, following renewed fierce fighting, the RCD, supported by Rwandan troops, succeeded in gaining control of the significant town of Pweto, in the south-eastern province of Katanga. The six countries and three rebel groups involved in the conflict subsequently signed an agreement in Harare, Zimbabwe, pledging to withdraw forces 15 km from positions of military engagement, prior to the deployment of MONUC troops (which was scheduled to take place within 45 days). Nevertheless, hostilities subsequently continued at Pweto, and in other eastern regions, while the RCD refused to withdraw its forces in accordance with the agreement until the Government entered into bilateral discussions with the rebels and permitted the complete deployment of MONUC troops. In mid-December the UN Security Council adopted a resolution in favour of extending the mandate of MONUC to mid-June 2001.

On 16 January 2001 Kabila was fatally injured by one of his bodyguards at his private residence in Kinshasa. (The circumstances of his assassination remained unclear, and a committee of investigation was established in early February.) The transitional Parliament approved the nomination by the political leadership of his son, Joseph (hitherto Chief of Staff), as interim President. Following his inauguration on 26 January, Maj.-Gen. Joseph Kabila immediately engaged in international diplomatic efforts to resolve the conflict and urged rebel leaders to attend peace discussions with him. Following a meeting with Kabila in early February, the President of Rwanda, Maj.-Gen. Paul Kagame, announced that Rwandan troops would be withdrawn from Pweto on condition that control of the town was transferred to MONUC. However, the UN Security Council continued to demand that the DRC Government demonstrate its commitment to peace prior to the deployment of MONUC troops and insisted that the implementation of the disengagement plan agreed in December was essential to this end. At a meeting of the UN Security Council in mid-February Kabila accepted the former Botswanan President, Sir Quett Ketumile Masire, as mediator to the conflict. (Laurent Kabila had previously opposed Masire's nomination to the post.) Following a further meeting of the UN Security Council later that month, attended by representatives of the six countries and three rebel factions involved in the conflict, it was agreed that the 15 km withdrawal of forces was to commence by mid-March.

The withdrawal from positions of military engagement duly commenced in mid-March 2001, in accordance with the UN-sponsored agreement, with the retreat from Pweto of the RCD and allied Rwandan troops. The first contingents of MONUC troops arrived in the DRC, and by the end of the month were stationed in the north-east of the country. At the beginning of April, however, the Ugandan-supported Forces pour la libération du Congo (FLC, which had been formed earlier that year by an amalgamation of the MLC and some factions of the RCD—ML) refused to proceed with the withdrawal from military positions near Kisangani until MONUC guaranteed security in the region. The deployment of MONUC troops in the east of the country was delayed, after the RCD initially prevented the peace-keeping forces from entering Kisangani. In mid-April Kabila appointed a new, enlarged Cabinet, which included only four members of the previous administration; it was reported that he had removed all ministers opposed to negotiating a settlement with the rebels.

In April 2001 a UN commission of experts issued a report, which accused Rwandan and Ugandan troops of systematic illegal exploitation of the DRC's mineral resources, and urged the Security Council to impose a trade embargo against the two countries. The Ugandan Government pledged to investigate the allegations of corruption (which implicated close members of the Ugandan President's family) and to complete the withdrawal of its forces from the DRC. In early May representatives of the DRC Government and the rebel factions, meeting in Lusaka, under the aegis of the OAU, the SADC and the UN, signed a declaration establishing the principles for an 'Inter-Congolese National Dialogue' (a formal process of national consultation, with the aim of reaching a permanent peace settlement). It was decided that Masire (as organizer of the dialogue) would visit each province to gather public opinion for a proposed agenda, prior to further preparatory discussions, which were scheduled for mid-June. Later in May Kabila ended the remaining restrictions on political activity (thereby removing a major impediment to conducting the Inter-Congolese National Dialogue) and ordered the release of a number of detained human rights activists. (The preliminary discussions were rescheduled for mid-July, and subsequently for August.)

In late May 2001 a report by the state prosecutor claimed that forces opposing the Government (the RCD and Rwandan and Ugandan troops) had conspired in the assassination of Laurent-Désiré Kabila, with the aim of seizing power. In June the UN Security Council approved a resolution extending the mandate of MONUC until mid-2002; the Council welcomed the progress towards negotiating a peace settlement, but reiterated demands that all foreign forces complete their withdrawal from the country. In early August, however, Kagame insisted that Kabila fulfil pledges to demobilize Rwandan Hutu militia, known as Interahamwe (who had become allied with DRC government forces, after participating in the genocide in Rwanda in 1994), as a precondition to withdrawing the Rwandan troops deployed in the country.

Preparatory discussions between Kabila and the leaders of the FLC and the RCD, mediated by Masire, which were for the first time attended by unarmed opposition groups and civic associations, were conducted in Gaborone, Botswana, in late August 2001. Agreement was reached on a number of significant issues for the organization of the Inter-Congolese National Dialogue, which was to commence in the Ethiopian capital, Addis Ababa, in mid-October and was expected to continue for 45 days. In early September the Namibian Government announced that it had withdrawn its troops (numbering some 1,850) from the DRC. However, further hostilities erupted in the east of the country, where government troops, supported by Mai-Mai militia, and RCD forces fought for control of the significant towns of Fizi and Kindu.

In mid-October 2001 the Inter-Congolese National Dialogue was convened in Addis Ababa; however, negotiations were suspended one week later, after the Government withdrew in protest at the absence of the allied Mai-Mai delegation. (The number of representatives had been significantly reduced, owing to the failure of donor governments to disburse much of the funds that had been pledged.) Later that year clashes intensified in the east of the country, while insufficient funds continued to present an impediment to the peace process. At the beginning of 2002, however, international donors pledged considerable development aid to support further efforts, in recognition of the progress achieved. In early January Ugandan troops were redeployed in the north-east of the country, near the town of Bunia, to prevent escalating fighting between the rebel factions from reaching the border with Uganda. In mid-January it was reported that the RCD had provisionally allowed the deployment of MONUC troops in Kindu, which was repeatedly under attack from Mai-Mai militia. Later that month RCD representatives, meeting with opposition parties and civil groups, reached consensus on a basis for political dialogue, including the establishment of a new transitional government, conditions under which elections would be conducted, and the length of the period of transition. The Inter-Congolese National Dialogue, which had been rescheduled several times, was to resume finally on 25 February.

The Inter-Congolese National Dialogue was reconvened in Sun City, South Africa, on 25 February 2002, as scheduled, but was initially boycotted by Bemba. On 18 April it was announced that the Government and the MLC had reached a compromise agreement, providing for the establishment of an administration of national unity: Kabila was to remain President and Bemba became Prime Minister for a transitional period, prior to general elections. The parties that signed the agreement commenced discussions in Matadi in May to draft a new constitution, while the RCD and the UDPS announced their intention to form a political alliance to oppose the accord between Kabila and Bemba. (In late August it was announced that some progress had been achieved in negotiations, with agreement reached on an arrangement that would allow the Kabila Government and the MLC to share control of a national armed force.) At the end of July, after discussions mediated by Mbeki and Annan, a peace agreement was signed by Kabila and President Kagame of Rwanda in Pretoria, South Africa. Under the accord, Kabila pledged to arrest and disarm the Interahamwe militia in the DRC, while the Rwandan Government was to withdraw all troops from the country (thereby also providing for the integration of the RCD into the peace process). President Robert Mugabe of Zimbabwe subsequently announced his intention of withdrawing the remaining Zimbabwean troops supporting the DRC Government. In August, however, following further fighting between Rwandan troops and armed groups in Sud-Kivu province, the DRC accused Rwanda of violating the cease-fire, while Rwanda, in turn, accused the Kabila Government of continuing to provide armaments to the Interahamwe militia. In early September the DRC and Uganda reached an accord in the Angolan capital, Luanda, providing for the normalization of relations between the two countries, and the full withdrawal of Ugandan troops in the DRC. The Ugandan and Zimbabwean Governments subsequently commenced the withdrawal of forces from the DRC (although the UN permitted some Ugandan troops provisionally to remain near the north-eastern town of Bunia to assist in the maintenance of security). At the end of September the withdrawal of Rwandan forces commenced, and it was announced that all 23,400 Rwandan troops had left the country by early October.

In mid-October 2002 Mai-Mai militia attacked RCD forces in the east of the country, following the departure of the Rwandan forces supporting the rebels. Later that month the five-member Panel of Experts on the exploitation of the DRC's mineral resources submitted a final report to the UN Security Council. Kabila subsequently suspended six ministers and a number of senior officials (including the head of the National Security Agency) who had been implicated in the report, and reorganized the Council of Ministers. (Several Zimbabwean ministers, and Ugandan and Rwandan military officers, were also cited in the report as being connected to illegal activities.) On 4 December the UN Security Council approved a resolution providing for the enlargement of MONUC to 8,700 personnel. (At the end of February 2003, however, the contingent continued to number only 4,414.) Following the convening of a peace conference in early December, in Pretoria, the Government and rebels signed an extensive power-sharing agreement on 17 of that month. Under the terms of this accord, Kabila was to remain as President, while four vice-presidential posts were to be allocated, respectively, to the incumbent Government, opposition parties, the main RCD faction and the MLC. The new 36-member transitional administration, to remain in power for a two-year period, was to comprise representatives of the Government, all three RCD factions, the MLC, the opposition and civil society. At the end of December the MLC and the two RCD factions signed a cease-fire agreement in Gbadolite, which was to allow the transportation of humanitarian assistance in the region. (However, all rebel factions subsequently failed to observe the cease-fire, and continued hostilities near the border with Uganda were reported.)

In early January 2003 a military court in Kinshasa imposed death sentences on 26 defendants, and custodial terms on a further 64, for their involvement in the assassination of President Laurent-Désiré Kabila. In the same month several members of the MLC were arrested in connection with atrocities perpetrated against civilians. Later in January the UN Security Council adopted a resolution extending the mandate of the Panel of Experts on the exploitation of the DRC's resources for a further six months. In February the Minister of Finance tendered his resignation, after the Council of Ministers rejected the proposed budget for that year (which had incorporated stringent IMF-recommended reforms). In early March the power-sharing agreement was endangered, when clashes erupted near Bunia between Ugandan forces and a small rebel group, known as Union des patriotes congolais (UPC), prompting the Ugandan Government to dispatch reinforcements to the region, while it was reported that large numbers of Rwandan troops had been redeployed at the border with the DRC. A further agreement to restore peace in the region was signed by the DRC and Ugandan Governments and local rebel groups later that month. Meanwhile, further discussions on constitutional and security issues for the transitional period were conducted in Pretoria; agreement was reached on the adoption of a draft constitution and the deployment of a neutral international force in the country, pending the establishment of a new national army (which would include former rebel combatants). All measures agreed by the participating groups under the December 2002 settlement were to be ratified at a final session of the Inter-Congolese National Dialogue. However, the Rwandan Government renewed threats to resume military engagement in eastern DRC if the UN failed to secure the total withdrawal of Ugandan forces. On 20 March 2003, in response to continuing violence near Bunia, in contravention of the cease-fire agreement, the UN Security Council adopted a resolution urging an increase in the number of military and humanitarian observers stationed in the DRC under the MONUC mandate, and an immediate withdrawal of the Ugandan troops. At the final peace conference, which was convened at Sun City on 2 April, government and rebel representatives endorsed the establishment of the two-year transitional administration. The official adoption of the Constitution on 4 April was followed by Kabila's inauguration as interim Head of State on 7 April. The Ugandan Government subsequently pledged to withdraw forces from the DRC by 24 April, in accordance with the peace agreement. Although the Ugandan troops failed to leave the country by that date, the departure of some 7,000 from the north-east commenced at the beginning of May. Despite the deployment of some 600 additional MONUC troops in the region of Bunia to compensate for the Ugandan withdrawal, fighting between ethnic militia forces erupted in the town (as Uganda and many international observers had predicted). Amid fears of a suspension of the peace process, UN officials conducted negotiations between the Hema and Lendu ethnic groups, which, it was reported, had been engaged in a longstanding land conflict in the region. Meanwhile, the nomination of the four Vice-Presidents to the new transitional Government was announced: these were Bemba; the Secretary-General of the main RCD faction, Azarias Ruberwa; a former minister (representing the incumbent administration), Abdoulaye Yerodia Ndombasi; and a former UN worker and prominent member of the political opposition, Arthur Zahidi Ngoma.

Zaire's relations with its neighbours have been complicated by the presence of large numbers of refugees in the border areas. From mid-1994 the credibility of Mobutu's Transitional Government was somewhat enhanced by its support for French and US initiatives to address the humanitarian crisis presented by the presence in Zaire of more than 2m. Rwandan refugees fleeing violence after the death of President Habyarimana. By August 1995, however, the security situation in refugee camps along the Zairean border had deteriorated to such an extent that the Zairean Government initiated a programme of forcible repatriation. Some 15,000 Rwandans were deported in a number of days, prompting widespread international concern for their welfare. In early September a formal agreement was concluded between the office of the UN High Commissioner for Refugees (UNHCR) and the Zairean Government for a more regulated and bilateral approach to the refugee crisis. By late 1996, however, little progress had been made in repatriating displaced Rwandans in Zaire. In October UNHCR warned that the distribution of food to the refugees was being prevented by the prevailing instability in eastern Zaire. In early November the AFDL declared a cease-fire for returning refugees, and later in the month announced the creation of a humanitarian corridor to the Rwandan border, in an effort to encourage the estimated 700,000 Rwandan refugees seeking shelter at the Mugunga camp, west of Goma, to return to Rwanda. An AFDL attack on extremist Hutu units operating from the camp finally prompted a large-scale return of refugees, although UNHCR continued to express concern over the welfare of repatriated Rwandans. As the AFDL advance continued as far west as Kisangani, reports began to emerge that relief supplies for the estimated 200,000 remaining refugees were being intercepted by the rebels, who were also accused of forcing refugees to flee nearby camps, and of refusing to allow aid workers to enter the camps. In late April 1997 the AFDL leader, Laurent Kabila, demanded that the UN complete full repatriation of the refugees within 60 days, after which time their return would be undertaken unilaterally by the rebels. By early May the AFDL had initiated an organized repatriation programme, which encountered almost immediate condemnation from the UN, owing to the overcrowded conditions in which the refugees were being transported. Allegations continued to emerge during 1997 that elements of the AFDL had committed massacres of Hutu refugees. In December the DRC and Rwandan Governments agreed procedures with UNHCR for the repatriation of DRC refugees from Rwanda. By March 1998 more than 40,000 DRC refugees had been repatriated from Tanzania, and in May UNHCR announced the repatriation of DRC refugees from Uganda. The outbreak of civil war in the DRC in August, however, caused a suspension of repatriation to this country, and further refugee movement in the region. Many Rwandan and Burundian refugees were evacuated to Burundi, while other groups of displaced people arrived in Tanzania from the DRC. Despite the partial restoration of peace, following a number of peace agreements (see above), hostilities continued in the DRC, particularly in the province of Equateur, and some 325,164 refugees remained in neighbouring countries at the end of September 2002 (principally 136,194 in Tanzania and 92,771 in the Republic of the Congo). The refugee population in the DRC at that time totalled 334,572, of whom 185,248 originated from Angola, 75,600 from Sudan, 23,145 from Uganda, 22,171 from Rwanda and 19,625 from Burundi.

Government

Under the terms of a constitutional decree, which was promulgated in May 1997, executive power is exercised by the President, in consultation with the Government. In October 1997 a 42-member Constitutional Commission was appointed to draft a new constitution. The resultant draft Constitution was referred, in March 1988, to a 300-member Constituent Assembly, which was to review the document and submit it to a national referendum. The Assembly was, however, unable to convene, owing to the outbreak of civil war, and the work was completed in October by a 12-member Institutional Reform Commission, appointed by Kabila. In mid-2000 a new 300-member transitional Parliament was established; 240 deputies were elected by a commission under the supervision of the Ministry of Internal Affairs, while the remaining 60 were nominated by Kabila. The new transitional legislature was inaugurated on 22 August.

Defence

Following the overthrow of Mobutu's regime in May 1997, the former Zairean armed forces were disbanded. In August 2002 government forces, known as the Alliance des forces démocratiques pour la libération du Congo-Zaïre (AFDL), were estimated to number 79,000, the navy 900 and the air force 1,500. A civil war began in August 1998 in the east of the country, with troops from a number of neighbouring countries becoming involved: Angolan and Zimbabwean troops supported the Government, and Burundian, Rwandan and Ugandan troops the rebel forces. After the Governments of the DRC and Rwanda signed a peace agreement in mid-2002, it was announced in early October that all 23,400 Rwandan troops had been withdrawn from the country. While an agreement was also reached with the Ugandan Government, some Ugandan troops were permitted to remain in north-eastern DRC to assist in maintaining national security; in March 2003, however, following continuing hostilities, the UN demanded a complete Ugandan withdrawal, and most forces were reported to have left the country by early May. At 28 February 2003 the Mission de l'organisation des nations unies en République démocratique du Congo (MONUC) comprised 4,414 troops, 49 civilian police, and 581 international and 682 local civilian personnel; MONUC had a total authorized strength of 8,700 personnel (including 500 military observers). The defence budget for 2000 was US $400m.

Economic Affairs

In 1998, according to estimates by the World Bank, the gross national income (GNI) of the DRC (formerly Zaire), measured at average 1996–98 prices, was US $5,433m., equivalent to $110 per head (or $733 per head on an international purchasing-power parity basis). During 1990–98, it was estimated, the population increased at an average annual rate of 3.4%, while gross domestic product (GDP) per head declined, in real terms, by an average of 8.1% per year. According to the IMF, the DRC's GDP decreased, in real terms, at an average annual rate of 8.1% in 1990–95 and of 5.5% in 1996–2000, declining by an estimated 6.2% in 2000 and by an estimated 4.4% in 2001.

Agriculture (including forestry, livestock, hunting and fishing) contributed an estimated 54.0% of GDP in 1999. About 59.4% of the working population were employed in agriculture at mid-2001. The principal cash crops are coffee (which accounted for 9.8% of export earnings in 1999), palm oil and palm kernels, sugar, tea, cocoa, rubber and cotton. Agricultural GDP increased at an average annual rate of 2.0% in 1990–95, but decreased by an average of 3.7% per year in 1996–2000, declining by an estimated 5.5% in 2000.

Industry (including mining, manufacturing, construction and public works, and power) contributed an estimated 17.0% of GDP in 1999. Some 15.9% of the working population were employed in industry in 1991. Industrial GDP decreased at an average annual rate of 15.9% in 1990–95 and of 12.8% in 1996–2000, declining by an estimated 10.2% in 2000.

Mining (including mineral processing) contributed about 8.2% of GDP in 1999. Mineral products accounted for about 87.4% of export earnings in 1999. Diamonds, of which the DRC has rich deposits, are the principal source of foreign exchange, accounting for 61.3% of export earnings in 1999. The most important minerals are copper and cobalt (of which the country has 65% of the world's reserves). Manganese, zinc, tin and gold are also mined. In 1998–2002 there was extensive illicit exploitation of the DRC's mineral resources by rebel factions (see Recent History). In 2001 illicit mining of the country's abundant resources of columbite-tantalite (coltan) exceeded that of diamonds in the east of the country (although international demand subsequently declined). There are also extensive off-shore reserves of petroleum (revenue from petroleum accounts for about 20% of total government income). The sector's GDP (including the processing of minerals) decreased at an average annual rate of 22.5% in 1990–95 and of 6.3% in 1996–2000, declining by an estimated 0.4% in 2000.

Manufacturing contributed an estimated 4.3% of GDP in 1999. The most important sectors are textiles, cement, engineering and agro-industries producing consumer goods. Manufacturing GDP declined at an average annual rate of 12.4% in 1990–95 and of 14.6% in 1996–2000. The GDP of the sector declined by 14.3% in 1999, but increased by an estimated 3.0% in 2000.

Energy is derived principally from hydroelectric power. In 1999 an estimated 99.7% of electricity production was generated by hydroelectric plants. In 1999 imports of petroleum comprised 5.1% of the value of total merchandise imports.

The services sector contributed an estimated 29.0% of GDP in 1999, and employed some 19.0% of the working population in 1991. The GDP of the services sector decreased at an average annual rate of 16.1% in 1990–95 and of 5.7% in 1996–2000, declining by an estimated 2.3% in 2000.

In 2001, according to provisional figures, the DRC recorded an estimated trade surplus of US $238m., but there was a deficit of $124m. on the current account of the balance of payments. In 1995 the principal source of imports (an estimated 16.6%) was Belgium-Luxembourg; other major suppliers were South Africa, Nigeria, Ecuador, the United Kingdom and Germany. In that year South Africa was the principal market for exports (taking an estimated 29.6% of the total); the USA, Belgium-Luxembourg and Angola were also important markets for exports. In 1999 the principal exports were mineral products (mainly industrial diamonds, crude petroleum, cobalt and copper) and agricultural products (primarily coffee). The principal import was petroleum.

In 2001 there was a budget deficit of 797m. new Congolese francs, equivalent to 0.1% of GDP. At the end of 2000 external debt totalled US $11,645m., of which $7,842m. was long-term public debt. In 1998 the cost of debt-servicing was equivalent to 1.2% of the value of exports of goods and services. At the end of 2001 external public debt was estimated at $12,880m. (of which

arrears amounted to $10,082m.). Annual inflation averaged 249.9% in 1996–2000. Consumer prices increased by 553.7% in 2000 and by an estimated 357% in 2001.

The DRC maintains economic co-operation agreements with its neighbours, Burundi and Rwanda, through the Economic Community of the Great Lakes Countries (see p. 340). The DRC is also a member of the International Coffee Organization (see p. 336) and of the Common Market for Eastern and Southern Africa (COMESA, see p. 162). In September 1997 the DRC became a member of the Southern African Development Community (SADC, see p. 311).

Potentially one of Africa's richest states, the DRC has extensive agricultural, mineral and energy resources. During the early 1990s, however, most foreign investment in the country was withdrawn, and by February 1994 government revenues had declined to such an extent that the World Bank declared the country 'insolvent', while in June it was suspended from the IMF. The administration of Laurent-Désiré Kabila, which came to power in May 1997, secured foreign investment to revive the highly lucrative mining sector and subsequently succeeded in restoring some financial stability. It was announced that a new currency, the Congolese franc, would replace the new zaire from June 1998. However, the outbreak of civil war in August resulted in a further deterioration in the financial situation, with repeated depreciation of the new currency, the resumption of hyperinflation and a widening of the budget deficit. Rebel factions gained control of much of the east of the country, where they systematically exploited mineral resources (thereby financing the continuing civil conflict). Ugandan and Rwandan forces supporting the rebels benefited significantly from gaining control of mineral concessions in the east, while Zimbabwe became involved in the conflict on behalf of the DRC Government, in return for significant control of the mining industry. Following the succession to the presidency of Joseph Kabila in January 2001 (see Recent History), significant progress in peace negotiations was achieved, although factional fighting continued in the east of the country. In that year the new Government implemented an IMF-monitored programme for the rehabilitation of public finances, which included the introduction of an official 'floating' exchange rate in May. The IMF subsequently commended the authorities' commitment to market reforms, which successfully ended hyperinflation, and allowed the organization to proceed with a three-year plan of poverty reduction and growth. In January 2002, in response to Kabila's urgent appeals for aid, international donors pledged to release considerable development assistance to support the continuation of the peace process. In August the World Bank also approved funding for the first stage of the DRC's emergency rehabilitation and reconstruction programme, which was to improve agricultural production and restore essential infrastructure. In September further progress towards post-conflict recovery was achieved, when the Paris Club of creditor Governments approved a large-scale rescheduling of the DRC's external debt. (The World Bank was expected to agree to a debt cancellation, conditional on the Government adhering to the IMF-approved economic programme.) A UN embargo on trade in unlicensed diamonds had been imposed in May 2001, and, following considerable progress in the peace process, most foreign troops were withdrawn from the DRC by October 2002 (see Recent History). An extensive power-sharing accord, which incorporated the principal rebel factions, was reached in December, although clashes involving the remaining Ugandan forces continued in the north-east of the country (see Recent History). In February 2003 the proposed budget for that year, which, in accordance with IMF recommendations, had aimed to maintain inflation at a low level through stringent fiscal measures, was rejected by a government consensus. In March the IMF granted further funds for reconstruction, but urged the Government to intensify efforts to control public expenditure.

Education

Primary education, beginning at six years of age and lasting for six years, is officially compulsory. Secondary education, which is not compulsory, begins at 12 years of age and lasts for up to six years, comprising a first cycle of two years and a second of four years. In 1998/99, according to UNESCO estimates, primary enrolment included 32.6% of students in the relevant age-group (33.4% of boys; 31.8% of girls), while the comparable ratio for secondary enrolment was 11.7% (14.8% of boys; 8.6% of girls). The country has four universities, situated at Kinshasa, Kinshasa/Limete, Kisangani and Lubumbashi. In the budget for

1997 a total of 144,000m. new zaires (0.2% of total expenditure by the central Government) was allocated to education.

Public Holidays

2003: 1 January (New Year's Day), 4 January (Commemoration of the Martyrs of Independence), 1 May (Labour Day), 24 June (Promulgation of the 1967 Constitution and Day of the Fishermen), 30 June (Independence Day), 1 August (Parents' Day), 14 October (Youth Day), 27 October (Naming Day), 17 November (Army Day), 24 November (Anniversary of the Second Republic), 25 December (Christmas Day).

2004: 1 January (New Year's Day), 4 January (Commemoration of the Martyrs of Independence), 1 May (Labour Day), 24 June (Promulgation of the 1967 Constitution and Day of the Fishermen), 30 June (Independence Day), 1 August (Parents' Day), 14 October (Youth Day), 27 October (Naming Day), 17 November (Army Day), 24 November (Anniversary of the Second Republic), 25 December (Christmas Day).

Weights and Measures

The metric system is in force.

Statistical Survey

Sources (unless otherwise stated): Département de l'Economie Nationale, Kinshasa; Institut National de la Statistique, Office Nationale de la Recherche et du Développement, BP 20, Kinshasa; tel. (12) 31401.

Area and Population

AREA, POPULATION AND DENSITY

Area (sq km)	2,344,885*
Population (census result)	
1 July 1984	
Males	14,543,800
Females.	15,373,000
Total	29,916,800
Population (UN estimates at mid-year)†	
1999	49,581,000
2000	50,948,000
2001	52,522,000
Density (per sq km) at mid-2001	22.4

* 905,365 sq miles.

† Source: UN *World Population Prospects: The 2000 Revision*. Figures are based on a UN-estimated mid-year population of 36,999,000 in 1990; according to official estimates, however, the population at mid-1990 was 35,562,000.

REGIONS*

	Area (sq km)	Population (31 Dec. 1985)†
Bandundu	295,658	4,644,758
Bas-Zaïre	53,920	2,158,595
Equateur	403,293	3,960,187
Haut-Zaïre	503,239	5,119,750
Kasaï Occidental	156,967	3,465,756
Kasaï Oriental	168,216	2,859,220
Kivu	256,662	5,232,442
Shaba (formerly Katanga). . .	496,965	4,452,618
Kinshasa (city)‡	9,965	2,778,281
Total.	**2,344,885**	**34,671,607**

* In October 1997 a statutory order redesignated the regions as provinces. Kivu was divided into three separate provinces, and several of the other provinces were renamed. There are now 11 provinces: Bandundu, Bas-Congo, Equateur, Kasaï Occidental, Kasaï Oriental, Katanga (formerly Shaba), Kivu-Maniema, Nord-Kivu, Province Orientale (formerly Haut-Zaïre), Sud-Kivu, Kinshasa (city).

† Provisional.

‡ Including the commune of Maluku.

Source: Département de l'Administration du Territoire.

PRINCIPAL TOWNS

(population at census of July 1984)

Kinshasa	2,664,309		Likasi	213,862
Lubumbashi . .	564,830		Boma	197,617
Mbuji-Mayi . .	486,235		Bukavu . . .	167,950
Kolwezi . . .	416,122		Kikwit. . . .	149,296
Kisangani. . .	317,581		Matadi . . .	138,798
Kananga . . .	298,693		Mbandaka . .	137,291

Source: UN, *Demographic Yearbook*.

BIRTHS AND DEATHS

(UN estimates, annual averages)

	1985–90	1990–95	1995–2000
Birth rate (per 1,000)	47.8	48.2	47.7
Death rate (per 1,000)	15.2	14.9	15.0

Source: UN, *World Population Prospects: The 2000 Revision*.

Expectation of life (WHO estimates, years at birth): 43.8 (males 42.1; females 45.5) in 2001 (Source: WHO, *World Health Report*).

ECONOMICALLY ACTIVE POPULATION

Mid-2001 (estimates in '000): Agriculture, etc. 13,353; Total labour force 21,286 (Source: FAO, *Production Yearbook*).

Health and Welfare

KEY INDICATORS

Total fertility rate (children per woman, 2001).	6.7
Under-5 mortality rate (per 1,000 live births, 2001) . .	205
HIV/AIDS (% of persons aged 15–49, 2001)	4.90
Physicians (per 1,000 head, 1996)	0.07
Hospital beds (per 1,000 head, 1990)	1.43
Health expenditure (2000): US $ per head (PPP) . . .	21.0
Health expenditure (2000): % of GDP	1.5
Health expenditure (2000): public (% of total) . . .	73.7
Access to water (% of persons, 2000).	45
Access to sanitation (% of persons, 2000)	20
Human Development Index (2000): ranking	155
Human Development Index (2000): value	0.431

For sources and definitions, see explanatory note on p. vi.

Agriculture

PRINCIPAL CROPS
('000 metric tons)

	1999	2000	2001
Rice (paddy)	350	338	326
Maize	1,199	1,184	1,169
Millet	33	34	35
Sorghum*	53	53	53
Potatoes	89	90	91
Sweet potatoes	246	237	228
Cassava (Manioc)	16,500	15,959	15,436
Taro (Coco yam)	60	62	64
Yams*	255	260	260
Other roots and tubers* . . .	52	56	56
Sugar cane	1,700	1,699	1,669*
Dry beans	130	122	114
Dry peas*	40	40	40
Groundnuts (in shell) . . .	396	382	368
Oil palm fruit*	950	950	990
Cabbages*	23	23	23
Tomatoes*	38	38	38
Onions (dry) *	53	53	53
Pumpkins*	38	38	38
Other vegetables*	274	274	274
Bananas	315	312	313
Plantains	577	527	530*
Oranges	192	185	185*
Grapefruit*	10	10	10
Avocados*	27	27	27
Mangoes	210	206	206*
Pineapples	200	196	196*
Papayas	220	213	213*
Other fruit*	64	64	64
Coffee (green)	49	42	37
Cocoa beans	7	6	6
Tea (made)	2	2	2
Tobacco (leaves)	4	4	4
Cotton (lint)	9	9	10
Natural rubber (dry weight) . .	7	7	7*

* FAO estimate(s).

Source: FAO.

LIVESTOCK
('000 head, year ending September)

	1999	2000	2001
Cattle	853	822	793
Sheep	939	925	911
Goats	4,197	4,131	4,067
Pigs	1,100	1,049	100
Poultry	22	22	21

Source: FAO.

LIVESTOCK PRODUCTS
('000 metric tons)

	1999	2000	2001
Beef and veal	14	14	13
Goat meat	19	19	19
Pig meat*	41	41	40
Poultry meat*	20	20	19
Game meat	91	90	90*
Other meat	57	56	57
Cows' milk*	5	5	5
Hen eggs*	7	7	7

* FAO estimate(s).

Source: FAO.

Forestry

ROUNDWOOD REMOVALS
(FAO estimates, '000 cubic metres, excl. bark)

	1999	2000	2001
Sawlogs, veneer logs and logs for sleepers	170	170	170
Other industrial wood . . .	3,483	3,483	3,483
Fuel wood	63,640	64,903	66,081
Total	67,293	68,556	69,734

Source: FAO.

SAWNWOOD PRODUCTION
('000 cubic metres, incl. railway sleepers)

	1997	1998	1999
Total (all broadleaved)	90	80	70

2000–01: Production as in 1999 (FAO estimates).

Source: FAO.

Fishing

(metric tons, live weight)

	1998	1999	2000
Capture	178,041	208,448	208,448
Aquaculture	500*	414	414
Total catch	178,541	208,862	208,862

* FAO estimate.

Source: FAO, *Yearbook of Fishery Statistics*.

Mining

(metric tons, unless otherwise indicated)

	1998	1999	2000
Hard coal	5,000*	—	—
Crude petroleum ('000 barrels) . .	9,444	8,650	10,300
Copper ore†	35,000	32,000*	21,000*
Zinc ore†	1,147	—	215
Tantalum and niobium (columbium) concentrates‡ . .	n.a.	n.a.	450*
Cobalt concentrates*† . .	5,000	6,000	7,000
Gold (kilograms)*†	4,800	4,000	4,000
Diamonds ('000 carats)§ . . .	26,083	20,116	17,700*

* Estimated production.

† Figures refer to the metal content of ores and concentrates.

‡ The estimated tantalum content in 2000 was 130 metric tons.

§ Of the total, the estimated production of gemstones (in '000 carats) was: 5,080 in 1998; 4,120 in 1999; 3,500 in 2000.

Source: US Geological Survey.

Industry

SELECTED PRODUCTS
('000 metric tons, unless otherwise indicated)

	1997	1998	1999
Maize flour	11.5	17.4	18.9
Wheat flour	131.6	113.4	88.8
Sugar	64.4	56.6	73.4
Cigarettes ('000 cartons)	3,555	3,848	3,200
Beer (million litres)	171.7	161.3	139.8
Soft drinks (million litres)	68.0	77.6	73.8
Soaps	25.7	29.2	17.5
Acetylene	35.2	24.4	12.8
Tyres ('000 units)	49.0	56.0	41.0
Cement	130.1	145.0	172.9
Steel	248	118	87
Explosives	435	513	300
Bottles ('000 units)	22.7	21.0	16.3
Gasoline ('000 barrels)*	89	434	431
Kerosene ('000 barrels)*	90	340	340
Jet fuel ('000 barrels)*	45	175	180
Distillate fuel oil ('000 barrels)*	90	457	460
Residual fuel oil ('000 barrels)*	280	874	880
Cotton fabrics ('000 sq metres)	10,568	1,563	3,143
Printed fabrics ('000 sq metres)	11,223	12,220	13,615
Footwear ('000 pairs)	1,742	1,609	848
Blankets ('000 units)	63	47	36
Matchets and wheels ('000 pieces)	304	245	207
Sheet metal ('000 pieces)	101	86	75
Motor cars (units)	156	94	84
Electric energy (million kWh)	4,835	4,520	5,087

* Estimates.

2000 (preliminary figures, '000 metric tons, unless otherwise indicated): Wheat flour 102.8; Sugar 72.9; Soaps 18.5; Acetylene 8.9; Cotton fabrics ('000 sq metres) 2,360; Printed fabrics ('000 sq metres) 3,710; Footwear ('000 pairs) 120.3.

Sources: IMF, *Democratic Republic of the Congo: Selected Issues and Statistical Appendix* (July 2001); US Geological Survey.

Finance

CURRENCY AND EXCHANGE RATES

Monetary Units
100 centimes = 1 new Congolese franc

Sterling, Dollar and Euro Equivalents (31 December 2002)
£1 sterling = 651.2 new Congolese francs
US $1 = 404.0 new Congolese francs
€1 = 423.7 new Congolese francs
1,000 new Congolese francs = £1.54 = $2.48 = €2.36

Average Exchange Rate (new Congolese francs per US $)
1998 1.607
1999 4.018
2000 21.818

Note: In June 1967 the zaire was introduced, replacing the Congolese franc (CF) at an exchange rate of 1 zaire = CF 1,000. In October 1993 the zaire was replaced by the new zaire (NZ), equivalent to 3m. old zaires. On 30 June 1998 a new Congolese franc, equivalent to NZ 100,000, was introduced. The NZ was withdrawn from circulation on 30 June 1999. Some of the figures in this Survey are still in terms of old or new zaires.

BUDGET
('000 million new zaires)*

Revenue†	1999	2000	2001
Taxation	1,793	10,270	61,420
Taxes on income and profits	408	1,299	10,239
Income taxes	273	846	5,611
Corporation tax	135	453	4,518
Taxes on goods and services	379	2,4462	14,451
Turnover taxes	155	562.	4,199
Excise duties	186	1,418.	9,085
Taxes on international trade	536	2,540	21,292
Import duties and taxes	513	2,406	20,670
Export duties	23	115	622
Other taxes	456	3,985	15,438
Other current revenue	803	823	5,224
Administrative fees and charges, etc.	126	593	4,736
Total	2,596	11,093	66,644

Expenditure	1999	2000	2001
Current expenditure	5,237	25,440	114,130
Expenditure on goods and services	4,623	22,078	65,530
Wages and salaries	2,080	6,964	24,030
Other goods and services	2,543	15,114	41,500
Interest on public debt	296	—	—
Transfers and subsidies	318	3,362	48,600
Transfers to other levels of national government	303	3,092	48,383
Capital expenditure‡	820	2,036	25,070
Total	6,058	27,476	139,200

* Figures refer to the consolidated accounts of the central Government.
† Excluding grants received ('000 million new zaires): 570 in 1999 (304 current; 266 capital); 4,397 in 2000 (3,092 current; 1,305 capital); 71,759 in 2001 (48,383 current; 23,376 capital).
‡ Including lending minus repayments.

Source: IMF, *Government Finance Statistics Yearbook*.

INTERNATIONAL RESERVES
(US $ million at 31 December)

	1993	1994	1995
Gold	8.59	10.71	10.83
Foreign exchange	46.20	120.69	146.60
Total	54.79	131.40	157.43

1996 (US $ million at 31 December): Foreign exchange 82.50.

1997 (US $ million at 31 December): Gold 15.80.

Source: IMF, *International Financial Statistics*.

MONEY SUPPLY
(million new Congolese francs at 31 December)

	1999	2000*
Currency outside banks	15,963	30,368
Demand deposits at deposit money banks	2,594	9,776
Total money	18,557	40,144

* Estimated figures.

Source: IMF, *Democratic Republic of Congo: Request for a Three-Year Arrangement Under the Poverty Reduction and Growth Facility and for the First Annual Program* (July 2002).

COST OF LIVING
(Consumer Price Index for Kinshasa; base: August 1995 = 100)

	1998	1999	2000
Food	3,820.7	12,909.6	75,943.0
Rent	3,143.7	11,086.5	73,439.8
Clothing	3,498.7	17,225.7	113,520.0
All items (incl. others)	3,259.0	12,069.0	78,899.0

Source: IMF, *Democratic Republic of the Congo: Selected Issues and Statistical Appendix* (July 2001).

NATIONAL ACCOUNTS
(million new Congolese francs at current prices)

Expenditure on the Gross Domestic Product

	1997	1998	1999
Government final consumption expenditure	624.1	809.2	3,173.3
Private final consumption expenditure	2,563.7	7,422.4	36,916.0
Gross capital formation	1,200.8	2,067.9	12,139.2
Total domestic expenditure	4,388.6	10,299.5	52,228.5
Exports of goods and services	1,380.5	2,976.0	11,033.0
Less Imports of goods and services	1,465.2	3,285.6	12,892.0
GDP in purchasers' values	4,303.9	9,989.9	50,369.5

Source: IMF, *Democratic Republic of the Congo: Selected Issues and Statistical Appendix* (July 2001).

Gross Domestic Product by Economic Activity

	1997	1998	1999
Agriculture, forestry, livestock, hunting, and fishing	343.8	4,645.3	27,138.2
Mining*	468.4	694.0	4,120.3
Manufacturing	465.2	593.7	2,144.0
Construction and public works	291.7	319.8	1,178.3
Electricity and water	378.4	435.3	1,089.4
Transportation and telecommunications	221.4	280.6	1,204.8
Trade and commerce	1,434.1	1,796.1	8,686.9
Public administration	177.0	359.4	2,096.3
Other services	563.0	715.0	2,589.4
Sub-total	4,343.0	9,839.2	50,247.6
Less Imputed bank service charges	145.0	55.9	413.1
GDP at factor cost	4,198.0	9,783.3	49,834.5
Import duties	105.9	206.6	535.0
GDP at market prices	4,303.9	9,989.9	50,369.5

* Including processing.

Source: IMF, *Democratic Republic of the Congo: Selected Issues and Statistical Appendix* (July 2001).

BALANCE OF PAYMENTS
(US $ million)

	2000	2001*
Exports of goods f.o.b.	892	940
Imports of goods f.o.b.	−669	−702
Trade balance	223	238
Services (net)	−165	−176
Balance on goods and services	58	62
Income (net)	−388	−414
Balance on goods, services and income	−330	−352
Current transfers (net)	136	228
Current balance	−194	−124
Capital account (net)	−388	−347
Net errors and omissions	−247	−216
Overall balance	−829	−686

* Provisional.

Source: IMF, *Democratic Republic of the Congo: Request for a Three-Year Arrangement Under the Poverty Reduction and Growth Facility and for the First Annual Program* (July 2002).

External Trade

PRINCIPAL COMMODITIES
(UN estimates, million old zaires)

Imports c.i.f.	1989	1990	1991
Food and live animals	63,380	121,824	2,172,956
Mineral fuels, lubricants, etc.	24,436	46,968	837,761
Chemicals	33,217	63,848	1,138,847
Basic manufactures	68,343	131,365	2,343,137
Machinery and transport equipment	102,706	197,414	3,521,243
Miscellaneous manufactured articles	16,418	31,557	562,877
Total (incl. others)	324,154	623,066	11,113,531

Exports f.o.b.	1989	1990	1991
Food and live animals	93,541	148,201	2,535,635
Mineral fuels, lubricants, etc.	36,064	57,138	977,599
Chemicals	49,024	77,672	1,328,924
Basic manufactures	100,866	159,807	2,734,207
Machinery and transport equipment	151,581	240,157	4,108,950
Miscellaneous manufactured articles	24,230	38,389	656,814
Total (incl. others)	478,409	757,967	12,968,384

Source: UN Economic Commission for Africa, *African Statistical Yearbook*.

1994 (US $ million): *Imports c.i.f.*: Mineral fuels 45.4; Total 628.8. *Exports f.o.b.*: Copper 42.8; Cobalt 140.3; Diamonds 293.6; Crude petroleum 123.5; Coffee 158.6; Total 1,271.6 (Source: IMF, *Zaire—Background Information and Statistical Data*, April 1996).

1996 (US $ million): *Imports c.i.f.*: Petroleum 79; Total 1,403. *Exports f.o.b.*: Copper 89; Cobalt 322; Diamonds 633; Crude petroleum 198; Coffee 263; Total 1,652 (Source: IMF, *Democratic Republic of the Congo: Selected Issues and Statistical Appendix*, July 2001).

1997 (US $ million): *Imports c.i.f.*: Petroleum 106; Total 1,133. *Exports f.o.b.*: Copper 83; Cobalt 119; Diamonds 611; Crude petroleum 177; Coffee 95; Total 1,189 (Source: IMF, *Democratic Republic of the Congo: Selected Issues and Statistical Appendix*, July 2001).

1998 (US $ million): *Imports c.i.f.*: Petroleum 126; Total 1,230. *Exports f.o.b.*: Copper 53; Cobalt 145; Diamonds 716; Crude petroleum 111; Coffee 67; Total 1,180 (Source: IMF, *Democratic Republic of the Congo: Selected Issues and Statistical Appendix*, July 2001).

1999 (US $ million): *Imports c.i.f.*: Petroleum 57; Total 1,108. *Exports f.o.b.*: Copper 48; Cobalt 80; Diamonds 572; Crude petroleum 116; Coffee 91; Total 933 (Source: IMF, *Democratic Republic of the Congo: Selected Issues and Statistical Appendix*, July 2001).

SELECTED TRADING PARTNERS
(US $ million)

Imports c.i.f.	1995
Belgium-Luxembourg	147.2
Canada	9.8
China, People's Repub.	26.8
Côte d'Ivoire	35.5
Ecuador	65.1
Germany	48.2
India	9.9
Iran	10.3
Italy	26.5
Japan	11.8
Kenya	22.5
Morocco	9.2
Netherlands	36.5
Nigeria	72.5
South Africa	89.3
Togo	22.5
United Kingdom	50.2
Zambia	9.4
Total (incl. others)	889.2

Exports f.o.b.	1995
Angola	51.0
Belgium-Luxembourg	90.9
Canada	11.6
Germany	8.7
Irael	17.2
Italy	29.6
Philippines	30.2
Senegal	9.5
South Africa	219.7
Switzerland	29.7
United Kingdom	29.7
USA	107.6
Total (incl. others)	742.8

Source: UN, *International Trade Statistics Yearbook*.

Transport

RAILWAYS
(Total traffic, million)

	1997	1998	1999
Passenger-km	235	242	9
Freight (net ton-km)	139	135	21

Source: UN, *Statistical Yearbook*.

ROAD TRAFFIC
(motor vehicles in use at 31 December)

	1994	1995*	1996*
Passenger cars	698,672	762,000	787,000
Buses and coaches	51,578	55,000	60,000
Lorries and vans	464,205	495,000	538,000
Total vehicles	1,214,455	1,312,000	1,384,000

* Estimates.

Source: International Road Federation, *World Road Statistics*.

SHIPPING

Merchant Fleet
(registered at 31 December)

	1999	2000	2001
Number of vessels	20	20	20
Total displacement ('000 grt)	12.9	12.9	12.9

Source: Lloyd's Register-Fairplay, *World Fleet Statistics*.

International Sea-borne Freight Traffic
(estimates, '000 metric tons)

	1988	1989	1990
Goods loaded	2,500	2,440	2,395
Goods unloaded	1,400	1,483	1,453

Source: UN, *Monthly Bulletin of Statistics*.

CIVIL AVIATION
(traffic on scheduled services)

	1997	1998	1999
Kilometres flown (million)	5	5	4
Passengers carried ('000)	237	241	132
Passenger-km (million)	305	321	263
Total ton-km (million)	44	44	39

Source: UN, *Statistical Yearbook*.

Tourism

FOREIGN TOURIST ARRIVALS BY ORIGIN

	1998	1999	2000
Africa	22,223	73,428	96,594
America	1,231	799	495
East Asia	1,333	1,400	—
Europe	7,975	4,295	5,681
Total (incl. others)	53,139	79,922	102,770

Tourism receipts (US $ million): 2 in 1998.

Source: World Tourism Organization, *Yearbook of Tourism Statistics*.

Communications Media

	1995	1996	1997
Radio receivers ('000 in use)	14,103	15,970	18,030
Television receivers ('000 in use)	3,679	5,051	6,478
Telephones ('000 main lines in use)*	36	36	21
Facsimile machines (number in use)*	5,000	5,000	n.a.
Mobile cellular telephones (subscribers)	8,500*	7,200	8,900
Daily newspapers	9	9	n.a.

* Provisional or estimated figure(s).

Source: International Telecommunication Union.

Book production (titles published): 64 in 1992.

Telephones ('000 main lines in use): 20 in 1998; 20 in 1999; 20 in 2000; 20 in 2001.

Mobile cellular telephones ('000 subscribers): 10,000 in 1998.

Personal computers ('000 in use): 200 in 1998; 500 in 1999.

Internet users: 500 in 1999; 6,000 in 2001.

Sources: UNESCO, *Statistical Yearbook*; UN Economic Commission for Africa, *African Statistical Yearbook*.

Education

(1998)

	Institu-tions	Teachers	Students Males	Students Females	Students Total
Primary	17,585	154,618	2,116,752	1,905,659	4,022,411
General secondary	6,007	89,461	554,895	307,830	862,725
Technical and vocational			256,313	115,490	371,803
Tertiary	n.a.	3,788	n.a.	n.a.	60,341*

* Estimate.

Source: UNESCO, *Statistical Yearbook*.

Adult literacy rate (UNESCO estimates): 61.4% (males 73.1%; females 50.2%) in 2000 (Source: UN Development Programme, *Human Development Report*).

Directory

The Constitution*

Following the proclamation of the Democratic Republic of the Congo, a 15-point constitutional decree was promulgated on 28 May 1997, which abrogated all previous constitutional dispositions. The decree declared the institutions of the Republic to be the President, the Government and the courts and tribunals; all institutions of the previous regime were suspended, except for the judiciary. All power was to be vested in the Head of State, pending the adoption of a new Constitution. In October 1997 President Kabila appointed a 42-member Constitutional Commission, which was to draft a new Constitution by March 1998. The resultant draft Constitution was subsequently referred to a 300-member Constituent Assembly, which was to review the document and submit it to a national referendum. The Assembly was, however, unable to convene, owing to the outbreak of civil war, and the work was undertaken in October by a 12-member Institutional Reform Commission, appointed by Kabila.

EXECUTIVE POWER

The President of the Republic exercises legislative power by decree, following consultation with the Cabinet; he is chief of the executive and of the armed forces and has the authority to issue currency; he has the power to appoint and dismiss members of the Government, ambassadors, provincial governors, senior army officers, senior civil servants and magistrates.

POLITICAL PARTIES

All political parties, with the exception of the Alliance des forces démocratiques pour la libération du Congo-Zaïre (AFDL), were banned by decree on 26 May 1997. In January 1999, however, President Kabila issued a decree legalizing the formation of political parties (see Recent History).

PROVINCIAL GOVERNMENTS

Local government in each province is administered by a provincial Governor and Deputy Governor, who are appointed and dismissed by the President.

*Following a power-sharing agreement between government and rebel representatives, reached in December 2002 (see Recent History), a new Constitution, providing for the installation of a two-year transitional authority, was officially adopted on 4 April 2003.

The Government

HEAD OF STATE

President: Maj.-Gen. Joseph Kabila (inaugurated 26 January 2001, 7 April 2003).

CABINET
(April 2003)

Minister of Agriculture: Salomon Banamuhere.

Minister of Communications and the Press: Kikaya Bin Karubi.

Minister of Culture and the Arts: Matuka Kavokisa.

Minister of Defence: Irung Awan.

Minister of the Economy: André Phillipe Futa.

Minister of Education: Kutumisan Kyota.

Minister of Energy: Georges Buse Falay.

Minister of Finance and the Budget: Albert Luhongwe.

Minister of Foreign Affairs and International Co-operation: Léonard She Okitundu.

Minister of Health: Mashako Mamba.

Minister of Human Rights: Ntumba Luaba.

Minister of Industry and Commerce: Ngalula Wafwana.

Minister of Internal Affairs: Théophile Mbemba.

Minister of Justice: Ngele Masudi.

Minister of Labour and Social Security: Marie Ange Lukiana Mufwankol.

Minister of Land Registration: Yuma Moota.

Minister of Mining and Petroleum: Nkulu Kikuku.

Minister of Posts, Telephones and Telecommunications: Mutombo Kyamakosa.

Minister of Public Administration: Benjamin Mukulungu.

Minister of Public Works: Kimbembe Mazungu.

Minister of Social Affairs: Jeanne Ebamba.

Minister of Transport: Pauni Wakale Kamanzi.

Minister of Youth and Sports: Thimothée Moleka Nzulama.

MINISTRIES

All ministries are in Kinshasa.

Office of the President: Hôtel du Conseil Exécutif, ave de Lemera, Kinshasa-Gombe; tel. (12) 30892.

Ministry of Agriculture: Immeuble Sozacom, 3rd floor, blvd du 30 juin, BP 8722 KIN I, Kinshasa-Gombe; tel. (12) 31821.

Ministry of Communications and the Press: ave du 24 novembre, BP 3171, KIN 1, Kinshasa-Kabinda; tel. (12) 23171.

Ministry of Culture and the Arts: BP 8541, Kinshasa 1; tel. (12) 31005.

Ministry of Defence: BP 4111, Kinshasa-Gombe; tel. (12) 59375.

Ministry of the Economy: Immeuble Onatra, blvd du 30 juin, BP 8500 KIN I, Kinshasa-Gombe.

Ministry of Education: Enceinte de l'Institut de la Gombe, BP 3163, Kinshasa-Gombe; tel. (12) 30098.

Ministry of Energy: Immeuble Snel, 239 ave de la Justice, BP 5137 KIN I, Kinshasa-Gombe; tel. (12) 22570.

Ministry of Finance and the Budget: blvd du 30 juin, BP 12998 KIN I, Kinshasa-Gombe; tel. (12) 31197.

Ministry of Foreign Affairs and International Co-operation: place de l'Indépendance, BP 7100, Kinshasa-Gombe; tel. (12) 32450.

Ministry of Health: blvd du 30 juin, BP 3088 KIN I, Kinshasa-Gombe; tel. (12) 31750.

Ministry of Internal Affairs: ave de Lemera, Kinshasa-Gombe; tel. (12) 23171.

Ministry of Justice: 228 ave de Lemera, BP 3137, Kinshasa-Gombe; tel. (12) 32432.

Ministry of Labour and Social Security: blvd du 30 juin, BP 3840, Kinshasa.

Ministry of Posts, Telephones and Telecommunications: Immeuble Kilou, 4484 ave des Huiles, BP 800 KIN I, Kinshasa-Gombe; tel. (12) 24854.

Ministry of Public Works: Immeuble Travaux Publics, Kinshasa-Gombe.

Ministry of Transport: Immeuble Onatra, blvd du 30 juin, BP 3304, Kinshasa-Gombe; tel. (12) 23660.

Ministry of Youth and Sports: 77 ave de la Justice, BP 8541 KIN I, Kinshasa-Gombe.

President

Following the assassination of President Laurent-Désiré Kabila on 16 January 2001, his son, Maj.-Gen. Joseph Kabila, was inaugurated as interim President on 26 January.

Legislature

The Head of State legislates by decree. In mid-2000 a 300-member transitional Parliament was formed; a selection committee, supervised by the Ministry of Internal Affairs, nominated candidates, who were subsequently approved by the President. Under a further presidential decree, signed in July, the Government was to be decentralized, with the legislature relocating to Lubumbashi. The new Parliament was inaugurated on 22 August in Lubumbashi.

Political Organizations

In January 1999 a ban on the formation of political associations was officially ended, and in May 2001 remaining restrictions on the registration and operation of political parties were removed. Despite a peace agreement, reached in December 2002, armed rebel movements remained active in the east of the country.

Comités du pouvoir populaire (CPP): f. 1999 as successor to **Alliance des forces démocratiques pour la libération du Congo-Zaïre (AFDL)**; committees formed in each village to devolve power to the people; to debate political policy.

Forces novatrices pour l'union et la solidarité (FONUS): Kinshasa; advocates political pluralism; Pres. JOSEPH OLENGHANKOY; Sec.-Gen. JOHN KWET.

Forces politiques du conclave (FPC): Kinshasa; f. 1993; alliance of pro-Mobutu groups, incl the UFERI, led by MPR; Chair. JEAN NGUZA KARL-I-BOND.

Forces pour le salut du Congo (FSC): f. June 2000 by fmr supporters of Pres. Mobutu; Leader JÉRÔME TSHISHIMBI.

Mouvement congolais pour la démocratie (MCD): Kinshasa; f. 1982; supports the aims of the late Patrice Lumumba; Sec.-Gen. JEAN-PIERRE MAKUNA WA KATENDA.

Mouvement pour la libération du Congo (MLC): f. 1998; Ugandan-supported rebel movement; numbers 32,000; Leader JEAN-PIERRE BEMBA.

Mouvement populaire de la révolution (MPR): f. 1966 by Pres. Mobutu; sole legal political party until Nov. 1990; advocates national unity and opposes tribalism; Leader (vacant); Sec.-Gen. KITHIMA BIN RAMAZANI.

Organistes des progressistes du Congo (Madaraka ya wendeliza wa Kongo—MWENDEKO): Kinshasa; e-mail mwendeko@mail.chez .com; internet www.chez.com/mwendeko.

Parti démocrate et social chrétien (PDSC): 32B ave Tombalbaye, Kinshasa-Gombe; tel. (12) 21211; f. 1990; centrist; Pres. ANDRÉ BO-BOLIKO; Sec.-Gen. TUYABA LEWULA.

Parti pour la réconciliation et le développement (PPRD): f. March 2002 by President Joseph Kabila.

Rassemblement congolais pour la démocratie (RCD): e-mail congorcd@congorcd.org; internet www.congorcd.org; f. 1998; advocates introduction of a democratic political system; split into two factions in 1999: Ilunga faction: Goma; supported by Rwanda; Pres. ADOLPHE ONUSUMBA.

Rassemblement congolais pour la démocratie—Mouvement de libération (RCD—ML): Bunia; broke away from main RCD in 1999; supported by Uganda; a number of groups were merged into the FLC (see above) in Jan. 2001; Pres. ERNEST WAMBA DIA WAMBA; Sec.-Gen. Dr JACQUES DEPELCHIN.

Rassemblement congolais pour la démocratie—National (RCD—N): Bafwasende; broke away from RCD—ML in Oct. 2000; Leader ROGER LUMBALA.

Rassemblement pour une nouvelle société (RNS): c/o 58 Hawthorne Court, Suite 1316, Washington, DC, 20017, USA; tel. (202) 4639373; fax (202) 4639374; e-mail info@congozaire.org.

Union des fédéralistes et républicains indépendants (UFERI): Kinshasa; f. 1990; seeks autonomy for province of Katanga; dominant party in the USOR; Pres. JEAN NGUZA KARL-I-BOND; Leader KOUYOUMBA MUCHULI MULEMBE.

Union des patriotes congolais (UPC): rebel group of 15,000 in conflict with Ugandan forces in north-east; Leader THOMAS LUBANGA.

Union pour la démocratie et le progrès social (UDPS): Twelfth St, Limete Zone, Kinshasa; e-mail udps@globalserve.net; internet www.udps.org/udps.html; f. 1982; Leader ETIENNE TSHISEKEDI WA MULUMBA; Sec.-Gen. Dr ADRIEN PHONGO KUNDA.

Union pour la République (UPR): Kinshasa; f. 1997 by fmr mems of the MPR; Leader CHARLES NDAYWEL.

Union sacrée de l'opposition radicale (USOR): Kinshasa; f. 1991, comprising c. 130 movements and factions opposed to Pres. Mobutu, in which the UDPS was the dominant party; a radical internal faction, known as the **Union sacrée de l'opposition radicale et ses alliés** (USORAL), emerged in 1994, led by FRÉDÉRIC KIBASSA MALIBA.

Union sacrée rénovée (USR): Kinshasa; f. 1993 by several ministers in fmr Govt of Nat. Salvation; Leader KIRO KIMATE.

Diplomatic Representation

EMBASSIES IN THE DEMOCRATIC REPUBLIC OF THE CONGO

Angola: 4413–4429 blvd du 30 juin, BP 8625, Kinshasa; tel. (12) 32415; Ambassador MAWETE JOÃO BAPTISTA.

Belgium: Immeuble Le Cinquantenaire, place du 27 octobre, BP 899, Kinshasa; tel. (12) 20110; fax (12) 22120; e-mail kinshasa@ diplobel.org; Ambassador RENIER NIJSKENS.

Benin: 3990 ave des Cliniques, BP 3265, Kinshasa-Gombe; tel. (98) 128659; e-mail abkin@raga.net; Ambassador GEORGES S. WHANNOU DE DRAVO.

Cameroon: 171 blvd du 30 juin, BP 10998, Kinshasa; tel. (12) 34787; Chargé d'affaires a.i. DOMINIQUE AWONO ESSAMA.

Canada: BP 8341, Kinshasa 1; tel. (88) 41277; e-mail knsha@ dfait-maeci.gc.ca; Ambassador ROLAND GOULET.

Central African Republic: 11 ave Pumbu, BP 7769, Kinshasa; tel. (12) 30417; Ambassador SISSA LE BERNARD.

Chad: 67–69 ave du Cercle, BP 9097, Kinshasa; tel. (12) 22358; Ambassador MAITINE DJOUMBE.

Congo, Republic: 179 blvd du 30 juin, BP 9516, Kinshasa; tel. (12) 30220; Ambassador MAURICE OGNAMY.

Côte d'Ivoire: 68 ave de la Justice, BP 9197, Kinshasa; tel. (12) 30440; Ambassador GILBERT DOH.

Cuba: 4660 ave Cateam, BP 10699, Kinshasa; tel. (12) 8803823; Ambassador JOSÉ SIVILA DE LA TORRE.

Egypt: 519 ave de l'Ouganda, BP 8838, Kinshasa; tel. (12) 34368; Ambassador AZIZ ABDEL HAMID HAMZA.

Ethiopia: BP 8435, Kinshasa; tel. (12) 23327; Ambassador DIEUDEONNE A. GANGA.

France: 97 ave de la République du Tchad, BP 3093, Kinshasa; tel. (12) 30513; Ambassador GILDAS LE LIDEC.

Gabon: ave du 24 novembre, BP 9592, Kinshasa; tel. (12) 68325; Ambassador MICHEL MADOUNGOU.

Germany: 82 ave Roi Baudouin, BP 8400, Kinshasa-Gombe; tel. (89) 48201; fax (satellite) 871-68-2623227; e-mail amballemagne@ic .cd; Ambassador DORETTA LOSCHELDER.

Greece: Immeuble de la Communauté Hellénique, 3ème étage, blvd du 30 juin, BP 478, Kinshasa; tel. (88) 44862; fax (88) 01002; e-mail grembkin@ic.cd; Ambassador SPYROS THEOCHAROPOULOS.

Holy See: 81 ave Goma, BP 3091, Kinshasa; tel. (12) 33128; fax (12) 33346; e-mail nuntius@raga.net; Apostolic Nuncio Most Rev. GIOVANNI D'ANIELLO (Titular Archbishop of Paestum).

Israel: 141 blvd du 30 juin, BP 8343, Kinshasa; tel. (99) 87218; fax (88) 07494; e-mail kinshasa@israel.org; Ambassador JAMAR F. GOLAN.

Japan: Immeuble Citibank, 2ème étage, ave Colonel Lukusa, BP 1810, Kinshasa; tel. (88) 45305; fax (satellite) 871-761-21-41-42; e-mail ambj@ic.cd; Ambassador YASUO TAKANO.

Kenya: 4002 ave de l'Ouganda, BP 9667, Kinshasa; tel. (88) 06834; Chargé d'affaires J. K. CHUMBA.

Korea, Democratic People's Republic: 168 ave de l'Ouganda, BP 16597, Kinshasa; tel. (12) 31566; Ambassador HAN PON CHUN.

Korea, Republic: 2A ave des Orangers, BP 628, Kinshasa; tel. (88) 20722; Ambassador CHUN SOON-KYU.

Lebanon: 3 ave de l'Ouganda, Kinshasa; tel. (12) 82469; Chargé d'affaires a.i. CHEHADE MOUALLEM.

Liberia: 3 ave de l'Okapi, BP 8940, Kinshasa; tel. (12) 82289; Ambassador JALLA D. LANSANAH.

Mauritania: BP 16397, Kinshasa; tel. (12) 59575; Ambassador Lt-Col M'BARECK OULD BOUNA MOKHTAR.

Netherlands: 11 ave Zongo Ntolo, BP 10299, Kinshasa; tel. (12) 7800142; fax (12) 7800155; e-mail kss@minbuza; Ambassador B. W. SCHORTINGHUIS.

Nigeria: 141 blvd du 30 juin, BP 1700, Kinshasa; tel. (12) 43272; Ambassador AHMED MOHAMMED KELE.

Portugal: 270 ave des Aviateurs, BP 7775, Kinshasa; tel. (88) 01309; Ambassador FRANCISCO FALCAO MACHADO.

Russia: 80 ave de la Justice, BP 1143, Kinshasa 1; tel. (12) 33157; fax (12) 45575; Ambassador VALERII GAMAIVNE.

South Africa: 17 ave Ngongo Lutete, BP 7829, Kinshasa-Gombe; tel. (88) 48287; fax (88) 04152; e-mail ambasud@raga.net; Ambassador S. NGOMBANE.

Sudan: 24 ave de l'Ouganda, Kinshasa; tel. (99) 37396; Chargé d'affaires a.i. ABDEL RA'OUF AMIR.

Sweden: 89 ave Roi Baudouin, BP 11096, Kinshasa-Gombe; tel. (81) 82528; fax (satellite) 870-761-971069; e-mail ambasuede@ic.cd; Ambassador ROBERT RYDBERG.

Togo: 3 ave de la Vallée, BP 10117, Kinshasa; tel. (12) 30666; Ambassador MAMA GNOFAM.

Tunisia: 67–69 ave du Cercle, BP 1498, Kinshasa; tel. and fax and fax (88) 03901; e-mail atkinshasa@ic.cd; Chargé d'affaires a.i. Azouz Ennifar.

Turkey: 18 ave Pumbu, BP 7817, Kinshasa; tel. (88) 01207; fax (88) 04740; e-mail tckinsbe@raga.net; Ambassador Deniz Uzmen.

United Kingdom: ave Roi Baudouin, BP 8049, Kinshasa; tel. (98) 169100; fax (88) 46102; e-mail ambrit@ic.cd; Ambassador James Atkinson.

USA: 310 ave des Aviateurs, BP 697, Kinshasa; tel. (88) 43608; fax (88) 43467; Ambassador Aubrey Hooks.

Zambia: 54–58 ave de l'Ecole, BP 1144, Kinshasa; tel. (12) 23038; Ambassador Ian Sikazwe.

Judicial System

The Minister of Justice is responsible for the organization and definition of competence of the judiciary; civil, penal and commercial law and civil and penal procedures; the status of persons and property; the system of obligations and questions pertaining to nationality; international private law; status of magistrates; organization of the legal profession, counsels for the defence, notaries and of judicial auxiliaries; supervision of cemeteries, non-profit-making organizations, cults and institutions working in the public interest; the operation of prisons; confiscated property.

There is a Supreme Court in Kinshasa, and there are also nine Courts of Appeal and 36 County Courts. A presidential decree, signed in July 2000, provided for government decentralization, with the Supreme Court relocating to Kisangani.

The Head of State is empowered to appoint and dismiss magistrates.

Supreme Court

Cnr ave de la Justice and ave de Lemera, BP 3382, Kinshasa-Gombe; tel. (12) 25104.

President of the Supreme Court: Bruno Mbiango.

Procurator-General of the Republic: Mongulu T'Apangane.

Religion

Many of the country's inhabitants follow traditional beliefs, which are mostly animistic. A large proportion of the population is Christian, predominantly Roman Catholic, and there are small Muslim, Jewish and Greek Orthodox communities.

CHRISTIANITY

The Roman Catholic Church

The Democratic Republic of the Congo comprises six archdioceses and 41 dioceses. An estimated 51% of the population are Roman Catholics.

Bishops' Conference

Conférence Episcopale de la République Démocratique du Congo, BP 3258, Kinshasa-Gombe; tel. (12) 34528; e-mail conf.episc.rdc@ic.cd; f. 1981; Pres. Cardinal Frédéric Etsou-Nzabi-Bamungwabi (Archbishop of Kinshasa).

Archbishop of Bukavu: Most Rev. Charles Kambale Mbogha, Archevêché, BP 3324, Bukavu; tel. (761) 470721; fax (762) 141148.

Archbishop of Kananga: Most Rev. Godefroid Mukeng'a Kalond, Archevêché, BP 70, Kananga; tel. 2477.

Archbishop of Kinshasa: Cardinal Frédéric Etsou-Nzabi-Bamungwabi, Archevêché, ave de l'Université, BP 8431, Kinshasa 1; tel. (12) 3723546.

Archbishop of Kisangani: Most Rev. Laurent Monsengwo Pasinya,, Archevêché, ave Mpolo 10B, BP 505, Kisangani; tel. (761) 608334; fax (761) 608336.

Archbishop of Lubumbashi: Most Rev. Floribert Songasonga Mwitwa, Archevêché, BP 72, Lubumbashi; tel. (2) 48601.

Archbishop of Mbandaka-Bikoro: Most Rev. Joseph Kumuondala Mbimba, Archevêché, BP 1064, Mbandaka; tel. 2234.

The Anglican Communion

The Church of the Province of the Congo comprises six dioceses.

Archbishop of the Province of the Congo and Bishop of Boga: Most Rev. Patrice Byankya Njojo, CAC-Boga, POB 25586, Nairobi, Kenya.

Bishop of Bukavu: Rt Rev. Fidèle Balufuga Dirokpa, CAC-Bukavu, POB 53435, Nairobi, Kenya.

Bishop of Katanga: Rt Rev. Isingoma Kahwa, BP 16482, Kinshasa; tel. (88) 06533; e-mail peac_isingoma@yahoo.fr.

Bishop of Kindu: Rt Rev. Zacharia Masimange Katanda, CAC-Kindu, POB 53435, Nairobi, Kenya; e-mail angkindu@antenna.nl.

Bishop of Kisangani: Rt Rev. Sylvestre Mugera Tibafa, CAC-Kisangani, BP 861, Kisangani.

Bishop of Nord Kivu: Rt Rev. Methusela Munzenda Musubaho, CAC-Butembo, POB 21285, Nairobi, Kenya; fax (satellite) 871-166-1121.

Kimbanguist

Eglise de Jésus Christ sur la Terre par le Prophète Simon Kimbangu: BP 7069, Kinshasa; tel. (12) 68944; f. 1921; officially est. 1959; c. 5m. mems (1985); Spiritual Head HE Salomon Dialungana Kiangani; Sec.-Gen. Rev. Luntadilla.

Protestant Churches

Eglise du Christ au Congo (ECC): ave de la Justice 75, BP 4938, Kinshasa-Gombe; f. 1902; a co-ordinating agency for all the Protestant churches, with the exception of the Kimbanguist Church; 62 mem. communities and a provincial org. in each province; c. 10m. mems (1982); Pres. Bishop Marini Bodho; includes:

Communauté Baptiste du Congo-Ouest: BP 4728, Kinshasa 2; f. 1970; 450 parishes; 170,000 mems (1985); Gen. Sec. Rev. Lusakweno-Vangu.

Communauté des Disciples du Christ: BP 178, Mbandaka; tel. 31062; f. 1964; 250 parishes; 650,000 mems (1985); Gen. Sec. Rev. Dr Elonda Efefe.

Communauté Episcopale Baptiste en Afrique: 2 ave Jason Sendwe, BP 2809, Lubumbashi 1; tel. and fax (2) 348602; e-mail kitobokabwe@yahoo.fr; f. 1956; 1,300 episcopal communions and parishes; 150,000 mems (2001); Pres. Bishop Kitobo Kabweka-Leza.

Communauté Evangélique: BP 36, Luozi; f. 1961; 50 parishes; 33,750 mems (1985); Pres. Rev. K. Lukombo Ntontolo.

Communauté Lumière: BP 10498, Kinshasa 1; f. 1931; 150 parishes; 220,000 mems (1985); Patriarch Kayuwa Tshibumbu Wa Kahinga.

Communauté Mennonite: BP 18, Tshikapa; f. 1960; 40,000 mems (1985); Gen. Sec. Rev. Kabangy Djeke Shapasa.

Communauté Presbytérienne: BP 117, Kananga; f. 1959; 150,000 mems (1985); Gen. Sec. Dr M. L. Tshihamba.

Eglise Missionaire Apostolique: 375 ave Commerciale, BP 15859, Commune de N'Djili, Kinshasa 1; tel. (98) 165927; e-mail buzi4@hotmail.com; f. 1986; 5 parishes; 2,600 mems; Apostle for Africa Rev. Lufanga-Ayimou Nanandana.

The Press

DAILIES

L'Analyste: 129 ave du Bas-Congo, BP 91, Kinshasa-Gombe; tel. (12) 80987; Dir and Editor-in-Chief Bongoma Koni Botahe.

Boyoma: 31 blvd Mobutu, BP 982, Kisangani; Dir and Editor Badriyo Rova Rovatu.

Elima: 1 ave de la Révolution, BP 11498, Kinshasa; tel. (12) 77332; f. 1928; evening; Dir and Editor-in-Chief Essolomwa Nkoy ea Linganga.

Mjumbe: BP 2474, Lubumbashi; tel. (2) 25348; f. 1963; Dir and Editor Tshimanga Koya Kakona.

Le Palmarès: 220 ave Mpolo, BP 63, Kinshasa-Gombe; supports Union pour la démocratie et le progrès social; Editor Michel Ladeluya.

Le Phare: bldg du 29 juin, ave Col Lukusa 3392, BP 15662, Kinshasa-Gombe; tel. (12) 45896; e-mail info@le-phare.com; f. 1983; Editor Polydor Muboyayi Mubanga; circ 4,000.

Le Potentiel: Immeuble Ruzizi, 873 ave du Bas-Congo, BP 11338, Kinshasa; tel. (12) 891053; e-mail potentiel@ic.cd; f. 1982; Editor Modeste Mutinga Mutuishayi; circ. 8,000.

La Référence Plus: BP 22520, Kinshasa; tel. (12) 45783; f. 1989; Dir André Ipakala.

PERIODICALS

Afrique Editions: Kinshasa; tel. (88) 43202; e-mail bpongo@raga.net.

Allo Kinshasa: 3 rue Kayange, BP 20271, Kinshasa-Lemba; monthly; Editor MBUYU WA KABILA.

L'Aurore Protestante: Eglise du Christ au Congo, BP 4938, Kinshasa-Gombe; French; religion; monthly; circ. 10,000.

BEA Magazine de la Femme: 2 ave Masimanimba, BP 113380, Kinshasa 1; every 2 weeks; Editor MUTINGA MUTWISHAYI.

Bingwa: ave du 30 juin, zone Lubumbashi no 4334; weekly; sport; Dir and Editor MATEKE WA MULAMBA.

Cahiers Economiques et Sociaux: BP 257, Kinshasa XI, (National University of the Congo); sociological, political and economic review; quarterly; Dir Prof. NDONGALA TADI LEWA; circ. 2,000.

Cahiers des Religions Africaines: Faculté de Théologie Catholique de Kinshasa, BP 712, Kinshasa/Limete; tel. (12) 78476; f. 1967; English and French; religion; 2 a year; circ. 1,000.

Le Canard Libre: Kinshasa; f. 1991; Editor JOSEPH CASTRO MULEBE.

Circulaire d'Information: Association Nationale des Entreprises du Congo, 10 ave des Aviateurs, BP 7247, Kinshasa 1; tel. (12) 22565; f. 1959; French; legal and statutory texts for the business community; monthly.

La Colombe: 32B ave Tombalbaye, Kinshasa-Gombe; tel. (12) 21211; organ of Parti démocrate et social chrétien; circ. 5,000.

Congo-Afrique: Centre d'Etudes pour l'Action Sociale, 9 ave Père Boka, BP 3375, Kinshasa-Gombe; tel. (12) 34245; e-mail cepas@raga.net; f. 1961; economic, social and cultural; monthly; Editors FRANCIS KIKASSA MWANALESSA, RENÉ BEECKMANS; circ. 2,500.

Le Conseiller Comptable: 51 rue du Grand Séminaire, Quartier Nganda, BP 308, Kinshasa; tel. (88) 01216; fax (88) 00075; f. 1974; French; public finance and taxation; quarterly; Editor TOMENA FOKO; circ. 2,000.

Documentation et Information Protestante (DIP): Eglise du Christ au Congo, BP 4938, Kinshasa-Gombe; tel. and fax (88) 46387; e-mail eccm@ic.cd; French and English; religion.

Documentation et Informations Africaines (DIA): BP 2598, Kinshasa 1; tel. (12) 33197; fax (12) 33196; e-mail dia@ic.cd; internet www.peacelink.it/dia/index.html; Roman Catholic news agency reports; 3 a week; Dir Rev. Père VATA DIAMBANZA.

L'Entrepreneur Flash: Association Nationale des Entreprises du Congo, 10 ave des Aviateurs, BP 7247, Kinshasa 1; tel. (12) 22565; f. 1978; business news; monthly; circ. 1,000.

Etudes d'Histoire Africaine: National University of the Congo, BP 1825, Lubumbashi; f. 1970; French and English; history; annually; circ. 1,000.

Horizons 80: Société Congolaise d'Edition et d'Information, BP 9839, Kinshasa; economic affairs; weekly.

JuriCongo: coin des aves commerce et plateau, Galerie du 24 Novembre, Kinshasa; fax (12) 20320; e-mail cavas@ic.cd; guide to judicial affairs; Pres. EMERY MUKENDI WAFWANA.

Les Kasaï: 161 9e rue, BP 575, Kinshasa/Limete; weekly; Editor NSENGA NDOMBA.

Kin-Média: BP 15808, Kinshasa 1; monthly; Editor ILUNGA KASAMBAY.

KYA: 24 ave de l'Equateur, BP 7853, Kinshasa-Gombe; tel. (12) 27502; f. 1984; weekly for Bas-Congo; Editor SASSA KASSA YI KIBOBA.

Libération: Kinshasa; f. 1997; politics; supports the AFDL; weekly; Man. NGOYI KABUYA DIKATETA M'MIANA.

Mambenga 2000: BP 477, Mbandaka; Editor BOSANGE YEMA BOF.

Le Moniteur de l'Economie (Economic Monitor): Kinshasa; Man. Editor FÉLIX NZUZI.

Mwana Shaba: Générale des Carrières et des Mines, BP 450, Lubumbashi; monthly; circ. 25,000.

Ngabu: Société Nationale d'Assurances, Immeuble Sonas Sankuru, blvd du 30 juin, BP 3443, Kinshasa-Gombe; tel. (12) 23051; f. 1973; insurance news; quarterly.

Njanja: Société Nationale des Chemins de Fer Congolais, 115 place de la Gare, BP 297, Lubumbashi; tel. (2) 23430; fax (2) 61321; railways and transportation; annually; circ. 10,000.

NUKTA: 14 chaussée de Kasenga, BP 3805, Lubumbashi; weekly; agriculture; Editor NGOY BUNDUKI.

Post: Immeuble Linzadi, 1538 ave de la Douane, Kinshasa-Gombe; e-mail thepostrdc@yahoo.com; internet www.congonline.com/thepost; 2 a week; Editor-in-Chief MUKEBAYI NKOSO.

Problèmes Sociaux Zaïrois: Centre d'Exécution de Programmes Sociaux et Economiques, Université de Lubumbashi, 208 ave Kasavubu, BP 1873, Lubumbashi; f. 1946; quarterly; Editor N'KASHAMA KADIMA.

Promoteur Congolais: Centre du Commerce International du Congo, 119 ave Colonel Tshatshi, BP 13, Kinshasa; f. 1979; international trade news; six a year.

Sciences, Techniques, Informations: Centre de Recherches Industrielles en Afrique Centrale (CRIAC), BP 54, Lubumbashi.

Le Sport Africain: 13è niveau Tour adm., Cité de la Voix du Congo, BP 3356, Kinshasa-Gombe; monthly; Pres. TSHIMPUMPU WA TSHIMPUMPU.

Taifa: 536 ave Lubumba, BP 884, Lubumbashi; weekly; Editor LWAMBWA MILAMBU.

Telema: Faculté Canisius, Kimwenza, BP 3724, Kinshasa-Gombe; f. 1974; religious; quarterly; edited by the Central Africa Jesuits; circ. 1,200.

Umoja: 23 Bunkeye Matonge, Kinshasa; weekly; Publr LÉON MOUKANDA LUNYAMA.

Vision: Kinshasa; 2 a week; independent; Man. Editor XAVIER BONANE YANGANZI.

La Voix des Sans-Voix: ave des Ecuries 3858, commune de Ngaliema, BP 11445, Kinshasa-Gombe; tel. (88) 40394; fax (88) 01826; e-mail vsv@ic.cd; internet www.congonline.com/vsv.

NEWS AGENCIES

Agence Congolaise de Presse (ACP): 44–48 ave Tombalbaye, BP 1595, Kinshasa 1; tel. (12) 22035; e-mail acpresse@rd-congo.com; internet www.rd-congo.com/acp.html; f. 1957; state-controlled; Dir-Gen. ALI KALONGA.

Documentation et Informations Africaines (DIA): BP 2598, Kinshasa 1; tel. (12) 34528; f. 1957; Roman Catholic news agency; Dir Rev. Père VATA DIAMBANZA.

Foreign Bureaux

Agence France-Presse (AFP): Immeuble Wenge 3227, ave Wenge, Zone de la Gombe, BP 726, Kinshasa 1; tel. (12) 27009; Bureau Chief JEAN-PIERRE REJETTE.

Agencia EFE (Spain): BP 2653, Lubumbashi; Correspondent KANKU SANGA.

Agência Lusa de Informação (Portugal): BP 4941, Kinshasa; tel. (12) 24437.

Agenzia Nazionale Stampa Associata (ANSA) (Italy): BP 2790, Kinshasa 15; tel. (12) 30315; Bureau Chief (vacant).

Pan-African News Agency (PANA) (Senegal): BP 1400, Kinshasa; tel. (12) 23290; f. 1983; Bureau Chief ADRIEN HONORÉ MBEYET.

Xinhua (New China) News Agency (People's Republic of China): 293 ave Mfumu Lutunu, BP 8939, Kinshasa; tel. (12) 25647; Correspondent CHEN WEIBIN.

PRESS ASSOCIATION

Union de la Presse du Congo: BP 4941, Kinshasa 1; tel. (12) 24437.

Publishers

Aequatoria Centre: BP 276, Mbandaka; f. 1980; anthropology, biography, ethnicity, history, language and linguistics, social sciences; Dir HONORÉ VINCK.

CEEBA Publications: BP 246, Bandundu; f. 1965; humanities, languages, fiction; Man. Dir (Editorial) Dr HERMANN HOCHEGGER.

Centre de Linguistique Théorique et Appliquée (CELTA): BP 4956, Kinshasa-Gombe; tel. (12) 30503; fax (12) 21394; f. 1971; language arts and linguistics; Gen. Man. N. KIKO; Dir NTITA NYEMBWE.

Centre de Documentation Agricole: BP 7537, Kinshasa 1; tel. (12) 32498; agriculture, science; Dir PIERTE MBAYAKABUYI; Chief Editor J. MARCELLIN KAPUKUNGESA.

Centre de Recherches Pédagogiques: BP 8815, Kinshasa 1; f. 1959; accounting, education, geography, language, science; Dir P. DETIENNE.

Centre de Vulgarisation Agricole: BP 4008, Kinshasa 2; tel. (12) 71165; fax (12) 21351; agriculture, environment, health; Dir-Gen. KIMPIANGA MAHANIAH.

Centre International de Sémiologie: 109 ave Pruniers, BP 1825, Lubumbashi.

Centre Protestant d'Editions et de Diffusion (CEDI): 209 ave Kalémie, BP 11398, Kinshasa 1; tel. (12) 22202; fax (12) 26730; f. 1935; fiction, poetry, biography, religious, juvenile; Christian tracts, works in French, Lingala, Kikongo, etc. Dir-Gen. HENRY DIRKS.

Commission de l'Education Chrétienne: BP 3258, Kinshasa-Gombe; tel. (12) 30086; education, religion; Man. Dir Abbé MUGADJA LEHANI.

Connaissance et Pratique du Droit Congolais Editions (CDPC): BP 5502, Kinshasa-Gombe; f. 1987; law; Editor DIBUNDA KABUINJI.

Facultés Catholiques de Kinshasa: 2 ave de l'Université, Kinshasa-Limete; tel. and fax (12) 46965; e-mail facakin@ic.cd; f. 1957; anthropology, art, economics, history, politics, computer science; Rector Prof. Mgr HIPPOLYTE NGIMBI NSEKA.

Editions Lokole: BP 5085, Kinshasa 10; state org. for the promotion of literature; Dir BOKEME SHANE MOLOBAY.

Editions Saint Paul: BP 8505, Kinshasa; tel. (12) 77726; fiction, general non-fiction, poetry, religion; Dir Sister FRANKA PERONA.

Les Editions du Trottoir: BP 1800, Kinshasa; tel. (12) 9936043; e-mail smuyengo@yahoo.fr; f. 1989; communications, fiction, literature, drama; Pres. CHARLES DJUNJU-SIMBA.

Librairie les Volcans: 22 ave Pres. Mobutu, BP 400, Goma, Nord-Kivu; f. 1995; social sciences; Man. Dir RUHAMA MUKANDOLI.

Presses Universitaires du Congo (PUC): 290 rue d'Aketi, BP 1800, Kinshasa 1; tel. (12) 9936043; e-mail smuyengo@yahoo.fr; f. 1972; science, arts and communications; Dir Abbé SÉBASTIEN MUYENGO.

Government Publishing House

Imprimerie du Gouvernement Central: BP 3021, Kinshasa-Kalina.

Broadcasting and Communications

TELECOMMUNICATIONS

Comcell: Commune de la Gombe, 6 ave du Port, BP 614, Kinshasa; tel. (12) 20241; fax (satellite) 377-97-990026; e-mail comcell@raga.net; provides satellite communications network; 4,000 subscribers.

Office Congolais des Postes et des Télécommunications (OCPT): Hôtel des postes, blvd du 30 juin, BP 13798, Kinshasa; tel. (12) 21871; fax (88) 45010; state-owned; 13,000 lines; 40,000 subscribers; Dir-Gen. KAPITAO MAMBWENI.

Telecel-Congo: Kinshasa; provides satellite communications network; largest private operator; 45% nationalized in 1998; 12,000 subscribers.

BROADCASTING

Radio-Télévision Nationale Congolaise (RTNC): BP 3171, Kinshasa-Gombe; tel. (12) 23171; state radio terrestrial and satellite television broadcasts; Dir-Gen. JOSE KAJANGUA.

Radio

Several private radio broadcasters operate in Kinshasa.

Radio Candip: Centre d'Animation et de Diffusion Pédagogique, BP 373, Bunia; state-controlled; under rebel control in late 1998.

La Voix du Congo: Station Nationale, BP 3164, Kinshasa-Gombe; tel. (12) 23175; state-controlled; operated by RTNC; broadcasts in French, Swahili, Lingala, Tshiluba, Kikongo; regional stations at Kisangani, Lubumbashi, Bukavu, Bandundu, Kananga, Mbuji-Mayi, Matadi, Mbandaka and Bunia.

Television

Several private television broadcasters operate in Kinshasa.

Antenne A: Immeuble Forescom, 2e étage, ave du Port 4, POB 2581, Kinshasa 1; tel. (12) 21736; private and commercial station; Dir-Gen. IGAL AVIVI NEIRSON.

Canal Z: ave du Port 6, POB 614, Kinshasa 1; tel. (12) 20239; commercial station; Dir-Gen. FRÉDÉRIC FLASSE.

Tele Kin Malebo (TKM): Kinshasa; private television station; nationalization announced 1997; Dir-Gen. NGONGO LUWOWO.

Télévision Congolaise: BP 3171, Kinshasa-Gombe; tel. (12) 23171; govt commercial station; operated by RTNC; broadcasts for 5 hours daily on weekdays and 10 hours daily at weekends.

Finance

(cap. = capital; res = reserves; dep. = deposits; m. = million; brs = branches; amounts in old zaires unless otherwise indicated)

BANKING

A reorganization of the banking sector was expected to follow the introduction as legal tender of a new currency unit, the Congolese franc (CF), which was completed on 30 June 1999.

Central Bank

Banque du Congo: 513 blvd Colonel Tshatshi au nord, BP 2697, Kinshasa; tel. (12) 20704; fax (12) 8805152; e-mail cabgouv@bcc.cd; internet www.bcc.cd; f. 1964; cap. and res 50,088.4m. (Dec. 1988); Gov. JEAN-CLAUDE MASANGU MULONGO; 8 brs.

Commercial Banks

African Trade Bank (ATB): ave Lemarinel, BP 3459, Kinshasa-Gombe; tel. (12) 33845; fax (12) 8846991; cap. and res NZ 67,893.3m., total assets NZ 406,946.6m. (Dec. 1996); Pres. ABDALLAH HASSAN WAZNI; Gen. Man. GHAZI ABDALLAH WAZNI.

Banque de Commerce et de Développement (BCD): 87 blvd du 30 juin, Kinshasa; tel. (88) 01768; fax (satellite) 1-703-3902716; e-mail bcd-kin@ic.cd; cap. and res CF 5.2m., total assets CF 29.1m. (Dec. 1998).

Banque Commerciale du Congo SARL (BCDC): blvd du 30 juin, BP 488, Kinshasa; tel. (88) 21776; fax (12) 21770; e-mail bcdc@raga.net; f. 1909 as Banque du Congo Belge, name changed as above 1997; cap. CF 210.6m., res CF 2,834.8m., dep. CF 15,963.0m. (Dec. 2001); Pres. NKEMA LILOO; Man. Dir HENRI LALOUX; 29 brs.

Banque Continentale Africaine (Congo) SARL: 4 ave de la Justice, BP 7613, Kinshasa-Gombe; tel. (12) 28006; fax (12) 25243; f. 1983; total assets 28,786.5m. (Dec. 1994); Pres. NASIR ABID; Dir-Gen. M. A. DOCHY.

Banque de Crédit Agricole: angle ave Kasa-Vubu et ave M'Polo, BP 8837, Kinshasa-Gombe; tel. (12) 21800; fax (12) 27221; f. 1982 to expand and modernize enterprises in agriculture, livestock and fishing, and generally to improve the quality of rural life; state-owned; in liquidation in 1999; cap. 5m. (Dec. 1991); Pres. MOLOTO MWA LOPANZA.

Banque Internationale de Crédit SARL (BIC): 191 ave de l'Equateur, BP 1299, Kinshasa 1; tel. (88) 43790; fax (88) 01125; e-mail bic@ic.cd; f. 1994; cap. CF 5.4m., res CF 73.2m., dep. CF 568.3m. (Dec. 2000); Pres. PASCAL KINDUELO LUMBU; Man. Dir THARCISSE K. M. MILEMBWE.

Banque Internationale pour l'Afrique au Congo (BIAC): Immeuble Nioki, ave de la Douane, Kinshasa 1; tel. (12) 20612; fax (12) 20120; e-mail biac-rj@raga.net; cap. and res US $1.4m., total assets US $17.4m. (Dec. 1998); Pres. ROBERT JONCHERAY.

Caisse Générale d'Epargne du Congo: 38 ave de la Caisse d'Epargne, BP 8147, Kinshasa-Gombe; tel. (12) 33701; f. 1950; state-owned; Chair. and Man. Dir NSIMBA M'VUEDI; 45 brs.

Citibank NA Congo: Immeuble Citibank Congo, angle aves Col Lukusa et Ngongo Lutete, BP 9999, Kinshasa 1; tel. (88) 46394; fax (12) 40015; e-mail singa.boyenge@citicorp.com; f. 1971; cap. and res NZ 199,425.2m., total assets NZ 1,928,804.9m. (Dec. 1996); Pres. ROBERT THORNTON; 1 br.

Fransabank (Congo) SARL: Immeuble Flavica 14/16, ave du Port, BP 9497, Kinshasa 1; tel. (12) 20119; fax (12) 20199; f. 1989; cap. and res NZ 7,351.7m., total assets NZ 174,809.7m. (Dec. 1996); Pres. ADNAN WAFIC KASSAR.

Nouvelle Banque de Kinshasa: 1 place du Marché, BP 8033, Kinshasa 1; tel. (12) 20562; fax (12) 496180043; f. 1969; nationalized 1975; control transferred to National Union of Congolese Workers in 1989; in liquidation in 1999; cap. NZ 2,000 (1990), res NZ 92,179.4m., dep. NZ 25,396.8m. (Dec. 1994); Pres. DOKOLO SANU; 15 brs.

Société Financière de Développement SARL (SOFIDE): Immeuble SOFIDE, 9–11 angle aves Ngabu et Kisangani, BP 1148, Kinshasa 1; tel. (12) 20676; fax (12) 20788; f. 1970; partly state-owned; provides tech. and financial aid, primarily for agricultural devt; cap. and res NZ 44,610.4m., total assets NZ 519,789.7m. (Dec. 1997); Pres. and Dir-Gen. KIYANGA KI-N'LOMBI; 4 brs.

Stanbic Bank Congo SARL: 12 ave de Mongala, BP 16297, Kinshasa 1; tel. (88) 48445; fax (88) 46216; e-mail sbiccongo@raga.net; internet www.stanbic.co.cd; f. 1973; subsidiary of Standard Bank Investment Corpn (South Africa); cap. 3.6m., res 6.4m., dep. 50.3m. (Dec. 1999); Chair. C. EVANS; Man. Dir R. L. GASKIN; 1 br.

Union de Banques Congolaises SARL (UBC): angle ave de la Nation et ave des Aviateurs 19, BP 197, Kinshasa 1; tel. (88) 41333;

fax (88) 46628; e-mail ubc@ic.cd; f. 1929; renamed as above in 1997; total assets US $59.3m. (Dec. 1997); Pres. NTUMBA MPOY; 13 brs.

INSURANCE

INTERAFF: Bldg Forescom, ave du Port 4, Kinshasa-Gombe; tel. (88) 01618; fax (320) 2091332; e-mail interaff@raga.net; internet www.ic.cd/interaff.

Société Nationale d'Assurances (SONAS): 3473 blvd du 30 juin, Kinshasa-Gombe; tel. (12) 23051; f. 1966; state-owned; cap. 23m.; 9 brs.

Trade and Industry

At November 1994 the Government's portfolio of state enterprises numbered 116, of which 56 were wholly owned by the Government.

DEVELOPMENT ORGANIZATIONS

Bureau pour le Développement Rural et Urbain: Mont Nga-fula, Kinshasa; e-mail bdru_kin@yahoo.fr.

Caisse de Stabilisation Cotonnière (CSCo): BP 3058, Kinshasa-Gombe; tel. (12) 31206; f. 1978 to replace Office National des Fibres Textiles; acts as an intermediary between the Govt, cotton ginners and textile factories, and co-ordinates international financing of cotton sector.

La Générale des Carrières et des Mines (GÉCAMINES): BP 450, Lubumbashi; tel. (2) 6768105; fax (2) 6768041; f. 1967 to acquire assets of Union Minière du Haut-Katanga; state-owned corpn engaged in mining and marketing of copper, cobalt, zinc and coal; also has interests in agriculture; privatization announced in 1994, subsequently delayed; Exec. Chair. GEORGE FORREST; operates the following enterprise.

  GÉCAMINES—Exploitation: mining operations.

Institut National pour l'Etude et la Recherche Agronomiques: BP 1513, Kisangani; f. 1933; agricultural research.

Office National du Café: ave Général Bobozo, BP 8931, Kinshasa 1; tel. (12) 77144; f. 1979; state agency for coffee and also cocoa, tea, quinquina and pyrethrum; Pres. FERUZA WA GHENDA.

Pêcherie Maritime Congolaise: Kinshasa; DRC's only sea-fishing enterprise.

CHAMBER OF COMMERCE

Chambre de Commerce, d'Industrie et d'Agriculture du Congo: 10 ave des Aviateurs, BP 7247, Kinshasa 1; tel. (12) 22286.

INDUSTRIAL AND TRADE ASSOCIATION

Association Nationale des Entreprises du Congo: 10 ave des Aviateurs, BP 7247, Kinshasa; tel. (12) 24623; f. 1972; represents business interests for both domestic and foreign institutions; Man. Dir EDOUARD LUBOYA DIYOKA; Gen. Sec. ATHANASE MATENDA KYELU.

EMPLOYERS' ASSOCIATION

Fédération des Entreprises du Congo (FEC): Kinshasa; e-mail feccongo@hotmail.com; Pres. PASCAL KINDUEL LUMBU; Sec.-Gen. JOSEPH MUKADULA KABUE.

UTILITIES

Electricity

Société Nationale d'Electricité (SNEL): 2831 ave de la Justice, BP 500, Kinshasa; tel. (12) 26893; fax (12) 33735; f. 1970; state-owned; Dir-Gen. MUYUMBA KALEMBE.

Water

Régie de Distribution d'Eau (REGIDESCO): 65 blvd du 30 juin, BP 12599, Kinshasa; tel. (12) 22792; water supply admin; Pres. LUBUNGU PENE SHAKO.

TRADE UNIONS

The Union Nationale des Travailleurs was founded in 1967 as the sole trade-union organization. In 1990 the establishment of independent trade unions was legalized, and by early 1991 there were 12 officially recognized trade-union organizations.

Union Nationale des Travailleurs du Congo: BP 8814, Kinshasa; f. 1967; comprises 16 unions; Pres. KATALAY MOLELI SANGOL.

Transport

Compagnie des Transports du Congo: ave Muzu 52/75, Kinshasa; tel. (88) 46249; fax (322) 7065718; e-mail ros@ic.cd; road transport; Dir ROGER SENGER.

Office National des Transports (ONATRA): BP 98, Kinshasa 1; tel. (12) 21457; fax (12) 1398632; e-mail onatradf@ic.cd; f. 1935; operates 10,077 km of waterways, 366 km of railways and road and air transport; administers ports of Kinshasa, Matadi, Boma and Banana; Pres. JULES IBULA MWANA KATAKANGA.

RAILWAYS

The main line runs from Lubumbashi to Ilebo. International services run to Dar es Salaam (Tanzania) and Lobito (Angola), and also connect with the Zambian, Zimbabwean, Mozambican and South African systems. In May 1997 the railway system was nationalized.

Kinshasa–Matadi Railway: BP 98, Kinshasa 1; 366 km operated by ONATRA; Pres. JACQUES MBELOLO BITWEMI.

Société Nationale des Chemins de Fer du Congo (SNCC): 115 place de la Gare, BP 297, Lubumbashi; tel. (2) 46306; fax (2) 342254; e-mail sncc01aie-lubum-cd; f. 1974; 3,606 km (including 858 km electrified); administers all internal railway sections as well as river transport and transport on Lakes Tanganyika and Kivu; man. contract concluded with a Belgian-South African corpn, Sizarail, in 1995 for the man. of the Office des Chemins de Fer du Sud (OCS) and the Société des Chemins de Fer de l'Est (SFE) subsidiaries, with rail networks of 2,835 km and 1,286 km respectively; assets of Sizarail nationalized and returned to SNCC control in May 1997; Pres. and Gen. Man. KIBWE MIBUYA KAKUDJI.

ROADS

In 1999 there were an estimated 157,000 km of roads, of which some 33,000 km were main roads. In general road conditions are poor, owing to inadequate maintenance. In August 1997 a rehabilitation plan was announced by the Government, under which 28,664 km of roads were to be built or repaired. The project was to be partly financed by external sources.

Office des Routes: Direction Générale, ave Ex-Descamp, BP 10899, Kinshasa-Gombe; tel. (12) 32036; construction and maintenance of roads.

INLAND WATERWAYS

The River Congo is navigable for more than 1,600 km. Above the Stanley Falls the Congo becomes the Lualaba, and is navigable along a 965-km stretch from Ubundu to Kindu and Kongolo to Bukama. The River Kasai, a tributary of the River Congo, is navigable by shipping as far as Ilebo, at which the line from Lubumbashi terminates. The total length of inland waterways is 14,935 km.

Régie des voies fluviales: 109 ave Lumpungu, Kinshasa-Gombe, BP 11697, Kinshasa 1; tel. (12) 26526; fax (12) 42580; administers river navigation; Gen. Man. NGIAM KIPOY.

Société Congolaise des Chemins de Fer des Grands Lacs: River Lualaba services: Bubundu–Kindu and Kongolo–Malemba N'kula; Lake Tanganyika services: Kamina–Kigoma–Kalundu–Moba–Mpulungu; Pres. and Gen. Man. KIBWE MBUYU KAKUDJI.

SHIPPING

The principal seaports are Matadi, Boma and Banana on the lower Congo. The port of Matadi has more than 1.6 km of quays and can accommodate up to 10 deep-water vessels. Matadi is linked by rail with Kinshasa. The country's merchant fleet numbered 20 vessels and amounted to 12,900 gross registered tons at 31 December 2001.

Compagnie Maritime du Congo SARL: USB Centre, place de la Poste, BP 9496, Kinshasa; tel. (88) 20396; fax (88) 26234; e-mail cmdckin@ic.cd; f. 1946; services: North Africa, Europe, North America and Asia to West Africa, East Africa to North Africa; Gen. Man. ALEX MUKENDI KAMAMA.

CIVIL AVIATION

International airports are located at Ndjili (for Kinshasa), Luano (for Lubumbashi), Bukavu, Goma and Kisangani. There are smaller airports and airstrips dispersed throughout the country.

Blue Airlines: BP 1115, Barumbu, Kinshasa 1; tel. (12) 20455; f. 1991; regional and domestic charter services for passengers and cargo; Man. T. MAYANI.

Business Aviation: 1345 ave de la Plaine, Kingabwa-Kinshasa; tel. (88) 45588; fax (99) 42260; e-mail businessaviation@ic.cd; internet www.businessaviation.cd; regional services.

Compagnie Africaine d'Aviation: 6ème rue, Limete, Kinshasa; tel. (88) 43072; fax (88) 41048; e-mail ltadek@hotmail.com; f. 1992; Pres. DAVID BLATTNER.

Congo Airlines: 1928 ave Kabambare, N'dolo-Kinshasa, BP 12847, Kinshasa; tel. (12) 43947; fax (12) 00235; e-mail cal-fih-dg@ic.cd; f. 1994 as Express Cargo, assumed present name in 1997; international, regional and domestic scheduled services for passengers and cargo; Pres. Jose Enduno; CEO Stavros Papaioannou.

Hewa Bora Airways: ave Kabambare 1928, BP 1284, Kinshasa; tel. (12) 20643; internet www.hba.cd; national and international services.

Lignes Aériennes du Congo (LAC): Air Terminus 4, ave du Port, Kinshasa-Gombe, BP 8552, Kinshasa 1; tel. (12) 20874; Pres. and Gen. Man. Paul Mukandila Mbayabu.

Malila Airlift: ave Basoko 188, Kinshasa-Gombe; tel. (88) 46428; fax (satellite) 1-5304817707; e-mail malila.airlift@ic.cd; internet www.malila.cd; f. 1996; regional services; Man. Véronique Malila.

Waltair Aviation: 9ème rue 206, Limete, Kinshasa; tel. (88) 48439; fax (satellite) 1-3094162616; e-mail waltair.rdc@ic.cd; regional services; Dir Vincent Gillet.

Zairean Airlines (Congo): 3555–3560 blvd du 30 juin, BP 2111, Kinshasa; tel. (88) 48103; f. 1981; international, regional and domestic services for passengers and cargo; Dir-Gen. Capt. Alfred Sommerauer.

Tourism

The country offers extensive lake and mountain scenery, although tourism remains largely undeveloped. In 2000 tourist arrivals totalled 102,770, while receipts from tourism amounted to an estimated US $2m. in 1998.

Office National du Tourisme: 2A/2B ave des Orangers, BP 9502, Kinshasa-Gombe; tel. (12) 30070; f. 1959; Man. Dir Botolo Magoza.

Société Congolaise de l'Hôtellerie: Immeuble Memling, BP 1076, Kinshasa; tel. (12) 23260; Man. N'Joli Balanga.

THE REPUBLIC OF THE CONGO

Introductory Survey

Location, Climate, Language, Religion, Flag, Capital

The Republic of the Congo is an equatorial country on the west coast of Africa. It has a coastline of about 170 km on the Atlantic Ocean, from which the country extends northward to Cameroon and the Central African Republic. The Republic of the Congo is bordered by Gabon to the west and the Democratic Republic of the Congo (formerly Zaire) to the east, while in the south there is a short frontier with the Cabinda exclave of Angola. The climate is tropical, with temperatures averaging 21°C–27°C (70°F–80°F) throughout the year. The average annual rainfall is about 1,200 mm (47 ins). The official language is French; Kituba, Lingala and other African languages are also used. At least one-half of the population follow traditional animist beliefs and about 45% are Roman Catholics. There are small Protestant and Muslim minorities. The national flag (proportions 2 by 3) comprises a yellow stripe running diagonally from lower hoist to upper fly, separating a green triangle at the hoist from a red triangle in the fly. The capital is Brazzaville.

Recent History

Formerly part of French Equatorial Africa, Middle Congo became the autonomous Republic of the Congo, within the French Community, in November 1958, with Abbé Fulbert Youlou as the first Prime Minister, and subsequently as President when the Congo became fully independent on 15 August 1960. Youlou relinquished office in August 1963, following a period of internal unrest, and was succeeded by Alphonse Massamba-Débat, initially as Prime Minister, and from December as President. In July 1964 the Mouvement national de la révolution (MNR) was established as the sole political party. In August 1968 Massamba-Débat was overthrown in a military coup, led by Capt. (later Maj.) Marien Ngouabi, who was proclaimed President in January 1969. A new Marxist-Leninist party, the Parti congolais du travail (PCT), replaced the MNR, and in January 1970 the country was renamed the People's Republic of the Congo. In March 1977 Ngouabi was assassinated, and in April Col (later Brig.-Gen.) Jacques-Joachim Yhombi-Opango, the head of the armed forces, became the new Head of State. In February 1979 Yhombi-Opango surrendered his powers to a Provisional Committee appointed by the PCT. In March the head of the Provisional Committee, Col (later Gen.) Denis Sassou-Nguesso, became Chairman of the PCT Central Committee and President of the Republic.

In July 1987 some 20 army officers were arrested for alleged complicity in a coup plot. Shortly afterwards fighting broke out in the north between government forces and troops led by Pierre Anga, a supporter of Yhombi-Opango. In September government troops suppressed the rebellion with French military assistance. Yhombi-Opango was transferred from house arrest to prison. Anga was subsequently killed by Congolese security forces.

In July 1989 Sassou-Nguesso, the sole candidate, was re-elected Chairman of the PCT and President of the Republic for a third five-year term. In August Alphonse Mouissou Poaty-Souchalaty, hitherto the Minister of Trade and Small- and Medium-sized Enterprises, was appointed Prime Minister. At legislative elections in September the PCT-approved single list of 133 candidates was endorsed by 99.2% of voters. The list included, for the first time, non-party candidates.

Progress towards political reform dominated the latter half of 1990. In August several political prisoners were released, among them Yhombi-Opango. In September the Central Committee of the PCT agreed to the immediate registration of new political parties. In December Poaty-Souchalaty resigned, the day before an extraordinary Congress of the PCT commenced. During the Congress the party abandoned Marxism-Leninism as its official ideology and formulated constitutional amendments legalizing a multi-party system, which took effect in January 1991. Gen. Louis Sylvain Goma was appointed Prime Minister (a position he had held between 1975 and 1984), to lead an interim Government.

A National Conference was convened in February 1991. Opposition movements were allocated seven of the 11 seats on the Conference's governing body. The Roman Catholic Bishop of Owando, Ernest N'Kombo, was elected as Chairman. Having voted to establish itself as a sovereign body, in April the Conference announced proposals to draft legislation providing for the abrogation of the Constitution and the abolition of the Assemblée nationale populaire and other national and regional institutions. In June a 153-member legislative Haut conseil de la République (HCR) was established, under the chairmanship of N'Kombo; this was empowered to supervise the implementation of the resolutions made by the Conference. From June the Prime Minister replaced the President as Chairman of the Council of Ministers, and the country's official name reverted to the Republic of the Congo. A new Prime Minister, André Milongo (a former World Bank official), was appointed in June. In December the HCR adopted a draft Constitution, which provided for legislative power to be vested in an elected Assemblée nationale and Sénat and for executive power to be held by an elected President.

The draft Constitution was approved by 96.3% of voters at a national referendum in March 1992. In May Milongo appointed a new Council of Ministers. At elections to the new Assemblée nationale, held in June and July, the Union panafricaine pour la démocratie social (UPADS) won 39 of the 125 seats, becoming the major party; the Mouvement congolais pour la démocratie et le développement intégral (MCDDI) took 29 seats and the PCT secured 18 seats. At indirect elections to the Sénat, held in July, the UPADS again won the largest share (23) of the 60 seats, followed by the MCDDI, with 13 seats. At the first round of presidential voting, in August, Pascal Lissouba, the leader of the UPADS (and Prime Minister in 1963–66), won the largest share of the votes cast (35.9%); of the 15 other candidates, his closest rival was Bernard Kolelas of the MCDDI (22.9%). Sassou-Nguesso took 16.9% of the votes cast. At a second round of voting, two weeks later, Lissouba defeated Kolelas, with 61.3% of the votes cast.

Lissouba took office as President in late August 1992. Maurice-Stéphane Bongho-Nouarra, of the UPADS, was appointed as Prime Minister. Meanwhile, the Union pour le renouveau démocratique (URD), a new alliance of seven parties, including the MCDDI, formed a coalition with the PCT (thereby establishing a parliamentary majority), which succeeded in winning a vote of 'no confidence' against the Government in October. In November the Government resigned, and shortly afterwards Lissouba dissolved the Assemblée nationale and announced that fresh legislative elections would be held in 1993. The URD-PCT coalition, which demanded the right to form the Government, commenced a campaign of civil disobedience. In December Claude Antoine Dacosta, a former FAO and World Bank official, was appointed Prime Minister and formed a transitional Government, comprising members of all the main political parties.

At the first round of elections to the Assemblée nationale, which took place in May 1993, the Mouvance présidentielle (MP), an electoral coalition of the UPADS and its allies, won 62 of the 125 seats, while the URD-PCT coalition secured 49. Protesting that serious electoral irregularities had occurred, the URD-PCT refused to contest the second round of elections in June (for seats where a clear majority had not been achieved in the first round) and demanded the repetition of some of the first-round polls. After the second round the MP had secured an absolute majority (69) of seats in the legislature. In June President Lissouba appointed a new Council of Ministers, with Yhombi-Opango as Prime Minister. During June Kolelas, now leader of the URD-PCT coalition, instigated a campaign of civil disobedience in an attempt to compel the Government to organize new elections. Violent conflict ensued between armed militiamen and the security forces. In late June the Supreme Court ruled that electoral irregularities had occurred at the first round of elections. By late July the Government and the opposition had negotiated a truce, and in August, following mediation by the Organization of African Unity (OAU, now the African Union (see p. 130), France and President Omar Bongo of Gabon, the two sides agreed to refer the disputed first-round election results to impartial international arbitration and to rerun the second round of elections.

Following the repeated second round of legislative elections, which took place in October 1993, the MP had 65 seats, retaining an overall majority in the Assemblée nationale. The URD-PCT coalition, which now held 57 seats, agreed to participate in the new Assemblée. Further confrontations between armed militias affiliated to political parties and the security forces reportedly resulted in at least 2,000 deaths in the second half of 1993. Although a cease-fire was agreed in January 1994, sporadic fighting continued.

In September 1994 six opposition parties formed an alliance, the Forces démocratiques unies (FDU), headed by Sassou-Nguesso and affiliated with the URD. In December Lissouba and the two main opposition leaders—Sassou-Nguesso and Kolelas—signed an agreement seeking a permanent end to hostilities between their supporters.

In January 1995 the Government resigned, and a new coalition Council of Ministers was appointed, including members of the MCDDI and headed by Yhombi-Opango. The FDU refused to participate in the new administration. In October the Government announced the impending restructuring of the armed forces; during 1994–96 some 4,000 militiamen were integrated into the defence and security forces.

In August 1996 Yhombi-Opango resigned as Prime Minister; he was replaced by David Charles Ganao, a former Minister of Foreign Affairs. In September Ganao appointed representatives of the URD to an expanded Council of Ministers. In October elections were held for 23 of the 60 seats in the Sénat, following which the MP retained its majority in the upper chamber.

In February 1997 19 opposition parties issued a number of demands, including the expedited establishment of republican institutions, the creation of an independent electoral commission, the disarmament of civilians and the deployment of a multinational peace-keeping force. In May further unrest erupted, and in June an attempt by the Government, in preparation for legislative and presidential elections scheduled for July and August, to disarm the 'Cobra' militia group associated with Sassou-Nguesso precipitated a fierce national conflict along ethnic and political lines, involving the militias and opposing factions within the regular armed forces. Barricades were erected in Brazzaville, which was divided into three zones, controlled by supporters of Lissouba, Sassou-Nguesso and Kolelas, respectively. The conflict soon became polarized between troops loyal to the Lissouba administration and the rebel forces of Sassou-Nguesso; both sides were allegedly reinforced by mercenaries and by foreign troops. Despite efforts to mediate—led by Kolelas, President Bongo of Gabon and by the joint UN-OAU special representative to the Great Lakes region—none of the numerous cease-fire agreements signed during mid-1997 endured. In June French troops assisted in the evacuation of foreign residents from Brazzaville, and later in the month themselves departed. Fighting intensified in August and spread to the north. In September Lissouba appointed a Government of National Unity, under the premiership of Kolelas, thereby compromising the latter's role as a national mediator. Sassou-Nguesso refused the offer of five ministerial positions for his allies. In September political organizations loyal to Lissouba formed the Espace républicain pour la défense de la démocratie et l'unité nationale (ERDDUN).

In October 1997 Sassou-Nguesso's forces, assisted by Angolan government troops, won control of Brazzaville and the strategic port of Pointe-Noire. Lissouba was ousted from the presidential palace, and, with Kolelas, found refuge in Burkina Faso. Sassou-Nguesso was inaugurated as President on 25 October, having retaken by force the office that he had lost at the 1992 presidential election, and appointed a new transitional Government in November. It was reported that some 10,000 people were killed during the civil war and that about 800,000 people were displaced, while the national infrastructure was severely disrupted.

A Forum for Unity and National Reconciliation was established in January 1998; notably, ERDDUN refused to participate. A Conseil national de transition (CNT) was to hold legislative power, pending the approval of a new constitution by referendum (scheduled for 2001), and subsequent legislative elections. Throughout 1998 clashes continued in the southern Pool region, a stronghold of the militia loyal to Kolelas, causing thousands to flee the area. Warrants were issued in November for the arrests of Lissouba, Kolelas and Yhombi-Opango, on charges of genocide and crimes against humanity.

Progress towards the restoration of democratic rule was impeded in December 1998, when a battle for control of Brazzaville broke out between forces loyal to Kolelas (who was in exile in the USA), reputedly supported by Angolan rebel groups, and Congolese government forces, augmented by Sassou-Nguesso's militia and Angolan government troops. Both sides claimed victory. More than 8,000 refugees were reported to have fled into the neighbouring Democratic Republic of the Congo (DRC). In late December government forces, aided by Angolan troops, launched offensives against Kolelas' forces in the south and west of the country.

On 12 January 1999 Sassou-Nguesso appointed a new Council of Ministers. Notably, Sassou-Nguesso ceded his defence portfolio to Itihi Ossetoumba Lekoundzou. In mid-January sporadic fighting continued between government forces and insurgents in Brazzaville. Fighting was also reported in the south-west, particularly around Loubomo (Dolisie). By early March the rebel militias had been obliged to withdraw to Pool, and further advances were made by government forces during mid-1999, permitting residents to return to evacuated districts. In August Sassou-Nguesso offered to grant an amnesty to any militiamen prepared to renounce violence and to surrender their weapons; by September some 600 militiamen loyal to Kolelas had reportedly surrendered to the authorities. In mid-November the Government announced that it had reached agreement with the militias loyal to Lissouba and Kolelas, although the two rebel leaders rejected the agreement, which included provision for a cease-fire and for a general amnesty. In December the CNT adopted legislation providing for an amnesty for those militiamen who surrendered their weapons to the authorities before 15 January 2000. The Government announced its intention to continue to seek the prosecution of Lissouba and Kolelas, who were excluded from the amnesty, for alleged war crimes.

In December 1999 President Bongo of Gabon was designated the official mediator in negotiations between the Government and the militias; at the end of the month he hosted further discussions in Libreville, Gabon. Representatives of the armed forces and of the rebel militias subsequently signed a second peace agreement, in the presence of Bongo and Sassou-Nguesso. Although militia leaders continued to demand the withdrawal of Angolan troops from the Congo, in late December a ceremony of reconciliation was held in Brazzaville between senior government figures and members of the previous Lissouba administration. In February 2000 the committee in charge of observing the implementation of the peace process announced, at a meeting with Bongo, that the civil war was definitively over. The Congolese Government subsequently appealed for funds from the international community to aid reconstruction. By that month it was estimated that around one-half of the estimated 810,000 people displaced by the conflict had returned to their homes.

In May 2000 Kolelas and his nephew, Col Philippe Bikinkita, the Minister of the Interior in the Lissouba administration, were convicted *in absentia* of operating personal prisons and of mistreating prisoners and causing their deaths during the 1997 civil war. Both men were sentenced to death and ordered to pay compensation to their victims. Kolelas denied the charges and demanded that an international team investigate the allegations.

In mid-November 2000 the Government adopted a draft Constitution, which included provisions for a presidential system of democratic government, with a bicameral legislature and independent judiciary. The Head of State, the sole holder of executive power, would be elected for a term of seven years, renewable only once. In early December it was announced that some 13,000 weapons had been surrendered and 12,000 militiamen disarmed in the past year, although UN sources suggested that this represented less than one-half of the total number of militiamen in the Congo. Also in December, the PCT rejected demands by the MCDDI for an amnesty for Lissouba and Kolelas. In late December it was announced that the PCT had signed an agreement with the Rassemblement pour la démocratie et le progrès social (RDPS), led by Jean-Pierre Thystère Tchicaya, to bring the latter party into the Government.

Internal and exiled opposition groups boycotted the opening ceremony of a period of national dialogue in mid-March 2001 and a series of regional debates, which took place later that month. Some 2,200 delegates from public institutions, civic associations and political parties attended the debates, reportedly reaching a consensus on the draft Constitution, despite some concerns regarding the extent of presidential power envisaged; notably, the President would have the power to appoint and dismiss ministers at will, while there would be no provision for a vote of censure against the Government. In April several returned exiles and opposition groups participated in a national convention in Brazzaville, although Kolelas and Lissouba were notably absent. The convention concluded, on 14 April, with the signature of a Convention for Peace and Reconstruction.

In July 2001 the families of some 353 missing Congolese citizens demanded a parliamentary inquiry into their disappearance; it was reported that these missing former refugees had been arrested by government forces following their voluntary repatriation to the Congo from the DRC in May 1999. In October–December, taking advantage of Belgian legislation permitting the country's courts to hear cases of international war crimes and crimes against humanity committed anywhere in the world, relatives of the missing filed three suits at courts in Belgium, accusing Sassou-Nguesso and other senior members of the Congolese Government of crimes against humanity with regard to the disappearances. (In 2002 a further case against a Congolese army inspector, Gen. Norbert Dabira, who had a second residence in France, was brought in that country. During an official visit to France in September of that year, a court in Meaux, near Paris, requested a written testimony from Sassou-Nguesso, who, however, maintained that the case was an internal Congolese affair.)

In July 2001 a grenade and rocket attack on the house of the Minister at the Presidency, responsible for National Defence, was attributed to persons dissatisfied with recently implemented and proposed military reforms and personnel changes; no injuries were reported in the attack. At the end of July a high-ranking official at the Ministry of the Interior, Security and Territorial Administration avoided injury in an armed attack. Also in July a coalition of opposition parties, the Alliance pour la démocratie et le progrès (ADP), was formed under the leadership of Milongo, with the intention of fielding a single candidate in the presidential election due to be held in 2002. Meanwhile, the FDU was expanded to comprise some 29 parties, with the purpose of uniting behind Sassou-Nguesso in the election (although the PCT was to contest the subsequent legislative elections independently of the FDU).

On 2 September 2001 the CNT approved the text of the proposed Constitution to be submitted to referendum, pending the compilation of an electoral census. Although the national convention had recommended that opposition parties participate in the electoral commission, only one such party, the ADP, was represented in the Commission nationale d'organisation des élections (CONEL), which was, moreover, to be responsible to the Ministry of the Interior, Security and Territorial Administration. In mid-December Lissouba, Kolelas and Yhombi-Opango issued a joint statement condemning the electoral process as detrimental to national unity and lacking impartiality, and urging the international community to assist in the establishment of an independent electoral commission. (Neither Lissouba nor Kolelas were permitted to contest the elections, as a result of their convictions for crimes against humanity.) Several opposition parties subsequently threatened to boycott the elections in protest at the composition of the CONEL.

In mid-December 2001 the electoral schedule was announced: the constitutional referendum was to be held on 20 January 2002, followed by the presidential election on 10 March (and 7 April, if a second round was necessary), elections to the Assemblée nationale on 12 May and 9 June, and indirect elections to the Sénat on 30 June. In mid-January 2002 a Congolese human rights organization urged the international community not to support the country's electoral process, citing numerous irregularities in the compilation of the electoral register. The constitutional referendum took place, as scheduled, on 20 January, without significant incident. According to official results, the new Constitution was approved by some 84.5% of votes cast, with a participation rate of some 77.5% of the electorate.

In mid-February 2002 10 presidential candidates were approved by the Supreme Court, including Sassou-Nguesso and Milongo. Six political parties supportive of Milongo, including Yhombi-Opango's Rassemblement pour la démocratie et le développement, formed an opposition alliance, the Convention pour la démocratie et le salut (CODESA), which effectively supplanted the ADP. None the less, in mid-February six of the 10 approved candidates, among them Milongo, threatened to withdraw from the polls unless the Supreme Court ruled that the electoral law conformed with the transitional fundamental law of 1997, which made no explicit provision for the holding of general elections. In early March 2002 two opposition candidates announced the withdrawal of their candidacies, having received no reply to their submission to the Supreme Court, and in protest at the perceived lack of transparency in the electoral arrangements. Two days later Milongo, who had been widely regarded as the sole credible challenger to Sassou-Nguesso, and who now headed the Union pour la démocratie et la République—Mwinda (UDR—Mwinda), also withdrew from the election and urged his supporters to boycott the poll, stating that his concerns about the transparency of electoral procedures and the impartiality of the CONEL remained unresolved.

With all the major opposition candidates thereby excluded, Sassou-Nguesso won an overwhelming victory in the presidential election (which was thus contested by seven candidates) on 10 March 2002, securing 89.41% of the votes cast. According to official figures, 69.36% of the electorate participated in the election. After the presidential election CODESA called for the postponement of the elections to the Assemblée nationale, so that amended electoral registers could be compiled. The Government subsequently delayed the elections until 26 May and 23 June; local elections were also postponed, until 30 June.

Meanwhile, in late March 2002 renewed violence erupted in the Pool region, apparently instigated by members of a 'Ninja' militia group, led by Rev. Frédéric Bitsangou Ntumi (who had been a co-signatory of the peace agreement reached in 1999), which attacked the town of Kindamba, prompting several thousand civilians to flee. The conflict widened in early April, when two people were killed in an attack on a train on the Congo-Océan railway by members of the militia, although Ntumi denied his forces had initiated the attack. Following further insurgency to the west of Brazzaville, government forces, reportedly assisted by Angolan troops, were dispatched to the region, and air attacks were launched against the rebels. By mid-April the unrest had spread to southern Brazzaville, and by late May some 50,000 people were reported to have been displaced. In late April government forces announced that they had regained control of the railway, facilitating a normalization in the supply of fuel and food to Brazzaville, although fighting continued in Pool. At the end of May government troops regained control of the rebel stronghold of Vindza, and in early June humanitarian assistance was finally permitted to reach the region.

The first round of elections to the 137-member Assemblée nationale, which was held on 26 May 2002, was contested by some 1,200 candidates from more than 100 parties; although more than one-half of the candidates had no party affiliation, it was reported than many of these nominally independent candidates were allies of Sassou-Nguesso. As a result of the unrest in Pool, voting was postponed indefinitely in eight constituencies, while disruption caused by protesters and administrative irregularities necessitated a rerun of polling in a further 12 constituencies on 28–29 May. Moreover, the CONEL subsequently announced the disqualification of 15 candidates, notably including Mathias Ndzon, the Minister of the Economy, Finance and the Budget. Turn-out in the first round, at which the PCT and its allies in the FDU won 38 of the 51 seats decided, was around 65%.

Prior to the second round of elections to the Assemblée, the security situation in Brazzaville deteriorated markedly. In mid-June 2002, while Sassou-Nguesso was in Italy, 'Ninja' rebels attacked the capital's main military base. In the subsequent fighting 72 rebels, three army officers and 15 civilians were killed, according to official reports, while some 100 rebel fighters were captured, and fighting subsequently spread to the regions around Brazzaville. In spite of requests by the UDR—Mwinda for a postponement of the elections in those areas where fighting had occurred, the elections went ahead on 23 June, although the rate of participation, at an estimated 30% nation-wide, was appreciably lower than in the first round, and was as low as 10% in some constituencies in Brazzaville and in Pointe-Noire. Following the polls, supporters of Sassou-Nguesso held an absolute majority in the new Assemblée; the PCT emerged as the largest party, with 53 seats, while the FDU alliance held a total of 30 seats. The UDR—Mwinda became the largest opposition party, with only six seats, while the UPADS held four seats. Notably, the MCDDI failed to secure representation in the Assemblée.

The local and municipal elections, held on 30 June 2002, were marked by a low turn-out and further entrenched Sassou-Nguesso's power; the success of the PCT and of constituent parties of the FDU ensured that supporters of the President held more than two-thirds of the elective seats. (CODESA had urged a boycott, citing allegations of widespread fraud in recent voting, although the UDR—Mwinda, the principal party in the alliance, encouraged its supporters to vote.) As the councillors elected on 30 June were those who would, in turn, elect the members of the Sénat on 7 July, the victory of those loyal to Sassou-Nguesso in the upper parliamentary chamber was also to be expected. Following these elections, the Sénat comprised 56 supporters of the President (44 from the PCT and 12 from the FDU), two representatives of civil society organizations, one independent and one member of the opposition. In mid-July it was reported that some 66,000 persons remained displaced as a result of the conflict in Pool.

In early August 2002 Tchicaya was elected as President of the Assemblée nationale, and the Secretary-General of the PCT, Ambroise-Edouard Noumazalay was elected as President of the Sénat. Sassou-Nguesso was inaugurated as elected President on 14 August 2002; later in the month he announced the formation of a new Government, which, notably, included no representatives of the opposition (although several representatives from civil society were appointed to ministerial positions). The new Government stated that its priority was to combat corruption within the state and the public sector.

At the end of December 2002 President Sassou-Nguesso announced the implementation of major structural and personnel changes in the military services; in particular, certain responsibilities that had formerly been held by the President, as the Supreme Commander of the Armed Forces, were to be transferred to a Deputy Chief of Defence Staff. In late January 2003 the 15 members of the High Court of Justice were named; among the eight parliamentarians appointed, there was one representative of the opposition, from the UPADS. Later in the month Gérard Bitsindou, a former cabinet director to Sassou-Nguesso, was appointed as the President of the Constitutional Court.

Meanwhile, during the second half of 2002 sporadic attacks by 'Ninja' militias in the Pool region, in particular against freight trains on the Congo-Océan railway, continued. In October unrest intensified, and several deaths of civilians were reported in clashes; up to 10,000 civilians were reported to have fled Pool, for Brazzaville, or the neighbouring Bouenza region, between early October and mid-November. In early November an *ad-hoc* presidential committee, comprising prominent citizens from the Pool region and politicians allied to Sassou-Nguesso or to Lissouba, proposed a cease-fire between government forces and the 'Ninja' forces allied to Ntumi, and the replacement of government army units in the region with gendarmerie patrols. In mid-November Sassou-Nguesso, rejecting the proposals of the committee, announced that a 'safe passage' would be provided from Pool to Brazzaville until mid-December for fighters who surrendered their arms, and reiterated that the terms of the peace agreement concluded in 1999 remained valid. However, following Sassou-Nguesso's announcement of the temporary amnesty, fighting intensified, and within one month only 371 rebels were reported to have surrendered (estimates of the number of rebels at large varied from 3,000–10,000). Although Sassou-Nguesso announced an extension of the amnesty, as a result of which a further 90 rebels surrendered in early January 2003, some 15 civilians were killed in an attack in Pool at the beginning of that month, and in early February the first outbreak of violence in the Bouenza region since 1999, in which a local police chief was killed, was reported. None the less, in mid-March 2003 the Government and Ntumi's 'Ninja' militia group signed a peace agreement, aimed at restoring peace to the Pool region. The rebels agreed to end hostilities and disarm, while the Government was to guarantee an amnesty for the rebels and integrate former combatants into the national armed forces.

Since the 1997 civil war the principal aim of Congolese foreign policy has been to gain international recognition for the legitimacy of the Sassou-Nguesso Government, and to ensure the continued support of the country's bilateral and multilateral donors. During the 1997 civil war President Lissouba accused France of favouring the rebel forces of Sassou-Nguesso (who was reported to have allied himself with French petroleum interests) over the elected administration. In May 1998 France extended its formal recognition to the Sassou-Nguesso Government, and in June resumed aid payments that had been suspended since the 1997 conflict. In September French military advisers were sent to Brazzaville to train the Congolese gendarmerie. Sassou-Nguesso made an official visit to Paris in September 2002, when he met President Jacques Chirac.

Prior to Sassou-Nguesso's seizure of power in 1997, relations with Angola were strained, as a result of the existence in the Congo of bases of an Angolan rebel, secessionist group, the Frente de Libertação do Enclave de Cabinda (FLEC). In the 1997 conflict Angolan government troops facilitated Sassou-Nguesso's victory by providing tactical support, including the occupation of Pointe-Noire, the Congo's main seaport and focus of the petroleum industry; Angolan troops also played an important role in the defeat of the rebel attack on Brazzaville in December 1998. In January 1999 the Heads of State of Angola, the Congo and the DRC met to agree a common policy on the conflicts in their countries. In December the interior ministers of the three countries met in Luanda, Angola, and signed a co-operation accord. The accord created a tripartite commission to ensure border security, the free movement of people and goods, the training of personnel, and the provision of assistance to displaced persons. In April 2000 further meetings were held in Kinshasa, the DRC, in order to discuss the implementation of the Luanda accord, which was expected to include the formation of joint military patrols. In the same month it was announced that the Angolan and Congolese Governments were to investigate the joint exploitation of offshore petroleum resources. Angolan troops assisted the Congolese Government in the renewed insurgency in the Pool region from early 2002, but the last contingent of Angolan soldiers was withdrawn from the Congo in December of that year. A further tripartite meeting of the Presidents of Angola, the Congo and the DRC was held in January 2002, when the Angolan President, José Eduardo dos Santos, urged the Governments of the Congo and the DRC to take further action against the operations of the FLEC in their territories.

Relations between the Republic of the Congo and the DRC steadily improved from the late 1990s. In December 1998 the two countries signed a non-aggression pact and agreed to establish a joint force to guarantee border security. In December 1999 Sassou-Nguesso met President Laurent-Désiré Kabila in order to discuss bilateral co-operation and the implementation of the tripartite Luanda accord, and further discussion on issues of common interest took place regularly between the two countries in 2000–02. In May 2001 19 DRC nationals suspected of involvement in the assassination of Laurent-Désiré Kabila in January were extradited from the Republic of the Congo to Kinshasa. In September 2002 Congolese authorities announced that, in accordance with a programme established in association with the International Organization for Migration (see p. 248), up to 4,000 soldiers from the DRC who had sought refuge or deserted in the Congo were to be repatriated.

Government

The 1992 Constitution was suspended following the assumption of power by Gen. Denis Sassou-Nguesso on 15 October 1997. A Conseil national de transition was subsequently appointed, with 75 designated members, to act as an interim legislative body. A new Constitution, which was approved by referendum on 20 January 2002, took effect following a presidential election in March–April and legislative elections in May–June. Under the terms of the 2002 Constitution, executive power is vested in a President, who is directly elected for a seven-year term, renewable only once. The President appoints a Council of Ministers. Legislative power is vested in a bicameral Parliament, comprising a 137-member Assemblée nationale, which is directly elected for a five-year term, and a 66-member Sénat, which is indirectly elected by local councils for a six-year term (with one-half of the membership renewable every three years).

For administrative purposes the country is divided into 10 regions, consisting of 76 districts (sous-préfectures) and six municipalities (communes urbaines).

Defence

In August 2002 the army numbered 8,000, the navy about 800 and the air force 1,200. In addition, there was a 2,000-strong Gendarmerie. An estimated 2,000 Angolan troops were also stationed in the Republic of the Congo at that time. National service is voluntary for men and women, and lasts for two years. The estimated defence budget for 2002 was 65,000m. francs CFA.

Economic Affairs

In 2001, according to estimates by the World Bank, the Congo's gross national income (GNI), measured at average 1999–2001 prices, was US $2,171m., equivalent to $700 per head (or $580 on an international purchasing-power parity basis). During 1990–2001, it was estimated, the population increased at an average annual rate of 3.1%, while gross domestic product

(GDP) per head declined, in real terms, by an average of 2.4% per year. Overall GDP increased, in real terms, at an average annual rate of 0.6% in 1990–2001; growth in 2001 was 2.9%.

Agriculture (including forestry and fishing) contributed 6.2% of GDP in 2001, and employed about 39.9% of the total labour force in that year. The staple crops are cassava and plantains, while the major cash crops are sugar cane, oil palm, cocoa and coffee. Forests cover about 57% of the country's total land area, and forestry is a major economic activity. Sales of timber provided an estimated 8.4% of export earnings in 1995, but in February 1998, to encourage local processing of wood, forestry companies were prohibited from exporting rough timber. Following the implementation of liberalization measures in the sector, output of timber was expected to increase significantly in the early 2000s. During 1990–2001 agricultural GDP increased at an average annual rate of 1.1%; growth in 2001 was 4.6%.

Industry (including mining, manufacturing, construction and power) contributed 67.4% of GDP in 2001, and employed an estimated 14.7% of the labour force in 1990. During 1990–2001 industrial GDP increased at an average annual rate of 2.3%; growth in 2001 was 0.6%.

Mining contributed 28.6% of GDP in 1989. The hydrocarbons sector is the only significant mining activity. In 1995 sales of petroleum and petroleum products provided an estimated 84.6% of export earnings. The real GDP of the petroleum sector (extraction and refining) increased by 6.1% in 1998 and by an estimated 4.3% in 1999. Annual petroleum production (an estimated 96.7m. barrels in 2000, according to the US Geological Survey) was expected to continue to grow, as a result of major exploration and development planned at various offshore deposits, in particular near to the maritime border with Angola. Deposits of natural gas are also exploited. Lead, zinc, gold and copper are produced in small quantities, and the large-scale mining of magnesium was expected to commence by 2004. There are also exploitable reserves of diamonds, phosphate, iron ore, bauxite and potash. In October 2001 the Government issued the Portuguese company Escom a licence to prospect for diamonds in the far north of the country.

Manufacturing contributed 4.7% of GDP in 2001. The most important industries, the processing of agricultural and forest products, were adversely affected by the civil conflict in the late 1990s, but began to recover in the early 2000s, as political stability was restored. The textile, chemical and construction materials industries are also significant. During 1990–2001 manufacturing GDP declined at an average annual rate of 5.8%; however, growth of 9.1% was recorded in 2001.

In 1999 some 97.9% of total electricity production was generated by hydroelectric plants. Imports of fuel and energy comprised an estimated 23.7% of the value of total imports in 2000.

The services sector contributed 26.3% of GDP in 2001. During 1990–2001, it was estimated, the GDP of the services sector declined at an average annual rate of 1.4%; however, growth of 5.5% was recorded in 2001.

In 2000 the Congo recorded a visible trade surplus of an estimated 1,319,700m. francs CFA., and there was an estimated surplus of 182,000m. francs CFA on the current account of the balance of payments. In 1995 the principal source of imports (32.0%) was France, while the USA was the principal market for exports (22.6%). Italy and the Netherlands are also important trading partners. The principal exports in 1996 were petroleum and petroleum products. The principal imports were machinery, chemical products, iron and steel and transport equipment.

The budget surplus for 2001 was estimated at 105,700m. francs CFA (equivalent to 5.1% of GDP). The country's external debt totalled US $4,887m. at the end of 2000, of which $3,758m. was long-term public debt. In that year the cost of debt-servicing was equivalent to 1.6% of the value of exports of goods and services. The annual rate of inflation averaged 6.5% in 1990–2001. Consumer prices declined by an average of 0.9% in 2000 and increased by 0.1% in 2001.

The Republic of the Congo is a member of the Central African organs of the Franc Zone (see p. 239) and of the Communauté économique des Etats de l'Afrique centrale (CEEAC, see p. 339).

Economic performance in the late 1990s was adversely affected by civil conflict and ensuing instability. An IMF-supported economic reform programme for 1996–99 was halted by the 1997 civil war. Moreover, in November 1997 the World Bank suspended relations with the Congo in response to the non-payment of debt arrears, while the outbreak of further hostilities in December 1998 led to the suspension of all donor activity. In recent years the high relative level of debt (which in 2000 was equivalent to 219% of GNI) has remained a major impediment to the resumption of aid. Moreover, weaknesses in the implementation of reforms and a lack of strict budget control have prevented the Congo from qualifying for relief under the Heavily Indebted Poor Countries initiative of the Bretton Woods institutions. None the less, in November 2000 the IMF approved a credit of some US $14m. for the Congo in emergency post-conflict assistance. Short-term economic objectives following the restoration of peace in late 1999 included the creation of sustainable economic growth, the continued rehabilitation of state infrastructure, the normalization of relations with external creditors and the strengthening of the non-petroleum sector, the real GDP of which had declined by 19% in 1997–99. Progress towards these aims in the early 2000s was hesitant, partially as a result of ongoing insecurity, particularly in the south, although major reforms, involving restructuring and privatization, were introduced in the banking and petroleum sectors in 2001–02. Furthermore, a new cement-producing company, the Nouvelle Société des Ciments du Congo commenced operations in 2002, as a joint enterprise between the Congolese Government and a Chinese company, to replace a state-owned company that had closed during the civil conflict; the production capacity of the company was expected to cover the entire national requirement for cement. A programme of post-conflict reconstruction initially emphasized infrastructural improvements, including the construction of a year-round river port at Lékéti and a new international airport in the north of the country. In August 2001 the World Bank declared that the Congo had cleared all of its overdue service payments and was again eligible for credit. In the longer term, however, the Congo's economic development was likely to depend on the successful implementation of credible privatization programmes, tighter budget control and the maintenance of political stability.

Education

Education is officially compulsory for 10 years between six and 16 years of age. Primary education begins at the age of six and lasts for six years. Secondary education, from 12 years of age, lasts for seven years, comprising a first cycle of four years and a second of three years. Enrolment at primary schools in 1999/2000 was equivalent to 83.8% of children in the relevant age-group (boys 88.2%; girls 79.5%). In 1998/99 114,450 pupils were receiving general secondary education. In 1997/98 16,862 students were attending vocational institutions. In 2000 there were some 20,000 students enrolled in the Marien Ngouabi University in Brazzaville. Some Congolese students also attend further education establishments abroad. Expenditure on education by all levels of government was 52,274m. francs CFA in 1995.

Public Holidays

2003: 1 January (New Year's Day), 18 April (Good Friday), 21 April (Easter Monday), 1 May (Labour Day), 9 June (Whit Monday), 15 August (Independence Day), 25 December (Christmas).

2004: 1 January (New Year's Day), 9 April (Good Friday), 12 April (Easter Monday), 1 May (Labour Day), 31 May (Whit Monday), 15 August (Independence Day), 25 December (Christmas).

Weights and Measures

The metric system is in force.

Statistical Survey

Source (unless otherwise stated): Direction Générale, Centre National de la Statistique et des Etudes Economiques, BP 2031, Brazzaville; tel. and fax 81-59-09.

Area and Population

AREA, POPULATION AND DENSITY

Area (sq km)	342,000*
Population (census results)	
22 December 1984	1,909,248
30 July 1996	2,591,271
Population (UN estimates at mid-year)†	
1998	2,845,000
1999	2,930,000
2000	3,018,000
Density (per sq km) at mid-2000	8.8

* 132,047 sq miles.

† Source: UN, *World Population Prospects: The 2000 Revision*.

ETHNIC GROUPS

1995 (percentages): Kongo 51.4; Téké 17.2; Mbochi 11.4; Mbédé 4.7; Punu 2.9; Sanga 2.5; Maka 1.8; Pygmy 1.4; Others 6.7 (Source: La Francophonie).

REGIONS
(population at 1996 census)

	Area (sq km)	Population	Capital
Bouenza	12,260	189,839	Madingou
Cuvette . . . . }	74,850 {	112,946	Owando
Cuvette ouest . . }		49,422	Ewo
Kouilou	13,650	77,048	Pointe-Noire
Lékoumou	20,950	75,734	Sibiti
Likouala	66,044	66,252	Impfondo
Niari	25,925	103,678	Loubomo (Dolisie)
Plateaux	38,400	139,371	Djambala
Pool	33,955	265,180	Kinkala
Sangha	55,795	39,439	Ouesso
Total*	341,829	1,118,909	

* Excluding the municipalities of Brazzaville (100 sq km, population 856,410), Pointe-Noire (45 sq km, population 455,131), Loubomo (Dolisie —18 sq km, population 79,852), Nkaya (8 sq km, population 46,727), Ouesso (population 17,784) and Mossendjo (population 16,458).

BIRTHS AND DEATHS
(UN estimates, annual averages)

	1985–90	1990–95	1995–2000
Birth rate (per 1,000)	44.3	44.6	44.5
Death rate (per 1,000)	15.0	14.9	14.7

Source: UN, *World Population Prospects: The 2000 Revision*.

Expectation of life (WHO estimates, years at birth): 52.9 (males 51.8; females 53.8) in 2001 (Source: WHO, *World Health Report*).

EMPLOYMENT
('000 persons at 1984 census)

	Males	Females	Total
Agriculture, etc.	105	186	291
Industry	61	8	69
Services	123	60	183
Total	289	254	543

Mid-2001 (FAO estimates, '000 persons): Agriculture, etc. 506; Total labour force 1,268 (Source: FAO).

Health and Welfare

KEY INDICATORS

Total fertility rate (children per woman, 2001)	6.3
Under-5 mortality rate (per 1,000 live births, 2001) . . .	108
HIV/AIDS (% of persons aged 15–49, 2001)	7.15
Physicians (per 1,000 head, 1995)	0.25
Hospital beds (per 1,000 head, 1990)	3.35
Health expenditure (2000): US $ per head (PPP)	25
Health expenditure (2000): % of GDP	2.2
Health expenditure (2000): public (% of total)	70.2
Access to water (% of persons, 2000)	51
Human Development Index (2000): ranking	136
Human Development Index (2000): value	0.512

For sources and definitions, see explanatory note on p. vi.

Agriculture

PRINCIPAL CROPS
('000 metric tons)

	1999	2000	2001
Sweet potatoes*	8.9	10.0	10.0
Cassava (Manioc)	811.9	828.1	844.7
Yams	8.9†	10.0	10.0*
Other roots and tubers*	38.9	39.4	39.4
Sugar cane	409.0	450.3	454.4
Groundnuts (in shell)	23.0	23.2	23.4
Oil palm fruit*	90	90	90
Vegetables (incl. melons)* . . .	39.7	39.8	39.8
Bananas	79.5	81.1	82.7
Plantains	67.6	70.3	70.3*
Citrus fruit	12.6	12.5	12.5
Mangoes*	23.5	23.5	23.5
Other fruit*	31.8	31.5	31.5

* FAO estimate(s).

† Unofficial figure.

Source: FAO.

LIVESTOCK
('000 head, year ending September)

	1999	2000	2001
Cattle	83	87	90
Pigs*	45	46	46
Sheep	115*	96	96*
Goats*	280	280	280
Poultry*	1,900	1,900	1,900

* FAO estimate(s).

Source: FAO.

LIVESTOCK PRODUCTS
(FAO estimates, '000 metric tons)

	1999	2000	2001
Beef and veal	1.6	1.6	1.7
Pig meat	2.0	2.0	2.0
Poultry meat	5.8	5.8	5.8
Game meat	16.0	16.0	16.0
Sheep and goat meat	1.1	1.1	1.1
Cows' milk	1.1	1.1	1.1
Hen eggs	1.1	1.2	1.2

Source: FAO.

Forestry

ROUNDWOOD REMOVALS
('000 cubic metres, excluding bark)

	1999	2000	2001
Sawlogs, veneer logs and logs for sleepers	520	520*	520*
Pulpwood	361	361	361*
Other industrial wood*	370	370	370
Fuel wood*	1,139	1,153	1,169
Total	2,340	2,404	2,420

* FAO estimate(s).
Source: FAO.

SAWNWOOD PRODUCTION
('000 cubic metres, including railway sleepers)

	1999	2000	2001
Total (all broadleaved)	74	93	95

Source: FAO.

Fishing

('000 metric tons, live weight)

	1998	1999	2000
Capture*	44.5	43.7	50.0
Freshwater fishes	25.5	25.5*	25.5*
Sardinellas*	11.6	11.2	15.0
Aquaculture	0.1*	0.2	0.2
Total catch*	44.6	43.9	50.2

* FAO estimate(s).

Source: FAO, *Yearbook of Fishery Statistics*.

Mining

	1998	1999	2000*
Crude petroleum ('000 barrels)	90,499	93,951	96,700
Gold (kg)†	10	10	10

* Estimates.
† Estimated metal content of ores.

Source: US Geological Survey.

Industry

SELECTED PRODUCTS
('000 metric tons, unless otherwise indicated)

	1996	1997	1998
Raw sugar*	43	40	43
Veneer sheets ('000 cu metres)	50	76	52
Jet fuels†	16	17	17
Motor spirit (petrol)†	55	55	56
Kerosene†	50	50	51
Distillate fuel oils†	92	95	96
Residual fuel oils†	260	262	262
Cement	43	20	—
Electric energy (million kWh)†	438	441	443†

1999: Raw sugar ('000 metric tons) 39.8; Veneer sheets ('000 cu metres) 19.

2000: Raw sugar ('000 metric tons) 41.6.

2001: Raw sugar ('000 metric tons) 42.9.

* FAO estimates.
† Provisional figure(s).

Sources: FAO; UN, *Industrial Commodity Statistics Yearbook*.

Finance

CURRENCY AND EXCHANGE RATES

Monetary Units
100 centimes = 1 franc de la Coopération financière en Afrique centrale (CFA)

Sterling, Dollar and Euro Equivalents (31 December 2002)
£1 sterling = 1,008.17 francs CFA
US $1 = 625.50 francs CFA
€1 = 655.96 francs CFA
10,000 francs CFA = £9.919 = $15.987 = €15.245

Average Exchange Rate (francs CFA per US $)
2000   711.98
2001   733.04
2002   696.99

Note: The exchange rate of 1 French franc = 50 francs CFA, established in 1948, remained in force until January 1994, when the CFA franc was devalued by 50%, with the exchange rate adjusted to 1 French franc = 100 francs CFA. The relationship to French currency remained in effect with the introduction of the euro on 1 January 1999. From that date, accordingly, a fixed exchange rate of €1 = 655.957 francs CFA has been in operation.

BUDGET
('000 million francs CFA)

Revenue*	1999	2000	2001†
Petroleum revenue	275.1	468.1	464.9
Other revenue	140.3	139.0	197.3
Domestic taxes	76.4	n.a.	n.a.
Customs receipts	21.7	n.a.	n.a.
Domestic petroleum taxes	7.8	n.a.	n.a.
Total	415.4	607.1	662.2

Expenditure	1999	2000	2001†
Current expenditure	376.8	416.5	450.6
Wages and salaries	100.7	106.7	118.1
Interest payments	159.4	160.4	155.4
External	148.4	150.8	145.7
Capital expenditure	80.0	159.6	205.4
Sub-total	456.8	576.1	656.0
Less Adjustment for payment arrears	305.2	256.4	95.8
Total (cash basis)	151.6	319.7	560.2

* Excluding grants received ('000 million francs CFA): 3.0 in 1999; 7.0 in 2000; 3.7 (estimate) in 2001.
† Estimates.

Source: mainly Banque des états de l'Afrique centrale.

INTERNATIONAL RESERVES
(US $ million at 31 December)

	2000	2001	2002
Gold*	3.03	3.09	3.81
IMF special drawing rights	0.04	0.19	3.23
Reserve position in IMF	0.70	0.67	0.73
Foreign exchange	221.27	68.05	27.67
Total	225.04	72.00	35.44

* National valuation.

Source: IMF, *International Financial Statistics*.

MONEY SUPPLY
(million francs CFA at 31 December)

	2000	2001	2002
Currency outside banks	123,867	142,910	129,002
Demand deposits at active commercial banks	171,742	81,360	129,772
Total money (incl. others)	309,578	238,077	271,235

Source: IMF, *International Financial Statistics*.

COST OF LIVING
(Consumer Price Index for Brazzaville; base: December 1977 = 100)

	1998	1999	2000
Food	376.6	394.7	374.3
Clothing	419.1	433.4	459.7
Housing	448.1	460.9	482.8
All items (incl. others)	403.7	420.4	416.7

NATIONAL ACCOUNTS
('000 million francs CFA at current prices)

Expenditure on the Gross Domestic Product

	1999	2000	2001*
Government final consumption expenditure	185.3	219.3	241.4
Private final consumption expenditure	516.9	485.8	663.0
Increase in stocks	51.0	5.0	8.0
Gross fixed capital formation	502.3	573.7	655.1
Total domestic expenditure	1,255.5	1,283.8	1,567.5
Exports of goods and services	1,050.5	1,954.2	1,549.6
Less Imports of goods and services	856.6	949.8	1,040.0
GDP in purchasers' values	1,449.4	2,288.1	2,077.2
GDP at constant 1990 prices	812.5	877.0	902.8

* Estimates.

Source: Banque des états de l'Afrique centrale.

Gross Domestic Product by Economic Activity

	1997	1998	1999*
Agriculture, hunting, forestry and fishing	123.9	126.0	119.8
Mining and quarrying†	} 740.7	499.6	771.6
Manufacturing†			
Electricity, gas and water	13.6	14.9	9.3
Construction	16.6	15.2	26.2
Trade, restaurants and hotels	132.9	139.3	116.7
Transport, storage and communication	77.5	77.7	72.0
Government services	122.0	119.2	122.2
Other services	98.3	108.3	91.1
GDP at factor cost	1,325.5	1,100.2	1,328.9
Import duties	30.2	49.9	36.4
GDP in purchasers' values	1,355.7	1,150.1	1,365.3

* Preliminary figures.

† Including petroleum sector ('000 million francs CFA): 666.7 in 1997; 419.6 in 1998; 692.3 (preliminary figure) in 1999.

Source: IMF, *Republic of Congo: Statistical Annex* (January 2001).

BALANCE OF PAYMENTS
('000 million francs CFA)

	1998	1999	2000*
Exports of goods f.o.b.	808.0	958.0	1,743.8
Imports of goods f.o.b.	−329.4	−321.8	−424.1
Trade balance	478.5	636.2	1,319.7
Services (net)	−436.4	−449.9	−478.5
Balance on goods and services	42.1	191.3	841.2
Other income (net)	−277.8	−436.5	−672.6
Balance on goods, services and income	−235.7	−245.2	168.6
Private unrequited transfers (net)	−6.3	−3.6	5.0
Public unrequited transfers (net)	4.5	0.4	8.4
Current balance	−237.5	−248.4	182.0
Capital account (net)	31.3	14.9	14.3
Direct investment (net)	24.1	319.5	340.2
Portfolio investment (net)	−7.5	−10.9	0.2
Other investment (net)	237.1	−51.9	−375.5
Net errors and omissions	−93.9	13.6	−41.1
Overall balance	−46.4	36.7	120.1

* Estimates.

Source: IMF, *Republic of Congo: Letter of Intent* (May 2002).

External Trade

PRINCIPAL COMMODITIES
(distribution by SITC, US $ million)

Imports c.i.f.	1993	1994	1995
Food and live animals	59.6	87.9	108.5
Meat and meat preparations	15.8	23.7	28.1
Fresh, chilled or frozen meat and edible offals	15.0	21.7	26.8
Fish and fish preparations	0.1	21.8	16.4
Cereals and cereal preparations	27.5	23.8	36.7
Flour of wheat or meslin	18.1	8.2	13.8
Mineral fuels, lubricants, etc.	2.9	4.9	108.7
Petroleum, petroleum products, etc.	2.8	4.9	106.0
Refined petroleum products	2.7	3.1	105.5
Motor spirit (gasoline) and other light oils	—	—	38.4
Motor spirit (incl. aviation spirit)	—	—	30.7
Kerosene and other medium oils	—	—	19.2
Gas oils	—	—	44.4
Chemicals and related products	54.6	54.7	77.0
Medicaments (incl. veterinary)	38.5	24.0	38.0
Basic manufactures	61.5	76.7	69.5
Iron and steel	17.8	20.5	15.6
Tubes, pipes and fittings	14.6	17.6	9.7
'Seamless' tubes and pipes; blanks for tubes and pipes	13.2	15.8	6.4
Iron or steel structures, etc.	0.2	21.6	1.0
Machinery and transport equipment	127.1	112.6	112.5
Machinery specialized for particular industries	10.7	17.3	17.2
Civil engineering and contractors' plant and equipment	7.2	11.9	10.0
General industrial machinery, equipment and parts	24.9	30.4	32.1
Electrical machinery, apparatus, etc.	11.7	23.7	19.0
Road vehicles and parts*	20.4	20.7	21.1
Other transport equipment and parts*	47.1	6.5	3.8
Tugs, special-purpose vessels and floating structures	46.7	2.8	0.3
Light-vessels, fire-floats, dredgers, floating cranes, etc.	45.7	—	—
Miscellaneous manufactured articles	24.2	36.3	65.2
Professional, scientific and controlling instruments, etc.	8.2	13.2	29.1
Measuring, checking, analysing and controlling instruments, etc.	7.5	11.6	26.3
Total (incl. others)	347.1	395.2	555.9

* Data on parts exclude tyres, engines and electrical parts.

Exports f.o.b.	1993	1994	1995
Crude materials (inedible) except fuels	18.4	124.5	94.2
Cork and wood	17.8	114.5	90.6
Non-coniferous sawlogs and veneer logs	8.7	106.0	80.3
Mineral fuels, lubricants, etc.	911.2	765.2	955.1
Petroleum, petroleum products, etc.	911.2	765.2	955.1
Crude petroleum oils, etc.	890.9	746.7	936.3
Total (incl. others)	965.3	917.8	1,089.8

Source: UN, *International Trade Statistics Yearbook*.

Imports c.i.f. (million francs CFA): 793,306 in 1996; 540,647 in 1997; 339,282 in 1998; 442,694 in 1999; 330,939 in 2000.

Exports (million francs CFA): 688,100 in 1996; 970,700 in 1997; 806,900 in 1998; 960,510 in 1999; 1,772,200 in 2000.

Source: IMF, *International Financial Statistics*.

PRINCIPAL TRADING PARTNERS
(US $ million)

Imports c.i.f.	1993	1994	1995*
Belgium-Luxembourg . . .	9.7	14.9	19.4
France (incl. Monaco) . . .	114.0	127.5	145.2
Germany	8.4	9.2	15.8
Hong Kong	4.5	4.0	3.7
Italy	66.2	17.1	20.8
Japan	11.1	10.2	12.3
Mauritania	—	0.7	5.9
Netherlands	27.5	24.6	30.7
Norway	1.7	4.0	2.4
Senegal	1.8	6.0	7.2
South Africa†	2.8	8.2	0.0
United Kingdom	9.0	12.7	16.6
USA	16.1	39.5	44.6
Total (incl. others)	347.1	395.2	555.9

Exports f.o.b.	1993	1994	1995
Angola	10.2	5.1	6.5
Brazil	0.1	14.0	—
Chile	—	15.6	—
France (incl. Monaco) . . .	79.5	56.3	107.3
Germany	2.6	8.1	11.5
Israel	12.8	11.8	—
Italy	226.3	191.8	189.6
Japan	14.4	3.2	3.4
Malta	—	—	31.3
Netherlands	16.6	11.0	130.7
Portugal	1.6	21.9	0.4
Spain	17.3	28.1	0.1
Switzerland-Liechtenstein . . .	12.3	—	—
USA	503.4	386.3	311.1
Total (incl others)	965.3	917.8	1,089.8

* Figures for individual countries exclude imports from free zones ($56.4 million) and stores and bunkers for ships and aircraft ($50.8 million).
† Including Botswana, Lesotho, Namibia and Swaziland.

Source: UN, *International Trade Statistics Yearbook*.

Transport

RAILWAYS
(traffic)

	1997	1998	1999
Passengers carried ('000) . . .	1,041	927	70
Freight carried ('000 metric tons) .	441	399	59
Passenger-km (million) . . .	235	242	9
Freight ton-km (million) . . .	139	135	21

Sources: partly UN, *Statistical Yearbook*; IMF, *Republic of Congo: Statistical Annex* (January 2001).

ROAD TRAFFIC
(estimates, '000 motor vehicles in use at 31 December)

	1994	1995	1996
Passenger cars	33.7	36.3	37.2
Goods vehicles	14.6	15.7	15.5

Source: IRF, *World Road Statistics*.

SHIPPING

Merchant Fleet
(registered at 31 December)

	1999	2000	2001
Number of vessels	20	18	18
Total displacement ('000 grt) . .	3.8	3.4	3.4

Source: Lloyd's Register-Fairplay, *World Fleet Statistics*.

Freight Traffic at Pointe-Noire
(metric tons)

	1996	1997	1998
Goods loaded	670,150	708,203	n.a.
Goods unloaded	584,376	533,170	724,000*

* Rounded figure.

Source: mainly Banque des états de l'Afrique centrale, *Etudes et Statistiques*.

CIVIL AVIATION
(traffic on scheduled services)*

	1997	1998	1999
Kilometres flown (million) . . .	5	5	4
Passengers carried ('000) . . .	237	241	132
Passenger-km (million)	305	321	263
Total ton-km (million)	44	44	39

* Including an apportionment of the traffic of Air Afrique.

Source: UN, *Statistical Yearbook*.

Tourism

	1998	1999	2000
Foreign tourist arrivals	25,082	4,753	26,000*
Tourism receipts (US $ million) .	9	12	11

* Rounded figure.

Source: World Tourism Organization.

Communications Media

	1999	2000	2001
Telephones ('000 main lines in use)	22	22	22
Mobile cellular telephones ('000 subscribers).	5	70	150
Personal computers ('000 in use) .	10	n.a.	12
Internet users ('000)	0.5	n.a.	n.a.

Source: International Telecommunication Union.

Radio receivers ('000 in use): 341 in 1997 (Source: UNESCO, *Statistical Yearbook*).

Television receivers ('000 in use): 33 in 1997 (Source: UNESCO, *Statistical Yearbook*).

Daily newspapers: 6 in 1996 (Source: UNESCO, *Statistical Yearbook*).

Non-daily newspapers: 15 in 1995 (average circulation 38,000 copies) (Source: UNESCO, *Statistical Yearbook*).

Education
(1998/99)

	Institutions	Teachers	Students Males	Students Females	Students Total
Pre-primary . .	95	606	2,338	3,695	6,033
Primary . . .	1,168	4,515	141,646	134,805	276,451
Secondary* . .	n.a.	5,094	71,169	43,281	114,450
Higher	n.a.	1,341†	n.a.	n.a.	16,862‡

* Figures refer to general secondary education only.
† 1995 figure.
‡ 1997/98 figure.

Sources: UNESCO Institute for Statistics; Ministry of Education, Brazzaville.

Adult literacy rate (UNESCO estimates): 80.7% (males 87.5%; females 74.4%) in 2000 (Source: UN Development Programme, *Human Development Report*).

Directory

The Constitution

The 1992 Constitution was suspended following the assumption of power by Gen. Denis Sassou-Nguesso on 15 October 1997. A new Constitution, which was approved by the Conseil national de transition (interim legislative body) on 2 September 2001 and endorsed by a public referendum on 20 January 2002, took effect following presidential and legislative elections in March–July 2002. Its main provisions are summarized below:

PREAMBLE

The Congolese people, having chosen a pluralist democracy as the basis for the development of the country, condemn the tyrannical use of power and political violence and declare that the fundamental principles proclaimed and guaranteed by the UN Charter, the Universal Declaration of Human Rights and other international treaties form an integral part of the present Constitution.

I. THE STATE AND SOVEREIGNTY

Articles 1–6: The Republic of the Congo is a sovereign, secular, social and democratic State. The principle of the Republic is government of the people, by the people and for the people. National sovereignty belongs to the people, who exercise it through universal suffrage by their elected representatives or by referendum. The official language of the Republic is French. The national languages of communication are Lingala and Kituba.

II. FUNDAMENTAL RIGHTS AND LIBERTIES

Articles 7–42: All citizens are equal before the law. Arbitrary arrest and all degrading forms of punishment are prohibited, and all accused are presumed innocent until proven guilty. Incitement to ethnic hatred, violence or civil war and the use of religion to political ends are forbidden. Equal access to education, which is compulsory until the age of 16, is guaranteed to all. The State is obliged to create conditions that enable all citizens to enjoy the right to work. All citizens, excluding members of the police and military forces, may participate in trade union activity. Slavery is forbidden, and forced labour permitted only as a judicial punishment.

III. DUTIES

Articles 43–50: All citizens have duties towards their family, society, the State and other legally recognized authorities. All citizens are obliged to conform to the Constitution, the laws of the Republic and to fulfil their obligations towards the State and society.

IV. POLITICAL PARTIES

Articles 51–55: Political parties may not be identified with an ethnic group, a region, a religion or a sect. They must protect and promote fundamental human rights, the rule of law, democracy, individual and collective freedoms, national territorial integrity and sovereignty, proscribe intolerance, ethnically based extremism, and any recourse to violence, and respect the secular form of the State.

V. EXECUTIVE POWER

Articles 56–88: The President of the Republic is the Head of State, Head of the Executive and Head of Government. The President is directly elected by an absolute majority of votes cast, for a term of seven years, renewable once. Presidential candidates must be of Congolese nationality and origin, aged between 40 and 70 years and have resided on national territory for at least 24 successive months prior to registering as a candidate. If required, a second round of voting takes place between the two highest-placed candidates in the first ballot. In the event of the death, resignation, or long-term incapacity of the President of the Republic, the President of the Sénat assumes limited executive functions for up to 90 days, pending an election, which he may not contest.

The President appoints ministers, senior civil servants, military staff and ambassadors. Ministers may not hold a parliamentary mandate or civic, public or military post, and their professional activity is restricted. The President of the Republic is the Supreme Head of the armed forces and the President of the Higher Council of Magistrates, and possesses the right of pardon. The President of the Republic chairs the Council of Ministers.

VI. LEGISLATIVE POWER

Articles 89–113: The Parliament is bicameral. Deputies are directly elected to the Assemblée nationale for a renewable term of five years. Senators are elected indirectly to the Sénat by local councils for a term of six years. One-half of the Sénat is elected every three years. Deputies and senators must be Congolese nationals, aged over 25 years in the case of deputies, or over 45 years in the case of senators, residing in national territory. A deputy or senator elected as a member of a political grouping may not resign from the grouping without simultaneously resigning his parliamentary position.

VII. RELATIONS BETWEEN THE LEGISLATIVE AND EXECUTIVE INSTITUTIONS

Articles 114–132: The President of the Republic may not dissolve the Assemblée nationale. The Assemblée nationale may not remove the President of the Republic. The legislative chambers consider proposed legislation in succession, with a view to adopting an identical text. If necessary, the President of the Republic may convene a joint commission to present a revised text to the two chambers. The President of the Republic may then call the Assemblée nationale to make a final decision. Special conditions apply to the passage of certain laws, including the national budget, and to a declaration of war or state of emergency.

VIII. JUDICIAL POWER

Articles 133–143: Judicial power is exercised by the Supreme Court, the Revenue and Budgetary Discipline Court, appeal courts and other national courts of law, which are independent of the legislature. The President of the Republic chairs a Higher Council of Magistrates, which guarantees the independence of the judiciary. The President of the Republic nominates judges to the Supreme Court and to the other courts of law, at the suggestion of the Higher Council of Magistrates. Judges of the Supreme Court may not be removed from office.

IX. CONSTITUTIONAL COURT

Articles 144–151: The Constitutional Court consists of nine members, each with a renewable mandate of nine years. One-third of the Court is renewed every three years. The President of the Republic nominates three members of the Constitutional Court independently, and the others at the suggestion of the President of each legislative chamber and of the Bureau of the Supreme Court. The President of the Republic nominates the President of the Constitutional Court. The Court ensures that laws, treaties and international agreements conform to the Constitution and oversees presidential elections.

X. HIGH COURT OF JUSTICE

Articles 152–156: The High Court of Justice is composed of an equal number of deputies and senators elected by their peers, and of members of the Supreme Court elected by their peers. It is chaired by the First President of the Supreme Court and is competent to try the President of the Republic in case of high treason. Members of the legislature, the Supreme Court and the Constitutional Court and government ministers are accountable to the High Court of Justice for crimes or offences committed in the execution of their duties, subject to a two-thirds' majority in a secret vote at a joint session of Parliament.

XI. ECONOMIC AND SOCIAL COUNCIL

Articles 157–160: The Economic and Social Council is a consultative assembly, which may become involved in any economic or social problem concerning the Republic, either of its own will or at the request of the President of the Republic or the President of either legislative chamber.

XII. HIGHER COUNCIL FOR THE FREEDOM OF COMMUNICATION

Articles 161–162: The Higher Council for the Freedom of Communication ensures freedom of information and communication, formulating recommendations on applicable issues.

XIII. MEDIATOR OF THE REPUBLIC

Articles 163–166: The Mediator of the Republic is an independent authority responsible for simplifying and humanizing relations between government and citizens, and may be addressed by any person dissatisfied with the workings of any public organization.

XIV. NATIONAL COMMISSION FOR HUMAN RIGHTS

Articles 167–169: The National Commission for Human Rights seeks to promote and protect human rights.

XV. POLICE AND MILITARY FORCES

Articles 170–173: The police and military bodies consist of the national police force, the national gendarmerie and the Congolese armed forces. These bodies are apolitical and subordinate to the civil authority. The creation of militia groups is prohibited.

XVI. LOCAL AUTHORITIES

Articles 174–177: The local administrative bodies of the Republic of the Congo are the department and the commune, and any others created by law.

XVII. INTERNATIONAL TREATIES AND AGREEMENTS

Articles 178–184: The President of the Republic negotiates, signs and, with the approval of Parliament, ratifies international treaties and agreements. Any proposed change to the territorial boundaries of the Republic must be submitted to popular referendum.

XVIII. ON REVISION

Articles 185–187: The Constitution may be revised at the initiative of the President of the Republic or members of Parliament. The territorial integrity of the Republic, the republican form of government, the secular nature of the State, the number of presidential terms of office permitted and the rights outlined in sections I and II (above) may not be the subject of any revision. Any constitutional amendments proposed by the President of the Republic are submitted directly to a referendum. Any constitutional changes proposed by Parliament must be approved by two-thirds of the members of both legislative chambers convened in congress, before being submitted to referendum. In both cases the Constitutional Court must have declared the acceptability of the proposals.

The Government

HEAD OF STATE

President: Gen. DENIS SASSOU-NGUESSO (assumed power 15 October 1997; inaugurated 25 October 1997; elected 10 March 2002).

COUNCIL OF MINISTERS
(April 2003)

Minister of State, Minister of Transport and Privatization, responsible for the Co-ordination of Government Action: ISIDORE MVOUBA.

Minister of Planning, Territorial Development and Economic Integration: PIERRE MOUSSA.

Minister of Foreign Affairs, Co-operation and Francophone Affairs: RODOLPHE ADADA.

Keeper of the Seals, Minister of Justice and Human Rights: JEAN-MARTIN MBEMBA.

Minister of Hydrocarbons: JEAN-BAPTISTE TATI LOUTARD.

Minister of the Economy, Finance and the Budget: ROGER RIGOBERT ANDELY.

Minister of Security and the Police: Brig.-Gen. PIERRE OBA.

Minister of Equipment and Public Works: Brig.-Gen. FLORENT NTSIBA.

Minister at the Presidency, responsible for State Control: SIMON MFOUTOU.

Minister of Agriculture, Livestock, Fishing and the Promotion of Women: JEANNE DAMBENZET.

Minister of Forestry and the Environment: HENRI DJOMBO.

Minister of Construction, Urban Development, and Housing and Land Reform: CLAUDE ALPHONSE NSILOU.

Minister of Territorial Administration and Decentralization: FRANÇOIS IBOVI.

Minister of Labour, Employment and Social Security: ANDRÉ OKOMBI SALISSA.

Minister of Posts and Telecommunications, responsible for New Technologies: JEAN DELLO.

Minister of Technical Education and Vocational Training: PIERRE MICHEL NGUIMBI.

Minister of Higher Education and Scientific Research: HENRI OSSEBI.

Minister of Industrial Development, Small- and Medium-sized Enterprises and Handicrafts: EMILE MABONZOT.

Minister of Trade, Consumption and Supplies: ADELAÏDE MOUNDELE-NGOLO.

Minister of Social Affairs, Solidarity, Humanitarian Action, Disabled Ex-servicemen and the Family: EMILIENNE RAOUL.

Minister of the Civil Service and the Reform of the State: GABRIEL ENTCHA-EBIA.

Minister of Mines, Energy and Water Resources: PHILIPPE MVOUO.

Minister of Health and Population: Dr ALAIN MOKA.

Minister of Primary and Secondary Education, responsible for Literacy: ROSALIE KAMA.

Minister of Culture, the Arts and Tourism: JEAN-CLAUDE GAKOSSO.

Minister of Communication, responsible for Relations with Parliament, Government Spokesman: ALAIN AKOUALAT.

Minister of Sports and Youth Redeployment: MARCEL MBANI.

Minister without Portfolio, Secretary-General to the Government: THOMAS DELLO.

Minister-delegate at the Presidency, responsible for National Defence: Brig.-Gen. JACQUES YVON NDOLOU.

Minister-delegate to the Minister of Construction, Urban Development and Housing and Land Reform, responsible for Land Reform: LAMYR NGUELE.

Minister-delegate to the Minister of Foreign Affairs, Co-operation and Francophone Affairs, responsible for Co-operation in Development and Francophone Affairs: JUSTIN BALLAY MEGOT.

Minister-delegate without Portfolio, Secretary-General to the Presidency: GABRIEL LONGOMBE.

In addition, there were four Secretaries of State

MINISTRIES

Office of the President: Palais du Peuple, Brazzaville; e-mail collgros@altranet.fr; internet www.presidence.cg.

Office of the Minister at the Presidency, responsible for State Control: Brazzaville; tel. 81-53-12; fax 81-27-16.

Office of the Minister-Delegate at the Presidency, responsible for National Defence: Brazzaville; tel. 81-45-60.

Ministry of Agriculture, Livestock, Fishing and the Promotion of Women: Brazzaville; tel. 81-41-31; fax 81-41-33.

Ministry of the Civil Service and the Reform of the State: Brazzaville; tel. 81-41-55; fax 81-41-49.

Ministry of Communication, responsible for Relations with Parliament: BP 114, Brazzaville; tel. 81-41-29; fax 81-41-28; e-mail depcompt@congonet.cg; internet www.gouv.cg.

Ministry of Construction, Urban Development and Housing and Land Reform: Brazzaville; tel. 81-58-39.

Ministry of Culture, the Arts and Tourism: BP 2480, Brazzaville; tel. 81-40-31; fax 81-40-30.

Ministry of the Economy, Finance and the Budget: Centre Administratif, Quartier Plateau, BP 2083, Brazzaville; tel. 81-41-43; fax 81-43-45.

Ministry of Equipment and Public Works: Brazzaville; tel. 81-13-72; fax 81-59-07.

Ministry of Foreign Affairs, Co-operation and Francophone Affairs: BP 2070, Brazzaville; tel. 81-41-62; fax 81-41-61.

Ministry of Forestry and the Environment: BP 98, Brazzaville; tel. 81-41-37; fax 81-41-34; e-mail secretariat@minifor.com; internet www.minifor.com.

Ministry of Health and Population: Palais du Peuple, Brazzaville; tel. 81-57-46; fax 81-12-95.

Ministry of Higher Education and Scientific Research: BP 169, Brazzaville; tel. 81-08-15; fax 81-52-65.

Ministry of Hydrocarbons: Brazzaville; tel. 81-56-14; fax 81-58-23.

Ministry of Industrial Development, Small- and Medium-sized Enterprises and Handicrafts: Centre Administratif, Quartier Plateau, BP 2093, Brazzaville; tel. 81-06-20.

Ministry of Mines, Energy and Water Resources: Brazzaville; tel. 81-02-95; fax 81-02-70.

Ministry of Justice and Human Rights: Brazzaville; tel. 81-41-67.

Ministry of Labour, Employment and Social Security: Brazzaville; tel. 81-100-67; fax 81-02-16.

Ministry of Planning, Territorial Development and Economic Integration: Brazzaville; tel. 81-06-56.

Ministry of Posts and Telecommunications, responsible for New Technologies: Brazzaville; tel. 81-41-18; fax 81-04-70.

Ministry of Primary and Secondary Education, responsible for Literacy: BP 169, Brazzaville; tel. 81-08-15; fax 81-52-65.

Ministry of Security and the Police: Brazzaville; tel. 81-59-98; fax 81-34-04.

Ministry of Social Affairs, Solidarity, Humanitarian Action, Disabled Ex-servicemen and the Family: Brazzaville.

Ministry of Sports and Youth Redeployment: Brazzaville.

Ministry of Technical Education and Vocational Training: Brazzaville; tel. 81-17-27.

Ministry of Territorial Administration and Decentralization: Brazzaville.

Ministry of Trade, Consumption and Supplies: BP 2098, Palais du Peuple, Brazzaville; tel. 81-41-57; fax 81-41-58.

Ministry of Transport and Privatization, responsible for the Co-ordination of Government Action: BP 2148, Brazzaville; tel. 81-45-50; fax 81-41-84.

President and Legislature

PRESIDENT

Presidential Election, 10 March 2002

Candidate	Votes	% of votes
Denis Sassou-Nguesso	1,075,247	89.41
Joseph Kignoumbi Kia Mbougou	33,154	2.76
Angèle Bandou	27,849	2.32
Jean Félix Demba Ntello	20,252	1.68
Luc Adamo Matéta	19,074	1.59
Côme Mankassa	15,054	1.25
Bonaventure Mizidi Bavouenza	11,981	1.00
Total	**1,202,611**	**100.00**

ASSEMBLÉE NATIONALE

Assemblée nationale: BP 2106, Brazzaville; tel. 81-11-12; fax 81-41-28; e-mail dsancongo@yahoo.fr.

President: JEAN-PIERRE THYSTÈRE TCHIKAYA.

General Election, 26 May and 23 June 2002*

Party	Seats
Parti congolais du travail (PCT)	53
Forces démocratiques unies (FDU)†	30
Union pour la démocratie et la République—Mwinda (UDR—Mwinda)	6
Union panafricaine pour la démocratie sociale (UPADS)	4
Independents	19
Others	17
Vacant‡	8
Total	**137**

* Including the results of voting in 12 constituencies where the elections were rerun on 28–29 May 2002, owing to procedural irregularities on 26 May.
† An alliance of 29 parties.
‡ Voting was postponed indefinitely in eight constituencies in the Pool region as a result of unrest.

SÉNAT

Sénat: Palais du Parlement, Brazzaville.

President: AMBROISE-EDOUARD NOUMAZALAY.

The upper chamber comprises 66 members, elected by representatives of local, regional and municipal authorities for a six-year term. After the first elections to the Sénat, held on 11 July 2002, the strength of the parties was as follows:

Party	Seats
Parti congolais du travail (PCT)	44
Forces démocratiques unies (FDU)*	12
Parti pour la reconstruction du Congo	1
Civil society organizations	2
Independent	1
Vacant†	6
Total	**66**

* An alliance of 29 parties.
† Six seats remained vacant, as unrest had led to the postponement, in June 2002, of local elections in the Pool region.

Advisory Council

The 2002 Constitution makes provision for the establishment of an Economic and Social Council.

Political Organizations

In early 2003 there were more than 100 political parties and organizations in the Republic of the Congo, of which the following were among the most important

Convention pour la démocratie et le salut (CODESA): Brazzaville; f. 2002; opposition alliance; Pres. ANDRÉ MILONGO.

Convention nationale pour la République et la solidarité (CNRS): Brazzaville; f. 2001; Leader MARTIN MBERI.

Parti pour la reconstruction du Congo: Brazzaville.

Rassemblement pour la démocratie et le développement (RDD): Brazzaville; f. 1990; advocates a mixed economy; Pres. JOACHIM YHOMBI OPANGO; Chair. SATURNIN OKABÉ.

Union pour la démocratie et le progrès social (UDPS): Brazzaville; f. 1994 by merger; Leader JEAN-MICHEL BOUKAMBA-YANGOUMA.

Union pour la démocratie et la République—Mwinda (UDR—Mwinda): Brazzaville; e-mail journalmwinda@presse-ecrite.com; internet www.mwinda.org; f. 1992; Leader ANDRÉ MILONGO.

Forces démocratiques unies (FDU): f. 1994; fmrly Forces démocratiques et patriotiques; 29 constituent parties in 2002; supports Govt of Pres. Sassou-Nguesso; Leader GABRIEL OBA APOUNOU.

Alliance pour le Congo (APC): Brazzaville; Leader JUSTIN COUMBA.

Alliance congolaise pour l'ouverture, le salut et la solidarité (ACOSS): Brazzaville; f. 1998; social-liberal; Pres. Dr LÉON-ALFRED OPIMBAT.

Club 2002: Brazzaville; f. 2002; Pres. WILFRID NGUESSO.

Rassemblement pour la démocratie et le progrès social (RDPS): Pointe-Noire; f. 1990; Pres. JEAN-PIERRE THYSTÈRE TCHIKAYA.

Rassemblement pour la démocratie et la République (RDR): Brazzaville; Leader Gen. (retd) RAYMOND DAMASE NGOLLO.

Union patriotique pour la démocratie et le progrès (UPDP): Brazzaville; Pres. AUGUSTE-CÉLESTIN GONGARAD-NKOUA.

Union pour le progrès (UP): Brazzaville; Pres. JEAN-MARTIN MBEMBA; Sec.-Gen. OMER DEFOUNDOUX.

Union pour le redressement national (URN): Mpila, Brazzaville; f. 1999; Pres. GABRIEL BOKILO.

Mouvement congolais pour la démocratie et le développement intégral (MCDDI): Brazzaville; e-mail info@mcddi.net; internet www.mcddi.org; f. 1990; Leader BERNARD KOLELAS (in exile); Pres. MICHEL MAMPOUYA.

Parti congolais du travail (PCT): Mpila, Brazzaville; f. 1969; sole legal political party 1969–90; fmrly member of FDU; Pres. Gen. DENIS SASSOU-NGUESSO; Sec.-Gen. AMBROISE-EDOUARD NOUMAZALAY.

Union congolaise des républicains (UCR): Brazzaville; Leader CÔME MANKASSA.

Union des forces démocratiques (UFD): Brazzaville; supports Govt; Pres. DAVID CHARLES GANOU.

Union panafricaine pour la démocratie sociale (UPADS): Brazzaville; e-mail courrier@upads.org; internet www.upads.org; Pres. PASCAL LISSOUBA (in exile); Leader ALPHONSE ONGAKO DATSOU.

Diplomatic Representation

EMBASSIES IN THE REPUBLIC OF THE CONGO

Algeria: BP 2100, Brazzaville; tel. 83-40-11; Ambassador ABDELAH LAOUARI.

Angola: BP 388, Brazzaville; tel. 81-14-71; Chargé d'affaires a.i. MANUEL JOÂO.

Belgium: ave Patrice Lumumba, face Congo pharmacie, BP 225, Brazzaville; tel. 66-26-14; fax 81-37-04; e-mail brazzaville@diplobel .org.

Cameroon: BP 2136, Brazzaville; tel. 83-34-04; fax 83-67-99.

Central African Republic: BP 10, Brazzaville; tel. 83-40-14.

Chad: BP 386, Brazzaville; tel. 83-22-22.

China, People's Republic: blvd Lyautey, BP 213, Brazzaville; tel. 83-11-32; fax 81-11-35; Ambassador YUAN GUOHOU.

Congo, Democratic Republic: Brazzaville; tel. 83-29-38; Ambassador FÉLIX MUMENGUI OTTHUW.

Cuba: 28 rue Lacien Fourneaux, BP 80, Brazzaville; tel. 81-45-16; e-mail ambacuba@congonet.cg; Ambassador LUIS DELGADO PÉREZ.

Egypt: Immeuble 15 Février, BP 917, Mpila, Brazzaville; tel. 83-44-28; Ambassador MEDHAT AL-KADI.

France: rue Alfassa, BP 2012, Brazzaville; tel. 81-55-41; fax 83-06-18; Ambassador GEORGES SERRE.

Guinea: Brazzaville; tel. 81-24-66.

Holy See: rue Colonel Brisset, BP 1168, Brazzaville; tel. 81-55-80; fax 81-55-81; e-mail nonapcg@yahoo.com; Apostolic Nuncio Most Rev. MARIO ROBERTO CASSARI (Titular Archbishop of Tronto).

Italy: 2 blvd Lyauté, BP 2484, Brazzaville; tel. and fax 81-11-52; e-mail ambitbra@congonet.cg; Ambassador ANNA FÉDÉLÉ RUBENS.

Korea, Democratic People's Republic: Brazzaville; tel. 83-41-98; Ambassador KIM RYONK.

Libya: BP 920, Brazzaville.

Nigeria: BP 790, Brazzaville; tel. 83-13-16; Ambassador GREG MBADIWE.

Russia: ave Félix Eboué, BP 2132, Brazzaville; tel. 81-19-23; fax 81-50-85; e-mail amrussie@congonet.cg; Ambassador SERGEI NENACHEV.

Judicial System

The 2002 Constitution provides for the independence of the judiciary from the legislature. Judges are to be accountable to the Higher Council of Magistrates, under the chairmanship of the President of the Republic. The constituent bodies of the judiciary are the Supreme Court, the Revenue and Budgetary Discipline Court and the appeal courts. The High Court of Justice is chaired by the First President of the Supreme Court and is competent to try the President of the Republic in case of high treason, and to try members of the legislature, the Supreme Court, the Constitutional Court and government ministers for crimes or offences committed in the execution of their duties.

Supreme Court: BP 597, Brazzaville; tel. 83-01-32; Pres. PLACIDE LENGA.

High Court of Justice: Brazzaville; f. 2001; Chair. Pres. of the Supreme Court.

Constitutional Court: Brazzaville; Pres. GÉRARD BITSINDOU.

Religion

At least one-half of the population follow traditional animist beliefs. Most of the remainder are Christians (mainly Roman Catholics).

CHRISTIANITY

The Roman Catholic Church

The Congo comprises one archdiocese, five dioceses and an apostolic prefecture. At 31 December 2000 there were an estimated 1.7m. Roman Catholics in the Republic of the Congo, accounting for some 47.2% of the population.

Bishops' Conference

Conférence Episcopale du Congo, BP 200, Brazzaville; tel. 83-06-29; fax 83-79-08.

f. 1992; Pres. Most Rev. ANATOLE MILANDOU (Archbishop of Brazzaville).

Archbishop of Brazzaville: Most Rev. ANATOLE MILANDOU, Archevêché, BP 2301, Brazzaville; tel. 81-53-63; fax 81-38-17; e-mail archebrazza@yahoo.fr.

Protestant Church

Eglise Evangélique du Congo: BP 3205, Bacongo-Brazzaville; tel. 81-43-64; fax 83-77-33; internet www.chez.com/ngouedippc/page3 .html; f. 1909; Presbyterian; autonomous since 1961; 135,811 mems (1993); 105 parishes (1998); Pres. Rev. ALPHONSE MBAMA.

ISLAM

In 1997 an estimated 2% of the population were Muslims. There were 49 mosques in the Congo in 1991.

Comité Islamique du Congo: 77 Makotipoko Moungali, BP 55, Brazzaville; tel. 82-87-45; f. 1988; Leaders HABIBOU SOUMARE, BACHIR GATSONGO, BOUILLA GUIBIDANESI.

BAHÁ'Í FAITH

Assemblée spirituelle nationale: BP 2094, Brazzaville; tel. 81-36-93; e-mail congolink1@aol.com.

The Press

In July 2000 legislation was adopted on the freedom of information and communication. The legislation, which confirmed the abolition of censorship and reduced the penalty for defamation from imprisonment to a fine, specified three types of punishable offence: the encouragement of social tension (including incitement to ethnic conflict), attacks on the authorities (including libels on the Head of State or on the judiciary), and libels against private individuals. The terms of the legislation were to be guaranteed by a regulatory body, the Higher Council for the Freedom of Communication.

DAILIES

ACI Actualité: BP 2144, Brazzaville; tel. and fax 81-01-98; publ. by Agence Congolaise d'Information; Dir-Gen. THÉODORE KIAMOSSI.

Aujourd'hui: BP 1171, Brazzaville; tel. and fax 83-77-44; f. 1991; Man. Dir and Editor-in-Chief FYLLA DI FUA DI SASSA.

Mweti: BP 991, Brazzaville; tel. 81-10-87; national news; Dir MATONGO AVELEY; Editor-in-Chief HUBERT MADOUABA; circ. 7,000.

PERIODICALS

L'Arroseur: Immeuble Boulangerie ex-Léon, BP 15021, Brazzaville; tel. 58-65-51; fax 58-37-60; e-mail larroseur@yahoo.fr; f. 2000; weekly; satirical; Dir GERRY-GÉRARD MANGONDO; Editor-in-Chief JEAN-MARIE KANGA.

L'Autre Vision: 48 rue Assiéné-Mikalou, BP 5255, Brazzaville; tel. 51-57-06; 2 a month; Dir JEAN PAULIN ITOUA.

Bulletin Mensuel de la Chambre de Commerce de Brazzaville: BP 92, Brazzaville; monthly.

Bulletin de Statistique: Centre Nationale de la Statistique et des Etudes Economiques, BP 2031, Brazzaville; tel. and fax 81-59-09; f. 1977; quarterly; Dir-Gen. DOROTHÉE OUISSIKA.

Capital: 3 ave Charles de Gaulle, Plateau Centre Ville, BP 541, Brazzaville; tel. 58-95-10; fax 51-37-48; e-mail capital@hotmail.com; 2 a month; economics and business; Dir SERGE-DENIS MATONDO; Editor-in-Chief HERVÉ SAMPA.

Le Chemin: Brazzaville; f. 1983; evangelical Christian; Editor RAYMOND BITEMO.

Le Choc: BP 1314, Brazzaville; tel. 41-25-39; fax 82-04-25; monthly; satirical; Dir ROMUALD MBEPA; Editor-in-Chief JEAN-BAPTISTE BAKOUVOUKA.

Co Co Ri Co: 201 rue Dolisie-Ouenzé, Brazzaville; tel. 66-39-80; fax 58-59-22; weekly; satirical; Dir AIMÉ-SERGE BAZOUNGOULA BISSEMO TURBO; Editor-in-Chief MOKABI DAWA.

Les Dépêches de Brazzaville: Résidence Méridien, BP 15457, Brazzaville; tel. and fax 81-28-13; e-mail belie@congonet.cg; internet www.brazzaville-adiac.com; 6 a year; publ. by Agence d'Information de l'Afrique Centrale; Dir-Gen. JEAN-PAUL PIGASSE; Dir and Editor-in-Chief BELINDA AYESSA.

Les Echos: Immeubles Fédéraux 036, Centre-ville, Brazzaville; tel. 51-57-09; e-mail gam7@raga.net; weekly; Dir-Gen. ADRIEN WAYI-LEWY; Editor-in-Chief INNOCENT OLIVIER TATY.

Le Flambeau: BP 1198, Brazzaville; tel. 66-35-23; e-mail congolink1@aol.com; weekly; independent; opposed to the Govt of Pres. Sassou-Nguesso; Dir and Man. Editor PRINCE-RICHARD NSANA.

Géopolitique Africaine: Brazzaville; f. 2000; quarterly; French- and English-language edns; Editor ANDRÉ SOUSSAN.

La Lettre de Brazzaville: Résidence Méridien, BP 15457, Brazzaville; tel. and fax 81-28-13; e-mail redaction@adiac.com; f. 2000; weekly; publ. by Agence d'Information de l'Afrique Centrale; Man. Dir JEAN-PAUL PIGASSE; Editor-in-Chief BELINDA AYESSA.

Le Monde du Travail: 45 rue Linzolo Talangai, BP 4020, Brazzaville; tel. 53-13-04; fax 56-74-44; 2 a month; Dir ANNE-MARIE NZILA; Editor-in-Chief MARC NKAZI-YANZINGA.

Le Nouveau Stade: BP 2159, Brazzaville; tel. 68-45-52; 2 a month; sports; Dir-Gen. LOUIS NGAMI; Editor-in-Chief S. F. KIMINA MAKUMBU.

La Nouvelle République: 3 ave des Ambassadeurs, BP 991, Brazzaville; tel. 81-00-20; pro-Govt; weekly; Dir-Gen. GASPARD NWAN; Editorial Dir HENRI BOUKOULOU.

L'Observateur: 165 ave de l'Amitié, BP 13370, Brazzaville; tel. 66-33-37; fax 81-11-81; weekly; independent; Dir GISLIN-SIMPLICE ONGOYUA.

Panorama: Brazzaville; tel. 66-15-07; fax 21-35-34; Editor FRANÇOIS OUDAÏ AKIÉRA.

Le Pays: BP 782, Brazzaville; tel. 61-06-11; fax 82-44-50; e-mail heblepays@yahoo.fr; f. 1991; weekly; Editorial Dir SYLVÈRE-ARSÈNE SAMBA.

La Référence: BP 13778, Brazzaville; tel. 56-11-37; fax 62-80-13; 2 a month; Dir PHILIPPE RICHET; Editor-in-Chief R. ASSEBAKO AMAIDJORE.

La Rue Meurt (Bala-Bala): BP 1258, Brazzaville; tel. 66-39-80; fax 81-02-30; f. 1991; weekly; satirical; opposes Sassou-Nguesso Govt; Publr MATTHIEU GAYELE; Editorial Dir JEAN-CLAUDE BONGOLO.

La Semaine Africaine: blvd Lyautey, face Chu, BP 2080, Brazzaville; tel. and fax 81-23-35; e-mail lasemaineafricaine@yahoo.fr; f. 1952; weekly; Roman Catholic; general news and social comment; circulates widely in francophone equatorial Africa; Dir JEAN-PIERRE GALLET; Editorial Dir JOACHIM MBANZA; circ. 7,500.

Le Soleil: f. 1991; weekly; organ of the Rassemblement pour la démocratie et le développement.

Le Stade: BP 114, Brazzaville; tel. 81-47-18; f. 1985; weekly; sports; Dir HUBERT-TRÉSOR MADOUABA-NTOUALANI; Editor-in-Chief LELAS PAUL NZOLANI; circ. 6,500.

Tam-Tam d'Afrique: 97 rue Moussana, Ouenzé, BP 1675, Brazzaville; tel. 51-03-95; e-mail tatafrique@yahoo.fr; weekly.

Le Temps: BP 2104, Brazzaville; weekly; owned by supporters of former Pres. Lissouba; Editor-in-Chief HENRI BOUKOULOU.

Vision pour Demain: 109 rue Bakongo Poto-Poto, BP 650, Brazzaville; tel. 41-14-22; 6 a year; Dir SAINT EUDES MFUMU FYLLA.

NEWS AGENCIES

Agence Congolaise d'Information (ACI): ave E. P. Lumumba, BP 2144, Brazzaville; tel. and fax 81-01-98; Gen. Man. THÉODORE KIAMOSSI.

Agence d'Information d'Afrique Centrale (ADIAC): Hôtel Méridien, BP 15457, Brazzaville; tel. and fax 81-28-13; e-mail belie@congonet.cg; internet www.brazzaville-adiac.com; f. 1997; Dirs JEAN-PAUL PIGASSE, BELINDA AYESSA; br. in Paris (France).

Foreign Bureaux

Agence France-Presse (AFP): c/o Agence Congolaise d'Information, BP 2144, Brazzaville; tel. 83-46-76.

Associated Press (AP) (USA): BP 2144, Brazzaville.

Inter Press Service (IPS) (Italy): POB 964, Brazzaville; tel. 810565.

Pan-African News Agency (PANA) (Senegal): BP 2144, Brazzaville; tel. 83-11-40; fax 83-70-15.

Xinhua (New China) News Agency (People's Republic of China): 40 ave Maréchal Lyauté, BP 373, Brazzaville; tel. 83-44-01.

Publishers

Editions ADIAC: Hôtel Méridien, BP 15457, Brazzaville; tel. and fax 81-28-13; e-mail belie@congonet.cg; internet www.brazzaville-adiac.com; f. 1997; publishes chronicles of current affairs; Dirs JEAN-PAUL PIGASSE, BELINDA AYESSA.

Editions 'Héros dans l'Ombre': BP 1678, Brazzaville; tel. 28-59-53; e-mail leopold_mamo@yahoo.fr; f. 1980; literature, criticism, poetry, essays, politics, drama; President LÉOPOLD PINDY-MAMONSONO.

Editions Renaissance Congolaise: Brazzaville.

Imprimerie Centrale d'Afrique (ICA): BP 162, Pointe-Noire; f. 1949; Man. Dir M. SCHNEIDER.

Government Publishing House

Imprimerie Nationale du Congo (INC): BP 58, Brazzaville; restructuring or privatization pending in 2003; Dir JULES ONDZEKI.

Broadcasting and Communications

TELECOMMUNICATIONS

Celtel Congo: Celtel House, BP 1267, Pointe-Noire; Brazzaville; tel. 94-86-02; fax 94-88-75; e-mail celtelcongo@yahoo.fr; internet www.msi-cellular.com; f. 1999; mobile cellular telephone operator; network covers Brazzaville, Pointe-Noire, Loubomo (Dolisie), Ouesso, Owando and other urban areas; subsidiary of MSI Cellular (United Kingdom); Man. Dir ROB GELDERLOOS; 30,000 subscribers (Dec. 2000).

Cyrus International (CYRTEL): Brazzaville; mobile cellular telephone operator; operates as jt venture between Nexus International (70%), a subsidiary of France Telecom and SOTELCO.

Libertis: 22 rue Behagle, BP 1150, Brazzaville; tel. 81-47-70; fax 81-44-16; f. 2000; mobile cellular telephone operator; network covers Brazzaville and Pointe-Noire; subsidiary of Orascom Telecom (Egypt).

Société de Télécommunications du Congo (SOTELCO): BP 39, Brazzaville; tel. 81-16-66; f. 2001 by division of postal and telecommunications services of the fmr Office National des Postes et Télécommunications; mobile cellular telephone system introduced in 1996; majority Govt-owned, part-owned by Atlantic TeleNetwork; further transfer to private ownership pending; Dir-Gen. RENÉ-SERGE BLANCHARD OBA (acting).

RADIO AND TELEVISION

Radio Brazzaville: face Direction Générale, SOTELCO, Brazzaville; tel. 51-60-73; f. 1999; official station; Man. JEAN PASCAL MONGO SLYM.

Canal FM: BP 60, Brazzaville; tel. 83-03-09; f. 1977 as Radio Rurales du Congo; present name adopted 2002; community stations established by the Agence de coopération culturelle et technique; transmitters in Brazzaville, Sembé, Nkayi, Etoumbi and Mossendjo; Dir ETIENNE EPAGNA-TOUA.

Radio Liberté: BP 1660, Brazzaville; tel. 81-57-42; f. 1997; operated by supporters of Pres. Sassou-Nguesso.

Radiodiffusion-Télévision Congolaise (RTC): BP 2241, Brazzaville; tel. 81-24-73; state-owned; Pres. JEAN-GILBERT FOUTOU; Dir-Gen. GILBERT-DAVID MUTAKALA.

Radio Congo: BP 2241, Brazzaville; tel. 81-50-60; radio programmes in French, Lingala, Kikongo, Subia, English and Portuguese; transmitters at Brazzaville and Pointe-Noire; Gen. Man. ALPHONSE BOUYA DIMI; Dir of Broadcasting THÉOPHILE MIETE LIKIBI.

Télévision congolaise (TVC): BP 975, Brazzaville; tel. 81-01-16; f. 1963; operates for 46 hours per week, with most programmes in French but some in Lingala and Kikongo; Gen. Man. WAMÉNÉ EKIAYE-ACKOLI.

Télédiffusion du Congo: BP 2912, Brazzaville; tel. 81-06-08; Gen. Man. MÉDARD BOKATOLA.

Finance

(cap. = capital; res = reserves; dep. = deposits; m. = million; br. = branch; amounts in francs CFA)

BANKING

Central Bank

Banque des Etats de l'Afrique Centrale (BEAC): BP 126, Brazzaville; tel. 81-10-73; fax 81-10-94; internet www.beac.int; HQ in Yaoundé, Cameroon; f. 1973; bank of issue for mem. states of the Communauté économique et monétaire en Afrique centrale (CEMAC, fmrly Union douanière et économique de l'Afrique centrale); comprising Cameroon, the Central African Repub., Chad, the Repub. of the Congo, Equatorial Guinea and Gabon; res 177,417m., total assets 2,034,793m. (Dec. 2001); Gov. JEAN-FÉLIX MAMALEPOT; Dir in Repub. of the Congo PACIFIQUE ISSOIBEKA; br. at Pointe-Noire.

Commercial Banks

BGFI Bank Congo: BP 14579, Angle rue Reims, face à Pairie de France, Brazzaville; tel. 81-40-50; fax 81-50-89; state-owned; cap. 1,000m. (2002); Pres. MATHIAS DZON; Dir-Gen. ALAIN MOUSSIROU MABIALA; 2 brs.

Compagnie de Financement et de Participation (COFIPA): ave Amílcar Cabral, BP 147, Brazzaville; tel. 81-58-33; fax 81-03-73; e-mail cofipabzv@caramail.com; f. 2001 on privatization of Union Congolaise de Banques; cap. 3,000m., total assets 121,818m. (Dec. 2000); Pres. BABER TOUNKARA; Dir-Gen. VAN THANH TRAN; 13 brs.

Crédit pour l'Agriculture, l'Industrie et le Commerce (CAIC): ave Amílcar Cabral, BP 2889, Brazzaville; tel. 81-09-78; fax 81-09-77; e-mail caic20@calva.com; fmrly Crédit Rural du Congo; state-owned; transfer to private sector pending in 2003; Pres. MATHIAS DZON; Dir-Gen. JEAN-PIERRE GRANGE; 4 brs.

Crédit Lyonnais-Congo: BP 33, Brazzaville; tel. 81-07-13; fax 81-16-69; f. 2002 to replace Banque Internationale du Congo; 90% owned by Crédit Lyonnais (France); 10% state-owned; cap. 2,000m. (2002); Dir-Gen. LUCIEN ELSENSOHN; 2 brs.

Co-operative Banking Institution

Mutuelle Congolaise de l'Epargne et de Crédit (MUCODEC): BP 13237, Brazzaville; tel. 81-07-57; fax 81-01-68; f. 1994; Chief Exec. JEAN-CLAUDE GARCIA; Pres. FRANÇOIS HYACINTHE NSIMOU; 45 brs.

Development Bank

Banque de Développement des Etats de l'Afrique Centrale: BP 1177, Brazzaville; tel. 81-17-61; fax 81-18-80; Chair. ERIC SORONGOPE; Gen. Man. ANICET G. DOLOGUÉLÉ.

Financial Institution

Caisse Congolaise d'Amortissement (CCA): ave Foch Beltrando, BP 2090, Brazzaville; tel. 81-57-35; fax 81-52-36; f. 1971; management of state funds; Dir-Gen. ROGER GOSSAKI.

INSURANCE

Assurances et Réassurances du Congo (ARC): BP 1033, Pointe-Noire; tel. 94-08-00; f. 1973; 50% state-owned; privatization pending; Dir-Gen. RAYMOND IBATA; brs at Brazzaville, Loubomo and Ouesso.

Gras Savoye Congo: Hôtel Novotel, ave Gén. de Gaulle, BP 1901, Pointe Noire; tel. 94-79-72; fax 94-79-74; e-mail grassavoye.congo1@cg.celtelplus.com; internet www.grassavoye.com; affiliated to Gras Savoye (France); insurance brokers and risk managers; Man. ERIC MANTOT.

Société de Courtage d'Assurances et de Réassurances (SCDE): BP 13177, Immeuble Foch, ave Maréchal Foch, Brazzaville; tel. 81-17-63.

Trade and Industry

GOVERNMENT AGENCY

Comité des Privatisations et de Renforcement des Capacités Locales: Immeuble ex-SCBO, 7ème étage, BP 1176, Brazzaville; tel. 81-46-21; fax 81-46-09; e-mail privat@aol.com; oversees and co-ordinates transfer of state-owned enterprises to the private sector.

DEVELOPMENT ORGANIZATIONS

Agence Française de Développement (AFD): rue Béhagle, BP 96, Brazzaville; tel. 81-53-30; fax 81-29-42; e-mail leclechn@afd.fr; internet www.afd.fr; French fund for economic co-operation; Dir ANDRÉ MEYER.

Mission Française de Coopération et d'Action Culturelle: BP 2175, Brazzaville; tel. 83-15-03; f. 1959; administers bilateral aid from France; Dir JEAN-BERNARD THIANT.

Société Nationale d'Elevage (SONEL): BP 81, Loutété, Massangui; f. 1964; development of semi-intensive stock-rearing; exploitation of cattle by-products; Man. Dir THÉOPHILE BIKAWA.

CHAMBERS OF COMMERCE

Chambre de Commerce, d'Agriculture, d'Industrie et des Métiers de Brazzaville: BP 92, Brazzaville; tel. and fax 81-16-08; f. 1935; Pres. PAUL OBAMBI; Sec.-Gen. GÉRARD DONGO.

Chambre de Commerce, d'Agriculture et d'Industrie de Kouilou: BP 665, Pointe-Noire; tel. 94-12-80; fax 94-07-13; f. 1948; fmrly Chambre de Commerce, d'Industrie et des Métiers de Pointe-Noire; Chair. NARCISSE POATY PACKA; Sec.-Gen. JEAN-BAPTISTE SOUMBOU.

Chambre de Commerce, d'Agriculture et d'Industrie de Loubomo: BP 78, Loubomo; tel. 91-00-17.

Chambre Nationale d'Industrie et d'Agriculture du Congo: BP 1119, Brazzaville; tel. 83-29-56; fmrly Conférence Permanente des Chambres de Commerce du Congo; Pres. PAUL OBAMBI.

TRADE ASSOCIATION

Office National de Commercialisation des Produits Agricoles (ONCPA): Brazzaville; tel. 83-24-01; f. 1964; marketing of agricultural products; promotion of rural co-operatives; Dir JEAN-PAUL BOCKONDAS.

EMPLOYERS' ORGANIZATIONS

Forum des Jeunes Entreprises du Congo (FJEC): BP 2080, Brazzaville; tel. 81-56-34; e-mail fjec@inmarsat.francetelecom.fr; f. 1996; Sec.-Gen. PAUL KAMPAKOL.

Union Nationale des Opérateurs du Congo (UNOC): BP 5187, Brazzaville; tel. 81-54-32; operates a professional training centre; Pres. El Hadj DJIBRIL ABDOULAYE BOPAKA.

Union Patronale et Interprofessionnelle du Congo (UNICONGO): BP 42, Brazzaville; tel. 81-47-68; fax 81-47-66; f. 1958; Nat. Pres. JEAN-CHRISTOPHE TRANCEPAIN; Sec.-Gen. JEAN-JACQUES SAMBA; membership of 10 federations, representing 400 enterprises, with a total work-force of 25,000 (2001).

UTILITIES

Electricity

Société Nationale d'Electricité (SNE): 95 ave Paul Doumer, BP 95, Brazzaville; tel. 81-38-58; f. 1967; transfer to private management proposed; operates hydroelectric plants at Bouenza and Djoué; Pres. JEAN BRUNO RICHARD ITOUA (acting); Dir-Gen. ALPHONSE BOUDONESA.

Water

Société Nationale de Distribution d'Eau (SNDE): rue du Sergent Malamine, BP 229, Brazzaville; tel. 83-73-26; fax 83-38-91; f. 1967; transfer to private-sector management pending in 2002; water supply and sewerage; holds monopoly over wells and import of mineral water; Dir-Gen. AMBROISE BONGOUANDÉ.

TRADE UNION FEDERATIONS

Independent trade unions were legalized in 1991.

Confédération Générale des Travailleurs du Congo (CGTC): Brazzaville; f. 1995; Chair. PAUL DOUNA.

Confédération Nationale des Syndicats Libres (CNASYL): Brazzaville; f. 1994; Sec.-Gen. MICHEL KABOUL MAOUTA.

Confédération Syndicale Congolaise (CSC): BP 2311, Brazzaville; tel. 83-19-23; f. 1964; 80,000 mems.

Confédération Syndicale des Travailleurs du Congo (CSTC): BP 14743, Brazzaville; tel. 61-47-35; f. 1993; fed. of 13 trade unions; Chair. MICHEL SOUZA; 40,000 mems.

Confédération des Syndicats Libres Autonomes du Congo (COSYLAC): BP 14861, Brazzaville; tel. 82-42-65; fax 83-42-70; e-mail b.oba@congonet.cg; Pres. RENÉ BLANCHARD SERGE OBA.

Transport

RAILWAYS

In 1999 there were 1,152 km of railway track in the Congo. A 286-km section of privately owned line was used until 1991 to link the manganese mines at Moanda (in Gabon) with the main line to Pointe-Noire. Rail traffic has been severely disrupted since the 1997 civil war. The main line (of some 518 km) between Brazzaville and Pointe-Noire reopened briefly in November 1998 for freight traffic, but was subsequently closed following further unrest and sabotage. In early 2000 the Government signed two agreements with the Société Nationale des Chemins de fer Français (France) relating to the repair of the line and associated infrastructure, and to the management of the network. Freight services resumed in August 2000, followed by passenger services in January 2001, although there was further disruption to the railways during unrest in mid-2002.

Chemin de Fer Congo-Océan (CFCO): BP 651, Pointe-Noire; tel. 94-11-84; fax 94-12-30; f. 1969; entered partnership with Rail Afrique International in June 1998; transfer to private management proposed in 2003; Pres. DOMINIQUE BEMBA; Dir-Gen. Adm. PIERRE GOMBÉ.

ROADS

In 2001 there were an estimated 17,244 km of roads, including 3,440 km of main roads and 4,150 km of secondary roads. Only about 7.0% of the total network was paved. The principal routes link Brazzaville with Pointe-Noire, in the south, and with Ouesso, in the north. A number of major construction projects initiated by President Sassou-Nguesso in 2000 and 2001 have involved the highways from Brazzaville to Kinkala, and from Brazzaville to the Pool region.

Régie Nationale des Transports et des Travaux Publics: BP 2073, Brazzaville; tel. 83-35-58; f. 1965; civil engineering, maintenance of roads and public works; Man. Dir HECTOR BIENVENU OUAMBA.

INLAND WATERWAYS

The Congo and Oubangui rivers form two axes of a highly developed inland waterway system. The Congo river and seven tributaries in the Congo basin provide 2,300 km of navigable river, and the Oubangui river, developed in co-operation with the Central African Republic, an additional 2,085 km.

Direction des Voies Navigables, Ports et Transports Fluviaux: BP 2048, Brazzaville; tel. 83-06-27; waterways authority; Dir MÉDARD OKOUMOU.

Transcap–Congo: BP 1154, Pointe-Noire; tel. 94-01-46; f. 1962; Chair. J. DROUAULT.

SHIPPING

The deep-water Atlantic seaport at Pointe-Noire is the most important port in Central Africa and Brazzaville is one of the principal ports on the Congo river. A major rehabilitation programme began in October 1999, with the aim of establishing Pointe-Noire as a regional centre for container traffic and as a logistics centre for offshore oil exploration. In 1997 708,203 metric tons of goods were loaded at the port of Pointe-Noire, and 533,170 tons were unloaded.

La Congolaise de Transport Maritime (COTRAM): Pointe-Noire; f. 1984; national shipping co; state-owned.

Maersk Congo: 10 rue Massabi, Zone Portuaire, Pointe-Noire; tel. 94-21-41; fax 94-23-25; e-mail pnrmkt@maersk.com; f. 1997; represents Maersk Sealand (Denmark).

Port Autonome de Brazzaville: BP 2048, Brazzaville; tel. 83-00-42; f. 2000; port authority; Dir JEAN-PAUL BOCKONDAS.

Port Autonome de Pointe-Noire: BP 711, Pointe-Noire; tel. 94-00-52; fax 94-20-42; e-mail papn@cg.celtelplus.com; internet www.congoport-papn.com; f. 2000; port authority; Dir-Gen. JEAN-MARIE ANIÉLÉ.

SAGA Congo: 18 rue du Prophète Lasse Zephirin, BP 674, Pointe Noire; tel. 94-10-16; fax 94-34-04; e-mail saga.congo@cg.dti.bollone.com.

Société Congolaise de Transports Maritimes (SOCOTRAM): BP 4922, Pointe Noire; tel. 94-49-21; fax 94-49-22; e-mail info@socotram.com; internet www.socotram.fr; f. 1990.

CIVIL AVIATION

There are international airports at Brazzaville (Maya-Maya) and Pointe-Noire (Agostinho Neto). There are also five regional airports, at Loubomo (Dolisie, Ngot-Nzounzoungou), Nkaye, Owando, Ouesso and Impfondo, as well as 12 smaller airfields. In early 2001 the construction of a new international airport at Ollombo, some 500 km north of Brazzaville, began; the airport was expected to open by 2008. The refurbishment of Brazzaville airport commenced in 2001.

Aéro-Service: ave Charles de Gaulle, BP 1138, Brazzaville; tel. 81-34-88; fax 83-09-47; e-mail info@aero-service.net; internet www.aero-service.net; f. 1967; scheduled and charter services; operates nationally and to regional destinations; Pres. and Dir-Gen. C. H. GRIESBAUM.

Trans Air Congo: Immeuble City Center, ave Amílcar Cabral, BP 2422, Brazzaville; tel. 81-10-46; fax 81-10-57; e-mail TAC10@calva.com; internet www.transaircongo.net; f. 1994; private airline operating internal scheduled and international charter flights; Dir BASSAM ELHAGE.

Tourism

The tourism sector has been severely disrupted by political instability and internal unrest. Tourist visitors numbered 4,753 in 1999 (compared with tourist arrivals of 25,082 in 1998). In 2000, however, the number of tourist arrivals increased to an estimated 26,000. In that year earnings from tourism were estimated at US $11m.

Direction Générale du Tourisme et des Loisirs: BP 456, Brazzaville; tel. 83-09-53; f. 1980; Dir-Gen. ANTOINE KOUNKOU-KIBOUILOU.

COSTA RICA

Introductory Survey

Location, Climate, Language, Religion, Flag, Capital

The Republic of Costa Rica lies in the Central American isthmus, with Nicaragua to the north, Panama to the south, the Caribbean Sea to the east and the Pacific Ocean to the west. The climate is warm and damp in the lowlands (average temperature 27°C (81°F)) and cooler on the Central Plateau (average temperature 22°C (72°F)), where two-thirds of the population live. The language spoken is Spanish. Almost all of the inhabitants profess Christianity, and the majority adhere to the Roman Catholic Church, the state religion. The national flag (proportions 3 by 5) has five horizontal stripes, of blue, white, red, white and blue, the red stripe being twice the width of the others. The state flag, in addition, has on the red stripe (to the left of centre) a white oval enclosing the national coat of arms, showing three volcanic peaks between the Caribbean and the Pacific. The capital is San José.

Recent History

Costa Rica was ruled by Spain from the 16th century until 1821, when independence was declared. The only significant interruption in the country's constitutional government since 1920 occurred in February 1948, when the victory of the opposition candidate, Otilio Ulate Blanco, in the presidential election was disputed. The legislature annulled the election in March but a civil war ensued. The anti-Government forces, led by José Figueres Ferrer, were successful, and a revolutionary junta took power in April. Costa Rica's army was abolished in December. After the preparation of a new Constitution, Ulate took office as President in January 1949.

Figueres, who founded the socialist Partido de Liberación Nacional (PLN), dominated national politics for decades, holding presidential office in 1953–58 and 1970–74. Under his leadership, Costa Rica became one of the most democratic countries in Latin America. Since the 1948 revolution, there have been frequent changes of power, all achieved by constitutional means. Figueres's first Government nationalized the banks and instituted a comprehensive social security system. The presidential election of 1958, however, was won by a conservative, Mario Echandi Jiménez, who reversed many PLN policies. His successor, Francisco Orlich Bolmarich (President from 1962 to 1966), was supported by the PLN but continued the encouragement of private enterprise. Another conservative, José Joaquín Trejos Fernández, held power in 1966–70. In 1974 the PLN candidate, Daniel Oduber Quirós, was elected President. He continued the policies of extending the welfare state and of establishing amicable relations with communist states. Communist and other left-wing parties were legalized in 1975. In 1978 Rodrigo Carazo Odio of the conservative Partido Unidad Opositora (PUO) coalition (subsequently the Coalición Unidad) was elected President. During Carazo's term of office increasing instability in Central America led to diplomatic tension, and in 1981 the President was criticized for his alleged involvement in illegal arms trafficking between Cuba and El Salvador.

At presidential and legislative elections in February 1982, Luis Alberto Monge Alvarez of the PLN won a comfortable majority when his party won 33 of the 57 seats in the Asamblea Legislativa (Legislative Assembly). Following his inauguration in May, President Monge announced a series of emergency economic measures, in an attempt to rescue the country from near-bankruptcy. A policy of neutrality towards the left-wing Sandinista Government of Nicaragua was continued. However, following a number of cross-border raids, a national alert was declared in May. The rebel Nicaraguan leader, Edén Pastora Gómez, was expelled in order to reduce Costa Rican involvement in the Nicaraguan conflict. Relations with Nicaragua deteriorated as guerrilla activity spread to San José. Thereafter Monge came under increasing pressure from liberal members of the Cabinet and PLN supporters to adopt a more neutral stance in foreign policy. Three leading members of the anti-Sandinista (Contra) movement were expelled from Costa Rica in May 1983, and 80 of Pastora's supporters were arrested in September. In addition, some 82 guerrilla camps were dismantled by the Civil Guard. In November Monge declared Costa Rica's neutrality in

an attempt to elicit foreign support for his country. This declaration was opposed by the USA and led to the resignation of the Costa Rican Minister of Foreign Affairs.

In early 1984 there were increasing reports of incursions into Costa Rica by the Sandinista forces. Public opposition to any renunciation of neutrality was emphasized by a demonstration in support of peace and neutrality, held in San José and attended by over 20,000 people. An attempt was made to defuse the tension with the establishment of a commission, supported by the Contadora group (Colombia, Mexico, Panama and Venezuela), to monitor events in the border area. In late May, however, the attempted assassination of Pastora near the Costa Rican border exacerbated the rift within the Cabinet concerning government policy towards Nicaragua. In December, following an incident involving a Nicaraguan refugee at the Costa Rican embassy in Managua, diplomatic relations with Nicaragua were reduced to a minimal level. Reports of clashes between Costa Rican Civil Guardsmen and Sandinista forces along the joint border became increasingly frequent. In 1985 the Government's commitment to neutrality was disputed when it decided to establish an anti-guerrilla battalion, trained by US military advisers.

During 1983 there were signs of increasing urban unrest in response to the Government's austerity measures and to the agrarian crisis, which had produced high levels of unemployment, principally among workers on banana plantations. By August 1984 the Government's position was regarded as unstable. The division within the Cabinet over policy towards Nicaragua, coupled with the effects of the unpopular austerity programme and a protracted strike by banana plantation workers, which had resulted in two deaths, led to fears of a coup. At Monge's request, the Cabinet resigned, and in the subsequent reshuffle four ministers were replaced.

At presidential and legislative elections in February 1986 Oscar Arias Sánchez, the candidate of the PLN, was elected President, with 52% of the votes cast. The PLN also obtained a clear majority in the Asamblea Legislativa. The new Government was committed to the development of a welfare state, the renegotiation of the country's external debt, and the conclusion of a social pact with the trade unions. Furthermore, Arias was resolved to maintain and reinforce Costa Rica's policy of neutrality.

In February 1986 diplomatic relations with Nicaragua were fully restored, and it was decided to establish a permanent inspection and vigilance commission at the common border. In accordance with the Government's pledge to protect neutrality, Costa Rica objected to the allocation of US $100m. in US aid to the Contra forces in mid-1986. In addition, the Government embarked on a series of arrests and expulsions of Contras resident in Costa Rica. A degree of Costa Rican complicity in anti-Sandinista activity became apparent, however, in 1986, when the existence of a secret airstrip in Costa Rica, which was used as a supply base for the Contras, was made public. The airstrip had been constructed by the USA during President Monge's administration but had been closed on Arias's accession to power.

Throughout 1986 and 1987 Arias became increasingly involved in the quest for peace in Central America. In August 1987 the Presidents of El Salvador, Nicaragua, Guatemala, Honduras and Costa Rica signed a peace agreement based on proposals presented by Arias, who was subsequently awarded the Nobel Peace Prize. In January 1988 Arias brought Nicaraguan government officials and Contra leaders together in San José for their first discussions concerning the implementation of a cease-fire. Prior to this meeting, Arias ordered three Contra leaders to leave Costa Rica or cease their military activities. Arias maintained his independent position by supporting discussions between the Contras and Sandinistas, held in Nicaragua in March, and by condemning any continuation of aid to the Contras. In November a border agreement was signed with Nicaragua.

In 1988 there were renewed indications of internal unrest as a result of the Government's economic policies. In March there were stoppages by public employees, to protest against concessions made to the IMF and the World Bank. In August there were strikes by farmers aggrieved at the Government's 'Agriculture for Change' policy of promoting the cultivation of cash crops, and thereby sacrificing the interests of many smallholders, to appease the IMF. Labour unrest increased throughout the country during 1989.

In September 1989 the Asamblea Legislativa's commission of inquiry into the extent of drugs-trafficking and related activities published its findings. As a result, a number of high-ranking public figures were asked to resign, including the former President (then a senior PLN official), Daniel Oduber Quirós.

At presidential and legislative elections in February 1990, Rafael Angel Calderón Fournier, the candidate of the Partido Unidad Social Cristiana (PUSC), was elected President, with 51.3% of the votes cast. The PUSC obtained a clear majority in the Asamblea Legislativa, with 29 seats. On assuming office in May, Calderón inherited a large fiscal deficit and was therefore forced to renege on his pre-election promise of improvements in welfare and income distribution. In an attempt to reduce the deficit, the Government introduced an adjustment programme of austerity measures. In October 70,000–100,000 public- and private-sector employees participated in a one-day national strike to protest against the Government's economic policies. Later that month the Minister of Labour resigned, stating that his decision to do so reflected the rift between 'economic and social groups' within the Cabinet.

In August 1991 the Minister of Public Security and the Minister of National Planning and Economic Policy resigned, following disagreements with President Calderón. The Minister of the Interior and Police, Luis Fishman, was subsequently appointed acting Minister of Public Security. The Civil Guard and the Rural Guard (which had previously been responsible to the Ministry of Public Security and the Ministry of the Interior and Police, respectively) therefore came under the sole charge of Fishman. Opposition groups expressed concern at this concentration of power, in view of the continuing decline in popular support for Calderón and the level of public unrest. In November, in response to pressure from student and public-sector unions, Calderón abandoned austerity measures involving a reduction in the education budget and the dismissal of thousands of public employees. This decision prompted the resignation of the Minister of Finance, who claimed that the President's action would make it impossible to curb the rapidly increasing fiscal deficit and thus attain IMF-agreed targets.

In January 1992 Calderón was summoned before the Asamblea Legislativa's commission on drugs-trafficking to answer allegations that the PUSC had been the recipient of the proceeds of illegal drugs-trafficking during its election campaign in 1990. Calderón denied any knowledge of such payments. Following the decision made by the Government in March 1992 to remove foreign-exchange controls, there was mounting concern that Costa Rican banking institutions were being used increasingly for the purposes of laundering money obtained from illegal drugs-trafficking.

In March 1993 some 25 people, including the Nicaraguan Ambassador to Costa Rica, were taken hostage at the Nicaraguan embassy in San José. The demands of the hostage-takers included the dismissals of the head of the Nicaraguan armed forces and the Nicaraguan President's chief adviser. The hostages were later released unharmed in return for a ransom and safe passage out of the country. A similar incident, which took place in April and involved members of the Supreme Court being taken hostage, served to heighten concern about the security situation in Costa Rica.

Presidential and legislative elections were held in February 1994. The presidential ballot was narrowly won by José María Figueres Olsen, the PLN candidate. The PLN failed to obtain an outright majority in the Asamblea Legislativa, securing only 28 of the 57 seats, while the PUSC won 25 seats and the Fuerza Democrática (FD) secured two seats. The remaining two seats were won by independent candidates. Figueres assumed office in early May.

In May 1994 industrial action by employees of the Geest banana company resulted in violent clashes with the security forces. The strike was organized in protest at the dismissal of some 400 workers for attempting to join a union. The dispute, which was resolved following government intervention, came in the wake of allegations by a US trade union body, the American Federation of Labor and Congress of Industrial Organizations, of violations of labour rights in Costa Rica. In late 1993 the

Costa Rican authorities avoided an investigation into the country's labour practices by the US trade representative office and the possible loss of trading benefits enjoyed under the Generalized System of Preferences by introducing legislation reforming the labour code.

In July 1995 some 50,000 teachers began strike action in protest at proposed reforms to the state pension system. Growing dissatisfaction among other public-sector employees at government economic policy, in particular proposals for the deregulation and privatization of state enterprises, resulted in an escalation of the unrest, which culminated, in August, in a 100,000-strong demonstration in the capital. Following the protest, the Government reached an accord with the teachers, under which it agreed to establish a commission, to include representatives of the teachers' unions, to debate the proposed reform of the pension system and to review certain other of the Government's economic policies.

In January 1996, in an incident that had serious repercussions for the country's important tourism sector, two European women were abducted from a hotel in San Carlos in northern Costa Rica, close to the border with Nicaragua. An insurgent group, the Viviana Gallardo Commando, claimed responsibility for the abduction and reportedly demanded a ransom of US $1m. The women were released unharmed in March. In November the Minister of Security resigned, following an investigation by the Comptroller-General's Office into allegations that he had been involved in corrupt practices.

Presidential and legislative elections were held in February 1998. Miguel Angel Rodríguez Echeverría, again the candidate of the PUSC, received 46.9% of the votes cast in the presidential contest, thus securing a narrow victory over the PLN candidate, José Miguel Corrales Bolaños, who obtained 44.4% of the votes. The PUSC failed to obtain an outright majority in the legislature, securing only 27 of the 57 seats, while the PLN won 23, the FD obtained three, the Partido Movimiento Libertario (PML) won two, and the Partido Integración Nacional (PIN) and the Partido Acción Laborista Agrícola (PALA) each secured one seat. In April the Minister of Labour and Social Security in the outgoing administration resigned in order to answer embezzlement charges. On 8 May Rodríguez was sworn in as President, and the new Cabinet was inaugurated.

The new President's attempts to alleviate the budget deficit through economic reform met with considerable opposition in 2000. In May of that year the Government was forced to withdraw proposed legislation on the privatization of the telecommunications and energy sectors, after the largest popular protests in the country in 30 years. In the same month a commission, comprising government, private-sector and trade-union representatives, was established to draft new proposals.

On 16 January 2001 Víctor Morales, the Minister of Labour, resigned his post in order to assist in the electoral campaign of Rodolfo Méndez Mata, who was attempting to secure the PUSC nomination in the presidential election that was scheduled to take place in February 2002 (Mata ultimately failed to secure the PUSC nomination); Morales was replaced by Bernardo Benavides Benavides. In June a constitutional commission was appointed to recommend a process of transformation from the presidential system of government to a semi-parliamentary one, in an attempt to improve the political decision-making process. On 3 July the Asamblea Legislativa approved legislation designed to improve tax efficiency: the new law would reduce tax on basic goods, while increasing duties on some luxury goods and services (for further details see Economic Affairs). On 21 August, following Alberto Dent Zeledon's appointment to the finance portfolio, where he replaced Leonel Baruch Goldberg, Alfredo Robert Polini became Minister of Agriculture and Livestock.

Presidential elections were held on 3 February 2002. According to preliminary results, Abel Pacheco, the candidate of the ruling PUSC, secured 38.5% of the votes cast. The second-placed candidate was Rolando Araya of the PLN, who attracted almost 31% of the ballot. Ottón Solís, representing the recently-formed Partido Acción Ciudadana (PAC), which campaigned against corruption, was third, with 26.3% of the votes. However, as no candidate gained 40% of the votes cast, for the first time in Costa Rican history a second round of voting was scheduled for 7 April, between the two leading candidates. Voter turn-out in the first round was an estimated 67.3%, lower than in previous elections. In concurrently-held legislative elections, the PAC again emerged as a strong third force in Costa Rican politics, gaining 13 seats at the expense of the two main parties: the number of PUSC deputies in the 57-seat Asamblea Legislativa fell from 27 to 19, while the PLN's parliamentary representation fell from 23 to 17. The PML gained seven seats, while the Partido Renovación Costarricense secured the remaining seat. The results, as well as the low voter turn-out, were a sign that the electorate had tired of two-party politics. Pacheo won the second round of the presidential ballot on 7 April, securing 58% of the votes cast. .

Pacheo was inaugurated as President on 8 May 2002. Upon assuming office, he pledged to reform the tax system and to seek ways to curb public-sector expenditure in order to reduce the budget deficit. In the previous month a report produced by a cross-party commission of former finance ministers recommended that higher taxes and reduced government spending were necessary to ensure the financial and social stability of the country by 2006. Among the proposals were the replacement of sales tax with value-added tax (VAT) for some goods and services, the extension of profits tax to export zones and the removal of 160 administrative positions in the civil service. However, the Government announced in mid-May that 40% of its non-priority spending would be diverted to repair damage caused by heavy flooding earlier in that month, which had left an estimated 5,100 people homeless.

In late 2002 a number of opposition groups made claims that Pacheco electoral campaign had benefited from contributions from illegal sources. The President accused the opposition PLN of trying to discredit him; in September he renounced his presidential immunity from prosecution to allow the Supreme Court to investigate allegations that he had neglected to declare to the electoral tribunal some US $125,000 in cheque payments. In November the Government intervened in the affairs of the state electricity and telecommunications company, Instituto Costarricense de Electricidad (ICE) when the Comptroller-General ordered its directors to annul contracts awarded to an equipment supplier, whose charges the Government considered to be too high. The following month the Government also announced that it would investigate a decision by the ICE to rescind a contract given to an Israeli company for the sale of telecommunications equipment. Meanwhile, in October plans for the construction of a new maximum security prison caused divisions between Pacheco's ministers. The project was to be supervised by a US company and it was proposed that staffing would also be controlled by a private firm. Following his objections to private-sector involvement in the scheme, the Minister of Justice, José Miguel Villalobos was dismissed.

In January 2003 the first direct local authority elections in Costa Rica took place. However, voter participation was estimated to be only 40%, owing to further heavy storms which isolated many communities and forced some 3,000 people to evacuate their homes.

In December 1998 a 10-year co-operation agreement was signed with the USA, allowing for US troops to enter Costa Rican territory in order to conduct joint operations with Costa Rican security forces against drugs-traffickers. An amended version of the agreement was finally approved by the Costa Rican legislature in August 1999, despite the efforts of opponents to the measure, who claimed that it would lead to the establishment of a US military base in Costa Rica. In the following month the legislature approved the creation of a coastguard to participate in joint patrols with US forces. In October 2002 a motorboat carrying some 200 kg of cocaine was intercepted by police off the Pacific coast of Costa Rica; five Colombians were subsequently arrested.

In August 1989, at a summit meeting in Honduras, the Presidents of Costa Rica, El Salvador, Guatemala, Honduras and Nicaragua ratified a plan, known as the Tela Agreement, to remove the Contra forces from base camps in Honduras, in exchange for the introduction of political reforms and the holding of free elections in Nicaragua. Peace proposals for El Salvador and Guatemala were also elaborated, as was an agreement on co-operation in the campaign against the trafficking and use of illicit drugs. In November, however, the conflicts in Nicaragua and El Salvador intensified. In December the deadline for the disbanding of Contra forces, agreed at Tela, passed unfulfilled, and the Presidents of the five Central American countries, meeting in Costa Rica, agreed on measures to revive the regional peace process. In February 1990, after being defeated in elections, Nicaragua's Sandinista Government decreed an immediate cease-fire. The Contras accepted this, and a cease-fire agreement was concluded in April.

In early 1995 relations with Nicaragua became strained, following a series of incidents concerning immigration and the policing of the countries' joint border. In February the Nicaraguan Government issued a formal protest at the allegedly violent manner in which a group of illegal Nicaraguan immigrants had been expelled from Costa Rica. A tightening of immigration policy in Costa Rica had led to the automatic expulsion of illegal immigrants who had previously been tolerated (providing, as they did, a source of cheap labour for agriculture and the construction industry). The change in government policy had been prompted by the excessive burden placed on Costa Rica's social services by a recent rapid increase in immigrant arrivals, and by a downturn in the country's economy. In 1998 the Costa Rican Government estimated the number of Nicaraguan immigrants living in the country at 400,000–500,000, of whom some 250,000 were residing illegally. In January of that year bilateral discussions were held regarding the continuing expulsion of Nicaraguan immigrants. Costa Rica demanded, as a condition for agreement on the issue, that Nicaragua grant concessions allowing Costa Rican artisan fishermen to operate in Nicaraguan territorial waters. Nicaragua, however, rejected the demand, and no agreement was reached. In July further antagonism developed between the two countries when Nicaragua prohibited Costa Rican civil guards from carrying arms while navigating the San Juan river, which forms the border between the two countries. According to a longstanding treaty, the river, which is Nicaraguan territory, was only to be used by Costa Rica for commercial purposes. Following protests by Costa Rica, the two sides reached an agreement allowing Costa Rican civil guards to carry arms on the river while under escort by the Nicaraguan authorities. Although in August Nicaragua annulled the accord and dismissed Costa Rican threats to appeal to the International Court of Justice on the issue, asserting that Nicaraguan sovereignty over the river was not open to dispute, in June 2000 both Governments agreed a procedure that would allow armed Costa Rican police officers to patrol the river. Nevertheless, in September 2001 Nicaragua disputed a ruling by the Costa Rican Constitutional Court that armed police officers were entitled to use the San Juan river without seeking prior permission from Nicaragua. Furthermore, in May 2001 a fresh dispute had arisen following the implementation of a US $25 charge for Costa Ricans using the river, and in July there were protests regarding the symbolism of a wall built on the joint frontier. In September 2002 the two countries appeared to have made some progress towards resolving the dispute. Nicaragua agreed to discontinue the fees charged to Costa Ricans crossing the river in exchange for the abolition of charges levied on visas and tourist permits required by Nicaraguans to enter Costa Rica. Costa Rica also announced that it would relinquish plans to refer the matter to the International Court of Justice. In July, however, the two Governments came into conflict over a separate issue when Nicaragua announced that it was to award concessions for petroleum exploration in an area of the Caribbean Sea and Pacific Ocean claimed by Costa Rica. Bilateral discussions aimed at solving the issue began in October.

On 1 February 1999 Costa Rica declared a six-month amnesty for all illegal Nicaraguan immigrants who had entered Costa Rica before 9 November 1998. All those who registered were to be issued with one-year renewable residence permits. However, by the expiry of the amnesty, on 31 July, only 160,000 immigrants had registered. While the Costa Rican authorities assured Nicaragua that the amnesty period would not be followed by mass deportations, they insisted that the law would be firmly applied.

In October 2000 Costa Rica ratified a maritime boundaries treaty with Colombia, recognizing their control over 500,000 sq km of the Pacific Ocean, including the Isla del Coco.

Government

Under the Constitution of 1949, executive power is vested in the President, assisted by two Vice-Presidents (or, in exceptional circumstances, one Vice-President) and an appointed Cabinet. The President is elected for a four-year term by compulsory adult suffrage, and a successful candidate must receive at least 40% of the votes. The legislative organ is the unicameral Asamblea Legislativa, with 57 members who are similarly elected for four years.

Defence

There have been no Costa Rican armed forces since 1948. In August 2002 Rural and Civil Guards totalled 2,000 and 4,400 men, respectively. In addition, there were 2,000 Border Security Police. In 1985 an anti-terrorist battalion was formed, composed of 750 Civil Guards; in 1994 it was superseded by the Immediate Action Unit. In September 1999 legislation was approved providing for the establishment of a coastguard to participate in joint anti-drugs patrols with units of the US coastguard, under the terms of a co-operation agreement with the USA, which had received legislative approval in the previous month. Expenditure on the security forces was budgeted at 33,900m. colones in 2001.

Economic Affairs

In 2001, according to estimates by the World Bank, Costa Rica's gross national income (GNI), measured at average 1999–2001 prices, was US $15,332m., equivalent to $3,950 per head (or $8,080 per head on an international purchasing-power parity basis). During 1990–2001, it was estimated, the population increased by an average of 2.2% per year, while gross domestic product (GDP) per head increased, in real terms, by an average of 2.6% per year. Overall GDP increased, in real terms, by an average annual rate of 4.8% in 1990–2001; growth in 2001 was 1.1%.

Agriculture (including hunting, forestry and fishing) contributed an estimated 8.3% of GDP in 2001 and employed 15.9% of the economically active population in 2002. In 2000 banana production employed some 40,000 people directly and a further 100,000 indirectly. The principal cash crops are bananas (which accounted for an estimated 10.0% of general export earnings in 2001), coffee (2.5% of general export earnings), flowers and tropical fruit. Seafood exports were also significant. Sugar cane, rice, maize and beans are also cultivated. According to the World Bank, the real GDP of the agricultural sector increased at an average annual rate of 3.6% during 1990–2001. Real agricultural GDP increased by an estimated 0.4% in 2000, but declined by 1.0% in 2001.

Industry (including mining, manufacturing, construction and power) employed 22.5% of the economically active population in 2002, and provided an estimated 28.7% of GDP in 2001. According to the World Bank, real industrial GDP increased at an average annual rate of 5.5% during 1990–2001. However, the GDP of the sector decreased by 2.0% in 2000 and grew by only 0.1% in 2001. Mining employed only 0.1% of the economically active population in 2002 and contributed an estimated 0.2% of GDP in 2001. In June 2002 open-cast mining was banned by presidential decree in order to preserve the environment and the future of eco-tourism in Costa Rica.

The manufacturing sector employed 14.3% of the employed work-force in 2002 and contributed an estimated 21.2% of GDP in 2001. In terms of the value of output, the principal branches of manufacturing in 1999 were food products (37.4%), chemical products (11.4%), beverages (8.4%) and paper and paper products (4.8%). Production of computer components by the US manufacturer Intel began in 1998. According to the World Bank, real GDP of the manufacturing sector increased at an average annual rate of 6.0% during 1990–2001. However, the sector's GDP remained stagnant in 2000 and increased by just 0.1% in 2001.

Energy is derived principally from petroleum and hydroelectric power. The Arenal hydroelectricity project was inaugurated in 1979; however, its full generating capacity of 1,974 MW did not fulfil Costa Rica's electricity requirements, and at the end of 1993 the state electricity company, Instituto Costarricense de Electricidad (ICE) began its third electricity development programme. The programme included a US $300m. hydroelectric power project on the Río Reventazón, completed in 2000, and the country's first wind-generated power plant. In 2000 the ICE announced plans to build a 1,250 MW hydroelectric plant at Boruca by 2011. In 1999 hydroelectric power accounted for 83.0% of total electrical energy generation. Imports of fuels and lubricants accounted for an estimated 7.4% of the total value of imports in 2000.

The services sector employed 61.3% of the economically active population in 2002, and provided an estimated 63.0% of GDP in 2001. According to the World Bank, the real GDP of this sector increased at an average annual rate of 4.3% during 1990–2001. Real GDP increased by 4.3% in 2000 and by 1.6% in 2001. Tourism is the country's most important source of foreign-exchange earnings, accounting for an estimated 24.7% of total export revenue in 1997. In 2000 receipts from tourism totalled an estimated US $1,140m. and the sector employed some 152,000 people. In 2002 the Costa Rican Tourism Institute requested assistance from the Government to aid future expansion of the sector, including exemption from land and import taxes.

In 2001 Costa Rica recorded a visible trade deficit of US $1,210.1m. and there was a deficit of $701.55m. on the current account of the balance of payments. In 2001 the principal source of imports (53.5%) was the USA; other major suppliers were Mexico, Venezuela and Japan. The USA was also the principal market for exports (51.8%) in that year; other significant purchasers were the Netherlands, Guatemala and the United Kingdom. The principal exports in 2000 were electrical components for microprocessors, textiles and bananas. The principal imports in 2000 were raw materials for industry, capital goods for industry and consumer non-durables.

In 2001 there was an estimated budgetary deficit of 156,709m. colones (equivalent to some 3.1% of GDP). Costa Rica's estimated total external debt at the end of 2000 was US $4,466m., of which $3,510m. was long-term public debt. The cost of debt-servicing in that year was $650m., equivalent to 8.2% of exports of goods and services. The annual rate of inflation averaged 15.9% in 1990–2000. Consumer prices increased by an annual average of 10.0% in 1999, and by an estimated 11.0% in 2000. Some 6.4% of the labour force were unemployed in 2002.

Costa Rica is a member of the Central American Common Market (CACM, see p. 160) and the Inter-American Development Bank (IDB, see p. 239). In May 2000 legislation was passed enhancing the Caribbean Basin Initiative, first introduced in 1983, granting North American Free Trade Agreement (NAFTA) parity to products from 24 states, including Costa Rica. In April 2001 the Government concluded a free trade agreement with Canada, which was promulgated in November 2002. In late January 2003 the first round of talks on the establishment of a Central American Free Trade Agreement with the USA were held in San José between representatives of the Governments of Costa Rica, El Salvador, Guatemala, Honduras, Nicaragua and the USA. Further negotiations were scheduled for later in 2003. Costa Rica was also expected to finalize the terms of a free trade agreement with the Caribbean Community and Common Market (CARICOM) by the end of March.

During the 1990s successive Governments adopted austerity measures aimed at addressing the country's high public-sector deficit. Measures promoting increased foreign investment and enabling private-sector participation in activities formerly confined to the state sector, including the deregulation of the banking system, were implemented in 1996. The IMF urged the incoming Rodríguez administration in 1998 to expedite the divestment of public assets, initiated by the previous Government, and to use the proceeds to reduce the country's public domestic debt, which was equivalent to 27.6% of GDP in 1997. However, the Government's efforts to end the state's monopoly in the telecommunications, energy and insurance sectors proved unsuccessful in 1999, owing to legislative opposition. A similar attempt in 2000 resulted in public protests, and in May a commission was established to draft new privatization proposals. In its draft budget for 1999 the Government proposed to allocate 38% of total expenditure to servicing the domestic debt. In March 1998 the US microprocessor manufacturer Intel began production at the first of four plants under construction in Costa Rica. Exports from the Intel plants, situated in a free-trade zone close to the capital, contributed some 3%–4% of GDP in 1999, superseding the traditional exports of bananas and coffee. However, despite expectations that it would remain the country's principal source of exports, in 2000 there was a significant decrease in microchip exports, owing to plant restructuring. In May 2001, following a brief closure for modernization, the Intel plant re-opened; however, sales of microchips fell by 60% in 2001. By June 2002 the company reported a 5% increase in sales in the first half of the year.

The agricultural sector was affected by fluctuations in the prices of coffee and bananas in the late 1990s. Although there was a slightly improved harvest of 152,000 metric tons in 1999/2000, international coffee prices reached a 30-year low in early 2001 and production suffered. In 1999 and 2000 exports totalled some US $280m., compared with the average of $404m. in 1995–98. In 2000 the Government channelled $23m. from the national coffee stabilization fund to aid small farmers. Central American producers, as well as Mexico, Colombia and Brazil, agreed to retain up to 10% of their stocks in 2001, in order to allow the price of coffee to rise; however, the arrangement proved difficult to enforce. Furthermore, the 2001 coffee crop was threatened by a plague. Despite precautionary measures, the plague was also expected to affect the crop in 2002 and in May of that year it was estimated that accumulated exports for the 2001/2002 season fell by 6.8% compared with the previous harvest. Costa Rican coffee producers announced in 2001 that the production of 'gourmet' beans was to be expanded, as demand for fine coffee was rapidly increasing. Subsequently, in July 2002 farmers destroyed 120,000 bags of low-quality coffee beans as part of a regional strategy to improve the quality of coffee on the world market.

In late 2000 the situation in the banana industry became critical, with the three principal exporters, Chiquita Brands, Banana Development Corporation and Standard Fruits Company, cancelling contracts. Exports in bananas fell by US $100m. in 2000, to $531.3m. (9% of total exports). Production in 2000 was an estimated 2.7m. metric tons. In April 2001, despite resistance from the multinationals, the Government fixed the price of a 40 lb box at $5.25. In July 2001 more than 1,000 ha of banana plantations were destroyed in an attempt to prevent the further spread of the 'sigatoka negra' blight. In early 1999, following years of protests from the USA and Latin American countries and the European Union's (EU, see p. 199) failure to satisfy the World Trade Organization that its banana-import regime complied with international trade regulations, the USA was permitted to impose compensatory tariffs on specific imports from the EU. These tariffs were removed, following an EU-USA accord in April 2001, under which the EU preferential market ended. From 1 July a transitional system, issuing licences according to historical trade patterns, was implemented, while the definitive tariff-only system was to enter into force on 1 January 2006. In May 2002 heavy rains destroyed some US $30m.-worth of banana crops on the country's Atlantic coast, causing revenue from banana exports to fall from $491m. in in 2001 to an estimated $451m. in 2002.

In May 2001 the Central American countries, including Costa Rica, agreed to establish, with Mexico, the 'Plan Puebla–Panamá'. This was a series of joint transport, industry and tourism projects intended to integrate the region. In an attempt to resolve the country's internal financial problems, in July the Asamblea Legislativa approved tax efficiency and simplification legislation, which would decrease tax on basic goods, while increasing tax on some luxury goods and services. The legislation came into force on 1 August, and in the same month the Government announced its intention to implement a 15% corporate tax in the free-trade zone from January 2003. However, the Asociación de Empresas de Zonas Francas opposed the decision, claiming that it would harm the free-trade zone's competitiveness.

In 2002 the new Pacheo Government pledged to reform the tax system and to seek ways to curb public-sector expenditure in order to reduce the budget deficit. Following the recommendations of an all-party commission earlier in the year, in December the Congreso approved further tax reforms aimed at reducing the fiscal deficit to 3% of GDP by the end of 2003 and eradicating it completely by 2006. These included changes to the tax code and the levying of VAT on a wider range of goods and services. The reforms were to be accompanied by a 5.9% limit on any increases in government spending and the reduction of the budgets of the national electricity institution, social security departments and the state petroleum refinery. In January 2003 the Minister of Finance, Jorge Bolaños, held talks with the IDB regarding the Government's request for a loan of US $500m. to fund improvements to the nation's infrastructure and health and transport systems. The IDB had already indicated that the terms of any loan agreement were likely to include a provision that the Government reduce fiscal deficit to within 1% of GDP. The Central Bank predicted that GDP would increase by between 2.7%–3.6% in 2002

Education

Education at all levels is available free of charge, and is officially compulsory for children between six and 15 years of age. Primary education begins at six years of age and lasts for six years. Secondary education consists of a three-year basic course, followed by a more highly specialized course of two years. In 1997 primary enrolment included an estimated 91.8% of children in the relevant age-group (males 91.1%; females 92.5%), while the comparable ratio for secondary enrolment was 55.8% (males 54.7%; females 56.9%). There are six universities, one of which is an open university. In 1999 total enrolment at primary, secondary and tertiary levels was 67% (males 67%; females 66%). Costa Rica has the highest adult literacy rate in Central America. Government expenditure on education in 1996 was 99,631m. colones (22.8% of total spending).

Public Holidays

2003: 1 January (New Year's Day), 19 March (Feast of St Joseph, San José only), 11 April (Anniversary of the Battle of Rivas), 17 April (Maundy Thursday), 18 April (Good Friday), 1 May (Labour Day), 19 June (Corpus Christi), 29 June (St Peter and St Paul), 25 July (Anniversary of the Annexation of Guanacaste Province), 2 August (Our Lady of the Angels), 15 August (Assumption), 15 September (Independence Day), 12 October (Columbus Day), 1 December (Abolition of the Armed Forces Day), 8 December (Immaculate Conception), 25 December (Christmas Day), 28–31 December (San José only).

2004: 1 January (New Year's Day), 19 March (Feast of St Joseph, San José only), 8 April (Maundy Thursday), 9 April (Good Friday), 11 April (Anniversary of the Battle of Rivas), 3 May (Labour Day), 10 June (Corpus Christi), 29 June (St Peter and St Paul), 26 July (Anniversary of the Annexation of Guanacaste Province), 2 August (Our Lady of the Angels), 16 August (Assumption), 15 September (Independence Day), 12 October (Columbus Day), 1 December (Abolition of the Armed Forces Day), 8 December (Immaculate Conception), 25 December (Christmas Day), 28–31 December (San José only).

Weights and Measures

The metric system is in force.

Statistical Survey

Sources (unless otherwise stated): Dirección General de Estadística y Censos, Ministry of the Economy, Industry and Commerce, Apdo 10.163, 1000 San José; tel. 221-0983; fax 223-0813; internet www.inec.go.cr ; Banco Central de Costa Rica, Avdas Central y Primera, Calles 2 y 4, Apdo 10.058, 1000 San José; tel. 233-4233; fax 223-4658; internet www.bccr.fi.cr.

Area and Population

AREA, POPULATION AND DENSITY

Area (sq km)	
Land	51,060
Inland water	40
Total	51,100*
Population (census results)	
11 June 1984†	2,416,809
28 June 2000	
Males	1,996,350
Females	1,928,981
Total	3,925,331
Population (official estimate at mid-year)	
2001	3,981,016
Density (per sq km) at mid-2001	78.0

* 19,730 sq miles.
† Excluding adjustment for underenumeration.

PROVINCES

(official estimates, 1 July 2001)

	Area (sq km)	Population (estimates)	Density (per sq km)	Capital (with population)
Alajuela	9,757.5	748,830	76.7	Alajuela (232,641)
Cartago	3,124.7	451,217	144.4	Cartago (137,747)
Guanacaste	10,140.7	276,070	27.2	Liberia (49,016)
Heredia	2,657.0	370,226	139.3	Heredia (108,335)
Limón	9,188.5	356,095	38.8	Limón (94,267)
Puntarenas	11,265.7	374,401	33.2	Puntarenas (107,095)
San José	4,965.9	1,404,177	282.8	San José (323,214)
Total	51,100.0	3,981,016	77.9	—

PRINCIPAL TOWNS

(estimates, 28 June 2000)

San José	309,672	San Francisco	40,840
Limón	56,719	Cartago	38,363
Ipís	52,922	Cinco Esquinas	36,627
Desamparados	52,283	Liberia	34,469
Alajuela	42,889	Puntarenas	32,460

Source: Thomas Brinkhoff, *City Population* (internet www.citypopulation.de).

BIRTHS, MARRIAGES AND DEATHS

	Registered live births		Registered marriages		Registered deaths	
	Number	Rate (per 1,000)	Number	Rate (per 1,000)	Number	Rate (per 1,000)
1994	80,391	24.6	21,520	6.5	13,313	4.0
1995	80,306	24.1	24,274	7.3	14,061	4.2
1996	79,203	23.3	23,574	6.9	13,993	4.1
1997	78,018	22.5	n.a.	n.a.	14,260	4.1
1998	76,982	21.8	24,831	7.0	14,708	4.2
1999	78,526	21.9	25,613	7.1	15,052	4.2
2000	78,178	20.5	n.a.	n.a.	14,944	3.9
2001	76,401	19.2	n.a.	n.a.	15,609	4.0

Expectation of life (WHO estimates, years at birth): 76.1 (males 73.1; females 73.8) in 2001 (Source: WHO, *World Health Report*).

ECONOMICALLY ACTIVE POPULATION*

('000 persons aged 12 years and over, household survey, July)

	2000	2001	2002
Agriculture, hunting and forestry	269.21	234.32	242.74
Fishing		7.57	8.77
Mining and quarrying	2.61	1.80	2.31
Manufacturing	190.26	232.91	226.28
Electricity, gas and water supply	10.88	19.56	21.86
Construction	89.72	107.89	106.58
Wholesale and retail trade	266.83	292.86	303.36
Hotels and restaurants	n.a.	85.96	82.46
Transport, storage and communications	78.83	86.04	90.24
Financial intermediation	64.26	29.25	32.02
Real estate, renting and business activities		92.74	103.19
Public administration activities		73.31	71.87
Education		85.01	91.90
Health and social work		59.44	53.00
Other community, social and personal service activities	337.09	60.90	58.53
Private households with employed persons		76.00	83.41
Extra-territorial organizations and bodies		2.17	2.55
Not classifiable by economic activity	n.a.	5.63	5.46
Total employed	1,318.63	1,552.92	1,586.49
Unemployed	71.94	100.40	108.53
Total labour force	1,390.56	1,653.32	1,695.02

* Figures for activities are rounded to the nearest 10 persons, and totals may not be equivalent to the sum of component parts as a result.

Source: ILO.

Health and Welfare

KEY INDICATORS

Total fertility rate (children per woman, 2001)	2.7
Under-5 mortality rate (per 1,000 live births, 2001)	11
HIV/AIDS (% of persons aged 15–49, 2000)	0.55
Physicians (per 1,000 head, 1997)	1.41
Hospital beds (per 1,000 head, 1998)	1.68
Health expenditure (2000): US $ per head (PPP)	481
Health expenditure (2000): % of GDP	6.4
Health expenditure (2000): public (% of total)	68.4
Access to water (% of persons, 2000)	98
Access to sanitation (% of persons, 2000)	96
Human Development Index (2000): ranking	43
Human Development Index (2000): value	0.820

For sources and definitions, see explanatory note on p. vi.

Agriculture

PRINCIPAL CROPS
('000 metric tons)

	1999	2000	2001
Rice (paddy)	294.7	296.0	211.6
Potatoes	76.7	78.0	89.2
Cassava (Manioc)*	152	159	159
Sugar cane*	3,860.0	3,550.0	3,750.0
Oil palm fruit	492.0	609.0	660.0
Watermelons	—	76.7	77.0*
Cantaloupes and other melons	176.8	194.0*	214.0*
Bananas*	2,420.0	2,250.0	2,130.0
Plantains	70.2	57.4*	81.9
Oranges	283.2	405.0	436.6
Pineapples*	445.0	475.0	550.0
Coffee (green)	163.9	180.5	166.0*

* FAO estimate(s).

Source: FAO.

LIVESTOCK
('000 head, year ending September)

	1999	2000	2001
Horses*	115	115	115
Mules*	5	5	5
Asses*	8	8	8
Cattle	1,428	1,358	1,229
Pigs*	390	440	485
Sheep*	3	3	3
Goats*	2	2	2
Poultry	17,000*	17,135	16,600

* FAO estimate(s).

Source: FAO.

LIVESTOCK PRODUCTS
('000 metric tons)

	1999	2000	2001
Beef and veal	84.4	83.2	80.7
Pig meat	28.7	30.8	35.7
Poultry meat	74.5	73.3	73.2
Cows' milk	707.0	772.0	778.0
Cheese*	7.3	6.7	6.7
Butter*	4.5	4.5	4.5
Hen eggs	38.2†	41.0	46.5
Honey*	1.3	1.3	1.3
Cattle hides (fresh)*	12.8	12.5	12.4

* FAO estimates.
† Unofficial figure.

Source: FAO.

Forestry

ROUNDWOOD REMOVALS
('000 cubic metres, excl. bark)

	1997	1998	1999
Sawlogs, veneer logs and logs for sleepers	1,400	1,400	1,400
Other industrial wood	260	266	273
Fuel wood	3,548	3,637	3,724
Total	5,216	5,303	5,397

2000–2001: Production as in 1999 (FAO estimates).

Source: FAO.

SAWNWOOD PRODUCTION
(FAO estimates, '000 cubic metres, incl. railway sleepers)

	1993	1994	1995
Coniferous (softwood)*	12	11	12
Broadleaved (hardwood)	786	735*	768*
Total	798	746*	780*

* FAO estimate(s).

1996–2001: Annual production as in 1995 (FAO estimates).

Source: FAO.

Fishing

('000 metric tons, live weight)

	1998	1999	2000
Capture	20.6	24.2	28.0
Freshwater fishes	1.0	1.0	1.0
Clupeoids	0.9	1.8	1.6
Tuna-like fishes	1.2	1.1	1.1
Sharks, rays, skates, etc.	3.5	3.8	5.5
Other marine fishes	7.9	10.0	13.0
Penaeus shrimps	1.4	1.7	1.1
Natantian decapods	0.7	1.0	1.0
Aquaculture	7.9	9.3	9.7
Tilapias	5.3	6.3	7.7
Whiteleg shrimp	2.3	2.5	1.4
Total catch	28.5	32.9	37.7

Source: FAO, *Yearbook of Fishery Statistics.*

Industry

SELECTED PRODUCTS
('000 metric tons, unless otherwise indicated)

	1995	1996	1997
Cigarettes (million units)	16	16	n.a.
Non-cellulosic continuous fibres	7.7	7.8	7.9
Jet fuels	37	30	35
Motor spirit (gasoline)	100	77	81
Naphthas	5	12	7
Kerosene	3	3	6
Distillate fuel oils	203	175	176
Residual fuel oils	369	310	325
Bitumen	25	23	26
Liquefied petroleum gas (refined)	2	2	2
Cement	990	n.a.	n.a.
Electric energy (million kWh)	4,840	4,894	5,589

Source: UN, *Industrial Commodity Statistics Yearbook.*

1999: Cement 1,100,000 metric tons; Electric energy 6,198 million kWh.

Finance

CURRENCY AND EXCHANGE RATES

Monetary Units
100 céntimos =1 Costa Rican colón

Sterling, Dollar and Euro Equivalents (31 December 2002)
£1 sterling = 610.4 colones
US $1 = 378.7 colones
€1 = 397.2 colones
1,000 Costa Rican colones = £1.638 = $2.640 = €2.518

Average Exchange Rate (colones per US $)
2000   308.19
2001   328.87
2002   359.82

GENERAL BUDGET
(million colones)

Revenue	1999	2000	2001
Taxation	538,867	603,748	712,944
Income tax	131,932	133,090	163,059
Social security contributions	17,694	18,677	21,151
Taxes on property	10,235	15,374	17,397
Taxes on goods and services	332,005	389,381	459,234
Taxes on international trade	47,002	47,226	52,104
Other current revenue	1,866	2,755	6,875
Current transfers	2,237	2,035	2,273
Capital transfers	20,257	1,600	3,472
Total	563,227	610,138	725,563

Expenditure	1999	2000	2001
Current expenditure	602,097	685,955	809,055
Wages and salaries	191,193	225,873	267,037
Social security contributions	20,894	29,480	38,954
Other purchases of goods and services	21,883	22,837	26,625
Interest payments	164,226	175,653	213,866
Internal	142,867	149,549	174,019
External	21,359	26,104	39,847
Current transfers	203,901	232,111	262,573
Capital expenditure	60,981	75,351	73,217
Investment	24,457	23,414	16,100
Capital transfers	36,524	51,937	57,117
Total	663,078	761,306	882,272

INTERNATIONAL RESERVES
(US $ million at 31 December)

	2000	2001	2002
Gold*	0.02	0.02	0.02
IMF special drawing rights	0.43	0.09	0.09
Reserve position in IMF	26.06	25.13	27.19
Foreign exchange	1,291.27	1,304.59	1,469.27
Total	1,317.78	1,329.83	1,496.57

* National valuation.

Source: IMF, *International Financial Statistics*.

MONEY SUPPLY
('000 million colones at 31 December)

	2000	2001	2002
Currency outside banks	141.4	156.5	169.7
Demand deposits at commercial banks	479.7	542.3	662.6
Total money (incl. others)	639.7	724.2	843.1

Source: IMF, *International Financial Statistics*.

COST OF LIVING
(Consumer Price Index; base: January 1995 = 100)

	1998	1999	2000
Food, beverages and tobacco	165.0	181.0	198.7
Clothing and footwear	135.8	145.2	152.4
Housing	138.2	153.8	173.9
All items (incl. others)	159.6	175.7	194.9

NATIONAL ACCOUNTS
(million colones at current prices)

Expenditure on the Gross Domestic Product

	1999	2000	2001*
Government final consumption expenditure	565,207	652,654	770,806
Private final consumption expenditure	2,916,434	3,290,353	3,690,394
Increase in stocks	−38,118	−34,637	108,873
Gross fixed capital formation	811,325	873,951	976,224
Total domestic expenditure	4,254,778	4,782,321	5,546,297
Exports of goods and services	2,330,567	2,384,640	2,238,773
Less Imports of goods and services	2,072,582	2,249,197	2,397,544
GDP in purchasers' values	4,512,763	4,917,764	5,387,526
GDP at constant 1991 prices	1,398,182	1,423,232	1,438,716

* Figures are provisional.

Gross Domestic Product by Economic Activity

	1999	2000	2001*
Agriculture, hunting, forestry and fishing	436,112	423,053	420,437
Mining and quarrying	6,172	7,383	8,458
Manufacturing	1,199,978	1,133,270	1,072,106
Electricity, gas and water	93,303	114,237	140,913
Construction	152,752	180,443	227,625
Trade, restaurants and hotels	772,719	860,980	958,188
Transport, storage and communications	314,376	375,969	409,865
Finance and insurance	182,999	226,398	255,964
Real estate	177,311	197,580	224,115
Other business services	109,787	148,775	207,049
Public administration	146,062	170,388	201,033
Other community, social and personal services	674,395	797,145	925,567
Sub-total	4,265,973	4,635,619	5,051,320
Less Imputed bank service charge	128,910	158,701	184,669
GDP at basic prices	4,137,063	4,476,918	4,866,651
Taxes, *less* subsidies, on products	375,700	440,846	520,875
GDP in purchasers' values	4,512,763	4,917,764	5,387,526

* Figures are provisional.

BALANCE OF PAYMENTS
(US $ million)

	1999	2000	2001
Exports of goods f.o.b.	6,576.8	5,813.7	4,907.8
Imports of goods f.o.b.	−5,996.3	−6,024.8	−6,117.9
Trade balance	580.5	−211.1	−1,210.1
Exports of services	1,660.4	1,900.0	2,051.0
Imports of services	−1,201.9	−1,286.7	−1,275.2
Balance on goods and services	1,309.0	402.2	−434.3
Other income received	198.2	243.0	560.6
Other income paid	−2,019.9	−1,495.0	−975.0
Balance on goods, services and income	−782.5	−849.8	−849.2
Current transfers received	190.8	192.0	248.9
Current transfers paid	−88.4	−100.0	−101.2
Current balance	−680.1	−757.8	−701.5
Direct investment abroad	−5.0	−5.2	−5.2
Direct investment from abroad	619.6	408.5	453.6
Portfolio investment assets	−10.8	−18.4	−81.3
Portfolio investment liabilities	−253.8	−350.4	−200.3
Other investment assets	161.7	−343.9	106.5
Other investment liabilities	56.3	225.3	109.8
Net errors and omissions	213.4	218.2	19.2
Overall balance	101.3	−614.9	−286.8

Source: IMF, *International Financial Statistics*.

External Trade

PRINCIPAL COMMODITIES
(US $ million)

Imports c.i.f.	1998	1999	2000
Raw materials for industry and mining	3,137.8	3,411.5	3,335.4
Consumer non-durables	743.3	770.7	807.7
Consumer durables	540.0	371.9	371.8
Capital goods for industry and mining	963.9	900.7	851.2
Capital goods for transport	205.4	195.5	178.7
Fuels and lubricants	260.8	320.2	472.1
Total (incl. others)	6,238.4	6,350.7	6,379.8

Exports f.o.b.	1998	1999	2000
Livestock and fishing products	350.8	168.5	159.7
Agricultural products (unprocessed)	1,588.9	1,422.2	1,270.9
Bananas	634.5	632.2	531.3
Coffee	409.4	289.5	277.8
Industrial products	3,569.1	5,129.4	4,466.8
Textiles	812.1	804.4	772.6
Electrical components for microprocessors	959.7	2,526.0	1,653.3
Products of food industry	378.4	387.3	382.3
Other products of Free Zone	344.3	668.3	886.3
Total	5,508.8	6,720.1	5,897.4

Source: Promotora del Comercio Exterior de Costa Rica.

2001 (US $ million): *Imports c.i.f.*: Agricultural products 478.0; Industrial products 6,068.3; Total 6,546.3. *Exports f.o.b.*: Agricultural products 1,561.7; Industrial products 3,481.0; Total 5,042.7.

PRINCIPAL TRADING PARTNERS
(US $ million)

Imports c.i.f.	1999	2000	2001
Brazil	99.9	113.7	110.8
Canada	74.1	72.7	73.5
China, People's Republic	60.5	78.4	100.5
Colombia	97.5	120.9	154.2
El Salvador	106.8	91.0	92.0
France	74.6	93.4	76.3
Germany	124.8	124.6	137.1
Guatemala	142.2	139.9	140.9
Italy	79.3	73.4	72.6
Japan	300.7	214.7	230.1
Korea, Republic	108.2	117.5	138.6
Mexico	345.6	392.7	381.7
Netherlands	45.0	96.0	128.7
Panama	86.0	91.1	110.7
Spain	89.1	143.9	104.6
Taiwan	68.7	65.4	68.3
USA	3,581.4	3,388.0	3,504.1
Venezuela	248.8	337.3	298.5
Total (incl. others)	6,350.7	6,373.3	6,546.3

Exports f.o.b.	1999	2000	2001
Belgium-Luxembourg	66.5	115.2	90.9
Canada	40.2	35.1	31.0
El Salvador	115.4	135.2	151.8
France	40.6	35.5	35.4
Germany	183.7	137.5	117.5
Guatemala	179.5	193.4	211.4
Honduras	102.4	115.8	123.3
Hong Kong	35.7	17.4	27.9
Italy	105.2	99.9	94.4
Japan	128.2	50.9	39.9
Malaysia	63.4	52.5	155.0
Mexico	144.2	98.2	87.3
Netherlands	452.3	394.9	275.2
Nicaragua	177.4	179.1	163.3
Panama	126.3	129.0	142.7
Puerto Rico	175.4	163.2	156.7
Singapore	75.0	43.7	12.1
Spain	68.6	24.2	22.6
United Kingdom	387.8	300.0	128.1
USA	3,452.1	3,056.7	2,504.8
Total (incl. others)	6,719.0	5,897.3	5,042.7

Source: Ministry of Foreign Commerce.

Transport

ROAD TRAFFIC
(motor vehicles in use at 31 December)

	1998*	1999*	2000
Private cars	316,844	326,524	341,990
Buses and coaches	11,102	11,441	11,983
Goods vehicles	164,796	169,831	177,875
Motorcycles and mopeds	79,446	81,564	85,427

* Estimates.

Source: IRF, *World Road Statistics*.

SHIPPING

Merchant Fleet
(registered at 31 December)

	1999	2000	2001
Number of vessels	15	15	12
Total displacement ('000 grt)	5.7	5.7	3.0

Source: Lloyd's Register-Fairplay, *World Fleet Statistics*.

International Sea-borne Freight Traffic
('000 metric tons)

	1996	1997	1998
Goods loaded	3,017	3,421	3,721
Goods unloaded	3,972	4,522	5,188

Source: Ministry of Public Works and Transport.

CIVIL AVIATION
(traffic on scheduled services)

	1997	1998	1999
Aircraft departures ('000)	n.a.	37	32
Passengers carried ('000)	992	1,170	1,055
Air freight ton-km (million)	55	96	85

Source: World Bank, *World Development Indicators*.

Tourism

FOREIGN TOURIST ARRIVALS BY COUNTRY OF ORIGIN

	1999	2000	2001
Canada	45,565	52,696	52,661
Colombia	26,704	40,458	47,547
El Salvador	28,572	31,149	35,054
Germany	24,622	26,475	23,995
Guatemala	33,677	33,191	32,574
Honduras	26,400	24,338	27,174
Italy	17,215	16,736	16,479
Mexico	31,875	33,432	36,841
Nicaragua	168,447	143,142	171,583
Panama	53,565	54,646	53,892
Spain	27,031	26,877	26,916
USA	392,556	429,725	429,093
Total (incl. others) . . .	1,031,585	1,088,075	1,131,406

Tourism receipts (US $ million): 1,036 in 1999; 1,229 in 2000; 1,278 in 2001.

Communications Media

	1999	2000	2001
Telephones ('000 main lines in use)	802.6	1,003.4	945.0
Mobile cellular telephones ('000 subscribers)	138.7	209.1	311.3
Personal computers ('000 in use)	400	n.a.	700
Internet users ('000)	150.0	250.0	384.0

Radio receivers ('000 in use): 3,045 in 1999.

Television receivers ('000 in use): 930 in 2000.

Facsimile machines (number in use): 8,500 in 1997.

Daily newspapers: 6 in 1996 (circulation 320,000 copies).

Non-daily newspapers: 12 in 1991 (average circulation 106,000 copies).

Book production: 1,034 titles (excluding pamphlets) in 1995.

Sources: UNESCO, *Statistical Yearbook*, UN, *Statistical Yearbook*, International Telecommunication Union.

Education

(1999)

	Institutions	Teachers	Students Males	Students Females	Students Total
Pre-primary . . .	1,821	3,604	40,015	37,952	77,967
Primary	3,768	20,185	275,976	259,081	535,057
Secondary . . .	468	11,891	115,443	119,982	235,425
General . . .	386	8,908	92,202	96,895	189,097
Vocational . . .	82	2,983	23,241	23,087	46,328
Tertiary	52	n.a.	n.a.	n.a.	59,947

Adult literacy rate (UNESCO estimates): 95.6% (males 95.5%; females 95.7%) in 2000 (Source: UN Development Programme, *Human Development Report*).

Directory

The Constitution

The present Constitution of Costa Rica was promulgated in November 1949. Its main provisions are summarized below:

GOVERNMENT

The government is unitary: provincial and local bodies derive their authority from the national Government. The country is divided into seven Provinces, each administered by a Governor who is appointed by the President. The Provinces are divided into Cantons, and each Canton into Districts. There is an elected Municipal Council in the chief city of each Canton, the number of its members being related to the population of the Canton. The Municipal Council supervises the affairs of the Canton. Municipal government is closely regulated by national law, particularly in matters of finance.

LEGISLATURE

The government consists of three branches: legislative, executive and judicial. Legislative power is vested in a single chamber, the Legislative Assembly, which meets in regular session twice a year—from 1 May to 31 July, and from 1 September to 30 November. Special sessions may be convoked by the President to consider specified business. The Assembly is composed of 57 deputies elected for four years. The chief powers of the Assembly are to enact laws, levy taxes, authorize declarations of war and, by a two-thirds' majority, suspend, in cases of civil disorder, certain civil liberties guaranteed in the Constitution.

Bills may be initiated by the Assembly or by the Executive and must have three readings, in at least two different legislative periods, before they become law. The Assembly may override the presidential vote by a two-thirds' majority.

EXECUTIVE

The executive branch is headed by the President, who is assisted by the Cabinet. If the President should resign or be incapacitated, the executive power is entrusted to the First Vice-President; next in line to succeed to executive power are the Second Vice-President and the President of the Legislative Assembly.

The President sees that the laws and the provisions of the Constitution are carried out, and maintains order; has power to appoint and remove cabinet ministers and diplomatic representatives, and to negotiate treaties with foreign nations (which are, however, subject to ratification by the Legislative Assembly). The President is assisted in these duties by a Cabinet, each member of which is head of an executive department.

ELECTORATE

Suffrage is universal, compulsory and secret for persons over the age of 18 years.

DEFENCE

A novel feature of the Costa Rican Constitution is the clause outlawing a national army. Only by a continental convention or for the purpose of national defence may a military force be organized.

The Government

HEAD OF STATE

President: ABEL PACHEO DE LA ESPRIELLA (took office 8 May 2002).

First Vice-President: LINETH SABORIO.

Second Vice-President: LUIS FISHMAN.

THE CABINET
(April 2003)

Minister of Finance: JORGE WALTER BOLAÑOS.

Minister of the Economy, Industry and Commerce: VILMA VILLALOBOS.

Minister of the Presidency: RINA CONTRERAS LÓPEZ.

Minister of Planning: LINETH SABORIO.

Minister of Foreign Relations: ROBERTO TOVAR FAJA.

Minister of Foreign Commerce: ALBERTO TREJOS.

Minister of Public Security: ROGELIO RAMOS MARTÍNEZ.

Minister of Agriculture and Livestock: RODOLFO COTO PACHEO.

Minister of the Environment and Energy: CARLOS MANUEL RODRÍGUEZ.

Minister of Justice: PATRICIA VEGA.

Minister of Labour and Social Security: OVIDIO PACHEO SALAZAR.

Minister of Public Education: ASTRID FISCHEL.

Minister of Public Health: MARÍA DEL ROCÍO SÁENZ.

Minister of Housing: HELIO FALLAS VENEGAS.

Minister of Public Works and Transport: JAVIER CHÁVEZ BOLAÑOS.

Minister of Science and Technology: ROGELIO PARDO EVANS.

Minister of Culture, Youth and Sports: GUIDO SÁENZ GONZÁLEZ.

Minister of Tourism: RUBÉN PACHEO.

Minister of Childhood: ROSALIA GIL.

Chargé of Conditions for Women (Ministerial Rank): ESMERALDA BRITTON.

MINISTRIES

Ministry of Agriculture and Livestock: Apdo 10.094, 1000 San José; tel. 231-2344; fax 231-2062; internet www.mag.go.cr.

Ministry of Childhood: San José.

Ministry of Culture, Youth and Sports: Avdas 3 y 7, Calles 11 y 15, frente al parque España, San José; tel. 255-3188; internet www.mcjdcr.go.cr.

Ministry of the Economy, Industry and Commerce: San José; tel. 235-2700; fax 222-2305; internet www.meic.go.cr.

Ministry of the Environment and Energy: Avdas 8 y 10, Calle 25, Apdo 10.104, 1000 San José; tel. 233-4533; fax 257-0697; e-mail root@ns.minae.go.cr; internet www.minae.go.cr.

Ministry of Finance: San José; tel. 257-9333; fax 255-4874; internet www.hacienda.go.cr.

Ministry of Foreign Commerce: Montes de Oca, Apdo 96, 2050 San José; tel. 256-7111; fax 255-3281; e-mail info@comex.go.cr; internet www.comex.go.cr.

Ministry of Foreign Relations: Apdo 10.027, 1000 San José; tel. 223-7555; fax 257-6597; e-mail desp_ministro@ns.rree.go.cr; internet www.rree.go.cr.

Ministry of Housing: Paseo de los Estudiantes, Apdo 222, 1002 San José; tel. 220-3831; fax 255-1976.

Ministry of Justice: Apdo 5.685, 1000 San José; tel. 256-6700; fax 223-3879; e-mail mnagel@gobnet.go.cr.

Ministry of Labour and Social Security: Apdo 10.133, 1000 San José; tel. 257-8211.

Ministry of the Presidency and of Planning: Avdas 3 y 5, Calle 4, Apdo 10.127, 1000 San José; tel. 281-2700; fax 253-6243; internet www.mideplan.go.cr.

Ministry of Public Education: Apdo 10.087, 1000 San José; tel. 233-9050; fax 233-0390; e-mail minieduc@sol.racsa.co.cr; internet www.mep.go.cr.

Ministry of Public Health: Apdo 10.123, 1000 San José; tel. 223-0333; fax 255-4997; internet www.netsalud.sa.cr/ms/.

Ministry of Public Security: Apdo 55, 4874 San José; tel. 227-4866; fax 226-6581; internet www.msp.go.cr.

Ministry of Public Works and Transport: Apdo 10.176, 1000 San José; tel. 257-7798; fax 227-1434.

Ministry of Science and Technology: Apdo 5589-1000, San José; tel. 290-1790; fax 290-4967; e-mail micit@micit.go.cr; internet www.micit.go.cr.

President and Legislature

PRESIDENT

Elections, 3 February and 7 April 2002

Candidate	First round % of votes	Second round % of votes
Abel Pacheco de la Espriella (PUSC) .	38.5	58.0
Rolando Araya Monge (PLN)	30.9	42.0
Ottón Solís (PAC)	26.3	—
Otto Guevara Guth (PML)	1.7	—
Total (incl. others)	100.0	100.0

ASAMBLEA LEGISLATIVA

General Election, 3 February 2002

Party	Seats
Partido Unidad Social Cristiana (PUSC)	19
Partido de Liberación Nacional (PLN)	17
Partido Acción Ciudadana (PAC)	14
Partido Movimiento Libertario (PML)	6
Partido Renovación Costarricense (PRC)	1
Total	57

Political Organizations

Alianza Nacional Cristiana (ANC): Calle Vargas Araya, Condominio UNI, 50 m norte Bazar Tere, Apdo 353, 2050 San José; tel. 253-2772; f. 1981; national party; Pres. VÍCTOR HUGO GONZÁLEZ MONTERO; Sec. SALVADOR ESTABAN BEATRIZ PORRAS.

Cambio 2000: 200 m al sur del Banco Popular de San José, Edif. esquinero, frente a la Sociedad de Seguros de Vida del Magisterio Nacional, San José; tel. 221-0694; f. 2000; Pres. WALTER COTO MOLINA; Sec. ROSA MARÍA ARTAVIA RODRÍGUEZ; Coalition comprising.

Acción Democrática Alajuelense: Frente al Liceo de San Carlos, Barrio San Roque, Ciudad Quesada, Alajuela; tel. 460-0075; f. 1978; provincial party; Pres. MARIANO BARQUERO FONSECA; Sec. JORGE ARROYO CASTRO.

Partido Pueblo Unido: 300 m sur de la Iglesia de Zapote, Apdo 4.565, 1000 San José; tel. 224-2364; fax 224-2364; e-mail upvargas@sol.racsa.co.cr; f. 1995; national party; Pres. TRINO BARRANTES ARAYA; Sec. HUMBERTO VARGAS CARBONELL.

Independiente Obrero: Edif. Multifamiliares, Hatillo 5, Apdo 179, 1000 San José; tel. 254-5450; fax 252-1107; e-mail cuberopio@racsa.co.cr; f. 1971; national party; Pres. JOSÉ ALBERTO CUBERO CARMONA; Sec. LUIS FERNANDO SALAZAR VILLEGAS.

Nuevo Partido Democrático: Central Barrio Naciones Unidas, detrás del Centro Comercial del Sur, Apdo 528, 2100 San José; tel. 227-1422; fax 283-4857; f. 1996; national party; Pres. RODRIGO GUTIÉRREZ SCHWANHAUSER; Sec. ROSA MARÍA ZELEDON GÓMEZ.

Partido Acción Ciudadana (PAC): Sede San José en San Pedro de Montes de Oca, de Ferreterias el Mar 200 m Sur 25 m Este y 350 m Sur; tel. 281-2727; fax 280-6640; e-mail accioncuidadana@amnet.co.cr; internet www.pac.or.cr; f. 2000; centre party; Leader OTTÓN SOLÍS.

Partido Acción Laborista Agrícola (PALA): 700m este y 50 norte del Palide Barva de Heredia, Apdo 698–1100 Tibás; tel. 236-6404; fax 240-6536; f. 1987; provincial party; Pres. FREDDY JESÚS MURILLO ESPINOZA; Sec. IRIS MARÍA RODRÍGUEZ VARGAS.

Partido Agrario Nacional: Frente al Banco Nacional, Guácimo, Limón; tel. 710-6330; fax 243-2212; f. 1988; provincial party; Pres. LUIS FRANCISCO SÁNCHEZ MOREIR; Sec. PEDRO CAMPOS PICADO.

Partido Auténtico Limonense: 70 m Oeste de la Escuela Rafael Yglesias, Apdo 1046, Limón; tel. 758-3563; f. 1976; provincial party; Pres. MARVIN WRIGHT LINDO; Sec. DELROY SEINOR GRANT.

Partido Cambio Ya: Farmacia la Cruz 2°, Ciudad Quesada, San Carlos, Alajuela; tel. 460-2501; fax 460-3855; f. 1995; provincial party; Pres. ANA PATRICIA GUILLÉN CAMPOS; Sec. MARÍA AURELIA ROJAS HERRERA.

Partido Convergencia Nacional: Del Restaurant Versalles, 50 m Oeste, Barrio Los Angeles, Cartago; tel. 551-4361; fax 552-3360; f. 1992; provincial party; Pres. EDUARDO CANTILLO ARIAS; Sec. SERGIO IZAGUIRRE CERDA.

Partido Demócrata (PD): Frente a las Oficinas del INVU, barrio Amón, contiguo a Restaurante La Criollita, Apdo 121, San José; tel.

256-4168; fax 256-0350; f. 1996; national party; Pres. Alvaro Gon-zález Espinoza; Sec. Ana María Pérez Granados.

Partido Fuerza Agraria de los Cartagineses: Comisión Campe-sina Asamblea Legislativa, Edif. Antiguo Sión, Cartago; tel. 551-8884; f. 1996; provincial party; Pres. Alicia Solano Bravo; Sec. Jorge Angulo Solano.

Partido Fuerza Democrática (FD): Edif. Colón, Apdo 1129-1007, San José; tel. 258-7207; fax 258-7204; f. 1992 as coalition; later became national party; Pes. Juan Carlos Chaves Mora; Sec. Marjorie Santamaría Monge.

Partido Guanacaste Independiente: Costado Norte de la Plaza de Fútbol, las Juntas, Guanacaste; tel. 662-0141; f. 1992; provincial party; Pres. José Angel Jara Chavarría; Sec. Teresita Salas Vindas.

Partido Integración Nacional (PIN): Del ferrocarril del Atlántico 100 m al sur, Edif. Nortesa 2°, Of. 4, San José; tel. 256-1836; fax 255-0834; e-mail waltermunoz@costarricense.cr; internet www.pin.co.cr; f. 1996; national party; Pres. Dr Walter Muñoz Céspedes; Sec.-Gen. Ana Lourdes Gölcher González.

Partido Liberación Nacional (PLN): Mata Redonda, 125 m oeste del Ministerio de Agricultura y Ganadería, Casa Liberacionista José Figueres Ferrer, Apdo 10.051, 1000 San José; tel. 232-5033; fax 231-4097; e-mail palina@sol.racsa.co.cr; internet www.pln.org; f. 1952; national social democratic party; affiliated to the Socialist Inter-national; 500,000 mems; Pres. (vacant); Sec.-Gen. Rolando González Ulloa.

Partido Movimiento Libertario (PML): Oficina de Cabinas San Isidro, Barrio Los Yoses Sur, Apdo 4.674, 1000 San José; tel. 283-4545; fax 221-6822; e-mail otto@libertario.org; internet www.libertario.org; f. 1994; national party; Pres. Otto Guevara Guth; Sec.-Gen. Raúl Costales Domínguez.

Partido Patriótico Nacional: Curridabat, Residencial Hacienda Vieja, de la entrada principal 200 m al sur y 200 m al este, Casa esquinera, Apdo 1.525, San José; tel. 272-0835; fax 253-5868; f. 1971; national party; Pres. Daniel Enrique Reynolds Vargas; Sec. Erick Delgado León.

Partido Renovación Costarricense (PRC): Centro Educativo Instituto de Desarrollo de Inteligencia, Hatillo 1, Avda Villanea, Apdo 31, 1300 San José; tel. 254-3651; fax 252-3270; f. 1995; national party; Gerardo Justo Orozco Alvarez; First Vice-Pres. Rafael Matamoro Mesén.

Partido Rescate Nacional: De la Iglesia Católica de San Pedro de Montes de Oca 150 m al oeste, contiguo al restaurante El Farolito, San José; tel. 234-9569; fax 225-0931; f. 1996; national party; Pres. Carlos Vargas Solano; Sec. Buenaventura Carlos Villalobos Brenes.

Partido Unidad Social Cristiana (PUSC): 100 m norte y 25 m este del costado este de Plaza de Sol, Apdo 10.095, 1000 San José; tel. 248-2470; fax 248-2179; internet www.pusc.or.cr; f. 1983; national party; Pres. Lorena Vásquez Badilla; Sec. Jorge Eduardo Sánchez Sibaja.

Partido Unión Agrícola Cartagines: Costado Este de la Iglesia, Cervantes, Frente al Estanco del CNP Alvarado, Apdo 534-4024, Cartago; f. 1969; provincial party; Pres. Juan Guillermo Brenes Castillo; Sec. Carolina Méndez Zamora.

Partido Unión General (PUGEN): Casa 256, Centro de Pérez Zeledón, Frente al Edif. de la Cámara de Comercio, Apdo 440-8000, Pérez Zeledón; tel. 771-0524; fax 771-0737; e-mail pugen@apc.c.co .cr; f. 1980; national party; Pres. Dr Carlos A. Fernández Vega; Sec. María Lourdes Rodríguez Morales.

Diplomatic Representation

EMBASSIES IN COSTA RICA

Argentina: Curridabat, Apdo 1963, 1000 San José; tel. 234-6520; fax 283-9983; e-mail embarg@sol.racsa.co.cr; Ambassador Juan José Arcuri.

Belgium: Los Yoses, 4a entrada, 25 m sur, Apdo 3725, 1000 San José; tel. 225-6255; fax 225-0351; e-mail sanjose@diplobel.org; Ambassador Robert Vanreusel.

Bolivia: Barrio Rohrmoser 669, Apdo 84.810, 1000 San José; tel. 296-3747; fax 232-7292; e-mail embolivia@rree.gov.bo; internet www.embajada-bolivia-costarica.com; Ambassador Jorge Monje Zapata.

Brazil: Edif. Torre Mercedes, °6, Apdo 10.132, 1000 San José; tel. 233-1544; fax 223-4325; e-mail embbsjo@sol.racsa.co.cr; Ambas-sador Joao Carlos de Souza de Gomes.

Canada: Oficentro Ejecutivo La Sabana, Edif. 5, 3°, detrás de la Contraloría, Centro Colón, Apdo 351, 1007 San José; tel. 296-4149;

fax 296-4270; e-mail canadacr@sol.racsa.co.cr; Ambassador Louise Léger.

Chile: De Autos Subarú en Los Yoses, 200 m. norte, Barrio Dent, San Pedro de Montes de Oca, Apdo. 10102-1000 San José; tel. 280-0037; fax 253-7016; e-mail echilecr@sol.racsa.co.cr; Ambassador Guillermo Yunge Bustamante.

China (Taiwan): 300 m al norte y 150 al este de la Iglesia Sta Teresita, Barrio Escalante, Apdo 676, 2010 San José; tel. 224-8180; fax 253-8333; e-mail embajroc@racsa.co.cr; internet www.cr .roe-taiwan.org.pa; Ambassador Steven F. Wang.

Colombia: Apdo 3.154, 1000 San José; tel. 283-6871; fax 283-6818; e-mail emcosric@sol.racsa.co.cr; Ambassador Julio Anibal Riaño Velandia.

Czech Republic: 75 m oeste de la entrada principal del Colegio Humboldt, Apdo 12.041, 1000 San José; tel. 296-5671; fax 296-5595; e-mail sanjose@embassy.mzv.cz; internet www.mzv.cz\sanjose; Ambassador Vladimír Eisenbruk Korselt.

Dominican Republic: McDonald's de Curridabat 400 sur, 90 m. este, Apdo 4746-1000 San José; tel. 283-8103; fax 280-7604; e-mail embdominicanacr@.racsa.co.cr; Ambassador Margarita Toribio de Aquino.

Ecuador: Edif. de la esquina sureste del Museo Nacional, 125 m al este, Avda 2, Calles 19 y 21, Apdo 1.374, 1000 San José; tel. 232-1503; fax 232-2086; e-mail embecuar@sol.racsa.co.cr; Ambassador Francisco Proaño Arandi.

El Salvador: Paseo Colón, Calle 30, Avda 1, No 53, Apdo 1.378, 1000 San José; tel. 222-3648; fax 258-1234; e-mail embasacr@sol.racsa.co .cr; Ambassador Hugo Roberto Carrillo Corleto.

France: Carretera a Curridabat, del Indoor Club 200 m sur y 25 m oeste, Apdo 10.177, 1000 San José; tel. 225-0733; fax 253-7027; e-mail sjfrance@sol.racsa.co.cr; Ambassador Norbert Carrasco-Saulnier.

Germany: Barrio Rohrmoser, de la Casa de Oscar Arias 200 m norte, 75 m este, Apdo 4.017, 1000 San José; tel. 232-5533; fax 231-6403; e-mail info@embajada-alemana-costarica.org; internet www .embajada-alemana-costarica.org; Ambassador Dr Friedrich Göckel.

Guatemala: De Pops Curridabat 500 m sur y 30 m este, 2a Casa Izquierda, Apdo 328, 1000 San José; tel. 283-2290; fax 283-2556; e-mail embcostarica@minex.gob.gt; Ambassador Jorge Mario García Laguardia.

Holy See: Urbanización Rohrmoser, Sabana Oeste, Centro Colón, Apdo 992, 1007 San José (Apostolic Nunciature); tel. 232-2128; fax 231-2557; e-mail nuapcr@sol.racsa.co.cr; Apostolic Nuncio Most Rev. Antonio Sozzo (Titular Archbishop of Concordia).

Honduras: Los Yoses sur, del ITAN hacia la Presidencia la primera entrada a la izquierda, 200 m norte y 100 m este, Apdo 2.239, 1000 San José; tel. 234-9502; fax 253-2209; e-mail emhondcr@sol.racsa.co .cr; Ambassador Aristides Mejía Castro.

Israel: Edif. Centro Colón, 11°, Calle 38 Paseo Colón, 1000 San José; tel. 221-6444; fax 257-0867; e-mail embofisr@sol.racsa.co.cr; Ambas-sador Alex Ben Zvi.

Italy: Los Yoses, 5a entrada, Apdo 1.729, 1000 San José; tel. 224-6574; fax 225-8200; e-mail ambiter@sol.racsa.co.cr; internet www .ambitcr.com; Ambassador Gioacchino Carlo Trizzino.

Japan: Oficentro Ejecutivo La Sabana, Edif. 7, 3°, detrás de la Contraloría, Sabana Sur, Apdo 501, 1000 San José; tel. 232-1255; fax 231-3140; e-mail embjapon@sol.racsa.co.cr; Ambassador Naotoshi Sugiuchi.

Korea, Republic: Oficentro Ejecutivo La Sabana, Edif. 2, 3°, Sabana Sur, Apdo 838, 1007 San José; tel. 220-3160; fax 220-3168; e-mail koreasec@sol.racsa.co.cr; Ambassador Shin Soon-chull.

Mexico: Avda 7, No 1371, Apdo 10.107, 1000 San José; tel. 257-0633; fax 258-2437; e-mail embamex@.racsa.co.cr; Ambassador Ricardo Francisco García Cervantes.

Netherlands: Los Yoses, Avda 8, Calles 35 y 37, Apdo 10.285, 1000 San José; tel. 296-1490; fax 296-2933; e-mail nethemb@sol.racsa.co .cr; Ambassador W. G. J. M. Wessels.

Nicaragua: Edif. Trianón, Avda Central 250, Barrio la California, Apdo 1.382, 1000 San José; tel. 222-2373; fax 221-5481; e-mail embanic@sol.racsa.co.cr; Ambassador Mauricio Díaz Dávila.

Panama: Del Centro Colón 275 m norte, Calle 38, Avda 5 y 7, Apdo 94, 1000 San José; tel. 257-3241; fax 257-4864; Ambassador Virginia I. Burgoa.

Peru: Barrio Pops de Curridabat, del Indoor Club 100 m sur y 50 m oeste, Apdo 4.248, 1000 San José; tel. 225-9145; fax 253-0457; Ambassador Alberto Varillas Montenegro.

Poland: De la Iglesia Santa Teresita 300 m este, 3307, Barrio Escalante, Apdo 664, 2010 San José; tel. 225-1481; fax 225-1592; e-mail polonia@sol.racsa.co.cr; Ambassador MIECZYSLAW BIERNACKI.

Russia: Curridabat, Lomas de Ayarco Sur, de la carretera a Cartago, 1a entrada, 100 m sur, Apdo 6.340, 1000 San José; tel. 272-1021; fax 272-0142; e-mail emrusa@sol.racsa.co.cr; Ambassador VLADIMIR N. KAZIMIROV.

Spain: Calle 32, Paseo Colón, Avda 2, Apdo 10.150, 1000 San José; tel. 222-1933; fax 222-4180; e-mail embespcr@correo.mae.es; Ambassador VICTOR IBÁNEZ-MARTIN MELLADO.

Switzerland: Paseo Colón, Centro Colón, Apdo 895, 1007 San José; tel. 221-4829; fax 255-2831; e-mail vertretung@sjc.rep.admin.ch; Ambassador Dr JEAN-DANIEL BIÉLER.

United Kingdom: Edif. Centro Colón, 11°, Apdo 815, 1007 San José; tel. 258-2025; fax 233-9938; e-mail britemb@sol.racsa.co.cr; Ambassador GEORGINA BUTLER.

Uruguay: Avda 14, Calles 35 y 37, Apdo 3.448, 1000 San José; tel. 253-2755; fax 234-9909; e-mail embajrou@sol.racsa.co.cr; Ambassador ANTONIO RICARDO MORELL BORDOLI.

USA: Pavas, frente Centro Comercial, Apdo 920, 1200 San José; tel. 220-3939; fax 220-2305; e-mail hdssjo@usia.gov; internet usembassy.or.cr; Ambassador JOHN J. DANILOVICH.

Venezuela: Avda Central, Los Yoses, 5a entrada, Apdo 10.230, 1000 San José; tel. 225-8810; fax 253-1335; Chargé d'affaires a.i. DULCE MARIA PARRA FUENTES.

Judicial System

Ultimate judicial power is vested in the Supreme Court, the justices of which are elected by the Assembly for a term of eight years, and are automatically re-elected for an equal period, unless the Assembly decides to the contrary by a two-thirds vote. Judges of the lower courts are appointed by the Supreme Court's five-member Supreme Council.

The Supreme Court may also meet as the Corte Plena, with power to declare laws and decrees unconstitutional. There are, in addition, four appellate courts, criminal courts, civil courts and special courts. The jury system is not used.

La Corte Suprema

Barrio González Lahmann Avdas 6–8, Calles 17–19, Circuito Judicial 1, San José; tel. 295-3000; fax 257-0801.

President of the Supreme Court: RODRIGO MONTENEGRO TREJOS.

Supreme Council

RODRIGO MONTENEGRO TREJOS, IFIGENIA BUSTAMANTE, JUAN DIEGO ROJAS, FRANCISCO CHAMBERLAIN TREJOS, SILVIA NAVARRO ROMANINI.

Justices of the Supreme Court: Dr RICARDO ZAMORA CARVAJAL, Dr HUGO PICADO ODIO, Dr RICARDO ZELEDÓN ZELEDÓN.

Justices of the Second Court: ORLANDO AGUIRRE GÓMEZ, BERNARDO VAN DER LAAT ECHEVERRÍA, ZARELA VILLANUEVA MONGE, ALVARO FERNÁNDEZ SILVA, Dr JORGE ROJAS SÁNCHEZ.

Justices of the Third Court: Dr DANIEL GONZÁLEZ ALVAREZ, Dr MARIO HOUED VEGA, JESÚS RAMÍREZ QUIRÓS, RODRIGO CASTRO MONGE, ALFONSO CHAVES RAMÍREZ.

Justices of the Constitutional Court: Dr LUIS PAULINO MORA MORA, ANA VIRGINIA CALZADA MIRANDA, CARLOS ARGUEDAS RAMÍREZ, Dr RODOLFO PIZA ESCALANTE, ADRIÁN VARGAS BENAVIDES, LUIS FERNANDO SOLANO CARRERA, EDUARDO SANCHO GONZÁLEZ.

Religion

Under the Constitution, all forms of worship are tolerated. Roman Catholicism is the official religion of the country. Various Protestant Churches are represented. There are an estimated 7,000 members of the Methodist Church.

CHRISTIANITY

The Roman Catholic Church

Costa Rica comprises one archdiocese and six dioceses. At 31 December 2001 Roman Catholics represented some 87% of the total population.

Bishops' Conference

Conferencia Episcopal de Costa Rica, Arzobispado, Apdo 497, 1000 San José; tel. 221-3053; fax 221-6662.

f. 1977; Pres. Most Rev. ROMÁN ARRIETA VILLALOBOS (Archbishop of San José de Costa Rica).

Archbishop of San José de Costa Rica: Most Rev. ROMÁN ARRIETA VILLALOBOS, Arzobispado, Apdo 497, 1000 San José; tel. 258-1015; fax 221-2427; e-mail curiam@sol.racsa.co.cr.

The Anglican Communion

Costa Rica comprises one of the five dioceses of the Iglesia Anglicana de la Región Central de América.

Bishop of Costa Rica: Rt Rev. CORNELIUS JOSHUA WILSON, Apdo 2.773, 1000 San José; tel. 225-0209; fax 253-8331; e-mail amiecr@sol.racsa.co.cr.

Other Churches

Federación de Asociaciones Bautistas de Costa Rica: Apdo 1.631, 2100 Guadalupe; tel. 253-5820; fax 253-4723; e-mail coven@racsa.co.cr; internet www.fabcr.org; f. 1946; represents Baptist churches; Pres. ALEJO QUESADA ULLOA.

Iglesia Evangélica Luterana de Costa Rica (Evangelical Lutheran Church of Costa Rica): Apdo 1.512, 1200 San José; tel. 231-3345; fax 291-0986; e-mail evkirche@sol.racsa.co.cr; f. 1966; 600 mems; Pres. Rev. RENÉ LAMMER.

Iglesia Evangélica Metodista de Costa Rica (Evangelical Methodist Church of Costa Rica): Apdo 5.481, 1000 San José; tel. 236-2171; fax 236-5921; autonomous since 1973; 6,000 mems; Pres. Bishop LUIS F. PALOMO.

BAHÁ'Í FAITH

Bahá'í Information Centre: Apdo 553, 1150 San José; tel. 231-0647; fax 296-1033; adherents resident in 242 localities.

National Spiritual Assembly of the Bahá'ís of Costa Rica: Apdo 553, 1150 La Uruca; tel. 231-0647; fax 296-1033; e-mail bahaiscr@sol.racsa.co.cr.

The Press

DAILIES

Al Día: Llorente de Tibás, Apdo 10138,1000, San José; tel. 247-4640; fax 247-4665; e-mail aldia@nacion.co.cr; f. 1992; morning; independent; Dir ARMANDO M. GONZÁLEZ RODICIO; circ. 60,000.

Boletín Judicial: La Uruca, Apdo 5.024, San José; tel. 231-5222; f. 1878; journal of the judiciary; Dir ISAÍAS CASTRO VARGAS; circ. 2,500.

Diario Extra: Edif. Borrasé, 2°, Calle 4, Avda 4, Apdo 177, 1009 San José; tel. 223-9505; fax 223-5921; internet www.diarioextra.com; f. 1978; morning; independent; Dir WILLIAM GÓMEZ VARGAS; circ. 120,000.

La Gaceta: La Uruca, Apdo 5.024, San José; tel. 231-5222; internet www.imprenal.go.cr; f. 1878; official gazette; Dir ISAÍAS CASTRO VARGAS; circ. 5,300.

El Heraldo: 400 m al este de las oficinas centrales, Apdo 1.500, San José; tel. 222-6665; fax 222-3039; e-mail info@elheraldo.net; internet www.elheraldo.net; f. 1994; morning; independent; Dir ERWIN KNOHR R; circ. 30,000.

La Nación: Llorente de Tibás, Apdo 10.138, 1000 San José; tel. 247-4747; fax 247-5002; e-mail cacortes@nacion.com; internet www.nacion.co.cr; f. 1946; morning; independent; Pres. MANUEL F. JIMÉNEZ ECHEVERRÍA; circ. 120,000.

La Prensa Libre: Calle 4, Avda 4, Apdo 10.121, San José; tel. 223-6666; fax 233-6831; e-mail plibre@prensalibre.co.cr; internet www.prensalibre.co.cr; f. 1889; evening; independent; Dir ANDRÉS BORRASÉ SANOU; circ. 56,000.

La República: Barrio Tournón, Guadalupe, Apdo 2.130, San José; tel. 223-0266; fax 255-3950; e-mail info@larepublica.co.cr; internet www.larepublica.net; f. 1950; reorganized 1967; morning; independent; Dir JULIO SUÑOL; circ. 61,000.

PERIODICALS

Abanico: Calle 4, esq. Avda 4, Apdo 10.121, San José; tel. 223-6666; fax 223-4671; weekly supplement of *La Prensa Libre*; women's interests; Editor MARÍA DEL CARMEN POZO C; circ. 50,000.

Acta Médica Costarricense: Colegio de Médicos y Cirujanos, Sabana Sur, Apdo 548-1000, San José; tel. 232-3433; fax 232-2406; e-mail medicos@racsa.co.cr; f. 1957; journal of the Colegio de Médicos; 3 issues per year; Editor Dr BAUDILIO MORA MORA; circ. 2,000.

El Cafetalero: Calle 1, Avdas 18 y 20, Apdo 37, 1000 San José; tel. 222-6411; fax 223-6025; e-mail evilla@icafe.go.cr; f. 1964 as Noticiero del Café; changed name in 2000; bi-monthly; coffee journal;

owned by the Instituto del Café de Costa Rica; Editor ERNESTO VILLALOBOS; circ. 10,000.

Contrapunto: La Uruca, Apdo 7, 1980 San José; tel. 231-3333; f. 1978; fortnightly; publication of Sistema Nacional de Radio y Televisión; Dir FABIO MUÑOZ CAMPOS; circ. 10,000.

Eco Católico: Calle 22, Avdas 3 y 5, Apdo 1.064, San José; tel. 222-6156; fax 256-0407; f. 1931; Catholic weekly; Dir ARMANDO ALFARO; circ. 20,000.

Mujer y Hogar: San José; f. 1943; weekly; women's journal; Editor and Gen. Man. CARMEN CORNEJO MÉNDEZ; circ. 15,000.

Perfil: Llorente de Tibás, Apdo 1.517, 1100 San José; tel. 247-4345; fax 247-5110; e-mail perfil@nacion.co.cr; f. 1984; fortnightly; women's interest; Dir CAROLINA CARAZO BARRANTES; circ. 16,000.

Polémica: San José; tel. 233-3964; f. 1981; every 4 months; leftwing; Dir GABRIEL AGUILERA PERALTA.

Rumbo: Llorente de Tibás, Apdo 10.138, 1000 San José; tel. 240-4848; fax 240-6480; f. 1984; weekly; general; Dir ROXANA ZÚÑIGA; circ. 15,000.

San José News: Apdo 7, 2730 San José; 2 a week; Dir CHRISTIAN RODRÍGUEZ.

Semanario Libertad: Calle 4, Avdas 8 y 10, Apdo 6.613, 1000 San José; tel. 225-5857; f. 1962; weekly; organ of the Partido del Pueblo Costarricense; Dir RODOLFO ULLOA B; Editor JOSÉ A. ZÚÑIGA; circ. 10,000.

Semanario Universidad: San José; tel. 207-5355; fax 207-4774; internet cariari.ucr.ac.cr; f. 1970; weekly; general; Dir THAIS AGUILAR; circ. 15,000.

The Tico Times: Calle 15, Avda 8, Apdo 4.632, 1000 San José; tel. 258-1558; fax 223-6378; e-mail info@ticotimes.net; internet www.ticotimes.net; weekly; in English; Dir DERY DYER; circ. 15,210.

Tiempos de Costa Rica: Casa 3372 Barrio Escalante, Avda 9, 480 m este, San José; tel. 280-2332; fax 280-6840; internet www.tdm.com; f. 1996; Costa Rican edition of the international *Tiempos de Mundo*; Dir WILLIAM COOK.

PRESS ASSOCIATIONS

Colegio de Periodistas de Costa Rica: Sabana Este, Calle 42, Avda 4, Apdo 5.416, San José; tel. 233-5850; fax 223-8669; f. 1969; 550 mems; Exec. Dir ADRIANA NÚÑEZ.

Sindicato Nacional de Periodistas: Sabana Este, Calle 42, Avda 4, Apdo 5.416, San José; tel. 222-7589; f. 1970; 200 mems; Sec.-Gen. ADRIÁN ROJAS JAÉN.

FOREIGN NEWS BUREAUX

ACAN-EFE (Central America): Costado Sur, Casa Matute Gómez, Casa 1912, Apdo 84.930, San José; tel. 222-6785; Correspondent WILFREDO CHACÓN SERRANO.

Agence France-Presse (France): Barrio Escalante, Del Farolito 175m al Este, Casa 3361, Apdo 5.276, San José; tel. 280-1773; fax 280-1755; Correspondent DOMINIQUE PETTIT.

Agencia EFE (Spain): Avda 10, Calles 19 y 21, No 1912, Apdo 84.930, San José; tel. 222-6785.

Agenzia Nazionale Stampa Associata (ANSA) (Italy): c/o Diario La República, Barrio Tournón, Guadalupe, Apdo 545, 1200 San José; tel. 231-1140; fax 231-1140; Correspondent LUIS CARTÍN S.

Associated Press (AP) (USA): San José; internet www.ap.org; Correspondent REID MILLER.

Deutsche Presse-Agentur (dpa) (Germany): Edif. 152, 3°, Calle 11, Avdas 1 y 3, Apdo 7.156, San José; tel. 233-0604; fax 233-0604; Correspondent ERNESTO RAMÍREZ.

Informatsionnoye Telegrafnoye Agentstvo Rossii—Telegrafnoye Agentstvo Suverennykh Stran (ITAR—TASS) (Russia): De la Casa Italia 1,000 m este, 50 m norte, Casa 675, Apdo 1.011, San José; tel. 224-1560; Correspondent ENRIQUE MORA.

Prensa Latina (Cuba): Avda 11, No 3185, Calles 31 y 33, Barrio Escalante (de la parrillada 25 m oeste), San José; tel. 253-1457; Correspondent FRANCISCO A. URIZARRI TAMAYO.

Rossiyskoye Informatsionnoye Agentstvo—Novosti (RIA-Novosti) (Russia): De la Casa Italiana 100 m este, 50 m norte, San José; tel. 224-1560.

Xinhua (New China) News Agency (People's Republic of China): Apdo 4.774, San José; tel. 231-3497; Correspondent XU BIHUA.

Publishers

Alef Editores: Apdo 146, 1017 San José 2000; tel. 256-7229; fax 258-2955; e-mail alefreading@racsa.co.cr.

Alfalit Internacional: Apdo 292, 4050 Alajuela; f. 1961; educational; Dirs GILBERTO BERNAL, OSMUNDO PONCE.

Antonio Lehmann Librería, Imprenta y Litografía, Ltda: Calles 1 y 3, Avda Central, Apdo 10.011, San José; tel. 223-1212; f. 1896; general fiction, educational, textbooks; Man. Dir ANTONIO LEHMANN STRUVE.

Ediciones Farben, SA: De la Sylvania 500 oeste, Condominio Industrial Pavas 19, Apdo 592-1200 Pavas; tel. 290-7125; fax 290-0061; e-mail fvanderlaat@farben.co.cr; Dir FERNANDO VANDERLAAT.

Editorial Caribe: Apdo 1.307, San José; tel. 222-7244; f. 1949; religious textbooks; Dir JOHN STROWEL.

Editorial Costa Rica: 100 m sur y 50 m este del Supermercado Periféricos en San Francisco de Dos Ríos, Apdo 10.010, San José; tel. 255-2323; fax 253-5091; e-mail editocr@racsa.co.cr; internet www.editorialcostarica.com; f. 1959; government-owned; cultural; Gen. Man. SHEILA DI PALMA GAMBOA.

Editorial Fernández Arce: Apdo 2410, 1000 San José; tel. 224-5201; fax 225-6109; f. 1967; textbooks for primary, secondary and university education; Dir Dr MARIO FERNÁNDEZ LOBO.

Editorial de la Universidad Autónoma de Centroamérica (UACA): Apdo 7.637, 1000 San José; tel. 234-0701; fax 224-0391; e-mail lauaca@sol.racsa.co.cr; f. 1981; Editor ALBERTO DI MARE.

Editorial de la Universidad Estatal a Distancia (EUNED): Apdo 474, 2050 San Pedro; tel. 253-2121; fax 234-9138; e-mail editoria@uned.ac.cr; internet www.uned.ac.cr; f. 1979; Dir AUXILIADORA PROTTI QUESADA.

Editorial Universitaria Centroamericana (EDUCA): Ciudad Universitaria Rodrigo Facio, San Pedro, Montes de Oca, Apdo 64, 2060 San Pedro; tel. 224-3727; fax 253-9141; e-mail educa@sp.cusa.ac.cr; f. 1969; organ of the CSUCA; science, literature, philosophy; Dir ANITA DE FORMOSO.

Mesén Editores: Urbanización El Cedral, 52, Cedros de Montes de Oca, Apdo 6.306, 1000 San José; tel. 253-5203; fax 283-0681; f. 1978; general; Dir DENNIS MESÉN SEGURA.

Trejos Hermanos Sucs, SA: Curridabat, Apdo 10.096, San José; tel. 224-2411; f. 1912; general and reference; Man. ALVARO TREJOS.

PUBLISHING ASSOCIATION

Cámara Costarricense del Libro: San José; e-mail ccl@libroscr.com; internet www.libroscr.com; f. 1978; Pres. MARIO CASTILLO MÉNDEZ.

Broadcasting and Communications

TELECOMMUNICATIONS

In 2002 there were plans to expand and modernize the telecommunications sector. The French company Alcatel was to oversee the project.

Cámara Costarricense de Telecomunicaciones: Edif. Centro Colón, Apdo 591, 1007 San José; tel. and fax 255-3422; Pres. EVITA ARGUEDAS MAKLOUF.

Cámara Nacional de Medios de Comunicación Colectiva (CANAMECC): San José; tel. 222-4820; f. 1954; Pres. ANDRÉS QUINTANA CAVALLINI.

Instituto Costarricense de Electricidad (ICE): govt agency for power and telecommunications (see Trade and Industry: Utilities below).

Radiográfica Costarricense, SA (RACSA): Avda 5, Calle 1, Frente al Edif. Numar, Apdo 54, 1000 San José; tel. 287-0087; fax 287-0379; e-mail mcruz@sol.sacsa.co.cr; f. 1921; state telecommunications co; Dir-Gen. MARCO A. CRUZ MIRANDA.

RADIO

Asociación Costarricense de Información y Cultura (ACIC): Apdo 365, 1009 San José; f. 1983; independent body; controls private radio stations; Pres. JUAN FEDERICO MONTEALEGRE MARTÍN.

Cámara Nacional de Radio (CANARA): Paseo de los Estudiantes, Apdo 1.583, 1002 San José; tel. 233-1845; fax 255-4483; e-mail canara@sol.racsa.co.cr; internet www.canara.org; f. 1947; Exec. Dir LUZMILDA VARGAS GONZÁLEZ.

Control Nacional de Radio (CNR): Dirección Nacional de Comunicaciones, Ministerio de Gobernación y Policia, Apdo 10.006, 1000

San José; tel. 221-0992; fax 283-0741; f. 1954; governmental supervisory department; Dir MELVIN MURILLO ALVAREZ.

Non-commercial

Faro del Caribe: Apdo 2.710, 1000 San José; tel. 226-2573; fax 227-1725; f. 1948; religious and cultural programmes in Spanish and English; Man. CARLOS ROZOTTO PIEDRASANTA.

Radio Costa Rica: De Autos Bohío, en barrio Córdoba, 100 m sur y 100 m este, Apdo 6.462, 1000 San José; tel. 227-4690; fax 231-3408; e-mail canalcr@sol.racsa.co.cr; f. 1988; broadcasts Voice of America news bulletins (in Spanish) and locally-produced educational and entertainment programmes; Gen. Man. ANTONIO ALEXANDRE GARCÍA.

Radio Fides: Avda 4, Curia Metropolitana, Apdo 5.079, 1000 San José; tel. 233-4546; fax 233-2387; f. 1952; Roman Catholic station; Dir Most Rev. ROMÁN ARRIETA VILLALOBOS.

Radio Nacional: 1 km oeste del Parque Nacional de Diversiones, La Uruca, Apdo 7, 1980 San José; tel. 231-7983; fax 220-0070; e-mail sinart@sol.racsa.co.cr; f. 1978; Dir RODOLFO RODRÍGUEZ.

Radio Santa Clara: Santa Clara, San Carlos, Apdo 221, Ciudad Quesada, Alajuela; tel. 479-1264; f. 1986; Roman Catholic station; Dir Rev. MARCO A. SOLÍS V.

Radio Universidad: Ciudad Universitaria Rodrigo Facio, San Pedro, Montes de Oca, Apdo 2.060, 1000 San José; tel. 207-5356; fax 207-5459; f. 1949; classical music; Dir CARLOS MORALES.

Commercial

There are about 40 commercial radio stations, including:

89 Ya!: Costado sur del Parque Desamparados, Apdo 301, San José; tel. 259-3657; fax 250-2376; f. 1995; Dir ALEXANDER RAMOS RODRÍGUEZ.

Cadena de Emisoras Columbia: San José; tel. 234-0355; fax 225-9275; operates Radio Columbia, Radio Uno, Radio Sabrosa, Radio Puntarenas; Dir C. ARNOLDO ALFARO CHAVARRA.

Cadena Musical: Apdo 854, 1000, San José; tel. 257-2789; fax 233-9975; f. 1954; operates Radio Musical, Radio Emperador; Gen. Man. JORGE JAVIER CASTRO.

Grupo Centro: Apdo 6.133, San José; tel. 240-7591; fax 236-3672; operates Radio Centro 96.3 FM, Radio 820 AM, Televisora Guanacasteca Channels 16 and 28; Dir ROBERTO HERNÁNDEZ RAMÍREZ.

Radio Chorotega: Apdo 92, 5175 Santa Cruz de Guanacaste; tel. 663-2757; fax 663-0183; f. 1983; Roman Catholic station; Dir Rev. EMILIO MONTES DE OCA CORDERO.

Radio Emaus: San Vito de Coto Brus; tel. and fax 773-3101; f. 1962; Roman Catholic station; Dir Rev. LUIS PAULINO CABRERA SOTO.

Radio Monumental: Avda Central y 2, Calle 2, Apdo 800, 1000 San José; tel. 222-0000; fax 222-8237; e-mail monument@sol.racsa.co.cr; internet www.novanet.co.cr/monumental; f. 1929; all news station; Gen. Man. TERESA MARÍA CHÁVES ZAMORA.

Radio Sinaí: Apdo 262, 8000 San Isidro de El General; tel. 771-0367; f. 1957; Roman Catholic station; Dir Mgr ALVARO COTO OROZCO.

Sistema Radiofónico: Edif. Galería La Paz, 3°, Avda 2, Calles 2 y 4, Apdo 341, 1000 San José; tel. 222-4344; fax 255-0587; operates Radio Reloj; Dir Dr HERNÁN BARQUERO MONTES DE OCA.

TELEVISION

Government-owned

Sistema Nacional de Radio y Televisión Cultural (SINART): 1 km al oeste del Parque Nacional de Diversiones La Uruca, Apdo 7, 1980 San José; tel. 231-0839; fax 231-6604; e-mail sinart@racsa.co.cr; f. 1977; cultural; Dir-Gen. GUIDO SÁENZ GONZÁLEZ.

Commercial

Alphavisión (Canal 19): Detrás Iglesia de Santa María y Griega, Carretera a Desamparados, Apdo 1490, San José; tel. 226-9333; fax 226-9095; f. 1987; Gen. Man. CECILIA RAMÍREZ.

Canal 2: Del Hospital México 300 m oeste, Antiguo Hotel Cristal, Apdo 2.860, San José; tel. 231-2222; fax 231-0791; f. 1983; Pres. RAMÓN COLL MONTERO.

Canal 54: De Plaza Mayot, en Rohrmoser, 50 m oeste, 50 m sur, Apdo 640, San José; tel. 232-6337; fax 231-3408; e-mail canalcr@sol.racsa.co.cr; f. 1996; Pres. ANTONIO ALEXANDRE GARCÍA.

Corporación Costarricense de Televisión, SA (Canal 6): Apdo 2.860, 1000 San José; tel. 232-9255; fax 232-6087; Gen. Man. MARIO SOTELA BLEN.

Multivisión de Costa Rica, Ltda (Canales 4 y 9): 150 m oeste del Centro Comercial de Guadelupe, Apdo 4.666, 1000 San José; tel. 233-4444; fax 221-1734; f. 1961; operates Radio Sistema Universal

A.M. (f. 1956) Channel 9 (f. 1962) and Channel 4 (f. 1964) and FM (f. 1980); Gen. Man. ARNOLD VARGAS V.

Televisora de Costa Rica (Canal 7), SA (Teletica): Costado oeste Estadio Nacional, Apdo 3.876, San José; tel. 232-2222; fax 231-6258; f. 1960; operates Channel 7; Pres. OLGA COZZA DE PICADO; Gen. Man. RENÉ PICADO COZZA.

Televisora Sur y Norte (Canal 11): Apdo 99, 1000 San José; tel. 233-4988; Gen. Man. FEDERICO ZAMORA.

Finance

(cap. = capital; p.u. = paid up; res = reserves; dep. = deposits; m. = million; brs = branches; amounts in colones, unless otherwise indicated)

BANKING

Banco Central de Costa Rica: Avdas Central y Primera, Calles 2 y 4, Apdo 10.058, 1000 San José; tel. 233-4233; fax 233-5930; internet www.bccr.fi.cr; f. 1950; cap. 5.0m., res 120,750.4m., total resources 1,404,932.1m. (1999); scheduled for privatization; Pres. EDUARDO LIZANO FAIT; Man. JOSÉ RAFAEL BRENES.

State-owned Banks

Banco de Costa Rica: Avdas Central y 2, Calles 4 y 6, Apdo 10.035, 1000 San José; tel. 287-9000; fax 255-0221; e-mail bcr@bcr.fi.cr; internet www.bcr.fi.cr; f. 1877; responsible for industry; total assets 10,353m. (1999); Pres. MARIANO GUARDIA CAÑAS; Gen. Man. MARIO BARRENECHEA; 44 brs and agencies.

Banco Nacional de Costa Rica: Calles 2 y 4, Avda Primera, Apdo 10.015, 1000 San José; tel. 221-2223; fax 233-3875; e-mail bconal@sol.racsa.co.cr; internet www.bncr.fi.cr; f. 1914; responsible for the agricultural sector; cap. 18,444.4m., res 8,367.1m., dep. 657,306.4m. (1999); Gen. Man. OMAR GARRO V; 125 brs and agencies.

Banco Popular y de Desarrollo Comunal: Calle 1, Avdas 2 y 4, Apdo 10.190, San José; tel. 257-5797; fax 255-1966; f. 1969; total assets 29,450m. (1999); Pres. Ing. RODOLFO NAVAS ALVARADO; Gen. Man. ALVARO UREÑA ALVAREZ.

Private Banks

Banco Bancrecen, SA: Oficentro La Sabana, Edif. 6 5°, Apdo 603, 1007 San José; tel. 296-5301; fax 296-5305; e-mail bancrecen@sol.racsa.co.cr; internet www.bancrecen.fi.cr; Pres. ROBERTO ALCANTARA ROJAS.

Banco BANEX, SA: Barrio Tournón, Diagonal a Ulacit, Apdo 7.983, 1000 San José; tel. 257-0522; fax 257-5967; e-mail interna@banex.co.cr; internet www.banex.co.cr; f. 1981 as Banco Agroindustrial y de Exportaciones, SA; adopted present name 1987; incorporated Banco Metropolitano in May 2001; cap. 9,590.9m., res. 1,250.2m., dep. 111,441.1m. (Dec. 2000); Pres. ALBERTO VALLARINO; Gen. Man. MARCO ANTONIO CUADRA; 9 brs.

Banco Bantec, SA: Frente antigua Canada Dry, La Uruca, Apdo 1.164, 1000 San José; tel. 290-8585; fax 290-2939.

Banco BCT, SA: Calle Central No. 160, Apdo 7.698, San José; tel. 257-0544; fax 233-6833; e-mail banco@bct.fi.cr; f. 1984; total assets 13,794m. (1999); merged with Banco del Comercio, SA in 2000; Pres. ANTONIO BURGUÉS; Gen. Man. LEONEL BARUCH.

Banco de Crédito Centroamericano, SA (Bancentro): Calles 26 y 38, Paseo Colón, de la Mercedes Benz 200 m norte y 150 m oeste, Apdo 5.099, 1000 San José; tel. 280-5555; fax 280-5090; f. 1974; cap. 492m. (1996); Pres. ROBERTO J. ZAMORA LLANES; Gen. Man GILBERTO SERRANO GUTIÉRREZ.

Banco Cuscatlan de Costa Rica, SA: Del Puente Juan Pablo II, 150 m norte, Canton Central, La Uruca, Apdo 6.531, 1000 San José; tel. 299-0299; fax 232-7476; e-mail cuscatlan@cuscatlancr.com; internet www.bfa.fi.cr; f. 1984 as Banco de Fomento Agrícola; changed name to Banco BFA in 1994; changed name to above in 2000; cap. 31.5m., dep. 86.6m. (Dec. 2000); Pres. ERNESTO ROHRMOSER; Gen. Man. and CEO MANUEL PÉREZ LARA.

Banco Elca, SA: Del Centro Colón, 200 m norte, Paseo Colón, Apdo 1.112, 1000 San José; tel. 258-3029; fax 233-8383; e-mail banelca@sol.racsa.co.cr; internet www.bancoelca.com; f. 1985 as Banco de la Industria; changed name to above in 2000; Pres. ROBERTO ALVARADO MOYA; Gen. Man. CARLOS ALVARADO MOYA.

Banco Finadesa, SA: Paseo Colón, Carmen, Apdo 5.336, 1000 San José; tel. 243-8900; fax 257-0051; e-mail finadesa@finadesa.com.

Banco Improsa, SA: 2985 Calle 29 y 31, Avda 5, Carmen, San José; tel. 257-0689; fax 223-7319; e-mail banimpro@sol.racsa.co.cr.

Banco Interfin, SA: Calle 3, Avdas 2 y 4, Apdo 6.899, San José; tel. 287-4000; fax 233-4823; f. 1982; total assets 11,139m. (1999); Pres. Ing. Luis Lukowiecki; Gen. Man. Dr Luis Liberman.

Banco Internacional de Costa Rica, SA: Edif. Inmobiliaria BICSA, Barrio Tournón, Apdo 6.116, San José; tel. 243-1000; fax 257-2378; f. 1987; Pres. Fernando Suñol Prego; Gen. Man. Marco Alfaro Chavarría.

Banco Promérica, SA: Edif. Promérica, Sabana oeste canal 7, Mata Redonda, Apdo 1.289, 1200 San José; tel. 296-4848; fax 232-5727; e-mail promeric@sol.racsa.co.cr.

Banco de San José, SA: Calle Central, Avdas 3 y 5, Apdo 5.445, 1000 San José; tel. 295-9595; fax 222-8208; e-mail info@ bancosanjose.fi.cr; internet www.bancodesanjose.fi.crf. 1968; fmrly Bank of America, SA; total assets US $350m.m. (2000); Pres. Ernesto Castegnaro Odio; Gen. Man. Mario Montealegre-Saborío.

Banco Santander: Edif. Centro Colon, Paseo Colon, Calles 38 y 40; Apdo 1147, 1000 San José; Apdo 1147, 1000 San José; tel. 233-8366; fax 233-8476.

Banco Uno, SA: Calle 28, Paseo Colón, Merced, Apdo 5.884, 1000 San José; tel. 257-1344; fax 257-2215; e-mail pacifico@cos.pibnet .com.

Citibank (Costa Rica), SA: Oficentro ejecutivo la Sabana, distrito Mata Redonda, Apdo 10.277, San José; tel. 296-1494; fax 296-2458.

Scotiabank Costa Rica: Avda Primera, Calles Central y 2, Apdo 5.395, 1000, San José; tel. 287-8700; fax 255-3076; f. 1995; Gen. Man. Brian W. Brady; 11 brs.

Credit Co-operatives

Federación Nacional de Cooperativas de Ahorro y Crédito (Fedecrédito, RL): Calle 20, Avdas 8 y 10, Apdo 4.748, 1000 San José; tel. 233-5666; fax 257-1724; f. 1963; 55 co-operatives, with 150,000 mems; combined cap. US $82m. Pres. Carlos Bonilla Ayub; Gen. Man. Mario Vargas Alvarado.

Banking Association

Asociación Bancaria Costarricense: San José; tel. 253-2889; fax 225-0987; e-mail abc@abc.fi.cr; internet www.abc.fi.cr; Pres. Gerardo Corrales Brenes.

STOCK EXCHANGE

Bolsa Nacional de Valores, SA: Edif. Cartagena, 4°, Calle Central, Avda Primera, Santa Ana, Apdo 6155, 1000 San José; tel. 204-4848; fax 204-4802; e-mail bnv@bnv.co.cr; f. 1976; Chair. Rodrigo Arias Sánchez; CEO Federico Carrillo Zürcher.

INSURANCE

In 1998 the Legislative Assembly approved legislative reform effectively terminating the state monopoly of all insurance activities.

Caja Costarricense de Seguro Social: Apdo 10105, San José; tel. 257-9122; fax 222-1217; accident and health insurance, state-owned; Pres. Dr Rodolfo Piza Rocafort.

Instituto Nacional de Seguros: Calles 9 y 9 bis, Avda 7, Apdo 10.061, 1000 San José; tel. 223-5800; fax 255-3381; internet www.ins .go.cr; f. 1924; administers the state monopoly of insurance; services of foreign insurance companies may be used only by authorization of the Ministry of the Economy, Industry and Commerce, and only after the Instituto has certified that it will not accept the risk; Exec. Pres. Jorge A. Hernández Castañeda; Gen. Man. Ana Ross Salazar.

Trade and Industry

GOVERNMENT AGENCIES

Instituto Nacional de Vivienda y Urbanismo (INVU): Apdo 2.534, San José; tel. 221-5266; fax 223-4006; housing and town planning institute; Exec. Pres. Ing. Victor Evelio Castro; Gen. Man. Pedro Hernández Ruiz.

Ministry of Planning: Avdas 3 y 5, Calle 4, Apdo 10.127, 1000 San José; tel. 221-9524; fax 253-6243; f. 1963; formulates and supervises execution of the National Development Plan; main aims: to increase national productivity; to improve distribution of income and social services; to increase citizen participation in solution of socio-economic problems; Pres. Dr Leonardo Garnier.

Promotora del Comercio Exterior de Costa Rica (PRO-COMER): Calle 40, Avdas Central y 3, Centro Colón, Apdo 1.278, 1007 San José; tel. 256-7111; fax 233-5755; e-mail info@procomer .com; internet www.procomer.com; f. 1968 to improve international competitiveness by providing services aimed at increasing, diversifying and expediting international trade.

DEVELOPMENT ORGANIZATIONS

Cámara de Azucareros: Calle 3, Avda Fernández Güell, Apdo 1.577, 1000 San José; tel. 221-2103; fax 222-1358; f. 1949; sugar growers; Pres. Rodrigo Arias Sánchez.

Cámara Nacional de Bananeros: Edif. Urcha, 3°, Calle 11, Avda 6, Apdo 10.273, 1000 San José; tel. 222-7891; fax 233-1268; f. 1967; banana growers; Pres. José Alvaro Sandoval; Exec. Dir Jorge Madrigal.

Cámara Nacional de Cafetaleros: Calle 3, Avdas 6 y 8, No. 652, Apdo 1.310, San José; tel. 221-8207; fax 257-5381; f. 1948; 70 mems; coffee millers and growers; Pres. Carlos R. Aubert Z; Exec. Dir Joaquín Valverde B.

Cámara Nacional de Ganaderos: Edif. Ilifilán, 4°, Calles 4 y 6, Avda Central, Apdo 5.539, 1000 San José; tel. 222-1652; cattle farmers; Pres. Ing. Alberto José Amador Zamora.

Cámara Nacional de Artesanía y Pequeña Industria de Costa Rica (CANAPI): Calle 17, Avda 10, detrás estatua de San Martín, Apdo 1.783 Goicoechea, 2100 San José; tel. 223-2763; fax 255-4873; e-mail canapi@sol.racsa.co.cr; f. 1963; development, marketing and export of small-scale industries and handicrafts; Pres. and Exec. Dir Rodrigo González.

Corporación Bananera Nacional: Apdo 6504, 1000 San José; tel. 224-4111; fax 253-9117; internet www.corbana.co.cr.

Costa Rican Investment and Development Board (CINDE): Apdo 7.170, 1000 San José; tel. 220-0366; fax 220-4750; e-mail cindes.m@sol.racsa.co.cr; internet www.cinde.co.cr; f. 1983; coalition for development of initiatives to attract foreign investment for production and export of new products; Chair. Emilio Bruce; CEO Enrique Egloff.

Instituto Costarricense de Pesca y Acuacultura (INCO-PESCA): San José; internet www.mag.go.cr/incopesca/.

Instituto del Café de Costa Rica: Calle 1, Avdas 18 y 20, Apdo 37, San José; tel. 222-6411; fax 222-2838; internet www.icafe.go.cr/ homepage.nsf; f. 1948 to develop the coffee industry, to control production and to regulate marketing; Pres. Luis Diego Escalante; Exec. Dir Guillermo Canet.

CHAMBERS OF COMMERCE

Cámara de Comercio de Costa Rica: Urbanización Tournón, 150 m noroeste del parqueo del Centro Comercial El Pueblo, Apdo 1.114, 1000 San José; tel. 221-0005; fax 233-7091; e-mail biofair@sol .racsa.co.cr; f. 1915; 900 mems; Pres. Emilio Bruce Jiménez; Exec. Dir Eugenio Pignataro Pacheco.

Cámara de Industrias de Costa Rica: 350 m sur de la Fuente de la Hispanidad, San Pedro de Montes de Oca, Apdo 10.003, San José; tel. 281-0006; fax 234-6163; e-mail cicr@cicr.com; internet www.cicr .com; Pres. Ing. Marco Vinicio Ruiz; Exec. Dir Mayi Antillon Guerrero.

Unión Costarricense de Cámaras y Asociaciones de la Empresa Privada (UCCAEP): 1002 Paseo de los Estudiantes, Apdo 539, San José; tel. 290-5595; fax 290-5596; f. 1974; business federation; Pres. Ing. Samuel Yankelewitz Berger; Exec. Dir Alvaro Ramírez Bogantes.

INDUSTRIAL AND TRADE ASSOCIATIONS

Asociación de Empresas de Zonas Francas (AZOFRAS): La Uruca San José, Apdo 162, 3006 Barreal de Heredia; tel. 293-7073; fax 293-7094; e-mail azofras@racsa.co.cr; internet www.azofras.com; Pres. Jorge Brenes.

Cámara Nacional de Agricultura y Agroindustria: Avda 10-10 bis, Cv. 23, Apdo 1.671, 1000 San José; tel. 221-6864; fax 233-8658; e-mail cnacr@sol.racsa.co.cr; f. 1947; Pres. Ing. Leonel Peralta; Exec. Dir José Carlos Barquero Arce.

Consejo Nacional de Producción: Calle 36 a 12, Apdo 2.205, San José; tel. 223-6033; fax 233-9660; f. 1948 to encourage agricultural and fish production and to regulate production and distribution of basic commodities; Pres. Ing. Javier Flores Galagarza; Man. Virginia Valverde de Molina.

Instituto de Desarrollo Agrario (IDA): Apdo 5.054, 1000 San José; tel. 224-6066; Exec. Pres. Ing. Roberto Solórzano Sanabria; Gen. Man. Ing. Jorge Angel Jiménez Calderón.

Instituto Mixto de Ayuda Social (IMAS): Calle 29, Avdas 2 y 4, Apdo 6.213, San José; tel. 225-5555; fax 224-8783; Pres. Clotilde Fonseca Quesada.

Instituto Nacional de Fomento Cooperativo: Apdo 10.103, 1000 San José; tel. 223-4355; fax 255-3835; f. 1973 to encourage the establishment of co-operatives and to provide technical assistance and credit facilities; Pres. Rafael Angel Rojas Jiménez; Exec. Dir Luis Antonio Monge Román.

UTILITIES

Electricity

Cía Nacional de Fuerza y Luz, SA: Calle Central y Primera, Avda 5, Apdo 10.026, 1000 San José; tel. 296-4608; fax 296-3950; internet www.cnfl.go.cr; f. 1941; electricity company; Pres. RAFAEL SEQUEIRA R; Gen. Man. PABLO COB SABORIO.

Instituto Costarricense de Electricidad (ICE) (Costa Rican Electricity Institute): Apdo 10.032, 1000 San José; tel. 220-7720; fax 220-1555; internet www.ice.co.cr; f. 1949; govt agency for power and telecommunications; Exec. Pres. Ing. RAFAEL SEQUEIRA RAMÍREZ; Gen. Man. INGRID HERRMAN.

Servicio Nacional de Electricidad: Apdo 936, 1000 San José; tel. 220-0102; fax 220-0374; co-ordinates the development of the electricity industry; Chair. LEONEL FONSECA.

Water

Instituto Costarricense de Acueductos y Alcantarillados: Avda Central, Calle 5, Apdo 5.120, 1000 San José; tel. 233-2155; fax 222-2259; water and sewerage; Pres. RAFAEL VILLALTA.

TRADE UNIONS

Central del Movimiento de Trabajadores Costarricenses (CMTC) (Costa Rican Workers' Union): Calle 20, Avdas 3 y 5, Apdo 4.137, 1000 San José; tel. 221-7701; fax 221-3353; e-mail cmtccr@solracsa.co.cr; Pres. DENNIS CABEZAS BADILLA.

Confederación Auténtica de Trabajadores Democráticos (Democratic Workers' Union): Calle 13, Avdas 10 y 12, Solera; tel. 253-2971; Pres. LUIS ARMANDO GUTIÉRREZ; Sec.-Gen. Prof. CARLOS VARGAS.

Confederación Costarricense de Trabajadores Democráticos (Costa Rican Confederation of Democratic Workers): Calles 3 y 5, Avda 12, Apdo 2.167, San José; tel. 222-1981; f. 1966; mem. ICFTU and ORIT; Sec.-Gen. LUIS ARMANDO GUTIÉRREZ R; 50,000 mems.

Confederación Unitaria de Trabajadores (CUT): Calles 1 y 3, Avda 12, Casa 142, Apdo 186, 1009 San José; tel. 233-4188; e-mail mcalde@racsa.co.cr; f. 1980; from a merger of the Federación Nacional de Trabajadores Públicos and the Confederación General de Trabajadores; 53 affiliated unions; Sec.-Gen. MIGUEL MARÍN CALDERÓN; c.75,000 mems.

Federación Sindical Agraria Nacional (FESIAN) (National Agrarian Confederation): Apdo 2.167, 1000 San José; tel. 233-5897; 20,000 member families; Sec.-Gen. JUAN MEJÍA VILLALOBOS.

The **Consejo Permanente de los Trabajadores** formed in 1986, comprises six union organizations and two teachers' unions

Transport

Ministry of Public Works and Transport: Apdo 10.176, 1000 San José; tel. 226-7311; fax 227-1434; the Ministry is responsible for setting tariffs, allocating funds, maintaining existing systems and constructing new ones.

Cámara Nacional de Transportes: San José; national chamber of transport.

RAILWAYS

Instituto Costarricense de Ferrocarriles (INCOFER): Calle 2, Avda 20, Apdo 1, 1009 San José; tel. 221-0777; fax 257-7220; e-mail incofer@sol.racsa.co.cr; f. 1985; government-owned; 471 km, of which 388 km are electrified.

INCOFER comprised:

División I: Atlantic sector running between Limón, Río Frío, Valle la Estrella and Siquirres. Main line of 109 km, with additional 120 km of branch lines, almost exclusively for transport of bananas; services resumed in 1999.

División II: Pacific sector running from San José to Puntarenas and Caldera; 116 km of track, principally for transport of cargo.

Note: In 1995 INCOFER suspended most operations, pending privatization, although some cargo transport continued.

ROADS

In 2000 there were 35,892 km of roads, of which 7,437 km were main roads and 28,455 km were secondary roads. An estimated 22% of the total road network was paved in that year. In 2001 the construction of four major roads across the country began; the first road to be built was 74 km long, running from San José to San Ramón.

SHIPPING

Local services operate between the Costa Rican ports of Puntarenas and Limón and those of Colón and Cristóbal in Panama and other Central American ports. The multi-million dollar project at Caldera on the Gulf of Nicoya is now in operation as the main Pacific port; Puntarenas is being used as the second port. The Caribbean coast is served by the port complex of Limón/Moín. International services are operated by various foreign shipping lines. The Caldera and Puntarenas ports were to be opened up to private investment and operation from 2002.

Junta de Administración Portuaria y de Desarrollo Económico de la Vertiente Atlántica (JAPDEVA): Calle 17, Avda 7, Apdo 5.330, 1000 San José; tel. 233-5301; state agency for the development of Atlantic ports; Exec. Pres. Ing. JORGE ARTURO CASTRO HERRERA.

Instituto Costarricense de Puertos del Pacífico (INCOP): Calle 36, Avda 3, Apdo 543, 1000 San José; tel. 223-7111; fax 223-9527; f. 1972; state agency for the development of Pacific ports; Exec. Pres. GERARDO MEDINA MADRIZ.

CIVIL AVIATION

Costa Rica's main international airport is the Juan Santamaría Airport, 16 km from San José at El Coco. Following a report by the US Federal Aviation Administration, the aviation sector was to undergo expansion and modernization from 2001. There is a second international airport, the Daniel Oduber Quirós Airport, at Liberia and there are regional airports at Limón and Pavas (Tobías Bolaños Airport).

Aero Costa Rica: San José; regional carrier; Chair. CALIXTO CHAVEL; Gen. Man. JUAN FERNÁNDEZ.

Líneas Aéreas Costarricenses, SA (LACSA) (Costa Rican Airlines): Edif. Lacsa, La Uruca, Apdo 1.531, San José; tel. 290-2727; fax 232-4178; internet www.flylatinamerica.com; f. 1945; operates international services within Latin America and to North America; Chair. ALONSO LARA; Pres. JOSÉ G. ROJAS.

Servicios Aéreos Nacionales, SA (SANSA): Paseo Colón, Centro Colón, Apdo 999, 1.007 San José; tel. 233-2714; fax 255-2176; subsidiary of LACSA; international, regional and domestic scheduled passenger and cargo services; Man. Dir CARLOS MANUEL DELGADO AGUILAR.

Servicios de Carga Aérea (SERCA): Aeropuerto Internacional Juan Santamaría, Apdo 6.855, San José; f. 1982; operates cargo service from San José.

Tourism

Costa Rica boasts a system of nature reserves and national parks unique in the world, which cover one-third of the country. The main tourist features are the Irazú and Poás volcanoes, the Orosí valley and the ruins of the colonial church at Ujarras. Tourists also visit San José, the capital, the Pacific beaches of Guanacaste and Puntarenas, and the Caribbean beaches of Limón. In 2001 there were numerous hotel and resort construction projects under way in the Guanacaste province. The project was being undertaken by the Instituto Costarricense de Turismo. In May 2001 one of the country's principal tourist sites, La Casona de Santa Rosa, was almost completely destroyed by fire. Some 1,131,406 tourists visited Costa Rica in 2001 and in 2000 tourism receipts totalled US $1,140m. Most visitors came from Canada (45.8% of the total in 2001) and the USA (37.9% in 2001). There were 27,103 hotel rooms in Costa Rica in 1998.

Cámara Nacional de Turismo (Canatur): tel. 234-6222; fax 253-8102; e-mail info@tourism.co.cr; internet www.costarica.tourism.co.cr.

Instituto Costarricense de Turismo: Edif. Genaro Valverde, Calles 5 y 7, Avda 4, Apdo 777, 1000 San José; tel. 223-3254; fax 223-3254; internet www.tourism-costarica.com; f. 1955; Exec. Pres. Ing. CARLOS ROESCH CARRANZA.

CÔTE D'IVOIRE
(THE IVORY COAST)

Introductory Survey

Location, Climate, Language, Religion, Flag, Capital

The Republic of Côte d'Ivoire lies on the west coast of Africa, between Ghana to the east and Liberia to the west, with Guinea, Mali and Burkina Faso to the north. Average temperatures vary between 21°C and 30°C (70°F and 86°F). The main rainy season, May–July, is followed by a shorter wet season in October–November. The official language is French, and a large number of African languages are also spoken. At the time of the 1998 census it was estimated that some 34% of the population were Christians (mainly Roman Catholics), 27% Muslims, 15% followed traditional indigenous beliefs, and 3% practised other religions, while 21% had no religious affiliation. (However, it was thought that the proportion of Muslims was, in fact, significantly higher, as the majority of unregistered foreign workers in Côte d'Ivoire were believed to be Muslims.) The national flag (proportions 2 by 3) has three equal vertical stripes, of orange, white and green. The political and administrative capital is Yamoussoukro, although most government ministries and offices remain in the former capital, Abidjan, which is the major centre for economic activity.

Recent History

Formerly a province of French West Africa, Côte d'Ivoire achieved self-government, within the French Community, in December 1958. Dr Félix Houphouët-Boigny, leader of the Parti démocratique de la Côte d'Ivoire—Rassemblement démocratique africain (PDCI—RDA), became Prime Minister in 1959. The country became fully independent on 7 August 1960; a new Constitution was adopted in October 1960, and Houphouët-Boigny became President in November.

Until 1990 the PDCI—RDA, founded in 1946, was Côte d'Ivoire's only legal political party, dspite constitutional provision for the existence of other political organizations. A high rate of economic growth, together with strong support from France, contributed, until the late 1980s, to the stability of the regime. The announcement in early 1990 of austerity measures, in compliance with an IMF-sponsored programme, precipitated an unprecedented level of unrest. In April Houphouët-Boigny appointed Alassane Ouattara, the Governor of the Banque centrale des états de l'Afrique de l'ouest (BCEAO, the regional central bank), to chair a special commission to formulate economic and political reforms. From May it was announced that hitherto unofficial political organizations were to be formally recognized, and many new parties were formed.

Côte d'Ivoire's first contested presidential election was held on 28 October 1990. Houphouët-Boigny—challenged by Laurent Gbagbo, the candidate of the socialist Front populaire ivoirien (FPI)—was re-elected for a seventh term with the support of 81.7% of votes cast. In November the legislature, the Assemblée nationale, approved two constitutional amendments. The first authorized the President of the legislature to assume the functions of the President of the Republic, in the event of the presidency becoming vacant, until the expiry of the previous incumbent's mandate (an arrangement that had existed, on an interim basis, since October 1985, following the abolition of the post of Vice-President of the Republic). The second amendment provided for the appointment of a Prime Minister, who would be accountable to the President; Ouattara was subsequently designated premier.

Almost 500 candidates, representing 17 political parties, contested legislative elections on 25 November 1990. The PDCI—RDA returned 163 deputies to the 175-member Assemblée nationale; Gbagbo and eight other members of the FPI were elected, along with the leader of the Parti ivoirien des travailleurs (PIT), Francis Wodié, and two independent candidates. Henri Konan Bédié, who had held the presidency of the legislature since 1980, was re-elected to that post. Ouattara's first Council of Ministers was named following the elections, in which the Prime Minister assumed personal responsibility for the economy.

The Government's response to the report of a commission of inquiry into student disturbances in May–June 1991, in which one student died, which was published in January 1992, provoked renewed violence. The disturbances were led by the outlawed Fédération estudiantine et scolaire de Côte d'Ivoire (FESCI), which remained a significant force of protest against the Government throughout the 1990s. Houphouët-Boigny refused to subject the armed forces Chief of the General Staff, Brig.-Gen. Robert Gueï, to disciplinary proceedings, despite the commission's conclusion that Gueï was ultimately responsible for violent acts perpetrated by forces under his command. In February Gbagbo was among more than 100 people arrested during a violent anti-Government demonstration in Abidjan, and in March was one of nine opposition leaders sentenced to two-year prison sentences under a new presidential ordinance that rendered political leaders responsible for violent acts committed by their supporters.

Houphouët-Boigny left Côte d'Ivoire in May 1993, in order to receive medical treatment in Europe. As the President's health failed, controversy intensified concerning the issue of succession. Many senior politicians, including Ouattara and Gbagbo (both of whom were known to have presidential aspirations), asserted that the process defined in the Constitution effectively endorsed an 'hereditary presidency', since Bédié, like Houphouët-Boigny, was a member of the Akan ethnic group. Houphouët-Boigny died on 7 December. Later the same day Bédié announced that, in accordance with the Constitution, he was assuming the duties of President of the Republic with immediate effect. Ouattara initially refused to recognize Bédié's right of succession, but tendered his resignation two days later. Daniel Kablan Duncan, hitherto Minister-delegate to the Prime Minister, with responsibility for the Economy, Finance and Planning, was appointed as Prime Minister.

In subsequent months Bédié appointed close associates to positions of influence in government, the judiciary and in the state-owned media.Bédié's position was further consolidated by his election to the chairmanship of the PDCI—RDA in April 1994, and by Ouattara's departure for the USA following his appointment to the post of Deputy Managing Director of the IMF. Disaffected members of the PDCI—RDA left the party in June to form what they termed a moderate, centrist organization, the Rassemblement des républicains (RDR); Ouattara formally announced his membership of the RDR in early 1995.

A new electoral code, adopted in December 1994, imposed new restrictions on eligibility for public office, notably stipulating that candidates for the presidency or for the Assemblée nationale be of direct Ivorian descent. The RDR protested that these restrictions would prevent Ouattara from contesting the presidency, since the former Prime Minister was of Burkinabè descent and would also be affected by the code's requirement that candidates have been continuously resident in Côte d'Ivoire for five years prior to seeking election. Opposition parties organized a series of demonstrations to demand the withdrawal of the electoral code, the establishment of an independent electoral commission and a revision of voters' lists.

In October 1995 the FPI (which was to have been represented by Gbagbo) and the RDR (whose Secretary-General, Djény Kobina, was to have replaced Ouattara as the party's candidate) announced their boycott of the forthcoming presidential election as long as the conditions were not 'clear and open'. Subsequent negotiations involving Bédié and opposition groups made no effective progress., and the presidential election took place, as scheduled, on 22 October 1995, following a week of violence in several towns. Bédié, with 95.25% of the valid votes cast, secured an overwhelming victory over Wodié, his sole challenger.

Prior to the legislative elections of 26 November 1995, representatives of both the FPI and the RDR were appointed to the electoral commission; both parties abandoned their threatened boycott of the poll. However, ongoing disturbances resulted in the postponement of polling in five constituencies, including the constituency that was to have been contested by Gbagbo; moreover, Kobina's candidacy was disallowed, on the grounds that he had been unable to prove direct Ivorian descent. In December the Constitutional Council annulled the results of the elections in three constituencies. The PDCI—RDA thus held 146 seats, the RDR 14, and the FPI nine, indicating a notable loss of support for the PDCI—RDA in the north in favour of the RDR.

In October 1995, shortly before the presidential election, Brig.-Gen. Gueï was replaced in his armed forces command and appointed as Minister of Employment and the Civil Service. In January 1996 Gueï became Minister of Sports, and the former Minister of Defence, Léon Konan Koffi, was appointed Minister of State, responsible for Religious Affairs and Dialogue with the Opposition. Reports emerged in May of a coup attempt by members of the armed forces at the time of the civil unrest that preceded the 1995 presidential election. These apparent demotions and the departure of Gueï and Koffi from the Government in August 1996 were interpreted as an indication of Bédié's desire to remove from positions of influence figures connected with the insecurity prior to the 1995 elections. In January 1997 Gueï was dismissed from the army, having been found to have committed serious disciplinary offences in the discharge of his duties.

Meanwhile, the RDR and the FPI refused to occupy their allotted seats on a commission of inquiry into the pre-election unrest, inaugurated in December 1996. By-elections for eight parliamentary seats, including those for which voting did not take place or was annulled in 1995, took place in December 1996; the FPI won five seats and the PDCI—RDA three. A number of attempts to incorporate representatives of the opposition into the Government were made in 1998. In March Adama Coulibaly's acceptance of the post of Minister of Transport was denounced by the RDR, of which he had been Deputy Secretary-General, and he was subsequently expelled from the party. In August Wodié was appointed as Minister of Higher Education and Scientific Research.

In June 1998 RDR and FPI deputies boycotted a vote in the Assemblée nationale that approved substantial amendments to the Constitution. The opposition objected, in particular, to provisions conferring wider powers on the Head of State, whose mandate was to be extended to seven years. Henceforth, candidates for public office were required to be Ivorian by birth, of direct Ivorian descent, and to have been continuously resident in Côte d'Ivoire for 10 years. The amendments included provisions for the establishment of an upper legislative chamber, the Sénat. In September Gbagbo and Kobina led a demonstration in Abidjan to denounce the amendments. Following the death of Kobina in October, Henriette Dagba Diabaté assumed the post of Secretary-General of the RDR.

The dismissal of the Minister of Public Health, in August 1999, was apparently connected to the misappropriation of aid from the European Union (EU, see p. 199). Much EU assistance to the country was consequently suspended. Meanwhile, suspicions of fraud at the state marketing body for cocoa and coffee contributed to an IMF decision to withhold funding to the country.

Alassane Ouattara returned to Côte d'Ivoire in July 1999 and, in August, was appointed to the newly created post of President of the RDR. Although Ouattara declared his intention to contest the 2000 presidential election, in October 1999 it was announced that his nationality certificate (which had been issued in September) had been annulled. Following protests in Abidjan, Diabaté was among several RDR activists found guilty of inciting violence and given custodial sentences. In December a warrant was issued for Ouattara's arrest on charges of fraudulently procuring identity papers, following the announcement that he would not, as previously intended, shortly return to Côte d'Ivoire from France, where he had spent much of the previous two months.

In late December 1999 a mutiny by soldiers demanding salary increases and the payment of outstanding arrears rapidly escalated into a *coup d'état*. Bédié initially sought to appease the soldiers by promising an amelioration of pay and conditions, but the protesters extended their demands to include the reinstatement of Brig.-Gen. Robert Gueï to the position of armed forces Chief of General Staff. On 24 December Gueï announced that he had assumed power at the head of a Comité national de salut public (CNSP), and that the Constitution and its institutions had been suspended. Constitutional review and fresh legislative elections were promised, and opposition parties were invited to submit nominations for an interim government, pending the restoration of constitutional order. In early January 2000 Bédié left Côte d'Ivoire for Togo and subsequently sought refuge in France.

Gueï encountered considerable difficulty in achieving his stated objective of forming a broad-based government. The CNSP, having released the imprisoned RDR leaders, was at first perceived as being supportive of Ouattara, particularly as one prominent member, Intendant-Gen. Lassana Palenfo, had previously served in Ouattara's Government. Consequently, the FPI (which had become increasingly distanced from the RDR) withdrew its nominees from the coalition Government appointed in early January 2000, although subsequent negotiations resulted in the party attaining a larger number of ministerial posts than any other. The PDCI—RDA declined to approve Gueï's appointment of two ministers from the party.

In late January 2000 a constitutional review body was inaugurated, and Gueï announced that presidential and legislative elections would be held by 31 October, following a constitutional referendum in July. The draft Constitution, presented in May, provoked considerable controversy, as it demanded that presidential candidates be of only Ivorian nationality and parentage. Following protests from the RDR, Gueï dismissed all ministers of that party, with the exception of Diabaté. Seydou Elimane Diarra, an experienced diplomat and a northern Muslim, was appointed Prime Minister.

In early July 2000 soldiers led two days of disturbances in Abidjan and Bouaké, demanding bonus payments in recognition of their role in the December coup. The authorities arrested 35 soldiers, accusing them of attempting to overthrow the CNSP; four members of the RDR were briefly detained on charges of complicity in the mutiny. The revised Constitution was endorsed by 86.5% of votes cast in a referendum on 23–24 July, with turnout estimated at 56%. Notably, all those involved in the *coup d'état* and members of the CNSP were granted immunity from prosecution.

In August 2000, in advance of the presidential election, which was scheduled for 17 September, Gueï announced that he would contest the election as an independent. The election was subsequently postponed until 22 October, owing to organizational difficulties. In September two members of the presidential guard were killed in an attack on Gueï's residence. Several days later Palenfo and Abdoulaye Coulibaly were dismissed in a government reshuffle. Believed to be allies of Ouattara, they were accused of involvement in the attack on Gueï's residence and subsequently sought refuge in the Nigerian Embassy in Abidjan. In November Palenfo and Coulibaly were arrested on charges related to the attack; in February 2001 further charges were brought against them. Meanwhile, following a further ministerial reorganization at the end of September 2000, the FPI became the sole political party to be represented in the transitional Government.

In early October 2000 the Supreme Court announced that only five of the 19 candidates for the presidential election complied with the conditions of eligibility. Those whose candidacies were rejected included Ouattara, Emile Constant Bombet, the candidate of the PDCI—RDA, and several unofficial representatives of that party, most notably Bédié. Of the five candidates permitted to stand, only Gueï and Gbagbo were regarded as capable of eliciting popular support; allegations that the two men had undertaken a private agreement of co-operation had been encouraged by the increasingly prominent role of the FPI in Gueï's Government. Leaders of the PDCI—RDA and the RDR urged an electoral boycott in protest at the Supreme Court's decision.

The two weeks preceding the presidential election were characterized by heightened unrest, and a state of emergency was imposed. Nevertheless, voting proceeded generally without incident on 22 October 2000. Preliminary results indicated that Gbagbo had received a greater percentage of votes cast than Gueï. However, on 24 October the Ministry of the Interior and Decentralization announced the dissolution of the national electoral commission and declared Gueï the winner of the election. The Government claimed that certain, unspecified, political parties had perpetrated electoral fraud, and announced that, following the readjustment of the results, Gueï, with 52.7% of the votes cast, had defeated Gbagbo, with 41.0%. These results were widely condemned as fraudulent, both domestically and internationally. Prime Minister Diarra resigned in protest on 23 October, and demonstrations were held across the country to demand that Gueï step down in favour of Gbagbo. Gueï declared a renewed state of emergency on 24 October, but on the following day soldiers joined the demonstrators, and the head of the presidential guard withdrew his support for Guéï. Following an outbreak of heavy fighting between rival army factions in the military barracks in Abidjan, and a declaration of support for Gbagbo by the Chief of Staff of the Armed Forces, Guéï fled, and Gbagbo declared himself President.

According to official figures released by the electoral commission, and confirmed by the Supreme Court, Gbagbo had secured 59.4% of the valid votes cast, while Guéï had received 32.7%; turn-out was estimated at 33.2%. Participation was notably low in the largely Muslim and RDR-supporting regions in the north, as well as in Yamoussoukro and other strongholds of the PDCI—RDA, casting doubt on the legitimacy of Gbagbo's victory. Additionally, concern was raised that Gbagbo had voiced support, during his campaign, for the notion of strengthening national identity, or *'ivoirité'*, in similar, potentially inflammatory, terms to those used previously by Bédié and Guéï. Gbagbo was inaugurated as President on 26 October.

Although the PDCI—RDA accepted Gbagbo's victory, the RDR continued to demand the annulment and reorganization of the election. In the three days following Gbagbo's accession to the presidency violent clashes between the security forces and RDR demonstrators resulted in 203 deaths, according to official figures. The majority of those killed were believed to be Muslims and members of the northern Dioula ethnic group. The discovery of a mass grave, containing the bodies of 57 people in Yopougon, a suburb of Abidjan, prompted the Government to announce an investigation into the violence. The UN subsequently established a commission of inquiry into the killings.

On 27 October 2000 Gbagbo appointed a new Council of Ministers, incorporating members of the FPI, the PDCI—RDA and the PIT. (The RDR stated that it would await legislative elections, subsequently scheduled to be held on 10 December, before participating in a coalition government.) Affi N'Guessan, the manager of Gbagbo's electoral campaign and a minister in the outgoing Government, was named as Prime Minister. In mid-November Guéï announced his recognition of Gbagbo as President.

In early December 2000 the Supreme Court ruled that the candidacy of Ouattara in the forthcoming legislative elections was invalid. The RDR urged an 'active boycott' of the legislative elections in protest and withdrew its members from the Comité de médiation pour la réconciliation nationale (CMRN), which Gbagbo had established in November. An estimated 30 people died in clashes between supporters of Ouattara and the police in early December, and several senior RDR officials were detained, as the Government accused the party of plotting a *coup d'état*. Following the death of his personal secretary, who had reportedly been beaten by police-officers, Ouattara fled to France. The UN, the Organization of African Unity (now the African Union, AU, see p. 130) and the EU announced that they would withdraw their observers from the legislative elections in response to the unrest and the exclusion of Ouattara.

Legislative elections proceeded on 10 December 2000, although violent clashes between RDR supporters and the security forces, in which 85 people were killed, prevented voting in 28 northern constituencies. Electoral turn-out was low, at 31.5%. The FPI secured 96 of the 225 seats in the Assemblée nationale, becoming the largest legislative party. The PDCI—RDA won 77 seats, the PIT four and independent candidates 17, while a 'moderate' faction of the RDR, which rejected the party's boycott of the elections, and two smaller parties each obtained one seat.

On the night of 7–8 January 2001 dissident soldiers seized control of the state radio and television station in Abidjan, in what was widely regarded as an attempted coup. Troops loyal to the Government suppressed the uprising, in which 15 people were killed, within several hours, and more than 30 arrests were made. The Government accused unspecified neighbouring countries of having encouraged the failed coup, prompting attacks on properties owned by foreigners. During early 2001 a number of RDR members and officials, including Diabaté, were arrested and accused of involvement in the coup attempt, although the RDR denied any involvement. In January 2001 Gbagbo announced that a warrant had been issued for the arrest of Guéï, although his whereabouts remained unknown.

Meanwhile, the remaining legislative elections took place on 14 January 2001, largely without incident. The PDCI—RDA secured 17 of the 26 contested seats, increasing their overall representation in the Assemblée nationale to 94 seats, only two

less than the FPI, which won no new seats. Independent candidates won five seats and the RDR faction four. Two seats in Kong, Ouattara's native town, remained uncontested. Only 13.3% of eligible voters participated in the elections. The legislative balance of power remained unclear. Mamadou Koulibaly of the FPI, hitherto Minister of the Economy and Finance, was elected President of the Assemblée nationale, with the support of both his own party and the PDCI—RDA. It soon emerged that seven of the 22 'independent' deputies had been financed by the PDCI—RDA and were to return to the party. A further 14 independents, PDCI—RDA dissidents who had left the party to support Guéï, formed a parliamentary alliance with the FPI and, in February, created a new centre-right party with some 50 other former members of the PDCI—RDA, the Union pour la démocratie et la paix de la Côte d'Ivoire (UDPCI).

N'Guessan was retained as Prime Minister in a new Council of Ministers appointed on 24 January 2001; of the 28 ministers, 18 were members of the FPI, while six were from the PDCI—RDA. Meanwhile, tensions between native Ivorians and Burkinabè migrants heightened, and, following a number of violent incidents, several thousand Burkinabè were reported to have returned to Burkina Faso from Côte d'Ivoire in January–February. The RDR performed well in municipal elections on 25 March, securing control of 64 of Côte d'Ivoire's 197 communes, more than any other party. In April, however, the leaders of 21 independently controlled communes announced their decision to join the PDCI—RDA, thereby giving that party control of 80 communes overall.

In July 2001 N'Guessan was elected leader of the FPI, replacing Gbagbo. In the same month the UN commission of inquiry issued a report implicating members of the gendarmerie in the killings of the 57 people whose bodies had been found in a mass grave at Yopougon in October 2000. In early August 2001, however, eight gendarmes were acquitted by a military tribunal on charges of murder in relation to these killings, on grounds of lack of evidence, although the conduct of the trial was widely criticized by human rights activists and by supporters of the RDR; in April 2002 Gbagbo announced that a civil tribunal was to be convened to reopen investigations into the killings. At the end of August 2001 a committee appointed by Gbagbo to investigate politically motivated violence in Côte d'Ivoire in the aftermath of the 2000 presidential election announced that, as a result of such violence, 303 people had died, 65 had disappeared and more than 1,500 had been injured.

Some 700 representatives of political, religious and civil society organizations participated in a national reconciliation forum, chaired by Diarra, which took place between 9 October and 18 December 2001, although a meeting between Gbagbo, Bédié, Guéï and Ouattara proved impossible to realize. Bédié returned to Côte d'Ivoire from France in late October, for the first time since December 1999, and participated in a meeting at the reconciliation forum in mid-November 2001. Guéï also returned from self-imposed seclusion in the west of Côte d'Ivoire to speak at the forum, stating that Gbagbo had won the presidential election fraudulently, and that the two men had entered into a secret pact to determine the election result in Guéï's favour, on condition that he contest no further elections. In mid-November Gbagbo admitted that certain clauses of the Constitution approved in July 2000 had been written in order to exclude Ouattara from future elections. Diabaté announced that the RDR would use all legal means to ensure that fresh presidential and legislative elections be held with the participation of Ouattara. At the beginning of December 2001 Ouattara, who had returned to Abidjan several days previously, addressed the forum, calling for a new constitution, in addition to fresh elections, to resolve the political crisis; he announced his intention of remaining in Côte d'Ivoire and reiterated his determination to be elected to the presidency. When the forum closed, in mid-December, it recommended, *inter alia*, that Ouattara be granted a nationality certificate and that a committee of legal experts be created to examine certain clauses in the Constitution; proposals on land reform and the judicial system were also made.

In late January 2002 a meeting took place in Yamoussoukro between Gbagbo, Bédié, Guéï and Ouattara. In a joint statement, issued in mid-February, the four leaders reviewed the resolutions of the reconciliation forum and made further recommendations. In April, at the national conference of the PDCI—RDA, Bédié was re-elected as leader of the party by a convincing majority. In May and June nine people were convicted of involvement in the coup attempt of January 2001 and sentenced to terms of up to 20 years' imprisonment, while a further 19 defendants were acquitted.

Ouattara was finally granted Ivorian citizenship in late June 2002, although he remained barred from contesting the presidency, as a result of his having held Burkinabè citizenship. None the less, renewed inter-ethnic unrest erupted prior to local elections in mid-July, particularly in Daloa, where clashes broke out between supporters of the RDR and the FPI. At the elections, the FPI and the PDCI—RDA secured the largest number of seats, although the RDR, with approximately 27% of votes cast, won the greatest share of votes cast. In early August the Secretary-General of the UDPCI, Balla Kéita, was assassinated in Burkina Faso.

A further attempt at reconciliation was evident in the appointment of four RDR ministers to a reshuffled Government of National Unity, under N'Guessan's premiership, in early August 2002. However, discontent at the membership of the Government became evident almost immediately; in particular, opposition parties expressed their dissatisfaction at the overruling of their preferred candidates for ministerial appointments by Gbagbo. Consequently, the UDPCI withdrew its support from the Government, although its sole minister remained in his post, in an independent capacity; similar disputes also arose within the PIT and the PDCI—RDA, while Gueï became an increasingly vocal critic of the Government. Moreover, the PDCI—RDA alleged that Gbagbo had sought to portray the party as representing factional interests by overruling its nomination of seven ministerial candidates from various ethnic groups in favour of a list including six members of the Akan ethnic group, to which Bedié belonged.

In the early hours of 19 September 2002, while Gbagbo was on a state visit to Italy, an apparently meticulously planned armed rebellion broke out, almost simultaneously, in Bouaké, Korhogo and Abidjan. The unrest in Abidjan culminated in an attack on a military barracks and the assassination of Emile Boga Doudou, the Minister of State, Minister of the Interior and Decentralization and a close ally of Gbagbo. Gueï was also killed, in unexplained circumstances, in Abidjan. Although some 300 people were killed in the city, government troops rapidly regained control of Abidjan. However, two ministers were held hostage for several days in the north, which remained under rebel control. The exact motivation and identity of the rebels was initially obscure; some reports suggested that the rebellion was led by groups of soldiers, recruited by Gueï in 2000, who were protesting against their imminent demobilization, while a presidential aide claimed Gueï had led the rebellion, although other sources indicated that opponents of Gueï within the army were responsible for the uprising. Gbagbo, following his return to Côte d'Ivoire on 20 September, implied that an unnamed foreign country (widely understood to refer to Burkina Faso) was implicated in the insurgency, which he described as an attempted *coup d'état*. Amid renewed inter-ethnic tension and an upsurge in violence directed against northern Muslims and citizens of neighbouring states, and following an attack on his residence in Abidjan, Ouattara sought refuge in the German embassy, before taking up residence in the French embassy.

Continuing unrest in the north, centred on Bouaké, prompted widespread concern across West Africa. In late September 2002 an emergency summit of the Economic Community of West African States (ECOWAS, see p. 187), which was convened in Accra, Ghana, resolved to dispatch a peace-keeping force to act as a 'buffer' between government and rebel troops, and mandated the Presidents of Ghana, Guinea-Bissau, Niger, Nigeria and Togo, in addition to the South African President, Thabo Mbeki, in his capacity as the Chairman of the AU, to form a 'contact group' to undertake negotiations between Gbagbo and the insurgents. In early October Master-Sgt Tou Fozié, who had been sentenced to 20 years' imprisonment *in absentia* earlier in the year for his purported role in the January 2001 attempted coup, emerged as a spokesman for the rebels, who identified themselves as the Mouvement patriotique de la Côte d'Ivoire (MPCI) and stated as their principal demand the removal of Gbagbo from the presidency and the holding of fresh presidential and legislative elections; the MPCI emphasized that, although elements within the group had returned to Côte d'Ivoire from exile in various countries, it had no connection with any government. Negotiations between the MPCI and ECOWAS mediators took place in early October. Meanwhile, Gbagbo announced that the Government was prepared to enter into a cease-fire with the rebels, subject to their disarmament and the nation-wide restoration of government authority. How-

ever, the signature of the proposed cease-fire accord by the Government, initially scheduled for 5 October, was delayed on two occasions, and subsequently cancelled, precipitating the departure of the ECOWAS 'contact group' from Côte d'Ivoire. Meanwhile, government forces unsuccessfully attempted to recapture Bouaké.

In mid-October 2002 Gbagbo appointed Moïse Lida Kouassi, hitherto Minister of State, Minister of Defence and Civil Protection, as Minister without Portfolio, Adviser to the Head of State, effectively assuming personal responsibility for defence (although a Minister-delegate at the Presidency, responsible for Defence and Civil Protection, Bertin Kadet, was appointed). On the following day the MPCI gained control of Daloa, although, following several days of clashes, in which at least 17 people were killed, government forces recaptured the city.

On 17 October 2002 Fozié signed a cease-fire agreement on behalf of the MPCI, to take effect from the following day; Gbagbo, speaking in a 'live' television broadcast, announced his acceptance of the accord. In late October, outside their base in Abidjan, French soldiers used tear gas to disperse pro-Government demonstrators, who were demanding the expulsion of Ouattara from the French embassy; both this demand, and calls for the rejection of government compromise with rebel groups, were increasingly expressed by the Coordination des jeunes patriotes, a mass youth movement led by Charles Blé Goudé, a former leader of the FESCI and an ally of Gbagbo. At the end of October the Government and the MPCI entered into further negotiations in Lomé, Togo, under the aegis of ECOWAS; the government delegation, led by Laurent Dona Fologo, the President of the Economic and Social Council, comprised representatives of the PFI, the PDCI—RDA, the UDPCI and the PIT, while the rebel delegation was headed by the Secretary-General of the recently formed political wing of the MPCI, Guillaume Soro Kigbafori, also a former leader of the FESCI.

At the beginning of November 2002 the Government announced an amnesty for the rebels and its acceptance of the eventual reintegration of rebels into the armed forces. However, two apparently politically motivated assassinations inhibited further efforts to resolve the crisis: in early November, following the decision of a co-founder of the FPI, Louis Dakoury-Tabley, to join the MPCI and the rebels' negotiating team, his brother was assassinated; earlier in the week Emile Téhé, the leader of the Mouvement populaire ivoirien, had been killed in Abidjan, following his arrest by gendarmes. Later in the month, responding to MPCI demands for constitutional change, Gbagbo announced that he was prepared to call a referendum, to be held in 2003 or early 2004, on the need for constitutional amendments. On 25 November the Minister of Transport, Marcel Amon Tanoh, of the RDR, resigned from the Government, in protest at alleged human rights abuses in which the Government was implicated (including the purported existence of 'death squads', comprising elements close to the Government and the gendarmerie, whose existence appeared to be subsequently confirmed in a report by the international human rights organization Amnesty International). On the following day the remaining three RDR representatives also withdrew from the Government. At the end of the month, following mediation by France, Ouattara left Côte d'Ivoire and sought refuge in Gabon.

In late October 2002 national security deteriorated further, with the emergence of two new rebel groups, apparently unconnected to the MPCI, in western regions. The Mouvement populaire ivoirien du grand ouest (MPIGO) and the Mouvement pour la justice et la paix (MJP) both announced their intention of taking vengeance for the death of Gueï, and by the end of the month had gained control of the cities of Man and Danane, near the border with Liberia. It was reported that the western rebel groups included mercenaries from Liberia. At the end of October clashes between French troops and MJP fighters were reported near Man, the first offensive action taken by French troops during the conflict. In early December Ivorian government forces attacked Danane and Man; in the ensuing clashes more than 150 people were killed. In early December the MPCI demanded an international inquiry following the discovery of a mass grave, containing some 120 corpses, at Monoko-Zohi, in central Côte d'Ivoire, where the rebels had recently taken control; the authorities subsequently ordered an international inquiry. Meanwhile, Kadet ordered a general mobilization of young men, with the intention of recruiting an additional 3,000 troops. On 9 December the MPCI acknowledged the existence of a further communal grave, containing the corpses of some 86 people, reportedly pro-Government soldiers and gendarmes, near Bouaké. In mid-December the French Minister of Defence, Michèle Alliot-Marie, announced that French troops in Côte d'Ivoire were henceforth to be permitted to use force to enforce the cease-fire; earlier in the month it was announced that France was to increase its contingent of troops in the country to number some 2,500, while the deployment of the ECOWAS peace-keeping force remained in abeyance. In mid-December two senior members of the UDPCI were kidnapped, reportedly by gendarmes, in Abidjan, and shot dead; their corpses were discovered several days later.

In early January 2003 the use of gunship helicopters by government troops to bombard rebel-controlled villages, resulting in the deaths of 24 civilians, provoked controversy. Meanwhile, MPIGO rebels, launching cross-border raids from eastern Liberia, gained control of territory at Mela, about 200 km north of the strategic port of San-Pédro. During January French-led diplomatic efforts to broker and maintain an enduring cease-fire, intensified; following a visit to Côte d'Ivoire by the French Minister of Foreign Affairs, Dominique Galouzeau de Villepin, it was announced that a summit was to be convened in Marcoussis, near Paris, France. None the less, clashes in the west continued, prompting the MPCI to threaten to withdraw from negotiations because of the involvement of French troops in skirmishes with the MPIGO and the MPJ. None the less, on 13 January a peace treaty was signed in Lomé by the leaders of the MPIGO and the MPJ, and by Fologo on behalf of the Government, although sporadic fighting continued to be reported in western regions.

Representatives of the Ivorian Government, seven political parties and the three rebel groups attended the Marcoussis summit, which commenced on 15 January 2003. On 18 January the first contingent of ECOMICI, as the ECOWAS peace-keeping force was known, comprising 179 Senegalese troops, arrived in Côte d'Ivoire. Although unrest continued, on 24 January unanimous agreement on a peace plan was reached by all parties involved in the negotiations. In accordance with this plan, Gbagbo was to remain as President, but was to share power with a new Prime Minister, appointed by consensus, as the head of a government of national reconciliation, prior to a presidential election, which the premier was to be forbidden to contest. Moreover, rebel groups and opposition parties were to receive government posts, while candidates for public office were to be required to have only one Ivorian parent, rather than two, as had hitherto been the case. An amnesty was to be granted for those charged with 'anti-state' crimes, although this was not to extend to those suspected of human rights abuses. On 25 January it was announced that Diarra was to be the Prime Minister in the government of national reconciliation.

The terms of the Marcoussis Accords, although welcomed internationally, provoked widespread protests in areas of Côte d'Ivoire under government control. Blé Goudé became a leading spokesman for those opposed to the sharing of power with rebel groups, and numerous attacks on French interests in Abidjan, including the embassy, occurred. Several members of the incumbent administration also expressed their opposition to the agreement; the assertion by the MPCI (which was not, however, contained in the text of the accords) that it was to gain control of the ministries responsible for defence and security was a particular source of grievance for parties with representatives in the Assemblée nationale and for the military. Further delays in the formation of the proposed government of national reconciliation resulted from the deteriorating security situation; in particular, Diarra refused to return to Côte d'Ivoire from Senegal until his safety could be assured. At the end of January 2003 eight people were killed in inter-ethnic clashes in Agboville, north of Abidjan. Meanwhile, the rebel groups expressed dissatisfaction at the delays in implementing the Accords, threatening a return to armed conflict if the formation of a new government were not expedited.

On 10 February 2003 Diarra was officially appointed as the new Prime Minister; he subsequently met representatives of the rebel groups in Accra and attended the Franco-African Summit in Paris. However, the formation of a new government continued to be delayed by the inability of all parties concerned to agree on acceptable candidates for the defence and interior portfolios, while intermittent clashes in the west, particularly near Toulepleu, were reported throughout February. Following an attack on Toulepleu in early March by a government helicopter gunship, in which some 20 civilians were reportedly killed, the leader of the MPIGO, Félix Doh, announced that the group was

to end its cease-fire, although this decision was subsequently rescinded.

On 8 March 2003 an ECOWAS summit in Accra resulted in an agreement on the allocation of ministerial portfolios; the FPI was to be given 10 posts, the PDCI—RDA eight, the RDR and the MPCI seven each, and the MJP and the MPIGO one each, while four smaller parties were to receive a total of six posts. The defence and security portfolios were to be excluded from these arrangements, with the agreement of the MPCI. Instead, a 15-member Conseil de la sécurité nationale (CSN), comprising the President, the Prime Minister, the Chief of Staff of the Armed Forces, the leaders of the gendarmerie and the police force, and representatives of the political parties and groups in the Government of National Reconciliation, was to be established to monitor the operations of these ministries, and to approve Diarra's nominees to these posts.

Further difficulties were encountered prior to the inaugural session of the Council of Ministers on 13 March 2003. The RDR announced that insecurity in Côte d'Ivoire continued to prevent its ministerial candidates from returning to the country from abroad. The MPCI, the MPIGO and the MJP also announced that that they would not attend the meeting, citing logistical difficulties. Following the session, the appointment of eight ministers of state and 15 ministers, from among those parties that attended, was announced. Prior to a further meeting of the Council of Ministers on 20 March, the appointees to 15 of the 18 unfilled posts were announced; however, representatives of the MPCI, the MPIGO and the MJP again failed to attend the meeting in Abidjan, expressing concern for their security in the south, and a delegation of the groups met the Prime Minister in Yamoussoukro to express their concerns regarding security and the functioning of the CSN. In late March Gbagbo issued a decree confirming a CSN decision that two existing ministers were to assume responsibility for the security and defence ministries, on an interim basis: the Minister of Water and Forestry, Adou Assou, of the FPI, was to serve additionally as Minister of Defence, while the Minister of Higher Education, Zémogo Fofana, of the RDR, was to serve as Minister of Security. Meanwhile, the position of Minister of Women, the Family and Children remained vacant, following Gbagbo's rejection of the RDR's appointee to that post. The appointment of Assou and Fofana to their additional roles was denounced by the MPCI, which denied that its representative on the CSN had consented to the measures.

At the end of April 2003 Doh was captured and killed, reportedly by pro-Government Liberian mercenary fighters operating in the west of Côte d'Ivoire. In early May the Chief of Staff of the Armed Forces, Gen. Mathias Doué, and the military leader of the MPCI, Col Michel Gueu, signed a cease-fire agreement, providing for the disarmament of rebels, which was intended to apply to all rebel groups operating within the country.

Relations with France, the country's principal trading partner and provider of bilateral assistance, have been close since independence. French reaction to Gbagbo's election as President in October 2000 was divided, largely along party lines. President Jacques Chirac and one of the minor parties in the governing coalition, Les Verts, demanded that the election be rerun, incorporating those candidates who had been excluded from participating. The leading party in the Government, the Parti socialiste, while critical of these exclusions, generally welcomed the accession to power of Gbagbo and the FPI. Following meetings between Gbagbo and Chirac in January 2001, France announced that full co-operation with Côte d'Ivoire, which had been suspended following the December 1999 *coup d'état*, would be restored. From late 2002 France dispatched additional troops to Côte d'Ivoire, to supplement the 550 already stationed in the country, and the French Government played an active role in the diplomatic efforts that led to the signature of the Marcoussis Accords in late January 2003 (see above). However, France appeared concerned to be regarded as a neutral force in the conflict between the Gbagbo Government and rebel groups. Notably, France stated that it regarded the civil conflict as an internal Ivorian matter, disregarding Gbagbo's statements relating to the alleged involvement of external forces in the rebellion; such involvement would have resulted in the invocation of a clause in a defence treaty between the two countries, necessitating the active military support of France for the Ivorian authorities. None the less, there was widespread anti-French feeling, particularly in Abidjan, following the conclusion of the Marcoussis Accords, and several thousand French citizens resident in Côte d'Ivoire reportedly left the country.

The emphasis on '*ivoirité*', or national identity, in the domestic policies of Bédié, Gueï and Gbagbo, has strained Côte d'Ivoire's relations with other West African states, particularly Burkina Faso; Burkinabè migrants in Côte d'Ivoire increasingly suffered from discrimination and became the victims of inter-ethnic violence, causing several thousand to flee the country in early 2001. As the process of national reconciliation advanced, tensions eased somewhat, and Gbagbo made his first visit as President to Burkina in December. However, following the onset of widespread civil unrest in Côte d'Ivoire in late 2002, thousands of citizens of Burkina and Mali left the country. Relations with Liberia were also strained from late 2002, as a result of the involvement, acknowledged by President Charles Taylor in January 2003, of Liberian mercenaries in civil unrest in western Côte d'Ivoire, both in alliance with the MPIGO and the MPG, and with Ivorian pro-Government troops. Tensions were further heightened by cross-border attacks from Côte d'Ivoire into the Liberian county of Grand Gedeh, in March, which the Liberian Minister of Defence, Daniel Chea, described as 'tantamount to a declaration of war'.

Government

Under the terms of the Constitution of July 2000, executive power is vested in the President, as Head of State, who is appointed by direct universal suffrage for a term of five years, renewable only once. The President appoints a Prime Minister, and on the latter's recommendation, a Council of Ministers. Legislative power is held by the Assemblée nationale, which is elected for a term of five years. The country is divided into 19 regions, and further sub-divided into 57 departments and 197 communes, each with its own elected council.

Defence

In August 2002 Côte d'Ivoire's active armed forces comprised an army of 6,500 men, a navy of about 900, an air force of 700, a presidential guard of 1,350 and a gendarmerie of 7,600. There was also a 1,500-strong militia. Reserve forces numbered 10,000 men. Military service is by selective conscription and lasts for 18 months. France supplies equipment and training, and increased its military presence in Côte d'Ivoire from 550 to some 2,500 in late 2002, in order to monitor and enforce the cease-fire signed in October of that year between the Ivorian Government and rebels of the Mouvement patriotique de Côte d'Ivoire; a further 500 French troops were dispatched in January 2003. The deployment by the Economic Community of West African States of a peace-keeping force (ECOMICI), eventually to number 3,200 troops commenced in Côte d'Ivoire from mid-January 2003. The defence budget for 2002 was an estimated 65,000m. francs CFA, prior to the armed rebellion that commenced in September of that year.

Economic Affairs

In 2001, according to estimates by the World Bank, Côte d'Ivoire's gross national income (GNI), measured at average 1999–2001 prices, was US $10,258m., equivalent to $630 per head (or $1,470 on an international purchasing-power parity basis). During 1990–2001, it was estimated, the population increased at an average annual rate of 3.0% per year, while gross domestic product (GDP) per head declined, in real terms, by an average of 0.8% per year. Overall GDP increased, in real terms, at an average annual rate of 2.2% per year in 1990–2001; real GDP declined by 2.3% in 2000 and by 0.9% in 2001.

Agriculture (including forestry and fishing) contributed 30.0% of GDP in 2001, and employed about 48.1% of the labour force in that year. Côte d'Ivoire is the world's foremost producer of cocoa, and exports of cocoa and related products contributed 28.1% of total export earnings in 2000. Côte d'Ivoire is also among the world's largest producers and exporters of coffee. Other major cash crops include cotton, rubber, bananas and pineapples. The principal subsistence crops are maize, yams, cassava, plantains and, increasingly, rice (although large quantities of the last are still imported). Excessive exploitation of the country's forest resources has led to a decline in the importance of this sector, although measures have now been instigated to preserve remaining forests. Abidjan is among sub-Saharan Africa's principal fishing ports; however, the participation of Ivorian fishing fleets is minimal. During 1990–2001 agricultural GDP increased at an average annual rate of 2.9% per year. Agricultural GDP increased by 12.9% in 2000, but declined by 1.6% in 2001.

Industry (including mining, manufacturing, construction and power) contributed an estimated 22.2% of GDP in 2001.

According to UN estimates, 11.5% of the labour force were employed in the sector in 1994. During 1990–2001 industrial GDP increased at an average annual rate of 2.6%. Industrial GDP declined by 9.5% in 2000 and by 2.4% in 2001.

Mining contributed only 0.3% of GDP in 2001. The sector's contribution was, however, expected to increase considerably following the commencement, in the mid-1990s, of commercial exploitation of important offshore reserves of petroleum and natural gas. Gold and diamonds are also mined, although illicit production of the latter has greatly exceeded commercial output. There is believed to be significant potential for the development of nickel deposits, and there are also notable reserves of manganese, iron ore and bauxite.

The manufacturing sector, which contributed 15.5% of GDP in 2001, is dominated by agro-industrial activities (such as the processing of cocoa, coffee, cotton, palm kernels, pineapples and fish). Crude petroleum is refined at Abidjan, while the tobacco industry uses mostly imported tobacco. During 1990–2001 manufacturing GDP increased by an average of 1.8% per year. The GDP of the sector declined by 7.2% in 2000 and by 2.7% in 2001.

Some 65.6% of Côte d'Ivoire's electricity generation in 1999 was derived from thermal sources, while 24.1% was derived from hydroelectric installations, and 10.3% from petroleum. Since 1995 the country has exploited indigenous reserves of natural gas, with the intention of becoming not only self-sufficient in energy, but also a regional exporter; the first stage of a major gas-powered turbine and power station in Abidjan commenced operations in 1999. Imports of fuel products accounted for some 33.8% of the value of total merchandise imports in 2000.

An important aim of economic policy in the late 1990s was the expansion of the services sector, which contributed 47.8% of GDP in 2001, and (according to UN estimates) employed 37.4% of the labour force in 1994. The transformation of Abidjan's stock market into a regional exchange for the member states of the Union économique et monétaire ouest-africaine (UEMOA, see p. 238) was expected to enhance the city's status as a centre for financial services. Abidjan's status as a major centre of regional communications and trade has been threatened by political unrest since the 1999 *coup d'état*, particularly since the commencement of the rebel uprising in September 2002. The GDP of the services sector increased by an average of 1.6% per year in 1990–2001. The GDP of the sector declined by 8.7% in 2000, but increased by 0.4% in 2000.

In 2001 Côte d'Ivoire recorded a visible trade surplus of US $1,539.6m., although there was a deficit of $57.7m. on the current account of the balance of payments. In 2000 the principal source of imports was Nigeria (which supplied 26.6% of total imports); France (20.3%) was also a notable supplier. France was the principal market for exports in 2000 (taking 14.9% of total exports), followed by the Netherlands, the USA and Mali. The principal exports in 2000 were cocoa and related products, petroleum and related products, coffee and coffee substitutes, and cork and wood. The principal imports in the same year were petroleum products, machinery and transport equipment, food and live animals (notably cereals and cereal preparations, and frozen fish), chemicals and related products, and basic manufactures.

Côte d'Ivoire's overall budget surplus in 2001 was estimated at 68,400m. francs CFA (equivalent to 1.0% of GDP). The country's total external debt was US $10,546m. at the end of 2000, of which $10,546m. was long-term public debt. In that year the cost of debt-servicing was equivalent to 22.4% of the value of exports of goods and services. The annual rate of inflation averaged 2.7% in 1990–93. Consumer prices increased by an average of 26.1% in 1994 (following the devaluation of the currency at the beginning of the year); the inflation rate slowed to an annual average of 14.3% in 1995, and averaged 3.2% in 1996–2001. Consumer prices increased by 4.3% in 2001. Some 114,880 persons were registered as unemployed at the end of 1992.

Côte d'Ivoire is a member of numerous regional and international organizations, including the Economic Community of West African States (ECOWAS, see p. 187), the West African organs of the Franc Zone (see p. 238), the African Petroleum Producers' Association (APPA, see p. 335), the International Cocoa Organization (ICCO, see p. 336), the International Coffee Organization (see p. 336) and the Conseil de l'Entente (see p. 339). The African Development Bank (see p. 128) has its headquarters in Abidjan; however, in February 2002 contingency measures for a 'temporary' relocation to Tunisia were announced, as a result of heightened instability in Côte d'Ivoire.

In 1995–99 Côte d'Ivoire enjoyed annual GDP growth in excess of the rate of population increase. However, in the late 1990s and early 2000s the country's economy was adversely affected by international economic and domestic political developments, including, notably, a sharp fall in international prices for cocoa. Furthermore, the failure to comply with targets set under an Enhanced Structural Adjustment Facility (ESAF) led to the suspension of IMF funding in late 1998, while revelations of the misappropriation of aid caused the European Union (EU) to suspend assistance. By the time of the *coup d'état* of December 1999 Côte d'Ivoire's financial situation was precarious; foreign budgetary assistance received in that year had totalled about 10% of the level originally forecast, and a further economic deterioration occurred under Gueï. In October 2000 the World Bank suspended assistance to Côte d'Ivoire, following a failure to repay debt totalling US $39.8m, and continuing political instability resulted in a decline in GDP in 2000. However, in September the IMF restored co-operation with Côte d'Ivoire. The World Bank resumed full co-operation in February 2002, after all outstanding debt had been paid, as did the EU. An expected return to economic growth was largely inhibited by the consequences of the rebellion of September 2002 and the loss of government control over northern cotton-growing regions, although cocoa-growing regions remained largely under government control. While world cocoa prices increased sharply in late 2002, the international trade of the country was severely disrupted. Abidjan's status as an *entrepôt* for trade with land-locked neighbouring countries was challenged by the effects of the uprising, and much trade was lost to Accra, Ghana, Cotonou, Benin, and Lomé, Togo, as communication links with Burkina Faso and Mali were impeded. An improvement in the economic position of Côte d'Ivoire remained largely dependent on the restoration of political order, as well as the resolution of tensions between different ethnic groups resident in the country, while further assistance from the IMF would be conditional on the effective implementation of structural reforms.

Education

Education at all levels is available free of charge. Primary education, which is officially compulsory for six years between the ages of seven and 13 years, begins at six years of age and lasts for six years. Total enrolment at primary schools in 1999/2000 included 58.4% of children in the relevant age-group (males 66.5%; females 50.2%), according to UNESCO estimates. The Ivorian Government's long-term objective is to provide primary education for all children by 2010. Secondary education, from the age of 12, lasts for up to seven years, comprising a first cycle of four years and a second cycle of three years. In 1998/99, according to UNESCO estimates, total enrolment at secondary schools was equivalent to 21.7% of children in the relevant age-group (males 28.3%; females 15.1%). The Université de Cocody (formerly the Université Nationale de Côte d'Ivoire) has six faculties, and there are two other universities, at Abodo-Adjamé (also in Abidjan) and at Bouaké. Some 47,187 students were enrolled at university-level institutions in 1997/98. Expenditure on education in 1999 was estimated at 303,700m. francs CFA, equivalent to 25.3% of total government expenditure (excluding spending on the public debt).

Public Holidays

2003: 1 January (New Year's Day), 12 February* (Id al-Adha, Feast of the Sacrifice), 18 April (Good Friday), 21 April (Easter Monday), 1 May (Labour Day), 29 May (Ascension Day), 9 June (Whit Monday), 7 August (National Day), 15 August (Assumption), 1 November (All Saints' Day), 26 November* (Id al-Fitr, end of Ramadan), 7 December (Félix Houphouët-Boigny Remembrance Day), 25 December (Christmas).

2004: 1 January (New Year's Day), 2 February* (Id al-Adha, Feast of the Sacrifice), 9 April (Good Friday), 12 April (Easter Monday), 1 May (Labour Day), 20 May (Ascension Day), 31 May (Whit Monday), 7 August (National Day), 15 August (Assumption), 1 November (All Saints' Day), 14 November* (Id al-Fitr, end of Ramadan), 7 December (Félix Houphouët-Boigny Remembrance Day), 25 December (Christmas).

* These holidays are dependent on the Islamic lunar calendar and may vary by one or two days from the dates given.

Weights and Measures

The metric system is in force.

Statistical Survey

Source (unless otherwise stated): Institut National de la Statistique, BP V55, Abidjan; tel. 20-21-05-38; fax 20-21-44-01.

Area and Population

AREA, POPULATION AND DENSITY

Area (sq km)	322,462*
Population (census results)	
1 March 1988.	10,815,694
20 December 1998	
Males	7,844,623
Females.	7,522,049
Total	15,366,672
Population (official estimate at mid-year)	
2000	16,398,000
Density (per sq km) at mid-2000	50.9

* 124,503 sq miles.

ETHNIC GROUPS

1998 census (percentages, residents born in Côte d'Ivoire): Akan 42*; Voltaïque 18†; Mandé du nord 17‡; Krou 11; Mandé du sud 10§; Naturalized Ivorians 1; Others 1.

* Comprising the Baoulé, Agni, Abrou, Ebrié, Abouré, Adioukrou and Appollonien groupings.
† Comprising the Sénoufo, Lobi, Koulango groupings.
‡ Comprising the Malinké and Dioula groupings.
§ Comprising the Yacouba and Gouro groupings.

NATIONALITY OF POPULATION

(numbers resident in Côte d'Ivoire at 1998 census)

Country of citizenship	Population	%
Côte d'Ivoire	11,366,625	73.97
Burkina Faso.	2,238,548	14.57
Mali	792,258	5.16
Guinea	230,387	1.50
Ghana	133,221	0.87
Liberia	78,258	0.51
Other	527,375	3.43
Total	15,366,672	100.00

POPULATION BY REGION
(1998 census)

Region	Population
Centre	1,001,264
Centre-Est	394,758
Centre-Nord	1,189,424
Centre-Ouest	2,169,826
Nord	929,686
Nord-Est	696,292
Nord-Ouest	740,175
Ouest	1,445,279
Sud	5,399,220
Sud-Ouest	1,400,748
Total	15,366,672

Note: In January 1997 the Government adopted legislation whereby Côte d'Ivoire's regions were to be reorganized. Further minor reorganizations were effected in April and July 2000. The new regions (with their regional capitals) are: Agnéby (Agboville), Bas-Sassandra (San-Pédro), Bafing (Touba), Denguélé (Odienné), 18 Montagnes (Man), Fromager (Gagnoa), Haut-Sassandra (Daloa), Lacs (Yamoussoukro), Lagunes (Abidjan), Marahoué (Bouaflé), Moyen-Cavally (Guiglo), Moyen-Comoé (Abengourou), N'zi-Comoé (Dimbokro), Savanes (Korhogo), Sud-Bandama (Divo), Sud-Comoé (Aboisso), Vallée du Bandama (Bouaké), Worodougou (Mankono) and Zanzan (Bondoukou).

PRINCIPAL TOWNS
(population at 1998 census)

Abidjan*	2,877,948	Korhogo	142,093
Bouaké	461,618	San-Pédro	131,800
Yamoussoukro*	299,243	Man	116,657
Daloa	173,107	Gagnoa	107,124

* The process of transferring the official capital from Abidjan to Yamoussoukro began in 1983.

BIRTHS AND DEATHS
(UN estimates, annual averages)

	1985–90	1990–95	1995–2000
Birth rate (per 1,000)	45.8	38.4	36.0
Death rate (per 1,000)	14.7	14.6	15.4

Source: UN, *World Population Prospects: The 2000 Revision*.

Expectation of life (WHO estimates, years at birth): 45.9 (males 45.0; females 47.0) in 2001 (Source: WHO, *World Health Report*).

ECONOMICALLY ACTIVE POPULATION*
(persons aged 6 years and over, 1988 census)

	Males	Females	Total
Agriculture, hunting, forestry and fishing	1,791,101	836,574	2,627,675
Mining and quarrying	} 78,768	6,283	85,051
Manufacturing			
Electricity, gas and water	13,573	1,092	14,665
Construction	82,203	2,313	84,516
Trade, restaurants and hotels	227,873	302,486	530,359
Transport, storage and communications	114,396	3,120	117,516
Other services	434,782	156,444	591,226
Activities not adequately defined	998	297	1,295
Total labour force	2,743,694	1,308,609	4,052,303

* Figures exclude persons seeking work for the first time, totalling 210,450 (males 142,688; females 67,762).

Source: UN, *Demographic Yearbook*.

Mid-2001 (estimates in '000): Agriculture, etc. 3,215; Total labour force 6,689 (Source: FAO).

Health and Welfare

KEY INDICATORS

Total fertility rate (children per woman, 2001)	4.8
Under-5 mortality rate (per 1,000 live births, 2001)	175
HIV/AIDS (% of persons aged 15–49, 2001)	9.65
Physicians (per 1,000 head, 1996)	0.09
Hospital beds (per 1,000 head, 1990)	0.8
Health expenditure (2000): US $ per head (PPP)	45
Health expenditure (2000): % of GDP	2.7
Health expenditure (2000): public (% of total)	36.9
Access to water (% of persons, 2000)	77
Human Development Index (2000): ranking	156
Human Development Index (2000): value	0.428

For sources and definitions, see explanatory note on p. vi.

Agriculture

PRINCIPAL CROPS
('000 metric tons)

	1999	2000	2001
Rice (paddy)	1,208.0	1,231.0	1,212.0
Maize	814.7	692.7	573.0
Millet	65*	70*	70†
Sorghum	24.7*	30.0*	30.0†
Sweet potatoes	42.1	43.0†	43.0†
Cassava (Manioc)	1,681.0	1,691.0	1,688.0
Taro (Coco yam)	364.6	370.0	369.0
Yams	2,944.0	2,950.0	2,938.0
Sugar cane†	1,250	1,300	1,300
Cashew nuts	40.8	78.0	78.0†
Kolanuts†	75	75	75
Groundnuts (in shell)	144.0	144.0	145.0
Coconuts	230.0	230.0†	230.0†
Oil palm fruit	1,242.0	1,771.0	1,400.0†
Karité nuts (Sheanuts)	35.8	36.0†	36.0†
Cotton seed	191.2	220.0†	162.0*
Tomatoes	130.0	159.0	159.0†
Aubergines (Eggplants)†	40	40	40
Chillies and green peppers†	21.3	21.3	21.3
Green corn (Maize)†	240	240	240
Other vegetables†	103	103	103
Bananas	252.0	279.6	250.0†
Plantains	1,402.0	1,418.0	1,410.0
Oranges†	29.4	29.4	29.4
Other citrus fruit†	29.7	29.7	29.7
Pineapples	257.0	225.7	225.7†
Other fruit†	27.6	29.1	29.1
Cotton (lint)	177.3	177.2	124.5
Coffee (green)	307.3	336.3	260.0*
Cocoa beans	1,306.2	1,396.0	1,200.0*
Natural rubber (dry weight)	118.9	123.4	108.0†

* Unofficial figure.

† FAO estimate(s).

Source: FAO.

LIVESTOCK
('000 head, year ending September)

	1998	1999	2000
Cattle	1,346	1,377	1,409
Pigs	278	327	336
Sheep	1,381	1,416	1,451
Goats	1,709	1,111	1,134
Poultry	22,790	30,810	29,400

Figures for 2001 assumed to be unchanged from 2000.

Source: FAO.

LIVESTOCK PRODUCTS
('000 metric tons)

	1999	2000	2001*
Beef and veal	46.8	48.3	43.7
Mutton and lamb.	5.8†	5.6†	5.6
Goat meat	4.7†	4.6†	4.6
Pig meat	13.0*	13.4†	13.4
Poultry meat*.	62.7	62.7	62.7
Game meat*	13	13	13
Other meat*	15	15	15
Cows' milk	24.2	21.8	21.8
Poultry eggs*	18	18	18
Cattle hides*	5.2	5.2	5.2
Sheepskins*	1.5	1.4	1.4
Goatskins*	1.2	1.2	1.2

* FAO estimate(s).
† Unofficial figure.
Source: FAO.

Forestry

ROUNDWOOD REMOVALS
('000 cubic metres, excluding bark)

	1999	2000	2001
Sawlogs, veneer logs and logs for sleepers .	2,222	2,500	2,615
Other industrial wood* . . .	916	916	916
Fuel wood*	8,569	8,529	8,552
Total	11,707	11,945	12,083

* FAO estimates.
Source: FAO.

SAWNWOOD PRODUCTION
('000 cubic metres, including railway sleepers)

	1999	2000	2001
Total (all broadleaved) . . .	611	603	630

Source: FAO.

Fishing

('000 metric tons, live weight)

	1998	1999	2000
Capture	72.5	78.3	80.3
Freshwater fishes* . . .	12.3	10.6	10.5
Bigeye grunt	1.6	4.0	5.2
Sardinellas	11.4	12.4	19.8
Bonga shad*	11.0	11.0	11.0
Frigate and bullet tunas . .	4.4	5.8	6.8
Little tunny (Atlantic black skipjack)	1.9	2.4	2.8
Skipjack tuna	1.7	2.2	2.5
Chub mackerel. . . .	1.3	2.5	0.3
Aquaculture	0.9	1.0	1.2
Total catch	73.4	79.3	81.5

* FAO estimates.
Source: FAO, *Yearbook of Fishery Statistics*.

Mining

	1999	2000	2001
Gold (kg)	2,967	3,444	3,672
Crude petroleum ('000 barrels). .	3,547	2,578	2,099

Source: Banque centrale des états de l'Afrique de l'ouest.

Diamonds ('000 carats): 117.3 in 1992; 98.4 in 1993; 84.3 in 1994.

Industry

SELECTED PRODUCTS
('000 metric tons, unless otherwise indicated)

	1996	1997	1998
Beer of barley*†	165	175	240
Salted, dried or smoked fish* . .	15.0	15.0	n.a.
Canned fish*	61.0	51.1	n.a.
Palm oil—unrefined*	297.0	248.9	268.6
Raw sugar*	120.9	120.3	108.1
Cocoa powder‡	1,053.7	992.9	895.4
Cocoa butter‡	26.6	29.0	30.3
Plywood ('000 cubic metres) . .	43	61	67
Jet fuel†	62	63	63
Motor gasoline (petrol)† . . .	432	434	437
Kerosene†	491	493	495
Gas-diesel (Distillate fuel) oils . .	696	706	708†
Residual fuel oils†	479	482	484
Cement‡§	1,000	1,100	650
Electric energy (million kWh) . .	3,221.5	3,975.5	3,987.9

1999: Beer of barley ('000 metric tons) 240*†; Palm oil—unrefined ('000 metric tons) 264.3*; Raw sugar ('000 metric tons) 151.3*; Cocoa powder ('000 metric tons) 1,132.2‡; Cocoa butter ('000 metric tons) 38.5‡; Plywood ('000 cubic metres) 59; Cement ('000 metric tons) 650†‡; Electric energy (million kWh) 4,785.2.

2000: Beer of barley ('000 metric tons) 240*†; Palm oil—unrefined ('000 metric tons) 278.0*; Raw sugar ('000 metric tons) 179.0*(unofficial figure).

2001: Beer of barley ('000 metric tons) 240*†; Palm oil—unrefined ('000 metric tons) 240.9*; Raw sugar ('000 metric tons) 177.0* (unofficial figure).

Cotton yarn (pure and mixed, '000 metric tons): 24.7 †in 1989.
* Data from FAO.
† Provisional or estimated figure(s).
‡ Data refer to exports.
§ Data from the US Geological Survey.
Source: mainly UN, *Industrial Commodity Statistics Yearbook*.

Finance

CURRENCY AND EXCHANGE RATES

Monetary Units
100 centimes = 1 franc de la Communauté financière africaine (CFA)

Sterling, Dollar and Euro Equivalents (31 December 2002)
£1 sterling = 1,008.17 francs CFA
US $1 = 625.50 francs CFA
€1 = 655.96 francs CFA
10,000 francs CFA = £9.992 = $15.987 = €15.245

Average Exchange Rate (francs CFA per US $)
2000   711.98
2001   733.04
2002   696.99

Note: An exchange rate of 1 French franc = 50 francs CFA, established in 1948, remained in force until January 1994, when the CFA franc was devalued by 50%, with the exchange rate adjusted to 1 French franc = 100 francs CFA. This relationship to French currency remained in effect with the introduction of the euro on 1 January 1999. From that date, accordingly, a fixed exchange rate of €1 = 655.957 francs CFA has been in operation.

BUDGET
('000 million francs CFA)

Revenue*	1999	2000	2001
Tax revenue	1,149.1	1,077.5	1,167.1
Direct taxes	322.3	334.4	325.9
Taxes on profits	143.6	143.3	n.a.
Individual income taxes . .	115.8	125.7	n.a.
Employers' contributions . .	27.8	23.6	n.a.
Indirect taxes	826.8	743.1	841.2
Taxes on goods and services .	241.2	254.2	289.1
Taxes on international transactions . . .	585.6	484.8	552.1
Taxes on imports . . .	408.7	321.4	355.6
Non-tax revenue	122.5	159.6	167.9
Social security contributions . .	83.7	102.8	114.2
Total (incl. others) . . .	1,271.6	1,237.1	1,335.0

Expenditure†	1999	2000	2001
Current expenditure.	1,169.1	1,140.8	1,150.2
Wages and salaries	425.3	454.1	484.1
Other operating expenses	445.2	392.4	406.4
Interest due on public debt	298.6	294.3	259.7
Internal	35.6	29.6	24.0
External	263.0	264.7	235.7
Capital expenditure .	352.5	210.4	147.1
Domestically funded	202.8	105.1	87.8
Funded from abroad	149.7	105.3	59.3
Total	1,521.6	1,351.2	1,297.3

* Excluding grants received ('000 million francs CFA): 64.9 in 1999; 33.5 in 2000; 40.3 in 2001.

† Excluding net lending ('000 million francs CFA): 0.0 in 1999; 9.0 in 2000; 9.6 in 2001.

Sources: IMF, *Republic of Côte d'Ivoire: Staff Report for the 2001 Article IV Consultation and Staff-Monitored Program* (September 2001), Banque centrale des états de l'Afrique de l'ouest.

INTERNATIONAL RESERVES
(US $ million at 31 December)

	2000	2001	2002
IMF special drawing rights.	1.3	0.7	1.2
Reserve position in IMF.	0.4	0.4	0.6
Foreign exchange.	666.2	1,017.9	1,861.5
Total	667.9	1,019.0	1,863.3

* Valued at market-related prices.

Source: IMF, *International Financial Statistics.*

MONEY SUPPLY
(million francs CFA at 31 December)

	2000	2001	2002
Currency outside banks .	620,739	774,673	1,146,480
Demand deposits at deposit money banks*	526,695	507,809	571,568
Total money (incl. others).	1,153,990	1,324,810	1,750,480

* Excluding the deposits of public establishments of an administrative or social nature.

Source: IMF, *International Financial Statistics.*

COST OF LIVING
(Consumer Price Index for African households in Abidjan; base: 1996 = 100)

	1998	1999	2000
Food, beverages and tobacco	117.8	112.5	112.5
Clothing and footwear	104.1	109.1	109.4
Housing, water, electricity and gas	101.8	105.9	107.6
All items (incl. others) .	108.9	109.7	112.5

2001: All items 117.3.

NATIONAL ACCOUNTS
('000 million francs CFA at current prices)

Expenditure on the Gross Domestic Product

	1999	2000	2001
Government final consumption expenditure.	910.1	831.1	863.7
Private final consumption expenditure.	4,149.6	4,269.7	4,435.9
Increase in stocks	−194.0	−30.0	65.0
Gross fixed capital formation	1,120.9	823.7	743.9
Total domestic expenditure.	5,986.6	5,894.5	6,108.5
Exports of goods and services	3,120.0	3,053.7	3,003.4
Less Imports of goods and services	2,273.6	2,277.1	2,359.4
GDP in purchasers' values .	6,833.3	6,671.1	6,752.5

Source: Banque centrale des états de l'Afrique de l'ouest.

Gross Domestic Product by Economic Activity

	1999	2000	2001
Agriculture, livestock-rearing, forestry and fishing	1,830.0	1,946.9	1,963.6
Mining and quarrying	19.0	24.8	22.7
Manufacturing	1,176.8	1,017.5	1,017.0
Electricity, gas and water	183.1	189.9	206.6
Construction and public works.	286.8	225.3	209.8
Transport, storage and communications	712.3	756.5	774.7
Trade	1,007.6	972.3	975.2
Non-market services.	536.4	567.3	588.6
Other services	841.0	781.7	796.5
Sub-total .	6,593.0	6,482.2	6,554.7
Import duties and taxes.	240.3	188.9	197.8
GDP in purchasers' values .	6,833.3	6,671.1	6,752.5

Source: Banque centrale des états de l'Afrique de l'ouest.

BALANCE OF PAYMENTS
(US $ million)

	1999	2000	2001
Exports of goods f.o.b.	4,661.4	3,888.1	3,947.4
Imports of goods f.o.b.	−2,766.0	−2,401.8	−2,407.8
Trade balance	1,895.4	1,486.3	1,539.6
Exports of services	586.0	482.5	487.4
Imports of services	−1,459.0	−1,226.9	−1,232.7
Balance on goods and services	1,022.4	741.9	794.4
Other income received	162.6	141.3	141.9
Other income paid	−919.4	−794.7	−719.2
Balance on goods, services and income	265.6	88.5	217.0
Current transfers received .	136.8	79.4	85.0
Current transfers paid .	−522.7	−409.4	−359.7
Current balance	−120.4	−241.6	−57.7
Capital account (net)	13.8	8.4	10.0
Direct investment from abroad.	323.7	234.7	245.7
Portfolio investment assets .	−28.7	−12.6	−12.7
Portfolio investment liabilities .	13.5	4.5	4.8
Financial derivatives liabilities	−3.1	−2.5	−2.6
Other investment assets	−350.5	−182.2	−170.1
Other investment liabilities	−532.1	−404.4	−88.5
Net errors and omissions	−24.0	−10.2	−23.0
Overall balance	−707.8	−605.9	−94.2

Source: IMF, *International Financial Statistics.*

External Trade

PRINCIPAL COMMODITIES
(US $ million)

Imports c.i.f.	1998	1999	2000
Food and live animals	568.2	488.3	377.9
Fish, crustaceans and molluscs, and preparations thereof	190.4	172.8	131.4
Fish, frozen, excluding fillets	188.4	169.4	127.9
Cereals and cereal preparations	233.1	181.7	153.4
Rice	141.8	111.6	97.5
Rice, semi-milled or wholly milled	139.3	107.9	91.2
Rice, semi-milled or milled (unbroken)	108.8	71.1	76.5
Crude materials (inedible) except fuels	96.0	48.9	45.0
Mineral fuels, lubricants, etc.	446.2	536.2	838.0
Petroleum, petroleum products, etc.	445.9	536.0	837.7
Crude petroleum and oils obtained from bituminous materials	331.6	391.8	679.5
Petroleum products, refined	110.8	140.1	154.9
Fuel oils	84.5	120.8	132.9
Chemicals and related products	513.1	444.5	352.1
Medicinal and pharmaceutical products	116.2	113.7	94.8
Medicaments (incl. veterinary medicaments)	107.7	103.8	89.3
Medicaments (incl. veterinary medicaments) containing other substances	89.8	86.5	75.1
Artificial resins and plastic materials, cellulose esters, etc.	125.9	96.4	90.7
Polymerization and copolymerization products	110.9	83.6	79.4
Basic manufactures	470.2	427.5	319.1
Non-metallic mineral manufactures	88.6	87.4	65.6
Iron and steel	107.0	87.0	64.7
Manufactures of metals	82.5	71.0	49.8
Machinery and transport equipment	694.3	740.3	406.6
General industrial machinery, equipment and parts	132.9	117.8	73.5
Electrical machinery, apparatus and parts	102.3	98.8	46.8
Road vehicles	202.1	178.7	104.7
Passenger motor vehicles (excl. buses)	93.5	83.3	52.5
Miscellaneous manufactured articles	124.3	127.1	84.6
Total (incl. others)	2,999.8	2,897.7	2,482.2

Exports f.o.b.	1998	1999	2000
Food and live animals	2,507.7	2,270.7	1,744.3
Fish, crustaceans and molluscs, and preparations thereof	215.9	152.3	128.9
Fish, prepared or preserved	206.5	141.2	120.1
Vegetables and fruit	148.7	224.5	179.5
Fruit and nuts, fresh, dried	142.3	210.3	171.6
Coffee, tea, cocoa, spices and manufactures thereof	2,037.9	1,782.1	1,327.2
Coffee and coffee substitutes	398.7	209.5	303.0
Coffee, green, roasted; coffee substitutes containing coffee	338.6	149.5	257.8
Coffee, not roasted; coffee husks and skins	320.7	141.9	244.1
Cocoa	1,630.9	1,567.1	1,017.9
Cocoa beans, raw, roasted	1,339.4	1,287.7	845.6
Cocoa butter and paste	289.0	275.0	160.7
Cocoa paste, whether or not defatted	174.1	151.9	98.2
Cocoa butter (fat or oil)	114.9	123.0	62.5
Crude materials (inedible) except fuels	496.4	435.6	511.6
Cork and wood	241.2	206.8	271.7
Wood, simply worked, and railway sleepers of wood	229.4	195.4	239.8
Wood, non-coniferous species, planed, tongued, grooved, etc.	227.0	192.7	237.2
Wood, non-coniferous species, sawn lengthwise, sliced or peeled	203.5	171.0	218.0
Cotton	168.1	151.1	148.2
Raw cotton, excl. linters, not carded or combed	167.7	150.9	148.0
Mineral fuels, lubricants, etc.	432.5	544.2	737.5
Petroleum, petroleum products, etc.	429.3	540.9	735.0
Petroleum products, refined	363.4	467.6	644.7
Gasoline and other light oils	170.4	209.9	294.2
Spirit type jet fuel	122.0	167.7	232.9
Gas oils	121.9	160.5	211.0
Chemicals and related products	208.1	191.1	142.9
Basic manufactures	275.7	322.2	244.3
Machinery and transport equipment	212.8	268.3	37.4
Miscellaneous manufactured articles	140.4	136.3	96.3
Total (incl. others)	4,407.4	4,313.8	3,627.9

Source: UN, *International Trade Statistics Yearbook.*

PRINCIPAL TRADING PARTNERS
(US $ million)

Imports c.i.f.	1998	1999	2000
Belgium	93.5*	110.6	100.3
Brazil	34.6	23.7	23.2
China, People's Republic	65.0	72.2	66.6
France (incl. Monaco)	856.5	751.6	504.7
Germany	136.5	123.5	89.5
India	64.6	32.9	17.6
Italy	156.9	162.0	90.5
Japan	103.0	125.5	72.2
Korea, Republic	50.5	39.6	24.6
Netherlands	111.6	100.5	76.0
Nigeria	319.6	396.3	659.8
Russia	89.0	74.3	62.5
Southern African Customs Union†	28.5	32.2	n.a.
Spain	107.5	102.0	81.4
Switzerland-Liechtenstein	58.4	68.2	15.6
Thailand	71.7	84.7	54.6
United Kingdom	80.9	69.1	56.3
USA	148.5	149.8	89.0
Venezuela	30.9	17.6	25.8
Total (incl. others)	2,999.8	2,897.7	2,482.2

Exports f.o.b.	1998	1999	2000
Argentina	23.6	36.6	39.6
Belgium	110.7*	88.8	138.7
Benin	52.2	53.6	43.2
Brazil	18.3	332.7	43.4
Burkina Faso	157.9	187.5	129.5
France (incl. Monaco)	752.4	623.5	540.5
Gabon	74.9	19.9	16.1
Germany	213.9	138.9	110.0
Ghana	253.0	137.1	134.9
Guinea	44.0	49.8	53.5
India	31.8	63.7	93.3
Italy	258.2	183.4	172.5
Mali	213.0	203.0	207.8
Netherlands	537.4	564.5	353.4
Niger	50.4	54.0	40.2
Nigeria	63.2	37.4	68.8
Poland	77.6	72.8	43.9
Russia	77.1	89.5	62.2
Senegal	46.4	67.0	145.8
Spain	162.5	159.2	136.5
Togo	63.3	71.3	88.6
United Kingdom	103.5	124.0	89.4
USA	398.2	365.7	301.3
Total (incl. others)	4,407.4	4,313.8	3,627.9

* Including trade with Luxembourg.

† Comprising Botswana, Lesotho, Namibia, South Africa and Swaziland.

Source: UN, *International Trade Statistics Yearbook*.

Transport

RAILWAYS
(traffic)

	1997	1998	1999
Passengers ('000)	379	269	243
Freight carried ('000 metric tons) .	596	643	806
Passenger-km (million) . . .	154.6	118.8	93.1
Freight ton-km (million) . .	504.8	527.2	537.6

Source: SITARAIL—Transport Ferroviare de Personnel et de Marchandises, Abidjan.

ROAD TRAFFIC
('000 motor vehicles in use)

	1996	1997	1998
Passenger cars	74.2	76.2	78.1
Commercial vehicles . . .	35.3	35.3	36.3

Source: UN, *Statistical Yearbook*.

SHIPPING

Merchant Fleet
(registered at 31 December)

	1999	2000	2001
Number of vessels	35	33	32
Total displacement ('000 grt) . .	9.5	9.2	8.6

Source: Lloyd's Register-Fairplay, *World Fleet Statistics*.

International Sea-borne Freight Traffic
(freight traffic at Abidjan, '000 metric tons)

	1999	2000	2001
Goods loaded	5,537	5,634	5,130
Goods unloaded	9,801	8,923	9,874

Source: Port Autonome d'Abidjan.

Freight traffic at San-Pédro ('000 metric tons, 1999): Goods loaded 851; Goods unloaded 365.

CIVIL AVIATION
(traffic on scheduled services)*

	1997	1998	1999
Kilometres flown (million) . . .	4	4	6
Passengers carried ('000) . . .	158	162	260
Passenger-km (million)	302	318	381
Total ton-km (million)	44	44	50

* Including an apportionment of the traffic of Air Afrique.

Source: UN, *Statistical Yearbook*.

Tourism

ARRIVALS BY COUNTRY OF RESIDENCE
('000)

	1996*	1997†	1998†
Belgium	4.3	4.2	4.5
Benin	12.5	11.1	14.3
Burkina Faso	11.0	11.9	17.1
Congo, Repub.	6.0	n.a.	7.6
France	66.7	69.0	73.2
Gabon	3.0	n.a.	5.4
Germany	3.2	3.8	3.9
Ghana	5.4	n.a.	6.7
Guinea	8.1	n.a.	12.5
Italy	5.0	14.0	7.6
Mali	10.7	n.a.	15.2
Niger	5.0	n.a.	5.4
Nigeria	7.9	n.a.	14.1
Senegal	13.0	12.1	16.6
Togo	8.7	8.2	10.8
United Kingdom	5.1	4.5	5.6
USA	15.3	17.0	18.8
Total (incl. others)	236.9	274.1	301.0

* Figures refer only to air arrivals at Abidjan—Félix Houphouët-Boigny airport.

† Figures refer only to air arrivals at Abidjan—Félix Houphouët-Boigny airport and to arrivals at land frontiers.

Source: World Tourism Organization: *Yearbook of Tourism Statistics*.

Tourism receipts (US $ million): 93 in 1996; 95 in 1997; 108 in 1998 (Source: World Bank).

Communications Media

	1999	2000	2001
Television receivers ('000 in use) .	944	887	n.a.
Telephones ('000 main lines in use)	219.3	263.7	293.6
Mobile cellular telephones ('000 subscribers).	257.1	473.0	728.5
Personal computers ('000 in use)	80	90	100
Internet users ('000)	20	40	70

Source: International Telecommunication Union.

Radio receivers ('000 in use): 2,260 in 1997 (Source: UNESCO, *Statistical Yearbook*).

Daily newspapers: 12 in 1996 (average circulation 231,000 copies) (Source: UNESCO, *Statistical Yearbook*).

Non-daily newspapers: 15 in 1996 (average circulation 251,000 copies) (Source: UNESCO, *Statistical Yearbook*).

Education

(1997/98, unless otherwise indicated)

	Institutions	Teachers	Students		
			Males	Females	Total
Pre-primary . .	207*	829*	17,129	17,780	34,909
Primary . . .	7,599†	40,529	1,032,989	774,514	1,807,503
Secondary: General . .	428*	15,959*	355,796	183,328	539,124
Secondary: Teacher training‡ . .	13§	538*	n.a.	n.a.	6,224*
Vocational¶ . .	n.a.	1,424	8,588	2,449	11,037
University level	n.a.	1,657¶	37,185	10,002	47,187

* 1995/96 figure.
† 1996/97 figure.
‡ Data refer only to schools attached to the Ministry of National Education.
§ 1993/94 figure.
¶ 1994/95 figure(s).

Source: Ministry of National Education, Abidjan.

1998/99: Primary: Students 1,910,820; General Secondary: Students 565,850.

2002/03: Primary: Students 2,118,501; General Secondary: Students 671,433.

Adult literacy rate (UNESCO estimates): 46.8% (males 54.5%; females 38.6%) in 2000 (Source: UN Development Programme, *Human Development Report*).

Directory

The Constitution

Following the *coup d'état* of 24 December 1999, the Constitution that had been in force, with amendments, since 1960 was suspended. A new Constitution was subsequently prepared by a consultative committee, and was approved by referendum in July 2000. The main provisions of the Constitution are summarized below

PREAMBLE

The people of Côte d'Ivoire recognize their diverse ethnic, cultural and religious backgrounds, and desire to build a single, unified and prosperous nation based on constitutional legality and democratic institutions, the rights of the individual, cultural and spiritual values, transparency in public affairs, and the promotion of sub-regional, regional and African unity.

FREEDOMS, RIGHTS AND DUTIES

Articles 1–28: The State guarantees the implementation of the Constitution and guarantees to protect the rights of each citizen. The State guarantees its citizens equal access to health, education, culture, information, professional training, employment and justice. Freedom of thought and expression are guaranteed to all, although the encouragement of social, ethnic and religious discord is not permitted. Freedom of association and demonstration are guaranteed. Political parties may act freely within the law, however, parties must not be created solely on a regional, ethnic or religious basis. The rights of free enterprise, the right to join a trade union and the right to strike are guaranteed.

NATIONAL SOVEREIGNTY

Articles 29–33: Côte d'Ivoire is an independent and sovereign republic. The official language is French. Legislation regulates the promotion and development of national languages. The Republic of Côte d'Ivoire is indivisible, secular, democratic and social. All its citizens are equal. Sovereignty belongs to the people, and is exercised through referendums and the election of representatives. The right to vote freely and in secret is guaranteed to all citizens over 18 years of age.

HEAD OF STATE

Articles 34–57: The President of the Republic is the Head of State. The President is elected for a five-year mandate (renewable once only) by direct universal suffrage. Candidates must be aged between 40 ĉnd 65, and be Ivorian citizens holding no other nationality, and

resident in the country, with Ivorian parents. If one candidate does not receive a simple majority of votes cast, a second round of voting takes place between the two most successful candidates. The President holds executive power, and appoints a Prime Minister to co-ordinate government action. The President appoints the Government on the recommendation of the Prime Minister. The President presides over the Council of Ministers, is the head of the civil service and the supreme head of the armed forces. The President may initiate legislation and call referendums. The President may not hold any other office or be a leader of a political party.

ASSEMBLÉE NATIONALE

Articles 58–83: The Assemblée nationale holds legislative power. The Assemblée nationale votes on the budget and scrutinizes the accounts of the nation. Deputies are elected for periods of five years by direct universal suffrage. Except in exceptional cases, deputies have legal immunity during the period of their mandate.

INTERNATIONAL AGREEMENTS

Articles 84–87: The President negotiates and ratifies treaties and international agreements. International agreements, which modify internal legislation, must be ratified by further legislation. The Constitution must be amended prior to the ratification of certain agreements if the Constitutional Council deems this necessary.

CONSTITUTIONAL COUNCIL

Articles 88–100: The Constitutional Council rules on the constitutionality of legislation. It also regulates the functioning of government. It is composed of a President, of the former Presidents of Côte d'Ivoire and of six councillors named by the President and by the President of the Assemblée nationale for mandates of six years. The Council supervises referendums and announces referendum and election results. It also examines the eligibility of candidates to the presidency and the legislature. There is no appeal against the Council's decisions.

JUDICIAL POWER

Articles 101–112: The judiciary is independent, and is composed of the High Court of Justice, the Court of Cassation, the Council of State, the National Audit Court, and regional tribunals and appeals courts. The Higher Council of Magistrates examines questions relating to judicial independence and nominates and disciplines senior magistrates. The High Court of Justice judges members of the Government in cases relating to the execution of their duties. The

High Court, which is composed of deputies elected by the Assemblée nationale, may only judge the President in cases of high treason.

CONSEIL ECONOMIQUE ET SOCIAL

Articles 113–114: The Conseil économique et social gives its opinion on proposed legislation or decrees relating to its sphere of competence. The President may consult the council on any economic or social matter.

THE MEDIATOR OF THE REPUBLIC

Articles 115–118: The Mediator is an independent mediating figure, appointed for a non-renewable six-year mandate by the President, in consultation with the President of the Assemblée nationale. The Mediator, who may not hold any other office or position, receives immunity from prosecution during the term of office.

OTHER ISSUES

Articles 119–133: Only the President or the Assemblée nationale, of whom a two-thirds' majority must be in favour, may propose amending the Constitution. Amendments relating to the nature of the presidency or the mechanism whereby the Constitution is amended must be approved by referendum; all other amendments may be enacted with the agreement of the President and of a four-fifths' majority of the Assemblée nationale. The form and the secular nature of the republic may not be amended. Immunity from prosecution is granted to members of the Comité national de salut public and to all those involved in the change of government of December 1999.

The Government

HEAD OF STATE

President of the Republic: Laurent Gbagbo (took office 26 October 2000).

COUNCIL OF MINISTERS
(April 2003)

A Government of National Reconciliation, comprising members of the Front populaire ivoirien (FPI), the Parti démocratique de la Côte d'Ivoire—Rassemblement démocratique africain (PDCI—RDA), the Rassemblement des républicains (RDR), the Mouvement patriotique de Côte d'Ivoire (MPCI), the Union pour la démocratie et pour la paix de la Côte d'Ivoire (UDPCI), the Parti ivoirien des travailleurs (PIT), the Mouvement des forces d'avenir (MFA), the Union démocratique citoyenne (UDCY), the Mouvement pour la justice et la paix (MJP), the Mouvement populaire ivoirien du grand ouest (MPIGO) and an Independent (Ind.).

Prime Minister: Seydou Elimane Diarra (Ind.).

Minister of State, Minister of Foreign Affairs: Bamba Mamadou (PDCI—RDA).

Minister of State, Minister of the Economy and Finance: Paul-Antoine Bohoun Bouabré (FPI).

Minister of State, Minister of Mines and Energy: Léon-Emmanuel Monnet (FPI).

Minister of State, Minister of Economic Infrastructure: Patrick Achi (PDCI—RDA).

Minister of State, Minister of Health and Population: Mabri Toikeuse (UDPCI).

Minister of State, Minister of Regional Integration and the African Union: Théodore Mel-Eg (UDCY).

Minister of State, Minister of Justice: Henriette Diabaté (RDR).

Minister of State, Minister of Agriculture: Amadou Gon Coulibaly (RDR).

Minister of State, Minister of the Environment: Angèle Gnonsoa (PIT).

Minister of State, Minister of Transport: Anaky Kobenan (MFA).

Minister of State, responsible for Communication: Guillaume Soro Kigbafori (MPCI).

Minister of State, responsible for Territorial Administration: Col Moussa Diakité (MPCI).

Minister of Defence: Assou Adou (FPI) (acting).

Minister of Security: Zémogo Fofana (RDR) (acting).

Minister of Religions: Désiré Gnonconté (PDCI—RDA).

Minister of Trade: Amadou Soumahoro (RDR).

Minister of Employment and the Civil Service: Hubert Oulaï (FPI).

Minister of Planning and Development: Britto Nama Boniface (PDCI—RDA).

Minister of Relations with the Institutions of the Republic: Alphonse Douaty (FPI).

Minister of Administrative Reform: Eric-Kahé Kplohourou (UDPCI).

Minister in charge of National Reconciliation: Sébastien Danon Djédjé (FPI).

Minister of Town Planning and Construction: Raymond Abouo-N'Dori (FPI).

Minister of Animal Production and Fisheries: Adjoumani Kobenan (PDCI—RDA).

Minister of Industry and the Development of the Private Sector: Jeannot Ahoussou Kouadio (PDCI—RDA).

Minister of Culture and Francophone Affairs: Madame Malan Messou (PDCI—RDA).

Minister of the Fight against AIDS: Christine Adjobi (FPI).

Minister of Higher Education: Zémogo Fofana (RDR).

Minister of Technical Education and Professional Training: Youssouf Soumahoro (MJP).

Minister of National Education: Michel Amani N'Guessan (FPI).

Minister of Scientific Research: Mamadou Koné (MPCI).

Minister of New Technologies and Telecommunications: Hamed Bakayoko (RDR).

Minister of Water and Forestry: Assou Adou (FPI).

Minister of Small- and Medium-sized Enterprises: Roger Banchi (MPIGO).

Minister of Crafts and the Training of the Informal Sector: Moussa Dosso (MPCI).

Minister of Solidarity and Social Security: Clotilde Ohouchi (FPI).

Minister of Human Rights: Victorine Wodié (PIT).

Minister of the Victims of War, the Displaced and the Exiled: Messamba Koné (MPCI).

Minister of Tourism: Marcel Amon Tanoh (RDR).

Minister of Sport and Leisure: Col Michel Gueu (MPCI).

Minister of Youth and Public Service: Master-Sgt Tuo Fozié (MPCI).

Minister of Women, the Family and Children: (vacant).

MINISTRIES

Office of the President: 01 BP 1354, Abidjan; tel. 20-22-02-22; fax 20-21-14-25; e-mail lepresident@pr.ci; internet www.presidence.gov.ci.

Office of the Prime Minister: blvd Angoulvant, 01 BP 1533, Abidjan 01; tel. 20-31-50-00; fax 20-22-18-33.

Ministry of Administrative Reform: Abidjan.

Ministry of Agriculture: Immeuble Caisse de Stabilisation, 25e étage, BP V82, Abidjan; tel. 20-21-38-58; fax 20-21-46-18; e-mail minagra@cimail.net.

Ministry of Animal Production and Fisheries: Abidjan.

Ministry of Communication: Abidjan.

Ministry of Crafts and the Training of the Informal Sector: Abidjan.

Ministry of Culture and Francophone Affairs: Tour E, 22e étage, BP V39, Abidjan; tel. 20-21-40-34; fax 20-21-33-59; e-mail culture.ci@ci.refer.org.

Ministry of Defence: Immeuble EECI, BP V241, Abidjan; tel. 20-21-26-82; fax 20-22-41-75.

Ministry of Economic Infrastructure: Immeuble Postel 2001, 18 BP 2203, Abidjan 18; tel. 20-34-42-73; fax 20-34-73-22.

Ministry of the Economy and Finance: Immeuble SCIAM, 16e étage, ave Marchand, BP V163, Abidjan; tel. 20-20-08-42; fax 20-21-32-08.

Ministry of Employment and the Civil Service: Immeuble Fonction Public, blvd Angoulvand, BP V93, Abidjan; tel. 20-21-42-90; fax 20-21-12-86.

Ministry of the Environment: BP V06, Abidjan; tel. 20-22-61-35; fax 20-22-20-50.

Ministry of the Fight against AIDS: Abidjan.

Ministry of Foreign Affairs: Bloc Ministériel, blvd Angoulvand, BP V109, Abidjan; tel. 20-22-71-50; fax 20-33-23-08.

Ministry of Health and Population: Abidjan.

Ministry of Higher Education: Tour C, 20e étage, Tours Administratives, BP V151, Abidjan; tel. 20-21-33-16; fax 20-21-22-25.

Ministry of Human Rights: Abidjan.

Ministry of Industry and the Development of the Private Sector: Immeuble CCI, 15e étage, BP V65, Abidjan; tel. 20-21-30-88.

Ministry of Justice: Bloc Ministériel, blvd Angoulvand A-17, BP V107, Abidjan-Plateau; tel. 20-21-17-27; fax 20-33-12-59.

Ministry of Mines and Energy: Immeuble Postel 2001, BP V40, Abidjan; tel. 20-34-48-51; fax 20-21-37-30.

Ministry of National Education: Tour D, 28e étage, Tours Administratives, BP V120, Abidjan; tel. 20-22-74-06; fax 20-22-93-22; e-mail menfb@ci.refer.org.

Ministry of National Reconciliation: Abidjan.

Ministry of New Technologies and Telecommunications: Tour C, Tours Administratives, BP V138, Abidjan; tel. 22-44-77-07; fax 22-44-78-47.

Ministry of Planning and Development: Abidjan.

Ministry of Regional Integration and the African Union: Abidjan.

Ministry of Relations with the Institutions of the Republic: Abidjan.

Ministry of Religions: Abidjan.

Ministry of Scientific Research: Abidjan.

Ministry of Security: Bloc Ministériel, blvd Angoulvand, BP V121, Abidjan; tel. 20-22-38-16; fax 20-22-36-48.

Ministry of Small- and Medium-sized Enterprises: Abidjan.

Ministry of Solidarity and Social Security: BP V241, Abidjan; tel. 20-21-19-50.

Ministry of Sport and Leisure: Abidjan; tel. 20-21-30-73.

Ministry of Technical Education and Professional Training: Abidjan.

Ministry of Territorial Administration: Abidjan.

Ministry of Tourism: BP V184, Abidjan 01; tel. 20-44-55-00; fax 20-44-55-80.

Ministry of Town Planning and Construction: Tour D, Tours Administratives, 20 BP 650, Abidjan; tel. 20-21-82-35; fax 20-21-35-68.

Ministry of Trade: Immeuble CCIA, 15e étage, rue Jean-Paul II, BP V65, Abidjan; tel. 20-21-64-73; fax 20-21-64-74.

Ministry of Transport: Immeuble Postel 2001, BP V06, Abidjan; tel. 20-34-73-15; fax 20-21-37-30.

Ministry of the Victims of War, the Displaced and the Exiled: Abidjan.

Ministry of Water and Forestry: Abidjan.

Ministry of Women, the Family and Children: Tour E, Tours Administratives, BP V200, Abidjan; tel. 20-21-76-26; fax 20-21-44-61.

Ministry of Youth and Public Service: BP V136, Abidjan; tel. 20-21-52-51; fax 20-22-48-21.

President and Legislature

PRESIDENT

Presidential Election, 22 October 2000

Candidate	Votes	% of votes
Laurent Gbagbo (FPI)	1,065,597	59.36
Robert Gueï (Ind.)	587,267	32.72
Francis Wodié (PIT)	102,253	5.70
Théodore Mel-Eg (UDCY)	26,331	1.47
Nicolas Dioulo (Ind.)	13,558	0.76
Total*	1,795,006	100.00

*Excluding invalid votes (25,413).

ASSEMBLÉE NATIONALE

Assemblée nationale: 01 BP 1381, Abidjan 01; tel. 20–21–60–69; fax 20–22–20–87.

President: MAMADOU KOULIBALY.

General Election, 10 December 2000*

Party	Seats
Front populaire ivoirien (FPI)	96
Parti démocratique de la Côte d'Ivoire—Rassemblement démocratique africain (PDCI—RDA)	94
Rassemblement des républicains (RDR)†	5
Parti ivoirien des travailleurs (PIT)	4
Union démocratique citoyenne (UDCY)	1
Mouvement des forces d'avenir (MFA)	1
Independents	22
Total‡	223

*These figures include the results of voting in 26 constituencies where elections were postponed until 14 January 2001, owing to unrest.

†The RDR officially boycotted the elections, and these seats were won by a faction within the party that did not participate in the boycott.

‡Voting for the remaining two seats was postponed indefinitely.

Advisory Councils

Constitutional Council: Abidjan; tel. 20-21-31-65; fax 20-21-31-54; f. 1994; Pres. TIA KONÉ.

Economic and Social Council: 04 BP 301, Abidjan 04; tel. 20-21-14-54; Pres. LAURENT DONA FOLOGO; Vice-Pres DIGBEU HILAIRE ANY, ETIENNE KOUDOU BOTI, NICOLE DEIGNA, MARTIN KOUAKOU N'GUESSA, VAKABA DEMOVALY TOURÉ; 120 mems.

Political Organizations

In early 2003 there were more than 100 registered political organizations, of which the following were among the most important:

Front populaire ivoirien (FPI): 22 BP 302, Abidjan 22; tel. 21-24-36-76; fax 22-22-19-18; e-mail infoservice@fpi-ci.org; internet www.fpi-ci.org; f. 1990; socialist; Pres. PASCAL AFFI N'GUESSAN; Sec.-Gen. SYLVAIN MIAKA OURETO.

Mouvement des forces d'avenir (MFA): 15 BP 794, Abidjan 15; f. 1995; Pres. INNOCENT KOBENA ANAKY.

Parti africain pour la renaissance ivoirienne (PARI): Abidjan; f. 1991; Sec.-Gen. DANIEL ANIKPO.

Parti démocratique de la Côte d'Ivoire—Rassemblement démocratique africain (PDCI—RDA): Maison du parti, Cocody, 01 BP 79, Abidjan 01; e-mail information@pdci-rda.org; f. 1946; Pres. HENRI KONAN BÉDIÉ; Sec.-Gen. ALPHONSE DJÉDJÉ MADY.

Parti ivoirien des travailleurs (PIT): 20 BP 43, Abidjan 20; e-mail pit@abc.ci; social-democratic; f. 1990; First Nat. Sec. FRANCIS WODIÉ.

Parti pour le progrès et le socialisme (PPS): Abidjan; f. 1993; Sec.-Gen. Prof. BAMBA MORIFÉRÉ.

Rassemblement des républicains (RDR): 8 rue Lepic, Cocody, 06 BP 1440, Abidjan 06; tel. 22-44-33-51; e-mail rdrci@rdrci.org; internet www.rdrci.org; f. 1994 following split from PDCI—RDA; officially boycotted the general election of Dec. 2000, except for a faction of some 60 candidates, led by ALPHONSE OULAÏ TOUSSÉA; Pres. Dr ALASSANE DRAMANE OUATTARA; Sec.-Gen. HENRIETTE DAGBA DIABATÉ.

Union démocratique citoyenne (UDCY): 01 BP 1410, Abidjan 01; f. 2000 following split from PDCI—RDA; Sec.-Gen. THÉODORE MEL-EG.

Union des sociaux-démocrates (USD): Abidjan; Sec.-Gen. Me JÉRÔME CLIMANLO COULIBALY.

Union pour la démocratie et pour la paix de la Côte d'Ivoire (UDPCI): Abidjan; f. 2001 following split from PDCI—RDA; Pres. (vacant); First Vice-Pres. PAUL AKOTO YAO; Sec.-Gen. ALASSANE SALIF N'DIAYE.

Note: Following the outbreak of civil conflict in northern Côte d'Ivoire, which subsequently spread to western regions, three 'politico-military' rebel groups emerged. In accordance with the Marcoussis Accords, agreed in late January 2003, the following groups were allocated posts in the Government of National Reconciliation that was formed in March of that year.

Mouvement patriotique de Côte d'Ivoire (MPCI): Bouaké; tel. 20-20-04-04; e-mail mpci-online@ifrance.com; internet www.mpci-online.fr.st; f. 2002; Sec.-Gen. GUILLAUME SORO KIGBAFORI.

Mouvement populaire ivoirien du grand ouest (MPIGO): Man; f. 2002 by supporters of the late fmr military ruler, Gen. Robert Gueï; Leader (vacant).

Mouvement pour la justice et la paix (MJP): Man; f. 2002 by supporters of the late fmr military leader, Gen. Robert Gueï; Leader Cmdr GASPARD DÉLI.

Diplomatic Representation

EMBASSIES IN CÔTE D'IVOIRE

Algeria: 53 blvd Clozel, 01 BP 1015, Abidjan 01; tel. 20-32-32-40; fax 20-22-37-12; Ambassador SALEH LEBDIOUI.

Angola: Lot 2461, rue des Jardins, Cocody-Deux-Plateaux, 01 BP 1734, Abidjan 01; tel. 22-41-38-79; fax 22-41-28-89; Ambassador BERNARDO MBALA NDOMBELE.

Austria: Immeuble N'Zarama, blvd Lagunaire, Plateau, 01 BP 1837, Abidjan 01; tel. 20-21-25-00; fax 20-22-19-23; Ambassador HEIDE KELLER.

Belgium: Immeuble Alliance, angle rue Lecoeur, 01 BP 1800, Abidjan 01; tel. 20-21-00-88; fax 20-22-41-77; Ambassador FRANK RECKER.

Benin: rue des Jasmins, Lot 1610, Cocody-Deux-Plateaux, 09 BP 283, Abidjan 09; tel. 22-41-44-13; fax 22-42-76-07; Ambassador RAYMOND VIVENAGBO.

Brazil: Immeuble Alpha 2000, rue Gourgas, 01 BP 3820, Abidjan 01; tel. 20-22-23-41; fax 22-22-64-01; Ambassador FAUSTO CARMELLO.

Burkina Faso: 2 ave Terrasson de Fougères, 01 BP 900, Abidjan 01; tel. 20-21-15-01; fax 20-21-66-41; Ambassador EMILE IBOUDO.

Cameroon: Immeuble le Général, blvd Botreau Roussel, 06 BP 326, Abidjan 06; tel. 20-21-33-31; fax 20-21-66-11; Ambassador (vacant).

Canada: Immeuble Trade Centre, ave Nogues, 01 BP 4104, Abidjan 01; tel. 20-21-20-09; fax 20-30-07-20; internet www.dfait-maeci.gc .ca/abidjan; Ambassador EMILE GAUVREAU.

Central African Republic: 9 rue des Jasmins, Cocody Danga Nord, 01 BP 3387, Abidjan 01; tel. 20-21-36-46; fax 22-44-85-16; Ambassador YAGAO-N'GAMA LAZARE.

China, People's Republic: Lot 45, ave Jacques Aka, Cocody, 01 BP 3691, Abidjan 01; tel. 22-44-59-00; fax 22-44-67-81; e-mail ambchine@aviso.ci; Ambassador ZHAO BAOZHEN.

Colombia: 01 BP 3874, Abidjan 01; tel. 20-33-12-44; fax 20-32-47-31; e-mail emcoci@africaonline.co.ci; Ambassador (vacant).

Czech Republic: Immeuble Tropique III, 01 BP 1349, Abidjan 01; tel. 20-21-20-30; fax 20-22-19-06; e-mail ambassade.tcheque@ globeaccess.net; Ambassador PETR LOM.

Egypt: Immeuble El Nasr, 01 BP 2104, Abidjan 01; tel. 20-32-79-25; fax 20-22-30-53; Ambassador AHMED TEWFIK RAGEB.

Ethiopia: Immeuble Nour Al-Hayat, 01 BP 3712, Abidjan 01; tel. 20-21-33-65; fax 20-21-37-09; e-mail ambethio@africaonline.co.ci; Ambassador TADELECH HAILE-MICHAEL.

France: rue Lecoeur, 01 BP 175, Abidjan 01; tel. 20-20-05-05; fax 20-22-42-54; e-mail presse@ambafrance-abidjan.org; internet www .ambafrance-abidjan.org; Ambassador GILDAS LE LIDEC.

Gabon: Cocody Danga Nord, 01 BP 3765, Abidjan 01; tel. 22-44-51-54; fax 22-44-75-05; Ambassador HENRI BEKALLE AKWE.

Germany: 39 blvd Hassan II, Cocody, 01 BP 1900, Abidjan 01; tel. 22-44-20-30; fax 22-44-20-41; e-mail d.bo.abj@africaonline.co.ci; internet www.allemagne.ci; Ambassador KARIN ELSA BLUMBERGER-SAUERTEIG.

Ghana: Lot 2393, rue J 95, Cocody-Deux-Plateaux, 01 BP 1871, Abidjan 01; tel. 20-33-11-24; fax 20-22-33-57; e-mail ghanaemb.abj@ aviso.ci; Ambassador YAW SAFO BOAFO.

Guinea: Immeuble Duplessis, 08 BP 2280, Abidjan 08; tel. 20-22-25-20; fax 20-32-82-45; Ambassador FODE CISSE.

Holy See: Apostolic Nunciature, 08 BP 1347, Abidjan 08; tel. 22-44-38-35; fax 22-44-72-40; e-mail nuntius@comete.ci; Apostolic Nuncio Most Rev. MARIO ZENARI (Titular Archbishop of Zuglio).

India: Cocody Danga Nord, 06 BP 318, Abidjan 06; tel. 22-42-37-69; fax 22-42-66-49; e-mail indeamadj@africaonline.co.ci; Ambassador NEELAM DEO.

Israel: Immeuble Nour Al-Hayat, 01 BP 1877, Abidjan 01; tel. 20-21-49-53; fax 20-21-87-04; Ambassador DANIEL KEDEM.

Italy: 16 rue de la Canebière, Cocody, 01 BP 1905, Abidjan 01; tel. 22-44-61-70; fax 22-44-35-87; e-mail ambitali@aviso.ci; Ambassador PAOLO SANNELLA.

Japan: Immeuble Alpha 2000, 01 BP 1329, Abidjan 01; tel. 20-21-28-63; fax 20-21-30-51; Ambassador YUJI KUROKAWA.

Korea, Republic: Immeuble le Mans, 01 BP 3950, Abidjan 01; tel. 20-32-22-90; fax 20-22-22-74; Ambassador KIM JONG-IL.

Lebanon: Immeuble Trade Center, ave Nogues, 01 BP 2227, Abidjan 01; tel. 20-33-28-24; fax 20-32-11-37; Ambassador MOSTAPHA ISSAM.

Libya: Immeuble Shell, 01 BP 5725, Abidjan 01; tel. 20-22-01-27; fax 20-22-01-30; Ambassador FATHI NASHAD.

Mali: Maison du Mali, 01 BP 2746, Abidjan 01; tel. 20-32-30-71; fax 20-21-55-14; Ambassador SADA SAMAKÉ.

Malta: 38 rue de la Canebière, Cocody, 01 BP 46, Abidjan 01; tel. 22-44-63-62; fax 22-44-19-78; Ambassador MARTHE BLOHORN.

Mauritania: blvd Latrille, rue Eglise St Jacques, 01 BP 2275, Abidjan 01; tel. 22-41-16-43; fax 22-41-05-77; Ambassador TIJANI OULD KERIM.

Morocco: Résidence Gyam, ave Clozel-Plateau D4, BP 1749, Abidjan 04; tel. 07-72-59-43; fax 22-44-60-58; e-mail khyate2001@ aviso.ci; Ambassador MOHAMED HAMA.

Netherlands: Immeuble Les Harmonies, blvd Carde, 01 BP 1086, Abidjan 01; tel. 20-21-31-10; fax 20-21-17-61; e-mail nlgovabi@ africaonline.co.ci; Ambassador PETER VAN LEEUWEN.

Niger: 6 blvd Achalme, Marcory, 01 BP 2743, Abidjan 01; tel. 21-26-28-14; fax 21-26-41-88; Ambassador ADAM ABDOULAYE DAN MARADI.

Nigeria: blvd de la République, 01 BP 1906, Abidjan 01; tel. 20-22-30-82; fax 20-21-30-83; Ambassador KEHINDE ONWAZU OLISEMEKA.

Norway: Immeuble N'Zarama, 01 BP 607, Abidjan 01; tel. 20-22-25-34; fax 20-21-91-99; Ambassador LARS TANGERAAS.

Poland: 04 BP 308, Abidjan 08; tel. 22-44-10-67; fax 22-44-12-25; e-mail polska@polamb.ci; internet www.polamb.ci; Chargé d'affaires BOGUSŁAW NOWAKOWSKI.

Portugal: Immeuble N'Zarama, blvd Lagunaire, 01 BP 3669, Abidjan 01; tel. 20-21-92-41; fax 20-25-57-05; e-mail ambport@ africaonline.co.ci; Ambassador JOSÉ MANUEL PESSANHA VIEGAS.

Russia: Riviera Golf, 01 BP 7646, Abidjan 01; tel. 22-43-09-59; fax 22-43-11-66; e-mail ambrus@globeaccess.net; Ambassador GEORGII A. CHERNOVOL.

Saudi Arabia: Plateau, Abidjan; Ambassador (vacant).

Senegal: Résidence Nabil, 01 BP 2165, Abidjan 01; tel. 20-33-28-76; fax 20-32-50-39; Ambassador OUSMANE CAMARA.

South Africa: Villa Marc André, rue Mgr René Kouassi, Cocody, 08 BP 1806, Abidjan 08; tel. 22-44-59-63; fax 22-44-74-50; e-mail ambafsudpol@aviso.ci; Ambassador G. DUMISANI GWADISO.

Spain: impasse Abla Pokou Cocody, Danga Nord, 01 BP 2589, Abidjan 01; tel. 20-21-47-27; fax 20-32-47-29; e-mail embespan@ aviso.ci; Ambassador FRANCISCO ELIAS DE TEJADA LOZANO.

Sweden: Immeuble N'Zarama, blvd Lagunaire, Plateau, 04 BP 992, Abidjan 04; tel. 20-21-24-10; fax 20-21-21-07; e-mail ambassaden .abidjan@foreign.ministry.se; Ambassador GÖRAN ANKARBERG.

Switzerland: Immeuble Botreau Roussel, 28 ave Delafosse, 01 BP 1914, Abidjan 01; tel. 20-21-17-21; fax 20-21-27-70; Ambassador JOHANNES KUNZ.

Tunisia: 01 BP 3906, Abidjan 01; tel. 20-22-61-23; fax 20-22-61-24; Ambassador ZINE EL ABIDINE TERRAS.

United Kingdom: Immeuble Les Harmonies, angle blvd Carde et ave Dr Jamot, Plateau, 01 BP 2581, Abidjan 01; tel. 20-30-08-00; fax 20-30-08-34; e-mail britemb@aviso.ci; internet www.britaincdi.com; Ambassador JEAN-FRANÇOIS GORDON.

USA: 5 rue Jesse Owens, 01 BP 1712, Abidjan 01; tel. 20-21-09-79; fax 20-22-32-59; e-mail cca_ci@pd.state.gov; internet usembassy .state.gov/abidjan; Ambassador ARLENE RENDER.

Judicial System

Since 1964 all civil, criminal, commercial and administrative cases have come under the jurisdiction of the courts of first instance, the assize courts and the Court of Appeal, with the Court of Cassation as the highest court of appeal.

Court of Cassation: rue Gourgas, BP V30, Abidjan; has four chambers: constitutional, judicial, administrative and auditing; Pres. TIA KONÉ.

Courts of Appeal: Abidjan and Bouaké; hear appeals from courts of first instance.

High Court of Justice: composed of deputies elected from and by the Assemblée nationale; has jurisdiction to impeach the President or other member of the Government.

Courts of First Instance: Abidjan: Pres. ANTOINETTE MARSOUIN; Bouaké: Pres. KABLAN AKA EDOUKOU; Daloa: Pres. WOUNE BLEKA; there are a further 25 courts in the principal centres.

Religion

The Constitution guarantees religious freedom, and this right is generally respected. Religious groups are required to register with the authorities, although no penalties are imposed on a group that fails to register. At the 1998 census it was estimated that about 34% of the population were Christians (mainly Roman Catholics), 27% of the population were Muslims, 15% followed traditional indigenous beliefs, 3% practised other religions, while 21% had no religious affiliation. It is, however, estimated that the proportion of Muslims is in fact significantly higher, as the majority of unregistered foreign workers are Muslims. Muslims are found in greatest numbers in the north of the country, while Christians are found mostly in the southern, central, western and eastern regions. Traditional indigenous beliefs are generally prevalent in rural areas.

ISLAM

Conseil National Islamique (CNI): Mosquée d'Aghien les deux Plateaux, BP 174 Cédex 03, Abidjan 08; tel. and fax 22-42-67-79; e-mail cni@africaonline.co.ci; internet www.cni-cosim.ci; f. 1993; groups more than 5,000 local communities organized in 13 regional and 78 local organizations; Chair. Imam El Hadj IDRISS KOUDOUSS KONÉ.

Conseil Supérieur Islamique (CSI): 11 BP 71, Abidjan 11; tel. 21-25-24-70; fax 21-24-28-04; f. 1978; Chair. El Hadj MOUSTAPHA KOWEÏT DIABY.

CHRISTIANITY

The Roman Catholic Church

Côte d'Ivoire comprises four archdioceses and 10 dioceses. At 31 December 2000 there were 2,604,896 Roman Catholics in the country, comprising about 16.0% of the total population.

Bishops' Conference: Conférence Episcopale de la Côte d'Ivoire, 01 BP 1287, Abidjan 01; tel. 20-33-22-56; f. 1973; Pres. Most Rev. VITAL KOMENAN YAO (Archbishop of Bouaké).

Archbishop of Abidjan: Cardinal BERNARD AGRÉ, Archevêché, ave Jean Paul II, 01 BP 1287, Abidjan 01; tel. 20-21-23-08; fax 20-21-40-22.

Archbishop of Bouaké: Most Rev. VITAL KOMENAN YAO, Archevêché, 01 BP 649, Bouaké 01; tel. and fax 31-63-24-59; e-mail archebke@aviso.ci.

Archbishop of Gagnoa: Most Rev. JEAN-PIERRE KUTWÂ, Archevêché, BP 527, Gagnoa; tel. 32-77-25-68; fax 32-77-20-96.

Archbishop of Korhogo: Most Rev. AUGUSTE NOBOU, Archevêché, BP 12, Korhogo; tel. 36-86-01-18; fax 36-86-05-26.

Protestant Churches

CB International: BP 109, Korhogo; tel. 36-86-01-07; fax 36-86-11-50; f. 1947; fmrly Conservative Baptist Foreign Mission Society; active in evangelism, medical work, translation, literacy and theological education in the northern area and in Abidjan.

Christian and Missionary Alliance: BP 585, Bouaké 01; tel. 31-63-23-12; fax 31-63-54-12; f. 1929; 13 mission stations; Dir Rev. DAVID W. ARNOLD.

Eglise du Nazaréen (Church of the Nazarene): 22 BP 623, Abidjan 22; tel. 22-41-07-80; fax 22-41-07-81; e-mail awfcon@compuserve .com; f. 1987; active in evangelism, ministerial training and medical work; Dir JOHN SEAMAN.

Eglise Evangélique des Assemblées de Dieu de Côte d'Ivoire: 04 BP 266, Abidjan 04; tel. 20-37-05-79; fax 20-24-94-65; f. 1960; Pres. JEAN-BAPTISTE NIELBIEN.

Eglise Harriste: Bingerville; f. 1913 by William Wade Harris; affiliated to World Council of Churches 1998; allows polygamous new converts; 100,000 mems, 1,400 preachers, 7,000 apostles; Sec.-Gen DOGBO JULES.

Eglise Protestante Baptiste Oeuvres et Mission: 03 BP 1032, Abidjan 03; tel. 23-45-20-18; fax 23-45-56-41; f. 1975; active in evangelism, teaching and social work; medical centre, 677 places of worship, 285 missionaries and 100,000 mems; Pres. YAYE ROBERT DION.

Eglise Protestante Méthodiste de Côte d'Ivoire: 41 blvd de la République, 01 BP 1282, Abidjan 01; tel. 20-21-17-97; fax 20-22-52-03; f. 1923; autonomous since 1985; c. 150,000 mems; Pres. BENJAMIN BONI.

Mission Evangélique de l'Afrique Occidentale: BP 822, Bouaflé; tel. and fax 30-68-93-70; e-mail wirci@aviso.ci; f. 1934; 25 missionaries, 25 staff at mission school; Field Dirs LINDA NAGEL, MARRY SCHOTTE; affiliated church: Alliance des Eglises Evangéliques de Côte d'Ivoire; 254 churches, 65 full-time pastors; Pres. KOUASSI ALAINGBRÉ PASCAL.

Mission Evangélique Luthérienne en Côte d'Ivoire (MELCI): BP 196, Touba; tel. 33-70-77-11; e-mail melci@aviso.ci; f. 1984; active in evangelism and social work; Dir GJERMUND VISTE.

Union des Eglises Evangéliques du Sud-Ouest de la Côte d'Ivoire and Mission Biblique: 08 BP 20, Abidjan 08; f. 1927; c. 250 places of worship.

The Press

DAILIES

Actuel: Cocody-les-Deux-Plateaux, 06 BP 2868, Abidjan 06; tel. 22-42-63-27; fax 22-42-63-32; f. 1996; organ of the FPI; Dir EUGÈNE ALLOU WANYOU; Editor-in-Chief DIABATÉ A. SIDICK.

L'Aurore: 18 BP 418, Abidjan 18; tel. 05-61-65-75; Editor-in-Chief EHOUMAN KASSY.

La Bombe: Abidjan; supports PDCI—RDA; Dir of Publication NAZAIRE BREKA.

Douze: rue Louis Lumière, zone 4c, 10 BP 2462, Abidjan 10; tel. 21-25-54-00; fax 21-24-47-27; e-mail douze@afnet.net; internet www .presseci.com/douze; publ. by Editions Olympe; f. 1994; sport; Dir MAZÉ SOUMAHORO; Editor-in-Chief FRANÇOIS BINI.

Fraternité Matin: blvd du Général de Gaulle, 01 BP 1807, Abidjan 01; tel. 20-37-06-66; fax 20-37-25-45; e-mail dangbeu@yahoo.fr; internet www.fratmat.co.ci; f. 1964; official newspaper; Dir-Gen. HONORAT DÉ YÉDAGNE; Editorial Dir ALFRED DAN MOUSSA; circ. 80,000.

L'Inter: rue Louis Lumière, Zone 4c, 10 BP 2462, Abidjan 10; tel. 21-25-32-77; fax 21-24-47-27; e-mail inter@afnet.net; internet www .presseci.com/linter; f. 1998; publ. by Editions Olympe; national and international politics and economics; Dir RAYMOND N'CHO NIMBA; Editor-in-Chief CHARLES A. D'ALMÉIDA.

Le JD (Jeune Démocrate): 23 BP 3842, Abidjan 23; tel. 23-51-62-45; fax 23-51-63-75; e-mail lejd@africaonline.co.ci; f. 1999; Dir IGNACE DASSOHIRI; Editor-in-Chief OCTAVE BOYOU.

Le Jour: 26 ave Chardy, Plateau, 01 BP 2432, Abidjan 01; tel. 20-21-95-78; fax 20-21-95-80; e-mail lejour@africaonline.co.ci; internet www.lejour.ci; f. 1994; publ. by Editions du Soleil; Dir BAILLY DIÉGOU; Editor-in-Chief ABDOULAYE SANGARÉ; circ. 12,000.

Le Libéral: 01 BP 6938, Abidjan 01; tel. and fax 22-52-21-41; e-mail leliberal@aviso.ci; internet www.leliberal.net; f. 1997; publication suspended Sept. 2002; Dir YORO KONÉ; Editor-in-Chief BAKARY NIMAGA.

Le National: Angré, Cocody 16 BP 165, Abidjan 16; tel. 22-52-27-43; fax 22-52-27-42; e-mail lenational@lenational.info; internet www .lenational.info; f. 1999; supports fmr President Bédié; Publr LAURENT TAPÉ KOULOU; Editor-in-Chief ASSÉ ALAFÉ.

Notre Chance: Immeuble SICOGI, 1er étage, porte escalier E, blvd du Gabon (Marcory), 10 BP 654, Abidjan 10; tel. 21-26-44-28; Dir MICHEL NAHOUA LEPREGNON.

Notre Voie: Cocody-les-Deux-Plateaux, 06 BP 2868, Abidjan 06; tel. 22-42-63-31; fax 22-42-63-32; e-mail gnh@africaonline.co.ci; internet www.notrevoie.ci; f. 1978; organ of the FPI; Dir WANYOU EUGÈNE ALLOU; Editor-in-Chief CÉSAR ETOU.

Le Nouveau Réveil: 220 Logements, Adjamé Sud-Tours SICOGI, face Frat-Mat, Bâtiment A, 2e étage P6, 04 BP 1947, Abidjan 04; tel. and fax 20-38-67-91; internet www.lenouveaureveil.com; f. 2001 to replace weekly *Le Réveil-Hebdo*; supports PDCI—RDA; Dir of Publication DENIS KAH ZION; Editor-in-Chief GUSTAVE N'GUESSAN; circ. 17,000 (2002).

Le Patriote: rue Marconi prolongée, Zone 4c, 22 BP 509, Abidjan 22; tel. 05-04-31-72; fax 20-22-59-26; e-mail lepatriote@globeaccess .net; internet www.eburneanews.net/lepatriote/lepatriote.asp; organ of the RDR; Dir PATRICE G. LENONHIN; Editor MÉITÉ SINDOU.

Le Populaire–Nouvelle Formule: 19 blvd Angoulvant, résidence Neuilly, Plateau, 01 BP 5496, Abidjan 01; tel. 21-36-34-15; fax 21-36-43-28; Dir RAPHAËL ORE LAKPÉ.

Soir Info: rue Louis Lumière, zone 4c, 10 BP 2462, Abidjan 10; tel. 21-25-32-77; fax 21-24-47-27; e-mail soirinfo@afnet.net; internet www.presseci.com/soirinfo; f. 1994; publ. by Editions Olympe; Dir MAURICE FERRO BI BALI; Editor-in-Chief ZOROMÉ LOSS; circ. 10,000–15,000.

Tassouman: Abidjan-Cocody, 22 BP 400, Abidjan 22; tel. 05-70-21-68; e-mail tassouman@globeaccess.net; internet www.tassouman.ci; f. 2000; satirical; supports RDR; publication suspended Sept. 2002; Dir and Editor-in-Chief ABOUBAKAR S. KONE.

La Voie: face Institut Marie-Thérèse Houphouët-Boigny, 17 BP 656, Abidjan 17; tel. 20-37-68-23; fax 20-37-74-76; organ of the FPI; Dir ABOU DRAHAMANE SANGARÉ; Man. MAURICE LURIGNAN.

SELECTED WEEKLIES

L'Agora: Immeuble Nana Yamoussou, ave 13, rue 38, Treichville, 01 BP 5326, Abidjan 01; tel. 21-34-11-72; f. 1997; Dir FERNAND DÉDÉ; Editor-in-Chief BAMBA ALEX SOULEYMANE.

Argument: 09 BP 3328, Abidjan 09; tel. 20-37-63-96; f. 1998; Dir GUY BADIETO LIALY; Editor-in-Chief JEAN-LOUIS PÉHÉ.

Citypoche: Immeuble Nour al-Ayat, 18 BP 3136, Abidjan 18; tel. 20-21-91-89; f. 1997; Dir ELIANE STROEHLIN.

Le Démocrate: Maison du Congrès, ave 2, Treichville, 01 BP 1212, Abidjan 01; tel. 21-24-45-88; fax 21-24-25-61; f. 1991; organ of the PDCI–RDA; Dir NOËL YAO.

Le Front: Immeuble Mistral, 3e étage, 220 Logts, Abidjan; tel. 20-38-13-24; fax 20-38-70-83; e-mail lefront@globeaccess.net; internet www.lefront.ci; 2 a week; Editorial Dir FATOUMATA COULIBALY; Editor KPOKPA BLÉ.

Gbich!: 10 BP 399, Abidjan 10; tel. and fax 21-26-31-94; e-mail gbich@assistweb.net; internet assistweb.net/gbich; satirical; Editor-in-Chief MATHIEU BLEDOU.

Le Nouvel Horizon: 220 Logements, blvd du Général de Gaulle, Adjamé, 17 BP 656, Abidjan 17; tel. 20-37-68-23; f. 1990; organ of the FPI; Dir ABOU DRAHAMANE SANGARÉ; circ. 15,000.

La Nouvelle Presse: rue des Jardins, Cocody-les-deux-Plateaux, 01 BP 8534, Abidjan 01; tel. 22-41-04-76; fax 22-41-04-15; e-mail jvieyra@africaonline.co.ci; f. 1992; publ. by Centre Africain de Presse et d'Edition; current affairs; Editors JUSTIN VIEYRA, JÉRÔME CARLOS; circ. 10,000.

Sports Magazine: Yopougon-SOGEFIHA, 01 BP 4030, Abidjan 01; tel. 23-45-14-02; f. 1997; Dir JOSEPH ABLE.

Téré: 220 Lgts, blvd du Général de Gaulle, Adjamé Liberté, 20 BP 43, Abidjan 20; tel. and fax 20-37-79-42; organ of the PIT; Dir ANGÈLE GNONSOA.

Top-Visages: 23 BP 892, Abidjan 23; tel. 20-33-72-10; fax 20-22-53-29; e-mail mam-camara@yahoo.fr; Editor-in-Chief BÉHI E. TONGA.

La Voie du Compatriote: Adjamé St-Michel; 09 BP 2008, Abidjan 09; tel. 20-37-50-13; f. 1998; Dir SINARI KAL.

SELECTED PERIODICALS

Côte d'Ivoire Magazine: Présidence de la République, 01 BP 1354, Abidjan 01; tel. 20-22-02-22; f. 1998; quarterly; Dir JEAN-NOËL LOUKO.

La Lettre de l'Afrique de l'Ouest: rue des Jardins, Cocody-les-Deux-Plateaux, 01 BP 8534, Abidjan 01; tel. 22-41-04-76; fax 22-41-04-15; e-mail jvieyra@africaonline.co.ci; f. 1995; publ. by Centre Africain de Presse et d'Edition; six a year; politics, economics, regional integration; Editors JUSTIN VIEYRA, JÉRÔME CARLOS.

Maisons et Matériaux: 08 BP 2150, Abidjan 08; tel. 22-42-92-17; monthly; Dir THIAM T. DJENEBOU.

Roots-Rock Magazine: Abidjan; tel. 22-42-84-74; f. 1998; monthly; music; Dir DIOMANDÉ DAVID.

RTI-Mag: 08 BP 663, Abidjan 08; tel. 20-33-14-46; fax 20-32-12-06; publ. by Radiodiffusion-Télévision Ivoirienne; listings magazine.

Sentiers: 26 ave Chardy, 01 BP 2432, Abidjan 01; tel. 20-21-95-68; fax 20-21-95-80; e-mail redaction@aviso.ci; Editor-in-Chief DIÉGOU BAILLY.

Stades d'Afrique: blvd du Général de Gaulle, 01 BP 1807, Abidjan 01; tel. 20-37-06-66; fax 20-37-25-45; e-mail fratmat@africaonline.co .ci; f. 2000; sports; monthly; Dir-Gen. EMMANUEL KOUASSI KOKORÉ; Editor-in-Chief HÉGAUD OUATTARA.

Le Succès: 21 BP 3748, Abidjan 21; tel. 20-37-71-64; monthly; Dir AKPLA PLAKATOU.

Univers jeunes: 01 BP 3713, Abidjan 01; tel. 20-21-20-00; fax 21-35-35-45; e-mail univers@africaonline.co.ci; monthly; Editor-in-Chief MOUSSA SY SAVANÉ.

La Voix d'Afrique: rue des Jardins, Cocody-les-Deux-Plateaux, 01 BP 8534, Abidjan 01; tel. 22-41-04-76; fax 22-41-04-15; e-mail jvieyra@africaonline.co.ci; publ. by Centre Africain de Presse et d'Edition; monthly; Editor-in-Chief GAOUSSOU KAMISSOKO.

NEWS AGENCIES

Agence Ivoirienne de Presse (AIP): ave Chardy, 04 BP 312, Abidjan 04; tel. 20-22-64-13; fax 20-21-35-39; e-mail aip@ci.refer.org; internet www.aip-ci.com; f. 1961; 14 regional bureaux; Dir DALLI DEBY.

Foreign Bureaux

Agence France-Presse (AFP): 18 ave du Docteur Crozet, 01 BP 726, Abidjan 01; tel. 20-21-90-17; fax 20-21-10-36; e-mail afp@aviso .ci; internet www.afp.com; Dir SERGE ARNOLD.

Associated Press (AP) (USA): 01 BP 5843, Abidjan 01; tel. 22-41-38-95; fax 22-41-28-94; e-mail iromauld@yahoo.fr; internet www.ap .org; Bureau Chief ELLEN KNICKMAYER.

PANA-Presse (Senegal): 09 BP 2744, Abidjan 09; tel. and fax 20-33-40-79; e-mail odji@bobley.africaonline.co.ci.

Reuters West Africa (United Kingdom): Résidence Les Acacias, 2e étage, appt 203–205, 20 blvd Clozel, 01 BP 2338, Abidjan 01; tel. 20-21-12-22; fax 20-21-30-77; e-mail abidjan.newsroom@reuters.com; West Africa Man. MICHEL CLÉMENT; Bureau Chief NICHOLAS PHYTHIAN.

Xinhua (New China) News Agency (People's Republic of China): Immeuble SGBCI, 4e étage, ave Lamblin, Plateau, 01 BP V321, Abidjan 01; tel. 20-32-52-20; fax 20-32-22-49; internet www.xinhua .org; Chief Correspondent LINGHU DAOCHENG.

PRESS ASSOCIATIONS

Association de la Presse Démocratique Ivoirienne (APDI): Abidjan; tel. 20-37-06-66; f. 1994; Chair. JEAN-BAPTISTE AKROU.

Union nationale des journalistes de Côte d'Ivoire (UNJCI): 06 BP 1675, Plateau, Abidjan 06; tel. 20-21-61-07; e-mail unjci@ globeaccess.net; internet www.unjci.ci; f. 1991; Pres. HONORAT NDJOMOU DE YÉDAGNE; 200 mems.

Publishers

Centre Africain de Presse et d'Edition (CAPE): rue des Jardins, Cocody-les-Deux-Plateaux, 01 BP 8534, Abidjan 01; tel. 22-41-04-76; fax 22-41-04-15; e-mail jvieyra@africaonline.co.ci; Man. JUSTIN VIEYRA.

Centre d'Edition et de Diffusion Africaines (CEDA): 17 rue des Carrossiers, 04 BP 541, Abidjan 04; tel. 20-24-65-10; fax 21-25-05-67; e-mail promotion@ceda-ci.com; internet www.ceda-ci.com; f. 1961; 20% state-owned; general non-fiction, school and children's books, literary fiction; Pres. and Dir-Gen. VENANCE KACOU.

Centre de Publications Evangéliques: 08 BP 900, Abidjan 08; tel. 22-44-48-05; fax 22-44-58-17; e-mail cpe@aviso.ci; f. 1970; reformed Christian; Dir JULES OUOBA.

Editions Bognini: 06 BP 1254, Abidjan 06; tel. 20-41-16-86; social sciences, literary fiction.

Editions Eburnie: 01 BP 1984, 01 Abidjan; tel. 20-21-64-65; fax 20-21-45-46; e-mail eburnie@aviso.ci; f. 2001; illustrated books for children, social sciences, poetry.

Editions Neter: 01 BP 7370, Abidjan 01; tel. 22-52-52-68; f. 1992; politics, culture, history, literary fiction; Dir RICHARD TA BI SENIN.

Nouvelles Editions Ivoiriennes: 1 blvd de Marseille, 01 BP 1818, Abidjan 01; tel. 21-24-07-66; fax 21-24-24-56; e-mail edition@nei-ci .com; internet www.nei-ci.com; f. 1972; literature, criticism, essays, drama, social sciences, history, in French and English; Dir GUY LAMBIN.

Presses Universitaires et Scolaires d'Afrique: 08 BP 177, Abidjan 08; tel. 22-41-12-71; mathematics, economics, medicine.

Université Nationale de Côte d'Ivoire: 01 BP V34, Abidjan 01; tel. 22-44-08-59; f. 1964; academic and general non-fiction and periodicals; Publications Dir GILLES VILASCO.

Government Publishing House

Imprimerie Nationale: BP V87, Abidjan; tel. 20-21-76-11; fax 20-21-68-68.

Broadcasting and Communications

TELECOMMUNICATIONS

Regulatory Authorities

Agence des Télécommunications de Côte d'Ivoire (ATCI): Immeuble Postel 2001, 4e étage, rue Lecoeur, 18 BP 2203, Abidjan

18; tel. 20-34-43-74; fax 20-34-43-75; e-mail courrier@atci.ci; internet www.atci.ci; f. 1995; Man. Dir LESAN BASILE GNON.

Conseil des Télécommunications de Côte d'Ivoire: 17 BP 110, Abidjan 17; tel. 20-34-43-04; f. 1995; deals with issues of arbitration.

Service Providers

CORA de Comstar: Immeuble Alpha 2000, 11e étage, Plateau, Abidjan; tel. 20-22-81-01; fax 20-22-81-05; f. 1996 as Comstar Wireless, present name adopted 2000; mobile cellular telephone operator in Abidjan and surrounding region; owned by Western Wireless Corpn (USA).

Côte d'Ivoire-Télécom (CI-Télécom): Immeuble Postel 2001, rue Lecoeur, 17 BP 275, Abidjan 17; tel. 20-34-40-00; fax 20-21-28-28; e-mail info@citelecom.ci; internet www.citelecom.ci; f. 1991; 51% owned by France Télécom; 49% state-owned; Pres. YAYA OUATTARA; Man. Dir ALAIN PETIT; 327,000 subscribers (June 2002).

Loteny Télécom—Télécel: 12 rue Crossons Duplessis, 01 BP 3685, Abidjan 01; tel. 20-32-32-32; fax 20-32-27-25; e-mail info@telecel .net; internet www.telecel.net; f. 1996; mobile cellular telephone operator in more than 60 urban centres; partnership between Telecel International, Access Télécom and Loteny Electronics; Pres. MIKO RWAYITARE; more than 300,000 subscribers (2002).

Orange Côte d'Ivoire: Immeuble Saha, blvd Valéry Giscard d'Estaing, Zone 4C, 11 BP 202, Abidjan 11; tel. 21-23-90-07; fax 21-23-90-11; internet www.orange.ci; f. 1996 as Société Ivoirienne de Mobiles (Ivoiris), present name adopted 2002; mobile cellular telephone operator in more than 60 urban centres; 85% owned by France Télécom; Man. Dir BERNARD CLIVET; 427,000 subscribers (June 2002).

BROADCASTING

Radio

In 1993 the Government permitted the first commercial radio stations to broadcast in Côte d'Ivoire; of the five licences initially granted, four were to foreign stations. Between 1998 and early 2001, a further 52 licences were granted, although strict regulations continue to restrict the operation of private radio stations.

Radiodiffusion-Télévision Ivoirienne (RTI): BP V 191, Abidjan 01; tel. 20-21-48-00; e-mail rti@rti.ci; f. 1962; state-owned; Pres. JOACHIM BONY; Dir-Gen. GEORGES ABOKE.

Fréquence 2: BP V 191, Abidjan 01; tel. 20-22-21-21; themed FM broadcasts; entertainment and youth; 147 hrs of programming weekly; transfer to private-sector management pending; Dir OULAÏ ELOI.

Radio-CI: BP V 191, Abidjan 01; tel. 20-21-48-00; fmrly La Chaîne Nationale; general FM broadcasts; 280 hours of programmes weekly; also broadcasts regional news in national languages; 10 studios (eight in Abidjan and two in Bouaké); Dir OULAÏ ELOI.

Africa N° 1: 09 BP 951, Abidjan 09; tel. 07-83-62-09; fax 22-42-70-07; internet www.africa1.com; FM station; Dir NOËL YAO.

BBC Afrique: 04 BP 563, Abidjan 04; tel. 20-22-18-05; fax 20-21-21-01; e-mail bbcafrique@bbc.co.uk; internet www.bbc.co.uk/french; broadcasts commenced 1994; FM station operated by British Broadcasting Corpn.

City FM: Immeuble Alpha Cissé, avant la piscine d'Etat, Treichville, 01 BP 7207, Abidjan 01; tel. 21-25-10-28; internet www .assistweb.net/cityfm; f. 1999; Pres. and Man. Dir. Me ALIOU SIBI.

Radio Espoir: 12 BP 27, Abidjan 12; tel. 21-27-60-01; fax 21-27-69-70; e-mail respoir@globeaccess.net; f. 1990; Roman Catholic; Dir Fr BASILE DIANÉ KOGNAN.

Radio France Internationale: Abidjan; tel. 05-60-92-00; e-mail biyack@hotmail.com; internet www.rfi.fr; Correspondent ALAIN BIYACK.

Radio Peleforo Gbon: Route Ferké km 2, BP 841, Korhogo; tel. 21-86-22-62; fax 21-86-20-33.

Radio Soleil: 16 BP 1179, Abidjan 16; tel. 21-99-17-64; fax 21-79-12-48; e-mail ebadouel@irisa.fr.

Television

Radiodiffusion-Télévision Ivoirienne (RTI): see above.

La Première Chaîne: 08 BP 331, Abidjan 08; tel. 22-44-90-39; general national and regional broadcasting; French and national languages; Dir FÉLICIEN KOFFI.

TV 2: 08 BP 883, Abidjan 08; tel. 22-44-90-39; f. 1991; operates in Abidjan and the southern region; local news and current affairs; transfer to private-sector management pending; Dir MAIXENT DEGNEY.

Canal Plus Horizons: Abidjan; e-mail abo.canal@aviso.ci; internet www.canalhorizons.com; broadcasts commenced 1994; subsidiary of Canal Plus (France); 15,000 subscribers (1995).

Finance

(cap. = capital; res = reserves; dep. = deposits; m. = million; br. = branch; amounts in francs CFA)

BANKING

Central Bank

Banque Centrale des Etats de l'Afrique de l'Ouest (BCEAO): 01 BP 1769, Abidjan 01; tel. 20-20-84-00; fax 20-22-28-52; internet www.bceao.int; f. 1962; HQ in Dakar, Senegal; bank of issue for the mem. states of the Union économique et monétaire ouest-africaine (UEMOA, comprising Benin, Burkina Faso, Côte d'Ivoire, Guinea-Bissau, Mali, Niger, Senegal and Togo); cap. and res 850,500m., total assets 5,157,700m. (Dec. 2001); Gov. CHARLES KONAN BANNY; Dir in Côte d'Ivoire LANSINA BAKARY; 5 brs.

Commercial Banks

Bank of Africa—Côte d'Ivoire (BOA—CI): Immeuble SMGL, 11 rue Joseph Anoma, 01 BP 4132, Abidjan 01; tel. 20-33-15-36; fax 20-32-89-93; e-mail ciboa@globeaccess.net; f. 1980; 64.7% owned by Groupe African Financial Holding; cap. and res 1,705m., total assets 38,835m. (Dec. 1999); Chair. PAUL DERREUMAUX; Man. Dir JEAN-PIERRE GALIBERT.

Banque Atlantique—Côte d'Ivoire: Immeuble Atlantique, ave Nogues, Plateau, 04 BP 1036, Abidjan 04; tel. 20-31-59-50; fax 20-21-68-52; e-mail baci1@baci.ci; f. 1978; cap. 7,000.0m., res 237.2m., dep. 31,162.7m. (Dec. 2000); Pres. SERGE GUETTA; Dir-Gen. JEAN-PIERRE COTI; 2 brs.

Banque de l'Habitat de Côte d'Ivoire (BHCI): 22 ave Joseph Anoma, 01 BP 2325, Abidjan 01; tel. 20-22-60-00; fax 20-22-58-18; f. 1993; cap. and res 1,755m., total assets 16,834m. (Dec. 1999); Chair. DAVID AMUAH; Man. Dir LANCINA COULIBALY.

Banque Internationale pour l'Afrique de l'Ouest—Côte d'Ivoire (BIAO—CI): 8–10 ave Joseph Anoma, 01 BP 1274, Abidjan 01; tel. 20-20-07-20; fax 20-20-07-00; e-mail biaosq@africaonline.co .ci; internet www.biao.co.ci; f. 1980; 80% owned by Banque Belgolaise (Belgium); cap. 5,000m., total assets 219,990m. (Dec. 2000); Pres. SEYDOU DIARRA; Man. Dir PAUL PEETERS; 32 brs.

Banque Internationale pour le Commerce et l'Industrie de la Côte d'Ivoire SA (BICI-CI): ave Franchet d'Espérey, 01 BP 1298, Abidjan 01; tel. 20-20-16-00; fax 20-20-17-00; e-mail m.lafont@bicici .com; internet www.bicici.org; f. 1962; 60.3% owned by BNP Paribas (France); cap. 16,666.7m., res 18,869.5m., dep. 257,368.1m. (Dec. 2001); Pres. and Dir-Gen. ANGE KOFFY; 37 brs.

Banque Paribas Côte d'Ivoire (Paribas—CI): 17 ave Terrasson de Fougères, 17 BP 09, Abidjan 17; tel. 20-21-86-86; fax 20-21-88-23; f. 1984; 85% owned by BNP Paribas (France); cap. and res 2,938m., total assets 30,697m. (Dec. 1999); Pres. and Dir-Gen. FRANÇOIS DAUGE.

Citibank Côte d'Ivoire: Immeuble Botreau Roussel, 28 ave Delafosse, 01 BP 3698, Abidjan 01; tel. 20-20-90-00; fax 20-21-76-85; e-mail citibank@odaci.net; dep. 55,155m., total assets 127,630m. (Dec. 1999); Dir-Gen. MARC H. WIESING.

Compagnie Bancaire de l'Atlantique Côte d'Ivoire (COBACI): Immeuble Atlantique, ave Nogues, 01 BP 522, Abidjan 01; tel. 20-21-28-04; fax 20-21-07-98; e-mail cobaci@africaonline.co.ci; 65% owned by Banque Atlantique—Côte d'Ivoire; cap. 2,572m., res 1,009m., dep. 16,082m. (Dec. 2000); Pres. and Dir-Gen. DOSSONGUI KONE; Man. Dir MICHEL FRANÇOIS KAHN.

Compagnie Financière de la Côte d'Ivoire (COFINCI): Tour BICI-CI, 15e étage, rue Gourgas, 01 BP 1566, Abidjan 01; tel. 20-21-27-32; fax 20-21-26-43; e-mail y.kouassi@bicici.com; f. 1974; 72% owned by BICI-CI; cap. and res 2,377m., total assets 8,893m. (Dec. 1999); Chair. ANGE KOFFY; Dir YAO KOUASSI.

Ecobank–Côte d'Ivoire: Immeuble Alliance, 1 ave Terrasson de Fougères, 01 BP 4107, Abidjan 01; tel. 20-21-10-41; fax 20-21-88-16; e-mail ecobankci@ecobank.com. internet www.ecobank.com; f. 1989; 94% owned by Ecobank Transnational Inc (Togo); cap. 3,226.0m., res 885.3m., dep. 90,330.6m. (Dec. 2000); Man. Dir FOGAN SOSSAH; 1 br.

Société Générale de Banques en Côte d'Ivoire (SGBCI): 5–7 ave Joseph Anoma, 01 BP 1355, Abidjan 01; tel. 20-20-12-34; fax 20-20-14-92; e-mail bhfm.mail@socgen.com; internet sgbci.groupe .socgen.com:8000/; f. 1962; 54.8% owned by Société Générale (France); cap. and res 49,573m., dep. 367,222m. (Dec. 2000); Pres. TIÉMOKO YADÉ COULIBALY; Man. Dir MICHEL MIAILLE; 52 brs.

Société Générale de Financement et de Participations en Côte d'Ivoire (SOGEFINANCE): 5–7 ave Joseph Anoma, 01 BP 3904, Abidjan 01; tel. 20-22-55-30; fax 20-32-67-60; f. 1978; 58% owned by SGBCI; cap. and res 2,050m., total assets 7,215m. (Dec. 1999); Pres. Jean Louis Mattei; Man. Dir Michel Miaille.

Société Ivoirienne de Banque (SIB): 34 blvd de la République, 01 BP 1300, Abidjan 01; tel. 20-20-00-00; fax 20-20-01-19; e-mail info@sib.ci; internet www.sib.ci; f. 1962; 51% owned by Crédit Lyonnais (France); 49% state-owned; reduction of state holding to 19% pending in 2002; cap. and res 12,497m., total assets 239,479m. (Dec. 2000); Man. Dir Pascal Fall; 14 brs.

Credit Institutions

Afribail—Côte d'Ivoire (Afribail—CI): 8–10 ave Joseph Anoma, 01 BP 1274, Abidjan 01; tel. 20-20-07-20; fax 20-20-07-00; 95% owned by BIAO—CI; cap. and res 776m., total assets 11,900m. (Dec. 1999); Chair. René Amany; Man. Dir Jacob Ahiwa Brou.

BICI Bail de Côte d'Ivoire: Tour BICI-CI, 5e étage, ave Franchet d'Espérey, 04 BP 6495, Abidjan 01; tel. 20-20-17-90; fax 20-22-93-95; e-mail m.djedjess@bicici.com; 75% owned by BICI-CI; cap. and res 1,707m., total assets 13,638m. (Dec. 1999); Pres. Ange Koffy; Man. Dir Martin Djedjess.

Coopérative Ivoirienne d'Epargne et de Crédit Automobile (CIECA): 04 BP 2084, Abidjan 04; tel. 20-22-77-13; fax 20-22-77-35; cap. and res 805m. (Dec. 1998), total assets 1,169m. (Dec. 1999); Dir-Gen. Dally Zabo.

Société Africaine de Crédit Automobilier (SAFCA): 1 rue des Carrossiers, Zone 3, 04 BP 27, Abidjan 04; tel. 21-24-91-77; fax 21-35-77-90; e-mail safca@aviso.ci; f. 1956; cap. 1,000m. (Dec. 2000), total assets 29,360m. (Dec. 1999); Pres. and Dir-Gen. Diack Diawar.

Société Africaine de Crédit-Bail (SAFBAIL): Immeuble SAFCA, 1 rue des Carrossiers, Zone 3, 04 BP 27, Abidjan 04; tel. 21-24-91-77; fax 21-35-77-90; e-mail safca@aviso.ci; f. 1971; cap. and res 2,922m., total assets 13,414m. (Dec. 1999); Chair. and Man. Dir Diack Diawar.

SOGEFIBAIL—CI: 26 ave Delafosse, 01 BP 1355, Abidjan 01; tel. 20-32-85-15; fax 20-33-14-93; 35% owned by GENEFITEC, 35% by SOGEFINANCE, 25% by SGBCI; cap. and res 2,145m., total assets 9,834m. (Dec. 1999); Pres. Jean-Louis Mattei; Dir Pierre Gabriel Siby.

Bankers' Association

Association Professionnelle des Banques et Etablissements Financiers de Côte d'Ivoire (APBEFCI): 01 BP 3810, Abidjan 01; tel. 20-21-20-08; affiliated to Conseil National du Patronat Ivoirien; q.v. Pres. Jean-Pierre Meyer.

Financial Institution

Caisse Autonome d'Amortissement de Côte d'Ivoire (CAA): Immeuble SCIAM, ave Marchand, 01 BP 670, Abidjan 01; tel. 20-20-98-00; fax 20-21-35-78; e-mail caadg@aviso.ci; f. 1959; management of state funds; Chair. Abdoulaye Koné; Man. Dir Sékou Bamba.

STOCK EXCHANGE

Bourse Régionale des Valeurs Mobilières (BRVM): 18 ave Joseph Anoma, 01 BP 3802, Abidjan 01; tel. 20-32-66-85; fax 20-32-66-84; e-mail brvm@brvm.org; internet www.brvm.org; f. 1998 to succeed Bourse des Valeurs d'Abidjan; regional stock exchange serving mem. states of UEMOA; Dir-Gen. Jean-Paul Gillet.

BRVM (Antenne Nationale de Côte d'Ivoire): 18 ave Joseph Anoma, 01 BP 1541, Abidjan 01; tel. 20-31-55-50; fax 20-32-47-77; e-mail tbah@brvm.org; Pres Tiémoko Tade Coulibaly; Man. Tidiane Amadou Bah.

INSURANCE

Abidjanaise d'Assurances: Immeuble Woodin Center, ave Noguès, 01 BP 2909, Abidjan 01; tel. 20-22-46-96; fax 20-22-64-81; e-mail abjassur@africaonline.co.ci; Dir-Gen. Marc Richmond.

African American Insurance Co (AFRAM): Immeuble ex-Monopris, 2 ave Noguès, 01 BP 7124, Abidjan 01; tel. 20-31-30-44; fax 20-32-69-72; Dir-Gen. Christian Casel.

Alliance Africaine d'Assurances (3A): 17 BP 477, Abidjan 17; tel. 20-32-42-52; fax 20-32-54-90; Pres. Dam Sarr; Dir-Gen. Corinne Sarr.

Assurances Générales de Côte d'Ivoire (AGCI): Immeuble AGCI, ave Noguès, 01 BP 4092, Abidjan 01; tel. 20-32-10-52; fax 20-33-25-79; e-mail agci@africaonline.co.ci; f. 1979; mem. of Groupe NSIA–AGCI since 1996; Chair. and Man. Dir Jean Kacou Diagou.

Assurances Générales de Côte d'Ivoire–Vie (AGCI–Vie): Immeuble AGCI, ave Noguès, 01 BP 4092, Abidjan 01; tel. 20-33-11-31; fax 20-33-25-79; f. 1988; mem. of Groupe NSIA–AGCI since 1996; life; Chair. and Man. Dir Jean Kacou Diagou.

AXA Assurances Côte d'Ivoire: ave Delafosse Prolongée, 01 BP 378, Abidjan 01; tel. 20-21-73-81; fax 20-22-12-43; f. 1981; fmrly l'Union Africaine–IARD; insurance and reinsurance; Chair. Joachim Richmond; Dir Alexandre Ahui Atte.

AXA Vie Côte d'Ivoire: 9 ave Houdaille, 01 BP 2016, Abidjan 01; tel. 20-22-25-15; fax 20-22-37-60; f. 1985; fmrly Union Africaine Vie; life assurance and capitalization; Chair. Joachim Richmond; Dir Patrice Desgranges.

Colina: Immeuble Colina, blvd Roume, 01 BP 3832, Abidjan 01; tel. 20-21-65-05; fax 20-22-59-05; e-mail c-dg@colina-sa.com; internet www.colina-sa.com; f. 1980; Chair. Michel Pharaon; Dir-Gen. Raymond Farhat.

Compagnie Nationale d'Assurances (CNA): Immeuble Symphonie, 30 ave du Général de Gaulle, 01 BP 1333, Abidjan 01; tel. 20-21-49-19; fax 20-22-49-06; f. 1972; cap. 400m. insurance and reinsurance; transfer to private ownership pending; Chair. Sounkalo Djibo; Man. Dir Richard Coulibaly.

Mutuelle Centrale d'Assurances: 15 Immeuble Ebrien, 01 BP 1217, Abidjan 01; tel. 20-21-11-24; fax 20-33-18-37.

Nouvelle Société Interafricaine d'Assurances (NSIA): rue Gourgas, Immeuble Alpha 2000, 01 BP 1571, Abidjan 01; tel. 20-22-76-21; fax 20-22-76-20; e-mail nsia@africaonline.co.ci; f. 1995; mem. of Groupe NSIA–AGCI; Chair. and Man. Dir Jean Kacou Diagou.

Société Africaine d'Assurances et de Réassurances en République de Côte d'Ivoire (SAFARRIV): 01 BP 1741, Abidjan 01; tel. 20-21-91-57; fax 20-21-82-72; e-mail groupe-safarriv@safarriv.ci; internet www.safarriv.ci; f. 1975; affiliated to AGF Afrique; Pres. Tiémoko Yadé Coulibaly; Man. Dir Christian Arrault.

Trade and Industry

GOVERNMENT AGENCIES

Autorité pour la Régulation du Café et du Cacao: Abidjan; f. 2001; implements regulatory framework for coffee and cocoa trade.

Bureau National d'Etudes Techniques et de Développement (BNETD): ancien hôtel 'Le Relais', blvd Hassan II, Cocody, 04 BP 945, Abidjan 04; tel. 22-44-28-05; fax 22-44-56-66; e-mail info@bnetd.sita.net; f. 1978 as Direction et Contrôle des Grands Travaux; management and supervision of major public works projects; Man. Dir Don-Mello Ahoua.

Comité de Privatisation: 6 blvd de l'Indénié, 01 BP 1141, Abidjan 01; tel. 20-22-22-31; fax 20-22-22-35; e-mail cpct@africaonline.co.ci; state privatization authority; Pres. Paul Agodio; Dir-Gen. Ahoua Don Mello.

Compagnie Ivoirienne pour le Développement des Cultures Vivrières (CIDV): Abidjan; tel. 20-21-00-79; f. 1988; production of food crops; Man. Dir Benoît N'Dri Brou.

Nouvelle PETROCI: Immeuble les Hévéas, 14 blvd Carde, BP V194, Abidjan 01; tel. 20-20-25-00; fax 20-21-68-24; e-mail petrociholding@globeaccess.net; f. 1975 as Société Nationale d'Opérations Pétrolières de la Côte d'Ivoire (PETROCI); restructured 2000 to comprise three companies—Petroci Exploration Production, SA, Petroci Gaz and Petroci Industries Services; all aspects of hydrocarbons development; Pres. Paul Gui Dibo; Man. Dir Koffi Ernest.

Société pour le Développement Minier de la Côte d'Ivoire (SODEMI): 31 blvd des Martyrs, 01 BP 2816, Abidjan 01; tel. 22-44-29-94; fax 22-44-08-21; e-mail sodemidg@aviso.cg; f. 1962; geological and mineral research; Pres. Nicolas Kouandi Angba; Man. Dir Jean-Yves Likane.

Société de Développement des Plantations Forestières (SODEFOR): blvd François Mitterrand, 01 BP 3770, Abidjan 01; tel. 22-44-46-16; fax 22-44-02-40; f. 1954; establishment and management of tree plantations, management of state forests, marketing of timber products; Pres. Minister of Agriculture and Animal Husbandry; Man. Dir Jean-Claude Aneh.

Société pour le Développement des Productions Animales (SODEPRA): 01 BP 1249, Abidjan 01; tel. 20-21-13-10; f. 1970; rearing of livestock; Man. Dir Paul Lamizana.

DEVELOPMENT AGENCIES

Agence Française de Développement (AFD): blvd François Mitterrand, 01 BP 1814, Abidjan 01; tel. 22-44-53-05; fax 22-44-21-78; e-mail afdci@aviso.ci; internet www.afd.fr; fmrly Caisse Française de Développement; Dir in Côte d'Ivoire Guy Terracol.

Centre de Promotion des Investissements en Côte d'Ivoire (CEPICI): Tour CCIA, 5e étage, BP V152, Abidjan 01; tel. 20-21-40-

70; fax 20-21-40-71; e-mail info@cepici.go.ci; internet www.cepici.go
.ci; f. 1993; investment promotion authority; Dir Pierre Dagbo Gode;
Gen. Man. M. Koffivi.

CHAMBERS OF COMMERCE

Chambre d'Agriculture de la Côte d'Ivoire: 11 ave Lamblin, 01
BP 1291, Abidjan 01; tel. 20-32-92-13; fax 20-32-92-20; Sec.-Gen.
Gauthier N'Zi.

Chambre de Commerce et d'Industrie de Côte d'Ivoire: 6 ave
Joseph Anoma, 01 BP 1399, Abidjan 01; tel. 20-33-16-00; fax 20-32-
39-42; e-mail cci@africaonline.co.ci; f. 1992; Pres. Jean-Louis Billon;
Dir-Gen. Yao Kouame.

TRADE ASSOCIATIONS

Bourse du Café et du Cacao (BCC): Abidjan; f. 2001 to replace
marketing, purchasing and certain other functions of La Nouvelle
Caistab (Caisse de Stabilisation et de Soutien des Prix des Productions Agricoles); Pres. Lucien Tapé Doh.

**Fédération Ivoirienne des Producteurs de Café et de Cacao
(FIPCC):** Yamoussoukro; f. 1998; coffee and cocoa growers' assoc.
Chair. Cissé Lociné; c. 3,000 mems.

**Organisation de Commercialisation de l'Ananas et de la
Banane (OCAB):** Abidjan; pineapple and banana growers' assoc;
Exec. Sec. Emmanuel Doli.

EMPLOYERS' ORGANIZATIONS

**Association Nationale des Producteurs de Café-Cacao de
Côte d'Ivoire (ANAPROCI):** Pres. Henri Amouzou; Sec.-Gen.
Thomas Eyimin.

Conseil National du Patronat Ivoirien: 01 BP 8666, Abidjan 01;
tel. 20-32-17-97; fax 20-32-39-73; e-mail cnpi@aviso.ci; f. 1993; Pres.
Diack Diawar; Sec.-Gen. Aboubakar Coulibaly; nine affiliated federations, including the following.

Fédération Maritime de la Côte d'Ivoire (FEDERMAR): 04
BP 723, Abidjan 04; tel. 20-21-25-83; f. 1958; Sec.-Gen. Vacaba
Touré de Movaly.

**Fédération Nationale des Industries de la Côte d'Ivoire
(FNICI):** 01 BP 1340, Abidjan 01; tel. 20-21-71-42; fax 20-21-72-
56; f. 1993; Pres. Pierre Magne; Sec.-Gen. Daniel Teurquetil; 280
mems.

Groupement Interprofessionnel de l'Automobile (GIPA): 01
BP 1340, Abidjan 01; tel. 20-21-71-42; fax 20-21-72-56; f. 1953;
Pres. Bouaké Fofana; Sec.-Gen. Daniel Teurquetil; 32 mems.

**Syndicat des Commerçants Importateurs et Exportateurs
(SCIMPEX):** 01 BP 3792, Abidjan 01; tel. 20-21-54-27; fax 20-32-
56-52; Pres. Jacques Rossignol; Sec.-Gen. M. Koffi.

**Syndicat des Entrepreneurs et des Industriels de la Côte
d'Ivoire (SEICI):** Immeuble Jean Lefèbvre, 14 blvd de Marseille,
01 BP 464, Abidjan 01; tel. 20-21-83-85; f. 1934; Pres. Abdel Aziz
Thiam.

**Syndicat des Exportateurs et Négociants en Bois de Côte
d'Ivoire:** Immeuble CCIA, 11e étage, 01 BP 1979, Abidjan 01; tel.
20-21-12-39; fax 20-21-26-42; Pres. Souleymane Coulibaly.

Syndicat des Producteurs Industriels du Bois (SPIB): Immeuble CCIA, 11e étage, 01 BP 318, Abidjan 01; tel. 20-21-12-39; fax 20-
21-26-42; f. 1943; Pres. Bruno Finocchiaro.

Union des Entreprises Agricoles et Forestières: Immeuble
CCIA, 11e étage, 01 BP 2300, Abidjan 01; tel. 20-21-12-39; fax 20-21-
26-42; f. 1952; Pres. Fulgence Koffy.

UTILITIES

Electricity

Compagnie Ivoirienne d'Electricité (CIE): ave Christiani, 01
BP 6932, Abidjan 01; tel. 21-23-33-00; fax 21-24-63-22; e-mail info@
cie.ci; f. 1990 to assume electricity distribution network fmrly oper-
ated by Energie Electrique de la Côte d'Ivoire; 71% controlled by
Société Bouygues group (France); Pres. Marcel Zadi Kessy; Dir-Gen.
Marcel Pelissou.

Compagnie Ivoirienne de Production d'Electricité (CIPREL):
Tour Sidom, 12e étage, ave Houdaille, 01 BP 4039, Abidjan 01; tel.
20-22-60-97; independent power production; Pres. Olivier Bouygues.

Gas

Gaz de Côte d'Ivoire (GDCI): 01 BP 1351, Abidjan; tel. 22-44-49-
55; f. 1961; transfer to majority private ownership pending; gas
distributor; Man. Dir Lambert Konan.

Water

Société de Distribution d'Eau de la Côte d'Ivoire (SODECI): 1
ave Christiani, Treichville, 01 BP 1843, Abidjan 01; tel. 21-23-30-00;
fax 21-24-20-33; f. 1959; production, treatment and distribution of
drinking water; 46% owned by Groupe Bouygues (France), 51%
owned by employees; Chair. Marcel Zadi Kessy; Man. Dir. Pierre le
Tareau.

TRADE UNIONS

Dignité: 03 BP 2031, Abidjan 03; tel. 21-39-26-02; fax 21-37-74-89;
Sec.-Gen. Basile Mahan-Gahe; 10,000 mems (2001).

**Fédération des Syndicats Autonomes de la Côte d'Ivoire
(FESACI):** Abidjan; breakaway group from the Union Générale des
Travailleurs de Côte d'Ivoire; Sec.-Gen. Marcel Etté.

Union Générale des Travailleurs de Côte d'Ivoire (UGTCI): 05
BP 1203, Abidjan 05; tel. 20-21-26-65; f. 1962; Sec.-Gen. Hyacinthe
Adiko Niamkey; 100,000 individual mems; 190 affiliated unions.

Transport

RAILWAYS

The rail network in Côte d'Ivoire totalled 1,316 km in 1999,
including 660 km of track from Abidjan to Niangoloko, on the border
with Burkina Faso; from there, the railway extends to Kaya, via the
Burkinabè capital, Ouagadougou.

**SITARAIL—Transport Ferroviaire de Personnel et de Mar-
chandises:** Résidence Memanou, blvd Clozel, Plateau, 16 BP 1216,
Abidjan 16; tel. 20-21-06-36; fax 20-22-48-47; f. 1995 to operate
services on Abidjan–Ouagadougou–Kaya (Burkina Faso) line; Man.
Dir Abdelaziz Thiam.

ROADS

There are about 68,000 km of roads, of which some 6,000 km are
paved. Some 68,000m. francs CFA was invested in the road network
in 1994–98; projects included the upgrading of 3,000 km of roads and
30,000 km of tracks. Tolls were introduced on some roads in the mid-
1990s, to assist in funding the maintenance of the network.

Société des Transports Abidjanais (SOTRA): 01 BP 2009,
Abidjan 01; tel. 21-24-90-80; fax 21-25-97-21; e-mail sotra@access
.net; f. 1960; 60% state-owned; urban transport; Dir-Gen. Philippe
Attey.

SHIPPING

Côte d'Ivoire has two major ports, Abidjan and San-Pédro, both of
which are industrial and commercial establishments with financial
autonomy. Abidjan, which handled some 15.0m. metric tons of goods
in 2001, is the largest container and trading port in West Africa.
Access to the port is via the 2.7-km Vridi Canal. The port at San-
Pédro, which handled 1.2m. tons of goods in 1999, remains the main
gateway to the south-western region of Côte d'Ivoire. As a result of
widespread civil unrest from September 2002, much international
freight transport that formerly left or entered the West African
region through ports in Côte d'Ivoire was transferred to neighbouring countries.

Port Autonome d'Abidjan (PAA): BP V85, Abidjan; tel. 21-23-80-
00; fax 21-23-80-80; e-mail info@paa-ci.org; internet www.paa-ci.org;
f. 1992; transferred to private ownership in 1999; Pres. Ange-
François Barry-Battesti; Man. Dir Allah Aboidjé.

Port Autonome de San-Pédro (PASP): BP 339/340, San-Pédro;
tel. 34-71-20-80; fax 34-71-27-85; internet ibs.africaonline.co.ci/
pasp; f. 1971; Man. Dir Ogou Attemene.

AMICI: Km 1, blvd de Marseille, 16 BP 643, Abidjan 16; tel. 21-35-
28-50; fax 21-35-28-53; e-mail amici.abj@aviso.ci; internet www
.amici-shipping.com; f. 1998; 45% owned by Ivorian interests, 25%
by Danish interests, 20% by German interests and 10% by French
interests.

Compagnie Maritime Africaine—Côte d'Ivoire (COMAF—CI):
rond-point du Nouveau Port, 08 BP 867, Abidjan 08; tel. 20-32-40-77;
f. 1973; navigation and management of ships; Dir Franco Bernardini.

SDV—Côte d'Ivoire (SDV—CI): 01 BP 4082, Abidjan 01; tel. 20-
20-20-20; fax 20-20-21-20; f. 1943; sea and air transport; storage and
warehousing; Pres. Gilles Cuche.

SAGA Côte d'Ivoire: rond-point du Nouveau Port, 01 BP 1727,
Abidjan 01; tel. 21-23-23-23; fax 21-24-25-06; f. 1959; merchandise
handling, transit and storage; privately owned; Pres. M. Georges;
Dir-Gen. David Charrier.

Société Agence Maritime de l'Ouest Africain—Côte d'Ivoire (SAMOA—CI): rue des Gallions, 01 BP 1611, Abidjan 01; tel. 20-21-29-65; f. 1955; shipping agents; Man. Dir CLAUDE PERDRIAUD.

Société Ivoirienne de Navigation Maritime (SIVOMAR): 5 rue Charpentier, zone 2B, Treichville, 01 BP 1395, Abidjan 01; tel. 20-21-73-23; fax 20-32-38-53; f. 1977; shipments to ports in Africa, the Mediterranean and the Far East; Dir SIMPLISSE DE MESSE ZINSOU.

Société Ouest-Africaine d'Entreprises Maritimes en Côte d'Ivoire (SOAEM-CI): 01 BP 1727, Abidjan 01; tel. 20-21-59-69; fax 20-32-24-67; f. 1978; merchandise handling, transit and storage; Chair. JACQUES PELTIER; Dir JACQUES COLOMBANI.

SOCOPAO–Côte d'Ivoire: Km 1, blvd de la République, 01 BP 1297, Abidjan 01; tel. 21-24-13-14; fax 21-24-21-30; e-mail socopao@africaonline.co.ci; shipping agents; Shipping Dir OLIVIER RANJARD.

CIVIL AVIATION

There are three international airports: Abidjan–Félix Houphouët-Boigny, Bouaké and Yamoussoukro. Work to expand and modernize Abidjan's airport began in mid-1996: the project, costing an estimated 14,000m. francs CFA, was scheduled for completion in late 2000. In addition, there are 25 domestic and regional airports, including those at Bouna, Korhogo, Man, Odienné and San-Pédro.

Agence Nationale de l'Aviation Civile: 07 BP 148, Abidjan 07; tel. 21-27-74-24; fax 21-27-63-46; civil aviation authority; Dir JEAN KOUASSI ABONOUAN.

Air Inter Ivoire: Aéroport de Port Boüet, 07 BP 62, Abidjan 07; tel. 21-27-84-65; internal flights.

Société Nouvelle Air Ivoire: Immeuble République, place de la République, 01 BP 7782, Abidjan 01; tel. 20-25-14-00; fax 20-25-14-25; e-mail info@airivoire.com; internet www.airivoire.com; f. 2000 to replace Air Ivoire; f. 1960; privatized in 2001; 76.42% owned by All Africa Airways, 23.58% state-owned; internal and regional flights.

Tourism

The game reserves, forests, lagoons, coastal resorts, rich ethnic folklore and the lively city of Abidjan are tourist attractions; Côte d'Ivoire also has well-developed facilities for business visitors, including golfing centres. Some 301,000 tourists visited Côte d'Ivoire in 1998; receipts from tourism in that year totalled US $108m. Tourism was negatively affected by instability resulting from the *coup d'état* in December 1999, the disputed elections of October 2000, and the widespread civil unrest that commenced in September 2002.

Office Ivoirien du Tourisme et de l'Hôtellerie: Immeuble ex-EECI, place de la République, 01 BP 8538, Abidjan 01; tel. 20-20-65-00; fax 20-20-65-31; e-mail oith@africaonline.co.ci; internet www.tourisme.ci; f. 1992; Dir CAMILLE KOUASSI.

CROATIA

Introductory Survey

Location, Climate, Language, Religion, Flag, Capital

The Republic of Croatia is situated in south-eastern Europe and has a long western coastline on the Adriatic Sea. It is bordered to the north-west by Slovenia, to the north-east by Hungary and to the east by the Vojvodina area of Serbia (Serbia and Montenegro). Bosnia and Herzegovina abuts into Croatia, forming a southern border along the Sava river. The Croatian territory of Dubrovnik (formerly known as Ragusa), which is situated at the southern tip of the narrowing stretch of Croatia (beyond a short coastal strip of Bosnia and Herzegovina), has a short border with Montenegro. The climate is continental in the hilly interior and Mediterranean on the coast. There is steady rainfall throughout the year, although summer is the wettest season. The average annual rainfall in Zagreb is 890 mm (35 ins). Both the ethnic Croats (who comprised 89.6% of the total population according to the 2001 census) and the Serb minority (4.5%) speak versions of Serbo-Croat, but the largely Roman Catholic Croats use the Latin script and the Eastern Orthodox Serbs use the Cyrillic script. Since 1991 the ethnic Croats have rejected the 1954 Novi Sad Agreement (which proclaimed Serbo-Croat to be one language with two scripts), and now claim the distinctness of a Croatian language (Croat). There are, in addition, a number of small minority communities in Croatia, notably the Muslim community (which comprised 0.5% of the total population in 2001). The national flag (proportions 1 by 2) consists of three horizontal stripes, of red, white and dark blue, with the arms of Croatia (a shield of 25 squares, alternately red and white, below a blue crown composed of five shields) fimbriated in red and white and set in the centre of the flag, overlapping all three stripes. The capital is Zagreb.

Recent History

From the 16th century the territory of what is now the Republic of Croatia was divided between the Ottoman (Turkish) and Habsburg (Austrian) Empires (although Dalmatia and Istria were dominated at different times by Venice and by France). After the Hungarian revolution of 1848–49, Croatia and Slavonia were made Austrian crown-lands. The Habsburg Empire became the Dual Monarchy of Austria-Hungary in 1867, and the territories were restored to the Hungarian Crown in the following year. Croatia gained its autonomy and was formally joined with Slavonia in 1881. However, Hungarian nationalism transformed traditional Croat-Serb rivalries into Southern Slav ('Yugoslav') solidarity. Following the collapse of the Austro-Hungarian Empire at the end of the First World War in October 1918, a Kingdom of Serbs, Croats and Slovenes (under the Serbian monarchy) was proclaimed on 4 December. The new Kingdom united Serbia, including Macedonia and Kosovo, with Montenegro and the Habsburg lands (modern Croatia, Slovenia and Vojvodina). The Kingdom was, however, dominated by the Serbs, and the Croats, as the second largest ethnic group, sought a greater share of power. Increasing unrest within the Kingdom culminated in the meeting of a separatist Croatian assembly in Zagreb in 1928. King Alexander imposed a royal dictatorship in January 1929, formally renaming the country Yugoslavia in October. In 1934 the King was assassinated in France by Croatian extremists.

Meanwhile, the Fascist Ustaša movement was gaining support among the discontented Croat peasantry. When German and Italian forces invaded Yugoslavia in 1941, many Croats welcomed the Axis powers' support for the establishment of an Independent State of Croatia. The new Croatian state, which included most of Bosnia and Herzegovina and parts of Serbia as well as modern-day Croatia, was proclaimed on 9 April 1941 and was led by the leader of the Ustaša, the 'Poglavnik' Ante Pavelić. During the Ustaša regime a vast number of Jews, Serbs, Roma (Gypsies) and political dissidents were murdered in extermination camps. At the same time fierce armed resistance was being waged by the Partisans, who were led by Josip Broz, known as Tito, the leader of the Communist Party of Yugoslavia (CPY). By 1943 the Fascist regime was beginning to lose control, and Tito's forces were able to proclaim a provisional government in a number of areas. The Ustaša state collapsed in 1944, and

Croatia was restored to Yugoslavia as one unit of a federal communist republic.

During the 1960s there was an increase in nationalism in Croatia. This 'mass movement' (*Maspok*) was supported by Croatian members of the ruling League of Communists (as the CPY had been renamed), as well as by non-communists. The movement encouraged the local communist leadership, which was associated with the reform wing of the party, to defy central policy in certain areas. In December 1971 Tito committed himself to opposing the nationalist movement, and the Croatian communist leaders were obliged to resign. Together with others prominent in *Maspok*, they were arrested, and a purge of the League of Communists of Croatia (LCC) followed. In 1974, however, Tito introduced a new Constitution, which enshrined the federal (almost confederal) and collective nature of the Yugoslav state.

When the power of the LCC (which contained a high proportion of Serbs) began to decline, particularly from 1989, Croatian nationalism re-emerged as a significant force. Dissidents of the 1970s and 1980s were the main beneficiaries. Dr Franjo Tudjman, who had twice been imprisoned for publicly criticizing repression in Croatia, formed the Croatian Democratic Union (CDU) in 1990. This rapidly became the main challenger to the ruling party, which had changed its name to the League of Communists of Croatia—Party of Democratic Reform (LCC—PDR). The communists introduced a plurality ('first-past-the-post') voting system for the multi-party elections to the republican legislature in April–May 1990. Tudjman campaigned as a nationalist, prompting considerable concern among the Serbs by advocating a 'Greater Croatia' (to include Bosnia).

At the elections to the tricameral republican Assembly (Sabor), which took place on 24 April and 6–7 May 1990, the CDU benefited from the new voting system, taking a majority of the seats, despite winning only about 42% of the votes cast in the second round (in both the Socio-Political Chamber and the Chamber of Counties). The CDU obtained 54 of the 80 seats in the Socio-Political Chamber, 68 of the 115 seats elected in the Chamber of Counties, and 83 of the 156 seats elected in the Chamber of Associated Labour; consequently, of the 351 seats of all three chambers of the Assembly (which had a possible maximum of 356), the CDU won 205. The next largest party was the LCC–PDR, with a total of 73 seats. Both the leading parties won further seats in alliance with other parties. Tudjman was elected President of Croatia, but he attempted to allay Serb fears by offering the vice-presidency of the Assembly to Dr Jovan Rašković, the leader of the Serbian Democratic Party (SDP). Although Rašković eventually refused the post, another Serb was appointed to it. However, Serb-dominated areas remained alienated by Tudjman's Croat nationalism. A 'Serb National Council', based at Knin (in Krajina), was formed in July and organized a referendum on autonomy for the Croatian Serbs. Despite attempts by the Croatian authorities to prohibit the referendum, it took place, amid virtual insurrection in some areas, in late August and early September. In October the Serb National Council announced the results of the referendum, and declared autonomy for the Krajina areas (the 'Serb Autonomous Region—SAR of Krajina').

Meanwhile, the new Croatian Government was intent on dismantling the structures of communist power. In August 1990 the Socialist Republic of Croatia became the Republic of Croatia. In the same month the Assembly voted to dismiss the republican member of the federal State Presidency, Dr Stipe Šuvar, and replace him with Stipe Mesić, then President of the Government (premier) of Croatia. His appointment was confirmed in October. In December the Assembly enacted a new republican Constitution, which declared Croatia's sovereignty, its authority over its own armed forces and its right to secede from the federation. Tensions increased when, in January 1991, the Croatian authorities refused to comply with an order by the federal State Presidency to disarm all paramilitary groups. The Croatian Minister of Defence was indicted on a charge of plotting armed rebellion, but the Croatian Government refused to arrest him and boycotted negotiations on the future of the federation. On 21 February Croatia asserted the primacy of its Constitution and laws over those of the federation and declared its conditions for participation in a confederation of sovereign states. Later that month the self-proclaimed SAR of Krajina declared its separation from Croatia and aim to unite with Serbia. In April the Croatian National Guard was formed, replacing the Territorial Defence Force, which had been under the jurisdiction of the Jugoslovenska Narodna Armija (JNA—Yugoslav People's Army). On 19 May some 94% of the voters participating in a referendum favoured Croatia's becoming a sovereign entity, possibly within a confederal Yugoslavia, and 92% rejected a federal Yugoslavia. Some 84% of the registered electorate voted in the referendum, which was largely boycotted by the Serb population.

On 25 June 1991 Croatia and Slovenia declared their independence and began the process of dissociation from the Yugoslav federation. (Two days later the SAR of Krajina declared its unification with the self-proclaimed Serb 'Municipal Community of Bosanska Krajina' in Bosnia and Herzegovina.) However, the federal and Serbian authorities were less prepared to accept the loss of Croatia than that of Slovenia, since Croatia contained a significant Serb minority. During July civil war effectively began in Croatia. In August an SAR of Western Slavonia was declared; the SAR of Slavonia, Baranja and Western Srem (Sirmium) also proclaimed its autonomy later that month. In September the UN placed an embargo on the delivery of all weapons and other military equipment to the territories of the former Yugoslavia. By November the JNA, supported by Serbian irregular troops, had secured about one-third of Croatian territory. The main area of conflict was Slavonia, in eastern Croatia, although Serbian and JNA attacks were also concentrated on the port of Zadar, in central Dalmatia. In October the JNA attacked and besieged the coastal city of Dubrovnik, prompting accusations that the forces were attempting to secure the borders of a 'Greater Serbian' state by linking the SAR to Serbia; among the main obstacles to this alleged goal, however, were the eastern Slavonian cities of Osijek, Vinkovci and Vukovar, the last of which finally surrendered on 18 November, after the 13th cease-fire agreement negotiated by the European Community (EC—known as the European Union, EU (see p. 199), from November 1993), which supervised the subsequent civilian evacuation. Both Croatia and Serbia indicated readiness to accept a UN peace-keeping force; military action continued, however, while negotiations on the terms for such a force were conducted. The 14th cease-fire agreement, therefore, involved the UN, although it did not bring an end to all the fighting. In mid-December the UN Security Council's Resolution 724 provided for observers to be sent to Yugoslavia, in addition to a small team of civilian and military personnel to prepare for a possible peace-keeping force. In the same month the 'Republic of Serb Krajina' (RSK), formed by the union of the three SARs, was proclaimed.

In August 1991 Tudjman appointed a coalition Government, which was dominated by the CDU; the SDP was not represented. The new Government continued to seek international recognition and to pursue negotiations at the EC-sponsored peace conference in The Hague, Netherlands. However, in October the Croatian Government refused to extend the three-month moratorium on the process of dissociation from the Yugoslav federation (which had been agreed during the first round of EC peace negotiations in July). In November, in accordance with the principles formulated at The Hague, the Assembly declared its readiness to enact legislation guaranteeing minority rights, to allay the anxieties of the Serbs. However, there were increasing allegations of atrocities on both sides. The CDU came under mounting pressure from its own right-wing and more extreme groups to make no concessions to the Serbs. One of the most prominent of the nationalist parties was the Croatian Party of Rights (CPR), of which the armed wing, the Croatian Defence Association, was actively involved in the fighting and was implicated in other anti-Serb incidents.

Despite such domestic and military pressures, the Croatian Government continued the process of dissociation, and in November 1991 the Supreme Council (a special war cabinet, chaired by the President of the Republic, which had been established in Croatia following the outbreak of civil conflict) ordered all Croatians to vacate any federal posts that they held and to place their services at the disposal of the Croatian state. On 5 December Stipe Mesić, Yugoslavia's nominal Head of State, resigned, followed by Ante Marković, the federal Prime Minister, on 19 December. On 23 December Germany recognized

Croatia, and on 15 January 1992 the other members of the EC initiated general international recognition of Croatia, which culminated in its accession to the UN in May.

With more than 6,000 dead, 23,000 wounded and 400,000 internally displaced in Croatia, a UN-sponsored unconditional cease-fire was signed by the Croatian National Guard and the JNA on 2 January 1992. In late February a 14,000-strong UN Protection Force (UNPROFOR) was entrusted with ensuring the withdrawal of the JNA from Croatia and the complete demilitarization of three Serbian-held enclaves, which were designated UN Protected Areas (UNPAs). In the same month UNPROFOR's mandate in Croatia was extended to cover the so-called 'pink zones' (areas occupied by JNA troops and with majority Serb populations, but outside the official UNPAs).

In mid-May 1992 the JNA began to withdraw from Croatia, in accordance with the UN demilitarization of Serb areas, and the siege of Dubrovnik ended on 28 May. Sporadic shelling continued, however, and UNPROFOR proved unable to prevent the expulsion of more than 1,000 non-Serbs by Serbian forces from Eastern Slavonia, and had only limited success in its enforcement of the demilitarization of the UNPAs. In June Croatian forces launched a series of offensives in Serbian areas, beginning with the shelling of Knin. This development provoked UN Security Council Resolution 762, adopted on 30 June, which required the Croats to withdraw to the positions that they had held prior to 21 June and to refrain from entering Serbian areas. Relations between Croatia and the UN remained strained.

In late July 1992 a military court in Split convicted 19 leading figures from the RSK for 'threatening the territorial integrity' of the Republic of Croatia. Shortly afterwards, however, as a precondition of their participation in the EC/UN peace conference on the former Yugoslavia, to be held in August, in London, United Kingdom, the leaders of the RSK renounced their claims to independence. In early September the Prime Minister of the Federal Republic of Yugoslavia (FRY, comprising Serbia and Montenegro), Milan Panić, announced Yugoslavia's willingness to recognize Croatia within the borders existing prior to the outbreak of civil war in mid-1991, on the condition that the Serbian enclaves be granted special status. During the London peace talks agreement was reached on economic co-operation between representatives of the Croatian Government and of the RSK, and at the end of September Presidents Tudjman of Croatia and Dobrica Ćosić of the FRY agreed to work towards a normalization of relations between their respective countries.

Presidential and legislative elections were held in Croatia on 2 August 1992. These were the first elections to be held under the new Constitution (promulgated in December 1990), which provided for a bicameral legislature composed of a Chamber of Representatives and a Chamber of Counties; however, the legislative election was to the former house only. The elections were contested by eight presidential candidates and 37 political parties. President Tudjman was re-elected, with 56% of the presidential votes cast, more than twice that of his nearest rival, Dražen Budiša of the Croatian Social-Liberal Party (CSLP), while the ruling CDU obtained an outright majority in the Chamber of Representatives, winning 85 of the 138 seats contested. The new Government, under the premiership of Hrvoje Šarinić (hitherto head of the President's office), was appointed shortly thereafter. In late November the Chamber of Representatives approved legislation providing for the reorganization of Croatia, for electoral purposes, into 21 counties, 420 municipalities and 61 towns, and in early January 1993 proportional representation was introduced to replace the former plurality electoral system. An election to the Chamber of Counties was held on 7 February. The CDU won 37 of the elective 63 seats, while the CSLP, together with allied parties, obtained 16 seats. The CPR boycotted the election.

In late January 1993 Croatian troops launched an offensive across the UN peace-keeping lines into Serb-held Krajina, an action that was provoked, they claimed, by the failure of the UN to restore the Maslenica bridge, a vital communications link between northern Croatia and the Dalmatian coast, to Croatian control. The Serbian forces in Krajina reclaimed weapons that they had earlier surrendered to UNPROFOR, in order to defend themselves. The UN responded by ordering Croatia to withdraw its troops and the Serbian forces to return their weapons. As Croatian forces advanced towards the coastal town of Zadar on 26 January, President Ćosić of Yugoslavia warned the UN that, if UNPROFOR did not intervene, Yugoslavia would dispatch troops to defend the Serbs in Croatia. Eight French UN troops were wounded, and two were killed, in fighting around Zadar on the following day; consequently the French Government dispatched an aircraft-carrier to the Adriatic Sea. The Croats regained control of the Maslenica bridge and Zemunik airport, and by the end of January the peace process in both Croatia and Bosnia and Herzegovina appeared to be in serious jeopardy.

There was extensive political unrest in Croatia throughout 1993. The issues of continuing civil strife in Krajina and of the quest for autonomy in the Istrian peninsula in the north-west of Croatia (see below) proved increasingly problematic for the Government and added to domestic dissatisfaction with the country's desperate economic circumstances and concern regarding Croatian involvement in the Bosnian conflict. In late March Šarinić's Government resigned, following a series of financial scandals and a rapid deterioration in the economic situation. A former executive of the Croatian state petroleum company, Nikica Valentić, was appointed Prime Minister. The new Government, which consisted only of members of the CDU, won a vote of confidence in the Chamber of Representatives in late April. Despite growing opposition to his policies within the party, Tudjman was re-elected Chairman of the CDU in October.

At local elections in Istria in early February 1993, the Istrian Democratic Assembly (IDA), a party advocating Istrian autonomy, obtained 72% of the total votes cast. The IDA subsequently proposed that Istria become a transborder region comprising Croatian, Slovenian and Italian areas. Tudjman and his Government, however, strongly opposed any suggestion of Istrian autonomy. In early April a UN-sponsored agreement guaranteed the reconstruction and reopening of the Maslenica bridge, Zemunik airport and the Peruca hydroelectric plant (all situated in Krajina), under UNPROFOR supervision. The Croats decided to reconstruct the bridge themselves, however, and it was duly reopened by President Tudjman in July. In the same month the Serbs, frustrated by the continued Croatian military presence in the area, launched an attack on Croatian forces. In mid-July the UN successfully negotiated the Erdut Agreement between the leaders of Croatia and Serbia, whereby Croat forces were to leave the Maslenica area (which would again be placed under the administration of UNPROFOR); in return, President Milošević of Serbia was to dissuade Serbian troops from attacking the bridge. However, the Croats failed to withdraw from Maslenica by the deadline of 31 July; the Croatian Government claimed that Serbian weapons had not been surrendered to UNPROFOR, and fighting resumed. In August the Croatian Minister of Foreign Affairs, Dr Mate Granić, declared the Erdut Agreement invalid. In the following month a full-scale mobilization was undertaken among the Serbs living in the SAR of Eastern Slavonia, Baranja and Western Sirmium, in response to the Croatian offensives in Krajina. Serb–Croat hostilities extended to Zagreb by mid-September. By this time most of the JNA had withdrawn from Croatia, and some Serb artillery had been placed under UN control, but UNPROFOR forces were not yet in effective control of Croatian borders.

On 4 October 1993, despite anti-UNPROFOR demonstrations in Croatia, the UN Security Council voted unanimously to extend UNPROFOR's mandate by Resolution 871. This Resolution also required the return to Croatian sovereignty of all 'pink zones', the restoration of all communications links between these regions and the remainder of Croatia, and the disarmament of Serb paramilitary groups. The UNPROFOR forces were empowered by the Resolution to act in self-defence while implementing the mandate. The Croat administration accepted the Resolution, but it was rejected by the assembly of the RSK, based in Beli Menastir, which proceeded to order the mobilization of all Serb conscripts in Krajina. Multi-party elections were held in the RSK in December, but these were declared illegal by the Constitutional Court of Croatia. In January 1994 Milan Martić, a candidate supported by President Milošević of Serbia, was elected to the post of 'President' of the RSK.

In mid-January 1994 Croatia and the FRY announced their intention to begin the normalization of relations, including the establishment of representative offices in Zagreb and Belgrade. A parallel agreement was also signed between representatives of the Bosnian Croats and the Bosnian Serbs. In the same month the Croatian Government indicated the possibility of direct Croatian intervention in central Bosnia and Herzegovina to support Bosnian Croat forces, prompting the US Permanent Representative to the UN, Madeleine Albright, to threaten the imposition of international sanctions. (Croatian army units had from 1992 supported the self-styled breakaway Croat state in Bosnia and Herzegovina, the 'Croat Union of Herzeg-Bosna'.) In

late February President Tudjman approved US proposals for a Muslim-Croat federation within Bosnia and Herzegovina, which would ultimately seek formal association with Croatia within a loose confederation (see chapter on Bosnia and Herzegovina). In the RSK, meanwhile, a cease-fire, which had been agreed between Croatia and the rebel Serbs in December 1993, was extended for a third time, until 31 March 1994. On 30 March a further cease-fire, agreed in Zagreb, provided for the establishment of a 'buffer' zone, to be monitored by UNPROFOR.

In April 1994 a long-standing public dispute between President Tudjman and Josip Manolić, the President of the Chamber of Municipalities and a leading member of the CDU, led to a division in the party. Manolić and other prominent liberals in the CDU (and in other parties) were displeased with Tudjman's perceived anti-Muslim views and his collusion with Gojko Šušak, the Minister of Defence, who was widely considered responsible for Croatia's involvement against the Muslims in the Bosnian conflict. Manolić demanded Šušak's resignation on the grounds that Tudjman could not hope to adhere to the Muslim-Croat federation accords with Šušak as Minister of Defence. Tudjman responded by suspending Manolić from his position within the CDU (also attempting, unsuccessfully, to dismiss him from his legislative office). On 5 April it was announced that Manolić, together with Stipe Mesić (now the President of the Chamber of Representatives), had left the CDU to form a new party, the Croatian Independent Democrats (CID). Formally established in late April, with Mesić as Chairman, the CID became the largest opposition party in the Assembly, with some 18 deputies. In June the principal opposition parties commenced a boycott of the Assembly, in protest at the appointment of two CDU deputies as Presidents of the parliamentary chambers (Manolić and Mesić having agreed to resign from their posts in mid-May); opposition deputies only returned to the Assembly in September.

Meanwhile, the cease-fire in the RSK continued precariously, as Croatian officials threatened to terminate the UN peace-keeping mandate in the area and forcibly reclaim Serb-held territory, unless the Krajina Serbs co-operated more fully in international peace negotiations. In late September 1994 the Chamber of Representatives voted to end the existing mandate of UNPROFOR in Croatia, offering a renewed mandate, on the condition that UNPROFOR disarm Serb troops in Krajina, facilitate the return of Croatian refugees to Krajina and protect Croatia's official borders. On 30 September, however, the Government withdrew its opposition to the continued presence of UN forces in Croatia, and on the same day the UN Security Council adopted a resolution renewing the UNPROFOR mandate in Croatia for a further six months.

In mid-October 1994 a new negotiating forum was established in Zagreb with the aim of resolving the Krajina question; known as the 'Zagreb Group', it comprised two representatives of the EU and the US and Russian ambassadors to Croatia. The group initially proposed that the RSK be reintegrated into Croatia, but receive extensive autonomy. In late October, however, the RSK 'Prime Minister', Borislav Mikelić, rejected any notion of Krajina's reintegration. Nevertheless, in December the two sides concluded an economic accord, which provided for the re-establishment of basic infrastructural links between the RSK and Croatia.

On 12 January 1995 President Tudjman, encountering pressure from nationalist factions of the CDU and public dissatisfaction at the Government's perceived failure to assert control over Croatian territory, announced that the Government would not renew the UNPROFOR mandate in Croatia upon its expiry at the end of March, claiming that the UN presence had merely reinforced the Serbs' position. In late January, amid growing fears of the outbreak of war throughout the former Yugoslavia, the 'Zagreb Group' presented a fresh peace plan to President Tudjman and the Krajina Serbs. The plan, which emphasized Croatia's territorial integrity, while affording rights to the Serb minority, envisaged the return of one-half of Serb-controlled territory to Croatia, in exchange for extensive regional autonomy for the Krajina Serbs. (The areas to be reintegrated into Croatia would be demilitarized, and administered by the UN for a minimum of five years.) The Krajina Serbs initially refused to consider the plan, but on 3 February Martić announced that the RSK would be willing to consider peace proposals if the UNPROFOR mandate were renewed and the RSK received guarantees of protection against Croatian aggression. A few days later the RSK suspended the economic accord concluded with Croatia in December 1994, following Croatia's decision to terminate UNPROFOR's mandate. However, on 12 March 1995 President Tudjman reversed his decision to expel UNPROFOR from Croatian territory, two weeks before the UN troops were due to begin their withdrawal. Croatia had agreed to a revised peace-keeping plan, following intensive diplomatic negotiations conducted by the international community (in particular, the USA), as a result of which a compromise UN mandate was to provide for a reduced peace-keeping force (to be known as the UN Confidence Restoration Operation—UNCRO), including several hundred troops to be deployed along Croatia's official frontiers with Bosnia and Herzegovina and the FRY (effectively isolating Serb-occupied territory in Croatia from sources of military aid).

In early March 1995, following talks in Zagreb, a formal military alliance was announced between the Croatian, Bosnian Croat and Bosnian government armies. (A similar agreement establishing a military alliance between the Croatian Serbs and the Bosnian Serbs had been drawn up in Banja Luka, Bosnia and Herzegovina, in February.) UN relief supplies to Serb-held enclaves in Croatia were suspended in March, following the disruption of aid convoys by Croatian Serbs and their rebel Muslim allies in Bosnia and Herzegovina. On 13 April Dubrovnik and its airport were attacked by Bosnian Serb artillery, resulting in one death and prompting Mate Granić to lodge a formal protest with the UN. On 1–2 May Croatian government forces seized the SAR of Western Slavonia; large numbers of Serb troops fled the area during the offensive. Government sources claimed that the attack was necessary in order to restore the Zagreb–Belgrade motorway (which was re-opened to civilian traffic on 3 May). The Croatian Serbs retaliated almost immediately with artillery attacks on Zagreb (where six civilians were killed), Karlovak and Sisak. The international community immediately intensified its efforts to achieve peace in Croatia, and on 3 May, under the mediation of the UN Special Envoy, Yasushi Akashi, the warring parties agreed a cease-fire, according to which Serb artillery was to be surrendered to the UN, in exchange for the safe passage of all Serb civilians and troops from Western Slavonia into Bosnia and Herzegovina (an evacuation was to be organized by the UN). Sporadic fighting continued in the enclave despite the cease-fire, however, and there were allegations of Croatian human rights abuses.

In early June 1995, following the expiry of UNCRO's mandate in Croatia on 31 October 1994, Tudjman threatened further offensives to seize Serb-held territories, prompting international criticism. In late July a joint offensive by Croatian government forces and Bosnian Croat troops resulted in the seizure of the strategic Serb-held town of Bosansko Grahovo, in south-western Bosnia and Herzegovina, thus blocking the principal supply route from Serb-held areas of Bosnia to Serb-held Krajina. On 4 August Croatian government troops launched a massive military operation and rapidly recaptured the Krajina enclave from the Croatian Serbs, prompting the largest exodus of refugees since the Yugoslav crisis began in 1991; about 150,000 Croatian Serbs either fled or were forcibly expelled from Krajina and took refuge in Serb-held areas in Bosnia or in Serbia itself. Following the capture of Krajina, it was reported that Serbian troops had been stationed along the Serbian border with Croatia (thus strengthening the position of the Serb-held enclave of Eastern Slavonia against possible Croatian attack). In early September the UN announced that some 10,500 peace-keeping troops were to be withdrawn from Croatia, in view of the reoccupation of Krajina. On 20 September the Croatian Chamber of Representatives voted to suspend sections of the law on minorities, which had provided the Krajina Serbs with special rights in areas where they had been a majority; this decision had been preceded two days earlier by a new electoral law reducing the representation of the Serb minority in the Croatian legislature from 13 seats to three. The law also provided for 12 seats in the Chamber of Representatives to represent some 470,000 Croatian emigrés, thus giving the right to vote to some 291,000 Bosnian Croats (many of whom supported the CDU's associated party in Bosnia and Herzegovina). At the end of September the Croatian Government, despite UN criticism, was reported to have resettled some 100,000 Bosnian refugees (both Croat and Muslim) in Krajina. In late September it was announced that an election to the Chamber of Representatives would take place on 29 October.

During October 1995 fighting continued in parts of Croatia despite the UN-brokered cease-fire. Heavy clashes were reported between Croatian troops and Serb forces in Eastern Slavonia, and President Tudjman continued to threaten the

recapture of the Eastern Slavonian enclave by force, as part of the CDU's electoral manifesto. On 3 October, however, an 'agreement on basic principles' was signed between Croatian government officials and Serb leaders in Eastern Slavonia, following talks in the Serb-held town of Erdut, conducted under the mediation of the US ambassador to Croatia, Peter Galbraith, and UN negotiator Thorvald Stoltenberg. The 11-point agreement provided for a 'transitional period', during which authority over the enclave would be invested in an interim administration established by the UN. The area would be demilitarized and a joint Serb-Croat police force would be created; the agreement also provided for the safe return of refugees.

The Croatian electoral campaign was marred by widespread allegations of media bias; in early October 1995 the state-owned television network banned opposition broadcasts. The election duly took place on 29 October; the CDU secured about 45% of the votes cast (although the party failed to obtain sufficient votes to achieve the two-thirds' parliamentary majority required to make constitutional amendments). A new Government was appointed in early November, under the premiership of the erstwhile Minister of the Economy, Zlatko Matesa.

On 12 November 1995 representatives of the Croatian Government and Eastern Slavonian Serbs signed an agreement in Erdut on the reintegration of the Eastern Slavonian enclave into Croatia. The signature of this accord followed peace negotiations between Tudjman, Milošević and the President of the Presidency of Bosnia and Herzegovina, Dr Alija Izetbegović, conducted in Dayton, Ohio, the USA (where the three leaders signed a comprehensive peace agreement, providing for the division of Bosnia and Herzegovina between a Muslim-Croat Federation and a Serb Republic—see chapter on Bosnia and Herzegovina). Under the terms of the accord, Eastern Slavonia was to be administered by a transitional administration appointed by the UN for a period of up to two years prior to its complete reintegration into Croatia. The interim administration and UN peace-keeping forces would supervise the demilitarization of the area and the return of refugees and displaced persons. Long-standing Serbian demands for a referendum to be held at the end of the transitional period, in which citizens would vote for the region's integration into either Croatia or Serbia, were not included in the agreement. On 15 January 1996, under Resolution 1037, the UN Security Council established the UN Transitional Administration for Eastern Slavonia, Baranja and Western Sirmium (UNTAES), with an initial one-year mandate; UNTAES, comprising some 5,000 troops, replaced UNCRO, the mandate of which expired on that day. A US diplomat, Jacques Paul Klein, was subsequently appointed Transitional Administrator of the region. The UN Security Council also authorized the UN Mission of Observers in Prevlaka (UNMOP) to assume responsibility for monitoring the demilitarization of the Prevlaka peninsula, south-east of Dubrovnik.

In April 1996 the Regional Executive Council of Eastern Slavonia appointed a former RSK 'President' (1992–94), Goran Hadžić, as President of the region. A new Regional Assembly (comprising representatives of Krajina and the five Eastern Slavonian municipalities) and Regional Executive Council were subsequently established. In the same month the Chamber of Representatives approved legislation on co-operation between Croatia and the UN International Criminal Tribunal for the Former Yugoslavia (ICTY—based in The Hague), which provided for the transfer of authority to conduct criminal proceedings to the Tribunal and the extradition of the accused.

In early May 1996 Tudjman dissolved the Zagreb City Assembly and appointed a Government Commissioner in its place (on the grounds that the Assembly had approved unconstitutional legislation), following a protracted dispute with an alliance of opposition parties that had won the local elections and held a majority in the Assembly.

In May 1996 the Croatian Chamber of Representatives adopted legislation granting amnesty for crimes committed during the civil conflict in Eastern Slavonia from August 1990, excepting 'war crimes'; the legislation was designed to expedite the return of displaced persons to the region. Later that month the demilitarization of Eastern Slavonia commenced; the process was completed within 30 days, as scheduled. In early July an international security force was installed in Eastern Slavonia for the transitional period. Later that month the Regional Assembly of Eastern Slavonia submitted an official request to the UN Security Council that the mandate of UNTAES, which was officially due to expire in January 1997, be extended for one further year. (The Croatian Government opposed the extension of the mandate for more than three months.)

In August 1996, following a meeting between Tudjman and Milošević in Athens, Greece, an agreement was signed, providing for the establishment of full diplomatic relations between Croatia and the FRY; remaining issues of contention, most notably the territorial dispute over the Prevlaka peninsula (which, under the terms of the Dayton agreement, was to be ceded to Bosnian Serb control), were to be resolved by further negotiations. In October the (Council of Europe, see p. 181) agreed to accept Croatia's application for membership, after the Government undertook to ratify the European Convention on Human Rights within one year of admission.

In November 1996 the UN Security Council announced that the mandate of UNTAES had been extended for an additional six months, to mid-July 1997. At the end of December 1996, following a meeting between Tudjman and Klein, it was announced that local government elections in Eastern Slavonia were to take place in March 1997, at the same time as an election to the upper house (Chamber of Counties) in Croatia. Serbs in Eastern Slavonia subsequently objected to elections taking place concurrently in Croatia and Eastern Slavonia (on the grounds that this pre-empted the reintegration of the region). In early February 1997 Tudjman announced that the election to the Chamber of Counties had been postponed until 13 April, apparently owing to difficulties in the organization of the concurrent local government elections in Eastern Slavonia. In March the Independent Democratic Serb Party (SDSS), headed by Vojislav Stanimirović (the President of the Regional Council of Eastern Slavonia), was established to contest the elections in the enclave.

In early April 1997 Serb officials in Eastern Slavonia conducted a referendum (which, however, the Croatian Government and UN officials declared to be illegitimate) regarding the future of the enclave; about 99.5% of the participating electorate voted in favour of Eastern Slavonia remaining a single administrative unit under Serb control after its return to Croatia. On 13 April elections to the Chamber of Counties and to a number of municipal and regional councils took place. Voting in the concurrent local government elections in Eastern Slavonia was extended for two days, owing to administrative irregularities. Nevertheless, election monitors from the Organization for Security and Co-operation in Europe (OSCE, see p. 283) declared that they had been largely 'free and fair'. The CDU secured 42 of the 63 elective seats in the Chamber of Counties, while the Croatian Peasants' Party took nine, the CSLP six, the Social Democratic Party (which had been reconstituted from the former LCC–PDR) four, and the IDA two seats. (A further five deputies were to be nominated by Tudjman, of whom two were to be members of the Serb community in Eastern Slavonia.) The SDSS obtained control of 11 of the 28 municipalities contested in the enclave. In May the CDU secured a narrow majority in the Zagreb City Assembly, following protracted negotiations, which resulted in the defection of two councillors from the Croatian Peasants' Party to the CDU.

In May 1997 the Government announced that the forthcoming presidential election was to take place on 15 June. Tudjman had been formally nominated as the presidential candidate of the CDU earlier that year (despite persistent reports, denied by government officials, that he was seriously ill). During a visit to Eastern Slavonia in early June Tudjman publicly offered reconciliation to all Serbs who were willing to accept Croatian citizenship, following continued pressure from Madeleine Albright, who had met Tudjman in late May. The presidential election took place as scheduled. Tudjman was re-elected with 61.4% of the votes cast; the Social Democratic Party candidate, Zdravko Tomac, secured 21.0% of the votes cast and the CSLP leader, Vlado Gotovac, 17.6%. However, OSCE monitors declared that the election had not been conducted fairly, on the grounds that opposition parties had not been permitted coverage in the state-controlled media during the electoral campaign. Later in June the Constitutional Court endorsed the results of the election.

At the end of June 1997 a former Serb mayor of Vukovar, Slavko Dokmanović, who had been indicted by the ICTY, was arrested for his alleged involvement in the killing of some 260 civilians in November 1991. (In June 1998 Dokmanović committed suicide in detention, while awaiting the verdict of the ICTY.) In early July 1997 the Government announced that the programme for the return of some 80,000 Croatian refugees to Eastern Slavonia had commenced; it was planned that about 40,000 displaced civilians would resettle in the region by the end

of that year. Despite previous objections from the Croatian Government, the UN Security Council adopted a resolution to extend the mandate of UNTAES (which had been due to expire in mid-July) until mid-January 1998, owing to UN concern over the continued stability of Eastern Slavonia, in view of the planned return of refugees to the enclave. (However, the size of the contingent was reduced from about 5,000 to 2,800.) Later in July the Croatian Government refused to comply with instructions from the ICTY to release official documents (which would be used as evidence in the trial of a former Bosnian Croat army officer) on the grounds of national security. In the same month the Bretton Woods institutions postponed the disbursement of financial assistance to Croatia, as a result of pressure from the Governments of the USA, the United Kingdom and Germany, which continued to criticize, in particular, the slow progress in the resettlement of refugees, the Croatian administration's failure to comply with extradition orders on suspects issued by the ICTY and continued state control of the media.

On 5 August 1997 Tudjman was officially inaugurated for a second presidential term. In the same month the President of the CPR, Dobroslav Paraga, submitted a proposal at the ICTY that Tudjman, Šušak and a number of Bosnian Croats be charged in connection with the former conflict in Bosnia and Herzegovina. Paraga and a human rights activist, Ivan Zvonimir Čičak, were subsequently charged by the Croatian authorities with disseminating false information, after publishing claims in a national newspaper that Tudjman had been involved in initiating the Bosnian conflict. In October the IMF approved the resumption of credit payments to Croatia. In November the legislature approved constitutional amendments, proposed by Tudjman, which, notably, prohibited the re-establishment of a union of Yugoslav states. In December Gotovac left the CSLP and formed a breakaway faction of the Party.

In mid-January 1998 the mandate of UNTAES expired and Eastern Slavonia was officially returned to Croatian authority, precipitating an increase in the number of ethnic Serbs leaving the former enclave. In the same month the UN Security Council voted to extend the mandate of the UNMOP contingent (at that time comprising 28 military observers) deployed in the Prevlaka peninsula until mid-July.

In February 1998 Tudjman was re-elected Chairman of the CDU at a party convention. In April, following the violent suppression of protests at poor economic conditions earlier that year, the Government adopted legislation regulating public gatherings and demonstrations, which, it claimed, was in accordance with the standards of Western authorities. In May the Government proposed a draft programme that relaxed conditions for the return of Serbian refugees to Croatia, following pressure from the international community (which had threatened to impose sanctions if the Croatian Government failed to allow the return of refugees); it was envisaged that some 220,000 displaced persons would be repatriated by 2003. Legislation providing for the new programme for the return of refugees was officially adopted by the Assembly in late June.

In early May 1998 Šušak died; Dr Andrija Hebrang (hitherto Minister of Health) was subsequently allocated the defence portfolio. In the same month the former Prime Minister, Hrvoje Sarinić, resigned from the post of head of the Office of the President, prompting speculation regarding increasing division within the CDU between moderates and nationalists.

In June 1998 Croatia submitted to the UN a proposal for a permanent settlement to the dispute over the Prevlaka peninsula; it was envisaged that a joint Croatian-Yugoslav commission would demarcate the borders between the two countries and that a demilitarized zone would be established for a period of five years. In mid-July the UN Security Council extended UNMOP's mandate for a further six months. In August Granić and the Yugoslav Minister of Foreign Affairs, meeting in Zagreb, agreed to conduct discussions on the issue of the Prevlaka peninsula. In September, following a meeting between Granić and the US ambassador in Croatia, it was agreed that joint Croatian-US commissions were to be established to further progress in the implementation of the Dayton peace agreement and Croatia's admission to NATO's 'Partnership for Peace' programme.

In September 1998 the trial of three Croats, who were charged, together with a further six Croats *in absentia*, with the massacre of hundreds of ethnic Serbs in 1991, commenced in Zagreb (the first trial of Croats accused of perpetrating human rights violations against Serbs to take place in Croatia). In early October Sarinić tendered his resignation from his remaining government and party offices, including the post of presidential Chief of Staff, claiming that Tudjman had failed to support his allegations that CDU nationalists, with connections to members of the intelligence service, were campaigning against him and other moderate members of the party. In the same month Hebrang resigned from his posts of Minister of Defence and Vice-President of the CDU, also as a result of disagreement with Tudjman. Gen. Pavao Miljavac, hitherto Chief of Staff of the army, was subsequently appointed Minister of Defence.

In January 1999 the UN Security Council adopted a resolution on UNMOP, stating that violations of the demilitarized zone in the Prevlaka peninsula had continued and that negotiations on the normalization of relations between the FRY and Croatia had not resulted in any significant progress. In March a US government report criticized the human rights situation in Croatia, citing, in particular, the state control of the media, the Government's lack of co-operation with the ICTY and the failure to reintegrate displaced ethnic Serbs. In April Milan Ramljak resigned from the posts of Deputy Prime Minister and Minister of Justice, in protest at the Government's increasingly authoritarian stance; the Government was subsequently reorganized.

In July 1999 Croatia submitted an application at the ICTY to institute legal proceedings against the FRY for crimes of genocide committed by Yugoslav forces in Croatia in 1991–95. In August the Croatian Government complied with a request by the ICTY for the extradition of Vinko Martinović, who had been indicted for crimes committed during the Croatian–Muslim conflict in 1993–94. However, the Croatian authorities' reluctance to extradite Mladen Naletilić, who had also been indicted for crimes perpetrated during the Croatian–Muslim conflict, prompted severe criticism from the Tribunal; the US Government threatened to initiate sanctions against Croatia, in response to its continued failure to comply with the ICTY. In early September the County Court in Zagreb ruled that there were no legal impediments to the extradition of Naletilić (following an earlier decision that he was unable to stand trial, on grounds of ill health). In mid-October the Supreme Court rejected an appeal by Naletilić against the ruling in favour of his extradition. Naletilić was finally extradited in March 2000.

In late October 1999 Tudjman announced that the election to the Chamber of Representatives would take place on 22 December. In early November, however, it was announced that Tudjman had undergone emergency medical treatment, after becoming seriously ill. He was consequently unable to confirm the election date, and on 26 November the Assembly declared him to be 'temporarily incapacitated' and provisionally transferred the powers of Head of State to the parliamentary Speaker, Vlatko Pavletić. On the following day the mandate of the Chamber of Representatives expired, and Pavletić rescheduled the election to take place on 3 January 2000. An alliance of six principal opposition parties, known as Opposition Six, pledged to establish a coalition government in the event of winning the parliamentary election; of the Opposition Six parties, the SDP and CSLP were to present one joint candidate, while the Croatian Peasants' Party, the Liberal Party (LP), the Croatian People's Party (CPP) and the IDA were to submit a second joint candidate to contest the elections. Meanwhile, Tudjman's medical condition deteriorated, and he died on 10 December. Later that month the Government announced that the election for his successor would take place on 24 January 2000 (in accordance with the Constitution, whereby an election was to be conducted within 60 days of the death of the President).

The election to the Chamber of Representatives, which took place on 3 January 2000 as scheduled, was contested by some 55 political associations. The coalition of the SDP and the CSLP (together with two minor parties) secured 47.0% of the votes cast and 71 of the 151 seats, defeating the CDU, with 30.5% of the votes cast and 45 seats; the alliance of the four other principal opposition parties, together with the Croatian Social Democrats' Action, won 15.9% of the total votes cast and 25 seats. The Chairman of the SDP, Ivica Račan, was subsequently designated as Prime Minister. Later in January nine candidates emerged to contest the forthcoming presidential election, including the CSLP leader, Dražen Budiša (who was to represent the SDP/CSLP alliance), and the former Yugoslav President Stipe Mesić, who was the joint candidate of the four other principal opposition parties. The CDU elected Mate Granić, hitherto Deputy Prime Minister and Minister of Foreign Affairs, as its presidential candidate, while Vladimir Šeks (who was reported to be a traditional party member) became acting leader,

pending a party congress. In the event that none of the candidates received more than 50% of the votes cast, a second round of voting, between the two candidates who received the most votes in the first ballot, was to take place within 15 days. In the first round of the election, which took place on 24 January, Mesić secured 41.1% of the votes cast, while Budiša won 27.7% and Granić 22.5%. Mesić and Budiša were consequently to contest a second round of voting, which was scheduled for 7 February. On 27 January Pavletić formally appointed Račan to the office of Prime Minister. Račan announced the establishment of a new coalition Government, comprising members of the Opposition Six parties. In the second presidential ballot, Mesić achieved an outright majority, with 56.2% of the votes cast; Budiša secured 43.8% of the votes. On 9 February the Assembly adopted a motion expressing confidence in the new Government headed by Račan. Following his inauguration as President on 18 February, Mesić pledged to support the return of ethnic Serbian refugees to Croatia.

In March 2000 the Government established a council for co-operation with the ICTY. In May, however, nationalists who had participated in the conflict of 1991–95 organized mass demonstrations in protest at the Government's policy of co-operation with the Tribunal. Meanwhile, in early April Granić left the CDU to form a new party, which became known as the Croatian Democratic Centre. In May a coalition of the SDP and the Croatian Pensioners' Party won the largest number of seats in the election to Zagreb City Assembly. In the same month the Chamber of Representatives approved constitutional amendments that guaranteed the educational and linguistic rights of minority groups, and representation in the legislature for those groups that constituted more than 8% of the total population. Later in May Croatia was officially admitted to NATO's 'Partnership for Peace' programme.

In August 2000 a Croat military officer, Milan Levar, who had testified at the ICTY in 1997 regarding the mass execution of Serbs in Gospić, in central Croatia, was killed in a bomb explosion at his private residence. In September the Croatian authorities detained 10 people on suspicion of involvement in Levar's murder; a further four suspects were arrested in connection with the massacre of some 100 Muslim civilians in the Bosnian village of Ahmici in 1993. Members of the armed forces and former supporters of Tudjman continued to condemn the Government's policy of co-operation with the ICTY, and in late September Mesić dismissed seven senior military officials who had publicly criticized the detention of war-crimes suspects. In early November the Chamber of Representatives adopted constitutional amendments that reduced the powers of the President and increased those of the legislature (which, henceforth, was to appoint the Government).

In March 2001 the Government submitted a proposal to the Chamber of Representatives for the abolition of the Chamber of Counties, in order to reduce expenditure. Despite the strenuous opposition of the CDU, which held a majority of seats in the upper house, the Chamber of Representatives accordingly approved a constitutional amendment converting the Assembly into a unicameral legislature. At local government elections, which took place on 20 May, the SDP-led coalition obtained control of 14 of the 21 County Assemblies (including those of Zagreb and Split). The CDU, despite receiving more votes than expected, secured a majority in only four County Assemblies (compared with 16 in the 1997 elections). In early June the IDA (which had held the European integration portfolio) withdrew from the Government, following differences with the other coalition parties, particularly with regard to the movement's aim to make Italian a second official language in Istria. The resignation of the Minister of Justice (an SDP representative) later that month was reported to be related to cabinet dissension over the Government's co-operation with the ICTY.

In early June 2001 the Rijeka County Court indicted a prominent Bosnian Muslim, Fikret Abdić (who had, notably, established an autonomous region in north-western Bosnia in 1993), for crimes against humanity, including the killing of civilians in a detention camp in 1993. In accordance with a bilateral agreement between the Croatian and Bosnian authorities, the trial of Abdić, who had obtained Croatian citizenship in 1995, commenced in the Croatian town of Karlovac in July; he was sentenced to 20 years' imprisonment at the end of July 2002. In early July 2001, following protracted argument, the Government voted in favour of extraditing two Croatian generals suspected of war crimes to the ICTY, in compliance with a secret indictment issued by the Tribunal. Four ministers belonging to the CSLP subsequently resigned in protest at the Government's decision. In mid-July, however, Račan's administration won an essential motion of confidence (by 93 votes to 36) in the Assembly, which also approved a statement reaffirming the Government's policy of co-operation with the ICTY. Following the forced resignation of Budiša (who had strongly opposed the extradition) from the leadership of the CSLP, the four representatives of that party rejoined the Government. Later in July one of the indicted suspects, Gen. Rahim Ademi, surrendered to the ICTY (thereby becoming the first Croat to be tried at The Hague), and denied charges relating to the killing of Serb civilians during a Croatian offensive to regain control of Krajina in 1993. The other suspect, Gen. Ante Gotovina, who had been indicted on similar charges, pertaining to an offensive in 1995, remained at large. (In February 2002 it was announced that Ademi was to be released provisionally from custody, pending his trial.)

In late September 2001 Milošević, who had been extradited to the ICTY in June on charges relating to Kosovo (see chapter on Serbia and Montenegro), was also formally indicted with crimes against humanity and violations of the Geneva Convention; Milošević was held responsible for the killing of large numbers of Croat civilians and the expulsion of some 170,000 non-Serbs from Croatian territory by Serb forces in 1991–92. In early October 2001 a former commander of the Yugoslav navy, together with three further Yugoslav military officers, were indicted by the ICTY for the killing of more than 40 civilians during the bombardment of Dubrovnik in 1991.

In early December 2001 the Assembly ratified Croatia's signature of a stabilization and association agreement with the EU (despite the opposition of the CDU and its allied parties). In early January 2002 the Government repeated its request for UNMOP to be withdrawn from the Prevlaka peninsula, in view of the improvement in relations with the FRY; nevertheless, the observer mission remained in place until December.

In early February 2002 Budiša (who had continued to express open antagonism to Račan) was re-elected to the presidency of the CSLP, defeating the party General Secretary and incumbent Minister of Defence, Jozo Radoš. At the end of that month the CSLP leadership decided to remove the First Deputy Prime Minister, Goran Granić, and a further two CSLP ministers from the Government; it was reported that Budiša questioned their loyalty to the party, owing to their failure to support his stance of opposition to Račan's co-operation with the ICTY. The remaining three CSLP members in the Cabinet (including Radoš) subsequently tendered their resignations to demonstrate disagreement with the party leadership. In early March, following lengthy discussions, the coalition parties in the Government reached agreement on a cabinet reorganization. Budiša became First Deputy Prime Minister, while Granić (henceforth an independent) and three of the CSLP representatives were reappointed to the Government. The issue of co-operation with the ICTY remained under discussion.

In April 2002 the Ministers of Foreign Affairs of Croatia and the FRY agreed to designate the boundary between Croatia and Montenegro (FRY) as the state border of the disputed Prevlaka region, in the first formal bilateral accord on Prevlaka to be reached since the dissolution of the Yugoslav federation. In May Milan Martić, the former President of the RSK, who had been indicted in 1996 for war crimes, in particular his alleged responsibility for the bombardment of Zagreb in 1995, surrendered to the ICTY. (The Yugoslav authorities had in April 2002 agreed to extradite Martić, then resident in Serbia, and a further 22 indicted suspects to the Tribunal.) He pleaded not guilty to all charges at the ICTY later in May. At the beginning of July Budiša finally withdrew the CSLP from the government coalition, after an agreement on joint ownership of the Krško nuclear power installation in Slovenia was ratified in the Sabor, despite the opposition of 17 of the CSLP's 23 deputies. He threatened to expel the six dissident CSLP deputies from the party. On 5 July Račan submitted his resignation to Mesić, following the collapse of his administration. Five days later, however, Račan was returned to the office of Prime Minister, after his nomination by Mesić was supported by 84 deputies in the Sabor. On 28 July Račan and the leaders of the other political parties belonging to the ruling coalition reached agreement on a new Council of Ministers, which was approved by the Sabor two days later.

In mid-July 2002 the Presidents of Croatia and the FRY met members of the Bosnian Presidency in Sarajevo (the first trilateral summit meeting since the dissolution of the former Yugoslavia). In September Gen. Janko Bobetko, the Croatian army Chief of Staff in 1991–95, was indicted by the ICTY on charges of crimes against humanity for his alleged involvement in the killing of some 100 Serbs in 1993. Račan rejected Bobetko's indictment, on the grounds that it violated the terms of the Constitution, thereby refusing for the first time to co-operate with the ICTY. EU officials responded by warning that failure to comply with the Tribunal could delay Croatia's admission to the organization (which was anticipated in 2007), and the British Government suspended the ratification of the stabilization and association agreement signed in December 2001. In October 2002 the Chief Prosecutor at the ICTY, Carla Del Ponte, visited Croatia to urge the authorities to extradite Bobetko, and the imposition of UN sanctions against the country was envisaged. The Government continued to contest the indictment against Bobetko (who was generally viewed in Croatia as a popular war veteran) and declared him unfit to be extradited to the ICTY owing to ill health, but subsequently pledged to abide by the decision of UN medical experts. Also in October Mesić, testifying against Milošević at the ICTY, declared that the Serbian leader had encouraged the Croatian conflict with the aim of creating a 'Greater Serbian' state. In December the Ministers of Foreign Affairs of Croatia and the FRY reached a provisional accord on the Prevlaka peninsula, thereby allowing the UN Security Council to end the mandate of UNMOP later that month; under the agreement, the peninsula was to remain demilitarized and joint maritime patrols were to be introduced.

In response to continued pressure from the EU, the Government indicated in early 2003 that it was prepared to demonstrate its full co-operation with the ICTY. In January, at a summit meeting in Zagreb, which was attended by the Prime Ministers of Croatia, Hungary, Italy and Slovenia, support was expressed for Croatian membership of the EU and NATO. In February Croatia submitted a formal application for membership of the EU. In March a former army commander, Gen. Mirko Norac (the most senior officer to be convicted by a Croatian court), was sentenced to 12 years' imprisonment for his involvement in the killing of some 50 Croatian Serb civilians in 1991; a further two defendants received terms of 15 years and 10 years, respectively.

Government

According to the 1990 Constitution (amended in March 2001), legislative power is vested in the 151-member unicameral Assembly (Sabor), which is elected for a four-year term. Executive power is held by the President, who is elected by universal adult suffrage for a period of five years. The Assembly appoints the Prime Minister, and (upon the recommendation of the Prime Minister) the ministers. The country is divided, for electoral purposes, into 21 counties, 420 municipalities and 61 towns.

Defence

Military service is compulsory for men and lasts for a period of 10 months. In August 2002 the estimated total strength of the armed forces was 51,000 (the number of reservists totalled 140,000), including an army of 45,000, a navy of 3,000 and an air force of 3,000. There were, in addition, 10,000 armed military police. The mandate of the UN Mission of Observers in Prevlaka, deployed in Croatia from 1996, ended in December 2002. Projected budgetary expenditure on defence by the central Government was estimated at 4,354.7m. kuna (6.0% of total spending) in 2002.

Economic Affairs

In 2001, according to estimates by the World Bank, Croatia's gross national income (GNI), measured at average 1999–2001 prices, was US $20,366m., equivalent to $4,550 per head (or $8,440 per head on an international purchasing-power parity basis). During 1990–2001, it was estimated, the population declined at an average annual rate of 0.8%, while gross domestic product (GDP) per head declined, in real terms, by an average of 0.1% per year. Overall GDP declined, in real terms, at an average annual rate of 0.9% in 1990–2001; however, GDP increased by 3.7% in 2000 and by 4.1% in 2001.

Agriculture (including hunting, forestry and fishing) contributed 8.3% of GDP in 2001. About 15.6% of the employed labour force were engaged in the sector in that year. The principal crops are maize, wheat, potatoes and sugar beet. (However, the civil conflict of 1991–95 destroyed much arable land.) The GDP of the agricultural sector declined, in real terms, at an average annual rate of 2.0% in 1990–2001; however, agricultural GDP increased by 1.3% in 2000 and by 2.5% in 2001.

Industry (including mining, manufacturing, construction and power) contributed 32.3% of GDP and engaged 30.0% of the employed labour force in 2001. Industrial GDP declined, in real terms, at an average annual rate of 4.4% during 1990–2001; however, GDP in the industrial sector increased by 1.5% in 2000 and by 5.2% in 2001.

The mining sector contributed 5.5% of GDP in 1998, and engaged only 0.6% of the employed labour force in 2001. Croatia has many exploitable mineral resources, including petroleum, coal and natural gas. The GDP of the mining sector declined by 2.4% in 1998; mining production increased by 1.9% in 1999.

The manufacturing sector contributed 20.7% of GDP and engaged 20.8% of the employed labour force in 2001. In 1992 the principal branches of the manufacturing sector, measured by the value of output, were food products (accounting for 19.2% of the total), chemicals (12.8%), textiles and clothing (8.5%), transport equipment and electrical machinery. The GDP of the manufacturing sector declined, in real terms, at an average annual rate of 4.4% per year during 1990–2001; however, manufacturing GDP increased by 4.1% in 2000 and by 5.1% in 2001.

Approximately 30% of Croatia's electricity-generating capacity was destroyed in the civil conflict. Of total electricity production in 1999, 53.8% was provided by hydroelectric power, 32.3% by petroleum and 9.6% by natural gas. However, the country remains dependent on imported fuel, which accounted for some 12.9% of total imports in 2001.

Services provided 59.5% of GDP and engaged 54.4% of the employed labour force in 2001. The virtual elimination of tourism in Croatia (which in the late 1980s accounted for some 82% of Yugoslavia's total tourism trade) represented the largest war-related economic loss. There was a significant recovery in the tourism sector in the 1990s; by 2001 tourist arrivals had increased to 6,544,000 (compared with 3,805,000 in 1999). According to World Bank estimates, the GDP of the services sector declined, in real terms, at an average annual rate of 0.2% in 1990–2001; however, the GDP of the sector increased by 5.0% in 2000 and by 6.6% in 2001.

In 2001 Croatia recorded a visible trade deficit of US $4,101.3m., while there was a deficit of $741.2m. on the current account of the balance of payments. In 2001 the principal source of imports was Italy (18.1%); other major sources were Germany, Slovenia, Russia and Austria. The principal market for exports in that year was Italy (23.7%); other important purchasers were Germany, Bosnia and Herzegovina and Slovenia. The principal exports in 2001 were machinery and transport equipment, miscellaneous manufactured articles (particularly clothing and accessories), basic manufactures, and chemical products. The main imports in that year were machinery and transport equipment (most notably road vehicles), basic manufactures, mineral fuels (particularly petroleum and petroleum products), miscellaneous manufactured articles, chemical products and foodstuffs.

Croatia's overall budgetary deficit for 2001 was 4,309.2m. kuna (equivalent to 3.2% of GDP). The country's total external debt was US $12,120m. at the end of 2000, of which $7,686m. was long-term public debt. In that year the cost of debt-servicing was equivalent to 25.5% of the value of exports of goods and services. Consumer prices increased at an average annual rate of 80.4% in 1990–2001. However, the average rate of inflation was only 5.3% in 2000 and 4.8% in 2001, and it declined further in 2002, to 2.0%. In 2001 the average annual rate of unemployment was estimated at 20.6%.

Croatia was admitted to the IMF in January 1993, and became a member of the European Bank for Reconstruction and Development (EBRD, see p. 193) in April of that year. In November 2000 Croatia was admitted to the World Trade Organization (WTO, see p. 323). In February 2003 Croatia made a formal application for membership of the EU. In early 2003 Croatia also joined the Central European Free Trade Association (CEFTA).

The outbreak of civil conflict in Croatia in the early 1990s resulted in a rapid deterioration of the economy. In 1993 the Government initiated an economic programme, which achieved some success in restraining inflation and public expenditure. A new national currency, the kuna, was introduced in May 1994. In October of that year the IMF extended its first stand-by loan to Croatia. The Government subsequently received reconstruction loans from other official creditors and concluded a rescheduling agreement with the 'Paris Club' of donor nations. In April 1996 an agreement was reached with the 'London Club' of commercial creditor banks, establishing Croatia's share of the foreign commercial bank debt incurred by the former Yugoslavia. In March 1997 the IMF approved a further three-year credit arrangement to finance the Government's economic reforms. Following the election of a new coalition Government in early 2000, relations with the USA and with western European Governments improved (resulting in increased financial aid). Despite a subsequent severe increase in the budgetary deficit, in early 2002 the IMF declared itself satisfied with Croatia's implementation of a stand-by arrangement (agreed in March 2001), concluding that it had met most of its economic targets, and exceeded those for growth, inflation and balance of payments. Significant progress had also been achieved in the privatization of state-owned enterprises, particularly in the financial sector. Following a period of political dissension, a new Government, which aimed to continue fiscal reforms, was approved in the legislature in July 2002. By the end of that year growth in real GDP had accelerated and monetary conditions further stabilized. In early 2003 the IMF approved a 14-month stand-by credit for Croatia (which, however, the Government viewed as precautionary), to support continued fiscal consolidation and structural reform, with emphasis on stabilizing the public-debt ratio, and accelerating progress in privatization. In addition, the continuing high rate of unemployment was to be addressed through increased labour-market flexibility. Croatia's application for membership of the EU, formally submitted in early 2003, and anticipated to take place in 2007, was, however, conditional on the continued implementation of reforms and the Government's co-operation with the International Criminal Tribunal for the Former Yugoslavia (see Recent History).

Education

Pre-school education, for children aged from three to six years, is available free of charge. Education is officially compulsory for eight years, between seven and 15 years of age. Primary education, which is provided free, begins at the age of seven and continues for four years. Enrolment at primary schools in 1998 was equivalent to 77% of children in the appropriate age-group. Special education in foreign languages is provided for children of non-Croat ethnic origin, since all national minorities in Croatia have the right to learn their minority language. Secondary education is available free (although private schools also exist) and lasts for up to eight years, comprising two cycles of four years each. There are various types of secondary school: grammar, technical and specialized schools and mixed-curriculum schools. Enrolment at secondary schools in 1998 was equivalent to 81% of the relevant age-group. In 2001/02 there were 102 institutions of higher education in Croatia, including four universities (in Zagreb, Rijeka, Osijek and Split). In that year a total of 111,782 students were enrolled in higher education establishments. Projected budgetary expenditure on education by the central Government in 2002 was 6,194.7m. kuna (8.5% of total spending).

Public Holidays

2003: 1 January (New Year's Day), 6 January (Epiphany), 21 April (Easter Monday), 1 May (Labour Day), 19 June (Corpus Christi), 22 June (Anti-Fascism Day), 5 August (National Day), 15 August (Assumption), 8 October (Independence Day), 1 November (All Saints' Day), 25–26 December (Christmas).

2004: 1 January (New Year's Day), 6 January (Epiphany), 12 April (Easter Monday), 1 May (Labour Day), 10 June (Corpus Christi), 22 June (Anti-Fascism Day), 5 August (National Day), 15 August (Assumption), 8 October (Independence Day), 1 November (All Saints' Day), 25–26 December (Christmas).

Weights and Measures

The metric system is in force.

Statistical Survey

Source (unless otherwise stated): Central Bureau of Statistics of the Republic of Croatia, 10000 Zagreb, Ilica 3; tel. (1) 4806111; fax (1) 4806148; e-mail stat.info@dzs.hr; internet www.dzs.hr.

Area and Population

AREA, POPULATION AND DENSITY

Area (sq km)	56,542*
Population (census results)	
31 March 1991	4,784,265
31 March 2001†	
Males	2,105,000
Females.	2,276,000
Total	4,381,000
Population (official estimates at mid-year)	
1998	4,501,000
1999	4,554,000
2000	4,381,000
Density (per sq km) at 31 March 2001	77.5

* 21,831 sq miles.

† Data are not directly comparable to those from the 1981 and 1991 censuses, owing to a change in the definition used to calculate total population.

POPULATION BY ETHNIC GROUP
(census of 31 March 2001)

	Number ('000)	%
Croat	3,977.2	89.6
Serb	201.6	4.5
Muslim	20.8	0.5
Italian	19.6	0.4
Hungarian	16.6	0.4
Albanian	15.1	0.3
Slovenian	13.2	0.3
Czech	10.5	0.2
Gypsy	9.5	0.2
Montenegrin	4.9	0.1
Slovak	4.7	0.1
Macedonian	4.3	0.1
Others*	139.5	3.3
Total	4,437.5	100.0

* Including other groups, ethnically non-declared persons and unknown ethnicity.

COUNTIES
(census of 31 March 2001)

Županije (County)	Area (sq km)	Population	Density (per sq km)
Zagreb	3,078	309,696	100.6
Krapina and Zagorje . . .	1,230	142,432	115.8
Sisak and Moslavina . . .	4,448	185,387	41.7
Karlovac	3,622	141,787	39.1
Varaždin	1,260	184,769	146.6
Koprivnica and Križevci . .	1,734	124,467	71.8
Bjelovar and Bilogora . . .	2,638	133,084	50.4
Primorje and Gorski Kotar . .	3,590	305,505	85.1
Lika and Senj	5,350	53,677	10.0
Virovitica and Podravina . .	2,021	93,389	46.2
Požega and Slavonia . . .	1,821	85,831	47.1
Slavonski Brod and Posavina	2,027	176,765	87.2
Zadar	3,643	162,045	44.5
Osijek and Baranja . . .	4,149	330,506	79.7
Šibenik and Knin . . .	2,994	112,891	37.7
Vukovar and Srem (Sirmium)	2,448	204,768	83.6
Split and Dalmatia . . .	4,524	463,676	102.5
Istria	2,813	206,344	73.4
Dubrovnik and Neretva . .	1,782	122,870	67.0
Meimurje	730	118,426	162.2
City of Zagreb	640	779,145	1,217.4
Total	56,542	4,437,460	78.5

PRINCIPAL TOWNS
(population at 2001 census)

Zagreb (capital) . .	691,724		Šibenik . . .	37,060
Split	175,140		Sisak	36,785
Rijeka	143,800		Velika Gorica. . .	33,339
Osijek	90,411		Vinkovci . . .	33,239
Zadar	69,556		Dubrovnik . . .	30,436
Slavonski Brod. . .	58,642		Vukovar . . .	30,126
Pula	58,594		Bjelovar . . .	27,783
Karlovac	49,082		Koprivnica . . .	24,809
Sesvete	44,914		Požega. . . .	20,943
Varaždin	41,434		Dakovo	20,912

BIRTHS, MARRIAGES AND DEATHS

	Registered live births		Registered marriages		Registered deaths	
	Number	Rate (per 1,000)	Number	Rate (per 1,000)	Number	Rate (per 1,000)
1994 . .	48,584	10.9	23,966	5.3	49,482	11.1
1995 . .	50,182	11.2	24,385	5.1	50,536	11.3
1996 . .	53,811	12.0	24,596	5.5	50,636	11.3
1997 . .	55,501	12.1	24,517	5.4	51,964	11.4
1998 . .	47,068	10.5	24,243	5.4	52,311	11.6
1999 . .	45,179	9.9	23,778	5.2	51,953	11.4
2000* . .	43,746	10.0	22,017	5.0	50,246	11.5
2001* . .	40,993	9.2	22,076	5.0	49,552	11.2

* Rates in 2000 and 2001 are calculated on the basis of the March 2001 census total of persons usually resident. Figures for earlier years were based on estimates of *de jure* population (permanent residents).

Expectation of life (WHO estimates, years at birth): 72.9 (males 68.9; females 77.1) in 2001 (Source: WHO, *World Health Report*).

EMPLOYMENT
(labour force surveys, '000 persons)

	1999	2000	2001
Agriculture, hunting and forestry	243.5	220.2	224.5
Fishing	3.9	5.0	3.9
Mining and quarrying	8.8	7.2	9.1
Manufacturing	325.0	310.9	305.6
Electricity, gas and water supply	26.2	29.7	29.1
Construction	97.1	99.9	96.6
Wholesale and retail trade; repairof motor vehicles, motorcycles and personal and household goods .	197.2	219.8	211.3
Hotels and restaurants	74.0	79.7	77.0
Transport, storage and communications	101.1	108.1	103.2
Financial intermediation . . .	34.6	37.2	28.5
Real estate, renting and business activities	56.6	68.2	59.8
Public administration and defence; compulsory social security . .	105.4	123.7	105.5
Education	80.8	88.0	76.4
Health and social work . . .	89.1	91.3	82.8
Other community, social and personal service activities . .	44.9	58.2	48.9
Private households with employed persons	3.4	3.4	3.9
Total employed (incl. others). .	1,491.6	1,553.0	1,469.5
Males	802.2	848.7	818.9
Females	689.5	704.3	650.6

Source: ILO.

Unemployed (sample surveys, '000 persons): 198.5 in 1998; 234.0 in 1999; 297.2 in 2000.

Registered unemployed (annual averages, '000 persons): 287.8 in 1998; 321.9 in 1999; 357.9 in 2000; 380.2 in 2001.

Health and Welfare

KEY INDICATORS

Total fertility rate (children per woman, 2001)	1.7
Under-5 mortality rate (per 1,000 live births, 2001) . . .	8
HIV/AIDS (% of persons aged 15–49, 2001)	<0.10
Physicians (per 1,000 head, 1998)	2.29
Hospital beds (per 1,000 head, 1994)	5.91
Health expenditure (2000): US $ per head (PPP) . . .	638
Health expenditure (2000): % of GDP	8.6
Health expenditure (2000): public (% of total) . . .	84.6
Human Development Index (2000): ranking	48
Human Development Index (2000): value	0.809

For sources and definitions, see explanatory note on p. vi.

Agriculture

PRINCIPAL CROPS
('000 metric tons)

	1999	2000	2001
Wheat	558.2	1,032.1	965.2
Barley	124.9	151.4	161.5
Maize	2,135.5	1,526.2	2,211.6
Rye	6.2	7.3	8.7
Oats	56.8	51.1	47.6
Potatoes	728.6	553.7	463.7
Sugar beet	1,114.0	482.2	964.9
Dry beans	22.3	9.9	16.5
Soybeans (Soya beans) . . .	115.9	65.3	91.9
Sunflower seed	72.4	54.0	43.0
Rapeseed	32.6	29.4	22.5
Cabbages	144.0	112.0	123.7
Tomatoes	70.8	69.6	73.9
Cucumbers and gherkins . .	37.9	28.0	36.0
Dry onions	55.6	44.8	58.1
Garlic	10.3	8.1	9.9
Carrots	29.9	24.2	28.2
Apples	66.8	81.3	32.5
Pears	10.0	10.1	6.7
Peaches and nectarines . . .	10.2	9.3	9.0
Plums	38.0	39.9	39.6
Grapes	394.1	353.5	359.0
Watermelons and melons . .	53.4	50.1	50.0
Tobacco (leaves)	10.1	9.7	10.5

LIVESTOCK
('000 head at 31 December)

	2000	2001	2002
Horses	11	10	8
Cattle	427	438	417
Pigs	1,233	1,234	1,286
Sheep	528	539	580
Goats	80	93	96
Poultry	11,256	11,747	11,665

LIVESTOCK PRODUCTS
('000 metric tons)

	1999	2000	2001
Beef and veal	19	19	16
Mutton and lamb	2	2	1
Pigmeat	64	52	33
Poultry meat	32	40	49
Cows' milk	622	606	654
Butter	2	2	3
Cheese (all kinds)	19	21	23
Hen eggs	49	47	47
Honey	1	2	2

Forestry

ROUNDWOOD REMOVALS
('000 cubic metres)

	1999	2000	2001
Sawlogs and veneer logs . . .	1,915	1,976	1,938
Pulpwood	311	551	561
Other industrial wood . . .	166	166*	222
Fuel wood	1,094	976	747
Total	3,486	3,669	3,468

* FAO estimate.

Source: FAO.

SAWNWOOD PRODUCTION
('000 cubic metres)

	1999	2000	2001
Coniferous (softwood) . . .	166	95	118
Broadleaved (hardwood) . . .	519	547	516
Total	685	642	634

Source: FAO.

Fishing

('000 metric tons, live weight)

	1999	2000	2001
Freshwater fishes	3.3	3.4	4.4
Marine fishes	19.3	21.6	20.5
Crustaceans and molluscs . .	2.5	2.7	5.2
Total catch	25.1	27.7	30.1

Mining

('000 metric tons, unless otherwise indicated)

	1999	2000	2001
Coal	15	n.a.	n.a.
Crude petroleum	1,292	1,214	1,121
Natural gas (million cu m) . . .	1,567	1,768	2,009
Bentonite	8.4	10.0	10.6
Ceramic clay	6.0	5.0	32.6
Salt (unrefined)	18.4	33.7	n.a.
Gypsum (crude)	188.0	150.8	130.9

Source: partly US Geological Survey.

Industry

SELECTED PRODUCTS

('000 metric tons, unless otherwise indicated)

	1999	2000	2001
Beer ('000 hectolitres) . . .	3,663	3,847	3,799
Spirits ('000 hectolitres). . . .	208	177	163
Cigarettes (million) . . .	12,785	13,692	14,716
Cotton fabric blankets ('000 sq metres)	13,179	13,873	14,059
Household linen ('000 sq metres) .	6,928	7,229	6,502
Ready-to-wear clothing ('000 sq metres)	24,704	24,397	24,468
Leather footwear ('000 pairs) . .	5,428	5,430	6,167
Paper and cardboard	181	228	234
Cardboard packaging	167	174	184
Motor spirit (petrol)	1,212	1,333	1,250
Gas oil (distillate fuels) . . .	1,006	1,050	1,036
Compound fertilizers	459	492	407
Synthetic materials and resin . .	92	57	64
Cement	2,712	2,852	2,303
Tractors (number)	2,325	1,751	2,386
Tankers ('000 gross registered tons)	203	144	225
Cargo ships ('000 gross registered tons)	131	147	224
Chairs ('000)	937	1,502	1,834
Electric energy (million kWh) . .	11,435	10,293	11,674

Finance

CURRENCY AND EXCHANGE RATES

Monetary Unit

100 lipa = 1 kuna.

Sterling, Dollar and Euro Equivalents (31 December 2002)

£1 sterling = 11.518 kuna
US $1 = 7.146 kuna
€1 = 7.494 kuna
1,000 kuna = £86.82 = $139.94 = €133.44.

Average Exchange Rate (kuna per US $)

2000   8.277
2001   8.340
2002   7.869

Note: The Croatian dinar was introduced on 23 December 1991, replacing (and initially at par with) the Yugoslav dinar. On 30 May 1994 the kuna, equivalent to 1,000 dinars, was introduced.

STATE BUDGET

(million kuna)

Revenue	2000	2001*	2002*†
Tax revenue	39,939.0	47,274.0	67,517.3
Taxes on personal income . .	4,094.6	3,404.4	3,567.4
Taxes on corporate income . .	1,673.8	1,987.2	2,035.1
General sales, turnover or value-added taxes	21,978.4	22,882.3	24,512.2
Excises	7,572.1	7,224.4	7,481.7
Excises on petroleum products	4,632.8	4,194.3	3,429.4
Excises on tobacco products .	2,073.7	2,094.7	2,700.0
Customs duties	3,896.5	4,229.9	3,928.2
Other current revenue . . .	1,595.9	1,632.3	2,479.6
Capital revenue	3,100.7	4,597.3	221.0
Proceeds of privatization . .	2,867.0	4,241.0	—
Total	44,635.7	53,503.6	70,217.9

Expenditure‡	2000	2001*	2002*†
General public services	2,933.2	2,978.3	3,040.9
Defence	5,479.5	4,338.6	4,354.7
Public order and safety . . .	5,185.3	4,761.2	4,890.7
Education	6,576.0	6,581.9	6,194.7
Health	332.4	270.3	10,790.5
Social security and welfare . .	14,947.3	25,153.7	32,339.3
Housing and community amenities	1,803.3	1,677.0	1,055.3
Recreational, cultural and religious affairs	904.1	955.7	963.3
Fuel and energy	0.3	7.7	8.7
Agriculture, forestry and fisheries	1,723.8	1,641.6	1,879.4
Mining and mineral resources manufacturing and construction	624.1	466.4	437.8
Transport and communications. .	4,953.2	3,113.1	1,356.7
Other economic affairs and services	813.2	832.2	876.8
Other purposes	3,291.8	3,945.6	4,665.7
Total	49,567.5	56,723.3	72,854.4

* From July 2001 includes social security funds, but excludes revenue and expenditure from Croatian Roads Company and Croatian Motorways.

† Projected figures.

‡ Excluding lending minus repayments (million kuna): 1,176.1 in 2000; 1,089.5 in 2001; 1,579.7 in 2002 (projected figure).

Source: Ministry of Finance, Zagreb.

INTERNATIONAL RESERVES

(US $ million at 31 December)

	2000	2001	2002
IMF special drawing rights . . .	147.2	107.4	1.5
Reserve position in IMF. . . .	0.2	0.2	0.2
Foreign exchange.	3,376.9	4,595.6	5,883.2
Total	3,524.4	4,703.2	5,884.9

Source: IMF, *International Financial Statistics*.

MONEY SUPPLY

(million kuna at 31 December)

	2000	2001	2002
Currency outside banks	6,636.7	8,507.4	9,680.9
Demand deposits at deposit money banks	11,386.0	15,180.6	21,166.2
Total (incl. others)	18,030.2	23,703.6	30,866.3

Source: IMF, *International Financial Statistics*.

COST OF LIVING

(Consumer price index; base: 1990 = 100)

	1999	2000	2001
Food	62,359.2	62,608.6	63,923.4
Fuel and light	58,798.1	64,677.9	72,698.0
Clothing (incl. footwear). . . .	69,816.8	74,424.7	77,104.0
Housing	56,473.4	60,426.5	64,293.8
All items (incl. others)	67,259.0	70,823.7	74,223.2

NATIONAL ACCOUNTS

Gross Domestic Product by Economic Activity
(million kuna at current prices)

	1998	1999	2000
Agriculture, hunting and forestry	10,661.6 ⎫	11,366	12,387
Fishing	238.9 ⎭		
Mining and quarrying	642.5 ⎫		
Manufacturing	24,661.2 ⎬	30,871	35,174
Electricity, gas and water supply	3,770.4 ⎭		
Construction	7,732.1	7,957	7,648
Wholesale and retail trade; repair of motor vehicles, motorcycles and personal and household goods	13,787.8	14,328	16,401
Hotels and restaurants . . .	3,581.2	3,452	4,232
Transport, storage and communications	9,777.2	10,507	12,596
Financial intermediation . . .	4,901.7 ⎫		
Real estate, renting and business activities	11,485.8 ⎭	17,396	18,502
Public administration and defence; compulsory social security	11,684.0		
Education	4,944.7		
Health and social work . .	5,702.4 ⎫	27,070	29,540
Other community, social and personal service activities . .	2,685.3 ⎬		
Private households with employed persons . . .	36.6 ⎭		
Sub-total	116,293.4	122,947	136,480
Less Financial intermediation services indirectly measured	5,232.4	5,603	6,037
GDP at basic prices . . .	111,061.0	117,344	130,443
Taxes, *less* subsidies, on products	26,542.7	25,356	27,068
GDP in purchasers' values .	137,603.7	142,700	157,511

BALANCE OF PAYMENTS
(US $ million)

	1999	2000	2001
Exports of goods f.o.b.	4,394.7	4,567.2	4,758.7
Imports of goods f.o.b.	−7,693.3	−7,770.9	−8,860.0
Trade balance	−3,298.6	−3,203.8	−4,101.3
Exports of services	3,723.1	4,095.9	4,874.6
Imports of services	−2,097.9	−1,828.0	−1,948.2
Balance on goods and services	−1,673.4	−935.8	−1,174.9
Other income received . . .	247.3	331.5	402.7
Other income paid	−604.3	−717.6	−934.7
Balance on goods, services and income	−2,030.3	−1,322.0	−1,706.9
Current transfers received . .	967.4	1,101.0	1,174.5
Current transfers paid . . .	−334.9	−217.8	−208.8
Current balance	−1,397.9	−438.8	−741.2
Capital account (net) . . .	24.9	20.9	133.0
Direct investment abroad . .	−44.8	0.2	−154.6
Direct investment from abroad .	1,458.1	1,077.0	1,578.4
Portfolio investment assets . .	−0.3	−0.2	−6.3
Portfolio investment liabilities .	570.5	722.3	729.4
Other investment assets . .	−117.7	−847.5	308.4
Other investment liabilities . .	891.9	841.3	−35.1
Net errors and omissions . .	−974.7	−764.5	−470.0
Overall balance	410.1	610.7	1,342.0

Source: IMF, *International Financial Statistics*.

External Trade

PRINCIPAL COMMODITIES
(distribution by SITC, US $ million)

Imports c.i.f.	1999	2000	2001
Food and live animals . . .	560.3	556.1	691.1
Mineral fuels, lubricants, etc. .	859.3	1,144.5	1,175.6
Petroleum and petroleum products	673.1	856.8	836.6
Chemicals and related products	939.8	1,004.8	1,038.5
Basic manufactures . . .	1,251.8	1,390.1	1,786.9
Textile yarn, fabrics, etc. . . .	160.2	249.2	355.8
Iron and steel	211.0	243.8	315.8
Machinery and transport equipment	2,732.5	2,568.3	3,102.7
Machinery specialized for particular industries . . .	257.1	250.5	236.5
General industrial machinery equipment and parts . . .	372.8	302.6	398.2
Telecommunications and sound equipment	155.3	209.5	297.5
Electrical machinery, apparatus etc. (excl. telecommunications and sound equipment) . .	338.8	326.0	427.5
Road vehicles and parts* . .	815.7	857.0	943.0
Other transport equipment and parts*	482.9	342.4	260.0
Miscellaneous manufactured articles	923.7	946.9	1,042.9
Clothing and accessories (excl. footwear)	212.8	278.5	258.0
Total (incl. others)	7,798.6	7,886.5	9,147.1

Exports f.o.b.	1999	2000	2001
Food and live animals . .	290.5	273.3	322.5
Crude materials (inedible) except fuels	243.0	251.3	241.4
Cork and wood	164.2	160.1	148.0
Mineral fuels, lubricants, etc. .	338.3	485.8	476.6
Petroleum and petroleum products	287.0	381.9	346.0
Chemicals and related products	515.0	553.8	494.3
Medicinal and pharmaceutical products	169.1	189.0	173.8
Plastics in primary forms . .	135.5	122.4	102.1
Basic manufactures . . .	572.2	669.2	663.7
Non-metallic mineral manufactures	152.7	169.0	183.0
Machinery and transport equipment	1,261.9	1,195.0	1,367.9
Electrical machinery, apparatus etc. (excl. telecommunications and sound equipment) . .	230.4	215.1	243.7
Transport equipment and parts (excl. road vehicles)* . . .	712.8	632.2	719.8
Miscellaneous manufactured articles	966.1	887.2	968.2
Clothing and accessories (excl. footwear)	525.2	469.2	491.8
Footwear	173.8	156.8	165.5
Total (incl. others)	4,302.5	4,431.6	4,665.9

* Data on parts exclude tyres, engines and electrical parts.

PRINCIPAL TRADING PARTNERS
(US $ million)

Imports c.i.f.	1999	2000	2001
Austria	557.6	528.7	631.2
Belgium	114.2	115.0	128.3
Bosnia and Herzegovina	116.8	81.6	126.7
China, People's Republic	75.6	87.3	144.3
Czech Republic	148.4	179.2	209.3
France	392.5	436.4	397.6
Germany	1,441.0	1,297.7	1,583.2
Hungary	174.1	183.8	238.0
Iraq	15.4	101.4	73.1
Italy	1,240.1	1,310.7	1,656.9
Japan	137.9	135.2	145.8
Korea, Republic	79.5	71.8	69.1
Libya	26.4	99.7	74.5
Netherlands	141.8	129.8	164.0
Russia	668.1	672.0	654.1
Slovenia	616.2	626.6	711.7
Spain	82.6	101.2	127.0
Sweden	115.7	111.6	110.4
Switzerland	157.9	150.7	149.9
United Kingdom	186.9	179.7	226.1
USA	240.9	239.0	297.0
Total (incl. others)	7,798.6	7,886.5	9,147.1

Exports f.o.b.	1999	2000	2001
Austria	276.0	292.4	267.9
Bosnia and Herzegovina	545.7	494.8	560.6
Cayman Islands	—	—	70.1
Cyprus	84.5	1.0	9.3
France	108.2	125.9	163.1
Germany	676.1	631.8	689.6
Greece	33.9	89.3	24.0
Hungary	39.6	60.0	56.9
Italy	774.7	989.0	1,105.4
Liberia	169.1	223.5	138.1
Macedonia, former Yugoslav republic	64.1	59.0	52.5
Malta	99.4	48.1	55.6
Netherlands	49.9	49.9	46.7
Norway	113.1	4.5	6.3
Poland	39.6	22.4	20.0
Russia	70.8	56.6	83.5
Slovenia	454.2	480.0	426.4
United Kingdom	79.9	76.2	67.3
USA	86.5	90.0	107.4
Yugoslavia	27.3	107.2	149.2
Total (incl. others)	4,302.5	4,431.6	4,665.9

* Including trade with Luxembourg.
† Including trade with Liechtenstein.
‡ Including trade with Puerto Rico.

Transport

RAILWAYS
(traffic)

	1999	2000	2001
Passenger journeys ('000)	17,537	17,611	17,431
Passenger-kilometres (million)	943	996	948
Freight carried ('000 metric tons)	11,491	11,053	11,963
Freight net ton-km (million)	1,849	1,928	2,249

ROAD TRAFFIC
(registered motor vehicles at 31 December)

	1999	2000	2001
Passenger cars	1,063,546	1,124,825	1,195,450
Buses	4,743	4,660	4,770
Lorries	109,387	113,134	119,899
Special vehicles			
Motorcycles and mopeds	58,109	65,292	73,766

INLAND WATERWAYS
(vessels and traffic)

	1999	2000	2001
Tugs	27	32	32
Motor barges	3	3	4
Barges	95	100	95
Goods unloaded (million metric tons)	1	1	1

SHIPPING

Merchant Fleet
(registered at 31 December)

	1999	2000	2001
Number of vessels	257	246	243
Total displacement ('000 grt)	868.9	734.3	775.2

Source: Lloyd's Register-Fairplay, *World Fleet Statistics*.

International Sea-borne Freight Traffic

	1999	2000	2001
Vessels entered (million grt)	20.8	24.8	30.6
Goods loaded ('000 metric tons)	3,728	5,471	5,847
Goods unloaded ('000 metric tons)	6,739	6,877	6,815
Goods in transit ('000 metric tons)	2,680	1,809	3,794

CIVIL AVIATION

	1999	2000	2001
Kilometres flown ('000)	11,434	12,178	13,225
Passengers carried ('000)	926	1,072	1,245
Passenger-kilometres (million)	643	763	922
Freight carried (metric tons)	4,858	5,697	6,007
Ton-kilometres ('000)	3,219	3,775	3,997

Tourism

FOREIGN TOURIST ARRIVALS BY COUNTRY OF ORIGIN
('000)

	1999	2000	2001
Austria	478	640	687
Bosnia and Herzegovina	157	182	172
Czech Republic	422	711	742
Germany	627	1,048	1,300
Hungary	147	250	280
Italy	630	1,011	1,060
Poland	108	285	392
Slovakia	110	188	203
Slovenia	717	849	877
Total (incl. others)	3,805	5,832	6,544

Nautical tourists ('000): 376 in 1999; 517 in 2000; 580 in 2001.

Receipts from tourism (US $ million): 2,493 in 1999; 2,758 in 2000.

Communications Media

	1999	2000	2001
Radio licences ('000)	1,110	1,120	1,150
Television licences ('000) . . .	1,083	1,093	1,080
Telephone licences ('000) . . .	1,641	1,646	1,783
Mobile cellular telephones ('000 subscribers)*	295.0	1,033.0	1,755.0
Personal computers ('000 in use)*	300	361	400
Internet users ('000)*	200	250	n.a.
Book production (titles)	2,768	2,969	3,832
Daily newspapers (number). . .	16	14	14

* Source: International Telecommunication Union.

Facsimile machines (number in use): 50,237 in 1997 (Source: UN, *Statistical Yearbook*).

Non-daily newspapers (1996): 767; Average circulation 584,000.

Other periodicals (1990): Number 352; Average circulation 6,357,000 (Source: UNESCO, *Statistical Yearbook*).

Education

(2001/02)

	Institutions	Teachers	Students
Pre-primary	1,051	6,566	87,592
Basic schools	2,134	27,502	400,100
Secondary schools	645	19,718	195,000
Higher education*	102	7,622	111,782

* Including post-graduate students.

Adult literacy rate (UNESCO estimates): 98.3% (Males 99.3%; Females 97.3%) in 2000 (Source: UN Development Programme, *Human Development Report*).

Directory

The Constitution

The Constitution of the Republic of Croatia was promulgated on 21 December 1990. Croatia issued a declaration of dissociation from the Socialist Federal Republic of Yugoslavia in June 1991, and formal independence was proclaimed on 8 October. Constitutional amendments, which were adopted in November 1997, included a prohibition on the re-establishment of a union of Yugoslav states.

The following is a summary of the main provisions of the Constitution:

GENERAL PROVISIONS

The Republic of Croatia is a democratic, constitutional state where power belongs to the people and is exercised directly and through the elected representatives of popular sovereignty.

The Republic of Croatia is an integral state, while its sovereignty is inalienable, indivisible and non-transferable. State power in the Republic of Croatia is divided into legislative, executive and judicial power.

All citizens of the Republic of Croatia over the age of 18 years have the right to vote and to be candidates for election to public office. The right to vote is realized through direct elections, by secret ballot. Citizens of the Republic living outside its borders have the right to vote in elections for the Assembly and the President of the Republic.

In a state of war or when there is a direct threat to the independence and unity of the Republic, as well as in the case of serious natural disasters, some freedoms and rights that are guaranteed by the Constitution may be restricted. This is decided by the Assembly of the Republic of Croatia by a two-thirds' majority of its deputies and, if the Assembly cannot be convened, by the President of the Republic.

BASIC RIGHTS

The following rights are guaranteed and protected in the Republic: the right to life (the death sentence has been abolished), fundamental freedoms and privacy, equality before the law, the right to be presumed innocent until proven guilty and the principle of legality, the right to receive legal aid, the right to freedom of movement and residence, the right to seek asylum, inviolability of the home, freedom and secrecy of correspondence, safety and secrecy of personal data, freedom of thought and expression of opinion, freedom of conscience and religion (all religious communities are equal before the law and are separated from the State), the right of assembly and peaceful association, the right of ownership, entrepreneurship and free trade (monopolies are forbidden), the right to work and freedom of labour, the right to a nationality, the right to strike, and the right to a healthy environment.

Members of all peoples and minorities in the Republic enjoy equal rights. They are guaranteed the freedom to express their nationality, to use their language and alphabet and to enjoy cultural autonomy.

GOVERNMENT

Legislature*

Legislative power resides with the unicameral Assembly (Sabor), which comprises the 151-member Chamber of Representatives (Zastupnički dom). The Assembly decides on the adoption and amendment of the Constitution, approves laws, adopts the state budgets, decides on war and peace, decides on the alteration of the borders of the Republic, calls referendums, supervises the work of the Government and other public officials responsible to the Assembly, in accordance with the Constitution and the law, and deals with other matters determined by the Constitution.

Members of the Assembly are elected by universal, direct and secret ballot for a term of four years, and their term is not mandatory. The Assembly may be dissolved, with the approval of the majority of all the deputies. The Assembly has the power to appoint and dismiss the Prime Minister and (upon his recommendation) the ministers.

President of the Republic

The President of the Republic is the Head of State of Croatia. The President represents the country at home and abroad and is responsible for ensuring respect for the Constitution, guaranteeing the existence and unity of the Republic and the regular functioning of state power. The President is elected directly for a term of five years.

The President is the Supreme Commander of the Armed Forces of the Republic of Croatia. In the event of war or immediate danger, the President issues decrees having the force of law. The President may convene a meeting of the Government and place on its agenda items that, in his opinion, should be discussed. The President attends the Government's meetings and presides over them.

Ministers

Executive power in the Republic resides with the President, the Prime Minister and the Ministers. The Government of the Republic consists of the Ministers and the Prime Minister. The Government issues decrees, proposes laws and the budget, and implements laws and regulations that have been adopted by the Assembly. In its work, the Government is responsible to the President of the Republic and the Assembly.

JUDICATURE

Judicial power is vested in the courts and is autonomous and independent. The courts issue judgments on the basis of the Constitution and the law. The Supreme Court is the highest court and is responsible for the uniform implementation of laws and equal rights of citizens. Judges and state public prosecutors are appointed and relieved of duty by the Judicial Council of the Republic, which is elected, from among distinguished lawyers, by the Assembly for a term of eight years.

*The Chamber of Counties, the upper chamber of the, hitherto, bicameral legislature, was abolished by a constitutional amendment adopted in March 2001.

The Government

HEAD OF STATE

President of the Republic: STIPE MESIĆ (elected 7 February 2000; inaugurated 18 February).

Office of the President: 10000 Zagreb, Banski Dvori.

GOVERNMENT
(April 2003)

A coalition of the Social Democratic Party (SDP), the Croatian People's Party (CPP), the Liberal Party (LP) and the Croatian Peasants' Party.

Prime Minister: IVICA RAČAN (SDP).

First Deputy Prime Minister: ANTE SIMONIĆ (Croatian Peasants' Party).

Deputy Prime Minister: GORAN GRANIĆ (Ind.).

Deputy Prime Minister, in charge of the Economy: SLAVKO LINIĆ (SDP).

Deputy Prime Minister, in charge of Social Affairs, and Minister of Defence: ŽELIJKA ANTUNOVIĆ (SDP).

Minister of Finance: MATO CRKVENAC (SDP).

Minister of the Interior: ŠIME LUČIN (SDP).

Minister of Foreign Affairs: TONINO PICULA (SDP).

Minister of Public Works, Reconstruction and Construction: RADIMIR ČAČIĆ (CPP).

Minister of the Economy: LJUBO JURČIĆ (SDP).

Minister of Croatian Homeland War Defenders: IVICA PANČIĆ (SDP).

Minister of Agriculture and Forestry: BOŽIDAR PANKRETIĆ (Croatian Peasants' Party).

Minister of Maritime Affairs, Transport and Telecommunications: ROLAND ŽUVANIĆ (SDP).

Minister of Justice, Administration and Local Self-Government: INGRID ANTIČEVIĆ-MARINOVIĆ (SDP).

Minister of Environmental Protection and Physical Planning: BOŽO KOVAČEVIĆ (LP).

Minister of Education and Sport: VLADIMIR STRUGAR (Croatian Peasants' Party).

Minister of Labour and Social Welfare: DAVORKO VIDOVIĆ (SDP).

Minister of Tourism: PAVE ŽUPAN RUSKOVIĆ (Ind.).

Minister of Health: ANDRO VLAHUŠIĆ (SDP).

Minister of Science and Technology: GVOZDEN FLEGO (SDP).

Minister of Culture: ANTUN VUJIĆ (SDP).

Minister of European Integration: NEVEN MIMICA (SDP).

Minister of Trades, Small and Medium Businesses: ŽELJKO PECEK (SDP).

Minister without Portfolio, in the Office of the Prime Minister: GORDANA SOBOL (SDP).

MINISTRIES

Office of the Prime Minister: Govt of the Republic of Croatia, 10000 Zagreb, trg sv. Marka 2; tel. (1) 4569201; fax (1) 432041.

Ministry of Agriculture and Forestry: 10000 Zagreb, Ave. Vukovar 78; tel. (1) 6133444; fax (1) 442070; internet www.mps.hr.

Ministry of Croatian Homeland War Defenders: Park Stara Trešnjevka 4, Zagreb; tel. (1) 3657800; fax (1) 3657852; e-mail pommin4@mhbdr.tel.hr.

Ministry of Culture: 10000 Zagreb, trg Burze 6; tel. (1) 4569000; fax (1) 410487; internet www.mini-kulture.hr.

Ministry of Defence: 10000 Zagreb, trg kralja Petra Krešimira IV 1; tel. (1) 4567111; e-mail infor@morh.hr; internet www.morh.hr.

Ministry of the Economy: 10000 Zagreb, trg sv. Marka 2; tel. (1) 4569207; fax (1) 4550606; e-mail info@mingo.hr; internet www.mingo.hr.

Ministry of Education and Sport: 10000 Zagreb, trg Hevatskih Velikana 6; tel. (1) 4569009; fax (1) 4569087; e-mail office@mips.hr; internet www.mips.hr.

Ministry of Environmental Protection and Physical Planning: 10000 Zagreb, Republike Austrije 20; tel. (1) 3782444; fax (1) 3772822; e-mail kabinet.ministra@zg.tel.hr; internet www.mzopu.hr.

Ministry of European Integration: 10000 Zagreb, ul. grada Vukovara 62; tel. (1) 4569335; fax (1) 6303182; e-mail info@mei.hr; internet www.mei.hr.

Ministry of Finance: 10000 Zagreb, ul. Katančićeva 5; tel. (1) 4591333; fax (1) 4922583; e-mail kabinet@mfin.hr; internet www.mfin.hr.

Ministry of Foreign Affairs: 10000 Zagreb, trg Nikole Šubića Zrinskog 7–8; tel. (1) 4569964; fax (1) 4569977; e-mail mvp@mvp.hr; internet www.mvp.hr.

Ministry of Health: 10000 Zagreb, ul. Baruna Tranka 6; tel. (1) 431068; fax (1) 431067; internet www.tel.hr/mzrh.

Ministry of the Interior: 10000 Zagreb, Savska cesta 39; tel. (1) 6122129; fax (1) 6122299; e-mail webinfo@vlada.hr; internet www.vlada.hr.

Ministry of Justice, Administration and Local Self-Government: 10000 Zagreb, Savska cesta 41; tel. (1) 535935; fax (1) 536321.

Ministry of Labour and Social Welfare: 10000 Zagreb, Prisavlje 14; tel. (1) 6169111; fax (1) 6169206; e-mail info@mrss.hr; internet www.mrss.hr.

Ministry of Maritime Affairs, Transport and Telecommunications: 10000 Zagreb, Prisavlje 14; tel. (1) 6169100; fax (1) 6196519; internet www.pomorstvo.hr.

Ministry of Public Works, Reconstruction and Construction: Zagreb, Savska cesta 41/12; tel. (1) 6176011; fax (1) 6176161; e-mail mpu@mpu.hr.

Ministry of Tourism: 10000 Zagreb, Ave. Vukovar 78; tel. (1) 6106300; fax (1) 6109300; e-mail ministarstvo.turizma@mint.hr; internet www.mint.hr.

Ministry of Trades, Small and Medium Businesses: 10000 Zagreb, Ksaver 200; tel. (1) 4698300; fax (1) 4698310; e-mail momsp@momsp.hr; internet www.momsp.hr.

President and Legislature

PRESIDENT

Presidential Election, First Ballot, 24 January 2000

	Votes	% of votes
Stipe Mesić*	1,100,671	41.11
Dražen Budiša†	741,837	27.71
Dr Mate Granić (Croatian Democratic Union)	601,588	22.47
Slaven Letica (Independent)	110,782	4.14
Ante Djapić (Croatian Party of Rights)	49,288	1.84
Ante Ledić (Independent)	22,875	0.85
Tomislav Mercep (Croatian People's Party)	22,672	0.85
Ante Prkacin (New Croatia)	7,401	0.28
Dr Zvonimir Šeparović (Independent)	7,235	0.27
Total	**2,664,349‡**	**100.00**

* Candidate of the Croatian Peasants' Party, the Liberal Party, the Croatian People's Party and the Istrian Democratic Assembly.
† Candidate of the Social Democratic Party and the Croatian Social-Liberal Party.
‡ Excluding 13,212 invalid votes (0.49% of the total votes).

Presidential Election, Second Ballot, 7 February 2000*

	% of votes
Stipe Mesić†	56.21
Dražen Budiša‡	43.79
Total	**100.00**

* Preliminary results.
† Candidate of the Croatian Peasants' Party, the Liberal Party, the Croatian People's Party and the Istrian Democratic Assembly.
‡ Candidate of the Social Democratic Party and the Croatian Social-Liberal Party.

SABOR
(Assembly)

President: ZLATKO TOMČIĆ, 10000 Zagreb, trg sv. Marka 617; tel. (1) 4569222; fax (1) 276483.

Vice-Presidents: MATO ARLOVIĆ, ZDRAVKO TOMAC, BALTAZAR JALSOVEC, VLATKO PAVLETIĆ, IVIĆ PASALIĆ.

Zastupnički dom
(Chamber of Representatives)

Election, 3 January 2000

	% of votes	Seats
Social Democratic Party		44
Croatian Social-Liberal Party . . .	47.0	24
Primorian-Goranian Union. . . .		2
Slavonian-Baranian Croatian Party .		1
Croatian Democratic Union . . .	30.5	45
Croatian Peasants' Party		16
Istrian Democratic Assembly . . .		4
Liberal Party	15.9	2
Croatian People's Party.		2
Croatian Social Democrats' Action .		1
Croatian Party of Rights	3.3	5
Others	3.3	1
Total	**100.0**	**151**

Political Organizations

Alternative for Rijeka (Alternativa za Rijeka): Rijeka, Trpimirova 2/10; tel. (51) 610726; e-mail azra_sna@hotmail.com; internet www.azra.2ya.com; Pres. GORANA TUŠKAN.

Christian People's Party (CPP) (Kršćanska Narodna Stranka—KNS): 10000 Zagreb, Degenova 7; tel. (1) 427258; fax (1) 273595; Pres. ZDRAVKO MRŠIĆ.

Croatian Bloc-Movement for a Modern Croatia: f. 2002; Chair. IVIC PASALIĆ.

Croatian Christian Democratic Union (CCDU) (Hrvatska Kršćanska Demokratska Unija—HKDU): 10000 Zagreb; tel. (1) 327233; fax (1) 325190; e-mail bihdem@posluh.hr; internet www.posluh.hr; Pres. MIJO IVANČIĆ.

Croatian Democratic Centre (Demokratski Centar): 10000 Zagreb; internet www.demokratski-centar.hr; f. March 2000 by a breakaway faction of the Croatian Democratic Union; pro-European, moderate; Pres. MATE GRANIĆ.

Croatian Democratic Party (CDP) (Hrvatska Demokratska Stranka—HDS): 10000 Zagreb; tel. (1) 431837; Pres. MARKO VESELICA.

Croatian Democratic Republican Party: f. Oct. 2000; by merger of Croatian Spring, National Democratic Party and Croatian Peasants' National Party; Leader JOSKO KOVAC.

Croatian Democratic Union (CDU) (Hrvatska Demokratska Zajednica—HDZ): 10000 Zagreb, trg hrvatskih velikana 4; tel. (1) 4553000; fax (1) 4552600; e-mail hdz@hdz.hr; internet www.hdz.hr; f. 1989; Christian Democrat; Chair. IVO SANADER; Sec.-Gen. JOSO SKARA.

Croatian Independent Democrats (CID) (Hrvatski Nezavisni Demokrati—HND): 10000 Zagreb; f. 1994 by a faction from the CDU; Chair. JOSIP MANOLIĆ.

Croatian Liberation Movement (Hrvatski Oslobodilački Pokret): 10000 Zagreb, Šenoina 27; fax (1) 4923035; e-mail ndh@hop.hr; internet www.hop.hr.

Croatian Muslim Democratic Party (CMDP) (Hrvatska Muslimanska Demokratska Stranka—HMDS): 10000 Zagreb; tel. (1) 421562.

Croatian Party of Rights (CPR) (Hrvatska Stranka Prava—HSP): 10000 Zagreb, ul. Šenoina 13; tel. and fax (1) 4839938; e-mail hsp1861@hsp1861.hr; internet www.hsp.hr; f. 1861; re-established 1990; right-wing, nationalist; armed br. was the Croatian Defence Asscn or Hrvatske Obrambene Snage (HOS); Pres. ANTE DJAPIĆ.

Croatian Party of Slavonia and Baranja (CPSB) (Slavonsko-Baranjska Hrvatska Stranka—SBHS): Osijek.

Croatian Peasants' Party (Hrvatska Seljačka Stranka—HSS): 10000 Zagreb, ul. Kralja Zvonimira 17; tel. and fax (1) 4553624; e-mail hss-sredisnjica@hss.hr; internet www.hss.hr; Pres. ZLATKO TOMČIĆ.

Croatian Peasants' Party Trogir (Hrvatska Seljačka Stranka—gradska organizacija Trogir): Trogir, ul. Blaža Jurjeva Trogiranina 4; tel. (21) 882449; fax (21) 884868; e-mail hss-trogir@inet.hr; internet www.hss-trogir.com; Pres. MILIVOJ ŠPIKA.

Croatian Pensioners' Party: 10000 Zagreb; contested local elections in 2000 in a coalition with the SDP.

Croatian People's Party (CPP) (Hrvatska Narodna Stranka—HNS): 10000 Zagreb, Tomićeva 2; tel. (1) 4877000; fax (1) 4877009; e-mail webmaster@hns.hr; internet www.hns.hr; Pres. VESNA PUSIĆ.

Croatian Republican Community (CRC) (Hrvatska Republikanska Zajednica—HRZ): 10000 Zagreb, Nalješkovićeva 11; tel. and fax (1) 4666740; e-mail hrz@zg.tel.hr; internet www.hrz.hr; Pres. BORKO JURIN.

Croatian Republicans' Party (Hrvatski Republikanci): 10000 Zagreb, trg bana Josipa Jelačića 1/III; tel. (1) 4812353; fax (1) 4811685; e-mail republikanci@zg.tel.hr; internet www.republikanci.hr; Pres. TOMISLAV BOGDANIĆ.

Croatian Social Democrats' Action (Akcija socijaldemokrata Hrvatske—ASH): Zagreb.

Croatian Social-Liberal Party (CSLP) (Hrvatska Socïjalno-Liberalna Stranka—HSLS): 10000 Zagreb, trg N. Š. Zrinskog 17; tel. (1) 4810401; fax (1) 4810404; e-mail hsls@hsls.hr; internet www.hsls.hr; f. 1989; Pres. DRAŽEN BUDIŠA.

Dalmatian Action (DA) (Dalmatinska Akcija): 21000 Split, ul. bana Jelačića 4/I; tel. (21) 344322; f. 1990; Pres. Dr MIRA LJUBIĆ-LORGER.

Independent Democratic Serb Party (Samostalne Demokratska Srpska Stranka—SDSS): 32000 Vukovar, Radnički dom 1–3; tel. and fax (32) 665116; f. 1997 by Serbs in Eastern Slavonia; Pres. Dr VOJISLAV STANIMIROVIĆ.

Istrian Democratic Assembly (IDA) (Istarski Demokratski Sabor—IDS): Pula, Splitska 3; tel. (52) 223316; fax (52) 213702; e-mail ids-ddi@pu.tel.hr; internet www.ids-ddi.com; Pres. IVAN JAKOVČIĆ.

Istrian People's Party (IPP) (Istarska Pučka Stranka—IPS): Pula, trg revolucije 3; tel. (52) 23863; fax (52) 23832; Pres. JOSIP FABRIS.

Liberal Party (Liberalna Stranka): 10000 Zagreb; e-mail liberali@bbm.hr; internet www.liberali.hr; f. 1998 by a breakaway faction of the Croatian Social-Liberal Party; Pres. IVO BANAC.

New Croatia: Zagreb; Pres. ANTE PRKACIN.

Party of Serbs: 10000 Zagreb; f. 1993 by mems of Serb cultural asscn Prosveta (Enlightenment) and Serb Democratic Forum; promotes liberal, democratic values; Leader MILORAD PUPOVAĆ.

Primorian-Goranian Union (Primorski-Goranski Savez): Zagreb; regionalist.

Programme for Croatian Identity and Prosperity: f. Nov. 2000 by former supporters of Pres. Dr Franjo Tudjman; Leader MIROSLAV TUDJMAN.

Rijeka Democratic Alliance (RDA) (Riječki Demokratski Savez—RDS): 51000 Rijeka, Žrtava fašizma 29; tel. (51) 423713; Pres. NIKOLA IVANIŠ; Sec. FRANJO BUTORAC.

Serb People's Party (SPP) (Srpska Narodna Stranka—SNS): 10000 Zagreb, trg Mažuranića 3; tel. and fax (1) 451090; promotes cultural and individual rights for ethnic Serbs in Croatia; 4,500–5,000 mems; Pres. MILAN DUKIĆ.

Slavonian-Baranian Croatian Party (Slavonsko-baranjska hrvatska stranka): Zagreb; internet www.osijek-online.com.

Social Democratic Party (SDP) (Socijaldemokratska Partija Hrvatske—SPH): 10000 Zagreb, trg Iblerov 9; tel. (1) 4552658; fax (1) 4552842; e-mail sdp@sdp.tel.hr; internet www.sdp.hr; formerly the ruling League of Communists of Croatia (Party of Democratic Reform), renamed as above in 1993; 20,000 mems; Chair. IVICA RAČAN.

Social Democratic Union of Croatia (SDUC) (Socijalno Demokratska Unija Hrvatske—SDUH): 10000 Zagreb, Tratinska 27; tel. and fax (1) 394055; f. 1992; Pres. VLADIMIR BEBIĆ.

Social Democrats of Croatia: 10000 Zagreb, Gunduliaeva 21A/III; tel. (1) 4854261; fax (1) 485428; e-mail ash@hinet.hr; internet www.hinet.hr/ash.

Socialist Party of Croatia (SPC) (Socijalistička Stranka Hrvatske—SSH): 10000 Zagreb, Prisavlje 14; tel. (1) 517835; fax (1) 510235; Pres. ŽELJKO MAŽAR.

Socialist Workers' Party of Croatia (SRPH) (Socijalističke Radničke Partije Hrvatske): 10000 Zagreb; tel. (1) 483958; e-mail srp@srp.hr; internet www.srp.hr; f. 1997; Leader STIPE SUVAR.

Zagreb Party (ZP) (Zagreb Stranka—ZS): Zagreb; f. April 2001; aimed to focus on local government issues; Leader MATE MESTROVIĆ.

Diplomatic Representation

EMBASSIES IN CROATIA

Albania: 10000 Zagreb, Jurišićeva 2A; tel. (1) 4810679; fax (1) 4810682; e-mail veleposlanstvo-albanije@zg.tel.hr; Ambassador ARBEN CICI.

Australia: 10000 Zagreb, Nova Ves 11; tel. (1) 4891200; fax (1) 4836606; internet www.auembassy.hr; Ambassador Frances Neil.

Austria: 10000 Zagreb, Jabukovač 39; tel. (1) 4834457; fax (1) 4834461; e-mail austrijsko-veleposlanstvo@alf.tel.hr; internet www.atembassy.hr; Ambassador Hans Knitel.

Belgium: 10000 Zagreb, Pantovčak 125; tel. (1) 4578901; fax (1) 4578902; Ambassador Luc Liebaut.

Bosnia and Herzegovina: 10001 Zagreb, Torbarova 9; tel. (1) 4683761; fax (1) 4683764; e-mail ambasada-bh-zg@zg.tel.hr; Ambassador Zlatko Diždarević.

Bulgaria: 10000 Zagreb, Novi Goljak 25; tel. (1) 4823336; fax (1) 4823338; e-mail veleposlanstvo-bugarske1@zg.hinet.hr; Ambassador Victor Valkov.

Canada: 10000 Zagreb, Prilaz Gjure Deželića; tel. (1) 4881200; fax (1) 4881230; e-mail zagreb@dfait-maeci.gc.ca; Ambassador Dennis A. Snider.

Chile: 10000 Zagreb, Smičiklasova 23/II; tel. (1) 4611958; internet www.clembassy.hr; Ambassador Jorge Dopouy Grez.

China, People's Republic: 10000 Zagreb, Mlinovi 132; tel. (1) 4637011; fax (1) 4637012; e-mail chnemb@zg.tel.hr; Ambassador Zhi Zhaolin.

Czech Republic: 10000 Zagreb, Savska cesta 41; tel. (1) 6177239; fax (1) 6176630; Ambassador Petr Burianek.

Egypt: 10000 Zagreb, Tuškanac 58A; tel. (1) 4834272; fax (1) 4834247; Ambassador Helmy Bedeier.

Finland: 10000 Zagreb, Berislavićeva 2/II; tel. (1) 4811662; fax (1) 4819946; internet www.finembassy.hr; Ambassador Ilpo Manninen.

France: 10000 Zagreb, Schlosserove stube 5; tel. (1) 4818110; fax (1) 4557765; e-mail presse@ambafrance.hr; internet www.ambafrance.hr; Ambassador Francis Bellanger.

Germany: 10000 Zagreb, ul. grada Vukovara 64; tel. (1) 6158100; fax (1) 6158103; internet www.deutschebotschaft-zagreb.hr; Ambassador Gerhardt Weiss.

Greece: 10000 Zagreb, Opatička 12; tel. (1) 4810444; fax (1) 4810419; internet www.grembassy.hr; Ambassador Christian Georges-Stavros Vassilopoulos.

Guinea-Bissau: 10000 Zagreb, Jurjevska 51; tel. (1) 4863500; fax (1) 4663502; Chargé d'affaires a.i. Desiderius Ostrogonac da Costa.

Holy See: 10000 Zagreb, Ksaverska cesta bb 10A; tel. (1) 4673996; fax (1) 4673997; e-mail apostolska.nuncijatura.rh@inet.hr; Apostolic Delegate Most Rev. Giulio Einaudi (Titular Archbishop of Villamagna in Tripolitania).

Hungary: 10000 Zagreb, Pantovcak 255–257A; tel. (1) 4890900; fax (1) 4579301; e-mail hungemb-tajnica@hungemb.tel.hr; internet www.hungemb.hr; Ambassador György Csóti.

India: 10000 Zagreb, ul. Boškovićeva 7A; tel. (1) 4873240; fax (1) 4817907; e-mail embassy.india@zg.tel.hr; Ambassador Kailasha Lal Agrawal.

Iran: 10000 Zagreb, Pantovčak 125c; tel. (1) 4578981; fax (1) 4578987; Ambassador Jafar Shamsian.

Italy: 10000 Zagreb, Medulićeva 22; tel. (1) 4846386; fax (1) 4846384; e-mail veleposlanstvo_italije@zg.tel.hr; Ambassador Fabio Pigliapoco.

Japan: 10000 Zagreb, Ksaver 211; tel. (1) 4677755; fax (1) 4677766; Ambassador Kaname Ikeda.

Macedonia, former Yugoslav republic: 10000 Zagreb, Petrinjska 29/I; tel. (1) 4922903; fax (1) 4922902; e-mail amb.makedonije.zgb@zg.tel.hr; Ambassador Servet Avziu.

Malaysia: 10000 Zagreb, Slavujevac 4A; tel. (1) 4834346; fax (1) 4834348; Ambassador Mohamad bin Sani.

Netherlands: 10000 Zagreb, Medveščak 56; tel. (1) 4684880; fax (1) 4684582; e-mail nlgovzag@zg.tel.hr; internet www.netherlandsembassy; Ambassador Lionel S. Veer.

Norway: 10000 Zagreb, Petrinjska 9; tel. (1) 4922829; fax (1) 4922828; Ambassador Knut Toraasen.

Poland: 10000 Zagreb, Krležin Gvozd 3; tel. (1) 4899444; fax (1) 4834576; Ambassador Jerzy Chmielewski.

Portugal: 10000 Zagreb, trg ban J. Jelačića 5/II; tel. (1) 4882210; fax (1) 4920663; Ambassador Ana Barata.

Romania: 10000 Zagreb, Srebrnjak 150A; tel. (1) 2430137; Ambassador Mihail Dinucu.

Russia: 10000 Zagreb, Bosanska 44; tel. (1) 3755038; fax (1) 3755040; e-mail veleposlanstvo-ruske-federacije@zg.tel.hr; Ambassador Eduard Leonidovich Kuzmin.

Serbia and Montenegro: 10000 Zagreb, Mesićeva 19; tel. (1) 4680552; fax (1) 4680770; e-mail ambasada-sav-rep-jugoslavije@zg.tel.hr; Ambassador Milan Simurdić.

Slovakia: 10000 Zagreb, Prilaz Djure Deželića 10; tel. (1) 4848941; fax (1) 4848942; e-mail velep-rep-slovacke-u-rh@zg.tel.hr; Ambassador Ján Petrík.

Slovenia: 10000 Zagreb, Savska cesta 41/II; tel. (1) 6311000; fax (1) 6177236; Ambassador Peter Andrej Bekeš.

Spain: 10000 Zagreb, Medulićeva 5; tel. (1) 4848603; fax (1) 4848605; Ambassador Sebastian de Erice Gomez-Acebo.

Sweden: 10000 Zagreb, Frankopanska 22; tel. (1) 4849322; fax (1) 4849244; e-mail swedish.embassy@zg.tel.hr; Ambassador Sture Theolin.

Switzerland: 10000 Zagreb, Bogovićeva 3; tel. (1) 4810891; fax (1) 4810890; e-mail swiemzag@zg.tel.hr; Ambassador Paul Widmer.

Turkey: 10000 Zagreb, Masarykova 3/II; tel. (1) 4855200; fax (1) 4855606; e-mail turembzag@zg.tel.hr; Ambassador Ufuk Tevfik Okyayuz.

Ukraine: 10000 Zagreb, Voćarska 52; tel. (1) 4616296; fax (1) 4633726; internet www.ukrembassy.hinet.hr; Ambassador Viktor A. Kyryk.

United Kingdom: 10000 Zagreb, Vlaska 121; tel. (1) 4555310; fax (1) 4551685; e-mail british-embassy@zg.tel.hr; Ambassador Nicholas Jarrold.

USA: 10000 Zagreb, Andrije Hebranga 2; tel. (1) 4555500; fax (1) 4558585; internet www.usembassy.hr; Ambassador Lawrence Rossin.

Judicial System

The judicial system of Croatia is administered by the Ministry of Justice. The Constitutional Court consists of 11 judges, elected by the Assembly for a period of eight years. The Supreme Court is the highest judicial body in the country, comprising 26 judges, also elected for a period of eight years.

Public Prosecutor: (vacant).

Ombudsman: 10000 Zagreb, Opatička 4; tel. (1) 4814893.

Constitutional Court of Croatia: 10000 Zagreb, Marka trg 4; tel. (1) 4851276; fax (1) 4550908; internet www.usud.hr; Pres. Smiljo Sokol.

Supreme Court: 10000 Zagreb, trg Nikole Zrinskog 3; tel. (1) 4810036; fax (1) 4810035; e-mail jsrh@jsrh.hr; Pres. Ivica Crnić.

Office of the Public Prosecutor: 10000 Zagreb, ul. Vinogradska 25; tel. (1) 3712700; fax (1) 3769302; e-mail dorh@zg.hinet.hr.

Religion

Most of the population are Christian, the largest denomination being the Roman Catholic Church, of which most ethnic Croats are adherents. The Archbishop of Zagreb is the most senior Roman Catholic prelate in Croatia. The Croatian Old Catholic Church does not acknowledge the authority of Rome or the papal reforms of the 19th century. There is a significant Serbian Orthodox minority. According to the 1991 census, 76.5% of the population of Croatia were Roman Catholics, 11.1% were Serbian Orthodox, 1.2% Muslims and there were small communities of Protestants and Jews.

CHRISTIANITY

The Roman Catholic Church

For ecclesiastical purposes, Croatia comprises four archdioceses (including one, Zadar, directly responsible to the Holy See) and 11 dioceses (including one for Catholics of the Byzantine rite). At 31 December 2000 there were an estimated 3.8m. adherents.

Latin Rite

Bishops' Conference

10000 Zagreb, Kaptol 22; tel. (1) 4811893; fax (1) 4811894; e-mail tanjnistvo@hbk.hr.

f. 1993; Pres. Mgr Josip Bozanić (Archbishop of Zagreb).

Archbishop of Rijeka: Dr Ivan Devčić, Nadbiskupski Ordinarijat, 51000 Rijeka, Slaviše Vajnera Čiče 2; tel. (51) 337999; fax (51) 215287; e-mail rijecka-nadbiskupija@ri.hinet.hr.

Archbishop of Split-Makarska: Marin Barišić, 21001 Split, pp 328, ul. Zrinsko-Frankopanska 14; tel. (21) 319523; fax (21) 319522; e-mail marin.barisic@hbk.hr.

Archbishop of Zadar: Ivan Prendja, Nadbiskupski Ordinarijat, 23000 Zadar, trg Zeleni 1; tel. (23) 315712; fax (23) 316299; e-mail nadbiskupija.zadarska@zd.te.hr.

Archbishop of Zagreb: Josip Bozanić, 10001 Zagreb, pp 553, Kaptol 31; tel. (1) 4894802; fax (1) 4816094; e-mail uzgnadb@zg .hinet.hr.

Byzantine Rite

Bishop of Križevci: Slavomir Miklovš, Ordinarijat Križevačke Eparhije, 10000 Zagreb, Kaptol 20; tel. (1) 270767; 48,975 adherents (1993).

Old Catholic Church

Croatian Catholic Church: Hrvatska Katolička Crkva Ordinariat, 10000 Zagreb, ul. Kneza Branimira 11; tel. (1) 4841361; f. 894; re-established 1923; Archbishop Mihovil Dubravčić.

Serbian Orthodox Church

Metropolitan of Zagreb and Ljubljana: Bishop Jovan, Srpska Biskupija, 10000 Zagreb.

The Press

PRINCIPAL DAILIES

Osijek

Glas Slavonije: 31000 Osijek, Hrvatske Republike 20; tel. (31) 223200; fax (31) 223203; e-mail glas@glas-slavonije.tel.hr; internet www.glas-slavonije.hr; morning; independent; Editor Sanja Marketić; circ. 25,000.

Pula

Glas Istre: 52100 Pula, Riva 10; tel. (52) 212969; fax (52) 211434; morning; Dir Željko Žmak; circ. 20,000.

Rijeka

Novi List: 51000 Rijeka, POB 130, Zvonimirova 20a; tel. (51) 32122; fax (51) 213654; morning; Editor Veljko Vicević; circ. 60,000.

La Voce del Popolo: 51000 Rijeka, Zvonimirova 20a; tel. (51) 211154; fax (51) 213528; e-mail lavoce@edit.hr; f. 1944; morning; Italian; Editor Rodolfo Segnan; circ. 4,000.

Split

Nedjeljna Dalmacija: 21000 Split, Gundulićeva 23; tel. (21) 362821; fax (21) 362526; f. 1972; weekly; politics and culture; Editor Dražen Gudić; circ. 45,000.

Slobodna Dalmacija: 21000 Split, ul. Hrvatske mornarice 4; tel. (21) 513888; fax (21) 551220; internet www.slobodnadalmacija.com; morning; Editor Josip Jović; circ. 102,000.

Zagreb

Nedjeljna Dalmacija: 10000 Zagreb, Ilica 24/II; tel. (1) 433716; fax (1) 433916; f. 1972; weekly; politics and culture; Editor-in-Chief Dubravko Grakalić; circ. 45,000.

Novi Vjesnik: 10000 Zagreb, Slavonska Ave. 4; tel. (1) 333333; fax (1) 341650; f. 1940; morning; Editor Radovan Stipetić; circ. 45,000.

Sportske novosti: 10000 Zagreb, Slavonska Ave. 4; tel. (1) 341920; fax (1) 341950; morning; Editor Darko Tironi; circ. 55,000.

Večernji list: 10000 Zagreb, Slavonska Ave. 4; tel. (1) 6500600; fax (1) 6500679; e-mail vecernji@vecernji.net.tel.hr; internet www .vecernji-list.hr; evening; Editor Ružica Cigler; circ. 200,000.

Vjesnik: 10000 Zagreb, Slavonska Ave. 4, POB 104; tel. (1) 342760; fax (1) 341602; internet www.vjesnik.com; morning; Editor Igor Mandić; circ. 50,000.

PERIODICALS

Arena: 10000 Zagreb, Slavonska Ave. 4; tel. (1) 6162795; fax (1) 6161572; e-mail arena@eph.hr; f. 1957; illustrated weekly; Editor Mladen Gerovac; circ. 135,000.

Feral Tribune: 21000 Split; e-mail webmaster@feral.hr; internet www.feral-tribune.com; weekly; satirical; Editor Viktor Ivancić.

Glasnik: 10000 Zagreb, trg hrvatskih velikana 4; tel. (1) 453000; fax (1) 453752; fortnightly; Editor Zdravko Gavran; circ. 9,000.

Globus: 10000 Zagreb, Slavonska Ave. 4; tel. (1) 6162057; fax (1) 6162058; e-mail globus@eph.hr; f. 1990; political weekly; Editor Mirko Galić; circ. 110,000.

Gloria: 10000 Zagreb, Slavonska Ave. 4; tel. (1) 6161288; fax (1) 6182042; e-mail gloria@eph.hr; weekly; Editor Dubravka Tomeković-Aralica; circ. 110,000.

Informator: 10000 Zagreb, Zelinska 3; tel. (1) 6111500; fax (1) 6111446; e-mail informator@informator.hr; internet www .informator.hr; f. 1952; economic and legal matters; Dir Dr Faruk Redžepagić.

Mila: 10000 Zagreb, Slavonska Ave. 4; tel. (1) 6161982; fax (1) 6162021; e-mail mila@eph.hr; weekly; Editor Zoja Padovan; circ. 110,000.

Nacionalni Oglasnik: 10000 Zagreb, Slavonska Ave. 4; tel. (1) 6162061; fax (1) 6161541; weekly; Editor Ivo Pukanić; circ. 55,000.

OK: Croatia: 10000 Zagreb, Slavonska Ave. 4; tel. (1) 6162127; fax (1) 6162125; e-mail ok@eph.hr; f. 1989; illustrated monthly; Editor Neven Kepeski; circ. 55,000.

Privredni vjesnik: 10000 Zagreb, Kačićeva 9a; tel. (1) 422182; fax (1) 422100; f. 1953; weekly; economic; Man. Ante Gavranović; Editor-in-Chief Franjo Žilić; circ. 10,000.

Republika: 10000 Zagreb, trg bana Josipa Jelačića; tel. (1) 274211; fax (1) 434790; f. 1945; monthly; published by Društvo hrvatskih književnika; literary review; Editor-in-Chief Velimir Visković.

Studio: 10000 Zagreb, Slavonska Ave. 4; tel. (1) 6162085; fax (1) 6162031; e-mail studio@eph.hr; f. 1964; illustrated weekly; Editor Robert Naprta; circ. 45,000.

Vikend: 10000 Zagreb, Slavonska Ave. 4; tel. and fax (1) 6162064; 2 a week; Editor Josip Mušnjak; circ. 50,000.

NEWS AGENCIES

HINA News Agency: 10000 Zagreb, trg Marulidev 16; tel. (1) 4808700; fax (1) 4808820; e-mail newsline@hina.hr; internet www .hina.hr; f. 1990; Man. Mirko Bolfek.

IKA (Catholic Information Agency): 10000 Zagreb, Kaptol 4; tel. (1) 4814951; fax (1) 4814957; e-mail ika-zg@zg.tel.hr; internet www.ika .hr; Man. Editor Anton Šuljić.

Publishers

AGM Publisher: 10000 Zagreb, Mihanovićeva 28; tel. (1) 4856307; fax (1) 4856316; Croatian and foreign literature, arts, economics, science; Gen. Dir Bože Čović.

Algoritam: 10000 Zagreb, Gajeva 12; tel. (1) 4803333; fax (1) 271541; e-mail mm@algoritam.hr; international bestsellers; Pres. Neven Antičević.

August Cesarec: 10000 Zagreb, Prilaz Gjure Deželića 57; tel. (1) 171071; fax (1) 573695; Croatian and foreign literature.

Books Trade and Services (BTS) Knjiga Trgovina: 10000 Zagreb, Donji prečac 19; tel. (1) 2421754; fax (1) 2421831; e-mail info@btsltd.com; internet www.btsltd.com; imports and exports publications; Gen. Man. Branko Vuković.

Ceres: 10000 Zagreb, Tomašićeva 13; tel. (1) 4558501; fax (1) 4550387; e-mail ceres@zg.tel.hr; internet www.ceres.hr; poetry, fiction, and philosophical and scientific writings; Gen. Dir Dragutin Dumančić.

Erasmus Publishing: 10000 Zagreb, Rakušina 4; tel. and fax (1) 433114; Croatian literature; Gen. Dir Srećko Lipovčan.

Europa Press: 10000 Zagreb, Slavonska Ave. 4; tel. (1) 6190011; fax (1) 6190033; Dir Marjan Jurleka.

Hena Com: 10000 Zagreb, Horvaćanska 65; tel. and fax (1) 3750206; e-mail hena-com@hena-com.hr; internet www.hena-com.hr; childrens' books; Gen. Man. Uzeir Husković.

Hrvatska Akademija Znanosti i Umjetnosti: 10000 Zagreb, trg Zrinski 11; tel. (1) 4819983; fax (1) 4819979; e-mail kabpred@ mahazu.hazu.hr; f. 1861; publishing dept of the Croatian Academy of Sciences and Arts; Pres. Dr Ivo Padovan.

Izvori: 10000 Zagreb, Trnjanska 64; tel. and fax (1) 6112576; e-mail izvori@iname.com; internet www.bakal.hr/izvori; scientific journalism, literature, comic books.

Kršćanska Sadašnjost: 10001 Zagreb, trg Marulićev 14, POB 434; tel. (1) 4828219; fax (1) 4828227; e-mail ks@zg.tel.hr; internet www .ks.hr; theological publications.

Leksikografski zavod 'Miroslav Krleža' (Miroslav Krleža Lexicographic Institute): 10000 Zagreb, Frankopanska 26; tel. (1) 4800333; fax (1) 4800399; f. 1951; encyclopedias, bibliographies and dictionaries; Pres. Dalibor Brozović.

Masmedia: 10000 Zagreb, ul. baruna Trenka 13; tel. (1) 4577400; fax (1) 4577769; e-mail masmedia@zg.tel.hr; business and professional literature; Gen. Dir Stjepan Andrašić.

Matica Hrvatska (Matrix Croatica): 10000 Zagreb, trg Strossmayerov 2; tel. (1) 4819310; fax (1) 4819319; arts and science; Pres. Prof. JOSIP BRATULIĆ.

Mladost: 10000 Zagreb, Ilica 30; tel. (1) 453222; fax (1) 434878; f. 1947; fiction, science, art, children's books; Gen. Dir BRANKO VUKOVIĆ.

Mosta: 10000 Zagreb, Majevička 12A; tel. (1) 325196; fax (1) 327898; popular fiction; Gen. Dir NLADIMIR VUĆUR.

Mozaik Knjiga: 10000 Zagreb, Tomićeva 5A; tel. (1) 425011; fax (1) 431291; educational books; Gen. Dir NIVES TOMAŠE, VIĆ.

Nakladni zavod Matice hrvatske: 10000 Zagreb, ul. Matice hrvatske 2; tel. (1) 4812422; fax (1) 4819317; e-mail nzm@zg.tel.hr; f. 1960; fiction, popular science, politics, economics, sociology, history; Dir NIKO VIDOVIĆ.

Naprijed: 10000 Zagreb, POB 1029, trg bana Jelacica 17; tel. (1) 432026; fax (1) 426897; e-mail naklada-napried@zg.tel.hr; f. 1946; philosophy, psychology, religion, sociology, medicine, dictionaries, children's books, art, politics, economics, tourist guides; Dir ZDENKO LJEVAK.

Naša Djeca: 10000 Zagreb, Gundulićeva 40; tel. (1) 4856046; fax (1) 4856613; e-mail nasa-djeca@zg.tel.hr; picture books, postcards, etc. Dir Prof. DRAGO KOZINA.

Nip Školske Novine: 10000 Zagreb, Hebranga 40; tel. (1) 4855709; fax (1) 4855712; education, religion, poetry, textbooks; Gen. Man. IVAN RODIĆ.

Sims: 10000 Zagreb, Ive Tijardovića 4; tel. (1) 3880500; fax (1) 3880731; e-mail info@sims-hr.com; internet www.simshr.com; exports Croatian and foreign language books; Gen. Man. IVAN MATLJEVIĆ.

Školska Knjiga: 10001 Zagreb, POB 1039, Masarykova 28; tel. (1) 420784; fax (1) 430260; e-mail skolska@skolskaknjiga.hr; education, textbooks, art; Dir Dr DRAGOMIR MADERIĆ.

Tehnička Knjiga: 10000 Zagreb, Jurišićeva 10; tel. (1) 278172; fax (1) 423611; f. 1947; technical literature, popular science, reference books; Gen. Man. ZVONIMIR VISTRIČKA.

Verbum: 21000 Split, Kraj zlatnih vrata 1; tel. and fax (21) 356770; e-mail verbum@st.tel.hr; religion, philosophy and humanism; Gen. Man. MIRO RADALJ.

Znanje: 10000 Zagreb, Zvonimirova 17; tel. (1) 4556000; fax (1) 4553652; e-mail znanje@zg.tel.hr; f. 1946; popular science, agriculture, fiction, poetry, essays; Pres. ŽARKO ŠEPETAVIĆ; Dir BRANKO JAZBEC.

PUBLISHERS' ASSOCIATION

Croatian Publishers' and Authors' Business Union (Poslovna Zajednica Izdavača i Knjižara Hrvatske): 10000 Zagreb, Klaićeva 7; fax (1) 171624.

Broadcasting and Communications

TELECOMMUNICATIONS

Croatian Telecommunications (Hrvatski Telekomunikacije—HT): 10000 Zagreb, Jurišićeva 13; tel. (1) 435435; fax (1) 429000; internet www.ht.hr/index.shtml; f. 1987; 51% owned by Deutsche Telekom (Germany); Pres. IVICA MUDRINIĆ.

BROADCASTING

Radio

Croatian Radio: 10000 Zagreb, HRT House, Dezmanova 6; tel. (1) 4807199; fax (1) 4807190; e-mail medjunrodni_hr@hrt.hr; internet www.hrt.hr; f. 1926; 3 radio stations; 8 regional stations (Sljeme, Osijek, Pula, Rijeka, Split, Zadar, Dubrovnik and Knin); broadcasts in Serbo-Croat, English and Spanish; Dir IVANKA LUCEV.

Radio 101: Zagreb; independent radio station; Editor-in-Chief ZRINKA VRABEC-MOJZES.

Radio Baranja: Beli Manastir; independent radio station; Dir KAROLJ JANESI.

Vaš Otvoreni Radio: 10000 Zagreb, Radnička cesta 27; tel. (1) 6154805; fax (1) 6154802; broadcasts nation-wide.

Television

Croatian Television: 10000 Zagreb, HRT House, Prisavlje 3; tel. (1) 6342634; fax (1) 6343712; e-mail program@hrt.hr; internet www .hrt.hr; f. 1956; 3 channels; broadcasts in Serbo-Croat; Head of TV MIRKO GALIĆ; Editor-in-Chief JASNA ULAGA VALIĆ.

Finance

(A new currency, the kuna (equivalent to 1,000 Croatian dinars), was introduced on 30 May 1994.(d.d. = dioničko društvo (joint-stock company); cap. = capital; res = reserves; dep. = deposits; m. = million; amounts in kuna, unless otherwise indicated; HRD = Croatian dinars; brs = branches))

BANKING

Central Bank

National Bank of Croatia: 10000 Zagreb, trg hrvatskih velikana 3; tel. (1) 4564555; fax (1) 4550726; e-mail webmaster@hnb.hr; internet www.hnb.hr; in 1991 it assumed the responsibilities of a central bank empowered as the republic's bank of issue; cap. 2,500.0m., res 3,311.7m., dep. 28,321.5m. (Dec. 2001); Gov. ŽELJKO ROHATINSKI.

Selected Banks

Croatia Banka d.d.: 10000 Zagreb, Kvaternikov trg 9; tel. (1) 2391111; fax (1) 2332470; e-mail marketing@crbanka.tel.hr; internet www.croatiabanka.hr; f. 1989; cap. 204.6m., res 75.3m., dep. 994.8m. (Dec. 2001); Chair. NIKOLA ŠEREMET; 29 brs.

Croatian Bank for Reconstruction and Development (Hrvatska Banka za Obnovu i Razvoj—HBOR): 10000 Zagreb, Strossmayerov trg 9; tel. (1) 4591696; fax (1) 4591689; e-mail dstimac@hbor.hr; internet www.hbor.hr; f. 1995; cap. 2,972.0m., res 1.1m., dep. 282.2m. (Dec. 2001); Pres. ANTON KOVAČEV.

Dresdner Bank d.d.: 10000 Zagreb, Gajeva 1; tel. (1) 4866777; fax (1) 4866779; e-mail contact.croatia@dresdner-bank.com; internet www.dresdner-bank.hr; f. 1997; cap. 100.0m., res 5.0m., dep. 507.2m. (Dec. 2001); Pres. Dr HANS-JOACHIM GERSMANN.

Dubrovačka Banka d.d., Dubrovnik (Bank of Dubrovnik): 20000 Dubrovnik, put Republike 9; tel. (20) 356333; fax (20) 356778; e-mail dubank@dubank.hr; internet www.dubank.hr; f. 1955; controlled by Dalmatinska Banka d.d. from Feb. 2002; cap. 185.0m., res 73.2m., dep. 2,516.9m. (Dec. 2001); Pres. VLAHO SUTIĆ.

Erste and Steiermärkische Bank d.d.: 10000 Zagreb, Varšavska 3–5; tel. (1) 4561999; fax (1) 4561900; e-mail esb@esb.hr; internet www.esb.hr; f. Sept. 2000; by merger of Bjelovarska Banka d.d., Cakoveka Banka d.d. and Trgovačka Banka d.d.; cap. 271.9m., res 149.5m., dep. 2,936.0m. (Dec. 2001); Chair. REINHARD ORTNER.

Hrvatska Poštanska Banka d.d.: 10000 Zagreb, Jurišićeva 4; tel. (1) 4804400; fax (1) 4810773; internet www.hpb.hr; f. 1991; cap. 584.8m., res 157.9m., dep. 1,990.1m. (Dec. 2001); Chair. JOSIP SLADE.

Hypo Alpe-Adria-Bank d.d.: 10000 Zagreb, Koturaška 47; tel. (1) 6103666; fax (1) 6103555; e-mail hypo@hypo.hr; internet www.hypo .hr; f. 1996; cap. 280.4m., res 26.2m., dep. 4,158.9m. (Dec. 2001); Chair. MAG GUENTER STRIEDINGER.

Istarska Kreditna Banka Umag d.d.: 52470 Umag, Ernesta Miloša 1; tel. (52) 702300; fax (52) 741275; e-mail marketing@ikb.hr; internet www.ikb.hr; f. 1956; commercial and joint-stock bank; controlled by Dalmatinska Banka d.d.; cap. 64.9m., res 46.3m., dep. 961.5m. (Dec. 2001); Chair. MIRO DODIĆ; 16 brs.

Karlovačka Banka d.d: 47000 Karlovac, Ivana Gorana Kovačića 1; tel. (47) 611540; fax (47) 614206; e-mail karlovacka.banka@hinet.hr; internet www.kaba.hr; f. 1955; cap. 57.4m., res 11.1m., dep. 730.6m. (2001); Pres. SANDA CVITESIĆ.

Kreditna Banka Zagreb d.d.: 10000 Zagreb, ul. grada Vukovara 74; tel. (1) 6167333; fax (1) 6116466; e-mail kbz-uprava@kbz.hr; internet www.kbz.hr/kbz; f. 1994; cap. 132.0m., res 24.1m., dep. 452.0m. (Dec. 2001); Pres. RUDO MIKULIĆ.

Medimurska Banka d.d., Čakovec: 40000 Čakovec, Valenta Morandinija 37; tel. (40) 370676; fax (40) 370505; e-mail info@mb.hr; internet www.mb.hr; f. 1954; cap. 127.9m., res 20.3m., dep. 1,074.4m. (Dec. 2000); Pres. MLADENA GOMBAR.

Nova Kreditna Banka Maribor d.d.: 2505 Maribor, Vita Kraigherja 4; tel. (2) 2292290; fax (2) 2524371; e-mail info@nkbm.si; internet www.nkbm.si; f. 1955 as Komunalna Banka Maribor; cap. 5,600m., res 33,859m., dep. 365,924m. (Dec. 2001); Pres. CRTOMIR MESARIĆ.

Privredna Banka Zagreb d.d.: 10000 Zagreb, POB 1032, Račkoga 6; tel. (1) 4723344; fax (1) 4723131; e-mail pbz@pbz.hr; internet www .pbz.hr; f. 1966; commercial bank; cap. 1,666m., res 368m., dep. 16,254m. (Dec. 2000); Chief Exec. BOZO PRKA; 28 brs.

Raiffeisenbank Austria d.d.: 10000 Zagreb, POB 651, ul. Petrinjska 59; tel. (1) 4566466; fax (1) 4811624; e-mail rba@rba.tel.hr; internet www.rba.hr; cap. 240.0m., res 24.8m., dep. 6,386.5m. (Dec. 2001); Chair. ZDENKO ADROVIĆ.

Riadria Banka d.d.: 51000 Rijeka, Đure Šporera 3; tel. (51) 3567777; fax (51) 211095; e-mail riadra-banka@ri.tel.hr; internet www.riab.hr; f. 1992; cap. 165.8m., res 20.4m., dep. 1,390.1m. (Dec. 2001); Pres. and CEO VESNA BADURINA.

Riječka Banka d.d.: 51000 Rijeka, POB 300, trg Jadranski 3A; tel. (51) 208211; fax (51) 330525; e-mail drazen.kurpisl@rbri.tel.hr; internet www.rbri.hr; f. 1954 as Komunalna banka i štedionica, renamed 1967; acquired by Erste Bank (Austria) in April 2002; cap. 503.3m., res 102.3m., dep. 7,910.4m. (Dec. 2001); Pres. CHRISTIAN CORETH; 15 brs.

Slavonska Banka d.d., Osijek (Bank of Slavonia): 31000 Osijek, POB 108, Kapucinska 29; tel. (31) 231231; fax (31) 201039; e-mail slbo@slbo.hr; internet www.slbo.hr; f. 1989; cap. 196.5m., res 165.0m., dep. 1,183.6m. (Dec. 2000); Pres. IVAN MIHALJEVIĆ; 9 brs.

Splitska Banka d.d. Split: 21000 Split, Boškovića 16; tel. (21) 312560; fax (21) 312586; e-mail info@splitskabanka.hr; internet www.splitskabanka.hr; f. 1966; cap. 363.5m., res 134.0m., dep. 6,989.8m. (Dec. 2001); Pres. ANTON KNETT.

Varaždinska Banka d.d.: 42000 Varaždin, POB 95, trg Kapucinski 5; tel. (42) 400000; fax (42) 400742; internet www.banka.hr; f. 1869; adopted current name 1981; cap. 164.7m., res 288.5m., dep. 2,711.1m. (Dec. 2001); Pres. MATO LUKINIĆ; 17 brs.

Volksbank d.d.: 10000 Zagreb, Varšavska 9; tel. (1) 4801300; fax (1) 4801365; e-mail info@volksbank.tel.hr; internet www.volksbank.hr; f. 1997; cap. 70.2m., res 10.6m., dep. 694.0m. (Dec. 2001); Chair. HEINRICH ANGELIDES.

Zagrebačka Banka Zagreb d.d. (Bank of Zagreb): 10000 Zagreb, Paromlinska 2; tel. (1) 6104000; fax (1) 6110555; e-mail zaba@zaba.hr; internet www.zaba.hr; f. 1913; cap. 1,096m., res 724m., dep. 37,903m. (Dec. 2001); Chair. FRANJO LUKOVIĆ; 150 brs.

Bankers' Organization

Croatian Banking Association: 10000 Zagreb, Centar Kaptol, Nova Ves 17; tel. (1) 4860080; fax (1) 4860081; e-mail info@hub.hr; internet www.hub.hr; Man. Dir Dr ZORAN BOHACEK.

STOCK EXCHANGE

Zagreb Stock Exchange: 10000 Zagreb, Ksaver 208; tel. (1) 428455; fax (1) 420293; e-mail zeljko.kardum@zse.hr; internet www.zse.hr; f. 1990; Gen. Man. MARINKO PAPUGA.

INSURANCE

Croatia Osiguranje: 35000 Slavonski Brod, Matije Gupca 29; tel. and fax (35) 214131; e-mail info@festung.hr; internet www.festung.hr; f. 1884; state-owned; scheduled for privatization in 2002.

Merkur Osiguranje: 10000 Zagreb, ul. grada Vukovara 237; tel. (1) 6308333; fax (1) 6157130; internet www.merkur.hr.

Trade and Industry

GOVERNMENT AGENCY

Croatian Investment Promotion Agency: 10000 Zagreb, World Trade Center Bldg, Ave. Dubrovnik 15; tel. (1) 6555333; fax (1) 6554563; e-mail hapu@zg.tel.hr; internet www.tel.hr.

Croatian Privatization Fund: 10000 Zagreb, Ivana Lučića 6; tel. (1) 4569111; fax (1) 4596294; e-mail hfp@hfp.hr; internet www.hfp.hr; f. 1994; by merger of the Croatian Fund for Development and the Restructuring and Development Agency; Chair. HRVOJE VOJKOVIĆ.

CHAMBERS OF COMMERCE

Croatian Chamber of Economy (Hrvatska Gospodarska Komora): 10000 Zagreb, trg Rooseveltov 2; tel. (1) 4561555; fax (1) 4828380; e-mail hgk@alf.hr; internet www.hgk.hr; Pres. NADAN VIDOŠEVIĆ.

Zagreb Chamber of Commerce: 10000 Zagreb, Draškovićeva 45; tel. (1) 4606777; fax (1) 4606813; e-mail hgk-zagreb@hgk.hr; internet www.hgk.hr; f. 1852.

UTILITIES

Electricity

HEP—Hrvatska Elektroprivreda d.d.: 10000 Zagreb, Ave. Vukovar 37; tel. (1) 6322111; fax (1) 6170430; e-mail ivo.covic@hep.hr; internet www.hep.hr; f. 1990; production and distribution of electricity; scheduled for privatization in 2002; Dir IVO COVIĆ.

Gas

Gradska Plinara: 10000 Zagreb, Radnička 1; tel. (1) 6302333; fax (1) 6184653; f. 1862; municipal and regional distribution of natural gas; Dir IVAN VULAS.

INA—Naftaplin: 10020 Zagreb, Većeslava Holjevca 10; tel. (1) 6450000; fax (1) 6452100; internet www.ina.hr; subsidiary of Industrija Nafte d.d. exploration of petroleum, natural-gas and geothermal energy; scheduled for privatization in 2003; Chair. TOMISLAV DRAGICEVIĆ.

Water

Hrvatske Vode: 10000 Zagreb, Vukovara 220; tel. (1) 6307333; fax (1) 6151388; e-mail du.vode@zg.hinet.hr; internet www.voda.hr; f. 1995; state water management organization; Dir ŠTEPAN ŠTURLAN.

TRADE UNIONS

Confederation of Independent Trade Unions of Croatia: 10000 Zagreb; f. 1990; 40,000 mems; Pres. DAVOR JURIĆ.

Croatian Association of Trade Unions: Zagreb; f. 1990; 200,000 mems; Pres. BERISLAV BELEC.

Union of Autonomous Trade Unions of Croatia: 10000 Zagreb, trg kralja Petra Krešimira 2; tel. (1) 4655013; fax (1) 4655040; e-mail sssh@sssh.hr; internet www.sssh.hr; f. 1990; 26 branch unions with some 500,000 mems; Pres. DAVOR JURIĆ.

Transport

RAILWAYS

In 2001 there were an estimated 2,726 km of railway lines in Croatia, and 36% of the rail network was electrified in 1995. In mid-1996 railway links between Croatia and Serbia, via Eastern Slavonia, were reopened. In May 2000 the Government announced plans for the modernization of railroad linking Rijeka and Budapest, Hungary.

Croatian Railways Ltd (Hrvatske Željeznice p.o.): 10000 Zagreb, Mihanovićeva 12; tel. (1) 4577111; fax (1) 4577730; f. 1990 as Hrvatsko Željezničko poduzeće, renamed 1992; state-owned; public railway transport, construction, modernization and maintenance of railway vehicles; Pres. DAVOR ŠTERN; Gen. Dir DRAGUTIN ŠUBAT.

ROADS

The Road Fund is responsible for the planning, construction, maintenance and rehabilitation of all interurban roads in Croatia. A project to construct a 75-km motorway linking Dragonje, near the Slovenian border, with Pula in southern Istria was completed in the late 1990s. In May 1996 the motorway between Zagreb and Belgrade, Yugoslavia, was reopened. In 2001 there were an estimated 28,275 km of roads in Croatia, of which 429 km were motorways; there were 7,427 km of main roads and 10,499 km of secondary roads in 2000. In October 2001 the European Bank for Reconstruction and Development (EBRD) pledged some US $80m. to Croatia for the construction of a Rijecka–Zagreb highway; the road was due for completion in 2004. In May 2000 the Croatian and Hungarian Governments agreed to draft a joint agreement on the construction by 2003 of a highway connecting Rijeka with the Hungarian capital, Budapest. In June Croatia and Bosnia and Herzegovina signed a statement on the construction of the Ploče–Budapest transport corridor, to link Croatia with Hungary, via Bosnia and Herzegovina. The construction of this 'C5' corridor was to end the isolation of Croatia's southern areas and ensure the optimal use of Ploče's port capacity. A project to construct a highway connecting Zagreb and Split was under way in mid-2002.

Croatian Roads Authority (Hrvatske Ceste): 10000 Zagreb, Vončinina 3; tel. (1) 445422; fax (1) 445215; f. 1991; state-owned; maintenance, construction and reconstruction of public roads; Pres. J. ZAVOREO; Man. Dir ALEKSANDAR ČAKLOVIĆ.

SHIPPING

Atlantska Plovidba d.d.: 20000 Dubrovnik, od sv. Mihajla 1; tel. (20) 412666; fax (20) 20384; f. 1974; Dir ANTE JERKOVIĆ.

Croatia Line: 51000 Rijeka, POB 379, Riva 18; tel. (51) 205111; fax (51) 335811; e-mail erc.hr@croatialine.com; internet www.croatialine.com; f. 1986; cargo and passenger services; chartering and tramp service; Gen. Man. DARIO VUKIĆ; 368 employees.

Jadrolinija (Adriatic Shipping Line): 51000 Rijeka, Riva 16; tel. (51) 666111; fax (51) 213116; e-mail jadrolinija@jadrolinija.hr; internet www.jadrolinija.hr; f. 1872; regular passenger and car-ferry services between Italian, Greek and Croatian ports; Pres. SLAVKO LONČAR.

Jadroplov: 21000 Split, Obala kneza Branimira 16; tel. (21) 302666; fax (21) 342198; f. 1984; fleet of 17 vessels and 1,500 containers engaged in linear and tramp service; Gen. Man. NIKŠA GIOVANELLI.

Slobodna Plovidba: 22000 Šibenik, Drage 2; tel. (22) 23755; fax (22) 27860; f. 1976; transport of goods by sea; tourism services; Dir VITOMIR JURAGA.

Tankerska Plovidba d.d.: 23000 Zadar, Božidara Petranovića 4; tel. (23) 202202; fax (23) 202375; internet www.tankerska.hr; f. 1976; Dir STANKO BANIĆ; 1,283 employees.

CIVIL AVIATION

There are 10 international airports in Croatia.

Croatia Airlines: 10000 Zagreb, Savska 41; tel. (1) 6160066; fax (1) 6176845; e-mail pr@ctn.tel.hr; internet www.croatiaairlines.com; f. 1989 as Zagreb Airlines; name changed 1990; operates domestic services and 16 international routes to European destinations; Pres. IVAN MIŠETIĆ.

Tourism

The attractive Adriatic coast and the country's 1,185 islands made Croatia a very popular tourist destination before the 1990s. However, the civil conflict of the early 1990s greatly reduced tourist activity in the country. The industry showed signs of recovery after 1992, with foreign tourist arrivals reaching some 4.1m. in 1998. Revenue generated by tourism in 1998 reached US $2,733m. In 1999, however, foreign tourist arrivals declined to 3.8m., owing to the conflict in Kosovo, the Federal Republic of Yugoslavia, in March–June. In that year income from tourism declined to $2,493m. In 2000 foreign tourist arrivals recovered to 5.8m. and revenue from tourism to $2,758m., and the number of foreign tourist arrivals increased further, to 6.5m., in 2001.

Croatian National Tourist Board: 10000 Zagreb, Ilica 1A; tel. (1) 4556455; fax (1) 4816757; e-mail info@htz.hr; internet www.htz.hr/text_e/htz.htm.

Generalturist: 10000 Zagreb, Praška 5; tel. (1) 4805555; fax (1) 4810420; e-mail generalturist@generalturist.com; f. 1923; renamed 1963; 17 brs.

Jadran-Turist d.d.: 55210 Rovinj, V. Nazora 6; tel. (52) 800300; fax (52) 800376; e-mail jadrantur-rovinj@pu.tel.hr; internet www.istra.com/rovinj/jadranturist; f. 1954; Dir IVAN SORIĆ.

CUBA

Introductory Survey

Location, Climate, Language, Religion, Flag, Capital

The Republic of Cuba is an archipelago of two main islands, Cuba and the Isla de la Juventud (Isle of Youth), formerly the Isla de Pinos (Isle of Pines), and about 1,600 keys and islets. It lies in the Caribbean Sea, 145 km (90 miles) south of Florida, USA. Other nearby countries are the Bahamas, Mexico, Jamaica and Haiti. The climate is tropical, with the annual rainy season from May to October. The average annual temperature is 25°C (77°F) and hurricanes are frequent. The language spoken is Spanish. Most of the inhabitants are Christians, of whom the great majority are Roman Catholics. The national flag (proportions 12 by 2) has five equal horizontal stripes, of blue, white, blue, white and blue, with a red triangle, enclosing a five-pointed white star, at the hoist. The capital is Havana (La Habana).

Recent History

Cuba was ruled by Spain from the 16th century until 1898, when the island was ceded to the USA following Spain's defeat in the Spanish–American War. Cuba became an independent republic on 20 May 1902, but the USA retained its naval bases on the island and, until 1934, reserved the right to intervene in Cuba's internal affairs. In 1933 an army sergeant, Fulgencio Batista Zaldívar, came to power at the head of a military revolt. Batista ruled the country, directly or indirectly, until 1944, when he retired after serving a four-year term as elected President.

In March 1952, however, Gen. Batista (as he had become) seized power again, deposing President Carlos Prío Socarrás in a bloodless coup. Batista's new regime soon proved to be unpopular and became harshly repressive. In July 1953 a radical opposition group, led by Dr Fidel Castro Ruz, attacked the Moncada army barracks in Santiago de Cuba. Castro was captured, with many of his supporters, but was later released. He went into exile and formed a revolutionary movement which was committed to Batista's overthrow. In December 1956 Castro landed in Cuba with a small group of followers, most of whom were captured or killed. However, 12 survivors, including Castro and the Argentine-born Dr Ernesto ('Che') Guevara, escaped into the hills of the Sierra Maestra, where they formed the nucleus of the guerrilla forces which, after a prolonged struggle, forced Batista to flee from Cuba on 1 January 1959. The Batista regime collapsed, and Castro's forces occupied Havana.

The assumption of power by the victorious rebels was initially met with great popular acclaim. The 1940 Constitution was suspended in January 1959 and replaced by a new 'Fundamental Law'. Executive and legislative power was vested in the Council of Ministers, with Fidel Castro as Prime Minister and his brother Raúl as his deputy. Guevara reportedly ranked third in importance. The new regime ruled by decree but promised to hold elections within 18 months. When it was firmly established, the Castro Government adopted a radical economic programme, including agrarian reform and the nationalization of industrial and commercial enterprises. These drastic reforms, combined with the regime's authoritarian nature, provoked opposition from some sectors of the population, including former supporters of Castro, and many Cubans went into exile.

All US business interests in Cuba were expropriated, without compensation, in October 1960, and the USA severed diplomatic relations in January 1961. A US-sponsored force of anti-Castro Cuban émigrés landed in April 1961 at the Bahía de Cochinos (Bay of Pigs), in southern Cuba, but the invasion was thwarted by Castro's troops. Later in the year, all pro-Government groups were merged to form the Organizaciones Revolucionarias Integradas (ORI). In December 1961 Fidel Castro publicly announced that Cuba had become a communist state, and he proclaimed a 'Marxist-Leninist' programme for the country's future development. In January 1962 Cuba was excluded from active participation in the Organization of American States (OAS). The USA instituted a full economic and political blockade of Cuba. Hostility to the USA was accompanied by increasingly close relations between Cuba and the USSR. In October 1962 the USA revealed the presence of Soviet missiles in Cuba but, after the imposition of a US naval blockade, the weapons were withdrawn. The missile bases, capable of launching nuclear weapons against the USA, were dismantled, thus resolving one of the most serious international crises since the Second World War. In 1964 the OAS imposed diplomatic and commercial sanctions against Cuba.

The ORI was replaced in 1962 by a new Partido Unido de la Revolución Socialista Cubana (PURSC), which was established, under Fidel Castro's leadership, as the country's sole legal party. Guevara resigned his military and government posts in April 1965, subsequently leaving Cuba to pursue revolutionary activities abroad. In October 1965 the PURSC was renamed the Partido Comunista de Cuba (PCC). Although ostracized by most other Latin American countries, the PCC Government maintained and consolidated its internal authority, with little effective opposition. Supported by considerable aid from the USSR, the regime made significant progress in social and economic development, including improvements in education and public health. At the same time, Cuba continued to give active support to left-wing revolutionary movements in Latin America and in many other parts of the world. Guevara was killed in Bolivia, following an unsuccessful guerrilla uprising under his leadership, in October 1967.

In July 1972 Cuba's links with the Eastern bloc were strengthened when the country became a full member of the Council for Mutual Economic Assistance (CMEA—dissolved in 1991), a Moscow-based organization linking the USSR and other communist states. As a result of its admission to the CMEA, Cuba received preferential trade terms and more technical advisers from the USSR and Eastern European countries.

In June 1974 the country's first elections since the revolution were held for municipal offices in Matanzas province. Cuba's first 'socialist' Constitution was submitted to the First Congress of the PCC, held in December 1975, and came into force in February 1976, after being approved by popular referendum. As envisaged by the new Constitution, elections for 169 municipal assemblies were held in October 1976. These assemblies later elected delegates to provincial assemblies and deputies to the Asamblea Nacional del Poder Popular (National Assembly of People's Power), inaugurated in December 1976 as 'the supreme organ of state'. The National Assembly chose the members of a new Council of State, with Fidel Castro as President. The Second Congress of the PCC was held in December 1980, when Fidel and Raúl Castro were re-elected First and Second Secretaries, respectively. In December 1981 Fidel Castro was re-elected by the Assembly as President of the Council of State, and Raúl Castro re-elected as First Vice-President.

Cuba continued to be excluded from the activities of the OAS, although the Organization voted in favour of allowing members to normalize their relations with Cuba in 1975. Relations with the USA deteriorated because of Cuban involvement in Angola in 1976 and in Ethiopia in 1977. The relaxation of restrictions on emigration in April 1980 resulted in the departure of more than 125,000 Cubans for Florida, USA. Antagonism continued as Cuba's military and political presence abroad increased, threatening US spheres of influence.

In 1981 Cuba expressed interest in discussing foreign policy with the USA, and declared that the shipment of arms to guerrilla groups in Central America had ceased. High-level talks between the two countries took place in November 1981 but US hostility increased. Economic sanctions were strengthened, the major air link was closed, and tourism and investment by US nationals was prohibited in April 1982. Cuba's support of Argentina during the 1982 crisis concerning the Falkland Islands improved relations with the rest of Latin America, and the country's legitimacy was finally acknowledged when it was elected to the chair of the UN General Assembly Committee on Decolonization in September 1982, while continuing to play a leading role in the Non-Aligned Movement (despite its firm alliance with the Soviet bloc).

An increase in US military activity in Honduras and the Caribbean region led President Castro to declare a 'state of national alert' in August 1983. The US invasion of Grenada in October, and the ensuing short-lived confrontation between US forces and Cuban personnel on the island, severely damaged hopes that the two countries might reach an agreement over the problems in Central America, and left Cuba isolated in the Caribbean, following the weakening of its diplomatic and military ties with Suriname in November.

In July 1984 official negotiations were begun with the USA on the issues of immigration and repatriation. In December agreement was reached on the resumption of Cuban immigration to the USA and the repatriation of 2,746 Cuban 'undesirables', who had accompanied other Cuban refugees to the USA in 1980. The repatriation of Cuban 'undesirables' began in February 1985, but, following the inauguration of Radio Martí (a radio station sponsored by the 'Voice of America' radio network, which began to broadcast Western-style news and other programmes to Cuba from Florida, USA), the Cuban Government suspended its immigration accord with the USA. Subsequently, all visits to Cuba by US residents of Cuban origin were banned. The US Government responded by restricting visits to the USA by PCC members and Cuban government officials. In September 1986, as a result of mediation by the Roman Catholic Church, more than 100 political prisoners and their families were permitted to leave Cuba for the USA.

Relations with the USA continued to deteriorate in 1987 when the US Government launched a campaign to direct public attention to violations of human rights in Cuba. In March a resolution to condemn Cuba's record on human rights was narrowly defeated at a meeting of the UN Commission on Human Rights. The Cuban Government subsequently allowed 348 current and former political prisoners to return to the USA. The restoration, in October 1987, of the 1984 immigration accord provoked rioting by Cuban exiles detained in US prisons. The accord allowed for the repatriation of 2,500 Cuban 'undesirables' in exchange for a US agreement to allow 23,000 Cubans to enter the USA annually. In 1988 the Government released some 250 political prisoners, and in the following January President Castro pledged to release the remaining 225 political prisoners acknowledged by the regime. In 1989 human rights activists formed a co-ordinating body and increased their operations. The Government responded in August by imprisoning leading activists for up to two years for having published allegedly false information. In September 1991 eight Cuban dissident organizations united to form a single democratic opposition group, the Concertación Democrática Cubana—CDC (Cuban Democratic Convergence), to campaign for political pluralism and economic reform.

At the Third Congress of the PCC in February 1986 drastic changes were made within the Central Committee; almost one-third of the 146 full members were replaced. A new Council of State was elected in December.

In June 1989 President Castro was confronted by Cuba's most serious political crisis since the 1959 Revolution. It was discovered that a number of senior military personnel were not only involved in smuggling operations in Angola but were also aiding Colombian drugs-traffickers from the infamous Medellín cartel, by enabling them to use Cuban airstrips as refuelling points (en route from Colombia to the USA) in return for bribes. Following court-martial proceedings, Gen. Arnaldo Ochoa Sánchez, who had led the military campaign in Angola, was found guilty of high treason and was executed. Three other officers were also executed. A further purge led to the imposition of harsh sentences on 14 senior officials, including the head of civil aviation and the Ministers of the Interior and of Transport, who had been found guilty of corruption. President Castro insisted that the bureaucracy in Cuba needed to undergo a process of 'purification', but not reform. However, the scandal had clearly undermined the regime's credibility at the international, as well as the domestic, level.

In Angola, where Cuban troops numbered an estimated 50,000, the peace process gathered momentum in 1988. In May a large Cuban offensive almost succeeded in expelling South African forces from Angola and lent new impetus to the peace negotiations. A cease-fire was implemented, and at discussions held in New York, USA, in October, agreement was reached on a phased withdrawal of Cuban troops over a period of 24–30 months. The withdrawal was completed in May 1991.

In April 1989 President Gorbachev of the USSR undertook the first official visit to Cuba by a Soviet leader since 1974. The two Heads of State discussed ways in which Cuba's dependence on Soviet aid might be reduced and Central American issues, and the talks culminated in the signing of a treaty of friendship and economic co-operation. Although, ostensibly, relations remained

good, tensions had arisen, owing to Castro's resistance to Soviet-style reforms. Gorbachev made it clear that, in future, general financial aid would be replaced by assistance for specific projects, thus giving the USSR greater power to influence policy decisions in Cuba. In July President Castro strongly attacked the ideas of *perestroika* and *glasnost*, which he blamed for the 'crisis in socialism'. He pledged to eradicate all market forms of economic activity, despite the fact that Cuba's failure to integrate into the new supply-and-demand system of many Eastern European factories had led to delays in imports and acute shortages.

In October 1990 President Castro announced plans to reduce the PCC's bureaucracy by as much as 50%, including the reassignment of thousands of employees to more productive sectors. In November rationing was extended to all products. Cubans were told to prepare for the possibility of a 'special wartime period' by the Minister of the Revolutionary Armed Forces, Gen. Raúl Castro, who warned of a possible US military attack if the currently intensified US economic blockade should fail. In spite of the gravity of Cuba's political and economic situation, President Castro was defiant in his rejection of recommendations that, as a condition for the removal of the blockade, Cuba should adopt a market economy and political pluralism.

In September 1991 the USSR announced that it intended to withdraw the majority of its military personnel (some 3,000 troops and advisers) from Cuba. The decision, which was condemned by Cuba as presenting a major threat to its national security, came as the result of US demands that the USSR reduce its aid to Cuba as a precondition to the provision of US aid to the USSR. Cuba's subsequent demands that the USA withdraw its troops from the naval base at Guantánamo were rejected. The Soviet withdrawal was completed in June 1993.

In 1992 President Castro's efforts to quiet internal dissent and bolster the country against the perceived US threat revealed an increasingly militant attitude, as several death sentences were imposed on Cuban dissidents. In the same year the USA began to implement a series of measures tightening its economic blockade against Cuba. In April US President Bush issued an executive order barring ships that were engaged in trade with Cuba from entering US ports. In October the Cuban Democracy Act, also known as the 'Torricelli Law', was adopted, making it illegal for foreign subsidiaries of US companies to trade with Cuba. These measures encountered widespread international criticism, including protests by the European Community (EC, later European Union—EU) that they violated international law. In November the UN General Assembly adopted a non-binding resolution demanding the cessation of the trade embargo.

In July 1992 the National Assembly approved a number of amendments to the Constitution. Under the reforms, President Castro was granted the authority to declare a state of emergency and, in such an event, to assume full control of the armed forces at the head of a National Defence Council. An electoral reform, which had originally been proposed at the Fourth Congress of the PCC in October 1991, was formally adopted, providing for elections to the National Assembly to be conducted by direct vote. The constitutional revisions also included an updating of the business law, legitimizing foreign investment in approved state enterprises and recognizing foreign ownership of property in joint ventures.

On 24 February 1993 elections to the National Assembly and the 14 provincial assemblies were, for the first time, conducted by direct secret ballot. Only candidates nominated by the PCC were permitted to contest the elections. According to official results, there was an abstention rate of only 1.2%, and 87.3% of the electorate cast a 'united' ballot (a vote for the entire list of candidates). Only 7.2% of votes cast were blank or spoilt. All 589 deputies of the National Assembly were elected with more than the requisite 50% of the votes. In the following month Fidel Castro and Gen. Raúl Castro were unanimously re-elected by the National Assembly to their respective posts as President and First Vice-President of the Council of State.

In July 1993, with the economic crisis deepening and international reserves exhausted, Castro announced that a 30-year ban on Cuban citizens' possessing foreign currency was to be lifted. The measure, which represented a significant departure from the country's centrally-planned socialist economy, was intended to attract the large sums of foreign currency (principally US dollars) in circulation on the black market into the economy, and to encourage remittances from Cuban exiles. Restrictions on Cuban exiles travelling to Cuba were also to be relaxed. Concerns that the measures were socially divisive, affording privileges to those receiving currency from relatives abroad, were acknowledged by the Government. In September, in a further move away from traditional economic policy, the Government authorized limited individual private enterprise in a range of 117 occupations. In the same month plans were announced for the introduction of agricultural reforms allowing for the decentralization and reorganization of state farms into 'Units of Basic Co-operative Production', to be managed and financed by the workers themselves.

In April 1994, in a reorganization of the Government, four new ministries were created and a number of state committees and institutes dissolved. The creation of the new ministries (of economy and planning, finance and prices, foreign investment and economic co-operation, and tourism) reflected a significant change in the economic management of the country. In early August, however, increasing discontent at deteriorating economic conditions resulted in rioting in the capital, precipitated by a confrontation between police and a large number of Cubans attempting to commandeer a ferry in order to take the vessel to the USA. In a public speech broadcast on the following day Castro indicated that, if the USA failed to halt the promotion of such illegal departures, Cuba would suspend its travel restrictions. The resultant surge of Cubans attempting to reach the USA by sea reached crisis proportions, and the US President, Bill Clinton, was forced to adopt measures to deter them. The automatic refugee status conferred on Cubans under the 1966 Cuban Adjustment Act was revoked, and Cubans were warned that those intercepted by the US Coast Guard would be transported to Guantánamo naval base and would not be allowed entry into the USA. Further measures imposed included the halting of cash remittances from Cuban exiles in the USA. However, these measures failed to stem the flow of Cubans seeking refuge in the USA, and in September the US and Cuban Governments held bilateral talks to resolve the crisis. As a result of the talks, the USA promised to grant visas allowing for the migration of a minimum of 20,000 Cubans annually (despite the 1984 immigration accord, a total of only 11,222 US entry visas had been granted to Cubans between December 1984 and July 1994). An additional 4,000–6,000 Cubans already on waiting lists for US visas would be granted them. In return, Cuba reintroduced border restrictions. More than 30,000 Cubans were estimated to have left the country during the period when travel restrictions were suspended, although the majority of these were detained by the US authorities and transported to camps in Guantánamo and the Panama Canal Zone. Talks continued with the USA throughout 1995. In May a further immigration accord was signed, bringing to an official end the automatic refugee status that had been revoked in August 1994. The accord also stated that all Cuban refugees intercepted at sea by the USA would thenceforth be repatriated. In addition, the USA agreed to grant visas to the majority of the approximately 20,000 Cuban refugees detained at Guantánamo, although the figure was to be deducted, over a period of four years, from the annual quota of visas granted under the September 1994 accord.

In early 1995 legislative proposals seeking to tighten the US embargo against Cuba were introduced to the US Congress by the Chairman of the Senate Foreign Relations Committee, Jesse Helms, and the Chairman of the House of Representatives Sub-Committee on the Western Hemisphere, Dan Burton. The proposals, referred to as the Helms-Burton bill, sought to impose sanctions on countries trading with or investing in Cuba, and threatened to reduce US aid to countries providing Cuba with financial assistance, notably Russia. The bill provoked international criticism, and a formal complaint was registered by the EU, which claimed that the legislation would be in violation of international law and the rules of the World Trade Organization (WTO, see p. 323). The legislation was approved by the House of Representatives in September but was considerably modified by the Senate.

In May 1995, following the first visit to Cuba by an international human rights mission since the 1959 Revolution, the Government authorized the release of six political prisoners. The mission had been co-ordinated by the human rights organization France-Libertés. According to Cuban human rights groups, however, more than 1,000 political prisoners remained in detention in the country.

In February 1996 Cuban MiG fighters shot down two US light aircraft piloted by members of the Cuban-American exile group Brothers to the Rescue, killing all four crew members. The action was vigorously condemned by the USA, which rejected Cuban claims that the aircraft had violated Cuban airspace. Further US sanctions were immediately implemented, including the indefinite suspension of charter flights to Cuba. In June, following an investigation, the International Civil Aviation Organization issued a report confirming US claims that the aircraft had been shot down over international waters. As a result of the incident, President Clinton reversed his previous opposition to certain controversial elements of the Helms-Burton bill, and on 12 March he signed the legislation, officially entitled the Cuban Liberty and Solidarity Act, thus making it law. However, Clinton was empowered to issue executive orders, at six-monthly intervals, postponing the implementation of a section of the law, Title IV, which allowed US citizens, including naturalized Cuban exiles, to prosecute through US courts any foreign corporation or investor with business dealings involving property that had been expropriated during the Castro regime. Title III of the Act, which made executives of companies investing in Cuba (and their dependants) liable to exclusion from the USA, was implemented selectively. Approval of the Helms-Burton bill prompted strenuous criticism from Cuba's major trading partners. The EU announced its intention to challenge the extra-territorial provisions of the Act through the WTO, while Mexico and Canada sought to dispute the law under the provisions of the North American Free Trade Agreement. International opposition to the Helms-Burton bill increased following the issue, in May, by the US State Department of letters to companies in Canada, Mexico and Italy, warning of possible prosecution. In June Canada initiated a series of legal measures to protect Canadian companies against the Act. Similar legislation was subsequently adopted by Mexico and the EU. In July Clinton imposed a six-month moratorium on Title IV of the Act, which had been due to come into force in August. In November, in its annual vote on the US embargo, the UN General Assembly voted for its repeal with the largest majority to date. Notably, the United Kingdom, Germany and the Netherlands, which had all previously abstained on this question, voted in favour of a repeal. In the same month the WTO adopted a resolution to establish a disputes panel to rule on the legality of the Helms-Burton-sponsored Act.

In December 1996 agreement was reached by the members of the EU to make the extent of economic co-operation with Cuba contingent upon progress towards democracy in the country. In that month the Cuban Government adopted legislation to counteract the application of the Cuban Liberty and Solidarity (Helms-Burton) Act in an attempt to protect foreign investment in the country. The Government also expressed its readiness to negotiate with the USA regarding the compensation of US citizens with property claims in Cuba. In early February 1997 the EU requested that the WTO postpone the appointment of a disputes panel in order that further discussions be conducted with the USA in an effort to reach a negotiated settlement. However, these efforts were not successful, and on 20 February a disputes panel was appointed and given six months to reach a decision on whether the extra-territorial provisions of the Act contravened WTO rules on multilateral trade, or whether, as the USA maintained, the Act was a matter of national security and therefore not within the jurisdiction of the WTO. In March, in a further attempt to avoid confrontation, the EU and the USA resumed discussions concerning the Act, and in the following month agreement was reached in principle on a resolution of the dispute. Under the terms of the agreement, the USA was to continue deferring the implementation of Title IV indefinitely, while the EU was to withdraw its petition to the WTO until October. In the interim, negotiations were to continue towards a multilateral accord defining investment principles, with particular emphasis on expropriated foreign assets. In a move widely interpreted as a concession to mounting domestic pressure to end restrictions on exports of food and medicines from the USA to Cuba, in March 1998 it was agreed that shipments of both commodities, via non-governmental organizations, were to be permitted. In addition, President Clinton announced an end to the ban on direct flights between the USA and Cuba (imposed in 1996) and on the transfer of cash remittances from the USA to Cuba. Henceforth, Cuban residents in the USA were to be permitted to send up to US $300 quarterly to relatives in Cuba. The process whereby applications for licences to sell medicines to Cuba were considered was also to be examined, with a view to accelerating procedures. However, the Cuban Government was extremely critical of a further outline agreement on extra-territorial legislation drafted by the US Government and the EU in May, which it considered to be highly concessionary on the part of the EU, at the expense of Cuban interests. Under the terms of the agreement, in return for a commitment from President Clinton to seek congressional consensus for a relaxation of the application of the Cuban Liberty and Solidarity Act, EU member states would participate in the compilation of a register of former US assets in Cuba (considered to have been illegally expropriated) and would observe firm US recommendations regarding their exclusivity. President Clinton repeatedly exercised his right to postpone the implementation of Title IV. His successor, George W. Bush, continued to suspend the implementation of Title IV at six-monthly intervals.

On 11 January 1998 elections to the National Assembly (enlarged from 589 to 601 seats) and to the 14 provincial assemblies were conducted. All 601 candidates who contested the legislative ballot were elected. Of the 7.8m. registered voters, 98.35% participated in the elections. Only 5% of votes cast were blank or spoilt. At the first meeting of the newly-constituted National Assembly on 24 February, the new Council of State was announced, confirming Fidel and Raúl Castro, and the five incumbent Vice-Presidents, in their positions for a further five-year term. Of the remaining 23 ordinary members of the Council, 14 were new appointments.

In January 1998 Cuba received its first ever papal visit. Pope John Paul II conducted four large-scale open-air masses throughout Cuba, and attended a private meeting with President Castro. During the visit the Pope was critical of the 'unjust and ethically unacceptable' US embargo against Cuba, and urged the reintegration of Cuba into the international community. In response, in late January, the Guatemalan Government announced that diplomatic relations were to be restored with Cuba, prompting a rebuke from the US Department of State. During February, moreover, it was announced that almost 300 Cuban prisoners were to be released, many as a result of a petition for clemency made by the papal delegation. In April, at a meeting of the UN Commission on Human Rights, the annual US-sponsored vote of censure against the Cuban Government for alleged abuses of human rights was defeated for the first time since 1991; the motion was supported by 16 countries and opposed by 19, while 18 abstained. Support for the annual UN General Assembly resolution urging an end to the US embargo against Cuba increased once again in October, receiving the support of 157 member nations. Twelve members abstained from the vote, while only two (the USA and Israel) voted against the resolution.

Following an announcement by the US Government that 10 Cubans had been arrested on charges of spying, in October 1998 Castro admitted that Cuban nationals had been deployed in the USA on espionage duties, charged with infiltrating counter-revolutionary organizations there.

In mid-March 1999 the Provincial Court in Havana sentenced four prominent political dissidents to prison terms of between three and a half and five years' duration. The decision followed the introduction, in February, of uncompromising new legislation to combat increasing criminal activity and to curb subversion and dissent. The incarceration of the dissidents, together with the imposition of death sentences in March on two Salvadorean nationals (see below), drew criticism of Cuba's respect for human rights from the international community in general, and resulted in a significant deterioration in relations with Canada (Cuba's largest trading partner) and Spain in particular.

In March 1999 two Salvadorean nationals were convicted (and subsequently sentenced to death) on terrorism charges relating to a spate of bomb attacks in mid-1997, allegedly organized by the anti-Castro Cuban-American National Foundation (CANF, based in Florida, USA). In December 1999 the US Department of Justice acquitted five Cuban exiles, including a member of the CANF executive, accused of plotting to assassinate President Castro in Venezuela in 1997. Three Guatemalan nationals, arrested in March 1998, stood trial in November 2001 on charges of terrorist action, allegedly organized and financed by the CANF.

Despite a further easing of restrictions relating to the US embargo in August 1999, and well-publicized visits to Cuba by several prominent US politicians, attempts by the US Government to appease the increasingly influential anti-embargo lobby were largely frustrated by an exchange of legal challenges. In March a US judge ruled that payments owed to the Cuban national telecommunications company, which were currently being withheld by a number of US telecommunications compa-

nies by judicial request, could be used to help honour a compensation award of US $187m. against the Cuban authorities, made in the USA in 1997 to benefit relatives of four pilots shot down by the Cuban air force in 1996 (see above). The US Government had made known its objection to the ruling, claiming that the decision amounted to interference in foreign policy. In response, in early June a new lawsuit was brought to the Cuban courts by a number of government-sponsored organizations, which were seeking some $181,100m. in compensation for more than 3,000 deaths and more than 2,000 injuries allegedly inflicted on Cuban nationals since the 1959 Revolution by the 'aggressive' policies of the US Government. (In early 2001 the US Administration authorized the transfer of these payments, to compensate relatives of the four pilots.) In September 1999 a unanimous declaration of the National Assembly condemned the US trade embargo as an act of 'genocide'. In October 2000 legislation was passed by the US Congress easing some aspects of the trade embargo, including the export of food and medicine. However, the Cuban Government declared that the conditions attached to the lifting of the restrictions were such that the legislation would tighten, rather than ease, the US embargo. In response, Cuba imposed a 10% tax on all telephone calls between the two countries and, in December, suspended telephone links with the USA, following the refusal of US telecommunications companies to pay the levy.

In the first six months of 2000 Cuban–US relations were dominated by the case of Elián González. In November 1999 Elián, a five-year-old Cuban boy, was rescued from the Atlantic Ocean off the coast of Florida, the sole survivor of a shipwrecked attempt to reach the USA, in which his mother had died. A dispute resulted between the boy's Miami-based relatives, who attempted to have him granted US citizenship, and his father in Cuba, who wanted his son repatriated. The US Department of Justice granted custody to Elián's father, but his Miami relatives refused to relinquish charge of the boy. In April armed Federal Bureau of Investigation agents seized Elián from his Miami relatives. He eventually returned to Cuba on 28 June, after the US Supreme Court had declined to hear further appeals from his US-based family. In Cuba the case prompted public demonstrations in protest at the USA's 'abduction' of the child. In November 2000, during a visit to Panama to attend the Ibero-American Summit, an alleged plot to assassinate President Castro was uncovered. Anti-Castro activist Luis Posada Carriles was arrested, along with three others. Posada Carriles had escaped from custody in Venezuela, where he was indicted for the bombing of a Cuban aeroplane near Barbados in 1976, and was also implicated in a series of hotel bombings in Havana in 1997. The Cuban Government's request for Posada Carriles' extradition was subsequently refused. In the same month the leaders of some 50 Cuban organizations opposed to the regime requested the aid of the leaders of 21 Ibero-American countries in achieving a peaceful transition to democracy. Also in November, the UN General Assembly, for the ninth time, passed a resolution by an overwhelming majority condemning the US trade embargo on Cuba; only Israel and the Marshall Islands supported the US vote in favour of continuing the sanctions. A report from an independent 'think tank' in the USA, the Council of Foreign Relations, advocated an easing of restrictions in relations with Cuba, while stopping short of an end to all sanctions. It emphasized that current policy served to alienate sectors of Cuban society that were important to the US Government, such as the Roman Catholic Church and certain dissident groups. On 25 July 2001 the US House of Representatives voted 240–186 to lift the ban on US citizens travelling to Cuba without prior permission. The motion moved to the Senate.

In January 2001 a former Czech finance minister and member of the Czech parliament, Ivan Pilip, and a Czech political activist, Jan Bubenik, were arrested in Cuba after meeting with anti-Castro dissidents and charged with counter-revolutionary plotting. They were released in February, after making a formal apology. On 18 April a UN motion, sponsored by the Czech Republic and supported by the USA, condemning Cuba for human rights violations, was narrowly approved. In response, Castro accused a number of Latin American countries of servility to the USA; as a result of the remarks, the Argentine Ambassador to Cuba was recalled by his Government.

On 30 June 2001 President Castro collapsed from heat exhaustion during a public speech. Despite suffering no ill effects, he subsequently announced that his brother Raúl would have the authority and experience to assume the presidency, were it necessary. In September the Havana representative of the Irish political party Sinn Féin, Niall Connolly, was one of three alleged Provisional Irish Republican Army (IRA) members arrested in Colombia, suspected of training members of the Colombian left-wing rebel group, the Fuerzas Armadas Revolucionarias de Colombia (FARC). In October a senior analyst with the US Defence Intelligence Agency, Ana Belen Montes, was accused of passing classified defence information to Cuba. (In October 2002, having been convicted of the charges against her by a US court, she was sentenced to a 25-year prison term.)

In November 2001 'Hurricane Michelle' struck west-central Cuba. Five people were killed and thousands were evacuated from the coastal areas. The country suffered serious damage to its infrastructure and to the agricultural sector. The USA lifted temporarily the trade embargo, allowing Cuba to purchase food and medicines necessary for the reconstruction and aid effort.

In December 2001 the USA announced that it was to hold Afghan war detainees at its naval base at Guantánamo Bay. The first prisoners arrived at the new maximum-security prison in January 2002. In the same month Gen. Raúl Castro Ruz, the Minister of the Revolutionary Armed Forces, announced Cuba's support for the use of the base for this purpose. At the beginning of 2003 those being held at the gaol continued to await trial, while the conditions in which the prisoners were being held provoked criticism from several human rights organizations.

In May 2002 former US President Jimmy Carter visited Cuba; he was the most prominent US political figure to have travelled to the country since 1928. In an unprecedented televised address Carter criticized the human rights record of the Cuban Government but stated that he believed that the USA should initiate moves towards the lifting of the trade embargo. However, in a speech given on 20 May, the centenary of Cuban independence from Spain, US President George W. Bush affirmed that the embargo and travel restrictions would remain in place until Cuba installed a government that would respect political and civil rights. Cuban–US relations were further strained when, in the same month, the US Administration added Cuba to the list of states it claimed formed an 'axis of evil' that supported international terrorism. The US Under-Secretary of State for Arms Control, John Bolton, claimed that Cuba was engaged in limited biological warfare research and development and that it had provided biotechnology that could be used for civilian and military purposes by so-called 'rogue states'. After visiting a Cuban biotechnology facility during his stay, however, Carter claimed that he had been assured by US intelligence agencies prior to his visit that there was no evidence that Cuba had engaged in such a practice. (In November 2002 Cuba finally acceded to the Treaty on the Non–Proliferation of Nuclear Weapons—NPT, see p. 82.) Meanwhile, in a gesture of goodwill, the Government released a leading political dissident who had been imprisoned since 1999 following his conviction on sedition charges.

Also in May 2002 an 11,000 signature petition—part of a dissident initiative known as the 'Varela Project'—was submitted to the National Assembly; it called for a referendum on basic civil and political liberties. In the following month the Government responded by initiating a drive to mobilize popular support for an amendment to the Constitution, declaring the socialist system to be 'untouchable' and ratifying that 'economic, diplomatic and political relations with any other state can never be negotiated in the face of aggression, threat or pressure from a foreign power'. The National Assembly subsequently voted unanimously to adopt a constitutional amendment declaring socialism in Cuba to be permanent and 'irrevocable'. In July Damador Peña Pentón was appointed as Minister of Public Health, replacing Carlos Dotres Martínez. Also in July, in an indication that the US legislature was moving towards a softening of its stance on Cuba, the US House of Representatives passed legislation easing both travel and trade restrictions to the country; the legislation awaited consideration by the Senate, although the Bush Administration stated its intention to veto any legislative provisions which might ease the embargo.

In November 2002 Vice-President Carlos Lage Dávila accused the US Government of encouraging 'terrorism against Cuba'. His remarks followed an incident in which eight Cuban citizens seized a government-owned aeroplane and flew it to Florida. Following an initial period of detention imposed by the US Immigration and Naturalization Service, the migrants were released. The Cuban Government then demanded that both the Cubans and the aircraft be returned to Cuba; the US Government, however, permitted the refugees to remain in the USA. In the same month a court in Florida ruled that the aeroplane could

be sold as part of a US $27m. judgment against the Cuban Government that had been won by the ex-wife of a Cuban spy. Meanwhile, the UN General Assembly passed its 10th resolution condemning the US embargo on Cuba; only Israel and the Marshall Islands, together with the USA, voted against the resolution. In December the Minister of Construction, Juan Mario Junco del Pino, was replaced by his deputy, Fidel Fernando Figueroa de la Paz, after his performance in the role was deemed to have been unsatisfactory.

On 19 January 2003 elections took place to the National Assembly (enlarged from 601 to 609 seats) and the 14 provincial legislatures. All the candidates elected were unopposed and voter turn-out was estimated to have been at least 97%.

Since 1985 Cuba has succeeded in establishing strong ties throughout Latin America and the Caribbean. Full diplomatic relations were restored with Colombia (suspended in 1981) in 1993, with Chile in 1995 and with Guatemala in 1998. Diplomatic relations were also re-established with the Dominican Republic in 1998 and with Honduras in 2002. In August 1998, during President Castro's first visit to the Dominican Republic, he attended a summit meeting of the Cariforum grouping of CARICOM (see p. 155) states and the Dominican Republic, at which the Statement of Santo Domingo was endorsed, envisaging full Cuban participation in any successor arrangement to Lomé IV. (Recent statements by the US and British Governments had indicated that pressure might be applied to EU member states to attach preconditions relating to human rights and democratic processes to Cuban participation in such an arrangement.) Cuba was afforded observer status at a meeting of the Council of Ministers of the Africa, Caribbean and Pacific (ACP) signatory nations to the Lomé Convention (which expired in February 2000 and was replaced by the Cotonou Agreement (see p. 234) in June) convened in Barbados in May 1998. In April 2000, following denunciation by the Office of the UN High Commissioner for Human Rights, for repression of religious groups and political dissent, Cuba withdrew its request to join the ACP-EU Joint Assembly. The Government claimed that the EU would impose selective and discriminatory conditions. However, following conciliatory moves by both sides, in 2001 Cuba confirmed that it had renewed its request to join the Assembly. Cuba signed an agreement with CARICOM in June designed to promote trade and co-operation. In November 1998 Cuba became the 12th full member of the Latin American Integration Association (LAIA, see p. 259), having enjoyed observer status since 1986. In December 2002 Cuba hosted a CARICOM summit meeting for the first time. In the same month it announced that it planned to renew its request to join the Cotonou Agreement; the ACP welcomed the decision.

In September 1988 diplomatic relations were established with the EC (restyled the European Union—EU—in late 1993). In the mid-1990s Spain played a significant role in advising Cuba on economic affairs and mediating in negotiations with the IMF, with a view to future co-operation. In 1994 Cuba and Spain concluded an agreement providing for the compensation of Spanish citizens whose property was expropriated during the Cuban Revolution of 1959. In 1996, however, following the transfer of power in Spain from a socialist government to the centre-right administration of José María Aznar, relations between the two countries became more strained. In November 2000 Cuba refused to support a special declaration condemning terrorism by the Basque separatist organization, Euskadi ta Askatasuna (ETA).

In 1992 Cuba signed a number of accords and protocols establishing diplomatic relations with republics of the former USSR, including Belarus, Georgia, Kyrgyzstan and Ukraine. In October 1989 Cuba was elected to the UN Security Council (for a two-year term from January 1990) for the first time in the 30 years of President Castro's rule. In April 2000 Cuba hosted the South G77 Summit of Developing Countries.

Cuba traditionally enjoyed good relations with Mexico (which was the only Latin American country not to suspend diplomatic relations with the Castro regime in 1961). Although relations deteriorated during the presidency of Ernesto Zedillo Ponce de León (1994–2000), his successor, Vicente Fox Quesada, pledged to strengthen bilateral relations. Several reciprocal agreements on investment, health and technical and scientific co-operation were signed during 2001, and in February 2002 Fox made an official visit to Cuba. However, in April bilateral relations were strained again when Mexico lent its support to a resolution sponsored by Uruguay condemning Cuba's human rights record at a meeting of the UN Human Rights Commission. Following the approval of the resolution (which also received support from the Governments of Argentina, Chile, Costa Rica, Guatemala and Peru) President Castro denounced the President of Uruguay, Jorge Batlle, as 'an abject Judas'; Uruguay subsequently severed diplomatic relations with Cuba. Meanwhile, Castro released to the media a tape recording of a private telephone conversation between himself and the Mexican President in which Fox apparently requested that Castro leave a UN meeting on financing development which had been held in February in Monterrey, Mexico, early in order to avoid a meeting with US President George W. Bush. In September the Mexican ambassador to Cuba, Ricardo Pascoe, resigned, citing his frustration at the deterioration of relations between the two countries. However, in November relations were improved somewhat when Mexico voted in favour of the annual UN resolution condemning the US trade embargo of Cuba. A new Mexican ambassador, Roberta Lajous Vargas, was appointed in the same month.

Government

Under the 1976 Constitution (the first since the 1959 Revolution, amended in July 1992), the supreme organ of state, and the sole legislative authority, is the Asamblea Nacional del Poder Popular (National Assembly of People's Power), with 609 deputies elected for five years by direct vote. The National Assembly elects 31 of its members to form the Council of State, the Assembly's permanent organ. The Council of State is the highest representative of the State, and its President is both Head of State and Head of Government. Executive and administrative authority is vested in the Council of Ministers, appointed by the National Assembly on the proposal of the Head of State. Municipal, regional and provincial assemblies have also been established. The Partido Comunista de Cuba (PCC), the only authorized political party, is 'the leading force of society and the State'. The PCC's highest authority is the Party Congress, which elects a Central Committee (150 members in 2003) to supervise the Party's work. To direct its policy, the Central Committee elects a Politburo (24 members in 2003).

Defence

Conscription for military service is for a two-year period, and conscripts also work on the land. In August 2002, according to Western estimates, the armed forces totalled 46,000 (including ready reserves serving 45 days per year to complete active and reserve units): the army numbered 35,000, the navy 3,000 and the air force 8,000. Army reserves were estimated to total 39,000. Paramilitary forces include 20,000 State Security troops, 6,500 border guards, a civil defence force of 50,000 and a Youth Labour Army of 70,000. A local militia organization (Milicias de Tropas Territoriales—MTT), comprising an estimated 1m. men and women, was formed in 1980. Expenditure on defence and internal security for 2001 was estimated at 692m. pesos (US $37.7m.). Despite Cuban hostility, the USA maintains a base at Guantánamo Bay, with 590 naval, 486 marine and 63 air force personnel in 2002. In June 1993, in accordance with the unilateral decision of the USSR in September 1991, the 3,000-strong military unit of the former USSR, which had been stationed in Cuba since 1962, was withdrawn. A number of Russian military personnel remained to operate military intelligence facilities. In December 2001 Russia closed the Lourdes military electronic surveillance base, first opened in 1964. Following the political changes in eastern Europe, previously high levels of military aid to Cuba were dramatically reduced in the early 1990s, and the size of the army was reduced by some 60,000 personnel.

Economic Affairs

In 2001 Cuba's gross domestic product (GDP), measured at constant 1981 prices, was an estimated 27,274m. pesos. During 1991–2000, it was estimated, GDP declined, in real terms, at an average annual rate of 1.4%. However, GDP increased by 6.2% in 1999, by 5.6% in 2000 and by 3.0% in 2001. In 2002, according to official figures, GDP grew by 1.1%. During 1990–2001 the population increased by an average of 0.1% per year.

Agriculture (including hunting, forestry and fishing) contributed 6.5% of GDP, measured at constant 1981 prices, in 2001 and employed 24.4% of the labour force in 2000. The principal cash crop is sugar cane, with sugar and its derivatives accounting for 27.4% of export earnings in 2000. The sugar crop in 1998 was the worst in 50 years, reaching only some 32.8m. metric tons. It recovered slightly in 1999 and 2000, amounting to 34.0m. tons, and 36.0m. tons, respectively, but fell short of expectations in 2001, owing to a drought and the destruction

caused by 'Hurricane Michelle'. In 2001 the Ministry of Sugar announced that the industry was to expand plantation acreage, following the poor harvests of recent years. In 2002, as a result of the damage caused by the hurricane, the Government announced that it would have to import sugar to meet domestic demand. In June 2002 the Government announced that, following recent production decreases, it intended to rationalize the sugar industry through a programme of restructuring—this would involve the closure of several sugar refineries and the loss of approximately 100,000 jobs in the sector. Approximately 60% of plantation area would be reallocated to other crops in an attempt to produce enough sugar to satisfy domestic needs, while sugar would only be exported while revenues continued to exceed production costs. In 2000 Cuba produced some 30,600 tons of tobacco and in 2001 it produced 330.3m. cigars. Other important crops are rice, citrus fruits (648,272 tons in 2000), plantains and bananas. Fishing exports in 2000 reached 87.8m. pesos. Cuba's principal seafood export markets were Japan, France, Spain, Italy and Canada. In real terms, the GDP of the agricultural sector declined at an average rate of 6.6% per year during 1990–98. Agricultural GDP increased by 10.4% in 1999 and by 11.6% in 2000, but decreased by 1.7% in 2001.

Industry (including mining, manufacturing, construction and power) contributed 28.0% of GDP, measured at constant 1981 prices, in 2001. The sector employed 24.0% of the labour force in 2000. Industrial GDP decreased, in real terms, at an average rate of 2.5% per year in 1990–98. The sector's GDP increased by 6.4% in 1999, by 5.6% in 2000 and by 2.9% in 2001.

Mining contributed 1.5% of GDP, measured at constant 1981 prices, in 2001 and employed 1.3% of the labour force in 2000. Nickel is the principal mineral export. In 2001 nickel and cobalt output reached 76,500 metric tons, an increase of some 7.1% compared with the previous year. Cuba also produces considerable amounts of chromium and copper, some iron and manganese, and there are workable deposits of gold and silver. The sector's GDP increased by only 1.0% in 1999, but by 14.4% in 2000 and by 3.1% in 2001.

Manufacturing contributed 17.4% of GDP, measured at constant 1981 prices, in 2001. The sector employed 16.0% of the labour force in 2000. The principal branches of manufacturing were food products, beverages and tobacco, machinery and industrial chemicals. In 2000 50% of the state citrus marketing company was purchased by a French-Spanish company, Altadis. During 1990–98 manufacturing GDP declined, in real terms, at an average annual rate of 1.0%. The sector's GDP increased by 7.1% in 1999, by 4.3% in 2000 and by 0.5% in 2001. The biomedical industry continued to expand in the 1990s and in July 1999 a joint venture was agreed with the pharmaceutical manufacturer SmithKline Beecham to market the Cuban meningitis vaccine.

Energy is derived principally from petroleum and natural gas. In 2002 total crude petroleum production was 3.6m. metric tons; production was expected to reach 4.2m. tons in 2003. In 2001 Cuba produced approximately 65,000 b/d of crude petroleum and 1.8m. cu m of natural gas per day. Imports of mineral fuels accounted for 24.0% of the total cost of imports in 2000. Formerly, some 13m. tons of petroleum were imported annually from the USSR, with 2m. tons being re-exported, but in 1990 imports were dramatically reduced. In 2002 the country generated 92% of its electricity requirement from domestically-produced petroleum and natural gas. Cuba expected to be self-sufficient in oil production by 2005. To this end, in 2001 Cuba began talks with Mexico on a possible bilateral agreement on energy efficiency, and in November Venezuela agreed to meet one-third of Cuba's petroleum requirements, on preferential terms, in exchange for medical and sports services. However, in 2002 petroleum shipments from Venezuela suffered some disruption owing to domestic unrest in that country (see chapter on Venezuela). In 2000 two oil-processing plants were planned for Santiago de Cuba and Cienfuegos and two power-generation plants were being built by Sherritt Power of Canada. In December Cuba announced that construction of the Juragua nuclear power plant, which had never been completed, was to be abandoned. However, in February 2001 the Slovakian engineering company, SES Tlmace, won a contract to reconstruct the oil-burning power-station in Santa Cruz. In June the construction of a 25 km petroleum pipeline between Matanzas province and Puerto Escondido was being finalized. When complete, it was to be operated by the state petroleum company.

Services accounted for 64.7% of GDP, measured at constant 1981 prices, in 2001. The sector employed 51.6% of the labour force in 2000. Tourism is one of the country's principal sources of foreign exchange, earning an estimated US $1,759m. in 2000, and development of the sector remains a priority of the Government. The country's 20 airports were modernized and expanded through state and foreign investment during the late 1990s. In real terms, the GDP of the service sector decreased at an average rate of 3.0% per year during 1990–98. The GDP of services increased by 5.6% in 1999, by 4.9% in 2000 and by 4.3% in 2001.

In 1999 Cuba recorded a trade deficit of US $600m., and a deficit of $350m. on the current account of the balance of payments. In 2000 the principal source of imports was Venezuela (18.6%). In 2000 Russia was the principal market for exports, accounting for 19.4% of the total. Other major trading partners were Spain and Canada. The principal imports in 2000 were mineral fuels, machinery and transport equipment. The principal exports in that year were food and live animals, and crude materials (excluding fuels).

In 2001 Cuba recorded an estimated budget deficit of 759m. pesos. According to the Central Bank, the country's external debt to Western creditor nations was US $11,078.0m. in 1999. Cuba's debt to the former USSR was estimated to be $20,000m. in 2000. In December of that year the Russian Government proposed writing off 70% of this debt and renegotiating the remainder through the 'Paris Club' of Western government creditors. However, the Cuban Government refused to negotiate with the Paris Club and disputed the size of the debt owed to Russia. Bilateral discussions with Russia took place in 2000–01 and included the possible conversion of debt to equity through joint-venture contracts. According to official figures, some 5.8% of the labour force were unemployed at the end of 2000. Although no index of consumer prices is published, official estimates put inflation at 2.9% in 1998 and at 0.3% in 1999.

Cuba is a member of the Latin American Economic System (see p. 340) and of the Group of Latin American and Caribbean Sugar Exporting Countries (see p. 336).

In the early 1990s Cuba suffered severe economic decline, prompted by the collapse of the USSR and by the consequent termination of the favourable aid and trade arrangements that had supported the Cuban economy. Resultant shortages, particularly of petroleum and basic raw materials, seriously affected production in all sectors and necessitated wide-ranging austerity measures. In 1994, in a significant departure from the country's traditional command economy, a series of adjustment measures was introduced. The measures included the introduction of new taxes and the drastic reduction (by some 40%) of subsidies to loss-making state enterprises. In December 1994 a new 'convertible peso' was introduced to regulate the circulation of foreign currency. A new investment law, approved in September 1995, opened all sectors of the economy, with the exception of defence, health and education, to foreign participation and introduced the possibility of 100% foreign ownership.

In 1996 the USA intensified its sanctions against Cuba with the introduction of the Cuban Liberty and Solidarity (Helms-Burton) Act. Denied access to medium- and long-term loans, Cuba's indebtedness increased substantially as high-interest short-term loans were contracted in order to finance production, most notably in the sugar industry. In 1997 three free-trade zones were opened to attract foreign investment. During 1999 the Central Bank made known its intention henceforth to prefer to conduct international transactions in euros, hoping thus to weaken the stranglehold of the US dollar on the Cuban economy. In October 2001 the Government announced that, thenceforth, only US paper currency would be accepted, owing to the high cost of handling and exporting US coin currency.

In 1999 the largest investments were in the mining (specifically nickel), tourism and telecommunications sectors. In December a 50% stake in Habanos, the state-owned cigar distributor, was sold for US $500m. In mid-2000 the EU called for a WTO disputes panel to rule on Section 211 of the 1998 US Omnibus Appropriations Act, under which trademarks used in connection with assets confiscated by the Cuban Government could not be registered without permission from the original owner. This followed a 1999 US court ruling against Havana Club International, a joint venture between Pernod Ricard of France and Cuba's Havana Rum and Liquors, concerning the use of the Havana Club rum brand name in the USA (the ruling was upheld by the US Supreme Court in October 2000). In response to the ruling, Cuba announced a new Bacardí brand, initiating a further dispute, this time with the Bacardí company in Bermuda. In January 2002 the WTO ruled that, in part, Section 211 violated the pact on protection of intellectual property and recommended that the USA bring its measures into conformity with the pact.

In October 2000, following an acrimonious passage through the US Congress, legislation was approved that allowed US food and medicine sales to Cuba. However, the potential for such trade was restricted by the conditions attached, such as a ban on financing by US banks or official credits. Imports of most Cuban goods remained illegal. Other sanctions legislation, such as the Torricelli and Helms-Burton Acts and the 'Trading with the Enemy' Act, remained operational, including a clause of the Torricelli Act that forbade ships to enter US ports within six months of entering a Cuban port for the purpose of trade. However, in February 2001 the USA granted the first licence to run a scheduled route to Cuba to the shipping company, Crowley Liner Services. In July further regulations regarding US sales to Cuba were introduced. The Cuban Government responded by refusing to trade with the USA under what it considered 'discriminatory and humiliating terms'. However, in November, in the wake of Hurricane Michelle, both Cuba and the USA allowed temporary trade in products necessary to the reconstruction and aid effort. In September 2002, although the trade and travel restrictions remained in operation, the first US food fair since 1959 was held in Havana as the business sector chose to take advantage of the easing of the embargo; Cuba purchased an estimated US $66m. of foodstuffs at the fair. In 2002 economic growth was estimated to have been 1.1%, compared with 3.0% in the previous year. The slowdown was believed to have resulted from a global economic contraction, together with a decline in tourism (partly a result of the ongoing effects of the terrorist attacks on the USA in September 2001), high crude petroleum prices, hurricane damage and a decrease in foreign direct investment (FDI).

Education

Education is universal and free at all levels. Education is based on Marxist-Leninist principles and combines study with manual work. Day nurseries are available for all children after their 45th day, and national schools at the pre-primary level are operated by the State for children of five years of age. Primary education, from six to 11 years of age, is compulsory, and secondary education lasts from 12 to 17 years of age, comprising two cycles of three years each. In 1998 primary enrolment included almost 100% of children in the relevant age-group, while secondary enrolment was equivalent to 87% of the population in the appropriate age-group. In 2001/02 there were an estimated 131,200 students in higher education. Workers attending university courses receive a state subsidy to provide for their dependants. Courses at intermediate and higher levels lay an emphasis on technology, agriculture and teacher training. In 2001 budgetary expenditure on education was estimated at 2,374m. pesos (15.3% of total spending).

Public Holidays

2003: 1 January (Liberation Day), 1 May (Labour Day), 25–27 July (Anniversary of the 1953 Revolution), 10 October (Wars of Independence Day), 25 December (Christmas Day).

2004: 1 January (Liberation Day), 1 May (Labour Day), 25–27 July (Anniversary of the 1953 Revolution), 10 October (Wars of Independence Day), 25 December (Christmas Day).

Weights and Measures

The metric system is in force.

Statistical Survey

Source (unless otherwise stated): Cámara de Comercio de la República de Cuba, Calle 21, No 661/701, esq. Calle A, Apdo 4237, Vedado, Havana; tel. (7) 55-1321; fax (7) 33-3042; internet www.camaracuba.cubaweb.cu; Oficina Nacional de Estadísticas, Calle Paseo 60, entre 3 y 5, Vedado, Havana; tel. (7) 30-0005; fax (7) 33-3083; internet www.cubagov.cu/otras_info/estadisticas.htm.

Area and Population

AREA, POPULATION AND DENSITY

Area (sq km)	110,860*
Population (census results)	
6 September 1970	8,569,121
11 September 1981	
Males	4,914,873
Females	4,808,732
Total	9,723,605
Population (official estimates at mid-year)	
1999	11,142,691
2000	11,187,673
2001	11,229,688
Density (per sq km) at mid-2001	101.3

* 42,803 sq miles.

PROVINCES
(31 December 2001)

	Population (estimates)
Camagüey	791,800
Ciego de Avila	413,500
Cienfuegos	398,600
Granma	835,200
Guantánamo.	516,300
La Habana	2,893,100
Holguín	1,035,800
Isla de la Juventud	80,600
Matanzas.	665,400
Pinar del Río	739,400
Sancti Spíritus	463,300
Santiago de Cuba	1,041,400
Las Tunas	532,600
Villa Clara	836,400
Total	11,243,400

PRINCIPAL TOWNS
(population in 1999)

La Habana (Havana, the capital). . .	2,189,716	Pinar del Río . . .	148,500
Santiago de Cuba .	441,524	Bayamo	143,600
Camagüey . . .	306,049	Cienfuegos . . .	137,513
Holguín . . .	259,300	Las Tunas . . .	137,331
Santa Clara . . .	210,100	Matanzas . . .	124,754
Guantánamo. . .	208,030	Sancti Spíritus *. .	103,591

* 1998 figure.
Source: UN Citydata.

BIRTHS, MARRIAGES AND DEATHS*

	Registered live births†		Registered marriages‡		Registered deaths	
	Number	Rate (per 1,000)	Number	Rate (per 1,000)	Number	Rate (per 1,000)
1993 . .	152,233	14.0	135,138	12.4	78,531	7.2
1994 . .	147,265	13.4	116,935	10.7	78,648	7.2
1995 . .	147,170	13.4	70,413	6.4	77,937	7.1
1996 . .	140,276	12.7	65,009	5.9	79,662	7.2
1997 . .	152,681	13.8	60,900	5.5	77,316	7.0
1998 . .	151,080	13.6	64,900	5.8	77,565	7.0
1999 . .	150,785	13.5	57,300	5.1	79,499	7.1
2000 . .	143,528	12.8	57,000	5.1	76,448	6.8

* Data are tabulated by year of registration rather than by year of occurrence.
† Births registered in the National Consumers Register, established on 31 December 1964.
‡ Including consensual unions formalized in response to special legislation.

Expectation of life (WHO estimates, years at birth): 76.9 (males 74.7; females 79.2) in 2001 (Source: WHO, *World Health Report*).

ECONOMICALLY ACTIVE POPULATION
('000 persons aged 17 years and over, with exception of 15 and 16 year olds with permission from relevant authorities)

	1998	1999	2000
Agriculture, hunting, forestry and fishing	921.6	912.6	937.9
Mining and quarrying . . .	53.7	42.3	50.5
Manufacturing	577.0	637.1	615.0
Electricity, gas and water . . .	57.9	65.5	53.2
Construction	224.9	208.1	204.5
Trade, restaurants and hotels . .	446.5	482.0	473.6
Transport, storage and communications	199.6	181.1	194.9
Financing, insurance, real estate and business services	59.8	69.7	55.0
Community, social and personal services	1,212.6	1,222.9	1,258.4
Total labour force (incl. others)	3,753.6	3,821.3	3,843.0

CIVILIAN EMPLOYMENT IN THE STATE SECTOR
('000 persons)

	1998	1999	2000
Agriculture, hunting, forestry and fishing	733.1	714.4	714.2
Mining and quarrying	47.3	20.8	20.8
Manufacturing	458.9	512.7	512.6
Electricity, gas and water . . .	46.0	51.0	51.0
Construction	178.9	167.1	167.8
Trade, restaurants and hotels . .	355.2	375.2	375.2
Transport, storage and communications	175.2	157.4	157.4
Financing, insurance, real estate and business services	47.6	54.3	54.3
Community, social and personal services	964.5	952.1	951.8
Total	3,006.7	3,005.0	3,005.1

Health and Welfare

KEY INDICATORS

Total fertility rate (children per woman, 2001)	1.6
Under-5 mortality rate (per 1,000 live births, 2001) . . .	9
HIV/AIDS (% of persons aged 15–49, 2001)	<0.10
Physicians (per 1,000 head, 1997)	5.30
Hospital beds (per 1,000 head, 1996)	5.13
Health expenditure (2000): US $ per head (PPP)	186
Health expenditure (2000): % of GDP	6.8
Health expenditure (2000): public (% of total)	89.2
Access to water (% of persons, 2000)	95
Access to sanitation (% of persons, 2000)	95
Human Development Index (2000): value	0.795

For sources and definitions, see explanatory note on p. vi.

Agriculture

PRINCIPAL CROPS

('000 metric tons)

	1999	2000	2001*
Rice (paddy)	368.6	305.9	350
Maize	185.3	203.8	205
Potatoes	344.2	367.9	350
Sweet potatoes	195.4	219.5	200
Cassava (Manioc)	280.9	333.9	300
Yautia (Cocoyam)	26.8	32.5	40
Sugar cane	34,000	36,400	35,000
Dry beans	38.1	59.6	25
Groundnuts (in shell)*	15	15	15
Coconuts*	26	26	26
Cabbages*	30	30	30
Tomatoes	129.6	153.9	150
Pumpkins, squash and gourds* . .	50	50	50
Cucumbers and gherkins* . . .	40	40	40
Dry onions	14.7	20.1	21
Other vegetables*	90.7	92.8	94
Bananas	151.9	185.1	180
Plantains	341.5	402.0	380
Oranges	440.6	440.8	350
Lemons and limes	21.1	18.7	15
Grapefruit and pomelos . . .	232.9	188.8	170
Mangoes	64.3	45.5	45
Pineapples*	19	19	19
Papayas	36.5	43.8	40
Other fruit*	89.7	91.2	91.7
Coffee (green)†	22.0	16.5	15
Fibre crops*	27.5	27.5	27.5
Tobacco (leaves)	30.6	38.0	35

* FAO estimates.
† Unofficial figures.

Source: FAO.

LIVESTOCK

('000 head, year ending September)

	1999	2000	2001*
Cattle	4,405.8	4,110.2	4,400
Horses	430.4	414.8	400
Mules	24.2	23.3	23
Pigs*	2,500	2,600	2,700
Sheep*	310	310	310
Goats	207.5	249.3	240
Poultry	13,151	13,232	13,300

* FAO estimates.

Source: FAO.

LIVESTOCK PRODUCTS

('000 metric tons)

	1999	2000	2001*
Beef and veal	72.7	72.6	77
Pig meat	103.4	103.1	112†
Chicken meat	60.1	59.4	60†
Cows' milk	617.8	614.1	614.1
Cheese*	14.5	14.5	14.5
Butter†	6.9	7.1	7.2
Hen eggs	69.8	65.4	67.5
Honey	6.7	6.9	7
Hides and skins	11.5	11.6	11.6

* FAO estimates.
† Unofficial figure(s).

Source: FAO.

Forestry

ROUNDWOOD REMOVALS

('000 cubic metres, excl. bark, FAO estimates)

	1999	2000	2001
Sawlogs, veneer logs and logs for sleepers	128	400	400
Other industrial wood	278	456	408
Fuel wood	1,187	963	888
Total	1,593	1,819	1,696

Source: FAO.

SAWNWOOD PRODUCTION

('000 cubic metres, incl. railway sleepers, FAO estimates)

	1999	2000	2001
Coniferous (softwood)	66	101	107
Broadleaved (hardwood)	80	78	83
Total	146	179	190

Source: FAO.

Fishing

('000 metric tons, live weight)

	1998	1999	2000*
Capture	67.1	67.4	56.1
Blue tilapia	5.1	4.6	4.5
Silver hake	6.3	3.9	—
Caribbean spiny lobster . . .	9.4	9.9	9.9
Aquaculture	46.7	55.2	52.7
Silver carp	25.7	32.0	30.0
Total catch	113.8	122.4	108.8

* FAO estimate(s).
Note: Figures exclude crocodiles, recorded by number rather than by weight. The number of spectacled caimans caught was: 5 in 1998; 2 in 1999. The number of Cuban crocodiles caught was: 3 in 1998. Also excluded are sponges (metric tons): 72.1 in 1998; 50.1 in 1999; 50.0 in 2000 (FAO estimate).

Source: FAO, *Yearbook of Fishery Statistics*.

Mining

('000 metric tons, unless otherwise indicated)

	1999	2000	2001
Crude petroleum	2,136.3	2,695.3	2,285.5
Natural gas (million cu metres) .	460.0	574.5	594.6
Nickel and cobalt (metal content) .	66.5	71.4	76.5
Crushed stone ('000 cu metres) .	2,950.3	3,301.3	n.a.

Industry

SELECTED PRODUCTS
('000 metric tons, unless otherwise indicated)

	1999	2000	2001
Crude steel	302.7	327.3	269.6
Grey cement	1,784.6	1,632.7	1,324.1
Detergent	12.9	13.4	15.9
Fertilizers	138.3	118.2	n.a.
Tyres ('000)	156.6	160.5	144.7
Woven textile fabrics (million sq metres)	51.0	47.4	46.9
Cotton yarn	3.2	2.2	n.a.
Cigarettes ('000 million)	12.3	12.1	11.8
Cigars (million)	284.0	240.9	330.3
Raw sugar	3,700.0	3,900.0	n.a.
Beer ('000 hectolitres)	2,008.5	2,136.1	2,196.5
Soft drinks ('000 hectolitres)	2,743.0	2,842.0	n.a.
Electric energy (million kWh)	14,487.5	15,028.8	15,301.3

Finance

CURRENCY AND EXCHANGE RATES

Monetary Units
100 centavos = 1 Cuban peso

Sterling, Dollar and Euro Equivalents (31 December 2002)
£1 sterling = 1.612 pesos
US $1 = 1.0000 pesos
€1 = 1.049 pesos
100 Cuban pesos = £62.04 = $100.00 = €95.36

Note: The foregoing information relates to official exchange rates. For the purposes of foreign trade, the peso was at par with the US dollar during each of the 10 years 1987–96. A 'convertible peso' was introduced in December 1994. The free market rate of exchange in September 1998 was US $1 = 23 Cuban pesos.

STATE BUDGET
(million pesos)

	2000	2001
Total revenue	14,915.2	14,774.0
Road tax	6,130.7	5,650.0
Social security contributions	1,181.2	1,242.0
Total expenditure	15,587.4	15,533.0
Entrepreneurial activity	3,075.7	2,625.0
Education	2,094.6	2,374.0
Health care	1,683.8	1,820.0
Social security	1,785.6	1,862.0
Management	509.1	570.0

Source: Ministry of Finance and Prices.

INTERNATIONAL RESERVES
(million pesos at 31 December)

	1987	1988
Gold and other precious metals	17.5	19.5
Cash and deposits in foreign banks (convertible currency)	36.5	78.0
Sub-total	54.0	97.5
Deposits in foreign banks (in transferable roubles)	142.5	137.0
Total	196.5	234.5

NATIONAL ACCOUNTS

Composition of Gross National Product
(million pesos at current prices)

	1998	1999	2000
Compensation of employees	10,328.3	11,146.9	11,965.8
Operating surplus			
Consumption of fixed capital	6,631.8	8,570.3	9,538.2
Gross domestic product (GDP) at factor cost	16,960.1	19,717.2	21,504.0
Indirect taxes *less* subsidies	6,940.7	5,786.4	6,130.7
GDP in purchasers' values	23,900.8	25,503.6	27,634.7
Less Factor income paid abroad (net)	599.2	514.1	693.0
Gross national product	23,301.6	24,989.5	26,941.7

Source: UN Economic Commission for Latin America and the Caribbean, *Statistical Yearbook*.

1999 (million pesos at current prices): GDP in purchasers' values 25,503.6.

Expenditure on the Gross Domestic Product
(million pesos at current prices)

	1998	1999	2000
Government final consumption expenditure	5,642.3	5,986.5	6,388.7
Private final consumption expenditure	17,109.0	17,949.0	19,227.0
Increase in stocks	−544.2	−395.8	−287.2
Gross fixed capital formation	2,431.4	2,646.7	2,979.9
Total domestic expenditure	24,638.5	26,186.4	28,308.4
Exports of goods and services	3,872.3	4,078.4	4,348.9
Less Imports of goods and services	4,610.0	4,761.2	5,022.6
GDP in purchasers' values	23,900.8	25,503.6	27,634.7
GDP at constant 1981 prices	14,754.0	15,674.4	16,556.4

Source: UN Economic Commission for Latin America and the Caribbean, *Statistical Yearbook*.

Gross Domestic Product by Economic Activity
(million pesos at current prices)

	1998	1999	2000
Agriculture, hunting, forestry and fishing	1,473.2	1,633.2	1,843.8
Mining and quarrying	360.5	370.8	478.5
Manufacturing	8,923.2	9,864.1	10,270.3
Electricity, gas and water	471.8	486.3	532.8
Construction	1,282.5	1,383.5	1,550.8
Wholesale and retail trade, restaurants and hotels	5,023.4	5,053.5	5,768.3
Transport, storage and communications	1,061.1	1,139.1	1,267.7
Finance, insurance, real estate and business services	546.6	579.5	614.8
Community, social and personal services	4,372.9	4,583.7	4,913.0
Sub total	23,515.0	25,094.0	27,240.0
Import duties	385.6	409.9	394.7
Total	23,900.8	25,503.6	27,637.7

Source: UN Economic Commission for Latin America and the Caribbean, *Statistical Yearbook*.

BALANCE OF PAYMENTS
(million pesos)

	1996	1997	1998
Exports of goods	1,866.2	1,823.1	1,444.4
Imports of goods	−3,656.5	−4,087.6	−4,229.7
Trade balance	−1,790.3	−2,264.5	−2,785.3
Services (net)	1,372.4	1,519.0	2,168.2
Balance on goods and services	−417.9	−745.5	−617.1
Other income (net)	−492.6	−482.9	−599.2
Balance on goods, services and income	−910.5	−1,228.4	−1,216.3
Current transfers (net)	743.7	791.7	820.0
Current balance	−166.8	−436.7	−396.3
Direct investment (net)	82.1	442.0	206.6
Other long-term capital (net)	225.8	344.9	426.1
Other capital (net)	−133.5	−329.5	−219.4
Overall balance	7.6	20.7	17.0

External Trade

PRINCIPAL COMMODITIES
('000 pesos)

Imports c.i.f.	1998	1999	2000
Food and live animals	704,200	722,396	671,801
Cereals and cereal preparations	348,260	313,755	285,541
Wheat and meslin (unmilled)	178,590	122,979	112,187
Rice	99,382	141,163	100,772
Mineral fuels, lubricants, etc.	687,030	730,763	1,158,071
Petroleum and petroleum products	664,844	710,881	1,137,418
Crude petroleum oils, etc.	65,358	88,087	279,901
Gas oils	151,819	198,056	301,551
Chemicals and related products	419,720	428,938	418,765
Basic manufactures	628,672	687,889	673,195
Iron and steel	117,098	150,889	111,940
Manufactures of metal	141,184	152,491	162,428
Machinery and transport equipment	1,130,414	1,144,441	1,202,330
Power-generating machinery and equipment	208,992	129,110	131,725
General industrial machinery and equipment and machine parts	249,889	269,441	259,300
Total (incl. others)	4,181,192	4,349,090	4,829,050

Exports f.o.b.	1998	1999	2000
Food and live animals	776,262	659,992	657,305
Fish, crustaceans and molluscs and preparations thereof	102,786	96,055	87,830
Fresh, chilled or frozen fish	102,661	95,267	87,176
Fruit and vegetables	35,201	74,980	89,618
Sugar, sugar preparations and honey	605,494	470,680	458,427
Raw beet and cane sugars (solid)	593,694	458,210	447,677
Beverages and tobacco	202,562	218,471	179,719
Manufactured tobacco	162,750	173,477	140,346
Crude materials (inedible) except fuels	358,781	436,808	623,089
Metalliferous ores and metal scrap	351,926	430,393	617,787
Nickel ores, concentrates, etc.	168,017	201,649	318,706
Petroleum, petroleum products and related materials	445	18,934	52,388
Chemicals and related products	45,566	39,662	41,235
Basic manufactures	97,202	94,268	99,230
Iron and steel	45,985	43,430	61,484
Total (incl. others)	1,512,197	1,495,783	1,675,868

PRINCIPAL TRADING PARTNERS
('000 pesos)

Imports c.i.f.	1998	1999	2000
Argentina	108,827	129,938	106,424
Brazil	63,630	75,761	130,129
Canada	321,046	339,642	311,074
China, People's Republic	336,496	432,241	445,769
Colombia	30,312	36,978	85,156
France	318,381	276,337	289,876
Germany	78,140	75,967	77,841
Italy	253,203	264,063	296,602
Mexico	342,796	321,772	298,527
Netherlands Antilles	74,397	84,312	25,788
Spain	608,210	721,771	743,589
Russia	134,881	124,545	111,300
United Kingdom	54,022	41,193	56,864
Venezuela	385,570	451,451	898,393
Total (incl. others)	4,181,192	4,349,090	4,829,050

Exports f.o.b.	1998	1999	2000
Belgium	41,407	43,978	48,289
Canada	230,169	229,185	277,728
China, People's Republic	81,855	49,491	80,532
Colombia	20,610	5,853	18,941
Dominican Republic	31,272	44,580	19,823
France	43,110	50,517	42,411
Germany	67,859	72,596	120,882
Iran	14,442	19,620	14,179
Italy	27,979	39,283	34,198
Japan	19,478	49,506	29,374
Korea, People's Democratic Republic	24,609	35,157	43
Mexico	45,134	25,049	39,285
Netherlands	53,074	93,037	116,842
Portugal	14,562	26,424	17,844
Russia	355,254	302,776	324,577
Spain	141,069	159,409	149,656
Sweden	31,346	35,240	50,426
Switzerland	21,466	24,329	22,602
Taiwan	23,343	2,422	11,210
Ukraine	22,614	1,199	478
United Kingdom	24,687	30,206	38,101
Total (incl. others)	1,512,197	1,495,783	1,675,868

Transport

RAILWAYS

	1998	1999	2000
Passenger-kilometres (million)	1,750	1,499	1,853
Freight ton-kilometres (million)	822	806	804

Source: UN, *Statistical Yearbook*.

Passengers ('000): 15,100 in 2000; 15,000 in 2001.

Freight carried ('000 metric tons): 6,006.0 in 2000; 5,380.2 in 2001.

ROAD TRAFFIC
(motor vehicles in use at 31 December)

	1996	1997
Passenger cars	216,575	172,574
Buses and coaches	28,089	28,861
Lorries and vans	246,105	156,634

Source: IRF, *World Road Statistics*.

SHIPPING

Merchant Fleet
(registered at 31 December)

	1999	2000	2001
Number of vessels	100	99	92
Total displacement ('000 grt)	130	120	101

Source: Lloyd's Register-Fairplay, *World Fleet Statistics*.

International Sea-borne Freight Traffic
('000 metric tons)

	1988	1989	1990
Goods loaded	8,600	8,517	8,092
Goods unloaded	15,500	15,595	15,440

Source: UN, *Monthly Bulletin of Statistics*.

CIVIL AVIATION
(traffic on scheduled services)

	1997	1998	1999
Kilometres flown (million) . . .	26	34	26
Passengers carried ('000) . . .	1,117	1,138	1,259
Passenger-kilometres (million) .	3,543	4,791	3,712
Total ton-kilometres (million) . .	388	524	421

Source: UN, *Statistical Yearbook*.

Passengers ('000): 1,700 in 1999; 1,400 in 2000; 1,300 in 2001.

Freight carried (metric tons): 13,300 in 1999; 10,700 in 2000; 10,800 in 2001.

Tourism

ARRIVALS BY NATIONALITY*

	1998	1999	2000
Argentina	47,579	42,612	54,185
Canada	215,644	276,346	307,725
France	101,604	123,607	132,089
Germany	148,987	182,159	203,403
Italy	186,688	160,843	175,667
Mexico	61,589	70,983	86,540
Spain	140,435	146,978	153,197
United Kingdom	64,276	85,829	90,972
USA	46,778	62,345	76,898
Total (incl. others)	1,415,832	1,602,781	1,773,986

* Figures include same-day visitors (excursionists).

Sources: World Tourism Organization, *Yearbook of Tourism Statistics*; World Bank, *World Development Indicators*.

Tourism arrivals ('000): 1,774 in 2000; 1,774.5 in 2001.

Tourism receipts (US $ million): 1,626 in 1998; 1,714 in 1999; 1,759 in 2000.

Communications Media

	1999	2000	2001
Telephones ('000 main lines in use)	433.8	488.6	572.6
Mobile cellular telephones ('000 subscribers)	5.1	6.5	8.1
Personal computers ('000 in use)	110	n.a.	220
Internet users ('000)	34.8	60.0	120.0
Book production (titles)	708	n.a.	1,004

Radio receivers ('000 in use): 3,900 in 1997.

Television receivers ('000 in use): 2,800 in 2000.

Facsimile machines (number in use): 392 in 1992.

Daily newspapers: 17 in 1996 (average estimated circulation 1.3m. copies).

Sources: UNESCO, *Statistical Yearbook*; UN, *Statistical Yearbook*; International Telecommunication Union.

Education

(2001/02)

	Institutions	Teachers	Students
Pre-primary	1,117	18,900	146,600
Primary	9,358	83,100	916,500
Secondary	2,015	83,100	949,800
Universities	49	24,200	131,200

Adult literacy rate (UNESCO estimates): 97% in 2000 (Source: UN Development Programme, *Human Development Report*).

Directory

The Constitution

Following the assumption of power by the Castro regime, on 1 January 1959, the Constitution was suspended and a Fundamental Law of the Republic was instituted, with effect from 7 February 1959. In February 1976 Cuba's first socialist Constitution came into force after being submitted to the first Congress of the Communist Party of Cuba, in December 1975, and to popular referendum, in February 1976; it was amended in July 1992. The main provisions of the Constitution, as amended, are summarized below:

Note: On 27 July 2002 the Constitution was further amended to enshrine the socialist system as irrevocable and to ratify that economic, diplomatic and political relations with another state cannot be negotiated in face of aggression, threat or pressure from a foreign power. A clause was also introduced making it impossible to remove these amendments from the Constitution.

POLITICAL, SOCIAL AND ECONOMIC PRINCIPLES

The Republic of Cuba is a socialist, independent, and sovereign state, organized with all and for the sake of all as a unitary and democratic republic for the enjoyment of political freedom, social justice, collective and individual well-being and human solidarity. Sovereignty rests with the people, from whom originates the power of the State. The Communist Party of Cuba is the leading force of society and the State. The State recognizes, respects and guarantees freedom of religion. Religious institutions are separate from the State. The socialist State carries out the will of the working people and guarantees work, medical care, education, food, clothing and housing. The Republic of Cuba bases its relations with other socialist countries on socialist internationalism, friendship, co-operation and mutual assistance. It reaffirms its willingness to integrate with and co-operate with the countries of Latin America and the Caribbean.

The State organizes and directs the economic life of the nation in accordance with a central social and economic development plan. The State directs and controls foreign trade. The State recognizes the right of small farmers to own their lands and other means of production and to sell that land. The State guarantees the right of citizens to ownership of personal property in the form of earnings, savings, place of residence and other possessions and objects which serve to satisfy their material and cultural needs. The State also guarantees the right of inheritance.

Cuban citizenship is acquired by birth or through naturalization.

The State protects the family, motherhood and matrimony.

The State directs and encourages all aspects of education, culture and science.

All citizens have equal rights and are subject to equal duties.

The State guarantees the right to medical care, education, freedom of speech and press, assembly, demonstration, association and privacy. In the socialist society work is the right and duty, and a source of pride for every citizen.

GOVERNMENT

National Assembly of People's Power

The National Assembly of People's Power (Asamblea Nacional del Poder Popular) is the supreme organ of the State and is the only organ with constituent and legislative authority. It is composed of deputies, over the age of 18, elected by free, direct and secret ballot, for a period of five years. All Cuban citizens aged 16 years or more, except those who are mentally incapacitated or who have committed a crime, are eligible to vote. The National Assembly of People's Power holds two ordinary sessions a year and a special session when requested by one-third of the deputies or by the Council of State. More than one-half of the total number of deputies must be present for a session to be held.

All decisions made by the Assembly, except those relating to constitutional reforms, are adopted by a simple majority of votes. The deputies may be recalled by their electors at any time.

The National Assembly of People's Power has the following functions:

to reform the Constitution;

to approve, modify and annul laws;

to supervise all organs of the State and government;

to decide on the constitutionality of laws and decrees;

to revoke decree-laws issued by the Council of State and the Council of Ministers;

to discuss and approve economic and social development plans, the state budget, monetary and credit systems;

to approve the general outlines of foreign and domestic policy, to ratify and annul international treaties, to declare war and approve peace treaties;

to approve the administrative division of the country;

to elect the President, First Vice-President, the Vice-Presidents and other members of the Council of State;

to elect the President, Vice-President and Secretary of the National Assembly;

to appoint the members of the Council of Ministers on the proposal of the President of the Council of State;

to elect the President, Vice-President and other judges of the People's Supreme Court;

to elect the Attorney-General and the Deputy Attorney-Generals;

to grant amnesty;

to call referendums.

The President of the National Assembly presides over sessions of the Assembly, calls ordinary sessions, proposes the draft agenda, signs the Official Gazette, organizes the work of the commissions appointed by the Assembly and attends the meetings of the Council of State.

Council of State

The Council of State is elected from the members of the National Assembly and represents that Assembly in the period between sessions. It comprises a President, one First Vice-President, five Vice-Presidents, one Secretary and 23 other members. Its mandate ends when a new Assembly meets. All decisions are adopted by a simple majority of votes. It is accountable for its actions to the National Assembly.

The Council of State has the following functions:

to call special sessions of the National Assembly;

to set the date for the election of a new Assembly;

to issue decree-laws in the period between the sessions of the National Assembly;

to decree mobilization in the event of war and to approve peace treaties when the Assembly is in recess;

to issue instructions to the courts and the Office of the Attorney-General of the Republic;

to appoint and remove ambassadors of Cuba abroad on the proposal of its President, to grant or refuse recognition to diplomatic representatives of other countries to Cuba;

to suspend those provisions of the Council of Ministers that are not in accordance with the Constitution;

to revoke the resolutions of the Executive Committee of the local organs of People's Power which are contrary to the Constitution or laws and decrees formulated by other higher organs.

The President of the Council of State is Head of State and Head of Government and for all purposes the Council of State is the highest representative of the Cuban state.

Head of State

The President of the Council of State is the Head of State and the Head of Government and has the following powers:

to represent the State and Government and conduct general policy;

to convene and preside over the sessions of the Council of State and the Council of Ministers;

to supervise the ministries and other administrative bodies;

to propose the members of the Council of Ministers to the National Assembly of People's Power;

to receive the credentials of the heads of foreign diplomatic missions;

to sign the decree-laws and other resolutions of the Council of State;

to exercise the Supreme Command of all armed institutions and determine their general organization;

to preside over the National Defence Council;

to declare a state of emergency in the cases outlined in the Constitution.

In the case of absence, illness or death of the President of the Council of State, the First Vice-President assumes the President's duties.

The Council of Ministers

The Council of Ministers is the highest-ranking executive and administrative organ. It is composed of the Head of State and

Government, as its President, the First Vice-President, the Vice-Presidents, the Ministers, the Secretary and other members determined by law. Its Executive Committee is composed of the President, the First Vice-President, the Vice-Presidents and other members of the Council of Ministers determined by the President.

The Council of Ministers has the following powers:

to conduct political, economic, cultural, scientific, social and defence policy as outlined by the National Assembly;

to approve international treaties;

to propose projects for the general development plan and, if they are approved by the National Assembly, to supervise their implementation;

to conduct foreign policy and trade;

to draw up bills and submit them to the National Assembly;

to draw up the draft state budget;

to conduct general administration, implement laws, issue decrees and supervise defence and national security.

The Council of Ministers is accountable to the National Assembly of People's Power.

LOCAL GOVERNMENT

The country is divided into 14 provinces and 169 municipalities. The provinces are: Pinar del Río, Habana, Ciudad de la Habana, Matanzas, Villa Clara, Cienfuegos, Sancti Spíritus, Ciego de Avila, Camagüey, Las Tunas, Holguín, Granma, Santiago de Cuba and Guantánamo.

Voting for delegates to the municipal assemblies is direct, secret and voluntary. All citizens over 16 years of age are eligible to vote. The number of delegates to each assembly is proportionate to the number of people living in that area. A delegate must obtain more than one-half of the total number of votes cast in the constituency in order to be elected. The Municipal and Provincial Assemblies of People's Power are elected by free, direct and secret ballot. Nominations for Municipal and Provincial Executive Committees of People's Power are submitted to the relevant assembly by a commission presided over by a representative of the Communist Party's leading organ and consisting of representatives of youth, workers', farmers', revolutionary and women's organizations. The President and Secretary of each of the regional and the provincial assemblies are the only full-time members, the other delegates carrying out their functions in addition to their normal employment.

The regular and extraordinary sessions of the local Assemblies of People's Power are public. More than one-half of the total number of members must be present in order for agreements made to be valid. Agreements are adopted by simple majority.

JUDICIARY

Judicial power is exercised by the People's Supreme Court and all other competent tribunals and courts. The People's Supreme Court is the supreme judicial authority and is accountable only to the National Assembly of People's Power. It can propose laws and issue regulations through its Council of Government. Judges are independent but the courts must inform the electorate of their activities at least once a year. Every accused person has the right to a defence and can be tried only by a tribunal.

The Office of the Attorney-General is subordinate only to the National Assembly and the Council of State and is responsible for ensuring that the law is properly obeyed.

The Constitution may be totally or partially modified only by a two-thirds majority vote in the National Assembly of People's Power. If the modification is total, or if it concerns the composition and powers of the National Assembly of People's Power or the Council of State, or the rights and duties contained in the Constitution, it also requires a positive vote by referendum.

The Government

Head of State: Dr FIDEL CASTRO RUZ (took office 2 December 1976; re-elected December 1981, December 1986, March 1993, February 1998 and March 2003).

COUNCIL OF STATE
(April 2003)

President: Dr FIDEL CASTRO RUZ.

First Vice-President: Gen. RAÚL CASTRO RUZ.

Vice-Presidents: JUAN ALMEIDA BOSQUE, Gen. ABELARDO COLOMÉ IBARRA, CARLOS LAGE DÁVILA, JUAN ESTEBAN LAZO HERNÁNDEZ, JOSÉ RAMÓN MACHADO VENTURA.

Secretary: Dr JOSÉ M. MIYAR BARRUECOS.

Members: José Ramón Balaguer Cabrera, Vilma Espín Guillois de Castro, Dr Armando Hart Dávalos, Orlando Lugo Fonte, Nidia Diana Martínez Piti, María T. Ferrer Madrazo, Marta Hernández Romero, Gen. Julio Casas Regueiro, Pedro Sáez Montejo, Gen. Roberto Ignacio González Planas, Francisco Soberón Valdés, Pedro Miret Prieto, Ramiro Valdés Menéndez, Julio Cristhian Jiménez Molina, Roberto Fernández Retamar, Felipe Ramón Pérez Roque, Marcos J. Portal León, Luis S. Herrera Martínez, Iris Betancourt Téllez, Pedro Ross Leal, Otto Rivero Torres, Carlos Manuel Valenciaga Díaz, Dra Rosa Elena Simeón Negrín.

COUNCIL OF MINISTERS

President: Dr Fidel Castro Ruz.

First Vice-President: Gen. Raúl Castro Ruz.

Secretary: Carlos Lage Dávila.

Vice-Presidents: Osmany Cienfuegos Gorriarán, Pedro Miret Prieto, José Luis Rodríguez García, José Ramón Fernández Alvarez.

Minister of Agriculture: Alfredo Jordán Morales.

Minister of Foreign Trade: Raúl de la Nuez Ramírez.

Minister of Internal Trade: Barbara Castillo Cuesta.

Minister of Computer Science and Communications: Gen. Roberto Ignacio González Planas.

Minister of Construction: Fidel Fernando Figueroa de la Paz.

Minister of Culture: Abel Enrique Prieto Jiménez.

Minister of Economy and Planning: José Luis Rodríguez García.

Minister of Education: Luis Ignacio Gómez Gutiérrez.

Minister of Higher Education: Fernando Vecino Alegret.

Minister of the Revolutionary Armed Forces: Gen. Raúl Castro Ruz.

Minister of Finance and Prices: José Manuel Millares Rodríguez.

Minister of the Food Industry: Alejandro Roca Iglesias.

Minister of Foreign Investment and Economic Co-operation: Martha Lomas Morales.

Minister of the Sugar Industry: Gen. Ulises Rosales del Toro.

Minister of Light Industry: Jesús D. Pérez Othón.

Minister of the Fishing Industry: Alfredo López Valdés.

Minister of the Iron, Steel and Engineering Industries: Fernando Acosta Santana.

Minister of Basic Industry: Marcos Javier Portal León.

Minister of the Interior: Gen. Abelardo Colomé Ibarra.

Minister of Justice: Roberto T. Díaz Sotolongo.

Minister of Foreign Relations: Felipe Ramón Pérez Roque.

Minister of Labour and Social Security: Alfredo Morales Cartaya.

Minister of Public Health: Damodar Peña Pentón.

Minister of Science, Technology and the Environment: Dra Rosa Elena Simeón Negrín.

Minister of Transportation: Alvaro Pérez Morales.

Minister of Tourism: Ibrahím Ferradaz García.

Minister of Auditing and Control: Lina Olinda Pedraza Rodríguez.

Minister, President of the Banco Central de Cuba: Francisco Soberón Valdés.

Ministers without Portfolio: Ricardo Cabrisas Ruiz, Wilfredo López Rodríguez.

MINISTRIES

Ministry of Agriculture: Avda Independencia, entre Conill y Sta Ana, Havana; tel. (7) 84-5770; fax (7) 33-5086; internet www.cubagob.cu.

Ministry of Auditing and Control: Havana; replaced the National Auditing Office in 2001.

Ministry of Basic Industry: Avda Salvador Allende 666, Havana; tel. (7) 70-7711.

Ministry of Construction: Avda Carlos M. de Céspedes y Calle 35, Havana; tel. (7) 81-8385; fax (7) 33-5585; e-mail dirinter@ceniai.inf .cu; internet www.cubagob.cu.

Ministry of Culture: Calle 2, No 258, entre 11 y 13, Plaza de la Revolución, Vedado, CP 10400, Havana; tel. (7) 55-2260; fax (7) 66-2053; e-mail atencion@min.cult.cu; internet www.ministerio.cult.cu.

Ministry of Economy and Planning: 20 de Mayo y Ayestarán, Plaza de la Revolución, Havana; fax (7) 33-3387.

Ministry of Education: Obispo 160, Havana; tel. (7) 61-4888.

Ministry of Finance and Prices: Calle Obispo 211, esq. Cuba, Havana; tel. (7) 57-3280; fax (7) 33-8050; e-mail sdinformacion@mfp .gov.cu; internet www.mfp.cu.

Ministry of the Fishing Industry: Avda 5 y 248 Jaimanitas, Santa Fé, Havana; tel. (7) 29-7034; fax (7) 24-9168; e-mail alvarez@ fishery.inf.cu.

Ministry of the Food Industry: Avda 41, No 4455, Playa, Havana; tel. (7) 23-6801; fax (7) 23-4052; e-mail minalvm1@ceniai.inf.cu.

Ministry of Foreign Relations: Calzada 360, esq. G, Vedado, Havana; tel. (7) 55-3537; fax (7) 33-3460; e-mail cubaminrex@ minrex.gov.cu; internet www.cubaminrex.cu.

Ministry of Foreign Investment and Economic Co-operation: 512 calle 30, entre 22 y 24, Miramar, Havana; tel. (7) 202-3873; fax (7) 204-2105; e-mail cpinv@minvec.cu.

Ministry of Foreign Trade: Infanta 16, esquina 23, Vedado, Havana; tel. (7) 55-0428; fax (7) 55-0376; e-mail cepecdir@infocex.cu; internet www.infocex.cu/cepec.

Ministry of Higher Education: Calle 23, No 565, esq. a F, Vedado, Havana; tel. (7) 3-; fax (7) 33-3090; e-mail develop@reduniv.edu.cu; internet www.mes.edu.cu.

Ministry of Computer Science and Communications: Plaza de la Revolución 'José Martí', Apdo 10600, Havana; tel. (7) 81-7654.

Ministry of the Interior: Plaza de la Revolución, Havana.

Ministry of Internal Trade: Calle Habana 258, Havana; tel. (7) 62-5790.

Ministry of the Iron, Steel and Engineering Industries: Avda Rancho Boyeros y Calle 100, Havana; tel. (7) 20-4861.

Ministry of Justice: Calle O, No 216, entre 23 y Humboldt, Vedado, Apdo 10400, Havana 4; tel. (7) 32-6319.

Ministry of Labour and Social Security: Calle 23, esq. Calles O y P, Vedado, Havana; tel. (7) 55-0071; fax (7) 33-5816; e-mail mtssmin@ceniai.inf.cu.

Ministry of Light Industry: Empedrado 302, Havana; tel. (7) 67-0387; fax (7) 67-0329; e-mail ministro@minil.org.cu; internet www .ligera.cu.

Ministry of Public Health: Calle 23, No 301, Vedado, Havana; tel. (7) 32-2561; internet www.infomed.sld.cu.

Ministry of the Revolutionary Armed Forces: Plaza de la Revolución, Havana.

Ministry of Science, Technology and the Environment: Havana.

Ministry of Sugar: Calle 23, No 171, Vedado, Havana; tel. (7) 30-5061.

Ministry of Tourism: Havana; internet www.cubatravel.cu.

Ministry of Transportation: Avda Independencia y Tulipán, Havana; tel. (7) 81-2076.

Legislature

ASAMBLEA NACIONAL DEL PODER POPULAR

The National Assembly of People's Power was constituted on 2 December 1976. In July 1992 the National Assembly adopted a constitutional amendment providing for legislative elections by direct vote. Only candidates nominated by the PCC were permitted to contest the elections. At elections to the National Assembly conducted on 19 January 2003 all 609 candidates were elected. Of the 8.2m. registered voters, 97.61% participated in the elections. Only 3.86% of votes cast were blank or spoilt.

President: Ricardo Alarcón de Quesada.

Vice-President: Jaime Crombet Hernández Maurell.

Secretary: Dr Ernesto Suárez Méndez.

Political Organizations

Partido Comunista de Cuba (PCC) (Communist Party of Cuba): Havana; internet www.pcc.cu; f. 1961 as the Organizaciones Revolucionarias Integradas (ORI) from a fusion of the Partido Socialista Popular (Communist), Fidel Castro's Movimiento 26 de Julio and the Directorio Revolucionario 13 de Marzo; became the Partido Unido de la Revolución Socialista Cubana (PURSC) in 1962; renamed as the Partido Comunista de Cuba in 1965; 150-member Central Committee, Political Bureau (23 mems in 2003), and five Commissions; 706,132 mems (1994).

Political Bureau

Dr FIDEL CASTRO RUZ; Gen. RAÚL CASTRO RUZ; JUAN ALMEIDA BOSQUE; JOSÉ RAMÓN MACHADO VENTURA; JUAN ESTEBAN LAZO HERNÁNDEZ; Gen. ABELARDO COLOMÉ IBARRA; PEDRO ROSS LEAL; CARLOS LAGE DÁVILA; ALFREDO JORDÁN MORALES; Gen. ULISES ROSALES DEL TORO; CONCEPCIÓN CAMPA HUERGO; YADIRA GARCÍA VALDÉS; ABEL ENRIQUE PRIETO JIMÉNEZ; Gen. JULIO CASAS REGUEIRO; Gen. LEOPOLDO CINTRA FRÍAS; RICARDO ALARCÓN DE QUESADA; JOSÉ RAMÓN BALAGUER CABRERA; MISAEL ENAMORADO DAGER; Gen. RAMÓN ESPINOSA MARTÍN; MARCOS JAVIER PORTAL LEÓN; JUAN CARLOS ROBINSON AGRAMONTE; PEDRO SÁEZ MONTEJO; JORGE LUIS SIERRA LÓPEZ.

There are a number of dissident groups operating in Cuba. These include:

Concertación Democrática Cubana (CDC): f. 1991; alliance of 11 dissident organizations campaigning for political pluralism and economic reform; Leader ELIZARDO SÁNCHEZ SANTA CRUZ.

Cuban Democratic Platform: f. 1990; alliance comprising three dissident organizations:

Coordinadora Social Demócrata.

Partido Demócrata Cristiano de Cuba (PDC): POB 558987, Miami, FL 33155, USA; tel. (305) 264-9411; fax (954) 489-1572; e-mail amayawarry@aol.com; internet www.pdc-cuba.org; Pres. MARCELINO MIYARES; Sec.-Gen. JULY HERNÁNDEZ.

Unión Liberal Cubana: Menéndez y Pelayo 83, 28007 Madrid, Spain; fax (91) 5011342; e-mail cubaliberal@mercuryin.es; internet www.cubaliberal.org; mem. of Liberal International; Founder and Chair. CARLOS ALBERTO MONTANER.

Partido Cubano Ortodoxo: f. 1999; Leader NELSON AGUIAR.

Partido Liberal Democrático de Cuba: Chair. OSVALDO ALFONSO VALDÉS.

Partido pro-Derechos Humanos: f. 1988 to defend human rights in Cuba; Pres. HIRAM ABI COBAS; Sec.-Gen. TANIA DÍAZ.

Partido Social Revolucionario Democrático de Cuba: POB 351081, Miami, FL 33135, USA; tel. and fax (305) 649-2886; e-mail psrdc@psrdc.org; internet www.psrdc.org; f. 1992; Pres. JORGE VALLS.

Partido Solidaridad Democrática (PSD): POB 310063, Miami, FL 33131, USA; tel. (305) 408-2659; e-mail gladyperez@aol.com; internet www.ccsi.com/~ams/psd; Pres. FERNANDO SÁNCHEZ LÓPEZ.

Solidaridad Cubana: Leader FERNANDO SÁNCHEZ LÓPEZ.

Diplomatic Representation

EMBASSIES IN CUBA

Algeria: Avda 5, No 2802, esq. 28, Miramar, Havana; tel. (7) 204-2835; fax (7) 204-2702; Ambassador RABAH KEROUAZ.

Angola: Avda 5, No 1012, entre 10 y 12, Miramar, Havana; tel. (7) 204-2474; fax (7) 204-2117; e-mail embangol@ceniai.inf.cu; Ambassador JOÃO MANUEL BERNARDO.

Argentina: Calle 36, No 511, entre 5 y 7, Miramar, Havana; tel. (7) 204–2565; fax (7) 204–2140; e-mail ecuba@enet.cu; Chargé d'affaires a.i. JOSÉ MARÍA ALLER.

Austria: Calle 4, No 101, entre 1 y 3, Miramar, Havana; tel. (7) 204-2824; fax (7) 204-1235; e-mail austria@ceniai.inf.cu; Ambassador Dr HELGA KONRAD.

Belarus: Avda 5, No 3802, entre 38 y 40, Miramar, Havana; tel. (7) 33-0341; fax (7) 33-0340; Chargé d'affaires a.i. VLADIMIR PISCHACO.

Belgium: Calle 8, No 309, entre 3 y 5, Miramar, Havana; tel. (7) 204-2410; fax (7) 204-1318; e-mail ambelhav@ceniai.inf.cu; Ambassador PATRICK DE BEYTER.

Belize: Avda 5, No 3608, entre 36 y 36A, Miramar, Havana; tel. (7) 204-3504; fax (7) 204-3506; e-mail belize.embassy@ip.etecsa.cu; Ambassador AMALIA MAI-RANCHARAN.

Benin: Calle 20, No 119, entre 1 y 3, Miramar, Havana; tel. (7) 204-2179; fax (7) 204-2334; Ambassador SIMPLICE GNANGUESSY.

Bolivia: Calle 26, No 113, entre 1 y 3, Miramar, Havana; tel. (7) 204-2426; fax (7) 204-2127; e-mail emboliviahabana@cubacel.net; Ambassador MARÍA EUGENIA SALINAS INARRA.

Brazil: Calle Lamparilla, No 2, 4°K, Miramar, Havana; tel. (7) 66-9052; fax (7) 66-2912; e-mail brasil@ceniai.inf.cu; Ambassador LUCIANO MARTINS DE ALMEIDA.

Bulgaria: Calle B, No 252, entre 11 y 13, Vedado, Havana; tel. (7) 33-3125; fax (7) 33-3297; e-mail embulhav@ceniai.inf.cu; Chargé d'affaires a.i. EMILIA STEFANOVA.

Burkina Faso: Calle 7, No 8401, Miramar, Havana; tel. (7) 204-2895; fax (7) 204-1942; e-mail ambfaso@ceniai.inf.cu; Ambassador SALIF NÉBIÉ.

Cambodia: Avda 5, No 7001, entre 70 y 72, Miramar, Havana; tel. (7) 204-1496; fax (7) 204-6400; e-mail cambodia@ceniai.inf.cu; Ambassador CHIM PRORNG.

Canada: Calle 30, No 518, entre 5 y 7, Miramar, Havana; tel. (7) 204-2516; fax (7) 204-2044; e-mail havan@dfait-maeci.gc.ca; internet www.dfait-maeci.gc.ca/cuba; Ambassador MICHAEL SMALL.

Cape Verde: Calle 20, No 2001, esq. 7, Miramar, Havana; tel. (7) 204-2979; fax (7) 204-1072; e-mail ecvc@ceniai.inf.cu; Ambassador FATIMA LIMA VEIGA.

Chile: Avda 33, No 1423, entre 16 y 18, Miramar, Havana; tel. (7) 204-1222; fax (7) 204-1694; e-mail echilecu@cubacel.net; Ambassador GERMÁN GUERRERO PAVEZ.

China, People's Republic: Calle 13, No 551, Vedado, Havana; tel. (7) 33-3005; fax (7) 33-3092; Ambassador WANG ZHIQUAN.

Colombia: Calle 14, No 515, entre 5 y 7, Miramar, Havana; tel. (7) 204-1246; fax (7) 204-1249; e-mail elahabana@minrelext.gov.co; Ambassador JULIO LONDOÑO PAREDES.

Congo, Republic: Avda 5, No 1003, Miramar, Havana; tel. and fax 204-9055; Ambassador PASCAL ONGUEMBY.

Czech Republic: Avda Kohly 259, entre 41 y 43, Nuevo Vedado, Havana; tel. (7) 33-3201; fax (7) 33-3596; e-mail havana@embassy.mzv.cz; Ambassador PETR STIEGLER.

Dominican Republic: Avda 5, No 9202, entre 92 y 94, Miramar, Havana; tel. (7) 204-8429; fax (7) 204-8431; Ambassador Dr DANIEL GUERRERO TAVERAS.

Ecuador: Avda 5A, No 4407, entre 44 y 46, Miramar, Havana; tel. (7) 204-2034; fax (7) 204-2868; e-mail embecuad@ceniai.inf.cu; Ambassador Dr FRANCISCO SUESCUM OTATTI.

Egypt: Avda 5, No 1801, esq. 18, Miramar, Havana; tel. (7) 204-2441; fax (7) 204-0905; e-mail emegipto@enet.cu; Ambassador HAZEM MUHAMMAD TAHER.

Ethiopia: Calle 6, No 318, Miramar, Havana; tel. (7) 22-1260; Ambassador ABEBE BELAYNEH.

France: Calle 14, No 312, entre 3 y 5, Miramar, Havana; tel. (7) 204-2132; fax (7) 204-1439; e-mail la-havane.amba@diplomatie.gouv.fr; internet www.ambafrance-cu.org; Ambassador JEAN LEVY.

Germany: Calle 13, No 652, esq. B, Vedado, Havana; tel. (7) 33-2539; fax (7) 33-1586; e-mail alemania@ip.etecsa.cu; internet www.deutschebotschaft-havanna.cu; Ambassador Dr BERND WULFFEN.

Ghana: Avda 5, No 1808, esq. 20, Miramar, Havana; tel. (7) 204-2153; fax (7) 204-2317; e-mail eghana@ceniai.inf.cu; internet www.ghanaembassy.cu; Ambassador Dr ISAAC ANTWI-OMANE.

Greece: Avda 5, No 7802, esq. 78, Miramar, Havana; tel. (7) 204-2995; fax (7) 204-1784; Ambassador GEORGE COSTOULAS.

Guatemala: Calle 16, No 505, entre 3 y 5, Miramar, Havana; tel. 204-3417; fax 204-3200; Ambassador HUGO RENÉ GUZMÁN MALDONADO.

Guinea: Calle 20, No 504, entre 5 y 7, Miramar, Havana; tel. (7) 204-2003; fax (7) 204-2380; Ambassador CHEICK ALIOUNE CONDÉ.

Guinea-Bissau: Calle 14, No 313, entre 3 y 5, Miramar, Havana; tel. (7) 204-2689; fax (7) 204-2794; Chargé d'affaires a.i. LIBERATO GOMES.

Guyana: Calle 18, No 506, entre 5 y 7, Miramar, Havana; tel. (7) 204-2249; fax (7) 204-2867; e-mail embguyana@ip.etecsa.cu; Ambassador Dr TIMOTHY N. CRICHLOW.

Haiti: No 6804, entre 68 y 70, Miramar, Havana; tel. (7) 204-5421; fax (7) 204-5423; Chargé d'affaires a.i. JEAN WILLIAM EXANTUS.

Honduras: Interests Section: Casa Palhero 112, Planta Baja, Calle 30, entre 1 y 3, Miramar, Havana; tel. (7) 204-5497; fax (7) 204-5496; e-mail embhocu@ip.etecsa.cu; Chargé d'affaires REYNIERI DAVID AMADOR.

Holy See: Calle 12, No 514, entre 5 y 7, Miramar, Havana (Apostolic Nunciature); tel. (7) 204-2700; fax (7) 204-2257; e-mail csa@pcn.net; Apostolic Nuncio Most Rev. LUIS ROBLES DÍAZ (Titular Archbishop of Stefaniaco).

Hungary: Calle G, No 458, entre 19 y 21, Vedado, Havana; tel. (7) 33-3365; fax (7) 33-3286; e-mail embhuncu@ceniai.inf.cu; Ambassador VILMOS KOPÁNYI.

India: Calle 21, No 202, esq. a K, Vedado, Havana; tel. (7) 33-3777; fax (7) 33-3287; e-mail eoihav@ceniai.inf.cu; internet www.indembassyhavana.cu; Ambassador RAMIAH RAJAGOPALAN.

Indonesia: Avda 5, No 1607, esq. 18, Miramar, Havana; tel. (7) 204-9618; fax (7) 204-9617; Ambassador Dr R. HARIDADI SUDJONO.

Iran: Avda 5, No 3002, esq. 30, Miramar, Havana; tel. (7) 204-2675; fax (7) 204-2770; e-mail embairan@ip.etecsa.cu; Ambassador AHMAD EDRISIAN.

Iraq: Avda 5, No 8201, entre 82 y 84, Miramar, Havana; tel. (7) 204-1607; fax (7) 204-2157; Ambassador MUHAMMED MAHMOUD K. H. AL-AMILI.

Italy: No 5, Avda 402, Calle 4, Miramar,, Havana; tel. (7) 204–5615; fax (7) 204–5659; e-mail ambitcub@enet.cu; Ambassador ELIO MENZIONE.

Jamaica: Calle 32, No 503, entre 5 y 7, Miramar,, Havana; tel. (7) 204-2908; fax (7) 204-2531; e-mail embjmcub@mail.infocom.etecsa.cu; Ambassador CARLYLE DUNKLEY.

Japan: Centro de Negocios Miramar, Avda 3, No 1, 5°, esq. 80, Miramar, Havana; tel. (7) 204-3355; fax (7) 204-8902; Ambassador MUTSUO MABUCHI.

Korea, Democratic People's Republic: Calle 17, No 752, Vedado, Havana; tel. (7) 66-2313; fax (7) 33-3073; Ambassador KIM KIL HWANG.

Laos: Avda 5, No 2808, esq. 30, Miramar, Havana; tel. (7) 204-1056; fax (7) 204-9622; e-mail embalao@ip.etecsa.cu; Ambassador CHANPHENG SIHAPHOM.

Lebanon: Calle 17A, No 16403, entre 164 y 174, Siboney, Havana; tel. (7) 28-6220; fax (7) 28-6432; e-mail lbcunet@ceniai.inf.cu; Ambassador SLEIMAN C. RASSI.

Libya: Avda 7, No 1402, esq. 14, Miramar, Havana; tel. (7) 204-2192; fax (7) 204-2991; Chargé d'affaires a.i. ABDULLATIF H. EL-KHAZMI.

Malaysia: Hotel Comodoro, Calle 84, Avda 3, Miramar, Havana; tel. (7) 204–5551; fax (7) 204–6888; e-mail mwhavana@enet.cu; Ambassador Dato' MOHD KAMAL BIN YAN YAHAYA.

Mexico: Calle 12, No 518, Miramar, Playa, Havana; tel. (7) 204-2553; fax (7) 204-2717; e-mail embamex@ip.etecsa.cu; Ambassador ROBERTA LAJOUS VARGAS.

Mongolia: Calle 66, No 505, esq. 5, Miramar, Havana; tel. (7) 204-2763; fax (7) 204-0639; Ambassador BALJIN NYAMAA.

Mozambique: Avda 7, No 2203, entre 22 y 24, Miramar, Havana; tel. (7) 204-2443; fax (7) 204-2232; e-mail embamoc@ceniai.inf.cu; Ambassador JULIO GONÇALO BRAGA.

Namibia: Avda 5, No 4406, entre 44 y 46, Miramar, Havana; tel. (7) 204-1430; fax (7) 204-1431; e-mail embnamib@ceniai.inf.cu; Ambassador ELÍA AKWAAKE.

Netherlands: Calle 8, No 307, entre 3 y 5, Miramar, Havana; tel. (7) 204-2511; fax (7) 204-2059; e-mail hav@minbuza.nl; Ambassador CORNELIA MINDERHOUD.

Nicaragua: Calle 20, No 709, entre 7 y 9, Miramar, Havana; tel. (7) 204-1025; fax (7) 204-6323; e-mail embanicc@enet.cu; Chargé d'affaires a.i. Dr MERCEDES RIVERA DE DE SEDAS.

Nigeria: Avda 5, No 1401, entre 14 y 16, Miramar, Havana; tel. (7) 204-2898; fax (7) 204-2202; Ambassador NGAM NWACHUKWU.

Panama: Calle 26, No 109, entre 1 y 3, Miramar, Havana; tel. (7) 204-1673; fax (7) 204-1674; Ambassador MARCO ANTONIO ALARCÓN PALOMINO.

Paraguay: Calle 34, No 503, entre 5 y 7, Miramar, Havana; tel. (7) 204-0884; fax (7) 204-0883; Chargé d'affaires a.i. AUGUSTO OCAMPOS CABALLERO.

Peru: Calle 30, No 107, entre 1 y 3, Miramar, Havana; tel. (7) 204-2477; fax (7) 204-2636; Ambassador JUAN ALVAREZ VITA.

Philippines: Avda 5, No 2207, esq. 24, Miramar, Havana; tel. (7) 204-1372; fax (7) 204-2915; e-mail philhavpe@ip.etecsa.cu; Ambassador REGINA IRENE P. SARMIENTO.

Poland: Calle G, No 452, esq. 19, Vedado, Havana; tel. (7) 66-2439; fax (7) 66-2442; e-mail ambhavpl@ceniai.inf.cu; internet www.embajadapolonia.cu; Ambassador TOMASZ TUROWSKI.

Portugal: Avda 7, No 2207, esq. 24, Miramar, Havana; tel. (7) 204-2871; fax (7) 204-2593; e-mail embport@enet.cu; Ambassador ALFREDO MANUEL SILVA DUARTE COSTA.

Romania: Calle 21, No 307, Vedado, Havana; tel. (7) 33-3325; fax (7) 33-3324; e-mail erumania@ceniai.inf.cu; Chargé d'affaires a.i. CONSTANTIN RUSEI.

Russia: Avda 5, No 6402, entre 62 y 66, Miramar, Havana; tel. (7) 204-2686; fax (7) 204-1038; e-mail embrusia@ceniai.inf.cu; Ambassador ANDREI VIKTOROVICH DIMITRIEV.

Serbia and Montenegro: Calle 42, No 115, entre 1 y 3, Miramar, Havana; tel. (7) 204-2488; fax (7) 204-2982; e-mail embyuhav@ceniai.inf.cu; Ambassador LJILJANA KADIC.

Slovakia: Calle 66, No 521, entre 5B y 7, Miramar, Havana; tel. (7) 204-1884; fax (7) 204-1883; e-mail embeslovaca@enet.cu; Ambassador IVAN PUŠKÁČ.

South Africa: Avda 5, No 4201, esq. 42, Miramar, Havana; tel. (7) 204-9658; fax (7) 204-1101; Ambassador NOEL MAKHAYA NDLOU JOHN MOSIA.

Spain: Cárcel No 51, esq. Zulueta, Havana; tel. (7) 33-8025; fax (7) 33-8006; e-mail embespcu@correo.mae.es; Ambassador JESÚS GRACIA ALDEZ.

Sri Lanka: Calle 32, No 307, entre 3 y 5, Miramar, Havana; tel. (7) 204-2562; fax (7) 204-2183; e-mail sri.lanka@ip.etecsa.cu; Chargé d'affaires a.i. DON BERNARD KALIDASA.

Sweden: Calle 34, No 510, entre 5 y 7, Miramar, Havana; tel. (7) 204-2831; fax (7) 204-1194; e-mail ambassaden.havanna@foreign.ministry.se; Ambassador EIVOR HALKJAER.

Switzerland: Avda 5, No 2005, entre 20 y 22, Miramar, Havana; tel. (7) 204-2611; fax (7) 204-1148; e-mail swissem@enet.cu; Ambassador JEAN-CAUDE RICHARD.

Syria: Avda 5, No 7402, entre 74 y 76, Miramar, Havana; tel. (7) 204-2266; fax (7) 204-2829; Chargé d'affaires Dr CHAHIN FARAH.

Turkey: Avda 5, No 3805, entre 36 y 40, Miramar, Havana; tel. (7) 204-1205; fax (7) 204-2899; e-mail turkemb@ip.etecsa.cu; Ambassador ATAMAN YALGIN.

Uganda: Calle 20, No 713, entre 7 y 9, Miramar, Havana; tel. (7) 204-0469; fax (7) 33-6668; Ambassador ELIZABETH PAULA NAPEYOK.

Ukraine: Avda 5, No 4405, entre 44 y 46, Miramar, Havana; tel. (7) 204-2586; fax (7) 204-2341; e-mail cubukrem@ceniai.inf.cu; Ambassador VICTOR PASCHUK.

United Kingdom: Calle 34, No 702/4, esq. 7, Miramar, Havana; tel. (7) 204-1771; fax (7) 204-8104; e-mail embrit@ceniai.inf.cu; Ambassador PAUL HARE.

USA (Relations severed in 1961): Interests Section: Calzada, entre L y M, Vedado, Havana; tel. (7) 33-3543; fax (7) 66-2095; Principal Officer JAMES C. CASON.

Uruguay: Calle 14, No 506, entre 5 y 7, Miramar, Havana; tel. (7) 204-2311; fax (7) 204-2246; e-mail urucub@ceniai.inf.cu; Ambassador ENRIQUE ESTRÁZULAS.

Venezuela: Avda 1601, No 5, entre 16 y 18, Miramar, Havana; tel. (7) 204–2612; fax (7) 204–2773; e-mail vencuba@enet.cu; Ambassador JULÍO MONTES PRADO.

Viet Nam: Avda 5, No 1802, Miramar, Havana; tel. (7) 204-1502; fax (7) 204-1041; e-mail embaviet@ceniai.inf.cu; internet www.vietnamembassy.cu; Ambassador PHAM TIEN TU.

Yemen: Calle 16, No 503, entre 5 y 7, Miramar, Havana; tel. (7) 204-1506; fax (7) 204-1131; Ambassador Dr AHMED ABDULLA ABDUL ELAH.

Zimbabwe: Avda 3, No 1001, esq. a 10, Miramar, Havana; tel. (7) 204-2857; fax (7) 204-2720; Ambassador JEVANA BEN MASEKO.

Judicial System

The judicial system comprises the People's Supreme Court, the People's Provincial Courts and the People's Municipal Courts. The People's Supreme Court exercises the highest judicial authority.

PEOPLE'S SUPREME COURT

The People's Supreme Court comprises the Plenum, the six Courts of Justice in joint session and the Council of Government. When the Courts of Justice are in joint session they comprise all the professional and lay judges, the Attorney-General and the Minister of Justice. The Council of Government comprises the President and Vice-President of the People's Supreme Court, the Presidents of each Court of Justice and the Attorney-General of the Republic. The Minister of Justice may participate in its meetings.

President: Dr RUBÉN REMIGIO FERRO.

Vice-Presidents: Dr MANUEL DE JESÚS PÉREZ PÉREZ, Dra GRACIELA PRIETO MARTÍN.

Criminal Court
President: Dr JORGE L. BODES TORRES.

Civil and Administrative Court
President: ANDRÉS BOLAÑOS GASSÓ.

Labour Court
President: Dr ANTONIO R. MARTÍN SÁNCHEZ.

Court for State Security
President: Dr GUILLERMO HERNÁNDEZ INFANTE.

Economic Court

President: Dr ELPIDIO PÉREZ SUÁREZ.

Military Court

President: Col JUAN MARINO FUENTES CALZADO.

Attorney-General: JUAN ESCALONA REGUERA.

Religion

There is no established Church, and all religions are permitted, though Roman Catholicism predominates. The Afro-Cuban religions of Regla de Ocha (Santéria) and Regla Conga (Palo Monte) also have numerous adherents.

CHRISTIANITY

Consejo Ecuménico de Cuba (Ecumenical Council of Cuba): Calle 14, No 304, entre 3 y 5, Miramar, Playa, Havana; tel. (7) 33-1792; fax (7) 33-178820; f. 1941; 11 mem. churches; Pres. Rev. ORESTES GON-ZÁLEZ; Exec. Sec. Rev. JOSÉ LÓPEZ.

The Roman Catholic Church

Cuba comprises three archdioceses and eight dioceses. At 31 December 2000 there were 5,755,652 adherents, representing 51.4% of the total population.

Conferencia de Obispos Católicos de Cuba—COCC (Bishops' Conference)

Calle 26, No 314, entre 3 y 5, Miramar, Apdo 594, Havana; tel. (7) 29-2395; fax (7) 204-2168; e-mail adjunto@cocc.co.cu; internet www.celam.org/sitios/ce_cuba/COCC.htm.

f. 1983; Pres. Cardinal JAIME LUCAS ORTEGA Y ALAMINO (Archbishop of San Cristóbal de la Habana).

Archbishop of Camagüey: JUAN GARCÍA RODRÍGUEZ, Calle Luaces, No 55, Apdo 105, Camagüey 70100; tel. (322) 92268; fax (322) 87143; e-mail dei@cocc.co.cu.

Archbishop of San Cristóbal de la Habana: Cardinal JAIME LUCAS ORTEGA Y ALAMINO, Calle Habana No 152, esq. a Chacón, Apdo 594, Havana 10100; tel. (7) 62-4000; fax (7) 33-8109; e-mail cocc@brigadoo.com.

Archbishop of Santiago de Cuba: PEDRO CLARO MEURICE ESTÍU, Sánchez Hechevarría No 607, Apdo 26, Santiago de Cuba 90100; tel. (226) 25480; fax (226) 86186.

The Anglican Communion

Anglicans are adherents of the Iglesia Episcopal de Cuba (Episcopal Church of Cuba).

Bishop of Cuba: Rt Rev. JORGE PERERA HURTADO, Calle 6, No 273, Vedado, Havana 10400; tel. (7) 832–1120; fax (7) 33-3293; e-mail episcopal@ip.etecsa.cu; internet cuba.anglican.org.

Protestant Churches

Convención Bautista de Cuba Oriental (Baptist Convention of Eastern Cuba): San Jerónimo, No 467, entre Calvario y Carnicería, Santiago; tel. 2-0173; f. 1905; Pres. Rev. Dr ROY ACOSTA; Sec. RAFAEL MUSTELIER.

Iglesia Metodista en Cuba (Methodist Church in Cuba): Calle K, No 502, 25 y 27, Vedado, Apdo 10400, Havana; tel. (7) 32-2991; fax (7) 33-3135; e-mail imecu@ip.etecsa.cu; autonomous since 1968; 6,000 mems; Bishop RICARDO PEREIRA DÍAZ.

Iglesia Presbiteriana-Reformada en Cuba (Presbyterian-Reformed Church in Cuba): Salud 222, entre Lealtad y Campanario, Havana 10200; tel. (7) 62–1219; fax (7) 33–8819; e-mail asel@ip.etecsa.cu; autonomous since 1967; 8,000 mems; Gen. Sec. Rev. Dr SERGIO ARCE.

Other denominations active in Cuba include the Apostolic Church of Jesus Christ, the Bethel Evangelical Church, the Christian Pentecostal Church, the Church of God, the Church of the Nazarene, the Free Baptist Convention, the Holy Pentecost Church, the Pentecostal Congregational Church and the Salvation Army.

The Press

DAILY

In October 1990 President Castro announced that, in accordance with other wide-ranging economic austerity measures, only one newspaper, *Granma* would henceforth be published as a nation-wide daily. The other national dailies were to become weeklies or were to cease publication.

Granma: Avda Gen. Suárez y Territorial, Plaza de la Revolución, Apdo 6187, Havana; tel. (7) 81-3333; fax (7) 33-5176; e-mail redac@granmai.get.cma.net; internet www.granma.cubaweb.cu; f. 1965 to replace *Hoy* and *Revolución*; official Communist Party organ; Dir FRANK AGÜERO GÓMEZ; circ. 400,000.

PERIODICALS

Adelante: Avda A, Rpto Jayamá, Camagüey; e-mail adelante@caonao.cmw.inf.cu; internet www.adelante.cu; f. 1959; Dir MIGUEL A. FEBLES HERNÁNDEZ; circ. 42,000.

Ahora: Salida a San Germán y Circunvalación, Holguín; e-mail ahoraweb@ahora.cu; internet www.ahora.cu; f. 1962; Dir RADOBALDO MARTÍNEZ PÉREZ; circ. 50,000.

ANAP: Línea 206, entre H e I, Vedado, Havana; f. 1961; monthly; information for small farmers; Dir LEONEL VÁLDEZ ALONSO; circ. 30,000.

Bastión: Territorial esq. a Gen. Suárez, Plaza de la Revolución, Havana; tel. (7) 79-3361; organ of the Revolutionary Armed Forces; Dir FRANK AGÜERO GÓMEZ; circ. 65,000.

Bohemia: Avda Independencia y San Pedro, Apdo 6000, Havana; tel. (7) 81-9213; fax (7) 33-5511; e-mail bohemia@bohemia.get.tor.cu; internet www.bohemia.cubaweb.cu; f. 1908; weekly; politics; Dir JOSÉ FERNÁNDEZ VEGA; circ. 100,000.

Boletín Alimentaria de Cuba: Amargura 103, 10100 Havana; tel. (7) 62-9245; f. 1996; quarterly; food industry; Dir ANTONIO CAMPOS; circ. 10,000.

El Caimán Barbudo: Paseo 613, Vedado, Havana; e-mail eabril@jcce.org.cu; internet www.caimanbarbudo.cu; f. 1966; monthly; cultural; Dir FIDEL DÍAZ CASTRO; circ. 47,000.

Casa de las Américas: 3 y G Vedado, 10400 Havana; tel. (7) 32-3587; fax (7) 33-4554; e-mail prensa@casa.cult.cu; internet www.casa.cult.cu; f. 1959; 6 a year; cultural.

Cinco de Septiembre: Calle 35, No 5609, entre 56 y 58, Cienfuegos; e-mail cip219@cip.etecsa.cu; internet www.5septiembre.cu; f. 1980; Dir FRANCISCO VALDÉS PETITÓN; circ. 18,000.

Cómicos: Calle 28, No 112, entre 1 y 3, Miramar, Havana; tel. (7) 22-5892; monthly; humorous; circ. 70,000.

Con la Guardia en Alto: Havana; f. 1961; monthly; for mems of the Committees for the Defence of the Revolution; Dir OMELIA GUERRA PÉREZ; circ. 60,000.

Cuba Internacional: Calle 21, No 406, Vedado, Havana 4, Apdo 3603 Havana 3; tel. (7) 32-3578; fax (7) 32-3268; f. 1959; monthly; political; Dir FÉLIX ALBISÚ; circ. 30,000.

Dedeté: Territorial y Gen. Suárez, Plaza de la Revolución, Apdo 6344, Havana; tel. (7) 82-0134; fax (7) 81-8621; e-mail ddt@jrebelde.cip.cu; internet www.dedete.cubaweb.cu; f. 1969; monthly; Dir ALEN LAUZÁN; circ. 70,000.

La Demajagua: Amado Estévez, esq. Calle 10, Rpto R. Reyes, Bayamo; e-mail cip225@cip.enet.cu; internet www.lademajagua.co.cu; f. 1977; Dir LUIS CARLOS FRÓMETA AGÜERO; circ. 21,000.

El Deporte, Derecho del Pueblo: Vía Blanca y Boyeros, Havana; tel. (7) 40-6838; f. 1968; monthly; sport; Dir MANUEL VAILLANT CARPENTE; circ. 15,000.

El Economista: Asociación Nacional de Economistas de Cuba, Calle 22, No 901 esq a 9, Miramar, Havana; tel. (7) 29-3303; fax (7) 22-3456; e-mail anec@info.get.cma.net; internet www.eleconomista.cubaweb.cu; monthly; business; Dir-Gen. ROBERTO VERRIER CASTRO.

Escambray: Adolfo del Castillo 10, Sancti Spíritus; tel. (41) 23003; e-mail cip220@cip.enet.cu; internet www.escambray.islagrande.cu; f. 1979; Dir JUAN ANTONIO BORREGO DÍAZ; circ. 21,000.

Girón: Avda Camilo Cienfuegos No 10505, P. Nuero, Matanzas; e-mail giron@giron.esimtz.co.cu; internet www.adelante.cu/periodicos/giron.htm; f. 1960; Dir DOMINGO ORTA VERA; circ. 25,000.

Guerrillero: Colón esq. Delicias y Adela Azcuy, Pinar del Río; e-mail cip216@cip.etecsa.cu; internet www.guerrillero.co.cu; f. 1969; Dir ERNESTO OSORIO ROQUE; circ. 33,000.

El Habanero: Gen. Suárez y Territorial, Plaza de la Revolución, Apdo 6269, Havana; tel. (7) 6160; e-mail internet@habanero.cip.cu; internet www.elhabanero.cubaweb.cu; f. 1987; Dir ANDRÉS HERNÁNDEZ RIVERO; circ. 21,000.

Industria Alimentica: Amargura 103, 10100 Havana; tel. (7) 61-8453; quarterly; food industry.

Invasor: Marcial Gómez 401, esq. Estrada Palma, Ciego de Avila; internet www.invasor.islagrande.cu; f. 1979; Dir MIGDALIA UTRERA PEÑA; circ. 10,500.

Juventud Rebelde: Territorial esq. Gen. Suárez, Plaza de la Revolución, Apdo 6344, Havana; tel. (7) 82-0155; fax (7) 33-8959; e-mail jrebelde@teleda.get.Cma.net; internet www.jrebelde.cubaweb.cu; f.

1965; organ of the Young Communist League; Dir ROGELIO POLANCO FUENTES; circ. 250,000.

Juventud Técnica: Prado 553, esq. Teniente Rey, Habana Vieja, Havana; tel. (7) 62-4330; e-mail eabril@jcce.org.cu; internet www .juventudtecnica.cu; f. 1965; every 2 months; scientific-technical; Dir MIRIAM ZITO VALDÉS; circ. 20,000.

Mar y Pesca: San Ignacio 303, Havana; tel. (7) 61-5518; fax 33-8438; f. 1965; quarterly; fishing; Dir GUSTAVO LÓPEZ; circ. 20,000.

El Militante Comunista: Calle 11, No 160, Vedado, Havana; tel. (7) 32-7581; f. 1967; monthly; Communist Party publication; Dir MANUEL MENÉNDEZ; circ. 200,000.

Moncada: Ministerio del Interior, Belasconia esq Zanja, Havana; tel. (7) 79-7109; f. 1966; monthly; government publication; Dir RICARDO MARTÍNEZ; circ. 70,000.

Muchacha: Galiano 264, esq. Neptuno, Havana; tel. (7) 61-5919; f. 1980; monthly; young women's magazine; Dir SILVIA MARTÍNEZ; circ. 120,000.

Mujeres: Galiano 264, esq. Neptuno, Havana; tel. (7) 61-5919; f. 1961; monthly; women's magazine; Dir REGLA ZULUETA; circ. 270,000.

El Muñe: Calle 28, No 112, entre 1 y 3, Mirimar, Havana; tel. (7) 22-5892; weekly; circ. 50,000.

Opciones: Territorial esq. Gen. Suárez, Plaza de la Revolucíon, Havana; e-mail cida@jrebelde.cip.cu; internet www.opciones .cubaweb.cu; weekly; finance, commerce and tourism; Dir ROGELIO POLANCO FUENTES.

Opina: Edif. Focsa, M entre 17 y 19, Havana; f. 1979; 2 a month; consumer-orientated; published by Institute of Internal Demand; Dir EUGENIO RODRÍGUEZ BALARI; circ. 250,000.

Pablo: Calle 28, No 112, entre 1 y 3, Mirimar, Havana; tel. (7) 22-5892; 16 a year; circ. 53,000.

Palante: Calle 21, No 954, entre 8 y 10, Vedado, Havana; tel. (7) 3-5098; f. 1961; weekly; humorous; Dir ROSENDO GUTIÉRREZ ROMÁN; circ. 235,000.

Pionero: Calle 17, No 354, Havana 4; tel. (7) 32-4571; internet www .pionero.cu; f. 1961; weekly; children's magazine; Dir PEDRO GON-ZÁLEZ (PÉGLEZ); circ. 210,000.

Prisma: Calle 21 y Avda G, No 406, Vedado, Havana; tel. (7) 8-7995; f. 1979; bimonthly; international news; Man. Dir LUIS MANUEL ARCE; circ. 15,000 (Spanish), 10,000 (English).

RIL: O'Reilly 358, Havana; tel. (7) 62-0777; f. 1972; 2 a month; technical; Dir Exec. Council of Publicity Dept, Ministry of Light Industry; Chief Officer MIREYA CRESPO; circ. 8,000.

Sierra Maestra: Avda de Los Desfiles, Santiago de Cuba; tel. (7) 2-2813; e-mail cip226@cip.etecsa.cu; internet www.sierramaestra.cu; f. 1957; weekly; Dir ARNALDO CLAVEL CARMENATY; circ. 45,000.

Sol de Cuba: Calle 19, No 60, entre M y N, Vedado, Havana 4; tel. (7) 32-9881; f. 1983; every 3 months; Spanish, English and French editions; Gen. Dir ALCIDES GIRO MITJANS; Editorial Dir DORIS VÉLEZ; circ. 200,000.

Somos Jóvenes: Calle 17, No 354, esq. H, Vedado, Havana; tel. (7) 32-4571; e-mail eabril@jcce.org.cu; internet www.somosjovenes.cu; f. 1977; monthly; Dir YARELIS RICO; circ. 200,000.

Trabajadores: Territorial esq. Gen. Suárez, Plaza de la Revolución, Havana; tel. (7) 79-0819; e-mail digital@trabaja.cip.cu; internet www.trabajadores.cubaweb.cu; f. 1970; organ of the trade-union movement; Dir JORGE LUIS CANELA CIURANA; circ. 150,000.

Tribuna de la Habana: Territorial esq. Gen. Suárez, Plaza de la Revolución, Havana; tel. (7) 81-5932; e-mail redac@tribuna.cip.cu; internet www.tribuna.islagrande.cu; f. 1980; weekly; Dir ANGEL RODRÍGUEZ ÁLVAREZ; circ. 90,000.

Vanguardia: Céspedes 5 (altos), Santa Clara, Matanzas; e-mail cip218@cip.enet.cu; internet www.vanguardia.co.cu; f. 1962; Dir PEDRO HERNÁNDEZ SOTO; circ. 24,000.

Venceremos: Carretera Jamaica, Km 1½, Guantánamo; tel. (7) 35980; e-mail cip227@cip.etecsa.cu; internet www.adelante.cu/ periodicos/venceremos.htm; f. 1962; Dir HAYDÉE LEÓN MOYA; circ. 28,000.

Ventiseis: Avda Carlos J. Finley, Las Tunas; f. 1977; Dir JOSÉ INFANTES REYES; circ. 21,000.

Verde Olivo: Avda de Rancho Boyeros y San Pedro, Havana; tel. (7) 79-8373; f. 1959; monthly; organ of the Revolutionary Armed Forces; Dir EUGENIO SUÁREZ PÉREZ; circ. 100,000.

Victoria: Carretera de la Fe, Km 1½, Plaza de la Revolución, Nueva Gerona, Isla de la Juventud; e-mail periodic@gerona.inf.cu; internet www.victoria.islagrande.cu; f. 1967; Dir SERGIO RIVERO CARRASCO; circ. 9,200.

PRESS ASSOCIATIONS

Unión de Periodistas de Cuba: Calle 23, No 452, esq. I, Vedado, 10400 Havana; tel. (7) 32-7098; fax (7) 33-3079; e-mail upec@jcce.org .cu; internet www.cubaperiodistas.cu; f. 1963; Pres. TUBAL PÁEZ HERNÁNDEZ.

Unión de Escritores y Artistas de Cuba: Calle 17, No 351, Vedado, Havana; tel. (7) 32-4571; fax (7) 33-3158; internet www .uneac.cult.cu; Pres. ABEL E. PRIETO JIMÉNEZ; Exec. Vice-Pres. LISANDRO OTERO.

NEWS AGENCIES

Agencia de Información Nacional (AIN): Calle 23, No 358, esq. a J, Vedado, Havana; tel. (7) 32-5541; fax (7) 66-2049; e-mail web@ ainch.ain.sld.cu; internet www.ain.cubaweb.cu; national news agency; Gen. Dir ESTEBAN RAMÍREZ ALONSO.

Prensa Latina (Agencia Informativa Latinoamericana, SA): Calle 23, No 201, esq. a N, Vedado, Havana; tel. (7) 32-5561; fax (7) 33-3069; e-mail dirdifu@prensa-latina.cu; internet www .prensa-latina.cu; f. 1959; Dir PEDRO MARGOLLES VILLANUEVA.

Foreign Bureaux

Agence France-Presse (AFP): Calle 17, No 4, 13°, entre N y O, Vedado, Havana; tel. (7) 33-3503; fax (7) 33-3034; e-mail mlsanz@ip .etecsa.cu; Bureau Chief MARIE SANZ.

Agencia EFE (Spain): Calle 36, No 110, entre 1 y 3, Miramar, Apdo 5, Havana; tel. (7) 33-2293; fax (7) 33-2272; Bureau Chief SOLEDAD MARÍN MARTÍN.

Agenzia Nazionale Stampa Associata (ANSA) (Italy): Edif. Fomeillán, Línea 5, Dpt 12, Vedado, Havana; tel. (7) 33-3542; Correspondent KATTY SALERNO.

Associated Press (AP) (USA): Lonja del Comercio, planta baja, Lamparilla 2, Local B, Habana Vieja, Havana; tel. (7) 33-0370; Correspondent ANITA SNOW.

Bulgarska Telegrafna Agentsia (BTA) (Bulgaria): Edif. Focsa, Calle 17, esq. M, Vedado, Apdo 22E, Havana; tel. (7) 32-4779; Bureau Chief VASIL MIKOULACH.

Česká tisková kancelář (ČTK) (Czech Republic): Edif. Fajardo, Calle 17 y M, Vedado, Apdo 3A, Vedado, Havana; tel. (7) 32-6101; Bureau Chief PAVEL ZOVADIL.

Deutsche Presse-Agentur (dpa) (Germany): Edif. Focsa, Calle 17 y M, Vedado, Apdo 2K, Havana; tel. (7) 33-3501; Bureau Chief VICTORIO COPA.

Informatsionnoye Telegrafnoye Agentstvo Rossii— Telegrafnoye Agentstvo Suverennykh Stran (ITAR—TASS) (Russia): Calle 96, No 317, entre 3 y 5, Miramar, Havana 4; tel. (7) 29-2528; Bureau Chief ALEKSANDR KANICHEV.

Inter Press Service (IPS) (Italy): Calle 36A, No 121 Bajos, esq. a 3, Miramar, Apdo 1, Havana; tel. (7) 22-1981; Bureau Chief CLAUDE JOSEPH HACKIN; Correspondent CARLOS BASTISTA MORENO.

Korean Central News Agency (Democratic People's Republic of Korea): Calle 10, No 613, esq. 25, Vedado, Apdo 6, Havana; tel. (7) 31-4201; Bureau Chief CHANG YON CHOL.

Magyar Távirati Iroda (MTI) (Hungary): Edif. Fajardo, Calle 17 y M, Apdo 2C, Havana; tel. (7) 32-8353; Bureau Chief ZOLTÁN TAKACS; Correspondent TIBOR CSÁSZÁR.

Novinska Agencija Tanjug (Serbia and Montenegro): Calle 5F, No 9801, esq. 98, Miramar, Havana; tel. (7) 22-7671; Bureau Chief DUŠAN DAKOVIĆ.

Polska Agencja Prasowa (PAP) (Poland): Calle 6, No 702, Apdo 5, entre 7 y 9, Miramar; Havana; tel. (7) 20-7067; Bureau Chief PIOTR SOMMERFED.

Reuters (United Kingdom): Edif. Someillán, Linea 5, 9°, Vedado, Havana 4; tel. (7) 33-3145; Bureau Chief FRANCES KERRY.

Rossiyskoye Informatsionnoye Agentstvo—Novosti (RIA—Novosti) (Russia): Calle 28, No 510, entre 5 y 7, Miramar, Havana; tel. (7) 22-4129; Bureau Chief YURII GOLOVIATENKO.

Viet Nam Agency (VNA): Calle 16, No 514, 1°, entre 5 y 7, Miramar, Havana; tel. (7) 2-4455; Bureau Chief PHAM DINH LOI.

Xinhua (New China) News Agency (People's Republic of China): Calle G, No 259, esq. 13, Vedado, Havana; tel. (7) 32-4616; Bureau Chief GAO YONGHUA.

Publishers

Casa de las Américas: Calle 3 y Avda G, Vedado, Havana; tel. (7) 32-3587; fax (7) 32-7272; e-mail casa@arsoft.cult.cu; f. 1960; Latin

American literature and social sciences; Dir ROBERTO FERNÁNDEZ RETAMAR.

Ediciones Unión: Calle 17, No 354 esq. a H, Vedado, Havana; tel. (7) 55-3112; fax (7) 33-3158; e-mail uneac@artsoft.cult.cu; f. 1962; publishing arm of the Unión de Escritores y Artistas de Cuba; Cuban literature, art; Dir MERCY RUIZ.

Editora Abril: Prado 553, esq. Teniente Rey, Habana Vieja, Havana; tel. (7) 62-7871; fax (7) 62-7871; e-mail eabril@tinored.cu; internet www.editoraabril.cu; f. 1980; attached to the Union of Young Communists; children's literature; Dir RAFAELA VALERINO ROMERO.

Editora Política: Belascoaín No 864, esq. a Desagüe y Peñalver, Havana; tel. (7) 79-8553; fax (7) 81-1084; e-mail editors@epol.cipcc .get.cma.net; f. 1963; publishing institution of the Communist Party of Cuba; Dir SANTIAGO DÓRQUEZ PÉREZ.

Editorial Academia: Industria No 452, esq. a San José, Habana Vieja, Havana; tel. (7) 62-9501; f. 1963; attached to the Ministry of Science, Technology and the Environment; scientific and technical; Dir MIRIAM RAYA HERNÁNDEZ.

Editorial de Ciencias Médicas y Centro Nacional de Información de Ciencias Médicas: Calle E, No 452, entre 19 y 21, Vedado, Apdo 6520, Havana 10400; tel. (7) 32-4519; fax (7) 32-5008; attached to the Ministry of Public Health; books and magazines specializing in the medical sciences; Dir AUGUSTO HERNÁNDEZ BATISTA.

Editorial Ciencias Sociales: Calle 14, No 4104, entre 41 y 43, Miramar, Playa, Havana; tel. (7) 23-3959; f. 1967; attached to the Cuban Book Institute; social and political literature, history, philosophy, juridical sciences and economics; Dir RICARDO GARCÍA PAMPÍN.

Editorial Científico-Técnica: Calle 2, No 58, entre 3 y 5, Vedado, Havana; tel. (7) 3-9417; f. 1967; attached to the Ministry of Culture; technical and scientific literature; Dir ISIDRO FERNÁNDEZ RODRÍGUEZ.

Editorial Gente Nueva: Palacio del Segundo Cabo, Calle O'Reilly, No 4, esq. a Tacón, Havana; tel. (7) 62-4753; f. 1967; books for children; Dir RUBÉN DEL VALLE LANTARÓN.

Editorial José Martí/Arte y Literatura: Calzada 259, entre I y J, Apdo 4208, Havana; tel. (7) 33-3541; fax (7) 33-8187; f. 1983; attached to the Ministry of Culture; foreign-language publishing; Dir CECILIA INFANTE GUERRERO.

Editorial Letras Cubanas: Calle O'Reilly, No 4, esq. Tacón, Habana Vieja, Havana; tel. (7) 62-4378; fax (7) 33-8187; e-mail elc@ icl.cult.cu; f. 1977; attached to the Ministry of Culture; general, particularly classic and contemporary Cuban literature and arts; Dir DANIEL GARCÍA SANTOS.

Editorial Oriente: Santa Lucía 356, Santiago de Cuba; tel. (226) 22496; fax (226) 42387; e-mail edoriente@cultstgo.cult.cu; internet www.cubaliteria.com; f. 1971; publishes works from the Eastern provinces; fiction, history, female literature and studies, art and culture, practical books and books for children; Dir AIDA BAHR.

Editorial Pueblo y Educación: Avda 3A, No 4601, entre 46 y 60, Playa, Havana; tel. (7) 22-1490; fax (7) 24-0844; e-mail epe@ceniai .inf.cu; f. 1971; textbooks and educational publications; publishes Revista Educación three times a year (circ. 2,200); Dir CATALINA LAJUD HERRERO.

Government Publishing Houses

Instituto Cubano del Libro: Palacio del Segundo Cabo, Calle O'Reilly, No 4, esq. a Tacón, Havana; tel. (7) 62-4789; fax (7) 33-8187; e-mail cclfilh@artsoft.cult.cu; printing and publishing organization attached to the Ministry of Culture which combines several publishing houses and has direct links with others; presides over the National Editorial Council (CEN); Pres. OMAR GONZÁLEZ JIMÉNEZ.

Oficina de Publicaciones: Calle 17, No 552, esq. a D, Vedado, Havana; tel. (7) 32-1883; fax (7) 33-5106; attached to the Council of State; books, pamphlets and other printed media on historical and political matters; Dir PEDRO ALVAREZ TABÍO.

Broadcasting and Communications

TELECOMMUNICATIONS

Empresa de Telecomunicaciones de Cuba, SA (ETECSA): Calle Egido, No 610, entre Gloria y Apodaca, Habana Vieja, Havana; tel. (7) 860-4848; fax (7) 860-5144; e-mail presidencia@etecsa.cu; internet www.etecsa.cu; Exec. Pres. JOSÉ ANTONIO FERNÁNDEZ.

Empresa de Telecomunicaciones Internacionales (EMTEL-CUBA): Zanja, No 855, 6°, Havana; tel. (7) 70-8794; fax (7) 78-3722; 50% sold to Mexico's Grupo Domor in 1994; Dir REGINO GONZÁLEZ TOLEDO.

Instituto de Investigación y Desarrollo de las Telecomunicaciones (LACETEL): Rancho Boyeros, Km 14½, Santiago de las Vegas, Rancho Boyeros, Havana; tel. (7) 20-2929; fax (7) 33-5812; Dir EDUARDO TRUFFÍN TRIANA.

Ministerio de Comunicaciones (Dirección General de Telecomunicaciones): Plaza de la Revolución, Havana; Dir CARLOS MARTÍNEZ ALBUERNE.

Teléfonos Celulares de Cuba, SA (CUBACEL): Calle 28, No 510, entre 5 y 7, Playa, Havana; tel. (7) 880-2222; fax (7) 880-1737; e-mail webmaster@cubacel.com; internet www.cubacel.com; Dir-Gen. RAFAEL GALINDO MIER.

BROADCASTING

Ministerio de la Informática y las Comunicaciones (Dirección de Frecuencias Radioeléctricas): Avda Independencia y 19 de Mayo, Plaza de la Revolución, Apdo 10600, Havana; tel. (7) 70-6932; Dir CARLOS MARTÍNEZ ALBUERNE.

Instituto Cubano de Radio y Televisión (ICRT): Edif. Radiocentro, Avda 23, No 258, entre L y M, Vedado, Havana 4; tel. (7) 32-1568; fax (7) 33-3107; e-mail icrt@cecm.get.tur.cu; f. 1962; Pres. ERNESTO LÓPEZ DOMÍNGUEZ.

Radio y Televisión Comercial: Calle 26, No 301, esq. 21, Vedado, Havana; tel. (7) 66-2719; fax (7) 33-3939; e-mail g.general@rtvc.com .cu; Dir RENÉ DUQUESNE LÓPEZ.

Radio

In 1997 there were five national networks and one international network, 14 provincial radio stations and 31 municipal radio stations, with a total of some 170 transmitters.

Radio Cadena Agramonte: Calle Cisneros, No 310, entre Ignacio Agramonte y General Gómez, Camagüey; tel. (322) 29-1195; e-mail cip240@cip.etecsa.cu; internet www.cadenagramonte.cubaweb.cu; digital radio; serves Camagüey; Dir GUILLERMO PAVÓN PACHECO.

Radio Enciclopedia: Calle N, No 266, entre 21 y 23, Vedado, Havana; tel. (7) 81-2809; e-mail enciclop@ceniai.inf.cu; internet www.radioenciclopedia.co.cu; f. 1962; national network; instrumental music programmes; 24 hours daily; Dir EDELSA PALACIOS GORDO.

Radio Habana Cuba: Infanta 105 esq. a 25, 6°, Apdo 6240, Havana; tel. (7) 77-6628; fax (7) 81-2927; e-mail radiohc@ip.etecsa .cu; internet www.radiohc.cu; f. 1961; shortwave station; broadcasts in Spanish, English, French, Portuguese, Arabic, Esperanto, Quechua, Guaraní and Creole; Dir-Gen. MILAGRO HERNÁNDEZ CUBA.

CMBF (Radio Musical Nacional): Infanta 105, esq. a 25, 6°, Havana; tel. (7) 79-8479; f. 1948; national network; classical music programmes; 17 hours daily; Dir LUIZ LÓPEZ-QUINTANA.

Radio Progreso: Infanta 105, esq. a 25, 6°, Apdo 3042, Havana; tel. (7) 70-4561; e-mail progreso@ceniai.inf.cu; internet www .radioprogreso.cu; f. 1929; national network; mainly entertainment and music; 24 hours daily; Dir MANUEL E. ANDRÉS MAZORRA.

Radio Rebelde: Edif. ICRT, Avda 23, No 258, entre L y M, Vedado, Apdo 6277, Havana; tel. (7) 31-3514; fax (7) 33-4270; e-mail rebelde@ ceniai.inf.cu; internet www.radiorebelde.com.cu; f. 1958; merged with Radio Liberación in 1984; national network; 24-hour news and cultural programmes, music and sports; Dir Gen. PEDRO PABLO FIGUEREDO RODRÍGUEZ.

Radio Reloj: Edif. Radiocentro, Avda 23, No 258, entre L y M, Vedado, Havana; tel. (7) 55-4185; e-mail radioreloj@rreloj.icrt.cu; internet www.radioreloj.cu; f. 1947; national network; 24-hour news service; Dir ISIDRO BETANCOURT SILVA.

Radio Taino: Edif. Radiocentro, Avda 23, No 258, entre L y M, Vedado, Havana; tel. (7) 31-2645; fax (7) 33-4270; internet radiotaino.cubasi.cu; broadcasts in English and Spanish.

Television

Instituto Cubano de Radiodifusión (Televisión Nacional): Calle M, No 313, entre 21 y 23, Vedado, Havana; tel. (7) 32-5000; broadcasts in colour on channel 6; Vice-Pres JOSEFA BRACERO TORRES, OVIDIO CABRERA, ERNESTO LÓPEZ.

Cubavisión: Calle M, No 313, Vedado, Havana; internet www .cubavision.cubaweb.cu.

Tele Rebelde: Mazón, No 52, Vedado, Havana; tel. (7) 32-3369; broadcasts on channel 2; Vice-Pres. GARY GONZÁLEZ.

CHTV: Habana Libre Hotel, Havana; f. 1990; subsidiary station of Tele-Rebelde; Dir ROSA MARÍA FERNÁNDEZ SOFÍA.

Finance

(cap. = capital; p.u. = paid up; res = reserves; dep. = deposits;
m. = million; brs = branches)

BANKING

All banks were nationalized in 1960. Legislation establishing the national banking system was approved by the Council of State in 1984. A restructuring of the banking system, initiated in 1995, to accommodate Cuba's transformation to a more market-orientated economy was proceeding in 2003. A new central bank, the Banco Central de Cuba (BCC), was created in 1997 to supersede the Banco Nacional de Cuba (BNC). The BCC was to be responsible for issuing currency, proposing and implementing monetary policy and the regulation of financial institutions. The BNC was to continue functioning as a commercial bank and servicing the country's foreign debt. The restructuring of the banking system also allowed for the creation of an investment bank, the Banco de Inversiones, to provide medium- and long-term financing for investment, and the Banco Financiero Internacional, SA, to offer short-term financing. A new agro-industrial and commercial bank was also to be created to provide services for farmers and co-operatives. The new banking system is under the control of Grupo Nueva Banca, which holds a majority share in each institution.

Central Bank

Banco Central de Cuba (BCC): Amargura y Lamparilla 402, Havana; tel. (7) 62–7601; fax (7) 66–6601; e-mail plascncia@bc.gov.cu; internet www.bc.gov.cu; f. 1997; sole bank of issue; Pres. Francisco Soberón Valdez.

Commercial Banks

Banco Financiero Internacional, SA: Edif. Someillán, Calle Línea y O, Vedado, Havana; tel. (7) 32-1518; fax (7) 33-3006; f. 1984; autonomous; cap. US $10m. (1985); finances Cuba's foreign trade; Chair. Eduardo Bencomo Zurdos; Gen. Man. Arnaldo Alayón.

Banco Internacional de Comercio, SA: 20 de Mayo y Ayestarán, Apdo 6113, Havana 10600; tel. (7) 55-5933; fax (7) 33-5112; e-mail bicsa@bicsa.columbus.cu; f. 1993; cap. US $82.0m., res $8.6m., dep. $431.9m. (Dec. 2001); Chair. Ernesto Medina.

Banco Metropolitano: Avda 5 y Calle 112, Playa, Havana; tel. (7) 204-3869; fax (7) 204-9193; e-mail bm@banco-metropolitano.com; internet www.banco-metropolitano.com; f. 1996; offers foreign currency and deposit account facilities; Pres. Manuel Vale Marrero; Dir Pedro de la Rosa González.

Banco Nacional de Cuba (BNC): Aguiar 456, entre Amargura y Lamparillla, Havana; tel. (7) 62-8896; fax (7) 66-9514; e-mail bancuba@bnc.cu; f. 1950; reorganized 1997; Chair. Diana Amelia Fernández Vila.

Foreign Banks

There are 16 foreign banks represented in Cuba, including Banco Bilbao Vizcaya Argentaria (Spain), Banco de Comercio Exterior de México, Banco Exterior de España, Banco Sabadell (Spain), ING Bank (Netherlands) and Société General de France.

Savings Bank

Banco Popular del Ahorro: Calle 16, No 306, entre 3 y 5, Playa, Havana; tel. (7) 22-2545; f. 1983; savings bank; cap. 30m. pesos; dep. 5,363.7m. pesos; Pres. Marisela Ferreyra de la Gándara; 520 brs.

Investment Bank

Banco de Inversiones, SA: 5 Avda 6802, entre 68 y 70, Miramar, Havana; tel. (7) 204–3374; fax (7) 204–3373; e-mail bdi@bdi.columbus.cu.

INSURANCE

State Organizations

Empresa del Seguro Estatal Nacional (ESEN): Calle 5, No 306, entre C y D, Vedado, Havana; tel. (7) 32–2500; fax (7) 33–8717; e-mail esen@esen.com.cu; internet www.esen.com.cu; f. 1978; motor and agricultural insurance; Man. Dir Pedro Manuel Roche Alvarez.

Seguros Internacionales de Cuba, SA—Esicuba: Cuba No 314, Apdo 79, Havana; tel. (7) 62-5051; fax (7) 33-8038; f. 1963; reorganized 1986; all classes of insurance except life; Pres. Ramón Martínez Carrera.

Trade and Industry

GOVERNMENT AGENCIES

Ministry of Foreign Investment and Economic Co-operation: Primera No 2203, entre 22 y 24, Miramar, Havana; tel. (7) 22-3873; fax (7) 204-2105; e-mail epinv@minuce.cu.

Free-Trade Zones National Office: Calle 22, No 528, entre 3 y 5, Miramar, Havana; tel. (7) 24-7636; fax (7) 24-7637.

CHAMBER OF COMMERCE

Cámara de Comercio de la República de Cuba: Calle 21, No 661, esq. Calle A, Apdo 4237, Vedado, Havana; tel. (7) 55-1321; fax (7) 33-3042; e-mail pdcia@camara.com.cu; internet www.camaracuba.cu; f. 1963; mems include all Cuban foreign trade enterprises and the most important agricultural and industrial enterprises; Pres. Antonio L. Carricarte Corona; Sec.-Gen. Sara Marta Díaz.

AGRICULTURAL ORGANIZATION

Asociación Nacional de Agricultores Pequeños (ANAP) (National Association of Small Farmers): Calle I, No 206, entre Linea y 13, Vedado, Havana; tel. (7) 32-4541; fax (7) 33-4244; f. 1961; 220,000 mems; Pres. Orlando Lugo Fonte; Vice-Pres. Evelio Pausa Bello.

STATE IMPORT-EXPORT BOARDS

Alimport (Empresa Cubana Importadora de Alimentos): Infanta 16, 3°, Apdo 7006, Havana; tel. (7) 54-2501; fax (7) 33-3151; e-mail precios@alimport.com.cu; f. 1962; controls import of foodstuffs and liquors; Man. Dir Pedro Alvarez Borrego.

Autoimport (Empresa Central de Abastecimiento y Venta de Equipos de Transporte Ligero): Galiano 213, entre Concordia y Virtudes, Havana; tel. (7) 61-5322; fax (7) 66-6549; e-mail eric@autoimport.com.cu; imports cars, light vehicles, motor cycles and spare parts; Dir José Arañaburu.

Aviaimport (Empresa Cubana Importadora y Exportadora de Aviación): Calle 182, No 126, entre 1 y 5, Reparto Flores, Playa, Havana; tel. (7) 21-7687; fax (7) 33-6234; e-mail aviaimcom@iacc3.get.sma.net; import and export of aircraft and components; Man. Dir Marcos Lago Martínez.

Caribex (Empresa Exportadora del Caribe): Aparthotel Las Brisas, Apdo 3c 41, Villa Panamericana, Havana; tel. (7) 95-1140; fax (7) 95-1142; e-mail direccion@caribex.fishnavy.inf.cu; internet www1.cubamar.cu/caribex/caribex.htm; import and export of seafood and marine products; Dir Pedro Suárez Gambe.

Construimport (Empresa Central de Abastecimiento y Venta de Equipos de Construcción y sus Piezas): Carretera de Varona, Km 1½, Capdevila, Havana; tel. (7) 45-2567; fax (7) 66-6180; e-mail construimport@colombus.cu; f. 1969; controls the import and export of construction machinery and equipment; Man. Dir Jesús Serrano Rodríguez.

Consumimport (Empresa Cubana Importadora de Artículos de Consumo General): Calle 23, No 55, 9°, Apdo 6427, Vedado, Havana; tel. (7) 54-3110; fax (7) 54-2142; e-mail comer@consumimport.infocex.cu; f. 1962; imports and exports general consumer goods; Dir Mercedes Rey Hechavarría.

Copextel (Corporación Productora y Exportadora de Tecnología Electrónica): Calle 194 y 7A, Siboney, Havana; tel. (7) 21-8400; fax (7) 33-1414; e-mail copextel@copextel.com.cu; internet www.copextel.com.cu; f. 1986; exports LTEL personal computers and microcomputer software; Dir Norma M. García Bruzón.

Coprefil (Empresa Comercial y de Producciones Filatélicas): Avda 49, No 2831, Reparto Kohly, Havana; tel. (7) 24-9668; fax (7) 24-5077; e-mail copredir@ip.etecsa.cu; imports and exports postage stamps, postcards, calendars, handicrafts, communications equipment, electronics, watches, etc. Dir Nelson Iglesias Fernández.

Cubaelectrónica (Empresa Importadora y Exportadora de Productos de la Electrónica): Calle 22, No 510, entre 5 y 7, Miramar, Havana; tel. (7) 24-0278; fax (7) 24-1233; f. 1986; imports and exports electronic equipment and devices; Man. Dir Luis Alberto de Aguero.

Cubaexport (Empresa Cubana Exportadora de Alimentos y Productos Varios): Calle 23, No 55, entre Infanta y P, 8°, Vedado, Apdo 6719, Havana; tel. (7) 54-3130; fax (7) 33-3587; e-mail cexport@infocex.cu; export of foodstuffs and industrial products; Man. Dir Milda Picos Rivers.

Cubafrutas (Empresa Cubana Exportadora de Frutas Tropicales): Calle 23, No 55, Apdo 6683, Vedado, Havana; tel. and fax (7) 79-

5653; f. 1979; controls export of fruits, vegetables and canned foodstuffs; Dir JORGE AMARO MOREJÓN.

Cubalse (Empresa para Prestación de Servicios al Cuerpo Diplomático): Avda 3 y Final, Miramar, Havana; tel. (7) 204-2284; fax (7) 204-2282; e-mail cubalse@cm.cubalse.cma.net; internet www .cubalse.cu; f. 1974; imports consumer goods for the diplomatic corps and foreign technicians residing in Cuba; exports beverages and tobacco, leather goods and foodstuffs; other operations include real estate, retail trade, restaurants, clubs, automobile business, state-of-the-art equipment and household appliances, construction, investments, wholesale, road transport, freight transit, shipping, publicity, photography and video, financing, legal matters; Pres. REIDAL RONCOURT FONT.

Cubametales (Empresa Cubana Importadora de Metales, Combustibles y Lubricantes): Infanta 16, 4°, Apdo 6917, Vedado, Havana; tel. (7) 70-4225; fax (7) 33-3477; controls import of metals (ferrous and non-ferrous), crude petroleum and petroleum products; also engaged in the export of petroleum products and ferrous and non-ferrous scrap; Dir PEDRO PEREZ RODRÍGUEZ.

Cubaniquel (Empresa Cubana Exportadora de Minerales y Metales): Calle 23, No 55, 8°, Apdo 6128, Havana; tel. (7) 33-5334; fax (7) 33-3332; f. 1961; sole exporter of minerals and metals; Man. Dir ARIEL MASÓ MARZAL.

Cubatabaco (Empresa Cubana del Tabaco): Calle O'Reilly, No 104, Apdo 6557, Havana; tel. (7) 61-5759; fax (7) 33-8214; f. 1962; controls export of leaf tobacco, cigars and cigarettes to France; Dir JUAN MANUEL DÍAZ TENORIO.

Cubatécnica (Empresa de Contratación de Asistencia Técnica): Calle 12, No 513, entre 5 y 7, Miramar, Havana; tel. (7) 22-3270; fax (7) 24-0923; e-mail info@cubatecnica.cu; internet www.cubatecnica .cu; f. 1976; controls export and import of technical assistance; Dir FÉLIX GONZÁLEZ NAVERÁN.

Cubatex (Empresa Cubana Importadora de Fibras, Tejidos, Cueros y sus Productos): Calle 23, No 55, Apdo 7115, Vedado, Havana; tel. (7) 70-2531; fax (7) 33-3321; controls import of fibres, textiles, hides and by-products and export of fabric and clothing; Dir LUISA AMPARO SESÍN VIDAL.

Cubazúcar (Empresa Cubana Exportadora de Azúcar y sus Derivados): Calle 23, No 55, 7°, Vedado, Apdo 6647, Havana; tel. (7) 54-2175; fax (7) 33-3482; e-mail producer@cubazucar.com; internet www.cubazucar.com; f. 1962; controls export of sugar, molasses and alcohol; Dir ALEJANDRO GUTÍERREZ MAIRIGAL.

Ecimact (Empresa Comercial de Industrias de Materiales, Construcción y Turismo): Calle 1c, entre 152 y 154, Miramar, Havana; tel. (7) 21-9783; controls import and export of engineering services and plant for industrial construction and tourist complexes; Dir OCTAVIO CASTILLA CANGAS.

Ecimetal (Empresa Importadora y Exportadora de Objetivos Industriales): Calle 23, No 55, esq. Plaza, Vedado, Havana; tel. (7) 55-0548; fax (7) 33-4737; e-mail ecimetal@infocex.cu; f. 1977; controls import and export of plant, equipment and raw materials for all major industrial sectors; Dir CONCEPCIÓN BUENO.

Ediciones Cubanas (Empresa de Comercio Exterior de Publicaciones): Obispo 527, Apdo 43, Havana; tel. (7) 63-1989; fax (7) 33-8943; e-mail edicuba@artsoft.cult.cu; controls import and export of books and periodicals; Dir NANCY MATOS LACOSTA.

Egrem (Estudios de Grabaciones y Ediciones Musicales): San Miguel 410, Havana; tel. (7) 33-1473; fax (7) 33-8043; f. 1964; controls the import and export of records, tapes, printed music and musical instruments; Dir Gen. JULIO BALLESTER GUZMÁN.

Emexcon (Empresa Importadora y Exportadora de la Construcción): Calle 25, No 2602, Miramar, Havana; tel. (7) 22-3694; fax (7) 24-1862; f. 1978; consulting engineer services, contracting, import and export of building materials and equipment; Dir CRISTOBAL E. MARTÍNEZ.

Emiat (Empresa Importadora y Exportadora de Suministros Técnicos): Calle 20, No 519, entre 5 y 7, Miramar, Havana; tel. (7) 22-1163; fax (7) 22-5176; f. 1983; imports technical materials, equipment and special products; exports furniture, kitchen utensils and accessories; Dir MARTA ALFONSO SÁNCHEZ.

Emidict (Empresa Especializada Importadora, Exportadora y Distribuidora para la Ciencia y la Técnica): Calle 16, No 102, esq. Avda 1, Miramar, Playa, 13000 Havana; tel. (7) 23-5316; fax (7) 204-1758; e-mail emidict@ceniai.inf.cu; internet www.emidict.com.cu; f. 1982; controls import and export of scientific and technical products and equipment, live animals; scientific information; Dir-Gen. CARLOS CANALES ENRÍQUEZ.

Energoimport (Empresa Importadora de Objetivos Electro-energéticos): Calle 7, No 2602, esq. a 26, Miramar, Havana; tel. (7) 23-8156; fax (7) 24-0148; f. 1977; controls import of equipment for electricity generation; Man. ANDRÉS MONTEZ PERRERA.

Eprob (Empresa de Proyectos para las Industrias de la Básica): Avda 31A, entre 18 y 20, Miramar, Playa, Apdo 12100, Havana; tel. (7) 33-2146; fax (7) 33-2146; f. 1967; exports consulting services and processing of engineering construction projects, consulting services and supplies of complete industrial plants and turn-key projects; Man. Dir RAÚL RIVERO MARTÍNEZ.

Eproyiv (Empresa de Proyectos para Industrias Varias): Calle 33, No 1815, entre 18 y 20, Playa, Havana; tel. (7) 24-2149; e-mail eproyiv@ceniai.inf.cu; f. 1967; consulting services, feasibility studies, development of basic and detailed engineering models, project management and turn-key projects; Dir MARTA ELENA HERNÁNDEZ DÍAZ.

Esi (Empresa de Suministros Industriales): Calle Aguiar, No 556, entre Teniente Rey y Muralla, Havana; tel. (7) 62-0696; fax (7) 33-8951; f. 1985; imports machinery, equipment and components for industrial plants; Dir-Gen. FRANCISCO DÍAZ CABRERA.

Fecuimport (Empresa Cubana Importadora y Exportadora de Ferrocarriles): Avda 7, No 6209, entre 62 y 66, Miramar, Apdo 6003, Havana; tel. (7) 79-7678; f. 1968; imports and exports railway equipment; Pres. DOMINGO HERRERA.

Ferrimport (Empresa Cubana Importadora de Artículos de Ferretería): Calle 23, No 55, 2°, Vedado, Apdo 6258, Havana; tel. (7) 70-6678; fax (7) 79-4417; importers of industrial hardware; Dir.-Gen. ALEJANDRO MUSTELIER.

Fondo Cubano de Bienes Culturales: Calle 36, No 4702, esq. Avda 47, Reparto Kohly, Playa, Havana; tel. (7) 23-6523; fax (7) 24-0391; e-mail fcbc@cubarte.cult.cu; f. 1978; controls export of fine handicraft and works of art; Dir-Gen. JOSÉ GONZÁLEZ FERNÁNDEZ-LARREA.

Habanos, S.A.: Avda 3, No 2006, entre 20 y 22, Miramar, Havana; tel. (7) 204-0510; fax (7) 204-0490; e-mail habanos@habanos.cu; internet www.habanos.net; f. 1994; controls export of leaf and pipe tobacco, cigars and cigarettes to all markets; jt venture with Altadis SA (Spain).

ICAIC (Instituto Cubano del Arte e Industria Cinematográficos): Calle 23, No 1155, Vedado, Havana 4; tel. (7) 55-3128; fax (7) 33-3032; f. 1959; production, import and export of films and newsreel; Dir ANTONIO RODRÍGUEZ RODRÍGUEZ.

Imexin (Empresa Importadora y Exportadora de Infraestructura): Avda 5, No 1007, esq. a 12, Miramar, Havana; tel. (7) 23-9293; f. 1977; controls import and export of infrastructure; Man. Dir RAÚL BENCE VIJANDE.

Imexpal (Empresa Importadora y Exportadora de Plantas Alimentarias, sus Complementos y Derivados): Calle 22, No 313, entre 3 y 5, Miramar, Havana; tel. (7) 29-1671; controls import and export of food-processing plants and related items; Man. Dir Ing. CONCEPCIÓN BUENO CAMPOS.

Maprinter (Empresa Cubana Importadora y Exportadora de Materias Primas y Productos Intermedios): Infanta 16, 2A, Apdo 2110, Havana; tel. (7) 55-0645-2971; fax (7) 33-3535; e-mail direccion@ maprinter.infocex.cu; f. 1962; controls import and export of raw materials and intermediate products; Dir-Gen. ANTONIO LUIS CARRICARTE CORONA.

Maquimport (Empresa Cubana Importadora de Maquinarias y Equipos): Calle 23, No 55, 6°, Vedado, Apdo 6052, Havana; tel. (7) 55-0639; fax (7) 33-5443; e-mail maquimport@infocex-cu; imports industrial goods and equipment; Dir JORGE MIGUEL HERNÁNDEZ.

Marpesca (Empresa Cubana Importadora y Exportadora de Buques Mercantes y de Pesca): Conill No 580, esq. Avda 26, Nuevo Vedado, Havana; tel. (7) 81-1846; fax (7) 33-6020; f. 1978; imports and exports ships and port and fishing equipment; Dir JOSÉ CEREIJO CASAS.

Medicuba (Empresa Cubana Importadora y Exportadora de Productos Médicos): Máximo Gómez 1, esq. a Egido, Havana; tel. (7) 62-4061; fax (7) 33-8516; e-mail alfonso@medicuba.sld.cu; enterprise for the export and import of medical and pharmaceutical products; Dir ALFONSO SÁNCHEZ DÍAZ.

Produimport (Empresa Central de Abastecimiento y Venta de Productos Químicos y de la Goma): Calle Consulado 262, entre Animas y Virtudes, Havana; tel. (7) 62-0581; fax (7) 62-9588; f. 1977; imports and exports spare parts for motor vehicles; Dir JOSÉ GUERRA MATOS.

Quimimport (Empresa Cubana Importadora y Exportadora de Productos Químicos): Calle 23, No 55, Apdo 6088, Vedado, Havana; tel. (7) 33-3394; fax (7) 33-3190; controls import and export of chemical products; Dir ARMANDO BARRERA MARTÍNEZ.

Suchel (Empresa de Jabonería y Perfumería): Calzada de Buenos Aires 353, esq. a Durege, Apdo 6359, Havana; tel. (7) 33-8008; fax (7) 33-5311; e-mail sie@columbus.cu; internet www.suchel.cu; f. 1985; exports and imports materials for the detergent, perfumery and cosmetics industry, exports cosmetics, perfumes, hotel amenities and household products; Dir José García Díaz.

Tecnoazúcar (Empresa de Servicios Técnicos e Ingeniería para la Agro-industria Azucarera): Calle 12, No 310, entre 3 y 5, Miramar, Playa, Havana; tel. (7) 29-5441; fax (7) 33-1218; e-mail promocion@ tecnoazucar.cu; imports machinery and equipment for the sugar industry, provides technical and engineering assistance for the sugar industry; exports sugar-machinery equipment and spare parts; provides engineering and technical assistance services for sugar-cane by-product industry; Gen. Man. Victor R. Hernández Martínez.

Tecnoimport (Empresa Importadora y Exportadora de Productos Técnicos): Edif. La Marina, Avda del Puerto 102, entre Justiz y Obrapía, Habana Vieja, Havana; tel. (7) 61-5552; fax (7) 66-9777; f. 1968; imports technical products; Dir Adel Izquierdo Rodríguez.

Tecnotex (Empresa Cubana Exportadora e Importadora de Servicios, Artículos y Productos Técnicos Especializados): Avda 47, No 3419, Playa, Havana; tel. (7) 81-3989; fax (7) 33-1682; f. 1983; imports specialized technical and radiocommunications equipment, exports outdoor equipment and geodetic networks; Dir Adel Izquierdo Rodríguez.

Tractoimport (Empresa Central de Abastecimiento y Venta de Maquinaria Agrícola y sus Piezas de Repuesto): Avda Rancho Boyeros y Calle 100, Apdo 7007, Havana; tel. (7) 45-2166; fax (7) 267-0786; e-mail direccion@tractoimport.colombus.cu; f. 1960 for the import of tractors and agricultural equipment; also exports pumps and agricultural implements; Dir Abdel García González.

Transimport (Empresa Central de Abastecimiento y Venta de Equipos de Transporte Pesados y sus Piezas): Calle 102 y Avda 63, Marianao, Apdo 6665, 11500 Havana; tel. (7) 20-0325; fax (7) 33-5338; f. 1962; controls import and export of vehicles and transportation equipment; Dir Ariel Mejías Pérez.

UTILITIES

Electricity

Empresa Consolidada de Electricidad: Avda Salvador Allende 666, Havana; public utility.

TRADE UNIONS

All workers have the right to become members of a national trade union according to their industry and economic branch.

The following industries and labour branches have their own unions: Agriculture, Chemistry and Energetics, Civil Workers of the Revolutionary Armed Forces, Commerce and Gastronomy, Communications, Construction, Culture, Defence, Education and Science, Food, Forestry, Health, Light Industry, Merchant Marine, Mining and Metallurgy, Ports and Fishing, Public Administration, Sugar, Tobacco and Transport.

Central de Trabajadores de Cuba (CTC) (Confederation of Cuban Workers): Palacio de los Trabajadores, San Carlos y Peñalver, Havana; tel. (7) 78-4901; fax (7) 55–5927; e-mail digital@ trabaja.cip.cu; internet www.trabajadores.cubaweb.cu; f. 1939; affiliated to WFTU and CPUSTAL; 19 national trade unions affiliated; Gen. Sec. Pedro Ross Leal; 2,767,806 mems (1996).

Transport

The Ministry of Transport controls all public transport.

RAILWAYS

The total length of railways in 1998 was 14,331 km, of which 9,638 km were used by the sugar industry. The remaining 4,520 km were public service railways operated by Ferrocarriles de Cuba. All railways were nationalized in 1960. In 2001 Cuba signed an agreement with Mexico for the maintenance and repair of rolling stock.

Ferrocarriles de Cuba: Edif. Estación Central, Egido y Arsenal, Havana; tel. (7) 70-1076; fax (7) 33-1489; f. 1960; operates public services; Dir-Gen. Fernando Pérez López; divided as follows:

División Occidente: serves Pinar del Río, Ciudad de la Habana, Havana Province and Matanzas.

División Centro: serves Villa Clara, Cienfuegos and Sancti Spíritus.

División Centro-Este: serves Camagüey, Ciego de Avila and Tunas.

División Oriente: serves Santiago de Cuba, Granma, Guantánamo and Holguín.

División Camilo Cienfuegos: serves part of Havana Province and Matanzas.

ROADS

In 1999 there were an estimated 60,858 km of roads, of which 4,353 km were highways or main roads. The Central Highway runs from Pinar del Río in the west to Santiago, for a length of 1,144 km. In addition to this paved highway, there are a number of secondary and 'farm-to-market' roads. A small proportion of these secondary roads is paved but many can be used by motor vehicles only during the dry season.

SHIPPING

Cuba's principal ports are Havana (which handles 60% of all cargo), Santiago de Cuba, Cienfuegos, Nuevitas, Matanzas, Antilla, Guayabal and Mariel. Maritime transport has developed rapidly since 1959, and at 31 December 2001 Cuba had a merchant fleet of 92 ships (with a total displacement of 100,685 grt). In 2000 a US $100m. renovation and enlargement project for the port of Mariel was announced.

Coral Container Lines, SA: Oficios 170, 1°, Habana Vieja, Havana; tel. (7) 67-0854; fax (7) 67-0850; e-mail info@coral.com.cu; internet www.coral.cubaweb.cu; f. 1994; liner services to Europe, Canada, Brazil and Mexico; 11 containers; Chair. and Man. Dir Evelio González González.

Empresa Consignataria Mambisa: San José No 65, entre Prado y Zulueta, Habana Vieja, Havana; tel. (7) 862-2061; fax (7) 33-8111; e-mail mercedes@mambisa.transnet.cu; shipping agent, bunker suppliers; Man. Dir Eduardo Denis Valcárcel; Commercial Operations Man. Mercedes Pérez Newhall.

Empresa Cubana de Fletes (Cuflet): Calle Oficios No 170, entre Teniente Rey y Amargura, Apdo 6755, Havana; tel. (7) 61-2604; freight agents for Cuban cargo; Man. Dir Carlos Sánchez Perdomo.

Empresa de Navegación Caribe (Navecaribe): San Martín, 4°, Agramonte y Pasco de Martí, Habana Vieja, Havana; tel. (7) 62-5878; fax (7) 33-8564; f. 1966; operates Cuban coastal fleet; Dir Ramón Durán Suárez.

Empresa de Navegación Mambisa: San Ignacio No 104, Apdo 543, Havana; tel. (7) 62-7031; fax (7) 61-0044; operates dry cargo, reefer and bulk carrier vessels; Gen. Man. Gumersindo González Feliú.

Naviera Frigorífica Marítima: Havana; tel. (7) 35743; fax (7) 33-5185.

Naviera Mar América: 5a Avda y 246, Barlovento, Playa; tel. (59)24-9053; fax (59) 24-8889; e-mail nubia@maramerica.fishnavy .inf.eu.

Naviera Poseidon: Altos de la Aduana, San Pedro 1, Habana Vieja, Havana; tel. (7) 29-8073; fax (7) 24-8627; e-mail ccom@poseidon .fishnavy.inf.cu.

Nexus Reefer: Avda de la Pesquera y Atarés, Puerto Pesquero de la Habana, Habana Vieja, Havana 1; tel. (7) 66-6561; fax (7) 33-8046; e-mail nexus@fishnavy.inf.cu; merchant reefer ships; Gen. Dir Quirino L. Gutiérrez López.

CIVIL AVIATION

There are a total of 16 civilian airports, with 11 international airports, including Havana, Santiago de Cuba, Camagüey, Varadero and Holguín. Abel Santamaría International Airport opened in Villa Clara in early 2001. In January 2003 the King's Gardens International Airport in Cayo Coco was opened. The airport formed part of a new tourist 'offshore' centre. The international airports were all upgraded and expanded during the 1990s and a third terminal was constructed at the José Martí International Airport in Havana. In November 2001 three North American airlines were permitted to commence direct flights from Miami and New York to Havana.

Aerocaribbean: Calle 23, No 64 esq. a P. Vedado, Havana; tel. (7) 33-4543; fax (7) 33-5016; e-mail vpcr@cacsa.avianet.cu; f. 1982; international and domestic charter services; Chair. Julián Alvarez Infiesta.

Aerogaviota: Avda 47, No 2814, entre 28 y 34, Reparto Kolhy, Havana; tel. (7) 203-0668; fax (7) 204-2621; e-mail vpcom@ aerogaviota.avianet.cu; f. 1994; operated by Cuban air force.

Empresa Consolidada Cubana de Aviación (Cubana): Calle 23, No 64 Vedado, La Rampa, Havana 4; tel. (7) 33-4949; fax (7) 33-4056; e-mail vpcom@cubana.avianet.cu; internet www.cubana.cu; f. 1929; international services to North America, Central America, the Caribbean, South America and Europe; internal services from Havana to 14 other cities; Gen. Dir Heriberto Prieto.

Instituto de Aeronáutica Civil de Cuba (IACC): Calle 23, No 64, La Rampa, Vedado, Havana; tel. (7) 33-4949; fax (7) 33-4553; e-mail iacc@avianet.cu; f. 1985; Pres. Rogelio Acevedo González.

Tourism

Tourism began to develop after 1977, with the easing of travel restrictions by the USA, and Cuba subsequently attracted European tourists. Receipts totalled an estimated US $1,759m. in 2000, when there were 1,773,986 visitors. The number of hotel rooms increased to 34,000 in 2000. In that year there were 189 hotels. In 2001 an estimated 1,774.5m. tourists visited the island. A number of hotel tourism complexes were under construction in the early 2000s.

Cubanacán: Calle 148, entre 11 y 13, Playa, Apdo 16046, Havana; tel. (7) 22-5512; fax (7) 22-8382; e-mail webmaster@coral.cha.cyt.cu;

internet www.cubanacan.cu; f. 1987; Pres. ABRAHAM MACIQUES MACIQUES.

Empresa de Turismo Internacional (Cubatur): Calle 23, No 156, entre N y O, Apdo 6560, Vedado, Havana; tel. (7) 35-4521; fax (7) 32-3157; e-mail erisbel@cubatur.cu; internet www.cubatur.cu; f. 1968; Dir JOSÉ PADILLA.

Empresa de Turismo Nacional (Viajes Cuba): Calle 20, No 352, entre 21 y 23, Vedado, Havana; tel. (7) 30-0587; internet www.viajes-cuba.com; f. 1981; Dir ANA ELIS DE LA CRUZ GARCÍA.

CYPRUS

Introductory Survey

Location, Climate, Language, Religion, Flag, Capital

The Republic of Cyprus is an island in the eastern Mediterranean Sea, about 100 km south of Turkey. The climate is mild, although snow falls in the mountainous south-west between December and March. Temperatures in Nicosia are generally between 5°C (41°F) and 36°C (97°F). About 75% of the population speak Greek and almost all of the remainder Turkish. The Greek-speaking community is overwhelmingly Christian, and nearly all Greek Cypriots adhere to the Orthodox Church of Cyprus, while most of the Turkish Cypriots are Muslims. The national flag of the Republic of Cyprus (proportions 3 by 5) is white, with a gold map of Cyprus, above two crossed green olive branches, in the centre. The national flag of the 'Turkish Republic of Northern Cyprus' (proportions 2 by 3) has a white field, with a red crescent and star to left of centre between two narrow horizontal bands of red towards the upper and lower edges. The capital is Nicosia.

Recent History

A guerrilla war against British rule in Cyprus was begun in 1955 by Greek Cypriots seeking unification (*Enosis*) with Greece. Their movement, the National Organization of Cypriot Combatants (EOKA), was led politically by Archbishop Makarios III, head of the Greek Orthodox Church in Cyprus, and militarily by Gen. George Grivas. Archbishop Makarios was suspected by the British authorities of being involved in EOKA's campaign of violence, and in March 1956 he and three other *Enosis* leaders were deported. After a compromise agreement between the Greek and Turkish communities, a Constitution for an independent Cyprus was finalized in 1959. Makarios returned from exile and was elected the country's first President in December 1959. Cyprus became independent on 16 August 1960, although the United Kingdom retained sovereignty over two military base areas.

A constitutional dispute resulted in the withdrawal of the Turks from the central Government in December 1963, and there was serious inter-communal violence. In March 1964 a UN Peace-keeping Force in Cyprus (UNFICYP, see p. 68) was established to prevent a recurrence of fighting between the Greek and Turkish Cypriot communities. The effective exclusion of the Turks from political power led to the creation of separate administrative, judicial and legislative organs for the Turkish community. Discussions with a view to establishing a more equitable constitutional arrangement began in 1968; these continued intermittently for six years without achieving any agreement, as the Turks favoured some form of federation while the Greeks advocated a unitary state. Each community received military aid from its mother country, and officers of the Greek Army controlled the Greek Cypriot National Guard.

In 1971 Gen. Grivas returned to Cyprus, revived EOKA, and began a terrorist campaign for *Enosis*, directed against the Makarios Government and apparently supported by the military regime in Greece. Grivas died in January 1974, and in June Makarios ordered a purge of EOKA sympathizers from the police, National Guard and civil service, accusing the Greek regime of subversion. On 15 July Makarios was deposed in a military coup led by Greek officers of the National Guard, who appointed as President Nikos Sampson, an extremist Greek Cypriot politician and former EOKA militant. Makarios escaped from the island the following day and travelled to the United Kingdom. At the request of Rauf Denktaş, the Turkish Cypriot leader, the Turkish army intervened to protect the Turkish community and to prevent Greece from using its control of the National Guard to take over Cyprus. Turkish troops landed on 20 July and rapidly occupied the northern third of Cyprus, dividing the island along what became the Attila Line, which runs from Morphou through Nicosia to Famagusta. Sampson resigned on 23 July, and Glavkos Klerides, the President of the House of Representatives, became acting Head of State. The military regime in Greece collapsed the same day. In December Makarios returned to Cyprus and resumed the presidency. However, the Turkish Cypriots established a *de facto* Government in the north, and in February 1975 declared a 'Turkish Federated State of Cyprus' ('TFSC'), with Denktaş as President.

Makarios died in August 1977. He was succeeded as President by Spyros Kyprianou, a former Minister of Foreign Affairs and the President of the House of Representatives since 1976. Following a government reorganization in September 1980 the powerful communist party, the Anorthotiko Komma Ergazomenou Laou (AKEL—Progressive Party of the Working People), withdrew its support from the ruling Dimokratiko Komma (DIKO—Democratic Party), and Kyprianou lost his overall majority in the legislature. At the next general election, held in May 1981, AKEL and the Dimokratikos Synagermos (DISY—Democratic Rally) each won 12 seats in the House. DIKO, however, won only eight seats, so the President remained dependent on the support of AKEL.

In the 'TFSC' a new Council of Ministers was formed in December 1978 under Mustafa Çağatay, a former minister belonging to the Ulusal Bırlık Partisi (UBP—National Unity Party). At elections held in June 1981 President Denktaş was returned to office, but his party, the UBP, lost its legislative majority, and the Government that was subsequently formed by Çağatay was defeated in December. In March 1982 Çağatay formed a coalition Government, comprising the UBP, the Demokratik Halk Partisi (Democratic People's Party) and the Türkiye Bırlık Partisi (Turkish Unity Party).

In September 1980 UN-sponsored intercommunal peace talks were resumed. The constitutional issue remained the main problem: the Turkish Cypriots demanded equal status for the two communities, with equal representation in government and strong links with the mother country, while the Greeks, although accepting the principle of an alternating presidency, favoured a strong central government and objected to any disproportionate representation for the Turkish community, who constituted less than 20% of the population. Discussions on a UN plan involving a federal council, an alternating presidency and the allocation of 70% of the island to the Greek community faltered in February 1982, when the Greek Prime Minister, Andreas Papandreou, proposed the withdrawal of all Greek and Turkish troops and the convening of an international conference rather than the continuation of intercommunal talks. Meanwhile, in April 1981 it was agreed to establish a Committee on Missing Persons in Cyprus, comprising one representative of each community and a representative of the International Committee of the Red Cross (ICRC), to investigate the fate of 1,619 Greek Cypriots and 803 Turkish Cypriots listed as missing since the 1974 invasion. In May 1983 the UN General Assembly voted in favour of the withdrawal of Turkish troops from Cyprus, whereupon Denktaş threatened to boycott any further intercommunal talks and to seek recognition for the 'TFSC' as a sovereign state; simultaneously it was announced that the Turkish lira was to replace the Cyprus pound as legal tender in the 'TFSC'.

On 15 November 1983 the 'TFSC' made a unilateral declaration of independence as the 'Turkish Republic of Northern Cyprus' ('TRNC'), with Denktaş as President. Çağatay subsequently resigned the premiership and as leader of the UBP, and an interim Government was formed in December under Nejat Konuk (Prime Minister of the 'TFSC' from 1976 to 1978 and President of the Legislative Assembly from 1981). Like the 'TFSC', the 'TRNC' was recognized only by Turkey, and the declaration of independence was condemned by the UN Security Council. The 'TRNC' and Turkey established diplomatic relations in April 1984, and the 'TRNC' formally rejected UN proposals for a suspension of its declaration of independence prior to further talks.

During 1984 a 'TRNC' Constituent Assembly drafted a new Constitution, which was approved by 70% of voters at a referendum in May 1985. At a presidential election in the 'TRNC' on 9 June Denktaş was returned to office with more than 70% of the vote. A general election followed on 23 June, at which the UBP, led by Dr Derviş Eroğlu, won 24 of the 50 seats in the Legislative Assembly. In July Eroğlu became 'TRNC' Prime Minister, leading a coalition Government formed by the UBP and the

Toplumcu Kurtuluş Partisi (TKP—Communal Liberation Party).

At elections held in February 1983 Kyprianou was returned to the Greek Cypriot presidency for a further five-year term, taking 56.5% of the votes. In November 1985, following a debate on his leadership, the House of Representatives was dissolved. A general election for an enlarged legislature proceeded in December, at which Kyprianou's DIKO secured 16 seats. DISY, which won 19 seats, and AKEL, with 15, did not secure the two-thirds' majority required to amend the Constitution and thus challenge the President's tenure of power. Kyprianou failed to secure a third presidential term in February 1988; the election was won at a second round of voting by Georghios Vassiliou, an economist who presented himself as an independent but who was unofficially supported by AKEL and the Socialistiko Komma Kyprou EDEK (EDEK—EDEK Socialist Party of Cyprus). Vassiliou undertook to restore a cross-party National Council (originally convened by President Makarios) to address the Cyprus issue.

Settlement plans proposed by the UN Secretary-General in July 1985 and in April 1986 were rejected by the Turkish Cypriots and the Greek Cypriots, respectively. Further measures concerning the demilitarization of the island, reportedly proposed by the Greek Cypriot Government, were rejected by Denktaş, who maintained that negotiations on the establishment of a two-zone, federal republic should precede any demilitarization. In March 1988 the new Greek Cypriot President rejected various proposals submitted by Denktaş, via the UN, including a plan to form committees to study the possibilities of intercommunal co-operation. Following a meeting with the revived National Council in June, however, Vassiliou agreed to a proposal by the UN Secretary-General that he and Denktaş should resume intercommunal talks, without pre-conditions, in their capacity as the leaders of two communities. Denktaş also approved the proposal, and a summit meeting took place, under UN auspices, in Geneva, Switzerland, in August; this was the first such meeting between Greek and Turkish Cypriot leaders since January 1985. Vassiliou and Denktaş subsequently began direct negotiations, under UN auspices, in September 1988. No real progress was made and, although Vassiliou and Denktaş resumed negotiations at the UN in February 1990, the talks were abandoned in March, chiefly because Denktaş demanded recognition of the right to self-determination for Turkish Cypriots.

In April 1988 Eroğlu resigned as 'TRNC' Prime Minister, following a disagreement between the UBP and its coalition partner (since September 1986), the Yeni Doğuş Partisi (New Dawn Party), which was demanding greater representation in the Government. At the request of Denktaş, Eroğlu formed a new Council of Ministers in May, comprising mainly UBP members but also including independents. In April 1990 Denktaş secured nearly 67% of the votes cast in an early presidential election. Eroğlu retained the office of Prime Minister after the UBP won 34 of the 50 seats in the 'TRNC' Legislative Assembly at elections in May. (Following by-elections for 12 seats in October 1991, the UBP increased its representation in the Assembly to 45 members.)

In July 1990 the Government of Cyprus formally applied to join the European Community (EC, now European Union—EU, see p. 199). Denktaş condemned the application, on the grounds that the Turkish Cypriots had not been consulted, and stated that the action would prevent the resumption of intercommunal talks. In June 1993, none the less, the European Commission approved the eligibility of Cyprus for EC membership, although it insisted that the application should be linked to progress in the latest UN-sponsored talks concerning the island.

At the May 1991 general election for the Greek Cypriot seats in the House of Representatives, the conservative DISY, in alliance with the Komma Phileleftheron (Liberal Party), received 35.8% of the votes cast, thereby securing 20 of the 56 seats in the legislature. AKEL unexpectedly made the most significant gains, obtaining 30.6% of the votes and 18 seats.

Following unsuccessful attempts to promote the resumption of discussions between Vassiliou and Denktaş by the UN, the EC and the USA during 1990–91, the new UN Secretary-General, Dr Boutros Boutros-Ghali, made the resolution of the Cyprus problem a priority. UN envoys visited Cyprus, Turkey and Greece in February 1992, and in January and March Boutros-Ghali himself held separate meetings in New York, USA, with Vassiliou and Denktaş. However, no progress was achieved on the fundamental differences between the two sides concerning territory and displaced persons. In mid-1992 the UN Secretary-General conducted a second round of talks in New York with Vassiliou and Denktaş, initially separately but subsequently involving direct discussions between the two leaders. The talks aimed to arrive at a draft settlement based on a 'set of ideas', compiled by Boutros-Ghali and endorsed by a UN Security Council resolution (No. 750), advocating 'uninterrupted negotiations' until a settlement was reached. Discussions centred on UN proposals for the demarcation of Greek Cypriot and Turkish Cypriot areas of administration under a federal structure. However, following the publication of what was described as a 'non-map' in the Turkish Cypriot press, which showed the proposed area of Turkish administration as being about 25% smaller than the 'TRNC', Denktaş asserted that the UN's territorial proposals were totally unacceptable to the 'TRNC' Government, while political opinion in the Greek Cypriot area was divided. The five weeks of talks came to an end in August, again without having achieved significant progress. A third round of UN-sponsored talks opened in New York in late October, but these were suspended in the following month with no discernible progress having been made on the key refugee, constitutional and territorial issues. The UN Security Council held Denktaş responsible for the lack of progress, and adjourned the talks.

At the election for the Greek Cypriot presidency held in February 1993 the DISY leader, Glavkos Klerides, narrowly defeated the incumbent Vassiliou at a second round of voting. Vassiliou subsequently formed a new party, the Kinema ton Eleftheron Dimokraton (KED—Movement of Free Democrats).

UN-sponsored negotiations were reconvened in New York in May 1993, focusing on the Secretary-General's plan to introduce a series of what were termed 'confidence-building measures' (CBMs). These included the proposed reopening, under UN administration, of the international airport at Nicosia, and the resettlement, also under UN directives, of a fenced suburb of Famagusta. Denktaş presented separate demands at the talks, among them the removal of the embargo against 'TRNC' airports, ports and sporting activities. The talks were abandoned in June, when the Turkish Cypriot negotiators declined to respond to the UN proposals.

In November 1993 Klerides and Andreas Papandreou, who had recently resumed the Greek premiership, agreed at a meeting in Athens that their countries would take joint decisions in negotiations for the settlement of the Cyprus problem. The two leaders also agreed on a common defence doctrine, whereby Greece was to provide Cyprus with a guarantee of air, land and naval protection.

An early general election was held in the 'TRNC' in December 1993, partly in response to increasing friction between President Denktaş and Prime Minister Eroğlu over the handling of the UN-sponsored peace talks. The UBP lost its majority in the Legislative Assembly, retaining only 17 of the 50 seats, and at the end of the month a coalition Government was formed by the Demokrat Parti (DP—Democrat Party), which had been supported by Denktaş, and the left-wing Cumhuriyetçi Türk Partisi (CTP—Republican Turkish Party). Together the DP and the CTP won 53.4% of the votes cast and 28 seats. The leader of the DP, Hakkı Atun (hitherto the Speaker of the Assembly), was appointed as Prime Minister of the new administration.

In February 1994, following the confirmation by both authorities of their acceptance, in principle, of the CBMs, UN officials undertook what were designated 'proximity talks' separately with the Greek and Turkish Cypriot leaders. However, Denktaş considered that the proposals under discussion differed from the intention of the measures originally agreed, and therefore refused to accept the document that was presented to both sides in March. A report issued at the end of May by Boutros-Ghali for consideration by the UN Security Council held the 'TRNC' authorities responsible for the breakdown of the process. In the following month the UN conducted negotiations to reclarify the CBMs. Denktaş accepted certain UN requests on the implementation of the measures, including the withdrawal of Turkish Cypriot troops from the access road to Nicosia international airport, but no substantive progress was made.

In July 1994 the UN Security Council adopted a resolution (No. 939), advocating a new initiative on the part of the Secretary-General to formulate a solution for peace, based on a single nationality, international identity and sovereignty. In response, in the following month the 'TRNC' Legislative Assembly approved measures seeking to co-ordinate future foreign and defence policies with those of Turkey, asserting that no peace solution based on the concept of a federation would be acceptable, and demanding political and sovereign status equal to that of Greek Cyprus. No tangible progress was made at informal UN-sponsored meetings between Klerides and Denktaş during October.

The issue of Cyprus's bid to accede to the EU had, furthermore, greatly unsettled the progress of negotiations. In June 1994 EU heads of government, meeting in Corfu, Greece, confirmed that Cyprus would be included in the next round of expansion of the Union. Denktaş remained adamant that any approach by the Greek Cypriots to the EU would prompt the 'TRNC' to seek further integration with Turkey. In early 1995 US officials commenced discussions with the two sides in an attempt to break the deadlock: while Denktaş insisted that the 'TRNC' would oppose Cyprus's EU membership application until a settlement for the island had been reached, the Greek Cypriot Government demanded 'TRNC' acceptance of the application as a pre-condition to pursuing the talks. In March the EU agreed to consider Cyprus's membership application without discrimination based on the progress (or otherwise) of settlement talks. This was ratified in June by a meeting of the EU-Cyprus Association Council, at which it was agreed to commence pre-accession 'structured dialogue'. In late June Klerides attended for the first time a summit meeting of EU heads of government.

Meanwhile, in February 1995 Hakkı Atun and the 'TRNC' Government resigned, following serious disagreements with Denktaş regarding the redistribution of Greek Cypriot-owned housing and land. However, the UBP failed to negotiate the formation of a new coalition, and in the following month Atun was reappointed Prime Minister. At a presidential election held in April Denktaş secured a conclusive victory only at a second round of voting (having taken 40.4% of votes cast in the first poll), winning 62.5% of the votes in a run-off contest with Eroğlu. Following protracted inter-party negotiations, a new coalition of the DP and CTP, under Atun's premiership, took office in June.

So-called 'secret' negotiations between representatives of the two Cypriot communities, held in May 1995 in London, United Kingdom, on a joint US-British initiative, achieved little in furthering agreement on the island's future or in securing agreement for direct talks between Denktaş and Klerides. Allegations, which emerged in July, that Turkish Cypriot construction work in the capital was, in fact, part of efforts to fortify the buffer zone presented a new political obstacle to intercommunal negotiations.

In August 1995 the 'TRNC' Legislative Assembly adopted legislation concerning compensation for Greek-owned property in the north (the issue that had provoked Atun's resignation earlier in the year). At the end of October Özker Özgür resigned as Deputy Prime Minister, reportedly owing to his disapproval of Denktaş's uncompromising attitude regarding the Cyprus issue. In the following month Atun submitted the resignation of his entire Government, after Denktaş rejected a new list of CTP ministers. A new DP-CTP coalition, again under Atun's leadership and with Mehmet Ali Talat (of the CTP) replacing Özgür as Deputy Prime Minister, took office in December.

Elections for the Greek Cypriot seats in the House of Representatives in May 1996 produced little change in the composition of the legislature. DISY retained its 20 seats, with 34.5% of the votes cast; AKEL took 19 seats, an increase of one, with 33.0% of the votes, while DIKO held 10 seats, a loss of one compared with the 1991 election, with 16.4%.

Persistent policy differences within the 'TRNC' coalition caused the Government to resign in July 1996. Negotiations to establish a new administration were undertaken by the DP and the UBP, and in August the two parties signed a coalition agreement whereby UBP leader Eroğlu became Prime Minister.

In April 1996 the UN Security Council endorsed a US initiative to promote a federal-based settlement for Cyprus. (The USA had in late 1995 declared its intention to strengthen efforts, led by Richard Holbrooke, the Assistant Secretary of State with responsibility for Europe, with the aim of achieving significant progress towards a final settlement in Cyprus during 1996.) In May the United Kingdom appointed Sir David Hannay, a former Permanent Representative to the UN, as its first special representative to Cyprus. In June, in advance of a visit to the island by the UN Secretary-General's newly appointed Special Representative in Cyprus, Han Sung-Joo, Boutros-Ghali held discussions, separately, with Denktaş and Klerides, with the intention of generating support for future direct bilateral negotiations. However, all efforts towards international mediation were diminished by a sharp escalation in intercommunal hostilities. At the end of October a military dialogue did commence, involving senior commanders of the Greek and Turkish Cypriot armed forces, with UN mediation, to consider proposals for reducing intercommunal tension. Further mediation efforts were undermined in November by alleged violations of Greek Cypriot airspace by Turkish military aircraft, as well as by efforts by the Greek Cypriot community to prevent tourists from visiting the 'TRNC' and the continued opposition of the 'TRNC' to the Cypriot application to join the EU.

In December 1996 the European Court of Human Rights (ECHR) ruled that Turkey was in breach of the European Convention on Human Rights by, as a result of its occupation in the north, denying a woman access to her property. The ruling implicated Turkey as fully responsible for activities in the 'TRNC' and for the consequences of the military action in 1974.

In January 1997 an agreement signed by the Greek Cypriot Government and Russia regarding the purchase of an advanced anti-aircraft missile system became the focus of political hostilities between the Greek and Turkish Cypriots, and the cause of considerable international concern. The purchase agreement was condemned by the 'TRNC' as an 'act of aggression', and the potential for conflict over the issue increased when Turkey declared its willingness to use military force to prevent the deployment of the system. Greece in turn reiterated that it would defend Cyprus against any Turkish attack. US mediators sought urgent meetings with the Cypriot leaders, and were assured by the Greek Cypriot Government that the system would not be deployed until May 1998 at the earliest, and that its deployment would be dependent upon the progress made in talks. In addition, both sides approved UN-supported measures to reduce tension in the border area, although the Greek Cypriots rejected a US proposal for a ban on all military flights over the island. Later in January Turkey threatened to establish air and naval bases in the 'TRNC' if Greece continued to promote plans for the establishment of military facilities in the Greek Cypriot zone, and at the end of the month Turkish military vessels arrived in the 'TRNC' port of Famagusta. Turkey and the 'TRNC' also declared their commitment to a joint military concept whereby any attack on the 'TRNC' would be deemed a violation against Turkey.

In June 1997, following proximity talks between Klerides and Denktaş which had begun in March, the Cypriot leaders agreed to take part in direct UN-sponsored negotiations in the USA in July, under the chairmanship of the UN Special Envoy for Cyprus, Dr Diego Córdovez. The talks took place under the auspices of the UN Secretary-General, Kofi Annan, and with the participation of Richard Holbrooke, whose appointment in June as US Special Envoy to Cyprus had been welcomed by both Klerides and Denktaş. Further private direct talks took place in Nicosia at the end of July, when agreement was reached to co-operate in efforts to trace persons missing since the hostilities in 1974. However, a second formal round of UN-sponsored negotiations, convened in Switzerland in August 1997, collapsed without agreement, as Denktaş demanded the suspension of Cyprus's application for EU membership—to which the Turkish Cypriot leader remained opposed on the grounds that accession negotiations, scheduled to begin in 1998, were to be conducted with the Greek Cypriot Government, ignoring the issue of Turkish Cypriot sovereignty. (The EU had in the previous month formally agreed that Cyprus would be included in the next phase of the organization's enlargement.) An agreement by the 'TRNC' and Turkey, prior to the latest round of UN-sponsored talks, to create a joint committee to co-ordinate the partial integration of the 'TRNC' into Turkey was widely regarded as a response to the EU's decision to negotiate future membership with the Greek Cypriot Government while excluding Turkey from EU expansion. Although negotiations concerning security issues were held under UN auspices in Nicosia in September, US and UN efforts during October and November to promote progress in the talks, including visits to Cyprus by both Holbrooke and Córdovez, achieved little success, partly owing to the imminence of the Greek Cypriot presidential election. Denktaş rejected Holbrooke's attempts to persuade the 'TRNC' to join the Greek Cypriot Government at EU accession talks in 1998, insisting on EU recognition of the 'TRNC' and the simultaneous admission of Turkey to EU membership. Meanwhile, tension remained high, as Turkish fighter aircraft violated Greek Cypriot airspace in October 1997 in retaliation for Greek participation in Greek Cypriot military manoeuvres.

In November 1997 DIKO voted to leave the Greek Cypriot ruling coalition in advance of the presidential election, and the party's five government members resigned their posts. On 15 February 1998, at the second round of voting in the presidential election, Klerides defeated Georghios Iacovou, an independent candidate supported by AKEL and DIKO, taking 50.8% of the votes cast. A new coalition Government, composed of members of DISY, EDEK, the Enomeni Dimokrates (EDE—United Democrats—formed in 1996 by a merger of Vassiliou's KED and the Ananeotiko Dimokratiko Socialistiko Kinema) and independents, was sworn in at the end of the month.

The Greek Cypriot Government began accession talks with the EU in March 1998, and in the following month Cyprus confirmed its application for associate membership of Western European Union (WEU, see p. 318). In May Holbrooke visited Cyprus and held discussions with Klerides and Denktaş, with the aim of relaunching formal negotiations. However, no progress was made; Holbrooke cited the principal obstacles as Denktaş' demands for recognition of the 'TRNC' and for the withdrawal of the Cypriot application to join the EU, and the decision of the EU further to delay Turkey's application for membership. In August Denktaş rejected a UN plan for the reunification of Cyprus, proposing instead, in a letter to the UN, a confederation of equal status; this was deemed unacceptable by Klerides on the grounds that it would legitimize the status of the 'TRNC'. The UN Special Envoy travelled to Cyprus for individual meetings with Klerides and Denktaş in October, but no progress was made.

In June 1998 a number of Greek military aircraft landed at the Paphos airfield in southern Cyprus for the first time since the airfield's completion in January. Shortly afterwards Turkish military aircraft made reciprocal landings in the 'TRNC'. In July the Greek Cypriot Government condemned the arrival of Turkish military naval vessels and aircraft in the 'TRNC' for the celebrations of the anniversary of the Turkish invasion of the island. During the course of the year Turkish aircraft were accused of violating Greek Cypriot airspace on a number of occasions, and in October Turkish fighter planes allegedly harassed Greek military aircraft that were participating in joint exercises with Greek-Cypriot forces. Earlier in the month, however, Denktaş had proposed a non-aggression treaty between the two sides. Joint Turkish-'TRNC' military exercises were held in November.

At the end of December 1998 it was formally announced that the contentious Russian missile system would not be deployed in Cyprus, and that negotiations would instead be held with a view to their installation on the Greek island of Crete. This decision followed diplomatic pressure from Greece, the EU (which threatened to suspend Cypriot accession talks if the deployment proceeded in Cyprus), the USA and the UN, and was influenced by the adoption earlier in the month of two resolutions by the UN Security Council (both of which were dismissed by Denktaş): the first renewed the UNFICYP mandate and appealed for the resumption of negotiations on reunification as a single sovereign state (apparently rejecting the 'TRNC' Government's proposed confederation), and the second expressed concern at the lack of progress towards a political settlement and advocated a phased reduction of military personnel and armaments on the island. The missiles were reportedly deployed in Crete in March 1999, following the signature in February of an agreement by the Greek and Greek Cypriot Government to the effect that Cyprus would own the missiles although they would be under Greek operational control.

Klerides' reversal of policy regarding the missiles' deployment provoked intense domestic criticism, and prompted the withdrawal of EDEK (to which party the Minister of Defence belonged) from the Greek Cypriot governing coalition.

Meanwhile, at legislative elections held in the 'TRNC' on 6 December 1998 the UBP increased its representation to 24 seats (from 16 in 1993), while the DP held only 13 seats. The TKP won seven of the 50 seats and the CTP the remaining six. At the end of the month a new UBP-TKP Council of Ministers received presidential approval. Eroğlu remained as Prime Minister, and the TKP leader, Mustafa Akıncı, became Minister of State and Deputy Prime Minister.

In June 1999 the UN Security Council, extending the mandate of UNFICYP for a further six months, adopted a resolution urging the Greek and Turkish Cypriot authorities to participate in UN-sponsored negotiations in late 1999 without preconditions or proscribed issues. In November, despite his earlier reluctance to attend the proposed meeting, Denktaş confirmed that he would attend proximity talks with Klerides in New York under the auspices of the UN. The UN Secretary-General acted as a mediator in the indirect talks in the first half of December, which aimed to facilitate meaningful negotiations leading to a comprehensive settlement in Cyprus. The talks were, however, undermined by a decision of that month's summit meeting of EU Heads of State and Government in Helsinki, Finland, that a political settlement for Cyprus was not a precondition to the accession of the Greek Cypriot Government to the EU. This decision was widely acknowledged to be a response to Greece's reversal of its opposition to Turkey's EU membership application, and the summit thus accorded Turkey formal status as a candidate for EU membership. Although Denktaş criticized the EU decision on Cyprus's accession, a second round of UN-sponsored proximity talks began in Geneva at the end of January 2000. The UN Secretary-General and his Special Adviser on Cyprus, Alvaro de Soto, held separate meetings with Klerides and Denktaş, but again there were no direct exchanges between the two Cypriot leaders, and the talks ended without any substantive progress. Meanwhile, after an interval of more than three years, the Committee on Missing Persons in Cyprus met from November 1999 to discuss resuming its investigative work; however, following the death, in January 2000, of the ICRC representative, it was emphasized that the appointment of a successor was contingent upon assurances that obstacles impeding investigations had been removed and that both the Greek and Turkish Cypriot parties were committed to the committee's task.

A first round of presidential voting in the 'TRNC' was held on 15 April 2000, contested by eight candidates. Denktaş took 43.7% of the votes cast, thus failing to secure the majority necessary for outright victory. A second round was scheduled for 22 April, to be contested by Denktaş and his closest rival, Eroğlu (who had polled 30.1% at the first round), but this was cancelled following Eroğlu's withdrawal on 19 April and Denktaş was thus declared elected for a fourth term as President.

In mid-June 2000 the UN Security Council adopted a resolution (No. 1303) extending the mandate of UNFICYP for a further six months. The resolution notably excluded any reference to the authority of the 'TRNC', citing only the Government of Cyprus, and at the end of the month the 'TRNC' instituted a number of retaliatory measures against UNFICYP including measures to impede the movement of UN forces and new tariffs for UN vehicles and for the use of utilities supplied by the north. 'TRNC' and Turkish forces also crossed into the buffer zone and established a check-point at a village inhabited by Greek Cypriots.

A third round of proximity talks—mediated by Alvaro de Soto and focusing on what were termed 'core' issues of territory, constitutional arrangements, property rights and guarantees—took place in Geneva in July–August 2000. Again, there were no direct exchanges between the Greek Cypriot and Turkish Cypriot representatives, and the talks ended without progress. A further round of indirect negotiations began in New York in September. Klerides boycotted the early stages of the talks, in protest at a statement in which the UN Secretary-General had, in the view of the Greek Cypriots, implied that the 'TRNC' was equal in authority to the internationally-recognized Cypriot Government, but the Greek Cypriot leader resumed attendance after he received assurances that the UN would act in accordance with earlier Security Council resolutions on the Cyprus issue. Although de Soto expressed cautious optimism regarding the outcome of the talks, the Greek and Turkish Cypriots remained apparently irreconcilable on the issue of a future structure for Cyprus—with the former advocating a reunified, bi-communal federation and the latter a looser confederation based on equal sovereignty. A fifth round of UN-sponsored proximity talks was convened in Geneva at the beginning of November. After separate meetings with both Klerides and Denktaş, Kofi Annan expressed his view that the negotiations had moved beyond procedure into substance, and both leaders were invited to a further round of contacts in January 2001. Later in November 2000, however, Denktaş condemned the process as 'a waste of time', stating that he would not return to the talks until such time as the 'TRNC' was accorded international recognition. His decision, taken with the support of the Government of Turkey, apparently reflected anger in the 'TRNC' that the UN Secretary-General had emphasized that any agreement on Cyprus must be based on the premise of a single sovereign entity, and in Turkey that the European Commission had, in a draft partnership agreement published earlier in November 2000, stipulated among preconditions for Turkish admission to the EU Turkey's willingness to promote a settlement for Cyprus based on UN resolutions. Alvaro de Soto visited Cyprus in December in an effort to foster a resumption of contacts, but Denktaş reiterated that the 'TRNC' would not take part in any further talks unless its sovereignty was recognized; he warned, furthermore, that in the absence of such recognition UNFICYP would no longer be welcome in the 'TRNC'. In the same month the UN Security Council adopted a resolution (No. 1331) extending the mandate of the force for a further six-month period; the resolution urged the 'TRNC' to revoke restrictive measures imposed against UNFICYP in June (see above), noting that these had undermined the operational effectiveness of the peace-keeping force. (This was reiterated in Resolutions 1354 and 1384, adopted in June and December 2001.)

The European Commission's Progress Towards Accession report on Cyprus, published in November 2000, assessed Cyprus as being among the candidate countries best equipped to join the union; the report also repeated the EU's invitation to the Turkish Cypriot community to participate in the accession negotiations.

In February 2001 Denktaş reiterated his determination not to participate in further UN proximity talks while the international community continued to regard the Greek Cypriot Government as the legitimate Government for the whole of Cyprus. He also criticized the EU for making a settlement to the Cyprus problem a condition for further progress on Turkey's application for EU membership. The divide between the two communities was further aggravated by an ECHR judgment in May that found Turkey guilty of extensive violations of human rights arising from its 1974 invasion and occupation of Northern Cyprus. Whereas the Greek Cypriot Government welcomed the ruling as 'historic', Denktaş claimed that it justified his refusal to participate in further talks.

At elections for the Greek Cypriot members of the House of Representatives, held on 27 May 2001, AKEL secured a narrow victory over DISY, taking 20 seats (with 34.7% of the votes cast) compared with the latter's 19 (34.0%). DIKO held nine seats (14.8%), one fewer than in 1996. In early June 2001 the AKEL leader, Demetris Christofias, was elected as the new president of the legislature, receiving crucial support from the DIKO members to defeat the DISY leader, Nicos Anastasiades.

The governing coalition of the 'TRNC' collapsed in late May 2001, following disagreement between the UBP and TKP on the issue of whether to rejoin talks on the future status of the island. In June the UBP and the DP agreed to form a new coalition administration, with Eroğlu continuing as Prime Minister. The DP leader, Salih Coşar, became Minister of State and Deputy Prime Minister in a Government that was expected to be more supportive than its predecessor of President Denktaş's policy on the Cyprus question.

In September 2001 Alvaro de Soto announced that a new round of talks between Greek Cypriot and 'TRNC' representatives was to take place later in the month. However, Denktaş described the announcement as premature, and insisted that 'TRNC' representatives would not attend. In early December, none the less, Presidents Klerides and Denktaş met briefly for the first time in four years; following the meeting, de Soto stated that the two leaders had agreed to recommence direct talks on the future of the island in January 2002 'without preconditions'. The following day Klerides became the first Greek Cypriot leader to visit the Turkish Cypriot northern sector since the island's partition, when he travelled to the 'TRNC' to dine with Denktaş. The resumption of contacts was broadly welcomed in the 'TRNC', but Greek Cypriot opposition parties and representatives of Greek Cypriots whose relatives had been 'missing' since the invasion, or who had been forced from their homes in the north, were critical of Klerides' visit. Denktaş made a reciprocal visit to dine with his Greek Cypriot counterpart at the end of December 2001. Formal direct negotiations commenced on 21 January 2002; three sessions were scheduled to take place per week, with a view to reaching agreement by June. The talks, on which strict reporting restrictions were imposed, were mediated by de Soto, who indicated that the focus of the discussions would be a power-sharing arrangement of Greek and Turkish regions within a proposed federal Cyprus. None the less, the political positions of the two parties remained apparently irreconcilable: the 'TRNC' continued to promote a solution based around a confederation of two separate states, while the Greek Cypriots—and the international community apart from Turkey —sought a united island with a high degree of communal

autonomy. In mid-May, amid growing pessimism regarding the progress of the talks, the UN Secretary-General travelled to Cyprus where he met separately with Klerides and Denktaş in an unsuccessful attempt to encourage a breakthrough before the target date of the end of June.

Talks continued during the remainder of 2002. In September the UN Secretary-General hosted Klerides and Denktaş in Paris, France, with de Soto in attendance. A further such meeting was held in New York, USA, in early October, but was disrupted when Denktaş underwent emergency heart surgery while there. Observers also noted that substantive progress was unlikely to be made in advance of the general election scheduled to take place in Turkey in November. On 11 November the UN presented a new peace plan to Klerides and Denktaş. The plan envisaged the creation of a common federal state with two equal components, but a single international legal personality. The state would have a joint six-member presidential council, with members holding a 10-month rotating presidency, and a bicameral legislature consisting of a 48-member senate with an equal number of members from both sides, and a 48-member, proportionally composed chamber of deputies. A common supreme court would have three judges from both sides, and three non-Cypriots. Dispossessed property owners would receive compensation, and the 'TRNC' would return territory to the Greek side, reducing the former's share of the island from 36% to 28.5%. This would allow 85,000 of the 162,000 Greek Cypriot refugees to return to their former homes, and would displace 42,000 Turkish Cypriots. Cyprus would be demilitarized, but both Greece and Turkey would be permitted to station up to 9,999 troops each on the island, and UNFICYP would retain its presence. The two leaders initially agreed to use the plan as a basis for future negotiations, but in early December Denktaş, who was in poor health, rejected a revised version of it.

The progress of EU accession talks meant that the need for a settlement to the Cyprus problem was increasingly urgent. At the EU summit held in Copenhagen, Denmark, in mid-December 2002, Cyprus was formally invited to join the EU in 2004. However, it was reiterated that if no peace agreement was forthcoming, then only the Greek part of the island would be admitted. Meanwhile, Greece, which assumed the presidency of the EU in January 2003, had earlier emphasized that it would veto the admission of other EU candidate countries if Cyprus was not admitted at the next round of expansion. Turkey, for its part, had warned in November 2001 that it might annex northern Cyprus if a divided island under a Greek Cypriot government was admitted to the EU.

Following the general election in Turkey in November 2002, Recep Tayyip Erdoğan, the leader of the Justice and Development Party (AKP) which formed the new Government, stated that a peace agreement for Cyprus would accelerate his country's chances of joining the EU. Denktaş's stance on the issue of agreement on Cyprus was not only at odds with Erdoğan's, but also, increasingly, with that of the Turkish Cypriot population: up to 30,000 demonstrated against their leader in late December, calling for his resignation, and some 50,000–70,000 Turkish Cypriots demonstrated in favour of the UN peace plan in mid-January 2003.

In the Greek Cypriot presidential election held on 16 February 2003 the DIKO leader, Tassos Papadopoulos (who was also supported by AKEL), was elected outright, with 51.5% of the votes cast. Klerides, who had sought a renewal of his mandate for 16 months, in order to oversee the peace process and Cyprus's accession, won 38.8% of the votes. There were concerns that Papadopoulos's victory would delay the implementation of the UN peace plan, as he was widely believed to favour a less compromising approach towards the Turkish Cypriots than his predecessor. The new President immediately demanded changes to the UN plan that would allow all Greek Cypriot refugees to return to the north. UN Secretary-General Kofi Annan extended, to 10 March, a deadline earlier set at 28 February for agreement on the island's future, which would thus allow a unified Cyprus to accede to the EU, and Papadopoulos and Denktaş held discussions in The Hague, Netherlands. However, the new deadline passed without agreement: Denktaş denounced the UN plan as unacceptable, and refused to continue discussions. The office of the UN Secretary-General's Special Adviser on Cyprus was subsequently closed down.

In early April 2003 the Greek Cypriot Government rejected an offer by Denktaş to return the eastern town of Varosha, stating that the UN plan should be the main basis for negotiation. Later in that month the Turkish Cypriot authorities announced that it would open its border to the Government-controlled area for the first time in 30 years, allowing Turkish Cypriots to visit the Greek part of the island for one-day trips and permitting Greek Cypriots to visit the north for up to three nights. Within days, more than 100,000 people had crossed the border.

Government

The 1960 Constitution provided for a system of government in which power would be shared by the Greek and Turkish communities in proportion to their numbers. This Constitution officially remains in force, but since the ending of Turkish participation in the Government in 1963, and particularly since the creation of a separate Turkish area in northern Cyprus in 1974, each community has administered its own affairs, refusing to recognize the authority of the other's Government. The Greek Cypriot administration claims to be the Government of all Cyprus, and is generally recognized as such, although it has no Turkish participation. The northern area is under the *de facto* control of the 'Turkish Republic of Northern Cyprus' (for which a new Constitution was approved by a referendum in May 1985). Each community has its own President, Council of Ministers, legislature (the Greek Cypriot community continues to elect members to the House of Representatives, as established by the 1960 Constitution, while the 'TRNC' elects its own legislative assembly) and judicial system.

Defence

The formation of the National Guard was authorized by the House of Representatives in 1964, after the withdrawal of the Turkish members. Men between 18 and 50 years of age are liable to 26 months' conscription. At 1 August 2002 the National Guard comprised an army of 10,000 regulars, mainly composed of Cypriot conscripts (some 8,700) but with an estimated 200 seconded Greek Army officers and NCOs, and 60,000 reserves. A further 1,250 Greek army personnel were stationed in Cyprus at that time. There is also a Greek Cypriot paramilitary police force of 750. In 2001 the defence budget for the Greek Cypriot area was C£212m.

At 1 August 2002 the 'TRNC' had an army of about 5,000 regulars and 26,000 reserves. There was also a paramilitary armed police force of about 150. Men between 18 and 50 years of age are liable to 24 months' conscription. The 'TRNC' forces were being supported by an estimated 36,000 Turkish troops. In 2001 the defence expenditure of the 'TRNC' was TL 34,870,000m.

The UN Peace-keeping Force in Cyprus (UNFICYP, see p. 68) consisted of 1,373 military and police personnel at 31 March 2003. There are British military bases (with personnel numbering 3,190 in August 2002) at Akrotiri, Episkopi and Dhekelia.

Economic Affairs

In 2000, according to estimates by the World Bank, Cyprus's gross national income (GNI), measured at average 1998–2000 prices, was US $9,361m., equivalent to $12,370 per head (or $20,780 per head on an international purchasing-power parity basis). During 1990–2000, it was estimated, the population increased at an average annual rate of 1.1%, while gross domestic product (GDP) per head increased, in real terms, by an average of 3.0% per year. Overall GDP increased, in real terms, by an estimated annual average of 4.1% in 1990–2000; growth in 2001 was 4.1%. In the 'TRNC' GNI was officially estimated at $963.9m., or $4,666 per head, in 1999. GNI increased, in real terms, at an average annual rate of 4.5% in 1994–99, while over the same period real GDP increased at an average annual rate of 4.8%. GDP growth of 5.2% and 7.5% was recorded in 1998 and 1999, respectively. However, GDP per head in the 'TRNC' remains only about one-third of that of the remainder of the island.

According to provisional figures, agriculture (including hunting, forestry and fishing) contributed 3.8% of GDP in 2001. In the government-controlled area 8.0% of the employed labour force were engaged in the sector in 2001. The principal export crops of the government-controlled area are citrus fruit (which accounted for 6.3% of domestic export earnings in 2001), potatoes (7.5% in the same year) and vegetables; grapes are cultivated notably for the wine industry, and barley is the principal cereal crop. In an effort to offset the island's vulnerability to drought, during the 1990s the Greek Cypriot authorities granted concessions for the construction and operation of several desalination plants. According to data published by the IMF, the GDP of the area's agricultural sector declined by an average of 0.3% per year in 1995–99. Agricultural output

increased by 5.5% in 1999, but declined by 3.2% in 2000. In the 'TRNC' 16.5% of the working population were employed in agriculture, forestry and fishing in 2001, and the sector contributed an estimated 7.9% of GDP in 2001. The principal crops of the 'TRNC' are citrus fruit, vegetables, potatoes, wheat and barley. The 'TRNC' imports water from Turkey in order to address the problem of drought. In early 2002 the Government of Turkey announced that it was to proceed with long-standing plans for the construction of a pipeline to transport fresh water to the 'TRNC'. The GDP of the agricultural sector increased by an average of 1.0% per year in 1994–99.

Industry (comprising mining, manufacturing, construction and utilities) engaged 21.5% of the employed labour force in the government-controlled area in 1999, and accounted for 20.0% of GDP in 2001. Industrial GDP increased by an average of 0.2% per year in 1995–99. In the 'TRNC' the industrial sector contributed 16.2% of GDP in 2001, and engaged 25.3% of the working labour force in the same year. Industrial GDP in the 'TRNC' increased at an annual average rate of 2.0% in 1994–99.

In the government-controlled area mining, principally the extraction of material for the construction industry, provided only 0.3% of GDP in 2001, and engaged just 0.2% of the employed labour force in that year. Minerals accounted for 5.5% of domestic exports (by value) from the government-controlled sector in 2000. In early 2001 it was announced that 25 foreign oil companies had expressed interest in acquiring exploration rights for potential petroleum and gas deposits in the eastern Mediterranean within Cyprus's economic zone. The GDP of the mining sector increased at an average annual rate of 6.1% in 1995–99. In the 'TRNC' mining and quarrying contributed 0.6% of GDP in 2001. The GDP of the 'TRNC' mining sector increased by an average of 1.3% per year in 1994–99.

Manufacturing accounted for 10.4% of GDP in the government-controlled area in 2001, and engaged 12.1% of the employed labour force in that year. Clothing represents the southern sector's main export commodity, providing 8.4% of domestic export earnings in 2001. The GDP of the manufacturing sector increased by an average of less that 0.1% per year in 1995–99. In the 'TRNC' the manufacturing sector provided 5.8% of GDP in 2001. The GDP of the 'TRNC' mining sector increased at an average annual rate of 1.4% in 1994–99.

Energy is derived almost entirely from imported petroleum, and mineral fuels and lubricants comprised 12.0% of total imports (including goods for re-export) in the government-controlled area in 2001. The Greek Cypriot Government is encouraging the development of renewable energy sources, including solar, wind and hydroelectric power. Mineral fuels, lubricants, etc. comprised 12.0% of total imports in the 'TRNC' in 2001.

The services sector in the government-controlled area contributed an estimated 76.2% of GDP in 2001, and engaged 70.5% of the employed labour force in that year. Within the sector, financial and business services provided an estimated 20.9% of overall GDP in 2001 and generated 10.1% of employment in that year. In 1999 there were 29 'offshore' banking units in the government-controlled area, and the number of registered 'offshore' enterprises was estimated to total more than 40,000. In the 'TRNC' the services sector contributed 75.9% of GDP in 2001, and engaged 58.2% of the employed labour force in that year. Both Cypriot communities have undertaken measures to expand their tourism industries, which are important generators of revenue and employment. Tourist arrivals to the government-controlled area increased from 2,686,205 in 2000 to 2,696,700 in 2001. Receipts from tourism in 2001 amounted to an estimated C£1,277m. In 2001 a total of 365,097 tourists (277,739 of whom were from Turkey) visited the 'TRNC'. Net tourism receipts in the 'TRNC' totalled US $93.7m. in 2001. Tourism in both sectors was expected to suffer a marked decline in response to the international instability following the suicide attacks on the USA in September 2001. The Greek Cypriot authorities are also attempting to enhance the island's status as an entrepôt for shipping and trade throughout the Eastern Mediterranean, while Cyprus's shipping registry has developed rapidly, to become the world's sixth largest by the end of 2000. In the government-controlled area the GDP of the services sector increased at an average annual rate of 4.7% in 1995–99. Services GDP in the 'TRNC' increased by an average of 5.8% per year in 1994–99.

In 2001 the government-controlled area recorded a visible trade deficit of US $2,544.9m. and a deficit of $394.1m. on the current account of the balance of payments. The 'TRNC' recorded a visible trade deficit in 2001 of $237.4m., while there was a deficit of $17.1m. on the current account of the balance of payments. In 2001 the principal sources of imports to the government-controlled area were the USA (which supplied 9.4% of merchandise imports) and Greece (8.9%); Italy, the United Kingdom, Germany and Japan were also important suppliers. The United Kingdom was the principal purchaser of Greek Cypriot exports in 2001, taking 20.6% of the total; Greece, Russia and Syria were also important markets. The principal domestic exports from the government-controlled area in 2001 were pharmaceutical products, clothing, cigarettes, citrus fruit and potatoes. The principal imports in that year were road vehicles, fuels and lubricants, manufactured goods, machinery and electrical equipment, foodstuffs, and beverages and tobacco. In 2001 the principal imports to the 'TRNC' were machinery and transport equipment, basic manufactures, food and live animals, chemicals, mineral fuels and lubricants, and beverages and tobacco; the principal exports were clothing, citrus fruit, barley and beverages and tobacco. Turkey is by far the principal trading partner of the 'TRNC', supplying 63.8% of imports and taking 37.0% of exports in 2001, although the United Kingdom purchased 33.2% of exports in that year.

In 2001 the government-controlled area recorded a budget deficit of an estimated C£152.5m., equivalent to 2.7% of GDP. External debt totalled C£1,796.0m. at the end of 1999, of which C£1,142.3m. was medium- and long-term public debt. In that year the cost of debt-servicing was equivalent to 5.8% of the value of exports of goods and services. The annual rate of inflation averaged 3.8% in 1990–2000. Consumer prices increased by an average of 4.1% in 2000 and by 2.0% in 2001. The average level of unemployment in the government-controlled area was 3.6% of the labour force in 1999. The 2001 budget of the 'TRNC' envisioned a balance of revenue and expenditure. In the 'TRNC' the average increase in prices for the 12 months to December averaged 72.3% in 1994–99; the rate of inflation in the 'TRNC' was 53.2% in the year to December 2000, 76.8% in the year to December 2001, and 24.5% in the year to December 2002. According to official figures, 1.6% of the 'TRNC' labour force were unemployed in 2001.

An application to become a full member of the European Union (EU, see p. 199), with which Cyprus has an association agreement, was submitted by the Greek Cypriot Government in July 1990; accession negotiations commenced in March 1998. In December 2002 Cyprus was formally invited to become a member of the EU from 1 May 2004. The 'TRNC' has guest status at the Economic Co-operation Organization (ECO, see p. 192).

By the beginning of the 21st century the Greek Cypriot economy was enjoying strong growth, owing in large part to continued advances in the services sector, notably in tourism. Other particular areas of investment promotion were in information technology, and in financial and medical services. Although the economy initially proved more resilient than had been anticipated following the terrorist attacks on the mainland USA in September 2001, with growth in that year almost attaining the targeted 4.5%, preliminary figures indicated that growth in 2002 was only 1.9%. However, a degree of recovery was forecast for 2003, with growth forecast at 3.7% for that year. The steady decline in the rate of inflation in the 1990s was reversed in 2000, as a period of enhanced consumer demand (reflecting in particular an increase of some 700% in the value of the Cyprus Stock Exchange in late 1999, following a period of intense trading activity), together with sustained increases in world petroleum prices at that time, coincided with the depreciation in the value of the euro (to which the Cyprus pound has been linked since January 1999) in relation to the US dollar. Recent economic policy has been shaped principally with a view to achieving the criteria required for EU membership. In July 2002 the Government raised the rate of value-added tax from 10% to 13%, and was expected to raise it further to 15% in 2003 —the lowest permissible rate for an EU member. As a result, inflation was expected to rise to 3.9% in that year. Furthermore, the budget deficit was progressively reduced in 1998–2002, and the out-turn was projected to be the equivalent of 2.7% of GDP in 2002 (comfortably below the EU 'ceiling' of 3%), owing to tighter fiscal policies, postponement of defence-related outlays, and more efficient tax collection. It was aimed to achieve a balanced budget in 2005. Meanwhile, the Government undertook a reform of tax arrangements for 'offshore' banks and other enterprises in order to comply with EU accession procedures: the EU is opposed to Cyprus's practice of charging 'offshore' companies less tax (4.5%) than domestic companies (25%). A new uniform tax rate of 10% was reportedly favourable enough to deter the more prestigious 'offshore' businesses from leaving, while also being attractive to new investors. Moreover, the Government pledged full compliance with efforts by the Organisation for Economic Co-operation and Development (of which Cyprus is not a member) to combat tax evasion and money-laundering. Despite the prospect of tighter regulation, the 'offshore' sector was continuing to expand. In early 2003 Cyprus also improved its prospects for energy development when it signed an agreement with Egypt delimiting its 200-mile exclusive economic zone, granting it rights to oil and gas deposits in more than 32,000 sq km of waters.

The economy of the 'TRNC', although substantially less prosperous and affected by diplomatic isolation, has also achieved significant growth since the 1980s, with considerable assistance from Turkey. By 2001/02 higher education had become one of the territory's most significant economic sectors, with 26,364 students, many from Turkey, attending private universities in the 'TRNC'; revenue from this sector was projected at US $250m. in 1999. The tourism sector was also expanding, although the development of the north as an international tourist destination remained hampered by the embargo on direct flights to the 'TRNC' (visitors must first land in Turkey). The close linkage with the Turkish economy, including the use of the Turkish lira as currency in the 'TRNC', has resulted in persistently high levels of inflation, and has rendered northern Cyprus particularly vulnerable to adverse economic developments in Turkey. Furthermore, there was evidence that the severe financial crisis affecting the Turkish economy from early 2001 (q.v.) was becoming detrimental to the 'TRNC', where the Government was obliged in late February to revise its budget for that year to include a 20% reduction in current expenditure. (Aid from Turkey contributed some 22.3% of budgetary revenue in 2001.) The new 'TRNC' coalition administration that took office in mid-2001 undertook to pursue free-market policies and to accelerate privatization. However, during 2001–02 13 banks and numerous businesses collapsed. The crisis further emphasized the economic divergence of the Turkish and Greek Cypriot communities, notably clear disparities in wealth between north and south, and also exacerbated long-term weaknesses in the 'TRNC' such as the comparative lack of diversification of the manufacturing sector and a high rate of emigration. Meanwhile, the loss of income in the form of essential grants and subsidies from Turkey adversely affected the public sector, which remains the largest employer in the 'TRNC', employing more than 20% of the working population. There was considerable evidence that the economic crisis in Turkey was encouraging Turkish Cypriot elements that favoured participation in Cyprus's accession negotiations with the EU and broader Cypriot reunification. This was particularly evident within the Turkish Cypriot business community, which feared a further loss of investment and increased economic isolation as a consequence of the collapse of peace talks in early 2003 (see Recent History). Anecdotal evidence suggested that many Turkish Cypriots were seeking to obtain Republic of Cyprus passports in order to acquire EU residency rights after 2004.

Education

In the Greek Cypriot sector elementary education, which is compulsory and available free of charge, is provided in six grades for children between five-and-a-half and 12 years of age. Enrolment at primary level in 1999/2000 was equivalent to 97% of children in the relevant age-group. Secondary education is free for all years of study and lasts six years, with three compulsory years at the Gymnasium being followed by three non-compulsory years at a technical school or a Lyceum. Comprehensive secondary schools were introduced in 1995. There are five options of specialization at the Lyceums: classical, science, economics, commercial/secretarial and foreign languages. In 1999/2000 enrolment in secondary education was equivalent to 97% of the relevant age-group. There are 11 three-year technical schools. Technical and vocational colleges provide higher education for teachers, technicians, engineers, hoteliers and caterers, foresters, nurses and health inspectors. The University of Cyprus was inaugurated in September 1992, and there were a further 33 post-secondary institutions in 1997/98. In that year the university had 2,311 enrolled students, while a total of 10,815 students from the Greek Cypriot area were studying at universities abroad. Budgetary expenditure on education by the central Government in the Greek Cypriot area was C£286.8m. (16.0% of total spending) in 1999.

Education in the Turkish Cypriot zone is controlled by the 'TRNC'. Pre-primary education is provided by kindergartens for children of 5 and 6 years of age. Primary education is free and compulsory: it comprises elementary schools for the 7–11 age-group, and secondary-junior schools for the 12–14 age-group. Secondary education, for the 15–17 age-group, is provided by high schools (Lycées) and vocational schools, including colleges of agriculture, nursing and hotel management. It is free, but not compulsory. In 2001/02 26,364 students were enrolled at eight higher education establishments in the 'TRNC', including five international universities.

Public Holidays

2003: 1 January (New Year's Day), 6 January (Epiphany)*, 11–13 February (Kurban Bayram—Feast of the Sacrifice)†, 10 March (Green Monday)*, 25 March (Greek Independence Day)*, 1 April (Anniversary of Cyprus Liberation Struggle), 23 April (National Sovereignty and Children's Day)†, 25–28 April (Easter)*, 1 May (May Day), 14 May (Birth of the Prophet)†, 19 May (Youth and Sports Day)†, 16 June (Pentecost)*, 20 July (Peace and Freedom Day, anniversary of the Turkish invasion in 1974)†, 1 August (Communal Resistance Day)†, 15 August (Assumption)*, 30 August (Victory Day)†, 1 October (Independence Day)*, 28 October (Greek National Day)*, 29 October (Turkish Republic Day)†, 15 November (TRNC Day)†, 26–28 November (Ramazam Bayram—end of Ramadan)†, 25–26 December (Christmas)*.

2004: 1 January (New Year's Day), 6 January (Epiphany)*, 1–3 February (Kurban Bayram—Feast of the Sacrifice)†, 23 February (Green Monday)*, 25 March (Greek Independence Day)*,

1 April (Anniversary of Cyprus Liberation Struggle), 9–12 April (Easter)*, 23 April (National Sovereignty and Children's Day)†, 1 May (May Day), 2 May (Birth of the Prophet)†, 19 May (Youth and Sports Day)†, 31 May (Pentecost)*, 20 July (Peace and Freedom Day, anniversary of the Turkish invasion in 1974)†, 1 August (Communal Resistance Day)†, 15 August (Assumption)*, 30 August (Victory Day)†, 1 October (Independence Day)*, 28 October (Greek National Day)*, 29 October (Turkish Republic Day)†, 14–16 November (Ramazam Bayram—end of Ramadan)†, 15 November (TRNC Day)†, 25–26 December (Christmas)*.

* Greek and Greek Orthodox.

† Turkish and Turkish Muslim.

Weights and Measures

Although the imperial and the metric systems are understood, Cyprus has a special internal system:

Weights
400 drams = 1 oke = 2.8 lb (1.27 kg.).
44 okes = 1 Cyprus kantar.
180 okes = 1 Aleppo kantar.

Capacity
1 liquid oke = 2.25 pints (1.28 litres).
1 Cyprus litre = 5.6 pints (3.18 litres).

Length and Area
1 pic = 2 feet (61 cm).

Area
1 donum = 14,400 sq ft (1,338 sq m).

Statistical Survey

Source (unless otherwise indicated): Department of Statistics and Research, Ministry of Finance, Nicosia; tel. (2) 309301; fax (2) 374830; internet www.pio.gov.cy/dsr/index.htm.

Note: Since July 1974 the northern part of Cyprus has been under Turkish occupation. As a result, some of the statistics relating to subsequent periods do not cover the whole island. Some separate figures for the 'TRNC' are also given.

AREA AND POPULATION

Area: 9,251 sq km (3,572 sq miles), incl. Turkish-occupied region; 5,896 sq km (2,276 sq miles), government-controlled area only.

Population: 703,529 (males 345,322; females 358,207), excl. Turkish-occupied region, at census of 1 October 2001; 793,100, incl. 87,600 in Turkish-occupied region, at 31 December 2001 (official estimate). Note: Figures for the Turkish-occupied region exclude settlers from Turkey, estimated at 115,000 in 2001.

Density (at census of 1 October 2001): 119.3 per sq km (government-controlled area).

Ethnic Groups (estimates, 31 December 2001): Greeks 639,400 (80.6%), Turks 87,600 (11.1%), Others 66,100 (8.3%); Total 793,100.

Principal Towns (population at 1 October 2001): Nicosia (capital) 205,633 (excl. Turkish-occupied portion); Limassol 160,733; Larnaca 71,740; Famagusta (Gazi Mağusa) 39,500 (mid-1974); Paphos 47,198; (estimated population at 31 December 2001): Nicosia 206,200 (excl. Turkish-occupied portion); Limassol 161,200; Larnaca 72,000; Paphos 47,300.

Births, Marriages and Deaths (government-controlled area, 2001): Registered live births 8,167 (birth rate 11.6 per 1,000); Registered marriages 10,574 (marriage rate 15.1 per 1,000); Registered deaths 4,827 (death rate 6.9 per 1,000).

Expectation of Life (WHO estimates, years at birth): 76.9 (males 74.6; females 79.2) in 2001. Source: WHO, *World Health Report*.

Employment (government-controlled area, provisional figures, '000 persons aged 15 years and over, excl. armed forces, 2001): Agriculture, hunting, forestry and fishing 24.7; Mining and quarrying 0.6; Manufacturing 37.2; Electricity, gas and water 1.5; Construction 26.9; Trade, restaurants and hotels 88.2; Transport, storage and communications 22.2; Financing, insurance, real estate and business services 31.1; Community, social and other services 66.2; Private households 9.2 Total 307.8. Figures exclude employment on British sovereign bases. Source: IMF, *Cyprus: Selected Issues and Statistical Appendix* (September 2000).

HEALTH AND WELFARE

Key Indicators

Total Fertility Rate (children per woman, 2001): 1.9.

Under-5 Mortality Rate (per 1,000 live births, 2001): 6.

HIV/AIDS (% of persons aged 15–49, 2001): 0.25.

Physicians (per 1,000 head, 2001): 2.62.

Hospital Beds (per 1,000 head, 2001): 4.37.

Health Expenditure (2001): US $ per head (PPP): 844 (provisional).

Health Expenditure (2001): % of GDP: 6.1.

Health Expenditure (2001): public (% of total): 33.4.

Human Development Index (2000): ranking: 26.

Human Development Index (2000): index: 0.883.

For sources and definitions, see explanatory note on p. vi.

AGRICULTURE, ETC.

Principal Crops (government-controlled area, '000 metric tons, 2001): Wheat 10.5; Barley 116.5; Potatoes 121.0; Olives 17.5; Cabbages 4.6; Tomatoes 37.5; Cucumbers and gherkins 17.5; Dry onions 6.9; Bananas 9.8; Oranges 36.5; Tangerines, mandarins, etc. 35.0; Lemons and limes 23.0; Grapefruit and pomelos 27.8; Apples 9.3; Grapes 88.0; Cantaloupes and other melons 10.1. Source: FAO.

Livestock (government-controlled area, '000 head, year ending September 2001): Cattle 53.6; Sheep 296.6; Goats 447.1; Pigs 445.3; Chickens 3,100; Asses 5.4 (estimate). Source: FAO.

Livestock Products (government-controlled area, '000 metric tons, 2001): Beef and veal 3.9; Mutton and lamb 4.2; Goat meat 6.8; Pig meat 50.7; Poultry meat 34.1; Cows' milk 141.5; Sheep's milk 21.8; Goats' milk 36.2; Cheese 4.4; Hen eggs 11.2. Source: FAO.

Forestry (government-controlled area, '000 cubic metres, 2000): Roundwood removals (excl. bark) 25.1; Sawnwood production (incl. railway sleepers) 8.7. Source: FAO.

Fishing (government-controlled area, metric tons, live weight, 2001): Capture 2,246 (Bogue 216, Picarels 671); Aquaculture 1,883 (European seabass 400, Gilthead seabream 1,325); Total catch 4,130.

MINING AND QUARRYING

Selected Products (government-controlled area, provisional figures, metric tons, 2001): Sand and gravel 9,980,000; Gypsum 144,000; Bentonite 115,460; Umber 7,817.

INDUSTRY

Selected Products (government-controlled area, provisional figures, 2001): Wine 29.6m. litres; Beer 40.7m. litres; Soft drinks 64.8m. litres; Cigarettes 3,745m.; Footwear 1,077,000 pairs; Bricks 46m.; Floor and wall tiles 843,000 sq m.; Cement 1,369,000 metric tons; Electricity 3,550 million kWh.

FINANCE

Currency and Exchange Rates: 100 cents = 1 Cyprus pound (Cyprus £). *Sterling, Dollar and Euro Equivalents* (31 December 2002): £1 sterling = 88.14 Cyprus cents; US $1 = 54.68 Cyprus cents; €1 = 57.35 Cyprus cents; Cyprus £100 = £113.46 sterling = $182.87 = €174.38. *Average Exchange Rate* (US $ per Cyprus £): 1.6107 in 2000; 1.5559 in 2001; 1.6431 in 2002.

Budget (government-controlled area, Cyprus £ million, 2001): *Revenue:* Taxation 1,659.4 (Direct taxes 659.4, Indirect taxes 722.0, Social security contributions 278.0); Other current revenue 410.5; Capital revenue 0.8; Total 2,070.7, excl. grants from abroad (2.5). *Expenditure:* Current expenditure 2,006.0 (Wages and salaries 559.7, Other goods and services 182.4, Social security payments 318.8, Subsidies 91.1, Interest payments 329.9, Other current expenditure 524.1); Capital expenditure 217.2 (Investments 155.6, Capital transfers 61.6); Total 2,223.2.

International Reserves (US $ million at 31 December 2002): Gold (national valuation) 149.2; IMF special drawing rights 2.1; Reserve position in IMF 66.8; Foreign exchange 2,953.2 (provisional); Total 3,171.3. Source: IMF, *International Financial Statistics*.

Money Supply (government-controlled area, Cyprus £ million at 31 December 2002, provisional): Currency outside banks 392.9; Demand deposits at deposit money banks 611.7; Total money (incl. others) 1,020.0. Source: IMF, *International Financial Statistics*.

Cost of Living (government-controlled area, Retail Price Index; base: 1995 = 100): 115.4 in 2000; 117.7 in 2001; 121.0 in 2002. Source: IMF, *International Financial Statistics*.

Gross Domestic Product in Purchasers' Values (government-controlled area, Cyprus £ million): *GDP at current prices:* 5,511.8 in 2000; 5,880.0 (provisional) in 2001; 6,191.5 (provisional) in 2002.

Expenditure on the Gross Domestic Product (government-controlled area, provisional, Cyprus £ million at current prices, 2001): Government final consumption expenditure 1,038.2; Private final consumption expenditure 3,999.4; Increase in stocks 60.0; Gross fixed capital formation 1,017.8; Statistical discrepancy 44.1; *Total domestic expenditure* 6,159.5; Exports of goods and services 2,751.7; *Less* Imports of goods and services 3,031.2; *GDP in purchasers' values* 5,880.0.

Gross Domestic Product by Economic Activity (government-controlled area, provisional, Cyprus £ million at current prices, 2001): Agriculture and hunting 214.7; Fishing 11.4; Mining and quarrying 17.4; Manufacturing 581.7; Electricity, gas and water supply 123.1; Construction 397.4; Wholesale and retail trade 720.7; Restaurants and hotels 544.7; Transport, storage and communications 557.8; Financial intermediation 391.6; Real estate, renting and business activities 781.1; Public administration and defence 515.2; Education 289.8; Health and social work 199.2; Other community, social and personal services 227.3; Private households with employed persons 30.5; *Sub-total* 5,603.6; Import duties 196.9; Value-added tax 344.7; *Less* Imputed bank service charges 265.2; *GDP in purchasers' values* 5,880.0.

Balance of Payments (government-controlled area, US $ million, 2001): Exports of goods f.o.b. 976.5, Imports of goods f.o.b.–3,526.9; *Trade balance* –2,550.4; Exports of services 3,352.9; Imports of services –1,185.2; *Balance on goods and services* –382.7; Other income received 563.8; Other income paid –597.6; *Balance on goods, services and income* –416.4; Current transfers received 49.3; Current transfers paid –27.7; *Current balance* –394.8; Direct investment abroad –217.7; Direct investment from abroad 163.3; Portfolio investment assets –443.2; Portfolio investment liabilities 524.0; Other investment assets –540.5; Other investment liabilities 1,359.8; Net errors and omissions 161.4; *Overall balance* 612.3. Source: IMF, *International Financial Statistics*.

EXTERNAL TRADE

Total Trade (government-controlled area, Cyprus £ million): Imports c.i.f.: 1,970.9 in 1999; 2,401.9 in 2000; 2,528.8 in 2001. Exports f.o.b. (incl. re-exports): 542.9 in 1999; 591.9 in 2000; 628.0 in 2001.

Principal Commodities (government-controlled area, Cyprus £ '000, 2001): *Imports c.i.f.:* Consumer goods 793,230 (Food and beverages 145,038; Other non-durable 358,208; Semi-durable 173,717; Durable 116,267); Intermediate inputs 736,702 (Construction and mining 124,724; Manufacturing 443,190); Capital goods 269,552; Transport equipment and parts thereof 328,872 (Passenger motor vehicles 160,398; Motor vehicles for the transport of goods 85,864); Fuels and lubricants 302,471; Total (incl. others) 2,528,752. *Exports f.o.b.:* Potatoes 17,511; Citrus fruit 14,717; Cheese 8,558; Cigarettes 10,768; Cement 8,396; Pharmaceutical products 39,411; Clothing 19,700; Total (incl. others) 233,944. Figures for exports exclude re-exports (Cyprus £ '000): 381,039. Also excluded are domestic exports of stores and bunkers for ships and aircraft (Cyprus £ '000): 13,046.

Principal Trading Partners (government-controlled area, Cyprus £ million, 2001): *Imports c.i.f.:* China, People's Repub. 91.0; France 127.3; Germany 172.7; Greece 225.2; Israel 99.7; Italy 223.2; Japan 153.7; Netherlands 52.8; Russia 78.9; Spain 96.5; Syria 96.6; Taiwan 27.3; Thailand 31.4; United Kingdom 222.2; USA 237.9; Total (incl. others) 2,528.8. *Exports f.o.b.* (incl. re-exports): Egypt 16.8; France 6.2; Germany 18.4; Greece 52.6; Iraq 9.5; Israel 8.8; Lebanon 23.3; Netherlands 10.7; Romania 6.5; Russia 54.1; Saudi Arabia 5.9; Spain 10.2; Syria 37.4; United Arab Emirates 49.0; United Kingdom 117.6; USA 10.7; Total (incl. others) 570.9, excluding stores and bunkers for ships and aircraft (57.1).

TRANSPORT

Road Traffic (government-controlled area, licensed motor vehicles, 31 December 2001): Private passenger cars 270,348; Taxis and self-drive cars 9,721; Buses and coaches 3,003; Lorries and vans 117,942; Motorcycles 41,985; Total (incl. others) 459,106.

Shipping (government-controlled area, freight traffic, '000 metric tons, 2001): Goods loaded 1,406, Goods unloaded 5,237. At 31 December 2001 a total of 1,407 merchant vessels (combined displacement 22,761,778 grt) were registered in Cyprus (Source: Lloyd's Register-Fairplay, *World Fleet Statistics*).

Civil Aviation (government-controlled area, 2001): Overall passenger traffic 6,415,225; Total freight transported 32,446 metric tons.

TOURISM

Foreign Tourist Arrivals (government-controlled area, '000): 2,434.3 in 1999; 2,686.2 in 2000; 2,696.7 in 2001.

Arrivals by Country of Residence (government-controlled area, 2001): Germany 214,153; Greece 89,763; Norway 61,620; Russia (incl. other ex-USSR countries) 128,532; Sweden 127,419; Switzerland 76,614; United Kingdom 1,486,703; Total (incl. others) 2,696,732. Source: Cyprus Tourism Organization.

Tourism Receipts (government-controlled area, Cyprus £ million): 1,025 in 1999; 1,194 in 2000; 1,277 in 2001.

COMMUNICATIONS MEDIA

Radio Receivers (government-controlled area, 1997): 310,000 in use.

Television Receivers (government-controlled area, 2000): 122,000 in use.

Telephones (main lines in use, 2001): 435,000.

Facsimile Machines (provisional or estimated figure, number in use, 1993): 7,000.

Mobile Cellular Telephones (subscribers, 2001): 314,400.

Personal Computers ('000 in use, 2001): 170.

Internet Users ('000, 2001): 150.

Book Production (government-controlled area, 1996): 930 titles and 1,776,000 copies.

Newspapers (1996): 9 daily (circulation 84,000 copies); 31 non-daily (circulation 185,000 copies).

Sources: mainly UNESCO, *Statistical Yearbook*, UN, *Statistical Yearbook,* and International Telecommunication Union.

EDUCATION

2000/01 (government-controlled area): Kindergarten: 642 institutions, 1,024 teachers, 26,455 pupils; Primary schools: 367 institutions, 3,759 teachers, 63,387 pupils; Secondary schools (Gymnasia and Lyceums): 123 institutions, 4,724 teachers, 59,526 pupils; Technical colleges: 11 institutions, 597 teachers, 4,497 pupils; University of Cyprus: 249 teachers, 2,866 students; Other post-secondary: 31 institutions, 885 teachers, 9,068 students.

Adult Literacy Rate (UNESCO estimate): 96.2% (males 98.1%; females 94.4%) in 2001. Source: UN Development Programme, *Human Development Report.*

'Turkish Republic of Northern Cyprus'

Sources: Statistics and Research Dept, State Planning Organization, Prime Ministry, Lefkoşa (Nicosia), Mersin 10, Turkey; tel. (22) 83141; fax (22) 85988; e-mail trnc-spo@management.emu.edu.tr; internet www.devplan.org; Office of the London Representative of the 'Turkish Republic of Northern Cyprus', 29 Bedford Sq., London WC1B 3EG; tel. (20) 7631-1920; fax (20) 7631-1948.

AREA AND POPULATION

Area: 3,355 sq km (1,295 sq miles).

Population (census, 15 December 1996): 200,587 (males 105,978; females 94,609). Official estimate at mid-2001: 211,191.

Density (2002): 63.3 per sq km.

Ethnic Groups (census, 15 December 1996): Turks 197,264, English 627, Greeks 384, Maronites 173, Russians 130, Germans 106, Others 1,903; Total 200,587.

Principal Towns (population within the municipal boundary, census, 15 December 1996): Lefkoşa (Nicosia) 42,767 (Turkish-occupied area only); Gazi Mağusa (Famagusta) 22,216; Girne (Kyrenia) 7,893.

Births, Marriages and Deaths (registered, 2001): Live births 2,550 (birth rate 15.0 per 1,000); Marriages 1,090 (marriage rate 5.2 per 1,000); Deaths 781 (death rate 8.0 per 1,000).

Expectation of life (years at birth, 2000): Males 70.9; Females 75.1.

Employment (2001): Agriculture, forestry and fishing 14,931; Industry 8,715; Construction 14,104; Trade and tourism 9,630; Transport and communications 8,104; Financial institutions 2,397; Business and personal services 14,401; Public services 18,084; *Total employed* 90,366. Total unemployed 1,500; *Total labour force* 91,866.

HEALTH AND WERLFARE

Key Indicators

Physicians (per 1,000 head, 2001): 1.7.

Hospital Beds (per 1,000 head, 2001): 5.2.

AGRICULTURE, ETC.

Principal Crops ('000 metric tons, 2001): Wheat 7.6; Barley 102.1; Potatoes 14.0; Legumes 2.5; Tomatoes 8.3; Onions 1.7; Artichokes 1.2; Watermelons 9.7; Melons 3.0; Cucumbers 2.1; Carobs 2.8; Olives 3.1; Lemons 10.7; Grapefruit 15.8; Oranges 61.6; Tangerines 2.0.

Livestock ('000 head, 2001): Cattle 34.2; Sheep 202.7; Goats 54.8; Chickens 4,238.

Livestock Products ('000 metric tons, unless otherwise indicated, 2001): Sheep's and goats' milk 11.4; Cows' milk 66.5; Mutton and lamb 3.3; Goat meat 0.8; Beef 2.1; Poultry meat 6.8; Wool 0.2; Eggs (million) 13.4.

Fishing (metric tons, 2001): Total catch 400.

FINANCE

Currency and Exchange Rates: Turkish currency: 100 kuruş = 1 Turkish lira (TL) or pound. *Sterling, Dollar and Euro Equivalents* (31 December 2002): £1 sterling = 2,649,314 liras; US $1 = 1,643,699 liras; €1 = 1,723,747 liras; 10,000,000 Turkish liras = £3.775 = $6.084 = €5.801. *Average Exchange Rate* (liras per US dollar): 625,218 in 2000; 1,225,590 in 2001; 1,507,230 in 2002.

Budget (provisional, '000 million Turkish liras, 2001): *Revenue:* Internal revenue 261,902.5 (Direct taxes 101,060.0, Indirect taxes 78,459.6, Other income 57,137.8, Fund revenues 25,245.0); Aid from Turkey 58,476.4; Aid from other countries 111.4; Loans 172,119.4; Total 492,609.7. *Expenditure:* Personnel 137,522.7; Other goods and services 24,760.9; Transfers 260,048.3; Investments 34,407.8; Defence 34,870.0; Total (incl. others) 492,609.7.

Cost of Living (Retail Price Index at December; base: December of previous year = 100): 153.2 in 2000; 176.8 in 2001; 124.5 in 2002.

Expenditure on the Gross Domestic Product (provisional, '000 million Turkish liras at current prices, 2001): Government final consumption expenditure 235,571; Private final consumption expenditure 627,327; Increase in stocks 15,700; Gross fixed capital formation 150,972; *Total domestic expenditure* 1,029,570; Exports of goods and services, *less* Imports of goods and services –58,538; *GDP in purchasers' values* 971,032; *GDP at constant 1977 prices* (million liras) 8,707.9.

Gross Domestic Product by Economic Activity ('000 million Turkish liras, 2001): Agriculture, forestry and fishing 78,627.2; Industry 121,736.4 (Mining and quarrying 5,973.2; Manufacturing 57,236.8; Electricity and water 58,526.4); Construction 38,923.3; Wholesale and retail trade 109,111.2; Restaurants and hotels 56,040.7; Transport and communications 133,453.3; Finance 92,763.0; Ownership of dwellings 28,508.8; Business and personal services 133,995.8; Government services 199,156.6; *Sub-total* 992,316.3; Import duties 76,836.1; *GDP in purchasers' values* 1,069,152.4.

Balance of Payments (US $ million, 2001): Merchandise exports f.o.b. 34.6; Merchandise imports c.i.f. –272.0; *Trade balance* –237.4; Services and unrequited transfers (net) 220.3; *Current balance* –17.1; Capital movements (net) 143.0; Net errors and omissions –35.2; *Total* (net monetary movements) 90.7.

EXTERNAL TRADE

Principal Commodities (US $ million, 2001): *Imports c.i.f.:* Food and live animals 46.2; Beverages and tobacco 19.3; Mineral fuels, lubricants, etc. 32.6; Chemicals 28.5; Basic manufactures 58.3; Machinery and transport equipment 59.0; Miscellaneous manufactured articles 20.6; Total (incl. others) 272.0. *Exports f.o.b.:* Agricultural products 18.1 (Citrus fruit 9.9, Potatoes 0.5); Beverages and tobacco 1.5; Crude materials (inedible), excluding fuels 2.1; Chemicals 1.3; Clothing 11.1; Total (incl. others) 34.6.

Principal Trading Partners (US $ million, 2001): *Imports c.i.f:* Germany 11.6; Italy 8.6; Japan 2.8; Netherlands 4.1; Turkey 173.5; United Kingdom 28.6; USA 4.1; Total (incl. others) 272.0. *Exports f.o.b.:* Germany 3.5; Israel 0.5; Kuwait 2.1; Netherlands 0.9; Russia 3.2; Turkey 12.8; United Kingdom 11.5; Total (incl. others) 34.6.

TRANSPORT

Road Traffic (registered motor vehicles, 2001): Saloon cars 76,850; Estate cars 9,168; Pick-ups 3,825; Vans 9,131; Buses 2,077; Trucks 1,593; Lorries 6,335; Motorcycles 16,424; Agricultural tractors 6,594; Total (incl. others) 134,454.

Shipping (2001): Freight traffic ('000 metric tons): Goods loaded 247.2, Goods unloaded 898.1; Vessels entered 3,220.

Civil Aviation: Kilometres flown (Turkish Cypriot Airlines) 1,126,848 (1985); Passenger arrivals and departures 691,431 (2001); Freight landed and cleared (metric tons) 4,297 (2001).

TOURISM

Visitors (2001): 365,097 (including 277,739 Turkish); Accommodation (2001): Hotels 120, Tourist beds (in all tourist accommodation, including pensions and hotel-apartments) 10,798; Net Receipts (US $ million, 2001): 93.7.

COMMUNICATIONS MEDIA

Radio Receivers (2001, provisional): 82,364 in use.

Television Receivers (2001, provisional): 70,960 in use.

Telephones (31 December 2001): 86,228 subscribers.

Mobile Cellular Telephones (31 December 2001): 143,178 subscribers.

EDUCATION

2001/02: *Primary and Pre-primary schools:* 257 institutions, 1,467 teachers, 20,169 pupils; *Secondary schools:* 29 institutions, 774 teachers, 9,867 students; *General high schools:* 23 institutions, 668 teachers, 5,764 students; *Vocational schools:* 13 institutions, 438 teachers, 2,177 students; *Universities:* 8 institutions, 26,364 students (of which 9,700 Turkish Cypriots, 16,664 from abroad).

Adult Literacy Rate (census, 15 December 1996): 93.5%.

Directory

The Constitution

The Constitution, summarized below, entered into force on 16 August 1960, when Cyprus became an independent republic.

THE STATE OF CYPRUS

The State of Cyprus is an independent and sovereign Republic with a presidential regime.

The Greek Community comprises all citizens of the Republic who are of Greek origin and whose mother tongue is Greek or who share the Greek cultural traditions or who are members of the Greek Orthodox Church.

The Turkish Community comprises all citizens of the Republic who are of Turkish origin and whose mother tongue is Turkish or who share the Turkish cultural traditions or who are Muslims.

The official languages of the Republic are Greek and Turkish.

The Republic shall have its own flag of neutral design and colour, chosen jointly by the President and the Vice-President of the Republic.

The Greek and the Turkish Communities shall have the right to celebrate respectively the Greek and the Turkish national holidays.

THE PRESIDENT AND VICE-PRESIDENT

Executive power is vested in the President and the Vice-President, who are members of the Greek and Turkish Communities respectively, and are elected by their respective communities to hold office for five years.

The President of the Republic as Head of the State represents the Republic in all its official functions; signs the credentials of diplomatic envoys and receives the credentials of foreign diplomatic envoys; signs the credentials of delegates for the negotiation of international treaties, conventions or other agreements; signs the letter relating to the transmission of the instruments of ratification of any international treaties, conventions or agreements; confers the honours of the Republic.

The Vice-President of the Republic, as Vice-Head of the State, has the right to be present at all official functions; at the presentation of the credentials of foreign diplomatic envoys; to recommend to the President the conferment of honours on members of the Turkish Community, which recommendation the President shall accept unless there are grave reasons to the contrary.

The election of the President and the Vice-President of the Republic shall be direct, by universal suffrage and secret ballot, and shall, except in the case of a by-election, take place on the same day but separately.

The office of the President and of the Vice-President shall be incompatible with that of a Minister or of a Representative or of a member of a Communal Chamber or of a member of any municipal council including a Mayor or of a member of the armed or security forces of the Republic or with a public or municipal office.

The President and Vice-President of the Republic are invested by the House of Representatives.

The President and the Vice-President of the Republic in order to ensure the executive power shall have a Council of Ministers composed of seven Greek Ministers and three Turkish Ministers. The Ministers shall be designated respectively by the President and the Vice-President of the Republic who shall appoint them by an instrument signed by them both. The President convenes and presides over the meetings of the Council of Ministers, while the Vice-President may ask the President to convene the Council and may take part in the discussions.

The decisions of the Council of Ministers shall be taken by an absolute majority and shall, unless the right of final veto or return

is exercised by the President or the Vice-President of the Republic or both, be promulgated immediately by them.

The executive power exercised by the President and the Vice-President of the Republic conjointly consists of:

Determining the design and colour of the flag.

Creation or establishment of honours.

Appointment of the members of the Council of Ministers.

Promulgation by publication of the decisions of the Council of Ministers.

Promulgation by publication of any law or decision passed by the House of Representatives.

Appointments and termination of appointments as in Articles provided.

Institution of compulsory military service.

Reduction or increase of the security forces.

Exercise of the prerogative of mercy in capital cases.

Remission, suspension and commutation of sentences.

Right of references to the Supreme Constitutional Court and publication of Court decisions.

Address of messages to the House of Representatives.

The executive powers which may be exercised separately by the President and Vice-President include: designation and termination of appointment of Greek and Turkish Ministers respectively; the right of final veto on Council decisions and on laws concerning foreign affairs, defence or security; the publication of the communal laws and decisions of the Greek and Turkish Communal Chambers respectively; the right of recourse to the Supreme Constitutional Court; the prerogative of mercy in capital cases; and addressing messages to the House of Representatives.

THE COUNCIL OF MINISTERS

The Council of Ministers shall exercise executive power in all matters, other than those which are within the competence of a Communal Chamber, including the following:

General direction and control of the government of the Republic and the direction of general policy.

Foreign affairs, defence and security.

Co-ordination and supervision of all public services.

Supervision and disposition of property belonging to the Republic.

Consideration of Bills to be introduced to the House of Representatives by a Minister.

Making of any order or regulation for the carrying into effect of any law as provided by such law.

Consideration of the Budget of the Republic to be introduced to the House of Representatives.

THE HOUSE OF REPRESENTATIVES

The legislative power of the Republic shall be exercised by the House of Representatives in all matters except those expressly reserved to the Communal Chambers.

The number of Representatives shall be 50, subject to alteration by a resolution of the House of Representatives carried by a majority comprising two-thirds of the Representatives elected by the Greek Community and two-thirds of the Representatives elected by the Turkish Community.

Out of the number of Representatives 70% shall be elected by the Greek Community and 30% by the Turkish Community separately from amongst their members respectively, and, in the case of a contested election, by universal suffrage and by direct and secret ballot held on the same day.

The term of office of the House of Representatives shall be for a period of five years.

The President of the House of Representatives shall be a Greek, and shall be elected by the Representatives elected by the Greek Community, and the Vice-President shall be a Turk and shall be elected by the Representatives elected by the Turkish Community.

THE COMMUNAL CHAMBERS

The Greek and the Turkish Communities respectively shall elect from amongst their own members a Communal Chamber.

The Communal Chambers shall, in relation to their respective Community, have competence to exercise legislative power solely with regard to the following:

All religious, educational, cultural and teaching matters.

Personal status; composition and instances of courts dealing with civil disputes relating to personal status and to religious matters.

Imposition of personal taxes and fees on members of their respective Community in order to provide for their respective needs.

THE PUBLIC SERVICE AND THE ARMED FORCES

The public service shall be composed as to 70% of Greeks and as to 30% of Turks.

The Republic shall have an army of 2,000 men, of whom 60% shall be Greeks and 40% shall be Turks.

The security forces of the Republic shall consist of the police and gendarmerie and shall have a contingent of 2,000 men. The forces shall be composed as to 70% of Greeks and as to 30% of Turks.

OTHER PROVISIONS

The following measures have been passed by the House of Representatives since January 1964, when the Turkish members withdrew:

The amalgamation of the High Court and the Supreme Constitutional Court (see Judicial System section).

The abolition of the Greek Communal Chamber and the creation of a Ministry of Education.

The unification of the Municipalities.

The unification of the Police and the Gendarmerie.

The creation of a military force by providing that persons between the ages of 18 and 50 years can be called upon to serve in the National Guard.

The extension of the term of office of the President and the House of Representatives by one year intervals from July 1965 until elections in February 1968 and July 1970 respectively.

New electoral provisions; abolition of separate Greek and Turkish rolls; abolition of post of Vice-President, which was re-established in 1973.

The Government*

HEAD OF STATE

President: Tassos Papadopoulos (took office 28 February 2003).

COUNCIL OF MINISTERS
(April 2003)

A coalition Government, comprising DIKO, AKEL, KISOS and Independents (Ind.).

Minister of Foreign Affairs: Georgios Iacovou (Ind.).

Minister of Defence: Kyriakos Mavronicolas (KISOS).

Minister of Finance: Markos Kyprianou (DIKO).

Minister of the Interior: Andreas Christou (AKEL).

Minister of Justice and Public Order: Doros Theodorou (KISOS).

Minister of Commerce, Industry and Tourism: Yiorgos Lillikas (AKEL).

Minister of Education and Culture: Pefkios Georgiades (DIKO).

Minister of Health: Constantina Akkelidou (AKEL).

Minister of Labour and Social Insurance: Iacovos (Makis) Keravnos (DIKO).

Minister of Communications and Works: Kyriakos Kazamias (AKEL).

Minister of Agriculture, Natural Resources and the Environment: Efthymios Efthymiou (Ind.).

Government Spokesman: Kypros Chrysostomides (DIKO).

Deputy Minister to the President: Christodoulos Pasiardis (Ind.).

Press Spokesman of the President of the Republic: Marios Karoyian (Ind.).

*Under the Constitution of 1960, the vice-presidency and three posts in the Council of Ministers are reserved for Turkish Cypriots. However, there has been no Turkish participation in the Government since December 1963. In 1968 President Makarios announced that he considered the office of Vice-President in abeyance until Turkish participation in the Government is resumed, but the Turkish community elected Rauf Denktaş Vice-President in February 1973.

MINISTRIES

Office of the President: Presidential Palace, Dem. Severis Ave, 1400 Nicosia; tel. (22) 661333; fax (22) 665016; internet www.pio.gov.cy/cygov/president.htm.

Ministry of Agriculture, Natural Resources and the Environment: Loukis Akritas Ave, 1411 Nicosia; tel. (22) 300807; fax (22) 781156; e-mail minagre@cytanet.com.

Ministry of Commerce, Industry and Tourism: 6 Andreas Araouzos St, 1424 Nicosia; tel. (22) 867100; fax (22) 375120; e-mail mcitrade@cytanet.com.cy.

Ministry of Communications and Works: 28 Achaion St, 1424 Nicosia; tel. (22) 800106; fax (22) 776248; e-mail permsec@mcw.gov.cy.

Ministry of Defence: 4 Emmanuel Roides Ave, 1432 Nicosia; tel. (22) 807622; fax (22) 675289.

Ministry of Education and Culture: Kimonos & Thoukydidou, Akropolis, 1434 Nicosia; tel. (22) 800600; fax (22) 427559; e-mail moec@moec.gov.cy; internet www.moec.gov.cy.

Ministry of Finance: Ex Secretariat Compound, 1439 Nicosia; tel. (22) 803640; fax (22) 302168; e-mail minfinresearch@cytanet.com.cy.

Ministry of Foreign Affairs: 18–19 Dem. Severis Ave, 1447 Nicosia; tel. (22) 300600; fax (22) 665778; e-mail minforeign1@cytanet.com.cy.

Ministry of Health: Byron Ave, 1448 Nicosia; tel. (22) 309526; fax (22) 305803.

Ministry of the Interior: Dem. Severis Ave, Ex Secretariat Compound, 1453 Nicosia; tel. (22) 867629; fax (22) 671465.

Ministry of Justice and Public Order: 125 Athalassa Ave, 1461 Nicosia; tel. (22) 805955; fax (22) 518356; e-mail registry@mjpo.gov.cy.

Ministry of Labour and Social Insurance: Byron Ave, 1463 Nicosia; tel. (22) 303481; fax (22) 670993.

President and Legislature

PRESIDENT

Election, 16 February 2003

Candidate	Votes	%
Tassos Papadopoulos (DIKO, with AKEL, KISOS and KEP support)	213,353	51.5
Glavkos Klerides (DISY, with EDI and ADIK support)	160,724	38.8
Alecos Markides (Independent) .	27,404	6.6
Nikos Koutsou (NEO)	8,771	2.1
Costas Kyriakou (Independent) .	1,840	0.4
Andreas Efstratiou (Independent)	606	0.2
Adamos Katsantonis (Independent)	558	0.1
Christos Josephides (Independent)	391	0.1
Georgios Mavrogenis (Independent)	337	0.1
Pantelis Sofokleous (Independent)	209	0.1
Total	**431,690**	**100.0**

HOUSE OF REPRESENTATIVES

The House of Representatives originally consisted of 50 members, 35 from the Greek community and 15 from the Turkish community, elected for a term of five years. In January 1964 the Turkish members withdrew and set up the 'Turkish Legislative Assembly of the Turkish Cypriot Administration' (see p. 1358). At the 1985 elections the membership of the House was expanded to 80 members, of whom 56 were to be from the Greek community and 24 from the Turkish community (according to the ratio of representation specified in the Constitution).

President: DEMETRIS CHRISTOFIAS.

Elections for the Greek Representatives, 27 May 2001

Party	Votes	% of Votes	Seats
AKEL (Progressive Party of the Working People). . . .	142,648	34.7	20
DISY (Democratic Rally). . .	139,721	34.0	19
DIKO (Democratic Party) . .	60,986	14.8	9
KISOS (Movement of Social Democrats)	26,767	6.5	4
NEO (New Horizons)	12,333	3.0	1
EDE (United Democrats) . .	10,635	2.6	1
ADIK (Fighting Democratic Movement)	8,860	2.2	1
Movement of Ecologist and Environmentalists	8,129	2.0	1
Independents	908	0.1	—
Total	**410,987**	**100.0**	**56**

Political Organizations

Agonistiko Dimokratiko Kinima (ADIK) (Fighting Democratic Movement): POB 216095, 80 Arch. Makariou III St, Flat 401, 1077 Nicosia; tel. (22) 765353; fax (22) 375737; e-mail info@adik.org.cy; internet www.adik.org.cy; f. 1999; centre-right; supports independent and united Cyprus and a settlement based on UN resolutions; advocates accession of Cyprus to the European Union; Pres. DINOS MICHAELIDES; Gen. Sec. YIANNIS PAPADOPOULOS.

Anorthotiko Komma Ergazomenou Laou (AKEL) (Progressive Party of the Working People): POB 21827, 4 E. Papaioannou St, 1513 Nicosia; tel. (22) 761121; fax (22) 761574; e-mail k.e.akel@cytanet .com.cy; internet www.akel.org.cy; f. 1941; successor to the Communist Party of Cyprus (f. 1926); Marxist-Leninist; supports united, sovereign, independent, federal (bi-zonal, bi-communal) and demilitarized Cyprus; over 14,000 mems; Sec.-Gen. DEMETRIS CHRISTOFIAS.

Dimokratiko Komma (DIKO) (Democratic Party): POB 23979, 50 Grivas Dhigenis Ave, 1080 Nicosia; tel. (22) 666002; fax (22) 666488; e-mail diko@diko.org.cy; internet www.diko.org.cy; f. 1976; absorbed Enosi Kentrou (Centre Union, f. 1981) in 1989; supports settlement of the Cyprus problem based on UN resolutions; Pres. TASSOS PAPADOPOULOS; Gen. Sec. ANDREAS ANGELIDES.

Dimokratikos Synagermos (DISY) (Democratic Rally): POB 25303, 25 Pindarou St, 1061 Nicosia; tel. (22) 883164; fax (22) 753821; e-mail epikinonia@disy.org.cy; internet www.disy.org.cy; f. 1976; absorbed Democratic National Party (DEK) in 1977, New Democratic Front (NEDIPA) in 1988 and Liberal Party in 1998; advocates entry of Cyprus into the European Union and greater active involvement by the EU in the settlement of the Cyprus problem; advocates market economy with restricted state intervention and increased state social role; 27,000 mems; Pres. NIKOS ANASTASIADES; Dir-Gen. GEORGE LIVERAS.

Enomeni Dimokrates (EDI) (United Democrats): POB 23494, 8 Iassonos St, 1683 Nicosia; tel. (22) 663030; fax (22) 664747; e-mail edicy@spidernet.com.cy; internet www.edi.org.cy; f. 1996 by merger of Ananeotiko Dimokratiko Socialistiko Kinema (ADISOK—Democratic Socialist Reform Movement) and Kinema ton Eleftheron Dimokraton (KED—Movement of Free Democrats); Pres. GEORGHIOS VASSILIOU; Gen. Sec. KOSTAS THEMISTOKLEOUS.

Epalxi Anasygrotisis Kentrou (EAK) (Political Forum for the Restructuring of the Centre): POB 22119, Lambousa St, 1095 Nicosia; tel. (22) 773564; fax (22) 779939; e-mail kchrysos@logos.cy .net; f. 1998; aims to achieve a wider grouping of all centrist social-democratic movements; supports a settlement to the Cyprus problem based on the principles of the Rule of Law, international law and respect for human rights for all citizens, and the establishment of a democratic federal system of government.

Kinima Ekologon-Perivallontiston (Movement of Ecologists and Environmentalists): POB 29682, 1722 Nicosia; tel. (22) 518787; fax (22) 512710; e-mail greenpar@cytanet.com.cy; internet www .cycentral.com/greens; f. 1996; opposed to any geographical division of the island; supports entry into the European Union; Gen. Co-ordinator SAVVAS PHILIPPOU.

Kinima Sosialdimokraton (KISOS) (Movement of Social Democrats): POB 21064, 40 Byron Ave, 1096 Nicosia; tel. (22) 670121; fax (22) 678894; e-mail info@kisos.org; internet www.kisos.org; f. 2000 as successor to Socialistico Komma Kyprou (EDEK—Socialist Party

of Cyprus, f. 1969); supports independent, non-aligned, unitary, demilitarized Cyprus; advocates accession of Cyprus to the European Union; Pres. Dr VASSOS LYSSARIDES; Dep. Pres. YIANNAKIS OMIROU.

Kinisi Politikou Eksychronismou (Movement for Political Reforms): 22 Stasikratous St, 1065 Nicosia; tel. (22) 668894; fax (22) 6698892; f. 1995; aims to contribute to realignment of the parties of the Centre; supports settlement of the Cyprus problem based on UN resolutions; supports accession of Cyprus to the European Union.

Komma Evrodimokratikis Ananeosis (KEA) (Eurodemocratic Renewal Party): 176 Athalassa Ave, Office 402, 2025 Nicosia; tel. (22) 514551; fax (22) 513565; f. 1998; supports entry into the European Union and federal settlement to the Cyprus problem based on UN resolutions; Pres. TAKIS HADJIOANNOU (acting).

Neoi Orizontes (NEO) (New Horizons): POB 22496, 3 Trikoupi St, 1522 Nicosia; tel. (22) 761476; fax (22) 761144; e-mail neo@ neoiorizontes.org; internet www.neoiorizontes.org; f. 1996; supports settlement of the Cyprus problem through political means and the establishment of a non-federal unitary state with single sovereignty throughout the whole territory of the island; Pres. NIKOS KOUTSOU; Gen. Sec. MARIA ROSSIDOU.

Diplomatic Representation

EMBASSIES AND HIGH COMMISSIONS IN CYPRUS

Australia: 4 Annis Komninis St, 2nd Floor, 1060 Nicosia; tel. (22) 753001; fax (22) 766486; e-mail auscomm@logos.cy.net; High Commissioner FRANZ JOHANN INGRUBER.

Bulgaria: POB 24029, 13 Konst. Paleologos St, 2406 Engomi, Nicosia; tel. (22) 672486; fax (22) 676598; e-mail bulgaria@cytanet .com.cy; Ambassador KRASSIMIR STEFANOV.

China, People's Republic: POB 4531, 28 Archimedes St, 2411 Engomi, Nicosia; tel. (22) 352182; fax (22) 353530; Ambassador SONG AIGUO.

Cuba: 7 Yiannis Taliotis St, Strovolos 2014, Nicosia; tel. (22) 512332; fax (22) 512331; e-mail embacuba@spidernet.com.cy; Ambassador MANUEL PARDIÑAS AJENO.

Czech Republic: POB 5202, 48 Arsinois St, 1307 Nicosia; tel. (22) 421118; fax (22) 421059; e-mail nicosia@embassy.mzv.cz; Ambassador VEŘA JEŘÁBIKOVÀ.

Egypt: POB 21752, 3 Egypt Ave, 1097 Nicosia; tel. (22) 680650; fax (22) 664265; Ambassador OMAR METWALLY.

France: POB 21671, 12 Ploutarchou St, Engomi, Nicosia; tel. (22) 779910; fax (22) 781052; e-mail ambachyp@spidernet.com.cy; internet www.ambafrancechypre.org; Ambassador JACQUES DESAIGNE.

Germany: POB 25705, 1311 Nicosia, 10 Nikitaras St, Ay. Omoloyitae, 1080 Nicosia; tel. (22) 451145; fax (22) 665694; e-mail info@ germanembassy-nicosia.org.cy; internet www .germanembassy-nicosia.org.cy; Ambassador Dr JOCHEN TREBESCH.

Greece: POB 1799, 8/10 Byron Ave, Nicosia; tel. (22) 680670; fax (22) 680649; Ambassador CHRISTOS PANAGOPOULOS.

Holy See: POB 21964, Holy Cross Catholic Church, Paphos Gate, 1010 Nicosia (Apostolic Nunciature); tel. (22) 662132; fax (22) 660767; e-mail holcross@logos.cy.net; Apostolic Nuncio Most Rev. PIETRO SAMBI (Titular Archbishop of Belcastro (with residence in Jerusalem)).

India: POB 25544, 3 Indira Gandhi St, Engomi, 2413 Nicosia; tel. (22) 351741; fax (22) 350402; e-mail india@spidernet.com.cy; High Commissioner SHYAMALA B. COWSIK.

Iran: POB 8145, 42 Armenias St, Akropolis, Nicosia; tel. (22) 314459; fax (22) 315446; Ambassador BAHMAN AGHA-RAZI.

Israel: POB 25159, 4 I. Gryparis St, Nicosia; tel. (22) 369500; fax (22) 666338; e-mail ambass-sec@nicosia.mfa.gov.il; Ambassador MICHAEL ELIGAL.

Italy: POB 27695, 11 25th March St, Engomi 2408, Nicosia; tel. (22) 357635; fax (22) 357616; e-mail ambnico@italianembassy.org.cy; internet www.italianembassy.org.cy; Ambassador FRANCESCO BASCONE.

Lebanon: POB 21924, 1 Vasilissis Olgas St, Nicosia; tel. (22) 776845; fax (22) 776662; Ambassador SAMIRA HANNA ED-DAHER.

Libya: POB 3669, 14 Estias St, 1041 Nicosia; tel. (22) 317366; fax (22) 316152; Ambassador KHALIFA AHMAD BAZELYA.

Poland: 11 Acharnon St, 2027 Strovolos, Nicosia; tel. (22) 427077; fax (22) 510611; Ambassador TOMASZ LIS.

Romania: POB 2210, 83 Kennedy Ave, 1077 Nicosia; tel. (22) 379303; fax (22) 379121; e-mail romemb@globalsoftmail.com; Ambassador COSTIN GEORGESCU.

Russia: Ay. Prokopias St and Archbishop Makarios III Ave, Engomi, Nicosia; tel. (22) 772141; fax (22) 774854; Ambassador VLADIMIR PRYGIN.

Serbia and Montenegro: 2 Vasilissis Olgas St, Nicosia; tel. (22) 445511; fax (22) 445910; Ambassador SVETISLAV BASARA.

Slovakia: POB 21165, 4 Kalamatas St, 2002 Strovolos, Nicosia; tel. (22) 879681; fax (22) 311715; e-mail skembassy@cytanet.com.cy; Ambassador JÁN VARŠO.

Switzerland: POB 20729, MEDCON Bldg, 6th Floor, 46 Themistoklis Dervis St, 1663 Nicosia; tel. (22) 766261; fax (22) 766008; e-mail swiemnic@spidernet.com.cy; Chargé d'affaires a.i. MARGRITH BIERI.

Syria: POB 21891, 24 Nikodimos Mylona St, Ay. Antonios, 1071 Nicosia; tel. (22) 764481; fax (22) 756963; Chargé d'affaires a.i. Dr AHMAD HAJ-IBRAHIM.

United Kingdom: POB 21978, Alexander Pallis St, 1587 Nicosia; tel. (22) 861100; fax (22) 861125; e-mail infobhc@cylink.com.cy; internet www.britain.org.cy; High Commissioner LYN PARKER.

USA: POB 24536, 7 Ploutarchou, 2407 Engomi, Nicosia; tel. (22) 776400; fax (22) 780944; e-mail amembass@spidernet.com.cy; internet www.americanembassy.org.cy; Ambassador DONALD K. BANDLER.

Judicial System

Supreme Council of Judicature: Nicosia; The Supreme Council of Judicature is composed of the President and Judges of the Supreme Court. It is responsible for the appointment, promotion, transfer, etc., of the judges exercising civil and criminal jurisdiction in the District Courts, the Assize Courts, the Family Courts, the Military Court, the Rent Control Courts and the Industrial Dispute Court.

SUPREME COURT

Supreme Court

Char. Mouskos St, 1404 Nicosia; tel. (22) 865716; fax (22) 304500.
The Constitution of 1960 provided for a separate Supreme Constitutional Court and High Court but in 1964, in view of the resignation of their neutral presidents, these were amalgamated to form a single Supreme Court
The Supreme Court is the final appellate court in the Republic and the final adjudicator in matters of constitutional and administrative law, including recourses on conflict of competence between state organs on questions of the constitutionality of laws, etc. It deals with appeals from Assize Courts, District Courts and other inferior Courts as well as from the decisions of its own judges when exercising original jurisdiction in certain matters such as prerogative orders of *habeas corpus, mandamus, certiorari* etc., and in admiralty cases.

President: GEORGHIOS M. PIKIS.

Judges: I. C. CONSTANTINIDES, T. ELIADES, CHR. C. ARTEMIDES, G. NIKOLAOU, P. KALLIS, FR. G. NIKOLAIDES, S. NIKITAS, P. CH. ARTEMIS, M. KRONIDES, A. KRAMVIS, R. GAVRIELIDES, Y. CHRYSOSTOMIS.

Attorney-General: ALEKOS MARKIDES.

OTHER COURTS

As required by the Constitution a law was passed in 1960 providing for the establishment, jurisdiction and powers of courts of civil and criminal jurisdiction, i.e. of six District Courts and six Assize Courts. In accordance with the provisions of new legislation, approved in 1991, a permanent Assize Court, with powers of jurisdiction in all districts, was established.
In addition to a single Military Court, there are specialized Courts concerned with cases relating to industrial disputes, rent control and family law.

'Turkish Republic of Northern Cyprus'

The Turkish intervention in Cyprus in July 1974 resulted in the establishment of a separate area in northern Cyprus under the control of the Autonomous Turkish Cypriot Administration, with a Council of Ministers and separate judicial, financial, police, military and educational machinery serving the Turkish community.

On 13 February 1975 the Turkish-occupied zone of Cyprus was declared the 'Turkish Federated State of Cyprus', and Rauf Denktaş declared President. At the second joint meeting held by the Executive Council and Legislative Assembly of the Autonomous Turkish Cypriot Administration, it was decided to set up a Constituent Assembly which would prepare a constitution for the 'Turkish Federated State of Cyprus' within 45 days. This Constitution, which was approved by the Turkish Cypriot population in a referendum held on 8 June 1975, was regarded by the Turkish Cypriots as a first step towards a federal republic of Cyprus. The main provisions of the Constitution are summarized below:
The 'Turkish Federated State of Cyprus' is a democratic, secular republic based on the principles of social justice and the rule of law. It shall exercise only those functions that fall outside the powers and functions expressly given to the (proposed) Federal Republic of Cyprus. Necessary amendments shall be made to the Constitution of the 'Turkish Federated State of Cyprus' when the Constitution of the Federal Republic comes into force. The official language is Turkish.
Legislative power is vested in a Legislative Assembly, composed of 40 deputies, elected by universal suffrage for a period of five years. The President is Head of State and is elected by universal suffrage for a period of five years. No person may be elected President for more than two consecutive terms. The Council of Ministers shall be composed of a prime minister and 10 ministers. Judicial power is exercised through independent courts.
Other provisions cover such matters as the rehabilitation of refugees, property rights outside the 'Turkish Federated State', protection of coasts, social insurance, the rights and duties of citizens, etc.
On 15 November 1983 a unilateral declaration of independence brought into being the 'Turkish Republic of Northern Cyprus', which, like the 'Turkish Federated State of Cyprus', was not granted international recognition.
The Constituent Assembly, established after the declaration of independence, prepared a new constitution, which was approved by the Turkish Cypriot electorate on 5 May 1985. The new Constitution is very similar to the old one, but the number of deputies in the Legislative Assembly was increased to 50.

HEAD OF STATE

President of the 'Turkish Republic of Northern Cyprus': RAUF R. DENKTAŞ (assumed office as President of the 'Turkish Federated State of Cyprus' 13 February 1975; became President of the 'TRNC' 15 November 1983; re-elected 1985, 1990, 1995 and 15 April 2000).

COUNCIL OF MINISTERS
(April 2003)

A coalition of the Ulusal Bırlık Partisi (UBP) and the Demokrat Parti (DP).

Prime Minister: Dr DERVIŞ EROĞLU (UBP).

Deputy Prime Minister and Minister of State for Economy: SALIH COŞAR (DP).

Minister of Foreign Affairs and Defence: TAHSIN ERTUĞRULOĞLU (UBP).

Minister of the Interior, Rural Affairs and Housing: Dr MEHMET ALBAYRAK (UBP).

Minister of Finance: MEHMET BAYRAM (UBP).

Minister of National Education and Culture: İLKAY KAMIL (UBP).

Minister of Agriculture and Forestry: İRSEN KÜÇÜK (UBP).

Minister of Public Works and Transport: SALIH MIROĞLU (UBP).

Minister of Tourism and Environment: SERDAR DENKTAŞ (DP).

Minister of Health and Social Welfare: Dr MUSTAFA ARABACIOĞLU (DP).

Minister of Labour, Social Security, Youth Affairs and Sports: Dr AHMET KAŞIF (DP).

MINISTRIES

Prime Minister's Office: Lefkoşa (Nicosia), Mersin 10, Turkey; tel. (22) 83141; fax (22) 75281; e-mail pressdpt@brimnet.com.

Ministry of State and Deputy Prime Minister's Office: Lefkoşa (Nicosia), Mersin 10, Turkey; tel. (22) 86838; fax (22) 85204; e-mail kktcb3@kktc.net; internet www.Turizm.TRNC.net.

Ministry of Agriculture and Forestry: Lefkoşa (Nicosia), Mersin 10, Turkey; tel. (22) 83735; fax (22) 86945.

Ministry of Communications and Works: Lefkoşa (Nicosia), Mersin 10, Turkey; tel. (22) 83666; fax (22) 81891.

Ministry of Finance: Lefkoşa (Nicosia), Mersin 10, Turkey; tel. (22) 83116; fax (22) 85204; e-mail ekonomi@ebim.com.tr.

Ministry of Foreign Affairs and Defence: Lefkoşa (Nicosia), Mersin 10, Turkey; tel. (22) 83241; fax (22) 84290; e-mail bakanlik@pubinfo.org; internet www.trncinfo.com.

Ministry of Health and Social Welfare: Lefkoşa (Nicosia), Mersin 10, Turkey; tel. (22) 78765; fax (22) 76349.

Ministry of the Interior, Rural Affairs and Housing: Lefkoşa (Nicosia), Mersin 10, Turkey; tel. (22) 85453; fax (22) 83043.

Ministry of Labour, Social Security, Youth Affairs and Sports: Lefkoşa (Nicosia), Mersin 10, Turkey; tel. (22) 83136; fax (22) 82334.

Ministry of National Education and Culture: Lefkoşa (Nicosia), Mersin 10, Turkey.

Ministry of Tourism and Environment: Lefkoşa (Nicosia), Mersin 10, Turkey; tel. (22) 83173; fax (22) 83893; e-mail turizm@dbby.trnc.net; internet www.tourism.trnc.net.

PRESIDENT

Election, 15 April 2000*

Candidates	Votes	%
Rauf R. Denktaş (Independent) . . .	42,819	43.67
Dr Derviş Eroğlu (UBP)	29,505	30.14
Mustafa Akinci (TKP)	11,469	11.70
Mehmet Ali Talat (CTP)	9,834	10.03
Arif Hasan Tahsin (YBH)	2,545	2.60
Sener Levet (Independent)	899	0.92
Turgut Afsaroglu (Independent) . . .	553	0.56
Ayhan Kaymak (Independent) . . .	369	0.38
Total	97,993†	100.00

* Although Denktaş did not gain the 50% of the votes necesary to be elected in the first round, he was declared the winner after Eroğlu withdrew from a second round of voting, scheduled for 22 April 2000.

† Excluding invalid votes.

LEGISLATIVE ASSEMBLY

Speaker: ERTUĞRUL HASIPOĞLU (UBP).

General Election, 6 December 1998

Party	% of votes	Seats
Ulusal Bırlık Partisi	40.3	24
Demokrat Parti	22.6	13
Toplumcu Kurtuluş Partisi	15.4	7
Cumhuriyetçi Türk Partisi	13.4	6
Others*	8.3	—
Total	100.0	50

* The other parties that contested the election were the National Revival Party, which won 4.6% of the votes; the Patriotic Unity Movement, which obtained 2.5%; and Our Party, which won 1.2%.

POLITICAL ORGANIZATIONS

Cumhuriyetçi Türk Partisi (CTP) (Republican Turkish Party): 99A Şehit Salahi, Şevket Sok., Lefkoşa (Nicosia), Mersin 10, Turkey; tel. (22) 73300; fax (22) 81914; e-mail ctp@cypronet.net; f. 1970 by members of the Turkish community in Cyprus; socialist principles with anti-imperialist stand; district organizations at Gazi Mağusa (Famagusta), Girne (Kyrenia), Güzelyurt (Morphou) and Lefkoşa (Nicosia); Leader MEHMET ALI TALAT; Gen. Sec. MUSTAFA FERD SOYER.

Demokrat Parti (DP) (Democrat Party): Lefkoşa (Nicosia), Mersin 10, Turkey; tel. (22) 83795; fax (22) 87130; e-mail yenidem@kktc.net; f. 1992 by disaffected UBP representatives; merged with the Yeni Doğuş Partisi (New Dawn Party; f. 1984) and Sosyal Demokrat Partisi (Social Democrat Party) in May 1993; Leader SALIH COŞAR; Sec.-Gen. HURSIT EMINER.

Hür Demokrat Parti (Free Democrat Party): Lefkoşa (Nicosia), Mersin 10, Turkey; f. 1991; Leader ÖZEL TAHSIN.

Toplumcu Kurtuluş Partisi (TKP) (Communal Liberation Party): 44 Ikinci Selim Sok., Lefkoşa (Nicosia), Mersin 10, Turkey; tel. (22) 72555; internet www.cm.gov.nc.tr/tkp; f. 1976; merged with the Atılımcı Halk Partisi (Progressive People's Party, f. 1979) in 1989; democratic left party; wants a solution of Cyprus problem as an independent, non-aligned, bi-zonal and bi-communal federal state; Leader MUSTAFA AKINCI; Gen. Sec. HÜSEYIN ANGOLEMLI.

Ulusal Bırlık Partisi (UBP) (National Unity Party): 9 Atatürk Meydanı, Lefkoşa (Nicosia), Mersin 10, Turkey; tel. (22) 73972; f.

1975; right of centre; based on Atatürk's reforms, social justice, political equality and peaceful co-existence in an independent, bi-zonal, bi-communal, confederate state of Cyprus; Leader Dr DERVIŞ EROĞLU; Sec.-Gen. SUHA TURKOZ.

Ulusal Dirilis Partisi (UDP) (National Revival Party): Lefkoşa (Nicosia), Mersin 10, Turkey; f. 1997; Leader ENVER EMIN.

Unity and Sovereignty Party (BEP): Lefkoşa (Nicosia), Mersin 10, Turkey; Leader ARIF SALIH KIRDAĞ.

Yeni Doğuş Partisi (YDP) (New Dawn Party): Lefkoşa (Nicosia); f. 1984; merged with DP in May 1993, revived 1997.

Yurtsever Bırlık Hareketi (YBH) (Patriotic Unity Movement): Lefkoşa (Nicosia), Mersin 10, Turkey; tel. (22) 74917; fax (22) 88931; e-mail ybh@north-cyprus.net; f. 1989; Leader RASIH KESKINER.

DIPLOMATIC REPRESENTATION

Embassy in the 'TRNC'

Turkey: Bedrettin Demirel Cad., T.C. Lefkoşa Büyükelçisi, Lefkoşa (Nicosia), Mersin 10, Turkey; tel. (22) 72314; fax (22) 85118; e-mail tclefkbe@cc.emu.edu.tr; Ambassador HAYATI GÜVEN.

Turkey is the only country officially to have recognized the 'Turkish Republic of Northern Cyprus'.

JUDICIAL SYSTEM

Supreme Court: Lefkoşa (Nicosia), Mersin 10, Turkey; tel. (22) 87535; fax (22) 85265; e-mail mahkeme@kktc.net; The highest court in the 'TRNC' is the Supreme Court. The Supreme Court functions as the Constitutional Court, the Court of Appeal and the High Administrative Court. The Supreme Court, sitting as the Constitutional Court, has exclusive jurisdiction to adjudicate finally on all matters prescribed by the Constitution. The Supreme Court, sitting as the Court of Appeal, is the highest appellate court in the 'TRNC'. It also has original jurisdiction in certain matters of judicial review. The Supreme Court, sitting as the High Administrative Court, has exclusive jurisdiction on matters relating to administrative law.

The Supreme Court is composed of a president and seven judges.

President: SALIH S. DAYIOĞLU.

Judges: CELÂL KARABACAK, TANER ERGINEL, METIN A. HAKKI, NEVVAR NOLAN, MUSTAFA ÖZKÖK, GÖNÜL ERÖNEN, SEYT A. BENSEN.

Subordinate Courts: Judicial power other than that exercised by the Supreme Court is exercised by the Assize Courts, District Courts and Family Courts.

Supreme Council of Judicature

The Supreme Council of Judicature, composed of the president and judges of the Supreme Court, a member appointed by the President of the 'TRNC', a member appointed by the Legislative Assembly, the Attorney-General and a member elected by the Bar Association, is responsible for the appointment, promotion, transfer and matters relating to the discipline of all judges. The appointments of the president and judges of the Supreme Court are subject to the approval of the President of the 'TRNC'.

Attorney-General: SAIT AKIN.

Religion

Greeks form 77% of the population and most of them belong to the Orthodox Church, although there are also adherents of the Armenian Apostolic Church, the Anglican Communion and the Roman Catholic Church (including Maronites). Most Turks (about 18% of the population) are Muslims.

CHRISTIANITY

The Orthodox Church of Cyprus

The Autocephalous Orthodox Church of Cyprus, founded in ad 45, is part of the Eastern Orthodox Church; the Church is independent, and the Archbishop, who is also the Ethnarch (national leader of the Greek community), is elected by representatives of the towns and villages of Cyprus. The Church comprises six dioceses, and in 1995 had an estimated 600,000 members.

Archbishop of Nova Justiniana and all Cyprus: Archbishop CHRYSOSTOMOS, POB 1130, Archbishop Kyprianos St, Nicosia; tel. (22) 430696; fax (22) 432470.

Metropolitan of Paphos: Bishop CHRYSOSTOMOS.

Metropolitan of Kitium: Bishop CHRYSOSTOMOS, POB 40036, 6300 Larnaca; tel. (24) 652269; fax (24) 655588; e-mail mlarnaca@logosnet.cy.net.

Metropolitan of Kyrenia: Bishop PAULUS.

Metropolitan of Limassol: Bishop ATHANASIOS.

Metropolitan of Morphou: Bishop NEOPHYTIOS.

The Roman Catholic Church

Latin Rite

The Patriarchate of Jerusalem covers Israel, Jordan and Cyprus. The Patriarch is resident in Jerusalem (see the chapter on Israel).

Vicar Patriarchal for Cyprus: Fr UMBERTO BARATO, Holy Cross Catholic Church, Paphos Gate, POB 21964, 1515 Nicosia; tel. (22) 662132; fax (22) 660767; e-mail holcross@logos.cy.net.

Maronite Rite

Most of the Roman Catholics in Cyprus are adherents of the Maronite rite. Prior to June 1988 the Archdiocese of Cyprus included part of Lebanon. At December 2000 the archdiocese contained an estimated 10,000 Maronite Catholics.

Archbishop of Cyprus: Most Rev. BOUTROS GEMAYEL, POB 22249, Maronite Archbishop's House, 8 Ayios Maronas St, Nicosia; tel. (22) 678877; fax (22) 668260.

The Anglican Communion

Anglicans in Cyprus are adherents of the Episcopal Church in Jerusalem and the Middle East, officially inaugurated in January 1976. The Church has four dioceses. The diocese of Cyprus and the Gulf includes Cyprus, Iraq and the countries of the Arabian peninsula.

Bishop in Cyprus and the Gulf, President Bishop of the Episcopal Church in Jeruselam and the Middle East: Most Rev. CLIVE HANDFORD, c/o POB 22075, Diocesan Office, 2 Grigoris Afxentiou St, 1517 Nicosia; tel. (22) 671220; fax (22) 674553; e-mail georgia@spidernet.com.cy.

Other Christian Churches

Among other denominations active in Cyprus are the Armenian Apostolic Church and the Greek Evangelical Church.

ISLAM

Most adherents of Islam in Cyprus are Sunni Muslims of the Hanafi sect. The religious head of the Muslim community is the Mufti.

Mufti of Cyprus: AHMET CEMAL İLKTAÇ (acting), PK 142, Lefkoşa (Nicosia), Mersin 10, Turkey.

The Press

GREEK CYPRIOT DAILIES

Alithia (Truth): POB 21695, 26A Pindaros and Androklis St, 1060 Nicosia; tel. (22) 763040; fax (22) 763945; e-mail alithia@spidernet .com.cy; f. 1952 as a weekly, 1982 as a daily; morning; Greek; right-wing; Dir SOCRATIS HASIKOS; Chief Editor ALEKOS KONSTANTINIDES; circ. 11,000.

Apogevmatini (Afternoon): POB 25603, 5 Aegaleo St, Strovolos, Nicosia; tel. (22) 353603; fax (22) 353223; f. 1972; afternoon; Greek; independent; Dirs EFTHYMIOS HADJIEFTHIMIOU, ANTONIS STAVRIDES; Chief Editor COSTAKIS ANTONIOY; circ. 8,000.

Cyprus Mail: POB 21144, 24 Vassilios Voulgaroktonos St, Nicosia; tel. (22) 818585; fax (22) 676385; e-mail mail@cyprus-mail.com; internet www.cyprus-mail.com; f. 1945; morning; English; independent; Dir KYRIACOS IAKOVIDES; Editor STEVEN MYLES; circ. 4,000.

Epilogi: 19 Nikitara St, Ay. Omologiles, Nicosia; tel. (22) 367345; fax (22) 367511; f. 1997; Greek; Chief Editor COSTAS ZACHARIADES.

Haravgi (Dawn): POB 21556, ETAK Bldg, 6 Ezekia Papaioannou St, Nicosia; tel. (22) 766666; fax (22) 765154; e-mail haravagi@ spidernet.com.cy; internet www.haravagi.com.cy; f. 1956; morning; Greek; organ of AKEL (Communist Party); Dir NIKOS KATSOURIDES; Chief Editor ANDROULLA GIOUROF; circ. 10,000.

Machi (Combat): POB 27628, 4A Danaes, Engomi, Nicosia; tel. (22) 356676; fax (22) 356701; f. 1961; morning; Greek; right-wing; Dir SOTIRIS SAMPSON; Chief Editor MINA SAMPSON; circ. 4,750.

O Phileleftheros (Liberal): POB 21094, Commercial Centre, 1 Diogenous St, 3rd, 6th–7th Floor, Engomi, 1501 Nicosia; tel. (22) 744000; fax (22) 590122; e-mail artemiou@phileleftheros.com; internet www.phileleftheros.com.cy; f. 1955; morning; Greek; independent, moderate; Dir N. PATTICHIS; Editorial Dir ANTHOS LYKAVGIS; Chief Editor TAKIS KOUNNAFIS; circ. 28,000.

Politis (Citizen): 12 Makhera St, Engomi, Nicosia; tel. (22) 861861; fax (22) 861871; e-mail info@politis-news.com; internet www .politis-news.com; f. 1999; morning; Greek; independent; Chief Editor ARISTOS MICHAELIDES.

Simerini (Today): POB 21836, 31 Archangelos Ave, Strovolos, Nicosia; tel. (22) 353532; fax (22) 352298; internet www.odyssey.com .cy/simerini; f. 1976; morning; Greek; right-wing; supports DISY party; Dir KOSTAS HADJIKOSTIS; Chief Editor SAVVAS IAKOVIDES; circ. 17,000.

TURKISH CYPRIOT DAILIES

Afrika: Lefkoşa (Nicosia), Mersin 10, Turkey; tel. (22) 71338; fax (22) 74585; e-mail avrupa@cc.emu.edu.tr; frmly Avrupa; independent; Editor ŞENER LEVENT; circ. 3,000.

Bırlık (Unity): 43 Yediler Sok., PK 841, Lefkoşa (Nicosia), Mersin 10, Turkey; tel. (22) 72959; fax (22) 83959; f. 1980; Turkish; organ of UBP; Editor LÜTFI ÖZTER.

Halkın Sesi (Voice of the People): 172 Kyrenia Sok., Lefkoşa (Nicosia), Mersin 10, Turkey; tel. (22) 73141; f. 1942; morning; Turkish; independent Turkish nationalist; Editor AKAY CEMAL; circ. 6,000.

Kıbrıs: Dr Fazil Küçük Bul., Lefkoşa (Nicosia), Mersin 10, Turkey; tel. (22) 52555; fax 52934; e-mail kibris@cypronet.net; Editor MEHMET ALI AKPINAR; circ. 13,000.

Ortam (Political Conditions): 158A Girne Cad., Lefkoşa (Nicosia), Mersin 10, Turkey; tel. (22) 74872; Turkish; organ of the TKP; Editor ÖZAL ZIYA; circ. 1,250.

Vatan (Homeland): 46 Mufti Ziyai Sok., PK 842, Lefkoşa (Nicosia), Mersin 10, Turkey; tel. (22) 77557; fax (22) 77558; e-mail vatan@ kktc.net; f. 1991; Editor ERTEN KASIMOĞLU.

Yeni Demokrat (New Democrat): 1 Cengiz Han Cad., Kösklüçiftlik, Lefkoşa (Nicosia), Mersin 10, Turkey; tel. (22) 81485; fax (22) 72558; Turkish; organ of the DP; Editor MUSTAFA OKAN; circ. 450.

Yeni Düzen (New System): Yeni Sanayi Sok., Lefkoşa (Nicosia), Mersin 10, Turkey; tel. (22) 56658; fax (22) 53240; e-mail yeniduzen@defne.net; Turkish; organ of the CTP; Editor BURHAN ERASUAN; circ. 1,250.

GREEK CYPRIOT WEEKLIES

Athlitiki tis Kyriakis: 5 Epias, Engomi, Nicosia; tel. (22) 352966; fax (22) 348835; f. 1996; Greek; athletic; Dir PANAYIOTIS FELLOUKAS; Chief Editor SAWAS KOSHARIS; circ. 4,000.

Cyprus Financial Mirror: POB 24280, 80B Thermopylon St, 2007 Nicosia; tel. (22) 495790; fax (22) 495907; e-mail shavasb@ financialmirror.com; internet www.financialmirror.com; f. 1993; English (with Greek-language supplement); independent; Dirs MASIS DER PARTHOGH, SHAVASB BOHDJALIAN; circ. 3,500.

Cyprus Weekly: POB 24977, Suite 102, Trust House, Gryparis St, 1306 Nicosia; tel. (22) 666047; fax (22) 668665; e-mail weekly@ spidernet.com.cy; internet www.cyprusweekly.com.cy; f. 1979; English; independent; Dirs GEORGES DER PARTHOGH, ALEX EFTHYVOULOS, ANDREAS HADJIPAPAS; Chief Editor MARTYN HENRY; circ. 18,000.

Ergatiki Phoni (Workers' Voice): POB 25018, SEK Bldg, 23 Alkeou St, Engomi, Nicosia; tel. (22) 441142; fax (22) 476360; f. 1947; Greek; organ of SEK trade union; Dir MICHALAKIS IOANNOU; Chief Editor XENIS XENOFONTOS; circ. 10,000.

Ergatiko Vima (Workers' Tribune): POB 21885, 31–35 Archemos St, Nicosia 1045; tel. (22) 349400; fax (22) 349382; f. 1956; Greek; organ of the PEO trade union; Chief Editor KOSTAS GREKOS; circ. 14,000.

Official Gazette: Printing Office of the Republic of Cyprus, Nicosia; tel. (22) 405811; fax (22) 303175; f. 1960; Greek; published by the Government of the Republic of Cyprus; circ. 5,000.

Paraskinio (Behind the Scenes): 6 Psichikou St, Strovolos, Nicosia; tel. (22) 322959; fax (22) 322940; f. 1987; Greek; Dir and Chief Editor D. MICHAEL; cir. 3,000.

Selides (Pages): POB 21094, 1501 Nicosia; tel. (22) 590000; fax (22) 590122; e-mail selides@phileleftheros.com; internet www .phileleftheros.com; f. 1991; Greek; Dir N. PATTICHIS; Chief Editor STAVROS CHRISTODOLOU; circ. 16,500.

Super Flash: POB 23647, 11 Kolokotronis St, Kaimakli, Nicosia; tel. (22) 316674; fax (22) 316582; f. 1979; youth magazine; Greek; Dir DEMETRIS ALONEFTIS; circ. 5,000.

Ta Nea (News): POB 4349, 40 Vyronos Ave, Nicosia; tel. (22) 476575; fax (22) 476512; f. 1968; Greek; organ of EDEK (Socialist Party); Chief Editor PHYTOS SOCRATOUS; circ. 3,000.

Tharros (Courage): POB 27628, 4A Danaes, Engomi, Nicosia; tel. (22) 356676; fax (22) 356701; f. 1961; Greek; right-wing; Dir SOTIRIS SAMPSON; Chief Editor MINA SAMPSON; circ. 5,500.

To Periodiko: POB 21836, Dias Bldg, 31 Archangelos Ave, Strovolos, Nicosia; tel. (22) 353646; fax (22) 352268; f. 1986; Greek; Dir KOSTAS HADJIKOSTIS; Chief Editor ANDREAS DEMETROPOULOS; circ. 16,000.

TURKISH CYPRIOT WEEKLIES

Cyprus Today: Dr Fazil Küçük Bul., PK 831, Lefkoşa (Nicosia), Mersin 10, Turkey; tel. (22) 52555; fax (22) 52934; e-mail cyprustoday@yahoo.com; f. 1991; English; political, social, cultural and economic; Editor GILL FRASER; circ. 5,000.

Ekonomi (The Economy): Bedrettin Demirel Cad. No.90, Lefkoşa (Nicosia), Mersin 10, Turkey; tel. (22) 83760; fax (22) 83089; f. 1958; Turkish; published by the Turkish Cypriot Chamber of Commerce; Editor-in-Chief SAMI TAŞARKAN; circ. 3,000.

Safak: PK 228, Lefkoşa (Nicosia), Mersin 10, Turkey; tel. (22) 71472; fax (22) 87910; f. 1992; Turkish; circ. 1,000.

Yeni Çağ: 28 Ramadan Cad., Lefkoşa (Nicosia), Mersin 10, Turkey; tel. (22) 74917; fax (22) 71476; e-mail yenicag@8m.com; internet www.north-cyprus.net/ybh; f. 1990; Turkish; publ. of the YBH; circ. 500.

OTHER WEEKLIES

The Blue Beret: POB 21642, HQ UNFICYP, 1590 Nicosia; tel. (22) 864550; fax (22) 864461; e-mail blueberetcyprus@hotmail.com; internet www.unficyp.org; English; circ. 1,500.

Lion: 55 AEC Episkopi, British Forces Post Office 53; tel. (25) 262445; fax (25) 263181; e-mail wolves1@cytanet.com.cy; distributed to British Sovereign Base Areas, United Nations Forces and principal Cypriot towns; weekly; includes British Forces Broadcasting Services programme guide; Editor SARA WOOTTON; circ. 5,000.

Middle East Economic Survey: Middle East Petroleum and Economic Publications (Cyprus), POB 24940, 1355 Nicosia; tel. (22) 665431; fax (22) 671988; e-mail info@mees.com; internet www.mees .com; f. 1957 (in Beirut, Lebanon); weekly review and analysis of petroleum, finance and banking, and political developments; Publr BASIM W. ITAYIM; Editor WALID KHADDURI.

GREEK CYPRIOT PERIODICALS

Cool: POB 8205, 86 Iphigenias St, 2091 Nicosia; tel. (22) 378900; fax (22) 378916; f. 1994; Greek; youth magazine; Chief Editor PROMETHEAS CHRISTOPHIDES; circ. 4,000.

Cypria (Cypriot Woman): POB 28506, 56 Kennedy Ave, 11th Floor, 1076 Nicosia; tel. (22) 494907; fax (22) 427051; f. 1983; every 2 months; Greek; Owner MARO KARAYIANNI; circ. 7,000.

Cyprus P.C.: POB 24989, 6th Floor, 1 Kyriakou Matsi St, 1306 Nicosia; tel. (22) 765999; fax (22) 765909; e-mail pc@infomedia.cy .net; internet www.infomedia.com.cy; f. 1990; monthly; Greek; computing magazine; Dir LAKIS VARNAVA; circ. 5,000.

Cyprus Time Out: POB 3697, 4 Pygmalionos St, 1010 Nicosia; tel. (22) 472949; fax (22) 360668; f. 1978; monthly; English; Dir ELLADA SOPHOCLEOUS; Chief Editor LYN HAVILAND; circ. 8,000.

Cyprus Today: c/o Ministry of Education and Culture, Nicosia; tel. (22) 800933; fax (22) 518042; e-mail cycult@cytanet.com.cy; f. 1963; quarterly; English; cultural and information review; published and distributed by Press and Information Office; Dir of Cultural Services Dr STELIOS ACH. HADJISTYLLIS; circ. 12,000.

Cyprus Tourism: POB 51697, Limassol; tel. (25) 337377; fax (25) 337374; f. 1989; bi-monthly; Greek; English; tourism and travel; Man. Dir G. EROTOKRITOU; circ. 250,000.

Dimosios Ypallilos (Civil Servant): 3 Dem. Severis Ave, 1066 Nicosia; tel. (22) 667260; fax (22) 665189; weekly; published by the Cyprus Civil Servants' Trade Union (PASYDY); circ. 14,000.

Enosis (Union): 71 Piraeus & Tombazis, Nicosia; tel. (22) 756862; fax (22) 757268; f. 1996; monthly; Greek; satirical; Chief Editor VASOS FTOCHOPOLILOS; circ. 2,000.

Eso-Etimos (Ever Ready): POB 4544, Nicosia; tel. (22) 443587; f. 1913; quarterly; Greek; publ. by Cyprus Scouts' Asscn; Editor TAKIS NEOPHYTOU; circ. 2,500.

Eva: 6 Psichikou St, Strovolos, Nicosia; tel. (22) 322959; fax (22) 322940; f. 1996; Greek; Dir DINOS MICHAEL; Chief Editors CHARIS PONTIKIS, KATIA SAVVIDOU; circ. 4,000.

Hermes International: POB 24512, Nicosia; tel. (22) 570570; fax (22) 581617; f. 1992; quarterly; English; lifestyle, business, finance, management; Chief Editor JOHN VICKERS; circ. 8,500.

I Kypros Simera (Present Day Cyprus): Apellis St, 1456 Nicosia; tel. (22) 801196; fax (22) 666123; e-mail pioxx@cytanet.com.cy; internet www.pio.gov.cy; f. 1983; fortnightly; Greek; published by the Press and Information Office of the Ministry of the Interior; Principal Officers E. HADJIPASCHALIS, A. LYRITSAS; circ. 3,500.

Nicosia This Month: POB 21015, Nikoklis Publishing House, Ledras and Pygmalionos St, Nicosia; tel. (22) 673124; fax (22) 663363; f. 1984; monthly; English; Chief Editor ELLADA SOPHOCLEOUS; circ. 4,000.

Omicron: POB 25211, 1 Commercial Centre Diogenous, 2nd Floor, 1307 Nicosia; tel. (22) 590110; fax (22) 590410; f. 1996; Greek; NIKOS CHR. PATTICHIS; Chief Editor STAVROS CHRISTODOULOU; circ. 8,000.

Paediki Chara (Children's Joy): POB 136, 18 Archbishop Makarios III Ave, 1065 Nicosia; tel. (22) 817585; fax (22) 817599; e-mail poed@ cytanet.com.cy; f. 1962; monthly; for pupils; publ. by the Pancyprian Union of Greek Teachers; Editor SOFOCLES CHARALAMBIDES; circ. 15,000.

Synergatiko Vima (The Co-operative Tribune): Kosti Palama 5, 1096 Nicosia; tel. (22) 680757; fax (22) 660833; e-mail coop .confeder@cytanet.com.cy; f. 1983; monthly; Greek; official organ of the Pancyprian Co-operative Confederation Ltd; circ. 5,000.

Synthesis (Composition): 6 Psichikou St, Strovolos, Nicosia; tel. (22) 322959; fax (22) 322940; f. 1988; every 2 months; Greek; interior decorating; Dir DINOS MICHAEL; circ. 6,000.

Tele Ores: POB 28205, 4 Acropoleos St, 1st Floor, 2091 Nicosia; tel. (22) 513300; fax (22) 513363; f. 1993; Greek; fortnightly; television guide; Chief Editor PROMETHEAS CHRISTOPHIDES; circ. 17,000.

TV Kanali (TV Channel): POB 25603, 5 Aegaleo St, Strovolos, Nicosia; tel. (22) 353603; fax (22) 353223; f. 1993; Greek; Dirs A. STAVRIDES, E. HADJIEFTHYMIOU; Chief Editor CHARIS TOMAZOS; circ. 13,000.

TURKISH CYPRIOT PERIODICALS

Güvenlik Kuvvetleri Magazine: Lefkoşa (Nicosia), Mersin 10, Turkey; tel. (22) 75880; publ. by the Security Forces of the 'TRNC'.

Halkbilimi: Has-Der, PK 199, Lefkoşa (Nicosia), Mersin 10, Turkey; tel. (22) 83146; fax (22) 84125; e-mail mesan@north-cyprus .net; internet www.cypnet.com/ncyprus/gifs/halkbil.gif; f. 1986; annual; publ. of Folk Arts Assoc. academic; Turkish; Chief Editor KANI KANOL; circ. 1,500 (2000).

Kıbrıs—Northern Cyprus Monthly: Ministry of Foreign Affairs and Defence, Lefkoşa (Nicosia), Mersin 10, Turkey; tel. (22) 83365; fax (22) 84847; e-mail pio@trncpio.org; internet www.trncpio.org; f. 1963; Editor GÖNÜL ATANER.

Kıbrısli Türkün Sesi: 44 Mecidiye St, Lefkoşa (Nicosia), Mersin 10, Turkey; tel. (22) 78520; fax (22) 87966; internet www.medyatext .com/kibrisli/; monthly; political; Exec. Dir DOGAN HARMAN; Gen. Co-ordinator CEVDET ALPARSLAN.

Kültür Sanat Dergisi: Girne Cad. 92, Lefkoşa (Nicosia), Mersin 10, Turkey; tel. (22) 83313; e-mail info@turkishbank.com; internet www .turkishbank.com; publ. of Türk Bankası; circ. 1,000.

Kuzey Kıbrıs Kültür Dergisi (North Cyprus Cultural Journal): PK 157, Lefkoşa (Nicosia), Mersin 10, Turkey; tel. (22) 31298; f. 1987; monthly; Turkish; Chief Editor GÜNSEL DOĞASAL.

NEWS AGENCIES

Cyprus News Agency: POB 23947, 1687 Nicosia; tel. (22) 499662; fax (22) 492697; e-mail cna@cytanet.com.cy; internet www.cna.org .cy; f. 1976; English and Greek; Dir THEMIS THEMISTOCLEOUS.

Kuzey Kıbrıs Haber Ajansı (Northern Cyprus News Agency): Alirizin Efendi Cad., Vakiflar Işhani, Kat 2, No. 3, Ortaköy, Lefkoşa (Nicosia), Mersin 10, Turkey; tel. (22) 81922; fax (22) 81934; f. 1977; Dir-Gen. M. ALI AKPINAR.

Papyrus General Press Distribution Agency: POB 12669, 5 Arch. Kyprianou, Latsia, Nicosia; tel. (22) 488855; fax (22) 488883; e-mail papyrus@spidernet.com.cy.

TürkAjansı-Kıbrıs (TAK) (Turkish News Agency of Cyprus): POB 355, 30 Mehmet Akif Cad., Lefkoşa (Nicosia), Mersin 10, Turkey; tel. (22) 71818; fax (22) 71213; e-mail tak@emu.edu.tr; internet kktc.gov .nc.tr/tak; f. 1973; Dir EMIR HÜSEYN ERSOY.

Foreign Bureaux

Agence France-Presse (AFP) (France): POB 7242, Loizides Centre, 7th Floor, 36 Kypranoros St, Nicosia; tel. (22) 754050; fax (22) 768977; e-mail nicosie.redaction@afp.com; Bureau Chief PIERRE TAILLEFER.

Agencia EFE (Spain): 64 Metochiou St, Office 401, Nicosia; tel. (22) 775725; fax (22) 781662; Correspondent DOMINGO DEL PINO.

Agenzia Nazionale Stampa Associata (ANSA) (Italy): Middle East Office, 10 Katsonis St, Ayii Omoloyites, Nicosia; tel. (22) 491699; fax (22) 492732; Rep. VITTORIO FRENQUELLUCCI.

Associated Press (AP) (USA): POB 4853, Neoelen Marina, 10 Katsonis St, Nicosia; tel. (22) 492599; fax (22) 491617; Correspondent ALEX EFTY.

Athinaikon Praktorion Eidiseon (Greece): Flat 64, Tryfonos Bldg, Eleftherias Sq., 1011 Nicosia; tel. (22) 441110; fax (22) 457418; Rep. GEORGE LEONIDAS.

Informatsionnoye Telegrafnoye Agentstvo Rossii—Telegrafnoye Agentstvo Suverennykh Stran (ITAR—TASS) (Russia): POB 2235, 5–6 Evangelias St, Archangelos, Nicosia; tel. (22) 382486; Rep. ALEXEI YEROVTCHENKOV.

Iraqi News Agency: POB 1098, Flat 201, 11 Ippocratous St, Nicosia; tel. (22) 472095; fax (22) 472096; Correspondent AHMAD SULEYMAN.

Jamahiriya News Agency (JANA) (Libya): Flat 203, 12 Kypranoros, Nicosia; tel. (22) 361129; Rep. MUHAMMAD ALI ESHOWEIHIDI.

Reuters (United Kingdom): POB 25725, 5th Floor, George and Thelma Paraskevaides Foundation Bldg, 36 Grivas Dhigenis Ave, Nicosia; tel. (22) 469607; fax (22) 662487; Correspondent MICHELE KAMBAS.

Sofia-Press Agency (Bulgaria): 9 Roumeli St, Droshia, Larnaca; tel. (4) 494484; Rep. IONKA VERESIE.

United Press International (UPI) (USA): 24A Heroes Ave, Nicosia 171; tel. (22) 456643; fax (22) 455998; Rep. GEORGES DER PARTHOGH.

Xinhua (New China) News Agency (People's Republic of China): 12 Byzantiou St, Flat 201, Ayios Dhometios, Nicosia; tel. (22) 590133; fax (22) 590146; Rep. HUANG JIANMING.

Publishers

GREEK CYPRIOT PUBLISHERS

Action Publications: POB 24676, 35 Ayiou Nicolaou St, Engomi, 1302 Nicosia; tel. (22) 590555; fax (22) 358443; e-mail chris.c@actionprgroup.com; f. 1971; travel; Pres. TONY CHRISTODOULOU.

Andreou Chr. Publications: POB 22298, 67A Regenis St, 1520 Nicosia; tel. (22) 666877; fax (22) 666878; e-mail andreou2@cytanet .com.cy; f. 1979; biography, literature, history, regional interest.

James Bendon Ltd: POB 56484, 3307 Limasol; tel. (25) 633181; fax (25) 632352; e-mail jbendon@attglobal.net; internet www .jamesbendon.com; philately; Pres. JAMES BENDON; Vice-Pres. RIDA BENDON.

Chrysopolitissa: 27 Al. Papadiamantis St, 2400 Nicosia; tel. (22) 353929; f. 1973; theatre, literature.

Costas Epiphaniou: Ekdoseis Antiprosopies Ltd, POB 2451, 1521 Nicosia; tel. (22) 750873; fax (22) 759266; f. 1973; Dir COSTAS EPIPHANIOU.

Foundation 'Anastasios G. Leventis': 40 Gladstonos St, POB 22543, 1095 Nicosia; tel. (22) 667706; fax (22) 675002; e-mail leventcy@zenon.logos.cy.net; internet www.leventisfoundation.org.

KY KE M: POB 4108, Nicosia; tel. (22) 450302; fax (22) 463624; Pres. NIKOS KOUTSOU.

MAM Ltd (The House of Cyprus and Cyprological Publications): POB 21722, 1512 Nicosia; tel. (22) 753536; fax (22) 375802; e-mail mam@mam.com.cy; internet www.mam.com.cy; f. 1965.

Nikoklis Publishing House: POB 23697, Nicosia; tel. (22) 672949; fax (22) 330218; ethnicity, travel; Man. ELLADA SOPHOCLEOUS.

Omilos Pnevmatikis Ananeoseos: 1 Omirou St, 2407 Engomi, Nicosia; tel. (22) 775854; literature.

Pierides Foundation: Larnaca; tel. (4) 651345; fax (4) 657227.

POLTE (Pancyprian Organization of Tertiary Education): c/o Higher Technical Institute, Nicosia; tel. (22) 305030; fax (22) 494953; Pres. KOSTAS NEOKLEOUS.

TURKISH CYPRIOT PUBLISHERS

Bırlık Gazetesi: Yediler Sok., Lefkoşa (Nicosia), Mersin 10, Turkey; tel. (22) 72959; f. 1980; Dir MEHMET AKAR.

Bolan Matbaası: 35 Pençizade Sok., Lefkoşa (Nicosia), Mersin 10, Turkey; tel. (22) 74802.

Devlet Basımevi (Turkish Cypriot Government Printing House): Şerif Arzik Sok., Lefkoşa (Nicosia), Mersin 10, Turkey; tel. (22) 72010; Dir S. KÜRŞAD.

Halkın Sesi Ltd: 172 Girne Cad., Lefkoşa (Nicosia), Mersin 10, Turkey; tel. (22) 73141.

Kema Matbaası: 1 Tabak Hilmi Sok., Lefkoşa (Nicosia), Mersin 10, Turkey; tel. (22) 72785.

North Cyprus Research and Publishing Centre (CYREP): PK 327, Lefkoşa (Nicosia), Mersin 10, Turkey; tel. (22) 78914; fax (22) 72592; Man. Editor AHMET C. GAZIOĞLU.

K. Rüstem & Bro.: 22–24 Girne Cad., Lefkoşa (Nicosia), Mersin 10, Turkey; tel. (22) 71418.

Sebil International Press: PK 421, Lefkoşa (Nicosia), Mersin 10, Turkey; tel. (22) 46805; fax (22) 310804; e-mail ics@analiz.net; f. 1985; technical and scientific; Principal Officer E. BAŞARAN.

Tezel Matbaası: 35 Şinasi Sok., Lefkoşa (Nicosia), Mersin 10, Turkey; tel. (22) 71022.

Broadcasting and Communications

TELECOMMUNICATIONS

Cyprus Telecommunications Authority (CYTA): POB 24929, 1396 Nicosia; tel. (22) 701000; fax (22) 494940; e-mail pr@cyta .cytanet.com.cy; internet www.cyta.com.cy; provides national, international and cellular services in Cyprus.

Telekomünikasyon Diaresi Müdürlügü (Directorate of Telecommunications): Lefkoşa (Nicosia), Mersin 10, Turkey; tel. (22) 81888; fax (22) 88666; f. 1963; state-owned; responsible to Ministry of Communications, Works and Tourism; admin. and operation of telecommunications services; Gen. Man. SALIH KARA.

BROADCASTING

Radio

British Forces Broadcasting Service, Cyprus: Akrotiri, British Forces Post Office 57; tel. (25) 252009; fax (25) 268580; e-mail Dusty .Miller@bfbs.com; internet www.bfbs.com; f. 1948; broadcasts a two-channel 24-hour radio service in English on VHF; Station Man. DUSTY MILLER; Engineering Man. JON FORDHAM.

Cyprus Broadcasting Corporation (CyBC): POB 24824, Broadcasting House, 1397 Nicosia; tel. (22) 422231; fax (22) 314050; e-mail rik@cybc.com.cy; internet www.cybc.com.cy; radio; f. 1952; Programme I in Greek, Programme II in Greek, Turkish, English and Armenian, Programme III in Greek; two medium-wave transmitters of 100 kW in Nicosia with relay stations at Paphos and Limassol; three 10-kW ERP VHF FM stereo transmitters on Mount Olympus; and three relay stations; Chair. MARIOS ELIADES; Dir-Gen. MICHAEL STYLIANOU; Head of Radio KYRIACOS CHARALAMBIDES.

Logos: Church of Cyprus, POB 27400, 1644 Nicosia; tel. (22) 355444; fax (22) 355737; e-mail director@logos.cy.net; Chair. ANDREAS PHILIPPOU; Dir-Gen. CHRISTODOULOS PROTOPAPAS.

Radio Astra: 145 Athalassas Ave, Strovolos, 2045 Nicosia; tel. (22) 313200; fax (22) 319261; e-mail info@astra.com.cy; internet www .astra.com.cy; Dir TAKIS HADJIGEORGIOU.

Radio Proto: POB 21836, 31 Archangelos St, Parissinos, 2054 Nicosia; tel. (22) 353545; fax (22) 352266; e-mail pavlos@radioproto .com; internet www.radioproto.com; Chair. KOSTAS HADJIKOSTIS; Gen. Man. PAVLOS PAPACHRISTODOULOU.

Bayrak Radio and TV Corpn (BRTK): Atatürk Sq., Lefkoşa (Nicosia), Mersin 10, Turkey; tel. (22) 85555; fax (22) 81991; e-mail brt@cc.emu.edu.tr; internet www.brt.gov.nc.tr; in July 1983 it became an independent Turkish Cypriot corpn, partly financed by the Govt; Radio Bayrak; f. 1963; home service in Turkish, overseas service in Turkish, Greek, English, Arabic and German; broadcasts 52.5 hours per day; Chair. GÜNAY YORGANCIOĞLU; Dir ISMET KOTAK; Head of Radio ŞIFA NESIM.

First FM and Interfirst FM: Lefkoşa (Nicosia), Mersin 10, Turkey; f. 1996.

Kıbrıs FM / Kıbrıs TV: Dr Fazil Küçük Blvd, Yeni Sanayi Bolgesi, Lefkoşa (Nicosia), Mersin 10, Turkey; tel. (22) 52555; fax (22) 53707; e-mail kibrisibrisgazetesi.com; Dir ERDINCH GUNDUZ.

Radio Emu: Gazi Mağusa (Famagusta), Mersin 10, Turkey; e-mail radioemu@cc.emu.edu.tr; internet www.emu.edu.tr/~radioemu.

Television

Greek Cypriot viewers have access to Greek television channels via satellite. Several Turkish channels are transmitted to the 'TRNC'.

Antenna T.V.: POB 20923, 1655 Nicosia; tel. (22) 311111; fax (22) 314959; Chair. LOUKIS PAPAPHILIPPOU; Man. Dir STELIOS MALEKOS.

British Forces Broadcasting Service, Cyprus: Akrotiri, British Forces Post Office 57; tel. (25) 252009; fax (25) 268580; e-mail dusty .miller@bfbs.com; f. 1948; broadcasts a daily TV service; Station Man. DUSTY MILLER; Engineering Man. JON FORDHAM.

Cyprus Broadcasting Corporation (CyBC): POB 24824, Broadcasting House, 1397 Nicosia; tel. (22) 422231; fax (22) 314050; e-mail rik@cybc.com.cy; internet www.cybc.com.cy; television; f. 1957; **Pik 1 (CyBC 1)** one Band III 100/10-kW transmitter on Mount Olympus. **Pik 2 (CyBC 2)** one Band IV 100/10-kW ERP transmitter on Mount Olympus. **ET 1** one Band IV 100/10-kW ERP transmitter on Mount Olympus for transmission of the ETI Programme received, via satellite, from Greece. The above three TV channels are also transmitted from 80 transposer stations; Chair. MARIOS ELIADES; Dir-Gen. MICHAEL STYLIANOU.

Lumiere TV Ltd: POB 25614, 2063 Nicosia; tel. (22) 357272; fax (22) 354622; e-mail administration@ltv.com.cy; internet www .lumieretv.com; f. 1992; encoded signal; Chair. and Man. Dir AKIS AVRAAMIDES; Gen. Man. GEORGE XINARIS.

MEGA TV: POB 27400, 1644 Nicosia; tel. (22) 477777; fax (22) 477737; e-mail info@megatv.com.cy; Gen. Man. GEORGE MAMALAKIS.

Sigma Radio TV Ltd: POB 21836, 2054 Nicosia; tel. (22) 357070; fax (22) 358640; island-wide coverage; Chair. and Dir KOSTAS HADJI-COSTIS; Man. DINOS ODYSSEOS; New Business Devt Dir ANDY HADJI-COSTIS.

Bayrak Radio and TV Corpn (BRTK): Atatürk Sq., Lefkoşa (Nicosia), Mersin 10, Turkey; tel. (22) 85555; fax (22) 81991; e-mail brt@cc.emu.edu.tr; internet www.brt.gov.nc.tr; in July 1983 it became an independent Turkish Cypriot corpn, partly financed by the Govt; Bayrak TV; f. 1976; transmits programmes in Turkish, Greek, English and Arabic on nine channels; Chair. GÜNAY YORGAN-CIOĞLU; Dir ISMET KOTAK; Head of Television TÜLIN URAL.

Gene TV: Bevel Yusuf Cad. 8, Yenişehir, Lefkoşa (Nicosia), Mersin 10, Turkey; tel. (22) 80790; fax (22) 76363; Dir ERTAN BIRINCI.

Kanal T: Dr Fazıl Küçük Cad. Foto Filiz Binaları, Göçmenköy, Lefkoşa (Nicosia), Mersin 10, Turkey; tel. (22) 37678; fax (22) 34257; Owner ERSIN FATAR.

Finance

(brs = branches; cap. = capital; res = reserves; dep. = deposits; m. = million; amounts in Cyprus pounds, except for Turkish Cypriot banks)

BANKING

Central Bank

Central Bank of Cyprus: POB 25529, 80 Kennedy Ave, 1395 Nicosia; tel. (22) 714100; fax (22) 378153; e-mail cbcinfo@ centralbank.gov.cy; internet www.centralbank.gov.cy; f. 1963; became fully independent from govt control in July 2002; cap. 15m., res 15m., dep. 1,209m. (Dec. 2000); Gov. CHRISTODOULOS CHRISTO-DOULOU.

Greek Cypriot Banks

Alpha Bank Ltd: POB 21661, Yiorkion Bldg, 1 Prodromou St, 1596 Nicosia; tel. (22) 888888; fax (22) 773766; e-mail secretariat@ alphabank.com.cy; internet www.alphabank.com.cy; f. 1960 as Lombard Banking (Cyprus) Ltd; name changed to Lombard NatWest Banking Ltd in 1989 and as above in 1998; locally incorporated although foreign-controlled; cap. 16.8m., res 50.8m., dep. 633.0m. (Dec. 2000); Chair. M. G. COLOCASSIDES; Dir ELEFTHERIOS IOANNOU; Man. Dir A. DEMETRIADES; 24 brs.

Bank of Cyprus Group: POB 21472, 51 Stassinos St, Ayia Paraskevi, 2002 Strovolos 140, 1599 Nicosia; tel. (22) 378000; fax (22) 378111; e-mail info@cy.bankofcyprus.com; internet www .bankofcyprus.com; f. 1899; reconstituted 1943 by the amalgamation of Bank of Cyprus, Larnaca Bank Ltd and Famagusta Bank Ltd; cap. 216.1m., res 254.9m., dep. 5,350.4m. (Dec. 2000); Chair. SOLON A. TRIANTAFYLLIDES; Group Chief Exec. CHR. S. PANTZARIS; 180 brs.

Co-operative Central Bank Ltd: POB 24537, 8 Gregoris Afxentiou St, 1389 Nicosia; tel. (22) 743000; fax (22) 670261; e-mail coopbank.gm@cytanet.com.cy; f. 1937 under the Co-operative Societies Law; banking and credit facilities to member societies, importer and distributor of agricultural requisites, insurance agent; cap. 3.6m., dep. 873.6m. (Dec. 2001); Chair. D. STAVROU; Sec.-Gen. D. PITSILLIDES; 4 brs.

The Cyprus Popular Bank Ltd: POB 22032, Laiki HQ, 154 Limassol Ave, 1598 Nicosia; tel. (22) 752000; fax (22) 811250; e-mail laiki.telebank@laiki.com; internet www.laiki.com; f. 1901; full commercial banking; cap. 149.1m., res 220.1m. dep. 3,438.5m. (Dec. 2000); Chair. and Pres. KIKIS N. LAZARIDES; 121 brs.

Hellenic Bank Ltd: POB 24747, 1394 Nicosia; tel. (22) 860000; fax (22) 754074; e-mail hellenic@hellenicbank.com; internet www .hellenicbank.com; f. 1974; financial services group; cap. 58.4m., res 123.8m., dep. 1,890.5m. (Dec. 2001); Chair. and Chief Exec. PANOS CHR. GHALANOS; 93 brs.

Housing Finance Corpn: POB 23898, 41 Themistoklis Dervis St, Hawaii Tower, Nicosia; tel. (22) 761777; fax (22) 762870; f. 1980; provides long-term loans for home-buying; cap. 12m., dep. 213m. (June 2000); Gen. Man. CH. SHAMBARTAS; 6 brs.

National Bank of Greece (Cyprus) Ltd: 15 Arch. Makarios III Ave, 1065 Nicosia; tel. (22) 840000; fax (22) 762080; e-mail cloizou@ nbg.com.cy; f. 1994 by incorporating all local business of the National Bank of Greece SA; full commercial banking; cap. 23m. (Nov. 2000); Chair. TH. KARATZAS; Man. Dir M. TAGAROULIAS; 30 brs.

Universal Bank: 6th Floor, Universal Tower, 85 Dhigeni Akrita Ave, 1070 Nicosia; tel. (22) 883333; fax (22) 358702; e-mail unimail@ usb.com.cy; internet www.universalbank.com.cy; f. 1925 as Yialousa Savings Ltd (closed 1974, reopened 1990), renamed as above 1996; cap. 15.0m., res 12.9m., dep. 91.1m. (Dec. 2000); Chair. GEORGE SYRIMIS; Gen. Man. Dr SPYROS EPISKOPOU; 15 brs.

Turkish Cypriot Banks
(amounts in Turkish liras unless otherwise indicated)

Akdeniz Garanti Bankası Ltd: PK 149, 2–4 Celaliye Sok. Inönu Meydan, Lefkoşa (Nicosia), Mersin 10, Turkey; tel. (22) 86742; fax (22) 86741; f. 1989 as Mediterranean Guarantee Bank; cap. and res 605,600m., dep. 22,867,000m. (Dec. 1999); Chair. ERDOĞAN NAIM.

Asbank Ltd: 8 Mecidiye Sok., PK 448, Lefkoşa (Nicosia), Mersin 10, Turkey; tel. (22) 83023; fax (22) 81244; internet www.asbank.com.tr; f. 1986; cap. 1,800,000m., res 2,754,759m. (Dec. 2001); Chair. ALTAY ADADEMIR; Dep. Gen. Man. T. M. ALTUNER; 7 brs.

First Merchant Bank OSH Ltd: 25 Serif Arzik Sok., Lefkoşa (Nicosia), Mersin 10, Turkey; tel. (22) 75373; fax (22) 75377; e-mail fmb@firstmerchantbank.com; internet www.firstmerchantbank .com; f. 1993; also provides offshore services; cap. US $10m., res US $6.2m., dep. US $2,123.8m. (Dec. 2000); Chair. and Gen. Man. Dr H. N. YAMAN.

Kıbrıs Altinbaş Bank Ltd (Cyprus Altinbaş Bank Ltd): PK 843, 2 Müftü Ziyai Efendi Sok., Lefkoşa (Nicosia), Mersin 10, Turkey; tel. (22) 88222; fax (22) 71623; e-mail kibrisaltinbasbank@yahu.com; internet www.altinbasbank.com.tr; f. 1993; cap. 748,100m., res 81,330m., dep. 7,822,563m. (Dec. 2000); Chair. VAKKAS ALTINBAŞ; Gen. Man. ÖZKAN TEKGUMUS.

Kıbrıs Endüstri Bankası Ltd (Industrial Bank of Cyprus Ltd): Bedrettin Demirel Cad., Başbakanlık Kavşağı, Lefkoşa (Nicosia), Mersin 10, Turkey; tel. (22) 83770; fax (22) 71830; administrators appointed in May 2000.

Kıbrıs Eurobank Ltd: PK 35, 18 Mecidiye Sok., Lefkoşa (Nicosia), Mersin 10, Turkey; tel. (22) 87550; fax (22) 87670; e-mail eurobank@ kktc.net; internet www.eurobank.cjb.net; f. 1993; cap. US $2.0m., dep. US $2.5m. (Dec. 1999); Pres. and Chair. BEDI TUNASOY; Gen. Man. NUR SENLET SELHEP.

Kıbrıs İktisat Bankası Ltd (Cyprus Economy Bank Ltd): 151 Bedreddin Demirel Cad., Lefkoşa (Nicosia), Mersin 10, Turkey; tel. (22) 85300; fax (22) 81311; e-mail info@iktisatbank.cc; internet www .iktisatbank.cc; f. 1990; cap. 900,000m., res 2,495,006m., dep. 32,696,936m. (Dec. 2001); Chair. and Gen. Man. METE ÖZMERTER; 12 brs.

Kıbrıs Kredi Bankası Ltd (Cyprus Credit Bank Ltd): 5–7 İplik Pazarı Sok., Lefkoşa (Nicosia), Mersin 10, Turkey; tel. (22) 83667; fax (22) 76999; f. 1978; administrators appointed in May 2000; cap. 30,930m., res 164,131m., dep. 2,628,193m. (Dec. 1994); Chair. SALIH BOYACI; Gen. Man. YÜKSEL YAZGIN; 12 local brs.

Kıbrıs Ticaret Bankası Ltd (Cyprus Commercial Bank Ltd): 111 Bedrettin Demirel Ave, Lefkoşa (Nicosia), Mersin 10, Turkey; tel. (22) 83180; fax (22) 82278; e-mail cycom@kktc.net; f. 1982; cap. 500,000m., res 833,934m., dep. 10,679,115m. (Dec. 1998); Chair. YÜKSEL AHMET RAŞIT; Gen. Man. HÜSEYIN HARMANCI; 8 brs.

Kıbrıs Türk Kooperatif Merkez Bankası Ltd (Cyprus Turkish Co-operative Central Bank): 49–55 Mahmut Paşa Sok., PK 823, Lefkoşa (Nicosia), Mersin 10, Turkey; tel. (22) 83207; fax (22) 76787; e-mail info@koopbank.com; internet www.koopcb.com; f. 1959; cap. and res 4,344,363m., dep. 117,722,019m. (Dec. 2000); banking and credit facilities to member societies and individuals; Chair. AHMET ALPER; Gen. Man. Dr TUNCER ARIFOĞLU; 12 brs.

Kıbrıs Vakiflar Bankası Ltd (Cyprus Vakiflar Bank Ltd): 58 Yediler Sok., PK 212, Lefkoşa (Nicosia), Mersin 10, Turkey; tel. (22) 75109; fax (22) 75169; e-mail kvb@kktc.net; f. 1982; cap. 300,000m., res 1,391,816m., dep. 46,475,912m. (Dec. 2000); Pres. and Chair. LATIF ARAN; Gen. Man. ALPAY R. ADANIR; 7 brs.

Limassol Turkish Co-operative Bank Ltd: 10 Orhaneli Sok., Kyrenia, PK 247, Mersin 10, Turkey; tel. (22) 8156786; fax (22) 8156959; e-mail fordept@kktc.net; internet www.limasolbank.com; f. 1939; cap. 6,993,213.8m., res 601,679.6m, dep. 96,734,104.4m. (Dec. 2001); Chair. GÜZEL HALIM; Gen. Man. TANER EKDAL.

Türk Bankası Ltd (Turkish Bank Ltd): 92 Girne Cad., PK 242, Lefkoşa (Nicosia), Mersin 10, Turkey; tel. (22) 83313; fax (22) 82432; e-mail info@turkishbank.netcom; internet www.turkishbank.com; f. 1901; cap. 19,530,381m., res 2,870,465m., dep. 422,689,723m. (Dec. 2001); Chair. M. TANJU ÖZYOL; Gen. Man. C. YENAL MUSANNIF; 12 brs.

Universal Bank Limited: POB 658, 57 Mehmet Akif ave, Lefkoşa (Nicosia), Mersin 10, Turkey; tel. (22) 86262; fax (22) 87826; e-mail univers@kktc.net; internet www.bankunivers.com; f. 1997; cap. 821,100.0m., res 261,023.3m., dep. 6,118,885.4m. (Dec. 2000); Chair. ILHAN KÖSEOĞLU; Gen. Man. MÜNIR ALTUNER.

Viyabank Ltd: Ataturk Cad., 16 Muhtar Yusuf Galleria, Lefkoşa (Nicosia), Mersin 10, Turkey; tel. (22) 88902; fax (22) 85878; e-mail viyabank@future.com.tr; internet www.viyabank.com; f. 1998; cap. US $0.6m., res US $0.4m., dep. US $2.8m. (Dec. 2000); Pres. SALVO TARAGANO; Chair. ERDOĞAN SEVINÇ; 3 brs.

Yakin Dogu Bank Ltd (Near East Bank Ltd): POB 47, 1 Girne Caddesi, Lefkoşa (Nicosia), Mersin 10, Turkey; tel. (22) 83834; fax (22) 84180; cap. 1,110,000.0m., res 331,051.6m., dep. 10,057,425.0m. (Dec 2000); Chair. Dr SUAT I. GÜNSEL; Gen. Man. KAZIM M. OLGU.

Yeşilada Bank Ltd: POB 626, 11 Atatürk ave, Lefkoşa (Nicosia), Mersin 10, Turkey; tel. (22) 81999; fax (22) 81962; e-mail yesilada@north-cyprus.net; cap. 599,550m., res 281,600m., dep. 4,520,516m. (Dec. 2000); Chair. and Pres. BURHAN YETKILI; Gen. Man. DERVIŞ TURKER.

Turkish Cypriot Bankers' Association

Northern Cyprus Bankers' Association: 92 Girne Cad., PK 242, Lefkoşa (Nicosia), Mersin 10, Turkey; tel. (22) 83180; fax (22) 82278; e-mail info@turkishbank.com; internet www.turkishbank.com; f. 1987; 31 mems (1998).

Investment Organization

The Cyprus Investment and Securities Corpn Ltd: POB 20597, 1660 Nicosia; tel. (22) 881700; fax (22) 338488; e-mail info@cisco.bankofcyprus.com; internet www.cisco-online.com.cy; f. 1982 to promote the development of capital market; brokerage services, fund management, investment banking; member of Bank of Cyprus Group; issued cap. 20m. (2001); Chair. S. A. TRIANTAFYLLIDES; Gen. Man. STELIOS CHRISTODOULOU.

Development Bank

The Cyprus Development Bank Ltd: POB 21415, Alpha House, 50 Archbishop Makarios III Ave, 1508 Nicosia; tel. (22) 846500; fax (22) 846603; e-mail info@cdb.com.cy; internet www.cyprusdevelopmentbank.com; f. 1963; cap. 12.4m., res 34.0m., dep. 16.5m. (Dec. 2001); aims to accelerate the economic development of Cyprus by providing medium- and long-term loans for productive projects, developing the capital market, encouraging joint ventures and providing technical and managerial advice to productive private enterprises; Chair. ANDREAS MOUSKOS; Gen. Man. JOHN G. JOANNIDES; 1 br.

Foreign Banks

Arab Bank PLC: POB 25700, 1 Santaroza Ave, 1393 Nicosia; tel. (22) 899100; fax (22) 760890; e-mail info@arabbank.com.cy; f. 1984; commercial; Area Exec. TOUFIC J. DAJANI; 15 brs.

Commercial Bank of Greece (Cyprus) Ltd: POB 25151, 1307 Nicosia; tel. (22) 663727; fax (22) 663923; e-mail gmoffice@combank.com.cy; f. 1992; Gen. Man. S. NIKAS.

Türkiye Cumhuriyeti Ziraat Bankası: Girnekapi Cad., Ibrahimpaşa Sok. 105, Lefkoşa (Nicosia), Mersin 10, Turkey; tel. (22) 83050; fax (22) 82041.

Türkiye Halk Bankası AŞ: Osman Paşa Cad., Ümit Office, Lefkoşa (Nicosia), Mersin 10, Turkey; tel. (22) 72145; fax (22) 72146.

Türkiye İş Bankası AŞ: Girne Cad. 9, Lefkoşa (Nicosia), Mersin 10, Turkey; tel. (22) 83133; fax (22) 78315; f. 1924; Man. KEMAL AĞANOĞLU.

'Offshore' (International) Banking Units

Cyprus-based Offshore Banking Units (OBUs) are fully-staffed units which conduct all forms of banking business from within Cyprus with other offshore or foreign entities and non-resident persons. (OBUs are not permitted to accept deposits from persons of Cypriot origin who have emigrated to the United Kingdom and taken up permanent residence there.) Although exempt from most of the restrictions and regulatory measures applicable to 'onshore' banks, OBUs are subject to supervision and inspection by the Central Bank of Cyprus. OBUs may conduct business with onshore and domestic banks in all banking matters which the latter are allowed to undertake with banks abroad. OBUs are permitted to grant loans or guarantees in foreign currencies to residents of Cyprus (conditional on obtaining an exchange control permit from the Central Bank of Cyprus). Interest and other income earned from transactions with residents is subject to the full rate of income tax (20%), but the Minister of Finance is empowered by law to exempt an OBU from the above tax liability if satisfied that a specific transaction substan-

tially contributes towards the economic development of the Republic. In 1999 there were 29 OBUs operating in Cyprus.

Agropromstroybank: POB 55297, Maximos Court B, 17 Leontiou St, Limassol; tel. (25) 384747; fax (25) 384858; Man. ALEXANDER MOKHONKO.

Allied Business Bank SAL: POB 54232, 3rd Floor, Flat 31, Lara Court, 276 Archbishop Makarios III Ave, Limassol; tel. (25) 363759; fax (25) 372711; Local Man. NAJIBA HAWILLA.

Arab Bank PLC: POB 25700, 1 Santaroza Ave, 1393 Nicosia; tel. (22) 899100; fax (22) 760890; e-mail arabbank@spidernet.com.cy; OBU licence granted 1997; Area Exec. TOUFIC J. DAJAN.

Arab Jordan Investment Bank SA: POB 54384, Libra Tower, 23 Olympion St, Limassol; tel. (25) 351351; fax (25) 360151; e-mail ajib@.cy.net; internet www.ajib.com; f. 1978; cap. and dep. US $388m., total assets US$410m. (Dec. 1999); Man. ABED ABU-DAYEH.

AVTOVAZBANK: POB 22025, Office 201, Stefanie Court, 301A Saint-Andrews, 3035 Limassol; tel. (25) 354594; fax (25) 362582; Local Man. A. TSELOUNOV.

Banca Română de Comerț Exterior (Bancorex) SA: POB 22538, Margarita House, 5th Floor, 15 Them. Dervis St, 1309 Nicosia; tel. (22) 677992; fax (22) 677945; Local Man. GRIGORE IOAN BUDISAN.

Bank of Beirut and the Arab Countries SAL: POB 56201, Emelle Bldg, 1st Floor, 135 Archbishop Makarios III Ave, Limassol; tel. (25) 381290; fax (25) 381584; Man. O. S. SAAB.

Banque du Liban et d'Outre-Mer SAL: POB 53243, P. Lordos Centre Roundabout, Byron St, Limassol; tel. (25) 376433; fax (25) 376292; Local Man. S. FARAH.

Banque Nationale de Paris Intercontinentale SA: POB 50058, Kanika Business Centre, 319 28th October St, 3600 Limassol; tel. (25) 840840; fax (25) 840698; e-mail bnpi.cyprus@bnpparibas.com; internet www.bnpi.com.cy; Local Man. CHRISTIAN ARLOT.

Banque SBA: 8C Iris House, Kanika Enaerios Complex, John Kennedy St, Limassol; tel. (25) 588650; fax (25) 581643; e-mail sba.ibu@banque-sba.com; branch of Banque SBA (fmrly Société Bancaire Arabe), Paris; Local Man. ADNAN NUWAYHED.

Barclays Bank PLC International Banking Unit: POB 27320, 88 Dhigenis Akritas Ave, 1644 Nicosia; tel. (22) 654400; fax (22) 754233; e-mail barclays@spidernet.co.cy; Cyprus Dir JONATHAN MILLS.

BEMO (Banque Européenne pour le Moyen-Orient SAL): POB 6232, Doma Court, 1st–2nd Floors, 227 Archbishop Makarios III Ave, Limassol; tel. (25) 583628; fax (25) 588611; e-mail bemolobu@spidernet.com.cy; Local Man. N. A. HCHAIME.

Byblos Bank SAL: POB 50218, Loucaides Bldg, 1 Archbishop Kyprianou St/St Andrew St, 3602 Limassol; tel. (25) 341433; fax (25) 367139; e-mail byblos@spidernet.com.cy; internet www.byblosbank.com.lb; Man. ANTOINE SMAIRA.

Commercial Bank of Greece SA: 1 Iona Nicolaou, POB 27587, Engomi, 2431 Nicosia; tel. (22) 663686; fax (22) 663688; Man. G. KANTIANIS.

Crédit Libanais SAL: POB 53492, Chrysalia Court, 1st Floor, 206 Archbishop Makarios III Ave, 3030 Limassol; tel. (25) 376444; fax (25) 376807; e-mail credub@inco.com.lb; Local Man. HAYAT HARFOUCHE.

Crédit Suisse First Boston (Cyprus) Ltd: POB 57530, 199 Christodolou Hadsipavlou Ave, 3316 Limassol; tel. (25) 341244; fax (25) 817424; internet www.csfb.com; f. 1996; OBU status granted 1997; Gen. Man. ANTONIS ROUVAS.

DePfa Investment Bank Ltd: POB 20909, 2nd Floor, 178 Athalassa Ave, 1665 Nicosia; tel. (22) 879300; fax (22) 318978; e-mail mail@depfacy.com; internet www.depfa.com; IBU licence granted 1998; Gen. Mans FRANK OTTERSBACH, LAMBROS CHARIDEMOU.

Federal Bank of the Middle East Ltd: POB 25566, J&P Bldg, 90 Archbishop Makarios III Ave, 1391 Nicosia; tel. (22) 888444; fax (22) 888555; e-mail mail@fbme.com; internet www.fbme.com; f. 1983; cap. US $46.0m., dep. $281.1m. (Dec. 2001); Chair. AYOUB-FARID M. SAAB; 2 brs.

First Investment Bank Ltd: POB 16023, cnr of Kennedy Ave & 39 Demofiritos St, 4th Floor, Flat 401, 2085 Nicosia; tel. (22) 760150; fax (22) 376560; Gen. Man. ENU NEDELE.

HSBC Republic Bank (Cyprus) Ltd: POB 25718, Para Bldg. Block C, 7 Dositheou St, 1311 Nicosia; tel. (22) 376116; fax (22) 376121; internet www.hsbc.com; f. 1984 as Wardley Cyprus Ltd; Man. Dir T. TAOUSHANIS; 1 br.

Jordan Kuwait Bank: Nicosia; business licence granted 2001.

Karić Banka: POB 26522, Flat 22, Cronos Court, 66 Archbishop Makarios III Ave, Nicosia; tel. (22) 374980; fax (22) 374151; Man. Dir O. ERDELIJANOVIĆ.

Lebanon and Gulf Bank SAL International Banking Unit: POB 40337, Akamia Centre, 3rd Floor, Flat 309, cnr of G. Afxentiou and Archbishop Makarios III Ave, 6303 Larnaca; tel. (4) 620500; fax (4) 620708; Local Man. F. SAADE.

Mega Euro Banka AD: c/o Tassos Papadopoulos and Co., Law Offices, 2 Safouli, Nicosia; OBU licence granted 1998.

Russian Commercial Bank (Cyprus) Ltd: POB 56868, 2 Ama-thuntos St, 3310 Limassol; tel. (25) 837300; fax (25) 342192; e-mail rcbib1@cytanet.com.cy; f. 1995; cap. US $10.8m., res US $5.2m., dep. US $497m. (Dec. 2000); Gen. Man. KONSTANTIN E. BUROWLEV.

Société Générale Cyprus Ltd: POB 25400, 7–9 Grivas Dhigenis Ave, 1309 Nicosia; tel. (22) 817777; fax (22) 764471; internet www.socgen.com; cap. US $2.0m., res US $5.9m., dep. US $105.2m. (Dec. 2000); Chair. MAURICE SEHNAOUI; Gen. Man. GÉRARD MALHAME.

STOCK EXCHANGE

Cyprus Stock Exchange: POB 5427, 54 Grivas Dhigenis Ave, 1309 Nicosia; tel. (22) 668782; fax (22) 668790; e-mail cyse@zenon.logos.cy.net; internet www.cse.com.cy; official trading commenced in March 1996; 60 companies listed in 1999; Chair. PAVLOS SAVVIDES; Gen. Man. NONDAS METAXAS.

INSURANCE

Insurance Companies Control Service: Ministry of Finance, POB 23364, 1682 Nicosia; tel. (22) 303256; fax (22) 302938; e-mail insurance.control@cytanet.co.cy; f. 1969 to control insurance compa-nies, insurance agents, brokers and agents for brokers in Cyprus.

Greek Cypriot Insurance Companies

Aegis Insurance Co Ltd: POB 23450, 7 Klimentos St, Ayios Antonios, 1061 Nicosia; tel. (22) 343644; fax (22) 343866; Chair. ARISTOS KAISIDES; Principal Officer PANTELAKIS SOUGLIDES.

Aetna Insurance Co Ltd: POB 8909, 19 Stavrou St, 2035 Stro-volos; tel. (22) 510933; fax (22) 510934; f. 1966; Chair. KONSTANTINOS L. PRODROMOU; Principal Officer KONSTANTINOS TSAN-GARIS.

Agrostroy Insurance Co Ltd: POB 6624, 89 Kennedy Ave, Office 201, 1077 Nicosia; tel. (22) 379210; fax (22) 379212; f. 1996; offshore captive company operating outside Cyprus; Chair. VALERIE V. USH-AKOV; Principal Officer IOANNIS ELIA.

Akelius Insurance Ltd: POB 23415, 36 Laodikias St, 1683 Nicosia; tel. (22) 318883; fax (22) 318925; e-mail info@akelius.com; internet www.akelius.com; f. 1987; offshore company operating outside Cyprus; Chair. ROGER AKELIOUS; CEO IOANNIS LOIZOU; Principal Officer DEMETRIS SYLLOURIS.

Allied Assurance & Reinsurance Co Ltd: POB 5509, 66 Grivas Dhigenis Ave, 1310 Nicosia; tel. (22) 672235; fax (22) 677656; f. 1982; offshore company operating outside Cyprus; Chair. HENRI J. G. CHAL-HOUB; Principal Officer DEMETRIOS DEMETRIOU.

Alpha Insurance Ltd: POB 26516, cnr Kennedy Ave and Stasinou St, 1640 Nicosia; tel. (22) 379999; fax (22) 379097; e-mail customer_service@alphainsurance.com.cy; f. 1993; Chair. DOUKAS PALEOLOGOS; Principal Officer EVANGELOS ANASTASIADES.

Antarctic Insurance Co Ltd: POB 613, 199 Archbishop Makarios III Ave, Neokleou Bldg, 3030 Limassol; tel. (25) 362818; fax (25) 359262; offshore captive company operating outside Cyprus; Prin-cipal Officer ANDREAS NEOKLEOUS.

Apac Ltd: POB 25403, 5 Mourouzi St, Apt 1, 1055 Nicosia; tel. (22) 343086; fax (22) 343146; f. 1983; captive offshore company operating outside Cyprus; Chair. KYPROS CHRYSOSTOMIDES; Principal Officer GEORGHIOS POYATZIS.

Asfalistiki Eteria I 'Kentriki' Ltd: POB 25131, Kentriki Tower, 33 Clementos St, 1061 Nicosia; tel. (22) 745745; fax (22) 745746; e-mail kentriki@logosnet.com.cy; internet www.kentriki.com.cy; f. 1985; Chair. ARISTOS CHRYSOSTOMOU; Principal Officer GEORGHIOS GEORGALLIDES.

Aspis Pronia Insurance Co Ltd: POB 25183, 101 Acropolis Ave, 2012 Strovolos; tel. (22) 871087; fax (22) 492402; e-mail aspis@spidernet.com.cy; f. 1996; Chair. P. PSOMIADES; Principal Officer CHRISTAKIS ELEFTHERIOU.

Atlantic Insurance Co Ltd: POB 24579, 37 Prodromou St, 2nd Floor, 1090 Nicosia; tel. (22) 664052; fax (22) 661100; e-mail atlantic@spidernet.com.cy; f. 1983; Chair. and Man. Dir ZENIOS PYR-ISHIS; Principal Officer EMILIOS PYRISHIS.

Axioma Insurance (Cyprus) Ltd: POB 24881, 2 Ionni Klerides St, Demokritos No. 2 Bldg, Flat 83, 1070 Nicosia; tel. (22) 374197; fax

(22) 374972; offshore company operating outside Cyprus; Principal Officer KONSTANTINOS KYAMIDES.

B & B Marine Insurance Ltd: POB 22545, 46 Gladstonos St, 1095 Nicosia; tel. (22) 666599; fax (22) 676476; f. 1996; offshore company operating outside Cyprus; Chair. DMITGRI MOLTCHANOV; Principal Officer GEORGHIOS YIANGOU.

Berytus Marine Insurance Ltd: POB 50132, 284 Archbishop Makarios III Ave, 3105 Limassol; tel. (25) 369404; fax (25) 377871; f. 1997; offshore company operating outside Cyprus; Principal Officer CHRIS GEORGHIADES.

Cathay Insurance Co Ltd: POB 54708, 21 Vasili Michailidi, 3727 Limassol; f. 1997; offshore captive company operating outside Cyprus; Principal Officer ARETI CHARIDEMOU.

Commercial Union Assurance (Cyprus) Ltd: POB 21312, Com-mercial Union House, 101 Archbishop Makarios III Ave, 1071 Nicosia; tel. (22) 377373; fax (22) 376155; e-mail mailbox@commercial-union.com.cy; internet www.commercial-union.com.cy; f. 1974; Chair. ANDREAS ARTEMIS; Man. Dir KONSTANTINOS P. DEKATRIS.

Cosmos (Cyprus) Insurance Co Ltd: POB 21770, 1st Floor, Flat 12, 6 Ayia Eleni St, 1060 Nicosia; tel. (22) 441235; fax (22) 457925; f. 1982; Chair. and Gen. Man. ANDREAS K. TYLLIS.

Crown Insurance Co Ltd: POB 24690, Royal Crown House, 20 Mnasiadou St, Nicosia 136; tel. (22) 673333; fax (22) 760757; f. 1992; Chair. W. R. ROWLAND; Principal Officer PHILIOS ZACHARIADES.

Cygnet Insurance Ltd: POB 58482, 56 Grivas Dhigenis Ave, Anna Tower, 4th Floor, Office 42, 3101 Limassol; tel. (25) 583253; fax (25) 584514; e-mail tcsl@logos.cy.net; f. 1997; offshore captive company operating outside Cyprus; Principal Officer MARIOS LOUKAIDES.

Cyprialife Ltd: POB 20819, 64 Archbishop Makarios III Ave and 1 Karpenisiou St, 1077 Nicosia; tel. (22) 887300; fax (22) 374450; e-mail cyprialife@cytanet.com.cy; f. 1995; Chair. KIKIS LAZARIDES; Principal Officer DIMIS MICHAELIDES.

Direct Insurance Company Ltd: POB 22274, 35–37 Byzantium St, 1585 Nicosia; tel. (22) 664433; fax (22) 665139; Chair. STAVROS DAVERONAS.

E.F.U. General Insurance Ltd: POB 1612, 3 Themistoklis Dervis St, Julia House, Nicosia; tel. (22) 453053; fax (22) 475194; offshore company; Chair. ROSHEN ALI BHIMJEE; Principal Officer CHARALAMBOS ZAVALLIS.

Emergency Market Insurance Ltd: POB 613, 199 Archbishop Makarios Ave, Neokleous Bldg, 3030 Limassol; tel. (25) 362818; fax (25) 359262; f. 1997; offshore captive company operating outside Cyprus; Principal Officer ANDREAS NEOKLEOUS.

Eurolife Ltd: POB 21655, Eurolife House, 4 Evrou, 1511 Nicosia; tel. (22) 474000; fax (22) 341092; internet www.bankofcyprus.com/eurolife; Chair. E. XENOPHONTOUS; Principal Officer ANDREAS KRITOTIS.

Eurosure Insurance Co Ltd: POB 21961, Eurosure Tower, 5 Limassol Ave, 2112 Aglantzia, 1515 Nicosia; tel. (22) 882500; fax (22) 882599; e-mail info@eurosure.com; internet www.eurosure.com; Chair. EFTHYVOULOS PARASKEVAIDES.

Excelsior General Insurance Co Ltd: POB 6106, 339 Ayiou Andreou St, Andrea Chambers, Of. 303, Limassol; tel. (25) 427021; fax (25) 312446; f. 1995; Chair. CLIVE E. K. LEWIS; Principal Officer MARIA HADJIANTONIOU.

FAM Financial and Mercantile Insurance Co Ltd: POB 50132, 284 Archbishop Makarios III Ave, Fortuna Bldg, Block 'B', 2nd Floor, 4007 Limassol; tel. (25) 362424; fax (25) 370055; f. 1993; offshore captive company operating outside Cyprus; Chair. VLADIMIR MOIS-SEEV; General Officer CHR. GEORGHIADES.

General Insurance of Cyprus Ltd: POB 21668, 2–4 Themistoklis Dervis St, 1066 Nicosia; tel. (22) 848700; fax (22) 671355; e-mail finance@gic.bankofcyprus.com; f. 1951; Chair. V. ROLOGIS; Gen. Man. A. STYLIANOU.

Geopolis Insurance Ltd: POB 8530, 6 Neoptolemou St, 2045 Strovolos, Nicosia; tel. (22) 490094; fax (22) 490494; f. 1993; Chair. MARIOS PROIOS; Principal Officer NIKOS DRYMIOTIS.

Granite Insurance Co Ltd: POB 613, 199 Archbishop Makarios III Ave, Neokleou Bldg, 3030 Limassol; tel. (25) 362424; fax (25) 359262; captive offshore company operating outside Cyprus; Chair. and Gen. Man. KOSTAS KOUTSOKOUMNIS; Principal Officer ANDREAS NEOKLEOUS.

Greene Insurances Ltd: POB 132, 4th Floor, Vereggaria Bldg, 25 Spyrou Araouzou St, 3036 Limassol; tel. (25) 362424; fax (25) 363842; f. 1987; Chair. GEORGHIOS CHRISTODOULOU; Principal Officer JOSIF CHRISTOU.

Hermes Insurance Ltd: POB 24828, 1st Floor, Anemomylos Bldg, 8 Michalakis Karaolis St, 1095 Nicosia; tel. (22) 666999; fax (22) 667999; e-mail cyprus-credit-insurance@cytanet.com.cy; f. 1980; Chair. and Man. Dir P. G. VOGAZIANOS.

I.G.R. Co Ltd: POB 21343, 20 Vasilissias Friderikis St, El Greco House, Office 104, 1066 Nicosia; tel. (22) 473688; fax (22) 455259; f. 1996; offshore company operating outside Cyprus; Principal Officer CHRISTODOULOS VASSILIADES.

Laiki Insurance Co Ltd: POB 22274, 45 Vyzantiou St, Strovolos, 1585 Nicosia; tel. (22) 664792; e-mail laiki.telebank@laiki.com; internet www.laiki.com; f. 1981; Chair. K. N. LAZARIDES; Gen. Man. STEPHIE DRACOS.

LCF Reinsurance Co Ltd: POB 60479, Abacus House, 58 Grivas Dhigenis Ave, 8103 Paphos, Nicosia; tel. (22) 555000; fax (22) 555001; f. 1984; Chair. ALAIN COPINE; Principal Officer SOPHIA XINARI.

Ledra Insurance Ltd: POB 23942, 66 Griva Dhigeui Ave, 1080 Nicosia; tel. (22) 743700; fax (22) 677656; f. 1994; Chair. CONSTANTINOS LOIZIDES; Principal Officer ALECOS PULCHERIOS.

Liberty Life Insurance Ltd: POB 26070, 75 Limassol Ave, 5th Floor, Nicosia; tel. (22) 319300; fax (22) 429134; f. 1994; Chair. KONSTANTINOS KITTIS; Principal Officer EURIPIDES NEOKLEOUS.

Marketrends Insurance Ltd: POB 24841, corner Kennedy Ave and 7 Epaninonda St, 1076 Nicosia; tel. (22) 796600; fax (22) 768065; e-mail markins@cytanet.com.cy; Man. Dir PANOS JOAHNOU.

Medlife Insurance Ltd: POB 21675, Themistoklis Dervis-Florinis St, 1512 Nicosia; tel. (22) 675181; fax (22) 671889; e-mail office@medlife.net; internet www.medlife.net; f. 1995; Chair. Dr WOLFGANG GOSCHNIK.

Minerva Insurance Co Ltd: POB 20866, 8 Epaminondas St, 1684 Nicosia 137; tel. (22) 445134; fax (22) 455528; f. 1970; Chair. and Gen. Man. K. KOUTSOKOUMNIS.

Pancyprian Insurance Ltd: POB 21352, Pancyprian Tower, 66 Grivas Dhigenis Ave, 1080 Nicosia; tel. (22) 743743; fax (22) 677656; e-mail picl@pancyprian.com; f. 1993; Chair. CONSTANTINOS ST. LOIZIDES; Principal Officer SOCRATES DEMETRIOU.

Paneuropean Insurance Co Ltd: POB 553, 88 Archbishop Makarios III Ave, 1660 Nicosia; tel. (22) 377960; fax (22) 377396; f. 1980; Chair. N. K. SHACOLAS; Gen. Man. POLIS MICHAELIDES.

Philiki Insurance Co Ltd: POB 22274, 35–37 Byzantium St, 2026 Strovolos, 1585 Nicosia; tel. (22) 664433; fax (22) 665139; f. 1982; Chair. NIKOS SHAKOLAS; Principal Officer DOROS ORPHANIDES.

Progressive Insurance Co Ltd: POB 22111, 44 Kallipoleos St, 1071 Nicosia; tel. (22) 758585; fax (22) 754747; e-mail progressive@cytanet.com.cy; Chair. ANDREAS HADJIANDREOU; Principal Officer TAKIS HADJIANDREOU.

Saviour Insurance Co Ltd: POB 23957, 8 Michalakis Karaolis St, Anemomylos Bldg, Flat 204, 1687 Nicosia; tel. (22) 675085; fax (22) 676097; f. 1987; Chair. ROBERT SINCLAIR; Principal Officer KONSTANTINOS KITTIS.

Technolink Insurance Services Ltd: POB 7007, 70 Kennedy Ave, Papavasiliou House, 1076 Nicosia; tel. (22) 496000; fax (22) 493000; f. 1996; offshore captive company operating outside Cyprus; Principal Officer GEORGHIOS YIALLOURIDES.

Tercet Insurance Ltd: POB 2545, 46 Gladstones St, 1095 Nicosia; tel. (22) 466456; fax (22) 466476; f. 1994; Chair. ANDREAS STYLIANOU; Principal Officer MARIA PIPINGA.

Triada Insurance Ltd: POB 21675, corner Themistoklis Dervis & Florinis St, Stadyl Bldg, 6th Floor, 1512 Nicosia; tel. (22) 675182; fax (22) 675926; f. 1996; offshore captive company operating outside Cyprus; Principal Officer ANDREAS STYLIANOU.

Trust International Insurance Co (Cyprus) Ltd: POB 54857, 284 Archbishop Makarios III Ave, Fortuna Bldg, 2nd Floor, 4007 Limassol; tel. (25) 369404; fax (25) 377871; f. 1992; Chair. GHAZI K. ABU NAHL; Principal Officer CHR. GEORGHIADES.

Universal Life Insurance Company Ltd: POB 21270, Universal Tower, 85 Dhigenis Akritas Ave, 1505 Nicosia; tel. (22) 882222; fax (22) 882200; e-mail unilife@unilife.com.cy; internet www.universallife.com.cy; f. 1970; Chair. ANDREAS GEORGHIOU.

UPIC Ltd: POB 57237, Nicolaou Pentadromos Centre, 10th Floor, Ayias Zonis St, 3314 Limassol; tel. (25) 347664; fax (25) 347081; e-mail upic@spidernet.com.cy; f. 1992; Principal Officer POLAKIS SARRIS.

Veritima Insurance Ltd: POB 956, 2b Orpheus St, Office 104, 1070 Nicosia; tel. (22) 375646; fax (22) 375620; f. 1996; offshore captive company operating outside Cyprus; Principal Officer SANDROS DIKEOS.

VTI Insurance Co Ltd: POB 50613, 199 Archbishop Makarios III Ave, Neokleou Bldg, 4004 Limassol; tel. (25) 362818; fax (25) 359262; f. 1994; Chair. SOTERIS PITTAS; Principal Officer ANDREAS NEOKLEOUS.

Turkish Cypriot Insurance Companies

Akfinans Sigorta Insurance AŞ: 16 Osman Paşa Cad., Lefkoşa (Nicosia), POB 451, Mersin 10, Turkey; tel. (22) 84506; fax (22) 85713; e-mail akfinans@akfinans.com; internet www.akfinans.com; f. 1996; Gen. Man. MEHMET KADER.

Altınbaş Sigorta Ltd: Müftü Ziya Sok. 2, Lefkoşa (Nicosia), Mersin 10, Turkey; tel. (22) 88222; fax (22) 76648.

Anadolu Anonim: 1-7-9 Girne Cad., Lefkoşa (Nicosia), Mersin 10, Turkey; tel. (22) 83133; fax (22) 79596.

Ankara Sigorta: PK 551, Bedrettin Demirel Cad., Lefkoşa (Nicosia), Mersin 10, Turkey; tel. (22) 85815; fax (22) 83099.

Başak Sigorta AŞ: Mehmet Akif Cad. 95, Lefkoşa (Nicosia), Mersin 10, Turkey; tel. (22) 80208; fax (22) 86160.

Bey Sigorta Ltd: Atatürk Cad. 5, Yenişehir, Lefkoşa (Nicosia), Mersin 10, Turkey; tel. (22) 88241; fax (22) 87362.

Birinci Sigorta Ltd: Tekin Yurdabak Cad., Tekin Birinci Binaları, Göçmenköy, Lefkoşa (Nicosia), Mersin 10, Turkey; tel. (22) 83200; fax (22) 83498.

Gold Insurance Ltd: Salih Mecit Sok. 12/B, Lefkoşa (Nicosia), Mersin 10, Turkey; tel. (22) 86500; fax (22) 86300.

Güneş Sigorta AŞ: Vakıflar İş Hanı 1C Girne Cad., Lefkoşa (Nicosia), Mersin 10, Turkey; tel. (22) 87333; fax (22) 81585.

Güven Sigorta (Kıbrıs) Sirketi AŞ: Mecidiye Sok. 8, Lefkoşa (Nicosia), Mersin 10, Turkey; tel. (22) 83023; fax (22) 81431.

İnan Sigorta TAŞ: Mehmet Akif Cad. 98, Kumsal, Lefkoşa (Nicosia), Mersin 10, Turkey; tel. (22) 83333; fax (22) 81976.

İşlek Sigorta: Bahçelievler Bul., Güzelyurt (Morphou), Mersin 10, Turkey; tel. (71) 42473; fax (71) 45507.

İsviçre Sigorta AŞ: Arkom Ltd, PK 693, Lefkoşa (Nicosia), Mersin 10, Turkey; tel. (22) 82125; fax (22) 88236.

Kıbrıs Sigorta: Osman Paşa Cad., Yağcıoğlu Işhanı 4, Lefkoşa (Nicosia), Mersin 10, Turkey; tel. (22) 83022; fax (22) 79277.

Limassol Sigorta Ltd: PK 267, Orhaneli Sok., Girne, Mersin 10, Turkey; tel. (81) 56786; fax (81) 58773.

Ray Sigorta AŞ: Bedrettin Demirel Cad. Arabacıoğlu Apt. 7, Lefkoşa (Nicosia), Mersin 10, Turkey; tel. (22) 70380; fax (22) 70383.

Saray Sigorta: 182 Girne Cad., Lefkoşa (Nicosia), Mersin 10, Turkey; tel. (22) 72976; fax (22) 79001.

Şeker Sigorta (Kıbrıs) Ltd: Mahmut Paşa Sok. 14/A, PK 664, Lefkoşa (Nicosia), Mersin 10, Turkey; tel. (22) 85883; fax (22) 74074.

Zirve Sigorta Ltd: Gültekin Şengör Sok., Abahorlu Türk Apt. 9, Lefkoşa (Nicosia), Mersin 10, Turkey; tel. (22) 75633; fax (22) 83600.

Trade and Industry

GREEK CYPRIOT CHAMBERS OF COMMERCE AND INDUSTRY

Cyprus Chamber of Commerce and Industry: POB 21455, 38 Grivas Dhigenis Ave, 1509 Nicosia; tel. (22) 889800; fax (22) 669048; e-mail chamber@ccci.org.cy; internet www.ccci.org.cy; f. 1927; Pres. VASSILIS ROLOGIS; Sec.-Gen. PANAYIOTIS LOIZIDES; 8,000 mems, 100 affiliated trade asscns.

Famagusta Chamber of Commerce and Industry: POB 53124, 339 Ayiou Andreou St, Andrea Chambers Bldg, 2nd Floor, Office No 201–202, 3300 Limassol; tel. (25) 370165; fax (25) 370291; e-mail chamberf@cytanet.com.cy; internet www.ccci.org.cy; f. 1952; Pres. PHOTIS PAPATHOMAS; Sec. IACOVOS HADJIVARNAVAS; 450 mems.

Larnaca Chamber of Commerce and Industry: POB 40287, 12 Gregoriou Afxentiou St, Skouros Bldg, Apt 43, 4th Floor, 6302 Larnaca; tel. (4) 655051; fax (4) 628281; e-mail lcci@spidernet.com.cy; Pres. ANDREAS LOUROUTZIATIS; Sec. GEORGE PSARAS; 450 mems.

Limassol Chamber of Commerce and Industry: POB 55699, 1st Floor, 166 Franklin Rossevelt, 3781 Limassol; tel. (25) 662556; fax (25) 661655; e-mail chamberl@cylink.com.cy; f. 1962; Pres. TONY ANTONIOU; Sec. and Dir CHRISTOS ANASTASSIADES; 770 mems.

Nicosia Chamber of Commerce and Industry: POB 21455, 38 Grivas Dhigenis Ave, Chamber Bldg, 1509 Nicosia; tel. (22) 889600; fax (22) 667433; e-mail ncci@ccci.org.cy; f. 1962; Pres. MANTHOS MAVROMATIS; Sec. SOCRATES HERACLEOUS; 1,200 mems.

Paphos Chamber of Commerce and Industry: POB 82, Athinon Ave & corner Alexandrou Papayou Ave, 8100 Paphos; tel. (6) 235115; fax (6) 244602; Pres. THEODOROS ARISTODEMOU; Sec. KENDEAS ZAMPIRINIS; 450 mems.

TURKISH CYPRIOT CHAMBERS OF COMMERCE AND INDUSTRY

Turkish Cypriot Chamber of Industry: 14 Osman Paşa Cad., PK

563, Köşklüçiftlik, Lefkoşa (Nicosia), Mersin 10, Turkey; tel. (22) 84596; fax (22) 84595; Pres. EREN ERTANIN.

Turkish Cypriot Chamber of Commerce: Bedrettin Demirel Cad., PK 718, Lefkoşa (Nicosia), Mersin 10, Turkey; tel. (22) 83645; fax (22) 83089; f. 1958; more than 6,000 regd mems; Chair. SALIH BOYACI; Sec.-Gen. JANEL BURCAN.

GREEK CYPRIOT EMPLOYERS' ORGANIZATION

Cyprus Employers' & Industrialists' Federation: POB 21657, 30 Grivas Dhigenis Ave, 1511 Nicosia; tel. (22) 665102; fax (22) 669459; e-mail oeb@cytanet.com.cy; internet www.oeb-eif.org; f. 1960; 45 member trade associations, 400 direct and 3,000 indirect members; Dir-Gen. MICHAEL PILIKOS; Chair. BYRON KRANDIDIOTIS; The largest of the trade association members are: Cyprus Building Contractors' Association; Land and Building Developers' Association; Association of Cyprus Tourist Enterprises; Cyprus Shipping Association; Cyprus Footwear Manufacturers' Association; Cyprus Metal Industries Association; Cyprus Bankers Employers' Association; Cyprus Association of Business Consultants; Mechanical Contractors Association of Cyprus; Union of Solar Energy Industries of Cyprus.

TURKISH CYPRIOT EMPLOYERS' ORGANIZATION

Kıbrıs Türk şverenler Sendikası (Turkish Cypriot Employers' Association): PK 674, Lefkoşa (Nicosia), Mersin 10, Turkey; tel. (22) 73673; fax (22) 77479; Chair. HASAN SUNGUR.

GREEK CYPRIOT UTILITIES

Electricity

Electricity Authority of Cyprus (EAC): POB 24506, 1399 Nicosia; tel. (22) 845000; fax (22) 767658; e-mail eac@eac.com.cy; internet www.eac.com.cy; generation, transmission and distribution of electric energy in government-controlled area; total installed capacity 988 MW in 2003.

Water

Water Development Department: Dem. Severis Ave, 1413 Nicosia; tel. (22) 803100; fax (22) 675019; e-mail waterdep@cytanet .com.cy; dam storage capacity 300m. cu m; Dir CHR. MARCOULLIS.

TURKISH CYPRIOT UTILITIES

Electricity

Cyprus Turkish Electricity Corpn: Lefkoşa (Nicosia), Mersin 10, Turkey; tel. (22) 83648; fax (22) 83851.

TRADE UNIONS

Greek Cypriot Trade Unions

Cyprus Civil Servants' Trade Union: 3 Dem. Severis Ave, Nicosia; tel. (22) 662337; fax (22) 665199; e-mail pasydy@spidernet .com.cy; f. 1949; registered 1966; restricted to persons in the civil employment of the Government and public authorities; 6 brs with a total membership of 15,383; Pres. ANDREAS CHRISTODOULOU; Gen. Sec. GLAFKOS HADJIPETROU.

Dimokratiki Ergatiki Omospondia Kyprou (DEOK) (Democratic Labour Federation of Cyprus): POB 21625, 40 Byron Ave, 1511 Nicosia; tel. (22) 676506; fax (22) 670494; e-mail deok@cytanet .com.cy; f. 1962; 5 workers' unions with a total membership of 7,316; Gen. Sec. DIOMEDES DIOMEDOUS.

Pankypria Ergatiki Omospondia (PEO) (Pancyprian Federation of Labour): POB 21885, 31–35 Archermos St, Nicosia 1045; tel. (22) 886400; fax (22) 349382; e-mail peo@cytanet.com.cy; internet www.cytanet.com.cy/peo; f. 1946; registered 1947; previously the Pancyprian Trade Union Committee f. 1941, dissolved 1946; 8 unions and 176 brs with a total membership of 75,000; affiliated to the WFTU; Gen. Sec. PAMBIS KYRITSIS.

Pankyprios Omospondia Anexartition Syntechnion (Pancyprian Federation of Independent Trade Unions): 4B Dayaes St, 2369 Ay. Dhometios; POB 7521, 2430 Nicosia; tel. (22) 356414; fax (22) 354216; f. 1956; registered 1957; has no political orientations; 8 unions with a total membership of 798; Gen. Sec. KYRIACOS NATHANAEL.

Synomospondia Ergaton Kyprou (Cyprus Workers' Confederation): POB 25018, 11 Strovolos Ave, 2018 Strovolos, 1306 Nicosia; tel. (22) 849849; fax (22) 849850; e-mail sek@org.cy.net; f. 1944; registered 1950; 7 federations, 5 labour centres, 47 unions, 12 brs with a total membership of 62,559; affiliated to the ICFTU and the ETUC; Gen. Sec. DEMETRIS KITTENIS; Deputy Gen. Sec. NIKOS MOESEOS.

Union of Cyprus Journalists: POB 23495, 2 Kratinos St, Strovolos, 1082 Nicosia; tel. (22) 664680; fax (22) 664598; e-mail cyjourun@logosnet.cy.net; f. 1959; Chair. ANDREAS KANNAOUROS.

Turkish Cypriot Trade Unions

In 1998 trade union membership totalled 24,864.

Devrimci İşçi Sendikaları Federasyonu (Dev-İş) (Revolutionary Trade Unions' Federation): 6 Serabioğlu Sok., 748 Lefkoşa (Nicosia), Mersin 10, Turkey; tel. (22) 86462; fax (22) 86463; e-mail devis@defne.net; f. 1976; four unions with a total membership of 1,850 (2002); affiliated to WFTU; Pres. ALI GULLE; Gen. Sec. MEHMET SEYIS.

Kıbrıs Türk İşçi Sendikaları Federasyonu (TÜRK-SEN) (Turkish Cypriot Trade Union Federation): POB 829, 7–7A Şehit Mehmet R. Hüseyin Sok., Lefkoşa (Nicosia), Mersin 10, Turkey; tel. (22) 72444; fax (22) 87831; f. 1954; regd 1955; 12 unions with a total membership of 5,250 (1998); affiliated to ICFTU, ETUC, CTUC and the Confederation of Trade Unions of Turkey (Türk-İş); Pres. ÖNDER KONULOĞLU; Gen. Sec. ASLAN BIÇAKLI.

Transport

RAILWAYS

There are no railways in Cyprus.

ROADS

In 1999, according to data published by the International Road Federation, there were 11,009 km of roads in the government-controlled areas, of which 216 km were motorway and 2,131 km were highways and other main roads; some 87.4% of the road network was paved. The Nicosia–Limassol four-lane dual carriageway, which was completed in 1985, was subsequently extended with the completion of the Limassol and Larnaca bypasses. Highways also connect Nicosia and Larnaca, Larnaca and Kophinou, Aradippo and Dhekelia, and Nicosia and Anthoupolis-Kokkinotrimithia. The first section of the Limassol–Paphos highway opened in 1997, and work on the remainder was scheduled to be completed in 2000. In 1997 work began on a Dhekelia–Ammochostos (Famagusta) highway. The north and south are now served by separate transport systems, and there are no services linking the two sectors.

SHIPPING

Until 1974 Famagusta, a natural port, was the island's most important harbour, handling about 83% of the country's cargo. Since its capture by the Turkish army in August 1974 the port has been officially declared closed to international traffic. However, it continues to serve the Turkish-occupied region.

The main ports that serve the island's maritime trade at present are Larnaca and Limassol, which were constructed in 1973 and 1974 respectively. Both ports have since been expanded and improved. There is also an industrial port at Vassiliko and there are three specialized petroleum terminals, at Larnaca, Dhekelia and Moni. A second container terminal became operational at Limassol in 1995.

In 1998 4,475 vessels, with a total net registered tonnage of 15,963,000, visited Cyprus, carrying 7,017,000 metric tons of cargo to and from Cyprus. In addition to serving local traffic, Limassol and Larnaca ports act as transhipment load centres for the Eastern Mediterranean, North Adriatic and Black Sea markets and as regional warehouse and assembly bases for the Middle East, North Africa and the Persian (Arabian) Gulf. Containerized cargo handled at Cypriot ports amounted to 1,722,300 metric tons in 1998.

Both Kyrenia and Karavostassi are under Turkish occupation and have been declared closed to international traffic. Karavostassi used to be the country's major mineral port, dealing with 76% of the total mineral exports. However, since the war minerals have been passed through Vassiliko which is a specified industrial port. A hydrofoil service operates between Kyrenia and Mersin on the Turkish mainland. Car ferries sail from Kyrenia to Taşucu and Mersin, in Turkey.

At 31 December 2001 the Greek Cypriot shipping registry comprised 1,407 vessels, with an aggregate displacement of 22.76m. grt.

Department of Merchant Shipping: POB 56193, Kyllinis St, Mesk Geitonia, 4405 Limassol; tel. (25) 848100; fax (25) 848200; e-mail dms@cytanet.com.cy; internet www.shipping.gov.cy; Dir SERGHIOS SERGHIOU.

Cyprus Ports Authority: POB 22007, 23 Crete St, 1516 Nicosia; tel. (22) 817200; fax (22) 765420; e-mail cpa@cpa.gov.cy; internet www.cpa.gov.cy; f. 1973; Chair. CHRISTOS HADJIMANOLIS; Gen. Man. Dr ANTONIS TOUMAZIS.

Cyprus Shipping Council: POB 56607, 3309 Limassol; tel. (25) 360717; fax (25) 358642; e-mail csc@csc-cy.org; internet www.csc-cy .org; Gen. Sec. THOMAS A. KAZAKOS.

Greek Cypriot Shipping Companies

Amer Shipping Ltd: POB 27363, 6th Floor, Ghinis Bldg, 58–60 Dhigenis Akritas Ave, 1061 Nicosia; tel. (22) 751707; fax (22) 751460; e-mail amer@spidernet.com.cy; internet www .amershipping.com; Man. Dir ANIL DESHPANDE.

C. F. Ahrenkiel Shipmanagement (Cyprus) Ltd: POB 53594, 4th Floor, O & A Tower, 25 Olympion St, 3033 Limassol; tel. (25) 854000; fax (25) 854001; Man. Dir VASSOS STAVROU.

Columbia Shipmanagement Ltd: POB 51624, Columbia House, Dodekanissou and Kolonakiou Corner, 3507 Limassol; tel. (25) 843100; fax (25) 320325; e-mail shipmanagement@csmcy.com; internet www.columbia.com.cy; f. 1978; Chair H. SCHOELLER; Man. Dir D. FRY.

Hanseatic Shipping Co Ltd: POB 127, 111 Spyrou Araouzou St, Limassol; tel. (25) 345111; fax (25) 342879; f. 1972; Man. Dirs A. J. DROUSSIOTIS, R. GROOL.

Interorient Navigation Co Ltd: POB 51309, 3 Thalia St, 3504 Limassol; tel. (25) 840300; fax (25) 575895; e-mail management@ interorient.com.cy; internet www.interorient.com; Man. Dir JAN LISSOW.

Louis Cruise Lines: POB 21301, 1506 Nicosia; 20 Amphipoleos St, 2025 Strovolos; tel. (22) 588002; fax (22) 442848; e-mail egavrielides@louisgroup.com; internet www.louiscruises.com; Exec. Chair. COSTAKIS LOIZOU; Man. Dir EURIPIDES GAVRIELIDES.

Marlow Navigation Ltd: POB 4077, Marlow Bldg, cnr 28th October St and Sotiris Michaelides St, Limassol; tel. (25) 348888; fax (25) 748222; e-mail marlow@marlow.com.cy; Gen. Man. ANDREAS NEOPHYTOU.

Oldendorff Ltd, Reederei 'Nord' Klaus E: POB 56345, Libra Tower, 23 Olympion St, 3306 Limassol; tel. (25) 841400; fax (25) 345077; e-mail rnkeo@spidernet.com.cy; internet www.rnkeo.com; Chair. and Man. Dir KLAUS E. OLDENDORFF.

Seatankers Management Co Ltd: POB 53562, Deana Beach Apartments, Block 1, 4th Floor, Promachon Eleftherias St, 4103 Limassol; tel. (25) 858300; fax (25) 323770; e-mail seatank@cytanet .com.cy; Dirs COSTAS PALLARIS, DIMITRIS HANNAS.

Turkish Cypriot Shipping Companies

Armen Shipping Ltd: Altun Tabya Yolu No. 10–11, Gazi Mağusa (Famagusta), Mersin 10, Turkey; tel. (36) 64086; fax (36) 65860; e-mail armen@armenshipping.com; Dir VARGIN VARER.

Compass Shipping Ltd: Seagate Court, Gazi Mağusa (Famagusta), Mersin 10, Turkey; tel. (36) 66393; fax (36) 66394.

Denko Koop Marine Cargo Department: PK 4, 12 Canbulat St, Gazi Mağusa (Famagusta), Mersin 10, Turkey; tel. (36) 65419; fax (36) 62773; e-mail info@koopbank.com; internet www.koopbank .com; Dir HASAN TRANSTURK.

Ertürk Ltd: Kyrenia (Girne), Mersin 10, Turkey; tel. (81) 55834; fax (81) 51808; Dir KEMAL ERTÜRK.

Fergun Maritime Co: Kyrenia (Girne), Mersin 10, Turkey; tel. (81) 54993; ferries to Turkish ports; Owner FEHIM KÜÇÜK.

Kıbrıs Türk Denizcilik Ltd, Şti (Turkish Cypriot Maritime Co Ltd): 3 Bülent Ecevit Bul., Gazi Mağusa (Famagusta), Mersin 10, Turkey; tel. (36) 65995; fax (36) 67840; e-mail cypship@superonline .com.

Medusa Marine Shipping Ltd: Aycan Apt, Gazi Mağusa (Famagusta), Mersin 10, Turkey; tel. (36) 63945; fax (36) 67800; Dir ERGÜN TOLAY.

Orion Navigation Ltd: Seagate Court, Gazi Mağusa (Famagusta), Mersin 10, Turkey; tel. (36) 62643; fax (36) 64773; e-mail orion@ analiz.net; f. 1976; shipping agents; Dir O. LAMA; Shipping Man. L. LAMA.

Özari Shipping Ltd: Seagate Court, Gazi Mağusa (Famagusta), Mersin 10, Turkey; tel. (36) 66555; fax (36) 67098; Dir YALÇIN RUHI.

Tahsin Transtürk ve Oğlu Ltd: 11 Kizilkule Yolu, Gazi Mağusa (Famagusta), Mersin 10, Turkey; tel. (36) 65409.

CIVIL AVIATION

There is an international airport at Nicosia, which can accommodate all types of aircraft, including jet-engined airliners. It has been closed since 1974, following the Turkish invasion. A new international airport was constructed at Larnaca, from which flights operate to Europe, the USA, the Middle East and the Gulf. Another international airport at Paphos began operations in 1983. A C£210m. expansion and modernization of Larnaca and Paphos airports was proposed in late 2001 and was due for completion by 2010.

Avistar: POB 5532, Nicosia; tel. (22) 459533; fax (22) 477367; f. 1990; freight; Chief Exec. Dr WALDEMAR HAAS.

Cyprus Airways: 21 Alkeou St, Engomi 2404, POB 21903, 1514 Nicosia; tel. (22) 663054; fax (22) 663167; e-mail marketing@ cyprusair.com.cy; internet www.cyprusair.com.cy; f. 1947; jointly owned by Cyprus Government (66%) and local interests; wholly-owned subsidiaries Cyprair Tours Ltd, Eurocypria Airlines Ltd, Duty Free Shops Ltd and Zenon NDC Ltd; Chair. HARIS LOIZIDES; Gen. Man. CHRISTOS KYRIAKIDES (services throughout Europe and the Middle East).

Eurocypria Airlines (ECA): POB 970, 97 Artemidos Ave, Artemis Bldg, Larnaca; tel. (4) 658001; fax (4) 658008; services to European destinations from Larnaca and Paphos; Chair. HARIS LOIZIDES; Gen. Man. GEORGE SOUROULLAS.

In 1975 the Turkish authorities opened Ercan (formerly Tymbou) airport, and a second airport was opened at Geçitkale (Lefkoniko) in 1986.

Kıbrıs Türk Hava Yolları (Cyprus Turkish Airlines): Bedrettin Demirel Cad., PK 793, Lefkoşa (Nicosia), Mersin 10, Turkey; tel. (22) 83901; fax (22) 81468; e-mail info@kthy.net; internet www.kthy.net; f. 1974; jointly owned by the Turkish Cypriot Community Assembly Consolidated Improvement Fund and Turkish Airlines Inc; services to Turkey and five European countries; Gen. Man. M. ZEKI ZIYQ.

Tourism

In 2001 a total of 2,696,732 foreign tourists visited the Greek Cypriot area and receipts from tourism amounted to C£1,277m., according to provisional figures. In the same year there were 88,302 hotel beds in the Greek-Cypriot area. In 2001 365,097 tourists visited the Turkish Cypriot area, and revenue from tourism amounted to $93.7m.

Cyprus Tourism Organisation (CTO): POB 24535, 19 Limassol Ave, 1390 Nicosia; tel. (22) 691100; fax (22) 331644; e-mail cytour@ cto.org.cy; internet www.visitcyprus.org.cy; Chair. CHRYSIS PRENTZAS; Dir-Gen. PHRYNE MICHAEL.

THE CZECH REPUBLIC

Introductory Survey

Location, Climate, Language, Religion, Flag, Capital

The Czech Republic lies in central Europe and comprises the Czech Lands of Bohemia and Moravia and part of Silesia. Its neighbours are Poland to the north, Germany to the north-west and west, Austria to the south and Slovakia to the east. The climate is continental, with warm summers and cold winters. The average mean temperature is 9°C (49°F). Czech, a member of the west Slavonic group, is the official language. There is a sizeable Slovak minority and also small Polish, German, Silesian, Romany, Hungarian and other minorities. The major religion is Christianity (about 40% of the population are Roman Catholics). The national flag (proportions 2 by 3) has two equal horizontal stripes, of white and red, on which is superimposed a blue triangle (half the length) at the hoist. The capital is Prague (Praha).

Recent History

In October 1918, following the collapse of the Austro-Hungarian Empire at the end of the First World War, the Republic of Czechoslovakia was established. The new state united the Czech Lands of Bohemia and Moravia, which had been incorporated into the Austrian Empire in the 16th and 17th centuries, and Slovakia, which had been under Hungarian rule for almost 1,000 years. After the Nazis came to power in Germany in 1933, there was increased agitation in the Sudetenland (an area in northern Bohemia that was inhabited by about 3m. German-speaking people) for autonomy within, and later secession from, Czechoslovakia. In 1938, to appease German demands, the British, French and Italian Prime Ministers concluded an agreement with the German leader, Adolf Hitler, whereby the Sudetenland was ceded to Germany, and other parts of Czechoslovakia were transferred to Hungary and Poland. The remainder of Czechoslovakia was invaded and occupied by Nazi armed forces in March 1939, and a German protectorate was established in Bohemia and Moravia. In Slovakia, which had been granted self-government in late 1938, a separate Slovak state was formed, under the pro-Nazi regime of Jozef Tiso.

After Germany's defeat in the Second World War (1939–45), the pre-1938 frontiers of Czechoslovakia were restored, although a small area in the east was ceded to the USSR in June 1945. Almost all of the German-speaking inhabitants of Czechoslovakia were expelled, and the Sudetenland was settled by Czechs from other parts of Bohemia. In response to Slovak demands for greater autonomy, a legislature (the Slovak National Council) and an executive Board of Commissioners were established in Bratislava, the Slovak capital. At elections in 1946 the Communist Party of Czechoslovakia (CPCz) emerged as the leading party, winning 38% of the votes cast. The CPCz's leader, Klement Gottwald, became Prime Minister in a coalition Government. After ministers of other parties resigned, communist control became complete on 25 February 1948. A People's Republic was established on 9 June. Gottwald replaced Edvard Beneš as President, a position that he held until his death in 1953. The country aligned itself with the Soviet-led Eastern European bloc, joining the Council for Mutual Economic Assistance (CMEA) and the Warsaw Pact.

Government followed a rigid Stalinist pattern, and in the early 1950s there were many political trials. Although these ended under Gottwald's successors, Antonín Zápotocký and, from 1956, Antonín Novotný, there was no relaxation of policy until 1963, when a new Government, with Jozef Lenárt as Prime Minister, was formed. Meanwhile, the country was renamed the Czechoslovak Socialist Republic, under a new Constitution, proclaimed in July 1960.

In January 1968 Alexander Dubček succeeded Novotný as CPCz Secretary, and in March Gen. Ludvík Svoboda succeeded Novotný as President. Oldřich Černík became Prime Minister in April. The new Government envisaged widespread reforms, including the introduction of a federal system of government, a more democratic electoral system, and a greater degree of separation between party and state. The Government's reformist policies were regarded by other members of the Eastern European bloc as endangering their unity and in August Warsaw Pact forces (numbering an estimated 600,000) invaded Czechoslovakia, occupying Prague and other major cities. Mass demonstrations in protest at the invasion were held throughout the country, and many people were killed in clashes with occupation troops. The Soviet Government exerted heavy pressure on the Czechoslovak leaders to suppress their reformist policies and in April 1969 Dubček was replaced by a fellow Slovak, Dr Gustáv Husák, as First (subsequently General) Secretary of the Central Committee of the CPCz. Under Husák's leadership, there was a severe purge of the CPCz membership and most of Dubček's supporters were removed from the Government. All the reforms of 1968 were duly abandoned, with the exception of the federalization programme. This was implemented in January 1969, when the unitary Czechoslovak state was transformed into a federation, with separate Czech and Slovak Republics, each having its own National Council (legislature) and Government. A Federal Government was established as the supreme executive organ of state power, and the country's existing legislature, the National Assembly, was transformed into a bicameral Federal Assembly. The first legislative election since 1964 was held in November 1971, and 99.81% of the votes cast were in favour of candidates of the National Front (the communist-dominated organization embracing all the legal political parties in Czechoslovakia).

In May 1975 Husák was appointed to the largely ceremonial post of President of Czechoslovakia, retaining his positions of Chairman of the National Front and General Secretary of the CPCz. He held the latter post until December 1987, when he was replaced by Miloš Jakeš, an economist and member of the Presidium of the party's Central Committee. However, Husák remained as President of the Republic.

Although Jakeš affirmed his commitment to the moderate programme of reform initiated by his predecessor, repressive measures against the Roman Catholic Church and dissident groups continued. Of the latter, the most influential was Charter 77, which had been established in January 1977 by intellectuals, former politicians and others to campaign for the observance of civil and political rights. Despite the regime's continued attempts to suppress the movement, its sphere of influence broadened and it played a leading role in anti-Government demonstrations, which began in 1988. In February 1989, following one such demonstration, the Czech playwright, Václav Havel (a leader of Charter 77), was sentenced to nine months' imprisonment. (He was released in May, following international condemnation.) Anti-Government demonstrations followed in May, August and October 1989.

In November 1989 the protest actions of preceding months evolved into a process of dramatic, yet largely peaceful, political change, which subsequently became known as the 'velvet revolution'. On 17 November an anti-Government demonstration in Prague, the largest public protest for 20 years, was violently dispersed by the police; large numbers of demonstrators (who were mainly students) were injured. Large-scale protests continued in Prague and in other towns throughout the country. Later that month a new opposition group, Civic Forum, was established as an informal alliance, which united several existing opposition and human rights organizations, including Charter 77, and rapidly gained widespread popular support. Meanwhile, Alexander Dubček addressed mass rallies in Bratislava and Prague, expressing his support for the opposition's demands for reform. On 24 November it was announced that Jakeš and the entire membership of the Presidium of the Central Committee had resigned. Karel Urbánek, a member of the Presidium, replaced Jakeš as General Secretary of the party, and a new Presidium was elected. The strength of Civic Forum and its Slovak counterpart, Public Against Violence (PAV), was demonstrated in discussions on reform, conducted between their leaders and the Federal Prime Minister, Ladislav Adamec. The opposition demands for the ending of censorship and the release of all political prisoners were accepted, and at the end of November the articles guaranteeing the CPCz's predominance were deleted from the Constitution.

In early December 1989 the Federal Government was reorganized. However, Civic Forum and PAV denounced the new Government, since the majority of its ministers had served in the previous administration, and it included only five non-communists. Adamec subsequently resigned as Prime Minister, and was replaced by Marián Čalfa, the newly appointed First Deputy Prime Minister. In the following week a new, interim Federal Government was formed, with a majority of non-communist members, including seven non-party supporters of Civic Forum. Husák resigned from the office of President of the Republic and at the end of December was replaced by Václav Havel. Alexander Dubček was elected Chairman of the Federal Assembly. At an emergency congress of the CPCz, held in December, Urbánek was dismissed from the post of General Secretary of the Central Committee and this position was abolished. Adamec was appointed to the new post of Chairman of the party.

In April 1990 the Federal Assembly voted to rename the country the Czech and Slovak Federative Republic (CzSFR). The decision, which followed intense controversy, satisfied Slovak demands that the new title should reflect the equal status of Slovakia within the federation. On 8–9 June the first democratic legislative elections since 1946 were held in Czechoslovakia. A total of 27 political associations contested representation to the Federal Assembly (now numbering 300 seats) and to the National Councils of each republic, with the participation of some 97% of the electorate. In the elections at federal level, the highest proportion of the total votes cast (about 46%) was secured by Civic Forum, in the Czech Lands, and by PAV, in Slovakia. The CPCz won a greater proportion of the votes (about 14%) than had been expected, obtaining the second highest representation in the Federal Assembly. The Christian Democratic Union (a coalition of the Czechoslovak People's Party, the Christian Democratic Party—Chr.DP— and the Slovak-based Christian Democratic Movement—CDM) obtained approximately 12% of votes cast. Contrary to expectations, two parties that had campaigned for regional autonomy or secession secured more than the 5% minimum required for representation in the legislature: the Movement for Autonomous Democracy–Society for Moravia and Silesia (MAD–SMS) and the separatist Slovak National Party (SNP). The newly elected Federal Assembly was to serve a transitional two-year term, during which period it was to draft new federal and republican constitutions and elect a new President of the Republic. In late June Alexander Dubček was re-elected Chairman of the Federal Assembly. A new Federal Government, announced in that month, comprised 16 members: four from Civic Forum, three from PAV, one from the CDM and eight independents. In early July Václav Havel was re-elected to the post of President.

In the latter half of 1990 there was increasing unrest in Slovakia, as several newly established parties and groups, most prominently the SNP, organized demonstrations and rallies as part of a campaign for Slovak autonomy. In an attempt to alleviate the increasing ethnic tension in the country, in December the Federal Assembly voted overwhelmingly to transfer broader powers to the Czech and Slovak Governments, while the Federal Government was to retain jurisdiction over defence, foreign affairs and monetary policy. None the less, the Slovak issue remained the dominant topic of political debate during 1991 and 1992. A widening division emerged between the more moderate Slovak movements, such as PAV and the CDM (which advocated the preservation of the federation, albeit in a looser form), and a minority of more radical parties, which campaigned for full independence. In early March 1991 Vladimír Mečiar, the Slovak Prime Minister and a founding member of PAV, announced the formation of a minority faction within PAV (the Movement for a Democratic Slovakia—MDS), in support of greater Slovak autonomy. However, leading officials in PAV and some of its representatives in the Slovak Government viewed Mečiar's policies and aggressive style of leadership as detrimental to the future of Czech-Slovak relations, and in April the Slovak National Council voted to remove Mečiar from the Slovak premiership. He was replaced by Ján Čarnogurský, the Chairman of the CDM. In response, Mečiar and his supporters left PAV, and the MDS was established as a separate political group. Meanwhile, disagreement over the direction of post-communist politics and economic management had led to a split within Civic Forum. Two main groups emerged in February 1991: the conservative Civic Democratic Party (CDP), led by Václav Klaus, and the liberal Civic Movement (CM), led by Jiří Dienstbier. However, it was announced that, in

the interests of national unity, the two new groups were to remain as coalition partners in the Federal Government, pending the next legislative elections, due to take place in June 1992.

In March 1991 representatives of all political forces in Czechoslovakia reached agreement on the framework of a new federal Constitution. This stipulated, *inter alia*, that the country would remain a federative state comprising two 'sovereign and equal republics, linked voluntarily and by the free will of their citizens'. However, by late 1991 the Federal Assembly's discussions on the new Constitution had reached an impasse, as deputies failed to agree on the status of the two republics within any future federation. President Havel repeatedly proposed the holding of a referendum on the possible division of Czechoslovakia into two separate states, as the only democratic means of resolving the issue. The constitutional debate continued in the first half of 1992, with increasing Slovak support for the loosest possible confederation, comprising two nominally independent states. The majority of Czech politicians, however, were in favour of preserving the existing state structure, and rejected Slovak proposals as impracticable. In March it was agreed that the constitutional talks would be postponed until after the legislative elections in June.

The legislative elections of 5–6 June 1992 proved to be decisive in the eventual dismantling of Czechoslovakia, particularly as the MDS, led by Mečiar, emerged clearly as the dominant political force in Slovakia. With about 34% of the total Slovak votes cast, the party obtained 57 seats (the second largest representation) in the 300-member Federal Assembly. The leading party in the Slovak Government, the CDM (which advocated a continued federation), won only 9% of the Slovak votes cast, securing 14 seats in the Federal Assembly, one seat less than the separatist SNP. As had been expected, Václav Klaus's party, the CDP (in coalition with the Chr.DP), won the largest proportion (about 34%) of the total votes cast in the Czech Lands. The CDP was one of only two parties to contest the election in both republics, and in Slovakia it received 4% of the votes cast. In total, the CDP won 85 seats in the Federal Assembly, thus becoming the largest party in the legislature. Two other splinter groups of the former Civic Forum—Dienstbier's CM and the Civic Democratic Alliance (CDA)—failed to win representation in the Federal Assembly, as did the Civic Democratic Union (formerly PAV), in Slovakia. The successor organizations to the communist parties of the two republics achieved considerable success: the Left Bloc (which included the Communist Party of Bohemia and Moravia, CPBM) won a total of 34 seats in the Federal Assembly, while the Slovak-based Party of the Democratic Left secured 23 seats. The representation of parties in the new republican legislatures did not differ greatly from that of the Federal Assembly, although the CDA and the MAD–SMS succeeded in winning seats in the Czech National Council.

Negotiations on the formation of a new federal government were initiated forthwith by the CDP and the MDS, but only served to emphasize the two leading parties' fundamental divergence of opinion on the future of the CzSFR. Nevertheless, a transitional Federal Government, dominated by members of the CDP and the MDS, was appointed in early July 1992. The new Prime Minister was Jan Stráský of the CDP, who had served as a Deputy Prime Minister in the outgoing Czech Government. There was increasing recognition by Czech politicians that the constitutional talks on the future of Czechoslovakia were no longer viable and that a complete separation was preferable to the compromise measures that most Slovak parties favoured. The principal task of the new Federal Government, it was acknowledged, was to supervise the eventual dissolution of the CzSFR. Meanwhile, in late June, the new Slovak Government was announced, with Mečiar as Prime Minister. All but one of the ministers were members of the MDS. A new coalition Czech Government, dominated by the CDP and with Klaus as Prime Minister, was appointed in early July. In three rounds of presidential elections, held in the same month, the Federal Assembly failed to elect any of the candidates. Havel's re-election as President had effectively been blocked by the MDS and the SNP, and in mid-July he resigned from the post. Further rounds of voting in August and October were abandoned, since no candidates presented themselves.

The events of June and July 1992 had ensured that the emergence of two independent states was now inevitable. On 17 July the Slovak National Council overwhelmingly approved a (symbolic) declaration of Slovak sovereignty, and in the following week the Czech and Slovak Prime Ministers agreed, in principle, to the dissolution of the CzSFR. In the following months extensive negotiations were conducted to determine the modalities of the division, which was to take effect from 1 January 1993. International observers expressed surprise not only that the dissolution of Czechoslovakia should be effected in so short a time, but also that the majority of Czechs and Slovaks (more than 60%, according to the results of public opinion polls) were still opposed to the country's division. Moreover, it appeared that Slovak leaders were less intent to leave the federation. Indeed, the Federal Assembly's failure, in early October 1992 and again in mid-November, to adopt legislation permitting the dissolution of the CzSFR was the result of opposition by (mainly) MDS deputies. However, the two republican Prime Ministers, supported by their respective governments, stressed that the process of partition was now irreversible. In late October the Czech and Slovak Governments ratified a number of accords, including a customs union treaty to abolish trade restrictions between the two republics following their independence. Finally, on 25 November the Federal Assembly adopted legislation providing for the constitutional disbanding of the federation, having secured the necessary three-fifths' majority by a margin of only three votes. Accordingly, the Federal Government accelerated the process of dividing the country's assets and liabilities as well as its armed forces. In most cases federal property was divided territorially (according to its location in either of the republics). It was agreed, however, that the two states would continue to share some federal infrastructure and would retain a single currency for the immediate future, although respective central banks were established. (Two separate currencies, the Czech and the Slovak koruna, were introduced in February 1993.)

On 17 December 1992 a treaty pledging cordial relations and co-operation was signed, followed by the establishment of diplomatic relations between the two republics. At midnight on 31 December all federal structures were dissolved and the Czech Republic and the Slovak Republic came into being. The dissolution of the CzSFR had thus been effected in an entirely peaceful fashion. As legal successors to Czechoslovakia, the two republics were quickly recognized by the states that had maintained diplomatic relations with the CzSFR, as well as by those international bodies of which the CzSFR had been a member. Existing treaties and agreements, to which the CzSFR had been a party, were to be honoured by both republics.

In anticipation of the establishment of the Czech Republic as an independent state, the existing legislature was replaced by a bicameral body, in accordance with the Czech Constitution (adopted in mid-December 1992); the Czech National Council was transformed into a Chamber of Deputies (lower house), which retained the Council's 200 members, and an upper house, or Senate, was to be elected at a later date. In late January 1993 the Chamber of Deputies elected Václav Havel to be the Czech Republic's first President. The composition of the Government remained largely unchanged. It included among its principal objectives the pursuance of the former Federal Government's economic reforms, including its programme of large-scale privatization.

Relations between the Czech Republic and Slovakia were troubled in early 1993 by disagreements over former Czechoslovak assets and property that still remained to be divided. In late 1993 the Czech Government was divided over the issue of the restitution of property that had been expropriated from Czech Jews during the period of Nazi occupation (1938–45). There were fears that any such restitution would lead to claims for compensation by those surviving Sudeten Germans who were expelled from Czechoslovakia in 1945 (see below). Nevertheless, in April 1994 the Chamber of Deputies adopted legislation permitting the restitution of Jewish property. At local elections in November, the CDP was confirmed as the party with the broadest support (receiving some 31% of the total votes cast), followed by the CPBM (with 13%); voter participation was about 60%. Renewed controversy emerged in 1995 over the so-called 'lustration', or screening, law, which had been adopted by the Czechoslovak Federal Assembly in October 1991. The law effectively banned former communist functionaries as well as members of the former state security service and the People's Militia (the CPCz's paramilitary force) from holding senior political, economic and judicial posts. In September 1995 the Chamber of Deputies voted to extend until 2000 the legislation on screening (which had been due to expire in late 1996). In the following month President Havel rejected the decision, but the Chamber

approved it for a second time, and the extension of the law entered into force.

The first general election since the dissolution of the CzSFR took place on 31 May and 1 June 1996. The CDP (which had merged with the Chr.DP in April) won 68 of the 200 seats in the Chamber of Deputies (with 29.6% of the total votes cast), while the Czech Social Democratic Party (CSDP), which had become a major force of the centre-left under the leadership of Miloš Zeman, almost quadrupled its parliamentary representation, winning 61 seats (26.4%). As a result, the coalition of the CDP, the Christian Democratic Union—Czechoslovak People's Party (CDU—CPP, which obtained 18 seats) and the CDA (13 seats) lost its overall majority, achieving a total of 99 seats. The CPBM and the Association for the Republic—Republican Party of Czechoslovakia were the only other parties to exceed the 5% minimum required for representation in the legislature, securing 22 seats and 18 seats, respectively. Despite losing its parliamentary majority, the governing coalition remained intact. The CSDP ruled out the possibility of joining the coalition, but agreed to give tacit support on most issues to a minority government. In early July Václav Klaus formed a new Government; in a major concession to the CSDP, Miloš Zeman was appointed Chairman of the Chamber of Deputies. The Government survived a vote of confidence in late July, despite CSDP opposition to government proposals to return some 175,000 ha of land, appropriated by the communists, to the Roman Catholic Church, without seeking the approval of the legislature. Voter participation in the elections to the 81-seat Senate, which took place in mid-November 1996, was low (35%), but the ruling coalition obtained a majority of the votes, winning 52 seats. The CSDP received 25 seats, and the CPBM two, while the remaining two seats were secured by the Democratic Union (DU) and an independent candidate.

In August 1997 the Government was forced to address the problems of the Romany population (unofficially estimated at some 300,000), as hundreds of Romanies, claiming to have suffered persecution in the Czech Republic, attempted to gain political asylum in Canada (which subsequently reimposed visa requirements for Czech visitors) and the United Kingdom. The Government established an interministerial commission for Romany community affairs in October and outlined further measures aimed at improving the situation of Romanies in the Czech Republic. In early 1998 the Government formed a second commission, headed by Romanies, to address issues affecting the Romany population, and a 40-year law restricting their nomadic way of life was revoked. None the less, large number of Romanies continued to seek political asylum abroad.

Meanwhile, three government ministers tendered their resignations in May 1997, as a result of economic problems and increasing divisions within the ruling coalition. Tension within the CDP and between the government coalition parties intensified in October. Josef Zieleniec resigned from his position as Minister of Foreign Relations and as Deputy Chairman of the CDP, citing a lack of consultation on important party decisions as the reason for his departure. In early November a large demonstration of trade union members was staged in Prague, in protest against the Government's social welfare and economic policies. At the end of that month allegations of impropriety in the funding of the CDP led to the resignation of the Klaus administration (which, nevertheless, denied the accusations), following the withdrawal of the CDU—CPP and the CDA from the coalition. In December Josef Lux, the Chairman of the CDU—CPP, was invited to lead talks on the formation of a new government. Klaus was re-elected Chairman of the CDP at the party's national conference later that month, defeating Jan Ruml, who subsequently formed a new faction within the party. Josef Tošovský, hitherto Governor of the Czech National Bank, was designated Prime Minister in December, and a new, interim Government, comprising seven non-political ministers, four CDP members, three CDU—CPP members and three CDA members, was appointed in January 1998. The CDP was divided over its participation in the new administration, and the party's four ministers subsequently defected to the Freedom Union (FU), a newly established breakaway party, which had 31 seats in the Chamber of Deputies by mid-February.

On 20 January 1998 Havel was narrowly re-elected to the presidency for a second five-year term. At the end of that month the Government won a vote of confidence when its policy statement was adopted in the Chamber of Deputies. In February Jiří Skalický resigned from the posts of Deputy Prime Minister and Minister of the Environment, and from the chairmanship of the

CDA, after admitting that, prior to the 1996 elections (when the CDA controlled the ministries responsible for privatization and industry), the party had received donations from a number of companies. Two further ministers subsequently resigned from the party, although they retained their positions in the Government. In April 1998 the Czech Republic's proposed membership of NATO was formally approved by the legislature, after the CSDP withdrew its demand for a referendum on the issue.

Early elections to the Chamber of Deputies were held on 19–20 June 1998. The CSDP retained its position (held since the defection of the CDP deputies to the FU earlier in the year) as the largest party in the Chamber of Deputies, winning 74 seats (with 32.3% of the votes cast), while the CDP secured 63 seats (with 27.7%). The remaining seats were divided between the CPBM (with 24 seats), the CDU—CPP (20 seats) and the FU (19 seats). The rate of voter participation was 74%. As leader of the CSDP, Zeman was given the task of attempting to form a government, but the parliamentary parties failed to reach agreement on a coalition grouping. In July Zeman and Klaus signed an agreement whereby the CDP pledged not to initiate or support a motion expressing 'no confidence' in a minority CSDP government, in exchange for a number of senior parliamentary posts, including the chairmanship of the Chamber of Deputies (to which Klaus was later elected), and a commitment to early constitutional reform. On 17 July Zeman was formally appointed Prime Minister, and a new Council of Ministers was subsequently formed.

Elections to renew one-third of the seats in the Senate were held in two rounds in November 1998. The CSDP performed poorly, winning only three of the 27 seats contested, while the CDP secured nine seats, and a four-party informal alliance, comprising the CDU—CPP, the CDA, the DU and the FU, won 13 seats. The CPBM doubled its representation to four seats. Voter participation was very low, reaching only 20.4% in the second round. In local elections, also held in November, independent candidates, followed by the CDU—CPP, obtained the largest number of seats on municipal councils, owing to strong support in smaller, rural communities. In terms of votes, however, the CDP received the greatest endorsement, with 24.3% of the total votes cast, although the party secured only 9.2% of seats, mainly in urban areas. The CSDP won 17.5% of the total votes (6.8% of seats). Observers largely attributed the CSDP's poor performance to its agreement with the CDP, which was deemed to be unpopular with the electorate.

In May 1999 a decision by the Council of Ministers to complete the construction of the controversial Temelín nuclear power plant in southern Bohemia, despite a resolution by the European Parliament opposing its completion, provoked international concern and strong criticism from President Havel and environmental groups. In June the Chamber of Deputies rejected a government proposal for constitutional amendments that would have enabled the Council of Ministers to issue decrees with the effect of law, but without the approval of the legislature. As anticipated, the CSDP Government had encountered difficulties in enacting new legislation, owing to its minority status. In July Ivo Svoboda was dismissed from the post of Minister of Finance, after it was announced that he was to be prosecuted for misconduct towards creditors of a bankrupt company of which he had been on the management board. In September the Council of Ministers approved a number of proposals for constitutional change that had been drafted by a joint CSDP-CDP commission. The amendments aimed to restrict presidential powers, including the right to appoint the Prime Minister and the heads of principal state institutions, and the right to grant amnesty. (The Chamber of Deputies approved the changes in January 2000, despite an opposition boycott of the vote.)

On 17 November 1999 celebrations commemorating the 10th anniversary of the 'velvet revolution' coincided with a protest against the current political system, organized by a group of former student leaders who had participated in the events of November 1989. Their appeal had been signed by some 150,000 supporters by early December 1999, when a large rally was staged in Prague. Jan Ruml subsequently resigned from the chairmanship of the FU, declaring that he considered himself responsible for the political situation. Meanwhile, Egon Lánský resigned from the post of Deputy Prime Minister for European Integration in December, citing ill health, although opposition parties had been demanding his resignation for several months, principally owing to dissatisfaction with preparations for entry to the European Union (EU, see p. 199). The Minister of Foreign

Affairs, Jan Kavan, was subsequently elevated to the position of Deputy Prime Minister. In late January 2000 the CSDP and the CDP extended their agreement on bilateral co-operation; the CSDP pledged to reorganize the Council of Ministers and to propose electoral reform measures, in return for the CDP's continued acceptance of the CSDP minority Government.

In accordance with the co-operation agreement between the CDP and the CSDP, the Council of Ministers was reorganized in March–April 2000 and four ministers were replaced. In early August, following the country's admission to NATO (see below), the Senate adopted a constitutional amendment permitting the Government to deploy peace-keeping forces abroad and to authorize the deployment of foreign troops on Czech territory without the prior approval of the legislature. At elections to one-third of seats in the Senate in November 2000, the alliance of the CDU—CPP, the CDA, the DU and the FU secured 16 seats, thereby increasing its overall representation to 39 seats (although narrowly failing to obtain a majority in the chamber). The CDP won eight seats, reducing its total number of seats held to 22, and the CSDP won only one seat, reducing its representation to 15.

In December 2000 employees of the state-owned Czech Television service began strike action, in protest at the appointment of the new Director-General, Jiří Hodac, who, it was feared, might influence editorial independence, owing to his affiliation to the CDP. Mass protests were staged in Prague in support of the striking journalists, who occupied part of the station's headquarters and initiated rival news broadcasts. At the end of the month the dismissal of 20 of the station's employees further increased tension. The dispute also prompted dissension between Havel, who expressed support for the protesters, and Zeman, who condemned their action. At the beginning of 2001 a mass demonstration (the largest since the fall of communism) was staged in support of the striking employees. Although the Council of Czech Television refused to comply with a ruling by the Chamber of Deputies that Hodac be removed from his post, he resigned in early January on the grounds of ill health. The Chamber of Deputies voted to dissolve the nine-member Council and approved a legislative amendment whereby the Council would, henceforth, comprise 15 members, selected by the Chamber from nominees of civic and professional organizations (rather than political parties). In early February the Chamber of Deputies elected a new (initially acting) Director-General of the state television company. The protesting television-station employees subsequently agreed to end their strike action and co-operate with a new Council.

In early April 2001 Vladimír Špidla, the Deputy Prime Minister and Minister of Labour and Social Affairs, was elected unopposed to the chairmanship of the CSDP; Zeman had agreed to relinquish the party leadership (although he was to remain Prime Minister pending legislative elections, scheduled to take place in June 2002). In the same month the Deputy Prime Minister for Economic Policies and Minister of Finance, Pavel Mertlik, tendered his resignation, citing criticism by other ministers of a number of financial measures, including the rapid privatization of state-owned enterprises. He was replaced by Jiří Rusnok, hitherto Deputy Minister of Employment and Social Affairs. In early May the Minister of Defence, Vladimír Vetchý, was dismissed by Zeman, owing to incompetence within the ministry; he was replaced by a senior military official, Jaroslav Tvrdik.

In November 2001 Lubomír Štrougal, the Prime Minister in 1970–88, was charged with having prevented investigations into secret police activities as Minister of the Interior in 1965; however, he was acquitted in February 2002, owing to lack of evidence. In early December 2001 the trial of another former Minister of the Interior, Jaromir Obzina, who was charged with organizing a campaign in the 1970s to force political dissidents to leave the country, commenced in Prague. Proceedings against Obzina were adjourned indefinitely in mid-2002, owing to serious illness, and he died in January 2003. In May 2002 a former Minister of Finance, Ivo Svoboda, was charged with having embezzled funds during his term in office. (His trial was under way in early 2003.)

Meanwhile, in late 2001 the FU and DU merged to form a single organization. In February 2002 it was announced that the electoral alliance of the CDU—CPP, CDA, and FU—DU had been dissolved, owing to inter-party disagreement; however, the CDU—CPP and FU—DU subsequently formed a further grouping, known as the Coalition. At elections to the Chamber of Deputies on 14–15 June, the CSDP was the most successful party (with 30.2% of the votes cast); a low rate of voter partic-ipation appeared to confirm suggestions of widespread popular disenchantment with the political establishment. President Havel invited Špidla to commence negotiations to form a govern-ment, and on 9 July a formal agreement establishing the terms of the new coalition administration was signed by the leaders of the CSDP and the Coalition. In mid-July a 17-member coalition Government, headed by Špidla and dominated by the CSDP, was officially appointed by Havel. In early August the new administration was approved by a narrow majority of 101 votes in the Chamber of Deputies. (The three main parties shared the aim for the Czech Republic to join the EU, although divisions remained over economic and social welfare issues.)

In August 2002 a state of emergency was declared in Prague and several other regions in the Czech Republic, following severe flooding (which affected much of central Europe). About 17 people were killed in the floods, and some 220,000 residents were evacuated from Prague, where extensive damage was caused in the historic centre of the capital. In mid-September Špidla threatened to expel the FU—DU from the ruling coali-tion, after legislation providing for tax increases to support the cost of reconstruction was rejected in the legislature (owing to the opposition of a prominent FU—DU member). Later that month, however, a further government coalition agreement was signed, and the emergency legislation was approved in the legislature. Also in September a former Prime Minister, Jozef Lenárt, and former leader of the CPCz, Miloš Jakeš, were acquitted of charges of collaborating with the Warsaw Pact troops that invaded Czechoslovakia in August 1968. Scheduled elections to 27 of the 81 seats in the Senate took place on 25–26 October and 1–2 November: the representation of the govern-ment coalition parties in the chamber was reduced to 34 seats, while that of the CDP increased from 22 to 26 seats. Local elections also took place on 1–2 November, in which the CDP won the largest proportion of the votes cast (25.2%).

Prior to the expiry of Havel's second term on 2 February 2003, voting took place in both legislative chambers to select a suc-cessor to the presidency. Following three inconclusive rounds in mid-January, later that month Klaus (who had relinquished the chairmanship of the CDP), contested further ballots against Zeman and Jaroslava Moserovo of the CDA, in which no candi-date received majority support. Klaus was finally elected Pres-ident on 28 February, defeating the candidate of the ruling coalition, Jan Sokol, with 142 of the 281 votes cast in both chambers. Klaus was inaugurated on 7 March. Four days later the Government survived a vote of 'no confidence' in the Chamber of Deputies (which had been requested by the Prime Minister); Špidla subsequently made efforts to assert his Gov-ernment's tenuous command in the legislature, and in March replaced the Minister for Industry and Trade (who had sup-ported Klaus). Later that month he survived a parliamentary motion of confidence, securing the support of all 101 deputies.

An important focus of the Czech Republic's foreign policy is to maintain close relations with Slovakia and other neighbouring Eastern European states. It is a member, with Slovakia, Hun-gary and Poland, of the Visegrad Group (established, following the collapse of communist rule, to promote economic, defence and other co-operation in the region). The Governments of the Czech Republic, Hungary and Poland agreed to co-ordinate preparations for accession to NATO and the EU (see below). Relations with Slovakia have been strained, mainly because of disagreements over the division of former federal property. In mid-September 1998, however, following talks between Miloš Zeman and Vladimír Mečiar, the Slovak Prime Minister, it was announced that a joint Czech-Slovak committee would meet in an attempt to further discussions on unresolved issues. The success of opposition parties in Slovak elections held at the end of that month, and the subsequent change of government, led to a further improvement in bilateral relations. Measures pro-viding for dual Czech-Slovak citizenship became fully effective in October 1999, and in November an agreement on the division of former federal property was signed in Bratislava by Zeman and Mikuláš Dzurinda, the Slovak Prime Minister. The agree-ment provided for the exchange of shares between the Czech Republic's Komerční banka and Slovakia's Všeobecná úverová banka and the restitution of gold reserves to Slovakia. The gold had been held by the Czech Central Bank as collateral for debts owed by Slovakia to the Czech Republic. These debts, totalling some 26,000m. koruny, had proved to be a major obstacle during negotiations, as they had never been recognized by Slovakia. The Czech Government consequently opted effectively to relieve Slovakia of its debts by buying the Central Bank's claim for a symbolic one koruna, despite the opposition of several Czech politicians. In May 2000 Zeman and Dzurinda signed an agree-ment that resolved remaining problems associated with the division of jointly held assets.

Since the end of the Second World War Czech-German rela-tions have been dominated by two issues: the question of com-pensation for Czech victims of Nazism, and demands for the restitution of property to the Sudeten Germans who were driven from Czechoslovakia in 1945–46. From 1993 negotiations were held to formulate a declaration on bilateral relations, but pro-gress was hampered by these unresolved issues. However, a joint declaration was finally signed by both Ministers of Foreign Affairs on 20 December 1996, and by Václav Klaus of the Czech Republic and Federal Chancellor Helmut Kohl of Germany on 21 January 1997. In the declaration, Germany admitted that it was to blame for the Nazi occupation and the partition of Czechoslo-vakia in 1939, while the Czech Republic apologized for the abuses of human rights that were committed during the depor-tation of ethnic Germans. The declaration did not, however, condemn the expulsion of the Sudeten Germans as a crime, which would have meant that those people expelled could have made claims for compensation. A Czech-German fund was established in January 1998 to finance joint projects, in partic-ular benefiting victims of the Nazis. Relations were strained somewhat in February and August, however, when the nomi-nation of Sudeten Germans to a Czech-German advisory council was rejected by Miloš Zeman, who claimed that the nominees had opposed the January 1997 declaration that had provided for the establishment of the council. In January 2002 a comment by Zeman, which described the German-speakers expelled from the Sudetenland as supporters of the Nazi regime, provoked strong protests from both Sudeten Germans and the German Govern-ment. The ensuing strain in relations between the two countries resulted in the postponement of a visit to Prague (originally scheduled for March) by the German Chancellor, Gerhard Schröder. In February Zeman and his Slovakian counterpart, Mikuláš Dzurinda, announced that they would not be attending a summit meeting of the Visegrad countries, scheduled to take place on 1 March, following a demand by the Hungarian Prime Minister, Viktor Orbán, for the abolition of the Beneš Decrees, which had provided for the expulsion of Germans from the Sudetenland. In April the Chamber of Deputies unanimously approved a resolution stipulating the inviolability of the Beneš Decrees.

The issue of the nuclear power installation at Temelín, in southern Bohemia, has continually impeded good relations between the Czech Republic and Austria. In September 2000 Austrian environmental protesters blockaded crossings at the Austrian–Czech border, following a decision by the Czech authorities that the power station was to commence operations; the demonstrations continued until mid-October. Despite pres-sure from the Austrian Government, which suspended imports of Czech electricity, the nuclear power plant commenced pro-duction in early October, after receiving authorization from the state nuclear safety office. In early November border protests were temporarily resumed, after discussions between Zeman and the Federal Chancellor of Austria, Wolfgang Schüssel, failed to resolve the ongoing dispute. In December, following further negotiations, the Czech Republic and Austria signed an agreement, whereby the plant was not to operate at commercial capacity until its safety and its environmental impact had been fully evaluated, under the supervision of the European Com-mission.

In August 2001 the European Commission issued a con-troversial report on the Temelín nuclear power installation. The Czech authorities maintained that the report demonstrated the safety of the plant and immediately commenced its reconnection with the national power network. However, Austrian anti-nu-clear movements announced that they were to submit a legal challenge to the resumption of operations at the plant, which was also strongly criticized by the Austrian authorities. In addition, the German Government expressed concern over safety at the nuclear installation; it was agreed that the Euro-pean commissioner responsible for the enlargement process was to mediate between the Governments of the Czech Republic, Austria and Germany over the issue. Later that year Schüssel threatened to veto the Czech Republic's accession to the EU unless the matter was satisfactorily resolved, on the grounds that the installation had failed to meet minimum safety require-ments. However, further safety issues were agreed, and in April

2003 the Temelín installation commenced production at full capacity for an 18-month trial period, prior to entering into commercial operations by the end of 2004.

In August 1993 the Czech Republic and Russia signed a treaty of friendship and co-operation (replacing the Russian-Czechoslovak treaty of 1992). In March 1994, despite Russia's apparent opposition, the Czech Republic joined NATO's 'Partnership for Peace' programme of military co-operation. In 1996 the Chamber of Deputies approved legislation prohibiting the storage of nuclear weapons on Czech territory, except where international treaties are concerned, thereby allowing for full membership of NATO. In July 1997 the Czech Republic, together with Hungary and Poland, was invited to commence membership negotiations. A protocol providing for the accession of the three states to NATO was signed in December and was subsequently ratified by the legislatures of member states. In March 1999 the Czech Republic, Hungary and Poland became full members of NATO. Associate membership of Western European Union (see p. 318) was subsequently granted. The Czech Republic is a member of the Council of Europe (see p. 181) and the Organization for Security and Co-operation in Europe (OSCE, see p. 283).

The Czech Republic was one of a number of Central and Eastern European states invited to commence negotiations in March 1998 on possible entry to the EU. In November more substantive talks commenced regarding the compliance of potential EU entrants with membership regulations. Earlier that month, however, the European Commission had criticized the slow pace of legislative reform in the Czech Republic. In October 1999 the Commission was again critical of the Czech Republic's lack of progress in adopting necessary EU legislation and expressed concern regarding the situation of the country's Romany minority. At an historic summit meeting in Copenhagen in December 2002, the Czech Republic was one of 10 nations that were formally invited to join the EU in May 2004. A plebiscite on EU membership was expected to be held in the Czech Republic in June 2003. However, continuing disagreement over the nuclear power installation at Temelín, the issue of the Beneš Decrees and alleged corruption and discrimination against the Romany minority remained potential impediments to accession.

Government

Legislative power is held by two chambers, the 200-member Chamber of Deputies (lower house) and the 81-member Senate. Members of the Chamber of Deputies and the Senate are elected for four and six years, respectively, by universal adult suffrage. The President of the Republic (Head of State) is elected for a term of five years by a joint session of the legislature. The President, who is also Commander of the Armed Forces, may be re-elected for a second consecutive term. He appoints the Prime Minister and, on the latter's recommendation, the other members of the Council of Ministers (the highest organ of executive power). For administrative purposes, the Czech Republic was divided into 72 districts; however, these were scheduled to be replaced by 14 self-governing units (regions) by the end of 2002.

Defence

In August 2002 total armed forces numbered 49,450 (including 25,000 conscripts): an army of 36,370 and an air force of 11,300; there were also some 1,780 troops attached to the Ministry of Defence and centrally-controlled formations. In addition, there were 5,600 border guards and 1,600 internal security forces. Military service is compulsory and lasts for 12 months. Of total consolidated expenditure by the central Government in 2001, 37,200m. koruny (1.7%) was allocated to defence. In March 1994 the Czech Republic joined NATO's (see p. 271) 'Partnership for Peace' programme of military co-operation, and in March 1999 it was formally admitted to NATO.

Economic Affairs

In 2001, according to estimates by the World Bank, the Czech Republic's gross national income (GNI), measured at average 1999–2001 prices, was US $54,108m., equivalent to $5,270 per head (or $14,550 per head on an international purchasing-power parity basis). During 1990–2001, it was estimated, the population decreased at an annual average rate of 0.1%, while gross domestic product (GDP) per head increased, in real terms, by an average of 0.4% per year. Overall GDP increased, in real terms, at an average annual rate of 0.3% in 1990–2001; annual growth was 3.3% in both 2000 and 2001.

Agriculture (including hunting, forestry and fishing) contributed 4.2% of GDP and engaged 4.2% of the employed labour force in 2001. The principal crops are wheat, sugar beet, barley, potatoes and hops (the Czech Republic is a major beer producer and exporter). According to estimates by the World Bank, the GDP of the agricultural sector increased at an average annual rate of 4.6% in 1990–2000. Agricultural GDP declined by 5.3% in 2001, according to IMF estimates.

Industry (including manufacturing, mining, construction and power) contributed 40.0% of GDP and engaged 39.7% of the employed labour force in 2001. According to estimates by the World Bank, the GDP of the industrial sector declined at an average annual rate of 2.7% in 1990–2000. According to IMF estimates, industrial GDP increased by 1.5% in 2001.

The principal minerals extracted are coal and lignite. In 2001 the mining sector engaged 1.3% of the employed labour force. According to the IMF, production of mining and quarrying increased by 1.4% in 1996, but declined by 2.9% in 1997, by 5.3% in 1998 and by 12.1% in 1999; however, growth in the sector was 9.2% in 2000, slowing to 1.9% in 2001.

The manufacturing sector engaged an estimated 29.2% of the employed labour force in 2001. Based on the value of output, the most important branches of manufacturing in 1996 were food products and beverages (accounting for 16.3% of the total), basic metals (12.7%), non-electric machinery and domestic appliances (9.0%), and metal products (7.6%). According to the IMF, manufacturing production increased by 3.0% in 1998, but declined by 2.6% in 1999; however, manufacturing output was estimated to have increased by 5.0% in 2000 and by 7.8% in 2001.

In 1999 coal provided 69.9% of total electricity production and nuclear power 20.8%. Imports of mineral fuels comprised 9.1% of the value of total imports in 2001.

The services sector contributed 55.8% of GDP and engaged 56.1% of the employed labour force in 2001. Tourism is an important source of revenue, providing receipts of US $2,982.0m. in 2000; tourist arrivals totalled some 5.2m. in 2001. According to the World Bank, the GDP of the services sector increased at an average annual rate of 2.0% in 1990–2000. Real GDP in the services sector increased by 2.8% in 2000 and by 6.4% in 2001.

In 2001 the Czech Republic recorded a visible trade deficit of US $3,078m., and there was a deficit of $2,624m. on the current account of the balance of payments. In 2001 the principal source of imports (32.9%) was Germany; other major sources were Russia, Slovakia and Italy. Germany was also the principal market for exports (38.2%) in that year; other important purchasers were Slovakia, Austria, the United Kingdom and Poland. The principal exports in 2001 were machinery and transport equipment, basic manufactures and miscellaneous manufactured articles. The principal imports in that year were machinery and transport equipment, basic manufactures, chemicals and related products, and miscellaneous manufactured articles.

In 2002 there was an estimated budgetary deficit of 45,600m. koruny. The Czech Republic's total external debt was US $21,299m. at the end of 2000, of which $8,132m. was long-term public debt. In that year the cost of debt-servicing was equivalent to 12.7% of the value of exports of goods and services. The annual rate of inflation averaged 12.5% in 1990–2001; consumer prices increased by 4.7% in 2001 and by 1.8% in 2002. In 2002 the rate of unemployment was estimated at 8.5%.

The Czech Republic is a member of the IMF and the World Bank and an associate member of the EU. In December 2002 it was formally invited to accede to the EU in May 2004. The Czech Republic is also a member of the European Bank for Reconstruction and Development (EBRD, see p. 193), and in late 1995 became the first post-communist state in Eastern Europe to be admitted to the Organisation for Economic Co-operation and Development (OECD, see p. 277).

Of all the post-communist states of Eastern Europe, for much of the 1990s the Czech Republic was considered to have undertaken the transition to a market economic system with greatest success. The country's programme of rapid privatization, price and currency stabilization and the establishment of a new banking system was highly successful during 1992–95, and attracted widespread foreign investment. In 1996, however, economic growth decelerated and the first budgetary deficit since the transition to a market economy was recorded. Several banks were subsequently forced to cease operations, and investor confidence was weakened by cases of embezzlement of investment funds. The imposition of tighter monetary policies in

1997 contributed to a worsening of the recession, however. In early 1999 the economy finally began to recover, following the Government's relaxation of monetary policies in late 1998 and significant progress in the restructuring of banks and state enterprises. The country subsequently benefited from strong export performance, and from a dramatic increase in foreign direct investment. After three years of decline, growth in GDP was recorded in 2000 and 2001. The Government continued to achieve considerable progress in privatization; however, the restructuring process resulted in a rapidly increasing overall fiscal deficit, and also contributed to a significant rise in the rate of unemployment. Following severe flooding in August 2002, the EU pledged considerable funds towards reconstruction. In September legislation providing for higher taxation was adopted and planned expenditure projects were abandoned, in order to finance reconstruction efforts. The total cost of funding damage reparation was estimated at US $3,600m.; moreover, the flooding adversely affected tourism in that year, and was likely to cause long-term damage to private industry. Consequently, the Government's plans for monetary restraint were thwarted, and the fiscal situation deteriorated in 2002, with a sharp increase in the projected budgetary deficit. It was announced that this position was likely to delay the Government's adoption of the common European currency, the euro, until at least 2007, owing to the EU's requirement that the public-finance deficit be restrained to below 3% of GDP. Planned government expenditure on restructuring was expected to increase the fiscal deficit further in 2003, prior to the adoption of a programme of spending reductions and tax increases.

Education

Pre-school education is available for children aged from three to six years. Education is officially compulsory for children aged from six to 15 years, who attend basic school, covering both primary (grades 1–5) and lower secondary (grades 6–9) levels. In 1999/2000 90.4% of children in the relevant age-group were enrolled in primary schools (boys 90.4%; girls 90.4%). Education continues at upper secondary schools, of which there are three types: gymnasia (providing general education and preparing students mainly for university entry), secondary vocational schools and secondary technical schools. Students follow three- to four-year courses. In 1999/2000 84.3% of children in the appropriate age-group attended secondary schools (83.9% of boys; 84.8% of girls). Tertiary education comprises higher professional schools, which offer three-year courses, and universities, at which most courses last from five to six years. Since 1990 many private schools, particularly at upper secondary level, have been established. In 2001/02 some 200,450 students attended 24 universities. Of total consolidated expenditure by the central Government in 2001/02, 92,300m. koruny (4.3%) was allocated to education.

Public Holidays

2003: 1 January (New Year's Day), 21 April (Easter Monday), 1 May (Labour Day), 8 May (Liberation Day), 5 July (Day of the Apostles St Cyril and St Methodius), 6 July (Anniversary of the Martyrdom of Jan Hus), 28 September (Czech Statehood Day), 28 October (Independence Day), 17 November (Freedom and Democracy Day), 24–25 December (Christmas), 26 December (St Stephen's Day).

2004: 1 January (New Year's Day), 12 April (Easter Monday), 1 May (Labour Day), 8 May (Liberation Day), 5 July (Day of the Apostles St Cyril and St Methodius), 6 July (Anniversary of the Martyrdom of Jan Hus), 28 September (Czech Statehood Day), 28 October (Independence Day), 17 November (Freedom and Democracy Day), 24–25 December (Christmas), 26 December (St Stephen's Day).

Weights and Measures

The metric system is in force.

Statistical Survey

Source: mainly Czech Statistical Office, Sokolovská 142, 186 04 Prague 8; tel. (2) 66042451; fax (2) 66310429; e-mail bondyova@gw.czso.cz; internet www .czso.cz.

Area and Population

AREA, POPULATION AND DENSITY

Area (sq km)	78,866*
Population (census results)	
3 March 1991.	10,302,215
1 March 2001	
Males	5,019,381
Females.	5,273,552
Total	10,292,933
Population (official estimates at 31 December)	
1999	10,278,098
2000	10,266,546
2001	10,206,436
Density (per sq km) at 31 December 2001	129.4

* 30,450 sq miles.

POPULATION BY NATIONALITY*
(census of 1 March 2001)

	Number	%
Czech (Bohemian)	9,270,615	90.1
Moravian	373,294	3.6
Slovak.	183,749	1.8
Polish	50,971	0.5
German	38,321	0.4
Roma (Gypsy)	11,716	0.1
Silesian	11,248	0.1
Others and unknown	353,019	3.4
Total	**10,292,933**	**100.0**

* Preliminary figures.

REGIONS
(31 December 2001)

	Area (sq km)	Population	Density (per sq km)
Praha (Prague, capital) . .	496	1,160,118	2,339
Středočeský.	11,014	1,123,931	102
Jihočeský	10,056	624,568	62
Plzeňský	7,560	549,600	73
Karlovarský	3,315	303,714	92
Ústecký	5,335	819,450	154
Liberecký	3,163	427,396	135
Královéhradecký	4,757	549,329	115
Pardubický	4,519	507,176	112
Vysočina	6,925	518,315	75
Jihomoravský	7,067	1,124,493	159
Olomoucký	5,139	638,374	124
Zlínský	3,965	594,060	150
Moravskoslezský	5,555	1,265,912	228
Total	**78,866**	**10,206,436**	**129**

PRINCIPAL TOWNS
(population at 31 December 2001)

Praha (Prague capital) . . .	1,160,118	Ústí nad Labem . .	94,871
Brno . . .	373,272	Pardubice. . . .	90,171
Ostrava . . .	315,442	Havířov	85,502
Plzeň (Pilsen). .	164,336	Zlín	80,581
Olomouc . . .	102,246	Kladno	70,702
Liberec . . .	98,380	Most	68,090
České Budějovice (Budweis) . .	96,742	Karviná	64,6531
Hradec Králové .	96,408	Opava	61,771
		Frýdek-Místek . .	61,736

BIRTHS, MARRIAGES AND DEATHS

	Registered live births		Registered marriages		Registered deaths	
	Number	Rate (per 1,000)	Number	Rate (per 1,000)	Number	Rate (per 1,000)
1994	106,579	10.3	58,440	5.7	117,373	11.4
1995	96,097	9.3	54,956	5.3	117,913	11.4
1996	90,446	8.8	53,896	5.2	112,782	10.9
1997	90,657	8.8	57,804	5.6	112,744	10.9
1998	90,535	8.8	55,027	5.3	109,527	10.6
1999	89,471	8.7	53,523	5.2	109,768	10.7
2000	90,910	8.8	55,321	5.4	109,001	10.6
2001	90,715	8.9	52,374	5.1	107,755	10.5

Expectation of life (WHO estimates, years at birth): 75.4 (males 71.9; females 78.8) in 2001 (Source: WHO, *World Health Report*).

ECONOMICALLY ACTIVE POPULATION

(persons aged 15 years and over)

	1999	2000	2001*
Agriculture, hunting, forestry and fishing	234,439	212,498	200,882
Mining and quarrying	64,604	58,687	57,074
Manufacturing	1,390,997	1,377,416	1,393,941
Electricity, gas and water	77,278	73,617	70,257
Construction	402,380	392,032	370,958
Trade, restaurants and hotels	861,420	891,472	901,299
Transport, storage and communications	350,251	344,410	348,458
Finance, insurance, real estate and business activities	489,292	501,982	516,937
Public administration, defence and compulsory social security	178,309	186,771	189,144
Education	300,721	297,558	296,291
Health and social welfare	265,506	264,819	268,255
Other community, social and personal services	145,021	150,195	152,818
Total	**4,760,218**	**4,751,457**	**4,766,314**

* Estimates.

Health and Welfare

KEY INDICATORS

Total fertility rate (children per woman, 2001)	1.2
Under-5 mortality rate (per 1,000 live births, 2001)	5
HIV/AIDS (% of persons aged 15–49, 2001)	<0.10
Physicians (per 1,000 head, 1998)	3.03
Hospital beds (per 1,000 head, 1999)	8.7
Health expenditure (2000): US $ per head (PPP)	1,031
Health expenditure (2000): % of GDP	7.2
Health expenditure (2000): public (% of total)	91.4
Human Development Index (2000): ranking	33
Human Development Index (2000): value	0.849

For sources and definitions, see explanatory note on p. vi.

Agriculture

PRINCIPAL CROPS

('000 metric tons)

	1999	2000	2001
Wheat	4,028	4,084	4,476
Barley	2,137	1,629	1,966
Maize	261	304	409
Rye*	202	150	149
Oats	179	136	136
Potatoes	1,407	1,476	1,131
Sugar beet	2,691	2,809	3,259
Dry peas	105	75	83
Rapeseed	931	844	973
Cabbages	133	134	104
Tomatoes	34	31	25
Cauliflowers	34	29	23
Cucumbers and gherkins	52	41	35
Dry onions	99	76	84
Carrots	79	59	52
Apples	264	339	221
Pears	23	25	16
Peaches	7	11	5
Plums	21	18	23
Grapes	67	67	68
Hops	6	5	7

* Including mixed crops of wheat and rye.

LIVESTOCK

('000 head at 1 March)

	1999	2000	2001
Horses	24	26	27
Cattle	1,574	1,582	1,466
Pigs	3,688	3,594	3,348
Sheep	84	90	97
Goats	32	28	26
Chickens	17,505	18,767	21,785
Ducks	446	451	279
Geese	132	127	28
Turkeys	669	723	887

LIVESTOCK PRODUCTS

('000 metric tons)

	1999	2000	2001
Beef and veal	120.7	107.4	126.1
Pig meat	451.6	416.6	474.8
Poultry meat	200.7	215.0	235.7
Milk	2,834.6	2,805.1	2,797.0
Cheese	138.2	142.3	139.8
Hen eggs	202.9	188.0	183.3

Source: FAO.

Forestry

LOGGING

('000 cubic metres)

	1999	2000	2001
Coniferous (softwood)	12,422	12,851	12,680
Broadleaved (hardwood)	1,781	1,590	1,694
Total	**14,203**	**14,441**	**14,374**

Fishing*

(metric tons)

	1999	2000	2001
Common carp	19,454	20,664	20,981
Others	3,511	3,465	3,763
Total catch	22,965	24,129	24,744

* Figures refer only to fish caught by the Fishing Association (formerly State Fisheries) and members of the Czech and Moravian Fishing Union.

Mining

('000 metric tons)

	1999	2000	2001
Hard coal	14,342	14,855	15,138
Brown coal and lignite	44,790	50,307	50,968
Crude petroleum*	176	n.a.	n.a.
Kaolin	1,049	1,242	1,140

* Source: US Geological Survey.

Industry

SELECTED PRODUCTS

('000 metric tons, unless otherwise indicated)

	1999	2000	2001
Wheat flour and meal	713	803	783
Refined sugar	420	367	482
Wine ('000 hectolitres)	560.8	538.2	605.2
Beer ('000 hectolitres)	17,946	17,796	17,734
Cotton yarn (metric tons)	56,118	58,871	65,124
Woven cotton fabrics ('000 metres)	265,461	226,088	231,917
Woollen fabrics ('000 metres)	17,445	14,297	13,517
Linen fabrics ('000 metres)	18,727	19,780	16,377
Paper and paperboard	184.5	170.4	182.9
Footwear ('000 pairs)	4,645	3,398	2,937
Nitrogenous fertilizers*	220	257	262
Soap	26.9	36.6	37.6
Motor spirit (petrol)	954	1,033	1,104
Gas-diesel (distillate fuel) oil	2,172	2,125	2,250
Residual fuel oils	1,128	911	773
Coke	3,332	3,411	3,522
Cement	4,241	4,093	3,591
Pig-iron†	4,022	4,621	n.a.
Crude steel†	5,613	5,700	n.a.
Trucks (number)	23,113	23,641	4,701
Motorcycles and mopeds (number)	4,814	6,389	10,602
Bicycles (number)	181,988	229,377	236,574
Electric energy (million kWh)	64,692	73,466	74,647

* Production in terms of nitrogen.
† Source: US: Geological Survey.

Finance

CURRENCY AND EXCHANGE RATES

Monetary Units

100 haléřů (singular: halér—heller) = 1 Czech koruna (Czech crown or Kč.; plural: koruny).

Sterling, Dollar and Euro Equivalents (31 December 2002)

£1 sterling =48.58 koruny
US $1 = 30.14 koruny
€1 = 31.61 koruny
1,000 koruny = £20.58 = $33.18 = €31.64.

Average Exchange Rate (koruny per US $)

2000	38.598
2001	38.035
2002	32.739

Note: In February 1993 the Czech Republic introduced its own currency, the Czech koruna, to replace (at par) the Czechoslovak koruna.

BUDGET

('000 million koruny, including local authorities)

Revenue	2000	2001*	2002†
Current revenue	770.3	840.4	880.1
Taxation	721.1	782.0	822.2
Personal income tax	98.3	104.4	117.2
Corporate profits tax	75.8	92.0	81.1
Value-added tax	145.9	150.9	160.5
Excises	70.9	76.3	82.4
Social security contributions	287.4	318.9	338.1
Other tax revenue	29.2	29.5	32.9
Other current revenue	49.2	58.4	57.9
Capital revenue	9.5	9.7	15.4
Total revenue ‡	779.8	850.1	895.5

Expenditure	2000	2001*	2002†
Current expenditure	751.7	843.1	971.4
Goods and services	171.0	175.0	206.7
Wages and salaries	70.3	76.3	73.8
Other goods and services	100.6	98.8	132.9
Interest payments	21.2	21.8	25.1
Subsidies and other current transfers	559.6	646.3	739.6
Subsidies	157.7	209.5	276.5
Transfers	401.8	436.8	463.1
To households and non-profit institutions	399.1	433.6	459.1
Social benefits	270.8	288.8	305.6
Capital expenditure	116.2	120.8	131.3
Acquisition of fixed capital assets	72.8	75.0	74.1
Capital transfers	39.3	41.7	57.2
Total expenditure §	867.9	963.9	1,102.7

* Preliminary figures.
† Projected figures.
‡ Excluding grants received ('000 million koruny): 1.2 in 2000; 2.8 in 2001 (preliminary figure).
§ Excluding lending minus repayments ('000 million koruny): −24.9 in 2000; −58.8 in 2001; −243.3 in 2002.

Source: IMF, Czech Republic: *Selected Issues and Statistical Appendix* (August 2002).

INTERNATIONAL RESERVES

(US $ million at 31 December)

	2000	2001	2002
Gold*	22	23	28
IMF special drawing rights	—	1	5
Reserve position in IMF	3	151	236
Foreign exchange	13,016	14,189	23,315
Total	13,041	14,364	23,584

* National valuation.

Source: IMF, *International Financial Statistics*.

MONEY SUPPLY

('000 million koruny at 31 December)

	2000	2001	2002
Currency outside banks	171.82	180.38	197.81
Demand deposits at deposit money banks	326.53	402.50	626.31
Total money (incl. others)	498.96	583.55	827.04

Source: IMF, *International Financial Statistics*.

COST OF LIVING

(Consumer Price Index; base: 1994 = 100)

	1999	2000	2001
Food, beverages and tobacco	127.5	129.0	133.1
Clothing and footwear	140.8	138.0	135.8
Housing, water, fuel and light	208.2	225.6	247.9
Furnishings, household equipment and maintenance	125.3	126.0	126.3
All items (incl. others)	145.6	151.3	158.4

NATIONAL ACCOUNTS
('000 million koruny at current prices)

Expenditure on the Gross Domestic Product

	1999	2000	2001
Government final consumption expenditure.	373.3	388.3	413.5
Private final consumption expenditure.	1,019.2	1,074.1	1,157.2
Increase in stocks	5.8	27.2	35.2
Gross fixed capital formation	528.3	561.5	610.9
Total domestic expenditure.	1,926.6	2,051.1	2,216.8
Exports of goods and services	1,152.6	1,385.9	1,539.4
Less Imports of goods and services	1,176.9	1,452.2	1,598.6
GDP in purchasers' values	1,902.3	1,984.8	2,157.8
GDP at constant 1995 prices	1,421.0	1,467.3	1,515.1

Source: IMF, *International Financial Statistics*.

Gross Domestic Product by Economic Activity

	1999	2000	2001
Agriculture, hunting, forestry and fishing	73.8	79.1	82.6
Mining and quarrying.			
Manufacturing }	560.3	593.7	652.1
Electricity, gas and water			
Construction	127.1	130.9	141.9
Trade, restaurants and hotels	287.8	303.9	337.4
Transport, storage and communications	141.8	149.5	162.9
Financial services	86.3	83.0	71.5
Business services*	212.7	223.2	239.9
Other services	272.7	277.0	296.9
Sub-total	1,762.5	1,840.3	1,985.2
Less Imputed bank service charge	66.2	69.7	49.5
GDP at basic prices	1,696.3	1,770.6	1,935.7
Taxes on products }	206.0	214.4	222.1
Less Subsidies on products }			
GDP in purchasers' values	1,902.3	1,984.8	2,157.8

* Including real estate, renting and business activities.

Source: IMF, *Czech Republic: Selected Issues and Statistical Appendix* (August 2002).

BALANCE OF PAYMENTS
(US $ million)

	1999	2000	2001
Exports of goods f.o.b.	26,259	29,019	33,404
Imports of goods f.o.b.	−28,161	−32,115	−36,482
Trade balance	−1,902	−3,095	−3,078
Exports of services	7,049	6,840	7,092
Imports of services	−5,850	−5,436	−5,568
Balance on goods and services	−704	−1,692	−1,554
Other income received	1,859	1,952	2,170
Other income paid	−3,209	−3,323	−3,710
Balance on goods, services and income	−2,053	−3,063	−3,094
Current transfers received	1,310	948	959
Current transfers paid	−722	−575	−489
Current balance	−1,466	−2,690	−2,624
Capital account (net)	−2	−5	−9
Direct investment abroad	−90	−43	−95
Direct investment from abroad.	6,313	4,987	4,924
Portfolio investment assets	−1,882	−2,236	125
Portfolio investment liabilities	500	482	798
Financial derivatives assets	—	−129	−254
Financial derivatives liabilities	—	89	168
Other investment assets	−2,688	984	−1,271
Other investment liabilities	928	−300	−337
Net errors and omissions	27	−297	362
Overall balance	1,639	844	1,787

Source: IMF, *International Financial Statistics*.

External Trade

COMMODITY GROUPS
(distribution by SITC, million koruny)

Imports f.o.b.	1999	2000	2001
Food and live animals	45,931	50,199	53,670
Beverages and tobacco	7,858	7,386	7,283
Crude materials (inedible) except fuels	31,047	39,381	40,045
Mineral fuels, lubricants, etc.	65,321	119,936	125,774
Chemicals and related products	119,746	139,101	151,098
Basic manufactures	205,008	257,870	280,317
Machinery and transport equipment	383,286	496,704	585,345
Miscellaneous manufactured articles	112,167	128,288	139,916
Total (incl. others)	973,169	1,241,924	1,386,938

Exports f.o.b.	1999	2000	2001
Food and live animals	26,281	32,998	34,416
Beverages and tobacco	7,833	8,396	8,743
Crude materials (inedible) except fuels	34,292	39,565	38,603
Mineral fuels, lubricants, etc.	26,476	34,245	38,151
Chemicals and related products	66,916	79,597	81,684
Basic manufactures	236,697	285,140	309,141
Machinery and transport equipment	385,390	498,402	601,427
Miscellaneous manufactured articles	122,982	140,486	154,890
Total (incl. others)	908,756	1,121,099	1,269,749

PRINCIPAL TRADING PARTNERS
(million koruny)

Imports f.o.b.	1999	2000	2001
Austria	55,676	61,332	63,302
China, People's Republic	19,527	26,813	40,600
France	47,915	61,643	66,602
Germany	331,889	400,549	456,761
Hungary	15,709	19,895	24,047
Italy	52,624	64,198	72,861
Japan	19,647	23,760	25,674
Netherlands	23,434	29,018	32,819
Poland	35,016	44,332	52,037
Russia	48,146	80,237	75,967
Slovakia	60,893	74,583	74,602
Switzerland	17,517	19,268	21,895
United Kingdom	37,742	51,342	55,401
USA	38,496	54,829	55,199
Total (incl. others)	973,169	1,241,924	1,386,938

Exports f.o.b.	1999	2000	2001
Austria	59,434	66,956	73,077
France	35,550	45,085	54,398
Germany	381,198	453,525	484,438
Hungary	16,246	21,010	23,991
Italy	33,307	42,389	51,552
Netherlands	22,199	25,781	35,394
Poland	50,756	60,902	65,791
Russia	13,186	14,915	18,536
Slovakia	75,329	86,070	101,934
Switzerland	12,348	14,934	17,478
United Kingdom	30,493	48,099	69,360
USA	21,497	31,608	38,017
Total (incl. others)	908,756	1,121,099	1,269,749

Transport

RAILWAYS
(traffic)

	1999	2000	2001
Passenger-km (million)	6,954	7,300	7,299
Freight net ton-km (million)	16,713	17,496	16,882

ROAD TRAFFIC
(motor vehicles in use at 31 December)

	1999	2000	2001
Passenger cars*	3,439,745	3,438,870	3,529,791
Buses and coaches	18,981	18,259	18,384
Commercial vehicles	268,259	275,617	296,412
Special-purpose commercial vehicles	85,726	70,838	67,106
Motorcycles	799,647	748,140	755,482

* Including vans.

INLAND WATERWAYS
(freight carried, '000 metric tons)

	1999	2000	2001
Imports	574	482	420
Exports	721	621	432
Internal	407	635	584
Total (incl. others)	1,877	1,906	1,594

AIR TRANSPORT

	1999	2000	2001
Kilometres flown ('000)	52,743	61,434	63,949
Passengers carried ('000)	2,904	3,484	3,946
Freight carried (metric tons)	17,359	18,950	16,079
Passenger-km ('000)	4,353,602	5,864,666	6,398,920
Freight ton-km ('000)	30,326	37,786	29,209

Tourism

FOREIGN TOURIST ARRIVALS*

Country of origin	1999	2000	2001
Austria	198,717	137,787	163,748
Denmark	160,189	161,593	137,927
France	171,669	151,989	187,118
Germany	1,654,400	1,493,958	1,551,353
Israel	119,753	189,876	n.a.
Italy	320,505	234,905	309,517
Netherlands	285,164	266,094	270,930
Poland	379,417	296,456	369,883
Russia	235,807	102,936	n.a.
Slovakia	242,396	134,095	209,348
Spain	169,277	129,413	156,568
Sweden	100,281	101,792	n.a.
United Kingdom	286,947	246,974	278,818
USA	240,830	224,418	218,139
Total (incl. others)	5,609,700	4,666,305	5,193,973

* Figures refer to visitors staying for at least one night at registered accommodation facilities.

Receipts from tourism (US $ million): 3,718.8 in 1998; 3,034.7 in 1999; 2,982.0 in 2000.

Communications Media

	1999	2000	2001
Radio receivers ('000 subscribers)	3,201.9	2,867.8	2,832.3
Television receivers ('000 subscribers)	3,438.3	3,288.7	3,209.5
Telephones ('000 main lines in public networks)	5,750.7	8,217.7	10,808.0
Mobile cellular telephones ('000 subscribers)*	1,944.6	4,346.0	6,947.2
Personal computers ('000 in use)*	1,100	1,250	n.a.
Internet users ('000)*	700	1,000	1,400
Book production (titles)	12,551	11,965	14,321
Daily newspapers (number)	n.a.	103	105
Other periodicals (number)	3,686	3,192	3,364

* Source: International Telecommunication Union.

Education

(2001/02)

	Institutions	Teachers	Students
Pre-primary	5,642	23,345	276,438
Basic:			
Primary	} 4,263	67,594	1,027,827
Lower secondary			
Upper secondary:			
General	346	11,665	136,729
Technical	804	19,581	210,387
Vocational	565	10,669	184,174
Tertiary:			
Higher professional schools	164	2,738	26,670
Universities	24	13,322	200,450

Directory

Note: All telephone lines in the Czech Republic were renumbered on 21–22 September 2002, becoming standardized at nine digits. Fourteen new nodal telephone areas (NTAs—to correspond to the 14 new administrative regions scheduled for the end of 2002 were introduced at the same time, replacing the 159 existing area codes.

The Constitution

The following is a summary of the main provisions of the Constitution of the Czech Republic, which was adopted on 16 December 1992 and entered into force on 1 January 1993:

GENERAL PROVISIONS

The Czech Republic is a sovereign, unified and democratic law-abiding state, founded on the respect for the rights and freedoms of the individual and citizen. All state power belongs to the people, who exercise this power through the intermediary of legislative, executive and judicial bodies. The fundamental rights and freedoms of the people are under the protection of the judiciary.

The political system is founded on the free and voluntary operation of political parties respecting fundamental democratic principles and rejecting force as a means to assert their interests. Political decisions derive from the will of the majority, expressed through the free ballot. Minorities are protected in decision-making by the majority.

The territory of the Czech Republic encompasses an indivisible whole, whose state border may be changed only by constitutional law. Procedures covering the acquisition and loss of Czech citizenship are determined by law. No one may be deprived of his or her citizenship against his or her will.

GOVERNMENT

Legislative Power

Legislative power in the Czech Republic is vested in two chambers, the Chamber of Deputies and the Senate. The Chamber of Deputies has 200 members, elected for a term of four years. The Senate has 81 members, elected for a term of six years. Every two years one-third of the senators are elected. Both chambers elect their respective Chairman and Deputy Chairmen from among their members. Members of both chambers of the legislature are elected on the basis of universal, equal and direct suffrage by secret ballot. All citizens of 18 years and over are eligible to vote.

The legislature enacts the Constitution and laws; approves the state budget and the state final account; and approves the electoral law and international agreements. It elects the President of the Republic (at a joint session of both chambers), supervises the activities of the Government, and decides upon the declaration of war.

President of the Republic

The President of the Republic is Head of State. He/she is elected for a term of five years by a joint session of both chambers of the legislature. The President may not be elected for more than two consecutive terms.

The President appoints, dismisses and accepts the resignation of the Prime Minister and other members of the Government, dismisses the Government and accepts its resignation; convenes sessions of the Chamber of Deputies; may dissolve the Chamber of Deputies; names the judges of the Constitutional Court, its Chairman and Deputy Chairmen; appoints the Chairman and Deputy Chairmen of the Supreme Court; has the right to return adopted constitutional laws to the legislature; initials laws; and appoints members of the Council of the Czech National Bank. The President also represents the State in external affairs; is the Supreme Commander of the Armed Forces; receives heads of diplomatic missions; calls elections to the Chamber of Deputies and to the Senate; and has the right to grant amnesty.

Council of Ministers

The Council of Ministers is the highest organ of executive power. It is composed of the Prime Minister, the Deputy Prime Ministers and Ministers. It is answerable to the Chamber of Deputies. The President of the Republic appoints the Prime Minister, on whose recommendation he/she appoints the remaining members of the Council of Ministers and entrusts them with directing the ministries or other offices.

JUDICIAL SYSTEM

Judicial power is exercised on behalf of the Republic by independent courts. Judges are independent in the exercise of their function. The judiciary consists of the Supreme Court, the Supreme Administrative Court, high, regional and district courts.

The Constitutional Court is a judicial body protecting constitutionality. It consists of 15 judges appointed for a 10-year term by the President of the Republic with the consent of the Senate.

The Government

HEAD OF STATE

President: VÁCLAV KLAUS (elected 28 February 2003; inaugurated 7 March 2003).

COUNCIL OF MINISTERS
(April 2003)

A coalition Government of the Czech Social Democratic Party (CSDP) and the Coalition, comprising the Christian Democratic Union—Czechoslovak People's Party (CDU—CPP) and the Freedom Union—Democratic Union (FU—DU).

Prime Minister: VLADIMÍR ŠPIDLA (CSDP).

Deputy Prime Minister and Minister of the Interior: STANISLAV GROSS (CSDP).

Deputy Prime Minister and Minister of Justice: PAVEL RYCHETSKÝ (CSDP).

Deputy Prime Minister and Minister of Foreign Affairs: CYRIL SVOBODA (CDU—CPP).

Deputy Prime Minister: PETR MAREŠ (FU—DU).

Minister of Defence: JAROSLAV TVRDÍK (CSDP).

Minister of Industry and Trade: MILAN URBAN (CSDP).

Minister of Agriculture: JAROSLAV PALAS (CSDP).

Minister of the Environment: LIBOR AMBROZEK (CDU—CPP).

Minister of Finance: BOHUSLAV SOBOTKA (CSDP).

Minister of Health: MARIE SOUČKOVÁ (CSDP).

Minister of Education, Youth and Sport: PETRA BUZKOVÁ (CSDP).

Minister of Transport: MILAN ŠIMONOVSKÝ (CDU—CPP).

Minister of Labour and Social Affairs: ZDENĚK ŠKROMACH (CSDP).

Minister of Culture: PAVEL DOSTÁL (CSDP).

Minister of Regional Development: PAVEL NĚMEC (FU—DU).

Minister of Information: VLADIMÍR MLYNAR (FU—DU).

MINISTRIES

Office of the Government of the Czech Republic: nábř. E. Beneše 4, 118 01 Prague 1; tel. (2) 24002111; fax (2) 24810231; e-mail www@vlada.cz; internet www.vlada.cz.

Ministry of Agriculture: Těšnov 17, 117 05 Prague 1; tel. (2) 2181111; fax (2) 24810478; e-mail vicenova@mze.cz; internet www.mze.cz.

Ministry of Culture: Milady Horákové 139, 160 41 Prague 6; tel. (2) 57085294; fax (2) 24324282; e-mail minkult@mkcr.cz; internet www.mkcr.cz.

Ministry of Defence: Tychonova 1, 160 01 Prague 6; tel. (2) 20201111; fax (2) 20212359; e-mail press.service@army.cz; internet www.army.cz.

Ministry of Education, Youth and Sport: Karmelitská 8, 118 12 Prague 1; tel. (2) 57193111; fax (2) 57193397; e-mail cink@msmt.cz; internet www.msmt.cz.

Ministry of the Environment: Vršovická 65, 100 10 Prague 10; tel. (2) 67121111; fax (2) 67310308; e-mail info@env.cz; internet www.env.cz.

Ministry of Finance: Lětenská 15, 118 00 Prague 1; tel. (2) 57041111; fax (2) 57042788; e-mail podatelna@mfcr.cz; internet www.mfcr.cz.

Ministry of Foreign Affairs: Loretánské nám. 5, 118 00 Prague 1; tel. (2) 24181111; fax (2) 24182044; e-mail info@mzv.cz; internet www.mzv.cz.

Ministry of Health: Palackého nám. 4, POB 81, 128 01 Prague 2; tel. (2) 24971111; fax (2) 24972111; e-mail mzcr@mzcr.cz; internet www.mzcr.cz.

Ministry for Industry and Trade: Na Františku 32, 110 15 Prague 1; tel. (2) 24851111; fax (2) 24811089; e-mail mpo@mpo.cz; internet www.mpo.cz.

Ministry of Information: Havelkova 2, 130 00 Prague 3; tel. (2) 21008111; fax (2) 22721745; e-mail posta@micr.cz; internet www.micr.cz.

Ministry of the Interior: Nad štolou 3, 170 34 Prague 7; tel. (2) 61432972; fax (2) 61433552; e-mail public@mvcr.cz; internet www.mvcr.cz.

Ministry of Justice: Vyšehradská 16, 128 10 Prague 2; tel. (2) 219977111; fax (2) 24919927; e-mail msp@msp.justice.cz; internet www.justice.cz.

Ministry of Labour and Social Affairs: Na poříčním právu 1, 128 01 Prague 2; tel. (2) 24918391; fax (2) 21922664; e-mail webmaster@mpsv.cz; internet www.mpsv.cz.

Ministry for Regional Development: Staroměstskě nám. 6, 110 15 Prague 1; tel. (2) 24861111; fax (2) 24861333; e-mail posta@mmr.cz; internet www.mmr.cz.

Ministry of Transport: nábř. L. Svobody 12, 110 15 Prague 1; tel. (2) 51411111; fax (2) 51431184; e-mail posta@mdcr.cz; internet www.mdcr.cz.

Legislature

The Czech Constitution, which was adopted in December 1992, provided for the creation of a bicameral legislature as the highest organ of state authority in the Czech Republic (which was established as an independent state on 1 January 1993, following the dissolution of the Czech and Slovak Federative Republic). The lower house, the Chamber of Deputies, retained the structure of the Czech National Council (the former republican legislature). The upper chamber, or Senate, was first elected in November 1996.

CHAMBER OF DEPUTIES
(Poslanecká sněmovna)

Chairman: LUBOMÍR ZAORALEK.

General election, 14–15 June 2002

Party	% of votes	Seats
Czech Social Democratic Party	30.2	70
Civic Democratic Party	24.5	58
Communist Party of Bohemia and Moravia	18.5	41
Coalition*	14.3	31
Green Party	2.4	—
Others	10.1	—
Total	100.0	200

* An informal electoral alliance of the Christian Democratic Union—Czechoslovak People's Party and the Freedom Union—Democratic Union.

SENATE
(Senát)

Chairman: PETR PITHART.

Party	Seats after elections* Nov. 2000	Oct. and Nov. 2002
Civic Democratic Party	22	26
Christian Democratic Union—Czechoslovak People's Party†	21	16
Freedom Union—Democratic Union†	18	15
Czech Social Democratic Party	15	11
Communist Party of Bohemia and Moravia	3	3
Others	—	8
Independents	2	2
Total	81	81

* One-third of the 81 seats are renewable every two years.
† Contested the 2000 and 2002 elections as an informal electoral alliance (in 2000 together with the Civil Democratic Alliance).

Political Organizations

Alternative 2000 (Alternativa 2000): POB 154, 718 00 Ostrava 18; e-mail kvazar@telecom.cz; f. 1998.

Association for the Republic—Republican Party of Czechoslovakia (Sdružení pro republiku–Republikánská strana Československa): Gerstnerova 5, 170 00 Prague 7; tel. (2) 20571450; fax (2) 20570075; f. 1989; extreme right-wing; Chair. MIROSLAV SLÁDEK; Vice-Chair. MARTIN SMETANA.

Christian Democratic Union—Czechoslovak People's Party (CDU—CPP) (Křestanská a demokratická uniei—Československá strana lidová): Karlovo náměstí 5, 12 801 Prague 2; tel. (2) 24923874; fax (2) 24917630; e-mail info@kdu.cz; internet www.kdu.cz; f. 1992; Chair. CYRIL SVOBODA.

Civic Democratic Alliance (CDA) (Občanská demokratická aliance): Štefánikova 21, 150 00 Prague 5; tel. (2) 57329855; fax (2) 57327072; e-mail usek@oda.cz; internet www.oda.cz; f. 1991 as a formal political party, following a split in Civic Forum (f. 1989); fmrly an informal group within Civic Forum; conservative; Chair. DANIEL KROUPA.

Civic Democratic Party (CDP) (Občanská demokratická strana): Sněmovní 3, 110 00 Prague 1; tel. (2) 3114809; fax (2) 24510731; e-mail info@ods.cz; internet www.ods.cz; f. 1991 following a split in Civic Forum (f. 1989); merged with Christian Democratic Party in 1996; liberal-conservative; c. 17,000 mems (March 1998); Chair. MIREK TOPOLANEK.

Communist Party of Bohemia and Moravia (Komunistická strana Čech a Moravy): Politických vězňů 9, 110 00 Prague 1; tel. (2) 22897428; fax (2) 22897449; e-mail leftnews@kscm.cz; internet www.kscm.cz; f. 1991 as a result of the reorganization of the fmr Communist Party of Czechoslovakia; c. 130,000 mems; Leader MIROSLAV GREBENÍČEK.

Communist Party of Czechoslovakia: f. 1995 as Party of Czechoslovak Communists renamed as above 1999; 19,980 mems; Sec.-Gen. MIROSLAV STEPAN.

Conservative Consensus Party (Strana konzervativní smlouvy): Čímská 26, 120 00 Prague 2; tel. (2) 250223; fax (2) 259424; e-mail skos@skos.cz; internet www.skos.cz; f. 1998 by fmr mems of right-wing faction in CDA.

Countryside Party: f. 1996 to promote interests of rural areas; c. 3,000 mems; Chair. JAN VELEBA.

Czech Right (Česká pravice): Pod Dívínem 34, 150 00 Prague 5; e-mail cp-praha@ceskapravice.cz; internet www.ceskapravice.cz; f. 1994; conservative.

Czech Social Democratic Party (CSDP) (Česká strana sociálně demokratická): Lidový dům, Hybernská 7, 110 00 Prague 1; tel. and fax (2) 24219911; e-mail info@socdem.cz; internet www.cssd.cz; f. 1878; prohibited 1948; re-established 1989; formerly the Czechoslovak Social Democratic Party; Chair. Ing. VLADIMÍR ŠPIDLA.

Democratic Left (Strana demokratická levice): Čitná 49, 110 00 Prague 1; tel. (2) 24221313; fax (2) 24221506; Chair. JOSEF MEĚL.

Democratic Socialist Party (Strana demokratického socialismu): e-mail mailto:secret@sds.cz; f. 1997 by merger of Left Bloc and Party of the Democratic Left; c. 9,000 mems; Chair. MARIE STIBOROVA.

European Democrats (ED): Prague; f. July 2002 by breakaway mems of Civic Democratic Party; Chair. JAN KASL.

Free Democrats—Liberal National Social Party (Svobodní demokraté—Liberální strana národně sociální): Republiky nám. 7, 111 49 Prague 1; tel. (2) 24223443; fax (2) 21618554; e-mail sdlsns@mbox.vol.cz; f. 1995; by merger of Free Democrats (fmrly Civic Movement) and Liberal National Social Party (fmrly Czechoslovak Socialist Party); Chair. JIŘÍ DIENSTBIER.

Freedom Union—Democratic Union (FU—DU) (Unie svobody—Demokratická unie): Legerova 72, 120 00 Prague 2; tel. (2) 24221291; fax (2) 24221215; e-mail info@unie.cz; internet www.unie.cz; Freedom Union; f. 1998 following a split in the Civic Democratic Party; merged with Democratic Union in 2001; Leader PETR MARES.

Green Party (Strana zelených): Murmanská 13, Prague 10; tel. and fax (2) 736580; f. 1989; Chair. EMIL ZEMAN.

Moravian Democratic Party: Starobrněnská 20, 60200 Brno; tel. (5) 42215290; e-mail modestr@seznam.cz; internet www.mujweb.cz/www/modestr; f. 1997 by merger of Bohemian-Moravian Union of the Centre and Moravian National Party; Chair. IVAN DRIMAL.

Union for Europe (Unie pro Evropu): Plzeň; f. 2000; c. 6,000 mems.

Workers' Party: Prague; f. Jan. 2003; Chair. JIŘÍ STEPANEK.

Diplomatic Representation

EMBASSIES IN THE CZECH REPUBLIC

Afghanistan: Na Kazance 7/634, 170 00 Prague 7; tel. (2) 8544228; fax (2) 8542009; Ambassador AZIZOLLAH KARZAI.

Albania: Pod kaštany 22, 160 00 Prague 6; tel. (2) 33370594; fax (2) 33377232; e-mail alembprg@mbox.vol.cz; Ambassador PIRO MILKANI.

Algeria: V tišině 10/483, POB 204, 160 41 Prague 6; tel. (2) 33371142; fax (2) 33371147; internet www.algeria.cz; Ambassador ABDERRAHMANE MEZIANE-CHERIF.

Argentina: Panska 6, 110 00 Prague 1; tel. (2) 24212448; fax (2) 22241246; e-mail embar@iol.cz; Ambassador JUAN EDUARDO FLEMING.

Austria: Viktora Huga 10, 151 15 Prague 5; tel. (2) 57090511; fax (2) 57316045; e-mail austrianembassy@vol.cz; internet www.austria.cz; Ambassador KLAUS DAUBLEBSKY.

Belarus: Sádky 626, 171 00 Prague 7; tel. (2) 6888216; fax (2) 6888217.

Belgium: Valdštejnská 6, 118 01 Prague 1; tel. (2) 57533524; fax (2) 57320753; e-mail prague@diplobel.org; Ambassador BERNARD PIERRE.

Brazil: Sušická 12, POB 79, 160 41 Prague 6; tel. (2) 24324965; fax (2) 24312901; e-mail chebrem@mbox.vol.cz; Ambassador FRANCISCO DE PAULA DE ALMEIDA N. JUNQUEIRA.

Bulgaria: Krakovská 6, 110 00 Prague 1; tel. (2) 22211259; fax (2) 22211728; e-mail bulvelv@mbox.vol.cz; Ambassador MARTIN TOMOV.

Canada: Mickiewiczova 6, 125 33 Prague 6; tel. (2) 72101800; fax (2) 72101890; e-mail prague@dfait-maeci.gc.ca; internet www.dfait-maeci.gc.ca; Ambassador MARGARET HUBER.

Chile: U Vorlíků 4/623, 160 00 Prague 6; tel. (2) 24315064; fax (2) 24316069; e-mail echilecz@mbox.vol.cz; internet www.eol.cz/chile; Ambassador RICARDO CONCHA GAZMURI.

China, People's Republic: Pelléova 22, 160 00 Prague 6; tel. (2) 24311323; fax (2) 24319888; e-mail tecoprag@mbox.vol.cz; Ambassador ROY Y. Y. WU.

Colombia: Washingtonova 25, 110 00 Prague 1; tel. (2) 21674200; fax (2) 24225538; e-mail emcol@mbox.vol.cz; Ambassador MARÍA MERCEDES RENGIFO DE DUQUE.

Congo, Democratic Republic: Kolínská 13, 130 00 Prague 3; tel. and fax (2) 71730212; Ambassador GOMEZ NDUBA KIMBAYA.

Croatia: V Průhledu 9, 162 00 Prague 6; tel. (2) 33355695; fax (2) 3123464; e-mail velrhprag@vol.cz; Ambassador ZORAN PIČULJAN.

Cuba: Sibiřské nám. 1, 160 00 Prague 6; tel. (2) 24311253; fax (2) 3121029; Ambassador DAVID PAULOVICH ESCALONA.

Cyprus: Sibiřské nám. 6, 160 00 Prague 6; tel. (2) 24316833; fax (2) 24317529; e-mail cyprusembass@mbox.vol.cz; Ambassador CHRISTO-PHOROS YIANGOU.

Denmark: Maltézské nám. 5, POB 25, 118 01 Prague 1; tel. (2) 57531600; fax (2) 57531410; e-mail danemb@terminal.cz; internet www.denmark.cz; Ambassador JØRGEN RUD HANSEN BØJER.

Egypt: Pelléova 14, 160 00 Prague 6; tel. (2) 24311506; fax (2) 24311157; e-mail embassyegypt@iol.cz; Ambassador ABDEL RAHMAN MOHAMED MOUSSA.

Estonia: Na Kampě 1, 118 00 Prague 1; tel. (2) 57530512; fax (2) 57530513; e-mail sekretar@estemb.cz; Ambassador MART LAANEMÄE.

Finland: Hellichova 1, Chotkův palác, 118 00 Prague 1; tel. (2) 57007130; fax (2) 57007132; e-mail sanomat.pra@formin.fi; Ambassador RISTO RÄNNÄLI.

France: Velkopřevorské nám. 2, POB 102, 118 01 Prague 1; tel. (2) 57532756; fax (2) 57532757; e-mail ambafrcz@vol.cz; internet www.france.cz; Ambassador PHILIPPE COSTE.

Germany: Vlašská 19, POB 88, 118 01 Prague 1; tel. (2) 57113111; fax (2) 57534056; e-mail d_botschaft@volny.cz; internet www.german-embassy.cz; Ambassador Dr MICHAEL LIBAL.

Ghana: V tišině 4, 160 00 Prague 6; tel. (2) 33377236; fax (2) 33375647; e-mail ghanaemb@mbox.vol.cz; Chargé d'affaires a.i. EDWIN NII ADJEI.

Greece: Helenska 2, 120 00 Prague 2; tel. (2) 22250943; fax (2) 22253686; Ambassador ELEFTHERIOS KARAYANNIS.

Holy See: Voršilská 12, 110 00 Prague 1; tel. (2) 24999811; fax (2) 24999833; e-mail nunciatgc@mbox.vol.cz; Apostolic Nuncio Most Rev. ERWIN JOSEF ENDER (Titular Archbishop of Germania di Numidia).

Hungary: Českomalínská 20, 160 00 Prague 6; tel. (2) 33324454; fax (2) 33322104; e-mail huembprg@vol.cz; Ambassador KRISTÓF JÁNOS FORRAI.

India: Valdštejnská 6, 118 00 Prague 1; tel. (2) 57533490; fax (2) 57533378; e-mail indembprague@bohem-net.cz; Ambassador Dr S. JAISHANKAR.

Indonesia: Nad Buďánkami II/7, 150 21 Prague 5; tel. (2) 57214388; fax (2) 57212105; e-mail informace@indoneske-velvyslanectvi.cz; internet www.indoneske-velvyslanectvi.cz; Ambassador SOENARTO SOEDARNO.

Iran: Na Zátorce 18, 160 00 Prague 6; tel. (2) 20570454; fax (2) 33380255; Chargé d'affaires MOHSEN SHARIF KHODAEI.

Iraq: Na Zátorce 10, 160 00 Prague 6; tel. (2) 24319810; fax (2) 24316706; Chargé d'affaires a.i. KANAAN I. HUSSAIN.

Ireland: Tržiště 13, 118 00 Prague 1; tel. (2) 57530061; fax (2) 57531387; e-mail hibernia@terminal.cz; Ambassador JOE HAYES.

Israel: Badeniho 2, 170 06 Prague 7; tel. (2) 33325109; fax (2) 33320092; e-mail israemba@bohem-net.cz; Ambassador ARTHUR AVNON.

Italy: Nerudova 20, 118 00 Prague 1; tel. (2) 33080111; fax (2) 57531522; e-mail italemba@mbox.vol.cz; internet www.italianembassy.cz; Ambassador PAOLO FAIOLA.

Japan: Maltézské nám. 6, 118 01 Prague 1; tel. (2) 57533546; fax (2) 57532377; Ambassador KOICHI TAKAHASHI.

Kazakhstan: Fetrovská 15, 160 00 Prague 6; tel. (2) 3114596; fax (2) 3112124; e-mail kzemb@bon.cz; Ambassador TULEUTAI SULEIMENOV.

Korea, Democratic People's Republic: Na Zátorce 6, 160 00 Prague 6; tel. (2) 24320783; fax (2) 24318817; Chargé d'affaires a.i. KIM SUNG NAM.

Korea, Republic: Slavíčkova 5, 160 00 Prague 6; tel. (2) 234090411; fax (2) 234090450; Ambassador LEE JOON-HEE.

Kuwait: Na Zátorce 26, 160 00 Prague 6; tel. (2) 205707813; fax (2) 20570787; Ambassador KHALED MUTLAQ ZAYED AL-DUWAILAH.

Latvia: Hradešínská 3, POB 54, 101 00 Prague 10; tel. (2) 24252454; fax (2) 24255099; Ambassador IVETA SULCA.

Lebanon: Masarykovo nábřeží 14, 110 00 Prague 1; tel. (2) 24930495; fax (2) 24919088; Ambassador ZOUHEIR KAZZAZ.

Libya: Na baště sv. Jiří 7, 160 00 Prague 6; tel. (2) 33324160; fax (2) 33322173; Chargé d'affaires a.i. IBRAHIM H. JABAH.

Lithuania: Pod Klikovkou 1916/2, 150 00 Prague 5; tel. (2) 57210122; fax (2) 57210124; e-mail ltembcz@mbox.vol.cz; internet www.ltembassycz.urrn.lt; Ambassador VYGINTAS GRINIS.

Mexico: Nad Kazankou 8, 171 00 Prague 7; tel. (2) 8555554; fax (2) 8550477; e-mail embamex@rep-checa.cz; Ambassador FEDERICO SALAS LOFTE.

Mongolia: Na Marně 5, 160 00 Prague 6; tel. (2) 24311198; fax (2) 24314827; e-mail monemb@bohem-net.cz; Ambassador ODONBAATAR SHIJEEKHUU.

Morocco: Ke starému Bubenči 4, 160 00 Prague 6; tel. (2) 33320267; fax (2) 33322634; Ambassador ABDESSELEM OUAZZANI.

Netherlands: Gotthardská 6/27, 160 00 Prague 6; tel. (2) 24312190; fax (2) 24312160; e-mail nlgovpra@mail.ti.cz; internet www.netherlandsembassy.cz; Ambassador IDA L. VAN VELDHUIZEN.

Nigeria: Před bateriemi 18, POB 27, 162 01 Prague 6; tel. (2) 24312065; fax (2) 24312072; e-mail embassy@nigeria.cz; Ambassador JULIE JOKE AYORINDE.

Norway: Na Ořechovce 69, 162 00 Prague 6; tel. (2) 3111411; fax (2) 3123797; e-mail noramb@noramb.cz; Ambassador LASSE SEIM.

Peru: Muchova 9, 160 00 Prague 6; tel. (2) 24316210; fax (2) 24314749; e-mail emba.peru@worldonline.cz; Ambassador RAÚL PATIÑO-ALVÍSTUR.

Philippines: Senovazne namesti 8, 110 00 Prague 1; tel. (2) 24216397; fax (2) 24216390; e-mail praguepe@phembassy.cz; Ambassador CARMELITA RODRÍGUEZ SALAS.

Poland: Valdštejnská 8, 118 01 Prague 1; tel. (2) 57530388; fax (2) 57530135; e-mail ambrpczechy@mbox.vol.cz; internet www.ambpol.cz; Ambassador ANDRZEJ KRAWCZYK.

Portugal: Kinských nám. 7, 150 00 Prague 5; tel. (2) 57311230; fax (2) 57311234; e-mail embport@mbox.vol.cz; Ambassador ANA MARTINHO.

Romania: Nerudova 5, POB 87, 118 01 Prague 1; tel. (2) 57534210; fax (2) 57531017; e-mail embrprg@mbox.vol.cz; Ambassador GHEORGHE TINCA.

Russia: Pod kaštany 1, 160 00 Prague 6; tel. (2) 33374100; fax (2) 33377235; e-mail rusembassy@cdnet.org; Ambassador IGOR SERGEJE-VICH SAVOLSKII.

Serbia and Montenegro: Mostecká 15, 118 00 Prague 1; tel. (2) 57532075; fax (2) 57533948; Ambassador ALEKSANDAR ILIĆ.

Slovakia: Pod hradbami 1, 160 00 Prague 6; tel. (2) 33321442; fax (2) 33324289; e-mail skembassy@pha.inecnet.cz; Ambassador LADI-SLAV BALLEK.

Slovenia: Pod hradbami 15, 160 41 Prague 6; tel. (2) 33081211; fax (2) 24314106; Ambassador DAMJAN PRELOVŠEK.

South Africa: Ruská 65, POB 133, 100 00 Prague 10; tel. (2) 67311114; fax (2) 67311395; e-mail saprague@terminal.cz; Ambassador NOEL NOA LEHOKO.

Spain: Pevnostní 9, 162 00 Prague 6; tel. (2) 24311222; fax (2) 33341770; e-mail embpraha@gts.cz; Ambassador CABANAS ANSORENA.

Sweden: Úvoz 13-Hradčany, POB 35, 160 12 Prague 612; tel. (2) 20313200; fax (2) 20313240; e-mail ambassaden.prag@foreign.ministry.se; Ambassador HARALD FÄLTH.

Switzerland: Pevnostní 7, POB 84, 162 01 Prague 6; tel. (2) 20400611; fax (2) 24311312; e-mail vertretung@pra.rep.admin.ch; Ambassador HANSRUDOLF HOFFMAN.

Syria: Pod kaštany 16, 160 00 Prague 6; tel. (2) 24310952; fax (2) 24317911; Chargé d'affaires a.i. HAYSSAM MASHFEJ.

Thailand: Romaina Rollanda 3, 160 00 Prague 6; tel. (2) 20571435; fax (2) 20570049; e-mail thai@thaiemb.cz; internet www.thaiemb.cz; Ambassador TAMNU TANGKANASING.

Tunisia: Nad Kostelem 8, 147 00 Prague 4; tel. (2) 44460652; fax (2) 44460825; e-mail atprague@vol.cz; Ambassador MONCEF LARBI.

Turkey: Pevnostní 3, 162 00 Prague 616; tel. (2) 24311402; fax (2) 24311279; Ambassador SABRI CENK DUATEPE.

Ukraine: Charlese de Gaulla 29, 160 00 Prague 6; tel. (2) 33342000; fax (2) 33344366; e-mail kosak@mbox.vol.cz; internet www.ukrembassy.cz; Ambassador SERHII USTYCH.

United Kingdom: Thunovská 14, 118 00 Prague 1; tel. (2) 57530278; fax (2) 57530285; e-mail info@britain.cz; internet www.britain.cz; Ambassador ANNE PRINGLE.

USA: Tržiště 15, 118 01 Prague 1; tel. (2) 57530663; fax (2) 57530583; internet www.usembassy.cz; Ambassador CRAIG ROBERTS STAPLETON.

Uruguay: Muchova 9, 160 00 Prague 6; tel. (2) 24314755; fax (2) 24313780; e-mail urupra@urupra.cz; Ambassador Dr PEDRO VIDAL SALABERRY.

Venezuela: Jánský vršek 2/350, 118 00 Prague 1; tel. (2) 57532211; fax (2) 57531376; e-mail embaven@mbox.vol.cz; internet www.vol.cz/embavenezuela; Ambassador ORLANDO SUÁREZ GALEANO.

Viet Nam: Plzeňská 214, 150 00 Prague 5; tel. (2) 57211540; fax (2) 57211792; Ambassador DOAN THANG.

Yemen: Pod hradbami 5, 160 00 Prague 6; tel. (2) 3111598; fax (2) 3112204; Ambassador ALI ABDULLAH ABO-LOHOM.

Judicial System

The judicial system comprises the Supreme Court, the Supreme Administrative Court, chief, regional and district courts. There is also a 15-member Constitutional Court.

Supreme Court: Buresova 20, 657 37 Brno; tel. (5) 41213293; fax (5) 41212917; e-mail sekretariat@nsoud.cz; internet www.nsoud.cz; Chair. IVA BROZOVA.

Office of the Attorney-General: Jezuitska 4, 660 55 Brno; tel. (5) 42512111; fax (5) 42219621; Attorney-Gen. MARIE BENESOVA.

Constitutional Court: Joštova 8, 660 83 Brno; tel. (5) 42161111; fax (5) 42218326; e-mail ivan@concourt.cz; internet www.concourt .cz; Chair. ZDENĚK KESSLER; Dep. Chair. MILOŠ HOLEČEK.

Religion

The principal religion in the Czech Republic is Christianity. The largest denomination in 2001 was the Roman Catholic Church. According to the results of the March 2001 national census, about 60% of the population profess no religious belief.

CHRISTIANITY

Ecumenical Council of Churches in the Czech Republic (Ekumenická rada církví v České republice): Donská 5/370, 101 00 Prague 10; tel. and fax (2) 71742326; e-mail ekumrada@iol.cz; internet www.ecumenicalcouncil.cz; f. 1955; 11 mem. churches; Pres. Bishop VLADISLAV VOLNÝ; Gen. Sec. JITKA KRAUSOVÁ.

The Roman Catholic Church

Latin Rite

The Czech Republic comprises two archdioceses and six dioceses. According to the results of the March 2001 national census, there were 2,740,780 adherents in the Czech Republic, equivalent to some 27% of the total population.

Czech Bishops' Conference (Česká biskupská konference): Thákurova 3, 160 00 Prague 6; tel. (2) 20181421; fax (2) 24310144; e-mail cbk2@ktf.cuni.cz; f. 1990; Pres. Most Rev. JAN GRAUBNER (Archbishop of Oloumouc).

Archbishop of Olomouc: Most Rev. JAN GRAUBNER, Biskupské nám. 2, 771 01 Olomouc; tel. 585500211; fax 585222244; e-mail arcibol@mbox.vol.cz.

Archbishop of Prague: Cardinal Dr MILOSLAV VLK, Hradčanské nám. 16, 119 02 Prague 1; tel. (2) 20392123; fax (2) 20514647; e-mail kancler@arcibiskpraha.cz.

Byzantine Rite

Apostolic Exarch in the Czech Republic: Rt Rev. IVAN LJAVINEC (Titular Bishop of Acalissus,), Haštalské nám. 4, 110 00 Prague 1; tel. and fax (2) 2312817; e-mail exarchat@volny.cz; 250,000 adherents (Dec. 2000).

The Eastern Orthodox Church

Orthodox Church (Pravoslavná církev): V jámě 6, 111 21 Prague 1; divided into two eparchies: Prague and Olomouc; Head of the Orthodox Church, Metropolitan of Prague and of all Czechoslovakia His Holiness Patriarch DOROTEJ.

Protestant Churches

Baptist Union in the Czech Republic: Na Topolce 14, 140 00 Prague 4; tel. and fax (2) 41434256; e-mail czechbaptist@iol.cz; f. 1994; 2,395 mems; Pres. Rev. MILOŠ SOLA; Sec. Rev. JAN TITERA.

Brethren Church: Soukenická 15, 110 00 Prague 1; tel. and fax (2) 2318131; e-mail pavel.cerny@cb.cz; internet www.cbchurch.cz; f. 1880; 8,331 mems, 46 churches; Pres. PAVEL ČERNÝ; Sec. KAREL FOJTÍK.

Christian Corps: nám. Konečného 5, 602 00 Brno; tel. (5) 756365; 3,200 mems; 123 brs; Rep. Ing. PETR ŽEMAN.

Evangelical Church of Czech Brethren (Presbyterian): Jungmannova 9, 111 21 Prague 1; tel. (2) 24999211; fax (2) 24999219; e-mail srcce@srcce.cz; f. 1781; united since 1918; activities extend over Bohemia, Moravia and Silesia; 138,616 adherents (1997) and 264 parishes (1995); Pres. Rev. PAVEL SMETANA; Synodal Curator Dr LYDIE ROSKOVCOVÁ.

Silesian Evangelical Church of the Augsburg Confession in the Czech Republic (Silesian Lutheran Church): Na nivách 7, 737 01 Český Těšín; tel. 558731804; fax 558731815; e-mail sceav@sceav .cz; internet www.sceav.cz; founded in the 16th century during the Lutheran Reformation, reorganized in 1948; 40,000 mems; Bishop VLADISLAV VOLNÝ.

United Methodist Church: Ječná 19, 120 00 Prague 2; tel. (2) 290623; fax (2) 290167; e-mail ecmradacz@mbox.vol.cz; 1,890 mems; 17 parishes; Supt JOSEF ČERVEŇÁK.

Unity of Brethren (Moravian Church): Kollárova 456, 509 01 Nová Paka; tel. and fax 493721258; e-mail jbmb@iol.cz; internet www .moravian.cz; f. 1457; 2,447 mems; 21 parishes; Pres. Rev. JAROSLAV PLEVA.

Other Christian Churches

Apostolic Church in the Czech Republic: V Zídkách 402, 280 02 Kolín; tel. 321720457; fax 321727668; e-mail hqbishopac@clever.cz; f. 1989; 4,277 mems; Bishop RUDOLF BUBIK.

Church of the Seventh-day Adventists: Zálesí 50, 142 00 Prague 4; tel. (2) 4723745; fax (2) 44471863; e-mail unie@casd.cz; internet www.casd.cz; f. 1919; 10,000 mems; 183 churches; Pres. KAREL NOWAK.

Czechoslovak Hussite Church: Wuchterlova 5, 166 26 Prague 6; tel. (2) 20398111; fax (2) 24320308; f. 1920; 101,000 mems; six dioceses, divided into 301 parishes; Bishop-Patriarch Dr JAN SCHWARZ.

Old Catholic Church: Na Baterinch 27, 162 00 Prague 6; tel. and fax (2) 24319528; e-mail stkat@comp.cz; 4,000 mems, 12 parishes; Bishop Mgr DUŠAN HEJBAL.

JUDAISM

Federation of Jewish Communities in the Czech Republic (Federace židovských obcí v České republice): Maiselova 18, 110 01 Prague 1; tel. (2) 24811090; fax (2) 24810912; 3,000 mems; Pres. Dr JAN MUNK; Chief Rabbi KAROL SIDON.

The Press

PRINCIPAL DAILIES

Brno

Brněnský večerník (Brno Evening Paper): Jakubské nám. 7, 658 44 Brno; tel. (5) 42321227; fax (5) 45215150; f. 1968; Editor-in-Chief PETR HOSKOVEC; circ. 16,000.

Rovnost (Equality): M. Horákové 9, 658 22 Brno; tel. (5) 45321121; fax (5) 45212873; f. 1885; morning; Editor-in-Chief LUBOMÍR SELINGER; circ. 62,000.

České Budějovice

Jihočeské listy (South Bohemia Paper): Vrbenská 23, 370 45 České Budějovice; tel. 7312682; f. 1991; morning; Editor-in-Chief VLADIMÍR MAJER; circ. 53,000.

Hradec Králové

Hradecké noviny (Hradec News): Škroupova 695, 501 72 Hradec Králové; tel. 495613511; fax 495615681; Editor-in-Chief JAROMÍR FRIDRICH; circ. 30,000.

Karlovy Vary

Karlovarské noviny (Karlovy Vary News): třída TGM 32, 360 21 Karlovy Vary; tel. 353224496; fax 353225115; f. 1991; Editor-in-Chief JIŘÍ LINHART; circ. 15,000.

Ostrava

Moravskoslezský den (Moravia-Silesia Daily): Novinářská 7, 700 00 Ostrava 1; tel. 5955134; fax 5957021; f. 1991; Editor-in-Chief VLADIMÍR VAVRDA; circ. 130,000.

Svoboda (Freedom): Mlýnská 10, 701 11 Ostrava; tel. 592472311; fax 592472312; f. 1991; morning; Editor-in-Chief JOSEF LYS; circ. 100,000.

Pardubice

Pardubické noviny (Pardubice News): Tříd Míru 60, 530 02 Pardubice; tel. 46517366; fax 46517156; f. 1991; Editor-in-Chief ROMAN MARČÁK; circ. 15,000.

Plzeň

Plzeňský deník (Plzeň Daily): Husova 15, 304 83 Plzeň; tel. 37551111; fax 37551234; f. 1991; (fmrly *Pravda*, f. 1919); Editor-in-Chief JAN PERTL; circ. 50,000.

Prague

Hospodářské noviny (Economic News): Dobrovského 25, 170 55 Prague 7; tel. (2) 33071111; fax (2) 33072307; e-mail data@hn .economia.cz; internet www.ihned.cz; f. 1957; morning; Editor-in-Chief PETR ŠTĚPÁNEK; circ. 97,000 (1999).

Lidové noviny (People's News): Pobřežni 20/224, 186 21 Prague 8; tel. (2) 67098700; fax (2) 67098799; e-mail inzerce@lidovky.cz; internet www.lidovenoviny.cz; f. 1893, re-established 1988; morning; Editor-in-Chief PAVEL ŠAFR; circ. 83,728.

Mladá fronta Dnes (Youth Front Today): Senovážná 4, 110 00 Prague 1; tel. (2) 22062111; fax (2) 22062229; e-mail mfdnes@mafra .cz; f. 1990; morning; independent; Editor-in-Chief PETR ŠABATA; circ. 350,000.

Právo (Right): Slezská 13, 120 00 Prague 2; tel. (2) 21001111; fax (2) 21001361; e-mail redakce@pravo.cz; internet www.pravo.cz; f. 1920 as *Rudé právo*: name changed as above 1995; morning; Editor-in-Chief ZDENĚK PORYBNÝ; circ. 250,000.

Slovo (Word): Václavské nám. 36, 112 12 Prague 1; tel. (2) 24227258; fax (2) 24229477; f. 1945; Editor-in-Chief LIBOR ŠEVČÍK; circ. 95,000.

Večerník Praha (Evening Prague): Na Florenci 19, 111 21 Prague 1; tel. (2) 24227625; fax (2) 2327361; f. 1991; (fmrly *Ve černí Praha*, f. 1955); evening; Editor-in-Chief IVAN ČERVENKA; circ. 130,000.

Ústí nad Labem

Severočeský deník (North Bohemia Daily): Ústí nad Labem; tel. 475220525; fax 475220587; f. 1920; Editor-in-Chief MARIE SRPOVÁ; circ. 95,000.

PRINCIPAL PERIODICALS

Czech Language

100+1 ZZ: Karlovo nám. 5, 120 00 Prague 2; tel. (2) 293291; fax (2) 299824; f. 1964; fortnightly foreign press digest; Editor-in-Chief VÁCLAV DUŠEK; circ. 85,000.

Amatérske Radio: Radnická 2, 150 00 Prague 5; tel. (2) 57317311; e-mail a-radio@mbok.inet.cz; internet www.aradio.cz; amateur radio technology and popular electronics; circ. 25,000 (2000).

Ateliér (Studio): Masarykovo nábř. 250, 110 00 Prague 1; tel. and fax (2) 221732338; e-mail atelier.art@volny.cz; f. 1988; visual arts; fortnightly; Editor-in-Chief BLANKA POLÁKOVÁ.

Auto Tip: Střelnična 1680/8, 182 21 Prague 8; tel. (2) 66193173; fax (2) 66193172; e-mail v.kodym@axelspringer.cz; f. 1990; fortnightly for motorists; Editor-in-Chief VÍTĚZSLAV KODYM; circ. 60,000.

Českomoravský profit (Czech–Moravia Profit): Domažlická 3, 130 00 Prague 3; tel. (2) 277084; fax (2) 278514; weekly; Editor-in-Chief JAN BALTUS.

Divadelní noviny (Theatre News): c/o Divadelní ústav, Celetná 17, 110 00 Prague 1; tel. and fax (2) 2315912; e-mail divadelni.noviny@ czech-theatre.cz; internet www.divadlo.cz/noviny; fortnightly; Editor-in-Chief JAN KOLÁŘ.

Ekonom (Economist): Dobrovského 25, 170 55 Prague 7; tel. (2) 33071301; fax (2) 33072002; e-mail ekonom@economia.cz; weekly; Editor-in-Chief BAYNEK FIALA.

Katolický týdeník (Catholic Weekly): Londýnská 44, 120 00 Prague 2; tel. (2) 24250385; fax (2) 24257041; e-mail tydenik@mbox .vol.cz; f. 1989; weekly; Editor-in-Chief NORBERT BADAL; circ. 70,000.

Květy (Flowers): Na Florenci 3, 117 14 Prague 1; tel. and fax (2) 24219549; f. 1834; illustrated family weekly; Editor-in-Chief JINDŘICH MAŘAN; circ. 320,000.

Mladý svět (Young World): Na Poříčí 30, 112 86 Prague 1; tel. (2) 24229087; fax (2) 24210211; f. 1956; illustrated weekly; Editor-in-Chief OLGA DOUBRAVOVÁ; circ. 110,000.

PC World: Seydlerova 2451, 155 00 Prague; tel. (2) 57088111; fax (2) 6520812; e-mail pcworld@idg.cz; internet www.idg.cz; monthly; Editor JAROSLAV VYDRA; circ. 28,000 (1997).

Reflex: Jeseniova 51, 130 00 Prague 3; tel. (2) 67097542; fax (2) 61216239; f. 1990; social weekly; Editor-in-Chief PETR BÍLEK; circ. 220,000.

Respekt: Sokolská 66, 120 00 Prague 2; tel. (2) 24941962; fax (2) 24941965; e-mail redakce@respekt.cz; f. 1990; political weekly; Editor-in-Chief PETER HOLUB; circ. 30,000.

Romano Hangos (Romany Voice): f. 1999; fortnightly; Editor-in-Chief KAREL HOLOMEK.

Romano Kurko (Romany Week): Černovické nábř. 7, 618 00 Brno; tel. and fax (5) 330785; f. 1991; weekly; in Czech with Romany vocabulary; Dir M. SMOLEŇ; circ. 8,000.

Sondy (Soundings): W. Churchilla 2, 130 00 Prague 3; tel. (2) 24462328; fax (2) 24462313; f. 1990; weekly; Editor-in-Chief JANA KAŠPAROVÁ; circ. 40,000.

Týdeník Rozhlas (Radio Weekly): Na Florenci 3, 112 86 Prague 1; tel. and fax (2) 2323261; f. 1923; Editor-in-Chief AGÁTA PILÁTOVÁ; circ. 170,000.

Vesmír (Universe): Národní 3, 111 42 Prague 1; tel. (2) 24229181; fax (2) 24240513; e-mail vesmir@mbox.cesnet.cz; f. 1871; monthly; popular science magazine; Editor IVAN M. HAVEL; circ. 8,000–10,000.

Vlasta: Žitná 18, 120 00 Prague 2; tel. (2) 298641; fax (2) 294535; f. 1947; weekly; illustrated magazine for women; Editor-in-Chief MARIE FORMÁČKOVÁ; circ. 380,000.

Výber: K. Rotunde 89/4, 120 00 Prague 2; tel. (2) 24232429; fax (2) 24233283; internet www.vyber.cz; f. 1993; monthly; general interest; Editor-in-Chief VERONIKA MAXOVA; circ. 180,000 (1998).

Zahrádkář (Gardener): Prague; tel. (2) 766346; fax (2) 768042; monthly; Editor-in-Chief ANTONÍN DOLEJŠÍ; circ. 200,000.

Zora: Krakovská 21, 115 17 Prague 1; tel. (2) 24228126; fax (2) 24228120; f. 1917; every two months; for the visually handicapped; Editor-in-Chief JIŘÍ REICHEL.

Other Languages

Amaro Lav (Our Word): Černovické nábř. 7, 618 00 Brno; tel. and fax (5) 330785; f. 1990; monthly; in Romany and Czech; Dir M. SMOLEŇ; circ. 3,000.

Czech Business and Trade: V jirchářích 8, 110 00 Prague 1; tel. (2) 24912185; fax (2) 24912355; e-mail journal@ppagency.cz; internet www.ppagency.cz; f. 1960; monthly; publ. in English, German, Spanish, Russian and French; Editor-in-Chief Dr PAVLA PODSKALSKÁ; circ. 15,000.

Prager Wochenblatt (Prague Weekly): Vítkovická 373, 199 00 Prague 9; tel. (2) 6282029; weekly; politics, culture, economy; in German; Editor-in-Chief FELIX SEEBAUER; circ. 30,000.

Prague Post: Štěpánská 20 Prague 1; tel. (2) 96334400; fax (2) 96334450; e-mail office@praguepost.cz; internet www.praguepost .cz; f. 1991; political, economic and cultural weekly in English; Editor-in-Chief ALAN LEVY; circ. 15,000.

Prognosis: Prague; tel. (2) 3167007; fax (2) 368139; f. 1991; political, economic and cultural fortnightly in English; Editor-in-Chief BEN SULLIVAN; circ. 10,000.

NEWS AGENCIES

Česká tisková kancelář (ČTK) (Czech News Agency): Opletalova 5–7, 111 44 Prague 1; tel. (2) 22098111; fax (2) 24220553; e-mail ctk@ mail.ctk.cz; internet www.ctk.cz; f. Nov. 1992, assuming control of all property and activities (in the Czech Lands) of the former Czechoslovak News Agency; news and photo-exchange service with all international and many national news agencies; maintains network of foreign correspondents; Czech and English general and economic news service; publishes daily bulletins in English; Gen. Dir Dr MILAN STIBRAL.

Foreign Bureaux

Agence France-Presse (AFP): Ječná 15, 120 00 Prague 2; tel. (2) 24921155; fax (2) 24919155; e-mail afp@mbox.vol.cz; Bureau Chief RENÉ PASCAL BIAGI.

Agencia EFE (Spain): Uhrineveska 65, 100 00 Prague 1; tel. (2) 71735816; fax (2) 74782319; e-mail efe@iol.cz; internet www.efe.es; Bureau Chief MIGUEL FERNÁNDEZ.

Agenzia Nazionale Stampa Associata (ANSA) (Italy): Prague; tel. and fax (2) 24222793.

Allgemeiner Deutscher Nachrichtendienst (ADN) (Germany): Milevská 835, 140 00 Prague 4; tel. (2) 6921911; fax (2) 6921627; Bureau Chief STEFFI GENSICKE.

Associated Press (AP) (USA): Prague; tel. (2) 24224346; fax (2) 24227445; Correspondent ONDŘEJ HEJMA.

Deutsche Presse-Agentur (dpa) (Germany): Petrské nám. 1, 110 00 Prague 1; tel. (2) 24810290; fax (2) 22315196; Bureau Chief WOLFGANG JUNG.

Informatsionnoye Telegrafnoye Agentstvo Rossii—Telegrafnoye Agentstvo Suverennykh Stran (ITAR—TASS) (Russia): Pevnostní 5, 162 00 Prague 6; tel. (2) 328307; fax (2) 327527; Bureau Chief ALEKSANDR YAKOVLEV.

Magyar Távirati Iroda (MTI) (Hungary): Prague; tel. and fax (2) 66710131; Bureau Chief GYÖRGY HARSÁNYI.

Novinska Agencija Tanjug (Yugoslavia): Prague; tel. (2) 2674401; Correspondent BRANKO STOŠIĆ.

Polska Agencja Prasowa (PAP) (Poland): Petrské nám. 1, 110 00 Prague 1; tel. and fax (2) 24812205; Correspondent ZBYGNIEW KRZYS-TYNJAK.

Rossiiskoye Informatsionnoye Agentstvo—Novosti (RIA—Novosti) (Russia): Italská 36, 130 00 Prague 3; tel. (2) 22253088; fax (2) 22253084; e-mail riapraha@bohem-net.cz; Bureau Chief VALERIJ ENIN.

Tlačová agentúra Slovenskej republiky (TASR) (Slovakia): Šmeralova 7, 170 00 Prague 7; tel. (2) 33372617; fax (2) 33379663; e-mail bkopcak@iol.cz; internet www.tasr.sk; Correspondent BOHDAN KOPČÁK.

Xinhua (New China) News Agency (People's Republic of China): Pelléova 22, 169 00 Prague 6; tel. and fax (2) 24311325; Correspondent SAN XI-YOU.

PRESS ASSOCIATION

Syndicate of Journalists of the Czech Republic: Pařížská 9, 116 30 Prague 1; tel. (2) 2325109; fax (2) 2327782; e-mail sncr@mbox.vol.cz; f. 1877; reorganized in 1990; 5,000 mems; Chair. IRENA VÁLOVÁ.

Publishers

Academia: Legerova 61, 120 00 Prague 2; tel. (2) 24942584; fax (2) 24941982; f. 1953; scientific books, periodicals; Dir ALEXANDER TOMSKÝ.

AkcentiBlok: Rooseveltova 4, 657 00 Brno; tel. and fax (5) 42214516; f. 1957; regional literature, fiction, general; Dir JAROSLAV NOVÁK.

Albatros: Truhlářská 9, 110 01 Prague 1; tel. (2) 24810704; fax (2) 24810850; internet www.albatros.cz; f. 1949; literature for children and young people; Dir MARTIN SLAVÍK.

Kalich, nakladatelství a knihkupectví, s.r.o.: Jungmannova 9, 111 00 Prague 1; tel. (2) 24947505; fax (2) 24947504; e-mail kalichknih@volny.cz; internet www.kalich.evangnet.cz; f. 1920; Dirs MICHAL PLZÁK, MARKÉTA LANGOUÁ.

Kruh (Circle): Dlouhá 108, 500 21 Hradec Králové; tel. 49522076; f. 1966; regional literature, fiction and general; Dir Dr JAN DVOŘÁK.

Melantrich: Václavské nám. 36, 112 12 Prague 1; tel. (2) 22093215; fax (2) 24213176; f. 1919; general, fiction, humanities, newspapers and magazines; Dir MILAN HORSKÝ.

Mladá fronta (Young Front): Mezi Vodami 1952/9, 143 00 Prague 4; tel. (2) 25276282; fax (2) 25276278; e-mail prodej@mf.cz; f. 1945; fiction, history, poetry, popular science, magazines; Dir MARTINA HARTOVA; Editor-in-Chief VLASTIMIL FIALA.

Nakladatelství dopravy a spojů (Transport and Communications): Hybernská 5, 115 78 Prague 1; tel. (2) 2365774; fax (2) 2356772; Dir Ing. ALOIS HOUDEK.

Nakladatelství Svoboda (Freedom): Na Florenci 3, POB 704, 113 03 Prague 1; tel. (2) 24224705; fax (2) 24226026; f. 1945 as the publishing house of the Communist Party; restructured in 1992–94 as a limited company; in voluntary liquidation since Sept. 1997; politics, history, philosophy, fiction, general; Dir STEFAN SZERYŃSKI.

Odeon: Prague; tel. (2) 24225248; fax (2) 24225262; f. 1953; literature, poetry, fiction (classical and modern), literary theory, art books, reproductions; Dir MILUŠE SLAPNIČKOVÁ.

Olympia: Klimentská 1, 110 15 Prague 1; tel. (2) 24810146; fax (2) 2315192; e-mail olympia@mbox.vol.cz; f. 1954; sports, tourism, encyclopaedias, fiction, illustrated books; Dir Ing. KAREL ZELNÍČEK.

Panton: Radlická 99, 150 00 Prague 5; tel. and fax (2) 548627; f. 1958; publishing house of the Czech Musical Fund; books on music, sheet music, records; Dir KAREL ČERNÝ.

Práce (Labour): Václavské nám. 17, 112 58 Prague 1; tel. (2) 24009100; fax (2) 2320989; f. 1945; trade-union movement, fiction, general, periodicals; Dir JANA SCHMIDTOVÁ.

Rapid, a.s.: 28. října 13, 112 79 Prague 1; tel. (2) 24195111; fax (2) 2327520; advertising; Dir-Gen. ČESTMÍR ČEJKA.

Severočeské nakladatelství (North Bohemian Publishing House): Ústí nad Labem; tel. 4728581; regional literature, fiction and general; Dir JIŘÍ ŠVEJDA.

Státní pedagogické nakladatelství: Ostrovní 30, 113 01 Prague 1; tel. and fax (2) 24912206; f. 1775; state publishing house; school and university textbooks, dictionaries, literature; Dir MILAN KOVÁŘ.

Vyšehrad: Bartolomějská 9, 110 00 Prague 1; tel. (2) 2326851; fax (2) 268390; e-mail vysehrad@login.cz; f. 1934; religion, philosophy, history, fiction; Dir PRAVOMIL NOVÁK; Chief Editor VLASTA HESOUNOVÁ.

PUBLISHERS' ASSOCIATION

Association of Czech Booksellers and Publishers: Jana Masaryka 56, 120 00 Prague 2; tel. (2) 90030150; fax (2) 22513198; e-mail sckn@mbox.vol.cz; internet www.sckn.cz; f. 1879; Chair. JAROSLAV CÍSAŇ.

WRITERS' UNION

Society of Writers (Obec spisovatelů): POB 669, 111 21 Prague 1; tel. and fax (2) 22220106; e-mail obecspis@volny.cz; f. 1989; 700 mems; Dir ANTONÍN JELÍNEK.

Broadcasting and Communications

TELECOMMUNICATIONS

Český Telecom: Olšanská 5, 130 34 Prague 3; tel. (2) 71411111; fax (2) 66316666; e-mail jindrich.trpisovsky@ct.cz; internet www.telecom.cz; fmrly SPT Telecom, renamed 2000; partially privatized 1995; 51% stat-owned, 27%-owned by Dutch/Swiss consortium; further privatization pending in 2003; monopoly operator of long-distance and international services; Chair. of Bd and CEO ONDREJ FELIX.

EuroTel: Sokolovská 225, POB 49, 190 00 Prague 9; tel. (2) 67011111; fax (2) 2327383; f. 1991; mobile telephone communications; launched GSM service July 1996; owned by SPT Telecom (51%) and West Atlantic (49%—consortium of US West and Bell Atlantic); Chief Exec. and Man. Dir EDWARD KINGMAN.

Český Mobil: Prague; 51% owned by Telesystem International Wireless (Canada); awarded licence to operate mobile telephone network in October 1999; Dir-Gen. ALEXANDER TOLSLTOY.

České Radiokomunikace, a.s.: U nákladového nádraži 4, 130 00 Prague 3; tel. (2) 67005111; fax (2) 71774885; e-mail info@cra.cz; internet www.cra.cz; f. 1994; privatized 2000; Dir-Gen. MIROSLAV ČUŘÍN.

Contactel: Vinohradská 174, 130 19 Prague 3; tel. (2) 33011111; fax (2) 33011112; e-mail press@contact.cz; internet www.contactel.cz; f. 1999; owned by České Radiokomunikace, a.s. (50%) and Tele Danmark A/S (50%); internet, data and voice services; Chief Exec. MICHAL ČUPA.

RadioMobil, a.s.: Londýnská 5759, 120 00, Prague 2; owned by České Radiokomunikace, a.s. (51%) and an international consortium, C-Mobil (49%); awarded 20-year licence to operate mobile telephone network in April 1996; launched GSM service Sept. 1996; Man. Dir KLAUS TEBBE.

RADIO

The national networks include Radio Prague (medium wave and VHF), Radio Vltava (VHF from Prague—programmes on Czech and world culture), Radio Regina (medium and VHF—programme of regional studios), and Interprogramme (medium and VHF—for foreign visitors to the Czech Republic, in English, German and French).

Local stations broadcast from Prague (Central Bohemian Studio), Brno, České Budějovice, Hradec Králové, Ostrava, Plzeň, Ústí nad Labem and other towns. By August 1993 44 private stations had been licensed, 37 of which were in operation (14 in Prague).

Český rozhlas (Czech Radio): Vinohradská 12, 120 99 Prague 2; tel. (2) 21551111; fax (2) 24222223; e-mail press@cro.cz; internet www.rozlas.cz; 4 nation-wide stations; Dir-Gen. VÁCLAV KASÍK.

Country Radio: Zenklová 34, 180 00 Prague 8; tel. (2) 5102411; fax (2) 51024224; e-mail country@ecn.cz; internet www.ecn.cz/country; commercial station; Man. Dir ZDENĚK PETERA.

Evropa 2: Nádražní 56, 150 05 Prague 5; tel. (2) 57001808; fax (2) 57001807; e-mail info@evropa2.cz; internet www.evropa2.cz; commercial station; Pres. MICHAEL FLEISCHMANN.

Frekvence 1: Nádražní 56, 150 05 Prague 5; tel. (2) 57001900; fax (2) 57314186; e-mail info@frekvence1.cz; internet www.frekvence1.cz; commercial station; Pres. MICHAEL FLEISCHMANN.

Radio Alfa: Na Poříčí 12, 110 00 Prague 1; tel. (2) 24872822; fax (2) 24872823; commercial station; Man. Dir V. KASÍK.

Radio FM Plus: POB 40, 320 90 Plzeň; tel. 37276666; fax 377422221; e-mail info@fmplus.cz; internet www.fmplus.cz; commercial station; Dir ZBYNĚK SUCHÝ.

Radio Free Europe/Radio Liberty: Vinohradská 1, 110 00 Prague 1; fax (2) 21123420; internet www.rferl.org; broadcasts in 23 languages.

TELEVISION

In 2000 there were five main television stations: the two state-run channels, ČT1 and ČT2, reached 98% and 71% of the population, respectively, while two private commercial stations, Nova TV and Prima TV, were received by 99% and approximately 50%, respectively. TV3, which began broadcasting in May 2000, was initially received by some 30% of the population and aimed to reach 45% by the end of that year.

Česká televize (Czech Television): Kavčí hory, 140 70 Prague 4; tel. (2) 61131111; fax (2) 6927202; e-mail jakub.puchalsky@czech-tv.cz; internet www.czech-tv.cz; f. 1992; state-owned; two channels; studios in Prague, Brno and Ostrava.

Nova TV: Vladislavova 20, 113 13 Prague 1; tel. (2) 21100111; fax (2) 21100565; f. 1994, through a joint venture with Central European Media Enterprises (CME—of the USA) as the Czech Republic's first independent commercial station; CME lost control of the station in 1999.

Prima TV: Na žertvách 24, 180 00 Prague 8; tel. (2) 66100111; fax (2) 66100201; e-mail kvizova@prima-televize.cz; internet www.prima-televize.cz; f. 1993; Gen. Dir KATEŘINA FRIČOVÁ.

TV3: Prague; e-mail info@tv3.cz; internet www.tv3.cz; f. 2000; independent commercial station; Dir JAN OBERMAN.

Finance

(cap. = capital; res = reserves; dep. = deposits; m. = million; brs = branches; amounts in Czech koruny)

BANKING

With the establishment of independent Czech and Slovak Republics on 1 January 1993, the State Bank of Czechoslovakia was divided and its functions were transferred to the newly-created Czech National Bank and National Bank of Slovakia. The Czech National Bank is independent of the Government.

At 31 March 2003 there were 37 banks operating in the Czech Republic, 11 of which were majority owned by Czech investors.

Central Bank

Czech National Bank (Česká národní banka): Na Příkopě 28, 115 03 Prague 1; tel. (2) 24411111; fax (2) 24413708; e-mail alice .frisaufova@cnb.cz; internet www.cnb.cz; f. 1993; bank of issue, the central authority of the Czech Republic in the monetary sphere, legislation and foreign exchange permission; central bank for directing and securing monetary policy, supervision of activities of other banks and savings banks; cap. 1,400m., res 4,229m., dep. 351,906m. (Dec. 2001); Gov. ZDENĚK TŮMA; 7 brs.

Commercial Banks

Banka Haná, a.s.: Prikop 8, POB 58, 602 00 Brno; tel. (5) 42219549; fax (5) 45215969; internet www.bhan.cz; f. 1990; cap. 5,101.2m., res 3,177.9m., dep. 17,506.7m. (Dec. 1998); banking licence surrendered in Dec. 2000; Chair. STANSLAV ZALMANEK; 2 brs.

Česká exportní banka as: Vodičkova 34, 111 221 Prague 1; e-mail ceb@ceb.cz; internet www.ceb.cz; f. 1994; cap. 1,650.0m., res 299.0m., dep. 21,196.54m. (Dec. 2001); Chair. LADISLAV ZELINKA.

Česká konsolidační agentura: Janovského 438/2, 170 06 Prague 7; tel. (2) 20141111; fax (2) 33370033; e-mail kobp@ms.aned.cz; internet www.kopb.cz; f. 1991; fmrly Konsolidační banka Praha, s.p.ú. current name adopted in Sept. 2001 following surrender of banking licence; cap. 5,950m., res 942.9m., dep. 106,661.5m. (Dec. 1998); Chair. KAMIL ZIEGLER.

Československá obchodní banka, a.s. (CSOB) (Czechoslovak Commercial Bank): Na Příkopě 14, 115 20 Prague 1; tel. (2) 24111111; fax (2) 24225049; e-mail webmaster@csob.cz; internet www.csob.cz; f. 1965; 66% state holding purchased by KBC Bank (Belgium) May 1999; commercial and foreign-trade transactions; cap. 5,105m., res 19,592m., dep. 506,930m. (Dec. 2001); Chair. and Gen. Man. PAVEL KAVÁNEK; 34 brs.

Investiční a Poštovní banka, a.s.: Senovážné nám. 32, POB 819, 114 03 Prague 1; tel. (2) 22041111; fax (2) 24244035; e-mail info@ipb.cz; internet www.ipb.cz; f. 1990; 36% state holding purchased by Nomura (Japan) March 1998; placed under central-bank administration and subsequently transferred to ownership of CSOB in June 2000; cap. 13,383m., res 1,755m., dep. 231,135m. (Dec. 1998); Chair. and Gen. Man. JAN KLACEK; 157 brs.

Komerční banka, a.s.: Na Příkopě 33, POB 839, 114 07 Prague 1; tel. (2) 22432111; fax (2) 24243020; e-mail mojebanka@koba.cz; internet www.koba.cz; f. 1990; 49% state-owned; agreement to sell 60% state holding to Société Générale (France) reached in June

2001; cap. 19,005m., res 5,922m., dep. 381,113m. (Dec. 2001); Chair. and Chief Exec. ALEXIS RAYMOND JUAN; 354 brs.

Volksbank CZ, a.s.: M-Palác Herspická 5, POB 226, 658 26 Brno; tel. (5) 43525111; fax (5) 43525555; e-mail mail@volksbank.cz; internet www.volksbank.cz; cap. 650.0m., res 27.1m., dep. 10,546.9m. (Dec. 2001); Chair. JOHANN LURF.

Foreign and Joint-Venture Banks

Citibank, a.s.: Evropská 178, 166 40 Prague 6; tel. (2) 33061111; fax (2) 33061617; internet www.citibank.com/czech; f. 1991; wholly-owned subsidiary of Citibank Overseas Investment Corpn (Delaware, USA); cap. 2,425.0m., res 2,821m., dep. 41,091.8m. (Dec. 2000); Chair. ATIF BAJWA; 6 brs.

Crédit Lyonnais Bank Praha, a.s.: Ovocný trh 8, 117 19 Prague 1; tel. (2) 22076111; fax (2) 22076119; e-mail crlytre@mbox.vol.cz; internet www.clbp.cz; wholly-owned subsidiary of Crédit Lyonnais Global Banking, Paris; cap. 500m., res 270.9m., dep. 16,252.4m. (Dec. 2000); Chair. and Gen. Man. CHRISTIAN RAMANOEL.

Dresdner Bank (CZ), a.s.: Vítězná 1, POB 229, 150 00 Prague 5; tel. (2) 57006111; fax (2) 57006200; internet www .bnp-dresdner-bank.cz; f. 1991; ownership: Banque Nationale de Paris (50%), Dresdner Bank (50%); cap. 1,000m., res 250.9m., dep. 19,500.1m. (Dec. 2001); Chair. MARKUA HERMANN.

GE Capital bank, a.s.: Vyskočilova 1422, BB Centrum, 140 28 Prague 4; tel. (2) 24441111; fax (2) 24441500; e-mail tomas.rajbr@ gecapital.com; internet www.gecb.cz; f. 1998, from purchase of Agrobanka Praha, a.s. wholly-owned by GE Capital International Holdings Corpn, Wilmington; cap. 500.0m., res 6,404.3m., dep. 68,751.7m. (Dec. 2001); Chair. PETR ŠMÍDA; 192 brs.

HypoVereinsbank CZ, a.s.: Namesti republiky 3a, POB 70, 110 00 Prague 1; tel. (2) 21112111; fax (2) 21112132; internet www.hvb.cz; f. 1999; by merger of HYPO-BANK CZ and Vereinsbank CZ; merged with Bank Austria Creditanstalt Czech Republic in Oct. 2001; cap. 5,047.0m., res 4,122.6m., dep. 129,234.7m. (Dec. 2001); Exec. Mems of Bd HANS-PETER HORSTER, Dr KAREL KRATINA, HARTMUT HAGEMANN.

Interbanka, a.s.: Václavské nám. 40, 110 00 Prague 1; tel. (2) 24406111; fax (2) 24215591; e-mail info@interbanka.cz; internet www.interbanka.cz; f. 1991; cap. 1,708.7m., res 22.2m., dep. 1,849.7m. (Dec. 2000); Chair. and Chief Exec. MANFRED JÜRGEN BAUMANN.

Raiffeisenbank, as: Vodičkova 38, 111 21 Prague 1; tel. (2) 24231270; fax (2) 24231278; e-mail raiffeisenbank@rb.cz; internet www.rb.cz; f. 1993; cap. 1,500.0m., res 38.5m., dep. 55,398.0m. (Dec. 2001); Chair. and Gen. Man. Ing. KAMIL ZIEGLER.

Živnostenská banka, a.s.: Na Příkopě 20, POB 421, 113 80 Prague 1; tel. (2) 24121111; fax (2) 24125555; e-mail info@zivnobanka.cz; internet www.zivnobanka.cz; f. 1868; cap. 1,360.4m., res 1,120.7m., dep. 56,878.3m. (Dec. 2001); Vice-Chair. of Bd JOSEF PITRA; 8 brs.

Savings Bank

Czech Savings Bank (Česká spořitelna, a.s.): Na Prikope 29, POB 838, 113 98 Prague 1; tel. (2) 61073492; fax (2) 61073006; e-mail csas@csas.cz; internet www.csas.cz; f. 1825; 52% holding purchased by Erste Bank AG (Austria) in February 2000; absorbed Erste Bank Sparkassen (ČR), a.s., in October 2000; accepts deposits and issues loans; total assets 491,605m., dep. 430,382m. (Dec. 2001); Chair. and Chief Exec. JOHN JAMES STACK; 684 brs.

Bankers' Organization

Association of Banks, Prague: Vodičkova 30, 110 00 Prague 1; tel. (2) 24225926; fax (2) 24225957; e-mail bank.asociace@mbox.vol.cz; Pres. JIŘÍ KUNERT; Vice-Pres. PAVEL KAVÁNEK.

STOCK EXCHANGE

Prague Stock Exchange (Burza cenných papírů Praha, a.s.): Rybná 14, 110 05 Prague 1; tel. (2) 21831111; fax (2) 21833040; e-mail info@pse.cz; internet www.pse.cz; f. 1992; Chair. GEORGE JEDLICKA; Vice-Chair. DUSAN BARAN.

Regulatory Authority

Czech Securities Commission: Prague; f. 1998; Chair. FRANTIŠEK JAKUB.

INSURANCE

Czech Co-operative Insurance Company (Kooperativa, a.s., pojišťovna, a.s.): Templová 747, 110 01 Prague 1; tel. (2) 21000111; fax (2) 2322562; e-mail info@koop.cz; internet www.koop.cz; f. 1993; Chair. and Gen. Man. Ing. VLADIMÍR MRÁZ.

Czech Insurance and Reinsurance Corporation (Česká Pojišťovna, a.s.): Spálená 16, 113 04 Prague 1; tel. (2) 24051111; fax

(2) 24052200; e-mail murban@cpoj.cz; internet www.cpoj.cz; f. 1827; many home brs and some agencies abroad; issues life, accident, fire, aviation, industrial and marine policies, all classes of reinsurance; Lloyd's agency; Chair. of Bd IVAN KOČÁRNÍK; Gen. Man. LADISLAV BARTONÍČEK.

ČS Zivnostenská pojišťovna, a.s.: Smilova 547, 530 02 Pardubice; tel. (40) 6051111; fax (40) 6051380; e-mail zivpo@zivpo.cz; internet www.zivpo.cz; f. 1992; Chair. and Gen. Dir Ing. JAROSLAV KLAPAL.

Trade and Industry

GOVERNMENT AGENCIES

Czech Trade Promotion Agency (Česká agentura na podporu obchodu): Vittrichova 21, POB 76, 128 01 Prague 2; tel. (2) 24907500; fax (2) 24907503; e-mail info@czechtrade.cz; internet www.czechtrade.cz; Gen. Dir MARTIN TLAPA.

Česká agentura pro zahraniční investice (CzechInvest): Štěpánská 15, 120 00 Prague 2; tel. (2) 96342500; fax (2) 96342502; e-mail marketing@czechinvest.org; internet www.czechinvest.org; f. 1992; foreign investment agency; Chief Exec. Ing. MARTIN JAHN.

National Property Fund: Rašínovo nábřeží 42, 128 00 Prague 2; tel. (2) 24991285; fax (2) 22718211; e-mail predseda@fnm.cz; internet www.fnm.cz; responsible for state property and state-owned companies in the period up to their privatization; Chair. JAN JUCHELKA.

CHAMBER OF COMMERCE

Economic Chamber of the Czech Republic (Hospodářská komora České republiky): Argentinská 38, 170 05 Prague 7; tel. (2) 66794939; fax (2) 875438; f. 1850; has almost 20,000 members (trading corporations, industrial enterprises, banks and private enterprises); Chair. Dr ZDENĚK SOMR.

EMPLOYERS' ORGANIZATIONS

Association of Entrepreneurs of the Czech Republic (Sdružení podnikatelů České republiky): Škrétova 6/44, 120 59 Prague 2; tel. and fax (2) 24230572; Chair. RUDOLF BARÁNEK.

Confederation of Industry of the Czech Republic (Svaz průmyslu a dopravy České republiky): Mikulandská 7, 113 61 Prague 1; tel. (2) 24915679; fax (2) 24919311; e-mail spcr@spcr.cz; internet www.spcr.cz; f. 1990; Dir-Gen. ZDENĚK LIŠKA.

UTILITIES

Electricity

Central Bohemian Electricity Distribution Company (Středočeská Energetická—STE a.s.): Vinohradská 325/8, 120 21 Prague 2; tel. (2) 22031111; fax (2) 22032555; e-mail inbox@ste.cz; internet www.ste.cz; f. 1994; Chair. and Gen. Man. JAROSLAV HÁBA.

České Energeticke Zavody (ČEZ): Hlavni Sprava, Jungmannova 29, 111 48 Prague 1; tel. (2) 24081111; fax (2) 24082440; e-mail info@hs.cez.cs; internet www.cez.cz; 68% state-owned; production co; Gen. Man. JAROSLAV MÍL; 7,600 employees.

Dukovany Nuclear Power Plant ČEZ, a.s.: 675 50 Dukovany; tel. 568811111; fax 568866360; e-mail sedlaj2.edu@mail.cez.cz; Dir JOSEF SEDLAK.

East Bohemian Electricity Company (Východočeská Energetika—VCE): Sladovského 215, 501 03 Hradec Králové; tel. 4955841111; fax 49530150; f. 1994; Chair. and Chief Exec. PETR ZEMAN; 2,094 employees.

Moravskoslezské Teplárny, a.s.: Října 152 28; 709 74 Ostrava; tel. 596609111; fax 596609158; f. 1992; Gen. Man. JAROSLAV VESELSKÝ.

North Bohemian Electricity (Severočeská Energetika—SČE a.s.): Teplická 8, 405 49 Děčín IV; tel. 412571111; fax 412572977; e-mail info@sce.cz; internet www.sce.cz; f. 1994; Chair. JIŘÍ ŠTASTNÝ.

North Moravian Electricity (Severomoravská Energetika—SME a.s.): 28 Října 152, 709 02 Ostrava; tel. 596671111; fax 596673284; internet www.sme.cz; distribution co; Dir-Gen. TOMÁŠ HÜNER.

Opatovice Electricity (Elektrarny Opatovice a.s.): Pardubice 0, 532 13 Opatovice nad Labem; tel. 466841111; fax 466536010; f. 1905; generation and distribution co; 48% owned by National Power (United Kingdom); Chair. and Man. Dir ARNOŠT POUL.

Prazská Energetika, a.s.: Na Hroudé 4, 100 05 Prague 10; tel. (2) 67051111; fax (2) 67310817; internet www.pre.cz; distribution; Chair. and Gen. Man. Ing DRAHOMÍR RUTA.

Prazská Teplárenská, a.s.: Partyzanska 7, 170 00 Prague 7; tel. (2) 66751111; fax (2) 876328; e-mail ptas@ptas.cz; internet www.ptas.cz; f. 1992; electricity supply; Chair. of Bd and Gen. Man. Ing. LUBOS PAVLAS.

South Bohemian Electricity (Jihočeská Energetika—JČE a.s.): Lannova 16, 370 49 České Budějovice; tel. 387312682; fax 386359803; e-mail info@jce.cz; internet www.jce.cz; majority-owned by Bayernwerk (Germany) and Raiffesenlandesbank (Austria); Pres. and Gen. Dir JAN ŠPIKA.

South Moravian Electricity (Jihomoravska Energetika—JME): Lidicka 36, POB 344, 659 44 Brno; tel. (5) 45141111; fax (5) 45142551; e-mail jme@jme.cz; internet www.jme.cz; f. 1994; Man. Dir ZDENĚK MACHALA.

State Office for Nuclear Safety (Státni úřad pro jadernou bezpečnost): Senovážné nám. 9, 110 00 Prague 1; tel. (2) 21624111; fax (2) 21624396; internet www.sujb.cz; state supervision of nuclear safety, co-ordination of international relations in the sphere of nuclear safety; Chair. DANA DRÁBOVÁ.

Gas

North Moravian Gas (Severomoravsjká Plynárenská—SMP): Plynární 6, POB 72/73, 702 00 Ostrava; tel. 596102525; fax 596113985; e-mail sek.gr@smpas.cz; internet www.smpas.cz; f. 1994; distribution co; Chair. of Bd KAREL MAZAL.

South Moravian Gas Company (Jihomoravská plynárenská—JMP a.s.): Plynárenská 1, 657 02 Brno; tel. (5) 45548111; fax (5) 578571; e-mail jmpas@jmpas.cz; internet www.jmpas.cz; distribution co; Chair. JÖRG SCHELER.

Transgas/Český Plynárensky Podnik: Limuzská 12, 100 98 Prague 10; tel. (2) 70771111; fax (2) 70776965; e-mail info@transgas.cz; internet www.transgas,cz; f. 1971; sale of majority stake to RWE Energie AG (Germany) approved in May 2002; import and distribution co; Chief Exec. TOMÁŠ TICHÝ.

Water

Prazske Vodovody a Kanalizace a.s.: Narodni 13, 112 65 Prague; tel. (2) 57320132; fax (2) 57535011; e-mail info@pvk.cz; internet www.pvk.cz; f. 1998; water supply and sewerage co; privatized in 2000.

TRADE UNIONS

Czech-Moravian Confederation of Trade Unions (Českomoravská konfederace odborových svazů): W. Churchilla nám. 2, 113 59 Prague 3; tel. (2) 24461111; fax (2) 22718994; f. 1990; 30 affiliated unions (1999); Pres. RICHARD FALBR.

Affiliated unions include the following:

Czech-Moravian Trade Union of Workers in Education (Českomoravský odborový svaz školství): W. Churchilla nám. 2, 113 59 Prague 3; tel. (2) 22721721; fax (2) 22722685; e-mail cmos.skolstvi@cmkos.cz; internet www.skolskeodbory.cz; Pres. JAROSLAV RÖSSLER; 80,000 mems.

Trade Union of the Health Service and Social Care of the Czech Republic (Odborový svaz zdravotnictví a sociální péče ČR): Koněvova 54, 130 00 Prague 3; tel. (2) 22714629; fax (2) 22718211; e-mail osz_cr@cmkos.cz; internet www.osz.cmkos.cz; Pres. JIŘÍ SCHLANGER; 65,000 mems.

Trade Union of Workers in Textile, Clothing and Leather Industry of Bohemia and Moravia (Odboroý svaz pracovníků textilního, oděvního a kožedělného průmyslu Čech a Moravy): W. Churchilla nám. 2, 113 59 Prague 3; tel. (2) 24222123; fax (2) 273589; Pres. KAREL NOCOTNY; 79,600 mems.

Trade Union of Workers in Woodworking Industry, Forestry and Management of Water Supplies in the Czech Republic (Odborový svaz pracovníků dřevozpracujícího odvětví, lesního a vodního hospodářství v České republice): W. Churchilla nám. 2, 113 59 Prague 3; tel. (2) 24462659; fax (2) 22716373; e-mail kyncl.rudolf@cmkos.cz; Pres. RUDOLF KYNCL; 43,000 mems.

TU UNIOS: W. Churchilla nám. 2, 113 59 Prague 3; tel. (2) 24463172; fax (2) 24463185; f. 1994 to succeed Czech-Moravian Trade Union of Workers in Services (f. 1990); Pres. KAREL SLADKOVSKÝ; 38,000 mems.

Transport

RAILWAYS

In 1998 the total length of the Czech railway network was 9,430 km.

České dráhy (Czech Railways): nábř. L. Svobody 1222/12, 110 15 Prague 1; tel. (2) 51431111; fax (2) 24812569; e-mail infoservis@gr

.cdrail.cz; internet www.cdrail.cz; f. 1993 as successor to Czecho-slovak State Railways; Gen. Dir Ing. DALIBOR ZELENÝ.

Prague Metropolitan Railway: Dopravní podnik hlavního města Prahy, a.s.-Metro, o.z., Sliačská 1, 141 41 Prague 4; tel. (2) 71763657; fax (2) 764762; e-mail pavlicar@dp-praha.cz; the Prague under-ground railway opened in 1974, and in 1998 50 km were operational; 50 stations; Chair. M. HEJL; Gen. Dir Ing. LADISLAV HOUDEK.

ROADS

In 2000 there were an estimated 55,408 km of roads in the Czech Republic, including 499 km of motorways.

INLAND WATERWAYS

The total length of navigable waterways in the Czech Republic is 663.6 km. The Elbe (Labe) and its tributary, the Vltava, connect the Czech Republic with the North Sea via the port of Hamburg (Ger-many). The Oder provides a connection with the Baltic Sea and the port of Szczecin (Poland). The Czech Republic's river ports are Prague Holešovice, Prague Radotín, Kolín, Mělník, Ústí nad Labem and Děčín, on the Vltava and Elbe.

Czechoslovak Elbe Navigation Ltd (Československá plavba labská, a.s.): K. Čapka 1, 405 91 Děčín; tel. 412561111; fax 412510140; f. 1922; river transport of goods to Germany, Poland, the Netherlands, Belgium, Luxembourg, France and Switzerland; Man. Dir KAREL HORYNA.

SHIPPING

Since August 1997 no ships have operated under the Czech flag. All Czech-owned ships operate under the Maltese and Cypriot flags.

Czech Ocean Shipping, Joint-Stock Company (Česká námořní plavba, akciová společnost): Počernická 168, 100 99 Prague 10; tel. (2) 778941; fax (2) 773962; e-mail coscompu@login.cz; internet www .cos.cz; f. 1959; six ships totalling 199,331 dwt; Man. Dir Capt. PAVEL TRNKA.

CIVIL AVIATION

There are main civil airports at Prague (Ruzyně), Brno, Karlovy Vary and Ostrava, operated by the Czech Airport Administration. The opening of a new terminal at Ruzyně in November 1997 in-creased the airport's capacity from 2.3m. passengers to 4.8m.

Air Ostrava: Ostrava International Airport, 742 51 Mosnov; tel. (69) 6659401; fax (69) 6659402; e-mail air.ostrava@ova.prtnet.cz; internet www.airostrava.cz; f. 1994; services to international, regional and domestic destinations; Pres. MILAN ROUSAR; Man. Dir PAVEL HRADEC.

ČSA (České aerolinie, a.s.) (Czech Airlines): Ruzyně Airport, 160 08 Prague 6; tel. (2) 20111111; fax (2) 20562266; e-mail info@uit.csa .cz; internet www.csa.cz; f. 1923; external services to most European capitals, the Near, Middle and Far East, North Africa and North America; scheduled for privatization; Pres. MIROSLAV KULA.

Tourism

The Czech Republic has magnificent scenery, with summer and winter sports facilities. Prague, Kutna Hora, Olomouc, Český Krumlov and Telč are among the best known of the historic towns, and there are famous castles and cathedrals and numerous resorts, as well as spas with natural mineral springs at Karlovy Vary (Carlsbad) and Mariánské Lázně (Marienbad). Registered accom-modation establishments recorded some 5.2m. stays of at least one night by foreigners in 2001. In 2000 tourism receipts totalled US $2,982.0m.

Czech Tourist Authority: Vinohradská 46, POB 32, 120 41 Prague 2; tel. (2) 22515078; fax (2) 24257145; e-mail kejvalova@cccr-cta.cz; internet www.visitczech.cz; f. 1993; Dir KAREL NEJDL.

Čedok Travel Corpn: Na Příkopě 18, 111 35 Prague 1; tel. (2) 24197111; fax (2) 2321656; internet www.cedok.cz; f. 1920; 80 domestic travel offices; eight branches throughout Europe; Pres. ČESTMÍR SAJDA.

DENMARK

Introductory Survey

Location, Climate, Language, Religion, Flag, Capital

The Kingdom of Denmark is situated in northern Europe. It consists of the peninsula of Jutland, the islands of Zealand, Funen, Lolland, Falster and Bornholm, and 401 smaller islands. The country lies between the North Sea, to the west, and the Baltic Sea, to the east. Denmark's only land frontier is with Germany, to the south. Norway lies to the north of Denmark, across the Skagerrak, while Sweden, the most southerly region of which is separated from Zealand by a narrow strait, lies to the north-east. Outlying territories of Denmark are Greenland and the Faroe Islands in the North Atlantic Ocean. Denmark is low-lying and the climate is temperate, with mild summers and cold, rainy winters. The language is Danish. Almost all of the inhabitants profess Christianity: the Evangelical Lutheran Church, to which some 85% of the population belong, is the established Church, and there are also small communities of other Protestant groups and of Roman Catholics. The national flag (proportions 28 by 37) displays a white cross on a red background, the upright of the cross being to the left of centre. The capital is Copenhagen (København).

Recent History

In 1945, following the end of German wartime occupation, Denmark recognized the independence of Iceland, which had been declared in the previous year. Home rule was granted to the Faroe Islands in 1948 and to Greenland in 1979. Denmark was a founder member of the North Atlantic Treaty Organization (NATO, see p. 271) in 1949 and of the Nordic Council (see p. 266) in 1952. In January 1973, following a referendum, Denmark entered the European Communities (including the EEC), later more commonly referred to as simply the European Community (EC), and from 1993 restyled as the European Union (EU, see p. 199).

In 1947 King Frederik IX succeeded to the throne on the death of his father, Christian X. Denmark's Constitution was radically revised in 1953: new provisions allowed for female succession to the throne, abolished the upper house of the Folketing (parliament) and amended the franchise. King Frederik died in January 1972, and his eldest daughter, Margrethe, became the first queen to rule Denmark for nearly 600 years.

The system of proportional representation, which is embodied in the 1953 Constitution, makes it difficult for a single party to gain a majority in the Folketing. The minority Government of Venstre (Liberals), led by Poul Hartling and formed in 1973, was followed in 1975 by a minority Government of the Social-demokratiet (Social Democrats) under Anker Jørgensen. Jørgensen led various coalitions and minority Governments until 1982. General elections in 1977, 1979 and 1981 were held against a background of growing unemployment and attempts to tighten control of the economy. By September 1982 Jørgensen's economic policy, including attempts to reduce the budget deficit by introducing new taxes, had once more led to disagreements within the Cabinet, and the Government resigned.

Det Konservative Folkeparti (the Conservative People's Party), which had been absent from Danish coalitions since 1971, formed a centre-right four-party Government—with Venstre, the Centrum-Demokraterne (Centre Democrats) and the Kristeligt Folkeparti (Christian People's Party)—led by Poul Schlüter, who became Denmark's first Conservative Prime Minister since 1894. Holding only 66 of the Folketing's 179 seats, the coalition narrowly avoided defeat in October 1982, when it introduced stringent economic measures, and again in September 1983, when larger reductions in public spending were proposed. In December the right-wing Fremskridtspartiet (Progress Party) withdrew its support for further cuts in expenditure, and the Government was defeated. A general election to the Folketing was held in January 1984, and Schlüter's Government remained in office, with its component parties holding a total of 77 seats, and relying on the support of members of Det Radikale Venstre (Social Liberals).

In January 1986 the left-wing parties in the Folketing combined to reject the ratification by Denmark of the Single Euro-pean Act (which amended the Treaty of Rome—the agreement that founded the EC—so as to establish the EC's single market and allow the EC Council of Ministers to take decisions by a qualified majority vote if a unanimous one was not achieved). Opponents of ratification, led by the Socialdemokratiet, argued that it would lead to a diminution of Denmark's power to maintain strict environmental controls. In a national referendum in February, however, 56.2% of the votes cast were in favour of ratification of the Act, and the Folketing formally approved it in May.

At a general election held in September 1987 Schlüter's co-alition retained only 70 seats in the Folketing while the opposition Socialdemokratiet lost two of their 56 seats. Jørgensen later resigned as leader of the latter party. Several of the smaller and extremist parties made considerable gains, with the result that the outgoing coalition was weakened, while the main opposition parties were unable to command a working majority. Schlüter eventually formed a new Cabinet comprising representatives of the former four-party governing coalition. However, Det Radikale Venstre had earlier declared that they would not support any administration that depended on the support of the Fremskridtspartiet. This therefore left a precarious balance of power within the Folketing.

In April 1988 the Folketing adopted an opposition-sponsored resolution requiring the Government to inform visiting warships of the country's ban on nuclear weapons. The British and US Governments were highly critical of the resolution. Schlüter consequently announced an early general election for May 1988, on the issue of Denmark's membership of NATO and defence policy. For the main parties the election result was inconclusive, and negotiations lasting three weeks were necessary before Schlüter was appointed to seek a basis for viable government. At the beginning of June a new minority coalition, comprising members of Det Konservative Folkeparti, Venstre and Det Radikale Venstre, formed a Cabinet under Schlüter. The new Government restored good relations with its NATO allies by adopting a formula that requested all visiting warships to respect Danish law in its territorial waters, while making no specific reference to nuclear weapons.

The Government proposed large reductions in social welfare provision for 1989, and attacked demands by the Fremskridtspartiet for less taxation as unrealistic. The Fremskridtspartiet, however, continued to increase in popularity, and in November 1989 its share of the vote rose significantly in municipal elections, while Det Konservative Folkeparti lost support. The Government therefore proposed to reduce the rates of taxation in 1990, despite opposition on the part of the Socialdemokratiet to the accompanying decreases in welfare expenditure. An early general election was organized for December 1990. Although the Socialdemokratiet retained the largest share of the vote (winning an additional 14 seats to bring their total to 69), Schlüter formed a minority coalition Government, comprising Det Konservative Folkeparti, which had lost five seats in the election, and Venstre, which had gained an additional seven seats. As expected, Det Radikale Venstre, while no longer part of the Government, continued to support the majority of the new coalition Government's policies.

In May 1992 the Folketing voted, by 130 votes to 25, to approve the Treaty on European Union (the Maastricht Treaty), which further expanded the scope of the Treaty of Rome. In a national referendum held in Denmark in June, however, 50.7% of the votes cast were against ratification of the Treaty, compared with 49.3% in favour. This unexpected result caused consternation among Denmark's European partners, and during the rest of the year discussions took place among representatives of EC countries, who sought to establish a formula that, without necessitating the renegotiation of the Treaty, would allow the Danish Government to conduct a second referendum with some hope of success. In December EC heads of government agreed that Denmark should be allowed exemption from certain provisions of the Treaty, namely the final stage of European monetary union (including the adoption of a single currency); participation in a common defence policy; common

European citizenship; and co-operation in legal and home affairs: all provisions that had been regarded as a threat to national sovereignty by Danish opponents of ratification. Despite uncertainty as to how far these exemptions were legally binding, the agreement was endorsed by seven of the eight parties represented in the Folketing (the exception being the Fremskridtspartiet), and in a second referendum, held in May 1993, 56.7% of the votes cast were in favour of ratification and 43.3% against. In June 1994 the Government announced that it would seek an amendment to the Maastricht Treaty to ensure that environmental safety took precedence over European free-trade initiatives.

Meanwhile, in January 1993 Schlüter resigned from the premiership after a judicial inquiry disclosed that he had misled the Folketing in April 1989 over a scandal that had its origin in 1987, when the then Minister of Justice, Erik Ninn-Hansen, had illegally ordered civil servants to delay issuing entry visas to the families of Tamil refugees from Sri Lanka. In subsequent negotiations between political parties, Poul Nyrup Rasmussen, the leader of the Socialdemokratiet, obtained sufficient support to form a new government, and in late January 1993 a majority coalition Government (the first majority administration in Denmark for 11 years, controlling 90 of the 179 seats in the legislature) took office: it comprised members of the Socialdemokratiet and three small centre parties (Det Radikale Venstre, the Centrum-Demokraterne and the Kristeligt Folkeparti). The new Government gave priority to securing an affirmative vote for the Maastricht Treaty (see above).

In a general election in September 1994, three months earlier than scheduled, the Socialdemokratiet won a reduced number of seats, although they retained the largest share of the vote. Venstre, led by Uffe Ellemann-Jensen, gained an additional 13 seats, but the Kristeligt Folkeparti, a member of the outgoing coalition, failed to secure representation in the new legislature. None the less, Nyrup Rasmussen was able to form a minority Government with his two remaining coalition partners, Det Radikale Venstre and the Centrum-Demokraterne, and denied that the Government would be dependent for support on the left-wing Socialistik Folkeparti (Socialist People's Party). In December 1996, however, the Centrum-Demokraterne withdrew from the coalition, following the Government's decision to seek support from left-wing parties in order to achieve parliamentary approval for legislation relating to the 1997 budget.

In late October 1997 Thorkild Simonsen was appointed as the new Minister of the Interior and of Health, following mounting public concern at reports of increasingly high levels of immigration. As expected, a new government initiative was launched in December, enforcing stricter immigration policies.

The results of local elections conducted in November 1997 indicated that the Socialdemokratiet, who received some 33% of the votes cast, were continuing to attract the largest share of popular support. In February 1998 Prime Minister Nyrup Rasmussen announced that an early general election would be conducted on 11 March, six months before the expiry of the mandate of the incumbent Government and in advance of a referendum on the Amsterdam Treaty on European integration (drafted at a meeting of EU members in the Netherlands in June 1997), which was scheduled to be held in late May. Despite the fact that the Centrum-Demokraterne supported an informal electoral alliance comprising Det Konservative Folkeparti and Venstre in the election, Nyrup Rasmussen's Government was returned to office with a narrow majority in the Folketing: the Socialdemokraterne, together with their coalition partner Det Radikale Venstre and other informal allies, secured a total of 90 of the 179 legislative seats, compared with 89 seats won by the centre-right opposition (led by Ellemann-Jensen). The right-wing Dansk Folkeparti (Danish People's Party), which campaigned for stricter immigration controls, performed strongly in its first general election, winning 7.4% of the total votes cast (13 seats). Following his defeat in the general election, Ellemann-Jensen resigned as leader of Venstre and was replaced by Anders Fogh Rasmussen.

On 28 May 1998 Danish voters narrowly endorsed the ratification of the Amsterdam Treaty by a margin of 55.1% in favour to 44.9% against. The referendum followed the rejection by the Danish Supreme Court early in the previous month of a legal challenge to the constitutional validity of the Maastricht Treaty, which had been brought by a group of private individuals who were opposed to further European integration.

In early November 1999 serious rioting erupted in a district of Copenhagen which housed a high concentration of immigrants.

The rioting, which was the most serious to occur in Denmark for six years, was reportedly provoked by the earlier announcement of a controversial judicial ruling, in accordance with which a man of Turkish origin became the first Danish-born person to receive an expulsion order from the country. (The man, convicted on charges of theft, had failed to apply for the Danish citizenship to which he was entitled.) The court decision was announced just days after the readmittance to the membership of the right-wing Fremskridtspartiet of the party's founder, Mogens Glistrup, who was renowned for his vociferous opposition to immigration; Glistrup's extreme racist sentiments, expressed following the court ruling, led, later in November, to the resignation from the party of all four of its representatives in the Folketing, leaving the Fremskridtspartiet with no parliamentary representation. (The four legislators subsequently founded a new political organization, Frihed 2000—Freedom 2000.)

On 28 September 2000 the Government held a national referendum to ascertain whether the population supported the adoption of the single European currency, the euro. Approval for the euro had been strong when the referendum was called in May, but had declined throughout the months preceding the vote, despite the support of the Government, the majority of the major political parties, the industrial sector, banks, trade unions, and the media. In the event Danish voters rejected membership of the single currency, with 53.1% opposed to the euro and 46.9% in favour; the rate of participation of the electorate was 87.5%. Immediately after the outcome of the referendum was revealed the central bank raised interest rates by 0.5% to defend the krone; opposition parties claimed the move was politically motivated in order to vindicate economic scaremongering by supporters of the euro prior to the referendum. Prime Minister Nyrup Rasmussen underlined the significance of the set-back by arguing that Europe now needed to develop a new and clearer delineation between policies to be decided nationally and those to be determined at a community level. Indications of a shift in Denmark's European policy became apparent when the Minister of Foreign Affairs, Niels Helveg Petersen, intimated that Denmark was no longer opposed to the creation of a 'two-speed' Europe, whereby countries ready for further economic and political integration progressed independently of the rest. (In January 2003 Prime Minister Fogh Rasmussen announced that Denmark would hold a second referendum on the euro in 2004, when the content of the EU's revised basic treaty would be known.)

A government reorganization took place in December 2000, prompted by the resignation of Petersen from the foreign affairs portfolio in protest at the result of the referendum on the euro and by the need to replace the Minister of Defence, Hans Hækkerup, who had been appointed as head of the UN mission in Kosovo. Five new ministers were appointed, some of whom were relatively inexperienced, in an attempt to revitalize the Government.

Following the terrorist attacks in the USA in September 2001, Prime Minister Nyrup Rasmussen announced that the general election, due to be held by mid-March 2002 at the latest, would be held early, on 20 November 2001, concurrently with local elections. He stated that, given the general unease and uncertainty generated by the attacks, and with major decisions to be made on security, four months of electoral campaigning would not be in the country's best interest. The Prime Minister also said that it was important to give the new government sufficient time to prepare to host the six-month rotating EU presidency, which Denmark was due to assume on 1 July 2002. There followed a brief period of uncharacteristically bitter campaigning, focusing mainly on the issue of immigration. At the general election the Socialdemokratiet won 52 of the 179 seats in the Folketing (with 29.1% of the valid votes cast), meaning that, for the first time since 1920, it was no longer the party with the largest representation in the legislature. Venstre won 56 seats (with 31.3% of the votes cast) and formed a minority coalition Government with Det Konservative Folkeparti, which secured 16 seats (9%). The Dansk Folkeparti performed well, winning 22 seats (12%); the leaders of Venstre stressed, however, that the far-right, anti-immigration party would not exert any influence over government policy. Nevertheless, by the end of November 2001 the Fogh Rasmussen Government had announced its intention to remove the legal right of refugees to bring their families to Denmark, to extend the period of residence required to obtain a residence permit from three to seven years, and to deport immediately all immigrants convicted of crimes—all of which was to be financed primarily by a privatization programme and a substantial reduction in development aid. A new Ministry of Refugees, Immigration and Integration Affairs was also created. The proposed legislation tightening the country's immigration and asylum regulations came into force, with the support of the Dansk Folkeparti, in July 2002. Following the 2001 general election there was a period of internecine struggle within the Socialdemokratiet, which culminated in Nyrup Rasmussen's resignation as party leader in November 2002 and his replacement by Mogens Lykketoft.

In March 2000 Svend Auken, the Minister of the Environment and Energy, demanded a moratorium on the reprocessing of spent nuclear fuel after safety fears at the Sellafield nuclear reprocessing plant in the United Kingdom. Together with ministers from other Nordic countries and from Ireland, he put proposals before the Oslo Paris Convention (Ospar—an international convention signed in July 1998, which controls marine pollution in the Irish Sea, north-east Atlantic and North Sea) in early June 2000, calling for the end of nuclear reprocessing in Europe.

In August 1988 the Danish Government submitted a dispute with Norway, concerning maritime economic zones between Greenland and Jan Mayen island, to the International Court of Justice (ICJ) at The Hague. A delimitation line was fixed by the ICJ in June 1993. In 1991 the construction of a bridge across the Great Belt, between the Danish islands of Zealand and Funen, was the subject of an objection presented by Finland to the ICJ that the proposed bridge's clearance would not allow Finland to move oil-drilling rigs through the strait and would, therefore, be in contravention of Denmark's international treaty obligations to permit the free passage of shipping through the Great Belt. In September 1992, however, the ICJ was informed by the parties that the dispute had been settled, and construction of the bridge was completed in mid-1998.

In August 1991 Denmark and Sweden signed an agreement on the proposed construction of a 15.9-km road and rail system across the Oresund strait between Copenhagen and Malmö. Although construction was initially delayed, owing to objections raised by environmentalists in Sweden and Germany, the agreement was finally ratified by the Swedish Government in 1994 and the project was completed in July 2000 at a total cost of approximately 23,400m. kroner.

In May 1999 the Danish Government signed a maritime boundary agreement with representatives of the Faroese Landsstýri and the British Government, thus ending a 30-year dispute over the location of the boundaries of a 42,000-sq km area in the North Sea, which was potentially rich in petroleum reserves.

Following the dissolution of the USSR at the end of 1991, Denmark rapidly established diplomatic relations with (and began investing in) the former Soviet Baltic states of Estonia, Latvia and Lithuania, and was a founder member of the Council of Baltic Sea States (see p. 179), established in 1992.

Denmark's relations with Russia deteriorated in October 2002, when Copenhagen hosted a World Chechen Forum, despite pressure from the Russian Government not to permit the event to proceed. During the event, which was attended by Chechen exiles, Danish police officers arrested Akhmed Zakayev, a senior aide to the Chechen separatist leader Aslan Maskhadov, after receiving information allegedly linking Zakayev to an armed siege in a theatre in Moscow some days earlier. Denmark subsequently refused to extradite Zakayev, however, claiming that the incriminatory evidence provided by the Russian authorities was insufficient. Zakayev was released in December 2002, whereupon he proceeded to the United Kingdom (where he was promptly rearrested).

Government

Denmark is a constitutional monarchy. Under the 1953 constitutional charter, legislative power is held jointly by the hereditary monarch (who has no personal political power) and the unicameral Folketing (parliament), which has 179 members, including 175 from metropolitan Denmark and two each from the Faroe Islands and Greenland. Members are elected for four years (subject to dissolution) on the basis of proportional representation. Executive power is exercised by the monarch through a Cabinet, which is led by the Prime Minister and is responsible to the Folketing. Denmark comprises 14 counties (amtskommuner), one city and one borough, all with elected councils.

Defence

In August 2002 Denmark maintained an army of 12,800 (including 5,000 conscripts), a navy of 4,000 (500 conscripts) and

an air force of 4,500 (125 conscripts). There were, in total, 64,900 reservists, and a volunteer Home Guard numbering some 59,300. Military service is for 4–12 months, although some ranks are required to serve for 24 months. Denmark abandoned its neutrality after the Second World War and has been a member of NATO since 1949. In 1992 Denmark assumed observer status in Western European Union (WEU, see p. 318). The defence budget for 2002 totalled 17,200m. kroner.

Economic Affairs

In 2001, according to estimates by the World Bank, Denmark's gross national income (GNI), measured at average 1999–2001 prices, was US \$166,345m., equivalent to \$31,090 per head (or \$27,950 per head on an international purchasing-power parity basis). During 1990–2001 Denmark's population grew at an average annual rate of 0.4%, while gross domestic product (GDP) per head increased, in real terms, at an average rate of 1.8% per year. Overall GDP increased, in real terms, at an average annual rate of 2.2% in 1990–2001; growth was 2.9% in 2000, falling to just 0.9% in 2001.

Agriculture (including forestry and fishing) employed 3.6% of the economically active population in 1998, and contributed an estimated 2.5% of GDP, measured at current prices, in 2000. In 1999 53.4% of Denmark's land area was used for agriculture. The principal activities are pig-farming and dairy farming; Denmark is a major exporter of pork products, and exports of live pigs and of pig meat accounted for an estimated 5.0% of total export revenue in 2000. Most of Denmark's agricultural production is exported, and the sector accounted for 18.1% of total exports in 2000. The fishing industry accounted for 3.7% of total export earnings in that year. Agricultural GDP increased, in real terms, at an average annual rate of 2.5% in 1990–2000; the GDP of the sector grew by 1.9% in 1999 and by 0.3% in 2000.

Industry (including mining, manufacturing, construction, power and water) employed 26.6% of the working population in 1998, and provided an estimated 25.3% of GDP, measured at current prices, in 2000. Industrial GDP increased, in real terms, at an average annual rate of 1.7% in 1990–2000; it decreased by 1.1% in 1999 and grew by 4.2% in 2000.

Mining accounted for only 0.1% of employment in 1998, and provided 2.1% of GDP, measured at current prices, in 2000. Denmark has few natural resources, but exploration for petroleum reserves in the Danish sector of the North Sea in the 1970s proved successful. Natural gas has also been extensively exploited. In 1989, in north-western Jutland, it was established that there was a significant reserve of sand which could be exploited for rich yields of titanium, zirconium and yttrium. The GDP of the mining sector increased, in real terms, at an average annual rate of 8.2% in 1990–99; the sector's GDP declined by 2.7% in 1998, but grew by 10.8% in 1999 and by 12.1% in 2000.

Manufacturing employed 19.2% of the working population in 1998, and contributed an estimated 16.7% of GDP, measured at current prices, in 2000. Measured by value of output, in 1998 the most important manufacturing industries were food products (accounting for 22.0% of the total), non-electric machinery and domestic appliances (12.8%), chemicals and pharmaceuticals (8.1%), metal products (7.0%), and furniture (4.1%). Manufacturing GDP increased, in real terms, at an average annual rate of 1.8% in 1990–2000; it decreased by 0.8% in 1999 before recovering to grow by 5.0% in 2000.

Energy is derived principally from petroleum and natural gas. Since 1996 Denmark has produced enough energy to satisfy its domestic consumption, and the degree of self-sufficiency in petroleum and natural gas production amounted to 203% and 160%, respectively, in 2000. In that year total petroleum production amounted to 21m. cu m and total gas output was 11,300m. cu m. In 2000 imports of mineral fuels accounted for 5.5% of the total cost of imports, while exports of mineral fuels contributed 8.3% of total export revenue. The use of renewable sources of energy (including wind power) has been encouraged. In 2000 Denmark derived 15% of its energy from wind-turbines, and planned to increase the share to 50% by 2030.

Services engaged 69.8% of the employed population in 1998, and provided 72.2% of GDP, measured at current prices, in 2000. In real terms, the combined GDP of the service sectors increased at an average rate of 2.5% per year in 1990–2000; it rose by 3.8% in 1999 and by 3.3% in 2000.

In 2001, according to the IMF, Denmark recorded a visible trade surplus of US \$6,780m., and a surplus of \$4,051m. on the current account of the balance of payments. Most Danish trade is with the other member states of the European Union (EU), which accounted for 69.1% of imports and 64.6% of exports in

2000. The principal source of imports in 2000 was Germany (21.3%); other major suppliers were Sweden (12.4%), the United Kingdom (8.6%), the Netherlands (7.4%) and France (5.1%). Germany was also the principal market for exports (18.9%); other major purchasers included Sweden (12.8%), the United Kingdom (10.0%), the USA (5.9%) and Norway (5.5%). The principal exports in 2000 were machinery and transport equipment (accounting for 27.8% of total export revenue), food and food products (18.1%), chemicals and related products (16.8%), and basic manufactures (10.6%). The principal imports in 2000 were machinery and transport equipment (accounting for 57.1% of total import costs), basic manufactures (16.8%), food and live animals (11.1%), and chemicals and related products (10.2%).

In 2000 the general government budget recorded a surplus equivalent to 2.4% of GDP, according to EU figures, compared with a budgetary deficit equal to almost 4% of GDP in 1993. The overall government gross debt was equivalent to 40% of GDP in 2000 (compared with 80% in 1993). The average annual rate of inflation was 2.0% in 1990–99. Consumer prices increased by 2.9% in 2000, by 2.3% in 2001 and by 2.4% in 2002. The rate of unemployment decreased from an average of 10.2% of the labour force in 1995 to 5.0% in 2000.

Denmark is a member of the EU (see p. 199), the Nordic Council (see p. 266) and the Nordic Council of Ministers (see p. 267).

In late 2002 the Danish Economic Council concluded that the Danish economy was 'rather robust'. After the economic slow-down of 2001, when GDP grew by a mere 1.0%, the rate of growth accelerated during the first half of 2002, mainly owing to higher private consumption and an increase in exports; the rate of growth of GDP was expected to stand at 1.7% for 2002 as a whole. A slight decrease in employment in 2002 was not viewed as the start of a sustained period of low economic growth rates. Rather, a marginal rise in the annual growth rate of GDP, to almost 2.0%, was projected for 2003–05, which was expected to lead to higher employment, albeit mitigated by some increase in the labour force. Growth for Denmark's trading partners was forecast to be around 1.3% in 2002 and about 2.0% in 2003. Despite this low international GDP growth, the performance of Danish exports improved in the first half of 2002. The growth rate for imports was also expected to be substantial in 2002, reflecting the increase in domestic demand. Hence, net exports were projected to contribute only slightly to overall GDP growth, which was expected to be primarily driven by domestic demand. The same pattern was expected to continue until 2005. Owing to the historical importance of foreign trade to Denmark's small-scale, open economy, the main objective of the country's economic policy has been to maintain a stable exchange rate. Denmark did not, however, participate in the EU's programme of economic and monetary union (EMU); this was decided by a referendum in 1993, and confirmed by a second plebiscite in September 2000. The Danish Government and the Central Bank subsequently released a joint declaration announcing the aim of maintaining a stable rate of exchange with the new common European currency, the euro. Consequently, Denmark has endeavoured to satisfy the so-called convergence criteria of the Treaty on European Union (Maastricht Treaty), which restricted the rate of increase of both consumer-price inflation and interest, and imposed strict conditions on public finances. The public sector plays an important role in the Danish economy: it employs around 33% of the work force, public expenditure amounts to almost 25% of GDP and the tax incidence is around 50% of GDP. Public budgets are therefore highly dependent on the development of economic activity and, accordingly, public finances improved markedly in the 'boom' years. Thus, in 2000, public finances showed a surplus of almost 3.0% of GDP, while public-sector debt was reduced to less than 50% of GDP—one of the lowest debt ratios in the EU. Future demographic changes, which will result in a smaller labour force and a larger number of elderly people in the population during the first half of the 21st century, will affect the sustainability of public finances. Under the assumption of some improvement in labour force participation rates, calculations indicate that the basic income tax rate should be raised by about 2.5% to ensure a sustainable fiscal policy from 2005. Naturally, these results are highly sensitive to changes in the underlying assumptions, not least the changes in the labour force and the projected spending on public consumption. However, because of relatively large future tax payments from pension funds, among other things, the Danish sustainability problem is smaller than in many other OECD countries.

Education

Education is compulsory for nine years between seven and 16 years of age. The State is obliged to offer a pre-school class and a tenth voluntary year. In 1999/2000 enrolment at pre-primary level was equivalent to 91.7% of children in the relevant age-group. State-subsidized private schools are available, but about 90% of pupils attend municipal schools. Primary and lower secondary education begins at seven years of age and lasts for nine (optionally 10) years. This includes at least six years at primary school. Enrolment at primary level included 99.3% of those in the relevant age-group in 1999/2000 (males 99.3%; females 99.4%). Secondary education is divided into two cycles of three years, the first beginning at 13 years of age, the second at the age of 16 or 17. Students may transfer to vocational courses at this stage. Total enrolment at secondary level in 1999/2000 included 89.5% of those in the relevant age-group (males 88.2%; females 90.8%). There are eight universities and many other institutions of further and higher education. The traditional folk high schools offer a wide range of further education opportunities, which do not confer any professional qualification. In 1999/2000 enrolment at tertiary level was equivalent to 56.1% of those in the relevant age-group (males 47.4%; females 65.2%). In 2001 proposed government expenditure on education totalled an estimated 29,773m. kroner, representing 7.3% of total budget spending.

Public Holidays

2003: 1 January (New Year's Day), 17–21 April (Easter), 16 May (General Prayer Day), 29 May (Ascension Day), 5 June (Constitution Day), 9 June (Whit Monday), 24–26 December (Christmas), 31 December (New Year's Eve).

2004: 1 January (New Year's Day), 8–12 April (Easter), 7 May (General Prayer Day), 20 May (Ascension Day), 31 May (Whit Monday), 5 June (Constitution Day), 24–26 December (Christmas), 31 December (New Year's Eve).

Weights and Measures

The metric system is in force.

Statistical Survey

Note: The figures in this survey relate only to metropolitan Denmark, excluding the Faroe Islands and Greenland, which are dealt with in separate chapters. (see pp. 1415 and 1420 respectively)

Source (unless otherwise stated): Danmarks Statistik, Sejrøgade 11, POB 2550, 2100 Copenhagen Ø; tel. 39-17-39-17; fax 39-17-39-99; e-mail dst@dst.dk; internet www.dst.dk.

Area and Population

AREA, POPULATION AND DENSITY

Area (sq km)	43,098*
Population (census results)	
1 January 1991	5,146,469
1 January 2001	
Males	2,644,319
Females.	2,704,893
Total	5,349,212
Population (official estimates at 1 January)	
1999	5,313,577
2000	5,330,020
2002	5,368,354
Density (per sq km) at 1 January 2002	124.6

* 16,640 sq miles.

PRINCIPAL TOWNS
(population at 1 January 2001)

København			
(Copenhagen, the		Kolding.	53,687
capital) 1,081,673*		Horsens	48,837
Århus (Aarhus) .	218,380	Vejle	48,402
Odense	144,849	Roskilde	43,210
Ålborg (Aalborg) .	119,996	Greve Strand . . .	41,441
Esbjerg.	73,046	Naestved	39,638
Randers	56,008	Sikeborg.	37,460

* Copenhagen metropolitan area, including Frederiksberg and 11 suburb municipalities. The estimated population of the Copenhagen municipality was 499,148 at 1 January 2001.

BIRTHS, MARRIAGES AND DEATHS

	Registered live births		Registered marriages		Registered deaths	
	Number	Rate (per 1,000)	Number	Rate (per 1,000)	Number	Rate (per 1,000)
1994 .	69,666	13.4	35,321	6.8	61,099	11.7
1995 .	69,771	13.3	34,736	6.6	63,127	12.1
1996 .	67,638	12.9	35,953	6.8	61,043	11.6
1997 .	67,636	12.8	34,244	6.5	59,898	11.3
1998 .	66,170	12.5	34,733	6.6	58,453	11.0
1999 .	66,232	12.5	35,459	6.7	59,156	11.1
2000 .	67,081	12.6	38,844	7.3	57,986	10.9
2001 .	65,450	12.2	n.a.	n.a.	58,338	10.9

Expectation of life (WHO estimates, years at birth): 77.2 (males 74.8; females 79.5) in 2001 (Source: WHO, *World Health Report*).

ECONOMICALLY ACTIVE POPULATION
(sample surveys, '000 persons aged 15 to 66 years, April–June)

	1996	1997	1998
Agriculture, hunting and forestry	98.1	93.6	91.9
Fishing	5.4	5.3	4.7
Mining and quarrying	3.5	3.0	3.2
Manufacturing	510.5	512.7	516.0
Electricity, gas and water supply	16.7	16.6	20.5
Construction	170.2	176.1	177.5
Wholesale and retail trade; repair of motor vehicles, motorcycles and personal and household goods	359.2	365.8	367.7
Hotels and restaurants	69.2	74.0	71.3
Transport, storage and communications	184.5	185.4	181.9
Financial intermediation . . .	83.3	79.8	79.2
Real estate, renting and business activities	189.1	209.1	227.9
Public administration and defence; compulsory social security .	167.5	168.3	168.3
Education	193.3	199.4	198.8
Health and social work . .	444.1	457.4	458.8
Other community, social and personal service activities . .	119.5	125.0	118.5
Private households with employed persons	7.2	4.7	5.4
Extra-territorial organizations and bodies	1.1	0.7	0.9
Activities not adequately defined .	5.0	5.1	5.2
Total employed	2,627.3	2,682.0	2,692.4
Unemployed	194.5	174.2	155.3
Total labour force	2,821.8	2,856.2	2,847.7
Males	1,528.3	1,539.5	1,528.5
Females	1,293.5	1,316.7	1,319.1

Source: ILO, *Yearbook of Labour Statistics*.

Health and Welfare

KEY INDICATORS

Total fertility rate (children per woman, 2001).	1.7
Under-5 mortality rate (per 1,000 live births, 2001) . . .	4
HIV/AIDS (% of persons aged 15–49, 2001).	0.15
Physicians (per 1,000 head, 1994)	2.9
Hospital beds (per 1,000 head, 1997)	4.6
Health expenditure (2000): US $ per head (PPP)	2,428
Health expenditure (2000): % of GDP	8.3
Health expenditure (2000): public (% of total)	82.1
Access to water (% of persons, 2000).	100
Human Development Index (2000): ranking	14
Human Development Index (2000): value	0.926

For sources and definitions, see explanatory note on p. vi.

Agriculture

PRINCIPAL CROPS

('000 metric tons)

	1998	1999	2000
Wheat	4,928	4,471	4,693
Barley	3,565	3,675	3,980
Rye	538	248	262
Oats	161	130	233
Triticale (wheat-rye hybrid)	142	250	245
Potatoes	1,546	1,502	1,645
Dry peas	386	193	139
Rapeseed	359	411	292
Sugar beet	3,486	3,545	3,345

LIVESTOCK

('000 head at May)

	1998	1999	2000
Horses	38.2	40.5	39.7
Cattle	1,977.4	1,887.1	1,867.9
Pigs	12,096.1	11,626.0	11,921.6
Sheep	156.0	142.9	145.5
Chickens	18,023.3	19,967.9	2,098.7
Turkeys	312.3	615.8	545.8
Ducks	328.9	410.0	296.0
Geese	9.3	16.2	6.8

LIVESTOCK PRODUCTS

('000 metric tons)

	1998	1999	2000
Beef and veal	164	159	156
Pig meat	1,698	1,709	1,677
Poultry meat	193	205	205
Cows' milk	4,668	4,655	4,720
Butter	49	48	46
Cheese	292	290	306
Hen eggs	84	78	74

Forestry

ROUNDWOOD REMOVALS

('000 cu m, excl. bark)

	1999	2000*	2001*
Sawlogs, veneer logs and logs for sleepers	658	1,322	630
Other industrial wood	313	573	259
Fuel wood	324	460	278
Total	1,295	2,355	1,167

* Unofficial figures.

Source: FAO.

SAWNWOOD PRODUCTION

('000 cu m, incl. railway sleepers)

	1999	2000	2001
Coniferous (softwood)	297	327	238
Broadleaved (hardwood)	47	37	43
Total	344	364	281

Source: FAO.

Fishing

('000 metric tons, live weight)

	1998	1999	2000
Capture	1,557.3	1,405.0	1,534.1
Atlantic cod	69.0	70.5	57.0
Norway pout	63.7	57.4	150.0
Blue whiting (Poutassou)	69.3	79.8	62.1
Sandeels (Sandlances)	646.9	528.6	567.4
European sprat	270.4	282.3	276.9
Capelin	40.3	3.8	20.8
Atlantic horse mackerel	32.6	32.0	25.1
Atlantic herring	139.7	137.6	153.9
Atlantic mackerel	27.4	29.7	31.6
Blue mussel	108.3	96.2	110.6
Aquaculture	42.4	42.7	43.6
Total catch	1,599.7	1,447.7	1,577.7

Note: Figures exclude aquatic mammals, recorded by number rather than by weight. The catch of whales and dolphins was: 2 in 1998.

Source: FAO, *Yearbook of Fishery Statistics*.

Mining

(sales-based estimates, '000 metric tons, unless otherwise indicated)

	1998	1999	2000
Crude petroleum (million barrels)	84	84	85
Natural gas (million cu metres)*	9,600	9,600	9,700
Limestone	950	950	950
Chalk	425	400	400
Salt (unrefined)	600	600	605
Peat	205	200	200

* Figures refer to gross output. Marketable production (estimates, million cu metres) was: 7,000 in 1998; 7,000 in 1999; 7,100 in 2000.

Source: US Geological Survey.

Industry

SELECTED PRODUCTS

('000 metric tons, unless otherwise indicated)

	1998	1999	2000
Pig meat:			
Fresh, chilled or frozen	1,072	1,183	1,176
Salted, dried or smoked	135	112	119
Poultry meat and offals	176	195	198
Fish fillets: fresh, chilled, frozen	37	37	45
Salami, sausages, etc	94	89	87
Meat in airtight containers:			
Hams	42	37	30
Other meat	143	137	141
Beet and cane sugar (solid)	573	654	443
Beer ('000 hectolitres)	8,044	8,205	7,455
Flours, meals and pastes of fish	352	305	328
Oil cake and meal	81	101	54
Cigarettes (million)	12,392	11,749	11,413
Cement	2,667	2,534	2,639
Motor spirit (Petrol)	2,636	2,571	2,829
Motor and fuel oils	1,921	1,780	1,726
Powder asphalt	907	816	1,203
Washing powders, etc	26	38	35
Refrigerators for household use ('000)	128	107	96

Finance

CURRENCY AND EXCHANGE RATES

Monetary Units
    100 øre = 1 Danish krone (plural: kroner)

Sterling, Dollar and Euro Equivalents (31 December 2002)
    £1 sterling = 11.4151 kroner
    US $1 = 7.0822 kroner
    €1 = 7.4271 kroner
    1,000 Danish kroner = £87.60 = $141.20 = €134.64

Average Exchange Rate (kroner per US $)
    2000   8.0831
    2001   8.3228
    2002   7.8947

BUDGET
(million kroner)

Revenue	1999*	2000*	2001†
Income and property taxes . . .	133,471	132,730	123,453
Customs and excise duties . . .	199,435	214,370	225,870
Other revenue . . . . }	74,422	85,765	90,498
Interest (net) . . . . }			
Total	407,328	432,865	439,821

Expenditure	1999*	2000*	2001†
Ministry of Social Affairs and			
Gender Equality	95,718	97,335	101,424
Ministry of Education . . .	26,445	26,968	29,773
Ministry of Defence	16,944	17,135	17,901
Public corporations	1,346	1,222	1,843
Ministry of Food, Agriculture and			
Fisheries	2,774	3,152	3,025
Ministry of Justice	8,704	9,257	9,820
Ministry of Finance	5,168	8,180	7,284
Other expenditure	236,844	234,763	239,696
Total	393,943	398,012	409,956

* Approved.
† Estimates.

2002 (budget proposals, million kroner): Revenue 443,778; Expenditure 420,408.

INTERNATIONAL RESERVES
(US $ million at 31 December)*

	2000	2001	2002
Gold†	569	557	703
IMF special drawing rights. . .	66	281	103
Reserve position in IMF. . . .	573	712	982
Foreign exchange.	14,469	16,117	25,901
Total	15,677	17,667	27,689

* Data referring to holdings of gold and foreign exchange exclude deposits made with the European Monetary Institute.
† Valued at market-related prices.

Source: IMF, *International Financial Statistics*.

MONEY SUPPLY
(million kroner at 31 December)

	2000	2001	2002
Currency outside banks . . .	37,430	39,210	38,980
Demand deposits at banks . . .	346,550	373,200	391,630
Total money (incl. others) . . .	385,980	414,850	430,820

Source: IMF, *International Financial Statistics*.

COST OF LIVING
(Consumer Price Index; base: 1980 = 100)

	1998	1999	2000
Food	191.4	192.7	197.3
Fuel and power	207.9	218.2	240.8
Clothing and footwear	182.6	185.3	179.9
Rent	242.1	248.6	255.7
All items (incl. others)	207.9	213.0	219.3

All items (base: 1995 = 100): 114.7 in 2001; 117.5 in 2002 (Source: IMF, *International Financial Statistics*).

NATIONAL ACCOUNTS
(provisional, million kroner at current prices)

National Income and Product

	1998	1999	2000
Compensation of employees. . .	623,044	656,014	687,091
Operating surplus	183,307	192,990	229,585
Domestic factor incomes. . .	806,351	849,004	916,676
Consumption of fixed capital . .	185,273	197,860	213,180
Gross domestic product at			
factor cost.	991,624	1,046,864	1,129,856
Indirect taxes.	213,069	221,342	222,816
Less Subsidies	35,697	38,621	37,146
GDP in purchasers' values . .	1,168,996	1,229,585	1,315,526
Factor income from abroad . .	80,311	76,742	104,990
Less Factor income paid abroad . .	93,020	81,929	122,706
Gross national product . . .	1,156,287	1,224,398	1,297,810
Less Consumption of fixed capital	185,273	197,860	213,180
National income in market			
prices	971,014	1,026,538	1,084,630
Other current transfers from			
abroad	14,481	13,839	14,510
Less Other current transfers paid			
abroad	34,304	40,148	46,817
National disposable income. .	951,191	1,000,229	1,052,323

Expenditure on the Gross Domestic Product

	1998	1999	2000
Government final consumption			
expenditure.	300,451	313,280	325,942
Private final consumption			
expenditure.	591,521	609,727	628,119
Increase in stocks	13,173	-2,009	-1,413
Gross fixed capital formation . .	240,971	250,138	285,583
Total domestic expenditure. .	1,146,116	1,171,136	1,238,231
Exports of goods and services . .	413,352	460,081	565,669
Less Imports of goods and services	390,473	401,633	488,375
GDP in purchasers' values . .	1,168,995	1,229,585	1,315,526
GDP at constant 1995 prices . .	1,095,260	1,118,618	1,154,514

Gross Domestic Product by Economic Activity

	1998	1999	2000
Agriculture and forestry	25,980	25,499	27,549
Fishing	2,409	2,544	2,326
Mining and quarrying	8,634	12,376	24,773
Manufacturing	175,720	181,686	195,395
Electricity, gas and water supply	22,890	23,011	23,088
Construction	48,829	49,761	52,637
Wholesale and retail trade	131,945	139,976	149,914
Restaurants and hotels	18,621	19,971	19,491
Transport, storage and communication	82,082	92,246	102,751
Finance and insurance	51,270	54,153	62,229
Real estate and renting activities	114,625	120,542	133,086
Business services	70,277	77,495	84,546
Public administration and defence; compulsory social security	74,702	77,326	75,938
Education	54,102	56,152	59,926
Health care activities	43,757	45,331	47,366
Social work activities	60,059	62,400	62,398
Other community, social and personal service activities	40,468	43,252	48,417
Sub-total	1,026,370	1,083,721	1,171,830
Less Imputed bank service charges	32,469	35,110	39,749
GDP at basic prices	993,901	1,048,611	1,132,081
Taxes on products	192,681	200,162	202,026
Less subsidies on products	17,586	19,188	18,581
GDP in purchasers' values	1,168,996	1,229,585	1,315,526

BALANCE OF PAYMENTS
(US $ million)

	1999	2000	2001
Exports of goods f.o.b.	49,932	50,754	50,449
Imports of goods f.o.b.	−43,533	−44,001	−43,670
Trade balance	6,399	6,754	6,780
Exports of services	20,090	24,385	26,956
Imports of services	−18,517	−22,082	−23,529
Balance on goods and services	7,972	9,056	10,206
Other income received	9,100	11,838	10,998
Other income paid	−11,426	−15,395	−14,546
Balance on goods, services and income	5,646	5,499	6,657
Current transfers received	4,156	3,303	3,650
Current transfers paid	−6,888	−6,296	−6,257
Current balance	2,915	2,507	4,051
Capital account (net)	1,083	−14	−25
Direct investment abroad	−17,039	−27,672	−9,623
Direct investment from abroad	16,076	35,532	7,367
Portfolio investment assets	−9,719	−23,623	−14,357
Portfolio investment liabilities	7,014	5,783	10,992
Financial derivatives liabilities	325	328	512
Other investment assets	−1,188	−1,677	10,118
Other investment liabilities	10,778	7,641	−8,545
Net errors and omissions	−808	−4,453	2,780
Overall balance	9,437	−5,649	3,270

Source: IMF, *International Financial Statistics*.

External Trade

PRINCIPAL COMMODITIES
(distribution by SITC, million kroner)

Imports c.i.f.	1998	1999	2000
Food and live animals	30,853.2	30,595.4	39,728.9
Crude materials (inedible) except fuels	11,898.1	10,914.0	12,175.5
Mineral fuels, lubricants, etc.	10,919.8	12,303.6	19,893.8
Petroleum, petroleum products, etc	8,257.0	10,170.0	17,563.0
Chemicals and related products	31,655.0	33,017.8	36,443.6
Basic manufactures	54,307.6	51,735.1	59,460.9
Paper, paperboard and manufactures	9,663.5	9,458.5	10,066.5
Iron and steel	11,291.7	8,832.9	10,882.7
Machinery and transport equipment	109,056.2	113,894.5	204,970.3
Machinery specialized for particular industries	9,907.8	10,316.8	12,182.8
General industrial machinery, equipment and parts	14,300.2	14,460.1	15,687.8
Office machines and automatic data-processing equipment	14,597.6	18,294.6	18,682.2
Telecommunications and sound equipment	13,927.9	15,263.4	19,506.9
Other electrical machinery, apparatus, etc.	16,543.4	17,421.6	21,950.7
Road vehicles (incl. air-cushion vehicles) and parts	25,923.2	25,260.6	23,051.4
Other transport equipment and parts	6,789.7	6,067.6	12,593.2
Miscellaneous manufactured articles	47,580.6	47,415.0	54,543.2
Clothing and accessories (excl. footwear)	15,656.0	15,572.5	21,455.5
Total (incl. others)	308,816.7	311,789.8	358,758.4

Exports f.o.b.	1998	1999	2000
Food and live animals	66,655.3	66,974.5	73,358.3
Meat and meat preparations	23,171.6	23,444.1	27,093.9
Dairy products and birds' eggs	9,961.3	10,337.0	10,545.8
Fish (not marine mammals), crustaceans, molluscs and aquatic invertebrates	13,869.7	14,999.8	15,177.1
Crude materials (inedible) except fuels	12,967.5	13,001.0	15,307.8
Mineral fuels, lubricants, etc.	10,894.4	15,247.9	33,812.1
Petroleum, petroleum products, etc.	7,687.8	12,478.5	29,725.5
Chemicals and related products	36,575.7	42,309.7	68,195.6
Medicinal and pharmaceutical products	16,853.6	21,110.0	24,075.3
Basic manufactures	37,136.5	38,876.6	43,086.9
Machinery and transport equipment	92,951.2	99,737.4	112,574.9
Machinery specialized for particular industries	12,980.4	12,893.8	15,247.7
General industrial machinery, equipment and parts	24,916.4	24,386.2	26,797.5
Telecommunications and sound equipment	13,427.6	15,543.8	18,107.2
Other electrical machinery, apparatus, etc.	12,334.7	12,397.0	15,344.9
Transport equipment and parts*	14,422.6	16,514.2	14,989.0
Miscellaneous manufactured articles	56,657.7	60,514.5	74,142.1
Furniture and parts	13,335.6	13,594.0	15,191.7
Clothing and accessories (excl. footwear)	11,444.9	12,366.5	15,996.0
Total (incl. others)	322,796.9	346,756.5	404,958.5

* Data on parts exclude tyres, engines and electrical parts.

PRINCIPAL TRADING PARTNERS
(million kroner)

Imports c.i.f.	1998	1999	2000
Austria.	3,116.0	3,386.8	3,833.9
Belgium-Luxembourg	11,150.3	11,084.9	12,111.4
China, People's Republic	6,396.5	8,237.7	10,561.3
Finland	8,193.1	8,556.0	9,757.3
France (incl. Monaco)	17,405.4	18,303.7	18,210.8
Germany	67,822.5	67,353.6	76,247.8
Ireland.	3,361.2	3,853.4	4,502.5
Italy	14,549.1	14,455.7	15,274.8
Japan	5,967.8	6,231.7	5,480.5
Korea, Republic	2,300.8	1,750.6	3,949.3
Netherlands	23,098.2	25,220.4	26,665.3
Norway	14,545.8	13,788.3	18,258.4
Poland.	5,308.3	5,543.9	6,585.3
Spain	4,430.4	4,652.2	5,065.4
Sweden	39,286.3	37,700.1	44,385.8
Switzerland	4,042.2	3,947.5	4,245.0
Taiwan.	2,508.3	2,611.2	3,740.2
United Kingdom	23,900.2	24,463.4	30,679.5
USA	15,292.9	14,871.4	14,659.8
Total (incl. others)	308,816.7	311,789.8	358,758.4

Exports f.o.b.	1998	1999	2000
Austria.	3,380.1	3,501.0	3,656.4
Belgium-Luxembourg	6,700.9	7,001.5	7,434.1
Finland	9,772.9	11,066.5	13,568.7
France (incl. Monaco)	16,702.1	18,227.9	20,305.0
Germany	66,971.1	68,869.7	76,637.8
Ireland.	2,352.3	4,814.4	5,469.6
Italy	12,666.0	12,749.6	13,111.0
Japan	9,428.2	11,805.6	14,563.6
Netherlands	14,948.9	15,986.9	20,184.3
Norway	19,875.9	20,943.5	22,454.1
Poland.	6,392.3	6,192.7	6,782.1
Russia.	4,856.9	2,939.6	4,126.1
Spain	7,183.5	8,244.0	9,148.0
Sweden	34,509.9	38,918.3	51,750.9
Switzerland	4,615.9	5,042.0	5,195.8
United Kingdom	30,567.2	32,909.2	40,448.2
USA	16,063.9	19,360.9	24,088.1
Total (incl. others)	322,796.9	346,756.5	404,958.5

Transport

RAILWAYS
(traffic)

	1998	1999	2000
Number of journeys ('000)	160,600	160,600	165,700
Passenger-kilometres (million).	5,365	5,318	5,591
Ton-kilometres (million).	2,066	1,974	2,118

ROAD TRAFFIC
(motor vehicles in use at 31 December)

	1998	1999	2000
Private cars	1,811,211	1,837,285	1,848,001
Taxis	5,936	5,969	6,059
Buses, coaches	13,911	13,909	13,968
Vans, lorries	347,136	362,002	373,293
Tractors	122,291	120,779	119,024
Trailers	473,334	502,616	531,250
Motorcycles	64,013	69,231	73,695

SHIPPING

Merchant Fleet
(registered at 31 December)

	1999	2000	2001
Number of vessels	914	942	904
Total displacement ('000 grt)	5,809.2	6,823.1	6,913.5

Source: Lloyd's Register-Fairplay, *World Fleet Statistics*.

Sea-borne Freight Traffic at Danish Ports*
('000 metric tons loaded and unloaded)

	1998	1999	2000
Ålborg	2,408	2,542	2,282
Århus	6,452	7,077	9,847
Copenhagen	8,713	6,068	8,223
Fredericia	13,619	14,539	16,172
Kalundborg	8,593	8,822	9,605
Skaelskør	783	964	881
Others	32,568	31,752	50,123
Total	73,136	71,764	96,533

* Including domestic traffic, excluding ferry traffic.

International Sea-borne Shipping*
(freight traffic, '000 metric tons)

	1998	1999	2000
Goods loaded	21,237	22,949	24,876
Goods unloaded	33,997	31,952	30,984

* Excluding international ferry traffic.

CIVIL AVIATION
(traffic on scheduled services)*

	1996	1997	1998
Kilometres flown (million)	75	80	81
Passengers carried ('000)	5,892	6,236	5,947
Passenger-kilometres (million).	5,466	5,669	5,658
Total ton-kilometres (million)	679	729	725

* Including an apportionment (2/7) of international operations by Scandinavian Airlines System (SAS).

Source: UN, *Statistical Yearbook*.

Tourism

FOREIGN TOURIST ARRIVALS
(at accommodation establishments)

Country of Residence	1998	1999	2000
Finland	38,221	41,062	43,034
Germany	437,666	401,498	380,703
Italy	50,120	49,274	46,738
Netherlands	84,494	82,018	81,612
Norway	290,301	285,670	295,134
Sweden	605,439	597,102	648,036
United Kingdom	82,627	89,161	103,194
USA	85,572	84,151	93,616
Total (incl. others)	2,072,800	2,023,056	2,087,681

Source: World Tourism Organization, *Yearbook of Tourism Statistics*.

Tourism receipts (million kroner): 21,652 in 1998; 25,162 in 1999; 32,526 in 2000.

Communications Media

	1998	1999	2000
Radio licences ('000)	2,218	2,222	2,241
Television receivers (estimates, '000 in use)	n.a.	4,100	4,300
Book production: titles*	13,175	14,455	14,959
Daily newspapers:			
Number	36	33	33
Average circulation ('000 copies)†	1,613	1,558	1,507
Telephones ('000 main lines in use)	3,496	3,638	3,835
Mobile cellular telephones ('000 subscribers).	1,931	2,629	3,364
Personal computers (estimates, '000 in use)	2,000	2,200	2,300
Internet users (estimates, '000) .	1,000	1,500	1,950

* Including pamphlets (4,274 titles in 1998; 4,828 titles in 1999; 4,711 titles in 2000).

† On weekdays.

2001: Telephones ('000 main lines in use): 3,882; Mobile cellular telephones ('000 subscribers): 3,954; Internet users (estimate, '000): 2,400.

Source: partly International Telecommunication Union.

Facsimile machines ('000 in use): 250 in 1995 (Source: UN, *Statistical Yearbook*).

Education

(1994/95)

	Institutions	Teachers	Students
Pre-primary.	4,395	19,200	201,571
Primary	n.a.	33,100	328,875
Secondary:			
General	n.a.	37,000	321,448
Vocational	n.a.	13,100	123,234
Higher	n.a.	9,600	169,783

1995/96: *Students*: Pre-primary 209,005; Primary 336,690.

Source: UNESCO, *Statistical Yearbook*.

1999: *Institutions*: Secondary (General) 1,990; Secondary (Vocational) 177; Higher 128. *Students*: Secondary (General) 716,689; Secondary (Vocational): 180,784; Higher 170,169.

Directory

The Constitution

The *Grundlov* (constitutional charter), summarized below, was adopted on 5 June 1953.

GOVERNMENT

The form of government is a limited (constitutional) monarchy. The legislative authority rests jointly with the Crown and the Folketing (parliament). Executive power is vested in the Crown, and the administration of justice is exercised by the courts. The Monarch can constitutionally 'do no wrong'. She exercises her authority through the Ministers appointed by her. The Ministers are responsible for the government of the country. The Constitution establishes the principle of Parliamentarism under which individual Ministers or the whole Cabinet must retire when defeated in the Folketing by a vote of 'no confidence'.

MONARCH

The Monarch acts on behalf of the State in international affairs. Except with the consent of the Folketing, she cannot, however, take any action that increases or reduces the area of the Realm or undertake any obligation, the fulfilment of which requires the co-operation of the Folketing or which is of major importance. Nor can the Monarch, without the consent of the Folketing, terminate any international agreement that has been concluded with the consent of the Folketing.

Apart from defence against armed attack on the Realm or on Danish forces, the Monarch cannot, without the consent of the Folketing, employ military force against any foreign power.

PARLIAMENT

The Folketing (parliament) is an assembly consisting of not more than 179 members, two of whom are elected in the Faroe Islands and two in Greenland. Danish nationals, having attained 18 years of age, with permanent residence in Denmark, have the franchise and are eligible for election. The members of the Folketing are elected for four years. Election is by a system of proportional representation, with direct and secret ballot on lists in large constituencies. A bill adopted by the Folketing may be submitted to referendum, when such referendum is claimed by not less than one-third of the mem-

bers of the Folketing and not later than three days after the adoption. The bill is void if rejected by a majority of the votes cast, representing not less than 30% of all electors.

The Government

HEAD OF STATE

Queen of Denmark: HM Queen MARGRETHE II (succeeded to the throne 14 January 1972).

THE CABINET
(April 2003)

A coalition of Venstre (V—Liberals) and Det Konservative Folkeparti (DKF—Conservative People's Party).

Prime Minister: ANDERS FOGH RASMUSSEN (V).

Deputy Prime Minister and Minister of Economic Affairs, Business and Trade: BENDT BENDTSON (DKF).

Minister of Foreign Affairs: Dr PER STIG MØLLER (DKF).

Minister of Finance: THOR PEDERSEN (V).

Minister of Employment: CLAUS HJORT FREDERIKSEN (V).

Minister of Justice: LENE ESPERSEN (DKF).

Minister of Cultural Affairs: BRIAN MIKKELSEN (DKF).

Minister of Refugees, Immigration and Integration Affairs and Minister without Portfolio (Minister of European Affairs): BERTEL HAARDER (V).

Minister of Taxation: SVEND ERIK HOVMAND (V).

Minister of Transport and of Nordic Affairs: FLEMMING HANSEN (DKF).

Minister of Science, Technology and Innovation: HELGE SANDER (V).

Minister of Food, Agriculture and Fisheries: MARIANN FISCHER BOEL (V).

Minister of Defence: SVEND AAGE JENSBY (V).

Minister of the Environment: HANS CHRISTIAN SCHMIDT (V).

Minister of Interior Affairs and Health: LARS LØKKE RASMUSSEN (V).

Minister of Ecclesiastical Affairs: TOVE FERGO (V).

Minister of Education: ULLA TØRNÆS (V).

Minister of Social Affairs and Gender Equality: HENRIETTE KJÆR (DKF).

MINISTRIES

Prime Minister's Office: Christiansborg, Prins Jørgens Gård 11, 1218 Copenhagen K; tel. 33-92-33-00; fax 33-11-16-65; e-mail stm@stm.dk; internet www.stm.dk.

Ministry of Culture: Nybrogade 2, POB 2140, 1015 Copenhagen K; tel. 33-92-33-70; fax 33-91-33-88; e-mail kum@kum.dk; internet www.kum.dk.

Ministry of Defence: Holmens Kanal 42, 1060 Copenhagen K; tel. 33-92-33-20; fax 33-32-06-55; e-mail fmn@fmn.dk; internet www.fmn.dk.

Ministry of Ecclesiastical Affairs: Frederiksholms Kanal 21, POB 2123, 1015 Copenhagen K; tel. 33-92-33-90; fax 33-92-39-13; e-mail km@km.dk; internet www.km.dk.

Ministry of Economic Affairs, Business and Trade: Slotsholmsgade 10–12, 1216 Copenhagen K; tel. 33-92-33-50; fax 33–12–37–78; e-mail oem@oem.dk; internet www.oem.dk.

Ministry of Education: Frederiksholms Kanal 21–25, 1220 Copenhagen K; tel. 33-92-50-00; fax 33-92-55-47; e-mail uvm@uvm.dk; internet www.uvm.dk.

Ministry of Employment: Ved Stranden 8, 1061 Copenhagen K; tel. 33-92-59-00; fax 33-12-13-78; e-mail bm@bm.dk; internet www.bm.dk.

Ministry of the Environment and Energy: Højbro Pl. 4, 1200 Copenhagen K; tel. 33-92-76-00; fax 33-32-22-27; e-mail mim@mim.dk; internet www.mim.dk.

Ministry of Finance: Christiansborg Slotspl. 1, 1218 Copenhagen K; tel. 33-92-33-33; fax 33-32-80-30; e-mail fm@fm.dk; internet www.fm.dk.

Ministry of Food, Agriculture and Fisheries: Holbergsgade 2, 1057 Copenhagen K; tel. 33-92-33-01; fax 33-14-50-42; e-mail fvm@fvm.dk; internet www.fvm.dk.

Ministry of Foreign Affairs: Asiatisk Pl. 2, 1448 Copenhagen K; tel. 33-92-00-00; fax 32-54-05-33; e-mail um@um.dk; internet www.um.dk.

Ministry of Justice: Slotsholmsgade 10, 1216 Copenhagen K; tel. 33-92-33-40; fax 33-93-35-10; e-mail jm@jm.dk; internet www.jm.dk.

Ministry of Refugees, Immigration and Integration Affairs: Holbergsgade 6, 1057 Copenhagen K; tel. 33-92-33-80; fax 33-11-12-39; e-mail inm@inm.dk; internet www.inm.dk.

Ministry of Science, Technology and Innovation: Bredgade 43, 1260 Copenhagen K; tel. 33-92-97-00; fax 33-32-35-01; e-mail vtu@vtu.dk; internet www.videnskabsministeriet.dk.

Ministry of Social Affairs and Gender Equality: Holmens Kanal 22, 1060 Copenhagen K; tel. 33-92-93-00; fax 33-93-25-18; e-mail sm@sm.dk; internet www.sm.dk.

Ministry of Taxation: Nicolai Eigtveds Gade 28, 1402 Copenhagen K; tel. 33-92-33-92; fax 33-14-91-05; e-mail skm@skm.dk; internet www.skm.dk.

Ministry of Transport: Frederiksholms Kanal 27, 1220 Copenhagen K; tel. 33-92-33-55; fax 33-12-38-93; e-mail trm@trm.dk; internet www.trm.dk.

Legislature

FOLKETING

Christiansborg, 1240 Copenhagen K; tel. 33-37-55-00; fax 33-32-85-36; e-mail folketinget@folketinget.dk; internet www.folketinget.dk.

President of the Folketing: (vacant).

Secretary-General: HENRIK TVARNØ.

General Election, 20 November 2001
(metropolitan Denmark only)

	Votes	% of votes	Seats
Venstre (Liberals)	1,077,734	31.3	56
Socialdemokratiet (Social Democrats)	1,002,986	29.1	52
Det Konservative Folkeparti (Conservative People's Party) .	312310	9.0	16
Socialistik Folkeparti (Socialist People's Party)	219,683	6.4	12
Det Radikale Venstre (Social Liberals)	179,121	5.2	9
Enhedslisten—De Rød-Grønne (Red-Green Alliance) . . .	82,224	2.4	4
Kristeligt Folkeparti (Christian People's Party)	78,475	2.4	4
Centrum-Demokraterne (Centre Democrats)	60,701	1.7	—
Fremskridtspartiet (Progress Party)	19,687	0.6	—
Independents	998	<0.1	—
Total	**3,447,410**	**100.0**	**175**

The Folketing also includes two members from Greenland and two from the Faroe Islands.

Political Organizations

Centrum-Demokraterne (Centre Democrats): Ny Vestergade 7, 1471 Copenhagen K; tel. 33-12-71-15; fax 33-12-01-15; e-mail landskontoret@centrumdemokraterne.dk; internet www.centrumdemokraterne.dk; f. 1973 ; opposes extreme ideologies, supports EU and NATO; Leader MIMI JAKOBSEN; Nat. Chair. INGER BORIIS.

Danmarks Kommunistiske Parti (Danish Communist Party): Studiestræde 24, 1455 Copenhagen K; tel. 33-91-66-44; fax 33-32-03-72; e-mail dkp@dkp.dk; internet www.dkp.dk; f. 1919; Chair. HENRIK STAMER HEDIN.

Danmarks Kommunistiske Parti/Marxister Leninister (Marxist-Leninist Party): Griffenfeldsgade 26, 2200 Copenhagen K; tel. 35-35-60-69; fax 35-37-20-39; e-mail dkp-ml@dkp-ml.dk; internet www.dkp-ml.dk; Sec.-Gen. JØRGEN PETERSEN.

Dansk Folkeparti (Danish People's Party): Christiansborg, 1240 Copenhagen K; tel. 33-37-51-99; fax 33-37-51-91; e-mail df@ft.dk; internet www.danskfolkeparti.dk; f. 1995 by defectors from the Progress Party; right-wing; Leader PIA KJAERSGAARD.

Enhedslisten—De Rød-Grønne (Red-Green Alliance): Studiestræde 24, 1455 Copenhagen K; tel. 33-93-33-24; fax 33-32-03-72; e-mail landskontoret@enhedslisten.dk; internet www.enhedslisten.dk; f. 1989; by three left-wing parties; membership of individual socialists; 21-mem. collective leadership.

Folkebevægelsen mod EU (Danish People's Movement Against the European Union): Sigurdsgade 39A, 2200 Copenhagen N; tel. 35-82-18-00; fax 35-82-18-06; e-mail folkebevaegelsen@folkebevaegelsen.dk; internet www.folkebevaegelsen.dk; opposes membership of the EU, in favour of self-determination for Denmark and all European countries; 21-mem. collective leadership.

Fremskridtspartiet (Progress Party): POB 180, 2630 Taastrup; tel. 70-26-20-27; fax 70-26-23-27; e-mail frp@frp.dk; internet www.frp.dk; f. 1972; right-wing; advocates gradual abolition of income tax, disbandment of most of the civil service, and abolition of diplomatic service and about 90% of legislation; Chair. JOHANNES SØRENSEN; Leader KIRSTEN JACOBSEN; Sec.-Gen. MARTIN IPSEN.

De Grønne/Økologisk-realistik Alternativ (Green Party/The Realistic Ecological Alternative): Copenhagen; tel. 31-38-00-97; f. 1983; reformed 1991.

Det Humanistiske Parti (The Humanist Party): Copenhagen; tel. 31-24-70-60; pro-democratic, non-violent; Chair. CHRISTIAN ADAMSEN.

JuniBevægelsen (June Movement): Kronprinsensegade 2, 1114 Copenhagen K; tel. 33-93-00-46; fax 33-93-30-67; e-mail jb@junibevaegelsen.dk; internet www.junibevaegelsen.dk; f. 1992; opposes the EU; Leaders JENS-PETER BONDE, HANNE DAHL, TRINE PERTOU-MACH.

Det Konservative Folkeparti (Conservative People's Party): Nyhavn 4, 1051 Copenhagen K; tel. 33-13-41-40; fax 33-93-37-73; e-mail info@konservative.dk; internet www.konservative.dk; f. 1916; advocates free initiative and the maintenance of private property, but recognizes the right of the State to take action to keep the economic and social balance; Leader BENDT BENDTSEN; Sec.-Gen. MORTEN BANGSGAARD.

Kristeligt Folkeparti (Christian People's Party): Allégade 24A, I., 2000 Frederiksberg; tel. 33-27-78-10; fax 33-21-31-16; e-mail krf@ krf.dk; internet www.krf.dk; f. 1970; emphasizes the need for political decisions based on Christian ethics; Chair. MARIANNE KARLMOSE NIELSEN; Sec.-Gen. BØRGE KLIT JOHANSEN.

Det Radikale Venstre (Social Liberals): Christiansborg, 1240 Copenhagen K; tel. 33-37-47-47; fax 33-13-72-51; e-mail radikale@ radikale.dk; internet www.radikale.dk; f. 1905; supports international *détente* and co-operation within regional and world organizations, social reforms without socialism, incomes policy, workers' participation in industry, state intervention in industrial disputes, state control of trusts and monopolies, strengthening private enterprise; Chair. SØREN BALD; Leader MARIANNE JELVED; Gen. Sec. ANDERS KLOPPENBORG.

Retsforbundet—Danmarks Retsforbund (Justice Party): Lyngbyvej 42, 2100 Copenhagen Ø; tel. 39-20-44-88; fax 39-20-44-50; internet www.retsforbundet.dk; f. 1919; programme is closely allied to Henry George's teachings (single tax, free trade); Chair. LARS BAEKGAARD.

Schleswigsche Partei (Schleswig Party): Vestergade 30, 6200 Abenrå; tel. 74-62-38-33; fax 74-62-79-39; e-mail sp@bdn.dk; internet www.schleswigsche-partei.dk; f. 1920; represents the German minority in North Schleswig; Chair. GERHARD D. MAMMEN.

Socialdemokratiet (Social Democrats): Thorvaldsensvej 2, 1780 Copenhagen V; tel. 35-39-15-22; fax 35-39-40-30; e-mail socialdemokratiet@net.dialog.dk; internet www.socialdemokratiet .dk; f. 1871; finds its chief adherents among workers, employees and public servants; 50,000 mems; Leader MOGENS LYKKETOFT; Gen. Sec. JENS CHRISTIANSEN.

Socialistisk Arbejderparti (Socialist Workers' Party): Studiestraede 24, 1, 1455 Copenhagen K; tel. 33-33-79-48; fax 33-33-32-17; e-mail sap@sap-fi.dk; internet www.sap-fi.dk.

Socialistisk Folkeparti (Socialist People's Party): Christiansborg, 1240 Copenhagen K; tel. 33-12-70-11; fax 33-32-72-48; e-mail sf@sf .dk; internet www.sf.dk; f. 1959; socialist; Chair. HOLGER K. NIELSEN; Parliamentary Leader AAGE FRANDSEN; Sec. OLE HVAS KRISTIANSEN.

Venstre (Liberals): Søllerødvej 30, 2840 Holte; tel. 45-80-22-33; fax 45-80-38-30; e-mail venstre@venstre.dk; internet www.venstre.dk; f. 1870; supports free trade, a minimum of state interference, and the adoption, in matters of social expenditure, of a modern general social security system; 79,182 mems; Pres. ANDERS FOGH RASMUSSEN; Sec.-Gen. CLAUS HJORT FREDERIKSEN.

Diplomatic Representation

EMBASSIES IN DENMARK

Algeria: Amaliegade 36, 1256 Copenhagen K; tel. 33-11-94-40; fax 33-11-58-50; e-mail ambalda@post10.tele.dk; Ambassador MOHAMOD BENHACINE.

Argentina: Borgergade 16, I., 1300 Copenhagen K; tel. 33-15-80-82; fax 33-15-55-74; e-mail embardin@vip.cybercity.dk; Ambassador JUAN CARLOS KRECKLER.

Austria: Sølundsvej 1, 2100 Copenhagen Ø; tel. 39-29-41-41; fax 39-29-20-86; e-mail kopenhagen-ob@bmaa.gv.at; Ambassador HELMUT WESSELY.

Belgium: Øster Allé 7, 2100 Copenhagen Ø; tel. 35-25-02-00; fax 35-25-02-11; e-mail copenhagen@diplobel.be; Ambassador MICHEL LASTCHENKO.

Bolivia: Amaliegade 16C, 2nd Floor, 1256 Copenhagen K; tel. 33-12-49-00; fax 33-12-49-03; e-mail embolivia_copenhagen@yahoo.es; Chargé d'affaires a.i. FERNANDO CALDERÓN.

Bosnia and Herzegovina: Nytorv 3, 1450 Copenhagen K; tel. 33-33-80-40; fax 33-33-80-17; e-mail ba-emb-dk-cph@mobilxnet.dk; internet www.embassybh.dk; Ambassador NUDŽEIM REČICA.

Brazil: Ryvangs Allé 24, 2100 Copenhagen Ø; tel. 39-20-64-78; fax 39-27-36-07; e-mail ambassade@denmark.dk; Ambassador VERA PEDROSA MARTINS DE ALMEIDA.

Bulgaria: Gamlehave Allé 7, 2920 Charlottenlund; tel. 39-64-24-84; fax 39-63-49-23; e-mail bg-embassy@mail.tdcadsl.dk; Ambassador DIMO VASSILEV DIMOV.

Burkina Faso: Svanemøllevej 20, 2100 Copenhagen Ø; tel. 39-18-40-22; fax 39-27-18-86; e-mail amba@burkina.dk; Ambassador CÉCILE YODA.

Canada: Kr. Bernikowsgade 1, 1105 Copenhagen K; tel. 33-48-32-00; fax 33-48-32-20; e-mail copen@dfait-maeci.gc.ca; internet www .canada.dk; Ambassador ALFONSO GAGLIANO.

Chile: Kastelsvej 15, 3rd Floor, 2100 Copenhagen Ø; tel. 35-38-58-34; fax 35-38-42-01; e-mail embassy@chiledk.dk; internet www .chiledk.dk; Ambassador JAIME LAGOS.

China, People's Republic: Øregårds Allé 25, 2900 Hellerup; tel. 39-46-08-89; fax 39-62-54-84; Ambassador YANG HEXIONG.

Côte d'Ivoire: Gersonsvej 8, 2900 Hellerup; tel. 39-62-88-22; fax 39-62-01-62; e-mail ambaivoire@mail.tele.dk; Ambassador LILIANE MARIE-LAURE BOA.

Croatia: Dronningens Tværgade 5, 1st Floor, 1302 Copenhagen K; tel. 33-91-90-95; fax 33-91-71-31; e-mail vpdk@koebenhavn.mail .telia.com; Ambassador ANA MARIJA BESKER.

Cuba: Carolinevej 12, Ground Floor left, 2900 Hellerup; tel. and fax 39-40-15-10; e-mail embadin@hotmail.com; Chargé d'affaires a.i. PEDRO PABLO PRADA.

Czech Republic: Ryvangs Allé 14–16, 2100 Copenhagen Ø; tel. 39-29-18-88; fax 39-29-09-30; e-mail copenhagen@embassy.mzv.cz; internet www.czechembassy.dk; Ambassador MARIE KOSTALOVA.

Egypt: Kristianiagade 19, 2100 Copenhagen Ø; tel. 35-43-70-70; fax 35-43-36-49; Ambassador Dr MUHAMMAD SHAABAN.

Estonia: Aurehøjvej 19, 2900 Hellerup; tel. 39-46-30-70; fax 39-46-30-76; e-mail sekretar@estemb.dk; internet www.estemb.dk; Ambassador TAAVI TOOM.

Finland: Skt Annæ Pl. 24, 1250 Copenhagen K; tel. 33-13-42-14; fax 33-32-47-10; e-mail sanomat.kob@formin.fi; internet www.finamb .dk; Ambassador PEKKA OJANEN.

France: Kongens Nytorv 4, 1050 Copenhagen K; tel. 33-67-01-00; fax 33-93-97-52; e-mail presse@amba-france.dk; internet www .amba-france.dk; Ambassador RÉGIS DE BELENET.

Germany: Stockholmsgade 57, POB 2712, 2100 Copenhagen Ø; tel. 35-45-99-00; fax 35-26-71-05; e-mail tyskeamba@email.dk; internet www.tyske-ambasssade.dk; Ambassador JOHANNES DOHMES.

Ghana: Egebjerg Allé 13, 2900 Hellerup; tel. 39-62-82-22; fax 39-62-16-52; e-mail ghana@mail.dk; Ambassador EMMANUEL K. ADU.

Greece: Borgergade 16, 1300 Copenhagen K; tel. 33-11-45-33; fax 33-93-16-46; e-mail greekembcop@post.tele.dk; Ambassador ANDONIOS NICOLAIDIS.

Hungary: Strandvejen 170, 2920 Charlottenlund; tel. 39-63-16-88; fax 39-63-00-52; e-mail huembcph@teliamail.dk; internet www .hungarianembassy.dk; Ambassador LÁSZLÓ DESEÖ.

Iceland: Dantes Pl. 3, 1556 Copenhagen V; tel. 33-18-10-50; fax 33-18-10-59; e-mail icemb.coph@utn.stjr.is; Ambassador PORSTEINN PÁLSSON.

India: Vangehusvej 15, 2100 Copenhagen Ø; tel. 39-18-28-88; fax 39-27-02-18; e-mail indemb@euroconnect.dk; Ambassador H. K. DUA.

Indonesia: Ørehøj Allé 1, 2900 Hellerup; tel. 39-62-44-22; fax 39-62-44-83; e-mail indon-dk@cybernet.dk; internet www.cybernet.dk/ users/indon.dk; Ambassador WITNAKSANA SOEGARDA.

Iran: Engskiftevej 6, 2100 Copenhagen Ø; tel. 39-16-00-71; fax 39-16-00-75; Chargé d'affaires a.i. NASSER JASBI.

Ireland: Østbanegade 21, 2100 Copenhagen Ø; tel. 35-42-32-33; fax 35-43-18-58; e-mail irlemb@email.dk; Ambassador JAMES BRENNAN.

Israel: Lundevangsvej 4, 2900 Hellerup; tel. 39-62-62-88; fax 39-62-19-38; e-mail info@embassy-of-israel.dk; internet www .embassy-of-israel.dk; Ambassador CARMI GILLON.

Italy: Gammel Vartov Vej 7, 2900 Hellerup; tel. 39-62-68-77; fax 39-62-25-99; e-mail italambcph@get2net.dk; Ambassador ANTONIO CATALANO di MELLI.

Japan: Pilestræde 61, 1112 Copenhagen K; tel. 33-11-33-44; fax 33-11-33-77; e-mail info@embjapan.dk; internet www.embjapan.dk; Ambassador SHOHEI NAITO.

Korea, Republic: Svanemøllevej 104, 2900 Hellerup; tel. 39-46-04-00; fax 39-46-04-22; Ambassador KIE-OK CHUNG.

Latvia: Rosbæksvej 17, 2100 Copenhagen Ø; tel. 39-27-60-00; fax 39-27-61-73; e-mail letambas@pip.dknet.dk; Ambassador AIVARS BAUMANIS.

Lesotho: Tuborg Nord, Strandvejen 64H, 2900 Hellerup; tel. 39-62-43-43; fax 39-62-15-38; e-mail ccc23925@vip.cybercity.dk; Ambassador RALECHATE LINCOLN MOKOSE.

Libya: Rosenvængets Hovedvej 4, 2100 Copenhagen Ø; tel. 35-26-36-11; fax 35-26-56-06; Ambassador Dr MOHAMED ELFANDI.

Lithuania: Bernstorffsvej 214, 2920 Charlottenlund; tel. 39-63-62-07; fax 39-63-65-32; e-mail mail@lit-embassy.dk; internet www.lit-embassy.dk; Ambassador DEIVIDAS MATULIONIS.

Luxembourg: Fridtjof Nansens Pl. 5, 1st Floor, 2100 Copenhagen Ø; tel. 35-26-82-00; fax 35-26-82-08; Ambassador FRANÇOIS BREMER.

Macedonia, former Yugoslav republic: Copenhagen; tel. 39-27-43-14; fax 39-27-43-15; Ambassador MUHAMED HALILI.

Mexico: Strandvejen 64E, 2900 Hellerup; tel. 39-61-05-00; fax 39-61-05-12; e-mail info@mexican-embassy.dk; internet www.mexican-embassy.dk; Ambassador HECTOR VASCONCELOS.

Morocco: Øregårds Allé 19, 2900 Hellerup; tel. 39-62-45-11; fax 39-62-24-49; Ambassador MENOUAR ALEM.

Netherlands: Toldbodgade 33, 1253 Copenhagen K; tel. 33-70-72-00; fax 33-14-03-50; e-mail nlgovkop@newmail.dk; internet www.nlembassy.dk; Ambassador HANS A. F. M. FÖRSTER.

Norway: Amaliegade 39, 1256 Copenhagen K; tel. 33-14-01-24; fax 33-14-06-24; e-mail emb.copenhagen@mfa.no; internet www.norsk.dk; Ambassador DAGFINN STENSETH.

Pakistan: Valeursvej 17, 2900 Hellerup; tel. 39-62-11-88; fax 39-40-10-70; e-mail parepcopenhagen@hotmail.com; Ambassador SALMAN BASHIR.

Peru: Copenhagen Ø; tel. 35-26-58-48; fax 35-26-84-06; e-mail embaperu@worldonline.dk; internet www.peruembassy.dk; Ambassador LILIANA CINO DE SILVA.

Poland: Richelieus Allé 12, 2900 Hellerup; tel. 39-46-77-00; fax 39-46-77-66; e-mail mail@ambpol.dk; internet www.ambpol.dk; Ambassador BARBARA TUGE-ERECINSKA.

Portugal: Hovedvagtsgade 6, 1103 Copenhagen K; tel. 33-13-13-01; fax 33-14-92-14; e-mail embport@get2met.dk; Ambassador JOSÉ ANTÓNIO MOYA RIBERA.

Romania: Strandagervej 27, 2900 Hellerup; tel. 39-40-71-77; fax 39-62-78-99; Ambassador Dr GRETE TARTLER TĂBĂRAŚI.

Russia: Kristianiagade 5, 2100 Copenhagen Ø; tel. 35-42-55-85; fax 35-42-37-41; e-mail emb.ru@get2net.dk; Ambassador NICOLAY BORDYUZHA.

Saudi Arabia: Lille Strandvej 27, 2900 Hellerup; tel. 39-62-12-00; fax 39-62-60-09; Ambassador (vacant).

Serbia and Montenegro: Svanevænget 36–38, 2100 Copenhagen Ø; tel. 39-29-71-61; fax 39-29-79-19; e-mail yuembdk@vip.cybercity.dk; Ambassador Dr BRANISLAV SRDANOVIĆ.

Slovakia: Vesterled 26–28, 2100 Copenhagen Ø; tel. 39-20-99-11; fax 39-20-99-13; e-mail slovakiskamb@vip.cybercity.dk; internet www.foreign.gov.sk; Ambassador ROMAN BUZEK.

South Africa: Gammel Vartov Vej 8, POB 128, 2900 Hellerup; tel. 39-18-01-55; fax 39-18-40-06; e-mail sa.embassy@inform-bbs.dk; Ambassador (vacant).

Spain: Kristianiagade 21, 2100 Copenhagen Ø; tel. 35-42-47-00; fax 35-26-30-99; Ambassador JOSÉ PONS IRAZAZÁBAL.

Swaziland: Kastelsvej 19, 2100 Copenhagen Ø; tel. 35-42-61-11; fax 35-42-63-00; e-mail embassy@swaziland.dk; Ambassador Prince DAVID DLAMINI.

Sweden: Skt Annæ Pl. 15A, 1250 Copenhagen K; tel. 33-36-03-70; fax 33-36-03-95; e-mail ambassaden.kopenhamn@foreign.ministry.se; internet www.sverigesambassad.dk; Ambassador CARL-MAGNUS HYLTENIUS.

Switzerland: Amaliegade 14, 1256 Copenhagen K; tel. 33-14-17-96; fax 33-33-75-51; e-mail vertretung@cop.rep.admin.ch; internet www.eda.admin.ch/copenhagen; Ambassador Dr JÜRG STREULI.

Thailand: Norgesmindevej 18, 2900 Hellerup; tel. 39-62-50-10; fax 39-62-50-59; e-mail thai-dk@inet.uni2.dk; Ambassador ADISAK PANUPONG.

Turkey: Rosbæksvej 15, 2100 Copenhagen Ø; tel. 39-20-27-88; fax 39-20-51-66; e-mail turkembassy@internet.dk; internet www.turkembassy.dk; Ambassador FÜGEN OK.

Uganda: Sofievej 15, 2900 Hellerup; tel. 39-62-09-66; fax 39-61-01-48; e-mail ug-embassy-denmark@inet.uni2.dk; internet www.ugandaembassy.suite.dk; Ambassador OMAR MIGADDE LUBULWA.

Ukraine: Toldbodgade 37A, 1st Floor, 1253 Copenhagen K; tel. 33-16-16-35; fax 33-16-00-74; Ambassador OLEKSANDR SLIPCHENKO.

United Kingdom: Kastelsvej 36–40, 2100 Copenhagen Ø; tel. 35-44-52-00; fax 35-44-52-93; e-mail info@britishembassy.dk; internet www.britishembassy.dk; Ambassador PHILIP S. ASTLEY.

USA: Dag Hammarskjölds Allé 24, 2100 Copenhagen Ø; tel. 35-55-31-44; fax 35-43-02-23; internet www.usembassy.dk; Ambassador STUART A. BERNSTEIN.

Venezuela: Holbergsgade 14, 3rd Floor, 1057 Copenhagen K; tel. 33-93-63-11; fax 33-37-76-59; e-mail emvendk@mail.dk; internet home7.inet.tele.dk/emvendk; Chargé d'affaires ZULAY RAMIREZ.

Judicial System

In Denmark the judiciary is independent of the Government. Judges are appointed by the Crown on the recommendation of the Minister of Justice and cannot be dismissed except by judicial sentence.

The ordinary courts are divided into three instances, the Lower Courts, the High Courts and the Supreme Court. There is one Lower Court for each of the 82 judicial districts in the country. These courts must have at least one judge trained in law and they hear the majority of minor cases. The two High Courts serve Jutland and the islands respectively. They serve as appeal courts for cases from the Lower Courts, but are also used to give first hearing to the more important cases. Each case must be heard by at least three judges. The Supreme Court, at which at least five judges must sit, is the court of appeal for cases from the High Courts. Usually only one appeal is allowed from either court, but in special instances the Board of Appeal may give leave for a second appeal, to the Supreme Court, from a case that started in a Lower Court. Furthermore, in certain minor cases, appeal from the Lower Courts to the High Courts is allowed only by leave of appeal from the Board of Appeal.

There is a special Maritime and Commercial Court in Copenhagen, consisting of a President and two Vice-Presidents with legal training and a number of commercial and nautical assessors; there is also a Labour Court, which deals with labour disputes.

An Ombudsman is appointed by Parliament after each general election, and is concerned with the quality and legality of the administration of the laws and administrative provisions. Although the Ombudsman holds no formal power to change decisions taken by the administration, he may, on a legal basis, express criticism of acts and decisions of administrative bodies. He is obliged to present an annual report to Parliament.

Supreme Court

Prins Jørgens Gård 13, 1218 Copenhagen K; tel. 33-63-27-50; fax 33-15-00-10.

President of the Supreme Court: JACQUES HERMANN.

President of the East High Court: SVEN ZIEGLER.

President of the West High Court: BJARNE CHRISTENSEN.

President of the Maritime and Commercial Court: JENS FEILBERG.

President of the Labour Court: MOGENS HORNSLET.

Ombudsman: HANS GAMMELTOFT-HANSEN.

Religion

CHRISTIANITY

Det Økumeniske Fællesraad i Danmark (Ecumenical Council of Denmark): Dag Hammarskjölds Allé 17/3, 2100 Copenhagen Ø; tel. 35-43-29-43; fax 35-43-29-44; e-mail oikoumene@oikoumene.dk; internet www.oikoumene.dk; f. 1939; associate council of the World Council of Churches; six mem. churches, one observer; Chair. Dr PETER LODBERG; Gen. Sec. HOLGER LAM.

The National Church

Den evangelisk-lutherske Folkekirke i Danmark (Evangelical Lutheran Church in Denmark)

Nørregade 11, 1165 Copenhagen K; tel. 33-13-35-08; fax 33-14-39-69.

The established Church of Denmark, supported by the State; no bishop exercises a presiding role, but the Bishop of Copenhagen is responsible for certain co-ordinating questions. The Church of Denmark Council on Inter-Church Relations (Vestergade 8, 1456 Copenhagen K; tel. 33-11-44-88 fax 33-11-95-88; e-mail interchurch@folkekirken.dk; internet www.folkekirken.dk) is responsible for ecumenical relations. Membership in 2001 was 4,532,635 (84.7% of the population).

Bishop of Copenhagen: ERIK NORMAN SVENDSEN.

Bishop of Helsingør: LISE LOTTE REBEL.

Bishop of Roskilde: B. WIBERG.

Bishop of Lolland-Falster: HOLGER JEPSEN.

Bishop of Odense: KRESTEN DREJERGAARD.

Bishop of Ålborg: SØREN LODBERG HVAS.

Bishop of Viborg: Karsten Nissen.

Bishop of Århus: Kjeld Holm.

Bishop of Ribe: Niels Holm.

Bishop of Haderslev: Niels Henrik Arendt.

The Roman Catholic Church

Denmark comprises a single diocese, directly responsible to the Holy See. At 31 December 2000 there were an estimated 34,369 adherents in the country. The Bishop participates in the Scandinavian Episcopal Conference (based in Sweden).

Bishop of Copenhagen: Czeslaw Kozon, Katolsk Bispekontor, Bredgade 69a, 1260 Copenhagen K; tel. 33-11-60-80; fax 33-14-60-86; e-mail bispekontor@katolsk.dk.

Other Churches

Apostolic Church in Denmark: Lykkegaardsvej 100, 6000 Kolding; tel. 79-32-16-00; fax 79-32-16-01; e-mail akd@apostolic.dk; internet www.apostolic.dk; Nat. Leader Johannes Hansen.

Baptistkirken i Danmark (Baptist Church of Denmark): Købnerhus, Lærdalsgade 7, 2300 Copenhagen S; tel. 32-59-07-08; fax 32-59-01-33; e-mail sekretariat@baptistkirken.dk; internet www.baptistkirken.dk; f. 1839; 5,400 mems; Pres. Ole Thorndal.

Church of England: St Alban's Church, Churchillparken 11, 1263 Copenhagen K; tel. 39-62-77-36; fax 39-62-77-35; e-mail chaplain@paradis.dk; f. 1728; Chaplain Rev. T. O. Mendel.

Church of Jesus Christ of Latter-day Saints (Mormons): Rødovre; tel. 31-70-90-43; in Denmark 1850; 4,500 mems.

Det Danske Missionsforbund (Danish Mission Covenant Church): Rosenlunden 17, 5000 Odense C; tel. 66-14-83-31; fax 66-14-83-00; e-mail ddm@email.dk; internet www.missionsforbundet.dk; Exec. Dir Palle Byg.

First Church of Christ, Scientist, Copenhagen: Nyvej 7, 1851 Frederiksberg C; tel. 33-13-08-91; e-mail cs.rr@email.dk; also in Århus; tel. 86-16-22-78.

German Lutheran Church: Skt Petri Church Office, Larslejsstræde 11, 1451 Copenhagen K; tel. 33-13-38-33; fax 33-13-38-35; e-mail kirchenbuero@sankt-petri.dk; internet www.sankt-petri.dk.

Methodist Church: Metodistkirkens Social Arbejde, Rigensgade 21A, 1316 Copenhagen K; tel. 33-93-25-96; e-mail msac@image.dk; f. 1910; Chair. Finn Uth.

Moravian Brethren: The Moravian Church, 6070 Christiansfeld; f. in Denmark 1773; Pastor Jorgen Bøytler; Lindegade 26, 6070 Christiansfeld; tel. 74-56-14-20; fax 74-56-14-21 e-mail boeytler@post7.tele.dk.

Norwegian Seamen's Church: Kong Håkons Kirke, Ved Mønten 9, 2300 Copenhagen S; tel. 32-57-11-03; fax 32-57-40-05; e-mail kobenhavn@sjomannskirken.no; internet www.sjomannskirken.no; f. 1958.

Reformed Church: Reformed Synod of Denmark, Nørrebrogade 32A, 7000 Fredericia; tel. 75-92-05-51; Rev. Sabine Hofmeister.

Russian Orthodox Church: Alexander Nevski Church, Bredgade 53, 1260 Copenhagen K; tel. 33-13-60-46; fax 33-13-28-85; e-mail ruskirke@worldonline.dk; internet www.rusmedia.dk; f. 1883; Rector Fr Sergy Plekhov.

Seventh-day Adventists: Syvende Dags Adventistkirken, POB 15, Concordiavej 16, 2850 Nærum; tel. 45-58-77-77; fax 45-58-77-78; e-mail adventistkirken@adventist.dk; internet www.adventist.dk; f. 1863; Pres. Carl-David Andreasen; Sec. Philip Philipsen.

Society of Friends: Danish Quaker Centre, Drejervej 17, 4., 1363 Copenhagen K; tel. and fax 35-83-09-76; internet www.kvaekerne.dk.

Swedish Lutheran Church: Svenska Gustafskyrkan, Folke Bernadottes Allé, 2100 Copenhagen Ø; tel. 33-15-54-58; fax 33-15-02-94.

The Salvation Army and the Unitarians are also active in the country.

BAHÁ'Í FAITH

Bahá'í: Det Nationale Åndelige Råd, Sofievej 28, 2900 Hellerup; tel. 39-62-35-18; e-mail sekretariat@bahai.dk; internet www.bahai.dk.

ISLAM

The Muslim Community: Nusrat Djahan Mosque (and Ahmadiyya Mission), Eriksminde Allé 2, 2650 Hvidovre; tel. 36-75-35-02; fax 36-75-00-07.

JUDAISM

Jewish Community: Mosaisk Trossamfund, Ny Kongensgade 6, 1472 Copenhagen K; tel. 33-12-88-68; fax 33-12-33-57; e-mail bent_lexner@hotmail.com; 5,000 mems; Chief Rabbi Bent Lexner.

The Press

There are more than 220 separate newspapers, including some 36 principal dailies. The average total circulation of daily newspapers in 2000 was 1,507,000 on weekdays.

Most newspapers and magazines are privately owned and published by joint concerns, co-operatives or limited liability companies. The main concentration of papers is held by the Berlingske Group, which owns *Berlingske Tidende, Weekendavisen* and *B.T.*, and the provincial *Jydskevestkysten* and *Århus Stiftstidende*.

There is no truly national press. Copenhagen accounts for 20% of the national dailies and about one-half of the total circulation. No paper is directly owned by a political party, although all papers show a fairly pronounced political leaning.

PRINCIPAL DAILIES

Aabenraa

Der Nordschleswiger: Skibbroen 4, POB 1041, 6200 Aabenraa; tel. 74-62-38-80; fax 74-62-94-30; e-mail redaktion@nordschleswiger.dk; internet www.nordschleswiger.dk; f. 1946; German; Editor-in-Chief Siegfried Matlok; circ. 2,573.

Ålborg

Nordjyske Stiftstidende: Langagervej 1, POB 8000, 9220 Ålborg Øst; tel. 99-35-35-35; fax 99-35-33-75; e-mail central@nordjyske.dk; internet www.nordjyske.dk; f. 1767; adopted present name in 1999, following the merger of six regional dailies; mornings; Liberal independent; Publr and Editor-in-Chief Per Lyngby; circ. weekdays 80,900, Sundays 95,699.

Århus

Århus Stiftstidende: Olof Palmes Allé 39, POB 1, 8200 Århus N; tel. 87-40-10-10; fax 87-40-14-04; e-mail redaktionen@stiften.dk; internet www.stiften.dk; f. 1794; evening and weekend mornings; Liberal independent; Editor-in-Chief Erik Frodelund; circ. weekdays 64,562, Sundays 74,422.

Copenhagen

Berlingske Tidende: Pilestræde 34, 1147 Copenhagen K; tel. 33-75-75-75; fax 33-75-20-20; e-mail redaktionen@berlingske.dk; internet www.berlingske.dk; f. 1749; morning; Conservative independent; Editor-in-Chief Karsten Madsen; circ. weekdays 153,681, Sundays 184,944.

Børsen: Møntergade 19, 1140 Copenhagen K; tel. 33-32-01-02; fax 33-12-24-45; e-mail redaktionen@borsen.dk; internet www.borsen.dk; f. 1896; morning; independent; business news; Editor-in-Chief Leif Beck Fallesen; circ. 56,020.

B.T.: Kr. Bernikowsgade 6, POB 200, 1006 Copenhagen K; tel. 33-75-75-33; fax 33-75-20-33; e-mail bt@bt.dk; internet www.bt.dk; f. 1916; morning; Conservative independent; Editor-in-Chief Kristian Lund; circ. weekdays 124,521, Sundays 170,929.

Dagbladet Arbejderen: Ryesgade 3F, 1. sal, 2200 Copenhagen N; tel. 35-35-21-93; fax 35-37-20-39; e-mail arbejderen@inform.dk; internet www.arbejderen.dk; Editor Birthe Sørensen.

Dagbladet Information: Store Kongensgade 40c, POB 188, 1006 Copenhagen K; tel. 33-69-60-00; fax 33-69-61-10; e-mail inf-dk@information.dk; internet www.information.dk; f. 1943; (underground during occupation), legally 1945; morning; independent; Editor Jørgen Steen Nielsen; circ. 20,834.

Ekstra Bladet: Rådhuspladsen 37, 1785 Copenhagen V; tel. 33-11-13-13; fax 33-14-10-00; e-mail post@ekstrabladet.dk; internet www.eb.dk; f. 1904; evening; Liberal independent; Editor-in-Chief Hans Engell; Man. Dir Lars Henrik Munch; circ. weekdays 132,828, Sundays 158,151.

Kristeligt Dagblad: Rosengården 14, 1174 Copenhagen K; tel. 33-48-05-00; fax 33-48-05-01; e-mail kristeligt-dagblad@kristeligt-dagblad.dk; internet www.kristeligt-dagblad.dk; f. 1896; morning; independent; Editor Erik Bjerager; circ. 20,000.

Politiken: Politikens Hus, Rådhuspladsen 37, 1785 Copenhagen V; tel. 33-11-85-11; fax 33-15-41-17; e-mail indland@pol.dk; internet www.politiken.dk; f. 1884; morning; Liberal independent; Editor-in-Chief Tøger Seidenfaden; circ. weekdays 138,177, Sundays 176,287.

Esbjerg

Jydskevestkysten: Banegårdspladsen, 6700 Esbjerg; tel. 75-12-45-00; fax 75-13-62-62; e-mail jydskevestkysten@jv.dk; internet www.jv.dk; f. 1917 as *Vestkysten*, merged with *Jydske Tidende* in 1991 to form present daily; morning; Liberal; Editor-in-Chief METTE BOCK; circ. weekdays 89,645, Sundays 101,595.

Helsingør

Helsingør Dagblad: Klostermosevej 101, 3000 Helsingør; tel. 49-22-21-10; fax 49-22-11-08; e-mail redaktionen@helsingordagblad.dk; internet www.helsingordagblad.dk; Editor-in-Chief JOHN BECH; circ. 6,738.

Herlev

Licitationen: Marienlundsvej 46 D, POB 537, 2730 Herlev; tel. 70-15-02-22; fax 44-85-89-19; e-mail licitationen@licitationen.dk; internet www.licitationen.dk; Editor-in-Chief KLAUS TØTTRUP; circ. 5,495.

Herning

Herning Folkeblad: Østergade 25, 7400 Herning; tel. 96-26-37-00; fax 97-22-36-00; e-mail hf@herningfolkeblad.dk; internet www.herningfolkeblad.dk; f. 1869; evening; Liberal; Editor-in-Chief FLEMMING LARSEN; circ. 14,298.

Hillerød

Frederiksborg Amts Avis: Milnersvej 44–46, 3400 Hillerød; tel. 48-24-41-00; fax 42-25-48-40; f. 1874; morning; Liberal; Editor TORBEN DALLEY LARSEN; circ. weekdays 38,000, Sundays 35,800.

Holbæk

Holbæk Amts Venstreblad: Ahlgade 1, 4300 Holbæk; tel. 59-48-02-00; fax 59-44-50-34; e-mail redaktion@venstrebladet.dk; internet www.venstrebladet.dk; f. 1905; evening; Social Liberal; Editor-in-Chief MOGENS FLYVHOLM; circ. 19,087.

Holstebro

Dagbladet Holstebro-Struer: Lægårdvej 86, 7500 Holstebro; tel. 99-12-83-00; fax 97-41-03-20; e-mail holstebro@de-bergske.dk; evening; Liberal independent; Editor ERIK MØLLER; circ. 11,801.

Horsens

Horsens Folkeblad: Søndergade 47, 8700 Horsens; tel. 76-27-20-00; fax 75-62-02-18; e-mail redaktionen@horsens-folkeblad.dk; internet www.horsens-folkeblad.dk; f. 1866; evening; Liberal; Editor JENS BEBE; circ. 19,375.

Kalundborg

Kalundborg Folkeblad: Skibbrogade 40, 4400 Kalundborg; tel. 56-21-24-60; fax 59-51-02-80; e-mail redaktion@kal-folkeblad.dk; internet www.kal-folkeblad.dk; Editor-in-Chief CLAUS SØRENSEN; circ. 8,637.

Kerteminde

Kjerteminde Avis: Ndr. Ringvej 54, 5300 Kerteminde; tel. 65-32-10-04; fax 65-32-39-04; e-mail info@kj-avis.dk; Editor JØRGEN WIND-HANSEN; circ. 1,693.

Næstved

Næstved Tidende: Dania 38, 4700 Næstved; tel. 72-45-11-00; fax 72-45-11-17; e-mail red@sj-medier.dk; internet www.sj-medier.dk; f. 1866; Liberal; 6 days a week; Editor SØREN BAUMANN; circ. 19,240.

Sjællands Tidende: Dania 38, 4700 Næstved; tel. 72-45-11-00; fax 72-45-11-17; e-mail red@sj-medier.dk; internet www.sj-medier.dk; f. 1815; morning; Liberal; for western part of Zealand; Editor SØREN BAUMANN; circ. 15,247.

Nykøbing

Lolland-Falsters Folketidende: Tværgade 14, 4800 Nykøbing F; tel. 54-88-02-00; fax 54-85-02-96; e-mail folketidende@indbakke.dk; internet www.folketidende.dk; f. 1873; evening; Liberal; Editor BO BISCHOFF; circ. 24,864.

Morsø Folkeblad: Elsøvej 105; 7900 Nykøbing M; tel. 97-72-10-00; fax 97-72-10-10; Editor-in-Chief LEIF KRISTIANSEN; circ. 6,021.

Odense

Fyens Stiftstidende: Blangstedgårdsvej 2–6, 5220 Odense SØ; tel. 66-11-11-11; fax 65-93-25-74; e-mail redaktion@fyens.dk; internet www.fyens.dk; f. 1772; morning; independent; Editor-in-Chief EGON TØTTRUP; circ. weekdays 63,349, Sundays 84,358.

Randers

Randers Amtsavis: Nørregade 7, 8900 Randers; tel. 87-12-20-00; fax 87-12-21-21; e-mail e-mail@amtsavisra.dk; f. 1810; evening; independent; Editor-in-Chief OLE C. JØRGENSEN; circ. 81,000.

Ringkøbing

Ringkøbing Amts Dagblad: Sankt Blichersvej 5, POB 146, 6950 Ringkøbing; tel. 99-75-73-00; fax 97-32-05-46; e-mail ringkoebing@de-bergske.dk; evening; Editor KRISTIAN SAND; circ. 15,389.

Rønne

Bornholms Tidende: Nørregade 11–13, 3700 Rønne; tel. 56-95-14-00; fax 56-95-31-19; e-mail redaktion@bornholmstidende.dk; internet www.bornholmstidende.dk; f. 1866; evening; Liberal; Editor-in-Chief BJARNE PEDERSEN; circ. 13,904.

Silkeborg

Midtjyllands Avis: Vestergade 30, 8600 Silkeborg; tel. 86-82-13-00; fax 86-81-35-77; e-mail silkeborg@midtjyllandsavis.dk; internet www.midtjyllandsavis.dk; f. 1857; daily except Sundays; Editor-in-Chief STEFFEN LANGE; circ. 17,644.

Skive

Skive Folkeblad: Gemsevej 7–9, 7800 Skive; tel. 97-51-34-11; fax 97-51-28-35; e-mail skivefol@post6.tele.dk; internet www.skivefolkeblad.dk; f. 1880; Social Liberal; Editor OLE DALL; circ. 13,153.

Svendborg

Fyns Amts Avis: Sankt Nicolai Gade 3, 5700 Svendborg; tel. 62-21-46-21; fax 62-22-06-10; e-mail post@fynsamtsavis.dk; internet www.fynsamtsavis.dk; f. 1863; Liberal; Editor OLE C. JØRGENSEN; circ. 20,255.

Thisted

Thisted Dagblad: Thisted; tel. 99-19-93-00; fax 97-91-07-20; e-mail thisted@de-bergske.dk; Liberal independent; Editor HANS PETER KRAGH; circ. 9,188.

Vejle

Vejle Amts Folkeblad: Bugattivej 8, 7100 Vejle; tel. 75-85-77-88; fax 75-85-72-47; e-mail vaf-fd@vaf-fd.dk; internet www.vejleonline.dk; f. 1865; evening; Liberal; Editor ARNE MARIAGER; circ. 27,755.

Viborg

Viborg Stifts Folkeblad: Sankt Mathiasgade 7, 8800 Viborg; tel. 89-27-63-00; fax 89-27-63-70; e-mail viborg@de-bergske.dk; f. 1877; evening; Liberal Democrat; also published: *Viborg Nyt* (weekly); Editor PER V. SUNESEN; circ.11,542.

Viby

Jyllands-Posten Morgenavisen: Grøndalsvej 3, 8260 Viby J; tel. 87-38-38-38; fax 87-38-31-99; e-mail jp@jp.dk; internet www.jp.dk; f. 1871; independent; Editor-in-Chief CARSTEN JUSTE; circ. weekdays 179,716, Sundays 240,057.

OTHER NEWSPAPERS

Den Blå Avis (East edition): Generatorvej 8D, 2730 Herlev; tel. 44-85-44-44; internet www.dba.dk; 2 a week; circ. 73,000.

Den Blå Avis (West edition): Marelisborg Havnevej 26, POB 180, 8100 Århus C; tel. 87-31-31-31; fax 86-20-20-02; internet www.dba.dk; Thursday; circ. 46,160.

Weekendavisen: Pilestræde 34, 3, 1147 Copenhagen K; tel. 33-75-25–33; fax 33-75-20-50; e-mail bwa@weekendavisen.dk; internet www.weekendavisen.dk; f. 1749; independent Conservative; Friday; Editor-in-Chief ANNE KNUDSEN; circ. 66,186.

POPULAR PERIODICALS

Ældre Sagen: Nyropsgade 45, 1602 Copenhagen V; tel. 33-96-86-86; fax 33-96-86-87; e-mail aeldresagen@aeldresagen.dk; internet www.aeldresagen.dk; 6 a year; for senior citizens; Editor SANNA KJAER HANSEN; circ. 360,000.

ALT for damerne: Hellerupvej 51, 2900 Hellerup; tel. 39-45-74-00; fax 39-45-74-80; e-mail alt@altfordamerne.dk; internet www.altfordamerne.dk; f. 1946; weekly; women's magazine; Editor-in-Chief HANNE HØIBERG; circ. 89,081.

Anders And & Co: Vognmagergade 11, 1148 Copenhagen K; tel. 33-30-50-00; fax 33-30-55-10; internet www.andeby.dk; weekly; children's magazine; Editor TOMMY MELLE; circ. 99,826.

Basserne: Hellerupvej 51, 2900 Hellerup; tel. 33-33-75-35; fax 33-33-75-05; fortnightly; children and youth; circ. 49,000.

Det Bedste fra Reader's Digest A/S: Jagtvej 169B, 2100 Copenhagen Ø; tel. 39-18-12-13; fax 39-18-12-36; e-mail det-bedste@internet.dk; monthly; Danish *Reader's Digest*; Editor YNGVE SKOVMAND; circ. 69,556.

Billed-Bladet: Vesterbrogade 16, 1620 Copenhagen V; tel. 31-23-16-11; fax 31-24-10-08; f. 1938; weekly; family picture magazine; Editor ANDERS THISTED; circ. 222,951.

Bo Bedre: Strandboulevarden 130, 2100 Copenhagen Ø; tel. 39-17-20-00; fax 39-17-23-02; e-mail bobedre@bp.bonnier.dk; monthly; homes and gardens; Editor-in-Chief ERIK RIMMER; circ. 99,894.

Camping: Silkeborg; tel. 86-82-55-00; fax 86-81-63-02; monthly; circ. 44,107.

Familie Journalen: Vigerslev Allé 18, 2500 Valby, Copenhagen; tel. 36-15-22-22; fax 36-15-22-99; e-mail redaktion@familiejournalen.dk; f. 1877; weekly; Editor-in-Chief PETER DALL; circ. 238,000.

Femina: Vigerslev Allé 18, 2500 Valby, Copenhagen; tel. 36-30-33-33; fax 36-44-19-79; f. 1873; weekly; Editor JUTTA LARSEN; circ. 93,866.

Gør Det Selv: Strandboulevarden 130, 2100 Copenhagen Ø; tel. 39-17-20-00; fax 39-17-23-07; e-mail gds@bp.bonnier.dk; internet www.goerdetselv.dk; f. 1975; 17 a year; do-it-yourself; Editor KÅRE OLOFSEN; circ. 150,000.

Helse—Familiens Lægemagasin: Østbanegade 55, 5. sal 2100 Copenhagen Ø; tel. 35-25-05-25; fax 35-26-87-60; e-mail helse@helse.dk; internet www.helse.dk; monthly; family health; circ. 300,000.

Hendes Verden: Hellerupvej 51, 2900 Hellerup; tel. 39-45-75-50; fax 39-45-75-99; f. 1937; weekly; for women; Editor IBEN NIELSEN; circ. 58,302.

Hjemmet (The Home): Vognmagergade 10, 1145 Copenhagen K; tel. 39-45-76-00; fax 39-45-76-60; weekly; Editor-in-Chief BJARNE RAUNSTED; circ. 207,087.

I form: Strandboulevarden 130, 2100 Copenhagen Ø; tel. 39-17-20-00; fax 39-17-23-11; e-mail iform@iform.dk; internet www.iform.dk; 17 a year; sport, health, nutrition, sex, psychology; Editor KAREN LYAGER HORVE; circ. 70,766.

Idé-nyt: Gl. Klausdalsbrovej 480, 2730 Herlev; tel. 44-53-40-00; fax 44-92-11-21; e-mail idenyt@idenyt.dk; internet www.idenyt.dk; f. 1973; 5 a year; free magazine (regional editions); homes and gardens; circ. 2,500,000.

Illustreret Videnskab: Strandboulevarden 130, 2100 Copenhagen Ø; tel. 39-17-20-00; fax 39-17-23-12; internet www.illustreretvidenskab.dk; 16 a year; popular science; Editor JENS E. MATTHIESEN; circ. 88,132.

Mad og Bolig: Vigersleu alle 18, 2500 Valby; tel. 36-15-20-00; f. 1991; 8 a year; gastronomy, wine, interiors and travel; Editor JETTE ØSTERLUND; circ. 61,293.

Månedsmagasinet IN: Vigerslev Allé 18, 2500 Valby; tel. 36-15-20-00; fax 36-15-27-94; e-mail in@in.dk; internet www.in.dk; fashion magazine; Editor-in-Chief CAMILLA LINDEMANN; circ. 50,000.

Motor: Firskovvej 32, POB 500, 2800 Lyngby; tel. 45-27-07-07; fax 45-27-09-89; e-mail motor@fdm.dk; internet www.fdm.dk; monthly; cars and motoring; circ. 210,000.

Rapport: Marielundvej 46E, 2730 Herlev; tel. 44-85-88-66; fax 44-85-88-67; e-mail rap@rapport.dk; internet www.rapport.dk; f. 1971; men's weekly; Editor-in-Chief JAN SCHIWE NIELSEN; circ. 36,964.

Samvirke: Roskildevej 65, 2620 Albertslund; tel. 43-86-43-86; fax 43-86-44-89; f. 1928; consumer monthly; Publr and Editor-in-Chief POUL DINES; circ. 500,000.

Se og Hør: Vigerslev Allé 18, 2500 Valby; tel. 36-15-24-00; fax 36-15-24-99; e-mail redaktionen@sh-online.dk; internet www.sh-online.dk; f. 1940; news and TV; Editor PETER SALSKOV; circ. 315,083.

Sofus' Lillebror: Copenhagen; tel. 33-33-75-35; fax 33-33-75-05; monthly; children and youth; circ. 44,000.

TIPS-bladet: Alsgarde Centret 2, 3140 Alsgarde; tel. 49-70-89-00; fax 49-70-88-30; weekly; sport; circ. 39,467.

Ud og Se: Allégade 8F, 2000 Frederiksberg; tel. 31-22-20-20; fax 31-22-99-59; travel monthly; circ. 290,000.

Ude og Hjemme: Vigerslev Allé 18, 2500 Valby, Copenhagen; tel. 36-15-25-25; fax 36-15-25-99; e-mail redaktionen@udeoghjemme.dk; internet www.udeoghjemme.dk; f. 1926; family weekly; Editor JØRN BAUENMAND; circ. 181,000.

Ugebladet Søndag: Otto Mønsteds Gade 3, 1505 Copenhagen V; tel. 36-15-34-00; fax 36-15-34-01; e-mail soendag@soendag.dk; f. 1921; weekly; family magazine; Editor JOHNNY JOHANSEN; circ. 103,603.

SPECIALIST PERIODICALS

ABF-Nyt: Carsten Ekström, Bagsværdhovedgade 296–298, 2880 Bagsværd; tel. 44-44-77-47; fax 44-44-67-47; e-mail abfnyt@announce-service.dk; 4 a year; Editor JAN HANSEN; circ. 60,185.

Aktive Kvinder: Niels Hemmingsensgade 10, 2. sal, 1153 Copenhagen K; tel. 33-13-12-22; fax 33-33-03-28; e-mail ddh@ddh-aktive-kvinder.dk; internet www.ddh-aktive-kvinder.dk; f. 1920; 6 a year; home management; Editor KIRSTEN WULFF; circ. 25,000.

Aktuel Elektronik: Copenhagen; tel. 31-21-68-01; fax 31-21-23-96; 22 a year; computing and information technology; circ. 21,642.

Alt om Data: St. Kongensgade 72, 1264 Copenhagen K; tel. 33-91-28-33; fax 33-91-01-21; e-mail redaktion@aod.dk; internet www.aod.dk/aod; f. 1983; monthly; Editor-in-Chief TORBEN OKHOLM; circ. 35,000.

Automatik: Algade 10, POB 80, 4500 Nykøbing; tel. 53-41-23-10; engineering; monthly; circ. 39,250.

Bådnyt (Boats): Marielundvej 46E, 2730 Herlev; tel. 44-85-89-55; fax 44-85-89-56; e-mail redaktionen@baadnyt.dk; monthly; Editor KNUT IVERSEN; circ. 18,500.

Beboerbladet: Allégade 8F, 2000 Frederiksberg; tel. 33-22-20-20; fax 33-22-99-59; e-mail jbmedia@post4.tele.dk; internet www.jbmedia.dk; quarterly; for tenants in public housing; circ. 475,000.

Beredskab: Meinungsgade 8D, 2200 Copenhagen N; tel. 35-24-00-00; fax 35-24-00-01; e-mail bf@beredskab.dk; internet www.beredskab.dk; f. 1934; 6 a year; civil protection and preparedness; publ. by the Danish Civil Protection League; circ. 4,000.

Bilsnak: Park Allé 355, 2605 Brøndby; tel. 43-28-82-00; fax 43-63-63-38; e-mail redaktion@bilsnak.dk; internet www.volkswagen.dk; f. 1976; 3 a year; cars; Editor JANNE DEGN SKALKAM; circ. 195,000.

Boligen: Studiestræde 50, 1554 Copenhagen V; tel. 33-76-20-21; fax 33-76-20-01; monthly; housing associations, architects; Editor HELGE MØLLER; circ. 30,000.

BygTek: Stationsparken 25, 2600 Glostrup; tel. 43-43-29-00; fax 43-13-28; e-mail odsgard@odsgard.dk; internet www.byggeri.dk; monthly; building and construction; circ. 25,000.

Computerworld: Carl Jacobsens Vej 25, 2500 Valby; tel. 77-30-03-00; fax 77-30-03-02; e-mail redaktionen@computerworld.dk; internet www.computerworld.dk; f. 1981; 2 a week; computing; Editors-in-Chief JAN HORSAGER, RUNE MICHAELSEN; circ. 28,000.

Cyklister: Dansk Cyklist Forbund, Rømersgade 7, 1362 Copenhagen K; tel. 33-32-31-21; fax 33-32-76-83; e-mail dcf@dcf.dk; internet www.dcf.dk; f. 1905; 6 a year; organ of Danish Cyclist Federation; Editor INGRID E. PETERSEN; circ. 19,000.

Effektivt Landbrug: Copenhagen; tel. 31-21-68-01; fax 31-21-53-50; 21 a year; farming; circ. 31,407.

FINANS: Langebrogade 5, 1411 Copenhagen K; tel. 32-96-46-00; internet www.finansforbundet.dk; 16 a year; for employees in the financial sector; circ. 53,000.

Folkeskolen: Vandkunsten 12, POB 2139, 1015 Copenhagen K; tel. 33-69-63-00; fax 33-69-64-26; e-mail folkeskolen@dlf.org; internet www.folkeskolen.dk; 43 a year; teaching; Editor THORKILD THEJSEN; circ. 84,461.

Foto Guiden: POB 239, 9900 Frederikshavn; tel. 98-42-90-60; fax 98-42-90-61; f. 1960; 2 a year; photography; Editor E. STEEN SØRENSEN; circ. 24,000.

Haber: Politiken, Rådhuspladsen 37, 1785 Copenhagen V; tel. 33-47-11-65; fax 33-47-11-66; e-mail haber@pol.dk; f. 2002; weekly; owned by Politiken; liberal independent; for the Turkish community in Denmark, articles in Danish and Turkish; Editor-in-Chief TØGER SEIDENFADEN; circ. 11,000.

Havebladet: Frederikssundsvej 304A, 2700 Brønshøj; tel. 38-28-87-50; fax 32-28-83-50; e-mail info@kolonihave.dk; internet www.kolonihave.dk; 5 a year; publ. by Kolonihaveforbundet for Danmark; gardening; circ. 40,500.

High Fidelity: Blegdamsvej 112A, 2100 Copenhagen Ø; tel. 70-23-70-01; fax 70-23-70-02; e-mail karen@hifi.dk; f. 1968; 8 a year; Editor-in-Chief MICHAEL MADSEN; circ. 24,833.

Hunden: Medichuset Wiegaarden, 9500 Hobro; tel. 98-51-20-66; fax 98-51-20-06; internet www.dansk-kennel-klub.dk; 10 a year; organ of the kennel club; circ. 30,000.

Ingeniøren: POB 373, Skelbækgade 4, 1503 Copenhagen V; tel. 33-26-53-00; fax 33-26-53-01; e-mail ing@ing.dk; internet www.ing.dk; f. 1892; weekly engineers' magazine; Editor PER WESTERGÅRD; circ. 82,300.

Jaeger: Hojnæsvej 56, 2610 Rødovre; tel. 36-72-42-00; fax 36-72-09-11; monthly except July; circ. 89,000.

Jern- og Maskinindustrien: Falkoner Allé 90, 2000 Frederiksberg; tel. 35-36-37-00; fax 35-36-37-90; e-mail jm@df-jm.dk; 22 a year; iron and metallic industries; circ. 25,295.

Jyllands Ringens program: Charlottenlund; tel. 31-64-46-92; 5 a year; cars and motorcycles; circ. 280,000.

Kommunalbladet: Park Allé 9, 8000 Aarhus C; tel. 86-76-13-22; fax 86-76-13-10; e-mail redaktionen@kommunalbladet.dk; internet www.kommunalbladet.dk; 22 a year; municipal administration, civil servants; Editor ULLA KRAG JESPERSEN; circ. 75,000.

Landsbladet Kvæg: Vester Farimagsgade 6, 1606 Copenhagen V; tel. 33-39-47-00; fax 33-39-47-49; monthly; for cattle-breeders and dairy-farmers; related titles *Landsbladet Mark* for arable farmers, *Landsbladet Svin* for pig-farmers; circ. 15,000.

Lederne: Vermlandsgade 65, 2300 Copenhagen S; tel. 32-83-32-83; fax 32-83-32-84; e-mail lh@lederne.dk; internet www.lederne.dk; 12 a year; for managers; circ. 80,136.

Metal: Nyropsgade 38, 1602 Copenhagen V; tel. 33-63-20-00; fax 33-63-21-00; 16 a year; metal industries; circ. 150,571.

Produktion: Axelborg, Vesterbrogade 4A, 1503 Copenhagen; tel. 33-69-87-00; fax 33-69-87-87; e-mail info@dlg.dk; internet www.dlg.dk; 6 a year; farming; Editor ELSE DAMSGAARD; circ. 63,000.

Spejd: The Danish Guide and Scout Association, Arsenalvej 10, 1436 Copenhagen K; tel. 32-64-00-50; fax 32-64-00-75; e-mail dds@dds.dk; internet www.dds.dk; 7 a year; organ of the Scout Movement; circ. 38,900.

Stat, Amt og Kommune Information: POB 162, 2600 Glostrup; tel. 43-43-31-21; fax 43-43-15-13; e-mail saki@saki.dk; internet www.saki.dk; monthly; public works and administration; circ. 21,000.

Sygeplejersken: Vimmelskaftet 38, POB 1084, 1008 Copenhagen K; tel. 33-15-15-55; e-mail redaktionen@dsr.dk; internet www.tfs.dk; 50 a year; nursing; circ. 74,000.

Tidsskrift for Sukkersyge—Diabetes: Rytterkasernen 1, 5000 Odense C; tel. 66-12-90-06; fax 65-91-49-08; e-mail df@diabetes.dk; internet www.diabetesforeningen.dk; f. 1940; 6 a year; diabetes; Dir FLEMMING KJERSGAARD JOHANSEN; circ. 50,000.

Ugeskrift for Læger: Trondhjemsgade 9, 2100 Copenhagen Ø; tel. 35-44-85-00; e-mail ufl@daol.dk; weekly; medical; Editors T. SCHROEDER, T. KITAJ; circ. 22,000.

NEWS AGENCY

Ritzaus Bureau I/S: Store Kongensgade 14, 1264 Copenhagen K; tel. 33-30-00-00; fax 33-30-00-01; e-mail ritzau@ritzau.dk; internet www.ritzau.dk; f. 1866; general, financial and commercial news; owned by all Danish newspapers; Chair. of Board of Dirs TORBEN DALBY LARSEN; Gen. Man. and Editor-in-Chief UFFE RIIS SØRENSEN.

Foreign Bureaux

Agence France-Presse (AFP): Store Kongensgade 14, 3rd floor, 1264 Copenhagen K; tel. 33-13-23-31; fax 33-14-32-06; e-mail afp@nitzau.dk; Bureau Chief SLIM ALLAGUI.

Agencia EFE (Spain): Copenhagen; Correspondent MARÍA CAMINO SÁNCHEZ.

Agenzia Nazionale Stampa Associata (ANSA) (Italy): Vestergade 2, 1456 Copenhagen K; tel. 33-32-03-59; fax 33-32-03-69; Correspondent DANIELA ROMITI.

Allgemeiner Deutscher Nachrichtendienst (ADN) (Germany): Copenhagen; Bureau Chief HERBERT HANSCH.

Associated Press (AP) (USA): Copenhagen; tel. 33-11-15-04; fax 33-32-36-60; Bureau Chief ED MCCULLOUGH.

Deutsche Presse-Agentur (dpa) (Germany): Store Kongensgade 14, 3rd Floor, 1264 Copenhagen K; tel. 33-14-22-19; fax 33-14-66-72; e-mail dpa@ritzau.dk; Chief Correspondent THOMAS BORCHERT.

Informatsionnoye Telegrafnoye Agentstvo Rossii— Telegrafnoye Agentstvo Suverennykh Stran (ITAR—TASS) (Russia): Uraniavej 9B, 1878 Frederiksberg C; tel. 31-31-88-48; Correspondent TARAS B. LARIOKHIN.

Reuters (UK): Badstuestræde 18, 1209 Copenhagen K; tel. 33-96-96-96; fax 33-12-32-72; e-mail copenhagen.newsroom@reuters.com; Bureau Chief PER BECH THOMSEN.

PRESS ASSOCIATIONS

Dansk Fagpresse (Association of the Danish Specialized Press): Pressens Hus, Skindergade 7, 1159 Copenhagen K; tel. 33-97-40-00; fax 31-91-26-70; e-mail df@danskfagpresse.dk; internet www.danskfagpresse.dk; Man. Dir CHRISTIAN KIERKEGAARD.

Dansk Magasinpresses Udgiverforening (Danish Magazine Publishers' Association): Hammerensgade 6, 1267 Copenhagen K; tel. 33-11-88-44; fax 33-15-01-86; e-mail dmu-mags@internet.dk; internet www.dmu-mags.dk; Chair. KJELD LUCAS; Dir FINN SKOVSGAARD.

Danske Dagblades Forening (Danish Newspaper Publishers' Association): Pressens Hus, Skindergade 7, 1159 Copenhagen K; tel. 33-97-40-00; fax 33-14-23-25; e-mail ddf@danskedagblade.dk; internet www.danskedagblade.dk; comprises managers and editors-in-chief of all newspapers; general spokesbody for the Danish press; Man. Dir EBBE DAL.

Publishers

Aarhus Universitetsforlag: Langelandsgade 177, 8200 Aarhus N; tel. 89-42-53-70; fax 89-42-53-80; e-mail unipress@au.dk; internet www.unipress.dk; reference, non-fiction and educational; Man. Dir CLAES HVIDBAK.

Forlaget åløkke A/S: Porskærvej 15, Nim, 8700 Horsens; tel. 75-67-11-19; fax 75-67-10-74; e-mail alokke@get2net.dk; internet www.alokke.dk; f. 1977; educational, children's books, audio-visual and other study aids; Pres. BERTIL TOFT HANSEN; Man. Dir EVA B. HANSEN.

Akademisk Forlag A/S (Danish University Press): Pilestrade 52, 3. sal, POB 54, 1002 Copenhagen K; tel. 33-43-40-80; fax 33-43-40-99; e-mail akademisk@akademisk.dk; internet www.akademisk.dk; f. 1962; history, health, linguistics, university textbooks, educational materials; Dir ESBEN ESBENSEN.

Forlaget Amanda: Rathsacksvej 7, 1862 Frederiksberg C; tel. 33-79-00-10; fax 33-79-00-11; e-mail forlag@dansklf.dk; art, culture, school books, non-fiction; Editorial Dir GERT EMBORG.

Forlaget Apostrof ApS: Berggreensgade 24, 2100 Copenhagen Ø; tel. 39-20-84-20; fax 39-20-84-53; e-mail info@apostrof.dk; internet www.apostrof.dk; f. 1980; psychotherapy and contemporary psychology, fiction and non-fiction for children; Publrs MIA THESTRUP, OLE THESTRUP.

Arkitektens Forlag: Strandgade 27A, 1401 Copenhagen K; tel. 32-83-69-00; fax 32-83-69-41; e-mail eksp@arkfo.dk; internet www.arkfo.dk; architecture, planning; Dir KIM DIRCKINCK-HOLMFELD.

Forlaget Artia (Ars Audiendi ApS): Vognmagergade 9, 1120 Copenhagen K; tel. 33-12-28-98; fax 33-14-12-63; fiction, non-fiction, science fiction, music, horror; Publr ERIK LÆSSØE STILLING; Dir PETER SCHANTZ.

Aschehoug Dansk Forlag A/S: Landemærket 8, POB 2179, 1017 Copenhagen K; tel. 33-30-55-22; fax 33-30-58-22; e-mail info@ash.egmont.com; internet www.aschehoug.dk; imprints: Aschehoug (fiction), Aschehoug Fakta (non-fiction, reference, children's books), Sesam (educational, children's books, history); Man. Dir (Aschehoug) ANETTE WAD.

Peter Asschenfeldt's nye Forlag A/S: Ny Adelgade 8–10, 1104 Copenhagen K; tel. 33-37-07-60; fax 33-91-03-04; fiction; Publr PETER ASSCHENFELDT.

Blackwell Munksgaard: Rosenørns Allé 1, POB 227, 1502 Copenhagen V; tel. 77-33-33-33; fax 77-33-33-77; e-mail headoffice@munksgaard.dk; internet www.blackwellmunksgaard.dk; f. 1917 as Munksgaard International Publishers Ltd, present name adopted 2000; scientific journals on medicine and dentistry; Man. Dir LISE BALTZER.

Thomas Bloms Forlag ApS: Skovenggaardsvej 8, 9490 Pandrup; tel. 98-24-85-25; fax 98-24-80-60; fiction, non-fiction, children's books, talking books; Publrs CONNIE BLOM, THOMAS BLOM.

Bogans Forlag: Kastaniebakken 8, POB 39, 3540 Lynge; tel. 48-18-80-55; fax 48-18-87-69; f. 1974; general paperbacks, popular science, non-fiction, humour, health; Publr EVAN BOGAN.

Borgens Forlag A/S: Valbygårdsvej 33, 2500 Valby; tel. 36-15-36-15; fax 36-15-36-16; e-mail post@borgen.dk; internet www.borgen.dk; f. 1948; fiction, poetry, children's books, humour, general non-fiction; Man. Dir NIELS BORGEN.

Bøornegudstjeneste-Forlaget: Korskærvej 25, 7000 Fredericia; tel. 75-93-44-55; fax 75-92-42-75; religion, children's books; Dir FINN ANDERSEN; Editorial Dir JØRGEN HEDAGER.

Carit Andersens Forlag A/S: Upsalagade 18, 2100 Copenhagen Ø; tel. 35-43-62-22; fax 35-43-51-51; e-mail info@caritandersen.dk; internet www.caritandersen.dk; illustrated books, non-fiction, fiction, science fiction; Publr ERIK ALBRECHTSEN.

Forlaget Carlsen A/S: Krogshøjvej 32, 2880 Bagsværd; tel. 44-44-32-33; fax 44-44-36-33; e-mail carlsen@carlsen.dk; internet www.carlsen.dk; children's books; Man. Dir JESPER HOLM.

Forlaget Centrum: Store Kongensgade 92, 3TV, 1264 Copenhagen K; tel. 33-32-12-06; fax 33-32-12-07; e-mail lmm@forlaget-centrum.dk; fiction, non-fiction; Man. Dir LISBETH MØLLER-MADSEN.

Cicero (Chr. Erichsens Forlag A/S): Vester Voldgade 83, 1552 Copenhagen V; tel. 33-16-03-08; fax 33-16-03-07; e-mail info@cicero .dk; internet www.cicero.dk; f. 1902; fiction, non-fiction, art, culture; Publrs NIELS GUDBERGSEN, ALIS CASPERSEN.

DA-Forlag/Dansk Arbejdsgiverforening: Vester Voldgade 113, 1552 Copenhagen V; tel. 33-38-94-63; fax 33-91-09-32; e-mail smh@ da.dk; non-fiction and reference; Publishing Dir SØREN MELDORF HANSEN.

Dafolo A/S: Suderbovej 22–24, 9900 Frederikshavn; tel. 96-20-66-66; fax 98-42-97-11; e-mail dafolo@dafolo.dk; internet www.dafolo .dk; educational books; Publr MICHAEL SCHELDE.

Dansk BiblioteksCenter A/S: Tempovej 7–11, 2750 Ballerup; tel. 44-86-77-77; fax 44-86-78-91; e-mail dbc@dbc.dk; internet www.dbc .dk; bibliographic data, information services, library systems, media; Man. Dir MOGENS BRABRAND JENSEN.

Dansk Historisk Håndbogsforlag A/S: Buddingevej 87A, 2800 Lyngby; tel. 45-93-48-00; fax 45-93-47-47; e-mail mrjensen@image .dk; f. 1976; genealogy, heraldry, law, culture and local history, facsimile editions, microfiches produced by subsidiary co; Owners and Man. Dirs RITA JENSEN, HENNING JENSEN.

Dansk psykologisk Forlag: Stockholmsgade 29, 2100 Copenhagen Ø; tel. 35-38-16-55; fax 35-38-16-65; e-mail dk-psych@dpf.dk; internet www.dpf.dk; educational books, health, psychology; Man. Dir HANS GERHARDT.

Det Danske Bibelselskabs Forlag/Det Kongelige Vajsenshus' Forlag: Frederiksborggade 50, 1360 Copenhagen K; tel. 33-12-78-35; fax 33-93-21-50; e-mail bibelselskabet@bibelselskabet.dk; internet www.bibelselskabet.dk; bibles, religious and liturgical books, children's books; Dir PETER BIRCH.

Christian Ejlers' Forlag ApS: Sølvgade 38/3, 1307 Copenhagen K; tel. 33-12-21-14; fax 33-12-28-84; e-mail liber@ce-publishers.dk; internet www.ejlers.dk; f. 1967; educational, academic and multimedia; Publr CHRISTIAN EJLERS.

Forlaget for Faglitteratur A/S: Copenhagen; tel. 33-13-79-00; fax 33-14-51-56; medicine, technology.

FinansSupport: Glostrup; tel. 43-44-04-44; fax 43-44-07-44; educational books; Pres. ERLING JENSEN.

Flachs: Øverødvej 98, 2840 Holte; tel. 45-42-48-30; fax 45-42-48-29; e-mail flachs@flachs.dk; internet www.flachs.dk; fiction, non-fiction, reference, educational and children's books; Publrs ALLAN FLACHS, ANETTE FLACHS.

Palle Fogtdal A/S: Østergade 22, 1100 Copenhagen K; tel. 33-15-39-15; fax 33-93-35-05; Danish history, photography; Man. Dir PALLE FOGTDAL.

Forum: Købmagergade 62, 1019 Copenhagen K; tel. 33-41-18-30; fax 33-41-18-31; f. 1940; history, fiction, biographies, quality paperbacks and children's books; Man. Dir OLE KNUDSEN.

Fremad: Købmagergade 62, POB 2252, 1019 Copenhagen K; tel. 33-41-18-10; fax 33-41-18-11; f. 1912; general trade, fiction, non-fiction, juveniles, reference, children's books; Man. Dir NIELS KØLLE.

G.E.C. Gad Publishers Ltd: Vimmelskaftet 32, 1161 Copenhagen K; tel. 33-15-05-58; fax 33-11-08-00; e-mail sekr@gads-forlag.dk; internet www.gads-forlag.dk; biographies, natural science, history, reference, fiction, educational materials, food and drink, travel guides; Man. Dir AXEL KIELLAND.

Gyldendalske Boghandel, Nordisk Forlag A/S: Klareboderne 3, 1001 Copenhagen K; tel. 33-75-55-55; fax 33-75-55-56; e-mail gyldendal@gyldendal.dk; internet www.gyldendal.dk; f. 1770; fiction, non-fiction, reference books, paperbacks, children's books, textbooks; Man. Dir STIG ANDERSEN.

P. Haase & Søns Forlag A/S: Løvstræde 8, 1152 Copenhagen K; tel. 33-14-41-75; fax 33-11-59-59; e-mail haase@haase.dk; internet www.haase.dk; f. 1877; educational books, audio-visual aids, children's books, humour, fiction, non-fiction; imprints: Natur og Harmoni, Rasmus Navers Forlag; Man. Dir MICHAEL HAASE.

Edition Wilhelm Hansen A/S: Bornholmsgade 1, 1266 Copenhagen K; tel. 33-11-78-88; fax 33-14-81-78; e-mail ewh@ewh.dk; internet www.ewh.dk; f. 1857; music books, school and educational books; Man. Dir TINE BIRGER CHRISTENSEN.

Hernovs Forlag: Nørrebakken 25, 2820 Gentofte; tel. 32-96-33-14; fax 32-96-04-46; e-mail admin@hernov.dk; internet www.hernov.dk; f. 1941; fiction, non-fiction, classic literature and children's; Man. FRANK HERNOV.

Holkenfeldt 3: Fuglevadsvej 71, 2800 Lyngby; tel. 45-93-12-21; fax 45-93-82-41; fiction, non-fiction, reference, sport, humour; Publr KAY HOLKENFELDT.

Høst & Søns Forlag: Købmagergade 62, POB 2212, 1018 Copenhagen K; tel. 33-38-28-88; fax 33-38-28-98; e-mail hoest@hoest.dk; internet www.hoest.dk; f. 1836; fiction, crafts and hobbies, languages, books on Denmark, children's books; Man. Dir ERIK C. LINDGREN.

Forlaget Hovedland: Elsdyvej 21, 8270 Højbjerg; tel. 86-27-65-00; fax 86-27-65-37; e-mail mail@hovedland.dk; internet www .hovedland.dk; fiction, non-fiction, environment, sport, health, crafts; Publr STEEN PIPER.

Forlaget Klematis: Østre Skovvej 1, 8240 Risskov; tel. 86-17-54-55; fax 86-17-59-59; fiction, non-fiction, crafts, children's books; Dir CLAUS DALBY.

Forlaget Per Kofod ApS: Kompagnistræde 4B, 1208 Copenhagen K; tel. 33-32-70-27; fax 33-32-70-78; fiction, non-fiction, art and culture; Publr PER KOFOD.

Krak: Virumgaardsvej 21, 2830 Virum; tel. 45-95-65-00; fax 45-95-65-65; e-mail krak@krak.dk; internet www.krak.dk; f. 1770; reference works, maps and yearbooks; Dir IB LE ROY TOPHOLM.

Egmont Lademann A/S: Gerdasgade 37, 2500 Valby; tel. 36-15-66-00; fax 36-44-11-62; internet www.lademann.dk; f. 1954; non-fiction, reference.

Lindhardt og Ringhof A/S: Frederiksborggade 1, 1360 Copenhagen K; tel. 33-69-50-00; fax 33-69-50-01; e-mail lr@ lindhardt-og-ringhof.dk; internet www.lindhardt-og-ringhof.dk; general fiction and non-fiction; Dir TRINE LICHT.

L & R FAKTA/Møntergården: Copenhagen; tel. 33-32-18-96; fax 33-37-71-38; e-mail montergaarden@borsen.dk; f. 1997; non-fiction, reference; Man. Dir HENRIK HJORTH; Publr ANNEMARIE ELKJÆR.

Lohses Forlag (incl. Forlaget Korskaer): Korskærvej 25, 7000 Fredericia; tel. 75-93-44-55; fax 75-92-42-75; e-mail finn@lohse.imh .dk; f. 1868; religion, children's, biographies, devotional novels; Man. Dir FINN ANDERSEN.

Forlaget Lotus: Ishøj; tel. 43-45-78-74; fax 43-45-97-71; e-mail fiolotus@post7.tele.dk; management, health, religion, the occult, educational; Publr FINN ANDERSEN.

Forlaget Magnus A/S Skattekartoteket: Informationskontor, Palægade 4, 1261 Copenhagen K; tel. 33-11-78-74; fax 33-93-80-09; e-mail magnus@cddk.dk; internet www.cddk.dk; f. 1962; guidebooks, journals, law; Man. Dir MORTEN ARNBERG.

Medicinsk Forlag ApS: Tranevej 2, 3650 Ølstykke; tel. and fax 47-17-65-02; astrology, medical and scientific books; Man. Dir ANNI LINDELØV.

Modtryk Forlaget: Anholtsgade 4, 8000 Århus C; tel. 87-31-76-00; fax 87-13-76-01; e-mail forlaget@modtryk.dk; internet www .modtryk.dk; f. 1972; children's and school books, fiction, thrillers and non-fiction; Man. Dir ILSE NØRR.

Nyt Nordisk Forlag-Arnold Busck A/S: Købmagergade 49, 1150 Copenhagen K; tel. 33-73-35-75; fax 33-73-35-76; e-mail nnf@ nytnordiskforlag.dk; internet www.nytnordiskforlag.dk; f. 1896; textbooks, school books, guidebooks, fiction and non-fiction; Man. Dir OLE A. BUSCK; Dir JESPER T. FENSVIG.

Jørgen Paludans Forlag ApS: 4 Straedet, 3100 Hornbæk; tel. 49-75-15-36; fax 49-75-15-37; language teaching, non-fiction, psychology, history, politics, economics, reference; Man. Dir JØRGEN PALUDAN.

C.A. Reitzels Boghandel og Forlag A/S: Nørregade 20, 1165 Copenhagen K; tel. 33-12-24-00; fax 33-14-02-70; f. 1819; reference books, philosophy, educational and academic books, Hans Christian Andersen, Kierkegaard; Dir SVEND OLUFSEN.

Hans Reitzels Forlag A/S: Købmagergade 62, POB 1073, 1008 Copenhagen K; tel. 33-38-28-00; fax 33-38-28-08; e-mail hrf@ hansreitzel.dk; internet www.hansreitzel.dk; f. 1949; education, philosophy, psychology, sociology, Hans Christian Andersen; Man. Dir ERIK C. LINDGREN.

Rhodos, International Science and Art Publishers: Niels Brocks Gård, Strandgade 36, 1401 Copenhagen K; tel. 32-54-30-20; fax 32-95-47-42; e-mail rhodos@rhodos.dk; internet www.rhodos.dk; f. 1959; university books, art, science, fiction, poetry; Man. Dir NIELS BLAEDEL; Dir RUBEN BLAEDEL.

Samlerens Forlag A/S: POB 2252, Købmagergade 62, 1019 Copenhagen K; tel. 33-41-18-00; fax 33-41-18-01; e-mail torben_madsen@ samleren.dk; internet www.samlerens.dk; Danish and foreign fiction, contemporary history and politics, biographies; Man. Dir TORBEN MADSEN.

Scandinavia Publishing House: Drejervej 11–21, 2400 Copenhagen NV; tel. 35-31-03-30; fax 35-31-03-34; e-mail jvo@ scanpublishing.dk; internet www.scanpublishing.dk; f. 1973; children's books, religion, Hans Christian Andersen; Dir JØRGEN VIUM OLESEN.

Det Schønbergske Forlag A/S: Landemærket 5, 1119 Copenhagen K; tel. 33-73-35-85; fax 33-73-35-86; f. 1857; fiction, humour, psychology, biography, children's books, paperbacks, textbooks; Dir JOAKIM WERNER; Editor ARVID HONORÉ.

Spektrum: Købmagergade 62, POB 2252, 1019 Copenhagen K; tel. 33-41-18-30; fax 33-41-18-31; non-fiction, history, biographies, science, psychology, religion, philosophy, arts; Man. Dir OLE KNUDSEN.

Strandbergs Forlag ApS: Vedbæk; tel. 42-89-47-60; fax 42-89-47-01; cultural history, travel; Publr HANS JØRGEN STRANDBERG.

Strubes Forlag og Boghandel ApS: Damhus Blvd 65, 2610 Rødovre; tel. 36-72-17-50; fax 36-72-17-52; health, astrology, philosophy, the occult; Man. Dir JONNA STRUBE.

Teknisk Forlag A/S: Copenhagen; tel. 33-43-65-00; fax 33-43-66-77; e-mail bogredaktion@tekniskforlag.dk; internet www.tekniskforlag.dk; f. 1948; computing, technical books, reference, business, educational, science; Man. Dir OLE SKALS PEDERSEN.

Tiderne Skifter: Købmagergade 62, 1019 Copenhagen K; tel. 33-41-18-20; fax 33-41-18-21; e-mail tiderneskifter@tiderneskifter.dk; fiction, sexual and cultural politics, psychology, science, religion, arts; Man. Dir CLAUS CLAUSEN.

Forlaget Thomson: Nytorv 5, 1450 Copenhagen K; tel. 33-74-07-00; fax 33-93-30-77; textbooks, legal, economic, financial, management, business, accounting; Editorial Dir VIBEKE CHRISTIANSEN.

Unitas Forlag: Valby Langgade 19, 2500 Valby; tel. 36-16-64-81; fax 36-16-08-18; e-mail forlag@unitas.dk; internet forlag.unitas.dk; religion, fiction, education, children's books; Man. PEDER GUNDERSEN.

Forlaget Vindrose A/S: Valbygaardsvej 33, 2500 Valby; tel. 36-15-36-15; fax 36-15-36-16; f. 1980; general trade, fiction and non-fiction; Man. Dir NIELS BORGEN.

Vitafakta ApS: Vedbæk; tel. and fax 45-16-11-50; health books, nutrition, school books; Dir INGER MARIE HAUT.

Wisby & Wilkens: Vesterled 45, 8300 Odder; tel. 70-23-46-22; fax 70-23-47-22; e-mail mail@wisby-wilkens.com; internet www.wisby-wilkens.com; f. 1986; children's books, crafts, fiction, health, humour, science, religion; imprint: Mikro (drama, poetry, humour); Publr JACOB WISBY.

Government Publishing House

Statens Information (State Information Service): Nørre Farimagsgade 65, POB 1103, 1009 Copenhagen K; tel. 33-37-92-00; fax 33-37-92-99; e-mail si@si.dk; f. 1975; acts as public relations and information body for the public sector; publishes Statstidende (Official Gazette), etc. Dir LEON ØSTERGAARD.

PUBLISHERS' ASSOCIATION

Den danske Forlæggerforening: Kompagnistræde 18, 1208 Copenhagen K; tel. 33-15-66-88; fax 33-15-65-88; e-mail publassn@webpartner.dk; internet www.danishpublishers.dk; f. 1837; 66 mems, 2 associate mems; Chair. JESPER HOLM; Man. Dir IB TUNE OLSEN.

Broadcasting and Communications

TELECOMMUNICATIONS

Telecommunications services are administered by the National IT and Telecom Agency.

Telecommunications links with the Faroe Islands are provided by satellite ground stations at Tórshavn and Herstedvester. The latter also provides international data communication links via the EUTELSAT system and the French Telecom 1 satellite system, while a station at Blåvand receives signals from INTELSAT.

Regulatory Organization

National IT and Telecom Agency: Holsteinsgade 63, 2100 Copenhagen Ø; tel. 45-35-00-00; fax 45-35-00-10; e-mail itst@itst.dk; internet www.itst.dk; f. 1991; under the Ministry of Science, Technology and Innovation, in charge of administration and regulation of the telecommunications sector as laid down in telecommunications legislation; works on legislation; government centre of expertise in telecommunications; Dir-Gen. JØRGEN ABILD ANDERSEN; Dep. Dir-Gens FINN PETERSEN, MICHAEL HENNEBERG PEDERSEN.

Major Service Providers

Eicon Networks, Danmark: Tuborg Blvd 12, 2900 Hellerup; tel. 44-77-00-00; fax 44-77-00-99; e-mail sales.nordic@eicon.com; internet www.eicon.dk; f. 1984.

GN Great Nordic Ltd: Kongens Nytorv 26, POB 2167, 1016 Copenhagen; tel. 72-11-18-88; fax 72-11-18-89; e-mail info@gn.com; internet www.gn.com; Pres. and CEO JORGEN LINDEGAARD.

LASAT Networks A/S: Nibe; tel. 96-71-10-00; fax 96-71-10-99; e-mail lasat@lasat.com; internet www.lasat.com; f. 1982; CEO CLAUS CHRISTENSEN.

Telecom A/S: Telegade 2, 2630 Tåstrup; tel. 42-52-91-11; fax 42-52-93-31; Man. Dir GREGERS MOGENSEN.

Tele Danmark A/S: Norregade 21, 0900 Copenhagen; tel. 33-43-77-77; fax 33-43-73-89; e-mail teledanmark@tdk.dk; internet www.teledanmark.dk; fmrly state-owned telecommunications company; transferred to private ownership in 1998; CEO HENNING DYREMOSE.

RADIO

DR RADIO: Radio House, Rosenørns Allé 22, 1999 Frederiksberg C; tel. 35-20-30-40; fax 35-20-26-44; e-mail webmaster@dr.dk; internet www.dr.dk; fmrly Danmarks Radio; independent statutory corpn; Dir-Gen. CHR. S. NISSEN; Dir of Radio Programmes LEIF LØNSMANN; operates a foreign service (Radio Denmark), nine regional stations and four national channels.

The four national channels are as follows:

Channel 1: broadcasts for 110 hours per week on FM, in Danish (Greenlandic programmes weekly); Head FINN SLUMSTRUP.

Channel 2: a music channel, broadcasts on FM, for 45 hours per week nationally, in Danish, as well as regional and special (for foreign workers) programmes; Head STEED FREDERIKSEN.

Channel 3: broadcasts on FM for 24 hours per day, in Danish; primarily a popular music channel, it also broadcasts news in Greenlandic, Faroese and in English; Head JESPER GRUNWALD.

Channel 4: broadcasts on FM for about 97 hours per week; news, entertainment and regional programmes.

There are also some 250 operators licensed for low-power FM transmissions of local and community radio, etc.

TELEVISION

DR TV: TV-Byen, 2860 Søborg; tel. 35-20-30-40; fax 35-20-26-44; e-mail dr-kontakten@dr.dk; internet www.dr.dk; operates two services, DR 1 and DR 2; Dir-Gen. CHR. S. NISSEN; Man. Dir JØRGEN RAMSKOV; Dir (News) LISBETH KMUDSEN.

DR 1: terrestrial television channel; Controller JØRGEN RAMSKOV.

DR 2: satellite television channel; Controller TORBEN FRØLICH.

TV 2/DANMARK: Rugaardsvej 25, 5100 Odense C; tel. 65-91-12-44; fax 65-91-33-22; e-mail tv2@tv2.dk; internet www.tv2.dk; began broadcasts in 1988; Denmark's first national commercial and public service TV station; 17% of its finances come from licence fees, the rest from advertising and sponsorship; CEO CRISTINA LAGE.

Viasat Broadcasting/TV 3: Wildersgade 8, 1408 Copenhagen K; tel. 35-25-90-00; fax 35-25-90-10; e-mail viasat@viasat.dk; internet www.tv3.dk; reaches 71% of the country via cable and satellite; Man. Dir LARS BO ANDERSEN; Dir of Programmes HENRIK RAVN.

There are some 50 operators licensed for local television transmission.

Finance

(cap. = capital; res = reserves; dep. = deposits; m. = million; brs = branches; amounts in kroner or euros (€))

BANKING

The first Danish commercial bank was founded in 1846. In 1975 restrictions on savings banks were lifted, giving commercial and savings banks equal rights and status, and restrictions on the establishment of full branches of foreign banks were removed. In 1988 all remaining restrictions on capital movements were ended. In 1998 there were some 187 banks and savings banks in operation. All banks are under government supervision, and public representation is obligatory on all bank supervisory boards.

Supervisory Authority

Finanstilsynet (Danish Financial Supervisory Authority): Gammel Kongevej 74A, 1850 Frederiksberg C; tel. 33-55-82-82; fax 33-55-82-00; e-mail finanstilsynet@ftnet.dk; internet www.ftnet.dk; agency of the Ministry of Economic Affairs, Business and Trade; Man. Dir HENRIK BJERRE-NIELSEN.

Central Bank

Danmarks Nationalbank: Havnegade 5, 1093 Copenhagen K; tel. 33-63-63-63; fax 33-63-71-03; e-mail nationalbanken@nationalbanken.dk; internet www.nationalbanken.dk; f. 1818; self-governing; sole right of issue; conducts monetary policy; administers reserves of foreign exchange; cap. 50m., res 46,655m., dep.

195,126m. (Dec. 2001); Gov. Bodil Nyboe Andersen; Chairs Torben Nielsen, Jens Thomsen.

Commercial Banks

Alm. Brand Bank: Jarmers Pl. 7, 1551 Copenhagen V; tel. 33-30-70-30; fax 33-93-15-88; e-mail almbrand-bank@almbrand.dk; internet www.almbrand-bank.dk; f. 1988; cap. 351m., res 74m., dep. 9,086m. (Dec. 2000); Chair. Christian N. B. Ulrich; Man. Dir Henrik Nordam; 24 brs.

Amagerbanken A/S: Amagerbrogade 25, 2300 Copenhagen S; tel. 32-66-66-66; fax 32-54-45-34; e-mail international@amagerbanken .dk; internet www.amagerbanken.dk; f. 1903; cap. 200m., res 95m., dep. 11,440m. (Dec. 2001); Chair. N. E. Nielsen; CEO and Man. Dir Knud Christensen; Man. Dir Bent Schøn Hansen; 26 brs.

Arbejdernes Landsbank A/S: Panoptikonbygningen, Vesterbrogade 5, 1502 Copenhagen V; tel. 33-38-80-00; fax 33-38-89-60; e-mail info@albank.dk; internet www.albank.dk; f. 1919; cap. 300m., res 95m., dep. 11,723m. (Dec. 2001); Chair. Povl Erik Skov Christensen; Gen. Mans E. Midtgaard, P. E. Leth, E. Castella; 59 brs.

Danske Bank A/S: Holmens Kanal 2–12, 1092 Copenhagen K; tel. 33-44-00-00; fax 70-12-10-80; internet www.danskebank.com; f. 1871 as Danske Landmandsbank; merged with Copenhagen Handelsbank and Provinsbanken in 1990 to form Den Danske Bank A/S; present name adopted 2000; the bank acquired the insurance group Danica in 1995, the Norwegian Fokus Bank in 1999, Real Denmark in 2000 and Bikubanken Girobank A/S in 2001; cap. 7,592m., res 28,655m., dep. 1,143,039m. (Dec. 2000); Chair. Peter Straarup; 650 brs.

Forstædernes Bank A/S: Malervangen 1, 2600 Glostrup; tel. 43-96-17-20; fax 43-63-32-36; e-mail finans@forbank.dk; internet www .forbank.dk; f. 1902; cap. 350m., res 52m., dep. 8,056m. (Dec. 2001); subsidiary, Den Fri Bank (f. 1994), provides telephone banking service to individual customers; Chair. Helmer Olsen; CEO Kjeld Mosebo Christensen; 19 brs.

Jyske Bank A/S: Vestergade 8–16, 8600 Silkeborg; tel. 89-22-22-22; fax 89-22-24-96; e-mail jyskebank@jyskebank.dk; internet www .jyskebank.dk; f. 1855; established in 1967; cap. 750m., res 2,798m., dep. 75,155m. (Dec. 2000); Chair. Leo Rasmussen; CEO Anders Dam; 133 brs.

Midtbank A/S: Østergade 2, 7400 Herning; tel. 96-26-26-26; fax 96-26-28-98; e-mail midtbank@midtbank.dk; internet www.midtbank .dk; f. 1965; cap. 260m., res 552m., dep. 6,240m. (Dec. 2000); Chair. Hans Christoffersen; Gen. Man. Steen Hove; 23 brs.

Nordea Bank Danmark A/S: Stranddegade 3, 1401 Copenhagen V; tel. 33-33-33-33; fax 33-33-63-63; internet www.nordea.dk; f. 1990 as Unibank A/S by merger of Andelsbanken, Privatbanken and SDS; in 1999 the bank merged with the insurance co Tryg-Baltica Forsikring A/S, but remained part of the Unidanmark A/S group, which became part of Nordea Group (Finland) in 2000; cap. €1,182m., res €5,927m., dep. €179,262m. (Dec. 2001); Man. Dir Peter Schütze; 353 brs.

Nordjyske Bank A/S: Jernbanegade 4–8, POB 701, 9900 Frederikshavn; tel. 99-21-22-23; fax 96-33-50-67; e-mail email@ nordjyskebank.dk; internet www.nordjyskebank.dk; f. 1970 as Egnsbank Nord A/S, current name adopted 2002 following merger with Vendsyssel Bank A/S; cap. 46m., res 402m., dep. 2,747m. (Dec. 2001); Chair. Hans Joergen Kaptain; Man. Dirs Jens Ole Jensen, Hans Jørn Vinther; 17 brs.

Nørresundby Bank A/S: Torvet 4, 9400 Nørresundby; tel. 98-17-33-33; fax 98-19-18-78; e-mail nbudland@nrsbank.dk; internet www .noerresundbybank.dk; f. 1898; cap. 50m., res 10m., dep. 3,581m. (Dec. 2000); Chair. Kjeld Kolind Jensen; Gen. Mans Andreas Rasmussen, Finn Øst Andersson; 16 brs.

Nykredit Bank A/S: Kalvebod Brygge 1–3, 1780 Copenhagen V; tel. 33-42-18-00; fax 33-42-18-01; e-mail nykredit-bank@nykredit.dk; internet www.nykredit.dk/bank; f. 1986; cap. 1,400m., res 1,078m., dep. 50,946m. (Dec. 2001); Chair. Henning Kruse Petersen; CEO/Man. Dir Kim Duus.

Ringkjøbing Bank A/S: Torvet 2, 6950 Ringkjøbing; tel. 99-75-32-00; fax 97-32-15-41; e-mail info@ringkjoebing-bank.dk; internet www.ringkjoebing-bank.dk; f. 1872; cap. 32m., res 0.7m., dep. 2,318m. (Dec. 2000); Chair. Leo Rønn Christensen; Man. Dir Preben Knudsgaard.

Ringkjøbing Landbobank A/S: Torvet 1, 6950 Ringkøbing; tel. 97-32-11-66; fax 97-32-18-18; e-mail post@landbobanken.dk; internet www.landbobanken.dk; f. 1886; cap. 25m., res 769m., dep. 3,881m. (Dec. 2001); Chair. Jens Kjeldsen; Gen. Mans Bent Naur Kristensen, John Bull Fisker; 16 brs.

Roskilde Bank A/S: Algade 14, POB 39, 4000 Roskilde; tel. 46-35-17-00; fax 46-34-83-52; f. 1884; cap. 100m., res 121m., dep. 5,982m.

(Dec. 2000); Chair. Jens Winther; Man. Niels Valentin Hansen; 17 brs.

Sparbank Vest: Adelgade 8, POB 505, 7800 Skive; tel. 97-52-33-11; fax 97-52-73-11; e-mail sp@rbankvest.dk; internet www .sparbankvest.dk; f. 1857; cap. 100m., res 144m., dep. 6,364m. (Dec. 2001); Chair. Jens Winther; Man. Dir Niels Valentin Hansen; 35 brs.

Sydbank A/S: Peberlyk 4, POB 169, 6200 Åbenrå; tel. 74-36-36-36; fax 74-36-35-49; e-mail info@sydbank.dk; internet www.sydbank .com; f. 1970; cap. 750m., res 2,685m., dep. 53,535m. (Dec. 2001); Chair. Kresten Philipsen; CEO Carsten Andersen; 120 brs.

Savings Banks

Amtssparekassen Fyn A/S: Vestre Stationsvej 7, POB 189, 5100 Odense C; tel. 66-14-04-74; fax 65-91-01-10; e-mail udland@ amtssparekassen.dk; internet www.amtssparekassen.dk; f. 1974; cap. 181m., res 761m., dep. 12,710m. (Dec. 2000); Chair. Claus Hansen; Man. Dir Finn B. Sorensen; 37 brs.

Lån & Spar Bank: Højbro Pl. 9–11, POB 2117, 1014 Copenhagen K; tel. 33-14-87-48; fax 33-14-18-48; e-mail lsb@lsb.dk; internet www .lsb.dk; f. 1880; present name 1990; cap. 281m., res 265m., dep. 5,991m. (Dec. 2000); Chair. Tommy Agerskov Thomsen; Man. Dir/CEO Peter Schou; 14 brs.

Spar Nord Bank: Karlskogavej 4, POB 162, 9100 Ålborg; tel. 96-34-40-00; fax 96-34-45-75; e-mail sparnord@sparnord.dk; internet www .sparnordbank.com; f. 1967; cap. 519m., res 1,171m., dep. 24,877m. (Dec. 2001); CEO Lasse Nyby; Man. Dirs Lars Møller, John Lundsgaard; 66 brs.

Bankers' Organization

Finansrådet: Finansrådets Hus, Amaliegade 7, 1256 Copenhagen K; tel. 33-70-10-00; fax 33-93-02-60; e-mail f@finansraadet.dk; internet www.finansraadet.dk; f. 1990; 169 mems; Chair. Peter Schütze; Man. Dir Jörgen Horwitz.

STOCK EXCHANGE

Københavns Fondsbørs (Copenhagen Stock Exchange): Nikolaj Pl. 6, POB 1040, 1007 Copenhagen K; tel. 33-93-33-66; fax 33-12-86-13; e-mail xcse@xcse.dk; internet www.xcse.dk; f. 1848; part of the Norex Alliance (launched June 1999); Pres. Hans-Ole Jochumsen; Chair. Hans Ejvind Hansen.

INSURANCE

Principal Companies

Alm. Brand af 1792: Lyngby Hovedgade 4, POB 1792, 2800 Lyngby; tel. 45-96-70-00; fax 45-93-05-46; e-mail almbrand@ almbrand.dk; internet www.almbrand.dk; f. 1792; subsidiaries: finance, life, non-life and reinsurance; Chief Gen. Man. Bent Knie-Andersen.

Codan Forsikring A/S: Codanhus, Gl. Kongevej 60, 1790 Copenhagen V; tel. 33-55-55-55; fax 33-55-21-22; f. 1915 as Forsikringsselskabet Codan A/S; adopted present name 2000; controlled by Royal and Sun Alliance Group Ltd (UK); acquired insurance operations of Hafnia Holdings in 1993; accident, life; CEO Jens Erik Christensen.

Danica Liv I, Livsforsikringsaktieselskab: Parallelvej 17, 2800 Lyngby; tel. 45-23-23-23; fax 45-23-20-20; e-mail servicecentre@ danica.dk; internet www.danica.dk; f. 1842 as state insurance co; privatized 1990; pensions, life and non-life.

GE Frankona Reinsurance A/S: Grønningen 25, 1270 Copenhagen K; tel. 33-97-95-93; fax 33-97-94-41; f. 1894 as ERC Frankona Reinsurance A/S; present name adopted 2000; reinsurance, life and non-life, international; Gen. Man. Walther Hammerstroem.

A/S Det Kjøbenhavnske Reassurance-Compagni (Copenhagen Re): Midtermolen 7, POB 325, 2100 Copenhagen Ø; tel. 35-47-45-45; fax 35-47-72-72; e-mail copre@copre.com; internet www .copre.com; f. 1915; reinsurance.

Købstædernes Forsikring: Grønningen 1, 1270 Copenhagen K; tel. 33-14-37-48; fax 33-32-06-66; e-mail kab@kab.dk; internet www .kab.dk; f. 1761; fire; Chair. Svend Erik Christensen; CEO Mogens N. Skov.

Kompas Rejseforsikring A/S: Klausdalsbrovej 601, 2750 Ballerup; tel. 44-68-81-00; fax 44-68-84-00; e-mail kompas@kompas.dk; internet www.kompas.dk; travel, health; Man. Per Guldbrandsen.

Max Levig & Cos Eft.: Klausdalsbrovej 601, 2750 Ballerup; tel. 44-20-39-60; fax 44-20-66-70; f. 1890; Gen. Man. Hugo Andersen.

PFA Pension: Marina Park, Sundkrogsgade 4, 2100 Copenhagen Ø; tel. 39-17-50-00; fax 39-17-59-50; f. 1917; life; non-life, property; Gen. Mans Henrik Heideby, A. Kühle.

Skandia: Stamholmen 159, 2650 Hvidovre; tel. 36-87-47-47; fax 36-87-47-87; f. 1798 as Kgl. Brand A/S; adopted present name 2000; all branches; subsidiaries: workers' liability, life; Gen. Man. JAN SVENSSON.

Topdanmark Forsikring A/S: Borupvang 4, 2750 Ballerup; tel. 44-68-33-11; fax 44-68-19-06; e-mail topdanmark@topdanmark.dk; internet www.topdanmark.dk; f. 1985; all classes, with subsidiaries; CEO MICHAEL PRAM RASMUSSEN.

Tryg Forsikring A/S: Klausdalsbrovej 601, 2750 Ballerup; tel. 44-20-20-20; fax 44-20-66-00; e-mail tryg@tryg.dk; internet www.tryg .dk; f. 1995; by merger of Tryg Forsikring A/S and Baltica Forsikring A/S; CEO HUGO ANDERSEN.

Insurance Association

Forsikring & Pension: Amaliegade 10, 1256 Copenhagen K; tel. 33-43-55-00; fax 33-43-55-01; e-mail fp@forsikringenshus.dk; internet www.forsikringenshus.dk; f. 1918 as Assurandør-Societetet; present name adopted 1999; Chair. HOLGER DOCK; Dir STEEN LETH JEPPESEN; 177 mems.

Trade and Industry

GOVERNMENT AGENCY

Dansk Industri (Confederation of Danish Industries): 1787 Copenhagen V; tel. 33-77-33-77; fax 33-77-33-00; e-mail di@di.dk; internet www.di.dk; f. 1992; Dir HANS SKOV CHRISTENSEN.

DEVELOPMENT ORGANIZATION

Det Økonomiske Råd (Danish Economic Council): Adelgade 13, 1304 Copenhagen K; tel. 33-13-51-28; fax 33-32-90-29; e-mail dors@ dors.dk; f. 1962 to supervise national economic development and help to co-ordinate the actions of economic interest groups; 26 members representing both sides of industry, the Government and independent economic experts; Co-Chairs Prof. TORBEN M. ANDERSEN, Prof. SØREN BO NIELSEN, Prof. JØRGEN BIRK MORTENSEN; Sec.-Gen. PEDER ANDERSEN.

CHAMBER OF COMMERCE

Det Danske Handelskammer (Danish Chamber of Commerce): Børsen, 1217 Copenhagen K; tel. 33-95-05-00; fax 33-32-52-16; e-mail handelskammeret@commerce.dk; internet www.commerce .dk; f. 1742; Pres. BENT LARSEN; Man. Dir LARS KROBAEK; approx. 2,000 mems.

INDUSTRIAL AND TRADE ASSOCIATIONS

Dansk Elvaerkers Forening (Association of Danish Electric Utilities): Rosenørns Allé 9, 1970 Frederiksberg C; tel. 31-39-01-11; f. 1923; promotes the interests of Danish producers and suppliers of electricity; 105 mem. cos.

Landbrugsradet (Danish Agricultural Council): Axelborg, Axeltorv 3, 1609 Copenhagen V; tel. 33-39-40-00; fax 33-39-41-41; e-mail agriculture@agriculture.dk; internet www.agriculture.dk; f. 1919; Pres. PETER GAEMELKE; Dir KLAUS BUSTRUP; 41 mems.

Mejeriforeningen (Danish Dairy Board): Frederiks Allé 22, 8000 Århus; tel. 87-31-20-00; fax 87-31-20-01; e-mail ddb@mejeri.dk; f. 1912; Chair. KAJ OLE PEDERSEN; Man. Dir K. THAYSEN; 30 mems.

Oliebranchens Fællesrepræsentation (OFR) (Danish Petroleum Industry Association): Vognmagergade 7, POB 120, 1004 Copenhagen K; tel. 33-45-65-70; fax 33-45-65-11; e-mail ofr@ oil-forum.dk; internet www.oil-forum.dk; representative organization for petroleum industry; Chair. K. M. OLESEN; Sec.-Gen. PER THORKILDSEN.

EMPLOYERS' ORGANIZATIONS

Bryggeriforeningen (Danish Brewers' Association): Frederiksberggade 11, 1459 Copenhagen K; tel. 33-12-62-41; fax 3314-25-13; e-mail info@bryggeriforeningen.dk; internet www .bryggeriforeningen.dk; f. 1899; Chair. LARS PÅHLSON; Dir NIELS HALD; 10 mems.

Dansk Arbejdsgiverforening (Danish Employers' Confederation): Vester Voldgade 113, 1790 Copenhagen V; tel. 33-38-90-00; fax 33-12-29-76; e-mail da@da.dk; internet www.da.dk; f. 1896; Chair. JØRGEN VORSHOLT; Dir-Gen. JØRN NEERGAARD LARSEN; 13 mem. orgs.

Dansk Landbrug (Danish Farmers): Axelborg, Vesterbrogade 4A 4., 1620 Copenhagen V; tel. 33-39-46-00; fax 33-39-46-06; e-mail dansklandbrug@dansklandbrug.dk; internet www.dansklandbrug .dk; f. 2003 by merger of Danske Landboforeninger (f. 1893) and

Dansk Familielandbrug (f. 1906); Chair. PETER GENAELHE; Sec.-Gen. CARL ANGE DEHL; 60,000 mems.

Dansk Pelsdyravlerforening (DPF) (Danish Fur Breeders' Association): Langagervej 60, POB 1479, 2600 Glostrup; tel. 43-26-10-00; fax 43-26-11-26; e-mail cfc@cfc.dk; internet www.cfc.dk; co-operative of 2,400 mems.

Håndværksrådet (Danish Federation of Small- and Medium-sized Enterprises): Islands Brygge 26, 2300 Copenhagen S; tel. 33-93-20-00; fax 33-32-01-74; e-mail hvr@hvr.dk; internet www.hvr.dk; f. 1879; Chair. POUL ULSØE; Man. LARS JØRGEN NIELSEN; 110 asscns with 25,000 mems.

Industriens Arbejdsgivere i København (The Copenhagen Employers' Federation): 1787 Copenhagen V; tel. 33-77-33-77; fax 33-77-33-00; e-mail di@di.dk; internet www.di.dk; Chair. JØRGEN E. TANDRUP; Sec. H. ENGELHARDT; 475 mems.

Provinsindustriens Arbejdsgiverforening (Federation of Employers in the Provincial Industry): 1787 Copenhagen V; tel. 33-77-33-77; fax 33-77-33-00; f. 1895; Chair. SVEND-AAGE NIELSEN; Sec. GLENN SØGÅRD.

Sammenslutningen af Landbrugets Arbejdsgiverforeninger (SALA) (Danish Confederation of Employers' Associations in Agriculture): Vester Farimagsgade 1, 1606 Copenhagen V; tel. 33-13-46-55; fax 33-11-89-53.

Skibsværftsforeningen (Association of Danish Shipbuilders): Store Kongensgade 128, 1264 Copenhagen K; tel. 33-13-24-16; fax 33-11-10-96; e-mail association@shipbuilders.dk; internet www .shipbuilders.dk.

UTILITIES

Danish Energy Authority: Amaliegade 44, 1256 Copenhagen K; tel. 33-92-67-00; fax 33-11-47-43; e-mail ens@ens.dk; internet www .ens.dk; f. 1976; govt agency under Ministry of Economic Affairs, Business and Trade; Dir IB LARSEN.

Electricity

Elektricitetsrådet (Electricity Council): Gothersgade 160, 1123 Copenhagen K; tel. 33-73-20-00; fax 33-73-20-99; e-mail er@elraadet .dk; internet www.elraadet.dk; f. 1907; responsible for the general planning, operation and safety of the electricity-supply industry in Denmark; Pres. TAGE DRAEBYE; Man. Dir HR. JARBY.

Elkraft Power Co Ltd: Lautruphøj 5, 2750 Ballerup; tel. 44-66-00-22; fax 44-65-61-04; e-mail elkraft@elkraft.dk; f. 1978; co-ordinates supply of electricity and co-generated heat to eastern Denmark; Man. Dir BENT AGERHOLM.

Københavns Belyningsvaesen (The Copenhagen Energy Department): Vognmagergade 8, 1149 Copenhagen K; tel. 33-12-72-90; fax 33-12-72-91; one of the largest distributors of electricity in Denmark; also supplier of gas, district-heating and public-lighting systems.

NESA A/S: Strandvejen 102, 2900 Hellerup; tel. 72-10-10-10; fax 72-10-10-11; e-mail nesa@nesa.dk; internet www.nesa.dk; f. 1902; largest distributor of electricity in Denmark; Man. Dir POUL LIND.

SK Power Company, Denmark: Strandvejen 102, 2900 Hellerup; tel. 39-47-39-47; fax 39-47-35-33; e-mail skpower@skpower.dk; internet www.skpower.dk; f. 1992; power production; owns and operates Asnæs, Avedøre, Kyndby, Masnedø and Stigsnæs power stations and a number of local stations.

Gas

Dansk Gasteknisk Forening (Danish Technical Gas Association): Rønnehaven 12, 5320 Agedrup; f. 1911; promotes the use of gas; 680 mems.

DONG (Dansk Olie og Naturgas A/S): Agern Allé 24–26, 2970 Hørsholm; tel. 45-17-10-22; fax 45-17-10-44; e-mail dong@dong.dk; internet www.dong.dk; f. 1972; petroleum and natural gas exploration, production and distribution; acts as consultant in other countries; agreed, in June 2001, to establish consortium with POGC of Poland to build a new pipeline, BalticPipe, to transport natural gas from the North Sea to Poland; Chair. SVEN RISKÆR.

CO-OPERATIVE

Fællesforeningen for Danmarks Brugsforeninger (Co-operative of Denmark): Roskildevej 65, 2620 Albertslund; f. 1896; Chair. EBBE LUNDGAARD; 1,113,506 mems.

TRADE UNIONS

Landsorganisationen i Danmark (LO) (Danish Confederation of Trade Unions): Islands Brugge 32D, 2300 Copenhagen S; tel. 35-24-60-00; fax 35-24-63-00; e-mail lo@lo.dk; internet www.lo.dk; Pres. HANS JENSEN; Vice-Pres. TINE A. BRØNDUM; 1,449,348 mems (2001); 1,031 brs.

Dansk Beklædnings- og Textilarbejderforbund (Textile and Garment Workers): Copenhagen; tel. 33-11-67-65; fax 33-32-99-94; Pres. ANNE M. PEDERSEN; 18,450 mems.

Dansk El-Forbund (Electricians' Union): Vodroffsvej 26, 1900 Frederiksberg C; tel. 33-29-70-00; fax 33-29-70-70; e-mail def@def .dk; internet www.def.dk; Pres. ERIK ANDERSSON; 30,269 mems (2000).

Dansk Funktionærforbund—Serviceforbundet (Danish Federation of Salaried Employees): Upsalagade 20, 2100 Copenhagen Ø; tel. 70-15-04-00; fax 70-15-04-05; e-mail dff-s@dff-s.dk; internet www.dff-s.dk; Pres. KARSTEN HANSEN; 22,001 mems (2002).

Dansk Metalarbejderforbund (Metalworkers): Nyropsgade 38, 1780 Copenhagen V; tel. 33-63-20-00; fax 33-63-21-50; e-mail metal@danskmetal.dk; internet www.danskmetal.dk; f. 1888; Pres. MAX BAHRING; 138,674 mems (2000).

Forbundet af Offentligt Ansatte (Public Employees): Staunings Pl. 1–3, 1790 Copenhagen V; tel. 33-43-46-00; fax 33-13-40-42; e-mail mailto:foa@foa.dk; internet www.foa.dk; Pres. DENNIS KRISTENSEN; 198,695 mems (2000).

Forbundet Trae-Industri-Byg i Danmark (Timber Industry and Construction Workers): Mimersgade 41, 2200 Copenhagen N; tel. 35-31-95-99; fax 35-31-94-52; Pres. ARNE JOHANSEN; 71,100 mems (2002).

Grafisk Forbund (Printing Workers): Copenhagen; tel. 31-81-44-89; fax 31-81-24-25; f. 1993 by merger; Pres. TOM DURBING; 24,025 mems.

Handels- og Kontorfunktionærernes Forbund i Danmark (Commercial and Clerical Employees): H. C. Andersens Blvd 50, POB 268, 1780 Copenhagen V; tel. 33-30-43-43; fax 33-30-40-99; e-mail hk@hk.dk; internet www.hk.dk; f. 1900; Pres. JOHN DAHL; 377,228 mems (2002).

Kvindeligt Arbejderforbund i Danmark (Female Workers): Applebys Pl. 5, 1411 Copenhagen K; tel. 32-83-83-83; fax 32-83-86-67; e-mail kad@kad.dk; internet www.kad.dk; f. 1901; Pres. LILLIAN KNUDSEN; 84,637 mems (2000).

Malerforbundet i Danmark (Painters): Lersø Parkallé 109, 2100 Copenhagen Ø; tel. 39-16-79-00; fax 39-19-79-10; e-mail maler@maler.dk; internet www.maler.dk; f. 1890; Pres. JØRN ERIK NIELSEN; 14,068 mems (2002).

Nærings- og Nydelsesmiddelarbejder Forbundet (Food, Sugar Confectionery, Chocolate, Dairy Produce and Tobacco Workers): C. F. Richsvej 103, POB 1479, 2000 Frederiksberg; tel. 38-18-72-72; fax 38-18-72-00; internet www.nnf.dk; Pres. HENRY HOLT JOCHUMSEN; 40,392 mems (2000).

Pædagogisk Medhjælper Forbund (Nursery and Child-care Assistants): Store Kongensgade 79, 1017 Copenhagen K; tel. 33-11-03-43; fax 33-11-31-36; f. 1974; Pres. JAKOB BANG; 29,193 mems (2000).

Restaurations Branchens Forbund (Restaurant Workers): Thoravej 29–33, 2400 Copenhagen NV; tel. 38-33-89-00; fax 38-33-67-91; e-mail faglig@rbf.dk; internet www.rbf.dk; Chair. PREBEN RASMUSSEN; 23,710 mems (2000).

Socialpædagogernes Landsforbund (National Federation of Social Educators in Denmark): Brolæggerstræde 9, 1211 Copenhagen K; tel. 33-96-28-00; fax 33-96-29-96; e-mail sl@sl-dk.dk; Pres. KIRSTEN NISSEN; 27,073 mems (2000).

Specialarbejderforbundet i Danmark (General Workers' Union in Denmark): Kampmannsgade 4, POB 392, 1790 Copenhagen V; tel. 33-14-21-40; fax 33-97-24-60; e-mail sid@sid.dk; internet www.sid.dk; Pres. POUL ERIK SKOV CHRISTENSEN; Int. Sec. SUNE BOEGH; 320,000 mems (2002).

Teknisk Landsforbund (Professional Technicians): Nørre Voldgade 12, 1358 Copenhagen K; tel. 33-43-65-00; fax 33-43-66-77; internet www.tl@tl.dk; f. 1919; Pres. OLE SKALS PEDERSEN; 32,850 mems (2001).

Telekommunikations Forbundet (Telecommunications): Rolfsvej 37B, 2000 Frederiksberg; tel. 38-15-55-00; fax 38-15-55-10; e-mail tkf@tkf.dk; internet www.tkf.dk; Pres. BO STENØR LARSEN; 13,331 mems (2002).

Akademikernes Centralorganisation (Danish Confederation of Professional Associations): Nørre Voldgade 29, POB 2192, 1017 Copenhagen K; tel. 33-69-40-40; fax 33-93-85-40; e-mail ac@ac.dk; internet www.ac.dk; 238,871 mems (2001).

Den Almindelige Danske Lægeforening (Danish Medical Association): Trondhjemsgade 9, 2100 Copenhagen Ø; tel. 35-44-85-00; fax 35-44-85-05; e-mail dadl@dadl.dk; internet www.dadl .dk; 20,469 mems (2001).

Civiløkonomerne (Association of Danish Business Economists): Søtorvet 5, POB 2043, 1012 Copenhagen K; tel. 33-14-14-46; fax 33-14-11-49; e-mail info@civiloekonomerne.org; internet www .civiloekonomerne.org; 16,500 mems (2001).

Danmark Jurist- og Økonomforbund (Association of Danish Lawyers and Economists): Gothersgade 133, POB 2126, 1015 Copenhagen K; tel. 33-95-97-00; fax 33-95-99-99; e-mail djoef@ djoef.dk; internet www.djoef.dk; 39,446 mems (2001).

Dansk Magisterforening (Danish Association of Masters and PhDs): Nimbusparken, Peter Bangs Vej 32, 2000 Frederiksberg; tel. 38-15-66-00; fax 38-15-66-66; e-mail dm@magister.dk; internet www.magister.dk; 33,000 mems (2001).

Erhvervssprogligt Forbund (Danish Association of Business Language Graduates): Skindergade 45–47, POB 2246, 1019 Copenhagen K; tel. 33-91-98-00; fax 33-91-68-18; e-mail esf@esf .dk; internet www.esf.dk.

Gymnasieskolernes Lærerforening (Danish National Union of Upper Secondary School Teachers): Vesterbrogade 16, 1620 Copenhagen V; tel. 33-29-09-00; fax 33-29-09-01; e-mail gl@gl.org; internet www.gl.org; 10,935 mems (2001).

Ingeniørforeningen i Danmark (Society of Danish Engineers): Ingeniørhuset, Kalvebod Brygge 31–33, 1780 Copenhagen V; tel. 33-18-48-48; fax 33-18-48-99; e-mail ida@ida.dk; internet www.ida .dk; 60,000 mems (2003).

Funktionærernes og Tjenestemændenes Fællesråd (Civil Servants' and Salaried Employees' Confederation): Niels Hemmingsens Gade 12, POB 1169, 1010 Copenhagen K; tel. 33-36-88-00; fax 33-36-88-80; f. 1952; Chair. ANKER CHRISTOFFERSEN; 350,255 mems (2000).

Transport

In June 1998 an 18-km combined tunnel-and-bridge road and rail link across the Great Belt, linking the islands of Zealand and Funen, was completed, at a cost of US $6,500m.; the project incorporated the world's second longest suspension bridge. A 15.9-km road and rail link across the Øresund strait, between Copenhagen and Malmö, was completed in July 2000 at a total cost of about 23,400m. kroner. In October 1992 a number of Danish railway companies, in conjunction with the German and Swedish state railways, announced a plan to develop a high-speed rail system linking Stockholm and Oslo with Copenhagen, and Copenhagen with Berlin, Hamburg and Köln. The plan, which was estimated to cost 40,000m.–50,000m. kroner, would include the bridge over the Øresund strait and would require new track between Copenhagen and Hamburg and the construction of a fixed link across the Fehmern Belt. In 1996 contracts were signed for the construction of a 22-km underground light railway system in Copenhagen, of which the first stage was expected to open in October 2002.

RAILWAYS

Banestyrelsen (Danish National Railway Agency): Pakhusvej 10, 2100 Copenhagen Ø; tel. 82-34-00-00; fax 82-34-20-38; e-mail bane@ bane.dk; internet www.bane.dk; f. 1997 to assume, from the DSB (see below), responsibility for the maintenance and development of the national rail network; controls 2,349 km of line, of which 602 km are electrified; also manages signalling and train control; CEO JENS ANDERSEN.

DSB (Danish State Railways): Sølvgade 40, 1349 Copenhagen K; tel. 33-14-04-00; fax 33-51-41-20; e-mail dsb@dsb.dk; internet www.dsb .dk; became an independent public corporation in Jan. 1999; operates passenger services; CEO KELD SENGELØV.

A total of 526 km, mostly branch lines, is run by 15 private companies.

ROADS

At 31 December 2000 Denmark had an estimated 71,663 km of paved roads, including 900 km of motorways, 718 km of national roads and 9,986 km of secondary roads.

SHIPPING

The Port of Copenhagen is the largest port in Denmark and the only one to incorporate a Free Port Zone. The other major ports are Århus, Fredericia, Ålborg and Esbjerg, all situated in Jutland. There are oil terminals, with adjacent refineries, at Kalundborg, Stigsnæs and Fredericia. Ferry services are provided by Scandlines (see below) and by various private companies.

Farvandsvæsenet (Royal Danish Administration of Navigation and Hydrography): Overgaden oven Vandet 62B, POB 1919, 1023 Copenhagen K; tel. 32-68-95-00; fax 31-57-43-41; e-mail frv@fomfrv .dk; internet www.fomfrv.dk.

Port Authorities

Århus: Port Authority of Århus, Mindet 2, POB 130, 8100 Århus; tel. 86-13-32-66; fax 86-12-76-62; e-mail port@aarhus.dk; Port Dir BJARNE MATHIESEN.

Associated Danish Ports A/S (ADP): Vesthavnsvej 33, 7000 Fredericia; tel. 79-21-50-00; fax 79-21-50-05; e-mail post@adp-as.dk; internet www.adp-as.dk; has authority for ports of Fredericia and Nyborg; Man. Dir JENS PETER PETERS.

Copenhagen: Copenhagen Malmö Port AB, Nordre Told bod 7, POB 9, 1001 Copenhagen K; tel. 35-46-11-11; fax 35-46-11-64; e-mail cmport@cmport.com; internet www.cmport.com; by merger of ports of Copenhagen and Malmö; Man. Dir LARS KARLSSON; Port Capt. S. ANDERSEN.

Esbjerg: Port of Esbjerg, Hulvejen 1, POB 2, 6701 Esbjerg; tel. 75-12-41-44; fax 75-13-40-50; e-mail adm@portesbjerg.dk; internet www.portesbjerg.dk; Habour Dir PER WISTOFT; Head of Maritime Dept KARL-JOHAN MADSEN.

Frederikshavn: Frederikshavn Havn, Oliepieren 7, POB 129, 9900 Frederikshavn; tel. 96-20-47-00; fax 96-20-47-11; e-mail info@frederikshavnhavn.dk; internet www.frederikshavnhavn.dk; Man.Dir PREBEN REINHOLT; Harbour Captain JESPER G. THOMSEN.

Kalundborg: Kalundborg Port Authority, Vestre Haunepl. 7, 4400 Kalundborg; tel. 59-51-01-88; fax 59-51-00-89; e-mail info@portofkalundborg.dk; internet www.portofkalundborg.dk.

Sønderborg: Sønderborg Havn, Norrebro 1, 6400 Sønderborg; tel. 74-42-27-65; fax 74-43-30-19; internet www.sonderborg.dk; Harbour Master LASS ANDERSEN.

Principal Shipping Companies

Corral Line A/S: Havnevej 18, 6320 Egernsund; e-mail info@corralline.com; tel. 74-44-14-35; fax 74-44-14-75; formerly Sønderborg Rederiaktieselskab; 8 livestock carriers of 19,302 grt; shipowners, managers, chartering agents; world-wide; Man. Dir B. CLAUSEN.

Rederiet Otto Danielsen: Kongevejen 272A, 2830 Virum; tel. 45-83-25-55; fax 45-83-17-07; e-mail od@ottodanielsen.com; f. 1944; 7 general cargo vessels, totalling 20,793 grt, under foreign flags; general tramp trade, chartering, ship sales; Fleet Man. JØRN STAUREBY.

Dannebrog Rederi A/S: Rungsted Strandvej 113, 2960 Rungsted Kyst; tel. 45-17-77-77; fax 45-17-77-70; e-mail dbrog@dannebrog.com; f. 1883; 3 ro-ro vessels, product chemical tanker services; liner service USA–Europe, US Gulf–Caribbean, Mediterranean–Caribbean; CEO JOHAN WEDELL-WEDELLSBORG.

DFDS A/S: Sankt Annæ Pl. 30, 1295 Copenhagen K; tel. 33-42-33-42; fax 33-42-33-41; e-mail dfds@dfds.dk; internet www.dfds.dk; f. 1866; 7 car/passenger ships of 166,233 grt and 21 ro-ro vessels of 390,812 grt (incl. Swedish and German subsidiaries); passenger and car ferry services between Denmark, Sweden, the UK, the Netherlands, Germany and Norway, liner trade between Denmark, Sweden, Norway, the UK, the Netherlands, eastern Europe and Belgium; J. Lauritzen Holding owns majority share; Man. Dir OLE FRIE.

The East Asiatic Co Ltd A/S: Asia House, Indiakaj 16, 2100 Copenhagen Ø; tel. 35-25-43-00; fax 35-25-43-13; e-mail eac@eac.dk; f. 1897; trading, industry, food processing, plantations, shipping; totally owned and managed tonnage: 4 bulk/log carriers of 94,400 grt and 2 tankers of 33,700 grt under foreign flags; world-wide services; Chair. JAN ERLUND; Man. Dir MICHAEL FIORINI.

Elite Shipping A/S: H.C. Andersens Blvd 12, 3rd Floor, 1553 Copenhagen V; tel. 33-15-32-33; fax 33-15-32-06; internet www.elite-shipping.dk; 29 dry cargo vessels of 80,200 grt; tramp, world-wide; Man. Dirs RINO LANGE, TORBEN PALLE HANSEN.

H. Folmer & Co: Fredericiagade 57, 1310 Copenhagen K; tel. 33-13-25-10; fax 33-13-54-64; f. 1955; 14 general cargo vessels of 14,100 grt; world-wide tramping; Man. Owners J. J. FOLMER, UFFE MARTIN JENSEN.

KIL Shipping A/S: 8 Smakkedalen, 2820 Gentofte; tel. 39-77-03-00; fax 39-76-03-99; e-mail kil@kil.dk; f. 1998; 13 container vessels totalling 121,800 dwt, 4 under the Danish Flag and 9 under a foreign flag, 16 chemical carriers totalling 130,400 dwt under foreign flags, and 6 gas carriers totalling 18,056 dwt under foreign flags; Man. Dir BJARNE TUILDE.

J. Lauritzen A/S: Skt Annæ Pl. 28, POB 2147, 1291 Copenhagen K; tel. 33-11-12-22; fax 33-11-85-13; e-mail info@j-lauritzen.com; internet www.j-lauritzen.com; f. 1884; operates reefer ships, LPG/C carriers and bulk ships; Pres. TORBEN JANHOLT.

Mercandia Rederierne: Prags Blvd 94, 2300 Copenhagen S; tel. 32-83-01-55; fax 32-83-01-50; e-mail mercandia@vip.cybercity.dk; internet www.mercandia.dk; f. 1964; 24 ro-ro vessels and car ferries

totalling 238,200 grt; tramp and liner services; Man. Owner PER HENRIKSEN.

A. P. Møller: Esplanaden 50, 1098 Copenhagen K; tel. 33-63-33-63; fax 33-14-15-15; internet www.maersk.com; f. 1904; fleet of 38 container vessels, 13 products tankers, 5 crude oil tankers, 13 gas carriers, 26 offshore vessels and 7 drilling rigs, totalling 3,081,900 grt under the Danish flag; further tonnage owned by subsidiary cos in Singapore and the UK; world-wide liner and feeder services under the name of **Maersk Line** , and world-wide tanker, bulk, offshore and rig services; Man. Owner JESS SØDERBERG.

Mortensen & Lange A/S: Kongevejen 2, 2480 Fredensborg; tel. 48-40-85-85; fax 42-28-00-57; f. 1961; general cargo vessels of 13,800 grt and 6 reefer vessels of 8,000 grt; world-wide tramping; Man. Dir (vacant).

Dampskibsselskabet Norden A/S: Amaliegade 49, 1256 Copenhagen K; tel. 33-15-04-51; fax 33-15-61-99; e-mail mail@ds-norden.com; internet www.ds-norden.com; f. 1871; operates about 60 tankers and bulk carriers; world-wide tramping; Man. Dir STEEN R. KRABBE.

Scandlines AG: Dampfaergevej 10, 2100 Copenhagen Ø; tel. 33-15-15-15; fax 35-29-02-01; e-mail scandlines@scandlines.dk; internet www.scandlines.dk; f. 1998 by merger of Scandlines A/S and Deutsche Fährgesellschaft Ostsee GmbH (Germany); maintains offices in Germany and Sweden; owned by Danish Govt and Deutsche Bahn; operates 20 ferry routes around Denmark and throughout the Baltic.

Corral Line A/S: Havnevej 18, 6320 Egernsund; e-mail info@corralline.com; tel. 74-44-14-35; fax 74-44-14-75; formerly Sønderborg Rederiaktieselskab; 8 livestock carriers of 19,302 grt; shipowners, managers, chartering agents; world-wide; Man. Dir B. CLAUSEN.

A/S Em. Z. Svitzer: Brøndby; tel. 43-43-43-71; fax 43-43-60-22; f. 1833; wholly-owned subsidiary of A. P. Møller; 22 tugs and salvage vessels and a barge fleet; salvage, towage and barge services; Gen. Man. KELD BALLE MORTENSEN.

Terkol-Rederierne: Jægergårdsvej 107, 8000 Århus C; tel. 86-13-36-88; fax 86-18-15-10; 2 container vessels of 21,100 grt and 17 chemical tankers of 42,400 grt; world-wide tanker services; Gen. Man. N. B. TERKILDSEN.

A/S Dampskibsselskabet Torm: Marina Park, Sundkrogsgade 10, 2100 Copenhagen Ø; tel. 39-17-92-00; fax 39-17-93-93; e-mail mail@torm.dk; internet www.torm.dk; f. 1889; 16 product carriers of 617,772 grt, 7 bulk carriers of 199,507 grt, 2 multipurpose vessels of 27,376 grt and 2 AHTs (1999); operator of a time-chartered fleet; Man. Dir KLAUS KJÆRULFF.

Shipping Association

Danmarks Rederiforening (Danish Shipowners' Asscn): Amaliegade 33, 1256 Copenhagen K; tel. 33-11-40-88; fax 33-11-62-10; e-mail info@danishshipping.com; internet www.danishshipping.com; f. 1884; 21 mems, representing 6.7m. grt (Jan. 2002); Chair. of the Bd KNUD PONTOPPIDAN; Man. Dir PETER BJERREGAARD.

CIVIL AVIATION

The main international airport is Copenhagen Airport, situated about 10 km from the centre of the capital. The following domestic airports have scheduled flights to European and Scandinavian destinations: Ålborg, Århus and Billund in Jutland. Other domestic airports include Roskilde (30 km south-west of Copenhagen); Esbjerg, Karup, Skrydstrup, Stauning, Sønderborg and Thisted in Jutland; Odense in Funen; and Bornholm Airport on the island of Bornholm.

Statens Luftfartsvæsen (Civil Aviation Administration): Luftfartshuset, POB 744, 2450 Copenhagen SV; tel. 36-18-60-00; fax 36-18-60-01; e-mail dcaa@slv.dk; internet www.slv.dk; Dir-Gen. OLE ASMUSSEN.

Det Danske Luftfartselskab A/S (DDL) (Danish Airlines): Industriens Hus, H. C. Andersens Blvd 18, 1553 Copenhagen V; tel. 33-14-13-33; fax 33-14-28-28; f. 1918; 50% govt-owned; Danish parent company of the designated national carrier, Scandinavian Airlines System—SAS (see below), SAS Commuter; Chair. HUGO SCHRØDER; Man. Dir GUNNAR TIETZ.

Scandinavian Airlines System (SAS): Head Office: Hedegårdsvej 88, POB 150, 2770 Kastrup; tel. 32-32-00-00; internet www.sas.dk; f. 1946; the national carrier of Denmark, Norway and Sweden. It is a consortium owned two-sevenths by SAS Danmark A/S, two-sevenths by SAS Norge ASA and three-sevenths by SAS Sverige AB. Each parent organization is a limited company owned 50% by its respective government and 50% by private shareholders. The SAS group includes the consortium and the subsidiaries in which the consortium has a majority or otherwise controlling interest; the Board consists of two members from each of the parent companies and the chairmanship rotates among the three national chairmen on an annual basis. SAS absorbed Linjeflyg AB (domestic passenger, newspaper and postal services in Sweden) in January 1993; strategic alliance with Lufthansa (Germany) formed in 1995; Chair. Bo BERGGREN; Pres. and CEO JAN STENBERG.

National Airlines

Cimber Air Denmark: Sønderborg Airport, Lufthavnsvej 2, 6400 Sønderborg; tel. 74-42-22-77; fax 74-42-65-11; e-mail marketing@cimber.dk; internet www.cimber.dk; f. 1950; operates domestic service in co-operation with Lufthansa and SAS; operates charter flights and total route systems for other cos throughout Europe; markets electronic data systems for airlines and industry; Pres., CEO JORGEN NIELSEN.

Maersk Air: Copenhagen Airport South, 2791 Dragør; tel. 32-31-44-44; fax 32-31-44-90; e-mail mail@maersk-air.dk; internet www.maersk-air.com; f. 1969; provides charter flights for Scandinavian tour operators, operates domestic services and international flights to Belgium, Germany, Sweden, the Netherlands, Norway, Italy, Greece and the UK; owned by Møller Group (see under Shipping); subsidiary: Maersk Air Cargo; Chair. BJARNE HANSEN; Pres. OLE DIETZ.

Premiair: Copenhagen Airport South, Hangar 276, 2791 Dragør; tel. 32-47-72-00; fax 32-45-12-20; internet www.premiair.com; f.

1994 by merger of Conair A/S (Denmark) and Scanair (Sweden); controlling stake acquired by Airtours (United Kingdom) in 1996; flights to major destinations in Europe; Pres. TOM CLAUSEN.

Star Air: Copenhagen Airport South, 2791 Dragør; tel. 32-31-43-43; fax 32-31-43-90; f. 1987; operates cargo services in Europe; Pres. OLE DIETZ.

Sun Air: Lufthansvej 33, 7190 Billund; tel. 76-50-01-00; fax 75-33-86-18; internet www.sunair.dk; f. 1978; also maintains offices at Århus and Thisted Airports; operates charter flights, sells and leases aircraft and operates aircraft maintenance services, operates a franchise of scheduled flights throughout northern Europe in co-operation with British Airways since 1996; Dir NIELS SUNDBERG.

Tourism

In 2000 there were 9.6m. overnight stays in all types of accommodation made by foreign visitors; in that year receipts from tourism totalled 32,526m. kroner.

Danmarks Turistråd (The Danish Tourist Board): Vesterbrogade 6D, 1620 Copenhagen V; tel. 33-11-14-15; fax 33-93-14-16; e-mail dt@dt.dk; internet www.visitdenmark.com; f. 1967; Dir LARS SANDAHL SØRENSEN.

DANISH EXTERNAL TERRITORIES

THE FAROE ISLANDS

Introductory Survey

Location, Climate, Language, Religion, Flag, Capital

The Faroe Islands are a group of 18 islands (of which 17 are inhabited) in the Atlantic Ocean, between Scotland and Iceland. The main island is Streymoy, where more than one-third of the population resides. The climate is mild in winter and cool in summer, with a mean temperature of 7°C (45°F). Most of the inhabitants profess Christianity: the majority of Faroese belong to the Evangelical Lutheran Church of Denmark. The principal language is Faroese, but Danish is a compulsory subject in all schools. The flag (proportions 16 by 22) displays a red cross, bordered with blue, on a white background, the upright of the cross being to the left of centre. The capital is Tórshavn, which is situated on Streymoy.

History and Government

The Faroe Islands have been under Danish administration since Queen Margrethe I of Denmark inherited Norway in 1380. The islands were occupied by the United Kingdom while Denmark was under German occupation during the Second World War, but they were restored to Danish control immediately after the war. The Home Rule Act of 1948 gave the Faroese control over all their internal affairs. The Faroe Islands did not join the European Community (EC—now European Union—EU, see p. 199) with Denmark in 1973. There is a local parliament (the Løgting), but the Danish legislature, the Folketing, to which the Faroese send two members, is responsible for defence and foreign policy, constitutional matters, and the judicial and monetary systems. The Faroes control fishing resources within their fisheries zone, and in September 1992 a long-standing dispute between Denmark and the Faroes was settled when the Danish Government agreed to give the Faroese authorities legislative and administrative power over mineral resources, including those beneath the bed of the sea in the area adjacent to the islands. This agreement removed one of the major obstacles to exploration for hydrocarbons off the Faroe Islands, where geologists consider that prospects for discovering reserves of petroleum and natural gas are favourable. In 1994 the Faroe Islands accordingly awarded a US company a licence to begin exploratory surveys, despite the existence of a long-standing dispute between Denmark and the United Kingdom over the demarcation of the continental shelf west of the Shetland Islands and south-east of the Faroe Islands, which had threatened to delay prospecting. This dispute was resolved in mid-1999, however, when representatives of the Faroese Government (the Landsstýri) signed an agreement with the Danish and British Governments regarding the location of the boundaries of the area concerned. The area, known as the 'golden corner' (formerly the White Zone), was believed to be potentially rich in petroleum reserves. Following the issue by the Faroese Government of a number of licences in mid-August 2000, exploratory drilling commenced in the 'golden corner' in mid-2001 (see Economy).

The centre-left coalition Government of the Social Democratic Party (SDP), Republicans and the People's Party, formed in 1975, collapsed in 1980 over a plan, opposed by the conservative People's Party, to extend through the winter months a government-owned ferry service linking the islands with Denmark, Norway and Scotland. At a general election, held in November, conservative political groups slightly increased their share of the popular vote. Although there was no material change in the balance of party representation in the Løgting, the Union Party formed a centre-right coalition with the People's Party and the Home Rule Party in January 1981. A general election was held in November 1984, and in December a four-party, centre-left coalition Government was formed under the premiership of Atli Dam, comprising his SDP, the Home Rule Party, the Republican Party and the Christian People's Party combined with the Progressive and Fishing Industry Party (CPP-PFIP).

Elections in 1988 demonstrated a shift to the right in the Faroes, to the benefit of the People's Party. Its one member in the Danish Folketing increased his support in the national elections of September 1987 and May 1988. At a Faroese general election in November 1988 the incumbent Government lost its majority, and the People's Party became the largest party in the Løgting. In January 1989, after 10 weeks of negotiations, a centre-right coalition, comprising the People's Party, the Republican Party, the Home Rule Party and the CPP-PFIP, and led by Jógvan Sundstein (Chairman of the People's Party), was formed. The coalition was committed to economic austerity and support for the fishing industry. In June, however, the CPP-PFIP and the Home Rule Party withdrew their support for the Government. After three weeks a new coalition was formed. Sundstein remained Prime Minister (Løgmaður), and his People's Party was supported by the Republican Party and the Union Party. In October 1990, however, these two parties withdrew their support for the coalition Government. As a result, an early general election was held in November. The SDP obtained the largest share of the vote, winning 10 seats (an increase of three), while the People's Party, which led the outgoing coalition, won seven seats (a loss of one seat).

In January 1991 a coalition between the SDP and the People's Party was formed, under the leadership of Atli Dam. He was replaced in January 1993 by Marita Petersen (also of the SDP). In April the People's Party withdrew from the coalition, and was replaced by the Republican Party and the Home Rule Party. At a general election, held in July 1994, the Union Party became the largest party in the Løgting, winning eight seats (an increase of two), while the SDP's allocation of seats was reduced from 10 to five. In September a coalition of the Union Party, the SDP, the Home Rule Party and the newly formed Labour Front took office. Edmund Joensen (Chairman of the Union Party) replaced Petersen as Prime Minister. In 1996 the People's Party replaced the SDP in the governing coalition. Joensen remained Prime Minister, while Anfinn Kallsberg succeeded Jóannes Eidesgaard as Minister of Finance and Economics. A general election was held on 30 April 1998, at which both the Republican Party and the People's Party each increased their allocation of seats to eight, while the number of seats secured by the SDP rose from five to seven; the parliamentary representation of the Union Party was reduced from eight seats to six. In mid-May a coalition Government was formed by members of the People's Party, the Republican Party and the Home Rule Party, under the premiership of Anfinn Kallsberg of the People's Party.

Tensions with the Danish Government in the early 1990s, the nationalistic persuasion of the new Government and the prospect of offshore petroleum discoveries revived Faroese ambitions for political and economic independence. (The Faroese had narrowly favoured independence from Denmark in a referendum in 1946, but the decision had been overturned by the Danish Folketing.) In October 1998 the Løgting adopted a resolution in support of the Government's intention (announced earlier that year) to seek status for the Faroe Islands as a 'sovereign nation' under the Danish monarchy, having a common monetary system with Denmark; it was envisaged by the Faroese Government that sovereignty for the islands would be most appropriately achieved through continued co-operation with Denmark within a new constitutional framework, based on a bilateral treaty between the two countries as equal, independent partners. A commission charged with the development of a proposal for a Faroese constitution was established by the Government in February 1999, and submitted its conclusions to the Løgting in June 2000. The Faroese envisaged retaining the Danish Queen Margrethe II as their Head of State and maintaining the link between their local currency and the Danish krone. The islands would seek to continue to co-operate with Denmark in social affairs, justice, health and air traffic control, and would also maintain present arrangements such as mutual rights of residence, employment and education. The Faroes would also seek to join NATO (see p. 271) and the UN.

Negotiations between the Danish and Faroese administrations concerning the future independence of the Faroe Islands began in March 2000, but swiftly stalled after the Danish Government confirmed that it would not oppose Faroese independence but would terminate annual subsidies (of about 1,000m. kroner) to the Faroes in four years time, compared with the 15 years envisaged by the Faroese. The Danish Prime Minister, Poul Nyrup Rasmussen, rejected an offer of mediation from the Icelandic premier, Davíð Oddsson. Discussions were resumed later in the year, but finally collapsed in late October, prompting Kallsberg to announce a plan to hold a referendum on independence in 2001. The Faroese had initially envisaged the successful negotiation of a treaty with the Danish Government prior to a referendum. The referendum, which in February was scheduled to be held on 26 May, was to include four issues: the full transfer of authority to the Faroese by 2012; the establishment of an economic fund to guarantee financial security during the transitional period; the gradual elimination of subsidies from Denmark; and the holding of a further referendum establishing the Faroe Islands as an independent state by 2012. The Danish Government reacted strongly to plans for a plebiscite, claiming that Denmark would regard it as a *de facto* referendum on sovereignty and that a vote in favour of the proposals for independence would result in the halting of Danish aid within four years. The reluctance of the Faroese population to lose Danish subsidies and disagreement within the Faroese coalition Government resulted in the cancellation of the referendum in early March 2001. Shortly afterwards agreement was reached within the Faroese Government on a plan for independence, which was subsequently submitted to the Danish authorities.

At the general election, held on 30 April 2002, the People's Party secured 20.8% of the votes cast and won seven seats in the Løgting; it subsequently formed a coalition Government with the Republican Party (which had secured 23.7% of the votes cast and eight seats), the Home Rule Party (4.4% and one seat) and the Centre Party (4.2% and one seat); the Union Party secured 26.0% of the votes cast, winning eight seats in the Løgting, and the Social Democratic Party secured 20.9% of the votes cast and seven seats.

The Minister of Fisheries, Jørgen Niclasen, resigned in January 2003 following revelations of financial improprieties regarding loans he had made to prawn trawlers using public funds; Anfinn Kallsberg assumed the portfolio.

Also in January 2003, the Faroese and Danish Governments began drafting legislation under which responsibility for several policy areas would be passed from Denmark to the Faroe Islands' Home Rule Government; these areas included matters of personal, estate and family law, and share, company and financial law. Independently of this process, further new legislation was being drafted that would govern relations between Denmark and the Faroe Islands, giving the latter greater access to and influence in policy areas directly affecting Faroese sovereignty, including defence, foreign policy and citizenship. Support for Faroese independence appeared to be increasing on the islands in early 2003.

In international affairs, the Faroe Islanders earned opprobrium for their traditional slaughter of pilot whales, an important source of food. After foreign journalists publicized the whaling in 1986, stricter regulations were imposed on whaling operations. In July 1992 the Faroese Government threatened to leave the International Whaling Commission (IWC, see p. 332), following the latter's criticism of whaling methods practised in the Faroe Islands. It was, however, claimed that the Faroese did not have the legal right to withdraw from the Commission independently of Denmark. In September the Faroe Islands, Greenland, Norway and Iceland agreed to establish the North Atlantic Marine Mammal Commission, in protest at what they viewed as the IWC's preoccupation with conservation.

Economic Affairs

In 1995 gross national product (GNP), estimated at 1990 prices, was US $829m., equivalent to $19,000 per head. Between 1973 and 1988, it was estimated, GNP increased, in real terms, at an average rate of 4.5% per year, with real GNP per head rising by 3.3% annually. Between 1989 and 1993, however, real GNP decreased dramatically, at an average rate of 9.4% per year. During 1994–95 real GNP increased by 4.2%. The population declined at an average annual rate of 1.6% in 1989–95, but increased by 1.1% per year in 1995–1999. Gross domestic product (GDP) increased, in real terms, by about 5% in 1997, 8% in 1998 and 3% in 1999.

Agriculture (principally sheep-farming) and fishing contributed 20.5% of GDP in 2000. Potatoes and other vegetables are the main crops. Only about 6% of the land surface is cultivated.

Fishing is the dominant industry. In 1999 fishing, aquaculture and fish-processing accounted for 25.1% of GDP; the sector employed 23% of the labour force in 1994. Fishing accounted for 93.1% of exports in 2000. Most fishing takes place within the 200-nautical-mile (370-km) fisheries zone imposed around the Faroes in 1977. In the 1980s fish farming began to be encouraged. The traditional hunting of pilot whales continues to provide an important source of meat for the Faroese.

Industry (including mining, manufacturing, construction and power) contributed 19.0% of GDP in 2000. The dominant sectors are fishing-related industries, such as fish-drying and -freezing, and ship maintenance and repairs.

Mining and quarrying contributed only 0.3% of GDP in 2000. 'Brown coal' (lignite) is mined on Suduroy. The potential for petroleum production around the islands is believed to be significant. Following the resolution of a boundary dispute with the United Kingdom in May 1999, in mid-2000 the Ministry of Petroleum issued seven exploration licences (of six to nine years' duration) to 12 oil companies, organized into five groups, in the 'golden corner' (formerly the White Zone), an area south-east of the Faroe Islands; exploratory drilling commenced in mid-2001. In November the US company Amerada Hess announced that it had discovered petroleum in considerable quantities (although it was calculated to take at least eight months to prove the commercial viability of the well). It was expected, however, that, owing to Faroese tax laws, the islands would not derive any substantial income from the reserves for 12 years. The Danish authorities also stated that they intended to renegotiate Denmark's subsidy agreement with the Faroe Islands should the latter start to make a profit from the petroleum reserves. In January 2002 the Faroes Oil and Gas Company (FOGC—Føroya Kolvetni) became the first Faroese company to be listed on the London Stock Exchange.

Manufacturing contributed 11.4% of GDP in 2000. The dominant sector is fish-processing, which accounted for 5.7% of GDP in 1999. Technical repairs and shipyards contributed 2.1% of GDP in 1999, while exports of vessels accounted for 6.9% of exports in 2000. A small textile industry exports traditional Faroese woollens.

The energy sector contributed 2.1% of GDP in 2000. About 48% of the islands' energy requirements are provided by a hydroelectric power plant. Imports of fuels and related products accounted for 12.1% of imports in 2000.

The services sector accounted for 60.6% of GDP in 2000.

In 2000 the Faroe Islands recorded a trade deficit of 404m. kroner, while there was a surplus of 317m. kroner on the current account of the balance of payments. Denmark was the Faroes' principal source of imports (29.5%) in 2001; other major suppliers were Norway (23.2%), Germany (8.0%) and Sweden (6.0%). Denmark was the principal market for exports (25.6%) in that year; other major purchasers were the United Kingdom (17.8%), Spain (11.8%) and France (including Monaco) (9.9%). In 1999 the European Union (EU, see p. 199) as a whole took 82.3% of exports and supplied 54.8% of imports. The principal imports in 2000 were products for industry (accounting for 22.9% of the total cost of imports), products for household consumption (22.3%) and vessels (16.5%). Principal exports in that year were chilled or frozen fish fillets (contributing 32.4% of total export revenue), chilled or frozen salmon and trout (17.5%), salted fish (14.3%) and vessels (6.9%).

Danish subsidies are an important source of income to the islands, and accounted for 27.9% of total government revenue in 2000. In that year, including the central government grant of 973m. kroner as revenue, the Faroese Government recorded a budget surplus of 605m. kroner; the surplus for 2001 was estimated at 710m. kroner. At the end of 1999 the net foreign debt was estimated at 447m. kroner. The annual rate of inflation was 4.3% in 2000 and 7.7% in 2001. In the 1980s there was an acute labour shortage in the Faroes, but by mid-1995 unemployment had increased to some 16% of the labour force. By August 2000, however, unemployment had declined to some 4% of the labour force.

The Faroe Islands did not join the European Community (now EU) with Denmark in 1973, but did secure favourable terms of trade with Community members and special concessions in Denmark and the United Kingdom. Agreements on free trade were concluded between the Faroe Islands and Iceland, Norway, Sweden, Finland and Austria in 1992–93. In international fisheries organizations, where Denmark is represented by the EU, the Kingdom maintains separate membership in respect of the Faroe Islands (and Greenland). The Faroe Islands is also a member of the Nordic Council (see p. 266).

During the 1980s the Faroes' principal source of income, the fishing industry, was expanded with the help of substantial investment and official subsidies, financed by external borrowing. However, depletion of stocks and the resulting decline in catches, together with a fall in export prices, led to a reduction in export earnings and a financial crisis in the early 1990s (GDP was estimated to have declined by some 20% in 1993). The Danish Government attempted to stabilize the economy by restructuring the banking sector and by extending significant loans (by the end of 1997 it was estimated that the Faroes owed some 5,500m. kroner to the Danish Government, equivalent to 140,000 kroner per head). The report of an independent commission of inquiry into Denmark's response to the crisis in the Faroes, which had been established by the islanders in 1995, was published in early 1998 and levelled accusations of serious mismanagement at Danish government officials, and at the Danish Den Danske Bank. In June 1998 an agreement was reached by the Faroese and Danish Governments regarding a reduction of Faroese debt to Denmark as a form of compensation. Denmark's annual subsidy (of 1,000m. kroner) provides nearly one-third of the Faroes' budget. However, a number of oil companies commenced exploratory offshore drilling in Faroese waters during 2001, and initial results proved promising (see above). The discovery of substantial and commercially-viable reserves of natural gas and petroleum would enable the Faroese economy to diversify, thereby reducing its overwhelming dependence on Danish subsidies as well as on the fisheries sector.

Education

The education system is similar to that of Denmark, except that Faroese is the language of instruction. Danish is, however, a compulsory subject in all schools. The Faroese Academy was upgraded to the University of the Faroe Islands in 1990.

In 2000 government expenditure on education represented 16.7% of total budgetary spending.

Public Holidays

Public holidays in the Faroe Islands are the same as those for Denmark. In addition, the Faroese also celebrate Flag Day on 25 April and St Ólavsøka on 28–29 July each year. Various regional holidays are also observed in May–July.

Statistical Survey

Sources (unless otherwise stated): Statistical Bureau of the Faroe Islands, POB 355, 110 Tórshavn; tel. 314636; fax 318696; e-mail farostat@olivant.fo; Statistics Faroe Islands, Traðagøta 39, POB 2068, 165 Argir; tel. 352028; fax 352038; e-mail hagstova@ hagstova.fo; internet www.hagstova.fo; Landsbanki Føroya, Müllers Hús-Gongin, POB 229, 110 Tórshavn; tel. 318305; fax 318537; e-mail landsbank@landsbank.fo; internet landsbank.fo; Faroese Government Office, Hovedvagtsgade 8, 2, 1103 Copenhagen K; tel. 33-14-08-66; fax 33-93-85-75 *Yearbook of Nordic Statistics.*

AREA AND POPULATION

Area: 1,398.9 sq km (540.1 sq miles).

Population: 45,412 at 31 December 1999; 46,196 at 31 December 2000; 46,996 (males 24,361; females 22,635) at 31 December 2001.

Density (31 December 2001): 33.6 per sq km.

Principal Towns (estimated population at 31 July 2000): Tórshavn (capital) 16,673; Klaksvík 4,762; Runavík 2,461. (Source: Thomas Brinkhoff, *City Population* (internet www.citypopulation.de); Tórshavn (capital), population 18,071 at 31 December 2001.

Births, Marriages and Deaths (2001): Registered live births 631 (birth rate 13.5 per 1,000); Registered marriages 274 (marriage rate 5.9 per 1,000); Deaths 361 (death rate 7.7 per 1,000).

Expectation of Life (years at birth, 1996–2000): Males 75.2; Females 81.4.

Economically Active Population (2001): Agriculture, etc. 1,000; Total labour force 24,000. Source: FAO.

HEALTH AND WELFARE

Key Indicators

Physicians (per 1,000 head, 1999): 1.8.

Hospital Beds (per 1,000 head, 1999): 6.6.

AGRICULTURE AND FISHING

Principal Crop (FAO estimate, 2001): Potatoes 1,500 metric tons. Source: FAO.

Livestock (FAO estimates, '000 head, year ending September 2001): Cattle 2; Sheep 68. Source: FAO.

Livestock Products (FAO estimates, metric tons, 2001): Beef and veal 77; Mutton and lamb 521; Sheepskins (fresh) 118. Source: FAO.

Fishing ('000 metric tons, live weight, 2000): Capture 365.8 (Atlantic cod 37.6, Haddock 23.2, Saithe (Pollock) 35.8 (FAO estimate), Blue whiting (Poutassou) 105.0 (FAO estimate), Capelin 24.5 (FAO estimate), Atlantic herring 56.5 (FAO estimate), Northern prawn 12.2); Aquaculture 29.3 (Atlantic salmon 28.3); Total catch 395.1. Figures exclude aquatic mammals, recorded by number rather than by weight. However, no whales or seals were caught in 2000. Source: FAO, *Yearbook of Fishery Statistics.*

INDUSTRY

Selected Products ('000 metric tons, unless otherwise indicated, 1996): Frozen or chilled fish 123; Salted and processed fish products 15; Aquamarine products 13; Oils, fats and meal of aquatic animals 124; Electric energy (million kWh) 182.

FINANCE

(Danish currency is in use)

Budget (million kroner, 2000): *Revenue:* Income taxes 1,309, Indirect taxes 1,116, Other domestic income 89, Danish state grant 973; Total 3,487. *Expenditure:* General public services 216, Defence and public safety 68, Education 482, Health 424, Social welfare 1,055, Housing and environment 89, Primary industry 87, Transport and communications 238, Interest payments 126; Total (incl. others) 2,882. *2001* (million kroner) Total revenue 4,165; Total expenditure 3,455.

Cost of Living (Consumer Price Index at 1 January; base: 1 January 1983 = 100): All items 176.4 in 1999; 183.9 in 2000; 198.0 in 2001.

Expenditure on the Gross Domestic Product (million kroner at current prices, 2000): Government final consumption expenditure 2,231; Private final consumption expenditure 4,560; Increase in stocks 370; Gross fixed capital formation 1,906; *Total domestic expenditure* 9,068; Exports of goods and services 4,332; *Less* Imports of goods and services 5,080; GDP *in purchasers' values* 8,320.

Gross Domestic Product by Economic Activity (million kroner at current prices, 2000): Agriculture, fishing, etc. 1,551; Mining and quarrying 21; Manufacturing 867; Electricity, gas and water 161; Construction 388; Trade, restaurants and hotels 835; Transport, storage and communications 601; Financing 434; Dwellings 756; Business services 216; Domestic services, etc. 97; Government services 1,651; *Sub-total* 7,580; *Less* imputed bank service charges 401; *GDP at factor cost* 7,179; Indirect taxes 1,352; *Less* Subsidies 211; *GDP in purchasers' values* 8,320.

Balance of Payments (million kroner, 2000): Exports of goods f.o.b. 3,789; Imports of goods c.i.f. –4,184; *Trade balance* –404; Exports of services 552; Imports of services –896; *Balance on goods and services* –748; Other income and current transfers (net) 1,165; Net errors and omissions –100; *Current balance* 317.

EXTERNAL TRADE

Principal Commodities (million kroner, 2000): *Imports c.i.f.:* Products for agriculture 298 (Animal fodder 277), Products for the construction industry 290, Products for other industries 669, Fuels and related products 508, Machinery and other capital goods 406, Vehicles 209, Products for household consumption 932, Vessels 690, Fish 132; Total (incl. others) 4,184. *Exports f.o.b.:* Chilled or frozen fish fillets 1,233, Chilled or frozen salmon and trout 667, Salted fish 545, Crustaceans and molluscs 236, Fish for reduction 240, Vessels 261; Total (incl. others) 3,804.

Principal Trading Partners (million kroner, 2001): *Imports c.i.f.:* Denmark 1,224, France (incl. Monaco) 121, Germany 330, Iceland 224, Italy 65, Japan 100, Netherlands 65, Norway 961, Russia 49, Sweden 247, United Kingdom 179, USA 109; Total (incl. others) 4,147. *Exports f.o.b.:* Canada 90, Denmark 1,097, France (incl. Monaco) 425, Germany 323, Greenland 58, Iceland 53, Italy 138, Japan 107, Norway 366, Spain 503, Sweden 45, United Kingdom 762, USA 121; Total (incl. others) 4,279.

TRANSPORT

Road Traffic (registered motor vehicles, 31 December 2001): Private motor cars 15,710 (incl. 95 taxis); Buses 176; Lorries and vans 3,522; Motorcycles 213.

Shipping: *Merchant Fleet* (31 December 2001): 150 vessels, Total displacement 195,465 grt (Source: Lloyd's Register-Fairplay, *World Fleet Statistics*). *International sea-borne freight traffic* (1996, '000 metric tons): Goods loaded 223, Goods unloaded 443.

COMMUNICATIONS MEDIA

Radio Receivers (1997): 26,000 in use (Source: UNESCO, *Statistical Yearbook*).

Television Receivers (1997): 15,000 in use (Source: UNESCO, *Statistical Yearbook*).

Book Production (2000): 170 titles.

Newspapers (2000): 6 titles (average circulation 8,520 copies per issue).

Telephones (main lines in use, 2000): 24,952 (Source: International Telecommunication Union).

Facsimile Machines (1993): 1,400 in use (Source: UN, *Statistical Yearbook*).

Mobile Cellular Telephones (subscribers, 2000): 16,971 (Source: International Telecommunication Union).

Internet Users ('000, 1999): 3 (Source: International Telecommunication Union).

EDUCATION

Institutions (2000/01): Basic schools 61 (Secondary schools 21); Upper secondary schools 3; Higher preparatory institutions 3.

Teachers (2000): 670 (full-time equivalent) in primary and secondary schools.

Students (2000/01, unless otherwise indicated): Pre-primary (1998/99) 59; Primary 5,570; Secondary 1,907; Upper secondary 600; Higher preparatory 181; Further education (1996/97) 2,166.

Directory

The Government

The legislative body is the Løgting (Lagting in Danish), which consists of 27 members, elected on a basis of proportional representation in seven constituencies, with up to five supplementary seats dependent upon the discrepancy between the distribution of seats among the parties and the numbers of people voting. All Faroese over the age of 18 years have the right to vote. Based on the strength of the parties in the Løgting, a Government, the Landsstýri, is formed. This is the administrative body in certain spheres, chiefly relating to Faroese economic affairs. The Løgmaður (Prime Minister) has to ratify all Løgting laws. Power is decentralized and there are about 50 local authorities. The Ríkisumboðsmaður, or High Commissioner, represents the Danish Government, and has the right to address the Løgting and to advise on joint affairs. All Danish legislation must be submitted to the Landsstýri before becoming law in the Faroe Islands.

The Danish Folketing (parliament), to which the Faroese send two members, is responsible for defence and foreign policy, constitutional matters and the judicial and monetary systems.

LANDSSTÝRI
(April 2003)

A coalition of the People's Party (PP), the Republican Party (RP), the Home Rule Party (HRP) and the Centre Party (CP).

Prime Minister (with responsibility for Constitutional Affairs, Foreign Affairs, Municipal Affairs and Administration, and Fisheries and Maritime Affairs): ANFINN KALLSBERG (PP).

Deputy Prime Minister and Minister of Self-governmental and Judicial Affairs and of Nordic Affairs: HØGNI HOYDAL (RP).

Minister of Finance: KARSTIN HANSEN (RP).

Minister of Trade and Industry: BJARNI DJURHOLM (PP).

Minister of Energy, Oil, the Extractive Industry and the Environment: EYÐUN ELTTØR (HRP).

Minister of Education and Culture: ANNLIS BJARKHAMAR (RP).

Minister of Health: BILL JUSTINUSSEN (CP).

Minister of Social Affairs: PÁLL Á REYNATÚGVU (RP).

Government Offices

Ríkisumboðsmaðurin (Danish High Commission): Amtmansbrekka 6, POB 12, 110 Tórshavn; tel. 351200; fax 310864; e-mail riomfr@fo.stm.dk; internet www.rigsombudsmanden.fo; High Commissioner BIRGIT KLEIS.

Løgtingsskrivstovan (Parliament Office): Erling Jalsgøtu 6, POB 208, 110 Tórshavn; tel. 310850; fax 310686; e-mail logting@logting.fo; internet www.logting.fo; Leader SÚSANNA DANIELSEN.

Faroese Government Office: Hovedvagtsgade 8, 2, 1103 Copenhagen K, Denmark; tel. 33-14-08-66; fax 33-93-85-75; e-mail faroes.mission.dk@mission.dk.

Løgmansskrivstovan (Prime Minister's Office): Tinganes, POB 64, 110 Tórshavn; tel. 351010; fax 351015; e-mail info@tinganes.fo; internet www.tinganes.fo.

Ministry of Finance: Traðagøta 39, POB 2039, 165 Argir; tel. 352020; fax 352025; e-mail figgjarmal@fms.fo; internet www.fms.fo.

Ministry of Fisheries and Maritime Affairs: Yviri við Strond 17, POB 347, 110 Tórshavn; tel. 353030; fax 353035; e-mail fisk@fisk.fo; internet www.fisk.fo.

Ministry of Education and Culture: Hoyvíksvegur 72, POB 3279, 110 Tórshavn; tel. 355050; fax 355055; e-mail mms@mms.fo; internet www.mms.fo.

Ministry of Energy, Oil, the Extractive Industry and the Environment: Brekkutún 1, POB 3050, 110 Tórshavn; tel. 357070; fax 357075; e-mail oms@oms.fo; internet www.oms.fo.

Ministry of Health and Social Affairs: Eirargarður 2, 110 Tórshavn; tel. 354050; fax 354045; e-mail ash@ahs.fo; internet www.ahs.fo.

Ministry of Trade and Industry: Tinganes, POB 377, 110 Tórshavn; tel. 356060; fax 356065; e-mail vms@vms.fo; internet www.vms.fo.

LØGTING

The Løgting has between 27 and 32 members, elected by universal adult suffrage.

Speaker: EDMUND JOENSEN (Union Party).

Election, 30 April 2002

	Votes	% of votes	Seats
Sambandsflokkurin (Union Party) . .	7,948	26.0	8
Tjóðveldisflokkurin (Republican Party). .	7,240	23.7	8
Javnaðarflokkurin (Social Democratic —Party)	6,371	20.9	7
Fólkaflokkurin (People's Party) . .	6,343	20.8	7
Sjálvstýrisflokkurin (Home Rule Party). .	1,349	4.4	1
Miðflokkurin (Centre Party)	1,286	4.2	1
Total	30,537	100.0	32

Political Organizations

Unless otherwise indicated, the address of each of the following organizations is: Áarvegur, POB 208, 110 Tórshavn; tel. 310850 fax 310686.

Fólkaflokkurin (People's Party): f. 1940; conservative-liberal party, favours free enterprise and wider political and economic autonomy for the Faroes; Chair. ÓLI BRECKMANN.

Hin Føroyski Flokkurin (The Føroyar Party): f. 1994; seeks to abolish Home Rule and fully to re-integrate the Faroes into the Kingdom of Denmark; Chair. ÓLAVUR CHRISTIANSEN.

Javnaðarflokkurin (Social Democratic Party—SDP): tel. 312493; fax 319397; e-mail javnadarflokkarin@logting.fo; internet www.javnadarflokkarin.fo; f. 1928; Chair. JÓANNES EIDESGAARD.

Kristiligi Fólkaflokkurin, Føroya Framburðs- og Fiskivinnuflokkurin (Christian People's Party, Progressive and Fishing Industry Party—CPP-PFIP): á Brekku 5, 700 Klaksvík; tel. 457580; fax 457581; f. 1954; centre party; Chair. NIELS PAULI DANIELSEN; Parliamentary Chair. LASSE KLEIN.

Miðflokkurin (Centre Party): POB 3237, 110 Tórshavn; tel. 314988; fax 312206; e-mail midflokk@post.olivant.fo; internet www.midflokkurin.fo; f. 1992; Chair. JENIS AV RANA.

Sambandsflokkurin (Union Party): Lucas Debersargøta 3, POB 1340, 110 Tórshavn; tel. 318870; fax 318910; e-mail samband@post.olivant.fo; internet www.samband.fo; f. 1906; favours the maintenance of close relations between the Faroes and the Kingdom of Denmark; conservative in internal affairs; Chair. EDMUND JOENSEN.

Sjálvstýrisflokkurin (Home Rule Party): Gamla Apotek, Tinghúsvegur, 100 Tórshavn; e-mail krossur@tingakrossur.fo; internet www.tingakrossur.fo/sfl; f. 1906; social-liberal party advocates eventual political independence for the Faroes within the Kingdom of Denmark; Chair. EYÐUN ELTOR.

Tjóðveldisflokkurin (Republican Party): Kongagøta 11, POB 143, 100 Tórshavn; tel. 312200; e-mail loysing@post.olivant.fo; internet www.tjodveldi.fo; f. 1948; left-wing party, advocates the secession of the Faroes from Denmark; Chair. HØGNI HOYDAL.

Verkmannafylkingin (Labour Front): f. 1994 by trade union leaders and former members of the SDP.

Religion

CHRISTIANITY

The Faroes Church (Evangelical Lutheran Church of Denmark) regained its diocese in November 1990, and the suffragan bishop became Bishop of the Faroe Islands. The largest independent group is the 'Plymouth Brethren'. There is also a small Roman Catholic community.

Evangelical Lutheran Church

Føroya Biskupur (Bishop of the Faroe Islands): J. Paturssonargøta 20, POB 8, 110 Tórshavn; tel. 311995; fax 315889; HANS J. JOENSEN.

BAHÁ'Í FAITH

Bahá'í: POB 1095, 110 Tórshavn; tel. 315025; internet www.bahai.fo.

The Press

In 2000 there were six general interest newspapers in the Faroe Islands.

Dagblaðið: Reynagøta 9, 100 Tórshavn; tel. 319833; fax 319823; weekly; People's Party.

Dimmalætting: Smyrilsvegur 13, POB 3019, 110 Tórshavn; tel. 341200; fax 341201; e-mail post@dimma.fo; internet www.dimma.fo; f. 1878; 5 a week; Union Party; circ. 11,000.

FF/FA-Blaðið: Vágsbotnur, POB 58, 110 Tórshavn; tel. 312169; fax 318769; weekly; Editor VILMUND JACOBSEN; circ. 2,500.

Norðlýsið: á Hædd, POB 58, 700 Klaksvík; tel. 456285; fax 456498; weekly; circ. 1,200.

Oyggjatíðinöi: R. C. Effersøesgøta 7, POB 3312, 110 Tórshavn; tel. 314411; fax 316410; 2 a week; circ. 4,500.

Tíðindablaðið Sosialurin: POB 76, 110 Tórshavn; tel. 311820; fax 314720; e-mail post@sosialurin.fo; internet www.sosialurin.fo; f. 1927; 5 a week; Social Democratic Party; Editor JAN MÜLLER; circ. 7,000.

NEWS AGENCY

Ritzaus Bureau: Gamli Vegur 3; tel. 316366; f. 1980; Man. RANDI MOHR.

Broadcasting and Communications

RADIO

Útvarp Føroya (Radio Faroe Islands): Norðari Ringvegur, POB 328, 110 Tórshavn; tel. 316566; fax 310471; internet www.uf.fo; f. 1957; Man. JÓGVAN JESPERSEN.

TELEVISION

Sjónvarp Føroya (Faroese Television): M. A. Winthersgøta 2, POB 21, 110 Tórshavn; tel. 340400; fax 340500; e-mail svf@svf.fo; internet www.svf.fo; f. 1984; Gen. Man. MIKKJAL HELMSDAL.

Finance

BANKS

(cap. = capital; res = reserves; dep. = deposits; m. = million; brs = branches; amounts in kroner)

Føroya Banki P/F: Húsagøta 3, POB 3048, 110 Tórshavn; tel. 311350; fax 315850; e-mail fbk@foroyabanki.fo; internet www.foroyabanki.fo; f. 1994 following merger of Føroya Banki (f. 1906) and Sjóvinnubankin (f. 1932); cap. 100m., res 0.2m., dep. 4,053m. (Dec. 2001); Chair. JÓHAN PÁLL JOENSEN; Man Dir and CEO JØRN ASTRUP HANSEN; Chair JÓHAN PÁLL JOENSEN; 24 brs.

Føroya Sparikassi (Faroese Savings Bank): Yviri við Strond 2, POB 34, 110 Tórshavn; tel. 348000; fax 348348; e-mail sparikassin@sparikassin.fo; internet www.sparikassin.fo; f. 1832; cap. 12m., dep. 4,064m. (Dec. 2001); res 3m. (Dec. 2000); Chair. PETER ZACHARIASSEN; Chief Man. Dir MARNER JACOBSEN.

Landsbanki Føroya: Müllers Hús, Gongin, POB 229, 110 Tórshavn; tel. 318305; fax 318537; e-mail landsbank@landsbank.fo; internet landsbank.fo; Man. SIGURÐ POULSEN.

Norðoya Sparikassi: Ósávegur 1, POB 149, 700 Klaksvík; tel. 475000; fax 476000; e-mail ns@ns.fo; internet www.ns.fo.

Suðuroya Sparikassi: POB 2, 900 Vágur; tel. 373064; fax 373340; e-mail sparsu@post.olivant.fo; internet www.sparsu.fo.

INSURANCE

Tryggingarfelagið Føroyar: Kongabrúgvin, POB 329, 110 Tórshavn; tel. 345600; fax 345601; e-mail tf@trigging.fr; internet www.trigging.fo; all non-marine; sole insurance co in islands; Man. GUNNAR í LIÐA.

Trade and Industry

GOVERNMENT AGENCY

Fiskivinnuumsitingin (Fisheries Administration): POB 87, 110 Tórshavn; tel. 313068; fax 314942.

INDUSTRIAL AND TRADE ASSOCIATIONS

L/F Føroya Fiskasøla—Faroe Seafood P/F: POB 68, 110 Tórshavn; tel. 345345; fax 345300; e-mail faroe@faroe.com; f. 1948; restructured 1995; joint stock company of fish producers; exports all seafood products; Man. Dir HANS JOHANNES A. BRUGV.

Føroya Reiðarafelag (Faroe Fishing Vessel-Owners' Association): R. C. Effersøesgøta, POB 179, 110 Tórshavn; tel. 311864; fax 317278.

Menningarstovan (Faroe Islands Trade Council): Bryggjubakki 12, POB 259, 110 Tórshavn; tel. 313028; fax 310459; e-mail trade@trade.fo; internet www.trade.fo; Man. KJARTAN KRISTIANSEN.

TRADE UNION

Føroya Arbeiðarafelag (Faroese Labour Organization): Tjarnðeild 5, POB 56, 110 Tórshavn; tel. 312101; fax 315374.

Transport

There are about 458 km of roads in the Faroe Islands. In August 2000 construction began on a 4.9-km tunnel running under the sea, linking Vágar to Streymoy. The tunnel was projected to cost 240m. kroner and was expected to open within three years.

The main harbour is at Tórshavn; the other ports are at Fuglafjorður, Klaksvík, Skálafjorður, Tvøroyri, Vágur and Vestmanna. Between mid-May and mid-September, a summer roll-on, roll-off ferry service links the Faroe Islands with Iceland, Shetland (United Kingdom), Denmark and Norway.

There is an airport on Vágar.

Atlantic Airways Faroe Islands: Vágar Airport, 380 Sørvágur; tel. 341000; fax 341001; e-mail info@atlantic.fo; internet www.atlantic.fo; f. 1987; owned by Faroese Govt; scheduled and charter passenger and cargo services to Copenhagen, Reykjavík and Aberdeen; Man. Dir MAGNI ARGE.

Smyril Line: Jonas Broncksgøta 37, POB 370, 110 Tórshavn; tel. 345900; fax 345950; e-mail office@smyril-line.com; internet www.smyril-line.com; ferry service.

Tourism

Ferðaráð Føroya (Faroe Islands Tourist Board): Bryggjubakka 17, POB 118, 100 Tórshavn; tel. 316055; fax 310858; e-mail tourist@tourist.fo; internet www.tourist.fo; f. 1984.

GREENLAND

Introductory Survey

Location, Climate, Language, Religion, Flag, Capital

Greenland (Kalaallit Nunaat) is the world's largest island, with a total area of 2,166,086 sq km, and lies in the North Atlantic Ocean, east of Canada. Most of the territory is permanently covered by ice, but 410,449 sq km of coastland are habitable. Greenlandic, an Inuit (Eskimo) language, and Danish are the official languages. The majority of the population profess Christianity and belong mainly to the Evangelical Lutheran Church of Denmark. There are also small communities of other Protestant groups and of Roman Catholics. The flag (proportions 2 by 3) consists of two equal horizontal stripes (white above red), on which is superimposed a representation of the rising sun (a disc divided horizontally, red above white) to the left of centre. Nuuk (Godthåb) is the capital.

Recent History

Greenland first came under Danish rule in 1380. In the revision of the Danish Constitution in 1953, Greenland became part of the Kingdom and acquired the representation of two members in the Danish Folketing (Parliament). In October 1972 the Greenlanders voted, by 9,658 to 3,990, against joining the European Community (EC—now European Union—EU, see p. 199) but, as part of Denmark, were bound by the Danish decision to join. Resentment of Danish domination of the economy, education and the professions continued, taking expression when, in 1977, the nationalist Siumut movement formed a left-wing party. In 1975 the Minister for Greenland appointed a commission to devise terms for Greenland home rule, and its proposals were approved, by 73.1% to 26.9%, in a referendum among the Greenland electorate in January 1979. Siumut, led by a Lutheran pastor, Jonathan Motzfeldt, secured 13 seats in the 21-member Landsting (the local legislature) at a general election in April, and a five-member Landsstyre (Home Rule Government), with Motzfeldt as Prime Minister, took office in May. From 1979 the island gradually assumed full administration of its internal affairs.

In February 1982 a referendum was held to decide Greenland's continued membership of the EC. This resulted in a 53% majority in favour of withdrawal. Negotiations were begun in May, with the Danish Government acting on Greenland's behalf, and were concluded in March 1984 (with effect from 1 February 1985): Greenland was accorded the status of an overseas territory in association with the Community, with preferential access to EC markets.

At the April 1983 general election to the Landsting (enlarged, by measures adopted in 1982, to between 23 and 26 seats, depending on the proportion of votes cast), Siumut and the conservative Atassut party won 12 seats each, while the Inuit Ataqatigiit (IA) obtained two seats. Siumut once again formed a Government, led by Motzfeldt, dependent on the support of the IA members in the Landsting: this support was withdrawn in March 1984, when the IA members voted against the terms of withdrawal from the EC, and Motzfeldt resigned. In the ensuing general election, held in June, Siumut and Atassut won 11 seats each, while the IA took three seats. Motzfeldt again formed a coalition Government, comprising Siumut and the IA.

In March 1987 the coalition Government collapsed, following a dispute between Siumut and the IA over policy towards the modernization of the US radar facility at Thule, which was claimed by the IA to be in breach of the 1972 US-Soviet Anti-Ballistic Missile Treaty. A general election was held in May. Siumut and Atassut retained 11 seats each in the Landsting (which had been enlarged in 1986, to 27 seats—23 of which were to be obtained by election in multi-member constituencies, while four were to be supplementary seats); the IA won four seats, and the remaining seat was secured by the newly formed Issittup Partiia, which was demanding the privatization of the trawler fleet. Motzfeldt eventually formed a new coalition Government with the IA. In May 1988, at elections to the Danish Folketing, Siumut was the most successful party. In June the coalition between Siumut and the IA collapsed, and Motzfeldt formed a new Siumut Government, with support from Atassut. In

December 1990, when Atassut withdrew its support for the Siumut administration (following allegations that government ministers had misused public funds), Motzfeldt organized an early general election for March 1991, at which both Siumut and Atassut obtained a reduced share of the vote, while the IA's quota rose. Accordingly, Siumut retained 11 seats in the Landsting, while Atassut's representation decreased to eight seats and the IA's increased to five. A new party, the liberal Akulliit Partiiat, won two seats, and the remaining place was taken by the Issittup Partiia. Siumut and the IA formed a coalition Government and elected the Chairman of Siumut, Lars Emil Johansen, as Prime Minister.

At the general election held in March 1995 Siumut increased its representation in the Landsting (enlarged to 31 seats) to 12 seats, while Atassut won 10 seats and the IA obtained six seats. A coalition Government was formed between Siumut and Atassut, following the withdrawal from negotiations of the IA, which failed to reach agreement with Siumut on the question of independence. Johansen retained the premiership, while Daniel Skifte, the leader of Atassut, was appointed Minister of Finance and Housing. In early 1997 Johansen asserted that Greenland could achieve economic independence from Denmark on the basis of its unexploited mineral resources. In September Motzfeldt replaced Johansen as Prime Minister at the head of the coalition. Johansen was reported to have taken a senior position with the Royal Greenland fishing group.

At the general election held in February 1999 Siumut received 35.3% of the votes cast, securing 11 seats in the Landsting. Atassut obtained 25.3% of the votes (eight seats), while the IA received 22.1% (seven seats). On 22 February a coalition Government was formed between Siumut and the IA; the two parties were to be represented in the Landsstyre by five and two ministers respectively. Jonathan Motzfeldt retained the premiership, while Josef Motzfeldt, the Chairman of the IA, was appointed Minister of Economy, Trade and Taxation.

In September 2001 Jonathan Motzfeldt was forced to resign as leader of Siumut during the party's annual congress, after he was held responsible for a deficit of 3,000m. kroner on the part of Royal Greenland (the island's main fish and seafood export company); Motzfeldt, however, retained his post as Prime Minister. In December the IA withdrew from the coalition Government, accusing Siumut of lacking direction in its policies. Siumut subsequently formed a new coalition Government with Atassut; the ministerial posts formerly held by the IA were taken over by members of Atassut, while there was no change in the ministries held by Siumut.

At the general election held on 3 December 2002 Siumut received 28.7% of the votes cast, winning 10 seats in the Landsting. The IA received 25.5% and won eight seats, Atassut 20.4% (seven seats) and Katusseqatigiit (Alliance of Independent Candidates) 5.3% (one seat); Demokraatit (the Democrats—a new party formed in October 2002) received 15.6% of the votes cast, securing five seats. Later that month Siumut and the IA formed a coalition Government, viewed by many as being strongly pro-independence, under the new Siumut Prime Minister, Hans Enoksen.

The Government was, however, extremely short-lived: the appointment to the top post of the civil service of Jens Lybeth, Enoksen's electoral campaign manager and close personal friend, prompted accusations of favouritism. Lybeth then engaged the services of Maannguaq Berthelsen, an Inuit 'healer', to 'chase away evil spirits' from government offices, urging some 600 civil servants to use similar methods to promote harmony between Greenlanders and Danes. In the ensuing furore, Enoksen was obliged to dismiss Lybeth. Josef Motzfeldt, the Deputy Prime Minister and Chairman of the IA, remained unsatisfied with the situation, and approached the Demokraatit to discuss ousting Enoksen and forming a new Government. Enoksen, again compelled to act, dissolved the coalition in mid-January 2003 and formed a new Government in coalition with Atassut.

Denmark remains responsible for Greenland's foreign relations. Greenland does, however, have separate representation on the Nordic Council (see p. 266), and is a member of the Inuit Circumpolar Conference (see p. 340). Denmark, a member of NATO (see p. 271), retains its responsibility for defence, and

Danish-US military co-operation in Greenland began in 1951. Under a 1981 agreement on the defence of Greenland, two US radar bases were established on the island, at Thule and at Kangerlussuaq (Søndre Strømfjord). An agreement between the USA and Denmark for the reduction of the bases from 325,000 ha to 160,000 ha took effect from October 1986, and the land thus available was returned to the Inuit. In March 1991 the USA agreed to transfer ownership and control of the base at Kangerlussuaq to the Greenland Government in September 1992, in exchange for the right to use it again in the future. In July 1996 it was announced that the base at Thule would be opened to aircraft. In August 1999 it was reported that the Danish Court of Appeal had ordered the Danish Government to pay compensation to Inuits who had been forced to leave their land in 1953 to allow for the expansion of the base at Thule.

Jonathan Motzfeldt and the Danish Minister for Foreign Affairs, Mogens Lykketoft, agreed in February 2001 not to adopt an official policy on the proposed US missile defence system, which would involve the upgrading of the early-warning radar station in the Thule base, pending an official request from the USA. Motzfeldt did, however, express personal concern at the plans, and called on the USA to discuss the proposals with its NATO allies. He added that Greenland would not accept the plans if they proved to be in breach of the 1972 Anti-Ballistic Missile Treaty, or if Russia opposed them. Josef Motzfeldt and the opposition parties of the Danish Folketing were already expressing strong opposition to the proposals, claiming that they risked provoking another 'arms race'. Public opinion in Greenland was also strongly opposed to the plans; many feared that they would make Greenland a target for nuclear strikes. Reports that a nuclear bomb could still be lying on the sea-bed south-west of the Thule base, following a crash involving a US B-52 aircraft in 1968, although unconfirmed and denied by both the USA and Denmark, did little to bolster public support for the US plans.

In January 2001 the newly inaugurated US President, George W. Bush, stated in a letter to Prime Minister Motzfeldt that Greenland 'should be open for dialogue' on the future of the Thule base. That the letter was sent directly to Motzfeldt rather than to Copenhagen caused consternation in Denmark, which still has control over Greenland's foreign policy. Motzfeldt, who had for years been seeking greater influence in foreign policy matters, was heartened by the development. The Greenland Government stated, in September 2001, that it welcomed the modernization of the Thule base, but sought an assurance from the USA that the base would not be used for any offensive purpose. In the previous month demonstrators from the environmental activist group Greenpeace had attempted to enter the base in order to deliver a letter of protest to the commanding officer; they were prevented from doing so by police-officers, who delivered the letter on their behalf. In September 2002 the USA returned the town of Dundas (also known as Uummannaq in Greenlandic) and its surroundings to Greenland; the USA had incorporated it into the Thule base some 50 years earlier.

In June 1980 the Danish Government declared an economic zone extending 200 nautical miles (370 km) off the east coast of Greenland. This, however, caused a dispute with Norway over territorial waters, owing to the existence of the small Norwegian island of Jan Mayen, 460 km off the east coast of Greenland. In 1988 Denmark requested the International Court of Justice (ICJ), based in The Hague, the Netherlands, to arbitrate on the issue of conflicting economic zones. A delimitation line was established by the ICJ in June 1993. A subsequent accord on maritime delimitation, agreed between the Governments of Norway, Greenland and Iceland in November 1997, established the boundaries of a 1,934-sq km area of Arctic sea that had been excluded from the terms of the 1993 settlement. In January 2002 Greenland and the Faroe Islands renewed an agreement granting the mutual right to fish in each other's waters.

Government

Greenland is part of the Kingdom of Denmark, and the Danish Government, which remains responsible for foreign affairs, defence and justice, is represented by the Rigsombudsmand, or High Commissioner, in Nuuk (Godthåb). Most functions of government are administered by the 'Home Rule Government', the Landsstyre. The formation of this executive is dependent upon support in the local legislature, the Landsting. The Landsting has 31 members elected for a maximum term of four years, on a basis of proportional representation. Greenland also elects two members to the Danish Folketing (Parliament). For admin-

istration purposes, Greenland is divided into 18 municipalities, of which the largest is Nuuk.

Defence

The Danish Government, which is responsible for Greenland's defence, co-ordinates military activities through its Greenland Command. The Greenland Command, which also undertakes fisheries control and sea rescues, is based at the Grønnedal naval base, in south-west Greenland. Greenlanders are not liable for military service. As part of the Kingdom of Denmark, Greenland belongs to NATO (see p. 271). The USA operates an air base, at Pituffik in Thule (see Recent History). In 2001 the Danish Government spent 260m. kroner (3.8% of total central government expenditure on Greenland) on the territory's defence (including the Fisheries Inspectorate).

Economic Affairs

In 1994, according to preliminary official estimates, Greenland's gross national product (GNP) was 6,381m. kroner, equivalent to some 114,800 kroner per head. The population increased at an average annual rate of 0.1% in 1990–2000. The economy enjoyed overall growth during the 1970s and 1980s, but gross domestic product (GDP) declined by 9%, in real terms, in 1990, and continued to decline significantly (owing to depleted fish stocks and the discontinuation of lead and zinc mining) until 1994 and 1995, when real growth rates of 5% and 3%, respectively, were recorded. GDP increased, in real terms, by 1.5% in 1996, 1.4% in 1997 and by 7.8% in 1998.

Fishing dominates the commercial economy, as well as being important to the traditional way of life. In 2000 the fishing industry accounted for 95.6% of Greenland's total export revenue. The industry, including the processing of the catch, employed 25.3% of the paid labour force in 1996. The cod catch has declined substantially, however, since 1989. The traditional occupation of the Greenlanders is seal-hunting, which remains important in the north. The only feasible agricultural activity in the harsh climate is livestock-rearing, and only sheep-farming has proved to be of any commercial significance. There are also herds of domesticated reindeer.

Industry (including mining, manufacturing, construction and public works) employed some 25% of those in paid employment in March 1987. Mining earned 13.0% of total export revenue in 1990. A Swedish company extracted lead, zinc and some silver at the important mine at Marmorilik in the north-west. The mine was closed, however, in 1990. In November 2001 an Australian company announced that it was to establish a mine to extract niobium (a metal used in the manufacture of electronic components) in Greenland. In recent years there have been several discoveries of petroleum, natural gas and other mineral deposits (including gold). However, in January 2002 the Norwegian state-owned oil company, Statoil, which had been drilling for petroleum off the coast of Greenland, announced that it had discovered insufficient amounts of petroleum and natural gas for commercial exploitation, and that it was to stop drilling operations.

Manufacturing is mainly dependent upon the fishing industry. Water power (melt water from the ice-cap and glaciers) is an important potential source of electricity. All mineral fuels are imported. Mineral fuels accounted for 18.7% of total imports in 2000.

In 2000 Greenland recorded a trade deficit of 742.3m. kroner. The principal trading partner remains Denmark, although its monopoly on trade ceased in 1950. Denmark supplied 73.2% of imports and received 86.0% of exports in 2000. Trade is still dominated by companies owned by the Home Rule Government. The principal exports are fish and fish products, and the principal imports are machinery and transport equipment.

Greenland is dependent upon large grants from the central Danish Government. In 2000 central government expenditure on Greenland included some 2,725m. kroner in the form of a direct grant to the Home Rule Government. Greenland has few debts, and also receives valuable revenue from the European Union (EU, see p. 199), for fishing licences. The annual rate of inflation averaged 0.9% in 1995–99, and stood at 0.7% in 1999, 1.7% in 2000 and 2.8% in 2001. In 2002 an estimated 6.5% of the labour force were unemployed.

Greenland, although a part of the Kingdom of Denmark, withdrew from the European Community (now EU) in 1985 (see Recent History). It remains a territory in association with the EU, however, and has preferential access to European markets. The loss of EU development aid has been offset by the annual payment (ECU 37.7m. during 1995–2000) for member countries to retain fishing rights in Greenlandic waters.

Greenland's economy is dominated by the fishing industry, but remains a subsistence, barter economy for a large part of the population. Migration to the towns and the rejection of a traditional life-style by many young people have, however, created new social and economic problems. Dependence on a single commodity leaves the economy vulnerable to the effects of depletion of fish stocks and fluctuating international prices. Any development or progress is possible only with Danish aid, which is already fundamental to Greenlandic finances. In an effort to generate revenue from the tourism industry, the Home Rule Government undertook, in 1990, to achieve a target of 35,000 tourist arrivals (equivalent to 500m. kroner) annually by 2005; by 1994 the campaign was showing positive results and tourist arrivals had doubled compared with levels in previous years.

Education

The educational system is based on that of Denmark, except that the main language of instruction is Greenlandic. Danish is, however, widely used. There is a school in every settlement. In 2000/01 there were 87 municipal primary and lower-secondary schools, with 11,316 pupils and 1,114 teachers (including 363 temporarily-employed teachers and 202 non-Greenlandic-speaking teachers). In 1999/2000 there were three secondary schools with 571 pupils. There is a teacher-training college in Nuuk, and a university centre opened in 1987. In 2000 current expenditure on education by the Home Rule Government represented 21.6% of total current budget spending (including allocations to the municipalities).

Statistical Survey

Sources: Statistics Greenland, *Statistical Yearbook;* Greenland Home Rule Government—Denmark Bureau, Pilestræde 52, POB 2151, 1122 Copenhagen K; tel. 33-13-42-24; fax 33-13-49-71; Statistics Greenland, POB 1025, 3900 Nuuk; tel. 345000; fax 322954; e-mail stat@gs.gh.gl; internet www.statgreen.gl.

AREA, POPULATION AND DENSITY

Area: Total 2,166,086 sq km (836,330 sq miles); Ice-free portion 410,449 sq km (158,475 sq miles).

Population: 56,542 (males 30,180; females 26,362) at 1 January 2002 (incl. 49,800 born in Greenland).

Density (1 January 2002): 0.026 per sq km.

Principal Towns (population at 1 January 2002): Nuuk (Godthåb, the capital) 13,889; Sisimiut 5,222; Ilulissat 4,285; Aasiaat 3,179; Qaqortoq 3,086; Maniitsoq 2,905.

Births, Marriages and Deaths (2000): Registered live births 885 (birth rate 15.7 per 1,000); Registered marriages (1999) 253 (marriage rate 4.5 per 1,000); Registered deaths 458 (death rate 8.2 per 1,000).

Expectation of Life (years at birth, 1996–2000): Males 62.8; Females 68.0.

Economically Active Population (1996): Fishing/fishing industry 6,380; Tourism 210; Public sector 10,080; Other land-based employment 8,500; Total 25,170.

Labour Force (census of 26 October 1976): Males 14,234; Females 7,144; Total 21,378. *2002* (provisional): Total 31,506 (incl. 29,467 employed).

HEALTH AND WELFARE

Key Indicators

Physicians (per 1,000 head, 2000): 1.6.

Health Expenditure (2000): Million kroner: 792; % of current budgetary expenditure: 18.4.

AGRICULTURE AND FISHING

Livestock (2001): Sheep 20,394, Horses 131, Beehives 18, Poultry 170, Cattle 5, Reindeer 2,480.

Livestock Products (metric tons, 2000): Mutton and lamb 357; Other meat 2.

Hunting (2000): Fox skins 87, Polar bears 49, Seals 103,369, Whales 2,602 (2001).

Fishing ('000 metric tons, live weight, 2000): Greenland halibut 21.5, Atlantic cod 4.7, Capelin 14.5; Other fishes 3.0, Crabs 6.8, Northern prawn 80.5, Clams 2.0; Total catch 133.0. The total excludes seals and whales, which are recorded by number rather than by weight (see Hunting, above).

MINING

Production (concentrates, '000 metric tons, 1989): Lead 36; Zinc 131. The estimated metal content ('000 metric tons) was: Lead 20.0; Zinc 71.5. Source: US Bureau of Mines. Note: The mine producing lead and zinc closed in 1990.

INDUSTRY

Selected Products: Frozen fish (1997) 15,100 metric tons; Electric energy (1998) 260 million kWh. Source: UN, *Industrial Commodity Statistics Yearbook.*

FINANCE

(Danish currency is in use)

Central Government Expenditure (by Ministry, million kroner, 2000): *Current:* Finance 2,725 (Grant to Home Rule Government 2,725), Defence (incl. Fisheries Inspection) 268, Environment and Energy 58, Transport 38, Research 7, Prime Minister's Office 8, Labour 3, Agriculture and Fisheries 1, Business and Industry 2, Total 3,274. *Capital:* 0. *Total:* 3,274.

Home Rule Government Accounts (million kroner, 2000): *Revenue:* Current 5,054 (Income tax 866, Import and production duties 687, Interests 240, Fishing licences 285, Danish central govt grant 2,725); Capital 0; Total 5,054. *Expenditure:* Current 4,299 (Administration 294, Education 930, Church and culture 183, Social security and welfare 1,054, Health 792, Housing 326, Business and Trade 286, Industry 139, Transport and communication 198, Energy 104, Fisheries, hunting and agriculture 133; Other (incl. Grants to municipalities) 443); Capital 583; Total 4,882.

Cost of Living (consumer price index; at July each year; base: July 1995 = 100): 103.5 in 1999; 105.3 in 2000; 108.2 in 2001.

Gross Domestic Product (provisional, million kroner at current market prices): 6,945 in 1996; 7,080 in 1997; 7,706 in 1998.

Gross National Product by Economic Activity (million kroner at factor cost, 1988): Agriculture and fisheries 971; Mineral resources 328; Manufacturing 171; Electricity, gas and heating 195; Construction 1,063, Other private services 1,989; Public sector 1,648; Total 6,365.

EXTERNAL TRADE

Principal Commodities (million kroner, 2000): *Imports c.i.f.:* Food and live animals 345.7 (Meat and meat preparations 99.7); Beverages and tobacco 102.1); Mineral fuels, lubricants, etc. 550.4 (Petroleum, petroleum products, etc. 550.3); Chemicals and related products 102.4; Basic manufactures 294.4; Machinery and transport equipment 782.9 (General industrial machinery, equipment and parts 106.5, Electrical machinery, apparatus, etc. 168.0, Transport equipment and parts 276.9); Miscellaneous manufactured articles 352.2; Total (incl. others) 2,947.5. *Exports f.o.b.:* Prawns 1,343.8; Greenland halibut 365.1; Crabs 228.7; Other fish, shellfish and products 168.1; Total (incl. others) 2,205.2.

Principal Trading Partners (million kroner, 2000): *Imports c.i.f.:* Denmark 2,158.5; Norway 246.4; Total (incl. others) 2,947.5. *Exports f.o.b.:* Denmark 1,895.9, Japan 146.4; Thailand 30.0; USA 103.1; Total (incl. others) 2,205.2.

TRANSPORT

Road Traffic (registered motor vehicles, 2001): Private cars 2,651 (incl. 166 taxis); Buses 72; Lorries 1,411; Motorcycles 8.

Shipping (2000): Number of vessels 162 (passenger ships 7, dry cargo ships 39, fishing vessels 110, others 6); Total displacement 59,938 grt (passenger ships 5,780 grt, dry cargo ships 6,411 grt, fishing vessels 47,046 grt, others 701 grt).

International Sea-borne Freight Traffic ('000 cubic metres, 1999): Goods loaded 175; Goods unloaded 332.

International Transport (passengers conveyed between Greenland, Denmark and Iceland): Ship (1983) 94; Aircraft (2001) 100,282.

TOURISM

Occupancy of Registered Hotel Accommodations (nights, 2001): 189,463 (incl. 64,059 by Danish visitors).

COMMUNICATIONS MEDIA

Radio Receivers (1997): 27,000 in use.

Television Receivers (1997): 22,000 in use.

Telephones ('000 subscribers, 2001): 26.2.

Facsimile Machines (1992): 1,153 in use.

Mobile Cellular Telephones ('000 subscribers, 2001): 17.

Internet Users ('000, 2001): 20.0.

Book Publishing (titles, 2001): 127.
Sources: UNESCO, *Statistical Yearbook,* International Telecommunication Union and UN, *Statistical Yearbook.*

EDUCATION

(municipal primary and lower-secondary schools only, 2000/01)

Institutions: 87.

Teachers: 1,114 (incl. 363 temporarily-employed teachers and 202 non-Greenlandic-speaking teachers).

Students: 11,316.

Directory

The Government

The legislative body is the Landsting, with 31 members elected for four years, on a basis of proportional representation. Greenlanders and Danes resident in Greenland for at least six months prior to an election and over the age of 18 years have the right to vote. Based on the strength of the parties in the Landsting, an executive, the Landsstyre, is formed. Since 1979 the Landsstyre has gradually assumed control of the administration of Greenland's internal affairs. Jurisdiction in constitutional matters, foreign affairs and defence remains with the Danish Government, the highest representative of which, in Greenland, is the Rigsombudsmand or High Commissioner. Greenland sends two representatives to the Danish legislature, the Folketing.

LANDSSTYRE
(April 2003)

A coalition of Siumut (S) and Atassut (A).

Prime Minister: HANS ENOKSEN (S).

Minister of Finance: AUGUSTA SALLING (A).

Minister of Infrastructure, Environment and Housing: MIKAEL PETERSEN (S).

Minister of Fisheriesand Hunting: SIMON OLSEN (S).

Minister of Industry: FINN KARLSEN (A).

Minister of Family and Health: RUTH HEILMANN (S).

Minister of Education: ARKALO ABELSEN (A).

Government Offices

Rigsombudsmanden i Grønland (High Commission of Greenland): POB 1030, 3900 Nuuk; tel. 321001; fax 324171; e-mail riomgr@gl.stm.dk; internet www.rigsombudsmanden.gl; High Commissioner PETER LAVRITZEN.

Grønlands Hjemmestyre (Greenland Home Rule Government): POB 1015, 3900 Nuuk; Denmark Bureau, Pilestræde 52, POB 2151, 1016 Copenhagen K; tel. 345000; fax 325002; e-mail homerule@gh .gl; internet www.nanoq.gl; tel. 33-69-34-00; fax 33-69-34-01.

LANDSTING

Chairman: DANIEL SKIFTE (Atassut).

Election, 3 December 2002

	Votes	%	Seats
Siumut (Forward)	8,151	28.7	10
Inuit Ataqatigiit (Inuit Brotherhood) .	7,234	25.5	8
Atassut (Solidarity)	5,845	20.4	7
Demokraatit (Democrats) . . .	4,558	15.6	5
Katusseqatigiit (Alliance of Independent Candidates) . . .	1,510	5.3	1
Arnat Partiiat (Women's Party) . .	686	2.4	—
Total	27,993	100.0	31

Political Organizations

Atassut (Solidarity): POB 399, 3900 Nuuk; tel. 323366; fax 325840; e-mail atassut.landsorganisation@partiit.centadm.gh.gl; f. 1978 and became political party in 1981; supports close links with Denmark and favours EU membership for Greenland; Leader DANIEL SKIFTE.

Demokraatit (Democrats—D): POB 164, 3900 Nuuk; tel. 345000; fax 346281; e-mail demokrat@greennet.gl; internet www.demokrat .gl; f. 2002; Chair. PER BERTHELSEN.

Inuit Ataqatigiit (Inuit Brotherhood—IA): POB 321, 3900 Nuuk; f. 1978; socialist organization, demanding that Greenland citizenship be restricted to those of Inuit parentage; advocates Greenland's eventual independence from Denmark; Chair. JOSEF MOTZFELDT.

Siumut (Forward): POB 357, 3900 Nuuk; tel. 322077; fax 322319; e-mail siumut@greennet.gl; f. 1971 and became political party in 1977; aims to promote collective ownership and co-operation, and to develop greater reliance on Greenland's own resources; favours greatest possible autonomy within the Kingdom of Denmark; social democratic party; Chair. HANS ENOKSEN.

Other registered parties include Arnat Partiiat (Women's Party) and Katusseqatigiit (Alliance of Independent Candidates).

Judicial System

The island is divided into 18 court districts and these courts all use lay assessors. For most cases these lower courts are for the first instance and appeal is to the Landsret, the higher court in Nuuk, which is the only one with a professional judge. This court hears the more serious cases in the first instance and appeal in these cases is to the High Court (Østre Landsret) in Copenhagen.

Religion

CHRISTIANITY

The Greenlandic Church, of which most of the population are adherents, forms an independent diocese of the Evangelical Lutheran Church in Denmark and comes under the jurisdiction of the Landsstyre and of the Bishop of Greenland. There are 17 parishes and in 1995 there were 23 ministers serving in Greenland.

Biskoppen over Grønlands Stift (Bishop of Greenland): SOFIE PETERSEN, Evangelical Lutheran Church, POB 90, 3900 Nuuk; tel. 321134; fax 321061; e-mail bispekontor@gh.gl.

There are also small groups of other Protestant churches and of Roman Catholics.

The Press

There are no daily newspapers in Greenland.

Atuagagdliutit/Grønlandsposten: POB 39, 3900 Nuuk; tel. 321083; fax 323147; e-mail redaktion@ag.gl; 2 a week; Editor JENS BRØNDEN.

Niviarsiaq: POB 357, 3900 Nuuk; tel. 322077; fax 322319; e-mail siumut@greennet.gl; organ of Siumut; monthly; Editor J. WÆVER JOHANSEN.

Sermitsiaq: Spindlers Bakke 10B, POB 150, 3900 Nuuk; tel. 321903; fax 322499; weekly; Editor POUL KRARUP.

Publisher

Atuakkiorfik/Greenland Publishers: Hans Egedesvej 3, POB 840, 3900 Nuuk; tel. 322122; fax 322500; e-mail greenpub@greennet .gl; f. 1956; general fiction and non-fiction, children's and textbooks, public relations; Man. HENRIETTE RASMUSSEN.

Broadcasting and Communications

TELECOMMUNICATIONS

TELE Greenland A/S: Nuuk; f. 1994; owned by Home Rule Govt.

BROADCASTING

Radio

Kalaallit Nunaata Radioa (KNR)—Grønlands Radio: POB 1007, 3900 Nuuk; tel. 325333; fax 325042; internet www.knr.gl; 5 AM stations, 45 FM stations; bilingual programmes in Greenlandic and Danish, 17 hours a day; Man. Dir PETER FREDERIK ROSING.

Avannaata Radioa: POB 223, 3952 Ilulissat; tel. 943633; fax 943618; e-mail avannaata@radio.knr.gl; regional station in north Greenland.

Kujataata Radioa: POB 158, 3920 Qaqortoq; regional station in south Greenland.

Thule Air Base Radio—50Z20: DAC POB 1117, 3970 Dundas; FM, non-commercial station; broadcasts 24 hours a day; news, music, etc. Station Man. KURT CHRISTENSEN.

Television

Kalaallit Nunaata Radioa TV: POB 1007, 3900 Nuuk; tel. 325333; fax 325042; internet www.knr.gl; broadcasts by VHF transmitter to all Greenland; commercial; most programmes in Danish; Man. Dir PETER FREDERIK ROSING.

Finance

BANK

(cap. = capital; res = reserves; dep. = deposits; m. = million; br. = branch; amounts in kroner)

The Bank of Greenland—GrønlandsBANKEN A/S: POB 1033, 3900 Nuuk; tel. 347700; fax 347706; e-mail banken@banken.gl; internet www.banken.gl; f. 1967 as The Bank of Greenland A/S; name changed as above following merger with Nuna Bank A/S in 1997; cap. 180.0m., res 339.9m., dep. 2,576.2m. (Dec. 2001); Pres. SVEND-ERIK DANIELSEN; Gen. Man. JESPER FLENSTED NIELSEN; Chair. JAKOB BROGAARD; 5 brs.

Trade and Industry

GOVERNMENT AGENCY

Government of Greenland, Bureau of Minerals and Petroleum: POB 930, 3900 Nuuk; tel. 346800; fax 324302; e-mail bmp@gh.gl; internet www.bmp.gl; f. 1998; performs the central administrative co-ordinating and regulatory tasks regarding exploration and production of mineral resources in Greenland; Dep. Min. HANS KRISTIAN SCHØNWANDT.

STATE-OWNED COMPANIES

Pilersuisoq A/S (KNI Service A/S)—Greenland Trade Service Ltd: POB 319, 3911 Sisimiut; tel. 862444; fax 866263; f. 1993; statutory wholesale and retail trading co, petroleum and fuel supply; Chair. ANDERS ANDERSEN; Pres. GERHARDT PETERSEN.

Pisiffik A/S Greenland TRADE RETAIL Ltd: POB 1009, 3911 Sisimiut; tel. 862444; fax 864175; e-mail nios@pisiffik.gl; f. 1993; statutory wholesale and retail trading co. Chair. KELD ASKÆR; Man. MICHAEL ØSTERGAARD.

Royal Greenland A/S: POB 1073, 3900 Nuuk; tel. 324422; fax 323349; internet www.royalgreenland.com; f. 1774; trade monopoly ended 1950; Home Rule Govt assumed control 1986; established as share company 1990 (all shares owned by Home Rule Govt); fishing group based in Greenland with subsidiaries in Japan, the United Kingdom, Scandinavia, the USA, Italy, France and Germany; main products are coldwater prawns and halibut; five trawlers; factories in Greenland, Denmark and Germany; Chair. UFFE ELLEMANN-JENSEN; Pres. and Chief Exec. KELD ASKÆR.

Transport

Domestic traffic is mainly by aircraft (fixed-wing and helicopter), boat and dog-sled. There are airports or heliports in all towns for domestic flights.

The main port is at Nuuk; there are also all-year ports at Paamiut (Frederikshåb), Maniitsoq (Sukkertoppen) and Sisimiut (Holsteinsborg). In addition, there are shipyards at Nuuk, Qaqortoq, Paamiut, Maniitsoq, Sisimiut and Aasiaat. Coastal motor vessels operate passenger services along the west coast from Upernavik to Nanortalik.

Shipping Company

Royal Arctic Line A/S: POB 1580, 3900 Nuuk; tel. 349100; fax 322450; e-mail info@ral.dk; internet www.ral.gl; f. 1993; owned by Home Rule Govt; four container vessels of 38,922 grt and one general cargo vessel of 4,209 grt; Pres. JENS ANDERSEN.

Airline

Grønlandsfly A/S (Greenlandair Inc.): POB 1012, Nuuk Airport, 3900 Nuuk; tel. 343434; fax 327288; e-mail glahq@greenlandair.gl; internet www.greenlandair.gl; f. 1960; air services to the 19 principal centres in Greenland, and to Copenhagen (Denmark); supply, survey, ice-reconnaissance services and helicopter/fixed-wing charters; owned by Danish Govt, Greenland Home Rule Govt and SAS; Chair. PETER GRØNVOLD SAMUELSEN; Pres. FINN ØELUND.

Tourism

Tourist arrivals traditionally did not exceed 5,000–7,000 per year. In order to stimulate increased revenue, it was decided in 1990 to set a target of 30,000–35,000 tourist arrivals per year (generating annual income of some 500m. kroner) to be achieved by 2005. The national tourist board of Greenland, Greenland Tourism, was established in 1992 in order to develop tourism in Greenland, and concentrates primarily on developing sustainable tourism projects. Some 13,000 tourist arrivals were registered in 1994.

Greenland Tourism: POB 1615, 3900 Nuuk; tel. 342820; fax 322877; e-mail info@visitgreenland.com; internet www.visitgreenland.com; f. 1992; Chair. NILS WILHJELM; Man. Dir STIG RØMER WINTHER.

DJIBOUTI

Introductory Survey

Location, Climate, Language, Religion, Flag, Capital

The Republic of Djibouti is in the Horn of Africa, at the southern entrance to the Red Sea. It is bounded on the north by Eritrea, on the north, west and south-west by Ethiopia, and on the south-east by Somalia. The land is mainly volcanic desert, and the climate hot and arid. There are two main ethnic groups, the Issa, who are of Somali origin and comprise 50% of the population, and the Afar, who comprise 40% of the population and are of Ethiopian origin. Both groups are Muslims, and they speak related Cushitic languages. The official languages are Arabic and French. The flag has two equal horizontal stripes, of light blue and light green, with a white triangle, enclosing a five-pointed red star, at the hoist. The capital is Djibouti.

Recent History

In 1945 the area now comprising the Republic of Djibouti (then known as French Somaliland) was proclaimed an overseas territory of France, and in 1967 was renamed the French Territory of the Afars and the Issas. The Afar and the Issa have strong connections with Ethiopia and Somalia respectively. Until the 1960s ethnic divisions were not marked; subsequently, however, internal tensions arose. Demands for independence were led by the Issa community, and, under pressure from the Organization of African Unity (OAU, now the African Union) to grant full independence to the territory, France acted to improve relations between the two communities. Following a referendum in May 1977, the territory became independent on 27 June. Hassan Gouled Aptidon, a senior Issa politician, became the first President of the Republic of Djibouti.

Initial intentions to maintain an ethnic balance in government were not sustained. In March 1979 Gouled formed a new political party, the Rassemblement populaire pour le progrès (RPP), which was declared the sole legal party in October 1981. In June 1981 Gouled was elected to a further six-year term as President. Legislative elections were held in May 1982, when candidates were chosen from a single list approved by the RPP. At the next presidential and legislative elections, held in April 1987, Gouled was re-elected, while RPP-sponsored candidates for all 65 seats in the legislaure were elected unopposed.

Until the mid-1980s there was little overt opposition to the RPP under Gouled's leadership. In May 1986 Aden Robleh Awalleh, a former political associate of Gouled, fled to Ethiopia and formed an opposition group, the Mouvement national djiboutien pour l'instauration de la démocratie (MNDID). Political tensions began to escalate during 1987, prompting Gouled to re-organize the Government. In April 1989 inter-tribal hostilities erupted in the capital and the Afar town of Tadjourah. Inter-ethnic tensions persisted, and in May 1990 fighting broke out between the Issa and the Gadabursi communities in the capital.

In April 1991 a new and powerful armed opposition group, the Front pour la restauration de l'unité et de la démocratie (FRUD), was formed by a merger of three insurgent Afar movements. In November the FRUD launched a full-scale insurrection against the Government. By late November the FRUD controlled many towns and villages in the north of the country and was besieging the northern towns of Tadjourah and Obock, which were held by the national army. The Government introduced mass conscription and requested military assistance from France (see below) to repel what it described as 'external aggression' by soldiers loyal to the deposed President Mengistu of Ethiopia. The FRUD denied that it constituted a foreign aggressor, claiming that its aim was to secure fair political representation for all ethnic groups in Djibouti.

In early 1992, under pressure from the French Government to accommodate opposition demands for democratic reform, President Gouled appointed a commission to draft a new constitution, which was to restore the multi-party system and provide for free elections. The FRUD stated its willingness to negotiate with Gouled and undertook to observe a cease-fire, subject to satisfactory progress on democratic reforms. Gouled, however, reasserted that the FRUD was controlled by 'foreign interests' and accused France of failing to honour its defence agreement. By late January most of northern Djibouti was under FRUD

control, although armed conflict between the FRUD and the Government continued. In June Ahmed Dini, who had been Djibouti's first Prime Minister after independence, assumed the leadership of the FRUD.

President Gouled's constitutional plan, which was announced in April 1992, conceded the principle of political pluralism, but proposed few other changes and retained a strong executive presidency. The plan was rejected by the opposition parties and by the FRUD, although cautiously welcomed by France. However, Gouled's intention that a constitutional referendum should take place in June, with legislative elections to follow in July, was recognized as unrealistic, especially with large areas of the country no longer under government control. The referendum, which was held in September, was boycotted by all the opposition groups; the Government, however, stated that, with 75% of the electorate participating, 97% of voters had endorsed the new Constitution. At the 30 September deadline for party registration, only the RPP and the Parti du renouveau démocratique (PRD), an opposition group formed earlier in 1992 under the leadership of Mohamed Djama Elabe, were granted legal status. The application for registration by the opposition Parti national démocratique (PND) was initially rejected, although it was allowed in October. Elections to the Assemblée nationale were held on 18 December, and all 65 seats were won by the RPP. More than 51% of the electorate abstained from voting, leading to charges from the PND that the legislature was unrepresentative.

Five candidates stood in Djibouti's first contested presidential election, which was held on 7 May 1993: Gouled, Elabe, Aden Robleh Awalleh (for the PND) and two independents. The election was again notable for a low level of participation (49.9%), but resulted in a clear victory for Gouled, who, according to official results, obtained 60.8% of the valid votes cast, compared with 22.0% for Elabe and 12.3% for Awalleh. The opposition alleged that there had been widespread electoral fraud.

Gouled's subsequent appeal to the FRUD to negotiate with the Government in Djibouti was rejected, as the FRUD insisted that it would only meet the Government abroad, in the presence of foreign mediators. In July 1993 the army launched a successful offensive on FRUD positions in the centre and north of the country, capturing the FRUD's headquarters, as well as other towns and areas held by the rebel group. Many of the rebels retreated into the mountains in the far north of the country. The FRUD continued its struggle, however, and began launching armed attacks on government forces. By July an estimated 80,000 civilians had been displaced by the fighting.

The extent of the military reverses inflicted on the FRUD was reflected in the intensification of political activity during late 1993. In October the PRD and the FRUD issued joint proposals for a cease-fire, to be followed by negotiations aimed at forming a transitional 'government of national unity' to supervise the implementation of democratic reforms. In December the PRD and the PND launched a co-ordinated campaign to persuade the Government to hold new parliamentary elections under the supervision of an independent electoral commission.

In March 1994 serious divisions emerged within the FRUD leadership. It was reported that the political bureau, led by Ahmed Dini, had been dissolved and that dissident members had formed an 'executive council', headed by Ougoureh Kifleh Ahmed. This dissident leadership (Ali Mohamed Daoud was subsequently declared President) sought support within the movement for a negotiated political settlement of the conflict. In June Kifleh Ahmed and the Government agreed terms for a cease-fire, and formal negotiations for a peace settlement began in July. Executive bodies of both FRUD factions continued to operate during the latter half of 1994, and parallel national congresses rejected the legitimacy of the opposing faction's leadership. In December an agreement signed by Kifleh Ahmed and the Minister of the Interior, Idris Harbi Farah, provided for a permanent cessation of hostilities, the incorporation of FRUD armed forces into the national force, the recognition of the FRUD as a legal political party, the multi-ethnic composition of a new council of ministers and the reform of electoral procedures prior to the next legislative elections. In accordance with the peace agreement, 300 members of the FRUD armed forces were integrated into the national army in March 1995. However, there was little further implementation of the accord, and there was considerable criticism of the agreement by the radical faction of the FRUD (which, under the leadership of Ahmed Dini, favoured a continuation of military operations and launched a number of small-scale attacks against government targets in late 1995) and other opposition groups. Nevertheless, Ali Mohamed Daoud and Kifleh Ahmed were appointed to posts in the Government in June. In March 1996 the Government granted legal recognition to the FRUD, which became the country's fourth and largest political party. However, Ibrahim Chehem Daoud, a former high-ranking official in the FRUD, who rejected the reconciliation between the Government and the group, formed a new group, FRUD-Renaissance.

In December 1995 President Gouled received medical treatment in France, where he remained in convalescence until March 1996. His prolonged absence from Djibouti prompted a succession crisis within the RPP, between the President's nephew and principal adviser, Ismael Omar Gelleh, and his private secretary, Ismael Gedi Hared. In February a prison riot in the capital provoked a confrontation between the Minister of Justice and Islamic Affairs, Moumin Bahdon Farah, and the Minister of the Interior, Idris Harbi Farah. In March Bahdon Farah, who was opposed to Gelleh, was dismissed from the Council of Ministers, together with Ahmed Bulaleh Barreh, the Minister of Defence. Both ministers had openly opposed the December 1994 peace agreement with the FRUD, on the grounds that it strengthened the position of Gelleh and his followers. In April 1996 Bahdon Farah established a splinter group of the RPP, the Groupe pour la démocratie de la république (RPP—GDR), which included 13 of the 65 members of the Assemblée nationale. The President of the Assemblée subsequently claimed that the RPP—GDR would remain banned while Bahdon Farah continued to hold his position as Secretary-General of the RPP. In May Gouled expelled Gedi Hared from the RPP's executive committee, together with Bahdon Farah and former ministers Barreh and Ali Mahamade Houmed, all of whom opposed Gelleh. In June Gedi Hared formed an opposition alliance, the Coordination de l'opposition djiboutienne, embracing the PND, the Front uni de l'opposition djiboutienne (a coalition of internal opposition groups) and the RPP—GDR. In August Gedi Hared, Bahdon Farah and Barreh were among five people sentenced to six months' imprisonment and the suspension of their civil rights for five years for 'insulting the Head of State'. The accused had reportedly signed a document in May, alleging that President Gouled ruled by force and terror. The detainees were released from prison in January 1997, following a presidential pardon, although their civil rights were not restored. (In early September 2001 it was announced that the Government had proposed an amnesty for the five, under which their civil rights would be restored and they would be entitled to stand in legislative elections scheduled for late 2002.)

Meanwhile, in September 1996 an internal dispute arose in the RPP, when Gelleh began a discreet campaign against the holding of several positions concurrently, which was aimed at the Prime Minister and Deputy Chairman of the RPP, Barkad Gourad Hamadou. In an apparent attempt to end these internecine disputes, President Gouled stated he would remain as Head of State until the expiry of his term of office in 1999, and in March 1997 was re-elected President of the RPP.

In April 1997 the FRUD faction led by Ali Mohamed Daoud announced its intention to participate in the forthcoming legislative elections (scheduled to be held in December) and to present joint electoral lists with the RPP. In October the armed forces of Djibouti and Ethiopia launched a joint offensive against FRUD rebels, and in February 1998 the Djiboutian security forces killed 12 members of the armed faction and arrested another 20. In March Ahmed Dini appealed to the Intergovernmental Authority on Development (IGAD) to mediate an end to the conflict. Shortly afterwards FRUD insurgents attacked several southern towns, and in November, following further FRUD assaults on the armed forces in the north, the authorities announced the creation of military zones around Tadjourah and Obock.

At the legislative elections, held on 19 December 1997, the RPP-FRUD alliance won all the seats in the Assemblée nationale. The rate of voter participation was officially recorded at 63.8%. The PRD and the PND presented candidates in some districts, but neither succeeded in gaining representation. The

PRD had suffered a split in May, when Abdillahi Hamareiteh was elected as the party's new President. A rival faction, led by Kaireh Allaleh Hared, was refused legal recognition. In late December President Gouled formed a new Council of Ministers; minor reshuffles had been effected in April and November.

In February 1999 President Gouled confirmed that he would not stand in the forthcoming presidential election; the RPP named Gelleh as its presidential candidate. At the election, held on 9 April, Gelleh won 74.4% of the votes cast, convincingly defeating his sole opponent, Moussa Ahmed Idris, who represented an opposition coalition, the Opposition djiboutienne unifiée (ODU), including the PND, the PRD and the Dini wing of the FRUD. Electoral participation was estimated at 60% of eligible voters. Following his inauguration as President on 7 May, Gelleh reappointed Hamadou as Prime Minister, at the head of a new Council of Ministers.

In early February 2000 the Government and the Dini wing of the FRUD signed a peace agreement in Paris, France. The accord provided for an end to hostilities, the reciprocal release of prisoners, the return of military units to positions held before the conflict, freedom of movement for persons and goods, the reintegration of FRUD insurgents into their previous positions of employment, and an amnesty for the rebels. In late March Dini returned to Djibouti from a self-imposed nine-year exile and announced his intention to assist in the implementation of the peace agreement. Meanwhile, earlier that month the RPP had convened its eighth congress, at which Gouled officially announced his retirement from active politics. Gelleh was elected to succeed him as President of the party. In April the commission for the implementation of the peace agreement between the Government and the Dini wing of the FRUD held its first meeting, during which four sub-commissions were established to organize disarmament and compensation, the rehabilitation of former combatants, the implementation of the decentralization programme and the strengthening of the democratic process. Meetings between the two sides continued during 2000. However, in October the FRUD demanded the revision of the Constitution, in order to curb the powers of the executive, the introduction of legislation to guarantee the independence of the magistrature, and the tribal rebalancing of the civil service. Furthermore, the FRUD leadership criticized Gelleh's apparent preoccupation with the Somali national reconciliation conference, and reports circulated that FRUD members were preparing to resume their armed struggle, if negotiations continued to be stalled.

In early February 2001 Barkad Gourad Hamadou resigned as Prime Minister on the grounds of ill health, after some 22 years in office. Dileita Mohamed Dileita, hitherto ambassador to Ethiopia, was appointed as Hamadou's replacement in March.

In May 2001 it was announced that an agreement bringing an official end to hostilities between the Government and the FRUD had been signed. The Government, for its part, pledged to establish a number of more representative local bodies and to introduce an 'unrestricted multi-party system' by September 2002. In early July 2001 President Gelleh effected a minor reorganization of the Council of Ministers, with moderate FRUD members allocated two portfolios.

On 4 September 2002, to coincide with the 10th anniversary of the approval of the new Constitution, the limit on the number of permitted political parties (previously fixed at four) was lifted. Henceforth, all parties would be recognized, subject to approval by the Ministry of the Interior and Decentralization, and, during the following months, a number of new parties registered with the intention of participating in the forthcoming legislative elections. At the elections, which were held on 10 January 2003, the Union pour la majorité présidentielle (UMP), a coalition comprising the RPP, the FRUD, the PND and the Parti populaire social démocrate, won 62.7% of the total votes cast; in accordance with the electoral laws, as it had won the majority of votes in each of the five constituencies, the UMP secured all 65 seats in the Assemblée nationale. Therefore, despite receiving 37.3% of votes cast, the opposition coalition, the Union pour l'alternance démocratique (UAD), comprising the Alliance républicaine pour la démocratie, the Mouvement du renouveau démocratique, the Parti djiboutien pour la démocratie, the Parti du renouveau démocratique and the Union djiboutienne pour la démocratie et la justice, failed to attain any legislative representation. However, for the first time in the country's history seven women were elected to the Assemblée nationale. According to official figures, the rate of voter participation was 48.4%. Later that month Idriss Arnaoud Ali, the deputy Secretary-General of the RPP, was appointed President of the Assemblée; the Council of Ministers remained unaltered.

Separate treaties of friendship and co-operation were signed in 1981 with Ethiopia, Somalia, Kenya and Sudan, with the aim of resolving regional conflicts. In August 1984 the Minister of Foreign Affairs reaffirmed Djibouti's policy of maintaining a neutral stance in the conflict between its neighbours in the Horn of Africa and expressed his Government's willingness to act as a mediator. A joint ministerial committee, which held its first session in mid-1985, was formed between Djibouti and Ethiopia, to strengthen existing relations and co-operation between the two countries. These relations, however, were overshadowed in 1986 by Ethiopia's support for the MNDID.

Djibouti's interest in promoting regional co-operation was exemplified by the creation, in February 1985, of the Intergovernmental Authority on Drought and Development (now IGAD (see p. 242) with six (now seven) member states; Djibouti was chosen as the site of its permanent secretariat, and President Gouled became its first Chairman.

Following the overthrow of the Ethiopian President, Mengistu Haile Mariam, in May 1991, Djibouti established good relations with the successor transitional Government in that country. In June Djibouti hosted a preliminary conference of groups from southern Somalia, aimed at forming a transitional Somali government. In October the borders between Djibouti and Somalia were reopened for the first time since May 1989, when they had been closed as a result of civil unrest in Somalia. In November 1997 Djibouti granted official recognition to the self-proclaimed 'Republic of Somaliland', which declared independence in 1991. In late 1999 President Gelleh drafted a peace plan aimed at reunifying Somali territory, to which the leaders of 'Somaliland' expressed their vehement opposition. Relations deteriorated further in April 2000 when the 'Somaliland' authorities closed the common border with Djibouti, following an incident in which a Djiboutian delegation was refused permission to leave its aircraft after landing at Hargeisa airport in 'Somaliland'. 'Somaliland' officials claimed that Djibouti was encouraging ethnic violence and had been responsible for a series of bomb attacks in Hargeisa. In response, Djibouti expelled three 'Somaliland' diplomats and closed the 'Somaliland' liaison office in Djibouti town. Furthermore, in May the 'Somaliland' authorities issued a ban on all flights from Djibouti to its territory; the Djibouti Government responded by prohibiting all flights to and from 'Somaliland'.The Djibouti-sponsored Somali national reconciliation conference, presided over by Gelleh, opened in May in Arta, about 40 km south of Djibouti town. The conference was attended by some 900 representatives of Somali clans and political and armed groups, and in August, following three months of extensive negotiations, the newly created Somali Transitional National Assembly elected Abdulkasim Salad Hasan President of Somalia. Relations between Djibouti and 'Somaliland' were further strained in April 2001 after the Djibouti authorities closed the common border and outlawed the transport of all goods and people between the two territories. Djibouti alleged that the administration in 'Somaliland' had stolen cigarettes worth US $800,000 from a Djibouti businessman at Berbera in 'Somaliland'. In October a delegation from 'Somaliland', led by its minister responsible for foreign affairs, held talks with Djibouti officials in an attempt to improve relations; although several bilateral agreements were concluded, the common border remained closed.

In December 1995 the Djibouti Government protested to the Eritrean authorities about alleged incursions by Eritrean troops into north-eastern Djibouti. These allegations were vehemently denied by Eritrea. Relations between the two countries were strained in April 1996, when President Gouled rejected a map of Eritrea submitted by the Eritrean Minister of Foreign Affairs, which reportedly included a 20-km strip of territory belonging to Djibouti. Relations between the two countries subsequently improved, but in November 1998 Djibouti suspended diplomatic relations with Eritrea, following accusations by that country that it was supporting Ethiopia in the Eritrea–Ethiopia border dispute. Gouled had been actively involved in an OAU committee mediating on the dispute, which earlier in the month had proposed a peace plan that was accepted by Ethiopia, but not by Eritrea. In 1999 relations between Djibouti and Ethiopia continued to improve, while those between Djibouti and Eritrea deteriorated further. In November President Gelleh visited Ethiopia and was praised by the Ethiopian President, Negasso Gidada, for his efforts in promoting a peace settlement in Somalia. Gelleh also criticized the Eritrean Government for its

aggressive attitude towards Ethiopia, and there were reports that French troops based in Djibouti were being stationed along the Eritrea–Djibouti border. In December the Djibouti and Ethiopian Governments signed a protocol of understanding on military co-operation, with the aim of establishing a further mutual defence pact. In March 2000, following Libyan mediation, Djibouti and Eritrea announced that they had resumed diplomatic relations. In December relations between Djibouti and Ethiopia temporarily deteriorated after plans were announced to increase handling charges at Djibouti port by more than 150%, which the Ethiopian authorities maintained violated a 1999 trade agreement between the two countries. However, in February 2001 the Dubai Port Authority, which had assumed control of Djibouti port in May 2000, agreed to reduce the tariffs, and bilateral relations subsequently improved.

In August 1986 a new scheme for repatriating Ethiopian refugees, under the auspices of the UN High Commissioner for Refugees (UNHCR), was begun. The burden that 'official' refugees imposed on the economy was exacerbated by an influx of illegal immigrants from Somalia and Ethiopia, and in June 1987 the Djibouti Government announced tighter controls on border crossings and identity papers. Following discussions in February 1988, Djibouti and Ethiopia agreed to control movements across their common border and to curb the influx of refugees into Djibouti. Although the Government maintained that by early 1993 the number of Somali refugees in Djibouti had reached 120,000, UNHCR argued that many of these were economic migrants. In September 1994 UNHCR initiated a programme of voluntary repatriation for Ethiopian refugees in Djibouti. According to UNHCR, some 35,000 Ethiopians returned voluntarily to their homes between early 1995 and April 1996. UNHCR estimated that at 31 December 2001 there were 23,200 refugees in Djibouti, of whom 21,700 were Somali.

President Gouled consistently fostered cordial relations with France and encouraged the maintenance of French troops in Djibouti. However, the French military presence became more controversial following Iraq's invasion of Kuwait in August 1990 and the onset of the 'Gulf crisis', during which Djibouti became the base of operations connected with France's participation in the multinational force deployed in Saudi Arabia. By supporting the UN resolutions that were formulated against Iraq, Djibouti jeopardized its future relations with that country, which was emerging as an important supplier of economic and military aid. However, Djibouti's stance during the Gulf War of January–February 1991 strengthened its ties with France, and in February the Djibouti and French Governments signed defence treaties, extending military co-operation, although France refused to intervene militarily in the conflict between the Government and the FRUD. The failure of the Government to conclude a peace agreement with the FRUD strained relations with France in 1993–94. Relations improved as a result of the peace accord of December 1994, but tensions remained between the two countries, largely owing to Djibouti's reluctance to adopt a strict programme of economic reform. In April 1998, during a visit to Djibouti by the French Minister of Defence, it was announced that France planned to reduce its military presence in the country from 3,200 troops to 2,600 by 2000. However, following a visit to Djibouti by the French army Chief of Staff, Gen. Jean-Pierre Kelche, in October 1999, the suspension of the troop reduction programme was announced. Furthermore, Gen. Kelche confirmed France's guarantees of Djibouti's territorial integrity. In July 2002, as part of a restructuring of the French forces in Djibouti, a new French army base was inaugurated

The attacks on the World Trade Center in New York and the Pentagon in Washington, DC, on 11 September 2001 resulted in a significant enhancement of Djibouti's strategic importance to the USA and its allies. In early October Djibouti demonstrated its support for the US-led coalition against terrorism by establishing a seven-member Comité national de lutte contre le terrorisme to monitor security conditions in Djibouti. Djibouti agreed to grant access to its port and airfields, and coalition members stated their intention to use Djibouti as a base from where to monitor developments in Somalia, Sudan and other countries in the region. In December a German military delegation discussed the possibility of establishing a base camp for German naval forces participating in the war on terrorism with Djibouti officials, and in January 2002 Djibouti and Germany signed a memorandum of understanding on the status of German military and civilian personnel in Djibouti. The accord granted German military personnel access to Djibouti's port and airfields to conduct surveillance missions in the region, and some 1,200 German naval personnel were subsequently stationed in Djibouti. This was the largest deployment of German forces to a foreign country since the Second World War.

Government

Executive power is vested in the President, who is directly elected by universal adult suffrage for a six-year term. Legislative power is held by the Assemblée nationale, consisting of 65 members elected for five years. The Council of Ministers, presided over by a Prime Minister, is responsible to the President. The Republic comprises five electoral districts.

Defence

Since independence, a large portion of the annual budget has been allocated to military expenditure, and defence (excluding demobilization) absorbed an estimated 12.9% of total government budgetary expenditure in 1998. In August 2002 there were about 3,200 French troops stationed in Djibouti. The total armed forces of Djibouti itself, in which all services form part of the army, was estimated at 9,850 (including 200 naval and 250 air force personnel, and 1,400 gendarmes), and there was a 2,500-strong national security force. In January 2002 Djibouti and Germany signed a memorandum of understanding on the status of German military and civilian personnel in Djibouti, granting German military personnel access to Djibouti's port and airfields to conduct surveillance missions in the region; some 1,200 German naval personnel were subsequently stationed in Djibouti. The defence budget for 2002 amounted to 4,000m. Djibouti francs.

Economic Affairs

In 2001, according to estimates by the World Bank, Djibouti's gross national income (GNI), measured at average 1999–2001 prices, was US $572m., equivalent to $890 per head. During 1990–2001, it was estimated, the population increased at an average annual rate of 2.9%, owing partly to the influx of refugees from neighbouring Ethiopia and Somalia, while gross domestic product (GDP) per head decreased, in real terms, by an average of 3.6% per year. Overall GDP remained constant, in real terms, during 1990–2001; growth in 2001 was 1.6%.

Agriculture (including hunting, forestry and fishing) provided some 4% of GDP in 2001, according to official figures, although some 78.7% of the labour force were engaged in the sector in mid-2001. There is little arable farming, owing to Djibouti's unproductive terrain, and the country is able to produce only about 3% of its total food requirements. More than one-half of the population are pastoral nomads, herding goats, sheep and camels. During 1990–2000, according to the World Bank, the real GDP of the agricultural sector increased at an average annual rate of 0.9%; agricultural GDP increased by 2.0% in 2000.

Industry (comprising manufacturing, construction and utilities) provided some 16% of GDP in 2001, according to official figures, and engaged 11.0% of the employed labour force in 1991. Industrial activity is mainly limited to a few small-scale enterprises. During 1990–2000, according to the World Bank, industrial GDP declined at an average annual rate of 5.6%; industrial GDP increased by 1.0% in 2000.

The manufacturing sector contributed some 3% of GDP in 2001. Almost all consumer goods have to be imported. Manufacturing GDP declined by an average of 9.8% per year in 1990–2000, according to the World Bank. However, the GDP of the sector increased by 1.0% in 2000.

In 1986 work commenced on a major geothermal exploration project, funded by the World Bank and foreign aid. In that year Saudi Arabia granted Djibouti US $21.4m. for the purchase and installation of three electricity generators, with a combined capacity of 15 MW. Total electricity generating capacity rose from 40 MW to 80 MW in 1988, when the second part of the Boulaos power station became operative. This figure continued to rise during the 1990s, and in 2001 Djibouti produced 235.2 MW of electricity. Nevertheless, imported fuels continued to satisfy a large proportion of Djibouti's energy requirements. Imports of petroleum products accounted for 18.5% of the value of total imports in 1999.

Djibouti's economic viability is based on trade through the international port of Djibouti, and on the developing service sector, which accounted for some 81% of GDP in 2001, according to official figures, and engaged 13.8% of the employed labour force in 1991. In May 2000 the Government and Dubai Ports International (DPI) signed an agreement providing DPI with a 20-year contract to manage the port of Djibouti. During 1990–2000, according to the World Bank, the GDP of the services sector declined at an average annual rate of 0.6%. Services GDP increased by 1.6% in 2000.

In 1998, according to provisional figures, Djibouti recorded a visible trade deficit of 33,297m. Djibouti francs, and there was a deficit of 2,365m. Djibouti francs on the current account of the balance of payments. According to the IMF, the principal sources of imports in 1999 were France (26.2%), Ethiopia and Saudi Arabia. The principal markets for exports in 1998 were Somalia (53.0%) and Yemen. The principal imports in 1999 were food and beverages, machinery and electrical appliances, qat (a narcotic leaf), petroleum products and vehicles and transport equipment. Most exports are unclassified.

Djibouti recorded a budget deficit of 839m. Djibouti francs in 2000 (equivalent to 0.9% of GDP). The country's total external debt was US $262.2m. at the end of 2000, of which $237.9m. was long-term public debt. In 2000 the cost of debt-servicing was equivalent to an estimated 5.5% of revenue from exports of goods and services. The annual rate of inflation averaged 4.8% during 1989–97. Consumer prices increased by an estimated 2.4% in 2000. In 1996 unemployment was estimated to affect some 58% of the labour force.

Djibouti is a member of the Intergovernmental Authority on Development (see p. 242) and numerous other international organizations, including the African Development Bank (see p. 128), the Arab Fund for Economic and Social Development (see p. 136) and the Islamic Development Bank (see p. 257). In 1995 Djibouti became a member of the World Trade Organization (see p. 323).

Djibouti is heavily dependent on foreign assistance, and the decline in foreign aid since 1986 has led to financial problems. Attempts by aid donors, notably France, to insist on structural reforms to the economy were initially resisted by the Government, but in mid-1995 considerable reductions in government spending were announced, and in April 1996 the IMF approved Djibouti's first stand-by credit, equivalent to US $6.7m. Djibouti agreed to implement a programme of austerity measures, concentrating on budgetary adjustment and structural reform. In October 1999 the IMF agreed a $26.5m. loan to support the Government's three-year economic reform programme. An initial payment of $3.8m. was released immediately. However, the payment of the balance was conditional on Djibouti implementing its 1999–2002 programme of economic and financial reform, which included reforms to tax, revenue administration and budget management; the completion of the army demobilization programme by the end of 2000; the reform of the civil service, thus lowering the wage bill; and the publication of a privatization programme for the six principal state-owned enterprises. Despite continued delays in the army demobilization programme and the reform of the civil service, in November 2001 the IMF disbursed a further $5.0m., and in December 2002, following the completion of the third policy review, the IMF released funds totalling $6.0m. In 2002 economic growth continued to be driven predominantly by activity in the expanding services sector, which benefited from the sizeable foreign military contingents stationed in Djibouti as part of the fight against international terrorism, as well as increased activity at the port of Djibouti. Meanwhile, inflation reached historically low levels, with price rises of just 0.1% recorded in the year to June 2002. The Government's economic priority remained, however, the reduction of expenditure on civil service and army wages, enabling increased investment in social programmes and the reduction of budgetary arrears.

Education

The Government has overall responsibility for education. Primary education generally begins at six years of age and lasts for six years. Secondary education, usually starting at the age of 12, lasts for seven years, comprising a first cycle of four years and a second of three years. In 1996 the total enrolment at primary and secondary schools was equivalent to 26% of the school-age population (31% of boys; 22% of girls). In 1999/2000 primary enrolment included 30.6% of pupils in the relevant age-group (34.9% of boys; 26.3% of girls), and secondary enrolment was equivalent to 14.7% of pupils in the relevant age-group (12.9% of boys; 16.6% of girls). Budgetary current expenditure on education in 1999 was 3,273m. Djibouti francs, equivalent to 10.0% of total government expenditure. As Djibouti has no university, students seeking further education travel abroad to study, mainly to France.

Public Holidays

2003: 1 January (New Year's Day), 12 February* (Id al-Adha, Feast of the Sacrifice), 5 March* (Muharram, Islamic New Year), 1 May (Workers' Day), 14 May* (Mouloud, Birth of the Prophet), 27 June (Independence Day), 26 November* (Id al-Fitr, end of Ramadan), 25 December (Christmas Day).

2004: 1 January (New Year's Day), 2 February* (Id al-Adha, Feast of the Sacrifice), 22 February* (Muharram, Islamic New

Year), 1 May (Workers' Day), 2 May* (Mouloud, Birth of the Prophet), 27 June (Independence Day), 14 November* (Id al-Fitr, end of Ramadan), 25 December (Christmas Day).

*These holidays are dependent on the Islamic lunar calendar and may vary by one or two days from the dates given.

Weights and Measures

The metric system is in force.

Statistical Survey

Source (unless otherwise stated): Ministère de l'Economie, des Finances et de la Planification, chargé de la Privatisation, BP 13, Djibouti; tel. 353331; internet www.mefpp.org.

AREA AND POPULATION

Area: 23,200 sq km (8,958 sq miles).

Population: 220,000 (1976 estimate), including Afars 70,000, Issas and other Somalis 80,000, Arabs 12,000, Europeans 15,000, other foreigners 40,000; 519,900 (including refugees and resident foreigners) at 31 December 1990 (official estimate); 644,000 (UN estimate) at mid-2001 (Source: UN, *Population and Vital Statistics Report*).

Density (mid-2001): 27.8 per sq km.

Principal Towns (estimated population in 2003): Djibouti (capital), 547,100; Ali-Sabieh 8,000; Tadjourah 7,500; Dikhil 6,500; Obock 5,000; Source: Stefan Helders, *World Gazetteer* (internet www.world-gazetteer.com).

Births and Deaths (UN estimates, 1995–2000): Average annual birth rate 40.7 per 1,000; Average annual death rate 18.0 per 1,000. Source: UN, *World Population Prospects: The 2000 Revision*.

Expectation of Life (WHO estimates, years at birth): 49.3 (males 47.9; females 50.4) in 2001. Source: WHO, *World Health Report*.

Economically Active Population (estimates, '000 persons, 1991): Agriculture, etc. 212; Industries 31; Services 39; *Total* 282 (males 167, females 115). Source: UN Economic Commission for Africa, *African Statistical Yearbook. 2000* ('000 persons, estimates): Agriculture, etc. 248; Total labour force 315. Source: FAO.

HEALTH AND WELFARE

Key Indicators

Total Fertility Rate (children per woman, 2001): 5.9.

Under-5 Mortality Rate (per 1,000 live births, 2001): 143.

HIV/AIDS (% of persons aged 15–49, 1999): 11.75.

Physicians (per 1,000 head, 1996): 14.0.

Hospital Beds (per 1,000 head, 1990): 2.54.

Health Expenditure (2000): US $ per head (PPP): 63.

Health Expenditure (2000): % of GDP: 5.0.

Health Expenditure (2000): public (% of total): 46.1.

Access to Water (% of persons, 2000): 100.

Access to Sanitation (% of persons, 2000): 91.

Human Development Index (2000): ranking: 149.

Human Development Index (1999): index: 0.445.
For sources and definitions, see explanatory note on p. vi.

AGRICULTURE, ETC.

Principal Crops (FAO estimates, '000 metric tons, 2001): Tomatoes 1.1; Other vegetables 23.2. Source: FAO.

Livestock (FAO estimates, '000 head, year ending September 2000): Cattle 269; Sheep 465; Goats 513; Asses 9; Camels 70. Source: FAO.

Livestock Products ('000 metric tons, 2000): Beef and veal 3.6; Mutton and lamb 2.1; Goat meat 2.4; Camel meat 0.7; Cows' milk 8.1; Camels' milk 5.9; Cattle hides 0.7; Sheepskins 0.4; Goatskins 0.5. Source: FAO.

Fishing (FAO estimates, metric tons, live weight, 2000): Groupers 100; Snappers and jobfishes 80; Porgies and seabreams 40; Barracudas 20; Carangids 20; Seerfishes 60; Other tuna-like fishes 15; Total catch (incl. others) 350. Source: FAO, *Yearbook of Fishery Statistics*.

INDUSTRY

Electric Energy (million kWh): 192.2 in 1999; 232.2 in 2000; 235.3 in 2001.

FINANCE

Currency and Exchange Rates: 100 centimes = 1 Djibouti franc. *Sterling, Dollar and Euro Equivalents* (31 December 2002): £1 sterling = 286.45 Djibouti francs; US $1 = 177.72 Djibouti francs; €1 = 186.38 Djibouti francs; 1,000 Djibouti francs = £3.491 = $5.627 = € 5.365. *Exchange Rate:* Fixed at US $1 = 177.721 Djibouti francs since February 1973.

Budget (million Djibouti francs, 2000): *Revenue:* Tax revenue 21,659 (Direct taxes 9,240, Indirect taxes 10,765; Registration fees, etc. 870); Other revenue (incl. property sales) 2,080; Total 23,739, excl. grants received from abroad (6,360) and loans (1,875). *Expenditure:* Current expenditure 30,195 (General administration 7,447, Defence 4,496, Education 3,273, Health 1,512, Economic services 952, Unallocable expenditure 7,444, Debt servicing 1,822, Transfers 3,123); Capital expenditure 2,618 (Foreign-financed 2,030); Total 32,813. *2001:* Total revenue 23,702; Total expenditure 30,215.

International Reserves (US $ million at 31 December 2001): IMF special drawing rights 0.13; Reserve position in IMF 1.38; Foreign exchange 66.80; Total 68.31. Source: IMF, *International Financial Statistics*.

Money Supply (million Djibouti francs at 31 December 2001): Currency outside banks 9,370; Demand deposits at commercial banks 19,275; Total money 28,645. Source: IMF, *International Financial Statistics*.

Cost of Living (Consumer Price Index for expatriates; base: 1989 = 100): All items 137.2 in 1995; 142.9 in 1996; 145.8 (estimate) in 1997. Source: IMF, *Djibouti: Statistical Annex* (August 1998).

Expenditure on the Gross Domestic Product (provisional, million Djibouti francs at current purchasers' values, 1998): Government final consumption expenditure 21,497; Private final consumption expenditure 72,466; Gross capital formation 13,958; *Total domestic expenditure* 107,921; Exports of goods and services 41,449; *Less* Imports of goods and services 58,172; *GDP in purchasers' values* 91,198. Source: IMF, *Djibouti: Statistical Annex* (December 1999).

Gross Domestic Product by Economic Activity (million Djibouti francs at current factor cost, 2001): Agriculture, hunting, forestry and fishing 3,184; Manufacturing (incl. mining) 3,030; Electricity and water 5,023; Construction and public works 6,170; Trade and hotels 14,332; Transport and communications 25,123; Finance and insurance 11,944; Public administration 19,489; Other services 1,749; Statistical discrepancy –300; *GDP at factor cost* 89,744; Indirect taxes *less* subsidies 12,188; *GDP in purchasers' values* 101,932. Source: Banque Centrale de Djibouti, *Rapport Annuel 2001*.

Balance of Payments (million Djibouti francs, 2001): Exports of goods f.o.b. 14,460; Imports of goods f.o.b. –46,757; *Trade balance* –33,297; Exports of services and other income 36,948; Imports of services and other income –15,206; *Balance on goods, services and income* –11,555; Official transfers (net) 10,238; Private transfers (net) –1,047; *Current balance* –2,365; Foreign direct investment 600; Public sector (net) 66; Private capital (net) and net errors and omissions 9,327; *Overall balance* 7,629. Source: Banque Centrale de Djibouti, *Rapport Annuel 2001*.

EXTERNAL TRADE

Principal Commodities: *Imports c.i.f.* (million Djibouti francs, 1999): Food and beverages 6,796; Qat 3,300; Petroleum products 2,944; Chemical products 1,620; Clothing and footwear 1,251; Metals and metal products 1,355; Machinery and electrical appliances 3,399; Vehicles and transport equipment 2,781; Total (incl. others) 27,131. *Exports f.o.b.* (distribution by SITC, US $ '000, 1992): Food and live animals 3,292 (Rice 726, Coffee and coffee substitutes 1,773); Crude materials (inedible) except fuels 867; Basic manufactures 771; Machinery and transport equipment 1,260 (Road vehicles and parts 585, Other transport equipment 501); Commodities not classified according to kind 9,481; Total (incl. others) 15,919. Source: UN, *International Trade Statistics Yearbook.*

Principal Trading Partners: *Imports c.i.f. (million Djibouti Francs, 1999):* Belgium-Luxembourg 612; China, Peoples Republic 640; Ethiopia 3,476; France 7,120; India 393; Italy 1,334; Japan 908; Kenya 301; Netherlands 1,231; Saudi Arabia 2,179; Singapore 633; Somalia 610; Spain 1,091; United Arab Emirates 1,861; United Kingdom 567; USA 559; Yemen 613; Total (incl. others) 27,131. *Exports f.o.b. (percentage of total trade, 1998):* Ethiopia 5.0; Somalia 53.0; Yemen 22.5. Source: IMF, *Direction of Trade Statistics in Djibouti: Statistical Annex* (December 1999).

TRANSPORT

Railways (traffic, 1998/99): Passengers ('000) 773; Passenger-km (million) 81; Freight carried ('000 metric tons) 266.1; Freight ton-km (million) 113.4.

Road Traffic (estimates, motor vehicles in use, 1996): Passenger cars 9,200; Lorries and vans 2,040. Source: International Road Federation, *World Road Statistics.*

Shipping: *Merchant Fleet* (registered at 31 December 2001): 10 vessels (displacement 2,493 grt). Source: Lloyd's Register-Fairplay, *World Fleet Statistics. Freight Traffic* ('000 metric tons, 1998): Goods loaded and unloaded 808. Source: IMF, *Djibouti: Statistical Annex* (December 1999).

Civil Aviation: Passengers carried (2001) 140,521670; Freight loaded and unloaded (2001) 6,361 metric tons. Source: Banque Centrale de Djibouti, *Rapport Annuel 2001.*

TOURISM

Tourist Arrivals ('000): 20 in 1996; 20 in 1997; 20 in 1998.

Receipts from Tourism (US $ million): 4 in 1996; 4 in 1997; 4 in 1998 (Source: World Bank).

COMMUNICATIONS MEDIA

Newspapers (1995): 1 non-daily (estimated circulation 1,000).

Periodicals (1989): 7 (estimated combined circulation 6,000).

Radio Receivers (1997): 52,000 in use.

Television Receivers (2000): 45,000 in use.

Telephones (2001): 9,900 main lines in use.

Facsimile Machines (1999): 69 in use.

Mobile Cellular Telephones (2001): 3,000 subscribers.

Personal Computers (2001): 7,000 in use.

Internet Users (2001): 3,300.
Sources: mainly UNESCO, *Statistical Yearbook;* UN, *Statistical Yearbook;* International Telecommunication Union.

EDUCATION

Pre-primary (1996/97): 2 schools; 247 pupils.

Primary (2000/01): 73 schools; 37,938 pupils; 1,127 teachers.

Secondary (2000/01): 16,121 pupils (general 14,803, vocational 1,318); 628 teachers (1995/96).

Higher (2000/01): 478 students.
Sources: UNESCO, *Statistical Yearbook;* Ministère de l'éducation nationale et de l'enseignement supérieur.

Adult Literacy Rate (UNESCO estimates): 64.6% (males 75.6%; females 54.4%) in 2000 (Source: UN Development Programme, *Human Development Report*).

Directory

The Constitution

A new Constitution was approved by national referendum on 4 September 1992 and entered into force on 15 September.
The Constitution of Djibouti guarantees the basic rights and freedoms of citizens; the functions of the principal organs of state are delineated therein.
The President of the Republic, who is Head of State and Head of Government, is directly elected, by universal adult suffrage, for a period of six years, renewable only once. The President nominates the Prime Minister and, following consultation with the latter, appoints the Council of Ministers. The legislature is the 65–member Assemblée nationale, which is elected, also by direct universal suffrage, for a period of five years.
The 1992 Constitution provided for the establishment of a maximum of four political parties. On 4 September 2002, however, this limit on the number of political parties was revoked.

The Government

HEAD OF STATE

President and Commander-in-Chief of the Armed Forces: ISMAEL OMAR GELLEH (inaugurated 7 May 1999).

COUNCIL OF MINISTERS
(April 2003)

Prime Minister: DILEITA MOHAMED DILEITA.

Minister of Justice, Muslim and Penal Affairs, and Human Rights: ISMAEL IBRAHIM HOUMED.

Minister of the Interior and Decentralization: ABOULKADER DOUALEH WAIS.

Minister of Defence: OUGOUREH KIFLEH AHMED.

Minister of Foreign Affairs, International Co-operation and Parliamentary Relations: ALI ABDI FARAH.

Minister of Economy, Finance and Planning, in charge of Privatization: YACIN ELMI BOUH.

Minister of Trade and Industry: SALEBAN OMAR OUDIN.

Minister of Agriculture, Livestock and Fishing: DINI ABDALLAH BILILIS.

Minister of Communication and Culture, in charge of Post and Telecommunications, and Government Spokesman: RIFKI ABDULKADER BAMAKHRAMA.

Minister of National and Higher Education: ABDI IBRAHIM ABSIEH.

Minister of Employment and National Solidarity: MOHAMED BARKAT ABDILLAHI.

Minister of Energy and Natural Resources: MOHAMED ALI MOHAMED.

Minister of Equipment and Transport: ELMI OBSIEH WAIS.

Minister of Health: Dr MOHAMED ALI KAMIL.

Minister of Presidential Affairs, in charge of Investment Promotion: OSMAN AHMED MOUSSA.

Minister of Urban Planning, Housing, the Environment, and National and Regional Development: ABDALLAH ABDILLAHI MIGUIL.

Minister of Youth, Sports, Leisure and Tourism: OTBAN GOITA MOUSSA.

Minister-delegate to the Prime Minister, in charge of the Promotion of Women's, Family and Social Affairs: HAWA AHMED YOUSSOUF.

Minister-delegate to the Minister of Foreign Affairs, International Co-operation and Parliamentary Relations, in charge of International Co-operation: MAHAMOUD ALI YOUSSOUF.

Minister-delegate to the Minister of Justice, Muslim and Penal Affairs, and Human Rights, in charge of Mosque Properties and Muslim Affairs: CHEIK MOGUEH DIRIR SAMATAR.

MINISTRIES

Office of the Prime Minister: BP 2086, Djibouti; tel. 351494; fax 355049.

Ministry of Agriculture, Livestock and Fishing: BP 453, Djibouti; tel. 351297.

Ministry of the Civil Service and Administrative Reform: BP 155, Djibouti; tel. 351464.

Ministry of Communication and Culture: Djibouti.

Ministry of Defence: BP 42, Djibouti; tel. 352034.

Ministry of the Economy, Finance and Planning: BP 13, Djibouti; tel. 353331; fax 356501.

Ministry of Employment and National Solidarity: Djibouti.

Ministry of Energy and Natural Resources: BP 175, Djibouti; tel. 350340.

Ministry of Equipment and Transport: BP 2501, Djibouti; tel. 350971.

Ministry of Foreign Affairs, International Co-operation and Parliamentary Relations: BP 1863, Djibouti; tel. 352471.

Ministry of Health: BP 296, Djibouti; tel. 353331; fax 356300.

Ministry of the Interior and Decentralization: BP 33, Djibouti; tel. 350791.

Ministry of Justice, Muslim and Penal Affairs, and Human Rights: BP 12, Djibouti; tel. 351506; fax 354012.

Ministry of Labour and Vocational Training: BP 170, Djibouti; tel. 350497.

Ministry of National and Higher Education: Cité Ministérielle, BP 16, Djibouti; tel. 350997; fax 354234; e-mail education.gov@intent.dj; internet www.education.dj.

Ministry of Presidential Affairs: Djibouti.

Ministry of Trade and Industry: BP 1846, Djibouti; tel. 351682.

Ministry of Urban Planning, Housing, the Environment, and National and Regional Development: Djibouti.

Ministry of Youth, Sports, Leisure and Tourism: BP 2506, Djibouti; tel. 355886; fax 356830.

President and Legislature

PRESIDENT

Presidential Election, 9 April 1999

Candidates	Votes	%
Ismael Omar Gelleh (RPP) .	70,993	74.44
Moussa Ahmed Idris (ODU)* .	24,375	25.56
Total .	95,368	100.00

* Opposition djiboutienne unifiée, an electoral coalition including the PND, the PRD and the Dini faction of the FRUD.

ASSEMBLÉE NATIONALE

President of the Assemblée: IDRISS ARNAOUD ALI.

General Election, 10 January 2003

Party	Valid votes	% of votes	Seats
Union pour la majorité présidentielle*.	53,293	62.73	65
Union pour l'alternance démocratique† .	31,660	37.27	—
Total .	84,953	100.00	65

* A coalition comprising the FRUD, the PND, the PPSD and the RPP.

† A coalition comprising the ARD, the MRD, the PDD, the PRD and the UDDJ.

Political Organizations

On 4 September 2002, to coincide with the 10th anniversary of the approval of the new Constitution, restrictions on the number of legally permitted political parties (hitherto four) were formally removed. The following organizations contested the legislative elections of January 2003:

Alliance républicaine pour la démocratie (ARD): BP 1488 Marabout, Djibouti; tel. 250919; f. 2002; Pres. AHMED DINI AHMED; Sec.-Gen. ADAN MOHAMED ABDOU.

Front pour la restauration de l'unité et de la démocratie (FRUD): BP 7236, rue Clochette, Djibouti; tel. 250279; f. 1991 by merger of three militant Afar groups; advocates fair representation in govt for all ethnic groups; commenced armed insurgency in Nov. 1991; split into two factions in March 1994; the dissident group, which negotiated a settlement with the Govt, obtained legal recognition in March 1996 and recognizes the following leaders; Pres. ALI MOHAMED DAOUD; Sec.-Gen. OUGOUREH KIFLEH AHMED; a dissident group, FRUD-Renaissance (led by IBRAHIM CHEHEM DAOUD), was formed in 1996.

Mouvement du renouveau démocratique (MRD): Djibouti; f. 2002; Pres. DAHER AHMED FARAH; Sec.-Gen. SOULEIMAN HASSAN FAIDAL.

Parti djiboutien pour la démocratie (PDD): Cité Einguela, Maison 22103, Djibouti; f. 2002; Pres. MOHAMED DAOUD CHEHEM; Sec.-Gen. ABDILLAHI MOHAMED SALAH.

Parti national démocratique (PND): BP 10204, Djibouti; tel. 342194; f. 1992; seeks formation of a 'govt of national unity' to supervise implementation of democratic reforms; Pres. ADEN ROBLEH AWALLEH.

Parti populaire social democrate (PPSD): BP 434, Route Nelson Mandela; f. 2002; Pres. MOUMIN BAHDON FARAH; Sec.-Gen. HASSAN IDRISS AHMED.

Parti du renouveau démocratique (PRD): BP 2198, Djibouti; tel. 356235; fax 351474; f. 1992; seeks to establish democratic parliamentary govt; Pres. ABDILLAHI HAMAREITEH; Sec.-Gen. MAKI HOUMED GABA.

Rassemblement populaire pour le progrès (RPP): Djibouti; f. 1979; sole legal party 1981–92; Pres. ISMAEL OMAR GELLEH; Sec.-Gen. MOHAMED ALI MOHAMED.

Union djiboutienne pour la démocratie et la justice (UDDJ): Djibouti.

The following organizations are banned:

Coordination de l'opposition djiboutienne: f. 1996; alliance of the PND, the FUOD and the RPP—GDR; Leader ISMAEL GEDI HARED.

Front des forces démocratiques (FFD): Leader OMAR ELMI KHAIREH.

Front de libération de la côte des Somalis (FLCS): f. 1963; Issa-supported; has operated from Somalia; Chair. ABDALLAH WABERI KHALIF; Vice-Chair. OMAR OSMAN RABEH.

Front uni de l'opposition djiboutienne (FUOD): f. 1992; based in Ethiopia; united front of internal opposition groups, incl. some fmr mems of the RPP; Leader MAHDI IBRAHIM A. GOD.

Groupe pour la démocratie de la république (RPP—GDR): f. 1996 by a dissident faction of the RPP; Leader MOUMIN BAHDON FARAH.

Mouvement de la jeunesse djiboutienne (MJD): Leader ABDOUL-KARIM ALI AMARKAK.

Mouvement pour l'unité et la démocratie (MUD): advocates political pluralism; Leader MOHAMED MOUSSA ALI 'TOURTOUR'.

Organisation des masses Afar (OMA): f. 1993 by mems of the fmr Mouvement populaire de libération; Chair. AHMED MALCO.

Parti centriste et des reformes démocratiques (PCRD): f. 1993 in Addis Ababa, Ethiopia, by a breakaway faction of the FRUD; seeks official registration as an opposition party; Chair. HASSAN ABDALLAH WATTA.

Parti populaire djiboutien (PPD): f. 1981; mainly Afar-supported; Leader MOUSSA AHMED IDRIS.

Union des démocrates djiboutiens (UDD): affiliated to the FUOD; Chair. MAHDI IBRAHIM AHMED.

Union démocratique pour le progrès (UDP): f. 1992; advocates democratic reforms; Leader FARAH WABERI.

Union des mouvements démocratiques (UMD): f. 1990 by merger of two militant external opposition groups; Pres. MOHAMED ADOYTA.

Diplomatic Representation

EMBASSIES IN DJIBOUTI

China, People's Republic: Djibouti; tel. 352246; Ambassador GUAN JINDI.

Egypt: BP 1989, Djibouti; tel. 351231; Ambassador IBRAHIM EL-CHOUMI.

Eritrea: BP 1944, Djibouti; tel. 354961; fax 351831; Ambassador MOHAMED ALI JABRA.

Ethiopia: rue Clochette, BP 230, Djibouti; tel. 350718; fax 354803; Ambassador SHEMSEDIN WORK ZEWDIE.

France: 45 blvd du Maréchal Foch, BP 2039, Djibouti; tel. 350963; fax 350272; e-mail ambfrdj@intnet.dj; Ambassador PATRICK ROUSSEL.

Iraq: BP 1983, Hai al-Eiron, Djibouti; tel. 356903; fax 356671; Ambassador FADEL ELEBI LAFTA.

Libya: BP 2073, Djibouti; tel. 350202; Ambassador KAMEL AL-HADI ALMARASH.

Oman: Djibouti; tel. 350852; Ambassador SAOUD SALEM HASSAN AL-ANSI.

Russia: BP 1913, Djibouti; tel. 350740; fax 355990; Ambassador MIKHAIL TSVIGOUN.

Saudi Arabia: BP 1921, Djibouti; tel. 351645; fax 352284; Ambassador ABDOULAZIZ MOHAMED AL-EIFAN.

Somalia: BP 549, Djibouti; tel. 353521; Ambassador ISE ALI AHMED.

Sudan: BP 4259, Djibouti; tel. 356404; fax 356662; Ambassador ABELWAHAB EL SAWI KHALAFALLA.

USA: Villa Plateau du Serpent, blvd du Maréchal Joffre, BP 185, Djibouti; tel. 353995; fax 353940; e-mail amembadm@bow.intnet.dj; Ambassador DONALD Y. YAMAMOTO.

Yemen: BP 194, Djibouti; tel. 352975; Ambassador MUHAMMAD ABDOUL WASSI HAMID.

Judicial System

The Supreme Court was established in 1979. There is a high court of appeal and a court of first instance in Djibouti; each of the five administrative districts has a 'tribunal coutumier'.

President of the Court of Appeal: KADIDJA ABEBA.

Religion

ISLAM

Almost the entire population are Muslims.

Qadi of Djibouti: MOGUE HASSAN DIRIR, BP 168, Djibouti; tel. 352669.

CHRISTIANITY

The Roman Catholic Church

Djibouti comprises a single diocese, directly responsible to the Holy See. There were an estimated 7,000 adherents in the country at 31 December 2000.

Bishop of Djibouti: GIORGIO BERTIN, Evêché, blvd de la République, BP 94, Djibouti; tel. 350140; fax 354831; e-mail evechcat@intnet.dj.

The Anglican Communion

Within the Episcopal Church in Jerusalem and the Middle East, Djibouti lies within the jurisdiction of the Bishop in Egypt.

Other Christian Churches

Eglise Protestante: blvd de la République, BP 416, Djibouti; tel. 351820; fax 350706; e-mail eped@intnet.dj; f. 1957; Pastor FRANCIS MULLER.

Greek Orthodox Church: blvd de la République, Djibouti; tel. 351325; c. 350 adherents; Archimandrite STAVROS GEORGANAS.

The Ethiopian Orthodox Church is also active in Djibouti.

The Press

L'Atout: Palais du peuple, Djibouti; twice a year; publ. by the Centre National de la Promotion Culturelle et Artistique.

Carrefour Africain: BP 393, Djibouti; fax 354916; fortnightly; publ. by the Roman Catholic mission; circ. 500.

La Nation de Djibouti: place du 27 juin, BP 32, Djibouti; tel. 352201; fax 353937; internet www.lanation.dj; weekly; Dir ABDOUL-RASHID IDRISS; circ. 4,300.

Le Progrès: Djibouti; weekly; publ. by the RPP; Publr ALI MOHAMED HUMAD.

Le Renouveau: Djibouti; weekly; independent; Editor-in-Chief DAHER AHMED FARAH.

La République: Djibouti; weekly; independent; Editor-in-Chief AMIR ADAWEH.

Revue de l'ISERT: BP 486, Djibouti; tel. 352795; twice a year; publ. by the Institut Supérieur d'Etudes et de Recherches Scientifiques et Techniques (ISERT).

Le Temps: Djibouti; opposition newspaper; Owners MOUSSA AHMED IDRIS, ALI MEIDAL WAIS.

NEWS AGENCIES

Agence Djiboutienne d'Information (ADJI): 1 rue de Moscou, BP 32, Djibouti; tel. 354013; fax 354037; e-mail adi@intent.dj; internet www.adi.dj; f. 1978.

Foreign Bureau

Agence France-Presse (AFP): BP 97, Djibouti; tel. 352294; Correspondent KHALID HAIDAR ABDALLAH.

Broadcasting and Communications

TELECOMMUNICATIONS

Djibouti Telecom: 3 blvd G. Pompidou, BP 2105, Djibouti; tel. 351110; fax 355757; e-mail Djibouti_telecom@intent.dj; internet www.intent.dj; f. 1999 to replace Société des Télécommunications Internationales; 100% state-owned; Dir-Gen. MOHAMED KAMIL ALI.

BROADCASTING

Radio and Television

Radiodiffusion-Télévision de Djibouti (RTD): BP 97, Djibouti; tel. and fax 352294; e-mail mo_hoche@hotmail.com; internet www.rtd.dj; f. 1957; state-controlled; programmes in French, Afar, Somali and Arabic; 17 hours radio and 5 hours television daily; Dir-Gen. (Radio) ABDI ATTEYEH ABDI; Dir-Gen. (Television) MOHAMED DJAMA ADEN.

Finance

(cap. = capital; res = reserves; dep. = deposits; m. = million; brs = branches; amounts in Djibouti francs)

BANKING

Central Bank

Banque Centrale de Djibouti: BP 2118, ave St Laurent du Var, Djibouti; tel. 352751; fax 356288; e-mail bndj@intnet.dj; internet www.banque-centrale.dj; f. 1977; bank of issue; cap. and res 2,179.2m. (Dec. 2001); Gov. DJAMA MAHAMOUD HAID; Dir AHMED OSMAN ALI.

Commercial Banks

Banque Indosuez—Mer Rouge (BIS—MR): 10 place Lagarde, BP 88, Djibouti; tel. 353016; fax 351638; e-mail indomr@intnet.dj; f. 1908; owned by Crédit Agricole Indosuez (France); cap. 1,500m., res 427.4m., dep. 18,784m. (Dec. 2000); Chair. and CEO JEAN-BERNARD ANGLADA.

Banque pour le Commerce et l'Industrie—Mer Rouge (BCI—MR): place Lagarde, BP 2122, Djibouti; tel. 350857; fax 354260; e-mail bcimr@intnet.dj; f. 1954; 51% owned by Banque Nationale de Paris Intercontinentale; cap. 3,000m.(Dec. 2001); Pres. VINCENT DE ROUX; Gen. Man. GUY CAZENAVE; 8 brs.

Investment Bank of Africa: Djibouti; f. 2000; subsidiary of AFH Holding (Luxembourg); cap. 300m. CEO ILIA KARAS.

Development Bank

Banque de Développement de Djibouti: angle ave Georges Clemenceau et rue Pierre Curie, BP 520, Djibouti; tel. 353391; fax 355022; f. 1983; 39.2% govt-owned; total assets 3,081m., cap. and res 1,233m. (Dec. 1997); Dir-Gen. ABDOURAHMAN ISMAEL GELLEH.

Banking Association

Association Professionnelle des Banques: c/o Banque pour le Commerce et l'Industrie—Mer Rouge, place Lagarde, BP 2122, Djibouti; tel. 350857; fax 354260; Pres. MOHAMED ADEN.

INSURANCE

Les Assureurs de la Mer Rouge et du Golfe Arabe (AMERGA): Djibouti; f. 2000; Dirs THIERRY MARILL, LUC MARILL, ABDURAHMAN BARKAT ABDILLAHI, MOHAMED ADEN ABUBAKER.

Boucher Assurances: AGF—Assurances Générales de France, rue Marchand, BP 200, Djibouti; tel. 353636; fax 353056; Country Man. CHRISTIAN BOUCHER.

Ethiopian Insurance Corpn: rue de Marseille, BP 2047, Djibouti; tel. 352306.

Trade and Industry

CHAMBER OF COMMERCE

Chambre Internationale de Commerce et d'Industrie: BP 84, Place de Lagarde, Djibouti; tel. 351070; fax 350096; e-mail cicid@ intent.dj; internet www.intnet.dj/public/cicid/index.html; f. 1906; 24 mems, 12 assoc. mems; Pres. SAID ALI COUBECHE; First Vice-Pres. ABDOURAHMAN MAHAMOUD BOREH.

TRADE ASSOCIATION

Office National d'Approvisionnement et de Commercialisation (ONAC): BP 119, Djibouti; tel. 350327; Chair. MOHAMED ABDULKADER.

UTILITIES

Electricity

Electricité de Djibouti (EdD): c/o Ministry of Trade and Industry, BP 1846, Djibouti; tel. 351682; Dir-Gen. DJAMA ALI GELLEH.

Water

Office National des Eaux de Djibouti (ONED): c/o Ministry of Trade and Industry, BP 1846, Djibouti; tel. 351682.

Société des Eaux de Tadjourah: c/o Ministry of Trade and Industry, BP 1846, Djibouti; tel. 351682.

TRADE UNION

Union Générale du Travail: Djibouti; f. 1992 to succeed Union Générale des Travailleurs de Djibouti; confed. of 22 trade unions; Chair. YUSSUF MOHAMED; Sec.-Gen. ADEN MOHAMED ARDOU.

Transport

RAILWAYS

Chemin de Fer Djibouti–Ethiopien (CDE): BP 2116, Djibouti; POB 1051, Addis Ababa; tel. 350280; fax 351256; tel. 517250; fax 513533; f. 1909; adopted present name in 1981; jtly-owned by Govts of Djibouti and Ethiopia; 781 km of track (121 km in Djibouti) linking Djibouti with Addis Ababa; Pres. SALEH OMAR HILDID; Dir-Gen. ALI ABDALLAH GADID.

ROADS

In 1996 there were an estimated 2,890 km of roads, comprising 1,090 km of main roads and 1,800 km of regional roads; some 12.6% of the roads were paved. Of the remainder, 1,000 km are serviceable throughout the year, the rest only during the dry season. About one-half of the roads are usable only by heavy vehicles. In 1981 the 40-km Grand Bara road was opened, linking the capital with the south.

In 1986 the Djibouti–Tadjourah road, the construction of which was financed by Saudi Arabia, was opened, linking the capital with the north. In 1996 the Islamic Development Bank granted Djibouti a loan of US $3.6m. to finance road construction projects.

SHIPPING

Djibouti, which was established as a free port in 1981, handled 808,000 metric tons of freight in 1998.

Port Autonome International de Djibouti: BP 2107, Djibouti; tel. 352331; fax 356187; e-mail luc.deruyver@port.dj; internet www .port.dj; Man. Dir LUC DERUYVER.

Maritime and Transit Service: rue de Marseille, BP 680, Djibouti; tel. 353204; fax 354149.

Principal Shipping Agents

Almis Shipping Line & Transport Co: BP 85, Djibouti; tel. 356996; fax 356998; Man. Dir MOHAMED NOOR.

Cie Générale Maritime: 3 rue Marchand, BP 182, Djibouti; tel. 353825; fax 354778; Gen. Man. HENRI FERRAND.

Cie Maritime et de Manutention de Djibouti: ave des Messageries Maritimes, BP 89, Djibouti; tel. 351028; fax 350466; e-mail comad@intnet.dj; internet www.intnet.dj/comad/index.htm; shipping agents and freight forwarders; Man. Dir ALI A. HETTAM.

Inchcape Shipping Services & Co (Djibouti) SA: 9–11 rue de Genève, BP 81, Djibouti; tel. 353844; fax 353294; e-mail iss@intnet .dj; f. 1942; Dir-Gen. AHMED OSMAN GELLEH.

J. J. Kothari & Co Ltd: rue d'Athens, BP 171, Djibouti; tel. 350219; fax 351778; e-mail kothari@intnet.dj; shipping agents; also ship managers, stevedores, freight forwarders; Dirs S. J. KOTHARI, NALIN KOTHARI.

Mitchell Cotts Djibouti SARL: blvd de la République, BP 85, Djibouti; tel. 351204; fax 355851; Dir FAHMY SAID CASSIM.

Société Maritime L. Savon et Ries: blvd Cheikh Osman, BP 2125, Djibouti; tel. 352351; fax 351103; Gen. Man. J. P. DELARUE.

CIVIL AVIATION

The international airport is at Ambouli, 6 km from Djibouti. There are six other airports providing domestic services.

Air Djibouti (Red Sea Airlines): BP 499, rue Marchand, Djibouti; tel. 356723; fax 356734; f. 1971; fmrly govt-owned, transferred to private ownership in 1997; internal flights and international services to destinations in Africa, the Middle East and Europe; Chair. SAAD BEN MOUSSA AL-JANAIBI.

Daallo Airlines: BP 2565, Djibouti; tel. 353401; fax 351765; internet www.daallo.com; f. 1992; operates services to Somalia, Saudi Arabia, the United Arab Emirates, France and the Netherlands; Man. Dir MOHAMED IBRAHIM YASSIN.

Djibouti Airlines (Puntavia Airline de Djibouti): BP 2240, place Lagarde, Djibouti; tel. 351006; fax 352429; f. 1996; scheduled and charter regional and domestic flights; Man. Dir Mr VABERI.

Tourism

Djibouti offers desert scenery in its interior and watersport facilities on its coast. A casino operates in the capital. There were about 20,000 tourist arrivals in 1998, when receipts from tourism totalled US $4m.

Office National du Tourisme de Djibouti (ONTD): place du 27 juin, BP 1938, Djibouti; tel. 353790; fax 356322; e-mail onta@intnet .dj; internet www.office-tourisme.dj; Dir MOHAMED ABDILLAHI WAIS.

DOMINICA

Introductory Survey

Location, Climate, Language, Religion, Flag, Capital

The Commonwealth of Dominica is situated in the Windward Islands group of the West Indies, lying between Guadeloupe, to the north, and Martinique, to the south. The climate is tropical, though tempered by sea winds which sometimes reach hurricane force, especially from July to September. The average temperature is about 27°C (80°F), with little seasonal variation. Rainfall is heavy, especially in the mountainous areas, where the annual average is 6,350 mm (250 ins), compared with 1,800 mm (70 ins) along the coast. English is the official language, but a local French patois, or Creole, is widely spoken. In parts of the north-east an English dialect, known as Cocoy, is spoken by the descendants of Antiguan settlers. There is a small community of Carib Indians on the east coast. Almost all of the inhabitants profess Christianity, and about 80% are Roman Catholics. The national flag (proportions 1 by 2) has a green field, with equal stripes of yellow, white and black forming an upright cross, on the centre of which is superimposed a red disc containing a parrot surrounded by ten five-pointed green stars (one for each of the island's parishes). The capital is Roseau.

Recent History

Dominica was first settled by Arawaks and then Caribs. Control of the island was fiercely contested by the Caribs, British and French during the 17th and 18th centuries. The British eventually prevailed and Dominica formed part of the Leeward Islands federation until 1939. In 1940 it was transferred to the Windward Islands and remained attached to that group until the federal arrangement was ended in December 1959. Under a new Constitution, effective from January 1960, Dominica (like each other member of the group) achieved a separate status, with its own Administrator and an enlarged Legislative Council.

At the January 1961 elections to the Legislative Council, the ruling Dominica United People's Party was defeated by the Dominica Labour Party (DLP), formed from the People's National Movement and other groups. Edward LeBlanc, leader of the DLP, became Chief Minister. In March 1967 Dominica became one of the West Indies Associated States, gaining full autonomy in internal affairs, with the United Kingdom retaining responsibility for defence and foreign relations. The House of Assembly replaced the Legislative Council, the Administrator became Governor and the Chief Minister was restyled Premier. At elections to the House in October 1970, LeBlanc was returned to power as Premier.

In July 1974 LeBlanc retired, and was replaced as DLP leader and Premier by Patrick John, formerly Deputy Premier and Minister of Finance. At elections to the enlarged House of Assembly in March 1975 the DLP was returned to power. Following a decision in 1975 by the Associated States to seek independence separately, Dominica became an independent republic within the Commonwealth on 3 November 1978. John became Prime Minister, and Frederick Degazon, formerly Speaker of the House of Assembly, was eventually elected President.

In May 1979 two people were killed by the Defence Force at a demonstration against the Government's attempts to introduce legislation that would restrict the freedom of the trade unions and the press. The deaths fuelled increasing popular opposition to the Government, and a pressure group, the Committee for National Salvation (CNS), was formed to campaign for John's resignation. Government opponents organized a general strike which lasted 25 days, with John relinquishing power only after all his cabinet ministers had resigned and President Degazon had gone into hiding abroad (there was a succession of Acting Presidents; Degazon finally resigned in February 1980). Oliver Seraphin, the candidate proposed by the CNS, was elected Prime Minister, and an interim Government was formed to prepare for a general election after six months.

A general election was eventually held in July 1980, when the Dominica Freedom Party (DFP) achieved a convincing victory, winning 17 of the 21 elective seats in the House of Assembly. Eugenia Charles, the party's leader, became the Caribbean's first female Prime Minister. Both John, who contested the election as leader of the DLP, and Seraphin, who stood as leader of the newly-formed Democratic Labour Party (DEMLAB), lost their seats. The DLP and DEMLAB had both suffered from major political scandals prior to the election.

Fears for the island's security dominated 1981. In January the Government disarmed the Defence Force (which was officially disbanded in April), following reports that weapons were being traded for marijuana. Against a background of increasing violence and the declaration of a state of emergency, however, there were two coup attempts involving former Defence Force members. John, the former Prime Minister, was also implicated and imprisoned. In June 1982 John and his fellow prisoners were tried and acquitted, but the Government secured a retrial in October 1985. John and the former Deputy Commander of the Defence Force each received a prison sentence of 12 years (they were released in May 1990). In 1986 the former Commander of the Defence Force was hanged for the murder of a police officer during the second coup attempt. The death sentences on five other soldiers were commuted to life imprisonment.

After his release in June 1982, John attempted to form a new left-wing coalition party. By 1985 the DLP, DEMLAB, the United Dominica Labour Party and the Dominica Liberation Movement had united to form a left-wing grouping, known as the Labour Party of Dominica (LPD). The new leader, however, was Michael Douglas, a former Minister of Finance. At a general election in July 1985 the DFP was returned to power, winning 15 of the 21 elective seats in the House of Assembly. The opposition LPD won five seats, with the remaining seat being won by Roosevelt (Rosie) Douglas, the brother of the LPD leader, whose candidature was not officially endorsed by the LPD. Following the election, the LPD began an 18-month boycott of the House, in protest at the Government's decision to curtail live broadcasts of parliamentary proceedings. By July 1987, the DFP's strength in the House had increased to 17 seats, with four seats still being held by the LPD.

Dissatisfaction at continued government austerity measures was offset by the success of the land reform programme. Since independence, the Government had acquired nearly all the large estates, often in an attempt to forestall violence. In 1986 the first of the estates was divided, and tenure granted to the former workers. Despite the success of this programme, the opposition LPD and the Dominica United Workers' Party (UWP—formed in 1988) bitterly denounced many other government policies and criticized Charles's style of leadership. The two opposition parties failed to agree on the formation of an electoral alliance, however, and the DFP was returned for a third term in government at a general election in May 1990. The DFP won a total of 11 seats, the UWP became the official opposition (with six seats) and the LPD won four seats. The results were reported to indicate the electorate's disenchantment with the traditional parties; participation and voting preferences were determined by personality rather than policy.

A programme, introduced in 1991, granting Dominican citizenship to foreigners in return for a minimum investment of US $35,000 in the country caused considerable controversy during 1992. The UWP expressed opposition to the policy, and a pressure group, 'Concerned Citizens', organized protests demanding that the programme be modified. In response to such pressure, the Government announced in July that the minimum investment was to be increased substantially, the number of applications was to be limited to 800 and restrictions were to be placed on the investors' right to vote in Dominica. By early 1995 some 615 people (mainly Taiwanese) had been granted citizenship under the scheme, and about US $7.1m. had been invested in the country.

In 1993, following the retirement of President Clarence Seignoret, Crispin Sorhaindo, formerly the Speaker of the House of Assembly, was appointed to the presidency. He assumed office in October.

At a general election in June 1995 the DFP's 15-year tenure was finally ended, with the party winning only five seats. The LPD also won five seats, while the UWP secured a narrow victory, with 11 seats. Some observers attributed the DFP's poor performance in the election to Charles's failure to give full support to her successor, Brian Alleyne, upon her retirement. The leader of the UWP, Edison James, was subsequently appointed as Prime Minister, and the LPD and DFP leaders agreed to occupy the position of Leader of the Opposition in alternate years, commencing with Alleyne. In July a legal dispute arose concerning the eligibility to serve in the House of Assembly of one of the DFP's members, Charles Savarin, owing to a potential conflict of interests. As a result of the dispute, the position of Leader of the Opposition was transferred to the LPD leader, Rosie Douglas. In April 1996, however, Savarin was elected leader of the DFP following Alleyne's resignation, which had been prompted by his appointment as a judge in Grenada. Government support for a long-term programme to privatize several state-owned enterprises and to implement structural adjustment measures (recommended by the International Monetary Fund—IMF) attracted criticism from the opposition in 1996–97, as well as from the Civil Service Association, which pledged its resistance to any retrenchment in the sector.

In April 1997 an investigation of the police force was conducted, following allegations of corruption. In November the Prime Minister announced that the Police Commissioner, Desmond Blanchard, his deputy and five other officers had been sent on leave, owing to the findings of the report. In April 1998 Rosie Douglas announced that he was taking legal action against the Government, on the grounds that it had acted unconstitutionally by failing to give him a copy of the report. Meanwhile, in 1997 the Government established a Constitutional Commission to examine several issues, including civil rights, standards in public service, the responsibility of politicians and public involvement in government.

In December 1997 the Government's citizenship programme (see above) again provoked controversy. *The Independent Newspaper* reported that, under the scheme, passports were being sold by agents for between US $15,000 and $20,000, and claimed that about 400 people (including 80 Russians and 50 Chinese) had acquired citizenship in 1997. The opposition LPD accused the Government of undermining the credibility of Dominican citizenship, and in August 1998 Rosie Douglas demanded an inquiry into the programme, following an administrative error which had allowed an Australian, who was sought by investigators in connection with a business collapse, to acquire citizenship. In late 1999 it was announced that the Dominican Government had stopped granting citizenship to Russians, following reports that up to 300 Russians had paid US $50,000 each to obtain a Dominican passport. In addition, there were complaints from the US Government that the trade in passports had increased 'suspicions of money laundering' in Dominica.

In early 1998 the LPD complained to the Electoral Boundaries Commission, accusing the Government of proposing changes to the boundaries of six electoral constituencies (four of which were regarded as LPD strongholds) purely for political gain. In November the High Court upheld the opposition's complaint, ruling that the proposed alterations were unconstitutional. (This judgment was endorsed by the Eastern Caribbean Court of Appeal in May 1999.)

In early October 1998 President Sorhaindo's five-year term in office ended. Following the failure of the Prime Minister and the Leader of the Opposition to agree on a joint nominee, the House of Assembly held a secret ballot to elect the new President. Vernon Shaw, a former cabinet secretary in the previous administration of Eugenia Charles, was duly elected and assumed the presidency on 6 October.

On 1 January 2000 the Prime Minister unexpectedly called a general election, to be held on 31 January. The DFP accused James of breaking a 1995 undertaking to give at least 90 days' notice of an election (which was not due constitutionally until June), and formed an electoral alliance with the LPD. The UWP suffered a narrow electoral defeat, while the LPD was returned to power after two decades in opposition, winning 10 of the 21 elective seats in the House of Assembly and receiving 42.9% of total votes cast. The UWP secured nine seats (with 43.4% of the votes), and the DFP won two. The leader of the LPD, Rosie Douglas, was named as Prime Minister and formed a coalition Government with the DFP (which was allocated two ministerial portfolios).

On taking office, the new Government immediately suspended the controversial citizenship programme. However, following a review, in April 2000 the Government announced that the programme should be resumed, claiming that changes had been made to ensure that passports would not be granted to those with a criminal record. The programme was relaunched in June 2002, with a fee of US $100,000 for individual applicants.

In July 2000 Atherton Martin, the Minister for Agriculture, Planning and the Environment, resigned from his post after the Government voted against the establishment of a South Pacific whaling sanctuary at a meeting of the International Whaling Commission in Australia. The vote was reported to be contrary to a cabinet agreement to abstain. Martin claimed that Japan had threatened to withdraw funding for two fish processing plants in Dominica if the Government abstained, and accused the Japanese Government of 'international extortion'. Lloyd Pascal, hitherto Dominica's whaling commissioner, replaced Martin.

On 1 October 2000 the Prime Minister, Rosie Douglas, died suddenly of a heart attack. Two days later, following a vote in the House of Assembly, Pierre Charles, previously the Minister of Communications and Works, was sworn in as premier. Reginald Austrie succeeded him as Minister of Communications and Works. On 11 December a by-election for Douglas's seat was won by his nephew, Ian Douglas, the candidate of the LPD, thus maintaining the Government's narrow parliamentary majority.

In December 2000 legislation was passed in the House of Assembly making the crime of money-laundering punishable by up to seven years' imprisonment and a fine of EC $1m. At the same time, the Government introduced stricter regulations governing its 'offshore' banking sector, following Dominica's inclusion on a blacklist published by the Financial Action Task Force (FATF) earlier in the year. Dominica was removed from the blacklist in October 2002, in light of the progress the Government had made in improving its anti-money-laundering measures. Part of these measures was the approval, in December 2001, of the Exchange of Information Bill, designed to give foreign authorities greater access to information about Dominica's offshore banks.

In March 2001 Charles was confirmed as leader of the DLP at the party's conference. Ambrose George, the Minister of Finance, was elected deputy leader. In June John Toussaint, the Minister of Health and Social Society, and Bernard Wilshire, the Attorney-General, were replaced by Herbert Sabroache and David Bruney (both of the DFP), respectively. However, Bruney resigned in October, citing differences with the Prime Minister as his main reason. Henry Dyer was sworn in as Bruney's replacement later that month.

In November 2001 Charles placed Ambrose George on two weeks' leave following the arrest on money-laundering charges of a businessman with whom he was travelling in Puerto Rico. Upon his return to government, and in the light of Dominica's place on the FATF blacklist, George was stripped of the finance portfolio, which passed to Charles, and given the post of Minister of Industry, Physical Planning and Enterprise Development. Osborne Riviere took over responsibility for foreign and Carib affairs, a portfolio hitherto held by the Prime Minister.

In June 2002 the Government announced its intention to reduce the size of the Cabinet by 1 August by revoking three ministries and five advisory positions, in an attempt to reduce expenditure. Consequently, the Minister of Industry, Planning and Physical Development, Ambrose George, and two ministers of state resigned. George's portfolios were shared between Charles Savarin and Reginald Austrie. In July the Public Service Union (PSU) organized a large-scale demonstration in the capital, Roseau, to protest against controversial tax increases introduced in a budget that was intended to engender economic recovery. In November a DFP deputy, dissatisfied with the Prime Minister's handling of the economic crisis, withdrew his support from the Government, leaving the governing coalition with a majority of one seat. Encouraged by this, the UWP attempted to force a vote of 'no confidence' in the Government; the motion failed, but the coalition's hold on power continued to look precarious in early 2003. In February 2003 the PSU, objecting to Government proposals to reduce the size of the public-sector work-force and to force workers to take two days of unpaid leave every month, organized an six-day strike. The strike ended after the Government agreed to review its proposal to reduce the public-sector wage bill. The industrial action further damaged the position of the embattled Government and possibly jeopardized the granting of a structural adjustment loan from the World Bank.

In foreign policy, Dominica has close links with France and the USA. France helped in suppressing the coup attempts against the DFP Government in 1981, and Dominica was the first Commonwealth country to benefit from the French aid agency FAC. In October 1983 Dominica, as a member of the Organisation of Eastern Caribbean States (OECS, see p. 341), contributed forces to the US-backed invasion of Grenada. In 1988 four countries of the Windward group (Dominica, Grenada, Saint Lucia and Saint Vincent and the Grenadines) decided to proceed with plans for the formation of a political union. In 1990 the four countries decided to convene a constituent assembly, which in early 1992 agreed a draft constitution, including provision for the election of an executive president by universal suffrage. Following its election in mid-1995, the Government of Edison James stated its commitment to further economic integration of the Windward Islands, leading to political union. In 2001 Libya granted Dominica, in common with other eastern Caribbean islands, access to a US $2,000m. development fund. It was also reported in September that Libya had agreed to purchase Dominican bananas at high prices and would provide the island with an immediate grant of US $4m. In October Charles and the Cuban Minister of Foreign Affairs, Felipe Pérez Roque, signed a bilateral accord on tourism; they also agreed to co-operate further in trade and commerce.

Government

Legislative power is vested in the unicameral House of Assembly, comprising 30 members (nine nominated and 21 elected for five years by universal adult suffrage). Executive authority is vested in the President, who is elected by the House, but in most matters the President is guided by the advice of the Cabinet and acts as the constitutional Head of State. He appoints the Prime Minister, who must be able to command a majority in the House, and (on the Prime Minister's recommendation) other ministers. The Cabinet is responsible to the House. The island is divided into 10 administrative divisions, known as parishes, and there is limited local government in Roseau, the capital, and in the Carib Territory.

Defence

The Dominican Defence Force was officially disbanded in 1981. There is a police force of about 300, which includes a coastguard service. The country participates in the US-sponsored Regional Security System.

Economic Affairs

In 2001, according to estimates by the World Bank, Dominica's gross national income (GNI), measured at average 1999–2001 prices, was US $224m., equivalent to US $3,060 per head (or $5,040 per head on an international purchasing-power parity basis). Between 1990 and 2001 the population increased by an average annual rate of of 0.1%, while gross domestic product (GDP) per head increased, in real terms, by an average of 1.0% per year. Overall GDP increased, in real terms, by an average of 1.1% per year in 1990–2001; GDP increased by 0.2% in 2000, but decreased by 4.7% in 2001.

Agriculture (including forestry and fishing) is the principal economic activity, accounting for an estimated 15.7% of GDP in 2001. In 1997 the sector engaged 23.7% of the employed labour force. The principal cash crop is bananas. The banana industry, which was already experiencing difficulties (owing to a decline in prices), was adversely affected by a September 1997 ruling of the World Trade Organization (WTO, see p. 323) against Dominica's preferential access to the European (particularly the British) market. In 1998 banana production decreased by some 27%, to some 30,000 metric tons, while receipts from banana exports fell by 8.9% to EC $42.2m. (some 24.8% of total domestic exports). In 1999, according to the FAO, banana output remained at the same level; however, production was estimated to have increased slightly in 2000 and 2001 (to 31,000 tons and 33,000 tons, respectively). In 2001 receipts from banana exports totalled US $8.2m. (some 18.1% of total domestic exports). Other important crops include coconuts (which provide copra for export as well as edible oil and soap), mangoes, avocados, papayas, ginger, citrus fruits and, mainly for domestic consumption, vegetables. Non-banana crops have grown in significance during recent years, from one-half of total crop production to about two-thirds in 2002. Livestock-rearing and fishing are also practised for local purposes. In early 2002 a US $10m., Japanese-funded renovation of the Roseau Fisheries Complex was near completion. In addition, 12 smaller, Japanese-funded, fisheries projects were also due to get under way later in the year, and research into the construction of another multi-purpose fisheries complex in Portsmouth was expected to commence in March. Dominica has extensive timber reserves

(more than 40% of the island's total land area is forest and woodland), and international aid agencies are encouraging the development of a balanced timber industry. The GDP of the agricultural sector decreased at an average annual rate of 4.3% in 1997–2001. In real terms, agricultural GDP declined by 1.1% in 2000 and by an estimated 11.5% in 2001.

Industry (comprising mining, manufacturing, construction and utilities) provided 20.9% of GDP in 2001, and employed 18.2% of the employed labour force in 1997. Real industrial GDP decreased at an average rate of 0.4% per year during 1997–2001; the sector increased by 4.3% in 2000, but decreased by an estimated 6.6% in 2001. Manufacturing activity is mainly small-scale and dependent upon agriculture. The mining sector contributed only 0.7% of GDP in 2001. There is some quarrying of pumice, and there are extensive reserves of limestone and clay. In 1996 an Australian mining company began investigations into the possible exploitation of extensive copper deposits in north-eastern Dominica. Pumice is useful to the construction industry, which accounted for 7.5% of GDP in 2001, and employed 8.4% of the employed labour force in 1997. Extensive infrastructure development by the Government has maintained high levels of activity in the construction sector in recent years. The GDP of the construction sector decreased at an average annual rate of 0.9%, in real terms, during 1997–2001; the sector's GDP increased by 2.0% in 2000, but decreased by an estimated 4.8% in 2001. The Government has also encouraged the manufacturing sector in an attempt to diversify the economy. In 2001 manufacturing contributed 7.2% of GDP and, in 1997, employed 8.8% of the employed work-force. Real manufacturing GDP decreased at an average rate of 2.8% per year during 1997–2001; it rose by 16.9% in 1998, largely owing to an 16.6% increase in the output of soap products, but also to the production of toothpaste, which began in November 1997. However, in 1999, a significant decline in soap production (of some 25.6%) resulted in a 3.0% contraction in the sector. In 2000 the manufacturing sector again increased strongly, by 8.2%; however, the sector's GDP decreased by an estimated 14.6% in 2001. There is a banana-packaging plant and factories for the manufacturing and refining of crude and edible vegetable oils and for the production of soap, canned juices and cigarettes. A brewery was established in 1995 to supply domestic requirements. Furniture, paint, cardboard boxes and candles are also significant manufactures.

In 2000 70% of Dominica's energy requirements were supplied by hydroelectric power. Investment in a hydroelectric development scheme and in the water supply system has been partially financed by the export of water, from Dominica's extensive reserves, to drier Caribbean islands such as Aruba. A hydroelectric power-station, with a generating capacity of 1.24 MW, began operation at Laudat in 1990. In 2000 Dominica's imports of mineral fuels totalled 9.7% of the cost of total imports. In 1998 a geothermal energy project in Soufrière began producing electricity, following investment of EC $25m. from a US company. In December 1996 the state-owned Dominica Electricity Services (Domlec) was privatized, with the British Government's overseas private finance institution, the Commonwealth Development Corporation (CDC), buying 72% of the company. The CDC outlined planned to increase electricity generation by 80% by 2000. Construction of a new 20-MW electric power plant, at an estimated cost of EC $80m., was scheduled for completion by early 2001. In November 2000 a demonstration took place outside Domlec's headquarters in protest at the company's failure to improve efficiency following its transfer to the private sector.

Services engaged 53.8% of the employed labour force in 1997, and provided 63.4% of GDP in 2001. The combined GDP of the service sectors increased at an average rate of 1.8% per year during 1997–2001; in 2000 the sector grew by 12.9%, but declined by an estimated 13.8% in 2001. The tourist industry is of increasing importance to the economy and exploits Dominica's natural history and scenery. Since 1998 the Government has placed considerable emphasis on the country's potential as an 'eco-tourism' destination, pursuing a development programme funded by the European Union (EU). The majority of tourists are cruise-ship passengers. Arrivals from cruise ships increased from 6,777 in 1990 to 64,762 in the following year, and by 1998 totalled 244,603. Following a decline in 1999, to 202,003, cruise-ship arrivals recovered strongly in 2000, to 239,544. However, this figure decreased again in 2001, to an estimated 207,627. In 2001 tourism receipts totalled an estimated EC $130.0m. In 1990 the Government decided to proceed with the construction of an international airport. However, in 2003 proposals for the project were still under review, although the Republic of China (Taiwan) had pledged US $35m.

In 2001 Dominica recorded a visible trade deficit of US $70.89m. and a deficit of US $48.86m. on the current account of the balance of payments. The principal source of imports in 2000 was the USA, which accounted for 37.5% of total imports, followed by Trinidad and Tobago (16.3%) and the United Kingdom (7.7%). The principal market for exports is the United Kingdom, which receives virtually all Dominica's banana production, taking 24.8% of total domestic exports in 2000, followed by Jamaica, which, received 23.7% of total exports. The principal imports in 2001 were machinery and transport equipment, food products and tobacco and basic manufactures (such as paper). The principal exports in the same year were soap and bananas.

In 2001, according to preliminary ECCB figures, there was an estimated budget deficit of EC $61m. At the end of 2000 Dominica's total external debt was US $108.2m., of which US $89.2m. was long-term public debt. In 1999 the cost of debt-servicing was equivalent to 7.3% of the value of exports of goods and services. The annual rate of inflation averaged 1.5% in 1995–2001; consumer prices increased by an average of 0.8% in 2000 and by 1.9% in 2001. An estimated 23.1% of the labour force were unemployed in 1997.

Dominica is a member of the Organization of American States (OAS, see p. 288), the Caribbean Community and Common Market (CARICOM (see p. 155), the OECS, and is a signatory of the Cotonou Agreement, the successor arrangement to the Lomé Conventions between the African, Caribbean and Pacific (ACP) countries and the European Union (see p. 199). Dominica is also a member of the Eastern Caribbean Securities Exchange (based in Saint Christopher and Nevis). Under the Charles administration, the island received considerable overseas aid.

The Dominican economy is heavily dependent on the production of coconut-based products and bananas, and their export to a limited market, and is thus vulnerable to adverse weather conditions, price fluctuations and economic conditions in its principal markets. The slowdown, and then contraction, in economic growth in 1999–2001 was largely attributable to the weak performance of the major productive sectors. In the 1990s growth in the economy slowed, owing to the uncertainty surrounding Dominica's preferential access to the European market and the devastation of the 1995 banana crop by a hurricane. Efforts to expand the country's economic base have been impeded by poor infrastructure and, in terms of tourism, a paucity of desirable beaches. During the 1990s the Government succeeded in expanding the tourist sector, aided by an 'eco-tourism' development programme with EU funding. None the less, according to preliminary figures, there was a decrease in both visitor arrivals and gross visitor expenditure in 2001. Tourist arrivals reportedly decreased by a further 29% in the first nine months of 2002. Banana exports decreased in both 1998 and 1999, owing to drought, a fall in producer prices and uncertainties caused by the continuing dispute over the EU's banana import regime. Many marginal farmers were unable to attain the new stringent quality standards of the industry, another contributing factor in the decline in banana output. Banana production failed to recover in 2001, owing to labour shortages and dry weather conditions and exports continued to fall in 2002. The end to the banana trade dispute in April 2001 was expected to have further adverse effects on the sector in the early years of the 21st century (from 2006 the EU's import regime was to be replaced by a universal tariff system). In 2002 the Government announced the proposed privatization of the Banana Marketing Corporation. In recent years the public

finances have weakened considerably, owing to an increase in expenditure caused by a rising wage bill and debt-servicing obligations, as well as a concurrent decrease in savings and foreign grants. In spite of the introduction, beginning in 1998, of value-added tax (VAT), in 2001 Dominica's tax system remained inefficient, with its narrow base, collection difficulties and substantial exemptions contributing to stagnating revenues. In 2002 structural reforms were planned in the areas of taxation policy and public administration, privatization and agricultural diversification. Austerity measures announced in July and contained in the 2002/03 budget included a reduction in the number of cabinet ministers, increases in fuel, sales and telephone-service taxes, and higher fees for passports and postage stamps. In addition, parliament approved an extra, reportedly temporary, 4% income tax, known as the 'Stabilization Levy', to be paid by virtually every earner. In August, in support of the reforms, the IMF agreed to provide a one-year US $4.3m. stand-by credit for Dominica, of which $2.7m. was to be available immediately. Furthermore, CARICOM leaders agreed to provide a $20m. support fund to the country to assist the stabilization programme. In the same month the EU made available $24.4m. for investment in eco-tourism, agriculture, road construction and development projects. Although the budget did not heed all of the recommendations made by the IMF (which had advised the Government to reduce the number of public employees by 10% and to cut public wages), nevertheless, proposed expenditure in 2002/03 was reduced by 15%, in an attempt to decrease the island's crippling fiscal deficit (estimated to be total some $30m. in 2002) and large external debt. According to reports, 2002 was likely to see a further, but less severe, contraction in real GDP.

Education

Education is free and is provided by both government and denominational schools. There are also a number of schools for the mentally and physically handicapped. Education is compulsory for 10 years between five and 15 years of age. Primary education begins at the age of five and lasts for seven years. Enrolment of children in the primary age-group was 70.7% in 1992. Secondary education, beginning at 12 years of age, lasts for five years. A teacher-training college and nursing school provide further education, and there is also a branch of the University of the West Indies on the island. In 1997 the Government announced plans to invest EC $17.9m., mainly financed by a World Bank loan, in a Basic Education Reform project. Estimated budgetary expenditure on schools was EC $4.1m. in 2001/02 (equivalent to 1.5% of total expenditure).

Public Holidays

2003: 1 January (New Year's Day), 2 January (Merchants' Holiday), 3–4 March (Masquerade, Carnival), 18 April (Good Friday), 21 April (Easter Monday), 5 May (May or Labour Day), 9 June (Whit Monday), 4 August (Emancipation, August Monday), 3 November (Independence Day), 4 November (Community Service Day), 25–26 December (Christmas).

2004: 1 January (New Year's Day), 2 January (Merchants' Holiday), 23–24 February (Masquerade, Carnival), 9 April (Good Friday), 12 April (Easter Monday), 3 May (May or Labour Day), 31 May (Whit Monday), 2 August (Emancipation, August Monday), 3 November (Independence Day), 4 November (Community Service Day), 25–26 December (Christmas).

Weights and Measures

The metric system is replacing the imperial system of weights and measures.

Statistical Survey

Sources (unless otherwise stated): Eastern Caribbean Central Bank, *Report and Statement of Accounts*.

AREA AND POPULATION

Area: 751 sq km (290 sq miles).

Population: 71,183 at census of 12 May 1991; 71,727 (males 36,434, females 35,293) at census of 12 May 2001.

Density (May 2001): 95.5 per sq km.

Population by Ethnic Group (*de jure* population, excl. those resident in institutions, 1981): Negro 67,272; Mixed race 4,433; Amerindian (Carib) 1,111; White 341; Total (incl. others) 73,795 (males 36,754, females 37,041). Source: UN, *Demographic Yearbook*.

Principal Town (population at 1991 census): Roseau (capital) 15,853. *Mid-2001:* (UN estimate, incl. suburbs): Roseau 26,000 (Source: UN, *World Urbanization Prospects: The 2001 Revision*).

Births, Marriages and Deaths (registrations, 2000): Live births 1,199 (birth rate 16.8 per 1,000); Marriages (1998) 336 (marriage rate 4.4 per 1,000); Deaths 503 (death rate 7.0 per 1,000). Source: UN, *Demographic Yearbook*.

Expectation of Life (WHO estimates, years at birth): 73.8 (males 71.6; females 76.0) in 2001. Source: WHO, *World Health Report*.

Economically Active Population (rounded estimates, persons aged 15 years and over, 1997): Agriculture, hunting, forestry and fishing 6,000; Fishing 100; Manufacturing 2,250; Electricity, gas and water supply 280; Construction 2,150; Wholesale and retail trade 4,050; Hotels and restaurants 980; Transport, storage and communications 1,500; Financial intermediation 540; Real estate, renting and business activities 850; Public administration, defence and social security 1,530; Education 1,260; Health and social work 1,110; Other community, social and personal service activities 930; Private households with employed persons 1,080; Not classifiable by economic activity 1,090; Total employed 25,690; Unemployed 7,720; Total labour force 33,420 (males 18,120; females 15,300). Source: ILO.

HEALTH AND WELFARE

Key Indicators

Total Fertility Rate (children per woman, 2001): 1.8.

Under-5 Mortality Rate (per 1,000 live births, 2001): 15.

Physicians (per 1,000 head, 1996): 49.3.

Hospital Beds (per 1,000 head, 1996): 2.64.

Health Expenditure (2000): US $ per head (PPP): 247.

Health Expenditure (2000): % of GDP: 6.1.

Health Expenditure (2000): public (% of total): 70.9.

Access to Water (% of persons, 2000): 97.

Human Development Index (2000): value: 0.779.

For sources and definitions, see explanatory note on p. vi.

AGRICULTURE, ETC.

Principal Crops (FAO estimates, '000 metric tons, 2001): Sweet potatoes 1.9; Cassava 1.0; Taro (Dasheen) 11.2; Yams 8.0; Other roots and tubers 4.8; Sugar cane 4.4; Coconuts 11.5; Cabbages 0.7; Pumpkins 0.8; Cucumbers 1.7; Carrots 0.5; Other vegetables 2.7; Bananas 33; Plantains 7.9; Oranges 7.2; Lemons and limes 1.0; Grapefruit 17.0; Mangoes 1.9; Avocados 0.6. Source: FAO.

Livestock (FAO estimates, '000 head, year ending September 2001): Cattle 13; Pigs 5; Sheep 8; Goats 10; Poultry 190. Source: FAO.

Livestock Products (FAO estimates, '000 metric tons, 2001): Beef and veal 0.5; Pig meat 0.4; Poultry meat 0.3; Cows' milk 6.1 (FAO estimate); Hen eggs 0.2. Source: FAO.

Fishing (FAO estimates, metric tons, live weight, 2000): Capture 1,150 (Wahoo 50, Skipjack tuna 85, Blackfin tuna 79, Yellowfin tuna 80); Aquaculture 7; Total catch 1,157. Source: FAO, *Yearbook of Fishery Statistics*.

MINING

Pumice ('000 metric tons, incl. volcanic ash): Estimated production 100 per year in 1988–2000. Source: US Geological Survey.

INDUSTRY

Production (preliminary, 2001, metric tons, unless otherwise indicated): Laundry soap 6,444; Toilet soap 3,749; Dental Cream 1,562; Hard surface cleansers 2,987; Crude coconut oil 855; Coconut meal 331; Electricity 39 million kWh (UN estimate, 1998). Sources: IMF, *Dominica: Statistical Appendix* (October 2002), and UN, *Industrial Commodity Statistics Yearbook*.

FINANCE

Currency and Exchange Rates: 100 cents = 1 Eastern Caribbean dollar (EC $). *Sterling, US Dollar and Euro Equivalents* (31 December 2002): £1 sterling = EC $4.351; US $1 = EC $2.700; €1 = EC $2.831; EC $100 = £22.98 = US $37.04 = €35.32. *Exchange Rate:* Fixed at US $1 = EC $2.70 since July 1976.

Budget (preliminary, EC $ million, 2001): *Revenue:* Tax revenue 161.9; Other current revenue 37.8; Capital revenue 3.2; Total 202.9, excl. grants received (34.3). *Expenditure:* Current expenditure 227.9 (Wages and salaries 123.3); Capital expenditure and net lending 70.2; Total 298.1.

International Reserves (US $ million at 31 December 2002): Reserve position in IMF 0.01; Foreign exchange 45.48; Total 45.49. Source: IMF, *International Financial Statistics*.

Money Supply (EC $ million at 31 December 2002): Currency outside banks 35.51; Demand deposits at commercial banks 92.51; Total money (incl. others) 128.90. Source: IMF, *International Financial Statistics*.

Cost of Living (Retail Price Index, base: 1995 = 100): All items 106.4 in 1999; 107.3 in 2000; 109.3 in 2001. Source: IMF, *International Financial Statistics*.

National Accounts (EC $ million at current prices): Gross domestic product in purchasers' values 722.6 in 1999; 728.0 in 2000; 710.4 (preliminary) in 2001. Source: IMF, *Dominica: Statistical Appendix* (October 2002).

Expenditure on the Gross Domestic Product (preliminary, EC $ million at current prices, 2001): Government final consumption expenditure 165.1; Private final consumption expenditure 483.5; Gross fixed capital formation (incl. increase in stocks) 151.6; *Total domestic expenditure* 800.2; Exports of goods and services 363.6; *Less* Imports of goods and services 453.4; GDP in purchasers' values 710.4. Source: IMF, *Dominica: Statistical Appendix* (October 2002).

Gross Domestic Product by Economic Activity (preliminary, EC $ million at current prices, 2001): Agriculture, hunting, forestry and fishing 103.3; Mining and quarrying 4.9; Manufacturing 47.2; Electricity and water 35.8; Construction 49.2; Wholesale and retail trade 71.7; Restaurants and hotels 14.9; Transport 53.9; Communications 44.2; Finance and insurance 71.6; Real estate and housing 21.3; Government services 128.4; Other services 9.7; Sub-total 656.1; *Less* imputed bank service charge 55.6; GDP at factor cost 600.5. Source: IMF, *Dominica: Statistical Appendix* (October 2002).

Balance of Payments (US $ million, 2001): Exports of goods f.o.b. 44.40; Imports of goods f.o.b. –115.29; *Trade balance* –70.89; Exports of services 75.75; Imports of services –51.65; *Balance on goods and services* –46.79; Other income received 3.64; Other income paid –23.18; *Balance on goods, services and income* –66.33; Current transfers received 24.77; Current transfers paid –7.30; *Current balance* –48.86; Capital account (net) 17.97; Direct investment from abroad 11.90; Portfolio investment assets 0.01; Portfolio investment liabilities –0.24; Other investment assets –5.03; Other investment liabilities 20.88; Net errors and omissions 7.91; *Overall balance* 4.54. Source: IMF, *International Financial Statistics*.

EXTERNAL TRADE

Principal Commodities (preliminary, US $ million, 2001): *Imports c.i.f.:* Food products and tobacco 26.0 (Meat and meat preparations 4.8; Cereals and cereal preparations 4.6); Mineral fuels 12.9; Miscellaneous oils and chemicals 9.7 (Essential oils and resinoids 4.3); Miscellaneous manufactures 23.5 (Paper products 4.4, Metal products 5.8); Miscellaneous primary products 5.4; Machinery and equipment 33.9 (Specialized industrial machines 4.2, Telecommunications and sound equipment 5.0, Electrical machinery 4.5, Vehicles 10.8); Other 19.2 (Miscellaneous manufactured articles 8.0); Total (incl. others) 130.6. *Exports f.o.b.:* Bananas 8.2; Other agricultural products 6.1; Soap 14.0; Other manufactures 17.1; Total 45.4. Source: IMF, *Dominica: Statistical Appendix* (October 2002).

Principal Trading Partners (US $ million, estimates, 2000): *Imports c.i.f.:* Barbados 4.7; Canada 6.2; France 2.8; Grenada 1.6; Guyana 1.7; Jamaica 1.7; Japan 9.3; Netherlands 3.2; Saint Lucia 2.4; Saint Vincent and the Grenadines 2.2; Trinidad and Tobago 24.0; United Kingdom 11.4; USA 55.2; Venezuela 2.7; Total (incl. others) 147.3. *Exports f.o.b.:* Antigua and Barbuda 4.0; Barbados 2.5; France 4.6; Guyana 3.4; Jamaica 12.8; Netherlands Antilles 0.5; Saint Christopher and Nevis 2.0; Saint Lucia 1.5; Saint Vincent and the Grenadines 0.6; Suriname 0.5; Trinidad and Tobago 2.8; United Kingdom 13.4; USA 4.0; Total (incl. others) 54.1. Source: UN, *International Trade Statistics Yearbook*.

TRANSPORT

Road Traffic (motor vehicles licensed in 1994): Private cars 6,491; Taxis 90; Buses 559; Motorcycles 94; Trucks 2,266; Jeeps 461; Tractors 24; Total 9,985. *2000* (motor vehicles in use): Passenger cars 8,700; Commercial vehicles 3,400. Source: partly UN, *Statistical Yearbook*.

Shipping: *Merchant Fleet* (registered at 31 December 2001): 7 vessels (total displacement 2,233 grt) (Source: Lloyd's Register-Fairplay, *World Fleet Statistics*); *International freight traffic* ('000 metric tons, estimates, 1993): Goods loaded 103.2; Goods unloaded 181.2.

Civil Aviation (1997): Aircraft arrivals and departures 18,672; Freight loaded 363 metric tons; Freight unloaded 575 metric tons.

TOURISM

Tourist Arrivals: *Stop-overs:* 70,791 in 1999; 64,439 in 2000; 63,600* in 2001. *Cruise-ship passengers:* 202,003 in 1999; 239,544 in 2000; 207,627* in 2001. *Excursionists:* 3,924 in 1999; 1,890 in 2000; 1,681* in 2001. Source: IMF, *Statistical Appendix* (October 2002). *Preliminary figure(s).

Tourism Receipts (EC $ million): 132.0 in 1999; 135.2 in 2000; 130.0 in 2001 (preliminary).

COMMUNICATIONS MEDIA

Radio Receivers (1997): 46,000 in use.

Television Receivers (1999): 17,000 in use.

Telephones (2001): 23,300 main lines in use.

Facsimile Machines (1996): 396 in use.

Mobile Cellular Telephones (2000): 1,200 in use.

Personal Computers (2001): 6,000 in use.

Internet Users (2000): 6,000.

Non-daily Newspapers (1996): 1.
Sources: mainly UNESCO, *Statistical Yearbook*, International Telecommunication Union and UN, *Statistical Yearbook*.

EDUCATION

Institutions (1994/95): Pre-primary 72 (1992/93); Primary 64; Secondary 14; Tertiary 2.

Teachers: Pre-primary 131 (1992/93); Primary 628 (1994/95); Secondary 269 (1994/95); Tertiary 34 (1992/93).

Pupils (1999): Pre-primary 3,000 (1992/93); Primary 12,885; Secondary 6,270; Tertiary 461 (1995/96).
Sources: UNESCO, *Statistical Yearbook*; Caribbean Development Bank, *Selected Indicators of Development*; UN Economic Commission for Latin America and the Caribbean, *Statistical Yearbook*.

Adult Literacy Rate (2000): 96.4%. Source: Secretariat of the Organisation of Eastern Caribbean States.

Directory

The Constitution

The Constitution came into effect at the independence of Dominica on 3 November 1978. Its main provisions are summarized below:

FUNDAMENTAL RIGHTS AND FREEDOMS

The Constitution guarantees the rights of life, liberty, security of the person, the protection of the law and respect for private property. The individual is entitled to freedom of conscience, of expression and assembly and has the right to an existence free from slavery, forced labour and torture. Protection against discrimination on the grounds of sex, race, place of origin, political opinion, colour or creed is assured.

THE PRESIDENT

The President is elected by the House of Assembly for a term of five years. A presidential candidate is nominated jointly by the Prime Minister and the Leader of the Opposition and on their concurrence is declared elected without any vote being taken; in the case of disagreement the choice will be made by secret ballot in the House of Assembly. Candidates must be citizens of Dominica aged at least 40 who have been resident in Dominica for five years prior to their nomination. A President may not hold office for more than two terms.

PARLIAMENT

Parliament consists of the President and the House of Assembly, composed of 21 elected Representatives and nine Senators. According to the wishes of Parliament, the latter may be appointed by the President—five on the advice of the Prime Minister and four on the advice of the Leader of the Opposition—or elected. The life of Parliament is five years.

Parliament has the power to amend the Constitution. Each constituency returns one Representative to the House who is directly elected in accordance with the Constitution. Every citizen over the age of 18 is eligible to vote.

THE EXECUTIVE

Executive authority is vested in the President. The President appoints as Prime Minister the elected member of the House who commands the support of a majority of its elected members, and other ministers on the advice of the Prime Minister. Not more than three ministers may be from among the appointed Senators. The President has the power to remove the Prime Minister from office if a resolution expressing 'no confidence' in the Government is adopted by the House and the Prime Minister does not resign within three days or advise the President to dissolve Parliament.

The Cabinet consists of the Prime Minister, other ministers and the Attorney-General in an ex officio capacity.

The Leader of the Opposition is appointed by the President as that elected member of the House who, in the President's judgement, is best able to command the support of a majority of the elected members who do not support the Government.

The Government

HEAD OF STATE

President: Vernon Lorden Shaw (assumed office 6 October 1998).

CABINET
(April 2003)

A coalition of the Labour Party of Dominica (LPD) and the Dominica Freedom Party (DFP).

Prime Minister and Minister of Finance and Carib Affairs: Pierre Charles (LPD).

Minister of Housing, Communications, Works and Physical Planning: Reginald Austrie (LPD).

Minister of Industry, Enterprise Development and Tourism: Charles Savarin (DFP).

Minister of Foreign Affairs and of Trade and Marketing: Osborne Riviere (LPD).

Minister of Community Development and Women's Affairs: Matthew Walter (LPD).

Minister of Agriculture and the Environment: Vince Henderson (LPD).

Minister of Sports and Youth Affairs: Roosevelt Skerrit (LPD).

Minister of Health and Social Security: Sen. Herbert Sabroache (DFP).

Attorney-General and Minister of Justice, Legal Affairs, Immigration and Labour: Henry Dyer (DFP).

MINISTRIES

Office of the President: Morne Bruce, Roseau; tel. 4482054; fax 4498366.

Office of the Prime Minister: Government Headquarters, Kennedy Ave, Roseau; tel. 4482401; fax 4485200.

All other ministries are at Government Headquarters, Kennedy Ave, Roseau; tel. 4482401.

CARIB TERRITORY

This reserve of the remaining Amerindian population is located on the central east coast of the island. The Caribs enjoy a measure of local government and elect their chief.

Chief: Garnet Joseph.

Waitukubuli Karifuna Development Committee: Salybia, Carib Territory; tel. 4457336.

Legislature

HOUSE OF ASSEMBLY

Speaker: Alix Boyd Knight.

Clerk: Alex F. Phillip.

Senators: 9.

Elected Members: 21.

General Election, 31 January 2000

Party	Votes cast	%	Seats
Labour Party of Dominica . .	15,362	42.9	10
Dominica United Workers' Party	15,555	43.4	9
Dominica Freedom Party . .	4,858	13.6	2
Independents	29	0.1	—
Total	35,804	100.0	21

Political Organizations

Dominica Freedom Party (DFP): Great George St, Roseau; tel. 4482104; Leader CHARLES SAVARIN.

Dominica United Workers' Party (UWP): 37 Cork St, Roseau; tel. 4485051; f. 1988; Leader EDISON JAMES; Chair. GARNET L. DIDIER.

Labour Party of Dominica (LPD): Cork St, Roseau; tel. 4488511; f. 1985 as a merger and reunification of left-wing groups, incl. the Dominica Labour Party (DLP; f. 1961); Leader PIERRE CHARLES.

Diplomatic Representation

EMBASSIES IN DOMINICA

China (Taiwan): Checkhall, Massacre, POB 56, Roseau; tel. 4491385; fax 4492085; e-mail rocemb@cwdom.dom; Ambassador MARIETTA KAO LIAU.

Venezuela: 20 Bath Rd, 3rd Floor, POB 770, Roseau; tel. 4483348; fax 4486198; e-mail embven@cwdom.dm; Ambassador CARMEN MARTINEZ DE GRIJALVA.

Judicial System

Justice is administered by the Eastern Caribbean Supreme Court (based in Saint Lucia), consisting of the Court of Appeal and the High Court. One of the six puisne judges of the High Court is resident in Dominica and presides over the Court of Summary Jurisdiction. The District Magistrate Courts deal with summary offences and civil offences involving limited sums of money (specified by law).

Religion

Most of the population profess Christianity, but there are some Muslims, Bahá'ís and Jews. The largest denomination is the Roman Catholic Church (with some 80% of the inhabitants in 1991).

CHRISTIANITY

The Roman Catholic Church

Dominica comprises the single diocese of Roseau, suffragan to the archdiocese of Castries (Saint Lucia). At 31 December 2001 there were an estimated 59,707 adherents in the country, representing a large majority of the inhabitants. The Bishop participates in the Antilles Episcopal Conference (currently based in Port of Spain, Trinidad).

Bishop of Roseau: Rt Rev. GABRIEL MALZAIRE, Bishop's House, Turkey Lane, POB 790, Roseau; tel. 4482837; fax 4483404; e-mail bishop@cwdom.dm.

The Anglican Communion

Anglicans in Dominica are adherents of the Church in the Province of the West Indies. The country forms part of the diocese of the North Eastern Caribbean and Aruba. The Bishop is resident in Antigua, and Archbishop of the Province is the Bishop of the Bahamas and the Turks and Caicos Islands.

Other Christian Churches

Christian Union Church of the West Indies: District 1, Rose St, Goodwill; tel. 4482725.

Other denominations include Methodist, Pentecostal, Baptist, Church of God, Presbyterian, the Assemblies of Brethren, Moravian and Seventh-day Adventist groups, and the Jehovah's Witnesses.

BAHÁ'Í FAITH

National Spiritual Assembly: 79 Victoria St, POB 136, Roseau; tel. 4483881; fax 4488460; e-mail nsa_dominica@yahoo.com.

The Press

The Chronicle: Wallhouse, POB 1724, Roseau; tel. 4487887; fax 4480047; e-mail thechronicle@cwdom.dm; internet www.news-dominica.com/new-index.cfm; f. 1996; Friday; progressive independent; Editor RASCHID OSMAN; Gen. Man. J. ANTHONY WHITE; circ. 3,000 (1997).

The Independent Newspaper: POB 462, 9 Great Marlborough St, Roseau; tel. 4480221; fax 4484368; internet www.delphis.dm/indpub; weekly.

Official Gazette: Government Printery, Roseau; tel. 4482401, ext. 330; weekly; circ. 550.

The Sun: Sun Inc., 50 Independence St, POB 2255, Roseau; tel. 4484744; fax 4484764; e-mail acsun@cwdom.dm; internet www.dominicasun.com; f. 1998; Editor CHARLES JAMES.

The Tropical Star: POB 1998, Roseau; tel. 4484634; fax 4485984; e-mail tpl@cwdom.dm; weekly; circ. 3,000.

Broadcasting and Communications

TELECOMMUNICATIONS

Regulatory Authority

Eastern Caribbean Telecommunications Authority: POB 1886, Castries, St Lucia; tel. (758) 4581701; fax (758) 4581698; e-mail info@ectel.int; internet www.ectel.info; f. 2000 to regulate telecommunications in Dominica, Grenada, Saint Christopher and Nevis, Saint Lucia and Saint Vincent and the Grenadines.

Major Service Providers

In April 2001 the Government signed an agreement to liberalize the telecommunications sector over the following 18 months. The monopoly of the sector hitherto enjoyed by Cable & Wireless was ended.

Cable & Wireless Dominica: Hanover St, POB 6, Roseau; tel. 4481000; fax 4481111; e-mail pr@cwdom.dm; internet www.tod.dm; Gen. Man. CARL ROBERTS.

Telecommunications of Dominica (TOD): Mercury House, Hanover St, Roseau; tel. 4481024.

BROADCASTING

Radio

In 2001 there were three radio stations operating in Dominica.

Dominica Broadcasting Corporation: Victoria St, POB 1, Roseau; tel. 4483283; fax 4482918; e-mail dbsradio@cwdom.dm; internet www.dbcradio.net; government station; daily broadcasts in English; 2 hrs daily in French patois; 10 kW transmitter on the medium wave band; FM service; programmes received throughout Caribbean excluding Jamaica and Guyana; Gen. Man. MARIETTE WARRINGTON; Programme Dir SHERMAINE GREEN-BROWN.

Kairi FM: Island Communications Corpn, Great George St, POB 931, Roseau; tel. 4487330; fax 4487332; e-mail kairfm@tod.dm; internet www.delphis.dm/kairi.htm; f. 1994; Owner FRANKEY BELLOT.

Voice of Life Radio (ZGBC): Gospel Broadcasting Corpn, Loubiere, POB 205, Roseau; tel. 4487017; fax 4487094; e-mail volbt@cwdom.dm; internet www.voiceoflife.com; linked to the US Christian Reformed Church; 112 hrs weekly AM, 24 hrs daily FM; Man. Dir BRENDA THOMAS-ST CLAIRE.

Television

There is no national television service, although there is a cable television network serving one-third of the island.

Marpin Telecom and Broadcasting: 5–7 Great Marlborough St, POB 2381, Roseau; tel. 4484107; fax 4482965; e-mail marpin@marpin.dm; internet www.marpin.dm; commercial; cable service; CEO RONALD ABRAHAM.

Finance

(cap. = capital; res = reserves; dep. = deposits; m. = million; amounts in East Caribbean dollars)

The Eastern Caribbean Central Bank (see p. 343), based in Saint Christopher, is the central issuing and monetary authority for Dominica.

BANKS

There were five commercial banks operating in Dominica in 2001.

Bank of Nova Scotia—Scotiabank (Canada): 28 Hillsborough St, POB 520, Roseau; tel. 4485800; fax 4485805; e-mail scotia@cwdom .dm; Man. C. Monte Smith.

Banque Française Commerciale (France): Queen Mary St, Roseau; tel. 4484040; fax 4485335; e-mail bfc@cwd.dom.dm; Man. Thierry Frey.

FirstCaribbean International Bank Ltd: Roseau; internet www .firstcaribbeaninternational.com; f. 2002 following merger of Caribbean operations of Barclays Bank PLC and CIBC; Exec. Chair. Michael Mansoor; CEO Charles Pink.

National Commercial Bank of Dominica: 64 Hillsborough St, POB 271, Roseau; tel. 4482571; fax 4483982; e-mail ncbdom@cwdom .dm; f. 1976; cap. 10.0m., res 10.0m., dep. 247.0m. (June 1999); 51% govt-owned; Chair. Nicholas Waldron; Gen. Man. Earl Edwards; 2 brs.

Royal Bank of Canada: Dame Mary Eugenia Charles Blvd, POB 19, Roseau; tel. 4482771; fax 4485398; Man. H. Pinard.

DEVELOPMENT BANK

Dominica Agricultural, Industrial and Development (DAID) Bank: cnr Charles Avenue and Rawles Lane, Goodwill, POB 215, Roseau; tel. 4482853; fax 4484903; e-mail aidbank@cwdom.dm; f. 1971; responsible to Ministry of Finance; planned privatization suspended in 1997; provides finance for the agriculture, tourism, housing, education and manufacturing sectors; cap. 9.5m. (1991); Chair. Crispin Sorhaindo; Man. Patricia Charles.

STOCK EXCHANGE

Eastern Caribbean Securities Exchange: based in Basseterre, Saint Christopher and Nevis; e-mail info@ecseonline.com; internet www.ecseonline.com; f. 2001; regional securities market designed to facilitate the buying and selling of financial products for the eight member territories—Anguilla, Antigua and Barbuda, Dominica, Grenada, Montserrat, Saint Christopher and Nevis, Saint Lucia and Saint Vincent and the Grenadines; Gen. Man. Baljit Vohra.

INSURANCE

In May 2001 there were 19 insurance companies operating in Dominica. Several British, regional and US companies have agents in Roseau. Local companies include the following:

First Domestic Insurance Co Ltd: 19–21 King George V St, POB 1931, Roseau; tel. 4488337; fax 4485778; e-mail insurance@cwdom .dm.

Insurance Specialists and Consultants: 19–21 King George V St, POB 20, Roseau; tel. 4482022; fax 4485778.

J. B. Charles and Co Ltd: Old St, POB 121, Roseau; tel. 4482876.

Tonge Inc Ltd: 19–21 King George V St, POB 20, Roseau; tel. 4484027; fax 4485778.

Windward Islands Crop Insurance Co (Wincrop): Vanoulst House, Goodwill, POB 469, Roseau; tel. 4483955; fax 4484197; f. 1987; regional; coverage for weather destruction of, mainly, banana crops; Man. Kerwin Ferreira; brs in Grenada, Saint Lucia and Saint Vincent.

Trade and Industry

DEVELOPMENT ORGANIZATIONS

National Development Corporation (NDC): Valley Rd, POB 293, Roseau; tel. 4482045; fax 4485840; e-mail ndc@cwdom.dm; internet www.ndcdominica.dm; f. 1988 by merger of Industrial Development Corpn (f. 1974) and Tourist Board; promotes local and foreign investment to increase employment, production and exports; promotes and co-ordinates tourism development; Chair. Desmond Carlisle; Gen. Man. Vincent Philbert.

Eastern Caribbean States Export Development and Agricultural Diversification Unit (EDADU): POB 769, Roseau; tel. 4482240; fax 4485554; e-mail oecsedu@cwdom.dm; internet www .oecs-edu.org; f. 1990 as Eastern Caribbean States Export Development Agency; reformed as above in 1997; OECS regional development org. Exec. Dir Colin Bully.

INDUSTRIAL AND TRADE ASSOCIATIONS

Dominica Association of Industry and Commerce (DAIC): POB 85, cnr Old St and Fields Lane, Roseau; tel. 4482874; fax 4486868; e-mail daic@marpin.dm; internet www.delphis.dm/daic .htm; f. 1972 by a merger of the Manufacturers' Association and the Chamber of Commerce; represents the business sector, liaises with the Government, and stimulates commerce and industry; 100 mems; Pres. Anthony Biscombe; CEO Jeanilia R. V. de Smet.

Dominica Banana Marketing Corporation (DBMC): Vanoulst House, POB 1620, Roseau; tel. 4482671; fax 4486445; e-mail dbmc@ cwdom-dm.com; internet www.dbmc-dm.com; f. 1934 as Dominica Banana Growers' Association; restructured 1984; state-supported, scheduled for privatization; Chair. Richard Charles; Gen. Man. Kervin Stephenson.

Dominica Export-Import Agency (DEXIA): Bay Front, POB 173, Roseau; tel. 4482780; fax 4486308; e-mail dexia@cwdom.dm; internet www.dexiaexport.com; f. 1986; replaced the Dominica Agricultural Marketing Board and the External Trade Bureau; exporter of Dominican agricultural products, trade facilitator and importer of bulk rice and sugar; Gen. Man. Gregoire Thomas.

EMPLOYERS' ORGANIZATION

Dominica Employers' Federation: 14 Church St, POB 1783, Roseau; tel. 4482314; fax 4484474; e-mail def@cwdom.dm; Pres. Lambert Lewis.

UTILITIES

Electricity

Dominica Electricity Services Ltd (Domlec): 18 Castle St, POB 1593, Roseau; tel. 4482681; fax 4485397; e-mail mansecdomlec@ cwdom.dm; national electricity service; 72%-owned by the Commonwealth Development Corporation (United Kingdom); Gen. Man. Murray Rogers.

Water

Dominica Water and Sewerage Co Ltd (DOWASCO): 3 High St, POB 185, Roseau; tel. 4484811; fax 4485813; e-mail dowasco@ cwdom.dm; state-owned; Chair. Don Christopher; Gen. Man. Damian Shillingford.

TRADE UNIONS

Dominica Amalgamated Workers' Union (DAWU): 5 Hillsborough St, POB 137, Roseau; tel. 4483048; fax 4485787; f. 1960; Gen. Sec. Fedaline M. Moulon; 500 mems (1996).

Dominica Association of Teachers: 7 Boyds Ave, Roseau; tel. 4488177; fax 4488177; e-mail dat@cwdom.dm; internet www .dateachers.4t.com; Pres. Celia Nicholas; 630 mems (1996).

Dominica Trade Union: 70–71 Independence St, Roseau; tel. 4498139; fax 4499060; f. 1945; Pres. Harold Sealey; Gen. Sec. Leo J. Bernard Nicholas; 400 mems (1995).

Media Workers' Association: Roseau; Pres. Matthias Peltier.

National Workers' Union: Independence St, cnr Church St and Old Market Sq., POB 387, Roseau; tel. 4485209; fax 4481934; e-mail icss@cwdom.dm; f. 1977; Pres. Rawlings F. A. Jemmott; Gen. Sec. Franklin Fabien; 450 mems (1996).

Public Service Union: cnr Valley Rd and Windsor Lane, Roseau; tel. 4482102; fax 4488060; e-mail dcs@cwdom.dm; f. 1940; registered as a trade union in 1960; representing all grades of civil servants, including firemen, prison officers, nurses, teachers and postal workers; Pres. Sonia D. Williams; Gen. Sec. Thomas Letang; 1,400 mems.

Waterfront and Allied Workers' Union: 43 Hillsborough St, POB 181, Roseau; tel. 4482343; fax 4480086; e-mail wawu@cwdom.dm; f. 1965; Pres. Louis Benoit; Gen. Sec. Kertist Augustis; 1,500 mems.

Transport

ROADS

In 1999 there were an estimated 780 km (485 miles) of roads, of which about 50.4% was paved; there were also numerous tracks. A road and bridge reconstruction project, costing an estimated EC $33m., was announced by the Government in 1997.

SHIPPING

A deep-water harbour at Woodbridge Bay serves Roseau, which is the principal port. Several foreign shipping lines call at Roseau, and there is a high-speed ferry service between Martinique and Guadeloupe which calls at Roseau eight times a week. Ships of the Geest Line call at Prince Rupert's Bay, Portsmouth, to collect bananas, and there are also cruise-ship facilities there. There are other specialized berthing facilities on the west coast.

Dominica Port Authority (DPA): POB 243, Roseau; tel. 4484431; fax 4486131; e-mail domport@cwdom.dm; f. 1972; responsible to the Ministry of Communications and Works; pilotage and cargo handling; Gen. Man. VINCENT ELWIN.

CIVIL AVIATION

Melville Hall Airport, 64 km (40 miles) from Roseau, and Canefield Airport, 5 km (3 miles) from Roseau, are the two airports on the island. Proposals for the construction of an international airport were under review. Construction of the new airport was to be funded by the European Union. The regional airline, LIAT (based in Antigua and Barbuda, and in which Dominica is a shareholder), provides daily services and, with Air Caraïbe, connects Dominica with all the islands of the Eastern Caribbean, including the international airports of Puerto Rico, Antigua, Guadeloupe and Martinique.

Tourism

The Government has designated areas of the island as nature reserves, to preserve the beautiful, lush scenery and the rich, natural heritage that constitute Dominica's main tourist attractions. Birdlife is particularly prolific, and includes several rare and endangered species, such as the Imperial parrot. There are also two marine reserves. Tourism is not as developed as it is among Dominica's neighbours, but the country is being promoted as an 'eco-tourism' and cruise destination. There were an estimated 272,908 visitors in 2001 (of whom 207,627 were cruise-ship passengers). Receipts from tourism decreased by 3.8% in 2001, to an estimated EC $130.0m.

National Development Corporation (NDC)—Division of Tourism: Valley Rd, POB 293, Roseau; tel. 4482045; fax 4485840; e-mail ndctourism@cwdom.dm; internet www.ndcdominica.dm; f. 1988 following merger of Tourist Board with Industrial Devt Corpn; Dir of Tourism SHARON PASCAL.

Dominica Hotel and Tourism Association (DHTA): POB 384, Roseau; tel. 4486565; fax 4480299; e-mail dhta@cwdom.dm; Pres. ATHERTON MARTIN; Treas. MAXINE ALLEYNE.

THE DOMINICAN REPUBLIC

Introductory Survey

Location, Climate, Language, Religion, Flag, Capital

The Dominican Republic occupies the eastern part of the island of Hispaniola, which lies between Cuba and Puerto Rico in the Caribbean Sea. The country's only international frontier is with Haiti, to the west. The climate is sub-tropical, with an average annual temperature of 27°C (80°F). In Santo Domingo, temperatures are generally between 19°C (66°F) and 31°C (88°F). The west and south-west of the country are arid. Hispaniola lies in the path of tropical cyclones. The official language is Spanish. Almost all of the inhabitants profess Christianity, and some 88% are Roman Catholics. There are small Protestant and Jewish communities. The national flag (proportions 5 by 8) is blue (upper hoist and lower fly) and red (lower hoist and upper fly), quartered by a white cross. The state flag has, in addition, the national coat of arms, showing a quartered shield in the colours of the flag (on which are superimposed national banners, a cross and an open Bible) between scrolls above and below, at the centre of the cross. The capital is Santo Domingo.

Recent History

The Dominican Republic became independent in 1844, although it was occupied by US military forces between 1916 and 1924. General Rafael Leónidas Trujillo Molina overthrew the elected President, Horacio Vázquez, in 1930 and dominated the country until his assassination in May 1961. The dictator ruled personally from 1930 to 1947 and indirectly thereafter. His brother, Héctor Trujillo, was President from 1947 until August 1960, when he was replaced by Dr Joaquín Balaguer Ricardo, hitherto Vice-President. After Rafael Trujillo's death, President Balaguer remained in office, but in December 1961 he permitted moderate opposition groups to participate in a Council of State, which exercised legislative and executive powers. Balaguer resigned in January 1962, when the Council of State became the Provisional Government. A presidential election in December 1962, the country's first free election for 38 years, was won by Dr Juan Bosch Gaviño, the founder and leader of the Partido Revolucionario Dominicano (PRD), who had been in exile since 1930. President Bosch, a left-of-centre democrat, took office in February 1963 but was overthrown in the following September by a military coup. The leaders of the armed forces transferred power to a civilian triumvirate, led by Emilio de los Santos. In April 1965 a revolt by supporters of ex-President Bosch overthrew the triumvirate. Civil war broke out between pro-Bosch forces and military units headed by Gen. Elías Wessin y Wessin, who had played a leading role in the 1963 coup. The violence was eventually suppressed by the intervention of some 23,000 US troops, who were formally incorporated into an Inter-American peace force by the Organization of American States (OAS). The peace force withdrew in September 1965.

Following a period of provisional government under Héctor García Godoy, a presidential election in June 1966 was won by Balaguer, the candidate of the Partido Reformista Social Cristiano (PRSC). The PRSC, founded in 1964, also won a majority of seats in both houses of the new National Congress. A new Constitution was promulgated in November. Despite his association with the Trujillo dictatorship, Balaguer initially proved to be a popular leader, and in May 1970 he was re-elected for a further four years. In February 1973 a state of emergency was declared when guerrilla forces landed on the coast. Captain Francisco Caamaño Deño, the leader of the 1965 revolt, and his followers were killed. Bosch and other opposition figures went into hiding. Bosch later resigned as leader of the PRD (founding the Partido de la Liberación Dominicana—PLD), undermining hopes of a united opposition in the May 1974 elections, when Balaguer was re-elected with a large majority.

In the May 1978 presidential election, Balaguer was defeated by the PRD candidate, Silvestre Antonio Guzmán Fernández. This was the first occasion in the country's history when an elected President yielded power to an elected successor. An attempted military coup in favour of Balaguer was prevented by pressure from the US Government. On assuming office in August, President Guzmán undertook to professionalize the armed forces by removing politically ambitious high-ranking officers. In June 1981 he declared his support for Jacobo Majluta Azar, his Vice-President, as his successor, but in November the PRD rejected Majluta's candidacy in favour of Dr Salvador Jorge Blanco, a left-wing senator, who was elected President in May 1982. In the congressional elections, held simultaneously, the PRD secured a majority in both the Senate and the Chamber of Deputies. Guzmán committed suicide in July after allegations of fraud were made against his Government and members of his family. Vice-President Majluta was immediately sworn in as interim President until Blanco assumed office in August. Although a member of the Socialist International, Blanco maintained good relations with the USA (on which the country is economically dependent) and declared that he would not resume relations with Cuba.

In April 1984 a series of public protests against substantial increases in the cost of essential items resulted in the deaths of more than 50 people. In May and August the Government responded to the prospect of further demonstrations by ordering the arrest of trade union and left-wing leaders. Further demonstrations, including one attended by 40,000 people in Santo Domingo, were held in protest at the continuing economic decline.

In February 1985 a further series of substantial price increases led to violent clashes between demonstrators and the security forces, during which four people died. Public unrest was exacerbated by the Government's decision, in April, to accept the IMF's terms for further financial aid. In June a 24-hour general strike was organized by trade unions, in protest at the Government's economic policy and its refusal to increase the minimum wage. In July, however, the threat of a 48-hour general strike prompted the Government to order an immediate increase in the minimum wage.

Further violence preceded the presidential and legislative elections of May 1986. The three principal candidates in the presidential election were all former Presidents: Balaguer of the PRSC; Majluta, who, having registered La Estructura, his right-wing faction of the PRD, as a separate political party in July 1985, nevertheless secured the candidacy of the ruling PRD; and Bosch of the PLD. The counting of votes was suspended twice, following allegations by Majluta of fraud by the PRSC and by the Junta Central Electoral (JCE—Central Electoral Board). Balaguer was finally declared the winner by a narrow margin of votes over Majluta, his closest rival. In the simultaneous legislative elections, the PRSC won 21 of the 30 seats in the Senate and 56 of the 120 seats in the Chamber of Deputies.

Upon taking office as President (for the fifth time) in August 1986, Balaguer initiated an investigation into alleged corrupt practices by members of the outgoing administration. Blanco, the outgoing President, was charged with embezzlement and the illegal purchase of military vehicles. (In August 1991 he was finally convicted of 'abuse of power' and misappropriation of public funds, and sentenced to 20 years' imprisonment. However, in September 1994 legislation granting him amnesty was approved by the Chamber of Deputies.) The financial accounts of the armed forces were examined, and the former Secretary of State for the Armed Forces was subsequently imprisoned. In September 1987 the Cabinet resigned, at the request of the President, to enable him to restructure the Government. Some 35,000 government posts were abolished, in an attempt to reduce public spending, and expenditure was to be redirected to a programme of public works projects, which were expected to create almost 100,000 new jobs. Nevertheless, strike action continued. In February 1988 demonstrations throughout the country to protest against the high cost of living, following an increase in the price of staple foods, resulted in the deaths of six people. Furthermore, prices continued to rise.

In 1989 opposition to the Government's economic policies intensified. Popular discontent was aggravated by the deterioration of public utilities, particularly water and electricity. In June a national strike committee called a 48-hour general strike. More than 300 organizations supported the action, which reportedly paralysed the country for two days. The major demands included the doubling of the minimum wage, a reduction in the prices of staple commodities, and the ending of interruptions in the supplies of water and electricity. Four people were killed and an estimated 3,000 were arrested during the protests. Despite mediation efforts by the Roman Catholic Church, the Government made no concessions to union demands. In October, following a 66% rise in fuel prices, there were further violent demonstrations.

With presidential and legislative elections due to take place in May 1990, Balaguer's prospects for re-election were impeded considerably by the continuing deterioration of the economy (particularly rapid inflation), the worsening energy crisis, and criticism of government spending on expansive public works programmes, which had resulted in a severe depletion of the country's reserves of foreign exchange. The principal contender for the presidency was the PLD candidate, Bosch, who concentrated his election campaign on seeking support from the private sector, promising privatization of state-owned companies. When the initial results indicated a narrow victory for Balaguer, Bosch accused the ruling PRSC and the JCE of fraud, necessitating a re-count, supervised by monitors from the OAS. Almost two months after the election, Balaguer was declared the official winner. The PRSC secured a narrow majority in the Senate, with 16 of the 30 seats; the PLD won 12 and the PRD two. At elections to the Chamber of Deputies the PLD obtained 44 of the 120 seats, while the PRSC won 42, the PRD 32 and the Partido Revolucionario Independiente (PRI) two. However, the lack of an outright majority in the Chamber of Deputies did not threaten seriously to impede government policies, in view of Balaguer's extensive powers to govern by decree.

In August 1990, in an attempt to reduce inflation by cutting government subsidies, the Government announced a programme of austerity measures, almost doubling the price of petrol and essential foodstuffs. In response the trade unions called a 48-hour general strike and in the ensuing conflict with the security forces some 14 people were killed. The price increases were partially offset by an increase of 30% in the salaries of army personnel and civilian employees in the public sector. The trade unions, however, rejected an identical offer by the private sector and threatened further strike action if their demands for basic food subsidies and considerable wage increases were not satisfied. In September a three-day general strike, organized by the Organizaciones Colectivas Populares (OCP), led to further arrests, injuries and at least one death. In the following month another general strike was called by the OCP and the Central General de Trabajadores (CGT), with the stated aim of ousting Balaguer from power. Violent clashes with the security forces in Santo Domingo resulted in a further four deaths. In August 1991 the Government concluded a stand-by agreement with the IMF, in spite of trade-union and public opposition.

In April 1992 47 high-ranking, and mainly left-wing, members announced their resignation from the PLD. In June more than 400 former PLD members held a 'national assembly' to form a new political movement, the Alianza por la Democracia (APD), which was officially established in August.

In late September 1992 a Dominican human rights leader, Rafael Efraín Ortiz, was shot dead by police during a demonstration in Santo Domingo in protest at the inordinate expense of the construction of the Columbus Lighthouse, estimated to have cost in excess of US $25m. Protesters also denounced the celebration of the Spanish conquest (the 500th anniversary of which the lighthouse had been built to commemorate), which had led to the enslavement and destruction of the indigenous Taino Indian population. In response to the killing of Efraín, general strikes were called in several cities, and violent protests broke out, resulting in one further death.

In April 1993 the APD split into two factions. In January 1994 the PLD announced it had formed an alliance with the right-wing Fuerza Nacional Progresista (FNP) in order to contest the forthcoming general election. In the same month Balaguer officially announced his intention to contest the forthcoming presidential election; his nomination received the support of the majority of the PRSC. However, his decision prompted 20 members of the PRSC executive to withdraw from the party in order to support the presidential candidate of the Unidad Democrática (UD), Fernando Alvarez Bogaert, himself a defecting member of the PRSC. The UD subsequently signed an electoral pact with the PRD.

The official results of the presidential and legislative elections of 16 May 1994 were delayed, amid accusations of widespread voting irregularities. Interim results, announced on 24 May, indicated a narrow victory for Balaguer in the presidential contest. However, the PRD claimed that polling stations had been issued with abbreviated electoral rolls and that the PRSC, which had effective control of the JCE, had removed the names of some 200,000 PRD supporters from the lists. A full recount began on 25 May. In June the JCE rejected a request, made by the US Department of State, that fresh elections be conducted wherever voting irregularities had been detected. In the same month Bosch resigned as leader of the PLD. In July an investigative commission confirmed that, as a result of serious irregularities, some 73,000 of the registered electorate had been denied a vote. Despite an atmosphere of growing political instability, Balaguer rejected opposition demands for the formation of a provisional government. Strike action in protest at the electoral irregularities was reported to have seriously affected several regions, including the capital, during that month. On 2 August the JCE announced the final election results, having apparently overlooked the findings of the electoral investigative commission. Balaguer was proclaimed the winner of the presidential election by a margin of less than 1% of the votes cast, with 43.6%. In the Senate the alliance of the PRD and the UD secured 15 seats, while the PRSC won 14 and the PLD one seat. In the Chamber of Deputies the PRD/UD alliance obtained 57 seats, while the PRSC won 50 and the PLD 13 seats.

Talks aimed at ending the political crisis caused by the election were held in early August 1994, with the mediation of the OAS and the Roman Catholic Church, and resulted in the signing of the Pact for Democracy. Under the terms of the accord (agreed by all the major parties), a fresh presidential election was to be held in November 1995 and a series of constitutional reforms would be adopted, providing for the prohibition of the re-election of a president to a consecutive term, a new electoral system for the head of state (see below), and the reorganization of the judiciary. Additionally, the legislative and municipal elections were to be held mid-way through the presidential term. As a result of the accord, José Francisco Peña Gómez, the PRD leader, cancelled a series of planned strikes and demonstrations organized by his party. However, at a session of the National Congress, held on 14 August, the deputies of the PRSC, with the support of those of the PLD, voted to extend Balaguer's mandate from 18 months to two years. The PRD withdrew from the legislature in protest, and Peña Gómez announced that his party would boycott Congress and resume strike action. The OAS also criticized Congress for violating the terms of the Pact for Democracy. The constitutional amendments that the Pact envisaged were, however, approved by Congress. On 16 August Balaguer was inaugurated as President for a seventh term, and a new Cabinet was appointed over the following days.

The year 1995 was marked by a series of protests and disturbances, largely provoked by the deteriorating standards of public services. In March a protest at increases in public transport fares resulted in four deaths (there were further protests in August after the Government increased fares by an additional 25%). In April, following the most severe electricity shortages since 1990, the administrator of the state electricity company, the Corporación Dominicana de Electricidad (CDE), was dismissed. In May a 24-hour general strike in protest at increases in food prices and at the deterioration of electricity and transport services took place, and in the following month there were renewed disturbances in Santo Domingo and other towns to the north of the capital. Violent confrontations occurred between security forces and workers in September at a sugar plantation in San Luis, where workers had been protesting the decision of the state sugar council, the Consejo Estatal de Azúcar, to dismiss some 12,700 of its work-force.

In April 1996 the energy shortfall again reached crisis proportions, with power cuts averaging between 14 and 20 hours per day. The crisis prompted renewed demands for Congress to expedite legislation enabling the privatization of CDE, which, owing largely to inefficiency and corruption, operated at a considerable loss.

The presidential election of 16 May 1996, the first for some 30 years in which Balaguer was not a candidate, was conducted according to a new system, introduced since 1994, whereby a second round of voting would be conducted between the two leading candidates should no candidate secure an absolute majority in the initial ballot. In the first round Peña Gómez won 45.9% of the votes, while the candidate of the PLD, Leonel Fernández Reyna, obtained 38.9%. The candidate of the PRSC, Jacinto Peynado (who had received only nominal support from Balaguer), obtained just 15.0% of the votes. At the second round of the presidential election, conducted on 30 June, Fernández secured a narrow victory, winning 51.25% of the votes, while Peña Gómez obtained 48.75%. The establishment, earlier in the month, of an electoral alliance between the PLD and PRSC, entitled the Frente Nacional Patriótico, had ensured Fernández the support of the PRSC voters. While the PRSC failed to retain the presidency, Balaguer appeared to have succeeded in retaining considerable influence in the new administration, since the PLD had only minority representation in Congress and would be dependent on the support of the PRSC to implement planned institutional reforms. However, in early August relations between Fernández and Balaguer appeared to have deteriorated when the PRSC signed an unexpected agreement with the PRD, which guaranteed the PRSC the presidency of the Senate while the PRD obtained that of the Chamber of Deputies. On 16 August Fernández was inaugurated, and the Cabinet, consisting almost exclusively of PLD members, was sworn in.

In 1997, as part of a campaign to eliminate deep-seated corruption in the country's institutions (which was estimated to cost the State some 30,000m. pesos per year), Fernández restructured both the police and the judiciary. In August Fernández, in his role as Chairman of the Consejo Nacional de la Magistratura, oversaw a restructuring of the Supreme Court, including the appointment of 15 new judges. Responsibility for appointing judges at all other levels of the judicial system was transferred from the Senate to the Supreme Court, principally to avoid appointments being influenced by political considerations.

Growing dissatisfaction with the continuing deterioration of public services and Fernández's failure to honour promises made during his election campaign provoked widespread disturbances and strike action throughout the country in 1997 and early 1998, with violent confrontations between demonstrators and the security forces resulting in several deaths. In October, in an effort to defuse the volatile social and political climate, Fernández introduced a recovery plan aimed at overcoming electricity and food shortages. However, in the following month a two-day general strike was organized by an 'umbrella' protest group, the Coordinadora de Organizaciones Populares, in support of demands for pay increases, reductions in the price of fuel and basic foodstuffs and improved public services.

At legislative elections held on 16 May 1998 the PRD won 83 seats in the 149-seat Chamber of Deputies (enlarged from 120 seats), while the PLD obtained 49 seats and the PRSC secured the remaining 17 seats. In the Senate the PRD won 24 seats, while the PLD won four and the PRSC two seats. The number of registered voters who abstained from participating in the poll was, at some 48%, the highest on record. As a result of the success of the opposition PRD, and the considerable losses incurred by the PRSC (on whom the PLD Government had hitherto depended for support in the legislature), it was considered likely that Fernández would encounter considerable difficulty in implementing his legislative programme for the remainder of his term of office, due to end in 2000. In July 1998 the outgoing Congress approved controversial legislation granting an amnesty to all public officials accused of corruption since 1978. The new legislature was inaugurated in August 1998. However, the PRD failed to secure the presidency of the Chamber of Deputies when a dissident group of PRD deputies joined forces with the PLD and the PRSC to re-elect the outgoing President of the Chamber, Héctor Rafael Peguero Méndez, to the post. Peguero had been expelled from the PRD in July, after refusing to accept the party's choice of candidate for the position.

In January 1999 conflict within the legislature threatened to jeopardize the disbursement of some US $216m. in reconstruction loans from the World Bank and the Inter-American Development Bank, which had been made available following the destruction caused by 'Hurricane Georges' in September 1998. The dispute concerned the election for the post of Secretary-General of the Liga Municipal Dominicana (LMD), an association of local government bodies with significant financial powers, which directed local government expenditure amounting to some 4% of the national budget. An accord was finally achieved in April, when it was agreed to appoint an impartial commission to manage the LMD pending a judicial decision on the control of the LMD.

Violent protests against electricity and water shortages and declining living standards continued in 1998 and 1999. In May 1999 the privatization of the CDE began. In October a general strike was organized in protest against the introduction of fuel price increases of up to 34% and a concomitant rise in transport

fares. The protest effectively paralysed the public transport sector before being abandoned on its second day.

In the first round of the presidential election, held on 16 May 2000, Rafael Hipólito Mejía Domínguez, the PRD candidate, received 49.9% of the votes cast, while the PRD candidate, Danilo Medina Sánchez, won 24.9%. Former President Joaquín Balaguer, standing as the PRSC's candidate for a potential eighth presidential term, won 24.6% of the ballot. Despite Mejía's failure to secure the constitutionally required 50%, a second ballot was not held and the JCE allowed Mejía to declare himself the winner. He was inaugurated as President on 16 August and a new Cabinet was officially appointed. The PRD crusade against the previous PLD administration's alleged corruption proved controversial, creating open hostility between the two parties. In November former President Fernández led a protest, following the arrest of various former senior government officials, including Diandino Peña, Haivanjoe Ng Cortinas and Feliz Bautista, on corruption charges. Fernández himself was later similarly accused and arrested; however, they were all subsequently released, owing to lack of evidence. With only 73 PRD deputies in the 149-seat lower house (10 of the 83 elected in May 1998 had been expelled from the party), Mejía lacked a parliamentary majority, and was dependent for support on the PRSC.

In early 2001 President Mejía initiated a series of fiscal measures, increasing value-added tax (VAT) from 8% to 12%, introducing taxes on luxury goods and obliging larger companies to pay corporation taxes of 1.5% in stages throughout the year. Petrol prices increased, following the implementation of a fixed tax on fuel, but there was no violent popular response. The Government also introduced a poverty mitigation programme, including training, infrastructural programmes and education, health and housing reforms. Social security legislation was introduced, aimed at providing employees with improved pensions and other benefits. The political programme also included decentralization of power and the restructuring of the public sector. There was some opposition to the measures, including a strike by hospital workers in protest at the proposed welfare reforms.

In May 2001 two people were shot dead by the police, and a further seven injured, during a public protest against police violence. President Mejía ordered an inquiry into the events leading up to the deaths. It was estimated that some 305 people had been killed by the police force in 2001. In January 2002 Mejía dismissed the national police chief, Pedro de Jesús Candelier, following further allegations of police brutality. He was replaced by Jaime Martes Martinez, to the appointment of whom a drop in the number of deaths to approximately one-third that of the previous year was accredited in 2002.

In November 2001 President Mejía declared three days of national mourning after an American Airlines Airbus bound for the Dominican Republic crashed soon after its take-off from New York, USA, killing all 255 people on board, including 175 Dominicans. In December Senator Darío Gómez of the PRD was assassinated by unidentified gunmen in his home; there was speculation that his death might be linked to his sponsorship of new legislation under consideration in the Senate to introduce more severe penalties in an effort to combat money laundering. (The legislation finally received assent in June 2002.) In March 2002 the Secretary of State for Finance, Fernando Alvarez Bogaert, resigned; he was replaced by José Luis Malkun.

In early December 2000 the Senate approved constitutional amendments to extend the presidential term to five years and the congressional term to six years, and to lower the minimum requirement of votes in a presidential election. The legislation was condemned by many politicians and, in order to appease opposition to the bill, Mejía subsequently appointed a Committee on Constitutional Reform to assess the situation. In October 2001 agreement was reached on the major clauses of a constitutional reform bill, which was then submitted to Congress. The proposed legislation included four principal points: a reduction in the proportion of votes needed to win a presidential election to 45% (or 40% if the leading candidate had at least a 10% majority); the abolition of 'closed' electoral stations; the election of representatives to the Central Andean Parliament to be decided by popular vote rather than by Congress; the establishment of a National Constituent Assembly, to draft a new constitution. However, in November the Senate voted to include in the constitutional amendments a clause permitting the re-election of a President. Mejía opposed the inclusion of this reform, claiming that it distracted from the main issues (he declared he would not seek re-election in 2004). Lower house deputies were also to vote on an extension of their mandates until 2004, to bring legislative elections back into line with the presidential contest. In December the Supreme Court ruled the proposed legislation to be unconstitutional. However, in January 2002 the Chamber of Deputies approved the formation of a National Constituent Assembly and in July, following re-examination, a bill of amendment permitting presidential re-election finally received assent from the National Assembly.

Legislative elections were held on 16 May 2002. The PRD secured 73 seats in the Chamber of Deputies, the PLD 41 (a reduction of its representation by eight seats) and the PRSC 36. The PRD also won 29 of 32 seats available in the Senate; the PLD obtained two and the PRSC the remaining seat. The failure of the PRD to secure an outright majority in the lower house ensured its contined dependence upon the support of the PRSC for the passage of legislation.

In July 2002 former President Joaquín Balaguer died at the age of 95. His death prompted speculation that there would be some political realignment within the legislature, following a formal proposal by the PLD that it enter into an alliance with the PRSC. However, in August the PRSC renewed its political alliance with the PRD, ensuring that the latter retained its dominance of the lower house. In September a fire started by protesting inmates at a prison in the town of La Vega resulted in the deaths of 29 prisoners, prompting criticism of the country's justice system and overcrowding in its prisons. In November Col. Pedro Julio Goico, a member of the armed forces and the head of presidential security, was detained following allegations that he had committed credit card fraud. President Mejía became involved in the scandal when it was discovered that he had reinstated Goico to the armed forces following his suspension in 1997 and had subsequently promoted him, as well as appointing him head of security, despite the charges that he faced. Meanwhile, former President Leonel Fernández launched a new political movement, Frente Independiente Leonel al Poder (FILA), to support his candidacy in the presidential elections scheduled to take place in 2004.

The continuing illegal import of plantation labour into the Dominican Republic from Haiti was a major issue for successive Governments. In June 1991, in reaction to increasing criticism of the Dominican Republic's human rights record (and, in particular, the Government's apparent acquiescence in the exploitation of Haitian child labourers), President Balaguer ordered the repatriation of all Haitian residents aged under 16 or over 60 years. Protests made by the Haitian Government that such a unilateral measure contravened normal diplomatic procedure were rejected by Balaguer. Following the army coup of September 1991 in Haiti, tens of thousands of Haitians fled to the Dominican Republic. However, few were granted refugee status, according to the UN High Commissioner for Refugees. In 1994 reports of large-scale smuggling from the Dominican Republic to Haiti, in defiance of UN sanctions against the Haitian military dictatorship, prompted the UN to seek assurances of co-operation from Balaguer. An agreement was reached, providing for a UN monitoring mission to observe the enforcement of the embargo until the lifting of UN sanctions (in October 1994). In 1997 relations with Haiti became strained following the expulsion from the Dominican Republic over a three-month period of some 20,000 Haitians who had been residing illegally in the country. In February Fernández and his Haitian counterpart agreed to put an immediate end to large-scale repatriations. Accord was also achieved providing for the repatriation process to be monitored by an international body to ensure the observance of human rights. In June 1998 Fernández became the first Dominican Head of State to visit Haiti since 1936. Fernández and the Haitian President met in Port-au-Prince, where they reached agreement on the establishment of joint border patrols to combat the traffic of drugs, arms and other contraband across the countries' joint border. In late 1999, following the summary deportation of some 8,000 Haitians, the two Governments signed a protocol limiting the repatriations.

In early 2001, following an increase in tensions in Haiti, a plan to protect Dominican territory was implemented; military forces deployed on the Dominican–Haitian border also were reinforced in an attempt to prevent both illegal immigration and drugs-trafficking. Relations improved during the presidency of Mejía, and there were proposals for joint Dominican-Haitian development programmes in the border region, to be financed by the European Union (EU). However, following the attempt by former Haitian police commissioners to take over the Haitian presidential palace, in December 2001, security along the Dominican–Haitian border was increased. In January 2002 the Haitian President, Jean-Bertrand Aristide, paid his first official visit to the Dominican Republic, during which he met with President Mejía. The two leaders signed an agreement pledging to discuss improved co-operation on border, immigration and economic issues. In April the inauguration of an industrial park at Ouanaminthe, spanning the shared border, was perceived to signal the start of an improved bilateral relationship. In late 2002 the USA pledged weapons, technical assistance and joint military exercises in order to help the Dominican armed forces patrol the border area.

Government

The Dominican Republic comprises 30 provinces, each administered by an appointed governor, and a Distrito Nacional (DN) containing the capital. Under the 1966 Constitution (as amended in 1994), legislative power is exercised by the bicameral National Congress, with a Senate of 32 members and a Chamber of Deputies (150 members). Members of both houses are elected for four years by universal adult suffrage. Executive power lies with the President, who is also elected by direct popular vote for four years. He is assisted by a Vice-President and a Cabinet comprising Secretaries of State.

Defence

Military service is voluntary and lasts for four years. In August 2002 the armed forces totalled 24,500 men: army 15,000, air force 5,500 and navy 4,000. Paramilitary forces numbered 15,000. The defence budget for 2001 was an estimated RD $2,500m.

Economic Affairs

In 2001, according to estimates by the World Bank, the Dominican Republic's gross national income (GNI), measured at average 1999–2001 prices, was US $18,955m., equivalent to $2,230 per head (or $5,870 per head on an international purchasing-power parity basis). During 1990–2001, it was estimated, the population increased by an average of 1.7% per year, while gross domestic product (GDP) per head increased, in real terms, by an average of 3.8% per year. Overall GDP increased, in real terms, by an average of 5.6% per year in 1990–2001. Real GDP increased by 2.7% in 2001. Growth was estimated at 4.0% in 2002.

Agriculture, including hunting, forestry and fishing, contributed an estimated 11.4% of GDP, at constant 1970 prices, in 2001, and employed an estimated 15.1% of the employed labour force in 2002. The principal cash crops are sugar cane (sugar and sugar derivatives accounted for an estimated 12.0% of total export earnings in 1999), coffee and cocoa beans and tobacco. Agricultural GDP increased, in real terms, by an average of 4.0% per year during 1990–2001. Real agricultural GDP increased by 5.0% in 2000 and by 5.1% in 2001. In 2001 the Government intended to implement a US $400m. development plan for fruit cultivation. In November 2002 it was reported that Japan was considering funding $400m. of agricultural and environmental projects in the country, including: a $70m. project to encourage the production of rice; a $10m. river basin reforestation project; and a $48m. loan intended to fund the sewer system in Santiago.

Industry (including mining, manufacturing, construction and power) employed 20.8% of the economically active population in 2002, and contributed an estimated 33.2% of GDP, at constant 1970 prices, in 2001. Industrial GDP increased, in real terms, by an average of 6.1% per year during 1990–2001. Real industrial GDP increased by 7.1% in 2000 but by only 0.1% in 2001.

Mining contributed an estimated 1.6% of GDP, at constant 1970 prices, in 2001, but employed only 0.3% of the economically active population in 2002. The major mineral export is ferro-nickel (providing 30.0% of total export earnings in 1995). Gold and silver are also exploited, and there are workable deposits of gypsum, limestone and mercury. The slump in world prices forced the ferro-nickel mine at Bonao to close in late 1998. Following an increase in prices in early 2000, the mine was reopened; however, it was closed again in October 2001 for three months, owing to a decrease in demand and prices. In February 2002 the Government reached agreement with Placer Dome of Canada on a 25-year concession to operate the Sulfuros de Pueblo Viejo mine. There were plans to develop other mines throughout the country. Real mining GDP decreased by an annual average of 1.4% during 1990–2001. The GDP of the mining sector increased, in real terms, by 13.3% in 2000, but decreased by 15.2% in 2001.

Manufacturing contributed an estimated 16.2% of GDP, at constant 1970 prices, in 2001, and employed 14.1% of the economically active population in 2002. Important branches of manufacturing in 1998 included beer and cigarettes. The most dynamic sector in 1999 was construction, in particular cement production. In mid-2001 there were 490 companies operating in 46 free-trade zones in the Dominican Republic, employing some 194,000 people. In 2001 a new free-trade zone was planned for San Pedro de Macorís. The passage of USA–Africa–Caribbean trade legislation in May 2000 gave Dominican apparel exports to the USA tariff-free status. The GDP of the manufacturing sector increased, in real terms, at an average rate of 4.6% per year during 1990–2001. Real manufacturing GDP increased by 7.5% in 2000, but decreased by 1.3% in 2001.

Energy is derived principally from petroleum; however, there is no domestic petroleum production. Imports of mineral fuels accounted for an estimated 13.2% of the total cost of imports in 1996. In 2002 construction was under way on a variety of energy projects, including: a 300 MW oil-fired power-station and a 300 MW gas-fired power-station, including a liquefied natural gas terminal; a regasification plant and a 500 MW gas-fired power-station; a hydroelectric dam in Altagracia, to supply drinking water and electricity to the province; and four mini-hydroelectric plants, together generating 16 MW. The Monción dam in Santiago Rodríguez, which included a 54 MW hydro-electric plant, was inaugurated in September 2001. York Caribbean Windpower, a subsidiary of York Research (USA), was to construct a US $160m. wind park in Puerto Plata; work was scheduled to begin in early 2003. In October 2000 the signing of the Caracas energy accord gave the Dominican Republic the option to buy petroleum from Venezuela under the preferential terms of the San José Agreement.

The services sector contributed an estimated 55.4% of GDP, at constant 1970 prices, in 2001, and employed 64.0% of the economically active population in 2002. The GDP of the services sector expanded at an average annual rate of 5.6% during 1990–2001. Real services GDP increased by 7.9% in 2000 and by 3.9% in 2001.

In 2001 the Dominican Republic recorded a visible trade deficit of US $3,451.3m., and there was a deficit of $838.9m. on the current account of the balance of payments. In 2000 the principal source of imports was the USA (49.8%); other major suppliers were Venezuela, Mexico and Japan. In the same year the USA was the principal market for exports (43.1% of the total); other significant purchasers were Belgium-Luxembourg and Puerto Rico. The principal exports in 1999 were iron and steel and sugar and sugar derivatives. In 1999 exports from the free-trade zones amounted to an estimated $3,200.4m. The principal imports in 1999 were petroleum and petroleum products, and food products. In 2001 banana exports totalled $35m., compared with $23m. in 2000.

In 2000 there was an estimated budgetary surplus of RD $3,449.5m. (equivalent to 1.1% of GDP). The Dominican Republic's total external debt at the end of 2000 was US $4,598m., of which $3,368m. was long term public debt. In that year the cost of debt-servicing was equivalent to 4.8% of total revenue from exports of goods and services. In 1990–2001 the average annual rate of inflation was 10.3%. Consumer prices increased by an average of 7.7% in 2000 and by 8.9% in 2001. An estimated 16.1% of the total labour force was unemployed in 1998.

In July 1984 the Dominican Republic was granted observer status in CARICOM (see p. 155). In December 1989 the country was accepted as a member of the ACP nations covered by the Lomé Convention (which expired in February 2000 and was replaced by the Cotonou Agreement, see p. 234, in June). In 1990 the Dominican Republic's application for full membership of CARICOM was threatened when ACP nations accused the Dominican Republic of breaking an agreement made under the Lomé Convention concerning the export of bananas to countries of the European Community (now the European Union). An agreement, originally signed on 22 August 1998, establishing a free-trade area between CARICOM countries and the Dominican Republic, came into effect on 1 December 2001.

In the 1990s the economy of the Dominican Republic was severely affected by the unstable nature of the country's electricity supply. Interruptions in the supply of electricity lasted up to 20 hours per day. The restructuring of the state electricity company (Corporación Dominicana de Electricidad—CDE) was repeatedly delayed. In May 1999 the generating and distribution operations of the CDE were partially privatized, with the divestment of 50%-shares producing revenue of US $644m. and saving the Government some $147m. per year in subsidies. In July 2001 President Rafael Hipólito Mejía Domínguez approved legislation that provided a framework for the electricity industry. However, there were widespread protests throughout 2001 and 2002 over continuing power cuts and the Government's failure to resolve the ongoing energy crisis. Trade unions called for the annulment of the privatization contracts that had been awarded to two electricity distribution companies—the US-owned company AES and the Spanish-owned Unión Fenosa—owing to allegations that since privatization the country's electricity service had become both more unreliable and more expensive. However, in October 2002 it was reported that the Government had instructed the power companies to raise their tariffs as it was no longer willing to subsidize electricity costs for any but the poorest areas of the country. In December the Senate approved a bill authorizing a sovereign bond issue of $750m., an increase from the $600m. originally proposed. The extra money was allegedly to be used to renationalize the privatized electricity companies. In 1999 it was announced that the Consejo Estatal de Azúcar (CEA) had accumulated debts totalling more than $250m. In September four private consortiums were granted 30-year contracts to manage the CEA's operations, providing the Government with a further $11m. per year in revenue. Despite the structural difficulties in the state power and sugar sectors, the economy continued to record significant growth in the late 1990s, based on expansion in tourism and the free-trade zones. Damages resulting from the impact of 'Hurricane Georges' in September 1998 were estimated by the Government at $2,000m.; the most adversely affected sectors were agriculture, manufacturing and tourism. A 3,500m. pesos emergency programme for reconstruction was partly financed by foreign grants. On 1 January 2001 a programme of fiscal measures, including an increase in consumer taxes, a rise in tariffs on imported luxury goods, a tax increase on cars, insurance, advertising, flights, security, commercial rents, gambling, cigarettes and beer, and a corporation tax of 1.5%, came into effect. In 2002 the peso experienced significant devaluation, reaching a record high of 25 pesos = US $1 in early December. The central bank implemented several attempts to stabilize the currency, investing over $500m. in the exchange-rate system during the year and imposing restrictions on banks and financial institutions, but with limited effectiveness. Meanwhile, the Government signed a 'Stability and Economic Development Pact' with members of the business sector, revising taxation measures and aiming to encourage economic growth and the stabilization of the currency. In February 2003 the Government announced several further emergency measures intended to limit spending and strengthen the peso, including the imposition of an additional 10% tariff on imports for at least three months; the measures attracted strong criticism from the business sector, which claimed that they contravened the terms of the pact. The budget for 2003, which awaited approval from the Congreso Nacional in January of that year, was some 83,000m. pesos. It proposed to freeze spending at current levels, while directing considerable resources into meeting public debt obligations and increasing health and education expenditure. In 2002 the tourist sector experienced a significant decline in revenue owing to a declining number of tourist arrivals and subsequent drop in hotel prices. Growth in GDP was estimated to have been approximately 4% in 2002.

Education

Education is, where possible, compulsory for children between the ages of six and 14 years. Primary education begins at the age of six and lasts for eight years. Secondary education, starting at 14 years of age, lasts for four years. In 1999 the total enrolment in primary, secondary and tertiary education was equivalent to 72% of the relevant age group (males 69%; females 75%). In 1997 primary enrolment included an estimated 91.3% of children in the relevant age-group (males 89.0%; females 93.6%), while secondary enrolment included an estimated 78.5% of children in the relevant age-group (males 74.9%; females 82.1%). In 1994/95 there were 4,001 primary schools, and in 1996/97 there were an estimated 1,737 secondary schools. There are eight universities. In October 2001 the Government announced the investment of US $52m. in the construction and repair of schools. Budgetary expenditure on education by the Secretariat of State for Education and Culture in 1997 was 5,114.7m. pesos, representing 14.3% of total government spending.

Public Holidays

2003: 1 January (New Year's Day), 6 January (Epiphany), 21 January (Our Lady of Altagracia), 26 January (Duarte), 27 February (Independence), 14 April (Pan-American Day), 18 April (Good Friday), 1 May (Labour Day), 16 July (Foundation of Sociedad la Trinitaria), 16 August (Restoration Day), 24 September (Our Lady of Mercedes), 12 October (Columbus Day), 24 October (United Nations Day), 1 November (All Saints' Day), 6 November (Constitution Day), 25 December (Christmas Day).

2004: 1 January (New Year's Day), 6 January (Epiphany), 21 January (Our Lady of Altagracia), 26 January (Duarte), 27

February (Independence), 9 April (Good Friday), 14 April (Pan-American Day), 1 May (Labour Day), 16 July (Foundation of Sociedad la Trinitaria), 16 August (Restoration Day), 24 September (Our Lady of Mercedes), 12 October (Columbus Day), 24 October (United Nations Day), 1 November (All Saints' Day), 6 November (Constitution Day), 25 December (Christmas Day).

Weights and Measures

The metric system is officially in force but the imperial system is often used.

Statistical Survey

Sources (unless otherwise stated): Oficina Nacional de Estadística, Edif. de Oficinas Gubernamentales, Avda México, esq. Leopoldo Navarro, Santo Domingo; tel. 682-7777; fax 685-4424; e-mail direccion@one.gov.do; internet www.one.gov.do; Banco Central de la República Dominicana, Calle Pedro Henríquez Ureña, esq. Leopoldo Navarro, Apdo 1347, Santo Domingo; tel. 221-9111; fax 686-7488; e-mail info@bancentral.gov.do; internet www.bancentral.gov.do.

Area and Population

AREA, POPULATION AND DENSITY

Area (sq km)	
Land	48,072
Inland water	350
Total	48,422*
Population (census results)†	
12 December 1981	5,647,977
24 September 1993	
Males	3,550,797
Females	3,742,593
Total	7,293,390
Population (official estimates at mid-year)‡	
1999	8,324,945
2000	8,518,483
2001	8,528,000§
Density (per sq km) at mid-2001	176.1§

* 18,696 sq miles.
† Excluding adjustment for underenumeration.
‡ Not adjusted to take account of the results of the 1993 census.
§ Preliminary figure.

PROVINCES

(estimated population, 2000)

Distrito Nacional	2,677,056		Maria Trinidad	
			Sánchez	142,030
Santiago	836,614		La Altagracia	128,627
San Cristóbal	519,906		Bahoruco	124,592
La Vega	390,314		Peravía	113,273
Duarte	318,151		San José de Ocoa	110,000
Puerto Plata	302,799		Salcedo	106,450
San Juan	265,562		El Seybo	105,447
San Pedro de Macorís	260,629		Monte Cristi	103,711
Azua	243,157		Hato Mayor	87,595
Espaillat	228,173		Samaná	82,135
La Romana	213,628		Dajabón	78,045
Valverde	198,979		Elias Piña	66,267
Sánchez Ramírez	194,282		Santiago Rodríguez	65,853
Barahona	179,945		Independencia	41,778
Monseñor Nouel	174,923		Pedernales	19,698
Monte Plata	174,126			

PRINCIPAL TOWNS

(estimated population, 2000)

Santo Domingo DN		San Felipe de Puerto	
(capital)	2,677,056	Plata	150,237
Santiago de los			
Caballeros	580,745	Moca	142,780
Concepción de la		San Juan de la	
Vega	241,917	Maguana	136,822
San Cristóbal	199,693	Bonao	134,443
San Francisco de			
Macorís	198,068	Bajos de Haina	119,732
La Romana	189,900	Baní	110,353
San Pedro de Macorís	179,686	Cotuí	103,089

Mid-2001 (UN estimate, incl. suburbs): Santo Domingo, 2,629,000 (Source: UN, *World Urbanization Prospects: The 2001 Revision*).

Births and deaths (1997): Registered live births 164,556 (birth rate 25.2 per 1,000); Registered deaths 26,301 (death rate 5.8 per 1,000).

Expectation of life (WHO estimates, years at birth): 67.0 (males 64.1; females 70.5) in 2001 (Source: WHO, *World Health Report*).

ECONOMICALLY ACTIVE POPULATION

('000 persons aged 10 years and over, national survey, April 2002)

	Males	Females	Total
Agriculture, hunting and forestry }	483.4	17.0	500.4
Fishing }			
Mining and quarrying	8.7	0.0	8.7
Manufacturing	304.1	163.7	467.8
Electricity, gas and water supply	23.3	6.3	29.5
Construction	180.5	3.4	183.9
Wholesale and retail trade	461.3	255.0	716.3
Hotels and restaurants	74.7	117.7	192.4
Transport, storage and			
communications	222.0	20.6	242.6
Financial intermediation }			
Real estate, renting and business }	32.9	33.4	66.4
activities }			
Public administration and			
defence	122.7	46.8	169.4
Education }			
Health and social work }			
Other community, social and }	258.7	473.0	731.6
personal service activities }			
Total employed	2,172.3	1,136.8	3,309.1
Unemployed	220.5	413.8	634.3
Total labour force	2,392.8	1,550.6	3,943.5

Health and Welfare

KEY INDICATORS

Total fertility rate (children per woman, 2001)	2.8
Under-5 mortality rate (per 1,000 live births, 2000) . . .	42
HIV/AIDS (% of persons aged 15–49, 2001)	2.5
Physicians (per 1,000 head, 1997)	2.16
Hospital beds (per 1,000 head, 1996)	1.5
Health expenditure (2000): US $ per head (PPP)	357
Health expenditure (2000): % of GDP	6.3
Health expenditure (2000): public (% of total)	28.0
Access to water (% of persons, 2000)	79
Access to sanitation (% of persons, 2000)	71
Human Development Index (2000): ranking	94
Human Development Index (2000): value	0.727

For sources and definitions, see explanatory note on p. vi.

Agriculture

PRINCIPAL CROPS
('000 metric tons)

	1999	2000	2001
Rice (paddy)	566.5	581.4	697.9
Maize	30.3	23.9	52.7
Potatoes	29.3	24.9	64.7
Sweet potatoes	53.0	36.8	32.3
Cassava (Manioc) . . .	126.5	126.5	123.9
Yautia (Cocoyam) . . .	48.5	49.0	39.5
Sugar cane	4,452.4	4,510.7	4,645.3
Dry beans	25.8	22.0	30.2
Coconuts	184.4	140.0*	140.0*
Oil palm fruit*	136.0	153.0	153.0
Tomatoes	280.7	285.6	203.0
Dry onions	39.4	31.6	41.2
Cantaloupes and other melons	41.3	39.6	52.0*
Other fresh vegetables* . . .	98.7	88.4	102.5
Bananas	432.0	343.3	445.4
Plantains	229.3	178.2	190.0*
Oranges	82.0	131.4	66.7
Mangoes*	180.0	180.0	185.0
Avocados	71.2	81.7	111.1
Pineapples	72.5	64.4	136.9
Papayas*	20.5	22.5	24.0
Other fresh fruit* . . .	49.7	49.7	49.5
Coffee (green)	34.6	45.5	35.5
Cocoa beans	25.9	37.1	44.9
Tobacco (leaves) . . .	15.8	17.2	17.5*

* FAO estimate(s).

Source: FAO.

LIVESTOCK
('000 head, year ending September)

	1999	2000	2001
Horses*	330	330	340
Mules*	138	138	140
Asses*	145	145	150
Cattle	1,954.2	2,018.3	2,106.8
Pigs	539.6	538.6	565.5
Sheep	105.5	105.5	106.0
Goats	163.5	178.4	187.4
Poultry	42,000	46,000	47,380

* FAO estimates.

Source: FAO.

LIVESTOCK PRODUCTS
('000 metric tons)

	1999	2000	2001
Beef and veal	65.5	68.9	70.8
Sheep and goat meat*	926.0	1,046.0	1,075.0
Pig meat	57.7	61.2	63.0
Poultry meat	182.7	211.0	203.4
Cows' milk	411.1	397.8	410.1
Cheese*	2.5	2.5	2.5
Butter*	1.5	1.5	1.5
Hen eggs	53.6	60.9	65.0
Honey	1.4	1.3	1.4
Cattle hides (fresh)*	8.7	8.1	8.8

* FAO estimates.

Source: FAO.

Forestry

ROUNDWOOD REMOVALS
('000 cubic metres, excl. bark)

	1983	1984	1985
Sawlogs, veneer logs and logs for sleepers	4	4	4
Other industrial wood	3	3	3
Fuel wood	531	543	556
Total	538	550	563

1986–2001: Annual production as in 1985 (FAO estimates).

Source: FAO.

Fishing

('000 metric tons, live weight)

	1998	1999	2000
Capture	10.2	8.5	11.0
Mozambique tilapia	0.4	—	—
Other tilapia	0.1	0.4	—
Groupers, seabasses	0.4	0.7	0.9
Southern red snapper	0.2	0.1	0.1
Yellowtail snapper	0.2	0.2	0.2
Other snappers and jobfishes	0.9	—	0.8
Grunts, sweetlips	0.2	0.4	0.3
Porgies	—	0.4	—
Wrasses, hogfishes, etc. . . .	0.1	0.1	0.1
Atlantic Spanish mackerel . . .	0.3	—	—
Northern bluefin tuna . . .	0.2	0.4	0.2
Nurse shark . . .	—	—	0.4
Caribbean spiny lobster . . .	0.9	0.8	1.3
Stromboid conchs	2.7	1.3	1.8
Aquaculture	0.8	0.7	2.1
Common carp	0.3	0.3	0.6
Total catch	11.0	9.3	13.2

Source: FAO, *Yearbook of Fishery Statistics*.

Mining

	1998	1999	2000
Ferro-nickel ('000 metric tons) . .	69	62	70*
Gold (kilograms)	1,424	651	—
Silver (kilograms)	7,409	3,140	—

* Estimate.

Source: US Geological Survey.

Industry

SELECTED PRODUCTS
('000 metric tons, unless otherwise indicated)

	1997	1998	1999
Wheat flour	438	498	391
Refined sugar	113	299	79
Cement	1,822	1,872	2,295
Beer ('000 hectolitres)	2,593	2,993	3,484
Cigarettes (million)	3,972	4,098	4,005
Motor spirit (gasoline)	370	n.a.	n.a.
Electricity (million kWh)	7,335	n.a.	n.a.

Source: UN, *Industrial Commodity Statistics Yearbook*.

Finance

CURRENCY AND EXCHANGE RATES

Monetary Units
100 centavos = 1 Dominican Republic peso (RD $ or peso oro)

Sterling, Dollar and Euro Equivalents (31 December 2002)
£1 sterling = 34.16 pesos
US $1 = 21.19 pesos
€1 = 22.23 pesos
1,000 Dominican Republic pesos = £29.27 = US $47.18 = €44.99

Average Exchange Rate (RD $ per US $)
2000   16.415
2001   16.952
2002   18.610

BUDGET
(RD $ million)

Revenue	1999	2000	2001*
Tax revenue	40,899.1	47,617.0	56,995.6
Taxes on income and profits	9,510.2	11,125.8	15,839.2
Taxes on goods and services	16,861.7	17,608.9	26,557.6
Taxes on international trade and transactions	13,292.6	17,262.3	12,856.2
Other current revenue	2,476.3	3,586.1	2,646.0
Property income	459.9	597.0	610.1
Fees and charges	1,427.1	1,845.5	1,638.5
Capital revenue	108.5	68.3	213.9
Total	43,483.9	51,271.4	59,855.5

Expenditure	1999	2000	2001*
Current expenditure	31,188.1	36,657.1	43,419.3
Wages and salaries	14,206.3	18,134.0	21,496.2
Other services	1,577.1	1,868.9	2,075.5
Materials and supplies	3,237.6	3,497.3	4,048.7
Current transfers	9,917.2	9,682.3	12,157.3
Interest payments	1,391.3	2,321.3	2,989.9
Internal debt	211.4	577.1	726.8
External debt	1,179.9	1,744.2	2,263.2
Capital expenditure	13,976.5	11,629.9	15,444.1
Machines and equipment	805.3	638.1	994.5
Construction of works and agricultural plantations	6,929.8	6,717.9	7,624.7
Capital transfers	4,876.2	3,460.5	6,196.0
Total (incl. others)	45,164.6	48,287.0	58,863.4

* Preliminary figures.

INTERNATIONAL RESERVES
(US $ million at 31 December)

	1999	2000	2001
Gold*	5.2	5.0	5.1
IMF special drawing rights	0.3	0.4	0.4
Foreign exchange	693.7	626.8	1,099.0
Total	699.2	632.2	1,104.5

* Valued at market-related prices.

Source: IMF, *International Financial Statistics*.

MONEY SUPPLY
(RD $ million at 31 December)

	2000	2001	2002
Currency outside banks	15,076	16,628	18,265
Demand deposits at commercial banks	20,290	24,529	25,341
Total money (incl. others)	35,445	41,258	43,765

Source: IMF, *International Financial Statistics*.

COST OF LIVING
(Consumer Price Index; base: 1990 = 100)

	1998	1999	2000
Food	225.5	237.6	238.5
Clothing	191.6	196.2	202.8
Rent	267.9	282.8	306.8
All items (incl. others)	235.3	250.5	269.9

2001: All items 293.8.

Source: ILO.

NATIONAL ACCOUNTS

National Income and Product
(RD $ million at current prices)

	1999	2000	2001
GDP in market prices	277,908	321,516	392,258
Net primary income from abroad	29,602	31,160	40,317
Gross national income (GNI)	307,510	352,676	432,575
Less Consumption of fixed capital	16,675	19,291	23,535
Net national income	290,835	333,385	409,040

Source: IMF, *International Financial Statistics*.

Expenditure on the Gross Domestic Product
(RD $ million at current prices)

	1999	2000	2001
Final consumption expenditure	231,275	275,126	336,785
Households			
Non-profit institutions serving households	208,725	247,984	300,187
General government	22,550	27,142	36,598
Gross capital formation	67,394	77,093	89,884
Gross fixed capital formation	66,593	76,166	88,753
Changes in inventories			
Acquisitions, *less* disposals, of valuables	801	927	1,131
Total domestic expenditure	298,669	352,219	426,669
Exports of goods and services	127,887	146,749	149,841
Less Imports of goods and services	148,647	177,451	184,251
GDP in market prices	277,909	321,517	392,259
GDP at constant 1970 prices	6,147	6,593	6,772

Source: IMF, *International Financial Statistics*.

Gross Domestic Product by Economic Activity
(RD $ million at constant 1970 prices)

	1999*	2000*	2001*
Agriculture, hunting, forestry and fishing	701.5	736.3	774.0
Mining and quarrying	109.8	124.4	105.5
Manufacturing	1,033.0	1,110.9	1,097.0
Electricity, gas and water†	130.5	139.5	165.2
Construction	826.2	872.8	881.1
Wholesale and retail trade restaurants and hotels	1,198.1	1,325.8	1,309.3
Transport, storage and communications	723.0	804.8	889.5
Finance, insurance and real estate	516.4	530.8	544.3
Community, social, personal and business services‡	908.7	947.6	1,006.2
Total	6,147.2	6,592.9	6,772.1

* Preliminary figures.
† Refers to electricity and water only.
‡ Including gas.

BALANCE OF PAYMENTS
(US $ million)

	1999	2000	2001
Exports of goods f.o.b	5,136.7	5,736.7	5,332.9
Imports of goods f.o.b.	−8,041.1	−9,478.5	−8,784.2
Trade balance	−2,904.4	−3,741.8	−3,451.3
Exports of services	2,850.3	3,227.6	2,998.8
Imports of services	−1,248.0	−1,373.3	−1,295.0
Balance on goods and services	−1,302.1	−1,887.5	−1,747.5
Other income received	218.3	299.7	271.2
Other income paid	−1,193.2	−1,341.0	−1,390.1
Balance on goods, services and income	−2,277.0	−2,928.8	−2,866.4
Current transfers received	1,997.1	2,095.6	2,232.0
Current transfers paid	−149.3	−193.3	−204.5
Current balance	−429.2	−1,026.5	−838.9
Direct investment from abroad	1,337.8	952.9	1,198.4
Portfolio investment assets	−433.0	268.4	123.5
Portfolio investment liabilities	−3.8	−3.9	480.2
Other investment assets	−53.4	−165.0	−155.5
Other investment liabilities	213.4	544.2	76.3
Net errors and omissions	−480.4	−618.5	−371.1
Overall balance	151.4	−48.4	512.9

Source: IMF, *International Financial Statistics*.

External Trade

PRINCIPAL COMMODITIES

Imports f.o.b. (US $ million)*	1998	1999	2000†
Consumer goods	2,178.3	2,368.9	3,329.7
Durable goods	541.1	542.8	662.4
Foodstuffs	208.2	237.1	250.6
Petroleum products	463.6	615.7	1,112.3
Raw materials	1,636.3	1,787.4	2,058.0
For food industry	158.3	111.5	96.5
For textile industry	136.5	189.5	130.9
Petroleum and petroleum products	184.3	255.3	442.2
Cast iron and steel	161.0	157.6	396.7
Capital goods	1,082.1	1,050.5	1,281.9
For transport	181.3	266.5	226.9
For industry	236.2	175.0	236.8
Machinery	344.1	242.1	342.2
Total (incl. others)	4,896.6	5,206.8	6,669.6

* Figures exclude imports into free-trade zones.
† Provisional figures.

Exports f.o.b. (US $ million)*	1998	1999	2000†
Primary products	370.3	230.8	275.9
Foodstuffs	344.1	209.3	254.0
Raw cane sugar	66.3	65.6	70.9
Green coffee beans	64.6	14.8	20.8
Cocoa beans	39.8	33.2	24.2
Intermediate products	210.7	202.0	286.3
Ferro-nickel	132.1	143.9	237.4
Consumer goods	299.1	372.4	403.9
Non-durables	288.7	341.2	364.1
Processed food	100.0	104.6	129.7
Tobacco substitutes	26.5	23.1	20.5
Other goods	188.7	236.6	234.4
Petroleum products	159.1	162.3	165.9
Total	880.2	805.2	966.1

* Figures exclude exports from free-trade zones.
† Provisional figures.

PRINCIPAL TRADING PARTNERS
(US $ '000)

Imports c.i.f.	1998	1999	2000
Argentina	60,697	40,687	24,808
Brazil	57,863	66,193	80,719
Canada	40,593	40,549	41,350
Colombia	45,434	65,040	75,199
Denmark	36,396	32,633	50,886
Germany	51,507	59,488	87,814
Italy	43,434	46,340	57,698
Japan	148,285	237,190	266,938
Korea, Democratic People's Republic	35,139	21,199	16,025
Mexico	245,284	265,894	436,254
Panama	80,808	124,101	157,221
Puerto Rico	131,209	72,388	88,813
Spain	125,141	143,688	243,198
Taiwan	46,847	72,018	79,221
USA	1,700,855	2,436,210	2,962,044
Venezuela	403,918	673,960	979,449
Total (incl. others)	3,446,603	4,635,545	5,953,829

Exports f.o.b.	1998	1999	2000
Belgium–Luxembourg	75,774	71,220	123,293
Canada	26,490	15,690	5,160
Cuba	2,422	4,604	10,114
France	10,805	11,930	11,227
Germany	30,236	28,467	26,908
Haiti	47,601	67,543	57,936
Italy	17,935	9,208	12,892
Japan	18,461	8,525	11,949
Korea, Republic	18,618	18,208	38,517
Mexico	9,356	4,897	3,343
Netherlands	12,526	11,668	17,340
Panama	9,960	17,923	18,879
Puerto Rico	74,012	91,948	97,505
Spain	17,262	16,931	15,300
United Kingdom	2,035	6,518	10,836
USA	448,509	327,875	373,462
Total (incl. others)	861,990	743,561	866,054

Source: Inter-American Development Bank.

Transport

ROAD TRAFFIC
(motor vehicles in use at 31 December, estimates)

	1997	1998
Passenger cars	305,477	353,177
Buses and coaches	27,380	32,619
Lorries and vans	147,523	167,728

SHIPPING

Merchant Fleet
(registered at 31 December)

	1999	2000	2001
Number of vessels	22	24	20
Total displacement ('000 grt)	10.1	10.4	9.4

Source: Lloyd's Register-Fairplay, *World Fleet Statistics*.

International Sea-borne Freight Traffic
('000 metric tons)

	1996	1997	1998
Goods loaded	112	152	139

Source: UN, *Monthly Bulletin of Statistics*.

CIVIL AVIATION
(traffic on scheduled services)

	1997	1998	1999
Kilometres flown (million) . . .	1	1	0
Passengers carried ('000) . . .	34	34	10
Passengers-km (million) . . .	16	16	5
Total ton-km (million)	1	1	0

Source: UN, *Statistical Yearbook*.

Tourism

ARRIVALS BY NATIONALITY

	2000	2001	2002
Argentina	74,659	59,107	13,497
Canada	245,732	283,490	313,612
France	174,258	194,090	242,027
Germany	451,920	333,559	240,603
Italy	135,295	113,826	113,574
Spain	138,281	138,281	135,526
United Kingdom	117,200	139,582	146,301
USA	643,748	666,290	710,971
Total (incl. others)	3,314,063	3,088,548	3,105,081

Receipts from Tourism (US $ million): 2,153.1 in 1998; 2,524.0 in 1999; 2,918 in 2000.

Communications Media

	1999	2000	2001
Telephones ('000 main lines in use)	826.7	894.2	939.5
Mobile cellular telephones ('000 subscribers).	424.4	705.4	1,073.3
Internet users ('000)	35.0	55.0	186.0

Daily newspapers: 10 in 1998 (average circulation 1.3m. copies).

Radio receivers ('000 in use): 1,440 in 1997.

Television receivers ('000 in use): 790 in 1998.

Facsimile machines (number in use): 2,300 in 1996.

Sources: UNESCO, *Statistical Yearbook*; UN, *Statistical Yearbook*; International Telecommunication Union.

Education

(1996/97)

	Institu-tions	Teachers	Students Males	Students Females	Students Total
Pre-primary*	n.a.	8,571	96,252	94,289	190,541
Primary . . .	4,001†	39,860	691,675	668,369	1,360,044
Secondary: General . .	1,737	11,033	145,560*	184,384*	329,944*
Secondary: Teacher-training† .	n.a.	86	549	743	1,292
Secondary: Vocational† .	n.a.	1,211	9,147	12,356	21,503
Higher . . .	n.a.	9,041	75,223	101,772	176,995

* 1997/98 figure(s).
† 1994/95 figure(s).

Source: UNESCO, *Statistical Yearbook*.

Adult literacy rate (UNESCO estimates): 83.6% (males 83.6%; females 83.6%) in 2000 (Source: UN Development Programme, *Human Development Report*).

Directory

The Constitution

The Constitution of the Dominican Republic was promulgated on 28 November 1966, and amended on 14 August 1994. Its main provisions are summarized below:

The Dominican Republic is a sovereign, free, independent state; no organizations set up by the State can bring about any act which might cause direct or indirect intervention in the internal or foreign affairs of the State or which might threaten the integrity of the State. The Dominican Republic recognizes and applies the norms of general and American international law and is in favour of and will support any initiative towards economic integration for the countries of America. The civil, republican, democratic, representative Government is divided into three independent powers: legislative, executive and judicial.

The territory of the Dominican Republic is as laid down in the Frontier Treaty of 1929 and its Protocol of Revision of 1936.

The life and property of the individual citizen are inviolable; there can be no sentence of death, torture nor any sentence which might cause physical harm to the individual. There is freedom of thought, of conscience, of religion, freedom to publish, freedom of unarmed association, provided that there is no subversion against public order, national security or decency. There is freedom of labour and trade unions; freedom to strike, except in the case of public services, according to the dispositions of the law.

The State will undertake agrarian reform, dedicating the land to useful interests and gradually eliminating the latifundios (large estates). The State will do all in its power to support all aspects of family life. Primary education is compulsory and all education is free. Social security services will be developed. Every Dominican has the duty to give what civil and military service the State may require. Every legally entitled citizen must exercise the right to vote,

i.e. all persons over 18 years of age and all who are or have been married even if they are not yet 18.

GOVERNMENT

Legislative power is exercised by Congress which is made up of the Senate and Chamber of Deputies, elected by direct vote. Senators, one for each of the 30 Provinces and one for the Distrito Nacional, are elected for four years; they must be Dominicans in full exercise of their citizen's rights, and at least 25 years of age. Their duties are to elect the President and other members of the Electoral and Accounts Councils, and to approve the nomination of diplomats. Deputies, one for every 50,000 inhabitants or fraction over 25,000 in each Province and the Distrito Nacional, are elected for four years and must fulfil the same conditions for election as Senators.

Decisions of Congress are taken by absolute majority of at least half the members of each house; urgent matters require a two-thirds' majority. Both houses normally meet on 27 February and 16 August each year for sessions of 90 days, which can be extended for a further 60 days.

Executive power is exercised by the President of the Republic, who is elected by direct vote for a four-year term. No President may serve more than one consecutive term. The successful presidential candidate must obtain at least 50% plus one vote of the votes cast; if necessary, a second round of voting is held 45 days later, with the participation of the two parties that obtained the highest number of votes. The President must be a Dominican citizen by birth or origin, over 30 years of age and in full exercise of citizen's rights. The President must not have engaged in any active military or police service for at least a year prior to election. The President takes office on 16 August following the election. The President of the Republic is Head of the Public Administration and Supreme Chief of the armed forces and police forces. The President's duties include nominating

Secretaries and Assistant Secretaries of State and other public officials, promulgating and publishing laws and resolutions of Congress and seeing to their faithful execution, watching over the collection and just investment of national income, nominating, with the approval of the Senate, members of the Diplomatic Corps, receiving foreign Heads of State, presiding at national functions, decreeing a State of Siege or Emergency or any other measures necessary during a public crisis. The President may not leave the country for more than 15 days without authorization from Congress. In the absence of the President, the Vice-President will assume power, or failing him, the President of the Supreme Court of Justice. The legislative and municipal elections are held two years after the presidential elections, mid-way through the presidential term.

LOCAL GOVERNMENT

Government in the Distrito Nacional and the Municipalities is in the hands of local councils, with members elected proportionally to the number of inhabitants, but numbering at least five. Each Province has a civil Governor, designated by the Executive.

JUDICIARY

Judicial power is exercised by the Supreme Court of Justice and the other Tribunals; no judicial official may hold another public office or employment, other than honorary or teaching. The Supreme Court is made up of at least 11 judges, who must be Dominican citizens by birth or origin, at least 35 years old, in full exercise of their citizen's rights, graduates in law and have practised professionally for at least 12 years. The National Judiciary Council appoints the members of the Supreme Court, who in turn appoint judges at all other levels of the judicial system. There are nine Courts of Appeal, a Lands Tribunal and a Court of the First Instance in each judicial district; in each Municipality and in the Distrito Nacional there are also Justices of the Peace.

Elections are directed by the Central Electoral Board. The armed forces are essentially obedient and apolitical, created for the defence of national independence and the maintenance of public order and the Constitution and Laws.

The artistic and historical riches of the country, whoever owns them, are part of the cultural heritage of the country and are under the safe-keeping of the State. Mineral deposits belong to the State. There is freedom to form political parties, provided they conform to the principles laid down in the Constitution. Justice is administered without charge throughout the Republic.

This Constitution can be reformed if the proposal for reform is supported in Congress by one-third of the members of either house or by the Executive. A special session of Congress must be called and any resolutions must have a two-thirds' majority. There can be no reform of the method of government, which must always be civil, republican, democratic and representative. Note: In July 2002 a National Constituent Assembly voted in favour of amending the Constitution to enable presidents serve two consecutive terms; a further proposal to allow presidential candidates to win an election with less than 50% of votes cast was also under discussion.

The Government

HEAD OF STATE

President: RAFAEL HIPÓLITO MEJÍA DOMÍNGUEZ (took office 16 August 2000).
Vice-President: Dra MILAGROS ORTIZ BOSCH.

CABINET
(April 2003)

Secretary of State to the Presidency: SERGIO GRULLÓN.
Secretary of State for External Relations: FRANK GUERRERO PRATS.
Secretary of State for the Interior and Police: Dr PEDRO FRANCO BADÍA.
Secretary of State for the Armed Forces: Maj.-Gen. JOSÉ MIGUEL SOTO JIMÉNEZ.
Secretary of State for Finance: RAFAEL CALDERÓN.
Secretary of State for Education: Dra MILAGROS ORTIZ BOSCH.
Secretary of State for Agriculture: Dr ELIGIO JAQUEZ CRUZ.
Secretary of State for Public Works and Communications: MIGUEL VARGAS MALDONADO.
Secretary of State for Public Health and Social Welfare: Dr JOSÉ RODRÍGUEZ SOLDEVILLA.
Secretary of State for Industry and Commerce: SONIA GUZMAN.
Secretary of State for Labour: Dr MILTON RAY GUEVARA.

Secretary of State for Tourism: Dr RAFAEL SUBERVÍ BONILLA.
Secretary of State for Sport, Physical Education and Recreation: CÉSAR CEDEÑO.
Secretary of State for Art and Culture: TONY RAFUL TEJADA.
Secretary of State for Higher Education, Science and Technology: ANDRES REYES.
Secretary of State for Women: Dra YADIRA HENRÍQUEZ.
Secretary of State for Youth: ROBERTO POLANCO.
Secretary of State for the Environment and Natural Resources: Dr FRANK MOYA PONS.
Technical Secretary of State to the Presidency: CARLOS DESPRADEL.
Administrative Secretary of State to the Presidency: SIQUIÓ NG DE LA ROSA.
Secretaries of State without Portfolio: ANGEL MIOLAN, RAMÓN EMILIO JIMÉNEZ, ANTONIO TORRES, ELIAS WESSIN Y WESSIN, DOMINGO MARIOTTI, ALBA MARIA CABRAL PEÑA GOMEZ.

SECRETARIATS OF STATE

Administrative Secretariat of the Presidency: Palacio Nacional, Avda México, esq. Dr Delgado, Santo Domingo, DN; tel. 686-4771; fax 688-2100; e-mail prensa@presidencia.gov.do; internet www.presidencia.gov.do.

Technical Secretariat of the Presidency: Avda México, esq. Dr Delgado, Santo Domingo, DN; tel. 221-5140; fax 221-8627; internet www.stp.gov.do.

Secretariat of State for Agriculture: Autopista Duarte, Km 6.5, Los Jardines del Norte, Santo Domingo, DN; tel. 547-3888; fax 227-1268; e-mail sec.agric@codetel.net.do; internet www.agricultura.gov.do.

Secretariat of State for the Armed Forces: Plaza de la Independencia, Avda 27 de Febrero, esq. Luperón, Santo Domingo, DN; tel. 530-5149; fax 531-1309; internet www.secffaa.mil.

Secretariat of State for Art and Culture: Avda Máximo Gómez 10, esq. Santiago, Santo Domingo, DN; tel. 688-9700; fax 689-8907.

Secretariat of State for Education: Avda Máximo Gómez 10, esq. Santiago, Santo Domingo, DN; tel. 688-9700; fax 689-8907; e-mail sub-administrativo@see.gov.do; internet www.see.gov.do.

Secretariat of State for External Relations: Avda Independencia 752, Santo Domingo, DN; tel. 535-6280; fax 533-5772; internet www.serex.gov.do.

Secretariat of State for the Environment and Natural Resources: Santo Domingo, DN.

Secretariat of State for Finance: Avda México 45, Santo Domingo, DN; tel. 687-5131; fax 688-6561.

Secretariat of State for Higher Education, Science and Technology: Centro de los Héroes, Avda Enrique Jiménez Moya, esq. Juan de Dios Ventura Simó, 5°, Santo Domingo, DN; tel. 533-3881; fax 535-4694; e-mail info@seescyt.gov.do; internet www.seescyt.gov.do.

Secretariat of State for Industry and Commerce: Edif. de Oficinas Gubernamentales, 7°, Avda Francia, esq. Leopoldo Navarro, Santo Domingo, DN; tel. 685-5171; fax 686-4741; e-mail ind.comercio@codetel.net.do; internet www.seic.gov.do.

Secretariat of State for the Interior and Police: Edif. de Oficinas Gubernamentales, 3°, Avda Francia, esq. Leopoldo Navarro, Santo Domingo, DN; tel. 686-6251; fax 221-8234.

Secretariat of State for Labour: Centro de los Héroes, Jiménez Moya 9, Santo Domingo, DN; tel. 535-4404; fax 535-4590; e-mail secret.trabajo@codetel.net.do; internet www.set.gov.do.

Secretariat of State for Public Health and Social Welfare: Avda Tiradentes, esq. San Cristóbal, Ensanche La Fe, Santo Domingo, DN; tel. 541-3121; fax 540-6445; internet www.saludpublica.gov.do.

Secretariat of State for Public Works and Communications: Avda San Cristóbal, esq. Tiradentes, Ensanche La Fe, Santo Domingo, DN; tel. 565-2811; fax 562-3382; e-mail info.seopc@codetel.net.do; internet www.seopc.gov.do.

Secretariat of State for Sport, Physical Education and Recreation: Avda Ortega y Gasset, Centro Olímpico, Santo Domingo, DN; tel. 540-4010; fax 563-6586; internet www.sedefir.gov.do.

Secretariat of State for Tourism: Bloque D, Edif. de Oficinas Gubernamentales, Avda México, esq. 30 de Marzo, Apdo 497, Santo Domingo, DN; tel. 221-4660; fax 682-3806; e-mail info@sectur.gov.do; internet www.sectur.gov.do.

Secretariat of State for Women: Bloque D, Edif. de Oficinas Gubernamentales, Avda México, esq. 30 de Marzo, Santo Domingo, DN; tel. 685-3755; fax 686-0911.

Secretariat of State for Youth: Santo Domingo, DN.

President and Legislature

PRESIDENT

Election, 16 May 2000

Candidate	% of votes cast
Rafael Hipólito Mejía Domínguez (PRD)	49.87
Danilo Medina Sánchez (PLD)	24.94
Dr Joaquín Balaguer Ricardo (PRSC)	24.60
Total (incl. others)	100.00

CONGRESO NACIONAL

The National Congress comprises a Senate and a Chamber of Deputies.

President of the Senate: ANDRÉS BAUTISTA GARCÍA (PRD).

President of the Chamber of Deputies: Dra RAFAELA ALBURQUERQUE DE GONZÁLEZ (PRSC).

General Election, 16 May 2002

	Seats	
	Senate	Chamber of Deputies
Partido Revolucionario Dominicano (PRD)	29	73
Partido de la Liberación Dominicana (PLD)	2	41
Partido Reformista Social Cristiano (PRSC)	1	36
Total	32	150

Political Organizations

Alianza por la Democracia (APD): Santo Domingo, DN; f. 1992 by breakaway group of the PLD; split into two factions (led, respectively, by Max Puig and Nélsida Marmolejos) in 1993; Sec.-Gen. VICENTE BENGOA.

Frente Independiente Leonel al Poder (FILA): Santo Domingo, DN; f. 2002; established by former Pres. Leonel Fernández to support his candidacy in 2004 presidential election; Leader LEONEL FERNÁNDEZ.

Fuerza Nacional Progresista (FNP): Santo Domingo, DN; rightwing; Leader MARIO VINICIO CASTILLO.

Fuerza de la Revolución: Avda Independencia 258, Apdo 2651, Santo Domingo, DN; e-mail fr@nodo50.ix.apc.org; internet www.nodo50.org/fr; f. 2000 by merger of the Partido Communista Dominicano, Movimiento Liberador 12 de Enero, Fuerza de Resistencia y Liberación Popular, Fuerza Revolucionaria 21 de Julio and other revolutionary groups; Marxist-Leninist.

Movimiento de Conciliación Nacional (MCN): Pina 207, Santo Domingo, DN; f. 1969; centre party; 659,277 mems; Pres. Dr JAIME M. FERNÁNDEZ; Sec. VÍCTOR MENA.

Movimiento de Integración Democrática (MIDA): Santo Domingo, DN; tel. 687-8895; centre-right; Leader Dr FRANCISCO AUGUSTO LORA.

Movimiento Popular Dominicano: Santo Domingo, DN; leftwing; Leader JULIO DE PEÑA VALDÉS.

Participación Ciudadana: Desiderio Arias 25, La Julia, Santo Domingo, DN; tel. 535-6200; fax 535-6631; e-mail p.ciudadana@codetel.net.do; internet www.pciudadana.com; f. 1993; Leaders JAVIER CABREJA POLANCO, RAMÓN TEJADA HOLGUÍN, JUAN BOLÍVAR DÍAZ.

Partido Demócrata Popular: Arz. Meriño 259, Santo Domingo, DN; tel. 685-2920; Leader LUIS HOMERO LÁJARA BURGOS.

Partido de la Liberación Dominicana (PLD): Avda Independencia 401, Santo Domingo, DN; tel. 685-3540; fax 687-5569; e-mail pldorg@pld.org.do; f. 1973 by breakaway group of PRD; left-wing; Leader LEONEL FERNÁNDEZ REYNA; Sec.-Gen. REINALDO PARED PÉREZ.

Partido Quisqueyano Demócrata (PQD): Bolivar 51, esq. Uruguay, Santo Domingo, DN; tel. 565-0244; internet www.geocities.com/CapitolHill/Senate/7090/; f. 1968; right-wing; 600,000 mems; Pres. Lic. PEDRO BERGÉS; Sec.-Gen. Dr ELÍAS WESSIN CHÁVEZ.

Partido Reformista Social Cristiano (PRSC): Avda San Cristóbal, Ensanche La Fe, Apdo 1332, Santo Domingo, DN; tel. 566-7089; f. 1964; centre-right party; Pres. (vacant).

Partido Revolucionario Dominicano (PRD): Espaillat 118, Santo Domingo, DN; tel. 687-2193; internet www.prd.partidos.com; f. 1939; democratic socialist; mem. of Socialist International; 400,000 mems; Pres. RAFAEL HIPÓLITO MEJÍA DOMÍNGUEZ; Sec.-Gen. HATUEY DECAMPS.

Partido Revolucionario Independiente (PRI): Santo Domingo, DN; f. 1985; after split by the PRD's right-wing faction; Pres. JOSÉ RAFAEL MOLINA UREÑA; Sec.-Gen. STORMI REYNOSO.

Partido Revolucionario Social Cristiano: Santo Domingo, DN; f. 1961; left-wing; Pres. Dr CLAUDIO ISIDORO ACOSTA; Sec.-Gen. Dr ALFONSO LOCKWARD.

Partido de los Trabajadores Dominicanos: Avda Duarte 69 (Altos), Santo Domingo, DN; tel. 685-7705; f. 1979; workers' party; Sec.-Gen. JOSÉ GONZÁLEZ ESPINOZA.

Unidad Democrática (UD): Santo Domingo, DN; Leader FERNANDO ALVAREZ BOGAERT.

Other parties include Unión Cívica Nacional (UCN), Partido Alianza Social Demócrata (ASD—Leader Dr JOSÉ RAFAEL ABINADER), Movimiento Nacional de Salvación (MNS—Leader LUIS JULIÁN PÉREZ), Partido Comunista del Trabajo de la República Dominicana (Sec.-Gen. RAFAEL CHALJUB MEJÍA), Partido de Veteranos Civiles (PVC), Partido Acción Constitucional (PAC), Partido Unión Patriótica (PUP—Leader ROBERTO SANTANA), Partido de Acción Nacional (right-wing) and Movimiento de Acción Social Cristiana (ASC).

Diplomatic Representation

EMBASSIES IN THE DOMINICAN REPUBLIC

Argentina: Avda Máximo Gómez 10, Apdo 1302, Santo Domingo, DN; tel. 682-2977; fax 221-2206; e-mail embarg@codetel.net.do; Ambassador CARLOS PIÑEIRO IÑÍGUEZ.

Brazil: Avda Winston Churchill 32, Edif. Franco-Acra y Asociados, 2°, Apdo 1655, Santo Domingo, DN; tel. 532-0868; fax 532-0917; e-mail e.brazil@codetel.net.do; Ambassador P. G. VILAS-BÔAS CASTRO.

Chile: Avda Anacaona 11, Mirador del Sur, Santo Domingo, DN; tel. 532-7800; fax 530-8310; e-mail embaj.chile@codetel.net.do; Ambassador RUBIO SANDOVAL CARLOS.

China (Taiwan): Edif. Palic, 1°, Avda Abraham Lincoln, esq. José Amado Soler, Apdo 4797, Santo Domingo, DN; tel. 562-5555; fax 563-4139; e-mail e.china@codetel.net.do; Ambassador PEDRO Y. C. HSIANG.

Colombia: Avda Abraham Lincoln 502, 2°, Santo Domingo, DN; tel. 562-1670; e-mail crdomini@minrelext.gov.co; Ambassador JOSÉ DEL CARMEN OLIVARES ROJAS.

Costa Rica: Malaquías Gil 11 Altos, Santo Domingo, DN; tel. 683-7209; fax 565-6467; e-mail emb.costarica@codetel.net.do; Ambassador EKHART PETERS SEEVERS.

Ecuador: Rafael Augusto Sánchez 17, Ensanche Naco, Apdo 808, Santo Domingo, DN; tel. 563-8363; fax 563-8153; e-mail mecuador@codetel.net.do; Ambassador LUIS NARVÁEZ RIVADENEIRA.

El Salvador: José A. Brea Peña 12, Ensanche Evaristo Morales, Santo Domingo, DN; tel. 565-4311; fax 541-7503; Ambassador Dr CARLOS ERNESTO MENDOZA C.

France: Las Damas 42, Zona Colonial, Santo Domingo, DN; tel. 657-5626; fax 657-5273; e-mail ambafrance@ambafrance-do.org; internet www.ambafrance-do.org; Ambassador JEAN-CLAUDE MOYRET.

Germany: Condominio Plaza Intercaribe, 5°, Rafael Augusto Sánchez 33, esq. Avda Lope de Vega, Ensanche Naco, Santo Domingo, DN; tel. 565-8811; fax 567-5014; e-mail embal@codetel.net.do; Ambassador EVA ALEXANDRA GRÄFIN KENDEFFY.

Guatemala: Calle Santiago 359, Gazcua, Santo Domingo, DN; tel. 689-5327; fax 689-5146; Ambassador Gen. BERNA RONALDO MÉNDEZ MARA.

Haiti: 33 Juan Sánchez Ramírez, Santo Domingo, DN; tel. 686-5778; fax 686-6096; Chargé d'affaires GUY G. LAMOTHE.

Holy See: Avda Máximo Gómez 27, Apdo 312, Santo Domingo, DN (Apostolic Nunciature); tel. 682-3773; fax 687-0287; Apostolic Nuncio Most Rev. TIMOTHY BROGLIO (Titular Archbishop of Amiternum).

Honduras: Calle Arístides García Mella, esq. Dolores Rodríguez Objío, Edif. El Buen Pastor VI, Apt 1-B, 1°, Mirador del Sur, Santo Domingo, DN; tel. 482-7992; fax 482-7505; e-mail e.honduras@codetel.net.do; Ambassador ANDRÉS VÍCTOR ARTILES.

Israel: Pedro Henríquez Ureña 80, Santo Domingo, DN; tel. 541-8974; fax 562-3555; e-mail emb.israel@codetel.net.do; Ambassador ELIAHU LÓPEZ.

Italy: Rodríguez Objío 4, Santo Domingo, DN; tel. 682-0830; fax 682-8296; e-mail ambital@codetel.net.do; internet www.iitalia.com/italambstdomingo; Ambassador STEFANO ALBERTO CANAVESIO.

Japan: Torre BHD, 8°, Avda Winston Churchill, esq. Luis F. Thomén, Santo Domingo, DN; tel. 567-3365; fax 566-8013; internet www.do.emb-japan.go.jp; Ambassador TAKEHISA NOGAMI.

Korea, Republic: Avda Sarasota 98, Santo Domingo, DN; tel. 532-4314; fax 532-3807; Ambassador KIM CHOU-UCK.

Mexico: Arzobispo Meriño No 265, Zona Colonial, Santo Domingo, DN; tel. 687-6444; fax 687-7872; e-mail embamex@codetel.net.do; Chargé d'affaires a.i. VICTOR HUGO RAMÍREZ LAVALLE.

Nicaragua: Avda México 152, Condominio Elsa María, Apdo 1, La Esperilla, Santo Domingo, DN; tel. 563-2311; fax 565-7961; e-mail embnicaragua@codetel.net.do; Ambassador LEOPOLDO RAMÍREZ EVA.

Panama: Calle Benito Moncion 255, Casi esq. Bolivar, Santo Domingo, DN; tel. 688-3789; fax 685-3665; Chargé d'affaires a.i. Lic. ALBERTO MAGNO CASTILLERO PINILLA.

Peru: Edif. Curvo Of., 485 Bella Vista, Pedro A. Bobea esq. Avda Anacaona, Santo Domingo, DN; tel. 532-6777; fax 532-6291; e-mail embaperu@codetel.net.do; Ambassador RAÚL GUTIÉRREZ.

Russia: Santo Domingo, DN; Ambassador VLADIMIR GONCHARENKO.

Spain: Avda Independencia 1205, Santo Domingo, DN; tel. 535-6500; fax 535-1595; e-mail embespdo@mail.mae.es; Ambassador RICARDO DÍEZ HOCHLEITNER.

United Kingdom: Edif. Corominas Pepin, 7°, Avda 27 de Febrero 233, Santo Domingo, DN; tel. 472-7111; fax 472-7574; e-mail brit.emb.sadom@codetel.net.do; Ambassador ANDY ASHCROFT.

USA: César Nicolás Pensón, esq. Leopoldo Navarro, Santo Domingo, DN; tel. 541-2171; e-mail usis.ic@codetel.net.do; internet santodomingo.usembassy.gov; Ambassador HANS H. HERTELL.

Uruguay: Baltasar Brum 7, Apt 1-B, Ensanche La Esperilla, Santo Domingo, DN; tel. 682-5565; fax 687-2167; e-mail embur@codetel.net.do; Ambassador JAIME WOLFSON KOT.

Venezuela: Cancillería, Avda Anacoana 7, Mirador Sur, Santo Domingo, DN; tel. 537-8578; fax 537-8780; e-mail embvenezuela@codetel.net.do; Ambassador FRANCISCO ALBERTO BELISARIO LANDIS.

Judicial System

The Judicial Power resides in the Suprema Corte de Justicia (Supreme Court of Justice), the Cortes de Apelación (Courts of Appeal), the Juzgados de Primera Instancia (Tribunals of the First Instance), the municipal courts and the other judicial authorities provided by law. The Supreme Court is composed of at least 11 judges (16 in February 2003) and the Attorney-General, and exercises disciplinary authority over all the members of the judiciary. The Attorney-General of the Republic is the Chief of Judicial Police and of the Public Ministry which he represents before the Supreme Court of Justice. The Consejo Nacional de la Magistratura (National Judiciary Council) appoints the members of the Supreme Court, which in turn appoints judges at all other levels of the judicial system.

Corte Suprema
Centro de los Héroes, Calle Hipolito Herrera Billini, esq. Juan B. Perez, Santo Domingo, DN; tel. 533-3191; e-mail suprema.corte@codetel.net.do; internet www.suprema.gov.do.

President: Dr JORGE SUBERO ISA.

Vice-President and President of First Court: Dr RAFAEL LUCIANO PICHARDO.

Second Vice-President: Dra EGLYS MARGARITA ESMURDOC.

President of Second Court: Dr HUGO ALVAREZ VALENCIA.

Justices: Dra MARGARITA A. TAVARES, VÍCTOR JOSÉ CASTELLANOS ESTRELLA, Dr JULIO IBARRA RÍOS, Dr EDGAR HERNÁNDEZ MEJÍA, Dra DULCE M. RODRÍGUEZ DE GORIS, Dra ANA ROSA BERGÉS DE FARRAY, Dr JUAN LUPERÓN VÁSQUEZ, Dr JULIO ANÍBAL SUÁREZ, Dra ENILDA REYES PÉREZ, Dr JOSÉ ENRIQUE HERNÁNDEZ MACHADO, Dr PEDRO ROMERO CONFESOR, Dr DARÍO OCTAVIO FERNÁNDEZ ESPINAL.

Attorney-General: Dr VICTOR MANUEL CESPEDES.

Religion

The majority of the inhabitants belong to the Roman Catholic Church, but freedom of worship exists for all denominations. The Baptist, Evangelist and Seventh-day Adventist churches and the Jewish faith are also represented.

CHRISTIANITY

The Roman Catholic Church
The Dominican Republic comprises two archdioceses and nine dioceses. At 31 December 2000 adherents represented about 88.06% of the population.

Bishops' Conference
Conferencia del Episcopado Dominicano, Apdo 186, Santo Domingo, DN; tel. 685-3141; fax 689-9454.

f. 1985; Pres. Cardinal NICOLÁS DE JESÚS LÓPEZ RODRÍGUEZ (Archbishop of Santo Domingo).

Archbishop of Santiago de los Caballeros: Most Rev. JUAN ANTONIO FLORES SANTANA, Arzobispado, Duvergé 14, Apdo 679, Santiago de los Caballeros; tel. 582-2094; fax 581-3580; e-mail arzobisp.stgo@codetel.net.do.

Archbishop of Santo Domingo: Cardinal NICOLÁS DE JESÚS LÓPEZ RODRÍGUEZ, Arzobispado, Isabel la Católica 55, Apdo 186, Santo Domingo, DN; tel. 685-3141; fax 688-7270; e-mail arzobispado@codetel.net.do.

The Anglican Communion
Anglicans in the Dominican Republic are under the jurisdiction of the Episcopal Church in the USA. The country is classified as a missionary diocese, in Province IX.

Bishop of the Dominican Republic: Rt Rev. JULIO CÉSAR HOLGUÍN KHOURY, Santiago 114, Apdo 764, Santo Domingo, DN; tel. 688-6016; fax 686-6364; e-mail igelpidom@codetel.net.do.

BAHÁ'Í FAITH

National Spiritual Assembly of the Bahá'ís of the Dominican Republic: Cambronal 152, esq. Beller, Santo Domingo, DN; tel. 687-1726; fax 687-7606; e-mail bahai.rd.aen@codetel.net.do; f. 1961; 402 localities.

The Press

Dirección General de Información, Publicidad y Prensa: Santo Domingo, DN; f. 1983; government supervisory body; Dir-Gen. LUIS GONZÁLEZ FABRA.

DAILIES

Santo Domingo, DN

El Caribe: Autopista Duarte, Km 7½, Apdo 416, Santo Domingo, DN; tel. 566-8161; fax 544-4003; f. 1948; morning; circ. 32,000; Editor ANTONIO EMILIO ORNÉS.

Diario Las Américas: Avda Tiradentes, Santo Domingo, DN; tel. 566-4577.

Hoy: Avda San Martín 236, Santo Domingo, DN; tel. 565-5581; fax 567-2424; f. 1981; morning; Dir MARIO ALVAREZ DUGAN; circ. 40,000.

Listín Diario: Paseo de los Periodistas 52, Ensanche Miraflores, Santo Domingo, DN; tel. 686-6688; fax 686-6595; e-mail webmaster@listindiario.com.do; internet www.listindiario.com.do; f. 1889; morning; Dir RAFAEL MOLINA MORILLO; circ. 88,050.

El Nacional: San Martín 236, Apdo 1402, Santo Domingo, DN; tel. 565-5581; fax 565-4190; f. 1966; evening and Sunday; Dir MARIO ALVAREZ DUGAN; circ. 45,000.

La Noticia: Julio Verne 14, Santo Domingo, DN; tel. 535-0815; f. 1973; evening; Pres. JOSÉ A. BREA PEÑA; Dir BOLÍVAR BELLO.

El Nuevo Diario: Ensanche Gazcue, Santo Domingo, DN; tel. 687-6205; fax 688-0763; morning; Dir PERSIO MALDONADO.

El Sol: Santo Domingo, DN; morning; Pres. QUITERIO CEDEÑO; Dir-Gen. MIGUEL ANGEL CEDEÑO.

Ultima Hora: Paseo de los Periodistas 52, Ensanche Miraflores, Santo Domingo, DN; tel. 688-3361; fax 688-3019; e-mail ultimahora@codetel.net.do; internet www.codetel.net.do/ultimahora; f. 1970; evening; Dir RUDDY L. GONZÁLEZ C; circ. 40,000.

Puerto Plata

El Porvenir: Imbert 5, Apdo 614, Puerto Plata; f. 1872; Dir Carlos Acevedo.

Santiago de los Caballeros, SD

La Información: Carretera Licey, Km 3, Santiago de los Caballeros, SD; tel. 581-1915; fax 581-7770; f. 1915; morning; Editor Fernando A. Pérez Memén; circ. 15,000.

PERIODICALS AND REVIEWS

Agricultura: Santo Domingo, DN; organ of the State Secretariat of Agriculture; f. 1905; monthly; Dir Miguel Rodríguez, Jr.

Agroconocimiento: Apdo 345-2, Santo Domingo, DN; monthly; agricultural news and technical information; Dir Domingo Marte; circ. 10,000.

¡Ahora!: San Martín 236, Apdo 1402, Santo Domingo, DN; tel. 565-5581; f. 1962; weekly; Dir Mario Alvarez Dugan.

La Campiña: San Martín 236, Apdo 1402, Santo Domingo, DN; f. 1967; Dir Ing. Juan Ulises García B.

Carta Dominicana: Avda Tiradentes 56, Santo Domingo, DN; tel. 566-0119; f. 1974; monthly; economics; Dir Juan Ramón Quiñones M.

Deportes: San Martín 236, Apdo 1402, Santo Domingo, DN; f. 1967; sports; fortnightly; Dir L. R. Cordero; circ. 5,000.

Eva: San Martín 236, Apdo 1402, Santo Domingo, DN; f. 1967; fortnightly; Dir Magda Florencio.

Horizontes de América: Santo Domingo, DN; f. 1967; monthly; Dir Armando Lemus Castillo.

Letra Grande, Arte y Literatura: Leonardo da Vinci 13, Mirador del Sur, Avda 27 de Febrero, Santo Domingo, DN; tel. 531-2225; f. 1980; monthly; art and literature; Dir Juan Ramón Quiñones M.

Renovación: José Reyes, esq. El Conde, Santo Domingo, DN; fortnightly; Dir Olga Quisqueya Viuda Martínez.

FOREIGN PRESS BUREAUX

Agencia EFE (Spain): Galerías Comerciales, 5°, Of. 507, Avda 27 de Febrero, Santo Domingo, DN; tel. 567-7617; Bureau Chief Antonio Castillo Urberuaga.

Agenzia Nazionale Stampa Associata (ANSA) (Italy): Leopoldo Navarro 79, 3°, Sala 17, Apdo 20324, Huanca, Santo Domingo, DN; tel. 685-8765; fax 685-8765; Bureau Chief Humber Andrés Suazo.

Inter Press Service (IPS) (Italy): Cambronal, No. 4-1, Ciudad Nueva, Santo Domingo, DN; tel. 593-5153; Correspondent Vianco Martínez.

United Press International (UPI) (USA): Carrera A. Manoguaybo 16, Manoguaybo, DN; tel. 689-7171; Chief Correspondent Santiago Estrella Veloz.

Publishers

Santo Domingo, DN

Arte y Cine, C por A: Isabel la Católica 42, Santo Domingo, DN.

Editora Alfa y Omega: José Contreras 69, Santo Domingo, DN; tel. 532-5577.

Editora de las Antillas: Santo Domingo, DN; tel. 685-2197.

Editora Dominicana, SA: 23 Oeste, No 3 Lup., Santo Domingo, DN; tel. 688-0846.

Editora El Caribe, C por A: Autopista Duarte, Km 7½, Apdo 416, Santo Domingo, DN; tel. 566-8161; fax 544-4003; f. 1948; Man. Dir Rafael Duarte.

Editora Hoy, C por A: San Martín, 236, Santo Domingo, DN; tel. 566-1147.

Editora Listín Diario, C por A: Paseo de los Periodistas 52, Ensanche Miraflores, Apdo 1455, Santo Domingo, DN; tel. 686-6688; fax 686-6595; f. 1889; Pres. Dr Rogelio A. Pellerano.

Editorama, SA: Justiniano Bobea, esq. Eugenio Contreras, Apdo 2074, Santo Domingo, DN; tel. 596-6669; fax 594-1421.

Editorial Padilla: San F. de Macorís 14, Santo Domingo, DN; tel. 682-3101.

Editorial Santo Domingo: Santo Domingo, DN; tel. 532-9431.

Editorial Stella: Santo Domingo, DN; tel. 682-2281.

Julio D. Postigo e Hijos: Santo Domingo, DN; f. 1949; fiction; Man. J. D. Postigo.

Publicaciones Ahora, C por A: Avda San Martín 236, Apdo 1402, Santo Domingo, DN; tel. 565-5580; fax 565-4190; Pres. Julio Castaño.

Publicaciones América: Santo Domingo, DN; Dir Pedro Bisonó.

Santiago de los Caballeros, SD

Editora el País, SA: Carrera Sánchez, Km 6½, Santiago de los Caballeros, SD; tel. 532-9511.

Broadcasting and Communications

Dirección General de Telecomunicaciones: Isabel la Católica 73, Santo Domingo, DN; tel. 682-2244; fax 682-3493; government supervisory body; Dir-Gen. Rubén Montas; Dir-Gen. of Television Nelson Arturo Marte.

Instituto Dominicano de Telecomunicaciones (INDOTEL): Santo Domingo, DN; Pres. Orlando Jorge Mera.

TELECOMMUNICATIONS

Compañía Dominicana de Teléfonos (Codetel): Avda Lincoln 1101, Apdo 1377, Santo Domingo, DN; tel. 220-2000; fax 543-1301; e-mail e.burri@codetel.net.do; internet www.codetel.net.do; f. 1930; Pres. Jorge Ivan Ramírez; Gen. Man. Guillermo Amore.

Tricom Telecomunicaciones de Voz, Data y Video: Avda Lope de Vega 95, Santo Domingo, DN; tel. 542-7556; fax 567-4412; internet www.tricom.net; Pres. Arturo Pellerano; Chief of Int. Relations César A. Franco.

BROADCASTING

Radio

There were some 130 commercial stations in 2000. The government-owned broadcasting network, Radio Televisión Dominicana, operates nine radio stations.

Asociación Dominicana de Radiodifusoras (ADORA): Paul Harris 3, Centro de los Héroes, Santo Domingo, DN; tel. 535-4057; Pres. Ivelise de Torres.

Television

Corporación Dominicana de Radio y Televisión, Canal 9: Emilio A. Morel, esq. Luis E. Pérez, Ensanche La Fe, Apdo 30043, Santo Domingo, DN; tel. 566-5876; fax 544-3607; commercial station; Channel 9; Dir-Gen. Manuel Quiroz Miranda.

Radio Televisión Dominicana: Dr Tejada Florentino 8, Apdo 869, Santo Domingo, DN; tel. 689-2120; government station; three channels, two relay stations; Dir-Gen. Nelson Arturo Marte; Gen. Man. Agustín Mercado.

Rahintel Televisión: Centro de los Héroes de Constanza, Avda Independencia, Apdo 1220, Santo Domingo, DN; tel. 532-2531; fax 535-4575; commercial station; two channels; Pres. Leonel Almonte V.

Teleantillas, Canal 2: Autopista Duarte, Km 7½, Los Prados, Apdo 30404, Santo Domingo, DN; tel. 567-7751; fax 540-4912; e-mail vbaez@corripio.com.do; Gen. Man. Hector Valentin Baez.

Telecentro, SA: Avda Pasteur 204, Santo Domingo, DN; tel. 687-9161; fax 542-7582; Channel 13 for Santo Domingo and east region; Pres. Jasinto Peynado.

Tele-Inde Canal 13: Avda Pasteur 101, Santo Domingo, DN; tel. 687-9161; commercial station; Dir Julio Hazim.

Telesistema, Canal 11: Avda 27 de Febrero 52, Sector Bergel, Santo Domingo, DN; tel. 563-6661; fax 472-1754; Pres. José L. Correpio.

Finance

(cap. = capital; dep. = deposits; m = million; p.u. = paid up; res = reserves; amounts in pesos)

BANKING

Supervisory Body

Superintendencia de Bancos: Avda México, esq. Leopoldo Navarro, Apdo 1326, Santo Domingo, DN; tel. 685-8141; fax 685-0859; f. 1947; Superintendent Lic. Alberto Elís Atala Lajan.

Central Bank

Banco Central de la República Dominicana: Pedro Henríquez Ureña, esq. Leopoldo Navarro, Apdo 1347, Santo Domingo, DN; tel. 689-7121; fax 687-7488; e-mail info@bancentral.gov.do; internet www.bancentral.gov.do; f. 1947; cap. 0.7m., res 92.3m., dep. 6,321.7m. (Dec. 1996); Gov. José Luis Malkun; Man. Rafael Alcántara.

Commercial Banks

Banco BHD, SA: Avda Winston Churchill, esq. Luis F. Thomen, Apdo 266-2, Santo Domingo, DN; tel. 243-3232; fax 562-4396; e-mail bhd@codetel.net.do; internet www.codetel.net.do.bhd; f. 1972; total assets 11,902m. (1999); Pres. José Antonio Caro; Gen. Man. Luis Molina A; 35 brs.

Banco Dominicano del Progreso, SA: Avda John F. Kennedy 3, Apdo 1329, Santo Domingo, DN; tel. 563-3233; fax 563-2455; f. 1974; total assets 9,947m. (1999); Chair. Tomás A. Pastoriza; Exec. Vice-Pres. Pedro E. Castillo L; 20 brs.

Banco del Exterior Dominicano, SA: Avda Abraham Lincoln 756, Santo Domingo, DN; tel. 565-5540; fax 565-5547.

Banco Gerencial y Fiduciario, SA: Avda 27 de Febrero 50, Santo Domingo, DN; tel. 473-9400; fax 565-7569; total assets 7,876m. (1999); f. 1983; Exec. Vice-Pres. George Manuel Hazoury Peña.

Banco Global, SA: Avda Rómulo Batancourt 1, esq. Avda A. Lincoln, Santo Domingo, DN; tel. 532-3000; fax 535-7070; total assets 11,486m. (1999).

Banco Industrial de Desarollo e Inversión, SA: Avda San Martín 40, esq. Dr Delgado, Santo Domingo, DN; tel. 685-3194; fax 689-3485.

Banco Intercontinental, SA: Avda 27 de Febrero, esq. Avda Winston Churchill, Santo Domingo, DN; tel. 535-5500; fax 535-3694; f. 1986; total assets 10,129m. (1999); Pres. Ramón Báez Figueroa.

Banco Mercantil: Avda Pastoriza 303, Santo Domingo, DN; tel. 567-4444; fax 549-6509; e-mail info@mercantil.com.do; internet www.mercantil.com.do; f. 1985; total assets 9,579m. (1999); Pres. Andrés Aybar Báez; Exec. Vice-Pres. Juan R. Oller; 21 brs.

Banco Metropolitano: Avda Lope de Vega, esq. Gustavo Mejía Ricart, Apdo 1872, Santo Domingo, DN; tel. 562-2442; fax 562-2464; f. 1974; total assets 12,055m. (1999); Pres. Agustín Verdeja; Gen. Dir Adalberto Pérez Perdomo; 7 brs.

Banco Nacional de Crédito, SA: Avda John F. Kennedy, esq. Tiradentes, Apdo 1408, Santo Domingo, DN; tel. 540-4441; fax 567-4854; e-mail info@bancredito.com; internet www.bancredito.com; f. 1981; cap. 686.8m., res 181.3m., dep. 7,911.3m. (Dec. 2000); Pres. Máximo Pellerano; Vice-Pres. Marina de Garrigó; 38 brs.

Banco Popular Dominicano: Avda John F. Kennedy 20, Torre Popular, Apdo 1441, Santo Domingo, DN; tel. 544-8000; fax 544-5899; e-mail abonilla@bpd.com.do; internet www.bpd.com.do; f. 1963; cap. 2,493.5m., res 714.4m., dep. 31,580.5m. (Dec. 2001); Pres. Manuel Alejandro Grullón; 135 brs.

Banco de Reservas de la República Dominicana: Isabel la Católica 201, Apdo 1353, Santo Domingo, DN; tel. 687-5366; fax 685-0602; e-mail sperdomo@brrd.com; internet www.banreservas.com.do; f. 1941; cap. 2,000.0m., res 762.4m., dep. 24,832.9m. (Dec. 2001); Pres. and Gen. Man. Manuel Antonio Lara Hernández; 24 brs.

Development Banks

Banco Agrícola de la República Dominicana: Avda G. Washington 601, Apdo 1057, Santo Domingo, DN; tel. 535-8088; fax 532-4645; e-mail bagricola.refor@codetel.net.do; f. 1945; government agricultural development bank; Pres. Lic. Rafael Angeles Suárez; Gen. Administrator Carlos A. Segura Foster.

Banco Continental de Desarollo, SA: Edif. Continental, Avda Pedro Henríquez Ureña 126, Santo Domingo, DN; tel. 472-2228; fax 472-3027; internet www.banco-continental.com; Pres. Hugo Giliano; Man. Dir Anton Yelari.

Banco de Desarollo Ademi, SA: Avda Pedro Henríquez Ureña 78, Santo Domingo, DN; tel. 683-0203; fax 227-8584.

Banco de Desarollo Agropecuario Norcentral, SA: Avda Independencia 801, esq. Avda Máximo Gómez, Santo Domingo, DN; tel. 686-0984; fax 687-0825.

Banco de Desarollo de Exportación, SA: Fatino Falco, entre Avda Lope de Vega y Tiradentes 201, Santo Domingo, DN; tel. 566-5841; fax 565-1769.

Banco de Desarollo Industrial, SA: Avda Sarasota 27, esq. La Julia, Santo Domingo, DN; tel. 535-8586; fax 535-6069.

Banco de Desarollo Intercontinental, SA: Edif. Lilian 5°, Avda Lope de Vega, esq. Gustavo Mejía Ricart, Santo Domingo, DN; tel. 544-0559; fax 563-6884.

Banco Nacional de la Construcción: Avda Alma Mater, esq. Pedro Henríquez Ureña, Santo Domingo, DN; tel. 685-9776; f. 1977; Gen. Man. Luis Manuel Pellerano.

Banco de la Pequeña Empresa, SA: Avda Bolivar 233, entre Avda Abraham Lincoln y Avda Winston Churchill, Santo Domingo, DN; tel. 534-8383; fax 534-8385.

Foreign Banks

Bank of Nova Scotia (Canada): Avda John F. Kennedy, esq. Lope de Vega, Apdo 1494, Santo Domingo, DN; tel. 544-1700; fax 567-5732; f. 1920; Vice-Pres. and Gen. Man. Ariel D. Pérez; 13 brs.

Citibank NA (USA): Avda John F. Kennedy 1, Apdo 1492, Santo Domingo, DN; tel. 566-5611; fax 567-2255; f. 1962; Vice-Pres. and Gen. Man. Henry Comber; 7 brs.

STOCK EXCHANGE

Santo Domingo Securities Exchange Inc: Edif. Disesa, Suite 302, Avda Abraham Lincoln, Santo Domingo, DN; tel. 567-6694; fax 567-6697; Pres. Felipe Auffant.

INSURANCE

Supervisory Body

Superintendencia de Seguros: Secretaría de Estado de Finanzas, Avda México, esq. Leopoldo Navarro, Santo Domingo, DN; tel. 688-1245; internet www.superseguro.gov.do; f. 1969; Superintendent Domingo Batista.

Insurance Companies

American Life and General Insurance Co, C por A: Edif. ALICO, 5°, Avda Abraham Lincoln, Santo Domingo, DN; tel. 533-7131; fax 533-5969; general; Gen. Man. Frank Cabreja.

La Americana, SA: Edif. La Cumbre, Avda Tiradentes, Apdo 25241, Santo Domingo, DN; tel. 567-1211; f. 1975; life; Pres. Marino Ginebra H.

Atlantica Insurance, SA: Avda 27 de Febrero 265A, 2°, Apdo 826, Santo Domingo, DN; tel. 565-5591; fax 565-4343; Pres. Lic. Rhina Ramírez.

Bankers Security Life Insurance Society: Gustavo Mejia Ricart 61, Apdo 1123, Santo Domingo, DN; tel. 544-2626; fax 567-9389; Pres. Viriato Fiallo.

Bonanza Compañía de Seguros, SA: Edif. Santanita I, Of. 201, Avda San Martín 253, Santo Domingo, DN; tel. 565-5525; fax 565-5630; e-mail bonanza.seg@codetel.net.do; internet www.bonanza.dominicana.com.do; Pres. Lic. Dario Lama.

Britanica de Seguros, SA: Max Henríquez Ureña 35, Apdo 3637, Santo Domingo, DN; tel. 542-6863; fax 544-4542; e-mail wharper@codetel.net.do; Pres. John Harper Saleta.

Centro de Seguros La Popular, C por A: Gustavo Mejía Ricart 61, Apdo 1123, Santo Domingo, DN; tel. 566-1988; fax 567-9389; f. 1965; general except life; Pres. Lic. Rosa Fiallo.

La Colonial, SA: Edif. Haché, 2°, Avda John F. Kennedy, Santo Domingo, DN; tel. 565-9926; f. 1971; general; Pres. Dr Miguel Feris Iglesias.

Compañía Nacional de Seguros, C por A: Avda Máximo Gómez 31, Apdo 916, Santo Domingo, DN; tel. 687-5390; fax 682-3269; e-mail infocns@bancredito.com; internet www.cns.com.do; f. 1964; general; Chair. Dr Máximo A. Pellerano.

Compañía de Seguros Palic, SA: Avda Abraham Lincoln, esq. José Amado Soler, Apdo 1132, Santo Domingo, DN; tel. 562-1271; fax 562-1825; e-mail cia.seg.palic2@codetel.net.do; Pres. Lic. Eduardo Tolentino.

Confederación del Canada Dominicana: Salvador Sturla 17, Santo Domingo, DN; tel. 544-4144; fax 540-4740; Pres. Lic. Moises A. Franco Llenas.

Federal Insurance Company: Edif. La Cumbre, 4°, Avda Tiradentes, esq. Presidente González, Santo Domingo, DN; tel. 567-0181; fax 567-8909; Pres. Diego Ramón Sosa.

General de Seguros, SA: Avda Sarasota 55, Bella Vista, Santo Domingo, DN; tel. 535-8888; fax 532-4451; f. 1981; general; Pres. Dr Fernando A. Ballista Díaz.

La Intercontinental de Seguros, SA: Plaza Naco, 2°, Avda Tiradentes, Apdo 825, Santo Domingo, DN; tel. 562-1211; general; Pres. Lic. Ramón Báez Romano.

Magna Compañía de Seguros, SA: Edif. Magna Motors, Avda Abraham Lincoln, esq. John F. Kennedy, Santo Domingo, DN; tel. 544-1400; fax 562-5723; f. 1974; general and life; Pres. E. Antonio Lama S; Man. Milagros de los Santos.

La Mundial de Seguros, SA: Avda Máximo Gómez, No 31, Santo Domingo, DN; tel. 685-2121; fax 682-3269; general except life and financial; Pres. PEDRO D'ACUNHA.

La Peninsular de Seguros, SA: Edif. Corp. Corominas Pepín, 3°, Avda 27 de Febrero 233, Santo Domingo, DN; tel. 472-1166; fax 563-2349; general; Pres. Lic. ERNESTO ROMERO LANDRÓN.

Reaseguradora Hispaniola, SA: Avda 27 de Febrero 205, Of. 202, Santo Domingo, DN; tel. 683-6150; fax 540-5288; Pres. MANUEL DE JESÚS COLÓN.

Seguros La Antillana, SA: Avda Lope de Vega 36, esq. Andres Julio Aybar y Ensanche Piantini, Santo Domingo, DN; tel. 541-3366; fax 567-9398; f. 1947; general and life; Pres. Lic. OSCAR LAMA.

Seguros La Isleña, C por A: Edif. Centro Coordinador Empresarial, Avda Nuñez de Caceres, esq. Guarocuya, Santo Domingo, DN; tel. 567-7211; fax 565-1448; Pres. MARÍA DEL PILAR RODRÍGUEZ.

Seguros Pepín, SA: Edif. Corp. Corominas Pepín, Avda 27 de Febrero 233, Santo Domingo, DN; tel. 472-1006; general; Pres. Dr BIENVENIDO COROMINAS.

Seguros San Rafael, C por A: Leopoldo Navarro 61, esq. San Francisco de Macorís, Santo Domingo, DN; tel. 688-2231; general; Admin. VÍCTOR RODRÍGUEZ.

El Sol de Seguros, SA: Torre Hipotecaria, 2°, Avda Tiradentes 25, Santo Domingo, DN; tel. 542-6063; general; Pres. GUILLERMO ARMENTEROS.

Sudamericana de Seguros, SA: El Conde 105, frente al Parque Colón, Santo Domingo, DN; tel. 685-0141; fax 688-8074; Pres. VINCENZO MASTROLILLI.

Transglobal de Seguros, SA: Avda Lope de Vega 36, esq. Andres Julio Aybar y Ensanche Piantini, Apdo 1869, Santo Domingo, DN; tel. 541-3366; fax 567-9398; e-mail transglobal@codetel.net.do; Dirs JOSÉ MANUEL VARGAS, OSCAR LAMA.

Universal América, C por A: Santo Domingo, DN; tel. 544-7200; fax 544-7999; internet www.universal.com.do; f. 1964 as La Universal de Seguros; merged with Grupo Asegurador América in 2000; general; Pres. Ing. ERNESTO IZQUIERDO.

Insurance Association

Cámara Dominicana de Aseguradores y Reaseguradores, Inc: Edif. Torre BHD, 5°, Luis F. Thomen, esq. Winston Churchill, Santo Domingo, DN; tel. 566-0019; fax 566-2600; e-mail cadoar@codetel.net.do; internet www.cadoar.org.do; f. 1972; Pres. Lic. NELSON HEDI HERNÁNDEZ.

Trade and Industry

GOVERNMENT AGENCIES

Comisión para la Reforma de la Empresa Pública: Santo Domingo, DN; commission charged with divestment and restructuring of state enterprises; Pres. JOSÉ DEL CARMEN MARCANO.

Consejo Estatal del Azúcar (CEA) (State Sugar Council): Centro de los Héroes, Apdo 1256/1258, Santo Domingo, DN; tel. 533-1161; fax 533-7393; f. 1966; management of operations contracted to private consortiums in 1999 and 2000; Dir-Gen. VÍCTOR MANUEL BÁEZ.

Corporación Dominicana de Empresas Estatales (CORDE) (Dominican State Corporation): Avda General Antonio Duvergé, Apdo 1378, Santo Domingo, DN; tel. 533-5171; f. 1966 to administer, direct and develop state enterprises; Dir-Gen. FÉLIX CALVO.

Instituto de Estabilización de Precios (INESPRE): Avda Luperón, Santo Domingo, DN; tel. 530-0020; fax 530-0343; f. 1969; price commission; Dir PABLO MERCEDES.

Instituto Nacional de la Vivienda: Antiguo Edif. del Banco Central, Avda Pedro Henríquez Ureña, esq. Leopoldo Navarro, Apdo 1506, Santo Domingo, DN; tel. 685-4181; f. 1962; low-cost housing institute; Dir-Gen. Ing. JUAN ANTONIO VARGAS.

DEVELOPMENT ORGANIZATIONS

Consejo Nacional de Desarrollo Minería: Santo Domingo, DN; f. 2000; encourages the development of the mining sector; Exec. Dir MIGUEL PENA; Sec.-Gen. PEDRO VÁSQUEZ.

Departamento de Desarrollo y Financiamento de Proyectos (DEFINPRO): c/o Banco Central de la República Dominicana, Pedro Henríquez Ureña, Apdo 1347, Santo Domingo, DN; tel. 221-9111; fax 687-7488; f. 1993; associated with AID, IDB, WB, KFW; encourages economic development in productive sectors of economy, excluding sugar; authorizes complementary financing to private sector for establishing and developing

industrial and agricultural enterprises and free-zone industrial parks; Dir ANGEL NERY CASTILLO PIMENTEL.

Fundación Dominicana de Desarrollo (Dominican Development Foundation): Mercedes No 4, Apdo 857, Santo Domingo, DN; f. 1962 to mobilize private resources for collaboration in financing small-scale development programmes; 384 mems; Dir Lic. ADA WISCOVICTH.

Instituto de Desarrollo y Crédito Cooperativo (IDECOOP): Centro de los Héroes, Apdo 1371, Santo Domingo, DN; tel. 533-8131; fax 535-5148; f. 1963 to encourage the development of co-operatives; Dir JAVIER PEÑA NUÑEZ.

CHAMBERS OF COMMERCE

Cámara de Comercio y Producción de Santo Domingo: Arz. Nouel 206, Zona Colonial, Apdo 815, Santo Domingo, DN; tel. 682-7206; fax 685-2228; e-mail camara.sto.dgo@codetel.net.do; f. 1910; 1,500 active mems; Pres. JOSÉ MANUEL ARMENTEROS; Exec. Dir MILAGROS J. PUELLO.

Cámara Americana de Comercio de la República Dominicana: Torre BHD, 4°, Avda Winston Churchill, Santo Domingo, DN; tel. 544-2222; fax 544-0502; e-mail amcham@codetel.net.do; internet www.amcham.org.do; Pres. ANDRÉS AYBAR BÁEZ.

There are official Chambers of Commerce in the larger towns.

INDUSTRIAL AND TRADE ASSOCIATIONS

Asociación Dominicana de Hacendados y Agricultores Inc: Santo Domingo, DN; tel. 565-0542; farming and agricultural org. Pres. Lic. CESARIO CONTRERAS.

Asociación de Industrias de la República Dominicana Inc: Avda Sarasota 20, Apdo 850, Santo Domingo, DN; tel. 535-9111; fax 533-7520; f. 1962; industrial org. Pres. NASSIM ALEMANY.

Centro Dominicano de Promoción de Exportaciones (CEDOPEX): Plaza de la Bandera, Apdo 199-2, Santo Domingo, DN; tel. 530-5505; fax 530-8208; e-mail cedopex@codetel.net.do; internet www.cedopex.gov.do; organization for the promotion of exports; Dir RAMÓN ALFREDO BORDAS.

Consejo Nacional de la Empresa Privada (CONEP): Santo Domingo, DN; Pres. Lic. MARINO GINEBRA.

Consejo Nacional de las Zonas Francas: Santo Domingo, DN; co-ordinating body for the free-trade zones; Exec. Dir JEANNETTE DOMÍNGUEZ ARISTY.

Consejo Promotor de Inversiones (Investment Promotion Council): Santo Domingo, DN; tel. 532-3281; fax 533-7029; Exec. Dir and CEO FREDERIC EMAM ZADÉ.

Corporación de Fomento Industrial (CFI): Avda 27 de Febrero, Plaza Independencia, Apdo 1452, Santo Domingo, DN; tel. 530-0010; fax 530-1303; f. 1962 to promote agro-industrial development; Dir-Gen. JOSÉ OVALLES.

Dirección General de Minería e Hidrocarburos: Edif. de Oficinas Gubernamentales, 10°, Avda México, esq. Leopoldo Navarro, Santo Domingo, DN; tel. 687-7557; fax 686-8327; f. 1947; government mining and hydrocarbon org. Dir-Gen. PEDRO VÁSQUEZ.

Instituto Agrario Dominicano (IAD): Avda 27 de Febrero, Santo Domingo, DN; tel. 530-8272; Dir-Gen. TOMÁS HERNÁNDEZ ALBERTO.

Instituto Dominicano de Tecnología Industrial (INDOTEC): Avda Nuñez de Caceres, esq. Olof Palme, Santo Domingo, DN; tel. 566-8121; fax 227-8808; e-mail indotec@codetel.net.do; internet www.indotec.gov.do; Dir ANTONIO ALMONTE REYNOSO.

Instituto Nacional del Azúcar (INAZUCAR): Avda Jiménez Moya, Apdo 667, Santo Domingo, DN; tel. 532-5571; internet www.inazucar.gov.do; sugar institute; f. 1965; Dir-Gen. RAFAEL MONTILLA.

EMPLOYERS' ORGANIZATIONS

Confederación Patronal de la República Dominicana: Edif. Mella, Cambronal/G. Washington, Santo Domingo, DN; tel. 688-3017; Pres. Ing. HERIBERTO DE CASTRO.

Consejo Nacional de Hombres de Empresa Inc: Edif. Motorámbar, 7°, Avda Abraham Lincoln 1056, Santo Domingo, DN; tel. 562-1666; Pres. JOSÉ MANUEL PALIZA.

Federación Dominicana de Comerciantes: Carretera Sánchez Km 10, Santo Domingo, DN; tel. 533-2666; Pres. IVAN GARCÍA.

UTILITIES

Electricity

Corporación Dominicana de Electricidad (CDE): Centro de los Héroes, Apdo 1428, Santo Domingo, DN; tel. 535-1100; fax 535-7472; f. 1955; state electricity company; partially privatized in 1999; Dir-Gen. MARCELO JORGE PÉREZ; Admin. CÉSAR DOMINGO SÁNCHEZ TORRES.

Superintendencia de Electricidad: Santo Domingo, DN; Superintendent José D. Ovalle Tejada.

Water

As part of the continuing programme of repair to the country's infrastructure, in 2001 construction began on aqueducts, intended to supply water to the provinces of Bahoruco, Barahona, Duarte, Espaillat, Independencia and Salcedo.

Instituto Nacional de Aguas Potables (INAPA): Santo Domingo, DN; Exec. Dir Juan Roberto Rodríguez Hernández.

Instituto Nacional de Recursos Hidráulicos: Centro de los Héroes, Santo Domingo, DN; tel. 532-3271; f. 1965; Dir Frank Rodríguez.

TRADE UNIONS

Central General de Trabajadores (CGT): Santo Domingo, DN; tel. 688-3932; f. 1972; 13 sections; Sec.-Gen. Francisco Antonio Santos; 65,000 mems.

Central de Trabajadores Independientes (CTI): Juan Erazo 133, Santo Domingo, DN; tel. 688-3932; f. 1978; left-wing; Sec.-Gen. Rafael Santos.

Central de Trabajadores Mayoritarias (CTM): Tunti Cáceres 222, Santo Domingo, DN; tel. 562-3392; Sec.-Gen. Nélsida Marmolejos.

Confederación Autónoma de Sindicatos Clasistas (CASC) (Autonomous Confederation of Trade Unions): J. Erazo 39, Santo Domingo, DN; tel. 687-8533; f. 1962; supports PRSC; Sec.-Gen. Gabriel del Río.

Confederación Nacional de Trabajadores Dominicanos (CNTD) (National Confederation of Dominican Workers): Santo Domingo, DN; f. 1988 by merger; 11 provincial federations totalling 150 unions are affiliated; Sec.-Gen. Julio de Peña Váldez; 188,000 mems (est.).

Confederación de Trabajadores Unitaria (CTU) (United Workers' Confederation): Santo Domingo, DN; f. 1991.

Transport

RAILWAYS

In April 2001 plans were announced for the construction of a passenger and freight railway from the coastal port of Haina to Santiago, with the possibility of subsequent extension to Puerto Plata and Manzanillo.

Dirección General de Tránsito Terrestre: Avda San Cristóbal, Santo Domingo, DN; tel. 565-2811; f. 1966; operated by Secretary of State for Public Works and Communications; Dir-Gen. Ing. Luis Emilio Pina.

Ferrocarriles Unidos Dominicanos: Santo Domingo, DN; government-owned; 142 km of track from La Vega to Sánchez and from Guayubín to Pepillo principally used for the transport of exports.

There are also a number of semi-autonomous and private railway companies for the transport of sugar cane, including:

Ferrocarril de Central Romana: La Romana; 375 km open; Pres. C. Morales.

Ferrocarril Central Río Haina: Apdo 1258, Haina; 113 km open.

ROADS

In 2000 there were an estimated 12,600 km of roads, of which about 6,225 km were paved. There is a direct route from Santo Domingo to Port-au-Prince in Haiti. The Mejía administration undertook an extensive road-building programme from 2000, aiming primarily to reduce traffic congestion in Santo Domingo. In July 2001 the Government announced that a Colombian-led consortium, Consorcio Dominico-Colombiano Autopista del Nordeste, was to construct a toll road between Boca and San Pedro de Macorís. A new bridge was to be constructed over the Ozama river in 2001.

Dirección General de Carreteras y Caminos Vecinales: Santo Domingo, DN; f. 1987; government supervisory body; Dir-Gen. Elizabeth Peralta Brito.

Autoridad Metropolitana de Transporte (AMET): Avda Expreso V Centenario, esq. Avda San Martín, Santo Domingo, DN; tel. 686-6520; fax 686-3447; e-mail info@amet.gov.do; internet www.amet.gov.do; Dir-Gen. Oneximo González.

SHIPPING

The Dominican Republic has 14 ports, of which Santo Domingo is by far the largest, handling about 80% of imports. In 2001 construction work was in progress on the conversion of Manzanillo port into a container terminal, and on Punta Caucedo and Haina ports. A new port and transhipment centre was being built near the Las Americas international airport, which was designed specifically for use by free-trade zone businesses.

A number of foreign shipping companies operate services to the island.

Agencias Navieras B&R, SA: Avda Abraham Lincoln 504, Apdo 1221, Santo Domingo, DN; tel. 544-2200; fax 562-3383; e-mail jperiche@navierasbr.com; internet www.navierasbr.com; f. 1919; shipping agents and export services; Man. Juan Periche Pidal.

Armadora Naval Dominicana, SA: Isabel la Católica 165, Apdo 2677, Santo Domingo, DN; tel. 689-6191; Man. Dir Capt. Einar Wettre.

Autoridad Portuaria Dominicana: Avda Máximo Gómez, Santo Domingo, DN; tel. 535-8462; Exec. Dir Prof. Aníbal García Duvergé.

Líneas Marítimas de Santo Domingo, SA: José Gabriel García 8, Apdo 1148, Santo Domingo, DN; tel. 689-9146; fax 685-4654; Pres. C. Lluberes; Vice-Pres. Juan T. Tavares.

CIVIL AVIATION

There are international airports at Santo Domingo (Aeropuerto Internacional de las Américas José Francisco Peña Gómez), Puerto Plata and Barahona (Aeropuerto Internacional María Móntez). A further international airport, at Samaná, was under construction. In December 2000 a new 421m.-peso international airport opened in La Romana. The international airports were undergoing privatization in 1999–2000. Most main cities have domestic airports.

Dirección General de Aeronáutica Civil: Bloque A, 2°, Edif. de Oficinas Gubernamentales, Avda México, esq. Dr Delgado, Apdo 1180, Santo Domingo, DN; tel. 221-7909; fax 221-8616; e-mail aeronautica.c@codetel.net.do; internet www.dgacdom.gov.do; f. 1955; government supervisory body; Dir-Gen. Gen. Trajano Moreta Cuevas.

Aerochago: Aeropuerto Internacional de las Américas, Santo Domingo, DN; tel. 549-0709; fax 549-0708; f. 1973; operates cargo and charter service in Central America and the Caribbean; Gen. Man. Pedro Rodríguez.

Aerolíneas Argo: Santo Domingo, DN; f. 1971; cargo and mail services to the USA, Puerto Rico and the US Virgin Islands.

Aerolíneas Dominicanas (Dominair): El Sol 62, Apdo 202, Santiago; tel. 581-8882; fax 582-5074; f. 1974; owned by Aeropostal (Venezuela); scheduled and charter passenger services.

Aerolíneas Santo Domingo: Edif. J.P., Avda 27 de Febrero 272, esq. Seminario, Santo Domingo, DN; e-mail asd@codetel.net.do; internet www.airsantodomingo.com; f. 1996; operates scheduled and charter internal, regional and international flights; Pres. Henry W. Azar.

Aeromar Airlines: Aeropuerto Internacional de las Américas, Santo Domingo, DN; tel. 549-0281; fax 542-0152; cargo services.

Compañía Dominicana de Aviación C por A: Avda Jiménez de Moya, esq. José Contreras, Apdo 1415, Santo Domingo, DN; tel. 532-8511; fax 535-1656; f. 1944; operates on international routes connecting Santo Domingo with the Netherlands Antilles, Aruba, the USA, Haiti and Venezuela; operations suspended 1995, privatization pending; Chair. Dr Rodolfo Rincón; CEO Marina Ginebra de Bonnelly.

Tourism

Strenuous efforts were made to improve the tourism infrastructure, with 200m. pesos spent on increasing the number of hotel rooms by 50%, road improvements and new developments. In 2001 tourist developments were under way in the south-western province of Pedernales, in Monte Cristi and in Cap Cana. The total number of visitors to the Dominican Republic in 2002 was 3,105,081. In 2000 receipts from tourism totalled US $2,918m. There were 52,000 hotel rooms in the Dominican Republic in 2001, with a further 7,000 rooms under construction.

Secretaría de Estado de Turismo: Bloque D, Edif. de Oficinas Gubernamentales, Avda México, esq. 30 de Marzo, Apdo 497, Santo Domingo, DN; tel. 221-4660; fax 682-3806; e-mail sectur@codetel.net.do.

Asociación Dominicana de Agencias de Viajes: Santo Domingo, DN; tel. 687-8984; Pres. Ramón Prieto.

Consejo de Promoción Turística: Edif. La Cumbre, 8°, Presidente González, esq. Tiradentes, Santo Domingo, DN; tel. 540-4676; fax 540-4727; e-mail cpt@codetel.net.do; internet www.drhotels.com.

ECUADOR

Introductory Survey

Location, Climate, Language, Religion, Flag, Capital

The Republic of Ecuador lies on the west coast of South America. It is bordered by Colombia to the north, by Peru to the east and south, and by the Pacific Ocean to the west. The Galápagos Islands, about 960 km (600 miles) off shore, form part of Ecuador. The climate is affected by the Andes mountains, and the topography ranges from the tropical rain forest on the coast and in the eastern region to the tropical grasslands of the central valley and the permanent snowfields of the highlands. The official language is Spanish, but Quechua and other indigenous languages are very common. Almost all of the inhabitants profess Christianity, and more than 90% are Roman Catholics. The national flag (proportions 1 by 2) has three horizontal stripes, of yellow (one-half of the depth), blue and red. The state flag has, in addition, the national emblem (an oval cartouche, showing Mt Chimborazo and a steamer on a lake, surmounted by a condor) in the centre. The capital is Quito.

Recent History

Ecuador was ruled by Spain from the 16th century until 1822, when it achieved independence as part of Gran Colombia. In 1830 Ecuador seceded and became a separate republic. A long-standing division between Conservatives (Partido Conservador), whose support is generally strongest in the highlands, and Liberals (Partido Liberal, subsequently Partido Liberal Radical), based in the coastal region, began in the 19th century. Until 1948 Ecuador's political life was characterized by a rapid succession of presidents, dictators and juntas. Between 1830 and 1925 the country was governed by 40 different regimes. From 1925 to 1948 there was even greater instability, with a total of 22 heads of state.

Dr Galo Plaza Lasso, who was elected in 1948 and remained in power until 1952, was the first President since 1924 to complete his term of office. He created a climate of stability and economic progress. Dr José María Velasco Ibarra, who had previously been President in 1934–35 and 1944–47, was elected again in 1952 and held office until 1956. A 61-year-old tradition of Liberal Presidents was broken in 1956, when a Conservative candidate, Dr Camilo Ponce Enríquez, took office. He was succeeded in 1960 by Velasco, who campaigned as a non-party Liberal. In the following year, however, President Velasco was deposed by a coup, and was succeeded by his Vice-President, Dr Carlos Julio Arosemena Monroy. The latter was himself deposed in 1963 by a military junta, led by Capt. (later Rear-Adm.) Ramón Castro Jijón, the Commander-in-Chief of the Navy, who assumed the office of President. In 1966 the High Command of the Armed Forces dismissed the junta and installed Clemente Yerovi Indaburu, a wealthy business executive and a former Minister of Economics, as acting President. Yerovi was forced to resign when the Constituent Assembly, elected in October, proposed a new Constitution which prohibited the intervention of the armed forces in politics. In November he was replaced as provisional President by Dr Otto Arosemena Gómez, who held office until the elections of 1968, when Velasco returned from exile to win the presidency for the fifth time.

In 1970 Velasco, with the support of the army, suspended the Constitution, dissolved the Congreso Nacional (National Congress) and assumed dictatorial powers to confront a financial emergency. In 1972 he was overthrown for the fourth time by a military coup, led by Brig.-Gen. Guillermo Rodríguez Lara, the Commander-in-Chief of the Army, who proclaimed himself Head of State. In 1976 President Rodríguez resigned, and power was assumed by a three-man military junta, led by Vice-Adm. Alfredo Poveda Burbano, the Chief of Staff of the Navy. The new junta announced its intention to lead the country to a truly representative democracy. A national referendum approved a newly drafted Constitution in January 1978 and presidential elections took place in July. No candidate achieved an overall majority, and a second round of voting was held in April 1979, when a new legislature was also elected. Jaime Roldós Aguilera of the Concentración de Fuerzas Populares was elected President and he took office in August, when the Congreso was inaugurated and the new Constitution came into force. Roldós

promised social justice and economic development, and guaranteed freedom for the press, but he encountered antagonism from both the conservative sections of the Congreso Nacional and the trade unions. In 1981 Roldós died and was replaced by the Vice-President, Dr Osvaldo Hurtado Larrea. Hurtado encountered opposition from left-wing politicians and trade unions for his efforts to reduce government spending and from right-wing and commercial interests, which feared encroaching state intervention in the private economic sector. In January 1982 the heads of the armed forces resigned and the Minister of Defence was dismissed, when they opposed Hurtado's attempts to settle amicably the border dispute with Peru (see below).

In March 1983 the Government introduced a series of austerity measures, which encountered immediate opposition from the trade unions and private-sector employees. Discontent with the Government's performance was reflected in the results of the presidential and congressional elections of January 1984, when the ruling party, Democracia Popular–Unión Demócrata Cristiana (DP–UDC), lost support. At a second round of voting in May León Febres Cordero, leader of the Partido Social Cristiano (PSC) and presidential candidate of the conservative Frente de Reconstrucción Nacional, unexpectedly defeated Dr Rodrigo Borja Cevallos, representing the left-wing Izquierda Democrática (ID), with 52.2% of the votes cast.

The dismissal of the Chief of Staff of the Armed Forces, Lt-Gen. Frank Vargas Pazzos, brought about a military crisis in 1986. Vargas and his supporters barricaded themselves inside the Mantas military base until they had forced the resignation of both the Minister of Defence and the army commander, who had been accused by Vargas of embezzlement. Vargas then staged a second rebellion at the military base where he had been detained. Troops loyal to the President made an assault on the base, captured Vargas and arrested his supporters. In January 1987 President Febres Cordero was abducted and, after being held for 11 hours, was released in exchange for Vargas, who was granted an amnesty. In July 58 members of the air force were sentenced to up to 16 years' imprisonment for involvement in the abduction of the President.

In June 1986 President Febres Cordero lost the majority that his coalition of parties had held in the Congreso Nacional. In May 1988 Dr Rodrigo Borja Cevallos (of the ID) won the presidential election, securing 46% of the votes cast in a second round of voting, defeating Abdalá Bucaram Ortiz of the Partido Roldosista Ecuatoriano (PRE), who won 41%. Borja took office as President in August, promising to act promptly to address Ecuador's increasing economic problems and to change the country's isolationist foreign policy. However, large demonstrations in protest against the rise in the price of fuel and against other anti-inflationary economic measures swiftly followed. In October the guerrilla organization Montoneros Patria Libre (MPL) proposed the establishment of dialogue between the Government and the rebels. In the same month the President of the Supreme Court of Justice was murdered in Quito by unknown assassins.

In February 1989 the Government conducted a campaign to confiscate weapons belonging to paramilitary organizations. In March Alfaro Vive ¡Carajo! (AVC), a leading opposition (hitherto guerrilla) group, urged paramilitary forces across the political spectrum to surrender their weapons. The Government agreed to guarantee the civil rights of AVC members and promised to initiate a national dialogue in return for the group's demobilization. (The AVC concluded the process of demobilization in February 1991 and was absorbed by the ID in October 1991.) The MPL dissociated itself from the agreement between the Government and the AVC and pledged to continue violent opposition.

At mid-term legislative elections in June 1990, the ID lost 16 seats and conceded control of the legislature to an informal alliance of the PSC and the PRE. In October a serious conflict arose between the Government and the legislature when the newly elected President of the Congreso Nacional, Dr Averroes Bucaram, attempted to stage a legislative coup against President Borja. Bucaram initially impeached several ministers, who were subsequently dismissed by the Congreso. The legislature then dismissed the Supreme Court justices and other high-ranking members of the judiciary, and appointed new courts with shortened mandates. Both the Government and the judiciary refused to recognize these actions, on the grounds that the Congreso had exceeded its constitutional powers. Bucaram then announced that the Congreso would initiate impeachment proceedings against Borja himself. However, this move was averted when three opposition deputies transferred their allegiance, so restoring Borja's congressional majority. Bucaram was subsequently dismissed as congressional President. None the less, impeachment proceedings against government ministers continued into 1991, and by August of that year a total of six ministers had been dismissed. The Government accused the opposition of using the proceedings as part of a deliberate campaign to undermine the prospects of the ID in the forthcoming elections.

In May 1990 about 1,000 indigenous Indians marched into Quito to demand official recognition of land rights for the indigenous population. In the following month the Confederación Nacional de Indígenas del Ecuador (CONAIE—National Confederation of the Indigenous Population of Ecuador) organized an uprising covering seven Andean provinces. Roads were blockaded, *haciendas* occupied, and supplies to the cities interrupted. Following the arrest of 30 Indians by the army, the rebels took military hostages. The Government offered to hold conciliatory negotiations with CONAIE, in exchange for the hostages. Among the demands made by the Indians were the return of traditional community-held lands, recognition of Quechua as an official language and compensation from petroleum companies for environmental damage. Discussions between CONAIE and President Borja collapsed in August. In January 1991 the Frente Unitario de Trabajadores (FUT) announced a joint anti-Government campaign with CONAIE. The FUT was protesting against the Government's decision on the level of increase of the minimum monthly wage. In February discussions between CONAIE and the Government were resumed, following the seizure by Indian groups in the Oriente of eight oil wells. As a result, the Government promised to consider the Indians' demands for stricter controls on the operations of the petroleum industry, and for financial compensation.

In April 1992 several thousand Amazon Indians marched from the Oriente to Quito to demand that their historical rights to their homelands be recognized. In May President Borja agreed to grant legal title to more than 1m. ha of land in the province of Pastaza to the Indians.

At legislative elections in May 1992 the PSC gained the highest number of seats in the enlarged Congreso Nacional, winning 21 of the 77 seats, while the PRE secured 13. The Partido Unidad Republicano (PUR) was formed prior to the elections by the former PSC presidential candidate, Sexto Durán Ballén, in order to contest the presidential election (since the PSC had nominated the President of the party, Jaime Nebot Saadi, as its candidate). The PUR won 12 seats, the ID only seven and the Partido Conservador (PC) six seats. In the second round of the presidential election, Durán secured 58% of the votes cast, defeating Nebot, who won 38%. The PUR was to govern with its ally, the PC. However, as the two parties' seats did not constitute a majority in the Congreso, support from other centre-right parties, particularly the PSC, was sought.

In September 1992 the Government's announcement of a programme of economic austerity measures, including the restructuring of the public sector, prompted violent demonstrations and several bomb attacks in Quito and Guayaquil and a general strike in May 1993. The 'Modernization Law', a crucial part of the controversial austerity programme (which was to provide for the privatization of some 160 state-owned companies and the reduction in the number of employees in the public sector by 100,000), was approved by the Congreso in August. In November striking teachers organized demonstrations throughout the country, demanding wage increases and reforms in the education system. During the protests two demonstrators were killed and many injured. Furthermore, the Government's decision in January 1994 to increase the price of fuel by more than 70% provoked violent demonstrations throughout the country and a general strike. In the following month the Tribunal of Constitutional Guarantees declared the rise to be unconstitutional, although President Durán refused to recognize the ruling. The unpopularity of Durán's PUR-PC governing alliance was demonstrated at mid-term congressional elections in May, when it won only nine of the 77 seats. The PSC secured

26 seats, while the PRE remained the second largest party in the Congreso, winning 11 seats.

Environmental concerns regarding the exploitation of the Oriente by the petroleum industry continued to be expressed by national and international groups during 1993. In November five Amazon Indian tribes began legal proceedings against the international company Texaco to claim compensation totalling US $1,500m. for its part in polluting the rain forest. (It was estimated that some 17m. barrels of oil had been spilt during the company's 25 years of operations in the region.) Protests intensified in January 1994, when the Government initiated a round of bidding for petroleum-exploration licences for 10 hydrocarbon regions, including sites in the eastern Oriente, previously withheld because of opposition from environmentalists and indigenous communities.

In June 1994 the increasingly vociferous indigenous movement organized large-scale demonstrations across the country, in protest at a recently approved Land Development Law. The law, which allowed for the commercialization of Amerindian lands for farming and resource extraction, provoked serious unrest and a general strike, during which a state of emergency was declared and the army mobilized. Seven protesters were killed, and many injured, in clashes with the security forces. The law was subsequently judged to be unconstitutional by the Tribunal of Constitutional Guarantees, although President Durán refused to accept the ruling. In July the law was modified to extend the rights of landowners and those employed to work on the land.

In August 1994 a national referendum on constitutional reform finally took place, at President Durán's instigation, following much disagreement between the Government and the judiciary and opposition parties. All but one of the eight proposed reforms (which included measures to alter the electoral system and the role of the Congreso Nacional, and the establishment of a bicameral legislature) were approved; however, only some 50% of eligible voters participated, of whom some 20% returned void ballot papers.

Protests against the Government's economic programme of austerity measures and privatizations in January 1995 resulted in the deaths of two students in Quito during clashes with riot police. In March the Minister of Finance resigned (the third to do so since the Government came to power), apparently because of differences within the Cabinet concerning economic policy. During May and June the FUT launched a national strike against a series of 'corrective' economic measures, introduced by the Government in an attempt to reduce the impact of the financial crisis caused by the border conflict with Peru (see below), and in July oil workers initiated a strike in protest at the impact of government policy on the petroleum industry. Later that month the country was plunged into a serious political crisis when Vice-President Alberto Dahik admitted giving funds from the state budget to opposition deputies (allegedly for use in local public-works projects) in return for their support for the Government's economic reform programme. Dahik refused to resign, despite the initiation of impeachment proceedings, and rejected the criminal charges against him. In a further development (believed by some observers to be an attempt to obstruct the case against Dahik) the President of the Supreme Court and two other justices were dismissed. Critics of the Government's action claimed that the dismissals themselves were unconstitutional, as they did not respect the separation of powers of the judiciary from the legislature and executive. In September impeachment proceedings began against the new Minister of Finance, Mauricio Pinto, for his role in various alleged financial irregularities. Meanwhile, the Superintendent of Banks resigned his post, following accusations that he had attempted to hinder the case against Dahik in the Supreme Court. Impeachment proceedings against Dahik began in October, and on 11 October, following an appeal by Durán, the Vice-President resigned. A further two cabinet ministers offered their resignations in support of Dahik, and on 13 October the entire Cabinet resigned in order that a reorganization of portfolios could take place.

In addition to the political crisis provoked by the scandal surrounding the Vice-President, the administration continued to be troubled by various industrial disputes and strikes in 1995. In September troops were dispatched to the Galápagos Islands, following disturbances among the islanders, who were demanding the Government's acceptance of a special law granting increased political and financial autonomy to the islands, in addition to some US $16m. in priority economic aid.

Concerned about the potentially disastrous effect of the protests on the country's important tourist industry, the Government quickly withdrew its opposition to the proposed legislation and agreed to establish a specialist commission to draft a new law acceptable to all parties. Moreover, in October petroleum workers resumed strike action in protest at the Government's privatization plans, and in one incident occupied the PETRO-ECUADOR building, taking two cabinet ministers hostage for several hours. The dispute ended following the resignation of the Minister of Energy and Mines at the end of the month. The strike, however, together with a severe drought, which halted production at the Paute hydroelectric plant (which, under normal circumstances, provided 60%–70% of the country's electricity), resulted in serious energy shortages in late 1995.

A referendum on government proposals for constitutional reform was held in November 1995. All of the proposed changes were rejected in the plebiscite, which was widely regarded as a reflection of the Government's continued unpopularity. Despite its decisive defeat, the Government announced its intention to pursue its programme of reforms. Widespread strikes and demonstrations by teachers and students in the same month, in which one student was killed in clashes with police, led to the resignation of the Minister of Education. The initiation of impeachment proceedings against a cabinet minister, and the resignation of another, further weakened the President's position, and pressure for him to resign intensified. Industrial action among employees in the energy sector continued, and in January 1996 army units were deployed at prominent sites throughout the country in order to prevent further unrest. An industrial dispute by transport workers in March resulted in serious disruption in the capital and prompted a series of strikes in other sectors.

A presidential election, held in May 1996, failed to produce an outright winner, thus necessitating a second round of voting for the two leading contenders. The PSC candidate, Jaime Nebot Saadi, secured 27.1% of the votes in the first round, while Abdalá Bucaram Ortiz of the PRE won 25.6%. An increasingly vocal and politically-organized indigenous movement resulted in the strong performance of Freddy Ehlers, the candidate for the newly formed Movimiento Nuevo País-Pachakútik (MNPP), a coalition of Amerindian and labour groups. Ehlers secured 21% of the votes. At legislative elections held concurrently, the PSC won 27 of the 82 seats in the enlarged Congreso Nacional, while the PRE secured 19 and Democracia Popular (DP—formerly DP-UDC) won 12. The MNPP emerged as a significant new force in the legislature, with a total of eight seats. At the second round of voting in the presidential election in July, Bucaram was the unexpected victor, receiving 54.5% of total votes. The success of Bucaram was widely interpreted as a rejection of the policies of the outgoing Government (which Nebot had promised to continue) and an expression of disenchantment with established party politics. Following his inauguration in August, Bucaram sought to allay the fears of the business community (prompted by his proposals for costly social reform) stating that existing economic arrangements would be maintained. Moreover, a team of prominent businessmen was assigned the role of advising the President on economic policy.

A 48-hour general strike began in January 1997, prompted by increases of up to 600% in the price of certain commodities and a climate of considerable dissatisfaction with the President's leadership. Protests intensified in early February when several hundred thousand demonstrators marched through Quito demanding Bucaram's resignation. The President responded by declaring a national holiday and a one-week closure of schools across the country, and stated his support for the strike. Meanwhile, troops were deployed in the capital as violent clashes erupted between protesters and security personnel and Bucaram was barricaded inside the presidential palace. On 6 February, at an emergency session, the Congreso Nacional voted by 44 votes to 34 to dismiss the President on the grounds of mental incapacity; by questioning the President's sanity, the Congreso was able to evade the normal impeachment requirements of a two-thirds' majority. A state of emergency was declared, and the erstwhile Speaker, Fabián Alarcón Rivera, who had assumed the presidency in an acting capacity, urged demonstrators to storm the presidential palace. Bucaram, however, refused to leave office and claimed that he would retain power by force if necessary. The situation was further complicated by the claim of the Vice-President, Rosalia Arteaga, to be the legitimate constitutional successor to Bucaram. Political confusion over the correct procedure led to fears of a military coup, despite a declaration of neutrality by the armed forces. Bucaram reportedly fled from the presidential palace on 9 February, and on the following day Arteaga was declared interim President after narrowly winning a congressional vote. However, by 11 February Arteaga had resigned, amid continued constitutional uncertainty, and Alarcón was reinstated as President. Alarcón, who sought political reform and the restoration of economic confidence, announced a reorganization of cabinet portfolios (which included no members of the two largest parties in the Congreso, the PSC and the PRE) and the creation of a commission to investigate allegations of corruption against Bucaram and his administration. In March Bucaram's extradition from Panama (where he had been granted political asylum) was requested in order that he face charges of misappropriating some US $90m. of government funds. In the following month the President of the Supreme Court announced that extradition would only be possible once a prison sentence had been issued. Furthermore, in May Bucaram declared his intention to stand as a presidential candidate at Ecuador's next elections. As a result, the legislature voted almost unanimously in favour of a motion to impose an indefinite ban on Bucaram's candidacy in any future presidential election. (In January 1998 the Supreme Court issued a four-year prison sentence to Bucaram for libel and in April 2001 he was indicted on corruption charges.) The legislature similarly voted to curtail the term of office of Rosalia Arteaga such that it would terminate, along with that of the interim President, in August 1998, when elections would take place.

In May 1997 a national referendum sought public opinion on a variety of matters, including electoral reform, the modernization of the judiciary and the authenticity of Alarcón's position. Although 40.7% of the electorate did not participate, the vote revealed considerable support for the decision to remove Bucaram from office (75.7%) and for the appointment of Alarcón as interim President (68.3%). Some 64.5% of voters also favoured the creation of a national assembly to consider constitutional reform. Alarcón's apparent success in the referendum, however, was undermined in June by the launch of an official congressional inquiry into allegations that leading drugs-traffickers in the country had contributed to political party funds, and, particularly, to Alarcón's Frente Radical Alfarista.

In July 1997 the Congreso Nacional dismissed all 31 judges of the Supreme Court, claiming that its action was in accordance with the views on the depoliticization of the judiciary (which is nominated by the legislature) expressed in the recent referendum. The President of the Supreme Court condemned the action as unconstitutional.

The announcement in August 1997 that a national assembly to review the Constitution (as proposed in the referendum of May 1997) would not be installed until August 1998 was widely opposed, and provoked a 48-hour strike in protest, which virtually paralysed the country by means of numerous roadblocks. The strike was supported most strongly by Indian and peasant organizations, which insisted that an assembly should be convened as soon as possible in order to discuss indigenous rights and the proposed privatization of key areas of the economy. In response to the apparent strength of public opinion, it was announced in September that elections for the 70 representatives to the assembly would take place in late November. However, 11 indigenous organizations demonstrated their lack of confidence in the Government to address their concerns by convening a mass rally in Quito to establish guide-lines for their own constitution.

In January 1998, following persistent pleas from international environmental and scientific organizations for greater protection of the Galápagos Islands, the Congreso Nacional approved a law which aimed to preserve the islands' unique environment more effectively. An element of the law, providing for an extension of the marine reserve around the islands from 15 to 40 nautical miles, attracted intense criticism from powerful fishing interests in the country and was, consequently, vetoed by Alarcón, prompting condemnation by environmentalists and small-scale fishing concerns, who claimed that the President had acceded to commercial pressures. (In January 2001 an environmental catastrophe was feared when an oil tanker ran aground less than one kilometre from the Galápagos Islands, leaking about 80% of its 240,000-gallon cargo into the sea. Although at least 76,000 gallons of petroleum were recovered and favourable winds and currents appeared to limit the extent of the ecological damage, it was feared that the spill would result in long-term detrimental effects.)

In February 1998 the recently established National Constituent Assembly (convened to review the Constitution) announced a number of institutional reforms, including the enlargement of the Congreso Nacional from 82 to 121 seats, the abolition of mid-term elections and the completion of a presidential term by the Vice-President in the case of the indefinite absence of the President. The new Constitution, which retained the majority of the provisions of the 1979 Constitution, officially came into force on 10 August.

At a presidential election on 31 May 1998 the DP candidate and mayor of Quito, Jamil Mahuad Witt, emerged as the strongest contender, securing 35.2% of total votes cast. Alvaro Noboa Pontón for the PRE, whose popularity was concentrated in Guayaquil and the coastal regions, received 26.5% of votes, while ex-President Borja and Freddy Ehlers won 15.6% and 14.3%, respectively. At concurrent elections to the newly-enlarged Congreso Nacional the DP secured 32 of the 121 seats, the PSC won 27, the PRE 24 and the ID 18 seats. At the second round of voting in the presidential election on 12 July, Mahuad narrowly defeated Noboa with 51.2% of total votes. Noboa rejected the result, alleging widespread voting irregularities, none of which was upheld by the Supreme Electoral Tribunal or the international observers present in the country. Mahuad was sworn in on 10 August and appointed a Cabinet consisting predominantly of independent members. The new President's stated objectives focused on the stimulation of economic recovery, following a series of serious reversals, including a decrease in world petroleum prices and the infrastructural and sociological damage caused by El Niño (a periodic warming of the tropical Pacific Ocean—see below). In addition, Mahuad proposed a number of social programmes (involving the creation of new jobs and the construction of low-cost homes), which prompted scepticism amongst observers, who doubted the feasibility of such plans.

A programme of severe adjustment measures, which included huge rises in the cost of domestic gas and electricity, as well as substantial increases in public transport fares and fuel prices, was introduced in September 1998, prompting a general strike, organized by FUT and CONAIE, in the following month. Subsequent rioting and violent confrontation between demonstrators and security personnel resulted in the deaths of four people. In February 1999 disagreement over economic policy led to the resignation of the Minister of Finance, and severe disruption arising from extensive fuel shortages prompted the resignation of the Minister of Energy and Mines. In the same month the leader of the left-wing Movimiento Popular Democrático and member of the Congreso Nacional, Jaime Hurtado González, was assassinated in Quito. The killing was linked to a right-wing Colombian paramilitary group. In March former interim President Alarcón was arrested on charges of illegally hiring personnel during his term in office as legislative Speaker.

In March 1999 a substantial decrease in the value of the sucre led President Mahuad to declare a week-long bank holiday in an attempt to prevent the withdrawal of deposits and reduce the pressure on the currency. A few days later a 60-day state of emergency was declared by the Government in response to a two-day strike, organized by leaders of the main trade unions and Indian groups. In addition, the Government announced an economic retrenchment programme in an attempt to restore investor confidence and prevent economic collapse. Measures included an increase in fuel prices of up to 160%, a number of tax reforms (notably a rise in value-added tax—VAT), the partial 'freezing' of bank accounts, and the planned privatization of certain state-owned companies. These prompted a further series of protests and the resignation of four of the five members of the board of the central bank (citing differences over government financial policies). The main opposition party, the PSC, similarly refused to endorse the austerity programme, thus compelling the President to compromise with the proposal of less severe economic measures, which were narrowly approved by the Congreso. These new measures included a partial reduction of fuel price increases, and the reinstatement of income tax; following their approval, Mahuad lifted the state of emergency. However, a further rise in prices and the collapse of a major bank (the Banco del Progreso) later in March led to renewed protests.

In April 1999 the Government announced an emergency plan entitled 'Ecuador 2000', which aimed to revive the economy and included a number of requisite measures to gain the support of the IMF. The plan incorporated numerous social and public works development schemes, tax reforms and moves towards less centralized government. The plan was approved by the IMF

and it was hoped that the Fund would provide an estimated US \$400m. in initial financing. However, in July taxi drivers and public transport workers took nation-wide industrial action in protest at increases in fuel prices and at the new economic retrenchment plan proposed by the IMF. In response to the ensuing massive disruption, the Government imposed a further state of emergency and called in the military. The state of emergency was lifted in mid-July, after President Mahuad agreed to 'freeze' fuel prices and allow co-operatives and transport companies access to 'frozen' bank deposits.

In August 1999 the Government announced its intention to default on US \$96m. in interest payments on \$6,000m. in outstanding foreign debt repayments (on so-called 'Brady bonds'—restructured commercial bank loans) for a period of 30 days, and to attempt to restructure its large external debts. The IMF-supported move was implemented owing to the country's inability to honour repayments on its foreign debt (which, at a total of more than \$13,000m., was equivalent to some 90% of GDP). In early September the Minister of Finance resigned, prompted by the unpopularity of the recent economic measures (her successor, however, remained in the post only six weeks before himself resigning). Nevertheless, at the end of September, the IMF signed a preliminary agreement with Ecuador which was expected to provide up to \$1,250m. in funding (comprising a \$400m. stand-by loan from the IMF and \$850m. in loans from other multilateral agencies).

President Mahuad imposed a state of emergency in early January 2000 in an attempt to curb increasing unrest, amid indications that the economic crisis was deteriorating. On 21 January Mahuad was forced to flee from the presidential palace, following large-scale protests in Quito by thousands of Indian demonstrators, who were supported by sections of the armed forces, over the President's perceived mismanagement of the economic crisis (including his controversial decision to replace the sucre with the US dollar). A three-man council was established to oversee the country. However, Gen. Carlos Mendoza, the Chief of Staff of the Armed Forces, disbanded the council within 24 hours of its creation, and announced the appointment of former Vice-President Gustavo Noboa Bejerano as President. This move followed talks with US officials, who had warned that foreign aid to Ecuador would be curtailed if power was not restored to the elected Government. The coup was widely condemned by governments around the world and by international organizations. Noboa, whose appointment as Head of State was endorsed by a large majority in the Congreso Nacional, promised to restore economic stability to the country. However, Indian activists who had supported the short-lived three-member council (one of whose members had been the leader of CONAIE, Antonio Vargas) continued to demonstrate against the assumption of the presidency by Noboa, whom they viewed as ideologically similar to Mahuad. Noboa appointed Pedro Pinto Rubianes as the new Vice-President on 27 January and formed a new Cabinet, comprising members of the DP, the PSC and the PRE, in February.

In February 2000 four members of the armed forces, who allegedly participated in the events leading up to Mahuad's removal from office, were apprehended on charges of insurrection. It was later announced that as many as 113 army officers were to be charged in connection with the previous month's events. In May the entire military high command was replaced, even though later that month the Congreso approved an amnesty for military officers and civilians arrested in connection with the coup.

Congressional approval for a controversial economic reform programme, the Ley de Transformación Económica (Economic Transformation Law), which included the adoption of the US dollar as the official currency, as well as fiscal adjustments and an acceleration in the privatization process, was secured in February 2000. CONAIE, which had returned to prominence following its role in the removal of President Mahuad, organized a series of demonstrations in protest at the dollarization policy and to demand a referendum on the dissolution of the Congreso Nacional and the Supreme Court. Palliative measures introduced by the Government, including an increase in the minimum wage, were rejected by trade unions and indigenous organizations. Nevertheless, the process of dollarization formally began in March and was completed in September, when the US dollar officially became Ecuador's sole currency. In late April the Minister of the Interior resigned, after he failed to secure an agreement with CONAIE to end the protests. The announcement by the Government in May of an IMF-approved economic adjustment package, which included a sharp increase in the price of fuel, not only provoked further antagonism between the Government and trade unions and indigenous organizations, but also resulted in the resignation of the Minister of Finance and Public Credit. However, in September CONAIE entered into renewed negotiations with the Government after its calls for mass demonstrations in the previous month had met with only moderate support. In the same month the Supreme Electoral Tribunal disallowed a petition from CONAIE requesting that a referendum on various aspects of the Ley de Transformación Económica be held, owing to irregularities in the collection of signatures.

Both the DP and the PSC performed well in municipal and provincial elections held throughout the country in May 2000, suggesting significant popular acceptance of the structural reforms (although the ID candidate, Paco Moncayo, won the strategically important mayoral election in Quito). However, relations between the DP and the PSC came under increasing strain in August when the independent Susana González was controversially elected legislative President for the remaining two years of the current presidential term (until August 2002). The PSC claimed that, as the second largest party in the Congreso Nacional, its nominee should fill the position and a Constitutional Tribunal was organized to determine the legality of the result. In the same month the Government offered to resign in support to the President after the governing coalition lost its majority in the Congreso (divisions within the DP had resulted in several of its members aligning themselves with the centre-left opposition). The coalition's lack of a parliamentary majority endangered the proposed reform (also known as Trole 11) of the labour and petroleum sectors, as well as the privatization process. At the end of August the impasse between the Government and the legislature was resolved after the Constitutional Tribunal ruled that a new election to the congressional presidency must be held; Hugo Quevado of the PSC was subsequently elected to the post. (Quevado resigned in June 2001 following allegations of corruption and was replaced by José Cordero.)

The relationship between the legislature and the executive was strained further in late August 2000 after President Noboa resorted to presidential decree to pass the proposed Trole 11 legislation. CONAIE and trade union organizations appealed to the Constitutional Tribunal to rule on the legality of such a move. In January 2001 the Constitutional Tribunal upheld almost one-third of the objections against Trole 11, and, most notably, declared unconstitutional the clause concerning the proposed privatization of state-owned companies.

In December 2000 two attacks on the trans-Ecuadorean oil pipeline resulted in at least 16 fatalities and 41 injuries. President Noboa attributed blame for the attack to terrorists attempting to destabilize the country and prevent economic modernization. In the same month the Minister of Finance and Public Credit submitted his resignation, apparently a result of his opposition to economic reforms advocated by the IMF, which included an increase in VAT from 12% to 15%. Popular resentment against the Government erupted in January 2001 after significant increases in fuel prices and transport costs were implemented. Thousands of Indian protesters occupied Quito and roadblocks were erected across the Andean highlands and the Amazon lowlands. In February the Government imposed a national state of emergency, which was lifted only after the Government acceded to the demands for a reduction in fuel prices in return for an end to the protests, which were marred by violence.

In March 2001 transport workers staged a 24-hour strike in protest at the Government's proposed tax reforms as well as a planned reduction in transportation costs. In the event, the Congreso Nacional rejected the proposals, which, in turn, resulted in a suspension of talks on debt relief with the IMF and international creditors. In May, in an extraordinary congressional session, the Government secured a 2% increase in VAT, as a result of which the IMF approved a US $48m. disbursement and an extension of the stand-by credit facility to the end of 2001. In August the Government suffered a further set-back when the Constitutional Tribunal ruled that the increase in VAT to 14% was unconstitutional, and it was therefore repealed.

A number of cabinet changes were implemented during 2001 and 2002, including the appointment, in September 2001, of Luis Maldonado Ruiz as Minister of Social Welfare. He was the first Indian to hold a portfolio that was not exclusively related to indigenous affairs. In October 2001 the Minister of Finance and

Public Credit, Jorge Gallardo, resigned after an order for his arrest was issued by the Attorney-General, following allegations of financial irregularities while he was President of Banco del Pacífico. Gallardo was succeeded by Carlos Julio Emanuel, who himself was forced to resign in June 2002 amid allegations that senior officials in his agency were implicated in a bribery scandal.

In February 2002 indigenous and civic groups in the northeast of the country occupied petroleum refineries, halted construction of a new oil pipeline and blocked major roads, prompting President Noboa to declare a state of emergency in the provinces of Sucumbíos and Orellana. In April, as a concession to the protesters, the Government pledged to direct funds to local infrastructure development. Meanwhile, the Government suffered an additional humiliation when it was forced to suspend the sale of state-owned electricity distribution facilities, owing to a lack of interested foreign buyers.

Presidential and legislative elections were held on 20 October 2002. In the congressional ballot, the PSC won 24 of the 100 contested seats, followed by the ID (15 seats), the PRE (14) and the right-wing Partido Renovador Institucional de Acción Nacional (PRIAN, 10 seats). The presidential election, held concurrently, was notable for a low rate of voter participation (62.9%) and for the electorate's rejection of candidates presented by traditional parties. None of the 11 candidates obtained sufficient votes to secure the presidency, and a second round of voting was scheduled for 24 November, at which the electorate would choose between Lucio Gutiérrez Borbua (a former colonel who had been imprisoned for participating in the coup against President Mahuad in 2000) and Alvaro Noboa Pontón (a banana magnate and founder of the PRIAN), who in the first round won 20.3% and 17.4% of the vote, respectively. Gutiérrez, who campaigned on a populist, anti-corruption platform, and whose own party (the Partido Sociedad Patriótica 21 de Enero) was supported by the MNPP, secured the presidency, winning 58.7% of the votes in the second round of the election, compared with Noboa's 41.3%.

As President-elect, Gutiérrez made clear his intention to honour Ecuador's debt obligations and continue negotiations with the IMF. He selected Mauricio Pozo, an orthodox economist, as Minister of Finance and Public Credit, and shortly after taking office on January 15 2003, President Gutiérrez announced a series of economic adjustment measures, including reductions in public-sector salaries and an increase in the price of fuel. Meanwhile, the opposition-led Congreso Nacional presented Gutiérrez with his first major obstacle prior to assuming the presidency, when the PSC, as the dominant congressional party, refused to preside over the legislature. In protest, Gutiérrez had initially threatened to boycott his own inauguration in the Congreso, although he later agreed to be sworn in while the post of congressional leader remained vacant.

Upon taking office, President Gutiérrez immediately decreed a series of measures intended to prevent a renewed fiscal crisis and to secure a new stand-by loan agreement with the IMF. These measures included a freeze on public-sector wages, a 35% increase in domestic petroleum prices and a 10% rise in electricity tariffs. In early February 2003, following the IMF's approval of Ecuador's draft budget, the Government announced a new US $500m. package of multilateral loans. The new lending was conditional upon the implementation of a series of fiscal and administrative reforms, and the allocation of a higher proportion of oil revenues towards the country's estimated $17,000m. foreign debt. However, in late February the opposition-controlled Congreso defied the President and reallocated intended debt repayments to health and education. Furthermore, in mid-March deputies again jeopardized the IMF funding by vetoing tax reform. By the end of that month, nevertheless, President Gutiérrez had succeeded in gaining legislative approval for the 2003 budget without any significant amendments, despite strong criticism from Gutiérrez's coalition allies, the MNPP (the congressional arm of CONAIE).

Another stated priority of the new President was the country's apparently endemic corruption. In March 2003 agreement was reached with the USA to repatriate allegedly corrupt financiers for prosecution in Ecuador. However, in the same month, the Minister of Urban Development and Housing, Nelson Álvarez, was dismissed, following allegations of fraudulent business dealings, and there remained persistent allegations of nepotism in the administration's appointments within the military and elsewhere in government.

Indeed, in his first few months in office President Gutiérrez faced considerable political opposition, despite his apparently favourable reception by a majority of the electorate. His announcement, in January 2003, that Ecuador was the 'best friend' of the USA, in addition to his pursuit of austere fiscal policies, caused some consternation among his political allies. In February CONAIE issued the President with a deadline of 30 days in which to reverse the IMF-approved policies, and protests in response to increased fuel costs and public-sector discontent also continued. However, with some democratic reforms (such as a reduction in the number of political parties) already in place, the most significant potential obstruction to the President's agenda of reforms continued to be posed by the main opposition parties inside the Congreso.

In April 1999 the World Trade Organization (WTO) upheld the complaint, put forward by the USA, Ecuador and four other Latin American countries, that the European Union (EU) unfairly favoured Caribbean banana producers, and authorized the USA to impose trade sanctions against EU goods. A two-tier tariff rate quota arrangement was agreed at a meeting between Ecuadorean government officials and leaders of Caribbean banana-producing countries in November, easing restrictions on Latin American banana exporters and consequently assisting Ecuadorean producers. In April 2001 the EU provided assurances to Ecuadorean producers over access to the EU market: quotas for Latin American producers were to be phased out by 2006 and replaced by a uniform tariff system.

The long-standing border dispute with Peru over the Cordillera del Cóndor erupted into war in January 1981. A cease-fire was declared a few days later under the auspices of the guarantors of the Rio Protocol of 1942 (Argentina, Brazil, Chile and the USA). The Protocol was not recognized by Ecuador as it awarded the area, which affords access to the Amazon river system, to Peru. Further clashes occurred along the border with Peru in December 1982 and January 1983. In January 1992 discussions on the border dispute were resumed. However, in January 1995 serious fighting broke out between the two sides, following reports of Peruvian incursions into Ecuadorean territory. Both Governments denied responsibility for initiating hostilities and issued contradictory reports concerning subsequent clashes. Following offers from the Organization of American States (OAS) and the four guarantor nations of the Rio Protocol, representatives of the two Governments met for negotiations in Rio de Janeiro, Brazil, and a cease-fire agreement was concluded in February. An observer mission, representing the four guarantor nations, was dispatched to the border, to oversee the separation of forces and demilitarization of the border area. Following intensive negotiations, agreement on the delimitation of the demilitarized zone in the disputed area was reached in July, and in October Ecuador finally repealed the state of emergency. A resumption of negotiations in September 1996 resulted in the signing of the Santiago Agreement by both sides in the following month, which was to provide a framework for a definitive solution on the border issue.

Following further negotiations in early 1998 a number of commissions were established to examine specific aspects of a potential agreement between Ecuador and Peru, including a trade and navigation treaty and the fixing of frontier markers on the ground in the Cordillera del Cóndor. Talks culminated in the signing of an accord in Brasília on 26 October by the Ministers of Foreign Affairs of Ecuador and Peru in the presence of the two countries' Presidents and of six other regional leaders. The accord confirmed Peru's claim regarding the delineation of the border, but granted Ecuador navigation and trading rights on the Amazon and its tributaries and the opportunity to establish two trading centres in Peru (although this was not to constitute sovereign access). Moreover, Ecuador was given 1 sq km of territory, as private property, at Tiwintza in Peru where many Ecuadorean soldiers, killed during the conflict in 1995, were buried. Although considerable opposition to the accord was expressed in Peru, international reaction was very favourable and resulted in several offers of finance from multilateral agencies for cross-border development projects.

An official ceremony in May 1999 marked the transfer of Tiwintza from Peru to Ecuador, and both parties confirmed that two ecological parks were to be created along the common border, where military personnel would not be allowed access. Presidents Mahuad and Alberto Fujimori reiterated their intention to seek US $3,000m. in funding, over a 10-year period, to finance a number of development projects (including the construction of new roads and health and education centres) and to organize the removal of land mines in the border area.

Following the suspected involvement of Colombian guerrillas in the murder of an Ecuadorean politician in Quito in February 1999 (see above) and reports (denied by the Ecuadorean Government) of the presence of Colombian paramilitary troops in the country, Ecuador's military presence was strengthened at its border with Colombia. In September 12 foreigners, several of whom were employees of a petroleum company operating in the region, were kidnapped by suspected Colombian guerrillas in the jungle near the Colombian border. In November an explosion which damaged an oil pipeline in the same area was linked to a Colombian rebel group, although any foreign involvement in the incident was denied by the Ecuadorean Government. As the internal conflict in Colombia escalated in 2000, Ecuador received an increasing number of Colombian refugees and experienced an intensification of violent incidents along its border. Between September 2000 and January 2001 about 2,100 Colombians sought refuge in the Ecuadorean border town of Lago Agrio. In February 2001 the Minister of Foreign Affairs, Heinz Moeller Freile, announced his intention to ask the US Government for financial aid to support the creation of an economic and military 'buffer' zone between Ecuador and Colombia. In March the Government assigned 10,000 troops to police the border with Colombia. In April the US Administration of George W. Bush proposed a US $882.3m. package of economic and counter-narcotics assistance for Colombia, Peru, Bolivia, Ecuador, Brazil, Panama and Venezuela, known as the Andean Regional Initiative (ARI). Under the ARI Ecuador would receive $56.5m. in socio-economic aid for border-area development, judicial reform and environmental programmes and $20m. for border security, law enforcement and sea and airport control efforts. In October Ecuador secured a further $266m. from the international donor community for alternative development programmes in the northern provinces that border Colombia. In November 2002 President-elect Gutiérrez announced his intention to meet with his Colombian counterpart to discuss measures to contain the activities of Colombian rebels. None the less, the new Government refused formally to classify the Fuerzas Armadas Revolucionarias de Colombia (FARC—Revolutionary Armed Forces of Colombia) as a terrorist organization, and reiterated its policy of military non-intervention in the Colombian conflict.

Government

Executive power is vested in the President, who is directly elected by universal adult suffrage for a four-year term (starting from 15 January of the year following his election). The President is not eligible for re-election. Legislative power is held by the 100-member unicameral Congreso Nacional (National Congress), which is also directly elected for a four-year term. Ecuador comprises 21 provinces, composed of 193 cantons, 322 urban parishes and 757 rural parishes. Each province has a Governor, who is appointed by the President. Measures to reform the structure of the Congreso Nacional were announced in January 2003.

Defence

Military service, which lasts one year, is selective for men at the age of 20. In August 2002 there were 59,500 men in the armed forces: army 50,000, navy 5,500 (including 1,700 marines) and air force 4,000. Defence expenditure in 2001 was estimated to be US $345m.

Economic Affairs

In 2001, according to estimates by the World Bank, Ecuador's gross national income (GNI), measured at average 1999–2001 prices, was US $15,952m., equivalent to $1,240 per head (or $3,070 per head on an international purchasing-power parity basis). During 1990–2001, it was estimated, the population increased at an average annual rate of 2.1%, while gross domestic product (GDP) per head decreased, in real terms, at an average annual rate of 0.1%. Overall GDP increased, in real terms, at an average annual rate of 2.1% in 1990–2001; growth in 2001 was 5.6%.

Agriculture (including hunting, forestry and fishing) contributed 10.8% of GDP in 2001. According to census figures, some 27.3% of the labour force were employed in the agricultural sector in 2001. The principal cash crops are bananas, coffee and cocoa. The seafood sector, particularly the shrimp industry, expanded rapidly in the 1980s, and by the 1990s Ecuador was the second largest producer of shrimps in the world. Ecuador's extensive forests yield valuable hardwoods, and the country is a leading producer of balsawood. Exports of cut flowers increased from US $0.5m. in 1985 to $155.6m. in 2000 (equivalent to 3.2% of the total value of exports). During 1990–2001 agricultural GDP increased at an average annual rate of 1.6%. It declined by 5.3% in 2000, but increased by 1.8% in 2001.

Industry (including mining, manufacturing, construction and power) employed 21.4% of the urban labour force in 1998, and provided 32.9% of GDP in 2001. During 1990–2001 industrial GDP increased at an average annual rate of 3.0%. The sector grew by 4.9% in 2000, and by a further 5.0% in 2001.

Mining contributed 21.5% of GDP in 2000, although the mining sector employed only 0.3% of the urban labour force in 1998. Petroleum and its derivatives remained the major exports in the early 21st century. In 2000 some 146.2m. barrels of crude petroleum were produced, of which about 60% was exported. Earnings from petroleum exports amounted to some US $2,442.3m. in 2000, equivalent to 50.7% of the total value of exports. Natural gas is extracted, but only a small proportion is retained. Gold, silver, copper, antimony and zinc are also mined. In real terms, the GDP of the mining sector increased at an average rate of 3.7% per year during 1991–2000. Mining GDP declined by 0.3% in 1999, but increased by 4.8% in 2000.

Manufacturing contributed 18.4% of GDP in 2001, and employed 14.7% of the labour force in urban areas in 1998. Measured by output in producers' prices, the most important branches of manufacturing in 1999 were food products (accounting for 27.0% of the total), petroleum refineries (10.5%), chemicals (7.3%) and pulp and paper products (7.2%). During 1990–2001 manufacturing GDP increased at an average annual rate of 2.3%. It increased by 5.2% in 2000 and by a further 5.0% in 2001.

Energy is derived principally from thermoelectric and hydro-electric plants. Imports of mineral fuels and lubricants comprised 8.2% of the value of total imports in 2000.

The services sector contributed 56.3% of GDP in 2001. Some 71.2% of the urban labour force were employed in services in 1998. The sector's GDP increased at an average annual rate of 1.6% during 1991–2000. It increased by 3.4% in 2000 and by a further 5.9% in 2001.

In 2001 Ecuador recorded a visible trade deficit of US $462m., and a deficit of $800m. on the current account of the balance of payments. In 2000 the principal source of imports was the USA (accounting for 25.6% of the total), which was also the principal market for exports (37.9%). Other major trading partners were Colombia, Germany, Italy, the Republic of Korea, Panama and Peru. The principal exports in 2000 were petroleum and petroleum derivatives (50.7%), bananas (17.0%) and seafood and seafood products (12.1%). The principal imports in 2000 were machinery and transport equipment (26.6%), chemicals (23.5%) and basic manufactures (19.9%).

In 2001 there was a budgetary surplus of about US $12m. In 1996 some 40% of government expenditure was financed by revenue from petroleum. Ecuador's total external debt was US $13,281m. at the end of 2000, of which $11,366m. was long-term public debt. In that year the cost of debt-servicing was equivalent to 17.6% of the total value of exports of goods and services. The average annual rate of inflation in 1990–2001 was 42.0%; the rate averaged 96.9% in 2000 and 37.6% in 2001. The rate of unemployment decreased from an average of 14.4% in 1999 to 9.0% in 2000.

Ecuador is a member of the Andean Community (see p. 133), the Organization of American States (OAS, see p. 288) and of the Asociación Latinoamericana de Integración (ALADI, see p. 259). In 1992 Ecuador withdrew from the Organization of the Petroleum Exporting Countries (OPEC, see p. 298) and announced its intention of seeking associate status. In 1995 Ecuador joined the World Trade Organization (WTO, see p. 323).

In the mid-1990s Ecuador's proven petroleum reserves almost tripled, following discoveries in the Amazon region, and the Government signed contracts with numerous companies for further exploration and drilling. In late 1997 work to expand the capacity of the trans-Ecuadorean pipeline from 330,000 b/d to 410,000 b/d began. Construction of a new pipeline for heavy crudes (Oleoducto para Crudos Pesados—OCP), financed by a consortium of private companies at a cost of US $594m., also began in 2002, despite concerted protests from indigenous groups and environmental activists. However, construction of the new pipeline, the completion of which was expected to double Ecuador's petroleum production, was suspended in early 2003 pending a ruling on its environmental impact. From 2000 attempts to privatize a number of state-owned industries were repeatedly impeded by political turmoil and trade union opposition. The programme suffered a major setback in May 2002 with the suspension of the sale of EMELEC, the state electricity utility, owing to a lack of interested investors. In the wake of Ecuador's default on its sovereign debt in August 1999, the country's relationship with the IMF continued to be of critical importance; in April 2000 a 12-month stand-by credit of US $304m. was approved to support the costly dollarization process, which was implemented in a bid to reduce inflation and to rebuild the country's fragile banking system. The loan was conditional on fiscal reforms, including the significant increase in fuel prices (in order to reduce costly subsidies), as well as structural reform in the labour and petroleum sectors and the privatization programme. However, opposition from the Congreso Nacional, as well as from indigenous organizations and trade unions, stalled the implementation of these policies, which also included a proposed increase in value-added tax (VAT). However, upon congressional approval of a 2% VAT increase in April 2001, the IMF disbursed a further $48m. In January 2003 the new President, Lucio Gutiérrez, secured a further $500m. in IMF loans, following government pledges of fiscal reforms. Significantly, however, the conditions of the loans included guarantees to channel some oil revenues towards debt repayment, projected at some 40% of the national budget in 2003. In 2002 government revenues were boosted by rising international oil prices, and production was expected to increase on completion of the new pipeline in the following year; however, the servicing requirements for the OCP were a major short-term factor in the reported $900m. trade deficit for 2002. Furthermore, despite expectations of growth in the sector, concerns continued as to the long-term viability of the oil industry, as would-be foreign investors remained unconvinced of the sector's transparency and accountability. In 2001 Ecuador's annual GDP increased by 5.6% (the biggest growth in the region in that year), and was expected to increase by 3.0% in 2002. However, by 2003 the number of people in poverty had increased to approximately 60% of the population. Despite dollarization, inflation levels remained high (average annual rate of 37.6% in 2001), and a further default on the country's debt obligations was widely feared in 2003.

Education

Education is compulsory for 10 years, to be undertaken between five and 15 years of age, and all state schools are free. Private schools continue to play a vital role in the educational system. Primary education begins at six years of age and lasts for six years. Secondary education, in general and specialized technical or humanities schools, begins at the age of 12 and lasts for up to six years, comprising two equal cycles of three years each. In 1997 the total enrolment at primary and secondary schools was equivalent to 89.5% of the school-age population. In 1999/2000 there were 3,502 secondary schools and 18,033 primary schools. University courses extend for up to six years, and include programmes for teacher training. Total expenditure on education by the central Government was estimated at 1,957,051m. sucres (equivalent to 3.5% of GNP) in 1996. In many rural areas, Quechua and other indigenous Indian languages are used in education.

Public Holidays

2003: 1 January (New Year's Day), 6 January (Epiphany), 3–4 March (Carnival), 17 April (Holy Thursday), 18 April (Good Friday), 19 April (Easter Saturday), 1 May (Labour Day), 24 May (Battle of Pichincha), 19 June (Corpus Christi), 24 July (Birth of Simón Bolívar), 10 August (Independence of Quito), 9 October (Independence of Guayaquil), 12 October (Discovery of America), 1 November (All Saints' Day), 2 November (All Souls' Day), 3 November (Independence of Cuenca), 6 December (Foundation of Quito), 25 December (Christmas Day).

2004: 1 January (New Year's Day), 6 January (Epiphany), 23–4 February (Carnival), 8 April (Holy Thursday), 9 April (Good Friday), 12 April (Easter Saturday), 1 May (Labour Day), 24 May (Battle of Pichincha), 10 June (Corpus Christi), 24 July (Birth of Simón Bolívar), 10 August (Independence of Quito), 9 October (Independence of Guayaquil), 12 October (Discovery of America), 1 November (All Saints' Day), 2 November (All Souls' Day), 3 November (Independence of Cuenca), 6 December (Foundation of Quito), 25 December (Christmas Day).

Weights and Measures

The metric system is in force.

Statistical Survey

Sources (unless otherwise stated): Banco Central del Ecuador, Quito; Ministerio de Industrias, Comercio, Integración y Pesquería, Quito; Instituto Nacional de Estadística y Censos, 10 de Agosto 229, Quito; tel. (2) 519-320; internet www.inec.gov.ec.

Area and Population

AREA, POPULATION AND DENSITY

Area (sq km)	272,045*
Population (census results)†	
25 November 1990	9,648,189
25 November 2001 (provisional results)	
Males	5,996,559
Females.	6,094,245
Total	12,090,804
Population (official estimates at mid-year)†	
1998	12,174,628
1999	12,411,232
2000	12,646,095
Density (per sq km) at 2001 census	44.4

* 105,037 sq miles.

† Figures exclude nomadic tribes of indigenous Indians. Census results also exclude any adjustment for underenumeration, estimated to have been 6.3% in 1990.

PROVINCES

(2001 census, provisional results)*

	Population	Capital
Azuay	598,504	Cuenca
Bolívar	168,874	Guaranda
Cañar	206,953	Azogues
Carchi	152,304	Tulcán
Chimborazo.	403,185	Riobamba
Cotopaxi	350,450	Latacunga
El Oro	515,664	Machala
Esmeraldas.	386,032	Esmeraldas
Guayas	3,256,763	Guayaquil
Imbabura	345,781	Ibarra
Loja	404,085	Loja
Los Ríos.	650,709	Babahoyo
Manabí	1,180,375	Portoviejo
Morona Santiago . . .	113,300	Macas
Napo.	79,610	Tena
Orellana	85,771	Puerto Francisco de Orellana (Coca)
Pastaza	61,412	Puyo
Pichincha	2,392,409	Quito
Sucumbíos	130,095	Nueva Loja
Tungurahua	441,389	Ambato
Zamora Chinchipe . . .	76,414	Zamora
Archipiélago de Colón (Galápagos)	18,555	Puerto Baquerizo (Isla San Cristóbal)
Total	12,090,804	

* Figures exclude persons in unspecified areas, totalling 72,170.

PRINCIPAL TOWNS

(2001 census, provisional results)

Guayaquil. . .	1,952,029	Ambato . . .	154,369
Quito (capital) . .	1,399,814	Riobamba . . .	124,478
Cuenca . . .	276,964	Quevedo . . .	119,436
Santo Domingo de los Colorados . . .	200,421	Loja	117,796
Machala . . .	198,123	Milagro . . .	110,093
Manta . . .	183,166	Ibarra . . .	108,666
Portoviejo . . .	170,326	Esmeraldas . . .	95,630
Eloy Alfaro . . .	167,784		

BIRTHS, MARRIAGES AND DEATHS

(excluding nomadic Indian tribes)*

	Registered live births		Registered marriages		Registered deaths	
	Number	Rate (per 1,000)	Number	Rate (per 1,000)	Number	Rate (per 1,000)
1995 . .	408,983	35.7	70,480	6.2	50,867	4.4
1996 . .	302,217	25.8	72,094	6.2	52,300	4.5
1997 . .	288,803	24.2	66,967	5.6	52,089	4.4
1998 . .	199,079	16.4	n.a.	n.a.	54,357	4.5
1999 . .	218,108	17.6	n.a.	n.a.	55,921	4.5
2000 . .	202,257	16.0	n.a.	n.a.	56,240	4.5

* Registrations incomplete.

Sources: partly UN, *Demographic Yearbook*.

Expectation of life (WHO estimates, years at birth): 70.3 (males 67.6; females 73.2) in 2001 (Source: WHO, *World Health Report*).

ECONOMICALLY ACTIVE POPULATION

(ISIC Major Divisions, urban areas only, '000 persons aged 10 and over, 1998)

	Males	Females	Total
Agriculture, hunting, forestry and fishing	202.4	28.2	230.6
Mining and quarrying	10.4	0.2	10.6
Manufacturing	303.7	159.3	463.0
Electricity, gas and water . . .	12.9	2.6	15.5
Construction	181.0	4.9	185.9
Trade, restaurants and hotels . .	489.9	462.6	952.5
Transport, storage and communications	181.3	17.7	198.9
Financing, insurance, real estate and business services	113.0	50.8	163.8
Community, social and personal services	425.3	502.6	927.8
Activities not adequately defined .	0.9	1.5	2.4
Total employed.	1,920.8	1,230.4	3,151.2
Unemployed	175.5	233.8	409.3
Total labour force	2,096.3	1,464.2	3,560.5

2001 (census figures): Agriculture, etc. 1,244.7; Total labour force 4,553.7.

Health and Welfare

KEY INDICATORS

Total fertility rate (children per woman, 2001)	2.9
Under-5 mortality rate (per 1,000 live births, 2001) . . .	30
HIV/AIDS (% of persons aged 15–49, 2001)	0.30
Physicians (per 1,000 head, 1997)	1.70
Hospital beds (per 1,000 head, 1996)	1.55
Health expenditure (2000): US $ per head (PPP) . . .	78
Health expenditure (2000): % of GDP	2.4
Health expenditure (2000): public (% of total)	50.4
Access to water (% of persons, 2000).	71
Access to sanitation (% of persons, 2000)	59
Human Development Index (2000): ranking	93
Human Development Index (2000): value	0.732

For sources and definitions, see explanatory note on p. vi.

Agriculture

PRINCIPAL CROPS
('000 metric tons)

	1999	2000	2001
Rice (paddy)	1,290	1,355	1,377
Barley	34	29	32
Maize	500	611	642
Potatoes	563	593	690
Cassava (Manioc)	319	292	361
Sugar cane	5,562	6,121	5,962
Dry beans	31	26	30
Soybeans (Soya beans) . . .	77	102	130
Oil palm fruit	952	1,400*	1,540*
Tomatoes	62	66	70
Pumpkins, squash and gourds* .	41	41	42
Onions and shallots (green) .	59	99	100*
Carrots	18	30	30
Bananas	6,392	6,477	7,561
Plantains	658	476	476*
Oranges	122	304	389
Tangerines, mandarins,			
clementines and satsumas . .	99	87	103
Lemons and limes	25	30	30
Watermelons	28	37	39
Mangoes	95	143	142
Pineapples	124	200	195
Papayas	112	86	101
Other fruit*	509	230	245
Coffee (green)	133	133	146
Cocoa beans	95	100	107

* FAO estimate(s).

Source: FAO.

LIVESTOCK
('000 head, year ending September)

	1999	2000	2001
Cattle	5,106	5,104	5,574
Sheep	2,196	1,919	1,976
Pigs	2,786	2,783	2,392
Horses*	521	521	525
Goats	277	280	273
Asses*	269	270	270
Mules*	157	158	158
Poultry	134,767	135,999	138,429

* FAO estimates.

Source: FAO.

LIVESTOCK PRODUCTS
('000 metric tons)

	1999	2000	2001
Beef and veal	164.3	174.0	179.0
Mutton and lamb	6.0*	6.3	6.4*
Pig meat	110.3	108.0	98.3*
Goat meat	1.1	1.5	1.4*
Poultry meat	146.1	148.2	152.2
Cows' milk	1,934.0	2,007.3	2,191.6
Sheep's milk	6.0	6.1	6.2
Goats' milk	2.4	2.5	2.5*
Butter	4.6	4.6*	n.a.
Cheese	7.2	7.3	n.a.
Hen eggs	55.5	56.8	56.9
Wool: greasy*	2.2	1.9	2.0
Cattle hides (fresh)*	32.8	35.1	36.5

* FAO estimate(s).

Source: FAO.

Forestry

ROUNDWOOD REMOVALS
('000 cubic metres, excluding bark)

	1999	2000	2001
Sawlogs, veneer logs and logs for			
sleepers	4,967	4,967*	4,967*
Pulpwood*	682	682	682
Other industrial wood* . . .	70	70	70
Fuel wood*	4,978	5,129	5,201
Total	10,697	10,848	10,920

* FAO estimate(s).

Source: FAO.

SAWNWOOD PRODUCTION
('000 cubic metres, including railway sleepers)

	1997	1998	1999
Coniferous (softwood) . . .	415	416	291
Broadleaved (hardwood) . . .	1,660	1,663	1,164
Total	2,075	2,079	1,455

2000–01: Production as in 1999 (FAO estimates).

Source: FAO.

Fishing

('000 metric tons, live weight)

	1998	1999	2000
Capture	310.0	497.9	592.5
Gurnards and searobins . . .	n.a.	22.6	27.1
Chilean jack mackerel . . .	25.9	19.1	7.1
South American pilchard . . .	1.0	8.8	51.6
Pacific thread herring	40.5	22.3	20.5
Pacific anchoveta	44.5	27.2	13.8
Frigate and bullet tunas . . .	4.2	48.9	9.6
Skipjack tuna	67.5	127.0	105.1
Yellowfin tuna	31.1	50.2	37.0
Bigeye tuna	17.9	22.3	29.4
Chub mackerel	44.7	28.3	84.3
Aquaculture	146.6	127.4	62.1
Blue shrimp	14.4	12.0	n.a.
Whiteleg shrimp	129.6	107.7	50.1
Total catch	456.6	625.2	634.1

Source: FAO, *Yearbook of Fishery Statistics*.

Mining

('000 barrels, unless otherwise indicated)

	1998*	1999	2000
Crude petroleum	136,875	136,291	146,180
Natural gas (million cu m) . .	190	964	1,057
Natural gasoline*	1,830	2,014	2,818
Gold (kilograms)†	3,500	2,026	2,823

* Estimates.
† Metal content of ore only.

Source: US Geological Survey.

Industry

SELECTED PRODUCTS
('000 barrels, unless otherwise indicated)

	1998*	1999	2000
Jet fuels	1,700	1,554	1,976
Kerosene	720	716	575
Motor spirit (gasoline)	10,800	9,783	9,272
Distillate fuel oils	10,700	8,361	12,161
Residual fuel oils	20,300	20,833	16,327
Liquefied petroleum gas	3,000	3,000	2,600
Crude steel ('000 metric tons)	46	53	50*
Cement ('000 metric tons)	2,600	2,300	2,800*
Electric energy (million kWh)	10,896*	n.a.	n.a.

* Provisional or estimated figure(s).

Sources: UN, *Industrial Commodity Statistics Yearbook*; US Geological Survey.

Finance

CURRENCY AND EXCHANGE RATES

Monetary Units
United States currency is used: 100 cents = 1 US dollar ($)

Sterling and Euro Equivalents (31 December 2002)
£1 sterling = US $1.6118
€1 = US $1.0487
US $100 = £62.04 = €95.36

Note: Ecuador's national currency was formerly the sucre. From 13 March 2000 the sucre was replaced by the US dollar, at an exchange rate of $1 = 25,000 sucres. Both currencies were officially in use for a transitional period of 180 days, but from 9 September sucres were withdrawn from circulation and the dollar became the sole legal tender. Some figures in this Survey are still in terms of sucres. The average exchange rate of sucres per dollar was: 5,446.6 in 1998; 11,786.8 in 1999; 24,988.4 in 2000.

BUDGET
(million sucres)

Revenue	1992	1993	1994
Petroleum revenue	1,537,698	2,069,852	2,345,187
Tax revenue	68,627	31,197	42,965
Non-tax revenue	1,469,071	2,038,655	2,302,222
Price increases on petroleum by-products for internal consumption	470,993	851,920	1,172,573
For export	998,078	1,186,735	1,129,649
Non-petroleum revenue	1,570,059	2,162,669	3,138,030
Tax revenue	1,368,994	2,034,925	2,808,630
External trade	274,413	392,470	606,631
Exports	—	—	—
Imports	274,413	392,470	606,631
Domestic taxes	1,094,581	1,642,455	2,201,999
Income tax	253,415	331,231	503,864
Taxes on financial transactions	66,246	43,013	110,576
Taxes on production and consumption	744,757	1,152,491	1,495,902
Other taxes	30,163	115,720	91,657
Non-tax revenue	201,065	127,744	329,400
Transfers	22,034	82,051	164,426
Total	**3,129,791**	**4,314,572**	**5,647,643**

Expenditure	1992	1993	1994
General services	736,416	1,144,175	1,679,092
Education and culture	605,075	746,993	1,066,535
Social welfare and labour	43,092	99,421	134,697
Health and community development	200,421	202,593	319,470
Farming and livestock development	88,631	146,023	230,227
Natural and energy resources	14,121	31,323	47,144
Industry and trade	43,041	25,507	33,674
Transport and communications	126,629	327,585	446,366
Public debt interest	473,826	500,841	898,153
Other purposes	216,730	539,389	677,075
Total	**2,547,982**	**3,763,850**	**5,532,433**

Source: Banco Central del Ecuador.

1995 (million US dollars): Total revenue 3,131.4; Total expenditure 3,295.2.

1996 (million US dollars): Total revenue 3,334.1; Total expenditure 3,422.7.

1997 (million US dollars): Total revenue 3,380.3; Total expenditure 3,671.7.

1998 (million US dollars): Total revenue 3,280.3; Total expenditure 3,211.6.

1999 (million US dollars): Total revenue 2,705.1; Total expenditure 2,804.1.

2000 (million US dollars): Total revenue 3,056.6; Total expenditure 2,966.6.

2001 (million US dollars): Total revenue 3,872.6; Total expenditure 3,860.6.

Source (for 1995–2001): IMF, *International Financial Statistics*.

INTERNATIONAL RESERVES
(US $ million at 31 December)

	2000	2001	2002
Gold*	232.7	233.8	293.3
IMF special drawing rights	0.3	2.3	1.9
Reserve position in IMF	22.3	21.6	23.3
Foreign exchange	924.3	815.9	689.4
Total	**1,179.6**	**1,073.6**	**907.9**

* National valuation $275 per ounce at 31 December 2000; $277 per ounce at 31 December 2001; $347 per ounce at 31 December 2002.

Source: IMF, *International Financial Statistics*.

MONEY SUPPLY
(US $ million at 31 December)

	1999	2000	2001
Currency outside banks	576.3	31.7	21.8
Demand deposits at deposit money banks	614.9	996.7	1,552.7
Total money *	**1,338.0**	**1,335.7**	**1,905.5**

* Includes private-sector deposits at the Central Bank.

Source: IMF, *International Financial Statistics*.

COST OF LIVING
(Consumer Price Index; base: 1990 = 100)

	1999	2000	2001
Food	1,579.9	3,486.6	4,575.0
Fuel (excl. light)	3,652.9	5,139.1	8,479.7
Clothing	1,243.8	2,727.7	3,562.7
Rent	1,612.9	2,101.3	2,720.5
All items (incl. others)	1,749.1	3,444.5	4,740.5

Source: ILO.

ECUADOR

NATIONAL ACCOUNTS

Expenditure on the Gross Domestic Product
(US $ million at current prices)

	1999	2000	2001
Government final consumption expenditure	1,419	1,275	1,649
Private final consumption expenditure	8,964	8,707	11,644
Increase in stocks	−260	124	162
Gross fixed capital formation	2,030	2,202	2,939
Statistical discrepancy	−1	—	—
Total domestic expenditure	12,152	12,308	16,394
Exports of goods and services	5,074	5,751	5,713
Less Imports of goods and services	3,537	4,131	4,990
GDP in purchasers' values	13,689	13,927	17,118
GDP at constant 1975 prices	8,445	8,642	9,130

Source: IMF, International Financial Statistics.

Gross Domestic Product by Economic Activity
('000 million sucres at current prices)

	1998	1999	2000
Agriculture, hunting, forestry and fishing	12,942	19,607	33,928
Petroleum and other mining	6,065	18,452	66,767
Manufacturing	23,501	34,291	57,518
Electricity, gas and water	303	441	848
Construction	5,290	7,296	11,500
Trade	21,691	29,632	58,046
Transport	10,260	15,109	31,144
Financial services	6,042	8,954	16,797
Government services	13,612	17,387	34,608
Sub-total	99,705	151,169	311,158
Adjustments	7,716	10,181	28,864
GDP in purchasers' values	107,421	161,350	340,022

BALANCE OF PAYMENTS
(US $ million)

	1999	2000	2001
Exports of goods f.o.b.	4,616	5,137	4,862
Imports of goods f.o.b.	−3,028	−3,743	−5,325
Trade balance	1,588	1,395	−462
Exports of services	730	849	911
Imports of services	−1,158	−1,256	−1,430
Balance on goods and services	1,159	988	−981
Other income received	75	71	48
Other income paid	−1,382	−1,482	−1,411
Balance on goods, services and income	−147	−424	−2,344
Current transfers received	1,188	1,437	1,550
Current transfers paid	−99	−85	−6
Current balance	942	928	−800
Capital account (net)	2	−1	−67
Direct investment from abroad	648	720	1,330
Portfolio investment liabilities	−46	−5,583	117
Other investment assets	−748	−1,288	−1,308
Other investment liabilities	−1,222	−469	868
Net errors and omissions	−521	−15	−399
Overall balance	−944	−5,707	−259

Source: IMF, International Financial Statistics.

External Trade

PRINCIPAL COMMODITIES
(distribution by SITC, US $ million)

Imports c.i.f.	1998	1999	2000
Food and live animals	582.2	283.8	261.4
Cereals and cereal preparations	221.5	134.8	109.1
Crude materials (inedible) except fuels	154.8	113.3	134.9
Mineral fuels, lubricants, etc.	335.4	248.8	282.3
Petroleum, petroleum products, etc.	236.4	143.1	115.5
Refined petroleum products	172.1	98.7	83.1
Kerosene and other medium oils	127.3	76.4	46.8
Liquefied petroleum gases, etc.	97.2	103.8	166.1
Chemicals and related products	881.5	663.8	809.3
Medicinal and pharmaceutical products	235.8	164.0	198.7
Medicaments (incl. veterinary)	196.2	136.7	167.4
Artificial resins, plastic materials etc.	141.2	99.2	145.0
Disinfectants, insecticides fungicides, etc.	112.6	91.6	104.9
Basic manufactures	995.9	498.4	684.6
Iron and steel	303.9	138.8	191.5
Machinery and transport equipment	1,954.3	869.8	914.9
Power-generating machinery and equipment	180.8	93.1	62.9
Machinery specialized for particular industries	262.6	89.8	133.0
General industrial machinery equipment and parts	335.3	191.1	182.9
Telecommunications and sound equipment	216.8	101.5	109.6
Other electrical machinery apparatus, etc.	284.5	109.4	146.5
Road vehicles and parts*	492.2	188.0	184.3
Passenger motor cars (excl. buses)	192.6	55.0	72.6
Motor vehicles for goods transport and special purposes	162.2	51.9	52.4
Miscellaneous manufactured articles	417.0	250.0	266.5
Total (incl. others)	5,575.4	3,017.2	3,445.9

* Data on parts exclude tyres, engines and electrical parts.

Exports f.o.b.	1998	1999	2000
Food and live animals	2,617.4	2,301.2	1,721.7
Fish, crustaceans and molluscs	1,215.8	944.2	568.3
Fresh, chilled, frozen, salted or dried crustaceans and molluscs	873.2	608.5	274.3
Prepared or preserved fish crustaceans and molluscs	253.9	262.9	213.3
Vegetables and fruit	1,173.1	1,087.1	938.2
Bananas and plantains	1,070.2	954.4	820.6
Coffee, tea, cocoa and spices	153.9	186.0	123.0
Crude materials (inedible) except fuels	216.0	232.0	199.0
Cut flowers and foliage	162.0	180.4	155.6
Mineral fuels, lubricants, etc.	992.9	1,479.6	2,442.3
Petroleum, petroleum products etc.	992.9	1,479.6	2,442.3
Crude petroleum oils, etc.	789.0	1,312.3	2,144.0
Refined petroleum products	107.6	139.5	231.5
Basic manufactures	161.6	170.8	177.6
Total (incl. others)	4,203.0	4,451.1	4,821.9

Source: UN, International Trade Statistics Yearbook.

www.europaworldonline.com

PRINCIPAL TRADING PARTNERS
(US $ million)

Imports c.i.f.	1998	1999	2000
Argentina	135.7	71.0	55.7
Aruba	17.4	0.0	0.0
Belgium-Luxembourg	62.4	n.a.	n.a.
Brazil	197.3	95.9	136.4
Canada	103.0	68.6	68.2
Chile	201.4	122.5	200.4
China, People's Republic	65.3	49.8	76.1
Colombia	592.2	363.4	488.2
France (incl. Monaco)	47.7	35.5	30.4
Germany	228.2	126.0	117.4
Italy	175.3	56.0	54.1
Japan	481.3	142.0	123.6
Korea, Republic	97.0	36.9	55.2
Mexico	156.1	96.1	116.0
Netherlands	57.7	32.3	35.1
Panama	184.9	87.9	98.9
Peru	98.3	48.1	72.6
Russia	70.4	46.3	36.5
Spain	112.2	76.5	58.6
United Kingdom	63.9	30.2	38.7
USA	1,680.2	918.5	883.6
Venezuela	269.4	193.2	271.7
Total (incl. others)	5,575.4	3,017.2	3,445.9

Exports f.o.b.	1998	1999	2000
Argentina	76.3	75.2	92.7
Belgium-Luxembourg	88.8	82.1*	—
Chile	139.8	195.1	220.7
China, People's Republic	52.2	83.7	57.7
Colombia	282.6	227.2	259.5
El Salvador	42.8	61.3	114.3
France (incl. Monaco)	94.7	75.1	30.8
Germany	130.0	124.3	123.4
Italy	257.2	208.1	159.6
Japan	124.4	112.1	129.2
Korea, Republic	95.2	213.5	317.0
Mexico	47.6	52.5	49.8
Netherlands	83.1	123.2	82.5
Panama	128.5	219.5	293.3
Peru	199.1	180.2	288.5
Russia	113.6	66.0	119.7
Spain	140.1	122.4	70.5
United Kingdom	60.7	55.9	32.6
USA	1,637.2	1,708.2	1,828.2
Venezuela	59.3	66.5	108.3
Total (incl. others)	4,203.0	4,451.1	4,821.9

* Excluding trade with Luxembourg.

Source: mainly UN, *International Trade Statistics Yearbook*.

2001 (US $ million): Total imports c.i.f. 5,325; Total exports f.o.b. 4,862 (Source: IMF, *International Financial Statistics*).

Transport

RAILWAYS
(traffic)

	1997	1998	1999
Passenger-kilometres (million)	47	44	5
Net ton-kilometres (million)	—	14	—

Source: UN, *Statistical Yearbook*.

ROAD TRAFFIC
(motor vehicles in use at 31 December)

	1997	1998	1999
Passenger cars	483,897	495,060	532,170
Buses and coaches	8,504	9,910	9,917
Lorries and vans	41,327	55,249	51,686
Road tractors	2,930	3,304	3,630
Motorcycles and mopeds	25,206	23,761	26,641

Source: IRF, *World Road Statistics*.

SHIPPING

Merchant Fleet
(registered at 31 December)

	1999	2000	2001
Number of vessels	174	171	175
Total displacement ('000 grt)	309.3	300.9	305.9

Source: Lloyd's Register-Fairplay, *World Fleet Statistics*.

International Sea-borne Freight Traffic
('000 metric tons)

	1988*	1989*	1990
Goods loaded	8,402	10,020	11,783
Goods unloaded	2,518	2,573	1,958

* Source: UN, *Monthly Bulletin of Statistics*.

CIVIL AVIATION
(traffic on scheduled services)

	1997	1998	1999
Kilometres flown (million)	18	18	11
Passengers carried ('000)	503	674	351
Passenger-km (million)	1,455	1,788	976
Total ton-km (million)	180	239	118

Source: UN, *Statistical Yearbook*.

Tourism

FOREIGN VISITOR ARRIVALS*

Country of residence	1998	1999	2000
Argentina	10,417	11,528	13,706
Chile	14,349	13,569	16,133
Colombia	165,596	142,047	168,889
France	16,034	14,167	16,844
Germany	21,701	18,340	21,806
Peru	29,821	53,190	63,241
Spain	12,306	13,215	15,712
United Kingdom	12,051	15,541	18,478
USA	113,155	124,526	148,057
Venezuela	12,255	10,540	12,532
Total (incl. others)	510,627	517,670	615,493

* Figures refer to total arrivals (including same-day visitors), except those of Ecuadorean nationals residing abroad.

Source: World Tourism Organization, *Yearbook of Tourism Statistics*.

Tourism receipts (US $ million): 291 in 1998; 343 in 1999; 402 in 2000 (Source: World Tourism Organization).

Communications Media

	1999	2000	2001
Television receivers ('000 in use)	2,640	2,760	n.a.
Telephones ('000 main lines in use)	1,129.5	1,265.2	1,335.8
Mobile cellular telephones ('000 subscribers)	383.2	482.2	859.2
Personal computers ('000 in use)	250	275	300
Internet users ('000)	100	180	328

Radio receivers ('000 in use): 5,040 in 1999.

Facsimile machines: 30,000 in use in 1996.

Daily newspapers: 11 in 1998; circulation 529,000.

Source: UNESCO, *Statistical Yearbook*; UN, *Statistical Yearbook*; International Telecommunication Union.

Education

(1999/2000)

	Institutions	Teachers	Students
Pre-primary	4,856	13,008	189,407
Primary	18,033	82,809	1,925,420
Secondary	3,502	80,511	938,910
Higher*	n.a.	12,856	206,541

* 1990/91 figures.

Sources: UNESCO, *Statistical Yearbook*; Ministerio de Educación y Cultura.

Adult literacy rate (UNESCO estimates): 91.6% (males 93.3%; females 90.6%) in 2000 (Source: UN Development Programme, *Human Development Report*).

Directory

The Constitution

The 1945 Constitution was suspended in June 1970. In January 1978 a referendum was held to choose between two draft Constitutions, prepared by various special constitutional committees. In a 90% poll, 43% voted for a proposed new Constitution and 32.1% voted for a revised version of the 1945 Constitution. The new Constitution came into force on 10 August 1979. In November 1997 a National Constituent Assembly was elected for the purpose of reviewing the Constitution, and a new Constitution, which retained many of the provisions of the 1979 Constitution, came into force on 10 August 1998. The main provisions of the Constitution are summarized below:

CHAMBER OF REPRESENTATIVES

The Constitution of 1998 states that legislative power is exercised by the Chamber of Representatives, which sits for a period of 60 days from 10 August. The Chamber is required to set up four full-time Legislative Commissions to consider draft laws when the House is in recess. Special sessions of the Chamber of Representatives may be called.

Representatives are elected for four years from lists of candidates drawn up by legally recognized parties. Twelve are elected nationally; two from each Province with over 100,000 inhabitants, one from each Province with fewer than 100,000; and one for every 200,000 citizens or fractions of over 150,000. Representatives are eligible for re-election.

In addition to its law-making duties, the Chamber ratifies treaties, elects members of the Supreme and Superior Courts, and (from panels presented by the President) the Comptroller-General, the Attorney-General and the Superintendent of Banks. It is also able to overrule the President's amendment of a bill that it has submitted for Presidential approval. It may reconsider a rejected bill after a year or request a referendum, and may revoke the President's declaration of a state of emergency. The budget is considered in the first instance by the appropriate Legislative Commission and disagreements are resolved in the Chamber.

PRESIDENT

The presidential term is four years (starting from 15 January of the year following his election), and there is no re-election. The President appoints the Cabinet, the Governors of Provinces, diplomatic representatives and certain administrative employees, and is responsible for the direction of international relations. In the event of foreign invasion or internal disturbance, the President may declare a state of emergency and must notify the Chamber, or the Tribunal for Constitutional Guarantees if the Chamber is not in session.

As in other post-war Latin-American Constitutions, particular emphasis is laid on the functions and duties of the State, which is given wide responsibilities with regard to the protection of labour; assisting in the expansion of production; protecting the Indian and peasant communities; and organizing the distribution and development of uncultivated lands, by expropriation where necessary.

Voting is compulsory for every Ecuadorean citizen who is literate and over 18 years of age. An optional vote has been extended to illiterates (under 15% of the population by 1981). The Constitution guarantees liberty of conscience in all its manifestations, and states that the law shall not make any discrimination for religious reasons.

The Government

HEAD OF STATE

President: LUCIO GUTIÉRREZ (assumed office on 15 January 2003).

Vice-President: ALFREDO PALACIO.

CABINET
(April 2003)

Minister of National Defence: Gen. (retd.) NELSON HERRERA.

Minister of the Interior: MARIO CANESSA ONETO.

Minister of Foreign Affairs: NINA PACARI VEGA.

Minister of Finance and Public Credit: MAURICIO POZO.

Minister of Foreign Trade, Industrialization and Fishing: IVONNE BAKI.

Minister of Labour and Social Action: FELIPE MANTILLA.

Minister of Energy and Mines: CARLOS ARBOLEDA.

Minister of Agriculture: LUIS MACAS AMBULUDÍ.

Minister of Urban Development and Housing: HERMEL FIALLO GRUNAVER.

Minister of Education and Culture: ROSA MARÍA TORRES.

Minister of Public Health: FRANCISCO ANDINO.

Minister of Planning: AUGUSTO BARRERA.

Minister of the Environment: EDGAR ISCH LÓPEZ.

Minister of Tourism: DORIS SOLIS CARRIÓN.

Minister of Public Works : ESTUARDO PEÑAHERRERA.

Minister of Social Welfare: PATRICIO ORTIZ JAMES.

Minister of Communications: ANTONIO TRAMONTANA.

The following are, *ex officio*, members of the Cabinet: the National Secretary of Administrative Development, the Co-ordinator of the Social Expenditure Fund (FISE), the State Comptroller-General, the State Procurator-General, the Chairman of the National Monetary Board, the General Manager of the State Bank, the General Manager of the Central Bank, the Secretary-General of the National Planning Council (CONADE), the President of the National Financial Corporation, the President of the National Modernization Council (CONAM), the Presidential Private Secretary, the Subsecretary-General of Public Administration and the Presidential Press Secretary.

MINISTRIES

Office of the President: Palacio Nacional, García Moreno 1043, Quito; tel. (2) 221-6300.

Office of the Vice-President: Manuel Larrea y Arenas, Edif. Consejo Provincial de Pichincha, 21°, Quito; tel. (2) 250-4953; fax (2) 250-3379.

Ministry of Agriculture: Avda Eloy Alfaro y Amazonas, Quito; tel. (2) 255-3472; fax (2) 256-4531; internet www.mag.gov.ec.

Ministry of Communications: Quito.

Ministry of Education and Culture: Mejía 322, Quito; tel. (2) 221-6224; fax (2) 258-0116; internet www.mec.edu.ec.

Ministry of Energy and Mines: Juan León Mera y Orellana, 5°, Quito; tel. (2) 255-0041; fax (2) 255-0018; e-mail menergia2@andinanet.net; internet www.menergia.gov.ec.

Ministry of the Environment: Avda Eloy Alfaro y Amazonas, edificio M.A.G., Quito; tel. (2) 256-3429; fax (2) 250-0041; e-mail mma@ambiente.gov.ec.

Ministry of Finance and Public Credit: Avda 10 de Agosto 1661 y Jorge Washington, Quito; tel. (2) 254-4500; fax (2) 253-0703; internet minfinanzas.ec-gov.net.

Ministry of Foreign Affairs: Avda 10 de Agosto y Carrión, Quito; tel. (2) 223-0100; fax (2) 256-4873; e-mail webmast@mmrree.gov.ec; internet www.mmree.gov.ec.

Ministry of Foreign Trade, Industrialization and Fishing: Avda Eloy Alfaro y Amazonas, Quito; tel. (2) 252-7988; fax (2) 250-3549.

Ministry of the Interior: Espejo y Benalcázar, Quito; tel. (2) 295-5666; fax (2) 295-8360; e-mail informacion@mingobierno.gov.ec; internet www.mingobierno.gov.ec.

Ministry of Labour and Social Action: Clemente Ponce 255 y Piedrahita, Quito; tel. (2) 256-6148; fax (2) 250-3122; e-mail mintrab@accessinter.net.

Ministry of National Defence: Exposición 208, Quito; tel. (2) 221-6150; fax (2) 256-9386; e-mail paginaweb@fuerzasarmadasecuador.org; internet www.fuerzasarmadasecuador.ec-gov.net.

Ministry of Public Health: Juan Larrea 444, Quito; tel. (2) 252-9163; fax 256-9786; e-mail msp@accessinter.net; internet www.msp.gov.ec.

Ministry of Public Works: Avda Juan León Mera y Orellana, Quito; tel. (2) 222-2749; fax (2) 222-3077; internet www.mop.gov.ec.

Ministry of Social Welfare: Quito.

Ministry of Tourism: Eloy Alfaro 32-300 y Carlos Tobar, Quito; tel. (2) 250-7559; fax (2) 222-9330; e-mail mtur1@ec-gov-net; internet www.vivecuador.com.

Ministry of Urban Development and Housing: Avda 10 de Agosto 2270 y Corotero, Quito; tel. (2) 223-8060; fax (2) 256-6785; e-mail mdesur2@ec-gov.net; internet www.miduvi.ec-gov.net.

Office for Public Administration: Palacio Nacional, García Morena 1043, Quito; tel. (2) 251-5990.

President and Legislature

PRESIDENT

Elections, 20 October and 24 November 2002

Candidate	% of votes cast in first ballot	% of votes cast in second ballot
Col Lucio Edwin Gutiérrez Borbua (PSP-MNPP)	20.3	58.7
Alvaro Fernando Noboa Pontón (PRIAN)	17.4	41.3
León Roldos Aguilera (PS-FA/DP/CFP)	15.5	—
Rodrigo Borja Cevallos (ID)	14.0	—
Antonio Xavier Neira Menendez (PSC)	12.2	—
Total (incl. others)	100.0	100.0

CONGRESO NACIONAL

Cámara Nacional de Representantes

President: GUILLERMO LANDAZURI.

Election, 20 October 2002

Political parties	Seats
Partido Social Cristiano (PSC)	24
Izquierda Democrática (ID)	15
Partido Roldosista Ecuatoriano (PRE)	14
Partido Renovador Institucional de Acción Nacional (PRIAN)	10
Movimiento Nuevo País-Pachakútik (MNPP)	8
Partido Sociedad Patriótica 21 de Enero (PSP)	8
Movimiento Popular Democrático (MPD)	7
Democracia Popular (DP)	5
Partido Socialista-Frente Amplio (PS-FA)	3
Independent	1
Total (incl. others)	100

Political Organizations

Acción Popular Revolucionaria Ecuatoriana (APRE): centrist; Leader Lt-Gen. FRANK VARGAS PAZZOS.

Coalición Nacional Republicana (CNR): Quito; f. 1986; fmrly Coalición Institucionalista Demócrata (CID).

Concentración de Fuerzas Populares (CFP): Quito; f. 1946; Leader GALO VAYAS; Dir Dr AVERROES BUCARAM SAXIDA.

Democracia Popular (DP): Calle Luis Saá 153 y Hnos Pazmiño, Casilla 17-01-2300, Quito; tel. (2) 254-7654; fax (2) 250-2995; f. 1978 as Democracia Popular-Unión Demócrata Cristiana; Christian democrat; Leader Lic. ABSALÓN ROCHA.

Frente Futuro de Ecuador (FFE): f. 2002 to contest the October 2002 presidential and legislative elections; Leader ANTONIO VARGAS.

Frente Radical Alfarista (FRA): Quito; f. 1972; liberal; Leader IVÁN CASTRO PATIÑO.

Izquierda Democrática (ID): Polonia 161, entre Vancouver y Eloy Alfaro, Quito; tel. (2) 256-4436; fax (2) 256-9295; f. 1977; absorbed Fuerzas Armadas Populares Eloy Alfaro—Alfaro Vive ¡Carajo! (AVC) (Eloy Alfaro Popular Armed Forces—Alfaro Lives, Damn It!) in 1991; Leader RODRIGO BORJA CEVALLOS; National Dir ANDRÉS VALLEJO.

Movimiento Independiente para una República Auténtica (MIRA): Quito; f. 1996; Leader Dra ROSALIA ARTEAGA SERRANO.

Movimiento Nuevo País-Pachakútik (MNPP): Quito; represents indigenous, environmental and social groups; Leader FREDDY EHLERS ZURITA.

Movimiento Popular Democrático (MPD): Maoist; Leader (vacant).

Partido Comunista Marxista-Leninista de Ecuador: Sec.-Gen. CAMILO ALMEYDA.

Partido Conservador (PC): Wilsón 578, Quito; tel. (2) 250-5061; f. 1855; incorporated Partido Unidad Republicano in 1995; centre-right; Leader SIXTO DURÁN BALLÉN.

Partido Demócrata (PD): Quito; Leader Dr FRANCISCO HUERTA MONTALVO.

Partido Liberal Radical (PLR): Quito; f. 1895; held office from 1895 to 1944 as the Liberal Party, which subsequently divided into various factions; perpetuates the traditions of the Liberal Party; Leader CARLOS JULIO PLAZA A.

Partido Renovador Institucional de Acción Nacional (PRIAN): Quito; right-wing, populist; Leader ALVARO FERNANDO NOBOA PONTÓN.

Partido Republicano (PR): Quito; Leader GUILLERMO SOTOMAYOR.

Partido Roldosista Ecuatoriano (PRE): Quito; f. 1982; populist; Dir ABDALÁ BUCARAM ORTIZ.

Partido Social Cristiano (PSC): Carrión 548 y Reina Victoria, Casilla 9454, Quito; tel. (2) 254-4536; fax (2) 256-8562; f. 1951; centre-right party; Pres. JAIME NEBOT SAADI; Leaders Dr LEÓN FEBRES CORDERO RIVADENEIRA, Lic. CAMILO PONCE GANGOTENA, HEINZ MOELLER FREILE, Lic. PASCUAL DEL CIOPPO ARAGUNDI.

Partido Socialista-Frente Amplio (PS-FA): Avda Gran Colombia y Yaguachi, Quito; tel. (2) 222-1764; fax (2) 222-2184; f. 1926; Pres. Dr MANUEL SALGADO TAMAYO.

Partido Sociedad Patriótica 21 de Enero (PSP): Quito; internet www.sociedadpatriotica.com; left-wing; contested the 2002 elections in alliance with the MNPP; Leader Col LUCIO EDWIN GUTIÉRREZ BORBUA.

Unión Alfarista-FRA: Quito; f. 1998; centrist; Leader CÉSAR VERDUGA VÉLEZ.

The following guerrilla groups are active:

Grupo de Combatientes Populares (GCP): claims to defend human rights and to fight poverty.

Montoneros Patria Libre (MPL): f. 1986; advocates an end to authoritarianism.

Partido Maoísta-Comunista 'Puka Inti': Sec.-Gen. RAMIRO CELI.

OTHER ORGANIZATIONS

Confederación de Nacionalidades Indígenas de Ecuador (CONAIE) (National Confederation of the Indigenous Population of Ecuador): Avda Los Granados 2553 y 6 de Diciembre, Quito; tel. and fax (2) 244-2271; internet conaie.org; f. 1986 to represent indigenous peoples; Pres. LEONIDAS IZA; Vice-Pres. TITO PONACHIR.

Frente Popular (FP): umbrella group of labour unions and other populist organizations; Pres. LUIS VILLACÍS.

Diplomatic Representation

EMBASSIES IN ECUADOR

Argentina: Avda Amazonas 22-147 y Roca, 8°, Quito; tel. (2) 256-2292; fax (2) 256-8177; e-mail embarge2@andinanet.net; Ambassador HERNÁN HIPÓLITO CORNEJO.

Belgium: Juan León Mera 23-103 y Wilson, Apdo. 17-21-532, Quito; tel. (2) 254-5340; e-mail quito@diplobel.org; Ambassador ROBERT VANREUSEL.

Bolivia: Avda Eloy Alfaro 2432 y Fernando Ayarza, Casilla 17-210003, Quito; tel. (2) 244-6652; fax (2) 224-4033; e-mail embolivia-quito@rree.gov.bo; Ambassador FERNANDO CÉSAR VARGAS MERCADO.

Brazil: Avda Amazonas 1429 y Colón, Apdo 231, Quito; tel. (2) 256-3846; fax (2) 250-9468; e-mail ebrasil@uio.satnet.net; Ambassador VERA PEDROSA MARTINS DE ALMEIDA.

Canada: Edif. Josueth Gonzales, Avda 6 de Diciembre 28-16 y Paul Rivet, 4°, Apdo 17-11-65-12, Quito; tel. (2) 250-6162; e-mail quito@dfait-maeci.gc.ca; Ambassador OTTFRIED VON FINCKENSTEIN.

Chile: Edif. Xerox, 4°, Juan Pablo Sanz y Amazonas, Quito; tel. (2) 224-9403; e-mail embchile@punto.net.ec; Ambassador RODRIGO ASENJO ZEGERS.

China, People's Republic: Avda Atahualpa y Amazonas, Quito; tel. (2) 245-8927; fax (2) 244-4364; e-mail embchina@uio.telconet.net; Ambassador LIU JUNXIU.

Colombia: Edif. Arista, Avda Colón 1133 y Amazonas, 7°, Apdo 17-07-9164, Quito; tel. (2) 222-8926; Ambassador MARÍA PAULINA ESPINOZA DE LÓPEZ.

Costa Rica: Rumipamba 692 y República, 2°, Apdo 17-03-301, Quito; tel. (2) 225-4945; e-mail embajcr@uiso.satnet.net; Ambassador LUZ ARGENTINA CALDERÓN DE AGUILAR.

Cuba: Mercurio 365, entre La Razón y El Vengador, Quito; tel. (2) 245-6936; fax (2) 243-0594; e-mail embquito@uio.satnet.net; Ambassador ILEANA DÍAZ-ARGÜELLES ALASÁ.

Dominican Republic: Edif. Albatros, Avda de los Shyris 1240 y Portugal, 2°, Apdo 17-01-387-A, Quito; Ambassador NOLBERTO LUIS SOTO.

Egypt: Edif. Araucaria, 9°, Baquedano 222 y Reina Victoria, Apdo 9355, Sucursal 7, Quito; tel. (2) 223-5046; Ambassador MOHAMED ELEISH.

El Salvador: Avda Republica de El Salvador 733 y Portugal, 201°, Quito; tel. (2) 243-3670; Ambassador RAFAEL A. ALFARO PINEDA.

France: Plaza 107 y Avda Patria, Apdo 536, Quito; tel. (2) 256-0789; fax (2) 256-6424; e-mail francie@uio.satnet.net; Ambassador SERGE PINOT.

Germany: Edif. Citiplaza, 14°, Avda Naciones Unidas y República de El Salvador, Casilla 17-17-536, Quito; tel. (2) 297-0820; fax (2) 297-0815; e-mail alemania@interactive.net.ec; Ambassador WALTER NOCKER.

Guatemala: Edif. Gabriela III, Avda República de El Salvador 733 y Portugal, Apdo 17-03-294, Quito; tel. (2) 245-9700; Ambassador ANGELA GAROZ CABRERA.

Holy See: Avda Orellana 692, Apdo 17-07-8980, Quito; tel. (2) 250-5200; fax (2) 256-4810; e-mail nunapec@impsat.net.ec; Apostolic Nunciature; Apostolic Nuncio Most Rev. ALAIN PAUL LEBEAUPIN (Titular Archbishop of Vico Equense).

Honduras: Edif. World Trade Centre, Torre A, 5°, Of. 501, Avda 12 de Octubre 1942 y Cordero, Apdo 17-03-4753, Quito; tel. (2) 222-3985; fax (2) 222-0441; e-mail embhondu@uio.satnet.net; Ambassador JORGE ALBERTO MILLA.

Israel: Edif. Plaza 2000, Avda 12 de Octubre y Fco. Salazar, Apdo 17-21-08, Quito; tel. (2) 223-7474; e-mail isremuio@uio.telconet.net; Ambassador YOSHEP HASEEN.

Italy: Calle La Isla 111 y Humberto Alborñoz, Casilla 17-03-72, Quito; tel. (2) 256-1077; fax (2) 256-1077; fax (2) 256-1074; e-mail ambital@ambitalquito.org; internet www.ambitalquito.org; Ambassador PAOLO LEGNAIOLI.

Japan: Juan León Mera 130 y Avda Patria, 7°, Quito; tel. (2) 256-1899; fax (2) 250-3670; e-mail japembec@uio.satnet.net; Ambassador MASANORI TODA.

Korea, Republic: Edif. Citiplaza, 8°, Avda Naciones Unidas y Avda de El Salvador, Quito; tel. (2) 297-0625; fax (2) 297-0630; e-mail ecemco@interactive.net.ec; Ambassador PIL-JOO SUNG.

Mexico: Avda 6 de Diciembre 4843 y Naciones Unidas, Casilla 17-11-6371, Quito; tel. (2) 245-7820; fax (2) 244-8245; e-mail embmxec@uio.satnet.net; Ambassador MANUEL MARTÍNEZ DEL SOBRAL Y PENICHET.

Netherlands: Edif. World Trade Centre, Torre A, 1°, Avda 12 de Octubre 1942 y Cordero, Quito; tel. (2) 222-9229; fax (2) 256-7917; e-mail nlgovqui@attglobal.net; internet www.embajadadeholanda.com; Ambassador FRANS G. BIJOUET.

Panama: Edif. Posada de las Artes, 3°, Diego de Almagro 1550 y Pradera, Apdo 17-07-9017, Quito; tel. (2) 256-5234; fax (2) 256-6449; e-mail pmaemecu@interactive.net.ec; Ambassador ALBA TEJADA DE ROLLA.

Paraguay: Avda Gaspar de Villarroel 2013 y Amazonas, Casilla 139A, Quito; tel. (2) 224-5871; fax (2) 225-1446; e-mail embapar@uio-telconet.net; Ambassador Dr CARLOS VILLAGRA MARSAL.

Peru: Avda República de El Salvador 495 e Irlanda, Quito; tel. (2) 246-8410; fax (2) 225-2560; e-mail embpeecu@uio.satnet.net; Ambassador OSCAR MAURTUA DE ROMAÑA.

Russia: Reina Victoria 462 y Roca, Quito; tel. (2) 256-1361; e-mail embrusia@accessinter.net; Ambassador GIORGII P. KOROLIOV.

Serbia and Montenegro: Gen. Francisco Salazar 958 y 12 de Octubre, Quito; tel. (2) 252-6218; Ambassador SAMUILO PROTIĆ.

Slovakia: Gen. Francisco Salazar 459 y Coruña, Quito.

Spain: La Pinta 455 y Amazonas, Casilla 9322, Quito; tel. (2) 223-7132; e-mail embespec@correo.mae.es; Ambassador EDUARDO CERRO GODINHO.

Switzerland: Edif. Xerox, 2°, Amazonas 3617 y Juan Pablo Sanz, Casilla 17-11-4815, Quito; tel. (2) 243-4949; fax (2) 244-9314; e-mail vertretung@qui.rep.admin.ch; Ambassador ROBERT REICH.

United Kingdom: Edif. Citiplaza, 14°, Avda Naciones Unidas y República de El Salvador, Casilla 17-01-314, Quito; tel. (2) 297-0800; fax (2) 297-0809; e-mail britembq@interactive.net.ec; internet www.britembquito.org.ec; Ambassador IAN GERKEN.

USA: Avda 12 de Octubre y Patria 120, Quito; tel. (2) 256-2890; fax (2) 250-2052; internet www.usembassy.org.ec; Ambassador KRISTIE KENNEY.

Uruguay: Edif. Josueth González, 9°, Avda 6 de Diciembre 2816 y James Orton, Casilla 17-12-282, Quito; tel. (2) 256-3762; fax (2) 256-3763; e-mail emburugl@emburuguay.int.ec; Ambassador DUNCAN B. CROCI DE MULA.

Venezuela: Avda Los Cabildos 115, Apdo 17-01-688, Quito; tel. (2) 226-8636; fax (2) 250-2630; e-mail embavene@impsat.net.ec; Ambassador CARLOS RODOLFO SANTIAGO MARTÍNEZ.

Judicial System

Attorney-General: JOSE MARÍA JIMÉNEZ BORJA GALLEGOS.

Supreme Court of Justice: Palacio de Justicia, Avda 6 de Diciembre y Piedrahita 332, Quito; tel. (2) 290-0424; fax (2) 290-0425; e-mail dni-cnj@access.net.ec; internet www.justiciaecuador.gov.ec; f. 1830; Pres. ARMANDO BERMEO CASTILLO.

Higher or Divisional Courts: Ambato, Azogues, Babahoyo, Cuenca, Esmeraldas, Guaranda, Guayaquil, Ibarra, Latacunga, Loja, Machala, Portoviejo, Quito, Riobamba and Tulcán. 90 judges.

Provincial Courts: there are 40 Provincial Courts in 15 districts. other courts include 94 Criminal, 219 Civil, 29 dealing with labour disputes and 17 Rent Tribunals.

Special Courts: National Court for Juveniles.

Religion

There is no state religion but more than 90% of the population are Roman Catholics. There are representatives of various Protestant Churches and of the Jewish faith in Quito and Guayaquil.

CHRISTIANITY

The Roman Catholic Church

Ecuador comprises four archdioceses, 11 dioceses, seven Apostolic Vicariates and one Apostolic Prefecture. At 31 December 2000 there were an estimated 12,275,813 adherents in the country, equivalent to some 91.4% of the population.

Bishops' Conference

Conferencia Episcopal Ecuatoriana, Avda América 1805 y La Gasca, Apdo 17-01-1081, Quito; tel. (2) 252-4568; fax (2) 250-1429; e-mail confepec@uio.satnet.net.

f. 1939; statutes approved 1999; Pres. José Mario Ruiz Navas (Archbishop of Porto viejo).

Archbishop of Cuenca: Vicente Rodrigo Cisneros Durán, Arzobispado, Calle Bolívar 7-64, Apdo 01-01-0046, Cuenca; tel. (7) 831-651; fax (7) 844-436; e-mail dicuenca@confep.org.ec.

Archbishop of Guayaquil: Juan Ignacio Larrea Holguín, Arzobispado, Calle Clemente Ballén 501 y Chimborazo, Apdo 09-01-0254, Guayaquil; tel. (4) 232-2778; fax (4) 232-9695.

Archbishop of Portoviejo: José Mario Ruiz Navas, Arzobispado, Avda Universitaria, Apdo 24, Portoviejo; tel. (5) 630-404; fax (5) 634-428; e-mail arzobis@ecua.net.ec.

Archbishop of Quito: Cardinal Antonio José González Zumárraga, Arzobispado, Calle Chile 1140 y Venezuela, Apdo 17-01-00106, Quito; tel. (2) 228-4429; fax (2) 258-0973.

The Anglican Communion

Anglicans in Ecuador are under the jurisdiction of Province IX of the Episcopal Church in the USA. The country is divided into two dioceses, one of which, Central Ecuador, is a missionary diocese.

Bishop of Littoral Ecuador: Rt Rev. Alfredo Morante, Calle Bogotá 1010, Barrio Centenario, Apdo 5250, Guayaquil.

Bishop of Central Ecuador: Rt Rev. José Neptalí Larrea Moreno, Apdo 17-11-6165, Quito; e-mail ecuacen@uio.satnet.net.

The Baptist Church

Baptist Convention of Ecuador: Casilla 3236, Guayaquil; tel. (4) 238-4865; Pres. Rev. Harolt Sante Mata; Sec. Jorge Moreno Chavarría.

The Methodist Church

Methodist Church: Evangelical United Church, Rumipamba 915, Casilla 17-03-236, Quito; tel. (2) 245-6714; fax (2) 252-92933; 800 mems, 2,000 adherents.

BAHÁ'Í FAITH

National Spiritual Assembly of the Bahá'ís: Apdo 869A, Quito; tel. (2) 256-3484; fax (2) 252-3192; e-mail ecua9nsa@uio.satnet.net; mems resident in 1,121 localities.

The Press

PRINCIPAL DAILIES

Quito

El Comercio: Avda Pedro Vicente Maldonado 11515 y el Tablón, Casilla 17-01-57, Quito; tel. (2) 267-0999; fax (2) 267-0466; e-mail elcomercio@elcomercio.com; internet www.elcomercio.com; f. 1906; morning; independent; Proprs Compañía Anónima El Comercio; Pres. Guadalupe Mantilla de Acquaviva; circ. 160,000.

Hoy: Avda Occidental N71-345, Casilla 17-07-09069, Quito; tel. (2) 249-0888; fax (2) 249-1881; e-mail hoy@hoy.com.ec; internet www .hoy.com.ec; f. 1982; morning; independent; Dir Benjamín Ortiz Brennan; Man. Jaime Mantilla Anderson; circ. 72,000.

El Tiempo: Avda América y Villalengua, Apdo 3117, Quito; f. 1965; morning; independent; Proprs Editorial La Unión, CA; Pres. Antonio Granda Centeno; Editor Eduardo Granda Garcés; circ. 35,000.

Ultimas Noticias: Avda Pedro Vicente Maldonado 11515 y el Tablón, Casilla 17-01-57, Quito; tel. (2) 267-0999; fax (2) 267-4923; f. 1938; evening; independent; commercial; Proprs Compañía Anónima El Comercio; Dir David Mantilla Cashmore; circ. 60,000.

Guayaquil

Expreso: Avda Carlos Julio Arosemena, Casilla 5890, Guayaquil; tel. (4) 220-1100; fax (4) 220-0291; internet www.diario-expreso.com; f. 1973; morning; independent; Editor Marcela Erazo; circ. 60,000.

El Extra: Avda Carlos Julio Arosemena, Casilla 5890, Guayaquil; tel. (4) 220-1100; fax (4) 220-0291; internet www.diario-extra.com; f. 1975; morning; Pres. Errol Cartwright Betancourt; Gen. Man. Galo Martínez Merchán; circ. 200,000.

La Razón: Avda Constitución y las Americas, Guayaquil; tel. (4) 228-0100; fax (4) 228-5110; f. 1965; morning; independent; Propr Roberto Isaías Dassum; Dir Jorge E. Pérez Pesantes; circ. 35,000.

La Segunda: Calle Colón 526 y Boyacá, Casilla 6366, Guayaquil; tel. (4) 232-0635; fax (4) 232-0539; f. 1983; morning; Propr Carlos Mansur; Dir Vicente Adum Antón; circ. 60,000.

El Telégrafo: Avda 10 de Agosto 601 y Boyacá, Casilla 415, Guayaquil; tel. (4) 232-6500; fax (4) 232-3265; e-mail cartas@telegrafo.com .ec; internet www.telegrafo.com.ec; f. 1884; morning; independent; commercial; Proprs El Telégrafo CA; Dir Dr Roberto Hanze Salem; circ. 45,000 (weekdays), 55,000 (Sundays).

El Universo: Avda Domingo Comín y Alban, Casilla 09-01-531, Guayaquil; tel. (4) 249-0000; fax (4) 249-1034; e-mail editores@ telconet.net; internet www.eluniverso.com; f. 1921; morning; independent; Pres. Nicolás Pérez Lapentti; Dir Carlos Pérez Barriga; circ. 174,000 (weekdays), 290,000 (Sundays).

There are local daily newspapers of low circulation in other towns.

PERIODICALS

Quito

La Calle: Casilla 2010, Quito; f. 1956; weekly; politics; Dir Carlos Enrique Carrión; circ. 20,000.

Cámara de Comercio de Quito: Avda Amazona y República, Casilla 202, Quito; tel. (2) 244-3787; fax (2) 243-5862; f. 1906; monthly; commerce; Pres. Andrés Pérez Espinosa; Exec. Dir Armando Tomaselli; circ. 10,000.

Carta Económica del Ecuador: Toledo 1448 y Coruña, Apdo 3358, Quito; f. 1969; weekly; economic, financial and business information; Pres. Dr Lincoln Larrea B; circ. 8,000.

El Colegial: Calle Carlos Ibarra 206, Quito; tel. (2) 221-6541; f. 1974; weekly; publ. of Student Press Association; Dir Wilson Almeida Muñoz; circ. 20,000.

Ecuador Guía Turística: Mejía 438, Of. 43, Quito; f. 1969; fortnightly; tourist information in Spanish and English; Propr Prensa Informativa Turística; Dir Jorge Vaca O; circ. 30,000.

Integración: Solano 836, Quito; quarterly; economics of the Andean countries.

Letras del Ecuador: Casa de la Cultura Ecuatoriana, Avda 6 de Diciembre, Casilla 67, Quito; f. 1944; monthly; literature and art; non-political; Dir Dr Teodoro Vanegas Andrade.

El Libertador: Olmedo 931 y García Moreno, Quito; f. 1926; monthly; Pres. Dr Benjamín Terán Varea.

Mensajero: Benalcázar 478, Apdo 17-01-4100, Quito; tel. (2) 221-9555; f. 1884; monthly; religion, culture, economics and politics; Man. Oswaldo Carrera Landázuri; circ. 5,000.

Nueva: Apdo 3224, Quito; tel. (2) 254-2244; f. 1971; monthly; left-wing; Dir Magdalena Jaramillo de Adoum.

Quince Dias: Sociedad Periodistica Ecuatoriana, Los Pinos 315, Panamericana Norte Km 51/2, Quito; tel. (2) 247-4122; fax (2) 256-6741; fortnightly; news and regional political analysis.

Solidaridad: Calle Oriente 725, Quito; tel. (2) 221-6541; f. 1982; monthly; publ. of Confederation of Catholic Office Staff and Students of Ecuador; Dir Wilson Almeida Muñoz; Man. Johny Merizalde; circ. 15,000.

Guayaquil

Análisis Semanal: Elizalde 119, 10°, Apdo 4925, Guayaquil; tel. (4) 232-6590; fax (4) 232-6842; e-mail wspurrie@gye.satnet.net; internet www.ecuadoranalysis.com; weekly; economic and political affairs; Editor Walter Spurrier Baquerizo.

Ecuador Ilustrado: Guayaquil; f. 1924; monthly; literary; illustrated.

El Financiero: Casilla 6666, Guayaquil; tel. (4) 230-4050; e-mail elfinanciero@elfinanciero.com; internet www.elfinanciero.com; weekly; business and economic news; Editor Xavier Pérez MacCollum.

Hogar: Aguirre 724 y Boyacá, Apdo 1239, Guayaquil; tel. (4) 232-7200; f. 1964; monthly; Man. Editor Rosa Amelia Alvarado; circ. 35,000.

Revista Estadio: Aguirre 730 y Boyacá, Apdo 1239, Guayaquil; tel. (4) 232-7200; fax (4) 232-0499; e-mail estadio@vistazo.com; f. 1962; fortnightly; sport; Editor LUIS SÁNCHEZ; circ. 70,000.

Vistazo: Aguirre 724 y Boyacá, Apdo 1239, Guayaquil; tel. (4) 232-7200; fax (4) 232-0499; e-mail vistazo@vistazo.com; f. 1957; fortnightly; general; Pres. XAVIER ALVARADO ROCA; circ. 85,000.

NEWS AGENCIES

Foreign Bureaux

Agencia EFE (Spain): Palacio Arzobispal, Chile 1178, Apdo 4043, Quito; tel. (2) 251-2427; Bureau Chief ÉMILIO CRESPO.

Agenzia Nazionale Stampa Associata (ANSA) (Italy): Calle Venezuela 1013 y esq. Mejía, Of. 26, Quito; tel. (2) 258-0794; fax (2) 258-0782; Correspondent FERNANDO LARENAS.

Associated Press (AP) (USA): Edif. Sudamérica, 4°, Of. 44, Calle Venezuela 1018 y Mejía, Quito; tel. (2) 257-0235; Correspondent CARLOS CISTERNAS.

Deutsche Presse-Agentur (dpa) (Germany): Edif. Atrium, Of. 5-7, González Suárez 894 y Gonnessiat, Quito; tel. (2) 256-8986; Correspondent JORGE ORTIZ.

Informatsionnoye Telegrafnoye Agentstvo Rossii—Telegrafnoye Agentstvo Suverennykh Stran (ITAR—TASS) (Russia): Calle Roca 328 y 6 de Diciembre, 2°, Dep. 6, Quito; tel. (2) 251-1631; Correspondent VLADIMIR GOSTEV.

Inter Press Service (IPS) (Italy): Urbanización Los Arrayanes Manzanas 20, Casa 15, Calle León Pontón y Pasaje E, Casilla 17-01-1284, Quito; tel. (2) 266-2362; fax (2) 266-1977; e-mail jfrias@uio.telconet.net; Correspondent KINTTO LUCAS.

Prensa Latina (Cuba): Edif. Sudamérica, 2°, Of. 24, Calle Venezuela 1018 y Mejía, Quito; tel. (2) 251-9333; Bureau Chief ENRIQUE GARCÍA MEDINA.

Reuters (United Kingdom): Avda Amazonas 3655, 2°, Casilla 17-01-4112, Quito; tel. (2) 243-1753; fax (2) 243-2949; Correspondent JORGE AGUIRRE CHARVET.

Xinhua (New China) News Agency (People's Republic of China): Edif. Portugal, Avda Portugal y Avda de la República del Salvador 730, 10°, Quito; Bureau Chief LIN MINZHONG.

Publishers

Artes Gráficas Ltda: Avda 12 de Octubre 1637, Apdo 533, Casilla 456a, Quito; Man. MANUEL DEL CASTILLO.

Centro de Educación Popular: Avda America 3584, Apdo 17-08-8604, Quito; tel. (2) 252-5521; fax (2) 254-2369; e-mail centro@cedep.ec; f. 1978; communications, economics; Dir DIEGO LANDÁZURI.

CEPLAES: Avda 6 de Diciembre 2912 y Alpallana, Apdo 17-11-6127, Quito; tel. (2) 254-8547; fax (2) 256-6207; f. 1978; agriculture, anthropology, education, health, social sciences, women's studies; Exec. Dir ALEXANDRA AYALA.

CIDAP: Hno Miguel 3-23, Casilla 01011943, Cuenca; tel. (7) 829-451; fax (7) 831-450; e-mail cidapl@cidap.org.ec; art, crafts, games, hobbies; Dir CLAUDIO MALO GONZALES.

CIESPAL (Centro Internacional de Estudios Superiores de Comunicación para América Latina): Avda Diego de Almagro 32-133 y Andrade Marin, Apdo 17-01-584, Quito; tel. (2) 254-8011; fax (2) 250-2487; e-mail ejaramillo@ciespal.net; internet www.ciespal.net; f. 1959; communications, technology; Dir EDGAR JARAMILLO.

Corporación de Estudios y Publicaciónes: Acuna 168 y J. Agama, Casilla 17-21-0086, Quito; tel. (2) 222-1711; fax (2) 222-6256; e-mail cep@accessinter.net; f. 1963; law, public administration.

Corporación Editora Nacional: Apdo 17-12-886, Quito; tel. (2) 255-4358; fax (2) 256-6340; e-mail cen@accessinter.net; f. 1978; archaeology, economics, education, geography, political science, history, law, literature, philosophy, social sciences; Pres. ERNESTO ALBÁN.

Cromograf, SA: Coronel 2207, Guayaquil; tel. (4) 234-6400; children's books, paperbacks, art productions.

Ediciones Abya-Yala: Avda 12 de Octubre 1430, Quito; tel. (2) 256-2633; fax (2) 250-6255; e-mail admin-info@abyayala.org; internet www.abyayala.org; f. 1975; anthropology, environmental studies, languages, theology; Dir Fr JUAN BOTTASSO.

Editorial de la Casa de la Cultura Ecuatoriana 'Benjamín Carrión': Avda 6 de Diciembre 679 y Patria, Apdo 67, Quito; tel. (2) 223-5611; f. 1944; general fiction and non-fiction, general science; Pres. MÍLTON BARRAGÁN DUMET.

Eguez-Pérez en Nombre Colectivo/Abrapalabra Editores: America 5378, Casilla 464A, Quito; tel. and fax (2) 254-4178; f. 1990; drama, education, fiction, literature, science fiction, social sciences; Man. IVAN EGUEZ.

Libresa SA: Murgeon 364 y Ulloa, Quito; tel. (2) 223-0925; fax (2) 250-2992; e-mail libresa@interactive.net.ec; f. 1979; education, literature, philosophy; Pres. FAUSTO COBA ESTRELLA.

Libros Técnicos Litesa Cía Ltda: Avda América 542, Apdo 456A, Quito; tel. (2) 252-8537; Man. MANUEL DEL CASTILLO.

Pontificia Universidad Católica del Ecuador, Centro de Publicaciones: Avda 12 de Octubre 1076 y Carrión, Apdo 17-01-2184, Quito; tel. (2) 252-9250; fax (2) 256-7117; e-mail puce@edu.ec; internet www.puce.edu.ec; f. 1974; literature, natural science, law, anthropology, sociology, politics, economics, theology, philosophy, history, archaeology, linguistics, languages and business; Rector Dr JOSÉ RIBADENEIRA ESPINOSA; Dir JESÚS AGUINAGA ZUMÁRRAGA.

Universidad Central del Ecuador: Departamento de Publicaciones, Servicio de Almacén Universitario, Ciudad Universitaria, Avda America y A. Perez Guerrero, POB 3291, Quito; tel. (2) 222-6080; fax (2) 250-1207.

Universidad de Guayaquil: Departamento de Publicaciones, Biblioteca General 'Luis de Tola y Avilés', Apdo 09-01-3834, Guayaquil; tel. (4) 251-6296; f. 1930; general literature, history, philosophy, fiction; Man. Dir LEONOR VILLAO DE SANTANDER.

Broadcasting and Communications

TELECOMMUNICATIONS

Andinatel: Edif. Zeta, Avda Amazonas y Veintimilla, Quito; tel. (2) 256-1004; fax (2) 256-2240; e-mail wmaster@andinatel.com; internet www.andinatel.com; Exec. Pres. Ing. ANDRÉS PÉREZ.

Asociación Ecuatoriana de Radiodifusión (AER): Guayaquil; tel. and fax (4) 256-2448; independent association; Pres. Abog. MARIO CANESSA ONETO.

Consejo Nacional de Telecomunicaciones (CONATEL): Avda Diego de Almagro 31-95 y Alpallana, Casilla 17-07-9777, Quito; tel. (2) 222-5614; fax (2) 222-5030; e-mail jpileggi@conatel.gov.ec; internet www.conatel.gov.ec; Pres. Dr JOSÉ PILEGGI VÉLIZ.

Pacifitel: Calle Panamá y Roca, Guayaquil; tel. (4) 230-8724; Exec. Pres. Ing. ANTONIO SAENZ FERNANDEZ.

Secretaría Nacional de Telecomunicaciones: Avda Diego de Almagro 31-95 y Alpallana, Casilla 17-07-9777, Quito; tel. (2) 250-2197; fax (2) 290-1010; Secretario Nacional de Telecomunicaciones Ing. CARLOS DEL POZO CAZAR.

Superintendencia de Telecomunicaciones: Edif. Olimpo, Avda 9 de Octubre 1645 y Berlín, Casilla 17-21-1797, Quito; tel. (2) 222-2449; fax (2) 256-6688; e-mail supertel@server.supertel.gov.ec; internet www.supertel.gov.ec; Superintendente de Telecomunicaciones Ing. HUGO RUIZ CORAL.

BROADCASTING

Regulatory Authority

Consejo Nacional de Radiodifusión y Televisión (CONARTEL): Calle La Pinta 225 y Rábida, Quito; tel. (2) 223-3492; fax (2) 252-3188; Pres. Ing. ALOO OTTATI PINO.

Radio

There are nearly 300 commercial stations, 10 cultural stations and 10 religious stations. The following are among the most important stations:

CRE (Cadena Radial Ecuatoriana): Edif. El Torreón, 9°, Avda Boyacá 642 y Padre Solano, Apdo 4144, Guayaquil; tel. (4) 256-4290; fax (4) 256-0386; e-mail aguerrero@cre.com.ec; Dir RAFAEL GUERRERO VALENZUELA.

Emisoras Gran Colombia: Calle Galápagos 112 y Guayaquil, Quito; tel. (2) 244-2951; fax (2) 244-3147; f. 1943; Pres. MARIO JOSÉ CANESSA ONETO.

Radio Católica Nacional: Avda América 1830 y Mercadillo, Casilla 17-03-540, Quito; tel. (2) 254-1557; fax (2) 256-7309; f. 1985; Pres. ANTONIO GONZÁLEZ.

Radio Centro: Avda República de El Salvador 836 y Portugal, Quito; tel. (2) 244-8900; fax (2) 250-4575; f. 1977; Pres. EDGAR YÁNEZ VILLALOBOS.

Radio Colón: Edif. Granda Centeno, Avda América OE4-22 y Villalengua, Casilla 17-08-8167, Quito; tel. (2) 224-7467; fax (2) 224-1994; f. 1934; Pres. JOSÉ ENRÍQUEZ ONTANEDA; Dir MARGARITA MOLINA GRANDA.

Radio Nacional del Ecuador: Mariano Echeverría 537 y Brasil, Casilla 17-01-82, Quito; tel. (2) 245-9555; fax (2) 245-5266; f. 1961; state-owned; Dir Ana Maldonado Robles.

Radio Quito: Avda 10 de Agosto 2441 y Colón, Casilla 17-21-1971, Quito; tel. (2) 250-8301; fax (2) 250-3311; f. 1940; Pres. Guadalupe Mantilla Mosquera.

Radio Sonorama (HCAEL): Eloy Alfaro 5400 y Los Granados, Casilla 130B, Quito; tel. (2) 244-8403; fax (2) 244-5858; f. 1975; Pres. Santiago Proaño.

Radio Sucre: Juan Tanca Marengo, Casilla 117114, Guayaquil; tel. (4) 268-0586; fax (4) 268-0592; e-mail rsucre@gye.satnet.net; internet www.radiosucre.com.ec; f. 1983; Pres. Vicente Arroba Ditto.

Radio Zacaray: Avda Quito 1424 y Pasaje Aguavil, Santo Domingo de los Colorados; tel. (2) 275-0140; fax (2) 244-9207; e-mail admizar@uio.satnet.net; internet ecuadormedia.com; f. 1959; Pres. Hólger Velasteguí Domínguez.

La Voz de los Andes (HCJB): Villalengua 884 y Avda 10 de Agosto, Casilla 17-17-691, Quito; tel. (2) 226-6808; fax (2) 226-7263; e-mail helpdesk@hcjb.org.ec; f. 1931; operated by World Radio Missionary Fellowship; programmes in 11 languages (including Spanish and English) and 22 Quechua dialects; private, non-commercial, cultural, religious; Dir, Int. Radio Curt Cole; Gen. Man. John E. Beck.

Television

Corporación Ecuatoriana de Televisión—Ecuavisa Canal 2: Cerro El Carmen, Casilla 1239, Guayaquil; tel. (4) 230-0150; fax (4) 230-3677; f. 1967; Pres. Xavier Alvarado Roca; Gen. Man. Francisco Arosemena Robles.

Cadena Ecuatoriana de Televisión—TC Televisión Canal 10: Avda de las Américas, frente al Aeropuerto, Casilla 09-01-673, Guayaquil; tel. (4) 239-7664; fax (4) 228-7544; e-mail tctvl@tctv.com.ec; f. 1969; commercial; Pres. Roberto Isaías; Gen. Man. Jorge Kronfle.

Televisora Nacional—Ecuavisa Canal 8: Bosmediano 447 y José Carbo, Bellavista, Quito; tel. (2) 244-6472; fax (2) 244-5488; commercial; f. 1970; Pres. Patricio Jaramillo.

Televisión del Pacífico, SA—Gamavisión: Eloy Alfaro 5400 y Rio Coca, Quito; tel. (2) 226-2222; fax (2) 244-0259; e-mail nicovega@gamavision.com; internet www.gamavision.com; f. 1978; Pres. Nicolás Vega.

Teleamazonas Cratel, CA: Granda Centeno y Brasil, Casilla 17-11-04844, Quito; tel. (2) 243-0350; fax (2) 245-1387; f. 1974; commercial; Pres. Eduardo Granda Garcés.

Teleandina Canal 23: Avda de la Prensa 3920 y Fernández Salvador, Quito; tel. (2) 259-9403; fax (2) 259-2600; f. 1991; Pres. Humberto Ortiz Flores; Dir Patricio Aviles.

Finance

(cap. = capital; p.u. = paid up; res = reserves; dep. = deposits; m. = million; amounts in sucres)

Junta Monetaria Nacional (National Monetary Board): Quito; tel. (2) 251-4833; fax (2) 257-0258; f. 1927; Pres. Francisco Swett.

Supervisory Authority

Superintendencia de Bancos y Seguros: Avda 12 de Octubre 561 y Madrid, Quito; tel. (2) 254-1326; fax (2) 250-6812; e-mail alejo@e-mail.superban.gov.ec; internet www.superban.gov.ec; f. 1927; supervises national banking system, including state and private banks and other financial institutions; Superintendent Miguel Dávila.

BANKING

Central Bank

Banco Central del Ecuador: Avda 10 de Agosto y Briceño, Plaza Bolívar, Casilla 339, Quito; tel. (2) 258-2577; fax (2) 295-5458; internet www.bce.fin.ec; f. 1927; cap. 1,482m., res 2,533m., dep. 666,608m. (Dec. 1987); Pres. José Luis Ycaza Pazmiño; Gen. Man. Leopoldo R. Báez Carrera; 2 brs.

Other State Banks

Banco del Pacífico: Francisco de P. Ycaza 200, Guayaquil; tel. (4) 566-010; fax (4) 564-636; internet www.bp.fin.ec; f. 1999; by merger of Banco del Pacífico and Banco Continental; Exec. Pres. Marcel J. Laniado.

Banco Ecuatoriano de la Vivienda: Avda 10 de Agosto 2270 y Cordero, Casilla 3244, Quito; tel. (2) 252-1311; f. 1962; cap. 5,006m., res 952m., dep. 7,389m. (Dec. 1986); Pres. Abog. Juan Pablo Moncagatta; Gen. Man. Dr Patricio Cevallos Morán.

Banco del Estado (BDE): Avda Atahualpa 628 y 10 de Agosto, Casilla 17-01-00373, Quito; tel. (2) 225-0800; fax (2) 225-0320; f. 1979; cap. 115,587.5m., res 8,481.5m. (Aug. 1991); Pres. Econ. César Robalino; Gen. Man. Luis Mejía Montesdeoca.

Banco Nacional de Fomento: Ante 107 y 10 de Agosto, Casilla 685, Quito; tel. (2) 257-2248; fax (2) 258-0910; e-mail bnf1@bnfomento.fin.ec; f. 1928; cap. 3,000m., res 14,914m., dep. 117,067m. (Dec. 1987); Pres. Dr Ignacio Hidalgo Villavicencio; Gen. Man. Marcelo Peña Durini; 70 brs.

Corporación Financiera Nacional (CFN): Avda Juan León Mera 130 y Patria, Casilla 163, Quito; tel. (2) 256-4900; fax (2) 256-2519; e-mail mbenitez@q.cfn.fin.ec; internet www.cfn.fin.ec; f. 1964; Pres. Milton Salgado; Gen. Man. Ing. Rafael Cuesta Alvarez.

Commercial Banks

Quito

Banco Amazonas, SA: Avda Amazonas 4430 y Villalengua, Casilla 121, Quito; tel. (2) 226-0400; fax (2) 225-5123; e-mail basacomp@porta.net; f. 1976; affiliated to Banque Paribas; cap. 21,400m., res 8,970m., dep. 145,740m. (Dec. 1994); Pres. Rafael Ferretti Benítez; Vice-Pres. Roberto Seminario.

Banco Caja de Crédito Agrícola Ganadero, SA: Avda 6 de Diciembre 225 y Piedrahita, Quito; tel. (2) 252-8521; f. 1949; cap. 132m., res 41m., dep. 592m. (Aug. 1984); Man. Hugo Grijalva Garzón; Pres. Nicolás Guillén.

Banco Consolidado del Ecuador: Avda Patria 740 y 9 de Octubre, Casilla 9150, Suc. 7, Quito; tel. (2) 256-0369; fax (2) 256-0719; e-mail jcalarco@gnb.fin.ec; f. 1981; cap. 2,874m., res 4,338m., dep. 5,545m. (Oct. 1998); Chair. Jaime Gilinski; Gen. Man. Antonio Coy; 2 brs.

Banco General Rumiñahui: Avda Orellana y Amazonas, Casilla 2952, Quito; tel. (2) 250-5446; fax (2) 250-5366; Gen. Man. Gen. Gustavo Herrera.

Banco Internacional, SA: Avda Patria E-421 y 9 de Octubre, Casilla 17-01-2114, Quito; tel. (2) 256-5547; fax (2) 256-5758; e-mail cromero@bancointernacional.com.ec; internet www.bancointernacional.com.ec; f. 1973; cap. US $8,600m. (Dec. 2000); Pres. Damián Vallejo; Gen. Man. Econ. Raúl Guerrero Andrade; 58 brs.

Banco Pacífico Popular (BPP): Avda Amazonas 3535 y Juan Pablo Sanz, Casilla 696, Quito; tel. (2) 244-4700; fax (2) 244-4794; f. 1998; by merger of Banco Popular del Ecuador, Banco del Pacífico and Banco COFIEC; cap. US $251m., dep. US $1,598m., total assets US $2,859m. (Nov. 1998); Chair. Arturo Quiros; Exec. Pres. Nicolás Landés; Pres. Francisco Rosales.

Banco del Pichincha, CA: Avda Amazonas 4560 y Pereira, Casilla 261, Quito; tel. (2) 298-0980; fax (2) 298-1187; internet www.pichincha.com; f. 1906; cap. 153,000m., dep. 6,773,832m. (Dec. 1998); Exec. Pres. and Chair. Dr Fidel Egas Grijalva; Gen. Man. Antonio Acosta Espinosa; 127 brs.

Produbanco: Avda Amazonas 3775 y Japón, Casilla 17-03-38-A, Quito; tel. (2) 226-0150; fax (2) 244-7319; internet www.produbanco.com; f. 1978 as Banco de la Producción; name changed as above in 1996; cap. 112,000m., res 64,840m., dep. 906,613.2m. (Dec. 1997); Exec. Pres. and Gen. Man. Econ. Abelardo Pachano Bertero; Exec. Vice-Pres. Fernando Vivero Loza.

UniBanco: Avda República 500 y Pasaje Carrion, Edif. Pucara, Primer Piso, Quito; tel. (2) 290–7576; fax (2) 222–5000; e-mail bermeojf@unibanco.fin.ec; f. 1964 as Banco de Co-operativas del Ecuador, name changed as above in 1995; Pres. Salvador Pedrero; Treas. Juan Fernando Bermeo.

Cuenca

Banco del Austro: Sucre y Borrero (esq.), Casilla 01-01-0167, Cuenca; tel. (7) 831-646; fax (7) 832-633; f. 1977; cap. 34,000m., dep. 141,000m. (July 1994); Pres. Juan Eljuri Antón; Gen. Man. Patricio Robayo Idrovo; 19 brs.

Guayaquil

Banco Bolivariano, CA: Junín 200 y Panamá, Casilla 09-01-10184, Guayaquil; tel. (4) 256-0799; fax (4) 256-6707; e-mail crivera@bolivariano.fin.ec; internet www.bolivariano.com; f. 1978; cap. US $11.3m., res $3.3m., dep. $161.7m. (Dec. 2000); Chair. José Salazar Barragán; Exec. Pres. Miguel Babra Lyon; 22 brs.

Banco Industrial y Comercial—Baninco: Pichincha 335 e Illingworth, Casilla 5817, Guayaquil; tel. (4) 232-3488; f. 1965; cap. and res 2m., dep. 10m. (June 1988); Pres. Ing. Carlos Manzur Peres; Gen. Man. Gabriel Martínez Intriago; 2 brs.

Banco Territorial, SA: Panamá 814 y V. M. Rendón, Casilla 09-01-227, Guayaquil; tel. (4) 256-6695; fax (4) 256-6695; f. 1886; cap. 3,800m., res 3,769m. (June 1993), dep. 516m. (Sept. 1991); Pres. ROBERTO GOLDBAUM; Gen. Man. Ing. GUSTAVO HEINERT.

Loja

Banco de Loja: esq. Bolívar y Rocafuerte, Casilla 11-01-300, Loja; tel. (4) 757-1682; fax (4) 753-3019; f. 1968; cap. 10,000m., res 4,207m., dep. 70,900m. (Dec. 1996); Pres. Ing. STEVE BROWN HIDALGO; Man. Ing. LEONARDO BURNEO MULLER.

Machala

Banco de Machala, SA: Avda 9 de Mayo y Rocafuerte, Casilla 711, Machala; tel. (4) 293-0100; fax (4) 292-2744; f. 1972; Pres. Dr RODOLFO VINTIMILLA FLORES; Exec. Pres. and Gen. Man. ESTEBAN QUIROLA FIGUEROA; 2 brs.

Portoviejo

Banco Comercial de Manabí, SA: Avda 10 de Agosto 600 y 18 Octubre, Portoviejo; tel. (4) 265-3888; fax (4) 263-5527; f. 1980; cap. 117m., res 21m., dep. 720m. (June 1985); Pres. Dr RUBÉN DARÍO MORALES; Gen. Man. ARISTO ANDRADE DÍAZ.

Foreign Banks

ABN AMBO Bank NV (Netherlands): Avda Amazonas 4272, Casilla 17-17-1534, Quito; tel. (2) 226-6666; fax (2) 244-3151; internet www.abnamro.com.ec; f. 1960; Gen. Man. SJEF MARTINOT; 6 brs.

Citibank, NA (USA): Juan León Mera 130 y Patria, Casilla 17-01-1393, Quito; tel. (2) 256-3300; fax (2) 256-6895; f. 1959; cap. 7,000m., res 1,000m., dep. 62,000m. (Dec. 1996); Gen. Man. BENJAMÍN FRANCO; 3 brs.

ING Bank NV (Netherlands): Edif. Centro Financiero, Avda Amazonas 4545 y Pereira, Quito; tel. (2) 298-1650; fax (2) 298-1665.

Lloyds TSB (BLSA) Ltd (United Kingdom): Avda Amazonas 580, esq. Jerónimo Carrión, Casilla 17-03-556, Quito; tel. (2) 256-4177; fax (2) 256-8997; e-mail lloydsec@interactive.net.ec; f. 1988; in succession to the Bank of London and South America, f. 1936; cap. US $1,500m., res US $8,300m., dep. US $80,000m. (Dec. 2000); Man. G. BELTRÁN M.

'Multibanco'

Banco de Guayaquil, SA: Plaza Ycaza 105 y Pichincha, Casilla 09-01-1300, Guayaquil; tel. (4) 251-7100; fax (4) 251-4406; e-mail servicios@bankguay.com; internet www.bankguay.com; f. 1923; absorbed the finance corpn, FINANSUR, in 1990 to become Ecuador's first 'multibanco', carrying out commercial and financial activities; cap. 145,000m., dep. 3,198,862m. (Dec. 1998); Exec. Pres. Dr GUILLERMO LASSO MENDOZA; Vice-Pres ANGELO CAPUTI, CARMEN SORIANO; 50 brs.

Finance Corporations

Financiera Guayaquil, SA: Carchi 702 y 9 de Octubre, 6°, Casilla 2167, Guayaquil; f. 1976; cap. 900m., res 142m. (June 1987); Gen. Man. Dr MIGUEL BABRA LYON.

FINANSA (Financiera Nacional, SA): Avda 6 de Diciembre 2417, entre Orellana y la Niña, Casilla 6420-CCI, Quito; tel. (2) 254-6200; f. 1976; cap. 694m., res 103.6m. (June 1986); Gen. Man. RICHARD A. PEARSE; Dir LEONARDO STAGG.

Associations

Asociación de Bancos Privados del Ecuador: Edif. Delta, 7°, Avda República de El Salvador 890 y Suecia, Casilla 17-11-6708, Quito; tel. (2) 246-6670; fax (2) 246-6701; e-mail echiribo@asobancos .org.ec; f. 1965; 36 mems; Pres. ANTONIO ACOSTA ESPINOSA; Exec. Pres. ERNESTO CHIRIBOGA BLONDET (acting).

Asociación de Compañías Financieras del Ecuador (AFIN): Robles 653 y Amazonas, 13°, Of. 1310-1311, Casilla 17-07-9156, Quito; tel. (2) 255-0623; fax (2) 256-7912; Pres. Ing. FRANCISCO ORTEGA.

STOCK EXCHANGES

Bolsa de Valores de Guayaquil: 9 de Octubre 110 y Pichincha, Guayaquil; tel. (4) 256-1519; fax (4) 256-1871; internet www.bvg.fin .ec; CEO ENRIQUE AROSEMENA; Dir of Operations ERNESTO MURILLO.

Bolsa de Valores de Quito: Avda Amazonas 540 y J. Carrión, Quito; tel. (2) 252-6805; fax (2) 252-6048; e-mail pazosc@ccbvq.com; internet www.ccbvq.com; f. 1969; volume of operations US $1,700m. (1995); Pres GONZALO CHIRIBOGA CHÁVEZ; Exec. Pres. ARTURO QUIROZ RIUMALLÓ.

INSURANCE

Instituto Ecuatoriano de Seguridad Social: Avda 10 de Agosto y Bogotá, Apdo 2640, Quito; tel. (2) 254-7400; fax (2) 250-4572; f. 1928; various forms of state insurance provided; directs the Ecuadorean social insurance system; provides social benefits and medical service; Dir-Gen. Dr RAÚL ZAPATER HIDALGO.

National Companies

The following is a list of the eight principal companies, selected by virtue of capital.

Amazonas Cía Anónima de Seguros: V. M. Rendón 401 y Córdova, Apdo 3285, Guayaquil; tel. (4) 256-6300; fax (4) 256-3192; e-mail contacto@segurosamazonas.com.ec; internet www .segurosamazonas.com.ec; f. 1966; Gen. Man. ANTONIO AROSEMENA.

Cía Reaseguradora del Ecuador, SA: Junín 105 y Malecón Simón Bolívar, Casilla 09-01-6776, Guayaquil; tel. (4) 256-6326; fax (4) 256-4454; e-mail oespinoz@ecuare.fin.ec; f. 1977; Man. Dir Ing. OMAR ESPINOSA ROMERO.

Cía de Seguros Condor, SA: Plaza Ycaza 302, Apdo 09-01-5007, Guayaquil; tel. (4) 256-5888; fax (4) 256-0144; f. 1966; Gen. Man. JAIME GUZMÁN ITURRALDE.

Cía de Seguros Ecuatoriano-Suiza, SA: Avda 9 de Octubre 2101 y Tulcán, Apdo 09-01-0937, Guayaquil; tel. (4) 237-2222; fax (4) 250-0209; f. 1954; Gen. Man. Econ. ENRIQUE SALAS CASTILLO.

La Nacional Cía de Seguros Generales, SA: Edif. World Trade Centre, Avda Francisco de Arellana, 5°, Guayaquil; tel. (4) 263-0170; fax (4) 263-0175; f. 1940; Gen. Man. Dr MIGUEL BABRA LEÓN.

Panamericana del Ecuador, SA: Calle Portugal 305 y Eloy Alfaro, Quito; tel. (2) 246-9460; fax (2) 246-9650; f. 1973; Gen. Man. GERMAN DAVILA.

Seguros Rocafuerte, SA: Plaza Carbo 505 y 9 de Octubre, Apdo 6491, Guayaquil; f. 1967; Gen. Man. Ing. DANIEL CAÑIZARES AGUILAR.

La Unión Cía Nacional de Seguros: Km 5½, Vía a la Costa, Apdo 09-01-1294, Guayaquil; tel. (4) 285-1500; fax (4) 285-1700; e-mail launion2@porta.net; f. 1943; Man. DAVID ALBERTO GOLDBAUM MORALES.

Trade and Industry

GOVERNMENT AGENCIES

Consejo Nacional de Modernización del Estado (CONAM): Edif. CFN, 9°, Avda Juan León Mera 130 y Patria, Quito; tel. (2) 250-9432; fax (2) 222-8450; e-mail cdelgado@uio.conam-pertal.gov.ec; f. 1994; responsible for overseeing the Government's privatization programme; Pres. Ing. RICARDO NOBOA; Exec. Dir Ing. ANTONIO PERÉ YCAZA.

Empresa de Comercio Exterior (ECE): Quito; f. 1980 to promote non-traditional exports; State owns 33% share in company; share capital 25m. sucres.

Fondo de Promoción de Exportaciones (FOPEX): Juan León Mera 130 y Patria, Casilla 163, Quito; tel. (2) 256-4900; fax (2) 256-2519; f. 1972; export promotion; Dir ELIANA SANTAMARÍA M.

Instituto Ecuatoriano de Reforma Agraria y Colonización (IERAC): f. 1973 to supervise the Agrarian Reform Law under the auspices and co-ordination of the Ministry of Agriculture; Dir LUIS LUNA GAYBOR.

Superintendencia de Compañías del Ecuador: Roca 660 y Amazonas, Casilla 17-21-0687, Quito; tel. (2) 254-1606; fax (2) 256-6685; e-mail superintcias@q.supercias.gov.ec; internet www .supercias.gov.ec; f. 1964; responsible for the legal and accounting control of commercial enterprises; Supt Dr XAVIER MUÑOZ CHÁVEZ.

DEVELOPMENT ORGANIZATIONS

Centro Nacional de Promoción de la Pequeña Industria y Artesanía (CENAPIA): Quito; agency to develop small-scale industry and handicrafts; Dir Econ. EDGAR GUEVARA (acting).

Centro de Reconversión Económica del Azuay, Cañar y Morona Santiago (CREA): Avda México entre Unidad Nacional y las Américas, Casilla 01-01-1953, Cuenca; tel. (7) 817-500; fax (7) 817-134; f. 1959; development organization; Dir Dr JUAN TAMA.

Consejo Nacional de Desarrollo (CONADE): Juan Larrea y Arenas, Quito; formerly Junta Nacional de Planificación y Coordinación Económica; aims to formulate a general plan of economic and social development and supervise its execution; also to integrate local plans into the national; Chair. GALO ABRIL OJEDA; Sec. PABLO LUCIO PAREDES.

Fondo de Desarrollo del Sector Rural Marginal (FOD-ERUMA): f. 1978 to allot funds to rural development programmes in poor areas.

Fondo Nacional de Desarrollo (FONADE): f. 1973; national development fund to finance projects as laid down in the five-year plan.

Instituto de Colonización de la Región Amazónica (INCREA): f. 1978 to encourage settlement in and economic development of the Amazon region; Dir Dr DIMAS GUZMÁN.

Instituto Ecuatoriano de Recursos Hidráulicos (INERHI): undertakes irrigation and hydroelectric projects; Man. Ing. EDUARDO GARCÍA GARCÍA.

Organización Comercial Ecuatoriana de Productos Artesanales (OCEPA): Carrión 1236 y Versalles, Casilla 17-01-2948, Quito; tel. (2) 254-1992; fax (2) 256-5961; f. 1964 to develop and promote handicrafts; Gen. Man. MARCELO RODRÍGUEZ.

Programa Nacional del Banano y Frutas Tropicales: Guayaquil; to promote the development of banana and tropical-fruit cultivation; Dir Ing. JORGE GIL CHANG.

Programa Regional de Desarrollo del Sur del Ecuador (PRE-DESUR): Pasaje María Eufrasia 100 y Mosquera Narváez, Quito; tel. (2) 254-4415; f. 1972 to promote the development of the southern area of the country; Dir Ing. LUIS HERNÁN EGUIGUREN CARRIÓN.

CHAMBERS OF COMMERCE AND INDUSTRY

Federación Nacional de Cámaras de Comercio del Ecuador: Avda Olmedo 414 y Boyacá, Guayaquil; tel. (4) 232-3130; fax (4) 232-3478; Pres. Ing. LUIS TRUJILLO BUSTAMANTE; Exec. Vice-Pres. Dr ROBERTO ILLINGWORTH.

Cámara de Comercio de Cuenca: Avda Federico Malo 1-90, Casilla 4929, Cuenca; tel. (7) 827-531; fax (7) 833-891; f. 1919; 5,329 mems; Pres. ENRIQUE MORA VÁZQUEZ.

Cámara de Comercio de Quito: Edif. Las Cámaras, 6°, Avda República y Amazonas, Casilla 17-01-202, Quito; tel. (2) 244-3787; fax (2) 243-5862; e-mail ccq@ccq.org.ec; internet www.ccp.org.ec; f. 1906; 8,000 mems; Chair. RAÚL GANGOTENA; Pres. FERNANDO NAVARRO.

Cámara de Comercio de Guayaquil: Avda Francisco de Orellana y V. H. Sicouret, Centro Empresarial 'Las Cámaras', 2° y 3°, Guayaquil; tel. (4) 268-2771; fax (4) 268—2725; e-mail info@lacamera.org; internet www.lacamara.org; f. 1889; 31,000 affiliates; Pres. Sr. JOAQUÍN ZEVALLOS MACCHIAVELLO; Exec. Vice-Pres. Dr ROBERTO ILLINGWORTH CABANILLA.

Federación Nacional de Cámaras de Industrias: Avda República y Amazonas, Casilla 2438, Quito; tel. (2) 245-2994; fax (2) 244-8118; f. 1974; Pres. Ing. PEDRO KOHN.

Cámara de Industrias de Cuenca: Edif. Cámara de Industrias de Cuenca, 12° y 13°, Avda Florencia Astudillo y Alfonso Cordero, Cuenca; tel. (7) 845–053; fax (7) 840-107; internet www.cainc.org.ec; f. 1936; Pres. Ing. FRANK TOSI IÑIGUEZ.

Cámara de Industrias de Guayaquil: Avda Francisco de Orellana y M. Alcivar, Casilla 09-01-4007, Guayaquil; tel. (4) 268-2618; fax (4) 268-2680; e-mail caindgye@cig.org.ec; internet www.cig.org.ec; f. 1936; Pres. FRANCISCO ALARCON.

INDUSTRIAL AND TRADE ASSOCIATIONS

Centro de Desarrollo Industrial del Ecuador (CENDES): Avda Orellana 1715 y 9 de Octubre, Casilla 2321, Quito; tel. (2) 252-7100; f. 1962; carries out industrial feasibility studies, supplies technical and administrative assistance to industry, promotes new industries, supervises investment programmes; Gen. Man. CLAUDIO CREAMER GUILLÉN.

Corporación de Desarrollo e Investigación Geológico-Minero-Metalúrgica (CODIGEM): Avda 10 de Agosto 5844 y Pereira, Casilla 17-03-23, Quito; tel. (2) 225-4673; fax (2) 225-4674; e-mail prodemi2@prodeminca.org.ec; f. 1991 to direct mining exploration and exploitation; Exec. Pres. Ing. JORGE BARRAGÁN G.

Corporación de Promoción de Exportaciones e Inversiones (CORPEI): Edif. Centro Empresarial Las Cámaras, Avda Francisco de Orellana y Miguel H. Alcívar, 2°, Guayaquil; tel. (4) 268-1550; fax (4) 268-1551; e-mail rcastelv@corpei.org.ec; internet www.corpei.org.ec; f. 1997 to promote exports and investment; CEO RICARDO ESTRADA ESTRADA.

Fondo Nacional de Preinversión (FONAPRE): Jorge Washington 624 y Amazonas, Casilla 17-01-3302, Quito; tel. (2) 256-3261; f. 1973 to undertake feasibility projects before investment; Pres. LUIS PARODÍ VALVERDE; Gen. Man. Ing. EDUARDO MOLINA GRAZZIANI.

Petróleos del Ecuador (PETROECUADOR): Avda 6 de Diciembre, Casilla 5007-8, Quito; tel. (2) 222-9043; internet www.petroecuador.com.ec; state petroleum co; operations in at least

seven oilfields were expected to be transferred to the private sector; Pres. GUSTAVO GUTIÉRREZ.

EMPLOYERS' ORGANIZATIONS

Asociación de Cafecultores del Cantón Piñas: García Moreno y Abdón Calderón, Quito; coffee growers' association.

Asociación de Comerciantes e Industriales: Avda Boyacá 1416, Guayaquil; traders' and industrialists' association.

Asociación de Industriales Textiles del Ecuador (AITE): Edif. Las Cámaras, 8°, Avda República y Amazonas, Casilla 2893, Quito; f. 1938; textile manufacturers' association; 40 mems; Pres. Ing. RAMIRO LEÓN PAEZ; Exec. Pres. Dr ANTONIO JOSÉ COBO.

Asociación de Productores Bananeros del Ecuador (APROBANA): Guayaquil; banana growers' association; Pres. NICOLÁS CASTRO.

Asociación Nacional de Empresarios (ANDE): Edif. España, 6°, Of. 67, Avda Amazonas 1429 y Colón, Casilla 17-01-3489, Quito; tel. (2) 223-8507; fax (2) 250-9806; e-mail ande@vio.satnet.net; internet www.ande.net; national employers' association.

Asociación Nacional de Exportadores de Cacao y Café (ANECAFE): Casilla 4774, Manta; tel. (2) 229-2782; fax (2) 229-2885; e-mail anacafe@uio.satnet.net; cocoa and coffee exporters' association.

Asociación Nacional de Exportadores de Camarones: Pres. LUIS VILLACÍS.

Cámara de Agricultura: Casilla 17-21-322, Quito; tel. (2) 223-0195; Pres. ALBERTO ENRÍQUEZ PORTILLA.

Consorcio Ecuatoriano de Exportadores de Cacao y Café: cocoa and coffee exporters' consortium.

Corporación Nacional de Exportadores de Cacao y Café: Guayaquil; cocoa and coffee exporters' corporation.

Federación Nacional de Cooperativas Cafetaleras del Ecuador (FENACAFE): Jipijapa; tel. (4) 260-0631; e-mail orgcafex@mnb.satnet.net; coffee co-operatives federation.

Unión Nacional de Periodistas: Joaquín Auxe Iñaquito, Quito; national press association.

There are several other coffee and cocoa organizations.

UTILITIES

Regulatory Authorities

Ministry of Energy and Mines: see section on The Government (Ministries).

Centro Nacional de Control de Energía (CENACE): Km 17.5 de la Panamericana Sur, Sector Cutuglahua, Casilla 17-21-1991, Quito; tel. (2) 269-1288; fax (2) 269-0469; e-mail gar@cenace.org.ec; f. 1999; co-ordinates and oversees national energy system; Exec. Dir GABRIEL ARGÜELLO RÍOS.

Comisión Ecuatoriana de Energía Atómica: Juan Larrea 15–36 y Riofrío, Casilla 17-01-2517, Quito; tel. (2) 254-5861; fax (2) 256-3336; e-mail comecen1@comecenat.gov.ec; atomic energy commission; Exec. Dir CELIANO ALMEIDA; Head of Information HIPSY CIFUENTES.

Consejo Nacional de Electricidad (CONELEC): Avda Amazonas 33-299 e Inglaterra, Quito; tel. (2) 226-8746; fax (2) 226-8737; e-mail conelec@conelec.gov.ec; internet www.conelec.gov.ec; f. 1999; supervises electricity industry following transfer of assets of the former Instituto Ecuatoriano de Electrificación (INECEL) to the Fondo de Solidaridad; pending privatization as six generating companies, one transmission company and 19 distribution companies; Exec. Pres. DIEGO PÉREZ PALLARES.

Directorate of Renewable Energy and Energy Efficiency (Ministry of Energy and Mines): J. L. Mera y Orellana, Edif. MOP, 6°, Quito; tel. (2) 255–0018; fax (2) 255–0018; e-mail jgalarza@menergia.gov.ec; internet www.menergia.gov.ec; f. 1995; research and development of new and renewable energy sources; Dir Ing. JUAN GALARZA.

Directorate-General of Hydrocarbons: Avda 10 de Agosto 321, Quito; supervision of the enforcement of laws regarding the exploration and development of petroleum.

Electricity

Empresa Eléctrica del Ecuador Inc: Urb. La Garzota, Sector 3, Manzana 47; tel. (4) 224-8006; fax (4) 224-8040; major producer and distributor of electricity, mostly using oil-fired or diesel generating capacity; privatization suspended in 2002.

Empresa Eléctrica Quito, SA: Avda 10 de Agosto y Las Casas, Quito; tel. (2) 254-3833; fax (2) 250-3817; internet www.eeq.com.ec;

f. 1894; produces electricity for the region around Quito, mostly from hydroelectric plants; Gen. Man. HERNÁN ANDINO ROMERO.

Empresa Eléctrica Regional El Oro, SA (EMELORO): e-mail mandrad@emeloro.gov.ec; internet www.eeq.com.ec; electricity production and generation in El Oro province; Pres. WILSON LAPO.

Empresa Eléctrica Regional del Sur, SA (EERSSA): internet www.eeq.com.ec; f. 1973; electricity production and generation in Loja and Zamora Chinchipe provinces; Man. DANIEL MAHAUAD ORTEGA.

Water

Instituto Ecuatoriano de Obras Sanitarias: Toledo 684 y Lérida, Troncal, Quito; tel. (2) 252-2738.

TRADE UNIONS

Frente Unitario de Trabajadores (FUT): f. 1971; left-wing; 300,000 mems; Pres. EDGAR PONCE; comprises:

> **Confederación Ecuatoriana de Organizaciones Clasistas (CEDOC):** Calle Río de Janeiro 407 y Juan Larrea, Casilla 3207, Quito; tel. (2) 254-8086; f. 1938; affiliated to CMT and CLAT; humanist; Pres. RAMIRO ROSALES NARVÁEZ; Sec.-Gen. JORGE MUÑOZ; 150,000 mems (est.) organized in 20 provinces.

> **Confederación Ecuatoriana de Organizaciones Sindicales Libres (CEOSL):** Casilla 17-01-1373, Quito; tel. (2) 252-2511; fax (2) 250-0836; e-mail ceosl@hoy.net; f. 1962; affiliated to ICFTU and ORIT; Pres. JAIME ARCINIEGA AGUIRRE; Sec.-Gen. GUILLERMO TOUMA GONZÁLEZ.

> **Confederación de Trabajadores del Ecuador (CTE)** (Confederation of Ecuadorean Workers): 9 de Octubre 1248 y Marieta de Veintimilla, Casilla 4166, Quito; tel. (2) 252-0456; fax (2) 252-0445; f. 1944; admitted to WFTU and CPUSTAL; Pres. CARLOS HUMBERTO LUZARDO; 1,200 affiliated unions, 76 national federations.

Central Católica de Obreros: Avda 24 de Mayo 344, Quito; tel. (2) 221-3704; f. 1906; craft and manual workers and intellectuals; Pres. CARLOS E. DÁVILA ZURITA.

A number of trade unions are not affiliated to the above groups. These include the Federación Nacional de Trabajadores Marítimos y Portuarios del Ecuador (FNTMPE—National Federation of Maritime and Port Workers of Ecuador) and both railway trade unions.

Transport

RAILWAYS

All railways are government-controlled. In 1997 the total length of track was 956 km.

Empresa Nacional de Ferrocarriles del Estado: Calle Bolívar 443, Casilla 159, Quito; tel. (2) 221-6180; Gen. Man. M. ARIAS SALAZAR.

There are divisional state railway managements for the following lines: Guayaquil–Quito, Sibambe–Cuenca and Quito–San Lorenzo.

ROADS

There were 43,197 km of roads in 2000, of which 18.9% were paved. The Pan-American Highway runs north from Ambato to Quito and to the Colombian border at Tulcán and south to Cuenca and Loja. Major rebuilding projects were undertaken in late 1998 with finance from several development organizations to restore roads damaged by the effects of El Niño (a periodic warming of the tropical Pacific Ocean).

SHIPPING

The following are Ecuador's principal ports: Guayaquil, Esmeraldas, Manta and Puerto Bolívar.

Acotramar, CA: General Gómez 522 y Coronel Guayaquil, Casilla 4044, Guayaquil; tel. (4) 240-1004; fax (4) 244-4852.

Ecuanave, CA: Junin 415 y Córdova, 4°, Casilla 09-01-30H, Guayaquil; tel. (4) 229-3808; fax (4) 228-9257; e-mail ecuanav@ecua.net.ec; Chair. Ing. P. ERNESTO ESCOBAR; Man. Dir A. GUILLERMO SERRANO.

Flota Bananera Ecuatoriana, SA: Edif. Gran Pasaje, 9°, Plaza Ycaza 437, Guayaquil; tel. (4) 230-9333; f. 1967; owned by Govt and private stockholders; Pres. DIEGO SÁNCHEZ; Gen. Man. JORGE BARRIGA.

Flota Mercante Grancolombiana, SA: Guayaquil; tel. (4) 251-2791; f. 1946; with Colombia and Venezuela; on Venezuela's withdrawal, in 1953, Ecuador's 10% interest was increased to 20%; operates services from Colombia and Ecuador to European ports, US

Gulf ports and New York, Mexican Atlantic ports and East Canada; offices in Quito, Cuenca, Bahía, Manta and Esmeraldas; Man. Naval Capt. J. ALBERTO SÁNCHEZ.

Flota Petrolera Ecuatoriana (FLOPEC): Edif. FLOPEC, Avda Amazonas 1188 y Cordero, Casilla 535-A, Quito; tel. (2) 256-4058; fax (2) 256-9794; e-mail g.general@flopec.com.ec; internet www .flopec.com.ec; f. 1972; Gen. Man. Vice-Adm. JORGE DONOSO MORAN.

Logística Marítima, CA (LOGMAR): Avda Córdova 812 y V. M. Rendón, 1°, Casilla 9622, Guayaquil; tel. (4) 230-7041; Pres. J. COELLOG; Man. IGNACIO RODRÍGUEZ BAQUERIZO.

Naviera del Pacífico, CA (NAPACA): El Oro 101 y La Ría, Casilla 09-01-529, Guayaquil; tel. (4) 234-2055; Pres. LUIS ADOLFO NOBOA NARANJO.

Servicios Oceánicos Internacionales, SA: Avda Domingo Comin y Calle 11, Casilla 79, Guayaquil; Pres. CARLOS VALDANO RAFFO; Man. FERNANDO VALDANO TRUJILLO.

Transfuel, CA: Junin 415 y Cordova, 4°, Casilla 09-01-30H, Guayaquil; tel. (4) 230-4142; Chair. Ing. ERNESTO ESCOBAR PALLARES; Man. Dir CARLOS MANRIQUE A.

Transportes Navieros Ecuatorianos (Transnave): Edif. Citibank, 4°–7°, Avda 9 de Octubre 416 y Chile, Casilla 4706, Guayaquil; tel. (4) 256-1455; fax (4) 256-6273; transports general cargo within the European South Pacific Magellan Conference, Japan West Coast South America Conference and Atlantic and Gulf West Coast South America Conference; Pres. Vice-Adm. YÉZID JARAMILLO SANTOS; Gen. Man. RUBÉN LANDÁZURI ZAMBRANO.

CIVIL AVIATION

There are two international airports: Mariscal Sucre, near Quito, and Simón Bolívar, near Guayaquil.

Ecuatoriana: Edif. Torres de Almagro, Avda Reina Victoria y Colón, Torres de Almagro, Casilla 17-07-8475, Quito; tel. (2) 256-3003; fax (2) 256-3920; e-mail eu@impsat.comec; internet www .ecuatoriana.com.ar; f. 1974 as Empresa Ecuatoriana de Aviación; nationalized 1974; ceased operations in 1993, aircraft subsequently sold or repossessed, and routes to the USA assigned to SAETA; airline reactivated in 1998 when VASP Brazilian Airlines acquired a 50.1% stake; placed under administration in 2001 following divestment by VASP.

SAETA Air Ecuador (Sociedad Anónima Ecuatoriana de Transportes Aereos): Avda. Carlos Julio Arosemena Km 2½, Guayaquil; tel. (4) 220-1152; fax (4) 220-1153; e-mail ehbuzon@saeta.com.ec; internet www.saeta.com.ec; f. 1967; domestic and regional scheduled flights; charter cargo services; suspended all activities in February 2000; Chair. ROBERTO DUNN BARREIRO; Exec. Dir ROBERTO D. SUÁREZ.

Servicios Aereos Nacionales (SAN): Km 2½, Avda Carlos Julio Arrosemena, Apdo 7138, Guayaquil; tel. (4) 220-2832; fax (4) 220-1152; f. 1964; scheduled passenger and cargo services linking Guayaquil with Quito and the Galápagos Islands and Quito with Cuenca; Dir of Operations Capt. LUGIEBRE JEPEZ.

Transportes Aéreos Militares Ecuatorianos (TAME): Avda Amazonas 1354 y Colón, 6°, Casilla 17-07-8736, Sucursal Almagro, Quito; tel. (2) 254-7000; fax (2) 250-0736; e-mail tame1@tame.com .ec; internet wwwpub4.ecua.net.ec/tame/; f. 1962; domestic scheduled and charter services for passengers and freight; Pres. WILLIAM BIRKETT.

The following airlines also offer national and regional services:

Aerotaxis Ecuatorianos, SA (ATESA); Cía Ecuatoriana de Transportes Aéreos (CEDTA); Ecuastol Servicios Aéreos, SA; Ecuavia Cía Ltda; Aeroturismo Cía Ltda (SAVAC).

Tourism

Tourism has become an increasingly important industry in Ecuador, with 615,493 foreign arrivals (including same-day visitors) in 2000. Of total visitors in that year, some 27% came from Colombia, 10% were from Peru, 12% from other Latin American countries, 24% from the USA and 21% from Europe. Receipts from the tourism industry amounted to US $402m. in 2000.

Asociación Ecuatoriana de Agencias de Viajes y Turismo (ASECUT): Edif. Banco del Pacífico, 5°, Avda Amazonas 720 y Veintimilla, Casilla 9421, Quito; tel. (2) 250-3669; fax (2) 228-5872; f. 1953; Pres. KATBE I. TOUMA ABUHAYAR.

Corporación Ecuatoriana de Turismo (CETUR): Avda Eloy Alfaro y Carlos Tobar, Quito; tel. (2) 250-7555; fax (2) 250-7565; e-mail mtur1@ec-gov.net; internet www.vivecuador.com; f. 1964; govt-owned; Exec. Dir KATBE I. TOUMA ABUHAYAR.

EGYPT

Introductory Survey

Location, Climate, Language, Religion, Flag, Capital

The Arab Republic of Egypt occupies the north-eastern corner of Africa, with an extension across the Gulf of Suez into the Sinai Peninsula, sometimes regarded as lying within Asia. Egypt is bounded to the north by the Mediterranean Sea, to the northeast by Israel, to the east by the Red Sea, to the south by Sudan, and to the west by Libya. The climate is arid, with a maximum annual rainfall of only 200 mm around Alexandria. More than 90% of the country is desert, and some 99% of the population live in the valley and delta of the River Nile. Summer temperatures reach a maximum of 43°C (110°F) and winters are mild, with an average day temperature of about 18°C (65°F). Arabic is the official language. More than 80% of the population are Muslims, mainly of the Sunni sect. The remainder are mostly Christians, principally Copts. The national flag (proportions 2 by 3) has three equal horizontal stripes, of red, white, and black; the white stripe has, in the centre, the national emblem (a striped shield superimposed on an eagle, with a cartouche beneath bearing the inscription, in Kufic script, 'Arab Republic of Egypt') in gold. The capital is Cairo (Al-Qahirah).

Recent History

Egypt, a province of Turkey's Ottoman Empire from the 16th century, was occupied by British forces in 1882. The administration was controlled by British officials, although Egypt remained nominally an Ottoman province until 1914, when a British protectorate was declared. The country was granted titular independence on 28 February 1922. Fuad I, the reigning Sultan, became King. He was succeeded in 1936 by his son, King Faruq (Farouk). The Anglo-Egyptian Treaty of 1936 recognized full Egyptian sovereignty, and after the Second World War British forces withdrew from Egypt, except for a military presence in the Suez Canal Zone. When the British mandate in Palestine was ended in 1948, Arab armies intervened to oppose the newly proclaimed State of Israel. A cease-fire was agreed in 1949, leaving Egyptian forces occupying the Gaza Strip.

On 23 July 1952 power was seized by a group of young army officers in a bloodless coup led by Lt-Col (later Col) Gamal Abd an-Nasir (Nasser). Farouk abdicated in favour of his infant son, Ahmad Fuad II, and went into exile. Gen. Muhammad Nagib (Neguib) was appointed Commander-in-Chief of the army and Chairman of the Revolution Command Council (RCC). In September Neguib was appointed Prime Minister and Military Governor, with Nasser as Deputy Prime Minister. In December the 1923 Constitution was abolished, and all political parties were dissolved in January 1953. The monarchy was abolished on 18 June 1953 and Egypt was proclaimed a republic, with Neguib as President and Prime Minister. In April 1954 Neguib was succeeded as Prime Minister by Nasser. In October Egypt and the United Kingdom signed an agreement providing for the withdrawal of all British forces from the Suez Canal by June 1956. President Neguib was relieved of all his remaining posts in November 1954, whereupon Nasser became acting Head of State.

The establishment of military rule was accompanied by wide-ranging reforms, including the redistribution of land, the promotion of industrial development and the expansion of social welfare services. In foreign affairs, the new regime was strongly committed to Arab unity, and Egypt played a prominent part in the Non-aligned Movement. In 1955, having failed to secure Western armaments on satisfactory terms, Egypt accepted military assistance from the USSR.

A new Constitution was approved by a national referendum in June 1956; Nasser was elected President unopposed, and the RCC was dissolved. In July, following the departure of British forces, the US and British Governments withdrew their offers of financial assistance for Egypt's construction of the Aswan High Dam. Nasser announced in response the nationalization of the Suez Canal Company, so that revenue from Canal tolls could be used to finance the dam's construction. The take-over of the Canal was a catalyst for Israel's invasion of the Sinai Peninsula on 29 October. British and French forces launched military operations against Egypt two days later. Strong pressure from the UN and the USA resulted in a cease-fire on 6 November, and supervision by the UN of the invaders' withdrawal.

Egypt and Syria merged in February 1958 to form the United Arab Republic (UAR), with Nasser as President. The new nation strengthened earlier ties with the USSR and other countries of the communist bloc. In September 1961 Syria seceded from the UAR, but Egypt retained this title until September 1971.

In December 1962 Nasser established the Arab Socialist Union (ASU) as the country's only recognized political organization. In May 1967 he secured the withdrawal of the UN Emergency Force from Egyptian territory. Egypt subsequently reoccupied Sharm esh-Sheikh, on the Sinai Peninsula, and closed the Straits of Tiran to Israeli shipping. This precipitated the so called Six-Day War, or June War, when Israel quickly defeated neighbouring Arab states, including Egypt. The war left Israel in control of the Gaza Strip and a large area of Egyptian territory, including the whole of the Sinai Peninsula. The Suez Canal was blocked, and remained closed until June 1975.

Nasser died suddenly in September 1970, and was succeeded by his Vice-President, Col Anwar Sadat. In September 1971 the UAR was renamed the Arab Republic of Egypt, and a new Constitution took effect. Egypt, Libya and Syria formed a Federation of Arab Republics in 1972, but this proved to be ineffective. In 1976 Egypt terminated its Treaty of Friendship with the USSR. Relations with the USA developed meanwhile, as President Sadat came to rely increasingly on US aid.

In October 1973 Egyptian troops crossed the Suez Canal to recover territory lost to Israel in 1967. After 18 days of fighting a cease-fire was achieved. In 1974–75 the US Secretary of State, Dr Henry Kissinger, negotiated disengagement agreements whereby Israel evacuated territory in Sinai and Israeli and Egyptian forces were separated by a buffer zone under the control of UN forces. In a dramatic peace-making initiative, opposed by many Arab countries, Sadat visited Israel in 1977 and addressed the Knesset (parliament). The leaders of Syria, Libya, Algeria, Iraq, the People's Democratic Republic of Yemen (PDRY) and the Palestine Liberation Organization (PLO) condemned Egypt, which responded by severing diplomatic relations with the five dissenting countries. In September 1978, following talks held at the US presidential retreat at Camp David, Maryland, Sadat and the Israeli Prime Minister, Menachem Begin, signed two agreements: the first provided for a five-year transitional period during which the inhabitants of the Israeli-occupied West Bank of Jordan and the Gaza Strip would obtain full autonomy and self-government; the second provided for a peace treaty between Egypt and Israel. The latter was signed in March 1979, whereafter Israel made phased withdrawals from the Sinai Peninsula, the last taking place in April 1982. The League of Arab States (the Arab League, see p. 260) expelled Egypt following the signing of the peace treaty, and imposed political and economic sanctions. Egypt continued to forge relations with Israel, and in February 1980 the two countries exchanged ambassadors for the first time.

In 1974 Sadat began to introduce a more liberal political and economic regime. Political parties (banned since 1953) were allowed to participate in the 1976 elections for the People's Assembly, and in July 1978 Sadat formed the National Democratic Party (NDP), with himself as leader. In 1979 the special constitutional status of the ASU was ended. In October 1981 Sadat was assassinated by members of Islamic Jihad, a group of militant fundamentalist Islamists. Sadat was succeeded by Lt-Gen. Hosni Mubarak, his Vice-President and a former Commander-in-Chief of the air force. A new electoral law required parties to receive a minimum of 8% of the total vote in order to secure representation in the People's Assembly. This prompted opposition parties to boycott elections to local councils and to the Shura (Advisory) Council. At legislative elections in May 1984 the ruling NDP won 72.9% of the total vote. Of the four other participating parties, only the New Wafd Party, with 15.1%, achieved representation. The campaign by Islamist fundamentalists for the Egyptian legal system fully to adopt the principles of the *Shari'a* (Islamic law) intensified in 1985. The

People's Assembly rejected proposals for immediate changes and advocated a thorough study of the small proportion of Egyptian law that did not conform to Islamic precepts.

Meanwhile, a division in the Arab world between a 'moderate' grouping (including Jordan, Iraq and the Gulf states), which viewed the participation of Egypt as indispensable to any diplomatic moves towards solving the problems of the region, and a 'radical' grouping, led by Syria, became increasingly evident. The PLO leader, Yasser Arafat, visited President Mubarak for discussions in December 1983, signifying the end of estrangement between Egypt and the PLO, and in 1984 Jordan resumed diplomatic relations with Egypt. These two developments led to the profound involvement of Egypt under Mubarak in the pursuit of a negotiated settlement of the Palestinian question. In November 1987, at a summit conference in Jordan attended by the majority of Arab leaders, President Hafiz Assad of Syria obstructed proposals to readmit Egypt to the Arab League. However, recognizing Egypt's support for Iraq in the Iran–Iraq War and acknowledging the influence that Egypt could exercise on the problems of the region, the conference approved a resolution placing the establishment of diplomatic links with Egypt at the discretion of member states.

The general election held in April 1987 resulted in a large majority for the ruling NDP. Of the 448 elective seats in the People's Assembly, the NDP won 346, the opposition parties together won 95, and independents seven. An electoral alliance of the Socialist Labour Party (SLP), the Liberal Socialist Party (LSP) and the Muslim Brotherhood won a combined total of 60 seats, of which the Brotherhood took 37 to become the largest single opposition group in the legislature. At a referendum held in October Mubarak was confirmed as President for a second six-year term of office by 97% of voters. In March 1988 the national state of emergency first declared after the assassination of President Sadat was renewed for a further three years.

A visit by King Fahd of Saudi Arabia to Cairo in March 1989 was a further indication of Egypt's improved status in the Arab world. Egypt was readmitted to the Arab League in May, with President Mubarak attending an emergency summit conference of the League convened to rally support for the diplomatic initiatives of Yasser Arafat following the Palestinian declaration of independence. Col Muammar al-Qaddafi of Libya attended the meeting and had separate discussions with President Mubarak. The border between the two countries was reopened in June, and in October Qaddafi visited Egypt for further discussions.

Following Iraq's invasion and annexation of Kuwait in August 1990, Egypt convened an emergency summit meeting of Arab leaders at which 12 of the 20 Arab League states supported a resolution demanding the withdrawal of Iraqi forces from Kuwait and, in response to Saudi Arabia's request for international assistance to deter potential aggression by Iraq, voted to send an Arab force to the Persian (Arabian) Gulf region. The Egyptian contingent within the multinational force eventually amounted to 35,000 troops. Egypt emerged from the Gulf conflict with its international reputation enhanced, largely as a result of what was regarded as Mubarak's firm leadership of 'moderate' Arab opinion.

Legislative elections in November and December 1990 were boycotted by the principal opposition parties, in protest at the Government's refusal to concede to demands that the elections be removed from the supervision of the Ministry of the Interior and that the state of emergency be repealed. The credibility of the polls was further undermined by the low rate of participation by voters, estimated at 20%–30% of the registered electorate. Of the 444 elective seats in the new Assembly, the NDP won 348, the National Progressive Unionist Party six, and independent candidates (the majority of whom were affiliated to the NDP) 83. Voting for the remaining seven seats was suspended. The national state of emergency was renewed for a further three-year period in June, in view of what the Government stated was the continued threat of internal and external subversion.

President Mubarak was formally proposed for a third term of office in July 1993, and in October his nomination was approved by some 94.9% of the valid votes cast at a national referendum. The official figure of an electoral turn-out of 84% was regarded with scepticism by many observers. The opposition parties, none of which had endorsed Mubarak's candidature, demanded reforms including amendment of the Constitution to allow direct presidential elections, the unrestricted formation of political parties, and the introduction of a two-term limit to the presidency.

At legislative elections held in November–December 1995, at which candidates of the NDP won 316 seats, thus retaining a decisive (albeit reduced) majority in the People's Assembly. The New Wafd Party took six seats, the National Progressive Unionist Party (NPUP) five and the LSP and the Nasserist Party one seat each. Of the 115 independent candidates elected, 99 were reported to have immediately joined or rejoined the NDP. Allegations of the intimidation of opposition supporters and of other electoral malpractices on the part of agents acting for the NDP were widespread. A new Council of Ministers was appointed in January 1996, with Kamal Ahmad al-Ganzouri, hitherto Minister of Planning, appointed Prime Minister (in place of Dr Atif Sidqi, who had held the post since 1986).

During 1998 domestic criticism of the Government resulted in the imposition of severe restrictions on the press (in place of more liberal legislation adopted in 1996). Dissenting editors of a number of newspapers were replaced with Government supporters, while six journalists were imprisoned on charges of libel between January and October. Moreover, a new law was introduced whereby individuals were prohibited from owning publishing companies, and in June stringent printing restrictions were imposed on two leading independent English-language newspapers.

In June 1999 Mubarak was formally nominated for a fourth presidential term; his nomination was approved by 93.8% of the valid votes cast in a national referendum held on 26 September. Voter turn-out was reported to be 79.2%. Of the four main legal opposition parties, only the Nasserist Party had refused to endorse Mubarak's candidature. In October Mubarak appointed Dr Atif Muhammad Obeid, previously Minister of the Public Enterprise Sector and responsible for the Government's privatization programme, to succeed al-Ganzouri as Prime Minister. Obeid's appointment was widely interpreted as an indication that economic reforms would be accelerated. None the less, although his Council of Ministers included 13 new ministers (among them Dr Midhat Hasanayn as Minister of Finance), most strategic portfolios did not change hands. Meanwhile, in September an assailant was killed by presidential escorts following an alleged attack in Port Said on President Mubarak, who sustained a slight injury in the incident.

In February 2000 the People's Assembly approved a presidential decree extending the state of emergency for a further three years. In the following month the Political Parties Committee approved the formation of a new political party, Hizb al-Wifaq al-Qawmi (or the National Accord Party), bringing the number of officially recognized parties to 15.

In June 2000 the Government ordered the closure of the Ibn Khaldoun Center for Social and Development Studies, and the centre's director, Prof. Sa'adeddin Ibrahim (a prominent academic and pro-democracy activist), was arrested on suspicion of collecting funds without prior authority and defaming Egypt through his work. It was alleged that Ibrahim had accepted more than US $220,000 from the European Commission to produce a video documentary on the electoral process in Egypt. Ibrahim was released on bail in August, but it was announced in September that he was to be tried on charges of receiving funds from abroad without official permission. Furthermore, in November military prosecutors announced that they were to investigate charges of espionage against Ibrahim. In May 2001 Ibrahim was sentenced to seven years' imprisonment with hard labour, having been convicted of receiving unauthorized funding from overseas, embezzlement and forgery; 27 employees of the Ibn Khaldoun Center also received custodial terms ranging from one to five years. The verdicts were widely criticized by many Western governments and national and international human rights organizations. Ibrahim was released from detention in early February 2002, after a retrial at the Supreme State Security Court was ordered. In July, however, following the conclusion of the second trial, Ibrahim again received a seven-year gaol sentence. The verdict again provoked fierce international criticism and the USA subsequently announced that it would suspend new aid, worth US $130m., to Egypt. In early December Ibrahim was released from prison after the Court of Cassation overturned his sentence and ordered a further retrial, and in mid-March 2003 Ibrahim and his 27 co-defendants were acquitted of all charges.

The Supreme Constitutional Court issued a judgment in July 2000 that the People's Assembly elected in 1995 was illegitimate (as was the Assembly elected in 1990), and that the existing electoral system was invalid since the constitutional requirement that the judiciary have sole responsibility for the supervision of elections had not been adhered to. President Mubarak subsequently convened an extraordinary session of the Assembly, at which two amendments to the existing electoral legislation were unanimously approved: these provided for judges to monitor voting in the impending general election, which was to be held over three stages in October–November 2000.

Almost 4,000 candidates contested the 444 elective seats in the People's Assembly at polls conducted in three rounds, each of two stages, beginning on 18 October, 29 October and 8 November 2000. According to figures published by the Ministry of the Interior in mid-November, the NDP increased its majority, with candidates of the ruling party taking 353 seats. Independent candidates secured 72 seats, but it was reported that 35 of these had either joined or rejoined the NDP shortly after the elections. The New Wafd Party won seven seats, the NPUP six, the Nasserist Party three and the LSP one seat. The rate of participation by voters at the various stages was officially stated to be between 15% and 40%. There were reports of outbreaks of violence in many parts of the country, primarily involving the security forces and members of the outlawed Muslim Brotherhood, and voting for the two seats in one constituency in Alexandria was postponed following the arrest of some 20 Muslim Brotherhood activists. At least 14 people were killed, and hundreds of others injured, during the voting period, while large numbers of Islamists were arrested for public order offences.

The summit meeting of the Arab League held in Jordan in March 2001 appointed Amr Moussa, Egypt's Minister of Foreign Affairs since 1991, as the organization's Secretary-General. Ahmad Maher was appointed to replace Moussa in his government post in May 2001. At partial elections to the Shura Council in that month 74 of the 88 contested seats were won by the NDP, while independent candidates took the remaining 14 seats. In mid-November President Mubarak effected a minor reorganization of the Council of Ministers. Most notably, the Ministry of Economics was abolished and responsibility for most of its functions was devolved to the new Governor of the Central Bank of Egypt.

Several high-profile court cases attracted considerable national and international attention from 2001. Early in the year a fundamentalist Islamist lawyer attempted to have a feminist writer, Nawal es-Sadawi, forcibly divorced from her husband on the grounds of apostasy after she had allegedly criticized aspects of orthodox Muslim beliefs in a newspaper interview. The case was, however, dismissed by the Prosecutor-General in April and by a family affairs tribunal in July. In September the editor of the independent weekly *An-Naaba* was sentenced to three years' imprisonment for undermining national security and inciting sectarian divisions. In June the newspaper had published an article in which it accused a former Coptic Christian monk of sexual misconduct and blackmail. The article, which was strongly criticized by President Mubarak, provoked days of angry protests in Cairo by several thousand Copts. The publication was prohibited the following month by the Administrative State Court. In mid-November 23 men, who had been among 52 individuals arrested as part of a campaign against homosexual activity following a police raid on a discothèque in May, were convicted by the State Security Court of engaging in immoral acts. Although homosexuality is not a crime under Egyptian law, the men were accused of practising 'habitual debauchery' and received terms of imprisonment ranging from one to five years. The remaining 29 defendants were acquitted. In May 2002, apparently in response to international pressure, President Mubarak overturned the sentences of 21 of the 23 men convicted of 'habitual debauchery' on the grounds that they had been tried by the wrong court and ordered the retrial of 50 of the 52 original defendants. However, Mubarak upheld gaol terms of five and three years, respectively, against two of the men, who had also been found guilty of 'scorning religion'. Upon completion of the retrial in March 2003, 21 of the accused were sentenced to three years' imprisonment; the other 29 defendants were again acquitted.

In February 2002 the worst rail disaster in Egypt's history, in which 373 people were killed after a train travelling from Cairo to Luxor caught fire, precipitated the resignation of the Minister of Transport and of the chairman of Egyptian National Railways. New ministers of transport, health and civil aviation

(responsibility for the last being devolved from the Ministry of Transport) were appointed in March.

At the eighth congress of the NDP held in Cairo in mid-September 2002, Mubarak was re-elected Chairman of the organization, while his son, Gamal, was elected Secretary-General for Policy, effectively making him the third most senior figure in the party and further fuelling speculation that he was being 'groomed' eventually to succeed his father. The Deputy Prime Minister and Minister of Agriculture and Land Reclamation, Dr Yousef Amin Wali, was replaced as the NPD's Secretary-General by the Minister of Information, Muhammad Safwat esh-Sharif, in a move widely regarded as an additional attempt to modernize the party.

Since 1992 the Government's attempts to suppress Islamist fundamentalism has dominated the domestic political agenda. During the early 1990s fundamentalist violence increasingly targeted foreign tourists visiting Egypt, as well as foreign investors, and there were frequent confrontations between Islamist militants and the security forces. In May 1993 a report published by a prominent human rights organization, Amnesty International, alleged that the Egyptian Government was systematically maltreating political detainees, and in November the organization accused the Government of breaching the UN Convention against Torture and Other Cruel, Inhuman or Degrading Treatment or Punishment.

In January 1994 the security forces were reported to have detained some 1,000 suspected fundamentalist activists in response to attacks on their members during that month. In March nine members of the Vanguard of Conquest (a faction of Islamic Jihad) were sentenced to death after having been convicted of conspiring to assassinate the Prime Minister in November 1993. In April 1994 the chief of the anti-terrorist branch of the State Security Investigation Section was assassinated by members of Jama'ah al-Islamiyah (one of Egypt's principal militant Islamist groups), prompting retaliatory security operations. Following the assassination emergency laws giving the security forces wide powers to arrest and detain suspects were renewed for a further three years. (The state of emergency was renewed in 1997 and again in 2000—see above.) In July 1994 a further five members of the Vanguard of Conquest were sentenced to death for the attempted assassination of the Minister of the Interior in August 1993.

In early 1995 the Government began to take steps to isolate the more moderate Muslim Brotherhood and to weaken its political influence in the approach to that year's legislative elections. Several leading members of the Brotherhood were arrested, and both President Mubarak and the Minister of the Interior claimed that there was evidence of links between the movement and Islamist extremists. The Government also acted to curb Islamist influence within professional organizations; in February the judiciary was accorded wide powers to intervene in union elections and to prevent Muslim Brotherhood members from standing. In January, meanwhile, clashes between extremists and security forces in Upper Egypt resulted in 87 deaths. In June Mubarak escaped an assassination attempt in Ethiopia while he was travelling to a summit meeting of the Organization of African Unity (OAU) in Addis Ababa; it was widely believed that the assailants were members of either Islamic Jihad or Jama'ah al-Islamiyah. Egypt's claim that the gunmen had been aided by Sudanese agents was denied by the Sudanese Government. (In September 1996 three Egyptians, reported to be members of unspecified Islamist groups, were sentenced to death by the Ethiopian Supreme Court for their involvement in the attempted assassination.)

In April 1996 12 prominent members of the Muslim Brotherhood were arrested and charged with attempting to revive the movement's activities and restore its links with extremist groups. For the first time the detainees included a member of the Brotherhood's Supreme Guidance Council. Three of those arrested were founder members of a new political organization, the Al-Wasat (Centre) Party, which the authorities claimed was serving as a 'front' for Brotherhood activities. The party's founders—who included Muslims, Christians, leftists and Nasserist activists—insisted, however, that they were seeking to create a political group that occupied the middle ground between the State and its fundamentalist Islamist opponents. (Twice in 1998 and again in June 1999 Al-Wasat was denied legal status by the authorities.)

In September 1997 a military court in Haekstep, north of the capital, conducted a military trial on an unprecedented scale of suspected Islamist militants; of 98 defendants convicted, four were sentenced to death and eight to life imprisonment. A few days later nine German tourists were killed, and 11 others injured, as a result of an attack on a tourist bus in Cairo. Although the perpetrators of the assault were widely believed to be members of Jama'ah al-Islamiyah, the Egyptian Government claimed, in an apparent attempt to protect the country's vital tourism industry, that the attack was an isolated incident unconnected with terrorism. (In May 1998 two men were hanged, having been convicted in October 1997 of the attack.) In November 1997 the massacre near Luxor of 70 people, including 58 foreign tourists, by members of Jama'ah al-Islamiyah severely undermined both the crucial tourism sector and the claims of the Government to have suppressed Islamist violence. Mubarak criticized the security forces' failure to protect tourists, and dismissed the Minister of the Interior, who had formulated the Government's uncompromising policies aimed at eradicating Islamist militancy. Mubarak ordered a heightened security presence at all tourist sites and placed the Prime Minister at the head of a special committee charged with devising a plan to safeguard the tourism sector. In December 1997 a number of Jama'ah al-Islamiyah's exiled leaders claimed that the Luxor massacre had been perpetrated by a 'rogue' element acting without the authorization of the group's central leadership; furthermore, the leaders in exile announced that Jama'ah al-Islamiyah (at least, those members under their specific authority) would no longer target tourists in their conflict with the Government. (In May 1999 security officials in Switzerland alleged that the Saudi Arabian-born militant Islamist, Osama bin Laden, had been responsible for the Luxor killings.)

New state security measures adopted by the Ministry of the Interior during 1998 included a relaxation of the criteria whereby affiliation to Islamist groups was assumed, and the release of some Islamist prisoners who had renounced connections with illegal organizations. By June 106 death sentences had been imposed upon Islamist fundamentalists since 1992, of which 72 had been exacted. In March 1998 Jama'ah al-Islamiyah declared a unilateral cease-fire and announced a new strategy of exerting maximum political pressure on the Government without the use of violence. Although the Government gave no formal acknowledgement of the apparent cease-fire, an acceleration in the release of imprisoned Islamist militants was subsequently evident. In April the Ministry of the Interior released some 1,200 Jama'ah al-Islamiyah detainees (reportedly among them two of the group's leaders who were involved in the assassination of President Sadat in 1981), and a further 1,200 were released in December. Nevertheless, government officials strongly denied that any deal had been concluded with the proscribed organization, and arrests and trials of suspected Islamist militants continued throughout 1999. In February it was reported that three men suspected of involvement in the 1997 Luxor attack had been arrested on the Uruguayan–Brazilian border and were expected to stand trial in Cairo. In the same month proceedings began against 107 alleged members of Islamic Jihad who were charged with conspiring to overthrow the Government. In April 1999 nine of the defendants were sentenced to death; 78 received sentences ranging from one year to life imprisonment, all with hard labour, while 20 were acquitted. In May the security services detained 23 suspects on the grounds that they were seeking to revive the activities in Egypt of the Vanguard of Conquest. In the following month 20 members of Jama'ah al-Islamiyah were given custodial sentences, having been convicted by a military court of planning a bomb attack on President Mubarak's Alexandria residence in 1996; that death sentences were not imposed was interpreted by the organization's lawyers as a positive response to the recent cease-fire declaration.

The unofficial truce between the Government and Jama'ah al-Islamiyah was apparently jeopardized in September 1999, when security forces in Giza shot dead four alleged members of the organization, including the commander of its military wing, in their first security action against the group since the implementation of the cease-fire in March. In November charges against 20 alleged members of the Muslim Brotherhood, who had been arrested in the previous month on charges of plotting to overthrow the Government and of infiltrating professional syndicates in order to undermine national security, were altered by the military court where they were standing trial from 'belonging' to the Muslim Brotherhood to 'participating in the founding and management' of the organization; any conviction under these charges was likely to result in much harsher sentences. The trial was initially postponed for procedural reasons but resumed in January 2000 (see below).

In January 2000 three days of violent clashes between Muslims and Copts in the southern village of el-Kosheh resulted in the deaths of 20 Christians and 1 Muslim. A subsequent inquiry conducted by the Egyptian Organization for Human Rights (EOHR) inferred that the primary cause of the violence was the 'economic inequalities' between the relatively prosperous Coptic majority and the poorer Muslim minority. There was a further outbreak of violence in el-Kosheh in late February. In February 2001 four Muslims were sentenced to custodial terms of up to 10 years for their part in the violence of early 2000; a further 92 defendants were acquitted. Later that month the Supreme State Prosecution Department announced that it would challenge the acquittal verdicts, and in late 2001 it was announced that the 92 acquitted were to be retried.

Meanwhile, in October 1999 there were newspaper reports that a new military leadership of Jama'ah al-Islamiyah had been established under Ala Abd ar-Raziq. It was rumoured later in the year that a power struggle was taking place within the group, and that the new Chairman of its Shura Council was Moustafa Hamzah, the chief suspect in the 1995 assassination attempt on President Mubarak. In February 2000 senior members of the leadership of Islamic Jihad publicly urged the cessation of the organization's armed activities, appealing to militants to concentrate their activities on the liberation of the al-Aqsa Mosque in Jerusalem; this, noted as the first time that the group's leaders had called for a cease-fire, followed recent reports that a 'coup' within Islamic Jihad had resulted in the removal from the high command of Dr Ayman az-Zawahri. Later in February eight prominent Islamists were arrested on charges of seeking to revive the Muslim Brotherhood, shortly after the proscribed organization had issued a statement denouncing the Government's decision to extend the state of emergency for a further three years. In March, none the less, between 500 and 1,000 Islamists, mostly members of Jama'ah al-Islamiyah or Islamic Jihad, were reportedly released from prison; a further 500 Islamists were freed in July. Despite regular releases of large numbers of militants since 1998, human rights organizations maintained that more than 15,000 remained in detention, many of whom were being held without charge under the country's emergency laws. Furthermore, during the approach to the 2000 legislative elections the authorities arrested increasing numbers of Muslim Brotherhood members, in what was widely acknowledged as an effort to prevent their standing as candidates for the People's Assembly. In mid-November the Higher Military Court in Cairo pronounced guilty verdicts on 15 of those arrested in late 1999 on charges of reviving the Brotherhood, sentencing them to between three and five years' imprisonment; the five other defendants were acquitted.

President Mubarak was swift to condemn the suicide attacks on New York and Washington, DC, of 11 September 2001. Several members of Egyptian Islamic Jihad were alleged to have assumed significant roles in the suicide attacks, held to have been perpetrated by the militant Islamist al-Qa'ida (Base) organization of Osama bin Laden. Ayman az-Zawahri, said to be one of bin Laden's closest associates, was presumed responsible for the organization of the attacks, and another Egyptian, Muhammad Atef, who was reportedly killed by US forces in Afghanistan in November, was, according to US intelligence, believed to have had the role of al-Qa'ida's chief military planner. Furthermore, an Egyptian national was suspected of having piloted one of the hijacked aircraft that hit the World Trade Center in New York. Following the events of 11 September more than 260 suspected Islamists were arrested in Egypt, and arrests Islamists continued on a large scale in mid-2002. In August 16 members of the Muslim Brotherhood were sentenced to terms of imprisonment ranging from three to five years after being convicted of inciting demonstrations against the Government. In the following month 51 militants, who had initially been arrested in May 2001, were sentenced to up to 15 years' imprisonment for conspiring to overthrow the Government.

In August 2002, meanwhile, a number of imprisoned senior members of Jama'ah al-Islamiyah reiterated their commitment to the cease-fire declared in 1998 and announced, in a series of interviews published in the weekly *al-Mussawar*, that they had completely renounced violence.

Egyptian mediation was prominent in the Middle East peace process throughout the 1990s. The country played an important role in the efforts leading to the convening of the Middle East peace conference in Madrid, Spain, in October 1991, and an Egyptian delegation attended the first, symbolic session of the conference. Egyptian mediators were influential in the secret negotiations between Israel and the PLO that led to the signing of the Declaration of Principles on Palestinian Self-Rule in September 1993, and PLO and Israeli delegations subsequently began to meet regularly in Cairo or at the Red Sea port of Taba to discuss the detailed implementation of the Declaration of Principles. In May 1994 an agreement on Palestinian self-rule in the Gaza Strip and the Jericho area (for full details, see the chapter on Israel) was signed in Cairo by the Israeli Prime Minister, Itzhak Rabin, and the PLO Chairman, Yasser Arafat, at a ceremony presided over by Mubarak. However, despite an official visit to Egypt by President Ezer Weizman in December (the first such visit by an Israeli Head of State), relations between Egypt and Israel began to deteriorate. Egypt hosted summit meetings of Arab leaders in December 1994 and February 1995, prompting censure from the Israeli Government, and further tension arose when Mubarak reiterated his warning that Egypt would not sign the Treaty on the Non-Proliferation of Nuclear Weapons (or Non-Proliferation Treaty—NPT, see p. 82), which was due for renewal in April 1995, unless Israel also agreed to sign it; he urged other states to do likewise. In March 1995 Israel offered to sign the NPT once it had concluded peace treaties with all of the Arab states and with Iran, and to allow Egypt to inspect its research nuclear reactor at Nahal Shorek (but not the nuclear facility at Dimona). Egypt rejected both offers, but adopted a more conciliatory line on the issue. Meanwhile, Egypt's stance with regard to the NPT antagonized the USA, which insisted that the continuation of US aid to Egypt depended on Egypt's signing the Treaty.

President Mubarak made his first visit to Jordan since the Gulf crisis in January 1995, when he met King Hussein at Aqaba. The visit was regarded as a sign of an improvement in relations between the two countries, following Jordan's signing of a peace treaty with Israel in July 1994.

Egypt continued its mediatory role in the complex negotiations that eventually led to the signing, in Washington, DC, of the Israeli-Palestinian Interim Agreement on the West Bank and the Gaza Strip in September 1995. In November Mubarak made his first presidential visit to Israel to attend the funeral of the assassinated Israeli Prime Minister, Itzhak Rabin. Egypt also participated in meetings leading to the resumption of peace negotiations between Israel and Syria at the end of 1995. In March 1996, following a series of Palestinian suicide bomb attacks in Israel, Egypt and the USA co-hosted a one-day 'Summit of Peacemakers' at the Red Sea resort of Sharm esh-Sheikh. Egypt's relations with Israel deteriorated again in April, as a consequence of Israeli military operations in Lebanon (q.v.). In June, in response to the apparently rejectionist stance of the new Israeli administration of Binyamin Netanyahu with regard to the exchange of land for peace, Mubarak convened an emergency summit meeting of the Arab League in Cairo—the first such meeting for six years. The summit's final communiqué reaffirmed the Arab states' commitment to peace, but warned that peace and any further *rapprochement* between them and Israel depended on Israel's returning all the Arab land that it occupied in 1967. The Arab League again met in emergency session in Cairo in September 1996, in response to a serious deterioration in Palestinian–Israeli relations. In March 1997 Egypt, in common with the other Arab League members, condemned the Israeli Government for ordering the start of construction work on the new Israeli settlement of Har Homa in East Jerusalem.

President Mubarak cautiously welcomed the Wye River Memorandum signed by Netanyahu and Arafat in October 1998 (see the chapter on Israel). However, in January 1999 Egypt suspended all contacts with the Israeli Government over its decision to suspend the implementation of the agreement. In March Egypt and Jordan made a joint declaration in support of the Palestinians' right to declare an independent state after the scheduled expiry of the Oslo accords in May. Subsequently, however, owing to an increasingly volatile security situation in the Israeli-Occupied Territories and in view of the forthcoming Israeli general election, Egypt and Jordan joined other countries in urging Yasser Arafat to postpone his planned declaration of statehood. The election, in May, of the leader of the One Israel alliance, Ehud Barak, to the Israeli premiership was generally welcomed in Egypt, but in July the Egyptian Minister of Foreign Affairs emphasized that there could be no normalization of Egyptian–Israeli relations prior to the resumption of compre-

hensive peace talks. Egyptian mediation was subsequently influential in discussions between Israeli and Palestinian negotiators that led to the signing of the Sharm esh-Sheikh Memorandum by Barak and Arafat in September 1999 (see the chapter on Israel).

In February 2000 Mubarak made his first ever visit to Lebanon. The main purpose of the visit was to demonstrate Egypt's solidarity with Lebanon following Israeli air attacks, condemned by Mubarak as 'criminal acts', on targets in Lebanon earlier in the month. None the less, Egypt continued to play an important role in the peace process during 2000. In March Arafat and Barak attended a summit meeting in Sharm esh-Sheikh, at which the two leaders agreed a formula for the resumption of peace talks, and Barak and Arafat both made brief visits to Cairo prior to the US-hosted summit at Camp David in July. Following the apparent failure of the summit, Mubarak emphasized that he would not pressure Arafat to make concessions regarding the central issue of the status of Jerusalem, and urged all Arab states to unite in support of the Palestinians until they regained all their legitimate rights in accordance with the pertinent UN resolutions.

Following the outbreak in Jerusalem in late September 2000 of violent clashes between Palestinians and Israeli security forces, which swiftly spread throughout the West Bank and Gaza, Mubarak assumed an important role in attempting to prevent the violence from escalating into a major regional crisis. Most notably, in mid-October, following mediation by UN Secretary-General Kofi Annan, Barak and Arafat agreed to lead delegations to a summit meeting at Sharm esh-Sheikh, brokered by US President Bill Clinton. Two days of intensive negotiations resulted in an agreement on the establishment of a fact-finding committee to investigate the causes of what had become known as the al-Aqsa *intifada*, but a tentative truce as part of the 'understanding' reached proved unviable and violence persisted. Later that month an emergency meeting of Heads of State of Arab League countries was convened in Cairo, at which Arab leaders held Israel solely to blame for the violence. In late November Egypt recalled its ambassador to Tel-Aviv, denouncing Israel's 'escalation of aggression and deliberate use of force against the Palestinian people'. Relations between the two countries deteriorated further at the end of that month when an Egyptian engineer, Sherif Filali, was charged with having gathered information regarding Egyptian economic and military projects for the Israeli overseas intelligence service. In mid-June 2001 Filali was acquitted of the charges by the State Security Court; however, in September President Mubarak invoked emergency legislation to reverse the acquittal and ordered a retrial. In March 2002 Filali was convicted of providing information to Israel with the intent of harming Egypt's national interests, and was sentenced to 15 years' imprisonment with hard labour.

In the approach to the premiership election scheduled to take place in Israel in February 2001, Mubarak and outgoing US President Clinton intensified their diplomatic attempts to secure an accommodation between Israel and the Palestinians ahead of the expected electoral victory of the right-wing Likud leader, Ariel Sharon. Following his election, it was alleged that Sharon had requested that the USA decrease military assistance to Egypt. Mubarak subsequently warned Sharon that he would interpret any such demand as a 'hostile action' and that it would significantly alter Egypt's attitude towards Israel. Nevertheless, at an Arab League summit on the Palestinian situation, held in Jordan in late March, Mubarak deflected demands (as he had at the Cairo emergency summit in October 2000) from more radical Arab states that Egypt and Jordan should sever diplomatic relations with Israel entirely. In April 2001 a joint Egyptian-Jordanian peace plan urged an immediate halt to Israeli construction of settlements and a withdrawal of Israeli forces to pre-*intifada* positions. The plan was supported by the new US Republican Administration of President George W. Bush, the European Union and the Arab world; however, Mubarak's claim, following a meeting in Cairo in late April with the Israeli Deputy Prime Minister and Minister of Foreign Affairs, Shimon Peres, to have secured the agreement of both Israel and the Palestinians to the Egyptian-Jordanian proposal proved premature, and diplomatic progress stalled as violence continued to escalate in subsequent months. At an emergency meeting of Arab League ministers of foreign affairs in Cairo in mid-May it was agreed to suspend all political contacts with Israel until its attacks on Palestinians halted. In early September Mubarak and King Abdullah of Jordan met to discuss the situation in the region, but their attempts to arrange talks between Peres and Arafat were unsuccessful. In December Egypt and Syria issued a joint condemnation of the conduct of Israel's military forces in the Palestinian territories following the escalation of violence there in that month. Egypt suspended all non-diplomatic contacts with Israel in April 2002, and in the same month Mubarak demanded Israel's immediate and unconditional withdrawal from the West Bank.

In mid-July 2002, following an Israeli air force attack on Gaza City, which resulted in the death of a senior Hamas military figure and a further 15 civilians, including nine children, Mubarak denounced the actions of the Israeli military and accused Sharon of deliberately ordering the attacks in order to sabotage Palestinian peace efforts. Earlier that month Mubarak had emphasized that he would not support calls from Israel and the USA to press for the removal of Arafat from power. During late 2002 and early 2003 Egypt hosted a number of meetings between the main Palestinian factions, although optimism that militant groups would agree to cease attacks within Israeli territory for a period of one year proved unfounded.

Although the USA announced in April 1996 that it would supply advanced military equipment to Egypt, including 21 F-16 fighter aircraft, in acknowledgement of the country's key role in the Middle East peace process, there have remained frequent tensions in relations between Egypt and the USA. In August 1998 Egypt was highly critical of US military air-strikes against targets in Afghanistan and Sudan held by the US administration to be associated with Osama bin Laden. Tensions were further exacerbated by the air-strikes undertaken against Iraq by US and British forces in December 1998, since Mubarak had consistently urged a diplomatic solution to the issue of weapons inspections. Differences persisted as the US Secretary of Defense, William Cohen, visited Cairo and other regional capitals in March 1999 to seek support for a renewed air campaign against Iraq. While in Egypt Cohen agreed to supply Egypt with US $3,200m. of US defence equipment, including a further 24 F-16 fighter aircraft. Following a further visit by Cohen, it was announced in April 2000 that the USA would supply short-range missiles in order to modernize Egypt's air-defence system. Meanwhile, Mubarak visited Washington in June 1999 and the two countries made significant progress on proposals for the resumption of Middle East peace talks, culminating in the signing of the Sharm esh-Sheikh Memorandum in September. In late 2000 the Egyptian and US leaders co-operated closely in their efforts to mediate in the Middle East crisis (see above). During a visit to the USA in early April 2001 President Mubarak met with President George W. Bush for the first time and urged the USA actively to support the Egyptian-Jordanian peace plan (see above). Meanwhile, Bush, who had indicated that Iraq would be his Administration's priority in terms of Middle East policy, expressed his unease at Egypt's lack of support for international sanctions against Saddam Hussain; he also urged Egypt to return its ambassador to Israel. Meanwhile, Mubarak was among Arab leaders to urge that the US-led military campaign against al-Qa'ida and the Taliban regime in Afghanistan should not be extended to target any Arab state. Relations between Egypt and the USA deteriorated in mid-2002 following the imprisonment of Sa'adeddin Ibrahim (see above) and the subsequent announcement by the Bush Administration that it would suspend any additional foreign aid to Egypt in protest at what it considered to be the country's poor treatment of pro-democracy campaigners and human rights organizations. It was emphasized, however, that existing aid programmes would not be affected (the USA provides Egypt with annual assistance worth some US $2,000m.). Bilateral relations were further strained in late September after David Welch, the US ambassador to Egypt, writing in the daily *al-Ahram*, criticized a number of Egyptian publications for suggesting that al-Qa'ida had not been responsible for the previous year's attacks on the mainland USA. Welch was subsequently declared *persona non grata* in a widely published open letter signed by a number of prominent Egyptian intellectuals.

As the likelihood of a US-led military campaign to oust the Iraqi regime of Saddam Hussain increased during the second half of 2002, President Mubarak was one of a number of Arab leaders who expressed their concern at the effects of military intervention in Iraq on the Middle East as a whole, as well as its implications for the unity of Iraq. In August he stated that he did not believe that a single Arab state supported military action against Iraq. In September Mubarak received the Iraqi Minister of Foreign Affairs and requested that Iraq comply with pertinent

UN resolutions and allow UN weapons inspectors to operate freely within the country. However, a series of Arab League meetings in early 2003 served to highlight the deepening divisions over the issue among Arab states.

Following the commencement of US-led hostilities against the Iraqi regime in mid-March 2003, there were a number of anti-war demonstrations in Cairo; these were suppressed by security forces and resulted in the arrest of some 800 protesters.

Egypt's relations with Libya improved steadily during the 1990s, and Egypt joined the Community of Sahel-Saharan States (CEN-SAD, see p. 339), which was established in Tripoli in 1997. Meanwhile, bilateral links were dominated by the repercussions of the Lockerbie bombing (see the chapter on Libya), with Egypt actively seeking to avert a confrontation between Libya and the USA and its Western allies. Following the suspension of UN sanctions against Libya in April 1999, the national carrier, EgyptAir, resumed regular flights to Tripoli in July 2000; Libyan air services to Egypt resumed later that month.

Egypt has a long-standing border dispute with Sudan concerning the so-called Halaib triangle. Relations deteriorated sharply in mid-1995, after Egypt accused Sudan of complicity in the attempted assassination of President Mubarak in Addis Ababa (see above). Egypt strengthened its control of the Halaib triangle, and subsequently (in contravention of a bilateral agreement concluded in 1978) imposed visa and permit requirements on Sudanese nationals visiting or resident in Egypt. In September 1995 the OAU accused Sudan of direct involvement in the assassination attempt, and in December the organization demanded that Sudan extradite immediately three individuals sought in connection with the attack. (It was reported in mid-1999 that one of the suspects had been extradited to Cairo.) In February 1996 the Sudanese authorities introduced permit requirements for Egyptian nationals resident in Sudan. President Mubarak met with his Sudanese counterpart, Omar al-Bashir, at the Arab League summit meeting in Cairo in May. In July, however, Egypt accused Sudan of harbouring Egyptian terrorists, contrary to an agreement concluded at the summit meeting. None the less, Egypt opposed the imposition by the UN of more stringent economic sanctions against Sudan (q.v.), on the grounds that they would harm the Sudanese people more than the regime. Bilateral security talks recommenced in August 1997 after a year-long suspension. In February 1998 river transport resumed between the Egyptian port of Aswan and Wadi Halfa in Sudan, and in April the two countries agreed to establish a joint ministerial committee (involving the Ministers of Higher Education, Defence and Irrigation). Although Sudan considered the presence of Sudanese opposition leaders in Egypt an obstacle to the normalization process, a meeting in Cairo, in May 1999, between representatives of the Sudanese Government and Sudan's former President Gaafar Mohammed Nimeri, to discuss arrangements for his return from exile, represented significant progress on this issue. In December Egypt and Sudan agreed to a full normalization of relations, and resolved to co-operate in addressing their border dispute. Taking up his post in Khartoum in March 2000, the new Egyptian ambassador to Sudan expressed optimism regarding the future of diplomatic relations between the two countries. In September the two countries signed a number of bilateral co-operation accords.

Government

Legislative power is held by the unicameral Majlis ash-Sha'ab (People's Assembly), which has 454 members: 10 nominated by the President and 444 directly elected for five years from 222 constituencies. The Assembly nominates the President, who is elected by popular referendum for six years (renewable). The President, who is Head of State, has executive powers and appoints one or more Vice-Presidents, a Prime Minister and a Council of Ministers. There is also a 210-member advisory body, the Shura Council. The country is divided into 27 governorates.

Defence

In August 2002 Egypt had total armed forces of 443,000 (army 320,000, air defence command 75,000, navy an estimated 19,000, air force 29,000), with 254,000 reserves. There is a selective three-year period of national service. Budgeted defence expenditure for 2001 was forecast at £E7,900m.

Economic Affairs

In 2001, according to estimates by the World Bank, Egypt's gross national income (GNI), measured at average 1999–2001 prices, was US $99,406m., equivalent to $1,530 per head (or $3,790 per head on an international purchasing-power parity basis). During 1990–2001, it was estimated, the population increased at an average annual rate of 2.0%, while gross domestic product (GDP) per head increased, in real terms, by 2.3% per year. Overall GDP increased, in real terms, at an annual average rate of 4.3% in 1990–2001. At factor cost, real GDP increased by 7.0% in the year ending 30 June 2001.

Agriculture (including forestry and fishing) contributed an estimated 16.8% of GDP in 2001/02, and employed an estimated 32.6% of the economically active population in 2001. The principal crops include sugar cane, maize, tomatoes and wheat. Exports of food and live animals accounted for 7.9% of total exports in 1999. During 1990–2000 agricultural GDP increased at an average annual rate of 3.1%. Agricultural GDP grew by 3.3% in 2000/01 and by an estimated 3.4% in 2001/02.

Industry (including mining, manufacturing, construction and power) engaged 22.6% of the employed labour force in 1999, and provided an estimated 33.0% of GDP in 2001/02. During 1990–2000 industrial GDP expanded at an average annual rate of 6.1%. Industrial GDP increased by 1.4% in 2000/01 and by an estimated 3.7% in 2001/02.

Mining and manufacturing (excluding hydrocarbons) together contributed an estimated 19.2% of GDP in 2001/02. Egypt's mineral resources include petroleum, natural gas, phosphates, manganese, uranium, coal, iron ore and gold. Although the mining sector employed only 0.3% of the working population in 1999, the petroleum industry contributed an estimated 7.7% of GDP in 2001/02, and petroleum and petroleum products accounted for 36.0% of total export earnings in 1999. Petroleum production averaged an estimated 758,000 barrels per day in 2001, and at the end of that year Egypt's oil reserves were estimated to total 2,900m. barrels (sufficient to sustain production at 2001 levels for a little over 11 years). At the end of 2001 Egypt's proven natural gas reserves totalled 1,000,000m. cu m, sustainable for almost 48 years at constant production levels (totalling 21,000m. cu m in 2001). In 2000 all the natural gas produced was consumed domestically, but the Government planned to begin exporting by 2003.

Manufacturing engaged 13.2% of the employed labour force in 1999. Based on the value of output, the main branches of manufacturing in 1997 were food products (accounting for 19.6% of the total), petroleum refining (15.4%), chemicals (12.4%), textiles (12.2%), metals and metal products (9.3%) and non-metallic mineral manufactures (7.6%). During 1990–2000 the real GDP of the manufacturing sector increased by an average of 6.3% per year. The combined GDP of the mining and manufacturing sectors expanded by 4.5% in 2000/01 and by an estimated 4.2% in 2001/02.

Energy is derived principally from natural gas (which provided 49.1% of total electricity output in 1999), petroleum (28.6%) and hydroelectric power (22.3%). In 1998 fuel imports accounted for about an estimated 6.1% of the value of merchandise imports.

Services contributed 50.2% of GDP in 2001/02, and employed 48.7% of the working population in 1998. By the late 1980s tourism had become one of the most dynamic sectors of the Egyptian economy. For much of the 1990s, however, the sector was severely undermined by the campaign of violence aimed by fundamentalist Islamists at tourist targets, and visitor numbers and tourism revenues declined significantly. By 1999, however, there were signs of a recovery in the sector, although this was reversed as a result of the regional insecurity arising from the violence between Israel and the Palestinians from the latter part of 2000 and also as a consequence of the terrorist attacks against the USA in September 2001. In 1990–2000 the real GDP of the services sector increased by an average of 3.7% per year. Services GDP increased by 4.5% in 2000/01 and by 2.7% in 2001/02.

In 2001 Egypt recorded a visible trade deficit of US $6,935m., while there was a deficit of $388m. on the current account of the balance of payments. In 1999 the principal source of imports (14.4%) was the USA; other major suppliers were Germany, Italy and France. The USA was also the principal market for exports (12.4%), followed by Italy (11.2%), the Netherlands, Israel, and India. Egypt's principal exports in 1999 were petroleum and petroleum products, basic manufactures, clothing, food and live animals and chemicals. The principal imports were machinery and transport equipment, food and live animals, basic manufactures and chemicals.

For the financial year 2000/01 there was a projected deficit of £E13,761m. in the state public budget (equivalent to 4.5% of

GDP). Egypt's external debt totalled US $28,957m. at the end of 2000, of which $24,279m. was long-term public debt. In that year the cost of servicing the foreign debt was equivalent to 8.4% of the value of exports of goods and services. The annual rate of inflation averaged 7.8% in 1990–2001. Consumer prices increased by an average of 2.7% in 2000, and by 2.2% in 2001. An estimated 9.0% of the total labour force were unemployed in mid-2002.

Egypt is a member of the Common Market for Eastern and Southern Africa (COMESA, see p. 162), the Council of Arab Economic Unity (see p. 178), the Organization of Arab Petroleum Exporting Countries (OAPEC, see p. 292), the African Petroleum Producers' Association (see p. 335), and the Co-operation Council for the Arab States of the Gulf (Arab Co-operation Council, see p. 175).

Following an impressive macro-economic performance during much of the 1990s, which resulted in strong GDP growth and low inflation, Egypt's economy suffered a series of major reverses from the late 1990s. A serious liquidity crisis during 1999 and early 2000, resulting primarily from a depletion in the main sources of hard currency (principally petroleum sales, tourism and Suez Canal revenues), prompted intervention by the Government and the Central Bank in mid-2000. The Egyptian pound's fixed exchange rate against the US dollar was informally abandoned, and in January 2001, under a series of fiscal reforms, control over the exchange rate was transferred to the Central Bank, which introduced a 'managed peg' system. Nevertheless, in 2001 the pound was devalued on a further three occasions, largely in an attempt to offset the effects of the loss of income from tourism in the aftermath of the suicide attacks against the USA in September, and in January 2003, in anticipation of further economic difficulties resulting from a likely US-led military campaign against the regime of Saddam Hussain in Iraq, the Government abandoned the pound's peg to the US dollar and allowed the currency to float freely. Meanwhile, the major reduction in tourism revenue after September 2001 resulted in a sharp decrease in the country's foreign reserves, although the effect on Egypt's balance of payments was not as adverse as had initially been feared, and government appeals to foreign donors in early 2002 for assistance were retracted later that year. None the less, growth slowed to 3.0% in the 2001/02 financial year. An increase of some 18% was recorded in the rate of unemployment in 2002, and Egypt's external debt amounted to an estimated 38% of GDP in that year. Resilience to regional instability was expected to be weak, and requests for emergency assistance from both the USA and the World Bank were made in early 2003 in order to offset negative economic repercussions from the conflict in Iraq.

Education

Education at all levels is available free of charge, and is officially compulsory for eight years between six and 14 years of age. Primary education, beginning at six years of age, lasts for five years. Secondary education, from 11 years of age, lasts for a further six years, comprising two cycles (the first being preparatory) of three years each. In 1997 total enrolment at primary and secondary schools was equivalent to 89% of the school-age population (males 94%; females 83%). In 1996 primary enrolment included 93% of children in the relevant age-group (males 98%; females 88%), while the comparable ratio for secondary enrolment was 67% (males 71%; females 64%). There are 14 universities. The Al-Azhar University and its various preparatory and associated institutes provide instruction and training in various disciplines, with emphasis on adherence to Islamic principles and teachings. Budget forecasts for 2000/01 allocated £E18,100m. (some 16.2% of total expenditure) to education.

Public Holidays

2003: 1 January (New Year), 12 February* (Id al-Adha, Feast of the Sacrifice), 5 March* (Muharram, Islamic New Year), 25 April (Sinai Day), 28 April (Sham an-Nessim, Coptic Easter Monday), 14 May* (Mouloud/Yum an-Nabi, Birth of Muhammad), 23 July (Revolution Day), 24 September* (Leilat al-Meiraj, Ascension of Muhammad), 6 October (Armed Forces Day), 24 October (Popular Resistance Day), 26 November* (Id al-Fitr, end of Ramadan), 23 December (Victory Day).

2004: 1 January (New Year), 2 February* (Id al-Adha, Feast of the Sacrifice), 22 February* (Muharram, Islamic New Year), 12 April (Sham an-Nessim, Coptic Easter Monday), 25 April (Sinai Day), 2 May* (Mouloud/Yum an-Nabi, Birth of Muhammad), 23 July (Revolution Day), 12 September* (Leilat al-Meiraj, Ascension of Muhammad), 6 October (Armed Forces Day), 24 October

(Popular Resistance Day), 14 November* (Id al-Fitr, end of Ramadan), 23 December (Victory Day).

*These holidays are dependent on the Islamic lunar calendar and may vary by one or two days from the dates given.

Coptic Christian holidays include: Christmas (7 January), Palm Sunday and Easter Sunday.

Weights and Measures

The metric system is in force, but some Egyptian measurements are still in use.

Statistical Survey

Sources (unless otherwise stated): Central Agency for Public Mobilization and Statistics, POB 2086, Cairo (Nasr City); tel. (2) 4024632; fax (2) 4024099; internet www.capmas.gov.eg; Research Department, National Bank of Egypt, Cairo.

Area and Population

AREA, POPULATION AND DENSITY

Area (sq km)	1,002,000*
Population (census results)†	
17–18 November 1986	48,254,238
31 December 1996	
Males	30,351,390
Females	28,961,524
Total	59,312,914
Population (official estimates at mid-year)	
2001	67,886,000
Density (per sq km) at mid-2001	67.8

* 386,874 sq miles. Inhabited and cultivated territory accounts for 55,039 sq km (21,251 sq miles).

† Excluding Egyptian nationals abroad, totalling an estimated 2,250,000 in 1986 and an estimated 2,180,000 in 1996.

GOVERNORATES

(estimated population at 1 January 2002)

Governorate	Area (sq km)*	Population ('000)	Density (per sq km)	Capital
Cairo	214.20	7,388	34,491.1	Cairo
Alexandria . . .	2,679.36	3,632	1,355.5	Alexandria
Port Said. . .	72.07	515	7,145.8	Port Said
Ismailia . . .	1,441.59	808	560.5	Ismailia
Suez	17,840.42	461	25.8	Suez
Damietta. . . .	589.17	1,015	1,772.8	Damietta
Dakahlia. . .	3,470.90	4,657	1,341.7	El-Mansoura
Sharkia . . .	4,179.55	4,798	1,148.0	Zagazig
Kalyoubia . . .	1,001.09	3,658	3,654.0	Banha
Kafr esh-Sheikh .	3,437.12	2,448	712.2	Kafr esh-Sheikh
Gharbia . . .	1,942.21	3,725	1,917.9	Tanta
Menoufia. . .	1,532.13	3,054	1,993.3	Shebien el-Kom
Behera . . .	10,129.48	4,428	437.1	Damanhour
Giza	85,153.56	5,319	62.5	Giza
Beni-Suef . . .	1,321.50	2,112	1,598.2	Beni-Suef
Fayoum . . .	1,827.10	2,264	1,239.1	El-Fayoum
Menia . . .	2,261.70	3,781	1,671.8	El-Menia
Asyout . . .	1,553.00	3,201	2,061.2	Asyout
Suhag . . .	1,547.20	3,569	2,306.7	Suhag
Qena	1,795.60	2,761	1,537.6	Qena
Luxor. . . .	55.00	400	7,272.7	Luxor
Aswan . . .	678.45	1,060	1,562.4	Aswan
Red Sea . . .	203,685.00	176	0.9	Hurghada
El-Wadi el-Gidid .	376,505.00	160	0.4	El-Kharga
Matruh . . .	212,112.00	247	1.2	Matruh
North Sinai . .	27,574.00	288	10.4	El-Areesh
South Sinai . .	33,140.00	61	1.8	Et-Tour

* The sum of these figures is 997,738.40 sq km, compared with the official national total of 1,002,000 sq km.

PRINCIPAL TOWNS

(population at 1996 census)*

Cairo (Al-Qahirah the capital). .	6,789,479	Asyout (Asyut) . .	343,498
		Zagazig (Az-Zaqaziq)	267,351
Alexandria (Al-Iskandariyah) . .	3,328,196	El-Fayum (Al-Fayyum) . . .	260,964
Giza (Al-Jizah) . .	2,221,868	Ismailia (Al-Ismailiyah). . .	254,477
Shoubra el-Kheima (Shubra al-Khaymah) . .	870,716	Kafr ed-Dawar (Kafr ad-Dawwar) . .	231,978
		Aswan	219,017
Port Said (Bur Sa'id)	469,533	Damanhour (Damanhur) . .	212,203
Suez (As-Suways) .	417,610	El-Menia (Al-Minya)	201,360
El-Mahalla el-Koubra (Al-Mahallah al-Kubra) . .	395,402	Beni-Suef (Bani-Suwayf). . .	172,032
Tanta	371,010	Qena (Qina) . . .	171,275
El-Mansoura (Al-Mansurah). . .	369,621	Suhag (Sawhaj) . .	170,125
Luxor (Al-Uqsor). .	360,503	Shebien el-Kom (Shibin al-Kawn) .	159,909

* Figures refer to provisional population. Revised figures include: Cairo 6,800,992; Alexandria 3,339,076; Port Said 472,335; Suez 417,527.

BIRTHS, MARRIAGES AND DEATHS

	Registered live births		Registered marriages		Registered deaths	
	Number	Rate (per 1,000)	Number	Rate (per 1,000)	Number	Rate (per 1,000)
1994 .	1,636,000	29.0	452,000	8.0	388,000	6.9
1995 .	1,605,000	27.9	471,000	8.2	385,000	6.7
1996 .	1,662,000	28.3	489,000	8.3	380,000	6.5
1997 .	1,655,000	27.5	493,000	8.2	389,000	6.5
1998 .	1,687,000	27.5	504,000	8.2	399,000	6.5
1999 .	1,693,000	27.0	520,000	8.3	401,000	6.4
2000 .	1,734,000	27.1	579,000	9.1	403,000	6.3
2001* .	1,744,000	26.7	513,000	7.9	410,000	6.3

* Provisional figures.

Expectation of life (WHO estimates, years at birth): 66.5 (males 65.3; females 67.8) in 2001 (Source: WHO, *World Health Report*).

ECONOMICALLY ACTIVE POPULATION

(sample surveys, '000 persons aged 15 years and over)

	1997	1998	1999
Agriculture, hunting and forestry	4,860.0	4,723.1	4,684.4
Fishing	90.9	99.6	122.6
Mining and quarrying	42.0	69.0	47.4
Manufacturing	2,133.5	2,042.2	2,207.6
Electricity, gas and water supply	192.7	203.4	207.0
Construction	1,152.9	1,287.1	1,320.1
Wholesale and retail trade; repair of motor vehicles, motorcycles and personal and household goods	1,745.8	1,949.9	2,020.2
Hotels and restaurants	217.1	277.0	299.6
Transport, storage and communications	923.2	954.1	1,060.2
Financial intermediation	180.0	174.3	185.2
Real estate, renting and business activities	207.0	266.2	273.0
Public administration and defence; compulsory social security	1,565.3	1,628.6	1,631.7
Education	1,715.1	1,665.2	1,764.5
Health and social work	410.4	485.8	531.1
Other community, social and personal service activities	304.4	316.3	356.5
Private households with employed persons	39.5	40.3	38.0
Activities not adequately defined	50.1	1.2	0.9
Total employed	15,830.0	16,183.0	16,750.2
Unemployed	1,446.4	1,447.5	1,480.5
Total labour force	17,276.4	17,630.5	18,230.7
Males	13,514.5	13,890.0	14,337.2
Females	3,761.9	3,740.5	3,893.5

Source: ILO, *Yearbook of Labour Statistics*.

Health and Welfare

KEY INDICATORS

Total fertility rate (children per woman, 2001)	3.0
Under-5 mortality rate (per 1,000 live births, 2001)	41
HIV/AIDS (% of persons aged 15–49, 2001)	0.10
Physicians (per 1,000 head, 1996)	20.2
Hospital beds (per 1,000 head, 1997)	2.1
Health expenditure (2000): US $ per head (PPP)	138
Health expenditure (2000): % of GDP	3.8
Health expenditure (2000): public (% of total)	46.1
Access to water (% of persons, 2000)	95
Access to sanitation (% of persons, 2000)	94
Human Development Index (2000): ranking	115
Human Development Index (2000): value	0.642

For sources and definitions, see explanatory note on p. vi.

Agriculture

PRINCIPAL CROPS

('000 metric tons)

	1999	2000	2001
Wheat	6,346.6	6,564.1	6,254.6
Rice (paddy)	5,817.0	6,000.5	5,226.7
Barley	114.0	99.4	93.9
Maize	6,143.4	6,474.5	6,842.3
Sorghum	954.2	941.2	862.3
Potatoes	1,808.9	1,769.9	1,903.1
Sweet potatoes	253.1	249.5	314.7
Taro (Coco yam)	47.1	42.4	44.6
Sugar cane	15,253.6	15,705.8	15,571.5
Sugar beet	2,559.7	2,890.4	2,857.7
Dry broad beans	307.1	353.9	439.5
Other pulses*	72.1	71.1	76.7
Groundnuts (in shell)	180.8	187.2	205.1
Olives	287.1	281.7	293.9
Cottonseed	367.6	329.5	367.6
Cabbages	497.9	564.0	562.4
Artichokes	43.8	88.0	65.3
Lettuce	159.6	174.6	179.6
Tomatoes	6,273.8	6,785.6	6,328.7
Cauliflowers	110.8	109.8	109.9
Pumpkins, squash and gourds	648.8	719.1	706.8
Cucumbers and gherkins	260.0*	260.0*	355.3
Aubergines (Eggplants)	562.0*	565.0*	703.1
Chillies and green peppers	388.1	428.1	386.7
Dry onions	889.8	763.0	628.4
Garlic	224.1	266.6	215.4
Green beans	200.0	201.6	214.9
Green peas	189.1	340.0	227.1
Carrots	122.1	128.2	111.2
Okra*	76.0	76.0	85.2
Other vegetables*	498.7	502.5	499.9
Bananas	729.0	760.5	849.3
Oranges	1,636.6	1,610.5	1,696.3
Tangerines, mandarins, clementines and satsumas	511.8	481.2	564.9
Lemons and limes	278.6	274.5	296.3
Apples	415.6	468.3	473.6
Peaches and nectarines	301.2	240.2	224.2
Strawberries	53.7	70.7	68.1
Grapes	1,009.6	1,075.1	1,078.9
Watermelons	1,670.3	1,785.1	1,446.9
Cantaloupes and other melons	773.6	850.0*	856.5
Figs	203.0	187.7	122.9
Mangoes	287.2	298.9	325.5
Dates	906.0	1,006.7	1,113.3
Other fruits and berries*	459.2	491.7	491.0
Cotton (lint)	233.1	228.0	228.0

* FAO estimate(s).

Source: FAO.

LIVESTOCK

('000 head, year ending September)

	1999	2000	2001
Cattle	3,417.6	3,529.7	3,801.1
Buffaloes	3,329.7	3,379.4	3,532.2*
Sheep	4,390.7	4,469.1	4,671.2
Goats	3,308.2	3,424.8	3,466.8
Pigs	29.0	29.5	29.5
Horses*	45.5	45.7	45.7
Asses*	3,000.0	3,050.0	3,050.0
Camels*	116.0	120.0	120.0
Rabbits*	9,200.0	9,250.0	9,250.0
Chickens*	87,000.0	88,000.0	88,000.0
Ducks*	9,200.0	9,200.0	9,200.0
Geese*	9,000.0	9,100.0	9,100.0
Turkeys*	1,800.0	1,850.0	1,850.0

* FAO estimate(s).

Source: FAO.

LIVESTOCK PRODUCTS

('000 metric tons)

	1999	2000	2001
Beef and veal	232.8	2.55.6*	246.8*
Buffalo meat	277.0	302.0*	306.0*
Mutton and lamb.	82.3	85.3*	85.3*
Goat meat	30.4	32.3*	32.7*
Pig meat*	3.0	3.0	3.0
Camel meat	33.6	36.5*	36.5*
Rabbit meat*	69.3	69.6	69.8
Poultry meat	591.1	620.4	646.6
Other meat*	9.7	9.9	9.9
Cows' milk	1,596.9	1,638.4	1,679.4
Buffaloes' milk	2,018.2	2,030.3	2,050.6*
Sheep's milk	93.0	93.0	93.0
Goats' milk*	15.0	15.0	15.0
Butter	96.1	96.7	96.7*
Cheese	464.3	466.0	467.5*
Hen eggs	168.3	176.7	199.6*
Honey	8.1	8.3	8.5
Wool: greasy	7.2	7.4	7.6
Wool: scoured*	3.3	3.4	3.5
Cattle hides*	27.4	30.0	28.8
Buffalo hides*	24.0	26.1	26.6
Sheepskins*	8.6	8.9	9.0
Goatskins	4.3	4.4*	4.6*

* FAO estimate(s).

Source: FAO.

Forestry

ROUNDWOOD REMOVALS

(FAO estimates, '000 cubic metres, excluding bark)

	1999	2000	2001
Industrial wood	134	134	134
Fuel wood	16,024	16,182	16,332
Total	16,176	16,316	16,466

Source: FAO.

SAWNWOOD PRODUCTION

('000 cubic metres, incl. railway sleepers)

	1999	2000	2001
Total	4	4	4*

* FAO estimate.
Source: FAO.

Fishing

('000 metric tons, live weight)

	1998	1999	2000
Capture	365.6	380.5	384.3
Grass carp	4.2	0.7	12.8
Nile tilapia	128.4	112.8	131.3
Lizardfishes	8.9	8.4	11.8
Mudfish	21.6	21.5	31.5
Other mullets	18.0	20.8	20.5
Sardinellas	28.9	44.9	25.4
Narrow-barred Spanish			
mackerel	9.9	7.4	14.9
Aquaculture	139.4	226.3	340.1
Common carp	12.4	22.4	16.4
Grass carp	38.3	51.3	66.2
Nile tilapia	52.8	104.0	157.4
Flathead grey mullet . . .	28.4	43.0	80.5
Total catch	505.0	606.8	724.4

Source: FAO, *Yearbook of Fishery Statistics*.

Mining

('000 metric tons, year ending 30 June)

	1998/99	1999/2000	2000/01*
Crude petroleum	4,000	n.a.	n.a.
Natural gas	11,872	14,500	n.a.
Iron ore†	3,002	2,932	3,226
Salt (unrefined)	2,588	1,990	2,578
Phosphate rock	1,165	1,177	1,295
Gypsum (crude)	2,666	3,027	2,229
Kaolin	314	205	226

* Figures are provisional.
† Figures refer to gross weight. The estimated iron content is 50%.

Industry

SELECTED PRODUCTS

('000 metric tons, unless otherwise indicated, year ending 30 June)

	1997/98	1998/99	1999/2000
Cottonseed oil (refined) . . .	306	290	260
Cigarettes (million)	52	51	53
Jute yarn	15	10	5
Jute fabrics	13	9	4
Wool yarn	12	12	15
Rubber tyres and tubes ('000)† .	3,502	3,598	2,662
Caustic soda (Sodium hydroxide) .	51	58	44
Phosphate fertilizers‡ . . .	365	378	390
Jet fuels	860	939	920
Kerosene	1,260	1,072	1,011
Distillate fuel oils	5,889	6,007	5,989
Residual fuel oil (Mazout) . .	12,700	12,773	11,785
Petroleum bitumen (asphalt) . .	714	954	957
Cement	21,225	21,232	18,932
Passenger motor cars—assembly			
(number)	13,337	11,629*	n.a.
Electric energy (million kWh) . .	62,300	62,300	70,600

* Estimate.
† Tyres and inner tubes for road motor vehicles (including motorcycles) and bicycles.
‡ Production in terms of phosphoric acid.

Finance

CURRENCY AND EXCHANGE RATES

Monetary Units

1,000 millièmes = 100 piastres = 5 tallaris = 1 Egyptian pound (£E)

Sterling, Dollar and Euro Equivalents (31 December 2002)

£1 sterling = £E7.253
US $1 = £E4.500
€1 = £E4.719
£E100 = £13.79 sterling = $22.22 = €21.19

Note: From February 1991 foreign-exchange transactions were conducted through only two markets, the primary market and the free market. With effect from 8 October 1991, the primary market was eliminated, and all foreign-exchange transactions are effected through the free market. In January 2001 a new exchange rate mechanism was introduced, whereby the value of the Egyptian pound would be allowed to fluctuate within narrow limits: initially, as much as 1% above or below a rate that was set by the Central Bank of Egypt but would be adjusted periodically in response to market conditions. For external trade purposes, the average value of the Egyptian pound was 29.452 US cents in 1999, 28.812 US cents in 2000 and 25.218 US cents in 2001.

STATE PUBLIC BUDGET
(£E million, year ending 30 June)

Revenue	1998/99	1999/2000*	2000/01†
Current revenue	67,207	71,898	86,294
Central Government	62,758	66,890	64,348
Tax revenue	48,096	50,869	62,909
Taxes on income and profits	15,641	17,550	27,788
Domestic taxes on goods and services	14,313	16,000	18,000
Customs duties	10,108	10,000	13,000
Stamp duties	3,342	3,324	4,121
Other current revenue	14,662	16,021	21,946
Profit transfers	9,802	10,856	13,406
Petroleum Authority	2,227	2,901	4,575
Suez Canal Authority	2,914	3,000	3,500
Central Bank of Egypt	3,222	3,500	3,200
Local government	4,449	2,879	1,404
Service authorities	1,576	2,129	35
Capital revenue	6,072	4,833	11,644
Total	73,279	76,731	97,938

Expenditure	1998/99	1999/2000*	2000/01†
Current expenditure	61,117	68,610	85,688
Wages	18,833	22,459	28,767
Pensions	5,009	6,228	8,090
Goods and services	3,888	3,946	3,884
Defence	8,290	8,321	3,727
Public debt interest	16,406	18,735	20,400
Local	14,081	16,435	18,400
Foreign	2,325	2,300	2,000
Subsidies	4,498	5,387	5,789
Capital expenditure (net)	24,892	20,452	26,011
Total	86,009	89,062	111,699

* Provisional figures.
† Projections.

INTERNATIONAL RESERVES
(US $ million at 31 December)

	2000	2001	2002
Gold*	511	488	571
IMF special drawing rights	48	35	91
Reserve position in IMF	156	0	0
Foreign exchange	12,913	12,891	13,151
Total	13,629	13,414	13,813

* Valued at market-related prices.

Source: IMF, *International Financial Statistics.*

MONEY SUPPLY
(£E million at 31 December)

	2000	2001	2002
Currency outside banks	37,902	40,548	45,281
Demand deposits at deposit money banks	21,747	23,515	27,021
Total money (incl. others)	62,195	67,078	75,781

Source: IMF, *International Financial Statistics.*

COST OF LIVING
(Consumer Price Index; base: 1990 = 100)

	1998	1999	2000
Food, beverages and tobacco	190.9	203.4	208.5
Fuel and light	324.1	313.6	336.1
Clothing and footwear	220.8	226.6	232.2
Rent	154.8	155.0	155.2
All items (incl. others)	207.5	218.4	224.4

Source: ILO, *Yearbook of Labour Statistics.*

2001: Food 210.7; All items 229.4 (Source: UN, *Monthly Bulletin of Statistics*).

NATIONAL ACCOUNTS
(£E million, year ending 30 June)

Expenditure on the Gross Domestic Product
(at current prices)

	1999/2000	2000/01	2001/02*
Government final consumption expenditure	33,000	36,500	39,900
Private final consumption expenditure	266,100	281,200	307,240
Increase in stocks	2,100	1,900	1,700
Gross fixed capital formation	60,000	59,400	63,900
Total domestic expenditure	361,200	379,000	412,740
Exports of goods and services	55,100	62,900	62,600
Less Imports of goods and services	77,600	80,100	87,800
GDP in purchasers' values	338,700	361,800	387,540

* Projected figures.

Source: Central Bank of Egypt.

Gross Domestic Product by Economic Activity
(at current prices)

	1999/2000	2000/01	2001/02*
Agriculture, hunting, forestry and fishing	52,845	56,861	60,955
Manufacturing and mining (excl. hydrocarbons)	61,211	65,128	69,769
Hydrocarbons	23,300	25,747	27,835
Electricity	4,936	5,300	5,825
Construction	15,140	15,760	16,470
Transport and communications	27,949	30,380	32,958
Tourism, restaurants and hotels	4,925	5,357	4,413
Trade, finance and insurance	70,624	73,373	76,962
Real estate	6,003	6,880	7,782
Government services and social insurance	24,426	27,039	29,279
Other services	25,045	26,775	30,611
GDP at factor cost	316,404	338,600	363,144

* Projected figures.

Source: Central Bank of Egypt.

BALANCE OF PAYMENTS
(US $ million)

	1999	2000	2001
Exports of goods f.o.b.	5,237	7,061	7,025
Imports of goods f.o.b.	−15,165	−15,382	−13,960
Trade balance	−9,928	−8,321	−6,935
Exports of services	9,494	9,803	9,042
Imports of services	−6,452	−7,513	−7,037
Balance on goods and services	−6,886	−6,031	−4,929
Other income received	1,788	1,871	1,468
Other income paid	−1,045	−983	−885
Balance on goods, services and income	−6,143	−5,143	−4,346
Current transfers received	4,564	4,224	4,056
Current transfers paid	−55	−52	−98
Current balance	−1,635	−971	−388
Direct investment abroad	−38	−51	−12
Direct investment from abroad	1,065	1,235	510
Portfolio investment assets	−22	−3	−2
Portfolio investment liabilities	617	269	1,463
Other investment assets	−1,805	−2,991	−1,261
Other investment liabilities	−1,240	−105	−509
Net errors and omissions	−1,558	587	−1,146
Overall balance	−4,614	−2,030	−1,345

Source: IMF, *International Financial Statistics.*

External Trade

Note: Figures exclude trade in military goods.

PRINCIPAL COMMODITIES
(distribution by SITC, US $ million)

Imports c.i.f.	1997	1998	1999
Food and live animals	2,698.6	2,658.3	2,917.5
Cereals and cereal preparations	1,257.6	1,253.4	1,298.2
Wheat and meslin (unmilled)	821.0	813.9	602.8
Maize (unmilled)	385.4	388.1	652.5
Crude materials (inedible) except fuels	1,119.8	1,182.0	1,068.3
Cork and wood	538.1	589.3	509.5
Simply worked wood and railway sleepers	502.2	553.3	473.2
Simply worked coniferous wood	410.3	444.8	369.6
Mineral fuels, lubricants, etc.	243.4	801.3	977.9
Petroleum, petroleum products, etc.	88.8	611.0	695.2
Crude petroleum oils, etc.	0.0	439.9	417.3
Animal and vegetable oils, fats and waxes	484.3	534.7	415.8
Fixed vegetable oils and fats	444.7	467.0	369.3
Chemicals and related products	1,727.2	1,785.6	1,830.9
Artificial resins, plastic materials, etc.	584.2	545.7	584.4
Products of polymerization, etc.	469.5	431.5	461.8
Basic manufactures	2,574.7	3,148.6	2,876.5
Paper, paperboard and manufactures	388.7	511.8	452.8
Iron and steel	919.8	1,162.8	887.7
Machinery and transport equipment	3,547.0	4,311.4	4,187.6
Machinery specialized for particular industries	768.0	1,143.9	936.5
General industrial machinery, equipment and parts	791.2	861.3	974.1
Electrical machinery, apparatus, etc.	796.2	1,063.2	1,143.3
Road vehicles and parts*	596.0	665.7	582.9
Miscellaneous manufactured articles	533.7	681.8	664.6
Total (incl. others)	13,168.5	16,478.6	15,962.1

* Excluding tyres, engines and electrical parts.

Exports f.o.b.	1997	1998	1999
Food and live animals	269.6	364.4	276.4
Cereals and cereal preparations	77.1	140.3	95.9
Rice	71.4	135.2	87.6
Vegetables and fruit	140.4	184.3	134.5
Crude materials (inedible) except fuels	202.9	240.4	315.4
Textile fibres (excl. wool tops) and waste	117.4	163.8	245.8
Cotton	111.1	158.3	239.5
Raw cotton (excl. linters)	110.2	158.2	239.5
Mineral fuels, lubricants, etc.	1,772.3	943.4	1,292.3
Petroleum, petroleum products, etc.	1,731.8	911.6	1,261.3
Crude petroleum oils, etc.	668.2	162.0	293.0
Refined petroleum products	968.4	733.5	960.3
Residual fuel oils	886.2	685.5	908.5
Chemicals and related products	197.8	265.5	264.0
Basic manufactures	1,003.9	825.6	697.2
Textile yarn, fabrics, etc.	533.4	440.9	355.1
Textile yarn	285.0	230.1	128.1
Cotton yarn	280.6	225.6	123.5
Other non-metal mineral manufactures	121.2	54.9	65.0
Iron and steel	108.5	113.8	72.6
Non-ferrous metals	151.1	137.7	117.8
Aluminium and aluminium alloys	148.7	136.1	115.4
Unwrought aluminium and alloys	125.5	120.9	100.8
Miscellaneous manufactured articles	395.2	428.0	423.3
Clothing and accessories (excl. footwear)	258.9	333.4	278.1
Total (incl. others)	3,908.0	3,195.3	3,500.9

Source: UN, *International Trade Statistics Yearbook*.

PRINCIPAL TRADING PARTNERS
(countries of consignment, US $ million)

Imports c.i.f.	1997	1998	1999
Argentina	339.4	373.4	196.3
Australia	480.3	291.3	435.0
Belgium	206.4	232.3	—
Brazil	257.3	332.5	318.2
China, People's Repub.	295.6	418.5	620.6
Finland	177.4	237.4	206.1
France (incl. Monaco)	805.4	923.6	786.6
Germany	1,141.8	1,408.0	1,382.1
India	223.1	296.7	269.2
Indonesia	95.9	192.7	196.4
Ireland	140.2	187.4	214.1
Italy	929.9	1,111.1	1,049.3
Japan	446.5	502.0	520.9
Korea, Republic	233.1	364.7	349.9
Malaysia	232.5	248.5	196.5
Netherlands	379.2	361.4	373.6
Romania	218.5	224.1	211.7
Russia	379.2	374.8	402.5
Saudi Arabia	440.3	612.7	698.4
Spain	221.4	252.2	334.1
Sweden	299.8	349.7	310.4
Switzerland-Liechtenstein	340.8	281.1	245.1
Turkey	174.1	487.1	356.6
Ukraine	230.9	299.4	224.0
United Kingdom	427.0	516.2	477.5
USA	1,719.8	2,073.9	2,295.8
Total (incl. others)	13,168.5	16,478.6	15,962.1

Exports f.o.b.	1997	1998	1999
Belgium-Luxembourg	62.8	65.0	—
France (incl. Monaco)	150.2	126.2	134.4
Germany	265.6	127.6	108.5
Greece	175.0	90.2	103.3
India	44.0	41.7	134.5
Iraq	20.0	38.5	59.9
Israel	327.9	140.4	186.9
Italy	438.0	319.9	352.5
Japan	90.8	55.6	44.5
Korea, Republic	60.4	48.0	33.7
Libya	69.6	75.0	42.1
Netherlands	264.4	249.3	249.3
Portugal	40.4	31.4	28.5
Romania	64.3	35.5	21.6
Saudi Arabia	138.5	176.3	97.7
Singapore	152.7	62.8	110.7
Spain	111.9	61.5	118.9
Syria	34.6	45.5	41.7
Turkey	96.6	117.5	96.5
United Arab Emirates . . .	34.2	40.5	33.2
United Kingdom	90.2	110.7	88.5
USA	447.2	389.7	435.7
Total (incl. others)	3,908.0	3,195.3	3,500.9

Source: UN, *International Trade Statistics Yearbook*.

International sea-borne freight traffic ('000 metric tons, incl. ships' stores, 1998): Goods loaded 23,868; Goods unloaded 31,152 (Source: UN, *Monthly Bulletin of Statistics*).

Suez Canal Traffic

	1998	1999	2000
Transits (number)	13,472	13,490	14,141
Displacement ('000 net tons) . .	386,069	384,994	438,962
Northbound goods traffic ('000 metric tons).	160,346	153,582	209,446
Southbound goods traffic ('000 metric tons).	118,107	153,088	158,535
Net tonnage of tankers ('000) . .	89,976	67,872	105,237

Source: Suez Canal Authority, *Yearly Report*.

CIVIL AVIATION
(traffic on scheduled services)

	1996	1997	1998
Kilometres flown (million) . . .	62	65	63
Passengers carried ('000) . . .	4,282	4,416	4,022
Passenger-km (million)	8,742	9,018	8,036
Total ton-km (million)	993	1,029	989

Source: UN, *Statistical Yearbook*.

Transport

RAILWAYS
(traffic, year ending 30 June)

	1998/99	1999/2000	2000/01
Passengers (million)	1,395	1,353	1,183
Passenger-km (million) . . .	n.a.	57,859	55,801

1995/96: Freight ton-km (million): 4,117 (Source: UN, *Statistical Yearbook*).

ROAD TRAFFIC
(licensed motor vehicles in use at 31 December)

	1995*	1996	1997
Passenger cars	1,280,000	1,099,583	1,154,753
Buses and coaches	36,630	39,781	43,740
Lorries and vans	387,000	489,542	510,766
Motorcycles and mopeds . . .	397,000	427,864	439,756

* Estimates from IRF, *World Road Statistics*.

SHIPPING

Merchant Fleet
(registered at 31 December)

	1999	2000	2001
Number of vessels	374	372	364
Displacement ('000 grt)	1,368.0	1,346.3	1,350.4

Source: Lloyd's Register-Fairplay, *World Fleet Statistics*.

Tourism

ARRIVALS BY NATIONALITY
('000*)

	1998	1999	2000
France	175.3	313.0	379.9
Germany	273.8	547.9	786.3
Israel	372.1	415.3	326.5
Italy	373.1	667.5	752.2
Jordan	78.2	72.4	78.5
Kuwait	69.8	70.2	64.0
Libya	186.0	145.7	152.5
Netherlands	107.6	123.6	142.1
Palestine	195.9	160.1	149.8
Saudi Arabia	233.6	240.7	240.2
Syria	74.2	60.2	67.4
United Kingdom	239.9	336.4	378.4
USA	153.6	196.1	235.3
Total (incl. others)	3,453.9	4,796.5	5,506.2

* Figures refer to arrivals at frontiers of visitors from abroad. Excluding same-day visitors (excursionists), the total number of tourist arrivals (in '000) was: 3,213 in 1998; 4,489 in 1999; 5,116 in 2000.

Source: World Tourism Organization, mainly *Yearbook of Tourism Statistics*.

Tourism receipts (US $ million): 2,564 in 1998; 3,903 in 1999; 4,345 in 2000 (Source: World Tourism Organization).

Communications Media

	1999	2000	2001
Television receivers ('000 in use)	11,400	12,000	n.a.
Telephones ('000 main lines in use)	4,686.4	5,483.6	6,650.0
Facsimile machines ('000 in use)	34.2	n.a.	n.a.
Mobile cellular telephones ('000 subscribers)	481.0	1,359.9	2,793.8
Personal computers ('000 in use)	750	1,400	1,000
Internet users ('000)	200	450	600

1995: Book production 2,215 titles; 92,353,000 copies.

1996: Daily newspapers 17 (average circulation 2,400,000 copies).

1997: Radio receivers ('000 in use) 20,500.

Sources: UNESCO, *Statistical Yearbook*; International Telecommunication Union.

Education

(provisional figures, 1999/2000, unless otherwise indicated)

	Schools	Teachers†	Students
Pre-primary	3,172†	14,894	289,995*
Primary	15,533	314,528	7,224,989
Preparatory	7,544	193,469	4,345,356
Secondary:			
General	1,595	79,218	1,039,958
Technical	1,826	145,050	1,913,022
Higher	356†‡	n.a.	1,316,491*

* 1996/97 figure. Source: partly UNESCO, *Statistical Yearbook*.
† 1998/99 figure(s).
‡ Official estimate.

Source: Ministry of Education.

Al-Azhar (provisional figures, 1999/2000): Primary: 2,631 schools; 707,633 students. Preparatory: 1,805 schools; 316,108 students. Secondary: 1,081 schools; 269,469 students.

Adult literacy rate (UNESCO estimates): 55.3% (males 66.6%; females 43.8%) in 2000 (Source: UNDP, *Human Development Report*).

Directory

The Constitution

A new Constitution for the Arab Republic of Egypt was approved by referendum on 11 September 1971.

THE STATE

Egypt is an Arab Republic with a democratic, socialist system based on the alliance of the working people and derived from the country's historical heritage and the spirit of Islam.

The Egyptian people are part of the Arab nation, who work towards total Arab unity.

Islam is the religion of the State; Arabic is its official language and the Islamic code is a principal source of legislation. The State safeguards the freedom of worship and of performing rites for all religions.

Sovereignty is of the people alone which is the source of all powers.

The protection, consolidation and preservation of the socialist gains is a national duty: the sovereignty of law is the basis of the country's rule, and the independence of immunity of the judiciary are basic guarantees for the protection of rights and liberties.

THE FUNDAMENTAL ELEMENTS OF SOCIETY

Social solidarity is the basis of Egyptian society, and the family is its nucleus.

The State ensures the equality of men and women in both political and social rights in line with the provisions of Muslim legislation.

Work is a right, an honour and a duty which the State guarantees together with the services of social and health insurance, pensions for incapacity and unemployment.

The economic basis of the Republic is a socialist democratic system based on sufficiency and justice in a manner preventing exploitation.

Ownership is of three kinds: public, co-operative and private. The public sector assumes the main responsibility for the regulation and growth of the national economy under the development plan.

Property is subject to the people's control.

Private ownership is safeguarded and may not be sequestrated except in cases specified in law nor expropriated except for the general good against fair legal compensation. The right of inheritance is guaranteed in it.

Nationalization shall only be allowed for considerations of public interest in accordance with the law and against compensation.

Agricultural holding may be limited by law.

The State follows a comprehensive central planning and compulsory planning approach based on quinquennial socio-economic and cultural development plans whereby the society's resources are mobilized and put to the best use.

The public sector assumes the leading role in the development of the national economy. The State provides absolute protection of this sector as well as the property of co-operative societies and trade unions against all attempts to tamper with them.

PUBLIC LIBERTIES, RIGHTS AND DUTIES

All citizens are equal before the law. Personal liberty is a natural right and no one may be arrested, searched, imprisoned or restricted in any way without a court order.

Houses have sanctity, and shall not be placed under surveillance or searched without a court order with reasons given for such action.

The law safeguards the sanctities of the private lives of all citizens; so have all postal, telegraphic, telephonic and other means of communication which may not therefore be confiscated, or perused except by a court order giving the reasons, and only for a specified period.

Public rights and freedoms are also inviolate and all calls for atheism and anything that reflects adversely on divine religions are prohibited.

The freedom of opinion, the Press, printing and publications and all information media are safeguarded.

Press censorship is forbidden, so are warnings, suspensions or cancellations through administrative channels. Under exceptional circumstances, as in cases of emergency or in wartime, censorship may be imposed on information media for a definite period.

Egyptians have the right to permanent or provisional emigration and no Egyptian may be deported or prevented from returning to the country.

Citizens have the right to private meetings in peace provided they bear no arms. Egyptians also have the right to form societies that have no secret activities. Public meetings are also allowed within the limits of the law.

SOVEREIGNTY OF THE LAW

All acts of crime should be specified together with the penalties for the acts.

Recourse to justice is a right of all citizens. Those who are financially unable will be assured of means to defend their rights.

Except in cases of *flagrante delicto* no person may be arrested or their freedom restricted unless an order authorizing arrest has been given by the competent judge or the public prosecution in accordance with the provisions of law.

SYSTEM OF GOVERNMENT

The President, who must be of Egyptian parentage and at least 40 years old, is nominated by at least one-third of the members of the People's Assembly, approved by at least two-thirds, and elected by popular referendum. His term is for six years and he 'may be re-elected for another subsequent term'. He may take emergency measures in the interests of the State but these measures must be approved by referendum within 60 days.

The People's Assembly, elected for five years, is the legislative body and approves general policy, the budget and the development plan. It shall have 'not less than 350' elected members, at least half of whom shall be workers or farmers, and the President may appoint up to 10 additional members. In exceptional circumstances the Assembly, by a two-thirds' vote, may authorize the President to rule by decree for a specified period but these decrees must be approved by the Assembly at its next meeting. The law governing the composition of the People's Assembly was amended in May 1979 (see People's Assembly, below, see p. 1494).

The Assembly may pass a vote of no confidence in a Deputy Prime Minister, a Minister or a Deputy Minister, provided three days' notice of the vote is given, and the Minister must then resign. In the case of the Prime Minister, the Assembly may 'prescribe' his responsibility and submit a report to the President: if the President disagrees with the report but the Assembly persists, then the matter is put to a referendum: if the people support the President the Assembly is dissolved; if they support the Assembly the President must accept the resignation of the Government. The President may dissolve the Assembly prematurely, but his action must be approved by a referendum and elections must be held within 60 days.

Executive Authority is vested in the President, who may appoint one or more Vice-Presidents and appoints all Ministers. He may also dismiss the Vice-Presidents and Ministers. The President has 'the right to refer to the people in connection with important matters related to the country's higher interests.' The Government is described as 'the supreme executive and administrative organ of the state'. Its members, whether full Ministers or Deputy Ministers, must be at least 35 years old. Further sections define the roles of Local Government, Specialized National Councils, the Judiciary, the Higher Constitutional Court, the Socialist Prosecutor-General, the Armed Forces and National Defence Council and the Police.

POLITICAL PARTIES

In June 1977 the People's Assembly adopted a new law on political parties, which, subject to certain conditions, permitted the formation of political parties for the first time since 1953. The law was passed in accordance with Article Five of the Constitution which describes the political system as 'a multi-party one' with four main parties: 'the ruling National Democratic Party, the Socialist Workers (the official opposition), the Liberal Socialists and the Unionist Progressive'. (The legality of the re-formed New Wafd Party was established by the courts in January 1984.)

1980 AMENDMENTS

On 30 April 1980 the People's Assembly passed a number of amendments, which were subsequently massively approved at a referendum the following month. A summary of the amendments follows:

(i) the regime in Egypt is socialist-democratic, based on the alliance of working people's forces.

(ii) the political system depends on multiple political parties; the Arab Socialist Union is therefore abolished.

(iii) the President is elected for a six-year term and can be elected for 'other terms'.

(iv) the President shall appoint a Consultative Council to preserve the principles of the revolutions of 23 July 1952 and 15 May 1971.

(v) a Supreme Press Council shall safeguard the freedom of the press, check government censorship and look after the interests of journalists.

(vi) Egypt's adherence to Islamic jurisprudence is affirmed. Christians and Jews are subject to their own jurisdiction in personal status affairs.

(vii) there will be no distinction of race or religion.

The Government

THE PRESIDENCY

President: MUHAMMAD HOSNI MUBARAK (confirmed as President by referendum, 13 October 1981, after assassination of President Anwar Sadat; re-elected and confirmed by referendum 5 October 1987, 4 October 1993 and 26 September 1999).

COUNCIL OF MINISTERS
(April 2003)

Prime Minister: Dr ATIF MUHAMMAD OBEID.

Deputy Prime Minister and Minister of Agriculture and Land Reclamation: Dr YOUSUF AMIN WALI.

Minister of Defence and Military Production: Field Marshal MUHAMMAD HUSSAIN TANTAWI.

Minister of Information: MUHAMMAD SAFWAT ESH-SHARIF.

Minister of Foreign Affairs: AHMAD MAHER ES-SAYED.

Minister of Justice: FAROUK MAHMOUD SAYF AN-NASR.

Minister of Culture: FAROUK ABD AL-AZIZ HOSNI.

Minister of Education: Dr HUSSAIN KAMAL BAHA ED-DIN.

Minister of Foreign Trade: Dr YOUSUF BOUTROS-GHALI.

Minister of Tourism: Dr MUHAMMAD MAMDOUH AHMAD EL-BELTAGI.

Minister of Housing, Utilities and New Urban Communities: Dr Eng. MUHAMMAD IBRAHIM SULAYMAN.

Minister of Labour and Migration: AHMAD AHMAD EL-AMAWI.

Minister of Awqaf (Islamic Endowments): Dr MAHMOUD HAMDI ZAKZOUK.

Minister of Health and Population: MUHAMMAD AWAD AFIFI TAG ED-DIN.

Minister of Higher Education and Scientific Research: Dr MUFID MAHMOUD SHEHAB.

Minister of Irrigation and Water Resources: Dr MAHMOUD ABD AL-HALIM ABU ZEID.

Minister of the Interior: Maj.-Gen. HABIB IBRAHIM EL-ADLI.

Minister of Local Development: MOUSTAFA MUHAMMAD ABD AL-QADIR.

Minister of Insurance and Social Affairs: Dr AMINAH HAMZEH MAHMOUD AL-JUNDI.

Minister of Industry and Technological Development: Dr ALI FAHMI IBRAHIM AS-SA'IDI.

Minister of Electricity and Energy: Eng. HASSAN YOUNIS.

Minister of Transport: HAMDY ASH-SHAYEB.

Minister of Youth: Dr ALI AD-DIN HELAL AD-DASUQI.

Minister of Supply and Internal Trade: Dr HASSAN ALI KHIDR.

Minister of Planning: Dr AHMAD MAHRUS AD-DARSH.

Minister of Public Enterprise: Dr MUKHTAR ABD AL-MUN'IM KHATTAB.

Minister of Finance: Dr MUHAMMAD MIDHAT ABD AL-ATTI HASANAYN.

Minister of Communications and Information Technology: Dr AHMAD MAHMOUD MUHAMMAD NAZIF.

Minister of Petroleum: Dr AMIN SAMIH SAMIR FAHMI.

Minister of Civil Aviation: Gen. AHMAD MUHAMMAD SHAFIQ ZAKI.

Minister of State for Parliamentary Affairs: KAMAL MUHAMMAD ASH-SHAZLI.

Minister of State for Foreign Affairs: FAIZA ABUL NAGA.

Minister of State for Administrative Development: Dr MUHAMMAD ZAKI ABU AMER.

Minister of State for Environmental Affairs: Eng. MAMDOUH RIAD TADROS.

Minister of State for Military Production: Dr SAID ABDUH MOUSTAFA MASH'AL.

Cabinet Secretary: AHMAD HASSAN ABU TALEB.

MINISTRIES

Office of the Prime Minister: Sharia Majlis ash-Sha'ab, Cairo; tel. (2) 7958014; fax (2) 7958016; e-mail primemin@idsc.gov.eg.

Ministry of Administrative Development: Sharia Salah Salem, Cairo (Nasr City); tel. (2) 4022910; fax (2) 2614126.

Ministry of Agriculture and Land Reclamation: Sharia Nadi es-Sayed, Cairo (Dokki), Giza; tel. (2) 3772566; fax (2) 3498128; e-mail sea@idsc.gov.eg; internet www.agri.gov.eg.

Ministry of Awqaf (Islamic Endowments): Sharia Sabri Abu Alam, Bab el-Louk, Cairo; tel. (2) 3929403; fax (2) 3900362; e-mail mawkaf@idsc1.gov.eg.

Ministry of Civil Aviation: Sharia Matar, Cairo; tel. (2) 3555566; fax (2) 3555564.

Ministry of Communications and Information Technology: 1 Sharia Mahmoud el-Hossary, Mohandessin, Cairo (Giza); tel. (2) 3444533; fax (2) 34446088; e-mail anazif@mcit.gov.eg; internet www .mcit.gov.eg.

Ministry of Culture: 2 Sharia Shagaret ed-Dor, Cairo (Zamalek); tel. (2) 7380761; fax (2) 7356449; e-mail mculture@idsc.gov.eg.

Ministry of Defence and Military Production: Sharia 23 July, Kobri el-Kobra, Cairo; tel. (2) 2602566; fax (2) 2916227; e-mail mod@ idsc.gov.eg.

Ministry of Education: 4 Sharia Ibrahim Nagiv, Cairo (Garden City); tel. (2) 5787643; fax (2) 7962952; e-mail moe@idsc.gov.eg; internet home.moe.edu.

Ministry of Electricity and Energy: Sharia Ramses, Abbassia, Cairo (Nasr City); tel. (2) 2616317; fax (2) 2616302; e-mail mee@idsc .gov.eg.

Ministry of Environmental Affairs: 30 Sharia Helwan, Cairo; tel. (2) 5256463; fax (2) 5256461.

Ministry of Finance: Justice and Finance Bldg, Sharia Majlis ash-Sha'ab, Lazoughli Sq., Cairo; tel. (2) 3541055; fax (2) 3551537; e-mail mofinance@idsc1.gov.eg.

Ministry of Foreign Affairs: Corniche en-Nil, Cairo (Maspiro); tel. (2) 5749820; fax (2) 5749533; e-mail minexter@idsc1.gov.eg; internet www.mfa.gov.eg.

Ministry of Foreign Trade: 8 Sharia Adly, Cairo; tel. (2) 3919661; fax (2) 3903029; e-mail moft@moft.gov.eg; internet www.moft.gov.eg.

Ministry of Health and Population: Sharia Majlis ash-Sha'ab, Lazoughli Sq., Cairo; tel. (2) 7941507; fax (2) 7953966; e-mail moh@idsc.gov.eg.

Ministry of Higher Education and Scientific Research: 101 Sharia Qasr el-Eini, Cairo; tel. (2) 7956962; fax (2) 7941005; e-mail mheducat@idsc.gov.eg; internet www.egy-mhe.gov.eg.

Ministry of Housing, Utilities and New Urban Communities: 1 Ismail Abaza, Sharia Qasr el-Eini, Cairo; tel. (2) 3553468; fax (2) 3557836; e-mail mhuuc@idsc1.gov.eg.

Ministry of Industry and Technological Development: 2 Sharia Latin America, Cairo (Garden City); tel. (2) 7946589; fax (2) 7955025; e-mail moindust@idsc.gov.eg.

Ministry of Information: Radio and TV Bldg, Corniche en-Nil, Cairo (Maspiro); tel. (2) 5748984; fax (2) 5748981; e-mail rtu@idsc.gov.eg.

Ministry of Insurance and Social Affairs: Sharia Sheikh Rihan, Bab el-Louk, Cairo; tel. (2) 3370039; fax (2) 3375390; e-mail msi@idsc.gov.eg.

Ministry of the Interior: Sharia Sheikh Rihan, Bab el-Louk, Cairo; tel. (2) 3557500; fax (2) 5792031; e-mail moi2@idsc.gov.eg.

Ministry of Irrigation and Water Resources: Sharia Corniche en-Nil, Imbaba, Cairo; tel. (2) 3123304; fax (2) 3123357; e-mail mpwwr@idsc.gov.eg; internet www.starnet.com.eg/mpwwr.

Ministry of Justice: Justice and Finance Bldg, Sharia Majlis ash-Sha'ab, Lazoughli Sq., Cairo; tel. (2) 7951176; fax (2) 7955700; e-mail mojeb@idsc1.gov.eg.

Ministry of Labour and Migration: 3 Sharia Yousuf Abbas, Abbassia, Cairo (Nasr City); tel. (2) 4042910; fax (2) 2609891; e-mail mwlabor@idsc1.gov.eg; internet www.emigration.gov.eg.

Ministry of Local Development: Sharia Nadi es-Seid, Cairo (Dokki); tel. (2) 3497470; fax (2) 3497788.

Ministry of Military Production: 5 Sharia Ismail Abaza, Qasr el-Eini, Cairo; tel. (2) 3552428; fax (2) 3548739.

Ministry of Parliamentary Affairs: Sharia Majlis ash-Sha'ab, Lazoughli Sq., Cairo; tel. (2) 3557750; fax (2) 3557681.

Ministry of Petroleum: Sharia el-Mokhayem ed-Dayem, Cairo (Nasr City); tel. (2) 2626060; fax (2) 2636060; e-mail mop@egyptonline.com.

Ministry of Planning: Sharia Salah Salem, Cairo (Nasr City); tel. (2) 4014615; fax (2) 4014733.

Ministry of Public Enterprise: Sharia Majlis ash-Sha'ab, Lazoughli Sq., Cairo; tel. (2) 3558026; fax (2) 3555882; e-mail mops@idsc.gov.eg.

Ministry of Supply and Internal Trade: 99 Sharia Qasr el-Eini, Cairo; tel. (2) 3557598; fax (2) 3544973; e-mail msit@idsc.gov.eg.

Ministry of Tourism: Misr Travel Tower, Abbassia Sq., Cairo; tel. (2) 2828439; fax (2) 2859551; e-mail mol@idsc.gov.eg; internet www.touregypt.net.

Ministry of Transport: 105 Sharia Qasr el-Eini, Cairo; tel. (2) 3555566; fax (2) 3555564; e-mail garb@idsc.gov.eg.

Legislature

MAJLIS ASH-SHA'AB
(People's Assembly)

There are 222 constituencies, which each elect two deputies to the Assembly. Ten deputies are appointed by the President, giving a total of 454 seats.

Speaker: Dr AHMAD FATHI SURUR.

Deputy Speakers: Dr ABD AL-AHAD GAMAL AD-DIN, AHMAD ABU ZEID, Dr AMAL UTHMAN.

Elections, 18 and 29 October and 8 November 2000

	Seats
National Democratic Party*	353
New Wafd Party	7
National Progressive Unionist Party	6
Nasserist Party	3
Liberal Socialist Party	1
Independents	72‡
Total†	442‡

* Official candidates of the National Democratic Party (NDP) won 353 seats in the three rounds of voting. However, after the elections it was reported that 35 of the 72 candidates who had successfully contested the elections as independents had either joined or rejoined the NDP.
† There are, in addition, 10 deputies appointed by the President.
‡ The results for the two seats in one constituency in Alexandria were annulled by a court ruling. (Elections were scheduled to be reheld there in 2001.).

MAJLIS ASH-SHURA
(Advisory Council)

In September 1980 elections were held for a 210-member **Shura (Advisory) Council,** which replaced the former Central Committee of the Arab Socialist Union. Of the total number of members, 140 are elected and the remaining 70 are appointed by the President. The opposition parties boycotted elections to the Council in October 1983, and again in October 1986, in protest against the 8% electoral threshold. In June 1989 elections to 153 of the Council's 210 seats were contested by opposition parties (the 'Islamic Alliance', consisting of the Muslim Brotherhood, the LSP and the SLP). However, all of the seats in which voting produced a result (143) were won by the NDP. NDP candidates won 88 of the 90 seats on the Council to which mid-term elections were held in June 1995. The remaining two elective seats were gained by independent candidates. On 21 June new appointments were made to 47 vacant, non-elective seats. Partial elections to the Council were held again in June 1998. The NDP won 85 of the 88 contested seats, while independent candidates won the remaining three seats. Most opposition parties chose not to contest the elections. In partial elections to the Council, held on 16 and 22 May 2001, the NDP won 74 of the 88 seats in question, while independent candidates won the remaining 14 seats.

Speaker: Dr MUSTAFA KAMAL HELMI.

Deputy Speakers: THARWAT ABAZAH, AHMAD AL-IMADI.

Political Organizations

Democratic People's Party: f. 1992; Chair. ANWAR AFIFI.

Democratic Unionist Party: f. 1990; Pres. IBRAHIM ABD AL-MONEIM TURK.

Et-Takaful (Solidarity): f. 1995; advocates imposition of 'solidarity' tax on the rich in order to provide needs of the poor; Chair. Dr USAMA MUHAMMAD SHALTOUT.

Green Party: f. 1990; Chair. Dr ABD AL-MONEIM EL-AASAR.

Hizb al-Wifaq al-Qawmi (National Accord Party): f. 2000.

Liberal Socialist Party (LSP): Cairo; f. 1976; advocates expansion of 'open door' economic policy and greater freedom for private enterprise and the press; Leader (vacant).

Misr el-Fatah (Young Egypt Party): f. 1990; Chair. GAMAL RABIE.

Nasserist Party: Cairo; f. 1991; Chair. DIAA ED-DIN DAOUD.

National Democratic Party (NDP): Cairo; f. 1978; government party established by Anwar Sadat; absorbed Arab Socialist Party; Leader MUHAMMAD HOSNI MUBARAK; Sec.-Gen. MUHAMMAD SAFWAT ESH-SHARIF; Political Bureau: Chair. MUHAMMAD HOSNI MUBARAK.

National Progressive Unionist Party (Tagammu): 1 Sharia Karim ed-Dawlah, Cairo; f. 1976; left-wing; Leader KHALED MOHI ED-DIN; Sec. Dr RIFA'AT ES-SAID; 160,000 mems.

New Wafd Party (The Delegation): Cairo; original Wafd Party; f. 1919; banned 1952; re-formed as New Wafd Party Feb. 1978; disbanded June 1978; re-formed 1983; Leader NU'MAN JUM'AH; Sec.-Gen. IBRAHIM FARAG.

Social Justice Party: f. 1993; Chair. MUHAMMAD ABD AL-AAL.

Socialist Labour Party (SLP): 12 Sharia Awali el-Ahd, Cairo; f. 1978; official opposition party; pro-Islamist; Leader IBRAHIM SHUKRI.

The following organizations are proscribed by the Government:

Islamic Jihad (al-Jihad—Holy Struggle): militant Islamist grouping established following the imposition of a ban on the Muslim Brotherhood; Leader AYMAN ZAWAHIRI.

Jama'ah al-Islamiyah (Islamic Group): militant Islamist group founded following the imposition of a ban on the Muslim Brotherhood; declared a cease-fire in March 1999; Spiritual Leader Sheikh OMAR ABD AR-RAHMAN; Chair. of the Shura Council MOUSTAFA HAMZAH; Mil. Cmmdr ALA ABD AR-RAQIL.

Muslim Brotherhood (Ikhwan al-Muslimun): internet www .ummah.org.uk/ikhwan; f. 1928; with the aim of establishing an Islamic society; banned in 1954; moderate; advocates the adoption of the *Shari'a*, or Islamic law, as the sole basis of the Egyptian legal system; Dep. Supreme Guide MA'MUN AL-HUDA BI.

Vanguards of Conquest: militant Islamist grouping; breakaway group from Islamic Jihad; Leader YASIR AS-SIRRI.

Diplomatic Representation

EMBASSIES IN EGYPT

Afghanistan: 59 Sharia el-Orouba, Cairo (Heliopolis); tel. (2) 666653; fax (2) 662262; Ambassador SAYED FAZLULLAH FAZIL.

Albania: 29 Sharia Ismail Muhammad, Cairo (Zamalek); tel. (2) 3415651; fax (2) 3413732; Ambassador ARBEN PANDI CICI.

Algeria: 14 Sharia Bresil, Cairo (Zamalek); tel. (2) 3418527; fax (2) 3414158; Ambassador MOUSTAFA CHERIF.

Angola: 12 Midan Fouad Mohi ed-Din, Mohandessin, Cairo; tel. (2) 3377602; fax (2) 708683; Ambassador HERMINO JOAQUIM ESCORCIO.

Argentina: 1st Floor, 8 Sharia es-Saleh Ayoub, Cairo (Zamalek); tel. (2) 7351501; fax (2) 7364355; e-mail argemb@idsc.gov.eg; Ambassador OSVALDO SANTIAGO PASCUAL.

Armenia: 20 Sharia Muhammad Mazhar, Cairo (Zamalek); tel. (2) 3424157; fax (2) 3424158; e-mail armenemb@idsc.gov.eg; Ambassador Dr EDWARD NALBANDIAN.

Australia: 11th Floor, World Trade Centre, Corniche en-Nil, Cairo 11111 (Boulac); tel. (2) 5750444; fax (2) 5781638; e-mail cairo .austremb@dfat.gov.au; Ambassador VICTORIA OWEN.

Austria: 5th Floor, Riyadh Tower, 5 Sharia Wissa Wassef, cnr of Sharia en-Nil, Cairo 11111 (Giza); tel. (2) 5702975; fax (2) 5702979; e-mail aec@gega.net; Ambassador FERDINAND TRAUTTMANSDORFF.

Bahrain: 15 Sharia Bresil, Cairo (Zamalek); tel. (2) 3407996; fax (2) 3416609; Ambassador EBRAHIM AL-MAJED.

Bangladesh: 47 Sharia Ahmad Heshmat, Cairo (Zamalek); tel. (2) 3412645; fax (2) 3402401; e-mail bdoot@wnet1.worldnet.com.eg; Ambassador RUHUL AMIN.

Belarus: 19–1 Sharia Muhammad el-Ghazali, Cairo (Dokki); tel. (2) 3375782; fax (2) 3375845; Ambassador IGOR LESHCHENYA.

Belgium: POB 37, 20 Sharia Kamal esh-Shennawi, Cairo 11511 (Garden City); tel. (2) 7947494; fax (2) 7943147; e-mail cairo@ diplobel.org; Ambassador PAUL PONJAERT.

Bolivia: 2 Sharia Hod el-Labban, Cairo (Garden City); tel. (2) 3546390; fax (2) 3550917; Ambassador HERNANDO VELASCO.

Bosnia and Herzegovina: 42 Sharia Sawra, Cairo (Dokki); tel. (2) 7499191; fax (2) 7499190; e-mail ebihebosnia@isdc.gov.eg; Ambassador SRBOLJUB LALOVIĆ.

Brazil: 1125 Corniche en-Nil, Cairo 11221 (Maspiro); tel. (2) 5756938; fax (2) 5761040; e-mail brasemb@soficom.com.eg; Ambassador CELSO MARCOS VIEIRA DE SOUZA.

Brunei: 24 Sharia Hassan Assem, Cairo (Zamalek); tel. (2) 7360097; fax (2) 7386375; e-mail ebdic@mail.link.net; Ambassador Dato' Paduka Haji ALI BIN HAJI HASSAN.

Bulgaria: 6 Sharia el-Malek el-Ajdal, Cairo (Zamalek); tel. (2) 7363025; fax (2) 7363826; e-mail bulembcai@link.net; Ambassador ALEXANDAR OLSHEVSKI.

Burkina Faso: POB 306, Ramses Centre, 9 Sharia el-Fawakeh, Mohandessin, Cairo; tel. (2) 3758956; fax (2) 3756974; Ambassador SOPHIE SOW.

Burundi: 22 Sharia en-Nakhil, Madinet ed-Dobbat, Cairo (Dokki); tel. (2) 3373078; fax (2) 3378431; Ambassador GERVAIS NDIKUMAGNEGE.

Cambodia: 2 Sharia Tahawia, Cairo (Giza); tel. (2) 3489966; Ambassador IN SOPHEAP.

Cameroon: POB 2061, 15 Sharia Muhammad Sedki Soliman, Mohandessin, Cairo; tel. (2) 3441101; fax (2) 3459208; Ambassador MOUCHILI NJI MFOUAYO ISMAILA.

Canada: POB 1667, 6 Sharia Muhammad Fahmi es-Said, Cairo (Garden City); tel. (2) 7943110; fax (2) 7963548; e-mail cairo@ dfait-maeci.gc.ca; Ambassador MICHEL DE SALABERRY.

Central African Republic: 41 Sharia Mahmoud Azmy, Mohandessin, Cairo (Dokki); tel. (2) 3446873; Ambassador HENRY KOBA.

Chad: POB 1869, 12 Midan ar-Refaï, Cairo 11511 (Dokki); tel. (2) 3373379; fax (2) 3373232; Ambassador AMIN ABBA SIDICK.

Chile: 5 Sharia Shagaret ed-Dor, Cairo (Zamalek); tel. (2) 3408711; fax (2) 3403716; e-mail chilemb@idsc.gov.eg; Ambassador NELSON HADAD HERESI.

China, People's Republic: 14 Sharia Bahgat Ali, Cairo (Zamalek); tel. (2) 3411219; fax (2) 3409459; e-mail chinaemb@idsc.gov.eg; Ambassador LUI XIAOMING.

Colombia: 6 Sharia Gueriza, Cairo (Zamalek); tel. (2) 3414203; fax (2) 3407429; e-mail colombemb@idsc.gov.eg; Ambassador JAIME GIRÓN DUARTE.

Congo, Democratic Republic: 5 Sharia Mansour Muhammad, Cairo (Zamalek); tel. (2) 3403662; fax (2) 3404342; Ambassador KAMIMBAYA WA DJONDO.

Côte d'Ivoire: 9 ave Shehab, rue Abdel Meguid Omar Mohandessine, Cairo; tel. (2) 3034373; fax (2) 3050148; Ambassador KONAN N. MARCEL.

Croatia: 3 Sharia Abou el-Feda, Cairo (Zamalek); tel. (2) 7383155; fax (2) 7355812; e-mail croem@soficom.com.eg; Ambassador Dr IVICA TOMIĆ.

Cuba: Apartment 1, 13th Floor, 14 Sharia Kamel Muhammad, Cairo (Zamalek); tel. (2) 7360651; fax (2) 7360656; e-mail cubaemb@ link.net; Ambassador LUIS E. MARISY FIGUEREDO.

Cyprus: 23A Sharia Ismail Muhammad, 1st Floor, Cairo (Zamalek); tel. (2) 3411288; fax (2) 3415299; Ambassador CHARALAMBOS KAPSOS.

Czech Republic: 1st Floor, 4 Sharia Dokki, Cairo 12511 (Giza); tel. (2) 3485531; fax (2) 3485892; e-mail caiembcz@intouch.com; Ambassador DANA HUŇÁTOVÁ.

Denmark: 12 Sharia Hassan Sabri, Cairo 11211 (Zamalek); tel. (2) 7396500; fax (2) 7396588; e-mail caiamb@um.dk; internet www .danemb.org.eg; Ambassador CHRISTIAN OLDENBURG.

Djibouti: 11 Sharia el-Gazaer, Aswan Sq., Cairo (Agouza); tel. (2) 3456546; fax (2) 3456549; Ambassador Sheikh MOUSSA MOHAMED AHMED.

Ecuador: Suez Canal Bldg, 4 Sharia Ibn Kasir, Cairo (Giza); tel. (2) 3496782; fax (2) 3609327; e-mail ecuademb@idsc.gov.eg; Ambassador FRANKLIN BAHAMONDE.

Ethiopia: 6 Sharia Abd ar-Rahman Hussein, Midan Gomhuria, Cairo (Dokki); tel. (2) 3353696; fax (2) 3353699; Ambassador GIRMA AMARE.

Finland: 13th Floor, 3 Sharia Abou el-Feda, 11511 Cairo (Zamalek); tel. (2) 7363722; fax (2) 7355170; e-mail fincairo@access.com.eg; internet www.finemb.org.eg; Ambassador HANNU MÄNTYVAARA.

France: POB 1777, 29 Sharia Giza, Cairo (Giza); tel. (2) 5703916; fax (2) 5710276; e-mail info@ambafrance-eg.org; internet www .diplo-france.org.eg/; Ambassador JEAN-CLAUDE COUSSERAN.

Gabon: 17 Sharia Mecca el-Moukarama, Cairo (Dokki); tel. (2) 3379692; Ambassador MAMBO JACQUES.

Germany: 8B Sharia Hassan Sabri, Cairo (Zamalek); tel. (2) 7399600; fax (2) 7360530; e-mail germemb@gega.net; internet www .german-embassy.org.eg; Ambassador PAUL VON MALTZAHN.

Ghana: 1 Sharia 26 July, Cairo (Zamalek); tel. (2) 3444455; fax (2) 3032292; Ambassador BON OHANE KWAPONG.

Greece: 18 Sharia Aicha at-Taimouria, Cairo (Garden City); tel. (2) 3551074; fax (2) 3563903; Ambassador GEORGE ASIMAKOPOULOS.

Guatemala: POB 346, 11 Sharia 10, Maadi, Cairo; tel. (2) 3802914; fax (2) 3802915; e-mail guatemb@infinity.com.eg; Ambassador FLORIDALMA FRANCO PAIZ.

Guinea: 46 Sharia Muhammad Mazhar, Cairo (Zamalek); tel. (2) 7358109; fax (2) 7361446; Ambassador el Hadj OUSMANE CAMARA.

Guinea-Bissau: 37 Sharia Lebanon, Madinet el-Mohandessin, Cairo (Dokki).

Holy See: Apostolic Nunciature, Safarat al-Vatican, 5 Sharia Muhammad Mazhar, Cairo (Zamalek); tel. (2) 7352250; fax (2) 7356152; e-mail nunteg@rite.com; Apostolic Nuncio Most Rev. MARCO DINO BROGI (Titular Archbishop of Citta Ducale).

Honduras: 21 Sharia Aicha at-Taimouria, Cairo (Garden City); tel. (2) 3409510; fax (2) 3413835.

Hungary: 29 Sharia Muhammad Mazhar, Cairo (Zamalek); tel. (2) 7358659; fax (2) 7358648; e-mail huembcai@soficom.com.eg; Ambassador LÁSZLÓ KÁDÁR.

India: 5 Sharia Aziz Abaza, Cairo (Zamalek); tel. (2) 3413051; fax (2) 3414038; e-mail indiaemb@idsc.gov.eg; Ambassador KENWAL GIBAL; also looks after Iraqi interests at 5 Sharia Aziz Abaza, Cairo (Zamalek) (tel. (2) 3409815).

Indonesia: POB 1661, 13 Sharia Aicha at-Taimouria, Cairo (Garden City); tel. (2) 3547200; fax (2) 3562495; Ambassador Dr BOER MAUNA.

Iraq: *Interests served by India.*

Ireland: POB 2681, 3 Sharia Abou el-Feda, Cairo (Zamalek); tel. (2) 7358264; fax (2) 7362863; e-mail irishemb@rite.com; Ambassador RICHARD O'BRIEN.

Israel: 6 Sharia Ibn el-Malek, Cairo (Giza); tel. (2) 7610380; fax (2) 7610414; Ambassador ZVI MAZEL.

Italy: 15 Sharia Abd ar-Rahman Fahmi, Cairo (Garden City); tel. (2) 7943194; fax (2) 7940657; e-mail ambcairo@brainy1.ie-eg.com; internet www.italembassy.org.eg; Ambassador MARIO SICA.

Japan: Cairo Centre Bldg, 2nd and 3rd Floors, 2 Sharia Abd al-Kader Hamza or 106 Sharia Qasr el-Eini, Cairo (Garden City); tel. (2) 7953962; fax (2) 7963540; e-mail center@embjapan.org.eg; internet www.mofa.go.jp/embjapan/egypt; Ambassador TAKAYA SUTO.

Jordan: 6 Sharia Juhaini, Cairo; tel. (2) 3485566; fax (2) 3601027; Ambassador NABIH AN-NIMR.

Kazakhstan: 4 Sharia Abay Kunanbayuli, New Maadi, Cairo; tel. and fax (2) 5194522; e-mail kazaemb@ids.gov.eg; Ambassador BOLAT-KHAN K. TAIZHANOV.

Kenya: POB 362, 7 Sharia el-Mohandes Galal, Cairo (Dokki); tel. (2) 3453628; fax (2) 3443400; Ambassador MUHAMMAD M. MAALIM.

Korea, Democratic People's Republic: 6 Sharia as-Saleh Ayoub, Cairo (Zamalek); tel. (2) 3408219; fax (2) 3414615; Ambassador JANG MYONG-SON.

Korea, Republic: 3 Sharia Boulos Hanna, Cairo (Dokki); tel. (2) 3611234; fax (2) 3611238; Ambassador SHIM KYOUNG-BO.

Kuwait: 12 Sharia Nabil el-Wakkad, Cairo (Dokki); tel. (2) 3602661; fax (2) 3602657; Ambassador ABD AR-RAZAK ABD AL-KADER AL-KANDRI.

Lebanon: 22 Sharia Mansour Muhammad, Cairo (Zamalek); tel. (2) 7382823; fax (2) 7382818; Ambassador SAMI KRONFOL.

Lesotho: 10 Sharia Bahr al-Ghazal, Sahafeyeen, Cairo; tel. (2) 3447025; fax (2) 3025495.

Liberia: 11 Sharia Bresil, Cairo (Zamalek); tel. (2) 3419864; fax (2) 3473074; Ambassador Dr BRAHIMA D. KABA.

Libya: 7 Sharia as-Saleh Ayoub, Cairo (Zamalek); tel. (2) 3401864; Ambassador JUM'AH AL-MAHDI AL-FAZZANI.

Lithuania: Cairo.

Malaysia: 29 Sharia Taha Hussein, Cairo (Zamalek); tel. (2) 3410863; fax (2) 3411049; Ambassador Dato RAJA MANSUR RAZMAN.

Mali: 3 Sharia al-Kawsar, Cairo (Dokki); tel. (2) 3371641; fax (2) 3371841; Ambassador ALLAYE ALPHADY CISSÉ.

Malta: 25 Sharia 12, Maadi, Cairo; tel. (2) 3804451; fax (2) 3804452; e-mail maltaemb@link.net; Ambassador GAETAN NAUDI ACIS.

Mauritania: 114 Mohi ed-Din, Abou-el Ezz, Mohandessin, Cairo; tel. (2) 3490671; fax (2) 3489060; Ambassador MUHAMMAD LEMINE OULD.

Mauritius: 156 Sharia es-Sudan, Mohandessin, Cairo; tel. (2) 7618102; fax (2) 7618101; e-mail embamaur@thewayout.net; Ambassador SOOROOJDEV PHOKEER.

Mexico: 5th Floor, 17 Sharia Port Said, 11431 Cairo (Maadi); tel. (2) 3500258; fax (2) 3511887; e-mail mexemb@idsc.gov.eg; Ambassador HÉCTOR CÁRDENAS.

Mongolia: 3 Midan en-Nasr, Cairo (Dokki); tel. (2) 3460670; Ambassador SONOMDORJIN DAMBADARJAA.

Morocco: 10 Sharia Salah ed-Din, Cairo (Zamalek); tel. (2) 3409849; fax (2) 3411937; e-mail morocemb@idsc.gov.eg; Ambassador ABD AL-LATIF MOULINE.

Mozambique: 9th Floor, 3 Sharia Abu el-Feda, Cairo (Zamalek); tel. (2) 3320647; fax (2) 3320383; e-mail emozcai@intouch.com; Ambassador DANIEL EDUARDO MONDLANE.

Myanmar: 24 Sharia Muhammad Mazhar, Cairo (Zamalek); tel. (2) 3404176; fax (2) 3416793; Ambassador U AUNG GYI.

Nepal: 9 Sharia Tiba, Madinet el-Kobah, Cairo (Dokki); tel. (2) 3603426; fax (2) 704447; Ambassador JITENDRA RAJ SHARMA.

Netherlands: 18 Sharia Hassan Sabri, Cairo (Zamalek); tel. (2) 7356434; fax (2) 7395500; e-mail az-cz@hollandemb.org.eg; internet www.hollandemb.org.eg; Ambassador SJOERD LEENSTRA.

Niger: 101 Sharia Pyramids, Cairo (Giza); tel. (2) 3865607; Ambassador MAMANE OUMAROU.

Nigeria: 13 Sharia Gabalaya, Cairo (Zamalek); tel. (2) 3406042; fax (2) 3403907; Chargé d'affaires a.i. P. S. O. EROMOBOR.

Norway: 8 Sharia el-Gezirah, Cairo (Zamalek); tel. (2) 7353340; fax (2) 7370709; e-mail embcai@mfa.no; internet www.norway.org.eg; Ambassador BJØRN FRODE ØSTERN.

Oman: 52 Sharia el-Higaz, Mohandessin, Cairo; tel. (2) 3036011; fax (2) 3036464; Ambassador ABDULLAH BIN HAMED AL-BUSAIDI.

Pakistan: 8 Sharia es-Salouli, Cairo (Dokki); tel. (2) 7487806; fax (2) 7480310; Ambassador ANWAR KEMAL.

Panama: POB 62, 4A Sharia Ibn Zanki, 11211 Cairo (Zamalek); tel. (2) 3400784; fax (2) 3411092; Chargé d'affaires a.i. ROY FRANCISCO LUNA GONZÁLEZ.

Peru: 8 Sharia Kamel esh-Shenawi, Cairo (Garden City); tel. (2) 3562973; fax (2) 3557985; Ambassador MANUEL VERAMENDI I. SERRA.

Philippines: 14 Sharia Muhammad Saleh, Cairo (Dokki); tel. (2) 7480396; fax (2) 7480393; e-mail cairope@dfa.gov.ph; Ambassador MENANDRO P. GALENZOGA.

Poland: 5 Sharia el-Aziz Osman, Cairo (Zamalek); tel. (2) 3409583; fax (2) 3405427; Ambassador ROMAN CZYZYCKI.

Portugal: 1 Sharia es-Saleh Ayoub, Cairo (Zamalek); tel. (2) 7350779; fax (2) 7350790; e-mail embpcai@link.com.eg; Ambassador MANUEL TAVARES DE SOUSA.

Qatar: 10 Sharia ath-Thamar, Midan an-Nasr, Madinet al-Mohandessin, Cairo; tel. (2) 3604693; fax (2) 3603618; Ambassador BADIR AD-DAFA.

Romania: 6 el-Khamel Muhammad, Cairo (Zamalek); tel. (2) 7360107; fax (2) 7360851; e-mail roembegy@access.com.eg; Ambassador DORU COSTEA.

Russia: 95 Sharia Giza, Cairo (Giza); tel. (2) 3489353; fax (2) 3609074; Ambassador VLADIMIR GOUDEV.

Rwanda: 23 Sharia Babel, Mohandessin, Cairo (Dokki); tel. (2) 3350532; fax (2) 3351479; Ambassador CÉLESTIN KABANDA.

San Marino: 5 Sharia Ramez, Mohandessin, Cairo; tel. (2) 3602718.

Saudi Arabia: 2 Sharia Ahmad Nessim, Cairo (Giza); tel. (2) 3490775; Ambassador ASSAD ABD AL-KAREM ABOU AN-NASR.

Senegal: 46 Sharia Abd al-Moneim Riad, Mohandessin, Cairo (Dokki); tel. (2) 3460946; fax (2) 3461039; Ambassador MAMADOU SOW.

Serbia and Montenegro: 33 Sharia Mansour Muhammad, Cairo (Zamalek); tel. (2) 3404061; fax (2) 3403913; Ambassador Dr IVAN IVEKOVIĆ.

Sierra Leone: *Interests served by Saudi Arabia.*

Singapore: 40 Sharia Babel, Cairo (Dokki); tel. (2) 7490468; fax (2) 7481682; e-mail singemb@link.com.eg; Ambassador TEE TUA BA.

Slovakia: 3 Sharia Adel Hussein Rostom, Dokki, Cairo (Giza); tel. (2) 3358240; fax (2) 3355810; e-mail zukahira@tedata.net.eg; Ambassador JOZEF CIBULA.

Slovenia: 5 es-Saraya el-Kobra Sq., Cairo (Garden City); tel. (2) 3555798; Ambassador ANDREJ ZLEBNIK.

Somalia: 27 Sharia es-Somal, Cairo (Dokki), Giza; tel. (2) 3374577; Ambassador ABDALLA HASSAN MAHMOUD.

South Africa: 18th Floor, Nile Tower Bldg, 21–23 Sharia Giza, Cairo (Giza); tel. (2) 5717203; fax (2) 5717241; e-mail saembcai@gega.net; Ambassador JUSTUS DE GOEDE.

Spain: 41 Sharia Ismail Muhammad, Cairo (Zamalek); tel. (2) 7356462; fax (2) 7352132; e-mail spainemb@startnet.com; Ambassador PEDRO LÓPEZ AGUIRREBENGOA.

Sri Lanka: POB 1157, 8 Sharia Sri Lanka, Cairo (Zamalek); tel. (2) 7350047; fax (2) 7367138; e-mail slembare@menanet.net; internet www.lankaemb-egypt.com; Ambassador D. SERASINGHE.

Sudan: 4 Sharia el-Ibrahimi, Cairo (Garden City); tel. (2) 3545043; fax (2) 3542693; Ambassador AHMAD ABD AL-HALIM.

Sweden: POB 131, 13 Sharia Muhammad Mazhar, Cairo (Zamalek); tel. (2) 3414132; fax (2) 3404357; e-mail sveamcai@link.com.eg; Ambassador CHRISTER SYLVÉN.

Switzerland: POB 633, 10 Sharia Abd al-Khalek Sarwat, Cairo; tel. (2) 5758284; fax (2) 5745236; e-mail vertretung@cai.rep.admin.ch; Ambassador BLAISE GODET.

Syria: 18 Sharia Abd ar-Rehim Sabry, POB 435, Cairo (Dokki); tel. (2) 3358806; fax (2) 3377020; Ambassador YUSUF AL-AHMAD.

Tanzania: 9 Sharia Abd al-Hamid Lotfi, Cairo (Dokki); tel. (2) 704155; Ambassador MUHAMMAD A. FOUM.

Thailand: 2 Sharia al-Malek el-Afdal, Cairo (Zamalek); tel. (2) 7358356; fax (2) 7360094; e-mail royalthai@link.net; Ambassador Dr WARAWIT KANITHASEN.

Tunisia: 26 Sharia el-Jazirah, Cairo (Zamalek); tel. (2) 3418962; Ambassador ABD AL-HAMID AMMAR.

Turkey: 25 Sharia Felaki, Cairo (Bab el-Louk); tel. (2) 3563318; fax (2) 3558110; Ambassador YAŞAR YAKIŞ.

Uganda: 9 Midan el-Messaha, Cairo (Dokki); tel. (2) 3486070; fax (2) 3485980; Ambassador IBRAHIM MUKIIBI.

Ukraine: 9 Sharia es-Saraya, Appt 31–32, Cairo (Dokki); tel. (2) 3491030; fax (2) 3360159; e-mail vlost@eis.com.eg.

United Arab Emirates: 4 Sharia Ibn Sina, Cairo (Giza); tel. (2) 3609721; e-mail uaeembassyca@online.com.eg; Ambassador AHMAD AL-MAHMOUD MUHAMMAD.

United Kingdom: 17 Sharia Ahmad Ragheb, Cairo (Garden City); tel. (2) 7940852; fax (2) 7940859; e-mail info@britishembassy.org.eg; internet www.britishembassy.org.eg; Ambassador JOHN SAWERS.

USA: 5 Sharia Latin America, Cairo (Garden City); tel. (2) 7973300; fax (2) 7973200; internet usembassy.egnet.net; Ambassador C. DAVID WELCH.

Uruguay: 6 Sharia Lotfallah, Cairo (Zamalek); tel. (2) 3415137; fax (2) 3418123; Ambassador JULIO CÉSAR FRANZINI.

Venezuela: 15ASharia Mansour Muhammad, Cairo (Zamalek); tel. (2) 3413517; fax (2) 3417373; e-mail eov@idsc.gov.eg; Ambassador DARIO BAUDER.

Viet Nam: 39 Sharia Kambiz, Cairo (Dokki); tel. (2) 3371494; fax (2) 3496597; Ambassador NGUYEN LE BACH.

Yemen: 28 Sharia Amean ar-Rafai, Cairo (Dokki); tel. (2) 3614224; fax (2) 3604815; Ambassador ABD AL-GHALIL GHILAN AHMAD.

Zambia: 6 Abd ar-Rahman Hussein, Mohandessin, Cairo (Dokki); tel. (2) 3610282; fax (2) 3610833; Ambassador Dr ANGEL ALFRED MWENDA.

Zimbabwe: 40 Sharia Ghaza, Mohandessin, Cairo; tel. (2) 3030404; fax (2) 3059741; e-mail zimcairo@thewayout.net; Ambassador Dr HENRY V. MOYANA.

Judicial System

The Courts of Law in Egypt are principally divided into two juridical court systems: Courts of General Jurisdiction and Administrative Courts. Since 1969 the Supreme Constitutional Court has been at the top of the Egyptian judicial structure.

THE SUPREME CONSTITUTIONAL COURT

The Supreme Constitutional Court is the highest court in Egypt. It has specific jurisdiction over: (i) judicial review of the constitutionality of laws and regulations; (ii) resolution of positive and negative jurisdictional conflicts and determination of the competent court between the different juridical court systems, e.g. Courts of General Jurisdiction and Administrative Courts, as well as other bodies exercising judicial competence; (iii) determination of disputes over the enforcement of two final but contradictory judgments rendered by two courts each belonging to a different juridical court system; (iv) rendering binding interpretation of laws or decree laws in the event of a dispute in the application of said laws or decree laws, always provided that such a dispute is of a gravity requiring conformity of interpretation under the Constitution.

COURTS OF GENERAL JURISDICTION

The Courts of General Jurisdiction in Egypt are effectively divided into four categories, as follows: (i) The Court of Cassation; (ii) The Courts of Appeal; (iii) The Tribunals of First Instance; (iv) The District Tribunals; each of the above courts is divided into Civil and Criminal Chambers.

Court of Cassation

Is the highest court of general jurisdiction in Egypt. Its sessions are held in Cairo. Final judgments rendered by Courts of Appeal in criminal and civil litigation may be petitioned to the Court of Cassation by the Defendant or the Public Prosecutor in criminal litigation and by any of the parties in interest in civil litigation on grounds of defective application or interpretation of the law as stated in the challenged judgment, on grounds of irregularity of form or procedure, or violation of due process, and on grounds of defective reasoning of judgment rendered. The Court of Cassation is composed of the President, 41 Vice-Presidents and 92 Justices.

President: Hon. ABD AL-BORHAN NOOR.

The Courts of Appeal: Each has geographical jurisdiction over one or more of the governorates of Egypt. Each Court of Appeal is divided into Criminal and Civil Chambers. The Criminal Chambers try felonies, and the Civil Chambers hear appeals filed against such judgment rendered by the Tribunals of First Instance where the law so stipulates. Each Chamber is composed of three Superior Judges. Each Court of Appeal is composed of President, and sufficient numbers of Vice-Presidents and Superior Judges.

The Tribunals of First Instance: In each governorate there are one or more Tribunals of First Instance, each of which is divided into several Chambers for criminal and civil litigations. Each Chamber is composed of: (a) a presiding judge, and (b) two sitting judges. A Tribunal of First Instance hears, as an Appellate Court, certain litigations as provided under the law.

District Tribunals: Each is a one-judge ancillary Chamber of a Tribunal of First Instance, having jurisdiction over minor civil and criminal litigations in smaller districts within the jurisdiction of such Tribunal of First Instance.

PUBLIC PROSECUTION

Public prosecution is headed by the Attorney-General, assisted by a number of Senior Deputy and Deputy Attorneys-General, and a sufficient number of chief prosecutors, prosecutors and assistant prosecutors. Public prosecution is represented at all levels of the Courts of General Jurisdiction in all criminal litigations and also in certain civil litigations as required by the law. Public prosecution controls and supervises enforcement of criminal law judgments.

Attorney-General: MAHIR ABD AL-WAHID.

Prosecutor-General: MUHAMMAD ABD AL-AZIZ EL-GINDI.

ADMINISTRATIVE COURTS SYSTEM (CONSEIL D'ETAT)

The Administrative Courts have jurisdiction over litigations involving the State or any of its governmental agencies. The Administrative Courts system is divided into two courts: the Administrative Courts and the Judicial Administrative Courts, at the top of which is the High Administrative Court. The Administrative Prosecutor investigates administrative crimes committed by government officials and civil servants.

President of Conseil d'Etat: Hon. MUHAMMAD HILAL QASIM.

Administrative Prosecutor: Hon. RIFA'AT KHAFAGI.

THE STATE COUNCIL

The State Council is an independent judicial body which has the authority to make decisions in administrative disputes and disciplinary cases within the judicial system.

THE SUPREME JUDICIAL COUNCIL

The Supreme Judicial Council was reinstituted in 1984, having been abolished in 1969. It exists to guarantee the independence of the judicial system from outside interference and is consulted with regard to draft laws organizing the affairs of the judicial bodies.

Religion

According to the 1986 census, some 94% of Egyptians are Muslims (and almost all of these follow Sunni tenets). According to government figures published in the same year, there are about 2m. Copts (a figure contested by Coptic sources, whose estimates range between 6m. and 7m.), forming the largest religious minority, and about 1m. members of other Christian groups. There is also a small Jewish minority.

ISLAM

There is a Higher Council for the Isamic Call, on which sit: the Grand Sheikh of al-Azhar (Chair); the Minister of Awqaf (Islamic Endowments); the President and Vice-President of Al-Azhar University; the Grand Mufti of Egypt; and the Secretary-General of the Higher Council for Islamic Affairs.

Grand Sheikh of al-Azhar: Sheikh MUHAMMAD SAYED ATTIYAH TANTAWI.

Grand Mufti of Egypt: AHMAD AT-TAYEB.

CHRISTIANITY

Orthodox Churches

Armenian Apostolic Orthodox Church: 179 Sharia Ramses, Cairo, POB 48-Faggalah; tel. (2) 5901385; fax (2) 906671; Archbishop ZAVEN CHINCHINIAN; 7,000 mems.

Coptic Orthodox Church: St Mark Cathedral, POB 9035, Anba Ruess, 222 Sharia Ramses, Abbassia, Cairo; tel. (2) 2857889; fax (2)

2825683; e-mail coptpope@tecmina.com; internet www.copticpope .org; f. AD 61; Patriarch Pope SHENOUDA III; c.13m. followers in Egypt, Sudan, other African countries, the USA, Canada, Australia, Europe and the Middle East.

Greek Orthodox Patriarchate: POB 2006, Alexandria; tel. (3) 4868595; fax (3) 4875684; e-mail goptalex@tecmina.com; internet www.greekorthodox-alexandria.org; f. AD 64; Pope and Patriarch of Alexandria and All Africa His Beatitude PETROS VII; 3m. mems.

The Roman Catholic Church

Armenian Rite

The Armenian Catholic diocese of Alexandria, with an estimated 1,276 adherents at 31 December 2000, is suffragan to the Patriarchate of Cilicia. The Patriarch is resident in Beirut, Lebanon.

Bishop of Alexandria: (vacant), Patriarcat Arménien Catholique, 36 Sharia Muhammad Sabri Abou Alam, 11121 Cairo; tel. (2) 3938429; fax (2) 3932025; e-mail pacal@gega.net.

Chaldean Rite

The Chaldean Catholic diocese of Cairo had an estimated 500 adherents at 31 December 2000.

Bishop of Cairo: Rt Rev. YOUSSEF IBRAHIM SARRAF, Evêché Chaldéen, Basilique-Sanctuaire Notre Dame de Fatima, 141 Sharia Nouzha, 11316 Cairo (Heliopolis); tel. and fax (2) 6355718.

Coptic Rite

Egypt comprises the Coptic Catholic Patriarchate of Alexandria and five dioceses. At 31 December 2000 there were an estimated 217,444 adherents in the country.

Patriarch of Alexandria: Cardinal STEPHANOS II (Andreas Ghattas), Patriarcat Copte Catholique, POB 69, 34 Sharia Ibn Sandar, Koubbeh Bridge, 11712 Cairo; tel. (2) 2571740; fax (2) 4545766.

Latin Rite

Egypt comprises the Apostolic Vicariate of Alexandria (incorporating Heliopolis and Port Said), containing an estimated 10,500 adherents at 31 December 2000.

Vicar Apostolic: Rt Rev. GIUSEPPE BAUSARDO (Titular Bishop of Ida in Mauretania), 10 Sharia Sidi el-Metwalli, Alexandria; tel. (3) 4876065; fax (3) 4838169; e-mail latinvic@link.net.

Maronite Rite

The Maronite diocese of Cairo had an estimated 5,000 adherents at 31 December 2000.

Bishop of Cairo: Rt Rev. JOSEPH DERGHAM, Evêché Maronite, 15 Sharia Hamdi, Daher, 11271 Cairo; tel. (2) 5939610.

Melkite Rite

His Beatitude Grégoire III Laham (resident in Damascus, Syria) is the Greek-Melkite Patriarch of Antioch, of Alexandria and of Jerusalem.

Patriarchal Exarchate of Egypt and Sudan: Patriarcat Grec-Melkite Catholique d'Alexandrie, 16 Sharia Daher, 11271 Cairo; tel. (2) 5904697; fax (2) 5935398; e-mail grecmelkitecath_egy@hotmail .com; 6,500 adherents (31 December 2000); Auxiliary Most Rev. JOSEPH JULES ZEREY (Titular Archbishop of Damietta).

Syrian Rite

The Syrian Catholic diocese of Cairo had an estimated 1,709 adherents at 31 December 2000.

Bishop of Cairo: Rt Rev. CLÉMENT-JOSEPH HANNOUCHE, Evêché Syrien Catholique, 46 Sharia Daher, 11271 Cairo; tel. (2) 5901234.

The Anglican Communion

The Anglican diocese of Egypt, suspended in 1958, was revived in 1974 and became part of the Episcopal Church in Jerusalem and the Middle East, formally inaugurated in January 1976. The Province has four dioceses: Jerusalem, Egypt, Cyprus and the Gulf, and Iran, and its President is the Bishop in Egypt. The Bishop in Egypt has jurisdiction also over the Anglican chaplaincies in Algeria, Djibouti, Eritrea, Ethiopia, Libya, Somalia and Tunisia.

Bishop in Egypt: Rt Rev. Dr MOUNEER HANNA ANIS, Diocesan Office, POB 87, 5 Sharia Michel Lutfalla, 11211Cairo (Zamalek); tel. (2) 7380829; fax (2) 7358941; e-mail diocese@intouch.com; internet www.geocities.com/dioceseofegypt.

Other Christian Churches

Coptic Evangelical Organization for Social Services: POB 162-11811, Panorama, Cairo; tel. (2) 2975901; fax (2) 2975878; e-mail gm@ceoss.org.eg.

Other denominations active in Egypt include the Coptic Evangelical Church (Synod of the Nile) and the Union of the Armenian Evangelical Churches in the Near East.

JUDAISM

The 1986 census recorded 794 Jews in Egypt.

Jewish Community: 13 Sharia Sebil el-Khazindar, Abbassia, Cairo; tel. (2) 4824613; internet www.geocities.com/rain/forest/ vines/5855; Office of the Community; President ESTHER WEINSTEIN.

The Press

Despite a fairly high illiteracy rate in Egypt, the country's press is well developed. Cairo is one of the region's largest publishing centres.

All newspapers and magazines are supervised, according to law, by the Supreme Press Council. The four major publishing houses of al-Ahram, Dar al-Hilal, Dar Akhbar al-Yawm and Dar at-Tahrir operate as separate entities and compete with each other commercially.

The most authoritative daily newspaper is the very long-established *Al-Ahram*.

DAILIES

Alexandria

Bareed ach-Charikat (Companies' Post): POB 813, Alexandria; f. 1952; Arabic; evening; commerce, finance, insurance and marine affairs; Editor S. BENEDUCCI; circ. 15,000.

Al-Ittihad al-Misri (Egyptian Unity): 13 Sharia Sidi Abd ar-Razzak, Alexandria; f. 1871; Arabic; evening; Propr ANWAR MAHER FARAG; Dir HASSAN MAHER FARAG.

Le Journal d'Alexandrie: 1 Sharia Rolo, Alexandria; French; evening; Editor CHARLES ARCACHE.

La Réforme: 8 Passage Sherif, Alexandria; French.

As-Safeer (The Ambassador): 4 Sharia as-Sahafa, Alexandria; f. 1924; Arabic; evening; Editor MUSTAFA SHARAF.

Tachydromos-Egyptos: 4 Sharia Zangarol, Alexandria; tel. (3) 35650; f. 1879; Greek; morning; liberal; Publr PENNY KOUTSOUMIS; Editor DINOS KOUTSOUMIS; circ. 2,000.

Cairo

Al-Ahram (The Pyramids): Sharia al-Galaa, Cairo 11511; tel. (2) 5801600; fax (2) 5786023; e-mail ahramdaily@ahram.org.eg; f. 1875; Arabic; morning, incl. Sundays; international edition published in London, United Kingdom; North American edition published in New York, USA; Chair. and Chief Editor IBRAHIM NAFEH; circ. 900,000 (weekdays), 1.1m. (Friday).

Al-Ahram al-Misaa' (The Evening Al-Ahram): Sharia al-Galaa, Cairo 11511; f. 1990; Arabic; evening; Editor-in-Chief MORSI ATALLAH.

Al-Ahrar: 58 Manshyet as-Sadr, Kobry al-Kobba, Cairo; tel. (2) 4823046; fax (2) 4823027; f. 1977; organ of Liberal Socialist Party; Editor-in-Chief SALAH QABADAYA.

Al-Akhbar (The News): Dar Akhbar al-Yawm, 6 Sharia as-Sahafa, Cairo; tel. (2) 5782600; fax (2) 5782520; f. 1952; Arabic; Chair. IBRAHIM ABU SADAH; Man. Editor GALAL DEWIDAR; circ. 780,000.

Arev: 3 Sharia Sulayman Halabi, Cairo; tel. (2) 754703; f. 1915; Armenian; evening; official organ of the Armenian Liberal Democratic Party; Editor AVEDIS YAPOUDJIAN.

The Egyptian Gazette: 24–26 Sharia Zakaria Ahmad, Cairo; tel. (2) 5783333; fax (2) 5781110; e-mail 100236.3241@compuserve.com; f. 1880; English; morning; Chair. SAMIR RAGAB; Editor-in-Chief MUHAMMAD ALI IBRAHIM; circ. 90,000.

Al-Gomhouriya (The Republic): 24 Sharia Zakaria Ahmad, Cairo; tel. (2) 5783333; fax (2) 5781717; f. 1953; Arabic; morning; mainly economic affairs; Chair. and Editor-in-Chief SAMIR RAGAB; circ. 900,000.

Al-Misaa' (The Evening): 24 Sharia Zakaria Ahmad, Cairo; tel. (2) 5781010; fax (2) 5784747; f. 1956; Arabic; evening; political, social and sport; Editor-in-Chief MUHAMMAD FOUDAH; Man. Dir ABD AL-HAMROSE; circ. 450,000.

Phos: 14 Sharia Zakaria Ahmad, Cairo; f. 1896; Greek; morning; Editor S. PATERAS; Man. BASILE A. PATERAS; circ. 20,000.

Le Progrès Egyptien: 24 Sharia Zakaria Ahmad, Cairo; tel. (2) (2) 5783333; fax (2) 5781110; f. 1890; French; morning including Sundays; Chair. SAMIR RAGAB; Editor-in-Chief KHALED ANWAR BAKIR; circ. 60,000.

Al-Wafd: 1 Sharia Boulos Hanna, Cairo (Dokki); tel. (2) 3482079; fax (2) 3602007; f. 1984; organ of the New Wafd Party; Editor-in-Chief GAMAL BADAWI; circ. 360,000.

PERIODICALS

Alexandria

Al-Ahad al-Gedid (New Sunday): 88 Sharia Said M. Koraim, Alexandria; tel. (3) 807874; f. 1936; Editor-in-Chief and Publr GALAL M. KORAITEM; circ. 60,000.

Alexandria Medical Journal: 4 G. Carducci, Alexandria; tel. (3) 4829001; fax (3) 4833076; e-mail alexmj@mail.com; internet www .who.sci.eg; f. 1922; English, French and Arabic; quarterly; publ. by Alexandria Medical Asscn; Editor Prof. TOUSSOUN ABOUL AZM.

Amitié Internationale: 59 ave el-Hourriya, Alexandria; tel. (3) 23639; f. 1957; publ. by Asscn Egyptienne d'Amitié Internationale; Arabic and French; quarterly; Editor Dr ZAKI BADAOUI.

L'Annuaire des Sociétés Egyptiennes par Actions: 23 Midan Tahrir, Alexandria; f. 1930; annually in Dec. French; Propr ELIE I. POLITI; Editor OMAR ES-SAYED MOURSI.

L'Echo Sportif: 7 Sharia de l'Archevêché, Alexandria; French; weekly; Propr MICHEL BITTAR.

Egyptian Cotton Gazette: POB 1772, 12 Sharia Muhammad Tala'at Nooman, Alexandria 21111; tel. (3) 4806971; fax (3) 4873002; e-mail alcotexa@idsc.gov.eg; internet www.alcotexa.org; f. 1947; organ of the Alexandria Cotton Exporters' Association; English; 2 a year; Chief Editor GALAI EL REFAI.

Informateur des Assurances: 1 Sharia Sinan, Alexandria; f. 1936; French; monthly; Propr ELIE I. POLITI; Editor SIMON A. BARANIS.

La Réforme Illustré: 8 Passage Sherif, Alexandria; French; weekly; general.

Sina 'at en-Nassig (L'Industrie Textile): 5 rue de l'Archevêché, Alexandria; Arabic and French; monthly; Editor PHILIPPE COLAS.

Voce d'Italia: 90 Sharia Farahde, Alexandria; Italian; fortnightly; Editor R. AVELLINO.

Cairo

Al-Ahali (The People): Sharia Kareem ad-Dawli, Tala'at Harb Sq., Cairo; tel. (2) 7786583; fax (2) 3900412; f. 1978; weekly; publ. by the National Progressive Unionist Party; Chair. LOTFI WAKID; Editor-in-Chief ABD AL-BAKOURY.

Al-Ahram al-Arabi: Sharia al-Galaa, Cairo 11511; f. 1997; Arabic; weekly; political, social and economic affairs; Chair. IBRAHIM NAFIE; Editor-in-Chief OSAMA SARAYA.

Al-Ahram Hebdo: POB 1057, Sharia al-Galaa, Cairo 11511; tel. (2) 5783104; fax (2) 5782631; e-mail hebdo@ahram.org.eg; internet www.ahram.org.eg/hebdo; f. 1993; French; weekly; Editor-in-Chief MUHAMMAD SALMAWI.

Al-Ahram al-Iqtisadi (The Economic Al-Ahram): Sharia al-Galaa, Cairo 11511; tel. (2) 5786100; fax (2) 5786833; Arabic; weekly (Monday); economic and political affairs; owned by Al-Ahram publrs; Chief Editor ISSAM RIFA'AT; circ. 93,798.

Al-Ahram Weekly (The Pyramids): Al-Ahram Bldg, Sharia al-Galaa, Cairo 11511; tel. (2) 5786100; fax (2) 5786833; e-mail weeklyweb@ahram.org.eg; internet www.ahram.org.eg/weekly; f. 1989; English; weekly; publ. by Al-Ahram publications; Editor-in-Chief HOSNI GUINDY; circ. 150,000.

Akhbar al-Adab: 6 Sharia as-Sahafa, Cairo; tel. (2) 5795620; fax (2) 5782510; e-mail akhbarelyom@akhbarelyom.org; internet www .akhbarelyom.org.eg/eladab; f. 1993; literature and arts for young people; Editor-in-Chief GAMAL AL-GHITANI.

Akhbar al-Hawadith: 6 Sharia as-Sahafa, Cairo; tel. (2) 5782600; fax (2) 5782510; f. 1993; weekly; crime reports; Editor-in-Chief MUHAMMAD BARAKAT.

Akhbar an-Nogoome: 6 Sharia as-Sahafa, Cairo; tel. (2) 5782600; fax (2) 5782510; f. 1991; weekly; theatre and film news; Editor-in-Chief AMAL OSMAN.

Akhbar ar-Riadah: 6 Sharia as-Sahafa, Cairo; tel. (2) 5782600; fax (2) 5782510; f. 1990; weekly; sport; Editor-in-Chief IBRAHIM HEGAZY.

Akhbar al-Yom (Daily News): 6 Sharia as-Sahafa, Cairo; tel. (2) 5782600; fax (2) 5782520; internet www.akhbarelyom.org.eg; f. 1944; Arabic; weekly (Saturday); Chair. and Editor-in-Chief IBRAHIM ABU SEDAH; circ. 1,184,611.

Akher Sa'a (Last Hour): Dar Akhbar al-Yawm, Sharia as-Sahafa, Cairo; tel. (2) 5782600; fax (2) 5782530; f. 1934; Arabic; weekly (Sunday); independent; consumer and news magazine; Editor-in-Chief MAHMOUD SALAH; circ. 150,000.

Aqidaty (My Faith): 24–26 Sharia Zakaria Ahmad, Cairo; tel. (2) 5783333; fax (2) 5781110; weekly; Muslim religious newspaper; Editor-in-Chief ABD AR-RAOUF ES-SAYED; circ. 300,000.

Al-Arabi an-Nassiri: Cairo; f. 1993; publ. by the Nasserist Party; Editor-in-Chief MAHMOUD EL-MARAGHI.

Al-Azhar: Idarat al-Azhar, Sharia al-Azhar, Cairo; f. 1931; Arabic; Islamic monthly; supervised by the Egyptian Council for Islamic Research of Al-Azhar University; Dir MUHAMMAD FARID WAGDI.

Al-Bitrul (Petroleum): Cairo; monthly; publ. by the Egyptian General Petroleum Corporation.

Cairo Today: POB 2098, 1079 Corniche en-Nil, Cairo (Garden City); monthly.

Computerworld Middle East: World Publishing Ltd (Egypt), 41A Masaken al-Fursan Bldg, Sharia Kamal Hassan Ali, Cairo 11361; tel. (2) 3460601; fax (2) 3470118; English; monthly; specialist computer information.

Contemporary Thought: University of Cairo, Cairo; quarterly; Editor Dr Z. N. MAHMOUD.

Ad-Da'wa (The Call): Cairo; Arabic; monthly; organ of the Muslim Brotherhood.

Ad-Doctor: 8 Sharia Hoda Sharawi, Cairo; f. 1947; Arabic; monthly; Editor Dr AHMAD M. KAMAL; circ. 30,000.

Droit al-Haqq: Itihad al-Mohameen al-Arab, 13 Sharia Itihad, Cairo; publ. by the Arab Lawyers' Union; 3 a year.

Echos: 1–5 Sharia Mahmoud Bassiouni, Cairo; f. 1947; French; weekly; Dir and Propr GEORGES QRFALI.

The Egyptian Mail: 24–26 Sharia Zakaria Ahmad, Cairo; weekly; Sat. edn of *The Egyptian Gazette*; English; circ. 40,000.

El-Elm Magazine (Sciences): 24 Sharia Zakaria Ahmad, Cairo; tel. (2) 5781010; fax (2) 5784747; f. 1976; Arabic; monthly; publ. with the Academy of Scientific Research in Egypt; circ. 70,000.

Al-Fusoul (The Seasons): 17 Sharia Sherif Pasha, Cairo; Arabic; monthly; Propr and Chief Editor SAMIR MUHAMMAD ZAKI ABD AL-KADER.

Al-Garidat at-Tigariyat al-Misriya (The Egyptian Business Paper): 25 Sharia Nubar Pasha, Cairo; f. 1921; Arabic; weekly; circ. 7,000.

Hawa'a (Eve): Dar al-Hilal, 16 Sharia Muhammad Ezz el-Arab, Cairo 11511; tel. (2) 3625450; fax (2) 3625469; f. 1892; women's magazine; Arabic; weekly (Sat.); Chief Editor EKBAL BARAKA; circ. 210,502.

Al-Hilal Magazine: Dar al-Hilal, 16 Sharia Muhammad Ezz el-Arab, Cairo 11511; tel. (2) 3625450; fax (2) 3625469; f. 1895; Arabic; literary monthly; Editor MOUSTAFA NABIL.

Horreyati: 24 Sharia Zakaria Ahmad, Cairo; tel. (2) 5781010; fax (2) 5784747; f. 1990; weekly; social, cultural and sport; Editor-in-Chief MUHAMMAD NOUR ED-DIN; circ. 250,000.

Huwa wa Hiya (He and She): Middle East Foundation, POB 525, Cairo 11511; tel. (2) 5167400; fax (2) 5167325; e-mail editor@ huwawahiya.com; f. 1977; monthly; news, leisure, sport, health, religion, women's issues; Dir GEORGE TAWFIK.

Industrial Egypt: POB 251, 26A Sharia Sherif Pasha, Cairo; tel. (2) 3928317; fax (2) 3928075; f. 1924; quarterly bulletin and year book of the Federation of Egyptian Industries in English and Arabic; Editor ALI FAHMY.

Informateur Financier et Commercial: 24 Sharia Sulayman Pasha, Cairo; f. 1929; weekly; Dir HENRI POLITI; circ. 15,000.

Al-Iza'a wat-Television (Radio and Television): 16 Sharia Muhammad Ezz el-Arab, Cairo 11511; tel. (2) 3643314; fax (2) 3543030; f. 1935; Arabic; weekly; Man. Editor MAHMOUD ALI; circ. 80,000.

Al-Kerazeh (The Sermon): Cairo; Arabic; weekly newspaper of the Coptic Orthodox Church.

Al-Kawakeb (The Stars): Dar al-Hilal, 16 Sharia Muhammad Ezz el-Arab, Cairo 11511; tel. (2) 3625450; fax (2) 3625469; f. 1952; Arabic; weekly; film magazine; Editor-in-Chief RAGAA AN-NAKKASH; circ. 86,381.

Kitab al-Hilal: Dar al-Hilal, 16 Sharia Muhammad Ezz el-Arab, Cairo 11511; tel. (2) 3625450; fax (2) 3625469; monthly; Founders EMILE, SHOUKRI ZEIDAN; Editor MOUSTAFA NABIL.

Al-Kora wal-Malaeb (Football and Playgrounds): 24 Sharia Zakaria Ahmad, Cairo; tel. (2) 5783333; fax (2) 5784747; f. 1976; Arabic; weekly; sport; circ. 150,000.

Al-Liwa' al-Islami (Islamic Standard): 11 Sharia Sherif Pasha, Cairo; f. 1982; Arabic; weekly; govt paper to promote official view of Islamic revivalism; Propr AHMAD HAMZA; Editor MUHAMMAD ALI SHETA; circ. 30,000.

Lotus Magazine: 104 Sharia Qasr el-Eini, Cairo; f. 1992; English, French and Arabic; quarterly; computer software magazine; Editor BEREND HARMENS.

Magallat al-Mohandessin (The Engineer's Magazine): 28 Sharia Ramses, Cairo; f. 1945; publ. by The Engineers' Syndicate; Arabic and English; 10 a year; Editor and Sec. MAHMOUD SAMI ABD AL-KAWI.

Al-Magallat az-Zira'ia (The Agricultural Magazine): Cairo; monthly; agriculture; circ. 30,000.

Mayo (May): Sharia al-Galaa, Cairo; f. 1981; weekly; organ of National Democratic Party; Chair. ABDULLAH ABD AL-BARY; Chief Editor SAMIR RAGAB; circ. 500,000.

Medical Journal of Cairo University: Qasr el-Eini Hospital, Sharia Qasr el-Eini, Cairo; tel. and fax (2) 3655768; f. 1933; Qasr el-Eini Clinical Society; English; quarterly; Editor SALEH A. BEDIR.

MEN Economic Weekly: Middle East News Agency, 4 Sharia Hoda Sharawi, Cairo; tel. (2) 3933000; fax (2) 3935055.

The Middle East Observer: 41 Sharia Sherif, Cairo; tel. (2) 3926919; fax (2) 3939732; e-mail meo@soficom.eg; internet www .meobserver.org; f. 1954; English; weekly; specializing in economics of Middle East and African markets; also publishes supplements on law, foreign trade and tenders; agent for IMF, UN and IDRC publications, distributor of World Bank publications; Man. Owner AHMAD FODA; Chief Editor HESHAM A. RAOUF; circ. 20,000.

Middle East Times Egypt: 2 Sharia el-Malek el-Afdal, Cairo (Zamalek); tel. (2) 3419930; fax (2) 3413725; e-mail met@ritsec1.com .eg; f. 1983; English; weekly; Man. Editor ROD CRAIG; circ. 6,000.

Al-Musawar: Dar al-Hilal, 16 Sharia Muhammad Ezz el-Arab, Cairo 11511; tel. (2) 3625450; fax (2) 3625469; f. 1924; Arabic; weekly; news; Chair. and Editor-in-Chief MAKRAM MUHAMMAD AHMAD; circ. 130,423.

Nesf ad-Donia: Sharia al-Galaa, Cairo 11511; tel. (2) 5786100; f. 1990; weekly; women's magazine; publ. by Al-Ahram Publications; Editor-in-Chief SANAA AL-BESI.

October: Dar al-Maaref, 1119 Sharia Corniche en-Nil, Cairo; tel. (2) 5777077; fax (2) 5744999; f. 1976; weekly; Chair. and Editor-in-Chief RAGAB AL-BANA; circ. 140,500.

Al-Omal (The Workers): 90 Sharia al-Galaa, Cairo; publ. by the Egyptian Trade Union Federation: Arabic; weekly; Chief Editor AHMAD HARAK.

PC World Middle East: World Publishing Ltd (Egypt), 41A Masaken al-Fursan Bldg, Sharia Kamal Hassan Ali, Cairo 11361; tel. (2) 34606; fax (2) 3470118; monthly; computers.

Le Progrès Dimanche: 24 Sharia al-Galaa, Cairo; tel. (2) 5781010; fax (2) 5784747; French; weekly; Sunday edition of *Le Progrès Egyptien*; Editor-in-Chief KHALED ANWAR BAKIR; circ. 35,000.

Rose al-Yousuf: 89A Sharia Qasr el-Eini, Cairo; tel. (2) 3540888; fax (2) 3556413; f. 1925; Arabic; weekly; political; circulates throughout all Arab countries; Chair. of Board and Editor-in-Chief MUHAMMAD ABD AL-MONEIM; circ. 35,000.

As-Sabah (The Morning): 4 Sharia Muhammad Said Pasha, Cairo; f. 1922; Arabic; weekly (Thurs.); Editor RAOUF TAWFIK.

Sabah al-Kheir (Good Morning): 89A Sharia Qasr el-Eini, Cairo; tel. (2) 3540888; fax (2) 3556413; f. 1956; Arabic; weekly (Thurs.); light entertainment; Chief Editor RAOUF TAWFIK; circ. 70,000.

Ash-Shaab (The People): 313 Sharia Port Said, Sayeda Zeinab, Cairo; tel. (2) 3909716; fax (2) 3900283; e-mail elshaab@idsc.gov.eg; f. 1979; organ of Socialist Labour Party; bi-weekly (Tues. and Fri.); Editor-in-Chief MAGDI AHMAD HUSSEIN; circ. 130,000.

Shashati (My Screen): 24 Sharia Zakaria Ahmad, Cairo; tel. (2) 5781010; fax (2) 5784747; weekly; art, culture, fashion and television news.

As-Siyassa ad-Dawliya: Al-Ahram Bldg, 12th Floor, Sharia al-Galaa, Cairo 11511; tel. (2) 5786022; fax (2) 5786833; e-mail siyassa@ahram.org.eg; quarterly; politics and foreign affairs; Editor-in-Chief Dr OSAMA AL-GHAZALI.

Tabibak al-Khass (Family Doctor): Dar al-Hilal, 16 Sharia Muhammad Ezz el-Arab, Cairo; tel. (2) 3625473; fax (2) 3625442; monthly.

At-Tahrir (Liberation): 5 Sharia Naguib, Rihani, Cairo; Arabic; weekly; Editor ABD AL-AZIZ SADEK.

At-Taqaddum (Progress): c/o 1 Sharia Jarim ed-Dawlah, Cairo; f. 1978; weekly; organ of National Progressive Unionist Party.

Tchehreh Nema: 14 Sharia Hassan el-Akbar (Abdine), Cairo; f. 1904; Iranian; monthly; political, literary and general; Editor MANUCHEHR TCHEHREH NEMA MOADEB ZADEH.

Up-to-Date International Industry: 10 Sharia al-Galaa, Cairo; Arabic and English; monthly; foreign trade journal.

Watani (My Country): 27 Sharia Abd al-Khalek Sarwat, Cairo; tel. (2) 3927201; fax (2) 3935946; e-mail watani@tecmina.com; internet www.watani.com.eg; f. 1958; Arabic and English; independent Sun. newspaper addressing Egyptians in general and the Christian Copts in particular; Editor-in-Chief YOUSSEF SIDHOM; circ. 60,000–100,000.

Yulio (July): July Press and Publishing House, Cairo; f. 1986; weekly; Nasserist; Editor ABDULLAH IMAM; and a monthly cultural magazine; Editor MAHMOUD AL-MARAGHI.

NEWS AGENCIES

Middle East News Agency (MENA): 17 Sharia Hoda Sharawi, Cairo; tel. (2) 3933000; fax (2) 3935055; e-mail newsroom@mena.org .eg; internet www.mena.org.eg; f. 1955; regular service in Arabic, English and French; Chair. and Editor-in-Chief MOUSTAFA NAGUIB.

Foreign Bureaux

Agence France-Presse (AFP): POB 1437-15511, 2nd Floor, 10 Misaha Sq., Cairo; tel. (2) 3481236; fax (2) 3603282; Chief SAMMY KETZ.

Agencia EFE (Spain): 35A Sharia Abou el-Feda, 4th Floor, Apt 14, Cairo (Zamalek); Correspondent DOMINGO DEL PIÑO.

Agenzia Nazionale Stampa Associata (ANSA) (Italy): 19 Sharia Abd al-Khalek Sarwat, Cairo; tel. (2) 3929821; fax (2) 3938642; Chief ANTONELLA TARQUINI.

Allgemeiner Deutscher Nachrichtendienst (ADN) (Germany): 17 Sharia el-Brazil, Apt 59, Cairo (Zamalek); tel. (2) 3404006; Correspondent RALF SCHULTZE.

Associated Press (AP) (USA): POB 1077, 1117 Sharia Corniche en-Nil, (Maspiro), Cairo 11221; tel. (2) 5784091; fax (2) 5784094; internet www.ap.org; Chief of Middle East Services EARLEEN FISHER.

Deutsche Presse-Agentur (dpa) (Germany): 1st Floor, 8 Sharia Dar esh-Shefaa, Cairo (Garden City); tel. (2) 7956842; fax (2) 7956318; e-mail dpa@gega.net; Chief ANN-BÉATRICE CLASMANN.

Informatsionnoye Telegrafnoye Agentstvo Rossii—Telegrafnoye Agentstvo Suverennykh Stran (ITAR—TASS) (Russia): 30 Sharia Muhammad Mazhar, Cairo (Zamalek); tel. (2) 3419784; fax (2) 3417268; Dir MIKHAIL I. KROUTIKHIN.

Jiji Press (Japan): 9 Sharia el-Kamal Muhammad, Cairo (Zamalek); tel. (2) 7356237; fax (2) 7355244; e-mail jijipresscairo@ yahoo.com; Chief TETSUYA KATAYAMA.

Kyodo News (Japan): Flat 301, 15 Sharia Hassan Sabri, Cairo 11211 (Zamalek); tel. (2) 7361756; fax (2) 7356105; e-mail kyodo@ intouch.com; Chief SHINGO KINIWA.

Reuters (United Kingdom): POB 2040, 21st Floor, Bank Misr Tower, 153 Sharia Muhammad Farid, Cairo; tel. (2) 5777150; fax (2) 5771133; e-mail cairo.newsroom@reuters.com; internet www .reuters.com; Chief ALISTAIR LYON.

United Press International (UPI) (USA): POB 872, 4 Sharia Eloui, Cairo; tel. (2) 3928106.

Xinhua (New China) News Agency (People's Republic of China): 2 Moussa Galal Sq., Mohandessin, Cairo; tel. (2) 3448950.

The Iraqi News Agency (INA) and the Saudi Press Agency (SPA) are also represented in Cairo.

PRESS ASSOCIATIONS

Egyptian Press Syndicate: Cairo; Chair. IBRAHIM NAFEH.

Foreign Press Association: Room 2037, Marriott Hotel, Cairo; tel. (2) 3419957.

Publishers

General Egyptian Book Organization: POB 1660, 117 Sharia Corniche en-Nil, Boulac, Cairo; tel. (2) 5775371; fax (2) 5754213; e-mail ssarhan@idsc.gov.eg; f. 1961; editing, publishing and distribution; organizer of Cairo International Book Fair; affiliated to the Ministry of Culture; Chair. Dr SAMIR SARHAN; Commercial Dir SAMIR SAAD KHALIL.

Alexandria

Alexandria University Press: Shatby, Alexandria.

Dar al-Matbo al-Gadidah: 5 Sharia St Mark, Alexandria; tel. (3) 4825508; fax (3) 4833819; agriculture, information sciences; social sciences.

Egyptian Printing and Publishing House: Ahmad es-Sayed Marouf, 59 Safia Zaghoul, Alexandria; f. 1947.

Maison Egyptienne d'Editions: Ahmad es-Sayed Marouf, Sharia Adib, Alexandria; f. 1950.

Maktab al-Misri al-Hadith li-t-Tiba wan-Nashr: 7 Sharia Noubar, Alexandria; also at 2 Sharia Sherif, Cairo; Man. AHMAD YEHIA.

Cairo

Al-Ahram Establishment: Al-Ahram Bldg, 6 Sharia al-Galaa, Cairo 11511; tel. (2) 5786100; fax (2) 5786023; e-mail ahram@ahram .org.eg; internet www.ahram.org.eg; f. 1875; publ. newspapers, magazines and books, incl. *Al-Ahram*; Chair. and Chief Editor IBRAHIM NAFEI; Dep. Chair. and Gen. Man. ALI GHONEIM.

Akhbar al-Yawm Publishing Group: 6 Sharia as-Sahafa, Cairo; tel. (2) 5748100; fax (2) 5748895; f. 1944; publ. *Al-Akhbar* (daily), *Akhbar al-Yawm* (weekly), and colour magazine *Akher Sa'a* (weekly); Pres. IBRAHIM SAAD.

Boustany's Publishing House: 29 Sharia Faggalah, Cairo 11271; tel. (2) 5915315; fax (2) 5908025; e-mail boustany@idsc.net.eg; internet www.boustanys.com; f. 1900; fiction, poetry, history, biography, philosophy, language, literature, politics, religion, archaeology, Egyptology; Chief Exec. FADWA BOUSTANY.

Cairo University Press: Al-Giza, Cairo; tel. (2) 846144.

Dar al-Gomhouriya: 24 Sharia Zakaria Ahmad, Cairo; tel. (2) 5781010; fax (2) 5784747; affiliate of At-Tahrir Printing and Publishing House; publications include the dailies, *Al-Gomhouriya, Al-Misaa', Egyptian Gazette* and *Le Progrès Egyptien*; Pres. SAMIR RAGAB.

Dar al-Hilal Publishing Institution: 16 Sharia Muhammad Ezz el-Arab, Cairo 11511; tel. (2) 3625450; fax (2) 3625469; f. 1892; publ. *Al-Hilal, Riwayat al-Hilal, Kitab al-Hilal, Tabibak al-Khass* (monthlies); *Al-Mussawar, Al-Kawakeb, Hawaa, Samir, Mickey* (weeklies); Chief Exec. MAKRAN MUHAMMAD AHMAD.

Dar al-Kitab al-Masri: POB 156, 33 Sharia Qasr en-Nil, Cairo 11511; tel. (2) 3922168; fax (2) 3924657; e-mail hlelzein@datum.com .eg; f. 1929; publishing, printing and distribution; publishers of books on Islam and history, as well as dictionaries, encyclopaedias, textbooks, children's books and books of general interest; Pres. and Man. Dir HASSAN EZ-ZEIN.

Dar al-Maaref: 1119 Sharia Corniche en-Nil, Cairo; tel. (2) 5777077; fax (2) 5744999; e-mail maaref@idselgov.eg; f. 1890; publishing, printing and distribution of wide variety of books in Arabic and other languages; publishers of *October* magazine; Chair. and Man. Dir RAGAB AL-BANA.

Dar an-Nahda al-Arabia: 32 Sharia Abd al-Khalek Sarwat, Cairo; tel. (2) 3926931; f. 1960; literature, law.

Dar an-Nashr (formerly Les Editions Universitaires d'Egypte): POB 1347, 41 Sharia Sherif, Cairo 11511; tel. (2) 3934606; fax (2) 3921997; f. 1947; university textbooks, academic works, encyclopaedia.

Dar ash-Shorouk Publishing House (Egyptian Publishers Association): 8 Sharia Sebaweh el-Masri, Rabaa el-Adawia; Nasr City, Cairo 11371; tel. (2) 4023399; fax (2) 4037567; e-mail imoallem@shorouk.com; f. 1968; publishing, printing and distribution; publishers of books on politics, history, Islamic studies, economics, literature, art and children's books; Chair. IBRAHIM EL-MOALLEM.

Dar ath-Thakafah al-Gadidah: 32 Sharia Sabry Abou Alam, Cairo; tel. (2) 42718; f. 1968; Pres. MUHAMMAD YOUSUF ELGUINDI.

Editions le Progrès: 6 Sharia Sherif Pasha, Cairo; Propr WADI SHOUKRI.

Egyptian Co for Printing and Publishing: 40 Sharia Noubar, Cairo; tel. (2) 21310; Chair. MUHAMMAD MAHMOUD HAMED.

Elias Modern Publishing House: 1 Sharia Kenisset ar-Rum el-Kathulik, Daher, Cairo; tel. (2) 5903756; fax (2) 5880091; e-mail eliaspub@tedata.net.eg; internet www.eliaspublishing.com; f. 1913; publishing, printing and distribution; publs dictionaries, children's books and books on linguistics, poetry and arts; Man. Dir LAURA KFOURY; Gen. Man. NADIM ELIAS.

Al-Khira Press: 8 Sharia Soliman el-Halabi, Cairo; tel. and fax (2) 5744809; Owner ABD AL-MEGUID MUHAMMAD.

Lagnat at-Taalif wat-Targama wan-Nashr (Committee for Writing, Translating and Publishing Books): 9 Sharia el-Kerdassi (Abdine), Cairo.

Librairie La Renaissance d'Egypte (Hassan Muhammad & Sons): POB 2172, 9 Sharia Adly, Cairo; f. 1930; religion, history, geography, medicine, architecture, economics, politics, law, philosophy, psychology, children's books, atlases, dictionaries; Man. HASSAN MUHAMMAD.

Maktabet Misr: POB 16, 3 Sharia Kamal Sidki, Cairo; tel. (2) 5898553; fax (2) 5907593; f. 1932; publs wide variety of fiction,

biographies and textbooks for schools and universities; Man. AMIR SAID GOUDA ES-SAHHAR.

Middle East Book Centre: 45 Sharia Qasr en-Nil, Cairo; tel. (2) 910980; f. 1954; biography, fiction, history, language, literature, religion, philosophy, sciences; Man. Dir Dr A. M. MOSHARRAFA.

National Centre for Educational Research and Development: 12 Sharia Waked, el-Borg el-Faddy, POB 836, Cairo; tel. (2) 3930981; f. 1956; formerly Documentation and Research Centre for Education (Ministry of Education); bibliographies, directories, information and education bulletins; Dir Prof. ABD EL-FATTAH GALAL.

National Library Press (Dar al-Kutub): Midan Ahmad Maher, Cairo; bibliographic works.

Senouhy Publishers: 54 Sharia Abd al-Khalek Sarwat, Cairo; f. 1956; history, poetry, regional interests, religion, non-fiction; Man. Dir LEILA A. FADEL.

At-Tahrir Printing and Publishing House: 24 Sharia Zakaria Ahmad, Cairo; tel. (2) 5781222; fax (2) 2784747; e-mail eltahrir@ eltahrir.net; internet www.eltahrir.net; f. 1953; affil. to Shura (Advisory) Council; Pres. and Chair. of Bd SAMIR RAGAB.

Watani (My Country): 27 Sharia Abd al-Khalek Sarwat, Cairo; tel. (2) 3927201; fax (2) 3935946; e-mail watani@tecmina.com; internet www.watani.com.eg; f. 1958; Arabic and English; Editor-in-Chief YOUSSEF SIDHOM.

Broadcasting and Communications

TELECOMMUNICATIONS

Telecommunications Regulatory Authority (TRA): 3 Burg Abu-el Feda, Cairo (Zamalek); e-mail tra@mcit.gov.eg; f. 2000.

Telecom Egypt: POB 2271, Sharia Ramses, Cairo 11511; tel. (2) 5793444; fax (2) 5744244; internet www.telecomegypt.com.eg; f. 1957; sole provider of fixed-line telephones; due to begin mobile telecommunications operations in 2002; partial privatization scheduled for 2002; Chair. AKIL HAMED BESHIR.

Egyptian Company for Mobile Services (MobiNil): Cairo; e-mail customercare@mobinil.com; internet www.mobinil.com; began operation of the existing state-controlled mobile telecommunications network in early 1998; owned by France Telecom and Orascom Telecom; CEO OSMAN SULTAN.

Orascom Telecom: 160 Sharia 26 July, POB 1191, Cairo (Agouza); tel. (2) 3026930; fax (2) 3440201; e-mail info@orascom.com; internet www.orascom.com; Chair. NAGUIB SAWARIS.

Vodafone Egypt: 7A Corniche en-Nil, Maadi, 11431 Cairo; tel. (2) 5292000; e-mail customer-service@vodafone.com.eg; internet www .vodafone.com/eg; f. 1998 by the MisrFone consortium; mobile telephone service provider; majority-owned by Vodafone International (UK); Chair. MUHAMMAD NOSSAIR; CEO and Man. Dir IAN GRAY.

BROADCASTING

Radio

Egyptian Radio and Television Union (ERTU): POB 11511, Cairo 1186; tel. (2) 5787120; fax (2) 746989; internet www.sis.gov.eg/ vidaudio/html/audiofm.htm; f. 1928; home service radio programmes in Arabic, English and French; foreign services in Arabic, English, French, Swahili, Hausa, Bengali, Urdu, German, Spanish, Armenian, Greek, Hebrew, Indonesian, Malay, Thai, Hindi, Pashtu, Farsi, Turkish, Somali, Portuguese, Fulani, Italian, Zulu, Shona, Sindebele, Lingala, Afar, Amharic, Yoruba, Wolof, Bambara; Pres. AMIN BASSIOUNI.

Middle East Radio: Société Egyptienne de Publicité, 24–26 Sharia Zakaria Ahmad, Cairo; tel. (2) 5781010; fax (2) 5784747; internet www.tahriv.net.

Television

Egypt had two direct television broadcast satellites. The second satellite, Nilesat 102, was launched in August 2000.

Egyptian Radio and Television Union (ERTU): see Radio.

Finance

(cap. = capital; res = reserves; dep. = deposits; m. = million;
brs = branches; amounts in Egyptian pounds unless otherwise
stated)

BANKING

Central Bank

Central Bank of Egypt: 31 Sharia Qasr en-Nil, Cairo; tel. (2)
3931514; fax (2) 3926361; e-mail research@cbe.org.eg; internet www
.cbe.org.eg; f. 1961; controls Egypt's monetary policy and supervises
the banking and insurance sectors; dep. 101,904m., total assets
146,001m. (June 2000); Gov. and Chair. ISMAIL HASSAN MUHAMMAD;
Dep. Gov. MAHMOUD IBRAHIM ABOUL-EIOUN; 3 brs.

Commercial and Specialized Banks

Alexandria Commercial and Maritime Bank, SAE: POB 2376,
85 ave el-Hourriya, Alexandria 21519; tel. (3) 3921237; fax (3)
3913706; f. 1981; cap. 84.1m., res 87.0m., dep. 1,386.2m. (Dec. 2001);
Chair. and Man. Dir MUHAMMAD ADEL EL-BARKOUKI; 6 brs.

Bank of Alexandria: 49 Sharia Qasr en-Nil, Cairo; tel. (2) 3911203
(Cairo); fax 3919805 (Cairo); e-mail foreign@alexbank.com;
internet www.alexbank.com; f. 1957; privatization pending; cap.
700m., res 486.8m., dep. 19,196.7m. (June 2000); Chair. MAHMOUD
ABD AS-SALAM OMAR; 184 brs.

Bank of Commerce and Development (At-Tegaryoon): POB
1373, 13 Sharia 26 July, Mohandessin, Cairo (Agouza); tel. (2)
7472063; fax (2) 3023963; f. 1980; cap. 205.9m., res 0.7m., dep.
734.2m. (Dec. 2000); Chair. and Man. Dir SAMIR MUHAMMAD FOUAD EL-
QASRI; 6 brs.

Banque du Caire, SAE: POB 1495, 30 Sharia Roushdy, Cairo
(Abdin); tel. (2) 3904554; fax (2) 3908992; e-mail foreign@bdc.com
.eg; internet www.bdc.com.eg; f. 1952; state-owned; cap. 750.0m., res
629.3m., dep. 30,785.0m. (June 2001); Chair. AHMAD MONIR EL-
BARDAI; Vice-Chair. MONA YASSEN; 239 brs in Egypt, 4 abroad.

Banque Misr, SAE: 151 Sharia Muhammad Farid, Cairo; tel. (2)
3912711; fax (2) 3919779; internet www.banquemisr.com; f. 1920;
privatization pending; cap. 1,000m., res 940.2m., dep. 50,687.4m.
(June 2000); Chair. BAHAA ED-DIN HELMY; 438 brs.

Commercial International Bank (Egypt), SAE: POB 2430, Nile
Tower Bldg, 21–23 Sharia Charles de Gaulle, Cairo (Giza); tel. (2)
5703043; fax (2) 5703172; e-mail info@cibeg.com; internet www
.cibeg.com; f. 1975 as Chase National Bank (Egypt) SAE; adopted
present name 1987; National Bank of Egypt has 19.91% interest,
Bankers Trust Co (USA) 18.76%, International Finance Corpn 5%;
cap. 650m., res 813.5m., dep. 12,152.1m. (Dec. 2000); Exec. Chair.
and Man. Dir HISHAM EZZ AL-ARAB; 27 brs.

Egyptian Arab Land Bank: 78 Sharia Gamet ad-Duwal al-Arabia,
Mohandessein, Cairo (Giza); tel. (2) 3383691; fax 3383561; e-mail
albcd@starnet.com.eg; internet www.ealb.com.eg; f. 1880; cap.
211.9m., res 162.8m., dep. 12,488.4m. (Dec. 2001); Chair. MUSTAFA
ABOUL-FUTTOUH; 26 brs in Egypt, 25 abroad.

Export Development Bank of Egypt (EDBE): 108 Mohyee el-
Din Abou al-Ezz, Cairo 12311 (Dokki); tel. (2) 7480587; fax (2)
3385940; f. 1983 to replace National Import-Export Bank; cap.
250.0m., res 257.8m., dep. 4,958.9m. (June 2000); Chair. MAHMOUD
MUHAMMAD MAHMOUD; Vice-Chair. SALAH ED-DIN FAHMY; 14 brs.

HSBC Bank Egypt, SAE: POB 126, Abou el-Feda Bldg, 3 Sharia
Abou el-Feda, Cairo (Zamalek); tel. (2) 3409186; fax (2) 3414010; f.
1982 as Hongkong Egyptian Bank; changed name to Egyptian
British Bank in 1994; changed name to above in 2001; the Hongkong
and Shanghai Banking Corporation has a 90% shareholding, other
interests 10%; cap. 168.2m., res 88.7m., dep. 3,188.4m. (Dec. 2000);
Chair. ANDREW DIXON; Deputy Chair. and Man. Dir ABD AS-SALAM EL-
ANWAR; 7 brs.

Mohandes Bank: 3–5 Sharia Mossadek, Cairo; tel. (2) 3362760; fax
(2) 3362741; internet www.mohandesbank.com; f. 1979; cap.
161.0m., res 5.8m., dep. 4,320.6m. (Dec. 1999); Pres. and Man. Dir
MUHAMMAD ADEL HASHISH; 10 brs.

National Bank for Development (NBD): POB 647, 5 Sharia el-
Borsa el-Gedida, Cairo 11511; tel. (2) 7963505; fax (2) 7964966;
e-mail nbd@internetegypt.com; internet www.nbdegypt.com; f.
1980; cap. 242.0m., res 183.0m., dep. 6,151.0m. (Dec. 2001); Chair.
MUHAMMAD ZAKI EL-ORABI; 67 brs; there are affiliated National Banks
for Development in 16 governorates.

National Bank of Egypt: POB 11611, National Bank of Egypt
Tower, 1187 Corniche en-Nil, Cairo; tel. (2) 5749101; fax (2)
5762672; e-mail nbe@nbe.com.eg; internet www.nbe.com.eg; f. 1898;
privatization pending; handles all commercial banking operations;

cap. 1,000m., res 2,698m., dep. 63,454m. (June 2000); Chair. AHMAD
DIAA ED-DIN FAHMY; Dep. Chair. HUSSEIN ABD AL-AZIZ HUSSEIN; 343 brs.

Principal Bank for Development and Agricultural Credit:
POB 11669, 110 Sharia Qasr el-Eini, Cairo; tel. (2) 7951204; fax (2)
7948337; f. 1976 to succeed former credit organizations; state-
owned; cap. 1,406m., res 275m., dep. 7,293m. (June 2001); Chair. Dr
YOUSSEF A. RAHMAN HOSNI; 167 brs.

Société Arabe Internationale de Banque (SAIB): POB 54, 56
Sharia Gamet ed-Dowal al-Arabia, Mohandessin, Cairo (Giza); tel.
(2) 3499463; fax (2) 3603497; f. 1976; the Arab International Bank
has a 41.1% share, other interests 58.9%; cap. US $42.0m., res
US $36.5m., dep. US $379.7m. (Dec. 2000); Chair. Dr HASSAN ABBAS
ZAKI; Man. Dir MUHAMMAD NOUR; 4 brs.

United Bank of Egypt (UBE): Cairo Center, 106 Sharia Kasr el-
Eini, Cairo; tel. (2) 7920146; fax (2) 7920153; e-mail info@ube.net;
internet www.ube.net; f. 1981 as Dakahlia National Bank for Development; current name adopted in 1997; cap. 200m., res 20.3m.,
dep 2,761.8m. (Dec. 2000); Chair. and Man. Dir SEIF COUTRY; 9 brs.

Social Bank

Nasser Social Bank: POB 2552, 35 Sharia Qasr en-Nil, Cairo; tel.
(2) 3924484; fax (2) 3921930; f. 1971; state-owned; interest-free
savings and investment bank for social and economic activities,
participating in social insurance, specializing in financing co-operatives, craftsmen and social institutions; cap. 20m. Chair. NASSIF
TAHOON.

Multinational Banks

Arab African International Bank: 5 Midan as-Saray el-Koubra,
POB 60, Majlis esh-Sha'ab, Cairo 11516 (Garden City); tel. (2)
7945094; fax (2) 7958493; internet www.aaibank.com; f. 1964 as
Arab African Bank, renamed 1978; cap. US $100.0m., res
US $231m., dep. US $789m. (Dec. 2001); commercial investment
bank; shareholders are Govts of Kuwait, Egypt, Algeria, Jordan and
Qatar, Bank Al-Jazira (Saudi Arabia), Rafidain Bank (Iraq), indi-
viduals and Arab institutions; Chair. Dr FAHED MOHAMMED AR-
RASHED; Vice-Chair. and Man. Dir HASSAN E. ABDALLA; 6 brs in Egypt,
3 abroad.

Arab International Bank: POB 1563, 35 Sharia Abd al-Khalek
Sarwat, Cairo; tel. (2) 3918794; fax (2) 3916233; internet www
.aib_egypt.com; f. 1971 as Egyptian International Bank for Foreign
Trade and Investment, renamed 1974; cap. US $262.0m., res
US $143.2m., dep. US $2,314.7m. (June 2001); offshore bank; aims
to promote trade and investment in shareholders' countries and
other Arab countries; owned by Egypt, Libya, UAE, Oman, Qatar
and private Arab shareholders; Chair. Dr MUSTAFA KHALIL; Man. Dir
ALI GAMAL AD-DIN DABBOUS; 7 brs.

Commercial Foreign Venture Banks

Alwatany Bank of Egypt: POB 63, 13 Sharia Semar, Dr Fouad
Mohi ed-Din Sq., Gameat ed-Dewal al-Arabia, Mohandessin, Cairo
12655; tel. (2) 3388816; fax (2) 3379302; e-mail watany@alwatany
.com.eg; internet www.alwatany.com.eg; f. 1980; cap. 157.5m., res
171.9m., dep. 3,568.3m. (Dec. 2000); Chair. ADEL HUSSEIN EZZI; Man.
Dir FATMA I. LOTFY; 13 brs.

BNP PARIBAS Le Caire: POB 2441, 3 Latin America St, Cairo
(Garden City); tel. (2) 7948323; fax (2) 7940619; e-mail bcpegypt@
bcpegypt.com; f. 1977 as Banque du Caire et de Paris SAE; name
changed in 2001; BNP Group Paribas has 76% interest and Banque
du Caire 19.8%; cap. 50.5m., res 30.6m., dep. 933.9m. (Dec. 2000);
Chair. JEAN THOMAZEAU; Man. Dir NOUR NAHAURI; 6 brs.

Cairo Barclays Bank, SAE: POB 110, 12 Midan esh-Sheikh
Yousuf, Cairo (Garden City); tel. (2) 3662600; fax (2) 3662810; f. 1975
as Cairo Barclays Int. Bank; name changed to Banque du Caire
Barclays International in 1983; renamed in 1999; Barclays Bank has
60%, Banque du Caire 40%; cap. 106.0m., res 118.5m., dep.
2,741.6m. (Dec. 2000); Chair. ANDREW ROBERT BUXTON; Man. Dir
COLIN McCORMACK; 5 brs.

Cairo Far East Bank, SAE: POB 757, 104 Corniche en-Nil, Cairo
(Dokki); tel. (2) 3362516; fax (2) 3483818; f. 1978; cap. 62.5m., res
13.6m., dep. 282.9m. (Dec. 2000); Chair. Dr HASSAN FAG EN-NOUR;
Man. Dir FAWZIA YOUSUF; 3 brs.

Crédit Agricole Indosuez (Egypt), SAE: 46 Sharia el-Batal
Ahmad Abd al-Aziz, Mohandessin, Cairo; tel. (2) 3361897; fax (2)
3608673; e-mail caie@eg.ca-indosuez.com; internet www
.ca-indosuez.com; f. 1978 as Crédit International d'Egypte; renamed
in 2001; Crédit Agricole Indosuez has 75% interest, el-Mansour & el-
Maghraby for Financial Investment 25%; cap. 60.2m., res 33.5m.,
dep. 634.9m. (Dec. 2001); Chair. MUHAMMAD LOTFI MANSOUR; Man. Dir
ADRIAN PHARES; 3 brs.

Delta International Bank: POB 1159, 1113 Corniche en-Nil,
Cairo; tel. (2) 5753492; fax (2) 5743403; e-mail dibbank@mst1.mist

.com.eg; f. 1978; cap. 300m., res 156m., dep. 1,556m. (Dec. 2001); Chair. and Man. Dir ALI MUHAMMAD NEGM; 17 brs.

Egyptian American Bank: POB 1825, 4 & 6 Sharia Hassan Sabri, Cairo (Zamalek); tel. (2) 7380126; fax (2) 7380609; e-mail ibadran@eab-online.com; internet www.eab-online.com; f. 1976; Amex Holdings Inc. has 40.8% interest, Bank of Alexandria 32.5%, others 26.7%; cap. 144.0m., res 381.0m., dep. 5,305.3m. (Dec. 2000); Chair. MAHMOUD ABD AS-SALAM OMAR; Man. Dir RODERICK RICHARDS; 30 brs.

Egyptian Commercial Bank: POB 92, 4th Floor, Evergreen Bldg, 10 Sharia Talaat Harb, Majlis ash-Sha'ab, Cairo; tel. (2) 5779766; fax (2) 5799862; f. 1978 as Alexandria-Kuwait International Bank, name changed as above in 1997; cap. 150m., res 15.4m., dep. 1,713.9m. (Dec. 2000); Chair. MUHAMMAD ABD AL-WAHAD; Gen. Man. AHMAD NABIL EL-MINOUFI; 6 brs.

Egyptian Gulf Bank: POB 56, El-Orman Plaza Bldg, 8–10 Sharia Ahmad Nessim, Cairo (Giza); tel. (2) 7606640; fax (2) 7606512; e-mail h.r.egb@mst1.mist.com.eg; f. 1981; Misr Insurance Co has 24.9% interest; cap. 217.7m., res 25.8m., dep. 1,675.1m. (Dec. 2000); Chair. JAWAD BU KHAMSEEN; Man. Dir MUHAMMAD BARAKAT; 5 brs.

Egyptian-Saudi Finance Bank: POB 445, 60 Sharia Mohy ad-Din Abu al-Ezz, Cairo (Dokki); tel. (2) 7481777; fax (2) 7611436; internet www.esf-bank.com; f. 1980 as Pyramids Bank; cap. 119.1m., res 24.5m., dep. 1,845.9m. (Dec. 2000); Chair. Sheikh SALEH ABDULLAH KAMAL; Man. Dir SOBHY BADAWY YAHIA; 7 brs.

Faisal Islamic Bank of Egypt, SAE: POB 2445, 1113 Corniche en-Nil, Cairo 11511; tel. (2) 5753109; fax (2) 777301; e-mail fisalbnk@internetegypt.com; f. 1977; all banking operations conducted according to Islamic principles; cap. 263.7m., res 80.6m., dep. 8,301.0m. (Dec. 2001); Chair. Prince MUHAMMAD AL-FAISAL AS-SA'UD; 14 brs.

Misr-America International Bank: POB 1003, 12 Sharia Nadi es-Seid, Cairo 11511 (Dokki); tel. (2) 7616623; fax (2) 7616610; e-mail maib@instinct.net; f. 1977; Misr Insurance Co has 50% interest, Banque du Caire 33%, Industrial Development Bank of Egypt 17%, S.A. for Investments, Luxembourg 1.2%; cap. 75.0m., res 37.9m., dep. 939.6m. (Dec. 2000); Chair. and Man. Dir AHMED MOUNIR EL-BARDAIE; 8 brs.

Misr Exterior Bank, SAE: Cairo Plaza Bldg, Corniche en-Nil, Boulaque, Cairo; tel. (2) 778701; fax (2) 762806; e-mail meb2@rite.com; internet www.misrext.com; f. 1981; Misr International Bank has 30.1% interest, Banque Misr 19.5%; cap. 51.1m., res 214.8m., dep. 5,026.2m. (Dec. 2000); Chair. and Man. Dir ABDULLAH TAYEL; 9 brs.

Misr International Bank, SAE: POB 218, 54 Sharia el-Batal Ahmad Abd al-Aziz, Mohandessin, Cairo 12411; tel. (2) 7497255; fax (2) 3489796; f. 1975; the Banque Misr has 26.0% interest, Banco di Roma 10%, UBAF London 8.5%, Europartners 7.9%; cap. 112.5m., res 792.1m., dep. 9,691.1m. (Dec. 2000); Chair. Dr BAHAA AD-DIN HELMY; 18 brs.

Misr Romanian Bank: 54 Sharia Lebanon, Mohandessin, Cairo (Giza); tel. (2) 3039825; fax (2) 3039804; e-mail mrbeg@ie-eg.com; internet www.mrb.com.eg; f. 1977; Banque Misr has 33% interest, Romanian Commercial Bank (Bucharest) 19%, Raiffeisen Bank (Bucharest) 15%, and Romanian Bank for Development (Groupe Societe Générale Bucharest) 15%; cap. 81.5m., res 219.0m., dep. 2,270.7m. (Dec. 2001); Chair. Dr AHMAD METWALLY HUSSAIN; 6 brs in Egypt, 3 in Romania.

Mohandes Bank: POB 170, 3–5 Sharia Mossadek, Cairo (Dokki); tel. (2) 3373110; fax (2) 3362741; internet www.mohandesbank.com; f. 1979; cap. 161.0m., res 5.9m., dep. 4,768.9m. (Dec. 2000); Chair. and Man. Dir MUHAMMAD ADEL HASHISH; 10 brs.

Nile Bank, SAE: POB 2741, 35 Sharia Ramses, Abd al-Moneim Riad Sq., Cairo; tel. (2) 5741417; fax (2) 5756296; e-mail nilebank@egyptonline.com; f. 1978; cap. 32.2m., res 88.3m., dep. 1,365.0m. (Dec. 2000); Chair. ISSA EL-AYOUTY; Man. Dir MUHAMMAD ES-SABAGH; 18 brs.

Suez Canal Bank, SAE: POB 2620, 7 Abd el-Kader Hamza St, Cairo (Garden City); tel. (2) 7943433; fax (2) 7942526; e-mail info@scbank.com.eg; internet www.scbank.com.eg; f. 1978; cap. 230.0m., res 505.4m., dep. 9,831.3m. (Mar. 2002); Chair. and Man. Dir MOUSTAFA FAYEZ HABLAS; 20 brs.

Non-Commercial Banks

Arab Banking Corporation—Egypt: 1 Sharia el-Saleh Ayoub, Cairo (Zamalek); tel. (2) 7362684; fax (2) 7363643; e-mail abcegypt@arabbanking.com.eg; internet www.arabbanking.com.eg; f. 1982 as Egypt Arab African Bank; acquired by Arab Banking Corporation (Bahrain) in 1999; Arab Banking Corporation has 93% interest, other interests 7%; cap. 75m., res 80m., dep. 1,220.6m. (Dec. 2000); merchant and investment bank services; Chair. EISSA MUHAMMAD AL SUWAIDI; Vice-Chair. FARAHAT O. EKDARA; 9 brs.

Arab Investment Bank: POB 826, Cairo Sky Center Bldg, 8 Sharia Abd al-Khalek Sarwat, Cairo; tel. (2) 768097; fax (2) 770329; e-mail arinbank@mst1.mist.com.eg; internet www.arab-investment-bank.egypt.com; f. 1978 as Union Arab Bank for Development and Investment; Egyptian/Syrian/Libyan joint venture; cap. 85.8m., res 2.5m., dep. 1,720.7m. (Dec. 2000); Chair. Prof. Dr MUHAMMAD AHMAD AR-RAZAZ; 14 brs.

Housing and Development Bank, SAE: POB 234, 12 Sharia Syria, Mohandessin, Cairo (Giza); tel. (2) 7492013; fax (2) 7600712; e-mail hdbank@internetegypt.com; internet www.hdb-eg.com; f. 1979; cap. 54m., res 213.6m., dep. 1,329.6m. (Dec. 2000); Chair. and Man. Dir MUHAMMAD TALA'AT ABOU SEDA; 24 brs.

Islamic International Bank for Investment and Development: POB 180, 4 Sharia Ali Ismail, Mesaha Sq., Cairo (Dokki); tel. (2) 7489983; fax (2) 3600771; e-mail ibid@infinitycom.eg; internet www.iibid.com; f. 1980; cap. 133.8m., res –25.3m., dep. 3,389.5m. (Dec. 2000); Chair. BADAWY HASAN HASSANAIN; Gen. Man. SAYED MUHAMMAD EL-MENSHAWY; 8 brs.

Misr Iran Development Bank: POB 219, Nile Tower Bldg, 21–23 Charles de Gaulle Ave, Cairo 12612 (Giza); tel. (2) 5727311; fax (2) 5701185; e-mail midb@mst1.mist.com.eg; f. 1975; the Bank of Alexandria has 39.73% interest, Misr Insurance Co 39.73%, Iran Foreign Investment Co 20.54%; cap. 211.9m., res 129.6m., dep. 1,077.1m. (Dec. 2000); Chair. and Man. Dir ISMAIL HASSAN MUHAMMAD; 7 brs.

National Société Générale Bank, SAE: POB 2664, Evergreen Bldg, 10 Sharia Tala'at Harb, Cairo; tel. (2) 5749376; fax (2) 5776249; e-mail nsgb.info@socgen.com; internet www.nsgb.co.eg; f. 1978; the Société Générale de Paris has 51% interest, National Bank of Egypt 18%, other interests 31%; cap. 220m., res 252.9m., dep. 4,615.8m. (Dec. 2000); Chair. MUHAMMAD MADBOULY; CEO JEROME GUIRAUD; 9 brs.

STOCK EXCHANGES

Capital Market Authority: 20 Sharia Emad ed-Din, Cairo; tel. (2) 5741000; fax (2) 5755339; e-mail cmauth@idsc.gov.eg; f. 1979; Chair. ABDELHAMID IBRAHIM; Dep. Chair. ASHRAF SHAMS ED-DIN.

Cairo and Alexandria Stock Exchanges (CASE): 4 Sharia esh-Sherifein, Cairo; 11 Sharia Talaat Harb, Menshia, Alexandria; tel. (2) 3921447; fax (2) 3928526; tel. (3) 4835432; fax (3) 4823039; internet www.egyptse.com; f. 1861; Chair. Dr SAMEH AT-TORGOMAN.

INSURANCE

Al-Ahly Insurance: Cairo; state-owned; scheduled for privatization.

Arab International Insurance Co: POB 2704, 28 Sharia Talaat Harb, Cairo; tel. (2) 5746322; fax (2) 5760053; e-mail aiic@aiic.com.eg; internet www.aiic.co.eg; f. 1976; a joint-stock free zone company established by Egyptian and foreign insurance companies; Chair. and Man. Dir HASSAN MUHAMMAD HAFEZ.

Ach-Chark Insurance Co: 15 Sharia Qasr en-Nil, Cairo; tel. (2) 5740455; fax (2) 5753316; e-mail ins_chark@frcu.eun.eg; f. 1931; scheduled for privatization; general and life; Chair. ANWAR ZEKRY.

Egyptian Reinsurance Co, SAE: POB 950, 7 Sharia Abd al-Latif Boltia, Cairo (Garden City); tel. (2) 3543354; fax (2) 3557483; e-mail egyptre@intouch.com; internet www.egyptre.com.eg; f. 1957; scheduled for privatization; Chair. MUHAMMAD HAMMAM BADR.

Al-Iktisad esh-Shabee, SAE: 11 Sharia Emad ed-Din, Cairo; f. 1948; Man. Dir and Gen. Man. W. KHAYAT.

Misr Insurance Co: POB 261, 44a Sharia Dokki, Cairo (Dokki); tel. (2) 3355350; fax (2) 3370428; e-mail micfin@frcu.eun.eg; internet www.frcu.eun.eg; f. 1934; all classes of insurance and reinsurance; scheduled for privatization; Chair. MOAWAD HASSANEIN.

Mohandes Insurance Co: POB 62, 3 El-Mesaha Sq., Cairo (Dokki); tel. (2) 3352162; fax (2) 3352697; e-mail mohandes@mist1.mist.com.eg; f. 1980; privately-owned; insurance and reinsurance; Chair. and Man. Dir SAMIR MOUSTAFA METWALLI.

Al-Mottahida: POB 804, 9 Sharia Sulayman Pasha, Cairo; f. 1957.

National Insurance Co of Egypt, SAE: POB 592, 41 Sharia Qasr en-Nil, Cairo; tel. (2) 3910731; fax (2) 3909133; e-mail omr-nice@eis.co.eg; f. 1900; cap. 100m. scheduled for privatization; Chair. MUHAMMAD ABUL-YAZEED.

Provident Association of Egypt, SAE: POB 390, 9 Sharia Sherif Pasha, Alexandria; f. 1936; Man. Dir G. C. VORLOOU.

Trade and Industry

GOVERNMENT AGENCY

Egyptian Geological Survey and Mining Authority (EGSMA): 3 Tarik Salah Salem, Abbassia, Cairo; tel. (2) 2855660; fax (2) 4820128; e-mail egsma@idsc.gov.eg; internet www.egsma.gov.eg; f. 1896; state supervisory authority concerned with geological mapping, mineral exploration and other mining activities; Chair. M. E. EL-HENAWY.

DEVELOPMENT ORGANIZATION

General Authority for Investment and Free Zones (GAFI): POB 1007, 8 Sharia Adly, Cairo; tel. (2) 3906163; fax (2) 3907315; e-mail gafi@idsc.gov.eg; internet www.gafi.gov.eg; Chair. Eng. Dr MUHAMMAD EL-GHAMRAWI DAWOUD.

CHAMBERS OF COMMERCE

Federation of Chambers of Commerce: 4 el-Falaki Sq., Cairo; tel. (2) 3551164; fax (2) 3557940; Pres. MAHMOUD EL-ARABY.

Alexandria

Alexandria Chamber of Commerce: 31 Sharia el-Ghorfa Altogariya, Alexandria; tel. (3) 809339; fax (2) 808993; Pres. MOUSTAFA EN-NAGGAR.

Cairo

American Chamber of Commerce in Egypt: Cairo; e-mail web@amcham.org.eg; internet www.amcham.org.eg.

Cairo Chamber of Commerce: 4 el-Falaki Sq., Cairo; tel. (2) 3558261; fax (2) 3563603; f. 1913; Pres. MAHMOUD EL-ARABY; Sec.-Gen. MOSTAFA ZAKI TAHA.

In addition, there are 20 local chambers of commerce.

EMPLOYERS' ORGANIZATION

Federation of Egyptian Industries: 1195 Cornich en-Nil, Ramlet Boulal, Cairo; and 65 Gamal Abd an-Nasser Ave, Alexandria; tel. (2) 5796950; fax (2) 5796953 (Cairo); tel. and fax (3) 4916121 (Alexandria); e-mail feind@idsc.net.eg; internet www.fei.org.eg; f. 1922; Pres. MUHAMMAD FARID KHAMIS; represents the industrial community in Egypt.

PETROLEUM AND GAS

Arab Petroleum Pipelines Co (SUMED): POB 158, Es-Saray, 431 El-Geish Ave, Louran, Alexandria; tel. (3) 5864138; fax (3) 5871295; f. 1974; Suez–Mediterranean crude oil transportation pipeline (capacity: 117m. metric tons per year) and petroleum terminal operators; Chair. and Man. Dir Eng. HAZEM AMIN HAMMAD.

Belayim Petroleum Co (PETROBEL): POB 7074, Sharia el-Mokhayam, Cairo (Nasr City); tel. (2) 2621738; fax (2) 2609792; f. 1977; capital equally shared between EGPC and International Egyptian Oil Co, which is a subsidiary of ENI of Italy; petroleum and gas exploration, drilling and production; Chair. and Man. Dir FAROUK KENAWY.

Egyptian General Petroleum Corporation (EGPC): POB 2130, 4th Sector, Sharia Palestine, New Maadi, Cairo; tel. (2) 7065956; fax (2) 7028813; e-mail info@egpc.com.eg; internet www.egpc.com.eg; state supervisory authority generally concerned with the planning of policies relating to petroleum activities in Egypt with the object of securing the development of the petroleum industry and ensuring its effective administration; Chair. MOUSTAFA SHAARAWI; Dep. Chair. HASAB EN-NABI ASAL.

General Petroleum Co (GPC): POB 743, 8 Sharia Dr Moustafa Abou Zahra, Cairo (Nasr City); tel. (2) 4030975; fax (2) 4037602; f. 1957; wholly-owned subsidiary of EGPC; operates mainly in Eastern Desert; Chair. HUSSEIN KAMAL.

Egyptian Natural Gas Holding Co: Cairo; f. 2001 as part of a restructuring of the natural gas sector; Chair. MUHAMMAD TAWILA.

GASCO: Sheraton Heliopolis, 6A Sharia Moustafa Rifaat, Cairo (Heliopolis); tel. (2) 2666458; fax (2) 2666469; e-mail gasco@gasco.com.eg; internet www.gasco.com.eg; f. 1997; Gen. Man. Eng. MUHAMMAD IBRAHIM.

Gulf of Suez Petroleum Co (GUPCO): POB 2400, 4th Sector, Sharia Palestine, New Maadi, Cairo 11511; tel. (2) 3520985; fax (2) 3531286; f. 1965; partnership between EGPC and BP Egypt (UK/USA); developed the el-Morgan oilfield in the Gulf of Suez, also holds other exploration concessions in the Gulf of Suez and the Western Desert; Chair. AHMED SHAWKY ABDINE; Man. Dir L. D. McVAY.

Western Desert Petroleum Co (WEPCO): POB 412, Borg eth-Thagr Bldg, Sharia Safia Zagloul, Alexandria; tel. (3) 4928710; fax (3) 4934016; f. 1967 as partnership between EGPC (50% interest) and Phillips Petroleum (35%) and later Hispanoil (15%); developed Alamein, Yidma and Umbarka fields in the Western Desert and later Abu Qir offshore gasfield in 1978 followed by NAF gas field in 1987; Chair. Eng. MUHAMMAD MOHI ED-DIN BAHGAT.

UTILITIES

Electricity

In 1998 seven new electricity generation and distribution companies were created, under the direct ownership of the Egyptian Electricity Authority (EEA). In 2000 the EEA was restructured into a holding company controlling five generation and seven distribution companies. A specialized grid company was to manage electricity transmission. The Government commenced partial privatizations of the generation and distribution companies in 2001–02, while retaining control of the hydroelectric generation and grid management companies.

Egypt Electricity Holding Co: Sharia Ramses, Cairo (Nasr City); tel. (2) 2616301; fax (2) 2616512; formerly the Egyptian Electricity Authority, renamed as above in 2000; Chair. NABIL YOUNES.

Alexandria Electricity Distribution: 9 Sharia Sidi el-Liban, Alexandria; tel. (3) 4935726; fax (3) 4933223.

Cairo Electricity Co: 53 Sharia 26 July, Cairo; tel. (2) 766612.

Cairo Electricity Distribution: 53 Sharia 26 July, Cairo; tel. (2) 766612; fax (2) 760383; Gen. Man. LOFTY EL-MOSHTLY.

Gas

Egypt Gas Company: Corniche en-Nil, 2 Geziret Muhammad, Warak-Imbaba, Cairo; tel. and fax (2) 3126081; e-mail egyptgas@hotmail.com; f. 1983; Chair and Man. Dir NABIL HASHEM.

Water

National Association for Potable Water and Sanitary Drainage (NOPWASD): 6th Floor, Mogamma Bldg, et-Tahrir Sq., Cairo; tel. (2) 3557664; fax (2) 3562869; f. 1981; water and sewerage authority; Chair. MUHAMMAD KHALED MOUSTAFA.

TRADE UNIONS

Egyptian Trade Union Federation (ETUF): 90 Sharia al-Galaa, Cairo; tel. (2) 5740362; fax (2) 5753427; f. 1957; 23 affiliated unions; 5m. mems; affiliated to the International Confederation of Arab Trade Unions and to the Organization of African Trade Union Unity; Pres. MUHAMMAD ES-SAYED RASHID; Gen. Sec. MUHAMMAD ES-SAYED MORSI.

General Trade Union of Air Transport: G2, Osman Ibn Affoun, Sofin Sq., Cairo; tel. (2) 2413165; fax (2) 6336149; 11,000 mems; Pres. Eng. CHEHATA MUHAMMAD CHEHATA; Gen. Sec. MUHAMMAD HUSSEIN.

General Trade Union of Banks and Insurance: 2 Sharia el-Kady el-Fadel, Cairo; 56,000 mems; Pres. MAHMOUD MUHAMMAD DABBOUR; Gen. Sec. ABDOU HASSAN MUHAMMAD ALI.

General Trade Union of Building and Wood Workers: 9 Sharia Emad ed-Din, Cairo; tel. (2) 5913486; fax (2) 5915849; e-mail gtubww@hotmail.com; 500,000 mems; Pres. SAYED TAHA HASSAN; Gen. Sec. MUHAMMAD BAHAA.

General Trade Union of Chemical Workers: 90 Sharia al-Galaa, Cairo; fax (2) 5750490; 120,000 mems; Pres. IBRAHIM EL-AZHARY; Gen. Sec. GAAFER ABD EL-MONEM.

General Trade Union of Commerce: 54DSharia el-Gomhouriya, Alfy Borg, Cairo; tel. (2) 5903159; fax (2) 5914144; f. 1903; 120,000 mems; Pres. FOUAD TOMA; Gen. Sec. SAMIR A. SHAFI.

General Trade Union of Food Industries: 3 Sharia Housni, Hadaek el-Koba, Cairo; 111,000 mems; Pres. SAAD M. AHMAD; Gen. Sec. ADLY TANOUS IBRAHIM.

General Trade Union of Health Services: 22 Sharia esh-Sheikh Qamar, es-Sakakiny, Cairo; 56,000 mems; Pres. IBRAHIM ABOU EL-MUTI IBRAHIM; Gen. Sec. AHMAD ABD AL-LATIF SALEM.

General Trade Union of Hotels and Tourism Workers: POB 606, 90 Sharia al-Galaa, Cairo; tel. and fax (2) 773901; 70,000 mems; Pres. MUHAMMAD HILAL ESH-SHARKAWI.

General Trade Union of Maritime Transport: 36 Sharia Sharif, Cairo; 46,000 mems; Pres. THABET MUHAMMAD ES-SEFARI; Gen. Sec. MUHAMMAD RAMADAN ABOU TOR.

General Trade Union of Military Production: 90 Sharia al-Galaa, Cairo; 64,000 mems; Pres. MOUSTAFA MUHAMMAD MOUNGI; Gen. Sec. FEKRY IMAM.

General Trade Union of Mine Workers: 5 Sharia Ali Sharawi, Hadaek el-Koba, Cairo; 14,000 mems; Pres. ABBAS MAHMOUD IBRAHIM; Gen. Sec. AMIN HASSAN AMER.

General Trade Union of Petroleum Workers: 5 Sharia Ali Sharawi, Hadaek el-Koba, Cairo; tel. (2) 4820091; fax (2) 4834551; 60,000 mems; Pres. FAUZI ABD AL-BARI; Gen. Sec. AMIR ABD ES-SALAM.

General Trade Union of Postal Workers: 90 Sharia al-Galaa, Cairo; 80,000 mems; Pres. HASSAN MUHAMMAD EID; Gen. Sec. SALEM MAHMOUD SALEM.

General Trade Union of Press, Printing and Information: 90 Sharia al-Galaa, Cairo; tel. (2) 740324; 55,000 mems; Pres. MUHAMMAD ALI EL-FIKKI; Gen. Sec. AHMAD ED-DESSOUKI.

General Trade Union of Public and Administrative Workers: 2 Sharia Muhammad Haggag, Midan et-Tahrir, Cairo; tel. (2) 5742134; fax (2) 5752044; e-mail mostommmostafa@hotmail.com; 250,000 mems; Pres. Dr AHMAD ABDELZAHER; Gen. Sec. MUKHTAR HAMOUDA.

General Trade Union of Public Utilities Workers: POB 194, 6 Sharia Ramsis, Cairo; tel. (2) 5799614; fax (2) 5799616; 290,000 mems; Pres. MUHAMMAD ES-SAYED MORSI ALY; Gen. Sec. USAMA GAMAL ABDUL SAMIEE.

General Trade Union of Railway Workers: POB 84 (el-Faggalah), 15 Sharia Emad ed-Din, Cairo; tel. (2) 5930305; fax (2) 5917776; 90,000 mems; Pres. SABER AHMAD HUSSAIN; Gen. Sec. YASIN SOLUMAN.

General Trade Union of Road Transport: 90 Sharia al-Galaa, Cairo; tel. (2) 5752955; fax (2) 5754919; 245,000 mems; Pres. SABRY EL-GUERIDI; Gen. Sec. SAYED RADURAN.

General Trade Union of Telecommunications Workers: POB 651, Cairo; 60,000 mems; Pres. KHAIRI HACHEM; Sec.-Gen. IBRAHIM SALEH.

General Trade Union of Textile Workers: 327 Sharia Shoubra, Cairo; 244,000 mems; Pres. ALI MUHAMMAD DOUFDAA; Gen. Sec. HASSAN TOULBA MARZOUK.

General Trade Union of Workers in Agriculture and Irrigation: 31 Sharia Mansour, Cairo (Bab el-Louk); tel. (2) 3541419; 150,000 mems; Pres. MUKHTAR ABD AL-HAMID; Gen. Sec. FATHI A. KURTAM.

General Trade Union of Workers in Engineering, Metal and Electrical Industries: 90 Sharia al-Galaa, Cairo; tel. (2) 742519; 160,000 mems; Pres. SAID GOMAA; Gen. Sec. MUHAMMAD FARES.

Transport

RAILWAYS

The area of the Nile Delta is well served by railways. Lines also run from Cairo southward along the Nile to Aswan, and westward along the coast to Salloum.

Egyptian National Railways: Station Bldg, Midan Ramses, Cairo 11794; tel. (2) 5751000; fax (2) 5740000; f. 1852; length 8,600 km; 42 km electrified; a 346-km line to carry phosphate and iron ore from the Bahariya mines, in the Western Desert, to the Helwan iron and steel works in south Cairo, was opened in 1973, and the Qena–Safaga line (length 223 km) came into operation in 1989; Chair. EID ABDELKADER.

Alexandria Passenger Transport Authority: POB 466, Aflaton, esh-Shatby, Alexandria 21111; tel. (3) 5975223; fax (3) 5971187; e-mail chrmapta@cns-egypt.com; f. 1860; controls City Tramways (28 km), Ramleh Electric Railway (16 km), suburban buses and minibuses (1,688 km); 121 tram cars, 42 light railway three-car sets; Chair. and Tech. Dir Eng. MEDHAT HAFEZ.

Cairo Metro: National Authority for Tunnels, POB 466, Ramses Bldg, Midan Ramses, Cairo 11794; tel. (2) 5742968; fax (2) 5742950; construction of the first electrified, 1,435 mm gauge underground transport system in Africa and the Middle East began in Cairo in 1982. Line 1 has a total of 35 stations (5 underground), connects el-Marg el Gedida with Helwan and is 44 km long with a 4.2-km tunnel beneath central Cairo; Line 2 links Shoubra el-Kheima with Giza, totalling 19km. (13 km in tunnel), and with 18 stations (12 underground), two of which interconnect with Line 1; Line 2 was to be extended a further 2.5 km south to el-Monib; construction of Line 3 which will connect Imbaba and Mohandeseen with Cairo International Airport and will total 34.2 km (30.3 km in tunnel) with 29 stations (27 underground) was due to commence in late 2003; Chair. Eng. SAAD HASSAN SHEHATA.

Cairo Transport Authority: POB 254, Madinet Nasr, Cairo; tel. (2) 830533; length 78 km (electrified); gauge 1,000 mm; operates 16 tram routes and 24 km of light railway; 720 cars; Chair. M. E. ABD ES-SALAM.

Lower Egypt Railway: El-Mansoura; f. 1898; length 160 km; gauge 1,000 mm; 20 diesel railcars.

ROADS

There are good metalled main roads as follows: Cairo–Alexandria (desert road); Cairo–Banha–Tanta–Damanhour–Alexandria; Cairo–Suez (desert road); Cairo–Ismailia–Port Said or Suez; Cairo–Fayoum (desert road); in 1997 there were some 41,300 km of roads, including 22,000 km of highways. The total length of road network at the end of 1999 was 44,000 km. The Ahmad Hamdi road tunnel (1.64 km) beneath the Suez Canal was opened in 1980. A 320-km macadamized road linking Mersa Matruh, on the Mediterranean coast, with the oasis town of Siwa was completed in 1986. A second bridge over the Suez Canal was completed in mid-2001.

General Authority for Roads, Bridges and Land Transport—Ministry of Transport: 105 Sharia Qasr el-Eini, Cairo; tel. (2) 3557429; fax (2) 3550591; e-mail garb@idsc.gov.eg; Chair. MUHAMMAD NABIL EL-KOUSSY.

SHIPPING

Egypt's principal ports are Alexandria, Port Said and Suez. A port constructed at a cost of £E315m., and designed to handle up to 16m. metric tons of grain, fruit and other merchandise per year (22% of the country's projected imports by 2000) in its first stage of development, was opened at Damietta in 1986. The second stage will increase handling capacity to 25m. tons per year. A ferry link between Nuweibeh and the Jordanian port of Aqaba was opened in 1985.

Alexandria Port Authority: 106 ave el-Horreia, Alexandria; Head Office: 106 Sharia el-Hourriya, Alexandria; tel. (3) 4871640; fax (3) 4869714; e-mail alexportinfo@internetalex.com; internet www .alexandriaportauthority.com; f. 1966; Chair. R. Adm. MUHAMMAD FARAG LOTRY; Vice-Chair. R. Adm. MUHAMMAD M. ZAKI.

Major Shipping Companies

Alexandria Shipping and Navigation Co: POB 812, 557 ave el-Hourriya, Alexandria; tel. (3) 62923; services between Egypt, N. and W. Europe, USA, Red Sea and Mediterranean; 5 vessels; Chair. Eng. MAHMOUD ISMAIL; Man. Dir ABD AL-AZIZ QADRI.

Arab Maritime Petroleum Transport Co (AMPTC): POB 143, 9th Floor, Nile Tower Bldg, 21 Sharia Giza, 12211 Giza; tel. (2) 5701311; fax (2) 3378080; e-mail amptc.cairo@amptc.net; internet www.amptc.net; 11 vessels; Chair. Dr RAMADAN ES-SANOUSSI BELHAG; Gen. Man. SULAYMAN AL-BASSAM.

Egyptian Navigation Co: POB 82, 2 Sharia en-Nasr, Alexandria 21511; tel. (3) 4800050; fax (3) 4871345; e-mail enc@dataxprs.com .eg; internet www.enc.com.eg; f. 1930; owners and operators of Egypt's mercantile marine; international trade transportation; 24 vessels; Chair. ABDALLA ALI FAHIM; Man. Dir ABU ZID ES-SAADANY.

Memnon Tours Co: POB 2533, 18 Sharia Hoda Sharawi, Cairo; tel. (2) 3930195; fax (2) 3917410; 7 vessels.

Misr Petroleum Co: POB 228, Misr Petroleum House, 6 Sharia Orabi, Cairo; tel. (2) 5755000; fax (2) 5745436; 8 vessels; Chair. Eng. SALAH ED-DIN HASSAN.

Misr Shipping Co: POB 157, 13 Sharia Masgid en-Nasr, Soumoha, Sidi Gaber, Alexandria; tel. (3) 4270227; fax (3) 4288425; e-mail insp@misrshipping.com; internet www.misrshipping.com; 9 vessels; Chair. and Man. Dir Adm. YOUSRI HANAFY.

National Navigation Co: 4 Sharia Ehegaz, Cairo (Heliopolis); tel. (2) 4525575; fax (2) 4526171; 11 vessels; Chair. and Man. Dir MUHAMMAD SHAWKI YOUNIS.

Pan-Arab Shipping Co: POB 39, 404 ave el-Hourriya, Rushdi, Alexandria; tel. (3) 5468835; fax (3) 5469533; f. 1974; Arab League Co; 5 vessels; Chair. Adm. MUHAMMAD SHERIF ES-SADEK; Gen. Man. Capt. MAMDOUH EL-GUINDY.

As-Salam Shipping & Trading Establishment: Apartment 203, 24 Sharia Ahmad Talceer, Cairo (Heliopolis); tel. (2) 908535; fax (2) 4175390; 6 vessels.

Samatour Shipping Co: As-Salam Bldg, 4 Sharia Naguib er-Rihani, Rami Station, Alexandria; tel. (3) 4822028; fax (3) 4832003; 5 vessels; Chair. SALEM A. SALEM.

Sayed Nasr Navigation Lines: 5 Sharia Dr Ahmad Amin, Cairo (Heliopolis); tel. (2) 2457643; fax (2) 2457736; 6 vessels.

Société Cooperative des Pétroles: Cooperative Bldg, 94 Sharia Qasr el-Eini, Cairo; tel. (2) 7360623; fax (2) 7956404; Chair. Dr TAMER ABU BAKR; Gen. Dir OSAMA IBRAHIM.

THE SUEZ CANAL

In 2000 a total of 14,141 vessels, with a net displacement of 439m. tons, used the Suez Canal, linking the Mediterranean and Red Seas.

Length of canal 190 km; maximum permissible draught: 17.68 m (58 ft); breadth of canal at water level and breadth between buoys defining the navigable channel at –11 m: 365 m and 225 m, respectively, in the northern section and 305 m and 205 m in the southern section.

Suez Canal Authority (Hay'at Canal as-Suways): Irshad Bldg, Ismailia; Cairo Office: 6 Sharia Lazoughli, Cairo (Garden City); tel. (64) 330000; fax (64) 320784; e-mail scanalb@idsc.net.eg; f. 1956; Chair. Adm. AHMAD ALI FADEL.

Suez Canal Container Handling Company: Cairo; f. 2000; with 30-year concession to operate the East Port Said container terminal, scheduled to begin operations in late 2002.

CIVIL AVIATION

The main international airports are at Heliopolis (23 km from the centre of Cairo) and Alexandria (7 km from the city centre). An international airport was opened at Nuzhah in 1983. In early 2001 the Ministry of Transport announced the restructure and modernization of the civil aviation sector. In that year airports were under construction at el-Alamein, west of Alexandria, and at Assiut, however, plans for the construction of a new airport in west Cairo were suspended in late 2001. The existing Cairo airport was to be expanded, with a third terminal and a new runway, while the Sharm esh-Sheikh airport was also scheduled for expansion.

In the 12-month period ending 30 June 1997 an estimated 14m. passengers and 109,000 metric tons of cargo passed through Egypt's airports.

Cairo Airport Authority (CAA): Cairo International Airport, Cairo (Heliopolis); tel. (2) 2474245; fax (2) 2432522; responsible for management of Cairo International Airport.

EgyptAir: Administration Complex, Cairo International Airport, Cairo (Heliopolis); tel. (2) 2674700; fax (2) 2663773; internet www .egyptair.com.eg; f. 1932 as Misr Airwork; known as United Arab Airlines 1960–1971; operates internal services in Egypt and external services throughout the Middle East, Far East, Africa, Europe and the USA; Chair. Eng. MUHAMMAD FAHIM RAYAN.

Egyptian Civil Aviation Holding Co: Cairo; f. 2001; responsible for management and development of all Egyptian airports, excluding Cairo International; Pres. ABD AL-FATTAH KATTU.

Egyptian Airports Co: Cairo; f. 2001; responsible for new airport projects; Pres. NAGI SAMUEL.

Egyptian Civil Aviation Authority: ECAA Complex, Sharia Airport, Cairo 11776; tel. (2) 2677610; fax (2) 2470351; e-mail egoca@ idsc.gov.eg; f. 2000; Chair. Dr IBRAHIM MUHAMMAD MUTAWALLI AD-DUMEIRI.

Tourism

Tourism is currently Egypt's second largest source of revenue, generating US $4,345m. in 2000. In that year some 5.1m. tourists (including excursionists) visited Egypt. Traditionally the industry has attracted tourists to the country's pyramids and monuments. Recently the industry has diversified; the Red Sea coastline has 1,000 km of beaches along which developments, including two international airports at Taba and Suba Bay, are under construction. A further luxury resort was planned for Port Ghaleb, equipped with a marina for 1,000 yachts and an airport. In early 2001 the Biblioteca Alexandrina opened in Alexandria. The tourism industry was adversely affected in the mid-1990s by the campaign of violence by Islamist fundamentalists; although some recovery in tourist numbers was recorded by the end of the decade, the sector was again adversely affected by the crisis in Israeli–Palestinian relations from late 2000, and by the repercussions of the suicide attacks on the USA in September 2001. There was considerable concern in early 2003 that recovery would be further impeded by the US-led military action to oust the regime of Saddam Hussein in Iraq.

Ministry of Tourism: Misr Travel Tower, Abbassia Sq., Cairo; tel. (2) 2828439; fax (2) 2859551; e-mail mol@idsc.gov.eg; internet www .touregypt.net; f. 1965; brs at Alexandria, Port Said, Suez, Luxor and Aswan; Minister of Tourism Dr MAMDOUH EL-BELTAGI.

Egyptian General Authority for the Promotion of Tourism: Misr Travel Tower, Abbassia Sq., Cairo; tel. (2) 2853576; fax (2) 2854363; Chair. ADEL ABD AL-AZIZ.

Egyptian General Co for Tourism and Hotels: 4 Sharia Latin America, Cairo (Garden City); tel. (2) 7942914; fax (2) 7964830; e-mail egoth@link.com.eg; f. 1961; affiliated to the holding co for Housing, Tourism and Cinema; Chair. MAHMOUD ABD EL-WAHAB IBRAHIM.

EL SALVADOR

Introductory Survey

Location, Climate, Language, Religion, Flag, Capital

The Republic of El Salvador lies on the Pacific coast of Central America. It is bounded by Guatemala to the west and by Honduras to the north and east. The climate varies from tropical on the coastal plain to temperate in the uplands. The language is Spanish. About 85% of the population are Roman Catholics, and other Christian churches are represented. The civil flag (proportions 2 by 3) consists of three equal horizontal stripes, of blue, over white, over blue. The state flag differs by the addition, in the centre of the white stripe, of the national coat of arms. The capital is San Salvador.

Recent History

El Salvador was ruled by Spain until 1821, and became independent in 1839. Since then the country's history has been one of frequent coups and outbursts of political violence. General Maximiliano Hernández Martínez became President in 1931, and ruthlessly suppressed a peasant uprising, with an alleged 30,000 killings (including that of Farabundo Martí, the leader of the rebel peasants), in 1932. President Hernández was deposed in 1944, and the next elected President, Gen. Salvador Castañeda Castro, was overthrown in 1948. His successor as President, Lt-Col Oscar Osorio (1950–56), relinquished power to Lt-Col José María Lemus, who was deposed by a bloodless coup in 1960. He was replaced by a military junta, which was itself supplanted by another junta in January 1961. Under this Junta, the conservative Partido de Conciliación Nacional (PCN) was established and won all 54 seats in elections to the Asamblea Legislativa (Legislative Assembly) in December. A member of the Junta, Lt-Col Julio Adalberto Rivera, was elected unopposed to the presidency in 1962. He was succeeded by the PCN candidate, Gen. Fidel Sánchez Hernández, in 1967.

In the 1972 presidential election Col Arturo Armando Molina Barraza, candidate of the ruling PCN, was elected. His rival, José Napoleón Duarte, the leader of the left-wing coalition party, Unión Nacional de Oposición, staged an abortive coup in March, and Col Molina took office in July, despite allegations of massive electoral fraud. Similar allegations were made during the 1977 presidential election, after which the PCN candidate, Gen. Carlos Humberto Romero Mena, took office.

Reports of violations of human rights by the Government were widespread in 1979. The polarization of left and right after 1972 was characterized by an increase in guerrilla activity. In October 1979 President Romero was overthrown and replaced by a Junta of civilians and army officers. The Junta, which promised to install a democratic system and to organize elections, declared a political amnesty and invited participation from the guerrilla groups, but violence continued between government troops and guerrilla forces, and elections were postponed. In January 1980 an ultimatum from progressive members of the Government resulted in the formation of a new Government, a coalition of military officers and the Partido Demócrata Cristiano (PDC). In March the country moved closer to full-scale civil war following the assassination of the Roman Catholic Archbishop of San Salvador, Oscar Romero y Galdames, an outspoken supporter of human rights.

In December 1980 José Napoleón Duarte, the 1972 presidential candidate and a member of the Junta, was sworn in as President. In January 1981 the guerrillas launched their 'final offensive' and, after initial gains, the opposition front, Frente Democrático Revolucionario—FDR (allied with the guerrilla front, the Frente Farabundo Martí para la Liberación Nacional —FMLN), proposed negotiations with the USA. The US authorities referred them to the Salvadorean Government, which refused to recognize the FDR while it was linked with the guerrillas. The USA affirmed its support for the Duarte Government and provided civilian and military aid. During 1981 the guerrilla forces unified and strengthened their control over the north and east of the country. Attacks on economic targets continued, while the army retaliated by acting indiscriminately against the local population in guerrilla-controlled areas. By December there were an estimated 300,000 Salvadorean refugees, many of whom had fled to neighbouring countries.

At elections to a National Constituent Assembly, conducted in March 1982, the PDC failed to win an absolute majority against the five right-wing parties, which, together having obtained 60% of the total votes, formed a Government of National Unity. Major Roberto D'Aubuisson Arrieta, leader of the extreme right-wing Alianza Republicana Nacionalista (ARENA), emerged as the most powerful personality within the coalition and became President of the National Constituent Assembly. In April a politically independent banker, Dr Alvaro Magaña Borja, was elected interim President of El Salvador, after pressure from the armed forces. However, the Assembly voted to award itself considerable power over the President. Military leaders then demanded that five ministerial posts be given to members of the PDC, fearing that, otherwise, US military aid would be withdrawn. A presidential election was scheduled for 1983, and a new constitution was to be drafted.

During 1982 about 1,600 Salvadorean troops were trained in the USA, and US military advisers were reported to be actively participating in the conflict. In November a military coup was forestalled by Gen. José Guillermo García, the Minister of Defence, who removed several right-wingers from important military posts. President Magaña's position was strengthened in December, when a division within the PCN resulted in the moderates achieving a majority in the Assembly.

The presidential election was postponed until March 1984, as a result of disagreement in the National Constituent Assembly over the new Constitution, which finally became effective in December 1983. The issue of agrarian reform caused a serious dispute between Maj. D'Aubuisson's ARENA party and the PDC, and provoked a campaign by right-wing 'death squads' against trade unionists and peasant leaders. (In 1980 the governing Junta had nationalized some 60% of the country's prime arable land as part of a three-phase agrarian reform initiative, which envisaged the eventual redesignation of 90% of El Salvador's farmland. However, subsequent phases of the expropriation and reallocation programme had been suspended in March 1981 and May 1982, prompting US Government threats to withdraw financial and military assistance.) In December 1983 ARENA secured the support of the Assembly for the reactivation of a severely compromised reform programme, which provided for a maximum permissible landholding of 245 ha (rather than 100 ha as originally envisaged). This represented an important victory for the ARENA party, which had been isolated in the Assembly following the collapse of its alliance with the PCN in February.

Following a period of intense activity by 'death squads' in September and October 1983, when the weekly total of murders exceeded 200, the US Government urged the removal of several high-level officials, military officers and political figures who were linked to the murders. The failure of the US-trained 'rapid reaction' battalions and frequent reports of army atrocities undermined both public confidence in the Government and US President Ronald Reagan's efforts to secure further US aid for El Salvador. In February 1984, following a number of strategic territorial advances, the FDR-FMLN proposed the formation of a broadly-based provisional government, as part of a peace plan without preconditions. The plan was rejected by the Government. The guerrillas refused to participate in the presidential election, conducted in March 1984, and attempted to prevent voting in various provinces. As no candidate emerged with a clear majority, a second round of voting was held in May, when José Napoleón Duarte, the candidate of the PDC, obtained 54% of the votes cast to defeat Maj. D'Aubuisson, the ARENA candidate.

Following his inauguration in June 1984, President Duarte instituted a purge of the armed forces and the reorganization of the police force, including the disbanding of the notorious Treasury Police. Both the FDR-FMLN and the President expressed their willingness to commence peace negotiations. Following pressure from the Roman Catholic Church and trade unions, the Government opened discussions with guerrilla leaders in Chalatenango in October. A second round of negotiations, held in November, ended amid accusations of intransigence from both sides.

At legislative and municipal elections in March 1985 the PDC won a convincing victory over the ARENA-PCN electoral alliance, thereby securing a clear majority in the new Asamblea Nacional (National Assembly). The PDC's victory, coupled with internal divisions within the right-wing grouping, precipitated a decline in the popularity and influence of the alliance, which culminated in the resignation of ARENA's leader, Roberto D'Aubuisson, in September.

Despite a perceived decline in political violence and abuses of human rights in 1985–86, the failure of the Government and the rebels to agree an agenda for renewed negotiations during this period prompted speculation that a military solution would be sought to end the civil war. Such speculation was supported by reports of the armed forces' growing domination of the conflict and by the success of the army's 'Unidos para reconstruir' campaign, a social and economic programme, launched in July 1986, to recover areas that had been devastated by the protracted fighting.

In March 1987 guerrillas carried out a successful attack on the army garrison at El Paraíso, which enabled them to take the military initiative in the civil war. Later in the year, however, the Salvadorean Government's participation in a peace plan for Central America, which was signed on 7 August in Guatemala City, encouraged hopes that a peaceful solution could be found to the conflict. Discussions between the Government and the FDR-FMLN were eventually held in October, when agreement was reached on the formation of two committees to study the possibility of a cease-fire and an amnesty.

Despite the inauguration, in September 1987, of a National Reconciliation Commission, appointed by the President in August, and the Government's proclamation, in November, of a unilateral cease-fire, no long-term cessation of hostilities was maintained by either side. The political situation deteriorated further in late 1987, following President Duarte's public denunciation of Roberto D'Aubuisson's complicity in the murder of Archbishop Romero y Galdames in March 1980. Furthermore, in 1988 there were increasing reports of the resurgence of 'death squads', and it was suggested that abuses of human rights were rapidly returning to the level reached at the beginning of the internal conflict.

In February 1988 the FMLN launched a campaign of bombings and transport disruptions, in order to undermine preparations for the forthcoming legislative and municipal elections. At the elections, in March, ARENA secured control of more than 200 municipalities, including San Salvador, hitherto held for more than 20 years by the PDC. However, a dispute developed over the distribution of seats in the legislature, with both ARENA and the PDC claiming the same seat in one region. Following protracted arguments, ARENA was able to resume an overall majority in the Asamblea, when a deputy of the PCN transferred allegiance to ARENA, thereby giving the party 31 seats, compared with the PDC's 23 seats.

By the end of 1988 it was estimated that as many as 70,000 Salvadoreans had died in the course of the civil war, while the US Administration had provided some US $3,000m. in aid to the Government. Moreover, by early 1989 many areas appeared to be without government, following the resignations of some 75 mayors and nine judges, purportedly because of death threats by the FMLN. In late January, however, radical new peace proposals were announced by the FMLN, which, for the first time, expressed its willingness to participate in the electoral process. The FMLN proposed that the presidential election be postponed from March to September, and offered a 60-day cease-fire (30 days on each side of a September election date). However, negotiations about this proposal failed to produce agreement. When Duarte announced that the election would proceed on the scheduled date of 19 March, the FMLN advocated a boycott of the election and intensified its campaign of violence, resulting in the deaths of more than 40 people on election day alone. The election resulted in victory for the ARENA candidate, Alfredo Cristiani Burkard. The level of abstention was estimated at almost 50%. Cristiani took office on 1 June 1989.

In August 1989 the Heads of State of five Central American countries signed an agreement in Tela, Honduras. The accord included an appeal to the FMLN to abandon its military campaign and to 'initiate dialogue' with the Salvadorean Government. In the spirit engendered by the Tela agreement, representatives of the Government and the FMLN began negotiations in Mexico City in September. A second round of discussions took

place in October and a third round was planned, in November. However, it was abandoned following a bomb attack in late October, allegedly perpetrated by the Salvadorean army, on the headquarters of the Salvadorean Workers' National Union Federation (FENASTRAS), in which 10 people were killed. On 7 November, in accordance with the Tela agreement, the UN Security Council authorized the creation of the UN Observer Group for Central America (ONUCA), a multinational military force, to monitor developments in the region.

On 11 November 1989 the FMLN launched a military offensive, and throughout the month the fiercest fighting for nine years took place. The Government declared a state of siege, and stability was further undermined when, on 16 November, gunmen murdered the head of a San Salvador Jesuit university and five other Jesuit priests. On 12 January 1990, however, the FMLN announced that it would accept an offer made by the Salvadorean Government whereby the UN Secretary-General, Javier Pérez de Cuéllar, was to arrange the reopening of peace talks. In March President Cristiani announced that he was willing to offer a comprehensive amnesty, territorial concessions and the opportunity to participate fully in political processes to members of the FMLN, as part of a broad-based peace proposal. Later in the year, however, hopes for the successful negotiation of a peaceful settlement were frustrated by the failure of the two sides to reach a consensus, at a series of UN-sponsored discussions, on the crucial issue of the future role, structure and accountability of the armed forces.

In May 1990 guerrilla forces had launched their first major offensive since November 1989, coinciding with demonstrations in San Salvador by some 40,000 trade unionists and opposition supporters in protest at economic austerity measures and the breakdown of peace negotiations. By the end of September all hopes for a cease-fire had been abandoned. A renewed FMLN offensive was undertaken by the newly-proclaimed National Army for Democracy (the establishment of which marked the reorganization of the FMLN's previous divisions into a more conventional army structure) in several departments in November. The conflict was considered to have entered into a new phase when, in the same month, a government aircraft was shot down by guerrilla forces armed with surface-to-air missiles (supplied by Nicaraguan military personnel). In January 1991 a US military helicopter, en route to operations in Honduras, was shot down by rebel forces in El Salvador.

Negotiations between the Government and the FMLN continued throughout 1991, interspersed by violent exchanges between the guerrillas and the security forces. On 10 March elections to the Asamblea (enlarged from 60 to 84 seats) and to 262 municipalities were conducted. While guerrilla forces refrained from disrupting the proceedings (the FMLN announced a three-day cease-fire), it was reported that many voters were intimidated by an escalation in military operations, and more than 50% of the electorate failed to cast a vote. The final results revealed that ARENA had lost its majority in the Asamblea, but continued to command considerable support, with 44.3% of the votes and 39 seats. The party also retained significant support in the local elections, with victories in 175 of the 262 municipalities.

In late March 1991 a new initiative for the negotiation of a peace settlement was presented by the FMLN in Managua, Nicaragua, following a meeting between foreign affairs ministers from Central America and the European Community (EC, now European Union—EU). This new proposal dispensed with previous stipulations put forward by the guerrillas that military and constitutional reforms should be effected prior to any cease-fire, and suggested that concessions on both sides could be adopted simultaneously. The constitutional requirement that amendments to the Constitution be ratified by two successive legislative assemblies lent impetus to negotiations in April, the current Asamblea being scheduled to dissolve at the end of the month. Despite the attempts of uncompromising right-wing members of the Asamblea to sabotage the proceedings, a last-minute agreement on human rights (including the creation of a three-member 'truth commission', to be appointed by the UN Secretary-General) and on judicial and electoral reform was reached by the Government and the FMLN, and was swiftly approved by the Asamblea, prior to its dissolution. The working structure of a cease-fire and the detailed reform and purge of the armed forces were set aside for negotiation at a later date.

In May 1991 the UN Security Council voted to create an observer mission to El Salvador (ONUSAL), to be charged with the verification of accords reached between the Government and the FMLN. Initially the mission was to be resident in six regional centres for a 12-month period, and was expected to participate in any future cease-fire and peaceful reintegration programme. The creation of ONUSAL was denounced by right-wing groups within El Salvador as unwarranted interference and as an insult to national sovereignty.

In August 1991, following a personal invitation from the UN Secretary-General, Javier Pérez de Cuéllar, both sides attended a round of discussions in New York, where a new framework for peace was agreed. A National Commission for the Consolidation of Peace (COPAZ) was to be created (comprising representatives of both sides, as well as of all major political parties), which would supervise the enforcement of guarantees for the political integration of the guerrillas. The FMLN also secured guaranteed territorial rights for peasants settled in guerrilla-controlled areas, and the participation of former FMLN members in a National Civilian Police, which was to be under the control of a new Ministry of the Interior and Public Security. At the same time, the Asamblea approved constitutional reforms, whereby the Central Electoral Commission would be replaced by a Supreme Electoral Tribunal, composed of five magistrates (one from each of the five most successful parties at the previous presidential election), to be elected by the Asamblea.

In December 1991, following renewed discussions between the Government and the guerrilla leaders in New York, a new peace initiative was announced. Under the terms of the agreement, a formal cease-fire was to be implemented on 1 February 1992, under the supervision of some 1,000 UN personnel. The FMLN was to begin a process of disarmament, to be implemented in five stages (simultaneous with the dissolution of the notorious, military-controlled, 17,000-strong rapid deployment battalions), leading to full disarmament by 31 October. The success of the cease-fire agreement was expected to be dependent upon the adequate implementation, by the Government, of previously agreed reforms to the judiciary, the electoral system, guarantees of territorial rights, human rights, and guerrilla participation in civil defence, and of newly agreed reforms whereby the armed forces would be purged of those most responsible for abuses of human rights during the previous 12 years, and would be reduced in size by almost one-half, over a 22-month period.

On 16 January 1992, at Chapultepec Castle in Mexico City, the formal peace accord was ratified and was witnessed by the new UN Secretary-General, Boutros Boutros-Ghali, the US Secretary of State, James Baker, Heads of State from Central America, South America and Europe, representatives of El Salvador's military high command and all 84 members of the Asamblea. On 1 February some 30,000 Salvadoreans gathered in San Salvador to celebrate the first day of the cease-fire and to attend the formal installation of COPAZ.

Although mutual allegations of failure to comply with the terms of the peace accord persisted during 1992, prompting the temporary withdrawal, in May, of the FMLN from COPAZ, and resulting in further UN mediation and the negotiation of a revised timetable for disarmament, the cease-fire was carefully observed by both sides. In San Salvador on 15 December (declared National Reconciliation Day), at a ceremony attended by President Cristiani, FMLN leaders, the UN Secretary-General and Central American Heads of State and government representatives, the conflict was formally concluded, the terms of the December 1991 agreement having been fulfilled to the satisfaction of both sides. On the same day the FMLN was officially registered and recognized as a legitimate political party.

In November 1992, in accordance with the terms of the December 1991 peace accord, the Comisión de la Verdad (Truth Commission) announced the names of more than 200 military personnel alleged to have participated in abuses of human rights during the civil war. By early 1993, however, despite the urgences of the UN Secretary-General, the reluctance of the Government to comply with the conditions of the peace accord, relating to the removal from the armed forces of those personnel (particularly officers) identified by the Commission, threatened the further successful implementation of the process of pacification, and prompted the FMLN to delay the demobilization of its forces and the destruction of its remaining arsenals. The situation was exacerbated in March by the publication of the report of the Commission, which attributed responsibility for the vast majority of the war's 75,000 fatalities to the counter-insurgency measures of the armed forces, including the systematic eradication, by the security forces, of civilians thought to harbour left-wing sympathies. Some 400 murders were attributed to the FMLN. Forty military personnel, identified by name as those responsible for various human rights atrocities, included the ARENA founder Roberto D'Aubuisson Arrieta (who died in 1992), who was identified as the authority behind the organization of 'death squads' in the early 1980s, and the murder of the Archbishop Romero y Galdames; also identified was the Minister of Defence and Public Security, Gen. René Emilio Ponce, his deputy, Gen. Orlando Zepeda, and the former air force chief, Gen. Juan Rafael Bustillo, who were believed to have ordered the murder of six prominent Jesuits in 1989. (In September 1991 Col Guillermo Benavides and an army lieutenant were found guilty of murder and sentenced to a maximum of 30 years' imprisonment; the seven other men charged were acquitted, on the grounds that they were simply following orders.) The report recommended that the judiciary should be reorganized, having failed to protect human rights during the war, and that all individuals identified by the report should be permanently excluded from all institutions of national defence and public security, and should be barred from holding public office for a period of 10 years.

While the conclusions of the report were welcomed by the FMLN, representatives of the Government and the armed forces challenged the legal validity of the document, despite the insistence of UN officials that the recommendations of the report were mandatory under the terms of the peace accord. However, later in March 1993, the strength of ARENA's representation in the Asamblea overcame opposition from the PDC, the Convergencia Democrática (CD, a left-wing alliance comprising two of the leading groups within the FDR-FMLN and the Partido Social Demócrata) and the Movimiento Nacional Revolucionario (MNR), and secured the approval of an amnesty law to extend to all political crimes committed before 1992, prompting widespread public outrage, which was compounded, in April 1993, by the release of the two prisoners sentenced in January 1992 for the murder of six prominent Jesuits, as the first beneficiaries of the amnesty. In June 1993 the Government compromised, to some extent, by announcing the compulsory retirement of several veteran military officers, including Gen. Ponce, although their immunity from prosecution was guaranteed.

The findings of the Truth Commission, together with the disclosure of information following the declassification by the US Administration, in November 1993, of hitherto confidential documents relating to the administrations of former US Presidents Ronald Reagan and George Bush, Sr, suggested that detailed knowledge of abuses of human rights was suppressed by US officials in order to continue to secure congressional funding for the Government in El Salvador in the 1980s. Evidence also emerged that US military training had been provided, in at least one instance, for a civilian group in El Salvador operating as a 'death squad'. In June 1998 three members of the National Guard, convicted in 1984 of the murder, in 1980, of three US nuns and a US lay worker, were granted a conditional release from prison on the grounds that they were simply following orders.

Meanwhile, in June 1993 the FMLN had agreed to comply with an ultimatum issued by the UN, that the location and destruction of all remaining arms caches in El Salvador and neighbouring countries should be swiftly implemented. In December, bowing to pressure from the UN, President Cristiani inaugurated a four-member commission of investigation (the Joint Group for the Investigation of Illegal Armed Groups), comprising representatives of the Government, the Office of the Ombudsman for Human Rights, and of ONUSAL, to examine allegations of political motivation behind an escalation in violent attacks against members of the FMLN in late 1993. The conclusions of the commission claimed that officials from numerous government departments, together with current and former members of the security forces, were continuing to participate in organized crime and in politically motivated acts of violence.

Voting to elect a new president, vice-president, legislature, 262 mayors and 20 members of the Central American parliament took place on 20 March 1994. ARENA's presidential candidate, Armando Calderón Sol, had been expected to win the presidential ballot. However, he failed to secure the clear majority needed for outright victory in the first poll, and was forced to contest a second round of voting against the second-placed candidate, Rubén Zamora Rivas, the joint CD-FMLN-MNR nominee, on 24 April 1994, which the ARENA candidate won with 68.2% of the votes. ARENA candidates also achieved considerable success in the legislative elections (retaining 39 seats in the Asamblea) and in the municipal poll (securing an estimated 200 municipalities). FMLN candidates were also considered to have performed well in the party's first electoral contest, winning 21 seats in the Asamblea and a number of rural municipalities. Calderón Sol was inaugurated on 1 June and a new Cabinet was installed. In late June, in response to a recent intensification of political violence and organized crime, President Calderón Sol announced a new initiative for national security, which attracted opposition for its virtual exclusion of the transitional National Civilian Police.

Meanwhile, serious divisions emerged within the FMLN during 1994. Members of two constituent parties, the Resistencia Nacional (RN) and the Expresión Renovadora del Pueblo (ERP—formerly the Fuerzas Armadas de la Resistencia Nacional and the Ejército Revolucionario Popular guerrilla groups, respectively) became increasingly alienated following a decision by the FMLN national council in May to suspend several prominent members of the two parties from their positions within the FMLN executive for failing to comply with a party directive to boycott elections to the new directorate of the Asamblea. In December the RN and the ERP announced their withdrawal from the FMLN, owing to a divergence of political interests. In March 1995 the Secretary-General of the ERP, Joaquín Villalobos (who had been highly critical of the predominance of political extremism), announced the formation of a new centre-left political force, the Partido Demócrata (PD), comprising the ERP, the RN, the MNR and a dissident faction of the PDC. The new party demonstrated an immediate willingness to co-operate with the country's most prominent political forces.

In September 1994 and January 1995, in protest at the Government's failure to honour the terms of the 1992 peace accord with regard to financial compensation and other benefits for demobilized military personnel, retired soldiers occupied the Asamblea and took a number of deputies hostage. On both occasions the occupation was ended swiftly and peacefully following the Government's agreement to enter into direct negotiations with the former soldiers. The Association of the Demobilized Armed Forces had earlier threatened to sabotage the economy by disrupting transport communications and foreign businesses throughout the country if the Government failed to meet its obligations, and had organized a series of co-ordinated protests throughout the country in January 1995. Further demonstrations by army veterans during March and November were forcibly curtailed by the security forces, prompting concern that such incidents might provoke a renewed escalation of armed conflict.

In May 1994 the UN Security Council voted to extend the ONUSAL mandate for a further six months in order to supervise the full implementation of the outstanding provisions of the peace agreement. Of particular concern were delays in the reform of the judiciary, the initiation of the land reform programme and the full integration and activation of the National Civilian Police. In September the UN Secretary-General appealed to the Government and to the international community for increased financial commitment to the peace process. In the same month, in the context of increasing levels of crime and social unrest, the ONUSAL mandate was further extended, pending the effective habilitation of the National Civilian Police; a further extension, until the end of April 1995, was approved by the UN Security Council in November. A small contingent of UN observers, MINUSAL, was mandated to remain in El Salvador until April 1996 (the revised deadline for the fulfilment of the outstanding terms of the peace accord). By this date, however, full implementation of those terms of the accord relating to land allocation for refugees and former combatants, and to the reform of the judiciary and the electoral code, had yet to be achieved. A reduced MINUSAL contingent was further mandated to oversee Government efforts to fulfil the outstanding terms of the agreement, and the mission was formally terminated on 31 December 1996.

Political manoeuvring in preparation for congressional and municipal elections scheduled for 16 March 1997, began in mid-1996 with the PD's announcement of its withdrawal from the legislative pact forged with ARENA in May 1995, owing to the Government's failure to honour pledges to increase spending on health and education and to safeguard the jobs of employees at state concerns scheduled for privatization. (The Government's divestment and rationalization programme had provoked industrial action in the public sector early in the year.) The PD subsequently announced that it would contest the elections in an alliance of the 'democratic centre', with the PDC. The results

of elections demonstrated a significant increase in support for the FMLN, particularly in the capital, where the party won seven of the 16 contested seats and secured the mayorality. The results of the legislative poll revealed a considerable erosion of ARENA's predominance in the Asamblea, with the party securing 29 seats, just one more than the FMLN. Widespread concern was expressed at the high level of voter abstention, estimated to be some 60%.

The presidential election of 7 March 1999 was won by Francisco Flores Pérez, the candidate of ARENA, who obtained 51.96% of the votes, thereby obviating the need for a second round of voting. Despite contesting the election in alliance with the Unión Social Cristiana, the candidate of the FMLN, Facundo Guardado, received only 29.05% of the votes, prompting him to resign as Co-ordinator of the party. He was succeeded by Fabio Castillo. Voter participation was the lowest recorded in the country's history, with more than 60% of the 3.2m. registered voters abstaining. President Flores was inaugurated on 1 June, when a new Council of Ministers was installed. Flores stated that his Government's priority was to address the problem of violent crime, and an initiative was unveiled that included provision for the restructuring of the National Civilian Police force and a revision of the penal code. However, economic measures announced later that month, which included the rationalization of public bodies, prompted a succession of strikes by public-sector workers demanding salary increases and job security. Furthermore, the Government was embarrassed by allegations that foreign funds, donated for disaster relief following the impact of 'Hurricane Mitch' in November 1998, had been diverted by ARENA to former paramilitaries in an attempt to buy votes for Flores in the presidential election. The issue was being investigated by the Comptroller-General's office.

Dissatisfaction with the ARENA Government was demonstrated in the results of the legislative elections of 12 March 2000, in which the FMLN became the largest single party in the Asamblea Nacional, winning 31 of the 84 seats. ARENA secured 29 seats, followed by the PCN (14 seats), the PDC (five seats), the Centro Democrático Unido (CDU—an electoral alliance comprising the CD and the Partido Social Demócrata, three seats) and the Partido Acción Nacional (PAN, two seats). Voter turnout was only 33%. In concurrently-held municipal elections the FMLN also performed well, gaining control of 78 of the 262 municipalities, while ARENA won 127. On 21 March the FMLN proposed a governability pact with ARENA. However, relations between the two parties immediately became strained, and on 1 May ARENA formed an alliance with the PCN and the PDC in order to prevent the FMLN claiming the presidency of the Asamblea. Although the party gaining the most seats was, traditionally, given the presidency, in order to prevent a political impasse it was decided that the post was to be rotated annually among the three largest parties, the PCN, ARENA and the FMLN.

On 22 November 2000 President Flores unexpectedly announced that, from 1 January 2001, the US dollar would be introduced as an official currency alongside the colón, anchored to the colón at a fixed rate of exchange. The 'dollarization' was an attempt to stabilize the economy, lower interest rates, and stimulate domestic and foreign investment. Despite opposition to the move from the FMLN, the so-called Law of Monetary Integration was approved by the Asamblea Nacional in December, and from 1 January 2001 the US dollar circulated freely with the colón at a fixed rate of 8.75.

On 13 January 2001 an earthquake, measuring 7.6 on the Richter scale, hit El Salvador. President Flores immediately declared a state of emergency and 87 medical and evacuee centres were established. Besides numerous aftershocks, a second earthquake, measuring 6.6 on the Richter scale, struck on 12 February, causing further damage and loss of life. More than 1,100 people were killed, an estimated 4,000 people were injured, and a further 1.5m. people were left homeless by the two earthquakes. Reconstruction costs were estimated at US $1,900m., representing around 14% of gross domestic product (GDP). The housing, health and education services, and communications sector were badly affected, while agriculture, industry and trade all suffered losses, particularly in the private sector. In March 2001 the Inter-American Development Bank (IDB) pledged some US $1,278.5m. in aid, mainly for economic, social and environmental development projects, and in September the IDB announced a $70m. loan to help rebuild the country's infrastructure. In the same month the US immigration authorities granted a one-year protective status to Salvadorean illegal immigrants residing in the USA and released those held in custody.

In May 2001 the PCN and the FMLN proposed legislation granting US $1,000 each to 37,708 former village guards recruited in the paramilitary civil defence unit during the civil war. However, the bill was vetoed by President Flores, who insisted that the country could not afford the compensation payments. In late October thousands of members of the unit, who had been campaigning for compensation for 10 years, rose in protest, laying siege to important public buildings and injuring three policemen. In October the professional qual-ifications of 70 serving judges came into question, when an official investigation revealed a series of irregularities. The Government's woes worsened in December when four days of nation-wide strikes were held following the Government's deci-sion to suspend state subsidies to bus operators. The Flores administration responded to the subsequent chaos by arresting leading protesters and confiscating buses.

During 2001 internal divisions deepened between the more orthodox and the reformist elements of the FMLN. In October the FMLN leader, Facundo Guardado, a reformist, was expelled from the party after he was accused of failing to support the party executive and of supporting government policies, such as the dollarization of the economy. In November, following internal elections, Salvador Sánchez Cerón, from the party's orthodox wing, became the new FMLN leader. Following Sán-chez's appointment, in January 2002 six reformist FMLN depu-ties announced their departure from the party and requested recognition as an independent bloc in the Asamblea Nacional. As a consequence, the FMLN's legislative representation was reduced to 25 seats, and ARENA, led by Roberto Murray Meza, became the largest parliamentary bloc, with 29 seats. In April the six FMLN dissidents joined with Guardado to form a new party, the Movimiento Renovador (Renewal Movement).

In February 2002 the UN Secretary-General, Kofi Annan, cancelled a visit to attend celebrations marking 10 years of peace in the country. It was thought that since many of the terms of the peace accords were yet to be fulfilled, such as the granting of land to former guerrillas, Annan had decided not to support the celebrations. However, the office of the UN Secre-tary-General maintained that the arrangements for the visit had never in fact been confirmed. In June two former army generals and defence ministers, Gen. (retd) Carlos Eugenio Vides Casanova and Gen. (retd) José Guillermo García, were convicted by a US court of 'crimes against humanity'. The case was brought by three El Salvadorean civilians who had been tortured by troops under the generals' commands during the civil war. In November 2000 Vides Casanova and García had been acquitted of charges of involvement in the 1980 murder of three US nuns and a US lay worker.

In September 2002 doctors at a hospital in San Salvador began a strike in protest at President Flores' plans to privatize sections of the health service, as well as in support of 10 colleagues who had been dismissed and a further 300 whose pay had been docked following their participation in earlier indus-trial action. The strikes spread to 11 other hospitals throughout the country and, on 23 October, medical workers organized a demonstration in San Salvador. The strike led to a dispute in the Asamblea Legislativa; in October deputies approved legislation that prevented the privatization of the social services. However, in November President Flores presented his own bill, which would allow private-sector participation in the healthcare industry. The President stressed that this would constitute reform of the health service, not privatization; nevertheless, the proposed legislation was subseqently rejected by the Asamblea. Meanwhile, the protest intensified towards the end of the month when strikers erected blockades on principal roads in the cap-ital. In November doctors announced that the strike would continue indefinitely until the Government abandoned privati-zation plans. In January 2003 20 protesters occupied the cathe-dral in San Salvador in order to bring pressure to bear on the Roman Catholic Church to mediate in the strike. The bishop of San Salvador, Gregorio Rosa Chávez, indicated his willingness to arbitrate in the dispute. However, it appeared unlikely that the conflict would be resolved before the legislative elec-tions that were scheduled for 16 March.

The search for a solution to the problems of the coffee industry was also a source of conflict between the Government and the Asamblea Nacional in the last months of 2002. In early October coffee growers' associations estimated that production had decreased by 65% in 2002, compared with the previous year's

harvest, owing to the effects of drought, earthquakes and low prices on the world market. As a result, the legislature approved a proposal to allow growers to defer repayments on a commerical loan of US $300m. made to the sector in 2001. However, the deferral angered banks and major coffee exporters, who urged the President to veto the decision. In mid-October, however, Flores announced that $192m. in government funds would be used to support the coffee industry over the next three years.

In legislative elections held on 16 March 2003, the FMLN won 33.8% of votes cast and retained its 31 seats in the Asamblea Nacional, while the ARENA secured 32.0% of votes and 27 seats. The PCN won 13.1% of votes and increased its number of seats from 14 to 16, while the PDC retained its five seats, thereby ensuring that the Government maintained its legislative majority.

In an attempt to resolve a territorial dispute between El Salvador and Honduras over three islands in the Gulf of Fonseca and a small area of land on the joint border, President Duarte and President Azcona of Honduras submitted the dispute to the International Court of Justice (ICJ) for arbitration in December 1986. In September 1992 both countries accepted the ruling of the ICJ, which awarded one-third of the disputed mainland and two of the three disputed islands to El Salvador. Following the ruling, negotiations began towards a protocol defining the nationality and property rights of the inhabitants of the redes-ignated land. Although the ICJ recommended that all those involved should be granted dual nationality, a provision of the Honduran Constitution precluded this possibility. A resolution of the issue, which had led to numerous disputes between the two countries, was finally achieved in January 1998, when the parties signed a convention specifying the rights and obligations of those affected, including the right to choose between Hon-duran and Salvadorean citizenship. In July 2001 El Salvador and Honduras signed a development plan for the border area between the two countries.

Government

Executive power is held by the President, assisted by the Vice-President and the Council of Ministers. The President is elected for a five-year term by universal adult suffrage. Legislative power is vested in the Asamblea Nacional (National Assembly), with 84 members elected by universal adult suffrage for a three-year term.

Defence

Military service is by compulsory selective conscription of men between 18 and 30 years of age for one year. In August 2002 the armed forces totalled 16,800 men, comprising the estimated army of 15,000, the navy 700 and the air force 1,100. The National Civilian Police force, created in 1991, numbered around 12,000 personnel by 2000 and there were plans for it to total some 16,000. The defence budget for 2002 totalled an estimated 956m. colones.

Economic Affairs

In 2001, according to estimates by the World Bank, El Salva-dor's gross national product (GNI), measured at average 1999–2001 prices, was US $13,088m., equivalent to $2,050 per head (or $4,500 per head on an international purchasing-power parity basis). Over the period 1990–2001, the population increased at an average annual rate of 2.1%, while gross domestic product (GDP) per head increased, in real terms, by an average of 2.2% per year. Overall GDP increased, in real terms, at an average annual rate of 4.3% in 1990–2001. GDP grew by 2.0% in 2001. GDP was estimated to have increased by 1.5% in 2002.

Agriculture (including hunting, forestry and fishing) con-tributed an estimated 9.8% of GDP in 2001 and employed some 24.7% of the employed labour force in 2000. The principal cash crops are coffee (which accounted for 22.4% of export earnings, excluding *maquila* zones, in 2000) and sugar cane. Maize, beans, rice and millet are the major subsistence crops. During 1990–2000 agricultural GDP increased at an average annual rate of 1.4%. The sector's GDP decreased by an estimated 3.1% in 2000, and by further estimated 2.1% in 2001. The agricultural sector was badly affected by the earthquakes that struck the country in early 2001. In March the Inter-American Development Bank (IDB) pledged some US $1,278.5m. in emergency assistance, of which US $132.6m. was intended for rehabilitation and develop-ment of agriculture; a further US $101.0m. was made available for redevelopment of the coffee industry, which had been partic-ularly badly affected. During May–August a serious drought in Central America destroyed crops, affecting some 150,000 Salvadoreans alone. Output of coffee, affected by the earthquakes and the drought, was reduced to 2.3m. 46 kg sacks in 2001/02, compared to 3.6m. sacks in 2000/01, and the sector decreased by an estimated 13% in 2001. In October 2002 the Government announced that it would loan some US $192m. to the coffee industry over the next three years. Despite this, many producers dismissed their workers or began to cultivate other crops. El Salvador's fishing catch was relatively small; however, in mid-2002 it was announced that a tuna-processing plant would be built at Punta Gorda to exploit the large stocks of the fish found off the country's Pacific coast. The project was to be funded by a Spanish firm, Grupo Calvo, which aimed to make tuna a major export commodity.

Industry (including mining, manufacturing, construction and power) contributed an estimated 30.5% of GDP in 2001 and the sector engaged 27.7% of the employed labour force in the previous year. During 1990–2000 industrial GDP increased at an average annual rate of 5.2%. The sector's GDP increased by an estimated 2.8% in 2000 and by an estimated 5.2% in 2001.

El Salvador has no significant mineral resources, and the mining sector employed less than 0.1% of the economically active population in 2000, and contributed only an estimated 0.5% of GDP in 2001. Small quantities of gold, silver, sea-salt and limestone are mined or quarried. The mining sector increased by 0.4% in 1999 and by 3.0% in 2000.

Manufacturing contributed an estimated 23.7% of GDP in 2001 and employed 21.5% of the active labour force in the same year. Measured by the gross value of output, the most important branches of manufacturing (excluding the in-bond industry) in 1996 were food products (about 23.5% of the total), chemical products (16.1%), petroleum products, textiles, apparel (excl. footwear) and beverages. During 1990–2000 manufacturing GDP increased at an average annual rate of 5.4%. The sector's GDP increased by an estimated 4.1% in 2000 and by an estimated 4.2% in 2001. By the late 1990s manufacturing had become the highest earning export sector, generating the equivalent of 53% of total exports in 1999. There is a thriving offshore (*maquila*) manufacturing sector, which in 2000 generated more than one-half of the country's total exports. However, in 2001 the *maquila* manufacturing sector declined, as a consequence of the natural disasters in El Salvador and the faltering US economy. Following the earthquakes in early 2001, the IDB pledged some US $62.2m. to the industry and commerce sector and a further $574.7m. to the housing sector to fund a renovation and reconstruction programme. In September the IDB announced a loan of $70m. and in December the World Bank pledged $270m. over three years, to help reconstruction efforts.

Energy is derived principally from imported fuel. Mineral products accounted for an estimated 13.5% of the cost of merchandise imports in 2001. In 1998 El Salvador derived almost one-half (46.8%) of its electricity from petroleum, compared with just 6.8% in 1990. An estimated further 46.6% of total electricity production in 1999 was contributed by hydroelectric installations. In 2001 construction began on an electricity interconnection between El Salvador and Honduras, part of a planned Central American regional power network.

The services sector contributed an estimated 60.0% of GDP in 2001 and employed 47.5% of the economically active population in 2000. The GDP of the services sector increased by an average of 4.7% per year in 1990–2000. The sector grew by an estimated at 3.1% in 2000 and by an estimated 1.0% in 2001. The promising tourism sector was severely damaged by the civil war, but recovered in the late 1990s. In 2000 receipts from tourism totalled US $254m., compared with $211m. in the previous year.

In 2001 El Salvador recorded a visible trade deficit of US $1,912.9m., while there was a deficit of $179.0m. on the current account of the balance of payments. Workers' remittances from abroad were equivalent to about 10% of annual GDP and totalled about $1,750m. in 2000. Following the earthquakes, remittances increased in 2001, with payments from the USA alone totalling some US $1,935m. that year. In 2001 almost one-half of total imports (49.0%) was provided by the USA; other major suppliers were Guatemala, Mexico, Costa Rica, Panama, Honduras and Ecuador. The USA was also the principal market for exports (taking 65.4% of exports, mostly from the *maquila* sector, in that year); other significant purchasers were the Guatemala, Nicaragua and Honduras. In 2001 the main exports were prepared foodstuffs, beverages, spirits and vinegar, tobacco and manufactures substitutes, chemicals and related products, vegetable products (76.3% of which was coffee) and mineral products. In the same year the principal imports were

machinery and electrical equipment, mineral products and chemicals and related products.

In 2001 there was an estimated budgetary deficit of 426.4m. colones, equivalent to some 3.1% of GDP. El Salvador's external debt totalled US $4,023m. at the end of 2000, of which $2,886m. was long-term public debt, in that year equivalent to 6.8% of GDP. In that year the cost of debt-servicing was $374m. The average annual rate of inflation was 6.8% in 1992–2001; consumer prices increased by an average of 3.70% in 2001 and by 1.9% in 2002. Some 7.9% of the labour force were unemployed in 2000.

El Salvador is a member of the Central American Common Market (CACM, see p. 160), which aims to increase trade within the region and to encourage monetary and industrial co-operation.

The Government of Calderón Sol (1994–99) achieved considerable progress in reducing financial imbalances and in addressing the problem of widespread poverty. The administration also made advances in the divestment of state assets in the sectors of electricity distribution and telecommunications. A private pensions system also began operating in 1998, intended to replace gradually the existing state system. The Flores administration, inaugurated in June 1999, announced a plan for economic reactivation designed to galvanize agricultural and industrial production. In particular, the introduction of value-added tax on imported consumer goods and the prospect of more easily available credit were expected to improve the competitiveness of the agricultural sector. A revision of the tax system was expected to produce a significant increase in revenue. Economic expansion of some 2.0% was recorded in both 2000 and 2001. The introduction, in January 2001, of the US dollar as an official currency alongside the colón, anchored to the colón at a fixed rate of exchange, was intended to stabilize the economy, to lower interest rates, and to stimulate domestic and foreign investment. In late 2002 the Central Bank estimated that US dollars accounted for 99% of money in El Salvador, including both currency in circulation and bank deposits. In February 2002 the Government announced plans to increase public investment by 23% in that year. The extra funds were intended to rebuild schools and roads damaged by the earthquakes of 2001 and were expected to generate some 30,000 jobs.

On 15 March 2001 the free-trade agreement previously agreed with Mexico was implemented. In May the Central American countries, including El Salvador, reached the basis of a deal with Mexico, the 'Plan Puebla–Panamá', to integrate the region through joint transport, industry and tourism projects. In November El Salvador, Guatemala, Honduras and Nicaragua (known as the CA-4 group of countries) began negotiations with Canada on a free-trade agreement.

Negotiations towards a further free-trade agreement, to be known as the Central American Free Trade Agreement, was expected to be concluded between the CA-4 group of countries, Costa Rica and the USA by the end of 2003. However, the World Bank warned that El Salvador would lose a substantial proportion of its customs revenue when the tariff barriers were removed, leading to an increase in the fiscal deficit by as much as 1.0% in 2004. The Minister of the Economy, Miguel Lacayo Argüello, announced that taxes would be reformed to counteract this increase. The economy was forecast to grow by 2.3% in 2003 and by 2.6% in 2004, although there was some concern in 2003 that the US-led military campaign against the regime of Saddam Hussein in Iraq could adversely affect economic prospects in the country, as the USA was El Salvador's major trading partner.

Education

There are two national universities and more than 30 private universities. Education is provided free of charge in state schools, and there are also numerous private schools. Primary education, beginning at seven years of age and lasting for nine years, is officially compulsory. In 1998/99 enrolment at primary schools was equivalent to 80.6% of children in the relevant age-group (males 74.3%; females 87.2%). Secondary education begins at the age of 16 and lasts for three years. In 1997 enrolment at secondary schools was equivalent to just 36.4% of students in the relevant age-group (males 36.1%; females 36.7%). In 1999 combined enrolment in primary, secondary and tertiary education was equivalent to 63% of students in the relevant age-group. Following the earthquakes in early 2001, the IDB pledged some US $43.6m. for infrastructure reconstruction and child protection. Budgetary expenditure on education by the central Government in 2001 was US $459.1m., equivalent to 23.3% of total expenditure.

Public Holidays

2003: 1 January (New Year's Day), 16–20 April (Easter), 1 May (Labour Day), 19 June (Corpus Christi), 4–6 August* (El Salvador del Mundo Festival), 15 September (Independence Day), 12 October (Discovery of America), 2 November (All Souls' Day), 5 November (First Call of Independence), 24–25 December (Christmas), 31 December (New Year's Eve).

2004: 1 January (New Year's Day), 7–11 April (Easter), 1 May (Labour Day), 10 June (Corpus Christi), 4–6 August* (El Salvador del Mundo Festival), 15 September (Independence Day), 12 October (Discovery of America), 2 November (All Souls' Day), 5 November (First Call of Independence), 24–25 December (Christmas), 31 December (New Year's Eve).

*5–6 August outside the capital.

Weights and Measures

The metric system is officially in force. Some old Spanish measures are also used, including:

25 libras = 1 arroba;
4 arrobas = 1 quintal (46 kg);
1 manzana = 0.699 ha.

Statistical Survey

Sources (unless otherwise stated): Banco Central de Reserva de El Salvador, Alameda Juan Pablo II y 17 Avda Norte, Apdo 01-106, San Salvador; tel. 271-0011; fax 271-4575 ; Dirección General de Estadística y Censos, Edif. Centro de Gobierno, Alameda Juan Pablo II y Calle Guadalupe, San Salvador; tel. 286-4260; fax 286-2505; internet www.minec.gob.sv.

Area and Population

AREA, POPULATION AND DENSITY

Area (sq km)	
Land	20,721
Inland water	320
Total	21,041*
Population (census results)†	
28 June 1971	3,554,648
27 September 1992	
Males	2,485,613
Females	2,632,986
Total	5,118,599
Population (official estimates at mid-year)	
1999	6,154,311
2000	6,276,037
2001	6,396,890
Density (per sq km) at mid-2001	304.0

* 8,124 sq miles.

† Excluding adjustments for underenumeration.

PRINCIPAL TOWNS

(official population estimates at mid-2001)*

San Salvador			
(capital).	485,847	Mejicanos	193,400
Soyapango	287,034	Apopa	179,122
Santa Ana	253,037	Nueva San Salvador.	163,794
San Miguel	245,428	Ciudad Delgado	157,094

* Figures refer to municipios, which may each contain rural areas as well as an urban centre.

BIRTHS, MARRIAGES AND DEATHS

	Registered live births		Registered marriages		Registered deaths	
	Number	Rate (per 1,000)	Number	Rate (per 1,000)	Number	Rate (per 1,000)
1992	154,014	28.1	23,050	4.2	27,869	5.1
1993	157,640	29.0	28,819	5.3	29,203	5.4
1994	160,772	29.0	27,761	5.0	29,407	5.3
1995	159,336	28.1	25,308	4.5	29,130	5.1
1996	163,007	28.2	27,130	4.7	28,904	5.0
1997	164,143	27.8	23,561	4.0	29,118	4.9
1998	158,350	26.3	25,937	4.3	29,919	5.0
1999	153,636	25.0	34,306	5.6	28,056	4.6

Expectation of life (WHO estimates, years at birth): 69.5 (males 66.3; females 72.7) in 2001 (Source: WHO, *World Health Report*).

Economically Active Population

ECONOMICALLY ACTIVE POPULATION

(ISIC Major Divisions, '000 persons aged 10 years and over)

	1999	2000
Agriculture, hunting, forestry and fishing	503.2	501.8
Mining and quarrying	1.8	1.5
Manufacturing	426.6	433.5
Electricity, gas and water	8.5	8.8
Construction	130.9	118.8
Trade, restaurants and hotels	578.5	610.9
Transport, storage and communication	100.3	109.4
Financing, insurance, real estate and business services	84.5	87.8
Community, social and personal services	140.1	154.9
Total employed	**1,974.4**	**2,027.5**
Unemployed	170.2	173.7
Total labour force	**2,144.7**	**2,201.1**

Health and Welfare

KEY INDICATORS

Total fertility rate (children per woman, 2001)	3.0
Under-5 mortality rate (per 1,000 live births, 2001)	39
HIV/AIDS (% of persons aged 15–49, 2001)	0.60
Physicians (per 1,000 head, 1997)	1.07
Hospital beds (per 1,000 head, 1996)	1.65
Health expenditure (2000): US $ per head (PPP)	338
Health expenditure (2000): % of GDP	8.8
Health expenditure (2000): public (% of total)	43.0
Access to water (% of persons, 2000)	74
Access to sanitation (% of prsons, 2000)	83
Human Development Index (2000): ranking	94
Human Development Index (2000): value	0.727

For sources and definitions, see explanatory note on p. vi.

Agriculture

PRINCIPAL CROPS
('000 metric tons)

	1999	2000	2001
Rice (paddy)	57.4	47.2	37.3
Maize	659.8	583.0	565.0
Sorghum	139.5	149.0	148.8
Yautia (Cocoyam)*	53	52	52.0
Sugar cane	5,306.6	5,071.2	4,589.5
Dry beans	66.5	68.2	74.1
Coconuts	87.4	85.0*	85.0*
Watermelons	50.6	78.8	75.0*
Other vegetables*	67.4	58.1	58.4
Bananas*	70	65	65
Plantains	66*	67	66*
Other fruit*	192.7	156.0	156.2
Coffee (green)	160.8	144.1	112.2

* FAO estimate(s).

Source: FAO.

LIVESTOCK
('000 head, year ending September)

	1999	2000	2001
Horses*	96	96	96
Asses*	3	3	3
Mules*	24	24	24
Cattle	1,141	1,212	1,216
Pigs	248	186	150
Sheep*	5	5	5
Goats*	15	15	15
Chickens*	8,760	8,100	8,100

* FAO estimates.

Source: FAO.

LIVESTOCK PRODUCTS
('000 metric tons)

	1999	2000	2001
Beef and veal	34.1	34.5	35.0†
Pig meat*	9.0	6.8	5.5
Poultry meat	46.2	47.6	48.0*
Sheep and goat meat*	0.1	0.1	0.1
Cows' milk	360.2	398.8	395.0
Cheese*	2.6	2.6	2.4
Butter*	0.2	0.2	0.2
Hen eggs	52.3	53.0	53.0*
Honey*	3.8	3.	3.5
Fresh cattle hides*	6.6	6.7	6.7

* FAO estimate(s).
† Unofficial figure.

Source: FAO.

Forestry

ROUNDWOOD REMOVALS
('000 cubic metres, excl. bark)

	1999	2000	2001
Sawlogs, veneer logs and logs for sleepers	650	682	682*
Fuel wood	4,520	4,518	4,518
Total	5,170	4,755	5,200

* FAO estimate.

Source: FAO.

SAWNWOOD PRODUCTION
(FAO estimates, '000 cubic metres, incl. railway sleepers)

	1995	1996	1997
Coniferous (softwood)	57	57	—
Broadleaved (hardwood)	14	14	58
Total	70	70	58

1998–2001: Annual production as in 1997 (FAO estimates).

Source: FAO.

Fishing

('000 metric tons, live weight)

	1998	1999	2000
Capture	11.0	9.9	9.6
Nile tilapia	1.0	1.2	1.1
Jaguar guapote	0.3	0.4	0.3
Other freshwater fishes	1.1	1.1	1.3
Croakers and drums	0.3	0.3	0.3
Sharks, rays, skates, etc.	0.3	0.2	3.6
Other marine fishes	1.6	1.8	1.9
Whiteleg shrimp	1.3	1.1	0.5
Other penaeus shrimps	0.6	0.2	0.1
Pacific seabobs	3.0	1.7	1.5
Marine molluscs	0.4	0.3	0.3
Aquaculture	0.4	0.3	0.3
Total catch	11.4	10.2	9.9

Source: FAO, *Yearbook of Fishery Statistics*.

Mining

(metric tons, unless otherwise specified)

	1999	2000	2001
Gold (kg)	71	—	—
Gypsum	5,600	5,600	5,600
Limestone	3,200	3,200	3,200
Salt (marine)	741,500	715,260	710,00*
Silver (kg)	20	—	—

* Estimate.

Source: US Geological Survey.

Industry

SELECTED PRODUCTS
('000 metric tons, unless otherwise indicated)

	1996	1997	1998
Raw sugar	310	423	502
Motor spirit (petrol)	202	149	134*
Distillate fuel oils	107	122	146
Residual fuel oils	309	382	497*
Cement	938	1,029	988
Electric energy (million kWh)	3,452	3,480	3,821*

1999: Raw sugar 500; Cement 1,032*.

* Estimate.

Source: UN, *Industrial Commodity Statistics Yearbook*.

Finance

CURRENCY AND EXCHANGE RATES

Monetary Units
100 centavos = 1 Salvadorean colón.

Sterling, Dollar and Euro Equivalents (31 December 2002)
£1 sterling = 14.103 colones
US $1 = 8.750 colones
€1 = 9.176 colones
1,000 Salvadorean colones = £70.91 = $114.29 = €108.98

Note: The foregoing information refers to the principal exchange rate, applicable to official receipts and payments, imports of petroleum and exports of coffee. In addition, there is a market exchange rate, applicable to other transactions. The principal rate was maintained at 8.755 colones per US dollar from May 1995 to December 2000. However, in January 2001, with the introduction of legislation making the US dollar legal tender, the rate was adjusted to $1 = 8.750 colones. Both currencies were to be accepted for a transitional period.

BUDGET
(million colones until 2000; US $ million from 2001)

Revenue*	1999	2000	2001
Current revenue	12,009.2	13,486.1	1,481.3
Taxation	11,723.8	12,484.9	1,387.3
Taxes on income, profits and capital gains	3,574.4	3,683.8	367.1
Individual	1,436.5	1,361.6	170.3
Corporate	2,137.9	2,322.2	196.8
Domestic taxes on goods and services	6,328.1	7,428.8	857.9
General sales or turnover taxes	5,795.7	7,003.8	808.6
Excises	453.2	425.0	49.3
Taxes on international trade and transactions	1,315.3	1,230.4	148.8
Customs duties	1,296.7	1,229.9	144.9
Other taxes	386.4	44.6	1.9
Non-tax revenue	253.2	1,001.2	93.6
Adjustment	32.2	—	0.2
Capital revenue	6.6	7.0	0.2
Total	12,015.8	13,493.1	1,481.5

Expenditure†	1999	2000	2001
General public services	1,419.3	1,613.5	250.2
Defence	872.9	839.3	250.2
Public order and safety	2,272.3	2,401.8	309.6
Education	2,380.4	2,775.0	459.1
Health	569.8	578.2	217.9
Social security and welfare	299.4	163.8	116.3
Housing and community services	62.8	194.4	149.0
Recreational, cultural and religious affairs	235.3	242.9	66.0
Economic affairs and services	1,525.2	2,074.0	289.0
Agriculture	169.4	644.9	48.3
Transportation and communications	1,072.2	1,122.6	193.1
Total (incl. others)	10,979.5	11,452.2	1,968.6
Adjustment	22.6	−834.4	−184.7
Current‡	9,579.3	10,262.9	1,681.9
Capital	1,377.6	2,023.7	471.4

* Excluding grants received: 18.9m. colones in 1999; 532.9m. colones in 2000; US $18.1m. in 2001.
† Excluding lending minus repayments: −31.7m. colones in 1999; −134.1m. colones in 2000; US $ −42.8m. in 2001.
‡ Including interest payments: 1,319.5m. colones in 1999; 1,360.2m. colones in 2000; US $165.3m. in 2001.
Source: IMF, *Government Finance Statistics Yearbook*.

INTERNATIONAL RESERVES
(US $ million at 31 December)

	2000	2001	2002
Gold*	19.8	19.8	19.8
IMF special drawing rights	32.6	31.4	34.0
Foreign exchange	1,889.8	1,709.6	1,588.8
Total	1,922.6	1,741.0	1,622.8

* Valued at US $42.22 per troy ounce.
Source: IMF, *International Financial Statistics*.

MONEY SUPPLY
(US $ million at 31 December)

	2000	2001	2002
Currency outside banks	451.5	220.2	60.6
Demand deposits at deposit money banks	630.2	977.7	1,027.1
Total money (incl. others)	1,093.0	1,198.1	1,090.4

Source: IMF, *International Financial Statistics*.

COST OF LIVING
(Consumer Price Index; base: 1990 = 100)

	1998	1999	2000
Food	248.3	246.2	246.6
Rent	171.9	176.7	181.8
Fuel and light	176.1	176.2	212.7
Clothing	153.0	151.4	149.8
All items (incl. others)	216.1	217.0	221.9

2001: All items 230.2.

Source: ILO.

NATIONAL ACCOUNTS

National Income and Product
(million colones at current prices)

	1998	1999	2000
Gross domestic product (GDP) at factor cost	97,557.7	101,354.7	107,542.1
Indirect taxes	7,543.0	7,788.0	8,095.0
Less subsidies	27.0	28.0	27.0
GDP in purchasers' values	105,073.7	109,114.7	115,610.1
Less Factor income from abroad (net)	1,426.3	2,563.8	2,190.1
Gross national product (GNP)	103,647.4	106,550.9	113,420.0

Source: UN Economic Commission for Latin America and the Caribbean, *Statistical Yearbook*.

Expenditure on the Gross Domestic Product
(million colones at current prices)

	1999	2000	2001
Government final consumption expenditure	10,928	11,406	12,068
Private final consumption expenditure	93,686	101,547	105,702
Increase in stocks	394	−50	−560
Gross fixed capital formation	17,522	19,460	19,851
Total domestic expenditure	122,530	132,363	136,971
Exports of goods and services	27,197	31,420	34,796
Less Imports of goods and services	40,661	48,816	51,552
GDP in purchasers' values	109,066	114,968	120,215
GDP at constant 1990 prices	55,980	57,099	58,214

Source: IMF, *International Financial Statistics*.

Gross Domestic Product by Economic Activity

(US $ million at current prices)

	1999	2000*	2001*
Agriculture, hunting, forestry and fishing	1,306.3	1,284.7	1,302.9
Mining and quarrying . . .	53.4	52.7	60.7
Manufacturing	2,815.4	3,030.8	3,161.7
Construction	533.3	572.1	637.6
Electricity, gas and water . .	248.5	222.4	216.3
Transport, storage and communications . . .	1,041.1	1,114.4	1,166.6
Wholesale and retail trade, restaurants and hotels . .	2,374.1	2,546.7	2,691.0
Finance and insurance . .	518.8	567.9	598.7
Real estate and business services	513.1	531.5	559.9
Owner-occupied dwellings . .	987.4	1,031.9	1,037.5
Community, social, domestic and personal services	819.7	881.8	927.0
Government services . . .	944.6	960.6	984.7
Sub-total	12,154.8	12,797.5	13,344.6
Import duties . . . . . }	810.6	862.0	947.1
Value-added tax . . . . }			
Less Imputed bank service charge	500.6	520.43	542.8
Total	12,464.7	13,139.1	13,738.9

* Preliminary figures.

BALANCE OF PAYMENTS

(US $ million)

	1999	2000	2001
Exports of goods f.o.b.	2,534.3	2,963.2	2,901.3
Imports of goods f.o.b. . . .	−3,890.4	−4,702.9	−4,813.9
Trade balance	−1,356.1	−1,739.7	−1,912.9
Exports of services . . .	640.5	698.4	1,075.8
Imports of services	−823.0	−933.3	−1,077.8
Balance on goods and services	−1,538.6	−1,974.7	−1,915.0
Other income received . . .	113.0	141.3	168.9
Other income paid	−395.1	−394.4	−434.7
Balance on goods, services and income	−1,820.7	−2,227.7	−2,180.7
Current transfers received . .	1,590.5	1,830.3	2,022.4
Current transfers paid . . .	−9.0	−33.2	−18.6
Current balance	−239.2	−430.6	−176.9
Capital account (net) . . .	78.6	109.0	197.7
Direct investment abroad . .	−53.8	5.0	9.7
Direct investment from abroad .	215.8	173.4185.4	267.8
Portfolio investment assets . .	−1.7	−8.9	−126.5
Portfolio investment liabilities .	75.2	−16.8	160.6
Other investment assets . .	−126.9	−245.4	−630.1
Other investment liabilities . .	465.8	380.0	464.2
Net errors and omissions . .	−205.9	−11.3	−344.2
Overall balance	207.8	−45.5	−177.7

Source: IMF, *International Financial Statistics.*

External Trade

PRINCIPAL COMMODITIES

(distribution by SITC, '000 US $)

Imports c.i.f.*	1999	2000	2001†
Live animals, animal products and vegetable products . .	279,590	311,923	332,868
Food, beverages and tobacco .	216,770	240,070	248,586
Mineral products	387,673	611,543	523,179
Crude petroleum oils . . .	114,905	210,405	168,836
Heavy refined oils	98,650	170,297	159,856
Chemicals and related products	357,083	460,388	471,361
Medicaments	80,888	125,419	117,811
Plastic materials, artificial resins, natural and synthetic rubber and similar manufactures	191,363	208,733	237,959
Plastics and resins . . .	145,498	164,979	189,328
Wood pulp, paper, paperboard and articles thereof . . .	154,030	171,983	197,047
Textiles and related products .	134,619	182,549	200,759
Base metals	229,201	246,618	311,907
Cast iron and steel . . .	89,745	96,472	158,485
Machinery and electrical equipment	593,649	752,671	701,567
Boilers, machinery and other mechanical products . . .	321,751	333,505	382,805
Electrical machinery and apparatus	271,898	419,166	318,762
Electric line telephonic and telegraphic apparatus . .	103,053	138,851	89,583
Transport equipment	271,633	251,192	249,578
Goods vehicles	105,479	85,228	78,353
Total (incl. others)	3,140,020	3,794,724	3,865,807

* Excluding imports into maquila zones ('000 US $): 954,700 in 1999; 1,152,700 in 2000; 1,161,600 in 2001.

† Preliminary figures.

Exports f.o.b.*	1999	2000	2001†
Live animals and animal products	46,996	47,173	39,213
Vegetable products	267,751	333,134	150,749
Coffee, including roasted and decaffinated coffee	245,093	297,971	115,095
Prepared foodstuffs beverages, spirits and vinegar, tobacco and manufactured substitutes	173,638	182,271	225,968
Unrefined sugar	37,263	39,970	70,031
Mineral products	66,873	69,600	74,557
Heavy refined oils . . .	24,443	37,816	44,814
Chemical products	151,234	151,397	151,817
Medicaments	49,612	53,698	52,089
Plastics, rubber and related products	44,254	54,731	60,213
Woodpulp, paper, paperboard and articles thereof . . .	80,034	80,900	99,573
Paper and cardboard packaging	29,588	33,695	37,040
Textiles and textile articles .	144,995	150,401	145,033
Clothing	42,826	47,676	54,415
Base metals and articles thereof	92,693	108,674	109,531
Electrical machinery and apparatus	39,875	50,817	56,303
Miscellaneous manufactured articles	32,846	54,003	61,953
Total (incl. others)	1,176,610	1,332,317	1,213,527

* Excluding exports from maquila zones ('000 US $): 1,333,400 in 1999; 1,609,000 in 2000; 1,651,600 in 2001.

† Preliminary figures.

PRINCIPAL TRADING PARTNERS
(US $ million)

Imports c.i.f.	1998	1999	2000
Brazil	26.0	33.5	40.2
China, People's Republic	53.4	20.1	63.7
Colombia	32.8	37.6	27.5
Costa Rica	115.1	116.3	143.2
Ecuador	85.5	83.2	151.4
Finland	3.3	3.1	61.1
France	18.8	23.0	37.9
Germany	89.7	74.6	75.8
Guatemala	346.8	368.9	488.2
Honduras	87.8	87.8	119.9
Italy	31.6	27.6	35.6
Japan	145.1	126.7	122.5
Korea, Republic	29.2	32.9	39.0
Mexico	238.4	264.3	255.7
Netherlands Antilles	37.0	54.5	175.6
Nicaragua	49.4	64.6	69.8
Panama	106.1	98.3	130.9
Russia	30.1	24.5	38.2
Spain	49.0	36.3	55.6
USA	1,197.6	1,173.1	1,322.0
Venezuela	41.8	43.5	63.0
Total (incl. others)	3,108.0	3,128.1	3,795.2

Exports f.o.b.*	1998	1999	2000
Belgium	24.7†	18.2	13.8
Costa Rica	110.3	91.9	85.6
Dominican Republic	13.4	14.2	12.2
France	13.2	12.1	12.2
Germany	139.9	104.7	94.4
Guatemala	282.5	272.3	322.5
Honduras	148.8	171.6	225.1
Japan	12.5	7.9	9.5
Mexico	17.3	14.3	10.8
Netherlands	21.9	6.7	4.2
Nicaragua	75.0	91.1	107.5
Panama	24.3	35.4	39.0
Russia	22.2	11.9	17.5
United Kingdom	19.4	14.1	14.5
USA	270.1	247.9	322.8
Total (incl. others)	1,257.1	1,164.2	1,341.4

* Excluding maquila zones.
† Including trade with Luxembourg.

Source: UN, *International Trade Statistics Yearbook.*

2001 (US $ million): *Imports c.i.f.:* Brazil 52.0; Costa Rica 163.4; Ecuador 127.4; Germany 89.0; Guatemala 435.4; Honduras 134.7; Japan 124.4; Mexico 312.4; Netherlands Antilles 42.5; Nicaragua 89.1; Panama 135.1*; Spain 54.8; USA 2,463.5†; Venezuela 82.3; Total (incl. others) 5,027.4. *Exports f.o.b.:* Costa Rica 94.6; Germany 48.8; Guatemala 323.2; Honduras 184.3; Nicaragua 120.3; Panama 48.9*; USA 1,874.8†; Total (incl. others) 2,865.1.
* Including Canal Zone.
† Including maquila zones.

Source: Banco Central de El Salvador, *Revista Trimestrial*, July–August 2002.

Transport

RAILWAYS
(traffic)

	1999	2000
Number of passengers ('000)	543.3	687.3
Passenger-kilometres (million)	8.4	10.7
Freight ('000 metric tons)	188.6	136.2
Freight ton-kilometres (million)	19.4	13.1

Source: Ferrocarriles Nacionales de El Salvador.

ROAD TRAFFIC
(motor vehicles in use at 31 December)

	1998	1999	2000
Passenger cars	187,440	197,374	207,259
Buses and coaches	34,784	36,204	37,554
Lorries and vans	166,065	177,741	189,812
Motorcycles and mopeds	32,271	35,021	37,139

Source: Servicio de Tránsito Centroamericano (SERTRACEN).

SHIPPING

Merchant Fleet
(registered at 31 December)

	1999	2000	2001
Number of vessels	13	13	12
Total displacement ('000 grt)	1.6	1.6	1.5

Source: Lloyd's Register-Fairplay, *World Fleet Statistics.*

CIVIL AVIATION
(traffic on scheduled services)

	1997	1998	1999
Kilometres flown (million)	17	22	28
Passengers carried ('000)	1,006	1,585	1,624
Passenger–km (million)	1,898	2,292	5,091
Total ton-km (million)	190	253	502

Source: UN, *Statistical Yearbook.*

Tourism

TOURIST ARRIVALS BY COUNTRY OF ORIGIN
(excluding Salvadorean nationals residing abroad)

	1996	1997	1998
Canada	8,855	9,052	9,282
Costa Rica	19,497	19,919	28,804
Guatemala	54,210	83,685	163,485
Honduras	20,644	36,515	84,299
Mexico	11,276	19,737	19,912
Nicaragua	14,104	24,546	60,735
Panama	9,050	6,883	10,498
Spain	8,242	8,779	7,631
USA	88,905	123,355	97,838
Total (incl. others)	282,835	387,052	541,863

Receipts from tourism (US $ million): 125 in 1998; 211 in 1999; 254 in 2000.

Arrivals ('000): 658 in 1999; 795 in 2000.

Sources: World Tourism Organization, *Yearbook of Tourism Statistics*, World Bank, *World Development Indicators.*

Communications Media

	1999	2000	2001
Television receivers ('000 in use) .	n.a.	1,260	n.a.
Telephones ('000 main lines in use)	493.3	625.8	598.0
Mobile cellular telephones ('000 subscribers)	511.4	743.6	800.0
Personal computers ('000 in use) .	100	100	140
Internet users ('000)	40.0	40.0	50.0

Radio receivers ('000 in use): 2,940 in 1999.

Daily newspapers: 4 in 1998 (total circulation 171,000).

Non-daily newspapers: 6 in 1996 (total circulation 52,000).

Sources: UNESCO, *Statistical Yearbook*, International Telecommunication Union.

Education

(2000)

	Institutions	Teachers	Students		
			Males	Females	Total
Pre-primary	4,272	3,185*	98,237*	95,806*	205,892
Primary	5,090	26,209	624,304*	581,693*	1,212,622
Secondary . . .	597	3,556*	70,767*	69,111*	147,867
Tertiary: University level	28	6,908	57,734	49,984	107,718
Tertiary: Other higher .	15	593	3,643	3,314	6,957

* 1999 figure.

Source: Ministry of Education.

Adult literacy rate (UNESCO estimates): 78.7% (males 81.6%; females 76.1%) in 2000 (Source: UN Development Programme, *Human Development Report*).

Directory

The Constitution

The Constitution of the Republic of El Salvador came into effect on 20 December 1983.

The Constitution provides for a republican, democratic and representative form of government, composed of three Powers—Legislative, Executive, and Judicial—which are to operate independently. Voting is a right and duty of all citizens over 18 years of age. Presidential and congressional elections may not be held simultaneously.

The Constitution binds the country, as part of the Central American Nation, to favour the total or partial reconstruction of the Republic of Central America. Integration in a unitary, federal or confederal form, provided that democratic and republican principles are respected and that basic rights of individuals are fully guaranteed, is subject to popular approval.

LEGISLATIVE ASSEMBLY

Legislative power is vested in a single chamber, the Asamblea Nacional, whose members are elected every three years and are eligible for re-election. The Asamblea's term of office begins on 1 May. The Asamblea's duties include the choosing of the President and Vice-President of the Republic from the two citizens who shall have gained the largest number of votes for each of these offices, if no candidate obtains an absolute majority in the election. It also selects the members of the Supreme and subsidiary courts; of the Elections Council; and the Accounts Court of the Republic. It determines taxes; ratifies treaties concluded by the Executive with other States and international organizations; sanctions the Budget; regulates the monetary system of the country; determines the conditions under which foreign currencies may circulate; and suspends and reimposes constitutional guarantees. The right to initiate legislation may be exercised by the Asamblea (as well as by the President, through the Council of Ministers, and by the Supreme Court). The Asamblea may override, with a two-thirds majority, the President's objections to a Bill which it has sent for presidential approval.

PRESIDENT

The President is elected for five years, the term beginning and expiring on 1 June. The principle of alternation in the presidential office is established in the Constitution, which states the action to be taken should this principle be violated. The Executive is responsible for the preparation of the Budget and its presentation to the Asamblea; the direction of foreign affairs; the organization of the armed and security forces; and the convening of extraordinary sessions of the Asamblea. In the event of the President's death, resignation, removal or other cause, the Vice-President takes office for the rest of the presidential term; and, in case of necessity, the Vice-President may be replaced by one of the two Designates elected by the Asamblea.

JUDICIARY

Judicial power is exercised by the Supreme Court and by other competent tribunals. The Magistrates of the Supreme Court are elected by the Legislature, their number to be determined by law. The Supreme Court alone is competent to decide whether laws, decrees and regulations are constitutional or not.

The Government

HEAD OF STATE

President: FRANCISCO FLORES PÉREZ (assumed office 1 June 1999).

Vice-President: CARLOS QUINTANILLA SCHMIDT.

COUNCIL OF MINISTERS
(April 2003)

Chief of Staff and Minister of the Treasury: Dr JUAN JOSÉ DABOUB ABDALÁ.

Minister of Foreign Affairs: MARÍA EUGENIA BRIZUELA DE AVILA.

Minister of the Interior: MARIO ERNESTO ACOSTA OERTEL.

Minister of Government: CONRADO LÓPEZ ANDREU.

Minister of the Economy: MIGUEL ERNESTO LACAYO ARGÜELLO.

Minister of Education: ROLANDO ERNESTO MARIN.

Minister of National Defence: Maj.-Gen. JUAN ANTONIO MARTÍNEZ VARELA.

Minister of Labour and Social Security: JORGE ISIDORO NIETO MENÉNDEZ.

Minister of Public Health and Social Welfare: Dr JOSÉ FRANCISCO LÓPEZ BELTRÁN.

Minister of Agriculture and Livestock: SALVADOR URRUTIA LOUCEL.

Minister of Public Works: JOSÉ ANGEL QUIROS.

Minister of the Environment and Natural Resources: WALTER JOKISCH.

MINISTRIES

Ministry for the Presidency: Avda Cuba, Calle Darió González 806, Barrio San Jacinto, San Salvador; tel. 221-8483; fax 771-0950; internet www.casapres.gob.sv.

Ministry of Agriculture and Livestock: 1a Avda Norte y 13 Calle Poniente, San Salvador; tel. 228-2070; fax 288-5153; internet www.go.to/mag.gob.sv.

Ministry of the Economy: Edif. C-1–C-2, Centro de Gobierno, Alameda Juan Pablo II y Calle Guadalupe, San Salvador; tel. 281-1122; fax 221-5446; internet www.minec.gob.sv.

Ministry of Education: Edif. A, Centro de Gobierno, Alameda Juan Pablo II y Calle Guadalupe, San Salvador; tel. 281-0044; fax 281-0077; e-mail atencion.publico@mined.gob.sv; internet www .mined.gob.sv.

Ministry of the Environment and Natural Resources: Edif. Torre El Salvador, 3°, Alameda Roosevelt y 55 Avda Norte, San Salvador; tel. 260-8900; fax 260-3115; e-mail medioambiente@marn .gob.sv; internet www.marn.gob.sv.

Ministry of Foreign Affairs: Calle Circunvalación 227, Col. San Benito, San Salvador; tel. 243-9648; fax 243-9656; internet www .rree.gob.sv.

Ministry of Government: Centro de Gobierno, Edif. B-1, Alameda Juan Pablo II y Avda Norte 17, San Salvador; tel. 221-3688; fax 221-3956.

Ministry of the Interior: Centro de Gobierno, Alameda Juan Pablo II y Calle Guadalupe, San Salvador; tel. 222-5000; e-mail informacion@minter.gob.sv; internet www.minter.gob.sv.

Ministry of Labour and Social Security: Paseo General Escalón 4122, San Salvador; tel. 263-5276; fax 263-5278; internet www.mtps .gob.sv.

Ministry of National Defence: Alameda Dr Manuel Enrique Araújo, Km 5, Carretera a Santa Tecla, San Salvador; tel. 223-0233; fax 998-2005; internet www.fuerzaarmada.gob.sv.

Ministry of Public Health and Social Welfare: Calle Arce 827, San Salvador; tel. 221-0966; fax 221-0991; internet www.mspas.gob .sv.

Ministry of Public Works: San Salvador; tel. 222-1505; fax 771-2881.

Ministry of the Treasury: Edif. Ministerio de Hacienda, Blvd Los Héroes 1231, San Salvador; tel. 244-3000; fax 226-8690; internet www.mh.gob.sv.

President and Legislature

PRESIDENT

Election, 7 March 1999

Candidates	% of votes cast
Francisco Flores Pérez (ARENA)	51.96
Facundo Guardado (FMLN/USC)	29.05
Rubén Ignacio Zamora (CD)	7.50
Rodolfo Parker (PDC)	5.68
Rafael Hernán Contreras (PCN)	3.82
Salvador Nelson García (LIDER)	1.63
Francisco Ayala de Paz (PUNTO)	0.36
Total	**100.00**

ASAMBLEA NACIONAL

President: WALTER ARAUJO.

General Election, 16 March 2003

Party	Seats
Frente Farabundo Martí para la Liberación Nacional (FMLN)	31
Alianza Republicana Nacionalista (ARENA)	27
Partido de Conciliación Nacional (PCN)	16
Partido Demócrata Cristiano (PDC)	5
Centro Democrático Unido (CDU)*	5
Total	**84**

* Electoral alliance comprising the Movimiento Nacional Revolucionario (MNR), the Movimiento Popular Social Cristiano (MPSC) and the Partido Social Demócrata (PSD).

Political Organizations

Alianza Republicana Nacionalista (ARENA): Prolongación Calle Arce 2423, entre 45 y 47 Avda Norte, San Salvador; tel. 260-4400; fax 260-5918; f. 1981; right-wing; Pres. JOSÉ SALAVERRIA.

Centro Democrática Unido (CDU): Blvd Tutunichapa y Calle Roberto Masferrer 1313, Urb. Médica, San Salvador; tel. 226-1928; fax 225-5883; f. 1987 as Convergencia Democrática (CD); electoral alliance of the Movimiento Nacional Revolucionario (MNR), the Movimiento Popular Social Cristiano (MPSC) and the Partido Social

Demócrata (PSD); changed name as above in 2000; became political party in 2001; Leader VINICIO PEÑATE; Sec.-Gen. RUBEN ZAMORA.

Frente Farabundo Martí para la Liberación Nacional (FMLN): 27 Calle Poniente 1316 y 9a Avda Norte 229, San Salvador; tel. 226-5236; internet www.fmln.org.sv; f. 1980 as the FDR (Frente Democrático Revolucionario-FMLN) as a left-wing opposition front to the PDC-military coalition Government; the FDR was the political wing and the FMLN was the guerrilla front; military operations were co-ordinated by the Dirección Revolucionaria Unida (DRU); achieved legal recognition 1992; comprised various factions, including Communist (Leader Shafik Handal), Renewalist (Leader Francisco Jovel) and Terceristas (Leader Manuel Melgar); Co-ordinator-Gen. SALVADOR SÁNCHEZ CERÉN.

Liga Democrática Republicana (LIDER): San Salvador; republican.

Movimiento Auténtico Cristiano (MAC): San Salvador; f. 1988; Leader JULIO ADOLFO REY PRENDES.

Movimiento Estable Republicano Centrista (MERECEN): San Salvador; f. 1982; centre party; Sec.-Gen. JUAN RAMÓN ROSALES Y ROSALES.

Movimiento Renovador: Calle a Motocross, Pasaje Los Bambués 6, San Salvador; tel. 284-7643; e-mail movimiento@renovadores .com; internet www.renovadores.com; f. 1944; Leader FACUNDO GUARDADO.

Partido Acción Democrática (AD): San Salvador; f. 1981; centre-right; observer mem. of Liberal International; Leader RICARDO GONZÁLEZ CAMACHO.

Partido Acción Nacional (PAN): 1 Avda Norte y 27 Calle Pte 114, San Salvador; tel. 274–9576; Dir TOMÁS MEJÍA.

Partido Acción Popular: 61 Calle Pte 3549, Col. Escalón; tel. 213-0759; Leader JOSÉ ALEJANDRO DUARTE.

Partido Auténtico Institucional Salvadoreño (PAISA): San Salvador; f. 1982; formerly right-wing majority of the PCN; Sec.-Gen. Dr ROBERTO ESCOBAR GARCÍA.

Partido de Conciliación Nacional (PCN): 15 Avda Norte y 3a Calle Poniente 244, San Salvador; tel. 221-3752; fax 281-9272; f. 1961; right-wing; Leader FRANCISCO JOSÉ GUERRERO; Sec.-Gen. CIRO CRUZ ZEPEDA.

Partido Convergenica Democratica: Final Blvd Tutnichapa y Calle Roberto Masferrer 1313, Urb. La Esperanza, San Salvador; tel. 226-1928; f. 1993; left-wing; Sec.-Gen. RÚBEN ZAMORA.

Partido Demócrata (PD): Blvd Héctor Silva 128, Urb. Médica, San Salvador; tel. 225-3166; f. 1995 by Movimiento Nacional Revolucionario and a dissident faction of the PDC, together with Expresión Renovadora del Pueblo (f. 1994, fmrly the ERP, see above) and Resistencia Nacional (f. 1994, fmrly the FARN, see above), following their withdrawal from the FMLN; centre-left; Leaders JORGE MELÉNDEZ, JUAN MEDRANO.

Partido Demócrata Cristiano (PDC): 3a Calle Poniente 924, San Salvador; tel. 222-8485; fax 998-1526; f. 1960; 150,000 mems; anti-imperialist, advocates self-determination and Latin American integration; Sec.-Gen. RENÉ NAPOLEÓN AGUILUZ.

Partido Fuerza Cristiano (FUERZA): Residencial Villa Olímpica, San Salvador; tel. 223-1216; fax 245-1600; formerly Futuro, Fuerza y Fortaleza; Dir-Gen. EDGAR MAURICIO MEYER BELTRAND.

Partido de Orientación Popular (POP): San Salvador; f. 1981; extreme right-wing.

Partido Liberal Democrático (PLD): Calle El Progreso, Pasaje El Rosal 11, Col. El Rosal, San Salvador; tel. 224-2143; f. 1994; right-wing; Leader KIRIO WALDO SALGADO.

Partido Nacional Liberal: Revisión de Firmes, 3 Avda Norte 325, San Salvador; Leader OSCAR SILDER CHÁVEZ HERNÁNDEZ.

Partido Popular Laborista (PPL): 23 Calle Pte 1518 Col. Layco, San Salvador; tel. 235-6260; f. 1997; Sec.-Gen. ERNESTO VILANOVA.

Partido Popular Salvadoreño (PPS): San Salvador; f. 1966; right-wing; represents business interests; Sec.-Gen. FRANCISCO QUIÑÓNEZ AVILA.

Partido Social Demócrata (PSD): Blvd Héctor Silva Romero 128, Urb. Clinicas Médicas, San Salvador; f. 1987; left-wing; contested 2000 elections as part of Centro Democrático Unido alliance; Sec.-Gen. JORGE MELÉNDEZ.

Partido Unificación Cristiana Democrática (UCD): 7a Calle Ote. 52, Col. Los Andes, San Marcos; tel. 213-0759; Sec.-Gen. JOSÉ ALEJANDRO DUARTE.

Partido Unionista Centroamericana (PUCA): San Salvador; advocates reunification of Central America; Pres. Dr GABRIEL PILOÑA ARAÚJO.

Pueblo Unido Nuevo Trato (PUNTO): San Salvador.

Unión Social Cristiana (USC): 12 Calle Pte y 31 Avda Sur, Col. Flor Blanca, San Salvador; tel. 222-0571; f. 1997; by merger of Movimiento de Unidad, Partido de Renovación Social Cristiano and Movimiento de Solidaridad Nacional; Leader CARLOS ABRAHAM RODRÍGUEZ.

Other parties include Partido Centrista Salvadoreño (f. 1985; Leader Tomás Chafoya Martínez); Partido de Empresarios, Campesinos y Obreros (ECO, Leader Dr Luis Rolando López); Partido Independiente Democrático (PID, f. 1985; Leader Eduardo García Tobar); Partido de la Revolución Salvadoreña (Sec.-Gen. Joaquín Villalobos); Patria Libre (f. 1985; right-wing; Leader Hugo Barrera).

OTHER GROUPS

The following groups were active during the internal disturbances of the 1980s and early 1990s:

Partido de Liberación Nacional (PLN): political-military organization of the extreme right; the military wing was the Ejército Secreto Anti-comunista (ESA); Sec.-Gen. and C-in-C AQUILES BAIRES.

The following guerrilla groups were dissident factions of the Fuerzas Populares de Liberación (FPL):

Frente Clara Elizabeth Ramírez: f. 1983; Marxist-Leninist group.

Movimiento Laborista Cayetano Carpio: f. 1983.

There were also several right-wing guerrilla groups and 'death squads', including the Fuerza Nacionalista Roberto D'Aubuisson (FURODA), not officially linked to any of the right-wing parties.

Diplomatic Representation

EMBASSIES IN EL SALVADOR

Argentina: 79 Avda Norte y 11 Calle Poniente 704, Col. Escalón, Apdo 384, San Salvador; tel. 263-3638; fax 263-3687; e-mail argensalv@saltel.net; Ambassador JORGE TELESFORO PEREIRA.

Belize: Calle el Bosque Norte y Calle Lomas de Candelaria, Col. Jardines de la Primera Etapa, San Salvador; tel. 248-1423; fax 273-6244; e-mail embelguat@guate.net; Ambassador DARWIN GABOUREL.

Brazil: Blvd de Hipódromo 305, Col. San Benito, San Salvador; tel. 298-2751; fax 279-3934; e-mail brasemb@es.com.sv; internet www.netcomsa.com/embbrasil; Ambassador VICTOR MANZOLLINO DE MORAES.

Canada: Centro Financiero Gigante, Alameda Roosevelt y Avda Sur, Torre A, Lobby 2, Col. Escalon, San Salvador; tel. 279-4655; fax 279-0765; e-mail ssal@dfait-maeci.gc.ca/Salvador; internet www.dfait-maeci.gc.ca; Ambassador JAMES LAMBERT.

Chile: Pasaje Bellavista 121, Entre 9a C.P. y 9a C.P. bis, Col. Escalón, San Salvador; tel. 263-4285; fax 263-4308; Ambassador VICTORIA EUGENIA MORALES.

China (Taiwan): Condominio Penthouse, 7°, Paseo General Escalón 5333, Col. Escalón, Apdo 956, San Salvador; tel. 263-1330; fax 263-1329; e-mail sinoemb@es.com.sv; Ambassador HOU PING-FU.

Colombia: Calle El Mirador 5120, Col. Escalón, San Salvador; tel. 263-1936; fax 263-1942; Ambassador GUILLERMO ORJUELA BERMEO.

Costa Rica: 85 Avda Sur y Calle Cuscatlán 4415, Col. Escalón, San Salvador; tel. 264-3863; fax 264-3866; e-mail embaricasal@sicanet.org.sv; Ambassador CARMEN DE MEJÍA.

Dominican Republic: Avda República Federal de Alemania 163, Col. Escalón, San Salvador; tel. 263-1816; fax 263-1816; Ambassador HECTOR PEREYRA ARIZA.

Ecuador: 77 Avda Norte 208, Col. Escalón, San Salvador; tel. 263-5323; fax 263-5258; Ambassador ENRIQUE GARCÉS FÉLIX.

Egypt: 9a Calle Poniente y 93 Avda Norte 12-97, Col. Escalón, San Salvador; tel. 211-5787; fax 263-2411; e-mail emebgip@telesal.net; Chargé d'affaires a.i. FAWZI MOHAMED ALSAID GOHAR.

France: 1 Calle Poniente 3718, Col. Escalón, Apdo 474, San Salvador; tel. 279-4016; fax 298-1536; e-mail ambafrance@es.com.sv; internet www.embafrancia.com.sv; Ambassador LYDIE GAZARIAN.

Germany: 7a Calle Poniente 3972, esq. 77a Avda Norte, Col. Escalón, Apdo 693, San Salvador; tel. 263-2088; fax 263-2091; e-mail embajada.alemana@web.de; internet www.sansalvador.diplo.de; Ambassador JOACHIM NEUKIRCH.

Guatemala: 15 Avda Norte 135, San Salvador; tel. 271-2225; fax 221-3019; Ambassador CARLOS ARTURO GONZÁLEZ ESTRADA.

Holy See: 87 Avda Norte y 7a Calle Poniente, Col. Escalón, Apdo 01-95, San Salvador (Apostolic Nunciature); tel. 263-2931; fax 263-

3010; e-mail nunels@telesal.net; Apostolic Nuncio Most Rev. GIACINTO BERLOCO (Titular Archbishop of Fidene).

Honduras: 89 Avda Norte, entre 7 y 9 Calle Poniente, Col. Escalón, San Salvador; tel. 263-2808; fax 263-2296; Ambassador JAIME GÜELL BOGRÁN.

Israel: Centro Financiero Gigante, Torre B, 11°, Alameda Roosevelt y Avda Sur 63, San Salvador; tel. 211-3434; fax 211-3443; Ambassador ARYEH ZUR.

Italy: Calle la Reforma 158, Col. San Benito, Apdo 0199, San Salvador; tel. 223-4806; fax 298-3050; e-mail ambitalia@ambasciatait.org.sv; internet www.ambasciatait.org.sv; Ambassador ROBERTO FALASCHI.

Japan: Calle Loma Linda 258, Col. San Benito, San Salvador; tel. 224-4740; fax 298-6685; Ambassador SABURO YUZAWA.

Korea, Republic: Calle Juan Santamaria 330, El Pedregal, Col. Escalón, San Salvador; tel. 263-0810; fax 263-0784; Chargé d'affaires a.i. OCK-JOO KIM.

Mexico: Calle Circunvalación y Pasaje 12, Col. San Benito, Apdo 432, San Salvador; tel. 243-3190; fax 243-0437; e-mail embamex@sv.inercomnet.net; Ambassador PABLO RUIZ LIMÓN.

Nicaragua: 71 Avda Norte y 1a Calle Poniente 164, Col. Escalón, San Salvador; tel. 223-7729; fax 223-7201; Chargé d'affaires a.i. DIANORA BALTONADO PADILLA.

Panama: Alameda Roosevelt 2838 y 55 Avda Norte, Altos de la Compañia Panameña de Aviación, San Salvador; tel. 298-0884; fax 298-5453; Ambassador RODERICK GUERRA BIANCO.

Peru: 7 Calle Poniente 4111, Col. Escalón, San Salvador; tel. 263-3326; fax 263-3310; e-mail embperu@telesal.net; Ambassador ANTONIO GRUTER VÁSQUEZ.

Spain: Calle La Reforma 167, Col. San Benito, San Salvador; tel. 257-5700; fax 257-5712; e-mail embajada@embespana.com.sv; Ambassador JUAN FRANCISCO MONTALBÁN CARRASCO.

United Kingdom: Edif. Inter-Inversiones, Paseo General Escalón 4828, Col. Escalón, Apdo 1591, San Salvador; tel. 263-6527; fax 263-6516; e-mail britemb.sansalv@fco.gov.uk; Ambassador PATRICK MORGAN.

USA: Blvd Santa Elena Sur, Antiguo Cuscatlán, San Salvador; tel. 278-4444; fax 278-6011; internet www.usinfo.org.sv; Ambassador ROSE M. LIKINS.

Uruguay: Edif. Gran Plaza 405, Blvd del Hipódromo, Col. San Benito, San Salvador; tel. 279-1627; fax 279-1626; Ambassador Dr ENRIQUE DELGADO GENTA.

Venezuela: 7a Calle Poniente, entre 75 y 77 Avda Norte, Col. Escalón, San Salvador; tel. 263-3977; fax 263-3979; e-mail venesal@amnetsal.com; Ambassador SOLIS ANTONIO MARTÍNEZ.

Judicial System

Supreme Court of Justice

Frente a Plaza José Simeón Cañas, Centro de Gobierno, San Salvador; tel. 271-8888; fax 271-3767; internet www.csj.gob.sv.

f. 1824; composed of 15 Magistrates, one of whom is its President. The Court is divided into four chambers: Constitutional Law, Civil Law, Penal Law and Litigation; Pres. AGUSTÍN GARCÍA CALDERÓN.

Chambers of 2nd Instance: 14 chambers composed of two Magistrates.

Courts of 1st Instance: 12 courts in all chief towns and districts.

Courts of Peace: 99 courts throughout the country.

Attorney-General: BELISARIO ARTIGA.

Secretary-General: ERNESTO VIDAL RIVERA GUZMÁN.

Attorney-General of the Poor: Dr VICENTE MACHADO SALGADO.

Religion

Roman Catholicism is the dominant religion, but other denominations are also permitted. In 1982 there were about 200,000 Protestants. Seventh-day Adventists, Jehovah's Witnesses, the Baptist Church and the Church of Jesus Christ of Latter-day Saints (Mormons) are represented.

CHRISTIANITY

The Roman Catholic Church

El Salvador comprises one archdiocese and seven dioceses. At 31 December 2000 Roman Catholics represented some 79.4% of the total population.

Bishops' Conference

Conferencia Episcopal de El Salvador, 15 Avda Norte 1420, Col. Layco, Apdo 1310, San Salvador; tel. 226 6344; fax 226-4979; e-mail arzfsl@vip.telesal.net.

f. 1974; Pres. Most Rev. FERNANDO SÁENZ LACALLE (Archbishop of San Salvador).

Archbishop of San Salvador: Most Rev. FERNANDO SÁENZ LACALLE, Arzobispado, Avda Dr Emilio Alvarez y Avda Dr Max Bloch, Col. Médica, Apdo 2253, San Salvador; tel. 226-6066; fax 226-4979; e-mail arzfsl@uip.telesat.net.

The Anglican Communion

El Salvador comprises one of the five dioceses of the Iglesia Anglicana de la Región Central de América.

Bishop of El Salvador: Rt Rev. MARTÍN DE JESÚS BARAHONA PASCACIO, 47 Avda Sur, 723 Col. Flor Blanca, Apdo 01-274, San Salvador; tel. 223-2252; fax 223-7952; e-mail martinba@gbm.net.

The Baptist Church

Baptist Association of El Salvador: Avda Sierra Nevada 922, Col. Miramonte, Apdo 347, San Salvador; tel. 226-6287; f. 1933; Exec. Sec. Rev. CARLOS ISIDRO SÁNCHEZ.

Other Churches

Sínodo Luterano Salvadoreño (Salvadorean Lutheran Synod): Iglesia Luterana Salvadoreña, Calle 5 de Noviembre 242, San Miguelito, San Salvador; tel. 225-2843; fax 273-1241; e-mail lutomg@netcomsa.com; Pres. Bishop MEDARDO E. GÓMEZ SOTO; 12,000 mems.

The Press

DAILY NEWSPAPERS

San Miguel

Diario de Oriente: Avda Gerardo Barrios 406, San Miguel.

San Salvador

Co Latino: 23a Avda Sur 225, Apdo 96, San Salvador; tel. 271-0671; fax 271-0971; e-mail colatino@es.com.sv; f. 1890; evening; Editor FRANCISCO ELÍAS VALENCIA; circ. 15,000.

El Diario de Hoy: 11 Calle Oriente 271, Apdo 495, San Salvador; tel. 271-0100; fax 271-2040; e-mail comedh@es.com.sv; internet www.elsalvador.com; f. 1936; morning; independent; Dir ENRIQUE ALTAMIRANO MADRIZ; circ. 115,000.

Diario Oficial: 4a Calle Poniente 829, San Salvador; tel. 221-9101; f. 1875; Dir LUD DREIKORN LÓPEZ; circ. 2,100.

El Mundo: 15 Calle Poniente y 2a Avda Norte 521, San Salvador; tel. 225-3300; fax 222-1490; e-mail aarguellop@elmundo.com.sv; internet www.elmundo.com; f. 1967; evening; Exec. Dir ERNESTO BORJA PAPINI; Gen. Man. ARTURO CHACÓN ANDRADE; circ. 40,215.

La Prensa Gráfica: 3a Calle Poniente 130, San Salvador; tel. 271-1010; fax 271-4242; e-mail lpg@gbm.net; internet www.laprensa.com.sv; f. 1915; general information; conservative, independent; Editor RODOLFO DUTRIZ; circ. 97,312 (weekdays), 115,564 (Sundays).

Santa Ana

Diario de Occidente: 1a Avda Sur 3, Santa Ana; tel. 441-2931; f. 1910; Editor ALEX E. MONTENEGRO; circ. 6,000.

PERIODICALS

Cultura: Concultura, Ministerio de Educación, 17 Avda Sur 430, San Salvador; tel. 222-0665; fax 271-1071; quarterly; educational; Dir Dr RICARDO ROQUE BALDOVINOS.

Orientación: 1a Calle Poniente 3412, San Salvador; tel. 998-6838; fax 224-5099; f. 1952; Catholic weekly; Dir P. FABIAN AMAYA TORRES; circ. 8,000.

Proceso: Universidad Centroamericana, Apdo 01-575, San Salvador; tel. 224-0011; fax 273-3556; f. 1980; weekly newsletter, published by the Documentation and Information Centre of the Uni-

versidad Centroamericana José Simeón Cañas; Dir LUIS ARMANDO GONZÁLEZ.

Revista del Ateneo de El Salvador: 13a Calle Poniente, Centro de Gobierno, San Salvador; tel. 222-9686; f. 1912; 3 a year; official organ of Salvadorean Athenaeum; Pres. Lic JOSÉ OSCAR RAMÍREZ PÉREZ; Sec.-Gen. Lic. RUBÉN REGALADO SERMEÑO.

Revista Judicial: Centro de Gobierno, San Salvador; tel. 222-4522; organ of the Supreme Court; Dir Dr MANUEL ARRIETA GALLEGOS.

PRESS ASSOCIATIONS

Asociación de Corresponsales Extranjeros en El Salvador: San Salvador; Dir CRISTINA HASBÚN.

Asociación de Periodistas de El Salvador (Press Association of El Salvador): Edif. Casa del Periodista, Paseo General Escalón 4130, San Salvador; tel. 223-8943; Pres. JORGE ARMANDO CONTRERAS.

FOREIGN NEWS AGENCIES

Agencia EFE (Spain): San Salvador; Bureau Chief CRISTINA HASBÚN DE MERINO.

Agenzia Nazionale Stampa Associata (ANSA) (Italy): Edif. 'Comercial 29', 29 Calle Poniente y 11 Avda Norte, San Salvador; tel. 226-8008; fax 774-5512; Bureau Chief RENÉ ALBERTO CONTRERAS.

Associated Press (AP) (USA): San Salvador; Correspondent ANA LEONOR CABRERA.

Deutsche Presse-Agentur (dpa) (Germany): San Salvador; Correspondent JORGE ARMANDO CONTRERAS.

Inter Press Service (IPS) (Italy): Apdo 05152, San Salvador; tel. 998-0760; Correspondent PABLO IACUB.

Reuters (United Kingdom): 5 Calle La Mascota, Carretera a Santa Tecla, San Salvador; tel. 223-4736; Bureau Chief ALBERTO BARRERA.

Publishers

Centro de Investigaciones Tecnológicas y Científicas (CENITEC): 85 Avda Norte 905 y 15c Pte, Col. Escalón, San Salvador; tel. 223-7928; f. 1985; politics, economics, social sciences; Dir IVO PRÍAMO ALVARENGA.

Clásicos Roxsil, SA de CV: 4a Avda Sur 2–3, Nueva San Salvador; tel. 229-6742; fax 228-1212; e-mail silviaa@navegante.com.sv; f. 1976; textbooks, literature; Dir ROSA VICTORIA SERRANO DE LÓPEZ.

Editorial Delgado: Universidad 'Dr José Matías Delgado', Km 8.5, Carretera a Santa Tecla, Ciudad Merliot; tel. 278-1011; f. 1984; Dir LUCÍA SÁNCHEZ.

Editorial Universitaria: Ciudad Universitaria de El Salvador, Apdo 1703, San Salvador; tel. 226-0017; f. 1963; Dir TIRSO CANALES.

Distribuidora de Textos Escolares (D'TEXE): Edif. C, Col., Paseo y Condominio Miralvalle, San Salvador; tel. 274-2031; f. 1985; educational; Dir JORGE A. LÓPEZ HIDALGO.

Dirección de Publicaciones e Impresos: Ministerio de Educación, 17a Avda Sur 430, San Salvador; tel. 222-0665; fax 271-1071; e-mail dpidireccion@sv.cciglobal.net; f. 1953; literary and general; Dir MIGUEL HUEZO MIXCO.

UCA Editores: Apdo 01-575, San Salvador; tel. 273-4400; fax 273-3556; f. 1975; social science, religion, economy, literature and textbooks; Dir RODOLFO CARDENAL.

PUBLISHERS' ASSOCIATIONS

Asociación Salvadoreña de Agencias de Publicidad: Centro Profesional Presidente Loc. 33a, Col. San Benito, San Salvador; tel. 243-3535; f. 1962; Dir ANA ALICIA DE GONZÁLEZ.

Cámara Salvadoreña del Libro: 4a Avda Sur 2–3, Apdo 2296, Nueva San Salvador; tel. 228-1832; fax 228-1212; f. 1974; Pres. ADELA CELARIÉ.

Broadcasting and Communications

TELECOMMUNICATIONS

Regulatory Authority

Superintendencia General de Electricidad y Telecomunicaciones (SIGET): Sexta Décima Calle Poniente y 37 Avda Sur 2001, Col. Flor Blanca, San Salvador; tel. 257-4438; internet www.siget.gob.sv/index.htm; f. 1996; Supt Lic. JOSÉ LUIS TRIGUEROS.

Major Service Providers

Digicel: San Salvador; provider of mobile telecommunications; owned by Digicel (USA).

Telecom El Salvador: Alameda Manuel Enrique Arajuo y Calle Nueva 1, 40°, Edif. Palic, San Salvador; tel. 800-8155; internet www .telecom.com.sv; terrestrial telecommunications network, fmrly part of Administración Nacional de Telecomunicaciones (Antel), which was divested in 1998; changed name from CTE Antel Telecom in 1999; became subsidiary of France Télécom in 2002; Pres. DOMINIQUE ST JEAN.

Telecom Personal: Alameda Manuel Enrique Arajuo y Calle Nueva 1, 40°, Edif. Palic, San Salvador; provider of mobile telecommunications; subsidiary of France Telecom.

Telefónica El Salvador: San Salvador; e-mail telefonica .empresas@telefonicamail.com.sv; internet www.telefonica.com.sv; manages sale of telecommunications frequencies; fmrly Internacional de Telecomunicaciones (Intel), which was divested in 1998; controlling interest owned by Telefónica de España; allied with Amzak International in March 2000 to form Telefónica Multiservicios, offering cable-based television, telephone and internet access; Dir-Gen. LUIS ANTÓN.

Telefónica Movistar: San Salvador; provider of mobile telecommunications; subsidiary of Telefónica (Spain).

Telemóvil: Avda Roosevelt, C. Financiero, Gigante Torre D, 9°, San Salvador; tel. 246-9977; fax 246-9999; internet www.telemovil.com; provider of mobile telecommunications; subsidiary of Millicom International Cellular (Sweden).

Tricom, SA: San Salvador; provider of mobile telecommunications; owned by Tricom, SA (Dominican Republic).

RADIO

Asociación Salvadoreña de Radiodifusores (ASDER): Avda Izalco, Bloco 6 No 33, Residencial San Luis, San Salvador; tel. 222-0872; fax 274-6870; f. 1965; Pres. MANUEL A. FLORES B.

YSSS Radio Nacional de El Salvador: Dirección General de Medios, Calle Monserrat, Plantel Ex-IVU, San Salvador; tel. 773-4170; e-mail webmaster@radioelsalvador.com.sv; internet www .radioelsalvador.com.sv; f. 1926; non-commercial cultural station; Dir-Gen. ALFONSO PÉREZ GARCÍA.

There are 64 commercial radio stations. Radio Venceremos and Radio Farabundo Martí, operated by the former guerrilla group FMLN, were legalized in April 1992. Radio Mayavisión (operated by FMLN supporters), began broadcasting in November 1993.

TELEVISION

Canal 2, SA: Carretera a Nueva San Salvador, Apdo 720, San Salvador; tel. 223-6744; fax 998-6565; commercial; Pres. BORIS ESERSKI; Gen. Man. SALVADOR I. GADALA MARÍA.

Canal 4, SA: Carretera a Nueva San Salvador, Apdo 720, San Salvador; tel. 224-4555; commercial; Pres. BORIS ESERSKI; Man. RONALD CALVO.

Canal 6, SA: Km 6, Carretera Panamericana a Santa Tecla, San Salvador; tel. 243-3966; fax 243-3818; e-mail tv6@gbm.net; internet www.elnoticiero.com.sv; f. 1972; commercial; Exec. Dir JUAN CARLOS ESERSKI; Man. Dr PEDRO LEONEL MORENO MONGE.

Canal 8 and 10 (Televisión Cultural Educativa): Avda Robert Baden Powell, Apdo 104, Nueva San Salvador; tel. 228-0499; fax 228-0973; f. 1964; government station; Dir TOMÁS PANAMEÑO.

Canal 12: Urb. Santa Elena 12, Antiguo Cuscatlán, San Salvador; tel. 278-0622; fax 278-0722; f. 1984; Pres. RICARDO SALINAS PLIEGO.

Canal 15: 4a Avda Sur y 5a Calle Oriente 301, San Miguel; tel. 661-3298; fax 661-3298; f. 1994; Gen. Man. JOAQUÍN APARICIO.

Canal 19 Sistemas de Video y Audio INDESI: Final Calle Los Abetos 1, Col. San Francisco, San Salvador; Gen. Man. MARIO CAÑAS.

Canal 21 (Megavisión): Final Calle Los Abetos 1, Col. San Francisco, Apdo 2789, San Salvador; tel. 298-5311; fax 298-6492; f. 1993; Pres. OSCAR ANTONIO SAFIE; Dir HUGO ESCOBAR.

Canal 25 (Auvisa de El Salvador): Final Calle Libertad 100, Nueva San Salvador; commercial; Gen. Man. MANUEL BONILLA.

Canal 33 (Teleprensa): Istmania 262, Col. Escalón, San Salvador; tel. 224-6040; fax 224-3193; f. 1957; Dir and Gen. Man. GUILLERMO DE LEÓN.

Finance

(cap. = capital; p.u. = paid up; res = reserves; dep. = deposits; m. = million; brs = branches; amounts in colones unless otherwise stated)

BANKING

The banking system was nationalized in March 1980. In 1994 the the transfer to private ownership of six banks and seven savings and loans institutions, as part of a programme of economic reform begun in 1991, was completed.

Supervisory Body

Superintendencia del Sistema Financiero: 7a Avda Norte 240, Apdo 2942, San Salvador; tel. 281-2444; fax 281-1621; internet www .ssf.gob.sv/princip.htm; Supt Lic. GUILLERMO ARGUMEDO.

Superintendencia de Valores: Antiguo Edif. BCR, 1a Calle Poniente y 7a Avda Norte, San Salvador; tel. 281-8900; fax 221-3404; e-mail info@superval.gob.sv; internet www.superval.gob.sv; Supt Lic. OMAR ERNESTO RODRÍGUEZ ALEMÁN.

Central Bank

Banco Central de Reserva de El Salvador: Alameda Juan Pablo II y 17 Avda Norte, Apdo 01-106, San Salvador; tel. 281-8000; fax 281-8011; e-mail comunicaciones@bcr.gob.sv; internet www.bcr.gob .sv; f. 1934; nationalized Dec. 1961; entered monetary integration process 1 Jan. 2001; cap. 1,000m., res 2,000m., dep. 6,500m. (Sept. 2000); Pres. LUZ MARÍA DE PORTILLO.

Commercial and Mortgage Banks

Banco Agrícola : Paseo General Escalón y 69 Avda Sur 3635, Col. Escalón, San Salvador; tel. 279-1033; fax 279-4202; internet www .bancoagricola.com; f. 1955; privately owned; cap. 324.0m., res 703.6m., dep. 11,947.9m. (Dec. 1998); merged with Banco Desarrollo in July 2000; merged with Banco Capital in November 2001; Pres. ARCHIE BALDOCCHI DUEÑAS; 150 brs world-wide.

Banco de Comercio: Edif. Ex Americana, 25 Avda Norte y 21 Calle Poniente, San Salvador; tel. 226-4577; fax 225-7767; f. 1949; privately owned; total assets 9,074m. (1999); Pres. JOSÉ GUSTAVO BELISMELIS VIDES; 23 brs.

Banco Cuscatlán de El Salvador, SA: Edif. Pirámide Cuscatlán, Km 10, Carretera a Santa Tecla, Apdo 626, San Salvador; tel. 212-3333; fax 228-5700; e-mail cuscatlan@bancocuscatlan.com; internet www.bancocuscatlan.com; f. 1972; privately owned; cap. 80m., res 85.9m., dep. 1,928.5m. (Dec. 2001); Pres. MAURICIO SAMAYOA RIVAS; Vice-Pres. ROBERTO ORTIZ; 31 brs.

Banco Hipotecario: Pasaje Senda Florida Sur, Col. Escalón, Apdo 999, San Salvador; tel. 298-3344; fax 298-1053; f. 1935; state-owned mortgage and commercial bank; cap. 104.0m., dep. 1,852m. (Dec. 1998); Pres. Ing. JOSÉ ROBERTO NAVARRO; 13 brs.

Banco Promérica: 71 Avda Sur y Paseo General Escalón 3669, Col. Escalón, San Salvador; tel. 243-3344; fax 245-2979; privately owned; Pres. Lic. EDUARDO ERNESTO VILANOVA.

Banco Salvadoreño, SA (BANCOSAL): Edif. Centro Financiero, Avda Olímpica 3550, Apdo 06-73, San Salvador; tel. 298-4444; fax 298-0102; internet www.bancosal.com; f. 1885; privately-owned commercial bank; cap. 12,000m., dep. 8,900m. (Aug. 2000); merged with Banco de Construcción y Ahorro, SA (BANCASA) in July 2000; Pres. and Chair. Lic. FÉLIX SIMÁN JACIR; Vice-Pres. Ing. MOISÉS CASTRO MACEDA; 53 brs.

Banco UNO: Paseo General Escalón y 69 Avda Sur 3563, Col. Escalón, San Salvador; tel. 245-0055; fax 245-0080; Pres. Ing. ALBINO ROMÁN.

Citibank, NA: Edif. Palic, Calle Nueva 1, Alameda Dr Manuel Enrique Araujo, Col. Escalón, San Salvador; tel. 224-3011; fax 245-1842; Pres. STEVEN J. PUIG; Vice-Pres. GIJF VELTMAN.

Financiera Calpiá: 37 Avda Sur 2, Col. Flor Blanca, San Salvador; tel. 260-6859; fax 260-6922; Pres. PEDRO DALMAU GORRITA.

First Commercial Bank: Centro Comercial Gigante, Torre Telefónica, 3°, 63 Avda Sur y Alameda Roosevelt, San Salvador; tel. 211-2121; fax 211-2130; Vice-Pres. PETER MING-FUNG LAN.

Scotiabank: Edif. Torre Ahorromet, Avda Olímpica y 63a Avda Sur 129, San Salvador; tel. 245-1211; fax 224-2815; internet www .scotiabank.com.sv; f. 1972; total assets 3,970.8m. Pres. Ing. LUIS IVANDIC.

UNIBANCO: Alameda Roosevelt, entre 47 y 49, Avda Sur 2511, San Salvador; tel. 245-0651; fax 298-5251; privately owned; Pres. Ing. JOSÉ ROBERTO NAVARRO.

Public Institutions

Banco de Fomento Agropecuario: Complejo Turístico 12, Nueva San Salvador; tel. 335-3028; fax 335-3158; e-mail rgprieto@gbm.net; f. 1973; state-owned; cap. 605.0m., dep. 872.0m. (Oct. 1997); Pres. Lic. GUILLERMO FUNES ARAUJO; 27 brs.

Banco Multisectoral de Inversiones: Alameda Manuel E. Araujo, Century Plaza, San Salvador; tel. 267-0000; fax 267-0038; f. 1994; Pres. Dr NICOLA ANGELUCCI.

Federación de Cajas de Crédito: 25 Avda Norte y 23 Calle Poniente, San Salvador; tel. 225-5922; fax 226-7059; f. 1943; Pres. Lic. MARCO TULIO RODRÍGUEZ MENA.

Fondo Social Para la Vivienda: Calle Rubén Darío y 17 Avda Sur, San Salvador; tel. 271-2774; Pres. Lic. EDGAR RAMIRO MENDOZA.

Banking Association

Asociación Bancaria Salvadoreña (ABANSA): Pasaje Senda Florida Norte 140, Col. Escalón, San Salvador; tel. 298-6938; fax 223-1079; Pres. Ing. MAURICIO SAMAYOA; Exec. Dir Dr CLAUDIO DE ROSA FERREIRA.

STOCK EXCHANGE

Mercado de Valores de El Salvador, SA de CV (Bolsa de Valores): San Salvador; tel. 298-4244; fax 223-2898; internet www .bolsavalores.com.sv; Pres. ROLANDO DUARTE SCHLAGETER.

INSURANCE

AIG Unión y Desarrollo, SA: Calle Loma Linda 265, Col. San Benito, Apdo 92, San Salvador; tel. 298-5455; fax 298-5084; e-mail aig.elsalvador@uni-desa.com; f. 1998; following merger of Unión y Desarrollo, SA and AIG; Pres. FRANCISCO R. DE SOLA.

American Life Insurance Co: Edif. Omnimotores, 2°, Km 4½, Carretera a Santa Tecla, Apdo 169, San Salvador; tel. 223-4925; f. 1963; Man. CARLOS F. PEREIRA.

Aseguradora Agrícola Comercial, SA: Alameda Roosevelt 3104, Apdo 1855, San Salvador; tel. 260-3344; fax 260-5592; internet www .acasal.com.sv; f. 1973; Pres. LUIS ALFREDO ESCALANTE; Gen. Man. FEDERICO PERAZA F.

Aseguradora Popular, SA: Paseo General Escalón 5338, Col. Escalón, San Salvador; tel. 263-0700; fax 263-1246; e-mail aseposapresi@telesal.net; f. 1975; Exec. Pres. Dr CARLOS ARMANDO LAHÚD.

Aseguradora Suiza Salvadoreña, SA: Calle la Reforma, Col. San Benito, Apdo 1490, San Salvador; tel. 298-5222; fax 298-5060; f. 1969; Pres. MAURICIO M. COHEN; Gen. Man. RODOLFO SCHILDKNECHT.

Internacional de Seguros, SA (Interseguros): Centro financiero Banco Salvadoreño, 5°, Avda Olímpica 3550, Col. Escalón, San Salvador; tel. 298-0202; fax 224-6935; internet www.interseguros .com.sv; f. 1958; Pres. FÉLIX JOSÉ SIMÁN JACIR; Gen. Man. ALEJANDRO CABRERA RIVAS.

La Centro Americana, SA: Alameda Roosevelt 3107, Apdo 527, San Salvador; tel. 223-6666; fax 223-2687; internet www.lacentro .com; f. 1915; Pres. RUFINO GARAY.

Compañía Anglo Salvadoreña de Seguros, SA: Paseo General Escalón 3848, San Salvador; tel. 224-2399; fax 224-4394; f. 1976; Pres. JOSÉ ARTURO GÓMEZ; Vice-Pres. JULIO E. PAYES.

Compañía General de Seguros, SA: Calle Loma Linda 223, Col. San Benito, Apdo 1004, San Salvador; tel. 779-2777; fax 998-2870; f. 1955; Pres. JOSÉ GUSTAVO BELISMELIS VIDES; Gen. Man. Lic. HERIBERTO PÉREZ AGUIRRE.

Seguros e Inversiones, SA (SISA): Alameda Dr Manuel Enrique Araújo 3530, Apdo 1350, San Salvador; tel. 998-1199; fax 998-2882; f. 1962; Pres. ALFREDO FÉLIX CRISTIANI BURKARD.

Seguros Universales, SA: Paseo Escalón y 81 Avda Norte 205, Col. Escalón, San Salvador; tel. 779-3533; fax 779-1830; Pres. Dr ENRIQUE GARCÍA PRIETO.

Trade and Industry

GOVERNMENT AGENCIES AND DEVELOPMENT ORGANIZATIONS

Consejo Nacional de Ciencia y Tecnología (CONACYT): Col. Médica, Avda Dr Emilio Alvarez, Pasaje Dr Guillermo Rodríguez Pacas 51, San Salvador; tel. 226-2800; fax 225-6255; internet www .conacyt.gob.sv; f. 1992; formulation and guidance of national policy on science and technology; Exec. Dir CARLOS FEDERICO PAREDES CASTILLO.

Corporación de Exportadores de El Salvador (COEXPORT): Condomínios del Mediterráneo, Edif. 'A', No 23, Col. Jardines de Guadalupe, San Salvador; tel. 243-1328; fax 243-3159; e-mail info@ coexport.com; internet www.coexport.com; f. 1973 to promote Salvadorean exports; Exec. Dir Lic. SILVIA M. CUÉLLAR.

Corporación Salvadoreña de Inversiones (CORSAIN): 1a Calle Poniente, entre 43 y 45 Avda Norte, San Salvador; tel. 224-4242; fax 224-6877; Pres. Lic. MARIO EMILIO REDAELLI.

Fondo de Financiamiento y Garantía para la Pequeña Empresa (FIGAPE): 9a Avda Norte 225, Apdo 1990, San Salvador; tel. 771-1994; f. 1994; government body to assist small-sized industries; Pres. Lic. MARCO TULIO GUARDADO.

Fondo Social para la Vivienda (FSV): Calle Rubén Darío y 17 Avda Sur 455, San Salvador; tel. 271-1662; fax 271-2910; internet www.fsv.gob.sv; f. 1973; Pres. EDGAR RAMIRO MENDOZA JEREZ; Gen. Man. FRANCISCO ANTONIO GUEVARA.

Instituto Salvadoreño de Transformación Agraria (ISTA): Km 5½, Carretera a Santa Tecla, San Salvador; tel. 224-6000; fax 224-0259; f. 1976 to promote rural development; empowered to buy inefficiently cultivated land; Pres. JOSÉ ROBERTO MOLINA MORALES.

CHAMBER OF COMMERCE

Cámara de Comercio e Industria de El Salvador: 9a Avda Norte y 5a Calle Poniente, Apdo 1640, San Salvador; tel. 771-2055; fax 771-4461; internet www.camarasal.com; f. 1915; 1,800 mems; Pres. EDUARDO OÑATE MUYHONDT; Exec. Dir Ing. ALBERTO PADILLA AQUINA; branch offices in San Miguel, Santa Ana and Sonsonate.

INDUSTRIAL AND TRADE ASSOCIATIONS

Asociación Cafetalera de El Salvador (ACES): 67 Avda Norte 116, Col. Escalón, San Salvador; tel. 223-3024; fax 223-7471; f. 1930; coffee growers' asscn; Pres. Ing. EDUARDO E. BARRIENTOS.

Asociación de Ganaderos de El Salvador: 1a Avda Norte 1332, San Salvador; tel. 225-7208; f. 1932; livestock breeders' asscn; Pres. Lic. CARLOS ARTURO MUYSHONDT.

Asociación Salvadoreña de Beneficiadores y Exportadores de Café (ABECAFE): 87a Avda Norte 720, Col. Escalón, Apdo A, San Salvador; tel. 223-3292; fax 223-3292; coffee producers' and exporters' asscn; Pres. VICTORIA DALTÓN DE DÍAZ.

Asociación Salvadoreña de Industriales: Calles Roma y Liverpool, Col. Roma, Apdo 48, San Salvador; tel. 279-2488; fax 279-2070; e-mail asi@asi.com.sv; internet www.asi.com.sv; f. 1958; 400 mems; manufacturers' asscn; Pres. NAPOLEÓN GUERRERO BERRIOS; Exec. Dir Lic. JORGE ARRIAZA.

Cooperativa Algodonera Salvadoreña, Ltda: San Salvador; f. 1940; 185 mems; cotton growers' asscn; Pres. ULISES FERNANDO GONZÁLEZ; Gen. Man. Lic. MANUEL RAFAEL ARCE.

Instituto Nacional del Azúcar: Paseo General Escalón y 87a Avda Norte, San Salvador; tel. 224-6044; fax 224-5132; national sugar institute, scheduled for privatization; Pres. Lic. JAIME ALVAREZ GOTÁN.

Instituto Nacional del Café (INCAFE): San Salvador; f. 1942; national coffee institute, scheduled for privatization; Pres. ROBERT SUÁREZ SUAY; Gen. Man. MIGUEL ÁNGEL AGUILAR.

UCAFES: San Salvador; union of coffee-growing co-operatives; Pres. FRANCISCO ALFARO CASTILLO.

EMPLOYERS' ORGANIZATIONS

There are several business associations, the most important of which is the Asociación Nacional de Empresa Privada.

Asociación Nacional de Empresa Privada (ANEP) (National Private Enterprise Association): 1a Calle Pte. y 71a Avda Norte 204, Col. Escalón, Apdo1204, San Salvador; tel. 224-1236; fax 223-8932; e-mail anep@telesal.net; internet www.anep.org.sv; national private enterprise association; Pres. MARIO SALAVERRIA; Exec. Dir Lic. FRANCISCO ARMANDO ARIAS.

UTILITIES

Electricity

Comisión Ejecutiva Hidroeléctrica del Río Lempa (CEL): 9a Calle Poniente 950, San Salvador; tel. 271-0855; fax 222-9359; e-mail naguilar@cel.gob.sv; internet www.cel.gob.sv; f. 1948; state energy agency dealing with electricity generation and transmission, and non-conventional energy sources; scheduled for privatization; Pres. GUILLERMO A. SOL BANG.

Superintendencia General de Electricidad y Telecomunicaciones (SIGET): Sexta Décima Calle Poniente y 37 Avda Sur 2001, Col. Flor Blanca, San Salvador; tel. 257-4438; internet www.siget .gob.sv/index.htm; f. 1996; Supt Lic. ERNESTO LIMA MENA.

Electricity Companies

In order to increase competition, the electricity-trading market was opened up in October 2000. Four companies (two domestic and two foreign) subsequently applied for licences to trade electricity in the wholesale market, from SIGET.

Cartotécnica: San Salvador; owned by Simán Group (El Salvador).

Comercializadora Eléctrica Centroamericana (CEC): San Salvador; licence approval pending.

CONEC: San Salvador; subsidiary of Energia Global (USA); provides electricity from sustainable sources, imported from Costa Rica.

Excelergy: San Salvador; joint US-Chilean owned.

Water

Administración Nacional de Acueductos y Alcantarillados (ANDA): Edif. ANDA, Final Avda Don Bosco, Col. Libertad, San Salvador; tel. 225-3534; fax 225-3152; f. 1961; maintenance of water supply and sewerage systems; Pres. Carlos Augusto Perla.

TRADE UNIONS

Asociación de Sindicatos Independientes (ASIES) (Association of Independent Trade Unions): San Salvador.

Central de Trabajadores Democráticos (CTD) (Democratic Workers' Confederation): Bulevar Maria Cristina 165, San Salvador; tel. 263-7768; fax 225-4130; Pres. Salvador Carazo.

Central de Trabajadores Salvadoreños (CTS) (Salvadorean Workers' Confederation): Calle Darío González 616, Barrio San Jacinto, San Salvador; f. 1966; Christian Democratic; 35,000 mems; Sec.-Gen. Miguel Angel Vásquez.

Confederación General de Sindicatos (CGS) (General Confederation of Unions): 3a Calle Oriente 226, San Salvador; f. 1958; admitted to ICFTU/ORIT; 27,000 mems.

Confederación General del Trabajo (CGT) (General Confederation of Workers): 2a Avda Norte 619, San Salvador; tel. 222-5980; f. 1983; 20 affiliated unions; Sec.-Gen. José Luis Grande Preza; 85,000 mems.

Coordinadora de Solidaridad de los Trabajadores (CST) (Workers' Solidarity Co-ordination): San Salvador; f. 1985; conglomerate of independent left-wing trade unions.

Federación Campesina Cristiana de El Salvador-Unión de Trabajadores del Campo (FECCAS-UTC) (Christian Peasant Federation of El Salvador—Union of Countryside Workers): Universidad Nacional, Apdo 4000, San Salvador; allied illegal Christian peasants' organizations.

Federación Nacional de Sindicatos de Trabajadores de El Salvador (FENASTRAS) (Salvadorean Workers' National Union Federation): San Salvador; f. 1975; left-wing; 35,000 mems in 16 affiliates.

Federación Revolucionaria de Sindicatos (Revolutionary Federation of Unions): San Salvador; Sec.-Gen. Salvador Chávez Escalante.

Federación Unitaria Sindical Salvadoreña (FUSS) (United Salvadorean Union Federation): Centro de Gobierno, Apdo 2226, San Salvador; tel. and fax 225-3756; f. 1965; left-wing; Sec.-Gen. Juan Edito Genovez.

MUSYGES (United Union and Guild Movement): San Salvador; labour federation previously linked to FDR; 50,000 mems (est.).

Unión Comunal Salvadoreña (UCS) (Salvadorean Communal Union): San Salvador; peasants' association; 100,000 mems; Gen. Sec. Guillermo Blanco.

Unidad Nacional de Trabajadores Salvadoreños (UNTS) (National Unity of Salvadorean Workers): San Salvador; f. 1986; largest trade union conglomerate; Leader Marco Tulio Lima; affiliated unions include:

    Unidad Popular Democrática (UPD) (Popular Democratic Unity): San Salvador; f. 1980; led by a committee of 10; 500,000 mems.

Unión Nacional Obrera-Campesina (UNOC) (Worker-Peasant National Union): San Salvador; f. 1986; centre-left labour organization; 500,000 mems.

Some unions, such as those of the taxi drivers and bus owners, are affiliated to the Federación Nacional de Empresas Pequeñas Salvadoreñas—Fenapes, the association of small businesses.

Transport

Comisión Ejecutiva Portuaria Autónoma (CEPA): Edif. Torre Roble, Blvd de Los Héroes, Apdo 2667, San Salvador; tel. 224-1133; fax 224-0907; f. 1952; operates and administers the ports of Acajutla (on Pacific coast) and Cutuco (on Gulf of Fonseca) and the El Salvador International Airport, as well as Ferrocarriles Nacionales de El Salvador; Pres. Ruy César Miranda; Gen. Man. Lic. Arturo Germán Martínez.

RAILWAYS

In 1998 there were 547 km of railway track in the country. The main track links San Salvador with the ports of Acajutla and Cutuco and with San Jerónimo on the border with Guatemala. The 429 km Salvadorean section of the International Railways of Central America runs from Anguiatú on the El Salvador–Guatemala border to the Pacific ports of Acajutla and Cutuco and connects San Salvador with Guatemala City and the Guatemalan Atlantic ports of Puerto Barrios and Santo Tomás de Castilla. A project to connect the Salvadorean and Guatemalan railway systems between Santa Ana and Santa Lucia (in Guatemala) is under consideration.

Ferrocarriles Nacionales de El Salvador (FENADESAL): Avda Peralta 903, Apdo 2292, San Salvador; tel. 271-5632; fax 271-5650; 562 km open; in 1975 Ferrocarril de El Salvador and the Salvadorean section of International Railways of Central America (429 km open) were merged and are administered by the Railroad Division of CEPA (see above); Gen. Man. Tulio O. Vergara.

ROADS

The country's highway system is well integrated with its railway services. There were some 10,029 km of roads in 1999, including: the Pan-American Highway (306 km). Following the earthquakes of early 2001, the Inter-American Development Bank (IDB) pledged some US $106.0m. to the transport sector for the restoration and reconstruction of roads and bridges.

SHIPPING

The port of Acajutla is administered by CEPA (see above). Services are also provided by foreign lines. The port of Cutuco has been inactive since 1996; however, it was being considered for privatization.

CIVIL AVIATION

The El Salvador International Airport is located 40 km (25 miles) from San Salvador in Comalapa. An expansion of the airport was completed in 1998, with a second expansion phase of hotel and commercial space to be completed early in the 21st century. The former international airport at Ilopango is used for military and private civilian aircraft; there are an additional 88 private airports, four with permanent-surface runways.

AESA Aerolíneas de El Salvador, SA de CV: San Salvador; cargo and mail service between San Salvador and Miami; Pres. E. Cornejo López; Gen. Man. José Roberto Santana.

TACA International Airlines: Edif. Caribe, 2°, Col. Escalón, San Salvador; tel. 339-9155; fax 223-3757; f. 1939; passenger and cargo services to Central America and the USA; Pres. Federico Bloch; Gen. Man. Ben Baldanza.

Tourism

El Salvador was one of the centres of the ancient Mayan civilization, and the ruined temples and cities are of great interest. The volcanoes and lakes of the uplands provide magnificent scenery, while there are fine beaches along the Pacific coast. The civil war, from 1979 to 1992, severely affected the tourism industry. However, in the late 1990s the number of tourist arrivals increased from 282,835 in 1996 to 795,000 in 2000. Tourism receipts in 2000 were US $254m. Following the earthquakes of early 2001, the IDB pledged some US $3.6m. to the tourism and historical and cultural heritage sectors, for the reconstruction and renovation of recreational centres, the promotion of tourism, and the development of culture and heritage.

Buró de Convenciones y Visitantes de la Ciudad de San Salvador: Edif. Olimpic Plaza, 73 Avda Sur 28, 2°, San Salvador; tel. 224-0819; fax 223-4912; f. 1973; assists in organization of national and international events; Pres. (vacant); Exec. Dir Rosy Mejía de Marchesini.

Cámara Salvadoreña de Turismo: San Salvador; tel. 223-9992; Pres. Arnoldo Jiménez; co-ordinates:

    Comité Nacional de Turismo (CONATUR): San Salvador; comprises hotels, restaurants, tour operators, airlines and Instituto Salvadoreño de Turismo; Sec. Mercedes Meléndez.

    Corporación de Turismo (CORSATUR): 508 Blvd del Hipódromo, Col. San Benito, San Salvador; tel. 243-7835; fax 243-0427;

e-mail corsatur@salnet.net; internet www.elsalvadorturismo.gob
.sv.

Feria Internacional de El Salvador (FIES): Avda La Revolución 222, Col. San Benito, Apdo 493, San Salvador; tel. 243-0244;
fax 243-3161; e-mail fies@es.com.sv; internet www.fies.gob.sv;
Pres. José Carlos Liévano.

Instituto Salvadoreño de Turismo (ISTU) (National Tourism
Institute): Calle Rubén Darío 619, San Salvador; tel. 222-0960; fax
222-1208; f. 1950; Pres. Carlos Hirlemann; Dir Eduardo López
Rivera.

EQUATORIAL GUINEA

Introductory Survey

Location, Climate, Language, Religion, Flag, Capital

The Republic of Equatorial Guinea consists of the islands of Bioko (formerly Fernando Póo and subsequently renamed Macías Nguema Biyogo under the regime of President Macías), Corisco, Great Elobey, Little Elobey and Annobón (previously known also as Pagalu), and the mainland region of Río Muni (previously known also as Mbini) on the west coast of Africa. Cameroon lies to the north and Gabon to the east and south of Río Muni, while Bioko lies offshore from Cameroon and Nigeria. The small island of Annobón lies far to the south, beyond the islands of São Tomé and Príncipe. The climate is hot and humid, with average temperatures higher than 26°C (80°F). The official languages are Spanish and French. In Río Muni the Fang language is spoken, as well as those of coastal tribes such as the Combe, Balemke and Bujeba. Bubi is the indigenous language on Bioko, although Fang is also widely used, and Ibo is spoken by the resident Nigerian population. An estimated 90% of the population are adherents of the Roman Catholic Church, although traditional forms of worship are also followed. The national flag (proportions 2 by 3) has three equal horizontal stripes, of green, white and red, with a blue triangle at the hoist and the national coat of arms (a silver shield, containing a tree, with six yellow stars above and a scroll beneath) in the centre of the white stripe. The capital is Malabo (formerly Santa Isabel).

Recent History

Portugal ceded the territory to Spain in 1778. The mainland region and the islands were periodically united for administrative purposes. In July 1959 Spanish Guinea, as the combined territory was known, was divided into two provinces: Río Muni, on the African mainland, and Fernando Póo (now Bioko), with other nearby islands. From 1960 the two provinces were represented in the Spanish legislature. In December 1963 they were merged again, to form Equatorial Guinea, with a limited measure of self-government.

After 190 years of Spanish rule, independence was declared on 12 October 1968. Francisco Macías Nguema, Equatorial Guinea's first President, formed a coalition Government from all the parties represented in the new National Assembly. In March 1969 the Minister for Foreign Affairs, Atanasio Ndongo Miyone, was killed by security forces during a failed coup attempt.

In February 1970 the President outlawed all existing political parties and formed the Partido Unico Nacional (PUN), which later became the Partido Unico Nacional de los Trabajadores (PUNT). Macías appointed himself Life President in July 1972. A new Constitution, giving absolute powers to the President was adopted in July 1973. Macías controlled both radio and press and all citizens were forbidden to leave the country, although many fled during his rule. During 1975–77 there were many arrests and executions. Nigerian workers were repatriated in 1976, following reports of maltreatment and forced labour. The Macías regime maintained close relations with the Soviet bloc.

In August 1979 President Macías was overthrown in a coup led by his nephew, Lt-Col (later Brig.-Gen.) Teodoro Obiang Nguema Mbasogo, hitherto the Deputy Minister of Defence. (Obiang Nguema subsequently ceased to use his forename.) Macías was found guilty of treason, genocide, embezzlement and violation of human rights, and was executed in September. The Spanish Government, which admitted prior knowledge of the coup, was the first to recognize the new regime, and remained a major supplier of financial and technical aid. Obiang Nguema appointed civilians to the Government for the first time in December 1981. In August 1982 he was reappointed President for a further seven years, and later that month a new Constitution, which provided for an eventual return to civilian government, was approved by 95% of voters in a referendum. At legislative elections held in August 1983 some 41 candidates, who had been nominated by the President, were elected (unopposed) to a new House of Representatives.

The imposition, from 1979 to 1991, of a ban on organized political activity within Equatorial Guinea, and persistent allegations against the Obiang Nguema regime of human rights abuses and corruption, resulted in the development of a sub-stantial opposition in exile. Opposition coalitions were formed in Spain and France during the 1980s.

During the 1980s Obiang Nguema's rule was threatened on a number of occasions. Attempted coups were reported in April 1981, May 1983 and November 1983. In January 1986 the President reinforced his control by assuming the post of Minister of Defence. An attempt in July by senior civilian and military officials to occupy the presidential palace in Malabo was quelled by loyalist forces. In the following month the alleged leader of the coup attempt, Eugenio Abeso Mondu (a former diplomat and a member of the House of Representatives), was sentenced to death and executed, while prison sentences were imposed on 12 others who had been convicted of complicity in the plot. In August 1987 Obiang Nguema announced the establishment of a 'governmental party', the Partido Democrático de Guinea Ecuatorial (PDGE), while continuing to reject demands for the legalization of opposition parties. At legislative elections held in July 1988, 99.2% of voters endorsed a single list of candidates who had been nominated by the President.

In June 1989, at the first presidential election to be held since independence, Obiang Nguema, the sole candidate, reportedly received the support of more than 99% of the electorate. Opposition groupings criticized the conduct of the election and declared the result invalid. Following his success, the President appealed to dissidents to return to Equatorial Guinea and declared an amnesty for political prisoners. However, Obiang Nguema reiterated his opposition to the establishment of a multi-party system, and in December 1990 it was reported that about 30 advocates of the introduction of a plural political system had been imprisoned. The human rights organization Amnesty International has frequently reiterated accusations against the Equato-Guinean authorities of detaining and torturing political opponents.

In April 1991 opposition groups in exile in Gabon formed a coalition, the Coordinación Democrática de los Partidos de Oposición de Guinea Ecuatorial. In early August the ruling PDGE held its first national extraordinary congress, at which delegates demanded the introduction of a new democratic constitution, the legalization of other political parties and the removal of restrictions on the media. Nevertheless, in mid-August a prominent opposition leader in exile was refused a passport to travel to Equatorial Guinea in order to campaign for democracy, and shortly afterwards it was reported that the Equato-Guinean Ambassador to Spain had been arrested during a return visit to Equatorial Guinea, for allegedly liaising with opposition movements. In the following month Amnesty International claimed that torture was 'accepted practice' in Equatorial Guinea, and reported the deaths in custody of at least six Equato-Guineans since 1988. Later in September the Government announced the formation of a human rights commission.

A new Constitution, containing provisions for a multi-party political system, was approved by an overwhelming majority of voters at a national referendum in November 1991. However, opposition movements rejected the Constitution, owing to the inclusion of clauses exempting the President from any judicial procedures arising from his tenure of office and prohibiting citizens who had not been continuously resident in Equatorial Guinea for 10 years from standing as election candidates, while requiring all political parties to submit an excessively large deposit (which could not be provided by funds from abroad) as a condition of registration. In addition, there was inadequate provision for the upholding of human rights. In January 1992 a transitional Government was formed (comprising only members of the PDGE), and, during that month, a general amnesty was extended to all political exiles. The UN published a report in January that adversely criticized the human rights record of the Equato-Guinean authorities and some of the provisions incorporated in the new Constitution. Throughout 1992 the security forces continued to arrest members of opposition parties. During November a new alliance of opposition organizations, the Plataforma de la Oposición Conjunta (POC), was created.

In January 1993 an electoral law was promulgated. In February the UN released another report in which it alleged a serious disregard for human rights by the Obiang Nguema regime. During February and March the Government and several opposition organizations negotiated a national pact which established conditions for the conduct of legislative elections that were due to take place in 1993, including the freedom to organize political activity and the provision of equal access to the media for all political parties. However, the Government was soon accused of violating the pact, and further arrests and mistreatment of its political opponents were reported. During August violent clashes occurred on the island of Annobón between anti-Government demonstrators and the security forces. Accusations by the Equato-Guinean authorities that Spain had incited the unrest were strongly denied by the Spanish Government.

Multi-party legislative elections took place in November 1993. The elections were, however, boycotted by most of the parties in the POC, in protest at Obiang Nguema's refusal to review contentious clauses of the electoral law or to permit impartial international observers to inspect the electoral register. The UN declined a request by the Equato-Guinean authorities to monitor the elections, contending that correct electoral procedures were evidently being infringed. Representatives of the OAU were present and estimated that 50% of the electorate participated. The PDGE won 68 of the 80 seats in the House of Representatives, while, of the six opposition parties that presented candidates, the Convención Socialdemocrática Popular obtained six seats, the Unión Democrática y Social de Guinea Ecuatorial (UDS) won five seats and the Convención Liberal Democrática (CLD) secured one. Widespread electoral irregularities were alleged to have occurred and, prior to the elections, opposition politicians were reportedly subjected to intimidation by the security forces. In early December the Government announced that all party political gatherings would henceforth be subject to prior official authorization. In mid-December Silvestre Siale Bileka, hitherto Prime Minister of the interim Government, was appointed Prime Minister of the new administration. Shortly afterwards Bileka nominated a Council of Ministers, which included no opposition representatives.

In April 1994 Severo Moto Nsa, the founding leader of one of the most influential exiled opposition parties, the Partido del Progreso de Guinea Ecuatorial (PPGE), based in Spain, returned to Equatorial Guinea. In June, in response to pressure from international aid donors, the Government agreed to amend the controversial electoral law and to conduct a preliminary electoral census prior to the holding of local elections. In September, however, the authorities began to compile a full population census, instead of preparing for the local elections, which had been scheduled for November. The census was boycotted by opposition parties, and many people were arrested in ensuing clashes with the security forces. The local elections were postponed. In October the Speaker and Deputy Speaker of the National Assembly resigned, accusing the Obiang Nguema administration of incompetence and disregard for human rights.

In early 1995 the Constitution and electoral law were amended to reduce from 10 to five the minimum number of years required for candidates to have been resident in Equatorial Guinea. In February several leading members of the PPGE, including Moto Nsa, were arrested for allegedly plotting to overthrow Obiang Nguema; in April they were found guilty by a military court and sentenced to terms of imprisonment. (Moto Nsa received a sentence of 28 years.) The convictions and sentences were widely condemned by foreign Governments and in August, following representations by President Chirac of France, Obiang Nguema unexpectedly pardoned all the convicted PPGE members.

Local elections (which had been postponed in 1994—see above) were staged, on a multi-party basis, in September 1995. According to the official results, the ruling PDGE won an overall victory, securing a majority of the votes cast in two-thirds of local administrations. Allegations by the opposition (which claimed to have obtained 62% of the votes) that serious electoral malpractice had occurred were supported by the Spanish Ambassador to Equatorial Guinea. A monitoring team of international observers agreed that some electoral irregularities had taken place.

At a presidential election held in February 1996 Obiang Nguema was returned to office, reportedly securing more than 90% of the votes cast. However, influential opposition leaders boycotted the contest, in protest at alleged electoral irregularities and official intimidation. In late March Obiang Nguema appointed a new Prime Minister, Angel Serafin Seriche Dougan

(hitherto a Deputy Minister); an enlarged Council of Ministers was announced in early April. Representatives of opposition parties had declined a presidential invitation to participate in the new administration. During March the POC was dissolved.

In August 1996 Obiang Nguema awarded himself the military rank of General. In November a military court found 11 army officers guilty of conspiring to overthrow the Government; all were sentenced to terms of imprisonment.

In April 1997 representatives of the Government and of 13 opposition parties concluded a new national pact. During the following month Moto Nsa was arrested by the Angolan authorities with a consignment of arms, which were reportedly intended for use in a planned coup in Equatorial Guinea. Following his release in June, Moto Nsa was granted refuge in Spain. Meanwhile, the PPGE was banned; the party subsequently divided into two factions, of which one was led by Moto Nsa. In August Moto Nsa and 11 others were convicted *in absentia* of treason; Moto Nsa was sentenced to 101 years' imprisonment. In September the Government protested strongly to Spain over its offer of political asylum to Moto Nsa. Shortly afterwards French was declared the second official national language. In January 1998 the Government resigned. Seriche Dougan was reappointed as Prime Minister, and a new, enlarged Council of Ministers was formed. In the following month a new electoral law was approved by the House of Representatives; this banned political coalitions, and was expected to disadvantage the opposition at the next legislative elections.

In late January 1998 armed protesters launched three successive attacks against military targets on Bioko, killing four soldiers and three civilians. The terrorist action was alleged to have been perpetrated by members of the secessionist Movimiento para la Autodeterminación de la Isla de Bioko (MAIB), which was founded in 1993 by ethnic Bubis (the original inhabitants of the island, who, following independence, had become outnumbered by the mainland Fang). Subsequently hundreds of Bubis and resident Nigerians were arrested; many were reportedly also severely tortured. In late May 1998 some 116 detainees were tried by a military court in connection with the January attacks, on charges including terrorism and treason. Fifteen of the defendants were found guilty of the most serious charges and sentenced to death; in response to international pressure, however, the death sentences were commuted to sentences of life imprisonment in September. In July Martin Puye, a prominent MAIB leader who had been sentenced to 27 years in prison following the May trial, died in detention, arousing widespread international condemnation of the conditions of imprisonment in Equatorial Guinea.

During early 1999 six unregistered opposition parties exiled in Spain, including the MAIB and Moto Nsa's faction of the PPGE, formed a new alliance, the Coordinadora de la Oposición Conjunta. Equatorial Guinea's second multi-party legislative elections took place in early March amid allegations of electoral malpractice and of the systematic intimidation of opposition candidates by the security forces. The elections were contested by 13 parties (excluding the divided PPGE, which had been banned in 1997—see above), and some 99% of the electorate was estimated to have voted. According to the official results, the ruling PDGE obtained more than 90% of the votes, increasing its representation from 68 to 75 of the 80 seats in the House of Representatives. Two opposition parties, the Unión Popular (UP) and the Convergencia para la Democracia Social (CPDS), secured four seats and one seat respectively. Both parties, however, refused to participate in the new administration, in protest at alleged violations of the electoral law. (This policy subsequently led to an internal crisis within the UP and a change of leadership was instigated in August 2000.) The UP, the CPDS and five other opposition organizations campaigned, without success, to have the election results annulled. Following the election, Seriche Dougan was reappointed to the premiership, and in late July a new Council of Ministers was announced.

The new administration dismissed hundreds of civil servants, including a number of high-ranking officials, during its first three months in office, as part of efforts to eradicate corruption. Furthermore, in January 2000 a number of judicial officials, including the President of the Supreme Court and the President of the Constitutional Court, were dismissed. Former Prime Minister Silvestre Siale Bileka was appointed to the presidency of the Supreme Court. Nevertheless, in March 2000 the new Special Representative for Equatorial Guinea at the UN Human Rights Commission condemned the Equatorial Guinean authorities for systematic and serious human rights violations. The Special Representative further stated that, despite some minor advances, real democracy did not exist in the country and accused the Government of refusing to authorize the formation of human rights non-governmental organizations. Following intense lobbying by several African countries, the mandate of the Special Representative was terminated in April 2002. However in December a new UN Human Rights Rapporteur arrived in Equatorial Guinea, with a mandate to investigate claims of human rights violations.

Meanwhile, municipal elections were held on 28 May 2000, but were boycotted by the CPDS, the UP and the Alianza Democrática Progresista (ADP). Consequently, the PDGE obtained 95.7% of the votes cast and secured control of all 30 municipal councils. The opposition dismissed the elections as invalid. In October Obiang Nguema reportedly urged Seriche Dougan to resign after the House of Representatives severely criticized the Prime Minister for failing to address adequately the problem of corruption in government. In November six opposition parties, including the CPDS, the UP and the ADP, formed the Frente de la Oposición Democrática in order to create a common front to promote democracy. Another coalition was created in March 2001 by eight opposition parties in exile in Spain (including the PPGE and the MAIB) and the CPDS and the UP in Equatorial Guinea.

In late February 2001 Seriche Dougan announced the resignation of his Government, in response to further pressure from the President and the legislature. Cándido Muatetema Rivas, formerly Deputy Secretary-General of the PDGE, was subsequently appointed as Prime Minister and formed a new Council of Ministers. Five members of the opposition were appointed to the new Government, including Jeremias Ondo Ngomo, the President of the UP, as Minister-delegate for Communications and Transport. In July Obiang Nguema was nominated as the PDGE candidate for the 2003 presidential election. In the same month the President made overtures to exiled political groups, urging them to legalize their political movements in Equatorial Guinea. In late July 2001 Florentino Ecomo Nsogo, the President of the Partido de Reconstrucción y Bienestar Social, became the first opposition leader to return from Spain in response to Obiang Nguema's request. In August the Government announced a programme of modernization for the army, to be financed by increased petroleum revenues.

In May and June 2002 some 144 members of opposition parties were tried on charges relating to an alleged plot to oust Obiang Nguema, following their arrest in March. In June 68 of the defendants received sentences of up to 20 years' imprisonment; those convicted included the Secretary-General of the CPDS, Plácido Micó Abogo, and Felipe Ondo Obiang, the Chairman of the Fuerza Demócrata Republicana. International concern regarding Equatorial Guinea's treatment of opposition groups increased further in July, following the death of Juan Ondo Nguema, a police-officer who had been convicted in June; opposition parties alleged that Ondo Nguema's death had resulted from injuries sustained during torture while in custody. None the less, also in July, the Secretary-General of the UP, Fabián Nsué Nguema, was imprisoned on charges of insulting the Head of State. In October, however, Nsué Nguema was released, along with some 120 others, although it was reported that only 12 of those convicted in June were included in the preidential pardon. In January 2003, apparently in response to international pressure, the Government announced a national conference on the judicial system.

In early November 2002 President Obiang Nguema announced that the presidential election would be brought forward to 15 December (from February 2003). A National Electoral Council was created, although international bodies were unwilling to monitor voting in view of the apparent weakness of the country's electoral institutions. Nevertheless, several leading members of both the exiled and resident opposition—including Celestino Bonifacio Bacale of the CPDS and Tomás Mecheba Fernández of the Partido Socialista de Guinea Ecuatorial—declared their intention to contest the election, albeit without agreeing to sign a written guarantee of their candidacy. Alfonso Nsué Mokuy of the CLD also agreed to participate in the election, as did the Deputy Minister of Public Works, Housing and Urban Affairs, Carmelo Modú Acusé Bindang (the President of the UDS), and the Deputy Minister of Communications and Transport, Jeremias Ondo Ngomo (of the UP).

On 15 December 2002, with voting already under way, Bacale and other opposition candidates announced their withdrawal from the election, alleging widespread irregularities in voting procedures. Their claims related to the apparent lack of secrecy in voting, the insufficient number of ballot papers for opposition candidates and voter intimidation. According to the official results, Obiang Nguema was re-elected to the presidency, with 97.1% of the votes cast. The conduct of the election was condemned by the European Union (EU), which urged the Government to grant an amnesty to opposition members. Despite the newly re-elected President's call for the opposition leaders to join the PDGE in a government of national unity, the CPDS and other 'radical' opposition parties continued to refuse to participate in Obiang Nguema's administration. In February 2003 Ondo Ngomo was appointed as Deputy Prime Minister in charge of Social Affairs and Human Rights. Cándido Muatetema Rivas was reappointed as Prime Minister, and two of President Obiang Nguema's sons, Teodoro Nguema Obiang Mangue and Gabriel Mbegha Obiang Lima, were appointed as Minister of State in charge of Infrastructure and Forests and Secretary of State for Mines and Hydrocarbon Fuels, respectively.

Equatorial Guinea enjoyed exceptionally high revenues from petroleum exports during the late 1990s; allegations emerged, however, that members of the Obiang Nguema regime were accruing private profits from national petroleum exports.

While Spain (the former colonial power) has traditionally been a major trading partner and aid donor, Equatorial Guinea's entry in 1983 into the Customs and Economic Union of Central Africa (replaced in 1999 by the Communauté économique et monétaire de l'Afrique centrale, see p. 239) represented a significant move towards a greater integration with neighbouring francophone countries. In 1985 Equatorial Guinea joined the Franc Zone (see p. 237), with financial assistance from France. Obiang Nguema has regularly attended Franco-African summit meetings. In 1989 the Spanish Government agreed to cancel one-third of Equatorial Guinea's public debt to Spain and in 1991 cancelled a further one-third of the bilateral debt. From mid-1993, however, Equato-Guinean-Spanish relations deteriorated, and in January 1994 the Spanish Government withdrew one-half of its aid to Equatorial Guinea in retaliation for the expulsion in December 1993 of a Spanish diplomat whom the Equato-Guinean authorities had accused of interfering in the country's internal affairs. In November 1994 the Equato-Guinean Government accused Spain of sponsoring the passage of a resolution adopted by the European Parliament condemning violations of human rights in Equatorial Guinea. In September 1997 the Obiang Nguema administration protested strongly to the Spanish Government over Spain's offer of political asylum to the opposition leader Severo Moto Nsa (see above). On several occasions in 1998 the Equato-Guinean Government accused Spain of attempting to destabilize Equatorial Guinea by providing funds to opposition organizations. However, in October 1999 the Spanish Government agreed to resume full assistance to its former colony, and during a visit to Madrid in March 2001 Obiang Nguema held talks with Spanish Prime Minister José María Aznar, who agreed to normalize relations with Equatorial Guinea in the economic field. Spain was willing to help strengthen the Equatorial Guinean institutions, in order to promote economic development, in exchange for the promotion and protection of human rights within Equatorial Guinea and legal guarantees for foreign investment.

In October 1999 the medical aid agency Médecins sans frontières withdrew its mission from Equatorial Guinea in protest against the alleged manipulation of humanitarian aid by the Government. During the 1990s the EU withdrew financial aid to Equatorial Guinea, and the UN Development Programme suspended some projects.

In November 1999 Equatorial Guinea, Angola, Cameroon, the Republic of the Congo, Gabon, Nigeria and São Tomé and Príncipe established an international committee to demarcate maritime borders in the Gulf of Guinea. The development of petroleum reserves in the region during the 1990s had revived long-standing frontier disputes. In September 2000 Equatorial Guinea and Nigeria formally resolved their maritime border dispute, reaching an agreement on the demarcation of the border, which was expected to encourage further petroleum exploration and development in that area. Both countries signed the agreement in December 2001, pending ratification by their respective national legislatures. In March 2003, however, relations between Equatorial Guinea and Gabon were strained, following the occupation of the small island of Mbagne by a contingent of Gabonese troops. Both countries have long claimed ownership of the island, which lies in potentially oil-rich waters north of the Gabonese capital, Libreville, and south-west of the Equato-Guinean mainland.

Government

In November 1991 a new Constitution was approved in a referendum, providing for the introduction of multi-party democracy. Executive power is vested in the President, whose seven-year term of office is renewable indefinitely. The President is immune from prosecution for offences committed before, during or after his tenure of the post. Legislative power is held by an 80-member House of Representatives, which serves for a term of five years. Both the President and the House of Representatives are directly elected by universal adult suffrage. The President appoints a Council of Ministers, headed by a Prime Minister, from among the members of the House of Representatives.

Defence

In August 2002 there were 1,100 men in the army, 120 in the navy and 100 in the air force. There was also a paramilitary force, trained by French military personnel. Military service is voluntary. The estimated defence budget for 2002 was US $4.5m. Spain has provided military advisers and training since 1979, and military aid has also been received from the USA.

Economic Affairs

In 2001, according to estimates by the World Bank, Equatorial Guinea's gross national income (GNI), measured at average 1999–2001 prices, was US $327m., equivalent to $700 per head (or $5,640 per head on an international purchasing-power parity basis). During 1990–2001, it was estimated, the population increased at an average annual rate of 2.6%, while gross domestic product (GDP) per head increased, in real terms, by an average of 15.2% per year. Overall GDP increased, in real terms, at an average annual rate of 18.3% in 1990–2001; GDP increased by 16.9% in 2000, but by only 1.3% in 2001.

Agriculture (including hunting, forestry and fishing) contributed 8.5% of GDP in 2001 (compared with 51.6% of GDP in 1995). The sector employed an estimated 70.1% of the labour force in 2001. The principal cash crop is cocoa, which contributed an estimated 1.5% of export earnings in 1998. Coffee is also a traditional export. The Government is encouraging the production of bananas, spices (vanilla, black pepper and coriander) and medicinal plants for export. The main subsistence crops are cassava and sweet potatoes. Exploitation of the country's vast forest resources (principally of okoumé and akoga timber) provided an estimated 9.2% of export revenue in 1998. Almost all industrial fishing activity is practised by foreign fleets, notably by those of countries of the Eurpean Union. During 1990–2000, according to the World Bank, the real GDP of the agricultural sector increased at an average annual rate of 5.8%; growth in 2001 was 6.6%.

Industry (including mining, manufacturing, construction and power) contributed 87.0% of GDP in 2001 (compared with 27.3% of GDP in 1995). During 1990–2001, according to the World Bank, industrial GDP increased at an average annual rate of 40.7%. Industrial GDP rose by 20.1% in 2000, but decreased by 1.2% in 2001.

Extractive activities were minimal during the 1980s, and the mining sector employed less than 0.2% of the working population in 1983. However, the development of onshore and offshore reserves of petroleum and of offshore deposits of natural gas led to unprecedented economic growth during the 1990s. Exports of petroleum commenced in 1992 and provided an estimated 94.4% of total export earnings by 2000. In 1998 exports of natural gas (which commenced in 1997) accounted for an estimated 1.6% of export earnings. The petroleum sector contributed an estimated 61.8% of GDP in 1998 (compared with 18.2% of GDP in 1995), and operations commenced at a new oilfield in November 2000. Petroleum production increased from 17,000 barrels per day (b/d) at the end of 1996 to an estimated 220,000 b/d at the end of 2002. The existence of deposits of gold, uranium, iron ore, titanium, tantalum and manganese has also been confirmed.

The manufacturing sector contributed only an estimated 0.4% of GDP in 1998. Wood-processing constitutes the main commercial manufacturing activity.

An estimated total of 20m. kWh of electric energy was generated in 1997. Bioko is supplied by a 3.6-MW hydroelectric installation, constructed on the Riaba river. There is a further 3.6-MW installation on the mainland. Imports of fuel products comprised 7.7% of the value of total imports in 1990, prior to the discovery of large reserves of petroleum in Equato-Guinean territory.

The services sector contributed 4.6% of GDP in 2001. The dominant services are trade, restaurants and hotels, and government services. During 1990–2001, according to the World Bank, the GDP of the services sector increased at an average annual rate of 10.5%; growth in 2001 was 10.8%.

According to IMF estimates, in 2000 there was a visible trade surplus of US $898.8m., while the deficit on the current account of the balance of payments was $365.9m. In 1998 the USA was both the principal source of imports (35.4%) and the main market for exports (62.0%). Other major trading partners were Spain, France, Cameroon and the People's Republic of China. In 1998 crude petroleum (87%), wood and cocoa constituted the principal sources of export revenue, while in 1990 the principal imports were ships and boats, petroleum and related products and food and live animals.

In 1998 the budget deficit was estimated at 3,754m. francs CFA. Equatorial Guinea's external debt was US $247.8m. at the end of 2000, of which $198.9m. was long-term public debt. In that year the cost of debt-servicing was equivalent to 0.2% of the value of exports of goods and services. The rate of inflation averaged 7.5% per year in 1990–98. Following the devaluation of the currency (see below), consumer prices rose by an estimated annual average of 38.9% in 1994; in 1998, however, prices increased by an estimated annual average of 7.8%. The annual average rate of inflation was only 0.6% in 1999 and 4.5% in 2000.

Equatorial Guinea is a member of the Central African organs of the Franc Zone (see p. 239), including the Communauté économique et monétaire de l'Afrique centrale (CEMAC, see p. 239).

Equatorial Guinea suffered a severe economic decline under the Macías regime. The Obiang Nguema administration has achieved some success in rehabilitating and diversifying the primary sector, and exceptional economic growth was recorded from the late 1990s, stimulated by the commencement in 1992 of petroleum exports. GNI per head nearly trebled in 1996–98. An economic development programme for 1994–96, supported by the IMF, was largely unsuccessful in its aim to restructure the public and financial sectors. Since 1996 Equatorial Guinea has had no formal arrangement with the IMF, which has repeatedly urged the Government to demonstrate greater fiscal control and to increase transparency in the management of petroleum contracts and revenue. Indeed, revenue from the profitable petroleum and timber sectors has been undermined by the country's inefficient taxation system and by poor budgetary discipline. In addition, it has been widely alleged that members of the Equato-Guinean regime have profited personally from national petroleum exports. Equatorial Guinea remains burdened by a large external debt. Spain and France have traditionally been important bilateral donors. However, economic relations with the USA have also strengthened in recent years as a result of major investments in the development of Equato-Guinean oilfields by US energy companies and the approval by the US Overseas Private Investment Corporation, in June 2000, of financing, worth US $373m., for the construction and operation of a methanol plant on Bioko. In 2001 and 2002 there were further discoveries of offshore natural gas and petroleum reserves. However, although construction and infrastructure projects proliferated from the 1990s, the levels of extreme poverty havenot been addressed. The absence of any visible improvement in living standards among the general population since the early 1990s has been variously attributed to corruption, the disadvantageous terms of many contracts negotiated by the state petroleum company, Guinea Ecuatorial de Petróleo (GEPetrol), and reduced international aid donations. Indeed, lower levels of foreign aid in recent years have led to a real reduction in the population's overall spending power and a consequent improvement in the country's trade balance. Equatorial Guinea's petroleum output was projected to increase to approximately 350,000 b/d in 2003, with GNI forecast to increase by 23.8% in 2002.

Education

Education is officially compulsory and free for five years between the ages of six and 11 years. Primary education starts at six years of age and normally lasts for five years. Secondary education, beginning at the age of 12, spans a seven-year period, comprising a first cycle of four years and a second cycle of three years. In 1982 the total enrolment at primary and secondary schools was equivalent to 81% of the school-age population. Total enrolment at primary schools in 1999/2000 included 79.0% of children in the relevant age-group (males 87.5%; females

70.4%), according to UNESCO estimates. In that year UNESCO estimated that total enrolment at secondary schools was equivalent to 31.2% of children in the relevant age-group (males 43.2%; females 19.2%). In 1990 there were 578 pupils in higher education. Since 1979, assistance in the development of the educational system has been provided by Spain. Two higher education centres, at Bata and Malabo, are administered by the Spanish Universidad Nacional de Educación a Distancia. The French Government also provides considerable financial assistance. In September 2002 a new National Plan for Education was ratified. The initiative aimed to improve basic literacy and introduce education on health-related topics. In 1993 budgetary expenditure on education by the central Government amounted to 734m. francs CFA (1.8% of total expenditure).

Public Holidays

2003: 1 January (New Year's Day), 5 March (Independence Day), 18–21 April (Easter), 1 May (Labour Day), 25 May (AU Day), 10 December (Human Rights Day), 25 December (Christmas).

2004: 1 January (New Year's Day), 5 March (Independence Day), 9–12 April (Easter), 1 May (Labour Day), 25 May (AU Day), 10 December (Human Rights Day), 25 December (Christmas).

Weights and Measures

The metric system is in force.

Statistical Survey

Source (unless otherwise stated): Dirección Técnica de Estadística, Secretaría de Estado para el Plan de Desarrollo Económico, Malabo.

AREA AND POPULATION

Area: 28,051 sq km (10,831 sq miles): Río Muni 26,017 sq km, Bioko 2,017 sq km, Annobón 17 sq km.

Population: 246,941 (Río Muni 200,106, Bioko 44,820, Annobón 2,015) at December 1965 census; 300,000 (Río Muni 240,804, Bioko 57,190, Annobón 2,006), comprising 144,268 males and 155,732 females, at census of 4–17 July 1983 (Source: Ministerio de Asuntos Exteriores, Madrid); 470,000 (UN estimate) at mid-2001.

Density (mid-2001): 16.8 per sq km.

Provinces (population, census of July 1983): Kié-Ntem 70,202, Litoral 66,370, Centro-Sur 52,393, Wele-Nzas 51,839, Bioko Norte 46,221, Bioko Sur 10,969, Annobón 2,006.

Principal Towns (population at 1983 census): Malabo (capital) 15,253, Bata 24,100. *2001:* (UN estimates, including suburbs): Malabo 33,000 (Source: UN, *World Urbanization Prospects: The 2001 Revision*).

Births and Deaths (UN estimates, annual averages): Birth rate 43.2 per 1,000 in 1995–2000; Death rate 16.5 per 1,000 in 1995–2000 Source: UN, *World Population Prospects: The 2000 Revision*.

Expectation of Life (WHO estimates, years at birth): 53.7 (males 52.3; females 55.1) in 2001. Source: WHO, *World Health Report*.

Economically Active Population (persons aged 6 years and over, 1983 census): Agriculture, hunting, forestry and fishing 59,390; Mining and quarrying 126; Manufacturing 1,490; Electricity, gas and water 224; Construction 1,929; Trade, restaurants and hotels 3,059; Transport, storage and communications 1,752; Financing, insurance, real estate and business services 409; Community, social and personal services 8,377; Activities not adequately defined 984; Total employed 77,740 (males 47,893, females 29,847); Unemployed 24,825 (males 18,040, females 6,785); Total labour force 102,565 (males 65,933, females 36,632). Note: Figures are based on unadjusted census data, indicating a total population of 261,779. The adjusted total is 300,000. Source: ILO, *Yearbook of Labour Statistics*.

HEALTH AND WELFARE

Key Indicators

Total Fertility Rate (children per woman, 2001): 5.9.

Under-5 Mortality Rate (per 1,000 live births, 2001): 153.

HIV/AIDS (% of persons aged 15–49, 2001): 3.38.

Physicians (per 1,000 head, 1990–99): 24.6.

Hospital Beds (per 1,000 head, 1988): 2.8.

Health Expenditure (2000): US $ per head (PPP): 103.

Health Expenditure (2000): % of GDP: 3.4.

Health Expenditure (2000): public (% of total): 67.6.

Access to Water (% of persons, 2000): 43.

Access to Sanitation (% of persons, 2000): 53.

Human Development Index (2000): ranking: 111.

Human Development Index (2000): value: 0.679.
For sources and definitions, see explanatory note on p. vi.

AGRICULTURE, ETC.

Principal Crops (FAO estimates, '000 metric tons, 2001): Sweet potatoes 36; Cassava 45; Coconuts 6; Oil palm fruit 35; Bananas 20; Plantains 31; Cocoa beans 5 (unofficial figure); Green coffee 4. Source: FAO.

Livestock (FAO estimates, '000 head, year ending September 2001): Cattle 5; Pigs 6; Sheep 38; Goats 9. Source: FAO.

Forestry (FAO estimates, 2000): Roundwood removals ('000 cubic metres): Fuel wood 447 (assumed to be unchanged since 1983); Sawlogs, veneer logs and logs for sleepers 364; Total 811. Source: FAO.

Fishing (FAO estimates, metric tons, live weight, 2000): Freshwater fishes 1,076,, Clupeoids 2,000, Sharks, rays, skates, etc. 100, Marine fishes 117; Total catch (incl. others) 3,634. Source: FAO, *Yearbook of Fishery Statistics*.

MINING

Production (estimates, 2001): Crude petroleum 69 million barrels; Natural gas 790 million cubic metres. Source: US Geological Survey.

INDUSTRY

Palm Oil ('000 metric tons): 4.5 in 1999; 4.5 in 2000 (FAO estimate); 4.5 in 2001 (FAO estimate). Source: FAO.

Veneer Sheets (FAO estimates, '000 cubic metres): 15 in 1999; 15 in 2000; 15 in 2001. Source: FAO.

Electric Energy (estimates, million kWh): 20 in 1996; 20 in 1997; 21 in 1998. Source: UN, *Industrial Commodity Statistics Yearbook*.

FINANCE

Currency and Exchange Rates: 100 centimes = 1 franc de la Coopération financière en Afrique centrale (CFA). *Sterling, Dollar and Euro Equivalents* (31 December 2002): £1 sterling = 1,008.17 francs CFA; US $1 = 625.49 francs CFA; €1 = 655.96 francs CFA; 10,000 francs CFA = £9.919 = $15.987 = €15.245. *Average Exchange Rate* (francs CFA per US dollar): 711.98 in 2000; 733.04 in 2001; 696.99 in 2002. *Note:* An exchange rate of 1 French franc = 50 francs CFA, established in 1948, remained in force until January 1994, when the CFA franc was devalued by 50%, with the exchange rate adjusted to 1 French franc = 100 francs CFA. This relationship to French currency remained in effect with the introduction of the euro on 1 January 1999. From that date, accordingly, a fixed exchange rate of €1 = 655.957 francs CFA has been in operation.

Budget (estimates, million francs CFA, 1998): *Revenue:* Petroleum sector 53,489; Taxation 14,608 (Taxes on income and profits 2,253; Taxes on domestic goods and services 6,501; Taxes on international trade 5,064; Other taxes 786); Other revenue 7,080; Total revenue 75,177, excl. grants from abroad (1,797). *Expenditure:* Current expenditure 33,788 (Wages and salaries 9,129; Other goods and services 12,917; Subsidies and transfers 7,284; Interest payments 4,458); Capital expenditure 29,410; Unclassified expenditure 17,530; Total expenditure 80,728. Source: IMF, *Equatorial Guinea: Recent Economic Developments* (October 1999).

International Reserves (US $ million at 31 December 2002): IMF special drawing rights 0.60; Foreign exchange 87.94; Total 88.54. Source: IMF, *International Financial Statistics*.

Money Supply (million francs CFA at 31 December 2002): Currency outside deposit money banks 25,951; Demand deposits at deposit money banks 46,524; Total money 72,475. Source: IMF, *International Financial Statistics.*

Cost of Living (Consumer Price Index; base: January 1990 = 100): 161.1 in 1996; 166.0 in 1997; 179.0 (estimate) in 1998. Source: IMF, *Equatorial Guinea: Recent Economic Developments* (October 1999).

Expenditure on the Gross Domestic Product ('000 million francs CFA at current prices, 1997): Government final consumption expenditure 32.0; Private final consumption expenditure 133.2; Gross capital formation 190.8; *Total domestic expenditure* 356.0; Exports of goods and services 292.9; *Less* Imports of goods and services 358.4; *GDP in purchasers' values* 290.5. Source: IMF, *Equatorial Guinea: Recent Economic Developments* (October 1999).

Gross Domestic Product by Economic Activity (million francs CFA at current prices, 1997): Agriculture, hunting, forestry and fishing 67,268; Petroleum sector 187,429; Manufacturing 962; Electricity, gas and water 3,121; Construction 5,768; Trade, restaurants and hotels 8,819; Transport and communications 1,920; Finance, insurance, real estate and business services 1,967; Government services 2,823; *Sub-total* 288,312; Import duties 2,205; *GDP in purchasers' values* 290,517. Source: IMF, *Equatorial Guinea: Recent Economic Developments* (October 1999).

Balance of Payments (US $ million, 1996): Exports of goods f.o.b. 175.31; Imports of goods f.o.b. −292.04; *Trade balance* −116.73; Exports of services 4.88; Imports of services −184.58; *Balance on goods and services* −296.43; Other income received 0.16; Other income paid −45.18; *Balance on goods, services and income* −341.44; Current transfers received 4.03; Current transfers paid −6.62; *Current balance* −344.04; Direct investment from abroad 376.18; Other investment liabilities −62.43; Net errors and omissions 24.82; *Overall balance* −5.46. Source: IMF, *International Financial Statistics.*

EXTERNAL TRADE

Principal Commodities (distribution by SITC, US $ '000, 1990): *Imports c.i.f.:* Food and live animals 4,340; Beverages and tobacco 3,198, (Alcoholic beverages 2,393); Crude materials (inedible) except fuels 2,589 (Crude fertilizers and crude minerals 2,102); Petroleum and petroleum products 4,738; Chemicals and related products 2,378; Basic manufactures 3,931; Machinery and transport equipment 35,880 (Road vehicles and parts 3,764, Ships, boats and floating structures 24,715); Miscellaneous manufactured articles 2,725; Total (incl. others) 61,601. *Exports f.o.b.:* Food and live animals 6,742 (Cocoa 6,372); Beverages and tobacco 3,217 (Tobacco and tobacco manufactures 2,321); Crude materials (inedible) except fuels 20,017 (Sawlogs and veneer logs 12,839, Textile fibres and waste 7,078); Machinery and transport equipment 24,574 (Ships, boats and floating structures 23,852); Total (incl. others) 61,705. Source: UN, *International Trade Statistics Yearbook.*

1997 (US $ '000): Imports c.i.f. 352,800; Exports f.o.b. 498,444. Source: IMF, *Equatorial Guinea: Recent Economic Developments* (October 1999).

2000 (US $ million): Imports c.i.f. 464.3; Exports f.o.b. 2,181.7 (Source: IMF, *International Financial Statistics*).

Principal Trading Partners (US $ '000, 1991): *Imports c.i.f.:* Cameroon 29,141; France 5,915; Italy 3,001; Liberia 22,032; Spain 11,640; USA 33,366; Total (incl. others) 113,545. *Exports f.o.b.:* Cameroon 47,212; Gabon 2,389; Netherlands 2,103; Nigeria 8,955; São Tomé and Príncipe 1,952; Spain 11,645; Total (incl. others) 86,151. Source: UN, *International Trade Statistics Yearbook.*

TRANSPORT

Road Traffic (estimates, motor vehicles in use at 31 December 1996): Passenger cars 1,520; Lorries and vans 540. Source: IRF, *World Road Statistics.*

Shipping: *Merchant Fleet* (at 31 December 2001): Vessels 60; Total displacement 37,225 grt. (Source: Lloyd's Register-Fairplay, *World Fleet Statistics.*). *International Sea-borne Freight Traffic* ('000 metric tons, 1990): Goods loaded 110; Goods unloaded 64. (Source: UN, *Monthly Bulletin of Statistics*).

Civil Aviation (traffic on scheduled services, 1998): Passengers carried ('000) 21; Passenger-km (million) 4. Source: UN, *Statistical Yearbook.*

COMMUNICATIONS MEDIA

1997: 180,000 radio receivers in use; 4,000 television receivers in use; 1 daily newspaper (1996, estimated circulation 2,000); Book production 17 titles (1988).

2001: 6,900 main telephone lines in use; 65 facsimile machines in use (1998); 15,000 mobile cellular telephone subscribers; 3,000 personal computers in use; 900 internet users. Sources: UNESCO, *Statistical Yearbook;* UN, *Statistical Yearbook;* International Telecommunication Union.

EDUCATION

Pre-primary (1998): Schools 180; Teachers 387; Pupils 16,645.

Primary (1998): Schools 483; Teachers 1,322; Pupils 74,940.

Secondary (1998): Teachers 763; Pupils 18,802.

Higher (1990/91): Teachers 58; Pupils 578 (Source: UNESCO Institute for Statistics).

Adult Literacy Rate (UNESCO estimates): 83.2% (males 92.5%; females 74.4%) in 2000 (Source: UN Development Programme, *Human Development Report*).

Directory

The Constitution

The present Constitution was approved by a national referendum on 16 November 1991 and amended in January 1995. It provided for the introduction of a plural political system and for the establishment of an 80-member legislative House of Representatives (Cámara de Representantes del Pueblo). The term of office of the President is seven years, renewable on an indefinite number of occasions. The President is immune from prosecution for offences committed before, during or after his tenure of the post. The Cámara de Representantes serves for a term of five years. Both the President and the Cámara de Representantes are directly elected by universal adult suffrage. The President appoints a Council of Ministers, headed by a Prime Minister, from among the members of the Cámara de Representantes.

The Government

HEAD OF STATE

President and Supreme Commander of the Armed Forces: Gen. (Teodoro) Obiang Nguema Mbasogo (assumed office 25 August 1979; elected President 25 June 1989; re-elected 25 February 1996 and 15 December 2002).

COUNCIL OF MINISTERS
(April 2003)

The nine parties represented in the Government are the Partido Democrático de Guinea Ecuatorial, the Unión Popular, Unión Democrática y Social de Guinea Ecuatorial, the Convención Social-democrática Popular, the Partido Socialista de Guinea Ecuatorial, the Convención Liberal Democrática, Partido Social Demócrata, the Partido de la Convergencia Social Democráta and the Alianza Democrática Progresista.

Prime Minister and Head of Government: Cándido Muatetema Rivas.

Deputy Prime Minister in charge of the Interior: Demetrio Elo Ndong Nsefumu.

Deputy Prime Minister in charge of Social Affairs and Human Rights: Jeremias Ondo Ngomo.

Minister of State for Presidential Missions: Alejandro Evuna Owono Asangono.

Minister of State, Secretary-General of the Presidency: Ignacio Milam Tang.

Minister of State for Parliamentary Relations and Judicial Affairs: Miguel Abia Biteo Borico.

Minister of State for Education and Science, Government Spokesman: Antonio Fernando Nvé Ngu.

Minister of State for Communications and Transport: MARCELINO OYONO NTUTUMU.

Minister of State for Information, Tourism and Culture: AGUSTIN NZÉ NFUMU.

Minister of State for the Civil Service and Administrative Co-ordination: RICARDO MANGUE OBAMA NFUBEA.

Minister of State for Infrastructure and Forests: TEODORO NGUEMA OBIANG MANGUE.

Minister of State for Youth and Sports: LUCAS NGUEMA ESONO MBANG.

Minister of State for Agriculture, Livestock and Rural Development: FRANCISCO PASCUAL OBAMA ASUÉ.

Minister of State for Industry, Commerce and Small- and Medium-sized Enterprises: CARMELO MODÚ ACUSÉ BINDANG.

Minister of Foreign Affairs, International Co-operation and Francophone Affairs: MICHA ONDO BILÉ.

Minister of Justice and Worship: RUBÉN MAYÉ NSUÉ.

Minister of the Interior and Local Corporations: CLEMENTE ENGONGA NGUEMA ONGUENE.

Minister of the Economy: BALTASAR ENGONGA EDJO.

Minister of Planning and Economic Development: ANTONIO NVÉ NSENG.

Minister of Finance and the Budget: MARCELINO OWONO EDU.

Minister of Mines and Energy: CRISTÓBAL MENANA ELA.

Minister of Health and Social Welfare: JUSTINO OBAMA NVÉ.

Minister of Labour and Social Security: MIGUEL EYANGA DJOBA MALANGO.

Minister of Social Affairs and Women's Development: TERESA EFUA ASANGONO.

Minister of Fishing and the Environment: FORTUNATO OFA MBO. In addition, there are 15 Ministers-delegate, five Deputy Ministers and five Secretaries of State.

MINISTRIES

All ministries are in Malabo.

Ministry of Agriculture, Livestock and Rural Development: Apdo 504, Malabo.

Ministry of the Economy: Malabo; tel. (9) 31-05; fax (9) 32-05.

Ministry of Foreign Affairs, International Co-operation and Francophone Affairs: Malabo; tel. (9) 32-20; fax (9) 31-32.

Ministry of the Interior and Local Corporations: Malabo; fax (9) 26-83.

Ministry of Justice and Worship: Malabo; fax (9) 21-15.

Ministry of Mines and Energy: Calle 12 de Octobre s/n, Malabo; tel. (9) 35-67; fax (9) 33-53.

Legislature

CÁMARA DE REPRESENTANTES DEL PUEBLO
(House of Representatives)

Speaker: SALOMON NGUEMA OWONO.

General Election, 7 March 1999

Party	Seats
Partido Democrático de Guinea Ecuatorial (PDGE) . .	75
Unión Popular (UP) . .	4
Convergencia para la Democracia Social (CPDS) . . .	1
Total	**80**

Political Organizations

Acción Popular (AP): Pres. MIGUEL ESONO.

Alianza Nacional para la Restauración Democrática de Guinea Ecuatorial (ANRD): 95 Ruperto Chapi, 28100 Madrid, Spain; tel. (91) 623-88-64; f. 1974; Sec.-Gen. LUIS ONDO AYANG.

Convención Liberal Democrática (CLD): Pres. ALFONSO NSUE MOKUY.

Convención Socialdemocrática Popular (CSDP): Leader SECUNDINO OYONO.

Coordinación Democrática de los Partidos de Oposición de Guinea Ecuatorial: coalition based in Libreville, Gabon; f. 1991.

Frente Democrático para la Reforma: Sec.-Gen. BIYONGO BITUNG.

Movimiento Nacional para la Nueva Liberación de Guinea Ecuatorial.

Partido Republicano.

Partido de Reunificación (PR).

Unión para la Democracia y el Desarrollo Social (UDDS): f. 1990; Sec.-Gen. ANTONIO SIBACHA BUEICHEKU.

Foro-Democracia Guinea Ecuatorial (FDGE).

Frente de la Oposición Democrática (FOD): f. 2000; alliance of six opposition groups.

Alianza Democrática Progresista (ADP): Pres. VICTORINO BOLEKIA.

Convergencia para la Democracia Social (CPDS): Pres. SANTIAGO OBAMA; Sec.-Gen. PLÁCIDO MICÓ ABOGO.

Fuerza Demócrata Republicana (FDR): f. 1995; Chair. FELIPE ONDO OBIANG.

Partido del Progreso de Guinea Ecuatorial (PPGE): f. 1983; Christian Democrat faction led by SEVERO MOTO NSA.

Partido Social Demócrata (PSD): Pres. BENJAMÍN BALINGA.

Unión Popular (UP): f. 1992; conservative; Pres. ANDRÉS MOISÉS MBA ADA.

Movimiento para la Autodeterminación de la Isla de Bioko (MAIB): f. 1993 by Bubi interests seeking independence of Bioko; Spokesman WEJA CHICAMPO.

Partido de la Convergencia Social Demócrata (PCSD): Pres. BUENAVENTURA MOSUY.

Partido Democrático de Guinea Ecuatorial (PDGE): Malabo; f. 1987; sole legal party 1987–92; Chair. Gen. (TEODORO) OBIANG NGUEMA MBASOGO.

Partido para el Desarrollo (PPD): based in Spain; f. June 2001; Pres. ELOY ELO MVE MBENGOMO.

Partido de Reconstrucción y Bienestar Social (PRBS): Pres. FLORENTINO ECOMO NSOGO.

Partido Socialista de Guinea Ecuatorial (PSGE): Sec.-Gen. TOMÁS MECHEBA FERNÁNDEZ.

Resistencia Nacional de Guinea Ecuatorial (RENAGE): f. 2000; alliance of seven opposition groups; Leader DANIEL M. OYONO.

Unión Democrática Independiente (UDI): Leader DANIEL OYONO.

Unión Democrática Nacional (UDEMA): Pres. JOSÉ MECHEBA.

Unión Democrática y Social de Guinea Ecuatorial (UDS): Pres. CARMELO MODÚ ACUSÉ BINDANG.

Unión Popular—Progresista (UP—Progresista): Leader PEDRO EKONG.

Unión para la Reconciliación y el Progreso (URP).

Diplomatic Representation

EMBASSIES IN EQUATORIAL GUINEA

Algeria: Malabo.

Angola: Malabo.

Cameroon: 37 Calle Rey Boncoro, Apdo 292, Malabo; tel. and fax (9) 22-63; Ambassador JOHN NCHOTU AKUM.

China, People's Republic: Carretera del Aeropuerto, Apdo 44, Malabo; tel. (9) 35-05; fax (9) 23-81; Ambassador HUAILONG CHEN.

Egypt: Malabo.

France: Carretera del Aeropuerto, Apdo 326, Malabo; tel. (9) 20-05; Ambassador GÉRARD BRUNET DE COURSSOU.

Gabon: Calle de Argelia, Apdo 18, Malabo; Ambassador JEAN-BAPTISTE MBATCHI.

Guinea: Malabo.

Korea, Democratic People's Republic: Malabo; Ambassador PAK MYONG HAK.

Morocco: Avda Enrique, Apdo 329, Malabo; tel. (9) 26-50; fax (9) 26-55; e-mail sifamambo@intnet.gq; Chargé d'affaires a.i. MOHAMED ABARGHAZ.

Nigeria: 4 Paseo de los Cocoteros, Apdo 78, Malabo; tel. (9) 23-86; Chargé d'affaires a.i. EDWARD NWADA.

Russia: Malabo; Ambassador Lev Aleksandrovich Vakhrameyev.

Spain: Parque de las Avenidas de Africa, Malabo; tel. (9) 20-20; fax (9) 26-11; Ambassador José Riera Sikuier.

Judicial System

The structure of judicial administration was established in 1981. The Supreme Tribunal in Malabo, consisting of a President of the Supreme Tribunal, the Presidents of the three chambers (civil, criminal and administrative), and two magistrates from each chamber, is the highest court of appeal. There are Territorial High Courts in Malabo and Bata, which also sit as courts of appeal. Courts of first instance sit in Malabo and Bata, and may be convened in the other provincial capitals. Local courts may be convened when necessary.

President of the Supreme Tribunal: Silvestre Siale Bileka.

Attorney-General: Antonio Nzambi.

Religion

An estimated 90% of the population are adherents of the Roman Catholic Church. Traditional forms of worship are also followed.

CHRISTIANITY

The Roman Catholic Church

Equatorial Guinea comprises one archdiocese and two dioceses. There were an estimated 384,534 adherents in the country at 31 December 2000.

Bishops' Conference

Arzobispado, Apdo 106, Malabo; tel. (9) 29-09; fax 21-76; e-mail arzobispadomalabo@hotmail.com.

f. 1984; Pres. Rt Rev. Ildefonso Obama Obono (Archbishop of Malabo).

Archbishop of Malabo: Most Rev. Ildefonso Obama Obono, Arzobispado, Apdo 106, Malabo; tel. (9) 29-09; fax (9) 21-76; e-mail arzobispadomalabo@hotmail.com.

Protestant Church

Iglesia Reformada Evangélica de Guinea Ecuatorial (Evangelical Reformed Church of Equatorial Guinea): Apdo 195, Malabo; f. 1960; c. 8,000 mems.

The Press

El Patio: Apdo 180, Malabo; tel. (9) 27-20; fax (9) 27-22; Spanish; cultural review; 6 a year; publ. by Centro Cultural Hispano-Guineano; Editor Gabriela Gómez-Pimpollo.

Hoja Parroquial: Malabo; weekly.

La Gaceta: Malabo; f. 1996; bi-weekly.

La Verdad: Malabo; publ. by the Convergencia para la Democracia Social; Editor Plácido Mikó Abogo.

Voz del Pueblo: Malabo; publ. by the Partido Democrático de Guinea Ecuatorial.

FOREIGN NEWS BUREAU

Agencia EFE (Spain): 50 Calle del Presidente Nasser, Malabo; tel. (9) 31-65; Bureau Chief Donato Ndongo-Bidyogo.

Publisher

Centro Cultural Hispano-Guineano: Apdo 180, Malabo; tel. (9) 27-20; fax (9) 27-22.

Broadcasting and Communications

RADIO

Radio Africa and Radio East Africa: Apdo 851, Malabo; e-mail pabcomain@aol.com; commercial station; owned by Pan American Broadcasting; music and religious programmes in English.

Radio Malabo: Malabo; Spanish and French programmes.

Radio Nacional de Guinea Ecuatorial: Apdo 749, Barrio Comandachina, Bata; and Apdo 195, 90 ave 30 de Agostó, Malabo; tel. (8) 25-92; fax (8) 20-93; tel. (9) 22-60; fax (9) 20-97; govt-controlled; commercial station; programmes in Spanish, French and vernacular languages; Dir (Bata) Sebastián Eló Aseko; Dir (Malabo) Juan Eyene Opkua Nguema.

Radio Televisión Asonga: Bata.

TELEVISION

Televisión Nacional: Malabo; broadcasts in Spanish and French; Dir Antonio Nkulu Oye.

Finance

(cap. = capital; res = reserves; dep. = deposits; m. = million; br. = branch; amounts in francs CFA)

BANKING

Central Bank

Banque des Etats de l'Afrique Centrale (BEAC): Apdo 510, Malabo; tel. (9) 20-10; fax (9) 20-06; HQ in Yaoundé, Cameroon; f. 1973; bank of issue for mem. states of the Communauté économique et monétaire de l'Afrique centrale (CEMAC, fmrly Union douanière et économique de l'Afrique centrale), comprising Cameroon, the Central African Repub., Chad, the Repub. of the Congo, Equatorial Guinea and Gabon; res 177,417m., total assets 2,034,793m. (Dec. 2001); Gov. Jean-Félix Mamalepot; Dir in Equatorial Guinea Francisco Garcia Bernikon.

Commercial Banks

Caisse Commune d'Epargne et d'Investissement Guinea Ecuatorial (CCEI-GE): Calle del Presidente Nasser, Apdo 428, Malabo; tel. (9) 31-21; fax (9) 33-11; e-mail cromw@hotmail.com; f. 1995; dep. 19,565m., total assets 34,947m. (Dec. 1999); Man. Dir Joseph Tindjou.

Société Générale des Banques GE (SGBGE): Avda de la Independencia, Apdo 686, Malabo; tel. (9) 93-37; fax (9) 27-43; internet groupe.socgen.com/sgbge; f. 1986; present name adopted 1998; 60% owned by Société Générale SA (France), 33% state-owned; cap. 1,740m., res 673m., dep. 24,390m. (Dec. 2000); Man. Dir Jean-Claude Robert; brs in Bata and Malabo.

Development Banks

Banco de Fomento y Desarrollo (BFD): Malabo; f. 1998; 30% state-owned; cap. 50m.

Banque de Développement des Etats de l'Afrique Centrale: see Franc Zone (see p. 239).

Financial Institution

Caja Autónoma de Amortización de la Deuda Pública: Ministry of the Economy, Malabo; tel. (9) 31-05; fax (9) 32-05; management of state funds; Dir-Gen. Rafael Tun.

Trade and Industry

GOVERNMENT AGENCIES

Cámaras Oficiales Agrícolas de Guinea: Bioko and Bata; purchase of cocoa and coffee from indigenous planters, who are partially grouped in co-operatives.

Empresa General de Industria y Comercio (EGISCA): Malabo; f. 1986; parastatal body jtly operated with the French Société pour l'Organisation, l'Aménagement et le Développement des Industries Alimentaires et Agricoles (SOMDIA); import-export agency.

Oficina para la Cooperación con Guinea Ecuatorial (OCGE): Malabo; f. 1981; administers bilateral aid from Spain.

DEVELOPMENT ORGANIZATION

Sociedad Anónima de Desarrollo del Comercio (SOADECO-Guinée): Malabo; f. 1986; parastatal body jtly operated with the French Société pour l'Organisation, l'Aménagement et le Développement des Industries Alimentaires et Agricoles (SOMDIA); development of commerce.

CHAMBER OF COMMERCE

Cámara de Comercio, Agrícola y Forestal de Malabo: Apdo 51, Malabo; tel. (9) 23-43.

INDUSTRIAL AND TRADE ASSOCIATIONS

Guinea Ecuatorial de Petróleo (GEPetrol): Malabo; f. 2001; state-owned petroleum company.

INPROCAO: Malabo; production, marketing and distribution of cocoa.

Total Ecuatoguineana de Gestion (GE—Total): Malabo; f. 1984; 50% state-owned, 50% by CFP-Total (France); petroleum marketing and distribution; Chair. of Bd of Dirs Minister of Public Works, Housing and Urban Affairs.

Unión General de Empresas Privadas de la República de Guinea Ecuatorial (UGEPRIGE): Apdo 138, Malabo.

UTILITIES

Electricity

ENERGE: Malabo; state-owned electricity board.

TRADE UNIONS

A law permitting the establishment of trade unions was introduced in 1992.

Transport

RAILWAYS

There are no railways in Equatorial Guinea.

ROADS

In 1996 there were an estimated 2,880 km of roads and tracks.

Bioko: a semi-circular tarred road serves the northern part of the island from Malabo down to Batete in the west and from Malabo to Bacake Grande in the east, with a feeder road from Luba to Moka and Bahía de la Concepción.

Río Muni: a tarred road links Bata with the town of Mbini (Río Benito) in the west; another road, partly tarred, links Bata with the frontier post of Ebebiyín in the east and then continues into Gabon; other earth roads join Acurenam, Mongomo and Anisok.

SHIPPING

The main ports are Bata (general cargo and most of the country's export timber), Malabo (general), Luba (bananas, timber), Mbini and Cogo (timber).

CIVIL AVIATION

There are two international airports, at Malabo (Santa Isabel Airport) and Bata (the latter was completed with Italian aid in 1995). The national carrier, EGA—Ecuato Guineana de Aviación (which has been in liquidation since 1990), continues to provide limited regional and domestic services, as well as a weekly service to Madrid. Scheduled services between Malabo and Madrid are operated by IBERIA and Líneas Aéreas de España. Cameroon Airlines (CAM-AIR) carries passengers between Malabo and Douala (Cameroon). Air Afrique operates a cargo service linking Equatorial Guinea with West African destinations.

EGA—Ecuato Guineana de Aviación: Apdo 665, Malabo; tel. (9) 23-25; fax (9) 33-13; regional and domestic passenger and cargo services; Exec. Dir J. LOWA.

Tourism

Tourism remains undeveloped. Future interest in this sector would be likely to focus on the unspoilt beaches of Río Muni and Bioko's scenic mountain terrain.

ERITREA

Introductory Survey

Location, Climate, Language, Religion, Flag, Capital

The State of Eritrea, which has a coastline on the Red Sea extending for almost 1,000 km, is bounded to the north-west by Sudan, to the south and west by Ethiopia, and to the south-east by Djibouti. Its territory includes the Dahlak islands, a low-lying coralline archipelago off shore from Massawa. Rainfall is less than 500 mm per year in lowland areas, increasing to 1,000 mm in the highlands. The temperature gradient is similarly steep: average annual temperatures range from 17°C (63°F) in the highlands to 30°C (86°F) in Massawa. The Danakil depression in the south-east, which is more than 130 m below sea-level in places, experiences some of the highest temperatures recorded, frequently exceeding 50°C (122°F). The major language groups in Eritrea are Afar, Bilien, Hedareb, Kunama, Nara, Rashaida, Saho, Tigre and Tigrinya. English is rapidly becoming the language of business and is the medium of instruction at secondary schools and at university. Arabic is also widely spoken. The population is fairly evenly divided between Tigrinya-speaking Christians (mainly Orthodox), the traditional inhabitants of the highlands, and the Muslim communities of the western lowlands, northern highlands and east coast; there are also systems of traditional belief adhered to by a small number of the population. The national flag (proportions 1 by 2) consists of a red triangle with its base corresponding to the hoist and its apex at the centre of the fly, in which is situated, towards the hoist, an upright gold olive branch with six clusters of three leaves each, framed by a wreath of two gold olive branches; the remainder of the field is green at the top and light blue at the base. The capital is Asmara.

Recent History

The Treaty of Ucciali, which was signed in 1889 between Italy and Ethiopia, gave the Italian Government control over what is today the State of Eritrea. Italian exploitation of the colony continued until the defeat of the Axis powers by the Allied powers in East Africa during the Second World War. During 1941–52 Eritrea was under British administration. The Eritrean national identity, which was established during the Italian colonial period, was further subjugated under British rule. As the Allied powers and the UN discussed the future of the former Italian colony, Ethiopian territorial claims helped to foment a more militant nationalism among the Eritrean population. In 1952 a compromise agreement was reached, whereby a federation was formed between Eritrea and Ethiopia. However, the absence of adequate provisions for the creation of federal structures allowed Ethiopia to reduce Eritrea's status to that of an Ethiopian province by 1962.

Resistance to the Ethiopian annexation was first organized in the late 1950s, and in 1961 the Eritrean Liberation Front (ELF) launched an armed struggle. In the mid-1970s a reformist group broke away from the ELF and formed the Popular Liberation Forces (renamed the Eritrean People's Liberation Front, EPLF, in 1977), and the military confrontation with the Ethiopian Government began in earnest. A major consequence of the split between the two groups was the civil war of 1972–74. After two phases of desertion from the ELF to the EPLF, firstly in 1977–78 and secondly in 1985 (following a second civil war), the ELF was left without a coherent military apparatus.

Following the 1974 revolution in Ethiopia and the assumption of power by Mengistu Haile Mariam in 1977, thousands of new recruits joined the EPLF, and the armed struggle transformed into full-scale warfare. The numerically and materially superior Ethiopian forces achieved significant victories over the EPLF, and, following defeat in the highlands, the EPLF was forced to retreat to its stronghold in the north of Eritrea. The EPLF launched counter-attacks throughout the late 1980s and slowly drove back the Ethiopian forces on all fronts. By 1989 the EPLF had gained control of the north and the west of the country, and in late 1989 the EPLF captured Massawa port, thereby severing a major supply-route to the Ethiopian forces, who were by now besieged in Asmara. In May 1991 units of the EPLF entered Asmara, after the Ethiopian troops had fled, and immediately established an interim EPLF administration.

Following the liberation of Asmara by the EPLF, and of Addis Ababa by the Ethiopian People's Revolutionary Democratic Front (EPRDF), a conference was convened in London, United Kingdom, in August 1991. Representatives of the EPLF attended in a delegation separate from the EPRDF, now in control of Ethiopia and sympathetic to Eritrean national aspirations. Both the USA and the Ethiopian delegation accepted the EPLF administration as the legitimate provisional Government of Eritrea, and the EPLF agreed to hold a referendum on independence in 1993. The provisional Government, which was to administer Eritrea during the two years prior to the referendum, drew most of its members from the EPLF. The Government struggled to rehabilitate and develop Eritrea's war-torn economy and infrastructure, and to feed a population of whom 80% remained dependent on food aid. The agricultural sector had been severely disrupted by the war, and urban economic activity was almost non-existent. The Government was confronted by the additional problem of how to reintegrate some 750,000 refugees, of whom approximately 500,000 lived in Sudan, mostly at subsistence level.

At the UN-supervised referendum on independence, held in April 1993, 99.8% of Eritreans who voted endorsed national independence. The anniversary of the liberation of Asmara, 24 May, was proclaimed Independence Day, and on 28 May Eritrea formally attained international recognition. In June Eritrea was admitted to the Organization of African Unity (OAU, now the African Union). Following Eritrea's accession to independence, a four-year transitional period was declared, during which preparations were to proceed for establishing a constitutional and pluralist political system. At the apex of the transitional Government were three state institutions: the Consultative Council (the executive authority formed from the ministers, provincial administrators and heads of government authorities and commissions); the National Assembly (the legislative authority formed from the Central Committee of the EPLF, together with 30 members from the Provincial Assemblies and 30 individuals selected by the Central Committee); and the judiciary. One of the National Assembly's first acts was the election as Head of State of Issaias Afewerki, the Secretary-General of the EPLF, by a margin of 99 votes to five.

In February 1994 the EPLF transformed itself into a political party, the People's Front for Democracy and Justice (PFDJ). An 18-member Executive Committee and a 75-member Central Committee were elected; President Afewerki was elected Chairman of the latter. In March the National Assembly adopted a series of resolutions whereby the former executive body, the Consultative Council, was formally superseded by a State Council. Other measures adopted included the creation of a 50-member Constitutional Commission and the establishment of a committee charged with the reorganization of the country's administrative divisions. It was decided that the National Assembly would henceforth comprise the 75 members of the PFDJ Central Committee and 75 directly elected members. However, no mechanism was announced for their election. All but eight of the 50 members of the Constitutional Commission were government appointees, and there was no provision for any opposition participation in the interim system.

A draft constitution was discussed at international conventions held by the Constitutional Commission in July 1994 and January 1995, and more than 1,000 popular meetings took place in the first six months of 1995 to allow wider discussion of the proposed constitution. In May the National Assembly approved proposals to create six administrative regions to replace the 10 regional divisions that had been in place since colonial rule. In November the Assembly approved new names for the regions and finalized details of their exact boundaries and sub-divisions.

In early 1997 the Government established a Constituent Assembly, comprising 527 members (150 from the National Assembly, with the remainder selected from representatives of Eritreans residing abroad or elected by regional assemblies), to discuss and ratify the draft constitution. On 23 May the Constituent Assembly adopted the Constitution, authorizing 'conditional' political pluralism and instituting a presidential regime, with a President elected for a maximum of two five-year terms. The President, as Head of State, would appoint a Prime Minister and judges of the Supreme Court; his or her mandate could be revoked should two-thirds of the members of the National Assembly so demand. The Constituent Assembly was disbanded, and a Transitional National Assembly (consisting of the 75 members of the PFDJ Central Committee, 60 members of the Constituent Assembly and 15 representatives of Eritreans residing abroad) was empowered to act as the legislature until the holding of elections to a new National Assembly.

It was initially announced that Eritrea's first post-independence elections, which were scheduled to have been held in 1998, but were postponed indefinitely following the outbreak of hostilities with Ethiopia (see below), would take place in December 2001. However, during 2001 the likelihood of elections taking place in that year diminished, as President Afewerki assumed an increasingly authoritarian position. In February he dismissed the Minister of Local Government, Mahmoud Ahmed Sherifo, who had previously been given the responsibility for drafting a law on political parties, and dissolved the electoral commission, which Sherifo had been appointed to head. Sherifo had reportedly distributed copies of his findings directly to the members of the National Assembly and had failed to seek presidential approval for a press conference at which he intended to publicize his report. In June Afewerki replaced the Ministers of Trade and Industry and of Maritime Resources. They were among a group of 15 senior PFDJ officials, including 11 former government ministers, who, in May, had signed a letter publicly accusing Afewerki of working in an 'illegal and unconstitutional manner'. Nevertheless, dissent from within the ruling party continued, and in August the Chief Justice of the Supreme Court was dismissed after he openly expressed his disapproval of Afewerki's continued interference in court operations. In mid-September six of the G-15, as the 15 signatories of the letter criticizing Afewerki had become known, were arrested, and the Government announced the 'temporary suspension' of the independent press. A few days later a further five members of the G-15 were detained. The Government justified the arrests on the grounds that the 11 were involved in 'illegal activities which endangered the country', although it refused to specify the charges they would face. In early October the Eritrean authorities expelled the Italian ambassador after he expressed concern at recent events in Eritrea on behalf of the European Union. The Italian Government responded by expelling the Eritrean ambassador in Rome, and later that month Denmark, France, Germany and the Netherlands recalled their ambassadors from Eritrea for consultations. The four returned to their posts in Asmara in mid-November, although Italy initially refused to reinstate its ambassador. In June 2002 Italy and Eritrea resumed diplomatic contacts and, following a meeting between Afewerki and the Italian Prime Minister, Silvio Berlusconi, agreed to the return of both countries' ambassadors.

Although no formal postponement of the legislative elections was announced, the failure of the National Assembly to convene to ratify legislation on the electoral system and on political pluralism by December 2001 made further delay inevitable. In late January 2002 the National Assembly ratified the electoral law, but failed to set an election date and postponed the formation of political parties. Meanwhile, President Afewerki replaced the Ministers of Information, Tourism, and Transport and Communications in September, October and November 2001, respectively. In January 2002 dissident members of the ruling PFDJ, including several members of the G-15, announced the formation, in exile, of a new political party, the Eritrean People's Liberation Front—Democratic Party. Furthermore, during early 2002 numerous senior Eritrean diplomats resigned from their posts in protest at Afewerki's increasingly autocratic tendencies. In late May a senior member of the PFDJ stated that legislative elections would eventually take place, but was unable to confirm that they would be held before the end of the year. Indeed, by April 2003 no date had been established for the holding of elections.

External relations have proved problematic. The transitional Government has attempted to consolidate good relations with Eritrea's neighbours and to develop stronger links with the USA, the People's Republic of China and other major powers. However, the complexity of regional relations, and of Eritrea's position therein, became evident in July 1993, when President Afewerki had to counter allegations, made during a visit to Saudi Arabia, that Israel was establishing a military presence in Eritrea. The Eritrean Government is keen to maintain good relations with its Arab neighbours (one of which, namely Saudi Arabia, had previously provided support to the ELF), but not to the detriment of what it regards as important ties with Israel.

Relations between the transitional Government and Sudan, which had supported the EPLF during the war, deteriorated in December 1993, following an incursion by members of an Islamist group, the Eritrean Islamic Jihad (EIJ), into Eritrea from Sudan, during which all the members of the group, and an Eritrean army commander, were killed. In response to the incident, President Afewerki stressed the links between the EIJ and the Sudanese National Islamic Front, led by Dr Hassan at-Turabi, implying that the latter had prior knowledge of the incursion. However, following a swift denial by the Sudanese Government that it would interfere in the affairs of neighbouring states, Afewerki reaffirmed his support for the Sudanese authorities and his commitment to improving bilateral relations.

In August 1994 Eritrea and Sudan signed an agreement concerning borders, security and the repatriation of refugees, and in November the office of the UN High Commissioner for Refugees (UNHCR) initiated a repatriation programme for Eritrean refugees currently in Sudan. Some 500,000 Eritreans had taken refuge in Sudan in the early 1990s as a result of separatist conflicts, although by 1995 an estimated 125,000 had returned spontaneously, particularly following Eritrea's accession to independence.

Relations between Eritrea and Sudan deteriorated in November 1994, when the Eritrean authorities accused Sudan of training 400 terrorists since August. Sudan accused Eritrea of training some 3,000 Sudanese rebels in camps within Eritrea. In December Eritrea severed diplomatic relations with Sudan. Further destabilization was provoked in early 1995 by attacks and infiltration in Barka Province by commandos of the military wing of the EIJ. The Eritrean authorities subsequently claimed to have identified six training camps on the Sudanese side of the border and also alleged that large numbers of Eritrean refugees in Sudan had been arrested by Sudanese security forces. Sudan responded by proposing Eritrea's suspension from the Intergovernmental Authority on Drought and Development (IGADD, now the Intergovernmental Authority on Development—IGAD, see p. 242), which had been attempting to mediate in Sudan's civil war. The Sudanese Government protested strongly against Eritrea's growing support for the Sudanese opposition grouping, the National Democratic Alliance (NDA), which held conferences in Asmara in December 1994, June 1995 and January 1996. In February 1996 Eritrea granted Sudanese opposition leaders permission to use Sudan's embassy in Asmara as their headquarters. In May 1997 Eritrean security forces announced that they had foiled a plot by the Sudanese Government to assassinate President Afewerki. In February 1998 Sudan closed the border with Eritrea in an attempt to prevent incursions into Sudan. Further attacks on Sudanese forces by Eritrean troops were reported during 1998, including an alleged offensive in eastern Sudan in October. In November the Ministers of Foreign Affairs of the two countries attended a mediation meeting in Qatar, at the conclusion of which they signed a memorandum of understanding to normalize relations. Tensions remained, however, and mutual recriminations regarding border incidents continued.

In early 1999 Sudan took steps to resolve its differences with Ethiopia, thus increasing the tension between Eritrea and Sudan. In March the Alliance of Eritrean National Forces (AENF) was launched in Khartoum by 10 Eritrean opposition organizations, with Ethiopia's support. Shortly afterwards the AENF announced its intention to establish an Eritrean government-in-exile. In the following month, however, Sudan indicated its willingness also to improve relations with Eritrea, and in May a reconciliatory agreement was signed in Qatar, which, *inter alia*, restored diplomatic relations between the two countries. In June Sudan accused Eritrea of violating the agreement by allowing a Sudanese opposition group to hold a rally in Asmara. However, relations improved further after President Afewerki ordered Sudanese anti-Government activists occupying the Sudanese embassy building to cease political activities and to vacate the premises. In January 2000 President al-Bashir of Sudan visited Afewerki in Asmara, where they pledged further to improve bilateral relations between the two countries. Following the renewed outbreak of hostilities between Eritrea and Ethiopia in May (see below), some 94,000 Eritreans fleeing the Ethiopian advances crossed the border into Sudan. After the cessation of fighting in June, many Eritrean refugees were repatriated with the assistance of UNHCR; however, an estimated 174,000 refugees remained in Sudan in early 2001. In May the voluntary repatriation of some 62,000 Eritrean refugees commenced, and it was expected that the repatriation would be completed by late 2002. By January of that year some 36,500 Eritreans had returned to their home country. Meanwhile, during 2000 the Eritrean Government assumed a mediatory role in the conflict between the Sudanese Government and opposition groups based in Eritrea. In August 2000 the two countries exchanged ambassadors, and in September al-Bashir travelled to Asmara where he met with the leader of the opposition NDA for the first time since 1989. In July 2001 Eritrea and Sudan signed an agreement on border security, which aimed to eradicate smuggling and illegal infiltration, as well as ensure the safe passage of people and goods across the common border. In October 2002 relations between the two countries again deteriorated after the Sudanese Government claimed that Eritrean forces had been involved in the NDA's capture of Hanashkoreb in eastern Sudan. Although Eritrea strenuously denied any involvement in the incident, Sudan closed the countries' common border with immediate effect.

In November 1995 there were reports that Eritrean troops had attempted to land on the Red Sea island of Greater Hanish, one of three islands (the others being Lesser Hanish and Zuqar) claimed by both Eritrea and Yemen. The incursion had reportedly been provoked by Yemen's announced intention to develop Greater Hanish as a tourist resort, and its subsequent refusal to comply with an Eritrean demand that the island be evacuated. The disputed islands had been used by Eritrea (with apparent Yemeni approval) during its struggle for independence from Ethiopia. Yemen had subsequently resumed its claims to the islands, because of both their strategic importance (located close to a principal shipping lane) and the possible existence of exploitable petroleum reserves in their surrounding waters. Negotiations in Eritrea and Yemen failed to defuse the crisis, and in mid-December fighting erupted between the two sides, resulting in several deaths. Two days later Eritrea and Yemen agreed to a cease-fire, but fighting resumed on the following day, and Eritrean forces succeeded in occupying Greater Hanish. The cease-fire was adhered to thenceforth, and some 180 captured Yemeni soldiers were released at the end of the month. The Ethiopian and Egyptian Governments attempted, unsuccessfully, to promote an agreement, and in January 1996 France assumed the mediatory role. In May representatives of Eritrea and Yemen signed an arbitration accord in Paris, France, whereby the two sides agreed to submit the dispute to an international tribunal. France subsequently undertook to observe and supervise military movements in the area around the disputed islands. In August, despite the accord, Eritrean troops occupied Lesser Hanish; however, later in the month Eritrea withdrew its soldiers after mediation by France and a UN Security Council instruction to evacuate the island forthwith. In October Eritrea and Yemen confirmed that they would submit the dispute to an international tribunal. In October 1998 the tribunal ruled that Yemen had sovereignty over Greater and Lesser Hanish, and all islands to their north-west, while Eritrea had sovereignty over the Mohabaka islands. The court recommended that the fishing traditions around the islands be maintained, thereby granting access to the Hanish islands to Eritrean and Yemeni fishermen. Both countries accepted the ruling, and shortly afterwards agreed to establish a joint committee to strengthen bilateral co-operation. In July 2001 Eritrea accused Yemen of disregarding the tribunal ruling by fishing in Eritrean waters and temporarily detained more than 100 Yemeni fishermen and their vessels. The two countries subsequently agreed to establish a committee to examine the issue of fishing in their territorial waters.

In November 1995 Eritrea and Djibouti pledged to enhance bilateral co-operation, following a meeting between Eritrea's Minister of Foreign Affairs, Petros Solomon, and Djibouti's President Gouled. Nevertheless, relations between the two countries were strained in April 1996, when Gouled reportedly rejected a map (produced by Italy in 1935) submitted by Solomon, which apparently indicated that a 20-km strip of land claimed by Djibouti was, in fact, Eritrean territory. Meanwhile, Eritrea denied reports of an attempted occupation of a border post in Djibouti (within the disputed territory) by Eritrean troops. Relations between the two countries subsequently improved; however, in November 1998 Djibouti suspended diplomatic relations with Eritrea, following allegations by the Eritrean authorities that it was supporting Ethiopia in the Eritrea–Ethiopia border conflict (see below). The two countries re-established diplomatic relations in March 2000, following Libyan mediation.

In September 1993 the first meeting of the Ethiopian-Eritrean joint ministerial commission was held in Asmara, during which agreement was reached on measures to allow the free movement of nationals between each country, and on co-operation regarding foreign affairs and economic policy. Meetings held between President Afewerki and the Ethiopian President, Meles Zenawi, in December underlined the good relations prevailing between the two Governments.

Relations with Ethiopia deteriorated in late 1997, following Eritrea's adoption of a new currency (the nakfa) to replace the Ethiopian birr and the subsequent disruption of cross-border trade. In early May 1998 fighting erupted between Eritrean and Ethiopian troops in the border region after both countries accused the other of having invaded their territory. Hostilities escalated in June around Badme, Zalambessa and Assab, resulting in numerous casualties for both sides. A peace plan devised by the USA and Rwanda in early June was unsuccessful, although later that month Eritrea and Ethiopia agreed to an aerial cease-fire, following mediation by the USA and Italy. However, a UN Security Council resolution adopted later that month, demanding the immediate cessation of hostilities, was not adhered to. The OAU, meanwhile, established a mediation committee in an attempt to resolve the crisis, and in July an OAU delegation visited the two countries. In August the committee presented its report to the Ministers of Foreign Affairs of Eritrea and Ethiopia at an OAU meeting in Ouagadougou, Burkina Faso. The OAU proposals, which endorsed the US-Rwandan peace plan, were rejected by Eritrea, which maintained that it would not withdraw its troops from the disputed territory prior to negotiations. In November President Afewerki and Prime Minister Meles of Ethiopia were present at different sessions of a special meeting of the OAU mediation committee in Ouagadougou, which was also attended by the Heads of State of Burkina Faso, Zimbabwe and Djibouti. The committee's peace proposals, which again stressed the need to demilitarize and demarcate the disputed territory, were accepted by Ethiopia, but rejected by Eritrea. Eritrea, moreover, demanded that Djibouti withdraw from the committee, accusing it of providing assistance to Ethiopia in the conflict. Djibouti suspended diplomatic relations with Eritrea, in protest at the allegations. Other international mediation attempts in late 1998 (including that of Anthony Lake, a former US national security adviser) failed to resolve the dispute, and in February 1999 the aerial cease-fire was broken and intense fighting resumed in the border region. In April both sides claimed that they were now prepared to accept and implement the OAU peace proposals, and at the OAU summit held in Algiers, Algeria, in July they confirmed their commitment to the OAU's Framework Agreement. Afewerki announced that Eritrean troops would be withdrawn from all territory captured from Ethiopia since 6 May 1998. Under the agreement, Ethiopia was also required to withdraw from all Eritrean territory captured since 6 February 1999, which, in effect, would see both sides return to their positions before the war. The UN subsequently announced it would demarcate the border using maps drawn up by Italy in around 1900. After requesting clarification of technical arrangements to end the war, Ethiopia informed the OAU in September that it had rejected the peace agreement, owing to inconsistencies contained therein. Eritrea accused Ethiopia of attempting to buy time, while secretly preparing for a fresh offensive.

Throughout late 1999 and early 2000 there were reports of numerous clashes between Eritrean and Ethiopian troops, and both countries continued to promote and assist opposition groups hostile to their foe. In March, with severe drought once again threatening widespread famine in the Horn of Africa, the Eritrean authorities agreed to allow large quantities of food aid destined for Ethiopia to be transported through the port of Assab. It was reported in the Ethiopian press, however, that this offer had been rejected by the Ethiopian Government. In late April delegations from both countries agreed to attend OAU-sponsored talks in Algiers, although they refused to meet directly, forcing Algerian diplomats to act as mediators. After six days of negotiations the talks collapsed, with representatives from both sides blaming the other for the breakdown. In mid-May hostilities between the two countries broke out again; Ethiopia launched a major offensive near the disputed towns of Badme and Zalambessa and succeeded in repulsing the Eritrean forces. The UN Security Council immediately adopted a resolution providing for the imposition of sanctions and an embargo on the sale of all military supplies to the two warring countries, if fighting was not halted within three days. Nevertheless, hostilities continued, despite fears of a grave humanitarian crisis in the region, and the UN Security Council unanimously approved the imposition of a 12-month arms embargo on Eritrea and Ethiopia. Ethiopian forces continued to drive deeper into Eritrean territory, capturing the strategically important town of Barentu and taking control of the western front. By late May Ethiopian forces had seized Zalambessa and the Eritrean authorities had announced that they would withdraw troops from the disputed areas, although Afewerki maintained that this was merely a 'gesture of goodwill' designed to revive the peace talks, which resumed in Algiers on 29 May. Two days later the Ethiopian Prime Minister, Meles Zenawi, stated that the war was over and that his troops had withdrawn from most of the territory it had captured from Eritrea. However, despite the ongoing discussions in Algiers, fighting continued, with each side accusing the other of resuming hostilities. Following extensive negotiations in early June, both sides expressed their readiness, in principle, to accept the OAU's cease-fire agreement, and on 18 June the Ethiopian and Eritrean Ministers of Foreign Affairs signed an agreement, which provided for an immediate cease-fire and the deployment of a UN peace-keeping force in a 25-km temporary security zone (TSZ) inside Eritrea until the issue of the demarcation of the border had been settled. It was estimated that about 100,000 people had been killed and up to 1.5m. Eritreans displaced since the conflict had begun in 1998. Indirect negotiations to discuss the technical issues of the peace accord, involving representatives from both countries, took place in Washington, DC, USA, in early July and continued in Algiers in October. Meanwhile, in September the UN Security Council approved the deployment of the UN Mission in Ethiopia and Eritrea (UNMEE, see p. 65), a 4,200-strong peace-keeping force, which was placed under the command of the Special Representative of the UN Secretary-General, Legwaila Joseph Legwaila. On 12 December Eritrea and Ethiopia signed an agreement in Algiers, which formally ended the conflict between the two countries. The agreement provided for a permanent cessation of all hostilities, the immediate return of all prisoners of war, the demarcation of the common border by an independent commission and the establishment of a Claims Commission to assess the issues of compensation and reparations. Furthermore, both countries pledged to co-operate with an independent investigation, which aimed to determine the origins of the conflict.

By late January 2001 the UNMEE force had been fully deployed and began making provisions for the establishment of a TSZ in a 25-km area along the Ethiopia–Eritrea border. In early February it was agreed that Ethiopian troops would be redeployed to the southern boundary of the prospective TSZ by 26 February, and that Eritrea would complete the redeployment of its forces to the northern boundary by 3 March. On 22 February the Ethiopian Government notified UNMEE that it had completed the redeployment of its troops; UNMEE verified the withdrawal as complete on 7 March. However, at the fourth meeting of the Military Co-ordination Commission (MCC), in late February, the Eritrean delegation had registered its objections to adjustments made to the original boundaries of the future TSZ, on which agreement had been provisionally reached at a previous MCC meeting. The Eritrean authorities subsequently informed UNMEE that they had suspended the withdrawal of their forces. Furthermore, in March Legwaila announced that UNMEE was still not permitted to fly directly from Asmara to Addis Ababa, despite both countries' commitment, as part of the Algiers agreement, to ensure the peacekeeping force's freedom of movement. In mid-March UNMEE's mandate was extended until September, and in early April, following intensive negotiations, Eritrea recommenced the redeployment of its troops. Nevertheless, Eritrea reiterated its dissatisfaction regarding the southern boundary of the prospective TSZ. On 16 April it was announced that the withdrawal of Eritrea's forces was complete, and two days later UNMEE declared the establishment of the TSZ, marking the formal separation of the Eritrean and Ethiopian forces. However, the UN Security Council again expressed concern that UNMEE did not have complete freedom of movement in the region. In mid-May the UN lifted the arms embargo imposed in May 2000. In late June UNMEE presented the final map of the TSZ to Ethiopia and Eritrea, although it emphasized that it would not

influence the work of the neutral boundary commission charged with determining the border between the two countries. Despite this announcement, the Ethiopian Government expressed its dissatisfaction with the map. Also that month UNMEE again complained that Eritrea was refusing to grant unrestricted movement to its members, thus impeding its ability to undertake its duties effectively. At the eighth MCC meeting in August both countries reiterated their objections to the current boundaries of the TSZ. In mid-September UNMEE's mandate was extended for a further six months, although Legwaila acknowledged that the mission faced an extremely difficult task in achieving lasting peace, as the two countries remained 'polarized', and also admitted that neither country had fully adhered to the terms of the agreement on the cessation of hostilities. In mid-December the two countries began presenting their cases for border demarcation to the five-member border commission at the International Court of Justice at The Hague, Netherlands. In mid-March 2002 UNMEE's mandate was extended until mid-September.

The Boundary Commission delivered its findings in April 2002. Both Ethiopia and Eritrea had committed themselves in advance to the acceptance of the Commission's report. However, the Commission did not identify on which side of the boundary line Badme lay, stating that it was awaiting delineation on the ground, which was expected to take up to one year, as extensive demining was required prior to placing boundary markers. In the absence of any decision by the Boundary Commission, both countries immediately claimed to have been awarded Badme. When UNMEE invited journalists to visit Badme in late April by entering through Eritrea, Ethiopia reacted by closing the border to UNMEE and demanding the removal of the UNMEE commander, Maj.-Gen. Patrick Cammaert. The border was reopened to UN personnel in early May. Later that month Ethiopia formally requested 'interpretation, correction and consultation' of the Boundary Commission's report, but this was rejected by the Commission in late June.

In early March 2003 the Border Commission reported to the UN Security Council that Ethiopia's requests for changes to the border ruling, in order to 'take better account of human and physical geography', threatened to undermine the peace process as a whole. Despite Ethiopia's claims that it had been promised that demarcations could be refined, later in March the Boundary Commission categorically ruled Badme to be Eritrean territory.

The repatriation of prisoners of war began in December 2000. By October 2001 856 Eritrean and 653 Ethiopian prisoners of war had been repatriated; however, it was reported that some 400 prisoners of war remained in Eritrea, and an estimated 1,800 Eritreans were still being held in Ethiopia. In November 2002 it was announced that Ethiopia had released all Eritrean prisoners of war and that their repatriation had commenced. All Ethiopian prisoners of war had been released in August. Other difficulties remained for the Eritrean authorities, primarily the need to repatriate the vast numbers of Eritreans who had been displaced during the conflict and the severe food shortages still affecting the nation, with relief agencies estimating that more than 1m. Eritreans (about one-quarter of the population) required food aid.

Government

In May 1991 the Eritrean People's Liberation Front (EPLF, restyled as the People's Front for Democracy and Justice—PFDJ —in February 1994) established a provisional Government to administer Eritrea, pending the holding of a national referendum on the issue of independence. The EPLF did not invite other organizations to participate, although it promised that free elections would be held following the referendum. The referendum was held in April 1993, and Eritrea was proclaimed an independent state in the following month. A transitional Government was established, at the apex of which were three state institutions: the Consultative Council (the executive authority formed from the ministers, provincial administrators and heads of government authorities and commissions); the National Assembly (the legislative authority comprising the Central Committee of the EPLF, 30 additional members from the Provincial Assemblies and 30 individuals selected by the Central Committee); and the judiciary. In March 1994 the Consultative Council was superseded by a State Council. At independence a four-year transitional period was declared, during which preparations were to proceed for the establishment of a constitutional and pluralist political system. Meanwhile, in March 1994 the National Assembly voted to alter its composition: it would thenceforth comprise the 75 members of the PFDJ Central Committee and 75 directly elected members. In May 1997, following the adoption of the Constitution, the Constituent Assembly empowered a Transitional National Assembly (comprising the 75 members of the PFDJ Central Committee, 60 members of the former Constituent Assembly and 15 representatives of Eritreans residing abroad) to act as the legislature until elections were held for a new National Assembly.

Defence

Eritrea's armed forces increased rapidly during the 1999–2000 border conflict with Ethiopia and in August 2002, despite the cessation of hostilities in June 2000, were estimated to number 172,200, including an army of about 170,000 (of which some 60,000 were scheduled to be demobilized), a navy of 1,400 and an air force of about 800. In July 2000 the UN Security Council adopted a resolution (No. 1312) establishing the UN Mission in Ethiopia and Eritrea (UNMEE, see p. 65), which was to supervise the cease-fire and the implementation of a peace agreement. At the end of August 2002 UNMEE numbered 4,154 uniformed personnel, including 214 military observers. National service is compulsory for all Eritrean citizens between 18 and 40 years of age (with certain exceptions), for a 16-month period, including four months of military training. Defence expenditure in 2000 was estimated at US $360m.

Economic Affairs

In 2001, according to estimates by the World Bank, Eritrea's gross national income (GNI), measured at average 1999–2001 prices, was US $792m., equivalent to $190 per head (or $970 per head on an international purchasing-power parity basis). During 1992–2001, it was estimated, the population increased at an average annual rate of 2.7% per year, while gross domestic product (GDP) per head declined, in real terms, by an average of 0.2% in per year. Overall GDP increased, in real terms, at an average annual rate of 2.4% in 1992–2001; it declined by 10.9% in 2000, but increased by 5.1% in 2001.

By far the most important sector of the economy is agriculture, which, despite a reduction in food production of roughly 40% between 1980 and 1990, still sustains 90% of the population. In 1999 agricultural production (including forestry and fishing) accounted for an estimated 16.0% of GDP. In 2001 the sector employed an estimated 77.2% of the economically active population. Most sedentary agriculture is practised in the highlands, where rainfall is sufficient to cultivate the main crops: teff (an indigenous grain), sorghum, millet, barley and wheat. The effects of successive crop failures in 1999 and 2000 were exacerbated by the outbreak of hostilities between Eritrea and Ethiopia, and in early 2002 it was estimated that more than 30% of the population was critically dependent on food aid. Although fishing activity is on a very small scale, the total catch increased considerably in the first half of the 1990s, reaching 3,267 metric tons in 1996. The total catch subsequently declined, but had risen to 12,612 tons by 2000. According to the UN, sustainable yields of as much as 70,000 tons per year may be possible.

As a result of serious environmental degradation (caused directly and indirectly by the war of independence), water scarcity and unreliable rainfall, projects have been undertaken to build water reservoirs and small dams, while badly eroded hillsides have been terraced and new trees planted in order to prevent soil erosion. Since 1994 several international organizations have granted loans for the development of the agricultural sector.

Eritrea's industrial base traditionally centred on the production of glass, cement, footwear and canned goods, but most industrial enterprises were badly damaged during the war of independence. In 1999 industrial production (comprising mining, manufacturing, construction and utilities) accounted for an estimated 27.3% of GDP. Some 5.0% of the labour force were employed in the industrial sector in 1990. Although some of the 42 public-sector factories—producing textiles, footwear, beverages and other light industrial goods—were operating in 1991, they were doing so at only one-third of capacity. By 1995 production had increased considerably, mostly as a result of substantial government aid. The Government has calculated that the cost of industrial recovery would be US $20m. for the private sector and $66m. for the state sector.

The manufacturing sector provided an estimated 13.9% of GDP in 1999. Until mid-1997 imported petroleum was processed at the Assab refinery, whose entire output of petroleum products was delivered to Ethiopia. The authorities announced that they would import refined petroleum for the immediate future. Eritrea purchases its own petroleum requirements from Ethiopia under a quota arrangement; however, trade between the two countries was disrupted by the outbreak of hostilities in May 1998.

Eritrea's mineral resources are believed to be of significant potential value, although in 1999 mining and quarrying accounted for only 0.1% of GDP. Of particular importance, in view of Eritrea's acute energy shortage, is the possibility of large reserves of petroleum and natural gas beneath the Red Sea. Production-sharing agreements for the exploration of petroleum and gas were signed with the Anadarko Petroleum Corpn of the USA in 1995 and 1997. However, Anadarko's first three deep drills were dry, and in May 1999 the company began reducing operations by removing most of its operational staff. Other mineral resources include potash, zinc, magnesium, copper, iron ore, marble and gold. New legislation on mining, adopted in 1995, declared all mineral resources to be state assets, but recognized an extensive role for private investors in their exploitation.

Most electric energy is provided by four thermal power stations, largely dependent on fuel imported from Ethiopia. Imports of fuel and energy comprised an estimated 8.9% of the total cost of imports in 2000. However, electricity is provided to only some 10% of the population, the remainder relying on fuelwood and animal products. In 1994 the Kuwait Fund for Arab Economic Development allocated US $158m. for improvements in electricity production and distribution. In mid-1999 the discovery of geothermal potential at the Alid volcanic centre raised hopes that Eritrea's energy problems could be alleviated.

The services sector contributed an estimated 56.6% of GDP in 1999. The dominant services are trade, public administration and transport.

In 1999, according to estimates by the IMF, Eritrea recorded a trade deficit of US $480.7m., and there was a deficit of $166.8m. on the current account of the balance of payments. In 1998 the principal sources of non-petroleum imports were Italy (accounting for 17.4% of the total), the United Arab Emirates (16.2%) and Germany (5.7%). Exports in that year were mostly to Sudan (27.2%) and Ethiopia (26.5%). The principal exports to these countries were crude materials (45.5% of the total), food and live animals, and basic manufactures. The main non-petroleum imports were machinery and transport equipment (38.3% of the total), basic manufactures, and food and live animals.

In 1999 it was estimated that Eritrea's budget deficit reached 2,551.9m. nakfa, equivalent to 43.8% of GDP. Eritrea's external debt at the end of 2000 totalled US $311.1m., of which $298.0m. was long-term public debt. The cost of debt-servicing represented 1.1% of the value of exports of goods and services in that year. The annual rate of inflation averaged 6.4% in 1995–99. Consumer prices increased by an average of 7.0% in 1998 and by 8.3% in 1999. Unemployment and underemployment are estimated to affect as many as 50% of the labour force.

In 1993 Eritrea was admitted to the group of African, Caribbean and Pacific (ACP) countries party to the Lomé Convention; in September 2001 Eritrea ratified the Cotonou Agreement (see p. 234), the successor of the Lomé Convention. Eritrea became a member of the IMF in 1994.

Since Eritrea achieved independence, the establishment of a strong market-based economy has been a government priority. Under a Recovery and Rehabilitation Programme, commenced in 1993 and funded by a series of loans on concessionary terms, emphasis was placed on improving agricultural productivity, promoting export-orientated industries, developing financial and tourism services, and restructuring the public administration. In November 1997 the Government introduced the nakfa as the national currency (Eritrea had retained the Ethiopian birr as its monetary unit since independence), initially at par with the birr. However, the adoption of the new currency led to tensions with Ethiopia, adversely affecting cross-border trade, and, following the outbreak of hostilities in May 1998, Ethiopia re-routed its maritime commerce via Djibouti. The conflict, which ended in December 2000, had a devastating effect on the Eritrean economy. Trade with Ethiopia, which previously accounted for two-thirds of Eritrean exports, virtually ceased, and Eritrea was estimated to have spent at least US $1m. per day on the war. This expenditure, coupled with the failure of successive harvests, increased Eritrea's already considerable reliance on donations from aid organizations, and the need to feed, clothe and shelter the vast numbers of people displaced during the war has placed a further strain on government finances. The planned demobilization of large numbers of the

Eritrean armed forces was slow to proceed, and President Afewerki's increasingly repressive tendencies during the early 2000s resulted in the cancellation and suspension of valuable development funding on which the country is heavily dependent. Indeed, the potential loss was estimated to total some $400m. Eritrea suffered severe food shortages in early 2003, when it was estimated that more than 1.4m. Eritreans were in need of food aid; the situation was expected to worsen considerably throughout the year, with agricultural production predicted to decrease by up to 70% from 2001 levels.

Education

Education is provided free of charge in government schools and at the University of Asmara. There are also some fee-paying private schools. Education is officially compulsory for children between seven and 13 years of age. Primary education begins at the age of seven and lasts for five years. Secondary education, beginning at 12 years of age, lasts for up to six years, comprising a first cycle of two years and a second of four years. In 1996 the total enrolment at primary and secondary schools was equivalent to 37% of the school-age population (males 41%; females 33%). In 1999/2000 primary enrolment included 40.3% of children in the relevant age-group (males 43.3%; females 37.4%),

while the comparable ratio for secondary enrolment was only 22.5% (males 25.0%; females 20.1%). Government expenditure on education and training in 1998 was 253.4m. nakfa (6.6% of total spending). In 1997 there were 3,096 students enrolled at the University of Asmara or at equivalent level institutions.

Public Holidays

2003: 1 January (New Year's Day), 6 January (Epiphany), 12 February* (Id al-Adha/Arafat), 24 May (Independence Day), 20 June (Martyrs' Day), 1 September (anniversary of the start of the armed struggle), 26 November* (Id al-Fitr, end of Ramadan), 25 December (Christmas).

2004: 1 January (New Year's Day), 6 January (Epiphany), 2 February* (Id al-Adha/Arafat), 24 May (Independence Day), 20 June (Martyrs' Day), 1 September (anniversary of the start of the armed struggle), 14 November* (Id al-Fitr, end of Ramadan), 25 December (Christmas).

* These holidays are dependent on the Islamic lunar calendar and may vary by one or two days from the dates given.

Weights and Measures

The metric system is in force.

Statistical Survey

Source (unless otherwise stated): Ministry of Trade and Industry, POB 1844, Asmara; tel. (1) 118386; fax (1) 120586.

Area and Population

AREA, POPULATION AND DENSITY*

Area (sq km)	121,144†
Population (census results)	
9 May 1984	
Males	1,374,452
Females	1,373,852
Total	2,748,304
Population (UN estimates at mid-year)‡	
1999	3,524,000
2000	3,659,000
2001	3,816,000
Density (per sq km) at mid-2001	31.5

* Including the Assab district.
† 46,774 sq miles.
‡ Source: UN, *World Population Prospects: The 2000 Revision.*

PRINCIPAL TOWNS

(estimated population at January 2003)

Asmara (capital)	400,000	Keren	38,000
Assab	56,300	Mitsiwa	30,700

Source: Stefan Helders, *World Gazetteer* (internet www.world-gazetteer.com).

BIRTHS AND DEATHS

(UN estimates, averages per year)

	1985–90	1990–95	1995–2000
Birth rate (per 1,000)	44.8	43.3	40.9
Death rate (per 1,000)	17.0	15.3	14.0

Source: UN, *World Population Prospects: The 2000 Revision.*

Expectation of life (WHO estimates, years at birth): 53.6 (males 53.6; females 55.0) in 2001 (Source: WHO, *World Development Report*).

Health and Welfare

KEY INDICATORS

Total fertility rate (children per woman, 2001)	5.4
Under-5 mortality rate (per 1,000 live births, 2001)	111
HIV/AIDS (% of persons aged 15–49, 2001)	2.80
Physicians (per 1,000 head, 1996)	0.03
Health expenditure (2000): US $ per head (PPP)	16
Health expenditure (2000): % of GDP	4.3
Health expenditure (2000): public (% of total)	65.6
Access to water (% of persons, 2000)	46
Access to sanitation (% of persons, 2000)	13
Human Development Index (2000): ranking	157
Human Development Index (2000): value	0.421

For sources and definitions, see explanatory note on p. vi.

Agriculture

PRINCIPAL CROPS

('000 metric tons)

	1999	2000	2001
Wheat	27.5	42.6	25.4
Barley	31.8	25.9	44.9
Maize	15.9	14.0*	9.3*
Millet	17.8	15.0*	18.2
Sorghum	207.2	62.0	78.8
Potatoes*	40.0	40.0	40.0
Other roots and tubers*	87.0	85.0	85.0
Dry beans	3.0	1.4	4.0
Dry broad beans*	2.0	1.8	1.8
Dry peas	1.8*	1.7	1.1
Chick-peas	2.8	3.0	8.2
Lentils*	4.0	3.0	3.0
Vetches*	5.0	5.0	5.0
Other pulses*	32.0	32.0	32.0
Groundnuts (in shell)	2.2†	1.3*	1.4*
Sesame seed*	4.2	4.0	4.0
Linseed	0.3	0.2	0.6
Vegetables*	29.0	28.0	28.0
Fruits and berries*	4.5	3.8	3.8

* FAO estimate(s).
† Unofficial figure.

Source: FAO.

LIVESTOCK

(FAO estimates, '000 head, year ending September)

	1999	2000	2001
Cattle	2,100	2,200	2,200
Sheep	1,570	1,570	1,570
Goats	1,700	1,700	1,700
Camels	75	75	75
Poultry	1,200	1,200	1,300

Source: FAO.

LIVESTOCK PRODUCTS

(FAO estimates, '000 metric tons)

	1999	2000	2001
Beef and veal	16.0	16.4	16.9
Mutton and lamb	5.7	5.7	5.7
Goat meat	5.8	5.8	5.8
Poultry meat	1.8	1.9	1.9
Camels' milk	5.1	5.1	5.1
Cows' milk	49.0	50.0	52.0
Goats' milk	8.5	8.5	8.5
Sheep's milk	3.9	3.9	3.9
Hen eggs	1.7	1.7	1.7
Wool: greasy	0.8	0.8	0.8
Wool: scoured	0.4	0.4	0.4
Cattle hides	3.1	3.2	3.2
Sheepskins	0.6	0.6	0.6
Goatskins	0.7	0.7	0.7

Source: FAO.

Fishing

(metric tons, live weight)

	1998	1999	2000
Lizardfishes	—	1,905	3,177
Sea catfishes	149	205	851
Groupers	67	257	378
Snappers	294	365	149
Threadfin breams	—	1,674	1,757
Grunts and sweetlips	45	594	536
Emperors (Scavengers)	104	371	443
Barracudas	57	150	684
Carangids	184	386	2,026
Narrow-barred Spanish mackerel	210	250	217
Tuna-like fishes	111	64	42
Penaeus shrimps	9	75	519
Total catch (incl. others)	1,629	6,891	12,612

Source: FAO, *Yearbook of Fishery Statistics*.

Mining

('000 metric tons, unless otherwise indicated)

	1998	1999*	2000*
Gold (kilograms)	573	570	500
Marble	200*	200	100
Limestone	4	4	4
Salt	114	114	100

* Estimates.

Source: US Geological Survey.

Finance

CURRENCY AND EXCHANGE RATES

Monetary Units

100 cents = 1 nakfa

Sterling, Dollar and Euro Equivalents (31 December 2002)

£1 sterling = 21.84 nakfa

US $1 = 13.55 nakfa

€1 = 14.21 nakfa

1,000 nakfa = £45.79 = $73.80 = €70.37

Note: Following its secession from Ethiopia in May 1993, Eritrea retained the Ethiopian currency, the birr. An exchange rate of US $1 = 5.000 birr was introduced in October 1992 and remained in force until April 1994, when it was adjusted to $1 = 5.130 birr. Further adjustments were made subsequently. In addition to the official exchange rate, the Bank of Eritrea applied a marginal auction rate (determined at fortnightly auctions of foreign exchange, conducted by the National Bank of Ethiopia) to aid-funded imports and to most trasactions in services. A more depreciated preferential rate applied to remittances of foreign exchange by Eritreans abroad, to proceeds from exports and to most payments for imports. On 1 April 1997 Eritrea unified the official and preferential exchange rates at $1 = 7.20 birr (which had been the preferential rate since January 1996). In November 1997 the Government introduced a separate national currency, the nakfa, replacing (and initially at par with) the Ethiopian birr. The exchange rate in relation to the US dollar was initially set at the prevailing unified rate, but from 1 May 1998 a mechanism to provide a market-related exchange rate was established.

BUDGET

(million birr/nakfa)

Revenue*	1997	1998	1999†
Tax revenue	959.4	976.9	982.5
Direct taxes	447.9	512.3	474.9
Taxes on personal income	117.2	128.0	132.5
Taxes on business profits	292.9	334.1	291.4
Rehabilitation tax	18.1	17.5	12.6
Domestic sales tax (incl. stamp duties)	212.8	198.5	243.3
Import duties and taxes	298.7	266.1	264.3
Port fees and charges	444.3	99.7	104.7
Other current revenue	619.1	499.5	361.8
Extraordinary revenue	—	175.3	251.1
Capital revenue	20.0	149.1	122.7
Total	2,042.8	1,900.5	1,822.9

Expenditure	1996	1997	1998
Current expenditure	1,883.3	1,445.5	2,336.7
General services	1,233.1	886.0	1,776.3
Internal affairs	74.7	56.6	21.1
Regional administration .	40.6	55.5	161.8
Foreign affairs	77.1	84.5	88.4
Defence‡	968.1	634.2	1,458.8
Economic services	186.4	140.8	66.3
Agriculture and natural resources	15.4	32.8	36.0
Mining and energy . . .	5.5	4.0	3.3
Construction and urban development . . .	61.8	9.7	3.0
Transport and communications . . .	85.4	85.0	12.8
Social services	188.0	279.5	323.0
Education and training. .	70.7	139.3	159.2
Health	56.0	81.1	99.4
Demobilization of ex-combatants	14.0	—	—
Capital expenditure	838.2	1,143.3	1,495.5
General services	163.9	99.6	188.3
Economic development . .	471.4	709.7	1,056.5
Agriculture and natural resources	256.1	180.6	410.6
Trade, industry and tourism .	35.0	83.1	76.7
Construction, transport and communications . . .	73.6	242.1	370.8
Social development	202.9	334.0	250.7
Education	49.3	99.3	94.2
Health	87.7	55.0	72.8
Total	2,721.5	2,588.8	3,832.2

* Excluding grants received (million birr/nakfa): 290.5 in 1997 (current 32.7, capital 257.8); 458.4 in 1998 (current 32.4, capital 426.0); 376.7 (preliminary) in 1999 (current 125.5, capital 251.2).
† Provisional figures.
‡ Including some demobilization costs.

1999: Total expenditure (million birr/nakfa, provisional): 4,628.7 (current 2,644.3, capital 1,984.4).

Source: IMF, *Eritrea: Statistical Appendix* (April 2000).

MONEY SUPPLY
(million birr/nakfa at 31 December)

	1996	1997	1998
Demand deposits at banks . . .	1,670.9	1,597.9	1,808.7

Source: IMF, *Eritrea: Statistical Appendix* (April 2000).

COST OF LIVING
(Consumer Price Index; base: 1995 = 100)

	1997	1998	1999
All items	110.8	118.6	128.4

Source: African Development Bank.

NATIONAL ACCOUNTS
(million birr/nakfa at current prices)

Gross Domestic Product by Economic Activity

	1997	1998	1999*
Agriculture, forestry and fishing .	390.3	734.9	853.6
Mining and quarrying . . .	4.5	3.8	4.7
Manufacturing†	656.0	644.7	741.2
Electricity and water . . .	65.1	71.7	84.0
Construction	515.4	530.5	624.9
Wholesale and retail trade . .	1,134.1	991.2	1,139.4
Transport and communications .	488.9	472.1	542.7
Financial services	85.7	97.6	114.4
Dwellings and domestic services .	103.7	115.8	135.1
Public administration and services	706.8	844.2	1,014.4
Other services	50.8	56.8	66.5
GDP at factor cost	4,201.4	4,563.4	5,320.7
Indirect taxes, *less* subsidies .	511.5	464.6	507.6
GDP in purchasers' values .	4,712.9	5,028.0	5,828.3

* Preliminary figures.
† Including handicrafts and small-scale industry.

Source: IMF, *Eritrea: Statistical Appendix* (April 2000).

BALANCE OF PAYMENTS
(US $ million)

	1997	1998	1999*
Exports of goods f.o.b.	53.5	27.9	26.3
Imports of goods c.i.f.	−494.6	−526.8	−506.9
Trade balance	−441.1	−498.9	−480.7
Exports of services	149.8	80.8	73.6
Imports of services	−94.4	−70.0	−55.2
Balance on goods and services	−385.7	−488.1	−462.3
Other income (net)	−3.4	4.4	3.4
Balance on goods, services and income	−389.1	−483.7	−458.9
Private unrequited transfers (net)	352.1	245.4	240.2
Official unrequited transfers (net)	51.4	62.9	51.9
Current balance	14.4	−175.4	−166.8
Direct investment (net) . . .	38.7	31.7	36.0
Official long-term capital (net) .	28.9	65.5	83.3
Portfolio investment (net). . .	—	3.1	16.4
Short-term capital (net) . . .	−142.7	−89.7	−39.1
Net errors and omissions . . .			
Overall balance	−60.7	−164.8	8.0

* Preliminary figures.

Source: IMF, *Eritrea: Statistical Appendix* (April 2000).

External Trade

PRINCIPAL COMMODITIES
(million birr/nakfa)

Imports c.i.f. (excl. petroleum)	1996	1997	1998
Food and live animals . . .	542.9	599.9	460.1
Crude materials (inedible) except fuels	116.5	67.7	43.7
Chemicals and related products .	209.7	182.8	152.2
Basic manufactures	733.8	678.5	642.4
Machinery and transport equipment	1,091.1	1,158.2	1,030.1
Miscellaneous manufactured articles	250.8	242.7	231.4
Total (incl. others)	3,062.8	3,062.0	2,693.0

Exports f.o.b.	1996	1997	1998
Food and live animals . . .	92.4	81.3	58.3
Beverages and tobacco . . .	26.2	8.9	0.2
Crude materials (inedible) except fuels	123.0	129.5	89.6
Basic manufactures	88.3	64.3	26.1
Machinery and transport equipment	27.7	10.8	4.7
Miscellaneous manufactured articles	146.6	70.9	13.8
Total (incl. others)	520.4	375.3	196.9

Source: IMF, *Eritrea: Statistical Appendix* (April 2000).

PRINCIPAL TRADING PARTNERS
(million birr/nakfa)

Imports c.i.f. (excl. petroleum)	1996	1997	1998
Belgium	84.1	26.8	47.3
Djibouti	78.6	79.0	57.3
Ethiopia	261.8	274.6	25.0
Germany	217.0	168.4	152.7
Italy	429.1	420.1	469.8
Japan	111.2	125.5	107.1
Korea, Repub.	126.0	—	118.4
Netherlands	49.4	51.2	60.1
Saudi Arabia	465.6	480.2	15.4
Sudan	97.9	20.3	22.0
United Arab Emirates . . .	365.9	402.0	436.8
United Kingdom	68.5	142.1	120.5
USA	83.1	96.4	113.9
Total (incl. others)	3,062.9	3,062.2	2,693.1

Exports f.o.b.	1996	1997	1998
Ethiopia	342.4	238.1	52.2
Italy	22.3	18.3	10.4
Japan	—	—	26.0
Saudi Arabia	20.0	7.3	2.3
Sudan	51.5	62.3	53.5
USA	39.9	3.2	4.0
Total (incl. others)	520.4	375.3	196.9

Source: IMF, *Eritrea: Statistical Appendix* (April 2000).

Transport

ROAD TRAFFIC
(motor vehicles in use)

	1996	1997	1998
Number of registered vehicles	27,013	31,276	35,942

SHIPPING

Merchant Fleet
(registered at 31 December)

	1999	2000	2001
Number of vessels	10	10	12
Displacement (grt)	15,913	15,913	20,686

Source: Lloyd's Register-Fairplay, *World Fleet Statistics*.

CIVIL AVIATION

	1996	1997	1998
Passengers ('000)	168.1	173.8	105.2

Tourism

ARRIVALS BY NATIONALITY

	1998	1999	2000
Belgium, Luxembourg and Netherlands	534	269	1,435
Ethiopia	117,087	73	35
Italy	2,570	1,360	1,691
Japan	178	1,256	1,214
Sudan	848	2,813	2,875
USA	1,749	665	1,464
Total (incl. others)	187,647	56,699	70,355

Source: World Tourism Organization, *Yearbook of Tourism Statistics*.

Tourism receipts (US $ million): 34 in 1998; 28 in 1999; 36 in 2000 (Source: World Tourism Organization).

Communications Media

	1999	2000	2001
Television receivers ('000 in use)	60	100	n.a.
Telephones ('000 main lines in use)	27.4	30.6	32.0
Facsimile machines (number in use)	1,660	1,771	n.a.
Personal computers ('000 in use)	5.6	6.2	7
Internet users ('000)	0.9	5.0	10.0

Radio receivers ('000 in use): 345 in 1997.

Book production (1993): 106 titles (including 23 pamphlets) and 420,000 copies (including 60,000 pamphlets). Figures for books, excluding pamphlets, refer only to school textbooks (64 titles; 323,000 copies) and government publications (19 titles; 37,000 copies).

Sources: mainly UNESCO, *Statistical Yearbook*; International Telecommunication Union.

Education

(1996/97)

	Institutions	Teachers	Pupils
Pre-primary	61	207	7,443
Primary	549	5,476	240,737
Secondary: General	n.a.	1,959	88,054
Secondary: Teacher-training	n.a.	33	359
Secondary: Vocational	n.a.	79	674
University and equivalent level*	n.a.	198	3,096

* Figures refer to 1997/98.

Source: UNESCO, *Statistical Yearbook*.

Adult literacy rate (UNESCO estimates): 55.7% (males 67.3%; females 44.5%) in 2000 (Source: UN Development Programme, *Human Development Report*).

Directory

The Constitution

On 23 May 1997 the Constituent Assembly unanimously adopted the Eritrean Constitution. A presidential regime was instituted, with the President to be elected for a maximum of two five-year terms. The President, as Head of State, has extensive powers and appoints, with the approval of the National Assembly (the legislature), the ministers, the commissioners, the Auditor-General, the President of the central bank and the judges of the Supreme Court. The President's mandate can be revoked if two-thirds of the members of the National Assembly so demand. 'Conditional' political pluralism is authorized. Pending the election of a new National Assembly, legislative power was to be held by a Transitional National Assembly, comprising the 75 members of the PFDJ Central Committee, 60 members of the former Constituent Assembly and 15 representatives of Eritreans residing abroad.

The Government

HEAD OF STATE

President: ISSAIAS AFEWERKI (assumed power May 1991; elected President by National Assembly 8 June 1993).

CABINET
(April 2003)

President: ISSAIAS AFEWERKI.

Minister of Defence: Gen. SEBHAT EPHREM.

Minister of Justice: FAWZIA HASHIM.

Minister of Foreign Affairs: ALI SAYYID ABDULLAH.

Minister of Information: NAIZGHI KIFLU.

Minister of Finance: BERHANE ABREHE.

Minister of Trade and Industry: Dr GIORGIS TEKLEMIKAEL.

Minister of Agriculture: AREFAINE BERHE.

Minister of Labour and Human Welfare: ASKALU MENKERIOS.

Minister of Marine Resources: AHMED HAJI ALI.

Minister of Construction: ABRAHA ASFAHA.

Minister of Energy and Mines: TESFAI GEBRESELASSIE.

Minister of Education: OSMAN SALIH MUHAMMAD.

Minister of Health: Dr SALIH MEKKI.

Minister of Transport and Communications: WOLDEMIKAEL ABRAHA.

Minister of Tourism: AMNA NUR HUSAYN.

Minister of Land, Water and the Environment: TESFAI GHIRMAZION.

MINISTRIES AND COMMISSIONS

Office of the President: POB 257, Asmara; tel. (1) 122132; fax (1) 125123.

Ministry of Agriculture: POB 1048, Asmara; tel. (1) 181499; fax (1) 181415.

Ministry of Construction: POB 841, Asmara; tel. (1) 119077; fax (1) 120661.

Ministry of Defence: POB 629, Asmara; tel. (1) 115493; fax (1) 124920.

Ministry of Education: POB 5610, Asmara; tel. (1) 113044; fax (1) 113866.

Ministry of Energy and Mines: POB 5285, Asmara; tel. (1) 116872; fax (1) 127652.

Ministry of Finance: POB 896, Asmara; tel. (1) 118131; fax (1) 127947.

Ministry of Marine Resources: POB 923, Asmara; tel. (1) 114271; fax (1) 112185.

Ministry of Foreign Affairs: POB 190, Asmara; tel. (1) 127838; fax (1) 123788; e-mail tesfai@wg.eol.

Ministry of Health: POB 212, Asmara; tel. (1) 117549; fax (1) 112899.

Ministry of Information: POB 242, Asmara; tel. (1) 117111; fax (1) 124647.

Ministry of Justice: POB 241, Asmara; tel. (1) 127739; fax (1) 126422.

Ministry of Labour and Human Welfare: POB 5252, Asmara; tel. (1) 181846; fax (1) 181649; e-mail mlhw@eol.com.er.

Ministry of Land, Water and the Environment: POB 976, Asmara; tel. (1) 118021; fax (1) 123285.

Ministry of Local Government: POB 225, Asmara; tel. (1) 127734.

Ministry of Tourism: POB 1010, Asmara; tel. (1) 126997; fax (1) 126949; e-mail ona@eol.com.er.

Ministry of Trade and Industry: POB 1844, Asmara; tel. (1) 118386; fax (1) 110586.

Ministry of Transport and Communications: POB 6465, Asmara; tel. (1) 123681; fax (1) 127048; e-mail motc.rez@eol.com.er.

Eritrean Relief and Refugee Commission: POB 1098, Asmara; tel. (1) 182222; fax (1) 182970; e-mail john@errec.er.punchdown.org.

Land and Housing Commission: POB 348, Asmara; tel. (1) 117400.

Provincial Administrators

There are six administrative regions in Eritrea, each with regional, sub-regional and village administrations.

Anseba Province: ALAMIN SHEIKH SALIH.

Debub Province: MESFIN HAGOS.

Debubawi Keyih Bahri Province: MUSA RAB'A.

Gash-Barka Province: MUSTAFA NUR HUSSEIN.

Maakel Province: SEMERE RUSOM.

Semenawi Keyih Bahri Province: IBRAHIM IDRIS TOTIL.

Legislature

NATIONAL ASSEMBLY

In accordance with transitional arrangements formulated in Decree No. 37 of May 1993, the National Assembly consists of the Central Committee of the People's Front for Democracy and Justice (PFDJ) and 60 other members: 30 from the Provincial Assemblies and an additional 30 members, including a minimum of 10 women, to be nominated by the PFDJ Central Committee. The legislative body 'outlines the internal and external policies of the government, regulates their implementation, approves the budget and elects a president for the country'. The National Assembly is to hold regular sessions every six months under the chairmanship of the President. In his role as Head of the Government and Commander-in-Chief of the Army, the President nominates individuals to head the various government departments. These nominations are ratified by the legislative body. In March 1994 the National Assembly voted to alter its composition: it would henceforth comprise the 75 members of the Central Committee of the PFDJ and 75 directly elected members. In May 1997, following the adoption of the Constitution, the Constituent Assembly empowered a Transitional National Assembly (comprising the 75 members of the PFDJ, 60 members of the former Constituent Assembly and 15 representatives of Eritreans residing abroad) to act as the legislature until elections were held for a new National Assembly.

Chairman of the Transitional National Assembly: ISSAIAS AFEWERKI.

Political Organizations

At independence in May 1993, many of the rival political organizations to the Eritrean People's Liberation Front (now the People's Front for Democracy and Justice) declared their support for the transitional Government.

Democratic Movement for the Liberation of Eritrea: opposition group; Leader HAMID TURKY.

Eritrean Islamic Jihad (EIJ): radical opposition group; in Aug. 1993 split into a mil. wing and a political wing, led by Sheikh MOHAMED ARAFA.

Eritrean Liberation Front (ELF): f. 1958; commenced armed struggle against Ethiopia in 1961; subsequently split into numerous factions (see below); mainly Muslim support; opposes the PFDJ; principal factions:

Eritrean Liberation Front—Central Command (ELF—CC): f. 1982; Chair. ABDALLAH IDRISS.

Eritrean Liberation Front—National Council (ELF—NC): Leader HASSAN ALI ASSAD.

Eritrean Liberation Front—Revolutionary Council (ELF—RC): Pres. SEYOUM OGBAMICHAEL; Leader AHMED MOHAMED NASSER.

Eritrean National Alliance (ENA): f. 1999 as the Alliance of Eritrean National Forces, adopted present name in 2002; Chair. ABDELLA IDRIS; Sec.-Gen. HIRUY TEDLA BAIRU.

Eritrean People's Liberation Front—Democratic Party (EPLF—DP): f. 2001; breakaway group from the PFDJ; Leader MESFIN HAGOS.

People's Front for Democracy and Justice (PFDJ): POB 1081, Asmara; tel. (1) 121399; fax (1) 120848; f. 1970 as the Eritrean Popular Liberation Forces, following a split in the Eritrean Liberation Front; renamed the Eritrean People's Liberation Front in 1977; adopted present name in Feb. 1994; Christian and Muslim support; in May 1991 took control of Eritrea and formed provisional Govt; formed transitional Govt in May 1993; Chair. ISSAIAS AFEWERKI; Sec.-Gen. ALAMIN MOHAMED SAID.

Red Sea Afar Democratic Organization: Afar opposition group; Sec.-Gen. AMIN AHMMAD.

Diplomatic Representation

EMBASSIES IN ERITREA

China, People's Republic: 16 Ogaden St, POB 204, Asmara; tel. (1) 185271; fax (1) 185275; Ambassador CHEN ZHANFU.

Denmark: Ras Dashan St 11, POB 6300, Asmara; tel. (1) 124346; fax (1) 124343; e-mail asmamb@um.dk; Chargé d'affaires a.i. PETER TRUELSEN.

Djibouti: POB 5589, Asmara; tel. (1) 354961; fax (1) 351831; Ambassador AHMAD ISSA.

Egypt: POB 5577, Asmara; tel. (1) 123603; fax (1) 123294; Ambassador Dr Rifat al-Ansari.

Ethiopia: Franklin D. Roosevelt St, POB 5688, Asmara; tel. (1) 116365; fax (1) 116144; Ambassador Awalom Woldu (recalled May 1998).

France: POB 209, Asmara; tel. (1) 126599; fax (1) 121036; e-mail af@gemel.com.er; Ambassador Gérard Sambrana.

Germany: 24 Ogaden Ave, POB 5589, Asmara; tel. (1) 182670; fax (1) 182900; Ambassador Elmar Timpe.

Israel: POB 5600, Asmara; tel. (1) 185626; fax (1) 185550; e-mail isremb@eol.com.er; Ambassador Uri Savir.

Italy: POB 220, Asmara; tel. (1) 120160; fax (1) 121115; e-mail iea@eol.com.er; Ambassador Emanuele Pignatelli.

Japan: Asmara; Ambassador Makoto Assami.

Libya: Asmara.

Russia: POB 5667, Asmara; tel. (1) 127172; fax (1) 127164; e-mail rusemb@eol.com.er; Ambassador Alexander Oblov.

Saudi Arabia: POB 5599, Asmara; tel. (1) 120171; fax (1) 121027; Ambassador Abdul R. Ibrahim at-Toelmi.

Sudan: Asmara; tel. (1) 202072; fax (1) 200760; e-mail sudanemb@eol.com.er; Ambassador Dr Mahjoub al-Basha.

United Kingdom: 24 Emperor Yohannes Ave, POB 5584, Asmara; tel. (1) 120145; fax (1) 120104; e-mail alembca@gemel.com.er; Ambassador Michael Murray.

USA: Franklin D. Roosevelt St, POB 211, Asmara; tel. (1) 120004; fax (1) 127584; Ambassador Donald J. McConnell.

Yemen: POB 5566, Asmara; tel. (1) 114434; fax (1) 117921; Ambassador Dr Akram Abd al-Marik al-Qabri.

Judicial System

The judicial system operates on the basis of transitional laws which incorporate pre-independence laws of the Eritrean People's Liberation Front, revised Ethiopian laws, customary laws and post-independence enacted laws. The independence of the judiciary in the discharge of its functions is unequivocally stated in Decree No. 37, which defines the powers and duties of the Government. It is subject only to the law and to no other authority. The court structure is composed of first instance sub-zonal courts, appellate and first instance zonal courts, appellate and first instance high courts, a panel of high court judges, presided over by the President of the High Court, and a Supreme Court presided over by the Chief Justice, as a court of last resort. The judges of the Supreme Court are appointed by the President of the State, subject to confirmation by the National Assembly.

Supreme Court: Asmara.

High Court: POB 241, Asmara; tel. (1) 127739; fax (1) 201828; e-mail prshict@eol.com.er.

Religion

Eritrea is almost equally divided between Muslims and Christians. Most Christians are adherents of the Orthodox Church, although there are Protestant and Roman Catholic communities. A small number of the population follow traditional beliefs.

CHRISTIANITY

The Eritrean Orthodox Church

In September 1993 the separation of the Eritrean Orthodox Church from the Ethiopian Orthodox Church was agreed by the respective church leaderships. The Eritrean Orthodox Church announced that it was to create a diocese of each of the country's then 10 provinces. The first five bishops of the Eritrean Orthodox Church were consecrated in Cairo in September 1994. In May 1998 Eritrea's first Patriarch (Abune) was consecrated in Asmara.

Patriarch (Abune): Archbishop Yacob.

The Roman Catholic Church

At 31 December 2000 there were an estimated 132,937 adherents in the country.

Bishop of Asmara: Rt Rev. Abba Menghisteab Tesfamariam, 19 Gonder St, POB 244, Asmara; tel. (1) 120206; fax (1) 126519.

Bishop of Barentu: Rt Rev. Luca Milesi, POB 9, Barentu; tel. and fax (1) 127283.

Bishop of Keren: Rt Rev. Tesfamariam Bedho, POB 460, Keren; tel. (1) 401907; fax (1) 401604; e-mail cek@gemel.com.er.

The Anglican Communion

Within the Episcopal Church in Jerusalem and the Middle East, Eritrea lies within the jurisdiction of the Bishop in Egypt.

Leader: Asfaha Mahary.

ISLAM

Eritrea's main Muslim communities are concentrated in the western lowlands, the northern highlands and the eastern coastal region.

Leader: Sheikh Al-Amin Osman al-Amin.

The Press

Business Perspective: POB 856, Asmara; tel. (1) 121589; fax (1) 120138; monthly; Tigrinya, Arabic and English; publ. by Eritrean National Chamber of Commerce; Editor Mohammed-Sfaf Hammed.

Chamber News: POB 856, Asmara; tel. (1) 120045; fax (1) 120138; monthly; Tigrinya, Arabic and English; publ. by Asmara Chamber of Commerce.

Eritrea Profile: POB 247, Asmara; f. 1994; weekly; English; publ. by the Ministry of Information.

Hadas Eritra (New Eritrea): Asmara; f. 1991; three times a week; in English, Tigrinya and Arabic; govt publ. Editor Yitbarek Zerom; circ. 25,000.

Meqahil: Asmara; Editor Mathewos Habeab.

Newsletter: POB 856, Asmara; tel. (1) 121589; fax (1) 120138; e-mail encc@aol.com.er; monthly; Tigrinya, Arabic and English; publ. by Eritrean National Chamber of Commerce; Editor Mohammed-Sfaf Hammed.

Broadcasting and Communications

Ministry of Transport and Communications (Communications Department): POB 4918, Asmara; tel. (1) 115847; fax (1) 126966; e-mail motc.rez@eol.com.er; Dir-Gen. Estifanos Afewerki.

TELECOMMUNICATIONS

Telecommunications Services of Eritrea: 11 Semaetat St, POB 234, Asmara; tel. (1) 117547; fax (1) 120938; f. 1991; Gen. Man. Goitom Ogbazghi.

Ericel: Asmara; f. 2001; operates mobile cellular telephone network.

BROADCASTING

Radio

Voice of the Broad Masses of Eritrea (Dimtsi Hafash): POB 242, Asmara; tel. (1) 120426; fax (1) 126747; govt-controlled; programmes in Arabic, Tigrinya, Tigre, Saho, Oromo, Amharic, Afar, Bilien, Nara, Hedareb and Kunama; Dir-Gen. Tesfai Keleta; Technical Dir Berhane Gerezgiher.

Television

ERI-TV: Asmara; f. 1992; govt station providing educational, tech. and information service; broadcasting began in 1993 in Arabic, Tigre and Tigrinya; transmissions limited to Asmara and surrounding areas; Dir-Gen. Ali Abdu.

Finance

(cap. = capital; dep. = deposits; m. = million; brs = branches; amounts in Ethiopian birr)

In November 1997 Eritrea adopted the nakfa as its unit of currency, replacing the Ethiopian birr, which had been Eritrea's monetary unit since independence.

BANKING

Central Bank

Bank of Eritrea: POB 849, 21 Victory Ave, Asmara; tel. (1) 123036; fax (1) 123162; e-mail tekieb@boe.gov.er; f. 1993; bank of issue; Gov. Tekie Beyene.

Other Banks

Commercial Bank of Eritrea: POB 219, Asmara; tel. (1) 121844; fax (1) 124887; f. 1991; dep. 5,100m. (Dec. 1996); Gen. Man. YAMANE TESFAI; 15 brs.

Eritrean Development and Investment Bank: POB 1266, Asmara; tel. (1) 123787; e-mail edib@gemel.com.er; f. 1996; cap. 45m. provides medium- to long-term credit; 13 brs.

Housing and Commerce Bank of Eritrea: POB 235, Asmara; tel. (1) 120350; fax (1) 120401; e-mail hcb@gemel.com.er; f. 1994; cap. 33m., total assets 1,824.7m. (Dec. 1999); finances residential and commercial construction projects and commercial loans; CEO Dr ARAIA TSEGGAI; 7 brs.

INSURANCE

National Insurance Corporation of Eritrea (NICE): NICE Bldg, POB 881, Asmara; tel. (1) 123000; fax (1) 123240; e-mail nice@eol.com.er; Gen. Man. ZERU WOLDEMICHAEL.

Trade and Industry

CHAMBER OF COMMERCE

Eritrean National Chamber of Commerce: POB 856, Asmara; tel. (1) 121388; fax (1) 120138; e-mail encc@aol.com.er.

TRADE ASSOCIATION

Red Sea Trading Corporation: 29/31 Ras Alula St, POB 332, Asmara; tel. (1) 127846; fax (1) 124353; f. 1983; import and export services; operated by the PFDJ; Gen. Man. KUBROM DAFLA.

UTILITIES

Electricity

Eritrean Electricity Authority (EEA): POB 911, Asmara; fax (1) 121468; e-mail eeahrg@eol.com.er.

Water

Dept of Water Resources: Asmara; tel. (1) 119636; fax (1) 124625.

Transport

Eritrea's transport infrastructure was severely damaged during the three decades of war prior to independence. International creditors have since provided loans for the repair and reconstruction of the road network and for the improvement of port facilities.

RAILWAYS

The 306-km railway connection between Agordat, Asmara and the port of Massawa was severely damaged during the war of independence and ceased operation in 1975. However, rehabilitation of the railway is underway: in 1999 an 81-km section of the Asmara–Massawa line (between Massawa and Embatkala) became operational, and in 2001 a further 18-km section of the railway, connecting Embatkala and Ghinda, was completed.

Eritrean Railway: POB 6081, Asmara; tel. (1) 123365; fax (1) 201785; Co-ordinator, Railways Rehabilitation Project AMANUEL GEBRESELLASIE.

ROADS

In 1999 there were an estimated 4,010 km of roads in Eritrea, of which some 874 km were paved. Roads that are paved require considerable repair, as do many of the bridges across seasonal water courses destroyed in the war. Road construction between Asmara and the port of Massawa was given particular priority in the Recovery and Rehabilitation Programme.

SHIPPING

Eritrea has two major seaports: Massawa, which sustained heavy war damage in 1990, and Assab, which has principally served Addis Ababa, in Ethiopia. Under an accord signed between the Ethiopian and Eritrean Governments in 1993, the two countries agreed to share the facilities of both ports. Since independence, activity in Massawa has increased substantially; however, activity at Assab declined following the outbreak of hostilities with Ethiopia in May 1998. In 1998 a total of 463 vessels docked at Massawa, handling 1.2m. metric tons of goods; 322 vessels docked at Assab, which handled 1.0m. tons of goods. At 31 December 2001 Eritrea's registered merchant fleet numbered 12 vessels, with a total displacement of 20,686 grt.

Dept of Maritime Transport: POB 679, Asmara; tel. (1) 121317; fax (1) 121316; e-mail motc.rez@eol.com.er; Dir-Gen. ALEM TZEHAIE.

Port and Maritime Transport Authority: POB 851, Asmara; tel. (1) 111399; fax (1) 113647; Dir WELDE MIKAEL ABRAHAM.

Eritrean Shipping Lines: 80 Semaetat Ave, POB 1110, Asmara; tel. (1) 120359; fax (1) 120331; f. 1992; provides shipping services in Red Sea and Persian (Arabian) Gulf areas and owns and operates four cargo ships; Gen. Man. TEWELDE KELATI.

CIVIL AVIATION

The international airport is at Asmara.

Civil Aviation Department: POB 252, Asmara; tel. (1) 124335; fax (1) 124334; e-mail motc.rez@eol.com.er; handles freight and passenger traffic for eight scheduled carriers which use Asmara airport; Dir-Gen. PAULOS KAHSAY.

Eri-Air: Asmara; weekly charter flights to Italy; Man. Dirs TEWOLDE TESFAMARIAM, HAILEMARIAM GEBRECHRISTOS.

Eritrean Airlines: POB 222, Asmara; tel. (1) 181822; fax (1) 181255; Man. Dir ABRAHA GHIRMAZION.

Tourism

The Ministry of Tourism is overseeing the development of this sector, although its advance since independence has been inhibited by the country's war-damaged transport infrastructure, and by subsequent conflicts with Ethiopia and other regional tensions. Eritrea possesses many areas of scenic and scientific interest, including the Dahlak Islands (a coralline archipelago rich in marine life), offshore from Massawa, and the massive escarpment rising up from the coastal plain and supporting a unique ecosystem. In 2000 tourist arrivals in Eritrea totalled 70,355, compared with 409,544 in 1997, and tourism receipts amounted to US $36m., compared with $90m. in 1997.

Eritrean Tourism Service Corporation: Asmara; operates govt-owned hotels.

ESTONIA

Introductory Survey

Location, Climate, Language, Religion, Flag, Capital

The Republic of Estonia (formerly the Estonian Soviet Socialist Republic) is situated in north-eastern Europe. The country is bordered to the south by Latvia, and to the east by Russia. Estonia's northern coastline is on the Gulf of Finland and its territory includes more than 1,520 islands, mainly off its western coastline in the Gulf of Rīga and the Baltic Sea. The largest of the islands are Saaremaa and Hiiumaa, in the Gulf of Rīga. The climate is influenced by Estonia's position between the Eurasian land mass and the Baltic Sea and the North Atlantic Ocean. The mean January temperature in Tallinn is –0.6°C (30.9°F); in July the mean temperature is 17.1°C (62.8°F). Average annual precipitation is 568 mm. The official language is Estonian, which is a member of the Baltic-Finnic group of the Finno-Ugric languages; it is written in the Latin script and is closely related to Finnish. Many of the Russian residents, who comprise nearly 30% of the total population, do not speak Estonian. Most of the population profess Christianity and, by tradition, Estonians belong to the Evangelical Lutheran Church. Smaller Protestant sects and the Eastern Orthodox Church are also represented. The national flag (proportions 7 by 11) consists of three equal horizontal stripes, of blue, black and white. The capital is Tallinn.

Recent History

The Russian annexation of Estonia, formerly under Swedish rule, was formalized in 1721. During the latter half of the 19th century, as the powers of the dominant Baltic German nobility declined, Estonians experienced a national cultural revival, which culminated in political demands for autonomy during the 1905 Russian Revolution, and for full independence after the beginning of the First World War. On 30 March 1917 the Provisional Government in Petrograd (St Petersburg), which had taken power after the abdication of Tsar Nicholas II in February, approved autonomy for Estonia. A Land Council was elected as the country's representative body. However, in October the Bolsheviks staged a coup in Tallinn, and declared the Estonian Soviet Executive Committee as the sole government of Estonia. As German forces advanced towards Estonia in early 1918, the Bolshevik troops were forced to leave. The major Estonian political parties united to form the Estonian Salvation Committee, and on 24 February an independent Republic of Estonia was proclaimed. A Provisional Government, headed by Konstantin Päts, was formed, but Germany refused to recognize Estonia's independence and the country was occupied by German troops until the end of the First World War. Following the capitulation of Germany in November, the Provisional Government assumed power. After a period of armed conflict between Soviet and Estonian troops, the Republic of Estonia and Soviet Russia signed the Treaty of Tartu on 2 February 1920, under the terms of which the Soviet Government recognized Estonia's independence and renounced any rights to its territory. Estonian independence was recognized by the major Western powers in January 1921, and Estonia was admitted to the League of Nations.

Independence lasted until 1940. During most of this time the country had a liberal-democratic political system, in which the Riigikogu (State Assembly) was the dominant political force. Significant social, cultural and economic advances were made in the 1920s, including radical land reform. However, the decline in trade with Russia and the economic depression of the 1930s, combined with the political problems of a divided parliament, caused public dissatisfaction. In March 1934 Prime Minister Päts seized power in a bloodless coup and introduced a period of authoritarian rule. The Riigikogu and political parties were disbanded, but in 1938 a new Constitution was adopted, which provided for a presidential system of government, with a bicameral legislature. In April 1938 Päts was elected President.

In August 1939 the USSR and Germany signed a non-aggression treaty (the Nazi-Soviet or Molotov-Ribbentrop Pact). The 'Secret Protocols' to the treaty provided for the occupation of Estonia by the USSR. In September Estonia was forced to sign an agreement that permitted the USSR to base Soviet troops in Estonia. In June 1940 the Government, in accordance with a Soviet ultimatum, resigned, and a new administration was appointed by the Soviet authorities, with Johannes Vares-Barbarus as Prime Minister. In July elections were held, in which only candidates approved by the Soviet authorities were permitted to participate. On 21 July the Estonian Soviet Socialist Republic was proclaimed by the new legislature, and on 6 August the republic was formally incorporated into the USSR. Soviet rule in Estonia lasted less than one year. In that short period, however, Soviet policy resulted in mass deportations of Estonians to Siberia, the expropriation of property, severe restrictions on cultural life and the introduction of Soviet-style government.

German forces entered Estonia in July 1941 and remained in occupation until September 1944. After a short-lived attempt to reinstate Estonian independence, Soviet troops occupied the whole of the country, and the process of 'sovietization' was continued. By the end of 1949 most Estonian farmers had been forced to join collective farms. Heavy industry was expanded, with investment concentrated on electricity generation and the chemicals sector. Structural change in the economy was accompanied by increased political repression, with deportations of Estonians continuing until the death of Stalin (Iosif V. Dzhugashvili), in 1953. The most overt form of opposition to Soviet rule was provided by the 'forest brethren' (*metsavennad*), a guerrilla movement, which continued to conduct armed operations against Soviet personnel and institutions until the mid-1950s. In the late 1960s, as in other Soviet republics, more traditional forms of dissent appeared, concentrating on cultural issues, provoked by the increasing domination of the republic by immigrant Russians and other Slavs.

During the late 1970s and the 1980s the issues of 'russification' and environmental degradation became subjects of intense debate in Estonia. The policy of *glasnost*, introduced by the Soviet leader, Mikhail Gorbachev, in 1986, allowed such discussion to spread beyond dissident groups. The success of the first major demonstrations of the 1980s, organized to oppose plans to increase open-cast phosphorite mining in north-eastern Estonia, prompted further protests. In August 1987 a demonstration attended by some 2,000 people commemorated the anniversary of the signing of the Nazi-Soviet Pact, and an Estonian Group for the Publication of the Molotov-Ribbentrop Pact (MRP-AEG) was subsequently formed. During 1988 the Nazi-Soviet Pact was duly published, and the MRP-AEG reformed as the Estonian National Independence Party (ENIP), proclaiming the restoration of Estonian independence as its political objective. Another opposition group, the Estonian Popular Front (EPF), was formally constituted at its first congress in October, and included many members of the ruling Communist Party of Estonia (CPE). The EPF was more cautious than the ENIP in its approach, advocating the transformation of the USSR into a confederal system; the CPE was forced to adapt its policies to retain a measure of public support. On 16 November the Estonian Supreme Soviet (legislature) adopted a declaration of sovereignty, which included the right to annul all-Union (USSR) legislation. The Presidium of the USSR Supreme Soviet declared the sovereignty legislation unconstitutional, but the Estonian Supreme Soviet affirmed its decision in December.

The adoption of Estonian as the state language was accepted by the Supreme Soviet in January 1989, and the tricolour of independent Estonia was reinstated as the official flag. Despite the successes of the opposition, differing political tactics were employed by the radical ENIP and the EPF. The ENIP refused to nominate candidates for elections to the all-Union Congress of People's Deputies in March. Instead, the ENIP leadership announced plans for the registration by citizens' committees of all citizens of the pre-1940 Republic of Estonia and their descendants. Voters on an electoral register, thus compiled, would elect a Congress of Estonia as the legal successor to the pre-1940 Estonian legislature. The EPF, however, participated in the elections to the Congress of People's Deputies and won 27 of the 36 contested seats. Five seats were won by the International Movement, a political group composed predominantly of

Russian immigrants, which was established in July 1988 to oppose the growing influence of the Estonian opposition movements in the republic. In October 1989 delegates at the second congress of the EPF, influenced by the growing popularity of the ENIP and the citizens' committees, voted to adopt the restoration of Estonian independence as official policy. In November the Estonian Supreme Soviet voted to annul the 1940 decision of its predecessor to enter the USSR, declaring that the decision had been reached under coercion from Soviet armed forces.

On 2 February 1990 a mass rally was held to commemorate the anniversary of the 1920 Treaty of Tartu. Deputies attending the rally later met to approve a declaration urging the USSR Supreme Soviet to begin negotiations on restoring Estonia's independence. On 22 February 1990 the Estonian Supreme Soviet approved the declaration, and on the following day it voted to abolish the constitutional guarantee of power enjoyed by the CPE. This formal decision permitted largely free elections to take place to the Estonian Soviet in March. The EPF won 43 of the 105 seats, and 35 were won by the Association for a Free Estonia and other pro-independence groups. The remainder were won by members of the International Movement. Candidates belonging to the CPE, which was represented in all these groups, won 55 seats.

At the first session of the new legislature, Arnold Rüütel, previously Chairman of the Presidium of the Supreme Soviet, was elected to the new post of Chairman of the Supreme Soviet, in which was vested those state powers that had been the preserve of the First Secretary of the CPE. On 30 March 1990 the Supreme Soviet adopted a declaration that proclaimed the beginning of a transitional period towards independence and denied the validity of Soviet power in the republic.

In late February and early March 1990 some 580,000 people took part in elections to the rival parliament to the Supreme Soviet, the Congress of Estonia. The Congress convened on 11–12 March and declared itself the constitutional representative of the Estonian people. The participants adopted resolutions demanding the restoration of Estonian independence and the withdrawal of Soviet troops from Estonia.

In early April 1990 the Supreme Soviet elected Edgar Savisaar, a leader of the EPF, as Prime Minister and on 8 May it voted to restore the first five articles of the 1938 Constitution, which described Estonia's independent status. The formal name of pre-1940 Estonia, the Republic of Estonia, was also restored, as were the state emblems, flag and anthem. On 16 May a transitional system of government was approved.

Although formal economic sanctions were not imposed on Estonia (as was the case with Lithuania), relations with the Soviet authorities were severely strained. In mid-May 1990 President Gorbachev annulled the republic's declaration of independence, declaring that it violated the USSR Constitution. The Estonian leadership's request for negotiations on the status of the republic was refused by Gorbachev, who insisted that the independence declaration be rescinded before negotiations could begin. There was also opposition within the republic, mostly from ethnic Russians affiliated to the International Movement.

When troops of the USSR's Ministry of Internal Affairs attempted military intervention in Latvia and Lithuania in January 1991, the Estonian leadership anticipated similar confrontation. Barricades and makeshift defences were erected, but no military action was taken. However, events in the other Baltic republics (Latvia and Lithuania) intensified popular distrust of Estonian involvement in a new union, which was being negotiated by other Soviet republics. Consequently, Estonia refused to participate in a referendum on the future of the USSR, which took place in nine of the republics in March 1991. The Estonian authorities had conducted a poll on the issue of independence earlier in the same month. According to the official results, 82.9% of the registered electorate took part, of which 77.8% voted in favour of Estonian independence.

When the State Committee for the State of Emergency announced that it had seized power in the USSR on 19 August 1991, Estonia, together with the other Baltic republics, expected military intervention to overthrow the pro-independence governments. Gen. Fyodor Kuzmin, the Soviet commander of the Baltic military district, informed Arnold Rüütel, the Chairman of the Supreme Council (as the legislature was now known), that he was taking full control of Estonia. Military vehicles entered Tallinn on 20 August, and troops occupied the city's television station. However, the military command did not prevent a session of the Estonian Supreme Council from convening on the same day. Deputies adopted a resolution declaring the full and immediate independence of Estonia, thus ending the transitional period that had begun in March 1990. Plans were also announced for the formation of a government-in-exile, should the Government and the Supreme Council be disbanded by Soviet troops. After it became evident, on 22 August 1991, that the Soviet coup had collapsed, the Government began to take measures against persons who had allegedly supported the coup. The anti-Government movements, the International Movement and the United Council of Work Collectives were banned, as was the Communist Party of the Soviet Union. Several directors of Soviet enterprises were dismissed, and the Committee of State Security (KGB) was ordered to terminate its activities in Estonia.

As the Estonian Government moved to assert its authority over former Soviet institutions, other countries quickly began to recognize its independence. On 6 September the USSR State Council finally recognized the re-establishment of Estonian independence. Later in the month Estonia, together with the other Baltic states, was admitted to the UN, as well as to the Conference on Security and Co-operation in Europe (CSCE), renamed the Organization for Security and Co-operation in Europe (OSCE, see p. 283) in December 1994. During the remainder of 1991 Estonia re-established diplomatic relations with most major states and was offered membership of leading international organizations. In internal politics there was hope for a cessation of conflict between the radical Congress of Estonia and the Supreme Council, with the establishment of a Constitutional Assembly, composed of equal numbers of delegates from each body, which was to draft a new constitution.

In January 1992, following a series of disputes with the Supreme Council concerning the issue of citizenship and the Government's failure to persuade the legislature to impose an economic state of emergency, Savisaar resigned as Prime Minister and was replaced by the erstwhile Minister of Transport, Tiit Vähi. A new Council of Ministers, which included seven ministers from the previous Government, was approved by the Supreme Council at the end of the month.

The draft Constitution that had been prepared by the Constitutional Assembly was approved by some 91% of the electorate in a referendum held in late June 1992. Under the recently adopted Citizenship Law, only citizens of pre-1940 Estonia and their descendants, or those who had successfully applied for citizenship, were entitled to vote. This ruling drew strong criticism from Russian leaders, concerned that the rights of the large Russian minority in Estonia, most of whom had not been granted citizenship and who were thus disenfranchised, were being violated. The new Constitution, which entered into force in early July 1992, provided for a parliamentary system of government, with a strong presidency. A new legislature, the Riigikogu, was to replace the Supreme Council (and the Congress of Estonia), and an election to the new body was to be held in September. A direct presidential election was to take place simultaneously (although subsequent presidents would be elected by the Riigikogu).

Legislative and presidential elections were duly held on 20 September 1992, with the participation of some 67% of the electorate. The country's Russian and other ethnic minorities, who represented 42% of the total population, were again barred from voting (with the exception of those whose applications for citizenship had been granted). The election to the 101-seat Riigikogu was contested by a total of 633 candidates, representing some 40 parties and movements, largely grouped into eight coalitions. The nationalist alliance Isamaa (Pro Patria, or Fatherland) emerged with the largest number of seats (29). The centrist Popular Front alliance (led by the EPF) won an unexpectedly low total of 15 seats. The Secure Home alliance, which comprised some former communists, obtained 17 seats. The Moderates electoral alliance obtained 12 seats and the ENIP, which was not part of a coalition, won 10 seats. None of the four candidates in the presidential election won an overall majority of the votes. It thus fell to the Riigikogu to choose from the two most successful candidates, Arnold Rüütel, now a leading member of the Secure Home alliance, and Lennart Meri, a former Minister of Foreign Affairs, who was supported by Isamaa. In early October the Isamaa-dominated Riigikogu elected Meri as Estonia's President.

A new coalition Government, with a large representation of Isamaa members, as well as members of the Moderates and the ENIP, was announced in mid-October 1992. Earlier in the month Mart Laar, a 32-year-old historian and the leader of Isamaa, had been chosen as Prime Minister. Laar indicated that the principal objectives of his administration would be to negotiate the withdrawal of all Russian troops remaining in Estonia, as well as to accelerate the country's privatization programme. In late November four of the five constituent parties of the Isamaa alliance united to form the National Fatherland Party (NFP), with Laar as its Chairman. In the same month the CPE was renamed the Estonian Democratic Labour Party.

The NFP suffered a considerable loss of support at local elections held in October 1993. In Tallinn the party secured only five of the 64 seats on the city council, and in the following month Laar survived a vote of 'no confidence' in the Riigikogu. In January 1994 Laar reshuffled four key portfolios in the Council of Ministers, overcoming initial opposition by President Meri to two of the nominees. Meanwhile, in November 1993, the EPF was disbanded; it was stated that the party had largely fulfilled its aims. The NFP continued to lose popular support in early 1994. At the same time the governing coalition, led by the NFP, was increasingly afflicted by internal divisions. In May–June four members of the Council of Ministers resigned. Defections from the Isamaa faction within the Riigikogu resulted in Laar's supporters retaining control of only 19 seats in the legislature by early September. Following the revelation, in that month, that Laar had secretly contravened an agreement with the IMF, a vote of 'no confidence' in the Prime Minister was endorsed by 60 members of the Riigikogu. In late October Andres Tarand, hitherto Minister of the Environment, was appointed to replace Laar. A new Council of Ministers, which included representatives of Isamaa and the Moderates, the ENIP and liberal and right-wing parties, was announced in the following month.

In early January 1995 seven electoral alliances and eight parties were registered to participate in the general election scheduled for 5 March. The result of the election reflected widespread popular dissatisfaction with the parties of the governing coalition. The largest number of seats in the Riigikogu (41 of the total of 101) was won by an alliance of the centrist Estonian Coalition Party (ECP, led by the former Prime Minister, Tiit Vähi) and the Rural Union (comprising various agrarian parties, most prominently Rüütel's Estonian Country People's Party). A coalition of the newly established Estonian Reform Party (ERP, led by Siim Kallas, the President of the Bank of Estonia) and liberal groups obtained 19 seats, followed by Edgar Savisaar's Estonian Centre Party (16). The NFP (in coalition with the ENIP) won only eight seats, while the Moderates alliance (which included Andres Tarand) obtained six seats. The 'Estonia is Our Home' pact (which united three new parties representing the Russian-speaking minority) also won six seats; this development was broadly welcomed as a potentially stabilizing factor in both the domestic and foreign affairs of the country. The participation rate was almost 70%.

Tiit Vähi was confirmed as Prime Minister by the legislature in early April 1995, and the new Government—a coalition of the ECP/Rural Union and the Estonian Centre Party—was appointed later in the month. The Government survived only until early October, when it was revealed that Edgar Savisaar, the Minister of the Interior, had made clandestine recordings of conversations that he had held with other politicians, following the general election in March, concerning the formation of a new coalition government. Although Savisaar was dismissed by Vähi, the Estonian Centre Party refused to accept his dismissal. As a result of the effective collapse of the coalition, Vähi and the remaining members of the Council of Ministers tendered their resignations. In mid-October President Meri reappointed Vähi as Prime Minister and charged him with the formation of a new Government. This emerged in late October, and represented a coalition of the ECP/Rural Union and the ERP. Meanwhile, Savisaar resigned as Chairman of the Estonian Centre Party. In December the NFP and the ENIP, which had campaigned jointly in the legislative election in March, merged to form the Pro Patria (Fatherland) Union. In March 1996 tension within the Estonian Centre Party, following the scandal surrounding Savisaar, resulted in the emergence of two factions: Andra Veidemann, the Chairman of the Party, and six deputies from the Riigikogu established the New Democratic Association, subsequently to become the liberal-centrist Development Party, and Savisaar was re-elected as Chairman of the Estonian Centre Party.

A presidential election was held in the Riigikogu on 26 August 1996, contested by the incumbent, Lennart Meri, and Arnold Rüütel of the Estonian Country People's Party. A two further inconclusive rounds of voting took place on the following day, and a larger electoral college, comprising the 101 deputies of the legislature and 273 representatives of local government, was therefore convened on 20 September. Five candidates contested the first round, but, as none of the contenders secured an overall majority of the votes, a second round of voting was held to choose between the leading candidates, Meri and Rüütel. The election was won by Meri, with some 52% of the votes cast, and in October he was duly sworn in as President for a second term.

In October 1996 local government elections were held, in which the ERP gained control of Tallinn city council. In November the ECP concluded a co-operation agreement with the Estonian Centre Party (excluded from the Government since October 1995), which pledged to seek to involve the centrists in the governing coalition. Disagreements among the coalition partners led to the collapse of the Tallinn council leadership, and Savisaar was appointed as the new Chairman of the council, replacing the newly elected ERP candidate. The ERP threatened to leave the Government unless the co-operation agreement with the Estonian Centre Party was cancelled, and on 22 November 1996 six ministers, including the Chairman of the ERP and the Minister for Foreign Affairs, Siim Kallas, resigned, thus causing the collapse of the ruling coalition. Following the failure of negotiations between the ECP, the Estonian Centre Party and the Development Party a minority Government, comprising the ECP, the Rural Union and independent members, was appointed, with the support of 41 deputies, in early December. In early 1997 a series of allegations of abuse of office were made against Tiit Vähi. A legislative motion of 'no confidence', presented by the leaders of four opposition parties, was defeated by a narrow margin, but Vähi, nevertheless, tendered his resignation at the end of that month, although he denied the allegations against him. Mart Siimann, the leader of the ECP parliamentary faction, was appointed Prime Minister, and was asked to form a new Government (the resignation of the Prime Minister automatically entailed that of the Government). In mid-March a new minority Government, which comprised a coalition of the ECP, the Rural Union and independent members, was appointed. In September Vähi announced his resignation from the ECP and his retirement from political life. His position as Chairman of the ECP was assumed by Siimann.

During 1998 there was considerable political consolidation and realignment in preparation for the legislative election expected in the following year. In January the Rural Union entered into a co-operation agreement with the opposition Estonian Centre Party, and in April the smaller Estonian Farmers' Party and People's Party of Republicans and Conservatives merged to form the People's Party, with Toomas Hendrik Ilves (formerly an independent) as leader. In May, in an attempt to broaden the appeal of both political platforms, the Estonian Green Party was absorbed by the Estonian Centre Party. Meanwhile, the six members of the Riigikogu representing the three major Russian-speaking minority parties announced that they were to present a united front in the legislature. In late September, following repeated criticism of his leadership of a party not represented in the governing coalition or the legislature, Ilves resigned his foreign affairs portfolio. In early December President Meri announced that the election to the Riigikogu would be conducted on 7 March 1999.

At the general election, held as scheduled, the Estonian Centre Party won 28 of the 101 seats in the legislature; the ERP and the Pro Patria (Fatherland) Union each secured 18 seats, the Moderates (in alliance with the People's Party) claimed 17 seats, the Estonian Country People's Party received seven seats and the United People's Party of Estonia won six seats. According to official sources, the level of participation was just 57.4% of the electorate. Although the Estonian Centre Party obtained the largest number of seats, it was unable to form a majority coalition. A centre-right coalition Government was thus formed by the ERP, the Pro Patria Union and the Moderates, with each party receiving five ministerial posts; Mart Laar, leader of the Pro Patria Union, was appointed Prime Minister (the post he had held in 1992–94). In May 1999 it was announced that non-native Estonians (numbering an estimated 300,000) were to be allowed to participate in local elections to be held in October.

At the local elections of October 1999 the governing ERP/Pro Patria (Fatherland) Union/Moderates alliance gained control of 13 of Estonia's 15 counties. The alliance joined four members of the People's Trust Party and one member of the People's Choice bloc (both representing the Russian-speaking population), to take control of Tallinn city council. Jüri Mõis was appointed Mayor of Tallinn, after resigning as Minister of Internal Affairs;

he was replaced by Tarmo Loodus. In November the Moderates' Party and the People's Party merged to form the People's Party Moderates. In mid-June 2000 a new party, the Estonian People's Union, was formed by the merger of the Estonian Rural People's Party, the Rural Union and the Pensioners' and Families' Party.

In February 2001 Prime Minister Laar was implicated in a scandal concerning an incident in 1999, when he and other officials had carried out informal shooting practice aimed at a picture of the Estonian Centre Party leader, Edgar Savisaar. Laar apologized for the incident, but a vote of 'no confidence' was brought against him in April 2001, which was defeated by eight votes; he had been accused of failing to act to combat increasing unemployment and of mismanaging the privatization of Estonian Railways. At the end of May Jüri Mõis resigned as Mayor of Tallinn, after being threatened with a fifth confidence vote. A member of the Pro Patria (Fatherland) Union, Tonis Palts, was elected as his successor, following a 'run-off' election, which was contested by Savisaar.

Inconclusive rounds of voting in the presidential election took place in the Riigikogu on 27–28 August 2001. The terms of the Constitution prevented the incumbent, Lennart Meri, from standing for a third term of office, and the first round of the election was contested by Andres Tarand of the People's Party Moderates and Peeter Kreitzberg of the opposition Estonian Centre Party, both of whom achieved substantially fewer than the 68 votes required to secure the necessary two-thirds' majority. Tarand was replaced as the candidate of the ruling coalition by Peeter Tulviste of the Pro Patria (Fatherland) Union in the second and third rounds of voting, but neither candidate emerged as the victor and, indeed, both candidates received an equal number of votes (33) in the third round. Responsibility for the election of the President was, therefore, transferred to an Electoral Body, composed of the 101 parliamentary deputies, and 266 representatives of local government, which was convened on 21 September. Kreitzberg and Tulviste were joined as candidates by Toomas Savi of the governing ERP (members of which had, hitherto, abstained from voting), and Arnold Rüütel, the honorary Chairman of the opposition Estonian People's Union, and the former Chairman of the Estonian Supreme Soviet. As no candidate received the necessary 185 votes in the first round of voting, a second round took place to choose between the two candidates with the greatest number of votes, Rüütel and Savi. Arnold Rüütel emerged as the victor in the 'run-off' election, in which he secured 186 votes. He was sworn in as President on 8 October, and pledged to combat unemployment, create equal opportunities for education, and restore population growth. The protracted electoral process had led to renewed demands for electoral reform, and some Estonians expressed concern at the election of a former communist President, and the effect that this might have on the country's relations with the West. It was observed that Rüütel had drawn strong support from those delegates representing the electorate in rural areas, with high levels of unemployment.

In late September 2001, satisfying long-standing opposition demands, Mikhel Pärnoja tendered his resignation as Minister of Economic Affairs, citing the unpopularity of decisions he had made regarding the privatization of Estonian Railways and the planned divestment of the Narva Power Plants. In early December the ERP announced that it was to leave the Government of Tallinn City Council, in protest at financial mismanagement. It subsequently signed a coalition agreement with the Estonian Centre Party, in what was widely regarded as an attempt to distance itself from the increasingly unpopular national Government of which it remained a part. Tonis Palts was forced to resign as Mayor, when a censure motion, brought by members of the Estonian Centre Party, was passed by a significant majority. His Pro Patria (Fatherland) Union left the City Government, and Edgar Savisaar was elected as Mayor of Tallinn in mid-December. These developments prompted Prime Minister Mart Laar to announce that he was to resign on 8 January 2002 (Laar delayed announcing his resignation until the 2002 budget, which committed his successor to increased spending, had been passed).

The resignation of Laar's Government on 8 January 2002, as planned, prompted fears that Estonia's prospects for rapid accession to the European Union (EU, see p. 199) and NATO (see p. 271) might be damaged by the country's lack of a stable government. On 17 January the Estonian Centre Party and the ERP signed an agreement on the formation of an interim, coalition government, despite their contrasting political ideals; eight ministers were to be appointed from the Estonian Centre

Party and six from the ERP. The coalition held fewer than one-half of the seats in the Riigikogu and, therefore, required the support of the Estonian People's Union. On 22 January Siim Kallas, the Chairman of the ERP and the former President of the Bank of Estonia, was approved as Prime Minister by 62 votes to 31, despite lacking the support of his former government allies, the Pro Patria (Fatherland) Union and the People's Party Moderates.

In July 2002, following a ruling by the Supreme Court prohibiting the formation of electoral blocs, the Riigikogu voted to permit their continued existence until 2005, in order to avoid a delay in holding the forthcoming local elections, scheduled to take place in October 2002. In August the Minister of Culture, Signe Kivi of the ERP, resigned her post, owing to a corruption scandal within a foundation that she chaired, and was subsequently replaced by Margus Allikmaa (also of the ERP). In mid-October the Ministries of Economic Affairs and of Transport and Communications (both headed by Liina Tõnisson) merged to form the Ministry of Economic Affairs and Communications, and the Ministry of Education assumed responsibility for science. The local elections took place on 20 October. Parties represented in the national government won the majority of the votes cast (in Tallinn the Estonian Centre Party secured 38.5% of the votes, and the ERP 15.2%), although the right-wing Union for the Republic Res Publica, founded in 2001, unexpectedly won 21% of the votes cast in the capital. At the beginning of November 2002 Edgar Savisaar was re-elected as Mayor of Tallinn. Meanwhile, owing to their parties' poor performance in the elections, in late October Toomas Hendrik Ilves resigned as Chairman of the People's Party Moderates and Mart Laar resigned the chairmanship of the Pro Patria (Fatherland) Union. At the end of November Ivari Padar became the new Chairman of the People's Party Moderates (Ilves was elected as one of the party's two Deputy Chairmen), and in early December Tunne Kelam, a Deputy Speaker of the Riigikogu, was elected to succeed Laar. In the same month the Estonian Russian-Baltic Party, the Estonian Unity Party and the Russian Unity Party were absorbed by the Russian Party in Estonia, and Stanislav Cherepanov (the former leader of the Estonian Russian-Baltic Party) was elected as its Chairman. In late January 2003 the New Estonia Party merged with the Estonian People's Union, under the name of the latter party. Meanwhile, in mid-December 2002 the Riigikogu had scheduled a referendum on EU membership for 14 September 2003; voters were to be asked whether they supported Estonia's planned accession to the EU in 2004, and the adoption of legislation amending the country's Constitution.

In February 2003 the Riigikogu approved an extension of the terms of local councils, from three years to four, in the first amendment to be made to the Constitution since its adoption. In early February the Minister of Internal Affairs, Ain Seppik of the Estonian Centre Party, resigned on the advice of the Prime Minister, following severe criticism of his actions as a judge at the Supreme Court during the Soviet era; a vote of 'no confidence' had failed at the end of January. Seppik was replaced by Toomas Varek, also a member of the Estonian Centre Party.

Eleven parties participated in the parliamentary election held on 2 March 2003, in which the Estonian Centre party received 25.4% of the votes cast and 28 seats in the 101-member Riigikogu, Union for the Republic Res Publica obtained 24.6% and 28 seats, and the ERP took 17.7% and 19 seats; the Estonian People's Union, the Pro Patria (Fatherland) Union and the People's Party Moderates also achieved more than the 5% of the votes required to achieve representation in parliament. The level of participation by the electorate was some 58.2%. Although the leftist Estonian Centre Party secured the largest number of votes cast in the election, Union for the Republic Res Publica refused to initiate talks with it on the formation of a new government, and instead invited the ERP, the Estonian People's Union and the Pro Patria (Fatherland) Union to join it in a four-member coalition. However, the ERP and the Estonian People's Union objected to the inclusion of the Pro Patria (Fatherland) Union, and on 27 March agreement was reached on the formation of a three-party government, which would hold a total of 60 seats in the Riigikogu. After Savisaar declined the President's offer to form a government, on 2 April Juhan Parts, the leader of Union for the Republic Res Publica, was nominated as Prime Minister. The new coalition Government, approved on 9 April, consisted of five members of that party, five members of the ERP and four representatives of the Estonian People's Union; Kristiina Ojuland retained the foreign affairs portfolio.

Since the restoration of Estonian independence in 1991, the republic's relations with its eastern neighbour, Russia, have been strained by a number of issues, most notably the presence of former Soviet troops (under Russian jurisdiction) and the rights of the large Russian minority in Estonia. Under the Citizenship Law of 1992 (a modified version of that adopted in 1938), non-ethnic Estonians who settled in the republic after its annexation by the USSR in 1940 were obliged to apply for naturalization (as were their descendants). Many of the requirements for naturalization—including two years' residency in Estonia as well as an examination in the Estonian language—were criticized by the Russian Government as being excessively stringent, and discriminatory against the Russian-speaking minority. A new citizenship law, adopted in January 1995, extended the residency requirement to five years. Non-citizens were given until 12 July to apply for residence and work permits, by which time almost 330,000 people (more than 80% of the total) had submitted applications. The deadline was extended until 30 November 1996, and by October some 110,000 people had taken Russian citizenship, while continuing to live in Estonia. In May 1997 the Ministry of Internal Affairs announced that Soviet passports were no longer valid in Estonia. An amendment to the Language Law, adopted by the Riigikogu in November, required parliamentary deputies and local government officials who had not received elementary education at an Estonian language school to demonstrate their knowledge of the language. The amendment, which was denounced by ethnic Russian members of the legislature as unconstitutional, was vetoed by President Meri in December and in January 1998. Meri's objections to the legislation were upheld by a ruling of the Supreme Court in early February. However, revised legislation requiring elected officials to demonstrate sufficient command of Estonian to participate in the basic bureaucratic procedures of office was approved by the Riigikogu in mid-December, despite opposition from the OSCE. The legislation became effective in May 1999, and on 1 July a further amendment to the Language Law came into force, which stipulated that those employed in the services sector be able to communicate with clients in Estonian. In April 2000, following a statement by the OSCE High Commissioner on National Minorities that the language legislation contradicted international standards on freedom of expression, the law was amended, to make knowledge of Estonian compulsory only where it was deemed necessary for the sake of public interest, for example, in areas such as public health and security. In November 2001 the requirement that electoral candidates be able to speak Estonian was abolished, although legislation was adopted in same month, which made Estonian the official language of parliament.

With the dissolution of the USSR in 1991, several thousand former Soviet troops remained stationed (under Russian command) on Estonian territory. Their withdrawal was commenced in 1992, but the Russian leadership increasingly linked the progress of the troop withdrawals with the question of the citizenship, and other rights, of the Russian-speaking minority in Estonia. Withdrawals of the troops were suspended temporarily on several occasions in response to allegations of violations of the Russian minority's rights. In November 1993 a resolution by the UN General Assembly demanded a complete withdrawal of the ex-Soviet troops, and the Russian Government proposed 31 August 1994 as the final deadline for the withdrawals. Negotiations were complicated by Russian demands that the 12,000 retired Russian military servicemen (and their dependants) living in Estonia be granted unqualified citizenship rights and social guarantees, but in July President Meri pledged that civil and social rights would be guaranteed to all Russian military pensioners in Estonia. The withdrawal of former Soviet troops was finally completed on 29 August. The agreements on the withdrawal of troops and on Russian military pensioners were ratified by the Russian and Estonian legislatures in 1995, despite opposition from many Estonian politicians who argued that, as Russia had been an occupying force, its servicemen should not be allowed to retire in Estonia. By December 1996 the Estonian Government had granted residence permits to over 20,000 retired servicemen and their dependants.

A further cause of tension in Estonian-Russian relations concerned Estonia's demand for the return of some 2,000 sq km (770 sq miles) of territory that had been ceded to Russia in 1944. This matter remained unresolved, with Estonia insisting that the Russian-Estonian state border be determined by the terms of the Treaty of Tartu of 1920, in which Russia recognized

Estonia's independence. In June 1994 President Yeltsin ordered the unilateral demarcation of Russia's border with Estonia according to the Soviet boundary, although no agreement with Estonia had been concluded. During 1995 Estonia abandoned its demand for the return of the disputed territories. Instead, the Estonian Government appealed only for minor amendments to be made to the existing line of demarcation, in order to improve border security; more importantly, it insisted that Russia recognize the Treaty of Tartu as the basis of future relations between the two countries. However, the Russian Government maintained that the Treaty had lost its legal force, having been superseded by the declaration on bilateral relations signed by Russia and Estonia in 1991.

Relations between Russia and Estonia deteriorated in 1996. The re-establishment of the Estonian Apostolic Orthodox Church (see section on Religion) was perceived by Russia as a threat to the rights of the Russian-speaking minority in Estonia, and the assertion of jurisdiction in Estonia by the Ecumenical Patriarch of Constantinople in February led to the temporary cessation of relations with the Moscow Patriarchate. Further negotiations concerning the adoption of the border agreement were held throughout 1996, but Russia continued to reject the inclusion in the agreement of the Treaty of Tartu, fearing that it would legitimize Estonia's claims on Russian territory (despite the fact that these had been abandoned by Estonia). In November it was announced that Estonia was prepared to omit the Treaty of Tartu from the border agreement. The Estonian Government approved the draft agreement in late November, and declared that it would be signed by Estonia and Russia at the Lisbon summit of the OSCE in December. However, the Russian Government refused to sign the agreement until other issues had been addressed, in particular the rights of the Russian-speaking minority in Estonia. Relations between the two countries remained strained, and in September 2000 Estonia decreed that from 2001 a full visa regime would come into effect between the two countries, despite Russian misgivings. None the less, in January 2002 a joint statement was issued by the Presidents of the three Baltic states on the development of stable and friendly relations with Russia.

Estonia actively pursues close relations with its Baltic neighbours, Latvia and Lithuania. In late 1991 the three states established a consultative interparliamentary body, the Baltic Assembly, with the aim of developing political and economic co-operation. In early 1992 it was agreed to abolish almost all trade restrictions between the three countries and to introduce a common visa policy, and a tripartite agreement on free trade and regional security was signed in late 1993. A customs agreement came into force in June 1996, which constituted the first stage of the establishment of a unified customs system. In November 1997 the three countries agreed to reject Russian overtures to provide unilateral security guarantees, and to remove all non-tariff customs barriers between them. In January 1998 the Presidents of the three states met President Clinton of the USA in Washington, DC, and all parties signed a Charter of Partnership. Estonia is a member of the Council of Baltic Sea States (see p. 179) established in March 1992. In July 1999 the Estonian, Latvian and Lithuanian Prime Ministers met in Palanga, Lithuania, where they agreed to develop the Baltic Common Economic Area and to remove obstacles to the further implementation of trilateral agreements on free trade.

An important focus of Estonia's foreign policy is the attainment of full membership of the EU. In July 1995 Estonia became an associate member, and in December it officially applied for full membership; formal accession negotiations began on 31 March 1998. Also in March, in accordance with the European Convention on Human Rights and Fundamental Freedoms, the Riigikogu voted to abolish the death penalty. In October 2002 the European Commission approved a report, which identified 10 countries, including Estonia, as ready to join the EU in 2004. Among the EU states, Estonia enjoys particularly cordial relations with Finland (its largest trading partner), with which it shares close cultural and linguistic ties. In addition, Estonia was pursuing the goal of membership of NATO (Estonia joined NATO's 'Partnership for Peace' programme of military co-operation in 1994). In November 2002, at a NATO summit meeting held in Prague, Czech Republic, Estonia was one of seven countries to be invited formally to accede to the Organization in 2004. Estonia is also a member of the Council of Europe (see p. 181. The OSCE closed its mission to Estonia at the end of 2001), upon fulfilment of its mandate (despite Russian objections).

Government

Legislative authority resides with the Riigikogu (State Assembly), which has 101 members, elected by universal adult suffrage for a four-year term. The Riigikogu elects the President (Head of State) for a term of five years. The President is also Supreme Commander of Estonia's armed forces. Executive power is held by the Council of Ministers, which is headed by the Prime Minister, who is nominated by the President. For administrative purposes, Estonia is divided into 15 counties (*maakonds*), six cities and 247 rural municipalities (*vald*) and towns (*linn*).

Defence

Before regaining independence in 1991, Estonia had no armed forces separate from those of the USSR. Following the establishment of its own Ministry of Defence in April 1992, Estonia began to form an independent army. By August 2002 its total armed forces numbered an estimated 5,510 (army 2,550, navy 440, air force 220, plus some 2,300 centrally controlled staff). There was also a reserve militia of some 24,000. There is a paramilitary border guard numbering 2,600 troops, under the command of the Ministry of Internal Affairs. In July 2000 the standard duration of military service was reduced from 12 to eight months. Also in 2000 a plan for the reform of the armed forces was approved. In February 1994 Estonia joined NATO's 'Partnership for Peace' programme of military co-operation. In 1998 the Baltic states agreed to establish a joint airspace observation system (BALTNET), a defence college and a peace-keeping battalion (BALTBAT); from 2001 this was to be divided into three national battalions. A Baltic naval unit (BALTRON) was established in mid-1998. In November 2002 Estonia was invited to join NATO, and it was scheduled to become a full member in 2004. The country had implemented measures to increase its defence expenditure, in line with NATO requirements that countries aspiring to membership should assign at least 2.0% of annual GDP for defence. Expenditure on defence in 2001 totalled 1,651m. kroons. The defence budget for 2002 assigned 2,019m. kroons to defence.

Economic Affairs

In 2001, according to World Bank estimates, Estonia's gross national income (GNI), measured at average 1999–2001 prices, was US $5,255m., equivalent to $3,810 per head (or $10,020 per head on an international purchasing-power parity basis). During 1990–2001, it was estimated, the population declined at an average annual rate of 1.3%, while gross domestic product (GDP) per head increased, in real terms, by an average of 0.4% per year. Overall GDP decreased, in real terms, at an annual average rate of 1.0% during 1990–2001. However, according to official figures, real GDP increased by 5.0% in 2001 and by 5.8% in 2002.

Agriculture (including hunting, forestry and fishing) contributed 5.4% of GDP in 2002. In that year the sector provided 7.3% of employment. Animal husbandry is the main activity in the agricultural sector. Some 27.4% of Estonia's land is cultivable. The principal crops are grains, potatoes and fruits and vegetables. Forestry products are also important. During 1990–2001, according to the World Bank, agricultural GDP declined, in real terms, at an average annual rate of 3.3%. The GDP of the sector increased by 1.5% in 2000 and by 1.4% in 2001.

Industry (including mining and quarrying, manufacturing, construction and power) contributed 29.3% of GDP in 2002. In that year the sector provided 33.0% of employment. The sector is dominated by machine-building, electronics and electrical engineering. During 1990–2001, according to the World Bank, industrial GDP declined at an average annual rate of 4.0%. Industrial GDP recorded an increase of 3.3% in 2000 and of 3.2% in 2001.

Mining and quarrying contributed 1.1% of GDP in 2002, when it provided 1.0% of employment. Estonia's principal mineral resource is oil-shale, and there are also deposits of peat and phosphorite ore. There are total estimated reserves of oil-shale of some 4,000 metric tons. However, annual extraction of oil-shale had declined to some 11.7m. tons by 2000, compared with some 31m. tons in 1980. Phosphorite ore is processed to produce phosphates for use in agriculture, but development of the industry has been accompanied by increasing environmental problems. According to official figures, the GDP of the mining and quarrying sector increased by 10.0% in 2001 and by 10.6% in 2002.

In 2002 the manufacturing sector accounted for 18.6% of GDP and engaged an estimated 23.0% of the employed labour force. The sector is based on products of food- and beverage-processing (especially dairy products), textiles and clothing, fertilizers and other chemical products, and wood and timber products (particularly furniture). The World Bank estimated that in 1992–2001 the GDP of the manufacturing sector declined, in real terms, at an annual average rate of 0.2%. However, according to official figures, real manufacturing GDP increased by 8.2% in 2001 and by 9.8% in 2002.

The country relies on oil-shale for over 90% of its energy requirements. In 2001 imports of mineral fuels accounted for 5.8% of total imports.

The services sector accounted for 65.3% of GDP in 2002, and engaged 59.7% of the employed population. During 1990–2001, according to the World Bank, the GDP of the services sector increased, in real terms, by an annual average of 1.5%. The GDP of the sector increased by 8.0% in 2000 and by 4.9% in 2001.

In 2001 Estonia recorded a visible trade deficit of US $786.9m., while there was a deficit of $339.0m. on the current account of the balance of payments. After 1991 trade with Western countries, particularly Scandinavia, increased considerably, while trade with former Soviet republics declined from about 90% of the pre-1991 total to some 30% by 1995. In 2001 Finland was Estonia's principal trading partner, accounting for 18.0% of imports and 33.9% of exports; other important trading partners were Sweden, Germany, Latvia, the People's Republic of China and Russia. In 2001 the principal exports were machinery and electrical goods (33.1% of total export revenue), wood and wood products (13.2%), textiles (11.5%), miscellaneous manufactured articles (8.1%) and base metals (6.9%). The principal imports were machinery and electrical goods (33.5%), transport vehicles (8.9%), base metals (8.1%), textiles (8.0%), chemical products (7.0%) and mineral products (6.1%).

In 2001, according to preliminary figures, there was a general consolidated budgetary surplus of 396.3m. kroons (equivalent to 0.4% of GDP). Estonia's external debt totalled US $3,280.4m. at the end of 2000, of which $206.3m. was long-term public debt. In the same year the cost of debt-servicing was equivalent to 8.7% of the value of exports of goods and services. The annual rate of inflation reached 1,069% in 1992. However, in 1993, following a programme of radical monetary reform, the average annual rate of inflation was reduced to 89%. During 1992–2000 the annual rate of inflation averaged 24.3%. Consumer prices increased by 5.8% in 2001 and by 3.6% in 2002. Some 67,200 people (approximately 10.3% of the labour force) were officially registered as unemployed in 2002.

In 1992 Estonia became a member of the IMF and the World Bank. It also joined the European Bank for Reconstruction and Development (see p. 193). In 1994 Estonia signed a free-trade agreement with the EU. It became an associate member of the EU in June 1995, and applied for full membership in December; Estonia was expected to accede to the EU in 2004. In November 1999 Estonia became a member of the World Trade Organization (WTO, see p. 323).

Even before it regained independence in mid-1991, Estonia had begun a transition to a market economy, and far-reaching economic reforms were continued in the early 1990s. However, despite Estonia's relative prosperity during the Soviet period, the collapse of the USSR and its internal economic system resulted in serious economic difficulties. In June 1992 Estonia introduced a new currency, the kroon, pegged at a rate of 8:1 against the German Deutsche Mark, enhancing international financial confidence in Estonia. The rate of annual inflation, which had reached 1,069% in 1992, had decreased to 10.6% by 1997. In 1999, however, largely owing to the adverse effects of the Russian financial crisis of the previous year, Estonia recorded negative growth, and unemployment increased dramatically. In 2000 the economy was aided by increased export trade to EU member countries, a recovery in industrial production and comparatively healthy domestic demand. Estonia's final stand-by arrangement with the IMF expired in August 2001; the World Bank's office in Estonia had closed earlier in the year. Owing to revenues exceeding those forecast, the Government introduced two supplementary budgets in 2002, contrary to the advice of the central bank and the IMF, and it planned to draw up another in 2003. The Government's budget for 2003 was the first to anticipate a deficit since independence. Following the general election in March 2003, a preliminary programme was agreed for the gradual diminution, by 2% per year, of the rate of personal income tax in 2004–06; the income-tax rate was 26% in 2003. Economic growth of 4.8% was predicted in 2003, and consumer prices were expected to rise by 3.2%. The large current-account deficit (which was reported to have increased by more than twofold in 2002) was regarded as the country's greatest economic obstacle, and was expected to represent 10.7% of GDP in 2003.

Education

The Estonian education system consists of pre-school, primary, secondary, vocational, university/higher, and adult education. Compulsory education begins at the age of seven and lasts for nine years: primary school (Grades 1–6) and lower secondary (Grades 7–9). Students may then attend either general secondary school (Grades 10–12) or vocational school. In 2000/01 there were 34 higher-education institutions in Estonia, including Tartu University (founded in 1632) and the Tallinn Technical University, with a total of 50,814 students enrolled. The language of instruction at all levels is either Estonian or Russian. In 1998 29% of students at general day schools took classes with Russian as the language of instruction. Estonian was to be the language of instruction in all secondary schools by 2007/08. In 1999 the enrolment at primary schools was equivalent to 96.6%

of the corresponding age group. At secondary school level, enrolment was equivalent to 77.2% of the school-age population and in tertiary education it was equivalent to 53.7%. Central government expenditure on education totalled 2,875.5m. kroons in 1999; local government expenditure amounted to 2,791.2m. kroons. Total public-sector expenditure on education in that year was equivalent to an estimated 7% of GDP.

Public Holidays

2003: 1 January (New Year's Day), 24 February (Independence Day), 18 April (Good Friday), 1 May (Spring Day), 23 June (Victory Day, anniversary of the Battle of Võnnu in 1919), 24 June (Midsummer Day, Jaanipäev), 20 August (Restoration of Independence Day), 25–26 December (Christmas).

2004: 1 January (New Year's Day), 24 February (Independence Day), 9 April (Good Friday), 1 May (Spring Day), 23 June (Victory Day, anniversary of the Battle of Võnnu in 1919), 24 June (Midsummer Day, Jaanipäev), 20 August (Restoration of Independence Day), 25–26 December (Christmas).

Weights and Measures

The metric system is in force.

Statistical Survey

Source (unless otherwise stated): Statistical Office of Estonia (Statiskaamet), Endla 15, Tallinn 0100; tel. 625-9202; fax 625-9370; e-mail stat@stat.ee; internet www.stat.ee.

Area and Population

AREA, POPULATION AND DENSITY

Area (sq km)	45,227*
Population (census results)†	
12 January 1989	1,565,662
31 March 2000	
Males	631,851
Females	738,201
Total	1,370,052
Population (official estimates at 1 January)†	
2001	1,366,959
2002	1,361,242
2003‡	1,356,000
Density (per sq km) at 1 January 2003	30.0

* 17,462 sq miles.

† Figures refer to permanent inhabitants. The *de facto* total was 1,572,916 at the 1989 census and 1,356,931 at the 2000 census.

‡ Rounded figure.

POPULATION BY NATIONALITY

(estimated permanent inhabitants at 1 January 2000)*

	Number	%
Estonian	939,310	65.3
Russian	403,925	28.1
Ukrainian	36,467	2.5
Belarusian	21,125	1.5
Finnish	12,762	0.9
Tatar	3,232	0.2
Latvian	2,638	0.2
Jewish	2,275	0.2
Polish	2,290	0.2
Lithuanian	2,188	0.2
German	1,228	0.1
Others	11,757	0.8
Total	**1,439,197**	**100.0**

* Based on the results of 1989 census and official estimates 1990–99.

POPULATION BY ADMINISTRATIVE COUNTY

(1 January 2002)

Harjumaa . . .	523,588	Pärnumaa . . .	90,507
Hiiumaa . . .	10,385	Raplamaa . . .	37,319
Ida-Virumaa . .	177,471	Saaremaa . . .	35,746
Jõgevamaa . . .	38,060	Tartumaa . . .	149,160
Järvamaa . . .	38,514	Valgamaa . . .	35,479
Läänemaa . . .	28,394	Viljandimaa . .	57,482
Lääne-Virumaa . .	67,364	Võrumaa . . .	39,465
Põlvamaa . . .	32,308	**Total**	**1,361,242**

PRINCIPAL TOWNS

(estimated population, excluding suburbs, at 1 January 2002)

Tallinn (capital) . .	398,434	Kohtla-Järve . .	47,106
Tartu	101,140	Pärnu	45,040
Narva	68,117	Viljandi	20,608

BIRTHS, MARRIAGES AND DEATHS*

	Registered live births		Registered marriages		Registered deaths	
	Number	Rate (per 1,000)	Number	Rate (per 1,000)	Number	Rate (per 1,000)
1994 . .	14,176	9.6	7,378	5.0	22,212	15.2
1995 . .	13,509	9.4	7,006	4.8	20,828	14.5
1996 . .	13,242	9.3	5,517	3.9	19,020	13.4
1997 . .	12,577	8.9	5,589	3.9	18,572	13.2
1998 . .	12,167	8.7	5,430	3.9	19,445	14.0
1999 . .	12,425	9.0	5,590	4.1	18,447	13.4
2000 . .	13,067	9.5	5,485	4.0	18,403	13.4
2001 . .	12,632	9.3	5,647	4.1	18,516	13.6

* Revised figures, based on the results of the 1989 and 2000 population censuses.

Expectation of life (WHO estimates, years at birth): 71.2 (males 65.7; females 76.5) in 2001 (Source: WHO, *World Health Report*).

EMPLOYMENT

(labour force sample surveys, annual averages, '000 persons aged 15–74 years, excl. armed forces)

	2000	2001	2002
Agriculture, hunting and forestry	38.3	37.3	38.8
Fishing	2.9	2.7	1.9
Mining and quarrying	7.2	5.8	5.7
Manufacturing	129.2	134.1	128.2
Electricity, gas and water supply	14.7	11.4	10.5
Construction	39.7	39.3	38.9
Wholesale and retail trade	79.3	83.6	86.3
Hotels and restaurants	19.9	17.4	17.9
Transport, storage and communications	56.9	53.7	54.5
Financial intermediation	7.7	7.2	7.9
Real estate, renting and business activities	40.0	38.2	44.3
Public administration and defence; compulsory social security	34.1	34.8	33.2
Education	44.6	51.0	55.6
Health and social work	28.5	30.9	31.6
Activities not adequately defined	29.6	30.4	30.1
Total employed	572.5	577.7	585.5

Unemployed (annual averages, '000 persons aged 15–74): 89.9 in 2000; 83.1 in 2001; 67.2 in 2002.

Health and Welfare

KEY INDICATORS

Total fertility rate (children per woman, 2001)	1.2
Under-5 mortality rate (per 1,000 live births, 2001)	12
HIV/AIDS (% of persons aged 15–49, 2001)	1.00
Physicians (per 1,000 head, 1998)	2.97
Hospital beds (per 1,000 head, 1997)	7.4
Health expenditure (2000): US $ per head (PPP)	556
Health expenditure (2000): % of GDP	6.1
Health expenditure (2000): public (% of total)	76.7
Human Development Index (2000): ranking	42
Human Development Index (2000): value	0.826

For sources and definitions, see explanatory note on p. vi.

Agriculture

PRINCIPAL CROPS

('000 metric tons)

	1999	2000	2001
Wheat	88.4	146.8	133.0
Barley	186.4	347.5	270.0
Rye	38.8	60.8	42.9
Oats	70.8	117.1	91.4
Other cereals	17.3	24.4	103.4
Potatoes	403.7	471.7	343.1
Dry peas	2.2	5.3	5.0
Rapeseed	29.8	38.8	41.3
Cabbages	18.9	21.5	16.7
Cucumbers and gherkins	6.1	5.6	11.5
Carrots	6.7	8.8	11.6
Other vegetables	17.1*	12.2†	9.4
Apples	11.4	18.5	15.1
Other fruits*	6.2	9.5	13.3

* FAO estimate(s).
† Unofficial figure.

Source: FAO.

LIVESTOCK

('000 head, year ending September)

	1999	2000	2001
Cattle	308	267	253
Pigs	326	286	300
Sheep	29	28	29
Chickens	2,636	2,462	2,366
Ducks	20*	20†	20†
Geese	8*	8†	8†
Turkeys	20*	20†	20†
Rabbits	20	21	55*

* Unofficial figure.
† FAO estimate.

Source: FAO.

LIVESTOCK PRODUCTS

('000 metric tons, unless otherwise indicated)

	1999	2000	2001
Beef and veal	21.7	15.4	14.2
Pig meat	31.3	30.3	33.6
Poultry meat	7.7	7.3	9.2
Cows' milk	625.5	628.9	683.2
Butter	10.9	8.7	6.9
Cheese	21.4	16.0	17.1
Hen eggs	17.2	16.5	18.1
Honey (metric tons)	336	334	291

Source: FAO.

Forestry

ROUNDWOOD REMOVALS

('000 cubic metres, excl. bark)

	1999	2000	2001
Sawlogs, veneer logs and logs for sleepers	2,200	2,850	3,260
Pulpwood	3,350	3,800	3,910
Other industrial wood	350	620	1,150
Fuel wood	804	1,640	1,880
Total	6,704	8,910	10,200

Source: FAO.

SAWNWOOD PRODUCTION

('000 cubic metres, incl. railway sleepers)

	1999	2000	2001
Coniferous (softwood)	1,100	1,346	1,536
Broadleaved (hardwood)	100	90	134
Total	1,200	1,436	1,670

Source: FAO.

Fishing

('000 metric tons, live weight)

	1998	1999	2000
Capture	118.7	111.8	113.1
Blue whiting	6.3	0	—
Atlantic redfishes	4.0	2.1	8.7
Atlantic herring	42.7	44.0	41.7
European sprat	32.2	36.4	41.4
Chub mackerel	7.2	3.4	—
Atlantic mackerel	7.4	3.6	2.7
Northern prawn	7.2	12.4	12.8
Aquaculture	0.3	0.2	0.2
Total catch	119.0	112.0	113.4

Source: FAO, *Yearbook of Fishery Statistics*.

Mining

('000 metric tons)

	1998	1999	2000
Oil-shale	12,463	10,685	11,726
Peat	365	1,299	586

Source: US Geological Survey.

Industry

SELECTED PRODUCTS

('000 metric tons, unless otherwise indicated)

	1998	1999	2000
Distilled spirits ('000 hectolitres)	102	66	86
Wine ('000 hectolitres)	31	24	33
Beer ('000 hectolitres)	744	957	950
Soft drinks ('000 hectolitres)	666	824	699
Woven cotton fabric ('000 sq metres)	127	95	121
Linen fabric ('000 sq metres)	1,444	3,910	n.a.
Carpets ('000 sq metres)	2,199	1,352	1,866
Footwear ('000 pairs)	1,226	1,347	1,443
Plywood ('000 cubic metres)	20	17	18
Particle board ('000 cubic metres)	176.6	147.8	175.8
Fibreboard (million sq metres)	17.7	17.0	17.7
Chemical wood pulp	44.1	49.5	54.4
Paper	42.6	47.9	52.4
Nitrogenous fertilizers*	31	41	38
Building bricks (million)	21	17	17
Cement	321	358	329
Electric energy (million kWh)	8,521	8,268	8,513

* In terms of nitrogen.

Electric energy (million kWh): 8,483 in 2001.

Finance

CURRENCY AND EXCHANGE RATES

Monetary Units
100 cents = 1 kroon

Sterling, Dollar and Euro Equivalents (31 December 2002)
£1 sterling = 24.07 kroons
US $1 = 14.94 kroons
€1 = 15.66 kroons
1,000 kroons = £41.54 = $66.95 = €63.84

Average Exchange Rate (kroons per US $)
2000	16.969
2001	17.564
2002	16.612

Note: In June 1992 Estonia reintroduced its national currency, the kroon, replacing the rouble of the former USSR, initially at a rate of one kroon per 10 roubles.

BUDGET
(million kroons)*

Revenue†	1999	2000	2001‡
Tax revenue	24,933.7	27,369.2	30,088.8
Taxes on income, profits and capital gains	8,166.9	7,448.9	7,847.4
Individual	6,531.8	6,594.4	7,099.1
Corporate	1,635.1	854.5	748.3
Social security contributions	7,247.3	8,419.3	9,546.0
Domestic taxes on goods and services	9,228.8	11,106.7	12,220.5
General sales, turnover or value-added taxes	6,419.9	8,156.2	8,642.5
Excises	2,686.5	2,819.2	3,434.1
Other current revenue	2,235.6	2,932.9	3,344.9
Entrepreneurial and property income	536.9	1,090.7	1,526.9
Administrative fees and charges, non-industrial and incidental sales	1,060.1	1,127.6	1,225.3
Capital revenue	356.7	468.2	834.0
Sales of land and intangible assets	143.8	150.4	169.1
Total	27,526.0	30,770.3	34,267.7

Expenditure§	1999	2000	2001‡
Current expenditure	27,966.5	29,206.9	31,405.4
Expenditure on goods and services	15,628.6	16,042.4	16,543.1
Wages and salaries	5,080.8	5,332.3	5,415.4
Interest payments	308.6	294.5	257.7
Subsidies and other current transfers	12,029.3	12,870.0	14,604.6
Subsidies	689.7	681.5	805.0
Transfers to non-profit institutions	2,432.3	2,482.2	3,298.0
Transfers to households	8,875.6	9,667.3	10,460.9
Capital expenditure	3,360.4	2,736.3	3,158.4
Acquisition of fixed assets	3,127.0	2,630.9	3,032.3
Total	31,326.9	31,943.2	34,563.8

* Figures represent a consolidation of the operations of the Government, comprising all central and local government accounts.
† Excluding grants received (million kroons): 303.9 in 1999; 267.2 in 2000; 629.5 in 2001.
‡ Preliminary data.
§ Excluding lending minus repayments (million kroons): −14.3 in 1999; −26.1 in 2000; −62.9 in 2001.

INTERNATIONAL RESERVES
(US $ million at 31 December)

	2000	2001	2002
Gold*	2.25	2.29	2.83
IMF special drawing rights	0.02	0.03	0.07
Reserve position in IMF	0.01	0.01	0.01
Foreign exchange	920.62	820.20	1,000.30
Total	922.90	822.53	1,003.21

* National valuation.

Source: IMF, *International Financial Statistics*.

MONEY SUPPLY
(million kroons at 31 December)

	2000	2001	2002
Currency outside banks	6,201.3	6,951.9	6,994.9
Demand deposits at banks	14,456.8	17,967.9	20,225.5
Total money (incl. others)	20,884.1	24,948.2	27,274.5

Source: IMF, *International Financial Statistics*.

COST OF LIVING
(Consumer price index; base: 1997 = 100)

	1999	2000	2001
Food (incl. beverages)	100.9	103.4	111.9
Alcohol and tobacco	119.8	123.8	127.3
Clothing (incl. footwear)	119.8	123.9	128.6
Housing	120.5	123.8	135.9
All items (incl. others)	111.8	116.3	123.0

NATIONAL ACCOUNTS
(million kroons at current prices)

Expenditure on the Gross Domestic Product

	2000	2001	2002
Government final consumption expenditure	18,108.7	19,562.6	21,269.2
Non-profit institutions	633.0	664.4	993.7
Private final consumption expenditure	48,584.4	53,793.9	60,292.6
Increase in stocks	2,059.8	1,567.2	3,580.4
Gross fixed capital formation	22,193.2	25,206.9	30,315.1
Total domestic expenditure	91,579.1	100,795.0	116,451.0
Exports of goods and services f.o.b.	81,831.7	87,533.6	90,579.5
Less Imports of goods and services f.o.b.	85,400.7	91,157.3	101,010.3
Statistical discrepancy	−774.6	−600.6	476.1
GDP in purchasers' values	87,235.5	96,570.7	106,496.3
GDP at constant 2000 prices	87,235.5	91,633.1	96,904.2

Gross Domestic Product by Economic Activity

	2000	2001	2002
Agriculture and hunting	2,682.8	2,867.9	2,800.7
Forestry	1,888.2	1,944.6	2,072.3
Fishing	217.2	214.9	219.8
Mining and quarrying	772.4	881.1	1,029.4
Manufacturing	14,092.9	15,921.3	17,592.3
Electricity, gas and water supply	2,586.5	2,834.3	3,005.7
Construction	4,762.1	5,122.4	6,103.9
Wholesale and retail trade; repair of motor vehicles, motorcycles and personal and household goods	10,830.7	12,284.7	13,783.9
Hotels and restaurants	1,137.4	1,220.3	1,460.4
Transport, storage and communications	12,693.2	14,193.3	15,013.2
Financial intermediation	3,234.0	3,692.9	10,521.0
Real estate, renting and business activities	8,586.7	9,743.8	4,167.8
Public administration and defence; compulsory social security	3,677.2	3,895.8	4,372.2
Education	4,410.7	4,684.3	5,175.2
Health and social work	2,819.6	2,910.7	3,107.3
Other community, social and personal service activities	3,610.6	3,916.8	4,214.1
Sub-total	78,002.2	86,329.1	94,639.2
Less Imputed bank service charge	1,249.9	1,450.4	1,676.0
GDP at factor cost	76,752.3	84,878.7	92,963.2
Net indirect taxes	10,483.2	11,692.0	13,533.1
GDP in purchasers' values	87,235.5	96,570.7	106,496.3

BALANCE OF PAYMENTS
(US $ million)

	1999	2000	2001
Exports of goods f.o.b.	2,453.1	3,311.4	3,338.1
Imports of goods f.o.b.	−3,330.6	−4,079.5	−4,125.0
Trade balance	−877.5	−768.1	−786.9
Exports of services	1,489.7	1,499.0	1,642.8
Imports of services	−917.6	−936.3	−1,064.9
Balance on goods and services	−305.4	−205.4	−209.0
Other income received	133.8	117.6	170.6
Other income paid	−235.5	−321.7	−451.8
Balance on goods, services and income	−407.1	−409.6	−490.1
Current transfers received	153.7	144.7	180.4
Current transfers paid	−41.2	−29.1	−29.3
Current balance	−294.6	−294.0	−339.0
Capital account (net)	1.2	16.5	5.1
Direct investment abroad	−82.9	−63.4	−199.6
Direct investment from abroad	305.2	387.3	539.4
Portfolio investment assets	−132.3	39.8	13.1
Portfolio investment liabilities	153.3	75.6	83.0
Financial derivatives assets	—	−4.7	−0.1
Financial derivatives liabilities	—	5.4	−2.0
Other investment assets	−110.3	−177.1	−297.7
Other investment liabilities	285.2	143.8	170.5
Net errors and omissions	−5.4	−1.6	−12.8
Overall balance	119.3	127.6	−40.3

Source: IMF, *International Financial Statistics*.

External Trade

PRINCIPAL COMMODITIES
(million kroons)

Imports c.i.f.	1999	2000	2001
Prepared foodstuffs; beverages spirits and vinegar; tobacco and manufactured substitutes	2,715.7	3,009.0	3,368.3
Mineral products	3,044.0	4,416.3	4,616.9
Mineral fuels, mineral oils and products of their distillation; bituminous substances, etc.	2,846.0	4,239.5	4,389.1
Products of chemical or allied industries	3,985.9	4,791.6	5,273.6
Plastics, rubber and articles thereof	2,456.7	3,258.0	3,586.1
Plastics and articles thereof	1,989.7	2,675.4	2,941.8
Paper-making material; paper and paperboard and articles thereof	1,586.3	2,174.2	2,213.1
Textiles and textile articles	4,493.9	5,416.3	5,962.2
Base metals and articles of base metal	4,121.3	5,867.8	6,087.8
Iron and steel	1,586.7	2,521.6	2,149.3
Machinery and mechanical appliances; electrical equipment; sound and television apparatus	15,474.3	27,788.5	25,134.4
Nuclear reactors, boilers machinery and mechanical appliances; parts thereof	5,069.9	6,426.2	7,180.6
Vehicles, aircraft, vessels and associated transport equipment	3,852.5	4,997.7	6,686.5
Vehicles other than railway or tramway rolling-stock, and parts and accessories	3,405.1	4,570.3	5,952.9
Total (incl. others)	50,452.1	72,717.2	75,074.6

Exports f.o.b.	1999	2000	2001
Live animals and animal products	1,389.4	1,967.9	2,423.1
Prepared foodstuffs; beverages spirits and vinegar; tobacco and manufactured substitutes . .	989.1	857.2	1,801.3
Products of chemical or allied industries	1,431.1	1,997.9	2,477.9
Wood and articles thereof; wood charcoal .	6,612.3	7,201.4	7,642.0
Textiles and textile articles. . .	4,929.9	6,094.6	6,633.7
Knitted and non-knitted clothing and accessories .	2,944.2	3,338.0	3,622.1
Base metals and articles of base metal	2,722.0	3,828.7	3,974.5
Articles of iron or steel . .	1,301.9	1,545.4	1,984.4
Machinery and mechanical appliances; electrical equipment; sound and television apparatus .	8,522.2	20,182.2	19,121.3
Nuclear reactors, boilers machinery and mechanical appliances; parts thereof . .	1,356.4	1,879.2	2,042.9
Electrical machinery equipment and parts; sound and television apparatus parts and accessories	7,165.8	18,302.9	17,078.4
Vehicles, aircraft, vessels and associated transport equipment .	1,061.7	1,383.6	1,860.5
Miscellaneous manufactured articles	2,757.0	3,578.6	4,665.8
Furniture; bedding, mattresses cushions, etc.; lamps and lighting fittings; prefabricated buildings	2,515.8	3,196.7	4,212.5
Total (incl. others)	35,408.9	53,892.4	57,829.9

PRINCIPAL TRADING PARTNERS
(million kroons)

Imports c.i.f.	1999	2000	2001
Belarus	346.3	569.9	824.4
Belgium	883.2	1,218.1	1,430.3
China, People's Repub. . . .	650.5	2,560.5	6,543.5
Czech Republic	379.2	686.4	894.8
Denmark	1,409.9	1,796.8	1,893.9
Finland	13,077.8	19,809.7	13,550.4
France	1,153.1	1,533.5	1,837.2
Germany	5,247.4	6,841.7	8,224.4
Hungary	335.0	205.4	778.1
Ireland	330.0	389.5	761.7
Italy	1,790.9	2,062.7	2,478.0
Japan	2,709.9	4,371.1	3,340.8
Latvia	1,192.4	1,856.7	1,681.4
Lithuania	903.0	1,184.5	1,950.8
Netherlands	1,308.2	1,524.6	1,851.2
Norway	522.1	981.2	801.4
Poland	1,048.8	1,313.8	1,691.9
Russia	4,043.7	6,123.9	6,097.2
Sweden	5,402.2	7,110.2	6,917.9
Switzerland	574.2	578.0	699.2
Ukraine	494.0	572.0	765.1
United Kingdom	1,293.4	1,650.5	1,772.6
USA	1,415.5	1,586.1	1,713.6
Total (incl. others)	50,452.1	72,217.2	75,074.6

Exports f.o.b.	1999	2000	2001
Belgium	416.4	479.9	387.2
Denmark	1,668.5	1,849.8	2,029.5
Finland	8,254.2	17,431.2	19,575.7
France	501.4	728.3	628.4
Germany	2,998.0	4,579.3	4,005.1
Italy	396.2	536.8	564.3
Latvia	2,936.9	3,789.5	4,014.4
Lithuania	1,200.9	1,511.1	1,732.1
Netherlands	913.9	1,324.0	1,601.8
Norway	915.2	1,267.7	1,617.6
Russia	1,187.0	1,278.1	1,593.9
Sweden	8,039.5	11,050.1	8,096.2
Ukraine	673.2	640.3	828.5
United Kingdom	1,993.7	2,351.5	2,434.4
USA	679.5	721.5	1,057.8
Total (incl. others)	35,408.9	53,892.4	57,829.9

Transport

DOMESTIC PASSENGER TRAFFIC
(million passenger-kilometres)

	1999	2000	2001
Railway traffic	238	263	183
Road traffic (bus traffic) . .	2,222	2,371	2,461
Sea traffic	433	455	376
Air traffic	298	303	310
Total public transport . .	3,191	3,392	3,330

DOMESTIC FREIGHT TRAFFIC
(million ton-kilometres)

	1999	2000	2001
Railway traffic	7,295	8,102	8,557
Road traffic	3,975	3,690	4,677
Sea traffic	19,221	4,304	2,943
Air traffic	4	5	4
Total public transport . .	30,495	16,101	16,181

ROAD TRAFFIC
('000 motor vehicles in use at 31 December)

	2000	2001	2002
Passenger cars	463.9	407.3	400.7
Buses and coaches . . .	6.1	5.5	5.3
Lorries and vans . . .	82.1	80.5	80.2
Motor cycles	6.7	6.8	7.3

SHIPPING

Merchant Fleet
(registered at 31 December)

	1999	2000	2001
Number of vessels	219	209	191
Total displacement (grt) . . .	452,648	379,110	346.6

Source: Lloyd's Register-Fairplay, *World Fleet Statistics*.

International Sea-borne Freight Traffic
('000 metric tons)

	2000	2001	2002
Goods loaded	36,037	37,435	41,835
Goods unloaded	4,513	4,084	5,439

CIVIL AVIATION
(traffic on scheduled services)

	1996	1997	1998
Kilometres flown (million) . . .	4	5	6
Passengers carried ('000) . . .	149	231	297
Passenger-km (million)	114	147	177
Total ton-km (million)	11	14	17

Source: UN, *Statistical Yearbook*.

1999: Passengers carried 336,200; Freight carried (incl. mail) 5,500 metric tons; Passenger-km 297.6m.

2000: Passengers carried 332,900; Freight carried (incl. mail) 5,700 metric tons; Passenger-km 302.5m.

2001: Passengers carried 362,300; Freight carried (incl. mail) 7,800 metric tons; Passenger-km 310.0m.

Tourism

FOREIGN TOURIST ARRIVALS BY COUNTRY OF ORIGIN

	1999	2000	2001
Finland	1,199,584	1,198,887	1,058,386
Germany	n.a.	22,825	26,903
Sweden	33,148	39,267	17,664
USA	32,065	43,522	54,138
Total (incl. others)	1,350,366	1,369,159	1,231,620

Receipts from tourism (US $ million): 560 in 1999; 505 in 2000 (Source: World Bank).

Communications Media

	1999	2000	2001
Television receivers ('000 in use)	800	850	n.a.
Telephones ('000 main lines in use)	515	523	504
Mobile cellular telephones ('000 subscribers)	388	557	651
Personal computers ('000 in use)	195	220	250
Internet users ('000)	200	367	430
Book production: titles . . .	3,265	3,466	3,506
Book production: copies ('000) . .	7,117	5,931	5,500*
Daily newspapers: number . . .	17	n.a.	14
Non-daily newspapers: number .	88	n.a.	95
Other periodicals: number . . .	930	956	1,088
Other periodicals: average annual circulation ('000 copies) . . .	19,453	19,843	20,400*

* Figures are rounded.

1996: Radio receivers in use 221,000.

Sources: partly UN, *Statistical Yearbook* and International Telecommunication Union.

Education

(2000/01)

	Institutions	Teachers	Students
Pre-primary	646	8,070*	50,600
Primary	400	17,896	117,300
General secondary	237		95,000
Special.	48		5,800
Vocational and professional .	78	1,779	30,872†
Universities, etc.	34	3,052‡	50,814†

* Figure refers to 1997/98. Including staff in child care and pre-school institutions. (Source: UNESCO, *Statistical Yearbook*).
† Including students enrolled in evening and correspondence courses.
‡ Figure refers to 1996/97.

Adult literacy rate (UNESCO estimates): 99.8% in 1995 (Source: UN Development Programme, *Human Development Report*).

Directory

The Constitution

A new Constitution, based on that of 1938, was adopted by a referendum held on 28 June 1992. It took effect on 3 July. The following is a summary of its main provisions

FUNDAMENTAL RIGHTS, LIBERTIES AND DUTIES

Every child with one parent who is an Estonian citizen has the right, by birth, to Estonian citizenship. Anyone who, as a minor, lost his or her Estonian citizenship has the right to have his or her citizenship restored. The rights, liberties and duties of all persons, as listed in the Constitution, are equal for Estonian citizens as well as for citizens of foreign states and stateless persons who are present in Estonia.

All persons are equal before the law. No one may be discriminated against on the basis of nationality, race, colour, sex, language, origin, creed, political or other persuasions. Everyone has the right to the protection of the state and the law. Guaranteeing rights and liberties is the responsibility of the legislative, executive and judicial powers, as well as of local government. Everyone has the right to appeal to a court of law if his or her rights or liberties have been violated.

The state organizes vocational education and assists in finding work for persons seeking employment. Working conditions are under state supervision. Employers and employees may freely join unions and associations. Estonian citizens have the right to engage in commercial activities and to form profit-making associations. The property rights of everyone are inviolable. All persons legally present in Estonia have the right to freedom of movement and choice of abode. Everyone has the right to leave Estonia.

Everyone has the right to health care and to education. Education is compulsory for school-age children. Everyone has the right to instruction in Estonian.

The official language of state and local government authorities is Estonian. In localities where the language of the majority of the population is other than Estonian, local government authorities may use the language of the majority of the permanent residents of that locality for internal communication.

THE PEOPLE

The people exercise their supreme power through citizens who have the right to vote by: i) electing the Riigikogu (legislature); ii) participating in referendums. The right to vote belongs to every Estonian citizen who has attained the age of 18 years.

THE RIIGIKOGU

Legislative power rests with the Riigikogu (State Assembly). It comprises 101 members, elected every four years in free elections on the principle of proportionality. Every citizen entitled to vote who has attained 21 years of age may stand as a candidate for the Riigikogu.

The Riigikogu adopts laws and resolutions; decides on the holding of referendums; elects the President of the Republic; ratifies or rejects foreign treaties; authorizes the candidate for Prime Minister to form the Council of Ministers; adopts the national budget and approves the report on its execution; may declare a state of emergency, or, on the proposal of the President, declare a state of war, order mobilization and demobilization.

The Riigikogu elects from among its members a Chairman (Speaker) and two Deputy Chairmen to direct its work.

THE PRESIDENT

The President of the Republic is the Head of State of Estonia. The President represents Estonia in international relations; appoints and recalls, on the proposal of the Government, diplomatic representatives of Estonia and accepts letters of credence of diplomatic representatives accredited to Estonia; declares regular (and early) elections to the Riigikogu; initiates amendments to the Constitution; nominates the candidate for the post of Prime Minister; and is the Supreme Commander of Estonia's armed forces.

The President is elected by secret ballot of the Riigikogu for a term of five years. No person may be elected to the office for more than two consecutive terms. Any Estonian citizen by birth, who is at least 40 years of age, may stand as a candidate for President.

Should the President not be elected after three rounds of voting, the Speaker of the Riigikogu convenes, within one month, an Electoral Body to elect the President.

THE GOVERNMENT

Executive power is held by the Government of the Republic (Council of Ministers). The Government implements national, domestic and foreign policies; directs and co-ordinates the work of government institutions; organizes the implementation of legislation, the resolutions of the Riigikogu, and the edicts of the President; submits draft legislation to the Riigikogu, as well as foreign treaties; prepares a draft of the national budget and presents it to the Riigikogu; administers the implementation of the national budget; and organizes relations with foreign states.

The Government comprises the Prime Minister and Ministers. The President of the Republic nominates a candidate for Prime Minister, who is charged with forming a new government.

JUDICIAL SYSTEM

Justice is administered solely by the courts. They are independent in their work and administer justice in accordance with the Constitution and laws. The court system is comprised of rural and city, as well as administrative, courts (first level); district courts (second level); and the Supreme Court of the Republic of Estonia (the highest court in the land).

The Government

HEAD OF STATE

President: ARNOLD RÜÜTEL (elected 21 September 2001; inaugurated 8 October).

COUNCIL OF MINISTERS
(April 2003)

A coalition of the Union for the Republic Res Publica, the Estonian Reform Party (ERP) and the Estonian People's Union.

Prime Minister: JUHAN PARTS (Res Publica).

Minister of Internal Affairs: MARGUS LEIVO (Estonian People's Union).

Minister of Foreign Affairs: KRISTIINA OJULAND (ERP).

Minister of Justice: KEN-MARTI VAHER (Res Publica).

Minister of Economic Affairs and Communications: MEELIS ATONEN (ERP).

Minister of Finance: TÕNIS PALTS (Res Publica).

Minister of the Environment: VILLU REILJAN (Estonian People's Union).

Minister of Culture: URMAS PAET (ERP).

Minister of Education and Science: TOIVO MAIMETS (Res Publica).

Minister of Agriculture: TIIT TAMMSAAR (Estonian People's Union).

Minister of Social Affairs: MARKO POMERANTS (Res Publica).

Minister of Defence: MARGUS HANSON (ERP).

Minister of Population and Ethnic Affairs: PAUL-EERIK RUMMO (Estonian People's Union).

Minister of Regional Affairs: JAAN ÕUNAPUU (Estonian People's Union).

MINISTRIES

Office of the Prime Minister: Rahukohtu 3, Tallinn 15161; tel. 631-6701; fax 631-6704; e-mail peaminister@rk.ee; internet www.riik.ee/primeminister/.

Ministry of Agriculture: Lai 39/41, Tallinn 15056; tel. 625-6101; fax 625-6200; e-mail pm@agri.ee; internet www.agri.ee.

Ministry of Culture: Suur Karja 23, Tallinn 15076; tel. 628-2222; fax 628-2200; e-mail info@kul.ee; internet www.kul.ee.

Ministry of Defence: Sakala 1, Tallinn 10141; tel. 640-6012; fax 640-6001; e-mail info@kmin.ee; internet www.mod.gov.ee.

Ministry of Economic Affairs and Communications: Harju 11, Tallinn 15072; tel. 625-6342; fax 631-3660; e-mail info@mkm.ee; internet www.mkm.ee.

Ministry of Education and Science: Munga 18, Tartu 50088; tel. 735-0222; fax 735-0250; e-mail hm@hm.ee; internet www.hm.ee.

Ministry of the Environment: Toompuiestee 24, Tallinn 15172; tel. 626-2800; fax 626-2801; e-mail min@ekm.envir.ee; internet www.envir.ee.

Ministry of Finance: Suur-Ameerika 1, Tallinn 15006; tel. 611-3558; fax 696-6810; e-mail info@fin.ee; internet www.fin.ee.

Ministry of Foreign Affairs: Islandi Väljak 1, Tallinn 15049; tel. 631-7000; fax 631-7099; e-mail vminfo@vm.ee; internet www.vm.ee.

Ministry of Internal Affairs: Pikk 61, Tallinn 15065; tel. 612-5001; fax 612-5087; e-mail sisemin@sisemin.gov.ee; internet www.sisemin.gov.ee.

Ministry of Justice: Tõnismägi 5A, Tallinn 15191; tel. 620-8100; fax 620-8109; e-mail sekretar@just.ee; internet www.just.ee.

Ministry of Population and Ethnic Affairs: Tallinn.

Ministry of Regional Affairs: Tallinn.

Ministry of Social Affairs: Gonsiori 29, Tallinn 15191; tel. 626-9700; fax 626-9802; e-mail smin@sm.ee; internet www.sm.ee.

President and Legislature

PRESIDENT

A presidential election was held on 27–28 August 2001 in the Riigikogu. The first round was contested by Andres Tarand and Peeter Kreitzberg, neither of whom achieved the necessary two-thirds' majority (68 votes). Tarand was subsequently replaced by Peeter Tulviste; Peeter Kreitzberg retained his candidacy. However, neither candidate secured the requisite majority after two further rounds of voting. A larger electoral college, comprising the 101 parliamentary deputies and 266 representatives from local government, was convened on 21 September. Four candidates contested the first round of the election and, as no candidate achieved the necessary 185 votes, the leading two candidates, Toomas Savi and Arnold Rüütel, proceeded to the second round of voting. The election was won by Arnold Rüütel, with 186 votes.

Election, 21 September 2001

Candidate	First round votes*	Second round votes†
Arnold Rüütel	114	186
Toomas Savi	90	155
Peeter Tulviste	89	—
Peeter Kreitzberg	72	—

* There was one abstention and one elector was absent.
† There were 23 abstentions and two invalid votes, with one elector absent.

RIIGIKOGU
(State Assembly)

Riigikogu: Lossi plats 1a, Tallinn 15165; tel. 631-6331; fax 631-6334; e-mail riigikogu@riigikogu.ee; internet www.riigikogu.ee.

Speaker: ENE ERGMA.

Deputy Speakers: TOOMAS SAVI, PEETER KREITZBERG.

General Election, 2 March 2003

Parties	% of votes	Seats
Estonian Centre Party	25.4	28
Union for the Republic Res Publica	24.6	28
Estonian Reform Party	17.7	19
Estonian People's Union	13.0	13
Pro Patria (Fatherland) Union	7.3	7
People's Party Moderates	7.0	6
Others	5.0	0
Total	**100.0**	**101**

Political Organizations

Democrats–Estonian Democratic Party: Ahdri 6 307, Tallinn 10151; tel. 625-9890; fax 625-9810; e-mail demokraatlik.partei@

mail.ee; internet www.demokraadid.ee; former Estonian Blue Party; Chair. JAAN LAAS.

Estonian Centre Party (Eesti Keskerakond): Toom-Rüütli 3/5, Tallinn 10130 POB 3737, Tallinn 0090; tel. 627-3460; fax 627-3461; e-mail keskerakond@keskerakond.ee; internet www.keskerakond .ee; absorbed the Estonian Green Party in mid-1998; f. 1991; Chair. EDGAR SAVISAAR; 5,000 mems.

Estonian Christian People's Party (Eesti Kristlik Rahvapartei): Narva mnt. 51, Tallinn 10152; tel. 504-5760; fax 678-2311; e-mail ekrp@ekrp.ee; internet www.ekrp.ee; f. 1998; Chair. ALDO VINKEL.

Estonian Conservative Party: Järva 19, Pärnu 80023; tel. 561-6207; fax (2) 422-969; e-mail konserfatiivid@hot.ee; internet www .hot.ee/konservatiivid; Leader ANDRO ROOS.

Estonian Independence Party: opposes EU membership; planned merger with the National Conservative Party-Farmers' Assembly; Chair. VELLO LEITO; 1,047 mems (2002).

Estonian People's Union (Eestimaa Rahvaliit): Marja 4D, Tallinn 10617; tel. 611-2909; fax 611-2908; e-mail erl@erl.ee; internet www .erl.ee; f. 2000; by merger of the Estonian Pensioners' and Families' Party and the Estonian Rural People's Union; merged with the New Estonia Party in Jan. 2003; right-wing; Hon. Chair. ARNOLD RÜÜTEL; Chair. VILLU REILJAN; 8,800 mems.

Estonian Reform Party (ERP) (Eesti Reformierakond): Tõnismagi 3A–15, Tallinn 0001; tel. 640-8740; fax 640-8741; e-mail info@ reform.ee; internet www.reform.ee; f. 1994; liberal; Gen. Sec. HEIKI KRANICH; Chair. SIIM KALLAS.

Estonian Social-Democratic Labour Party (Eesti Sotsiaaldemokraatlik Tööpartei): Rävala puiestee 8, POB 4102, Tallinn 10143; tel. 661-2406; fax 661-2402; e-mail esdtp@solo.ee; internet www .esdtp.ee; f. 1920 as the Communist Party of Estonia; renamed Estonian Democratic Labour Party in 1992 and as above in 1997; left-wing; Chair. TIIT TOOMSALU; Dep. Chair. ENDEL PAAP; 1,250 mems (2003).

Estonian United People's Party (Eestimaa Ühendatud Rahvapartei): Estonia pst. 3/5, Tallinn 10143; tel. 645-5335; fax 645-5336; e-mail eurp@eurp.ee; internet www.eurp.ee; f. 1994; represents the Russian-speaking minority in Estonia; Chair. VIKTOR ANDREYEV.

Farmers' Union (Põllumeeste Kogu): POB 543, Tallinn 0010; tel. (2) 437-733; f. 1992; Chair. ELDUR PARDER.

Moderates' Women's Assembly (Mõõdukad Naiskogu): Tallinn; e-mail moodukad@datanet.ee; f. 1996 to encourage women to take part in politics; Pres. HELJO PIKHOF.

National Conservative Party-Farmers' Assembly: Tallinn; f. 2002 by former mems of the Pro Patria (Fatherland) Union; Chair. MART HELME; approx. 1,700 mems (2002).

People's Party Moderates (Mõõdukad): Vana–Viru 4, Tallinn 10111 POB 3437, Tallinn 19090; tel. 641-2227; fax 644-4605; e-mail kirjad@moodukad.ee; internet www.moodukad.ee; f. 1999 by merger of the People's Party and the Moderates' Party; social-democratic party; Chair. IVARI PADAR; Sec.-Gen. TONU KOIV.

Progressive Party (Arengupartei): Tallinn; e-mail arengupartei@ online.ee; internet www.arengupartei.ee; f. 1996 following a split in the Estonian Centre Party; Chair. ANDRA VEIDEMANN; Sec.-Gen. TOIVO KEVA; 1,300 mems.

Pro Patria (Fatherland) Union (Isamaaliit): Wismari 11, Tallinn 10136; tel. 669-1070; fax 660-1071; e-mail info@isamaaliit.ee; internet www.isamaaliit.ee; f. 1995; by merger of the National Fatherland Party Isamaa; f. 1992; and the Estonian National Independence Party; f. 1988; right-wing party; Chair. TUNNE KELAM; Sec.-Gen. TARMO LOODUS; 2,900 mems.

Republican Party (Vabariiklik Partei): Kuperjanovi 56-5, Tartu 50409; tel. 521-4512; e-mail leping.vp@mail.ee; internet www .vabariiklikpartei.ee; f. 1999; Chair. KRISTJAN-OLARI LEPING.

Russian Democratic Movement: Tallinn; tel. (2) 440-421; fax (2) 441-237; f. 1991 to promote domestic peace and mutual understanding between Estonians and Russians living in Estonia.

Russian Party in Estonia: Tallinn; f. 1994; merged with the Russian People's Party of Estonia in early 1996; represents the Russian-speaking minority in Estonia; opposed to NATO membership; absorbed the Estonian Unity Party, the Russian-Baltic Party and the Russian Unity Party in Dec. 2002; Chair. STANISLAV CHEREPANOV.

Union for the Republic Res Publica: Hobujaama 12/Narva mnt. 9E, Tallinn 10151; tel. (2) 610-9244; fax (2) 610-9243; e-mail respublica@respublica.ee; internet www.respublica.ee; f. 2001; right-wing; Chair. JUHAN PARTS; 2,500 mems.

Diplomatic Representation

EMBASSIES IN ESTONIA

Austria: Vambola 6, Tallinn 14114; tel. 627-8740; fax 631-4365; e-mail embassy@austrianembassy.ee; internet www.austrian embassy.ee; Ambassador Dr JAKUB FORST-BATTAGLIA.

Belarus: Magdaleena 3, Section B, Tallinn 11312; tel. and fax 655-8001; Gen. Consul PETR KRECHKO.

Canada: Toom-Kooli 13, Tallinn 10130; tel. 627-3311; fax 627-3310; e-mail tallinn@canada.ee; internet www.canada.ee; Ambassador ROBERT ANDRIGO.

China, People's Republic: Narva mnt. 98, Tallinn 15009; tel. 601-5830; fax 601-5833; e-mail office@chinaembassy.ee; internet www .chinaembassy.ee; Ambassador CONG JUN.

Czech Republic: Roosikrantsi 11, Tallinn 10119; tel. 627-4400; fax 631-4716; e-mail tallinn@embassy.mzv.cz; internet www.mfa.cz/ tallinn; Ambassador VLADISLAV LABUDEK.

Denmark: Wismari 5, Tallinn 15047; tel. 630-6400; fax 630-6421; e-mail tllamb@um.dk; internet www.denmark.ee; Ambassador JØRGEN MUNK RASMUSSEN.

Finland: Kohtu 4, Tallinn 15180; tel. 610-3200; fax 610-3281; e-mail info@datanet.ee; internet www.finemb.ee; Ambassador JAAKKO BLOMBERG.

France: Toom-Kuninga 20, Tallinn 15185; tel. 631-1492; fax 631-1385; e-mail france@datanet-ee.org; internet www.ambafrance-ee .org; Ambassador CHANTAL DE GHAISNE DE BOURMONT.

Germany: Toom-Kuninga 11, Tallinn 15048; tel. 627-5300; fax 627-5304; e-mail deutschland@online.ee; internet www.germany.ee; Ambassador JÜRGEN DRÖGE.

Hungary: Narva mnt. 122, Tallinn 10127; tel. 605-1880; fax 605-4088; e-mail huembtal@mfa.neti.ee; Ambassador LÁSZLÓ NIKICSER.

Ireland: Demini Bldg, Virui/Vene 2, 2nd Floor, Tallinn 10123; tel. 681-1888; fax 681-1889; e-mail embassytallinn@eircom.net; Ambassador SEAN FARRELL.

Italy: Vene 2, 3rd Floor, Tallinn 10123; tel. 627-6160; fax 631-1370; e-mail italemb1@online.ee; internet www.italembtallinn.ee; Ambassador RUGGERO VOZZI.

Japan: Harju 6, Tallinn 10130; tel. 631-0531; fax 631-0533; e-mail jaapansk@online.ee; Chargé d'affaires a.i. KEIICHI HASEGAWA.

Latvia: Tõnismägi 10, Tallinn 10119; tel. 646-1313; fax 631-1366; Ambassador EDGARS SKUJA.

Lithuania: Uus tn. 15, Tallinn 15070; tel. 631-4030; fax 641-2013; e-mail amber@anet.ee; internet www.hot.ee/lietambasada; Ambassador ANTANAS VINKUS.

Netherlands: Harju 6, Tallin 10130; tel. 631-0580; fax 631-0583; e-mail neth.gov@delfi.ee; internet www.netherlandsembassy.ee; Ambassador JOANNA M. P. F. VAN VLIET.

Norway: Harju 6, Tallinn 15054; tel. 627-1000; fax 627-1001; e-mail emb.tallinn@mfa.no; Ambassador PER K. PEDERSEN.

Poland: Pärnu mnt. 8, Tallinn 10503; tel. 627-8206; fax 644-5221; e-mail ambrptal@netexpress.ee; internet www.poola.ee; Ambassador WOJCIECH WRÓBLEWSKI.

Russia: Pikk 19, Tallinn 10133; tel. 646-4175; fax 646-4178; e-mail vensaat@online.ee; internet www.estonia.mid.ru; Ambassador KONSTANTIN PROVALOV.

Sweden: Pikk 28, Tallinn 15055; tel. 640-5600; fax 640-5695; e-mail swedemb@estpak.ee; internet www.sweden.ee; Ambassador ELISABET BORSIIN BONNIER.

Turkey: Narva mnt. 30, Tallinn 10152; tel. 627-2880; fax 627-2885; e-mail tallinn.be@mfa.gov.tr; Ambassador ÖMER ALTUG.

Ukraine: Lahe 6, Tallinn 15170; tel. 601-5815; fax 601-5816; e-mail embukr@eol.ee; internet www.uninet.ee/~embukra; Ambassador MYKOLA MAKAREVYCH.

United Kingdom: Wismari 6, Tallinn 10136; tel. 667-4700; fax 667-4755; e-mail information@britishembassy.ee; internet www .britishembassy.ee; Ambassador SARAH SQUIRE.

USA: Kentmanni 20, Tallinn 15099; tel. 668-8100; fax 668-8134; e-mail tallinn@usemb.ee; internet www.usemb.ee; Ambassador JOSEPH M. DETHOMAS.

Judicial System

Supreme Court of the Republic of Estonia

Lossi 17, Tartu 50093; tel. (7) 309-002; fax (7) 309-003; e-mail nc@nc .ee; internet www.nc.ee.

Chief Justice and Chairman of the Constitutional Review Chamber: Uno Lõhmus.

Chairman of the Civil Chamber: Jaano Odar.

Chairman of the Criminal Chamber: Jüri Ilvest.

Chairman of the Administrative Law Chamber: Tõnu Anton.

Legal Chancellor's Office

Tõnismägi 16, Tallinn 15193; tel. 693-8400; fax 693-8401; e-mail info@lc.gov.ee; internet www.oiguskantsler.ee.

f. 1993; reviews general application of legislative and executive powers and of local governments for conformity with the constitution, supervises activities of state agencies in guaranteeing constitutional rights and freedoms; Legal Chancellor Allar Joks.

Public Prosecutor's Office

Wismari 7, Tallinn 15188; tel. 631-3002; fax 645-1475; e-mail info@prokuratuur.ee; internet www.prokuratuur.ee.

State Prosecutor-Gen.: Raivo Sepp.

Religion

CHRISTIANITY

Protestant Churches

Consistory of the Estonian Evangelical Lutheran Church of Estonia: Kiriku plats 3, Tallinn 10130; tel. 627-7350; fax 627-7352; e-mail konsistoorium@eelk.ee; internet www.eelk.ee; Archbishop Jaan Kiivit.

Estonian Conference of Seventh-day Adventists: Lille 18, Tartu 51010; tel. (7) 343-211; fax (7) 343-389; e-mail office@advent.ee; internet www.advent.ee; f. 1917; Chair. Ülo Pärna.

Union of Evangelical Christian and Baptist Churches of Estonia: Pargi 9, Tallinn 11620; tel. 670-0698; fax 650-6008; e-mail eekbl@ekklesia.ee; internet www.ekklesia.ee; Pres. Helari Puu.

United Methodist Church in Estonia: Apteegi 3, Tallinn 10146; tel. (2) 445-447; fax 631-3482; e-mail keskus@emk.edu.ee; internet www.metodistikirik.ee; f. 1907; Superintendent Olav Pärnamets.

The Eastern Orthodox Church

Between 1923 and 1940 the Estonian Apostolic Orthodox Church (EAOC) was subordinate to the Constantinople Ecumenical Patriarchate (based in İstanbul, Turkey). Following the Soviet occupation of Estonia in 1940, the EAOC was banned and its churches and communities were placed under the jurisdiction of the Moscow Patriarchate. The leaders of the EAOC went into exile in Stockholm, Sweden. After the restoration of Estonian independence, in 1993 Estonia recognized the EAOC as the legal successor of the Orthodox Church in operation before the Second World War, and in February 1996 the Constantinople Patriarchate restored the EAOC to its jurisdiction. The Estonian Orthodox Church of the Moscow Patriarchate was officially registered in April 2002.

Estonian Apostolic Orthodox Church (EAOC): Tallinn; Chair. of Synod Nikolai Suuresoot; 59 congregations.

Estonian Orthodox Church of Moscow Patriarchate (EOCMP): Pikk 64/4, Tallinn 10133; tel. 641-1301; fax 641-1302; Archbishop Kornelius; 32 congregations.

The Roman Catholic Church

At 31 December 2001 there were an estimated 3,500 Roman Catholic adherents in Estonia.

Office of the Apostolic Administrator: Jaan Poska 47, Tallinn 10150; tel. 601-3079; fax 601-3190; e-mail admapost@online.ee; Apostolic Administrator Most Rev. Most Rev. Peter Stephan Zurbriggen (Titular Archbishop of Glastonia (Glastonbury), Apostolic Nuncio to Lithuania, Estonia and Latvia (resident in Vilnius, Lithuania)).

Roman Catholic Parish of St Peter and St Paul in Tallinn: Vene 18, Tallinn 0001; tel. 644-6367; fax 644-4678; Parish Priest Fr Zbigniew Piłat.

Tallinn Parish of the Ukrainian Catholic (Uniate) Church: Võrgu 13–6, Tallinn; tel. 632-4306; Chair. of Bd Anatolii Lyutyuk.

ISLAM

Estonian Islamic Congregation: Sütiste 52–76, Tallinn 0034; tel. (2) 522-403; f. 1928; Chair. of Bd Timur Seifullen.

JUDAISM

Hineirry Jewish Progressive Community of Narva: Pk 955, Narva 5; tel. (35) 426-26; Chair. of Bd Aleksandr Spivak.

Jewish Community of Estonia: Karu 16, Tallinn; POB 3576, Tallinn 10507; tel. and fax 662-3034; e-mail community@jewish.ee; internet www.jewish.ee; Chair. Cilja Laud.

Jewish Progressive Community in Tallinn: POB 200, Tallinn; Chair. of Bd David Slomka.

The Press

In 2001 there were 14 officially registered daily newspapers and 95 non-daily newspapers published in Estonia. In that year 10 daily newspapers and 80 non-daily newspapers were published in Estonian. In 2001 1,088 periodicals were published; 881 of which were published in Estonian.

PRINCIPAL NEWSPAPERS

In Estonian except where otherwise stated.

Äripäev (Business Daily): Pärnu mnt. 105, Tallinn 19094; tel. 667-0222; fax 667-0165; e-mail mbp@mbp.ee; internet www.mbp.ee; f. 1989; five days a week; business and finance; Editor-in-Chief Igor Rõtov; circ. 17,200.

Den za Dujan (Day After Day): Pärnu mnt. 130, Tallinn 11313; tel. 678-8288; fax 678-8290; e-mail ambre@dd.ee; internet www.dd.ee; f. 1991; weekly; in Russian; Editor-in-Chief Jana Litvinova; circ. 20,000.

Eesti Ekspress (Estonian Express): Narva mnt. 11E, Tallinn 10151; tel. 669-8080; fax 669-8154; e-mail ekspress@ekspress.ee; internet www.ekspress.ee; f. 1989; weekly; Editor-in-Chief Aavo Kokk; circ. 49,300.

Eesti Kirik (Estonian Church): Ülikooli, Tartu 51003; tel. (7) 431-437; fax (7) 433-243; f. 1923; weekly; Editor-in-Chief Sirje Semm; circ. 2,100.

Eesti Päevaleht (Estonian Daily): Pärnu mnt. 67A, POB 433, Tallinn 10151; tel. 614-4498; fax 614-4334; e-mail mail@epl.ee; internet www.epl.ee; f. 1905; daily; Editor-in-Chief Priit Hõbemägi; circ. 37,000.

Estonija: Madala 16, Tallinn 10315; tel. 665-1100; fax 665-1111; e-mail vestimg@teleport.ee; internet www.vesti.ee; f. 1940; five days a week in Russian (with Estonian edn Mon.); Editor-in-Chief Sergei Sergeyev; circ. 7,700.

Maaleht (Country News): Toompuiestee 16, Tallinn 10137; tel. 661-3718; fax 662-2292; e-mail ml@maaleht.ee; internet www.maaleht.ee; f. 1987; weekly; problems and aspects of politics, culture, agriculture and country life; Editor-in-Chief Sulev Valner; circ. 42,000.

ME: POB 120, Kentmanni 18, Tallinn 10502; tel. 628-6123; fax 646-1623; e-mail moles@infonet.ee; three days a week; in Russian; Editor-in-Chief Arkadii Prisjazhnõi; circ. 5,100.

Meie Meel (Our Mind): POB 104, Tallinn 0090; tel. (2) 681-253; fax 646-1625; e-mail meiemeel@zzz.ee; f. 1991; weekly; youth paper; Editor-in-Chief Mare Vetemaa; circ. 20,700.

Postimees (Postman): Maakri 23A, Tallinn 10145; tel. 666-2302; fax 666-2301; e-mail erik.roose@postimees.ee; internet www.postimees.ee; f. 1857; daily; Editor-in-Chief Urmas Klaas; circ. 60,200.

Sirp: POB 388, Tallinn 10503; tel. 640-5770; fax 640-5771; e-mail sirp@sirp.ee; internet www.sirp.ee; f. 1940; weekly; cultural; Editor-in-Chief Mihkel Mutt; circ. 3,500.

SL Õhtuleht (Evening Gazette): Narva mnt. 13, POB 106, Tallinn 10501; tel. 614-4805; fax 614-4001; e-mail priit@sloleht.ee; internet www.sloleht.ee; f. 2000; by merger of Õhtuleht and Sõnumileht newspapers; daily; Editor-in-Chief Väino Koorberg; circ. 67,200.

PRINCIPAL PERIODICALS

Akadeemia: Ülikooli 21, Tartu 51007; tel. (7) 423-050; fax (7) 423-146; e-mail akadeemia@akad.ee; internet www.akad.ee; f. 1989; monthly; journal of the Union of Writers; Editor-in-Chief Toomas Kiho; circ. 2,500.

Eesti Arst (Estonian Physician): Pepleri 32, Tartu 51010; tel. and fax (7) 427-825; e-mail ea@gennet.ee; internet www.eestiarst.ee; f. 1922; monthly; Editor-in-Chief Väino Sinisalu; circ. 3,500.

Eesti Loodus (Estonian Nature): Veski 4, POB 110, Tartu 50002; tel. (7) 421-186; fax (7) 421-143; e-mail toimetus@el.loodus.ee; internet www.loodus.ee/el; f. 1933; monthly; popular science; illustrated; Editor-in-Chief Toomas Kukk; circ. 5,200.

Eesti Naine (Estonian Woman): Maakri 23A, Tallinn 10145; tel. 666-2627; fax 666-2557; e-mail katrin.streimann@kirjastus.ee;

internet www.kirjastus.ee/eestinaine; f. 1924; monthly; Editor-in-Chief KATRIN STREIMANN; circ. 24,000.

Hea Laps (Good Kid): Harju 1, Tallinn 10146; tel. 631-4428; monthly; for children; Editor-in-Chief LEELO TUNGAL.

Horisont (Horizon): Narva mnt. 5, Tallinn 0117; tel. 661-6163; fax 641-8033; e-mail horisont@horisont.ee; f. 1967; 6 a year; popular scientific; Editor-in-Chief INDREK ROHTMETS; circ. 3,000.

Keel ja Kirjandus (Language and Literature): Roosikrantsi 6, Tallinn 10119; tel. 644-9228; fax 644-1800; e-mail kk@eki.ee; f. 1958; monthly; joint edition of the Academy of Sciences and the Union of Writers; Editor-in-Chief MART MERI; circ. 1,100.

Kodukiri (Your Home): Maakri 23A, Tallinn 10145; tel. 666-2550; fax 666-2558; e-mail velve.saar@kirjastus.ee; f. 1992; monthly; Editor-in-Chief KATRIN KUUSEMÄE; circ. 50,000.

Linguistica Uralica: Roosikrantsi 6, Tallinn 10119; tel. 644-0745; e-mail lu@eki.ee; internet www.gaid.gi.ee/eap/l.-u.htm; f. 1965; Editor-in-Chief VÄINO KLAUS; circ. 400.

Looming (Creation): Harju 1, Tallinn 10146; tel. (2) 627-6420; e-mail looming@hot.ee; f. 1923; journal of the Union of Writers; fiction, poetry, literary criticism; Editor-in-Chief UDO UIBO; circ. 1,800.

Loomingu Raamatukogu (Library of Creativity): Harju 1, Tallinn 10146; tel. 627-6425; e-mail loominguraamatukogu@hot.ee; f. 1957; journal of the Union of Writers; poetry, fiction and non-fiction by Estonian and foreign authors; Editor-in-Chief TOOMAS HAUG; circ. 1,600.

Maakodu (Country Home): Toompuiestee 16, Tallinn 10137; tel. 660-5306; fax 662-2292; e-mail meelim@maaleht.ee; internet www.maaleht.ee; f. 1989; monthly; Editor-in-Chief MEELI MÜÜRIPEAL; circ. 12,000.

Maamajandus (Country Economy): Toompuiestee 16, Tallinn 10137; tel. 660-5305; fax 662-2292; e-mail ylo@maaleht.ee; internet www.maaleht.ee; f. 2000; monthly; Editor-in-Chief ÜLO KALM; circ. 2,000.

Oil Shale: Estonia pst. 7, Tallinn 10143; tel. 646-7512; fax 646-6026; e-mail aili@kirj.ee; internet www.kirj.ee/oilshale; f. 1984; quarterly; geology, chemistry, mining, oil-shale industry; Editor-in-Chief JÜRI KANN; circ. 350.

Põllumajandus (Agriculture): Lai 39, Tallinn 0001; tel. 641-1161; f. 1932; monthly; Editor-in-Chief ARVO SIRENDI; circ. 1,000.

Täheke (Little Star): Pärnu mnt. 67A, Tallinn 10134; tel. 646-3697; e-mail tell@tallpost.ee; f. 1960; monthly; illustrated; for 6–10-year-olds; Editor-in-Chief ELJU SILD; circ. 3,500.

Teater, Muusika, Kino (Theatre, Music, Cinema): POB 3200, Narva mnt. 5, Tallinn 10117; tel. 660-1828; fax (2) 660-1887; e-mail tmk@estpak.ee; f. 1982; monthly; Editor-in-Chief JÜRI AARMA; circ. 1,500.

Vikerkaar (Rainbow): Voorimehe 9, Tallinn 10146; tel. 646-4059; fax (2) 442-484; e-mail vikerkaar@teleport.ee; f. 1986; monthly; fiction, poetry, critical works; in Estonian and Russian; Editor-in-Chief MÄRT VÄLJATAGA; circ. 1,500.

NEWS AGENCY

BNS (Baltic News Service): Pärnu mnt. 105, Tallinn 15043; tel. 610-8800; fax 610-8811; e-mail bns@bns.ee; internet www.bns.ee; f. 1990; Chief Exec. GEORGE SHABAD.

PRESS ORGANIZATIONS

Estonian Journalists' Union: Gonsiori 21-409, Tallinn 10147; tel. 646-3699; fax 646-3672; e-mail eal@eal.ee; internet www.eal.ee; f. 1919; Chair. ALLAN ALAKÜLA.

Estonian Newspaper Association (Eesti Ajalehtede Liit): Pärnu mnt. 67A, Tallinn 10134; tel. 646-1005; fax 631-1210; e-mail eall@eall.ee; internet www.eall.ee; f. 1990; 39 mem. newspapers; Chair. IGOR RÕTOV.

Estonian Press Council (Avaliku Sõna Nõukogu): Gonsiori 21, Tallinn 15020; tel. and fax 646-3699; e-mail asn@asn.org.ee; internet www.asn.org.ee; Chair. URMAS LOIT.

Publishers

Eesti Raamat (Estonian Book): Laki 26, Tallinn 12915; tel. and fax 658-7889; e-mail georg.grynberg@mail.ee; f. 1940; fiction; Dir ANNE-ASTRI KASK.

Estonian Encyclopaedia Publishers Ltd: Narva mnt. 4, Tallinn 10117; tel. 699-9620; fax 699-9621; e-mail encyclo@ene.ee; internet www.ene.ee; f. 1991; Man. Dir ANTO RAUKAS.

Huma: Vene 14, Tallinn 10123; tel. and fax 644-0955; e-mail huma@online.ee; fiction, non-fiction, children's books, art, calendars; Dir LIIVI KESKPAIK.

Ilmamaa: Vanemuise 19, Tartu 51014; tel. (7) 427-290; fax (7) 427-320; e-mail ilmamaa@ilmamaa.ee; internet www.ilmamaa.ee; general fiction, philosophy, cultural history, electronic publishing; Dir MART JAGOMÄGI.

Koolibri: Pärnu mnt. 10, Tallinn 10148; tel. 644-5223; fax 644-6813; e-mail koolibri@koolibri.ee; internet www.koolibri.ee; f. 1991; textbooks, dictionaries, children's books; Dir ANTS LANG.

Kunst (Fine Art): Lai 34, Tallinn 10133; POB 105, Tallinn 10502; tel. 641-1764; fax 641-1762; e-mail kunst.lai@mail.ee; internet www.kirjastused.com/kunst/; f. 1957; fine arts, fiction, tourism, history, biographies; Dir SIRJE HELME.

Kupar: Pärnu mnt. 67A, Tallinn 10134; tel. 628-6174; fax 646-2076; e-mail kupar@netexpress.ee; f. 1987; contemporary fiction; Dir IVO SANDRE.

Logos: Toompuiestee 23, Tallinn 10137; tel. and fax 661-3712; e-mail logos@logos.ee; internet www.logos.ee; f. 1991; religious publications; Chair. INGMAR KURG.

Monokkel: POB 311, Tallinn 10503; tel. 501-6307; fax 656-9176; f. 1988; history, fiction; Dir ANTS ÕÕBIK.

Olion: Laki 26, Tallinn 12915; tel. 655-0175; fax 655-0173; e-mail olion@hot.ee; internet www.kirjastused.com/olion/; f. 1989; politics, reference, history, biographies, children's books; Dir HÜLLE UNT.

Õllu: Harju 1, Tallinn 10146; tel. 652-2038; fiction; Chair. of Bd HEINO KIIK.

Olympia: Pikk 2, Tallinn 10123; tel. 644-2549; fax 661-2853; e-mail olympia@online.ee; sports; Editor-in-Chief PAAVO KIVINE.

Perioodika (Periodicals): Voorimehe 9, Tallinn 10146; POB 3648, Tallinn 10507; tel. 644-1252; fax 644-2484; f. 1964; newspapers, guidebooks, periodicals, fiction, children's books in foreign languages; Dir UNO SILLAJÕE.

Publishing House ILO: Madara 14, Tallinn 10612; tel. 661-0553; fax 661-0556; e-mail ilo@ilo.ee; internet www.ilo.ee; dictionaries, encyclopaedias, business, management and law; Dir SILVI-AIRE VILLO.

Tartu University Press: Tiigi 78, Tartu 50410; tel. (7) 375-961; fax (7) 375-944; e-mail tyk@psych.ut.ee; internet www.psych.ut.ee/tup; f. 1958; science, textbooks, etc; Chair. VAIKO TIGANE.

Tiritamm: Laki 26, Tallinn 12915; tel. and fax 656-3570; e-mail tiritamm@hot.ee; internet www.kirjastused.com/tiritamm/; f. 1991; children's books; Dir SIRJE SAIMRE.

Valgus Publishers: Tulika 19, Tallinn 10613; tel. 650-5025; fax 650-5104; e-mail info@kirjastusvalgus.ee; internet www.kirjastusvalgus.ee; f. 1965; scientific literature, resource materials and textbooks; Man. Dir MARIKA TAMM.

PUBLISHERS' ASSOCIATION

Estonian Publishers' Association: Laki 17, Tallinn 0006; POB 3366, Tallinn 0090; tel. 650-5592; fax 650-5590; f. 1991; unites 31 publishing houses; Chair. of Bd TÕNU KOGER.

Broadcasting and Communications

TELECOMMUNICATIONS

Regulatory Authorities

Broadcasting Council: Gonsiori 21, Tallinn 15020; tel. 611-4305; fax 611-4457; e-mail rhn@er.ee.

National Communications Board: Ädala 4D, Tallinn 10614; tel. 693-1154; fax 693-1155; e-mail postbox@sa.ee; internet www.sa.ee; Dir JÜRI JÕEMA.

Major Provider

Eesti Telekom AS (Estonian Telecom Ltd): Roosikrantsi 2, Tallinn 10119; tel. 631-1212; fax 631-1224; e-mail mailbox@telekom.ee; internet www.telekom.ee; f. 1992 as Eesti Telefon; privatized in 1999; operates national telecommunications system; Dir-Gen. TOOMAS SOMERA; Chief Exec. JAAN MÄNNIK.

Eesti Mobiltelefon AS: Lasnamäe 64, Tallinn 19095; tel. 639-7111; fax 611-1897; e-mail emt@emt.ee; internet www.emt.ee; f. 1991; Man. Dir PEET PAVIKSO.

BROADCASTING

Radio

In 2001 there were 25 private radio broadcasters operating in Estonia (one with an international broadcasting licence, 14 with regional licences and 10 with local licences), in addition to the public broadcaster, Eesti Raadio (Estonian Radio).

Eesti Raadio (Estonian Radio): Gonsiori 21, Tallinn 15020; tel. 611-4115; fax 611-4457; e-mail raadio@er.ee; internet www.er.ee; f. 1926; five 24-hour channels (three in Estonian, one in Russian and one in English, French and German); external service in English; Chair. and Dir-Gen. AIN SAARNA.

Raadio Elmaar: Õpetaja 9A, Tartu 51003; tel. (7) 427-927; fax (7) 742-044; owned by AS Radio Elmaar; Dir JAAN HABICHT.

Raadio Kuku: Narva mnt. 63, Tallinn 20606; tel. 630-7660; fax 601-5759; internet www.kuku.ee; owned by AS Trio LSL; Chair. of Council REIN LANG.

Raadio Sky Plus: Pärnu mnt. 139c, Tallinn 11317; tel. 678-8777; fax 678-8710; e-mail sky@sky.ee; internet www.skyplus.fm; owned by Taevaraadio AS; Chief Exec. ILMAR KOMPUS.

Raadio Uuno: Narva mnt. 63, Tallinn 20606; tel. 630-7660; fax 601-5759; internet www.uuno.ee; owned by AS Trio LSL; Chair. of Council REIN LANG.

Star FM: Peterburi tee 81, Tallinn 11415; tel. 622-0288; fax 622-0294; internet www.starfm.ee; owned by AS Mediainvest Holding; Chair. SVEN NUTMANN.

Tartu Pereraadio Ühing (Tartu Family Radio Corpn): Annemõisa 8, Tartu 50718; tel. and fax (7) 488-458; e-mail tartu@pereraadio.ee; internet www.pereraadio.ee; f. 1994; Christian radio broadcasting; Pres. JOEL LUHAMETS; Exec. Dir PAAVO PIHLAK.

Television

There are three national commercial television stations in Estonia. In addition, five cable television licences have been issued. The commercial stations are:

Eesti Televisioon (Estonian Television): Faehlmanni 12, Tallinn 15029; tel. 628-4113; fax 628-4155; e-mail etv@etv.ee; internet www.etv.ee; f. 1955; state-owned; one channel; programmes in Estonian and Russian; Chair. ILMAR RAAG.

Kanal 2 (Channel 2): Maakri 23A, Tallinn 10145; tel. 666-2450; fax 666-2451; e-mail info@kanal2.ee; internet www.kanal2.ee; f. 1993; commercial station; owned by AS Kanal 2; Chair. HANS ERIK MATRE.

TV3: Peterburgi tee 81, Tallinn 11415; tel. 622-0200; fax 622-0201; e-mail tv3@tv3.ee; internet www.tv3.ee; f. 1996; owned by AS TV3; Exec. Dir TOOMAS VARA.

Broadcasting Association

Association of Estonian Broadcasters (AEB): Ülemiste tee 3A, Tallinn 11415; tel. and fax 606-1701; e-mail erl@online.ee; internet www.ringhliit.ee; 19 mems.

Finance

(cap. = capital; res = reserves; dep. = deposits; m. = million; brs = branches; amounts in kroons, unless otherwise stated)

BANKING

The bank of Estonia was re-established in 1990, as was a private banking system. During a crisis in the financial sector in 1992 a number of weaker banks collapsed and others merged. New legislation was subsequently enacted to strengthen the sector, with increased supervision. A currency board became responsible for monetary supervision in 1992.

Central Bank

Bank of Estonia (Eesti Pank): Estonia pst. 13, Tallinn 15095; tel. 668-0719; fax 668-0836; e-mail info@epbe.ee; internet www.ee/epbe; f. 1918; re-established 1990; central bank of Estonia; bank of issue; cap. and res 2,356.2m., dep. 3,873.5m. (Dec. 2001); Pres. VAHUR KRAFT.

Commercial Banks

Estonian Credit Bank (Eesti Krediidipank): Narva mnt. 4, Tallinn 15014; tel. 669-0900; fax 661-6037; e-mail krediidipank@ekp.ee; internet www.krediidipank.ee; f. 1992; cap. 85.6m., res 20.9m., dep. 777.1m. (Dec. 2001); Pres. REIN OTSASON; Chair. of Bd ANDRUS KLUGE; 12 brs.

Hansapank: Liivalaia 8, Tallinn 15040; tel. 613-1310; fax 613-1410; e-mail hansa@hansa.ee; internet www.hansa.ee; f. 1991; cap.

50.4m., res 201.6m., dep.1,958.8m. (Dec. 2001); merged with Estonian Savings Bank (Eesti Hoiupank) in 1998; Chair. of Bd INDREK NEIVELT; 103 brs.

Sampo Bank: Narva mnt. 11, POB 19, Tallinn 15015; tel. 630-2100; fax 630-2200; e-mail info@sampopank.ee; internet www.sampo.ee; f. 1992 as Estonian Forexbank; merged with Estonian Investment Bank in 1998 to form Optiva Bank; name changed as above in 2000; wholly owned by Sampo Plc; cap. 323.1m., res 17.1m., dep. 4,446.6m. (Dec. 2001); Chair. HÄRMO VÄRK; 7 brs.

Tallinn Business Bank Ltd (Tallinna Äripanga AS): Estonia pst. 3–5, Tallinn 15097; tel. 668-8000; fax 668-8001; e-mail info@tbb.ee; internet www.tbb.ee; f. 1991; cap. 76.8m., res 9.5m., dep. 445.0m. (Dec. 2001); Chair. of Bd VALERI HARITONOV.

Union Bank of Estonia (Eesti Ühispank): Tornimäe 2, Tallinn 15010; tel. 665-5100; fax 665-5102; e-mail postkast@eyp.ee; internet www.eyp.ee; f. 1992; cap. 665.6m., res 1,271.1m., dep. 14,638.2m. (Dec. 2001); merged with North Estonia Bank in Jan. 1997 and with Tallinna Pank in July 1998; Pres. AIN HANSCHMIDT; 90 brs.

Foreign Bank

Nordea Bank Estonia (Finland): Hobujaama 4, Tallinn 15068; tel. 628-3200; fax 628-3201; e-mail tallinn@nordea.com; internet www.nordea.ee; f. 1995 as Merita Bank Ltd; name changed in 1999; owned by Nordea AB (Finland).

Banking Association

Estonian Banking Association (Eesti Pangaliit): Ahtri 12, Tallinn 10151; tel. 611-6567; fax 611-6568; e-mail post@pangaliit.ee; internet www.pangaliit.ee; f. 1992; Chair. HÄRMO VÄRK; Man. Dir VIKTOR HÜTT.

STOCK EXCHANGE

Tallinn Stock Exchange: Pärnu mnt. 12, Tallinn 10148; tel. 640-8840; fax 640-8801; e-mail hex@hex.ee; internet www.hex.ee; f. 1995; strategically owned by the HEX stock exchange (Finland) from April 2001; Chair. GERT TIIVAS.

INSURANCE

Estonian Financial Supervisory Authority: Sakala 4, Tallinn 15030; tel. 668-0500; fax 668-0501; e-mail info@fi.ee; internet www.fi.ee; f. 1993; Chair. of Bd ANDRES TRINK.

Principal non-life companies include Balti Kindlustus (BICO) Ltd, Eesti Varakindlustus Ltd, ETAS Kindlustus Ltd, Hansa Kindlustus Ltd, Inges Kindlustus Ltd, Kalju Ltd, Leks Kindlustus Ltd, Nordika Kindlustus Ltd, Polaris-Vara Ltd, Salva Kindlustus Ltd, Sampo Kindlustus Ltd, Seesam Rahvusvaheline Kindlustus Ltd and Ühiskindlustus.

Principal life companies include AB Elukindlustus Ltd, Bico Elukindlustus Ltd, Eesti Elukindlustus Ltd, Hansapanga Kindlustus Ltd, Leks Elukindlustus Ltd, Nordika Elukindlustus Ltd, Polaris-Elu Ltd and Seesam Elukindlustus Ltd.

Trade and Industry

GOVERNMENT AGENCIES

Consumer Protection Board: Kiriku 4, Tallinn 15071; tel. 620-1700; fax 620-1701; e-mail info@consumer.ee; internet www.consumer.ee; f. 1994; Dir-Gen. HELLE ARUNIIT.

Enterprise Estonia: Roosikrantsi 11, Tallinn 10119; tel. 627-9279; fax 627-9427; e-mail info@eia.ee; internet www.eia.ee; Chair. URMAS VAHUR.

Estonian Centre for Standardization: Aru 10, Tallinn 10317; tel. 605-5050; fax 605-5070; e-mail info@evs.ee; internet www.evs.ee; Man. Dir SVEN KASEMAA.

Estonian Competition Board: Kohtu 8, Tallinn 15184; tel. 611-3942; fax 611-3943; e-mail compet@konkurentsiamet.ee; internet www.konkurentsiamet.ee; Dir-Gen. PEETER TAMMISTU.

Estonian Grain Board: Hobujaama 1, Tallinn 0001; tel. (2) 432-815; fax 641-9075; Dir-Gen. AGO SOOTS.

Estonian Investment Agency: Roosikrantsi 11, Tallinn 10119; tel. 627-9420; fax 627-9427; e-mail info@eas.ee; internet www.investinestonia.com; Dir ANDRUS VIIRG.

Estonian Privatization Agency (Eesti Erastamisagentuur): Rävala 6, Tallinn 0105; tel. 630-5600; fax 630-5699; e-mail eea@eea.ee; internet www.eea.ee; Dir-Gen. VÄINO SARNET.

Estonian Trade Council: Liimi 1-503, Tallinn 10621; tel. 656-3299; fax 656-3923; e-mail etc@etc.ee; internet www.etc.ee; f. 1991; Chair. of Bd TAMBET MADE; Dir AARE PUUR.

Estonian Trade Promotion Agency: Roosikrantsi 11, Tallinn 10119; tel. 627-9440; fax 627-9427; e-mail trade@eas.ee; internet www.export.ee; f. 1997.

CHAMBERS OF COMMERCE

Estonian Chamber of Agriculture and Commerce: Vilmsi 53B, Tallinn 10147; tel. 600-9349; fax 600-9350; e-mail info@epkk.ee; internet www.epkk.ee; Chair. ALAR OPPAR.

Estonian Chamber of Commerce and Industry (ECCI): Toom-Kooli 17, Tallinn 10130; tel. 646-0244; fax 646-0245; e-mail koda@koda.ee; internet www.koda.ee; f. 1925; Pres. TOOMAS LUMAN; Gen. Dir MART RELVE.

INDUSTRIAL AND TRADE ASSOCIATIONS

Association of Construction Material Producers of Estonia (Eesti Ehitusmaterjalide Tootjate Liit): Kiriku 6, Tallinn 10130; tel. 620-1918; fax 648-9062; e-mail eetl@hot.ee; internet www.hot.ee/eetl; Pres. TOOMAS VAINOLA.

Association of Estonian Electrotechnical and Electronic Industry: Pirita 20, Tallinn 0001; tel. (2) 238-981; fax (2) 237-827; Pres. GUNNAR TOOMSOO.

Association of Estonian Food Industry: Gonsiori 29, Tallinn 10147; tel. 648-6073; fax 631-2718; e-mail info@toiduliit.ee; internet www.toiduliit.ee; f. 1993; Man. Dir HELVE REMMEL.

Association of Estonian International Road Carriers (Eesti Rahvusvaheliste Autovedajate Assotsiatsioon): Narva mnt. 91, Tallinn 10127; tel. 627-3740; fax 627-3741; e-mail info@eraa.ee; internet www.eraa.ee; Sec.-Gen. TOLVO KULDKEPP.

Association of Estonian Local Industry: Tallinn; tel. (2) 422-367; fax (2) 424-962; Chair. HEINO VASAR.

Estimpex Foreign Trade Association: Uus 32/34, Tallinn 0101; tel. (2) 601-462; fax (2) 602-184; import and export of household fixtures, foodstuffs, souvenirs and oil-based products; Gen. Dir OSVALD KALDRE.

Estonian Agricultural Producers Central Union (Eestimaa Pollumajandustootjate Keskliit): Lai 39/41, Tallinn 10133; tel. and fax 641-1113; e-mail epk.epk@mail.ee; Chair. of Bd VIKTOR SARTAKOV.

Estonian Asphalt Pavement Association (Eesti Asfaldiliit): Parnu 24, Tallinn 10141; tel. 611-9365; fax 611-9360; f. 1991; co-ordinates Estonian asphalt paving and mixing companies; Chair. of Bd ALEKSANDER KALDAS.

Estonian Association of Construction Entrepreneurs (Eesti Ehitusettevõtjate Liit): Kiriku 6, Tallinn 10130; tel. and fax 641-0071; e-mail eeel@eeel.ee; internet www.hot.ee/eeel; Man. Dir ILMAR LINK.

Estonian Association of Fisheries: Gonsiori 29-502, Tallinn 10147; tel. 648-4537; fax 641-9006; e-mail kalaliit@online.ee; Chair. JAAN JALAKAS; Man. Dir VALDUR NOORMÄGI.

Estonian Association of Small and Medium-sized Enterprises (EVEA): Pronksi 3, Tallinn 10124; tel. 640-3935; fax 631-2451; e-mail sme@evea.ee; internet www.evea.ee; f. 1988; Pres. RIIVO SINIJÄRV; Man. Dir MARGIT KALLASTE.

Estonian Business Association: Liivalaia 9, 10118 Tallinn; tel. 646-2030; fax 646-2031; e-mail easa@esea.ee; internet www.esea.ee; f. 1996; Chair. AADU LUUKAS; Man. Dir JAAK SAARNIIT.

Estonian Clothing and Textile Association (Eesti Rõivaja Tekstiililiit): Tartu mnt. 63, Tallinn 10115; tel. 611-5567; fax 611-5568; e-mail ertl@online.ee; internet www.online.ee/~ertl; Chair. MADIS VÕÕRAS.

Estonian Dairy Association (Eesti Piimaliit): Vilmsi 53, Tallinn 10147; tel. 600-9357; fax 600-9355; e-mail eestipl@online.ee; Chair. of Bd ENN SOKK; Man. Dir REIN REISSON.

Estonian Forest Industries Federation (Eesti Metsatööstuse Liit): Marja 9, Tallinn 10617; tel. 656-7643; fax 656-7644; e-mail info@emtl.ee; internet www.forestindustries.ee; Man. Dir ANDRES TALIJÄRV.

Estonian Gas Association (Eesti Gaasiliit): Liivalaia 9, Tallinn 0001; tel. 646-1571; fax 631-4340; Chair. of Bd ANDRES SAAR.

Estonian Hotel and Restaurant Association (Easti Hotellide ja Restoranide Liit): Kiriku 6, Tallinn 10130; tel. 641-1428; fax 641-1425; e-mail info@ehrl.ee; Chair. of Bd TARMO SUMBERG.

Estonian Meat Association (Eesti Lihaliit): Lai 39/41, Tallinn 10133; tel. 641-1179; fax 641-1035; e-mail lihaliit@hot.ee; f. 1989; 18 mem. companies (2002); Chair. of Bd AIGAR PINDMAA; Man. Dir PEETER GRIGORJEV.

Estonian Oil Association (Eesti Õliühing): Kiriku 6, Tallinn 10130; tel. 620-1930; fax 620-1935; e-mail maimu@oilunion.ee;

internet www.oilunion.ee; f. 1993; represents more than 70% of the fuel market; Chair. RAIVO VARE.

Estonian Society of Merchants: Kiriku 6, Tallinn 10130; tel. 620-1914; fax 620-1935; e-mail info@kaupmeesteliit.ee; internet www.kaupmeesteliit.ee; Chair. of Bd PEETER RAUDSEPP; Man. Dir MARIKA MERILAI.

Estonian Woodworking Federation: Pärnu mnt. 158B, Tallinn 11317; tel. 655-8525; fax 655-8524; e-mail info@furnitureindustry.ee; internet www.furnitureindustry.ee; Chair. AIN SAARMANN; Man. Dir MÄRT RAHAMÄGI.

ETK Managers' Club: Narva mnt. 7, Tallinn 10117; tel. 630-2324; fax 630-2333; f. 1991; Pres. GEORG ILVEST.

Federation of the Estonian Chemical Industry: Kiriku 6, Tallinn 10130; tel. and fax 648-9004; e-mail info@keemia.ee; internet www.keemia.ee; f. 1991; 32 mem. enterprises; Chair. ILMAR VESIALIIK; Man. Dir HALLAR MEIBAUM.

Federation of the Estonian Engineering Industry: Mustamäe 4, Tallinn 10621; tel. 611-5893; fax 656-6640; e-mail eml@ltnet.ee; f. 1991; 80 mem. enterprises; Chair. of Bd MIKHEL PIKNER.

Union of Estonian Automobile Enterprises (Eesti Autoettevõtete Liit): Magasini 31, Tallinn 10138; tel. 643-9476; fax 644-3345; e-mail al@autoettevoteliit.ee; Pres. MATI MÄGI.

Union of Estonian Breweries (Eesti Õlletootjate Liit): Tähtvere 58/62, Tartu 2400; tel. (7) 434-330; fax (7) 431-193; Chair. of Bd MADIS PADDAR.

Union of Estonian Paper Manufacturers (Eesti Paberitööstuse Liit): Tööstuse 19, Kohila 3420; tel. (48) 33-564; fax (48) 32-132; e-mail kohilapv@netexpress.ee; Chair. of Bd HENNO PAVELSON.

Union of Estonian Wine Producers (Eesti Veinitootjate Liit): Karksi, Karksi vald, Vilijandi mk. 69104; tel. and fax (43) 54-022; e-mail veinilitt@hot.ee; Chair. of Bd JÜRI KERT.

EMPLOYERS' ORGANIZATION

Estonian Employers' Confederation (Eesti Tööandjate Kesliit): Kiriku 6, Tallinn 10130; tel. 699-9301; fax 699-9310; e-mail ettk@ettk.ee; internet www.ettk.ee; f. 1991 as Confederation of Estonian Industry; Chair. of Bd MEELIS VIRKEBAU; Man. Dir TIIT LAJA.

UTILITIES

Electricity

Eesti Energia AS (Estonian Energy Ltd): Estonia pst 1, Tallinn 10143; tel. 625-2222; fax 625-2200; e-mail kaja.malts@energia.ee; internet www.energia.ee; f. 1939; producer of thermal and electric energy; manufacture of electric motors; electrical engineering; Chair. GUNNAR OKK; 8,000 employees.

Gas

Eesti Gaas AS (Estonian Gas Association): Liivalaia 9, Tallinn 10118; tel. 646-1571; fax 631-4340; e-mail egl@online.ee; internet www.gaas.ee; f. 1993; purchases and transports natural gas, constructs pipelines, calibrates gas meters; Chair. AARNE SAAR; 255 employees.

Water

Tallinn Water Ltd (AS Tallinna Vesi): Ädala 10, POB 174, Tallinn 10502; tel. 626-2200; fax 626-2300; e-mail tvesi@tvesi.ee; internet www.tallvesi.ee; f. 1997; supply and treatment of water; collection and treatment of waste water; 50.4% owned by British International Water UU; Chair. BOB GALLIENE; Dir-Gen. ENNO PERE; 685 employees.

TRADE UNIONS

Association of Estonian Chemical Industry Workers' Trade Unions: Kohtla-Järve; tel. (33) 478-28; fax (33) 457-98; f. 1990; Chair. MIHKEL ISKÜL.

Association of Estonian Radio and Electronics Industry Workers' Trade Unions: Rävala 4, Tallinn 0100; tel. (2) 432-318; Chair. LYUBOV SEROVA.

Confederation of Estonian Food and Landworkers' Unions: 32 Raua Str, Tallinn 10152; tel. and fax 641-0249; e-mail aare.etmk@mail.ee; f. 1989; Chair. AARE-LEMBIT NEEVE.

Confederation of Estonian Trade Unions: Rävala 4, Tallinn 10143; tel. 661-2383; fax 661-2542; e-mail eakl@eakl.ee; f. 1990; Chair. KADI PARNITS.

Estonian Communication Workers' Trade Union (Eesti Sidetöötajate Ametiühingute Liit—ESAL): Masti 2/5, Tallinn 11911; tel. 601-1124; e-mail esal@uninet.ee; internet www.esal.org.ee.

Estonian Light Industry Workers' Trade Union: Rävala 4, Tallinn 0100; tel. and fax (2) 431-640; Chair. EVI JAAGURA.

Estonian Transportation and Roadworkers' Union (Eesti Transpordi-ja Teetöötajate Ametiühing—ETTA): Tallinn; tel. 641-3131; fax 641-3129; e-mail etta@online.ee; internet www.online.ee/~etta.

Society of Estonian Economy Workers' Trade Unions: Rävala 4, Tallinn 10143; tel. and fax 661-2414; e-mail emal@online.ee.

Trade Union of Oil-Shale Industry Workers: Jaama 10, Jõhvi 41502; tel. (33) 70575; e-mail ental@en.ee; Chair. ENDEL PAAP.

Transport

RAILWAYS

In 2000 there were 968 km of railway track in use, of which 132 km were electrified. Main lines link Tallinn with Narva and St Petersburg (Russia), Tartu and Pskov (Russia), Tartu and Valga (Latvia), and Pärnu and Rīga (Latvia). In December 2001 the World Bank disbursed a loan of 870m. kroons to Estonian Railways for the upgrading of engines and infrastructural repairs.

Estonian Railway Administration: Lastekodu 31, Tallinn 10113; tel. 605-7401; fax 605-7410; e-mail raudteeamet@rdtamet.ee; internet www.rdtamet.ee; f. 1999; Dir-Gen. OLEG EPNER.

Estonian Railways Ltd (AS Eesti Raudtee): Pikk 36, Tallinn 15073; tel. 615-8610; fax 615-8710; e-mail raudtee@evr.ee; www.evr.ee; f. 1918; privatized in 2001; freight carriers; Chair. and Man. Dir HERBERT PAYNE; 4,000 employees.

ROADS

In 2002 Estonia had a total road network of 51,410 km, of which 1,455 km were main roads, 12,442 km were secondary roads, 2,496 were basic roads and 34,975 km were local roads. The motorway network totalled 87 km in 1999. In 2000 there were plans to construct an international motorway, to be known as the Via Baltica, between Tallinn and Warsaw, Poland. The project was to be partly funded by the EU. In 2000 51.5% of the total road network was asphalted.

Estonian Road Administration: Pärnu Road 24, Tallinn 10141; tel. 611-9300; fax 611-9360; e-mail estroad@mnt.ee; internet www.mnt.ee; f. 1990; Gen. Dir RIHO SÖRMUS; 15 county offices.

INLAND WATERWAYS

In 2000 there were 320 km of navigable inland waterways.

SHIPPING

Tallinn is the main port for freight transportation. There are regular passenger services between Tallinn and Helsinki, Finland. A service between Tallinn and Stockholm, Sweden, was inaugurated in 1991.

Estonian National Maritime Board: Sadama 29, Terminal B, Tallinn 10111; tel. 620-5500; fax 620-5506; e-mail eva@enmb.ee; internet www.enmb.ee; f. 1990; administers and implements state maritime safety policies, ship-control, pilot, lighthouse and hydrography services; Gen. Dir ANDRUS MAIDE; 375 employees.

Shipowning Company

Estonian Shipping Company Ltd (ESCO) (AS Eesti Merelaevandus): Estonia Blvd 3/5, Tallinn 15096; tel. 640-9500; fax 640-9595; internet www.eml.ee; f. 1940; transferred to private ownership in mid-1997; liner services, ship chartering and cargo shipping; Chair. of Supervisory Bd OLEV SCHULTS; Man. Dir TOM STAGE PETERSEN; 2,000 employees.

Shipowners' Association

Estonian Shipowners' Association (Eesti Laevaomanike Liit): Luise 1A, Tallinn 10142; tel. and fax 646-0109; e-mail reeder@teleport.ee; Pres. REIN MERISALU.

Port Authority

Port of Tallinn: Sadama 25, Tallinn 15051; tel. 631-8002; fax 631-8166; e-mail portoftallinn@portoftallinn.com; internet www.portoftallinn.ee; f. 1991; Chair. of Bd RIHO RASMANN; Harbour Master E. HUNT; 990 employees.

CIVIL AVIATION

Estonia has air links with several major cities in the former USSR, including Moscow and St Petersburg (Russia), Kiev (Ukraine), Minsk (Belarus), Rīga (Latvia) and Vilnius (Lithuania), and with several western European destinations.

Estonian Civil Aviation Administration: Rävala pst. 8, Tallinn 10143; tel. 694-9666; fax 694-9667; e-mail info@ecaa.ee; internet www.ecaa.ee; f. 1990; Dir-Gen. TOOMAS PETERSON.

Elk Airways (Estonian Aviation Company Ltd): Eesti Vabariik, Majaka 26, Tallinn 11416; tel. 638-0972; fax 638-0975; e-mail elk@infonet.ee; internet www.elk.ee; f. 1992; international and domestic passenger and cargo flights to Europe and the CIS; Man. Dir VLADIMIR SLONTCHEVSH.

Estonian Air: Lennujaama 13, Tallinn 11101; tel. 640-1101; fax 601-6092; e-mail ov@estonian-air.ee; internet www.estonian-air.ee; f. 1991; passenger and cargo flights to Europe, the CIS and North Africa; Chair. OLEV SCHULTS; Pres. JØRN ERIKSEN.

Tourism

Estonia has a wide range of attractions for tourists, including the historic towns of Tallinn and Tartu, extensive nature reserves and coastal resorts. In 1990 the National Tourism Board was established to develop facilities for tourism in Estonia. In 2001 there were 1,231,620 visitors to Estonia, with Finland the main source of tourists.

Estonian Association of Travel Agents (Eesti Turismifirmade Liit): Kiriku 6, Tallinn 10130; tel. 631-3013; fax 631-3622; e-mail info@etfl.ee; internet www.etfl.ee; f. 1990; Pres. DAISY JÄRVA.

Estonian Marine Tourism Association: Regati pst. 1, 6K, Tallinn 11911; tel. 639-8933; fax 639-8899; e-mail helle.hallika@mail.ee; f. 1990; Man. Dir HELLE HALLIKA.

Estonian Tourist Board: Roosikrantsi 11, Tallinn 10119; tel. 627-9770; fax 627-9777; e-mail info@visitestonia.com; internet www.visitestonia.com; f. 1990; Dir RIINA LÕHMUS.

ETHIOPIA

Introductory Survey

Location, Climate, Language, Religion, Flag, Capital

The Federal Democratic Republic of Ethiopia is a land-locked country in eastern Africa; it has a long frontier with Somalia near the Horn of Africa. Sudan lies to the west, Eritrea to the north, Djibouti to the north-east and Kenya to the south. The climate is mainly temperate because of the high plateau terrain, with an average annual temperature of 13°C (55°F), abundant rainfall in some years and low humidity. The lower country and valley gorges are very hot and subject to recurrent drought. The official language is Amharic, but many other local languages are also spoken. English is widely used in official and commercial circles. The Ethiopian Orthodox (Tewahido) Church, an ancient Christian sect, has a wide following in the north and on the southern plateau. In much of the south and east the inhabitants include Muslims and followers of animist beliefs. The national flag (proportions 2 by 3) has three equal horizontal stripes, of green, yellow and red. The capital is Addis Ababa.

Recent History

Haile Selassie, who became Regent in 1916, King in 1928 and Emperor in 1930, was deposed by the armed forces in September 1974. He died, a captive of the military regime, in August 1975. The 1974 revolution was organized by an Armed Forces Co-ordinating Committee, known popularly as the Dergue (Shadow), which established a Provisional Military Administrative Council (PMAC), led by Brig.-Gen. Teferi Benti. In December Ethiopia was declared a socialist state. A radical programme of social and economic reforms led to widespread unrest, however, and in February 1977 Lt-Col Mengistu Haile Mariam executed Teferi and his closest associates, and replaced him as Chairman of the PMAC and as Head of State.

During 1977–78, in an attempt to end opposition to the regime, the Government imprisoned or killed thousands of its opponents. Political power was consolidated in a Commission for Organizing the Party of the Working People of Ethiopia (COPWE), largely dominated by military personnel. In September 1984, at the COPWE's third congress, the Workers' Party of Ethiopia (WPE) was formally inaugurated. Mengistu was unanimously elected Secretary-General of the party, which modelled itself on the Communist Party of the Soviet Union. In mid-1986, in preparation for the eventual transfer of power from the PMAC to a civilian government, a draft Constitution was published. In February 1987 it was endorsed by a referendum, obtaining the support of some 81% of the votes cast. In June national elections were held to an 835-seat legislature, the National Shengo (Assembly). In September, at the inaugural meeting of the new legislature, the PMAC was abolished, and the People's Democratic Republic of Ethiopia was declared. The National Shengo unanimously elected Mengistu as President of the Republic, and a 24-member Council of State was also elected, to act as the Shengo's permanent organ.

Numerous groups, encouraged by the confusion resulting from the 1974 revolution, launched armed insurgencies against the Government. Of these, the most effective were based in the Ogaden, Eritrea and Tigrai regions. Somalia laid claim to the Ogaden, which is populated mainly by ethnic Somalis. Somali troops supported incursions by forces of the Western Somali Liberation Front, and in 1977 the Somalis made major advances in the Ogaden. In 1978, however, they were forced to retreat, and by the end of 1980 Ethiopian forces had gained control of virtually the whole of the Ogaden region.

The former Italian colony of Eritrea was merged with Ethiopia, in a federal arrangement, in September 1952, and annexed to Ethiopia as a province in November 1962. A secessionist movement, the Eritrean Liberation Front (ELF), was founded in Egypt in 1958. In the late 1960s and early 1970s the ELF enjoyed considerable success against government troops, but eventually split into several rival factions, the largest of which was the Eritrean People's Liberation Front (EPLF). In 1978 government troops re-established control in much of Eritrea, and the EPLF retreated to the northern town of Nakfa. In 1982 an offensive by government troops failed to capture Nakfa, and in 1984 the EPLF made several successful counter-attacks.

In mid-1986 government forces abandoned the north-east coast to the rebels.

An insurgent movement also emerged in Tigrai province in the late 1970s. The Tigrai People's Liberation Front (TPLF) was armed and trained by the EPLF, but relations between the two groups deteriorated sharply in the mid-1980s. The TPLF was weakened by conflict with other anti-Government groups, and in 1985 and 1986 government forces had considerable success against the TPLF.

The conflict in the north of the country during 1984–85 compounded difficulties being experienced in areas of Ethiopia already severely affected by famine. In 1984 the rains failed for the third consecutive crop season, and in May it was estimated that 7m. people could suffer starvation. Emergency food aid was received from many Western nations, but distribution was hampered, both by the continuing conflict and by the inadequacy of Ethiopia's infrastructure.

In September 1987 the newly elected National Shengo announced that five areas, including Eritrea and Tigrai, were to become 'autonomous regions' under the new Constitution. Eritrea was granted a considerable degree of self-government, but both the EPLF and the TPLF rejected the proposals. In March 1988 EPLF forces captured the town of Afabet; the TPLF took advantage of the movement of government forces from Tigrai to Eritrea and overran all the garrisons in north-western and north-eastern Tigrai. In May the Government declared a state of emergency in Eritrea and Tigrai, and in June government troops regained control of some of the captured garrison towns in Tigrai, suffering heavy losses in the process. However, in early 1989, following major defeats in north-west Tigrai, government forces abandoned virtually the whole region to the TPLF.

US-sponsored negotiations held in late 1989 between representatives of the Ethiopian Government and the EPLF proved inconclusive. Negotiations between the TPLF and the Ethiopian Government, in late 1989 and early 1990, were also unsuccessful. A third round of negotiations, held in Rome, Italy, in March 1990, collapsed over the TPLF's insistence that substantive negotiations should involve a joint delegation of the TPLF and their allies, the Ethiopian People's Democratic Movement (EPDM).

Following the capture of Massawa port by the EPLF in February 1990 (presenting a direct threat to the continued survival of the Ethiopian army in Eritrea), President Mengistu was obliged to make a number of concessions. In March Ethiopian socialism was virtually abandoned, when the WPE was renamed the Ethiopian Democratic Unity Party, and membership was opened to non-Marxists. Mengistu began introducing elements of a market economy and dismantling many of the economic structures that had been established after the 1974 revolution. However, heavy defeats of government forces continued during 1990 and early 1991. Peace negotiations held in the USA in February 1991 between representatives of the EPLF and the Ethiopian Government failed to end the military conflict.

By late April 1991, troops of the Ethiopian People's Revolutionary Democratic Front (EPRDF—an alliance of the TPLF and the EPDM, formed in September 1989) had captured Ambo, a town 130 km west of Addis Ababa, while EPLF forces were 50 km north of Assab, Ethiopia's principal port. On 21 May, faced with the prospect of the imminent defeat of his army, Mengistu fled the country. Lt-Gen. Tesfaye, the Vice-President, assumed control. On 28 May, following the failure of negotiations in the United Kingdom, and with the public support of the USA, units of the EPRDF entered Addis Ababa. They encountered little resistance, and the EPRDF established an interim Government, pending the convening, in July, of a multi-party conference, which was to elect a transitional government. Meanwhile, the EPLF had gained control of the Eritrean capital, Asmara, and announced the establishment of a provisional Government to administer Eritrea until the holding of a referendum, within two years, on the issue of independence.

In July 1991 a national conference adopted amendments to a national charter, presented by the EPRDF, and elected an 87-member Council of Representatives, which was to govern for a transitional period of two years, after which free national elections were to be held. The national charter provided guarantees for freedom of association and expression, and for self-determination for Ethiopia's various ethnic groups. The EPLF was not officially represented at the conference, but came to an agreement with the EPRDF, whereby the EPRDF accepted the formation of the EPLF's provisional Government of Eritrea and the determination by referendum of the future of the region. In late July the Council of Representatives established a commission to draft a new constitution and elected Meles Zenawi, the leader of the EPRDF (and of the TPLF), as Chairman of the Council, a position that made him President of the transitional Government and Head of State, and in August it appointed a Council of Ministers.

In November 1991, in accordance with the national charter's promise of self-determination for Ethiopia's peoples, the transitional Government announced the division of the country into 14 regional administrations, which would have autonomy in matters of regional law and internal affairs. A transitional economic policy, designed to accelerate economic reform, was also approved.

In early 1992 skirmishes continued between forces of the EPRDF and the Oromo Liberation Front (OLF) in the south and east of the country, severely hampering the distribution of food aid to some 6.5m. people affected by drought and to a further 1.4m. people displaced during the continuing conflict. In April a cease-fire between the two sides was agreed, under the auspices of the USA and the EPLF. Local elections were held in many parts of the country in April and May, and regional elections in June. An international observer group, including representatives of the UN, the Organization of African Unity (OAU, now the African Union) and the European Community (EC, now the European Union—EU), indicated that claims of electoral malpractice at the regional polls by the EPRDF in many areas were, at least in part, justified. Shortly after the elections, in which the EPRDF and associated parties obtained 90% of the votes cast, the OLF withdrew its support from the transitional Government. In July 10 political organizations that were signatories to the national charter of July 1991 demanded the annulment of the results of the regional elections. The transitional Government established a board 'to correct election errors' at the end of the month, but by late August the regional councils were functioning in all parts of the country except the Afar and Somali areas, where the elections had been postponed.

In June 1992 OLF troops reportedly captured the town of Asbe Teferi, about 150 km from Addis Ababa; however, the EPRDF's numerically superior forces ensured that the transitional Government's control of the capital was secure. In October talks between the EPRDF and the OLF ended in failure, with the OLF continuing to demand the annulment of the June election results, while the EPRDF urged the OLF to rejoin the transitional Government. Hostilities continued in various parts of the country, with the EPRDF taking prisoners in massive numbers.

In November 1992 the provisional Government of Eritrea announced that a UN-supervised referendum on the area's status would be held in April 1993. The Sudanese Government expressed its readiness to assist the Eritrean Referendum Commission in conducting a plebiscite among some 250,000 Eritrean refugees still residing in Sudan. The referendum revealed overwhelming support for Eritrean independence, which was duly proclaimed on 24 May 1993.

Elections to a Constituent Assembly were conducted in Ethiopia in June 1994, in which the EPRDF won 484 of the 547 seats. The elections were boycotted by the All-Amhara People's Organization, the recently formed Council of Alternative Forces for Peace and Democracy in Ethiopia (CAFPDE—incorporating 30 opposition groups) and the OLF, whose leaders alleged that the Meles administration had intimidated their supporters and refused opposition parties permission to open offices. The Constituent Assembly was inaugurated in October to debate a draft Constitution, which it ratified in December. The new Constitution provided for the establishment of a federal government and the division of the country (renamed the Federal Democratic Republic of Ethiopia) into nine states and two chartered cities. It provided for regional autonomy, including the right of secession. A new legislature, the Federal Parliamentary Assembly, was to be established, comprising two chambers: the House of People's Representatives (consisting of no more than 550 directly elected members) and the House of the Federation (composed of 117 deputies, elected by the new state assemblies).

The EPRDF and its allies won an overwhelming victory in elections to the House of People's Representatives and state assemblies in May 1995. In Tigrai region the TPLF won all the seats in both the federal and state assemblies; EPRDF parties were equally successful in Amhara and Oromia regions. The EPRDF itself won all 92 local assembly seats in Addis Ababa. The largest opposition party to participate in the elections, the Ethiopian National Democratic Movement, contested 80 seats, but none of its candidates was elected. Elections in Afar and Somali regions, where opposition to the EPRDF was strong, were postponed until June, when pro-EPRDF parties won narrow victories. Most opposition parties boycotted the poll. International observers accepted that the elections were conducted in a largely free and fair manner. In July EU ambassadors to Ethiopia expressed concern that the overwhelming victory of the EPRDF would impede the further development of political pluralism in the country.

On 21 August 1995 legislative power was transferred from the transitional Council of Representatives to the Federal Parliamentary Assembly. On 22 August the transitional administration was terminated, and the country's new Constitution and designation as the Federal Democratic Republic of Ethiopia were formally instituted. Later that day Dr Negasso Gidada (formerly the Minister of Information), a member of the Oromo People's Democratic Organization (OPDO, which was in alliance with the EPRDF) and the nominee of the EPRDF, was elected President of the Federal Republic. A new Prime Minister, ex-President Meles Zenawi, was elected from among the members of the House of People's Representatives; Meles nominated a 17-member Council of Ministers, which was duly approved by the Federal Parliamentary Assembly.

During late 1995 and early 1996 the Meles administration was criticized for its harsh treatment of opposition activists. In June 1996 Dr Taye Wolde Semayat, the Secretary-General of the Ethiopian Teachers' Association, was arrested with several associates and accused of leading a clandestine political organization (the Ethiopian National Patriotic Front—ENPF), which had allegedly been responsible for several terrorist acts. The arrests were strongly criticized by human rights groups, which claimed that the detainees were guilty only of expressing discontent at certain government policies. Meanwhile, the Somali-based al-Ittihad al-Islam (Islamic Union Party—which sought independence for Ethiopia's Ogaden province) claimed responsibility for bomb explosions at hotels in Addis Ababa and Dire Dawa in early 1996, and for the attempted assassination in July of Dr Abdul-Mejid Hussen, the Minister of Transport and Communications. Government forces launched reprisal attacks on al-Ittihad bases in Somalia on numerous occasions during 1996–98, resulting in the deaths of several hundred al-Ittihad members.

Attempts by the authorities to stifle the opposition continued during 1997–98, with the arrest of numerous journalists and the closure of several independent periodicals. In September 1998 some 30 delegates attended a meeting in Paris, France, of Ethiopian opposition movements, during which eight groups agreed to establish a new bloc, the Coalition of Ethiopian Opposition Political Organizations (CEOPO). The delegates (who included representatives of the CAFPDE, the Southern Ethiopian People's Democratic Coalition (SEPDC) and Ethiopians in exile) urged the Ethiopian authorities to facilitate national dialogue. A CEOPO-organized demonstration held in Addis Ababa in January 1999 was attended by some 5,000 people.

Meanwhile, the trial of 69 former government officials, including Mengistu, opened in Addis Ababa in December 1994, although proceedings were adjourned on numerous occasions. The defendants, 23 of whom were being tried *in absentia* (including Mengistu, who was in exile in Zimbabwe) and five of whom had died while awaiting trial, were accused of crimes against humanity and of genocide, perpetrated during 1974–91. In February 1997 the office of the Special Prosecutor announced that an additional 5,198 people would be indicted for war crimes and genocide, of whom nearly 3,000 would be tried *in absentia*. In November 1999 South Africa refused a request from the Ethiopian Government to extradite ex-President Mengistu, after it emerged that he was receiving medical treatment in that country. In March 2001 Mengistu was granted permanent residence in Zimbabwe, thus removing any possibility of his extradition to Ethiopia. In April the Ethiopian High Court found 37 people (13 *in absentia*) guilty of crimes against humanity and genocide; they were sentenced to up to 20 years' 'rigorous' imprisonment.

Elections to the House of People's Representatives and the House of the Federation were held concurrently on 14 May 2000, except in the Somali regional state, where voting was postponed until 31 August, owing to severe drought. Voting was also repeated in several constituencies after accusations of irregularities were upheld by the National Electoral Board (NEB). According to results published by the NEB in September, the OPDO won the largest number of seats in the House of People's Representatives, taking 178 of the 546 available. The OPDO's major partners in the EPRDF coalition, the Amhara National Democratic Movement (as the EPDM had been renamed in 1994) and the TPLF, gained 134 and 38 seats, respectively, while a number of smaller groups in the EPRDF won a further 19 seats. The EPRDF thus comfortably retained its large majority in the lower chamber. In mid-October the new legislature was sworn in, and Meles was re-elected as Prime Minister.

In March 2001 Prime Minister Meles dismissed numerous high-ranking TPLF members, including Siye Abraha, a former Minister of Defence, and Gebru Asrat, President of Tigrai regional state, from their party posts. (Asrat was also dismissed as President of Tigrai in April.) This followed the emergence of major divisions within the TPLF between pro-Meles reformists and conservatives critical of the Prime Minister's handling of the conflict with Eritrea (see below) and of the country's economy. It was claimed later in April that several dissident members of the TPLF were being detained in the capital and that Abraha had been accused of illicitly obtaining commission from weapons-handling and siphoning hard currency into foreign bank accounts. In late May Abraha was among a group of 20 former senior government officials and business executives arrested on suspicion of corruption; their trial was repeatedly postponed during late 2001, in order to allow the prosecution further time to prepare its case.

Meanwhile, in mid-April 2001 violence erupted in Addis Ababa, when thousands of students from the capital's university held a protest against the presence of armed police-officers on campus and the prohibition of their newspaper by the university administration. The demonstrators were forcibly dispersed by riot police, resulting in injuries to some 50 students. The Ministry of Education temporarily closed the university and issued a deadline by which it insisted all protests should cease. However, the deadline was not met, and, as police units again entered the university to break up the protests, rioting quickly spread to other parts of the capital. It was reported that more than 30 people were killed and some 250 injured during the disturbances. The university was again closed, and as many as 3,000 students were arrested for their role in the violence. Despite the prompt release of more than 2,000 detainees and the subsequent reopening of the university, many students insisted that they would not return to classes until all of those held in police stations and detention camps had been released. In early May two prominent Ethiopian academics, Prof. Mesfin Woldemariam, a former head of the Ethiopian Human Rights Council, and Dr Berhanu Nega, a respected economist, were arrested in connection with the riots in the capital, after the authorities claimed that they had made inflammatory speeches at a student meeting and were, in part, responsible for inciting the violence. In the following month the two men were charged with 'attempting to change the constitutional order of Ethiopia by force' and with belonging to a proscribed clandestine organization. Their detention was fiercely criticized by international human rights organizations, and after they entered pleas of not guilty to the charges they were released on bail.

During 2001 the Meles administration suffered a number of internal set-backs. In May Ethiopia's Head of Security and Intelligence, Kinfe Gebremedhin, a staunch supporter of the Prime Minister, was assassinated in Addis Ababa. In late June President Gidada was dismissed from the executive committee of the OPDO, after it was alleged that he had refused to accept the party's programme of reform and was providing support to dissidents opposed to Meles. Gidada, in turn, accused the Government of embarking on a campaign of propaganda against him. Gidada was also expelled from the EPRDF, after leaving an EPRDF council meeting, complaining of pressure from Meles. The President remained insistent, however, that he would complete his presidential term, which was scheduled to end in October. In August relations between the Prime Minister and the President were further strained by Gidada's criticism of the appointment of the army Chief-of-Staff, Abedula Gemeda, to the leadership of the OPDO. Earlier that month the Speaker of the

House of the Federation, Almaz Meko, had accused the Tigraian-dominated Government of persecuting the Oromo people and the TPLF of plundering the resources of the Oromo people in order to develop the Tigrai region. She subsequently resigned from her post, relinquished her membership of both the OPDO and the central committee of the EPRDF, and defected to the OLF. Nevertheless, by mid-September it appeared that Meles had succeeding in re-establishing control over the TPLF, and therefore the EPRDF, following his re-election as Chairman of the party.

On 8 October 2001 Lt Girma Wolde Giorgis, a former President of the parliament during Haile Selassie's reign and a member of the House of People's Representatives since 1995, was elected by the legislature to replace Gidada as President of Ethiopia. Later that month Prime Minister Meles effected a major reorganization of the Council of Ministers and created several new ministries, including a Ministry of Federal Affairs; only eight of the members of the previous Council of Ministers were retained.

In mid-March 2002 violence erupted in the Tepi region of the Southern Nations, Nationalities and Peoples State (SNNPS) between rival ethnic groups and the security forces, following a series of protests regarding the outcome of local elections, held in December 2001. According to official figures, 128 people were killed in the disturbances, although opposition sources claimed the number was as high as 1,000, and there were reports that a number of villages had been razed to the ground. The EU subsequently demanded a 'transparent, public and open' inquiry into the incidents and expressed its concern that a large number of those believed to have been killed were the victims of 'revenge attacks' by local police-officers. In May as many as 38 people were killed in Awasa after police violently suppressed a demonstration against plans to remove the city's status as the capital of the SNNPS. Human rights organizations condemned the actions of the security forces, claiming that they had fired indiscriminately on unarmed civilians. In August some 90 state employees, including 41 police-officers and 11 administrative officials, were arrested by the state authorities for their roles in the March riots and charged with human rights violations, instigation of violence and abuses of office.

In late 2002 Ethiopia was again threatened by widespread famine, following the failure of rains for the second successive year. Prime Minister Meles stated in November that the scale of the disaster was likely to be much more serious than the great famine of 1984 and that some 6m. Ethiopians were already in need of food aid; he expected this total to rise to as many as 15m. by mid-2003. International aid agencies immediately appealed for donations of aid for the country.

In December 2002 Nestlé, a multinational food and beverages company, revealed that it was seeking US $6m. from the Government of Ethiopia to compensate for the nationalization of its business interests in that country by the Mengistu administration in 1975. Furthermore, it was announced that a number of other private creditors were seeking compensation totalling almost $500m. for assets nationalized during Mengistu's tenure. The Ethiopian Government offered Nestlé payment of $1.5m.; however, Nestlé stated that it would continue to seek payment in full and that it was 'in the interest of Ethiopia to reach a deal to ensure continued flows of direct investment in the country'. Nestlé's stance was subject to fierce international criticism, and in January 2003 the company appeared to bow to public opinion and announced that it would accept the $1.5m. and reinvest it in famine-relief projects in Ethiopia

Ethiopia's foreign affairs after Mengistu's coup in 1977 were dominated by relations with the USSR, which replaced the USA as the principal supplier of armaments to Ethiopia and provided military advisers and economic aid. In the late 1980s, however, changes in Soviet foreign policy weakened the relationship, and the Soviet Government began to urge a political, rather than military, solution to Ethiopia's regional conflicts.

In April 1989 Ethiopia sought to upgrade its diplomatic relations with the USA, receiving a cautious initial response. The USA subsequently encouraged the EPRDF's seizure of power in May 1991 and expressed its approval of proposals for a transition to a multi-party democratic system. In 1993 Ethiopia and the USA signed an agreement on economic and technical co-operation, the first such agreement for 17 years.

Relations with Somalia have been problematic since the Ogaden War of 1977–78. However, in April 1988 Ethiopia and Somalia agreed to re-establish diplomatic relations, to withdraw troops from their common border and to exchange prisoners of war. During 1988–91 an estimated 600,000 Somali refugees entered Ethiopia from northern Somalia, of whom more than 150,000 arrived in the first half of 1991. The transitional Government of Ethiopia declared a policy of non-interference in the affairs of neighbouring states and adopted a neutral stance in Somalia's civil conflict. In August 1998 Ethiopia's Minister of Foreign Affairs held discussions with Hussein Aidid, the leader of the Somali National Alliance (SNA), on resolving Somalia's conflict. Aidid was also requested to cease providing support to al-Ittihad and Oromo organizations opposed to the Ethiopian administration. In February 1999 tensions escalated when Aidid accused the Ethiopian Government of interfering in Somali affairs and supplying arms to three anti-SNA factions. In April heavily armed Ethiopian forces, which claimed to be pursuing OLF insurgents, entered Somalia. Aidid appealed to the UN and the OAU to take action against Ethiopia. In June the Somali-based Rahawin Resistance Army (RRA), assisted by some 3,000 Ethiopian troops, captured the town of Baidoa, which had been controlled by Aidid, after heavy fighting. Aidid's continuing support of the Eritrean Government and Ethiopian insurgent groups led many observers to believe that the conflict between Eritrea and Ethiopia was in danger of spreading elsewhere in the Horn of Africa. The Ethiopian Government claimed, however, that its actions were merely attempts to protect the border from attacks initiated by Somali-based rebel opposition groups. Following mediation attempts in October, Ethiopia withdrew its forces from Somalia, although the Ethiopian Government reiterated its demand that the SNA sever its connections with Eritrea and the Oromo rebels. In November 2000 the President of Somalia, Abdulkassim Salad Hasan, visited Ethiopia for the first time since his election in August. This followed a visit to Ethiopia by the President of the self-proclaimed 'Republic of Somaliland' earlier that month. During his visit Hasan held talks with senior Ethiopian officials, but, although relations between the two countries were reported to have improved as a result of the discussions, the Ethiopian authorities continued to refuse to recognize officially the Hasan administration and urged it to reach agreements with its opponents. In January 2001 relations between the countries deteriorated after the Somali Prime Minister accused Ethiopia of continuing to assist the RRA, which had taken control of a number of towns in south-west Somalia, and maintained that Ethiopia was behind an assassination attempt on the Speaker of Somalia's transitional legislature. The accusations were strenuously denied by the Ethiopian authorities, which stated that no Ethiopian troops were in Somali territory. In June the Somali Minister of Defence accused Ethiopia of again dispatching heavily armed troops into Somali territory; however, later that month a delegation from Somalia, led by the Deputy Prime Minister, visited Ethiopia and admitted that its claims had been mistaken. Ethiopia subsequently agreed to mediate between the Somali Transitional National Government (TNG) and the Somali Reconciliation and Restoration Council, which had been established in Ethiopia in March to rival the TNG. In April 2002 five members of al-Ittihad were sentenced to death by an Ethiopian court for their roles in a series of terrorist attacks in Ethiopia in 1995, in which 27 people were killed and a further 16 injured. The Ethiopian Prime Minister, Meles Zenawi, claimed that Ethiopia had obtained proof of links between al-Ittihad and the al-Qa'ida (Base) organization, which was believed to have been responsible for the devastating suicide attacks of 11 September 2001 in the USA. In February 2003 Meles admitted that Ethiopian troops had, on occasion, been dispatched into Somali territory in pursuit of suspected members of al-Ittihad. Relations between Somalia and Ethiopia were further strained by Meles' claim that a number of al-Ittihad members were represented in the Somali TNG; the accusation was, however, strenuously denied by Hasan.

Following the military coup in Sudan in April 1985, full diplomatic relations were restored between Ethiopia and Sudan. Relations between the two countries were strained, however, by the influx into Ethiopia, in the late 1980s, of thousands of Sudanese refugees, fleeing from famine and civil war in southern Sudan. The vast majority of an estimated 380,000 refugees were reported to have returned to Sudan by early 1991, as a result of the civil war in Ethiopia. The change of government in Ethiopia in May 1991 led to a considerable improvement in relations between Ethiopia and Sudan, and in October President Meles and Sudan's leader, Lt-Gen. al-Bashir, signed an agreement on friendship and co-operation. In September 1995 the Ethiopian administration adopted a number of sanctions against Sudan, including the suspension of air flights between the two countries and a reduction in Sudanese diplomatic representation in Ethiopia, after the Sudanese authorities refused to extradite to Ethiopia three men allegedly involved in an assassination attempt on President Mubarak of Egypt in Addis Ababa in June. Accusations of border incursions intensified during 1996–97. Although attacks against Sudanese positions were known to have been launched by the Sudan People's Liberation Army (SPLA), operating from Ethiopia, the Ethiopian authorities denied any knowledge of their activities. Relations between the two countries subsequently improved, and in October 1998 Ethiopia reportedly resumed air flights to Sudan. The Ethiopian authorities were also reported to have closed the SPLA offices in western Ethiopia, while Sudan closed the OLF base in Khartoum. In November 1999 Prime Minister Meles received Lt-Gen. al-Bashir in Addis Ababa, where they discussed the possible reactivation of the Ethio-Sudan Joint Ministerial Commission and announced their intent to form closer economic ties between the two countries.

In November 1991 the leaders of Ethiopia and Kenya signed a co-operation agreement, although in October 1992 it was reported that the Kenyan Government was secretly giving asylum to Ethiopian dissidents. In April 1997 the two countries agreed to strengthen border controls following an attack by Ethiopian tribesmen in Kenya's frontier region, in which 41 civilians and 16 security personnel were killed. Additional security measures were agreed in late 1998, following an incursion by Ethiopian tribesmen into Kenya, which resulted in some 140 fatalities. In March 1999 Kenyan security forces exchanged fire with Ethiopian troops pursuing OLF rebels across the border. Kenya accused Ethiopia of violating international law, and relations between the two countries became further strained after Ethiopian soldiers attacked villages along the border. Bilateral relations deteriorated yet further during late 2000 and early 2001 after it was reported that some 50 Kenyans had been killed by Ethiopian militia forces. In January 2001 representatives from both countries met in Nairobi, Kenya, and agreed to take steps aimed at ending disputes along the common border.

After May 1991 the EPLF governed Eritrea as a *de facto* independent state and conducted its affairs with foreign countries accordingly. Ethiopia and the newly independent Eritrea signed a treaty of co-operation during a visit by the Eritrean President, Issaias Afewerki, to Addis Ababa in July 1993. The agreement included provisions on the joint utilization of resources and co-operation in the energy, transport, defence and education sectors. A further agreement, signed in late 1994, provided for the free movement of goods between the two countries without payment of customs dues.

In late 1997 relations with Eritrea deteriorated, following that country's adoption of a new currency (to replace the Ethiopian birr) and the subsequent disruption of cross-border trade. Fighting between Ethiopian and Eritrean troops erupted in early May 1998, with both countries accusing the other of having invaded their territory. Eritrea rejected a peace plan drafted by the USA and Rwanda in early June, as it refused to comply with a precondition to withdraw its troops from the disputed region. In mid-June the USA and Italy successfully mediated an aerial cease-fire, but a resolution passed by the UN Security Council later that month, demanding that Ethiopia and Eritrea cease hostilities forthwith, was ignored. The OAU established a mediation committee in June in an attempt to end the dispute, and in July an OAU delegation visited the two countries. The committee presented its report to the Ethiopian and Eritrean Ministers of Foreign Affairs at a meeting in Ouagadougou, Burkina Faso, in August; however, its proposals were rejected by Eritrea, necessitating the convening of a special meeting of the mediation committee in Ouagadougou in November. Ethiopia welcomed the committee's proposals, which stressed the need to demilitarize and demarcate the disputed region, but Eritrea rejected the plans. Other international mediation attempts continued in late 1998 (including that of Anthony Lake, a former US national security adviser), but failed to resolve the dispute.

In February 1999, after two weeks of intense fighting, Ethiopia recaptured the disputed town of Badme, and the Eritrean Government announced that it had accepted the OAU peace plan that it had rejected in late 1998. However, Ethiopia appeared eager to maximize its opportunity to secure access to the coast, ignoring appeals by the UN Security Council for an immediate cease-fire. Fighting erupted again in March 1999, as the two sides continued to blame each other for obstructing the

OAU's peace efforts. Ethiopia insisted on Eritrea's unilateral withdrawal from its territory; however, Eritrea repeatedly rejected this demand and insisted that it did not form part of the OAU peace agreement. Mutual distrust persisted on both sides, with the deadlock continuing into May, as Eritrea steadfastly refused to withdraw from the territory that it occupied, and, despite the UN Security Council's repeated insistence on an immediate cessation of fighting, Ethiopian military aircraft bombed the Eritrean port of Massawa.

In July 1999 the deadlock between Ethiopia and Eritrea appeared to have been broken at the OAU summit meeting in Algiers, when the two warring countries confirmed their commitment to the OAU peace proposals, under which both sides would withdraw from all territory captured since the outbreak of the conflict, thus effectively returning both sides to their pre-war frontiers. However, the situation was complicated by Eritrean demands for war reparations and Ethiopian requests for clarification of the technical arrangements regarding the withdrawal of troops from the disputed territory. In August Eritrea formally accepted the latest OAU peace plan; however, in the following month Ethiopia announced that it had rejected the proposals, as the technical arrangements did not guarantee a return to the *status quo ante*. In February 2000 Lake and Prime Minister Ahmed Ouyahia of Algeria, the OAU's special envoy, visited Addis Ababa and Asmara, but failed to persuade the two warring parties to accept the OAU's peace proposals. By March it was evident that the Horn of Africa was on the verge of widespread famine, and the Eritrean authorities offered to allow large quantities of food aid destined for Ethiopia to be transported through the port of Assab. This offer was, however, rejected by the Ethiopian Government, which claimed that about 100,000 metric tons of food aid destined for Ethiopia in May 1998 had been looted by Eritreans at Assab. In April 2000 it was announced that some 8m. people in Ethiopia were in danger of starvation, and both the Ethiopian and Eritrean Governments were strongly criticized by aid agencies for continuing to spend vast amounts on funding their war efforts, while millions of their citizens endured severe food shortages. Later that month delegations from both countries agreed to attend OAU-sponsored talks in Algiers, although neither side would agree to a direct meeting, and after six days of negotiations the talks collapsed.

In mid-May 2000 Ethiopian troops launched a major offensive near the disputed towns of Badme and Zalambessa, repelling the Eritrean forces. An announcement by the UN Security Council that it would impose sanctions and an embargo on the sale of all military supplies to the two countries, if fighting did not cease within three days, provoked violent protests outside the British and US embassies in Addis Ababa. However, hostilities continued, and on 18 May the UN Security Council unanimously approved the imposition of a 12-month arms embargo on Ethiopia and Eritrea. Shortly afterwards Ethiopian forces captured the strategically vital town of Barentu, thus taking control of the western front. Zalambessa subsequently fell to the Ethiopian forces, and on 25 May the Eritrean Government announced the withdrawal of its troops from all disputed areas. Despite the resumption of peace talks in Algiers on 29 May, Ethiopian forces continued to capture Eritrean towns, and on 30 May Ethiopian aircraft bombed the military airfield in Asmara. The following day Prime Minister Meles stated that Ethiopia had no territorial claims over Eritrea and that the war between the two countries was over. Nevertheless, sporadic fighting continued to take place. Following extensive indirect negotiations in Algiers during early June, both sides expressed their willingness, in principle, to accept the OAU's peace proposals. On 18 June the Ethiopian and Eritrean Ministers of Foreign Affairs signed an agreement, which provided for an immediate cease-fire and the establishment of a 25-km temporary security zone (TSZ) on the Eritrean side of the common border until the issue of the final demarcation of the border had been settled. It was estimated that as many as 120,000 people had been killed since the beginning of the conflict in 1998, and that more than 350,000 Ethiopians had been internally displaced. Indirect negotiations involving representatives from both countries, at which the technical issues of the peace agreement were to be discussed, commenced in Washington, DC, USA, in early July and continued in Algiers in October. Meanwhile, in mid-September the UN Security Council approved the deployment of a 4,200-strong UN Mission in Ethiopia and Eritrea (UNMEE).

On 12 December 2000 Ethiopia and Eritrea signed an agreement in Algiers, which formally brought an end to the conflict.

The agreement provided for a permanent cessation of all hostilities, the return of all prisoners of war, the demarcation of the common border by an independent commission, and the establishment of a Claims Commission to assess the issues of compensation and reparations. Furthermore, both countries pledged to co-operate with an independent investigation into the origins of the conflict. Later that month the first exchange of prisoners of war between the two countries took place. By late January 2001 the UNMEE force had arrived in the region, and, in compliance with the provisions for the establishment of a TSZ along the Ethiopia–Eritrea border, Ethiopian troops commenced their withdrawal from the territory they had captured from Eritrea. On 22 February Ethiopia informed UNMEE that it had completed the redeployment of its troops to the southern boundary of the prospective TSZ. However, at the fourth meeting of the Military Co-ordination Commission (MCC), later that month, the Eritrean delegation registered its objections to adjustments made to the original boundaries of the future TSZ, on which agreement had been provisionally reached at a previous MCC meeting. The Eritrean authorities subsequently announced that they had suspended the withdrawal of their forces, which had been scheduled to be completed by 3 March. In mid-March the UN Security Council extended UNMEE's mandate (which was about to expire) until 15 September. Despite reiterating its dissatisfaction at the southern boundary of the prospective TSZ, in early April Eritrea recommenced the redeployment of its troops. On 16 April it was announced that the withdrawal of Eritrea's forces was complete. Two days later UNMEE declared the establishment of the TSZ, marking the formal separation of the Eritrean and Ethiopian forces. In mid-May the arms embargo imposed on the two countries by the UN in May 2000 was lifted. In late June 2001 UNMEE presented the final map of the TSZ to Ethiopia and Eritrea, although it emphasized that it would not influence the work of the neutral Boundary Commission charged with determining the border between the two countries. Despite this announcement, the Ethiopian Government expressed its dissatisfaction with the map, and at the eighth MCC meeting in August both countries again stated their objections to the current boundaries of the TSZ. In mid-September UNMEE's mandate was extended for a further six months, although the head of the mission, Legwaila Joseph Legwaila, acknowledged that UNMEE faced an extremely difficult task in achieving lasting peace, as the two countries remained 'polarized', and also admitted that neither country had fully adhered to the terms of the agreement on the cessation of hostilities.

In mid-December 2001 Ethiopia and Eritrea began presenting their cases for border demarcation to the five-member Boundary Commission at the International Court of Justice at The Hague, Netherlands. In mid-March 2002 UNMEE's mandate was extended until mid-September. The Boundary Commission delivered its findings in April. Both Ethiopia and Eritrea had committed themselves in advance to the acceptance of the report, which was carefully balanced, thus allowing both sides to claim success. However, the Commission did not identify on which side of the boundary line Badme lay, stating that it was awaiting delineation on the ground, which was expected to take up to one year, as extensive demining was required prior to placing boundary markers. In the absence of any decision by the Boundary Commission, both countries immediately claimed to have been awarded Badme. When UNMEE invited journalists to visit Badme in late April by entering through Eritrea, Ethiopia reacted by closing the border to UNMEE and demanding the removal of the UNMEE commander, Maj.-Gen. Patrick Cammaert. The border was reopened to UN personnel in early May. Later that month Ethiopia formally requested 'interpretation, correction and consultation' of the Boundary Commission's report, but this was rejected by the Commission in late June.

In early March 2003 the Border Commission reported to the UN Security Council that Ethiopia's requests for changes to the border ruling, in order to 'take better account of human and physical geography', threatened to undermine the peace process as a whole. Despite Ethiopia's claims that it had been promised that demarcations could be refined, later in March the Boundary Commission categorically ruled Badme to be Eritrean territory, thus rejecting Ethiopia's territorial claim over the town.

Government

In August 1995 the Council of Representatives, a body established in 1991 to govern the country during the transitional period after the overthrow of the Mengistu regime, formally transferred power to a newly elected legislature, the Federal Parliamentary Assembly. Under the provisions of a new Constitution, adopted in December 1994, the country became a federation, consisting of nine states and two chartered cities, the capital, Addis Ababa, and Dire Dawa. The states have their own parliamentary assemblies, which also elect representatives to the House of the Federation, the upper chamber of the Federal Parliamentary Assembly. The lower chamber, the House of People's Representatives, consists of no more than 550 directly elected deputies. The Federal Parliamentary Assembly elects a President as Head of State. However, the President fulfils mainly ceremonial functions, executive power being the preserve of the Prime Minister. The Prime Minister, who is elected by the House of People's Representatives, appoints the Council of Ministers (subject to approval by the legislature), and acts as Commander-in-Chief of the armed forces.

Defence

In December 1991 Ethiopia's transitional Government announced that a 'national defence army', based on already active EPRDF troops, would constitute Ethiopia's armed forces during the transitional period. In October 1993 the Minister of Defence announced that preparations were under way to create a 'multi-ethnic defence force', comprising members of all the different ethnic groups in Ethiopia. Extensive demobilization of former members of the TPLF has since taken place. In September 1996 the Government sold its naval assets. Owing to the war with Eritrea during 1999–2000, there was a large increase in the size of the armed forces and in defence expenditure. In August 2002 Ethiopia's active armed forces numbered an estimated 252,500, comprising an army of about 250,000 and an air force of some 2,500. The defence budget for 2000 was estimated at 3,700m. birr. In July 2000 the UN Security Council adopted a resolution (No. 1312) establishing the UN Mission in Ethiopia and Eritrea (UNMEE—see p. 65), which was to supervise the cease-fire and the implementation of a peace agreement between the two countries. At the end of August 2002 UNMEE numbered 4,154 uniformed personnel, including 214 military observers.

Economic Affairs

In 2001, according to estimates by the World Bank, Ethiopia's gross national income (GNI), measured at average 1999–2001 prices, was US $6,767m., equivalent to $100 per head (or $710 per head on an international purchasing-power parity basis): one of the lowest recorded levels of GNI per head for any country in the world. During 1990–2001, it was estimated, the population increased at an average annual rate of 2.3%, while gross domestic product (GDP) per head increased, in real terms, by an average of 1.9% per year. Overall GDP increased, in real terms, at an average annual rate of 4.2%; growth in 2001 was 7.9%.

Agriculture (including forestry and fishing) contributed an estimated 45.1% of GDP (at constant 1980/81 prices) in 2000/01, and employed an estimated 82.0% of the economically active population in 2001. The principal cash crop is coffee (which accounted for 53.0% of export earnings in 2000). The principal subsistence crops are cereals (barley, maize, sorghum and teff) and sugar cane. During 1990–2001 agricultural GDP increased at an average annual rate of 2.9%; growth in 2001 was 13.2%.

Industry (including mining, manufacturing, construction and power) employed 2.0% of the labour force in 1995, and provided an estimated 10.6% of GDP (at constant 1980/81 prices) in 2000/01. During 1990–2001 industrial GDP increased by an average of 4.1% per year. It rose by 5.1% in 2001.

Mining contributed only an estimated 0.5% of GDP (at constant 1980/81 prices) in 2000/01, and employed less than 0.1% of the labour force in 1995. During 1996/97–2000/01 mining GDP increased by an estimated average of 7.4% per year; growth in 2000/01 was an estimated 8.4%. Ethiopia has reserves of petroleum, although these have not been exploited, and there are also deposits of copper and potash. Gold, tantalite, soda ash, kaolin, dimension stones, precious metals and gemstones, salt, and industrial and construction materials are mined. In April 2000 a US company discovered large petroleum deposits in the west of the country.

Manufacturing employed only 1.6% of the labour force in 1995 and contributed 4.3% of GDP (at constant 1980/81 prices) in 2000/01. During 1990–2001 manufacturing GDP increased at an average annual rate of 3.7%. It increased by 4.3% in 2000 and by 6.3% in 2001.

In years of normal rainfall, energy is derived principally from Ethiopia's massive hydroelectric power resources. In 1999 97.3%

of Ethiopia's electricity was produced by hydroelectric power schemes. Imports of mineral fuels accounted for an estimated 20.1% of the cost of total imports in 2000. In 1993 agreement was reached with the World Bank on the financing of a project to construct a liquefied gas unit to exploit gas reserves in the Ogaden. In late 1995 the Government announced plans to develop geothermal energy sources at 15 sites in various regions of the country. Ethiopia's electricity generating capacity is expected to be doubled (to 713 MW) by 2005.

Services, which consisted mainly of wholesale and retail trade, public administration and defence, and transport and communications, employed 9.5% of the labour force in 1995, and contributed an estimated 44.3% of GDP (at constant 1980/81 prices) in 2000/01. The combined GDP of the service sectors increased, in real terms, at an average rate of 5.4% per year during 1990–2001. It rose by 3.4% in 2001.

In 2000 Ethiopia recorded a visible trade deficit of US $1,192.8m., and there was a deficit of $476.9m. on the current account of the balance of payments. In 2000 the principal source of imports (19.1%) was Yemen; other major suppliers were Italy, Japan, the People's Republic of China and India. The principal market for exports in that year were Germany (19.6%), Japan, Djibouti, Saudi Arabia, Italy, Somalia and Switzerland. The principal exports in 2000 were food and live animals, coffee, and leather and leather products. The principal imports in that year were machinery and transport equipment, mineral fuels and related products, and basic manufactures.

In the fiscal year 2001/02 it was estimated that Ethiopia's budgetary deficit reached 5,190.6m. birr. Ethiopia is the principal African recipient of concessionary funding, and the largest recipient of EU aid. At the end of 2000 Ethiopia's total external debt was $5,481m., of which $5,325m. was long-term public debt. In that year the cost of debt-servicing was equivalent to an estimated 13.9% of total earnings from the export of goods and services. The annual rate of inflation averaged 10.1% in 1990–96, but slowed to average –0.3% in 1997–2001. Consumer prices increased by 1.9% in 2000, but declined by 7.2% in 2001. There were 28,350 persons registered as applicants for work in the 12 months to June 1996.

Ethiopia is a member of the African Development Bank (see p. 128) and the Common Market for Eastern and Southern Africa (see p. 162). In July 2001 Ethiopia ratified the Cotonou Agreement (see p. 234), the successor of the Lomé Convention of the EU.

Ethiopia remains one of the poorest countries in the world, and the country's economy continues to suffer from the effects of recurrent, catastrophic drought, which severely disrupts agricultural production (the country's economic base). The Ethiopian economy is heavily dependent on assistance and grants from abroad, particularly in times of drought. However, many donors suspended aid for the duration of the war with Eritrea, and Ethiopia's economic difficulties were further exacerbated by its vast military expenditure and the renewed failure of crop harvests in 1999 and 2000. The conflict was estimated to have cost the country some US $2,900m. Following the cessation of fighting between Ethiopia and Eritrea in mid-2000 (see above), the World Bank agreed to resume development assistance to Ethiopia and, in December, approved a credit of $400.6m. to support the Ethiopian Government's planned recovery and rehabilitation projects. Furthermore, from early 2001 Ethiopia benefited from significant IMF assistance under the Poverty Reduction and Growth Facility and also qualified for additional debt relief from the Heavily Indebted Poor Countries initiative. A sustained recovery in the agricultural sector ended in late 2002, when a lack of rainfall again threatened severe famine across the country and prompted the country to appeal to donors for food assistance. The Government introduced value added tax on certain goods at a rate of 10% in January 2003, which was expected to increase government revenues, thus enabling greater expenditure on health, education and infrastructural projects. GDP growth of 5.0% was recorded in 2001/02, although this was somewhat lower than earlier predictions, owing to a decline in the prices of coffee and cereals.

Education

Education in Ethiopia is available free of charge up to grade 10, and, after a rapid growth in numbers of schools, it became compulsory between the ages of seven and 13 years. Since 1976 most primary and secondary schools have been controlled by local peasant associations and urban dwellers' associations. In 1994 Ethiopia adopted a new Education and Training Policy and Strategy, which restructured the education system and aimed to improve the quality of education. Primary education begins at seven years of age and lasts for eight years. Secondary education, beginning at 15 years of age, lasts for a further four years, comprising two cycles of two years each, the second of which provides preparatory education for entry to the tertiary level. A system of vocational and technical education also exists parallel to the preparatory programme. In 2000 total enrolment at primary schools was equivalent to 51.0% of children in the appropriate age-group (60.9% of boys; 40.7% of girls); enrolment at secondary schools was equivalent to 10.3% of children in the relevant age-group (12.0% of boys; 8.5% of girls). There are 21 institutions of higher education in Ethiopia, including six universities (in Addis Ababa, Bahir Dar, Alemanya, Jimma, Awassa and Makele). A total of 67,682 students were enrolled in higher education in 1999/2000. The 1999/2000 budget allocated an estimated 11.3% (2,304m. birr) of total expenditure to education.

Public Holidays

2003: 7 January* (Christmas), 19 January* (Epiphany), 12 February† (Id al-Adha/Arafat), 2 March (Battle of Adowa), 18

April* (Good Friday), 21 April* (Easter Monday), 1 May (May Day), 5 May (Patriots' Victory Day), 14 May† (Mouloud, Birth of the Prophet), 28 May (Downfall of the Dergue), 11 September (New Year's Day), 27 September* (Feast of the True Cross), 26 November† (Id al-Fitr, end of Ramadan).

2004: 7 January* (Christmas), 19 January* (Epiphany), 2 February† (Id al-Adha/Arafat), 2 March (Battle of Adowa), 9 April* (Good Friday), 12 April* (Easter Monday), 1 May (May Day), 2 May† (Mouloud, Birth of the Prophet), 5 May (Patriots' Victory Day), 28 May (Downfall of the Dergue), 11 September (New Year's Day), 27 September* (Feast of the True Cross), 14 November† (Id al-Fitr, end of Ramadan).

* Coptic holidays.

† These holidays are dependent on the Islamic lunar calendar and may vary by one or two days from the dates given.

Note: Ethiopia uses its own solar calendar; the Ethiopian year 1995 began on 11 September 2002.

Weights and Measures

The metric system is officially in use. There are also many local weights and measures.

Statistical Survey

Source (unless otherwise stated): Central Statistical Authority, POB 1143, Addis Ababa; tel. (1) 553010; fax (1) 550334.

Note: Unless otherwise indicated, figures in this Survey refer to the territory of Ethiopia after the secession of Eritrea in May 1993.

Area and Population

AREA, POPULATION AND DENSITY

Area (sq km)	1,133,380*
Population (census results)	
9 May 1984†	39,868,501
11 October 1994	
Males	26,910,698
Females	26,566,567
Total	53,477,265
Population (official estimates at mid-year)	
1999	61,672,000
2000	63,495,000
2001	65,370,000
Density (per sq km) at mid-2001	57.7

* 437,600 sq miles.

† Including an estimate for areas not covered by the census.

ADMINISTRATIVE DIVISIONS

(estimated population at mid-1999)

	Population ('000)		
	Males	Females	Total
Regional States			
1 Tigrai	1,767	1,826	3,593
2 Afar	667	521	1,188
3 Amhara	7,938	7,912	15,850
4 Oromia	10,833	10,861	21,694
5 Somali	1,952	1,650	3,602
6 Benishangul/Gumuz	264	259	523
7 Southern Nations, Nationalities and Peoples. . . .	6,029	6,103	12,132
8 Gambela. . . .	105	101	206
9 Harari	78	76	154
Chartered Cities			
1 Dire Dawa . . .	154	152	306
2 Addis Ababa . .	1,169	1,255	2,424
Total	30,956	30,716	61,672

PRINCIPAL TOWNS

(census results of October 1994)

Addis Ababa (capital)	2,084,588	Jimma.	119,717
Dire Dawa . . .	164,851	Dessie	117,268
Nazret.	127,842	Bahir Dar . . .	115,531
Harar	122,932	Debrezit . . .	105,963
Mekele	119,779		

Source: UN, *Demographic Yearbook.*

BIRTHS AND DEATHS

(UN estimates, annual averages)

	1985–90	1990–95	1995–2000
Birth rate (per 1,000)	47.2	45.6	44.6
Death rate (per 1,000)	19.4	18.4	19.0

Source: UN, *World Population Prospects: The 2000 Revision.*

Expectation of life (WHO estimates, years at birth): 48.0 (males 46.8; females 49.2) in 2001 (Source: WHO, *World Health Report*).

ECONOMICALLY ACTIVE POPULATION

(official estimates, ISIC Major Divisions, persons aged 10 years and over, mid-1995)*

	Males	Females	Total
Agriculture, hunting, forestry and fishing	12,681,037	8,924,280	21,605,317
Mining and quarrying . . .	12,114	4,426	16,540
Manufacturing	224,106	160,889	384,995
Electricity, gas and water . .	14,799	2,267	17,066
Construction	55,906	5,326	61,232
Trade, restaurants and hotels . .	335,353	600,584	935,937
Transport, storage and communications	87,975	15,179	103,154
Financing, insurance, real estate and business services . . .	14,513	4,938	19,451
Community, social and personal services	777,907	474,317	1,252,224
Total labour force	14,203,710	10,192,206	24,395,916

* The figures exclude persons seeking work for the first time, totalling 210,184 (males 100,790; females 109,394), but include other unemployed persons.

Source: ILO, *Yearbook of Labour Statistics.*

Mid-2001 (estimates in '000): Agriculture, etc. 23,294; Total labour force 28,416 (Source: FAO).

Health and Welfare

KEY INDICATORS

Total fertility rate (children per woman, 2001)	5.4
Under-5 mortality rate (per 1,000 live births, 2001) . . .	172
HIV/AIDS (% of persons aged 15–49, 2001)	6.41
Hospital beds (per 1,000 head, 1990)	0.24
Health expenditure (2000): US $ per head (PPP)	17
Health expenditure (2000): % of GDP	4.6
Health expenditure (2000): public (% of total) . . .	65.6
Access to water (% of persons, 2000)	24
Access to sanitation (% of persons, 2000)	15
Human Development Index (2000): ranking	168
Human Development Index (2000): value	0.313

For sources and definitions, see explanatory note on p. vi.

Agriculture

PRINCIPAL CROPS

('000 metric tons)

	1999	2000	2001
Wheat	1,237	1,212.6	1,571.2
Barley	813.4	741.9	845.4
Maize	2,685.3	2,525.5	3,138.4
Oats	50.7	430.2	49.6
Millet (Dagusa)	320.3	317.7	316.2
Sorghum	1,184.1	1,332.9	1,538.3
Other cereals	1,721.9	1,749.6	1,749.6*
Potatoes*	370	385	385
Sweet potatoes*	165	175	170
Yams*	267	270	270
Other roots and tubers* . . .	3,450	3,480	3,480
Sugar cane*	2,200	2,200	2,400
Dry beans	102.5	110.0*	110.0*
Dry broad beans	388.7	452.8	452.8*
Dry peas	121.2	116.0	141.4
Chick-peas	164.6	211.9	175.7
Lentils	49.8*	55.3	55.3*
Vetches	107.5	99.4	99.4*
Other pulses	10.8	8.0	8.5*
Tree nuts*	68	70	70
Soybeans (Soya beans)* . . .	25	25	25
Groundnuts (in shell)* . . .	11.9	15.0*	15.2
Castor beans*	15.5	14.0	14.0
Rapeseed	13.9	14.7	15.0*
Safflower seed*	37	37	37
Sesame seed	15.6	18.9	22.0*
Cottonseed†	45.5	45.5	45.5
Linseed	35.3	64.1	64.1*
Cabbages*	52	48	48
Tomatoes*	54	50	50
Green onions and shallots* . .	19	16	16
Dry onions*	45	40	40
Other vegetables*	428.5	420.5	420.5
Bananas*	81	78	78
Oranges*	13.5	12.5	12.5
Other fruit*	136.5	130.0	130.0
Coffee (green)	217.5	230.0†	228.0†
Pimento and allspice* . . .	113	110	110

* FAO estimate(s).
† Unofficial figure(s).

Source: FAO.

LIVESTOCK

('000 head, year ending September)

	1999	2000	2001
Cattle	35,095	35,480*	34,500*
Sheep*	22,000	22,500	22,500
Goats*	16,950	17,000	17,000
Asses*	5,200	5,200	5,200
Horses*	2,750	2,750	2,750
Mules*	630	630	630
Camels*	1,050	1,060	1,070
Pigs*	25	25	25
Poultry*	55,400	55,600	55,800

* FAO estimate(s).

Source: FAO.

LIVESTOCK PRODUCTS

('000 metric tons)

	1999	2000	2001
Beef and veal	290	298*	298*
Mutton and lamb*	81.4	83.0	83.0
Goat meat*	63.4	63.5	63.5
Pig meat*	1.4	1.4	1.4
Poultry meat*	73.6	73.8	73.8
Game meat*	74	74	74
Other meat	59.7	59.9*	59.9*
Cows' milk	960.6	970.0*	970.0*
Goats' milk*	94.0	95.0	95.0
Sheep's milk*	55.0	56.3	56.3
Butter*	1.3	1.3	1.3
Ghee*	10.6	10.6	10.6
Cheese	3.9	4.0	4.0
Hen eggs*	75.2	75.6	75.6
Honey	28.5	29.0*	29.0*
Wool: greasy*	11.7	11.1	11.1
Wool: scoured*	6.1	5.8	5.8
Cattle hides*	56.3	57.8	57.8
Sheepskins*	14.7	14.9	14.9
Goatskins*	13.4	13.5	13.5

* FAO estimate(s).

Source: FAO.

Forestry

ROUNDWOOD REMOVALS

('000 cubic metres, excl. bark)

	1999	2000	2001
Sawlogs, veneer logs and logs for sleepers	2	7	6
Pulpwood*	7	7	7
Other industrial wood* . . .	2,445	2,445	2,445
Fuel wood*	85,785	87,471	88,825
Total	88,239	89,925	91,283

* FAO estimates.

Source: FAO.

SAWNWOOD PRODUCTION

(FAO estimates, '000 cubic metres, incl. railway sleepers)

	1999	2000	2001
Coniferous (softwood) . . .	25	25	25
Broadleaved (hardwood) . . .	35	35	35
Total	60	60	60

Source: FAO.

Fishing

(metric tons, live weight)

	1998	1999	2000
Capture	14,000	15,858	15,681
Rhinofishes	3,168	3,621	3,451
Other cyprinids	918	1,050	1,045
Tilapias	7,952	9,088	7,000
North African catfish	1,677	1,917	4,000
Nile perch	191	75	65
Aquaculture*	14	—	—
Total catch	14,014	15,858	15,681

* FAO estimates.

Source: FAO, *Yearbook of Fishery Statistics.*

Mining

('000 metric tons, unless otherwise indicated, year ending 7 July)

	1998/99	1999/2000	2000/2001
Gold (kilograms)	4,960	5,177	5,200
Marble ('000 cu m)	152	n.a.	n.a.
Limestone	846*	1,197*	1,300
Gypsum and anhydrite	36	47	51
Pumice*	135	156	169

* Estimated production.

Sources: US Geological Survey.

Industry

SELECTED PRODUCTS

('000 metric tons, unless otherwise indicated; year ending 7 July)

	1996/97	1997/98	1998/99
Wheat flour	140	105	168
Macaroni and pasta	18	20	24
Raw sugar	172	173	235
Wine ('000 hectolitres)	35	26	20
Beer ('000 hectolitres)	843	831	921
Mineral waters ('000 hectolitres)	374	390	421
Soft drinks ('000 hectolitres)	669	655	667
Cigarettes (million)	2,024	2,029	1,829
Cotton yarn	3	3	3
Woven cotton fabrics ('000 sq m)	35,000	38,000	43,000
Nylon fabrics ('000 sq m)	4,200	4,700	4,000
Footwear (excluding rubber, '000 pairs)	6,925	6,252	7,477
Soap	14.3	10.9	26.1
Tyres ('000)	151	152	148
Clay building bricks ('000)	20	20	19
Quicklime	7	7	14
Cement	775	497	470

Beer of millet ('000 hectolitres): 1,782 in 1998; 2,664 in 1999; 2,222 in 2000 (Source: FAO).

Finance

CURRENCY AND EXCHANGE RATES

Monetary Units
100 cents = 1 birr

Sterling, Dollar and Euro Equivalents (29 November 2002)
£1 sterling = 13.313 birr
US $1 = 8.578 birr
€1 = 8.516 birr
1,000 birr = £75.11 = $116.57 = €117.43

Average Exchange Rate (birr per US $)
2000   8.2173
2001   8.4575
2002   8.5678

GENERAL BUDGET

(preliminary figures, million birr, year ending 7 July)

Revenue*	1999/2000	2000/01	2001/02
Taxation	7,640.0	6,052.0	6,473.4
Taxes on income and profits	2,333.1	1,592.6	1,555.5
Personal income	508.2	318.4	333.8
Business profits	1,372.6	1,115.3	1,221.7
Domestic indirect taxes	1,458.1	1,135.5	1,247.6
Import duties	3,685.0	3,230.6	3,280.2
Export duties	163.8	93.3	28.1
Other revenue	4,449.8	2,702.7	1,971.5
Government investment income	1,144.9	1,345.8	1,005.6
Reimbursements and property sales	204.4	n.a.	n.a.
Sales of goods and services	372.0	n.a.	n.a.
Total	12,089.8	8,754.7	8,444.9

* Excluding grants received from abroad (million birr): 2,101.8 in 1999/2000; 977.0 in 2000/01; 305.7 in 2001/02.

Expenditure	1999/2000	2000/01	2001/02
Current expenditure	13,801.6	5,899.5	5,637.8
General services	8,339.5	3,988.1	3,450.0
Economic services	801.5	306.6	360.4
Social services	2,107.0	503.3	805.9
Interest and charges	1,118.7	1,079.8	1,004.7
External assistance (grants)*	1,289.5	n.a.	n.a.
Capital expenditure	3,425.5	2,685.1	3,484.9
Economic development	2,079.3	1,852.7	2,441.0
Social development	708.2	639.7	564.8
General services and compensation	233.5	192.7	479.1
External assistance (grants)*	404.7	n.a.	n.a.
Regional transfers	n.a.	3,548.1	3,847.6
Total	17,227.1	12,532.7†	13,941.2†

* Imputed value of goods and services provided mainly in kind.
† Including adjustment.

Source: National Bank of Ethiopia.

INTERNATIONAL RESERVES

(US $ million, at 31 December)

	2000	2001	2002
Gold*	0.3	0.3	0.3
IMF special drawing rights	—	0.2	0.1
Reserve position in IMF	9.2	9.0	9.7
Foreign exchange	297.1	424.1	871.9
Total	306.3	433.6	882.0

* National valuation.

Source: IMF, *International Financial Statistics.*

MONEY SUPPLY

(million birr, at 31 December)

	2000	2001	2002
Currency outside banks	4,591	4,870	5,686
Demand deposits at commercial banks	6,819	7,027	7,975
Total money	11,409	11,898	13,662

Source: IMF, *International Financial Statistics.*

COST OF LIVING

(General Index of Retail Prices for Addis Ababa; base: 1997 = 100)

	1999	2000	2001
Food	111.2	110.0	93.2
Clothing (incl. footwear)	89.2	n.a.	n.a.
All items (incl. others)	104.7	106.7	99.0

Sources: ILO, *Yearbook of Labour Statistics*; UN, *Monthly Bulletin of Statistics.*

NATIONAL ACCOUNTS
(million birr at current prices; year ending 7 July)

Expenditure on the Gross Domestic Product

	1998/99	1999/2000	2000/01*
Government final consumption expenditure	8,945	12,053	9,115
Private final consumption expenditure	38,819	39,859	41,693
Gross capital formation	7,878	7,914	9,375
Total domestic expenditure	55,643	59,826	60,182
Exports of goods and services	6,877	8,020	7,982
Less Imports of goods and services	14,098	15,976	16,202
GDP in purchasers' values	48,422	51,869	51,962

* Estimated figures.

Source: IMF, *Ethiopia: Statistical Appendix* (September 2002).

Gross Domestic Product by Economic Activity
(at constant 1980/81 factor cost)

	1998/99	1999/2000	2000/01*
Agriculture, hunting, forestry and fishing	6,874	7,025	7,831
Mining and quarrying	75	83	90
Manufacturing	982	1,015	1,068
Electricity, gas and water	226	235	243
Construction	418	399	431
Trade, hotels and restaurants	1,344	1,397	1,469
Transport, storage and communications	910	1,027	1,081
Finance, insurance and real estate	1,046	1,144	1,207
Public administration and defence	2,138	2,449	2,513
Education	356	388	427
Health	188	187	202
Domestic and other services	738	766	795
Total	15,294	16,112	17,357

* Estimated figures.

Source: IMF, *Ethiopia: Statistical Appendix* (September 2002).

BALANCE OF PAYMENTS
(US $ million)

	1999	2000	2001
Exports of goods f.o.b.	467.4	486.0	433.3
Imports of goods f.o.b.	−1,387.2	−1,131.4	−1,626.1
Trade balance	−919.8	−645.4	−1,192.8
Exports of services	473.6	506.2	522.9
Imports of services	−466.3	−490.7	525.6
Balance on goods and services	−912.5	−629.9	−1,195.5
Other income received	16.6	16.2	16.3
Other income paid	−50.4	−50.4	−48.3
Balance on goods, services and income	−946.3	−664.1	−1,227.5
Current transfers received	500.8	697.9	774.6
Current transfers paid	−19.7	−17.7	−24.0
Current balance	−465.2	16.2	−476.9
Investment assets	−85.3	116.1	60.5
Investment liabilities	−93.2	−93.3	−200.1
Net errors and omissions	407.2	−233.0	51.6
Overall balance	−236.3	−195.6	−564.9

Source: IMF, *International Financial Statistics*.

External Trade

PRINCIPAL COMMODITIES
(distribution by SITC, US $ '000)

Imports c.i.f.	1998	1999	2000
Food and live animals	70.2	100.1	57.1
Cereals and cereal preparations	55.9	86.3	39.5
Unmilled wheat and meslin	47.6	73.4	18.1
Unmilled durum wheat	38.6	63.7	9.6
Mineral fuels, lubricants, etc.	359.7	154.0	253.4
Petroleum and petroleum products	354.7	153.1	252.6
Refined petroleum products	327.2	148.0	247.2
Chemicals and related products	154.1	174.3	142.6
Basic manufactures	305.8	255.7	243.8
Textile yarn, fabrics, etc.	59.3	54.3	55.9
Iron and steel	96.2	60.4	70.8
Universals, plates and sheets	50.5	29.1	40.8
Machinery and transport equipment	420.0	534.7	402.0
Machinery specialized for particular industries	83.3	89.9	67.0
General industrial machinery equipment and parts	44.9	45.1	44.4
Telecommunications, sound recording and reproducing equipment	53.8	59.6	41.1
Electrical machinery, apparatus, etc.*	62.6	66.2	48.7
Road vehicles and parts†	116.1	223.8	151.4
Passenger motor cars (excl. buses)	41.3	53.7	39.9
Lorries and special purposes motor vehicles	41.9	115.1	72.2
Motor vehicles for goods transport, etc.	38.4	102.1	70.3
Miscellaneous manufactured articles	99.7	108.9	109.8
Total (incl. others)	1,458.7	1,385.8	1,260.4

* Excluding telecommunications and sound equipment.
† Excluding tyres, engines and electrical parts.

Exports f.o.b.	1998	1999	2000
Food and live animals	410.1	298.8	291.0
Vegetables and fruit	14.9	18.6	13.8
Coffee, tea, cocoa and spices	386.4	271.8	258.8
Coffee, not roasted, coffee husks and skins	381.9	269.1	255.4
Crude materials (inedible) except fuels	99.6	109.2	114.0
Oil seeds and oleaginous fruit	33.8	31.7	28.7
Sesame seeds	31.2	23.0	22.2
Miscellaneous manufactured articles	36.5	34.9	47.4
Leather	30.5	26.4	41.0
Sheep and lamb skin leather	26.2	21.9	31.7
Other commodities	6.9	2.8	27.7
Total (incl. others)	560.3	448.6	482.0

Source: UN *International Trade Statistics Yearbook.*.

2000/01 (million birr): Total imports 12,967.7; Total exports 3,679.8 (Source: National Bank of Ethiopia).

PRINCIPAL TRADING PARTNERS
(US $ million)

Imports c.i.f.	1998	1999	2000
Belgium*	23.1	18.1	18.2
China, People's Repub. . . .	67.5	76.5	96.7
Denmark	9.4	16.6	12.3
Egypt	10.8	16.6	16.2
France (incl. Monaco) . . .	40.0	60.2	39.7
Germany	91.4	93.2	65.3
Greece	13.0	14.8	6.1
India	81.6	62.9	65.6
Indonesia	20.7	29.9	23.6
Italy	114.5	115.5	111.6
Japan	90.6	131.9	103.0
Kenya	17.4	15.4	20.4
Korea, Repub..	49.8	47.9	39.2
Malaysia	9.6	11.9	14.2
Netherlands	16.0	25.6	16.0
Saudi Arabia	356.8	53.6	20.6
Spain	9.8	20.4	8.5
Sweden	32.4	31.5	30.7
Switzerland-Liechtenstein . .	11.7	33.8	10.2
Turkey	26.3	25.0	23.1
United Arab Emirates . . .	26.5	27.7	29.6
United Kingdom	69.2	84.0	54.8
USA	80.6	90.6	60.9
Yemen	8.3	111.8	240.6
Total (incl. others)	1,458.7	1,385.8	1,260.4

Exports f.o.b.	1998	1999	2000
Belgium*	23.5	15.4	16.8
Djibouti	55.3	49.2	51.4
Egypt	11.7	11.4	6.4
France	20.3	21.7	14.2
Germany	138.3	76.9	94.3
India	0.3	1.8	7.9
Indonesia	1.1	3.5	5.8
Israel	7.2	12.6	15.5
Italy	38.0	30.1	32.2
Japan	68.1	57.9	56.3
Netherlands	11.0	6.0	10.1
Poland	5.9	3.3	2.2
Saudi Arabia	55.4	51.5	38.9
Somalia	3.5	20.4	29.3
Sweden	6.0	1.7	1.6
Switzerland	3.1	4.1	28.8
United Kingdom	14.0	10.6	10.4
USA	37.8	21.9	17.6
Yemen	5.9	6.6	6.2
Total (incl. others)	560.3	448.6	482.0

* Figures for 1998 include trade with Luxembourg.

Source: UN, *International Trade Statistics Yearbook*.

Transport

RAILWAYS
(traffic, year ending 7 July)*

	1996/97	1997/98	1998/99
Addis Ababa–Djibouti:			
Passenger-km (million) . . .	157	167	150
Freight (million net ton-km) . .	106	90	116

* Including traffic on the section of the Djibouti–Addis Ababa line which runs through the Republic of Djibouti. Data pertaining to freight include service traffic.

Source: former Ministry of Transport and Communications, Addis Ababa.

ROAD TRAFFIC
(motor vehicles in use, year ending 7 July)

	1998	1999	2000
Passenger cars	57,666	58,528	59,048
Buses and coaches	12,603	14,205	9,334
Lorries and vans	24,761	25,364	34,355
Motorcycles and mopeds . . .	1,432	1,743	n.a.
Road tractors	6,421	6,010	6,809
Total	102,883	105,850	109,546

Source: IRF, *World Road Statistics*.

SHIPPING

Merchant Fleet
(registered at 31 December)

	1999	2000	2001
Number of vessels	13	12	9
Displacement (grt)	96,154	92,434	81,933

Sources: Ethiopian Shipping Lines Corporation; Lloyd's Register-Fairplay, *World Fleet Statistics*.

International Sea-borne Shipping
(freight traffic, '000 metric tons, year ending 7 July)

	1996/97	1997/98	1998/99
Goods loaded	242	201	313
Goods unloaded	777	1,155	947

Source: former Ministry of Transport and Communications, Addis Ababa.

CIVIL AVIATION
(traffic on scheduled services, year ending 7 July)

	1996/97	1997/98	1998/99
Kilometres flown (million) . . .	28	n.a.	n.a.
Passengers carried ('000) . . .	808	807	779
Passenger-km (million) . . .	1,915	1,944	1,999
Total ton-km (million) . . .	129	149	115

Source: former Ministry of Transport and Communications, Addis Ababa.

Tourism

TOURIST ARRIVALS BY COUNTRY OF ORIGIN

	1998	1999	2000
Canada	2,990	2,289	2,597
Djibouti	2,377	3,442	14,512
France	3,159	2,592	5,856
Germany	4,418	3,888	4,665
India	1,642	1,755	3,480
Italy	4,815	4,024	4,395
Japan	3,355	3,756	1,193
Kenya	4,588	5,006	3,437
Netherlands	1,704	1,664	2,717
Saudi Arabia	7,928	7,922	1,967
Sudan	352	1,290	4,723
United Kingdom	5,393	4,321	7,074
USA	11,916	13,637	11,318
Yemen	2,192	1,767	3,897
Total (incl. others)*	90,847	91,859	135,954

* Including Ethiopian nationals residing abroad.

Source: World Tourism Organization, *Yearbook of Tourism Statistics*.

Receipts from tourism (US $ million): 16 in 1998; 16 in 1999; 24 in 2000 (Source: World Tourism Organization).

Communications Media

	1999	2000	2001
Television receivers ('000 in use)	350	367	n.a.
Telephones ('000 main lines in use)	194.5	231.9	310.0
Facsimile machines (number in use)	3,090	3,594	n.a.
Mobile cellular telephones ('000 subscribers).	6.7	17.8	27.5
Personal computers ('000 in use)	45	60	75
Internet users ('000)	8.0	10.0	25.0

Book production: 240 titles (including 93 pamphlets) in 1991.

Non-daily newspapers: 17 in 1995 (average combined circulation 159,000).

Daily newspapers: 4 in 1996 (average circulation 89,000 copies).

Radio receivers ('000 in use): 11,750 in 1997.

Sources: UNESCO, *Statistical Yearbook*; International Telecommunication Union.

Education

(1999/2000)

	Institutions	Teachers	Students
Pre-primary	834	2,877	99,710
Primary	11,490	115,777	6,462,503
Secondary: general	410	13,154	571,719
Secondary: teacher training	12	294	4,813
Secondary: skill development centres	25	367	2,474
Secondary: technical and vocational (government)	16	523	3,427
Secondary: technical and vocational (non-government)	9	125	1,837
University level	6	1,779	40,894
Other higher:			
Government	11	578	18,412
Non-government	4	140	8,376

Source: Ministry of Education, Addis Ababa.

Adult literacy rate (UNESCO estimates): 39.1% (males 47.2%; females 30.9%) in 2000 (Source: UN Development Programme, *Human Development Report*).

Directory

The Constitution

The Constitution of the Federal Democratic Republic of Ethiopia was adopted by the transitional Government on 8 December 1994. The following is a summary of the main provisions of the Constitution, which came into force on 22 August 1995.

GENERAL PROVISIONS

The Constitution establishes a federal and democratic state structure and all sovereign power resides in the nations, nationalities and peoples of Ethiopia. The Constitution is the supreme law of the land. Human rights and freedoms, emanating from the nature of mankind, are inviolable and inalienable. State and religion are separate and there shall be no state religion. The State shall not interfere in religious matters and vice versa. All Ethiopian languages shall enjoy equal state recognition; Amharic shall be the working language of the Federal Government.

FUNDAMENTAL RIGHTS AND FREEDOMS

All persons are equal before the law and are guaranteed equal and effective protection, without discrimination on grounds of race, nation, nationality, or other social origin, colour, sex, language, religion, political or other opinion, property, birth or other status. Everyone has the right to freedom of thought, conscience and religion and the freedom, either individually or in community with others, and in public or private, to manifest his religion or belief in worship, observance, practice and teaching. Every person has the inviolable and inalienable right to life, privacy, and the security of person and liberty.

DEMOCRATIC RIGHTS

Every Ethiopian national, without discrimination based on colour, race, nation, nationality, sex, language, religion, political or other opinion, or other status, has the following rights: on the attainment of 18 years of age, to vote in accordance with the law; to be elected to any office at any level of government; to freely express oneself without interference; to hold opinions without interference; to engage in economic activity and to pursue a livelihood anywhere within the national territory; to choose his or her means of livelihood, occupation and profession; and to own private property.

Every nation, nationality and people in Ethiopia has the following rights: an unconditional right to self-determination, including the right to secession; the right to speak, to write and to develop its own language; the right to express, to develop and to promote its culture, and to preserve its history; the right to a full measure of self-government which includes the right to establish institutions of government in the territory that it inhabits. Women shall, in the enjoyment of rights and protections provided for by this Constitution, have equal right with men.

STATE STRUCTURE

The Federal Democratic Republic of Ethiopia shall have a parliamentarian form of government. The Federal Democratic Republic shall comprise nine States. Addis Ababa shall be the capital city of the Federal State.

STRUCTURE AND DIVISION OF POWERS

The Federal Democratic Republic of Ethiopia comprises the Federal Government and the member States. The Federal Government and the States shall have legislative, executive and judicial powers. The House of People's Representatives is the highest authority of the Federal Government. The House is responsible to the people. The State Council is the highest organ of state authority. It is responsible to the people of the State. State government shall be established at state and other administrative levels deemed necessary. Adequate power shall be granted to the lowest units of government to enable the people to participate directly in the administration of such units. The State Council has legislative power on matters falling under state jurisdiction. Consistent with the provisions of this Constitution, the Council has the power to draft, adopt and amend the state constitution. The state administration constitutes the highest organ of executive power. State judicial power is vested in its courts. The States shall respect the powers of the Federal Government. The Federal Government shall likewise respect the powers of the States. The Federal Government may, when necessary, delegate to the States powers and functions granted to it by the Constitution.

THE FEDERAL HOUSES

There shall be two Federal Houses: the House of People's Representatives and the House of the Federation.

Members of the House of People's Representatives shall be elected by the people for a term of five years on the basis of universal suffrage and by direct, free and fair elections held by secret ballot. Members of the House, on the basis of population and special representation of minority nationalities and peoples, shall not exceed 550; of these, minority nationalities and peoples shall have at least 20 seats. The House of People's Representatives shall have legislative power in all matters assigned by this Constitution to federal jurisdiction. The political party or coalition of political parties that has the greatest number of seats in the House of People's Representatives shall form and lead the Executive. Elections for a new House shall be concluded one month prior to the expiry of the House's term.

The House of the Federation is composed of representatives of nations, nationalities and peoples. Each nation, nationality and people shall be represented in the House of the Federation by at least one member. Each nation or nationality shall be represented by one additional representative for each one million of its population. Members of the House of the Federation shall be elected by the State

Councils. The State Councils may themselves elect representatives to the House of the Federation, or they may hold elections to have the representatives elected by the people directly. The House of the Federation shall hold at least two sessions annually. The term of mandate of the House of the Federation shall be five years. No one may be a member of the House of People's Representatives and of the House of the Federation simultaneously.

PRESIDENT OF THE REPUBLIC

The President of the Federal Democratic Republic of Ethiopia is the Head of State. The House of People's Representatives shall nominate the candidate for President. The nominee shall be elected President if a joint session of the House of People's Representatives and the House of the Federation approves his candidacy by a two-thirds' majority vote. The term of office of the President shall be six years. No person shall be elected President for more than two terms. The President's duties include the opening of the Federal Houses; appointing ambassadors and other envoys to represent the country abroad; granting, upon recommendation by the Prime Minister and in accordance with law, high military titles; and granting pardons.

THE EXECUTIVE

The highest executive powers of the Federal Government are vested in the Prime Minister and in the Council of Ministers. The Prime Minister and the Council of Ministers are responsible to the House of People's Representatives. In the exercise of state functions, members of the Council of Ministers are collectively responsible for all decisions they make as a body. Unless otherwise provided in this Constitution, the term of office of the Prime Minister is the duration of the mandate of the House of People's Representatives. The Prime Minister is the Chief Executive, the Chairman of the Council of Ministers, and the Commander-in-Chief of the national armed forces. The Prime Minister shall submit for approval to the House of People's Representatives nominees for ministerial posts from among members of the two Houses or from among persons who are not members of either House and possess the required qualifications. The Council of Ministers is responsible to the Prime Minister and, in all its decisions, is responsible to the House of People's Representatives. The Council of Ministers ensures the implementation of laws and decisions adopted by the House of People's Representatives.

STRUCTURE AND POWERS OF THE COURTS

Supreme Federal judicial authority is vested in the Federal Supreme Court. The House of People's Representatives may, by a two-thirds' majority vote, establish nation-wide, or in some parts of the country only, the Federal High Court and First-Instance Courts it deems necessary. Unless decided in this manner, the jurisdictions of the Federal High Court and of the First-Instance Courts are hereby delegated to the state courts. States shall establish State Supreme, High and First-Instance Courts. Judicial powers, both at federal and state levels, are vested in the courts. Courts of any level shall be free from any interference or influence of any governmental body, government official or from any other source. Judges shall exercise their functions in full independence and shall be directed solely by the law. The Federal Supreme Court shall have the highest and final judicial power over federal matters. State Supreme Courts shall have the highest and final judicial power over state matters. They shall also exercise the jurisdiction of the Federal High Court.

MISCELLANEOUS PROVISIONS

The Council of Ministers of the Federal Government shall have the power to decree a state of emergency in the event of an external invasion, a breakdown of law and order that endangers the constitutional order and cannot be controlled by the regular law enforcement agencies and personnel, a natural disaster or an epidemic. State executives can decree a state-wide state of emergency should a natural disaster or an epidemic occur.

A National Election Board independent of any influence shall be established, to conduct free and fair elections in federal and state constituencies in an impartial manner.

The Government

HEAD OF STATE

President: Lt GIRMA WOLDE GIORGIS (took office 8 October 2001).

COUNCIL OF MINISTERS
(April 2003)

Prime Minister: MELES ZENAWI.

Deputy Prime Minister and Minister of Rural Development: ADDISO LEGGESE.

Minister of Foreign Affairs: SEYOUM MESFIN.

Minister of Health: Dr KEBEDE TADESSE.

Minister of Capacity Building: TEFERA WALWA.

Minister of Infrastructure: Dr KASSA YLALA.

Minister of Defence: Gen ABEDULA GEMEDA.

Minister of Energy and Mines: MOHAMMED DIRIR.

Minister of Finance and Economic Development and Co-operation: SUFYAN AHMED.

Minister of Information: BEREKET SIMEON.

Minister of Education: GENET ZEWDE.

Minister of Agriculture: Dr MULATU TESHOME.

Minister of Trade and Industry: GIRMA BIRU.

Minister of Justice: HARIKA HAROYE.

Minister of Federal Affairs: ABBAY TSEHAYE.

Minister of Labour and Social Affairs: HASAN ABDELA.

Minister of Water Resources: SHIFERAW JARSO.

Minister of Revenues: GETACHEW BELAY.

Minister of Youth, Culture and Sport: TESHOME TOGA.

MINISTRIES

Office of the Prime Minister: POB 1013, Addis Ababa; tel. (1) 552044.

Ministry of Agriculture: POB 62347, Addis Ababa; tel. (1) 152816; fax (1) 512984.

Ministry of Capacity Building: Addis Ababa.

Ministry of Defence: POB 125, Addis Ababa; tel. (1) 445555.

Ministry of Education: POB 1367, Addis Ababa; tel. (1) 553133.

Ministry of Energy and Mines: POB 486, Addis Ababa; tel. (1) 518250; fax (1) 517874.

Ministry of Federal Affairs: Addis Ababa.

Ministry of Finance, Economic Development and Co-operation: Addis Ababa; tel. (1) 552800; fax (1) 551355.

Ministry of Foreign Affairs: POB 393, Addis Ababa; tel. (1) 447345; fax (1) 514300; internet www.mfa.gov.et.

Ministry of Health: POB 1234, Addis Ababa; tel. (1) 518031; fax (1) 519366.

Ministry of Information: Addis Ababa; tel. (1) 517020.

Ministry of Infrastructure: POB 1238, Addis Ababa; tel. (1) 516166; fax (1) 515665.

Ministry of Justice: POB 1370, Addis Ababa; tel. (1) 517390.

Ministry of Labour and Social Affairs: POB 2056, Addis Ababa; tel. (1) 517080.

Ministry of Revenues: Addis Ababa.

Ministry of Rural Development: Addis Ababa.

Ministry of Trade and Industry: POB 704, Addis Ababa; tel. (1) 518025; fax (1) 515411.

Ministry of Water Resources: POB 5744, Addis Ababa; tel. (1) 611111; fax (1) 610885.

Ministry of Youth, Culture and Sport: Addis Ababa.

Regional Governments

Ethiopia comprises nine regional governments, one chartered city (Addis Ababa) and one Administrative Council (Dire Dawa), which are vested with authority for self-administration. The executive bodies are respectively headed by Presidents (regional states) and Chairmen (Addis Ababa and Dire Dawa).

PRESIDENTS

Tigrai: TSEGAYE BERHE.

Afar: ESMAEL ALISERO.

Amhara: YOSEF RETA.

Oromia: JUNEIDI SADO.

Somali: ABDULRASHID DULENI RAFLE.

Benishangul/Gumuz: YAREGAL AYSHESHIM.

Southern Nations, Nationalities and Peoples: HAILEMARIAM DESALEGNE.

Gambela: OKALO GNIGELO.

Harari: FUAD IBRAHIM.

CHAIRMEN

Dire Dawa: SOLOMON HAILU.

Addis Ababa: ARKEBE OQUBAY MITIKU.

Legislature

FEDERAL PARLIAMENTARY ASSEMBLY

The legislature comprises an upper house, the House of the Federation (Yefedereshn Mekir Bet), with 108 seats (members are selected by state assemblies and are drawn one each from 22 minority nationalities and one from each professional sector of the remaining nationalities, and serve for a period of five years), and a lower house of no more than 550 directly elected members, the House of People's Representatives (Yehizbtewekayoch Mekir Bet), who are also elected for a five-year term.

Speaker of the House of the Federation: MULATU TESHOME.

Yehizbtewekayoch Mekir Bet
(House of People's Representatives)

Speaker: DAWIT YOHANES.

Deputy Speaker: PETROS OLANGO.

General Election, 14 May and 31 August* 2000

Party	Seats
Oromo People's Democratic Organization (OPDO)	178
Amhara National Democratic Movement (ANDM)	134
Tigrai People's Liberation Front (TPLF)	38
Walayta, Gamo, Gofa, Dawro, and Konta People's Democratic Organization (WGGPDO)	30
Ethiopian People's Revolutionary Democratic Front (EPRDF)	19
Somali People's Democratic Party (SPDP)	19
Sidama People's Democratic Organization (SPDO)	18
Gurage Nationalities' Democratic Movement (GNDM)	15
Kafa Shaka People's Democratic Organization (KSPDO)	10
Afar National Democratic Party (ANDP)	8
Gedeyo People's Revolutionary Democratic Front (GPRDF)	7
South Omo People's Democratic Movement (SOPDM)	7
Benishangul Gumuz People's Democratic Unity Front (BGPDUF)	6
Kembata, Alabea and Tembaro (KAT)	6
Bench Madji People's Democratic Organization (BMPDO)	5
Hadiya Nation Democratic Organization (HNDO)	5
Gambela People's Democratic Front (GPDF)	3
South Ethiopia People's Democratic Front (SEPDF)	3
Council of Alternative Forces for Peace and Democracy in Ethiopia (CAFPDE)	2
Derashe People's Democratic Organization (DPDO)	2
Ethiopian Democratic Party (EDP)	2
Hadiya People's Democratic Organization (HPDO)	2
Southern Ethiopian People's Democratic Union (SEPDU)	2
All Amhara People's Organization (AAPO)	1
Argoba People's Democratic Movement (APDM)	1
Burgi People's Democratic Union (BPDU)	1
Gambella People's Democratic Congress (GPDC)	1
Konso People's Democratic Organization (KPDO)	1
Kore Nationality Democratic Organization (KNDO)	1
Oromo Liberation Unity Front (OLUF)	1
Oromo National Congress (ONC)	1
Oyda Nationality Democratic Organization (ONDO)	1
Sidama Hadicho People's Democratic Organization (SHPDO)	1
Silte People's Democratic Unity Party (SPDUP)	1
Yem People's Democratic Unity Party (YPDUP)	1
Independents	13
Total*	**546**

* Owing to irregularities and violence at some polling stations, voting was reheld in 16 constituencies. Furthermore, voting in the Somali regional state was postponed until 31 August because of severe drought affecting the area.

Political Organizations

Afar People's Democratic Organization (APDO): fmrly Afar Liberation Front (ALF); based in fmr Hararge and Wollo Admin. Regions; Leader ISMAIL ALI SIRRO.

Council of Alternative Forces for Peace and Democracy in Ethiopia (CAFPDE): f. 1993 as a broadly-based coalition of groups opposing the EPRDF; split into two factions in Dec. 1999, led by former Vice-Chair. KIFLE TIGNEH ABATE and by Dr BEYENE PETROS.

Coalition of Ethiopian Democratic Forces (COEDF): f. 1991 in the USA by the Ethiopian People's Revolutionary Party–EPRP (the dominant member), together with a faction of the Ethiopian Democratic Union (EDU) and the Ethiopian Socialist Movement (MEISON); opposes the EPRDF; Chair. MERSHA YOSEPH.

Coalition of Ethiopian Opposition Political Organizations (CEOPO): f. 1998 in France as a coalition of groups opposing the EPRDF; Chair. NEGEDE GOBEZIE; Chair. (Ethiopia) KIFLEH TIGNEH ABATE.

Ethiopian Democratic Unity Party (EDUP): Addis Ababa; f. 1984 as Workers' Party of Ethiopia; adopted present name in 1990, when its Marxist-Leninist ideology was relaxed and membership opened to non-Marxist and opposition groups; sole legal political party until May 1991; Leader RAS MENGESHA; Sec.-Gen. Lt-Gen. TESFAYE GEBRE KIDAN.

Ethiopian National Congress (ENC): USA-based organization aims to form a unified opposition among anti-Govt parties; Chair. GEBEYEHU IJUGU.

Ethiopian National Democratic Party (ENDP): f. 1994 by merger of five pro-Govt orgs with mems in the Council of Representatives; comprises: the Ethiopian Democratic Organization, the Ethiopian Democratic Organization Coalition (EDC), the Gurage People's Democratic Front (GPDF), the Kembata People's Congress (KPC), and the Wolaita People's Democratic Front (WPDF); Chair. FEKADU GEDAMU.

Ethiopian People's Revolutionary Democratic Front (EPRDF): Addis Ababa; f. 1989 by the TPLF as an alliance of insurgent groups seeking regional autonomy and engaged in armed struggle against the EDUP Govt; Chair. MELES ZENAWI; Vice-Chair. ADDISO LEGGESE; in May 1991, with other orgs, formed transitional Govt; alliance comprises:

Amhara National Democratic Movement (ANDM): based in Tigrai; represents interests of the Amhara people; fmrly the Ethiopian People's Democratic Movement (EPDM); adopted present name in 1994; Sec.-Gen. TEFERA WALWA.

Oromo People's Democratic Organization (OPDO): f. 1990 by the TPLF to promote its cause in Oromo areas; based among the Oromo people in the Shoa region; Leader Gen. ABEDULA GEMEDA.

Tigrai People's Liberation Front (TPLF): f. 1975; the dominant org. within the EPRDF; Chair. MELES ZENAWI; Vice-Chair. SEYOUM MESFIN.

Gambela People's Democratic Front (GPDF): pro-Govt group based in the Gambela region; Chair. AKILO NIGILIO.

Oromo Liberation Front (OLF): seeks self-determination for the Oromo people; participated in the Ethiopian transitional Govt until June 1992; Chair. KATABE MAYU (acting); Vice-Chair. ABDULFATTAH A. MOUSSA BIYYO.

Somali Abo Liberation Front (SALF): operates in fmr Bale Admin. Region; has received Somali military assistance; Sec.-Gen. MASURAD SHU'ABI IBRAHIM.

Somali People's Democratic Party: f. 1998 by merger of Ogaden National Liberation Front (ONLF) and the Ethiopian Somali Democratic League (ESDL—an alliance comprising the Somali Democratic Union Party, the Issa and Gurgura Liberation Front, the Gurgura Independence Front, the Eastern Gabooye Democratic Organization, the Eastern Ethiopian Somali League, the Horyal Democratic Front, the Social Alliance Democratic Organization, the Somali Abo Democratic Union, the Shekhash People's Democratic Movement, the Ethiopian Somalis' Democratic Movement and the Per Barreh Party); Chair. MOHAMOUD DIRIR GHEDDI; Sec.-Gen. SULTAN IBRAHIM.

Southern Ethiopian People's Democratic Coalition (SEPDC): opposition alliance; Chair. Dr BEYENE PETROS.

Southern Ethiopian People's Democratic Union (SEPDU): f. 1992 as an alliance of 10 ethnically-based political groups from the south of the country; was represented in the transitional Council of Representatives, although five of the participating groups were expelled from the Council in April 1993.

United Oromo Liberation Forces (UOLF): f. 2000 in Asmara, Eritrea, as a common Oromo Front seeking to overthrow the Ethiopian Government; Chair Waqo Cutu; Sec.-Gen. Galasa Dilbo; alliance comprises:

Islamic Front for the Liberation of Oromia: Leader Abdelkarim Ibrahim Hamid.

Oromo Liberation Council (OLC).

Oromo Liberation Front (OLF): see above.

Oromo People's Liberation Front (OPLF).

Oromo People's Liberation Organization (OPLO).

United Oromo People's Liberation Front (UDPLF): Chair. Waqo Cutu.

Western Somali Liberation Front (WSLF): POB 978, Mogadishu, Somalia; f. 1975; aims to unite the Ogaden region with Somalia; maintains guerrilla forces of c. 3,000 men; has received support from regular Somali forces; Sec.-Gen. Issa Shaykh Abdi Nasir Adan.

The following parties all have parliamentary representation: **Afar National Democratic Party (ANDP); All Amhara People's Organization (AAPO):** Pres. Hailu Shawel; **Argoba People's Democratic Movement (APDM); Bench Madji People's Democratic Organization (BMPD); Benishangul Gumuz People's Democratic Unity Front (BGPDUF); Burgi People's Democratic Union (BPDU); Derashe People's Democratic Organization (DPDO); Ethiopian Democratic Party (EDP):** Pres. Admassu Gebeyehu; Sec.-Gen. Lidetu Ayalew; **Gambella People's Democratic Congress (GPDC); Gedeyo People's Revolutionary Democratic Front (GPRDF); Gurage Nationalities' Democratic Movement (GNDM); Hadiya Nation Democratic Organization (HNDO); Hadiya People's Democratic Organization (HPDO); Kafa Shaka People's Democratic Organization (KSPDO); Kembata Alabaa and Tembaro (KAT); Konso People's Democratic Organization (KPDO); Kore Nationality Democratic Organization (KNDO); Oromo Liberation Unity Front (OLUF); Oromo National Congress (ONC):** Leader Merera Gudina; **Oyda Nationality Democratic Organization (ONDO); Sidama Hadicho People's Democratic Organization (SHPDO); Sidama People's Democratic Organization (SPDO); Silte People's Democratic Unity Party (SPDUP); South Ethiopia People's Democratic Front (SEPDF); South Omo People's Democratic Movement (SOPDM); Southern Ethiopian People's Democratic Union (SEPDU); Walayta, Gamo, Gofa, Dawro, and Konta People's Democratic Organization (WGGPDO); Yem People's Democratic Organization Unity Party (YPDUP).**

Diplomatic Representation

EMBASSIES IN ETHIOPIA

Algeria: POB 5740, Addis Ababa; tel. (1) 652300; fax (1) 650187; e-mail algemb@telecom.net.et; Ambassador Smail Chergui.

Angola: Kebele 18, House No. 26, POB 2962, Addis Ababa; tel. (1) 710118; fax (1) 514922; e-mail angola.embassy@telecom.net.et; Ambassador Miguel Neto.

Austria: POB 1219, Addis Ababa; tel. (1) 712144; fax (1) 712140; Ambassador Thomas Michael Baier.

Belgium: POB 1239, Addis Ababa; tel. (1) 611813; fax (1) 613646; e-mail embel.et@telecom.net.et; Ambassador Leopold Carrewyn.

Bulgaria: POB 987, Addis Ababa; tel. (1) 610032; fax (1) 613373; Chargé d'affaires a.i. Miroslav Komarov.

Burkina Faso: POB 19685, Addis Ababa; tel. (1) 615863; fax (1) 612094; e-mail ambfet@telecom.net.et; Ambassador Zeondre B. Bassole.

Burundi: POB 3641, Addis Ababa; tel. (1) 651300; e-mail burundi .emb@telecom.net.et; Ambassador Melchior Bwakira.

Cameroon: Bole Rd, POB 1026, Addis Ababa; tel. and fax (1) 504488; Ambassador Jean-Hilaire Mbéa Mbéa.

Canada: Old Airport Area, Higher 23, Kebele 12, House No. 122, POB 1130, Addis Ababa; tel. (1) 713022; fax (1) 713033; Ambassador John R. Schram.

Chad: POB 5119 Addis Ababa; tel. (1) 613819; fax (1) 612050; Ambassador Mahamat Abdelkerim.

China, People's Republic: POB 5643, Addis Ababa; tel. (1) 711960; fax (1) 712457; e-mail chinesembassy@telecom.net.et; Ambassador Ai Ping.

Congo, Democratic Republic: Makanisa Rd, POB 2723, Addis Ababa; tel. (1) 710111; fax (1) 713466; e-mail rdca@telecom.net.et; Chargé d'affaires a.i. Margret Rashid Kabamba.

Congo, Republic: POB 5639, Addis Ababa; tel. (1) 514188; Chargé d'affaires a.i. Casimir Mpiera.

Côte d'Ivoire: POB 3668, Addis Ababa; tel. (1) 712178; e-mail coted .aa@telecom.net.et; Ambassador Pierre Yéré.

Cuba: Jimma Road Ave, POB 5623, Addis Ababa; tel. (1) 620459; fax (1) 620460; Ambassador Angel Arzuaga Reyes.

Czech Republic: POB 3108, Addis Ababa; tel. (1) 516132; fax (1) 513471; e-mail czech.emba@telecom.net.et; Ambassador Miroslav Křenek.

Djibouti: POB 1022, Addis Ababa; tel. (1) 613200; fax (1) 612786; Ambassador (vacant).

Egypt: POB 1611, Addis Ababa; tel. (1) 553077; fax (1) 552722; Ambassador Marwan Badr.

Equatorial Guinea: POB 246, Addis Ababa; tel. (1) 615973; Ambassador Aplinar Moihe Echek.

Eritrea: POB 2571, Addis Ababa; tel. (1) 512844; fax (1) 514911; Chargé d'affaires a.i. Sahih Omer.

Finland: Higher 17, Kebele 19, House No. 163, POB 1017, Addis Ababa; tel. (1) 611575; fax (1) 615964; e-mail finland.embassy@ telecom.net.et; Chargé d'affaires a.i. Kari Toiviainen.

France: Kabana, POB 1464, Addis Ababa; tel. (1) 550066; fax (1) 551441; e-mail ambfrance@telecom.net.et; Ambassador Josette Dallant.

Gabon: POB 1256, Addis Ababa; tel. (1) 611090; fax (1) 613760; Ambassador Emmanuel Mendoume-nze.

Germany: Kabana, POB 660, Addis Ababa; tel. (1) 550433; fax (1) 551311; Ambassador Helga Grafin Strachwitz.

Ghana: POB 3173, Addis Ababa; tel. (1) 711402; fax (1) 712511; e-mail ghmfa24@telecom.net.et; Ambassador John Evonlah Aggrey.

Greece: off Debre Zeit Rd, POB 1168, Addis Ababa; tel. (1) 654911; fax (1) 654883; e-mail greekembassy@telecom.net.et; internet www .telecom.net.et/~greekemb; Ambassador Spyros Aliagas.

Guinea: POB 1190, Addis Ababa; tel. (1) 651308; fax (1) 651250; Ambassador Mamadi Diawara.

Holy See: POB 588, Addis Ababa (Apostolic Nunciature); tel. (1) 712100; fax (1) 711499; e-mail vatican.embassy@telecom.net.et; Apostolic Nuncio Most Rev. Silvano M. Tomasi (Titular Archbishop of Asolo).

Hungary: Abattoirs Rd, POB 1213, Addis Ababa; tel. (1) 651850; Ambassador Dr Sándor Robel.

India: Kabena, POB 528, Addis Ababa; tel. (1) 552394; fax (1) 552521; e-mail indembassy@podis.gn.apc.org; Ambassador Kadakath Pathrose Ernest.

Indonesia: Mekanisa Rd, POB 1004, Addis Ababa; tel. (1) 710122; fax (1) 710873; e-mail kbriadis@telecom.net.et; Ambassador Haditmo Harsojo.

Iran: POB 70488, Addis Ababa; tel. (1) 200794; fax (1) 711915; e-mail csiri@telecom.net.et; internet www.telecom.net.et/~iranet/; Ambassador Morteza Damanpak Jami.

Ireland: POB 9585, Addis Ababa; tel. (1) 665050; fax (1) 665020; e-mail ireland.emb@telecom.net.et; Chargé d'affaires a.i. Pauline Conway.

Israel: POB 1266, Addis Ababa; tel. (1) 610998; fax (1) 612456; e-mail israel.embassy@telecom.net.et; Ambassador Ariel Kerem.

Italy: Villa Italia, POB 1105, Addis Ababa; tel. (1) 553042; fax (1) 550218; e-mail italembadd@telecom.net.et; Ambassador Marcello Ricoveri.

Jamaica: National House, Africa Ave, POB 5633, Addis Ababa; tel. (1) 613656; Ambassador Owen A. Singh.

Japan: Sunshine Bldg, Bole Rd, POB 5650, Addis Ababa; tel. (1) 511088; fax (1) 511350; e-mail japan-embassy@telecom.net.et; Ambassador Hiroyoshi Ihara.

Kenya: Fikre Mariam Rd, POB 3301, Addis Ababa; tel. (1) 610033; fax (1) 611433; e-mail kenya.embassy@telecom.net.et; Ambassador George Agoi.

Korea, Democratic People's Republic: POB 2378, Addis Ababa; tel. (1) 182828; fax (1) 625417; Ambassador O. Nam Jung.

Korea, Republic: Jimma Rd, Old Airport Area, POB 2047, Addis Ababa; tel. (1) 655230; Ambassador Ja Chol-Hahn.

Kuwait: Higher 20, Kebele 17, House No. 128, Bole Rd, Addis Ababa; tel. (1) 615411; fax (1) 612621; Ambassador Muhammad al-Awadhi.

Lesotho: POB 7483, Addis Ababa; tel. (1) 614368; fax (1) 612837; Ambassador Mashula H. Leteka.

Liberia: POB 3116, Addis Ababa; tel. (1) 513655; Ambassador MARCUS M. KOFA.

Libya: POB 5728, Addis Ababa; tel. (1) 511077; fax (1) 511383; Ambassador ALI ABDALLA AWIDA.

Madagascar: POB 60004, Addis Ababa; tel. (1) 612555; fax (1) 610127; e-mail amba.mad.addis@telecom.net.et; Ambassador CHRISTIAN RÉMI RICHARD.

Malawi: POB 2316, Addis Ababa; tel. (1) 615866; fax (1) 615436; e-mail malemb@telecom.net.et; Ambassador WILLIE CHAKANI.

Mali: POB 4561, Addis Ababa; tel. (1) 201528; fax (1) 712601; Ambassador AL MAAMOUN KEITA.

Mexico: Tsige Mariam Bldg 292/21, 4th Floor, Churchill Rd, POB 2962, Addis Ababa; tel. (1) 443456; Ambassador CARLOS FERRER.

Morocco: 210 Bole Rd, POB 60033, Addis Ababa; tel. (1) 531700; fax (1) 511828; e-mail morocco.emb@telecom.net.et; Ambassador SIDI MUHAMMAD RAHHALI.

Mozambique: POB 5671, Addis Ababa; tel. (1) 710020; fax (1) 613824; e-mail embamoc-add@telecom.net.et; Ambassador ALEXANDRE ZANDAMELA.

Namibia: Higher 17, Kebele 19, House No. 002, POB 1443, Addis Ababa; tel. (1) 611966; fax (1) 612677; e-mail embassy@telecom.net.et; Ambassador GEORGE OBANGA.

Netherlands: POB 1241, Addis Ababa; tel. (1) 711100; fax (1) 711577; e-mail netherlands.emb@telecom.net.et; internet www.telecom.net.et/~nethemb/body.htm; Ambassador PIETER J. T. MARRES.

Niger: Debrezenit Rd, Higher 18, Kebele 41, House No. 057, POB 5791, Addis Ababa; tel. (1) 651305; Ambassador ASSANE IGODOE.

Nigeria: POB 1019, Addis Ababa; tel. (1) 552307; Ambassador J. K. SHINKAYE.

Norway: POB 8383, Addis Ababa; tel. (1) 710799; fax (1) 711255; e-mail ambassade-addis@telecom.net.et; Ambassador S. OSKARSSON.

Romania: 17 Woreda, Kebele 19, 10 Bole Rd, POB 2478, Addis Ababa; tel. (1) 610156; fax (1) 611191; Chargé d'affaires a.i. VASILE BONDARET.

Russia: POB 1500, Addis Ababa; tel. (1) 612060; fax (1) 613795; e-mail russemb@telecom.net.et; Ambassador VALERY N. LIPNYAKOV.

Rwanda: Africa House, Higher 17, Kebele 20, POB 5618, Addis Ababa; tel. (1) 610300; fax (1) 610411; e-mail rwanda.emb@telecom.net.et; Ambassador Dr NGOGA PASCAL.

Saudi Arabia: Old Airport Area, POB 1104, Addis Ababa; tel. (1) 712952; fax (1) 711799; Ambassador SAOUD A. M. AL-YAHAYA.

Senegal: Africa Ave, POB 2581, Addis Ababa; tel. (1) 611376; fax (1) 610020; Ambassador PAPA LOUIS FALL.

Serbia and Montenegro: POB 1341, Addis Ababa; tel. (1) 517804; fax (1) 514192; e-mail yugoslav.embassy@telecom.net.et; Ambassador VOJISLAV VUCIEVIC.

Sierra Leone: POB 5619, Addis Ababa; tel. (1) 710033; fax (1) 711911; e-mail sleon.et@telecom.net.et; Ambassador MELVIN H. CHALOBAH.

Somalia: Addis Ababa; Ambassador ABRAHIM HAJI NUR.

South Africa: POB 1091, Addis Ababa; tel. (1) 713034; fax (1) 711330; e-mail sa.embassy.addis@telecom.net.et; Ambassador JEREMIAH N. MAMABOLO.

Spain: Entoto St, POB 2312, Addis Ababa; tel. (1) 550222; fax (1) 551131; e-mail embespet@mail.mae.es; Ambassador PABLO ZALDIVAR MIQUELARENA.

Sudan: Kirkos, Kebele, POB 1110, Addis Ababa; tel. (1) 516477; fax (1) 518141; e-mail sudan.embassy@telecom.net.et; Ambassador OSMAN AS-SAYED.

Swaziland: Addis Ababa; Ambassador SOLOMON DLAMINI.

Sweden: Ras Ababa Aregaye Ave, POB 1142, Addis Ababa; tel. (1) 511255; fax (1) 515830; e-mail sweden.embassy@telecom.net.et; Ambassador JOHAN HOLMBERG.

Switzerland: Jimma Rd, Old Airport Area, POB 1106, Addis Ababa; tel. (1) 711107; fax (1) 712177; e-mail swissemadd@telecom.net.et; Ambassador PAOLO BROGINI.

Tanzania: POB 1077, Addis Ababa; tel. (1) 511063; fax (1) 517358; Ambassador CHARLES S. KILEO.

Togo: Addis Ababa; Ambassador KATI OHARA KORGA.

Tunisia: Wereda 17, Kebele 19, Bole Rd, POB 100069, Addis Ababa; tel. (1) 612063; fax (1) 614568; e-mail embassy.tunisia@telecom.net.et; Ambassador ZOUHEIR ALLAGUI.

Turkey: POB 1506, Addis Ababa; tel. (1) 613161; fax (1) 611688; e-mail turk.emb@telecom.net.et; Ambassador KENAN TEPEDELEN.

Uganda: Addis Ababa; tel. (1) 513088; fax (1) 514355; Ambassador Dr ALEX KAMUGISHA.

United Kingdom: POB 858, Addis Ababa; tel. (1) 612354; fax (1) 610588; e-mail b.emb4@telecom.net.et; Ambassador MYLES WICKSTEAD.

USA: Entoto St, POB 1014, Addis Ababa; tel. (1) 550666; fax (1) 551328; e-mail usembassy@telecom.net.et; internet www.telecom.net.et/~usemb-et/; Ambassador TIBOR P. NAGY, Jr.

Venezuela: Debre Zeit Rd, POB 5584, Addis Ababa; tel. (1) 654790; Chargé d'affaires a.i. ALFREDO HERNÁNDEZ-ROVATI.

Viet Nam: POB 1288, Addis Ababa; Ambassador NGUYEN DUY KINH.

Yemen: POB 664, Addis Ababa; Ambassador MANSUR ABD AL-JALIL ABD AL-RAB.

Zambia: POB 1909, Addis Ababa; tel. (1) 711302; fax (1) 711566; Ambassador SIMATAA AKAPELWA.

Zimbabwe: POB 5624, Addis Ababa; tel. (1) 613877; fax (1) 613476; e-mail zimbabwe.embassy@telecom.net.et; Ambassador NEVILLE NDONDO.

Judicial System

The 1994 Constitution stipulates the establishment of an independent judiciary in Ethiopia. Judicial powers are vested in the courts, both at federal and state level. The supreme federal judicial authority is the Federal Supreme Court. This court has the highest and final power of jurisdiction over federal matters. The federal states of the Federal Democratic Republic of Ethiopia can establish Supreme, High and First-Instance Courts. The Supreme Courts of the federal States have the highest and the final power of jurisdiction over state matters. They also exercise the jurisdiction of the Federal High Court. According to the Constitution, courts of any level are free from any interference or influence from government bodies, government officials or any other source. In addition, judges exercise their duties independently and are directed solely by the law.

Federal Supreme Court: Addis Ababa; tel. (1) 448425; comprises civil, criminal and military sections; its jurisdiction extends to the supervision of all judicial proceedings throughout the country; the Supreme Court is also empowered to review cases upon which final rulings have been made by the courts (including the Supreme Court) where judicial errors have occurred; Pres. KEMAL BEDRI.

Federal High Court: POB 3483, Addis Ababa; tel. (1) 751911; fax (1) 755399; e-mail fedhc@telecom.net.et; hears appeals from the state courts; has original jurisdiction; Pres. WOUBISHET KIBRU.

Awraja Courts: regional courts composed of three judges, criminal and civil.

Warada Courts: sub-regional; one judge sits alone with very limited jurisdiction, criminal only.

Religion

About 45% of the population are Muslims and about 40% belong to the Ethiopian Orthodox (Tewahido) Church. There are also significant Evangelical Protestant and Roman Catholic communities. The Pentecostal Church and the Society of International Missionaries carry out mission work in Ethiopia. There are also Hindu and Sikh religious institutions. Virtually all of Ethiopia's small Jewish population had been evacuated by the Israeli Government by mid-1999. It has been estimated that 5%–15% of the population follow animist rites and beliefs.

CHRISTIANITY

Ethiopian Orthodox (Tewahido) Church

The Ethiopian Orthodox (Tewahido) Church is one of the five oriental orthodox churches. It was founded in AD 328, and in 1989 had more than 22m. members, 20,000 parishes and 290,000 clergy. The Supreme Body is the Holy Synod and the National Council, under the chairmanship of the Patriarch (Abune). The Church comprises 25 archdioceses and dioceses (including those in Jerusalem, Sudan, Djibouti and the Western Hemisphere). There are 32 Archbishops and Bishops. The Church administers 1,139 schools and 12 relief and rehabilitation centres throughout Ethiopia.

Patriarchate Head Office: POB 1283, Addis Ababa; tel. (1) 116507; Patriarch (Abune) Archbishop PAULOS; Gen. Sec. L. M. DEMTSE GEBRE MEDHIN.

The Roman Catholic Church

At 31 December 2000 Ethiopia contained an estimated 66,972 adherents of the Alexandrian-Ethiopian Rite and 376,407 adherents of the Latin Rite.

Bishops' Conference: Ethiopian and Eritrean Episcopal Conference, POB 21322, Addis Ababa; tel. (1) 550300; fax (1) 553113; f. 1966; Pres. Most Rev. Berhane-yesus Demerew Souraphiel (Archbishop of Addis Ababa).

Alexandrian-Ethiopian Rite

Adherents are served by one archdiocese (Addis Ababa) and one diocese (Adigrat).

Archbishop of Addis Ababa: Most Rev. Berhaneyesus Demerew Souraphiel, Catholic Archbishop's House, POB 21903, Addis Ababa; tel. (1) 111667; fax (1) 553113.

Latin Rite

Aherents are served by the five Apostolic Vicariates of Awasa, Harar, Meki, Nekemte and Soddo-Hosanna, and by the Apostolic Prefectures of Gambela and Jimma-Bonga.

Other Christian Churches

The Anglican Communion: Within the Episcopal Church in Jerusalem and the Middle East, the Bishop in Egypt has jurisdiction over seven African countries, including Ethiopia.

Armenian Orthodox Church: St George's Armenian Church, POB 116, Addis Ababa; f. 1923; Deacon Vartkes Nalbandian.

Ethiopian Evangelical Church (Mekane Yesus): POB 2087, Addis Ababa; tel. (1) 531919; fax (1) 534148; e-mail eecmy.co@telecom.net.et; Pres. Rev. Yadesa Daba; f. 1959; affiliated to Lutheran World Fed., All Africa Conf. of Churches and World Council of Churches; c. 3.2m. mems (1999).

Greek Orthodox Church: POB 571, Addis Ababa; Metropolitan of Axum Most Rev. Petros Yiakoumelos.

Seventh-day Adventist Church: POB 145, Addis Ababa; tel. (1) 511319; e-mail sdaeum@telecom.net.et; f. 1907; Pres. Tinsae Tolessa; 130,000 mems.

ISLAM

Leader: Haji Mohammed Ahmad.

JUDAISM

A phased emigration to Israel of about 27,000 Falashas (Ethiopian Jews) took place during 1984–91. An estimated further 4,000 Falashas were assisted to emigrate to Israel in mid-1999, leaving only a small number remaining in the country.

The Press

DAILIES

Addis Zemen: POB 30145, Addis Ababa; f. 1941; Amharic; publ. by the Ministry of Information; Editor-in-Chief (vacant); circ. 40,000.

The Daily Monitor: POB 22588, Addis Ababa; tel. (1) 611880; fax (1) 518409; f. 1993; English; Editor-in-Chief Lullit Mickael; circ. 6,000.

Ethiopian Herald: POB 30701, Addis Ababa; tel. (1) 119050; f. 1943; English; publ. by the Ministry of Information; Editor-in-Chief Kiflom Hadgoi; circ. 37,000.

PERIODICALS

Abyotawit Ethiopia: POB 2549, Addis Ababa; fortnightly; Amharic.

Addis Tribune: Tambek International, POB 2395, Addis Ababa; tel. (1) 615228; fax (1) 615227; e-mail tambek@telecom.net.et; internet www.addistribune.ethiopiaonline.com; f. 1993; weekly; English; Editor-in-Chief (vacant); circ. 6,000.

Addis Zimit: POB 2395, Addis Ababa; tel. (1) 118613; fax (1) 552110; f. 1993; weekly; Amharic; Editor-in-Chief (vacant); circ. 8,000.

Al-Alem: POB 30232, Addis Ababa; tel. (1) 158046; fax (1) 516819; f. 1941; weekly; Arabic; publ. by the Ministry of Information; Editor-in-Chief Telsom Ahmed; circ. 2,500.

Berisa: POB 30232, Addis Ababa; f. 1976; weekly; Oromogna; publ. by the Ministry of Information; Editor Bulo Siba; circ. 3,500.

Beza: Addis Ababa; weekly; Editor-in-Chief Yared Kemfe.

Birhan Family Magazine: Addis Ababa; monthly; women's magazine.

Birritu: National Bank of Ethiopia, POB 5550, Addis Ababa; tel. (1) 517430; fax (1) 514588; e-mail nbe.excd@telecom.net.et; f. 1968; quarterly; Amharic and English; banking, insurance and macro-economic news; circ. 2,000; Editor-in-Chief Semeneh Adge.

Ethiopis Review: Editor-in-Chief Tesfera Asmare.

Mabruk: Addis Ababa; weekly; Editor-in-Chief Tesahalenne Mengesha.

Maebel: Addis Ababa; weekly; Amharic; Editor-in-Chief Abera Wogi.

Meskerem: Addis Ababa; quarterly; theoretical politics; circ. 100,000.

Negarit Gazzetta: POB 1031, Addis Ababa; irregularly; Amharic and English; official gazette.

Nigdina Limat: POB 2458, Addis Ababa; tel. (1) 513882; fax (1) 511479; e-mail aachamber1@telecom.net.et; monthly; Amharic; publ. by the Addis Ababa (Ethiopia) Chamber of Commerce; circ. 6,000.

Press Digest: POB 12719, Addis Ababa; tel. (1) 504200; fax (1) 513523; e-mail phoenix.universal@telecom.net.et; internet pressdigest.phoenixuniversal.com; f. 1993; weekly.

Tequami: Addis Ababa; weekly; Editor-in-Chief Samson Seyum.

Tinsae (Resurrection): Addis Ababa; tel. (1) 116507; Amharic and English; publ. by the Ethiopian Orthodox Church.

Tobia Magazine: POB 22373, Addis Ababa; tel. (1) 556177; fax (1) 552654; e-mail akpac@telecom.net.et; monthly; Amharic; Man. Goshu Moges; circ. 30,000.

Tobia Newspaper: POB 22373, Addis Ababa; tel. (1) 556177; fax (1) 552654; e-mail akpac@telecom.net.et; weekly; Amharic; Man. Goshu Moges; circ. 25,000.

Tomar: Benishangul; weekly; Amharic; Editor-in-Chief Befekadu Moreda.

Wetaderna Alamaw: POB 1901, Addis Ababa; fortnightly; Amharic.

Yezareitu Ethiopia (Ethiopia Today): POB 30232, Addis Ababa; weekly; Amharic and English; publ. by the Ministry of Information; Editor-in-Chief Imiru Worku; circ. 30,000.

NEWS AGENCIES

Ethiopian News Agency (ENA): Patriot St, POB 530, Addis Ababa; tel. (1) 550011; fax (1) 551609; e-mail ena@telecom.net.et; internet www.telecom.net.et/~ena; Chair Netsanet Asfaw.

Foreign Bureaux

Agence France-Presse (AFP): POB 3537, Addis Ababa; tel. (1) 511006; Chief Saba Seyoum.

Agenzia Nazionale Stampa Associata (ANSA) (Italy): POB 1001, Addis Ababa; tel. (1) 111007; Chief Brahame Ghebrezghi-Abiher.

Associated Press (AP): Addis Ababa; tel. (1) 161726; Correspondent Abebe Andualam.

Deutsche Presse-Agentur (dpa) (Germany): Addis Ababa; tel. (1) 510687; Correspondent Ghion Hagos.

Informatsionnoye Telegrafnoye Agentstvo Rossii—Telegrafnoye Agentstvo Suverennykh Stran (ITAR—TASS) (Russia): Addis Ababa; tel. (1) 181255; Bureau Chief Gennadii G. Gabrielyan.

Prensa Latina (Cuba): Gen. Makonnen Bldg, 5th Floor, nr Ghion Hotel, opp. National Stadium, Addis Ababa; tel. (1) 519899; Chief Hugo Rius Blein.

Reuters (UK): Addis Ababa; tel. (1) 156505; Correspondent Tsegaye Tadesse.

Rossiiskoye Informatsionnoye Agentstvo—Novosti (RIA—Novosti) (Russia): POB 239, Addis Ababa; Chief Vitalii Polikarpov.

Xinhua (New China) News Agency (People's Republic of China): POB 2497, Addis Ababa; tel. (1) 515676; fax (1) 514742; Correspondent Chen Cailin.

PRESS ASSOCIATIONS

Ethiopian Free Press Journalists' Association (EFJA): POB 31317, Addis Ababa; tel. (1) 555021; fax (1) 922939; e-mail efja@telecom.net.et; internet www.ifex.org/members/efja; f. 1993; granted legal recognition in 2000; Pres. Kifle Mulat.

Ethiopian Journalists' Association: POB 30288, Addis Ababa; tel. (1) 117852; fax (1) 513365; Pres. Kefale Mammo.

Publishers

Addis Ababa University Press: POB 1176, Addis Ababa; tel. (1) 119148; fax (1) 550655; e-mail aau.pres@telecom.net.et; f. 1968; educational and reference works in English, general books in English and Amharic; Editor MESSELECH HABTE.

Berhanena Selam Printing Enterprise: POB 1241 Addis Ababa; tel. (1) 553233; fax (1) 553939; e-mail bspe@telecom.net.et; f. 1921; fmrly Government Printing Press; publishes and prints newspapers, periodicals and books; Gen. Man. MULUWORK G. HIOWT.

Ethiopia Book Centre: POB 1024, Addis Ababa; tel. (1) 116844; f. 1977; privately-owned; publr, importer, wholesaler and retailer of educational books.

Kuraz Publishing Agency: POB 30933, Addis Ababa; tel. (1) 551688; state-owned.

Broadcasting and Communications

TELECOMMUNICATIONS

Ethiopian Telecommunications Corpn (ETC): POB 1047, Addis Ababa; tel. (1) 510500; fax (1) 515777; e-mail etc-hq@telecom.net.et; internet www.telecom.net.et; Man. Dir TESFAYE BIRU.

BROADCASTING

Radio

Radio Ethiopia: POB 1020, Addis Ababa; tel. (1) 121011; f. 1941; Amharic, English, French, Arabic, Afar, Oromifa, Tigre, Tigrinya and Somali; Gen. Man. KASA MILOKO.

Radio Torch: Addis Ababa; f. 1994; Amharic; autonomous station; Gen. Man. SEIFU TURE GETACHEW.

Radio Voice of One Free Ethiopia: Amharic; broadcasts twice a week; opposes current Govts of Ethiopia and Eritrea.

Voice of the Revolution of Tigrai: POB 450, Mekele; tel. (4) 400600; fax (4) 405485; e-mail vort@telecom.net.et; f. 1985; Tigrinya and Afargna; broadcasts 57 hours per week; supports Tigrai People's Liberation Front.

Television

Ethiopian Television: POB 5544, Addis Ababa; tel. (1) 155326; fax (1) 512685; f. 1964; semi-autonomous station; accepts commercial advertising; programmes transmitted from Addis Ababa to 26 regional stations; Chair. BEREKET SIMON.

Finance

(cap. = capital; res = reserves; dep. = deposits; m. = million; brs = branches; amounts in birr)

BANKING

Central Bank

National Bank of Ethiopia: POB 5550, Addis Ababa; tel. (1) 517430; fax (1) 514588; e-mail nbe.vgov@telecom.net.et; internet www.telecom.net/~nbe; f. 1964; bank of issue; cap. and res 1,117.5m., dep. 6,022.8m. (May 1999); Gov. TEKLEWOLD ATNAFU; Vice-Gov. LEGESSE MOTTA; 4 brs.

Other Banks

Awash International Bank SC: Africa Ave, POB 12638, Addis Ababa; tel. (1) 612771; fax (1) 614477; e-mail awash.bank@telecom .net.et; internet www.awash-bank.com; f. 1994; cap. 110.1m., res 18.1m., dep. 1,063.9m. (Dec. 2002); Chair. BULCHA DEMEKSA; Gen. Man. LEIKUN BERHANU; 25 brs.

Bank of Abyssinia: POB 12947, Addis Ababa; tel. (1) 530663; fax (1) 510409; e-mail abyssinia@telecom.net.et; internet www .bankofabyssinia.com; f. 1905; closed 1935 and reopened 1996; commercial banking services; cap. and res 139m., dep. 795m. (Jan. 2002); Chair. ADDIS ANTENEH; CEO TEKLE ALEMNEH; 15 brs.

Commercial Bank of Ethiopia: Unity Sq., POB 255, Addis Ababa; tel. (1) 511271; fax (1) 514522; e-mail cbe/ibd@telecom.net.et; internet www.combanketh.com; f. 1943; reorg. 1996; state-owned; cap. and res 995.7m., dep. 14,931.0m. (June 1999); Pres. GELAHEGN YILMA; 168 brs.

Construction and Business Bank: Higher 21, Kebele 04, POB 3480, Addis Ababa; tel. (1) 512300; fax (1) 515103; e-mail cbb@ telecom.net.et; f. 1975 as Housing and Savings Bank; provides credit for construction projects and a range of commercial banking services; state-owned; total assets 933.1m. (June 2001); Chair. HAILE ASEGIDE; Gen. Man. ADMASSU TECHANE; 20 brs.

Dashen Bank: POB 12752, Garad Bldg, Debre Zeit Rd, Addis Ababa; tel. (1) 661380; fax (1) 653037; e-mail dashen.bank@telecom .net.et; cap. 50.0m., dep. 861.2m. (June 2001); CEO LULSEGED TEFERI; 22 brs.

Development Bank of Ethiopia: POB 1900, Addis Ababa; tel. (1) 511188; fax (1) 511606; e-mail dbe@telecom.net.et; provides devt finance for industry and agriculture, technical advice and assistance in project evaluation; state-owned; cap. and res 385.2m., dep. 727.7m. (March 1999); Chair. GIRMA BIRRU; Gen. Man. MOGES CHEMERE; 32 brs.

NIB International Bank SC: POB 2439, Africa Avenue, Dembel City Centre, Addis Ababa; tel. (1) 503288; fax (1) 504349; e-mail nibbank@telecom.net.et; f. 1999; cap. 51.8m., res 3.3m., dep. 233.2m. (June 2001); Chair and Gen. Man LEGASSE TICKEHER.

United Bank: POB 19963, Addis Ababa; tel. (1) 655222; fax (1) 655243; f. 1998; commercial banking services; cap. and res 41.6m., dep. 70.6m. (June 2000); Chair. GEBREYES BEGNA; Gen. Man. KEBEDE TEMESGEN; 7 brs.

Wegagen Bank: POB 1018, Addis Ababa; tel. (1) 655015; fax (1) 653330; e-mail wegagen@telecom.net.et; f. 1997; commercial banking services; cap. 44.9m., total assets 679.5m. (June 2000); CEO KIDANE NIKODEMOS; 13 brs.

Bankers' Association

Ethiopian Bankers' Association: Addis Ababa; f. 2001; Pres. LEIKUN BERHANU.

INSURANCE

Africa Insurance Co: POB 12941, Addis Ababa; tel. (1) 517861; fax (1) 510376; Gen. Man. ALEM TESFATSION.

Awash Insurance Co: POB 12637, Addis Ababa; tel. (1) 614420; fax (1) 614419; Gen. Man. TSEGAYE KEMAS.

Ethiopian Insurance Corpn: POB 2545, Addis Ababa; tel. (1) 512400; fax (1) 517499; e-mail eic.md@telecom.net.et; internet www .telecom.net.et/~eic; f. 1976; Man. Dir TEWODROS TILAHUN (acting).

Global Insurance SC: POB 180112, Addis Abba; tel. (1) 567400; fax (1) 566200; e-mail globalinsu@telecom.net.et; f. 1997; Gen. Man. MASRESHA G. MESKEL.

Lion Insurance SC: POB 661, Addis Ababa; tel. (1) 513305; fax (1) 534799; f. 1998; Gen. Man. ALMAZ MOGES.

National Insurance Co of Ethiopia: POB 12645, Addis Ababa; tel. (1) 661129; fax (1) 650660; e-mail nice@telecom.net.et; Man. Dir and CEO HABTEMATIAM SHUMGIZAW.

Nile Insurance Co: POB 12836, Addis Ababa; tel. (1) 537709; fax (1) 514592; e-mail nileinsu@mail.telecom.net.et; f. 1995; Gen. Man. MAHTSENTU FELEKE.

Nyala Insurance SC: POB 12753, Addis Ababa; tel. (1) 626707; fax (1) 626706; e-mail nisco@telecom.net.et; Man. Dir NAHU-SENAYE ARAYA.

United Insurance Co SC: POB 1156, Addis Ababa; tel. (1) 515656; fax (1) 513258; e-mail united.insurance@telecom.net.et; Man. Dir IYESUSWORK ZAFU.

Trade and Industry

CHAMBERS OF COMMERCE

Ethiopian Chamber of Commerce: Mexico Sq., POB 517, Addis Ababa; tel. (1) 518240; fax (1) 517699; e-mail ethchamb@telecom.net .et; f. 1947; city chambers in Addis Ababa, Asella, Awasa, Bahir Dar, Dire Dawa, Nazret, Jimma, Gondar, Dessie, Mekele and Shashemene; Pres. ASCHALEW HAILE; Sec.-Gen. ANDU ALEM TEGEGNE.

Addis Ababa Chamber of Commerce: POB 2458, Addis Ababa; tel. (1) 513882; fax (1) 511479; e-mail AAchamber1@telecom.net.et; internet www.addischamber.com; Chair. BERHANE MEWA; Vice-Chair. IYESUSWORK ZAFU.

INDUSTRIAL AND TRADE ASSOCIATIONS

Ethiopian Beverages Corpn: POB 1285, Addis Ababa; tel. (1) 186185; Gen. Man. MENNA TEWAHEDE.

Ethiopian Cement Corpn: POB 5782, Addis Ababa; tel. (1) 552222; fax (1) 551572; Gen. Man. REDI GEMAL.

Ethiopian Chemical Corpn: POB 5747, Addis Ababa; tel. (1) 184305; Gen. Man. Asnake Sahlu.

Ethiopian Coffee Export Enterprise: POB 2591, Addis Ababa; tel. (1) 515330; fax (1) 510762; f. 1977; Gen. Man. Derga Gurmessa.

Ethiopian Food Corpn: Addis Ababa; tel. (1) 518522; fax (1) 513173; f. 1975; produces and distributes food items, including edible oil, ghee substitute, pasta, bread, maize, wheat flour etc. Gen. Man. Bekele Haile.

Ethiopian Fruit and Vegetable Marketing Enterprise: POB 2374, Addis Ababa; tel. (1) 519192; fax (1) 516483; f. 1980; sole wholesale domestic distributor and exporter of fresh and processed fruit and vegetables, and floricultural products; Gen. Man. Kaknu Pewonde.

Ethiopian Grain Trade Enterprise: POB 3321, Addis Ababa; tel. (1) 653166; fax (1) 652792; e-mail egte@telecom.net.et; Gen. Man. Girma Bekele.

Ethiopian Handicrafts and Small-Scale Industries Development Agency: Addis Ababa; tel. (1) 157366; f. 1977.

Ethiopian Import and Export Corpn (ETIMEX): Addis Ababa; tel. (1) 511112; fax (1) 515411; f. 1975; state trading corpn under the supervision of the Ministry of Trade and Industry; import of building materials, foodstuffs, stationery and office equipment, textiles, clothing, chemicals, general merchandise, capital goods; Gen. Man. Aschenaki G. Hiwot.

Ethiopian National Metal Works Corpn: Addis Ababa; fax (1) 510714; Gen. Man. Alula Berhane.

Ethiopian Oil Seeds and Pulses Export Corpn: POB 5719, Addis Ababa; tel. (1) 550597; fax (1) 553299; f. 1975; Gen. Man. Abdouruhman Mohammed.

Ethiopia Peasants' Association (EPA): f. 1978 to promote improved agricultural techniques, home industries, education, public health and self-reliance; comprises 30,000 peasant asscns with c. 7m. mems; Chair. (vacant).

Ethiopian Petroleum Enterprise: POB 3375, Addis Ababa; fax (1) 512938; e-mail ethpetroleum@telecom.net.et; f. 1976; Gen. Man. Yigzaw Mekonnen.

Ethiopian Pharmaceuticals and Medical Supplies Corpn (EPHARMECOR): POB 21904, Addis Ababa; tel. (1) 134577; fax (1) 752555; f. 1976; manufacture, import, export and distribution of pharmaceuticals, chemicals, dressings, surgical and dental instruments, hospital and laboratory supplies; Gen. Man. Girma Bepasso.

Ethiopian Sugar Corpn: POB 133, Addis Ababa; tel. (1) 519700; fax (1) 513488; Gen. Man. Abate Lemengh.

Green Star Food Co LLC: POB 5579, Addis Ababa; tel. (1) 526588; fax (1) 526599; e-mail greenstar@telecom.net.et; f. 1984; fmrly the Ethiopian Livestock and Meat Corpn; production and marketing of canned and frozen foods; Gen. Man. Dawit Bekele.

National Leather and Shoe Corpn: POB 2516, Addis Ababa; tel. (1) 514075; fax (1) 513525; f. 1975; produces and sells semi-processed hides and skins, finished leather, leather goods and footwear; Gen. Man. Girma W. Aregai.

National Textiles Corpn: Addis Ababa; tel. (1) 157316; fax (1) 511955; f. 1975; production of yarn, fabrics, knitwear, blankets, bags, etc. Gen. Man. Fikre Hugiane.

Natural Gums Processing and Marketing Enterprise: POB 62322, Addis Ababa; tel. (1) 159930; fax (1) 518110; e-mail natgum@telecom.net.et; f. 1976; Gen. Man. Teklemasinanot Nigatu.

UTILITIES

Electricity

Ethiopian Electric Power Corpn (EEPCO): De Gaulle Sq., POB 1233, Addis Ababa; tel. (1) 111443; fax (1) 551324; Chair. Haile Selassie Asegide; Gen. Man. Mihret Debebe.

Water

Addis Ababa Water Sewerage Authority: POB 1505; Addis Ababa; tel. (1) 550422; fax (1) 553793; e-mail aawsa.ha@telecom.net.et.

Water Resources Development Authority: POB 1045, Addis Ababa; tel. (1) 612999; fax (1) 611245; Gen. Man. Getachew Gizaw.

TRADE UNIONS

Ethiopian Trade Union (ETU): POB 3653, Addis Ababa; tel. (1) 514366; f. 1975; comprises nine industrial unions and 22 regional unions with a total membership of 320,000 (1987); Chair. (vacant).

Transport

RAILWAYS

Djibouti-Ethiopian Railway (Chemin de Fer Djibouti-Ethiopien) (CDE): POB 1051, Addis Ababa; tel. (1) 517250; fax (1) 513533; e-mail cde@telecom.net.et; f. 1909; adopted present name in 1981; jtly-owned by Govts of Ethiopia and Djibouti; 781 km of track (681 km in Ethiopia), linking Addis Ababa with Djibouti; Pres. Saleh Omar Hildid; Dir-Gen. Ali Abdallah Gadid.

ROADS

In 2000 the total road network comprised an estimated 31,571 km of primary, secondary and feeder roads, of which 3,789 km were paved, the remainder being gravel roads. In addition, there are some 30,000 km of unclassified tracks and trails. A highway links Addis Ababa with Nairobi in Kenya, forming part of the Trans-East Africa Highway. In early 1998 the World Bank granted Ethiopia a loan of US \$309.2m. to help finance the first five-year phase of an ambitious 10-year government programme to rebuild and upgrade rural and urban roads.

Comet Transport Enterprise: POB 2402, Addis Ababa; tel. (1) 151864; fax (1) 514254; e-mail cometrans@telecom.net.et; f. 1994; Gen. Man. Feleke Yimer.

Ethiopian Freight Transport Corpn: Addis Ababa; restructured into five autonomous enterprises in 1994.

Ethiopian Road Transport Authority: POB 2504, Addis Ababa; tel. (1) 510244; fax (1) 510715; enforcement of road transport regulations, registering of vehicles and issuing of driving licences; Gen. Man. Kasahun H. Mariam.

Ethiopian Roads Authority: POB 1770, Addis Ababa; tel. (1) 517170; fax (1) 514866; f. 1951; construction and maintenance of roads, bridges and airports; Gen. Man. Tesfa Michael Nahusenai.

Public Transport Corpn: POB 5780, Addis Ababa; tel. (1) 153117; fax (1) 510720; f. 1977; urban bus services in Addis Ababa and Jimma, and services between towns; restructured into three autonomous enterprises in 1994 and scheduled for privatization; Man. Dir Ahmed Nuru.

SHIPPING

The formerly Ethiopian-controlled ports of Massawa and Assab now lie within the boundaries of the State of Eritrea (q.v.). Although an agreement exists between the two Governments allowing Ethiopian access to the two ports, which can handle more than 1m. metric tons of merchandise annually, in mid-1998 Ethiopia ceased using the ports, owing to the outbreak of hostilities. Ethiopia's maritime trade currently passes through Djibouti (in the Republic of Djibouti), and also through the Kenyan port of Mombasa. At 31 December 2001 Ethiopia's registered merchant fleet numbered nine vessels, with a total displacement of 81,933 grt.

Ethiopian Shipping Lines Corpn: POB 2572, Addis Ababa; tel. (1) 518280; fax (1) 519525; e-mail esl@telecom.net.et; f. 1964; serves Red Sea, Europe, Mediterranean, Gulf and Far East with its own fleet and chartered vessels; Chair. G. Tsadkan Gebre Tensay; Gen. Man. Ambachew Abraha.

Marine Transport Authority: Maritime Dept, POB 1861, Addis Ababa; tel. (1) 158227; fax (1) 515665; f. 1993; regulates maritime transport services; Chair. Teshome Woldegiorgis.

Maritime and Transit Services Enterprise: POB 1186, Addis Ababa; tel. (1) 518197; fax (1) 514097; e-mail mtse@telecom.net.et; internet www.telecom.net/~mtse; f. 1979; services include stevedoring, bagging, forwarding and transporting; Chair. Desta Amare; Gen. Man. Ahmed Yassin.

CIVIL AVIATION

Ethiopia has two international airports (at Addis Ababa and Dire Dawa) and around 40 airfields. Bole International Airport in the capital handles 95% of international air traffic and 85% of domestic flights. A programme to modernize the airport, at an estimated cost of 819m. birr (US \$130m.), was to be undertaken during 1997–2001. Construction of airports at Aksum, Lalibela and Gonda was completed in April 2000, while renovation work continued at a further seven domestic airports during 2002.

Ethiopian Airlines: Bole International Airport, POB 1755, Addis Ababa; tel. (1) 612222; fax (1) 611474; e-mail eal@telecom.net.et; internet www.flyethiopian.com; f. 1945; operates regular domestic services and flights to 47 international destinations in Africa, Europe, Middle East, Asia and the USA; Chair. Seyoum Mesfin; CEO Bisrat Nigatu.

Ethiopian Civil Aviation Authority: POB 978, Addis Ababa; tel. (1) 610277; fax (1) 612533; e-mail civilaviation@telecom.net.et; constructs and maintains airports; provides air navigational facilities; Dir-Gen. TEFERA MEKONEN (acting).

Tourism

Ethiopia's tourist attractions include the early Christian monuments and churches, the ancient capitals of Gondar and Axum, the Blue Nile Falls and the National Parks of the Semien and Bale Mountains. Tourist arrivals in 2000 totalled 135,954, and in that year receipts from tourism amounted to US $24m.

Ethiopian Tourism Commission: POB 2183, Addis Ababa; tel. (1) 517470; fax (1) 513899; e-mail tour.com@telecom.net.et; internet www.visitethiopia.org; f. 1964; formulates national tourism policy, publicizes tourist attractions and regulates standards of tourist facilities; Commr YOUSUF ABDULLAHI SUKKAR.

FIJI

Introductory Survey

Location, Climate, Language, Religion, Flag, Capital

The Republic of Fiji comprises more than 300 islands, of which 100 are inhabited, situated about 1,930 km (1,200 miles) south of the equator in the Pacific Ocean. The four main islands are Viti Levu (on which almost 70% of the country's population lives), Vanua Levu, Taveuni and Kadavu. The climate is tropical, with temperatures ranging from 16°C to 32°C (60°F–90°F). Rainfall is heavy on the windward side. Fijian and Hindi are the principal languages but English is also widely spoken. In 1986 about 53% of the population were Christians (mainly Methodists), 38% Hindus and 8% Muslims. The national flag (proportions 1 by 2) is light blue, with the United Kingdom flag as a canton in the upper hoist. In the fly is the main part of Fiji's national coat of arms: a white field quartered by a red upright cross, the quarters containing sugar canes, a coconut palm, a stem of bananas and a dove bearing an olive branch; in chief is a red panel with a yellow crowned lion holding a white cocoa pod. The capital is Suva, on Viti Levu.

Recent History

The first Europeans to settle on the islands were sandalwood traders, missionaries and shipwrecked sailors, and in October 1874 Fiji was proclaimed a British possession. In September 1966 the British Government introduced a new Constitution for Fiji. It provided for a ministerial form of government, an almost wholly elected Legislative Council and the introduction of universal adult suffrage. Rather than using a common roll of voters, however, the Constitution introduced an electoral system that combined communal (Fijian and Indian) rolls with cross-voting. In September 1967 the Executive Council became the Council of Ministers, with Ratu Kamisese Mara, leader of the multiracial (but predominantly Fijian) Alliance Party (AP), as Fiji's first Chief Minister. Following a constitutional conference in April–May 1970, Fiji achieved independence, within the Commonwealth, on 10 October 1970. The Legislative Council was renamed the House of Representatives, and a second parliamentary chamber, the nominated Senate, was established. The British-appointed Governor became Fiji's first Governor-General, while Ratu Sir Kamisese Mara (as he had become in 1969) took office as Prime Minister.

Fiji was, however, troubled by racial tensions. Although the descendants of indentured Indian workers who were brought to Fiji in the late 19th century had grown to outnumber the native inhabitants, they were discriminated against in political representation and land ownership rights. A new electoral system was adopted in 1970 to ensure a racial balance in the legislature.

At the general election held in March and April 1977 the National Federation Party (NFP), traditionally supported by the Indian population, won 26 of the 52 seats in the House of Representatives, but was unable to form a government and subsequently split into two factions. The AP governed in a caretaker capacity until the holding of a further general election in September, when it was returned with its largest-ever majority. While the two main parties professed multiracial ideas, the Fijian Nationalist Party campaigned in support of its 'Fiji for the Fijians' programme in order to foster nationalist sentiment.

In 1980 Ratu Sir Kamisese Mara's suggestion that a Government of National Unity be formed was overshadowed by renewed political disagreement between the AP and the NFP (whose two factions had drawn closer together again) over land ownership. Fijians owned 83% of the land and were strongly defending their traditional rights, while the Indian population was pressing for greater security of land tenure. The general election held in July 1982 was also dominated by racial issues. The AP retained power after winning 28 seats, but its majority had been reduced from 20 to four. The NFP won 22 seats and the Western United Front (WUF), which professed a multiracial outlook, took the remaining two seats.

A meeting of union leaders in May 1985 represented the beginning of discussions that culminated in the founding of the Fiji Labour Party (FLP), officially inaugurated in Suva in July. Sponsored by the Fiji Trades Union Congress (FTUC), and under the presidency of Dr Timoci Bavadra, the new party was formed with the aim of presenting a more effective parliamentary opposition, and declared the provision of free education and a national medical scheme to be among its priorities. The FLP hoped to work through farmers' organizations to win votes among rural electorates, which traditionally supported the NFP. During 1985–86 disagreements between the Government and the FTUC over economic policies became increasingly acrimonious, leading to an outbreak of labour unrest and the withdrawal, in June 1986, of government recognition of the FTUC as the unions' representative organization.

At a general election in April 1987 a coalition of the FLP and NFP won 28 seats (19 of which were secured by ethnic Indian candidates) in the House of Representatives, thus defeating the ruling AP, which won only 24 seats. The new Government, led by Bavadra, was therefore the first in Fijian history to contain a majority of ministers of Indian, rather than Melanesian, origin. Bavadra, himself, was of Melanesian descent. On 14 May, however, the Government was overthrown by a military coup, led by Lt-Col (later Maj.-Gen.) Sitiveni Rabuka. The Governor-General, Ratu Sir Penaia Ganilau, responded by declaring a state of emergency and appointed a 19-member advisory council, including Bavadra and Rabuka. However, Bavadra refused to participate in the council, denouncing it as unconstitutional and biased in its composition.

Widespread racial violence followed the coup, and there were several public demands for Bavadra's reinstatement as Prime Minister. In July 1987 the Great Council of Fijian Chiefs, comprising the country's 70 hereditary Melanesian leaders, approved plans for constitutional reform. In September negotiations began, on the initiative of Ganilau, between delegations led by the two former Prime Ministers, Bavadra and Mara, to resolve the political crisis. On 22 September it was announced that the two factions had agreed to form an interim bipartisan Government.

On 25 September 1987, however, before the new plan could be implemented, Rabuka staged a second coup and announced his intention to declare Fiji a republic. Despite Ganilau's refusal to recognize the seizure of power, Rabuka revoked the Constitution on 1 October and proclaimed himself Head of State, thus deposing the Queen. Ganilau conceded defeat and resigned as Governor-General. At a meeting in Canada, Commonwealth Heads of Government formally declared that Fiji's membership of the Commonwealth had lapsed. An interim Cabinet, comprising mainly ethnic Fijians, was installed by Rabuka. In late October Rabuka announced that he would resign as Head of State as soon as he had appointed a new President of the Republic. Several cases of violations of human rights by the Fijian army were reported, as the regime assumed powers of detention without trial and suspended all political activity.

On 6 December 1987 Rabuka resigned as Head of State. Although he had previously refused to accept the post, Ganilau, the former Governor-General, became the first President of the Fijian Republic. Mara was reappointed Prime Minister, and Rabuka became Minister of Home Affairs. A new interim Cabinet was announced on 9 December, containing 11 members of Rabuka's administration, but no member of Bavadra's deposed Government.

In February 1988 Rotuma (the only Polynesian island in the country), which lies to the north-west of Vanua Levu, declared itself politically independent of Fiji, whose newly acquired republican status it refused to recognize. Fijian troops were dispatched to the island, however, and soon quelled the dissent.

A new draft Constitution was approved by the interim Government in September 1988. The proposed Constitution was rejected, however, by a multiracial constitutional committee, which considered unnecessary the specific reservation of the principal offices of state for ethnic Fijians. In September 1989 the committee published a revised draft, which was still, however, condemned by Bavadra and the FLP-NFP coalition. In November Bavadra died and was replaced as leader of the FLP-NFP coalition by his widow, Adi Kuini Bavadra.

In January 1990 Rabuka resigned from the Cabinet and returned to his military duties. Mara agreed to remain as Prime Minister until the restoration of constitutional government. In June the Great Council of Chiefs approved the draft Constitution. At the same time, the Great Council of Chiefs stated its intention to form a new party, the Soqosoqo ni Vakavulewa ni Taukei (SVT) or Fijian Political Party, to advocate the cause of ethnic Fijians. The new Constitution was finally promulgated on 25 July by President Ganilau, and was immediately condemned by the FLP–NFP coalition, which announced that it would boycott any elections held in accordance with the Constitution's provisions. Angered by the fact that a legislative majority was guaranteed to ethnic Fijians (who were reserved 37 of the 70 elective seats, compared with 27 Indian seats), and that the Great Council of Chiefs was to nominate ethnic Fijians to 24 of the 34 seats in the Senate and to appoint the President of the Republic, the opposition organized anti-Constitution demonstrations. The new Constitution was similarly condemned for its racial bias by India, New Zealand and Australia at the UN General Assembly, meeting in New York in October. In May 1991 the Commonwealth stated that Fiji would not be re-admitted to the organization until it changed its Constitution.

In July 1991 Rabuka resigned as Commander of the Armed Forces in order to rejoin the Cabinet as Deputy Prime Minister and Minister of Home Affairs, although towards the end of 1991, he relinquished the post in order to assume the leadership of the SVT.

Disagreements between the Government and the FTUC re-emerged at the beginning of 1991. In February a strike by more than 900 members of the Fijian Miners' Union over union recognition, pay and poor working conditions led to the dismissal of some 400 of the workers. In May the Government announced a series of reforms to the labour laws, including the abolition of the minimum wage, restrictions on strike action and derecognition of unions that did not represent at least two-thirds of the work-force. A significant political development announced by the Government in late 1992 was the official recognition of the FTUC (withheld since 1986) as the sole representative of workers in Fiji.

At legislative elections in May 1992 the SVT secured 30 of the 37 seats reserved for ethnic Fijians, while the NFP won 14 and the FLP 13 of the seats reserved for Indian representatives. Following the election, the FLP agreed to participate in Parliament and to support Rabuka in his campaign for the premiership, in return for a guarantee from the SVT of a full review of the Constitution and of trade union and land laws. Rabuka was, therefore, appointed Prime Minister and formed a coalition Government (consisting of 14 members of the SVT and five others).

Remarks made by the Prime Minister in an Australian television interview in October 1992, expressing his implicit support for the repatriation of Fijian Indians, attracted controversy and prompted renewed fears that any reform of the Constitution would be merely superficial. Nevertheless, in December Rabuka formally invited the opposition leaders, Jai Ram Reddy of the NFP and Mahendra Chaudhry of the FLP (formerly the National Secretary of the FTUC), to form a Government of National Unity. The move was largely welcomed, but Indian politicians expressed reluctance to take part in a government whose political control remained fundamentally vested with ethnic Fijians. Rabuka was criticized equally by nationalist extremists of the Taukei Solidarity Movement, who accused him of conceding too much political power to Fijian Indians. Following the appointment of a new Cabinet in June, all 13 of the FLP legislative members began an indefinite boycott of Parliament, in protest at Rabuka's failure to implement the reforms, which he had agreed to carry out in return for their support for his election to the premiership in June 1992.

In December 1993 President Ganilau died, following a long illness, and was replaced by Ratu Sir Kamisese Mara, who took office on 18 January 1994 (re-elected on 18 January 1999).

At legislative elections held in February 1994 the SVT increased the number of its seats in the House of Representatives to 31, while the Fijian Association Party (FAP, established in January by former members of the SVT) secured only five seats, of a total of 37 reserved for ethnic Fijians. Of the 27 seats reserved for ethnic Indian representatives, 20 were secured by the NFP. The SVT subsequently formed a governing coalition with the General Voters' Party (GVP, which represented the interests of the General Electors—i.e. the minority Chinese and European communities and people from elsewhere in the Pacific

region resident in Fiji) and an independent member, under the premiership of Rabuka, who announced the formation of a new Cabinet composed entirely of ethnic Fijians. In response to international concern regarding the continued existence of Fiji's racially-biased Constitution, Rabuka announced in June that a Constitutional Review Commission had been established, which, it was hoped, would have completed a review of the Constitution by 1997.

In January 1995 the Government announced that it was to recommend that Parliament vote to repeal the Sunday observance law (imposed after the coups of 1987), which prohibited work, organized entertainment and sport on that day. It was believed that the law had become increasingly unpopular, particularly among the Indian community. However, the announcement aroused intense opposition from nationalist politicians and Methodist church leaders, who organized demonstrations in three cities, attended by more than 12,000 people. In February, however, the House of Representatives voted in favour of removing the regulations. The Senate narrowly rejected the proposal, thus effectively delaying the implementation of any changes. The Sunday observance law was finally repealed in November.

The issue of independence for the island of Rotuma was revived in September 1995 with the return of the King of Rotuma from exile in New Zealand. King Gagaj Sa Lagfatmaro, who had fled to New Zealand following death threats made against him during the military coups of 1987, appeared before the Constitutional Review Commission to petition for the island's independence within the Commonwealth, reiterating his view that Rotuma remained a British colony rather than a part of Fiji.

In September 1995 the Government decided to transfer all state land (comprising some 10% of Fiji's total land area), hitherto administered by the Government Lands Department, to the Native Land Trust Board. The decision was to allow the allocation of land to indigenous Fijians on the basis of native custom. However, concern among the Fijian Indian population increased following reports in early 1996 that many would not be able to renew their land leases (most of which were due to expire between 1997 and 2024) under the Agricultural Landlords and Tenants Act (ALTA). The reports were strongly denied by the Government, despite statements by several Fijian land-owning clans that Indians' leases would not be renewed. Moreover, a recently-formed sugar cane growers' association solely for ethnic Fijians, the Taukei Cane Growers' Association, announced its intention to campaign for ethnic Fijian control of the sugar industry, largely by refusing to renew land leases to ethnic Indians (who held some 85% of sugar farm leases). Concern was expressed that mounting tensions between land-owners and tenants could lead to violence, and that the situation was affecting investor confidence. By the end of 2000 almost 2,000 land leases had expired, leaving many tenant farmers and their families homeless. Some 70 farmers, who had expressed a wish not to be resettled, received rehabilitation grants of $F28,000 in December 2000, although the authorities were criticized for their apparent slowness in processing the applications. In January 2001 the administration of native land leases was transferred from ALTA to the Native Lands Trust Act (NLTA), prompting fears of increased bias in favour of ethnic Fijian landowners and further instability in the sugar industry. A further 1,500 leases expired during 2001.

Meanwhile, racial tension intensified in October 1995, following the publication of the SVT's submission to the Constitutional Review Commission. In its report the party detailed plans to abandon the present multiracial form of government, recommending instead the adoption of an electoral system based on racial representation, in which each ethnic group would select its own representatives. The expression of numerous extreme anti-Indian sentiments in the document was widely condemned (by both ethnic Fijians and ethnic Indians) as offensive.

A rift within the GVP in early 1996, which resulted in two of the four GVP members of the House of Representatives withdrawing their support for the Government, prompted Rabuka to seek alternative coalition partners from among the opposition, in an attempt to establish a more secure majority. However, the Prime Minister was unsuccessful in persuading parliamentary members of the FAP (which had strongly criticized the SVT's submission to the Constitutional Review Commission the previous year) to join the Government. The administration's troubles during 1996 contributed to the defeat of the SVT in virtually every municipality at local elections, which took place in September.

Existing divisions within the Government were further exacerbated by the presentation to the House of Representatives, in September 1996, of the Constitutional Review Commission's report. The report included recommendations to enlarge the House of Representatives to 75 seats, with 25 seats reserved on a racial basis (12 for ethnic Fijians, 10 for Fijian Indians, two for General Electors and one for Rotuma Islanders), and also proposed that the size of the Senate should be reduced from 34 to 32 members (and the number of nominated ethnic Fijian senators be reduced from 24 to 15), and that the Prime Minister should be a Fijian of any race, while the President should continue to be an indigenous Fijian. Rabuka and Mara both endorsed the findings of the report, while several nationalist parties, including the Vanua Independent Party, the Fijian Nationalist United Front Party (FNUFP) and the Taukei Solidarity Movement, expressed extreme opposition to the proposals, and formed a coalition in an attempt to further their influence within Parliament. In addition, a number of SVT members of the House of Representatives aligned themselves with the nationalists, and in early 1997 were reported to be responsible for a series of political manoeuvres within the Cabinet, aimed at undermining Rabuka's position. The parliamentary committee reviewing the report agreed on a majority of the 700 recommendations, but proposed that the House of Representatives be enlarged to only 71 seats, with 46 seats reserved on a racial basis (23 for ethnic Fijians, 19 for Indians, three for General Electors and one for Rotuma Islanders) and 25 seats open to all races. The committee's modified proposals were presented in May to the Great Council of Chiefs, which officially endorsed the recommendations in early June. The Constitution Amendment Bill was approved unanimously by the House of Representatives and the Senate in the following month. Rabuka was anxious to reassure extremist nationalist Fijians, who had vociferously opposed the reforms throughout the debate, that their interests would be protected under the amended Constitution (which was not due to take effect until July 1998) and that indigenous Fijians would continue to play a pre-eminent role in the government of the country.

Despite opposition from both the FLP and the nationalist parties, Fiji was readmitted to the Commonwealth at a meeting of member states in October 1997. In the same month Rabuka was granted an audience with Queen Elizabeth II in London, at which he formally apologized for the military coups of 1987. Events in early 1998 were dominated by political reaction to the imminent promulgation of the new Constitution. An extremist nationalist group of former SVT supporters, including senior church, military and police officials, were rumoured to be planning to overthrow Rabuka's Government. Meanwhile, it was reported that opponents of the Constitution were discussing the establishment of several new political parties. The new Constitution, none the less, came into effect on 27 July 1998.

A dispute between tribal landowners and the Government over compensation payments for land flooded by the Monosavu hydroelectric power station erupted into violence in July 1998. Landowners, who had been demanding compensation worth some $30m. since the plant was constructed in 1983, seized control of the station (which supplies 90% of Fiji's electricity) and carried out a series of arson attacks on Fiji Electricity Authority property. In October the Government agreed to pay the landowners compensation totalling some $A12m., although many involved in the dispute rejected the offer and announced their intention of pursuing a legal claim against the Government.

The prospect of legislative elections, to be held in early May 1999, prompted reports of political manoeuvring as parties sought to increase their influence by forming alliances. In addition, a number of changes in the country's political organizations occurred in late 1998. Following the death of Josefata Kamikamica, Adi Kuini Vuikaba Speed (widow of ex-President Bavadra) was elected leader of the FAP. Meanwhile, the GVP and the General Electors' Party merged to form the United General Party (UGP) under the leadership of the Minister for Tourism, Transport and Civil Aviation, David Pickering, and Rabuka was re-elected leader of the SVT (despite the party being required to amend its constitution in order for this to be possible). The formation of a new party, the Veitokani ni Lewenivanua Vakarisito (VLV, Christian Democratic Alliance), by several senior church and military leaders and former members of the nationalist Taukei Solidarity Movement, was widely criticized for its extremist stance and refusal to accept the newly formed, multiracial Constitution.

At legislative elections held on 8–15 May 1999, the first to be held under the new Constitution, Rabuka's coalition Government was defeated by Mahendra Chaudhry, leader of the Indian-dominated FLP, who thus became Fiji's first ethnic Indian Prime Minister. Chaudhry's broad-based Government (a coalition of the FLP, FAP, VLV and the Party of National Unity—PANU) initially seemed threatened by the reluctance of FAP members to serve under an Indian Prime Minister. The leaders were persuaded to remain in the coalition in the interests of national unity, after the intervention of President Mara. Political stability after the elections was further marred by demands for Chaudhry's resignation by the Fijian Nationalist Vanua Takolavo Party (NVTLP), and by a number of arson attacks, allegedly linked to the outgoing SVT (although these allegations were denied by Rabuka). Following the SVT's decisive defeat in the elections, Rabuka resigned as party leader; he was replaced by Ratu Inoke Kubuabola, the former Minister for Communications, Works and Energy. Rabuka was later appointed the first independent Chairman of the newly autonomous Great Council of Chiefs. The NVTLP was widely suspected to have been responsible for three bomb explosions in Suva in August 1999. In the same month a parliamentary vote of 'no confidence' against Prime Minister Chaudhry was overwhelmingly defeated. In the latter half of 1999 there were persistent demands by various nationalist groups (including the SVT) that Chaudhry be replaced by a leader of indigenous Fijian descent, and a number of demonstrations were organized, expressing disillusionment with the Government. In October the opposition coalition was successful in gaining control of a majority of councils in local elections, while the FLP won control of four municipal councils (having previously been in charge of none).

The Government's decision to disband the Fiji Intelligence Service from December 1999 was criticized by the opposition as 'foolish' and racially motivated. An announcement by the Chief Justice in December of a project to amend a number of laws that did not comply with the terms of the new Constitution, together with reports that the Government was planning to withdraw state funds previously provided to assist indigenous Fijian business interests, prompted further accusations of racism by the Government against ethnic Fijians. Consequently, the SVT and the VLV held talks to discuss ways of consolidating the ethnic Fijian political base. Proposed legislation, which would alter the distribution of power between the President and the Prime Minister, attracted further criticism from the opposition, and in February 2000 a faction of the FAP announced its withdrawal from the governing coalition, citing dissatisfaction with Chaudhry's leadership. Of greater significance, however, was the announcement in April that the extremist nationalist Taukei Movement (which had been inactive for several years) had been revived with the sole intention of removing the Prime Minister from office. The group subsequently publicized a campaign of demonstrations and civil disobedience, prompting the army to issue a statement distancing itself from any anti-Government agitation and pledging loyalty to Chaudhry. The campaign attracted considerable public support, however, and culminated in a march through Suva by some 5,000 people in early May.

On 19 May 2000 a group of armed men, led by businessman George Speight, invaded the parliament building and ousted the Government, taking hostage Chaudhry and 30 other members of the governing coalition. President Mara condemned the coup and declared a state of emergency as Speight's supporters rampaged through the streets of Suva, looting and setting fire to Indian businesses. Speight declared that he had reclaimed Fiji for indigenous Fijians and had dissolved the Constitution. Moreover, he threatened to kill the hostages if the military intervened. On 22 May Mara formally invited Rabuka, in his role as chairman of the Great Council of Chiefs, to seek a resolution of the crisis. In the following days the Great Council of Chiefs convened to discuss the situation and proposed the replacement of Chaudhry's Government with an interim administration, an amnesty for Speight and the rebels, and the amendment of the Constitution. Speight rejected the proposals, demanding that Mara also be removed from office. Meanwhile, violent clashes erupted at the headquarters of Fiji Television when the rebels stormed the building following the broadcast of an interview with an opponent of the coup. A police-officer was shot dead, television equipment was destroyed and the station's employees were taken hostage. On 29 May Mara resigned and the Commander of the Armed Forces, Frank Bainimarama, announced the imposition of martial law and a curfew, in an attempt to restore calm and stability to the country. In an expression of his apparent reluctance to assume the role, Bainimarama gave Mara a whale's tooth, a traditional Fijian symbol of regret.

Negotiations between the newly installed Military Executive Council and the Great Council of Chiefs continued throughout June 2000. Failure to reach a conclusive outcome seemed to be the result of inconsistencies in Speight's demands and an ambivalent attitude on the part of the military towards the coup. Regular patrols by the security forces curbed rioting in Suva, although outbreaks of violence in rural areas (mostly in the form of attacks on Indian Fijians, the looting and burning of Indian-owned farms and the occupation of several tourist resorts) were reported. On 25 June the four female hostages were released from the parliament building. The Military Executive Council announced its intention to appoint an interim government without consulting Speight and demanded that the rebel leader release the remaining hostages. Speight reiterated his threat to kill all those held if any rescue attempts were made.

An interim administration of 19 indigenous Fijians led by Laisenia Qarase (the former managing director of the Merchant Bank of Fiji) was sworn in on 4 July 2000. Minutes after the ceremony a gun battle erupted outside the parliament building in which four civilians and one rebel were injured; the rebel subsequently died. Speight announced that he not recognize the interim authority, and most of Fiji's mainstream political parties similarly denounced it, although the Methodist Church declared its support for the body. On 12 July a further nine hostages were released and on the following day the remaining 18, including Chaudhry, were liberated. In accordance with Speight's wishes, Ratu Josefa Iloilo, hitherto the First Vice-President, was then installed as President. In the same month Chandrika Prasad, a farmer, quickly brought a legal challenge to the abrogation of the 1997 Constitution in the High Court of Fiji. Chaudhry launched an international campaign to reinstate both the Constitution and the People's Coalition Government.

Incidents of civil unrest (including the occupation of the hydroelectric dam at Monosavu and of the army barracks on Vanua Levu) continued throughout July 2000 as Speight sought to manipulate existing grievances, particularly disputes over land ownership, in order to mobilize additional support. On 29 July, however, Speight was finally arrested, along with dozens of his supporters, for breaking the terms of his amnesty by refusing to relinquish weapons. Armed rebels responded violently to the arrest, and in Labasa Indian Fijians were rounded up and detained in army barracks by supporters of Speight. In early August more than 300 rebels appeared in court on a variety of firearms and public order offences. Speight was similarly charged with several minor offences. On 11 August Speight and 14 of his supporters were formally charged with treason. During September Speight made several applications for bail, all of which were refused. Meanwhile, the suspended police commissioner, Isikia Savua, revealed that police were conducting an investigation into a commercial deal involving the Fijian mahogany trade, which, it was believed, might have precipitated the coup; Speight had been chairman of both Fiji Pine Corporation and Fiji Hardwood Corporation before being dismissed in 1999. This view was reiterated by the deposed Prime Minister on an overseas tour during October, when Chaudhry expressed his commitment to the restoration of democracy and constitutional rule and stated his belief that the coup had been motivated by commercial vested interests rather than by concern over indigenous rights.

In early November 2000 about 40 soldiers staged a mutiny at army headquarters in Suva. Troops loyal to Bainimarama, who narrowly escaped capture, retook the barracks following an eight-hour assault in which five rebels and four loyal soldiers were killed. It was later revealed that a number of the rebel soldiers had been involved in the coup in May and speculation spread that the mutiny had been another attempted coup. The chairman of the Great Council of Chiefs, Sitiveni Rabuka, denied allegations by New Zealand's Minister of Foreign Affairs and Trade, Phil Goff, that he had been involved in the mutiny. In November 2002 Capt. Shane Stevens was sentenced to life imprisonment after he was found guilty of leading the mutiny two years earlier. Fourteen other soldiers received lesser sentences for their part in the uprising. Bainimarama criticized the majority of the sentences for being too lenient.

On 15 November 2000 the High Court ruled that the existing Constitution remained valid and that the elected Parliament, ousted in the coup, remained Fiji's legitimate governing authority. Laisenia Qarase responded by lodging an appeal against the ruling and by declaring that the interim authority, of which he was leader, would continue as the country's national government until new elections could be organized and a new constitution drafted within 18 months.

In mid-December 2000 Chaudhry's campaign to re-establish his Government suffered a significant set-back when the ministers of foreign affairs of Australia and New Zealand announced that they were abandoning their appeal for its reinstatement, although they would continue to support a return to the 1997 Constitution. However, within Fiji, supporters of a return to democracy formed the Fiji First Movement, which aimed to consolidate opposition to the post-coup regime. The group organized a series of protests across the country in late 2000 and early 2001.

In February 2001 an international panel of judges at the Court of Appeal began the hearing against the November 2000 ruling, which found the abrogation of the 1997 Constitution to be illegal. In its final judgment the court ruled that the 1997 Constitution remained the supreme law of Fiji, that the interim civilian government could not prove that it had the support of a majority of Fijian people and was therefore illegal and that, following Mara's resignation, the office of President remained vacant. The ruling was welcomed by many countries in the region, including Australia and New Zealand, and appeared to be accepted by the interim authority, which announced that it would organize elections as soon as possible. However, on 14 March Iloilo informed Chaudhry in a letter that he had been dismissed as Prime Minister, claiming that by advising Iloilo to dissolve the authority in preparation for elections he had accepted that he no longer had the mandate of Parliament. Chaudhry rejected the decision as unconstitutional and unlawful. Ratu Tevita Momoedonu was appointed Prime Minister on the same day. On the following day, however, Iloilo dismissed Momoedonu, on the advice of the Great Council of Chiefs, and reinstated Laisenia Qarase as head of the interim authority. It was announced that a general election would be held in August–September 2001, and would be conducted under the preferential voting system, similar to that of Australia, as used in Fiji's 1999 election.

There followed a period of factionalism and fragmentation among Fiji's political parties. George Speight had already been appointed President of the new Matanitu Vanua (MV—Conservative Alliance Party), despite facing the charge of treason for his part in the 2000 coup. In May 2001 Qarase formed the Soqosoqo Duavata ni Lewenivanua (SDL—Fiji United Party), a new contender for the indigenous Melanesian vote, thus rivalling the established SVT. Another indigenous party, the Bai Kei Viti, was launched in June. Tupeni Baba, former Deputy Prime Minister in Chaudhry's Government, left the FLP and formed the New Labour United Party (NLUP). The election took place between 25 August and 1 September. Qarase's SDL was victorious, but failed to obtain an overall majority. The SDL secured 31 seats in the House of Representatives (increasing to 32 of the 71 seats after a by-election on 25 September). The FLP won 27 seats, the MV six seats and the NLUP two seats. International monitors were satisfied that the election had been contested fairly.

Following the election, however, by refusing to allow the FLP any representation in his new Cabinet, Qarase was accused of contravening a provision of the Constitution whereby a party winning more than 10% of the seats in the House of Representatives was entitled to a ministerial post. Two members of George Speight's MV were included in the Cabinet. Qarase claimed that Mahendra Chaudhry had not accepted that the Government should be based fundamentally on nationalist Fijian principles. In October 2001, when members of the House of Representatives were sworn in, Chaudhry refused to accept the position of Leader of the Opposition, a title that consequently fell to Prem Singh, leader of the NFP. In December Parliament approved the Social Justice Bill, a programme of affirmative action favouring Fijians and Rotumans in education, land rights and business-funding policies.

The Prime Minister defended himself against demands for his resignation in January 2002 following allegations that he had broken the Electoral Act by pledging some $F25m. of funds from the Ministry of Agriculture to pro-indigenous Fijian businesses during the 2001 election campaign. In February 2002, furthermore, an appeal court ruled that the Prime Minister had violated the Constitution by failing to incorporate any member of the opposition FLP in his Cabinet. Qarase had previously declared that he would resign if the legal challenge against him were to be successful. (The newly appointed Chief Justice, Daniel Fatiaki, was himself under scrutiny in mid-2002—the Chief Justice being appointed on the advice of the Prime Minister and the Leader of the Opposition, and being responsible for assembling the Supreme Court.) In September the High Court ruled that Prem Singh, the NFP leader, was not entitled to retain his parliamentary seat (the validity of certain votes cast at the 2001 election having been questioned). The disputed seat was therefore allocated to a member of the FLP. Also in September, in advance of the ruling by the Supreme Court on the issue of the inclusion of the FLP in the Cabinet, the Prime Minister effected a ministerial reorganization, assuming personal responsibility for a number of additional portfolios.

Meanwhile, in June 2002 the Prime Minister and the FLP leader co-operated briefly in addressing the issue of expiring land leases that were threatening Fiji's sugar industry. A committee, comprising members of both the SDL and FLP, was established to try to negotiate land leases that would satisfy both Indian Fijian tenants and their predominantly ethnic Fijian landowners. Most of the 30-year leases drawn up under the ALTA (see above) were expiring, and both tenants and the FLP were opposed to its replacement by the Native Land Trust Act (NLTA), which they saw as disproportionately favouring landowners. Two parliamentary bills had been approved by the Senate in April, reducing the land under state control to around 1% of the total and increasing the amount under the Native Land Trust Board to over 90%.

In August 2002, however, the FLP abandoned a second round of land lease discussions and announced that it would boycott most of the proceedings in the current session of Parliament. Chaudhry accused the Government of attempting to accelerate the passage of six bills through Parliament without regard for the mandatory 30 days' notice of a bill being tabled. He also complained that the Government had not given the FLP the full details of the proposed NLTA. The Prime Minister protested that this would compel the Government to accept the decision of the Great Council of Chiefs regarding the leases. Tensions between the ruling SDL and the FLP and, furthermore, between Fijians and Indian Fijians had been further exacerbated by anti-Indian comments made by the Minister for Women, Social Welfare and Land Resettlement, Asenaca Caucau, which the Prime Minister had not denounced. In September Qarase effected a reorganization of cabinet portfolios in which he assumed direct responsibility for the reform of the sugar industry and restated his commitment to resolve the long-standing issue of land leases.

The trial of George Speight and his accomplices on charges of treason opened in May 2001. (Speight was refused bail to enable him to occupy the seat that he won in the legislative election later in the year.) All the accused pleaded guilty to their involvement in the coup of May 2000, and at the conclusion of the trial in February 2002 Speight received the death sentence. Within hours of the verdict, however, President Iloilo signed a decree commuting the sentence to life imprisonment. Prison sentences of between 18 months and three years were imposed on 10 of Speight's accomplices, the charges of treason having been replaced by lesser charges of abduction. The trial of two other defendants on charges of treason began in July and, after being suspended as a result of technical problems, resumed in November, following the rejection of protests from the defendants that they were protected by an Immunity Decree promulgated by the Commander of the Fiji Military Forces, Frank Bainimarama.

In November 1989, meanwhile, the Fijian Government expelled the Indian ambassador to Fiji for allegedly interfering in Fiji's internal affairs, and the status of the Indian embassy was downgraded to that of a consulate. Relations between Fiji and India deteriorated following the coup of May 1987, when many ethnic Indians emigrated. In January 1989 statistical information, released by the interim Government, indicated that the islands' ethnic Fijians were in a majority for the first time since 1946. Following the adoption of significant constitutional reforms in 1997 diplomatic relations improved considerably, and in October the Indian Government invited Fiji to open a High Commission in New Delhi. In February 1999 India lifted its trade embargo against Fiji (which had been in force for 10 years), and in May India reopened its High Commission in Suva. However, Fiji's relations with the international community suffered a major reversal following the coup of May 2000, which was condemned by the UN, the Commonwealth, the United Kingdom, Australia, New Zealand and several other nations in the region. In June Fiji was partially suspended from the Commonwealth (having been readmitted in October 1997 following its expulsion after the coups of 1987) and a delegation of ministers of foreign affairs from the organization visited the islands to demand the reinstatement of the 1997 Constitution. Australia, New Zealand and the Commonwealth withheld formal recognition of Qarase's Government when Parliament opened in October 2001, but in December the Commonwealth Ministerial Action Group recommended that Fiji be readmitted to meetings of the Commonwealth. In November 2002 Qarase's Government confirmed its intention to reopen the Fijian High Commission in India, claiming that it was needed to cater for the new business and diplomatic links being fostered by the administration. It was reported that Indian business concerns had expressed interest in reviving Fiji's kava industry and that Indian film companies were interested in using Fiji as a location for filming. The sanctions imposed by the European Union (EU) remained in place until early 2002.

Relations with France meanwhile, were severely strained from 1995 by that country's decision to resume nuclear testing in the region. In January 2002 the French Government removed its sanctions against Fiji, following the islands' democratic election of the previous year.

Government

Fiji has a parliamentary form of government with a bicameral legislature, comprising the elected 71-seat House of Representatives and the appointed Senate, with 32 members. The Constitution states that 46 seats in the House are reserved on a racial basis (23 for ethnic Fijians, 19 for Indians, three for other races—General Electors—and one for Rotuma Islanders) and 25 seats are open to all races. The Senate is appointed by the President of the Republic, 14 members on the advice of the Great Council of Chiefs (a 70-member traditional body comprising every hereditary chief (Ratu) of a Fijian clan), nine on the advice of the Prime Minister, eight on the advice of the Leader of the Opposition and one on the advice of the Rotuma Island Council. In November 2002 the Prime Minister announced that he supported attempts by the Great Council of Chiefs to acquire legislative powers and indicated that these might be granted during 2003.

Defence

The Fiji Military Forces consist of men in the regular army, the Naval Squadron, the conservation corps and the territorials. The conservation corps was created in 1975 to make use of unemployed labour in construction work. In August 2002 the total armed forces numbered 3,500 men: 3,200 in the army and 300 in the navy. Budgetary expenditure on defence in 2001 was projected at $F58m.

Economic Affairs

In 2001, according to estimates by the World Bank, Fiji's gross national income (GNI), measured at average 1999–2001 prices, was US $1,755m, equivalent to $2,130 per head (or $5,140 on an international purchasing-power parity basis). During 1990–2001, it was estimated, the population increased at an average annual rate of 1.0%, while gross domestic product (GDP) per head increased, in real terms by an average of 1.4%. According to the Asian Development Bank (ADB), overall GDP increased, in real terms, at an average annual rate of 2.4% in 1990–2001. Following a contraction of 2.8% in 2000, the ADB estimated that Fiji's GDP had increased by 2.6% in 2001.

In 2000 agriculture (including forestry and fishing) contributed an estimated 15.9% of GDP. In that year, according to FAO, the sector engaged 39.8% of the economically active population. The principal cash crop is sugar cane, which normally accounts for about 80% of total agricultural production and 30% of the country's GDP. Following the successful implementation of a crop rehabilitation programme in the late 1990s, the sugar industry subsequently experienced a sharp decline in output owing to problems arising from the coup in May 2000 and from the issue of expiring land leases (see above). In 2001 sugar accounted for 21.0% of total export earnings. Sugar production declined by 25.9% in 2001 and was expected to remain at a similar level in 2002. Other important export crops are coconuts and ginger, while the most significant subsistence crop is paddy rice. Fishing became an increasingly important activity from the mid-1990s. In 2001 fish products earned some $98.3m in export revenue (8.0% of domestic export receipts) and accounted for some 10.8% of agricultural GDP. During 1990–2001, according to ADB estimates, agricultural GDP rose by an average annual rate of just 0.1%. Having increased by 16.1% in 1999, the sector's GDP was estimated to have declined by 1.2% in 2000 and by 2.4% in 2001.

Industry (including mining, manufacturing, construction and power) engaged 33.8% of the total number of paid employees in 1998, and provided an estimated 24.2% of GDP in 2000. The GDP of the industrial sector, according to the ADB, increased at an average rate of 3.0% per year during 1990–2001. The industrial sector's GDP was estimated to have decreased by 7.4% in 2000, before rising by 2.3% in 2001.

Mining contributed an estimated 2.4% of GDP in 2000, and engaged 1.8% of those in paid employment in 1999. Gold and silver are the major mineral exports. Production of gold declined from 3,794 kg in 2000 to 2,823 kg in 2001, when exports earned $F85.4m, equivalent to 7.0% of total export earnings. Gold exploration activity had increased dramatically in the mid-1990s (with the number of prospecting licences totalling 49 in late 1998). A copper-mining project in Namosi, central Viti Levu, began operations in 1997. The mining sector's GDP, however, declined in real terms at an estimated average annual rate of 0.6% between 1990 and 2001, a particularly sharp decrease of 14.1% being recorded in 2000.

Manufacturing contributed an estimated 13.7% of GDP in 2000 and engaged 26.0% of paid employees in 1999. The sector's GDP increased at an estimated average rate of 3.0% per year during 1990–2001. Compared with the previous year, manufacturing GDP decreased by 6.2% in 2000 but rose by an estimated 1.8% in 2001. The most important branch of the sector is food-processing, in particular sugar, molasses and coconut oil. The ready-made garment industry is also important and has particularly benefited from the tax-exemption scheme implemented by the Government in 1987. In 1997 there were 156 tax-exempt factories operating in the country, of which 96 were dedicated to garment manufacture. The sector engaged 85.8% of the 13,400 people employed in the tax-free sector in 1994. In late 1998 the Government sought to increase its trade quota with the USA, with the aim of exporting more garments to that country. Output from the garment industry increased by some 10% in 1999 owing to the introduction of preferential trade arrangements with Australia and New Zealand, but declined considerably in the following year as a result of the sanctions imposed by those countries in protest at the coup of May 2000. Garments represented 25.6% of export earnings in 2001.

Energy is derived principally from hydroelectric power, which provided some 90% of Fiji's electricity in the late 1990s. The electricity, gas and water sector accounted for 4.1% of GDP in 2000. Imports of mineral fuels represented 15.0% of the total cost of imports in 2001.

The services sector contributed an estimated 59.9% of GDP in 2000. During 1990–2001 the sector's GDP rose by an average annual rate of 2.5%, according to ADB estimates. The GDP of the services sector contracted by an estimated 1.1% in 2000 before rising by 4.2% in 2001. Tourism is Fiji's largest source of foreign exchange. In 2000, however, arrivals fell to 294,070 and earnings to $F426.3m., as a result of the events surrounding the coup of May of that year. Tourist numbers recovered somewhat in 2001 when 348,014 visited the country and the industry earned $F495.5m. Most visitors are from Australia (28.2% of total arrivals in 2001), followed by New Zealand (19.1%), the USA (16.6%), the United Kingdom (8.8%) and Japan (5.9%).

In 1999 Fiji recorded a visible trade deficit of US $115.6m., but a surplus of US $12.7m. on the current account of the balance of payments. According to the ADB, export earnings decreased from $F672.0m. in 2000 to $F650m. in 2001, while the cost of imports increased from $F755.5m. to $F812.3m. in the same period.. In 2001 the principal sources of imports were Australia (47.7%), New Zealand (13.8%) and Singapore (7.8%). The principal markets for exports were Australia (20.5%), the USA (27.8%) and the United Kingdom (12.1%). The principal imports in that year were basic manufactured goods (23.1% of total imports) and machinery and transport equipment (22.9%). The principal exports were sugar, gold, fish, re-exported petroleum products and ready-made garments.

In 2002 there was a projected budgetary deficit equivalent to some 6% of GDP. In 2002/03 Fiji received financial assistance from Australia totalling $A19.7m., and in the same period New Zealand contributed $NZ3.9m. in development aid. Fiji's total external debt was US $135.9m. at the end of 2000, of which US $101.2m. was long-term public debt. In that year the cost of debt-servicing was equivalent to 2.5% of the revenue from goods and services. The average annual rate of inflation was 3.4% in 1990–2000, decreasing to 1.1% in 2000. According to the ADB, the inflation rate increased to 4.3% in 2001. An estimated 12.1% of the total labour force were unemployed in 2000. Since 1987 Fiji has suffered a very high rate of emigration, particularly of skilled and professional personnel. Between January 1987 and December 1995 72,688 citizens emigrated from Fiji, of whom some 90% were Fijian Indians, with an estimated 30% described as professional or semi-professional workers. Emigration of professional and technical workers decreased by 2.8% in 2001, although the number of emigrants from the services sector increased by 28.2%.

Fiji is a member of the UN Economic and Social Commission for Asia and the Pacific, the Pacific Islands Forum (see p. 306), the Pacific Community (see p. 304), the Colombo Plan (see p. 339) and the International Sugar Organization (see p. 337). Fiji is also a signatory of the South Pacific Regional Trade and Economic Co-operation Agreement—SPARTECA (see p. 308) and the Lomé Conventions and successor Cotonou Agreement with the European Union (EU, see p. 199). In 1996 Fiji was admitted to the Melanesian Spearhead Group.

The overthrow of the Government during a coup in May 2000 and the subsequent installation of an unelected authority had a severe impact on Fiji's economy. A significant amount of that year's sugar crop was not harvested, and a large proportion of tourist bookings were cancelled. In addition, the islands lost a considerable sum of revenue owing to the withdrawal of foreign aid and faced further hardship through the imposition of economic sanctions and trade union boycotts from abroad (which particularly affected the mining sector and garment manufacture). It was estimated that 6,700 people lost their jobs in the second half of 2000, the overwhelming majority of these having been engaged either in tourist-related activities or in manufacturing. In response to the economic difficulties following the coup, the Government introduced an emergency interim budget in July 2000, including austerity measures which were successful in keeping government debt at a manageable level. The 2001 budget, announced in November 2000, reduced business taxes, as a way of stimulating investment in the economy. The Government signalled a yet more interventionist policy in the 2002 budget, with all income derived from exports in the 2001/02 financial year to be tax-exempt, with the percentage of export income taxed to rise gradually to 100% during 2003–09. Budgeted expenditure for 2002 was F$1,255m. This included $F283m. in capital expenditure for investment, and the Government established the Fiji Investment Corporation to manage and promote investment in tourism, forestry, fisheries and inter-island shipping services. The budget projected an increase in economic growth to 3.5% in 2002, compared with an estimated GDP growth rate of 1.5% in 2001. The 2003 budget, announced in November 2002, was widely criticized for its proposal to increase value-added tax from 10% to 12.5%. Opponents claimed that the higher tax would increase inflationary pressures and contribute towards the continued emigration of skilled workers from Fiji.

Education

Education in Fiji is compulsory at primary level. The Government planned to extend the duration of compulsory free education in 2002. Primary education begins at six years of age, lasts for eight years and is provided free of charge. Secondary education, beginning at the age of 14, lasts for a further three years. State subsidies are available for secondary and tertiary education in cases of hardship. In 1995 there were 709 primary schools (with a total enrolment of 142,912 pupils in 2000), 146 secondary schools (with an enrolment of 66,905 pupils in 2000), and in 1998 there were 33 vocational and technical institutions (with 1,730 enrolled students in 2000). In 1999 Fiji had four teacher-training colleges (with 1,003 students in 2000). In 1999 a total of 4,014 students were enrolled on campus at the University of the South Pacific and there were a further 5,194 extension students. Budgetary expenditure on education by the central Government in 2000 was projected at $F123.1m., representing 11.4% of total spending. The budget proposals for 2002 allocated $F217m. for education, an increase of $F39m.

Public Holidays

2003: 1 January (New Year's Day), 12 April (National Youth Day), 18–21 April (Easter), 12 May* (Birth of the Prophet

Muhammad), 2 June (Ratu Sir Lala Sukuna Day), 16 June (Queen's Official Birthday), 10 October (Fiji Day), 25 October (Diwali), 25–26 December (Christmas).

2004 (provisional): 1 January (New Year's Day), 9–12 April (Easter), 2 May* (Birth of the Prophet Muhammad), 3 May (National Youth Day), May/June (Ratu Sir Lala Sukuna Day), 15

June (Queen's Official Birthday), 7 October (Fiji Day), 12 November (Diwali), 25–26 December (Christmas).

*This Islamic holiday is dependent on the lunar calendar and may vary by one or two days from the dates given.

Weights and Measures

The metric system is in force.

Statistical Survey

Sources (unless otherwise stated): Bureau of Statistics, POB 2221, Government Bldgs, Suva; tel. 315144; fax 303656; internet www.statsfiji .gov.fj ; Reserve Bank of Fiji, POB 1220, Suva; tel. 313611; fax 301688; e-mail rbf@reservebank.gov.fj; internet www.reservebank.gov.fj.

AREA AND POPULATION

Area (incl. the Rotuma group): 18,376 sq km (7,095 sq miles). Land area of 18,333 sq km (7,078 sq miles) consists mainly of the islands of Viti Levu (10,429 sq km—4,027 sq miles) and Vanua Levu (5,556 sq km—2,145 sq miles).

Population: 715,375 at census of 31 August 1986; 775,077 (males 393,931, females 381,146) at census of 25 August 1996; 844,330 (estimate) at mid-2001.

Density (mid-2001): 45.9 per sq km.

Principal Towns (population at 1996 census): Suva (capital) 77,366; Lautoka 36,083; Nadi 9,170; Labasa 6,491; Ba 6,314.

Ethnic Groups (1996 census): Fijians 393,575; Indians 338,818; Part-European 11,685; European 3,103; Rotuman 9,727; Chinese 4,939; Other Pacific Islanders 10,463; Others 2,767; Total 775,077.

Births, Marriages and Deaths (registrations, 1998): Live births 17,944 (birth rate 22.5 per 1,000); Marriages 8,058 (marriage rate 10.1 per 1,000); Deaths 5,241 (death rate 6.6 per 1,000). Source: UN, *Demographic Yearbook*.

Expectation of Life (WHO estimates years at birth): 69.7 (males 67.8; females 71.8) in 2001. Source: WHO, *World Health Report*.

Economically Active Population (persons aged 15 years and over, census of 31 August 1986): Agriculture, hunting, forestry and fishing 106,305; Mining and quarrying 1,345; Manufacturing 18,106; Electricity, gas and water 2,154; Construction 11,786; Trade, restaurants and hotels 26,010; Transport, storage and communications 13,151; Financing, insurance, real estate and business services 6,016; Community, social and personal services 36,619; Activities not adequately defined 1,479; Total employed 222,971 (males 179,595, females 43,376); Unemployed 18,189 (males 10,334, females 7,855); Total labour force 241,160 (males 189,929, females 51,231). *1999* (total labour force, provisional): 330,800 (unemployed 25,100). *2000* (total labour force, provisional): 341,700 (unemployed 41,700).

HEALTH AND WELFARE

Key Indicators

Total Fertility Rate (children per woman, 2001): 3.0.

Under-5 Mortality Rate (per 1,000 live births, 2001): 21.

HIV/AIDS (% of persons aged 15–49, 2001): 0.07.

Physicians (per 1,000 head, 1997): 0.48.

Health Expenditure (2000): US $ per head (PPP): 194.

Health Expenditure (2000): % of GDP: 3.9.

Health Expenditure (2000): public (% of total): 65.2.

Access to Water (% of persons, 2000): 47.

Access to Sanitation (% of persons, 2000): 43.

Human Development Index (2000): ranking: 72.

Human Development Index (2000): value: 0.758.
For sources and definitions, see explanatory note on p. vi.

AGRICULTURE, ETC.

Principal Crops (mostly FAO estimates, '000 metric tons, 2001): Sugar cane 3,076; Coconuts 240; Copra 13 (2000); Cassava 33; Rice (paddy) 16; Sweet potatoes 6; Bananas 7; Yams 5; Taro 38. Source: FAO.

Livestock (FAO estimates, '000 head, year ending September 2001): Cattle 340; Pigs 137; Goats 246; Horses 44; Chickens 3,700. Source: FAO.

Livestock Products (mostly FAO estimates, metric tons, 2001): Poultry meat 7,874; Beef and veal 8,942; Goat meat 950; Pig meat 3,870; Hen eggs 3,773; Cows' milk 51,600; Butter and ghee 1,800; Honey 103. Source: FAO.

Forestry ('000 cubic metres, 2001): *Roundwood removals* (excl. bark): Sawlogs and veneer logs 200; Fuel wood 37; Pulpwood 273; Total 510. *Sawnwood production* (incl. sleepers): 79. Source: FAO, *Yearbook of Forest Products*.

Fishing (FAO estimates, '000 metric tons, live weight, 2000): Capture 37.6 (Groupers 1.4, Snappers 1.6, Emperors 2.7, Barracudas 2.7, Mullets 2.8, Narrow-barred Spanish mackerel 2.0, Albacore 5.2, Freshwater molluscs 5.0, Anadara clams 2.7, Other marine molluscs 3.0); Aquaculture 1.8; *Total catch* 39.4. Figures exclude aquatic plants ('000 metric tons): 0.6 (Capture 0.1, Aquaculture 0.5). Also excluded are trochus shells (158 metric tons), pearl oyster shells (12 tons) and corals (1,000 tons). Source: FAO, *Yearbook of Fishery Statistics*.

MINING

Production (kg, 2001): Gold 3,865; Silver 1,934.

INDUSTRY

Production (metric tons, 2001, unless otherwise indicated): Sugar 310,000; Molasses 142,000 (1997); Flour 59,569; Soap 5,341; Cement 98,000; Paint ('000 litres) 2,789; Beer ('000 litres) 18,000; Soft drinks ('000 litres) 24,160; Cigarettes 442; Matches ('000 gross boxes) 128; Electric energy (million kWh) 535 (1998 estimate); Ice cream ('000 litres) 1,257; Toilet paper ('000 rolls) 20,225. Source: UN, *Industrial Commodity Statistics Yearbook*.

FINANCE

Currency and Exchange Rates: 100 cents = 1 Fiji dollar ($F). *Sterling, US Dollar and Euro Equivalents* (31 December 2002): £1 sterling = $F3.3281; US $1 = $F2.0648; €1 = $F2.1654; $F100 = £30.47 = US $48.43 = €46.18. *Average Exchange Rate* ($F per US $): 2.8479 in 2000; 2.9017 in 2001; 2.8072 in 2002.

General Budget (provisional, $F million, 2000): *Revenue:* Current revenue 894 (Taxes 713, Non-taxes 181); Capital revenue 16; Total 910. *Expenditure:* General public services 125.1; Defence 60.2; Education 123.1; Health 72.8; Social security and welfare 1.6; Housing and community amenities 6.3; Economic services 109.4 (Agriculture 9.1, Industry 27.6, Electricity, gas and water 9.0, Transport and communications 21.4); Other purposes 583.5; Total 1,082 (Current 936, Capital 146. Source: Asian Development Bank, *Key Indicators of Developing Asian and Pacific Countries*. *2001* ($F million): Total revenue 921.7; Total expenditure 935.7.

International Reserves (US $ million at 31 December 2002): Gold (valued at market-related prices) 0.29; IMF special drawing rights 6.83; Reserve position in IMF 20.49; Foreign exchange 331.50; Total 359.11. Source: IMF, *International Financial Statistics*.

Money Supply ($F million at 31 December 2002): Currency outside banks 202.6; Demand deposits at commercial banks 495.9; Total money (incl. others) 712.0. Source: IMF, *International Financial Statistics*.

Cost of Living (Consumer Price Index; base: 1995 = 100): 114.8 in 1999; 116.1 in 2000; 121.0 in 2001. Source: IMF, *International Financial Statistics*.

Expenditure on the Gross Domestic Product ($F million at current prices, 1999): Government final consumption expenditure 588.2; Private final consumption expenditure 2,105.3; Increase in stocks 40.0; Gross fixed capital formation 390.2; *Total domestic expenditure* 3,123.7; Exports of goods and services 2,062.8; *Less* Imports of goods and services 1,818.5; Statistical discrepancy 220.4; *GDP in purchasers' values* 3,588.4. Source: IMF, *International Financial Statistics*.

Gross Domestic Product by Economic Activity ($F million at constant 1989 prices, 2000, preliminary): Agriculture, forestry and fishing 342.1; Mining and quarrying 51.1; Manufacturing 295.9; Electricity, gas and water 87.6; Building and construction 88.4; Wholesale and retail trade 331.8; Hotels and restaurants 50.2; Transport and communications 270.0; Finance, real estate, etc. 248.3; Community, social and personal services 376.4; Other services 16.3; Sub-total 2,158.1; *Less* Imputed bank service charges 125.8; GDP at factor cost 2,032.2. Source: Fiji Islands Trade and Investment Bureau.

Balance of Payments (US $ million, 1999): Exports of goods f.o.b. 537.7; Imports of goods f.o.b. –653.3; *Trade balance* –115.6; Exports of services 525.1; Imports of services –389.8; *Balance on goods and services* 19.7; Other income received 47.3; Other income paid–82.8; *Balance on goods, services and income* –15.8; Current transfers received 42.7; Current transfers paid –14.2; *Current balance* 12.7; Capital account (net) 14.0; Direct investment abroad–53.0; Direct investment from abroad –33.2; Other investment assets –62.2; Other investment liabilities 44.4; Net errors and omissions 32.5; *Overall balance* –44.9. Source: IMF, *International Financial Statistics.*

EXTERNAL TRADE

Principal Commodities ($F million, 2001): *Imports c.i.f.* (distribution by SITC): Food and live animals 310.8; Mineral fuels, lubricants, etc. 271.7; Chemicals and related products 143.3; Basic manufactures 417.4; Machinery and transport equipment 414.0; Miscellaneous manufactured articles 200.2; Total (incl. others) 1,807.9. *Exports f.o.b.:* Food and live animals 398.9; Beverages and tobacco 29.3; Crude materials (inedible) except fuels 52.2; Basic manufactures 65.8; Miscellaneous manufactured articles 354.1; Total (incl. others) 1,007.8. Source: Fiji Islands Trade and Investment Bureau.

Principal Trading Partners (US $ million, 2001): *Imports c.i.f.:* Australia 387.3; China, People's Republic 27.3; Hong Kong 25.8; India 16.2; Japan 29.1; Malaysia 12.0; New Zealand 112.1; Singapore 63.6; Thailand 16.2; USA 21.3; Total (incl. others) 812.3. *Exports:* Australia 133.0; Hong Kong 10.9; Japan 32.0; Kiribati 9.3; New Zealand 22.0; Portugal 16.4; Samoa 31.0; Tonga 15.0; United Kingdom 79.0; USA 181.0; Total (incl. others) 650.0. Source: Asian Development Bank, *Key Indicators of Developing Asian and Pacific Countries.*

TRANSPORT

Road Traffic (motor vehicles registered at 31 December 1998): Passenger cars 47,053; Goods vehicles 34,182; Buses 1,801; Taxis 2,956; Rental vehicles 4,714; Motorcycles 4,409; Tractors 5,404; Total (incl. others) 104,760.

Shipping: *Merchant Fleet* (registered at 31 December 2001): Vessels 50; Total displacement ('000 grt) 28.7. (Source: Lloyd's Register-Fairplay, *World Fleet Statistics.*) *International Freight Traffic* ('000 metric tons, 1990): Goods loaded 568; Goods unloaded 625. (Source: UN, *Monthly Bulletin of Statistics*).

Civil Aviation (traffic on scheduled services, 1999): Passengers carried 525,000; Passenger-kilometres 2,159 million; Total ton-kilometres 218 million. Source: UN, *Statistical Yearbook.*

TOURISM

Foreign Visitors by Country of Residence (excluding cruise-ship passengers, 2001): Australia 98,213, Canada 10,752, Japan 20,411, New Zealand 66,472, Pacific Islands 23,608, United Kingdom 30,508, USA 57,711; Total (incl. others) 348,014.

Tourism Receipts ($F million): 558.6 in 1999; 413.5 in 2000; 495.5 in 2001.

COMMUNICATIONS MEDIA

Radio Receivers (1999): 545,000 in use*.

Television Receivers (2000): 92,000 in use†.

Telephones (2001): 90,400 main lines in use†.

Facsimile Machines (1999): 2,815 in use†.

Mobile Cellular Telephones (2001): 76,000 subscribers†.

Personal Computers (2001): 50,000 in use†.

Internet Users (2001): 15,000†.

Book Production (1980): 110 titles (84 books, 26 pamphlets); 273,000 copies (229,000 books, 44,000 pamphlets).

Daily Newspaper (2001): 3 (estimated combined circulation 49,124)‡.

Non-daily Newspapers (provisional, 1988): 7 (combined circulation 99,000)*.

* Source: UNESCO, *Statistical Yearbook.*
† Source: International Telecommunication Union.
‡ Source: Audit Bureau of Circulations, Australia.

EDUCATION

Primary (2000): 709 schools (1995); 5,082 teachers; 142,912 pupils.

General Secondary (2000): 146 schools (1995); 3,696 teachers; 66,905 pupils.

Vocational and Technical (2000): 33 institutions (1998); 1,024 teachers (including special schools); 1,730 students.

Teacher Training (2000): 4 institutions (1999); 97 teachers; 1,003 students.

Medical (1989): 2 institutions; 493 students.

University (1999): 1 institution; 277 teachers (1991); 9,208 students.
Source: mainly UNESCO, *Statistical Yearbook*, and UN, *Statistical Yearbook for Asia and the Pacific.*

Adult Literacy Rate (UNESCO estimates): 92.9% (males 94.9%, females 90.8%) in 2000 (Source: UN Development Programme, *Human Development Report*).

Directory

The Constitution

On 1 March 2001 President Iloilo reinstated the 1997 Constitution, after the Great Council of Chiefs (Bose Levu Vakaturaga—a traditional body, with some 70 members, consisting of every hereditary chief or Ratu of each Fijian clan) had approved the draft. The Constitution Amendment Bill that was approved in July 1997 included provisions to ensure of a multi-racial Cabinet. The following is a summary of the main provisions:

The Constitution, which declares Fiji to be a sovereign, democratic republic, guarantees fundamental human rights, a universal, secret and equal suffrage and equality before the law for all Fijian citizens. Citizenship may be acquired by birth, descent, registration or naturalization and is assured for all those who were Fijian citizens before 6 October 1987. Parliament may make provision for the deprivation or renunciation of a person's citizenship. Ethnic Fijians, and the Polynesian inhabitants of Rotuma, receive special constitutional consideration. The Judicial and Legal Services Commission, the Public Service Commission and the Police Service Commission are established as supervisory bodies.

THE GREAT COUNCIL OF CHIEFS

The Great Council of Chiefs (Bose Levu Vakaturaga) derives its authority from the status of its members and their chiefly lineage. The Great Council appoints the President of the Republic and selects the 14 nominees for appointment to the Senate, the upper chamber of the Parliament.

The Great Council became fully independent of the Government in mid-1999.

THE EXECUTIVE

Executive authority is vested in the President of the Republic, who is appointed by the Great Council of Chiefs, for a five-year term, to be constitutional Head of State and Commander-in-Chief of the armed forces. The Presidential Council advises the President on matters of national importance. The President, and Parliament, can be empowered to introduce any necessary measures in an emergency or in response to acts of subversion which threaten Fiji.

In most cases the President is guided by the Cabinet, which conducts the government of the Republic. The Cabinet is led by the Prime Minister, who is a Fijian of any ethnic origin and is appointed by the President from among the members of Parliament, on the basis of support in the legislature. The Prime Minister selects the other members of the Cabinet (the Attorney-General, the minister responsible for defence and security and any other ministers) from either the House of Representatives or the Senate on a multi-party and multiracial basis. The Cabinet is responsible to Parliament.

THE LEGISLATURE

Legislative power is vested in the Parliament, which comprises the President, the appointed upper house or Senate and an elected House of Representatives. The maximum duration of a parliament is five years.

The Senate has 32 members, appointed by the President of the Republic for the term of the Parliament. A total of 14 senators are nominated by the Great Council of Chiefs, nine are appointed on the advice of the Prime Minister, eight on the advice of the Leader of the Opposition, and one on the advice of the Rotuma Island Council. The Senate is a house of review, with some powers to initiate legislation, but with limited influence on financial measures. The Senate is important in the protection of ethnic Fijian interests, and its consent is essential to any attempt to amend, alter or repeal any provisions affecting ethnic Fijians, their customs, land or tradition.

The House of Representatives has 71 elected members, who themselves elect their presiding officials and the Speaker from outside the membership of the House, and Deputy Speaker from among their number (excluding ministers). Voting is communal, with universal suffrage for all citizens of the Republic aged over 21 years. Seats are reserved on a racial basis: 23 for ethnic Fijians, 19 for Indians, three for other races (General Electors), one for Rotuma Islanders and 25 open seats. Elections must be held at least every five years and are to be administered by an independent Supervisor of Elections. An independent Boundaries Commission determines constituency boundaries.

THE JUDICIARY

The judiciary is independent and comprises the High Court, the Fiji Court of Appeal and the Supreme Court. The High Court and the Supreme Court are the final arbiters of the Constitution. The establishment of Fijian courts is provided for, and decisions of the Native Lands Commission (relating to ethnic Fijian customs, traditions and usage, and on disputes over the headship of any part of the Fijian people, with the customary right to occupy and use any native lands) are declared to be final and without appeal.

The Government

HEAD OF STATE

President: Ratu JOSEFA ILOILO (appointed 12 July 2000 by an interim authority established following the coup of 19 May 2000).

Vice-President: Ratu JOPE SENILOLI.

THE CABINET
(April 2003)

Prime Minister, Minister for Fijian Affairs, Culture and Heritage, National Reconciliation and Unity: LAISENIA QARASE.

Minister for Foreign Affairs and External Trade: KALIOPATE TAVOLA.

Minister for Finance, National Planning and Communications: Ratu JONE KUBUABOLA.

Attorney-General and Minister for Justice: QORINIASI BALE.

Minister for Lands and Mineral Resources: Ratu NAIQAMA LALABALAVU.

Minister for Works and Energy: SAVENACA DRAUNIDALO.

Minister for Education: RO TEIMUMU VUIKABA KEPA.

Minister for Tourism: PITA NACUVA.

Minister for Transport and Civil Aviation: JOSEFA VOSANIBOLA.

Minister for Labour, Industrial Relations and Productivity: KENNETH ZINCK.

Minister for Commerce, Business Development and Investment: TOMASI VUETILOVONI.

Minister for Information and Media Relations: SIMIONE KAITANI.

Minister for Local Government, Housing, Squatter Settlement and Environment: MATAIASI VAVE RAGIGIA.

Minister of Health: SOLOMONE NAIVALU.

Minister for Agriculture, Sugar and Land Resettlement: JONETANI GALUINADI.

Minister for Regional Development: ILAITIA TUISESE.

Minister for Women, Social Welfare and Poverty Alleviation: ASENACA CAUCAU.

Minister for Youth, Employment Opportunities and Sports: ISIRELI LEWENIQILA.

Minister for Home Affairs and Immigration: JOKETANI COKANASIGA.

Minister for Fisheries and Forests: KONISI YABAKI.

Minister for Public Enterprises and Public Sector Reform: IRAMI MATAIRAVULA.

Minister for Multi-Ethnic Affairs: GEORGE SHIU RAJ.

MINISTRIES

Office of the President: Government Bldgs, POB 2513, Suva; tel. 3314244; fax 3301645.

Office of the Prime Minister: Government Bldgs, POB 2353, Suva; tel. 3211201; fax 3306034; e-mail pmsoffice@is.com.fj; internet www.fiji.gov.fj.

Office of the Attorney-General and Ministry of Justice: Government Bldgs, Victoria Parade, POB 2213, Suva; tel. 3309866; fax 3305421.

Ministry of Agriculture, Sugar and Land Resettlement: PMB, POB 358, Raiwaqa; tel. 3384233; fax 3385048; e-mail maffinfo@is.com.fj.

Ministry of Commerce, Business Development and Investment: Government Bldgs, POB 2118, Suva; tel. 3305411; fax 3302617.

Ministry of Education: Marela House, Thurston St, PMB, Suva; tel. 3314477; fax 3303511.

Ministry of Fijian Affairs: Government Bldgs, POB 2100, Suva; tel. 3304200; fax 3302585.

Ministry of Finance and National Planning: Government Bldgs, POB 2212, Suva; tel. 3307011; fax 3300834.

Ministry of Fisheries and Forests: POB 2218, Government Bldgs, Suva; tel. 3301611; fax 3301595; e-mail forestry-hq@msd.gov.fj.

Ministry of Foreign Affairs and External Trade: Government Bldgs, POB 2220, Suva; tel. 3211458; fax 3301741; e-mail info@foreignaffairs.gov.fj; internet www.foreignaffairs.gov.fj.

Ministry of Health: Government Bldgs, POB 2223, Suva; tel. 3306177; fax 3306163; e-mail info@health.gov.fj.

Ministry of Home Affairs and Immigration: Government Bldgs, POB 2349, Suva; tel. 3211401; fax 3300346.

Ministry of Labour, Industrial Relations and Productivity: Government Bldgs, POB 2216, Suva; tel. 3211640; fax 3304701; e-mail minlabour@is.com.fj.

Ministry of Lands and Mineral Resources: Government Bldgs, POB 2222, Suva; tel. 3211556; fax 330437; e-mail mbaravilala@lands.gov.fj.

Ministry of Local Government, Housing, Squatter Settlement and Environment: *National Planning* : Government Bldgs, POB 2351, Suva; *Local Government* : Government Bldgs, POB 2131; *Environment* : Government Bldgs, POB 2131; tel. 3313411; fax 3304809; tel. 3211310; fax 3303515; tel. 3311069; fax 3312879; e-mail msovaki@govnet.gov.fj.

Ministry of National Reconciliation, Information and Media Relations: Government Bldgs, POB 2645, Suva; tel. 3211250; fax 3303146; e-mail info@fiji.gov.fj.

Ministry of Public Enterprise and Public Sector Reform: Government Bldgs, POB 2278, Suva; tel. 3315577; fax 3315035; e-mail achandoo2@govnet.gov.fj.

Ministry of Regional Development: Government Bldgs, POB 2219, Suva; tel. 3313400; fax 3313035.

Ministry of Tourism: Third Floor, Civic Tower, POB 1260, Suva; tel. 3312788; fax 3302060; e-mail infodesk@fijivb.gov.fj; internet www.bulafiji.com.

Ministry of Transport and Civil Aviation: POB 1260, Suva; tel. 3312788; fax 3302060; e-mail infodesk@fijifvb.gov.fj; internet www.bulafiji.com.

Ministry of Women, Social Welfare and Poverty Alleviation: POB 14068, Suva; tel. 3312199; fax 3303829; e-mail slomaloma@govnet.gov.fj.

Ministry of Works and Energy: POB 2493, Government Bldgs, Suva; tel. 3384111; fax 3383198.

Ministry of Youth, Employment Opportunities and Sports: Government Bldgs, POB 2448, Suva; tel. 3315960; fax 3305348.

Legislature

PARLIAMENT

Senate

The Senate is also known as the House of Review. The upper chamber comprises 32 appointed members (see The Constitution).

House of Representatives

The lower chamber comprises 71 elected members: 23 representing ethnic Fijians, 19 representing ethnic Indians, three representing other races (General Electors), one for Rotuma Islands and 25 seats open to all races.

Speaker: Ratu EPELI NAILATIKAU.

General Election, 25 August–1 September 2001

	Communal Seats			Open Seats	Total Seats
	Fijian	Indian	Other*		
Fiji United Party (SDL) . .	18	—	1	13	32
Fiji Labour Party (FLP) . .	—	19	—	8	27
Conservative Alliance Party (MV)	5	—	—	1	6
New Labour Unity Party (NLUP)	—	—	1	1	2
National Federation Party (NFP)	—	0	—	1	1
United General Party (UGP)	—	—	1	—	1
Independents	—	—	1	1	2
Total	23	19	4	25	71

* One Rotuman and three General Electors' seats.
Notes: The total includes one seat won by the Fiji United Party in a by-election held on 25 September 2001. In September 2002, following a court ruling, the one NFP seat was awarded to the FLP, thus bringing the latter's representation to 28 seats.

Political Organizations

Bai Kei Viti: Suva; f. 2001; Sec. Ratu TEVITA MOMOEDONU.

Fiji Indian Congress: POB 3661, Samabula, Suva; tel. 3391211; fax 3340117; f. 1991; Gen. Sec. VIJAY RAGHWAN.

Fiji Indian Liberal Party: Rakiraki; f. 1991; represents the interests of the Indian community, particularly sugar-cane farmers and students; Sec. SWANI KUMAR.

Fiji Labour Party (FLP): POB 2162, Government Bldgs, Suva; tel. 3305811; fax 3305317; e-mail flp@connect.com; internet www.flp.org.fj; f. 1985; Pres. JOKAPECI KOROI; Sec.-Gen. MAHENDRA PAL CHAUDHRY.

Fijian Association Party (FAP): Suva; f. 1995 by merger of Fijian Association (a breakaway faction of the SVT) and the multiracial All Nationals Congress; Leader Ratu TU'UAKITAU COKANAUTO (acting); Pres. Ratu VILIAME DREUNIMISIMISI.

Fijian Conservative Party: Suva; f. 1989 by former mems of the Fiji Nationalist Party and the Alliance Party; Leader ISIRELI VUIBAU.

Fijian Nationalist United Front Party (FNUFP): POB 1336, Suva; tel. 3362317; f. 1992 to replace Fijian Nationalist Party; seeks additional parliamentary representation for persons of Fijian ethnic origin, the introduction of other pro-Fijian reforms and the repatriation of ethnic Indians; Leader SAKEASI BAKEWA BUTADROKA.

Janata Party: Suva; f. 1995 by former mems of NFP and FLP.

Matanitu Vanua (MV) (Conservative Alliance Party): c/o House of Representatives, Suva; f. 2001; Leader GEORGE SPEIGHT.

National Federation Party (NFP): POB 13534, Suva; tel. 3305811; fax 3305317; f. 1960 by merger of the Federation Party, which was multiracial but mainly Indian, and the National Democratic Party; Leader PREM SINGH; Pres. SHIU CHARAN; Gen. Sec. ATTAR SINGH.

Nationalist Vanua Takolavo Party (NVTLP): c/o House of Representatives, Suva; Leader SAULA TELAWA.

New Labour Movement: Suva; Gen. Sec. MICHAEL COLUMBUS.

New Labour United Party (NLUP): Suva; f. 2001 by Tupeni Baba.

Party of National Unity (PANU): Ba; f. 1998 to lobby for increased representation for the province of Ba; Leader MELI BOGILEKA.

Soqosoqo Duavata ni Lewenivanua (SDL) (Fiji United Party): c/o House of Representatives, Suva; f. 1990; Leader LAISENIA QARASE.

Soqosoqo ni Vakavulewa ni Taukei (SVT) (Fijian Political Party): Suva; f. 1990 by Great Council of Chiefs; supports constitutional dominance of ethnic Fijians but accepts multiracialism; Pres. Ratu EPELI MATAITIUI.

Taukei Movement: POB 505, Lautoka; f. 1987, following merger of Taukei Liberation Front and Domo Ni Taukei group; right-wing indigenous Fijian nationalist group; Pres. Ratu TEVITA BOLOBOLO; Vice-Pres. Ratu INOKE KUBUABOLA; Gen. Sec. APISAI TORA.

United General Party (UGP): Suva; f. 1998 by the merger of the General Electors' Party and the General Voters' Party (fmrly the General Electors' Association, one of the three wings of the Alliance Party—AP, the ruling party 1970–87); represents the interests of the minority Chinese and European communities and people from other Pacific Islands resident in Fiji, all of whom are classed as General Electors under the 1998 Constitution; Pres. DAVID PICKERING.

Vanua Independent Party: Leader ILIESA TUVALOVO; Sec. URAIA TUISOVISOVI.

Veitokani ni Lewenivanua Vakarisito (VLV) (Christian Democratic Alliance): c/o House of Representatives, Suva; f. 1998 in opposition to constitutional reforms and to defend Christian and Melanesian interests; Leader POESCI WAQALEVU BUNE; Sec. TANIELA TABU.

Other minor parties that contested the 2001 election included the Justice and Freedom Party, the Dodonu ni Taukei Party, the Girmit Heritage Party, the General Voters' Party, the Lio'on Famor Rotuma Party and the Party of the Truth.

Supporters of secession are concentrated in Rotuma.

Diplomatic Representation

EMBASSIES AND HIGH COMMISSIONS IN FIJI

Australia: 37 Princes Rd, POB 214, Suva; tel. 3382211; fax 3382065; e-mail public-affairs-suva@dfat.gov.au; High Commissioner SUSAN BOYD.

China, People's Republic: 147 Queen Elizabeth Dr., PMB, Nasese, Suva; tel. 3300215; fax 3300950; e-mail chinaemb@is.com.fj; Ambassador ZHANG JUNSAI.

France: Dominion House, 7th Floor, Thomson St, Suva; tel. 3312233; fax 3301894; e-mail vidon@ambafrance.org.fj; Ambassador JEAN-PIERRE VIDON.

India: POB 471, Suva; tel. 3301125; fax 3301032; e-mail hicomindsuva@is.com.fj; High Commissioner ISHWAR SINGH CHAUHAN.

Japan: Dominion House, 2nd Floor, POB 13045, Suva; tel. 3304633; fax 3302984; e-mail eojfiji@is.com.fj; Ambassador HISATO MURAYAMA.

Korea, Republic: Vanua House, 8th Floor, PMB, Suva; tel. 3300977; fax 3303410; Ambassador LIM DAE-TAEK.

Malaysia: Pacific House, 5th Floor, POB 356, Suva; tel. 3312166; fax 3303350; e-mail mwsuva@is.com.fj; High Commissioner MOHAMMED TAKWIR DIN.

Marshall Islands: 41 Borron Rd, Government Bldgs, POB 2038, Suva; tel. 3387899; fax 3387115; Ambassador MACK KAMINAGA.

Micronesia, Federated States: 37 Loftus St, POB 15493, Suva; tel. 304566; fax 3300842; e-mail fsmsuva@sopacsun.sopac.org.fj; Ambassador KODARO MARTIN GALLEN.

Nauru: Ratu Sukuna House, 7th Floor, Government Bldgs, POB 2420, Suva; tel. 3313566; fax 3302861; High Commissioner CAMILLA SOLOMON.

New Zealand: Reserve Bank of Fiji Bldg, 10th Floor, Pratt St, POB 1378, Suva; tel. 3311422; fax 3300842; e-mail nzhc@is.com.fj; High Commissioner ADRIAN SIMCOCK.

Papua New Guinea: Credit Corporation House, 3rd Floor, Government Bldgs, POB 2447, Suva; tel. 3304244; fax 3300178; e-mail kundufj@is.com.fj; High Commissioner BABANI MARAGA.

Tuvalu: 16 Gorrie St, POB 14449, Suva; tel. 3301355; fax 3308479; High Commissioner TAUKELINA FINIKASO.

United Kingdom: Victoria House, 47 Gladstone Rd, POB 1355, Suva; tel. 3311033; fax 3301406; e-mail ukinfo@bhc.org.fj; internet www.ukinthepacific.bhc.org.fj; High Commissioner CHARLES MOCHAN.

USA: 31 Loftus St, POB 218, Suva; tel. 3314466; fax 3300081; e-mail usembsuva@is.com.fj; internet www.amembassy-fiji.gov; Ambassador DAVID LYON.

Judicial System

Justice is administered by the Supreme Court, the Fiji Court of Appeal, the High Court and the Magistrates' Courts. The Supreme Court of Fiji is the superior court of record presided over by the Chief Justice. The 1990 Constitution provided for the establishment of Fijian customary courts and declared as final decisions of the Native Lands Commission in cases involving Fijian custom, etc.

Supreme Court

Suva; tel. 3211524; fax 3300674.

Chief Justice: Daniel Fatiaki.

President of the Fiji Court of Appeal: Jai Ram Reddy.

Director of Public Prosecutions: Peter Ridgway.

Solicitor-General: Nainendra Nand.

Religion

CHRISTIANITY

Most ethnic Fijians are Christians. Methodists are the largest Christian group, followed by Roman Catholics. In the census of 1986 about 53% of the population were Christian (mainly Methodists).

Fiji Council of Churches: POB 2300, Government Bldgs, Suva; tel. (1) 3313798; f. 1964; seven mem. churches; Pres. Most Rev. Apimeleki Qilio; Gen. Sec. Benjamin Bhagwan.

The Anglican Communion

In April 1990 Polynesia, formerly a missionary diocese of the Church of the Province of New Zealand, became a full and integral diocese. The diocese of Polynesia is based in Fiji but also includes Wallis and Futuna, Tuvalu, Kiribati, French Polynesia, Cook Islands, Tonga, Samoa and Tokelau.

Bishop of Polynesia: Rt Rev. Jabez Leslie Bryce, Bishop's Office, 8 Desvoeux Rd, Suva; e-mail episcopus@connect.com.fj; tel. 3304716; fax 3302687.

The Roman Catholic Church

Fiji comprises a single archdiocese. At 31 December 1999 there were an estimated 86,141 adherents in the country.

Bishops' Conference: Episcopal Conference of the Pacific Secretariat (CEPAC), 14 Williamson Rd, POB 289, Suva; tel. 3300340; fax 3303143; e-mail cepac@is.com.fj; f. 1968; 17 mems; Pres. Most Rev. Michel Marie Calvet (Archbishop of Nouméa, New Caledonia); Gen. Sec. (vacant); Admin. Officer Thomas Tavutonivalu.

Regional Appeal Tribunal for CEPAC

14 Williamson Rd, POB 289, Suva; tel. 300340; fax 3303143; e-mail cepac@is.com.fj.

f. 1980; 17 mems; Judicial Vicar Rev. Theo Koster.

Archbishop of Suva: Most Rev. Petero Mataca, Archdiocesan Office, Nicolas House, Pratt St, POB 109, Suva; tel. 3301955; fax 3301565.

Other Christian Churches

Methodist Church in Fiji (Lotu Wesele e Viti): Epworth Arcade, Nina St, POB 357, Suva; tel. 3311477; fax 3303771; f. 1835; autonomous since 1964; 215,416 mems (1999); Pres. Rev. Tomasi Kanailagi; Gen. Sec. Rev. Laisiasa Ratabacaca.

Other denominations active in the country include the Assembly of God (with c. 7,000 mems), the Baptist Mission, the Congregational Christian Church and the Presbyterian Church.

HINDUISM

Most of the Indian community are Hindus. According to the census of 1986, 38% of the population were Hindus.

ISLAM

In 1993 some 8% of the population were Muslim. There are several Islamic organizations:

Fiji Muslim League: POB 3990, Samabula, Suva; tel. 3384566; fax 3370204; e-mail fijimuslim@is.com.fj; f. 1926; Nat. Pres. Hafizud Dean Khan; Gen. Sec. Nisar Ahmad Ali; 26 brs and 3 subsidiary orgs.

SIKHISM

Sikh Association of Fiji: Suva; Pres. Harkewal Singh.

BAHÁ'Í FAITH

National Spiritual Assembly: National Office, POB 639, Suva; tel. 3387574; fax 3387772; e-mail nsafijiskm@suva.is.com.fj; mems resident in 490 localities; national headquarters for consultancy and co-ordination.

The Press

NEWSPAPERS AND PERIODICALS

Coconut Telegraph: POB 249, Savusavu, Vanua Levu; f. 1975; monthly; serves widely-scattered rural communities; Editor Lema Low.

Fiji Calling: POB 12095, Suva; tel. 3305916; fax 3301930; publ. by Associated Media Ltd; every 6 months; English; Publr Yashwant Gaunder.

Fiji Cane Grower: POB 12095, Suva; tel. 3305916; fax 3305256.

Fiji Daily Post: 10–16 Toorak Rd, POB 2071, Govt Bldgs, Suva; f. 1987 as *Fiji Post* , daily from 1989; English; 45% govt-owned; Gen. Man. Anura Bandara (acting); Editor Jale Moala.

Fiji Magic: POB 12095, Suva; tel. 3305916; fax 3301930; e-mail review@is.com.fj; publ. by The Review Ltd; monthly; English; Publr Yashwant Gaunder.

Fiji Republic Gazette: Printing Dept, POB 98, Suva; tel. 3385999; fax 3370203; f. 1874; weekly; English.

Fiji Sun: Suva; re-established 1999; daily; Editor Mark Garret.

Fiji Times: 20 Gordon St, POB 1167, Suva; tel. 3304111; fax 3301521; f. 1869; publ. by Fiji Times Ltd; daily; English; Man. Dir Tony Ianni; Editor Samisoni Kakaiualu; circ. 34,000.

Fiji Trade Review: The Rubine Group, POB 12511, Suva; tel. 3313944; monthly; English; Publr George Rubine; Editor Mabel Howard.

Islands Business Magazine: 46 Gordon St, POB 12718, Suva; tel. 3303108; fax 3301423; e-mail editor@ibi.com.fj; internet www .pacificislands.cc; fmrly *Pacific Magazine* ; regional monthly news and business magazine featuring the Fiji Islands Business supplement; English; Publr Robert Keith-Reid; Editor-in-Chief Laisa Taga; circ. 8,500.

Na Tui: 422 Fletcher Rd, POB 2071, Govt Bldgs, Suva; f. 1988; weekly; Fijian; Publr Taniela Bolea; Editor Samisoni Bolatagici; circ. 7,000.

Nai Lalakai: 20 Gordon St, POB 1167, Suva; tel. 3304111; fax 3301521; e-mail fijitimes@is.com.fj; f. 1962; publ. by Fiji Times Ltd; weekly; Fijian; Editor Samisoni Kakaivalu; circ. 18,000.

Pacific Business: POB 12095, Suva; tel. 3305916; fax 3301930; publ. by Associated Media Ltd; monthly; English; Publr Yashwant Gaunder.

Pacific Telecom: POB 12095, Suva; tel. 3300591; fax 3302852; e-mail review@is.com.fj; publ. by Associated Media Ltd; monthly; English; Publr Yashwant Gaunder.

Pactrainer: PMB, Suva; tel. 3303623; fax 3303943; e-mail pina@is .com.fj; monthly; newsletter of Pacific Journalism Development Centre; Editor Peter Lomas.

PINA Nius: Pacific Islands News Association, 46 Gordon St, PMB, Suva; tel. 3303623; fax 3303943; e-mail pina@is.com.fj; internet www.pinarius.org; monthly newsletter of Pacific Islands News Association; Editor Nina Ratulele.

The Review: POB 12095, Suva; tel. 3305916; fax 3301930; e-mail review@is.com.fj; publ. by Associated Media Ltd; monthly; English; Publr Yashwant Gaunder.

Sartaj: John Beater Enterprises Ltd, Raiwaqa, POB 5141, Suva; f. 1988; weekly; Hindi; Editor S. Daso; circ. 15,000.

Shanti Dut: 20 Gordon St, POB 1167, Suva; f. 1935; publ. by Fiji Times Ltd; weekly; Hindi; Editor Nilam Kumar; circ. 12,000.

Top Shot: Suva; f. 1995; golf magazine; monthly.

Volasiga: 10–16 Toorak Rd, POB 2071, Suva; f. 1988; weekly; Fijian; Gen. Man. Anura Bandara (acting); Editor Samisoni Bolatagici.

The Weekender: 2 Dension Rd, POB 15652, Suva; tel. 3315477; fax 3305346; publ. by Media Resources Ltd; weekly; English; Publr Josefata Nata.

PRESS ASSOCIATIONS

Fiji Islands Media Association: c/o Vasiti Ivaqa, POB 12718, Suva; tel. 3303108; fax 3301423; national press asscn; operates Fiji

Press Club and Fiji Journalism Training Institute; Sec. NINA RATU-LELE.

Pacific Islands News Association: 46 Gordon St, PMB, Suva; tel. 3303623; fax 3303943; e-mail pina@is.com.fj; internet www.pinarius .org; regional press asscn; defends freedom of information and expression, promotes professional co-operation, provides training and education; Administrator NINA RATULELE; Pres. JOHNSON HON-IMAE.

Publishers

Fiji Times Ltd: POB 1167, Suva; tel. 3304111; fax 3302011; e-mail tyianni@fijitimes.com.fj; f. 1869; Propr News Corpn Ltd; largest newspaper publr; also publrs of books and magazines; Man. Dir TONY IANNI.

Lotu Pasifika Productions: POB 2401, Suva; tel. 3301314; fax 3301183; f. 1973; cookery, education, poetry, religion; Gen. Man. SERU L. VEREBALAVU.

University of the South Pacific: University Media Centre, POB 1168, Suva; tel. 3313900; fax 3301305; e-mail austin_l@usp.ac.fj; f. 1986; education, natural history, regional interests.

Government Publishing House

Printing and Stationery Department: POB 98, Suva; tel. 3385999; fax 3370203.

Broadcasting and Communications

TELECOMMUNICATIONS

Fiji International Telecommunicatons Ltd (FINTEL): 158 Victoria Parade, POB 59, Suva; tel. 3312933; fax 3300750; e-mail prichards@fintelfiji.com; 51% govt-owned; 49% C&W plc; CEO PHILIP RICHARDS.

Telcom Fiji Ltd: Private Mail Bag, Suva; tel. 3304019; fax 3301765; internet www.tfl.com.fj/; Chair. LIONEL YEE; CEO WINSTON THOMPSON.

Vodafone Fiji Ltd: Private Mail Bag, Suva; tel. 3312000; fax 3312007; e-mail aslam.khan@vodafone.com.fj; 51% owned by Telecom Fiji, 49% by Vodafone International Holdings BV; Man. Dir ASLAM KHAN.

BROADCASTING

Radio

Fiji Broadcasting Commission—FBC (Radio Fiji): Broadcasting House, POB 334, Suva; tel. 3314333; fax 3301643; f. 1954; statutory body; jointly funded by govt grant and advertising revenue; Chair. DANIEL WHIPPY; CEO SIRELI KINI.

Radio Fiji 1 broadcasts nationally on AM in English and Fijian;

Radio Fiji 2 broadcasts nationally on AM in English and Hindi;

Radio Fiji Gold broadcasts nationally on AM and FM in English;

104 FM and Radio Rajdhani 98 FM, mainly with musical programmes, broadcast in English and Hindi respectively, but are received only on Viti Levu;

Bula FM, musical programmes, broadcasts in Fijian, received only on Viti Levu.

Communications Fiji Ltd: 231 Waimanu Rd, PMB, Suva; tel. 3314766; fax 3303748; e-mail cfl@fm96.com.fj; f. 1985; operates three commercial stations; Man. Dir WILLIAM PARKINSON; Gen. Man. IAN JACKSON.

FM 96, f. 1985, broadcasts 24 hours per day, on FM, in English;

Navtarang, f. 1989, broadcasts 24 hours per day, on FM, in Hindi;

Viti FM, f. 1996, broadcasts 24 hours per day, on FM, in Fijian.

Radio Light: Shop 11B, Pacific Harbour Culture Centre, POB 319, Pacific Harbour; tel. and fax 3450007; e-mail radiolight@connect .com.fj; f. 1990; non-profit religious organization; broadcasts on FM 106 and FM 93.6; Station Man. and Programmes Dir DOUGLAS ROSE.

Radio Pasifik: POB 1168, University of the South Pacific, Suva; tel. 3313900; fax 3312591; e-mail schuster@usp.ac.fj; Gen. Man. ALFRED SCHUSTER.

Television

Film and Television Unit (FTU): c/o Ministry of Information and Communications, Govt Bldgs, POB 2225, Suva; tel. 3314688; fax 3300196; video library; production unit established by Govt and

Hanns Seidel Foundation (Germany); a weekly news magazine and local documentary programmes.

Fiji Television Ltd: 20 Gorrie St, POB 2442, Govt Bldgs, Suva; tel. 3305100; fax 3305077; e-mail fijitv@is.com.fj; internet www.fijitv .com; f. 1994; operates two services, Fiji 1, a free channel, and Sky Fiji, a three-channel subscription service; Chair. OLOTA ROKOVUNISEI; CEO KEN CLARK; Head of Programming RICHARD BROADBRIDGE.

Fiji Vision Ltd: Suva; f. 1997; subscription television; jointly-owned by Yasana Holdings Ltd and a Hawaiian consortium.

In 1990 two television stations were constructed at Suva and Monsavu, with aid from the People's Republic of China. A permanent television station became operational in July 1994.

Finance

In 1996 the Ministry of Finance announced that it had secured financial assistance for the undertaking of a study to investigate the possibility of developing an 'offshore' financial centre in Fiji.

BANKING

(cap. = capital; res = reserves; dep. = deposits; m. = million; brs = branches; amounts in Fiji dollars)

Central Bank

Reserve Bank of Fiji: Pratt St, PMB, Suva; tel. 3313611; fax 3301688; e-mail rbf@reservebank.gov.fj; internet www.reservebank .gov.fj; f. 1984 to replace Central Monetary Authority of Fiji; bank of issue; administers Insurance Act; cap. 2.0m., res 95.2m., dep. 226.0m. (Dec. 2001); Chair. and Gov. SAVENACA NARUBE.

Commercial Bank

Colonial National Bank : 3 Central St, POB 1166, Suva; tel. 3314400; fax 3302190; f. 1974 as National Bank of Fiji; 51% acquired from Fiji Govt by Colonial Ltd in 1999; 51% owned by Commonwealth Bank of Australia, 49% owned by Govt of Fiji; cap. 15.0m., res 0.3m., dep. 213.5m. (June 2001); Chair. MALAKAI NAIYAGA; Gen. Man. MIKE UPPERTON; 13 brs; 66 agencies.

Development Bank

Fiji Development Bank: 360 Victoria Parade, POB 104, Suva; tel. 3314866; fax 3314886; f. 1967; finances the development of natural resources, agriculture, transportation and other industries and enterprises; statutory body; cap. 50.8m., res 14.0m., dep. 182.6m. (June 1993); Chair. CHARLES WALKER; 9 brs.

Merchant Banks

Merchant Bank of Fiji Ltd: 231 Waimanu Rd, POB 14213, Suva; tel. 3314955; fax 3300026; e-mail merchantbk@connect.com.fj; f. 1986; owned by the Fijian Holdings Ltd (80%), South Pacific Trustees (20%); Man. Dir S. WETEILAKEBA; 3 brs.

National MBf Finance (Fiji) Ltd: Burns Philp Bldg, 2nd Floor, POB 13525, Suva; tel. 302232; fax 3305915; e-mail mbf@is.com.fj; f. 1991; 51% owned by the National Bank of Fiji, 49% by MBf Asia Capital Corpn Holding Ltd (Hong Kong); Chief Operating Officer SIEK KART; 4 brs.

Foreign Banks

Agence Française de Développement (ADF) (France): Suva; licensed to operate in Fiji in 1997.

Australia and New Zealand (ANZ) Banking Group Ltd: ANZ House, 25 Victoria Parade, POB 179, Suva; tel. 3213000; fax 3312527; bought Bank of New Zealand in Fiji (8 brs) in 1990; Gen. Man. (Fiji) DAVID BELL; 17 brs; 9 agencies.

Bank of Baroda (India): Bank of Baroda Bldg, Marks St, POB 57, Suva; tel. 3311400; fax 3302510; f. 1908; CEO S. K. BAGCHI; 7 brs; 2 agencies.

Bank of Hawaii (USA): 67–69 Victoria Parade, POB 273, Suva; tel. 3312144; fax 3312464; f. 1993; Gen. Man. BRIAN BLISS; 3 brs.

Habib Bank (Pakistan): Narsey's Bldg, Renwick Rd, POB 108, Suva; tel. 3304011; fax 3304835; e-mail hblfibas@is.com.fj; Chief Man. (Fiji) ABDUL MATIN; licensed to operate in Fiji 1990; 3 brs.

Westpac Banking Corporation (Australia): 1 Thomson St, Suva; tel. 3300666; fax 3301813; Chief Man. (Pacific Islands region) TREVOR WISEMANTEL; 12 brs; 9 agencies.

STOCK EXCHANGE

South Pacific Stock Exchange: Level 2, Plaza One, Provident Plaza, 33 Ellery St, POB 11689, Suva; tel. 3304130; fax 3304145; e-mail suvastockex@is.com.fj; internet www.suvastockex.com; formerly Suva Stock Exchange; name changed as above in 2000; Chair. FOANA T. NEMANI; Man. MESAKE NAWARI.

INSURANCE

Blue Shield (Pacific) Ltd: Parade Bldg, POB 15137, Suva; tel. 3311733; fax 3300318; Fijian co; subsidiary of Colonial Mutual Life Assurance Society Ltd; medical and life insurance; Chief Exec. SIALENI VUETAKI.

Colonial Mutual Life Assurance Society Ltd: Colonial Bldg, PMB, Suva; tel. 314400; fax 3303448; f. 1876; inc in Australia; life; Gen. Man. SIMON SWANSON.

Dominion Insurance Ltd: Civic House, POB 14468, Suva; tel. 3311055; fax 3303475; partly owned by Flour Mills of (Fiji) Ltd; general insurance; Man. Dir GARY S. CALLAGHAN.

FAI Insurance (Fiji) Ltd: Suva.

Fiji Reinsurance Corpn Ltd: RBF Bldg, POB 12704, Suva; tel. 3313471; fax 3305679; 20% govt-owned; reinsurance; Chair. Ratu JONE Y. KUBUABOLA; Man. PETER MARIO.

Fijicare Mutual Assurance: 41 Loftus St, POB 15808, Suva; tel. 3302717; fax 3302119; f. 1992; CEO JEFF PRICE.

Insurance Trust of Fiji: Loftus St, POB 114, Suva; tel. 3311242; fax 3302541; Man. SAMUEL KRISHNA.

National Insurance Co of (Fiji) Ltd: McGowan Bldg, Suva; tel. 3315955; fax 3301376; owned by New Zealand interests; Gen. Man. GEOFF THOMPSON.

New India Assurance Co Ltd: Harifam Centre, POB 71, Suva; tel. 3313488; fax 3302679; Man. MILIND A. KHARAT.

Queensland Insurance (Fiji) Ltd: Queensland Insurance Center, Victoria Parade, POB 101, Suva; tel. 3315455; fax 3300285; owned by Australian interests; Gen. Man. PETER J. NICHOLLS.

There are also two Indian insurance companies operating in Fiji.

Trade and Industry

GOVERNMENT AGENCIES

Fiji National Training Council (FNTC): Beaumont Rd, POB 6890, Nasinu; tel. 3392000; fax 3340184; e-mail gen-enq@fntc.ac.fj; internet www.fntc.ac.fj; Dir-Gen. NELSON DELAILOMALOMA.

Fiji Trade and Investment Board: Civic House, 6th Floor, Victoria Parade, Suva; tel. 3315988; fax 3301783; e-mail ftibinfo@ftib .org.fj; internet www.ftib.org.fj; f. 1980, restyled 1988, to promote and stimulate foreign and local economic development investment; Chair. JAMES DATTA; CEO JESONI VITUSAGAVULU.

Mineral Resources Department: Private Mail Bag, Suva; tel. 3381611; fax 3370039; e-mail director@mrd.gov.fj; internet www .mrd.gov.fj/index.html.

DEVELOPMENT ORGANIZATIONS

Fiji Development Company Ltd: POB 161, FNPF Place, 350 Victoria Parade, Suva; tel. 3304611; fax 3304171; e-mail hfc@is.com .fj; f. 1960; subsidiary of the Commonwealth Development Corpn; Man. F. KHAN.

Fiji-United States Business Council: CI-FTIB; POB 2303; Suva; f. 1998 to develop and expand trade links between the two countries; Pres. RAMENDRA NARAYAN.

Fijian Development Fund Board: POB 122, Suva; tel. 3312601; fax 3302585; f. 1951; funds derived from payments of $F20 a metric ton from the sales of copra by indigenous Fijians; deposits receive interest at 2.5%; funds used only for Fijian development schemes; Chair. Minister for Fijian Affairs; CEO VINCENT TOVATA.

Land Development Authority: c/o Ministry for Agriculture, Sugar and Land Resettlement, POB 5442, Raiwaqa; tel. 33384900; fax 33384058; f. 1961 to co-ordinate development plans for land and marine resources; Chair. JONETANI GALUINADI.

CHAMBERS OF COMMERCE

Ba Chamber of Commerce: POB 99, Ba; tel. 6670134; fax 6670132; Pres. DIJENDRA SINGH.

Labasa Chamber of Commerce: POB 121, Labasa; tel. 8811262; fax 8813009; Pres. SHIVLAL NAGINDAS.

Lautoka Chamber of Commerce and Industry: POB 366, Lautoka; tel. 6661834; fax 6662379; e-mail vaghco@connect.com.fj; Pres. NATWARLAL VAGH.

Levuka Chamber of Commerce: POB 85, Levuka; tel. 3440248; fax 3440252; Pres. ISHRAR ALI.

Nadi Chamber of Commerce: POB 2735, Nadi; tel. 6701704; fax 6702314; e-mail arunkumar@is.com.fj; Pres. VENKAT RAMANI AIYER.

Nausori Chamber of Commerce: POB 228, Nausori; tel. 3478235; fax 3400134; Pres. ROBERT RAJ KUMAR.

Sigatoka Chamber of Commerce: POB 882, Sigatoka; tel. 6500064; fax 6520006; Pres. NATWAR SINGH.

Suva Chamber of Commerce and Industry: 37 Viria Rd, Vatuwaqa Industrial Estate, POB 337, Suva; tel. 3380975; fax 3380854; f. 1902; Joint Sec. VERONIKA HANSRAJ; 150 mems.

Tavua-Vatukoula Chamber of Commerce: POB 698, Tavua; tel. 6680390; fax 6680390; Pres. SOHAN SINGH.

INDUSTRIAL AND TRADE ASSOCIATIONS

Fiji Forest Industries (FFI): Suva; Deputy Chair. Ratu SOSO KATONIVERE.

Fiji National Petroleum Co Ltd: Suva; f. 1991; govt-owned, distributor of petroleum products.

Fiji Sugar Corporation Ltd: Western House, 2nd and 3rd Floors, Cnr of Bila and Vidilo St, PMB, Lautoka; tel. 6662655; fax 6664685; nationalized 1974; buyer of sugar-cane and raw sugar mfrs; Chair. HAFIZUD D. KHAN; Man. Dir JONETANI K. GALUINADI.

Fiji Sugar Marketing Co Ltd: Dominion House, 5th Floor, Thomson St, POB 1402, Suva; tel. 3311588; fax 3300607; Man. Dir JONETANI GALUINADI.

Mining and Quarrying Council: 42 Gorrie St, Suva; tel. 33313188; fax 3302183; e-mail employer@is.com.fj; Chief Exec. K. A. J. ROBERTS.

National Trading Corporation Ltd: POB 13673, Suva; tel. 3315211; fax 3315584; f. 1992; a govt-owned body set up to develop markets for agricultural and marine produce locally and overseas; processes and markets fresh fruit, vegetables and ginger products; CEO APIAMA CEGUMALINA.

Native Lands Trust Board: POB 116, Suva; e-mail info@nltb.com .fj; internet www.nltb.com.fj; manages holdings of ethnic Fijian landowners; Gen. Man. KALIVATI BAKANI.

Pacific Fishing Co: Suva; fish-canning; govt-owned.

Sugar Cane Growers' Council: Canegrowers' Bldg, 3rd Floor, 75 Drasa Ave, Lautoka; tel. 6650466; fax 6650624; e-mail canegrower@ is.com.fj; f. 1985; aims to develop the sugar industry and protect the interests of registered growers; CEO JAGANNATH SAMI; Chair. RUSIATE MUSUDROKA.

Sugar Commission of Fiji: POB 5993, Lautoka; tel. 6664866; fax 6664051; e-mail scof@is.com.fj; Chair. GERALD BARRACK.

EMPLOYERS' ORGANIZATIONS

Fiji Employers' Federation: 42 Gorrie St, POB 575, Suva; tel. 3313188; fax 3302183; e-mail employer@fef.com.fj; represents 206 major employers; Pres. D. Y. AIDNEY; CEO KENNETH A. J. ROBERTS.

Fiji Manufacturers' Association: POB 1308, Suva; tel. 9212223; fax 3302567; e-mail volau-m@usp.ac.fj; internet www.fijibusiness .com; f. 1902; Pres. DESMOND WHITESIDE; 55 mems.

Local Inter-Island Shipowners' Association: POB 152, Suva; fax 3303389; Pres. VITI G. WHIPPY.

Textile, Clothing and Footwear Council: POB 10015, Nabua; tel. 3384777; fax 3370446; Sec. R. DUNSTAN.

UTILITIES

Electricity

Fiji Electricity Authority (FEA): PMB, Suva; e-mail ceo@fea.com .fj; tel. 3311133; fax 3311882; f. 1966; govt-owned; responsible for the generation, transmission and distribution of electricity throughout Fiji; CEO NIZAM UD-DEAN.

Water

Water and Sewerage Section: Public Works Dept, Ministry of Works and Energy, Nasilivata House, Kings Rd, PMB, Samabula; tel. 3384111; fax 3383013; e-mail rsshandil@fijiwater.gov.fj; Dir RAM SUMER SHANDIL.

TRADE UNIONS

Fiji Trades Union Congress (FTUC): 32 Des Voeux Rd, POB 1418, Suva; tel. 3315377; fax 3300306; e-mail ftucl@is.com.fj; f. 1951; affiliated to ICFTU and ICFTU—APRO; 35 affiliated unions; more than 42,000 mems; Pres. DANIEL URAI; Gen. Sec. FELIX ANTHONY.

Principal affiliated unions:

Association of USP Staff: POB 1168, Suva; tel. 3313900; fax 3301305; f. 1977; Pres. GANESH CHAND; Sec. D. R. RAO.

Federated Airline Staff Association: Nadi Airport, POB 9259, Nadi; tel. 6722877; fax 6790068; Sec. RAM RAJEN.

Fiji Aviation Workers' Association: FTUC Complex, 32 Des Voeux Rd, POB 5351, Raiwaqa; tel. 3303184; fax 3311805; Pres. VALENTINE SIMPSON; Gen. Sec. ATTAR SINGH.

Fiji Bank and Finance Sector Employees' Union: 101 Gordon St, POB 853, Suva; tel. 3301827; fax 3301956; e-mail fbeu@connect.com.fj; Nat. Sec. DIWAN C. SHANKAR.

Fiji Electricity and Allied Workers Union: POB 1390, Lautoka; tel. 6666353; e-mail feawu@is.com.fj; Pres. LEONE SAKETA; Sec. J. A. PAUL.

Fiji Garment, Textile and Allied Workers' Union: c/o FTUC, Raiwaqa; f. 1992.

Fiji Nursing Association: POB 1364, Suva; tel. 3305855; Gen. Sec. KUINI LUTUA.

Fiji Public Service Association: 298 Waimanu Rd, POB 1405, Suva; tel. 3311922; fax 3301099; e-mail fpsa@is.com.fj; f. 1943; 3,434 mems; Pres. AISEA BATISARESARE; Gen. Sec. RAJESHWAR.SINGH.

Fiji Sugar and General Workers' Union: 84 Naviti St, POB 330, Lautoka; tel. 6660746; fax 664888; 25,000 mems; Pres. SHIU LINGAM; Gen. Sec. FELIX ANTHONY.

Fiji Teachers' Union: 1–3 Berry Rd, Govt Bldgs, POB 2203, Suva; tel. 3314099; fax 3305962; e-mail ftn@is.com.fj; f. 1930; 3,200 mems; Pres. BALRAM; Gen. Sec. AGNI DEO SINGH.

Fijian Teachers' Association: POB 14464, Suva; tel. 3315099; fax 3304978; e-mail fta@.com.fj; Pres. TARITA KOREI; Gen. Sec. MAIKA NAMUDU.

Insurance Officers' Association: POB 71, Suva; tel. 3313488; Pres. JAGDISH KHATRI; Sec. DAVID LEE.

Mineworkers' Union of Fiji: POB 876, Tavua; f. 1986; Pres. HENNESY PETERS; Sec. KAVEKINI NAVUSO.

National Farmers' Union: POB 522, Labasa; tel. 8811838; 10,000 mems (sugar-cane farmers); Pres. DEWAN CHAND; Gen. Sec. M. P. CHAUDHRY; CEO MOHAMMED LATIF SUBEDAR.

National Union of Factory and Commercial Workers: POB 989, Suva; tel. 3311155; 3,800 mems; Pres. CAMA TUILEVEUKA; Gen. Sec. JAMES R. RAMAN.

National Union of Hotel and Catering Employees: Nadi Airport, POB 9426, Nadi; tel. 670906; fax 6700181; Pres. EMOSI DAWAI; Sec. TIMOA NAIVAHIWAQA.

Public Employees' Union: POB 781, Suva; tel. 3304501; 6,752 mems; Pres. SEMI TIKOICINA; Gen. Sec. FILIMONE BANUVE.

Transport and Oil Workers' Union: POB 903, Suva; tel. 3302534; f. 1988 following merger of Oil and Allied Workers' Union and Transport Workers' Union; Pres. J. BOLA; Sec. MICHAEL COLUMBUS.

There are several independent trade unions, including Fiji Registered Ports Workers' Union (f. 1947; Pres. Jioji Taholosale).

Transport

RAILWAYS

Fiji Sugar Corporation Railway: Rarawai Mill, POB 155, Ba; tel. 6674044; fax 670505; for use in cane-harvesting season, May–Dec. 595 km of permanent track and 225 km of temporary track (gauge of 600 mm), serving cane-growing areas at Ba, Lautoka and Penang on Viti Levu and Labasa on Vanua Levu; Gen. Man. ADURU KUVA.

ROADS

At the end of 1996 there were some 3,440 km of roads in Fiji, of which 49.2% were paved. A 500-km highway circles the main island of Viti Levu.

SHIPPING

There are ports of call at Suva, Lautoka, Levuka and Savusavu. The main port, Suva, handles more than 800 ships a year, including large passenger liners. Lautoka handles more than 300 vessels and liners and Levuka, the former capital of Fiji, mainly handles commercial fishing vessels. In 1996 a feasibility study into the possible establishment of a free port at Suva was commissioned. In May 1997 the Government approved 14 new ports of entry in the northern, western and central eastern districts of Fiji.

Maritime and Ports Authority of Fiji (MPAF): Administration Bldg, Princes Wharf, POB 780, Suva; tel. 3312700; fax 3300064; corporatized in 1998; Chair. DANIEL ELISHA; Port Master Capt. GEORGE MACOMBER.

Ports Terminals Ltd: POB S13, Suva; tel. 3304725; fax 3304769; e-mail herbert@suv.ptl.com.fj; f. 1998; stevedore, pilotage, storage and warehousing; CEO H. HAZELMAN; Port Manager E. KURUSIGA.

Burns Philp Shipping (Fiji) Ltd: Rodwell Rd, POB 15832, Suva; tel. 3315444; fax 3302754; e-mail burshipfiji@is.com.fj; shipping agents, customs agents and international forwarding agents; Gen. Man. DANNY REES.

Consort Shipping Line Ltd: Muaiwalu Complex, Rona St, Walubay, POB 152, Suva; tel. 3313344; fax 3303389; CEO HECTOR SMITH; Man. Dir JUSTIN SMIT.

Fiji Maritime Services Ltd: c/o Fiji Ports Workers and Seafarers Union, 36 Edinburgh Drive, Suva; f. 1989 by PAF and the Ports Workers' Union; services between Lautoka and Vanua Levu ports.

Inter-Ports Shipping Corpn Ltd: 25 Eliza St, Walu Bay; POB 152, Suva; tel. 3313638; f. 1984; Man. Dir JUSTIN SMITH.

Transcargo Express Fiji Ltd: POB 936, Suva; f. 1974; Man. Dir LEO B. SMITH.

Wong's Shipping Co Ltd: Suite 647, Epworth House, Nina St, POB 1269, Suva; tel. 3311867.

CIVIL AVIATION

There is an international airport at Nadi (about 210 km from Suva), a smaller international airport at Nausori (Suva) and 15 other airfields. Nadi is an important transit airport in the Pacific and in 1990 direct flights to Japan also began.

Airports Fiji Ltd: Nadi International Airport, Nadi; tel. 6725777; fax 6725 161; e-mail info@afl.com.fj; Chair. VILIAME S. J. GONELEVU; CEO JONE KOROITAMANA.

Air Fiji Ltd: 219 Victoria Parade, POB 1259, Suva; tel. 3314666; fax 3300771; internet www.airfiji.net; operates 65 scheduled services daily to 15 domestic destinations; daily service to Tonga and Tuvalu and direct flights to Auckland and Sydney commenced in 1999; charter operations, aerial photography and surveillance also conducted; partly owned by the Fijian Govt, which was expected to sell a majority of its shares in 2001; Chair. DOUG HAZARD; CEO KEN MACDONALD.

Air Pacific Ltd: Air Pacific Centre, POB 9266, Nadi International Airport, Nadi; tel. 6720777; fax 6720512; internet www.airpacific.com; f. 1951 as Fiji Airways, name changed in 1971; domestic and international services from Nausori Airport (serving Suva) to Nadi and international services to Tonga, Solomon Islands, Cook Islands, Vanuatu, Samoa, Japan, Australia, New Zealand and the USA; 51% govt-owned, 46.05% owned by Qantas (Australia); Chair. GERALD BARRACK; Man. Dir and CEO MICHAEL MCQUAY.

Fijian Airways International: POB 10138, Nadi International Airport, Nadi; tel. 6724702; fax 6724654; f. 1997; service to London via Singapore and Mumbai (India) planned; Chair. NEIL UNDERHILL; CEO ALAN LINDREA.

Hibiscus Air Ltd: Nadi International Airport, Nadi; domestic airline operating charter and non-scheduled flights around Fiji.

Sunflower Airlines Ltd: POB 9452, Nadi International Airport, Nadi; tel. 6723555; fax 6720085; e-mail sun@is.com.fj; internet www.fiji.to; f. 1980; scheduled flights to domestic destinations, also charter services; Man. Dir DON IAN COLLINGWOOD.

Vanua Air Charters: Labasa; f. 1993; provides domestic charter and freight services; Proprs Ratu Sir KAMISESE MARA, CHARAN SINGH.

Tourism

Scenery, climate, fishing and diving attract visitors to Fiji, where tourism is an important industry. The number of foreign tourist arrivals increased from 294,070 in 2000 to 348,014 in 2001 (excluding cruise-ship passengers who numbered 6,858 in 2001). In 2001 some 28.2% of visitors came from Australia, 19.1% from New Zealand, 16.6% from the USA, 8.8% from the United Kingdom and 5.9% from Japan. A total of 5,542 rooms in 187 hotels were available in 2001. Receipts from tourism increased from $F413.5m. in 2000 to $F495.5m. in 2001. The South Pacific Tourism Organization (formerly the Tourism Council of The South Pacific) is based in Suva. In 1998 the Government announced its intention further to develop the tourist industry in Fiji through the establishment of the Fiji Tourism Development Plan: 1998–2005. In April 1999 construction began on a new luxury resort at Korotoga, situated half-way between Suva and Nadi. The industry was severely affected by the coup of May 2000. However, tourism expanded significantly during 2002 and was expected to contribute substantially to high economic growth rates in the following years.

Fiji Hotel Association (FHA): 42 Gorrie St, GPOB 13560, Suva; tel. 3302980; fax 3300331; e-mail fha@connect.com.fj; represents 76 hotels; Pres. DIXON SEETO; Chief Exec. OLIVIA PARETI.

Fiji Visitors' Bureau: POB 92, Suva; tel. 3302433; fax 3300986; e-mail infodesk@fijifvb.gov.fj; internet www.bulafiji.com; f. 1923; Chair. SITIVENI WELEILAKEBA; Chief Exec. VILIAME GAVOKA; Dir of Tourism ERONI LUVENIYALI.

FINLAND

Introductory Survey

Location, Climate, Language, Religion, Flag, Capital

The Republic of Finland lies in northern Europe, bordered to the far north by Norway and to the north-west by Sweden. Russia adjoins the whole of the eastern frontier. Finland's western and southern shores are washed by the Baltic Sea. The climate varies sharply, with warm summers and cold winters. The mean annual temperature is 5°C (41°F) in Helsinki and –0.4°C (31°F) in the far north. There are two official languages: more than 93% of the population speak Finnish and 6% speak Swedish. There is a small Lapp population in the north. Almost all of the inhabitants profess Christianity, and about 85% belong to the Evangelical Lutheran Church. The national flag (proportions 11 by 18) displays an azure blue cross (the upright to the left of centre) on a white background. The state flag has, at the centre of the cross, the national coat of arms (a yellow-edged red shield containing a golden lion and nine white roses). The capital is Helsinki.

Recent History

Finland formed part of the Kingdom of Sweden until 1809, when it became an autonomous Grand Duchy under the Russian Empire. During the Russian revolution of 1917 the territory proclaimed its independence. Following a brief civil war, a democratic Constitution was adopted in 1919. The Soviet regime that came to power in Russia attempted to regain control of Finland but acknowledged the country's independence in 1920.

Demands by the USSR for military bases in Finland and for the cession of part of the Karelian isthmus, in south-eastern Finland, were rejected by the Finnish Government in November 1939. As a result, the USSR attacked Finland, and the two countries fought the 'Winter War', a fiercely contested conflict lasting 15 weeks, before Finnish forces were defeated. Following its surrender, Finland ceded an area of 41,880 sq km (16,170 sq miles) to the USSR in March 1940. In the hope of recovering the lost territory, Finland joined Nazi Germany in attacking the USSR in 1941. However, a separate armistice between Finland and the USSR was concluded in 1944.

In accordance with a peace treaty signed in February 1947, Finland agreed to the transfer of about 12% of its pre-war territory (including the Karelian isthmus and the Petsamo area on the Arctic coast) to the USSR, and to the payment of reparations, which totalled about US $570m. when completed in 1952. Meanwhile, in April 1948 Finland and the USSR signed the Finno-Soviet Treaty of Friendship, Co-operation and Mutual Assistance (the YYA treaty), which was extended for periods of 20 years in 1955, 1970 and again in 1983. A major requirement of the treaty was that Finland repel any attack made on the USSR by Germany, or its allies, through Finnish territory. (The treaty was replaced by a non-military agreement in 1992, see below.)

Since independence in 1917, the politics of Finland have been characterized by coalition governments (including numerous minority coalitions) and the development of consensus between parties. The Social Democratic Party (Sosialidemokraattinen Puolue, SDP) and the Centre Party (Keskusta—Kesk) have usually been the dominant participants in government. The conservative opposition gained significant support at a general election in March 1979, following several years of economic crises. A new centre-left coalition Government was formed in May, however, by Dr Mauno Koivisto, a Social Democratic economist and former Prime Minister. This four-party Government, comprising Kesk, the SDP, the Swedish People's Party (Svenska Folkpartiet, SFP) and the Finnish People's Democratic League (Suomen Kansan Demokraattinen Liitto, SKDL—an electoral alliance, which included the communists, continued to pursue deflationary economic policies, although there were disagreements within the Council of State (Cabinet) in 1981, over social welfare policy and budgetary matters.

Dr Urho Kekkonen, who had been President since 1956, resigned in October 1981. Dr Koivisto was elected President in January 1982. He was succeeded as head of the coalition by a former Prime Minister, Kalevi Sorsa, a Social Democrat. Towards the end of 1982 the SKDL refused to support austerity measures or an increase in defence spending. This led to the reformation of the coalition in December, without the SKDL, until the general election of March 1983.

At this election the SDP won 57 of the 200 seats in the Eduskunta (Parliament), compared with 52 in the 1979 election; while the conservative opposition National Coalition Party (Kansallinen Kokoomus—Kok) lost three seats. In May Sorsa formed another centre-left coalition, comprising the SDP, the SFP, Kesk and the Finnish Rural Party (Suomen Maaseudun Puolue, SMP): the coalition parties held a total of 122 parliamentary seats.

At a general election held in March 1987, the combined non-socialist parties gained a majority in the Eduskunta for the first time since the election of 1945. Although the SDP remained the largest single party, losing one seat and retaining 56, the system of modified proportional representation enabled Kok to gain an additional nine seats, winning a total of 53, while increasing its share of the votes cast by only 1%. President Koivisto eventually invited Harri Holkeri, a former Chairman of Kok, to form a coalition Government comprising Kok, the SDP, the SFP and the SMP, thus avoiding a polarization of the political parties within the Eduskunta. The four parties controlled 131 of the 200 seats. Holkeri became the first conservative Prime Minister since 1946, and Kesk joined the opposition for the first appreciable length of time since independence.

In February 1988 Koivisto retained office after the first presidential election by direct popular vote (in accordance with constitutional changes adopted in the previous year), following his campaign for a reduction in presidential power. He did not win the required absolute majority, however, and an electoral college was convened. Koivisto was re-elected after an endorsement by the Prime Minister, Holkeri, who had also contested the presidency and who had received the third highest number of direct votes (behind Paavo Väyrynen, the leader of Kesk).

At a general election held in March 1991, Kesk obtained 55 of the 200 seats in the Eduskunta, the SDP gained 48 seats, and Kok 40 seats. In April a coalition Government, comprising Kesk, Kok, the SFP and the Finnish Christian Union (Suomen Kristillinen Liitto, SKL), took office. The new coalition constituted the country's first wholly non-socialist Government for 25 years. The Chairman of Kesk, Esko Aho, was appointed Prime Minister. In March 1993 President Koivisto announced that he would not present himself as a candidate for a third term in the forthcoming presidential election. In the first stage of the election, which took place in January 1994, the two most successful candidates were Martti Ahtisaari (the SDP candidate and a senior United Nations official), with 25.9% of the votes cast, and Elisabeth Rehn (the SFP candidate and Minister of Defence), with 22%. The Kesk candidate (Paavo Väyrynen) obtained 19.5% of the votes cast, and the Kok candidate 15.2%. Both of the leading candidates were firm supporters of Finland's application for membership of the European Union (EU, see p. 199), as the European Community (EC) had been restyled in late 1993. In accordance with constitutional changes adopted since the previous election (stipulating that, if no candidate gained more than 50% of the votes cast, the electorate should choose between the two candidates with the most votes), a second stage of the election took place in February 1994. It was won by Ahtisaari (with 53.9% of the votes cast), who took office in March.

At a general election held in March 1995, the SDP obtained 63 of the 200 seats in the Eduskunta, Kesk secured 44 seats, Kok 39 seats, and the Vasemmistoliitto (Left Alliance), formed in 1990 by a merger of the communist parties and the SKDL 22 seats. A new coalition Government was formed in April, comprising the SDP, Kok, the SFP, the Vasemmistoliitto and the Vihreä Liitto (VL—Green League). Paavo Lipponen, the leader of the SDP, replaced Aho as Prime Minister, and Sauli Niinistö, the Chairman of Kok, was appointed Deputy Prime Minister.

Following a general election held on 21 March 1999, the SDP remained the largest party in the Eduskunta, gaining 51 of the 200 seats. Kesk won 48 seats and Kok 46 in an election that was characterized by the second lowest rate of voter participation—

68%—since 1945. In April the five parties of the outgoing Government—the SDP, Kok, the SFP, the Vasemmistoliitto and the VL—agreed to form a new coalition. The terms of the new coalition agreement stipulated that the SDP leader, Paavo Lipponen, should remain in office as Prime Minister, while the leader of Kok, Sauli Niinistö, was reappointed as Minister of Finance. The remaining portfolios of the Council of State were redistributed among the coalition partners. Another element of the coalition agreement was that there should be no increase (in real terms) in public expenditure during the term in office of the new legislature.

Presidential elections were held in January and February 2000, at which Ahtisaari did not seek re-election, following his failure to secure the nomination of the SDP. In mid-January seven candidates contested the first round of the ballot, which was won by Tarja Halonen (the SDP candidate and Minister of Foreign Affairs), who received 40% of the votes cast; the second largest share of the vote (34.4%) was obtained by Esko Aho (the Kesk candidate). As Halonen had failed to win 50% of the vote, a second round of voting was held on 6 February, contested by Halonen and Aho. This second stage of the election was won by Halonen (with 51.6% of the votes cast), who took office as the first female President of Finland on 1 March. Following the conclusion of the elections, a minor reorganization of the Council of State was effected, in which Halonen was replaced as Minister of Foreign Affairs by Erkki Tuomioja, the former Minister of Trade and Industry.

A new Constitution entered into force on 1 March 2000, under the provisions of which the executive power of the President was significantly reduced while the real authority of the Eduskunta was increased, with the power of decision-making being divided more equally between the Eduskunta, the Council of State and the President. According to the 1919 Constitution, the President appointed the Prime Minister and the other ministers; however, under the new Constitution, the Eduskunta elects the Prime Minister (who is then officially appointed by the President) and the other government ministers are appointed by the President on the basis of nominations by the Prime Minister. In addition, according to new constitutional provisions, the President was to co-operate more closely with the Council of State with regard to issues of foreign policy.

Following his defeat in the presidential election, the Chairman of the opposition Kesk, Aho, took leave from domestic politics for one year from August 2000 to lecture at Harvard University in the USA. His decision was believed to reflect the perceived stability of the coalition, which, despite its disparate composition, seemed likely to carry out its full four-year term in government. Anneli Jäättenmäki, a former Minister of Justice, was elected to replace Aho during his sabbatical. At municipal elections that were held on 22 October 2000, however, the two principal parties in the coalition (the SDP and Kok) suffered losses, whilst Kesk, under the leadership of Jäätteenmäki, secured the largest gains, winning 23.8% of the votes cast to become the largest municipal party. Voter participation in the local elections was only 55.8% of the electorate (compared with 61.3% in 1996). Popular support for Jäätteenmäki's leadership prompted Aho's resignation in mid-2002 and the election of Jäätteenmäki as Chairman.

In November 2000, the stability of the coalition Government was threatened by a controversial proposal by a Finnish electricity company to build a fifth nuclear reactor in Finland, the first such proposal in western Europe since the mid-1980s. The Government was divided over the issue, with the SDP Minister of Trade and Industry, Sinikka Mönkäre, in favour of the proposal, while the VL was strongly opposed to nuclear expansion and threatened to leave the coalition should the proposal be accepted. In January 2002 the proposal was approved by the Council of State, despite the opposition of seven ministers, led by the Chairman of the VL and Minister of Health and Social Services, Osmo Soininvaara. The Eduskunta approved the construction of the reactor in May by 107 votes to 92, prompting the resignation of the VL from the coalition Government; the coalition retained a majority in the Eduskunta with 130 seats.

In November 2002 the opposition proposed a motion of 'no confidence' in the Government over its role in the unprofitable investments of the telecommunications company, Sonera. Sonera, which was 53% owned by the Government, had invested €8,400m. in a German third generation mobile telephone licence in 2000; in July 2002 it announced its intention to write off a debt of €4,300m. A government inquiry into the affair, which was launched in August, published its findings in October,

exonerating the Prime Minister and the Council of State from any responsibility for the corporate error. The Government survived the motion by 106 voted to 64.

Legislative elections were held on 16 March 2003; 69.6% of the electorate participated in the poll. The opposition Kesk, which had campaigned on a platform of improvements to public health-care, promoting employment by lowering social contributions and income taxes for low paid jobs and relaxing legislation for small businesses, won the largest representation in the new Parliament with 24.7% of the votes cast, securing 55 seats in the Eduskunta. The SDP won 24.5% of the votes cast and 53 seats, an increase of two seats compared with the last election. Although the SDP made gains, the three other members of the former government coalition lost seats, with Kok suffering the worst reverse with the loss of six seats (winning 18.5% of the votes and 40 seats). Lipponen's coalition tendered its resignation to the President but continued as a caretaker administration pending the formation of a new government. The Eduskunta met at the end of March and named Jäätteenmäki as its Speaker. Under the new Constitution the party with the largest representation would lead negotiations for a coalition government. In early April Kesk formed a coalition Government with the SDP and the SFP (which won 4.6% of the vote and thus 8 seats) with Jäätteenmäki as Prime Minister.

In foreign affairs, Finland has traditionally maintained a neutral stance, although the pursuance of friendly relations with the USSR, and latterly Russia, has generally been regarded as a priority. In October 1989 Mikhail Gorbachev became the first Soviet Head of State to visit Finland since 1975, and recognized Finland's neutral status. The 1948 Finno-Soviet Treaty of Friendship, Co-operation and Mutual Assistance, which bound Finland to a military defence alliance with the USSR and prevented the country from joining any international organization (including the EC) whose members posed a military threat to the USSR, was replaced in January 1992 by a 10-year agreement, signed by Finland and Russia, which involved no military commitment. The agreement was to be automatically renewed for five-year periods unless annulled by either signatory. The new treaty also included undertakings by the two countries not to use force against each other and to respect the inviolability of their common border and each other's territorial integrity. In 1998 a Russian diplomat to Finland, who had reportedly been involved in an incident of espionage, left the country at the request of the Finnish authorities; a second Russian diplomat, who had also allegedly been involved in the incident, left the country voluntarily, while an official from the Finnish Ministry of Foreign Affairs was suspended. In June 2000 the Finnish official was found guilty of espionage and of having passed confidential EU documents to the Russian diplomats; the details of the case were declared secret for 30 years. In the same month the Finnish President, Halonen, paid an official visit to Russia and held a cordial meeting with his Russian counterpart, Vladimir Putin. Good bilateral relations continued with Russian into 2003 when in March the Finnish Minister of Foreign Affairs, Erkki Tuomioja visited Moscow for discussions with his Russian counterpart.

Finland joined the United Nations and the Nordic Council (see p. 266) in 1955 but became a full member of the European Free Trade Association (EFTA, see p. 195) only in 1986. In 1989 Finland joined the Council of Europe (see p. 181). A free-trade agreement between Finland and the EC took effect in 1974. In March 1992 the Finnish Government formally applied to join the EC, despite opposition from farmers, who feared the impact of membership on Finland's strongly-protected agricultural sector. In a referendum on the question of Finland's accession to membership of the EU, which was held on 16 October 1994, 56.9% of the votes cast were in favour of membership, and in November the treaty of accession was ratified after protracted debate in the Eduskunta. Opponents of EU membership highlighted the benefits of Finland's traditional policy of neutrality, particularly with regard to Russian national security considerations, and warned that the country would now be increasingly forced to identify with Western security policy. The Government declared, however, that Finland's neutral stance would not be compromised either by joining the EU or by its stated intention to participate in NATO's 'Partnership for Peace' programme, and announced that it would not seek full membership of NATO (see p. 271) or Western European Union (WEU, see p. 318). The decision not to apply for membership of NATO was reiterated in May 1995 by the new Prime Minister, Paavo Lipponen. Finland left EFTA and joined the EU, as scheduled, on 1 January 1995. Following the devastating terrorist attacks of 11 September 2001 in the USA, Finland did not participate in the US-led retaliatory military action against the Taleban regime in Afghanistan. Finnish military personnel did, however, take part in the subsequent peace-keeping operation in Afghanistan as part of a wider UN-authorized multinational body (the International Security Assistance Force—ISAF) including NATO forces. In January 2003 Lipponen commissioned a report into the possible economic effects of Finnish entry into NATO; a security policy report was scheduled to be compiled in 2004. Finland was opposed to military action in Iraq in early 2003 without a UN Security Council resolution but indicated that it would be prepared to take part in military action under UN auspices and in possible humanitarian and peace-keeping operations.

Finland has proved its commitment to European integration. For instance, the so-called 'rainbow coalition', formed in 1995 and renewed in 1999, ensured the country's adherence to the economic 'convergence' criteria for Stage III of economic and monetary union (EMU), which commenced on 1 January 1999. In July of that year Finland assumed the presidency of the EU for the first time. During its six-month incumbency the Government had intended to promote economic and cultural links in the so-called 'Northern Dimension'—the Nordic countries, the Baltic states and Russia. In the event, this agenda was superseded by the conflict over the Serbian region of Kosovo and Metohija in Yugoslavia (now Serbia and Montenegro), which led to Western military intervention from March. Finland was deemed to have distinguished itself through its diplomacy, in particular the role of the Finnish President, which was important in securing an end to the hostilities in Yugoslavia.

A joint Finnish-Norwegian survey of the two countries' border in Arctic Lapland concluded in January 2002 that the Inarijoki River, the deepest point of which is taken to mark the border, had changed its course. Consequently, an unnamed island in the middle of the river, which had previously been Norwegian, was found to be part of Finland. Norway accordingly transferred the island to Finland.

Government

Finland has a republican Constitution, under the provisions of which executive power is divided between the Eduskunta (Parliament), the Council of State (Cabinet) and the President. The unicameral Eduskunta has 200 members, elected by universal adult suffrage for four years on the basis of proportional representation. The President is elected for six years by direct popular vote. Legislative power is exercised by the Eduskunta. The Eduskunta elects the Prime Minister, who is then appointed by the President. The other government ministers are appointed by the President on the basis of nominations by the Prime Minister. Finland is divided into 452 municipalities, which are guaranteed self-government and are entitled to levy taxes. The province of Ahvenanmaa (the Åland Islands) has rights of legislation in internal affairs.

Defence

In August 2002 the armed forces of Finland numbered 31,850 (of whom 15,500 were conscripts serving up to 12 months), comprising an army of 24,550 (11,500 conscripts), an air force of 2,700 (1,500 conscripts) and a navy of 4,600 (2,200 conscripts). There were also some 485,000 reserves (to be reduced to 430,000) and a 3,100-strong frontier guard (under the Ministry of the Interior). The proposed defence budget for 2003 was 1,945m. euros (equivalent to 5.4% of total proposed budgetary expenditure).

Economic Affairs

In 2001, according to estimates by the World Bank, Finland's gross national income (GNI), measured at average 1999–2001 prices, was US $124,171m., equivalent to $23,940 per head (or $25,180 per head on an international purchasing-power parity basis). During 1990–2001, it was estimated, the population increased at an average annual rate of 0.4%, while gross domestic product (GDP) per head increased, in real terms, by an average of 1.7% per year. Overall GDP increased, in real terms, at an average annual rate of 2.0% per year in 1990–2001; growth in 2001 was 0.7%.

Agriculture (including hunting, forestry and fishing) contributed an estimated 3.6% of GDP in 2000 and employed 5.4% of the working population in 2002. Forestry is the most important branch of the sector, with products of the wood and paper industries providing about 20.7% of export earnings in 2000.

Animal husbandry is the predominant form of farming. The major crops are barley, oats and sugar beet. During 1990–2000 agricultural GDP increased, in real terms, by an average of 0.5% per year; agricultural GDP declined by 2.2% in 1999, but increased by 7.3% in 2000.

Industry (including mining, manufacturing, construction and power), provided 33.3% of GDP in 2000 and employed 26.9% of the working population in 2002. Industrial GDP increased, in real terms, by an average of 3.9% per year during 1990–2000; industrial GDP grew by 6.2% in 1999 and by 10.9% in 2000.

Mining and quarrying contributed 0.2% of GDP in 2000 and employed 0.2% of the working population in the same year. The GDP of the mining sector increased, in real terms, at an average rate of 3.4% per year during 1995–99; mining GDP declined by 17.8% in 1998, but increased by 18.0% in 1999. Gold is the major mineral export, and zinc ore, copper ore and lead ore are also mined in small quantities.

Manufacturing provided 25.7% of GDP in 2000, and in the same year employed 20.0% of the working population. The most important branches of manufacturing are the electronics industry (particularly mobile telephones), transport equipment, metal products and food and beverages. The GDP of the manufacturing sector increased, in real terms, at an average rate of 4.6% per year during 1990–99; the sector's GDP increased by 9.6% in 1998 and by 7.1% in 1999.

Of total energy generated in 1999 33.1% was derived form nuclear energy, 20.9% from coal, 18.4% from hydroelectric power, 13.7 from natural gas and 1.3% from petroleum. At the end of 2000 there were four nuclear reactors in operation; plans for a fifth reactor were approved by the Eduskunta in 2002. Imports of mineral fuels comprised 11.9% of the total cost of imports in 2000.

Services provided 63.1% of GDP in 2000 and engaged 67.7% of the employed labour force in 2002. In real terms, the combined GDP of the services sector increased at an average rate of 1.7% per year during 1990–2000; growth in the sector's GDP was recorded at 3.8% in 1999 and 3.2% in 2000.

In 2001 Finland recorded a visible trade surplus of US $12,657m., and there was a surplus of $8,631m. on the current account of the balance of payments. In 2000 the principal source of imports was Germany (providing 14.3% of total imports); other major sources were Sweden (10.3%), the USA (10.1%), Russia (9.4%) and the United Kingdom (6.5%). Germany was also the principal market for exports in the same year (accounting for 12.5% of total exports); other major purchasers were Sweden (9.3%), the United Kingdom (9.1%), the USA (7.4%) and France (5.2%). The EU accounted for some 51.8% of exports and 68.8% of imports in 2000. The principal exports in 2000 were machinery and transport equipment (mainly electronic products, notably mobile telephones), basic manufactures (mainly paper, paperboard and manufactures) and crude materials (mainly wood and pulp). The principal imports were machinery and transport equipment, basic manufactures, chemicals and related products and miscellaneous manufactured articles.

In 2001 Finland recorded an overall budget surplus of 1,006m. euros (equivalent to 0.7% of GDP). At the end of September 1999 Finland's gross public debt amounted to some €49,340m. The average annual rate of inflation was 1.8% during 1990–99. Consumer prices increased by 2.6% in 2001, and by 1.8% in 2002. The rate of unemployment declined from 15.4% in 1995 to 9.1% in 2001.

Finland is a member of the Nordic Council (see p. 266) and the Organisation for Economic Co-operation and Development (see p. 277). In January 1995 it left the European Free Trade Association (see p. 195) and joined the European Union (EU, see p. 199).

Throughout the 1990s the Finnish economy expanded consistently faster than the European average. The loss of control over monetary policy under European economic monetary union (EMU) became a problem for Finland as its economic cycle demanded higher interest rates than those set by the European Central Bank, to prevent the risk of rising inflation. However, strict fiscal policy proved effective and although inflation in 2000 was higher than in most European countries, it remained moderate. By 2003 Finland felt threatened by a possible relaxation of the EU's Stability and Growth Pact: Finland had managed to balance its budget despite consistently high levels of unemployment, and resented the possibility of higher interest rates and a weakened currency owing to a lack of fiscal discipline in some of its larger neighbours. Much of Finland's success was due to the mobile telephone manufacturer, Nokia, which alone accounted for more than 20% of exports in 1999, representing a divergence away from the traditional industries of pulp and paper production and metal engineering. However, by 2002 the downturn in the global telecommunications market slowed growth for Nokia and, as a consequence, for Finland as a whole. Nokia's losses were reflected on the Helsinki stock exchange, which performed poorly throughout the year. While this did little to affect consumer demand, it was expected to have an impact on government finances which had, until recently, benefited greatly from the tax income from Nokia and the windfall gains from the company's option schemes. Nevertheless, a budget surplus equivalent to 3.3% of GDP was forecast for 2002. Inflation was expected to remain low, and unemployment levels were forecast to start to decline; growth in both exports and internal demand was expected to accelerate by the end of 2003, with Finland's current-account surplus projected at 7% of GDP. Despite the deceleration in GDP growth, Finland's prospects for future economic progress remained promising. The country's stable economic climate, sound policy and clear legal structures prompted the World Economic Forum to rank Finland as the country with the best prospects for economic growth over the next five years.

Education

Compulsory education was introduced in 1921. By the 1977/78 school year, the whole country had transferred to a new comprehensive education system. Tuition is free and the core curriculum is the same for all students. Compulsory attendance lasts for nine years, and is divided into a six-year lower stage, beginning at the age of seven, and a three-year upper stage (or lower secondary stage), beginning at the age of 13. After comprehensive school, the pupil may continue his or her studies, either at a general upper secondary school, or a vocational upper secondary school. The upper secondary school curriculum is designed for three years but may be completed in two or four years. Courses leading to basic vocational qualifications take three years to complete. The matriculation examination taken at the end of three years of general upper secondary school gives eligibility for higher education as do three-year vocational diplomas. Higher education is provided by 20 universities and 25 polytechnics. Of total budgetary expenditure by the central Government in 2002, 5,810m. euros (16.3%) was allocated to the Ministry of Education.

Public Holidays

2003: 1 January (New Year's Day), 6 January (Epiphany), 18 April (Good Friday), 21 April (Easter Monday), 30 April–1 May (May Day), 29 May (Ascension Day), 9 June (Whitsun), 21–22 June (Midsummer Day), 1 November (All Saints' Day), 6 December (Independence Day), 24–26 December (Christmas).

2004: 1 January (New Year's Day), 6 January (Epiphany), 9 April (Good Friday), 12 April (Easter Monday), 30 April–1 May (May Day), 20 May (Ascension Day), 31 May (Whitsun), 21–22 June (Midsummer Day), 1 November (All Saints' Day), 6 December (Independence Day), 24–26 December (Christmas).

Weights and Measures

The metric system is in force.

Statistical Survey

Source (unless otherwise specified): Statistics Finland, 00022 Helsinki; tel. (9) 17342220; fax (9) 17342279; e-mail kirjasto.tilastokeskus.fi; internet www .tilastokeskus.fi.

Note: Figures in this Survey include data for the autonomous Åland Islands.

Area and Population

AREA, POPULATION AND DENSITY

Area (sq km)	
Land	304,473
Inland water	33,672
Total	338,145*
Population (census results)	
31 December 1995	5,116,826
31 December 2000	
Males	2,529,341
Females	2,651,774
Total	5,181,115
Population (official estimates at 31 December)	
1998	5,159,646
1999	5,171,302
2001	5,194,901
Density (per sq km) at 31 December 2001†	17.1

* 130,559 sq miles.

† Excluding inland waters.

REGIONS
(estimated population at 31 December 2001)*

	Land area (sq km)†	Population	Density (per sq km)
Uusimaa (Nyland)	6,366	1,318,324	207.1
Itä-Uusimaa (Östra Nyland)	2,747	90,201	32.8
Varsinais-Suomi (Egentliga Finland)	10,624	449,293	42.3
Satakunta	8,289	236,308	28.5
Kanta-Häme (Egentliga Tavastland)	5,204	165,509	31.8
Pirkanmaa (Birkaland)	12,272	450,745	36.7
Päijät-Häme (Päijänne-Tavastland)	5,133	197,656	38.5
Kymenlaakso (Kymmenedalen)	5,106	186,707	36.6
Etelä-Karjala (Södra Karelen)	5,618	137,019	24.4
Etelä-Savo (Södra Savolax)	14,137	164,471	11.6
Pohjois-Savo (Norra Savolax)	16,808	252,842	15.0
Pohjois-Karjala (Norra Karelen)	17,782	170,793	9.6
Keski-Suomi (Mellersta Finland)	16,582	264,762	16.0
Etelä-Pohjanmaa (Södra Österbotten)	13,458	194,542	14.5
Pohjanmaa (Österbotten)	7,675	173,083	22.6
Keski-Pohjanmaa (Mellersta Österbotten)	5,286	70,848	13.4
Pohjois-Pohjanmaa (Norra Österbotten)	35,290	368,029	10.4
Kainuu (Kajanaland)	21,567	88,473	4.1
Lappi (Lappland)	93,004	189,288	2.0
Ahvenanmaa (Åland)	1,527	26,008	17.0
Total	**304,473**	**5,194,901**	**17.1**

* According to the regional division of 1 January 2002.

† Excluding inland waters, totalling 33,672 sq km.

PRINCIPAL TOWNS
(estimated population at 31 December 2001)*

Helsinki (Helsingfors) (capital)	559,718	Kuopio	87,347
Espoo (Esbo)	216,836	Jyväskylä	80,372
Tampere (Tammerfors)	197,774	Pori (Björneborg)	75,955
Vantaa (Vanda)	179,856	Lappeenranta (Villmanstrand)	58,401
Turku (Åbo)	173,686	Vaasa (Vasa)	57,014
Oulu (Uleåborg)	123,274	Kotka	54,768
Lahti	97,543	Joensuu	52,140

* According to the regional division of 1 January 2002.

BIRTHS, MARRIAGES AND DEATHS

	Registered live births* Number	Rate (per 1,000)	Registered marriages† Number	Rate (per 1,000)	Registered deaths* Number	Rate (per 1,000)
1994	65,231	12.8	24,898	4.9	48,000	9.4
1995	63,067	12.3	23,737	4.6	49,280	9.6
1996	60,723	11.8	24,464	4.8	49,167	9.6
1997	59,329	11.5	23,444	4.6	49,108	9.6
1998	57,108	11.1	24,023	4.7	49,262	9.6
1999	57,574	11.1	24,271	4.7	49,345	9.6
2000	56,742	11.0	26,150	5.1	49,339	9.5
2001	56,189	10.8	24,830	4.8	48,550	9.4

* Including Finnish nationals temporarily outside the country.
† Data relate only to marriages in which the bride was domiciled in Finland.

Expectation of life (WHO estimates, years at birth): 77.9 (males 74.5; females 81.2) in 2001 (Source: WHO, *World Health Report*).

ECONOMICALLY ACTIVE POPULATION*
(annual averages, '000 persons aged 15 to 74 years)

	2000	2001	2002
Agriculture, forestry and fishing	142	135	127
Mining and quarrying	4		
Manufacturing	467	497	491
Electricity, gas and water	22		
Construction	149	145	148
Trade, restaurants and hotels	354	357	363
Transport, storage and communications	171	174	169
Finance, insurance, real estate and business services	287	301	308
Community, social and personal services	732	750	759
Activities not adequately defined	6	7	7
Total employed	2,335	2,367	2,372
Unemployed	253	238	237
Total labour force	2,589	2,605	2,610

* Excluding persons on compulsory military service (21,000 in 1999; 20,000 in 2000; 15,500 in 2001).

Health and Welfare

KEY INDICATORS

Total fertility rate (children per woman, 2001)	1.6
Under-5 mortality rate (per 1,000 live births, 2001)	5
HIV/AIDS (% of persons aged 15–49, 2001)	<0.10
Physicians (per 1,000 head, 2001)	3.13
Hospital beds (per 1,000 head, 1998)	7.8
Health expenditure (2000): US $ per head (PPP)	1,667
Health expenditure (2000): % of GDP	6.6
Health expenditure (2000): public (% of total)	75.1
Access to water (% of persons, 2000)	100
Access to sanitation (% of persons, 2000)	100
Human Development Index (2000): ranking	10
Human Development Index (2000): value	0.930

For sources and definitions, see explanatory note on p. vi.

Agriculture

PRINCIPAL CROPS
('000 metric tons; farms with arable land of 1 hectare or more)

	1999	2000	2001
Wheat	254	538	489
Barley	1,568	1,985	1,786
Rye	24	108	64
Oats	990	1,413	1,287
Mixed grain*	44	56	44
Potatoes	791	785	733
Rapeseed*	88	87	101
Sugar beet	1,172	1,046	1,070

* Source: FAO.

LIVESTOCK
('000 head at 1 May; farms with arable land of 1 hectare or more)

	1999	2000	2001
Horses*	54.5	56.7	59
Cattle	1,086.8	1,056.7	1,037
Sheep	106.6	99.6	96
Reindeer	195.0	203.0	186
Pigs†	1,351.3	1,295.8	1,261
Poultry	4,386.6	4,024.4	4,245‡

* Including horses not on farms.
† Including piggeries of dairies.
‡ Provisional figure.

LIVESTOCK PRODUCTS
('000 metric tons)

	1999	2000	2001
Beef	90	90	89
Veal	0.2	0.3	n.a.
Pig meat	182	172	176
Poultry meat	66	64	76
Cows' milk*	2,325	2,371	2,378
Butter†	60	62	61
Cheese‡	88	93	98
Hen eggs	59	59	n.a.

* Millions of litres.
† Including amount of butter in vegetable oil mixture.
‡ Excluding curd.

Forestry

ROUNDWOOD REMOVALS
('000 cu m, excl. bark)

	1999	2000	2001
Sawlogs, veneer logs and logs for sleepers	25,090	25,994	23,359
Pulpwood	24,503	24,153	24,368
Fuel wood	4,044	4,115	4,483
Total	53,637	54,262	52,210

Source: FAO.

SAWNWOOD PRODUCTION
('000 cu m, incl. railway sleepers)

	1999	2000	2001
Coniferous (softwood)	12,708	13,320	12,670
Broadleaved (hardwood)	60*	100	100
Total	12,768	13,420	12,770

* FAO estimate.

Source: FAO.

Fishing

('000 metric tons, live weight)

	1998	1999	2000
Capture	171.7	160.6	162.9
Roaches	6.8	6.8	6.8
Northern pike	11.6	11.7	11.6
European perch	14.7	14.7	14.7
Atlantic herring	86.4	83.0	81.5
European sprat	27.0	18.9	23.1
Aquaculture	16.0	15.4	15.4
Rainbow trout	15.9	15.3	15.3
Total catch	187.7	176.0	178.3

Note: Figures exclude aquatic mammals, recorded by number rather than by weight. The catch of grey seals was 4 in 1998; 30 in 1999; 62 in 2000.

Source: FAO, *Yearbook of Fishery Statistics*.

Mining

('000 metric tons, unless otherwise indicated)

	1998	1999	2000
Copper ore*	9.5†	10.5†	11.6
Nickel ore (metric tons)*	1,967	8,079	2,600†
Zinc ore*†	30.7	20.0	16.2
Chromium ore†‡	610	635	640
Cobalt (metric tons)§	5,250	6,200	7,700
Mercury (metric tons)	54	40†	45†
Silver (metric tons)†§	29.7	31.5	23.6
Gold (kilograms)†§	5,000	5,900	5,000
Platinum (kilograms)†§	50	50	50
Palladium (kilograms)†§	150	150	150
Phosphate rock (incl. apatite)‖	716	724	750†
Talc	350†	469	360†
Peat: for fuel	1,700†	4,140	7,000†
Peat: for horticulture	150†	1,595	400†

* Figures refer to the metal content of ores.

† Estimated production.

‡ Figures refer to the gross weight of chromite. The estimated chromic oxide content (in '000 metric tons) was: 230 in 1998; 230 in 1999; 235 in 2000.

§ Figures refer to production of metal and (for cobalt) powder and salts.

‖ Figures refer to gross weight. The phosphoric acid content (in '000 metric tons) was: 260 in 1998; 268 (estimate) in 1999; 277 (estimate) in 2000.

Source: US Geological Survey.

Industry

SELECTED PRODUCTS

('000 metric tons, unless otherwise indicated)

	1998	1999*	2000*
Cellulose	6,385	6,482	7,383
Newsprint	1,594	1,579	1,394
Other paper, boards and cardboards	10,790	10,809	12,116
Plywoods and veneers ('000 cubic metres)	910	1,015	1,196
Cement	1,232	1,310	1,382
Pig iron and ferro-alloys	2,920	2,954	2,983
Electricity (net, million kWh)	67,324	62,555	67,899
Sugar	125	161	n.a.
Rolled steel products (metric tons)	3,715	3,783	3,902
Copper cathodes (metric tons)	122,894	114,700	n.a.
Cigarettes (million)	5,510	n.a.	n.a.

* Preliminary data.

Finance

CURRENCY AND EXCHANGE RATES

Monetary Units

100 cent = 1 euro (€)

Sterling and Dollar Equivalents (31 December 2002)

£1 sterling = 1.5370 euros

US $1 = 0.9536 euros

100 euros = £65.06 = $104.87

Average Exchange Rate (euros per US $)

2000	1.0854
2001	1.1175
2002	1.0626

Note: The national currency was formerly the markka (Finnmark). From the introduction of the euro, with Finnish participation, on 1 January 1999, a fixed exchange rate of €1 = 5.94573 markkaa was in operation. Euro notes and coins were introduced on 1 January 2002. The euro and local currency circulated alongside each other until 28 February, after which the euro became the sole legal tender. Some of the figures in this Survey are still in terms of markkaa.

BUDGET

(million euros)*

Revenue	2001	2002†	2003‡
Taxes and other levies	29,365	30,819	30,398
on income and property	12,743	13,545	13,327
on turnover	10,225	10,342	10,283
Excise duties	4,572	4,519	4,892
Miscellaneous revenues	4,491	4,056	4,131
Sub-total	33,856	34,875	34,529
Interest on investments and profits received	1,372	817	892
Loans receivable	198	134	301
Total	35,426	35,326	35,722

Expenditure	2001	2002†	2003‡
President of the Republic	5	6	7
Parliament	77	88	118
Council of State	39	37	39
Ministry of Foreign Affairs	663	712	722
Ministry of Justice	543	564	629
Ministry of the Interior	1,284	1,313	1,384
Ministry of Defence	1,653	1,715	1,945
Ministry of Finance	5,194	5,689	5,058
Ministry of Education	5,152	5,478	5,810
Ministry of Agriculture and Forestry	2,395	2,466	2,565
Ministry of Transport and Communications	1,763	1,318	1,638
Ministry of Trade and Industry	918	875	976
Ministry of Social Affairs and Health	7,606	8,147	8,471
Ministry of Labour	1,779	2,083	2,160
Ministry of the Environment	601	622	639
Public debt	6,400	4,211	3,562
Total	36,072	35,326	35,722

* Figures refer to the General Budget only, excluding the operations of the Social Insurance Institution and of other social security funds with their own budgets.

† Projections.

‡ Proposals.

INTERNATIONAL RESERVES

(US $ million at 31 December)

	2000	2001	2002
Gold*	430.0	436.0	541.0
IMF special drawing rights	138.7	234.1	199.9
Reserve position in IMF	497.5	551.7	648.3
Foreign exchange	7,341.0	7,198.0	8,347.0
Total	8,407.2	8,419.8	9,736.2

* Valued at market-related prices.

Source: IMF, *International Financial Statistics*.

MONEY SUPPLY
(million euros at 31 December)

	2000	2001	2002
Currency in circulation . . .	3,336	2,687	6,258
Demand deposits at banking institutions	37,129	39,014	40,960

* Of which only 3,446 million were put into circulation by the Bank of Finland.

Source: IMF, *International Financial Statistics*.

COST OF LIVING
(Consumer Price Index; base: 1995 = 100)

	1998	1999	2000
Food	101.3	101.0	102.0
Beverages and tobacco . . .	106.0	107.8	110.5
Clothing and footwear . . .	98.5	99.5	99.7
Rent, heating and lighting . .	104.8	106.1	111.8
Furniture, household equipment	101.2	102.4	103.2
All items	103.2	104.4	108.0

2002: All items 112.7 (Source: IMF, *International Financial Statistics*).

NATIONAL ACCOUNTS
(million markkaa at current prices)

National Income and Product

	1998	1999	2000*
Compensation of employees . .	330,758	347,072	368,550
Operating surplus	161,991	163,485	195,031
Domestic factor incomes . .	492,975	510,557	563,581
Consumption of fixed capital . .	111,656	116,255	124,628
Gross domestic product at factor cost	604,631	626,812	688,206
Indirect taxes	100,838	105,320	109,196
Less Subsidies	15,946	15,762	17,147
GDP in purchasers' values .	689,523	716,370	780,255
Factor income received from abroad. . . . . }	−16,829	−11,632	−11,680
Less Factor income paid abroad . }			
Gross national product . .	672,694	704,738	768,575
Less Consumption of fixed capital	111,656	116,255	124,625
National income in market prices.	561,038	588,483	643,950

* Provisional figures.

Expenditure on the Gross Domestic Product

	1998	1999	2000*
Government final consumption expenditure.	149,428	155,327	160,939
Private final consumption expenditure.	346,021	363,556	385,873
Increase in stocks	6,816	−636	5,620
Gross fixed capital formation . .	128,913	135,749	150,359
Statistical discrepancy . . .	−2,472	2,178	4,452
Total domestic expenditure. .	628,706	656,174	707,243
Exports of goods and services . .	267,467	270,974	334,831
Less Imports of goods and services	206,650	210,778	261,819
GDP in purchasers' values .	689,523	716,370	780,255

* Provisional figures.

Gross Domestic Product by Economic Activity

	1998	1999	2000*
Agriculture, hunting, forestry and fishing	22,986	23,446	25,281
Mining and quarrying	1,643	1,707	1,379
Manufacturing	153,040	155,271	178,584
Electricity, gas and water . . .	14,131	13,072	12,025
Construction	30,298	34,358	39,687
Trade, restaurants and hotels . .	73,274	74,891	78,205
Transport, storage and communication.	60,890	64,768	71,336
Finance, insurance and business services	56,120	57,627	68,642
Owner-occupied dwellings . . .	54,326	57,811	61,879
Public administration and welfare	107,975	111,884	117,798
Other community, social and personal services	35,031	38,243	40,956
Sub-total	609,714	633,078	695,772
Less Imputed bank service charge	14,439	15,526	17,946
GDP in basic values	595,275	617,552	677,826
Commodity taxes	99,354	103,723	107,589
Less Commodity subsidies . . .	5,106	4,905	5,160
GDP in purchasers' values . .	689,523	716,370	780,255

* Provisional figures.

BALANCE OF PAYMENTS
(US $ million)

	1999	2000	2001
Exports of goods f.o.b.	41,983	45,703	42,980
Imports of goods f.o.b.	−29,815	−32,019	−30,323
Trade balance	12,168	13,684	12,657
Exports of services	6,522	6,177	5,832
Imports of services	−7,952	−8,440	−8,105
Balance on goods and services.	10,738	11,421	10,385
Other income received . . .	5,664	7,265	8,503
Other income paid	−7,712	−8,989	−9,573
Balance on goods, services and income	8,690	9,698	9,315
Current transfers received . .	1,608	1,715	1,549
Current transfers paid	−2,641	−2,334	−2,233
Current balance	7,657	9,079	8,631
Capital account (net)	113	92	65
Direct investment abroad . . .	−6,739	−23,898	−8,458
Direct investment from abroad. .	4,649	9,125	3,739
Portfolio investment assets . . .	−15,699	−18,920	−11,594
Portfolio investment liabilities . .	13,550	17,116	5,985
Financial derivatives liabilities .	−419	−631	38
Other investment assets . . .	−3,324	−5,636	−10,117
Other investment liabilities . .	1,567	14,001	9,712
Net errors and omissions . . .	−1,761	−609	2,447
Overall balance	13	351	410

Source: IMF, *International Financial Statistics*.

External Trade

PRINCIPAL COMMODITIES
(distribution by SITC, million markkaa)

Imports c.i.f.	1998	1999	2000
Food and live animals	9,268.5	9,042.4	9,357.9
Crude materials (inedible) except fuels	11,202.7	11,625.9	14,570.5
Metalliferous ores and metal scrap	4,665.0	5,162.0	7,266.3
Mineral fuels, lubricants, etc.	12,735.3	14,944.0	25,941.9
Petroleum, petroleum products, etc.	7,964.6	11,128.6	20,969.3
Crude petroleum oils, etc.	5,803.6	8,177.4	15,651.0
Chemicals and related products	19,276.7	19,530.3	22,980.3
Basic manufactures	22,484.4	20,907.8	25,347.1
Iron and steel	5,610.5	4,880.8	6,619.0
Machinery and transport equipment	75,234.5	76,297.1	91,942.4
Non-electric machinery	29,832.5	28,017.3	30,091.0
Electrical machinery, apparatus, etc.	26,830.0	29,168.3	43,411.1
Transport equipment	18,571.9	19,111.5	18,440.2
Road vehicles and parts*	13,992.8	14,276.7	15,015.7
Passenger motor cars (excl. buses)	7,185.8	7,507.0	7,485.2
Miscellaneous manufactured articles	17,705.6	18,818.8	21,407.6
Total (incl. others)	172,819.2	176,535.6	218,152.5

* Excluding tyres, engines and electrical parts.

Exports f.o.b.	1998	1999	2000
Crude materials (inedible) except fuels	16,046.0	16,324.9	20,127.4
Wood, lumber and cork	8,983.6	9,159.9	9,971.1
Shaped or simply worked wood	8,522.1	8,665.7	8,541.0
Sawn coniferous lumber	7,433.4	8,364.2	8,386.4
Mineral fuels, lubricants, etc.	4,292.3	5,632.0	10,115.9
Petroleum, petroleum products, etc.	4,136.6	5,536.3	10,001.5
Refined petroleum products	4,096.4	5,490.7	9,891.2
Chemicals and related products	14,287.7	14,592.8	17,503.4
Basic manufactures	78,710.6	77,204.2	90,972.7
Paper, paperboard and manufactures	48,317.5	47,825.1	55,377.1
Paper and paperboard	44,027.5	43,957.2	50,799.2
Printing and writing paper in bulk	31,251.5	31,051.0	35,898.1
Iron and steel	10,402.4	9,593.3	12,222.6
Machinery and transport equipment	96,271.2	99,747.5	132,877.4
Non-electric machinery	35,672.3	32,547.8	37,813.7
Electrical machinery, apparatus, etc.	47,217.4	53,524.4	72,972.1
Transport equipment	13,381.4	13,675.3	16,091.7
Miscellaneous manufactured articles	13,715.6	13,473.8	15,313.4
Total (incl. others)	230,568.7	233,343.3	293,643.2

PRINCIPAL TRADING PARTNERS
(million markkaa)*

Imports c.i.f.	1998	1999	2000
Belgium	4,550.3†	4,223.9	4,588.6
China, People's Republic	3,171.7	4,092.4	6,616.7
Denmark	6,175.1	6,466.9	8,434.7
Estonia	3,045.4	3,213.9	6,117.3
France	8,433.2	7,566.2	8,515.7
Germany	26,191.7	26,940.3	31,172.4
Italy	7,137.4	6,590.1	6,972.3
Japan	9,768.2	11,026.6	11,636.9
Netherlands	7,302.6	7,213.3	8,435.8
Norway	6,016.1	6,331.8	7,675.9
Russia	11,360.3	12,750.8	20,524.7
Spain	2,922.3	2,793.4	3,309.0
Sweden	20,243.4	19,782.6	22,545.9
United Kingdom	12,552.1	11,667.2	14,087.1
USA	14,148.1	13,933.4	21,854.4
Total (incl. others)	172,819.2	176,535.6	218,152.5

Exports f.o.b.	1998	1999	2000
Belgium	5,759.8†	6,041.6	6,556.9
China, People's Republic	6,766.0	5,823.5	8,580.4
Denmark	6,464.2	6,591.8	7,420.8
Estonia	7,597.2	7,057.8	9,012.6
France	11,732.1	12,296.7	15,207.8
Germany	27,277.0	30,471.2	36,782.6
Italy	8,863.2	8,842.8	12,822.4
Netherlands	10,441.3	10,129.5	5,085.8
Norway	7,552.5	6,518.2	11,637.0
Russia	13,804.4	9,549.8	7,675.9
Spain	5,805.7	6,287.4	12,800.4
Sweden	21,770.8	23,177.8	7,623.1
United Kingdom	21,255.5	21,344.7	27,259.8
USA	16,845.3	18,427.9	26,816.5
Total (incl. others)	230,568.7	233,343.7	293,643.2

* Imports by country of production; exports by country of consumption.
† Including trade with Luxembourg.

Transport

RAILWAYS
(traffic)

	1999	2000	2001
Passengers ('000 journeys)	53,209	54,783	54,987
Passenger-km (million)	3,415	3,405	3,282
Freight carried ('000 metric tons)	39,979	40,501	41,678
Freight ton-km (million)	9,753	10,107	9,857

ROAD TRAFFIC
(registered motor vehicles at 31 December)

	1999	2000	2001
Passenger cars	2,082,580	2,134,728	2,160,603
Buses and coaches	9,487	9,852	n.a.
Lorries and vans	293,707	304,318	312,557
Motorcycles	80,178	90,877	102,811
Snowmobiles*	88,022	90,511	93,486

* Excluding Åland Islands.

SHIPPING

Merchant Fleet
(registered at 31 December)

	1999	2000	2001
Number of vessels	279	280	284
Total displacement ('000 grt)	1,658.4	1,620.4	1,595.4

Source: Lloyd's Register-Fairplay, *World Fleet Statistics*.

International Sea-borne Freight Traffic

	1999	2000	2001
Number of vessels entered	27,705	29,041	29,246
Goods ('000 metric tons):			
Loaded	39,307	39,502	39,634
Unloaded	38,196	41,093	44,895

CANAL TRAFFIC

	1998	1999	2000
Vessels in transit*	49,319	50,819	56,919
Timber rafts in transit	1,181	n.a.	n.a.
Goods carried ('000 metric tons)	4,493	4,230	4,273
Passengers carried ('000)	n.a.†	n.a.	113

* Excludes vessels on self-service lock canals.
† In 2000 some lock canals were converted into self-service lock canals, for which only the total number of lock uses can be included. These figures are therefore no longer available.

CIVIL AVIATION
(traffic on scheduled services, '000)

	1998	1999	2000
Kilometres flown	108,000	108,000	117,000
Passenger-kilometres	13,096,000	12,916,000	12,683,000
Cargo ton-kilometres	295,654	336,375	301,886

Tourism

FOREIGN TOURIST ARRIVALS
(at accommodation establishments)

Country of residence	1998	1999	2000
Denmark	46,891	55,755	54,964
Estonia	52,163	47,216	56,699
France	61,539	63,888	66,634
Germany	232,566	235,977	228,891
Italy	58,473	63,954	67,513
Japan	70,305	73,359	81,750
Netherlands	76,859	80,658	80,304
Norway	87,297	96,201	99,561
Russia	253,045	165,122	185,246
Sweden	329,496	328,200	360,750
Switzerland	41,433	44,472	45,072
United Kingdom	135,011	145,519	162,197
USA	94,621	95,567	105,085
Total (incl. others)	1,866,842	1,830,560	1,970,817

Tourism receipts (US $ million): 1,631 in 1998; 1,517 in 1999; 1,401 in 2000.

Source: World Tourism Organization, mainly *Yearbook of Tourism Statistics*.

2001: Tourism receipts 1,615.1 million euros.

Communications Media

	1999	2000	2001
Newspapers: number*	220	213	208
total circulation ('000 copies)	3,314	3,325	3,246
Other periodicals: number	5,129	5,104	5,158
Book production: titles	13,173	11,764	12,090
Television receivers (estimates, '000 in use)†	3,320	3,580	n.a.
Telephones ('000 main lines in use)	2,850.3	2,848.8	2,806.1
Mobile cellular telephones ('000 subscribers)	3,273.4	3,728.6	4,175.6
Personal computers (estimates, '000 in use)†	1,860	2,050	2,200
Internet users ('000 aged 15 years and over)†	1,667	1,927	2,235

* Comprising 56 dailies and 160 non-dailies in 1999; 55 dailies and 158 non-dailies in 2000; 54 dailies and 154 non-dailies in 2001.
† Source: International Telecommunication Union.

Radio receivers ('000 in use): 7,700 in 1997 (Source: UNESCO, *Statistical Yearbook*).

Facsimile machines ('000 in use): 198 in 1997 (Source: UN, *Statistical Yearbook*).

Education
(1999)

	Institutions	Teachers	Students
Comprehensive schools*	4,101	42,142	594,500
Senior secondary schools	456	6,802	139,100
Vocational and professional institutions	366	14,121	225,400
Polytechnics	25	3,861	90,500
Universities	20	7,255	151,900

Students enrolled (2001): Comprehensive schools* 595,727; Senior secondary schools 128,642; Vocational and professional institutions 160,115; Polytechnics 118,013; Universities 162,939.
* Comprising six-year primary stage and three-year lower secondary stage.

Directory

The Constitution

The Constitution of Finland entered into force on 1 March 2000, amending the Constitution of July 1919. Its main provisions are summarized below:

FUNDAMENTAL PROVISIONS

Finland is a sovereign republic. The powers of the State are vested in the people, who are represented by the Eduskunta (parliament). Legislative power is exercised by the Eduskunta, which also decides on state finances, governmental power is held by the President of the Republic and the Council of State, and judicial power is exercised by independent courts of law. The basic rights and liberties of the individual are guaranteed in the Constitution.

PARLIAMENT

The unicameral Eduskunta comprises 200 representatives, who are elected for a term of four years by a direct, proportional and secret vote. For the parliamentary elections the country is divided, on the basis of the number of Finnish citizens, into at least 12 and at most 18 constituencies. In addition, the Åland Islands form their own constituency for the election of one representative. Registered political parties, and groups of persons who have the right to vote, are entitled to nominate candidates in parliamentary elections. The President of the Republic, in response to a proposal by the Prime Minister, may order that extraordinary parliamentary elections be held. The Eduskunta elects from among its members a Speaker and two Deputy Speakers for each parliamentary session. The proposal for the enactment of legislation is initiated in the Eduskunta either by the Government or through a motion submitted by a representative.

PRESIDENT

The President of the Republic is elected by a direct vote for a term of six years (with the same person restricted to a maximum of two consecutive terms in office). The President will be a native-born Finnish citizen. The candidate who receives more than one-half of the votes cast in the election will be elected President. If none of the candidates receives a majority of the votes cast, a further election will be held between the two candidates who have received the most votes. The right to nominate a candidate in the presidential election is held by any registered political party from which at least one representative was elected to the Eduskunta in the most recent elections, as well as by any group of 20,000 persons who have the right to vote. The President of the Republic makes decisions on the basis of proposals submitted by the Council of State. The foreign policy of Finland is directed by the President of the Republic in co-operation with the Council of State.

COUNCIL OF STATE

The Council of State comprises the Prime Minister and the necessary number of ministers. The Eduskunta elects the Prime Minister, who is thereafter appointed to the office by the President of the Republic. The President appoints the other ministers on the basis of nominations made by the Prime Minister.

JUDICIARY

The Supreme Court, the Courts of Appeal and the District Courts are the general courts of law. The Supreme Administrative Court and the regional Administrative Courts are the general courts of administrative law. Justice in civil, commercial and criminal matters in the final instance is administered by the Supreme Court, while justice in administrative matters in the final instance is administered by the Supreme Administrative Court. The High Court of Impeachment deals with charges brought against a member of the Government, the Chancellor of Justice, the Parliamentary Ombudsman or a member of the supreme courts for unlawful conduct in office. Tenured judges are appointed by the President of the Republic.

ADMINISTRATION AND SELF-GOVERNMENT

In addition to the Government, the civil administration of the State may consist of agencies, institutions and other bodies. The Åland Islands are guaranteed self-government. Finland is divided into municipalities, which are guaranteed self-government, and are entitled to levy tax. In their native region the Sámi have linguistic and cultural autonomy.

The Government

HEAD OF STATE

President: TARJA HALONEN (elected 6 February 2000; took office 1 March 2000).

COUNCIL OF STATE
(Valtioneuvosto)
(April 2003)

A coalition of the Centre Party (Kesk), the Social Democratic Party (SDP) and the Swedish People's Party (SFP).

Prime Minister: ANNELI JÄÄTTEENMÄKI (Kesk).

Deputy Prime Minister and Minister of Finance: ANTTI KALLIO-MÄKI (SDP).

Minister of Foreign Affairs: ERKKI TUOMIOJA (SDP).

Minister of Foreign Trade and Development: PAULA LEHTOMÄKI (Kesk).

Minister of Justice: JOHANNES KOSKINEN (SDP).

Minister of the Interior: KARI RAJAMÄKI (SDP).

Minister of Regional and Municipal Affairs: HANNES MANNINEN (Kesk).

Minister of Defence: MATTI VANHANEN (Kesk).

Minister at the Ministry of Finance: ULLA-MAJ WIDEROOS (SFP).

Minister of Education: TUULA HAATAINEN (SDP).

Minister of Culture: TANJA KARPELA (Kesk).

Minister of Agriculture and Forestry: JUHA KORKEAOJA (Kesk).

Minister of Transport and Communications: LEENA LUHTANEN (SDP).

Minister of Trade and Industry: MAURI PEKKARINEN (Kesk).

Minister of Social Affairs and Health: SINIKKA MÖNKÄRE (SDP).

Minister of Health and Social Services: LIISA HYSSÄLÄ (Kesk).

Minister of Labour: TARJA FILATOV (SDP).

Minister of the Environment: JAN-ERIK ENESTAM (SFP).

MINISTRIES

Prime Minister's Office: Snellmaninkatu 1A, 00170 Helsinki; POB 23, 00023 Government; tel. (9) 16001; fax (9) 16022165; e-mail kirjaamo@vnk.vn.fi; internet www.vnk.fi.

Ministry of Agriculture and Forestry: Hallituskatu 3A, 00170 Helsinki; POB 30, 00023 Government; tel. (9) 16001; fax (9) 16054202; e-mail tiedotus@mmm.fi; internet www.mmm.fi.

Ministry of Defence: Eteläinen Makasiinikatu 8, POB 31, 00131 Helsinki; tel. (9) 16001; fax (9) 653254; e-mail tiedotus@plm.vn.fi; internet www.puolustusministerio.fi.

Ministry of Education: Meritullinkatu 10, 00171 Helsinki; POB 29, 00023 Government; tel. (9) 16004; fax (9) 1359335; e-mail pia .ekqvist@minedu.fi; internet www.minedu.fi.

Ministry of the Environment: Kasarmikatu 25, 00131 Helsinki; POB 35, 00023 Government; tel. (9) 16007; fax (9) 16039545; e-mail kirjaamo.ym@ymparisto.fi; internet www.ymparisto.fi.

Ministry of Finance: Snellmaninkatu 1A, 00170 Helsinki; POB 28, 00023 Government; tel. (9) 16001; fax (9) 16033123; internet www .vn.fi/vn.

Ministry of Foreign Affairs: Merikasarmi, Laivastokatu 22, Merikasarminkatu 5F, POB 176, 00161 Helsinki; tel. (9) 16005; fax (9) 629840; e-mail kirjaamo.um@formin.fi; internet formin.finland.fi.

Ministry of the Interior: Kirkkokatu 12, 00170 Helsinki; POB 26, 00023 Government; tel. (9) 16001; fax (9) 16042927; e-mail sm .kirjaamp@sm.intermin.fi; internet www.intermin.fi.

Ministry of Justice: Eteläesplanadi 10, 00170 Helsinki; POB 25, 00023 Government; tel. (9) 16003; fax (9) 16067730; e-mail om-tiedotus@om.fi; internet www.om.fi.

Ministry of Labour: Eteläesplanadi 4, 00101 Helsinki; POB 34, 00023 Government; tel. (9) 16006; fax (9) 16047590; internet www .mol.fi.

Ministry of Social Affairs and Health: Meritullinkatu 8, 00170 Helsinki; POB 33, 00023 Government; tel. (9) 16001; fax (9) 16074126; e-mail kirjaamo.stm@stm.vn.fi; internet www.stm.fi.

Ministry of Trade and Industry: Aleksanterinkatu 4, 00171 Helsinki; POB 32, 00023 Government; tel. (9) 16001; fax (9) 16063666; e-mail tiedotus@ktm.fi; internet www.ktm.fi.

Ministry of Transport and Communications: Eteläesplanadi 16–18, 00131 Helsinki; POB 31, 00023 Government; tel. (9) 16002; fax (9) 16028596; e-mail info@mintc.fi; internet www.mintc.fi.

President and Legislature

PRESIDENT

Elections of 16 January and 6 February 2000

	Popular vote (%)	
	First Round	Second Round
Tarja Halonen (SDP)	40.0	51.6
Esko Aho (Kesk)	34.4	48.4
Riitta Uosukainen (Kok)	12.8	—
Märta Elisabeth Rehn (SFP)	7.9	—
Heidi Hautala (VL)	3.3	—
Ilkka Hakalehto (PS)	1.0	—
Risto Kuisma (REM)	0.6	—
Total	100.0	100.0

EDUSKUNTA
(Parliament)

Suomen Eduskunta

Mannerheimintie 30, 00102 Helsinki; tel. (9) 4321; fax (9) 4322274; e-mail parliament@parliament.fi; internet www.eduskunta.fi.

Speaker: PAAVO LIPPONEN (SDP).

Secretary-General: SEPPO TIITINEN.

General Election, 16 March 2003

	Number of votes	% of votes	Seats
Keskusta (Kesk— Centre Party) .	689,147	24.7	55
Sosialidemokraattinen Puolue (SDP— Social Democratic Party)	682,819	24.5	53
Kansallinen Kokoomus (Kok— National Coalition Party) . .	517,171	18.5	40
Vasemmistoliitto (V—Left Alliance)	276,756	9.9	19
Vihreä Liitto (Green League) . .	223,267	8.0	14
Kristillisdemokraatit (Christian Democrats)	148,965	5.3	7
Svenska Folkpartiet (SFP— Swedish People's Party) . .	128,617	4.6	8
Perussuomalaiset/Sannfinländarna (PerusS—True Finns) . . .	43,791	1.6	3
Suomen Kommunistinen Puolue (Finnish Communist Party) .	21,111	0.8	—
Others*	57,970	2.1	1
Total	2,789,614	100.0	200

* Including the representative of the Åland Islands.

Political Organizations

Eco-Diverse Party: Helsinki; tel. (9) 4323566; fax (9) 4322717; Chair. PERTTI VIRTANEN; Sec. JUKKA WALLENIUS.

Kansallinen Kokoomus (Kok) (National Coalition Party): Pohjoinen Rautatiekatu 21B, 00100 Helsinki; tel. (9) 1603004; fax (9)

1603004; e-mail jori.arvonen@kokoomus.fi; internet www.kokoomus .fi; f. 1918; moderate conservative political ideology; Chair. VILLE ITÄLÄ; Sec.-Gen. MATTI KANKARE; Chair. Parliamentary Group BEN ZYSKOWICZ; 50,000 mems.

Keskusta (Kesk) (Centre Party): Apollonkatu 11A, 00100 Helsinki; tel. (9) 75144200; fax (9) 75144240; e-mail puoluetoimisto@keskusta .fi; internet www.keskusta.fi; f. 1906; a radical centre party founded to promote the interests of the rural population, now a reformist 'green' movement favouring individual enterprise, equality and decentralization; Chair. ANNELI JÄÄTTEENMÄKI; Sec.-Gen. EERO LANKIA; Chair. Parliamentary Group MAURI PEKKARINEN; 220,000 mems.

Kristillisdemokraatit (KD) (Christian Democrats): Karjalankatu 2C, 7 krs, 00520 Helsinki; tel. (9) 34882200; fax (9) 34882228; e-mail kd@kristillisdemokraatit.fi; internet www.kristillisdemokraatit.fi; f. 1958 as Suomen Kristillinen Liitto, present name adopted 2001; Chair. BJARNE KALLIS; Sec. EIJA-KIITTA KORHOLA; Chair. Parliamentary Group JOUKO JÄÄSKELÄINEN; 14,700 mems.

Liberaalit r.p. (Liberal Party of Finland): Vehkatie 29, 01300 Vantaa; tel. (9) 85168401; fax (9) 85168402; e-mail liberaalit@ liberaalit.fi; internet www.liberaalit.fi; f. 1965 as a coalition of the Finnish People's Party and the Liberal Union; Chair. TOMI RIIHIMÄKI; Sec.-Gen. KIMMO ERIKSSON; 4,000 mems.

Perussuomalaiset/Sannfinländarna rp (PerusS) (True Finns): Mannerheimintie 40 B 56, 00100 Helsinki; tel. (9) 4540411; fax (9) 4540466; e-mail peruss@perussuomalaiset.fi; internet www .perussuomalaiset.fi; f. 1995; Chair. TIMO SOINI; Sec. HANNU PURHO.

Reform Group (REM): Mannerheimintie 40A, 00100 Helsinki; tel. (9) 4143352; fax (9) 645379; Chair. RISTO KUISMA; Sec. SEIJA LAHTI.

Sosialidemokraattinen Puolue (SDP) (Social Democratic Party): Saariniemenkatu 6, 00530 Helsinki; tel. (9) 478988; fax (9) 712752; e-mail palaute@sdp.fi; internet www.sdp.fi; f. 1899; constitutional socialist programme; mainly supported by the urban working and middle classes; Chair. PAAVO LIPPONEN; Sec. EERO HEINÄLUOMA; Chair. Parliamentary Group ANTTI KALLIOMÄKI; 59,000 mems.

Suomen Kommunistinen Puloue (SKP) (Finnish Communist Party): Petter Wetterin tie 1A, 00810 Helsinki; tel. (09) 77438150; fax (09) 77438160; e-mail skp@skp.fi; internet www.skp.fi; f. 1918; refounded by breakaway group after the SKP formed the Vasemmistoliitto (Left Alliance) with other left-wing groups in 1990.

Svenska Folkpartiet (SFP) (Swedish People's Party): Simonsgatan 8A, 00100 Helsinki; tel. (9) 693070; fax (9) 6931968; internet www.sfp.fi; f. 1906; a liberal party representing the interests of the Swedish-speaking minority; Chair. JAN-ERIK ENESTAM; Sec. BERTH SUNDSTRÖM; Chair. Parliamentary Group ULLA-MAJ WIDEROOS; 35,700 mems.

Vasemmistoliitto (V) (Left Alliance): Viherniemenkatu 5A, 00530 Helsinki; tel. (9) 774741; fax (9) 77474200; e-mail vas@ vasemmistoliitto.fi; internet www.vasemmistoliitto.fi; f. 1990 as a merger of the Finnish People's Democratic League (f. 1944), the Communist Party of Finland (f. 1918), the Democratic League of Finnish Women, and left-wing groups; Chair. SUVI-ANNE SIIMES; Sec.-Gen. AULIS RUUTH; Chair. Parliamentary Group OUTI OJALA; 14,000 mems.

Vihreä Liitto (VL) (Green League): Runeberginkatu 5B, 00100 Helsinki; tel. (9) 58604160; fax (9) 58604161; e-mail vihreat@ vihrealiitto.fi; internet www.vihrealiitto.fi; f. 1988; Chair. OSMO SOININVAARA; Sec. ARI HEIKKINEN.

Young Finns: Helsinki; tel. (9) 6856211; fax (9) 6856233; Chair. RISTO E. J. PENTTILÄ; Sec. MARITA VUORINEN.

Diplomatic Representation

EMBASSIES IN FINLAND

Argentina: Bulevardi 5A11, 00120 Helsinki; tel. (9) 42428700; fax (9) 42428701; e-mail embassy@embargentina.fi; Ambassador ALFREDO CORTI.

Austria: Keskuskatu 1A, 00100 Helsinki; tel. (9) 171322; fax (9) 665084; e-mail helsinki-ob@bmaa.gv.at; Ambassador Dr CHRISTOPH QUERNER.

Belgium: Kalliolinnantie 5, 00140 Helsinki; tel. (9) 170412; fax (9) 628842; e-mail ambel.helsinki@kolumbus.fi; Chargé d'affaires a.i. NATHALIE CASSIERS.

Brazil: Itäinen puistotie 4B1, 00140 Helsinki; tel. (9) 177922; fax (9) 650084; e-mail brasemb.helsinki@kolumbus.fi; Ambassador LUIZ HENRIQUE PEREIRA DA FONSECA.

Bulgaria: Kuusisaarentie 2B, 00340 Helsinki; tel. (9) 4584055; fax (9) 4584550; e-mail bulembfi@icon.fi; Chargé d'affaires a.i. KIRIL DIMITROV.

Canada: Pohjoisesplanadi 25B, 00100 Helsinki; tel. (9) 228530; fax (9) 601060; internet www.canada.fi; Ambassador ADÈLE DION.

Chile: Erottajankatu 11, 00130 Helsinki; tel. (9) 6126780; fax (9) 61267825; e-mail echilefi@kolumbus.fi; Ambassador IGNACIO GONZALEZ SERRANO.

China, People's Republic: Vanha Kelkkamäki 9–11, 00570 Helsinki; tel. (9) 22890110; fax (9) 22890168; Ambassador ZHANG ZHIJIAN.

Colombia: Ratakatu 1B A1, 00120 Helsinki; tel. (9) 6802799; fax (9) 6802180; e-mail emcolhel.emba@kolumbus.fi; Chargé d'affaires a.i. CARMEN LUCIA TRISTANCHO-CEDIEL.

Croatia: Eteläesplanadi 12, 1., 00130 Helsinki; tel. (9) 6222232; fax (9) 6222221; e-mail croatia@embassy.inet.fi; Ambassador LJILJANA PANCIROV.

Cuba: Uudenmaankatu 26 A 3, 00120 Helsinki; tel. (9) 6802022; fax (9) 643163; e-mail cuba@embacuba.inet.fi; internet personal.inet.fi/ business.cuba; Chargé d'affaires MANUEL VIÑAS BARREDO.

Cyprus: Bulevardi 5A, 19, 00120 Helsinki; tel. (9) 6962820; fax (9) 69628230; e-mail mail@cyprusembassy.fi; internet www .cyprusembassy.fi; Ambassador LORIA MARKIDES.

Czech Republic: Armfeltintie 14, 00150 Helsinki; tel. (9) 171169; fax (9) 630655; e-mail helsinki@embassy.mzv.cz; Ambassador ALENA PROUZOVÁ.

Denmark: Keskuskatu 1A, POB 1042, 00101 Helsinki; tel. (9) 6841050; fax (9) 68410540; e-mail danmark@kolumbus.fi; internet www.denmark.fi; Ambassador NIELS HELSKOV.

Egypt: Munkkiniemen puistotie 25, 00330 Helsinki; tel. (9) 4777470; fax (9) 47774721; Ambassador SAMAH MOHAMED SOTOUBI.

Estonia: Itäinen puistotie 10, 00140 Helsinki; tel. (9) 6220260; fax (9) 62202610; e-mail sekretar@estemb.fi; internet www.estemb.fi; Ambassador MATTI MAASIKAS.

France: Itäinen puistotie 13, 00140 Helsinki; tel. (9) 618780; fax (9) 618783923; e-mail ambassade.france@kolumbus.fi; Ambassador JEAN-JACQUES SUBRENAT.

Germany: POB 5, 00331 Helsinki; tel. (9) 458580; fax (9) 45858258; e-mail saksa@germanembassy.fi; internet www.germanembassy.fi; Ambassador Dr CORNELIUS SOMMER.

Greece: Maaneesikatu 2A4, 00170 Helsinki; tel. (9) 2781100; fax (9) 2781200; e-mail info@greekembassy.fi; internet www.greekembassy .fi; Ambassador LYSANDER MIGLIARESSIS-PHOCAS.

Hungary: Kuusisaarenkuja 6, 00340 Helsinki; tel. (9) 484144; fax (9) 480497; e-mail unkarin.suurianetysto@kolumbus.fi; Ambassador JÓZSEF VIG.

Iceland: Pohjoisesplanadi 27C, 00100 Helsinki; tel. (9) 6122460; fax (9) 61224620; e-mail icemb.helsinki@utn.stjr.is; internet www .islanti.fi; Ambassador JÓN BALDVINN HANNIBALSSON.

India: Satamakatu 2A8, 00160 Helsinki; tel. (9) 608927; fax (9) 6221208; e-mail eoihelsinki@indianembassy.fi; Ambassador OM PRAKASH GUPTA.

Indonesia: Kuusisaarentie 3, 00340 Helsinki; tel. (9) 4470370; fax (9) 4582882; e-mail info@indonesian-embassy.fi; internet www .indonesian-embassy.fi; Ambassador AHMAD FAUZIE GANI.

Iran: Kulosaarentie 9, 00570 Helsinki; tel. (9) 6869240; fax (9) 68692410; e-mail embassy@iran.fi; internet www.iran.fi; Ambassador SEYED ABBAS ARAGHCHI.

Iraq: Lars Sonckin tie 2, 00570 Helsinki; tel. (9) 6849177; fax (9) 6848977; Chargé d'affaires a.i. GHAZI Y. KHUDHAIR.

Ireland: Erottajankatu 7A, 00130 Helsinki; tel. (9) 646006; fax (9) 646022; e-mail embassy.ireland@welho.com; Chargé d'affaires a.i. LORRAINE CHRISTIAN.

Israel: Vironkatu 5A, 00170 Helsinki; tel. (9) 6812020; fax (9) 1356959; e-mail helsinki@israel.org; internet www.mfa.gov.il; Ambassador MIRYAM SHOMRAT.

Italy: Itäinen puistotie 4, 00140 Helsinki; tel. (9) 6811280; fax (9) 6987829; e-mail info@italia.fi; internet www.italia.fi; Ambassador PIETRO LONARDO.

Japan: Eteläranta 8, 00130 Helsinki; tel. (9) 6860200; fax (9) 633012; e-mail webmaster@jpnembassy.fi; internet www.fi .emb-japan.go.jp; Ambassador NORIMASA HASEGAWA.

Korea, Republic: Annankatu 32A, 00100 Helsinki; tel. (9) 6866230; fax (9) 68662355; e-mail koreanembassy@kolumbus.fi; Ambassador YOUNG-GIL LEE.

Latvia: Armfeltintie 10, 00150 Helsinki; tel. (9) 47647244; fax (9) 47647288; e-mail embassy.finland@mfa.gov.lv; Ambassador VALDIS KRASTINS.

Lithuania: Rauhankatu 13A, 00170 Helsinki; tel. (9) 608210; fax (9) 608220; e-mail embassy@liettua.pp.fi; Ambassador AUDRIUS BRŪZGA.

Mexico: Simonkatu 12A, 00100 Helsinki; tel. (9) 5860430; fax (9) 6949411; e-mail mexican.embassy@co.inet.fi; Ambassador CRISTINA DE LA GARZA.

Morocco: Mikonkatu 8A, 00100 Helsinki; tel. (9) 635740; fax (9) 635160; e-mail embassyofmorocco@co.inet.fi; Chargé d'affaires a.i. AZIZ OUARRAK.

Netherlands: Eteläesplanadi 24A, 00130 Helsinki; tel. (9) 661737; fax (9) 654734; e-mail nlgovhel@kolumbus.fi; internet www .netherlands.fi; Ambassador NIEK PETER VAN ZUTPHEN.

Norway: Rehbinderintie 17, 00150 Helsinki; tel. (9) 6860180; fax (9) 657807; e-mail emb.helsinki@mfa.no; Ambassador TOM VRAALSEN.

Peru: Annankatu 31–33C44, 00100 Helsinki; tel. (9) 6933681; fax (9) 6933682; e-mail embassy.peru@peruemb.inet.fi; Ambassador MARTHA CHAVARRI DUPUY.

Poland: Armas Lindgrenin tie 21, 00570 Helsinki; tel. (9) 6848077; fax (9) 6847477; e-mail amb.poland@helsinki.inet.fi; internet www .embassyofpoland.fi; Ambassador STANISŁAW STEBELSKI.

Portugal: Itäinen puistotie 11B, 00140 Helsinki; tel. (9) 68243715; fax (9) 663550; e-mail emb.port@kolumbus.fi; Ambassador FILIPE GUTERRES.

Romania: Stenbäckinkatu 24, 00250 Helsinki; tel. (9) 2413624; fax (9) 2413272; e-mail romamb@clinet.fi; Ambassador NAAGU UDROIU.

Russia: Tehtaankatu 1B, 00140 Helsinki; tel. (9) 661876; fax (9) 661006; Ambassador ALEKSANDR K. PATSEV.

Serbia and Montenegro: Kulosaarentie 36, 00570 Helsinki; tel. (9) 6848522; fax (9) 6848783; Ambassador RADOJE Z. ZEČEVIĆ.

Slovakia: Annankatu 25, 00100 Helsinki; tel. (9) 68117810; fax (9) 68117820; e-mail skemb.hels@sci.fi; Ambassador Dr EMIL KUCHÁR.

Slovenia: POB 9, 00101 Helsinki; Chargé d'Affaires a.i. ALAIN BERGANT.

South Africa: Rahapajankatu 1A5, 00160 Helsinki; tel. (9) 68603100; fax (9) 68603160; e-mail saembfin@welno.com; Ambassador FRANKI VERWEY.

Spain: Kalliolinnantie 6, 00140 Helsinki; tel. (9) 6877080; fax (9) 170923; e-mail embespfi@mail.mae.es; Ambassador FERNANDO CARDERERA.

Sweden: Pohjoisesplanadi 7B, 00171 Helsinki; tel. (9) 6877660; fax (9) 655285; e-mail ambassaden.helsingfors@foreign.ministry.se; internet www.sverige.fi; Ambassador ULF HJERTONSSON.

Switzerland: Uudenmaankatu 16A, 00120 Helsinki; tel. (9) 6229500; fax (9) 62295050; e-mail vertretung@hel.rep.admin.ch; Ambassador PIERRE CHRZANOVSKI.

Turkey: Puistokatu 1B A 3, 00140 Helsinki; tel. (9) 6811030; fax (9) 655011; e-mail turkish.embassy@welho.com; Ambassador ILHAN YIGITBASIOGLU.

Ukraine: Vähäniityntie 9, 00570 Helsinki; tel. (9) 2289000; fax (9) 2289001; e-mail ukrainian.embassy@kolumbus.fi; Ambassador PETRO SARDACHUK.

United Kingdom: Itäinen puistotie 17, 00140 Helsinki; tel. (9) 22865100; fax (9) 22865262; e-mail info@ukembassy.fi; internet www.ukembassy.fi; Ambassador MATTHEW KIRK.

USA: Itäinen puistotie 14A, 00140 Helsinki; tel. (9) 171931; fax (9) 174681; e-mail webmaster@usembassy.fi; internet www.usembassy .fi; Ambassador BONNIE MCELVEEN-HUNTER.

Venezuela: Bulevardi 1A, POB 285, 00101 Helsinki; tel. (9) 641522; fax (9) 640971; e-mail embavene.finland@dlc.fi; Ambassador JOSÉ E. LÓPEZ CONTRERAS.

Judicial System

The administration of justice is independent of the Government and judges can be removed only by judicial sentence. The compulsory retirement age for judges is 67.

SUPREME COURT

Korkein oikeus/Högsta domstolen

Pohjoisesplanadi 3, POB 301, 00171 Helsinki; tel. (9) 12381; fax (9) 1238354; e-mail korkein.oikeus@om.fi; internet www.kko.fi.

Consists of a President and at least 15 Justices appointed by the President of the Republic. Final court appeal in civil and criminal cases, supervises judges and executive authorities.

President: LEIF SEVÓN.

SUPREME ADMINISTRATIVE COURT

Korkein hallinto-oikeus/Högsta förvaltningsdomstolen

Unioninkatu 16, POB 180, 00131 Helsinki; tel. (9) 18531; fax (9) 1853382; e-mail korkein.hallinto-oikeus@om.fi; internet www.kho .if.

Consists of a President and 20 Justices appointed by the President of the Republic. Highest tribunal for appeals in administrative cases.

President: PEKKA HALLBERG.

COURTS OF APPEAL

There are Courts of Appeal at Turku, Vaasa, Kuopio, Helsinki, Kouvola, and Rovaniemi, consisting of a President and an appropriate number of members.

ADMINISTRATIVE COURTS

There are eight Administrative Courts, which hear the appeals of private individuals and corporate bodies against the authorities in tax cases, municipal cases, construction cases, social welfare and health-care cases and other administrative cases. In certain of these, the appeal must be preceded by a complaint to a separate lower appellate body. The State and municipal authorities also have a right of appeal in certain cases.

DISTRICT COURTS

Courts of first instance for almost all suits. Appeals lie to the Court of Appeal, and then to the Supreme Court. The composition of the District Court is determined by the type of case to be heard. Civil cases and 'ordinary' criminal cases can be considered by one judge. Other criminal cases and family law cases are heard by a judge and a panel of three lay judges (jurors). Other civil cases are heard by three legally-qualified judges. There are 66 District Courts.

SPECIAL COURTS

In addition there are a number of special courts with more restricted jurisdictions. These are: the High Court of Impeachment, the Insurance Court, the Labour Court and the Market Court. There is no constitutional court in Finland, but the Constitutional Committee of Parliament has been entrusted with the process of verifying the compatibility of new legislation with the Constitution.

CHANCELLOR OF JUSTICE

The Oikeuskansleri is responsible for ensuring that authorities and officials comply with the law. He is the chief public prosecutor, and acts as counsel for the Government.

Chancellor of Justice: PAAVO NIKULA.

Chancellor of Justice's Office: Snellmaninkatu 1A, 00170 Helsinki; POB 20, 00023 Government; tel. (9) 16001; fax (9) 16023975; e-mail kirjaamo@okv.vn.fi; internet www.vn.fi/okv.

PARLIAMENTARY OMBUDSMAN

The Eduskunnan Oikeusasiamies is the Finnish Ombudsman appointed by the Eduskunta to supervise the observance of the law.

Parliamentary Ombudsman: LAURI LEHTIMAJA.

Parliamentary Ombudsman's Office: Aurorankatu 6, 00102 Helsinki; tel. (9) 4321; fax (9) 4322268; e-mail eoa-kirjaamo@eduskunta .fi; internet www.ombudsman.fi.

In addition to the Chancellor of Justice and the Parliamentary Ombudsman, there are also specialized authorities that have similar duties in more limited fields. These include the Consumer Ombudsman, the Ombudsman for Equality, the Data Protection Ombudsman, the Ombudsman for Aliens and the Bankruptcy Ombudsman.

Religion

CHRISTIANITY

Suomen ekumeeninen neuvosto/Ekumeniska rådet i Finland (Finnish Ecumenical Council): Katajanokankatu 7, POB 185, 00161 Helsinki; tel. (9) 18021; fax (9) 174313; e-mail sen@kolumbus.fi; f. 1917; 12 mem. churches; Pres. Archbishop JUKKA PAARMA (Archbishop of Karelia and All Finland, Evangelical Lutheran Church of Finland); Gen. Sec. Rev. JAN EDSTRÖM.

National Churches

Suomen evankelis-luterilainen kirkko (Evangelical Lutheran Church of Finland): Dept for International Relations, Satamakatu 11, POB 185, 00161 Helsinki; tel. (9) 18021; fax (9) 1802230; about

84.8% of the population are adherents; Leader Archbishop Dr JUKKA PAARMA.

Suomen Ortodoksinen Kirkko (Orthodox Church of Finland): Karjalankatu 1, 70110 Kuopio; tel. (17) 2872230; fax (17) 2872231; e-mail archbishop@ort.fi; internet www.ort.fi; 58,000 mems; Leader LEO (Archbishop of Karelia and all Finland).

The Roman Catholic Church

Finland comprises the single diocese of Helsinki, directly responsible to the Holy See. At 31 December 2000 there were an estimated 7,835 adherents in the country. The Bishop participates in the Scandinavian Episcopal Conference (based in Sweden).

Bishop of Helsinki: JÓZEF WRÓBEL, Rehbinderintie 21, 00150 Helsinki; tel. (9) 6877160; fax (9) 639820; e-mail curia@catholic.fi.

Other Churches

Finlands svenska baptistmission (Finland Swedish Baptist Union): POB 54, 65101 Vasa; tel. (6) 3178559; fax (6) 3178550; e-mail fsb@baptist.fi; internet www.baptist.fi; 1,353 mems.

Jehovan Todistajat (Jehovah's Witnesses): Puutarhatie 60, 01300 Vantaa; tel. (9) 825885; fax (9) 82588285; 20,120 mems.

Myöhempien Aikojen Pyhien Jeesuksen Kristuksen Kirkko (Church of Jesus Christ of Latter-day Saints—Mormon): Neitsytpolku 3A, 00140 Helsinki; tel. (9) 177311; 3,101 mems.

Suomen Adventtikirkko (Seventh-day Adventist Church in Finland): POB 94, 33101 Tampere; tel. (3) 3611111; fax (3) 3600454; e-mail advent@sdafin.org; internet www.sdafin.org; f. 1894; 5,469 mems; Pres. ERKKI HAAPASALO; Sec. SIBRINA KALLIOKOSKI.

Suomen Baptistiyhdyskunta (Baptists—Finnish-speaking): Kissanmaankatu 19, 33530 Tampere; tel. (3) 2530901; fax (3) 2530913; e-mail kharis@sci.fi; 1,821 mems; Pres. Rev. JORMA LEMPINEN.

Suomen Vapaakirkko (Evangelical Free Church of Finland): POB 198, 13101 Hämeenlinna; tel. (3) 6445150; fax (3) 6122153; e-mail svk@svk.fi; internet www.svk.fi; f. 1923; 14,100 mems; Pres. Rev. OLAVI RINTALA.

Svenska Kyrkan i Finland (Church of Sweden in Finland): Minervagatan 6, 00100 Helsinki; tel. (9) 443831; fax (9) 4546059; e-mail forsamlingen@olauspetri.inet.fi; f. 1919; 1,300 mems; Rector Dr JARL JERGMAR.

United Methodist Church in Northern Europe: Helsinki; tel. (9) 4542620; fax (9) 45426226; e-mail umc.vaxby@kolumbus.fi; Leader Bishop HANS VÄXBY.

Finlands svenska metodistkyrka (United Methodist Church in Finland—Swedish-speaking): Apollonkatu 5, 00100 Helsinki; tel. (9) 449874; fax (9) 406098; internet www.metodistkyrkan.org; 1,000 mems; District Superintendents Rev. FREDRIK WEGELIUS, Rev. HANS VÄXBY.

Suomen Metodistikirkko (United Methodist Church—Finnish-speaking): Punavuorenkatu 2, 00120 Helsinki; tel. (9) 628135; e-mail suomen.metodistikirkko@kolumbus.fi; 770 mems; District Superintendent Rev. TAPANI RAJAMAA.

The Anglican Church and the Salvation Army are also active in the country.

BAHÁ'Í FAITH

Suomen Bahá'í-yhteisö (Bahá'í Community of Finland): POB 423, 00600 Helsinki; tel. (9) 790875; fax (9) 790058; e-mail secretariat@bahai.fi; f. 1953; 600 mems.

JUDAISM

Helsingin Juutalainen Seurakunta (Jewish Community of Helsinki): Synagogue and Community Centre, Malminkatu 26, 00100 Helsinki; tel. (9) 5860310; fax (9) 6948916; e-mail srk@jchelsinki.fi; internet www.jchelsinki.fi; 1,200 mems; Pres. GIDEON BOLOTOWSKY; Exec. Dir DAN KANTOR.

ISLAM

Suomen Islamilainen Yhdyskunta (Islamic Community of Finland): POB 87, 00101 Helsinki; tel. (9) 3512190; fax (9) 6121156; 936 mems; Imam ENVER YILDIRIM.

The Press

In 2001 there were 200 daily newspapers in Finland (including 27 printed seven days a week), with a total circulation of some 3.2m. A number of dailies are printed in Swedish. The most popular daily papers are *Helsingin Sanomat*, *Ilta-Sanomat*, *Aamulehti* and *Ilta-* *lehti*. Most respected for its standard of news coverage and commentary is *Helsingin Sanomat*, an independent paper.

PRINCIPAL DAILIES

Espoo

Hevosurheilu: Tulkinkuja 3, 02600 Espoo; tel. (9) 51100300; fax (9) 51100390; e-mail hevosurheilu@hevosurheilulehti.fi; internet www .hippos.fi/hu; independent; Man. Dir JUKKO AHONEN; Editor-in-Chief JORMA KEMILÄINEN; circ. 27,589.

Helsinki

Helsingin Sanomat: Töölönlahdenkatu 2, POB 77, 00089 Sanomat; tel. (9) 1221; fax (9) 605709; e-mail janne.virkkunen@ sanomat.fi; internet www.helsinginsanomat.fi; f. 1889; independent; Publr SEPPO KIEVARI; Senior Editor-in-Chief JANNE VIRKKUNEN; circ. 436,009 weekdays, 507,011 Sunday.

Hufvudstadsbladet: Mannerheimvägen 34, POB 217, 00101 Helsinki; tel. (9) 12531; fax (9) 642930; e-mail nyheter@hbl.fi; internet www.hbl.fi; f. 1864; Swedish language; independent; Editors-in-Chief MAX ARHIPPAINEN, BARBRO TEIR; circ. 52,175 weekdays, 54,542 Sunday.

Iltalehti: Aleksanterinkatu 9, 4., 00100 Helsinki; tel. (9) 507721; fax (9) 177313; e-mail il.toimitus@iltalehti.fi; internet www.iltalehti .fi; f. 1981; afternoon; independent; Man. Dir VELI-MATTI ASIKAINEN; Editor-in-Chief PETRI HAKALA; circ. 132,836 weekdays, 165,528 Saturday.

Ilta-Sanomat: POB 45, 00089 Sanomat; tel. (9) 1221; fax (9) 1223419; e-mail iltasanomat@sanoma.fi; f. 1932; afternoon; independent; Man. Dir SEPPO KIEVARI; Editor-in-Chief VESA-PEKKA KOLJONEN; circ. 214,610 weekdays, 243,443 weekend.

Kansan Uutiset: Fabianinkatu 7, 00131 Helsinki; tel. (9) 759601; f. 1957; organ of the Left Alliance; Editor YRJÖ RAUTIO; circ. 9,749.

Kauppalehti (The Commercial Daily): POB 189, 00101 Helsinki; tel. (9) 50781; fax (9) 5078419; internet www.kauppalehti.fi; f. 1898; morning; Man. Dir JUHA BEMSTER; Editor-in-Chief LAURI HELVE; circ. 84,626.

Maaseudun Tulevaisuus: Simonkatu 6, POB 440, 00100 Helsinki; tel. (9) 131151; fax (9) 6944766; internet www .maaseuduntulevaisuus.fi; f. 1916; independent; Man. Dir KIMMO VARJORAARA; Editor-in-Chief LAURI KONTRO; circ. 91,172.

Uutispöivä Demari: Haapaniemenkatu 7–9B, POB 338, 00531 Helsinki; tel. (9) 701041; fax (9) 7010570; e-mail toimitus@demari.fi; internet www.demari.fi; f. 1895; chief organ of the Social Democratic Party; Man. Dir HEIKKI NYKANEN; Editor-in-Chief KARI AROLA; circ. 23,021.

Hämeenlinna

Hämeen Sanomat: Vanajantie 7, POB 530, 13111 Hämeenlinna; tel. (3) 61511; fax (3) 6151492; internet www.hameensanomat.fi; f. 1879; independent; Man. Dir MATTI VIHERVUORI; Editor-in-Chief OLLI-PEKKA BEHM; circ. 30,076.

Joensuu

Karjalainen: Kosti Aaltosentie 9, POB 99, 80141 Joensuu; tel. (13) 2551; fax (13) 2552363; e-mail toimitus@karjalainen.fi; internet www.karjalainen.fi; f. 1874; independent; Man. Dir RAIMO PUUSTINEN; Editor PEKKA SITARI; circ. 47,636.

Jyväskylä

Keskisuomalainen: Aholaidantie 3, POB 159, 40101 Jyväskylä; tel. (14) 622000; fax (14) 622272; e-mail tiepal@keskisuomalainen.fi; internet www.keskisuomalainen.fi; f. 1871; Man. Dir ERKKI PORANEN; Editor ERKKI LAATIKAINEN; circ. 77,475.

Kajaani

Kainuun Sanomat: Viestitie 2, POB 150, 87101 Kajaani; tel. (8) 61661; fax (8) 6166307; e-mail toimitus@kainuunsanomat.fi; internet www.kainuunsanomat.fi; f. 1918; independent; Man. Dir JUHA RUOTSALAINEN; Editor-in-Chief MATTI PIIRAINEN; circ. 23,454.

Kemi

Pohjolan Sanomat: Sairaalakatu 2,94100 Kemi; tel. (16) 2911; fax (16) 291300; e-mail ps.toimitus@pohjolansanomat.fi; internet www .pohjolansanomat.fi; f. 1915; Man. Dir MARTTI NIKKANEN; Editor-in-Chief HEIKKI LÄÄKKÖLÄ; circ. 23,483.

Kokkola

Keskipohjanmaa: Kosila, POB 45, 67101 Kokkola; tel. (6) 8272000; fax (6) 8220208; internet www.keskipohjanmaa.net; f. 1917; independent; Man. Dir EINO LAUKKA; Editor LASSI JAAKKOLA; circ. 28,385.

Kotka

Kymen Sanomat: POB 27, 48101 Kotka; tel. (5) 210015; fax (5) 21005206; e-mail uutiset@kymensanomat.fi; internet www .kymensanomat.fi; f. 1902; independent; Man. Dir ANTTI MÄKELÄ; Editor MARKKU ESPO; circ. 27,408.

Kouvola

Kouvolan Sanomat: POB 40, 45101 Kouvola; tel. (5) 828911; fax (5) 3115335; e-mail ks.toimitus@kouvolansanomat.fi; internet www .kouvolansanomat.fi; f. 1909; independent; Man. Dir ANTTI MÄKELA; Editor-in-Chief VILLE POHJONEN; circ. 29,974.

Kuopio

Savon Sanomat: POB 68, 70101 Kuopio; tel. (17) 303111; fax (17) 303347; e-mail lukijansanomat@iwn.fi; internet www .savonsanomat.fi; f. 1907; independent; Man. Dir HEIKKI AURASMAA; Editor-in-Chief TAPANI LEPOLA; circ. 67,185.

Lahti

Etelä-Suomen Sanomat: Ilmarisentie 7, POB 80, 15101 Lahti; tel. (3) 75757; fax (3) 7575466; internet www.ess.fi; f. 1900; independent; Man. Dir JUKKA OTTELA; Editor-in-Chief HEIKKI HAKALA; circ. 62,218.

Lappeenranta

Etelä-Saimaa: POB 3, 53501 Lappeenranta; tel. (5) 677111; fax (5) 4516936; internet www.esaimaa.fi; f. 1885; independent; Man. Dir ANTERO JUNTTILA; Editor JORMA HERNESMAA; circ. 34,419.

Mikkeli

Länsi-Savo: POB 6, 50101 Mikkeli; tel. (15) 3501; fax (15) 350337; e-mail toimitus@lansi-savo.fi; internet www.lansi-savo.fi; independent; Man. Dir JUKKA TIKKA; Editor-in-Chief KARI JUUTILAINEN; circ. 26,149.

Oulu

Kaleva: POB 170, 90401 Oulu; tel. (8) 5377111; fax (8) 5377195; e-mail kaleva@kaleva.fi; internet www.kaleva.fi; f. 1899; independent; Man. Dir TAISTO RISKI; Editor-in-Chief RISTO UIMONEN; circ. 84,106.

Pori

Satakunnan Kansa: POB 58, 28101 Pori; tel. (2) 6228111; fax (2) 6228392; e-mail sk.toimitus@satakunnankansa.fi; internet www .satakunnankansa.fi; f. 1873; independent; Man. Dir TUOMO SAAR-INEN; Editor-in-Chief ERKKI TEIKARI; circ. 56,781.

Rauma

Länsi-Suomi: Susivuorentie 2, 26100 Rauma; tel. (2) 83361; fax (2) 8420959; f. 1905; independent; Man. Dir and Editor-in-Chief PAULI UUSI-KILPONEN; circ. 17,171.

Rovaniemi

Lapin Kansa: Veitikantie 2–8, 96100 Rovaniemi; tel. (16) 320011; fax (16) 3200345; e-mail lktoimitus@lapinkansa.fi; internet www .lapinkansa.fi; f. 1928; independent; Man. Dir HEIKKI OLLILA; Editor-in-Chief HEIKKI TUOMI-NIKULA; circ. 35,887.

Salo

Salon Seudun Sanomat: Örninkatu 14, POB 117, 24101 Salo; tel. (2) 77021; fax (2) 7702300; internet www.sss.fi; independent; Man. Dir KIRSTI KIRJONEN; Editor-in-Chief JARMO VÄHÄSILTA; circ. 21,913.

Savonlinna

Itä-Savo: POB 101, 57101 Savonlinna; tel. (15) 51740; organ of the Keskusta (Centre) Party; Man. Dir PAAVO SARRANEN; Editor KYÖSTI PILAIMÄKI; circ. 20,821.

Seinäjoki

Ilkka: POB 60, 60101 Seinäjoki; tel. (6) 4186555; fax (6) 4186500; e-mail ilkka.toimitus@ilkka.fi; internet www.ilkka.fi; f. 1906; independent; Man. Dir MATTI KORKIATUPA; Editor-in-Chief KARI HOK-KANEN; circ. 54,976.

Tampere

Aamulehti: POB 327, 33101 Tampere; tel. (3) 2666111; fax (3) 2666259; internet www.aamulehti.fi; f. 1881; Editor MATTI APUNEN; circ. 133,779 weekdays, 142,157 Sunday.

Turku

Turun Sanomat: POB 95, 20101 Turku; tel. (2) 2693311; fax (2) 2693274; e-mail ts.toimitus@ts-group.fi; internet www .turunsanomat.fi; f. 1904; independent; Man. Dir KEIJO KETONEN; Editors-in-Chief ARI VALJAKKA, RAIMO VAHTERA, AIMO MASSINEN; circ. 114,086 weekdays, 125,318 Sunday.

Tuusula

Keski-Uusimaa: POB 52, 04301 Tuusula; tel. (9) 273000; fax (9) 27300205; e-mail toimitus@keskiuusimaa.fi; internet www .kcskiuusimaa.fi; independent; Man. Dir JORMA HÄMÄLÄINEN; Editor-in-Chief EERO LEHTINEN; circ. 21,851.

Vaasa

Pohjalainen: Pitkäkatu 37, POB 37, 65101 Vaasa; tel. (6) 3249111; fax (6) 3249351; e-mail kari.mantila@pohjalainen.fi; internet www .pohjalainen.fi; f. 1903; independent; Man. Dir MATTI KORKIATUPA; Editor MARKU MANTILA; circ. 33,491.

Vasabladet: Sandögatan 6, POB 52, 65101 Vaasa; tel. (6) 3260211; fax (6) 3129003; e-mail tips@vasabladet.fi; internet www.vasabladet .fi; f. 1856; Swedish language; Liberal independent; Man. Dir HANS BOIJE; Editor-in-Chief DENNIS RUNDT; circ. 26,500.

PRINCIPAL PERIODICALS

7 päivää: POB 124, 00151 Helsinki; tel. (9) 177777; fax (9) 177477; weekly; television and radio; circ. 127,810.

Ahjo: POB 107, 00531 Helsinki; tel. (9) 77071; fax (9) 7707400; e-mail ahjo@metalliliitto.fi; fortnightly; for metal industry employees; Editor-in-Chief HEIKKI PISKONEN; circ. 164,000.

Aku Ankka (Donald Duck): POB 40, 00040 Helsinki; tel. (9) 1201; fax (9) 1205569; f. 1951; weekly; children's; Editor-in-Chief MARKKU KIVEKÄS; circ. 283,334.

Apu: Hitsaajankatu 10, 00081 Helsinki; tel. (9) 75961; fax (9) 781911; e-mail matti.saari@apu.fi; internet www.apu.fi; f. 1933; weekly; family journal; Editor-in-Chief MATTI SAARI; circ. 254,696.

Avotakka: Hitsaajankatu 7/6, 00081 A-lehdet, Helsinki; tel. (9) 75961; fax (9) 7591268; e-mail avotakka@a-lehdet.fi; internet www .a-lehdet.fi/avotakka; f. 1967; monthly; interior decorating; Editor-in-Chief SOILI UKKOLA; circ. 102,162.

Birka: Köydenpunojankatu 2A, 00180 Helsinki; tel. (9) 15668510; fax (9) 15668525; 10 a year; trade; in Swedish; circ. 64,189.

Diabetes: Kirjoniementie 15, 33680 Tampere; tel. (3) 2860111; fax (3) 3600462; e-mail lehdet@diabetes.fi; internet www.diabetes.fi; f. 1949; monthly; health; circ. 56,120.

Eeva: Hitsaajankatu 7/7, 00081 A-lehdet, Helsinki; tel. (9) 75961; fax (9) 786858; e-mail eeva@a-lehdet.fi; internet www.a-lehdet.fi/ eeva; f. 1933; monthly; women's; Editor-in-Chief LIISA JÄPPINEN; circ. 99,678.

Erä: Esterinportti 1, 00015 Kuvalehdet, Helsinki; tel. (9) 15661; fax (9) 15666210; e-mail era@kuvalehdet.fi; internet www.kuvalehdet .fi; monthly; sport fishing and outdoor leisure; Editor SEPPO SUUR-ONEN; circ. 52,088.

ET-lehti: POB 100, 00040 Helsinki; tel. (9) 1201; fax (9) 1205428; e-mail kaisa.larmela@helsinkimedia.fi; monthly; over 50s magazine; Editor-in-Chief KAISA LARMELA; circ. 250,000.

Gloria: POB 100, 00040 Helsinki; tel. (9) 1201; fax (9) 1205427; e-mail gloria@helsinkimedia.fi; monthly; women's; Editor-in-Chief RIITTA LINDEGREN; circ. 64,000.

Hippo: POB 308, 00101 Helsinki; tel. (9) 4041; fax (9) 4042165; 4 a year; Editor-in-Chief STINA SUOMINEN; circ. 188,141.

Hymy: Maistraatinportti 1, 00240 Helsinki; tel. (9) 15661; fax (9) 15666206; monthly; family journal; Editor ESKO TULUSTO; circ. 94,527.

Hyvä Terveys: POB 100, 00040 Sanoma Magazines; tel. (9) 1201; fax (9) 1205456; e-mail hyva.terveys@sanomamagazines.fi; internet www.hyvaterveys.fi; 11 a year; health; Editor-in-Chief JALI RUUS-KANEN; circ. 102,000.

IT-Invalidityö: Kumpulantie 1A, 00520 Helsinki; tel. (9) 613191; fax (9) 1461443; e-mail it-lehti@invalidiliitto.fi; internet www .it-lehti.fi; 12 a year; for handicapped people; Editor-in-Chief PEKKA HUOLMAN; circ. 51,611.

Kaksplus: Maistraatinportti 1, 00015 Kuvalehdet; tel. (9) 1566591; fax (9) 1566550; e-mail kaksplus@kuvalehdet.fi; internet www

.kaksplus.fi; f. 1969; monthly; for families with young children; Editor-in-Chief MARI IKONEN; circ. 46,740.

Katso: Hitsaajankatu 7/5, 00081 A-lehdet, Helsinki; tel. (9) 75961; fax (9) 7596342; e-mail katso@a-lehdet.fi; internet www.a-lehdet.fi/katso; f. 1960; weekly; TV, radio, film and video; Editor-in-Chief MARKKU VEIJALAINEN; circ. 70,388.

Kauneus ja terveys: Hitsaajankatu 10, 00081 Helsinki; tel. (9) 75961; fax (9) 786858; monthly; health and beauty; circ. 61,647.

Kirkko ja kaupunki: POB 137, 00201 Helsinki; tel. (9) 613021; fax (9) 61302342; weekly; church and community; Editor-in-Chief SEPPO SIMOLA; circ. 207,528.

Kodin Kuvalehti: POB 100, 00040 Helsinki; tel. (9) 1201; fax (9) 1205468; e-mail kodin.kuvalehti@helsinkimedia.fi; fortnightly; family magazine; Editor LEENA KARO; circ. 180,068.

Kotilääkäri: Maistraatinportti 1, 00240 Helsinki; tel. (9) 15661; fax (9) 1566507; e-mail kotilaakari@kuvalehdet.fi; f. 1889; monthly; health and beauty; Editor-in-Chief TARJA HURME; circ. 64,769.

Kotiliesi: Maistraatinportti 1, 00240 Helsinki; tel. (9) 15661; fax (9) 147724; f. 1922; fortnightly; women's; Editor-in-Chief ELINA SIMONEN-HYVÄRINEN; circ. 200,474.

Kotivinkki: Kalevankatu 56, 00180 Helsinki; tel. (9) 773951; fax (9) 77395399; monthly; women's; Editor-in-Chief ANNELI MYLLER; circ. 207,550.

Me Naiset: POB 100, 00040 Helsinki; tel. (9) 1201; fax (9) 1205414; internet www.menaiset.fi; f. 1952; weekly; women's; Editor ULLA-MAIJA PAAVILAINEN; circ. 115,000.

Metsälehti: Soidinkj 4, 00700 Helsinki; tel. (9) 1562333; fax (9) 1562335; e-mail paavo.seppanen@metsalehti.mailnet.fi; internet www.metsalehti.fi; f. 1933; fortnightly; forestry; Editor PAAVO SEPPÄNEN; circ. 37,606.

MikroPC: POB 920, 00101 Helsinki; tel. (9) 148801; fax (9) 6856631; 20 a year; computers; circ. 39,000.

Nykyposti: Maistraatinportti 1, 00240 Helsinki; tel. (9) 15661; fax (9) 144595; f. 1977; monthly; family journal; Editor JAANA LAUKKANEN; circ. 107,375.

Partio: Kylänvanhimmantie 29, 00640 Helsinki; tel. (9) 25331100; fax (9) 25331160; e-mail jaana.kivipelto@sp.partio.fi; six a year; the Scout movement; circ. 57,188.

Pellervo: POB 77, 00101 Helsinki; tel. (9) 4767501; fax (9) 6948945; e-mail toimisto@pellervo.fi; internet www.pellervo.fi; f. 1899; monthly; agricultural and co-operative journal; organ of the central organization of co-operatives; Editor-in-Chief KAISU RÄSÄNEN; circ. 35,188.

PerusSuomalainen: Mannerheimintie 40 B 56, 00100 Helsinki; tel. (9) 4540411; fax (9) 4540466; e-mail peruss@perussuomalaiset.fi; f. 1936; 12 a year; organ of the Perussuomalaiset-Sannfinländarna rp (PerusS—True Finns); Editor ROLF (FRED) SORMO; circ. 75,000.

Pirkka: Kanavakatu 3B, 00160 Helsinki; tel. (9) 1053010; fax (9) 105336235; 10 a year; Swedish; trade; Editor-in-Chief KAISA PEUTERE; circ. 2,278,939.

Reserviläinen: Döbelninkatu 2, 00260 Helsinki; tel. (9) 40562018; fax (9) 499875; e-mail reservilainen@maanpuolustusyhtio.fi; nine a year; military; circ. 60,000.

Sähköviesti/Elbladet: POB 1427, 00101 Helsinki; tel. (9) 53052700; fax (9) 53052801; e-mail ari.vesa@energia.fi; f. 1939; quarterly; publ. by Asscn of Finnish Electric Utilities; Editor-in-Chief ARI J. VESA; circ. 101,575.

Sampovisio: POB 2, 00040 Helsinki; tel. (9) 1205964; fax (9) 1205999; six a year; business, finance; circ. 65,000.

Seura: Maistraatinportti 1, 00240 Helsinki; tel. (9) 15661; fax (9) 1496472; f. 1934; weekly; family journal; Editor-in-Chief JOUNI FLINKKILÄ; circ. 268,553.

STTK—lehti: POB 248, 00171 Helsinki; tel. (9) 131521; fax (9) 652367; e-mail matti.hynynen@sttk.fi; eight a year; organ of Finnish Confederation of Salaried Employees; Editor-in-Chief MATTI HYNYNEN; circ. 40,000.

Suomen Kuvalehti: Maistraatinportti 1, 00015 Kuvalehdet; tel. (9) 15661; fax (9) 144076; e-mail suomen.kuvalehti@kuvalehdet.fi; internet www.suomenkuvalehti.fi; f. 1916; weekly; illustrated news; Editor-in-Chief TAPANI RUOKANEN; circ. 102,715.

Suosikki: Maistraatinportti 1, 00015 Yhtyneet Kuvalehdet; tel. (9) 1566553; fax (9) 1445595; e-mail suosikki@kuvalehdet.fi; internet www.suosikki.fi; monthly; pop music; Editor-in-Chief JYRKI HÄMÄLÄINEN; circ. 75,000.

Suuri Käsityölehti: POB 100, 00040 Helsinki; tel. (9) 1201; fax (9) 1205428; f. 1974; monthly; needlework, knitting and dress-making magazine; Editor KRISTINA TÖTTERMAN; circ. 126,858.

Talouselämä: Malminkatu 30, POB 920, 00101 Helsinki; tel. 2044240; fax 204424108; e-mail te@talentum.fi; internet www.talouselama.fi; f. 1938; 43 a year; economy, business; Man. Dir HARRI ROSCHIER; Editor-in-Chief PEKKA SEPPÄNEN; circ. 78,804.

Tekniikan Maailma: Esterinportti 1, 00240 Helsinki; tel. (9) 15661; fax (9) 15666313; e-mail tekniikan.maailma@kuvalehdet.fi; internet www.tekniikanmaailma.fi; f. 1953; 20 a year; technical review; Editor-in-Chief MARTTI J. MERILINNA; circ. 140,838.

Trendi: Kalevankatu 56A, 00180 A-lehdet, Helsinki; tel. (9) 773951; fax (9) 77395399; 10 a year; women's lifestyle; circ. 62,063.

Tuulilasi: Hitsaajankatu 7/6, 00081 A-lehdet; tel. (9) 75961; fax (9) 787311; e-mail tuulilasi@a-lehdet.fi; internet www.tuulilasi.fi; f. 1963; monthly; motoring; Editor-in-Chief LAURI LARMELA; circ. 87,777.

Työ Terveys Turvallisuus: Topeliuksenkatu 41A, 00250 Helsinki; tel. (9) 47471; fax (9) 47472478; f. 1971; 12 a year; occupational safety and health; Editor-in-Chief MATTI TAPIAINEN; circ. 69,923.

Valitut Palat: POB 46, 00441 Helsinki; tel. (9) 503441; fax (9) 5034499; monthly; Finnish Reader's Digest; Editor-in-Chief TOM LUNDBERG; circ. 354,103.

Voi Hyvin: Hitsaajankatu 7, 00081 Helsinki; tel. (9) 75961; fax (9) 786858; e-mail voihyvin@a-lehdet.fi; six a year; health; circ. 75,000.

Yhteishyvä: Fleminginkatu 34, POB 171, 00511 Helsinki; tel. (9) 1882621; fax (9) 1882626; e-mail elo@sok.fi; internet www.yhteiashyva.fi; f. 1905; monthly; free to members of co-operative group; Editor-in-Chief PENTTI TÖRMÄLÄ; circ. 848,000.

NEWS AGENCIES

Oy Suomen Tietotoimisto-Finska Notisbyrån Ab (STT-FNB): Albertinkatu 33, POB 550, 00101 Helsinki; tel. (9) 695811; fax (9) 69581335; e-mail toimitus@stt.fi; internet www.stt.fi; f. 1887; nine provincial branches; independent national agency distributing domestic and international news in Finnish and Swedish; Chair. SEPPO KIEVARI; Gen. Man. and Editor-in-Chief MIKAEL PENTIKÄINEN.

Foreign Bureaux

Agence France-Presse (AFP) (France): Hämeentie 101B, 38, 00500 Helsinki; tel. (9) 737693; fax (9) 27095339; Correspondent PASCAL ZERLING.

Agenzia Nazionale Stampa Associata (ANSA) (Italy): Albertinkatu 33, 00180 Helsinki; tel. 503075115; fax (9) 69581335; e-mail anna.torvalds@stt.fi; Correspondent ANNA TORVALDS.

Associated Press (AP) (USA): Erottasankatu 9A, 00130 Helsinki; tel. (9) 6802394; fax (9) 6802310; Correspondent MATTI HUUHTANEN.

Informatsionnoye Telegrafnoye Agentstvo Rossii—Telegrafnoye Agentstvo Suverennykh Stran (ITAR—TASS) (Russia): Ratakatu 1A B 10, 00120 Helsinki; tel. (9) 601877; fax (9) 601151; e-mail ryhels@hotmail.com; internet www.itar-tass.com; Dir YURI ROMANTSOV.

Inter Press Service (IPS) (Italy): Helsinki; tel. (9) 7536954; fax (9) 7536964; e-mail ips@kaapeli.fi; Editor MILLA SUNDSTRÖM.

Reuters (UK): Yrjönkatu 23B7, POB 550, 00100 Helsinki; tel. (9) 68050247; fax (9) 6802284; Correspondent ADAM JASSER.

Rossiyskoye Informatsionnoye Agentstvo—Novosti (RIA-Novosti) (Russia): Lönnrotinkatu 25A, 00180 Helsinki; tel. (9) 6820580; fax (9) 6942357; Dir LEONID LAAKSO; Correspondent RUDOLF HILTUNEN.

Xinhua (New China) News Agency (People's Republic of China): Hopeasalmentie 14, 00570 Helsinki; tel. (9) 6847587; fax (9) 6848629; Correspondents ZHENG HUANGING, QIE SHUANGTAO.

PRESS ASSOCIATIONS

Aikakauslehtien Liitto (Periodical Publishers' Association): Lönnrotinkatu 11, 00120 Helsinki; tel. (9) 22877280; fax (9) 603478; internet www.aikakaus.fi; f. 1946; aims to further the interests of publishers of magazines and periodicals, to encourage co-operation between publishers, and to improve standards; Man. Dir MATTI AHTOMIES.

Suomen Journalistiliitto—Finlands Journalistförbund r.y. (Union of Journalists): Hietalahdenkatu 2B22, 00180 Helsinki; tel. (9) 6122330; fax (9) 644120; e-mail eila.hypponen@journalistiliito.fi; internet www.journalistiliito.fi; f. 1921; 12,703 mems; Pres. PEKKA LAINE; Sec.-Gen. EILA HYPPÖNEN.

Sanomalehtien Liitto—Tidningarnas Förbund (Finnish Newspapers Association): Lönnrotinkatu 11, 00120 Helsinki; tel. (9) 22877300; fax (9) 607989; e-mail info@sanomalehdet.fi; internet www.sanomalehdet.fi; f. 1908; represents the press in relations with Government and advertisers; undertakes technical research; promotes newspaper advertising; 202 mems; Dir KRISTIINA MARKKULA.

Publishers

Art House Oy: Bulevardi 19c, 00120 Helsinki; tel. (9) 6932727; fax (9) 6949028; f. 1975; Finnish and foreign fiction, non-fiction, popular science, horror, fantasy, science fiction, detective fiction; Publr Paavo Haavikko.

Gummerus Kustannus Oy: Arkadiankatu 23b, POB 749, 00101 Helsinki; tel. (9) 584301; fax (9) 58430200; e-mail publisher@gummerus.fi; internet www.gummerus.fi/kustannus; f. 1872; fiction, non-fiction, encyclopaedias, dictionaries; Man. Dir Ahti Sirkiä.

Helsinki Media Oy: POB 100, 00040 Helsinki; tel. (9) 1201; fax (9) 1205171; internet www.helsinkimedia.fi; f. 1993; magazines, directories, children's books, comics, non-fiction; Pres. Eija Ailasmaa.

Karisto Oy: Paroistentie 2, POB 102, 13101 Hämeenlinna; tel. (3) 63151; fax (3) 6161565; f. 1900; non-fiction and fiction, the printing industry; Man. Dir Simo Moisio.

Kirjapaja: POB 137, 00201 Helsinki; tel. (9) 613021; fax (9) 61302341; e-mail mira.pitkanen@kirjapaja.fi; internet www.kirjapaja.fi; f. 1942; Christian literature, general fiction, non-fiction, reference, juvenile; Man. Dir Mira Pitkänen.

Kustannus-Mäkelä Oy: POB 14, 03601 Karkkila; tel. (9) 2257995; fax (9) 2257660; f. 1971; juvenile, fiction; Man. Dir Orvo Mäkelä.

Oy Like Kustannus Ltd: Meritullinkatu 21, 00170 Helsinki; tel. (9) 1351385; fax (9) 1351372; e-mail likekustannus@dlc.fi; f. 1987; film literature, fiction, non-fiction, comics; Man. Dir Hannu Paloviita.

Otava Publishing Co Ltd: Uudenmaankatu 10, 00120 Helsinki; tel. (9) 19961; fax (9) 643136; e-mail otava@otava.fi; internet www.otava.fi; f. 1890; non-fiction, fiction, the printing industry, science, juvenile, and textbooks; Man. Dir Antti Reenpää.

Schildts Förlags Ab: Rusthållargatan 1, 02270 Espoo; tel. (9) 8870400; fax (9) 8043257; e-mail schildts@schildts.fi; f. 1913; subjects mainly in Swedish; Man. Dir Johan Johnson.

Söderström & Co Förlags Ab: Georgsgatan 29a, 00100 Helsinki; tel. (9) 68418620; fax (9) 68418621; e-mail soderstr@soderstrom.fi; f. 1891; all subjects in Swedish only; Man. Dir Marianne Bargum.

Suomalaisen Kirjallisuuden Seura, SKS (Finnish Literature Society): POB 259, 00171 Helsinki; tel. (9) 131231; fax (9) 13123220; internet www.finlit.fi; f. 1831; Finnish and other Finno-Ugric languages, Finnish literature, literary scholarship, folklore, comparative ethnology and history; Publishing Dir Päivi Vallisaari.

Tammi Publishers: Urho Kekkosen katu 4–6e, 00100 Helsinki; tel. (9) 6937621; fax (9) 69376266; e-mail tammi@tammi.net; internet www.tammi.net; f. 1943; fiction, non-fiction, juvenile; Man. Dir Pentti Molander.

Weilin & Göös Oy: Kappelitie 8, 02200 Espoo; tel. (9) 43771; fax (9) 4377270; e-mail weegee@wg.fi; internet www.wg.fi; f. 1872; non-fiction, encyclopaedias.

Werner Söderström Corporation (WSOY): Bulevardi 12, 00120 Helsinki; tel. (9) 61681; fax (9) 61683560; internet www.wsoy.fi; f. 1878; fiction and non-fiction, science, juvenile, textbooks, reference, comics, the printing industry; Pres. Antero Siljola.

PUBLISHERS' ASSOCIATION

Suomen Kustannusyhdistys (Finnish Book Publishers' Association): POB 177, 00121 Helsinki; tel. (9) 22877258; fax (9) 6121226; e-mail veikko.sonninen@skyry.net; internet www.skyry.net; f. 1858; Chair. Olli Arrakoski; Man. Dir Veikko Sonninen; 97 mems.

Broadcasting and Communications

TELECOMMUNICATIONS

Finnish Communications Regulatory Authority: Itämerenkatu 3a, POB 313, 00181 Helsinki; tel. (9) 69661; fax (9) 6966410; e-mail info@ficora.fi; internet www.ficora.fi; affiliated to Ministry of Transport and Communications; CEO Rauni Hagman.

Elisa Communications: Korkeavuorenkatu 35–37, POB 10, 00061 Elisa; tel. (9) 1026000; fax (9) 1026060; internet www.elisa.com; Pres. and CEO Matti Mattheiszen.

Finnet International Ltd: Itämerenkatu 1, POB 999, 00181 Helsinki; tel. (9) 695500; fax (9) 69550300.

Nokia Oyj: Keilalahdentie 4, 02150 Espoo; POB 226, 00045 Nokia Group; tel. (0)718008000; fax (0)718038226; internet www.nokia.com; Pres. and CEO Jorma Ollila.

Sonera Ltd: Teollisuuskatu 15, POB 106, 00051 Sonera; tel. (9) 20401; fax (9) 204060025; internet www.sonera.fi; fmrly Telecom Finland Ltd; 52.8% state-owned; Pres. and CEO Harri Koponen.

Telecon Ltd: POB 110, Teollisuuskatu 15, 00511 Helsinki; tel. (9) 20405390; fax (9) 20405389; e-mail telecon@telecon.fi; Man. Dir Yrjö Sirkeinen.

RADIO

Yleisradio Oy (YLE) (Finnish Broadcasting Company): POB 90, 00024 Yleisradio; tel. (9) 14801; fax (9) 14803216; e-mail fbc@yle.fi; internet www.yle.fi/fbc; f. 1926; 99.9% state-owned, with management appointed by the Administrative Council; Dir-Gen. Arne Wessberg; Dir of Radio and Deputy Dir-Gen. Seppo Härkönen; Dir of Television Olli-Pekka Heinonen; Dir of Swedish-language Radio and Television Programmes Ann Sandelin.

Digita Oy: POB 135, 00521 Helsinki; tel. (9) 20411711; fax (9) 204117234; e-mail pauli.heikkila@digita.fi; internet www.digita.fi; f. 1999; 100%-owned by Yleisradio Oy (YLE); provides transmission services to YLE, MTV3, Channel Four Finland and Radio Nova; Man. Dir Pauli Heikkilä.

YLE R1 (Radio Ylen Ykkönen): 24-hour arts and culture in Finnish; Dir Olli Alho.

YLE R2 (Radiomafia): 24-hour popular culture for young people in Finnish; Dir Jukka Haarma.

YLE R3 (Radio Suomi): 24-hour news, current affairs, sport, regional programmes in Finnish; Dir Raimo Vanninen.

YLE R4 (Radio Extrem): Swedish-language channel for young people; Dir Richard Nordgren.

YLE R5 (Radio Vega): news, current affairs, art, culture and regional programmes in Swedish; Dir Peik Henrichson.

Capital FM: 24-hour local service in the Helsinki area combining broadcasts by YLE and several foreign radio stations.

Radio Finland: broadcasts in Finnish, Swedish, English, German, French, Russian and Classical Latin.

Radio Peili: Finland's first digital radio service, began operations in 1998.

Sámi Radio: Sámi-language network covering northern Lapland.

Experimental Finnish local radio began operations in 1984, and in 1995 there were 61 local radio stations, of which two were broadcasting on a semi-national basis.

TELEVISION

Oy Yleisradio Ab (YLE): (see above) operates two national networks, TV 1 and TV 2, and leases the third network to the commercial company MTV Finland (see below).

YLE/TV 1: POB 97, 00024 Helsinki; tel. (9) 14801; fax (9) 14803424; internet www.yle.fi/tv1; f. 1957; programmes in Finnish.

YLE/TV 2: POB 196, 33101 Tampere; tel. (3) 3456111; fax (3) 3456892; internet www.yle.fi/tv2; f. 1964; programmes in Finnish and Swedish; Dir Jyrki Pakarinen.

YLE/TV 4: relays programmes from Sweden for coastal areas in southern Finland.

MTV Finland: 00033 MTV3; 00240 Helsinki; tel. (9) 15001; fax (9) 1500707; e-mail palaute@mtv3.fi; internet www.mtv3.fi; f. 1957; independent nation-wide commercial television company producing programmes on the third national network (MTV3), leased from YLE, the state broadcasting company (see above); became part of Alma Media Corpn in 1998; broadcasts about 120 hours per week; Pres. and CEO Pekka Karhuvaara.

Oy Ruutunelonen Ab: POB 40, 00521 Helsinki; tel. (9) 45451; fax (9) 1482323; e-mail juha-pekka.louhelainen@nelonen.fi; internet www.nelonen.fi; independent commercial television co reaching 81% of households via terrestrial, satellite and cable broadcasting; 90.6% owned by Swelcom Oy; CEO Juha-Pekka Louhelainen.

Finance

The Bank of Finland is the country's central bank and the centre of Finland's monetary and banking system. It functions 'under guarantee and supervision of the Eduskunta (Parliament) and the Bank supervisors delegated by the Eduskunta'.

At the end of 2000 there were a total of 355 domestic banks operating in Finland, of which eight were commercial banks. There were 244 co-operative banks belonging to the OKO Bank Group, 43 local co-operative banks and 40 savings banks. There were six foreign credit institutions, with a total of 27 branches.

In addition to the above, there were finance and credit card companies, mortgage banks and special credit institutions. Insurance companies (numbering over 60) also grant credit.

BANKING

(cap. = capital; res = reserves; dep. = deposits; m. = million; brs = branches; amounts in euros (€))

Supervisory Authority

Financial Supervision Authority: Snellmaninkatu 1, POB 159, 00101 Helsinki; tel. (9) 18351; fax (9) 1835328; e-mail rahoitustarkastus@bof.fi; internet www.rata.bof.fi; f. 1993; maintains confidence in the financial markets by supervising the markets and the bodies working within them. It functions administratively in connection with the Bank of Finland, but operates as an independent decision-making body; Dir-Gen. KAARLO JÄNNÄRI.

Central Bank

Suomen Pankki/Finlands Bank (The Bank of Finland): Snellmaninaukio, POB 160, 00101 Helsinki; tel. (9) 1831; fax (9) 174872; e-mail info@bof.fi; internet www.bof.fi; f. 1811; Bank of Issue under the guarantee and supervision of Parliament; cap. €841m., res €309m., dep. €4,222 (Dec. 2001); Gov. MATTI VANHALA; 4 brs.

Commercial Banks

Nordea Bank Finland: Aleksanterinkatu 36, 00100 Helsinki; tel. (9) 1651; fax (9) 16554500; internet www.nordea.fi; cap. €1,182m., res 9,069m., dep. €179,262m. (Dec. 2001); CEO THORLEIF KRARUP.

Sampo Bank PLC: Unioninkatu 22, Helsinki, 00075 Sampo; tel. 1051515; fax 105140051; e-mail viestinta@sampo.fi; internet www .sampo.fi; subsidiary of financial holding co Sampo PLC (formed by merger of Leonia Bank PLC—f. 1886 as Postipankki Ltd—with insurance company Sampo PLC in 2001); cap. €106m., res €690m., dep. €14,642m. (Dec. 2001); CEO BJÖRN WAHLROOS; 63 brs.

Co-operative Banks

Association of Finnish Local Co-operative Banks: Yrjöninkatu 23A, POB 1290, 00101 Helsinki; tel. (9) 6811700; fax (9) 68117070; internet www.paikallisosuuspankit.fi; f. 1997; central organization of local co-operative banking group, which comprises 43 local co-operatives; cap. €200m., dep. €1,600m., total assets €2,062m. (Dec. 2000); 241 brs.

OKO Osuuspankkien Keskuspankki Oyj (OKO Bank): Teollisuuskatu 1B, POB 308, 00101 Helsinki; tel. (9) 4041; fax (9) 4042002; internet www.okobank.com; f. 1902; cap. €618m., dep. €2,659m., total assets €12,650m. (Dec. 2001); Chair. and CEO ANTTI TANSKANEN; Pres. MIKAEL SILVENNOINEN; 693 brs.

Savings Banks

Aktia Sparbank Abp (Aktia Savings Bank PLC): Mannerheimintie 14, 00100 Helsinki; tel. 102475000; fax 102476356; e-mail kommunikation@aktia.fi; internet www.aktia.fi; f. 1852; current name adopted 1997; cap. €71m., res €67m., dep. €2,941m. (Dec. 2001); Chair. PATRICK ENCKELL; Man. Dir ERIK ANDERSON; 62 brs.

Mortgage Banks

OP-Asuntoluottopankki: POB 308, 00101 Helsinki; tel. (9) 4041; fax (9) 4042620; f. 2000; part of OKO Bank Group.

Suomen Asuntoluottopankki (Housing Loan Bank of Finland): Unioninkatu 22, 00075 Sampo; tel. 105135789; fax 105134616; f. 2000; part of Sampo Group; cap. €6m., total assets €25m. (Dec. 2000).

Investment Banks

Nordiska Investeringsbanken (Nordic Investment Bank): Fabianinkatu 34, POB 249, 00171 Helsinki; tel. (9) 18001; fax (9) 1800210; e-mail info@nib.fi; internet www.nib.int; f. 1976; owned by Govts of Denmark, Finland, Iceland, Norway and Sweden; cap. €404m., res €997m., dep. €12,552m. (Dec. 2001); Pres. and CEO JON SIGURÐSSON.

Banking Associations

Säästöpankkiliitto (Finnish Savings Banks Association): Mannerheimintie 14A, 00100 Helsinki; tel. (9) 618440; fax 206029108; internet www.savings-banks.fi; f. 1906; 40 mems; Chair. JOUKO TUOMOLA; Man. Dir MARKKU RUUTU; 256 brs.

Suomen Hypoteekkiyhdistys (Mortgage Society of Finland): Yrjönkatu 9, POB 509, 00101 Helsinki; tel. (9) 228361; fax (9) 647443; e-mail hypo@hypoteekkiyhdistys.fi; internet www .hypoteekkiyhdistys.fi; f. 1860; cap. €36m., total assets €336.m (Dec. 2000); Pres. MATTI INHA.

Suomen Pankkiyhdistys r.y. (The Finnish Bankers' Association): Museokatu 8A, POB 1009, 00101 Helsinki; tel. (9) 4056120; fax (9) 40561291; e-mail info@fba.fi; internet www.fba.fi; f. 1914; Chair. KARI JORDAN; Man. Dir MARKUS FOGELHOLM.

Suomen Rahoitusyhtiöiden Yhdistys r.y. (Finnish Finance Houses' Association): Museokatu 8A, POB 1009, 00101 Helsinki; tel.

(9) 4056120; fax (9) 40561291; internet www.rahoitusyhtiot.fi; f. 1974; Chair. JUKKA M. S. SALONEN.

STOCK EXCHANGE

Helsinki Exchanges (HEX Ltd, Helsinki Securities and Derivatives Exchange, Clearing House): Fabianinkatu 14, POB 361, 00131 Helsinki; tel. (9) 616671; fax (9) 61667366; e-mail juhani .erma@hex.fi; internet www.hex.fi; f. 1912; current name adopted following merger between Helsinki Stock Exchange Ltd and SOM Ltd in 1997; from 1999 Finnish derivatives were to be traded within the Swiss–German exchange, the Eurex, and from 2000 the cash market was to use the German Xetra trading system; 132 listed cos at end of December 1998; Chair. of Bd of Dirs JUSSI LAITINEN; CEO JUHANI ERMA.

INSURANCE

A list is given below of some of the more important insurance companies:

A-Vakuutus keskinäinen yhtiö (A-Vakuutus Mutual Insurance Co): Hietalahdenranta 3, POB 165, 00151 Helsinki; tel. 105040; fax 105045200; non-life; Man. Dir ESKO RINKINEN.

Aurum Life Insurance Co. Ltd: POB 308, 00101 Helsinki; tel. (9) 4042528; fax (9) 4043501; Man. Dir JUKKA RUUSKANEN.

Eurooppalainen Insurance Co Ltd: Lapinmäentie 1, 00013 Pohjola; tel. 1055911; fax 105592205; non-life; Man. Dir JOUNI AALTONEN.

Garantia Insurance Co Ltd: Salomonkatu 17A, POB 600, 00101 Helsinki; tel. (9) 685811; fax (9) 68581301; internet www.garantia.fi; non-life; Man. Dir MIKAEL ENGLUND.

Henkivakuutusosakeyhtiö Pohjola (Pohjola Life Assurance Co Ltd): POB 1068, 00101 Helsinki; tel. 1055911; fax 105596799; internet www.pohjola.fi; Man. Dir JARMO KUISMA.

Henkivakuutusosakeyhtiö Veritas (Veritas Life Insurance Co Ltd): Olavintie 2, POB 133, 20101 Turku; tel. 1055010; fax 105501690; internet www.veritas.fi; Man. Dir MATTI RUOHONEN.

Keskinäinen Eläkevakuutusyhtiö Ilmarinen (Ilmarinen Mutual Pension Insurance Co): Porkkalankatu 1, 00018 Ilmarinen; tel. 1028411; fax 102843445; e-mail info@ilmarinen.fi; internet www .ilmarinen.fi; f. 1961; statutory employment pensions; Man. Dir KARI PURO.

Keskinäinen Eläkevakuutusyhtiö Tapiola (Tapiola Mutual Pension Insurance Co): 02010 Tapiola; tel. (9) 4531; fax (9) 4532146; internet www.tapiola.fi; Pres. ASMO KALPALA; Man. Dir OLLI-PEKKA LAINE.

Keskinäinen Eläkevakuutusyhtiö Varma-Sampo (Varma-Sampo Mutual Pension Insurance Company): POB 1, 00098 Varma-Sampo; tel. 1051513; fax 105144752; e-mail information@ varma-sampo.fi; internet www.varma-sampo.fi; Man. Dir PAAVO PITKÄNEN.

Keskinäinen Henkivakuutusosakeyhtiö Suomi (Suomi Mutual Life Assurance Co): Lönnrotinkatu 5, 00120 Helsinki; tel. 1055911; fax 105596799; Man. Dir JUKKA RANTALA.

Keskinäinen Henkivakuutusyhtiö Tapiola (Tapiola Mutual Life Assurance Co): 02010 Tapiola; tel. (9) 4531; fax (9) 4532146; internet www.tapiola.fi; Pres. ASMO KALPALA; Man. Dir JUHA-PEKKA HALMEERMAKI.

Keskinäinen Vakuutusyhtiö Kaleva (Kaleva Mutual Insurance Co): Bulevardi 56, 00075 Sampo; tel. 10515225; fax 105144229; internet www.sampo.fi; Man. Dir MATTI RANTANEN.

Keskinäinen Vakuutusyhtiö Tapiola (Tapiola General Mutual Insurance Co): 02010 Tapiola; tel. (9) 4531; fax (9) 4532146; internet www.tapiola.fi; non-life; Pres. ASMO KALPALA; Man. Dir JUHA SEPPÄNEN.

Keskinäinen Yhtiö Yrittäjäinvakuutus—Fennia (Enterprise Fennia Mutual Insurance Co): Asemamiehenkatu 3, 00520 Helsinki; tel. 105031; fax 105035300; non-life; Man. Dir KARI ELO.

Lähivakuutus Keskinäinen Yhtiö (Local Insurance Mutual Co): Lintuvaarantie 2, POB 50, 02610 Espoo; tel. (9) 511011; fax (9) 51101335; e-mail myynti@lahivakuutus.fi; internet www .lahivakuutus.fi; non-life; Man. Dir HARRI KAINULAINEN.

Leonia Henkivokuutus Oy (Leonia Life Insurance Co Ltd): Fabianinkatu 7 00007 Helsinki; tel. 204256099; fax 204256299; Man. Dir ARTO JURTTILA.

Merita Henkivakaatus Oy (Merita Life Insurance Ltd): Asemakuja 2, 00020 Merita; tel. (9) 16527601; fax (9) 8594622; internet www.merita.fi/selekta; Man. Dir SEPPO ILVESSALO.

Palonvara Mutual Insurance Co: Saimaankatu 20, 15140 Lahti; tel. (3) 873300; fax (3) 8733050; e-mail palvelu@palonvara.fi; internet www.palonvara.fi; f. 1912; non-life; Man. Dir JUKKA HERTTI.

Pankavara Insurance Co Ltd: Kanavaranta 1, POB 309, 00101 Helsinki; tel. 2046131; fax 204621447; non-life; Man. Dir JUKKA KÄHKÖNEN.

Pohjanti Keskäinen Vakuutusyhtiö (Pohjantähti Mutual Insurance Co): Raatihuoneenkatu 19, POB 164, 13101 Hämeenlinna; tel. (3) 62671; fax (3) 6169303; e-mail polvelu@pohjantahti.fi; internet www.pohjantahti.fi; f. 1895; non-life; Man. Dir EERO YLÄ-SOININMÄKI.

Spruce Insurance Ltd: POB 330, 00101 Helsinki; tel. 108611; fax 108621107; e-mail leena.laakso@kemira.com; non-life; Man. Dir LEENA LAAKSO.

Teollisuusvakuutus Oy (Industrial Insurance Co Ltd): Vattuniemenkuja 8A, 00035 Helsinki; tel. 1051512; fax 105145232; internet www.sampo.fi; non-life; Man. Dir JUHA TOIVOLA.

Vakuutusosakeyhtiö Pohjola (Pohjola Insurance Co Ltd): Lapinmäentie 1, 00013 Pohjola; tel. 1055911; fax 105592205; non-life; Man. Dir JOUKKO BERGIUS.

Insurance Associations

Federation of Accident Insurance Institutions: Bulevardi 28, POB 275, 00121 Helsinki; tel. (9) 680401; fax (9) 68030389; e-mail tapani.miettinen@vakes.fi; internet www.tvl.fi; f. 1920; Man. Dir TAPANI MIETTINEN.

Federation of Finnish Insurance Companies: Bulevardi 28, 00120 Helsinki; tel. (9) 680401; fax (9) 68040216; e-mail esko.kivisaari@vakes.fi; internet www.vakes.fi/svk; f. 1942; Chair. ASMO KALPALA; Man. Dir ESKO KIVISAARI; 52 mems.

Finnish Atomic Insurance Pool, Finnish Pool of Aviation Insurers, Finnish General Reinsurance Pool: Ratakatu 9, 00120 Helsinki; tel. (9) 680149; Man. Dir K. M. STRÖMMER.

Finnish Motor Insurers' Centre: Bulevardi 28, 00120 Helsinki; tel. (9) 680401; fax (9) 68040391; e-mail lvk@vakes.fi; internet www.vakes.fi/lvk; f. 1938; Man. Dir ULLA NIKU-KOSKINEN.

Finnish Pension Alliance TELA: Lastenkodinkuja 1, 00180 Helsinki; tel. (9) 695560; fax (9) 69556200; f. 1964; Man. Dir ESA SWANLJUNG.

Trade and Industry

GOVERNMENT AGENCIES

Finpro: Arkadiankatu 2, POB 908, 00101 Helsinki; tel. (204) 6951; fax (204) 695535; e-mail info@finpro.fi; internet www.finpro.fi; f. 1919 as Finnish Foreign Trade Association; Chair. ANTTI PIIPPO; Chair. of Bd JOHANNES KOROMA; CEO TAPANI KASKEALA.

Invest in Finland Bureau: Aleksanterinkatu 17, POB 800, 00101 Helsinki; tel. (9) 6969125; fax (9) 69692530; e-mail investinfinland@wtc.fi; internet www.investinfinland.fi.

DEVELOPMENT ORGANIZATION

Altia Group: Salmisaarenranta 7, POB 350, 00101 Helsinki; tel. (9) 13311; fax (9) 1333361; e-mail viestinta@altiagroup.com; internet www.altiagroup.com; f. 1932; development, manufacture, import, export, wholesale and marketing of alcoholic beverages; 100% state-owned; Pres. and CEO VEIKKO KASURINEN.

CHAMBERS OF COMMERCE

Helsinki Chamber of Commerce: Kalevankatu 12, 00100 Helsinki; tel. (9) 228601; f. 1917; Pres. KURT NORDMAN; Man. Dir HEIKKI HELIÖ; 4,100 mems.

Keskuskauppakamari (The Central Chamber of Commerce of Finland): Aleksanterinkatu 17, POB 1000, 00101 Helsinki; tel. (9) 696969; fax (9) 650303; internet www.chamber.fi; f. 1918; Gen. Man. KARI JALAS; represents 21 regional chambers of commerce.

INDUSTRIAL AND TRADE ASSOCIATIONS

Kalatalouden Keskusliitto (Federation of Finnish Fisheries Associations): Köydenpunojankatu 7B23, 00180 Helsinki; tel. (9) 6844590; fax (9) 68445959; e-mail kalastus@ahven.net; internet www.ahven.net; f. 1891; Sec. M. MYLLYLÄ; 616,000 mems.

Kaukomarkkinat Oy: Kutojantie 4, 02630 Espoo; tel. (9) 5211; fax (9) 5216641; e-mail kari.ansio@kaukomarkkinat.fi; internet www.kaukomarkkinat.fi; f. 1947; export, import and international trade; Pres. KARI ANSIO.

Kaupan Keskusliitto (Federation of Finnish Commerce and Trade): Mannerheimintie 76A, 00250 Helsinki; tel. (9) 43156122; fax (9) 43156302; e-mail e-mail@kaupankl.fi; internet www.kaupankl.fi; f. 1992; Man. Dir GUY WIRES; 40 mem. asscns with more than 14,000 firms.

Kesko Oyj (Retailers' Wholesale Co): Satamakatu 3, 00160 Helsinki; tel. (10) 5311; fax (10) 174398; internet www.kesko.fi; f. 1941; retailer-owned wholesale corporation, trading in foodstuffs, textiles, shoes, consumer goods, agricultural and builders' supplies, and machinery; Pres. MATTI HONKALA.

Oy Labor Ab (Agricultural Machinery): Helsinki; tel. (9) 7291; f. 1898; Gen. Man. KIMMO VARJOVAARA.

Maa- ja metsataloustuottajain Keskusliitto MTK r.y. (Central Union of Agricultural Producers and Forest Owners): Simonkatu 6, 00100 Helsinki; tel. (0) 204131; fax (0) 204132425; e-mail paavo.makinen@mtk.fi; internet www.mtk.fi; f. 1917; Chair. of Bd of Dirs ESA HÄRMÄLÄ; Sec.-Gen. PAAVO MÄKINEN; 179,000 mems.

Metsäteollisuus r.y. (Finnish Forest Industries' Federation): Snellmaninkatu 13, POB 336, 00171 Helsinki; tel. (9) 13261; fax (9) 1324445; e-mail timo-poranen@forestindustries.fi; internet www.forestindustries.fi; f. 1918; Man. Dir TIMO PORANEN; mems: 120 cos in the forestry industry and sales or trade asscns.

Suomalaisen Työn Liitto (Association for Finnish Work): Mikonkatu 17, POB 429, 00101 Helsinki; tel. (9) 6962430; fax (9) 6924333; e-mail stl@avainlippu.fi; internet www.avainlippu.fi; f. 1978; public relations for Finnish products and for Finnish work; Chair. of Council JARI VILÉN; Chair. of Bd of Dirs HANNU JAAKKOLA; Man. Dir LARS COLLIN; c. 1,200 mems.

Suomen Betoniteollisuuden Keskusjärjestö r.y. (Association of the Concrete Industry of Finland): Helsinki; tel. (9) 648212; fax (9) 642597; f. 1929; Chair. ERKKI INKINEN; Man. Dir ERKKI TIKKANEN; 78 mems.

Suomen Osuuskauppojen Keskusliitto (SOKL) r.y. (Finnish Co-operative Union): POB 171, 00511 Helsinki; tel. (9) 1882222; fax (9) 1882580; f. 1908; Chair. JUKKA HUISKONEN; Man. Dir TAPIO PELTOLA; 44 mems.

Svenska lantbruksproducenternas centralförbund (Central Union of Swedish-speaking Agricultural Producers): Fredriksgatan 61A, 00100 Helsinki; tel. (9) 5860460; fax (9) 6941358; internet www.slc.fi; f. 1945; Chair. H. FALCK; 18,000 mems.

Teknisen Kaupan Liitto (Association of Finnish Technical Traders): Sarkiniementie 3, 00210 Helsinki; tel. (9) 6824130; fax (9) 68241310; e-mail tekninen.kauppa@tkl.fi; internet www.tkl.fi; f. 1918; organization of the main importers dealing in steel and metals, machines and equipment, heavy chemicals and raw materials; Chair. HEIMO AHO; Man. Dir KLAUS KATARA; 225 mems.

EMPLOYERS' ORGANIZATIONS

Autoliikenteen Työnantajaliitto r.y. (Employers' Federation of Road Transport): Nuijamiestentie 7A, 00400 Helsinki; tel. (9) 47899480; fax (9) 5883995; internet www.altnet.fi; Chair. MIKKO VÄHÄLÄ; Man. Dir HANNU PARVELA; c. 1,000 mems.

Kultaseppien Työnantajaliitto r.y. (Employers' Association of Goldsmiths): Eteläranta 10, 00130 Helsinki; tel. (9) 172841; fax (9) 179588; e-mail sari.vannela@ryhma.ttliitot.fi; Chair. ILKKA RUOHOLA; Exec. Dir SARI VANNELA.

Palvelutyönantajat r.y. (Employers' Confederation of Service Industries): Eteläranta 10, 00130 Helsinki; tel. (9) 172831; fax (9) 655588; internet www.palvelutyonantajat.fi; f. 1945; 13 mem. asscns consisting of about 8,900 enterprises with 362,200 employees; Man. Dir ARTO OJALA.

Suomen Tiiliteollisuusliitto r.y. (Finnish Brick Industry Association): POB 381, 00131 Helsinki; tel. (9) 12991; fax (9) 1299214; e-mail juha.lukanka@rakeuuusteollisuusrt.fi; Chair. MAGNUS HOLM.

Teollisuuden ja Työnantajain Keskusliitto (TT) (Confederation of Finnish Industry and Employers): Eteläranta 10, POB 30, 00131 Helsinki; tel. (9) 68681; fax (9) 68682812; e-mail tt@tt.fi; internet www.tt.fi; f. 1907; renamed 1992; aims to promote co-operation between cos and mem. organizations and to protect the interests of mems in employment issues; 30 asscns consisting of about 5,600 enterprises with 500,000 employees; Chair. JURKI JUUSELA; Dir-Gen. (vacant).

Elintarviketeollisuusliitto r.y. (Finnish Food and Drink Industries' Federation): Pasilankatu 2, 00240 Helsinki; tel. (9) 148871; fax (9) 14887201; e-mail info@etl.fi; internet www.etl.fi; Chair. BERTEL PAULIG; Dir-Gen. KALEVI HEMILÄ.

Kemianteollisuus (KT) r.y. (Chemical Industry Federation): Eteläranta 10, POB 4, 00131 Helsinki; tel. (9) 172841; fax (9) 630225; internet www.chemind.fi; Chair. GEORGE BERNER; Man. Dir HANNU VORNAMO.

Kenkä- ja Nahkateollisuus r.y. (Association of Finnish Shoe and Leather Industries): Eteläranta 10, 00130 Helsinki; tel. (9) 172841; fax (9) 179588; e-mail sari.vannela@ryhma.ttliitot.fi; Chair. OLAVI VILJANMAA; Exec. Dir SARI VANNELA.

Kumiteollisuus r.y. (Rubber Manufacturers' Association): Eteläranta 10, 00130 Helsinki; tel. (9) 6220410; fax (9) 176135; e-mail tuula.rantalaiho@kumi.ttliitot.fi; internet www.kumiteollisuus.fi; Chair. Kim Gran; Man. Dir Tuula Rantalaiho.

Lääketeollisuus r.y. (Pharma Industry Finland—PIF): Sörnä isten rantatie 23, POB 108, 00501 Helsinki; tel. (9) 5842400; fax (9) 58424728; e-mail pif@pif.fi; internet www.pif.fi; Chair. Kari Järvinen; Man. Dir Jarmo Lehtonen.

Metalliteollisuuden Keskusliitto r.y. (Federation of Finnish Metal, Engineering and Electrotechnical Industries): Eteläranta 10, POB 10, 00131 Helsinki; tel. (9) 19231; fax (9) 624462; internet www.met.fi; f. 1903; Chair. Matti Alahuhta; Man. Dir Martti Mäenpää.

Muoviteollisuus r.y. (Finnish Plastics Industries' Federation): Eteläranta 10, 00130 Helsinki; tel. (9) 172841; fax (9) 171164; Chair. Antti Pohjonen; Man. Dir Kari Teppola.

Palvelualojen Toimialaliitto r.y. (Association of Support Service Industries): Eteläranta 10, 00130 Helsinki; tel. (9) 172841; fax (9) 176877; internet www.palvelualojentoimialaliitto.com; Chair. Pyry Lautsuo; Man. Dir Peter Forsström.

PT Työnantajaliitto r.y. (PT Employers' Federation): Mannerheiminaukio 1A, 00100 Helsinki; tel. (9) 613151; fax (9) 61315082; Chair. Pekka Vennamo; Man. Dir Juha Kivinen.

Puusepänteollisuuden Liitto r.y. (Association of the Finnish Furniture and Joinery Industries): Snellmaninkatu 13, POB 336, 00171 Helsinki; tel. (9) 13261; fax (9) 1324447; e-mail jukka .nevala@forestindustries.fi; internet www.finfurniture.org; f. 1917; Chair. Pekka Sairanen; Man. Dir Jukka Nevala; 90 mems.

Rakennusteollisuus RT r.y. (Confederation of Finnish Construction Industries): Unioninkatu 14 VI, 00130 Helsinki; tel. (9) 12991; fax (9) 628264; e-mail rt@rakennusteollisuusrt.fi; internet www.rakennusteollisuusrt.fi; f. 2001; Chair. Lauri Ratia; Man. Dir Terho Salo.

Rannikko- ja Sisävesiliikenteen Työnantajaliitto (RASILA) r.y. (Coastal and Inland Waterway Employers' Association): Satamakatu 4A, 00160 Helsinki; tel. (9) 62267312; fax (9) 669251; Chair. Stefan Håkans; Man. Dir Henrik Lönnqvist.

Sähkö- ja telealan työnantajaliitto r.y. (Finnish Association of Electrical and Telecommunications Employers): Yrjönkatu 13, 00120 Helsinki; tel. (9) 695900; fax (9) 69590111; Chair. Risto Rinta Mänty; Man. Dir Matti Höysti; 110 mems.

Suomen Kiinteistöliitto r.y. (Finnish Real-Estate Association): Annankatu 24, 00100 Helsinki; tel. (9) 166761; fax (9) 16676400; internet www.kliitto.fi; f. 1907; Chair. Asko Salminen; Man. Dir Ukko Laurila.

Suomen Lastauttajain Liitto (SLL) r.y. (Federation of Finnish Master Stevedores): Köydenpunojankatu 8, 00180 Helsinki; tel. (9) 6949800; fax (9) 6944585; f. 1906; Chair. Hans Martin; Man. Dir Harri Tuulensu.

Suomen Varustamoyhdistys r.y. (Finnish Shipowners' Association): see under Shipping.

Suunnittelu- ja konsulttitoimistojen liitto (SKOL) r.y. (Finnish Association of Consulting Firms—SKOL): Pohjantie 12A, 02100 Espoo; tel. (9) 460122; fax (9) 467642; e-mail skolry@skolry .fi; internet www.skolry.fi; Chair. Kari Lautso; Man. Dir Timo Myllys; 255 mems.

Teknokemian Yhdistys r.y. (Finnish Cosmetic, Toiletry and Detergent Association): Eteläranta 10, 00130 Helsinki; tel. (9) 172841; fax (9) 666561; e-mail stig.granqvist@ty.ttliitot.fi; internet www.teknokem.fi; Chair. Jarl Storgårds; Man. Dir Stig Granqvist.

Tekstiili- ja vaatetusteollisuus r.y. (Federation of Finnish Textile and Clothing Industries): Aleksis Kivenkatu 10, POB 50, 33211 Tampere; tel. (3) 3889111; fax (3) 3889120; internet www .finatex.fi; f. 1905; Chair. Hannu Jaakkola; Man. Dir Matti Järventie.

Toimistoteknisen Kaupan Yhdistys (TTK) r.y. (Finnish Association of Office Technology Traders): Mannerheimintie 76A, 00250 Helsinki; tel. (9) 441651; fax (9) 496142; Chair. Kari Solala; Man. Dir Eero Peritalo.

Tupakkateollisuusliitto r.y. (Finnish Tobacco Industries' Federation): POB 115, 00241 Helsinki; tel. (9) 644373; fax (9) 14887201; e-mail asta.morsky@etl.fi; Chair. Matti Rihko.

Työnantajain Yleinen Ryhmä r.y. (Finnish Employers' General Group): Eteläranta 10, 00130 Helsinki; tel. (9) 172841; fax (9) 179588; e-mail sari.vannela@ryhma.ttliitot.fi; Chair. Markku Jokinen; Exec. Dir Sari Vannela.

Viestintätyönantajat VTA (Media Employers' Association): Lönnrotinkatu 11A, 00120 Helsinki; tel. (9) 22877200; fax (9) 603527; Chair. Keijo Ketonen; Man. Dir Juhana Hintsanen.

Yleinen Teollisuusliitto r.y. (General Industry Association): Eteläranta 10, 00130 Helsinki; tel. (9) 6220410; fax (9) 176135; Chair. Markku Talonen; Man. Dir Markku Käppi.

UTILITIES

Finnish Energy Industries Federation (Finergy): Etelaranta 10, POB 21, 00131 Helsinki; tel. (9) 686161; fax (9) 6861630; e-mail info@finergy.fi; internet www.energia.fi/finergy.

Fortum Oyj: POB 1, 00048 Fortum; tel. 104511; fax 104524798; internet www.fortum.com; f. 1998; following merger of the Imatran Voima Group and the Neste Group; international energy co with core businesses in oil, gas, power and heat; listed on the Helsinki exchanges in December 1998; Exec. Chair. Matti Vuoria; CEO Mikael Lilius.

Helsingin Kaupungin Energialaitos (Helsinki Energy Board): POB 469, 00101 Helsinki; tel. (9) 6171; fax (9) 6172360; f. 1909; municipal undertaking; generates and distributes electrical power and district heating; distributes natural gas.

Electricity

Kemijoki Oy: Valtakatu 9–11, POB 8131, 96101 Rovaniemi; tel. (16) 7401; fax (16) 7402325; e-mail info@kemijoki.fi; internet www .kemijoki.fi; f. 1954; electric power; 66.99% state-owned; Chair. of Supervisory Bd Kalervo Nurmimäki; Chair. of Bd of Management Tapio Kuula; 344 employees.

Sähköenergialiitto r.y. (Finnish Electricity Association): POB 100, 00101 Helsinki; tel. (9) 530520; fax (9) 53052100; internet www .energia.fi; f. 1926; 100 mems; development of technical, economic and administrative functions of utilities; consultant services in electricity supply; educational activities; research and advice on electrical applications; collection and publication of electricity statistics; publishes consumer magazine *Sähköviesti/Elbladet*; domestic and international co-operation; safety at work and environmental conservation.

Water

Helsinki Water: Iimalankuja 2A, 00240 Helsinki; POB 1100, 00099 Helsinki; tel. (9) 47371; fax (9) 47342010; responsible for water supply and sewerage of the greater Helsinki area.

CO-OPERATIVES

Pellervo (Confederation of Finnish Co-operatives): Simonkatu 6, POB 77, 00101 Helsinki; tel. (9) 4767501; fax (9) 6948845; e-mail toimisto@pellervo.fi; internet www.pellervo.fi; f. 1899; central organization of co-operatives; CEO Samuli Skurnik; 430 mem. societies (incl. 7 central co-operative societies).

Munakunta (Co-operative Egg Producers' Association): POB 6, 20761 Piispanristi; tel. 2214420; fax 22144222; internet www .kultamuna.fi; f. 1921; Man. Dir Jan Lähde; 500 mems.

Valio Ltd (Finnish Co-operative Dairies' Association): POB 10, 00039 Valio; tel. 10381121; fax 103812059; internet www.valio.com; f. 1905; production and marketing of dairy products; Pres. and CEO Olavi Kuusela.

TRADE UNIONS

AKAVA (Confederation of Unions for Academic Professionals): Rautatieläisenkatu 6, 00520 Helsinki; tel. (9) 141822; fax (9) 142595; internet www.akava.fi; f. 1950; 32 affiliates, incl. asscns of doctors, engineers, social workers and teachers; total membership 409,000; Pres. Risto Piekka.

Suomen Ammattiliittojen Keskusjärjestö (SAK) r.y. (Central Organization of Finnish Trade Unions): Siltasaarenkatu 3A, POB 157, 00531 Helsinki; tel. (9) 77211; fax (9) 7721447; internet www .sak.fi; f. 1907; 25 affiliated unions; 1,110,000 mems (1996); Pres. Lauri Ihalainen; Dirs Tuulikki Kannisto, Pekka Ahmavaara.

Principal affiliated unions:

Auto- ja Kuljetusalan Työntekijäliitto (AKT) r.y. (Transport Workers): John Stenbergin ranta 6, POB 313, 00531 Helsinki; tel. (9) 613110; fax (9) 739287; e-mail juhani.koivunen@akt.fi; internet www.akt.fi; f. 1948; Pres. Timo Räty; Secs Matti Vehkaoja, Juhani Koivunen; 50,474 mems.

Kemianliitto-Kemifacket r.y. (Chemical Workers): Haapaniemenkatu 7–9B, POB 324, 00531 Helsinki; tel. (9) 773971; fax (9) 7538040; internet www.kemianliitto.fi; f. 1993; Pres. Timo Vallittu; Sec. Sulo Korhonen; 35,000 mems.

Kunta-alan Ammattiliitto (KTV) r.y. (Municipal Sector): Kolmas linja 4, POB 101, 00531 Helsinki; tel. (9) 77031; fax (9) 7703397; internet www.ktv.fi; f. 1931; Pres. TUIRE SANTAMÄKI-VUORI; 211,031 mems.

Metallityöväen Liitto r.y. (Metalworkers): Siltasaarenkatu 3–5A, POB 107, 00531 Helsinki; tel. (9) 77071; fax (9) 7707277; internet www.metalliliitto.fi; f. 1899; Pres. PER-ERIK LUNDH; Sec. ERIK LINDFORS; 164,000 mems.

Palvelualojen ammattiliitto PAM r.y. (Service Union United): Paasivuorenkatu 4–6, POB 54, 00531 Helsinki; tel. (9) 77571; fax (9) 7011119; internet www.pamliitto.fi; f. 1987 as Liikealan ammattiliitto r.y. present name adopted 2000; Pres. ANN SELIN; Vice-Pres. ANSSI VUORID, KAARLO JULKUNEN; 210,000 mems.

Paperiliitto r.y. (Paperworkers): Paasivuorenkatu 4–6A, POB 326, 00531 Helsinki; tel. (9) 70891; fax (9) 7012279; f. 1906; Pres. JARMO LÄHTEENMÄKI; Gen. Sec. ARTTURI PENNANEN; 48,569 mems.

Puu- ja erityisalojen Liitto r.y. (Wood and Allied Workers): Haapaniemenkatu 7–9B, POB 318, 00531 Helsinki; tel. (9) 615161; fax (9) 736069; e-mail puuliitto@puuliitto.fi; internet www .puuliitto.fi; f. 1993 by merger of two unions; Pres. KALEVI VANHALA; 50,000 mems.

Rakennusliitto r.y. (Construction Workers): Siltasaarenkatu 4, POB 307, 00531 Helsinki; tel. (9) 77021; fax (9) 7702241; e-mail info@rakennusliitto.fi; internet www.rakennusliitto.fi; f. 1930; Pres. PEKKA HYNÖNEN; 89,000 mems.

Sähköalojen ammattiliitto r.y. (Electrical Workers): Aleksanterinkatu 15, POB 747, 33101 Tampere; tel. (3) 2520111; fax (3) 2520210; e-mail lauri.lyly@sahkoliitto.fi; internet www .sahkoliitto.fi; f. 1955; Pres. LAURI LYLY; Sec. HEIMO RINNE; 31,500 mems.

Suomen Elintarviketyöläisten Liitto (SEL) r.y. (Food Workers): Siltasaarenkatu 6, POB 213, 00531 Helsinki; tel. (9) 393881; fax (9) 712059; internet www.selry.fi; f. 1905; Pres. RITVA SAVTSCHENKO; 41,000 mems.

Suomen Merimies-Unioni r.y. (Seamen): Uudenmaankatu 16B, POB 249, 00121 Helsinki; tel. (9) 6152020; fax (9) 61520227; e-mail forename.surname@smury.fi; internet www.smury.fi; f. 1916; Pres. SIMO ZITTING; Sec. ERKKI UKKONEN; 10,099 mems.

Tekstiili- ja vaatetustyöväen liitto Teva r.y. (Textile and Garment Workers): Salhojankatu 27, POB 87, 33101 Tampere; tel. (3) 2593111; fax (3) 2593343; e-mail tevaliitto@tevaliitto.fi; internet www.tevaliitto.fi; f. 1970; Pres. AULI KORHONEN; 19,000 mems.

Valtion yhteisjärjestö (VTY) r.y. (Joint Organization of State Employees): Haapaniemenkatu 7–9B, POB 317, 00531 Helsinki; tel. (9) 584211; fax (9) 739513; e-mail raimo.rannisto@valry.fi; internet www.vty.fi; f. 1946; Pres. RAIMO RANNISTO; Sec.-Gen. JAAN VINGISAAR; 35,000 mems.

Viestintäalan ammattiliitto r.y. (Media Union): Stiltasaarenkatu 4, POB 303, 00531 Helsinki; tel. (9) 616581; fax (9) 61658333; e-mail pertti.raitoharju@viestintaliito.fi; internet www .viestintaliitto.fi; f. 1894; Pres. PERTTI RAITOHARJU; Sec. IRENE HÄMÄLÄINEN; 32,000 mems.

STTK (Finnish Confederation of Salaried Employees): Pohjoisranta 4A, POB 248, 00171 Helsinki; tel. (9) 131521; fax (9) 652367; internet www.sttk.fi.

The principal independent trade unions (formerly affiliated to the now-dissolved Confederation of Salaried Employees—TVK, f. 1922) include the following:

Erityisalojen Toimihenkilöliitto ERTO r.y. (Special Service and Clerical Employees): Asemamiehenkatu 4, 00520 Helsinki; tel. (9) 0201130200; fax (9) 0201130201; e-mail info.erto@erto.fi; internet www.erto.fi; f. 1968; Chair. MATTI HELLSTEN; 20,000 mems.

Hallintovirkailijoiden Keskusliitto (HVK) (Civil Servants): Ratamestarinkatu 11, 00520 Helsinki; tel. (9) 1551; f. 1992; Chair. HEIKKI KUJANPÄÄ; 12,500 mems.

Kunnallisvirkamiesliitto r.y. (KVL) (Municipal Officers): Asemamiehenkatu 4, 00520 Helsinki; tel. (9) 1551; fax (9) 1552333; f. 1918; Chair. MARKKU JALONEN; 74,000 mems.

Maanpuolustuksen ja Turvallisuuden Ammattijärjestöt (MTAJ) r.y. (Defence and Security Employees): Ratamestarinkatu 11, 00520 Helsinki; tel. (9) 1551; f. 1992; Chair. PIRKKO MATTILA; 7,800 mems.

Suomen Perushoitajaliitto (Enrolled Nurses): Asemamiehenkatu 2, 00520 Helsinki; tel. (9) 141833; f. 1948; Chair. KAARINA MUHLI; 36,000 mems.

Suomen Poliisijärjestöjen Liitto (Police): Asemamiehenkatu 2, 00520 Helsinki; tel. (9) 1551; f. 1990; Chair. MATTI KRATS; 13,600 mems.

Suomen Rahoitus- ja Erityisalojen ammattiliitto r.y. (Financial Sector Union): Ratamestarinkatu 12, 00520 Helsinki; tel. (9) 229141; fax (9) 22914300; f. 1931; Pres. CHRISTINA HOLMLUND; Sec.-Gen. SIMO LEIVO; 40,000 mems.

Tehy (Union of Health and Social-Care Professionals): POB 10, 00060 Helsinki; tel. (9) 1551; fax (9) 1483038; e-mail tehy .international@tehy.fi; f. 1982; Chair. JAANA LAITINEN-PESOLA; 110,000 mems.

Vakuutusväen Liitto r.y. (Insurance Employees): Asemamiehenkatu 2, 00520 Helsinki; tel. (9) 85672400; fax (9) 85672401; e-mail sirpa.spoljari@jttpalvelut.fi; internet www.vvl.fi; f. 1945; Chair. SIRPA KOMONEN; Gen. Sec. SIRPA SPOLJARI; 11,000 mems.

Valtion Laitosten ja Yhtiöiden Toimihenkilöliitto (Employees in State-owned Institutions and Companies): Topparikuja 7, 00520 Helsinki; tel. (9) 348050; fax (9) 145135; e-mail joan.vingisar@vty.fi; f. 1945; Gen. Sec. PEKKA ELORANTA; 10,000 mems.

Transport

RAILWAYS

Finland has 5,854 km of railways, providing internal services and connections with Sweden and Russia. As part of an initiative to upgrade the existing rail network a high-speed rail link was planned between Helsinki and St Petersburg, Russia; it was scheduled to be operational in 2008. An underground railway service has been provided by Helsinki City Transport since 1982.

Ratahallintokeskus (RHK) (Finnish Rail Administration): POB 185, 00101 Helsinki; tel. (9) 58405111; fax (9) 58405100; e-mail info@ rhk.fi; internet www.rhk.fi; f. 1995; civil service department under the Ministry of Transport and Communications; owns the rail network, together with its equipment, structures and land holdings; wide gauge (1,524 mm); 2,372 km of route are electrified; responsible for management, maintenance and development of railways; Chief Dir O. NIEMIMUUKKO.

Karhula Railway: Ratakatu 8, 48600 Karhula; tel. (5) 298221; fax (5) 298225; f. 1937; goods transport; operates 10 km of railway (1,524 mm gauge); Man. PERTTI HONKALA.

VR Group: Vilhonkatu 13, POB 488, 00101 Helsinki; tel. (307) 10; fax (307) 21500; internet www.vr.fi; began operating 1862; joint-stock co since 1995; operates 5,854 km of railways; Pres. and CEO HENRI KUITUNEN; Exec. Vice-Pres. JUHANI KOPPERI.

ROADS

Finland had 78,059 km of public roads in 2001, of which 550 km are motorways, 12,700 km other main roads, 28,500 km secondary or regional roads and 36,250 other roads.

In early 2001 Tielaitos (National Road Administration) was divided into the following organizations:

Tiehallinto (Finnish Road Administration): POB 33, 00521 Helsinki; tel. (204) 2211; fax (204) 222202; e-mail info@tiehallinto.fi; internet www.tiehallinto.fi; f. 1799; government agency; divided into nine road districts; manages the public road network, including bridges and ferries; organizes bids for road construction and maintenance; Dir-Gen. EERO KARJALUOTO.

Tieliikelaitos (Finnish Road Enterprise): POB 73, 00521 Helsinki; tel. (204) 4411; e-mail name.familyname@tieliikelaitos.fi; internet www.tieliikelaitos.fi; unincorporated state enterprise; provides transport infrastructure and transport environment services; Man. Dir HEIKKI KOIVISTO.

INLAND WATERWAYS

Lakes cover 33,350 sq km. The inland waterway system comprises 7,842 km of buoyed-out channels, 40 open canals and 37 lock canals. The total length of canals is 116 km. In 2000 cargo vessel traffic on inland waterways amounted to 2.3m. metric tons (including traffic on the Saimaa Canal), timber floating amounted to 1m. tons and passenger traffic to 480,000 passengers.

In 1968 the southern part of the Saimaa Canal, which was leased to Finland by the USSR for 50 years, was opened for vessels. In 2000 a total of 1.8m. metric tons of goods were transported along the canal.

SHIPPING

The chief port of export is Kotka. Reclamation of land is currently under way to build a second container port in Kotka. It was scheduled to open in 2001 and was to have the capacity to handle 500,000 20-ft equivalent units (TEUs) of cargo per year. The main port of import is Helsinki, which has three specialized harbours. The West Harbour handles most of the container traffic, the North Harbour cargo ferry (ro-ro) traffic and the South Harbour passenger traffic. Other important international ports are Turku (Åbo), Rauma and Hamina. The ports handled 90m. metric tons of cargo in 1999.

Port Authority Association

Suomen Satamaliitto (Finnish Port Association): Toinen Linja 14, 00530 Helsinki; tel. (9) 7711; fax (9) 7530474; e-mail matti.aura@ satamaliitto.fi; internet www.finnports.com; f. 1923; 29 mems; Man. Dir MATTI AURA.

Port Authorities

Hamina: POB 14, 49401 Hamina; tel. (5) 2255400; fax (5) 22554101; e-mail office@portofhamina.fi; internet www.portofhamina.fi; Port Man. SEPPO HERRALA; Harbour Master MARKKU KOSKINEN.

Helsinki: Port of Helsinki, POB 800, 00099 Helsinki; tel. (9) 173331; fax (9) 17333232; e-mail port.helsinki@hel.fi; internet www .portofhelsinki.fi; Man. Dir HEIKKI NISSINEN; Harbour Master KARI WALLIN.

Kotka: Port of Kotka Ltd, Laivurinkatu 7, 48100 Kotka; tel. (5) 2344280; fax (5) 2181375; e-mail marketing@portofkotka.fi; internet www.portofkotka.fi; Man. Dir KIMMO NASKI.

Rauma: Port of Rauma, Hakunintie 19, 26100 Rauma; tel. (2) 8344712; fax (2) 8226369; e-mail harbour.office@portofrauma.com; internet www.portofrauma.com; Dir HANNU ASUMALAHTI.

Turku: Turku Port Authority, Linnankatu 90, 20100 Turku; tel. (2) 2674111; fax (2) 2674125; e-mail pekka.rasanen@turku.fi; internet www.port.turku.fi; Harbour Master PEKKA RÄSÄNEN.

Shipowners' Association

Suomen Varustamoyhdistys r.y. (Finnish Shipowners' Association): Satamakatu 4, POB 155, 00161 Helsinki; tel. (9) 6226730; fax (9) 669251; e-mail office@varustamoyhdistys.fi; f. 1932; Chair. JUKKA LAAKSOVIRTA; Man. Dir HENRIK LÖNNQVIST (acting); 6 mems.

Principal Companies

ESL Shipping Oy: Suolakivenkatu 10, 00810 Helsinki; tel. (9) 7595777; fax (9) 787315; world-wide tramp services; Man. Dir E. YRJOLA.

FG Shipping Oy Ab: Lönnrotinkatu 21, POB 406, 00121 Helsinki; tel. 1021640; fax (9) 2164243; e-mail fgs@fg-shipping.fi; f. 1947; until 1989 Oy Finnlines Ltd; ship management, marine consulting; Pres. ESKO MUSTAMÄKI.

Finnlines PLC: Salmisaarenkatu 1, POB 197, 00181 Helsinki; tel. 1034350; fax 103435200; e-mail info@finnlines.fi; internet www .finnlines.fi; f. 1949; liner and contract services between Finland and other European countries; overland and inland services combined with direct sea links; Pres. and CEO ANTTI LAGERROOS; 85 cargo ferries.

Fortum Oil and Gas Oy: POB 100, 00048 Fortum Keilaniemi, 02150 Spoo; tel. 104511; fax 104524777; internet www.fortum.com; Senior Vice-Pres. JUKKA LAAKSOVIRJA.

Alfons Håkans Oy Ab: Linnankatu 36c, 20100 Turku; tel. (2) 515500; fax (2) 2515873; e-mail office.turku@alfonshakans.fi; 30 tugs.

Nurminen Maritime Oy: POB 124, 00241 Helsinki; tel. (0) 1054500; fax (0) 105452000; e-mail info@johnnurminen.com; internet www.johnnurminen.com; liner and port agency services; Man. Dir JAN LÖNNBLAD.

Rederi Ab Engship: Linnankatu 33B, 20100 Turku; tel. (2) 5125500; fax (2) 2502087; e-mail engship@engship.fi; internet www .engship.fi; Man. Dir BENGT ENGBLOM; 15 dry cargo vessels; 96,800 dwt.

Rettig Oy Ab Bore: Veistämönaukio 1–3, POB 144, 20101 Turku; tel. (2) 2813600; fax (2) 2534036; e-mail info@boret.com; internet www.boreship.com; f. 1897; Man. Dir KAJ ERIKSSON; 4 cargo ferries; 32,751 dwt.

RG Line Oy Ab: Vaskiluodon Satama, 65170 Vaasa; tel. (6) 3200300; fax (6) 3194545; e-mail info@rgline.com; internet www .rgline.com; operates ferry services across the Gulf of Bothnia from Vaasa to Umeå.

Silja Line Oy: POB 880, 00101 Helsinki; tel. (9) 18041; fax (9) 1804484; internet www.silja.com; f. 1883; cruise and ferry services in the Baltic; Man. Dir NILS-GUSTAF PALMGREN; 7 passenger vessels.

CIVIL AVIATION

An international airport is situated at Helsinki-Vantaa, 19 km from Helsinki. International and domestic services also operate to and from airports at Ivalo, Joensuu, Jyväskylä, Kajaani, Kemi-Tornio, Kruunupyy, Kuopio, Lappeenranta, Mariehamn, Oulu, Pori, Rovaniemi, Savonlinna, Tampere-Pirkkala, Turku, Vaasa and Varkaus. Domestic services are available at airports at Enontekiö, Kittilä, Kuusamo and Mikkeli.

In 2001 13.8m. passengers passed through Finnish airports.

Ilmailulaitos (Civil Aviation Administration): POB 50, 01531 Vantaa; tel. (9) 82771; fax (9) 82772099; e-mail ilmailulaitos@fcaa.fi; internet www.ilmailulaitos.com; Dir-Gen. MIKKO TALVITIE.

Principal Airlines

Air Botnia: POB 168, 01531 Vantaa; tel. (9) 61512900; fax (9) 61512919; e-mail airbotnia@sas.se; internet www.airbotnia.fi; f. 1994; intra-nordic services; acquired by Scandinavian Airlines System in 1998; Pres. and CEO KJELL FREDHEIM.

Finnair Oyj: Tietotie 11A, POB 15, 01053 Vantaa; tel. (9) 81881; fax (9) 8184401; internet www.finnair.com; f. 1923; 58.4% state-owned; 17 domestic services and 30 European services and 6 international services (to North America, the Middle East and the Far East); Pres. and CEO KEIJO SUILA.

Tourism

Europe's largest inland water system, vast forests, magnificent scenery and the possibility of holiday seclusion are Finland's main attractions. Most visitors come from other Nordic countries, Germany, Russia, the United Kingdom and the USA. Registered accommodation establishments recorded 4,183,206 overnight stays by foreigners in 2001.

Matkailun edistämiskeskus (Finnish Tourist Board): Töölönkatu 11, POB 625, 00101 Helsinki; tel. (9) 4176911; fax (9) 41679333; e-mail mek@mek.fi; internet www.mek.fi; f. 1973; Chair. BO GÖRAN ERIKSSON; Dir JAAKKO LEHTONEN.

FINNISH EXTERNAL TERRITORY

THE ÅLAND ISLANDS

Introductory Survey

Location, Language, Religion, Flag, Capital

The Åland Islands are a group of 6,554 islands (of which some 60 are inhabited) in the Gulf of Bothnia, between Finland and Sweden. About 94% of the inhabitants are Swedish-speaking, and Swedish is the official language. The majority profess Christianity and belong to the Evangelical Lutheran Church of Finland. The flag displays a red cross, bordered with yellow, on a blue background, the upright of the cross being to the left of centre. The capital is Mariehamn, which is situated on Åland, the largest island in the group.

History and Government

For geographical and economic reasons, the Åland Islands were traditionally associated closely with Sweden. In 1809, when Sweden was forced to cede Finland to Russia, the islands were incorporated into the Finnish Grand Duchy. However, following Finland's declaration of independence from the Russian Empire, in 1917, the Ålanders demanded the right to self-determination and sought to be reunited with Sweden. Their demands were supported by the Swedish Government and people. In 1920 Finland granted the islands autonomy but refused to acknowledge their secession, and in 1921 the Åland question was referred to the League of Nations. In June the League granted Finland sovereignty over the islands, while directing that certain conditions pertaining to national identity be included in the autonomy legislation offered by Finland and that the islands should be a neutral and non-fortified region. Elections were held in accordance with the new legislation, and the new provincial parliament (Landsting) held its first plenary session on 9 June 1922. The revised Autonomy Act of 1951 provided for independent rights of legislation in internal affairs and for autonomous control over the islands' economy. This Act could not be amended or repealed by the Finnish Eduskunta (Parliament) without the consent of the Åland Landsting.

In 1988 constitutional reform introduced the principle of a majority parliamentary government, to be formed by the Lantrådskandidat, the member of the Landsting nominated to conduct negotiations between the parties. These negotiations may yield two alternative outcomes: either the nominee will submit a proposal to create a new government or the nominee will fail to reach agreement on a new government (in which case renewed negotiations will ensue). The first formal parliamentary government and opposition were duly established. The governing coalition consisted of the three largest parties that had been elected to the Landsting in October 1987 (the Centre Party, the Liberals and the Moderates), which together held 22 seats in the 30-member legislature.

At a general election held in October 1991 the Centre Party increased its share of the seats in the Landsting to 10, while the Liberal Party secured seven seats and the Moderates and Social Democrats won six and four seats respectively. The parties forming the new coalition Government included the Centre and Moderate Parties, as before, while the Liberal Party was replaced by the Social Democratic Party.

A revised Autonomy Act, providing Åland with a greater degree of autonomous control, was adopted in 1991 and took effect on 1 January 1993. The rules regarding legislative authority were modernized, and the right of the Åland legislature (henceforth known as the Lagting) to enact laws was extended. Åland was given greater discretion with respect to its budget, and the revised Act also introduced changes in matters such as right of domicile, land ownership regulations and administrative authority. The Autonomy Act contains a provision that, in any treaty which Finland may conclude with a foreign state and to which Åland is a party, the Lagting must consent to the statute implementing the treaty in order for the provision to enter into force in Åland. This procedure gave Åland the opportunity not to consent to membership of the European Union (EU, see p. 199). A referendum on the issue of Åland's proposed accession to membership of the EU in 1995 was held in November 1994, immediately after similar referendums in Finland and Sweden had shown a majority in favour of membership. (A small majority of Åland citizens had supported Finland's membership.) Despite low participation in the referendum, 73.7% of the votes cast supported membership and Åland duly joined the EU, together with Finland and Sweden, on 1 January 1995. Under the terms of the treaty of accession, Åland was accorded special exemption from tax union with the EU in order to stimulate the ferry and tourism industries. (In 1998 two of Europe's largest ferry operators, Silja and Viking—both Finnish, re-routed their major services via Åland in order to continue to conduct duty-free sales, which were later abolished within the rest of the EU.)

A general election was held in October 1995. The Centre Party secured nine seats and the Liberal Party won eight seats, while the Moderates and Social Democrats maintained the representation that they had achieved in the previous parliament. The new coalition Government was composed of members of the Centre and Moderate Parties and one independent.

At a general election held on 17 October 1999 the Centre Party and the Liberal Party each won nine seats. The Moderate Party, meanwhile, secured only four seats, compared with six at the previous election, while the Social Democrats maintained their level of representation, with three seats. Independents grouped together in the Obunden samling won four seats. A coalition Government was formed comprising the Centre Party, the Moderate Party and the Independents. In March 2001, following a 'no-confidence' motion in the Lagting, the Chairman (Lantråd) of the Government, Roger Nordlund of the Centre Party, dissolved the coalition and formed a new administration comprising members of the Centre Party and the Liberal Party.

Economic Affairs

In 1998 the gross domestic product (GDP) of the Åland Islands, measured at current prices, was 4,428m. markkaa. In 2000 6.2% of the working population were employed in the agriculture sector. Forests covered 57.4% of the islands in 2001, and only 8.9% of the total land area was arable. The principal crops are cereals, sugar beet, potatoes and fruit. Dairy-farming and sheep-rearing are also important.

Since 1960 the economy of the islands has expanded and diversified. Fishing has declined as a source of income, and shipping (particularly the operation of ferry services between Finland and Sweden), trade and tourism have become the dominant economic sectors. In 2000 services engaged 77.7% of the employed labour force. The transport sector, including shipping, employed 18.6%. The political autonomy of the islands and their strategic location between Sweden and Finland have contributed to expanding banking and trade sectors; financial services engaged 7.8% of the employed labour force in 2000, while trade and hotels employed 13.3%. Tourist arrivals totalled 1,718,404 in 2002. Consumer prices increased at an average annual rate of 1.3% in 1996–99; prices rose by 2.9% in 2000, by 2.3% in 2001 and by 2.0% in 2002. Unemployment stood at 2.2% in 2001, compared with 5.2% in 1996.

Education

The education system is similar to that of Finland, except that Swedish is the language of instruction and Finnish an optional subject.

Statistical Survey

Source: Statistics Åland, POB 1187, 22111 Mariehamn; tel. (18) 25490; fax (18) 19495; internet www.asub.aland.fi.

AREA, POPULATION AND DENSITY

Area: 6,784 sq km (2,619 sq miles), of which 1,527 sq km (589 sq miles) is land and 5,258 sq km (2,030 sq miles) is water.

Population (31 December 2001): 26,008 (males 12,800; females 13,208).

Density per sq km (31 December 2001): 17.0.

Principal Towns (31 December 2001): Mariehamn (capital) 10,609; Jomala 3,356; Finström 2,304; Saltvik 1,721; Lumparland 1,618; Hammarland 1,373.

Vital Statistics (2001): Registered live births 283 (birth rate 10.9per 1,000); Marriages 99 (marriage rate 3.8 per 1,000); Deaths 228 (death rate 8.8 per 1,000).

Expectation of Life (years at birth): 80.8 (males 77.2; females 84.7) in 2001.

Employed Labour Force (1999): Agriculture 807; Manufacturing 1,287; Construction 787; Trade 1,715; Transport 2,410; Financial services 1,012; Public services 4,439; Other services 475; Total employed 12,932.

HEALTH AND WELFARE

Physicians (1997): 51.

Hospital Beds (2001): 148.

AGRICULTURE AND FISHING

Agricultural Production (metric tons, 2001): Milk 14,161; Beef 530; Pork 101; Poultry 1,425; Wheat 3,152; Barley and oats 4,913; Sugar beet 39,561; Potatoes 13,436; Onions 6,418; Chinese cabbage and head lettuce 2,094; Apples 1,485.

Livestock (2001): Cattle 7,617; Pigs 1,654; Hens 8,335; Sheep 5,073; Horses 254.

Forestry Production (cu m, roundwood, 2001): Logs 49,081; Pulp 92,935.

Fishing (metric tons, live weight, 2001): Capture 5,460 (Baltic herring 4,254, Whitefish 148, Perch 120, Pike-perch 49, Pike 42, Other fish 847); Aquaculture 5,322; Total catch 10,782.

FINANCE

Currency: Finnish currency was used until the end of 2001. Euro notes and coins were introduced on 1 January 2002, and the euro became the sole legal tender from 1 March. Some of the figures in this Survey are still in terms of Finnish markkaa. For details of exchange rates, see the chapter on Finland.

Government Accounts ('000 euros, 2001): Revenue 239,564; Expenditure 226,336.

Cost of Living (consumer price index; base: 1995 = 100): All items 106.8 in 2000; 109.3 in 2001; 111.5 in 2002.

Gross Domestic Product by Economic Activity (million markkaa at current prices, 1998): Agriculture, hunting, forestry and fishing 151; Manufacturing 296; Construction 127; Trade, restaurants and hotels 335; Transport, storage and communications 1,962; Financing, insurance, real estate and business services 653; Government services 738; Other community, social and personal services 136; Non-profit institutions 30; *Sub-total* 4,428; *Less* Imputed bank service charge 121; *GDP at factor cost* 4,307; Indirect taxes 699; *Less* Subsidies 148; *GDP in purchasers' values* 4,858.

EXTERNAL TRADE

1996 (million markkaa): Imports 3,473; Exports 4,250.

TRANSPORT AND TOURISM

Road Traffic (registered motor vehicles, 31 December 2001): Private motor cars 14,360; Vans 2,863; Lorries 424; Buses 39; Motorcycles 672; Tractors 3,337.

Shipping (2000): Merchant fleet 49 vessels (car and passenger ferries 10, archipelago ferries 8); Total displacement 870,371 grt (car and passenger ferries 262,598 grt, archipelago ferries 6,641). Note: Figures include 11 vessels registered under flags other than Åland or Finland, total displacement 449,000 grt.

Tourist Arrivals (2002): 1,718,404.

EDUCATION

Primary and Secondary Schools (2001): Institutions 27 (Comprehensive schools 26, Upper-stage schools 9); Pupils 3,012 (Comprehensive schools 2,038, Upper-stage schools 974). Note: Seven schools offer both comprehensive and upper-stage education.

Pupils Enrolled in Education After Comprehensive Schools (2001): Preparatory study programme 498 (males 206; females 292); Vocational programme 533 (males 306; females 227); Advanced vocational programme 316 (males 198; females 118); Other 87 (males 20; females 67).

Directory

Government and Legislature

The legislative body is the Lagting, comprising 30 members, elected every four years on a basis of proportional representation. All Ålanders over the age of 18 years, possessing Åland regional citizenship, have the right to vote and to seek election. An Executive Council (Landskapsstyrelse), consisting of five to seven members, is elected by the Lagting, and its Chairman (Lantråd) is the highest-ranking politician in Åland after the Speaker (Talman) of the Lagting. The President has the right to veto Lagting decisions only when the Lagting exceeds its legislative competence, or when there is a threat to the security of the country. The Governor of Åland represents the Government of Finland and is appointed by the Finnish President (with the agreement of the Speaker of the Åland legislature).

Governor: PETER LINDBÄCK.

LANDSKAPSSTYRELSE
(Executive Council)
(April 2003)

The governing coalition comprises members of the Centre Party and the Liberal Party.

Chairman (Lantråd): ROGER NORDLUND (Centre Party).

Deputy Chairman (Vicelantråd): OLOF ERLAND (Liberal Party).

Members: SUNE ERIKSSON (Liberal Party), RUNAR KARLSSON (Centre Party), RITVA SARIN-GRUFBERG (Liberal Party), GUN CARLSSON (Centre Party).

LAGTING
(Parliament)

Speaker (Talman): VIVEKA ERIKSSON (Liberal Party).

Election, 17 October 1999

	% of votes cast	Seats
Liberalerna på Åland (Liberal Party) . .	28.7	9
Åländsk Center (Centre Party) . . .	27.3	9
Frisinnad samverkan (Moderate Party) .	14.5	4
Obunden samling (Independents) . . .	12.8	4
Ålands socialdemokrater (Social Democratic Party)	11.8	3
Ålands Framstegsgrupp (Progress Group) .	4.8	1
Total	100.0	30

Political Organizations

Unless otherwise indicated, the address of each of the following organizations is: Ålands Lagting, POB 69, 22101 Mariehamn; tel. (18) 25000; fax (18) 13302; internet www.lagtinget.aland.fi.

Åländsk Center (Centre Party): e-mail centern@lagtinget.aland.fi; internet www.centern.aland.fi; Chair. ROGER NORDLUND; Leader JAN-ERIK MATTSSON; Sec. ROBERT BRANÉR.

Ålands Framstegsgrupp (Progress Group): e-mail ronald.boman@ lagtinget.aland.fi; internet www.afg.aland.fi; Chair. and Leader RONALD BOMAN.

Ålands socialdemokrater (Social Democratic Party): e-mail socialdemokraterna@lagtinget.aland.fi; internet www.social demokraterna.aland.fi; Chair. BARBRO SUNDBACK.

Frisinnad samverkan (Moderate Party): e-mail fs@lagtinget .aland.fi; internet www.fs.aland.fi; Chair. ROGER JANSSON; Leader JÖRGEN STRAND; Sec.-Gen. NINA DANIELSSON.

Liberalerna på Åland (Liberal Party): tel. (18) 25362; fax (18) 16075; e-mail liberalerna@lagtinget.aland.fi; internet www .liberalerna.aland.fi; Chair. OLOF ERLAND; Leader LEO SJÖSTRAND; Gen. Sec. SOLVEIG GESTBERG.

Obunden samling (Independents): tel. (18) 25368; fax (18) 16370; e-mail info@obundet.nu; internet www.obundet.nu; f. 1987; Chair. GUN-MARI LINDHOLM; Leader BERT HÄGGBLOM.

Religion

CHRISTIANITY

In 1998 93.3% of the population were adherents of the Lutheran National Church.

The Press

Åland: POB 50, 22101 Mariehamn; tel. (18) 26026; fax (18) 15505; internet www.tidningen.aland.net; 5 a week; circ. 10,876.

Nya Åland: POB 21, 22101 Mariehamn; tel. (18) 23444; fax (18) 23449; 4 a week; circ. 7,768.

Broadcasting and Communications

RADIO

Ålands Radio och TV: POB 140, 22101 Mariehamn; tel. (18) 26060; fax (18) 26520; e-mail redaktion@radiotv.aland.fi; internet www.radiotv.aland.fi; f. 1996; broadcasts radio programmes in Swedish, 115.5 hours a week; Man. Dir PIA ROTHBERG-OLOFSSON; Editor-in-Chief ASTRID OLHAGEN.

Finance

BANKS

(cap. = capital; res = reserves; dep. = deposits; m. = million; amounts in euros; brs = branches)

Ålandsbanken Abp (Bank of Åland PLC): Nygatan 2, POB 3, 22101 Mariehamn; tel. (204) 29011; fax (204) 29228; e-mail info@alandsbanken.fi; internet www.alandsbanken.fi; f. 1919 as Ålands Aktiebank; name changed to Bank of Åland Ltd 1980, changed as above in 1998; merged with Ålands Hypoteksbank Ab in November 1995; cap. 20m., res 50m., dep. 1,519m. (Dec. 2001); Man. Dir FOLKE HUSELL; 28 brs.

Andelsbanken för Åland: POB 34, 22101 Mariehamn; tel. (18) 26000; Dirs HÅKAN CLEMES, ROLAND KARLSSON.

Lappo Andelsbank: 22840 Lappo; tel. (18) 56621; fax (18) 56699; Dir TORSTEN NORDBERG.

Merita Bank: Torggatan 10, 22100 Mariehamn; tel. (18) 5330; fax (18) 12499; Dirs ERLING GUSTAFSSON, JAN-ERIK RASK.

Postbanken: Sampo Bank, Torggatan 7, 22100 Mariehamn; tel. (18) 6360; fax (18) 636608.

INSURANCE

Alandia Group: Ålandsvägen 31, POB 121, 22101 Mariehamn; tel. (18) 29000; fax (18) 12290; e-mail mhamn@alandiabolagen.com; internet www.alandiabolagen.com; f. 1938; life, non-life and marine; comprises three subsidiaries; Gen. Man. JOHAN DAHLMAN.

Ålands Ömsesidiga Försäkringsbolag (Åland Mutual Insurance Co): Köpmansgatan 6, POB 64, 22101 Mariehamn; tel. (18) 27600; fax (18) 27610; f. 1866; property; Man. Dir BJARNE OLOFSSON.

Cabanco Insurance Co Ltd: Köpmansgatan 6, POB 64, 22101 Mariehamn; tel. (18) 27690; fax (18) 27699; Man. Dir BO-STURE SJÖLUND.

Hamnia Reinsurance Co Ltd: Köpmansgatan 6, POB 64, 22101 Mariehamn; tel. (18) 27690; fax (18) 27699; Man. Dir BO-STURE SJÖLUND.

Trade and Industry

CHAMBER OF COMMERCE

Ålands Handelskammare: Torggatan 5, 22100 Mariehamn; tel. (18) 29029; fax (18) 21129; e-mail info@hk.aland.fi; internet www.hk.aland.fi; f. 1945; Chair. ANDERS NORDLUND; Man. Dir JOHAN ERIKSSON.

TRADE ASSOCIATION

Ålands Företagareförening (Åland Business Asscn): Skarpansvägen 17, 22100 Mariehamn; tel. (18) 23277; fax (18) 23288; e-mail ombudsman@aff.aland.fi; internet www.aff.aland.fi; f. 1957; Chair. CHRISTER KULLMAN; Sec. JONNY MATTSSON.

EMPLOYERS' ORGANIZATIONS

Ålands Arbetsgivareförening (Åland Employers' Asscn): Nygatan 9, 22100 Mariehamn; tel. (18) 291474; fax (18) 21129; f. 1969; Chair. ERIK SUNDBLOM; Man. Dir ANDERS KULVES.

Ålands Fiskodlarförening (Åland Fish Farmers' Asscn): Storagatan 14, 22100 Mariehamn; tel. (18) 17834; fax (18) 17833; e-mail al.fishfarm@pb.alcom.aland.fi; Chair. MARCUS ERIKSSON; Sec. OLOF KARLSSON.

Ålands köpmannaförening (Åland Businessmen's Asscn): Ålandsvägen 34, 22100 Mariehamn; tel. (18) 13650; fax (18) 12145; e-mail kopmannaforeningen@aland.net; f. 1927; Chair. TOM FORSBOM; Sec. STEFAN BLOMQVIST.

Ålands producentförbund (Åland Agricultural Producers' Asscn): Ålands Landsbygdscentrum, 22150 Jomala; tel. (18) 329640; fax (18) 329631; e-mail henry.lindstrom@landsbygd.aland.fi; f. 1946; Chair. ANDERS ENGLUND; Man. Dir HENRY LINDSTROM.

Fraktfartygsföreningen r.f. (Cargo Ship's Asscn): Norragatan 7A, 22100 Mariehamn; tel. (18) 23662; fax (18) 23644; e-mail small.ton@aland.net; internet www.fraktfartygsforeningen.fi; f. as Utrikesfartens Småtonnageförening; present name adopted 2000; Chair. OLOF WIDÉN.

TRADE UNIONS

AKAVA-Åland (Professional Asscn): Storagatan 14, 22100 Mariehamn; tel. (18) 16348; fax (18) 12125; e-mail akava-a@aland.net; Chair. PEKKA ERÄMETSÄ; Gen. Sec. MARIA HAGMAN.

Fackorgan för offentliga arbetsomraden på Åland (FOA-Å) (Joint Organization of Civil Servants and Workers (VTY) in Åland): Norragatan 7A 1, 22100 Mariehamn; tel. (18) 16976; e-mail info@foa.inet.fi; Chair. ULLA ANDERSSON; Gen. Sec. ULLA BRITT DAHL.

FFC-facken på Åland: POB 108, 22101 Mariehamn; tel. (18) 16207; fax (18) 17207; e-mail kurt.gustafsson@sak.fi; internet www.facket.aland.fi; Chair. HELGE FREDRIKSSON; Gen. Sec. KURT GUSTAFSSON.

Tjänstemannaorganisationerna på Åland, TCÅ r.f. (Union of Salaried Employees in Åland): Strandgatan 23, 22100 Mariehamn; tel. (18) 16210; e-mail tca@aland.net; Chair. ANNE SJÖLUND; Dir TUULA MATTSSON.

Transport

The islands are linked to the Swedish and Finnish mainlands by ferry services and by air services from Mariehamn airport.

ROADS

In 1999 there was a road network of 912.7 km, of which 646.8 km was paved.

SHIPPING

Ålands Redarförening r.f. (Åland Shipowners' Association): Hamngatan 8, 22100 Mariehamn; tel. (18) 13430; fax (18) 22520; e-mail info@alship.aland.fi; f. 1934; Chair. WIKING JOHANSSON; Man. Dir HANS AHLSTRÖM; seven mems.

Principal Companies

Birka Line Abp: POB 175, 22101 Mariehamn; tel. (18) 27027; fax (18) 27343; e-mail info@birkaline.com; internet www.birkaline.com; f. 1971; shipping service; Man. Dir WIKING JOHANSSON.

Birka Cargo Ab Ltd: Storagatan 11, POB 175, 22101 Mariehamn; tel. (18) 27320; fax (18) 23223; e-mail info@birkacargo.com; internet www.birkacargo.com; f. 1990 as United Shipping Ltd Ab; 7 ro-ro vessels; Man. Dir STEFAN AXBERG.

Lundqvist Rederierna: Norra Esplanadgatan 9B, 22100 Mariehamn; tel. (18) 26050; fax (18) 26428; e-mail info@lundqvist.aland.fi; f. 1927; tanker and ro-ro services; Pres. BEN LUNDQVIST; total tonnage 1.0m. dwt.

Rederi Ab Eckerö (Eckerö Linjen): Torggatan 2, POB 158, 22101 Mariehamn; tel. (18) 28000; fax (18) 12011; e-mail info@eckerolinjen.fi; internet www.eckerolinjen.fi; f. 1980; operates ferry routes between the Åland Islands and Sweden, and between Finland and Estonia; Man. Dir JARL DANIELSSON.

Rederi Ab Lillgaard: Nygatan 5, POB 136, 22101 Mariehamn; tel. (18) 13120; fax (18) 17220.

Rederiaktiebolaget Gustaf Erikson: POB 49, 22101 Mariehamn; tel. (18) 27070; fax (18) 12670; e-mail gustaf.erikson@geson.aland.fi; f. 1913; Man. Dir GUN ERIKSON-HJERLING; manages dry cargo and refrigerated vessels.

Viking Line Abp: Norragatan 4, 22100 Mariehamn; tel. (18) 27000; fax (18) 16977; e-mail nn@vikingline.fi; internet www.vikingline.fi; f. 1963; operates cruise and ferry services between Finland and Sweden and throughout the Baltic Sea; Chair. BEN LUNDQVIST; Man. Dir NILS-ERIK EKLUND; 7 car/passenger vessels; total tonnage 212,257 grt.

Tourism

In 2002 tourist arrivals totalled 1,718,404.

Ålands Turist Förbund (Åland Tourist Asscn): Storagatan 8, 22100 Mariehamn; tel. (18) 24000; fax (18) 24265; internet www .goaland.net; f. 1989; Chair. MAGNUS LUNDBERG; Man. Dir GUNILLA G. NORDLUND.

FRANCE

Introductory Survey

Location, Climate, Language, Religion, Flag, Capital

The French Republic is situated in western Europe. It is bounded to the north by the English Channel (la Manche), to the east by Belgium, Luxembourg, Germany, Switzerland and Italy, to the south by the Mediterranean Sea and Spain, and to the west by the Atlantic Ocean. The island of Corsica is part of metropolitan France, while four overseas departments, one overseas collectivité départementale, one overseas 'collectivité territoriale', three overseas territories and one overseas country also form an integral part of the Republic. The climate is temperate throughout most of the country, but in the south it is of the Mediterranean type, with warm summers and mild winters. The principal language is French, which has numerous regional dialects, and small minorities speak Breton and Basque. Almost all French citizens profess Christianity, and about 79% are adherents of the Roman Catholic Church. Other Christian denominations are represented, and there are also Muslim and Jewish communities. The national flag (proportions 2 by 3) has three equal vertical stripes, of blue, white and red. The capital is Paris.

Recent History

In September 1939, following Nazi Germany's invasion of Poland, France and the United Kingdom declared war on Germany, thus entering the Second World War. In June 1940 France was forced to sign an armistice, following a swift invasion and occupation of French territory by German forces. After the liberation of France from German occupation in 1944, a provisional Government took office under Gen. Charles de Gaulle, leader of the 'Free French' forces during the wartime resistance. The war in Europe ended in May 1945, when German forces surrendered at Reims. In 1946, following a referendum, the Fourth Republic was established and Gen. de Gaulle announced his intention to retire from public life.

France had 26 different Governments from 1946 until the Fourth Republic came to an end in 1958 with an insurrection in Algeria (then an overseas department) and the threat of civil war. In May 1958 the President, René Coty, invited Gen. de Gaulle to form a government. In June the Assemblée nationale (National Assembly) invested de Gaulle as Prime Minister, with the power to rule by decree for six months. A new Constitution was approved by referendum in September and promulgated in October; thus the Fifth Republic came into being, with Gen. de Gaulle taking office as President in January 1959. The new system provided for a strong presidency, the authority of which would be strengthened by national referendums and a stable executive.

France was a founder member of the European Community (EC—now European Union—EU, see p. 199) and of the North Atlantic Treaty Organization (NATO, see p. 271). In 1966 it withdrew from the integrated military structure of NATO, but remained a member of the alliance.

The early years of the Fifth Republic were overshadowed by the Algerian crisis. De Gaulle granted Algeria independence in 1962, withdrew troops and repatriated French settlers. In May 1968 students and workers joined in a revolt against the Government's authoritarian education and information policies, low wage rates and lack of social reform. For a time the republic appeared threatened, but the student movement collapsed and the general strike was settled by large wage rises. In April 1969 President de Gaulle resigned following his defeat in a referendum on regional reform.

Georges Pompidou, Prime Minister between April 1962 and July 1968, was elected President in June 1969. Although the Parti Socialiste (PS) and the Parti Communiste Français (PCF) agreed on a common programme for contesting legislative elections, the Gaullist government coalition was returned at a general election in March 1973. Pompidou died in April 1974. In the presidential election held in May, Valéry Giscard d'Estaing, formerly leader of the centre-right Républicains Indépendants (RI) narrowly defeated François Mitterrand, the First Secretary of the PS. A coalition Government was formed from members of the RI, the Union des Démocrates pour la Republique (UDR) and the centrist parties. In August 1976 Jacques Chirac resigned as Prime Minister and subsequently undertook to transform the UDR into a new Gaullist party, the Rassemblement pour la République (RPR). In February 1978 the governing non-Gaullist parties formed the Union pour la Démocratie Française (UDF) to compete against RPR candidates in the Assemblée nationale elections held in March, when the governing coalition retained a working majority.

In the April/May 1981 presidential elections Mitterrand defeated Giscard d'Estaing. At elections for a new Assembly, held in June, the PS and associated groups, principally the Mouvement des Radicaux de Gauche (MRG), won an overall majority of seats, following which four members of the PCF were appointed to the Council of Ministers. The new Government introduced a programme of social and labour reforms, including the transfer of several major industrial enterprises and financial institutions to state control.

A legislative election took place in March 1986, using a party-list based system of proportional representation for the first time. Although the PS remained the largest single party in the new Assemblée nationale, the centre-right parties, led by the RPR-UDF alliance, commanded a majority of seats. The PCF suffered a severe decline in support, while the far-right Front National (FN) won legislative seats for the first time. A period of political 'cohabitation' ensued as Mitterrand invited the RPR leader, Chirac, to form a new Council of Ministers.

In April 1986 Chirac introduced legislation that allowed his Government to legislate by decree on economic and social issues and on the proposed reversion to a voting system comprising single-member constituencies for legislative elections. However, Mitterrand insisted on exercising the presidential right to withhold approval of decrees that reversed the previous Government's social reforms. In July Chirac thus resorted to the 'guillotine' procedure (setting a time-limit for consideration of legislative proposals) to gain parliamentary consent for legislation providing for the transfer to the private sector of 65 state-owned companies, which, since it had been approved by the predominantly right-wing Sénat (Senate) and the Constitutional Council, the President was legally bound to approve.

Mitterrand was re-elected as President in May 1988, defeating Chirac in the second round of voting. The PS-dominated Government under the premiership of Michel Rocard failed to command a reliable majority in the 577-seat Assemblée nationale. A general election took place in June, with a reintroduced single-seat majority voting system. An alliance of the PS and the MRG secured 276 seats, whilst an alliance of the RPR, the UDF and other right-wing candidates won 272. The PCF won 27 seats, and the FN one (compared with the 35 deputies it held in the previous legislature). Rocard, who had been reappointed as Prime Minister, formed an administration in which members of the previous Government retained the principal portfolios, although six UDF members and a number of independents were also included.

Rocard resigned in May 1991, weakened by disunity within the PS and by his failure to negotiate the passage of three government bills. Edith Cresson, France's first female Prime Minister, succeeded him. Cresson, who had resigned eight months previously from her post as Minister of European Affairs, undertook to increase government control over economic and industrial planning.

In April 1992 Mitterrand replaced Cresson as Prime Minister, appointing Pierre Bérégovoy, hitherto the Minister of State for the Economy, Finance and the Budget, as her successor. In June the Assemblée nationale approved constitutional changes allowing the ratification of the EC's Treaty on European Union (the 'Maastricht Treaty'), subject to approval by referendum. In the referendum, held in September, 69.7% of the electorate voted, of whom 51.1% were in favour of the ratification of the Treaty.

Elections to the Assemblée nationale in March 1993 resulted in a clear defeat for the PS; notably, several government ministers failed to retain their seats. In the first round of voting the RPR and the UDF (which had presented joint candidates, as the

Union pour la France, in some 500 constituencies) together received 39.5% of total votes cast, while the PS obtained 17.6%. Following the second round of voting, the RPR won 247 of the 577 seats in the Assemblée, the UDF 213 and the PS 54. Chirac, as the leader of the largest party in the new legislature, had made it known that he intended to concentrate on his candidacy in the 1995 presidential election, and consequently was not available for the post of Prime Minister. Mitterrand therefore asked another RPR member, Edouard Balladur, a former Minister of Finance, to form a government. Balladur's centre-right coalition enacted stricter laws on immigration and the conferral of French citizenship during 1993–94, together with controversial legislation giving the police wider powers to make random security checks.

In the first round of voting in the presidential election, on 23 April 1995, Lionel Jospin, the candidate of the PS, won 23% of the votes, while Chirac and Balladur, both representing the RPR, took 21% and 19% respectively. Jean-Marie Le Pen, the leader of the FN, won 15%. In the second round, on 7 May, Chirac (with 53% of the votes) defeated Jospin. Balladur resigned as Prime Minister, and Chirac appointed Alain Juppé (Minister of Foreign Affairs in the previous Government) as his successor. Juppé formed an administration in which the principal portfolios were evenly shared between the RPR and the UDF. In October Juppé was elected President of the RPR, while Jospin was elected First Secretary of the PS, a position he had held in 1981–88.

In April 1997 Chirac announced that legislative elections would take place in May–June, some 10 months earlier than required, a decision that was widely viewed as an attempt to secure a mandate for a number of policies relating to economic and monetary union (EMU, see p. 225) within the EU. In the first round of voting, held on 25 May, the PS secured 23.5% of total votes cast, the RPR 15.7%, the FN 14.9% and the UDF 14.2%. Following the second round of voting, held on 1 June, the PS secured 241 seats, the RPR 134, the UDF 108 and the PCF 38. Despite its strong performance in the first round, the FN won only one seat.

The unexpected victory of the PS, which began a further period of 'cohabitation', was widely attributed to dissatisfaction with Juppé's administration and the imposition of economic austerity measures necessitated under the terms of EMU. Jospin, leader of the PS, became Prime Minister, and formed a 'plural left' coalition.

In October 1997 the trial of Maurice Papon, a former civil servant and senior official in the pro-Nazi Vichy regime (1940–44), opened in Bordeaux. Papon was accused of deporting some 1,560 Jews to Germany, where almost all were killed in Nazi concentration camps, in 1943–44; he also served as a government minister at various times between 1935–81. Defence lawyers for Papon, who denied the charges against him, argued that their client was unfit to stand trial, owing to ill health. In April 1998 Papon was sentenced to 10 years' imprisonment, having been found guilty of complicity in crimes against humanity. However, Papon was exempt from imprisonment, on the grounds of ill health. In October 1999, however, on the eve of his appeal, it became clear that Papon, who had been due to surrender into custody, had absconded, and had thus forfeited any right to appeal. An international warrant was issued for his arrest, and Papon was subsequently apprehended and expelled from Switzerland, where he had been in hiding, and returned to begin sentence in France. In June 2001 the European Court of Human Rights dismissed an appeal for Papon's release, stating that both the general health and state of mind of the detainee did not warrant an end to his detention, which Papon had claimed was 'inhuman and degrading', and hence in breach of the European Convention of Human Rights. In September 2002 Papon's release from imprisonment, on the grounds of ill health, precipitated a public outcry. Consequently, the Ministry of Justice sought to return Papon to prison, stating that his release constituted a threat to public order. However, in February 2003 the Court of Cassation ruled that there were no legal grounds for Papon's renewed incarceration.

In February 1998 legislation shortening the maximum working week from 39 to 35 hours, regarded as central to the Government's policy of creating some 700,000 new jobs, was approved by the Assemblée nationale.

At regional council elections held in March 1998, the governing socialist coalition won 39.4% of the total vote, the centre-right opposition secured 35.6%, and the FN 15.5%. A subsequent offer by the FN to form alliances with the RPR and the UDF in

order to secure control of a number of councils caused much controversy. Both parties instructed their members to ignore the proposal; however, five members of the UDF defied their leadership and consequently obtained council presidencies. Two later resigned, while the remaining three were expelled from the party; one of these, Charles Millon, subsequently formed a new political organization called La Droite (later renamed La Droite Libérale Chrétienne). A further two senior UDF members left the party in protest at the expulsions, amid serious criticism of party President, François Léotard's, management of the crisis; moreover, one of the constituent parties of the UDF, Démocratie Libérale (DL—formerly the Parti Républicain—PR), led by Alain Madelin, announced its departure from the Union, partly as a result of its agreement to form alliances with the FN in regional councils, and partly as a result of its support for a more market-orientated economic policy. Later in the year the UDF reconstituted itself as a unified party. In an attempt to counteract the increasing fragmentation of the country's political centre-right, the RPR and the UDF announced the formation in May of a loose umbrella organization, the Alliance pour La France, although this grouping collapsed in February 1999, following the decision of the UDF to present a separate list of candidates at forthcoming elections to the European Parliament. In late June the Assemblée nationale voted to reform the system of regional elections, largely as a result of the problems experienced following the elections in March. The changes, which aimed to ensure coherent majorities in the regional councils, included the replacement of the previous one-round system with a two-round poll in which a party with an outright majority in the first round of voting would automatically receive 25% of the seats available.

At a by-election in May 1998 the FN narrowly lost its only seat in the Assemblée nationale. In April a court banned Le Pen from holding or seeking public office for two years (reduced to one year on appeal) and gave him a three-month suspended prison sentence after finding him guilty of physical assault on a PS candidate in the 1997 general election. The selection of a potential replacement for Le Pen, necessitated by the ban, to lead the FN list of candidates in the following year's elections to the European Parliament (of which the FN leader was a member), resulted in a major dispute within the party and the creation of two rival factions. Deepening divisions between supporters of Le Pen and those of Bruno Mégret, the party's second-in-command, led, in December, to Mégret's suspension, and later expulsion, from the party, together with six other senior party officials. In January 1999 Mégret launched his own party, which subsequently became known as the Mouvement National Républicain (MNR), and which appeared to follow harsher anti-immigrant policies than the FN. Although a significant proportion of FN members subsequently transferred their allegiance or membership to the MNR, the electoral performance of the new party was in general somewhat poorer than that of the depleted FN. In October 2000 Le Pen was expelled from his seat in the European Parliament, following the rejection of his final appeal against his 1998 conviction in the European Court of Human Rights. However, in January 2001 the European Court of Justice ruled that the President of the European Parliament had illegally excluded Le Pen from the legislature as the expulsion had been predicated on French national law.

In March 1999 Roland Dumas took leave of absence from the presidency of the Constitutional Council, following the reopening that month of a magistrate's inquiry into his involvement in the corruption scandals at the formerly state-owned petroleum company, Elf Aquitaine, including allegations of fraudulent handling of commission payments, estimated at US $500m., on the sale of six frigates to Taiwan in 1991. Also in March 1999 a Paris public prosecutor upheld a ruling of the Constitutional Court, issued in January, that Chirac enjoyed immunity from prosecution for all crimes, other than high treason, for the duration of his presidential term. This decision, which was confirmed by an appeal court ruling in January 2000, followed the disclosure of documentation purporting to show that Chirac had been aware of the existence of at least 300 fictitious employees on the payroll of the Paris city council under his tenure as mayor; a significant proportion of these fictitious employees, whose existence had first been revealed in mid-1998, were reputed to be RPR members or supporters.

In April Philippe Séguin resigned as President of the RPR, citing his dissatisfaction with Chirac's leadership. His interim replacement, Nicolas Sarkozy, in turn resigned, following poor results for the party in elections to the European Parliament held in June. The RPR, in alliance with DL, gained 12.8% of the votes cast, less than both the PS, which won 22.0% of votes cast, and a breakaway Gaullist group, opposed to the terms of the Maastricht Treaty, the Rassemblement pour la France (RPF), led by Charles Pasqua, which gained 13.1% of the votes cast. In December Michèle Alliot-Marie was elected President of the RPR.

In November 1999 Dominique Strauss-Kahn resigned as Minister of the Economy, Finance and Industry, following allegations that he had received payments from a students' mutual fund in respect of a fictitious job, although these charges were subsequently reduced to the falsification of documents related to this employment, and were dismissed in November 2001; other charges against Strauss-Kahn in relation to his alleged involvement in other cases of financial corruption were dismissed in mid-2001.

In March 2000 Jospin carried out the first major reorganization of the Council of Ministers since taking office. Laurent Fabius, PS Prime Minister in 1984–86, returned to office as Minister of the Economy, Finance and Industry, in which role he was regarded as a supporter of reform and greater economic liberalization. The hitherto First Vice-President of the Assemblée nationale, Raymond Forni, replaced Fabius as its President. Jack Lang, a former Minister of Culture under President Mitterrand, returned to senior office as Minister of National Education.

Dumas resigned in March 2000 as President of the Constitutional Council when it was announced that he would stand trial for his alleged participation in reputedly corrupt practices at Elf Aquitaine; the trial was subsequently postponed until January 2001.

In August 2000 the Minister of the Interior, Jean-Pierre Chevènement, the leader and sole minister of the Mouvement des Citoyens (MDC), resigned in protest at government policy towards Corsica (see below). Daniel Vaillant of the PS was appointed in his place. A further ministerial reshuffle was implemented in October.

Evidence of Chirac's apparent knowledge and tolerance of corrupt practice within government deepened in September 2000, when a transcript of a video-cassette made by Jean-Claude Méry, a former RPR official who had been imprisoned on charges of embezzlement in the mid-1990s, was published posthumously in *Le Monde*. In the recording Méry stated that Chirac had personally ordered him to arrange for funds of the Paris city council to be diverted to political parties. In December 2000 Michel Roussin, who had been Chirac's principal private secretary from 1989 to 1993, was arrested, while the former unofficial treasurer for the RPR was remanded for questioning. Their testimony, which was 'leaked' to the press, included details of the systematic levying of an illegal 2% commission on public works contracts awarded by the Paris administration. The RPR, the PR and the PS were all reportedly implicated in this scheme.

Throughout 2000 the tensions caused by a prolonged period of 'cohabitation' promoted moves towards constitutional change. In May Valéry Giscard d'Estaing submitted proposals to reduce the presidential term from seven to five years, in order to bring it into line with the life of a parliament. In June 2000 the Assemblée nationale voted conclusively in favour of the proposed constitutional amendment, which was now apparently supported by both the Prime Minister and the President. Amid concerns that the more conservative Sénat might not support the bill by the two-thirds' majority required for a constitutional change to be approved, Chirac called for a referendum, to be held on 24 September. The referendum attracted only a 30.6% participation rate, by far the lowest in any constitutional referendum held in metropolitan France. Of those who voted, 73.2% were in favour of the change, which was thereby enacted, to take effect from the 2002 presidential elections.

Following this constitutional change, a proposal previously raised by the UDF leader, François Bayrou, to the effect that presidential elections be held in advance of the parliamentary elections due in May 2002, gained in popularity, particularly among deputies of the UDF and PS, as it was felt that the proposed arrangement would be more likely to prevent a further period of 'cohabitation'. The RPR opposed the proposal as a partisan move intended to benefit Jospin and the PS, while the PCF and DL rejected the proposed change as granting an unacceptable increase in power to the President. Following a series of votes in the two legislative chambers, the Constitutional Council finally approved the proposal in May 2001.

Following inconclusive municipal and cantonal elections in March 2001, several ministers resigned from the mayorships that they had won in these elections and two Secretaries of State resigned from their government positions, following Jospin's insistence that henceforth members of the Government would not be permitted simultaneously to hold more than one elected position. In April officials from the RPR, UDF, and DL, although not including the senior leadership of the two latter parties, announced their intention to form a unified centre-right platform, which subsequently became known as the Union en Mouvement (UEM), prior to the legislative elections of 2002.

In early April 2001 Chirac refused to attend court to give evidence pertaining to the reputedly illegal use of funds in the Paris city council. At the end of the month the investigating judge in the case, Eric Halphen, announced the existence of consistent evidence implicating Chirac, but stated that the doctrine of presidential immunity prevented Chirac from being brought to trial. Although Jospin and the hierarchy of the PS opposed bringing Chirac to trial, the socialist deputy Arnaud Montebourg launched a campaign to being the case against Chirac to the High Court of Justice, which was the only court constitutionally able to bring charges against the President.

In June 2001 Chevènement resigned as leader of the MDC, in order to concentrate on building support for his anticipated presidential campaign as a candidate supporting 'republican' values, although his candidacy was not officially announced until early September.

Meanwhile, the trial of Dumas on charges of having misappropriated public funds was further delayed, in February 2001, following the extradition to France, from the Philippines, in relation to further charges of corruption within Elf Aquitaine, of the company's former Deputy Chairman, Alfred Sirven, who refused to co-operate with the trial when brought to court in March 2001. At the end of May Dumas and Sirven were among four people found guilty on charges relating to fraudulent practice within Elf Aquitaine; Dumas was sentenced to six months in prison, while Sirven received a sentence of four years; none-the-less all four were released on bail, pending an appeal, which was expected to necessitate the investigation of further alleged instances of corruption within Elf Aquitaine.

In mid-June 2001 Jospin admitted reports that he had been a member of a Trotskyist organization, the Organisation communiste internationale (OCI) in the 1960s, but rebutted suggestions that he had 'infiltrated' the PS on behalf of the OCI, and denied allegations that he had maintained connections with the OCI until 1987. New revelations concerning Chirac's alleged involvement in financial malpractice also emerged, including the first implications that Chirac had personally benefited from malpractice; the President was alleged to have spent up to 2.4m francs (a figure subsequently increased to 3.1m francs) of state 'secret funds'—issued annually by the Office of the Prime Minister for the security services, to pay bonuses to staff, and as a contingency fund—on airline tickets and luxury hotel bills for himself and his family in 1992–1995, although suspicions were voiced that the finance for these holidays may have originated from the alleged illicit commission payments made by building firms to the Paris city council. In mid-June 2001 the Assemblée nationale approved a bill, supported by the PS, that proposed removing judicial immunity from the President for acts committed outside his official role; however, the bill was regarded as having a purely symbolic function, as it was regarded as unlikely to gain the support of the Sénat or the President. At the end of the month a judicial investigation into the airline tickets and hotel bills affair was initiated, during the course of which Chirac's daughter, Claude Chirac, was called to testify. In early July Jospin demanded that a comprehensive audit be carried out into the use of the 'secret funds', which totalled some 400m. francs annually. Further ambiguity about the extent of presidential immunity was engendered in July following contradictory announcements by two Chief Prosecutors in Paris: the Chief Prosecutor of Paris, Jean-Pierre Dintilhac, declared that Chirac could legitimately be summonsed as a potential suspect, while the Chief Prosecutor of the Appeal Court, Jean-Louis Nadal, questioned the legitimacy of this ruling.

In a television interview broadcast on 14 July 2001, President Chirac declared himself innocent of all charges made against him, and confirmed that he would not participate in any court case. A few days later another three judges declared themselves constitutionally incompetent to try the President. At the end of the month a parliamentary committee agreed to a demand by magistrates to see the statements of personal financial wealth made by Chirac between 1988 and 1995; these statements made no reference to the large sums of money with which Chirac had purchased the holidays. Additional revelations concerning Chirac's reputed malpractice as the treasurer of a charity in the late 1970s also emerged at this time.

In August 2001 Jospin announced changes to the 35-hour working-week law, a scheme aimed at lowering unemployment levels. The amendments permitted companies with up to 20 employees legally to institute a longer working week, apparently in response to protests by employers at the restrictions engendered by the law. Previous concessions had already been made, after the implementation of the first stage of the legislation was greeted with widespread protests in February 2000.

In September 2001 the Appeal Court dismissed Halphen as the leading investigator into the case regarding the illicit transfer of funds from building contractors to political parties at the Paris city council; Halphen was ruled to have exceeded his powers by calling the President as a witness, and by introducing certain items of evidence, including the video-cassette of Méry. Although the case could be tried again, under a different judge, this decision effectively ruled out any development in the case until after the presidential election in 2002. (Halphen announced his retirement from the judiciary in January 2002, stating his dissatisfaction with the judicial system.)

Following partial senatorial elections held on 23 September 2001, the upper chamber of Parliament remained dominated by the Gaullist parties, although the Groupe socialiste increased its representation from 78 to 83 seats.

In mid-October 2001 the Court of Cassation confirmed the Constitutional Court's ruling that an incumbent President could not be prosecuted; additionally, the court ruled that a Head of State could not undergo formal investigation while in power, even for offences allegedly committed prior to taking office. The court also suspended the statute of limitations, as a consequence of which Montebourg ended his campaign to bring Chirac to trial. In the same month the President of the Audit Court presented a report to Jospin which recommended that henceforth, unspent funds from the Prime Minister's Office should be returned to the state budget each year, that bonuses paid to staff should be subject to taxation, and that the 'secret funds', as such, should be reserved solely for the secret security services.

In February 2002 Jean Glavany resigned as Minister of Agriculture and Fisheries, in order to organize Jospin's presidential campaign; he was replaced by François Patriat. Jospin formally announced his intention to contest the presidency on 21 February; Chirac had announced his candidacy earlier in the month. In late February Bayrou provoked controversy at a conference of the UEM in Toulouse when he stated his opposition to the notion that members of the UEM should support Chirac's candidature for the presidency. Several days later, some 109 UDF and DL deputies announced their support for Chirac in the presidential election, despite both Bayrou and Madelin also having announced their candidacies.

The first round of the presidential election, held on 21 April 2002, was contested by an unprecedented 16 candidates. Prior to the first round, Chirac and Jospin had been widely expected to progress to second round, with the remaining candidates regarded as liable to benefit predominately from 'protest' votes. Apparently partly as a result of the wide choice of candidates, a relatively low rate of participation (only 69.2% of the electorate cast valid votes), and a campaign focus on issues related to 'insecurity' and law and order, Jospin polled only 16.2% of the valid votes cast, while Chirac accounted for 19.9% and Le Pen 16.9%. The splintering of the governmental 'plural left' coalition was to prove detrimental for Jospin, as four of the parties hitherto represented in that coalition, other than the PS, presented individual candidates for the presidency, obtaining 16.3% of votes cast in total. Moreover, three Trotskyite candidates together polled some 10.4% of votes cast. The unexpected qualification of the FN leader for the second-round poll precipitated widespread demonstrations, and the majority of the defeated candidates rallied around Chirac as a candidate that represented 'republican values', although Chirac's first-round vote, in both percentage and actual terms, had been the lowest of any outgoing President of the Fifth Republic. In the second round, the first to be held without a left-wing candidate since 1969, on 5 May, the turn-out increased slightly—75.4% of the electorate cast valid votes. Although Le Pen's share of the vote rose marginally, Chirac's victory, with 82.2% of the valid votes cast, was widely interpreted as a resounding defeat for the far-right. On 6 May, following Jospin's resignation as Prime Min-

ister, Chirac appointed Jean-Pierre Raffarin, of the DL, as Prime Minister. On 7 May Raffarin appointed an interim Government, consisting of members of the DL, the UDF and the RPR, in addition to several independent ministers, which was to remain in office pending the legislative elections that were due to be held in June; among the principal appointments were Sarkozy as Minister of the Interior, Interior Security and Local Freedoms, Alliot-Marie as Minister of Defence and Dominique Galouzeau de Villepin as Minister of Foreign Affairs. In the period between the presidential elections and those to the Assemblée nationale, Chirac was instrumental in the organization of a new centre-right electoral alliance to replace the RPR, and to build on the informal alliances forged within the UEM with the intention of avoiding a further period of 'cohabitation'; this alliance was initially titled the Union pour la Majorité Présidentielle (UMP), and was provisionally led by Alain Juppé.

At the elections to the Assemblée nationale held on 9 and 16 June 2002 the UMP, which incorporated the greater part of the RPR and DL, and significant elements of the UDF, succeeded in becoming the largest grouping in the new Assemblée, with 355 of the 577 seats, whilst a further 43 representatives of other parties of the centre-right and right were elected, thus ensuring a clear working majority for the pro-presidential grouping in the assembly. Of the 176 seats awarded to parties of the broad left, the PS was the most successful, with 140 deputies; of the other left-wing parties, the PCF was the most successful, with only 21 deputies. Notably, a number of high-profile political figures from the previous administration failed to gain re-election to the Assemblée nationale. The FN obtained 11.34% of votes cast in the first round of polling, but did not receive any deputies. The new Government, appointed shortly after the conclusion of the legislative elections, retained substantially the same members as the interim Government appointed in May, but several new Ministers-Delegate and Secretaries of State were appointed. The new Government cited law and order as one of its principal concerns, and expressed the intention of implementing various administrative reforms, including a programme of decentralization (see below), further privatizations, and a reduction in levels of taxation. Concern about the degree of support for the far-right in France, which had heightened following Le Pen's progression to the second round of the presidential election, intensified further, following an attempt, on the national day, July 14, to assassinate President Chirac during a procession in Paris; it subsequently emerged that the assailant, Maxime Brunerie, was a member of a small neo-fascist grouping, Unité Radicale (UR), and had, moreover, contested a municipal election as a candidate of the MNR in 2001; UR was formally proscribed in early August, and Brunerie was subsequently interned in a psychiatric hospital.

In the aftermath of the legislative elections, political parties of both the left and the right underwent restructuring; on the centre-right the UMP consolidated its position, formally constituting itself as the Union pour un Mouvement Populaire in November 2002. The UMP absorbed the RPR and DL, in addition to factions of the UDF and the RPF; Juppé was elected as President of the party. In mid-December a UMP group was formed in the Sénat; with 166 of 321 seats, the group had an absolute majority in the chamber. Meanwhile, the future ideological direction of the PCF and, particularly, the PS became a subject of intense debate within the respective parties, and in January 2003 Les Verts elected a new executive committee, with Gilles Lemaire as the new National Secretary. Following the unexpectedly low share of the vote received by Chevènement (5.3%) at the presidential polls, and of his Pôle Républicain (which, temporarily, supplanted the MDC) at the legislative elections (when the party obtained only 1.2% of votes cast in the first round, and in which Chevènement lost his position as a deputy), the movement was reconstituted as the Mouvement Républicain et Citoyen (MRC) in January 2003.

In late January 2003 Dumas was cleared of all charges against him in the Elf Aquitaine case; although his conduct was described as 'blameable', he was not charged with any crime. However, the former Elf employees charged alongside Dumas were found guilty on appeal; the former President of Elf, Loik Le Floch-Prigent was sentenced to 30 months' imprisonment, while former Deputy President of Elf, Alfred Sirven, received three years' imprisonment, whilst Dumas's former mistress, Christine Deviers-Joncour, was sentenced to 18 months' imprisonment, with an additional suspended sentence of 12 months. (In late March Cresson was charged by a Belgian investigating magistrate with corruption in relation to her period as European Commissioner for Education in 1995–99; in January 2003 the European Commission commenced a parallel inquiry into allegations that Cresson had, during that period, been involved in the creation of falsified documents relating to a fictive employee.)

On 17 March 2003 the two houses of Parliament, meeting in congress, approved several constitutional changes relating to the proposed decentralization programme; the amendments provided for the eventual possibility of territorial units receiving varying degrees of autonomy and powers, to be decided in each case by law, for the institution of deliberative assemblies and for the holding of local referendums in such territories; these measures were approved by the UMP and UDF, but opposed by the PS and PCF. Moreover, the amendments permitted the introduction of legislation pertaining to decentralization on a temporary, or experimental, basis. Notably, the first article of the Constitution was amended to assert that the organization of the Republic was decentralized. Further organic laws, which would mark a further stage in the decentralization process, were expected to be brought before the parliamentary assemblies later in the year. A further constitutional amendment, relating to the implementation of the European arrest warrant, was also approved on 17 March.

As a result of decentralization legislation of 1982, the status of Corsica was elevated to that of a 'collectivité territoriale' (territorial community), with its own directly-elected 61-seat Assembly, and an administration with augmented executive powers. In April 1991 the Assemblée nationale adopted legislation, which granted greater autonomy to Corsica; a seven-member executive council was to be formed, chosen from a 51-member Assemblée de Corse, which would be elected in 1992. In early February 1998 the Préfet of Corsica, Claude Erignac, was assassinated by separatist extremists. The killing was condemned by the pro-independence Fronte di Liberazione Naziunale di a Corsica (FLNC). Despite sustained attempts to locate and arrest the suspected assassin of Erignac, the chief suspect, Yvan Colonna, remained in hiding in early 2003, although eight others, suspected of being accomplices in the killing, were to be brought to trial in that year.

In January 1999 the FLNC declared a cease-fire, on Corsican territory only. In regional assembly elections, held in March, the position of Corsican nationalist parties was strengthened, with the moderate Corsica Nazione coalition winning 17% of votes cast. An arson attack on a bar in the island's capital, Ajaccio, in April led to the arrest and dismissal of the island's Préfet, Bernard Bonnet, and the disbandment of the security unit that had been established after the murder of Erignac. Bonnet's arrest was made in response to allegations that the head of the unit, Henri Mazères, had ordered the attack on the bar; Bonnet, Mazères and an aide, Gerard Pardini, received custodial sentences in January 2002 for ordering the arson attacks, although Bonnet denied any involvement and announced that he would appeal. (At the appeal, which commenced in Bastia in November, the President of the Appeal Court rejected a request by Bonnet to call Jospin as a witness.)

Meanwhile, talks involving the Government and representatives of the island commenced in Paris in December 1999. Four groups of Corsican militants called an unconditional cease-fire, and pledged to disarm should their aims, including the recognition of the Corsican people as a nation, and the granting of official status to the Corsican language on the island, be achieved. The peace process resulted in agreement on a number of proposals known as the Matignon Accords. In July 2000 the proposals were approved in the territorial Assemblée by an overwhelming majority. Under the proposals, subject to the maintenance of peace on Corsica, and the approval of the Assemblée nationale, a referendum would be held on eventual revisions to the Constitution in 2004, prior to the introduction of a single political and administrative body for the island with formal, but limited, legislative powers, replacing the two existing administrative departments. The proposals also provided for instruction in the Corsican language to take place in all primary schools. The Minister of the Interior, Jean-Pierre Chevènement, resigned in protest over the proposals, claiming that they represented a surrender to the demands of terrorist groups, as well as a weakening of the republican structure of government. President Chirac and other leading figures in the RPR also expressed their opposition to this proposed act of decentralization.

Although most dissident groups maintained a cease-fire following the signature of the Matignon Accords, a prominent separatist, Jean-Michel Rossi was assassinated in the northwest of Corsica in August 2000. Rossi and another high-profile separatist, François Santoni, were believed to have been the co-founders of Armata Corsa, which had broken away from a faction of the FLNC in mid-1999, and had co-written a book that revealed purported associations between separatist groups and organized crime in Corsica. Armata Corsa ended its observance of a cease-fire following Rossi's assassination. The attacks by Corsican activists continued following a visit to the island by the new Minister of the Interior, Daniel Vaillant, in November 2000, during which he presented a draft document outlining the additional powers that were intended to be devolved to the Assemblée de Corse from January 2002. Following the announcement in October 2000 that groups in support of greater autonomy or independence for other regions of the French Republic had formed an alliance in response to what they regarded as a positive resolution of Corsica's status; Chirac used his constitutional prerogative to delay the submission of the relevant bill to the Council of Ministers in February 2001.

In mid-May 2001 the Assemblée nationale began to examine the bill to amend the status of Corsica. On 22 May the Assemblée nationale approved a more moderate version of the bill than that which had initially been envisaged, with the view to presenting a text that would be acceptable to the Constitutional Council; consequently, Corsican language instruction at primary schools was to be optional, rather than compulsory, and the French Parliament would be required to pass enabling legislation before local legislation approved by the Assemblée de Corse could take effect. Corsican separatists expressed disapproval of the amendments.

In June 2001 a journalist and writer, Nicolas Giudici, who had criticized the increasing significance of organized crime on the island, was assassinated. In July two explosions at police barracks outside Bastia, in which 22 people were injured, were attributed to a new, unknown group. In mid-August Santoni was assassinated, reportedly in revenge for having publicized details of organized crime among nationalist groups. Two other separatists were killed in attacks in August and September.

In late September 2001 the process envisaged by the Matignon Accords appeared to be stalling; the moderate nationalist leader, Jean-Guy Talamoni, who had been involved in negotiating the Matignon Accords, announced that Corsica Nazione had decided, by an almost unanimous vote of its militants and representatives, to withdraw from the provisions of the accords.

Before the bill on greater autonomy was submitted to the Sénat in early November 2001, further amendments to the bill were presented. On 19 December the final bill was approved, by the Assemblée nationale. The Gaullist parties, which generally opposed the legislation, announced that they would bring the bill before the Constitutional Council. In mid-January 2002 the Constitutional Council ruled that the section of the bill that permitted the Assemblée de Corse to amend national legislation on the island was illegitimate, although the section of the law that permitted the optional use of Corsican language in primary schools was approved. Following the defeat of Jospin in the first round of presidential elections in April 2003, and a statement by Chirac to the effect that Corsican aspirations for greater autonomy were insignificant, nationalists on the island announced their withdrawal from the Matignon process. In early May the FLNC announced that it was to resume its dissident campaign, although the organization stated its preference for a negotiated settlement.

The new centre-right Government appointed in May 2002, led by Raffarin, unexpectedly announced, following the conclusion of legislative elections in June, that it was to seek several amendments to the Constitution, that would permit the eventual decentralization of a number of powers, and that, moreover, Corsica would be one region which could be expected to be affected by these measures. Corsican nationalists expressed concern that the proposed measures would fail to take into account the specific characteristics of Corsica. In late July Sarkozy visited Corsica, where he spoke to the territorial Assemblée and announced efforts to relaunch a dialogue with nationalists. Following the generally positive reception of these efforts, and of Sarkozy's assurance that the Government recognized the specificity of Corsica, to which the granting of greater autonomy, he stated, could serve as a precursor for other regions, Raffarin also travelled to the island. In spite of this apparent demonstration of the Government's interest in Corsican affairs, and the subsequent announcement by Sarkozy that he intended to visit the island on a regular basis, the FLNC remained sceptical as to the willingness of the Government to resolve the issue of Corsica's status, and the number of small-scale bomb attacks on the island increased sharply in 2002, to reach the highest annual total recorded (in excess of 220) since 1997. In mid-October 2002 the Government announced that a detention centre was to be built on the island, and that Corsican nationalists imprisoned in continental France would, eventually, be transferred to Corsica. (Similar plans to fulfil this long-held demand had been announced by Vaillant in late 2001, although these proposals were subsequently withdrawn.) In late December 2002 Sarkozy announced various measures intended to benefit the economy of the island; in particular, both the Free Zone status granted to Corsica in 1996, and the tax credits for enterprises and investment granted by Jospin earlier in 2002 were to be extended; in early January 2003 Sarkozy attended the European Commission in Brussels, with elected representatives of Corsica, excepting those of the PCF, when the Government gained approval for the implementation of these measures. In early April Raffarin announced that a referendum would be held in July on the future staus of the island.

In June 1995 Chirac announced that France was to end a moratorium on nuclear testing imposed by Mitterrand in 1992. Six tests were subsequently conducted in French Polynesia, in the Pacific Ocean. The announcement caused widespread outrage in the international community.

In November 1998, following a lengthy campaign for the independence of the Pacific overseas territory of New Caledonia (see p. 1724) by indigenous Melanesian (Kanak) separatists, a referendum on self-determination was held. At the referendum a gradual transfer of powers to local institutions was approved, and the Republican Constitution amended accordingly. In October 1999 the Sénat approved legislation granting New Caledonia the new status of 'pays d'outre-mer' (overseas country). By February 2003, however, the constitutional amendment was still awaiting final ratification. Notably, the constitutional amendments that sought to permit other communities to, eventually, gain increased autonomy approved in March 2003 were not to apply to New Caledonia.

France granted independence to most of its former colonies after the Second World War. In Indo-China, after prolonged fighting, Laos, Cambodia and Viet Nam became fully independent in 1954. In Africa most of the French colonies in the West and Equatorial regions attained independence in 1960, but, with the notable exception of Guinea, retained their close economic and political ties with France (particularly within the framework of the Franc Zone (see p. 237). From the second half of the 1990s, France has sought closer relations with a number of former British colonies in Africa and has been active in promoting the establishment of regional peace-keeping forces in Africa.

In the early 1990s a contingent of French troops was dispatched to Rwanda to train forces of the Rwandan Government and to supply military equipment, following the outbreak of armed conflict between the Government and the opposition Front patriotique rwandais (FPR, or Inkotanyi). In April 1994 French troops re-entered Rwanda to establish a 'safe humanitarian zone' for refugees fleeing the civil war. Although France declared its presence to be restricted to a transitional period prior to the arrival of UN peace-keeping forces, the FPR accused France of using the operation secretly to transport alleged war criminals out of the country. In January 1998 new evidence emerged in support of allegations that France had sold arms to Rwanda during the massacres in 1994, after the imposition of a UN embargo on the delivery of military equipment to any party in the conflict, although the Government denied the accusations. A commission of inquiry, established to investigate the affair, effectively exonerated France but implicated the international community (and particularly the USA) for failing to provide adequate support for UN forces in the country, although the Rwandan Government rejected these findings.

From late 2002, more than 2,000 French troops were dispatched to Côte d'Ivoire to assist the 600 French troops permanently based there, initially to protect French citizens resident in the country from civil unrest that erupted in September, and subsequently to monitor a cease-fire, signed in mid-October, between Ivorian government troops and rebel forces in the north of the country; the troops were subsequently granted authority to enforce the cease-fire, and also that signed with other rebel groups in the west, where the French troops became involved in

various clashes; it was intended that by mid-2003 that the French peace-keeping forces would be replaced by those of the Economic Community of West African States (ECOWAS, see p. 187)

In September 1994, following the killing by Islamist extremists of five officials at the French embassy in Algiers, Algeria, the French Government initiated an extensive security operation, the results of which included the detention and subsequent expulsion from France of a number of alleged Islamist activists. In December members of the French security forces killed four Islamist extremists on board an Air France aircraft, which had been hijacked in Algiers and flown, initially, to Marseille. The following day four Roman Catholic priests, three of them French citizens, were killed in Algeria, in apparent reprisal. Eight people were killed in the second half of 1995 in a series of bombings in France, for which the Groupe islamique armé (GIA), an extremist Algerian organization, was widely believed to be responsible. In 1998 some 36 militant Islamists received custodial sentences for providing logistical support to the GIA during its bombing campaign, and in late 1999 a further 24 militants were found guilty of involvement in the bombing campaign. Meanwhile, in December 1996 four people were killed and up to 100 injured in an explosion on a crowded commuter train in Paris. Although no organization claimed responsibility for the attack it was speculated that the bombing might be in protest against the imminent trial in Paris of 30 young men of north African extraction who were accused of involvement in extremist activities in Morocco in 1994. In December 1996 the GIA warned that it would continue its campaign of violence in France, unless the French Government undertook to sever ties with the Algerian Government. France has been accused by Algerian Islamist groups of providing covert military assistance to the Algerian Government following the suspension of the 1992 general election in Algeria. Diplomatic contacts between the Algerian President, Abdelaziz Bouteflika, and the French Minister of Foreign Affairs, Hubert Védrine, resulted in the reopening of a number of French consulates in Algeria, and in the state visit of Bouteflika to Paris in May 2000, and a reciprocal visit by Védrine to Algiers in February 2001. Chirac visited Algeria in December 2001, as part of a tour of Maghreb countries, and following a further improvement in relations between France and Algeria that country's Prime Minister, Ali Benflis, visited Paris in January 2003. Moreover, in March, Chirac became the first French President to participate in an official state visit to Algeria since that country's independence, and Chirac and Bouteflika signed a declaration providing for increased economic and cultural co-operation between the countries.

France's relations with the USA have frequently been marked by a desire to establish French independence of action, particularly with regard to military concerns. Although France had been a participant, alongside the USA and the United Kingdom, in maintaining a 'no-fly' zone (the so-called 'Southern Watch') in southern Iraq following the conclusion of the Persian (Arabian) Gulf war in 1991, it withdrew from these duties in December 1998 and criticized aerial raids on Iraq by US and British forces in February 2001. In that month France also announced that it was opposed to the continuation of UN sanctions against Iraq implemented in connection with that country's alleged arsenal of weapons of mass destruction. In June France recommended to the UN Security Council, during discussions on the sanctions regime against Iraq, that foreign investment be permitted in the Iraqi petroleum industry, but, none the less, declared its full support for the 'smart sanctions' proposed by the USA and the United Kingdom at this time. In the aftermath of the attacks in New York and Washington, DC, attributed to the al-Qa'ida (Base) organization of the militant Islamist Osama bin Laden on 11 September 2001, France offered full military and logistical support, including the dispatch to Afghanistan of marines, engineers and members of the Special Forces to the USA in its campaign against al-Qa'ida. However, France remained a prominent critic of the perceived unilateralism of the foreign policy of the administration of US President George W. Bush. Although France supported the UN Security Council resolution 1441 (presented by the USA and the United Kingdom) in November 2002, which demanded the expedited admittance of weapons inspectors of UNMOVIC to Iraq, the French Minister of Foreign Affairs, Dominique Galouzeau de Villepin, maintained opposition to any UN Security Council resolution which would authorize any automatic resort to force against Iraq. Moreover, as Spain, the USA and the United Kingdom sought to gain support for a further UN Security Council resolution regarding Iraq's non-compliance with the requirements of Resolution 1441, in March 2003, President Chirac reiterated that France would, at that stage, veto any resolution that would have the effect of legitimizing military action against that country, although the French ambassador to the USA, Jean-David Levitte stated that, in the event that Iraq utilized chemical or biological weapons in the conflict against US-led troops that commenced later that month, France would be prepared to join the conflict on the side of the US-led coalition.

In May 1992 France and Germany announced that they would establish a joint defence force of 50,000 troops, the 'Eurocorps', which was intended to provide a basis for a European army under the aegis of Western European Union (WEU, see p. 318), and which became operational on 30 November 1995. Belgium, Spain and Luxembourg also agreed to participate in the force. In January 1993 an agreement was signed between NATO and the French and German Governments, establishing formal links between the corps and NATO's military structure. In December 1995 it was announced that France would rejoin the military structure of NATO, although it would not initially become a full member of NATO's integrated military command and would retain control of its independent nuclear forces. France's proposed re-entry into the integrated military command has been delayed as a result of an ongoing dispute with the USA over command of the alliance troops in southern Europe, which France insists must be under the command of a European officer. In February 2003 France, in addition to Belgium and Germany, objected to proposals for the deployment of additional NATO resources to Turkey, in advance of any US-led attack against neighbouring Iraq, on the grounds that such a deployment would imply the inevitability of any such attack. However, later in the month, following the withdrawal of objections by Belgium and Germany (which, unlike France, were represented in the integrated military command of NATO), additional resources intended to enhance Turkey's defensive capabilities, were dispatched. In late 2000 it was announced that France would contribute 12,000 troops, of a total of 66,000 that would form a European rapid reaction force, to participate in peace-keeping missions from 2003.

Government

Under the 1958 Constitution, legislative power is held by the bicameral Parliament, comprising a Sénat (Senate) and an Assemblée nationale (National Assembly). The Sénat has 321 members (296 for metropolitan France, 13 for the overseas departments, 'collectivités territoriales', the overseas country and territories, and 12 for French nationals abroad). Senators are elected for a nine-year term by an electoral college composed of the members of the Assemblée nationale, delegates from the Councils of the Departments and delegates from the Municipal Councils. One-third of the Sénat is renewable every three years, and election is by a system of proportional representation in those constituencies represented by three or more senators (five or more prior to the elections held in September 2001). The Assemblée nationale has 577 members, with 555 for metropolitan France and 22 for overseas departments, the overseas country, 'collectivités territoriales' and territories. Members of the Assemblée are elected by universal adult suffrage, under a single-member constituency system of direct election, using a second ballot if the first ballot failed to produce an absolute majority for any one candidate. The term of the Assemblée is five years, subject to dissolution. Executive power is held by the President. Since 1962 the President had been directly elected by popular vote (using two ballots if necessary) for seven years, although a constitutional amendment passed on 2 October 2000 shortened the term of office to five years. The President appoints a Council of Ministers, headed by the Prime Minister, which administers the country and is responsible to Parliament. Under constitutional amendments and legislation instituted in 1998–2000, political parties are penalized financially if they do not ensure parity of men and women in candidatures for elections.

Metropolitan France comprises 21 administrative regions containing 96 departments. Under the decentralization law of March 1982, administrative and financial power in metropolitan France was transferred from the Préfets, who became Commissaires de la République, to locally-elected departmental assemblies (Conseils généraux) and regional assemblies (Conseils régionaux). The special status of a 'collectivité territoriale' was granted to Corsica, which has its own directly-elected legislative assembly (the Assemblée de Corse). There are four overseas departments (French Guiana, Guadeloupe, Martinique and Réunion), one overseas collectivité départementale (Mayotte), one overseas 'collectivité territoriale' (St Pierre and Miquelon), three overseas territories (French Polynesia, the French Southern and Antarctic Territories, and the Wallis and Futuna Islands) and one overseas country (New Caledonia), all of which are integral parts of the French Republic. Each overseas department is administered by an elected Conseil général and Conseil régional, each 'collectivité territoriale' by an appointed government commissioner, each overseas territory by an appointed high commissioner, and New Caledonia by its Government. In 1998 a referendum granted a transfer of powers to local institutions in New Caledonia over a period of 15–20 years. In early 2001 the Assemblée nationale approved a proposal to change the status of Mayotte to that of 'collectivité départementale'.

Defence

French military policy is decided by the Supreme Defence Council. Military service was compulsory, and lasted for a period of 10 months, until November 2001, when proposals to create fully professional armed forces, which were submitted to the Assemblée nationale in 1996, took effect.. In August 2002 the total active armed forces numbered 260,400, including an army of 137,000, a navy of 45,600, an air force of 64,000, central service staff numbering 5,200and a medical corps of 8,600. In addition, there was a paramilitary gendarmerie of 101,399. Total reserves stood at 100,000 (army 28,000; navy 6,500; air force 8,000, gendarmerie 50,000, medical service 7,000, others 500) in August 2002. Government expenditure on defence in 2001 amounted to 246,000m. francs. Defence expenditure was budgeted at €28,900m. for 2002. Although a member of NATO, France withdrew from its integrated military organization in 1966, and possesses its own nuclear weapons. In 1995, however, it was announced that France was to rejoin NATO's defence committee, and in 1996 President Chirac declared France's intention to rejoin NATO's integrated military command; by early 2003, however, there had been no firm indication as to when or if this latter move was likely to occur. In mid-2000 France announced that it would be the third largest contributor of troops, behind Germany and the United Kingdom, to the European rapid reaction force, which was to enter service, primarily on peace-keeping missions, in 2003.

Economic Affairs

In 2001, according to estimates by the World Bank, France's gross national income (GNI), measured at average 1999–2001 prices, was US $1,377,389m., equivalent to $22,690 per head (or $25,280 on an international purchasing-power parity basis). During 1990–2001, it was estimated, the population increased by an average of 0.4% per year, while gross domestic product (GDP) per head increased, in real terms, by an average of 1.4% per year. Overall GDP increased, in real terms, by an average annual rate of 1.8% per year in 1990–2001. Real GDP increased by 3.1% in 2000 and by 2.0% in 2001. Growth of 1.2% was recorded in 2002, according to preliminary figures, the lowest annual growth since 1996.

Agriculture (including forestry and fishing) contributed 2.9% of GDP in 2000, and engaged 3.2% of the economically active population in 2001. The principal crops are wheat, sugar beet, maize and barley. Livestock, dairy products and wine are also important. Agricultural GDP increased, in real terms, by an average of 1.6% per year in 1990–2000; it increased by 2.9% in 1999 and remained constant in 2000. The sector was adversely affected in 2000–01 by the outbreak of Bovine Spongiform Encephalopathy (BSE—'Mad Cow Disease') and its human variant, Creutzfeldt-Jakob Disease, v-CJD); by the end of 2000 a number of the country's major export markets for beef had placed restrictions on the export of meat from France. More than 30,000 cattle suspected to be infected with BSE were destroyed in January 2001.

Industry (including mining, manufacturing, construction and power) provided 26.1% of GDP in 2000, and employed 26.6% of the working population in 1994. Industrial GDP increased, in real terms, by an average of 1.3% per year during 1990–2000; it increased by 2.3% in 1999 and by 3.1% in 2000.

Mining and quarrying contributed 0.4% of GDP in 1997 and employed 0.3% of the working population in 1994. Coal is the principal mineral produced, while petroleum and natural gas are also extracted. In addition, metallic minerals, including iron ore, copper and zinc, are mined. In real terms, the GDP of the mining sector increased by 3.8% in 1996, but declined by 8.6% in 1997.

Manufacturing provided 18.9% of GDP in 1999 and employed 18.8% of the working population in 1994. Measured by the value of output, the most important branches of manufacturing in 1995 were machinery and transport equipment (accounting for 31% of the total), food, beverages and tobacco (17%), chemicals (10%) and fabricated metal products (6%). According to the World Bank, manufacturing GDP increased, in real terms, at an average annual rate of 2.4% in 1991–2001.

France has only limited fossil fuel resources, and in the early 2000s was the world's largest producer of nuclear power per head of population. In 2000 nuclear power provided 76.5% of total electricity production and hydroelectric power 18.1%; 9.7% of energy produced was from thermal sources. In the 1990s the Government abandoned a policy, by which almost all electricity in France was to have been generated by nuclear power. Imports of fuel products comprised 9.9% of the value of total merchandise imports in 2000; in the early 2000s the major sources of petroleum imported to France were Saudi Arabia and Norway. In late 1998 the NorFra pipeline, which connected Norway's Troll gas field in the North Sea to the French national gas grid, opened, becoming the first pipeline to link a foreign production field to France. By 2005 it was anticipated that this pipeline would supply one-third of France's total national gas requirements The GDP of the energy sector increased, in real terms, at an average rate of 1.5% per year in 1990–99.

Services accounted for 70.9% of GDP in 2000 and employed 68.7% of the working population in 1994. In the late 1990s and early 2000s France was consistently the country with the largest quantity of tourist visitors in the world; there were an estimated 75,595,000 tourist arrivals in 2000, and in that year tourism receipts totalled US $29,900m. The combined GDP of all service sectors increased, in real terms, at an average rate of 2.0% per year in 1990–2000; it increased by 3.3% in 1999 and by 3.1% in 2000.

In 2001 France recorded a trade surplus of US $2,853m. and there was a surplus of $21,359m. on the current account of the balance of payments. In 2000 the principal source of imports (providing 16.3% of the total) was Germany; other major sources were the USA (8.8%), Italy (8.7%), and the United Kingdom (8.0%). Germany was also the principal market for exports (accounting for 15.2% of the total); other major trading partners were the United Kingdom (9.9%), Spain (9.7%) and Italy (8.9%). The EU as a whole provided 59.2% of imports in 1998 and took 62.6% of exports. The principal exports in 2000 were machinery and transport equipment, basic manufactures, chemicals and miscellaneous manufactured articles. The principal imports were machinery and transport equipment, basic manufactures and miscellaneous manufactured articles.

The budget deficit for 2002 amounted to €47,446m., equivalent to 3.1% of GDP. In 2002 gross state debt was equivalent to 59.1% of annual GDP. The average annual rate of inflation in 1990–2001 was 1.7%. Consumer prices increased by 1.6% in 2001 and by 1.9% in 2002.. The rate of unemployment declined from 12.3% in 1997 to 8.8% in 2001, but increased to 9.1%, by December 2002.

France is a member of the European Union (EU, see p. 199), and of the Organisation for Economic Co-operation and Development (see p. 277), and presides over the Franc Zone (see p. 237).

As one of the initial 11 member countries of the EU that had chosen to participate in a single currency under economic and monetary union (EMU, see p. 225), France adopted the euro in January 1999 as a single currency unit for transactions throughout the euro zone and as an internationally traded currency, and as legal tender in cash from 1 January 2002. The French economy exhibited vigorous growth from 1997 to 2000, although in 2001 growth decelerated somewhat, largely as a result of a downturn in investor and consumer confidence, and as part of the general global economic decline in that year. The implementation, by the Jospin administration, from January 2000 of legislation reducing the duration of the working week from 39 to 35 hours, was initially regarded as contributing to an appreciable reduction in unemployment. However, in response to concerns that this system inhibited flexibility for enterprises and necessitated additional costs, the Raffarin administration, in January 2003, announced amendments to the system, permitting additional overtime to workers; legislation, approved in that month, introduced further flexibility to the system, particularly for enterprises with less than 20 employees, which had only been required to implement the reduced working hours legislation from January 2002. A number of major state-owned corporations have been wholly or partially privatized since 1993,

and while France remained the euro-zone country with the highest general government expenditure and revenue as a share of GDP in 2001 (in both cases in excess of 50%), privatization programmes have led to the increasing liberalization of the economy. France has, however, been slow to implement European Commission requirements on opening markets to competition and on restricting state subsidies, particularly in the energy sector. In June 2000 the European Commission commenced legal proceedings against France for failing to ensure that competition in electricity markets, permitted since February of that year, would be fair, and in May 2001 legal proceedings against France began with regard to its failure to create competition in gas markets. Moreover, in October 2002 the European Commission ruled that the state electricity company, Electricité de France (EdF), was obliged to repay some €900m. that it had received as a subsidy from the state. However, in November 2002 France approved a directive of the European Union Council of Ministers, to the effect that the electricity and gas markets were to be fully liberalized by July 2004 for enterprises, and by July 2007, for individual customers. In July 2002, Raffarin announced that the capital of both EdF and Gaz de France, was progressively to be opened to private investors, although both companies would remain within the public sector.

The announcement, in March 2003, that the anticipated budget deficit for 2003, had increased to the equivalent of 3.4% of GDP, in excess of the 3.0% limit permitted by the euro-zone Growth and Stability Pact, as a result of lower than expected growth, resulted in France being issued with a formal warning by the European Commission for failing to fulfil its obligations with regard to fiscal consolidation. The Commission subsequently launched its excessive deficit procedure, in accordance with which France could be fined by an amount equivalent to up to 0.5% of GDP, although no decision on this matter was expected to be taken before mid-2003. As a consequence of an ageing population, the public-sector pension system, and the development of a complementary private pension sector, represent a further area in which France will be required to implement reforms during the early 2000s.

Education

France is divided into 27 educational districts, called Académies, each responsible for the administration of education, from primary to higher levels, in its area. Education is compulsory and free for children aged six to 16 years. Primary education begins at six years of age and lasts for five years. At the age of 11 all pupils enter the first cycle of the Enseignement secondaire, with a four-year general course. At the age of 15 they may then proceed to the second cycle, choosing a course leading to the baccalauréat examination after three years or a course leading to vocational qualifications after two or three years, with commercial, administrative or industrial options. From 1963 junior classes in the Lycées were gradually abolished in favour of new junior comprehensives, called Collèges. Alongside the collèges and lycées, technical education is provided in the Lycées professionnels and the Lycées techniques. About 17% of children attend France's 10,000 private schools, most of which are administered by the Roman Catholic Church.

Educational reforms, introduced in 1980, aimed to decentralize the state school system: the school calendar now varies according to three zones, and the previously rigid syllabus has been replaced by more flexibility and choice of curricula. Further decentralization measures included, from 1986, the transfer of financial responsibility for education to the local authorities.

The minimum qualification for entry to university faculties is the baccalauréat. There are three stages of university education. The first level, the Diplôme d'études universitaires générales (DEUG), is reached after two years of study, and the first degree, the Licence, is obtained after three years. The master's degree (Maîtrise) is obtained after four years of study, while the doctorate requires six or seven years' study and the submission of a thesis. The prestigious Grandes Ecoles complement the universities; entry to them is by competitive examination, and they have traditionally supplied France's administrative élite. The 1968 reforms in higher education aimed to increase university autonomy and to render teaching methods less formal. Enrolment at schools in 1996 included 100% of children in the relevant age-group for primary education and 95% (males 94%; females 95%) for secondary education. Expenditure on education by all levels of government in 1999 totalled an estimated €92,600m. (7.2% of GDP). Proposed budgetary expenditure on education by the central Government amounted to 334,378m. francs in 1998 (21.1% of total budgetary expenditure).

Public Holidays

2003: 1 January (New Year's Day), 21 April (Easter Monday), 1 May (Labour Day), 8 May (Liberation Day), 29 May (Ascension Day), 9 June (Whit Monday), 14 July (National Day, Fall of the Bastille), 15 August (Assumption), 1 November (All Saints' Day), 11 November (Armistice Day), 25 December (Christmas Day).

2004: 1 January (New Year's Day), 12 April (Easter Monday), 1 May (Labour Day), 8 May (Liberation Day), 20 May (Ascension Day), 31 May (Whit Monday), 14 July (National Day, Fall of the Bastille), 15 August (Assumption), 1 November (All Saints' Day), 11 November (Armistice Day), 25 December (Christmas Day).

Weights and Measures

The metric system is in force.

Statistical Survey

Unless otherwise indicated, figures in this survey refer to metropolitan France, excluding Overseas Departments and Territories

Source (unless otherwise stated): Institut national de la statistique et des études économiques, 18 boulevard Adolphe Pinard, 75675 Paris Cédex 14; tel. 1-45-17-50-50; internet www.insee.fr.

Area and Population

AREA, POPULATION AND DENSITY

Area (sq km)	543,965*
Population (census results, *de jure*)†	
5 March 1990	56,615,155
8 March 1999‡	
Males	28,419,419
Females	30,101,269
Total	58,520,688
Population (official estimates at mid-year)	
2000	58,893,601
2001	59,188,189
2002	59,481,919
Density (per sq km) at mid-2002	109.3

* 210,026 sq miles.

† Excluding professional soldiers and military personnel outside the country with no personal residence in France.

‡ Data are provisional. The revised total is 58,518,395. Figures include double counting.

NATIONALITY OF THE POPULATION

(numbers resident in France at 1999 census, revised figures)

Country of citizenship	Population	%
France	55,257,502	94.42
Portugal	553,663	0.95
Morocco	504,096	0.86
Algeria	477,482	0.82
Turkey	208,049	0.36
Italy	201,670	0.34
Spain	161,762	0.28
Tunisia	154,356	0.26
Germany	78,381	0.31
Belgium	66,666	0.11
Yugoslavia*	50,543	0.09
Poland	33,758	0.06
Others	772,760	1.32
Total	**58,520,688**	**100.00**

* The successor states of the former Socialist Federal Republic of Yugoslavia, comprising Bosnia-Herzegovina, Croatia, the Former Yugoslav Republic of Macedonia, Slovenia and the Federal Republic of Yugoslavia (now Serbia and Montenegro).

REGIONS

(population at 1999 census, revised figures)

	Area (sq km)	Population	Density (per sq km)	Principal city
Alsace	8,280.2	1,734,145	209.4	Strasbourg
Aquitaine	41,308.4	2,908,359	70.4	Bordeaux
Auvergne	26,012.9	1,308,878	50.3	Clermont-Ferrand
Basse-Normandie .	17,589.3	1,422,193	80.9	Caen
Bourgogne (Burgundy) . .	31,582.0	1,610,067	51.0	Dijon
Bretagne (Brittany) . .	27,207.9	2,906,197	106.8	Rennes
Centre	39,150.9	2,440,329	62.3	Orléans
Champagne–Ardenne	25,605.8	1,342,363	52.4	Châlons-sur-Marne
Corse (Corsica) . .	8,679.8	260,196	30.0	Ajaccio
Franche-Comté .	16,202.3	1,117,059	68.9	Besançon
Haute-Normandie .	12,317.4	1,780,192	144.5	Rouen
Ile-de-France . .	12,012.3	10,952,011	911.7	Paris
Languedoc–Roussillon . .	27,375.8	2,295,648	83.9	Montpellier
Limousin	16,942.3	710,939	42.0	Limoges
Lorraine	23,547.4	2,310,376	98.1	Nancy
Midi–Pyrénées . .	45,347.9	2,551,687	56.3	Toulouse
Nord–Pas-de-Calais	12,414.1	3,996,588	321.9	Lille
Pays de la Loire . .	32,081.8	3,222,061	100.4	Nantes
Picardie (Picardy) . .	19,399.5	1,857,481	95.7	Amiens
Poitou–Charentes .	25,809.5	1,640,068	63.5	Poitiers
Provence–Alpes–Côte d'Azur . .	31,399.6	4,506,151	143.5	Marseille
Rhône–Alpes . .	43,698.2	5,645,407	129.2	Lyon
Total	**543,965.4**	**58,518,395**	**107.6**	

PRINCIPAL TOWNS*

(population at 1999 census, revised figures)

Paris (capital) . . .	2,125,246	Brest	149,634
Marseille (Marseilles) .	798,430	Le Mans	146,105
Lyon (Lyons) . . .	445,452	Clermont-Ferrand . .	137,140
Toulouse	390,350	Amiens	135,501
Nice	342,738	Aix-en-Provence . .	134,222
Nantes	270,251	Limoges	133,968
Strasbourg	264,115	Nîmes	133,424
Montpellier	225,392	Tours	132,820
Bordeaux	215,363	Villeurbanne . . .	124,215
Rennes	206,229	Metz	123,776
Le Havre	190,905	Besançon	117,733
Reims (Rheims) . .	187,206	Caen	113,987
Lille	184,493	Orléans	113,126
Saint-Etienne . . .	180,210	Mulhouse	110,359
Toulon	160,639	Rouen	106,592
Grenoble	153,317	Boulogne-Billancourt .	106,367
Angers	151,279	Perpignan	105,115
Dijon	149,867	Nancy	103,605

* Figures refer to the population of communes (municipalities).

BIRTHS, MARRIAGES AND DEATHS*

	Registered live births		Registered marriages		Registered deaths	
	Number	Rate (per 1,000)	Number	Rate (per 1,000)	Number	Rate (per 1,000)
1995	729,609	12.6	254,651	4.4	531,618	9.2
1996	734,338	12.7	280,072	4.8	535,775	9.2
1997	726,768	12.5	283,984	4.9	530,319	9.1
1998	738,080	12.6	271,361	4.6	534,005	9.1
1999	744,791	12.7	286,191	4.9	537,661	9.2
2000†	774,782	13.2	297,922	5.1	535,066	9.1
2001†	770,945	13.0	288,255	4.9	531,845	9.0
2002†	762,700	12.8	280,600	4.7	539,700	9.1

* Including data for national armed forces outside the country.
† Provisional figures.

Expectation of life (WHO estimates, years at birth): 79.3 (males 75.6; females 82.9)in 2001 (Source: WHO, *World Health Report*).

ECONOMICALLY ACTIVE POPULATION*
(annual averages, '000 persons aged 15 years and over)

	1992	1993	1994
Agriculture, hunting, forestry and fishing	1,150.3	1,100.8	1,048.4
Mining and quarrying	72.0	69.9	65.9
Manufacturing	4,479.0	4,269.3	4,162.2
Electricity, gas and water	204.0	204.9	203.7
Construction	1,568.3	1,487.8	1,443.1
Trade, restaurants and hotels	3,715.2	3,680.5	3,715.7
Transport, storage and communications	1,418.4	1,403.1	1,397.0
Financing, insurance, real estate and business services	2,295.2	2,265.1	2,340.4
Community, social and personal services†	7,405.4	7,596.2	7,733.8
Total employed	22,307.6	22,078.2	22,110.0
Persons on compulsory military service	221.1	219.9	212.4
Unemployed	2,590.7	2,929.0	3,163.8
Total labour force	25,119.4	25,227.1	25,486.2

* Figures are provisional. The revised totals (in '000) are: Employed 22,320.1 in 1992, 22,039.1 in 1993, 22,024.6 in 1994; Unemployed 2,560.2 in 1992, 2,891.5 in 1993, 3,053.9 in 1994; Total labour force 24,480.4 (males 13,567.6, females 11,312.8) in 1992, 24,930.6 (males 13,511.2, females 11,419.4) in 1993, 25,078.6 (males 13,478.6, females 11,600.0) in 1994. These figures exclude those on compulsory miltary service (annual average, '000): 225.1 in 1992, 219.9 in 1993, 212.4 in 1994.
† Figures include regular members of the armed forces, officially estimated at 304,200 (males 286,000; females 18,200) in 1986.

Source: mainly ILO, *Yearbook of Labour Statistics*.

1995 (annual averages, '000 persons ages 15 years and over): Total employed 22,233.2; Unemployed 2,887.1; Total labour force 25,120.3 (males 13,481.2, females 11,639.1).

1996 (annual averages, '000 persons aged 15 years and over): Total employed 22,317.6; Unemployed 3,088.7; Total labour force 25,406.2 (males 13,604.6, females 11,801.6).

1997 (annual averages, '000 persons aged 15 years and over): Total employed 22,432.4; Unemployed 3,170.1; Total labour force 25,770.1 (males 13,661.6, females 11,915.5).

1998 (annual averages, '000 persons aged 15 years and over): Total employed 22,766.6; Unemployed 3,003.5; Total labour force 25,770.1 (males 13,736.9, females 12,033.2).

1999 (annual averages, '000 persons aged 15 years and over): Total employed 20,789.8; Unemployed 2,870.5; Total labour force 26,131.0 (males 13,849.7, females 12,281.3).

2000 (annual averages, '000 persons ages 15 years and over, provisional): Total employed 23,871.4; Unemployed 2,517.6; Total labour force 26,389.0 (males 14,051.9, females 12,337.1).

Note: Figures do not specify the status of those on compulsory military service (annual averages, '000): 206.1 in 1995; 199.6 in 1996; 170.1 in 1997; 127.8 in 1998; 83.5 in 1999; 51.6 in 2000.

Health and Welfare

KEY INDICATORS

Total fertility rate (children per woman, 2001)	1.8
Under-5 mortality rate (per 1,000 live births, 2001)	6
HIV/AIDS (% of persons aged 15–49, 2001)	0.33
Physicians (per 1,000 head, 1997)	3.03
Hospital beds (per 1,000 head, 1998)	8.5
Health expenditure (2000): US $ per head (PPP)	2,335
Health expenditure (2000): % of GDP	9.5
Health expenditure (2000): public (% of total)	76.0
Human Development Index (2000): ranking	12
Human Development Index (2000): value	0.928

For sources and definitions, see explanatory note on p. vi.

Agriculture

PRINCIPAL CROPS
('000 metric tons)

	1999	2000	2001
Wheat	37,050.0	37,358.0	31,572.0
Rice (paddy)	110.3	116.0	103.0
Barley	9,377.6	9,716.5	9,806.0
Maize*	15,356.7	16,073.0	16,476.0
Rye	164.9	145.7	116.0
Oats	513.7	459.2	485.0
Sorghum	320.7	372.0	395.0
Triticale (wheat-rye hybrid)	1,212.8	1,261.4	1,123.0
Potatoes	6,645	6,652	6,259
Sugar beet	32,919	31,131	26,841
Pulses†	2,715	2,053	1,873
Soybeans (Soya beans)	261.5	201.0	306.4
Sunflower seed	1,929.9	1,833.0	1,621.2
Rapeseed	4,391.6	3,480.5	2,874.0
Cabbages	238.6	239.8	249.4
Artichokes†	75.0	64.3	59.0
Lettuce	490.5	513.2	514.6
Spinach	127.6	132.1	112.3
Tomatoes	921.5	897.6	844.8
Cauliflowers	425.4	385.5	392.1
Pumpkins, squash and gourds	192.1	196.2	213.7
Cucumbers and gherkins	147.1	150.0	127.4
Onions (dry)	349.2	360.7	437.4
Beans (green)	125.0	108.3	104.5
Peas (green)	557.4	550.1	474.0
Carrots	672.0	681.0	670.8
Apples	2,165.8	2,156.9	2,397.0
Pears	287.4	261.6	259.5
Apricots	180.9	146.0	108.9
Peaches and nectarines	477.5	475.8	460.4
Plums	185.0	214.2	281.0
Strawberries‡	67.7	70.5	63.4
Grapes	8,137.3	7,626.6	7,281.6
Canteloupes and other melons	322.3	313.0	318.3
Kiwi fruit	73.1	77.1	74.1
Tobacco (leaves)	26.2	25.5	24.8

* Figures refer to main, associated and catch crops.
† FAO estimates.
‡ Unofficial figures.

Source: FAO.

LIVESTOCK
('000 head, year ending 30 September)

	1999	2000	2001
Cattle	20,265	20,527	20,338
Pigs	14,682	14,635	14,762
Sheep	10,240	9,509	9,324
Goats	1,199	1,191	1,202
Horses	348	349	350*
Asses*	16	16	16
Mules	14	15	15*
Chickens	241,150	232,970	230,000*
Ducks	23,756	23,800*	23,500*
Turkeys	43,533	42,017	42,000*

* FAO estimate(s).

Source: FAO.

LIVESTOCK PRODUCTS
('000 metric tons)

	1999	2000	2001
Beef and veal	1,609.0	1,514.0	1,565.7
Mutton and lamb	132.1	133.4	133.1
Pig meat	2,353.0	2,312.0	2,317.0
Chicken meat	1,275.0	1,242.0	1,208.1
Duck meat	224.8	235.7	238.0
Turkey meat	682.5	738.0	750.1
Other meat	307.2	310.5	314.5
Cows' milk	24,892.0	24,898.0	24,791.0
Sheep's milk	243.9	246.7	245.7
Goats' milk	495.8	485.4	486.3
Butter	447.6	448.5	448.8
Cheese	1,675.6	1,722.4	1,770.7
Honey	18.1	18.0*	18.0*
Hen eggs	1,054	1,039	1,034
Wool: greasy*	22	22	22
Wool: scoured*	12	12	12
Cattle hides*	151	150	150
Sheepskins*	17.5	16.0	15.2

* FAO estimate(s).
Source: FAO.

Forestry

ROUNDWOOD REMOVALS
('000 cubic metres, excluding bark)

	1999	2000	2001
Sawlogs, veneer logs and logs for sleepers	22,185	30,619	25,715
Pulpwood	10,575	12,341	10,110
Other industrial wood	477	480	480
Fuel wood	9,771	2,388	2,500
Total	43,008	45,828	38,805

Source: FAO.

SAWNWOOD PRODUCTION
('000 cubic metres, including railway sleepers)

	1999	2000	2001
Coniferous (softwood)	7,257	7,568	7,670
Broadleaved (hardwood)	2,979	2,968	3,030
Total	10,236	10,536	10,700

Source: FAO.

Fishing*

('000 metric tons, live weight)

	1998	1999	2000
Capture	544.3	588.5	596.9
Pollocks	21.6	27.6	30.3
European pilchard (Sardine)	18.6	38.9	29.6
European anchovy	25.5	24.7	26.3
Skipjack tuna	48.7	63.0	57.9
Yellowfin tuna	53.1	62.0	67.8
Atlantic horse mackerel	28.1	27.1	22.5
Crustaceans	17.3	18.3	19.3
Molluscs	55.1	68.2	71.0
Aquaculture	267.8	264.8	267.7
Rainbow trout	44.5	38.6	41.1
Pacific cupped oyster	136.2	137.0	133.5
Blue mussel	50.8	51.6	58.0
Total catch	812.1	853.4	864.7

* Figures exclude aquatic plants ('000 metric tons): 127.0 (capture 67.0, aquaculture 60.0) in 1998; 107.3 (capture 87.3, aquaculture 20.0) in 1999; 90.3 (capture 70.3, aquaculture 20.0) in 2000; coral (metric tons): 4.5 in 1998; 3.8 in 1999; 3.6 in 2000; and sponges (metric tons, FAO estimates): 5.0 in 1998; 4.0 in 1999; 3.0 in 2000. Also excluded are aquatic mammals, recorded by number rather than by weight. The number of toothed whales caught was: 50 in 1998, 192 in 1999, 213 in 2000.

Source: FAO, *Yearbook of Fishery Statistics*.

Mining

('000 metric tons, unless otherwise indicated)

	1998	1999	2000
Hard coal	5,300	4,033	3,166
Brown coal (incl. lignite)	800	894	297
Crude petroleum ('000 barrels)	13,000*	13,380	13,476
Natural gas (million cu metres)	2,600*	2,500*	1,040
Silver (kilograms)†	1,027*	1,140*	720
Uranium (metric tons)†	468	625*	302
Gold (kilograms)†	3,793	3,570*	2,632
Kaolin and kaolinitic clay‡	333*	330*	380
Potash salts‡§	453	345*	360
Fluorspar‡	105	106	105
Barite (Barytes)	75*	76*	51
Salt*	7,000	6,787	6,830
Gypsum and anhydrite (crude)*	4,500	4,500	4,500
Pozzolan and lapilli*	460	450	450
Mica*	10	10	10
Talc (crude)	391	405*	350*

* Estimate(s).
† Figures refer to the metal content of ores and concentrates.
‡ Figures refer to marketable production.
§ Figures refer to potassium oxide (K_2O) content.

Source: US Geological Survey.

Industry

SELECTED PRODUCTS
('000 metric tons, unless otherwise indicated)

	1998	1999	2000
Margarine	138	130	n.a.
Wheat flour	6,167	6,152	n.a.
Raw sugar*	4,637	4,914	4,601†
Wine*	5,427	6,294	5,974
Beer of barley*	1,655	1,662	1,599
Cigarettes (million)	43,304	42,405	n.a.
Cotton yarn (metric tons)	111,168	103,020	89,508
Woven cotton fabrics (metric tons)	83,124	88,764	83,508
Wool yarn (metric tons)	8,820	10,284	7,560
Woven woollen fabrics (metric tons)	5,436	4,404	3,684
Artificial or synthetic fibres (metric tons)	80,256	73,320	66,036
Woven fabrics of artificial or synthetic fibres (metric tons)	109,404	111,252	111,936
Mechanical and semi-chemical wood pulp	881	885	771
Chemical wood pulp	1,793	1,705	1,697
Newsprint	922	1,099	1,039
Other printing and writing paper	3,102	3,247	3,432
Other paper and paperboard	5,137	5,255	5,534
Synthetic rubber	605	571	668
Rubber tyres ('000)‡	59,748	58,860	60,242
Sulphuric acid	2,214	2,177	2,181
Caustic soda (Sodium hydroxide)	1,578	1,601	1,690
Fertilizers	4,412	3,845	3,710
Liquefied petroleum gas ||	2,828§	n.a.	n.a.
Motor gasolene (petrol)	19,717§	n.a.	n.a.
Jet fuels	6,689§	n.a.	n.a.
Kerosene	66§	n.a.	n.a.
Distillate fuel oils	36,050§	n.a.	n.a.
Residual fuel oils	12,171§	n.a.	n.a.
Petroleum bitumen (asphalt)	3,448§	n.a.	n.a.
Coke-oven coke	5,500§	n.a.	n.a.
Cement (excl. clinker)	19,434	20,302	20,652
Pig-iron	13,602	13,558	13,622
Crude steel	20,126	20,200	20,954
Aluminium (unwrought): primary	424	455	441
secondary (incl. alloys)	245	n.a.	n.a.
Refined copper—unwrought	22.4		
Lead (unwrought): primary	155.9	n.a.	n.a.
secondary	134.3	n.a.	n.a.
Zinc (unwrought)	333	331	348
Radio receivers ('000)	4,586	2,961	3,831

— continued	1998	1999	2000
Television receivers ('000) . .	5,856	4,705	5,079
Merchant ships launched ('000 gross reg. tons). . . .	105	255	291
Passenger motor cars ('000)¶ .	3,932	4,265	2,652
Lorries and vans ('000)¶ . .	608.4	627.6	741.8
Electric energy (million kWh) . .	486,955	500,306	516,672§

2001 ('000 metric tons): Raw sugar 4,007*†; Wine 5,601*; Beer of barley 1,572*.

* Data from FAO. Data refer to production during crop year ending 30 September.
† Unofficial figure.
‡ Rubber tyres for passenger motor vehicles and similar.
| Excluding production in natural gas processing plants ('000 metric tons): 252 (estimate) in 1998.
§ Estimate.
¶ Including manufactured components, to be assembled in other territories.

Source: partly UN, *Industrial Commodity Statistics Yearbook.*

Finance

CURRENCY AND EXCHANGE RATES

Monetary Units
100 cent = 1 euro

Sterling and Dollar Equivalents (31 December 2002)
£1 sterling = 1.5370 euros
US $1 = 1.0487 euros
100 euros = £65.06 = $104.87

Average Exchange Rate (euros per US $)
2000   1.0854
2001   1.1175
2002   1.0626

Note: The national currency was formerly the French franc. From the introduction of the euro, with French participation, on 1 January 1999, a fixed exchange rate of €1 = 6.55957 French francs was in operation. Euro notes and coins were introduced on 1 January 2002. The euro and local currency circulated alongside each other until 17 February, after which the euro became the sole legal tender. Some of the figures in this Survey are still in terms of French francs.

GENERAL BUDGET
(million euros)

Revenue	2000	2001
Tax revenue	236,482	248,823
Income tax	51,496	52,445
Corporation tax	40,757	42,814
Other direct taxation	22,245	23,985
Domestic tax on petroleum products . .	25,480	25,305
Value-added tax	103,855	108,967
Stamp duty, etc.	16,161	15,803
Non-tax revenue	27,951	29,077
Sub-total	250,522	277,900
Deductions for local communities . . .	−28,894	−31,669
Deductions for EU	−15,016	−15,169
Total	220,522	231,062

Expenditure*	2000	2001
General non-salary disbursements (net) . . .	53,916	51,050
Agriculture and fisheries	4,427	5,107
Culture and communications . . .	2,452	2,549
Defence	37,019	37,309
Economy, finance and industry . . .	13,834	14,143
Employment and solidarity. . . .	32,673	31,947
Equipment, transport and housing . .	20,945	21,363
Foreign affairs	3,196	3,368
Interior	13,175	16,980
Justice.	4,162	4,435
National education	55,030	59,166
Overseas territories, etc.	972	1,040
Research and technology	6,077	6,157
War veterans	3,672	3,627
Total (incl. others)	253,806	260,900

* Expenditure by ministry, according to initial budgetary law.

Source: Ministry of the Economy, Finance and Industry, Paris.

INTERNATIONAL RESERVES
(US $ million at 31 December)*

	2000	2001	2002
Gold†	26,514	26,888	33,331
IMF special drawing rights . . .	402	492	622
Reserve position in IMF. . .	4,522	4,894	5,778
Foreign exchange.	32,114	26,363	21,965
Total	63,552	58,637	61,696

* Excluding deposits made with the European Monetary Institute (now the European Central Bank).
† Valued at market-related prices.

Source: IMF, *International Financial Statistics.*

MONEY SUPPLY
(million euros at 31 December)

	2000	2001	2002
Currency outside banks . . .	49,187	34,575	74,105*
Demand deposits at banking institutions	269,174	305,546	296,045

* Of which 41,588 million were put into circulation by the Banque de France.

Source: IMF, *International Financial Statistics.*

COST OF LIVING
(Consumer Price Index for Urban Households, average of monthly figures; base: 1990 = 100)

	1998	1999	2000
Food (incl. beverages) . . .	110.7	111.4	113.7
Fuel and light	104.3	101.4	108.7
Clothing and household linen . .	108.6	108.7	108.9
Rent	128.3	130.6	130.4
All items (incl. others) . . .	116.0	116.6	118.6

Source: ILO.

2001: Food 119.4; All items 120.5 (Source: UN, *Monthly Bulletin of Statistics*).

NATIONAL ACCOUNTS

National Income and Product
(million francs at current prices)

	1995	1996	1997
Compensation of employees. . .	3,980,473	4,115,718	4,221,754
Operating surplus	1,721,333	1,746,683	1,830,390
Domestic factor incomes. . .	5,701,806	5,862,401	6,052,144
Consumption of fixed capital . .	983,997	1,000,996	1,031,616
Gross domestic product (GDP) at factor cost	6,685,803	6,863,397	7,083,760
Indirect taxes	1,155,070	1,221,100	1,275,264
Less Subsidies	178,482	212,766	221,939
GDP in purchasers' values . .	7,662,391	7,871,731	8,137,085
Factor income received from abroad	374,333	364,131	454,771
Less Factor income paid abroad .	405,112	392,724	440,958
Gross national product (GNP) .	7,631,612	7,843,138	8,150,898
Less Consumption of fixed capital	983,997	1,000,996	1,031,616
National income in market prices	6,647,615	6,842,142	7,119,282
Other current transfers from abroad	183,024	176,827	169,7022
Less Other current transfers paid abroad	218,681	232,190	241,194
National disposable income	6,611,958	6,786,779	7,047,110

Source: UN, *National Accounts Statistics.*

Expenditure on the Gross Domestic Product

('000 million euros at current prices)

	1999	2000	2001
Government final consumption expenditure	315.7	329.9	341.1
Private final consumption expenditure	734.4	764.6	796.3
Increase in stocks*	5.6	11.0	−3.1
Gross fixed capital formation*	259.9	285.1	296.0
Total domestic expenditure	1,315.6	1,390.6	1,430.3
Exports of goods and services	350.3	404.9	413.5
Less Imports of goods and services	320.1	386.1	388.3
GDP in purchasers' values†	1,354.3	1,418.1	1,464.9
GDP at constant 1995 prices	1,300.7	1,354.9	1,379.5

* Includes construction of non-residential buildings.
† Including adjustment.

Source: IMF, *International Financial Statistics*.

Gross Domestic Product by Economic Activity

(million euros at current prices)

	1997	1998	1999
Agriculture, hunting, forestry and fishing	36,226	37,515	36,281
Mining and quarrying	2,006	2,165	2,178
Manufacturing	212,028	220,032	227,268
Electricity, gas and water	24,724	27,357	26,264
Construction	51,236	51,966	55,347
Trade, restaurants and hotels	147,115	155,141	157,395
Transport, storage and communications	71,655	76,325	78,354
Finance, insurance, real estate and business services*	330,371	341,553	361,598
Public administration and defence; compulsory social security	99,865	101,910	104,738
Education, health and social work; other community, social and personal services	166,685	174,718	178,437
Private households with employed persons	8,102	8,426	8,937
Sub-total	1,150,014	1,197,107	1,236,798
Less Financial intermediation services indirectly measured	36,426	34,988	35,281
Gross value added in market prices	1,113,588	1,162,119	1,201,517
Taxes, *less* subsidies on products	137,574	143,733	148,643
GDP in market prices	1,251,163	1,305,851	1,350,159

* Including imputed rents of owner-occupied dwellings.

Source: UN, *National Accounts Statistics*.

2000 (million euros at current prices): Gross value added in market prices: 1,288,286; *Less* Financial intermediation services indirectly measured 35,521; Gross value added in market prices 1,252,765; Taxes, *less* Subsidies on products 152,010; GDP in market prices 1,404,775 (Source: UN, *National Accounts Statistics*).

BALANCE OF PAYMENTS

(US $ million)*

	1999	2000	2001
Exports of goods f.o.b.	300,052	295,533	291,410
Imports of goods f.o.b.	−282,064	−294,402	−288,557
Trade balance	17,988	1,132	2,853
Exports of services	82,387	81,740	80,386
Imports of services	−64,449	−62,628	−62,476
Balance on goods and services	35,926	20,244	20,763
Other income received	64,962	71,358	79,575
Other income paid	−53,025	−57,648	−64,191
Balance on goods, services and income	47,863	33,954	36,147
Current transfers received	18,880	17,346	17,162
Current transfers paid	−31,704	−30,873	−31,950
Current balance	35,039	20,428	21,359
Capital account (net)	1,572	1,395	−121
Direct investment abroad	−119,494	−169,481	−83,193
Direct investment from abroad	46,625	43,173	52,504
Portfolio investment assets	−126,809	−96,803	−83,665
Portfolio investment liabilities	117,517	132,964	102,243
Financial derivatives liabilities	−2,226	4,135	947
Other investment assets	−26,625	963	−55,905
Other investment liabilities	74,878	54,765	35,503
Net errors and omissions	−1,870	6,027	4,861
Overall balance	−1,392	−2,433	−5,466

* Figures refer to transactions of metropolitan France, Monaco and the French Overseas Departments and Territories with the rest of the world.

Source: IMF, *International Financial Statistics*.

External Trade

(Note: Figures refer to the trade of metropolitan France, French Overseas Departments (French Guiana, Guadeloupe, Martinique and Réunion) and Monaco with the rest of the world, excluding trade in war materials, goods exported under the off-shore procurement programme, war reparations and restitutions and the export of sea products direct from the high seas. The figures include trade in second-hand ships and aircraft, and the supply of stores and bunkers for foreign ships and aircraft.)

PRINCIPAL COMMODITIES

(distribution by SITC, US $ million)

Imports c.i.f.	1998	1999	2000
Food and live animals	22,687.9	21,541.6	20,424.6
Mineral fuels, lubricants, etc. (incl. electric current)	16,818.2	18,973.1	30,878.2
Petroleum, petroleum products, etc.	11,997.8	14,455.9	24,547.3
Crude petroleum oils, etc.	8,694.6	10,382.6	17,997.3
Chemicals and related products	34,980.3	35,008.6	37,154.3
Basic manufactures	45,531.2	43,186.0	45,855.5
Iron and steel	8,982.0	7,704.2	8,944.5
Machinery and transport equipment	111,869.0	114,205.6	121,673.4
Power-generating machinery and equipment	9,724.0	9,822.7	10,085.5
General industrial machinery, equipment and parts	12,663.7	12,704.9	12,918.8
Office machines and automatic data-processing equipment	15,597.1	15,033.7	15,982.0
Automatic data-processing machines and units	9,579.1	8,920.1	9,393.0
Telecommunications and sound equipment	8,549.0	9,009.1	10,914.6
Other electrical machinery, apparatus, etc.	20,109.4	20,077.5	23,920.7
Road vehicles and parts*	28,121.4	30,240.8	30,205.5
Passenger motor cars (excl. buses)	14,835.1	16,457.7	16,815.5
Miscellaneous manufactured articles	40,571.2	40,889.5	42,087.6
Clothing and accessories (excl. footwear)	11,658.5	11,569.2	11,484.7
Total (incl. others)	286,035.9	286,592.9	310,896.8

* Data on parts exclude tyres, engines and electrical parts.

Exports f.o.b.	1998	1999	2000
Food and live animals . . .	26,866.4	25,631.0	23,628.3
Beverages and tobacco . . .	9,206.0	9,399.3	8,479.2
Beverages	8,833.6	9,013.8	8,103.6
Chemicals and related products	38,312.7	39,646.6	40,769.6
Medicinal and pharmaceutical products.	9,314.5	10,043.3	10,321.2
Basic manufactures . . .	45,374.3	43,124.9	43,299.7
Iron and steel.	10,015.4	9,182.3	9,892.6
Machinery and transport equipment.	131,663.8	130,196.8	135,692.9
Power-generating machinery and equipment	11,102.7	11,617.9	10,470.0
General industrial machinery, equipment and parts . . .	14,564.8	13,949.2	12,991.9
Office machines and automatic data-processing equipment . .	10,830.9	10,047.7	10,079.7
Telecommunications and sound equipment	10,364.9	10,923.2	13,917.7
Other electrical machinery, apparatus, etc.	22,213.1	21,472.9	22,700.4
Road vehicles and parts* . .	36,144.0	36,977.5	37,740.1
Passenger motor cars (excl. buses).	19,414.4	19,309.2	19,388.3
Parts and accessories for cars, buses, lorries, etc.* . . .	10,894.6	11,921.7	12,479.1
Other transport equipment and parts*	17,074.6	16,773.6	19,500.6
Aircraft, associated equipment and parts*	15,053.9	15,101.6	16,605.5
Miscellaneous manufactured articles.	28,885.2	29,125.6	29,136.5
Total (incl. others)	300,571.2	296,025.3	302,248.0

* Data on parts exclude tyres, engines and electrical parts.

Source: UN, *International Trade Statistics Yearbook*.

PRINCIPAL TRADING PARTNERS
(US $ million)

Imports c.i.f.	1998	1999	2000
Belgium	22,114.7*	19,617.7	20,772.0
China, People's Republic . .	7,218.6	8,047.1	9,866.6
Germany	49,342.7	49,222.1	50,388.3
Ireland.	5,203.6	4,999.5	6,389.4
Italy	28,406.4	27,574.3	27,050.6
Japan	9,517.2	10,240.7	11,750.9
Netherlands	14,490.1	14,604.9	14,896.3
Norway	3,992.2	4,165.5	7,246.5
Portugal	3,149.9	3,085.7	2,935.0
Russia	2,786.7	2,989.3	4,428.8
Saudi Arabia	1,787.9	1,974.4	3,244.7
Spain	20,335.6	20,335.4	21,120.1
Sweden	4,088.3	4,311.9	4,370.2
Switzerland-Liechtenstein . .	7,104.0	7,000.7	7,018.7
United Kingdom	23,996.2	24,013.7	24,762.6
USA	25,348.8	25,186.5	27,364.3
Total (incl. others)	286,035.9	286,592.9	310,896.8

Exports f.o.b.	1998	1999	2000
Austria	3,294.4	3,348.9	3,146.3
Belgium	23,279.8*	21,278.4	20,955.5
Canada	2,297.1	3,041.5	2,426.8
China, People's Republic . .	3,308.1	3,263.8	3,039.5
Germany	48,001.1	46,587.4	45,500.2
Greece	2,473.0	3,003.7	2,404.1
Hong Kong	3,105.8	1,915.5	2,210.3
Italy	27,506.4	27,037.6	26,944.5
Japan	4,666.4	4,542.1	5,099.4
Netherlands	13,849.3	13,911.3	13,223.0
Portugal	4,471.0	4,624.5	4,436.7
Spain	26,216.6	27,913.5	29,234.4
Sweden	4,394.7	4,331.2	4,659.7
Switzerland-Liechtenstein . .	10,347.1	10,956.0	10,075.2
Turkey.	2,849.9	3,039.8	3,456.8
United Kingdom	30,107.6	30,548.6	29,755.2
USA	22,273.6	23,026.6	26,543.2
Total (incl. others)	300,571.2	296,025.3	302,248.0

* Including trade with Luxembourg.

Source: UN, *International Trade Statistics Yearbook*.

Transport

RAILWAYS
(traffic)

	1998	1999	2000
Paying passengers ('000 journeys)	823,000	861,000	941,000
Freight carried ('000 metric tons)	136,100	134,000	142,000
Passenger-km (million) . . .	64,500	66,590	n.a.
Freight ton-km (million)* . .	53,800	52,110	n.a.

* Including passengers' baggage.

Sources: UN, *Statistical Yearbook*; Société Nationale des Chemins de fer Français, Paris.

ROAD TRAFFIC
('000 motor vehicles in use at 31 December)

	1998	1999	2000
Passenger cars	26,810	27,480	28,060
Lorries and vans	5,057	5,530	5,673
Buses and coaches	82	80	80
Motorcycles	2,321	n.a.	n.a.

Source: International Road Federation, *World Road Statistics*.

INLAND WATERWAYS

	1997	1998	1999
Freight carried ('000 metric tons)	48,493	50,793	54,991
Freight ton-km (million) . . .	5,682	6,207	6,829

Source: Voies navigables de France.

SHIPPING

Merchant Fleet
(registered at 31 December)

	1999	2000	2001
Number of vessels	713	700	699
Total displacement ('000 grt) . .	1,813.5	1,502.5	1,406.8

Source: Lloyd's Register-Fairplay, *World Fleet Statistics*.

Sea-borne Freight Traffic
('000 metric tons)

	1996	1997	1998
Goods loaded (excl. stores) . . .	82,409	94,987	95,987
International	74,489	86,545	85,995
Coastwise	7,920	8,442	9,993
Goods unloaded (excl. fish) . . .	215,916	229,016	240,629
International	204,275	216,511	226,675
Coastwise	11,641	12,505	13,953

Source: Ministère de l'Equipement, du Logement, des Transports et du Tourisme, Direction du Transport maritime, des Ports et du Littoral.

CIVIL AVIATION
(revenue traffic on scheduled services)*

	1997	1998	1999
Kilometres flown (million) . . .	669	726	819
Passengers carried ('000) . . .	42,344	43,826	48,693
Passenger-km (million)	84,037	90,225	101,449
Total ton-km (million)	13,750	14,033	14,279

* Including data for airlines based in French Overseas Departments and Territories.

Source: UN, *Statistical Yearbook*.

Tourism

FOREIGN TOURIST ARRIVALS BY COUNTRY OF ORIGIN
('000, estimates)

	1998	1999	2000
Belgium and Luxembourg . . .	8,364	9,073	9,482
Germany	14,770	15,180	15,420
Italy	5,836	6,276	6,464
Netherlands	10,203	11,457	11,819
Spain	2,875	3,119	3,228
Switzerland	3,682	3,551	3,785
United Kingdom and Ireland . .	11,359	11,890	12,127
USA	2,911	2,936	3,259
Total (incl. others)	70,040	73,042	75,595

* Estimates.

Source: World Tourism Organization, *Yearbook of Tourism Statistics*.

Tourism receipts (US $ million): 29,931 in 1998; 31,507 in 1999; 29,900 in 2000 (Source: World Tourism Organization).

Communications Media

	1999	2000	2001
Book production (titles)	49,767	51,837	n.a.
Television receivers ('000 in use) .	36,500	37,000	n.a.
Telephones ('000 main lines in use)	34,100.0	34,114.0	34,032.9
Mobile cellular telephones ('000 subscribers).	21,433.5	29,052.4	35,922.3
Personal computers ('000 in use) .	15,680	17,920	20,000
Internet users ('000)	5,370	8,500	15,653

Radio receivers ('000 in use): 55,300 in 1997.

Facsimile machines ('000 in use): 2,800 in 1997.

Daily newspapers (1999): 93 titles (combined circulation 2,895.1m.).

Non-daily newspapers (1995): 278 titles (circulation 1,714,000 copies).

Other periodicals (1993): 2,683 titles (circulation 120,018,000 copies in 1991).

Sources: mainly UN, *Statistical Yearbook*; UNESCO, *Statistical Yearbook*; International Telecommunication Union.

Education

(2000/01, unless otherwise indicated)

	Institu-tions*	Tea-chers	Students Males	Females	Total
Pre-primary . .	18,428	106,581	n.a.	n.a.	2,461,800†
Primary . . .	39,131	211,192	1,970,343	1,869,427	3,839,770
Secondary: .					
Lower . . .			1,679,362	1,602,283	3,281,645
Upper— Professional .	11,052	483,493	n.a.	n.a.	666,596
Upper— General/ Technical . .			650,072	801,120	1,451,192
Higher:					
Universities . .	n.a.	46,196	650,553	774,840	1,405,393
Other	n.a.	6,467	n.a.	n.a.	705,755

* Figures are for 1996/97.
† Figure for 1999/2000, rounded.

Source: partly UNESCO, *Statistical Yearbook*.

Directory

The Constitution

The Constitution of the Fifth Republic was adopted by referendum on 28 September 1958, promulgated on 6 October 1958 and subsequently amended as indicated below.

PREAMBLE

The French people hereby solemnly proclaims its attachment to the Rights of Man and to the principles of national sovereignty as defined by the Declaration of 1789, confirmed and complemented by the Preamble of the Constitution of 1946.

By virtue of these principles and that of the free determination of peoples, the Republic hereby offers to the Overseas Territories that express the desire to adhere to them, new institutions based on the common ideal of liberty, equality and fraternity and conceived with a view to their democratic evolution.

Article 1. (As amended by legislation of 4 August 1995 and 17 March 2003.) France shall be a Republic, indivisible, secular, democratic and social. It shall ensure the equality of all citizens before the law, without distinction of origin, race or religion. It shall respect all beliefs. Its organization shall be decentralized.

I. ON SOVEREIGNTY

Article 2. (As amended by legislation of 25 June 1992.) The language of the Republic shall be French.

The national emblem shall be the tricolour flag, blue, white and red.

The national anthem shall be the 'Marseillaise'.

The motto of the Republic shall be 'Liberty, Equality, Fraternity'.

Its principle shall be government of the people, by the people, and for the people.

Article 3. (As amended by legislation of 8 July 1999.) National sovereignty belongs to the people, who shall exercise this sovereignty through their representatives and through the referendum.

No section of the people, nor any individual, may arrogate to themselves or himself the exercise thereof.

Suffrage may be direct or indirect under the conditions stipulated by the Constitution. It shall always be universal, equal and secret.

All French citizens of both sexes who have reached their majority and who enjoy civil and political rights may vote under the conditions to be determined by law.

The law shall promote equal access by women and men to elective offices and positions.

Article 4. (As amended by legislation of 8 July 1999.) Political parties and groups are instrumental in the exercise of suffrage. They may form and carry on their activities freely. They must respect the principles of national sovereignty and of democracy. They shall contribute to the implementation of the principle set out in the last paragraph of Article 3 as provided by the law.

II. THE PRESIDENT OF THE REPUBLIC

Article 5. (As amended by legislation of 4 August 1995.) The President of the Republic shall see that the Constitution is respected. He shall ensure, by his arbitration, the regular functioning of the governmental authorities, as well as the continuity of the State.

He shall be the guarantor of national independence, of the integrity of the territory, and of respect for treaties.

Article 6. (As amended by legislation of 6 November 1962 and 2 October 2000.) The President of the Republic shall be elected for five years by direct universal suffrage. The method of implementation of the present Article shall be determined by an organic law.

Article 7. (As amended by legislation of 6 November 1962, 18 June 1976 and 17 March 2003.) The President of the Republic shall be elected by an absolute majority of the votes cast. If such a majority is not obtained at the first ballot, a second ballot shall take place 14 days later. Those who may stand for the second ballot shall be only the two candidates who, after the possible withdrawal of candidates with more votes, have gained the largest number of votes on the first ballot.

Voting shall begin at the summons of the Government. The election of the new President of the Republic shall take place not less than 20 days and not more than 35 days before the expiry of the powers of the President in office. In the event that the Presidency of the Republic has been vacated for any reason whatsoever, or impeded in its functioning as officially declared by the Constitutional Council, after the matter has been referred to it by the Government and which shall give its ruling by an absolute majority of its members, the functions of the President of the Republic, with the exception of those covered by Articles 11 and 12 hereunder, shall be temporarily exercised by the President of the Sénat (Senate) or, if the latter is in his turn unable to exercise his functions, by the Government.

In the case of vacancy or when the impediment is declared to be permanent by the Constitutional Council, the voting for the election of the new President shall take place, except in case of *force majeure* officially noted by the Constitutional Council, not less than 20 days and not more than 35 days after the beginning of the vacancy or of the declaration of the final nature of the impediment.

If, in the seven days preceding the latest date for the lodging of candidatures, one of the persons who, at least 30 days prior to that date, publicly announced his decision to be a candidate dies or is impeded, the Constitutional Council may decide to postpone the election.

If, before the first ballot, one of the candidates dies or is impeded, the Constitutional Council orders the postponement of the election.

In the event of the death or impediment, before any candidates have withdrawn, of one of the two candidates who received the greatest number of votes in the first ballot, the Constitutional Council shall declare that the electoral procedure must be repeated in full; the same shall apply in the event of the death or impediment of one of the two candidates standing for the second ballot.

All cases shall be referred to the Constitutional Council under the conditions laid down in paragraph 2 of Article 61 below, or under those determined for the presentation of candidates by the organic law provided for in Article 6 above.

The Constitutional Council may extend the periods stipulated in paragraphs 3 and 5 above provided that polling shall not take place more than 35 days after the date of the decision of the Constitutional Council. If the implementation of the provisions of this paragraph results in the postponement of the election beyond the expiry of the powers of the President in office, the latter shall remain in office until his successor is proclaimed.

Articles 49 and 50 and article 89 of the Constitution may not be put into application during the vacancy of the Presidency of the Republic or during the period between the declaration of the final nature of the impediment of the President of the Republic and the election of his successor.

Article 8. The President of the Republic shall appoint the Prime Minister. He shall terminate the functions of the Prime Minister when the latter presents the resignation of the Government.

At the suggestion of the Prime Minister, he shall appoint the other members of the Government and shall terminate their functions.

Article 9. The President of the Republic shall preside over the Council of Ministers.

Article 10. The President of the Republic shall promulgate laws within 15 days following the transmission to the Government of the finally adopted law.

He may, before the expiry of this time limit, ask Parliament for a reconsideration of the law or of certain of its Articles. This reconsideration may not be refused.

Article 11. (As amended by legislation of 4 August 1995.) The President of the Republic, on the proposal of the government during [Parliamentary] sessions, or on joint motion of the two Assemblies published in the *Journal Officiel*, may submit to a referendum any bill dealing with the organization of the governmental authorities, with reforms related to the economic or social policy of the nation and to the public services contributing thereto or providing for authorization to ratify a treaty that, without being contrary to the Constitution, might affect the functioning of the institutions.

Where the referendum is held in response to a proposal by the Government, the latter shall make a statement before each Assembly, which shall be followed by a debate.

Where the referendum decides in favour of the government bill, the President of the Republic shall promulgate the law within 15 days following the proclamation of the results of the vote.

Article 12. (As amended by legislation of 4 August 1995.) The President of the Republic may, after consultation with the Prime Minister and the Presidents of the Assemblies, declare the dissolution of the Assemblée nationale (National Assembly).

A general election shall take place 20 days at the least and 40 days at the most after the dissolution.

The Assemblée nationale shall convene by right on the second Thursday following its election. If this meeting takes place between the period provided for the ordinary session, a session shall, by right, be opened for a 15-day period.

There may be no further dissolution within a year following this election.

Article 13. (As amended by legislation of 17 March 2003) The President of the Republic shall sign the ordinances and decrees decided upon in the Council of Ministers.

He shall make appointments to the civil and military posts of the State.

Councillors of State, the Grand Chancellor of the Legion of Honour, Ambassadors and Envoys Extraordinary, Master Councillors of the Audit Court, prefects, representatives of the State in the Overseas communities governed by Article 74 and in New Caledonia, general officers, rectors of academies [regional divisions of the public educational system] and directors of central administrations shall be appointed in meetings of the Council of Ministers.

An organic law shall determine the other posts to be filled by decision of the Council of Ministers, as well as the conditions under which the power of the President of the Republic to make appointments to office may be delegated by him to be exercised in his name.

Article 14. The President of the Republic shall accredit Ambassadors and Envoys Extraordinary to foreign powers; foreign Ambassadors and Envoys Extraordinary shall be accredited to him.

Article 15. The President of the Republic shall be commander of the armed forces. He shall preside over the higher councils and committees of national defence.

Article 16. When the institutions of the Republic, the independence of the nation, the integrity of its territory or the fulfilment of its international commitments are threatened in a grave and immediate manner and the regular functioning of the constitutional governmental authorities is interrupted, the President of the Republic shall take the measures required by these circumstances, after official consultation with the Prime Minister and the Presidents of the Assemblies, and the Constitutional Council.

He shall inform the nation of these measures in a message.

These measures must be prompted by the desire to ensure to the constitutional governmental authorities, in the shortest possible time, the means of accomplishing their mission. The Constitutional Council shall be consulted with regard to such measures.

Parliament shall meet by right.

The Assemblée nationale may not be dissolved during the exercise of exceptional powers.

Article 17. The President of the Republic shall have the right of pardon.

Article 18. The President of the Republic shall communicate with the two Assemblies of Parliament by means of messages, which he shall cause to be read, and which shall not be the occasion for any debate.

Between sessions, the Parliament shall be convened especially to this end.

Article 19. Official decisions of the President of the Republic, other than those provided for under Articles 8 (first paragraph), 11, 12, 16, 18, 54, 56 and 61, shall be counter-signed by the Prime Minister and, where applicable, by the appropriate ministers.

III. THE GOVERNMENT

Article 20. The Government shall determine and conduct the policy of the nation.

It shall have at its disposal the administration and the armed forces.

It shall be responsible to the Parliament under the conditions and according to the procedures stipulated in articles 49 and 50.

Article 21. The Prime Minister shall direct the operation of the Government. He shall be responsible for national defence. He shall ensure the execution of the laws. Subject to the provisions of Article 13, he shall have regulatory powers and shall make appointments to civil and military posts.

He may delegate certain of his powers to the ministers.

He shall replace, should the occasion arise, the President of the Republic as the Chairman of the councils and committees provided for under article 15.

He may, in exceptional instances, replace him as the chairman of a meeting of the Council of Ministers by virtue of an explicit delegation and for a specific agenda.

Article 22. The official decisions of the Prime Minister shall be counter-signed, when circumstances so require, by the ministers responsible for their execution.

Article 23. The functions of Members of the Government shall be incompatible with the exercise of any parliamentary mandate, with the holding of any office, at the national level, in business, professional or labour organizations, and with any public employment or professional activity.

An organic law shall determine the conditions under which the holders of such mandates, functions or employments shall be replaced.

The replacement of the members of Parliament shall take place in accordance with the provisions of article 25.

IV. THE PARLIAMENT

Article 24. The Parliament shall comprise the Assemblée nationale and the Sénat.

The deputies to the Assemblée nationale shall be elected by direct suffrage.

The Sénat shall be elected by indirect suffrage. It shall ensure the representation of the territorial communities of the Republic. French nationals living outside France shall be represented in the Sénat.

Article 25. An organic law shall determine the term for which each Assembly is elected, the number of its members, their emoluments, the conditions of eligibility, and the offices incompatible with membership of the Assemblies.

It shall likewise determine the conditions under which, in the case of a vacancy in either Assembly, persons shall be elected to replace the deputy or senator whose seat has been vacated until the holding of new complete or partial elections to the Assembly concerned.

Article 26. (As amended by legislation of 4 August 1995.) No Member of Parliament may be prosecuted, subjected to inquiry, arrested, detained or tried as a result of the opinions expressed or votes cast by him in the exercise of his functions.

No Member of Parliament shall be subjected, in regard to any criminal or correctional matter, to arrest or any other custodial or semi-custodial measures other than with the authorization of the Assembly of which he is a member. Such authorization shall not be required in the case of a serious crime or other major offence committed *in flagrante delicto* or a final conviction.

The detention, subjection to custodial or semi-custodial measures, or prosecution of a Member of Parliament shall be suspended for the duration of the session if the Assembly of which he is a member so requires.

The Assembly concerned shall convene as of right for additional sittings in order to permit the preceding paragraph to be applied should circumstances so require.

Article 27. Any compulsory vote shall be null and void.

The right to vote of the members of Parliament shall be personal.

An organic law may, under exceptional circumstances, authorize the delegation of a vote. In this case, no member may be delegated more than one vote.

Article 28. (As amended by legislation of 4 August 1995.) Parliament shall convene by right in one ordinary session a year, which shall start on the first working day of October and shall end on the last working day of June.

The number of days for which each Assembly may sit during the ordinary session shall not exceed one hundred and twenty. The sitting weeks shall be determined by each Assembly.

The Prime Minister, after consulting the President of the Assembly concerned, or the majority of the members of each Assembly, may decide to meet for additional sitting days.

The days and hours of sittings shall be determined by the rules of procedure of each Assembly.

Article 29. Parliament shall convene in extraordinary session at the request of the Prime Minister or of the majority of the members comprising the Assemblée nationale, to consider a specific agenda.

When an extraordinary session is held at the request of the members of the Assemblée nationale, the closure decree shall take effect as soon as the Parliament has exhausted the agenda for which it was called, and at the latest 12 days from the date of its meeting.

Only the Prime Minister may ask for a new session before the end of the month following the closure decree.

Article 30. Apart from cases in which Parliament meets by right, extraordinary sessions shall be opened and closed by decree of the President of the Republic.

Article 31. The members of the Government shall have access to the two Assemblies. They shall be heard when they so request.

They may call for the assistance of Commissioners of the Government.

Article 32. The President of the Assemblée nationale shall be elected for the duration of the legislature. The President of the Sénat shall be elected after each partial re-election [of the Sénat].

Article 33. The meetings of the two Assemblies shall be public. An *in extenso* report of the debates shall be published in the *Journal Officiel*.

Each Assembly may sit in secret committee at the request of the Premier or of one-tenth of its members.

V. ON RELATIONS BETWEEN PARLIAMENT AND THE GOVERNMENT

Article 34. (As amended by legislation of 22 February 1996 and 17 March 2003.) Laws shall be voted by Parliament.

Legislation shall establish the regulations concerning:

Civil rights and the fundamental guarantees granted to the citizens for the exercise of their public liberties; the obligations imposed by the national defence upon the person and property of citizens;

Nationality, status and legal capacity of persons; marriage contracts, inheritance and gifts;

Determination of crimes and misdemeanours as well as the penalties imposed therefor; criminal procedure; amnesty; the creation of new juridical systems and the status of magistrates;

The basis, the rate and the methods of collecting taxes of all types; the issue of currency.

Legislation likewise shall determine the regulations concerning:

The electoral system of the Parliamentary Assemblies and the local assemblies;

The establishment of categories of public institutions;

The fundamental guarantees granted to civil and military personnel employed by the State;

The nationalization of enterprises and the transfers of the property of enterprises from the public to the private sector.

Legislation shall determine the fundamental principles of:

The general organization of national defence;

The free administration of territorial communities, of their competencies and their resources;

Education;

Property rights, civil and commercial obligations;

Legislation pertaining to employment unions and social security.

The financial laws shall determine the financial resources and obligations of the State under the conditions and with the reservations to be provided for by an organic law.

Social security finance bills shall determine the general conditions for the financial balance of social security and, taking account of their revenue forecasts, shall determine expenditure targets in the manner and under the reserves provided for by an organic law.

Laws pertaining to national planning shall determine the objectives of the economic and social action of the State.

The provisions of the present Article may be detailed and supplemented by an organic law.

Article 35. Parliament shall authorize the declaration of war.

Article 36. Martial law shall be decreed in a meeting of the Council of Ministers.

Its extension beyond 12 days may be authorized only by Parliament.

Article 37. Matters other than those that fall within the domain of law shall be of a regulatory character.

Legislative texts concerning these matters may be modified by decrees issued after consultation with the Council of State. Those legislative texts which shall be passed after the entry into force of the present Constitution shall be modified by decree only if the Constitutional Council has stated that they have a regulatory character as defined in the preceding paragraph.

Article 37-1. (Appended by legislation of 17 March 2003). Law and regulations may include, for a limited duration and object, dispositions of an experimental character.

Article 38. The Government may, in order to carry out its programme, ask Parliament for authorization to take through ordinances, during a limited period, measures that are normally within the domain of law.

The ordinances shall be enacted in meetings of Ministers after consultation with the Council of State. They shall come into force upon their publication but shall become null and void if the bill for their ratification is not submitted to Parliament before the date set by the enabling act.

At the expiry of the time limit referred to in the first paragraph of the present Article, the ordinances may be modified only by the law in respect of those matters which are within the legislative domain.

Article 39. (As amended by legislation of 22 February 1996 and 17 March 2003.) The Prime Minister and the Members of Parliament alike shall have the right to initiate legislation.

Government bills shall be discussed in the Council of Ministers after consultation with the Council of State and shall be filed with the secretariat of one of the two Assemblies. Finance bills shall be submitted first to the Assemblée nationale. Finance bills and social security finance bills shall be submitted first to the Assemblée nationale. Without prejudice to the first paragraph of Article 44, projects of law having for their principal object the organization of territorial communities, and projects of law related to the representative authorities of French nationals living outside France shall be submitted in the first instance to the Sénat.

Article 40. Private members' bills and amendments shall be inadmissible when their adoption would have as a consequence either a diminution of public financial resources or an increase in public expenditure.

Article 41. If it shall appear in the course of the legislative procedure that a Parliamentary bill or an amendment is not within the domain of law or is contrary to a delegation granted by virtue of Article 38, the Government may declare its inadmissibility.

In case of disagreement between the Government and the President of the Assembly concerned, the Constitutional Council, upon the request of one or the other, shall rule within a time limit of eight days.

Article 42. The discussion of bills shall pertain, in the first Assembly to which they have been referred, to the text presented by the Government.

An Assembly given a text passed by the other Assembly shall deliberate on the text that is transmitted to it.

Article 43. Government and private members' bills shall, at the request of the Government or of the Assembly concerned, be sent for study to committees especially designated for this purpose.

Government and private members' bills for which such a request has not been made shall be sent to one of the permanent committees, the number of which is limited to six in each Assembly.

Article 44. Members of Parliament and of the Government have the right of amendment.

After the opening of the debate, the Government may oppose the examination of any amendment which has not previously been submitted to committee.

If the Government so requests, the Assembly concerned shall decide, by a single vote, on all or part of the text under discussion, retaining only the amendments proposed or accepted by the Government.

Article 45. Every government or private member's bill shall be considered successively in the two Assemblies of Parliament with a view to the adoption of an identical text.

When, as a result of disagreement between the two Assemblies, it has been impossible to adopt a Government or private member's bill after two readings by each Assembly, or, if the Government has declared the matter urgent, after a single reading by each of them, the Prime Minister shall have the right to bring about a meeting of a joint committee composed of an equal number from both Assemblies charged with the task of proposing a text on the matters still under discussion.

The text elaborated by the joint committee may be submitted by the Government for approval of the two Assemblies. No amendment shall be admissible except by agreement with the Government.

If the joint committee does not succeed in adopting a common text, or if this text is not adopted under the conditions set forth in the preceding paragraph, the Government may, after a new reading by the Assemblée nationale and by the Sénat, ask the Assemblée nationale to rule definitively. In this case, the Assemblée nationale may reconsider either the text elaborated by the joint committee, or the last text voted by it, modified when circumstances so require by one or several of the amendments adopted by the Sénat.

Article 46. The laws that the Constitution characterizes as organic shall be passed and amended under the following conditions:

A Government or private member's bill shall be submitted to the deliberation and to the vote of the first Assembly notified only at the expiration of a period of 15 days following its introduction;

The procedure of article 45 shall be applicable. Nevertheless, lacking an agreement between the two Assemblies, the text may be adopted by the Assemblée nationale on final reading only by an absolute majority of its members;

The organic laws relative to the Sénat must be passed in the same manner by the two Assemblies;

The organic laws may be promulgated only after a declaration by the Constitutional Council on their constitutionality.

Article 47. The Parliament shall pass finance bills under the conditions to be stipulated by an organic law.

Should the Assemblée nationale fail to reach a decision on first reading within a time limit of 40 days after a bill has been filed, the Government shall refer it to the Sénat, which must rule within a time limit of 15 days. The procedure set forth in article 45 shall then be followed.

Should Parliament fail to reach a decision within a time limit of 70 days, the provisions of the bill may be enforced by ordinance.

Should the finance bill establishing the resources and expenditures of a fiscal year not be filed in time for it to be promulgated before the beginning of that fiscal year, the Government shall urgently request Parliament for authorization to collect taxes and shall make available by decree the funds needed to meet the Government commitments already voted.

The time limits stipulated in the present Article shall be suspended when the Parliament is not in session.

The Audit Court shall assist Parliament and the Government in supervising the implementation of the finance laws.

Article 47–1. (Appended by legislation of 22 February 1996.) Parliament shall pass social security finance bills in the manner provided for by an organic law.

Should the Assemblée nationale fail to reach a decision on first reading within twenty days following the introduction of a bill, the Government shall refer the bill to the Sénat, which must rule within fifteen days. The procedure set out in Article 45 shall then apply.

Should Parliament fail to reach a decision within fifty days, the provisions of the bill may be implemented by ordinance.

The time limits set by this Article shall be suspended when Parliament is not in session and, as regards each assembly, during the weeks when it has decided not to sit in accordance with the second paragraph of Article 28.

The Audit Court shall assist Parliament and the Government in monitoring the implementation of social security finance Acts.

Article 48. (As amended by legislation of 4 August 1995.) Without prejudice to the application of the last three paragraphs of Article 28, the discussion of the bills tabled or agreed upon by the Government shall have priority on the agenda of the Assemblies in the order determined by the Government.

At least one meeting a week shall be reserved, by priority, for questions asked by Members of Parliament and for answers by the Government.

One meeting a month shall be reserved, by priority, for the agenda determined by each Assembly.

Article 49. (As amended by legislation of 4 August 1995.) The Prime Minister, after deliberation by the Council of Ministers, shall make the Government responsible, before the Assemblée nationale, for its programme or, should the occasion arise, for a declaration of general policy.

The Assemblée nationale may challenge the responsibility of the Government by a motion of censure. Such a motion is admissible only if it is signed by at least one-tenth of the members of the Assemblée nationale. The vote may not take place before 48 hours after the motion has been filed. Only the votes that are favourable to a motion of censure shall be counted; the motion of censure may be adopted only by a majority of the members comprising the Assembly. Except as provided for in the following paragraph, a Deputy shall not sign more than three motions of censure during a single ordinary session and more than one during a single extraordinary session.

The Prime Minister may, after deliberation by the Council of Ministers, make the Government responsible before the Assemblée nationale for the adoption of a bill. In this case, the text shall be considered as adopted unless a motion of censure, filed during the twenty-four hours that follow, is carried under the conditions provided for in the preceding paragraph.

The Prime Minister shall have the right to request the Sénat for approval of a declaration of general policy.

Article 50. When the Assemblée nationale adopts a motion of censure, or when it disapproves the programme or a declaration of general policy of the Government, the Prime Minister must hand the resignation of the Government to the President of the Republic.

Article 51. (As amended by legislation of 4 August 1995.) The closure of the ordinary or of extraordinary sessions shall by right be delayed, should the occasion arise, in order to permit the application of article 49. Additional sittings shall by right be held for the same purpose.

VI. ON TREATIES AND INTERNATIONAL AGREEMENTS

Article 52. (As amended by legislation of 4 August 1995.) The President of the Republic shall negotiate and ratify treaties.

He shall be informed of all negotiations leading to the conclusion of an international agreement not subject to ratification.

Article 53. Peace treaties, commercial treaties, treaties or agreements relative to international organization, those that commit the finances of the State, those that modify provisions of a legislative nature, those relative to the status of persons, those that call for the cession, exchange or addition of territory may be ratified or approved only by a law.

They shall go into effect only after having been ratified or approved.

No cession, no exchange, or addition of territory shall be valid without the consent of the populations concerned.

Article 53–1. (Appended by legislation of 25 November 1993.) The Republic may conclude, with European states that are bound by commitments identical with its own in the matter of asylum and the protection of human rights and fundamental liberties, agreements determining their respective competence in regard to the consideration of requests for asylum submitted to them.

However, even if the request does not fall within their competence under the terms of these agreements, the authorities of the Republic shall remain empowered to grant asylum to any foreigner who is persecuted for his action in pursuit of liberty or who seeks the protection of France for some other reason.

Article 53–2. (Appended by legislation of 8 July 1999.) The Republic may recognize the jurisdiction of the International Criminal Court as provided for by the treaty signed on 18 July 1998.

Article 54. (As amended by legislation of 25 June 1992.) If the Constitutional Council, the matter having been referred to it by the President of the Republic, by the Prime Minister, by the President of one or the other Assembly, or by any 60 Deputies or 60 Senators, shall declare that an international commitment contains a clause contrary to the Constitution, the authorization to ratify or approve the commitment in question may be given only after amendment of the Constitution.

Article 55. Treaties or agreements duly ratified or approved shall, upon their publication, have an authority superior to that of laws, subject, for each agreement or treaty, to its application by the other party.

VII. THE CONSTITUTIONAL COUNCIL

Article 56. The Constitutional Council shall consist of nine members, whose mandates shall last nine years and shall not be renewable. One-third of the membership of the Constitutional Council shall be renewed every three years. Three of its members shall be appointed by the President of the Republic, three by the President of the Assemblée nationale, three by the President of the Sénat.

In addition to the nine members provided for above, former Presidents of the Republic shall be members *ex officio* for life of the Constitutional Council.

The President shall be appointed by the President of the Republic. He shall have the deciding vote in case of a tie.

Article 57. The office of member of the Constitutional Council shall be incompatible with that of minister or Member of Parliament. Other incompatibilities shall be determined by an organic law.

Article 58. The Constitutional Council shall ensure the regularity of the election of the President of the Republic.

It shall examine complaints and shall announce the results of the vote.

Article 59. The Constitutional Council shall rule, in the case of disagreement, on the regularity of the election of deputies and senators.

Article 60. (As amended by legislation of 17 March 2003.) The Constitutional Council shall ensure the regularity of the referendum procedure, as provided for in Articles 11 and 89, and shall announce the results thereof.

Article 61. (As amended by legislation of 29 October 1974.) Organic laws, before their promulgation, and regulations of the Parliamentary Assemblies, before they come into application, must be submitted to the Constitutional Council, which shall rule on their constitutionality.

To the same end, laws may be submitted to the Constitutional Council, before their promulgation, by the President of the Republic, the Prime Minister, the President of the Assemblée nationale, the President of the Sénat, or any 60 deputies or 60 senators.

In the cases provided for by the two preceding paragraphs, the Constitutional Council must make its ruling within a time limit of one month. Nevertheless, at the request of the Government, in case of urgency, this period shall be reduced to eight days.

In these same cases, referral to the Constitutional Council shall suspend the time limit for promulgation.

Article 62. A provision declared unconstitutional may not be promulgated or implemented.

The decisions of the Constitutional Council may not be appealed to any jurisdiction whatsoever. They shall be binding on the governmental authorities and on all administrative and juridical authorities.

Article 63. An organic law shall determine the rules of organization and functioning of the Constitutional Council, the procedure to be followed before it, and in particular of the periods of time allowed for laying disputes before it.

VIII. ON JUDICIAL AUTHORITY

Article 64. The President of the Republic shall be the guarantor of the independence of the judicial authority.

He shall be assisted by the High Council of the Judiciary.

An organic law shall determine the status of the judiciary.

Judges may not be removed from office.

Article 65. (As amended by legislation of 27 July 1993.) The High Council of the Judiciary shall be presided over by the President of the Republic. The Minister of Justice shall be its Vice-President *ex officio*. He may preside in place of the President of the Republic.

The High Council of the Judiciary shall consist of two sections, one with competence for judges, the other for public prosecutors.

The section with competence for judges shall include, in addition to the President of the Republic and the Minister of Justice, five judges and one public prosecutor, one senior member of the Council of State appointed by the Council of State, and three prominent citizens who are neither members of Parliament nor the judiciary, appointed respectively by the President of the Republic, the President of the Assemblée nationale and the President of the Sénat.

The section with jurisdiction for public prosecutors shall include, in addition to the President of the Republic and the Minister of Justice, five public prosecutors and one judge, the senior member of the Council of State and the three prominent citizens referred to in the preceding paragraph.

The section of the High Council of the Judiciary with jurisdiction for judges shall make nominations for the appointment of judges in the Court of Cassation, for the First Presidents of the courts of appeal and the presidents of the tribunaux de grande instance. Other judges shall be appointed with its assent.

It shall serve as the disciplinary council for judges. When acting in that capacity, it shall be presided over by the First President of the Court of Cassation.

The section of the High Council of the Judiciary with jurisdiction for public prosecutors shall give its opinion on the appointment of public prosecutors, with the exception of posts to be filled in the Council of Ministers. It shall give its opinion on disciplinary penalties with regard to public prosecutors. When acting in that capacity, it shall be presided over by the Chief Public Prosecutor at the Court of Cassation.

An organic law shall determine the manner in which this Article is to be implemented.

Article 66. No one may be arbitrarily detained.

The judicial authority, guardian of individual liberty, shall ensure the respect of this principle under the conditions stipulated by law.

IX. THE HIGH COURT OF JUSTICE

Article 67. A High Court of Justice shall be instituted.

It shall be composed, in equal number, of members elected, from among their membership, by the Assemblée nationale and by the Sénat after each general or partial election to these Assemblies. It shall elect its President from among its members.

An organic law shall determine the composition of the High Court, its rules, as well as the procedure to be applied before it.

Article 68. (As amended by legislation of 27 July 1993.) The President of the Republic shall not be held accountable for actions performed in the exercise of his office except in the case of high treason. He may be indicted only by the two Assemblies ruling by identical vote in open balloting and by an absolute majority of the members of said Assemblies. He shall be tried by the High Court of Justice.

X. ON THE CRIMINAL LIABILITY OF MEMBERS OF GOVERNMENT

(title and section appended by legislation of 27 July 1993)

Article 68–1. The members of the Government shall be criminally liable for actions performed in the exercise of their office and rated as crimes or misdemeanours at the time they were committed.

They shall be tried by the Court of Justice of the Republic.

The Court of Justice of the Republic shall be bound by such definition of serious crimes and other major offences and such determination of penalties as are laid down by the law.

Article 68–2. The Court of Justice of the Republic shall consist of 15 members: 12 Members of Parliament, elected in equal number from among their ranks by the Assemblée nationale and the Sénat after each general or partial election to these Assemblies, and three judges of the Court of Cassation, one of whom shall preside over the Court of Justice of the Republic.

Any person claiming to be a victim of a crime or misdemeanour committed by a member of the Government in the exercise of his duties may lodge a complaint with a commission of requests.

This committee shall order either the closure of the case or that it be forwarded to the chief public prosecutor at the Court of Cassation for referral to the Court of Justice of the Republic.

The Chief Public Prosecutor at the Court of Cassation may also make a reference *ex officio* to the Court of Justice of the Republic with the assent of the commission of requests.

An organic law shall determine the manner in which this Article is to be implemented.

Article 68–3. (Appended by legislation of 4 August 1995.) The provisions of this title shall apply to acts committed before its entry into force (*on 27 July 1993*).

XI. THE ECONOMIC AND SOCIAL COUNCIL

Article 69. The Economic and Social Council, at the referral of the Government, shall give its opinion on the Government bills, draft ordinances and decrees, as well as on the private members' bills submitted to it.

A member of the Economic and Social Council may be designated by the Council to present, before the Parliamentary Assemblies, the opinion of the Council on the Government or private members' bills that have been submitted to it.

Article 70. (As amended by legislation of 4 August 1995.) The Economic and Social Council may likewise be consulted by the Government on any problem of an economic or social character. Any plan, or any bill dealing with a plan, of an economic or social character shall be submitted to it for advice.

Article 71. The composition of the Economic and Social Council and its rules of procedure shall be determined by an organic law.

XII. ON TERRITORIAL COMMUNITIES

Article 72. (As amended by legislation of 17 March 2003.) The territorial communities of the Republic shall be the communes, the departments, regions, communities granted with a particular status and overseas communities regulated by Article 74. Any other territorial community shall be created by law, if need be, at the place of one or more of the communities mentioned in this paragraph.

The territorial communities shall serve the purpose of taking decisions for the entirety of competencies which may be best made at their level of jurisdiction.

In conditions provided for by law, these communities shall administer themselves freely by means of elected councils and dispose of a regulatory power for the exercise of their competencies.

In conditions provided for by organic law, and provided that the essential conditions exist for the exercise of a public liberty or a constitutionally guaranteed right, territorial communities or groupings thereof may, depending on the case, as provided for by law or regulations, exercise, in an experimental manner and for a limited object and duration, legislative or regulatory dispositions which govern the exercise of their competencies.

No territorial community may exercise any tutelage over any other. However, when the exercise of a competency necessitates the participation of several territorial units, the law may authorize one of the communities, or one grouping thereof, to organize the modalities of their common action.

In the territorial communities of the Republic, the representative of the State, representative of each member of the Government, shall be responsible for national interests, administrative control and the respect of the law.

Article 72–1. (Appended by legislation of 17 March 2003.) Law shall determine the conditions under which voters of each territorial community may, by exercising the right of petition, demand the inclusion in the agenda of the Deliberative Assembly of that community a question relating to its competencies.

In conditions provided for by organic law, projects of deliberation or of an act relating to the competency of a territorial community may, at the initiative of that community, be submitted, by means of a referendum, to the decision of the voters of that same community.

When the creation of a territorial community granted with a particular status or the modification of the organization thereof is envisaged, the law may approve the consultation of voters registered in the communities concerned. The modification of the boundaries of territorial communities may also follow from the consultation of voters in conditions provided for by law.

Article 72-2. (Appended by legislation of 17 March 2003.) Territorial communities shall benefit from resources which they may dispose of freely in conditions determined by law.

They may receive all or part of the product of taxation of every kind. The law may authorize them to set the basis and levels of taxation within limits determined by law.

The fiscal receipts and other resources belonging to the territorial communities shall represent, for each category of community, a determining share of the sum of their resources. Organic law shall determine the conditions under which this rule is implemented.

Any transfer of competencies between the State and territorial communities shall be accompanied by the attribution of equivalent resources to those which were dedicated to their exercise. Any creation or extension of competencies which necessitates an increase in expenditure by territorial communities shall be accompanied by resources determined by law.

The law shall provide for mechanisms of adjustment intended to promote equality between territorial communities.

Article 72-3. (Appended by legislation of 17 March 2003.) The Republic recognizes, among the French people, the overseas populations, sharing a common ideal of liberty, equality and fraternity.

Guadeloupe, French Guiana, Martinique, Réunion, Mayotte, St Pierre and Miquelon, Wallis and Futuna and French Polynesia shall be governed by Article 73 with regard to Overseas Departments and Regions, and for the territorial communities created by the applica-

tion of the last paragraph of Article 73, and by Article 74 with regard to other communities.

The status of New Caledonia shall be governed by Title XIII.

The law shall determine the legislative regime and the particular organization of the French Southern and Antarctic Territories.

Article 72–4. (Appended by legislation of 17 March 2003.) No change, for part or the whole of any of the communities referred to in the second paragraph of Article 72-3, from one to the other of the regimes provided for in Articles 73 and 74, may take place without the prior consent having been obtained of the voters of the community, or of that part of the community concerned, in conditions determined by the following paragraph. Any such change of regime shall be determined by organic law.

The President of the Republic, on the proposal of the Government during [Parliamentary] sessions, or on joint motion of the two Assemblies published in the *Journal Officiel*, may decide to consult the voters of a territorial community located overseas on a matter related to its organization, its competencies or its legislative regime. When this consultation relates to a proposed change as provided for in the previous paragraph and is organized in response to the request of the Government, the President shall make a declaration to that end before each Assembly, which shall be followed by a debate.

Article 73. (As amended by legislation of 17 March 2003.) In the overseas departments and regions, laws and regulations shall be fully applicable. They may be subject to adaptations which take account of the particular characteristics and constraints of these communities.

These adaptations may be decided by the communities with regard to subjects in which they exercise competency and should they be so authorized by the law.

By special dispensation referred to in the first paragraph, and in order to take account of their specific qualities, the communities governed by the present Article may be authorized by law to themselves determine the rules applicable on their territory, in a limited number of subjects which fall under the domain of the law.

These rules may not concern nationality, civic rights, guarantees of public liberties, the State and the capacity of persons, the organization of justice, penal law, the penal procedure, foreign policy, defence, security and public order, money, credit and exchange, or electoral law. This list may be clarified and completed by an organic law.

The dispositions provided for in the previous two paragraphs shall not be applicable to either the Department or the Region of Réunion.

The authorizations provided for in the second and third paragraphs shall be decided, at the request of the community concerned, under conditions and reserves provided for in an organic law. They may not be applied should the essential conditions for the exercise of a public liberty or of a constitutionally guaranteed right be brought into question.

The creation by law of a community in replacement of an overseas department or region, or the institution of a single Deliberative Assembly for these two communities shall not occur without the prior consent, received in the form provided for in the second paragraph of Article 72-4, of the voters registered in the totality of those communities.

Article 74. (As amended by legislation of 25 June 1992 and 17 March 2003. The overseas communities governed by the present Article shall have a status which takes account of their proper interests within the Republic

This status shall be defined by an organic law, adopted after the advice of the Deliberative Assembly, which shall determine:

the conditions under which the laws and regulations shall be applicable in that community;

the competencies of that community; excepting those already so exercised, the transfer of competencies from the State shall not include those subjects enumerated in the fourth paragraph of Article 73, clarified and completed, if need be, by an organic law;

the rules of the organization and functioning of institutions of the community, and the electoral regime of its Deliberative Assembly;

the conditions under which the institutions of that community shall be consulted upon projects and propositions of law and projects of edict or of decree including dispositions particular to that community, as well as regarding the ratification or approval of international engagements concluded within subjects relating to its competency.

Organic law may also determine, for those communities granted with autonomy, the conditions under which:

the Council of State shall exercise judicial control specific to certain categories of acts of the Deliberative Assembly intervening in the scope of activities exercised by the assembly within the domain of the law;

the Deliberative Assembly may modify a law promulgated prior to the entry into force of the status of the community, when the Constitutional Council, referred by the authorities of the community, has stated that the law has intervened in the domain of the competency of this community;

measures justified by local necessities may be taken by the community in favour of its population, with regard to the access to employment, the right of establishment for the exercise of a professional activity or for the protection of property;

the community may participate, under the control of the State, in the exercise of the competencies it maintains, with respect to guarantees accorded to the entirety of the national territory for the exercise of public liberties.

Article 74–1. (Appended by legislation of 17 March 2003.) In those overseas communities to which Article 74 applies and in New Caledonia, the Government may, within those areas which remain within the competence of the State, extend by the means of edicts, with any necessary adaptations, the dispositions of a legislative nature in force in metropolitan France, except where the law shall expressly preclude, for the dispositions concerned, the recourse to this procedure.

Any such edicts shall be taken to the Council of Ministers following the advice of the Deliberative Assemblies concerned and of the Council of State. They enter into force from the time of their publication. They become null and void should they not be ratified by Parliament within a period of eighteen months following this publication.

Article 75. Citizens of the Republic who do not have ordinary civil status, the only status referred to in Article 34, may keep their personal status as long as they have not renounced it.

XIII. TRANSITIONAL PROVISIONS RELATING TO NEW CALEDONIA
(Section appended by legislation of 20 July 1998)

Article 76. The population of New Caledonia is called upon to vote by 31 December 1998 on the provisions of the agreement signed at Nouméa on 5 May 1998, and published in the *Journal Officiel* of the French Republic on 27 May 1998.

Persons satisfying the requirements laid down in Article 2 of Act No. 88-1028 of 9 November 1988 shall be eligible to take part in the vote.

The measures required to organize the ballot shall be taken by decree adopted after consultation with the *Conseil d'Etat* and discussion in the Council of Ministers.

Article 77. After approval of the agreement by the vote provided for in Article 76, the organic law passed after consultation with the Deliberative Assembly of New Caledonia shall determine, in order to ensure the development of New Caledonia in accordance with the guidelines set out in that agreement and as required for its implementation:

the competencies of the State which are to be transferred definitively to the institutions of New Caledonia, at what time and in what manner such transfers are to be made, and how the costs incurred thereby are to be apportioned

the rules for the organization and operation of the institutions of New Caledonia, including the circumstances in which certain categories of instrument passed by the Deliberative Assembly may be referred to the Constitutional Council for review before publication

the rules concerning citizenship, the electoral system, employment, and ordinary civil status

the circumstances and the time limits within which the population concerned in New Caledonia is to vote on the attainment of full sovereignty.

Any other measures required to give effect to the agreement referred to in Article 76 shall be determined by law.

[A former Article 76, permitting Overseas Territories to retain their former status within the Republic and a section 'On the Community' (Articles 77–87), providing for a community of autonomous states of common citizenship, were repealed by legislation of 4 August 1995.]

XIV. ON AGREEMENTS OF ASSOCIATION

Article 88. The Republic may make agreements with States that wish to associate themselves with it in order to develop their own civilizations.

XV. ON THE EUROPEAN COMMUNITIES AND THE EUROPEAN UNION
(Section appended by legislation of 25 June 1992)

Article 88–1. The Republic shall participate in the European Communities and in the European Union constituted by States that have freely chosen, by virtue of the treaties that established them, to exercise some of their powers in common.

Article 88–2 (Amended by legislation of 25 January 1999 and 17 March 2003.) Subject to reciprocity and in accordance with the terms of the Treaty on European Union signed on 7 February 1992, France agrees to the transfer of competencies necessary for the establishment of European economic and monetary union.

Subject to the same reservation and in accordance with the terms of the Treaty establishing the European Community, as amended by the treaty signed on 2 October 1997, the transfer of competencies necessary for the determination of rules concerning freedom of movement for persons and related areas may be agreed.

The law shall determine the rules relative to the European mandate of arrest with regard to acts taken on the basis of the treaty of the European Union.

Article 88–3. Subject to reciprocity and in accordance with the terms of the Treaty on European Union signed on 7 February 1992, the right to vote and stand as a candidate in municipal elections shall be granted only to citizens of the Union residing in France. Such citizens shall neither exercise the office of mayor or deputy mayor nor participate in the designation of Sénat electors or in the election of Senators. An organic law passed in identical terms by the two Assemblies shall determine the manner of implementation of this Article.

Article 88–4. (Amended by legislation of 25 January 1999.) The Government shall present to the Assemblée nationale and the Sénat any proposals for or drafts of acts of the European Communities or the European Union containing provisions of a legislative nature as soon as they have been transmitted to the Council of the European Union. It may also present to them other proposals or drafts of acts or any document emanating from a European Union institution.

In the manner laid down by the rules of procedure of each Assembly, resolutions may be passed, even if Parliament is not in session, on the drafts, proposals or documents referred to in the preceding paragraph.

XVI. ON AMENDMENT

Article 89. The initiative for amending the Constitution shall belong both to the President of the Republic on the proposal of the Prime Minister and to the Members of Parliament.

The Government or private member's bill for amendment must be passed by the two Assemblies in identical terms. The amendment shall become definitive after approval by a referendum.

Nevertheless, the proposed amendment shall not be submitted to a referendum when the President of the Republic decides to submit it to Parliament convened in Congress; in this case, the proposed amendment shall be approved only if it is accepted by a three-fifths majority of the votes cast. The Secretariat of the Congress shall be that of the Assemblée nationale.

No amendment procedure may be undertaken or followed if it is prejudicial to the integrity of the territory.

The republican form of government shall not be the object of an amendment.

ELECTORAL LAW, JULY 1986

The 577 Deputies of the Assemblée nationale are to be directly elected under the former single-member constituency system (in force before the implementation of a system of proportional representation imposed by the electoral law of 1985). Participating parties can nominate only one candidate and designate a reserve candidate, who can serve as a replacement if the elected Deputy is appointed a Minister or a member of the Constitutional Council, or is sent on a government assignment scheduled to last more than six months, or dies. A candidate must receive an absolute majority and at least one-quarter of registered votes in order to be elected to the Assemblée nationale. If these conditions are not fulfilled, a second ballot will be held a week later, for voters to choose between all candidates receiving 12.5% of the total votes on the first ballot. The candidate who receives a simple majority of votes on the second ballot will then be elected. Candidates polling less than 5% of the votes will lose their deposit.

The Government

HEAD OF STATE

President: JACQUES CHIRAC (took office 17 May 1995; re-elected 5 May 2002).

COUNCIL OF MINISTERS
(April 2003)

Prime Minister: JEAN-PIERRE RAFFARIN.

Minister of the Interior, Internal Security and Local Freedoms: NICOLAS SARKOZY.

Minister of Social Affairs, Labour and Solidarity: FRANÇOIS FILLON.

Keeper of the Seals, Minister of Justice: DOMINIQUE PERBEN.

Minister of Foreign Affairs: DOMINIQUE GALOUZEAU DE VILLEPIN.

Minister of Defence: MICHÈLE ALLIOT-MARIE.

Minister of Youth, National Education and Research: LUC FERRY.

Minister of the Economy, Finance and Industry: FRANCIS MER.

Minister of Capital Works, Transport, Housing, Tourism and the Sea: GILLES DE ROBIEN.

Minister of Ecology and Sustainable Development: ROSELYNE BACHELOT-NARQUIN.

Minister of Health, the Family and Handicapped Persons: JEAN-FRANÇOIS MATTÉI.

Minister of the Civil Service, the Reform of the State and Land Management: JEAN-PAUL DELEVOYE.

Minister of Agriculture, Food, Fisheries and Rural Affairs: HERVÉ GAYMARD.

Minister of Culture and Communication: JEAN-JACQUES AILLAGON.

Minister of the Overseas Departments, Territories and Country: BRIGITTE GIRARDIN.

Minister of Sport: JEAN-FRANÇOIS LAMOUR.

Minister-Delegate attached to the Minister of the Interior, Internal Security and Local Freedoms:

Local Freedoms: PATRICK DEVEDJIAN.

Ministers-Delegate attached to the Minister of Social Affairs, Labour and Solidarity:

Towns and Urban Redevelopment: JEAN-LOUIS BORLOO.

Parity and Professional Equality: NICOLE AMELINE.

Ministers-Delegate attached to the Minister of Foreign Affairs:

European Affairs: NOËLLE LENOIR.

Co-operation and La Francophonie: PIERRE-ANDRÉ WILTZER.

Ministers-Delegate attached to the Minister of Youth, National Education and Research:

School-teaching: XAVIER DARCOS.

Research and New Technologies: CLAUDIE HAIGNERE.

Ministers-Delegate attached to the Minister of the Economy, Finance and Industry:

The Budget and Budgetary Reform: ALAIN LAMBERT.

Industry: NICOLE FONTAINE.

External Trade: FRANÇOIS LOOS.

Minister-Delegate attached to the Minister of Health, the Family and Handicapped Persons:

The Family: CHRISTIAN JACOB.

SECRETARIES OF STATE

Attached to the Prime Minister:

Relations with Parliament, Government Spokesman: JEAN-FRANÇOIS COPÉ.

Attached to the Minister of Social Affairs, Labour and Solidarity:

The Battle Against Precariousness and Exclusion: DOMINIQUE VERSINI;

Elderly Persons: HUBERT FALCO.

Attached to the Keeper of the Seals, Minister of Justice:

Property Programmes of Justice: PIERRE BÉDIER.

Attached to the Minister of Foreign Affairs:

Foreign Affairs: RENAUD MUSELIER.

Attached to the Minister of Defence:

Former Combatants: HAMLAOUI MEKACHERA.

Attached to the Minister of the Economy, Finance and Industry:

Small- and Medium-sized Enterprises, Trade, Crafts, the Liberal Professions and Consumption: RENAUD DUTREIL.

Attached to the Minister of Capital Works, Transport, Housing, Tourism and the Sea:

Transport and the Sea: DOMINIQUE BUSSEREAU;

Tourism: LÉON BERTRAND.

Attached to the Minister of Ecology and Sustainable Development:

Sustainable Development: TOKIA SAÏFI.

Attached to the Minister of Health, the Family and Handicapped Persons:

Handicapped Persons: MARIE-THÉRÈSE BOISSEAU.

Attached to the Minister of the Civil Service, the Reform of the State and Land Management:

Reform of the State: HENRI PLAGNOL.

MINISTRIES

Office of the President: Palais de l'Elysée, 55–57 rue du Faubourg Saint Honoré, 75008 Paris; tel. 1-42-92-81-00; fax 1-47-42-24-65; internet www.elysee.fr.

Office of the Prime Minister: Hôtel Matignon, 57 rue de Varenne, 75007 Paris; tel. 1-42-75-80-00; fax 1-42-75-75-04; e-mail premier-ministre@premier-ministre.gouv.fr; internet www .premier-ministre.gouv.fr.

Ministry of Agriculture, Food, Fisheries and Rural Affairs: 78 rue de Varenne, 75349 Paris 07; tel. 1-49-55-49-55; fax 1-49-55-40-39; e-mail webmaster@agriculture.gouv.fr; internet www .agriculture.gouv.fr.

Ministry of Capital Works, Transport, Housing, Tourism and the Sea: 246 blvd Saint-Germain, 75007 Paris; tel. 1-40-81-31-59; fax 1-40-81-31-64; e-mail webmestre@equipement.gouv.fr; internet www.equipement.gouv.fr.

Ministry of the Civil Service, the Reform of the State and Land Management: 72 rue de Varenne, 75007 Paris; tel. 1-42-75-80-00; fax 1-42-75-89-70; e-mail maryline.pilorge@cab.fpre.gouv.fr; internet www.fonction-publique.gouv.fr.

Ministry of Culture and Communication: 3 rue de Valois, 75001 Paris; tel. 1-40-15-80-00; fax 1-42-61-35-77; e-mail atelier-internet .dic@culture.gouv.fr; internet www.culture.gouv.fr.

Ministry of Defence: 14 rue Saint Dominique, 75007 Paris; tel. 1-42-19-30-11; fax 1-47-05-40-91; internet www.defense.gouv.fr.

Ministry of Ecology and Sustainable Development: 20 ave de Ségur, 75302 Paris Cédex 07; tel. 1-42-19-20-21; e-mail ministere@ environnement.gouv.fr; internet www.environnement.gouv.fr.

Ministry of the Economy, Finance and Industry: 139 rue de Bercy, 75572 Paris Cédex 12; tel. 1-40-04-04-04; fax 1-43-43-75-97; internet www.minefi.gouv.fr.

Ministry of Foreign Affairs: 37 quai d'Orsay, 75007 Paris; tel. 1-43-17-53-53; fax 1-43-17-52-03; internet www.diplomatie.gouv.fr.

Ministry of Health, the Family and Handicapped Persons: 8 ave de Ségur, 75007 Paris; tel. 1-40-56-60-00; internet www .famille-enfance.gouv.fr.

Ministry of the Interior, Internal Security and Local Freedoms: place Beauvau, 75008 Paris; tel. 1-49-27-49-27; fax 1-43-59-89-50; e-mail sirp@interieur.gouv.fr; internet www.interieur.gouv .fr.

Ministry of Justice: 13 place Vendôme, 75042 Paris Cédex 01; tel. 1-44-77-60-60; fax 1-44-77-70-20; e-mail cyberjustice@justice.gouv .fr; internet www.justice.gouv.fr.

Ministry of the Overseas Departments, Territories and Country: 27 rue Oudinot, 75007 Paris; tel. 1-53-69-20-00; internet www.outre-mer.gouv.fr.

Ministry of Social Affairs, Labour and Solidarity: 127 rue de Grenelle, 75007 Paris; tel. 1-44-38-38-38; fax 1-44-38-20-10; internet www.emploi-solidarite.gouv.fr.

Ministry of Sport: 78 rue Olivier de Serres, 75015 Paris; tel. 1-40-45-90-00; fax 1-42-50-42-49; e-mail arnaud.beuron@jeunesse-sports .gouv.fr; internet www.jeunesse-sports.gouv.fr.

Ministry of Youth, National Education and Research: 110 rue de Grenelle, 75357 Paris 07; tel. 1-55-55-10-10; fax 1-45-51-53-63; internet www.education.gouv.fr.

President and Legislature

PRESIDENT

Elections of 21 April and 5 May 2002

First Ballot, 21 April 2002

Candidates	Votes	% of votes
Jacques Chirac (Rassemblement pour la République)	5,665,855	19.88
Jean-Marie Le Pen (Front National)	4,804,713	16.86
Lionel Jospin (Parti Socialiste)	4,610,113	16.18
François Bayrou (Union pour la Démocratie Française)	1,949,170	6.84
Arlette Laguiller (Lutte Ouvrière)	1,630,045	5.72
Jean-Pierre Chevènement (Mouvement des Citoyens)	1,518,528	5.33
Noël Mamère (Les Verts)	1,495,724	5.25
Olivier Besancenot (Ligue Communiste Révolutionnaire)	1,210,562	4.25
Jean Saint-Josse (Chasse Pêche Nature Traditions)	1,204,689	4.23
Alain Madelin (Démocratie Libérale)	1,113,484	3.91
Robert Hue (Parti Communiste Français)	960,480	3.37
Bruno Mégret (Mouvement National Républicain)	667,026	2.34
Christiane Taubira (Parti guyanais de centre-gauche/Parti Radical de Gauche)	660,447	2.32
Corinne Lepage (Citoyenneté, Action, Participation pour le 21ème siècle)	535,837	1.88
Christine Boutin (Forum des républicains sociaux)	339,112	1.19
Daniel Gluckstein (Parti des Travailleurs)	132,686	0.47
Total	28,498,471	100.00

Second Ballot, 5 May 2002

Candidate	Votes	% of votes
Jacques Chirac (Rassemblement pour la République)	25,537,956	82.21
Jean-Marie Le Pen (Front National)	5,525,032	17.79
Total	31,062,988	100.00

PARLEMENT
(Parliament)

ASSEMBLEE NATIONALE
(National Assembly)

126 rue de l'Université, 75377 Paris Cédex 07; tel. 1–40–63–60–00; fax 1–45–55–75–23; e-mail infos@assemblee-nat.fr; internet www.assemblee-nat.fr.

President: JEAN-LOUIS DEBRÉ.

General Election, 9 June and 16 June 2002

Party	% of votes cast in first ballot	% of votes cast in second ballot*	Seats
Union pour la Majorité Présidentielle	33.30	47.26	355†
Parti Socialiste (PS)	24.11	35.26	140
Union pour la Démocratie Française (UDF)	4.85	3.92	29†
Parti Communiste Français (PCF)	4.82	3.26	21
Parti Radical de Gauche (PRG)	1.54	2.15	8
Les Verts	4.51	3.19	3
Démocratie Libérale (DL)	0.41	—	2†
Rassemblement pour la France (RPF)	0.37	0.29	3
Mouvement pour la France (MPF)	0.80	—	2
Front National (FN)	11.34	1.85	—
Pôle Républicain (PR)	1.19	0.06	—

Party — *continued*	% of votes cast in first ballot	% of votes cast in second ballot*	Seats
Chasse Pêche Nature Traditions (CPNT)	1.67	—	—
Ligue Communiste Révolutionnaire (LCR)	1.27	—	—
Lutte Ouvrière (LO)	1.20	—	—
Mouvement National Républicain (MNR)	1.09	—	—
Various right-wing candidates‡	3.65	1.29	7
Various left-wing candidates	1.09	1.27	5
Regionalist candidates	0.26	0.14	1
Various ecologist candidates§	1.17	—	—
Various far-left candidates‖	0.32	—	—
Various far-right candidates¶	0.24	—	—
Others**	0.77	0.06	1
Total	100.00	100.00	577

* Held where no candidate had won the requisite overall majority in the first ballot, between candidates who had received at least 12.5% of the votes in that round. The total number of valid votes cast was 25,246,045 in the first round, and 21,221,026 in the second round.

† In November 2002 the Union pour un Mouvement Populaire (UMP) was formed on the basis of the Union pour la Majorité Présidentielle, Démocratie Libérale and other right-wing and centrist factions, including elements of the Union pour la Démocratie Française.

‡ Including, notably, candidates of the Droite Libérale Chrétienne and the Centre National des Indépendants et Paysans.

§ Including, notably, candidates of Génération Ecologie-Les Bleus and the Mouvement Ecologiste Indépendant.

‖ Including, notably, candidates of the Parti des Travailleurs, Les Motivé-e-s and Les Alternatifs.

¶ Including, notably, candidates of the Parti National Républicain, La France aux Français and the Parti Nationaliste Français.

** Including, notably, candidates of the Rassemblement des Contribuables Français, the Parti de la Loi Naturelle and the Union pour la Semaine de Quatre Jours.

SENAT
(Senate)

15 rue de Vaugirard, 75291 Paris Cédex 06; tel. 1–42–34–20–00; fax 1–42–34–26–77; e-mail communication@senat.fr; internet www.senat.fr.

President: CHRISTIAN PONCELET.

Members of the Senate are indirectly elected for a term of nine years, with one-third of the seats renewable every three years

After the most recent election, held on 23 September 2001, the Senate had 321 seats: 296 for metropolitan France; 13 for the overseas departments and territories; and 12 for French nationals abroad. The strength of the parties was as follows:

	Seats
Groupe du Rassemblement pour la République	95*
Groupe Socialiste	83
Groupe de l'Union Centriste	53*
Groupe de l'Union des Républicains et des Indépendants	41*
Groupe Communiste Républicain et Citoyenne	23
Groupe du Rassemblement Démocratique et Social Européen	20*
Non-attached	6*
Total	**321**

* On 11 December 2002 a new grouping, the Groupe Union pour un Mouvement Populaire was formed, on the basis of the Groupe du Rassemblement pour la République, the Groupe de l'Union des Républicains et des Indépendants, both of which thereby ceased to exist; a number of senators from the Groupe de l'Union Centriste, the Groupe du Rassemblement Démocratique et Social Européen, and one hitherto non-attached senator also joined the new grouping. On that date, the strength of the groupings was as follows: *Groupe Union pour un Mouvement Populaire* 167, *Groupe Socialiste* 82, *Groupe de l'Union Centriste* 27, *Groupe Communiste Républicaine et Citoyenne* 23, *Groupe du Rassemblement Démocratique et Social Européen* 17, *Non-attached* 5.

Political Organizations

Centre National des Indépendants et Paysans (CNI): 6 rue Quentin Bauchart, 75008 Paris; tel. 1-47-23-47-00; fax 1-47-23-47-03; f. 1949; right-wing; Pres. ANNICK DU ROSCOAT; Sec.-Gen. BRUNO COTTARD.

Chasse Pêche Nature Traditions (CPNT): Centre d'Affaires Praxis, 245 blvd de la Paix, 64000 Pau; tel. 5-59-14-71-71; fax 5-59-14-71-72; e-mail cpnt@cpnt.asso.fr; internet www.cpnt.asso.fr; f. 1989 as Chasse-Pêche-Traditions; emphasizes defence of rural traditions, field sports; Pres. JEAN SAINT-JOSSE; Sec.-Gen. JEAN-LOUIS BERNIÉ.

Corsica Nazione: Assemblée de Corse, 22 Cours Grandval, BP 215, 21087 Ajaccio Cédex 01; tel. 4-95-51-64-85; fax 4-95-50-08-22; e-mail corsica-nazione@corsica-nazione.com; internet www.corsica-nazione.com; f. 1992; supports the establishment of an independent state in Corsica; Leader JEAN-GUY TALAMONI.

Droite Libérale Chrétienne (DLC): 29 rue Sully, 69006 Lyon; tel. 4–72–69–67–67; fax 4–72–69–67–66; e-mail contact@d-l-c.org; internet d-l-c.org; f. 1998 as La Droite by breakaway faction of UDF that favoured the formation of coalitions with FN candidates in regional councils; present name adopted 1999; right-wing; Pres. CHARLES MILLON.

Front National (FN): 4 rue Vauguyon, 92210 Saint-Cloud; tel. 1-41-12-10-00; fax 1-41-12-10-86; e-mail vizier@frontnational.com; internet www.frontnational.com; f. 1972; extreme right-wing nationalist; Pres. JEAN-MARIE LE PEN; Sec.-Gen. CARL LANG.

Génération Ecologie-Les Bleus: 7 villa Virginie, 75014 Paris; tel. 1-56-53-53-73; fax 1-56-53-53-70; e-mail generation.ecologie@wanadoo.fr; internet www.generation-ecologie.com; f. 1990; ecologist; Leader BRICE LALONDE.

Ligue Communiste Révolutionnaire (LCR): 2 rue Richard Lenoir, 93100 Montreuil; tel. 1-48-70-42-20; fax 1-48-59-23-28; e-mail lcr@lcr-rouge.org; internet www.lcr-rouge.org; f. 1974; Trotskyist; 2,450 mems (2001); Leaders ALAIN KRIVINE, OLIVIER BESANCENOT.

Lutte Ouvrière (LO): BP 233, 75865 Paris Cédex 18; tel. 1-44-83-08-93; e-mail contact@lutte-ouvriere.org; internet www.lutte-ouvriere.org; f. 1968; Trotskyist; Leaders ARLETTE LAGUILLER, F. DUBURG, GEORGES KALDY, ROBERT BARCIA HARDY.

Mouvement Ecologiste Indépendant (MEI): 26 rue Nicolaï, 75012 Paris; tel. and fax 2-33-45-37-82; e-mail contact@mei-fr.org; internet www.mei-fr.org; f. 1994; ecologist; 3,000 mems; Pres. ANTOINE WAECHTER; Nat. Sec. DOMINIQUE BAUDUIN.

Mouvement National Républicain (MNR): 15 rue de Cronstadt, 75015 Paris; tel. 1-56-56-64-34; fax 1-56-56-52-47; e-mail m-n-r@m-n-r.com; internet m-n-r.com; f. 1999 by breakaway faction of FN; extreme right-wing nationalist; Pres. BRUNO MÉGRET.

Mouvement pour la France (MPF): 35 ave de la Motte-Piquet, 75007 Paris; tel. 1-44-42-02-42; fax 1-44-42-02-43; e-mail mpf@mpf-villiers.org; internet www.mpf-villiers.org; f. 1994; right-wing, nationalist; Pres. PHILIPPE DE VILLIERS.

Mouvement Républicain et Citoyen (MRC): 9 rue du Faubourg Poissonnière, 75009 Paris; tel. 1-44-83-83-00; fax 1–44-83–83–10; e-mail contact@pole-republicain.org; internet mrc-france.org; f. 2002 as Pôle Républicain on the basis of the Mouvement des Citoyens; present name adopted 2003; socialist; sceptical of increased European integration or devolution of powers from the nation-state; Pres. JEAN-PIERRE CHEVÈNEMENT; First Sec. JEAN-LUC LAURENT; 4,000 mems (2002).

Parti Communiste Français (PCF): 2 place du Colonel Fabien, 75019 Paris; tel. 1-40-40-12-12; fax 1-40-40-13-56; e-mail pcf@pcf.fr; internet www.pcf.fr; subscribed to the common programme of the United Left (with the Parti Socialiste) until 1977; advocates independent foreign policy; Pres. ROBERT HUE; Nat. Sec. MARIE-GEORGE BUFFET.

Parti Radical de Gauche (PRG): 13 rue Duroc, 75007 Paris; tel. 1-45-66-67-68; fax 1-45-66-47-93; e-mail prg-nat@club-internet.fr; internet www.planeteradicale.org; f. 1972 as the Mouvement des Radicaux de Gauche; left-wing; Pres. JEAN-MICHEL BAYLET; Sec.-Gen. ELISABETH BOYER.

Parti Socialiste (PS): 10 rue de Solférino, 75333 Paris Cédex 07; tel. 1-45-56-77-00; fax 1-47-05-15-78; e-mail infops@parti-socialiste.fr; internet www.parti-socialiste.fr; f. 1971; 147,300 mems (2002); First Sec. FRANÇOIS HOLLANDE.

Rassemblement pour la France (RPF): 129 ave Charles de Gaulle, 92200 Neuilly-sur-Seine; tel. 1-55-62-24-24; fax 1-55-62-24-44; e-mail rpfie@rpfie.org; internet www.rpfie.org; f. 1999; right-wing, nationalist; Pres. CHARLES PASQUA; Gen.-Sec. ERIC CESARI.

Union pour la Démocratie Française (UDF): 133 bis rue de l'Université, 75007 Paris; tel. 1-53-59-20-00; fax 1-53-59-20-59; e-mail communication@udf.org; internet www.udf.org; f. 1978 to unite for electoral purposes non-Gaullist 'majority' candidates; frequently formed electoral alliances with Gaullist Rassemblement des Républicains; reconstituted as a unified party in 1998; in 2002 elections to Assemblée nationale some elements formed electoral alliances with UMP, and subsequently were absorbed into that party; Pres. FRANÇOIS BAYROU; Sec.-Gen. ANNE-MARIE IDRAC.

Union pour un Mouvement Populaire (UMP): 11 rue St Dominque, 75007 Paris; internet www.u-m-p.org; f. 2002; as Union pour la Majorité Presidentielle by members of the former Rassemblement pour la République and Démocratie Liberale parties, in conjunction with elements of the UDF (q.v.) ; centre-right grouping formed to ensure that President Jacques Chirac had a majority grouping in the Assemblée nationale; Pres. ALAIN JUPPÉ; Sec.-Gen. PHILIPPE DOUSTE-BLAZY.

Parti Radical: 1 place de Valois, 75001 Paris; tel. 1-42-61-56-32; fax 1-42-61-49-65; e-mail radical@partiradical.net; internet www.partiradical.net; f. 1901; democratic socialist; frmly affiliated to UDF, joined UMP in 2002; Pres. FRANÇOIS LOOS; Sec.-Gen. ARLETTE FRUCTUS.

Les Verts: 25 rue Mélingue, 75019 Paris; tel. 1-53-19-53-19; fax 1-53-19-03-93; e-mail verts@les-verts.org; internet www.les-verts.org; f. 1984; ecologist; Spokespersons MARIE-HÉLÈNE AUBERT, YVES CONTASSOT, MIREILLE FERRI, YANN WEHRLING; Nat. Sec. GILLES LEMAIRE.

Diplomatic Representation

EMBASSIES IN FRANCE

Afghanistan: 32 ave Raphaël, 75016 Paris; tel. 1-45-25-05-29; fax 1-45-24-60-68; e-mail webmaster@ambafghane.com; internet membres.lycos.fr/ambafgh/index1.html; Ambassador Prof ZALMAÏ HAQUANI.

Albania: 57 ave Marceau, 75116 Paris; tel. 1-45-53-51-32; fax 1-45-53-89-38; e-mail ambassade.albanie@wanadoo.fr; Ambassador FERIT HOXHA.

Algeria: 50 rue de Lisbonne, 75008 Paris; tel. 1-53-93-20-20; fax 1-42-25-10-25; e-mail ambassadealgerie@free.fr; Ambassador MOHAMED GHOUALMI.

Andorra: 30 rue d'Astorg, 75008 Paris; tel. 1-40-06-03-30; fax 1-40-06-03-64; e-mail ambaixada@andorra.ad; internet www.amb-andorre.fr; Ambassador IMMA TOR FAUS.

Angola: 19 ave Foch, 75116 Paris; tel. 1-45-01-58-20; fax 1-45-00-33-71; e-mail barreira.ramiro_manuel_ @libertysurf.fr; internet www.amb-angola.fr; Ambassador ASSUNÇÃO DOS ANJOS.

Antigua and Barbuda: 43 ave de Friedland, 75008 Paris; tel. 1-53-96-93-96; fax 1-53-96-93-97; e-mail ronald@antiguahc.sonnet.co.uk ; Ambassador Sir RONALD MICHAEL SANDERS.

Argentina: 6 rue Cimarosa, 75116 Paris; tel. 1-44-05-27-00; fax 1-45-53-46-33; Ambassador JUAN ARCHIBALDO LANÚS.

Armenia: 9 rue Viète, 75017 Paris; tel. 1-42-12-98-01; fax 1-42-12-98-03; e-mail ambarmen@wanadoo.fr; Ambassador EDUARD NAUBANDIAN.

Australia: 4 rue Jean Rey, 75724 Paris Cédex 15; tel. 1-40-59-33-00; fax 1-40-59-33-10; e-mail information.paris@dfat.gov.au; internet www.austgov.fr; Ambassador WILLIAM NORMAN FISHER.

Austria: 6 rue Faber, 75007 Paris; tel. 1-40-63-30-63; fax 1-45-55-63-65; e-mail paris-ob@bmaa.gv.at; internet www.amb-autriche.fr; Ambassador ANTON PROHASKA.

Azerbaijan: 209 rue de l'Université, 75007 Paris; tel. 1-44-18-60-20; fax 1-44-18-60-25; e-mail ambazer@wanadoo.fr; Ambassador ELÉONORA HUSSEÏNOVA.

Bahrain: 3 bis place des Etats-Unis, 75116 Paris; tel. 1-47-23-48-68; fax 1-47-20-55-75; Ambassador Sheikha HAYA RASHED AL-KHALIFA.

Bangladesh: 5 sq. Pétraque, 75016 Paris; tel. 1-45-53-41-20; fax 1-47-04-72-41; e-mail bdootpar@club-internet.fr; Ambassador JAHANGIR SAADAT.

Belarus: 38 blvd Suchet, 75016 Paris; tel. 1-44-14-69-79; fax 1-44-14-69-70; Ambassador VLADIMIR SENKO.

Belgium: 9 rue de Tilsitt, 75017 Paris; tel. 1-44-09-39-39; fax 1-47-54-07-64; e-mail paris@diplobel.org; internet www.diplobel.org/france/home.htm; Ambassador PIERRE-ETIENNE CHAMPENOIS.

Benin: 87 ave Victor Hugo, 75116 Paris; tel. 1-45-00-98-82; fax 1-45-01-82-02; e-mail ambassade@ambassade-benin.org; internet www.ambassade-benin.org; Ambassador ANDRÉ-GUY OLOGOUDOU.

Bolivia: 12 ave Président Kennedy, 75016 Paris; tel. 1-42-24-93-44; fax 1-45-25-86-23; Ambassador PEDRO RIVERO-MERCADO.

Bosnia and Herzegovina: 174 rue de Courcelles, 75017 Paris; tel. 1-42-67-34-22; fax 1-40-53-85-22; Ambassador SLOBODAN ŠOJA.

Brazil: 34 cours Albert 1er, 75008 Paris; tel. 1-45-61-63-00; fax 1-42-89-03-45; e-mail imprensa@bresil.org; internet www.bresil.org; Ambassador MARCOS CASTRIOTO DE AZAMBUJA.

Brunei: 7 rue de Presbourg, 75116 Paris; tel. 1-53-64-67-60; fax 1-53-64-67-83; e-mail embruneip@libertysurf.fr; Ambassador Pengiran Hajjah MASRAINAH binti Pengiran Haji AHMAD.

Bulgaria: 1 ave Rapp, 75007 Paris; tel. 1-45-51-85-90; fax 1-45-51-18-68; e-mail bulgamb@wanadoo.fr; internet www.amb-bulgarie.fr; Ambassador MARIN RAYKOV.

Burkina Faso: 159 blvd Haussmann, 75008 Paris; tel. 1-43-59-90-63; fax 1-42-56-50-07; e-mail amba.burkina.faso@wanadoo.fr; Ambassador FILIPPE SAWADOGO.

Burundi: 24 rue Raynouard, 75016 Paris; tel. 1-45-20-60-61; fax 1-41-12-99-42; Ambassador LIBOIRE NGENDAHAYO.

Cambodia: 4 rue Adolphe Yvon, 75116 Paris; tel. 1-45-03-47-20; fax 1-45-03-47-40; e-mail ambcambodgeparis@mangoosta.fr; Ambassador PRAK SOKHONN.

Cameroon: 73 rue d'Auteuil, 75116 Paris; tel. 1-47-43-98-33; fax 1-46-51-24-52; Ambassador PASCAL BILOA TANG.

Canada: 35 ave Montaigne, 75008 Paris; tel. 1-44-43-29-00; fax 1-44-43-29-99; internet www.amb-canada.fr; Ambassador RAYMOND CHRÉTIEN.

Cape Verde: 80 rue Jouffroy d'Abbans, 75017 Paris; tel. 1-42-12-73-50; fax 1-40-53-04-36; e-mail ambassade-cap-vert@wanadoo.fr; Ambassador ARNALDO ANDRADE RAMOS.

Central African Republic: 30 rue des Perchamps, 75116 Paris; tel. 1-42-24-42-56; fax 1-46-51-00-21; Ambassador NESTOR KOMBOT-NAGUEMON.

Chad: 65 rue des Belles Feuilles, 75116 Paris; tel. 1-45-53-36-75; fax 1-45-53-16-09; Ambassador MAHMOUD HISSEIN MAHMOUD.

Chile: 2 ave de la Motte-Picquet, 75007 Paris; tel. 1-44-18-59-60; fax 1-44-18-59-61; e-mail echile@amb-chili.fr; internet www.amb-chili.fr; Ambassador MARCELO SCHILLING.

China, People's Republic: 11 ave George V, 75008 Paris; tel. 1-47-23-36-77; fax 1-47-20-24-22; e-mail xinwen@clubobs.com; internet www.amb-chine.fr; Ambassador WU JIANMIN.

Colombia: 22 rue de l'Elysée, 75008 Paris; tel. 1-42-65-46-08; fax 1-42-66-18-60; e-mail embcolombia@wanadoo.fr; Ambassador MARTA LUCIA RAMIREZ DE RINCON.

Comoros: 20 rue Marbeau, 75116 Paris; tel. 1-40-67-90-54; fax 1-40-67-72-87; Chargé d'affaires a.i. SAID ABASSE ALLOUI.

Congo, Democratic Republic: 32 cours Albert 1er, 75008 Paris; tel. 1-42-25-57-50; fax 1-43-59-30-21; e-mail amb.rdc.paris@wanadoo.fr; Ambassador EDDYI ANGULU MABENGI.

Congo, Republic: 37 bis rue Paul Valéry, 75116 Paris; tel. 1-45-00-60-57; fax 1-45-00-34-26; Ambassador HENRI LOPES.

Costa Rica: 78 ave Emile Zola, 75015 Paris; tel. 1-45-78-96-96; fax 1-45-78-99-66; Ambassador ANI RAMOS DE ANAYA.

Côte d'Ivoire: 102 ave Raymond Poincaré, 75116 Paris; tel. 1-53-64-62-62; fax 1-45-00-47-97; Ambassador RAYMOND KOUDOU KESSIÉ.

Croatia: 39 ave Georges Mandel, 75116 Paris; tel. 1-53-70-02-80; fax 1-53-70-02-90; e-mail secretariat@amb-croatie.fr; internet www.amb-croatie.fr; Ambassador BOŽIDAR GAGRO.

Cuba: 16 rue de Presles, 75015 Paris; tel. 1-45-67-55-35; fax 1-45-66-80-92; e-mail embacu@club-internet.fr; Ambassador EUMELIO CABALLERO RODRÍGUEZ.

Cyprus: 23 rue Galilée, 75116 Paris; tel. 1-47-20-86-28; fax 1-40-70-13-44; e-mail embrecyp@worldnet.fr; Ambassador MINAS A. HADJMICHAEL.

Czech Republic: 15 ave Charles Floquet, 75007 Paris; tel. 1-72-76-13-00; fax 1-72-76-13-13; e-mail paris@embassy.mzv.cz; internet www.mzv.cz/paris; Ambassador PETR JANYŠKA.

Denmark: 77 ave Marceau, 75116 Paris; tel. 1-44-31-21-21; fax 1-44-31-21-88; e-mail paramb@um.dk; internet www.amb-danemark.fr; Ambassador HANS HENRIK BRUUN.

Djibouti: 26 rue Emile Ménier, 75116 Paris; tel. 1-47-27-49-22; fax 1-45-53-50-53; e-mail ambassadeur@ambdjibouti.org; internet www.ambdjibouti.org; Ambassador MOHAMED GOUMANEH GULRREH.

Dominican Republic: 45 rue de Courcelles, 75008 Paris; tel. 1-53-53-95-95; fax 1-45-63-35-63; e-mail embajadom@amba-dominicaine-paris.com; internet www.amba-dominicaine-paris.com; Chargé d'affaires a.i. PABLO IGNACIO GOMEZ BORBON.

Ecuador: 34 ave de Messine, 75008 Paris; tel. 1-45-61-10-21; fax 1-42-56-06-64; e-mail embajadaenfrancia@ambassade-equateur.fr; internet www.ambassade-equateur.fr; Ambassador JOSÉ AYALA-LASSO.

Egypt: 56 ave d'Iéna, 75116 Paris; tel. 1-53-67-88-30; fax 1-47-23-06-43; e-mail boustane.paris@free.fr; Ambassador HATEF SEIF EL-NASR.

El Salvador: 12 rue Galilée, 75116 Paris; tel. 1-47-20-42-02; fax 1-40-70-01-95; e-mail embparis@club-internet.fr; Ambassador PEDRO LUIS APOSTOLO.

Equatorial Guinea: 29 blvd de Courcelles, 75008 Paris; tel. 1-47-66-44-33; fax 1-47-09-26-38; Ambassador NARCISO NTUGU ABESO OYANA.

Estonia: 46 rue Pierre Charron, 75008 Paris; tel. 1-56-62-22-00; fax 1-49-52-05-65; e-mail embassy.paris@mfa.ee; internet www.est-emb.fr; Ambassador ANDRES TALVIK.

Ethiopia: 35 ave Charles Floquet, 75007 Paris; tel. 1-47-83-83-95; fax 1-43-06-52-14; e-mail embethe@starnet.fr; Ambassador SAHLE-WORK ZEWDE.

Finland: 1 pl. de Finlande, 75007 Paris; tel. 1-44-18-19-20; fax 1-45-55-51-57; e-mail sanomat.par@formin.fi; internet www.amb-finlande.fr; Ambassador ESKO HAMILO.

Gabon: 26 bis ave Raphaël, 75116 Paris; tel. 1-44-30-22-30; fax 1-42-24-62-42; Ambassador JEAN-MARIE ADZÉ.

The Gambia: 117 rue St Lazare, 75008 Paris; tel. 1-42-94-09-30; fax 1-42-94-11-91; Ambassador WILLIAM JOHN JOOF.

Georgia: 104 ave Raymond Poincaré, 75116 Paris; tel. 1-45-02-16-16; fax 1-45-02-16-01; e-mail sophieko@cybercable.fr; Ambassador GOTCHA TCHOGOVADZE.

Germany: 13–15 ave Franklin D. Roosevelt, 75008 Paris; tel. 1-53-83-45-00; fax 1-43-59-74-18; e-mail ambassade@amb-allemagne.fr; internet www.amb-allemagne.fr; Ambassador FRITJÖF VON NORDENSKJÖED.

Ghana: 8 Villa Saïd, 75116 Paris; tel. 1-45-00-09-50; fax 1-45-00-81-95; e-mail embassy.of.ghana1@libertysurf.fr; Ambassador Prof. ALBERT OWUSU-SARPONG.

Greece: 17 rue Auguste Vacquerie, 75116 Paris; tel. 1-47-23-72-28; fax 1-47-23-73-85; e-mail ambgrpar@wanadoo.fr; internet www.amb-grece.fr/presse; Ambassador DIMITRIS KARAÏTIDIS.

Guatemala: 73 rue de Courcelles, 75008 Paris; tel. 1-42-27-78-63; fax 1-47-54-02-06; e-mail embguatefrancia@wanadoo.fr; Ambassador ANTONIO PALLARES BUONAFINA.

Guinea: 51 rue de la Faisanderie, 75116 Paris; tel. 1-47-04-81-48; fax 1-47-04-57-65; e-mail ambagiu.paris@laposte.net; Ambassador LANSANA KÉITA.

Guinea-Bissau: 94 rue Saint Lazare, 75009 Paris; tel. 1-45-26-18-51; fax 1-45-26-60-59; Ambassador JOÃO SOARES DA GAMA.

Haiti: 10 rue Théodule Ribot, 75017 Paris; tel. 1-47-63-47-78; fax 1-42-27-02-05; e-mail haiti01@francophonie.org; Ambassador MARC A. TROUILLOT.

Holy See: 10 ave du Président Wilson, 75116 Paris (Apostolic Nunciature); tel. 1-47-23-01-50; fax 1-47-23-65-44; e-mail noncapfr@worldnet.fr; Apostolic Nuncio Most Rev. FORTUNATO BALDELLI (Titular Archbishop of Bevagna).

Honduras: 8 rue Crevaux, 75116 Paris; tel. 1-47-55-86-45; fax 1-47-55-86-48; e-mail ambassade.honduras@noos.fr; Ambassador MARIO CARIAS ZAPATA.

Hungary: 7 sq. Vergennes, 75015 Paris; tel. 1-56-36-07-54; fax 1-56-36-02-68; e-mail ambassade-de-hongrie@wanadoo.fr; internet www.hongrie.org; Ambassador ANDRÉ ERDÖS.

Iceland: 8 ave Kléber, 75116 Paris; tel. 1-44-17-32-85; fax 1-40-67-99-96; e-mail icemb.paris@utn.stjr.is; internet www.iceland.org/fr; Ambassador SIGRÍDUR ÁSDÍS SNÆVARR.

India: 15 rue Alfred Dehodencq, 75016 Paris; tel. 1-40-50-70-70; fax 1-40-50-09-96; e-mail pic@amb-inde.fr; internet www.amb-inde.fr; Ambassador SAVITRI KUNADI.

Indonesia: 47–49 rue Cortambert, 75116 Paris; tel. 1-45-03-07-60; fax 1-45-04-50-32; e-mail kasubpen@amb-indonesie.fr; internet www.amb-indonesie.fr; Ambassador ADIAN SILALAHI.

Iran: 4 ave d'Iéna, 75116 Paris; tel. 1-40-69-79-00; fax 1-40-70-01-57; internet www.ambassade-iran.com; Ambassador SEYED MOHAMMAD SADEGH KHARAZI.

Iraq (Interests Section): 53 rue de la Faisandrie, 75016 Paris; tel. 1-45-53-33-70; fax 1-45-53-33-80; e-mail paris@embassyiraq.com; internet www.embassyiraq.com.

Ireland: 4 rue Rude, 75116 Paris; tel. 1-44-17-67-00; fax 1-44-17-67-60; e-mail irembparis@wanadoo.fr; Ambassador PÁDRAIC MAC KERNAN.

Israel: 3 rue Rabelais, 75008 Paris; tel. 1-40-76-55-00; fax 1-40-76-55-55; e-mail ambassade@par.mfa.gov.il; internet www.amb-israel.fr; Ambassador NISSIM ZVILI.

Italy: 51 rue de Varenne, 75343 Paris Cédex 07; tel. 1-49-54-03-00; fax 1-45-49-35-81; e-mail ambasciata@amb-italie.fr; Ambassador GIOVANNI DEMINEDO.

Japan: 7 ave Hoche, 75008 Paris; tel. 1-48-88-62-00; fax 1-42-27-50-81; e-mail i-richard@amb-japon.fr; internet www.amb-japon.fr; Ambassador KAZUO OGOURA.

Jordan: 11 rue Alfred Dehodencq, 75016 Paris; tel. 1-55-74-73-73; fax 1-55-74-73-74; e-mail amb.jor@wanadoo.fr; Ambassador DINA KAWAR.

Kazakhstan: 59 rue Pierre Charron, 75008 Paris; tel. 1-45-61-52-00; fax 1-45-61-52-01; e-mail amb.kaz4@wanadoo.fr; internet www.amb-kazakhstan.fr; Ambassador AKMARAL ARYSTANBEKOVA.

Kenya: 3 rue Freycinet, 75116 Paris; tel. 1-56-62-25-25; fax 1-47-20-44-41; e-mail kenparis@wanadoo.fr; internet www.kenyaembassyparis.org; Ambassador BOAZ K. MBAYA.

Korea, Republic: 125 rue de Grenelle, 75007 Paris; tel. 1-47-53-01-01; fax 1-47-53-00-41; e-mail koremb-fr@mofat.go.kr; internet www.amb-coreesud.fr; Ambassador JANG JAI-RYONG.

Kuwait: 2 rue de Lübeck, 75116 Paris; tel. 1-47-23-54-25; fax 1-47-20-33-59; Ambassador AHMAD AL-EBRAHIM.

Laos: 74 ave Raymond Poincaré, 75116 Paris; tel. 1-45-53-02-98; fax 1-47-57-27-89; Ambassador SOUTSAKHORU PATHAMMAVONG.

Latvia: 6 villa Saïd, 75016 Paris; tel. 1-53-64-58-10; fax 1-53-64-58-19; e-mail embassy.france@mfa.gov.lv; Ambassador ROLANDS LAPPUKE.

Lebanon: 3 villa Copernic, 75116 Paris; tel. 1-40-67-75-75; fax 1-40-67-16-42; e-mail ambliban@club-internet.fr; Ambassador ELYSÉ ALAM.

Liberia: 12 place du Général Catroux, 75017 Paris; tel. 1-47-63-58-55; fax 1-42-12-76-14; e-mail libem.paris@wanadoo.fr; Ambassador CHRISTOPHER TUGBA MOSES MINIKON.

Libya: 2 rue Charles Lamoureux, 75116 Paris; tel. 1-47-04-71-60; fax 1-47-55-96-25; Ambassador Dr ABDESSALEM EL-MAZOUGHI.

Lithuania: 14 blvd Montmartre, 75009 Paris; tel. 1-48-01-00-33; fax 1-48-01-03-31; e-mail amb.lituanie@magic.fr; internet www.amb-lituanie-paris.fr; Ambassador ASTA SKAISGIRYTÉ-LIAUŠKIENĖ.

Luxembourg: 33 ave Rapp, 75007 Paris; tel. 1-45-55-13-37; fax 1-45-51-72-29; Ambassador JEAN-MARC HOSCHEIT.

Macedonia, former Yugoslav republic: 21 rue Sébastian Mercier, 75015 Paris; tel. 1-45-77-10-50; fax 1-45-77-14-84; e-mail amb-mk@wanadoo.fr; Ambassador JORDAN PLEVNEŠ.

Madagascar: 4 ave Raphaël, 75016 Paris; tel. 1-45-04-62-11; fax 1-45-03-58-70; internet www.ambamad-france.com; Ambassador JEAN-PIERRE RAZAFY-ANDRIAMIHAINGO.

Malawi: 20 rue Euler, 75008 Paris; tel. 1-40-70-18-46; fax 1-47-23-62-48; e-mail malawi.embassy@libertysurf.fr; Ambassador Dr AHMED I. KHARODIA.

Malaysia: 2 bis rue Bénouville, 75116 Paris; tel. 1-45-53-11-85; fax 1-47-27-34-60; e-mail mw paris@wanadoo.fr; Ambassador Tunku Datuk NAZIHAH Tunku MOHD RUS.

Mali: 89 rue du Cherche-Midi, 75263 Paris Cédex 06; tel. 1-45-48-58-43; fax 1-45-48-55-34; Ambassador MOUSSA COULIBALY.

Malta: 92 ave des Champs Elysées, 75008 Paris; tel. 1-56-59-75-90; fax 1-45-62-00-36; e-mail salvino.busuttil@gov.mt; Ambassador Prof. SALVINO BUSUTTIL.

Mauritania: 5 rue de Montévidéo, 75116 Paris; tel. 1-45-04-88-54; fax 1-40-72-82-96; e-mail ambassade.mauritanie@wanadoo.fr; Ambassador SIDNEY SOKHONA.

Mauritius: 127 rue de Tocqueville, 75017 Paris; tel. 1-42-27-66-70; fax 1-40-53-02-91; e-mail amb-maurice-paris@gofornet.com; Ambassador ABDOOL RAOUF BUNDHUN.

Mexico: 9 rue de Longchamp, 75116 Paris; tel. 1-53-70-27-70; fax 1-47-55-65-29; e-mail embfrancia@sre.gob.mx; internet www.sre.gob.mx/francia; Ambassador CLAUDE HELLER.

Moldova: 1 rue de Sfax, 75116 Paris; tel. 1-40-67-11-20; fax 1-40-67-11-23; e-mail ambassade.moldavie@free.fr; Ambassador MIHAI POPOV.

Monaco: 22 blvd Suchet, 75116 Paris; tel. 1-45-04-74-54; fax 1-45-04-45-16; Ambassador CHRISTIAN ORSETTI.

Mongolia: 5 ave Robert Schuman, 92100 Boulogne-Billancourt; tel. 1-46-05-28-12; fax 1-46-05-23-18; e-mail esyam@ambassademongolie.fr; Ambassador TS. BATBUYAN.

Morocco: 3–5 rue Le Tasse, 75116 Paris; tel. 1-45-20-69-35; fax 1-45-20-92-90; Ambassador HASSAN ABOUYOUB.

Mozambique: 82 rue Laugier, 75017 Paris; tel. 1-47-64-91-32; fax 1-44-15-90-13; e-mail embamocparis@compuserve.com; Ambassador FERNANDA LICHALE.

Myanmar: 60 rue de Courcelles, 75008 Paris; tel. 1-42-25-56-95; fax 1-42-56-49-41; Ambassador U WUNNA MAUNG LWIN.

Namibia: 80 ave Foch, 75016 Paris; tel. 1-44-17-32-65; fax 1-44-17-32-73; e-mail namparis@club-internet.fr; Ambassador WILFRIED I. EMVULA.

Nepal: 45 bis rue des Acacias, 75017 Paris; tel. 1-46-22-48-67; fax 1-42-27-08-65; e-mail nepal@worldnet.fr; Ambassador INDRA BAHADUR SINGH.

Netherlands: 7–9 rue Eblé, 75007 Paris; tel. 1-40-62-33-00; fax 1-40-62-34-56; e-mail ambassade@amb-pays-bas.fr; internet www.amb-pays-bas.fr; Ambassador CHRISTIAAN M. J. KRÖNER.

New Zealand: 7 ter rue Léonard de Vinci, 75116 Paris; tel. 1-45-01-43-43; fax 1-45-01-43-44; e-mail nzembassy.paris@wanadoo.fr; internet www.nzembassy.com/France; Ambassador ADRIAN HENRY MACEY.

Nicaragua: 34 ave Bugeaud, 75116 Paris; tel. 1-44-05-90-42; fax 1-44-05-92-42; e-mail embanifr@noos.fr; Ambassador MARIO SALVO HORVILLEUR.

Niger: 154 rue de Longchamp, 75116 Paris; tel. 1-45-04-80-60; fax 1-45-04-62-26; Ambassador ADAMOU SEYDOU.

Nigeria: 173 ave Victor Hugo, 75116 Paris; tel. 1-47-04-68-65; fax 1-47-04-47-54; e-mail embassy@nigeriaparis.com; internet www.nigeriaparis.com; Ambassador E. A. AINA.

Norway: 28 rue Bayard, 75008 Paris; tel. 1-53-67-04-00; fax 1-53-67-04-40; e-mail emb.paris@mfa.no; internet www.amb-norvege.fr; Ambassador ROLF TROLLE ANDERSEN.

Oman: 50 ave d'Iéna, 75116 Paris; tel. 1-47-23-01-63; fax 1-47-23-77-10; Ambassador JAIFER SALIM AL-SAID.

Pakistan: 18 rue Lord Byron, 75008 Paris; tel. 1-45-62-23-32; fax 1-45-62-89-15; e-mail pakemb_paris@yahoo.com; Ambassador MUSA JAVED CHONAN.

Panama: 145 ave de Suffren, 75015 Paris; tel. 1-45-66-42-44; fax 1-45-67-99-43; Ambassador ANEL ENRIQUE BELIZ.

Paraguay: 1 rue St Dominique, 75007 Paris; tel. 1-42-22-85-05; fax 1-42-22-83-57; e-mail embaparf@noos.fr; Ambassador RUBÉN BAREIRO SAGUIER.

Peru: 50 ave Kléber, 75116 Paris; tel. 1-53-70-42-00; fax 1-47-55-98-30; e-mail perou.ambassade@amb-perou.fr; internet www.amb-perou.fr; Ambassador JAVIER PÉREZ DE CUÉLLAR.

Philippines: 4 Hameau de Boulainvilliers, 75016 Paris; tel. 1-44-14-57-00; fax 1-46-47-56-00; e-mail parispe@wanadoo.fr; Ambassador HECTOR K. VILLARROEL.

Poland: 1–3 rue de Talleyrand, 75343 Paris Cédex 07; tel. 1-43-17-34-05; fax 1-43-17-35-07; e-mail info@ambassade.pologne.net; internet www.ambassade.pologne.net; Ambassador JAN TOMBINSKI.

Portugal: 3 rue de Noisiel, 75116 Paris; tel. 1-47-27-35-29; fax 1-44-05-94-02; e-mail mailto@embaixada-portugal-fr.org; internet www.embaixada-portugal-fr.org; Ambassador ANTÓNIO MONTEIRO.

Qatar: 57 quai d'Orsay, 75007 Paris; tel. 1-45-51-90-71; fax 1-45-51-77-07; Ambassador MOHAMED ABDULLAH MUTAAB AL-RUMAIHI.

Romania: 5 rue de l'Exposition, 75007 Paris; tel. 1-47-05-10-46; fax 1-45-56-97-47; e-mail secretariat@amb-roumanie.fr; internet www.amb-roumanie.fr; Ambassador OLIVIU GHERMAN.

Russia: 40–50 blvd Lannes, 75116 Paris; tel. 1-45-04-05-50; fax 1-45-04-17-65; e-mail ambrus@wanadoo.fr; Ambassador ALEKSANDR AVDEYEV.

Rwanda: 12 rue Jadin, 75017 Paris; tel. 1-42-27-36-31; fax 1-42-27-74-69; Ambassador JACQUES BIHOZAGARA.

San Marino: 4 rue de Cerisoles, 75116 Paris; tel. and fax 1-47-23-04-75; Ambassador Countess ISA CORINALDI DE BENEDETTI.

Saudi Arabia: 5 ave Hoche, 75008 Paris; tel. 1-56-79-40-00; fax 1-56-79-40-01; e-mail fremb@mofa.gov.sa; Ambassador FAISAL ABDULAZIZ ALHEGELAN.

Senegal: 14 ave Robert Schuman, 75007 Paris; tel. 1-47-05-39-45; fax 1-45-56-04-30; e-mail repsen@wanadoo.fr; internet www.ambassenparis.com; Ambassador DOUDOU DIOP SALLA.

Serbia and Montenegro: 54 rue de la Faisanderie, 75116 Paris; tel. 1-40-72-24-24; fax 1-40-72-24-11; e-mail pariz@compuserve.com; Ambassador RADOMIR DIKLIĆ.

Seychelles: 51 ave Mozart, 75016 Paris; tel. 1-42-30-57-47; fax 1-42-30-57-40; e-mail ambsey@aol.com; Ambassador CALLIXTE D'OFFAY.

Singapore: 12 sq. de l'ave Foch, 75116 Paris; tel. 1-45-00-33-61; fax 1-45-00-61-79; e-mail ambsing@club-internet.fr; internet www.mfa.gov.sg/paris-french; Ambassador THAMBYNATHAN JASUDASEN.

Slovakia: 125 rue du Ranelagh, 75016 Paris; tel. 1-44-14-56-00; fax 1-42-88-76-53; e-mail paris@amb-slovaquie.fr; internet www.amb-slovaquie.fr; Ambassador MÁRIA KRASNOHORSKÁ.

Slovenia: 28 rue Bois le Vent, 75016 Paris; tel. 1-44-96-50-60; fax 1-45-24-67-05; Ambassador MAGDALENA TOVORNIK.

Somalia: 26 rue Dumont d'Urville, 75116 Paris; tel. 1-45-00-88-98; Ambassador Said Hajgi MOHAMOUD FARAH.

South Africa: 59 quai d'Orsay, 75343 Paris Cédex 07; tel. 1-53-59-23-23; fax 1-53-59-23-33; e-mail info@afriquesud.net; internet www.afriquesud.net; Ambassador THUTHUKILE E. SKWEYIYA.

Spain: 22 ave Marceau, 75008 Paris; tel. 1-44-43-18-00; fax 1-47-23-59-55; e-mail ambespfr@mail.mae.es; internet www.amb-espagne.fr; Ambassador FRANCISCO JAVIER ELORZA.

Sri Lanka: 16 rue Spontine, 75016 Paris; tel. 1-55-73-31-31; fax 1-55-73-18-49; e-mail sl.france@wanadoo.fr; Ambassador CHANDRA GEMUNU WICKRAMASINGHE.

Sudan: 56 ave Montaigne, 75008 Paris; tel. 1-42-25-55-71; fax 1-54-63-66-73; e-mail ambassade-du-soudan@wanadoo.fr; internet www.ambassade-du-soudan.org; Ambassador ABDELBASIT BADAWI ALI ELSANOUSI.

Sweden: 17 rue Barbet-de-Jouy, 75007 Paris; tel. 1-44-18-88-00; fax 1-44-18-88-40; e-mail presseinfo@amb-suede.fr; internet www.amb-suede.fr; Ambassador FRANK BELFRAGE.

Switzerland: 142 rue de Grenelle, 75007 Paris; tel. 1-49-55-67-00; fax 1-49-55-67-67; e-mail vertretung@par.rep.admin.ch; internet www.amb-suisse.fr; Ambassador FRANÇOIS NORDMANN.

Syria: 20 rue Vaneau, 75007 Paris; tel. 1-40-62-61-00; fax 1-47-05-92-73; e-mail ambassade-syrie@wanadoo.fr; Ambassador SIBA NASSER.

Tanzania: 13 ave Raymond Poincaré, 75116 Paris; tel. 1-53-70-63-66; fax 1-47-55-05-46; e-mail ambtanzanie@wanadoo.fr; internet amb-tanzanie.fr; Ambassador JUMA V. MWAPACHU.

Thailand: 8 rue Greuze, 75116 Paris; tel. 1-56-26-50-50; fax 1-56-26-04-46; e-mail thaipar@wanadoo.fr; Ambassador SAROJ CHAVANAVIRAJ.

Togo: 8 rue Alfred Roll, 75017 Paris; tel. 1-43-80-12-13; fax 1-43-80-90-71; Ambassador KONDI CHARLES MADJOME AGBA.

Tunisia: 25 rue Barbet-de-Jouy, 75007 Paris; tel. 1-45-55-95-98; fax 1-45-56-02-64; Ambassador FAÏZA KEFI.

Turkey: 16 ave de Lamballe, 75016 Paris; tel. 1-53-92-71-22; fax 1-45-20-41-91; e-mail paris.be@mfa.gov.tr; Ambassador ULUÇ ÖZÜLKER.

Turkmenistan: 13 rue Picot, 75116 Paris; tel. 1-47-55-05-36; fax 1-47-55-05-68; e-mail turkmenamb@aol.com; Ambassador TCHARY G. NIYAZOV.

Ukraine: 21 ave de Saxe, 75007 Paris; tel. 1-43-06-07-37; fax 1-43-06-02-94; e-mail emb_fr@mfa.gov.ua; Ambassador YURIY A. SERHEYEV.

United Arab Emirates: 3 rue de Lota, 75116 Paris; tel. 1-44-34-02-00; fax 1-47-55-61-04; e-mail ambassade.emirats@wanadoo.fr; Ambassador SAIF SULTAN MUBARAK AL-ARYANI.

United Kingdom: 35 rue du Faubourg Saint Honoré, 75383 Paris Cédex 08; tel. 1-44-51-31-00; fax 1-44-51-41-27; internet www.amb-grandebretagne.fr; Ambassador Sir JOHN HOLMES.

USA: 2 ave Gabriel, 75382 Paris Cédex 08; tel. 1-43-12-22-22; fax 1-42-66-97-83; internet www.amb-usa.fr; Ambassador HOWARD H. LEACH.

Uruguay: 15 rue Le Sueur, 75116 Paris; tel. 1-45-00-81-37; fax 1-45-01-25-17; e-mail urugali@fr.inter.net; internet www.amb-uruguay-france.com; Ambassador MIGUEL ANGEL SEMINO.

Uzbekistan: 22 rue d'Aguesseau, 75008 Paris; tel. 1-53-30-03-53; fax 1-53-30-03-54; e-mail ambssade.ouzbekistan@wanadoo.fr; internet www.oaric.com/ouzbekistan.htm; Ambassador TOKHIRJON MAMAJANOV.

Venezuela: 11 rue Copernic, 75116 Paris; tel. 1-45-53-29-98; fax 1-47-55-64-56; e-mail info@amb-venezuela.fr; internet www.embavenez-paris.com; Ambassador JÉSUS ARNALDO PÉREZ.

Viet Nam: 62 rue Boileau, 75016 Paris; tel. 1-44-14-64-00; fax 1-45-24-39-48; e-mail pchi@imaginet.fr; Ambassador NGUYÊN MANH DUNG.

Yemen: 25 rue Georges Bizet, 75116 Paris; tel. 1-53-23-87-87; fax 1-47-23-69-41; Ambassador MOHAMED AHMED BA-SALAMA.

Zimbabwe: 12 rue Lord Byron, 75008 Paris; tel. 1-56-88-16-00; fax 1-56-88-16-09; e-mail zim.paris@wanadoo.fr; Ambassador JOEY MAZORODZE BIMHA.

Judicial System

The Judiciary is independent of the Government. Judges of the Court of Cassation and the First President of the Court of Appeal are appointed by the executive from nominations of the High Council of the Judiciary.

Subordinate cases are heard by Tribunaux d'instance, of which there are 471, and more serious cases by Tribunaux de grande instance, of which there are 181. Parallel to these Tribunals are the Tribunaux de commerce, for commercial cases, composed of judges elected by traders and manufacturers among themselves. These do not exist in every district. Where there is no Tribunal de commerce, commercial disputes are judged by Tribunaux de grande instance.

The Conseils de Prud'hommes (Boards of Arbitration) consist of an equal number of workers or employees and employers ruling on the differences that arise over Contracts of Work.

The Tribunaux correctionnnels (Correctional Courts) for criminal cases correspond to the Tribunaux de grande instance for civil cases. They pronounce on all graver offences (délits), including those involving imprisonment. Offences committed by juveniles of under 18 years go before specialized tribunals for children.

From all these Tribunals appeal lies to the Cours d'appel (Courts of Appeal).

The Cours d'assises (Courts of Assize) have no regular sittings, but are called when necessary to try every important case, for example, murder. They are presided over by judges who are members of the Cours d'appel, and are composed of elected judges (jury). Their decision is final, except where shown to be wrong in law, and then recourse is had to the Cour de cassation (Court of Cassation). The Cour de cassation is not a supreme court of appeal but a higher authority for the proper application of the law. Its duty is to see that judgments are not contrary either to the letter or the spirit of the law; any judgment annulled by the Court involves the trying of the case anew by a court of the same category as that which made the original decision.

A programme of extensive reforms in the judicial system, which aimed to reduce political control of the Judiciary and to increase citizens' rights, was introduced in stages between 1997 and 2001. A notable innovation introduced by these reforms was the introduction of the convention that a person accused of a crime is presumed innocent unless otherwise proven.

COUR DE CASSATION

5 quai de l'Horloge, 75055 Paris RP; tel. 1-44-32-50-50; fax 1-44-32-78-29; e-mail webmaster@courdecassation.fr; internet www.courdecassation.fr.

First President: GUY CANIVET.

Presidents of Chambers: JACQUES LEMONTEY (1ère Chambre civile), JEAN-PIERRE ANGEL (2ème Chambre civile), JEAN-FRANÇOIS WEBER (3ème Chambre civile), JEAN-PIERRE DUMAS (Chambre commerciale), PIERRE SARGOS (Chambre sociale), BRUNO COTTE (Chambre criminelle).

Solicitor-General: JEAN-FRANÇOIS BURGELIN.

There are 85 Counsellors, two First Attorneys-General and 27 Attorneys-General.

Chief Clerk of the Court: MARLÈNE TARDI.

Council of Advocates at Court of Cassation

Pres. ELISABETH BARADUC.

COUR D'APPEL DE PARIS

34 quai des Orfèvres, 75001 Paris; tel. 1-44-32-52-52; internet www.ca-paris.justice.fr.

First President: JEAN-MARIE COULON.

There are also 69 Presidents of Chambers.

Solicitor-General: JEAN-LOUIS NADAL.

There are also 121 Counsellors, 24 Attorneys-General and 38 Deputies.

TRIBUNAL DE GRANDE INSTANCE DE PARIS

4 blvd du Palais, 75055 Paris RP; tel. 1-44-32-51-51; fax 1-43-29-12-55; internet www.tgi-paris.justice.fr.

President: JEAN-CLAUDE MAGENDIE.

Solicitor of the Republic of Paris: YVES BOT.

TRIBUNAL DE COMMERCE DE PARIS

1 quai de Corse, 75181 Paris Cédex 04; e-mail eric.labonne@greffe-tc-paris.fr; internet www.greffe-tc-paris.fr.

President: GILBERT COSTES.

TRIBUNAUX ADMINISTRATIFS

Certain cases arising between civil servants (when on duty) and the Government, or between any citizen and the Government are judged by special administrative courts.

The Tribunaux administratifs, of which there are 22, are situated in the capital of each area; the Conseil d'Etat (see below) has its seat in Paris.

TRIBUNAL DES CONFLITS

Decides whether cases shall be submitted to the ordinary or administrative courts.

President: The Minister of Justice, Keeper of the Seals.

Vice-President: YVES ROBINEAU.

There are also four Counsellors of the Cour de cassation and three Counsellors of State.

COUR DES COMPTES

13 rue Cambon, 75100 Paris RP; tel. 1-42-98-95-00; fax 1-42-60-01-59; internet www.ccomptes.fr.

An administrative tribunal (Audit Court) competent to judge the correctness of public accounts. It is the arbiter of common law of all public accounts laid before it. The judgments of the Court may be annuled by the Conseil d'Etat.

First President: FRANÇOIS LOGEROT.

Presidents of Chambers: FRANÇOIS DELAFOSSE, BERTRAND FRAGONARD, JEAN-FRANÇOIS COLLINET, JEAN-PIERRE GASTINEL, JEAN MARMOT, BERNARD CIEUTAT, BERNARD MENASSEYRE.

Solicitor-General: HÉLÈNE GISSEROT.

CHAMBRES RÉGIONALES DES COMPTES

In 1983 jurisdiction over the accounts of local administrations (Régions, Départements and Communes) and public institutions (hospitals, council housing, etc.) was transferred from the Cour des comptes to local Chambres régionales. The 25 courts are autonomous but under the jurisdiction of the State. Appeals may be brought before the Cour des comptes.

CONSEIL D'ETAT

Place du Palais-Royal, 75100 Paris 01 SP; tel. 1-40-20-80-00; fax 1-40-20-80-08; e-mail webmestre@conseil-etat.fr; internet www.conseil-etat.fr.

The Council of State is a council of the central power and an administrative tribunal, with 201 members in active service. As the consultative organ of the Government, it gives opinions in the legislative and administrative domain (interior, finance, public works and social sections). In administrative jurisdiction it has three functions: to judge in the first and last resort such cases as appeals against excess of power laid against official decrees or individuals; to judge appeals against judgments made by Tribunaux administratifs and resolutions of courts of litigation; and to annul decisions made by various specialized administrative authorities that adjudicate without appeal, such as the Cour des comptes.

President: The Prime Minister.

Vice-President: RENAUD DENOIX DE SAINT-MARC.

Presidents of Sections: MARIE-EVE AUBIN, JEAN-MICHEL BELORGEY, JEAN-LOUIS DEWOST, OLIVER FOUQUET, BRUNO GENEVOIS, DANIEL LABETOULLE.

General Secretary: PATRICK FRYDMAN.

CONSEIL CONSTITUTIONNEL

2 rue de Montpensier, 75001 Paris; tel. 1-40-15-30-00; fax 1-40-20-93-27; e-mail relations-exterieures@conseil-constitutionnel.fr; internet www.conseil-constitutionnel.fr.

President: YVES GUÉNA.

Members: MICHEL AMELLER, PIERRE MAZEAUD, SIMONE VEIL, JEAN-CLAUDE COLLIARD, MONIQUE PELLETIER, OLIVIER DUTHEILLET DE LAMOTHE, DOMINIQUE SCHNAPPER, PIERRE JOXE.

Religion

CHRISTIANITY

Conseil d'Eglises Chrétiennes en France: 80 rue de l'Abbé-Carton, 75014 Paris; tel. 1-53-90-25-50; fax 1-45-42-03-07; e-mail unite.chretiens.revue@wanadoo.fr; f. 1987; ecumenical organization comprising representatives from all Christian denominations to express opinions on social issues; 21 mems; Pres. Most Rev. JEAN-PIERRE RICARD, Pastor JEAN-ARNOLD DE CLERMONT, Most Rev. JÉRÉMIE CALIGIORGIS; Secs Pastor GILL DAUDÉ, Fr CHRISTIAN FORSTER, Fr MICHEL EVDOKIMOV.

The Roman Catholic Church

For ecclesiastical purposes, France comprises nine Apostolic Regions, together forming 19 archdioceses (of which two, Marseille and Strasbourg, are directly responsible to the Holy See), 95 dioceses (including one, Metz, directly responsible to the Holy See) and one Territorial Prelature. The Archbishop of Paris is also the Ordinary for Catholics of Oriental Rites. At the end of 2000 there were an estimated 46.3m. adherents of the Roman Catholic Church in France, equivalent to some 79.2% of the population.

Bishops' Conference: Conférence des Evêques de France, 106 rue du Bac, 75341 Paris Cédex 07; tel. 1-45-49-69-90; fax 1-45-49-69-95; e-mail cef@cef.fr; internet www.cef.fr; Pres. Most Rev. JEAN-PIERRE RICARD (Archbishop of Bordeaux); Sec.-Gen. Rev. STANISLAS LALANNE.

Latin Rite

Archbishop of Lyon and Primate of Gaul: Most Rev. PHILIPPE BARBARIN, Archevêché, 1 place de Fourvière, 69321 Lyon Cédex 05; tel. 4-72-38-80-90; fax 4-78-36-06-00; e-mail dioceselyon@wanadoo.fr; internet catholique-lyon.cef.fr.

Archbishop of Aix: Most Rev. CLAUDE FEIDT.

Archbishop of Albi: Most Rev. PIERRE-MARIE CARRÉ.

Archbishop of Auch: Most Rev. MAURICE FRÉCHARD.

Archbishop of Avignon: Most Rev. JEAN-PIERRE CATTENOZ.

Archbishop of Besançon: Most Rev. LUCIEN DALOZ.

Archbishop of Bordeaux: Most Rev JEAN-PIERRE RICARD.

Archbishop of Bourges: Most Rev. HUBERT BARBIER.

Archbishop of Cambrai: Most Rev. FRANÇOIS GARNIER.

Archbishop of Chambéry: Most Rev. LAURENT ULRICH.

Archbishop of Marseille: Most Rev. BERNARD PANAFIEU.

Archbishop of Paris: Cardinal JEAN-MARIE LUSTIGER.

Archbishop of Reims: Most Rev. THIERRY JORDAN.

Archbishop of Rennes: Most Rev. FRANÇOIS SAINT-MACARY.

Archbishop of Rouen: Most Rev. JOSEPH DUVAL.

Archbishop of Sens: Most Rev. GEORGES EDMOND ROBERT GILSON.

Archbishop of Strasbourg: Most Rev. JOSEPH DORÉ.

Archbishop of Toulouse: Most Rev. EMILE MARCUS.

Archbishop of Tours: Most Rev. ANDRÉ VINGT-TROIS.

Armenian Rite

Bishop of Sainte-Croix-de-Paris: GRÉGOIRE GHABROYAN, 10 bis rue Thouin, 75005 Paris; tel. 1-40-51-11-90; fax 1-40-51-11-99; e-mail epaparis@francenet.fr; 30,000 adherents (2002).

Ukrainian Rite

Apostolic Exarch in France: Most Rev. MICHEL HRYNCHYSHYN (Titular Bishop of Zygris), 186 blvd Saint-Germain, 75006 Paris; tel. 1-45-48-48-65; fax 1-48-08-34-05; 16,000 adherents (1989).

Protestant Churches

There are some 950,000 Protestants in France.

Eglise Méthodiste: 3 rue Paul Verlaine, 30100 Alès; tel. 4-66-86-20-72; the total Methodist community was estimated at 1,000 mems in 2001.

Fédération Protestante de France: 47 rue de Clichy, 75311 Paris Cédex 09; tel. 1-44-53-47-00; fax 1-42-81-40-01; e-mail fpf@protestants.org; internet www.protestants.org; f. 1905; Pres. Pastor JEAN-ARNOLD DE CLERMONT; Gen. Sec. Pastor CHRISTIAN SEYTRE.

The Federation includes:

Armée du Salut: 60 rue des Frères Flavien, 75976 Paris Cédex 20; tel. 1-43-62-25-95; fax 1-43-62-25-98; e-mail info@armeedusalut.fr; internet www.armeedusalut.fr; f. 1881; Pres. Col GLEN SHEPHERD.

Communauté protestante évangélique de Vannes: 18 blvd Edouard Herriot, 56000 Vannes; tel. 2-97-47-16-75; fax 2-97-42-44-93; Pres. Pastor JEAN-MARC THOBOIS.

Eglise de la Confession d'Augsbourg d'Alsace et de Lorraine: 1b quai St Thomas, 67081 Strasbourg Cédex; tel. 3-8825-90-05; fax 3-88-25-90-99; e-mail epal-directoire@protestants.org; internet www.protestants.org/epal; 218,000 mems; Pres. Prof. MARC LIENHARD.

Eglise évangélique de Rochefort: 30 Quéreux de la Laiterie, 17300 Rochefort; tel. 5-46-99-63-79; Pres. Pastor PIERRE ROCHAT.

Eglise évangélique luthérienne de France: 16 rue Chauchat, 75009 Paris; tel. 1-44-79-04-73; fax 1-44-79-05-81; e-mail usynparis@aol.com; 40,000 mems; f. 1872; Pres. JEAN-FRANÇOIS NARDIN; Sec. CHRISTIANE LAURENT.

Eglise réformée d'Alsace et de Lorraine: 1 quai St Thomas, 67081 Strasbourg Cédex; tel. 3-88-25-90-10; fax 3-88-25-90-80; e-mail eral@protestants.org; internet www.protestants.org/epal; 33,000 mems; Pres. Pastor JEAN-PAUL HUMBERT.

Eglise réformée de France: 47 rue de Clichy, 75311 Paris Cédex 09; tel. 1-48-74-90-92; fax 1-42-81-52-40; internet www.eglise-reformee-fr.org; 350,000 mems; Pres. Nat. Council Pastor MARCEL MANOËL; Gen. Sec. Pastor BERTRAND DE CAZENOVE.

Fédération des Eglises évangéliques baptistes de France: 47 rue de Clichy, 75311 Paris Cédex 09; tel. 1-53-20-15-40; fax 1-53-20-15-41; e-mail feebf@aol.com; internet www.feebf.com; 6,000 mems; f. 1910; Pres. MICHEL CHARLES; Gen. Sec. Pastor ETIENNE LHERMENAULT.

Mission évangélique tzigane de France: 'Les Petites Brosses', 45500 Neuvoy; tel. 2-38-67-38-00; 70,000 mems; f. 1946; Pres. Pastor GEORGES MEYER.

Mission populaire évangélique de France: 47 rue de Clichy, 75311 Paris Cédex 09; tel. 1-48-74-98-58; fax 1-48-78-52-37; e-mail mpef@free.fr; 4,000 mems; f. 1871; Pres. JEAN-JACQUES DEMOUVEAUX; Gen. Sec. Pastor JEAN-FRANÇOIS FABA.

Union des Eglises évangéliques libres de France: 12 rue Claude-Perrault, 31500 Toulouse; tel. 5-61-26-06-18; fax 5-61-99-92-82; internet www.ueel.org; 2,500 mems; Pres. Pastor PIERRE LACOSTE; Sec. RAYMOND CHAMARD.

Union Nationale des Eglises réformées évangéliques indépendantes de France: 74 rue Henri Revoil, 30900 Nîmes; tel. 4-66-23-95-05; e-mail unerei@wanadoo.fr; internet erei.free.fr; f. 1938; 12,000 mems; Pres. ANTOINE SCHLUCHTER; Sec.-Gen. GÉRARD FINES.

The Orthodox Church

There are about 200,000 Orthodox believers in France, of whom 100,000 are Russian Orthodox and 50,000 Greek Orthodox. There are 85 parishes and eight monasteries.

Administration of Russian Orthodox Churches in Western Europe (Jurisdiction of the Ecumenical Patriarchate): Cathédrale St Alexandre-Nevski, 12 rue Daru, 75008 Paris; tel. 1-46-22-38-91; internet www.russie.net/orthodoxie/nevsky.htm; Pres. Most Rev. SERGE (KONOVALOV) (Archbishop of Russian Orthodox Churches in Western Europe and Exarch of the Ecumenical Patriarch).

Assembly of the Orthodox Churches of France (Greek Orthodox Church): Cathédrale St Stéphane, 7 rue Georges Bizet, 75116 Paris; tel. 1-47-20-82-35; fax 1-47-20-83-15; f. 1997; Pres. Most Rev. JÉRÉMIE (KALIGIORGIS) (Metropolitan of France, Exarch of Spain and Portugal).

The Anglican Communion

Within the Church of England, France forms part of the diocese of Gibraltar in Europe. The Bishop is resident in London (United Kingdom).

Archdeacon of France: Ven. ANTHONY WELLS, St. Michael's Church, 5 rue d'Aguesseau, 75008 Paris; tel. 1-47-42-70-88; e-mail office@saintmichaelsparis.org; internet www.saintmichaelsparis.org.

Other Christian Denominations

Centre Quaker International: 114 rue de Vaugirard, 75006 Paris; tel. 1-45-48-74-23; e-mail jeannehenriette@ifrance.com; internet quaker.chez.tiscali.fr; f. 1920; 10 meetings nationwide; Clerk JEANNE HENRIETTE-LOUIS.

ISLAM

In numerical terms, Islam is the second most important religion in France; in 2001 there were about 5m. adherents, of whom some 35% resided in the Ile-de-France region. Approximately one-half of Muslims resident in France at this time were of French nationality, with the majority of the remainder being of Maghreb origin. In early 2002 there were an estimated 1,500 Islamic places of worship in France. A Conseil français du culte musulman, which was to be responsible for representing Islamic interests to the public authorities, was established in 2003.

Conseil français du culte musulman: Paris; f. 2003 to represent Islamic interests to the public authorities; Pres. Dr DALIL BOUBAKEUR; Vice-Pres MOHAMED BECHARI, FOUAD ALAOUI; Sec.-Gen. HAYDAR DEMIRYUREK.

Fédération Nationale des Musulmans de France (FNMF): Paris; f. 1985; 20 asscns; Pres. DANIEL YOUSSOF LECLERQ.

Institut Musulman de la Grande Mosquée de Paris: 2 bis place du Puits de l'Ermite, 75005 Paris; tel. 1-45-35-97-33; fax 1-45-35-16-23; e-mail boubakeur@mosquee-de-paris.com; internet www.mosquee-de-paris.com; f. 1926; cultural, diplomatic, social, judicial and religious sections; research and information and commercial annexes; Rector Dr DALIL BOUBAKEUR.

Ligue nationale des Musulmans de France: BP 39, 91103 Corbeil-Essones Cédex; tel. 8-92-68-18-30; e-mail inscription@lnmf.net; internet www.lnmf.net.

JUDAISM

There are about 650,000 Jews in France.

Conseil représentatif des institutions juives de France (CRIF): 39 rue Broca, 75005 Paris; tel. 1-42-17-11-11; e-mail info@crif.org; internet www.crif.org; 61 asscns; Pres. ROGER CUKIERMAN.

Consistoire Central—Union des Communautés Juives de France: 19 rue Saint Georges, 75009 Paris; tel. 1-49-70-88-00; fax 1-42-81-03-66; e-mail consis@wanadoo.fr; f. 1808; 230 asscns; Chief Rabbi of France JOSEPH SITRUK; Pres. JEAN KAHN; Dir-Gen. FRÉDÉRIC ATTALI.

Consistoire Israélite de Paris: 17 rue Saint Georges, 75009 Paris; tel. 1-40-82-76-76; internet www.consistoire.org; f. 1808; 40,000 mems; Pres. MOÏSE COHEN; Chief Rabbi of Paris DAVID MESSAS; Chief Rabbi of the Consistoire Israélite de Paris ALAIN GOLDMANN.

Fonds social juif unifié (FSJF): Espace Rachi, 39 rue Broca, 75005 Paris; tel. 1-42-17-10-10; fax 1-42-17-10-45; e-mail fsju@col.fr; internet www.amyisrael.co.il/europe/france/fsju.htm; f. 1950; unites the principal organizations supporting Jewish cultural, educational and social activity in France, and seeks to establish closer links between French Jewry and Israel; Pres. DAVID DE ROTHSCHILD; Dir DAVID SAADA.

BAHÁ'Í FAITH

Centre National Bahá'í: 45 rue Pergolèse, 75116 Paris; tel. 1-45-00-90-26; internet www.bahai-fr.org.

BUDDHISM

World Federation of Buddhists, French Regional Centre: 98 chemin de la Calade, 06250 Mougins; Sec. TEISAN PERUSAT STORK.

The Press

Most major daily newspapers are owned by individual publishers or by the powerful groups that have developed round either a company or a single personality. The major groups are as follows:

Amaury Group: 25 ave Michelet, 93408 Saint Ouen Cédex; tel. 1-40-10-30-30; fax 1-40-11-15-26; owns *Le Parisien*, *Aujourd'hui en France*, the sports daily *L'Equipe*, the weeklies *L'Equipe Magazine* and *France-Football*, and the monthly *Vélo*; Man. Dir PHILIPPE AMAURY.

Bayard Presse: 3–5 rue Bayard, 75393 Paris Cédex 08; tel. 1-44-35-60-60; fax 1-44-35-61-61; e-mail communication@bayard-presse.com; internet www.bayardpresse.fr; f. 1873; Roman Catholic press group; owns 100 publs world-wide (43 within France), incl. the national *La Croix*, *Pèlerin Magazine*, *Panorama*, *Notre Temps* magazines for young people and the over 50s, and several specialized religious publications; Pres. ALAIN CORDIER.

Emap France: 19–21 rue Emile Duclaux, 92284 Suresnes Cédex; tel. 1-41-33-50-01; fax 1-41-33-57-19; internet www.emapfrance.com; fmrly Editions Mondiales; owns several popular magazines, incl. *Nous Deux*, *FHM*, *Studio*, *Télé-Star*, *Top Santé*, *Télé-Poche*, *Auto Plus* and also specialized magazines; Man. Dir ARNAUD DE PUYFONTAINE.

Hachette Filipacchi Médias (HFM): 149 rue Anatole-France, 92534 Levallois-Peret Cédex; tel. 1-41-34-60-00; e-mail commint@hfp.fr; internet www.hachette-filipacchi.com; f. 1999 by merger of Filipacchi Groupe and Hachette Groupe Presse; controls 42 magazines in France incl. *Paris-Match*, *Echo des Savanes*, *Pariscope*, *Jeune et Jolie*, *Photo*, *France-Dimanche*, *Elle*, *Télé 7 Jours* and holds stake in seven regional daily newspapers, including *Var Matin*; also owns 158 magazines world-wide; Pres. and Dir-Gen. GÉRALD DE ROQUEMAUREL.

Socpresse: 12 rue de Presbourg, 75116 Paris; one of the largest of the provincial daily press groups; fmrly Hersant Group; owns 20 dailies, numerous weeklies, fortnightlies and periodicals; dailies incl. *Le Progrès, Le Figaro, France-Soir, Le Dauphiné Libéré, Nord-Matin* and *Nord-Eclair*; acquired Groupe Express-Expansion in 2003; Chair. and Man. Dir YVES DE CHAISEMARTIN.

DAILY PAPERS (PARIS)

La Croix: 3–5 rue Bayard, 75393 Paris Cédex 08; tel. 1-44-35-60-60; fax 1-44-35-60-01; internet www.la-croix.com; f. 1883; Catholic; Dir BRUNO FRAPPAT; circ. 90,000 (2000).

Les Echos: 46 rue la Boétie, 75381 Paris Cédex 08; tel. 1-49-53-65-65; fax 1-45-61-48-92; internet www.lesechos.fr; f. 1908; economic and financial; Chair. DANIEL GUNAUEL; Editor NICOLAS BEYTOUT; circ. 153,048 (2001).

L'Equipe: 4 rue Rouget-de-l'Isle, 92130 Issy-les-Moulineaux Cédex; tel. 1-40-93-20-20; fax 1-40-93-20-08; e-mail emortureux@lequipe.fr; internet www.lequipe.fr; f. 1946; sport; Chair. LOUIS GILLET; Editorial Dir CLAUDE DROUSSENT; circ. 373,886 (2001).

Le Figaro: 37 rue du Louvre, 75002 Paris; tel. 1-42-21-62-00; fax 1-42-21-64-05; e-mail contact@lefigaro.fr; internet www.lefigaro.fr; f. 1828; morning; news and literary; magazine on Saturdays; three weekly supplements; Editor-in-Chief JEAN DE BELOT; circ. 372,661 (2001).

France-Soir: 37 rue du Louvre, 75002 Paris; tel. 1-44-82-87-00; f. 1941 as *Défense de la France*; present title adopted 1944; Dir PHILIPPE BOUVARD; circ. 87,000 (2001).

L'Humanité: 32 rue Jean Jaurès, 93528 Saint-Denis Cédex; tel. 1-49-22-72-72; fax 1-49-22-73-00; internet www.humanite.presse.fr; f. 1904 by Jean Jaurès; communist; morning; Dir PATRICK LE HYARIC; Editor-in-Chief PIERRE LAURENT.

International Herald Tribune: 6 bis rue des Graviers, 92521 Neuilly-sur-Seine Cédex; tel. 1-41-43-93-00; fax 1-41-43-93-38; e-mail iht@iht.com; internet www.iht.com; f. 1887; present name adopted 1966; 100% owned by The New York Times Co (USA); English language; Chief Exec. PETER GOLDMARK; Exec. Editor WALTER WELLS (acting); circ. 230,000.

Le Journal Officiel de la République Française: 26 rue Desaix, 75727 Paris Cédex 15; tel. 1-40-58-75-00; fax 1-45-79-17-84; e-mail info@journal-officiel.gouv.fr; internet www.journal-officiel.gouv.fr; f. 1870; official journal of the Government; publishes laws, decrees, parliamentary proceedings, and economic bulletins; Dir JEAN-PAUL BOLUFER.

Libération: 11 rue Béranger, 75154 Paris Cédex 03; tel. 1-42-76-17-89; fax 1-42-72-94-93; e-mail webmaster@liberation.fr; internet www.liberation.fr; f. 1973; 65%-owned by the Chargeurs group from 1996; independent; Pres. and Dir-Gen. EVENCE-CHARLES COPPÉE; Editorial Dir ANTOINE DE GAUDEMAR; circ. 174,310 (2001).

Le Monde: 21 bis rue Claude-Bernard, 75242 Paris Cédex 05; tel. 1-42-17-20-00; fax 1-42-17-21-21; e-mail lemonde@lemonde.fr; internet www.lemonde.fr; f. 1944; independent; Chair. of Supervisory Bd ALAIN MINC; Pres.and Dir. of Publication JEAN-MARIE COLOMBANI; Editorial Dir. EDWY PLENEL; circ. 415,323 (2001).

Paris-Turf: Société des Editions France Libre, 65 rue de Bercy, 75012 Paris; e-mail info@paris-turf.com; internet www.paris-turf .com; horse-racing; Editorial Dir FRANÇOIS HALLOPÉ; circ. 105,000 (2000).

Le Parisien: 25 ave Michelet, 93405 Saint-Ouen Cédex; tel. 1-40-10-30-30; fax 1-40-10-35-16; e-mail infoat@leparisien.fr; internet www.leparisien.fr; f. 1944; morning; sold in Paris area and surrounding départements; Man. Dir JACQUES GUERIN; Editorial Dir CHRISTIAN DE VILLENEUVE; circ. 367,892 (2001).

   Aujourd'hui en France: f. 1994; national version of *Le Parisien*; circ. 145,796 (2001).

Le Quotidien du Médecin: 140 rue Jules Guesde, 92593 Levallois-Perret Cédex; tel. 1-41-40-75-00; fax 1-41-40-75-75; e-mail quotidien@wanadoo.fr; internet www.quotimed.com; medical journal; Pres. and Dir-Gen. Dr GÉRARD KOUCHNER; Editorial Dir RICHARD LISCIA; circ. 82,000.

La Tribune: 46 rue Notre Dame des Victoires, 75095 Paris Cédex 02; tel. 1-44-82-16-16; fax 1-44-82-17-92; e-mail directiondelaredaction@latribune.fr; internet www.latribune.fr; economic and financial; Pres. and Dir-Gen. CHRISTIAN BREGOU; Editorial Dir PHILIPPE MUDRY; circ. 102,097 (2001).

SUNDAY PAPERS (PARIS)

Le Journal du Dimanche: 149 rue Anatole France, 92534 Levallois-Perret Cédex; tel. 1-41-34-60-00; fax 1-41-34-97-16; e-mail jcmaurice@hfp.fr; Dir JEAN-CLAUDE MAURICE; Editors-in-Chief CHRISTIAN SAUVAGE, PATRICE TRAPICK; circ. 303,000 (2002).

Le Parisien Dimanche: 25 ave Michelet, 93405 Saint Ouen Cédex; tel. 1-40-10-30-30; fax 1-40-10-35-16; e-mail infoat@leparisien.fr; internet www.leparisien.fr.

PRINCIPAL PROVINCIAL DAILY PAPERS

Amiens

Le Courrier Picard: 29 rue de la République, BP 1021, 80010 Amiens Cédex 01; tel. 3-22-82-60-00; fax 3-22-82-60-12; e-mail jquemere@courier-picard.fr; internet www.courier-picard.fr; f. 1944; Chair./Man. DOMINIQUE FONTAINE; Editor-in-Chief FRANÇOIS PERRIER; circ. 72,820 (2001).

Angers

Le Courrier de l'Ouest: 4 blvd Albert Blanchoin, BP 728, 49007 Angers Cédex 01; tel. 2-41-68-86-88; fax 2-41-44-31-43; f. 1944; Pres. and Man. Dir CHRISTIAN COUSTAL; Editor-in-Chief JACQUES BOSSEAU; circ. 103,202 (2001).

Angoulême

La Charente Libre: ZI No 3, BP 1025, 16001 Angoulême Cédex; tel. 5-45-94-16-00; fax 5-45-94-16-19; e-mail charente@charente.com; internet www.charentelibre.com; Pres. and Man. Dir MICHEL LÉPINAY; Editors-in-Chief JEAN-LOUIS HERVOIS, JACQUES GUYON; circ. 40,142 (2001).

Auxerre

L'Yonne Républicaine: 8-12 ave Jean Moulin, 89025 Auxerre; tel. 3-86-49-52-00; fax 3-86-46-99-90; e-mail gdelorme@lyonne-republicaine.fr; internet www.lyonne-republicaine.fr; f. 1944; Dir-Gen. JOËL LOUBERT; Editor-in-Chief GÉRARD DELORME; circ. 44,496 (2001).

Bordeaux

Sud-Ouest: 101 place J. Lemoine, 33094 Bordeaux Cédex; tel. 5-56-00-33-33; fax 5-56-00-33-01; e-mail contact@sudouest.com; internet www.sudouest.com; f. 1944; independent; Chair./Man. Dir PIERRE JEANTET; Editor-in-Chief PATRICK VENRIES; circ. 344,837 (2001).

Chalon-sur-Saône

Le Journal de Saône-et-Loire: 9 rue des Tonneliers, BP 134, 71100 Chalon-sur-Saône; tel. 3-85-44-68-68; fax 3-85-93-02-96; e-mail jslmediatheque@le-journal-de-saone-et-loire.fr; internet jsl .sdv.fr; f. 1826; Dir FRANÇOIS PRETET; circ. 83,000 (2000).

Chartres

L'Echo Républicain: 37 rue de Châteaudun, BP 189, 28000 Chartres; f. 1929; Pres. and Dir-Gen. JACQUES CAMUS; Sec.-Gen. J. P. COUSIN; circ. 35,000.

Clermont-Ferrand

La Montagne: 28 rue Morel Ladeuil, BP 83, 63000 Clermont-Ferrand Cédex 1; tel. 4-73-17-17-17; fax 4-73-17-18-19; e-mail lamontagne@centrefrance.com; f. 1919; independent; Man. Dir JEAN-PIERRE CAILLARD; Editor-in-Chief JEAN-LOUP MANOUSSI; circ. 220,494 (2001).

Dijon

Le Bien Public-Les Dépêches: 7 blvd du Chanoine Kir, BP 550, 21015 Dijon Cédex; tel. 3-80-42-42-42; fax 3-80-42-42-40; e-mail redaction@lebienpublic.fr; internet www.bienpublic.fr; f. 1850 as Le Bien Public; merged with Les Dépêches 2001; Dir-Gen. FRANÇOIS PRETET; Editor-in-Chief JEAN-LOUIS PIERRE; circ. 56,268 (2001).

Epinal

Liberté de l'Est: 40 quai des Bons Enfants, 88026 Epinal Cédex 07; tel. 3-29-82-98-00; fax 3-29-82-99-29; e-mail contact@lalibertedelest .fr; internet www.lalibertedelest.fr; f. 1945; Chair./Man. Dir ALAIN GARROUY; Editor-in-Chief GÉRARD NOEL; circ. 30,630 (1998).

Grenoble

Le Dauphiné Libéré: Les Iles-Cordées, 38913 Veurey-Voroize Cédex; tel. 4-76-88-71-00; fax 4-76-88-70-96; e-mail redaction@ledauphine.com; internet www.ledauphinelibere.com; f. 1945; Chair./Man. Dir/Editor-in-Chief HENRI-PIERRE GUILBERT; circ. 268,379 (2001).

Lille

La Voix du Nord: 8 place du Général de Gaulle, BP 549, 59023 Lille Cédex; tel. 3-20-78-40-40; fax 3-20-78-42-44; e-mail webvdn@ lavoixdunord.fr; internet www.lavoixdunord.fr; f. 1944; Chair./Man. Dir JEAN-LOUIS PRÉVOST; Editor-in-Chief PHILIPPE CARON; circ. 330,070 (2001).

Limoges

L'Echo du Centre: 29 rue C. H. Gorceix, 87022 Limoges Cédex 9; tel. 5-55-04-49-99; fax 5-55-04-49-78; f. 1943; five edns; Communist; Man. Dir CHRISTIAN AUDOUIN; Editor-in-Chief BERNARD CUNY; circ. 26,853 (2001).

Le Populaire du Centre: 7 rue du Général Catroux, BP 541, 87011 Limoges Cédex; tel. 5-55-58-59-60; fax 5-55-58-69-79; f. 1905; Chair./Man. Dir MARCEL TOURLONIAS; Editor-in-Chief SERGE JOFFRE; circ. 50,842 (2001).

Lyon

Le Progrès: 93 ave du Progrès, 69680 Chassieu; tel. 4-72-22-23-23; fax 4-78-90-52-40; internet www.leprogres.fr; f. 1859; Pres. and Dir-Gen. MICHEL NOZIÈRE; Editor-in-Chief JEAN PAUL LARDY; circ. 272,728 (2001).

Le Mans

Le Maine Libre: 28–30 place de l'Eperon, BP 299, 72013 Le Mans Cédex; tel. 2-43-83-72-50; fax 2-43-83-72-59; Chair./Man. Dir GÉRARD CHOL; Editor-in-Chief RAYMOND MAUDET; circ. 50,368 (2001).

Marseille

La Marseillaise: 19 cours Honoré d'Estienne d'Orves, BP 1862, 13222 Marseille Cédex 01; tel. 4-91-57-75-00; fax 4-91-57-75-25; f. 1944; Communist; Man. Dir PAUL BIAGGINI; Editor-in-Chief CHRISTIAN DIGNE; circ. 78,900 (2001).

MarseillePlus: 248 ave Roger-Salengro, 13015 Marseille; tel. 4-91-84-00-00; e-mail redaction@marseilleplus.com; internet www .marseilleplus.com; f. 2002; Mon.–Fri. mornings; distributed free of charge.

La Provence: 248 ave Roger-Salengro, 13015 Marseille; tel. 4-91-84-45-45; fax 4-91-84-49-95; e-mail redaction@laprovence-presse.fr; internet www.laprovence-presse.fr; f. 1996 following merger of *Le Provençal* with *Le Méridional*; Chair./Man. Dir GHISLAIN LELEU; Editor-in-Chief LAURENT GILARDINO; circ. 176,070 (2001).

Metz

Le Républicain Lorrain: 3 ave des Deux Fontaines, 57777 Metz Cédex 9; tel. 3-87-34-17-89; fax 3-87-33-28-18; e-mail pm.pernet@ republicain-lorrain.fr; internet www.republicain-lorrain.fr; f. 1919; independent; Chair. CLAUDE PUHL; Editor-in-Chief MAURICE PADIOU; circ. 172,994 (2001).

Montpellier

Midi-Libre: 'Le Mas de la Grille', 34063 Montpellier Cédex 02; tel. 4-67-07-67-07; fax 4-67-07-68-13; internet www.midilibre.fr; f. 1944; Pres. and Man. Dir NOËL-JEAN BERGEROUX; Editor-in-Chief ALAIN PLOMBAT; circ. 168,312 (2001).

Morlaix

Le Télégramme: 7 voie d'Accès au Port, BP 243, 29205 Morlaix Cédex; tel. 2-98-62-11-33; fax 2-98-88-76-65; e-mail telegramme@ bretagne-online.com; internet www.letelegramme.com; f. 1944; fmrly Le Télégramme de Brest et de l'Ouest; Pres. and Man. Dir EDOUARD COUDURIER; Editor-in-Chief JEAN-CLAUDE CASSENAC; circ. 195,042 (2001).

Mulhouse

L'Alsace: 18 rue de Thann, 68945 Mulhouse Cédex 9; tel. 3-89-32-70-00; fax 3-89-32-11-26; e-mail redaction@alsapresse.com; internet www.alsapresse.com; f. 1944; Chair. JEAN-DOMINIQUE PRETET; Editor-in-Chief JEAN-MARIE HAEFFELLE; circ. 117,371 (2001).

Nancy

L'Est Républicain: rue Théophraste-Renaudot, Nancy Houdemont, 54185 Heillecourt Cédex; tel. 3-83-59-80-54; fax 3-83-59-80-13; e-mail er-secretariat-general@wanadoo.fr; internet www .estrepublican.fr; f. 1889; Chair./Man. Dir GÉRARD LIGNAC; Editor-in-Chief PIERRE TARIBO; circ. 217,002 (2001).

Nantes

Presse Océan: 5 rue Santeuil, BP 22418, 44024 Nantes Cédex 1; tel. 2-40-44-24-00; fax 2-40-44-24-59; f. 1944; Chair. CHRISTIAN COUSTAL; Editor-in-Chief JEAN-PIERRE CHAMPIAT; circ. 58,522 (2001).

Nevers

Le Journal du Centre: 3 rue du Chemin de Fer, BP 106, 58001 Nevers; tel. 3-86-71-45-00; fax 3-86-71-45-20; e-mail lejournalducentre@centrefrance.com; f. 1943; Man. Dir LOUIS COTTIER; Editor-in-Chief FRANÇOIS GILARDI; circ. 34231 (2001).

Nice

Nice-Matin: 214 route de Grenoble, BP 4, 06290 Nice Cédex 3; tel. 4-93-18-28-38; fax 4-93-83-93-97; internet www.nicematin.fr; f. 1945; Chair./Man. Dir MICHEL COMBOUL; Editor-in-Chief HUBERT PERRIN; circ. 287,538 (2001, including regional editions, *Corse-Matin* and *Var-Matin*.

Orléans

La République du Centre: 31 rue de la Hatte, BP 93035, 45403 Fleury-les-Aubrais Cédex; tel. 2-38-78-79-80; fax 2-38-78-79-79; f. 1944; Chair./Man. Dir JACQUES CAMUS; Editor-in-Chief DENIS LEGER; circ. 57,784 (2001).

Perpignan

L'Indépendant: 'Le Mas de la Garrigue', 2 ave Alfred Sauvy, 66605 Rivesaltes Cédex; tel. 4-68-64-88-88; fax 4-68-64-88-38; e-mail redaction.steno@lindependant.com; f. 1846; also **Indépendant-Dimanche** (Sunday); Dir-Gen. YVES CHAVANON; circ. 82,595.

Reims

L'Union: 5 rue de Talleyrand, 51083 Reims Cédex; tel. 3-26-50-50-50; fax 3-26-50-51-69; e-mail dirgen@journal-lunion.fr; internet www.lunion.presse.fr; f. 1944; Chair. DANIEL HUTIER; Editor-in-Chief THIERRY DE CABARRUS; circ. 124,250 (2001).

Rennes

Ouest-France: 10 rue du Breil, 35051 Rennes Cédex 09; tel. 2-99-32-60-00; fax 2-99-32-60-25; internet www.ouest-france.fr; f. 1944; publ. by non-profit making Société civile pour le soutien des principes de la démocratie humaniste; 42 local editions (weekdays), 9 editions (Sundays); the largest circulation of any daily newspaper in France; Chair./Man. Dir FRANÇOIS-RÉGIS HUTIN; Editor-in-Chief DIDIER PILLET; circ. 796,376 (weekdays—2001), 252,010 (Sundays—2001).

Roubaix

Nord-Eclair: 42 rue du Général Sarrail, 59052 Roubaix Cédex 1; tel. 3-20-25-02-50; fax 3-20-82-83-63; f. 1944; Chair./Man. Dir MICHEL PROUVOT; Editor-in-Chief ANDRÉ FARINE; circ. 60,231 (2001).

Rouen

Paris-Normandie: 19 place du Général de Gaulle, BP 563, 76187 Rouen Cédex; tel. 2-35-14-56-56; fax 2-35-14-56-15; internet www .paris-normandie.com; f. 1944; Chair./Man. Dir PHILIPPE HERSANT; Editor-in-Chief GILLES DAUXERRE; circ. 85,539 (2001).

Strasbourg

Les Dernières Nouvelles d'Alsace: 17–21 rue de la Nuée Bleue, BP 406/R1, 67077 Strasbourg Cédex; tel. 3-88-21-55-00; fax 3-88-21-56-41; e-mail dnasug@sdv.fr; internet www.dna.fr; f. 1877; non-party; Chair./Man. Dir GÉRARD LIGNAC; Editor-in-Chief ALAIN HOWILLER; circ. 206,684 (2001).

Toulon

Var Matin: 214 route de Grenoble, BP 4, 06290 Nice Cédex 3; tel. 4-94-06-91-91; fax 4-94-63-49-98; internet www.varmatin.com; f. 1975; Pres. and Dir-Gen. MICHEL COMBOUL; Editorial Dir PATRICK ANDRIEU; circ. 93,000.

Toulouse

La Dépêche du Midi: ave Jean Baylet, 31095 Toulouse Cédex; tel. 5-62-11-33-00; fax 5-61-44-74-74; internet www.ladepeche.com; f. 1870; Chair./Man. Dir JEAN-MICHEL BAYLET; Editors-in-Chief GUY-MICHEL EMPOCIELLO, HENRI AMAR; circ. 214,067 (2001).

Tours

La Nouvelle République du Centre-Ouest: 232 ave de Grammont, 37048 Tours Cédex; tel. 2-47-31-70-00; fax 2-47-31-70-70; e-mail admin@nrco.com; internet www.nrco.com; f. 1944; non-party; Pres. JACQUES SAINT-CRICQ; Editor-in-Chief PASCAL ARNAUD; circ. 249,266 (2001).

Troyes

L'Est-Eclair: 71 ave du Maréchal Leclerc, 10120 St André les Vergers; tel. 3-25-71-75-75; fax 3-25-79-58-54; e-mail redaction@lest-eclair.fr; f. 1945; Dir François Le Saché; circ. 33,000.

SELECTED PERIODICALS

General, Current Affairs and Politics

Annales—Histoire, Sciences sociales: 54 blvd Raspail, 75006 Paris; tel. 1-49-54-23-77; fax 1-49-54-26-88; e-mail annales@ehess .fr; f. 1929; every 2 months.

Armées d'Aujourd'hui: Délégation à l'Information et à la Communication de la Défense, BP 33, 00445 Armées; tel. 1-44-42-48-93; fax 1-44-42-31-42; e-mail adamag@caramail.com; 10 a year; military and technical; produced by the Délégation à l'Information et à la Communication de la Défense; circ. 100,000.

Le Canard Enchaîné: 173 rue Saint Honoré, 75051 Paris Cédex 01; tel. 1-42-60-31-36; fax 1-42-27-97-87; f. 1915; weekly; political satire; Dir Michel Gaillard; circ. 520,000.

Commentaire: 116 rue du Bac, 75007 Paris; tel. 1-45-49-37-82; fax 1-45-44-32-18; e-mail infos@commentaire.fr; internet www .commentaire.fr; f. 1978; quarterly; Dir Jean-Claude Casanova.

Courrier International: 64–68 rue du Dessous-des-Berges, 75647 Paris Cédex 13; tel. 1-46-46-16-00; fax 1-46-46-16-01; e-mail communication@courrierinternational.com; internet www .courrierint.com; f. 1990; weekly; current affairs and political; Pres. and Editorial Dir. Philippe Thureau-Dangin; circ. 143,000 (2001).

L'Evénement: 32 rue René Boulanger, 75467 Paris Cédex 10; tel. 1-53-72-00-00; f. 1984 as L'Evénement du jeudi; weekly; current affairs; Dir Jean-François Kahn; Editor-in-Chief Bernard Poulet; circ. 169,820 (1998).

L'Express: 17 rue de l'Arrivée, 75733 Paris Cédex 15; tel. 1-53-91-11-11; fax 1-53-91-12-05; e-mail dired@lexpress.fr; internet www .lexpress.fr; f. 1953; weekly; Dir Denis Jeambar.

L'Humanité Hebdo: 32 rue Jean Jaurès, 93528 Saint-Denis Cedex; tel. 1-49-22-72-72; fax 1-49-22-73-00; current affairs; Editor Martine Bulard.

Ici-Paris: 10 rue Thierry le Luron, 92592 Levallois-Perret Cédex; tel. 1-49-53-49-53; fax 1-42-89-31-78; f. 1941; weekly; Dir Ghislain Le Leu; Editor Robert Madjar; circ. 372,386.

Marianne: 32 rue René Boulanger, 75484 Paris Cédex 10; tel. 1-53-72-29-00; fax 1-53-72-29-72; e-mail journal@marianne-en-ligne.fr; internet www.marianne-en-ligne.fr; f. 1997; weekly; current affairs; Dir Jean-François Kahn; Editorial Dir Laurent Neumann.

Le Monde Diplomatique: 1 ave Stephen Pichon, 75013 Paris; tel. 1-53-94-96-15; fax 1-53-94-96-26; e-mail secretariat@monde-diplomatique.fr; internet www.monde-diplomatique.fr; f. 1954; international affairs; Dir Ignacio Ramonet; circ. 210,000 (2001).

Le Nouvel Observateur: 10–12 place de la Bourse, 75002 Paris; tel. 1-44-88-34-34; e-mail direction@nouvelobs.com; internet permanent.nouvelobs.com; f. 1964; weekly; left-wing political and literary; Chair. Claude Perdriel; Dir Jean Daniel; circ. 432,433.

Paris-Match: 151 rue Anatole-France, 92598 Levallois-Perret Cédex; tel. 1-41-34-62-43; fax 1-41-34-75-29; e-mail lesommire@parismatch.com; internet www.parismatch.com; f. 1949; weekly; magazine of French and world affairs; Gen. Dir. Alain Genestar; Editor-in-Chief Gilles Martin Chauffier; circ. 776,700.

Passages: 17 rue Simone Weil, 75013 Paris; tel. 1-45-86-30-02; fax 1-44-23-98-24; e-mail passages@club-internet.fr; internet perso .club-internet.fr/passages; f. 1987; 6 a year; multidisciplinary discussions of geostrategic issues, seeking to present major contemporary events in an ethical and historical perspective; Dir Emile Malet; circ. 75,000.

Le Peuple: 263 rue de Paris, Case 432, 93514 Montreuil Cédex; tel. 1-48-18-83-05; fax 1-48-59-28-31; e-mail lepeuple@cgt.fr; internet www.lepeuple-cgt.com; f. 1921; fortnightly; official organ of the Confédération Générale du Travail (trade union confederation); Dir Daniel Prada; Editor-in-Chief Françoise Duchesne.

Le Point: 74 ave du Maine, 75014 Paris; tel. 1-44-10-10-10; fax 1-43-21-43-24; e-mail courrier@lepoint.tm.fr; internet www.lepoint.fr; f. 1972; weekly; politics and current affairs; Man. Dir Bernard Wouts; Editor-in-Chief Michel Colomes; circ. 339,331.

Point de Vue: 142 rue du Bac, 75007 Paris; tel. 1-44-39-11-11; fax 1-42-84-17-34; e-mail contact@pointdevue.fr; internet www .pointdevue.fr; weekly; general illustrated; Dir and Editor Laure Boulay de la Meurthe; circ. 370,311.

Politique Internationale: 11 rue du Bois de Boulogne, 75116 Paris; tel. 1-45-00-15-26; fax 1-45-00-38-79; f. 1978; quarterly; Dir and Editor-in-Chief Patrick Wajsman.

Regards: 120 rue Lafayette, 75010 Paris; tel. 1-49-49-08-49; e-mail regards@regards.fr; internet www.regards.fr; monthly; communist, politics, current affairs, culture; Editor-in-Chief Jackie Viruega.

Revue 'Défense Nationale': Ecole Militaire, 1 place Joffre, 75325 Paris Cédex 07; tel. 1-44-42-31-90; fax 1-44-42-31-89; e-mail redac@rdn.com.fr; internet www.rdn.com.fr; f. 1939; monthly; publ. by Committee for Study of National Defence; military, economic, political and scientific problems; Chair. Gen. Quesnot; Editor Adm. Girard.

Revue des Deux Mondes: 97 rue de Lille, 75007 Paris; tel. 1-47-53-61-92; fax 1-47-53-61-98; e-mail contact@revuedesdeuxmondes.fr; internet www.revuedesdeuxmondes.fr; f. 1829; monthly; current affairs; Dir. Véronique Morali; Editor-in-Chief Michel Crepu.

Rivarol: 1 rue St Hauteville, 75010 Paris; tel. 1-53-34-97-97; fax 1-53-34-97-98; e-mail galic@rivarol.com; internet www.rivarol.com; f. 1951; weekly; conservative, political, literary and satirical; Dir and Editor-in-Chief Camille-Marie Galic; circ. 12,000.

Technikart: 156/2 rue de la Roquette, 75011 Paris; tel. 1-43-14-36-08; e-mail redaction@technikart.com; internet www.technikart.com; monthly; cultural review; Dir Thomas Coutheillas; Editor-in-Chief Nicolas Santolaria.

La Vie: 163 blvd Malesherbes, 75859 Paris Cédex 17; tel. 1-48-88-46-00; fax 1-48-88-46-01; e-mail vie.forum@mp.com.fr; internet www .lavie.presse.fr; f. 1945; weekly; general, Christian; Editorial Dir Max Armanet; circ. 218,000 (2001).

VSD (Vendredi-Samedi-Dimanche): 15 rue Galvani, 75809 Paris Cédex 17; tel. 1-56-99-47-00; fax 1-56-99-51-28; e-mail lecteurs@vsd .fr; internet www.vsd.fr; f. 1977; weekly; current affairs, leisure; Editors-in-Chief Marc Dolisi, Christian Moguerou; circ. 225,238 (1999).

The Arts

L'Architecture d'Aujourd'hui: 6 rue Lhomond, 75005 Paris; tel. 1-44-32-18-66; e-mail sowa@jmplace.com; internet www .architecture-aujourdhui.presse.fr; f. 1930; publ. by Editions J-M. Place; Editor-in-Chief Axel Sowa; circ. 16,000.

Art et Décoration: 16–18 rue de l'Amiral Mouchez, 75686 Paris Cédex 14; tel. 1-45-65-48-48; e-mail info@art-decoration.fr; internet www.art-decoration.fr; f. 1897; 8 a year; Dir Jean Massin; Editor-in-Chief Daniel Soubeyrand; circ. 451,443.

Critique: 7 rue Bernard Palissy, 75006 Paris; tel. 1-45-44-23-16; fax 1-42-84-08-63; f. 1946; monthly; general review of French and foreign literature, philosophy, art, social sciences and history; Dir Philippe Roger; Editor Isabelle Chave.

Diapason: 9–13 rue du Col Pierre Avia, 75754 Paris Cédex 15; tel. 1-46-62-20-00; fax 1-46-62-25-33; f. 1956; monthly; classical music; Pres. and Dir-Gen. Claude Pommereau; Editor-in-Chief Yves Petit de Voize; circ. 70,000.

Esprit: 212 rue St. Martin, 75003 Paris; tel. 1-48-04-92-90; fax 1-48-04-50-53; e-mail redaction@esprit.presse.fr; internet www.esprit .presse.fr; f. 1932; 10 a year; philosophy, history, sociology; Dir Olivier Mongin; Editor-in-Chief Marc-Olivier Padis.

Gazette des Beaux-Arts: 140 rue du Faubourg Saint Honoré, 75008 Paris; tel. 1-45-61-61-70; fax 1-45-61-61-71; e-mail gazette.des .beaux.arts@wanadoo.fr; f. 1859; monthly; the oldest review of the history of art; Dir Guy Wildenstein.

Les Inrockuptibles: 144 rue du Rivoli, 75001 Paris; tel. 1-42-44-16-16; fax 1-42-44-16-00; e-mail mediator@inrocks.com; internet www.lesinrocks.com; weekly; music, cinema, literature; Editorial Dir Christian Fevret.

Lire: BP 38, 33 ave du Maine, 75755 Paris Cédex 15; tel. 1-53-91-11-11; fax 1-53-91-11-04; internet www.lire.fr; f. 1975; monthly; literary review; Editorial Dir Pierre Assouline; circ. 120,000 (2001).

Livres-Hebdo: 35 rue Grégoire-de-Tours, 75006 Paris; tel. 1-44-41-28-00; fax 1-43-29-77-85; e-mail livreshebdo@electre.com; f. 1979; 46 a year; Editor-in-Chief Pierre-Louis Rozynès.

Livres de France: 35 rue Grégoire de Tours, 75006 Paris; tel. 1-44-41-28-00; fax 1-43-29-77-85; f. 1979; 11 a year; Dir Jean-Marie Doublet.

Magazine littéraire: 40 rue des Saints-Pères, 75007 Paris; tel. 1-45-44-14-51; fax 1-45-48-86-36; e-mail magazine@magazine-litteraire.com; internet www.magazine-litteraire.com; f. 1966; monthly; literature; Dir Nicky Fasquelle; Editor Jean-Louis Hue; circ. 100,000.

Le Matricule des Anges: BP 225, 34004 Montpellier Cédex; tel. and fax 4-67-92-29-33; e-mail lmda@lmda.net; internet www.lmda .net; f. 1992; literary criticism; Editor THIERRY GUICHARD.

Le Monde de l'Education: 21 bis rue Claude-Bernard, 75242 Paris Cédex 05; tel. 1-42-17-20-00; fax 1-42-17-21-21; e-mail roulier@ lemonde.fr; internet www.lemonde.fr/mde; f. 1974; monthly; education; Editor-in-Chief BRIGITTE PERUCCA; circ. 40,000.

Poétique: Editions du Seuil, 27 rue Jacob, 75261 Paris Cédex 06; tel. 1-40-46-50-50; fax 1-40-46-51-43; f. 1970; quarterly; literary review.

La Quinzaine Littéraire: 135 rue Saint-Martin, 75194, Paris Cédex 04; tel. 1-48-87-75-87; fax 1-48-87-13-01; e-mail selis@ wanadoo.fr; internet www.quinzaine-litteraire.net; f. 1966; fortnightly; Dir MAURICE NADEAU; circ. 20,000.

La République Internationale des Lettres: 11 Rue du Clos, 75020 Paris; e-mail editeur@republique-des-lettres.com; internet www.republique-des-lettres.com; f. 1994; monthly; literature; Dir and Editor NOËL BLANDIN; circ. 20,000.

Les Temps Modernes: 4 rue Férou, 75006 Paris; tel. 1-43-29-08-47; fax 1-40-51-83-38; f. 1945 by J.-P. Sartre; four a year; literary review; publ. by Gallimard; Dir CLAUDE LANZMANN.

Economic and Financial

Challenges: 10–12 place de la Bourse, 75002 Paris; e-mail redaction@challenges.fr; internet www.challenges-eco.com; fortnightly; economics and politics; Chair. CLAUDE PERDRIEL.

L'Expansion: 14 blvd Poissonnière, 75308 Paris Cédex 09; tel. 1-53-24-40-40; fax 1-53-24-41-04; internet www.lexpansion.com; f. 1967; monthly; economics and business; Editorial Dir GEORGES VALANCE; circ. 147,602 (2000).

Marchés Tropicaux et Méditerranéens: 11 rue du Faubourg Poissonnière, 75009 Paris; tel. 1-49-49-07-49; fax 1-49-49-07-45; e-mail webmaster-mtm@moreux.fr; internet www .marches-tropicaux.com; f. 1945; weekly; analysis and information on Africa and the Indian Ocean and on tropical products; Pres. SERGE MARPAUD; Editor SÉBASTIEN DE DIANOUS.

Mieux Vivre Votre Argent: 32 rue Notre-Dame-des-Victoires, 75002 Paris; tel. 1-53-00-20-00; fax 1-42-33-44-98; e-mail jpviallon@ mieuxvivre.fr; internet www.mieuxvivre.fr; monthly; f. 1918; investment, economics; Editorial Dir JEAN-ANTOINE BOUCHEZ; Editor-in-Chief FRANÇOIS DE WITT; circ. 257,994 (2001).

Le Monde-Initiatives: 46 rue du Fer à Moulin, 75005 Paris; tel. 1-55-43-69-00; fax 1-55-43-69-19; e-mail sec.ini2@lemonde.fr; f. 2002; monthly; Dir ALAIN LEBAUBE; circ. 50,000 (2002).

Le Nouvel Economiste: 10 rue du Faubourg Montmartre, 75009 Paris; tel. 1-55-33-30-00; fax 1-55-33-30-31; e-mail abonnements@ nouveleco.com; internet www.nouveleco.com; f. 1975; two a month; Pres. and Dir-Gen.. CLAUDE POSTERNAK; Editorial Dir YANNICK LE BOURDONNEC; circ. 117,090.

L'Usine Nouvelle: 12–14 rue Médéric 75815 Paris Cédex 17; tel. 1-56-79-41-00; fax 1-56-79-42-34; internet www.usinenouvelle.com; f. 1945; weekly; technical and industrial journal; Dir JEAN-LÉON VANDOOME; Editor-in-Chief JEAN-LOUIS MARROU; circ. 63,100 (2002).

Valeurs Actuelles: 10 place du Général Catroux, 75858 Paris Cédex 17; tel. 1-40-54-11-00; fax 1-40-54-12-85; internet www .valeursactuelles.com; f. 1966; weekly; politics, economics, international affairs; Editor FRANÇOIS D'ORCIVAL; circ. 100,000.

La Vie Financière: 14 blvd Poissonnière, 75308 Paris Cédex 09; tel. 1-53-24-40-40; fax 1-53-24-41-10; e-mail jl.champetier@ groupe-expansion.com; internet www.laviefinanciere.com; f. 1945; weekly; economics and finance; Publishing Dir DENIS JEAMBAR; Editorial Dir NASSER OUZEGDOUH; circ. 98,623 (2001).

History and Geography

Annales de géographie: 21 rue de Montparnasse, 75298 Paris; tel. 1-44-39-51-24; fax 1-40-46-62-21; e-mail dazzarotti@vuef.fr; f. 1891; every 2 months.

Cahiers de civilisation médiévale: 24 rue de la Chaine, 86022 Poitiers; tel. 5-49-45-45-63; fax 5-49-45-45-73; e-mail marie-helene .debies@mshs-univ-poitiers.fr; f. 1958; quarterly; pluri-disciplinary medieval studies, concentrating on the 10th–12th centuries; Dir MARTIN AURELL; circ. 1,500 (2002).

La Géographie: 184 blvd Saint Germain, 75006 Paris; tel. 1-45-48-54-62; fax 1-42-22-40-93; e-mail socgeo@socgeo.org; internet www .socgeo.org; f. 1821; quarterly of the Société de Géographie; Chair. JEAN BASTIÉ.

L'Histoire: 4 rue de Texel, 75014 Paris; tel. 1-40-47-44-00; fax 1-40-47-44-40; e-mail courrier@histoire.presse.fr; internet www.histoire .presse.fr; f. 1978; monthly; Dir-Gen. STÉPHANE KHÉMIS; Editor-in-Chief VALÉRIE HANNIN.

Historia: 74 ave du Maire, 75014 Paris; tel. 1-44-10-12-90; fax 1-44-10-12-94; e-mail pczete@tallandier.fr; internet www.historia.presse .fr; f. 1909; monthly; Dirs BERNARD WOUTS; circ. 104,097.

Revue d'histoire diplomatique: 13 rue Soufflot, 75005 Paris; tel. 1-43-54-05-97; fax 1-46-34-07-60; f. 1887; quarterly; Dirs MAURICE VAISSE, GEORGES-HENRI SOUTOU.

Revue Historique: Archives Nationales, 60 rue des Francs Bourgeois, 75003 Paris; f. 1876; quarterly; Dirs CLAUDE GAUVARD, JEAN-FRANÇOIS SIRINELLI.

Revue de synthèse: Centre International de Synthèse, 4 rue Lhomand, 75005 Paris; tel. 1-55-42-83-11; fax 1-55-42-83-19; e-mail revuedesynthese@ens.fr; f. 1900; quarterly; anthropology, economics, social sciences; Dir ERIC BRIAN.

Leisure Interests and Sport

Cahiers du Cinéma: 9 passage de la Boule-Blanche, 75012 Paris; tel. 1-53-44-75-75; fax 1-43-43-95-04; e-mail courrier@ cahiersducinema.com; internet www.cahiersducinema.com; f. 1951; monthly; film reviews; Editors-in-Chief CHARLES TESSON, JEAN-MARC LALANNE; circ. 30,000 (2002).

Le Chasseur Français: 19 rue d'Orléans, 92200 Neuilly-sur-Seine; tel. 1-41-43-42-00; fax 1-41-43-42-90; internet www .lechasseurfrancais.com; f. 1885; monthly; hunting, shooting, fishing; Dir JEAN-MARIE SIMON; Editor THIERRY MASSÉ; circ. 552,461 (2000).

France-Football: 4 rue Rouget de Lisle, 92793 Issy-les-Moulineaux Cédex 9; tel. 1-40-93-20-20; fax 1-40-93-24-05; f. 1947; twice weekly; owned by Amaury Group; Editor GÉRARD ERNAULT; circ. 230,000 (Tues.), 135,000 (Fri.—2002).

Pariscope: 149 ave Anatole France, 92534 Levallois-Perret Cédex; tel. 1-41-34-43-47; fax 1-41-34-78-30; internet www.pariscope.fr; f. 1965; listings and reviews of events in Paris and Ile-de-France; weekly; Dir-Gen. ANNE-MARIE COUDERC; Editorial Dir PASCALE DACBERT-LEMAIRE; circ. 125,300.

Photo: 149 rue Anatole France, 92534 Levallois-Perret; tel. 1-41-34-73-27; fax 1-41-34-71-52; e-mail photo@hfp.fr; internet www.photo .fr; f. 1967; monthly; specialist photography magazine; circ. 87,400; Editorial Dir ERIC COLMET-DAAGE.

Télépoche: 19–21 rue Emile Duclaux, 92284 Suresnes; tel. 1-41-33-50-02; fax 1-41-33-57-48; e-mail felix.droissart@emw.fr; internet www.telepoche.fr; f. 1966; weekly; publ. by EMAP France; TV; Pres. and Dir-Gen. ARNAUD ROY DE PUYFONTAINE; Editor FÉLIX DROISSART; circ. 1,027,240 (2002).

Vélo Magazine: 4 rue Rouget de Lisle, 92793 Issy-les-Moulineaux; tel. 1-40-93-20-20; fax 1-40-93-20-09; e-mail velomag@lequipe .presse.fr; monthly; cycling; Editorial Dir CLAUDE DROUSSENT.

Voiles et Voiliers: 13 rue du Breil, 35063 Rennes Cédex; tel. 2-99-32-58-80; fax 2-99-41-89-57; internet www.voilesetvoiliers.com; monthly; sailing and nautical sports; publ. by Ouest-France group; Dir. CHARLES DE FREMINVILLE; circ. 70,388 (2001).

Maritime

Le Droit Maritime Français: 190 blvd Haussmann, 75008 Paris; tel. 1-44-95-99-50; fax 1-42-89-08-72; f. 1949; monthly; maritime law; Editor STÉPHANE MIRIBEL.

Le Journal de la Marine Marchande et du Transport Multimodal: 1 ave Edouard Belion, 92500 Rueil-Malmaison; tel. 1-41-29-75-95; fax 1-41-29-75-98; e-mail marine-marchande@groupeliaisons .fr; f. 1919; weekly shipping publication; Pres. S. TSCHANZ; Editor-in-Chief M. AYSONNAVE.

Le Marin: 13 rue du Breil, 35063 Rennes Cédex; tel. 2-99-32-58-80; fax 2-99-41-89-57; internet www.lemarin.fr; f. 1946; weekly; publ. by Infomer; subsidiary of Ouest-France group; Dir-Gen. RODOLPHE DE LOYNES; Editor-in-Chief YANN BESSOULE; circ. 13,203 (2001).

Religion and Philosophy

Actualité des Religions: 163 blvd Malesherbes, 75017 Paris; tel. 1-48-88-46-00; fax 1-42-27-04-19; e-mail actualite.religions@mpfr .com; f. 1999; Editor JEAN-PAUL GUETNY; circ. 40,000.

Actualité Juive: 14 rue Raymond Salez, 93260 Les Lilas; tel. 1-43-60-20-20; fax 1-43-60-20-21; e-mail info@actuj.com; internet www .actuj.com; Dir SERGE BENATTAR.

Études: 14 rue d'Assas, 75006 Paris; tel. 1-44-39-48-48; fax 1-44-39-48-17; e-mail etudes@free.fr; internet perso.wanadoo.fr/ assas-editions; f. 1856; monthly; general interest; Editor-in-Chief HENRI MADELIN.

France Catholique: 60 rue de Fontenay, 92350 Le Plessis Robinson; tel. 1-46-30-79-01; fax 1-46-30-04-64; e-mail francecath@aol .com; internet www.france-catholique.com; weekly; Dir ANNIE CHABADEL; circ. 20,000.

Pèlerin Magazine: 3–5 rue Bayard, 75008 Paris; tel. 1-44-35-60-60; fax 1-44-35-60-21; e-mail rene.poujol@bayard-presse.com; f. 1873; weekly; Dir Pascal Ruffenach; Editor-in-Chief René Poujol; circ. 317,800 (1999).

Prier: 163 blvd Malesherbes, 75017 Paris; tel. 1-48-88-46-00; fax 1-42-27-29-03; e-mail o.sauvaget@mp.com.fr; internet www.prier.org; f. 1978; monthly; review of modern prayer and contemplation; circ. 62,611.

Réforme: 53–55 ave du Maine, 75014 Paris; tel. 1-43-20-32-67; fax 1-43-21-42-86; e-mail reforme@reforme.net; internet www.reforme.net; f. 1945; weekly; considers current affairs from a protestant Christian perspective; Dir Jean-Paul Willaime; Editor-in-Chief Rémy Hebding; circ. 7,000.

Revue des sciences philosophiques et théologiques: Librairie J. Vrin, 6 place de la Sorbonne, 75005 Paris; tel. 1-43-54-03-47; fax 1-43-54-48-18; e-mail contact@vrin.fr; internet www.vrin.fr; f. 1907; quarterly.

Silence: Ecologie, Alternatives, Non-violence: 9 rue Dumenge, 69004 Lyon; tel. 4-78-39-55-33; e-mail francisvengier@free.fr; f. 1982; monthly; circ. 6,000.

Témoignage Chrétien: 49 rue du Faubourg Poissonnière, 75009 Paris; tel. 1-44-83-82-82; fax 1-44-83-82-88; e-mail interactif@tc-hebdo.com; f. 1941; weekly; Christianity and politics; Dir Michel Cool.

Tribune Juive: Les Montalets, 2 rue de Paris, 92190 Meudon; tel. 1-46-90-20-63; fax 1-46-20-90-19; e-mail abonnement@tribune-juive.com; internet www.tribune-juive.com; weekly; Jewish affairs; Editorial Dir and Chief Exec. Jacob Abbou; circ. 12,000.

La Voix Protestante: 14 rue de Trévise, 75009 Paris; tel. 1-47-70-23-53; fax 1-48-01-09-13; e-mail la.voix.protestante@wanadoo.fr; monthly review of Protestant churches; Editor Didier Weil.

Science and Technology

Action Auto-Moto: 1 rue du Colonel Pierre Avia, 75015 Paris; tel. 1-46-48-48-48; fax 1-46-48-49-90; internet www.auto-moto.com; monthly; cars; Dir Paul Dupuy; Editor-in-Chief Jean Savary.

Air et Cosmos: 1 bis ave de la République, 75011 Paris; tel. 1-49-29-30-00; fax 1-49-29-32-01; e-mail aerospacemedia@aerospacemedia.com; internet www.air-cosmos.com; f. 1962; weekly; aerospace; Pres. and Dir-Gen. Pierre Condom; Editor-in-Chief Oliver Sutton.

Annales de Chimie—Science des Matériaux: Editions Scientifiques et Médicales Elsevier, 23 rue Linois, 75747 Paris Cédex 15; tel. 1-45-58-90-67; fax 1-45-58-94-24; e-mail haidore@elsevier.fr; f. 1789; six a year; chemistry and material science.

L'Argus de l'Automobile: 1 place Boieldieu, 75082 Paris Cédex 02; tel. 1-53-29-11-00; fax 1-49-27-09-50; e-mail emichel@argusauto.com; internet www.argusauto.com; f. 1927; motoring weekly; Man. Dir Christophe Dupontavice.

Astérisque: Société Mathématique de France, Institut Henri Poincaré, 11 rue Pierre et Marie Curie, 75231 Paris Cédex 05; tel. 1-44-27-67-99; fax 1-40-46-90-96; e-mail revues@smf.ens.fr; internet smf.emath.fr/Publications/Asterisque; f. 1973; 7–9 a year; mathematics; Editor-in-Chief P. Colmez; Sec. Nathalie Christiaën.

L'Astronomie: 3 rue Beethoven, 75016 Paris; tel. 1-42-24-13-74; fax 1-42-30-75-47; e-mail saf@fr.inter.net; internet www.iap.fr/saf; f. 1887; monthly; publ. by Société Astronomique de France; Chair. Patrick Guibert.

L'Auto Journal: 37–43 rue du Colonel Pierre Avia, 75015 Paris; tel. 1-41-33-50-00; fax 1-41-33-57-04; e-mail olivier.bernis@emapfrance.com; internet www.autojournal.fr; fortnightly; cars; Editor-in-Chief Olivier Bernis.

Biochimie: Centre universitaire des Saints Pères, 45 rue des Saints Pères, 75270 Paris Cédex 06; tel. 1-40-20-04-12; fax 1-40-20-04-22; e-mail redaction.biochimie@ibpc.fr; f. 1914; monthly; biochemistry; Editor-in-Chief M. Grunberg-Manago.

Electronique pratique: 2–12 rue de Bellevue, 75940 Paris Cédex 19; tel. 1-44-84-84-84; fax 1-44-84-85-45; e-mail redaction@electroniquepratique.com; internet www.electroniquepratique.com; monthly; electronics; Editorial Dir Bernard Fighiera.

Industries et techniques: 12–14 rue Méderic, 75017 Paris; tel. 1-56-79-41-00; fax 1-45-58-15-19; e-mail webmaster-it@industries-techniques.com; internet www.industries-techniques.com; monthly; Editorial Dir Paul Wagner.

Ingénieurs de l'Automobile: Le Chêne d'Antin, 15 rue du 19 Janvier, 92380 Garches; tel. 1-47-01-44-74; fax 1-47-01-48-25; e-mail didier.rose@lcda.fr; internet www.lcda.fr/html/ingenieurs.htm; f. 1927; 8 a year; technical automobile review, in French and Engslih; Editor-in-Chief Didier Rose.

Matériaux et Techniques: SIRPE Editeur, 76 rue de Rivoli, 75004 Paris; tel. 1-42-78-52-20; fax 1-42-74-40-48; e-mail sirpe@noos.fr; internet www.sirpe.com; f. 1913; monthly; review of engineering research and progress on industrial materials; publ. by La Société d' Ingénierie, de Recherche, de Prospective et d'Edition; Editor-in-Chief R. Drouhin.

Le Monde Informatique: IDG Communications France, 5 rue Chantecoq, 92808 Puteaux Cédex; tel. 1-41-97-61-61; fax 1-49-04-79-04; e-mail lmihebdo@idg.fr; internet www.weblmi.com; weekly; information science; Publr Michel Crestin; Editor-in-Chief François Jeanne.

Le Moniteur des Travaux Publics et du Bâtiment: 17 rue d'Uzès, 75108 Paris Cédex 02; tel. 1-40-13-30-30; fax 1-40-41-94-95; e-mail redac@groupemoniteur.fr; internet www.lemoniteur-expert.com; f. 1903; weekly; construction; Chair. Jacques Guy; Editor-in-Chief Bertrand Fabré; circ. 67,000.

Psychologie française: Université Nancy II, B.P. 3397, 54015 Nancy Cédex; e-mail nicole.dubois@univ-nancy2.fr; internet perso.wanadoo.fr/sfpsy/psy_fr.htm; f. 1956; quarterly; review of the Société Française de Psychologie; Editor Nicole Dubois.

La Recherche: 4 rue de Texel, 75014 Paris; tel. 1-40-47-44-00; fax 1-40-47-44-02; e-mail courrier@larecherche.fr; internet www.larecherche.fr; monthly; review of the Société d'éditions scientifiques; Dir. Stéphane Khémis; Editor-in-Chief Olivier Postel-Vinay.

Science et vie: 1 rue du Colonel Pierre Avia, 75015 Paris; tel. 1-46-48-48-48; fax 1-46-48-48-67; e-mail svmems@excelsior.fr; internet www.science-et-vie.com; f. 1913; monthly; Pres. Paul Dupuy; circ. 350,000.

Women's, Home and Fashion

Cosmopolitan: 10 blvd des Frères Voisin, 92792 Issy-les-Moulineaux Cédex 9; tel. 1-41-46-88-88; fax 1-41-48-84-93; Dir Evelyne Prouvost-Berry; Editor Anne Chabrol.

Côté Femme: 3–5 rue Bayard, 75008 Paris; tel. 1-44-35-60-60; fax 1-44-35-60-37; e-mail micheline.noel@bayard-presse.com; f. 1922; weekly; Editor-in-Chief Claudine Litaud; circ. 234,637 (2002).

Elle: 11 rue de Cambrai, 75019 Paris; tel. 1-41-34-60-11; fax 1-41-34-74-94; e-mail ellemagazine@hfp.fr; internet www.elle.fr; f. 1945; monthly; Dir Anne-Marie Périer-Sardou; Editor-in-Chief Valérie Toranian; circ. 358,400.

Femme Actuelle: 73–75 rue La Condamine, 75854 Paris Cédex 17; tel. 1-44-90-67-00; fax 1-44-90-67-14; e-mail femactu@prisma-presse.com; f. 1984; weekly; Editor Maryse Bonnet; circ. 2,100,000 (2002).

Le Journal de la Maison: 20 rue de Billancourt, BP 406, 92103 Boulogne-Billancourt Cédex; tel. 1-41-10-13-55; fax 1-41-10-13-01; e-mail ccorvaisier@hfp.fr; monthly; home; Editor Caroline Corvaisier.

Marie-Claire: 10 blvd des Frères Voisin, 92792 Issy-les-Moulineaux Cédex 9; tel. 1-41-46-88-88; fax 1-41-46-86-86; e-mail webgmc@gmc.tm.fr; internet www.marieclaire.presse.fr; f. 1954; monthly; Publr Monique Majerowicz; Editor Tina Kieffer; circ. 506,466 (2000); also *Marie-France*.

Modes et travaux: 152 rue Galliéni, 92644 Boulogne-Billancourt Cédex; tel. 1-41-86-84-31; fax 1-41-86-85-32; f. 1919; monthly; Editor Jeanne Thiriet; circ. 710,389.

Notre Temps: 3–5 rue Bayard, 75393 Paris Cédex 08; tel. 1-44-35-60-60; fax 1-44-35-60-31; e-mail notre.temps@bayardweb.net; internet www.notretemps.bayardweb.com; monthly; for retired people; Dir Patrick Darde; Editor Rémy Michel.

Nous Deux: 152 rue Galliéni, 92644 Boulogne-Billancourt Cédex; tel. 1-41-86-86-86; fax 1-41-86-84-02; e-mail nous-deux@emapfrance.com; internet www.nousdeux.com; f. 1947; weekly; Editor Anne-Marie Lesage; circ. 352,137 (2002).

Parents: 10 rue Thierry-le-Luron, 92592 Levallois-Perret Cédex; tel. 1-41-34-61-88; fax 1-41-34-70-79; magazine for parents; Editorial Dir. Catherine Lilièvre; circ. 378,100.

Pleine Vie: 152 rue Galliéni, 92644 Boulogne-Billancourt Cédex; tel. 1-41-86-84-15; fax 1-41-86-85-63; e-mail annick.alombert@emapfrance.com; f. 1981; monthly; intended for women aged 50 and over; Dir Annick Alombert; circ. 1,105,000.

Questions de femmes: 117 rue de la Tour, 75116 Paris; tel. 1-45-03-80-00; fax 1-45-03-80-20; e-mail fialaix@groupe-ayache.com; internet www.questionsdefemmes.com; f. 1996; monthly; Editor-in-Chief Geneviève Leroy.

Santé Magazine: 110 rue Marius Aufan, BP 318, 92304 Levallois-Perret Cédex; tel. 1-41-49-41-49; fax 1-40-89-04-30; e-mail direction@santemagazine.fr; internet santemagazine.fr; f. 1976; monthly; health; Editor André Giovanni.

Vogue: 56A rue du Faubourg Saint Honoré, 75008 Paris; tel. 1-41-49-41-49; fax 1-40-89-04-30; e-mail magazine@vogueparis.com; internet www.vogueparis.com; monthly; Publr GARDNER BELLANGER; Editor-in-Chief JOAN JULIET BUCK.

NEWS AGENCIES

In 1995 there were some 216 news agencies in France.

Agence France-Presse (AFP): 13 place de la Bourse, 75002 Paris; tel. 1-40-41-46-46; fax 1-40-41-73-99; e-mail contact@afp.com; internet www.afp.fr; f. 1944; 24-hour service of world political, financial, sporting news, and photographs; 165 agencies and 2,000 correspondents world-wide; Pres. BERTRAND EVENO; Editor-in-Chief ERIC WISHART.

Agence Parisienne de Presse: 18 rue Saint Fiacre, 75002 Paris; tel. 1-42-36-95-59; fax 1-42-33-83-24; f. 1949; Man. Dir MICHEL BURTON.

Infomedia M.C.: 8 rue de la Michodière, 75002 Paris; tel. 1-47-42-14-33; fax 1-47-42-14-39; f. 1988; economic and financial news; Dir FRANÇOIS COUDURIER.

Foreign Bureaux

Agence Maghreb Arabe Presse (MAP) (Morocco): 9 blvd la Madeleine, 75001 Paris; tel. 1-42-44-24-30; fax 1-42-44-24-40; e-mail hasna.daoudi@wanadoo.fr; internet www.map.co.ma; f. 1959; Correspondent HASNA DAOUDI.

Agence de Presse Xinhua (People's Republic of China): 27 rue Médéric, 92110 Clichy-la-Garenne; tel. 1-41-06-97-33; fax 1-42-70-65-38; internet www.xinhua.org; Bureau Chief QI YANG.

Agencia EFE (Spain): 10 rue Saint-Marc, 75002 Paris; tel. 1-44-82-65-40; fax 1-40-39-91-78; e-mail efeparis@wanadoo.fr; internet www.efe.es; f. 1939; Bureau Chief ANNE LEROUX.

Agenzia Nazionale Stampa Associata (ANSA) (Italy): 29 rue Tronchet, 75008 Paris; tel. 1-42-65-55-16; fax 1-42-65-12-11; e-mail ansa.paris@noos.fr; internet www.ansa.it; Bureau Chief PIER ANTONIO LACQUA.

Associated Press (AP) (USA): 162 rue du Faubourg Saint Honoré, 75008 Paris; tel. 1-43-59-86-76; fax 1-40-74-00-45; e-mail apmail@associatedpress.fr; internet www.ap.org; Bureau Chief KEVIN COSTELLOE.

Deutsche Presse-Agentur (dpa) (Germany): 30 rue Saint Augustin, 75002 Paris; tel. 1-47-42-95-02; fax 1-47-42-51-75; Bureau Chief HANNS-JOCHEN KAFFSACK.

Informatsionnoye Telegrafnoye Agentstvo Rossii-Telegrafnoye Agentstvo Suverennykh Stran (ITAR-TASS) (Russia): 27 ave Bosquet, 75007 Paris; tel. 1-44-11-31-80; fax 1-47-05-33-98; internet www.itar-tass.com; Chief Correspondent and Head of ITAR-TASS Western European Regional Office VITALII MAKARCHEV.

IPS—Inter Press Service: Paris; tel. 1-45-49-81-62; e-mail rameshjaura@visto.com; internet www.ips.org; European Co-ordinator RAMESH JAURA.

Jiji Tsushin (Japan): 27 blvd des Italiens, 75002 Paris; tel. 1-42-66-96-57; fax 1-42-66-96-61; internet www.jiji.co.jp; Bureau Chief YUKIO YOSHINAGA.

Magyar Távirati Iroda (MTI) (Hungary): 365 rue de Vaugirard, 75015 Paris; tel. 1-45-33-22-59; fax 1-45-33-32-06; e-mail mtiparis@yahoo.fr; internet hirek.mti.hu; Correspondent ANSAF HILU.

Middle East News Agency (Egypt): Paris; tel. 1-47-42-16-03; fax 1-47-42-44-52; internet www.mena.org.eg; f. 1956; Dir MOHAMED EL-SHAMY.

Reuters (UK): 618 blvd Haussmann, 75009 Paris Cédex 02; tel. 1-42-21-50-00; fax 1-40-26-69-70; internet www.reuters.fr; Dir CHRISTIAN LEVESQUE; Editor-in-Chief G. REGENSTREIF.

Rossiyskoye Informatsionnoye Agentstvo—Novosti (RIA—Novosti) (Russia): 14 place du Général Catroux, 75017 Paris; tel. 1-42-27-79-21; fax 1-43-80-96-83; internet www.rian.ru; Bureau Chief N. VIKHLAEV.

United Press International (UPI) (USA): Paris; tel. 1-42-60-23-68; fax 1-42-60-30-98; internet www.upi.com.

PRESS ASSOCIATIONS

Comité de Liaison de la Presse: Paris; tel. 1-53-20-90-56; liaison organization for press, radio and cinema.

Fédération Française des Agences de Presse (FFAP): Paris; tel. 1-42-93-42-57; fax 1-42-93-15-32; e-mail info@agencesdepresse.fr; internet www.ffap.fr; comprises five syndicates (news, photographs, television, general information and multimedia) with a total membership of 109 agencies; Pres. ARNAUD HAMELIN; Dir JACQUES MORANDAT.

Fédération Nationale de la Presse Française (FNPF): 13 rue La Fayette, 75009 Paris; tel. 1-53-20-90-50; fax 1-53-20-90-51; e-mail contact@portail-presse.com; internet www.portail-presse.com; f. 1944; mems: Syndicat de la Presse Parisienne, Syndicat Professionnel de la Presse, Magazine et d'Opinion, Syndicat de la Presse Quotidienne Régionale, Syndicat de la Presse Quotidienne Départementale, Fédération de la Presse Périodique Régionale, Fédération Nationale de la Presse d'Information Spécialisée; Pres. XAVIER ELLIE.

Fédération Nationale de la Presse d'Information Spécialisée: 37 rue de Rome, 75008 Paris; tel. 1-44-90-43-60; fax 1-44-90-43-72; e-mail contact@fnps.fr; internet www.fnps.fr; comprises Syndicat National de la Presse Agricole et Rurale (SNPAR), Syndicat National de la Presse Médicale et des Professions de Santé (SNPM), Syndicat de la Presse Culturelle et Scientifique (SPCS), Syndicat de la Presse Economique, Juridique et Politique (SPEJS), Syndicat de la Presse Professionnelle (SP—PRO, Syndicat de la Presse d'Informations Spécialisées (SPIS) and Syndicat de la Presse Sociale (SPS), representing some 1,350 specialised or professional publications. CEO JEAN-MICHEL HUAN.

Fédération de la Presse Périodique Régionale: 72 rue d'Hauteville, 75010 Paris; tel. 1-45-23-98-00; fax 1-45-23-98-01; e-mail sphr@presse-hebdo.com; internet www.press-hebdo.com; f. 1970; present name adopted 1992; mems: Syndicat de la Presse Hebdomadaire Régionale, Syndicat National des Publications Régionales, Syndicat de la Presse Judiciaire de Province, Syndicat National de la Presse Judiciaire; represents 250 regional periodical publications; Pres. BERNARD BIENVENU; Sec.-Gen. JEAN-PIERRE BONIS.

Syndicat de la Presse Quotidienne Régionale: 17 place des Etats-Unis, 75116 Paris; tel. 1-40-73-80-20; fax 1-47-20-48-94; internet www.spqr.fr; f. 1986; regional dailies; Pres. JEAN-LOUIS PRÉVOST; Dir-Gen. BRUNO HOCQUART DE TURTOT.

PRESS INSTITUTE

Institut Français de Presse et des Sciences de l'Information: 92 rue d'Assas, 75006 Paris; tel. 1-44-41-57-93; fax 1-44-41-59-49; e-mail ifp@u-paris2.fr; f. 1951; studies and teaches all aspects of communication and the media; maintains research and documentation centre; open to research workers, students, journalists; Dir NADINE TOUSSAINT-DESMOULINS.

Publishers

Actes Sud: Le Méjan, place Nina-Berberova, BP 38, 13633 Arles; tel. 4-90-49-86-91; fax 4-90-96-95-25; e-mail contact@actes-sud.fr; internet www.actes-sud.fr; f. 1978; French and translated literature, music, theatre, studies of Arabic and Islamic civilisations; Pres. FRANÇOISE NYSSEN; Editorial Dir BERTRAND PY.

Editions Albin Michel: 22 rue Huyghens, 75680 Paris Cédex 14; tel. 1-42-79-10-00; fax 1-43-27-21-58; e-mail virginie.caminade@albin-michel.fr; internet www.albin-michel.fr; f. 1901; general, fiction, history, classics; Pres. FRANCIS ESMÉNARD; Man. Dir RICHARD DUCOUSSET.

Editions de l'Atelier/Editions Ouvrières: 12 ave Soeur Rosalie, 75013 Paris; tel. 1-44-08-95-15; fax 1-44-08-95-00; e-mail editions.atelier@wanadoo.fr; internet www.maitron.org/maitron/Dico/atelier1.htm; f. 1929; religious, educational, political and social, including labour movement; Man. Dirs BERNARD STEPHAN, PATRICK MERRANT.

Editions Aubier—Montaigne: 13 quai de Conti, 75006 Paris; tel. 1-40-51-31-00; fax 1-43-29-71-04; f. 1924; psychoanalysis, literature, philosophy, history and sociology; Man. Dir M. AUBIER-GABAIL.

Editions Balland: 33 rue Saint André des Arts, 75006 Paris; tel. 1-43-25-74-40; fax 1-46-33-56-21; e-mail balland@club-internet.fr; f. 1967; literature, non-fiction; Chair. and Man. Dir DENIS BOURGEOIS.

Bayard Editions—Centurion: 3 rue Bayard, 75393 Paris Cédex 08; tel. 1-44-35-60-60; fax 1-44-35-61-61; e-mail communication@bayard-presse.com; internet www2.bayardpresse.com; f. 1870; children's books, religion, human sciences; Man. Dir JEAN-CLAUDE DUBOST.

Beauchesne Editeur: 7 cité du Cardinal Lemoine, 75005 Paris; tel. 1-53-10-08-18; fax 1-53-10-85-19; e-mail beauchesne@wanadoo.fr; f. 1900; scripture, religion and theology, philosophy, religious history, politics, encyclopaedias; Man. Dir JEAN-ETIENNE MITTELMANN.

Editions Belfond: 12 ave d'Italie, 75627 Paris; tel. 1-44-16-05-00; fax 1-44-16-05-06; f. 1963; fiction, poetry, documents, history, arts; Chair. JÉRÔME TALAMON; Man. Dir FABIENNE DELMOTE.

Berger-Levrault: 17 rue Rémy Dumoncel, 75014 Paris; tel. 1-40-64-42-32; fax 1-40-64-42-30; e-mail blc@berger-levrault.fr; internet www.berger-levrault.fr; f. 1976; fine arts, health, social and economic sciences, law; Chair. MARC FRIEDEL; Man. Dir BERNARD AJAC.

De Boccard, Edition-Diffusion: 11 rue de Médicis, 75006 Paris; tel. 1-43-26-00-37; fax 1-43-54-85-83; e-mail deboccard@deboccard.com; internet www.deboccard.com; f. 1866; history, archaeology, religion, orientalism, medievalism; Man. Dir DOMINIQUE CHAULET.

Bordas: 89 blvd Blanqui, 75013 Paris; tel. 1-44-39-54-45; fax 1-43-22-85-18; e-mail asotty@vuef.fr; internet www.editions-bordas.com; f. 1946; encyclopaedias, dictionaries, history, geography, arts, children's and educational; Pres. and Dir-Gen. PATRICE MAUBOURGUET.

Editions Bornemann: 62 rue Blanche, 75009 Paris; tel. 1-42-82-08-16; fax 1-48-74-14-88; f. 1829; art, fiction, sports, nature, easy readers; Chair. and Man. Dir PIERRE C. LAHAYE.

Buchet-Chastel: 18 rue de Condé, 75006 Paris; tel. 1-44-32-05-60; fax 1-44-32-05-61; e-mail buchet_chastel@wanadoo.fr; f. 1929; literature, music, crafts, religion, practical guides; Chair. SARA MICHALSKI; Gen. Man. HENRY MARCELLIN.

Calmann-Lévy: 3 rue Auber, 75009 Paris; tel. 1-47-42-38-33; fax 1-47-42-77-81; f. 1836; French and foreign literature, history, social sciences, economics, sport, leisure; Chair. JEAN-ETIENNE COHEN-SEAT.

Editions Casterman: 36 rue du Chemin Vert, 75011 Paris; tel. 1-55-28-12-00; fax 1-55-28-12-60; e-mail info@casterman.com; internet www.casterman.com; f. 1857; juvenile, comics, fiction, education, leisure, art; Chair. and Man. Dir SIMON CASTERMAN.

Editions du Cerf: 29 blvd de Latour Maubourg, 75340 Paris Cédex 07; tel. 1-44-18-12-12; fax 1-45-56-04-27; e-mail cerf.diffusion@wanadoo.fr; internet www.editionsducerf.fr; f. 1929; religion, social science; Chair. MICHEL BON; Man. Dir NICOLAS SED.

Editions Champ Vallon: 01420 Seyssel; tel. 4-50-56-15-51; fax 4-50-56-15-64; e-mail info@champ-vallon.com; internet www.champ-vallon.com; f. 1980; social sciences, literary history, literary criticism; Dirs MYRIAM MONTEIRO-BRAZ, PATRICK BEAUNE.

Chiron (Editions): 10 rue Léon-Foucault, 78184 Saint-Quentin-en-Yveline; tel. 1-30-14-19-30; fax 1-30-14-19-46; f. 1907; sport, education, fitness, health, dance, games; Dir MARINUS VISSER.

Editions Climats: 470 chemin des Pins, 34170 Castelnau-le Lez; tel. 4-99-58-30-91; fax 4-99-58-30-92; e-mail contact@editions-climats.com; internet www.editions-climats.com; f. 1988; literature, arts, political science; Dir ALAIN MARTIN.

Armand Colin Editeur: 21 rue du Montparnasse, 75283 Paris Cédex 06; tel. 1-44-39-54-47; fax 1-44-39-43-43; e-mail infos@armand-colin.com; internet www.armand-colin.com; f. 1870; literature, fine arts, history, science, school and university textbooks; Man. Dir JEAN-MAX LECLERC.

Dalloz-Sirey: 31–35 rue Froidevaux, 75685 Paris Cédex 14; tel. 1-40-64-54-54; fax 1-40-64-54-62; e-mail ventes@dalloz.fr; internet www.dalloz.fr; f. 1824; law, philosophy, political science, business and economics; subsidiary of Vivendi Universal Publishing; Pres. CHARLES VALLÉE; Dir-Gen. PHILIPPE CHAGNON.

Dargaud: 15–27 rue Moussorgski, 75895 Paris Cédex 18; tel. 1-53-26-32-32; fax 1-53-26-32-00; e-mail contact@dargaud.fr; internet www.dargaud.fr; f. 1943; juvenile, cartoons, comics, video, graphic novels; Chair. and Man. Dir CLAUDE DE SAINT-VINCENT.

La Découverte: 9 bis rue Abel Hovelacque, 75013 Paris; tel. 1-44-08-84-00; fax 1-44-08-84-39; e-mail decouverte@dial.oleane.com; f. 1959; economic, social and political science, literature, history; Man. Dir FRANÇOIS GÈZE.

Denoël Editeur: 9 rue du Cherche-Midi, 75006 Paris; tel. 1-44-39-73-73; fax 1-44-39-73-79; f. 1929; general literature, science fiction, crime, history; imprint of Editions Gallimard; Man. Dir OLIVIER RUBINSTEIN.

Editions des Femmes Antoinette Fouque: 6 rue de Mézières, 75006 Paris; tel. 1-42-22-60-74; fax 1-42-22-62-73; e-mail info@desfemmes.fr; internet www.desfemmes.fr; f. 1973; mainly women authors; fiction, essays, art, history, politics, psychoanalysis, talking books; Dir ANTOINETTE FOUQUE.

Desclée De Brouwer: 76 bis rue des Saints Pères, 75007 Paris; tel. 1-45-49-61-92; fax 1-42-22-61-41; e-mail info@descleedebrouwer.com; internet www.descleedebrouwer.com; f. 1877; religion, philosophy, arts, human sciences; Dir MARC LEBOUCHER.

Diderot Editeur: 22 rue Malher, 75004 Paris; tel. 1-48-04-91-45; f. 1995; science, fine arts, history of art and culture.

La Documentation Française: 29 quai Voltaire, 75344 Paris Cédex 07; tel. 1-40-15-70-00; fax 1-40-15-72-30; e-mail depcom@ladocumentationfrancaise.fr; internet www.ladocumentationfrancaise.fr; f. 1945; government publs; politics, law, economics, culture, science; Man. Dir SOPHIE MOATI.

Dunod Editeur: 5 rue Laromiguière, 75005 Paris Cédex; tel. 1-40-46-35-00; fax 1-40-46-61-11; e-mail infos@dunod.com; internet www.dunod.com; f. 1800; science, computer science, electronics, economics, accountancy, management, psychology and humanities;

subsidiary of Vivendi Universal Publishing; Chair. CHARLES VALLÉE; Dir-Gen. PHILIPPE CHAGNON.

Edilarge Editions Ouest-France: 13 rue du Breil, BP 6339, 35063 Rennes Cédex; tel. 2-99-32-58-27; fax 2-99-32-58-30; internet www.edilarge.com; history, guides; subsidiary of Ouest-France group; fmrly Editions Ouest-France; Chair. FRANÇOIS-XAVIER HUTIN; Dir-Gen. SERVANE BIGUAIS.

Edisud: 3120 Route d'Avignon, 13090 Aix-en-Provence; tel. 4-42-21-61-44; fax 4-42-21-56-20; e-mail info@edisud.com; internet www.edisud.com; f. 1971; Dir CHARLY-YVES CHAUDOREILLE.

Eyrolles: 61 blvd Saint Germain, 75005 Paris; tel. 1-44-41-11-11; fax 1-44-41-11-44; e-mail librairie@eyrolles.com; internet www.eyrolles.com; f. 1918; science, computing, technology, electronics, management, law; Man. Dir JEAN-PIERRE TISSIER.

Fayard: 75 rue des Saints Pères, 75278 Paris Cédex 06; tel. 1-45-49-82-00; fax 1-42-22-40-17; e-mail rights@editions-fayard.fr; internet www.editions-fayard.fr; f. 1857; literature, biography, history, religion, essays, music; Chair. CLAUDE DURAND.

Librairie Ernest Flammarion: 26 rue Racine, 75006 Paris; tel. 1-40-51-31-00; fax 1-43-29-76-44; e-mail basquin@easynet.fr; internet www.flammarion.com; f. 1875; general literature, art, human sciences, sport, children's books, medicine; Chair. CHARLES-HENRI FLAMMARION; Man. Dir FRÉDÉRIC MOREL.

Groupe Fleurus: 15–27 rue Moussorgski, 75895 Paris Cédex 18; tel. 1-53-26-33-35; fax 1-53-26-33-36; e-mail m.daigne@fleurus-mame.fr; f. 1944; arts, education, leisure; Chair. VINCENT MONTAGNE; Man. Dir PIERRE-MARIE DUMONT; also Fleurus Idées, Fleurus Enfants, Fleurus Jeunesse, Mame, Tardy, Critérion, Desclée, Droguet et Ardant.

Fleuve Noir: 12 ave d'Italie, 75627 Paris Cédex 13; tel. 1-44-16-05-07; e-mail beatrice.duval@havaspoche.com; fax 1-44-16-05-11; subsidiary of Vivendi Universal Publishing; crime and science fiction; Chair. JEAN-CLAUDE DUBOST; Man. Dir BÉATRICE DUVAL.

Editions Foucher: 31 rue du Fleurus, 75278 Paris Cédex 06; tel. 1-49-54-35-35; fax 1-49-54-35-00; e-mail cfages@editions-foucher.fr; internet www.editions-foucher.fr; f. 1936; science, economics, law, medicine textbooks; Chair. and Man. Dir BERNARD FOULON.

Editions Gallimard: 5 rue Sébastien-Bottin, 75328 Paris Cédex 7; tel. 1-49-54-42-00; fax 1-45-44-94-03; e-mail pub@gallimard.fr; internet www.gallimard.fr; f. 1911; general fiction, literature, history, poetry, children's, philosophy; Dir ANTOINE GALLIMARD; Editorial Dir TERESA CREMISI.

Editions Grasset et Fasquelle: 61 rue des Saints-Pères, 75006 Paris; tel. 1-44-39-22-00; fax 1-42-22-64-18; e-mail afarges@edition-grasset.fr; internet www.edition-grasset.fr; f. 1907; contemporary literature, criticism, general fiction and children's books; Pres. OLIVIER NORA.

Librairie Gründ: 60 rue Mazarine, 75006 Paris; tel. 1-43-29-87-40; fax 1-43-29-49-86; internet www.grund.fr; f. 1880; art, natural history, children's books, guides; Chair. ALAIN GRÜND.

Hachette Livre: 43 quai de Grenelle, 75905 Paris Cédex 15; tel. 1-43-92-30-00; fax 1-43-92-30-30; internet www.hachette.com; f. 1826; group includes Hachette Education, Hachette Jeunesse, Hachette Littératures, Hachette Référence; Chair. and Man. Dir JEAN-LOUIS LISIMACHIO.

L'Harmattan Edition: 7 rue de l'Ecole Polytechnique, 75005 Paris; tel. 1-40—46-79-20; fax 1-43-25-82-03; e-mail harmat@worldnet.fr; internet www.editions-harmattan.fr; f. 1975; politics, human sciences, developing countries; Dir DENIS PRYEN.

Editions Hatier: 8 rue d'Assas, 75278 Paris Cédex 06; tel. 1-49-54-49-54; fax 1-40-49-00-45; e-mail mnmalapert@editions-hatier.fr; internet www.editions-hatier.fr; f. 1880; children's books, fiction, history, science, nature guides; Chair. BERNARD FOULON.

Hermann: 293 rue Lecourbe, 75015 Paris; tel. 1-45-57-45-40; fax 1-40-60-12-93; e-mail hermann.sa@wanadoo.fr; f. 1870; sciences and art, humanities; Chair. PIERRE BERÈS.

Editions Ibolya Virag: 11 rue du Grand-Prieuré, 75011 Paris; tel. and fax 1-43-38-56-05; fax 1-43—38—43–14; e-mail ibovirag@aol.com; f. 1996; fiction, history, Central and Eastern Europe, Russia and Central Asia; Dir IBOLYA VIRAG.

J'ai Lu: 84 rue de Grenelle, 75007 Paris; tel. 1-44-39-34-70; fax 1-45-44-65-52; e-mail ajasmin@jailu.com; internet www.jailu.com; f. 1958; fiction, paperbacks; subsidiary of Flammarion; Chair. CHARLES-HENRI FLAMMARION; Man. Dir BERTRAND LOBRY.

Julliard: 24 ave Marceau, 75008 Paris; tel. 1-53-67-14-00; fax 1-53-67-14-14; internet www.lafont.fr/julliard/index.htm; f. 1931; general literature, biography, essays; imprint of Editions Robert Laffont; subsidiary of Vivendi Universal Publishing.

Karthala Editions: 22–24 blvd Arago, 75013 Paris; tel. 1-43-31-15-59; fax 1-45-35-27-05; e-mail www.karthala.com; e-mail karthala@wanadoo.fr; politics, history, developing countries.

Jeanne Laffitte: 25 Cours d'Estienne d'Orves, BP 1903, 13225 Marseille Cédex 01; tel. 4-91-59-80-49; fax 4-91-54-76-33; e-mail librairie@les-arcenaulx.com; internet www.jeanne-laffitte.com; f. 1972; art, geography, culture, medicine, history; Chair. and Man. Dir JEANNE LAFFITTE.

Editions Robert Laffont: 24 ave Marceau, 75381 Paris Cédex 08; tel. 1-53-67-14-00; fax 1-53-67-14-14; e-mail bvernet@robert.laffont.fr; internet www.laffont.fr; f. 1941; literature, history, translations; subsidiary of Vivendi Universal Publishing; Chair. LEONELLO BRANDOLINI.

Larousse-Bordas: 21 rue du Montparnasse, 75298 Paris Cédex 06; tel. 1-44-39-44-00; fax 1-44-39-43-43; internet www.larousse.net; f. 1852; general, specializing in dictionaries, illustrated books on scientific subjects, encyclopaedias, classics, textbooks and periodicals; subsidiary of Vivendi Universal Publishing; Chair. and Man. Dir CHRISTIAN BREGOU.

Editions JC Lattès: 17 rue Jacob, 75006 Paris; tel. 1-44-41-74-00; fax 1-43-25-30-47; e-mail mpageix@editions-jclattes.fr; internet www.editions-jclattes.fr; f. 1968; general fiction and non-fiction, biography; Man. Dir ISABELLE LAFFONT.

Letouzey et Ané: 87 blvd Raspail, 75006 Paris; tel. 1-45-48-80-14; fax 1-45-49-03-43; e-mail letouzey@free.fr; f. 1885; theology, religion, archaeology, history, ecclesiastical encyclopaedias and dictionaries, biography; Man. Dir FLORENCE LETOUZEY.

LGDJ—Montchrestien: 31 rue Falguière, 75741 Paris Cédex 15; e-mail info@eja.fr; internet www.lgdj.fr; tel. 1-56-54-16-00; fax 1-56-54-16-47; f. 1836; law and economy; Chair. LIONEL GUÉRIN; Man. Dir VINCENT MARTY.

Editions Litec: 141 rue de Javel, 75747 Paris Cédex 01; tel. 1-45-58-93-76; fax 1-45-58-94-00; e-mail commercial@litec.fr; internet www.litec.fr; f. 1927; member of Groupe Lexis-Nexis (ReedElsevier); law, economics, taxation; Dirs ANJER HOLL, MARIELLE BERNARD.

Livre de Poche: 43 quai de Grenelle, 75905 Paris Cédex 15; tel. 1-43-92-30-00; fax 1-43-92-35-90; internet www.livredepoche.com; general literature, dictionaries, encyclopaedias; f. 1953; Chair. DOMINIQUE GOUST.

Editions Magnard: 20 rue Berbier-du-Mets, 75647 Paris Cédex 13; tel. 1-44-08-85-85; fax 1-44-08-49-79; e-mail l.breton@magnard.fr; internet www.magnard.fr; f. 1933; children's and educational books; subsidiary of Editions Albin Michel; Man. Dir LOUIS MAGNARD.

Masson Editeur: 120 blvd Saint Germain, 75006 Paris; tel. 1-40-46-60-00; fax 1-40-46-60-01; e-mail infos@masson.fr; internet www.masson.fr; f. 1804; medicine and science, books and periodicals; publrs for various academies and societies; subsidiary of Medimedia; Pres. GÉRARD KOUCHNER.

Mercure de France: 26 rue de Condé, 75006 Paris; tel. 1-55-42-61-90; fax 1-43-54-49-91; internet www.mercuredefrance.fr; f. 1893; general fiction, history, biography, sociology; Pres. and Man. Dir ISABELLE GALLIMARD; Editor NICOLAS BREHAL.

Editions de Minuit: 7 rue Bernard Palissy, 75006 Paris; tel. 1-44-39-39-20; fax 1-45-44-82-36; e-mail contact@leseditionsdeminuit.fr; internet www.leseditionsdeminuit.fr; f. 1945; general literature; Man. Dir IRÈNE LINDON.

Nathan Education: 9 rue Méchain, 75014 Paris; tel. 1-45-87-50-00; fax 1-47-07-57-57; internet www.nathan.fr; f. 1881; educational books for all levels; Chair. BERTRAND EVENO; Man. Dir JEAN-PAUL BAUDOIN.

Editions Payot-Rivages: 106 blvd Saint Germain, 75006 Paris; tel. 1-44-41-39-90; fax 1-44-41-39-69; e-mail payotrivages@wanadoo.com; f. 1917; literature, human sciences, philosophy; Chair. and Dir JEAN-FRANÇOIS LAMUNIÈRE.

A. et J. Picard: 82 rue Bonaparte, 75006 Paris; tel. 1-43-26-96-73; fax 1-43-26-42-64; e-mail livres@librairie-picard.com; internet www.abebooks.com/home/libpicard; f. 1869; archaeology, architecture, history of art, history, pre-history, auxiliary sciences, linguistics, musicological works, antiquarian books; Chair. and Man. Dir CHANTAL PASINI-PICARD.

Plon-Perrin: 76 rue Bonaparte, 75284 Paris Cédex 06; tel. 1-44-41-35-00; fax 1-44-41-35-01; e-mail nicolas.roche@plon-perrin.com; internet www.editions-perrin.fr; f. 1884; fiction, travel, history, anthropology, human sciences, biography; Chair. OLIVIER ORBAN.

Editions P.O.L.: 33 rue Saint-André-des-Arts, 75006 Paris; tel. 1-43-54-21-20; fax 1-43-54-11-31; e-mail pol@pol-editeur.fr; internet www.pol-editeur.fr; literature; arts.

Presses de la Cité: 12 ave d'Italie, 75625 Paris Cédex 13; tel. 1-44-16-05-00; internet www.pressesdelacite.com; f. 1944; fiction and factual literature for general audience; Dir JEAN ARCACHE.

Presses de Sciences Po: 44 rue du Four, 75006 Paris; tel. 1-44-39-39-60; fax 1-45-48-04-41; e-mail info@presses.sciences-po.fr; internet www.sciences-po.fr/edition; f. 1975; history, politics, linguistics, economics, sociology; Dir BERTRAND BADIE.

Presses Universitaires de France: 6 ave Reille, 75014 Paris; tel. 1-58-10-31-00; fax 1-58-10-31-80; e-mail info@puf.com; internet www.puf.com; f. 1921; philosophy, psychology, psychoanalysis, psychiatry, education, sociology, theology, history, geography, economics, law, linguistics, literature, science; Chair. MICHEL PRIGENT.

Presses Universitaires de Grenoble: Saint Martin-d'Hères, 38040 Grenoble Cédex 09; tel. 4-76-82-56-51; fax 4-76-82-78-35; e-mail pug@pug.fr; internet www.pug.fr; f. 1972; psychology, law, economics, management, history, statistics, literature, medicine, science, politics; Man. Dir BERNARD WIRBEL.

Presses Universitaires de Nancy: 42–44 ave de la Libération, BP 3347, 54014 Nancy Cédex; tel. 3-83-96-84-30; fax 3-83-96-84-39; e-mail pun@univ-nancy2.fr; internet www.univ-nancy2.fr/PUN; f. 1976; literature, history, law, social sciences, politics; Chair. and Man. Dir ALAIN TROGNON.

Editions Privat: 10 rue des arts, BP 828, 31000 Toulouse Cédex 06; tel. 5-34-31-81-81; fax 5-34-31-64-44; e-mail privat@intelcom.fr; f. 1839; regional, national and international history, heritage, health; Dir DOMINIQUE PORTÉ.

Le Serpent à Plumes: 20 rue des Petits Champs, 75002 Paris; tel. 1-55-35-95-85; fax 1-42-61-17-46; e-mail contact@serpentaplumes.com; internet www.serpentaplumes.com; f. 1993; world literature; Dir PIERRE ASTIER.

Editions du Seuil: 27 rue Jacob, 75261 Paris Cédex 06; tel. 1-40-46-50-50; fax 1-40-46-43-00; e-mail contact@seuil.com; internet www.seuil.com; f. 1936; modern literature, fiction, illustrated books, non-fiction; Chair. and Man. Dir CLAUDE CHERKI.

Editions du Signe: 1 rue Alfred Kastler, BP 94, Eckbolsheim, 67038 Strasbourg Cédex 02; tel. 3-88-78-91-91; fax 3-88-78-91-99; e-mail info@editionsdusigne.fr; internet www.editionsdusigne.fr; f. 1987; Christianity; Chair. and Man. Dir CHRISTIAN RIEHL.

Editions Stock: 31 rue de Fleurus, 75006 Paris; tel. 1-49-54-36-55; fax 1-49-54-36-62; e-mail prey@editions-stock.fr; internet www.editions-stock.fr; f. 1710; literature, translations, biography, human sciences, guides; Chair. and Editorial. Dir JEAN-MARC ROBERTS.

Succès du Livre: 60 rue St André des Arts, 75006 Paris; tel. 1-43-29-82-82; fax 1-43-29-60-75; f. 1987; fiction, biography; Chair. JACQUES DOMAS.

Editions de la Table Ronde: 7 rue Corneille, 75006 Paris; tel. 1-43-26-03-95; fax 1-44-07-09-30; f. 1944; fiction, essays, religion, travel, theatre, youth; Pres. DENIS TILLINAC.

Editions Tallandier: 18 rue Dauphine, 75006 Paris; tel. 1-40-46-43-88; fax 1-40-46-43-99; e-mail atalland@st2.tallandier.fr; internet www.tallandier.com; f. 1909; history, reference; Dir HENRI BOVET.

Editions Vigot Frères: 23 rue de l'Ecole de Médecine, 75006 Paris; tel. 1-43-29-54-50; fax 1-46-34-05-89; f. 1890; medicine, pharmacology, nature, veterinary science, sport; Chair. CHRISTIAN VIGOT; Man. Dir DANIEL VIGOT.

Vivendi Universal Publishing (VU Publishing): 31 rue du Colisée, 75383 Paris Cédex 08; tel. 1-53-53-30-00; fax 1-53-53-37-37; e-mail benoit.liva@vupublishing.net; internet www.vivendiuniversalpublishing.com; fmrly Havas; f. 1835; renamed 2000; education, literature, reference; imprints include Bordas, Dunod, Fleuve Noir, Harrap, Laffont, Larousse, Le Robert; 100% owned by Vivendi Universal; Pres. and Dir-Gen. AGNÈS TOURAINE.

Librairie Philosophique J. Vrin: 6 place de la Sorbonne, 75005 Paris; tel. 1-43-54-03-47; fax 1-43-54-48-18; e-mail contact@vrin.fr; internet www.vrin.fr; f. 1911; university textbooks, philosophy, education, science, law, religion; Chair. and Man. Dir A. PAULHAC-VRIN.

Librairie Vuibert: 20 rue Berbier-du-Mets, 75647 Paris Cédex 13; tel. 1-44-08-49-00; fax 1-44-08-49-03; e-mail laurence.brunel@vuibert.fr; internet www.vuibert.com; f. 1877; school and university textbooks, psychology, law; subsidiary of Editions Albin Michel.

PUBLISHERS' AND BOOKSELLERS' ASSOCIATIONS

Cercle de la Librairie (Syndicat des Industries et Commerces du Livre): 35 rue Grégoire de Tours, 75006 Paris Cédex; tel. 1-44-41-28-00; fax 1-44-41-28-40; f. 1847; a syndicate of the book trade, grouping the principal asscns of publishers, booksellers and printers; Chair. CHARLES-HENRI FLAMMARION; Man. Dir JEAN-MARIE DOUBLET.

Chambre Syndicale des Editeurs de Musique de France: 4–6 place de la Bourse, 75080 Paris Cédex 02; tel. 1-44-88-73-74; fax 1-44-88-73-89; e-mail cemf@bmg.com; f. 1873; music publishers' asscn; Chair. BERNARD BROSSOLLET; Sec. NELLY QUEROL.

Chambre Syndicale de l'Edition Musicale (CSDEM): 62 rue Blanche, 75009 Paris; tel. 1-48-74-09-29; fax 1-42-81-19-87; e-mail csdem@club-internet.fr; internet www.csdem.org; f. 1978 by merger; music publishers.

Fédération Française Syndicale de la Librairie: 49 rue de Châteaudun, 75009 Paris; tel. 1-42-82-00-03; fax 1-42-82-10-51; f. 1892; booksellers' asscn; 2,000 mems; Chair. JEAN LEGUÉ; Gen. Man. JEAN-BAPTISTE DAELMAN.

Syndicat National de l'Edition: 115 blvd Saint-Germain, 75006 Paris; tel. 1-44-41-40-50; fax 1-44-41-40-77; internet www.sne.fr; f. 1892; publishers' asscn; 550 mems; Chair. SERGE EYROLLES; Man. Dir JEAN SARZANA.

Syndicat National de la Librairie: 40 rue Grégoire de Tours, 75006 Paris; tel. 1-46-34-74-20; fax 1-44-07-14-73; booksellers' asscn; Pres. ALAIN DIART.

Broadcasting and Communications

TELECOMMUNICATIONS

Regulatory Authorities

Agence Nationale des Fréquences (ANFR): 78 ave du Général de Gaulle, BP 400, 94704 Maisons-Alfort Cédex; tel. 1-45-18-72-72; fax 1-45-18-72-00; e-mail parmentier@anfr.fr; internet www.anfr.fr; Pres. JEAN-CLAUDE GUIGUET; Gen. Man. JEAN-MARC CHADUC.

Autorité de Régulation des Télécommunications (ART): 7 sq. Max Hymans, 75730 Paris Cédex 15; tel. 1-40-47-70-00; fax 1-40-47-71-98; internet www.art-telecom.fr; Pres. JEAN-MICHEL HUBERT; Gen. Man. JEAN MARIMBERT.

Direction des Postes et Télécommunications (DPT): 20 ave de Ségur, 75354 Paris 07; tel. 1-43-19-19-39; fax 1-43-19-63-00; e-mail emmanuel.gabla@industrie.gouv.fr; Dir PATRICK DE GUERRE.

Major Service Providers

Bouygues Telecom: Arcs de Seine, 20 quai du Point du Jour, 92100 Boulogne-Billancourt; tel. 8-10-63-01-00; internet www.bouygtel .com; f. 1994; mobile cellular telecommunications; Pres. PHILIPPE MONTAGNER; Dir-Gen. GILLES PÉLISSON.

Cegetel: 1 place Carpeaux, Tour Séquoia, 92915 Paris La Défense Cédex; tel. 1-71-07-07-07; fax 1-71-07-75-22; internet www .cegetel-entreprises.fr; f. 1996; Pres. and Dir-Gen. FRANK ESSER; Dir-Gen. OLIVIER HUART.

France Telecom: 6 place d'Alleray, 75505 Paris Cédex 15; tel. 1-44-44-89-34; fax 1-44-44-03-59; internet www.francetelecom.fr; 54% state-owned; acquired Orange (UK) in 2000; Chair. THIERRY BRETON.

OrangeFrance: 41–45 blvd Romain Rolland, 92120 Montrouge; tel. 1—55–22—22—22; fax 1—55–22—25—50; internet www.orange.fr; f. 1992 as Itineris; present name adopted 2001; mobile cellular telecommunications; 19.2m. subscribers (Dec. 2002); Pres. THIERRY BRETON; Dir-Gen. SOLOMON TRUJILLO.

SFR: 1 place Carpeaux, Tour Séquoia, 92915 Paris La Défense Cédex; tel. 8–05–77–66–66; internet www.sfr.fr; f. 1993; mobile cellular telecommunications; 13.5m. subscribers (Dec. 2002); Pres. and Dir-Gen FRANK ESSER; Dir-Gen. PIERRE BARDON.

BROADCASTING

Conseil Supérieur de l'Audiovisuel (CSA): Tour Mirabeau, 39–43 quai André Citroën, 75739 Paris Cédex 15; tel. 1-40-58-38-00; fax 1-45-79-00-06; internet www.csa.fr; f. 1989 as replacement for the Commission Nationale de la Communication et des Libertés (CNCL); supervises all French broadcasting; awards licences to private radio and television stations, allocates cable networks and frequencies, appoints heads of state-owned radio and television cos, monitors programme standards; consists of nine members, appointed for six years: three nominated by the Pres. of the Republic; three by the Pres. of the National Assembly; and three by the Pres. of the Senate; Pres. DOMINIQUE BAUDIS; Gen. Man. LAURENT TOUVET.

Institut National de l'Audiovisuel: 4 ave de l'Europe, 94366 Bry-sur-Marne Cédex; tel. 1-49-83-26-74; fax 1-49-83-23-89; e-mail dtixiergallix@ina.fr; internet www.ina.fr; f. 1975; research and professional training in the field of broadcasting; radio and TV archives, TV production; Pres. EMMANUEL HOOG.

Télédiffusion de France (TDF): 10 rue d'Oradour-sur-Glane, 75732 Paris Cédex 15; e-mail e-tdf@tdf.fr; internet www.tdf.fr; f. 1975; partly privatized 1987; restructured in 2002; responsible for broadcasting programmes produced by the production companies, for the organization and maintenance of the networks, for study and research into radio and television equipment; operates a cable television network; broadcasts digital terrestrial television.

Radio

State-controlled Radio

Public radio services are provided by three entities: Radio France for the domestic audience; Radio-Télévision Française d'Outre-Mer for the French overseas departments and territories; and Radio France International for foreign countries (and those of foreign origin in France). Radio France began the digital broadcasting of certain of its channels in early 2000.

Société Nationale de Radiodiffusion (Radio France: 116 ave du Président Kennedy, 75786 Paris Cédex 16; tel. 1-42-30-22-22; fax 1-42-30-14-88; internet www.radio-france.fr; f. 1975; planning and production of radio programmes; provides five national services, 47 local stations and two European services; Chair. JEAN-MARIE CAVADA; Man. Dir CLAUDE NOREK.

    France Bleu: domestic, nation-wide service; for older people; Dir MICHEL MEYER.

    France Inter: domestic, nation-wide service; general programmes, for entertainment and information; Dir JEAN-LUC HEES.

    France Culture: domestic, nation-wide service; Dir LAURE ADLER.

    France Info : domestic, nation-wide service; continuous news and information; f. 1978; Dir PASCAL DELANNOY.

    France Musiques: domestic, nation-wide service; Dir PIERRE BOUTEILLER.

    Le Mouv': domestic, nation-wide service; music and general interest for people aged 18–35; f. 1997; Dir MARC GARCIA.

    France Inter: comprises 38 decentralized local radio stations; Dir PATRICK PÉPIN.

    Réseau FIP: comprises nine local stations; continuous music; Dir DOMINIQUE PENSEC.

    Hector: European service, broadcast by TDF1/TDF2 satellite; mainly classical music.

    France Culture Europe: European service, broadcast by TDF1/TDF2 satellite; cultural and information; Dir LAURE ADLER.

Radio France Internationale (RFI): 116 ave du Président Kennedy, BP 9516, 75786 Paris Cédex 16; tel. 1-42-30-12-12; fax 1-42-30-47-59; internet www.rfi.fr; broadcasts on MW and FM transmitters, mainly to Africa, Eastern Europe, North America, the Caribbean, South-East Asia and the Middle East, in French and 18 other languages; Pres. JEAN-PAUL CLUZEL; Dir-Gen. CHRISTIAN CHARPY.

Réseau France Outre-mer (RFO): 35–37 rue Danton, 92240 Malakoff; tel. 1-55-22-71-00; fax 1-55-22-74-76; e-mail rfo@rfo.fr; internet www.rfo.fr; controls broadcasting in the French overseas territories; 10 local stations providing two radio networks, two television channels, the latter broadcasting material from various state and private channels as well as local programmes, and one satellite television channel; Pres. ANDRÉ-MICHEL BESSE.

Independent Radio

BFM: 12 rue d'Oradour sur Glane, 75015 Paris; tel. 1-56-97-27-70; fax 1–56–97–27–61; e-mail nrepa@radiobfm.com; internet bfm.iside .net; f. 1992; broadcasts on cable and 14 FM frequencies; politics, economics; Pres. ALAIN WEILL.

Europe 1: 26 bis rue François 1er, 75008 Paris; tel. 1-42-32-90-00; fax 1-47-23-19-00; internet www3.europeinfos.com; owned by Groupe Lagardère, which also owns Europe 2 and RFM; broadcasting on long wave and 99 FM frequencies; Chair. ARNAUD LAGARDÈRE; Man. Dir JÉRÔME BELLAY.

Radio Monte-Carlo (RMC): 12 rue d'Oradour sur Glane, 75015 Paris; tel. 1-56-97-29-18; fax 1-56-97-29-05; internet www.rmcinfo .fr; broadcasting on long wave and 102 FM frequencies; information, talk and sports programmes; Pres. ALAIN WEILL.

RTL: 22 rue Bayard, 75008 Paris; tel. 1-40-70-40-70; fax 1-40-70-42-72; internet www.rtl.fr; broadcasting on long wave and 150 FM frequencies; Chair. and Man. Dir RÉMY SAUTTER.

Television

State-controlled Television

France Télévisions: 1 place Henri de France, 75015 Paris; tel. 1-44-31-60-00; fax 1-47-20-24-54; f. 1992 as supervisory authority for the national public television networks (France 2, France 3 and France 5: see below); Pres. MARC TESSIER; Sec.-Gen. FRANÇOIS GUILBEAU.

Société Nationale de Télévision—France 2 (F2): 7 Esplanade Henri de France, 75907 Paris Cédex 15; tel. 1-56-22-42-42; e-mail contact@france2.fr; internet www.france2.fr; f. 1975 as Antenne 2 (A2); general programmes for a nation-wide audience; Dir-Gen. MICHÈLE COTTA.

Société Nationale de Programmes—France 3 (F3): 7 Esplanade Henri de France, 75907 Paris Cédex 15; tel. 1-56-22-30-30; internet www.france3.fr; f. 1975 as France Régions 3 (FR3); general programmes for a nation-wide audience (with a larger proportion of cultural and educational programmes than F2), and regional programmes transmitted from 13 regional stations; Dir-Gen. RÉMY PFLIMLIN.

Société Nationale de Programmes—France 5 (F5): 10 rue Horace Vernet, 92785 Issy-les-Moulineaux Cédex 09; tel. 1-56-22-93-93; e-mail telespectateurs@france5.fr; internet www.france5.fr; f. 1994 as La Cinquième; present name adopted 2002; educational programmes and documentaries; Pres. MARC TESSIER; Dir-Gen. JEAN-PIERRE COTTET.

Arte France: 8 rue Marceau, 92785 Issy-les-Moulineaux Cédex 09; tel. 1-55-00-77-77; internet www.arte-tv.com; f. 1992 to replace La Sept; arts, cultural programmes, in French and German; Pres. JÉRÔME CLÉMENT; Dir-Gen. JEAN ROZAT.

Television programmes for France's overseas departments and territories are provided by Réseau France Outre-mer (see under Radio).

Independent Television

Canal Plus: 85–89 quai André Citroën, 75711 Paris Cédex 15; tel. 1-44-25-10-00; fax 1-44-25-12-34; e-mail contact_web@cplus.fr; internet www.cplus.fr; f. 1984; 34% owned by Vivendi, 15% by Richemont, and the remainder by other cos; coded programmes financed by audience subscription; uncoded programmes financed by advertising sold by Canal Plus; specializes in drama (including cinema films) and sport; launched a 'pay-per-view' service for sports events 1996; produces 21 theme channels in six countries; Pres. and Dir-Gen BERTRAND MÉHEUT.

Demain!: 1 rue Patry, 92220 Bagneux; fax 1-44-25-72-00; internet www.demain.fr; f. 1997; owned by Canal Plus; information about employment for job-seekers; Dir-Gen. MARTINE MAULÉON.

LCI (La Chaîne Info): 54 ave de la Voie Lactée, 92656 Boulogne-Billancourt Cédex; tel. 1-41-41-37-37; e-mail comm-lci@lci.fr; internet www.lci.fr; f. 1994; news, information; Pres. ETIENNE MOUGEOTTE; Dir-Gen. JEAN-CLAUDE DASSIER.

M6: 89 ave Charles de Gaulle, 92523 Neuilly-sur-Seine Cédex; tel. 1-41-92-66-66; fax 1-41-92-66-10; internet www.m6.fr; f. 1986 as TV6, re-formed as M6 1987; 46% owned by RTL Group, 37% by Groupe Suez; specializes in drama, music and magazines; Chair. of Bd JEAN DRUCKER; CEO NICOLAS DE TAVERNOST.

Télévision Française 1 (TF1): 1 quai du Point du Jour, 92656 Boulogne-Billancourt Cédex; tel. 1-41-41-12-34; fax 1-41-41-28-40; internet www.tf1.fr; f. 1975; as a state-owned channel, privatized 1987; 40.1% owned by Bouygues SA, 3.0% by Société Générale, and smaller percentages by other shareholders, including 2.4% by TF1 employees; general programmes; Pres. and Dir-Gen. PATRICK LE LAY.

Satellite Television

In 1984 TV5 began broadcasting programmes relayed from French, Belgian and Swiss television stations by satellite. In the same year, the French Government reached an agreement with Luxembourg to finance jointly a communal direct-broadcasting satellite television system (TDF1). TDF1 was inaugurated in 1988, and another satellite television system, TDF2 (financed by private investors), was launched in 1989. In 1993 the TDF1/TDF2 satellites were transmitting television programmes for Arte, Canal Plus and the MCM-Euromusique music channel, and radio programmes for Radio France (Hector and Elisa). Two telecommunications satellites, Télécom 2A and Télécom 2B, were also transmitting programmes for the principal television channels. In 1995 the Astra, Eutelsat and Télécom satellites were transmitting to the majority of the 1.0m. households that were able to receive satellite television. In 1996, with the advent of digital television programming, three new satellites, Canal Satellite, Télévision par satellite and AB Sat, were launched.

Cable Television

In 1999 a total of 116 television channels were available in France, including terrestrial, cable and pay-per-view channels. This compared with a total of 68 channels available in 1995, or 26 in 1990. The channels available to subscribers of cable television included the specialized national channels: Canal J for children, Ciné-Cinémas, providing cinema films, Planète, specializing in documentaries, and Eurosport France, local channels and foreign channels. The following are the principal cable television service providers:

Est Vidéocommunication: 26 blvd du Président Wilson, 67954 Strasbourg Cédex 9; tel. 3-88-76-44-60; fax 3-88-76-44-69; e-mail estvideo@evc.net; internet www.evc.net; f. 1988; 137,500 subscribers (2001); affiliated to Electricité de Strasbourg; Dir-Gen. FRANÇOIS HOLVECK.

France Télécom Cable: 3 rue Danton, 92240 Malakoff; tel. 1-55-58-34-00; fax 1-55-58-34-06; e-mail ftc.communication@wanadoo.fr;

internet www.francetelecomcable.fr; f. 1993; 753,900 subscribers (1998); Chair. PATRICK PINOCHET.

NC Numéricâble: 12–16 rue Guynemer, 92445 Issy-les-Moulineaux; tel. 1-55-92-46-00; fax 1-55-92-46-90; e-mail communication@ncnumericable.com; internet www.ncnumericable.com; f. 1997; affiliated to Canal Plus; 602,937 subscribers (1998); Pres. BERNARD COTTIN; Dir-Gen. CHRISTIAN KOZAR.

Noos: 20 place des vins de France, 75614 Paris Cédex 12; tel. 1-53-44-81-81; fax 1-53-44-80-98; e-mail webmaster@noos.com; internet www.noos.com; f. 1986; as Lyonnaise Communications, affiliated to Groupe Suez; 633,405 subscribers (1998); Chair FRANÇOIS JACLOT; Dir-Gen. FRANÇOIS GUICHARD.

Finance

(cap. = capital; res = reserves; dep. = deposits; m. = million; brs = branches; amounts in euros or French francs—FF)

BANKING

Central Bank

Banque de France: 31 rue Croix-des-Petits-Champs, 75001 Paris; tel. 1-42-92-42-92; fax 1-42-92-45-00; internet www.banque-france.fr; f. 1800; nationalized 1946; became independent 1994; acts as banker to the Treasury, issues bank notes, controls credit and money supply and administers France's gold and currency assets; in 1993 the National Assembly approved legislation to make the Banque de France an independent central bank, with a General Council to supervise activities and appoint the principal officials, and a nine-member monetary policy committee, independent of government control, to be in charge of French monetary policy; a member of the European System of Central Banks since June 1998; cap. and res 27,710.3m., dep. 46,720.2m., total assets 127,725.7m. (Dec. 2001); Gov. JEAN-CLAUDE TRICHET; Dep. Govs HERVÉ HANNOUN, JEAN-PAUL REDOUIN; 211 brs.

State Savings Bank

Caisse des depôts et consignations: 56 rue de Lille, 75356 Paris Cédex 07; tel. 1-40-49-56-78; fax 1-40-49-88-99; internet www.caissedesdepots.fr; f. 1816; manages state savings system, holds widespread investments in industrial cos; res 11,587m., dep. 206,941m., total assets 328,253m. (Dec. 2001); Pres. and CEO DANIEL LEBÈGUE; 1 br.

Commercial Banks

Banca Commerciale Italiana (France): BP 21009, 2 rue Meyerbeer, 75009 Paris; tel. 1-45-23-72-22; fax 1-45-23-70-90; internet www.bcif.fr; 99.99% owned by IntesaBci SpA (Italy); cap. 188.0m., res 3.8m., dep. 2,710.8m. (Dec, 2001); Chair. GIORGIO WINTELER; Gen. Man. GIAN BERTO.

Banque AGF: 14 rue Halévy, 75009 Paris; tel. 1-53-24-47-70; fax 1-53-24-45-54; e-mail serviceclient@banqueagf.fr; internet www.banqueagf.fr; f. 1991; by merger as Banque du Phénix; affiliated to Group Allianz; cap. €202.0m. (Dec. 2001), res 0.8m. FF, dep. 20,479.7m. FF (Dec. 1995); Pres. PHILIPPE TOUSSAINT.

Banque de Bretagne: 18 quai Duguay-Trouin, 35084 Rennes Cédex; tel. 2-99-01-75-75; fax 2-99-01-75-00; internet www.banque-de-bretagne.com; f. 1909; 100% owned by BNP Paribas; cap. 52.9m., res 14.8m., dep. 1,359.5m. (Dec. 2001); Pres. GERARD UZEL; 69 brs.

Banque CIAL—Crédit Industriel d'Alsace et de Lorraine: 31 rue Jean Wenger-Valentin, 67000 Strasbourg; tel. 3-88-37-61-23; fax 3-88-37-71-81; internet www.banquecial.fr; f. 1919; 99.99% owned by Crédit Industriel et Commercial; cap. 26.8m., res 527.8m., dep. 12,267.0m. (Dec. 2001); Chair. PHILIPPE VIDAL; Gen. Man. PIERRE JACHEZ; 170 brs and sub-brs.

Banque Commerciale pour l'Europe du Nord—Eurobank (BCEN—Eurobank): 79–81 blvd Haussmann, 75382 Paris Cédex 08; tel. 1-40-06-43-21; fax 1-40-06-48-48; f. 1921; present name adopted 1972; 87% owned by Central Bank of the Russian Federation; cap. 185.3m., res –119.8m., dep. 748.3m. (Dec. 2001); Chair. YURII PONOMAREV.

Banque de l'Economie du Commerce et de la Monétique: 34 rue du Wacken, 67913 Strasbourg Cédex 9; tel. 3-88-14-74-74; fax 3-88-14-75-10; e-mail becm@becm.creditmutuel.fr; internet www.becm.fr; f. 1992 as Banque de l'Economie—Crédit Mutuel; cap. 199.7m., dep. 1,167.0m., total assets 5,716.7m. (2001); CEO BERNARD BARTELMANN; 34 brs.

Banque Espírito Santo et de la Vénétie: 45 ave Georges Mandel, 75116 Paris; tel. 1-44-34-48-00; fax 1-44-34-48-48; e-mail besv@besv

.fr; internet www.besv.fr; f. 1945; present name adopted 1998; absorbed Via Banque in 2002; 42% owned by Espirito Santo Financial Group SA (Luxembourg); cap. 52.2m., res 1.3m., dep. 339.9m. (Dec. 2001); Chair. JEAN-CHRISTIAN P. MENARD.

Banque Fédérative du Crédit Mutuel: 34 rue du Wacken, 67913 Strasbourg Cédex 9; tel. 3-88-14-88-14; fax 3-88-14-67-00; internet www.bfcm.creditmutuel.fr; f. 1933; cap.1,296.5m., res 1,607.6m., dep. 151,022.5m. (Dec. 2001); Chair. ETIENNE PFLIMLIN; Gen. Man. MICHEL LUCAS.

Banque Française de l'Orient: 30 ave George V, 75008 Paris; tel. 1-49-52-17-00; fax 1-49-52-18-00; f. 1989 by merger; 98.6% owned by Crédit Agricole Indosuez; cap. 500.0m. FF, res 264.9m. FF, dep. 21,146.9m. FF (Dec. 1999); Chief Exec. BERNARD CALVET UNGER; Chair. HENRI GUILLEMIN.

Banque Hervet: 127 ave Charles de Gaulle, 92200 Neuilly-sur-Seine; tel. 1-46-40-92-87; fax 1-46-40-96-51; e-mail marketing@ banque-hervet.fr; internet www.banque-hervet.fr; f. 1830; 97.9% owned by Crédit Commercial de France (CCF); dep. 1,854m., total assets 5,266m. (Dec. 2000); Chair.of Bd and Pres. PATRICK CAREIL; Chief Exec. and Gen. Man. JEAN-PIERRE LECLERC; 86 brs.

Banque Intercontinentale Arabe: 67 ave Franklin D. Roosevelt, 75008 Paris; tel. 1-53-76-62-62; fax 1-42-89-09-59; e-mail bia-paris@ wanadoo.fr; f. 1975; 50% owned by Banque Extérieure d'Algérie, 50% by Libyan Arab Foreign Bank; cap. 102.0m., res 0.3m., dep. 679.8m. (Dec. 2001); Pres. MOHAMED TERBECHE.

Banque Nationale de Paris Intercontinentale: 1 rue Taitbout, 75009 Paris; tel. 1-40-14-22-11; fax 1-40-14-69-34; f. 1940; present name adopted 1972; 100% owned by BNP Paribas; cap. 30.5m., res. 406.0m., dep. 3,029.9m. (Dec. 2000); Chair. PIERRE MARIANI; Man. and CEO VINCENT DE ROUX.

Banque de Neuflize, Schlumberger, Mallet, Demachy (Banque NSMD): 3 ave Hoche, 75410 Paris Cédex 08; tel. 1-56-21-70-00; fax 1-56-21-84-60; e-mail webmaster@fr.abnamro.com; internet www.banque-nsmd.fr; f. 1966 by merger; 96.5% owned by ABN AMRO France; cap. 197.2m., res 109.0m., dep. 7,194.9m. (Dec. 2001); Chair. Supervisory Bd ROGER PAPAZ; Chair. Man. Bd JEAN-LOUIS MILIN; 18 brs.

Banque OBC—Odier Bungener Courvoisier: 57 ave d'Iéna, BP 195, 75783 Paris Cédex 16; tel. 1-45-02-40-00; fax 1-45-00-77-79; e-mail severine.cheyppe@fr.abnamro.com; internet www .banque-obc.fr; f. 1960 by merger; present name adopted 1987; 99.99% owned by ABN AMRO France; cap. 60.0m., res 11.5m., dep. 877.4m. (Dec. 2001); Chair. and Chief Exec. MAGGIEL SCALONGNE.

Banque Régionale de l'Ouest, SA: BP 49, 7 rue Gallois, 41003 Blois; tel. 2-54-56-54-56; fax 2-54-56-54-00; e-mail brostoi@bro.cic.fr; internet www.bro.fr; f. 1913; 100% owned by Crédit Industriel et Commercial; cap. 217.2m. FF, res 381.4m. FF, dep. 13,444.0m. FF (Dec. 2000); Chair. and CEO MICHEL MICHENKO; Gen. Man. JEAN-PIERRE BICHON; 95 brs.

Banque Sanpaolo: 52 ave Hoche, 75382 Paris Cédex 08; tel. 1-47-54-40-40; fax 1-47-54-46-57; e-mail info@sanpaolo.fr; internet www .sanpaolo.fr; f. 1971 by merger; 100% owned by Sanpaolo IMI SpA (Italy); cap. 350.0m., res 46.6m., dep. 5,621.9m. (Dec. 2001; Chair. LANFRANCO VIVARELLI; 60 brs.

Banque Scalbert-Dupont: 33 ave le Corbusier, BP 567, 59800 Lille; tel. 3-20-12-64-64; fax 3-20-12-64-05; e-mail bsdinter@bsd.cic .fr; internet www.bsd.tm.fr; f. 1977 by merger; 100% owned by Crédit Industriel et Commercial; cap. 80.0m., res 112.9m., dep. 5,656.3m. (Dec. 2001); Chair. GÉRARD ROMEDEMME; Gen. Man. JÉRÔME GUILLEMARD; 150 brs.

Banque Sudameris: 4 rue Meyerbeer, 75009 Paris; tel. 1-48-01-77-77; fax 1-42-46-32-13; e-mail webmaster@sudameris.com; internet www.sudameris.com; f. 1910; present name adopted 1978; cap. 545.2m., res 1,117.8m., dep. 16,500.9m. (Dec. 2001); active principally in South America; Chair. L. BENASSI.

Banque Worms: Le Voltaire, 1 place des Degrés, Puteaux, 92059 Paris La Défense Cédex; tel. 1-49-07-50-50; fax 1-49-07-59-11; internet www.banque-worms.fr; f. 1928; 100% owned by Deutsche Bank; cap. 335.3m., res –87.5m., dep. 4,250.1m. (Dec. 2000); Chair. JÉRÔME MEYSSONNIER; 18 brs.

Barclays Bank PLC France: 183 ave Daumesnil, 75575 Paris Cédex 12; tel. 1-55-78-78-78; fax 1-55-78-70-00; e-mail contact.fr@ barclays.co.uk; internet www.barclays.fr; f. 1968; subsidiary of Barclays Bank PLC (United Kingdom); Gen. Man. HENRI-PAUL PELLEGRINO; 43 brs.

BNP Paribas: 16 blvd des Italiens, 75009 Paris; tel. 1-40-14-45-46; fax 1-40-14-69-40; internet www.bnpparibas.com; f. 2000 by merger of Banque Nationale de Paris and Paribas; cap. 1,772m., res 18,820m., dep. 524,255 (Dec. 2001); Chair. and Chief Exec. MICHEL PÉBEREAU.

CCF: 103 ave des Champs Elysées, 75419 Paris Cédex 08; tel. 1-40-70-70-40; fax 1-40-70-70-09; internet www.ccf.com; 99.99% owned by HSBC Bank PLC (United Kingdom); f. 1894; fmrly Crédit Commercial de France; present name adopted 2002; cap. 377.0m., res 2,100.5m., dep. 44,208.2m. (Dec. 2001); Chair. and Chief Exec. CHARLES DE CROISSET; 184 brs in France.

Caisse d'Epargne Ile de France Paris: BP 9401, 19 rue du Louvre, 75021 Paris Cédex 01; tel. 1-40-41-30-31; fax 1-42-33-45-18; f. 1818; present name adopted 1991; cap. 266.6m., res 384.3m., dep. 22,888.6m. (Dec. 2001); Pres. NICOLE MOREAU; Chair. BERNARD COMOLET; 301 brs.

Compagnie Financière du Crédit Mutuel (CFCM): 32 rue Mirabeau, 29480 Le Relecq-Kerhuon; tel. 2-98-00-22-22; fax 2-98-60-27-24; internet www.cmb.fr; f. 1960; present name adopted 2001; 100% owned by Caisse Interfederale de Credit Mutuel, Brest; cap. 715.0m., res 71.5m., dep. 12,578.6m. (Dec. 2001); Chair. YVES LE BAQUER; Gen. Man. LOUIS ECHELARD; 300 brs.

CPR: 30 rue Saint Georges, 75312 Paris Cédex 09; tel. 1-45-96-20-00; fax 1-45-96-25-55; e-mail dircom@cpr.fr; internet www.cpr.fr; f. 1928 as Compagnie Parisienne de Réescompte; present name adopted 1997; discount bank; 88.53% owned by Crédit Agricole Indosuez; cap. 93.9m., res 350.7m., dep. 6,538.2m. (Dec. 2000); Chair. ROBERT RAYMOND; Gen. Man. ALEC DE LEZARDIÈRE; 2 brs.

Crédit Agricole Indosuez: 9 quai Paul Doumer, 92920 Paris La Défense Cédex; tel. 1-41-89-00-00; fax 1-41-89-15-22; internet www .ca-indosuez.com; f. 1975 as Banque Indosuez; 100% owned by Crédit Agricole; merchant and offshore banking; cap. 920m., res 2,180m., dep. 126,430m. (Dec. 2001); Chair. JEAN LAURENT; 13 brs in France, 44 outside France.

Crédit Coopératif: 33 rue des Trois Fontanot, BP 211, 92002 Nanterre Cédex; tel. 1-47-24-85-00; fax 1-47-24-89-25; e-mail din@ coopanet.com; internet www.credit-cooperatif.fr; f. 1893; fmrly Banque Française de Crédit Coopératif; present name adopted 2001; cap. 124.8m., res 36.4m., dep. 5,402.6m. (Dec. 2001); Pres. JEAN-CLAUDE DETILLEUX; Gen. Man. PIERRE LAJUGIE; 63 brs.

Crédit Foncier de France: 19 rue des Capucines, 75050 Paris Cédex 01; tel. 1-42-44-80-00; fax 1-42-44-86-99; e-mail communication@creditfoncier.fr; internet www.creditfoncier.fr; f. 1852; 90.6% owned by Caisse Nationale d'Epargne et de Prévoyance; mortgage banking; cap. 381.5m., res 216.5m., dep. 33,742.5m. (Dec. 2001); Gov. FRANÇOIS LEMASSON.

Crédit Industriel et Commercial (CIC): 6 ave de Provence, 75452 Paris Cédex 09; tel. 1-45-96-96-96; fax 1-45-96-96-66; internet www.cic-banques.fr; f. 1990 by merger; present name adopted 2000; 68.6% owned by Banque Fédérative du Crédit Mutuel; cap. 560m., res 2,708m., dep. 108,254m. (Dec. 2001); Pres. ETIENNE PFIMLIN; Chair. MICHEL LUCAS.

Crédit Industriel de Normandie (Banque CIN): BP 3026X, 15 place de la Pucelle d'Orléans, 76041 Rouen; tel. 2-35-08-64-00; fax 2-35-08-64-38; internet www.cin.fr; f. 1932; 100% owned by Crédit Industriel et Commercial; cap. 64.0m., res 14.0m., dep. 2,390.0m. (Dec. 2001); Chair. GÉRARD ROMEDENNE; Gen. Man. JÉRÔME GUILLEMARD; 7 brs and 71 sub-brs.

Crédit Industriel de l'Ouest (Banque CIO): BP 84001, 2 ave Jean-Claude Bonduelle, 44040 Nantes Cédex 1; tel. 2-40-12-91-91; fax 2-40-12-92-07; e-mail cio-teleconseil@cio.cic.fr; internet www.cio .fr; f. 1957; 100% owned by Crédit Industriel et Commercial; cap. 45.0m., res 254.5m., dep. 5,835.2m. (Dec. 2001); Chair. BENOÎT DE LA SEIGLIÈRE; Man. Dir GÉRARD GOULET; 13 brs and 181 sub-brs.

Crédit Lyonnais: 19 blvd des Italiens, 75002 Paris; tel. 1-42-95-70-00; fax 1-53-02-73-83; internet www.creditlyonnais.com; f. 1863; privatized 1999; merger with Crédit Agricole agreed 2003; cap. 1,767m., res 5,749m., dep. 173,807m. (Dec. 2000); Chair. JEAN PEYRELEVADE; Chief Exec. DOMINIQUE FERRARO; 2,100 brs.

Crédit du Nord: 28 place Rihour, BP 569, 59023 Lille Cédex; tel. 1-40-22-40-22; fax 1-40-22-55-83; internet www.cdn.fr; f. 1974 by merger; 80% owned by Société Générale; cap. 740.3m., res 135.7m., dep. 15,028.5m. (Dec. 2001); Pres. ALAIN RY; Gen. Man. BERNARD BEAUFILS; 614 brs.

Dresdner Bank Gestions France: 108 blvd Haussmann, 75008 Paris; tel. 1-44-70-80-80; fax 1-42-93-03-30; e-mail webmaster-paris@dresdner-bank.de; internet www.dresdner-kb.fr; f. 1979; fmrly Dresdner Kleinwort Benson (Marchés); present name adopted 2001; Chair. ALEXIS PILLET-WILL; Dir KONSTANTIN VON SCHWEINITZ.

Entenial: 33–37 blvd Vauban, Guyancourt, 78066 St Quentin-en-Yvelines Cédex; tel. 1-39-41-10-10; fax 1-39-41-10-55; internet www .entenial.com; f. 2000 by merger of Banque La Henin, COCEFI and Comptoir de Banque; total assets 11,445m. (June 2001); Pres. JACQUES LEBHAR.

Fortis Banque France: 56 rue de Châteaudun, 75009 Paris; tel. 1-42-80-68-68; fax 1-42-81-53-35; e-mail courrier@fr.fortisbanque .com; internet www.fr.fortisbank.com; f. 1920; 99.94% owned by Fortis Bank (Belgium); cap. 35.2m., res 179.0m., dep. 3,301.5m. (Dec. 2001); Pres. and Chair. of Bd LUCAS WILLEMYNS; 79 brs.

HSBC Bank France: 20 Place Vendôme, 75332 Paris Cédex 07; tel. 1-44-86-18-61; fax 1-42-60-05-62; f. 1966; 100% owned by HSBC Europe BV; present name adopted 1999; merged with HSBC Republic Bank (France) 2000; cap. 1,077.5m., res 809.3m., dep. 5,342.0m. (Dec. 2001); Chair. MARK McCOMBE.

ING Bank (France): 89–91 rue du Faubourg Saint-Honoré, 75008 Paris; tel. 1-55-27-70-00; fax 1-55-27-77-77; internet www.ingbank .fr; f. 1953; fmrly Banque Bruxelles Lambert France; present name adopted 2000; 100% owned by Bank Brussels Lambert (Belgium); cap. 320.0m., res 158.2m., dep. 4,541.3m. (Dec. 2001); Chair. MICHEL TILMANT; 1 br.

Lyonnaise de Banque: 8 rue de la République, 69001 Lyon; tel. 4-78-92-02-12; fax 4-78-92-03-00; e-mail ddi@lb.cicomore.fr; internet www.l-b.fr; f. 1865; 100% owned by Crédit Industriel and Commercial; cap. 211.4m., res 217.2m., dep. 11,623.9m. (Dec. 2001); Chair. and Chief Exec. D. SAMUEL-LAJEUNESSE; Gen. Man. RÉMY WEBER; 368 brs.

Natexis Banques Populaires: 45 rue Saint-Dominique, 75007 Paris; tel. 1-48-00-48-00; fax 1-48-00-41-51; internet www.nxbp .banquepopulaire.fr; f. 1999; 76% owned by Banque Fédérale des Banques Populaires; cap. 709m., res 2,668m., dep. 73,299m. (Dec. 2001); Chair. PHILIPPE DUPONT; Chief Exec. PAUL LORIOT.

Société Bordelaise de CIC: 42 cours du Chapeau Rouge, 33000 Bordeaux; tel. 5-57-85-55-00; fax 5-57-85-57-50; internet www.sb.cic .fr; f. 1880; 100% owned by Crédit Industrial et Commercial; cap. 363.3m., res 105.2m., dep. 11,266.4m. (Dec. 2000); Chair.and Man. Dir JEAN-PAUL ESCANDE; 93 brs.

Société Générale: Tour Société Générale, 17 Cours Valmy, 92972 Paris La Défense; tel. 1-42-14-20-00; fax 1-40-98-20-99; internet www.societegenerale.fr; f. 1864; cap. 539m., res 13,057m., dep. 350,261m. (Dec. 2001); Chair. and Chief Exec. DANIEL BOUTON; 2,000 brs in France.

Société Marseillaise de Crédit: 75 rue Paradis, 13006 Marseille; tel. 4-91-13-33-33; fax 4-91-13-55-15; e-mail infos@smc.fr; internet www.smc.fr; f. 1865; 97.0% owned by Cie Financière Ile-du-Rhône; cap. 16.0m., res 36.3m., dep. 2,998.8m. (Dec. 2001); Chair. and Chief Exec. JOSEPH PEREZ; Gen. Mans MAURICE DADONNE, EMMANUEL BARTHELEMY; 165 brs (incl. 3 in Monaco).

Société Nancéienne Varin-Bernier (CIC Banque SNVB): 4 place André Maginot, 54074 Nancy; tel. 3-83-34-50-00; fax 3-83-34-50-99; e-mail snvbinter@snvb.cic.fr; internet www.snvb.fr; f. 1881; 100% owned by Crédit Industriel et Commercial; cap. 60.0m., res 200.3m., dep. 5,963.7m. (Dec. 2001); Chair. PHILIPPE VIDAL; Gen. Man. LUC DYMARSKI; 148 brs.

Union de Banques à Paris: 17–19 place Etienne Pernet, 75738 Paris Cédex 15; tel. 1-45-30-44-44; fax 1-45-30-44-57; internet www .ubp.fr; f. 1935; 99.4% owned by Crédit Industriel et Commercial; cap. 331.3m. FF, res 13.0m. FF, dep. 11,213.1m. FF (Dec. 1999); Chair. RAYMOND BERT; Chief Exec. and Gen. Man. JEAN-FRANÇOIS LE TREIS; 54 brs.

Union de Banques Arabes et Françaises (UBAF): 190 ave Charles de Gaulle, 92523 Neuilly-sur-Seine; tel. 1-46-40-61-01; fax 1-47-38-13-88; e-mail info@ubafrance.com; internet www.ubafrance .com; f. 1970; 43.9% owned by Crédit Lyonnais, 56.1% by Arab interests; cap. 228.3m., res 89.6m., dep. 2,139.0m. (Dec. 2001); Chair. PATRICK LEGAIT.

Co-operative Banks

Banque Populaire Bourgogne Franche-Comté: 14 blvd de la Trémouille, BP 310, 21008 Dijon Cédex; internet www.bpbfc .banquepopulaire.fr; f. 2002 by merger of Banque Populaire de Bourgogne and Banque Populaire de Franche-Comté, du Mâconnais et de l'Ain; Pres. ALAIN JACQUIER; Dir-Gen. BERNARD JEANNIN; 150 brs.

Banque Populaire de la Côte d'Azur (BPCA): BP 241, 457 Promenade des Anglais, 06024 Nice; tel. 4-93-21-52-00; fax 4-93-21-54-45; e-mail contact@cotedazur.banquepopulaire.fr; internet www .cotedazur.banquepopulaire.fr; f. 1986; cap. 315.8m. FF, res 231.4m. FF, dep. 16,121.5m. FF (Dec. 2000); Pres BERNARD FLEURY; Gen. Man. JEAN-FRANÇOIS COMAS; 67 brs.

Banque Populaire Loire et Lyonnais: 141 rue Garibaldi, 69003 Lyon; tel. 4-89-95-55-55; fax 4-78-71-03-99; internet www .loirelyonnais.banquepopulaire.fr; f. 2000 by merger of Banque Populaire de Lyon and Banque Populaire de la Loire; cap. 113.1m., res 88.6m., dep. 3,218.3m.

Banque Populaire de la Région Economique de Strasbourg: BP 401 R/1, 5–7 rue du 22 novembre, 67001 Strasbourg; tel. 3-88-62-77-11; fax 3-88-62-70-35; e-mail international.bpres@strasbourg .banquepopulaire.fr; internet www.strasbourg.banquepopulaire.fr; f. 1909; present name adopted 1945; cap. 74.1m., res 63.9m., dep. 2,255.3m. (Dec. 2001); Pres. CHRISTIAN BREVARD; Gen. Man. DOMINIQUE DIDON; 50 brs.

Banque Populaire du Massif Central: BP 53, 18 blvd Jean Moulin, 63000 Clermont-Ferrand; tel. 4-73-23-46-23; fax 4-73-23-47-99; internet www.massifcentral.banquepopulaire.fr; f. 1920; cap. 56.4m., res 82.0m., dep. 2,060.6m. (Dec. 2001); Chair. of Bd MAX SEROR; Gen. Man. DOMINIQUE DIDON.

BRED Banque Populaire: 18 quai de la Rapée, 75604 Paris Cédex 12; tel. 1-48-98-60-00; fax 1-40-04-71-57; e-mail webmaster@bred.fr; internet www.bred.fr; f. 1919; fmrly Banque Régionale d'Escompte et de Dépôts; present name adopted 1994; cap. 220.0m. , res 260.0m., dep. 16,371.4m. (Dec. 2001); Chair. STEVE GENTILI; Gen. Man. and Chief Exec. FRANÇOIS-XAVIER DE FOURNAS; 244 brs (including 52 in the French Overseas).

Crédit Agricole: 91–93 blvd Pasteur, 75015 Paris; tel. 1-43-23-52-02; fax 1-43-23-20-28; internet www.credit-agricole.fr; f. 1920; central institution for co-operative banking group comprising 53 Caisses Regionales and a central bank (CNCA); emphasis on agri-business; merger with Crédit Lyonnais agreed 2003; cap. 2,911m., res 11,016m., dep. 352,601m. (Dec. 2001); Pres. RENÉ CARRON; Chief Exec. JEAN LAURENT; 7,971 brs.

Supervisory Body

Association Française des Etablissements de Crédit (AFEC): 36 rue Taitbout, 75009 Paris; tel. 1-48-24-34-34; fax 1-48-24-13-31; f. 1983; advises Govt on monetary and credit policy and supervises the banking system; Pres. MICHEL FREYCHE; Gen. Man. ROBERT PELLETIER.

Banking Association

Association Française des Banques: 18 rue La Fayette, 75440 Paris Cédex 09; tel. 1-48-00-52-52; fax 1-42-46-76-40; e-mail afb@afb .fr; internet www.afb.fr; f. 1941; 430 mems; Pres. MICHEL PEBEREAU; Dir-Gen. GILLES GUITTON.

STOCK EXCHANGES

The Paris Stock Exchange (Bourse) was established in 1725. There are provincial exchanges at Bordeaux, Lille, Lyon, Marseille, Nancy and Nantes. During the 1980s the Paris Bourse underwent extensive changes and deregulation and a fully computerized clearing and settlement system, called Relit, was installed. The reforms allowed member firms to open their capital to banks, insurance companies and other financial institutions.

In September 2000 Euronext, the largest stock exchange in the euro zone, was formed by the merger of the stock exchanges of Paris (Bourse de Paris), Brussels, Belgium (Brussels Exchanges) and Amsterdam, the Netherlands (Amsterdam Exchanges); in February 2002 the Bolsa de Valores de Lisboa e Porta in Lisbon, Portugal, merged with Euronext, and adopted the name Euronext Lisbonne.

Euronext Paris: 39 rue Cambon, 75001 Paris; tel. 1-49-27-10-00; fax 1-49-27-14-33; e-mail d.lande@euronext.fr; internet www .euronext.fr; Chair. JEAN-FRANÇOIS THÉODORE.

Marché à Terme International de France (MATIF): 39 rue Cambon, 75001 Paris; tel. 1-49-27-10-00; fax 1-49-27-11-15; e-mail a.darpy@euronext.fr; internet www.matif.fr; f. 1986; financial and commodities futures exchange.

Le Marché des Options Négociables de Paris (MONEP): 39 rue Cambon, 75001 Paris; internet www.monep.fr; f. 1987; derivatives and options trading.

Stock Exchange Associations

Commission des Opérations de Bourse (COB): 17 place de la Bourse, 75002 Paris; tel. 1-53-45-60-25; fax 1-53-45-61-00; e-mail rel-pub@cob.fr; internet www.cob.fr; f. 1967; 266 mems; Chair. MICHEL PRADA.

Fédération Française des Clubs d'Investissement (FFCI): 39 rue Cambon, 75001 Paris; tel. 1-42-60-12-47; fax 1-42-60-10-14; e-mail fnaci@club-internet.fr; internet www.ffci.org; f. 1968; fmrly Fédération Nationale des Associations de Clubs d'Investissement (FNACI); represents investment clubs in matters concerning public and political institutions; Pres. CLAUDE VALLON.

INSURANCE

Abeille Vie: 57 rue Taitbout, 75009 Paris; tel. 1-55-50-55-50; fax 1-55-50-55-60; e-mail catherine_charrier@cgu.fr; internet www .abeille-assurances.fr; subsidiary of CGU France; Pres. BERNARD POTTIER; Dir BRUNO ROSTAIN.

Assurances du Crédit Mutuel IARD, SA: BP 373 R 10, 34 rue du Wacken, 67010 Strasbourg Cédex; tel. 3-88-14-90-90; fax 3-88-14-90-01; internet www.creditmutuel.fr; Pres. MICHEL LUCAS; Dir ALAIN SCHMITTER.

Assurances Générales de France (AGF): 87 rue de Richelieu, 75113 Paris Cédex 02; tel. 1-44-86-20-00; fax 1-49-27-99-57; internet www.agf.fr; f. 1968 by merger; affiliated to Groupe Allianz (Germany); insurance and reinsurance; Pres. ANTOINE JEANCOURT-GALI-GNANI; Gen. Mans JEAN-FRANÇOIS DEBROIS, YVES MANSION.

Aviva: 52 rue de la Victoire, 75009 Paris; e-mail veronique_eriaud@aviva.fr; internet www.aviva.fr; f. 1998 as CGU France by merger; present name adopted 2002; affiliated to CGNU Group (United Kingdom).

AXA Assurances IARD: 21 rue de Châteaudun, 75441 Paris Cédex 09; tel. 1-53-21-16-00; fax 1-53-21-17-96; internet www.axa.com; Pres. CLAUDE TENDIL; Dir JEAN-LUC BERTOZZI.

Caisse Centrale des Assurances Mutuelles Agricoles: 8 rue d'Astorg, 75383 Paris Cédex 08; tel. 1-44-56-77-77; fax 1-44-56-79-46; affiliated to Groupama; Pres. JEAN BALIGAND; CEO JEAN AZEMA.

Caisse Nationale de Prévoyance-Assurances (CNP): 4 place Raoul Dautry, 75716 Paris Cédex 15; tel. 1-42-18-88-88; fax 1-42-34-70-14; general insurance; Pres GILLES BENOIST, EDMOND ALPHANDERY.

Cardif: 4 rue des Frères Caudron, 92858 Rueil-Malmaison Cédex; tel. 1-41-42-83-00; fax 1-41-42-84-17; internet www.cardif.fr; general insurance; Pres. PAUL VILLEMAGNE; Dir-Gens DANIEL DERRÉ, PHILIPPE MATHOUILLET, PIERRE DE VILLENEUVE.

Ecureuil Vie: 5 rue Masseran, 75007 Paris; tel. 1-58-40-64-00; fax 1-58-40-64-91; e-mail jean.baby@ecuvie.caisse-epargne.fr; life insurance; Pres. PHILIPPE WAHL; Dir JEAN BABY.

ERISA: Immeuble Ile de France, 4 pl. de la Pyramide, 92800 Paris La Défense; tel. 1-41-02-40-40; fax 1-41-02-49-84; life insurance; affiliated to HSBC France; Pres. PATRICK POLLET; Dir JOËLLE DURIEUX.

La Fédération Continentale: 11 blvd Haussmann, 75009 Paris; tel. 1-55-32-74-00; fax 1-55-32-74-01; e-mail webmastre@federation-continentale.fr; internet www.federation-continentale.fr; f. 1961; life insurance; Pres. HENRI MOULARD; Dir-Gen. DANIEL COLLIGNON.

Garantie Mutuelle des Fonctionnaires: 76 rue de Prony, 75857 Paris Cédex 17; tel. 1-47-54-10-10; fax 1-47-54-18-97; internet www.gmf.fr; f. 1934; Pres. YVES CAZAUX; Dir CHRISTIAN SASTRE.

Generali France Assurances: 5 rue de Londres, 75456, Paris Cédex 09; tel. 1-55-32-40-00; fax 1-55-32-40-05; e-mail webmaster@agence.generali.fr; internet www.gfa.generali.fr; Pres. CLAUDE TENDRIL; Dir ERIC LE GENTIL.

GPA Assurances—Groupe Generali: 18 place des Cinq Martyrs du Lycée Buffon, 75695 Paris Cédex 14; tel. 1-40-47-15-15; fax 1-43-27-10-90; internet www.gpa.fr; Pres. CLAUDE TENDRIL; Dir-Gen. JEAN-YVES HERMENIER.

Groupama Vie: 5 rue du Centre, 93199 Noisy Le Grand Cédex; tel. 1-49-31-31-31; fax 1-49-31-31-98; e-mail webmaster@groupama.fr; internet www.groupama.fr; life insurance; Pres. JEAN BALIGAND.

Groupe des Assurances Nationales (GAN): 8–10 rue d'Astorg, Paris 75008; tel. 1-42-47-50-00; fax 1-42-47-67-66; e-mail gan.rimbault.philippe@wanadoo.fr; internet www.gan.fr; f. 1820; fire; f. 1830; life; f. 1865; accident; affiliated to Groupama; Pres. JEAN-FRANÇOIS LEMOUX; Dir HENRI GUS.

La Mondiale: 32 ave Emile Zola, Mons en Baroeul, 59896 Lille Cédex 9; tel. 3-20-67-37-00; fax 3-20-47-70-90; internet www.lamondiale.com; f. 1905; life insurance; Pres. and Dir-Gen. PATRICK PEUGEOT.

La Mutuelle d'Assurances du Commerce et de l'Industrie (MACI): BP 609, 8 rue de Dammartin, 59671 Roubaix Cédex 1; tel. 3-20-45-72-00; fax 3-20-45-72-36; Pres. GILBERT TOULEMONDE; Dir LUCIEN CATRY.

La Mutuelle du Mans Assurances IARD: 19 rue Chanzy, 72030 le Mans Cédex 09; tel. 2-43-41-72-72; fax 2-43-42-60-85; internet www.mma.fr; life and general insurance; f. 1828; Pres. JEAN-CLAUDE SEYS; Dir-Gen. JACQUES LENORMAND.

Predica: 50 rue de la Procession, 75724 Paris Cédex 15; tel. 1-43-23-58-00; fax 1-43-23-03-47; internet www.predica.com; affiliated to Caisse Nationale du Crédit Agricole; general insurance; Pres. MAURICE GRANGEY; Dir MICHEL VILLATTE.

Préservatrice Foncière Assurances Vie (PFA Vie): Immeuble Athena, Cédex 43, 92076 Paris La Défense; tel. 1-42-91-10-10; fax 1-42-91-19-19; general insurance; Pres. ANTOINE JEANCOURT-GALIGNANI; Dir YVES MANSION.

Previposte: BP 7162, 4 Place Raoul Dautry, 75716 Paris Cédex 15; tel. 1-42-18-91-80; fax 1-42-18-94-94; life insurance; Pres. JACQUES OUVAROFF; Dir GILLES ARTAUD.

Socapi: 42 rue des Mathurins, 75008 Paris; tel. 1-44-71-52-00; fax 1-40-17-02-33; internet www.socapi.fr; f. 1985; 55% owned by Groupe Crédit Industriel et Commercial, 45% by Groupe des Assurances Nationales; life insurance; Pres. JEAN-PAUL GUILLOU; Gen. Man. JEAN VECCHIERINI.

Suravenir: BP 103, 232 rue Général Paulet, 29802 Brest Cédex 09; tel. 2-98-34-65-00; fax 2-98-34-65-11; internet www.suravenir.fr; f. 1984; general insurance; Pres. DENIS GUYARD; Dir HUMBERT DE FRESNOYE.

Union des Assurances Fédérales (UAF): 27 ave Claude Vellefaux, 75499 Paris Cédex 10; tel. 1-40-03-10-00; fax 1-40-18-36-93; internet www.uafdirect.fr; life insurance; affiliated to Crédit Lyonnais; Chair. and CEO JEAN-PIERRE WIEDMER.

Insurance Associations

Fédération Française des Courtiers d'Assurances et de Réassurances (FCA): 91 rue Saint Lazare, 75009 Paris; tel. 1-48-74-19-12; fax 1-42-82-91-10; e-mail ffca@wanadoo.fr; internet www.ffca.fr; f. 1991; Chair. RÉGIS FABRE; c. 700 mems.

Fédération Française des Sociétés d'Assurances (FFSA): 26 blvd Haussmann, 75009 Paris; tel. 1-42-47-90-00; fax 1-42-47-93-11; internet www.ffsa.fr; f. 1937; Chair. DENIS KESSLER; Sec.-Gen. GILLES WOLKOWITSCH.

Fédération Nationale des Syndicats d'Agents Généraux d'Assurances de France: 104 rue Jouffroy d'Abbans, 75847 Paris Cédex 17; tel. 1-44-01-18-00; fax 1-46-22-76-29; Chair. JEAN-CLAUDE LECHANOINE.

Syndicat Français des Assureurs-Conseils: 14 rue de la Grange Batelière, 75009 Paris; tel. 1-55-33-51-51; fax 1-48-00-93-01; internet www.sfac-assurance.fr; Chair. HERVÉ DE WAZIÈRES.

Trade and Industry

GOVERNMENT AGENCIES

Centre Français du Commerce Extérieur: 10 ave d'Iéna, 75783 Paris Cédex 16; tel. 1-40-73-38-88; fax 1-40-73-39-79; e-mail orientation@cfce.fr; internet www.cfce.fr; Pres. ARIANE OBOLENSKY; CEO JEAN-DANIEL GARDÈRE.

Conseil du Commerce de France: 14 rue de Castiglione, 75001 Paris; tel. 1-40-15-03-03; fax 1-40-15-97-22; Pres. BAUDOUIN MONNOYEUR.

DEVELOPMENT ORGANIZATIONS

Agence Pour la Création d'Entreprises (APCE): 14 rue Delambre, 75682 Paris Cédex 14; tel. 1-42-18-58-58; fax 1-42-18-58-00; e-mail info@apce.com; internet www.apce.com; Pres. MICHEL HERVÉ.

Groupe IDI: 18 ave Matignon, 75008 Paris; tel. 1-55-27-80-00; fax 1-40-17-04-44; f. 1970 as Institut de Développement Industriel; provides venture capital, takes equity shares in small and medium-sized businesses; Chair. CHRISTIAN LANGLOIS MEURINNE; CEO F. MARMISSOLLE.

CHAMBERS OF COMMERCE

There are Chambers of Commerce in all the larger towns for all the more important commodities produced or manufactured.

Assemblée des Chambres Françaises de Commerce et d'Industrie: 45 ave d'Iéna, 75116 Paris; tel. 1-40-69-37-00; e-mail contactsweb@acfci.cci.fr; internet www.acfci.cci.fr; f. 1964; unites 160 local and 20 regional chambers of commerce and industry; Pres. JEAN-FRANÇOIS BERNARDIN.

Chambre de Commerce et d'Industrie de Paris: 27 ave de Friedland, 75382 Paris Cédex 08; tel. 1-55-65-55-65; fax 1-55-65-78-68; e-mail webmestre@ccip.fr; internet www.ccip.fr; f. 1803; 307,000 mems in Paris and surrounding regions (Hauts de Seine, Seine-Saint-Denis and Val de Marne); Chair. MICHEL FRANCK.

INDUSTRIAL AND TRADE ASSOCIATIONS

Assemblée Permanente des Chambres d'Agriculture (APCA): 9 ave George V, 75008 Paris; tel. 1-53-57-10-10; fax 1-53-57-10-05; e-mail accueil@apca.chambagri.fr; internet paris.apca.chambagri.fr; f. 1929; Chair. LUC GUYAU; Dir-Gen. (vacant).

Association Nationale des Industries Alimentaires (ANIA): 155 blvd Haussmann, 75008 Paris; tel. 1-53-83-86-00; fax 1-45-61-96-64; e-mail infos@ania.net; internet www.ania.net; f. 1971; food produce; Chair. VICTOR SCHERRER.

Chambre Syndicale de l'Ameublement, Négoce de Paris et de l'Ile de France: 15 rue de la Cerisaie, 75004 Paris; tel. 1-42-72-13-79; fax 1-42-72-02-36; e-mail info@meubleparis.com.fr; internet www.meubleparis.com.fr; f. 1860; furnishing; Chair. NICOLE PHILIBERT; 350 mems.

Chambre Syndicale des Céramistes et Ateliers d'Art de France: 4 passage Roux, 75017 Paris; tel. 1-44-01-08-30; fax 1-44-01-08-35; internet www.ateliersdart.com; f. 1886; craft and design trades; Chair. VICTOR DESCHANG.

Chambre Syndicale des Constructeurs de Navires: 47 rue de Monceau, 75008 Paris; tel. 1-53-89-52-01; fax 1-53-89-52-15; e-mail cscn@club-internet.fr; internet www.cscn.fr; shipbuilding; Chair. PATRICK BOISSIER; Gen. Man. FABRICE THEOBALD.

Comité Central des Armateurs de France: 47 rue de Monceau, 5008 Paris; tel. 1-53-89-52-52; fax 1-53-89-52-53; e-mail caf@ccaf.asso.fr; internet www.ccaf.asso.fr; f. 1903; shipping; Pres. ALAIN WILS; Delegate-Gen. EDOUARD BERLET; 110 mems.

Comité des Constructeurs Français d'Automobiles: 2 rue de Presbourg, 75008 Paris; tel. 1-49-52-51-00; fax 1-49-52-51-88; e-mail cmory@ccfa.fr; internet www.ccfa.fr; f. 1909; motor manufacturing; Chair. YVES DE BELABRE; 9 mems.

Comité National des Pêches Maritimes et des Elevages Marins (CNPMEM): 51 rue Salvador Allende, 92027 Nanterre Cédex; tel. 1-47-75-01-01; fax 1-49-00-06-02; e-mail cnpmem@comite-peches.fr; internet www.comite-peches.fr; marine fisheries.

Comité Professionnel du Pétrole: 212 ave Paul Doumer, 92508 Rueil-Malmaison Cédex; tel. 1-47-16-94-60; fax 1-47-08-10-57; e-mail cpdp@cpdp.org; internet www.cpdp.org; f. 1950; petroleum industry; 80 mems; Pres. JACQUES CHAUMAS.

Commissariat à l'Energie Atomique (CEA) (Atomic Energy Commission): 31–33 rue de la Fédération, 75752 Paris Cedex 15; tel. 1-40-56-10-00; fax 1-40-56-29-70; e-mail dcom@aramis.cea.fr; internet www.cea.fr; f. 1945; promotes the uses of nuclear energy in science, industry and national defence; involved in research of nuclear materials; reactor development; fundamental research; innovation and transfer of technologies; military applications; bio-technologies; robotics; electronics; new materials; radiological protection and nuclear safety; Gen. Administrator PASCAL COLOMBANI; High Commissioner RENÉ PELLAT.

Confédération des Industries Céramiques de France: 3 rue La Boétie, 75008 Paris; tel. 1-58-18-30-40; fax 1-42-66-09-00; e-mail cicf@ceramique.org; f. 1937; ceramic industry; Chair. JACQUES RUSSEIL; Man. Dir FRANÇOIS DE LA TOUR; 85 mems, 5 affiliates.

Fédération des Chambres Syndicales de l'Industrie du Verre: 3 rue La Boétie, 75008 Paris; tel. 1-42-65-60-02; e-mail fedeverre@wanadoo.fr; internet www.verre-avenir.org; f. 1874; glass industry; Chair. JACQUES DEMARTY.

Fédération des Chambres Syndicales des Minerais, Minéraux Industriels et Métaux non-Ferreux: 30 ave de Messine, 75008 Paris; tel. 1-45-63-02-66; fax 1-45-63-61-54; e-mail fmmnfx@aol.com; e-mail www.mineraux-et-metaux.org; f. 1945; minerals and non-ferrous metals; Chair. BERTRAND DURRANDE; Delegate-Gen. G. JOURDAN; 16 affiliated syndicates.

Fédération des Exportateurs des Vins et Spiritueux de France: 95 rue de Monceau, 75008 Paris; tel. 1-45-22-75-73; fax 1-45-22-94-16; e-mail contact@fevs.com; f. 1921; exporters of wines and spirits; Pres. PATRICK RICARD; Delegate-Gen. LOUIS RÉGIS AFFRE; 450 mems.

Fédération Française de l'Acier: Immeuble Pacific, 11-13 Cours Valmy, 92070 Paris La Défense Cédex; tel. 1-41-25-58-00; fax 1-41-25-59-81; e-mail svp.clients@ffa.fr; internet www.ffa.fr; f. 1945; steel-making; Chair. GUY DOLLÉ; Delegate-Gen. GEORGES CHACORNAC.

Fédération Française du Bâtiment: 33 ave Kléber, 75784 Paris Cédex 16; tel. 1-40-69-51-00; fax 1-45-53-58-77; e-mail ffbbox@ffb.fr; internet www.ffbatiment.fr; f. 1906; building trade; Chair. ALAIN SIONNEAU; Dir-Gen. BERTRAND SABLIER; 50,000 mems.

Fédération Française des Industries Lainière et Cotonnière (FFILC): BP 121, 37–39 rue de Neuilly, 92113 Clichy Cédex; tel. 1-47-56-30-40; fax 1-47-37-06-20; e-mail ffilc@fedcoton-laine.com; internet www.fedcoton-laine.com; f. 1902; manufacturing of wool, cotton and associated textiles; Chair. YVES DUBIEF; Vice-Chair. CAMILLE AMALRIC; 400 mems.

Fédération Française du Négoce de Bois (FFNB): 18 rue des Pyramides, 75001 Paris; tel. 1-44-55-35-09; fax 1-42-86-01-83; e-mail bois@cgi-cf.fr; internet www.bois.tm.fr; timber trade; Pres. ANDRÉ TALON; Dir-Gen. LIONEL THOMAS D'ANNEBAULT.

Fédération Française de la Tannerie-Mégisserie: 122 rue de Provence, 75008 Paris; tel. 1-45-22-96-45; fax 1-42-93-37-44; e-mail fftm@leatherfrance.com; f. 1885; leather industry; 100 mems.

Fédération de l'Imprimerie et de la Communication Graphique: 68 blvd Saint Marcel, 75005 Paris; tel. 1-44-08-64-46; fax 1-43-36-09-51; e-mail pressecom@ficg.fr; printing, communication and design; Pres. FRANÇOIS GUTLÉ.

Fédération des Industries de la Parfumerie (France): 33 Champs Elysées, 75008 Paris; tel. 1-56-69-67-89; fax 1-56-69-67-90; makers of perfume, cosmetics and toiletries; Pres. ALAIN GRANGÉ CABANE.

Fédération des Industries Electriques, Electroniques et de Communication (FIEEC): 11–17 rue Hameline, 75783 Paris Cédex 16; tel. 1-45-05-70-70; fax 1-45-53-03-93; e-mail comm@fieec.fr; internet www.fieec.fr; f. 1925; electrical and electronics industries; Chair. HENRI STARCK; Delegate-Gen. JEAN-CLAUDE KARPELÈS; c. 1,000 mems.

Fédération des Industries Mécaniques: 39–41 rue Louis Blanc, 92400 Courbevoie; tel. 1-47-17-60-27; fax 1-47-17-64-37; e-mail ppoisson@mail.fimeca.com; internet www.fim.net; f. 1840; mechanical and metal-working; Chair. YVON JACOB; Man. Dir ALAIN POIX.

Fédération des Industries Nautiques: Port de Javel Haut, 75015 Paris; tel. 1-44-37-04-00; fax 1-45-77-21-88; e-mail info@fin.fr; internet www.fin.fr; f. 1965; pleasure-boating; Pres. ANNETTE ROUX; Man. Dir TIBOR SILLINGER; 600 mems.

Fédération Nationale du Bois: 6 rue François 1er, 75008 Paris; tel. 1-56-69-52-00; fax 1-56-69-52-09; e-mail infos@fnbois.com; internet www.fnbois.com; f. 1884; timber and wood products; Chair. DOMINIQUE JUILLOT; 1,850 mems.

Fédération Nationale des Chambres Syndicales des Horlogers, Bijoutiers, Joailliers et Orfèvres (HBJO): 249 rue Saint Martin, 75003 Paris; tel. 1-44-54-34-00; fax 1-44-54-34-07; e-mail fedhbjo@wanadoo.fr; internet www.fedehbjo.com; jewellery, watch- and clock-making; Pres. GÉRARD ATLAN; 1,200 mems.

Fédération Nationale de l'Industrie Hôtelière (FNIH): 22 rue d'Anjou, 75008 Paris; tel. 1-44-94-19-94; fax 1-42-65-16-21; e-mail fnih@imagenet.fr; Chair. ANDRÉ DAGUIN.

Fédération Nationale de l'Industrie Laitière: 42 rue de Châteaudun, 75314 Paris Cédex 09; tel. 1-49-70-72-86; fax 1-42-80-63-94; e-mail fnil@atla.asso.fr; f. 1946; dairy products; Pres. XAVIER PAUL-RENARD; Sec.-Gen. HUGUES TRIBALLAT.

Fédération Nationale des Industries Électrométallurgiques, Éléctrochimiques et Connexes: 30 ave de Messine, 75008 Paris; tel. 1-45-61-06-63; fax 1-45-63-61-54; Chair. JACQUES GANI.

Fédération Nationale de la Musique: 62 rue Blanche, 75009 Paris; tel. 1-48-74-09-29; fax 1-42-81-19-87; f. 1964; includes Chambre Syndicale de la Facture Instrumentale, Syndicat National de l'Edition Phonographique and other groups; musical instruments, publications and recordings; Chair. PIERRE HENRY; Sec.-Gen. FRANÇOIS WELLEBROUCK.

Les Fondeurs de France: 45 rue Louis Blanc, 92038 Paris La Défense Cédex; tel. 1-43-34-76-30; fax 1-43-34-76-31; e-mail contact@fondeursdefrance.org; internet www.fondeursdefrance.org; f. 1897; metal casting; Chair. ANDRÉ ROBERT-DEHAULT; Man. Dir OLIVIER DUCRU; 300 mems.

Groupe Intersyndical de l'Industrie Nucléaire (GIIN): 39–41 rue L. Blanc, 92400 Courbevoie Cédex; tel. 1-47-17-62-78; f. 1958; aims to promote the interests of the French nuclear industry; 200 member firms.

Groupement des Industries Françaises Aéronautiques et Spatiales (GIFAS): 4 rue Galilée, 75782 Paris Cédex 16; tel. 1-44-43-17-00; fax 1-40-70-91-41; e-mail infogifas@gifas.asso.fr; internet www.gifas.asso.fr; aerospace industry; Pres. PHILIPPE CAMUS.

Syndicat Général des Cuirs et Peaux: Bourse de Commerce, 2 rue de Viarmes, 75040 Paris Cédex 01; tel. 1-45-08-08-54; fax 1-40-39-97-31; e-mail syndicuir@free.fr; f. 1977; untreated leather and hides; Chair. ANDRÉ LECOMTE; 30 mems.

Syndicat Général des Fabricants d'Huile et de Tourteaux de France: 118 ave Achille Peretti, 92200 Neuilly-sur-Seine; tel. 1-46-37-22-06; fax 1-46-37-15-60; f. 1928; edible oils; Pres. HENRI RIEUX; Sec.-Gen. JEAN-CLAUDE BARSACQ.

Syndicat National de l'Industrie Pharmaceutique (SNIP): 88 rue de la Faisanderie, 75782 Paris Cédex 16; tel. 1-45-03-88-88; fax 1-45-04-47-71; e-mail dcre@snip.fr; internet www.snip.fr; pharmaceuticals; Chair. JEAN-PIERRE CASSAN.

Syndicat National des Industries de la Communication Graphique et de l'Imprimerie-Francaises (SICOGIF): 8 rue de Berri, 75008 Paris; tel. 1-53-53-96-96; fax 1-53-53-96-97; e-mail info@sicogif.com; internet www.sicogif.com; f. 1991; printers' asscn; 310 mems; Chair. JEAN-RAOUL ROSAY; Sec.-Gen. PHILIPPE QUEINEC.

Union des Armateurs à la Pêche de France: 59 rue des Mathurins, 75008 Paris; tel. 1-42-66-32-60; fax 1-47-42-91-12; e-mail uapf75@wanadoo.fr; f. 1945; fishing-vessels; Chair. JEAN-YVES LABBE; Delegate-Gen. MICHEL DION.

Union des Fabricants de Porcelaine de Limoges: 7 bis rue du Général Cérez, 87000 Limoges; tel. 5-55-77-29-18; fax 5-55-77-36-81; e-mail ufpl@porcelainelimoges.org; porcelain manufacturing; Chair. MICHEL BERNARDAUD; Sec.-Gen. MARIE-THÉRÈSE PASQUET.

Union des Industries Chimiques: Paris La Défense; tel. 1-47-78-50-00; e-mail uicgeneral@uic.fr; internet www.uic.fr; f. 1860; chemical industry; Chair. J.-C. ACHILLE; Dir-Gen. C. MARTIN; 58 affiliated unions.

Union des Industries Métallurgiques et Minières (UIMM): 56 ave de Wagram, 75017 Paris; tel. 1-40-54-20-20; fax 1-47-66-22-74; e-mail uimm@uimm.fr; internet www.uimm.fr; metallurgy and mining; Chair. DANIEL DEWAVRIN; 223 mems.

Union des Industries Papetières pour les Affaires Sociales (UNIPAS): 154 blvd Haussmann, 75008 Paris; tel. 1-53-89-25-25; fax 1-53-89-25-26; e-mail unipas@aol.com; f. 1864; paper, cardboard and cellulose; Chair. MICHEL SORIANO; Sec.-Gen. JEAN-PIERRE DELPOPOLO.

Union des Industries Textiles (Production): BP 121, 37–39 rue de Neuilly, 92113 Clichy Cédex; tel. 1-47-56-31-00; fax 1-47-30-25-28; e-mail thierry_noblot.uit@textile.fr; internet www.textile.fr; f. 1901; Chair. GUILLAUME SARKOZY; 2,500 mems.

Union professionnelle artisanale (UPA): 79 ave de Villiers, 75017 Paris; tel. 1-47-63-31-31; fax 1-47-63-31-10; e-mail UPA@wanadoo.fr; internet www.upa.fr; f. 1975; unites crafts and other manual workers in three trade bodies and more than 100 regional organizations; Chair. ROBERT BUGUET.

EMPLOYERS' ORGANIZATIONS

Association Française des Entreprises Privées (AGREF): Paris; represents the interests of 81 of the largest enterprises in France; Chair. BERTRAND COLLOMB.

Centre des Jeunes Dirigeants d'Entreprise (CJD): 19 ave Georges V, 75008 Paris; tel. 1-53-23-92-50; fax 1-40-70-15-66; e-mail cjd@cjd.net; internet www.cjd.net; f. 1938; asscn for young entrepreneurs (under 45 years of age); Pres. SYLVAIN BREUZARD; 2,300 mems (2002).

Confédération Générale des Petites et Moyennes Entreprises (CGPME): 10 terrasse Bellini, 92806 Puteaux Cédex; tel. 1-47-62-73-73; fax 1-47-73-08-86; e-mail contact@cgpme.org; internet www.cgpme.org; small and medium-sized cos; Chair. JEAN-FRANÇOIS ROUBAUD; 1,600,000 mems (2001).

Les Entrepreneurs et Dirigeants Chrétiens (Les EDC): 24 rue Hamelin, 75016 Paris; tel. 1-45-53-09-01; fax 1-47-27-43-32; e-mail lesedc@lesedc.org; internet www.lesedc.org; fmrly Centre Français du Patronat Chrétien; asscn of Christian employers; Pres. JEAN BRUNET LECOMTE.

Entreprise et Progrès: 11 rue Anatole de la Forge, 75017 Paris; tel. 1-45-74-52-62; fax 1-45-74-52-63; e-mail progres@noos.fr; internet www.entreprise-progres.net; f. 1970; represents 110 enterprises; Pres. PAUL DUBRULE; Sec.-Gen. ODILE DELORT-MAIXANDEAU.

Entreprises de Taille Humaine Indépendantes et de Croissance (ETHIC): 6 Villa Thoréton, 75015 Paris; tel. 1-56-82-20-75; fax 1-56-82-20-37; e-mail l.michon@ethic.fr; internet www.ethic.fr; represents small enterprises and promotes ethical values in business; Pres. SOPHIE DE MENTHON.

Mouvement des Entreprises de France (MEDEF): 31 ave Pierre I de Serbie, 75784 Paris Cédex 16; tel. 1-40-69-44-44; fax 1-47-23-47-32; internet www.medef.fr; f. 1998 to replace Conseil National du Patronat Français; employers' asscn grouping 700,000 cos from all sectors of activity in 85 professional feds and 152 regional orgs; Chair. ERNEST-ANTOINE SEILLIÈRE DE LABORDE.

UTILITIES

Electricity

Alcatel: 54 rue la Boétie, 75382 Paris Cedex 08; tel. 1-40-76-10-10; fax 1-40-76-14-00; internet www.alcatel.com; f. 1898; telecommunications and business systems, terrestrial and submarine optical networks; 110,000 employees; Chair. SERGE TCHURUK; Man. Dir. JEAN-PIERRE HALBRON.

Charbonnages de France (CdF): 110 ave Albert 1er, BP 220, 92508 Rueil-Malmaison Cédex; tel. 1-47-52-35-00; fax 1-47-51-31-63; e-mail cdf.com@wanadoo.fr; internet www.groupecharbonnages .fr; established under the Nationalization Act of 1946; responsible for coal mining, sales and research in metropolitan France; there are also engineering and electricity divisions; 9,957 employees; Chair. and Dir-Gen. PHILIPPE DE LADOUCETTE.

Electricité de France (EDF): 22–30 ave de Wagram, 75382 Paris Cédex 8; tel. 1-40-42-46-37; fax 1-40-42-72-44; e-mail masteredf@ edfgdf.fr; internet www.edf.fr; established under the Electricity and Gas Industry Nationalization Act of 1946; responsible for generating and supplying electricity for distribution to consumers in metropolitan France; 120,000 employees; Chair. FRANÇOIS ROUSSELY.

Gas

Gaz de France: 23 rue Philibert Delorme, 75840 Paris Cédex 17; tel. 1-47-54-20-20; fax 1-47-54-21-87; internet www.gdf.fr; established under the Electricity and Gas Industry Nationalization Act of 1946; responsible for distribution of gas in metropolitan France; about 10% of gas was produced in France (Aquitaine) in 1993 and the rest imported from Algeria, the Netherlands, Norway and the territories constituting the former USSR; Chair. PIERRE GADONNEIX.

Water

Générale des Eaux: 52 rue d'Anjou, 75384 Paris Cédex 08; tel. 1-49-24-33-77; fax 1-49-24-34-44; e-mail anne.froger@ generale-des-eaux.net; internet www.generale-des-eaux.com; f. 1853; subsidiary of Vivendi Water; provides water and other environmental services, as well as telecommunications and construction; Chair. JEAN-MARIE MESSIER.

Lyonnaise des Eaux: 1 rue d'Astorg, 75008 Paris; internet www .lyonnaise-des-eaux.fr; f. 1858; fmrly Suez-Lyonnaise des Eaux; present name adopted 2001; subsidiary of Ondeo (Groupe Suez); Pres. and CEO GÉRARD MESTRALLET.

TRADE UNIONS

In late 1995 it was estimated that some 8% of the French labour force belonged to trade unions (compared with 18% in 1980).

There are three major trade union organizations:

Confédération Générale du Travail (CGT): Complexe Immobilier Intersyndical CGT, 263 rue de Paris, 93516 Montreuil Cédex; tel. 1-48-18-80-00; fax 1-49-88-18-57; e-mail info@cgt.fr; internet www.cgt.fr; f. 1895; National Congress is held every three years; Sec.-Gen. BERNARD THIBAULT; 650,000 mems.

Affiliated unions:

Agro-Alimentaire et Forestière (FNAF): 263 rue de Paris, Case 428, 93514 Montreuil Cédex; tel. 1-48-18-83-27; fax 1-48-51-57-49; Sec.-Gen. FREDDY HUCK.

Bois Ameublement (Woodworkers): 263 rue de Paris, Case 414, 93514 Montreuil Cédex; tel. 1-48-18-81-61; fax 1-48-51-59-91; Sec.-Gen. HENRI SANCHEZ.

Cheminots CGT (Railway Workers): 263 rue de Paris, Case 546, 93510 Montreuil Cédex; tel. 1-49-88-61-00; fax 1-48-57-95-65; e-mail coord@cheminotcgt.fr; internet www.cheminotcgt.fr; Sec.-Gen. DIDIER LERESTE.

Chimie (Chemical Industries): 263 rue de Paris, Case 429, 93514 Montreuil Cédex; tel. 1-48-18-80-36; fax 1-48-18-80-35; e-mail fnic@cgt.fr; internet www.fnic.cgt.fr; Sec.-Gen. JEAN-MICHEL PETIT.

Commerce: 263 rue de Paris, Case 425, 93514 Montreuil Cédex; tel. 1-48-18-83-11; fax 1-48-18-83-19; e-mail commerce@cgt.fr; Sec.-Gen. JACQUELINE GARCIA.

Construction (Building): 263 rue de Paris, Case 413, 93514 Montreuil Cédex; tel. 1-48-18-81-60; fax 1-48-59-10-37; e-mail construction@cgt.fr; Sec.-Gen. ERIC AUBIN.

Equipement: 263 rue de Paris, Case 543, 93515 Montreuil Cédex; tel. 1-48-18-82-81; fax 1-48-51-62-50; e-mail equipement@cgt.fr; Sec.-Gen. DANIEL SALANDRI.

Education Recherche Culture (FERC-CGT): 263 rue de Paris, Case 544, 93515 Montreuil Cédex; tel. 1-48-18-82-44; fax 1-49-88-07-43; e-mail ferc@cgt.fr; internet www.ferc.cgt.fr; Sec.-Gen. CHRISTIAN DUBOT.

Finances: 263 rue de Paris, Case 540, 93515 Montreuil Cédex; tel. 1-48-18-82-21; fax 1-48-18-82-52; e-mail finances@cgt.fr; internet www.finances.cgt.fr; Sec.-Gen. PIERRETTE CROSEMARIE.

Fonctionnaires (UGFF) (Civil Servants): 263 rue de Paris, Case 542, 93515 Montreuil Cédex; tel. 1-48-18-82-31; fax 1-48-18-82-11; e-mail ugff@cgt.fr; internet www.ugff.cgt.fr; groups National Education, Finance, Technical and Administrative, Civil Servants, Police, etc. mems of about 70 national unions covered by six federations; Sec.-Gen. BERNARD LHUBERT.

Industries Chimiques (Chemical Industries): 263 rue de Paris, Case 429, 93514 Montreuil Cédex; tel. 1-48-18-80-36; fax 1-48-18-80-35; e-mail fnic@cgt.fr; internet www.fnic.cgt.fr; Sec.-Gen. JEAN-MICHEL PETIT.

Industries du Livre, du Papier et de la Communication (FILPAC) (Printing, Paper Products and Media): 263 rue de Paris, Case 426, 93514 Montreuil Cédex; tel. 1-48-18-80-24; fax 1-48-51-99-07; e-mail filpac@cgt.fr; internet www.filpac-cgt.fr; Sec.-Gen. MICHEL MULLER.

Ingénieurs, Cadres et Techniciens (UGICT-CGT) (Engineers, Managerial Staff and Technicians): 263 rue de Paris, Case 408, 93514 Montreuil Cédex; tel. 1-48-18-81-25; fax 1-48-51-64-57;

e-mail ugict@cgt.fr; internet www.ugict.cgt.fr; f. 1963; Secs-Gen. MARIE-JO KOTLICKI, JEAN-FRANÇOIS BOLZINGER.

Intérimaires (Temporary Workers): 263 rue de Paris, Case 460, 93514 Montreuil Cédex; tel. 1-48-18-84-16; fax 1-48-18-82-59; Pres. SAMUEL GAULTIER.

Journalistes: 263 rue de Paris, Case 570, 93514 Montreuil Cédex; tel. 1-48-18-81-78; fax 1-48-51-58-08; e-mail snf@cgt.fr; Sec.-Gen. MICHEL DIARD.

Marine Marchande (Merchant Marine): Cercle Franklin, 119 Cours de la République, 76600 Le Havre; tel. 2-35-25-04-81; fax 2-35-24-23-77; e-mail fedeoffmarmaugict.cgt@wanadoo.fr; Sec.-Gen. CHARLES NARELLI.

Maritimes (Seamen): 263 rue de Paris, Case 420, 93514 Montreuil Cédex; tel. 1-48-18-84-21; fax 1-48-51-59-21; e-mail synd-mar@cgt.fr; Sec.-Gen. ALAIN MERLET.

Métallurgie (FTM) (Metalworkers): 263 rue de Paris, 93514 Montreuil Cédex; tel. 1-48-18-21-21; fax 1-48-59-80-66; e-mail ftm@ftm-cgt.fr; internet www.ftm-cgt.fr; f. 1891; Sec.-Gen. DANIEL SANCHEZ.

Mines-Energie: 263 rue de Paris, Case 535, 93515 Montreuil Cédex; tel. 1-48-18-82-25; fax 1-48-51-60-36; e-mail international@fnme-cgt.fr; internet www.fnme-cgt.fr; Sec.-Gen. DENIS COHEN.

Organismes Sociaux: 263 rue de Paris, Case 536, 93515 Montreuil Cédex; tel. 1-48-18-83-56; fax 1-48-59-24-75; e-mail fede@orgasociaux.cgt.fr; internet www.orgasociaux.cgt.fr; Sec.-Gen. PHILIPPE HOURCADE.

Pénitentiares (Prison workers): 263 rue de Paris, Case 542, 93514 Montreuil Cédex; tel. 1-48-18-82-42; fax 1-48-18-82-50; e-mail ugspcgt@aol.com; Sec-Gen. FRANÇOIS HULOT.

Police: 263 rue de Paris, Case 550, 93514 Montreuil Cédex; tel. 1-48-18-81-85; fax 1-48-51-14-43; e-mail police@cgt.fr; internet perso.wanadoo.fr/cgt-police; f. 1906; Sec.-Gen. PASCAL MARTINI.

Ports et Docks: 263 rue de Paris, Case 424, 93514 Montreuil Cédex; tel. 1-48-18-82-96; fax 1-48-18-82-94; Sec.-Gen. DANIEL LEFÈVRE.

Postes et Télécommunications: 263 rue de Paris, Case 545, 93515 Montreuil Cédex; tel. 1-48-18-54-00; fax 1-48-59-25-22; e-mail fede@cgt-ptt.fr; internet www.cgt-ptt.fr; Sec.-Gen. MARYSE DUMAS.

Santé, Action Sociale (SAS-CGT) (Health and Social Services): 263 rue de Montreuil, Case 538, 93514 Montreuil Cédex; tel. 1-48-18-20-99; fax 1-48-18-29-80; e-mail santeas@cgt.fr; internet www.cgt.fr/santeas; f. 1907; Sec.-Gen. NADINE PRIGENT.

Secteurs Financiers: 263 rue de Paris, Case 537, 93515 Montreuil Cédex; tel. 1-48-18-83-40; fax 1-49-88-16-36; e-mail sect-fin@cgt.fr; internet www.fnpsf.cgt.fr; Sec.-Gen. PHILIPPE BOURGALE.

Services Publics (Community Services): 263 rue de Paris, Case 547, 93514 Montreuil Cédex; tel. 1-48-18-83-74; fax 1-48-51-98-20; e-mail serv-pub@cgt.fr; internet www.spterritoriaux.cgt.fr; Sec.-Gen. VINCENT DEBEIR.

Sociétés d'études (Research, Service-sector Workers, Translators, Accountants, Notaries): 263 rue de Paris, Case 421, 93514 Montreuil Cédex; tel. 1-48-18-84-34; fax 1-48-18-84-86; e-mail fsetud@cgt.fr; internet www.soc-etudes.cgt.fr; Pres. NOËL LECHAT.

Sous-sol (Miners): 263 rue de Paris, Case 535, 93514 Montreuil Cédex; tel. 1-48-18-82-25; fax 1-48-51-60-36; Sec.-Gen. JACKY BERNARD.

Spectacle, Audio-Visuel et Action Culturelle (Theatre, Media and Culture): 14–16 rue des Lilas, 75019 Paris; tel. 1-48-03-87-60; fax 1-42-40-90-20; e-mail info@fnsac-cgt.com; internet www.fnsac-cgt.com; Sec.-Gen. JEAN VOIRIN.

Tabac et Allumettes (Tobacco and Matches): 263 rue de Paris, Case 422, 93514 Montreuil Cédex; tel. 1-48-18-84-19; fax 1-48-51-54-53; e-mail cgt.tabacs.allumettes@wanadoo.fr; Sec.-Gen. BERTRAND PAGE.

Textiles, Habillement, Cuir (THC) (Textiles): 263 rue de Paris, Case 415, 93514 Montreuil Cédex; tel. 1-48-18-82-98; fax 1-48-18-83-01; e-mail thc@cgt.fr; Sec.-Gen. CHRISTIAN LAROSE.

Transports: 263 rue de Paris, Case 423, 93514 Montreuil Cédex; tel. 1-48-18-80-82; fax 1-48-18-82-54; e-mail transports@cgt.fr; Sec.-Gen. ALAIN RENAULT.

Travailleurs de l'Etat (State Employees): 263 rue de Paris, Case 541, 93515 Montreuil Cédex; tel. 1-48-18-86-86; fax 1-48-18-86-87; e-mail trav-etat@cgt.fr; Sec.-Gen. JEAN-LOUIS NAUDET.

Verre-Céramique (Glassworkers, Ceramics): 263 rue de Paris, Case 417, 93514 Montreuil Cédex; tel. 1-48-18-80-13; fax 1-48-18-80-11; e-mail ver-ceram@cgt.fr; Sec.-Gen. JACQUES BEAUVOIR.

Voyageurs-Représentants (Commercial Travellers): Bourse du Travail, 3 rue du Château d'eau, 75010 Paris; tel. 1-42-39-02-99; fax 1-42-39-09-11; e-mail prof-vente@cgt.fr; Sec.-Gen. ALAIN SERRE.

Force Ouvrière: 141 ave du Maine, 75680 Paris Cédex 14; tel. 1-40-52-82-00; fax 1-40-52-82-02; e-mail mblondel@force-ouvriere.fr; internet www.force-ouvriere.fr; f. 1948 by breakaway from the more left-wing CGT (above); Force Ouvrière is a member of ICFTU and of the European Trade Union Confederation; Sec.-Gen. MARC BLONDEL; c. 1m. mems.

Affiliated federations:

Action Sociale: 7 passage Tenaille, 75680 Paris Cédex 14; tel. 1-40-52-85-80; fax 1-40-52-85-79; e-mail mpinaud@force-ouvriere.fr; Sec.-Gen. MICHEL PINAUD.

Administration Générale de l'État: 46 rue des Petites Ecuries, 75010 Paris; tel. 1-42-46-40-19; fax 1-42-46-19-57; e-mail flamarque@force-ouvriere.fr; f. 1948; Sec.-Gen. FRANCIS LAMARQUE; 20,000 mems.

Agriculture, Alimentation et Tabacs (Agriculture, Food and Tobacco): 7 passage Tenaille, 75680 Paris Cédex 14; tel. 1-40-52-85-10; fax 1-40-52-85-12; e-mail fgtafo@fgta-fo.org; internet www.fgtafo.fr; Sec.-Gen. RAFAËL NEDZYNSKI.

Cadres et Ingénieurs (UCI) (Managers, Engineers): 2 rue de la Michodière, 75002 Paris; tel. 1-47-42-39-69; fax 1-47-42-03-53; e-mail hbouchet@force-ouvriere.fr; internet www.uci-fo.com; Sec.-Gen. HUBERT BOUCHET.

Cheminots (Railway Workers): 61 rue de la Chapelle, 75018 Paris; tel. 1-55-26-94-00; fax 1-55-26-94-01; e-mail federation@fo-cheminots.com; internet www.fo-cheminots.com; f. 1948; Sec.-Gen. ERIC FALEMPIN; 10,000 mems.

Coiffeur, Esthétique, Parfumerie (Hairdressers, Beauticians and Perfumery): 3 rue de la Croix Blanche, 18350 Nerondes; tel. 2-48-78-89-32; fax 2-48-74-81-26; e-mail fcoiffure@force-ouvriere.fr; Sec.-Gen. GUY MARIN.

Communications: 60 rue Vergniaud, 75640 Paris Cédex 13; tel. 1-40-78-31-50; fax 1-40-78-30-58; e-mail federation@fo-com.com; internet www.fo-com.com; f. 1947; Sec.-Gen. JACQUES LEMERCIER.

Cuirs, Textiles, Habillement (Leather, Textiles and Clothing): 7 passage Tenaille, 75680 Paris Cédex 14; tel. 1-40-52-83-00; fax 1-40-52-82-99; e-mail fvanderosieren@force-ouvriere.fr; Sec.-Gen. FRANCIS VAN DE ROSIEREN.

Défense, Industries de l'Armement et Secteurs Assimilés (Defence and Arms Manufacture): 46 rue des Petites Ecuries, 75010 Paris; tel. 1-42-46-00-05; fax 1-45-23-12-89; e-mail fediasa@force-ouvriere.fr; Sec.-Gen. CHARLES SISTACH.

Employés et Cadres (Office Workers and Private Sector Managerial Staff): 28 rue des Petits Hôtels, 75010 Paris; tel. 1-48-01-91-91; fax 1-48-01-91-92; e-mail rboutaric@force-ouvriere.fr; internet www.fec-fo.com; Sec.-Gen. ROSE BOUTARIC.

Energie et Mines (Energy and Mines): 60 rue Vergniaud, 75640 Paris Cédex 13; tel. 1-44-16-86-20; fax 1-44-16-86-32; e-mail federation@fnem-fo.fr; internet www.fnem-fo.fr; Sec.-Gen. GABRIEL GAUDY.

Enseignement, Culture et Formation Professionnelle (Teaching): 6–8 rue Gaston-Lauriau, 93513 Montreuil Cédex; tel. 1-56-93-22-22; fax 1-56-93-22-20; e-mail fchaintron@force-ouvriere.fr; Sec.-Gen. FRANÇOIS CHAINTRON; 50,000 mems.

Equipements, Transports et Services (Transport and Public Works): 46 rue des Petites Ecuries, 75010 Paris; tel. 1-44-83-86-20; fax 1-48-24-38-32; e-mail contact@fets-fo.fr; internet www.fets-fo.fr; f. 1932; Sec.-Gen. YVES VEYRIER; 50,000 mems.

Fédéchimie (Chemical Industries): 60 rue Vergniaud, 75640 Paris Cédex 13; tel. 1-45-80-14-90; fax 1-45-80-08-03; e-mail mdecayeux@force-ouvriere.fr; f. 1948; Sec.-Gen. MICHEL DECAYEUX.

Finances: 46 rue des Petites Ecuries, 75010 Paris; tel. 1-42-46-75-20; fax 1-47-70-23-92; e-mail fo.finances@wanadoo.fr; internet financesfo.fr; Sec.-Gen. JACKY LESUEUR.

Fonctionnaires (Civil Servants): 46 rue des Petites Ecuries, 75010 Paris; tel. 1-44-83-65-55; fax 1-42-46-97-80; e-mail rgaillard@force-ouvriere.fr; internet www.fo-fonctionnaires.fr; Sec.-Gen. ROLAND GAILLARD.

Générale (Building, Public Works, Wood, Ceramics, Paper, Cardboard and Building Materials): 170 ave Parmentier, 75010 Paris; tel. 1-42-01-30-00; fax 1-42-39-50-44; e-mail mdaudigny@force-ouvriere.fr; internet www.federationgeneralefo.com; Sec.-Gen. MICHEL DAUDIGNY.

Livre (Printing Trades): 7 passage Tenaille, 75680 Paris Cédex 14; tel. 1-40-52-85-00; fax 1-40-52-85-01; e-mail livre.fo@wanadoo.fr; Sec.-Gen. PATRICE SACQUÉPÉE.

Métaux (Metals): 9 rue Baudouin, 75013 Paris; tel. 1-53-94-54-00; fax 1-45-83-78-87; e-mail contact@fo-metaux.fr; internet www.fo-metaux.com; Sec.-Gen. MICHEL HUC.

Mineurs, Miniers et Similaires (Mine Workers): 7 passage Tenaille, 75014 Paris; tel. 1-40-52-85-50; fax 1-40-52-85-48; e-mail federation@fnem-fo.org; internet www.fnem-fo.org; Sec.-Gen. BERNARD FRAYSSE.

Pharmacie, Officine-Industrie VM, Droguerie-Répartition, Laboratoire d'Analyse (Pharmacists, Druggists and Analytical Laboratories): 7 passage Tenaille, 75680 Paris Cédex 14; tel. 1-40-52-85-60; fax 1-40-52-85-61; e-mail fopharma@wanadoo.fr; internet www.fo-pharmacie.com; Sec.-Gen. GILBERT LEBRUMENT.

Police: 146–148 rue Picpus, 75013 Paris; tel. 1-53-46-11-00; fax 1-44-68-07-41; e-mail xbeugnet@force-ouvriere.fr; internet www.fsgp-fo.com; f. 1948; Sec.-Gen. XAVIER BEUGNET; 11,000 mems.

Services des Départements et Régions (Local and Regional Government): 46 rue des Petits Ecuries, 75010 Paris; tel. 1-42-46-50-52; fax 1-47-70-26-06; e-mail msimonnin@force-ouvriere.fr; Sec.-Gen. MICHÈLE SIMONNIN.

Services Publics et de Santé (Health and Public Services): 153–155 rue de Rome, 75017 Paris; tel. 1-44-01-06-00; fax 1-42-27-21-40; e-mail fedespsfo@wanadoo.fr; internet www.fo-publics-sante.org; f. 1947; Sec.-Gen. JEAN-MARIE BELLOT; 130,000 mems (2002).

Spectacles, Presse, Audiovisuel (Theatre and Media): 2 rue de la Michodière, 75002 Paris; tel. 1-47-42-35-86; fax 1-47-42-39-45; e-mail fasap-fo@wanadoo.fr; Sec.-Gen. BERTRAND BLANC.

Transports: 7 passage Tenaille, 75680 Paris Cédex 14; tel. 1-40-52-85-45; fax 1-40-52-85-09; e-mail fotransports@force-ouvriere.fr; Gen. Sec. GÉRARD APRUZZESE.

Voyageurs-Représentants-Placiers (Commercial Travellers): 6–8 rue Albert Bayet, 75013 Paris; tel. 1-45-82-28-28; fax 1-45-70-93-69; e-mail fovrp@force-ouvriere.fr; f. 1930; Sec.-Gen. LOIC LOUVEL.

Confédération Française Démocratique du Travail (CFDT): 4 blvd de la Villette, 75955 Paris Cédex 19; tel. 1-42-03-80-00; fax 1-42-03-81-44; e-mail confederation@cfdt.fr; internet www.cfdt.fr; f. 1919 as Confédération Française des Travailleurs Chrétiens—CFTC, present title and constitution adopted 1964; moderate; co-ordinates 1,500 trade unions, 95 departmental and overseas unions, 3 confederal unions and 17 affiliated professional federations, all of which are autonomous. There are 22 regional orgs; 830,601 mems (2001); affiliated to European Trade Union Confederation and to ICFTU; Sec.-Gen. FRANÇOIS CHEREQUE.

Affiliated federations:

Agroalimentaire (FGA-CFDT): 47–49 ave Simon Bolivar, 75950 Paris Cédex 19; tel. 1-56-41-50-50; fax 1-56-41-50-30; e-mail fga@cfdt.fr; internet www.fga-cfdt.fr; f. 1980; Sec.-Gen. HERVÉ GARNIER; 50,000 mems (2001).

Banques et Sociétés Financières: 47–49 ave Simon Bolivar, 75950 Paris Cédex 19; tel. 1-44-52-71-20; fax 1-44-52-71-21; e-mail federation@cfdt-banques.fr; internet www.cfdt-banques.fr; Sec.-Gen. BERNARD DUFIL.

Chimie-Energie (FCE-CFDT): 47–49 ave Simon Bolivar, 75950 Paris Cédex 19; tel. 1-44-84-86-00; fax 1-44-84-86-05; e-mail fce@cfdt.fr; internet www.fce.cfdt.fr; f. 1946; Sec.-Gen. JACQUES KHELIFF; 57,000 mems (1996).

Communication et Culture (FTILAC): 47–49 ave Simon Bolivar, 75950 Paris Cédex 19; tel. 1-56-41-53-80; fax 1-56-41-53-90; e-mail federation@folt-ftilac.fr; internet www.fcc-cfdt.net; Sec.-Gen. DANIÈLE RIVED.

Construction-Bois (FNCB-CFDT) (Builders, Wood-workers, Architects, Town-planners): 47–49 ave Simon Bolivar, 75950 Paris Cédex 19; tel. 1-56-41-55-60; fax 1-56-41-55-61; e-mail fncb@cfdt.fr; internet www.cfdt-construction-bois.fr; f. 1934; Sec.-Gen. JOSEPH MURGIA.

Education Nationale (SGEN-CFDT) (National Education): 47–49 ave Simon Bolivar, 75950 Paris Cédex 19; tel. 1-56-41-51-00; fax 1-56-41-51-11; e-mail fede@sgen-cfdt.org; internet www.sgen-cfdt.org; f. 1937; Sec.-Gen. JEAN-LUC VILLENEUVE.

Etablissements et Arsenaux de l'Etat: 47–49 ave Simon Bolivar, 75950 Paris Cédex 19; tel. 1-42-52-55-33; fax 1-44-52-55-44; e-mail feae@cfdt.fr; Sec.-Gen. JACQUES LEPINARD.

Finances et Affaires Economiques (Finance): 47–49 ave Simon Bolivar, 75950 Paris Cédex 19; tel. 1-56-41-55-55; fax 1-56-41-55-59; e-mail federation@cfdt-finances.fr; internet www.cfdt-finances .fr; f. 1936; civil servants and workers within government financial departments; Sec.-Gen. PHILIPPE LECLEZIO.

Fonctionnaires et Assimilés (UFFA-CFDT) (Civil Servants): 47–49 ave Simon Bolivar, 75950 Paris Cédex 19; tel. 1-56-41-54-40; fax 1-56-41-54-44; e-mail uffa@cfdt.fr; f. 1932; Sec.-Gen. MARIE-CLAUDE KERVELLA.

Formation et Enseignement Privés (Independent education): 47–49 ave Simon Bolivar, 75950 Paris Cédex 19; tel. 1-56-41-54-70; fax 1-56-41-54-71; e-mail contact@fep-cfdt.fr; internet www.fep-cfdt.fr; Sec.-Gen. XAVIER NAU.

Habillement, Cuir et Textile (HACUITEX-CFDT) (Clothing Industry): 47–49 ave Simon Bolivar, 75950 Paris Cédex 19; tel. 1-56-41-55-90; fax 1-56-41-55-95; e-mail hacuitex@cfdt.fr; f. 1963; Sec.-Gen. MARTIAL VIDET.

Ingénieurs et Cadres (CFDT Cadres) (Managers, Professionals, Engineers): 47–49 ave Simon Bolivar, 75950 Paris Cédex 19; tel. 1-53-38-95-70; fax 1-42-02-48-58; e-mail contact@cfdt-cadres .fr; internet www.cadres-plus.net; Sec.-Gen. FRANÇOIS FAYOL.

Interco (Local Government Workers): 47–49 ave Simon Bolivar, 75950 Paris Cédex 19; tel. 1-40-40-85-50; fax 1-42-06-86-86; e-mail interco@cfdt.fr; internet www.interco-cfdt.fr; Sec.-Gen. ALEXIS GUÉNÉGO.

Métallurgie et Mines (Miners, Machinery and Metal Workers): 47–49 ave Simon Bolivar, 75950 Paris Cédex 19; tel. 1-44-52-20-20; fax 1-44-52-20-52; e-mail fgmm@cfdt.fr; internet www.fgmm.cfdt.fr; Sec.-Gen. MARCEL GRIGNARD.

Postes et Télécoms CFDT (FUPT-CFDT) (Post and Telecommunications Workers): 47–49 ave Simon Bolivar, 75950 Paris Cédex 19; tel. 1-56-41-54-00; fax 1-56-41-54-01; e-mail fupt@cfdt .fr; internet www.cfdt-postes-telecoms.org; Sec.-Gen. HERVÉ MORLAND.

Protection Sociale, Travail, Emploi (Social Security): 47–49 ave Simon Bolivar, 75950 Paris Cédex 19; tel. 1-40-18-77-72; fax 1-40-18-77-79; e-mail pste@cfdt.fr; internet www.pste-cfdt.org; Sec.-Gen. JEAN-LOUIS TARDIVAUN.

Retraités (UCR) (Retired People): 47–49 ave Simon Bolivar, 75950 Paris Cédex 19; tel. 1-56-41-55-20; fax 1-56-41-55-21; e-mail union-retraites@cfdt.fr; Sec.-Gen. JACQUES SENSE.

Services: Tour Essor, 14 rue Scandicci, 93508 Pantin Cédex; tel. 1-48-10-65-90; fax 1-48-10-65-95; e-mail services@cfdt.fr; internet www.cfdt-services.fr; Sec.-Gen. DIDIER BRULÉ.

Services de Santé et Services Sociaux (Health and Social Workers): 47–49 ave Simon Bolivar, 75950 Paris Cédex 19; tel. 1-56-41-52-00; fax 1-42-02-48-08; e-mail santesociaux@cfdt.fr; internet www.fed-cfdt-sante-sociaux.org; Sec.-Gen. YOLANDE BRIAND.

Transports-Equipement: 47–49 ave Simon Bolivar, 75950 Paris Cédex 19; tel. 1-44-84-29-50; fax 1-42-02-49-96; e-mail fgte@cfdt .fr; f. 1977; Sec.-Gen. BRUNO DALBERTO.

Confédération Française de l'Encadrement (CFE—CGC): 59–63 rue du Rocher, 75008 Paris; tel. 1-55-30-12-12; fax 1-55-30-13-13; e-mail presse@cfecgc.fr; internet www.cfecgc.fr; f. 1944; organizes managerial staff, professional staff and technicians; co-ordinates unions in every industry and sector; Chair. JEAN-LUC CAZETTES; Vice-Chair. CLAUDE CAMBUS; 192,842 mems.

Confédération Française des Travailleurs Chrétiens (CFTC): 13 rue des Ecluses Saint Martin, 75483 Paris Cédex 10; tel. 1-44-52-49-00; fax 1-44-52-49-18; e-mail eurint@cftc.fr; internet www.cftc.fr; f. 1919; present form in 1964 after majority CFTC became CFDT (see above); mem. European Trade Union Confederation, World Confederation of Labour; Chair. ALAIN DELEU; Gen. Sec. JACKY DINTINGER; 250,000 mems.

Confédération des Syndicats Libres (CSL): 37 rue Lucien Sampaix, 75010 Paris; tel. 1-55-26-12-12; fax 1-55-26-12-00; e-mail csl@ifrance.com; internet www.ifrance.com/csl; f. 1947; fmrly Confédération française du Travail; Sec.-Gen. GEORGES LENGLET; 250,000 mems.

Fédération Nationale des Syndicats Autonomes: Paris; f. 1952; groups unions in the private sector; Sec.-Gen. MICHEL-ANDRÉ TILLIÈRES.

Fédération Nationale des Syndicats d'Exploitants Agricoles (FNSEA) (National Federation of Farmers' Unions): 11 rue de la Baume, 75008 Paris; tel. 1-53-83-47-47; fax 1-53-83-48-48; e-mail fnsea@fnsea.fr; internet www.fnsea.fr; f. 1946; comprises 92 departmental federations and 32,000 local unions; Chair. JEAN-MICHEL LEMÉTAYER; Dir-Gen. PATRICK FERRERE; 600,000 mems.

Fédération Syndicale Unitaire (FSU): 3–5 rue de Metz, 75010 Paris; tel. 1-44-79-90-30; fax 1-48-01-02-52; e-mail webmaster@fsu .fr; internet www.fsu.fr; f. 1993; federation of civil service and education workers' unions; Sec.-Gen. GÉRARD ASCHIERI; 230,000 mems (2002).

Syndicat National Unitaire des Instituteurs (SNUIPP): 128 blvd Blanqui, 75013 Paris; tel. 1-44-08-69-30; fax 1-44-08-69-40; e-mail snuipp@snuipp.fr; internet www.snuipp.fr; f. 1993; primary-school teachers; Secs-Gen. BERNADETTE GROISON, LAURENT ZAPPI, NICOLE GENEIX.

UNSA Education: 87 bis ave Georges Gosnat, 94853 Ivry-sur-Seine Cédex; tel. 1-56-20-29-52; fax 1-56-20-29-89; e-mail national@unsa-education.org; internet www.unsa-education.org; f. 1948; federation of teachers' unions; fmrly Fédération de l'Education Nationale; Sec.-Gen. PATRICK GONTHIER.

Transport

RAILWAYS

Most of the French railways are controlled by the Société Nationale des Chemins de fer Français (SNCF), established in 1937, and the Réseau Ferré de France (f. 1997) manages track and infrastructure. The SNCF is divided into 22 régions (areas). In 2003 the SNCF operated 31,385 km of track, of which 14,464 km were electrified. High-speed services (trains à grande vitesse—TGV) operate between Paris and various other destinations: Lyon (TGV Sud-Est), extending to Marseille or Nîmes (TGV Méditerranée), Bordeaux or Nantes (TGV Atlantique), and Lille (TGV Nord Europe). The TGV network covered 1,540 km of track in 2003. A further TGV line, linking Paris with Strasbourg (TGV Est), was expected to open in 2006. The Parisian transport system is controlled by a separate authority, the Régie Autonome des Transports Parisiens (RATP). A number of small railways in the provinces are run by independent organizations. In 1994 a rail link between France and the United Kingdom was opened, including a tunnel under the English Channel (la Manche), from Calais to Folkestone.

Réseau Ferré de France (RFF): Tour Pascal A, 92045 Paris La Défense Cédex; tel. 1-46-96-90-00; fax 1-46-96-52-99; e-mail mama .jebbari@rff.fr; internet www.rff.fr; f. 1997 to assume ownership and financial control of national rail infrastructure; state-owned; Pres. JEAN-PIERRE DUPORT; Gen. Man. JEAN-FRANÇOIS BERTRAND.

Société Nationale des Chemins de fer Français (SNCF): 34 rue du Commandant Mouchotte, 75699 Paris Cédex 14; tel. 1-53-25-60-00; fax 1-53-25-61-08; e-mail webcom@sncf.fr; internet www.sncf.fr; f. 1937; Pres. LOUIS GALLOIS; Sec.-Gen. PAUL MINGASSON.

Channel Tunnel (Le Tunnel sous la Manche)

Groupe Eurotunnel: BP 69, Coquelles Cédex; tel. 3-21-00-65-43; internet www.eurotunnel.fr; Anglo-French consortium contracted to design, finance and construct the Channel Tunnel under a concession granted for a period up to 2052 (later extended to 2086); receives finance exclusively from the private sector, including international commercial banks; the Channel Tunnel was formally opened in May 1994; operates a series of road vehicle 'shuttle' trains and passenger and freight trains through the Channel Tunnel; Group Chair. CHARLES MACKAY; Chief Exec. PHILIPPE LAZARE.

Metropolitan Railways

Régie Autonome des Transports Parisiens (RATP): 54 quai de la Rapée, 75599 Paris Cédex 12; tel. 1-44-68-20-20; fax 1-44-68-31-60; internet www.ratp.fr; f. 1949; state-owned; operates the Paris underground (comprising 16 lines totalling 212 km, and 297 stations in 2001), suburban railways (totalling 327 km in 2001), 2 suburban tram lines, and buses; Chair. and Dir-Gen. ANNE-MARIE IDRAC.

Four provincial cities also have underground railway systems: Marseille, Lyon, Lille and Rennes.

ROADS

At 31 December 2000 there were 11,500 km of motorways (autoroutes). There were also 27,500 km of national roads (routes nationales), 355,000 km of secondary roads and 500,000 km of major local roads.

Fédération Nationale des Transports Routiers (FNTR): 6 rue Ampère, 75017 Paris; tel. 1-44-29-04-29; fax 1-44-29-04-01; e-mail fntr@fntr.fr; internet www.fntr.fr; road transport; Chair. RENÉ PETIT.

INLAND WATERWAYS

At 31 December 2000 there were 8,500 km of navigable waterways, of which 1,686 km were accessible to craft of 3,000 metric tons.

Voies navigables de France: 175 rue Ludovic Boutleux, BP 820, 62408 Béthune Cédex; tel. 3-21-63-24-42; e-mail direction-generale@vnf.fr; internet www.vnf.fr; f. 1991; management and development

of France's inland waterways; Pres. F. BORDRY; Gen. Man. A. BOROWSKI.

SHIPPING

In 1998 the principal ports, in terms of quantity of cargo, were Marseille, Le Havre and Dunkerque, and the principal passenger port was Calais. The six major seaports (Marseille, Le Havre, Dunkerque, Rouen, Nantes–Saint-Nazaire and Bordeaux) are operated by autonomous authorities, although the State retains supervisory powers.

Conseil National des Communautés Portuaires: 3 sq. Desaise, 75007 Paris; tel. 1-40-81-86-11; f. 1987; central independent consultative and co-ordinating body for ports and port authorities; more than 50 mems, including 10 trade union mems; Pres. JACQUES DUPUY-DAUBY; Sec.-Gen. M. DE ROCQUIGNY DU FAYEL.

Port Autonome Atlantique—Nantes-Saint Nazaire: Nantes; tel. 2-40-44-20-26; fax 2-40-44-21-81; e-mail ser.com@nantes.port.fr; internet www.nantes.port.fr; f. 1966; Pres. MICHEL QUIMBERT.

Port Autonome de Bordeaux: 3 pl. Gabriel, 33075 Bordeaux; tel. 5-56-90-58-00; e-mail postoffice@bordeaux-port.fr; internet www .bordeaux-port.fr; Pres. MICHEL SAMMARCELLI.

Port Autonome de Dunkerque: terre-plein Guillain, 59386 Dunkerque Cédex 01; tel. 3-28-28-78-78; fax 3-28-28-78-77; e-mail info@portdedunkerque.fr; internet www.portdedunkerque.fr; Pres. JEAN-PIERRE TROTIGNON; Dir-Gen. BRUNO VERGOBBI.

Port Autonome de Marseille: 23 pl. de la Joliette, BP 1965, 13226 Marseille Cédex 02; tel. 4-91-39-40-00; fax 4-91-39-57-00; e-mail pam@marseille-port.fr; internet www.marseille-port.fr; Pres. CLAUDE CARDELLA; Dir-Gen. ERIC BRASSART.

Port Autonome du Havre: BP 1413, 76067 Le Havre Cédex; tel. 2-32-74-74-00; fax 2-32-74-74-29; e-mail pahmail@havre-port.fr; internet www.havre-port.fr; Chair. JEAN-PIERRE LECOMTE; Sec.-Gen. MICHEL BAUX.

Port Autonome de Rouen—Vallée de Seine: 34 blvd de Boisguilbert, BP 4075, 76022 Rouen Cédex 03; tel. 2-35-52-54-30; fax 2-35-52-54-95; e-mail dg@rouen.port.fr; internet www.rouen.port.fr; Pres. GHISLAIN DE BOISSIEU; Dir-Gen. RENÉ GENEVOIS.

Port de Calais: pl. de l'Europe, 62226 Calais Cédex; tel. 3-21-96-31-20; fax 3-21-34-08-92; e-mail ccic@calais.cci.fr; internet www .calais-port.com; Pres. HENRI RAVISSE.

Principal Shipping Companies

Note: Not all the vessels belonging to the companies listed below are registered under the French flag.

Brittany Ferries: Port du Bloscon, BP 72, 29688 Roscoff Cédex; tel. 2-98-29-28-00; fax 2-98-29-27-00; e-mail compay@brittany-ferries.fr; internet www.brittany-ferries.fr; f. 1972 as BretagneAngleterre-Irlande (BAI); transport between France, Ireland, Spain and the United Kingdom; Chair. ALEXIS GOURVENNEC; Man. Dir MICHEL MARAVAL.

Broström Tankers, SA: 5 ave Percier, 75008 Paris; tel. 1-42-99-66-66; fax 1-42-99-66-20; e-mail brotank.paris@brostrom.fr; internet www.brostroms.se/tankers; subsidiary of Broström AB (Sweden); fmrly Van Ommeren Tankers; oil product and chemical coastal tankers and tramping.

Compagnie Maritime Marfret: 13 quai de la Joliette, 13002 Marseille; tel. 4-91-56-91-00; fax 4-91-56-91-01; e-mail mfmedsea@marfret.fr; internet www.marfret.fr; freight services to the Mediterranean, South America, the Caribbean, Canada and northern Europe; Chair. RAYMOND VIDIL; displacement 8,711 grt.

Consortium Européen de Transports Maritimes (CETRAMAR): 87 ave de la Grande Armée, 75782 Paris Cédex 16; tel. 1-40-66-11-11; fax 1-45-00-77-35; Chair. PHILIPPE POIRIER D'ANGÉ D'ORSAY; Man. Dir ANDRÉ MAIRE; displacement 564,291 grt.

Corsica Ferries: 5 bis rue Chanoine Leschi, 20296 Bastia; tel. 4-95-32-95-95; fax 4-95-32-14-71; internet www.corsicaferries.com; affiliated to Groupe Lota Maritime; passenger and freight ferry services between Corsica, Sardinia, mainland France, and mainland Italy; Pres. PASCAL LOTA.

Esso France: 2 rue des Martinets, 92569 Rueil-Malmaison Cédex; tel. 1-47-10-60-00; fax 1-47-10-60-44; internet www.esso.com/eaff/essofrance; f. 1952; Chair. and Man. Dir PATRICK HEINZLE.

Groupe CMA—CGM: 4 quai d'Arenc, BP 2409, 13215 Marseille Cédex 02; tel. 4-91-39-30-00; fax 4-91-39-30-95; e-mail webmaster@cma-cgm.com; internet www.cma-cgm.com; f. 1996; by merger of Compagnie Générale Maritime and Compagnie Maritime d'Affrètement; freight services to USA, Canada, the Caribbean, Central and South America, the Mediterranean, the Middle East, the Far East, India, Australia, New Zealand, Indonesia, East Africa and other Pacific and Indian Ocean areas; 25 ships owned; Chair. JACQUES R.

SAADÉ; Man. Dir FARID T. S. ALEM, ALAIN WILS; displacement 1,300,000 grt (1999).

Louis-Dreyfus Armateurs (SNC): 87 ave de la Grande Armée, 75782 Paris Cédex 16; tel. 1-40-66-11-11; fax 1-45-00-23-97; internet www.lda.fr; gas and bulk carriers; Pres. PHILIPPE LOUIS-DREYFUS.

Mobil Oil Française: Tour Septentrion, 92081 Paris La Défense Cédex; tel. 1-41-45-42-41; fax 1-41-45-42-93; bulk petroleum transport; refining and marketing of petroleum products; Chair. G. DUPAS-QUIER; displacement 281,489 grt.

Navale Française SA: 8 blvd Victor Hugo, 34000 Montpellier; tel. 4-67-58-82-12; fax 4-67-92-98-34; Chair. MARC CHEVALLIER.

SeaFrance: 3 rue Ambroise Paré, 75010 Paris; tel. 1-49-95-58-92; fax 1-48-74-62-37; e-mail presse@seafrance.net; internet www .seafrance.fr; frmly Société Nouvelle d'Armement Transmanche; vehicle and passenger services between France and the United Kingdom, Ireland and the Channel Islands; Man. Dir EUDES RIBLIER.

Société d'Armement et de Transport (Socatra): 9 allées de Tourny, 33000 Bordeaux; tel. 5-56-00-00-47; fax 5-56-48-51-23; e-mail direction@socatra.com; internet www.socatra.com; Chair. F. BOZZONI; Man. Dir M. DUBOURG.

Société Européenne de Transport Maritime: 9 allées de Tourny, 33000 Bordeaux; tel. 5-56-00-00-56; fax 5-56-48-51-23; Man. Dirs GILLES BOUTHILLIER, FERNAND BOZZONI; displacement 53,261 grt.

Société Nationale Maritime Corse-Méditerranée: 61 blvd des Dames, BP 1963, 13226 Marseille Cédex 02; tel. 4-91-56-32-00; fax 4-91-56-34-94; e-mail info@sncm.fr; internet www.sncm.fr; passenger and roll on/roll off ferry services between France and Corsica, Sardinia, North Africa; also subsidiary *Corsica Maritima*; Chair. PIERRE VIEU; displacement 141,454 grt.

Société Navale Caennaise: Caen; tel. 2-31-72-54-00; fax 2-31-78-04-94; e-mail veluma@mail.cpod.fr; internet perso.normandnet.fr/navale; f. 1901; cargo services to Europe and West Africa; Chair. and Man. Dir A. LABAT; displacement 59,680 grt.

Société Services et Transports: route du Hoc Gonfreville-L'Orcher, 76700 Harfleur; tel. 2-35-24-72-00; fax 2-35-53-36-25; petroleum and gas transport, passenger transport; Chair. YVES ROUSIER; Man. Dir JACQUES CHARVET; displacement 118,274 grt.

CIVIL AVIATION

There are international airports at Orly and Roissy-Charles de Gaulle (Paris), Bordeaux, Lille, Lyon, Marseille, Nice, Strasbourg and Toulouse.

Aéroports de Paris: 291 blvd de Raspail, 75675 Paris Cédex 14; tel. 1-43-35-70-00; fax 1-43-35-72-19; e-mail webmaster@adp.fr; internet www.adp.fr; state authority in charge of Paris airports at Orly and Roissy-Charles de Gaulle; Chair. PIERRE CHASSIONEUX; Man. Dir HUBERT DU MESNIL.

Airlines

Air France: 45 rue de Paris, 95747 Roissy Cédex; tel. 1-41-56-78-00; fax 1-41-56-70-29; internet www.airfrance.net; f. 1933; 56% state-owned; internal, international, European and inter-continental services; flights to Africa, the Americas, Middle and Far East and West Indies; Chair. JEAN-CYRIL SPINETTA; Pres. P. H. GOURGEON.

Air Littoral: Le Millénaire II, 417 rue Samuel Morse, 34000 Montpellier; tel. 4-67-20-67-20; e-mail information@airlittoral.fr; internet www.airlittoral.fr; f. 1972; flights to domestic destinations, Algeria

and the Mediterranean region; Pres. MARC DUFOUR; Dir-Gen. JEAN DURAND.

Brit Air: Aérodrome de Ploujean, BP 156, 29204 Morlaix; tel. 2-98-62-10-22; fax 2-98-62-77-66; internet www.britair.com; f. 1973; European flights; 99% owned by Air France; Pres. MARC LAMIDEY.

Hex Air: Aéroport Le Puy, 43320 Loudes; tel. 4-71-08-62-28; fax 4-71-08-04-10; f. 1991; domestic services; Pres. BERNARD GUICHON.

Regional Airlines: Aéroport Nantes Atlantique, 44345 Bougenais Cédex; tel. 2-40-13-53-00; fax 2-40-13-53-08; e-mail contact@ regional.com; internet www.regional.com; f. 1992; operates European and domestic flights; 99% owned by Air France Finance; Pres. JEAN-PAUL DUBREUIL; Man. Dir GUY LE SANN.

TAT European Airlines: 47 rue Christiaan-Huygens, BP 7237, 37072 Tours Cédex 02; tel. 2-47-42-30-00; fax 2-47-54-29-50; f. 1968; wholly-owned by British Airways; Pres. RODOLPHE MARCHAIS; Chair. MARC ROCHET.

Airlines Association

Fédération Nationale de l'Aviation Marchande (FNAM): 28 rue de Châteaudun, 75009 Paris; tel. 1-45-26-23-24; fax 1-45-26-23-95; e-mail info@fnam.fr; internet www.fnam.fr; f. 1991; Chair. CÉDRIC PASTOUR; Delegate-Gen. JEAN-PIERRE LE GOFF.

  Chambre Syndicale du Transport Aérien (CSTA): 28 rue de Châteaudun, 75009 Paris; tel. 1-45-26-23-24; fax 1-45-26-23-95; e-mail info@fnam.fr; internet www.fnam.fr/syndicats/csta.asp; f. 1946 to represent French airlines at national level; Chair. CÉDRIC PASTOUR; Delegate-Gen. JEAN-PIERRE LE GOFF.

Tourism

France attracts tourists from all over the world. Paris is famous for its boulevards, historic buildings, theatres, art treasures, fashion houses, restaurants and night clubs. The Mediterranean and Atlantic coasts and the French Alps are the most popular tourist resorts. Among other attractions are the many ancient towns, the châteaux of the Loire, the fishing villages of Brittany and Normandy, and spas and places of pilgrimage, such as Vichy and Lourdes. The theme park, Disneyland Paris, also attracts large numbers of tourists. There were an estimated 75,595,000 tourist arrivals in 2000; estimated tourist receipts in that year totalled US $29,900m. Most visitors are from the United Kingdom, Germany, Belgium, the Netherlands and Italy.

Direction du Tourisme: 2 rue Linois, 75740 Paris Cédex 15; tel. 1-44-37-36-00; fax 1-44-37-36-36; internet www.tourisme.gouv.fr; Dir BRUNO FARENIAUX.

Maison de la France: 20 ave de l'Opéra, 75041 Paris Cédex 01; tel. 1-42-96-70-00; fax 1-42-96-70-11; internet www.franceguide.com; f. 1987; Pres. GÉRARD BRÉMOND; Dir-Gen. JEAN-PHILIPPE PÉROL.

Observatoire National du Tourisme: 8 ave de l'Opéra, 75001 Paris; tel. 1-44-77-95-40; fax 1-44-77-95-50; e-mail isabelle .chevassut@ont-tourisme.com; internet www.ont.asso.fr; f. 1991; conducts studies and publishes information on all aspects of tourism in France; Pres. MAURICE BERNADET; Dir ALAIN MONFERRAND.

There are Regional Tourism Committees in the 23 regions and 4 overseas départements. There are more than 3,200 Offices de Tourisme and Syndicats d'Initiative (tourist offices operated by the local authorities) throughout France.

FRENCH OVERSEAS POSSESSIONS

Ministry of Overseas Departments, Territories and Country: 27 rue Oudinot, 75007, Paris, France; tel. 1-53-69-20-00; internet www.outre-mer.gouv.fr.

Minister of the Overseas Departments, Territories and Country: BRIGITTE GIRARDIN.

The national flag of France, proportions two by three, with three equal vertical stripes, of blue, white and red, is used in the Overseas Possessions.

French Overseas Departments

The four Overseas Departments (départements d'outre-mer) are French Guiana, Guadeloupe, Martinique and Réunion. They are integral parts of the French Republic. Each Overseas Department is administered by a Prefect, appointed by the French Government, and the administrative structure is similar to that of the Departments of metropolitan France. Overseas Departments, however, have their own Courts of Appeal (Cour d'Appel). In 1974 each of the Overseas Departments was granted the additional status of a Region (a unit devised for the purpose of economic and social planning, presided over by a Conseil Régional—Regional Council). Under the decentralization law of March 1982, the executive power of the Prefect in each Overseas Department was transferred to the locally-elected Conseil Général (General Council). As a compromise between autonomy and complete assimilation into France, the responsibility of the Conseil Régional for economic, social and cultural affairs was increased in 1983. In February of that year the first direct elections for the Conseils Régionaux were held. Government proposals regarding the institutional future and socio-economic development of the Departments were provisionally accepted by the

Assemblée Nationale in May 2000 and, following a number of alterations, were subsequently adopted by the Sénat. Changes proposed by the French Government included the creation on Réunion of a second department; the establishment on French Guiana, Guadeloupe and Martinique of congresses of the Conseils Régionaux and Généraux, which would discuss issues of common interest and formulate proposals concerning institutional reform and economic and social development; the transfer to the Regions of responsibilities in areas such as roads, territorial development, water resources and housing; and measures to increase the Departments' autonomy in conducting relations with neighbouring countries and territories. The amended proposals were definitively approved by the Assemblée Nationale in November (although the creation of a second department on Réunion was rejected) and by the Cour de Cassation (Constitutional Council) in December. The Overseas Departments continue to send elected representatives to the Assemblée Nationale and to the Sénat in Paris, and also to the European Parliament in Strasbourg.

FRENCH GUIANA

Introductory Survey

Location, Climate, Language, Religion, Capital

French Guiana (Guyane) lies on the north coast of South America, with Suriname to the west and Brazil to the south and east. The climate is humid, with a season of heavy rains from April to July and another short rainy season in December and January. Average temperature at sea-level is 27°C (85°F), with little seasonal variation. French is the official language, but a creole patois is also spoken. The majority of the population belong to the Roman Catholic Church, although other Christian churches are represented. The capital is Cayenne.

Recent History

French occupation commenced in the early 17th century. After brief periods of Dutch, English and Portuguese rule, the territory was finally confirmed as French in 1817. The colony steadily declined, after a short period of prosperity in the 1850s as a result of the discovery of gold in the basin of the Approuague river. French Guiana, including the notorious Devil's Island, was used as a penal colony and as a place of exile for convicts and political prisoners before the practice was halted in 1937. The colony became a Department of France in 1946.

French Guiana's reputation as an area of political and economic stagnation was dispelled by the growth of pro-independence sentiments, and the use of violence by a small minority, compounded by tensions between the Guyanais and large numbers of immigrant workers. In 1974 French Guiana was granted regional status, as part of France's governmental reorganization, thus acquiring greater economic autonomy. In that year, none the less, demonstrations against unemployment, the worsening economic situation and French government policy with regard to the Department led to the detention of leading trade unionists and pro-independence politicians. In 1975 the French Government announced plans to increase investment in French Guiana, but these were largely unsuccessful, owing partly to the problems of developing the interior (about 90% of the territory is

covered by forest). Further industrial and political unrest in the late 1970s prompted the Parti Socialiste Guyanais (PSG), then the strongest political organization, to demand greater autonomy for the Department. In 1980 there were several bomb attacks against 'colonialist' targets by an extremist group, Fo nou Libéré la Guyane. Reforms introduced by the French Socialist Government in 1982–83 devolved some power over local affairs to the new Conseil Régional (Regional Council). In the February 1983 elections to the Conseil Régional the left-wing parties gained a majority of votes, but not of seats, and the balance of power was held by the separatist Union des Travailleurs Guyanais (UTG), the political wing of which became the Parti National Populaire Guyanais (PNPG) in November 1985. At elections to the Conseil Général (General Council) held in March 1985, the PSG and left-wing independents secured 13 seats out of a total of 19.

For the general election to the Assemblée Nationale in March 1986, French Guiana's representation was increased from one to two deputies. The incumbent PSG deputy was re-elected, the other seat being won by the Gaullist Rassemblement pour la République (RPR). At simultaneous elections to the Conseil Régional, the PSG increased its strength on the Conseil from 14 to 15 members, and Georges Othily of the PSG was re-elected President of the Conseil. The RPR won nine seats, and the centre-right Union pour la Démocratie Française (UDF) three, while the remaining four seats were secured by Action Démocratique Guyanaise.

Of the votes cast in the Department at the 1988 French presidential election, the incumbent François Mitterrand of the Parti Socialiste (PS) defeated Jacques Chirac of the RPR. In the legislative elections held in June, the RPR none the less retained a seat in the Assemblée Nationale. In September–October the left-wing parties won 14 of the 19 seats at elections to the Conseil Général. In September 1989 Othily, the President of the Conseil Régional, was elected to take French Guiana's seat in the French Sénat (Senate). Othily had recently been expelled from the PSG for having worked too closely with the opposition parties. However, he attracted support from those who regarded the party's domination of French Guiana as corrupt, and his victory over the incumbent senator, a PSG member, was believed to reflect the level of dissatisfaction within the party.

In March 1992 elections were held to both the Conseil Général and the Conseil Régional. In the former, the PSG retained 10 seats, while other left-wing candidates took five seats. The PSG leader, Elie Castor, retained the presidency of the Conseil Général. The party also won 16 seats in the Conseil Régional, and the PSG Secretary-General, Antoine Karam, was subsequently elected as the body's President. In a referendum in September, 67.3% of voters in French Guiana approved ratification of the Treaty on European Union (see p. 199), although a high abstention rate was recorded.

At the March 1993 elections to the Assemblée Nationale Léon Bertrand of the RPR was re-elected, along with Christiane Taubira-Delannon, the founder of the independent left-wing Walwari movement and an outspoken critic of existing policies for the management of French Guiana's natural resources; she subsequently joined the République et liberté grouping in the Assemblée Nationale.

The PSG's representation in the Conseil Général declined to eight seats following the March 1994 cantonal elections; none the less, one of its members, Stéphan Phinéra-Horth, was subsequently elected President of the Conseil (Elie Castor having left the party). Taubira-Delannon, defeated by Karam, failed to secure election, although another member of the Walwari movement did enter the Conseil. Taubira-Delannon was elected to the European Parliament in June, as a representative of the Energie radicale grouping—which secured the greatest percentage of the votes (36.3%) in the Department, ahead of the government list and a combined list of the parties of the left of the four Overseas Departments.

At the first round of voting in the 1995 presidential elections, on 23 April, there was a considerable increase in support in French Guiana for Chirac, who took 39.8% of the votes cast, at the expense of the candidate of the PS, Lionel Jospin, who received the support of 24.2% of voters. The level of support for Jean-Marie Le Pen, of the extreme right-wing Front National, almost doubled (to 8.1%), compared with that at the 1988 election. At the second round, on 7 May, Chirac won 57.4% of the valid votes cast.

Beginning in late October 1996 a boycott of classes by secondary-school pupils, who were demanding improved conditions of study, escalated in the following month into a crisis that was regarded as exemplifying wider social tensions between the Department and metropolitan France. The refusal of the Prefect, Pierre Dartout, to receive schools' representatives prompted protests in Cayenne, which swiftly degenerated into rioting and looting, apparently as the protesters were joined by disaffected youths from deprived areas. Considerable material damage was caused to government and commercial property during two nights of violence. The central Government dispatched anti-riot police to assist the local security forces, and it was announced that Jean-Jacques de Peretti and the Minister of National Education, François Bayrou, would visit French Guiana. However, the conviction, shortly afterwards, of several people implicated in the rioting provoked further protests and clashes with security forces, and a one-day general strike in Cayenne, organized by the UTG, resulted in the closure of most businesses and government departments. The extent of the security forces' actions in suppressing the demonstrations was criticized both by those involved in the schools' protest and by local politicians, while the competence of the Department's administrators in their approach to the crisis was the focus of considerable scrutiny. Local officials, meanwhile, denounced the role in the violence not only of unemployed youths but also of separatist groups, alleging that the latter were seeking to exploit the crisis for their own ends. Bayrou and de Peretti subsequently arrived in Cayenne to meet those involved in the crisis. Local administrators and schools' representatives had already reached agreement on the students' material demands, but, to considerable local acclaim, the ministers announced the establishment, effective from the beginning of 1997, of separate Academies for French Guiana, Guadeloupe and Martinique. The creation was also announced of additional primary educational facilities, and a programme was declared to improve academic standards in secondary schools. In all, the measures were to cost the French Government more than 500m. francs.

Elie Castor died in France in June 1996; prior to his death he had been under investigation in connection with allegations including fraud and abuse of influence during his time in public office. In May 1997 further details of irregularities in the Conseil Général's administration of French Guiana during Elie Castor's presidency were revealed in a letter from the Antilles–Guyane Chambre régionale des comptes (responsible for monitoring public finances in the region) to Phinéra-Horth, Castor's successor as President of the Conseil.

In April 1997 violent incidents followed the arrest of five pro-independence activists suspected of setting fire to the home of the public prosecutor during the disturbances of November 1996. Five others, including leading members of the UTG and the PNPG, were subsequently detained in connection with the arson incident. The transfer of all 10 detainees to Martinique prompted further violent protests in Cayenne. Police reinforcements were dispatched by the central Government to help suppress the violence, as nine gendarmes reportedly received gunshot wounds during two nights of rioting. In July one of the detainees, Jean-Victor Castor, a prominent member of the UTG and the pro-independence Mouvement pour la Décolonisation et l'Emancipation Sociale (MDES), who had been released the previous month, was rearrested and accused of assaulting a policeman during the April riots. Following the announcement, in August, that Castor was to remain in custody, some 200 demonstrators clashed with riot police in Cayenne. Castor was released shortly afterwards, and in September a further four separatists, who had been held on remand since April, were also freed.

In late May and early June 1997 Léon Bertrand, securing 63.3% of votes cast, and Christiane Taubira-Delannon, winning 64.8% of votes, were both re-elected to the Assemblée Nationale in elections that were marked by a high rate of abstention. Candidates from pro-independence parties notably gained increased support, winning slightly more than 10% of the votes cast in both constituencies.

Elections to the Conseil Régional and the Conseil Général were held in March 1998. The PSG's representation in the former declined to 11 seats, with other left-wing candidates securing a further 11 seats (including two won by Walwari). Antoine Karam was re-elected to the presidency of the Conseil. The PSG also lost seats in the Conseil Général, retaining only five of the 19 seats, while other left-wing candidates took a further five, and independent candidates won seven seats. André Lecante, an independent left-wing councillor, was elected as the body's President, defeating the incumbent, Phinéra-Horth. In late September 1998 Othily was re-elected to the Sénat.

In January 1999 representatives of 10 separatist organizations from French Guiana, Guadeloupe and Martinique, including the MDES and the PNPG, signed a joint declaration denouncing 'French colonialism', in which they stated their intention to campaign for the reinstatement of the three Caribbean Overseas Departments on a UN list of territories to be decolonized. In February members of the Conseil Régional and the Conseil Général held a congress to discuss the political, economic and social future of French Guiana; the participants proposed the replacement of the two Conseils with a single body, to which responsibility in several areas, such as economic development, health and education, would be transferred. Several RPR councillors boycotted the meeting. In October, however, during a visit to Guadeloupe and Martinique, Lionel Jospin, the Prime Minister, precluded from future legislation any merger of the Conseil Régional and Conseil Général. Following a series of meetings held in late 1999, in December the Presidents of the regional councils of French Guiana, Guadeloupe and Martinique signed a joint declaration in Basse-Terre, Guadeloupe, affirming their intention to propose, to the President and the Government, a legislative amendment, possibly constitutional, aimed at creating a new status of overseas region. The declaration, however, was dismissed by the Secretary of State for Overseas Departments and Territories, Jean-Jack Queyranne, in February 2000 as unconstitutional and exceeding the mandate of politicians responsible. In March, during a visit to the Department by Queyranne, rioting broke out following Queyranne's refusal to meet a delegation of separatist organizations. Later that month the Conseil Régional rejected, by 23 votes to seven, reforms proposed by Queyranne in February, which included the creation of a Congress in French Guiana, as well as the extension of the Departments' powers in areas such as regional co-operation. Nevertheless, the proposals were provisionally accepted by the Assemblée Nationale in May, and were subsequently adopted, by a narrow margin, by the Sénat, following a number of modifications. In November the Assemblée Nationale approved the reforms, and in December they were ratified by the Constitutional Council. At a referendum held in September, French Guiana voted overwhelmingly in favour (80%) of reducing the presidential mandate from seven years to five.

In late November 2000 several people were injured following riots in Cayenne. The demonstrations followed a march, organized by the UTG, demanding greater autonomy for French Guiana, as well as immediate negotiations with the new Secretary of State for Overseas Departments and Territories, Christian Paul. Protesters claimed they had been excluded from talks on French Guiana's status (Paul had invited leaders of various political parties in French Guiana to attend a meeting to be held in France in December, but the offer was rejected by MDES activists, who demanded the meeting be held in Cayenne). Nevertheless, discussions were held in mid-December in Paris at which Paul, various senior politicians from French Guiana and representatives from the PSG, the RPR, Walwari, and the Forces Démocratiques Guyanaises (FDG) were present. It was agreed that further talks were to be held between the Conseil Régional and the Conseil Général of French Guiana before the end of 2001, eventually to be followed by a referendum in the Department. In early January 2001, following further consultations, it was agreed that a document detailing proposals for increased autonomy for French Guiana was to be drawn up by local officials and was to be presented to the French Government for approval. Following a meeting of members of both Conseils in late June 2001, a series of proposals on greater autonomy, to be presented to the French Government, was agreed upon. These included: the division of the territory into four districts; the creation of a 'collectivité territoriale' (territorial community), governed by a 41-member Assembly elected for a five-year term; and the establishment of an independent executive council. Furthermore, the proposals included a request that the territory be given control over legislative and administrative affairs, as well as legislative authority on matters concerning French Guiana alone. In November the French Government announced itself to be in favour of the suggested constitutional developments, although no further steps had been effected by early 2003.

At municipal elections held in March 2001, the PSG candidate for the mayorship of Cayenne, Jean-Claude Lafontaine, defeated the Walwari candidate, Christiane Taubira-Delannon. At concurrently-held elections to the presidency of the Conseil Général the left-wing independent candidate Joseph Ho-Ten-You defeated André Lecante.

In September 2001 the Secretary of State for Overseas Departments and Territories, Christian Paul, announced the establishment of a number of measures designed to improve security in the Department. Plans included a 20% increase in the police force, the creation of a small 'peace corps' and a continuous police presence in the town of Maripasoula and its surrounding region, following concerns over the security of gold prospectors in the area. In the first round of the presidential election, held on 21 April 2002, Taubira-Delannon received 52.7% of the votes cast in the Department, followed by Chirac, who attracted 19.0%. In the second round, held on 5 May, Chirac overwhelmingly defeated Jean-Marie Le Pen, receiving 89.1% of the vote and thereby winning a second presidential term. At the legislative elections held in June, Taubira-Delannon was re-elected to the Assemblée Nationale with 65.3% of the vote, and Bertrand with 64.0%; about two-thirds of registered voters abstained. Following the elections the RPR merged to become the Union pour un Mouvement Populaire. In July 2002 Ange Mancini was appointed Prefect, replacing Henri Masse.

In 1986–87 French Guiana's relations with neighbouring Surinam deteriorated as increasing numbers of Surinamese refugees fled across the border to escape rebel uprisings in their own country. In late 1986 additional French troops were brought in to patrol the border, as a result of which the Surinamese Government accused the French Government of preparing an invasion of Suriname via French Guiana. It was also reported that Surinamese rebels were using French Guiana as a conduit for weapons and supplies. In 1992 the French Government implemented a programme under which all of the refugees from Suriname were to be repatriated. In mid-2001 the French President, Jacques Chirac, rejected a joint request by French Guiana, Guadeloupe and Martinique that they be permitted to join, as associate members, the Association of Caribbean States.

Government

France is represented in French Guiana by an appointed Prefect. There are two councils with local powers: the Conseil Général, with 19 members, and the Conseil Régional, with 31 members. Both are elected by universal adult suffrage for a period of six years. French Guiana elects two representatives to the Assemblée Nationale in Paris, and sends one elected representative to the Sénat. French Guiana is also represented at the European Parliament.

Defence

At 1 August 2002 France maintained military forces of 3,000 in French Guiana, as well as a gendarmerie of 600.

Economic Affairs

In 1999 French Guiana's gross domestic product (GDP), measured at current prices, was US $1,490m., equivalent to $9,342 per head. Between 1990 and 1999, according to UN estimates, GDP increased, in real terms, at an average rate of 4.2% per year; growth in 1999 was 1.6%. Between the censuses of 1990 and 1999, according to provisional figures, the population increased at an average annual rate of 3.5%.

Agriculture (including fishing) engaged 6.6% of the employed labour force in 1999 and, according to official sources, contributed 5.2% of GDP. The dominant activities are fisheries and forestry, although the contribution of the latter to export earnings has declined in recent years. In 1998 exports of shrimps provided some 22.4% of total export earnings. The principal crops for local consumption are cassava, vegetables and rice, and sugar cane is grown for making rum. Rice, pineapples and citrus fruit are cultivated for export. According to UN estimates, agricultural GDP decreased at an average annual rate of 0.8% in 1990–98; in 1998 agricultural GDP increased by an estimated 0.3%.

Industry, including construction, engaged about 15.6% of the employed labour force in 1999 and, according to official sources, contributed 18.7% of GDP. The mining sector is dominated by the extraction of gold, which involves small-scale alluvial operations as well as larger local and multinational mining concerns. Exploration activity intensified in the mid-1990s, and the proposed construction of a major new road into the interior of the Department was expected to encourage further development. Officially-recorded gold exports were estimated at 4,857 kg in 1999 (actual production levels and sales are believed to be higher than published levels). In 2000 3.4 metric tons (109,310 troy oz) of gold were mined. Crushed rock for the construction industry is the only other mineral extracted in significant quantities, although exploratory drilling of known diamond deposits began in 1995. Deposits of bauxite, columbotantalite and kaolin are also present. There is little manufacturing activity, except for the processing of fisheries products (mainly shrimp-freezing) and the distillation of rum. In 1990–98 industrial GDP (excluding construction) increased at an average annual rate of 7.8%. The construction sector expanded at an average of 2.0% per year in the same period.

French Guiana was heavily dependent on imported fuels for the generation of energy prior to the flooding of the Petit-Saut hydroelectric dam on the River Sinnamary, in 1994. Together with existing generating plants, the 116-MW dam was expected to satisfy the territory's electrical energy requirements for about 30 years. Fuel imports accounted for 11.3% of total imports in 2000.

The services sector engaged 77.7% of the employed labour force in 1999 and, according to official sources, contributed 76.1% of GDP. The European Space Agency's satellite-launching centre at Kourou (established in 1964 and expanded during the 1990s) has provided a considerable stimulus to the economy, most notably the construction sector (which engaged 7.5% of the employed labour force in 1999). The tourist sector expanded in the last two decades of the 20th century, although its potential is limited by the lack of infrastructure away from the coast. In 1999 68,211 visitor arrivals were recorded.

In 2000 French Guiana recorded a trade deficit of 499m. euros. In that year the principal source of imports was metropolitan France (which supplied 55.8% of total imports in 2000); the Department's other major suppliers were Trinidad and Tobago, Italy and Japan. Metropolitan France was also the principal market for exports in 2000 (63.6%); other important purchasers were Switzerland, Guadeloupe and the USA. The principal imports in 2000 were food and agricultural products and road vehicles and parts. The principal exports were metals and metal products and food and agricultural products.

Under the 1998 regional budget it was envisaged that expenditure would total €67m., while revenue was €63m. By September 1988 French Guiana's external debt had reached US $1,200m. The annual rate of inflation averaged 1.4% in

1990–2001; consumer prices increased by an average of 1.4% in 2000 and by 1.6% in 2001. Unemployment in mid-2002 was estimated at 23% of the total labour force. However, there is a shortage of skilled labour, offset partly by immigration.

As an integral part of France, French Guiana is a member of the European Union (EU, see p. 199).

Economic development in French Guiana has been hindered by the Department's location, poor infrastructure away from the coast and lack of a skilled indigenous labour force, although there is considerable potential for further growth in the fishing, forestry and tourism (notably 'eco-tourism') sectors. A particular concern throughout the 1990s was the rapid rise in the rate of unemployment; youth unemployment and related social problems were widely interpreted as having contributed to the violence in Cayenne in late 1996 (see Recent History). French Guiana's geographical characteristics—large parts of the territory are accessible only by river—have resulted in difficulties in regulating key areas of the economy, such as gold-mining and forestry. Considerable concern has been expressed regarding the ecological consequences of such a lack of controls; moreover, the flooding of a large area of forest (some 340 sq km), as part of the Petit-Saut barrage project, has prompted disquiet among environmental groups, as has uncertainty regarding the ecological implications of the satellite-launching programme at Kourou. Proposals for the creation of a national park, covering 2.5m. ha of the south of French Guiana, with the aim of protecting an expanse of equatorial forest, were hindered in the early 2000s by the need to reconcile ecological concerns with economic priorities and the needs of the resident communities, notably the demands of gold prospectors. The budget deficit represents a significant obstacle to growth, while high demand for imported consumer goods (much of which is generated by relatively well-remunerated civil servants, who constitute about two-thirds of the working population) undermines progress in reducing the trade deficit. In mid-2001 the decision by the French Government to abandon a sugar cane plantation project was met with disappointment by local politicians. The plantation of some 8,000 ha of sugar cane, with an estimated annual output of 65,000 tons of raw sugar, had been expected to generate significant employment opportunities. However, the project was considered to be too costly by the Government, which subsequently pledged to undertake a plan for the development of the agricultural sector in French Guiana.

Education

Education is modelled on the system in metropolitan France, and is compulsory for 10 years between the ages of six and 16 years. Primary education begins at six years of age and lasts for five years. Secondary education, beginning at 11 years of age, lasts for up to seven years, comprising a first cycle of four years and a second of three years. Education at state schools (which accounted for more than 92% of total enrolment in 2000/01) is provided free of charge. In 2000/01 there were 32,365 pupils attending primary and pre-primary schools in French Guiana, while 20,585 students were enrolled in secondary education. In 1999/2000 there were 125 primary and pre-primary schools and, in 2000/01, there were 35 institutes of secondary education. Higher education in law, administration and French language and literature is provided by a branch of the Université des Antilles et de la Guyane in Cayenne (the university as a whole had some 11,328 enrolled students in the 2000/01 academic year), and one department of a technical institute opened at Kourou in 1988. There is also a teacher-training college and an agricultural college. Total government expenditure on education amounted to 851m. French francs in 1993. The French Government announced its decision to increase expenditure in the education sector in 2000–06, including €71m. on the construction of new school buildings. An Academy for French Guiana was established in January 1997.

Public Holidays

2003: 1 January (New Year's Day), 3–4 March (Lenten Carnival), 5 March (Ash Wednesday), 18–21 April (Easter), 1 May (Labour Day), 29 May (Ascension Day), 9 June (Whit Monday), 10 June (Slavery Day), 14 July (National Day), 11 November (Armistice Day), 25 December (Christmas Day).

2004: 1 January (New Year's Day), 23–24 February (Lenten Carnival), 25 February (Ash Wednesday), 9–12 April (Easter), 1 May (Labour Day), 20 May (Ascension Day), 30 May (Whit

Monday), 10 June (Slavery Day), 14 July (National Day), 11 November (Armistice Day), 25 December (Christmas Day).

Weights and Measures

The metric system is in use.

Statistical Survey

Sources (unless otherwise stated): Institut national de la statistique et des études économiques (INSEE), Service Régional de Guyane, ave Pasteur, BP 6017, 97306 Cayenne Cédex; tel. 5-94-29-73-00; fax 5-94-29-73-01; internet www.insee.fr/fr/insee_regions/GUYANE ; Chambre de Commerce et d'Industrie, Hôtel Consulaire, pl. de l'Esplanade, BP 49, 97321 Cayenne Cédex; tel. 5-94-29-96-00; fax 5-94-29-96-34; internet www.guyane .cci.fr.

AREA AND POPULATION

Area: 83,534 sq km (32,253 sq miles).

Population: 114,808 (males 59,799, females 55,009) at census of 15 March 1990; 156,790 (males 78,963, females 77,827) at census of 8 March 1999.

Density (at 1999 census): 1.9 per sq km.

Principal Towns (population at 1999 census, provisional): Cayenne (capital) 50,594; Saint-Laurent-du-Maroni 19,211; Kourou 19,107; Matoury 18,032; Remire-Montjoly 15,555; Mana 5,445; Macouria 5,050; Maripasoula 3,710. *2001* (UN estimate, including suburbs): Cayenne 53,000 (Source: UN, *World Urbanization Prospects: The 2001 Revision*).

Births, Marriages and Deaths (1999): Registered live births 4,907 (birth rate 31.0 per 1,000); Registered marriages 548 (marriage rate 3.5 per 1,000); Registered deaths 648 (death rate 4.1 per 1,000). *2001* Registered live births 5,140; Registered marriages 553; Registered deaths 679.

Expectation of Life (years at birth, 1999): Males 71.7; Females 79.2.

Economically Active Population (persons aged 15 years and over, 1999): Agriculture, forestry and fishing 2,888; Construction 3,256; Industry 3,524; Trade 4,573; Transport 1,616; Education, health and social services 8,990; Public administration 10,337; Other services 8,259; Total employed 43,443 (males 25,703; females 17,740). *Mid-2001* (estimates): Agriculture, etc. 13,000; Total labour force 72,000 (males 48,000, females 24,000) (Source: FAO).

HEALTH AND WELFARE

Key Indicators

Access to Water (% of persons, 2000): 84.

Access to Sanitation (% of persons, 2000): 79.
For sources and definitions, see explanatory note on p. vi.

AGRICULTURE, ETC.

Principal Crops (FAO estimates, '000 metric tons, 2001): Rice (paddy) 19.9; Cassava 10.4; Sugar cane 5.3; Cabbages 6.4; Tomatoes 3.8; Cucumbers and gherkins 3.7; Green beans 3.3; Other fresh vegetables 7.7; Bananas 4.5; Plantains 3.2. Source: partly FAO.

Livestock (FAO estimates, '000 head, year ending September 2001): Cattle 9.2; Pigs 10.5; Sheep 2.6. Source: FAO.

Livestock Products (FAO estimates, metric tons, unless otherwise indicated, 2001): Beef and veal 460; Pig meat 1,245; Poultry meat 560; Cows' milk 268; Hen eggs 460. Source: FAO.

Forestry (FAO estimates, '000 cubic metres, 2001): *Roundwood removals* (excl. bark): Sawlogs, veneer logs and logs for sleepers 51; Other industrial wood 9; Fuel wood 79; Total 139. *Sawnwood production* (incl. railway sleepers): Total 15. Source: FAO.

Fishing (metric tons, live weight, 2000): Capture 5,237 (Marine fishes 2,500, Shrimps 2,737); Aquaculture 31; Total catch 5,268. Source: FAO, *Yearbook of Fishery Statistics*.

MINING

Production ('000 metric tons unless otherwise indicated, estimates, 2001): Cement 50,000; Gold (metal content of ore, kilograms) 3,000; Sand 1,500. Source: US Geological Survey.

INDUSTRY

Production: Rum 3,072 hl in 2000; Electric energy 453 million kWh in 1998. Source: partly UN, *Industrial Commodity Statistics Yearbook*.

FINANCE

Currency and Exchange Rates: 100 cent = 1 euro (€). *Sterling and Dollar Equivalents* (31 December 2002): £1 sterling = 1.5370 euros; US $1 = 0.9536 euros; 1,000 euros = £650.64 = $1,048.70. *Average Exchange Rate* (euros per US dollar): 1.0854 in 2000; 1.1175 in 2001; 1.0626 in 2002. Note: The national currency was formerly the French franc. From the introduction of the euro, with French participation, on 1 January 1999, a fixed exchange rate of €1 = 6.55957 French francs was in operation. Euro notes and coins were introduced on 1 January 2002. The euro and French currency circulated alongside each other until 17 February, after which the euro became the sole legal tender. Some of the figures in this Survey are still in terms of francs.

Budget (million French francs, 1992): *French Government:* Revenue 706; Expenditure 1,505. *Regional Government:* Revenue 558; Expenditure 666. *Departmental Government:* Revenue 998; Expenditure 803. *Communes:* Revenue 998; Expenditure 982. *1998* (million euros): *Regional Budget:* Revenue 63; Expenditure 67. *Departmental Budget:* Revenue 137; Expenditure 15.

Money Supply (million French francs at 31 December 1996): Currency outside banks 3,000; Demand deposits at banks 1,621; Total money 4,621.

Cost of Living (Consumer Price Index for Cayenne; base: 1990 = 100): 113.7 in 1999; 115.3 in 2000; 117.1 in 2001. Source: UN, *Monthly Bulletin of Statistics*.

Expenditure on the Gross Domestic Product (million French francs at current prices, 1995): Government final consumption expenditure 4,042; Private final consumption expenditure 5,898; Increase in stocks 121; Gross fixed capital formation 2,542; *Total domestic expenditure* 12,603; Exports of goods and services 7,746; *Less* Imports of goods and services 9,577; *GDP in purchasers' values* 10,772.

Gross Domestic Product by Economic Activity (million French francs at current prices, 1995): Agriculture, hunting, forestry and fishing 572; Mining, quarrying and manufacturing 988; Electricity, gas and water 139; Construction 858; Trade, restaurants and hotels 1,895; Transport, storage and communications 1,241; Finance, insurance, real estate and business services 815; Public administration 1,492; Other services 2,451; *Sub-total* 10,449; *Less* Imputed bank service charge 310; *GDP at basic prices* 10,139; Taxes, less subsidies, on products 633; *GDP in purchasers' values* 10,772.

EXTERNAL TRADE

Principal Commodities: *Imports* (million euros, 2000): Food and agricultural products 120; Clothing and leather 21; Chemicals and related products 33; Household goods 44; Road vehicles and parts 87; Boats, aeroplanes, trains, motorbikes 21; Machinery 61; Electrical equipment 39; Plastic or rubber chemical products 35; Metals and metal products 22; Fuels 70; Total (incl. others) 620. *Exports f.o.b.:* (million euros, 2000): Food and agricultural products 25; Road vehicles and parts 5; Electrical equipment 12; Metals and metal products 64; Total (incl. others) 121.

Principal Trading Partners (million euros, 2000): *Imports c.i.f.:* Belgium-Luxembourg 10; France (metropolitan) 346; Germany 15; Italy 18; Japan 18; Martinique 11; Netherlands 12; Spain 9; Trinidad and Tobago 66; USA 12; Total (incl. others) 620. *Exports f.o.b.:* Brazil 5; France (metropolitan) 77; Guadeloupe 6; Italy 2; Martinique 4; Netherlands 3; Spain 3; Switzerland 6; USA 9; Total (incl. others) 121.

TRANSPORT

Road Traffic ('000 motor vehicles in use, 1997): Passenger cars 28.2; Commercial vehicles 9.4 (Source: UN, *Statistical Yearbook*). *2000:* 38,340 motor vehicles in use.

International Sea-borne Shipping (traffic, 1999): Vessels entered 240; Goods loaded 65,000 metric tons; Goods unloaded 501,000 metric tons; Passengers carried 275,300 (1998). *2000:* Goods loaded 26,135 metric tons; Goods unloaded 406,054 metric tons.

Civil Aviation (2000): Freight carried 7,179 metric tons; Passengers carried 449,014.

TOURISM

Tourist Arrivals (1999): 68,211. Source: Comité du Tourisme de la Guyane.

Receipts from Tourism (US $ million): 51 in 1998; 50 in 1999. Source: World Tourism Organization.

COMMUNICATIONS MEDIA

Radio Receivers ('000 in use): 104 in 1997.

Television Receivers ('000 in use): 37 in 1998.

Telephones ('000 main lines in use): 49.2 in 1999.

Facsimile Machines (number in use): 185 in 1990.

Mobile Cellular Telephones ('000 subscribers): 39.8 in 2000.

Personal Computers ('000 in use): 23 in 1999.

Internet Users ('000): 2 in 1999.

Daily Newspaper: 1 in 1996 (average circulation 2,000 copies). Sources: UNESCO, *Statistical Yearbook*; UN, *Statistical Yearbook*; International Telecommunication Union.

EDUCATION

Pre-primary: 39 institutions (1999/2000); 11,188 students (2000/01).

Primary* (2000/01): 86 institutions (79 state, 7 private) (1999/2000); 1,718 teachers; 20,826 students (19,237 state, 1,589 private).

Secondary (2000/01): 35 institutions (29 state, 6 private); 1,385 teachers; 20,585 students (18,938 state, 1,647 private).

Higher (2000/01): 666 students (1998/99); 42 teachers.

*Figures for teachers in primary education include pre-primary education.

Directory

The Government

(April 2003)

Prefect: ANGE MANCINI, Préfecture, rue Fiedmont, BP 7008, 97307 Cayenne Cédex; tel. 5-94-39-45-00; fax 5-94-30-02-77; e-mail sgaer1.prefect.guyane@wanadoo.fr; internet www.guyane.pref.gouv.fr.

President of the General Council: JOSEPH HO-TEN-YOU (Independent left), Hôtel du Département, place Léopold Héder, BP 5021, 97305 Cayenne Cédex; tel. 5-94-29-55-00; fax 5-94-29-55-25.

President of the Economic and Social Committee: ROGER MICHEL LOUPEC, 35 ave Léopold Héder, 97300 Cayenne; tel. 5-94-30-81-00; fax 5-94-30-73-65.

Deputies to the French National Assembly: CHRISTIANE TAUBIRA (Walwari), LÉON BERTRAND (Union pour la Majorité Présidentielle).

Representative to the French Senate: GEORGES OTHILY (Rassaemblement démocratique et social européen).

CONSEIL RÉGIONAL

Conseil Regional, 66 ave du Général de Gaulle, BP 7025, 97307 Cayenne Cédex; tel. 5-94-29-20-20; fax 5-94-31-95-22.

President: ANTOINE KARAM (PSG).

Election, 15 March 1998

	Seats*
Parti Socialiste Guyanais (PSG)	11
Rassemblement pour la République (RPR)	6
Walwari	2
Others	12†
Total	31

*Three independents and nine left-wing candidates.

†In 2000 one PSG and one RPR candidate defected from their respective parties; thus the new distribution of seats changed to PSG 10, RPR five, Walwari two and Others 14.

Political Organizations

Forces Démocratiques Guyanaises (FDG): Cayenne; f. 1989 by a split in the PSG; Leader GEORGES OTHILY.

Front National: Cayenne; internet www.frontnational.com; extreme right-wing.

Mouvement pour la Décolonisation et l'Emancipation Sociale (MDES): Cayenne; f. 1991; pro-independence party; Sec.-Gen. MAURICE PINDARD.

Parti National Populaire Guyanais (PNPG): Cayenne; f. 1985; pro-independence party; Leader JOSÉ DORCY.

Parti Socialiste Guyanais (PSG): 1 Cité Césaire, Cayenne; f. 1956; left-wing; Sec.-Gen. MARIE-CLAUDE VERDANT.

Union pour la Démocratie Française (UDF): Cayenne; tel. 5-94-31-17-10; f. 1979; local branch of the national party; centre-right; Leader GEORGES HABRAN-MERY.

Union pour un Mouvement Populaire: Cayenne; internet www .u-m-p.org; f. 2002 by members of the former Rassemblement pour la République and Démocratie Liberal parties; successor party to the Union pour la Majorité Présidentielle party.

Union Socialiste Démocratique (USD): Cayenne; Leader THÉO-DORE ROUMILLAC.

Les Verts Guyane: Cayenne; tel. 5-94-31-02-96; local branch of national green party.

Walwari: Cayenne; f. 1993; left-wing; Leader CHRISTIANE TAUBIRA.

Judicial System

Courts of Appeal: see Judicial System, Martinique (see p. 1691).

Tribunal de Grande Instance: Palais de Justice, 9 ave du Général de Gaulle, 97300 Cayenne; Pres. J. FAHET; Procurator-Gen. ANNE KAYANAKIS.

Religion

CHRISTIANITY

The Roman Catholic Church

French Guiana comprises the single diocese of Cayenne, suffragan to the archdiocese of Fort-de-France, Martinique. At 31 December 2000 there were an estimated 150,000 adherents in French Guiana, representing some 75% of the total population. French Guiana participates in the Antilles Episcopal Conference, currently based in Port of Spain, Trinidad and Tobago.

Bishop of Cayenne: Rt Rev. LOUIS SANKALÉ, Evêché, 24 rue Madame Payé, BP 378, 97328 Cayenne Cédex; tel. 5-94-31-01-18; fax 5-94-30-20-33.

The Anglican Communion

Within the Church in the Province of the West Indies, French Guiana forms part of the diocese of Guyana. The Bishop is resident in Georgetown, Guyana.

Other Churches

Assembly of God: 1051 route de Raban, 97300 Cayenne; tel. 5-94-25-62-22; fax 5-94-35-23-05; Pres. JACQUES RHINO.

Church of Jesus Christ of Latter-day Saints (Mormons): allée des Cigales, route de Montabo, 97300 Cayenne; tel. 5-94-31-21-86; Br. Pres. FRANÇOIS PRATIQUE.

Seventh-day Adventist Church: Mission Adventiste de la Guyane, 39 rue Schoëlcher, BP 169, 97324 Cayenne Cédex; tel. 5-94-25-64-26; fax 5-94-37-93-02; e-mail mission.adventiste@wanadoo.fr.

The Jehovah's Witnesses are also represented.

The Press

France-Guyane: 88 bis ave du Général de Gaulle, 97300 Cayenne; tel. 5-94-31-48-80; fax 5-94-31-11-57; daily; Publishing Dir PHILIPPE HERSANT; Local Dir JEAN-NOËL BIRE; circ. 5,500.

Rot Koze: 21 rue Nassin, 97300 Cayenne; tel. 5-94-30-55-97; fax 5-94-30-97-73; weekly; Dir MAURICE PINDARD.

La Semaine Guyanaisee: 6 ave Pasteur, 97300 Cayenne; tel. 5-94-31-09-83; fax 5-94-31-95-20; e-mail semaine.guyanaise@nplus.gf; weekly; Dir ALAIN CHAUMET.

La Presse de Guyane: Place Léopold Héder, 97300 Cayenne; tel. 5-94-29-55-55; fax 5-94-29-55-54; Editor TCHISSÉKA LOBELT; 4 a week; circ. 1,000.

NEWS AGENCIES

Agence France Presse: 22 réseau St. Antoine, 97300 Cayenne; tel. and fax 5-94-29-34-72; Rep. ALEXANDRE ROZIGA.

Foreign Bureau

Reuters (UK): Impasse du 8 Mai 1945, 97300 Cayenne; tel. 5-94-30-44-26; fax 5-94-31-93-24; Rep. ALEXANDER MILES.

Broadcasting and Communications

TELECOMMUNICATIONS

France Telecom: 76 ave Voltaire, 97300 Cayenne; tel. 5-94-39-91-14; fax 5-94-39-93-02; local branch of national telecommunications co.

BROADCASTING

Réseau France Outre-mer (RFO): 43 rue du Dr Devèze, BP 7013, 97305 Cayenne; tel. 5-94-29-99-00; fax 5-94-30-26-49; e-mail rfosaf@ nplus.gf; internet www.rfo.fr; fmrly Société Nationale de Radio-Télévision Française d'Outre-mer, renamed as above 1998; Radio-Guyane Inter: broadcasts 18 hours daily; Téléguyane: 2 channels, 32 hours weekly; Pres. ANDRÉ-MICHEL BESSE; Regional Dir ANASTASIE BOURQUIN.

Radio

Six private FM radio stations are in operation.

Radio Gabrielle: Rue Montravel, 97311 Roura; tel. 5-94-27-00-47; fax 5-94-28-01-28.

Radio Ouassaille: Rue Maurice Demongeot, 97360 Mana; tel. 5-94-34-80-96.

Radio Pagani: Ave Léopold Héder, 97355 Macouria; tel. 5-94-38-85-90.

Radio U.D.L. (Union Défense des Libertés): Ave Félix Eboué, 97323 Saint-Laurent-du-Maroni; tel. 5-94-34-27-90.

RCI Guyane: 33 rue Madame Payé, 97300 Cayenne; tel. 5-94-37-80-88; fax 5-94-30-60-00.

RFM 90: Annexe Hôtel des Roches, Le Manguier, 97310 Kourou; tel. 5-94-32-07-90.

RTM 102 (Radio Tout 'Moun): Centre Socio-Culturel Guyanais, rond point de Mirza, 97300 Cayenne; tel. 5-94-30-09-18; fax 5-94-30-91-19; f. 1982; private station; broadcasts 24 hours a day; Pres. R. BATHILDE; Dir GUY SAINT-AIME.

Television

Antenne Guyane Créole: 31 ave Louis Pasteur, 97300 Cayenne; tel. 5-94-31-20-20; fax 5-94-30-51-57; private television station; Dir. FRÉDÉRIC LANCRI.

Finance

(cap. = capital; res = reserves; dep. = deposits; m. = million; brs = branches; amounts in French francs)

BANKING

Central Bank

Institut d'Emission des Départements d'Outre-mer (IEDOM): 8 rue Christophe Colomb, BP 6016, 97306 Cayenne Cédex; tel. 5-94-29-36-50; fax 5-94-30-02-76; e-mail d.grebert@iedom-guyane.fr; internet www.iedom.com; f. 1959; Dir DIDIER GREBERT.

Commercial Banks

Banque Française Commerciale Antilles-Guyane (BFC Antilles-Guyane): 8 pl. des Palmistes, BP 111, 97345 Cayenne; tel. 5-94-30-35-77; fax 5-94-30-13-12; see chapter on Guadeloupe; Regional Dir PHILIPPE BISSAINTE.

BNP Paribas Guyane SA: 2 pl. Victor Schoëlcher, BP 35, 97300 Cayenne; tel. 5-94-39-63-00; fax 5-94-30-23-08; e-mail bnpg@arias .fr; f. 1855; fmrly BNP Guyane; name changed July 2000; cap. 71.7m., res 100.0m., dep. 2,007m. (Dec. 1994); Dir and Gen. Man FRANÇOIS DU PEUTY; 5 brs.

BRED-Banque Populaire: 5 ave du Général de Gaulle, 97300 Cayenne; tel. 5-94-25-56-80.

Crédit Martiniquais: 76 ave Général de Gaulle, 97300 Cayenne; tel. 5-94-31-57-00; fax 5-94-31-48-01.

Development Bank

Société financière pour le développement économique de la Guyane (SOFIDEG): PK 3, route de Baduel, BP 860, 97339 Cayenne Cédex; tel. 5-94-29-94-29; fax 5-94-30-60-44; f. 1982; part of the Agence Française de Développment (AFD—see entry below); Dir FRANÇOIS CHEVILLOTTE.

Trade and Industry

GOVERNMENT AGENCY

Direction Régionale de l'Industrie, de la Recherche et de l'Environnement (DRIRE): impasse Buzaré, BP 7001, 97307 Cayenne; tel. 5-94-29-75-30; fax 5-94-29-07-34; e-mail drire-antilles-guyane@industrie.gouv.fr; internet www.ggm.drire.gouv.fr; mining authority; responsible for assessing applications for and awarding exploration and exploitation rights; Regional Dir PHILIPPE COMBE.

DEVELOPMENT ORGANIZATION

Agence Française de Développement (AFD): Lotissement les Héliconias, Route de Baduel, BP 1122 97345, Cayenne Cédex; tel. 5-94-29-90-90; fax 5-94-30-63-32; e-mail afd.cayenne@outremeronline.com; fmrly Caisse Française de Développement; Man. GENEVIÈVE JAVALOYES.

CHAMBERS OF COMMERCE

Chambre d'Agriculture: 8 ave du Général de Gaulle, Cayenne; tel. 5-94-29-61-95; fax 5-94-31-00-01; Pres. PATRICK LABRANCHE.

Chambre de Commerce et d'Industrie: Hôtel Consulaire, pl. de l'Esplanade, BP 49, 97321 Cayenne Cédex; tel. 5-94-29-96-00; fax 5-94-29-96-34; internet www.guyane.cci.fr; Pres. JEAN-PAUL LE PELLETIER.

Chambre de Métiers: Jardin Botanique, blvd de la République, BP 176, 97324 Cayenne Cédex; tel. 5-94-30-21-80; fax 5-94-30-54-22; Pres. ALEX LASHLEY.

Jeune Chambre Economique de Cayenne: Cité A. Horth, route de Montabo, BP 683, Cayenne; tel. 5-94-31-62-99; fax 5-94-31-76-13; internet http://cayenne.jcef.org; f. 1960; Pres. FRANCK VERSET.

EMPLOYERS' ORGANIZATIONS

Organisation des Producteurs Guyanais de Crevettes (OPG): Kourou; tel. 5-94-32-27-26; fax 5-94-32-19-18; shrimp producers' asscn and export business; Man. ROBERT COTONNEC.

Syndicat des Exploitants Forestiers et Scieurs de la Guyane (SEFSEG): Macouria; tel. 5-94-31-72-50; fax 5-94-30-08-27; f. 1987; asscn of 14 forestry developers (450 employees); timber processers; Man. M. POMIES.

Syndicat des Exportateurs de la Guyane: Z. I. de Dégrad-des-Cannes, 97354 Rémire-Montjoly; tel. 5-94-35-40-78; Pres. JEAN PATOZ.

Union Patronale de la Guyane (UPDG): c/o SOFIDEG, km 3 route de Baduel, BP 820, 97338 Cayenne Cédex; tel. 5-94-31-17-71; fax 5-94-30-32-13; e-mail updg@nplus.gf; Pres. ALAIN CHAUMET.

UTILITIES

Electricity

Électricité de France Guyane (EDF): blvd Jubelin, BP 6002, 97300 Cayenne; tel. 5-94-39-64-00; fax 5-94-30-10-81; state-owned; Gen. Man. GUY EHRMANN.

Water

SGDE: PK 3 route de Montabo, 97305 Cayenne; tel. 5-94-30-32-32; fax 5-94-30-59-60; Gen. Man. MARC THEPOT.

TRADE UNIONS

Centrale Démocratique des Travailleurs de la Guyane (CDTG): 99-100 Cité Césaire, BP 383, 97300 Cayenne; tel. 5-94-31-50-72; fax 5-94-31-81-05; Sec.-Gen. GÉRARD FAUBERT.

SE/FEN (Syndicat des enseignants): 52 rue F. Arago, Cayenne; Sec.-Gen. GEORGINA JUDICK-PIED.

Union Départementale Force Ouvrière de Guyane (FO): 25, Cité Mirza, rue des Acajous, 97300 Cayenne; Sec.-Gen. M. XAVERO.

Union des Travailleurs Guyanais (UTG): 7 ave Ronjon, Cayenne; tel. 5-94-31-26-42; Sec.-Gen. CHRISTIAN RAVIN.

Transport

RAILWAYS

There are no railways in French Guiana.

ROADS

In 1988 there were 1,137 km (707 miles) of roads in French Guiana, of which 371 km were main roads. Much of the network is concentrated along the coast, although proposals for a major new road into the interior of the Department were under consideration.

SHIPPING

Dégrad-des-Cannes, on the estuary of the river Mahury, is the principal port, handling 80% of maritime traffic in 1989. There are other ports at Le Larivot, Saint-Laurent-du-Maroni and Kourou. Saint-Laurent is used primarily for the export of timber, and Larivot for fishing vessels. There are river ports on the Oyapock and on the Approuague. There is a ferry service across the Maroni river between Saint-Laurent and Albina, Suriname. The rivers provide the best means of access to the interior, although numerous rapids prevent navigation by large vessels.

Direction Départementale des Affaires Maritimes: 2 bis rue Mentel, BP 307, 97305 Cayenne Cédex; tel. 5-94-31-00-08; Dir PIERRE-YVES ANDRIEUX.

Société de Transport Maritime Guyanes: 13 ave Pt Gaston Monnerville, Cayenne.

Somarig: Z. I. de Dégrad-des-Cannes, Remire, BP 81, 97322 Cayenne Cédex; tel. 5-94-35-42-00; fax 5-94-35-53-44; joint venture between the Compagnie Générale Maritime and Delmas; Dir DANIEL DOURET.

CIVIL AVIATION

Rochambeau International Airport, situated 17.5 km (11 miles) from Cayenne, is equipped to handle the largest jet aircraft. Access to remote inland areas is frequently by helicopter.

Air Guyane: Aéroport de Rochambeau, 97300 Matoury; tel. 5-94-35-65-55; f. 1980; operates internal and international services.

Tourism

The main attractions are the natural beauty of the tropical scenery and the Amerindian villages of the interior. In 2000 there were 28 hotels with 1,272 rooms; in 1999 68,211 tourist arrivals were recorded.

Comité du Tourisme de la Guyane: Pavillon du Tourisme, Jardin Botanique, 12 rue Lallouette, BP 801, 97338 Cayenne Cédex; tel. 5-94-29-65-00; fax 5-94-29-65-01; internet www.tourisme-guyane.gf.

Délégation Régionale au Tourisme, au Commerce et à l'Artisanat pour la Guyane: 9 rue Louis Blanc, BP 7008, 97307 Cayenne Cédex; tel. 5-94-28-92-90; fax 5-94-31-01-04; e-mail drtca973@nplus.gf; Delegate PAUL RENAUD.

Fédération des Offices de Tourisme et Syndicats d'Initiative de la Guyane (FOTSIG): 12 rue Lallouette, 97300 Cayenne; tel. 5-94-30-96-29; fax 5-94-31-23-41; e-mail fotsig@nplus.gf; internet www.guyanetourisme.com; Pres. ARMAND HILDAIRE.

Office Culturel de la Région Guyane: 82 ave du Général de Gaulle, BP 6007, 97306 Cayenne Cédex; tel. 5-94-28-94-00; fax 5-94-28-94-04.

GUADELOUPE

Introductory Survey

Location, Climate, Language, Religion, Capital

Guadeloupe is the most northerly of the Windward Islands group in the West Indies. Dominica lies to the south, and Antigua and Montserrat to the north-west. Guadeloupe is formed by two large islands, Grande-Terre and Basse-Terre, separated by a narrow sea channel (but linked by a bridge), with a smaller island, Marie-Galante, to the south-east, and another, La Désirade, to the east. There are also a number of small dependencies, mainly Saint-Barthélemy and the northern half of Saint-Martin (the remainder being part of the Netherlands Antilles), among the Leeward Islands. The climate is tropical, with an average temperature of 26°C (79°F), and a more humid and wet season between June and November. French is the official language, but a creole patois is widely spoken. The majority of the population profess Christianity, and belong to the Roman Catholic Church. The capital is the town of Basse-Terre; the other main town and the principal commercial centre is Pointe-à-Pitre, on Grande-Terre.

Recent History

Guadeloupe was first occupied by the French in 1635, and has remained French territory, apart from a number of brief occupations by the British in the 18th and early 19th centuries. It gained departmental status in 1946.

The deterioration of the economy and an increase in unemployment provoked industrial and political unrest during the 1960s and 1970s, including outbreaks of serious rioting in 1967. Pro-independence parties (which had rarely won more than 5% of the total vote at elections in Guadeloupe) resorted, in some cases, to violence as a means of expressing their opposition to the economic and political dominance of white, pro-French landowners and government officials. In 1980 and 1981 there was a series of bomb attacks on hotels, government offices and other targets by a group called the Groupe Libération Armée, and in 1983 and 1984 there were further bombings by a group styling itself the Alliance Révolutionnaire Caraïbe (ARC). The Government responded by outlawing the ARC and reinforcing the military and police presence throughout Guadeloupe. (The ARC merged with the Mouvement Populaire pour une Guadeloupe Indépendante—MPGI—in 1984). Further sporadic acts of violence continued in 1985–87, and in January 1988 responsibility for bomb explosions in various parts of the territory was claimed by a previously unknown pro-independence group, the Organisation Révolutionnaire Armée.

In 1974 Guadeloupe was granted the status of a Region, and an indirectly-elected Conseil Régional (Regional Council) was formed. In direct elections to a new Conseil Régional in February 1983, held as a result of the recent decentralization reforms, the centre-right coalition succeeded in gaining a majority of the seats and control of the administration. In January 1984 Lucette Michaux-Chevry, the President of the Conseil Général (General Council), formed a new conservative centre party, Le Parti de la Guadeloupe, which remained in alliance with the right-wing Rassemblement pour la République (RPR). However, at the elections for the Conseil Général held in March 1985, the left-wing combination of the Parti Socialiste (PS) and the Parti Communiste Guadeloupéen (PCG) gained a majority of seats on the enlarged Conseil, and the PS leader, Dominique Larifla, was elected its President. In July demonstrations and a general strike, organized by pro-separatist activists in order to obtain the release of a leading member of the MPGI, quickly intensified into civil disorder and rioting in the main commercial centre, Pointe-à-Pitre.

For the March 1986 general election to the Assemblée Nationale, Guadeloupe's representation was increased from three to four deputies. The local branches of the RPR and the centre-right Union pour la Démocratie Française (UDF), which had campaigned jointly at the 1981 general election and the 1983 regional elections, presented separate candidates. Ernest Moutoussamy and Frédéric Jalton, respectively the incumbent PCG and PS members of the Assemblée, were re-elected, but the UDF deputy was not; the two remaining seats were won by RPR candidates (Michaux-Chevry and Henri Beaujean). In the concurrent elections for the 41 seats on the Conseil Régional, the two left-wing parties together won a majority of seats (PS 12, PCG 10). As a result, José Moustache of the RPR was replaced as President of the Conseil by Félix Proto of the PS. At the 1988 French presidential elections the incumbent President François Mitterrand of the PS defeated Jacques Chirac of the RPR. At elections to the Assemblée Nationale in June, Larifla (for the PS) defeated Beaujean, while the three other deputies to the Assemblée retained their seats. In September–October the left-wing parties won 26 of the 42 seats at elections to the Conseil Général, and Larifla was re-elected President of the Conseil.

In April 1989 the separatist Union Populaire pour la Libération de la Guadeloupe (UPLG) organized protests in Port Louis to demand the release of 'political prisoners', which led to violent clashes with the police. A number of activists of the now disbanded ARC (including its leader, Luc Reinette) staged a hunger strike while awaiting trial in Paris, accused in connection with politically-motivated offences in the Overseas Departments. In the following month the Comité Guadeloupéen de Soutien aux Prisonniers Politiques united 11 organizations in demonstrations against the Government. Demands included the release of the prisoners held in France, a rejection of the Single European Act and the granting of a series of social demands. In June the Assemblée Nationale approved legislation granting an amnesty for crimes that had taken place before July 1988, and that were intended to undermine the authority of the French Republic in the Overseas Departments. The agreement of those seeking greater independence in Guadeloupe to work within the democratic framework had gained parliamentary support for the amnesty. However, when the freed activists returned to Guadeloupe in July 1989, they urged increased confrontation with the authorities in order to achieve autonomous rule. In March 1990 the UPLG declared that it would henceforth participate in elections, and would seek associated status (rather than full independence) for Guadeloupe.

In March 1992 concurrent elections were held to the Conseil Général and the Conseil Régional. Larifla was re-elected as President of the former, despite his refusal to accept part of the local official PS list of candidates and his leadership of a group of 'dissident' PS members. (The division was not recognized at national level.) In the elections to the Conseil Régional the official PS list (headed by Jalton) secured nine seats and the dissident PS members seven. Former members of the PCG, who had formed a new organization, the Parti Progressiste Démocratique Guadeloupéen (PPDG), won five seats, compared with only three for the PCG. The RPR, the UDF and other right-wing candidates formed an electoral alliance, Objectif Guadeloupe, to contest the elections, together securing 15 of the 41 seats in the Conseil Régional. Jalton's refusal to reach an agreement with the 'dissident' PS members prompted Larifla's list to support the presidential candidacy of Michaux-Chevry. Thus, despite an overall left-wing majority in the Conseil Régional, the right-wing Michaux-Chevry was elected as President with 21 votes. In December 1992, however, the French Conseil d'Etat declared the election to the Conseil Régional invalid, owing to the failure of Larifla's list to pay a deposit on each seat prior to the registration of its candidates. Seven other heads of lists, including Moutoussamy of the PPDG, were subsequently found to have submitted incomplete documents to the election commission, and (although malpractice was discounted) the electoral code necessitated that they be declared ineligible for election to the Conseil Régional for one year. Fresh elections took place in January 1994, at which Objectif Guadeloupe took 22 seats, while the PS and 'dissident' PS retained a total of only 10 seats.

In a referendum on 20 September 1992 67.5% of voters in Guadeloupe endorsed ratification of the Treaty on European Union (see p. 199), although a high abstention rate was recorded.

The persistence of divisions between the socialists was evident at the March 1993 elections to the Assemblée Nationale. Michaux-Chevry of the RPR was re-elected, as were Moutoussamy (for the PPDG) and Jalton (representing the anti-Larifla faction of the PS). Larifla, meanwhile, was defeated by Edouard Chammougon, a candidate of the independent right, who was elected (despite his implication in several corruption scandals—see below) with the assistance of votes in the second round of those socialists who resented Larifla's support for Michaux-Chevry in 1992. Michaux-Chevry was appointed to the position of Minister-Delegate, with responsibility for human rights and humanitarian action, in Edouard Balladur's centre-right coalition Government.

The left retained control of the Conseil Général following cantonal elections in March 1994. Larifla was subsequently re-elected President of the Conseil. At elections to the European Parliament in June, a combined list of parties of the left of the French Overseas Departments, including the PPDG (the list was headed by Moutoussamy), won the greatest share of the votes cast (37.2%) in Guadeloupe.

Meanwhile, local political affairs were dominated by scandals involving prominent public figures. Twice during 1993 the Antilles-Guyane Chambre régionale des comptes—the body responsible for overseeing public finances in the region—rejected budget figures submitted by Guadeloupe's Conseil Régional, deeming that the Conseil's deficit projections were severely underestimated. In January 1994 an administrative tribunal in Basse-Terre ruled that Michaux-Chevry had been unjustified in dismissing (following the first rejection of the budget) the Conseil Régional's director of finances, who had submitted departmental accounts, as required by law, to the Chambre régional des comptes; this judgment was upheld at an appeal in Paris in April 1995. In January 1993 Chammougon, the Mayor of Baie-Mahault, was sentenced to three years' imprisonment, fined and deprived of his civic and civil rights for 10 years, following his conviction on corruption charges dating as far back as 1980. He remained at liberty pending an appeal and also, after March 1993, benefited from parliamentary immunity; the prison sentence was suspended and the fine lowered in November 1993, and in October 1994 a higher appeal reduced the deprivation of rights to five years. In September 1993 an investigation of alleged corruption among several of Chammougon's close associates resulted in the deputy's implication in further charges of 'passive corruption' and the abuse and misappropriation of public funds. In November 1994 the French Constitutional Council revoked Chammougon's membership of the Assemblée Nationale. In January 1995 Chammougon's wife was elected to succeed him in the Conseil Général, although Léo Andy, the candidate of the 'dissident' PS, was elected to the vacant seat in the Assemblée Nationale, defeating the candidate supported by both Chammougon and Michaux-Chevry.

In the 1995 presidential elections, held on 23 April and 7 May, Lionel Jospin emerged as the winner, securing 55.1% of the second-round votes, having benefited from the expressed support of all the parties of the left. At municipal elections in June, Michaux-Chevry became mayor of Basse-Terre, defeating the incumbent PPDG candidate. Jalton, who was supplanted as mayor of Les Abymes by a candidate of the 'dissident' PS, died in November. Michaux-Chevry and Larifla were elected to the Sénat in September; the defeat of one of the incumbents, Henri Bangou of the PPDG, was attributed to the continuing divisions within the left. Philippe Chaulet of the RPR was subsequently elected to take Michaux-Chevry's seat in the Assemblée Nationale.

At elections to the Assemblée Nationale in late May and early June 1997, Moutoussamy, Andy and Chaulet all retained their seats, while Daniel Marsin, a candidate of the independent left, was elected in the constituency of Les Abymes, Pointe-à-Pitre. The RPR performed strongly in elections to the Conseil Régional in March 1998, securing 25 of the 41 seats, while the PS won 12; Michaux-Chevry was re-elected as President of the Conseil. The composition of the Conseil Général remained largely unchanged following concurrent cantonal elections, with the left retaining a majority of 28 seats, although the RPR doubled its representation to eight seats; Marcellin Lubeth, of the PPDG, was elected to the presidency, defeating Larifla.

In January 1999 representatives of 10 separatist organizations from French Guiana, Guadeloupe and Martinique, including the UPLG, signed a joint declaration denouncing 'French colonialism', in which they stated their intention to campaign for the reinstatement of the three Caribbean Overseas Departments on a UN list of territories to be decolonized.

Social and industrial unrest intensified in Guadeloupe in late October 1999, prior to a two-day visit by Lionel Jospin, the Prime Minister. Demonstrations escalated into rioting in Pointe-à-Pitre, following the sentencing of Armand Toto, a leading member of the Union Générale des Travailleurs de la Guadeloupe (UGTG), to four months' imprisonment for assaulting two policemen and threatening to kill another while occupying the premises of a motor vehicle company in support of a dismissed worker. Further protests ensued a few days later when an appeal against Toto's sentence failed. Moreover, banana producers demonstrated around the port of Basse-Terre, demanding the disbursement of 100m. French francs, and additional assistance for the restructuring of their businesses, as compensation for a significant decline in banana prices on the European market. Meanwhile, an indefinite strike by hospital workers, organized by the UGTG, affected Guadeloupe's 16 private clinics. However, calls issued by several trade union and political organizations for a 48-hour general strike during Jospin's visit were largely ignored, and the Prime Minister announced an emergency plan for the banana sector.

The institutional future of the Overseas Departments provoked much discussion in 1999 and 2000. Following a series of meetings, in December 1999 the Presidents of the Conseils Régionaux of French Guiana, Guadeloupe and Martinique signed a joint declaration in Basse-Terre, affirming their intention to propose, to the President and the Government, a legislative amendment, possibly constitutional, aimed at creating a new status of overseas region. The declaration, however, was dismissed by the Secretary of State for Overseas Departments and Territories, Jean-Jack Queyranne, in February 2000 as unconstitutional and exceeding the mandate of politicians responsible. Proposals regarding the institutional evolution of Guadeloupe were provisionally accepted by the Assemblée Nationale in May, and were subsequently adopted, by a narrow margin, by the Sénat, following a number of modifications. In November the Assemblée Nationale approved the amended proposals, and in December they were ratified by the Constitutional Council. At a referendum held in September, Guadeloupe voted overwhelmingly in favour of reducing the presidential mandate from seven years to five.

In municipal elections held in March 2001 Michaux-Chevry was re-elected mayor of Basse-Terre, despite corruption charges against her. (Michaux-Chevry had been acquitted of charges of forgery in January; however, she was still under investigation for charges of embezzlement.) Following her election, Michaux-Chevry relinquished the post to Pierre Martin, in order to comply with regulations that no official may hold more than two elected posts simultaneously (she already held the positions of Senator and President of the Conseil Régional). Henri Bangou of the PPDG was also re-elected to the mayoralty of Pointe-à-Pitre. In the concurrently-held election to the presidency of the Conseil Général, Jacques Gillot of Guadeloupe Unie, Socialisme et Réalité (GUSR) defeated Marcellin Lubeth of the PPDG.

In early June 2001 riots occurred in Pointe-à-Pitre in which a number of people were injured. The riots were in protest at the arrest of the leader of the UGTG, Michel Madassamy, who had been charged in late May with vandalizing a number of shops that had remained open on the day of the anniversary of the abolition of slavery in Guadeloupe, in defiance of the UGTG's recommendations. The General Secretary of the UGTG subsequently called for a general strike to be held for the duration of Madassamy's incarceration. A period of severe drought, necessitating the rationing of water supplies, served to exacerbate the deteriorating social situation on the island in 2001.

Following a meeting of members of the Conseil Régional and the Conseil Général in late June 2001, a series of proposals on greater autonomy, to be presented to the French Government, was agreed upon. These included: the division of the territory into four districts; the creation of a 'collectivité territoriale' (territorial community), governed by a 41-member Assembly elected for a five-year term; and the establishment of an independent executive council. Furthermore, the proposals included a request that the territory be given control over legislative and administrative affairs, as well as legislative authority on matters concerning Guadeloupe alone. In November the French Government announced itself to be in favour of the suggested constitutional developments, and a vote on enacting the proposals was due to take place in March 2003.

In mid-2001 the French President, Jacques Chirac, rejected a joint request by French Guiana, Guadeloupe and Martinique that they be permitted to join, as associate members, the Association of Caribbean States. In the first round of the presidential election, held on 21 April 2002, Christine Taubira won 37.2% of the vote in the Department (although she was eliminated nationally), ahead of Chirac, who obtained 28.9%. In the second round, held on 5 May, Chirac overwhelmingly defeated Jean-

Marie Le Pen of the extreme right-wing Front National, receiving 91.3% of the vote. In June all four incumbent deputies were defeated in elections to the Assemblée Nationale; they were replaced by Gabrielle Louis-Carabin and Joël Beaugendre, both representing the Union pour la Majorité Présidentielle (UMP), a right-wing alliance that included the Objectif Guadeloupe, Eric Jalton, also of a right-wing coalition, and Victorin Lurel of the PS. The RPR subsequently merged into the successor party to the UMP, the Union pour un Mouvement Populaire (also known as the UMP). In August Dominique Vian replaced Jean-François Carenco as Prefect.

Government

France is represented in Guadeloupe by an appointed prefect. There are two councils with local powers: the 42-member Conseil Général (General Council) and the 41-member Conseil Régional. (Regional Council) Both are elected by universal adult suffrage for a period of up to six years. Guadeloupe elects four deputies to the Assemblée Nationale in Paris, and sends two indirectly-elected representatives to the Sénat. The Department is also represented at the European Parliament.

Defence

At 1 August 2002 France maintained a military force of 4,000 and a gendarmerie of 860 in the Antilles, with headquarters in Fort-de-France (Martinique).

Economic Affairs

In 1999 Guadeloupe's gross domestic product (GDP), measured at current prices, was US $4,650m., equivalent to $10,953 per head. During 1990–99, according to UN estimates, GDP increased, in real terms, at an average annual rate of 1.8%; growth in 1999 was 0.6%. Between the censuses of 1990 and 1999, according to provisional figures, the population increased at an average annual rate of 1.0%.

Agriculture, hunting, forestry and fishing contributed an estimated 4.1% of GDP in 1999 and, according to FAO estimates, engaged an estimated 2.9% of the economically active population in mid-2001. The principal cash crops are bananas and sugar cane; exports of the former provided 21.9% of total export earnings in 1997, while exports of raw sugar accounted for 23.7% of the total in that year. Yams, sweet potatoes and plantains are the chief subsistence crops. Fishing, mostly at an artisanal level, fulfilled about two-thirds of domestic requirements in the 1990s; shrimp-farming was developed during the 1980s. According to UN estimates, agricultural GDP decreased at an average annual rate of 0.3% in 1990–98; the sector increased by 4.1% in 1998.

The industrial sector (including mining, manufacturing, construction and power) contributed an estimated 15.9% of GDP in 1999 and engaged 11.5% of the total labour force in 1998. Manufacturing, mining and power provided some 6.8% of GDP in 1998, while construction contributed 9.1%. The main manufacturing activity is food processing, particularly sugar production, rum distillation, and flour-milling. The sugar industry was in decline in the 1990s, owing to deteriorating equipment and a reduction in the area planted with sugar cane (from 20,000 ha in 1980 to 9,600 ha in 1999). Industrial GDP (excluding construction) increased at an average annual rate of 5.2% in 1990–98. Construction expanded at an average rate of 2.2% per year in the same period.

Of some 700,000 tons of petroleum imported annually, about one-third is used for the production of electricity. Efforts are currently being concentrated on the use of renewable energy resources—notably solar, geothermal and wind power—for energy production; there is also thought to be considerable potential for the use of sugar cane as a means of generating energy in Guadeloupe. Imports of mineral fuels accounted for 5.8% of total expenditure on imports in 1995.

The services sector engaged 52.8% of the total labour force in 1998 and provided an estimated 80% of GDP in 1999. Tourism superseded sugar production in 1988 as the Department's principal source of income, and there is significant potential for the further development of the sector, particularly 'eco-tourism'. In 1999 tourist arrivals totalled 847,131, and receipts from tourism amounted to US $418m. in 2000. In 1999 82.3% of arrivals came from metropolitan France or dependent territories.

In 1998 Guadeloupe recorded a trade deficit of 9,999.7m. French francs. In 1997 the principal source of imports (62.9%) was metropolitan France, which was also the principal market for exports (60.7%). Martinique, the USA and Germany are also important trading partners. The principal exports in 1997 were sugar, bananas, boats and rum. The principal imports in 1995 were machinery and transport equipment (mainly road vehicles), food and live animals, miscellaneous manufactured articles, basic manufactures and chemicals.

Guadeloupe's budget deficit was estimated by the metropolitan authorities to amount to some 800m. French francs (including arrears) in 1993. Under the 1997 regional budget it was envisaged that expenditure would total 1,700m. French francs. The annual rate of inflation averaged 1.7% in 1990–2001; consumer prices remained constant in 2000, and increased by 2.6% in 2001. Some 25.7% of the labour force were unemployed in mid-2002.

As an integral part of France, Guadeloupe belongs to the European Union (EU, see p. 199).

Economic growth in Guadeloupe has been restricted by certain inherent problems: its location; the fact that the domestic market is too narrow to stimulate the expansion of the manufacturing base; the lack of primary materials; and the inflated labour and service costs compared with those of neighbouring countries. Economic activity was severely disrupted in 1989, when 'Hurricane Hugo' struck the islands. The French Government undertook to provide more than 2,000m. French francs for reconstruction, and additional aid for the modernization of the sugar industry. The banana-growing sector and the tourist industry, both of which were particularly adversely affected, recovered well. However, Hurricanes Luis and Marilyn, which struck in September 1995, caused severe infrastructural damage. In the late 1990s Guadeloupe's banana sector was adversely affected by declining prices on the European market, while a dispute between the USA and four major Latin American producers and the EU over the latter's banana import regime also threatened the sector. This dispute was resolved in April 2001 when it was agreed that the quota system currently employed by the EU was to be replaced by a universal tariff system from 2006. Concern was expressed that tourism in the Guadeloupean dependency of Saint-Martin (an island shared with the Dutch territory of St Maarten) would be adversely affected by the decision of AOM Compagnie Aérienne Française (now Air Liberté) to cease flights to St Maarten in March 2001. Moreover, it was thought that a renewed monopoly on flights by Air France would further affect the tourism sector (the deregulation of air transport in 1986, ending Air France's monopoly on flights to Guadeloupe, was a major factor in attracting more visitors to the main island). In November 2002 the French hotel group Accor announced that it would close its five hotels in Martinque and Guadeloupe, citing high operating costs, poor industrial relations and decreasing tourist arrivals.

Education

The education system is similar to that of metropolitan France (see chapter on French Guiana). In 1996 secondary education was provided at 40 junior comprehensives, or collèges, 10 vocational lycées, 10 general and technological lycées and one agricultural lycée. A branch of the Université Antilles-Guyane, at Pointe-à-Pitre, has faculties of law, economics, sciences, medicine and Caribbean studies. The university in Guadeloupe had 5,800 enrolled students in 1997. There is also a teacher training college. An Academy for Guadeloupe was established in January 1997. Total government expenditure on education amounted to 2,776m. French francs in 1993.

Public Holidays

2003: 1 January (New Year's Day), 3–4 March (Lenten Carnival), 18–21 April (Easter), 1 May (Labour Day), 8 May (Victory Day), 29 May (Ascension Day), 9 June (Whit Monday), 14 July (National Day), 21 July (Victor Schoëlcher Day), 15 August (Assumption), 1 November (All Saints' Day), 11 November (Armistice Day), 25 December (Christmas Day).

2004: 1 January (New Year's Day), 23–24 February (Lenten Carnival), 9–12 April (Easter), 1 May (Labour Day), 8 May (Victory Day), 20 May (Ascension Day), 30 May (Whit Monday), 14 July (National Day), 21 July (Victor Schoëlcher Day), 15 August (Assumption), 1 November (All Saints' Day), 11 November (Armistice Day), 25 December (Christmas Day).

Weights and Measures

The metric system is in use.

Statistical Survey

Sources (unless otherwise stated): Institut national de la statistique et des études économiques (INSEE), ave Paul Lacavé, BP 96,97102 Basse-Terre; tel. 99-0250; internet www.insee.fr/fr/insee_regions/guadeloupe ; Service de Presse et d'Information, Ministère des départements et territoires d'outre-mer,27 rue Oudinot, 75700 Paris 07 SP, France; tel. 1-53-69-20-00; fax 1-43-06-60-30; internet www.outre-mer.gouv.fr.

AREA AND POPULATION

Area: 1,705 sq km (658.3 sq miles), incl. dependencies (La Désirade, Les Saintes, Marie-Galante, Saint-Barthélemy, Saint-Martin).

Population: 327,002 (males 160,112, females 166,890) at census of 9 March 1982; 387,034 (males 189,187, females 197,847) at census of 15 March 1990; 422,496 at census of 8 March 1999.

Density (at 1999 census): 247.8 per sq km.

Principal Towns (population at 1999 census): Les Abymes 63,054; Saint-Martin 29,078; Le Gosier 25,360; Baie-Mahault 23,389; Pointe-à-Pitre 20,948; Le Moule 20,827; Petit Bourg 20,528; Sainte Anne 20,410. *2001:* Basse-Terre (capital) 12,410 at 1999 census.

Births, Marriages and Deaths (1997, provisional figures): Registered live births 7,554 (birth rate 17.4 per 1,000); Registered marriages 1,936 (marriage rate 4.7 per 1,000); Registered deaths 2,441 (death rate 5.6 per 1,000). *2001:* Registered live births 7,658; Registered marriages 1,926; Registered deaths 2,775.

Expectation of Life (UN estimates, years at birth): 77.3 (males 73.6; females 80.9) in 1995–2000. Source: UN, *World Population Prospects: The 2000 Revision.*

Economically Active Population (persons aged 15 years and over, 1990 census): Agriculture, hunting, forestry and fishing 8,391; Industry and energy 9,630; Construction and public works 13,967; Trade 15,020; Transport and telecommunications 6,950; Financial services 2,802; Other marketable services 26,533; Non-marketable services 34,223; Total employed 117,516 (males 68,258, females 49,258); Unemployed 54,926 (males 25,691, females 29,235); Total labour force 172,442 (males 93,949, females 78,493). *1998* Agriculture 8,200; Industry 7,900; Construction 13,000; Services 96,200; Not available 1,000; Total employed 126,300; Unemployed 55,900; Total labour force 182,200. *1999:* Total labour force 191,362 (males 97,329, females 94,033). *Mid-2001* (estimates): Agriculture, etc. 6,000; Total labour force 204,000 (males 112,000, females 92,000) (Source: FAO).

HEALTH AND WELFARE

Key Indicators

Physicians (per 1,000 head, 1996): 1.6.

Hospital Beds (per 1,000 head, 1996): 29.1.
For sources and definitions, see explanatory note on p. vi.

AGRICULTURE, ETC.

Principal Crops (FAO estimates, '000 metric tons, 2001): Sweet potatoes 4.3; Yams 10; Other roots and tubers 4.2; Sugar cane 798.1; Lettuce 3.1; Tomatoes 3.1; Cucumbers and gherkins 3.9; Other fresh vegetables 15.1; Bananas 115.5; Plantains 9.2; Cantaloupes and other melons 4.1; Pineapples 7.0. Source: FAO.

Livestock (FAO estimates, '000 head, year ending September 2001): Cattle 85; Goats 28; Pigs 19; Sheep 3.2. Source: FAO.

Livestock Products (FAO estimates, '000 metric tons, 2001): Beef and veal 3.4; Pig meat 1; Hen eggs 1.7. Source: FAO.

Forestry ('000 cubic metres, 2001): *Roundwood removals* (excl. bark): Sawlogs, veneer logs and logs for sleepers 0.3; Fuel wood 15.0; Total 15.3. *Sawnwood Production* (incl. railway sleepers): Total 1.0. Source: FAO.

Fishing (metric tons, live weight, 2000): Capture 10,100 (Common dolphinfish 700 (FAO estimate), Blackfin tuna 500, Other mackerel-like fishes 1,600 (FAO estimate), Marine fishes 6,600 (FAO estimate), Stromboid conchs 550; Aquaculture 14; Total catch 10,114. Source: FAO, *Yearbook of Fishery Statistics.*

MINING

Production ('000 metric tons, 2000, estimates): Pozzolan 210.0. Source: US Geological Survey.

INDUSTRY

Production: Raw sugar 65,200 metric tons in 2001; Rum 62,679 hl in 1998; Cement (estimate) 230,000 metric tons in 2000; Electric energy (million kWh) 1,211 in 1998. Source: mainly UN, *Industrial Commodity Statistics Yearbook.*

FINANCE

Currency and Exchange Rates: The French franc was used until the end of February 2002. Euro notes and coins were introduced on 1 January 2002, and the euro became the sole legal tender from 18 February. Some of the figures in this Survey are still in terms of francs. For details of exchange rates, see French Guiana.

Budget (million French francs): *State budget* (1990): Revenue 2,494; Expenditure 4,776. *Regional budget* (1997): Expenditure 1,700. *Departmental budget* (million euros, 1998): Revenue 332; Expenditure 318.

Money Supply (million French francs at 31 December 1996): Currency outside banks 1,148; Demand deposits at banks 6,187; Total money 7,335.

Cost of Living (Consumer Price Index for urban areas; base: 1990 = 100): 117.6 in 1999; 117.6 in 2000; 120.6 in 2001. Source: UN, *Monthly Bulletin of Statistics.*

Expenditure on the Gross Domestic Product (million French francs at current prices, 1994): Government final consumption expenditure 5,721; Private final consumption expenditure 16,779; Increase in stocks 161; Gross fixed capital formation 5,218; *Total domestic expenditure* 27,879; Exports of goods and services 912; *Less* Imports of goods and services 9,040; *GDP in purchasers' values* 19,751.

Gross Domestic Product by Economic Activity (million French francs at current prices, 1992): Agriculture, hunting, forestry and fishing 1,206.9; Mining, quarrying and manufacturing 1,237.5; Electricity, gas and water 307.5; Construction 1,164.4; Trade, restaurants and hotels 2,907.9; Transport, storage and communications 1,415.4; Finance, insurance, real estate and business services 2,023.0; Government services 4,769.7; Other community, social and personal services 2,587.7; Other services 348.0; *Sub-total* 17,968.0; Import duties 699.4; Value-added tax 615.7; *Less* Imputed bank service charge 1,311.2; *GDP in purchasers' values* 17,972.0. Source: UN, *National Accounts Statistics. 1999* (million euros): GDP in purchasers' values 5,328.

EXTERNAL TRADE

Principal Commodities: *Imports c.i.f.* (US $ million, 1995): Food and live animals 302.8 (Meat and meat preparations 74.7, Dairy products and birds eggs 51.9, Cereals and cereal preparations 55.6, Vegetables and fruit 51.4); Beverages and tobacco 88.1 (Beverages 78.8); Mineral fuels, lubricants, etc. 110.7 (Petroleum, petroleum products, etc. 52.5, Gas, natural and manufactured 58.0); Chemicals and related products 172.8 (Medicinal and pharmaceutical products 78.1); Basic manufactures 259.5 (Paper, paperboard and manufactures 39.3); Machinery and transport equipment 607.0 (Office machines and automatic data-processing equipment 40.7, Telecommunications and sound equipment 43.0, Road vehicles and parts 217.7, Other transport equipment 100.0); Miscellaneous manufactured articles 282.6 (Furniture and parts 47.2, Clothing and accessories, excl. footwear, 52.6, Printed matter 39.5); Total (incl. others) 1,901.3. Source: UN, *International Trade Statistics Yearbook. Exports f.o.b.* (million French francs, 1997): Bananas 179.7; Melons and fresh papayas 33.8; Sugar 193.9; Rum 40.2; Wheaten or rye flour 35.3; Yachts and sports boats 50.7; Total (incl. others) 819.4. *1998* (million french francs): *Imports:* 10,703.9; *Exports:* 704.2.

Principal Trading Partners (million French francs, 1997): *Imports c.i.f.:* Belgium-Luxembourg 161.8; Curaçao (Netherlands Antilles) 212.6; France (metropolitan) 6,435.7; Germany 445.5; Italy 395.0; Japan 247.6; Martinique 114.0; Spain 190.2; Trinidad and Tobago 189.3; United Kingdom 151.7; USA 315.4; Total (incl. others) 10,236.6. *Exports f.o.b.:* Belgium-Luxembourg 23.0; France (metropolitan) 497.2; French Guiana 20.6; Italy 21.7; Martinique 152.2; United Kingdom 18.7; USA 36.6; Total (incl. others) 819.4.

TRANSPORT

Road Traffic ('000 motor vehicles in use, 1998): Passenger cars 108.7; Commercial vehicles 35.6. Source: UN, *Statistical Yearbook.*

Shipping: *Merchant Fleet)* (vessels registered, '000 grt at 31 December 1992): Total displacement 6. (Source: Lloyd's Register of Shipping). *International Sea-borne Traffic* (1999): Vessels entered 2,988; Goods loaded 428,000 metric tons; Goods unloaded 2,747,000 metric tons; Passengers carried 1,296,000.

Civil Aviation (1998): Passengers carried 1,978,200; Freight carried 16,500 metric tons.

TOURISM

Tourist Arrivals: 849,237 in 1997; 849,671 in 1998; 847,131 in 1999.

Tourist arrivals by country (1999): Canada 18,435; France 697,128; Italy 33,349; Switzerland 30,025; USA 29,128; Total (incl. others) 847,131. Source: World Tourism Organization, *Yearbook of Tourism Statistics*.

Receipts from Tourism (US $ million): 466 in 1998; 375 in 1999; 418 in 2000. Source: World Tourism Organization.

COMMUNICATIONS MEDIA

Radio Receivers ('000 in use): 113 in 1997.

Television Receivers ('000 in use): 118 in 1997.

Telephones ('000 main lines in use): 204.9 in 2000.

Facsimile Machines (number in use): 3,400 in 1996.

Mobile Cellular Telephones ('000 subscribers): 292.5 in 2001.

Personal Computers ('000 in use): 100 in 2000.

Internet Users ('000): 8.0 in 2000.

Daily Newspaper: 1 (estimate) in 1996 (estimated average circulation 35,000 copies).
Sources:: UNESCO, *Statistical Yearbook*; UN, *Statistical Yearbook*; International Telecommunication Union.

EDUCATION

Pre-primary (1993/94): 121 institutions; 760 teachers; 22,678 students (1994/95) (Source: UNESCO, *Statistical Yearbook*).

Primary* (2000/01): 219 institutions (1992/93); 3,020 teachers; 64,165 students (Source: UNESCO, *Statistical Yearbook*).

Secondary (2000/01): 3,778 teachers; 52,277 students (Source: UNESCO, *Statistical Yearbook*).
* Figures for teachers and students in primary education include pre-primary education.

Higher (1997): 5,800 students (Université Antilles-Guyane).

Adult Literacy Rate: 90.1% (males 89.7%; females 90.5%) in 1992.

Directory

The Government

(April 2003)

Prefect: DOMINIQUE VIAN, Préfecture, Palais d'Orléans, rue Lardenoy, 97109 Basse-Terre Cédex; tel. 5-90-99-39-00; fax 5-90-81-58-32; internet www.guadeloupe.pref.gouv.fr.

President of the General Council: JACQUES GILLOT (GUSR), Hôtel du Département, blvd Félix Eboué, 97109 Basse-Terre; tel. 5-90-99-77-77; fax 5-90-99-76-00; e-mail info@cg971.com; internet www.cg971.com.

President of the Economic and Social Committee: GUY FRÉDÉRIC.

Deputies to the French National Assembly: ÉRIC JALTON (PCG), GABRIELLE LOUIS-CARABIN (Objectif Guadeloupe), JOËL BEAUGENDRE (Objectif Guadeloupe), VICTORIN LUREL (Gauche Plurielle).

Representatives to the French Senate: LUCETTE MICHAUX-CHEVRY (UMP), DOMINIQUE LARIFLA (Rassemblement démocratique et social européen).

CONSEIL RÉGIONAL

Ave Paul Lacavé, Petit-Paris, 97109 Basse-Terre; tel. 5-90-80-40-40; fax 5-90-81-34-19; internet www.cr-guadeloupe.fr.

President: LUCETTE MICHAUX-CHEVRY (UMP).

Election, 15 March 1998

	Seats
Rassemblement pour la République (RPR)	25
Parti Socialiste (PS)	12
Parti Communiste Guadeloupéen (PCG)	2
Others*	2
Total	**41**

* Other right-wing candidates.

Political Organizations

Gauche Plurielle: Pointe-à-Pitre; electoral alliance; f. 2001; comprising the PS and various other left-wing parties.

Guadeloupe Unie, Socialisme et Réalité (GUSR): Pointe-à-Pitre; 'dissident' faction of the Parti Socialiste; Leader DOMINIQUE LARIFLA.

Konvwa pou Liberayson Nasyon Gwadloup (KLNG): Pointe-à-Pitre; pro-independence; Leader LUC REINETTE.

Lutte Ouvrière: Pointe-à-Pitre; internet www.lutte-ouvriere.org; extreme left-wing.

Mouvement Guadeloupéen Écologiste: Pointe-à-Pitre; green party.

Mouvement National Républicain: Pointe-à-Pitre; internet www.m-n-r.com; extreme right-wing.

Objectif Guadeloupe: Pointe-à-Pitre; f. 2001; electoral alliance comprising the RPR, UDF and other right-wing parties.

Parti Communiste Guadeloupéen (PCG): 119 rue Vatable, 97110 Pointe-à-Pitre; tel. 5-90-82-19-45; fax 5-90-83-69-90; f. 1944; Sec.-Gen. CHRISTIAN CÉLESTE.

Parti Radical de Gauche: Bergette, 97150 Petit Bourg; tel. 5-90-95-72-83; f. 1902; Pres. FLAVIEN FERRANT.

Parti Socialiste (PS): 801 Residence Collinette, Grand Camp, 97139 Les Abymes; tel. and fax 5-90-82-19-32; divided into two factions to contest the March 1992 and March 1993 elections; First Sec. GEORGES LOUISOR.

Union pour un Mouvement Populaire (UMP): Lotissement SIG, Sainte-Anne; f. 2002 by mems of the former Rassemblement pour la République and Démocratie Liberale parties; Departmental Sec. ALDO BLAISE.

Les Verts: 32 rue Alsace-Lorraine, 97110 Pointe-à-Pitre; tel. 5-90-35-41-90; fax 5-90-25-02-62; internet www.les-verts.org; green party; Regional Dirs HARRY DURIMEL, MARIE LINE PIRBAKAS.

Judicial System

Cour d'Appel: Palais de Justice, 4 blvd Félix Eboué, 97100 Basse-Terre; tel. 5-90-80-63-17; fax 5-90-80-63-39; First Pres. JEAN-PIERRE ATTHENONT; Procurator-Gen. M. ZIRNHELT; two Tribunaux de Grande Instance, four Tribunaux d'Instance.

Religion

The majority of the population belong to the Roman Catholic Church.

CHRISTIANITY

The Roman Catholic Church

Guadeloupe comprises the single diocese of Basse-Terre, suffragan to the archdiocese of Fort-de-France, Martinique. At 31 December 2000 there were an estimated 355,000 adherents, representing some 81.5% of the total population. The Bishop participates in the Antilles Episcopal Conference, currently based in Port of Spain, Trinidad and Tobago.

Bishop of Basse-Terre: Rt Rev. ERNEST MESMIN LUCIEN CABO, Evêché, pl. Saint-François, BP 369, 97106 Basse-Terre Cédex; tel. 5-90-81-36-69; fax 5-90-81-98-23; e-mail eveche@catholique-guadeloupe.info.

Other Denominations

Apostles of Infinite Love: Plaines, 97116 Pointe-Noire; tel. 5-90-98-01-19.

Mission Baptiste: 101 Belcourt, 97122 Baie-Mahault; tel. and fax 5-90-26-15-71; e-mail al.gary@wanadoo.fr.

The Press

L'Etincelle: 119 rue Vatable, 97110 Pointe-à-Pitre; tel. 5-90-91-12-77; fax 5-90-83-69-90; f. 1944; weekly; organ of the PCG; Dir RAYMOND BARON; circ. 5,000.

France-Antilles: 1 rue Hincelin, BP 658, 97159 Pointe-à-Pitre; tel. 5-90-5-90-90-25-25; fax 5-90-91-78-31; daily; Dir FRANÇOIS MERCADER; circ. 25,000.

Match: 33 rue Peyrier, 97110 Pointe-à-Pitre; tel. and fax 5-90-82-01-87; fortnightly; Dir MARIE ANTONIA JABBOUR; circ. 6,000.

Newsmagazine Guadeloupéen: Résidence Vatable, Bâtiment B, BP 1286, 97178 Pointe-à-Pitre; tel. 5-90-91-16-94; fax 5-90-82-22-38;

f. 1994; fmrly *Magwa*; fortnightly; independent; Editor DANNICK ZANDRONIS; circ. 4,000.

Le Progrès social: rue Toussaint L'Ouverture, 97100 Basse-Terre; tel. 5-90-81-10-41; weekly; Dir JEAN-CLAUDE RODES; circ. 5,000.

7 Mag: Immeuble SOCOGAR, 97122 Baie-Mahault; Dir JACQUES CANNEVAL.

TV Magazine Guadeloupe: 1 rue Paul Lacavé, BP 658, 97169 Pointe-à-Pitre; tel. 5-90-90-25-25; weekly.

Broadcasting and Communications

BROADCASTING

Réseau France Outre-mer (RFO): BP 180, 97122 Baie Mahault Cédex; tel. 5-90-60-96-96; fax 5-90-60-96-82; internet www.rfo.fr; fmrly Société Nationale de Radio-Télévision Française d'Outre-mer, renamed as above 1998; 24 hours radio and 24 hours television broadcast daily; Pres. ANDRÉ-MICHEL BESSE; Regional Dir ROBERT MOY.

Radio

More than 30 private FM radio stations are in operation.

Radio Actif: Baie-Mahault; commercial; satellite link to Radio Monte-Carlo (Monaco and France).

Radio Caraïbes International (RCI): BP 1309, 97187 Point-à-Pitre Cédex; tel. 5-90-83-96-96; fax 5-90-83-96-97; two commercial stations broadcasting 24 hours daily; Dir JEAN-FRANÇOIS FERANDIER-SICARD.

Radio Saint-Martin: Port de Marigot, 97150 Saint-Martin; commercial station broadcasting 94 hours weekly; Man. H. COOKS.

Radio Voix Chrétiennes de Saint-Martin: BP 103, Marigot, 97150 Saint-Martin; tel. 5-90-87-13-59; religious; Man. Fr CORNELIUS CHARLES.

Television

Canal Antilles: 2 Lotissement Les Jardins de Houelbourg, 97122 Baie-Mahault; tel. 5-90-26-81-79; private 'coded' station.

TCI Guadeloupe: Montauban, 97190 Grosier; commercial station.

Finance

(cap. = capital; res = reserves; dep. = deposits;
m. = million; brs = branches; amounts in French francs unless
otherwise indicated)

BANKING

Central Bank

Institut d'Emission des Départments d'Outre-mer (IEDOM): blvd Légitimus, BP 196, 97155 Pointe-à-Pitre; tel. 5-90-93-74-00; fax 5-90-93-74-25; internet www.iedom-ieom.com; Dir THIERRY CORNAILLE.

Commercial Banks

Banque des Antilles Françaises: pl. de la Victoire, BP 696, 97110 Pointe-à-Pitre Cédex; tel. 5-90-26-80-07; fax 5-90-26-74-48; internet www.bdaf.gp; f. 1853; cap. €7.5m., res €4.6m., dep. €428.9m. (Dec. 2000); Chair. JACQUES GIRAULT; Gen. Man. JEAN TAUZIES.

Banque Française Commerciale Antilles-Guyane (BFC Antilles-Guyane): BP 13, 97151 Baie-Mahault; tel. 5-90-25-19-50; fax 5-90-25-19-49; internet www.cosmobay.com/demo/bfcag; f. 1976 as branch of Banque Française Commerciale SA, separated 1984; total assets 3,609.1m (1998); Dir EDOUARD BEAUCHET.

BNP Paribas, SA: pl. de la Rénovation, 97110 Pointe-à-Pitre; tel. 5-90-90-58-58; fax 5-90-90-04-07; Dir HENRI BETBEDER; 6 further brs in Guadeloupe.

BRED Banque Populaire: 10 rue Achille René Boisneuf, BP 35, 97110 Pointe-à-Pitre; tel. 5-90-89-67-00.

Crédit Agricole de la Guadeloupe: Petie Pérou-les-Abymes, 97159 Pointe-à-Pitre Cédex; tel. 5-90-90-65-65; fax 5-90-90-65-89.

Société Générale de Banque aux Antilles (SGBA): 30 rue Frébault, BP 55, 97152 Pointe-à-Pitre; tel. 5-90-25-49-77; fax 5-90-25-49-78; e-mail sgba@wanadoo.fr; f. 1979; cap. 63.5m., res 2.7m., dep. 1,510.6m. (2001); Chair. JEAN-LOUIS MATTEI; Gen. Man. JEAN-MAURICE BEAUX; 5 brs in French West Indies.

Development Bank

Société de crédit pour le développement de Guadeloupe (SODEGA): Pointe-à-Pitre; part of the Agence Française de Développment (AFD—see entry below).

Foreign Companies

Some 30 of the principal European insurance companies are represented in Pointe-à-Pitre, and another six companies have offices in Basse-Terre.

Trade and Industry

GOVERNMENT AGENCY

Direction Régionale de l'Industrie, de la Recherche et de l'Environnement (DRIRE): 20 rue de la Chapell, Z. I. Jarry, 97122 Baie-Mahault; tel. 5-90-38-03-47; fax 5-90-38-03-50; e-mail drire-antilles-guyane@industrie.gouv.fr; internet www.ggm.drire .gouv.fr/Guadeloupe/; mining authority; responsible for assessing applications for and awarding exploration and exploitation rights; Departmental Co-ordinator GILLES LEDOUX.

DEVELOPMENT ORGANIZATIONS

Agence Française de Développement (AFD): blvd Légitimus, BP 160, 97159 Pointe-à-Pitre Cédex; tel. 5-90-89-65-65; fax 5-90-83-03-73; e-mail afd.gpe@wanadoo.fr; internet www.afd.fr; fmrly Caisse Française de Développement; Man. CHRISTIAN SZERSNOVICZ.

Agence pour la Promotion des Investissements en Guadeloupe (APRIGA): BP 514, 97165 Pointe-à-Pitre; tel. 5-90-83-48-97; fax 5-90-82-07-09; e-mail apriga@apriga.com; internet www.apriga .com; f. 1979 as Agence pour la Promotion de l'Industrie de la Guadeloupe; Pres. PATRICK DOQUIN; Dir CHARLY BLONDEAU.

Centre Technique Interprofessionnel de la Canne et du Sucre: Morne Epingle, Les Abymes, BP 397, 97162 Pointe-à-Pitre Cédex; tel. 5-90-82-94-70; fax 5-90-20-97-84; Pres. MICHEL MONTEIRO; Dir MICHEL MARCHAT.

CHAMBERS OF COMMERCE

Chambre d'Agriculture de la Guadeloupe: Rond Point Destreland, 97122 Baie-Mahault; tel. 5-90-25-17-17; fax 5-90-26-07-22.

Chambre de Commerce et d'Industrie de Pointe-à-Pitre: Hôtel Consulaire, rue Félix Eboué, 97159 Pointe-à-Pitre Cédex; tel. 5-90-93-76-00; fax 5-90-90-21-87; e-mail contacts@cci-pap.org; internet www.cci-pap.org; Pres. FÉLIX CLAIREVILLE; Dir-Gen. JACQUES GARRETA.

Chambre de Commerce et d'Industrie de Basse-Terre: 6 rue Victor Hugues, 97100 Basse-Terre; tel. 5-90-99-44-44; fax 5-90-81-21-17; internet www.basse-terre.cci.fr; f. 1832; 24 mems; Pres. JEAN-JACQUES FAYEL; Sec.-Gen. JEAN-CLAUDE BAPTISTIDE.

Chambre de Métiers de la Guadeloupe: route Choisy, BP 61, 97120 Saint-Claude; tel. 5-90-80-23-33; fax 5-90-80-12-13; Dir MAURICE SONGEONS.

EMPLOYERS' ORGANIZATIONS

Union Patronale de la Guadeloupe (UPRG): Immeuble SCI, BTB Voie principale, Z. I. Jarry, 97122 Baie-Mahault; tel. 5-90-26-83-58; fax 5-90-26-83-57; e-mail uprg@wanadoo.fr.

Syndicat des Producteurs-Exportateurs de Sucre et de Rhum de la Guadeloupe et Dépendances: Zone Industrielle de la Pointe Jarry, 97122 Baie-Mahault, BP 2015, 97191 Pointe-à-Pitre; tel. 5-90-26-62-12; fax 5-90-26-86-76; f. 1937; 4 mems; Pres. AMÉDÉE HUYGHUES-DESPOINTES.

TRADE UNIONS

Centrale des Travailleurs Unis (CTU): Logement Test 14, BP 676, Bergevin, 97169 Pointe-à-Pitre; tel. 5-90-83-16-50; fax 5-90-91-78-02; affiliated to the Confédération Française Démocratique du Travail; Sec.-Gen. HENRI BERTHELOT.

Confédération Générale du Travail de la Guadeloupe (CGTG): 4 cité Artisanale de Bergevin, BP 779, 97173 Pointe-à-Pitre Cédex; tel. 5-90-82-34-61; fax 5-90-91-04-00; f. 1961; Sec.-Gen. CLAUDE MORVAN; 5,000 mems.

Union Départementale de la Confédération Française des Travailleurs Chrétiens: BP 245, 97159 Pointe-à-Pitre; tel. 5-90-82-04-01; f. 1937; Sec.-Gen. ALBERT SARKIS; 3,500 mems.

Union Départementale des Syndicats CGT-FO: 59 rue Lamartine, 97110 Pointe-à-Pitre; Gen. Sec. FERDINAND QUILLIN; 1,500 mems.

Union Générale des Travailleurs de la Guadeloupe (UGTG): rue Paul Lacavé, 97110 Pointe-à-Pitre; tel. 5-90-83-10-07; confederation of pro-independence trade unions; Leader MICHEL MADASSAMY; Gen. Sec. GABY CLAVIER; 4,000 mems.

Transport

RAILWAYS
There are no railways in Guadeloupe.

ROADS
In 1990 there were 2,069 km (1,286 miles) of roads in Guadeloupe, of which 323 km were Routes Nationales.

SHIPPING
The major port is at Pointe-à-Pitre, and a new port for the export of bananas has been built at Basse-Terre.

Compagnie Générale Maritime Antilles-Guyane: Z.I. de la Pointe Jarry, BP 92, 97100 Baie-Mahault; tel. 5-90-26-72-39; fax 5-90-26-74-62.

Direction Départementale des Affaires Maritimes de la Guadeloupe: 1 Quai Layrle, BP 473, 97164 Pointe-à-Pitre Cédex; tel. 5-90-82-03-13; fax 5-90-90-07-33; Dir RENÉ GOALLO.

Port Autonome de la Guadeloupe: Gare Maritime, BP 485, 97165 Pointe-à-Pitre Cédex; tel. 5-90-21-39-00; fax 5-90-21-39-00; e-mail webmaster@port-guadeloupe.com; internet www .port-guadeloupe.com; port authority; Gen. Man. PATRICK LAMBERT.

Société Guadeloupéenne de Consignation et Manutention (SGCM): 8 rue de la Chapelle, BP 2360, 97001 Jarry Cédex; tel. 5-90-38-05-55; fax 5-90-26-95-39; e-mail sgcm@outremer.com; f. 1994; shipping agents, stevedoring; Chair. LUC EMY; Gen. Man. BERTRAND KERGUELEN.

Société de Transport Maritimes Brudy Frères: 78 Centre St John Perse, 97110 Pointe-à-Pitre; tel. 5-90-82-52-25; fax 5-90-93-00-79.

CIVIL AVIATION
Raizet International Airport is situated 3 km (2 miles) from Pointe-à-Pitre and is equipped to handle jet-engined aircraft. There are smaller airports on the islands of Marie-Galante, La Désirade and Saint-Barthélémy.

Air Caraïbe: Immeuble Le Caducée, Morne Vergain, 97139 Abymes; tel. 5-90-82-47-47; fax 5-90-82-47-49; e-mail info@ aircaraibes.com; internet www.aircaraibes.com; f. 2000 following merger of Air St Martin, Air St Barts, Air Guadeloupe and Air Martinique; operates inter-island and regional services within the Eastern Caribbean and flights to Miami (USA).

Tourism

Guadeloupe is a popular tourist destination, especially for visitors from metropolitan France (who account for some 82% of tourists) and the USA. The main attractions are the beaches, the mountainous scenery and the unspoilt beauty of the island dependencies. In 1999 847,131 tourists visited Guadeloupe, and receipts from tourism totalled US $418m. In 1998 there were 168 hotels, with 8,371 rooms.

Delégation Régionale au Tourisme: 5 rue Victor Hugues, 97100 Basse-Terre; tel. 5-90-81-15-60; fax 5-90-81-94-82; Dir HUGUES JONNIAUX.

Office du Tourisme: 5 square de la Banque, BP 1099, 97110 Pointe-à-Pitre Cédex; tel. 5-90-82-09-30; fax 5-90-83-89-22; e-mail office.tourisme.guadeloupe@wanadoo.fr; Pres. DANIEL ARNOUX.

Syndicat d'Initiative de la Guadeloupe: Pointe-à-Pitre; Pres. Dr EDOUARD CHARTOL.

MARTINIQUE

Introductory Survey

Location, Climate, Language, Religion, Capital
Martinique is one of the Windward Islands in the West Indies, with Dominica to the north and Saint Lucia to the south. The island is dominated by the volcanic peak of Mont Pelée. The climate is tropical, but tempered by easterly and north-easterly breezes. The more humid and wet season runs from July to November, and the average temperature is 26°C (79°F). French is the official language, but a creole patois is widely spoken. The majority of the population profess Christianity and belong to the Roman Catholic Church. The capital is Fort-de-France.

Recent History
Martinique has been a French possession since 1635. The prosperity of the island was based on the sugar industry, which was devastated by the volcanic eruption of Mont Pelée in 1902. Martinique became a Department of France in 1946, when the Governor was replaced by a Prefect, and an elected Conseil Général (General Council) was created.

During the 1950s there was a growth of nationalist feeling, as expressed by Aimé Césaire's Parti Progressiste Martiniquais (PPM) and the Parti Communiste Martiniquais (PCM). However, economic power remained concentrated in the hands of the *békés* (descendants of white colonial settlers), who owned most of the agricultural land and controlled the lucrative import-export market. This provided little incentive for innovation or self-sufficiency, and fostered resentment against lingering colonial attitudes.

In 1974 Martinique, together with Guadeloupe and French Guiana, was given regional status as part of France's governmental reorganization. An indirectly-elected Regional Council (Conseil Régional) was created, with some control over the local economy. In 1982 and 1983 the socialist Government of President François Mitterrand, which had pledged itself to decentralizing power in favour of the Overseas Departments, made further concessions towards autonomy by giving the local councils greater control over taxation, local police and the economy. At the first direct elections to the new Conseil Régional, held in February 1983, left-wing parties (the PPM, the PCM and the Fédération Socialiste de la Martinique—FSM) won 21 of the 41 seats. This success, and the election of Aimé Césaire as the Conseil's President, strengthened his influence against the pro-independence elements in his own party. (Full independence for Martinique attracted support from only a small minority of the population; the majority sought reforms that would bring greater autonomy, while retaining French control.) The Mouvement Indépendantiste Martiniquais (MIM), the most vocal of the separatist parties, fared badly in the elections, obtaining less than 3% of the total vote. At elections to the enlarged Conseil Général, held in March 1985, the left-wing parties increased their representation, but the centre-right coalition of the Union pour la Démocratie Française (UDF) and the Rassemblement pour la République (RPR) maintained their control of the administration.

For the general election to the Assemblée Nationale in March 1986, Martinique's representation was increased from three to four deputies. Césaire and a member of the FSM were elected from a unified list of left-wing candidates, while the RPR and the UDF (which had also presented a joint list) each won one seat. For the concurrent elections to the Conseil Régional the left-wing parties (including the PPM, the FSM and the PCM) won 21 of the 41 seats, and the RPR and the UDF together won the remaining seats. Césaire retained the presidency of the Council until 1988, when he relinquished the post to Camille Darsières (the Secretary-General of the PPM). In September 1986 indirect elections were held for Martinique's two seats in the Sénat. As in the March elections, the left-wing parties united, and, as a consequence, Martinique acquired a left-wing senator for the first time since 1958, a PPM member, while the other successful candidate belonged to the UDF.

Following the recent trend in Martinique, the incumbent, François Mitterrand of the Parti Socialiste (PS), won a decisive majority of the island's votes at the 1988 French presidential election. Left-wing candidates secured all four seats at elections to the Assemblée Nationale in June. Furthermore, in September–October, for the first time in 40 years, the parties of the left achieved a majority at elections to the Conseil Général. Emile Maurice of the RPR was, none the less, elected President of the Conseil Général for a seventh term.

In June 1990 the results of the 1986 election to the Conseil Régional were annulled because of a technicality, and another election was held in October. Pro-independence candidates won nearly 22% of the votes, and secured nine seats (of which seven were won by the MIM). The PPM, the FSM and the PCM again formed a joint electoral list, but won only 14 seats, and consequently lost their absolute majority on the Conseil; Camille Darsières was, however, re-elected to the presidency of the Conseil. The success of the pro-independence candidates was attributed to local apprehension concerning the implications of plans within the European Community (EC, known as the European Union, EU, see p. 199, from November 1993) for a single market, which would, it was feared, expose Martinique's economy to excessive competition.

At elections to the Conseil Général in March 1992, left-wing parties secured 26 seats and right-wing organizations 19. Claude Lise, a PPM deputy to the Assemblée Nationale, was elected President of the Conseil Général. In concurrent elections to the Conseil Régional the RPR and the UDF, contesting the election as the Union pour la France (UPF), won 16 seats, the MIM (which contested the election under the title Patriotes Martiniquais) and the PPM secured nine seats each, and the PCM (under the title Pour une Martinique au Travail) and the FSM (as the Nouvelle Génération Socialiste) won four and three seats, respectively. Following three rounds of voting, Emile Capgras of the PCM was finally elected President of the Conseil Régional.

In September 1992 72.3% of voters in Martinique approved ratification of the Treaty on European Union (see p. 199), although the abstention rate was high. In November of that year banana-growers in Guadeloupe and Martinique suspended economic activity in their respective Departments by obstructing access to ports and airports and blocking roads, in protest at the threatened loss of special advantages under the Single European Act. Order was restored after four days, however, following assurances that subsidies would be maintained and that certain products, such as bananas (one of Martinique's principal exports), would be protected under EC proposals.

At the March 1993 elections to the Assemblée Nationale there was a marked swing in favour of the parties of the right: André Lesueur and Pierre Petit were elected to represent the RPR, while a third right-wing candidate, Anicet Turinay, campaigned successfully on behalf of the UPF. Césaire did not seek re-election, and was replaced at the Assemblée Nationale by Camille Darsières.

The composition of the Conseil Général remained largely unchanged following cantonal elections in March 1994, at which the PPM retained 10 seats, the RPR seven and the UDF three; Lise was subsequently re-elected President of the Council. At elections to the European Parliament in June, the government list secured the greatest proportion (36.6%) of the votes cast. A combined list of parties of the left of the four Overseas Departments (which included the PPM and the Parti Martiniquais Socialiste) took 20.2% of the votes.

At the first round of voting in the 1995 presidential election, on 23 April, Martinique was the only French overseas possession in which the candidate of the PS, Lionel Jospin, received the greatest proportion of the valid votes cast (34.4%). Jospin, supported by all the parties of the left, took 58.9% of the votes cast at the second round on 7 May. At municipal elections in June the PPM retained control of Martinique's principal towns. In September Lise was elected to the Sénat, while the incumbent PPM representative, Rodolphe Désiré, was returned to office.

At elections to the Assemblée Nationale in May and June 1997, Turinay and Petit, representing the RPR, were re-elected, together with Darsières of the PPM. Alfred Marie-Jeanne, the

First Secretary and a founding member of the MIM, was elected in a constituency hitherto held by the RPR. At elections to the Conseil Régional in March 1998, the left retained its majority. The pro-independence MIM performed well, increasing its representation by four seats, to 13, while the PPM secured seven seats, the RPR six and the UDF five. Marie-Jeanne was elected President of the Conseil Régional. In concurrent elections to the Conseil Général the left again increased its majority, from 26 to 29 seats, with right-wing candidates winning 14 seats and independents two. Lise was re-elected to the presidency of the Conseil.

In January 1999 representatives of 10 separatist organizations from French Guiana, Guadeloupe and Martinique, including the MIM, signed a joint declaration denouncing 'French colonialism', in which they stated their intention to campaign for the reinstatement of the three Caribbean Overseas Departments on a UN list of territories to be decolonized.

A two-month strike by workers in the banana sector, which had severely disrupted economic activity around the port of Fort-de-France, was ended in January 1999, when a pay agreement was reached. The social climate deteriorated further in May, as two companies were affected by strike action. Workers at the Toyota motor company were demanding substantial pay increases and a reduction in working hours, while employees of the Roger Albert distribution group were protesting against the dismissal of two colleagues. In early October tension escalated as trade unions took sympathetic action, blocking access to the main industrial and commercial zones around the capital for two days. Subsequent negotiations between the local authorities and a trade union delegation resulted in the removal of the blockades and an agreement to hold talks on the resolution of the two conflicts. The dispute at Roger Albert was concluded shortly afterwards, following the intervention of Marie-Jeanne, but, despite mediation efforts, industrial action at Toyota continued. In mid-October trade unions organized a week-long blockade of the port of Fort-de-France in protest against proposed redundancies at Toyota. Later that month, prior to a two-day visit to Martinique by Jospin, the Prime Minister, banana producers occupied the headquarters of the French naval forces for several days, demanding the disbursement of exceptional aid to compensate for the adverse effect on their industry of a dramatic decline in prices on the European market. Marie-Jeanne, who was opposed to the limited nature of the Government's plans for institutional reform, refused to participate in the events organized for Jospin's stay. The Prime Minister announced an emergency plan for the banana sector and, while attending a conference on regional co-operation, agreed, in principle, to a proposal for greater autonomy for the local authorities in conducting relations with neighbouring countries and territories. In November, following two weeks of direct negotiations between trade union representatives and the management of Toyota, a protocol was signed, marking the end of the five-month dispute; a pay increase was awarded and dismissal proceedings against 12 employees were annulled.

Following a series of meetings, in December 1999 the Presidents of the Conseils Régionaux of French Guiana, Guadeloupe and Martinique signed a joint declaration in Basse-Terre, Guadeloupe, affirming their intention to propose, to the President and the Government, a legislative amendment aimed at creating a new status of overseas region, despite an earlier statement by Jospin indicating that the Government did not envisage a change in status for the Departments. Further meetings of the three regional Presidents were held in January and February 2000. Proposals regarding the institutional future and socio-economic development of the Departments were provisionally accepted by the French Assemblée Nationale in May 2000, and a modified version of the proposals was subsequently adopted, by a narrow margin, by the Sénat. In November the Assemblée Nationale approved the proposals and in December they were ratified by the Constitutional Council. Following a meeting of members of the Conseil Régional and the Conseil Général in late June 2001, a series of proposals on greater autonomy, to be presented to the French Government, was agreed upon. These included: the division of the territory into four districts; the creation of a 'collectivité territoriale' (territorial community), governed by a 41-member Assembly elected for a five-year term; and the establishment of an independent executive council. Furthermore, the proposals included a request that the territory be given control over legislative and administrative affairs, as well as legislative authority on matters concerning Martinique alone. In November the French Government announced itself to be in favour of the suggested constitutional developments, and a vote on enacting the proposals was due to be held in March 2003.

At a referendum held in September 2000, Martinique voted overwhelmingly in favour of reducing the presidential mandate from seven years to five. In municipal elections held in March 2001 the PPM retained control of the majority of municipalities (including Fort-de-France, where Césaire, retiring as mayor after 55 years, was succeeded by a fellow PPM member, Sérge Letchimy, who defeated Marie-Jeanne, President of the Conseil Régional). In the concurrently-held election to the Conseil Général, Lise was re-elected President. In mid-2001 the French President, Jacques Chirac, rejected a joint request by French Guiana, Guadeloupe and Martinique that they be permitted to join, as associate members, the Association of Caribbean States. In the first round of the presidential election, held on 21 April 2002, Chirac obtained 33.0% of the votes cast in the Department, followed by Jospin with 29.2%, who was, however, eliminated nationally. In the second round, held on 5 May, Chirac overwhelmingly defeated Jean-Marie Le Pen of the extreme right-wing Front National, securing 96.1% of the votes cast. At elections to the Assemblée Nationale in June, Marie-Jeanne was re-elected, while Turinay lost his seat to Louis-Joseph Mansour of the PS, and Darsière lost his to Pierre-Jean Samot of the left-wing Bâtir le Pays Martinique; Alfred Almont, representing the right-wing alliance of the Union pour la Majorité Présidentielle (UMP) and the RPR, secured the remaining seat. The RPR subsequently merged into the successor party to the UMP, the Union pour un Mouvement Populaire (also known as the UMP).

Government

France is represented in Martinique by an appointed prefect. There are two councils with local powers: the 45-member Conseil Général (General Council) and the 41-member Conseil Régional (Regional Council). Both are elected by universal adult suffrage for a period of up to six years. Martinique elects four deputies to the Assemblée Nationale in Paris, and sends two indirectly-elected representatives to the Sénat. The Department is also represented at the European Parliament.

Defence

At 1 August 2002 France maintained a military force of 4,000 and a gendarmerie of 860 in the Antilles, with headquarters in Fort-de-France.

Economic Affairs

In 1999 Martinique's gross domestic product (GDP), measured at current prices, was estimated at US $4,570m., equivalent to about $11,979 per head. During 1990–99, according to UN estimates, GDP increased, in real terms, at an average rate of 1.3% per year; growth in 1999 was 0.6%. Between the censuses of 1990 and 1999, according to provisional figures, the population increased at an average annual rate of 0.7%.

Agriculture, hunting, forestry and fishing contributed an estimated 5% of GDP in 1998, and according to FAO figures, engaged an estimated 3.7% of the labour force in mid-2001. The principal cash crops are bananas (which accounted for some 36.6% of export earnings in 1997), sugar cane (primarily for the production of rum), limes, melons and pineapples. The cultivation of cut flowers is also of some significance. Roots and tubers and vegetables are grown for local consumption. Agricultural production increased at an average rate of 1.3% per year during 1990–98. It increased by 6.7% in 1997, but declined by 0.2% in 1999.

The industrial sector (including construction and public works) contributed an estimated 15% of GDP in 1998, and engaged 10.6% of the total labour force in the same year. Mining, manufacturing and power provided some 10% of GDP in 1998. The most important manufacturing activities are petroleum refining (exports of refined petroleum products accounted for some 16.0% of the value of total exports in 1997) and the processing of agricultural products—the production of rum being of particular significance. Exports of rum provided some 10.0% of export earnings in 1997. Martiniquais rum was accorded the designation of Appellation d'origine contrôlée (AOC) in 1996 (the first AOC to be designated outside metropolitan France). Other areas of activity include metals, cement, chemicals, plastics, wood, printing and textiles. Energy is derived principally from mineral fuels. Imports of mineral fuels (including crude petroleum destined for the island's refinery) accounted for 7.5% of the value of total imports in 1995.

The services sector engaged 55.2% of the total labour force in 1998 and provided an estimated 80% of GDP in the same year.

Tourism is a major activity on the island and one of the most important sources of foreign exchange. In 2001 506,104 tourists visited the island. In 2001 earnings from the tourism industry totalled an estimated €226.6m.

In 2000 Martinique recorded a trade deficit of 9,495.5m. French francs. In 2000 the principal source of imports (63.5%) was metropolitan France, which was also the principal market for exports (57.8%). Guadeloupe, Germany, Venezuela and Belgium-Luxembourg were also significant trading partners. The principal exports in 1997 were bananas, refined petroleum products, rum, flavoured or sweetened water and boats. The principal imports in 1995 were machinery and transport equipment (especially road vehicles), food and live animals, miscellaneous manufactured articles, basic manufactures, chemicals and mineral fuels.

In 2001 the departmental budget was expected to balance. The annual rate of inflation averaged 2.0% in 1990–2001; consumer prices increased by 1.0% in 2000 and by 2.1% in 2001. Some 26.3% of the labour force were unemployed in 2002. In 1990 the level of emigration from the island was estimated at about 15,000 per year; most of the emigrants were under 25 years of age.

As an integral part of France, Martinique belongs to the European Union (EU, see p. 199).

Martinique's economic development has created a society that combines a relatively high standard of living with a weak economic base in agricultural and industrial production, as well as a chronic trade deficit. Levels of unemployment and emigration are high (in 1990 some 30% of Martiniquais nationals were resident in France), although the rate of growth of both these factors has slowed since the mid-1980s. The linking of wage levels to those of metropolitan France, despite the island's lower level of productivity, has increased labour costs and restricted development. In the late 1990s the value of banana exports declined owing to a significant fall in prices on the European market, while an ongoing dispute between the USA and four Latin American countries and the EU over the latter's banana import regime also threatened Martinique's banana-growing sector. This dispute was resolved in April 2001 when it was agreed that the quota system currently employed by the EU was to be replaced by a universal tariff system from 2006. Moreover, a succession of industrial disputes severely disrupted economic activity in 1999. In November 2002 the French hotel group Accor announced that it would close its five hotels in Martinque and Guadeloupe, citing high operating costs, poor industrial relations and decreasing tourist arrivals.

Education

The educational system is similar to that of metropolitan France (see chapter on French Guiana). Higher education in law, French language and literature, human sciences, economics, medicine and Creole studies is provided in Martinique by a branch of the Université Antilles-Guyane. The university as a whole had 11,755 enrolled students in 2001. There are also two teacher-training institutes, and colleges of agriculture, fisheries, hotel management, nursing, midwifery and child care. Separate Academies for Martinique, French Guiana and Guadeloupe were established in January 1997, replacing the single Academy for the Antilles-Guyane (which was based in Fort-de-France). Departmental expenditure on education and culture was estimated at 111.5m. French francs in 2001.

Public Holidays

2003: 1 January (New Year's Day), 3–4 March (Carnival), 5 March (Ash Wednesday), 18–21 April (Easter), 1 May (Labour Day), 8 May (Victory Day), 29 May (Ascension Day), 9 June (Whit Monday), 14 July (National Day), 15 August (Assumption), 1 November (All Saints' Day), 11 November (Armistice Day), 25 December (Christmas Day).

2004: 1 January (New Year's Day), 23–24 February (Carnival), 25 February (Ash Wednesday), 9–12 April (Easter), 1 May (Labour Day), 8 May (Victory Day), 20 May (Ascension Day), 30 May (Whit Monday), 14 July (National Day), 15 August (Assumption), 1 November (All Saints' Day), 11 November (Armistice Day), 25 December (Christmas Day).

Weights and Measures

The metric system is in use.

Statistical Survey

Sources (unless otherwise stated): Institut national de la statistique et des études économiques (INSEE), Service Régional de Martinique, Centre Delgrès, blvd de la Pointe des Sables, Les Hauts de Dillon, BP 641, 97262 Fort-de-France Cédex; tel. 60-73-60; fax 60-73-50; internet www.insee.fr/fr/insee_regions/ martinique ; Ministère des départements et territoires d'outre-mer, 27 rue Oudinot, 75700 Paris 07 SP; tel. 1-53-69-20-00; fax 1-43-06-60-30; internet www.outre-mer.gouv.fr.

AREA AND POPULATION

Area: 1,100 sq km (424.7 sq miles).

Population: 326,717 (males 158,415; females 168,302) at census of 9 March 1982; 359,579 (males 173,878; females 185,701) at census of 15 March 1990; 381,427 at census of 8 March 1999.

Density (at 1999 census): 346.8 per sq km.

Principal Towns (at 1999 census): Fort-de-France (capital) 94,049; Le Lamentin 35,460; Le Robert 21,240; Schoelcher 20,845; Sainte-Marie 20,098; Le François 18,559; Saint-Joseph 15,785; Ducos 15,240. *2001* (UN estimate, incl. suburbs): Fort-de-France 93,000 (Source: UN, *World Urbanization Prospects: The 2001 Revision*).

Births, Marriages and Deaths (1999): Birth rate 15.1 per 1,000; Registered marriages 1,548 (marriage rate 4.1 per 1,000, 1997 figure, provisional); Death rate 6.2 per 1,000. *2001:* Registered births 5,774; Registered marriages 1,571; Registered deaths 2,734.

Expectation of Life (years at birth, 1997): Males 75.2; Females 81.7.

Economically Active Population (persons aged 15 years and over, 1998): Agriculture and fishing 7,650; Industry 7,103; Construction and public works 10,405; Trade 16,196; Transport 4,383; Financial services and real estate 3,354; Business services 8,376; Public services 14,179; Education 14,991; Health and social security 10,676; Administrative services 18,742; Total employed 116,055 (males 62,198; females 53,857); Unemployed 48,537 (males 22,628; females 25,909); Total labour force 164,592 (males 84,826; females 79,766). *1999* Total employed 119,900; Unemployed 46,900; Total labour force 166,800. *2000* Total employed 123,300; Unemployed 44,100; Total labour force 167,400. *Mid-2001* (estimates): Agriculture, etc. 7,000; Total labour force 189,000 (males 100,000; females 89,000) (Source: FAO).

HEALTH AND WELFARE

Key Indicators

Number of Physicians (1995): 680.

Number of Hospital Beds (1995): 2,100.
For definitions, see explanatory note on p. vi.

AGRICULTURE, ETC.

Principal Crops (FAO estimates, '000 metric tons, 2001): Yams 7.5; Other roots and tubers 13.3; Sugar cane 207; Lettuce 7.8; Tomatoes 6.1; Cucumbers and Gherkins 4; Other fresh vegetables 8.7; Bananas 310; Plantains 16; Pineapples 20.8. Source: FAO.

Livestock (FAO estimates, '000 head, year ending September 2001): Cattle 25; Sheep 34; Pigs 35; Goats 17. Source: FAO.

Livestock Products (FAO estimates, '000 metric tons, 2001): Beef and veal 2.3; Pig meat 1.7; Poultry meat 1; Cows' milk 2.2; Hen eggs 1.5. Source: FAO.

Forestry: Roundwood removals ('000 cu m, excluding bark, 1999): Sawlogs, veneer logs and logs for sleepers 2; Fuel wood 10; Total 12. *2001:* Production as in 1999 (FAO estimates). Source: FAO.

Fishing (metric tons, live weight, 2000, estimates): Capture 6,314 (Clupeoids 3,504, Common dolphinfish 250, Atlantic bonito 610, Blackfin tuna 540, Caribbean spiny lobster 200, Clams, etc. 1,100); Aquaculture 51; Total catch 6,365. Source: FAO, *Yearbook of Fishery Statistics*.

MINING

Production (estimates, 2000, '000 metric tons, unless otherwise indicated): Pumice 130.0; Petroleum ('000 barrels) 4,800; Salt 200. Source: US Geological Survey.

INDUSTRY

Production (1998, '000 metric tons, unless otherwise indicated): Pineapple juice 3.2 (1994); Canned or bottled pineapples 18.4 (1994); Raw sugar 6 (estimate, 2001); Rum (hl) 69,458; Motor spirit (petrol) 153 (estimate); Kerosene 133 (estimate); Gas-diesel (distillate fuel) oils 160 (estimate); Residual fuel oils 275 (estimate); Liquefied petroleum gas 21; Cement 350 (estimate, 1999); Electric energy (million kWh) 1,080 (1999). Source: mainly UN, *Industrial Commodity Statistics Yearbook*.

FINANCE

Currency and Exchange Rates: The French franc was used until the end of 2001. Euro notes and coins were introduced on 1 January 2002, and the euro became the sole legal tender from 18 February. Some of the figures in this Survey are still in terms of francs. For details of exchange rates, see French Guiana.

Budget (forecasts, million French francs, 2001): *Revenue*: Tax revenue 836.9 (Departmental taxes 332.0, Fuel tax 295.0, Transfer taxes, etc. 58.0, Motor vehicle tax 68.0, Fiscal subsidy 53.0); Other current revenue 886.6 (Refunds of social assistance 65.0, Operational allowance 315.0, Decentralization allowance 477.0); Capital revenue 499.5 (EU development funds 71.0, Capital allowances 59.0, Other receipts 101.4, Borrowing 270.0); Total 2,223.0. *Expenditure*: Current expenditure 1,482.2 (Finance service 57.1, Permanent staff 394.7, General administration 65.1, Other indirect services 69.0, Administrative services 108.4, Public health 49.9, Social assistance 503.6, Support costs of minimum wage 99.8, Economic services 114.7); Capital expenditure 740.8 (Road system 139.5, Networks 47.9, Education and culture 111.5, Other departmental programmes 101.6, Other public bodies 83.7, Other programmes 96.3, Non-programme expenditure 162.3); Total 2,223.0. Note: Figures refer only to the departmental budget.

State budget (million francs, 1998): Revenue 4,757, Expenditure 8,309.

Regional budget (million euros, 2000): Revenue 237, Expenditure 237.

Money Supply (million French francs at 31 December 1998): Currency outside banks 924; Demand deposits at banks 6,330; Total money 7,254.

Cost of Living (Consumer Price Index; base: 1990 = 100): 120.5 in 1999; 121.7 in 2000; 124.2 in 2001. Source: UN, *Monthly Bulletin of Statistics*.

Expenditure on the Gross Domestic Product (million French francs at current prices, 1994): Government final consumption expenditure 6,962; Private final consumption expenditure 20,133; Increase in stocks 20; Gross fixed capital formation 5,102; *Total domestic expenditure* 32,217; Exports of goods and services 1,439; *Less* Imports of goods and services 9,150; *GDP in purchasers' values* 24,506.

Gross Domestic Product by Economic Activity (million French francs at current prices, 1992): Agriculture, hunting, forestry and fishing 1,106.3; Mining, quarrying and manufacturing 1,770.6; Electricity, gas and water 483.6; Construction 1,145.3; Trade, restaurants and hotels 4,022.1; Transport, storage and communications 1,427.6; Finance, insurance, real estate and business services 2,590.1; Government services 5,416.0; Other community, social and personal services 3,576.4; Other services 330.5; Sub-total 21,868.5; Import duties 791.0; Value-added tax 640.9; *Less* Imputed bank service charge 1,207.1; *GDP in purchasers' values* 22,093.4. Source: UN, *National Accounts Statistics*.

EXTERNAL TRADE

Principal Commodities: *Imports c.i.f.* US $ million, 1995): Food and live animals 319.6 (Meat and meat preparations 82.8, Dairy products and birds' eggs 53.6, Fish and fish preparations 38.6, Cereals and cereal preparations 45.6, Vegetables and fruit 49.1); Beverages and tobacco 52.0 (Beverages 45.0); Mineral fuels, lubricants, etc. 148.0 (Petroleum and petroleum products 146.2); Chemicals and related products 189.5 (Medicinal and pharmaceutical products 83.9); Basic manufactures 260.1 (Paper, paperboard and manufactures 45.1); Machinery and transport equipment 637.6 (Power-generating machinery and equipment 62.8, General industrial machinery, equipment and parts 83.2, Telecommunications and sound equipment 41.1, Road vehicles and parts 240.7, Ships and boats 50.3); Miscellaneous manufactured articles 288.5 (Furniture and parts 46.2, Clothing and accessories, excl. footwear 62.6); Total (incl. others) 1,969.8 (Source: UN, *International Trade Statistics Yearbook*). Exports f.o.b. (million French francs, 1997): Bananas 462.2; Rum 126.7; Flavoured or sweetened water 78.8; Refined petroleum products 201.9; Yachts and sports boats 74.4; Total (incl. others) 1,263.3. *1997* (million French francs): *Imports*: 9,947.0; *Exports*: 1,239.0. *1998* (million French francs): *Imports*: 10,046.8; *Exports*: 1,701.4. *1999* (million French francs): *Imports*: 10,605.6; *Exports*: 1,715.1. *2000* (million French francs): *Imports*: 1,759; *Exports*: 294. Source: Direction Générale des Douanes.

Principal Trading Partners (million euros, 2000): *Imports c.i.f.*: France (metropolitan) 1,117; Germany 69; Italy 55; Japan 36; Netherland Antilles 41; USA 36; Venezuela 102; Total (incl. others) 1,759; *Exports f.o.b.*: Belgium-Luxembourg 8; France (metropolitan) 170; French Guiana 11; Guadeloupe 63; United Kingdom 10; Total (incl. others) 294.

TRANSPORT

Road Traffic ('000 motor vehicles in use, 1995): Passenger cars 95.0; Commercial vehicles 21.5. Source: UN, *Statistical Yearbook*.

Shipping Merchant Fleet (vessels registered '000 grt at 31 December, 1992): Source: Lloyd's Register of Shipping. *International Sea-borne Traffic* (2000): Goods loaded 853,000 metric tons; Goods unloaded 1,991,000 metric tons. Source: Direction Départementale de l'Equipement.

Civil Aviation (2000): Passengers carried 1,731,065; Freight carried 15,754 metric tons. Source: Chambre de Commerce et d'Industrie de la Martinique.

TOURISM

Tourist Arrivals (excl. same-day visitors and cruise-ship arrivals): 564,303 in 1999; 526,290 in 2000; 506,104 in 2001.

Tourist Arrivals by Country (excl. same-day visitors and cruise-ship arrivals, 1999): France 447,730, USA 15,047, Canada 5,244; Total (incl. others) 564,303.

Receipts from Tourism (US $ million): 384 in 1995; 382 in 1996; 400 in 1997. *2001* (million euros): Total receipts 226.6. Source: mainly World Tourism Organization, *Yearbook of Tourism Statistics*.

COMMUNICATIONS MEDIA

Radio Receivers ('000 in use): 82 in 1997.

Television Receivers ('000 in use): 62 in 1999.

Telephones ('000 main lines in use): 172.0 in 2001.

Facsimile Machines (number in use): 5,200 in 1997.

Mobile Cellular Telephones ('000 subscribers): 286.1 in 2001.

Personal Computers ('000 in use): 45 in 1999.

Internet Users ('000): 5.0 in 1999.

Daily Newspaper: 1 (estimate) in 1996 (estimated average circulation 30,000 copies).
Sources: UNESCO, *Statistical Yearbook*; UN, *Statistical Yearbook*; International Telecommunication Union.

EDUCATION

Pre-primary (1996/97): 84 institutions; 660 teachers; (1998/99) 21,445 students.

Primary* (2001/02): 273 institutions (258 state, 15 private); 3,260 teachers (3,022 state, 238 private); 53,347 students.

Secondary (2001/02): 78 institutions (60 state, 18 private); 4,257 teachers (3,918 state, 339 private); 51,057 students.

Vocational (1998/99): 15 institutions (9 state, 6 private); 7,661 students (7,101 state, 560 private).

Higher (2001): 11,755 students (Université Antilles-Guyane).
* Includes pre-primary.
Sources: UNESCO, *Statistical Yearbook*, and Académie de la Martinique.

Directory

The Government

(April 2003)

Prefect: MICHEL CADOT, Préfecture, 82 rue Victor Sévère, BP 647–648, 97262 Fort-de-France Cédex; tel. 5-96-63-18-61; fax 5-96-71-40-29.

President of the General Council: CLAUDE LISE (PPM), Conseil Général de la Martinique, blvd Chevalier Sainte-Marthe, 97200 Fort-de-France Cédex; tel. 5-96-55-26-00; fax 5-96-73-59-32; internet www.cg972.fr.

Deputies to the French National Assembly: LOUIS-JOSEPH MANSCOUR (PS), ALFRED ALMONT (UMP), PIERRE-JEAN SAMOT (Bâtir le Pays Martinique), ALFRED MARIE-JEANNE (MIM).

Representatives to the French Senate: CLAUDE LISE (Socialiste), RODOLPHE DÉSIRÉ (Rassemblement démocratique et social européen).

CONSEIL RÉGIONAL

Hôtel de Région, rue Gaston Deferre, BP 601, 97200 Fort-de-France Cédex; tel. 5-96-59-63-00; fax 5-96-72-68-10; e-mail Crg72.com-ext@wanadoo.fr; internet www.cr-martinique.fr.

President: ALFRED MARIE-JEANNE (MIM).

Election, 15 March 1998

	Seats
Mouvement Indépendantiste Martiniquais (MIM) . .	13
Parti Progressiste Martiniquais (PPM) .	7
Rassemblement pour la République (RPR) . . .	6
Union pour la Démocratie Française (UDF)*	5
Parti Martiniquais Socialiste (PMS)	3
Others†	7
Total	**41**

* Re-established as the Forces Martiniquaises de Progrès in October 1998.
† Three of those elected were candidates of the right.

Political Organizations

Bâtir le Pays Martinique: Fort-de-France; f. 1998; left-wing; Leader PIERRE-JEAN SAMOT.

Fédération Socialiste de la Martinique (FSM): 52 rue du Capitaine Pierre-Rose, 97200 Fort-de-France; tel. 5-96-60-14-88; e-mail psmq@ais.mq; internet www.socialiste-martinique.mq; local branch of the **Parti Socialiste (PS)**; Sec.-Gen. JEAN CRUSOL.

Forces Martiniquaises de Progrès: f. 1998 to replace the local branch of the Union pour la Démocratie Française; Pres. ANICET TURINAY.

Mouvement des Démocrates et Écologistes pour une Martinique Souveraine (MODEMAS): Fort-de-France.

Mouvement Indépendantiste Martiniquais (MIM): Fort-de-France; f. 1978; pro-independence party; First Sec. ALFRED MARIE-JEANNE.

Mouvement Populaire Franciscain: Fort-de-France; left-wing.

Osons Oser: Fort-de-France; f. 1998; right-wing; Pres. PIERRE PETIT.

Parti Progressiste Martiniquais (PPM): Fort-de-France; tel. 5-96-71-86-83; f. 1957; left-wing; Sec.-Gen. PIERRE SUÉDILE.

Parti Radical de Gauche: 16 allée de la Corniche La Colline, 97233 Schoelcher; tel. 5-96-61-94-38; e-mail milard.albert@PRGM@wanadoo.fr; f. 1902; Pres. DIDIER SAINT-LOUIS.

Judicial System

Cour d'Appel de Fort-de-France: BP 634, 97262 Fort-de-France Cédex; tel. 5-96-70-62-62; fax 5-96-63-52-13; e-mail ca-fort-de-france@justice.fr; highest court of appeal for Martinique and French Guiana; First Pres. RENÉ SALOMON; Procurator-Gen. GÉRARD LOUBENS.

There are two Tribunaux de Grande Instance, at Fort-de-France and Cayenne (French Guiana), and three Tribunaux d'Instance (two in Fort-de-France and one in Cayenne).

Religion

The majority of the population belong to the Roman Catholic Church.

CHRISTIANITY

The Roman Catholic Church

Martinique comprises the single archdiocese of Fort-de-France, with an estimated 297,515 adherents (some 78% of the total population) at 31 December 2000. The Archbishop participates in the Antilles Episcopal Conference, currently based in Port of Spain, Trinidad and Tobago.

Archbishop of Fort-de-France: Most Rev. MAURICE MARIE-SAINTE, Archevêché, 5–7 rue du Révérend Père Pinchon, BP 586, 97207 Fort-de-France Cédex; tel. 5-96-63-70-70; fax 5-96-63-75-21; e-mail diocesef@ais.mq.

Other Churches

Among the denominations active in Martinique are the Assembly of God, the Evangelical Church of the Nazarene and the Seventh-day Adventist Church.

The Press

Antilla: BP 46, Lamentin; tel. 5-96-75-48-68; fax 5-96-75-58-46; e-mail antilla@wanadoo.fr; weekly; Dir ALFRED FORTUNE.

Aujourd'hui Dimanche: Presbytère de Bellevue, Fort-de-France; tel. 5-96-71-48-97; weekly; Dir Père GAUTHIER; circ. 12,000.

Carib Hebdo: 97200 Fort-de-France; f. 1989; Dir GISÈLE DE LA FARGUE.

Combat Ouvrier: BP 213, 97156 Pointe-à-Pitre Cédex; e-mail combatouvrier@fr.fm; internet www.chez.com/combatouvrier; weekly; communist; Dir M. G. BEAUJOUR.

France-Antilles: pl. Stalingrad, 97200 Fort-de-France; tel. 5-96-59-08-83; fax 5-96-60-29-96; f. 1964; daily; Dir HENRI MERLE; circ. 30,000 (Martinique edition).

Justice: rue Andrè Aliker, 97200 Fort-de-France; tel. 5-96-71-86-83; fax 5-96-63-13-20; e-mail ed.justice@wanadoo.fr; weekly; organ of the PCM; Dir FERNAND PAPAYA; circ. 8,000.

Le Naif: Fort-de-France; weekly; Dir R. LAOUCHEZ.

Le Progressiste: Fort-de-France; weekly; organ of the PPM; Dir PAUL GABOURG; circ. 13,000.

Télé Sept Jours: rond-point du Vietnam Héroïque, 97200 Fort-de-France; tel. 5-96-63-75-49; weekly.

Broadcasting and Communications

BROADCASTING

Réseau France Outre-mer (RFO): La Clairière, BP 662, 97263 Fort-de-France; tel. 5-96-59-52-00; fax 5-96-63-29-88; internet www.rfo.fr; fmrly Société Nationale de Radio-Télévision Française d'Outre-mer, renamed as above 1998; broadcasts 24 hours of radio programmes daily and 37 hours of television programmes weekly; Pres. ANDRÉ-MICHEL BESSE; Regional Dir MARIJOSÉ ALIE-MONTHIEUX; Editor-in-Chief GÉRARD LE MOAL.

Radio

There are some 40 licensed private FM radio stations.

Radio Caraïbe International (RCI): 2 blvd de la Marne, 97200 Fort-de-France Cédex; tel. 5-96-63-98-70; fax 5-96-63-26-59; internet www.fwinet.com/rci.htm; commercial station broadcasting 24 hours daily; Dir YANN DUVAL.

Television

ATV Antilles Télévision: 28 rue Arawaks, 97200 Fort de France; tel. 5-96-75-44-44; fax 5-96-75-55-65; commercial station; Dir DANIEL ROBIN.

Canal Antilles: Centre Commerciale la Galléria, 97232 Le Lamentin; tel. 5-96-50-57-87; private commercial station.

Finance

(cap. = capital; res = reserves; dep. = deposits; m. = million; brs = branches; amounts in French francs)

BANKING

Central Bank

Institut d'Emission des Départements d'Outre-mer (IEDOM): 8 blvd du Général de Gaulle, BP 512, 97206 Fort-de-France Cédex; tel. 5-96-59-44-00; fax 5-96-59-44-04; internet www.iedom-ieom.com; Dir JEAN-PIERRE DERANCOURT.

Major Commercial Banks

Banque des Antilles Françaises: 28–34 rue Lamartine, BP 582, 97207 Fort-de-France Cédex; tel. 5-96-73-93-44; fax 5-96-63-58-94; internet www.bdaf.gp; f. 1853; Dir ALBERT CLERMONT.

Banque Française Commerciale Antilles Guyane: 6–10 rue Ernest Deproge, BP 986, 97200 Fort-de-France; tel. 5-96-63-82-57; fax 5-96-70-51-15; Man. EDDY MANGATTALE.

BRED Banque Populaire: 5 Place Monseigneur Romero, 97200 Fort-de-France; tel. 5-96-63-77-63; internet www.bred.fr; Chair. STEVE GENTILI.

Crédit Agricole: rue Case Nègre–Place d'Armes, 97232 Le Lamentin Cédex 2; tel. 5-96-66-59-39; fax 5-96-66-59-67; internet www.credit-agricole.fr; Chair MARC BUÉ.

Crédit Martiniquais: 17 rue de la Liberté, 97200 Fort-de-France; tel. 5-96-59-93-00; fax 5-96-60-29-30; f. 1922; associated since 1987 with Chase Manhattan Bank (USA) and, since 1990, with Mutuelles du Mans Vie (France); cap. 185.4m. (1998); Administrator ALAIN DENNHARDT; 10 brs.

Fédération du Crédit Mutuel Antilles-Guyane: rue du Professeur Raymond Garcin, 97200 Fort-de-France.

Société Générale de Banque aux Antilles: 19 rue de la Liberté, BP 408, 97200 Fort-de-France; tel. 5-96-71-69-83; f. 1979; cap. 15m. Dir MICHEL SAMOUR.

Development Bank

Société de crédit pour le développement de Martinique (SODEMA): 12 blvd du Général de Gaulle, BP 575, 97242 Fort-de-France Cédex; tel. 5-96-72-87-72; fax 5-96-72-87-70; e-mail sodema@compuserve.com; f. 1970; part of the Agence Française de Développement (AFD—see entry below, see p. 1692); cap. 25m. frs; medium- and long-term finance; Dir-Gen. JACKIE BATHANY.

INSURANCE

Caraïbe Assurances: 11 rue Victor Hugo, BP 210, 97202 Fort-de-France; tel. 5-96-63-92-29; fax 5-96-63-19-79.

Groupement Français d'Assurances Caraïbes (GFA Caraïbes): 46–48 rue Ernest Desproges, 97205 Fort-de-France; tel. 5-96-59-04-04; fax 5-96-73-19-72.

La Nationale (GAN): 30 blvd Général de Gaulle, BP 185, Fort-de-France; tel. 5-96-71-30-07; Reps MARCEL BOULLANGER, ROGER BOULLANGER.

Le Secours: 74 ave Duparquet, 97200 Fort-de-France; tel. 5-96-70-03-79; Dir Y. ANGANI.

Trade and Industry

GOVERNMENT AGENCY

Direction Régionale de l'Industrie, de la Recherche et de l'Environnement (DRIRE): see chapter on French Guiana (see p. 1480).

DEVELOPMENT ORGANIZATIONS

Agence Française de Développement (AFD): Immeuble AFD/IEDOM, 12 blvd du Général de Gaulle, BP 804, 97244 Fort-de-France Cédex; tel. 5-96-59-44-73; fax 5-96-59-44-88; e-mail afdfdf@wanadoo.fr; internet www.afd.fr; fmrly Caisse Française de Développement; Man. ALAIN DAHLEM.

Bureau du Développement Economique: Préfecture, 97262 Fort-de-France; tel. 5-96-39-36-00; fax 5-96-71-40-29; research, documentation and technical and administrative advice on investment in industry and commerce; Chief VICTOR VÉLAIDOMESTRY.

Société de Développement Régional Antilles-Guyane (SODERAG): 111–113 rue Ernest Desproges, BP 450, 97205 Fort-de-France Cédex; tel. 5-96-59-71-00; fax 5-96-63-38-88; Dir-Gen. FULVIO MAZZEO; Sec.-Gen. OLYMPE FRANCIL.

CHAMBERS OF COMMERCE

Chambre d'Agriculture: pl. d'Armes, BP 312, 97286 Le Lamentin; tel. 5-96-51-75-75; fax 5-96-51-76-77; Pres. GUY OVIDE-ETIENNE.

Chambre de Commerce et d'Industrie de la Martinique: 50–54 rue Ernest Desproge, BP 478, 97241 Fort-de-France; tel. 5-96-55-28-00; fax 5-96-60-66-68; e-mail ccim.doi@martinique.cci.fr; internet www.martinique.cci.fr; f. 1907; Pres. JEAN-CLAUDE LUBIN; Dir-Gen. FERNAND LERYCHARD.

Chambre des Métiers de la Martinique: 2 rue du Temple, Morne Tartenson, BP 1194, 97200 Fort-de-France; tel. 5-96-71-32-22; fax 5-96-70-47-30; f. 1970; Pres. CHRISTIAN CAYOL; 8,000 mems.

EMPLOYERS' ORGANIZATIONS

Groupement de Producteurs d'Ananas de la Martinique: Fort-de-France; f. 1967; Pres. C. DE GRYSE.

Ordre des Médecins de la Martinique: 80 rue de la République, 97200 Fort-de-France; tel. 5-96-63-27-01; Pres. Dr RENÉ LEGENDRI.

Ordre des Pharmaciens de la Martinique: BP 587, 97207 Fort-de-France Cédex; tel. 5-96-52-23-67; fax 5-96-52-20-92; e-mail ordrepharmacienmartinik@wanadoo.fr.

Société Coopérative d'Intérêt Collectif Agricole Bananière de la Martinique (SICABAM): Domaine de Montgéralde, La Dillon, 97200 Fort-de-France; f. 1961; Pres. ALEX ASSIER DE POMPIGNAN; Dir GÉRARD BALLY; 1,000 mems.

Syndicat des Distilleries Agricoles: Fort-de-France; tel. 5-96-71-25-46.

Syndicat des Producteurs de Rhum Agricole: La Dillon, 97200 Fort-de-France.

Union Départementale des Coopératives Agricoles de la Martinique: Fort-de-France; Pres. M. URSULET.

TRADE UNIONS

Centrale Démocratique Martiniquaise des Travailleurs: BP 21, 97201 Fort-de-France; tel. 5-96-70-19-86; fax 5-96-71-32-25; Sec.-Gen. CATHERINE FELIX.

Confédération Générale des Travailleurs de la Martinique (1936): Maison des Syndicats, porte no 14, Jardin Desclieux, 97200 Fort-de-France; tel. 5-96-60-45-21; f. 1936; affiliated to World Federation of Trade Unions; Sec.-Gen. LUC BERNABÉ; c. 12,000 mems.

Syndicat des Enseignants SE—UNSA Martinique: 8 Ter rue Félix Eboué, 97200 Fort-de-France; tel. 5-96-70-24-52; fax 5-96-63-74-36; e-mail se-gen-972@cgit.com.

Union Départementale des Syndicats (FO): BP 1114, 97248 Fort-de-France Cédex; affiliated to International Confederation of Free Trade Unions; Sec.-Gen. ALBERT SABEL; c. 2,000 mems.

Transport

RAILWAYS

There are no railways in Martinique.

ROADS

There were 2,077 km of roads in 1998, of which 261 km were motorways and first-class roads.

SHIPPING

Direction des Concessions Services Portuaires: Quai de l'Hydro Base, BP 782, 97244 Fort-de-France Cédex; tel. 5-96-59-00-00; fax 5-96-71-35-73; e-mail port@martinique.cci.fr; port services management; Dir FRANTZ THODIARD; Operations Man. VICTOR EUSTACHE.

Direction Départementale des Affaires Maritimes: blvd Chevalier de Sainte-Marthe, BP 620, 97261 Fort-de-France Cédex; tel. 5-96-71-90-05; fax 5-96-63-67-30; Dir FRANÇOIS NIHOUL.

Alcoa Steamship Co, Alpine Line, Agdwa Line, Delta Line, Raymond Witcomb Co, Moore MacCormack, Eastern Steamship Co: c/o Etablissements Ren, Cottrell, Fort-de-France.

American President Lines: c/o Compagnie d'Agence Multiples Antillaise (CAMA), 44 rue Garnier Pages, 97205 Fort-de-France Cédex; tel. 5-96-71-31-00; fax 5-96-63-54-40.

CMA-CGM CGM Antilles-Guyane: 8 ave Maurice Bishop, BP 574, 97242 Fort-de-France Cédex; tel. 5-96-55-32-05; fax 5-96-60-47-84; e-mail fdf.jdurand@cma-cgm.com; internet www.cma-cgm.com; also represents other passenger and freight lines; Dir. JEAN-LUC DURAND.

Compagnie de Navigation Mixte: Immeuble Rocade, La Dillon, BP 1023, 97209 Fort-de-France; Rep. R. M. MICHAUX.

CIVIL AVIATION

Martinique's international airport is at Le Lamentin, 6 km from Fort-de-France.

Direction des Services Aéroportuaires: BP 279, 97285 Le Lamentin; tel. 5-96-42-16-00; fax 5-96-42-18-77.

Air Caraïbe: see chapter on Guadeloupe (Civil Aviation, see p. 1687).

Tourism

Martinique's tourist attractions are its beaches and coastal scenery, its mountainous interior, and the historic towns of Fort-de-France and Saint Pierre. In 2000 tourist arrivals totalled 526,290. Tourism receipts in 1998 totalled 1,580.4m. French francs. In 2000 there were 117 hotels, with some 5,115 rooms.

Agence Régionale pour le Développement du Tourisme en Martinique: Anse Gouraud, 97233 Schoelcher; tel. 5-96-61-61-77; fax 5-96-61-22-72.

Délégation Régionale au Tourisme: 41 rue Gabriel Périé 97200 Fort-de-France; tel. 5-96-63-18-61; Dir GILBERT LECURIEUK.

Fédération Martiniquaise des Offices de Tourisme et Syndicats d'Initiative (FMOTSI): Maison du Tourisme Vert, 9 blvd du Général de Gaulle, BP 491, 97207 Fort-de-France Cédex; tel. 5-96-63-18-54; fax 5-96-70-17-61; f. 1984; Pres. VICTOR GRANDIN.

Office Départemental du Tourisme de la Martinique: 2 rue Ernest Desproges, BP 520, 97206 Fort-de-France; tel. 5-96-63-79-60; fax 5-96-73-66-93.

RÉUNION

Introductory Survey

Location, Climate, Language, Religion, Capital

Réunion is an island in the Indian Ocean, lying about 800 km (500 miles) east of Madagascar. The climate varies greatly according to altitude: at sea-level it is tropical, with average temperatures between 20°C (68°F) and 28°C (82°F), but in the uplands it is much cooler, with average temperatures between 8°C (46°F) and 19°C (66°F). Rainfall is abundant, averaging 4,714 mm annually in the uplands, and 686 mm at sea-level. The population is of mixed origin, including people of European, African, Indian and Chinese descent. The official language is French. A large majority of the population are Christians belonging to the Roman Catholic Church. The capital is Saint-Denis.

Recent History

Réunion was first occupied by France in 1642, and was ruled as a colony until 1946, when it received full departmental status. In 1974 it became an Overseas Department with the status of a region.

In 1978 the Organization of African Unity (OAU, now the African Union, see p. 130) adopted a report recommending measures to hasten the independence of the island, and condemned its occupation by a 'colonial power'. However, this view seemed to have little popular support in Réunion. Although the left-wing political parties on the island advocated increased autonomy (amounting to virtual self-government), few people were in favour of complete independence.

In 1982 the French Government proposed a decentralization scheme, envisaging the dissolution of the General and Regional Councils in the Overseas Departments and the creation in each department of a single assembly, to be elected on the basis of proportional representation. As a result of considerable opposition in Réunion and the other Overseas Departments, the Government was eventually forced to abandon the project. Revised legislation on decentralization in the Overseas Departments, however, was approved by the French National Assembly (Assemblée Nationale) in December 1982. Elections to the Regional Council (Conseil Régional) took place in Réunion in February 1983, when left-wing candidates won 50.8% of the votes cast.

In elections to the Assemblée Nationale in March 1986, Réunion's representation was increased from three to five deputies. The Parti Communiste Réunionnais (PCR) won two seats, while the Union pour la Démocratie Française (UDF), the Rassemblement pour la République (RPR) and a newly formed right-wing party, France-Réunion-Avenir (FRA), each secured one seat. In the concurrent elections to the Conseil Régional, an alliance between the RPR and the UDF obtained 18 of the 45 seats, while the PCR secured 13 and the FRA eight. The leader of the FRA, Pierre Lagourgue, was elected as President of the Conseil Régional.

In the second round of the French presidential election in May 1988, François Mitterrand, the incumbent President and a candidate of the Parti Socialiste (PS), received 60.3% of the votes cast in Réunion, while Jacques Chirac, the RPR Prime Minister, obtained 39.7%. At elections to the Assemblée Nationale in June, the PCR won two of the seats allocated to Réunion, while the UDF and the RPR (which contested the elections jointly as the Union du Rassemblement du Centre—URC), and the FRA each won one seat. (The RPR and FRA deputies later became independents, although they maintained strong links with the island's right-wing groups.) Relations between the PCR and the PS subsequently deteriorated, following mutual recriminations concerning their failure to co-operate in the general election.

In the elections for the newly enlarged 44-member General Council (Conseil Général) in September and October 1988, the PCR and the PS won nine and four seats respectively, while left-wing independent candidates obtained two seats. The UDF secured six seats and right-wing independent candidates 19, but the RPR, which had previously held 11 seats, won only four. Later in October, Eric Boyer, a right-wing independent candidate, was elected as President of the Conseil Général. The results of the municipal elections in March 1989 represented a slight decline in support for the left-wing parties; for the first time since the 1940s, however, a PS candidate, Gilbert Annette, became mayor of Saint-Denis.

In September 1990, following the restructuring of the RPR under the new local leadership of Alain Defaud, several right-wing and centrist movements, including the UDF and the RPR, established an informal alliance, known as the Union pour la France (UPF), to contest the regional elections in 1992. During a visit to Réunion in November 1990 the French Minister for Overseas Departments and Territories, Louis Le Pensec, announced a series of proposed economic and social measures, in accordance with the pledges made by Mitterrand in 1988 regarding the promotion of economic development and social equality between the Overseas Departments and metropolitan France. However, the proposals were criticized as insufficient by right-wing groups and by the PCR. Following a meeting in Paris between Le Pensec and a delegation from Réunion, the adoption of a programme of social and economic measures was announced in April 1991.

In March 1990 violent protests took place in support of an unauthorized television service, Télé Free-DOM, following a decision by the French national broadcasting commission, the Conseil Supérieur de l'Audiovisuel (CSA), to award a broadcasting permit to a rival company. In February 1991 the seizure by the CSA of Télé Free-DOM's broadcasting transmitters prompted renewed demonstrations in Saint-Denis. Some 11 people were killed in ensuing riots, and the French Government dispatched police reinforcements to restore order. Le Pensec, who subsequently visited Réunion, ascribed the violence to widespread discontent with the island's social and economic conditions. In March a commission of enquiry attributed the riots in February to the inflammatory nature of television programmes that had been broadcast by Télé Free-DOM in the weeks preceding the disturbances, and cited the station's director, Dr Camille Sudre, as responsible. However, the commission refuted allegations by right-wing and centrist politicians that the PCR had orchestrated the violence.

In March 1992 Annette expelled Sudre, who was one of the deputy mayors of Saint-Denis, from the majority coalition in the municipal council, after Sudre presented a list of independent candidates to contest the forthcoming regional elections. In the elections to the Conseil Régional, which took place on 22 March, Sudre's list of candidates (known as Free-DOM) secured 17 seats, while the UPF obtained 14 seats, the PCR nine seats and the PS five seats. In concurrent elections to the Conseil Général (newly enlarged to 47 seats), right-wing independent candidates won 20 seats, although the number of PCR deputies increased to 12, and the number of PS deputies to six; Boyer retained the presidency of the Conseil. Following the elections, the Free-DOM list of candidates formed an alliance with the PCR, thereby obtaining a narrow majority of 26 of the 45 seats in the Conseil Régional. Under the terms of the agreement, Sudre was to assume the presidency of the Conseil Régional. Sudre was accordingly elected as President of the Conseil Régional by a

majority of 27 votes, with the support of members of the PCR. The PS subsequently appealed against the results of the regional elections on the grounds of media bias; Sudre's privately owned radio station, Radio Free-DOM, had campaigned on his behalf prior to the elections. Following his election to the presidency of the Conseil Régional, Sudre announced that Télé Free-DOM was shortly to resume broadcasting. The CSA indicated, however, that it would continue to regard transmissions by Télé Free-DOM as illegal, and liable to judicial proceedings. Jean-Paul Virapoullé, a deputy to the Assemblée Nationale, subsequently proposed the adoption of legislation that would legalize Télé Free-DOM and would provide for the establishment of an independent media sector on Réunion. In April Télé Free-DOM's transmitters were returned, and at the end of May a full broadcasting service was resumed (without the permission of the CSA).

In June 1992 a delegation from the Conseil Régional met President Mitterrand to submit proposals for economic reforms, in accordance with the aim of establishing parity between Réunion and metropolitan France. In early July, however, the French Government announced increases in social security benefits that were substantially less than had been expected, resulting in widespread discontent on the island. In September the PCR demanded that the electorate refuse to participate in the forthcoming French referendum on ratification of the Treaty on European Union (see p. 199), in protest at the alleged failure of the French Government to recognize the requirements of the Overseas Departments. At the referendum, which took place later that month, the ratification of the Treaty was approved by the voters of Réunion, although only 26.3% of the registered electorate voted.

At the end of September 1992 Boyer and the former President of the Conseil Régional, Pierre Lagourgue, were elected as representatives to the French Senate (Sénat). (The RPR candidate, Paul Moreau, retained his seat.) In October the investigation of allegations that members of the Conseil Général had misappropriated funds and obtained contracts by fraudulent means commenced. In December increasing discontent with deteriorating economic conditions on Réunion prompted violent rioting in Saint-Denis and in the town of Le Port.

In March 1993 Sudre announced that he was to contest Virapoullé's seat on behalf of the Free-DOM–PCR alliance in the forthcoming elections to the Assemblée Nationale. However, at the elections, which took place later that month, Sudre was defeated by Virapoullé in the second round of voting, while another incumbent right-wing deputy, André Thien Ah Koon (who contested the elections on behalf of the UPF), also retained his seat. The PCR, the PS and the RPR each secured one of the remaining seats.

In May 1993 the French Conseil d'Etat declared the results of the regional elections in March 1992 to be invalid, and prohibited Sudre from engaging in political activity for a year, on the grounds that programmes broadcast by Radio Free-DOM prior to the elections constituted political propaganda. Sudre subsequently nominated his wife, Margie, to assume his candidacy in further elections to the Conseil Régional. In the elections, which took place in June 1993, the Free-DOM list of candidates, headed by Margie Sudre, secured 12 seats, while the UDF obtained 10 seats, the RPR eight seats, the PCR nine seats and the PS six seats. Margie Sudre was subsequently elected as President of the Conseil Régional, with the support of the nine PCR deputies and three dissident members of the PS, obtaining a total of 24 votes.

In April 1993 a number of prominent business executives were arrested in connection with the acquisition of contracts by fraudulent means; several senior politicians, including Boyer and Pierre Vergès (the mayor of Le Port and son of Paul Vergès), were also implicated in malpractice, following the investigation into their activities. Both Boyer and Pierre Vergès subsequently fled in order to evade arrest. In August Boyer, who had surrendered to the security forces, was formally charged with corruption and placed in detention. (Joseph Sinimalé, a member of the RPR, temporarily assumed the office of President of the Conseil Général.)

In January 1994 Jules Raux, a deputy mayor of Saint-Denis who was also the local treasurer of the PS, was arrested on charges of corruption: it was alleged that both local and French enterprises had obtained contracts from the Saint-Denis municipality in exchange for a share in profits (which was apparently used, in part, to finance PS activities on the island). In February two municipal councillors from Saint-Denis were arrested on suspicion of involvement in the affair. In the same month a French citizen was arrested on Réunion on charges of having transferred the funds that had been illegally obtained by the Saint-Denis municipality to enterprises in Djibouti. In March Annette, who was implicated in the affair, resigned as mayor of Saint-Denis, and was subsequently charged with corruption. Later that month Boyer and Moussa were convicted and sentenced to terms of imprisonment.

At elections to the Conseil Général, which took place in March 1994, the PCR retained 12 seats, while the number of PS deputies increased to 12. The number of seats held by the RPR and UDF declined to five and 11 respectively. The RPR and UDF subsequently attempted to negotiate an alliance with the PCR; however, the PCR and PS established a coalition (despite the long-standing differences between the two parties), thereby securing the support of 24 of the 47 seats in the Conseil Général. In April a member of the PS, Christophe Payet, was elected President of the Conseil Général (obtaining 26 votes), defeating Sinimalé; the right-wing parties (which had held the presidency of the Conseil Général for more than 40 years) boycotted the poll. The PS and PCR signed an agreement whereby the two parties were to control the administration of the Conseil Général jointly, and indicated that centrist deputies might be allowed to join the alliance. In July, following a judicial appeal, Boyer's custodial sentence was reduced to a term of one year.

In November 1994 an official visit to Réunion by the French Prime Minister, Edouard Balladur (who intended to contest the French presidential election in early 1995), prompted strike action in protest at his opposition to the establishment of social equality between the Overseas Departments and metropolitan France. Jacques Chirac, who was the official presidential candidate of the RPR, visited the island in December; the organ of the PCR, *Témoignages* (which had criticized Balladur), declared its approval of Chirac's stated commitment to the issue of social equality. In the second round of the presidential election, which took place in May 1995, the socialist candidate, Lionel Jospin, secured 56% of votes cast on Réunion, while Chirac won 44% of the votes (although Chirac obtained the highest number of votes overall); the PCR and Free-DOM had urged their supporters not to vote for Balladur in the first round, owing to his opposition to the principle of social equality between the Overseas Departments and metropolitan France. Following Chirac's election to the French presidency, Margie Sudre was nominated Minister of State with responsibility for Francophone Affairs, prompting concern among right-wing organizations on Réunion.

In August 1995 Pierre Vergès was sentenced *in absentia* to a custodial term of 18 months; an appeal was rejected in July 1996. In September the mayor of Salazie, who was a member of the RPR, was also charged with corruption. In November 1995 Boyer lost an appeal against his 1994 conviction and was expelled from the Sénat.

With effect from the beginning of 1996 the social security systems of the Overseas Departments were aligned with those of metropolitan France. In February Alain Juppé, the French Prime Minister, invited representatives from the Overseas Departments to Paris to participate in discussions on social equality and development. The main issue uniting the political representatives from Réunion was the need to align the salaries of civil servants on the island with those in metropolitan France. Several trade unionists declared themselves willing to enter into negotiations, on condition that only new recruits would be affected. Paul Vergès, joint candidate of the PCR and the PS, was elected to the Sénat in April, securing 51.9% of the votes cast. Fred K/Bidy won 40.0% of the votes, failing to retain Eric Boyer's seat for the RPR. In the by-election to replace Paul Vergès, which took place in September, Claude Hoarau, the PCR candidate, was elected as a deputy to the Assemblée Nationale with 56.0% of the votes cast, while Margie Sudre obtained 44.0%. A new majority alliance between Free-DOM, the RPR and the UDF was subsequently formed in the Conseil Régional, with the re-election of its 19-member permanent commission in October.

In October 1996 the trial of a number of politicians and business executives, who had been arrested in 1993–94 on charges of corruption, took place, after three years of investigations. Gilbert Annette and Jules Raux were convicted and, in December 1996, received custodial sentences, although Annette's sentence was reduced on appeal in December 1997. Jacques de Châteauvieux, the Chairman of Groupe Sucreries de Bourbon, was found guilty of bribery, and was also imprisoned. Two senior executives from the French enterprise, Compagnie

Générale des Eaux, were given suspended sentences, although the public prosecutor subsequently appealed for part of the sentences to be made custodial. Some 20 others were also found guilty of corruption. Pierre Vergès surrendered to the authorities in December and appeared before a magistrate in Saint-Pierre, where he was subsequently detained; in February 1997 he was released by the Court of Appeal. Also in December 1996 voting on the regional budget for 1997 was postponed three times, as a result of the abstention of eight Free-DOM councillors, led by the first Vice-President of the Conseil Régional, Jasmin Moutoussamy, who demanded the dismissal of Gilbert Payet, a Sub-Prefect and special adviser to Sudre, and greater delegation of power to the Vice-Presidents. They also objected to Sudre's alliance with the RPR-UDF majority. In late March 1997 the regional budget was eventually adopted, although Sudre and many right-wing councillors abstained from voting because of the opposition's insistence on a number of amendments, most significantly to the composition of the Conseil's permanent commission, in which it had no representation. Following the vote, Sudre suspended the session to allow for discussion between the political organizations.

Meanwhile, civil servants and students protested violently against a French government proposal, made earlier in March 1997, to undertake reform of the civil service, including a reduction in the incomes of new recruits to bring them closer to those in metropolitan France. Senator Pierre Lagourgue was designated to mediate between the French Government and the civil servants' trade unions, but strike action and demonstrations continued into April, leading to violent clashes with the security forces.

Four left-wing candidates were successful in elections to the Assemblée Nationale held in May and June 1997. Claude Hoarau (PCR) retained his seat and was joined by Huguette Bello and Elie Hoarau, also both from the PCR, and Michel Tamaya (PS), while Thien Ah Koon, representing the RPR-UDF coalition, was re-elected.

In February 1998 the PCR (led by Paul Vergès), the PS and several right-wing mayors presented a joint list of candidates, known as the Rassemblement, to contest forthcoming elections. In the elections to the Conseil Régional, which took place on 15 March, the Rassemblement secured 19 seats, while the UDF obtained nine seats and the RPR eight, with various left-wing candidates representing Free-DOM winning five. Vergès was elected President of the Conseil Régional on 23 March, with the support of the deputies belonging to the Rassemblement and Free-DOM groups. In concurrent elections to an expanded 49-member Conseil Général, right-wing candidates (including those on the Rassemblement's list) secured 27 seats, while left-wing candidates obtained 22 seats, with the PCR and the PS each winning 10 seats. At the end of the month Jean-Luc Poudroux, of the UDF, was elected President of the Conseil Général, owing to the support of two left-wing deputies.

In October 1998 Réunion's three PCR deputies to the Assemblée Nationale proposed legislation providing for the division of the island into two departments, with Saint-Pierre to join Saint-Denis as a departmental town. In December 1999, whilst attending the heads of state summit of the Indian Ocean Commission (IOC, see p. 340) on the island, President Chirac announced that he supported the creation of a second department on Réunion, as part of a number of proposed changes to the institutional future and socio-economic development of the French Overseas Departments. In March 2000 the French Secretary of State for Overseas Departments, Jean-Jack Queyranne, declared that Réunion was to be divided into two departments, Réunion South and Réunion North, as of 1 January 2001. However, both the proposed date and the geographical division of the island were rejected by the PS, although it stated that it remained in favour of the creation of a second department. The leader of the UDF, Virapoullé, expressed his opposition to the proposals. Demonstrations both for and against the division of the island took place in March 2000. It was subsequently agreed that the proposals would not be effected until 1 January 2002, and changes were made to the initial plans regarding the division of the island. However, on 15 June 2000 the creation of a second department was rejected by the Sénat by 203 votes to 111. In November the Assemblée Nationale definitively rejected the creation of a second department, but approved the changes to the institutional future of the Overseas Departments, which were finally ratified by the Constitutional Council in December. Also in that month Paul Vergès was arrested on charges of forgery and fraud in connection with his election to the Sénat in 1996.

At municipal elections, held in March 2001, the left-wing parties experienced significant losses. Notably, the PS mayor of Saint-Denis, Michel Tamaya, was defeated by the RPR candidate, René-Paul Victoria. The losses were widely interpreted as a general rejection of Jospin's proposals to create a second department on the island. At elections to the Conseil Général, held concurrently, the right-wing parties also made substantial gains, obtaining 38 of the 49 seats; the UDF retained its majority, and Poudroux was re-elected as President. In July Elie Hoarau was obliged to resign from the Assemblée Nationale, following his condemnation on charges of electoral fraud, as a result of which he received a one-year prison sentence and was banned from holding public office for a period of three years.

In January 2002 Réunion's infrastructure was severely damaged by Cyclone Dina, which also destroyed a large proportion of the crops on the island. The French Government later pledged some €32.5m. in aid to assist in the island's rehabilitation. In the first round of the presidential election, which was held on 21 April, Jospin secured 39.0% of the valid votes cast in the department (although he was eliminated nationally), followed by Chirac, who received 37.1%. In the second round, on 5 May, Chirac overwhelmingly defeated the candidate of the extreme right-wing Front National, Jean-Marie Le Pen, with 91.9% of the vote. At elections to the Assemblée Nationale in June, Thien Ah Koon, allied to the new Union pour la Majorité Présidentielle (UMP, which had recently been formed by the merger of the RPR, the Démocratie Libérale and elements of the UDF), and Bello were re-elected. Tamaya lost his seat to Victoria of the UMP, Claude Hourau lost to Bertho Audifax of the UMP, while Elie Hourau, who was declared ineligible to stand for re-election, was replaced by Christophe Payet of the PS.

In January 1986 France was admitted to the IOC, owing to its sovereignty over Réunion. Réunion was given the right to host ministerial meetings of the IOC, but would not be allowed to occupy the presidency, owing to its status as a non-sovereign state.

Government

France is represented in Réunion by an appointed Prefect. There are two councils with local powers: the 49-member Conseil Général and the 45-member Conseil Régional. Both are elected for up to six years by direct universal suffrage. Réunion sends five directly elected deputies to the Assemblée Nationale in Paris and three indirectly elected representatives to the Sénat. The Department is also represented at the European Parliament.

Defence

Réunion is the headquarters of French military forces in the Indian Ocean. At 1 August 2002 there were 4,700 French troops stationed on Réunion and Mayotte, as well as a gendarmerie of 850.

Economic Affairs

Réunion's gross national income (GNI) in 1995 was estimated at 29,200m. French francs, equivalent to about 44,300 francs per head. During 1990–97, according to World Bank estimates, Réunion's population increased at an average annual rate of 1.7%. In 1999, according to the UN, Réunion's gross domestic product (GDP) was US $7,180m., equivalent to $10,116 per head. GDP increased, in real terms, at an average annual rate of 3.0% in 1990–99; growth in 1999 was 3.0%.

Agriculture (including hunting, forestry and fishing) contributed 3.4% of GDP in 1996, and engaged 3.0% of the labour force in mid-2001. The principal cash crops are sugar cane (sugar accounted for 48.1% of export earnings in 2000), maize, tobacco, vanilla, and geraniums and vetiver root, which are cultivated for the production of essential oils. Fishing and live-stock production are also important to the economy. According to the UN, agricultural GDP increased at an average annual rate of 3.9% during 1990–2000; growth in 1998 was 3.0%.

Industry (including mining, manufacturing, construction and power) contributed 13.2% of GDP in 1996, and employed 14.1% of the working population in 1999. The principal branch of manufacturing is food-processing, particularly the production of sugar and rum. Other significant sectors include the fabrication of construction materials, mechanics, printing, metalwork, textiles and garments, and electronics. According to the UN, industrial GDP increased at an average annual rate of 4.3% during 1990–98; growth in 1998 was 3.6%.

There are no mineral resources on the island. Energy is derived principally from thermal and hydroelectric power. Imports of petroleum products comprised 7.4% of the value of total imports in 2000.

Services (including transport, communications, trade and finance) contributed 83.4% of GDP in 1996, and employed 80.4% of the working population in 1999. The public sector accounts for about one-half of employment in the services sector. Tourism is also significant; in 2001 424,000 tourists visited Réunion, and tourism revenue totalled €271.5m.

In 2000 Réunion recorded a trade deficit of €2,494.6m. The principal source of imports (63.5%) in 1997 was metropolitan France; other major suppliers are Italy and Bahrain. Metropolitan France is also the principal market for exports (taking 72.1% of the total in 1997); other significant purchasers are Japan and Belgium-Luxembourg. The principal exports in 2000 were sugar and capital equipment. The principal imports in that year were prepared foodstuffs, road motor vehicles and parts, and chemical products.

In 1998 there was an estimated state budgetary deficit of 8,048.9m. French francs. The annual rate of inflation averaged 2.2% in 1990–2001; consumer prices increased by 2.3% in 2001. An estimated 31.0% of the labour force were unemployed in March 2002.

Réunion is represented by France in the Indian Ocean Commission (IOC, see p. 340). As an integral part of France, Réunion belongs to the European Union (EU, see p. 199).

Réunion has a relatively developed economy, but is dependent on financial aid from France. The economy has traditionally been based on agriculture, and is therefore vulnerable to poor climatic conditions. During the 1990s the production of sugar cane (which dominates this sector) was adversely affected by increasing urbanization, which resulted in a decline in agricultural land. In 1994 the Government indicated that it intended to give priority to the reduction of unemployment and announced a programme of economic and social development. However, Réunion's rate of unemployment remained the highest of all the French Departments in 1997, with youth unemployment of particular concern. In November of that year the French Government and the authorities on Réunion signed an agreement that was designed to create nearly 3,500 jobs for young people over a period of three years. Although favourable economic progress was reported in 1998, sustained largely by tourism, economists have identified Réunion's need to expand external trade, particularly with fellow IOC members, if the island's economy is to continue to prosper. In May 2000 the French Government announced that it had agreed to equalize the minimum taxable wage in the Overseas Departments with that of metropolitan France within a period of three years; the current minimum taxable wage in Réunion was 20% lower than that of metropolitan France. This measure was approved by the French Senate in June. In early 2001 the French Government announced that it was to spend €84m. on improving educational facilities on Réunion, as part of a major programme of investment in the Overseas Territories and Departments.

Education

Education is modelled on the French system, and is compulsory for 10 years between the ages of six and 16 years. Primary education begins at six years of age and lasts for five years. Secondary education, which begins at 11 years of age, lasts for up to seven years, comprising a first cycle of four years and a second of three years. For the academic year 2001/02 there were 44,262 pupils enrolled at 174 pre-primary schools, 77,792 at 354 primary schools, and 98,848 at 118 secondary schools. There is a university, with several faculties, providing higher education in law, economics, politics, and French language and literature, and a teacher-training college.

Public Holidays

2003: 1 January (New Year's Day), 21 April (Easter Monday), 1 May (Labour Day), 8 May (Liberation Day), 29 May (Ascension Day), 9 June (Whit Monday), 14 July (National Day, Fall of the Bastille), 15 August (Assumption), 1 November (All Saints' Day), 11 November (Armistice Day), 20 December (Abolition of Slavery Day), 25 December (Christmas Day).

2004: 1 January (New Year's Day), 12 April (Easter Monday), 1 May (Labour Day), 8 May (Liberation Day), 20 May (Ascension Day), 30 May (Whit Monday), 14 July (National Day, Fall of the Bastille), 15 August (Assumption), 1 November (All Saints'

Day), 11 November (Armistice Day), 20 December (Abolition of Slavery Day), 25 December (Christmas Day).

Weights and Measures

The metric system is in use.

Statistical Survey

Source (unless otherwise indicated): Institut National de la Statistique et des Etudes Economiques, Service Régional de la Réunion, 15 rue de l'Ecole, 97490 Sainte-Clotilde; tel. 48-81-00; fax 41-09-81; internet www.insee.fr/fr/insee_regions/reunion.

AREA AND POPULATION

Area: 2,507 sq km (968 sq miles).

Population: 597,828 (males 294,256, females 303,572) at census of 15 March 1990; 706,180 (males 347,076, females 359,104) at census of 8 March 1999; 741,300 (official estimate) at 1 January 2002.

Density (1 January 2002): 295.7 per sq km.

Principal Towns (population at census of March 1999): Saint-Denis (capital) 131,557; Saint-Paul 87,712; Saint-Pierre 68,915; Le Tampon 60,323; Saint-Louis 43,519; Saint-André 43,174.

Births, Marriages and Deaths (provisional figures, 2000): Registered live births 14,587 (birth rate 20.2 per 1,000); Registered marriages 3,468 (marriage rate 4.8 per 1,000); Registered deaths 3,781 (death rate 5.2 per 1,000). *2001:* Registered live births 14,541; Registered marriages 3,577; Registered deaths 3,829.

Expectation of Life (provisional figures, years at birth, 2001): Males 71.0; Females 79.4.

Economically Active Population (persons aged 15 years and over, 1999 census): Agriculture, hunting, forestry and fishing 9,562; Mining, manufacturing, electricity, gas and water 13,424; Construction 11,003; Wholesale and retail trade 24,658; Transport, storage and communications 5,494; Financing, insurance and real estate 4,851; Business services 11,225; Public administration 39,052; Education 23,325; Health and social work 17,376; Other services 13,707; Total employed 173,677 (males 100,634, females 73,043); Unemployed 124,203 (males 63,519, females 60,684); Total labour force 297,880 (males 164,153, females 133,727). Figures exclude 967 persons on compulsory military service (males 945, females 22). *2000* (estimates, '000 persons aged 15 years and over): Total employed 179.5; Unemployed 130.4; Total labour force 309.9. *Mid-2002* (estimates): Agriculture, etc. 9,000; Total labour force 303,000. (Source: FAO).

HEALTH AND WELFARE

Key Indicators

Total Fertility Rate (children per woman, 2001): 2.5.

Physicians (per 1,000 head, 2001): 2.2.

Hospital Beds (per 1,000 head, 2000): 3.7.

For definitions, see explanatory note on p. vi.

AGRICULTURE, ETC.

Principal Crops (FAO estimates, '000 metric tons, 2001): Maize 17; Potatoes 6; Sugar cane 1,812 (unofficial figure); Cabbages 14; Lettuce 4.5; Tomatoes 7; Cauliflower 8; Onions and shallots (green) 5; Bananas 6.5; Tangerines, mandarins, clementines and satsumas 7.2; Pineapples 12. Source: FAO.

Livestock (FAO estimates, '000 head, year ending September 2001): Cattle 28; Pigs 77; Sheep 1.8; Goats 38; Chickens 12,000. Source: FAO.

Livestock Products (FAO estimates, '000 metric tons, 2001): Beef and veal 1.6; Pig meat 13 (unofficial figure); Poultry meat 18.2; Cow's milk 22.5 (unofficial figure); Hen eggs 5.8. Source: FAO.

Forestry ('000 cubic metres, 1991): *Roundwood removals:* Sawlogs, veneer logs and logs for sleepers 4.2; Other industrial wood 0.9 (FAO estimate); Fuel wood 31.0 (FAO estimate); Total 36.1. *Sawnwood production:* 2.2. *1992–2001:* Annual production as in 1991 (FAO estimates). Source: FAO.

Fishing (metric tons, live weight, 2000): Capture 5,091 (Albacore 579, Yellowfin tuna 656, Bigeye tuna 167, Swordfish 1,744, Common dolphinfish 194, Marine fishes 1,084); Aquaculture 142; Total catch 5,233875. Source: FAO, *Yearbook of Fishery Statistics*.

INDUSTRY

Selected Products (metric tons, 2000, unless otherwise indicated): Sugar 203,557; Oil of geranium 6.25 (1998); Oil of vetiver root 0.24 (1998); Rum (hl) 80,888; Electric energy (million kWh) 1,757 (net production).

FINANCE

Currency and Exchange Rates: The French franc was used until the end of February 2002. Euro notes and coins were introduced on 1 January 2002, and the euro became the sole legal tender from 18 February. Some of the figures in this Survey are still in terms of francs. For details of exchange rates, see French Guiana.

Budget (million francs, 1998): *State Budget:* Revenue 7,432.1, Expenditure 15,481.0; *Regional Budget:* Revenue 2,118, Expenditure 2,090; *Departmental Budget:* Revenue 4,624, Expenditure 4,300. *2001* (forecasts, million francs): Departmental Budget: *Revenue* 4,159.8 (State revenue 2,248.6, Direct and indirect taxation 1,107.8, Loans received 350.0, Investment funds and other interests 409.5, Other revenue 43.8); *Expenditure* 4,159.8 (Public health and welfare 1,133.2, Construction 655.7, Economic affairs and employment 495.6, Local development 167.1, Education, transport, sport and culture 308.1, Public debt 551.4, Other expenditure 848.8).

Money Supply (million francs at 31 December 1996): Currency outside banks 4,050; Demand deposits at banks 7,469; Total money 11,519.

Cost of Living (Consumer Price Index for urban areas, average of monthly figures; base: 1990 = 100): All items 121.9 in 1999; 124.2 in 2000; 127.1 in 2001. Source: UN, *Monthly Bulletin of Statistics*.

Expenditure on the Gross Domestic Product (million euros at current prices, 1996): Collective final consumption expenditure 717; Individual final consumption expenditure 6,787; Increase in stocks −54; Gross fixed capital formation 1,182; *Total domestic expenditure* 8,632; Exports of goods and services 400; *Less* Imports of goods and services 2,279; *GDP in purchasers' values* 6,753. *1997* (million euros): GDP 7,615.

Gross Domestic Product by Economic Activity (million euros at current prices, 1996): Agriculture, forestry and fishing 219; Mining, manufacturing, electricity, gas and water 451; Construction 396; Wholesale and retail trade 738; Hotels and restaurants 94; Transport and communications 339; Finance and insurance 317; Public administration 838; Education, health and social work 1,645; Other marketable services 797; Other non-market services 580; *Subtotal* 6,414; *Less* Imputed bank service charge 281; *GDP at basic prices* 6,133; Taxes on products, *less* subsidies on products 620; *GDP in purchasers' values* 6,753.

EXTERNAL TRADE

Principal Commodities (million euros, 2000): *Imports c.i.f.:* Prepared foodstuffs 407.6; Articles of clothing and furs 111.6; Road motor vehicles and parts 354.1; Machinery and mechanical appliances 200.6; Radio, television and communications equipment 115.0; Chemical products 290.3; Products of cokeries, petroleum refineries and nuclear industries 202.7; Total (incl. others) 2,721.4. *Exports f.o.b.:* Crops and livestock products (unprocessed) 8.9; Prepared foodstuffs 158.0 (Sugar 109.0); Other consumer goods 11.2; Road motor vehicles and parts 11.2; Other capital goods 24.6; Intermediate goods 11.6; Total (incl. others) 226.8.

Principal Trading Partners (million francs, 1996): *Imports c.i.f.:* Bahrain 519.4; Belgium-Luxembourg 302.0; France (metropolitan) 9,348.2; Germany 466.0; Italy 515.6; Japan 299.0; South Africa 291.5; Total (incl. others) 14,251.5. *Exports f.o.b.:* Belgium-Luxembourg 56.8; France (metropolitan) 759.3; Japan 56.1; Madagascar 34.1; Mauritius 36.2; Mayotte 48.7; United Kingdom 26.6; Total (incl. others) 1,071.2.

TRANSPORT

Road Traffic (1 Jan. 2001): Motor vehicles in use 258,400.

Shipping: *Merchant Fleet* (total displacement at 31 December 1992): 21,000 grt (Source: UN, *Statistical Yearbook*); *Traffic* (2000): Vessels entered 754; Freight unloaded 2,783,700 metric tons; Freight loaded 482,300 metric tons; Passenger arrivals 13,302; Passenger departures 13,449.

Civil Aviation (commercial flights, 2001): Passenger arrivals 747,044; Passenger departures 744,788; Freight unloaded 17,945 metric tons; Freight loaded 8,881 metric tons.

TOURISM

Tourist Arrivals ('000): 394 in 1999; 430 in 2000; 424 in 2001.

Arrivals by Country of Residence (2001): France (metropolitan) 328,135; Madagascar 8,515; Mauritius 37,290; Total (incl. others) 424,000.

Tourism Receipts (million euros, excl. advance payments): 242.7 in 1999; 276.2 in 2000; 271.5 in 2001.
Source: mainly Comité du Tourisme de la Réunion.

COMMUNICATIONS MEDIA

Radio Receivers (1997): 173,000 in use. Source: UNESCO, *Statistical Yearbook*.

Television Receivers (1998): 130,000 in use. Source: UNESCO, *Statistical Yearbook*.

Telephones (main lines, 1999): 268,496. Source: International Telecommunication Union.

Facsimile Machines (1996): 9,164 in use. Source: UN, *Statistical Yearbook*.

Mobile Cellular Telephones (2000): 276,100 subscribers. Source: International Telecommunication Union.

Personal Computers ('000 in use, 1999): 32. Source: International Telecommunication Union.

Internet Users ('000, 2000): 130.0. Source: International Telecommunication Union.

Book Production (1992): 69 titles (50 books; 19 pamphlets). Source: UNESCO, *Statistical Yearbook*.

Daily Newspapers (1996): 3 (estimated average circulation 55,000 copies). Source: UNESCO, *Statistical Yearbook*.

Non-daily Newspapers (1988, estimates): 4 (average circulation 20,000 copies). Source: UNESCO, *Statistical Yearbook*.

EDUCATION

Pre-primary and Primary: Schools (2000/01) 528 (pre-primary 174, primary 354); teachers (2001/02) 6,349; pupils (2001/02) 122,054 (pre-primary 44,262, primary 77,792).

Secondary (2001/02): Schools 118; teachers 7,868; pupils 98,848.

University (2001/02): Institution 1; teaching staff 343; students 10,637.

Teacher-Training (2001/02): Institution 1; teaching staff 82; students 1,288.

Other Higher (2001/02): Students 2,945.
Source: mainly Académie de la Réunion.

Directory

The Government

(April 2003)

Prefect: GONTHIER FRIEDERICI, Préfecture, Place du Barachois, 97405 Saint-Denis Cédex; tel. 40-77-77; fax 41-73-74; e-mail prefet974@guetali.fr.

President of the General Council: JEAN-LUC POUDROUX (UDF), Hôtel du Département, 2 rue de la Source, 97400 Saint-Denis; tel. 90-30-30; fax 90-39-99.

Deputies to the French National Assembly: BERTHO AUDIFAX (UMP), HUGUETTE BELLO (PCR), CHRISTOPHE PAYET (PS), ANDRÉ THIEN AH KOON (independent right-wing, allied to the UMP), RENÉ-PAUL VICTORIA (UMP).

Representatives to the French Senate: EDMOND LAURET (UMP), LILIAN PAYET (Union Centriste), PAUL VERGÈS (PCR).

GOVERNMENT OFFICES

Direction de l'Agriculture et de la Forêt: blvd de la Providence, 97489 Saint-Denis Cédex; tel. 48-61-00; fax 48-61-99.

Direction du Développement Économique et de l'Économie Solidaire: ave de la Victoire, 97488 Saint-Denis Cédex; tel. 90-31-90; fax 90-39-89.

Direction du Développement Local, des Actions Sociales, de Santé: 2 rue de la Source, 97488 Saint-Denis Cédex; tel. 90-33-33; fax 90-39-96.

Direction de l'Environnement: 60 rue Fénélon, 97488 Saint-Denis Cédex; tel. 90-24-00; fax 90-24-19.

Direction des Finances: ave de la Victoire, 97488 Saint-Denis Cédex; tel. 90-39-39; fax 90-39-92.

Direction Générale des Services: 2 rue de la Source, 97488 Saint-Denis Cédex; tel. 90-30-30; fax 90-39-99.

Direction de l'Informatique: 19 route de la Digue, 97488 Saint-Denis Cédex; tel. 90-32-00; fax 90-32-99; e-mail fneyra@cg974.fr.

Direction des Infrastructures Départementales: 1A rue Charles Gounaud, 97488 Saint-Denis Cédex; tel. 41-56-52; fax 21-73-19; e-mail did-eau@cg974.fr.

Direction de la Logistique: 2 rue de la Source, 97488 Saint-Denis Cédex; tel. 90-31-38; fax 90-39-91.

Direction du Patrimoine: 6b rue Rontaunay, 97488 Saint-Denis Cédex; tel. 90-86-86; fax 90-86-90.

Direction de la Presse et de la Communication: 42 rue du Général de Gaulle, 97488 Saint-Denis Cédex; tel. 21-86-30; fax 21-39-45.

Direction de la Promotion Culturelle et Sportive: 18 rue de Paris, 97488 Saint-Denis Cédex; tel. 90-35-35; fax 20-26-03.

Direction de la Promotion de l'Enfance, de la Famille et de la Santé: 2 rue de la Source, 97488 Saint-Denis Cédex; tel. 90-33-33; fax 90-39-96.

Direction des Resources Humaines: 2 rue de la Source, 97488 Saint-Denis Cédex; tel. 90-37-37; fax 90-34-90.

Direction des Transports: 34 rue Notre Dame de la Source, 97488 Saint-Denis Cédex; tel. 20-38-08; fax 41-72-88.

Direction de la Vie Éducative: ave de la Victoire, 97488 Saint-Denis Cédex; tel. 90-31-31; fax 90-39-98.

CONSEIL RÉGIONAL

Hôtel de la Région Pierre Lagourgue, ave René Cassin, Le Moufia BP 402, 97494 Sainte-Clotilde Cédex; tel. 48-70-00; fax 48-70-71; e-mail emmanuelle.ganne@guetali.fr; internet www.region-reunion.com.

President: PAUL VERGÈS (PCR).

Election, 15 March 1998

Party	Seats
Le Rassemblement*	19
UDF	9
Rassemblement pour la République†	8
Free-DOM	5
Réunion France Europe	4
Total	**45**

* An alliance comprising the PCR, the PS and the MDLFT (a right-wing group).
† Merged with the Démocratie Libérale and elements of the UDF prior to elections to the Assemblée Nationale in June 2002, to form the Union pour la Majorité Présidentielle (later renamed the Union pour un Mouvement Populaire).

Political Organizations

Front National (FN)—Fédération de la Réunion: Saint-Denis; tel. 51-38-97; e-mail fatna@frontnational.com; internet www.frontnational.com; f. 1972; extreme right-wing; Sec. RICHARD ALAVIN.

Mouvement pour l'Indépendance de la Réunion (MIR): f. 1981 to succeed the fmr Mouvement pour la Libération de la Réunion; grouping of parties favouring autonomy.

Mouvement National Républicain (MNR)—Fédération de la Réunion: tel. 22-34-69; Sec. RÉMI BERTIN.

Parti Communiste Réunionnais (PCR): Saint-Denis; f. 1959; Pres. PAUL VERGÈS; Sec.-Gen. ELIE HOARAU.

Mouvement pour l'Egalité, la Démocratie, le Développement et la Nature: affiliated to the PCR; advocates political unity; Leader RENÉ PAYET.

Parti Radical de Gauche (PRG)—Fédération de la Réunion: 18 rue des Demoiselles, Hermitage les Bains, 97434 Saint-Gilles-les-Bains; tel. 33-94-73; internet www.radical-gauche.org; f. 1977; fmrly Mouvement des Radicaux de Gauche; advocates full independence and an economy separate from, but assisted by, France; Pres. RÉMY MASSAIN.

Parti Socialiste (PS)—Fédération de la Réunion: 18 ave Stanislas Gimard, 97490 Saint-Denis; tel. 97-46-42; fax 28-53-03; e-mail fede974@parti-socialiste.fr; internet www.parti-socialiste.fr; left-wing; Sec. MICHEL VERGOZ.

Rassemblement des Démocrates pour l'Avenir de la Réunion (RADAR): Saint-Denis; f. 1981; centrist.

Rassemblement des Socialistes et des Démocrates (RSD): Saint-Denis; Sec.-Gen. DANIEL CADET.

Réunion France Europe: Saint-Denis.

Union pour la Démocratie Française (UDF): Saint-Denis; internet www.udf.org; f. 1978; centrist; Pres. JEAN-PAUL VIRAPOULLÉ.

Union pour un Mouvement Populaire (UMP)—Fédération de la Réunion: 6 bis blvd Vauban, BP 11, 97461 Saint-Denis Cédex; tel. 20-21-18; fax 41-73-55; f. 2002 as Union pour la Majorité Présidentielle by mems of the fmr Rassemblement pour la République and Démocratie Libérale parties, in conjunction with elements of the UDF; Departmental Sec. RENÉ-PAUL VICTORIA.

Les Verts Réunion: BP 31, 97429 Petite île; tel. and fax 31-61-74; e-mail verts.reunion@voila.fr; internet www.chez.com/rayonvert; ecologist; Sec. V. DENES.

Judicial System

Cour d'Appel: Palais de Justice, 166 rue Juliette Dodu, 97488 Saint-Denis; tel. 40-58-58; fax 21-95-32; Pres. JEAN CLAUDE CARRIÉ.

There are two **Tribunaux de Grande Instance**, one **Tribunaux d'Instance**, two **Tribunaux pour Enfants** and two **Conseils de Prud'hommes**.

Religion

A substantial majority of the population are adherents of the Roman Catholic Church. There is a small Muslim community.

CHRISTIANITY

The Roman Catholic Church

Réunion comprises a single diocese, directly responsible to the Holy See. At 31 December 2000 there were an estimated 595,000 adherents, equivalent to some 92.2% of the population.

Bishop of Saint-Denis de la Réunion: Mgr GILBERT AUBRY, Evêché, 36 rue de Paris, BP 55, 97461 Saint-Denis Cédex; tel. 94-85-70; fax 94-85-71; e-mail evechediocesereunion@wanadoo.fr; internet www.diocese_reunion.com.

The Press

DAILIES

Journal de l'Ile de la Réunion: 357 rue du Maréchal Leclerc, BP 166, 97463 Saint-Denis Cédex; tel. 90-46-00; fax 90-46-01; f. 1956; Dir JACQUES TILLIER; circ. 35,000.

Quotidien de la Réunion et de l'Océan Indien: BP 303, 97712 Saint-Denis Cédex 9; tel. 92-15-15; fax 28-43-60; f. 1976; Dir MAXIMIN CHANE KI CHUNE; circ. 38,900.

PERIODICALS

AGRI-MAG Réunion: Chambre d'Agriculture, 24 rue de la Source, BP 134, 97463 Saint-Denis Cédex; tel. 94-25-94; fax 21-06-17; e-mail chambagri.cda-97@wanadoo.fr; f. 2001; monthly; Dir Guy Derand; Chief Editor HERVÉ CAILLEAUX; circ. 8,000.

Al-Islam: Centre Islamique de la Réunion, BP 437, 97459 Saint-Pierre Cédex; tel. 25-45-43; fax 35-58-23; e-mail info@centre-islamique.com; internet www.centre-islamique.com; f. 1975; 4 a year; Dir SAÏD INGAR.

Cahiers de la Réunion et de l'Océan Indien: 24 blvd des Cocotiers, 97434 Saint-Gilles-les-Bains; monthly; Man. Dir CLAUDETTE SAINT-MARC.

L'Economie de la Réunion: c/o INSEE, 15 rue de l'Ecole, BP 13 Le Chaudron, 97408 Saint-Denis; tel. 48-89-00; fax 48-89-89; 6 a year; Dir RENÉ JEAN; Editor-in-Chief COLETTE PAVAGEAU.

L'Eglise à la Réunion: 18 rue Montreuil, 97469 Saint-Denis; tel. 41-56-90; fax 40-92-17; e-mail eglise-reunion@wanadoo.fr; monthly; Dir ELIE CADET.

L'Enjeu: Saint-Denis; tel. 21-75-76; fax 41-60-62; Dir BLANDINE ETRAYEN; Editor-in-Chief JEAN-CLAUDE VALLÉE; circ. 4,000.

Le Journal de la Nature: Saint-Denis; tel. 29-45-45; fax 29-00-90; Dir J. Y. CONAN.

Le Memento Industriel et Commercial Réunionnais: 80 rue Pasteur, 97400 Saint-Denis; tel. 21-94-12; fax 41-10-85; e-mail memento@oceanes.fr; internet www.memento.fr; f. 1970; monthly; Dir CATHERINE LOUAPRE POTTIER; Editor GEORGES-GUILLAUME LOUAPRE POTTIER; circ. 10,000.

974 Ouest: Montgaillard, 97400 Saint-Denis; monthly; Dir DENISE ELMA.

Télé 7 Jours Réunion: 6 rue Montyon, BP 405, 93200 Saint-Denis; weekly; Dir MICHEL MEKDOUD; circ. 25,000.

Témoignage Chrétien de la Réunion: 21 bis rue de l'Est, BP 192, 97465 Saint-Denis; weekly; Dir RENÉ PAYET; circ. 2,000.

Témoignages: 21 bis rue de l'Est, BP 192, 97465 Saint-Denis; tel. 21-13-07; f. 1944; publ. of the PCR; weekly; Dir ELIE HOARAU; circ. 6,000.

Visu: 97712 Saint-Denis Cédex 9; tel. 90-20-60; fax 90-20-61; weekly; Editor-in-Chief GUY LEBLOND; circ. 53,000.

NEWS AGENCY

Imaz Press Réunion: Saint-Denis; tel. 20-05-65; fax 20-05-49; e-mail ipr@iprenunion.com; internet www.ipreunion.com.

Broadcasting and Communications

TELECOMMUNICATIONS

Cegetel: Saint-Denis; sole cellular telephone operator on Réunion; 93,000 subscribers.

BROADCASTING

Réseau France Outre-mer (RFO): 1 rue Jean Chatel, 97716 Saint-Denis Cédex; tel. 40-67-67; fax 21-64-84; internet www.rfo.fr; fmrly Société Nationale de Radio-Télévision Française d'Outre-mer; home radio and television relay services in French; operates two television channels and two radio frequencies; Pres. ANDRÉ-MICHEL BESSE; Regional Dir DOMINIQUE RICHARD; Dir of Television GÉRARD CHRISTIAN HOARAU; Dir of Radio JEAN-PAUL MELADE.

Radio

Radio Free-DOM: BP 666, 97473 Saint-Denis Cédex; tel. 41-51-51; fax 21-68-64; e-mail freedom@guetali.fr; internet www.freedom.fr; f. 1981; privately owned radio station; Dir Dr CAMILLE SUDRE.

In February 1998 there were a total of 44 authorized radio stations broadcasting in Réunion.

Television

Antenne Réunion: BP 80001, 97801 Saint-Denis Cédex 9; tel. 48-28-28; fax 48-28-29; f. 1991; broadcasts 10 hours daily; Dir PHILIPPE ROUSSEL.

Canal Réunion: 35 chemin Vavangues, 97490 Sainte-Clotilde; tel. 29-02-02; fax 29-17-09; subscription television channel; broadcasts a minimum of 19 hours daily; Chair. DOMINIQUE FAGOT; Dir JEAN-BERNARD MOURIER.

TV-4: 8 chemin Fontbrune, 97400 Saint-Denis; tel. 52-73-73; broadcasts 19 hours daily.

TV Sud: 10 rue Aristide Briand, 97430 Le Tampon; tel. 57-42-42; commenced broadcasting in 1993; broadcasts 4 hours daily.

Other privately owned television services include TVB, TVE, RTV, Télé-Réunion and TV-Run.

Finance

(cap. = capital; res = reserves; dep. = deposits; m. = million; brs = branches; amounts in French francs, unless otherwise stated)

BANKING

Central Bank

Institut d'Emission des Départements d'Outre-mer: 4 rue de la Compagnie, 97487 Saint-Denis Cédex; tel. 90-71-00; fax 21-41-32; Dir GUY DEBUYS.

Commercial Banks

Banque Française Commerciale Océan Indien (BFCOI): 60 rue Alexis de Villeneuve, BP 323, 97468 Saint-Denis Cédex; tel. 40-55-55; fax 20-09-07; Chair. PHILIPPE BRAULT; Dir PHILIPPE LAVIT D'HAUTEFORT; 8 brs.

Banque Nationale de Paris Intercontinentale: 67 rue Juliette Dodu, BP 113, 97463 Saint-Denis; tel. 40-30-30; fax 41-39-09; e-mail bnpipmv@guetali.fr; internet www.bnpgroup.com; f. 1927; 100% owned by BNP Paribas; Chair. MICHEL PEBEREAU; Man. Dir JEAN TABARIES; 11 brs.

Banque de la Réunion (BR), SA: 27 rue Jean Chatel, 97711 Saint-Denis Cédex; tel. 40-01-23; fax 40-00-61; e-mail webmestre@banquedelareunion.fr; internet www.banquedelareunion.fr; f. 1849; cap. €50.0m., res €52.0m., dep. €1,120.7m. (Dec. 2001); Pres. SERGE ROBERT; Gen. Man. MICHEL DUMAS; 12 brs.

BRED-Banque Populaire: 33 rue Victor-Mac-Auliffe, 97461 Saint-Denis; tel. 90-15-60; fax 90-15-99.

Crédit Agricole de la Réunion: Les Camélias, Cité des Lauriers, BP 84, 97462 Saint-Denis Cédex; tel. 40-81-81; fax 40-81-40; internet www.credit-agricole.fr; f. 1949; Chair. CHRISTIAN DE LA GIRODAY; Dir ERIC PRADEL.

Development Bank

Banque Populaire Fédérale de Développement: 33 rue Victor MacAuliffe, 97400 Saint-Denis; tel. 21-18-11; Dir OLIVIER DEVISME; 3 brs.

Société financière pour le développement économique de la Réunion (SOFIDER): 3 rue Labourdonnais, BP 867, 97477 Saint-Denis Cédex; tel. 40-32-32; fax 40-32-00; part of the Agence Française de Développpment; Dir-Gen. CLAUDE PÉRIOU.

INSURANCE

More than 20 major European insurance companies are represented in Saint-Denis.

Trade and Industry

DEVELOPMENT ORGANIZATIONS

Agence Française de Développement (AFD): 44 rue Jean Cocteau, 97488 Saint-Denis Cédex; tel. 90-00-90; fax 21-74-58; e-mail afdstdenis@re.groupe-afd.org.

Association pour le Développement Industriel de la Réunion: 8 rue Philibert, BP 327, 97466 Saint-Denis Cédex; tel. 94-43-00; fax 94-43-09; e-mail adir@guetali.fr; f. 1975; 190 mems; Pres. MAURICE CERISOLA.

Chambre d'Agriculture de la Réunion: 24 rue de la Source, BP 134, 97463 Saint-Denis Cédex; tel. 21-25-88; fax 21-06-17; e-mail chambagri.cda-97@wanadoo.fr; Pres. JEAN-YVES MINATCHY; Dir-Gen. FATMA BADAT.

Direction de l'Action Economique: Secrétariat Général pour les Affaires Economiques, ave de la Victoire, 97405 Saint-Denis; tel. 40-77-10; fax 40-77-01.

Jeune Chambre Economique de Saint-Denis de la Réunion: 25 rue de Paris, BP 1151, 97483 Saint-Denis; f. 1963; 30 mems; Chair. JEAN-CHRISTOPHE DUVAL.

Société de Développement Economique de la Réunion (SODERE): 26 rue Labourdonnais, 97469 Saint-Denis; tel. 20-01-68; fax 20-05-07; f. 1964; Chair. RAYMOND VIVET; Man. Dir ALBERT TRIMAILLE.

CHAMBERS OF COMMERCE

Chambre de Commerce et d'Industrie de la Réunion: 15 route de la Balance, 97410 Saint Pierre; tel. 96-96-96; fax 94-22-90; internet www.reunion.cci.fr; f. 1830; Pres. ALAIN MACÉ.

Chambre de Métiers: 42 rue Jean Cocteau, 97490 Sainte-Clotilde; tel. 21-04-35; fax 21-68-33; internet www.cm-reunion.fr.

INDUSTRIAL AND TRADE ASSOCIATIONS

Fedération Réunionnaise du Bâtiment et des Travaux Publics: BP 108, 97462 Saint-Denis Cédex; tel. 41-70-87; fax 21-55-07; Pres. J. M. LE BOURVELLEC.

Syndicat des Exportateurs d'Huiles Essentielles, Plantes Aromatiques et Medicinales de Bourbon: Saint-Denis; tel. 20-10-23; exports oil of geranium, vetiver and vanilla; Pres. RICO PLOENIÈRES.

Syndicat des Fabricants de Sucre de la Réunion: 46 rue Labourdonnais, BP 284, 97466 Saint-Denis Cédex; tel. 90-45-00; fax 41-24-13; e-mail prestsuc@groupemace.com; Chair. XAVIER THIEBLIN.

Syndicat des Producteurs de Rhum de la Réunion: 46 rue Labourdonnais, BP 284, 97466 Saint-Denis Cédex; tel. 90-45-00; fax 41-24-13; e-mail prestsuc@groupemace.com; Chair. XAVIER THIEBLIN.

TRADE UNIONS

Confédération Générale du Travail de la Réunion (CGTR): 144 rue du Général de Gaulle, BP 1132, 97482 Saint-Denis Cédex; Sec.-Gen. GEORGES MARIE LEPINAY.

Réunion also has its own sections of the major French trade union confederations, **Confédération Française Démocratique du Travail (CFDT)**, **Force Ouvrière (FO)**, **Confédération Française de l'Encadrement** and **Confédération Française des Travailleurs Chrétiens (CFTC)**.

Transport

ROADS

A route nationale circles the island, generally following the coast and linking the main towns. Another route nationale crosses the island from south-west to north-east linking Saint-Pierre and Saint-Benoît. In 1994 there were 370 km of routes nationales, 754 km of departmental roads and 1,630 km of other roads; 1,300 km of the roads were bituminized.

SHIPPING

In 1986 work was completed on the expansion of the Port de la Pointe des Galets, which was divided into the former port in the west and a new port in the east (the port Ouest and the port Est). In 2000 some 2.8m. metric tons of freight were unloaded and 482,300 tons loaded at the two ports.

Groupe CMA—CGM La Réunion: 85 rue Jules Verne, ZI no 2, BP 2007, 97822 Le Port Cédex; tel. 55-10-10; fax 43-23-04; e-mail felce.gmc-cgm@stor.fr; internet www.cma-cgm.com; f. 1996 by merger of Compagnie Générale Maritime and Compagnie Maritime d'Affrètement; shipping agents; Dir HENRI FELCE.

Réunion Maritime: f. 1991; consortium of 15 import cos; freight only.

Shipping Mediterranean Co: Le Port.

Société de Manutention et de Consignation Maritime (SOMACOM): BP 7, Le Port; shipping agents.

Société Réunionnaise de Services Maritimes: Zac 2000, BP 2006, 97822 Le Port Cédex; tel. 55-17-57; fax 55-17-58; e-mail jj.rene@dti-Reunion.com; freight only; Man. JEAN JACQUES RENÉ.

CIVIL AVIATION

Réunion's international airport, Roland Garros-Gillot, is situated 8 km from Saint-Denis, and serves daily flights to metropolitan France. A programme to develop the airport was completed in 1994, and in 1997 work commenced on the extension of its terminal, at a cost of some 175m. French francs. The Pierrefonds airfield, 5 km from Saint-Pierre, commenced operating as an international airport in December 1998, serving daily flights to Mauritius, following its development at an estimated cost of nearly 500m. French francs. An extension to the runway was planned for 2000 to enable flights to Madagascar.

Air Austral: Zone Aéroportuaire, Aéroport de la Réunion Roland Garros, 97438 Sainte-Marie, BP 611, 97472 Saint-Denis; tel. 93-10-10; fax 29-28-95; e-mail info@air-austral.com; internet www.airaustral.com; f. 1975; subsidiary of Air France; scheduled regional services; Dir-Gen. GÉRARD ETHEVE.

Air Liberté: Saint-Denis; merged with Air Outre-Mer in 2001; scheduled services to Paris; Chair. RENÉ MICAUD.

Tourism

Tourism is being extensively promoted. Réunion's attractions include spectacular scenery and a pleasant climate. In March 2001 the island had some 2,790 hotel rooms. In 2001 424,000 tourists visited Réunion, and revenue from tourism totalled €271.5m.

Comité du Tourisme de la Réunion (CTR): Place du 20 Décembre 1848, BP 615, 97472 Saint-Denis Cédex; tel. 21-00-41; fax 21-00-21; e-mail ctr@la-reunion-tourisme.com; internet www.la-reunion-tourisme.com; Pres. MARGIE SUDRE.

Délégation Régionale au Commerce, à l'Artisanat et au Tourisme: Préfecture de la Réunion, 97400 Saint-Denis; tel. 40-77-58; fax 50-77-15; e-mail DRCAT974@wanadoo.fr; Dir PHILIPPE JEAN LEGLISE.

Office du Tourisme Intercommunal du Nord: 53 rue Pasteur, 97400 Saint-Denis; tel. 41-83-00; fax 21-37-76; e-mail otinord@wanadoo.fr; Pres. JEAN-MARIE DUPUIS.

French Overseas Collectivité Départementale

The overseas Collectivité Départementale is Mayotte. It is an integral part of the French Republic and is currently administered by a Prefect, who is appointed by the French Government. The Prefect is assisted by an elected General Council (Conseil Général). Under the terms of its status, which was approved by the French Parliament in July 2001, executive power in Mayotte was to be transferred from the Prefect to the President of the Conseil Général in March 2004, and the position of Prefect dissolved by 2007. The Collectivité Départementale is represented in the French National Assembly (Assemblée Nationale) and in the Senate (Sénat) in Paris, and also in the European Parliament in Strasbourg.

MAYOTTE

Introductory Survey

Location, Climate, Language, Religion, Capital

Mayotte forms part of the Comoros archipelago, which lies between the island of Madagascar and the east coast of the African mainland. The territory comprises a main island, Mayotte (Mahoré), and a number of smaller islands. The climate is tropical, with temperatures averaging between 24°C and 27°C (75°F to 81°F) throughout the year. The official language is French, and Islam is the main religion. The capital is Dzaoudzi, which is connected to the island of Pamandzi by a causeway.

Recent History

Since the Comoros unilaterally declared independence in July 1975, Mayotte has been administered separately by France. The independent Comoran state claims sovereignty of Mayotte, and officially represents it in international organizations, including the UN. In December 1976 France introduced the special status of Collectivité Territoriale for the island. Following a coup in the Comoros in May 1978, Mayotte rejected the new Government's proposal that it should rejoin the other islands under a federal system, and reaffirmed its intention of remaining linked to France. In December 1979 the Assemblée Nationale approved legislation that extended Mayotte's special status for another five years, during which the islanders were to be consulted. In October 1984, however, the Assemblée Nationale further prolonged Mayotte's status, and the referendum on the island's future was postponed indefinitely. The UN General Assembly has adopted a number of resolutions in support of the sovereignty of the Comoros over the island. Until 1999 the main political party on Mayotte, the Mouvement Populaire Mahorais (MPM), demanded full departmental status for the island (as held by Réunion), but France was reluctant to grant this in view of Mayotte's lack of development.

At the general election to the Assemblée Nationale in March 1986, Henry Jean-Baptiste, a member of the Centre des Démocrates Sociaux (CDS), which was affiliated to the Union pour la Démocratie Française (UDF), was elected as deputy for Mayotte. During a visit to Mayotte in October the French Prime Minister, Jacques Chirac, assured the islanders that they would remain French citizens for as long as they wished. Relations between the MPM and the French Government rapidly deteriorated after the Franco-African summit in November 1987, when Chirac expressed reservations concerning the elevation of Mayotte to the status of an Overseas Department (despite his announcement, in early 1986, that he shared the MPM's aim to upgrade Mayotte's status).

In the second round of the French presidential election, which took place in May 1988, François Mitterrand, the incumbent President and the candidate of the Parti Socialiste (PS), received 50.3% of the votes cast on Mayotte, defeating Chirac, the candidate of the Rassemblement pour la République (RPR). At elections to the Assemblée Nationale, which took place in June, Jean-Baptiste retained his seat. (Later that month, he joined the newly formed centrist group in the Assemblée Nationale, the Union du Centre—UDC.) In elections to the Conseil Général in September and October, the MPM retained the majority of seats. In November the Conseil Général demanded that the French Government introduce measures to restrict immigration to Mayotte from neighbouring islands, particularly from the Comoros.

In 1989–1990 concern about the number of Comoran immigrants seeking employment on the island resulted in an increase in racial tension. In 1989 more than 150 Comoran refugees were prevented from landing on Mayotte by security forces. In January 1990 demonstrators in the town of Mamoudzou protested against illegal immigration to the island. A paramilitary organization, known as Caiman, was subsequently formed in support of the expulsion of illegal immigrants, but was refused legal recognition by the authorities.

At elections to the Conseil Général, which took place in March 1991, the MPM secured an additional three seats, although Younoussa Bamana, the President of the Conseil Général and leader of the MPM, was defeated in his canton, Keni-Keli, by the RPR candidate. In April, however, Bamana secured the majority of votes cast in a partial election, which took place in the canton of Chicani, and was subsequently re-elected to the presidency of the Conseil Général.

In June 1992 increasing resentment resulted in further attacks against Comoran immigrants resident in Mayotte. In early September representatives of the MPM met the French Prime Minister, Pierre Bérégovoy, to request the reintroduction of entry visas to restrict immigration from the Comoros. Later that month the MPM organized a boycott of Mayotte's participation in the French referendum on the Treaty on European Union (see p. 199), in support of the provision of entry visas. In December the Prefect, Jean-Paul Costes, and a number of other prominent officials were charged in connection with the deaths of six people in domestic fires, which had been caused by dangerous fuel imported from Bahrain. In February 1993 a general strike, which was staged in support of claims for wage increases, culminated in protracted violent rioting. Security forces were subsequently dispatched from Réunion to restore order, while trade unions agreed to end the strike. Later that month Costes was replaced as Prefect.

At elections to the Assemblée Nationale, which took place in March 1993, Jean-Baptiste was returned, securing 53.4% of votes cast, while the Secretary-General of the RPR, Mansour Kamardine, received 44.3% of the votes. Kamardine (who contested the elections as an independent candidate) subsequently accused Jean-Baptiste of illegally claiming the support of an electoral alliance of the RPR and the UDF, known as the Union pour la France, by forging the signatures of party officials on a document. Jean-Baptiste, however, denied the allegations, and began legal proceedings against Kamardine for calumny.

Elections to the Conseil Général (which was enlarged from 17 to 19 members) took place in March 1994: the MPM retained 12 seats, while the RPR secured four seats, and independent candidates three seats. During an official visit to Mayotte in November, the French Prime Minister, Edouard Balladur, announced the reintroduction of entry visas as a requirement for Comoran nationals, and the adoption of a number of security measures, in an effort to reduce illegal immigration to the island. In January 1995 the reimposition of visa requirements prompted widespread protests on the Comoros; the Comoran Government suspended transport links between Mayotte and the Comoros in response to the measure. In the first round of the French presidential election in April, Balladur received the highest number of votes on Mayotte (although Chirac subsequently won the election).

In elections to the Sénat in September, the incumbent MPM representative, Marcel Henry, was returned by a large majority. During a visit to Mayotte in October, the French Secretary of State for Overseas Departments and Territories pledged that a referendum on the future status of the island would be conducted by 1999. In October 1996 he confirmed that two commissions, based in Paris and Mayotte, were preparing a consultation document, which would be presented in late 1997, and announced that the resulting referendum would take place before the end of the decade.

Partial elections to fill nine seats in the Conseil Général were held in March 1997; the MPM secured three seats (losing two that it had previously held), the RPR won three seats, the local PS one seat, and independent right-wing candidates two seats. In elections to the Assemblée Nationale Jean-Baptiste, representing the alliance of the UDF and the Force Démocrate (FD, formerly the CDS), defeated Kamardine, securing 51.7% of votes cast in the second round of voting, which took place in June.

In July 1997 the relative prosperity of Mayotte was believed to have prompted separatist movements on the Comoran islands of Nzwani and Mwali to demand the restoration of French rule, and subsequently to declare their independence in August. Illegal immigration from the Comoros continued to prove a major concern for the authorities on Mayotte; during January–February 1997 some 6,000 Comorans were expelled from the island, with many more agreeing to leave voluntarily.

Meanwhile, uncertainty remained over the future status of Mayotte. In April 1998 one of the commissions charged with examining the issue submitted its report, which concluded that the present status of Collectivité Territoriale was no longer appropriate, but did not advocate an alternative. In May the MPM declared its support for an adapted form of departmental administration, and urged the French authorities to decide on a date for a referendum. In July Pierre Bayle succeeded Philippe Boisadam as Prefect. In December two rounds of preparatory talks on the island's future constitutional status took place between local political organizations and senior French government officials. However, further negotiations, which were to be held in February 1999, were suspended, owing to France's concerns over the political instability in the Comoros. In May Bamana made an appeal that the inhabitants of Mayotte be allowed to organize their own vote on their future, and later that month Jean-Baptiste introduced a draft piece of legislation to the Assemblée Nationale, which proposed the holding of a referendum regarding the island's future before the end of 1999. In August, following negotiations between the French Secretary of State for Overseas Departments and Territories, Jean-Jack Queyranne, and island representatives, Mayotte members of the RPR and the PS and Bamana (the leader of the MPM) signed a draft document providing for the transformation of Mayotte into a Collectivité Départementale, if approved at a referendum. However, both Henry and Jean-Baptiste rejected the document. The two politicians subsequently announced their departure from the MPM and formed a new political party entitled the Mouvement Départementaliste Mahorais (MDM), while reiterating their demands that Mayotte be granted full overseas departmental status.

Following the approval of Mayotte's proposed new status by the Conseil Général (by 14 votes to five) and the municipal councils, an accord to this effect was signed by Queyranne and political representatives of Mayotte on 27 January 2000. On 2 July a referendum was held, in which the population of Mayotte voted overwhelmingly in favour of the January accord, granting Mayotte the status of Collectivité Départementale for a period of 10 years. In November the commission established to define the terms of Mayotte's new status published a report, which envisaged the transfer of executive power from the Prefect to the Conseil Général by 2004, the dissolution of the position of Prefect by 2007 and the concession of greater powers to the local Government, notably in the area of regional co-operation.

At elections to the Conseil Général, held in March 2001, no party established a majority. The MPM experienced significant losses, with only four of its candidates being elected, while the RPR won five seats, the Mouvement des Citoyens two, the MDM one, the PS one, and various right-wing independent candidates six seats. Bamana was re-elected as President of the Conseil Général. The French Parliament approved Mayotte's status as a Collectivité Départementale in July 2001. In September Philippe de Mester succeeded Bayle as Prefect.

In the first round of the French presidential election, which was held on 21 April 2002, Chirac received the highest number of votes on Mayotte, winning 43.0% of the valid votes cast; the second round, held on 5 May, was also won resoundingly by Chirac, who secured 88.3% of votes cast on the island, defeating the candidate of the extreme right-wing Front National, Jean-

Marie Le Pen. At elections to the Assemblée Nationale, held in June, Jean-Baptiste did not stand. Kamardine, representing the recently formed Union pour la Majorité Présidentielle (UMP, which incorporated the RPR, the Démocratie Libérale and significant elements of the UDF), defeated the MDM-UDF candidate, Siadi Vita. Jean-Jacques Brot replaced de Mester as Prefect in July. In November the UMP was renamed the Union pour un Mouvement Populaire.

(For further details of the recent history of the island, see the chapter on the Comoros.)

Government

The French Government is currently represented in Mayotte by an appointed Prefect. There is a Conseil Général, with 19 members, elected by universal adult suffrage. Mayotte elects one deputy to the Assemblée Nationale, and one representative to the Sénat. Mayotte is also represented at the European Parliament. Under the terms of its status as a Collectivité Départementale, which was approved by the French Parliament in July 2001, executive power in Mayotte was to be transferred from the Prefect to the Conseil Général in March 2004, and the position of Prefect dissolved by 2007.

Defence

At 1 August 2002 there were 4,700 French troops stationed in Mayotte and Réunion.

Economic Affairs

Mayotte's gross domestic product (GDP) per head in 1991 was estimated at 4,050 French francs. Between the censuses of 1991 and 2002 the population of Mayotte increased at an average annual rate of 10.1%.

The economy is based mainly on agriculture. In 1997 18.6% of the employed labour force were engaged in this sector. The principal export crops are ylang-ylang and vanilla. Rice, cassava and maize are cultivated for domestic consumption. Livestock-rearing and fishing are also important activities. However, Mayotte imports large quantities of foodstuffs, which comprised 27.0% of the value of total imports in 2001.

Industry (which is dominated by the construction sector) engaged 21.5% of the employed population in 1997. There are no mineral resources on the island. Imports of mineral products comprised 5.0% of the value of total imports in 1997; in 2001 base metals and metal products comprised 7.4% of the value of total imports.

Services engaged 59.8% of the employed population in 1997. The annual total of tourist arrivals (excluding cruise-ship passengers) increased from 6,700 in 1995 to 21,000 in 1999. Receipts from tourism in 1999 totalled 50m. French francs.

In 1998 Mayotte recorded a trade deficit of 896m. French francs. The principal source of imports in 1997 was France (60%); the other major supplier was South Africa. France was also the principal market for exports (taking 68% of exports in that year); the other significant purchaser was Réunion. The principal exports in 1997 were oil of ylang-ylang, transport equipment and foodstuffs. In that year falling prices and increased competition led to a significant decline in exports of vanilla (usually one of Mayotte's principal exports). The principal imports in 2001 were foodstuffs, electrical machinery, apparatus and appliances, transport equipment, chemicals and related products, and base metals and metal products.

In 1997 Mayotte's total budgetary revenue was estimated at 1,022.4m. French francs, while total expenditure was estimated at 964.2m. French francs. Official debt was 435.7m. French francs at 31 December 1995. The rate of inflation in the year to December 2002 was 5.4%. Some 35.5% of the labour force were unemployed in 2000.

Mayotte suffers from a persistently high trade deficit, owing to its reliance on imports, and is largely dependent on French aid. From the late 1980s the French Government granted substantial aid to finance a number of construction projects, in an attempt to encourage the development of tourism on the island. Mayotte's remote location, however, continued to prove an impediment to the development of the tourist sector. A five-year Development Plan (1986–91) included measures to improve infrastructure and to increase investment in public works; the Plan was subsequently extended to the end of 1993. In 1995 Mayotte received credit from France to finance further investment in infrastructure, particularly in the road network. As Mayotte's labour force has continued to increase (mostly owing to a high birth rate and continued illegal immigration), youth unemployment has caused particular concern. In 1997 37.8% of the unemployed population were under 25 years of age. In September 2000 an economic and social development agreement was signed with the French Government for the period 2000–04; Mayotte was to receive 4,386m. French francs to assist in its development. It was hoped that as well as improving regional transport links, the establishment of Air Mayotte International in early 2002 would increase tourist arrivals to the island.

Education

Education is compulsory for children aged six to 15 years, and comprises five years' primary and five years' secondary schooling. In 2001/02 there were 112 primary schools on the island. In the same year there were 14 secondary schools, comprising 12 collèges (junior comprehensives) and two lycées. There were also two vocational and technical institutions. Some 9,606 pre-primary school pupils, 28,591 primary school pupils and 15,626 secondary school pupils were enrolled in 2002/03. A further 1,733 students were enrolled at the vocational and technical institutions. In December 1996 the Caisse Française de Développement (now Agence Française de Développement) provided 21.6m. French francs for the construction of pre-primary and primary schools on Mayotte.

Public Holidays

The principal holidays of metropolitan France are observed.

Statistical Survey

Source (unless otherwise indicated): Institut National de la Statistique et des Etudes Economiques; 51 hauts des Jardins du Collège, BP 1369, 97600 Mamoudzou; tel. 61-36-65; fax 61-39-56; internet www.insee.fr/mayotte.

AREA AND POPULATION

Area: 374 sq km (144 sq miles).

Population: 94,410 (census of August 1991); 131,368 (males 66,600; females 64,768) at census of 5 August 1997; 160,265 at census of 30 July 2002.

Principal Towns (population of communes at 2002 census): Mamoudzou 45,485, Koungou 15,383, Dzaoudzi (capital) 12,308.

Density (30 July 2002): 428.5 per sq km.

Births and Deaths (1997): Registered live births 5,326 (birth rate 40.6 per 1,000); Death rate 5.6 per 1,000.

Economically Active Population (persons aged betweeen 15 and 64 years, census of August 1997): Agriculture and fishing 4,672; Electricity, gas and water 399; Industry 1,164; Construction and engineering 3,843; Wholesale and retail trade 2,717; Transport and telecommunications 1,563; Other marketable services 1,530; Finance and insurance 97; Other non-marketable services 9,108; Total employed 25,093 (males 18,200, females 6,893); Persons on compulsory military service 143 (males 139, females 4); Unemployed 17,660 (males 8,982, females 8,678); Total labour force 42,896 (males 27,321, females 15,575).

HEALTH AND WELFARE

Key Indicators

Total Fertility Rate (children per woman, 1997): 5.0.

Physicians (per 1,000 head, 1997): 0.4.

Hospital Beds (per 1,000 head, 1997): 1.4.
For definitions see explanatory note on p. vi.

AGRICULTURE, ETC.

Livestock (1995): Cattle 15,000; Sheep 2,700; Goats 23,000.

Fishing (metric tons, live weight, 1999): Capture (Marine fishes) 5,000 (FAO estimate); Aquaculture (FAO estimate) 3; Total catch 5,003. Source: FAO, *Yearbook of Fishery Statistics*.

FINANCE

Currency and Exchange Rates: The French franc was used until the end of February 2002. Euro notes and coins were introduced on 1 January 2002, and the euro became the sole legal tender from 18 February. Some of the figures in this Survey are still in terms of francs. For details of exchange rates, see French Guiana.

Budget (million French francs, 1997): Total revenue 1,022.4 (current 783.7, capital 238.7); Total expenditure 964.2 (current 725.4, capital 238.7).

Money Supply (million French francs at 31 December 1997): Currency outside banks 789; Demand deposits 266; Total money 1,055.

Cost of Living (Consumer Price Index; base: December 1996 = 100): 103.9 in December 2000; 103.5 in December 2001; 109.1 in December 2002.

EXTERNAL TRADE

Total Trade (million euros): *Imports:* 181.8 in 2001. *Exports:* 6.3 in 2001.

Principal Commodities (million French francs, 1997): *Imports:* Foodstuffs 188.1 (Beef and veal 19.2, Poultry and rabbit meat 26.4, Rice 33.6); Mineral products 41.0 (Hydraulic cements 31.4); Chemicals and related products 63.1 (Medicinal and pharmaceutical products 21.6); Plastic materials, ethers and resins 29.1; Wood, charcoal and wickerwork 25.5 (Sawnwood 16.2); Paper-making material, paper and paper products 20.8; Textiles 22.9; Base metals and metal products 84.6; Electrical machinery, apparatus and appliances 168.5; Transport equipment 101.1 (Passenger motor cars 44.3, Road motor vehicles for goods transport 25.2); Optical and photographic apparatus 21.4; Miscellaneous goods 20.1; Total (incl. others) 823.4. *Exports:* Foodstuffs 2.4 (Vanilla 0.8); Chemicals and related products 5.8 (Ylang-ylang 5.6); Paper-making materials, paper and paper products 1.5; Base metals and metal products 1.9; Electrical machinery, apparatus and appliances 2.2; Transport equipment 4.6 (Passenger motor cars 1.0, Road motor vehicles for goods transport 1.9); Total (incl. others) 20.2. *2001* (million euros): *Imports:* Foodstuffs 49.1; Chemicals and related products 15.9; Base metals and metal products 13.5; Electrical machinery, apparatus and appliances 34.4; Transport equipment 29.3; Total 181.8. *Exports:* Vanilla 0.2; Ylang-ylang 0.7; Total 6.3.

Principal Trading Partners (percentage of trade, 1997): *Imports:* France 60; South Africa 8. *Exports:* France 68; Réunion 7.

TRANSPORT

Road Traffic (1998): Motor vehicles in use 8,213.

Shipping: *Traffic* (metric tons, 2001): Goods unloaded 229,715; Goods loaded 92,393.

Civil Aviation (1998): *Passenger arrivals:* 42,260; *Passenger departures:* 45,774; *Freight carried:* 1,240 metric tons (2001).

TOURISM

Visitor Arrivals (excluding cruise-ship passengers): 9,500 in 1997; 11,400 in 1998; 21,000 in 1999.

Tourism Receipts (million French francs): 50 in 1999.

COMMUNICATIONS MEDIA

Telephones ('000 main lines in use, 2001): 10.0. Source: International Telecommunication Union.

EDUCATION

Pre-primary (2001/02): 50 schools; 9,606 pupils (2002/03).

Primary (2001/02): 112 schools; 28,591 pupils (2002/03).

Primary (pre-vocational) (2001/02): 13 schools; 798 pupils (2002/03).

General Secondary (2001/02): 14 schools (1997); 15,626 pupils (2002/03).

Vocational and Technical (2001/02): 2 institutions (1997); 1,733 students (2002/03).

Directory

The Constitution

Mayotte has an elected General Council (Conseil Général), comprising 19 members, which assists the Prefect in the administration of the island. Under the status of Collectivité Départementale, which was adopted by the French Parliament in July 2001, executive power was to be transferred from the Prefect to the President of the Conseil Général in March 2004, and the position of Prefect dissolved by 2007.

The Government

(April 2003)

Prefect: Jean-Jacques Brot.

Secretary-General: André Dorso.

Deputy to the French National Assembly: MANSOUR KAMARDINE (UMP).

Representative to the French Senate: MARCEL HENRY (MDM, Union Centriste).

Economic and Social Adviser: IBRAHIM ABUBACAR (PS).

GOVERNMENT DEPARTMENTS

Department of Agriculture and Forestry: BP 103, 15 rue Mariazé, 97600 Mamoudzou; tel. 61-12-13; fax 61-10-31; e-mail daf .mayotte@wanadoo.fr.

Department of Education: BP 76, 97600 Mamoudzou; tel. 61-10-24; fax 61-09-87; e-mail vice-rectorat@ac-mayotte.fr; internet www .ac-mayotte.fr.

Department of Health and Social Security: BP 104, rue de l'Hôpital, 97600 Mamoudzou; tel. 61-12-25; fax 60-19-56.

Department of Public Works: BP 109, rue Mariazé, 97600 Mamoudzou; tel. 61-12-54; fax 61-18-19.

Department of Work, Employment and Training: BP 174, Place Mariazé, 97600 Mamoudzou; tel. 61-16-57; fax 61-03-37; e-mail dtefp@wanadoo.fr.

Department of Youth and Sports: BP 94, rue Mariazé, 97600 Mamoudzou; tel. 61-10-87; fax 61-01-26; e-mail mayotte.djs@ wanadoo.fr.

CONSEIL GÉNÉRAL

(Conseil Général, BP 101, 108 rue de l'Hôpital, 97600 Mamoudzou; tel. 61-12-33; fax 61-10-18; e-mail conseil-general-de-mayotte@wanadoo.fr)

The Conseil général comprises 19 members. At elections in March 2001, the Fédération de Mayotte du Rassemblement pour la République (known as the Fédération de Mayotte de l'Union pour un Mouvement Populaire since November 2002) secured five seats, the Mouvement populaire mahorais (MPM) four, the Mouvement des citoyens (MDC) two, the Mouvement départementaliste mahorais (MDM) one, the Parti socialiste (PS) one, and independent right-wing candidates six seats.

President: YOUNOUSSA BAMANA.

Political Organizations

Fédération de Mayotte de l'Union pour un Mouvement Populaire: 97610 Dzaoudzi; local branch of the French (Gaullist) Union pour un Mouvement Populaire (UPM); Sec.-Gen. MANSOUR KAMARDINE.

Front national: 7 rue du Collège, BP 1331, 97600 Mamoudzou; tel. and fax 60-00-30; e-mail fatna@frontnational.com; Regional Sec. HAMADA OUSSENI.

Mouvement des citoyens (MDC): Collège Tsim Koura, BP 04, 97620 Chirongui; Leader JEAN-CLAUDE MAHINC.

Mouvement départementaliste mahorais (MDM): 97610 Dzaoudzi; f. 1999 by former members of the MPM; seeks full overseas departmental status for Mayotte; Leader HENRY JEAN-BAPTISTE.

Fédération du mouvement national républicain (MNR) de Mayotte: 15 rue des Réfugiers, 97615 Pamandzi; tel. 60-33-21; fax 60-33-21; Departmental Sec. ABDOU MIHIDJAY.

Mouvement populaire mahorais (MPM): 97610 Dzaoudzi; seeks departmental status for Mayotte; Leader YOUNOUSSA BAMANA.

Parti socialiste (PS): Dzaoudzi; local branch of the French party of the same name; Leader IBRAHIM ABUBACAR.

Judicial System

Palais de Justice: BP 106 (Kawéni), 34 rue de l'Hôpital, 97600 Mamoudzou; tel. 61-11-15; fax 61-19-63.

Tribunal Supérieur d'Appel

16 rue de l'Hôpital, BP 106, 97600 Mamoudzou; tel. 61-11-15; fax 61-19-63.

Pres. JEAN-BAPTISTE FLORI; Prosecutor JEAN-LOUIS BEC.

Procureur de la République: PATRICK BROSSIER.

Tribunal de Première Instance: Pres. ARLETTE MEALLONNIER-DUGUE.

Religion

Muslims comprise about 98% of the population. Most of the remainder are Christians, mainly Roman Catholics.

CHRISTIANITY

The Roman Catholic Church

Mayotte is within the jurisdiction of the Apostolic Administrator of the Comoros.

Office of the Apostolic Administrator: BP 1012, 97600 Mamoudzou; tel. and fax 61-11-53.

The Press

Flash-Infos: BP 60, 97600 Mamoudzou; tel. 61-54-45; fax 61-54-47; e-mail flash-infos@wanadoo.fr; daily e-mail bulletin; Dir LAURENT CANAVATE.

Le Kwezi: BP 05, ZI Nel, 97600 Mamoudzou; tel. 61-30-00; fax 61-19-91; e-mail kwezi@wanadoo.fr; f. 1996; biweekly; Dir ZAÏDOU BAMANA; Editor-in-Chief LAURENT CANAVATE.

Mayotte Hebdo: BP 60, 97600 Mamoudzou; tel. 61-20-04; fax 60-35-90; e-mail mayotte.hebdo@wanadoo.fr; weekly; Dir LAURENT CANAVATE; circ. 2,000.

Broadcasting and Communications

TELECOMMUNICATIONS

France Télécom Mayotte: BP 299 (Kawéni), Place Mariazé, 97600 Mamoudzou; tel. 61-00-14; fax 61-19-02; e-mail richard.roques@ francetelecom.com.

RADIO AND TELEVISION

Réseau France Outre-mer (RFO): BP 103, 1 rue du Jardin, 97615 Pamandzi; tel. 60-10-17; fax 60-18-52; e-mail bernard.joyeux@rfo.fr; internet www.rfo.fr; fmrly Société Nationale de Radio-Télévision Française d'Outre-mer; f. 1977; govt-owned; radio broadcasts in French and Mahorian; television transmissions began in 1986; plans for a satellite service were announced in 1998; Pres. ANDRÉ-MICHEL BESSE; Regional Dir. BERNARD JOYEUX.

Finance

BANKS

Issuing Authority

Institut d'Emission d'Outre-mer: BP 500, ave de la Préfecture, 97600 Mamoudzou; tel. 61-05-05; fax 61-05-02; e-mail iedom .mayotte@wanadoo.fr; Dir MAX REMBLIN.

Commercial Bank

Banque Française Commerciale Océan Indien: BP 322, route de l'Agriculture, 97600 Mamoudzou; tel. 61-10-91; fax 61-17-40; e-mail mayotte@bfcoi.com; br. at Dzaoudzi.

Banque de la Réunion: BP 29, 29 Place Mariazé, 97600 Mamoudzou; tel. 61-20-30; fax 61-20-28; e-mail br.mayotte@ wanadoo.fr.

BRED Banque Populaire: Place Mariazé, ZI 3, 97600 Mamoudzou; tel. 60-89-90; fax 60-68-69.

INSURANCE

AGF: BP 184, Place Mariazé, 97600 Mamoudzou; tel. 61-16-37; fax 61-14-89; e-mail jl.henry@wanadoo.fr; Gen. Man. JEAN-LUC HENRY.

Groupama: BP 665, ZI Nel, Lot 7, 97600 Mamoudzou; tel. 62-59-92; fax 60-76-08; e-mail groupama.assurance.mayotte@wanadoo.fr.

Prudence Créole: BP 480, Immeuble Sana, rue du Commerce, 97600 Mamoudzou; tel. 61-11-10; fax 61-11-21; e-mail prudencecreolemayotte@wanadoo.fr.

Vectra Paic Océan Indien: BP 65, 97680 Combani; tel. 62-44-54; fax 62-46-97; e-mail cfonteneau@wanadoo.fr.

Trade and Industry

DEVELOPMENT ORGANIZATION

Agence Française de Développement (AFD): Ave de la Préfecture, BP 500, 97600 Mamoudzou; tel. 61-05-05; fax 61-05-02.

UTILITIES

Electricity

Electricité de Mayotte (EDM): BP 333, ZI Kawéni, 97600 Kawéni; tel. 61-44-44; fax 60-10-92; e-mail edm.mayotte@wanadoo.fr.

Water

Syndicat des Eaux: BP 289, 97600 Mamoudzou; tel. 62-11-11; fax 62-10-31.

TRADE UNION

Confédération Inter-Syndicale de Mayotte (CISMA): 18 rue Mahabou, BP 1038, 97600 Mamoudzou; tel. 61-12-38; fax 61-36-16; Gen. Sec. SAID BOINALI.

Transport

ROADS

In 1998 the road network totalled approximately 230 km, of which 90 km were main roads.

SHIPPING

Coastal shipping is provided by locally owned small craft. There is a deep-water port at Longoni.

Affaires Maritimes: Zone Industrielle de Kaweni, BP 333, 97600 Mamoudzou; tel. 61-44-44; fax 60-10-92.

Service des Transports Maritimes (STM): BP 186, 97610 Dzaoudzi; tel. 60-10-69; fax 60-80-25; e-mail info@mayotte-stm.com; internet www.mayotte_stm.com.

CIVIL AVIATION

There is an airfield at Dzaoudzi, serving four-times weekly commercial flights to Réunion, twice-weekly services to Madagascar, Njazidja, Nzwani and Mwali, and a weekly service to Kenya. A direct service to Paris, expected to commence in 1999, was postponed, owing to the inadequacy of facilities at the island's airfield. The establishment of Air Mayotte International in early 2002 was expected to improve transport links to Réunion, Mauritius, the Seychelles and the Comoros.

Air Mayotte International: Mamoudzou; e-mail philippe.parot@airmayotte.com; internet www.airmayotte.com; f. 2002; Chair. SERGE CASTEL.

Tourism

Tropical scenery provides the main tourist attraction. In 1999 the island had six hotels, providing 118 rooms, five guest houses and eight apartments and lodges. Excluding cruise-ship passengers, Mayotte received 21,000 visitors in 1999, and tourism receipts totalled 50m. French francs in that year.

Comité du Tourisme de Mayotte: rue de la Pompe, BP 1169, 97600 Mamoudzou; tel. 61-09-09; fax 61-03-46; e-mail ctm@mayotte-tourisme.com; internet www.mayotte-tourisme.com.

French Overseas Collectivité Territoriale

The overseas Collectivité Territoriale is St Pierre and Miquelon. It is an integral part of the French Republic and is administered by a Prefect, who is appointed by the French Government. The Prefect is assisted by an elected General Council (Conseil Général). The Col-lectivité Territoriale is represented in the French National Assembly (Assemblée Nationale) and in the Senate (Sénat) in Paris, and also in the European Parliament in Strasbourg.

ST PIERRE AND MIQUELON

Introductory Survey

Location, Climate, Language, Religion, Capital

The territory of St Pierre and Miquelon (Iles Saint-Pierre-et-Miquelon) consists of a number of small islands which lie about 25 km (16 miles) from the southern coast of Newfoundland and Labrador, Canada, in the North Atlantic Ocean. The principal islands are St Pierre, Miquelon (Grande Miquelon) and Lan-glade (Petite Miquelon)—the last two being linked by an isthmus of sand. Winters are cold, with temperatures falling to –20°C (–4°F), and summers are mild, with temperatures aver-aging between 10° and 20°C (50° and 68°F). The islands are particularly affected by fog in June and July. The language is French, and the majority of the population profess Christianity and belong to the Roman Catholic Church. The capital is Saint-Pierre, on the island of St Pierre.

Recent History

The islands of St Pierre and Miquelon are the remnants of the once extensive French possessions in North America. They were confirmed as French territory in 1816, and gained departmental status in July 1976. The departmentalization proved unpopular with many of the islanders, since it incorporated the territory's economy into that of the European Community (EC, now Euro-pean Union, see p. 199), and was regarded as failing to take into account the islands' isolation and dependence on Canada for supplies and transport links. In March 1982 socialist and other left-wing candidates, campaigning for a change in the islands' status, were elected unopposed to all seats in the Conseil Gén-éral (General Council). St Pierre and Miquelon was excluded from the Mitterrand administration's decentralization reforms, undertaken in 1982.

In 1976 Canada imposed an economic interest zone extending to 200 nautical miles (370 km) around its shores. Fearing the loss of traditional fishing areas and thus the loss of the live-lihood of the fishermen of St Pierre, the French Government claimed a similar zone around the islands. Hopes of discovering valuable reserves of petroleum and natural gas in the area heightened the tension between France and Canada.

In December 1984 legislation was approved giving the islands the status of a Collectivité Territoriale with effect from 11 June 1985. This was intended to allow St Pierre and Miquelon to receive the investment and development aid suitable for its position, while allaying Canadian fears of EC exploitation of its offshore waters. Local representatives, however, remained apprehensive about the outcome of negotiations between the French and Canadian Governments to settle the dispute over coastal limits. (France continued to claim a 200-mile fishing and economic zone around St Pierre and Miquelon, while Canada wanted the islands to have only a 12-mile zone.) The dispute was submitted to international arbitration. Discussions began in March 1987, and negotiations to determine quotas for France's catch of Atlantic cod over the period 1988–91 were to take place simultaneously. In the mean time, Canada and France agreed on an interim fishing accord, which would allow France to increase its cod quota. The discussions collapsed in October, however, and French trawlers were prohibited from fishing in Canadian waters. In February 1988 Albert Pen and Gérard Grignon, St Pierre's elected representatives to the French legis-lature, together with two members of the St Pierre admin-istration and 17 sailors, were arrested for fishing in Canadian waters. This episode, and the arrest of a Canadian trawler captain in May for fishing in St Pierre's waters, led to an unsuccessful resumption of negotiations in September. An agreement was reached on fishing rights in March 1989, whereby France's annual quotas for Atlantic cod and other species were determined for the period until the end of 1991. (Further quotas were subsequently stipulated for the first nine months of 1992.) At the same time the Governments agreed upon the composition of an international arbitration tribunal which would delineate the disputed maritime boundaries and exclusive economic zones.

In July 1991 the international arbitration tribunal began its deliberations in New York, USA. The tribunal's ruling, issued in June 1992, was generally deemed to be favourable to Canada. France was allocated an exclusive economic zone around the territory totalling 2,537 square nautical miles (8,700 sq km), compared with its demand for more than 13,000 square nautical miles. The French authorities claimed that the sea area granted would be insufficient to sustain the islands' fishing community. Talks on new fishing quotas for the area off Newfoundland (known as Newfoundland and Labrador from December 2001) failed, and, in the absence of a new agreement, industrial fishing in the area was effectively halted until November 1994, when the Governments of the two countries signed an accord speci-fying new quotas for a period of 10 years. In the following month deputies in the Assemblée Nationale expressed concern that the terms of the agreement would be detrimental to St Pierre and Miquelon's interests, although the Government asserted that the accord recognized the islanders' historic fishing rights in Canadian waters. Meanwhile, in January of that year St Pierre and Miquelon protested at what it alleged was an unauthorized entry into the islands' waters by Canadian coastguards (who had been attempting to intercept goods being smuggled from Saint-Pierre to Newfoundland).

At the March 1986 election to the Assemblée Nationale the islands' incumbent deputy, Pen of the Parti Socialiste (PS), was re-elected. Pen was also the sole candidate at the indirect election to choose the islands' representative in the Sénat in September. A fresh election for a deputy to the Assemblée Nationale was held in November, when Gérard Grignon, repre-senting the centre-right Union pour la Démocratie Française (UDF), was elected. At the 1988 French presidential election Jacques Chirac of the right-wing Rassemblement pour la Répub-lique (RPR) received 56% of the votes cast by the islanders in the second round, in May, against the successful PS incumbent, François Mitterrand. In June Grignon was re-elected to the Assemblée National, taking 90.3% of the valid votes. In Sep-tember–October, however, the parties of the left won a majority at elections to the Conseil Général, securing 13 of the 19 seats.

In September 1992 64.2% of voters approved ratification of the Treaty on European Union (see p. 199), although only a small percentage of the electorate participated in the referendum. Grignon was re-elected to the Assemblée Nationale in March 1993; some 83% of the electorate participated in the poll. At the 1995 presidential election Chirac was the winning candidate at the second round on 7 May, taking 66.9% of the votes cast. At elections to the Sénat in September, Pen was narrowly defeated at a second round of voting by Victor Reux of the RPR, since 1994 the Secretary of the islands' Economic and Social Council. Grignon was re-elected to the Assemblée Nationale at a second round of voting on 1 June 1997, with 52.34% of the votes cast.

A number of government proposals regarding the socio-eco-nomic and institutional development of the Overseas Depart-ments, certain provisions of which were also to be applied to St Pierre and Miquelon, were provisionally accepted by the Assem-blée Nationale in May 2000, and subsequently adopted by the Sénat (following a number of modifications). The proposals were definitively approved by the Assemblée Nationale in November and were ratified by the Constitutional Council in December. Measures included provisions for improving and supporting the economic development of the islands, as well the introduction of proportional representation in elections to the Conseil Général. In the first round of the presidential election, held on 5 May 2002, Chirac won 30.8% of the vote on the islands, followed by Jospin, with 13.7%, who was, however, eliminated nationally. In the second round, held on 5 May, Chirac overwhelmingly defeated Jean-Marie Le Pen of the Front National, with 90.0% of the vote. Grignon, representing an alliance of the Union pour la Majorité Présidentielle and the UDF, was re-elected to the Assemblée Nationale in June, with 69% of the valid votes cast on the islands in the second round. In October Claude Valleix replaced Jean-François Tallec as Prefect.

Government

The French Government is represented in St Pierre by an appointed Prefect. There is a Conseil Général (General Council), with 19 members (15 for St Pierre and four for Miquelon), elected by adult universal suffrage for a period of six years. St Pierre and Miquelon elects one deputy to the Assemblée Nationale and one representative to the Sénat in Paris.

Defence

France is responsible for the islands' defence.

Economic Affairs

The soil and climatic conditions of St Pierre and Miquelon do not favour agricultural production, which is mainly confined to smallholdings, except for market-gardening and the production of eggs and chickens.

The principal economic activity of the islands is traditionally fishing and related industries, which employed some 18.5% of the working population in 1996. However, the sector has been severely affected by disputes with Canada regarding territorial waters and fishing quotas; the absence of quotas in 1992–94 effectively halted industrial fishing. New arrangements have been to the detriment of St Pierre and Miquelon, although there is some optimism regarding potential for the exploitation of shellfish, notably mussels and scallops, in the islands' waters. However, the total fish catch increased from 747 metric tons in 1996 to 6,485 tons in 2000.

Processing of fish provides the basis for industrial activity, which engages about 41% of the labour force. It is dominated by one major company, which produces frozen and salted fish, and fish meal for fodder. Following a sharp decrease in production in the late 1980s, much of the fish processed is now imported. Electricity is generated by two thermal power-stations, with a combined capacity of 23 MW. In 2000 plans were well advanced for the construction of a wind power-station, which, it was hoped, would generate some 40% of the islands' electricity requirements. The resolution of a boundary dispute between the Canadian provinces of Nova Scotia and Newfoundland and Labrador in 2002 accorded the islands about 500 sq miles of waters over the Gulf of St Lawrence basin, believed to contain substantial reserves of petroleum and gas.

The replenishment of ships' (mainly trawlers') supplies was formerly an important economic activity, but has now also been adversely affected by the downturn in the industrial fishing sector. Efforts were made to promote tourism, and the opening of the St Pierre–Montréal air route in 1987 led to an increase in air traffic in the 1990s. Tourist arrivals in 1998 were estimated at 11,994. In 1999 the completion of a new airport capable of accommodating larger aircraft further improved transport links.

In 1997 St Pierre and Miquelon recorded a trade deficit of 356m. French francs; total exports were 29m. francs. Most trade is with Canada and France and other countries of the European Union. The only significant exports are fish and fish meal. The principal imports in 1994 were fuel, building supplies and food from Canada. Items such as clothing and other consumer goods are generally imported from France.

The annual rate of inflation averaged 3.2% in 1997–2001; consumer prices increased by 8.5% in 2000 and by 2.3% in 2001. Some 12.8% of the labour force were unemployed at the 1999 census.

Given the decline of the fishing sector, the development of the port of Saint-Pierre and the expansion of tourism (particularly from Canada and the USA) are regarded by St Pierre and Miquelon as the principal means of maintaining economic pro-

gress. The islands will, none the less, remain highly dependent on budgetary assistance from the French central Government.

Education

The education system is modelled on the French system, and education is compulsory for children between the ages of six and 16 years. In 1997 there were nine primary schools, three secondary schools (one of which is private and has a technical school annex) and one technical school.

Public Holidays

2003: 1 January (New Year's Day), 18–21 April (Easter), 1 May (Labour Day), 29 May (Ascension Day), 9 June (Whit Monday), 14 July (National Day), 11 November (Armistice Day), 25 December (Christmas Day).

2004: 1 January (New Year's Day), 9–12 April (Easter), 1 May (Labour Day), 20 May (Ascension Day), 30 May (Whit Monday), 14 July (National Day), 11 November (Armistice Day), 25 December (Christmas Day).

Weights and Measures

The metric system is in use.

Statistical Survey

Source: Préfecture, Place du Lieutenant-Colonel Pigeaud, BP 4200, 97500 Saint-Pierre; tel. 41-10-10; fax 41-47-38.

AREA AND POPULATION

Area: 242 sq km (93.4 sq miles): St Pierre 26 sq km, Miquelon-Langlade 216 sq km.

Population: 6,392 at census of 15 March 1990: Saint-Pierre 5,683, Miquelon-Langlade 709; 6,316 (males 3,147, females 3,169) at census of 8 March 1999.

Density (1999): 26.1 per sq km.

Births, Marriages and Deaths (1997): Live births 92; Marriages 36; Deaths 51.

Economically Active Population (1992): Fish and fish-processing 540; Construction 333; Transport 192; Dockers 44; Trade 409; Restaurants and hotels 154; Business services 417; Government employees 727; Activities not adequately defined 106; Total labour force 2,922. *1999:* Total economically active population 3,198 (of which government employees 825).

FISHING

Total Catch (metric tons, live weight, 2000): Capture 6,485 (Atlantic cod 4,682, Lumpfish 536, Queen crab 511). Source: FAO, *Yearbook of Fishery Statistics*.

FINANCE

Currency and Exchange Rates: French currency was used until the end of 2001. Euro notes and coins were introduced on 1 January 2002, and the euro became the sole legal tender from 18 February. Some of the figures in this Survey are still in terms of French francs. For details of exchange rates, see French Guiana.

Expenditure by Metropolitan France (1997): 280 million francs.

Budget (estimates, million francs, 1997): Expenditure 244 (current 128; capital 116).

Money Supply (million francs at 31 December 1997): Currency outside banks 281; Demand deposits at banks 897; Total money 1,178.

Cost of Living (Consumer price index; base: 1997 = 100): 110.8 in 2000; 113.3 in 2001. Source: UN, *Monthly Bulletin of Statistics*.

EXTERNAL TRADE

Total (million francs, 1997): *Imports*: 385; *Exports*: 29. Most trade is with Canada, France (imports), other countries of the European Union (exports) and the USA.

TRANSPORT

Road Traffic (1997): 3,876 motor vehicles in use.

Shipping (1995): Ships entered 884; Freight entered 20,400 metric tons. *1997:* Ships entered 918.

Civil Aviation (1997): Passengers carried 30,341, Freight carried 105 metric tons.

TOURISM

Tourist Arrivals (estimate, 1998): 11,994. Source: Agence Régionale du Tourisme.

COMMUNICATIONS MEDIA

Radio Receivers (estimate, '000 in use): 5.0 in 1997.

Television Receivers (estimate, '000 in use): 3.5 in 1997.

EDUCATION

Primary (1997): 9 institutions; 50 teachers (1987); 877 students.

Secondary (1997): 3 institutions; 55 teachers (1987); 562 students.

Technical (1997): 1 institution; 194 students.

Directory

The Government

(April 2003)

Prefect: CLAUDE VALLEIX, Place du Lieutenant-Colonel Pigeaud, BP 4200, 97500 Saint-Pierre; tel. 41-10-10; fax 41-47-38.

Deputy to the French National Assembly: GÉRARD GRIGNON (UMP-UDF).

Representative to the French Senate: VICTOR REUX (UMP).

CONSEIL RÉGIONAL

Place de l'Eglise, 97500 Saint-Pierre; tel. 41-46-22; fax 41-22-97. The General Council has 19 members (St Pierre 15, Miquelon four).

President: MARC PLANTEGENEST.

Political Organizations

Centre des Démocrates Sociaux (CDS): 97500 Saint-Pierre.

Parti Socialiste (PS): BP 984, 97500 Saint-Pierre; tel. 41-35-74; fax 41-78-90; e-mail psspm@altavista.net; f. 1996.

Union pour la Démocratie Française (UDF): 97500 Saint-Pierre; centrist.

Union pour un Mouvement Populaire (UMP): BP 113, 97500 Saint-Pierre; e-mail vicreux@cheznoo.net; tel. 41-35-73; fax 41-29-97; Gaullist.

Judicial System

Tribunal Supérieur d'Appel: 97500 Saint-Pierre; tel. 41-47-26; fax 41-49-45; e-mail tsaspm@cheznoo.net; Pres. FRANÇOIS BILLON.

Tribunal de Première Instance: 14 rue Emile Sasco, BP 4215, 97500 Saint-Pierre; tel. 41-47-26; fax 41-49-45; e-mail tsaspm@cheznoo.net; Presiding Magistrate CAROL CHAPALAIN.

Religion

Almost all of the inhabitants are adherents of the Roman Catholic Church.

CHRISTIANITY

The Roman Catholic Church

The islands form the Apostolic Vicariate of the Iles Saint-Pierre et Miquelon. At 31 December 1999 there were an estimated 6,310 adherents.

Vicar Apostolic: LUCIEN FISCHER (Titular Bishop of Avioccala), Vicariat Apostolique, BP 4245, 97500 Saint-Pierre; tel. 41-02-40; fax 41-47-09; e-mail mission-catho.spm@wanadoo.fr.

The Press

L'Echo des Caps Hebdo: rue Georges Daguerre, BP 4213, 97500 Saint-Pierre; tel. 41-41-01; fax 41-49-33; e-mail echohebd@cheznoo .net; f. 1982; weekly; circ. 2,500.

Recueil des Actes Administratifs: 4 rue du Général Leclerc, BP 4233, 97500 Saint-Pierre; tel. 41-24-50; fax 41-20-85; f. 1866; monthly; Dir E. DEROUET.

Trait d'Union: BP 113, 97500 Saint-Pierre; tel. 41-35-73; fax 41-29-97; e-mail vicreuz@cheznoo.net; 10 a year; organ of the senator and the local branch of the UMP.

Le Vent de la Liberté: 1 rue Amiral Muselier, BP 1179, 97500 Saint-Pierre; tel. 41-42-19; fax 41-48-06; e-mail archipel@cheznoo .net; weekly; circ. 550; Dir GÉRARD GRIGNON.

Broadcasting and Communications

RADIO AND TELEVISION

Réseau France Outre-mer (RFO): BP 4227, 97500 Saint-Pierre; tel. 41-11-11; fax 41-22-19; internet www.rfo.fr; fmrly Société Nationale de Radio-Télévision Française d'Outre-mer, renamed as above 1998; broadcasts 24 hours of radio programmes daily and 195 hours of television programmes weekly on two channels; Pres. ANDRÉ-MICHEL BESSE; Dir JEAN-FRANÇOIS MOENNAN.

Radio Atlantique: BP 1282, 97500 Saint-Pierre; tel. 41-24-93; fax 41-56-33; e-mail contact@radioatlantique.com; internet www .radioatlantique.com; private; broadcasts 24 hours of radio programmes daily; Pres. and Dir ROGER GUICHOT.

Finance

(cap. = capital, res = reserves, dep. = deposits; m. = million; amounts in French francs)

BANKING

Central Bank

Institut d'Emission des Départements d'Outre-mer (IEDOM): 22 place du Général de Gaulle, BP 4202, 97500 Saint-Pierre; tel. 41-43-57; fax 41-58-55; internet www.iedom-ieom.com; Dir FRANCIS ROCHE TOUSSAINT.

MAJOR BANKS

Banque des Iles Saint-Pierre-et-Miquelon: 2 rue Jacques Cartier, BP 4223, 97500 Saint-Pierre; tel. 41-25-43; fax 41-25-31; e-mail bdispm@cancom.net; f. 1889; cap. 25m., res 10.2m., dep. 336.4m. (Dec. 2000); Pres. and Gen. Man. GUILLAUME DE CHALUS; Man. BERNARD DURDILLY.

Crédit Saint Pierrais: 20 place du Général de Gaulle, BP 4218, 97500 Saint-Pierre; tel. 41-22-49; fax 41-25-96; f. 1962; cap. 36.5m., res 3m., dep. 286m. (Dec. 1998); Pres. GEORGES HARAN; Man. PIERRE SPIETH.

PRINCIPAL INSURANCE COMPANIES

Mutuelle des Iles: 5 rue Maréchal Foch, BP 1112, 97500 Saint-Pierre; tel. 41-28-69; fax 41-51-13.

Paturel Assurances SARL, Agence PFA Athéna: 31 rue Maréchal Foch, BP 4288, 97500 Saint-Pierre; tel. 41-32-98; fax 41-51-65; Gen. Agent GUY PATUREL; Man. NATHALIE PATUREL.

Trade and Industry

GOVERNMENT AGENCY

Comité Economique et Social: 4 rue Borda, 97500 Saint-Pierre; tel. 41-45-50; fax 41-42-45.

DEVELOPMENT ORGANIZATIONS

Agence Française de Développement (AFD): 4 rue de la Roncière, BP 4202, 97500 Saint-Pierre; tel. 41-43-57; fax 41-25-98; e-mail jolya@afd.fr; internet www.afd.fr; fmrly Caisse Française de Développement; Man. FRANCIS ROCHE-TOUSSAINT.

SODEPAR: Palais Royal, rue Borda, BP 4365, 97500 Saint-Pierre; tel. 41-15-15; fax 41-15-16; e-mail sodepar@cancom.net; internet www.cancom.net/~sodepar; f. 1989; economic development agency; Chair. MARC PLANTEGENEST; Dir FRANCK CALDERINI.

CHAMBER OF COMMERCE

Chambre de Commerce, d'Industrie et de Métiers: 4 rue Constant-Colmay, BP 4207, 97500 Saint-Pierre; tel. 41-45-12; fax 41-32-09; e-mail ccim975@cheznoo.net; Pres. JEAN LEBAILLY.

TRADE UNIONS

Union Interprofessionnelle CFDT (SPM): BP 4352, 97500 Saint-Pierre; tel. 41-23-20; fax 41-27-99; affiliated to the Confédération Française Démocratique du Travail; Sec.-Gen. PHILIPPE GUILLAUME.

Union Interprofessionnelle CFTC: BP 1117, 97500 Saint-Pierre; tel. 41-37-19; affiliated to the Confédération Française des Travailleurs Chrétiens.

Union Intersyndicale CGT de Saint-Pierre et Miquelon: 97500 Saint-Pierre; tel. 41-41-86; affiliated to the Confédération Générale du Travail; Sec.-Gen. RONALD MANET.

Union des Syndicats CGT-FO de Saint-Pierre et Miquelon: 15 rue Dr Dunan, BP 4241, 97500 Saint-Pierre; tel. 41-25-22; fax 41-46-55; affiliated to the Confédération Générale du Travail-Force Ouvrière; Sec.-Gen. MAX OLAISOLA.

Transport

SHIPPING

Packet boats and container services operate between Saint-Pierre, Halifax, Nova Scotia, and Boston, MA. The seaport at Saint-Pierre has three jetties and 1,200 metres of quays.

SPM Express: Agence Hôtel Robert, 10 rue du 11 novembre, 97500 Saint-Pierre; tel. 41-24-26; daily service between St-Pierre and Newfoundland.

CIVIL AVIATION

There is an airport on St Pierre, served by airlines linking the territory with France and Canada. Construction of a new airport, able to accommodate larger aircraft and thus improve air links, was completed in 1999.

Air Saint-Pierre: 18 rue Albert Briand, Saint-Pierre, BP 4225, 97500 Saint-Pierre; tel. 41-00-00; fax 41-00-02; e-mail asp@cancom.net; internet http://209.205.50.254/aspweb; f. 1964; connects the territory directly with Newfoundland, Nova Scotia and Québec; Pres. RÉMY L. BRIAND; Man. THIERRY BRIAND.

Tourism

There were an estimated 11,994 tourist arrivals in 1998.

Service Loisirs Accueil: Place du Général de Gaulle, BP 4274, 97500 Saint-Pierre; tel. 41-22-22; fax 41-33-55; e-mail tourispm@cheznoo.net; internet www.st-pierre-et-miquelon.com; f. 1989; Pres. FRANÇOISE DUPONT; Dir JEAN-HIGUES DETCHEVERRY.

French Overseas Territories

The three Overseas Territories (territoires d'outre-mer) are French Polynesia, the French Southern and Antarctic Territories, and the Wallis and Futuna Islands. They are integral parts of the French Republic. Each is administered by a High Commissioner or Chief Administrator, who is appointed by the French Government. Each permanently inhabited Territory also has a Territorial Assembly or Congress, elected by universal adult suffrage. Certain members of the Territorial Assembly or Congress sit in the French National Assembly and the Senate of the Republic in Paris. The Territories have varying degrees of internal autonomy.

FRENCH POLYNESIA

Introductory Survey

Location, Climate, Language, Religion, Flag, Capital

French Polynesia comprises several scattered groups of islands in the South Pacific Ocean, lying about two-thirds of the way between the Panama Canal and New Zealand. Its nearest neighbours are the Cook Islands, to the west, and the Line Islands (part of Kiribati), to the north-west. French Polynesia consists of the following island groups: the Windward Islands (Iles du Vent—including the islands of Tahiti and Moorea) and the Leeward Islands (Iles Sous le Vent—located about 160 km north-west of Tahiti) which, together, constitute the Society Archipelago; the Tuamotu Archipelago, which comprises some 80 atolls scattered east of the Society Archipelago in a line stretching north-west to south-east for about 1,500 km; the Gambier Islands, located 1,600 km south-east of Tahiti; the Austral Islands, lying 640 km south of Tahiti; and the Marquesas Archipelago, which lies 1,450 km north-east of Tahiti. There are 35 islands and 83 atolls in all. The average monthly temperature throughout the year varies between 20°C (68°F) and 29°C (84°F), and most rainfall occurs between November and April, the average annual precipitation being 1,625 mm (64 ins). The official languages are French and Tahitian. Polynesian languages are spoken by the indigenous population. The principal religion is Christianity; about 55% of the population are Protestant and some 34% Roman Catholic. The official flag is the French tricolour. Subordinate to this, there is a territorial flag (proportions 2 by 3), comprising three horizontal stripes, of red, white (half the depth) and red, with, in the centre, the arms of French Polynesia, consisting of a representation in red of a native canoe, bearing a platform supporting five stylized persons, on a circular background (five wavy horizontal dark blue bands, surmounted by 10 golden sunrays). The capital is Papeete, on the island of Tahiti.

Recent History

Tahiti, the largest of the Society Islands, was declared a French protectorate in 1842, and became a colony in 1880. The other island groups were annexed during the last 20 years of the 19th century. The islands were governed from France under a decree of 1885 until 1946, when French Polynesia became an Overseas Territory, administered by a Governor in Papeete. A Territorial Assembly and a Council of Government were established to advise the Governor.

Between May 1975 and May 1982 a majority in the Territorial Assembly sought independence for French Polynesia. Following pressure by Francis Sanford, leader of the largest autonomist party in the Assembly, a new Constitution for the Territory was negotiated with the French Government and approved by a newly elected Assembly in 1977. Under the provisions of the new statute, France retained responsibility for foreign affairs, defence, monetary matters and justice, but the powers of the territorial Council of Government were increased, especially in the field of commerce. The French Governor was replaced by a High Commissioner, who was to preside over the Council of Government and was head of the administration, but had no vote. The Council's elected Vice-President, responsible for domestic affairs, was granted greater powers. An Economic, Social and Cultural Council, responsible for all development matters, was also created, and French Polynesia's economic zone was extended to 200 nautical miles (370 km) from the islands' coastline.

Following elections to the Territorial Assembly in May 1982, the Gaullist Tahoeraa Huiraatira, led by Gaston Flosse, which secured 13 of the 30 seats, formed successive ruling coalitions, first with the Ai'a Api party and in September with the Pupu Here Ai'a Te Nunaa Ia Ora party. Seeking self-government, especially in economic matters, elected representatives of the Assembly held discussions with the French Government in Paris in 1983, and in September 1984 a new statute was approved by the French National Assembly. This allowed the territorial Government greater powers, mainly in the sphere of commerce and development; the Council of Government was replaced by a Council of Ministers, whose President was to be elected from among the members of the Territorial Assembly. Flosse became the first President of the Council of Ministers.

At elections held in March 1986 the Tahoeraa Huiraatira gained the first outright majority to be achieved in the Territory, winning 24 of the 41 seats in the Territorial Assembly. Leaders of opposition parties subsequently expressed dissatisfaction with the election result, claiming that the Tahoeraa Huiraatira victory had been secured only as a result of the allocation of a disproportionately large number of seats in the Territorial Assembly to one of the five constituencies. The constituency at the centre of the dispute comprised the Mangareva and Tuamotu islands, where the two French army bases at Hao and Mururoa constituted a powerful body of support for Flosse and the Tahoeraa Huiraatira, which, in spite of winning a majority of seats, had obtained a minority of individual votes in the election. At the concurrent elections for French Polynesia's two seats in the National Assembly in Paris, Flosse and Alexandre Léontieff, the candidates of the Rassemblement pour la République (RPR—to which Tahoeraa Huiraatira is affiliated), were elected, Flosse subsequently ceding his seat to Edouard Fritch. Later in March the French Prime Minister, Jacques Chirac, appointed Flosse to a post in the French Council of Ministers, assigning him the portfolio of Secretary of State for South Pacific Affairs.

In April 1986 Flosse was re-elected President of the Council of Ministers. However, he faced severe criticism from leaders of the opposition for his allegedly inefficient and extravagant use of public funds, and was accused, in particular, of corrupt electoral practice. Flosse resigned as President of the Territory's Council of Ministers in February 1987, and was replaced by Jacques Teuira.

In December 1987, amid growing discontent over his policies, Teuira and the entire Council of Ministers resigned and were replaced by a coalition of opposition parties and the Te Tiaraama party (a breakaway faction of the Tahoeraa Huiraatira) under the presidency of Alexandre Léontieff. The Léontieff Government survived several challenges in the Territorial Assembly to its continuation in office during 1988–89. Amendments to the Polynesian Constitution, which were approved by the French Parliament and enacted by July 1990, augmented the powers of the President of the Territorial Council of Ministers and increased the competence of the Territorial Assembly. The major purpose of these amendments was to clarify the areas of responsibility of the State, the Territory and the judiciary, which was considered particularly necessary following various disputes about the impending single market of the European Community (EC—now European Union, EU, see p. 199). In June 1989, in protest, 90% of the electorate refused to vote in the elections to the European Parliament.

At territorial elections in March 1991 the Tahoeraa Huiraatira won 18 of the 41 seats. Flosse then formed a coalition with the Ai'a Api, thereby securing a majority of 23 seats in the

Territorial Assembly. Emile Vernaudon, leader of the Ai'a Api, was elected President of the Assembly and Flosse was elected President of the Council of Ministers. In September Flosse announced the end of the coalition between his party and the Ai'a Api, accusing Vernaudon of disloyalty, and signed a new alliance with the Pupu Here Ai'a Te Nunaa Ia Ora led by Jean Juventin.

In April 1992 Flosse was found guilty of fraud (relating to an illegal sale of government land to a member of his family) and there were widespread demands for his resignation. In November Juventin and Léontieff were charged with 'passive' corruption, relating to the construction of a golf course by a Japanese company. In the following month the French Court of Appeal upheld the judgment against Flosse, who received a six-month, suspended prison sentence. The case provoked a demonstration by more than 3,000 people in January 1993, demanding the resignation of Flosse and Juventin. In September 1994 Flosse succeeded in having the conviction overturned, on a procedural issue, in a second court of appeal. In October 1997, however, Léontieff was found guilty of accepting substantial bribes in order to facilitate a business venture and was sentenced to three years in prison (half of which was to be suspended). In May 1998 Léontieff was sentenced to a further three years' imprisonment (two of which were to be suspended) for corruption.

French presidential elections took place in April/May 1995. During the second round of voting in the Territory, the socialist candidate, Lionel Jospin, received 39% of the total votes, while the RPR candidate, Jacques Chirac, won 61%. (Chirac was elected to the presidency with 52.6% of votes cast throughout the republic.)

In November 1995 the Territorial Assembly adopted a draft statute of autonomy, which proposed the extension of the Territory's powers to areas such as fishing, mining and shipping rights, international transport and communications, broadcasting and the offshore economic zone. France, however, would retain full responsibility for defence, justice and security in the islands. Advocates of independence for French Polynesia criticized the statute for promising only relatively cosmetic changes, while failing to increase the democratic rights of the islanders. The statute was approved by the French National Assembly in December and came into force in April 1996.

At territorial elections held on 13 May 1996 the Gaullist Tahoeraa Huiraatira achieved an outright majority, although the principal pro-independence party, Tavini Huiraatira/Front de Libération de la Polynésie (FLP), made considerable gains throughout the Territory (largely owing to increased popular hostility towards France since the resumption of nuclear-weapons tests at Mururoa Atoll—see below). Tahoeraa Huiraatira secured 22 of the 41 seats in the Territorial Assembly, with 38.7% of total votes cast, while Tavini Huiraatira won 10 seats, with 24.8% of votes. Other anti-independence parties won a total of eight seats and an additional pro-independence grouping secured one seat. Flosse defeated the independence leader, Oscar Temaru, by 28 votes to 11 to remain as President of the Council of Ministers later in the month, and Justin Arapari was elected President of the Territorial Assembly. Allegations of voting irregularities led to legal challenges, which overturned the results in 11 constituencies. Following by-elections in May 1998 for the 11 seats, Tahoeraa Huiraatira increased its representation by one seat. Tavini Huiraatira again claimed that the elections had not been fairly conducted.

At elections for French Polynesia's two seats in the French National Assembly in May 1997 Michel Buillard and Emile Vernaudon, both supporters of the RPR, were elected with 52% and 59% of total votes cast, respectively. However, the pro-independence leader, Oscar Temaru, was a strong contender for the western constituency seat, securing 42% of the votes. Flosse was re-elected as the Territory's representative to the French Senate in September 1998.

In March 1999 proposals to increase French Polynesia's autonomy, as part of constitutional reforms, were announced in Paris. These proposals followed an initial agreement between the Territory and the French Government in late 1998, on the future of French Polynesia. In October 1999 the French Senate adopted a constitutional amendment granting French Polynesia a greater degree of autonomy. According to the bill (which had also been approved by the National Assembly in June), the status of the islands was to be changed from that of overseas territory to overseas country, and a new Polynesian citizenship was to be created. Although France was to retain control over

areas such as foreign affairs, defence, justice and electoral laws, French Polynesia would have the power to negotiate with other Pacific countries and sign its own international treaties. The constitutional amendment was presented to a joint session of the French Senate and National Assembly for final ratification in late January 2000, although no decision on the matter was taken.

In November 1999 Flosse was found guilty of corruption, on charges of accepting more than 2.7m. French francs in bribes from the owner of an illegal casino, allegedly to help fund his party. Flosse was sentenced to a two-year suspended prison term, a large fine, and a one-year ban on seeking office. Demonstrations, organized by the pro-independence FLP, took place in Tahiti, in protest at Flosse's refusal to resign from his post as President of the Territorial Council of Ministers. In October 2000 Flosse lodged an appeal with the High Court, which reversed the ruling in May 2001. In November 2002 the Court of Appeal in Paris announced that Flosse should be pardoned.

In December 2000 some 2,000 workers went on strike in Papeete, protesting against low wages, and demanding that their pay be raised to a level commensurate with the prosperous state of the Territory's economy. In that month provision was made for the number of seats in the Territorial Assembly to be increased from 41 to 49, in an attempt to reflect demographic changes in the Territory more accurately. At the elections, held on 6 May 2001, Tahoeraa Huiraatira won 28 seats, securing a fifth successive term in office. The pro-independence Tavini Huiraatira took 13 seats. Flosse was subsequently re-elected President of the Territorial Assembly, and a government reorganization ensued.

In January 2002 representatives of state and local government met to review the first five years of the Restructuring Fund, an agreement implemented in 1996 to further the economic autonomy of Polynesia and to regulate financial subsidies to the Territory following the cessation of nuclear testing. The President and Prime Minister of France took part in further such meetings in June and July. It was agreed that funding would be extended for a further 10 years after 2006. The French delegation supported the proposal for a new autonomy statute to grant more powers of self-government to French Polynesia. In December the French Senate approved a bill providing for a constitutional amendment that would allow French Polynesia (along with Wallis and Futuna) to become an Overseas Country; both chambers of the National Assembly in Paris were to debate proposed amendments to the Constitution in March 2003. Meanwhile, at elections to the National Assembly in June 2002, Michel Buillard and Béatrice Vernaudon of the Tahoeraa Huiraatira were elected as deputies.

The testing of nuclear devices by the French Government began in 1966 at Mururoa Atoll, in the Tuamotu Archipelago. In July 1985 the *Rainbow Warrior*, the flagship of the anti-nuclear environmentalist group, Greenpeace, which was to have led a protest flotilla to Mururoa, was sunk in Auckland Harbour, New Zealand, in an explosion that killed one crew member. Two agents of the French secret service, the Direction générale de sécurité extérieure (DGSE), were subsequently convicted of manslaughter and imprisoned in New Zealand, and relations between France and New Zealand were seriously affected by the resultant dispute, especially regarding the treatment of the two agents (see chapter on New Zealand for further details). In May 1991, during a visit to New Zealand, the French Prime Minister, Michel Rocard, formally apologized for the bombing of the *Rainbow Warrior*; however, in July tension between France and the region was exacerbated by the French Government's decision to award a medal for 'distinguished service' to one of the agents convicted for his role in the bombing. Between 1975 and 1992 France performed 135 underground and 52 atmospheric nuclear tests in the Territory.

In April 1992 the French Government announced that nuclear tests would be suspended until the end of the year. Although the decision was welcomed throughout the South Pacific, concern was expressed in French Polynesia over the economic implications of the move, because of the Territory's dependence on income received from hosting the nuclear-test programme. Similarly, it was feared that unemployment resulting from the ban would have a serious impact on the economy. A delegation of political leaders subsequently travelled to Paris to express its concerns, and in January 1993 accepted assistance worth 7,000m. francs CFP in compensation for lost revenue and in aid for development projects.

Shortly after his election in May 1995, President Jacques Chirac announced that France would resume nuclear testing, with a programme of eight tests between September 1995 and May 1996. The decision provoked almost universal outrage in the international community, and was condemned for its apparent disregard for regional opinion, as well as for undermining the considerable progress made by Western nations towards a worldwide ban on nuclear testing. Scientists also expressed concern at the announcement; some believed that further explosions at Mururoa could lead to the collapse of the atoll, which had been weakened considerably. Large-scale demonstrations and protest marches throughout the region were accompanied by boycotts of French products and the suspension of several trade and defence co-operation agreements. Opposition to the French Government intensified in July 1995, when French commandos violently seized *Rainbow Warrior II*, the flagship of Greenpeace, and its crew, which had been protesting peacefully near the test site. Chirac continued to defy mounting pressure from within the EU, from Japan and Russia, as well as from Australia, New Zealand and the South Pacific region, to reverse the decision to carry out the tests.

French Polynesia became the focus of world attention when the first test took place in September 1995. The action attracted further statements of condemnation from Governments around the world, and provoked major demonstrations in many countries. In Tahiti hitherto peaceful protests soon developed into full-scale riots, as several thousand demonstrators rampaged through the capital, demanding an end to French rule. Meanwhile, violent clashes with police, and the burning of dozens of buildings in Papeete during the riots, left much of the capital in ruins. In defiance of world opinion, a further five tests were carried out, the sixth and final one being conducted in January 1996. In early 1996 the French Government confirmed reports by a team of independent scientists that radioactive isotopes had leaked into the waters surrounding the atoll, but denied that they represented a threat to the environment. However, following the election of a new socialist administration in France in mid-1997, the French Minister of the Environment demanded in August 1998 that the matter be investigated further, stating that she had not been reassured by the initial reports. Work to dismantle facilities at the test site began in 1997 and was completed in July 1998.

In September 1998 the trial of more than 60 people charged with offences relating to the riots and protests of September 1995 began in Papeete. Hiro Tefaare, a pro-independence member of the Territorial Assembly and former police officer, was found guilty of instigating the riots and was sentenced to three years' imprisonment (of which 18 months were to be suspended). Furthermore, in September 1999 the French Government was ordered by the Administrative Tribunal to pay 204m. francs CFP in compensation for failing to maintain law and order.

In early 1999 a study by the French Independent Research and Information Commission reported that there was serious radioactive leakage into underground water, lagoons and the ocean at Mururoa and Fangataufa atolls. These claims were dismissed by a New Zealand scientist who had taken part in an earlier study by the International Atomic Energy Agency, which had claimed that radiation levels were nearly undetectable. In May a French government official admitted that fractures had been found in the coral cone at the Mururoa and Fangataufa nuclear testing sites. The reports, by Greenpeace, that the atoll was in danger of collapsing had always been previously denied by France. However, France's claim that no serious long-term damage had been done was contested by Greenpeace, which also suggested the need for an urgent independent study of the test sites. In January 2000, in what was considered to be a significant development, the commander of the French armed forces in French Polynesia admitted that there were significant cracks in the coral reef surrounding Mururoa, and that these could lead to the occurrence of a tsunami.

Government

The French Government is represented in French Polynesia by its High Commissioner to the Territory, and controls various important spheres of government, including defence, foreign diplomacy and justice. A local Territorial Assembly, with 49 members, is elected for a five-year term by universal adult suffrage. The Assembly may elect a President of an executive body, the Territorial Council of Ministers, who, in turn, submits a list of between six and 12 members of the Assembly to serve as ministers, for approval by the Assembly.

In addition, French Polynesia elects two deputies to the French National Assembly in Paris and one representative to the French Senate, all chosen on the basis of universal adult suffrage. French Polynesia is also represented at the European Parliament.

Defence

France tested nuclear weapons at Mururoa Atoll, in the Tuamotu Archipelago, between 1966 and 1996. In August 2002 France maintained a force of 2,600 military personnel in the Territory, as well as a gendarmerie of 600.

Economic Affairs

In 2000, according to World Bank estimates, French Polynesia's gross national income (GNI), measured at average 1998–2000 prices, was US$4,064m., equivalent to US$17,290 per head (or US$23,340m. per head on an international purchasing-power parity basis). During 1990–2000, it was estimated, GNI per head increased, in real terms, at an average annual rate of 0.6%. Over the same period, the population increased at an average annual rate of 1.8%. French Polynesia's gross domestic product (GDP) increased, in real terms, at an average annual rate of 2.3% in 1990–2000. Real GDP increased by 4.0% in both 1999 and 2000.

Agriculture, forestry and fishing contributed only 4.7% of GDP in 2000, but provided most of French Polynesia's exports. The sector engaged 14.6% of the employed labour force in 1996. Coconuts are the principal cash crop, and in 2000 the estimated harvest was 82,000 metric tons. Vegetables, fruit (especially pineapples and citrus fruit), vanilla and coffee are also cultivated. Most commercial fishing, principally for tuna, is conducted, under licence, by Japanese and Korean fleets. Another important activity is the production of cultured black pearls, of which the quantity exported increased from 112 kg in 1984 to 8,182 kg in 1999. In 2000 the Territory was expected to export some 7,116 kg of black pearls, earning some 21,000m. francs CFP (compared with 16,429m. francs CFP and 19,100m. francs CFP in 1998 and 1999 respectively), and during the mid-1990s was estimated to have produced more than 95% of the world's cultured black pearls. Japan is the biggest importer of black pearls from the Territory, and in 1998 purchased an estimated 65% of black pearls produced in that year. The development of the black pearl industry appeared to have decelerated by 2001. Auctions early in the year raised less revenue than expected, with a marked reduction in the number of buyers from Japan in particular, largely owing to the downturn in that country's economy, as well as in Europe and the USA. In 2000 French Polynesia's pearl producers embarked on a 'clean-up' operation aimed at preserving high standards and deterring the sale of cheaper, poor-quality pearls. In December 2001 the industry lowered prices to maintain the level of sales, while at the same time forming a centralized buying syndicate, ensuring minimum prices. Meanwhile, the Territory's largest producer of black pearls, announced the suspension of operations at five farms and a reduction in staff levels for six months, in the hope that pearl prices would rise. In early 2003 the Government allocated some francs CFP 150m. for the promotion of the black pearl industry overseas. The aquaculture sector produced only 41 metric tons of shrimps in 2000.

Industry (comprising manufacturing, construction and utilities) engaged 16.6% of the working population in 1998, and provided 15.5% of GDP in 1997. There is a small manufacturing sector, which is heavily dependent on agriculture. Coconut oil and copra are produced, as are beer, dairy products and vanilla essence. Important deposits of phosphates and cobalt were discovered during the 1980s. The manufacturing sector engaged 8.2% of the employed labour force in 1998, and provided 7.0% of GDP in 1997. Construction is an important industrial activity, contributing 5.3% of GDP in 1997, and engaging 8.4% of the employed labour force in 1998.

Hydrocarbon fuels are the main source of energy in the Territory, with the Papeete thermal power station providing about three-quarters of the electricity produced. Hydroelectric and solar energy also make a significant contribution to French Polynesia's domestic requirements. Hydroelectric power dams, with the capacity to generate the electricity requirements of 36% of Tahiti's population, have been constructed. Solar energy is also increasingly important, especially on the less-populated islands.

Tourism is the Territory's major industry. In 1990 the trade, restaurants and hotels sector contributed 22.7% of GDP. In 2001 some 227,660 tourists visited French Polynesia, compared with

252,000 in the previous year. Receipts from tourism totalled an estimated 45,000m. francs CFP in 2000. French Polynesia's hotel capacity amounted to 3,357 rooms in 2000. The services sector engaged 69.8% of the employed labour force in 1996, and provided 80.4% of GDP in 1997.

In 2000, according to the Institut d'Émission d'Outre-Mer (IEOM—the French overseas reserve bank), French Polynesia recorded a visible trade deficit of 81,052m. francs CFP. On the current account of the balance-of payments there was a surplus of 45,660m. francs CFP, equivalent to 11% of GDP and an increase of 75.8% compared with the previous year. In 2001 imports reached 140,939.3m. francs CFP and exports totalled 25,979.3m. francs CFP. In 2000 the principal sources of imports were France (which provided 36.0% of total imports), the USA (13.9%), Australia (9.3%) and New Zealand (7.4%). The principal markets for exports in that year were Hong Kong (accounting for 20.8% of the total), France (13.8%) and the USA (13.1%). The principal imports in 2001 included machinery and mechanical appliances (9.9% of the total) and road vehicles (12.1%). In 2001 the principal commodity exports were cultured black pearls (providing 58.8% of total export revenue).

A budgetary deficit of 44,579m. francs CFP was projected in 2000. In that year expenditure by the French State in the Territory totalled 124,800m. francs CFP, 28.4% of which was on the military budget. In 2002 France allocated budgetary aid of €929,682m., compared with €905,545m. in 2001. The total external debt was estimated at US $390m. in 1992. The annual rate of inflation averaged 1.2% in 1990–2000, standing at 1.1% in 2000. A high unemployment rate (recorded at 13.2% of the labour force in 1996) is exacerbated by the predominance of young people in the population (in 1996 some 43% of the population were under the age of 20 years).

French Polynesia forms part of the Franc Zone (see p. 237), and is a member of the Pacific Community (see p. 304), which provides technical advice, training and assistance in economic, cultural and social development to countries in the region.

French Polynesia's traditional agriculture-based economy was distorted by the presence of large numbers of French military personnel (in connection with the nuclear-testing programme which began in 1966), stimulating employment in the construction industry and services at the expense of agriculture, and encouraging migration from the outer islands to Tahiti, where 75% of the population currently reside. These dramatic changes effectively transformed French Polynesia from a state of self-sufficiency to one of import dependency in less than a generation. The development of tourism had a similar effect. The Contract for Development, an agreement for metropolitan France to provide the Territory with 28,300m. francs CFP annually between 1996 and 2006, was concluded in 1995 and took effect upon completion of the last series of nuclear tests in early 1996. It was hoped that the arrangement would enable French Polynesia to establish an economy that was more reliant upon local resources and would consequently create greater employment, thereby enhancing the Territory's potential for durable independence. In an attempt to increase revenue, the Territorial Government announced the introduction of a value-added tax (VAT) from October 1997. French Polynesia's steady economic growth has partly been as a result of the development of the services sector, notably in hotel construction and other tourism-related services, which has led to significant employment creation. Other sectors of the economy, such as pearl farming, however, have not expanded as rapidly, principally because of regional economic conditions (notably the recession in Japan, one of the largest importers of black pearls). The continued expansion of GDP throughout the late 1990s was principally due to the financial support provided by France, but also to a significant rise in the number of tourists visiting the Territory (a 16.8% increase between 1997 and 1999). It was hoped that revenue from tourism would eventually replace the grants provided by the French State. In 2001 customs duties were decreased, while VAT rates were maintained at similar levels, as the Government continued the anti-inflationary policy that it had instigated in 1996. The principal aim of the 2002 budget, however, was to avoid recession and to counter the repercussions of the deteriorating global economic situation. VAT rates were increased by an average of 3.3%, and total VAT receipts for the year were expected to reach 36,600m. francs CFP. The 2002 budget also introduced new taxes on alcohol, soft drinks, sugar and new road vehicles. The Government defended the introduction of these new taxes by citing the 'economic uncertainties' faced by French Polynesia. Of total budgetary expenditure of 139,000m. francs CFP, some 50,000m. francs CFP was allocated for investment purposes. The tourism sector, meanwhile, proved vulnerable in the wake of the terrorist attacks on the USA on 11 September 2001. The number of visitor arrivals declined sharply in late 2001, and by early 2002 many of French Polynesia's hotels were reporting occupancy rates as low as 35%.

Education

Education is compulsory for eight years between six and 14 years of age. It is free of charge for day pupils in government schools. Primary education, lasting six years, is financed by the territorial budget, while secondary and technical education are supported by state funds. In 2000/01 there were 54 kindergartens, with 13,720 children enrolled, and 173 primary schools, with 26,249 pupils. Secondary education is provided by both church and government schools. In 2000/01 there were 26,249 pupils at general secondary schools. A total of 3,730 secondary pupils were enrolled at vocational institutions in 1992/93. The French University of the Pacific was established in French Polynesia in 1987. In 1999 it was divided into two separate branches, of which the University of French Polynesia is now based in Papeete. In 1995 the Papeete branch had 50 teachers and, in 1998/99, some 1,685 students. Total government expenditure on education in the Territory was 40,300m. francs CFP in 1999.

Public Holidays

2003: 1 January (New Year's Day), 5 March (Arrival of the Gospel), 18–21 April (Easter), 1 May (Labour Day), 8 May (Liberation Day), 29 May (Ascension Day), 9 June (Whit Monday), 14 July (Fall of the Bastille), 15 August (Assumption), 8 September (Internal Autonomy Day), 1 November (All Saints' Day), 11 November (Armistice Day), 25 December (Christmas Day).

2004: 1 January (New Year's Day), 5 March (Arrival of the Gospel), 9–12 April (Easter), 1 May (Labour Day), 8 May (Liberation Day), 20 May (Ascension Day), 30 May (Whit Monday), 14 July (Fall of the Bastille), 15 August (Assumption), 8 September (Internal Autonomy Day), 1 November (All Saints' Day), 11 November (Armistice Day), 25 December (Christmas Day).

Weights and Measures

The metric system is in force.

Statistical Survey

Source (unless otherwise indicated): Institut Statistique de la Polynésie Française, Immeuble UUPA, rue Edouard Ahne, BP 395, 98713 Papeete; tel. 473434; fax 427252; e-mail ispf@ispf.pf; internet www.ispf.pf.

AREA AND POPULATION

Area: Total 4,167 sq km (1,609 sq miles); Land area 3,521 sq km (1,359 sq miles).

Population: 188,814 at census of 6 September 1988; 219,521 (males 113,934, females 105,587) at census of 3 September 1996; 245,405 (provisional figure) at census of 7 November 2002.

Population by island group (provisional figures, 2002 census): Society Archipelago 214,445 (Windward Islands 184,224, Leeward Islands 30,221); Marquesas Archipelago 8,712; Austral Islands 6,386; Tuamotu-Gambier Islands 15,862.

Density (provisional figure, November 2002): 58.9 per sq km.

Ethnic Groups (census of 15 October 1983): Polynesian 114,280; 'Demis' 23,625 (Polynesian-European 15,851, Polynesian-Chinese 6,356, Polynesian-Other races 1,418); European 19,320; Chinese 7,424; European-Chinese 494; Others 1,610; Total 166,753. *1988 census* ('000 persons): Polynesians and 'Demis' 156.3; Others 32.5.

Principal Towns (population at 2002 census, provisional figures): Faaa 28,339; Papeete (capital) 26,181; Punaauía 23,706; Pirae 14,499; Moorea-Maiao 14,550; Mahina 13,334; Paea 12,276.

Births, Marriages and Deaths (1999, provisional): Registered live births 4,580 (birth rate 20.0 per 1,000); Marriages (1997) 1,176 (marriage rate 5.3 per 1,000). *2001* (marriage rate 3.9 per 1,000); Registered deaths 1,003 (death rate 4.4 per 1,000).

Expectation of Life (years at birth, provisional, 2000): Males 72.5; Females 77.2. Source: UN, *Statistical Yearbook for Asia and the Pacific*.

Economically Active Population (persons aged 14 years and over, 1996 census): Agriculture, hunting, forestry and fishing 10,888; Mining and manufacturing 6,424; Electricity, gas and water 459; Construction 4,777; Trade, restaurants and hotels 9,357; Transport, storage and communications 3,788; Financial services 1,482; Real estate 383; Business services 3,710; Private services 9,033; Education, health and social welfare 10,771; Public administration 13,475; Total employed 74,547 (males 46,141, females 28,406); Persons on compulsory military service 1,049 (all males); Unemployed 11,525 (males 6,255, females 5,270); Total labour force 87,121 (males 53,445, females 33,676).

HEALTH AND WELFARE

Key Indicators

Physicians (per 1,000 head, 2001): 1.8.
For definitions, see explanatory note on p. vi.

AGRICULTURE, ETC.

Principal Crops (FAO estimates, metric tons, 2001): Roots and tubers 12,400; Vegetables and melons 7,210; Pineapples 3,500; Other fruit 4,120; Coconuts 82,000; Vanilla 20; Coffee (green) 18. Source: FAO.

Livestock (FAO estimates, year ending September 2001): Cattle 9,100; Horses 2,200; Pigs 37,000; Goats 16,500; Sheep 440; Chickens 300,000; Ducks 33,000. Source: FAO.

Livestock Products (FAO estimates, metric tons, 2001): Beef and veal 170; Pig meat 1,300; Goat meat 75; Poultry meat 729; Cows' milk 1,305; Hen eggs 1,600; Other poultry eggs 85. Source: FAO.

Fishing ('000 metric tons, live weight, 2000): Capture 13.9 (Common dolphinfish 0.4, Skipjack tuna 1.2; Albacore 3.6, Yellowfin tuna 1.8, Marlins and sailfishes 0.6, Sharks, rays, skates, etc. 0.6); Aquaculture 0.1; Total catch 14.0. Note: Figures exclude trochus shells (FAO estimate, metric tons): 35. Source: FAO, *Yearbook of Fishery Statistics*.

INDUSTRY

Production: Copra 8,262 metric tons (sales, 2001); Coconut oil 5,000* metric tons (2001); Oilcake 2,500* metric tons (2001); Beer 129,000 hectolitres (1992); Printed cloth 200,000 m (1979); Japanese sandals 600,000 pairs (1979); Electric energy 495.2m. kWh (2001). *FAO estimate.

FINANCE

Currency and Exchange Rates: 100 centimes = 1 franc de la Communauté française du Pacifique (franc CFP or Pacific franc). *Sterling, Dollar and Euro Equivalents* (31 December 2002): £1 sterling = 183.41 francs CFP; US $1 = 113.79 francs CFP; €1 = 119.33 francs CFP; 1,000 francs CFP = £5.452 = $8.788 = €8.380. *Average Exchange Rate* (francs CFP per US $): 129.52 in 2000; 133.35 in 2001; 126.80 in 2002. Note: Until 31 December 1998 the value of the franc CFP was fixed at 5.5 French centimes (1 French franc = 18.1818 francs CFP). Since the introduction of the euro, on 1 January 1999, an official exchange rate of 1,000 francs CFP = €8.38 (€1 = 119.332 francs CFP) has been in operation. Accordingly, the value of the franc CFP has been adjusted to 5.4969 French centimes (1 French franc = 18.1920 francs CFP), representing a 'devaluation' of 0.056%.

Territorial Budget (million francs CFP, 2001): *Revenue:* Current 108,036 (Indirect taxation 59,523). *Expenditure:* Current 95,796, Capital 44,913; Total 140,709.

French State Expenditure (million francs CFP, 1996): Civil budget 61,706 (Current 56,564, Capital 5,142); Military budget 46,119 (Current 37,160, Capital 8,959); Pensions 10,458; Total (incl. others) 123,774 (Current 109,060, Capital 14,714). *1998* (million francs CFP): 121,788 (incl. military budget 37,982). *1999* (million francs CFP): 120,631 (incl. military budget 34,343). *2000* (million francs CFP): 124,800 (incl. military budget 35,400). *2001* (million francs CFP): 128,480 (incl. military budget 36,774).

Money Supply (million francs CFP at 31 December 2001): Currency in circulation 9,366; Demand deposits 100,617; Total money 109,983. Source: Institut d'Emission d'Outre-Mer.

Cost of Living (Consumer Price Index; base: 1990 = 100): All items 111.7 in 1999; 112.9 in 2000; 114.0 in 2001. Source: UN, Monthly Bulletin of Statistics.

Gross Domestic Product (million francs CFP at current prices): 378,501 in 1997; 404,886 in 1998; 412,100 in 1999; 446,100 in 2000.

Expenditure on the Gross Domestic Product (million francs CFP at current prices, 1993): Government final consumption expenditure 126,127; Private final consumption expenditure 202,563; Increase in stocks -536; Gross fixed capital formation 53,494; *Total domestic expenditure* 381,648; Exports of goods and services 34,523; *Less* Imports of goods and services 86,905; *GDP in purchasers' values* 329,266. Source: UN, *National Accounts Statistics*.

Gross Domestic Product by Economic Activity (million francs CFP at current prices, 1997): Agriculture, forestry and fishing 15,534; Manufacturing 26,360*; Electricity, gas and water 12,221*; Construction 20,104; Trade 81,854; Transport and telecommunications 27,832. Other private services 96,714; Government services 97,238; Domestic services 646; *GDP in purchasers' values* 378,503. *Manufacturing of energy-generating products is included in electricity, gas and water. Source: UN, *National Accounts Statistics*.

EXTERNAL TRADE

Principal Commodities (million francs CFP, 2001): *Imports c.i.f.*: Live animals and animal products 9,617.3 (Meat and edible meat offal 6,188.0); Prepared foodstuffs; beverages, spirits and vinegar; tobacco and manufactured substitutes 13,890.5; Mineral products 13,257.9 (Mineral fuels, mineral oils and products of their distillation; bituminous substances; mineral waxes 11,725.0); Products of chemical or allied industries 9,871.5 (Pharmaceutical products 4,675.7); Plastics, rubber and articles thereof 5,313.2; Paper-making materials; paper and paperboard and articles thereof 4,266.3; Textiles and textile articles 4,751.3; Base metals and articles thereof 8,177.2; Machinery and mechanical appliances; electrical equipment; sound and television apparatus 24,524.1 (Nuclear reactors, boilers, machinery, mechanical appliances and parts 14,007.9, Electrical machinery, equipment, etc. 10,516.2); Vehicles, aircraft, vessels and associated transport equipment 24,955.2 (Road vehicles, parts and accessories 17,087.7); Miscellaneous manufactured articles 5,689.9; Total (incl. others) 140,939.3. *Exports f.o.b.*: Live animals and animal products 1,627.9 (Fish and crustaceans, molluscs and other aquatic invertebrates 1,458.2); Prepared foodstuffs; beverages, spirits and vinegar; tobacco and manufactured substitutes 950.1 (Preparations of vegetables, fruit, nuts or other parts of plants 862.8); Natural or cultured pearls, precious or semi-precious stones, precious metals and articles thereof; imitation jewellery; coin 15,281.3; Machinery and mechanical appliances; electrical equipment; sound and television apparatus 1,746.1 (Nuclear reactors, boilers, machinery, mechanical appliances and parts 1,213.2); Vehicles, aircraft, vessels and associated transport equipment 4,851.8 (Aircraft, spacecraft and parts 4,324.3); Total (incl. others) 25,979.3.

Principal Trading Partners (million francs CFP, 2000): *Imports*: Australia 11,763; Belgium 6,004; China, People's Republic 3,566; France 45,531; Germany 1,775; Italy 3,828; Japan 5,116; Korea, Republic 1,544; New Zealand 9,338; Singapore 2,445; Spain 1,707; Taiwan 1,634; United Kingdom 2,447; USA 17,594; Total (incl. others) 126,407. *Exports*: France 3,989; Germany 499; Hong Kong 6,010; Japan 349; New Caledonia 1,440; New Zealand 297; USA 3,768; Total (incl. others) 28,829. Source: ISPF—Service des Douanes.

TRANSPORT

Road Traffic (1987): Total vehicles registered 54,979; (1996 census): Private cars 47,300.

Shipping (1990): *International traffic*: Passengers carried 47,616; Freight handled 642,314 metric tons. *Domestic traffic*: Passengers carried 596,185; Freight handled 261,593 metric tons. (2001): Goods unloaded 904,727 metric tons; Goods loaded 32,658 metric tons.

Civil Aviation (2001): *International traffic*: Passengers carried 560,701; Freight handled 8,717 metric tons. *Domestic traffic*: Passengers carried 833,086; Freight handled 2,992 metric tons.

TOURISM

Visitors (excluding cruise passengers and excursionists): 210,800 in 1999; 252,000 in 2000; 227,660 in 2001.

Tourist Arrivals by Country of Residence (2001): Australia 6,420; Canada 3,648; France 50,466; Germany 5,448; Italy 9,351; Japan 19,031; New Zealand 5,435; United Kingdom 6,496; USA 93,363; Total (incl. others) 227,658.

Tourism Receipts (US $ million): 359 in 1997; 354 in 1998; 394 in 1999 (Source: World Tourism Organization).

2000: 49,900m. francs CFP.
Source: Ministère du Tourisme.

COMMUNICATIONS MEDIA

Radio Receivers (1997): 128,000 in use*.

Television Receivers (2000): 44,000 in use†.

Telephones (2001): 52,600 main lines in use†.

Facsimile Machines (1998): 3,000 in use†.

Mobile Cellular Telephones (subscribers, 2001): 67,000†.

Internet Users (2001): 16,000†.

Daily Newspapers (2000): 2.

* Source: UNESCO, *Statistical Yearbook*.
† Source: International Telecommunication Union.

EDUCATION

Pre-primary (2000/01): 54 schools; 408 teachers (1996/97); 13,720 pupils.

Primary (2000/01): 173 schools; 2,811 teachers (1996/97); 26,249 pupils.

General Secondary (2000/01): 2,035 teachers (1998/99); 24,743 pupils.

Vocational (1992): 316 teachers; 3,730 students.

Tertiary (1993): 34 teachers; 892 students.
Source: partly UNESCO, *Statistical Yearbook*.

Directory

The Constitution

The constitutional system in French Polynesia is established under the aegis of the Constitution of the Fifth French Republic and specific laws of 1977, 1984 and 1990. The French Polynesia Statute 1984, the so-called 'internal autonomy statute', underwent amendment in a law of July 1990. A further extension of the Territory's powers under the statute was approved by the French National Assembly in December 1995. A constitutional amendment granting French Polynesia a greater degree of autonomy was presented to a joint session of the French Senate and National Assembly for final ratification in January 2000 (see History). By early 2002, however, no decision had been taken on the matter.

French Polynesia is declared to be an autonomous Territory of the French Republic, of which it remains an integral part. The High Commissioner, appointed by the French Government, exercises the prerogatives of the State in matters relating to defence, foreign relations, the maintenance of law and order, communications and citizenship. The head of the local executive and the person who represents the Territory is the President of the Territorial Government, who is elected by the Territorial Assembly from among its own number. The Territorial President appoints and dismisses the Council of Ministers and has competence in international relations as they affect French Polynesia and its exclusive economic zone, and is in control of foreign investments and immigration. The Territorial Assembly, which has financial autonomy in budgetary affairs and legislative authority within the Territory, is elected for a term of up to five years on the basis of universal adult suffrage. There are 49 members: 32 elected by the people of the Windward Islands (Iles du Vent—Society Islands), seven by the Leeward Islands (Iles Sous le Vent—Society Islands), four by the Tuamotu Archipelago and the Gambier Islands and three each by the Austral Islands and by the Marquesas Archipelago. The Assembly elects a Permanent Commission of between seven and nine of its members, and itself meets for two ordinary sessions each year and upon the demand of the majority party, the Territorial President or the High Commissioner. Local government is conducted by the municipalities. There is an Economic, Social and Cultural Council (composed of representatives of professional groups, trade unions and other organizations and agencies which participate in the economic, social and cultural activities of the Territory), a Territorial Audit Office and a judicial system which includes a Court of the First Instance, a Court of Appeal and an Administrative Court. The Territory, as a part of the French Republic, also elects two deputies to the National Assembly and one member of the Senate, and may be represented in the European Parliament.

The Government

(April 2003)

High Commissioner: MICHEL MATHIEU (appointed October 2001).

Secretary-General: CHRISTIAN MASSIMON.

COUNCIL OF MINISTERS

President and Minister for Foreign Affairs, the Pearl Culture Industry and Urban Development: GASTON FLOSSE.

Vice-President and Minister for Employment and Training, Outer Island Development, New Technologies and Post: EDOUARD FRITCH.

Minister for Economy and Finance: GEORGES PUCHON.

Minister for Housing, Land Use, Urban Affairs, Town Humanization and Government Spokesman: JEAN-CHRISTOPHE BOUISSOU.

Minister for Lands, Land Redistribution and Valuation: GASTON TONG SANG.

Minister for Education and Technical Training: NICOLAS SANQUER.

Minister for Ports and Utilities: JONAS TAHUAITU.

Minister for Environment and City Policy: BRUNO SANDRAS.

Minister for Tourism and Transport: BRIGITTE VANIZETTE.

Minister for Fisheries, Industry and Small and Medium Businesses: NINA VERNAUDON.

Minister for Agriculture and Livestock: FRÉDÉRIC RIVETA.

Minister for Solidarity and Family: PIA FAATOMO.

Minister for Youth and Sports, Youth Opportunities and Associative Affairs, responsible for Relations with the Territorial Assembly and the Economic, Social and Cultural Council: REYNALD TEMARII.

Minister for Health, Public Service and Administrative Decentralization: ARMELLE MERCERON.

Minister for Culture and Higher Education, responsible for the Promotion of Women's Affairs and Polynesian Languages: LOUISE PELTZER.

Minister for Arts and Crafts: PASCALE HAITI.

GOVERNMENT OFFICES

Office of the High Commissioner of the Republic: Bureau du Haut Commissaire, ave Bruat, BP 115, 98713, Papeete; tel. 468686; fax 468689; e-mail courrier@haut-commissariat.pf.

Office of the President of the Territorial Government: BP 2551, 98713 Papeete; tel. 472000; fax 419781; e-mail presid@mail.pf; internet www.presidence.pf.

Territorial Government of French Polynesia: BP 2551, Papeete; 28 blvd Saint-Germain, 75005 Paris, France; tel. 472000; fax 419781; e-mail presid@mail.pf; tel. 1-55-42-65-10; fax 1-55-42-64-09; all ministries; Delegation in Paris.

Economic, Social and Cultural Council: ave Bruat, BP 1657, 98716 Papeete; tel. 416500; fax 419242; e-mail cesc@cesc.gov.pf; Pres. BRUNO SANDRAS.

Ministry of Agriculture: Papeete; internet www.agriculture.gov.pf.

Ministry of Craft Industry: Papeete; internet www.artisanat.gov.pf.

Ministry of Culture: Papeete; internet www.culture.gov.pf.

Ministry of the Economy and Finance: Papeete; e-mail cabinet@economie.gov.pf; internet www.finances.gov.pf.

Ministry of Education: Papeete; internet www.education.gov.pf.

Ministry of Environment: Papeete.

Ministry of Fisheries: Papeete; internet www.mer.gov.pf.

Ministry of Health: Papeete; internet www.sante.gov.pf.

Ministry of Housing: Papeete; internet www.logement.gov.pf.

Ministry of Land Affairs: Papeete; internet www.foncier.gov.pf.

Ministry of the Pearl Industry: Papeete; internet www.perle.gov.pf.

Ministry of Public Works and Harbours: Papeete; internet www.equipement.gov.pf.

Ministry of Solidarity and Family Affairs: Papeete; internet www.solidarite.gov.pf.

Ministry of Tourism and Transportation: BP 2551, 98713 Papeete; tel. 472440; fax 426136; e-mail dircab.mtt@tourisme.gov.pf; internet www.tourisme.gov.pf.

Ministry of Youth: Papeete; internet www.jeunesse.gov.pf.

Legislature

ASSEMBLÉE TERRITORIALE

President: LUCETTE TAERO.

Territorial Assembly: Assemblée Territoriale, BP 28, Papeete; tel. 416100; fax 416160.

Election, 6 May 2001

Party	Seats
Tahoeraa Huiraatira/RPR	28
Tavini Huiraatira	13
Fe'tia Api	7
Tapura Amui No Tuhaa Pae	1
Total	49

PARLEMENT

Deputies to the French National Assembly: Michel Buillard (Tahoeraa Huiraatira/RPR), Béatrice Vernaudon (Tahoeraa Huiraatira/RPR).

Representative to the French Senate: Gaston Flosse (Tahoeraa Huiraatira/RPR).

Political Organizations

Ai'a Api (New Land): BP 11055, Mahina, Tahiti; tel. 481135; f. 1982; after split in Te E'a Api; Leader Emile Vernaudon.

Alliance 2000: c/o Assemblée Territoriale, BP 28, Papeete; pro-independence grouping.

Fe'tia Api (New Star): c/o Assemblée Territoriale, BP 140 512, Arue; Leader Boris Léontieff.

Haere i Mua: Leader Alexandre Léontieff.

Heiura-Les Verts: BP 44, Borabora; tel. and fax 677174; e-mail heiura@mail.pf.

Ia Mana Te Nunaa: rue du Commandant Destrémau, BP 1223, Papeete; tel. 426699; f. 1976; advocates 'socialist independence'; Sec.-Gen. Jacques Drollet.

Polynesian Union Party: Papeete; Leader Jean Juventin.

Pupu Here Ai'a Te Nunaa Ia Ora: BP 3195, Papeete; tel. 420766; f. 1965; advocates autonomy; 8,000 mems.

Te Hono e Tau I te Honu Hui: Papeete; f. 2002; Leader Stanley Cross.

Te Tiaraama: Papeete; f. 1987 by split from the RPR; Leader Alexandre Léontieff.

Pupu Taina/Rassemblement des Libéraux: rue Cook, BP 169, Papeete; tel. 429880; f. 1976; seeks to retain close links with France; associated with the French Union pour la Démocratie Française (UDF); Leader Michel Law.

Taatiraa No Te Hali: BP 2916, Papeete; tel. 437494; fax 422546; f. 1977; Pres. Robert Tanseau.

Tahoeraa Huiraatira/Rassemblement pour la République (RPR): rue du Commandant Destrémau, BP 471, Papeete; tel. 429898; fax 450004; f. 1958; supports links with France, with internal autonomy; Pres. Gaston Flosse; Hon. Pres. Jacques Teuira.

Tapura Amui No Tuhaa Pae: c/o Assemblée Territoriale, BP 28, Papeete; represents the Austral Islands; Leader Chantal Flores.

Tavini Huiraatira/Front de Libération de la Polynésie (FLP): independence movement; anti-nuclear; Leader Oscar Temaru.

Te Avei'a Mau (True Path): c/o Assemblée Territoriale, BP 28, Papeete; Leader Tinomana Ebb.

Te e'a No Maohi Nui: Leader Jean-Marius Raapoto.

Te Henua Enata Kotoa: c/o Assemblée Territoriale, BP 28, Papeete; Leader Lucien Kimitete.

Judicial System

Court of Appeal: Cour d'Appel de Papeete, BP 101, 98713 Papeete; tel. 415553; fax 424416; Pres. Patrick Michaux; Attorney-General François Deby.

Court of the First Instance: Tribunal de Première Instance de Papeete, BP 101, Papeete; tel. 415500; fax 454012; internet www.polynesie-francaise.gouv.fr; e-mail pr.tpi-papeete@justice.pf; Pres. Jean-Louis Thiolet; Procurator Michel Marotte; Clerk of the Court Carole Vairaaroa.

Court of Administrative Law: Tribunal Administratif, BP 4522, Papeete; tel. 509025; fax 451724; e-mail tapapeete@mail.pf; Pres. Alfred Poupet; Cllrs Raoul Aureille, Marie-Christine Lubrano, Alain Levasseur, Hélène Rouland.

Religion

About 54% of the population are Protestants and 30% are Roman Catholics.

CHRISTIANITY

Protestant Church

L'Eglise évangélique en Polynésie française (Etaretia Evaneria i Porinetia Farani): BP 113, Papeete; tel. 460600; fax 419357; e-mail eepf@mail.pf; f. 1884; autonomous since 1963; c. 95,000 mems; Pres. of Council Rev. Jacques Terai Ihorai; Sec.-Gen. (vacant).

The Roman Catholic Church

French Polynesia comprises the archdiocese of Papeete and the suffragan diocese of Taiohae o Tefenuaenata (based in Nuku Hiva, Marquesas Is). At 31 December 1999 there were an estimated 83,000 adherents in the Territory, representing about 37% of the total population. The Archbishop and the Bishop participate in the Episcopal Conference of the Pacific, based in Fiji.

Archbishop of Papeete: Most Rev. Hubert Coppenrath, Archevêché, BP 94, Vallée de la Mission, 98713 Papeete; tel. 502351; fax 424032; e-mail catholic@mail.pf.

Other Churches

There are small Sanito, Church of Jesus Christ of Latter-day Saints (Mormon), and Seventh-day Adventist missions.

The Press

La Dépêche de Tahiti: Société Océanienne de Communication, BP 50, Papeete; tel. 464343; fax 464350; e-mail journalistes@france-antilles.pf; internet www.ladepechedetahiti.com; f. 1964; daily; French; Editor-in-Chief Daniel Pardon; Dir-Gen. Pascal Heems; circ. 15,000.

Les Nouvelles de Tahiti: place de la Cathédrale, BP 629, Papeete; tel. 508100; fax 508109; e-mail nouvelles@mail.pf; f. 1956; daily; French; Editor Muriel Pontarollo; Dir-Gen. Pascal Heems; Publr Philippe Hersant; circ. 6,500.

Le Semeur Tahitien: BP 94, 98713 Papeete; tel. 502350; e-mail catholic@mail.pf; f. 1909; bi-monthly; French; publ. by the Roman Catholic Church.

Tahiti Beach Press: BP 887, 98713 Papeete; tel. 426850; fax 423356; e-mail tahitibeachpress@mail.pf; f. 1980; weekly; English; Publr G. Warti; circ. 3,500.

Tahiti Pacifique Magazine: BP 368, Maharepa, Moorea; tel. 562894; fax 563007; e-mail tahitipm@mail.pf; internet www.tahiti-pacifique.com; monthly; French; Editor Alex du Prel; circ. 5,000.

Tahiti Rama: Papeete; weekly.

Tahiti Today: BP 887, 98713 Papeete; tel. 426850; fax 423356; f. 1996; quarterly; Publr G. Warti; circ. 3,000.

La Tribune Polynésienne: place du Marché, BP 392, Papeete; tel. 481048; fax 481220; weekly; Dir Louis Bresson.

Ve'a Katorika: BP 94, 98713 Papeete; f. 1909; monthly; publ. by the Roman Catholic Church.

Ve'a Porotetani: BP 113, Papeete; tel. 460623; fax 419357; e-mail eepf@mail.pf; f. 1921; monthly; French and Tahitian; publ. by the Evangelical Church; Dir Ihorai Jacques; circ. 5,000.

NEWS AGENCIES

Tahitian Press Agency (ATP): Papeete; f. 2001; bilingual French and English news service providing pictures and radio reports.

Foreign Bureaux

Agence France-Presse (AFP): BP 629, Papeete; tel. 508100; fax 508109; e-mail international@france-antilles.pf; Correspondent Christian Bretault.

Associated Press (AP) (USA): BP 912, Papeete; tel. 437562; Correspondent Al Prince.

Reuters (UK): BP 50, Papeete; tel. 464340; fax 464390; e-mail danielpardon@mail.pf; Correspondent Daniel Pardon.

Publishers

Haere Po No Tahiti: BP 1958, Papeete; fax 582333; f. 1981; travel, history, botany, linguistics and local interest.

Au Vent des Îles: BP 5670, 98716 Pirae; tel. 509595; fax 509597; e-mail mail@auventdesiles.pf; internet www.auventdesiles.pf; f. 1992; Gen. Man. CHRISTIAN ROBERT.

Government Printer

Imprimerie Officielle: 43 rue des Poilus-Tahitiens, BP 117, 98713 Papeete; tel. 500580; fax 425261; e-mail compta.clients@imprimerie.gov.pf; f. 1843; printers, publrs; Dir (acting) MARC LAUGHLIN.

Broadcasting and Communications

TELECOMMUNICATIONS

Office des Postes et Télécommunications: 8 rue de la Reine Pomare IV, Papeete; tel. 414242; fax 436767; Dir-Gen. GEFFRY SALMON.

France Cables et Radio (FCR): Télécommunications extérieures de la Polynésie française, BP 99, Papeete; tel. 415400; fax 437553; e-mail fcr@mail.pf.

BROADCASTING

Radio

RFO Polynésie: 410 rue Dumont d'Urville, POB 60, Pamatai; tel. 861616; fax 861611; e-mail jrbodin@mail.pf; internet www.rfo.fr.html; public service radio and television station operated by Réseau France Outre-Mer (RFO), Paris; daily programmes in French and Tahitian; Area Man. WALLES KOTRA; Communications Man. JEAN-RAYMOND BODIN.

Private Stations

NRJ Radio: Papeete; tel. and fax 464346; e-mail nrj@mail.pf; French.

Radio Bleue: Papeete; tel. 483436; fax 480825; e-mail redaction@radiobleue.pf; affiliated to the political party Ai'a Api; French.

Radio Maohi: Maison des Jeunes, Pirae; tel. 819797; fax 825493; e-mail tereo@mail.pf; owned by the political party Tahoeraa Huiraatira; French and Tahitian.

Radio One: Fare Ute, BP 3601, Papeete; tel. 434100; fax 423406; e-mail infos@radio1.pf.

Radio Tefana: Papeete; tel. 819797; fax 825493; e-mail tereo@mail.pf; affiliated to the political party Tavini Huiraatira; French and Tahitian.

Radio Tiare: Fare Ute, Papeete; tel. 434100; fax 423406; e-mail contact@tiarefm.pf.

Television

Radio-Télé-Tahiti: see Radio.

Canal Plus Polynésie: Immeuble Pomare, blvd Paofai, BP 20051, 98713 Papeete; tel. 540754; fax 540755; e-mail serge.lamagnere@canal-caledonie.com; privately owned; Dir SERGE LAMAGNÈRE.

Telefenua: Centre Commercial Le Lotus, Punaauia 98717; tel. 461111; fax 501275; internet www.telefenua.com; paying cable channel broadcasting in French, Tahitian and English; Pres. ALAIN DIETER.

TNTV (Tahiti Nui Television): BP 348 98713, Papeete; tel. 473636; e-mail tntv@tntv.pf; internet www.tntv.pf; broadcasts in French and Tahitian; Gen. Man. DANIEL FRANCO.

TNS (Tahiti Nui Satellite): see TNTV; French.

Finance

(cap. = capital; res = reserves; dep. = deposits; m. = million; brs = branches; amounts in CFP francs)

BANKING

Commercial Banks

Banque de Polynésie SA: 355 blvd Pomare, BP 530, 9713 Papeete; tel. 466666; fax 466664; e-mail sec.gen@sg-bdp.pf; internet www.sg-bdp.pf; f. 1973; 80% owned by Société Générale (France); cap. and res 4,536.5m., dep. 83,005.9m. (Dec. 2001); Pres. JEAN-LOUIS MATTEI; Gen. Man. CHRISTIAN DESBORDES; 14 brs.

Banque de Tahiti SA: rue François Cardella, BP 1602, Papeete; tel. 417000; fax 423376; e-mail dirgene@bt.pf; internet www.banque-tahiti.pf; f. 1969; owned by Caisse Nationale (96%); merged with Banque Paribas de Polynésie, Aug. 1998; cap. 1,336.5m., res 5,169.2m., dep. 84,249.3m. (Dec. 2001); Pres. JEAN-CHRISTOPHE IRRMANN; Exec. Vice-Pres. MICHEL DUPIEUX; 17 brs.

Banque SOCREDO—Société pour le Crédit et le Développement en Océanie: 115 rue Dumont d'Urville, BP 130, 98713 Papeete; tel. 415123; fax 433661; f. 1959; public body; affiliated to Banque Nationale de Paris (France); cap. 7,000m. (Dec. 1993), dep. 76,610m. (Dec. 1995); Pres. JEAN VERNAUDON; Dir ERIC POMMIER; 24 brs.

Trade and Industry

DEVELOPMENT ORGANIZATIONS

Agence pour l'Emploi et la Formation Professionnelle: BP 540, Papeete; tel. 426375; fax 426281.

Agence Française de Développement (ACFD): BP 578, Papeete; tel. 544600; fax 544601; public body; development finance institute.

Conseil Economique, Social et Culturel: ave Bruat, BP 1657, 98716 Papeete; tel. 416500; fax 419242; e-mail cesc@cesc.gov.pf; Dir BRUNO SANDRAS.

Service de l'Artisanat Traditionnel: BP 4451, Papeete 98713; tel. 423225; fax 436478; Dir TEURA IRITI.

Service du Développement de l'Industrie et des Métiers: BP 9055, 98713 Papeete; tel. 502880; fax 412645; e-mail self.service@industrie.gov.pf; industry and small business development administration.

Société pour le Développement de l'Agriculture et de la Pêche: BP 1247, Papeete; tel. 836798; fax 856886; agriculture and marine industries.

SODEP (Société pour le Développement et l'Expansion du Pacifique): BP 4441, Papeete; tel. 429449; f. 1961 by consortium of banks and private interests; regional development and finance co.

CHAMBERS OF COMMERCE

Chambre de Commerce, d'Industrie, des Services et des Métiers de Polynésie Française: 41 rue du Docteur Cassiau, BP 118, Papeete 98713; tel. 472700; fax 540701; e-mail info@cci.pf; internet www.ccism.pf; f. 1880; 36 mems; Pres. STÉPHANE CHIN LOY.

Chambre d'Agriculture et de la Pêche Lagonaire: route de l'Hippodrome, BP 5383, Pirae; tel. 425393; fax 438754; f. 1886; 10 mems; Pres. CLAUDE HAUATA.

Jeune Chambre Economique de Tahiti: BP 2576, Papeete; tel. 454542; fax 466070; internet www.jce.pf; Pres. CATHY GOURBAULT.

EMPLOYERS' ORGANIZATIONS

Chambre Syndicale des Entrepreneurs du Bâtiment et des Travaux Publics: BP 2218, Papeete; tel. 438898; fax 423237; Pres. GEORGES TRAMINI.

Conseil des Employeurs: Immeuble Farnham, rue Clappier, BP 972, Papeete; tel. 541040; fax 423237; internet cepf@cepf.pf; f. 1983; Pres. ANTONIMA MAMBRIDGE; Sec.-Gen. CÉDRIC VIDAL.

Fédération Générale du Commerce (FGC): angle rue Albert Leboucher et rue Clappier, BP 1607, 98713 Papeete; tel. 541042; fax 422359; Pres. GILLES YAU.

Fédération Polynésienne de l'Agriculture et de l'Elevage: Papara, Tahiti; Pres. MICHEL LEHARTEL.

Union Interprofessionnelle du Tourisme de la Polynésie Française: BP 4560, Papeete; tel. 439114; f. 1973; 1,200 mems; Pres. PAUL MAETZ; Sec.-Gen. JEAN CORTEEL.

Union Patronale: BP 317, Papeete; tel. 438898; fax 423237; f. 1948; 63 mems; Pres. DIDIER CHOMER.

UTILITES

Electricity

Electricité de Tahiti: route de Puurai, BP 8021, Faaa-Puurai; tel. 867777.

Water

Société Polynésienne des Eaux et Assainissements: Papeete, Tahiti.

Syndicat Central de l'Hydraulique: Tahiti.

TRADE UNIONS

Confédération Syndicale A Tia I Mua: Immeuble la Ora, BP 4523, Papeete; tel. 544010; fax 450245; e-mail atiaimua@ifrance.com; affiliated to CFDT (France); Gen. Sec. TU YAN.

Fédération des Syndicats de la Polynésie Française: BP 1136, Papeete; Pres. MARCEL AHINI.

Syndicat Territorial des Instituteurs et Institutrices de Polynésie: BP 3007, Papeete; Sec.-Gen. WILLY URIMA.

Union des Syndicats Affiliés des Travailleurs de Polynésie/Force Ouvrière (USATP/FO): BP 1201, Papeete; tel. 426049; fax 450635; Pres. COCO TERAIEFA CHANG; Sec.-Gen. PIERRE FRÉBAULT.

Union des Syndicats de l'Aéronautique: Papeete; Pres. JOSEPH CONROY.

Union des Travailleurs de Tahiti et des Iles: BP 3366, Papeete.

Transport

ROADS

French Polynesia has 792 km of roads, of which about one-third are bitumen-surfaced and two-thirds stone-surfaced.

SHIPPING

The principal port is Papeete, on Tahiti.

Port Authority: Port Autonome de Papeete, Motu Uta, BP 9164, 98715 Papeete; tel. 505454; fax 421950; e-mail portppt@mail.pf; internet www.portoftahiti.com; Harbour Master Commdt CLAUDE VIGOR; Port Man. BÉATRICE CHANSIN.

Agence Maritime Internationale de Tahiti: BP 274, Papeete, Tahiti; tel. 428972; fax 432184; e-mail amitahiti@mail.pf; services from Asia, the USA, Australia, New Zealand, American Samoa and Europe.

CGM Tour du Monde SA: 80 rue du Général de Gaulle, BP 96, Papeete; tel. 420890; fax 436806; shipowners and agents; freight services between Europe and many international ports; Dir HENRI C. FERRAND.

Compagnie de Développement Maritime des Tuamotu (CODEMAT): POB 1291, Papeete.

Compagnie Française Maritime de Tahiti: 2 rue de Commerce, POB 368, Papeete; tel. 426393; fax 420617; Man. M. GARBUTT.

Compagnie Maritime des Iles Sous le Vent: BP 9012, Papeete.

Compagnie Polynésienne de Transport Maritime: BP 220, Papeete; tel. 426240; fax 434889; e-mail aranui@mail.pf; internet www.aranui.com; Dir JEAN WONG.

Leprado Valere SARL: POB 3917, Papeete; tel. 450030; fax 421049.

Richmond Frères SARL: POB 1816, Papeete.

Société de Navigation des Australes: BP 1890, Papeete; tel. 509609; fax 420609.

Société de Transport Insulaire Maritime (STIM): BP 635, Papeete; tel. 452324.

Société de Transport Maritime de Tuamotu: BP 11366, Mahina; tel. 422358; fax 430373.

CIVIL AVIATION

There is one international airport, Faaa airport, 6 km from Papeete, on Tahiti, and there are about 40 smaller airstrips. International services are operated by Air France, Air New Zealand, LAN-Chile, Air Outre Mer, Air Calédonie International, Corsair and Hawaiian Airlines (USA).

Service d'État de l'Aviation Civile: Papeete; internet www.seac.pf; Dir GUY YEUNG.

Air Moorea: BP 6019, Faaa; tel. 864100; fax 864269; f. 1968; operates internal services between Tahiti and Moorea Island and charter flights throughout the Territory; Pres. MARCEL GALENON; Dir-Gen. FREDDY CHANSEAU.

Air Tahiti: BP 314, 98713 Papeete; tel. 864000; fax 864009; e-mail direction.generale@airtahiti.pf; f. 1953; Air Polynésie 1970–87; operates domestic services to 39 islands; Chair. CHRISTIAN VERNAUDON; Gen. Man. MARCEL GALENON.

Air Tahiti Nui: BP 1673, Papeete; tel. 460200; fax 460290; e-mail fly@airtahitinui.pf; internet www.airtahitinui-usa.com; f. 1996; commenced operations 1998; scheduled services to the USA, France, Japan and New Zealand; Chair. and CEO NELSON LEVY.

Tourism

Tourism is an important and developed industry in French Polynesia, particularly on Tahiti, and 227,658 people visited the Territory in 2001. In that year some 22.2% of arrivals were from France and 41.0% from the USA. There were a total of 3,650 hotel rooms in Tahiti in 2000. In 1999 the tourism industry earned an estimated 47,300m. francs CFP.

GIE Tahiti Tourisme: Immeuble Paofai, bâtiment D, blvd Pomare, BP 65, 98713 Papeete; tel. 505700; fax 436619; e-mail tahiti-tourisme@mail.pf; internet www.tahiti-tourisme.com; f. 1966 as autonomous public body, transformed into private corpn in 1993; tourist promotion; CEO DANY PANERO.

Service du Tourisme: Fare Manihini, blvd Pomare, BP 4527, Papeete; tel. 476200; fax 476201; govt dept; manages Special Fund for Tourist Development; Dir CLARISSE GODEFROY.

Syndicat d'Initiative de la Polynésie Française: BP 326, Papeete; Pres. PIU BAMBRIDGE.

FRENCH SOUTHERN AND ANTARCTIC TERRITORIES

Introduction

The French Southern and Antarctic Territories (Terres australes et antarctiques françaises) form an Overseas Territory but are administered under a special statute. The territory comprises Adélie Land, a narrow segment of the mainland of Antarctica together with a number of offshore islets, and three groups of sub-Antarctic islands (the Kerguelen and Crozet Archipelagos and Saint-Paul and Amsterdam Islands) in the southern Indian Ocean.

Under the terms of legislation approved by the French Government on 6 August 1955, the French Southern and Antarctic Territories were placed under the authority of a chief administrator, responsible to the government member responsible for Overseas Departments and Territories. The Chief Administrator is assisted by a Consultative Council, which meets at least twice annually. The Council is composed of seven members who are appointed for five years by the Minister of Defence and the government member responsible for Overseas Departments and Territories (from among members of the Office of Scientific Research and from those who have participated in scientific missions in the sub-Antarctic islands and Adélie Land) and by other designated ministers. Under the terms of a decree issued in February 1997, administration of the French Southern and Antarctic Territories was formally transferred from Paris to Saint-Pierre, Réunion, in April 2000.

From 1987 certain categories of vessels were allowed to register under the flag of the Kerguelen Archipelago, provided that 25% of their crew (including the captain and at least two officers) were French. These specifications were amended to 35% of the crew and at least four officers in April 1990. At 31 December 2001 there were 108 registered vessels.

In 1992 the French Government created a 'public interest group', the Institut Français pour la Recherche et la Technologie Polaires (IFRTP), to assume responsibility for the organization of scientific and research programmes in the French Southern and Antarctic Territories. France is a signatory to the Antarctic Treaty (see p. 492).

Statistical Survey

Area (sq km): Kerguelen Archipelago 7,215, Crozet Archipelago 515, Amsterdam Island 58, Saint-Paul Island 8, Adélie Land (Antarctica) 432,000.

Population (the population, comprising members of scientific missions, fluctuates according to season, being higher in the summer; the figures given are approximate): Kerguelen Archipelago, Port-aux-Français 80; Amsterdam Island at Martin de Viviès 30; Adélie Land at Base Dumont-d'Urville 27; the Crozet Archipelago at Alfred Faure (on Ile de la Possession) 35; Saint-Paul Island is uninhabited. Total population (April 2000): 172.

Fishing (catch quotas in metric tons, 2001/02): Crayfish (spiny lobsters) in Amsterdam and St Paul: 340; Patagonian toothfish (caught by French and foreign fleets) in the Kerguelen and Crozet Archipelagos: 6,500.

Currency: French currency was used until the end of 2001. Euro notes and coins were introduced on 1 January 2002, and the euro became the sole legal tender from 18 February. For details of exchange rates, see French Guiana.

Budget: Projected at €163.2m. in 2002, of which official subventions comprised €45.2m.

External Trade: Exports consist mainly of crayfish and other fish to France and Réunion. The Territories also derive revenue from the sale of postage stamps and other philatelic items.

Directory

Government: e-mail taaf.com@wanadoo.fr; internet www.taaf.fr. the central administration is in Saint-Pierre, Réunion.
Chief Administrator FRANÇOIS GARDE.

Consultative Council: Pres. JEAN-PIERRE CHARPENTIER.

Transport:
An oceanographic and supply vessel, the *Marion Dufresne II*, operated by the French Government, provides regular links between Réunion and the sub-Antarctic islands. Another specialized vessel, the *Astrolabe*, owned by the Groupe Bourbon and operating from Hobart, Tasmania, calls five times a year at the Antarctic mainland.

Research Stations:
There are meteorological stations and geophysical research stations on Kerguelen, Amsterdam, Adélie Land and Crozet. Research in marine microbiology is conducted from the Crozet and Kerguelen Archipelagos, and studies of atmospheric pollution are carried out on Amsterdam Island. The French atomic energy authority, the Commissariat à l'énergie atomique, also maintains a presence on Crozet, Kerguelen and Adélie Land.

WALLIS AND FUTUNA ISLANDS

Introductory Survey

Location, Climate, Language, Religion, Capital

The Territory of Wallis and Futuna comprises two groups of islands: the Wallis Islands, including Wallis Island (also known as Uvea) and 19 islets *(motu)* on the surrounding reef, and, to the south-west, Futuna (or Hooru), comprising the two small islands of Futuna and Alofi. The islands are located north-east of Fiji and west of Samoa. Temperatures are generally between about 23°C (73°F) and 30°C (86°F), and there is a cyclone season between December and March. French and Wallisian (Uvean), the indigenous Polynesian language, are spoken in the Territory, and nearly all of the population is nominally Roman Catholic. The capital is Mata'Utu, on Wallis Island.

Recent History

The Wallis and Futuna Islands were settled first by Polynesian peoples, Wallis from Tonga and Futuna from Samoa. Futuna was subsequently discovered by the Dutch navigators, Schouten and Le Maire, in 1616, and Uvea was discovered by Samuel Wallis in 1767. Three kingdoms later emerged, and in 1837 the first Marist missionaries arrived. By 1842 the majority of the population had been converted to Christianity. In April 1842 the authorities requested French protection, coinciding with a similar proclamation in Tahiti (now French Polynesia). In 1851 a *fakauvea* war between the Catholic majority and the Methodist minority assisted by Tonga (which had commenced in 1843) came to an end when 500 Wallisians left for Tonga. Protectorate status was formalized in 1887 for Wallis and in 1888 for the two kingdoms of Futuna, but domestic law remained in force. The islands were never formally annexed, and nor were French law or representative institutions introduced, although Wallis and Futuna were treated as a dependency of New Caledonia. During the Second World War, Wallis was used as an airforce base by the USA. In 1959 the traditional Kings and chiefs requested integration into the French Republic. The islands formally became an Overseas Territory in July 1961, following a referendum in December 1959, in which 94.4% of the electorate requested this status (almost all the opposition was in Futuna, which itself recorded dissent from only 22.2% of the voters; Wallis was unanimous in its acceptance).

Although there is no movement in Wallis and Futuna seeking secession of the Territory from France (in contrast with the situation in the other French Pacific Territories, French Poly-

nesia and New Caledonia), the two Kings whose kingdoms share the island of Futuna requested in November 1983, through the Territorial Assembly, that the island groups of Wallis and Futuna become separate Overseas Territories of France, arguing that the administration and affairs of the Territory had become excessively concentrated on Uvea (Wallis Island).

At elections to the 20-member Territorial Assembly in March 1982, the Rassemblement pour la République (RPR) and its allies won 11 seats, while the remaining nine were secured by candidates belonging to, or associated with, the Union pour la Démocratie Française (UDF). Later that year one member of the Lua Kae Tahi, a group affiliated to the metropolitan UDF, defected to the RPR group. In November 1983, however, three of the 12 RPR members joined the Lua Kae Tahi, forming a new majority. In the subsequent election for President of the Territorial Assembly, this 11-strong bloc of UDF-associated members supported the ultimately successful candidate, Falakiko Gata, even though he had been elected to the Territorial Assembly in 1982 as a member of the RPR.

In April 1985 Falakiko Gata formed a new political party, the Union Populaire Locale (UPL), which was committed to giving priority to local, rather than metropolitan, issues.

In 1987 a dispute broke out between two families both laying claim to the throne of Sigave, the northern kingdom on the island of Futuna. The conflict arose following the deposition of the former King, Sagato Keletaona, and his succession by Sosefo Vanaï. The intervention of the island's administrative authorities, who attempted to ratify Vanaï's accession to the throne, was condemned by the Keletaona family as an interference in the normal course of local custom, according to which such disputes are traditionally settled by a fight between the protagonists.

At elections to the Territorial Assembly held in March 1987, the UDF (together with affiliated parties) and the RPR each won seven seats. However, by forming an alliance with the UPL, the RPR maintained its majority, and Falakiko Gata was subsequently re-elected President. At elections for the French National Assembly in June 1988, Benjamin Brial was re-elected Deputy. However, when the result was contested by an unsuccessful candidate, Kamilo Gata, the election was investigated by the French Constitutional Council and the result declared invalid, owing to electoral irregularities. When the election was held again in January 1989, Kamilo Gata was elected Deputy, obtaining 57.4% of total votes.

Statistical information, gathered in 1990, showed that the emigration rate of Wallis and Futuna islanders had risen to over

50%. In October of that year 13,705 people (of whom 97% were Wallisians and Futunians) lived in the Territory, while 14,186 were resident in New Caledonia. At the 1996 census the number of Wallisians and Futunians resident in New Caledonia had increased to 17,563. According to the results, a proportion of the islanders had chosen to emigrate to other French Overseas Possessions or to metropolitan France. The principal reason for the increase was thought to be the lack of employment opportunities in the islands.

At elections to the Territorial Assembly in March 1992 the newly founded Taumu'a Lelei secured 11 seats, while the RPR won nine. The new Assembly was remarkable for being the first since 1964 in which the RPR did not hold a majority. At elections to the French National Assembly in March 1993, Kamilo Gata was re-elected Deputy, obtaining 52.4% of total votes cast to defeat Clovis Logologofolau. In June 1994 the Union Locale Force Ouvrière organized a general strike in protest at the increasing cost of living in the Territory and the allegedly inadequate education system. It was reported that demonstrations continued for several days, during which the Territorial Assembly building was damaged in an arson attack.

In October 1994 it was reported that the King of Sigave, Lafaele Malau, had been deposed by a unanimous decision of the kingdom's chiefs. The action followed the appointment of two customary leaders to represent the Futunian community in New Caledonia, which had led to unrest among the inhabitants of Sigave. He was succeeded by Esipio Takasi.

At elections to the Territorial Assembly in December 1994 the RPR secured 10 seats, while a coalition group, Union Populaire pour Wallis et Futuna (UPWF), won seven, and independent candidates three. Mikaele Tauhavili was subsequently elected President of the Assembly.

The refusal by 10 of the 20 members of the Territorial Assembly to adopt budgetary proposals in January 1996, led to appeals for the dissolution of the Government by France and the organization of new elections. The budget (which, at US $20m., was some US $4.5m. smaller than the previous year) aroused opposition for its apparent lack of provision for development funds, particularly for the islands' nascent tourist industry.

Elections to the Territorial Assembly took place on 16 March 1997. A participation rate of 87.2% was recorded at the poll, in which RPR candidates secured 14 seats and left-wing candidates (including independents and members of various political groupings) won six seats. Victor Brial, a representative of the RPR, was elected President of the Territorial Assembly. At the second round of elections to the French National Assembly, on 1 June, Brial defeated Kamilo Gata, obtaining 3,241 votes (51.3% of the total).

Allegations that electoral irregularities had occurred in the elections to the Territorial Assembly of March 1997 were investigated and upheld for 11 of the seats. As a result, new elections were organized for the 11 seats on 6 September 1998, at which the RPR's representation in the Assembly was reduced to 11 seats overall, while left-wing and independent members increased their share of seats to nine. Also in September 1998, in a second round of voting, Fr Robert Laufoaulu was elected to the French Senate, defeating Kamilo Gata in a vote by the Territorial Assembly. Laufoaulu, a priest and director of Catholic education in the islands, stood as a left-wing candidate, nominated by RPR candidates, but was elected with the support of right-wing politicians.

In late March 1999 festivities were held to commemorate the 40th anniversary of the accession of the King of Wallis Island, Lavelua Tomasi Kulimoetoke. From March 2000 delegations from Wallis and Futuna visited New Caledonia to discuss mutual arrangements concerning free trade and employment rights between the two Territories.

In January 2001 two candidates of the RPR contested the presidency of the Territorial Assembly. Patalione Kanimoa was elected by the majority of the RPR (eight votes) and of the UPWF (four votes). Soane Muni Uhila, the previous President of the Territorial Assembly, then formed a new party, La Voix des Peuples Wallisiens et Futuniens, along with five other RPR dissidents. The new majority RPR-UPWF grouping elected Albert Likuvalu (of the UPWF) president of the permanent commission.

In June 2001 senior officials from Wallis and Futuna and from New Caledonia agreed on a project to redefine their bilateral relationship under the Nouméa Accord on greater autonomy, signed in 1998. The Accord gave the New Caledonian authorities the power to control immigration from Wallis and Futuna;

following decades of migration, the population of Wallis and Futuna was 15,000, while the number of migrants and descendants from the islands in New Caledonia had risen to 20,000. In exchange for controlling immigration, New Caledonia stated that it would make a financial contribution to economic development in Wallis and Futuna. The Nouméa Accord also called for a separate arrangement allowing for open access to New Caledonia for residents of Wallis and Futuna. The French State was to address the issue of financial aid before the two territories' assemblies approved the deal.

In January 2002 a delegation from Wallis and Futuna met President Jacques Chirac in Paris to discuss the status of members of their community living in New Caledonia. Under the Nouméa Accord, New Caledonia was to have signed a separate agreement with Wallis and Futuna better to define their status, with particular regard to the job market.

A general election was held on 10 March 2002 for the 20 seats of the Territorial Assembly. The RPR won 12 of the seats, whilst socialist candidates, or affiliated independents, won eight. An unprecedented 82.7% of some 9,500 registered voters cast their vote. The election campaign was the first to give parties coverage on television and radio, provided by the national broadcasting company.

At elections to the National Assembly in June 2002, Victor Brial, representing a coalition of the Union pour la Majorité Présidentielle and the RPR, was re-elected as the Territory's deputy to the French legislature, winning 50.4% of the votes cast in the first round. However, in December the Constitutional Council ruled that the result was invalid as certain ballot papers had been improperly marked; Brial subsequently won the by-election in March 2003. Meanwhile, Christian Job replaced Alain Waquet as Chief Administrator of the islands in August 2002. In December the French Senate approved a bill providing for a constitutional amendment that would allow Wallis and Futuna (along with French Polynesia) to become an Overseas Country; both houses of the National Assembly in Paris ratified the amendments to the Constitution in March 2003.

Government

The Territory of Wallis and Futuna is administered by a representative of the French Government, the Chief Administrator, who is assisted by the Territorial Assembly. The Assembly has 20 members and is elected for a five-year term. The three traditional kingdoms, from which the Territory was formed, one on Wallis and two sharing Futuna, have equal rights, although the kings' powers are limited. In addition, the Territory elects one Deputy to the French National Assembly in Paris and one representative to the French Senate. The islands may also be represented at the European Parliament.

Economic Affairs

In 1995 it was estimated that Wallis and Futuna's gross domestic product (GDP) was US $28.7m., equivalent to some $2,000 per head. Most monetary income in the islands is derived from government employment and remittances sent home by islanders employed in New Caledonia and also in Metropolitan France.

Agricultural activity is of a subsistence nature. Yams, taro, bananas, cassava and other food crops are also cultivated. Tobacco is grown for local consumption. In 1998 almost all the cultivated vegetation on the island of Wallis, notably the banana plantations, was destroyed by a cyclone. In response to the cyclone damage, the French Government provided exceptional aid of 80m. francs CFP to alleviate the situation. An estimated 25,000 pigs a year are reared on the islands. Three units rear 800, 500 and 450 hens a year respectively, which are used principally for eggs, and meet an estimated 80% of the territory's commercial needs. Apiculture was revived in 1996, and in 2000 honey production was sufficient to meet the demands of the local market. Fishing activity in the Territory's exclusive economic zone increased during the 1990s; the total catch was estimated at 300 metric tons in 2000, compared with 70 tons in 1991. The Territorial Assembly accorded Japan deep-water fishing rights to catch 3,000 tons of fish a year in the islands' exclusive economic zone, a broad area of 200 miles (370 km) around Wallis and Futuna over which France exerts sovereignty.

Mineral fuels are the main source of electrical energy, although it is hoped that hydroelectric power can be developed, especially on Futuna. There is a 4,000-KW thermal power station on Wallis, and a 2,600-KW thermal power station was completed on Futuna in 2000. Electricity output in 2001 totalled 14.6m. kWh on Wallis and 3.0m. kWh on Futuna.

There were 291 businesses in the Territory in 2000, of which 24 were in the industrial and artisanal sector, 68 in construction and 199 in the service and commercial sectors; 47 of those businesses were located on Futuna. A new commercial centre was to open in Wallis in 2002. In August 1989 a new earth station for satellite communications was inaugurated. The islands also benefited from an increase in building activity and public works in the early 1990s. The tourism sector, however, is very limited. In 2002 Wallis had four hotels and Futuna two.

In 2000 the cost of the islands' imports reached 4,735.7m. francs CFP. Road vehicles, parts and accessories accounted for 10.0% of the total value of imports, followed by mineral fuels and products (9.8%), electrical machinery and sound and television apparatus (7.4%) and meat products (6.4%). Exports totalled only 22.4m. francs CFP. Traditional food products, mother of pearl (from the Trochus shell) and handicrafts are the only significant export commodities. Exports of copra from Wallis ceased in 1950, and from Futuna in the early 1970s. The principal sources of imports in 2000 were France, which supplied 28.7% of the total, and Australia (22.6%). Most of the islands' exports were purchased by Italy. In August 2001 the frequency of supplies to Wallis and Futuna was significantly improved when the Sofrana shipping company, based in Auckland, began operating a new route linking New Zealand, Tonga and the Samoas to Wallis and Futuna.

French aid to Wallis and Futuna totalled 7,048m. francs CFP in 1999, increasing to 10,329m. francs CFP in 2002. The islands' budgetary expenditure in 2001 totalled an estimated US $25.0m. Budgetary aid from France was to rise from €83,178m. in 2001 to €86,610m. in 2002. The annual rate of inflation in 1989–2000 averaged 1.2%.

Education

In 2002/03 there were 19 state-financed primary schools (including three pre-primary, 14 primary and two homecraft centres), with an enrolment of 2,938 pupils at the 14 primary schools, and seven secondary schools (including two vocational schools) in Wallis and Futuna, with a total of 2,293 pupils. In 1999/2000, 361 students attended various universities overseas.

Public Holidays

2003: 1 January (New Year's Day), 5 March (Missionary Day), 21 April (Easter Monday), 1 May (Labour Day), 8 May (Liberation Day), 29 May (Ascension Day), 9 June (Whit Monday), 14 July (Fall of the Bastille), 8 September (Internal Autonomy Day), 24 September (anniversary of possession by France), 1 November (All Saints' Day), 11 November (Armistice Day), 25 December (Christmas Day).

2004: 1 January (New Year's Day), 5 March (Missionary Day), 12 April (Easter Monday), 1 May (Labour Day), 8 May (Liberation Day), 20 May (Ascension Day), 30 May (Whit Monday), 14 July (Fall of the Bastille), 8 September (Internal Autonomy Day), 24 September (anniversary of possession by France), 1 November (All Saints' Day), 11 November (Armistice Day), 25 December (Christmas Day).

Weights and Measures

The metric system is in force.

Statistical Survey

Source (unless otherwise indicated): Service Territorial de la Statistique et des Etudes Economiques, Centre de Havelu, Mata' Utu, 98600 Uvea, Wallis Islands, Wallis and Futuna, via Nouméa, New Caledonia; tel. and fax 722403; e-mail stats@wallis.co.nc; internet www.wallis.co.nc/stats.

AREA AND POPULATION

Area (sq km): 160.5. *By island:* Uvea (Wallis Island) 77.5, Other Wallis Islands 18.5; Futuna Island 45, Alofi Island 19.5.

Population (census of 15 February 1983): 12,408: Wallis Islands 8,084, Futuna Island 4,324, Alofi Island uninhabited; (October 1990 census): 13,705 (males 6,829, females 6,876): Wallis Islands 8,973, Futuna Island 4,732 (Alo 2,860, Sigave 1,872); 14,186 Wallisians and Futunians resided in New Caledonia. Total population 14,166 (males 6,984, females 7,182) at census of 1996; 17,563 Wallisians and Futunians resided in New Caledonia. Total population 14,600 (estimate) at mid-2000.

Density (estimate, mid-2000): 91.0 per sq km.

Principal Town: Mata'Utu (capital), population 1,137 at 1996 census.

Births and Deaths (estimates, 2000): Birth rate 21.7 per 1,000; Death rate 5.6 per 1,000.

Expectation of Life (estimates, years at birth): 73.8 (males 73.2; females 74.4) in 1998.

AGRICULTURE, ETC.

Principal Crops (FAO estimates, '000 metric tons, 2001): Cassava 2.4; Taro (coco yam) 1.6; Yams 0.5; Other roots and tubers 1.0; Coconuts 2.3; Vegetables 0.5; Bananas 4.1; Other fruits (excl. melons) 4.6. Source: FAO.

Livestock (FAO estimates, '000 head, year ending September 2001): Pigs 25; Goats 7; Poultry 63. Source: FAO.

Livestock Products (FAO estimates, metric tons, 2001): Pig meat 315; Goat meat 15; Poultry meat 46; Cows' milk 30; Hen eggs 33; Honey 11. Source: FAO.

Fishing (FAO estimates, metric tons, live weight, 2000): Total catch 300 (Marine fishes 294). Note: Figures exclude trochus shells (FAO estimate, metric tons); 25. Source: FAO, *Yearbook of Fishery Statistics.*

INDUSTRY

Electricity Production (million kWh, 2001): 14.6 in Wallis; 3.0 in Futuna.

FINANCE

Currency and Exchange Rates: see French Polynesia.

Territorial Budget (million francs CFP): 2,444.2 in 2000; 3,271.1 in 2001.

Aid from France (million francs CFP, 2002): 10,329. Source: Institut d'Emission d'Outre-Mer.

Money Supply (million francs CFP at 30 Sept. 2001): Currency in circulation 759; Demand deposits 1,595; Total money 2,355. Source: Institut d'Emission d'Outre-Mer.

Cost of Living (Consumer Price Index; base: July–Sept. 1989 = 100): All items 114.3 in 2000; 119.9 in 2001.

EXTERNAL TRADE

Principal Commodities (million francs CFP, 2000): *Imports c.i.f.:* Meat and edible meat offal 302.1; Preparations of meat, of fish or of crustaceans, molluscs or other aquatic invertebrates 178.2; Beverages, spirits and vinegar 199.0; Mineral fuels, mineral oils and products of their distillation; bituminous substances; mineral waxes 462.5; Articles of iron or steel 153.9; Boilers, machinery, mechanical appliances and parts 281.2; Electrical machinery, equipment and parts; sound and television apparatus 350.4; Road vehicles, parts and accessories 474.2; Total (incl. others) 4,735.7. *Exports f.o.b.:* Total 22.4.

Principal Trading Partners (million francs CFP, 2000): *Imports c.i.f.:* Australia 1,068.9; China, People's Republic 84.5; Fiji 174.3; France (incl. Monaco) 1,360.5; Japan 270.1; New Caledonia 307.2; New Zealand 643.2; Singapore 107.0; United Kingdom 76.1; USA 99.9; Total (incl. others) 4,735.7. *Exports f.o.b.:* French Polynesia 0.6; Italy 21.6; Total (incl. others) 22.4.

TRANSPORT

Shipping: *Merchant Fleet* (31 December 2001): Vessels registered 7; displacement ('000 grt) 183.0. Source: Lloyd's Register-Fairplay, World Fleet Statistics.

Civil Aviation (2001): aircraft arrivals and departures 1,310; freight handled 131.1 metric tons; passenger arrivals and departures 32,445; mail loaded and unloaded 58.3 metric tons.

TOURISM

Visitors: 400 in 1985.

COMMUNICATIONS MEDIA

Telephones (2000): 1,705 main lines in use. Source: International Telecommunication Union.

Facsimile Machines (1993): 90 in use. Source: UN, *Statistical Yearbook.*

Internet Users (2001): 268.

EDUCATION

Pre-primary (2002/03): 3 institutions.

Primary (2002/03): 14 institutions; 2,938 students (incl. pre-primary); 271 teachers.

Secondary (2002/03): 7 institutions (2 vocational); 2,293 students; 191 teachers.
Source: Vice-Rectorat de Wallis & Futuna.

Directory

The Constitution

The Territory of the Wallis and Futuna Islands is administered according to a statute of 1961, and subsidiary legislation, under the Constitution of the Fifth Republic. The Statute declares the Wallis and Futuna Islands to be an Overseas Territory of the French Republic, of which it remains an integral part. The Statute established an administration, a Council of the Territory, a Territorial Assembly and national representation. The administrative, political and social evolution envisaged by, and enacted under, the Statute is intended to effect a smooth integration of the three customary kingdoms with the new institutions of the Territory. The Kings are assisted by ministers and the traditional chiefs. The Chief Administrator, appointed by the French Government, is the representative of the State in the Territory and is responsible for external affairs, defence, law and order, financial and educational affairs. The Chief Administrator is required to consult with the Council of the Territory, which has six members: three by right (the Kings of Wallis, Sigave and Alo) and three appointed by the Chief Administrator upon the advice of the Territorial Assembly. This Assembly assists in the administration of the Territory; there are 20 members elected on a common roll, on the basis of universal adult suffrage, for a term of up to five years. The Territorial Assembly elects, from among its own membership, a President to lead it. The Territory elects national representatives (one Deputy to the National Assembly, one Senator and one Economic and Social Councillor) and votes for representatives to the European Parliament in Strasbourg.

The Government

(April 2003)

Chief Administrator (Administrateur Supérieur): CHRISTIAN JOB (appointed 2002).

CONSEIL DU TERRITOIRE

Chair: Chief Administrator.

Members by Right: King of Wallis, King of Sigave, King of Alo.

Appointed Members: MIKAELE HALAGAHU (Faipule), ATOLOTO UHILA (Kulitea), KELETO LAKALAKA (Sous réserves).

GOVERNMENT OFFICE

Government Headquarters: Bureau de l'Administrateur Supérieur, Havelu, BP 16, Mata'Utu, 98600 Uvea, Wallis Islands, Wallis and Futuna; tel. 722727; fax 722324; all departments.

Legislature

ASSEMBLÉE TERRITORIALE

The Territorial Assembly has 20 members and is elected for a five-year term. The most recent general election took place on 10 March 2002, at which RPR candidates secured a total of 12 seats and various left-wing candidates (including independents) won eight seats.

President: PATALIONE KANIMOA (UMP).

Territorial Assembly: Assemblée Territoriale, Havelu, BP 31, Mata'Utu, 98600 Uvea, Wallis Islands, Wallis and Futuna; tel. 722504; fax 722054.

PARLEMENT

Deputy to the French National Assembly: VICTOR BRIAL (UMP).

Representative to the French Senate: Fr ROBERT LAUFOAULU (UMP).

Social and Economic Adviser: KAMILO GATA (UPWF).

The Kingdoms

WALLIS
(Capital: Mata'Utu on Uvea)

Lavelua, King of Wallis: TOMASI KULIMOETOKE.

Council of Ministers: Prime Minister (Kivalu) and five other ministers; Kivalu TISIMASI HEAFALA.

The Kingdom of Wallis is divided into three districts (Hihifo, Hahake, Mua), and its traditional hierarchy includes three district chiefs (Faipule) and 20 village chiefs (Pule).

SIGAVE
(Capital: Leava on Futuna)

Keletaona, King of Sigave: PASILIO KELETAONA.

Council of Ministers: six ministers, chaired by the King.

The Kingdom of Sigave is located in the north of the island of Futuna; there are five village chiefs.

ALO
(Capital: Ono on Futuna)

Tuigaifo, King of Alo: SAGATO ALOFI.

Council of Ministers: five ministers, chaired by the King.

The Kingdom of Alo comprises the southern part of the island of Futuna and the entire island of Alofi. There are nine village chiefs.

Political Organizations

Taumu'a Lelei (Bright Future): c/o Assemblée Territoriale; f. 1992; Leader SOANE MUNI UHILA.

Union pour la Démocratie Française (UDF): c/o Assemblée Territoriale; centrist; based on Uvean (Wallis) support.

Union Populaire pour Wallis et Futuna (UPWF): c/o Assemblée Territoriale; affiliated to the Parti Socialiste of France in 1998; f. 1994; Leader KAMILO GATA.

Union pour un Mouvement Populaire (UMP): c/o Assemblée Territoriale; f. 2002 by members of the former Rassemblement pour la République and Démocratie Liberale parties; Territorial Leader CLOVIS LOGOLOGOFOLAU.

La Voix des Peuples Wallisiens et Futuniens: c/o Assemblée Territoriale; f. 2001 by dissident RPR mems.

Religion

Almost all of the inhabitants profess Christianity and are adherents of the Roman Catholic Church.

CHRISTIANITY

The Roman Catholic Church

The Territory comprises a single diocese, suffragan to the archdiocese of Nouméa (New Caledonia). The diocese estimated that there were 14,192 adherents (99.0% of the population) at 31 December 1999. The Bishop participates in the Catholic Bishops' Conference of the Pacific, currently based in Fiji.

Bishop of Wallis and Futuna: Mgr LOLESIO FUAHEA, Evêché Lano, BP G6, 98600 Mata'Utu, Uvea, Wallis Islands, Wallis and Futuna; tel. 722932; fax 722783; e-mail eveche.wallis@wallis.co.nc.

The Press

Te-Fenua Fo'ou: BP 435, 98600 Mata'Utu, Uvea, Wallis Islands, Wallis and Futuna; tel. 721746; e-mail tff@wallis.co.nc; f. 1995; weekly; French, Wallisian and Futurian; ceased publication in April 2002.

Broadcasting and Communications

TELECOMMUNICATIONS

France Telecom (FCR): Télécommunications extérieures de Wallis et Futuna, BP 54, 98600 Mata'Utu, Uvea, Wallis Islands, Wallis and Futuna; tel. 722436; fax 722255; e-mail admin@wallis.co.nc.

Service des Postes et Télécommunications: Administration Supérieure des Iles Wallis et Futuna, BP 00, 98600 Mata'Utu, Uvea, Wallis Islands, Wallis and Futuna; tel. 722121; fax 722500; e-mail adminspt.get@wallis.co.nc.

BROADCASTING

Radio and Television

Radio Wallis et Futuna: BP 102, 97911 Mata'Utu, Uvea, Wallis Islands, Wallis and Futuna; tel. 722020; fax 722346; internet www .rfo.fr; fmrly Radiodiffusion Française d'Outre-mer (RFO); transmitters at Mata'Utu (Uvea) and Alo (Futuna); programmes broadcast 24 hours daily in Uvean (Wallisian), Futunian and French; a television service on Uvea, transmitting for 12 hours daily in French, began operation in 1986; a television service on Futuna was inaugurated in December 1994; satellite television began operation in March 2000; Man. JOSEPH BLASCO; Head of Information BERNARD JOYEUX.

Finance

BANKING

Bank of Issue

Institut d'Emission d'Outre-Mer: 98600 Mata'Utu, Uvea, Wallis Islands, Wallis and Futuna; tel. 722505; f. 1998.

Other Banks

Agence Française de Développement: 98600 Mata'Utu, Uvea, Wallis Islands, Wallis and Futuna; tel. 722505; fmrly Caisse Française de Développement; development bank.

Banque de Wallis et Futuna: BP 59, 98600 Mata'Utu, Uvea, Wallis Islands, Wallis and Futuna; tel. 722124; fax 722156; f. 1991; 51% owned by BNP Paribas (New Caledonia).

Paierie de Wallis et Futuna: 98600 Mata'Utu, Uvea, Wallis Islands, Wallis and Futuna, via Nouméa, New Caledonia.

Trade and Industry

GOVERNMENT AGENCY

Economie Rurale et Pêche: BP 05, 98600 Mata'Utu, Uvea, Wallis Islands, Wallis and Futuna; Antenne de Futuna, BP 05, 98620 Sigave, Futuna, Wallis and Futuna; tel. 720400; fax 720404; e-mail ecoru@wallis.co.nc; tel. 723214; fax 723402.

UTILITIES

Electricité et Eau de Wallis et Futuna: 98600 Mata'Utu, Uvea, Wallis Islands, Wallis and Futuna; 32.3% owned by the territory and 66.64% owned by EEC of New Caledonia.

TRADE UNIONS

Union Interprofessionnelle CFDT Wallis et Futuna (UI CFDT): BP 178, 98600 Mata'Utu, Uvea, Wallis Islands, Wallis and Futuna; tel. 721880; Sec. Gen. KALOLO HANISI.

Union Territoriale Force Ouvrière: BP 325, Mata-Utu, 98600 Wallis and Futuna; tel. 721732; fax 720132; Sec.-Gen. CHRISTIAN VAAMEI.

Transport

ROADS

Uvea has a few kilometres of road, one route circling the island, and there is also a partially surfaced road circling the island of Futuna; the only fully surfaced roads are in Mata'Utu.

SHIPPING

Mata'Utu serves as the seaport of Uvea and the Wallis Islands, while Sigave is the only port on Futuna. A total of 45 general freight ships and 17 gas and petroleum tankers docked in Wallis in 1999.

Services des Douanes et Affaires Maritimes: Aka'aka, 98600 Mata'Utu, Uvea, Wallis Islands, Wallis and Futuna; tel. 722571; fax 722986.

AMACAL (General Agent): POB 1080, Nouméa, New Caledonia; tel. 232910; fax 287388; e-mail amb.noumea@offratel.nc.

CIVIL AVIATION

There is an international airport in Hihifo district on Uvea, about 5 km from Mata'Utu. Air Calédonie International (New Caledonia) operates five flights a week from Wallis to Futuna, one flight a week from Wallis to Tahiti (French Polynesia) and two flights a week from Wallis to Nouméa (New Caledonia). The airport on Futuna is at Vele, in the south-east, in the Kingdom of Alo.

Tourism

Tourism remains undeveloped. There are four small hotels on Uvea, Wallis Islands. In 1985 there were some 400 tourist visitors, in total, to the islands. There are two small guest-houses for visitors on Futuna.

French Overseas Country

New Caledonia was formerly an Overseas Territory of France. The Nouméa Accord, concluded in 1998, provides for a gradual transfer of powers to New Caledonia. The Territory became an Overseas Country of France in 1999.

NEW CALEDONIA

Introductory Survey

Location, Climate, Language, Religion, Capital

New Caledonia comprises one large island and several smaller ones, lying in the South Pacific Ocean, about 1,500 km (930 miles) east of Queensland, Australia. The main island, New Caledonia (la Grande-Terre), is long and narrow, and has a total area of 16,372 sq km. Rugged mountains divide the west of the island from the east, and there is little flat land. The nearby Loyalty Islands, which are administratively part of New Caledonia, are 1,981 sq km in area, and a third group of islands, the uninhabited Chesterfield Islands, lies about 400 km north-west of the main island. The climate is generally mild, with an average temperature of about 24°C (75°F) and a rainy season between December and March. The average rainfall in the east of the main island is about 2,000 mm (80 ins) per year, and in the west about 1,000 mm (40 ins). French is the official language and the mother tongue of the Caldoches (French settlers); the indigenous Kanaks (Melanesians) also speak Melanesian languages. Other immigrants speak Polynesian and Asian languages. New Caledonians almost all profess Christianity; about 59% are Roman Catholics, and there is a substantial Protestant minority. The capital is Nouméa, on the main island.

Recent History

New Caledonia became a French possession in 1853, when the island was annexed as a dependency of Tahiti. In 1860 a separate administration was established, and in 1885 a Conseil Général was elected to defend the local interests before metropolitan France. France took possession of Melanesian land and began mining nickel and copper in 1864, displacing the indigenous Kanak population. This provoked a number of rebellions, including the Kanak revolt of 1878. From 1887 two separate administrations existed, for Melanesian Kanaks and expatriates, until New Caledonia became an Overseas Territory of the French Republic in 1946. In 1956 the first Territorial Assembly, with 30 members, was elected by universal adult suffrage, although the French Governor effectively retained control of the functions of government. New Caledonian demands for a measure of self-government were answered in 1976 by a new statute, which gave the Council of Government, elected from the Territorial Assembly, responsibility for certain internal affairs. The post of Governor was replaced by that of French High Commissioner to the Territory. In 1978 the Kanak-supported, pro-independence parties obtained a majority of the posts in the Council of Government. In early 1979, however, the French Government dismissed the Council, following its failure to support a proposal for a 10-year 'contract' between France and New Caledonia, because the plan did not acknowledge the possibility of New Caledonian independence. The Territory was then placed under the direct authority of the High Commissioner. A general election was held in July, but a new electoral law, which affected mainly the pro-independence parties, ensured that minor parties were not represented in the Assembly. Two parties loyal to France (Rassemblement pour la Calédonie dans la République—RPCR, and Fédération pour une Nouvelle Société Calédonienne—FNSC) together won 22 of the 36 seats.

Following the election of François Mitterrand as President of France, tension increased in September 1981 after the assassination of Pierre Declercq, the Secretary-General of the pro-independence party, Union Calédonienne (UC). In December of that year the French Government made proposals for change that included equal access for all New Caledonians to positions of authority, land reforms and the fostering of Kanak cultural institutions. To assist in effecting these reforms, the French Government simultaneously announced that it would rule by decree for a period of at least one year. In 1982 the FNSC joined with the opposition grouping, Front Indépendantiste (FI), to form a government that was more favourable to the proposed reforms.

In November 1983 the French Government proposed a five-year period of increased autonomy from July 1984 and a referendum in 1989 to determine New Caledonia's future. The statute was opposed in New Caledonia, both by parties in favour of earlier independence and by those against, and it was rejected by the Territorial Assembly in April 1984. However, the proposals were approved by the French National Assembly in September 1984. Under the provisions of the statute, the Territorial Council of Ministers was given responsibility for many internal matters of government, its President henceforth being an elected member instead of the French High Commissioner; a second legislative chamber, with the right to be consulted on development planning and budgetary issues, was created at the same time. All of the main parties seeking independence (except the Libération Kanak Socialiste (LKS) party, which left the FI) boycotted elections for the new Territorial Assembly in November 1984 and, following the dissolution of the FI, formed a new movement called the Front de Libération Nationale Kanak Socialiste (FLNKS). On 1 December, the FLNKS Congress established a 'provisional government', headed by Jean-Marie Tjibaou. The elections to the Territorial Assembly attracted only 50.1% of the electorate, and the anti-independence party Rassemblement pour la Calédonie dans la République (RPCR) won 34 of the 42 seats. An escalation of violence began in November, and in the following month three settlers were murdered by pro-independence activists and 10 Kanaks were killed by *métis* settlers.

In January 1985 Edgard Pisani, the new High Commissioner, announced a plan by which the Territory might become independent 'in association with' France on 1 January 1986, subject to the result of a referendum in July 1985. Kanak groups opposed the plan, insisting that the indigenous population be allowed to determine its own fate. At the same time, the majority of the population, which supported the RPCR, demonstrated against the plan and in favour of remaining within the French Republic. A resurgence of violence followed the announcement of Pisani's plan, and a state of emergency was declared after two incidents in which a leading member of the FLNKS was killed by security forces and the son of a French settler was killed by Kanak activists.

In April 1985 the French Prime Minister, Laurent Fabius, put forward new proposals for the future of New Caledonia, whereby the referendum on independence was deferred until an unspecified date not later than the end of 1987. Meanwhile, the Territory was to be divided into four regions, each to be governed by its own elected autonomous council, which would have extensive powers in the spheres of planning and development, education, health and social services, land rights, transport and housing. The elected members of all four councils together would serve as regional representatives in a Territorial Congress (to replace the Territorial Assembly).

The 'Fabius plan' was well received by the FLNKS, although the organization reaffirmed the ultimate goal of independence. It was also decided to maintain the 'provisional Government' under Tjibaou at least until the end of 1985. The RPCR, however, condemned the plan, and the proposals were rejected by the predominantly anti-independence Territorial Assembly in May. However, the necessary legislation was approved by the

French National Assembly in July, and the Fabius plan came into force. Elections were held in September, and, as expected, only in the region around Nouméa, where the bulk of the population is non-Kanak, was an anti-independence majority recorded. However, the pro-independence Melanesians, in spite of their majorities in the three non-urban regions, would be in a minority in the Territorial Congress.

The FLNKS boycotted the general election to the French National Assembly in March 1986, in which only about 50% of the eligible voters in New Caledonia participated. In May the French Council of Ministers approved a draft law providing for a referendum to be held in New Caledonia within 12 months, whereby voters would choose between independence and a further extension of regional autonomy. In December, in spite of strong French diplomatic opposition, the UN General Assembly voted to reinscribe New Caledonia on the UN list of non-self-governing territories, thereby affirming the population's right to self-determination.

The FLNKS decided to boycott the referendum on 13 September 1987, at which 98.3% votes were cast in favour of New Caledonia's continuation as part of the French Republic and only 1.7% were cast in favour of independence. Of the registered electorate, almost 59% voted, a higher level of participation than was expected, although 90% of the electorate abstained in constituencies inhabited by a majority of Kanaks.

In October 1987 seven pro-French loyalists were acquitted on a charge of murdering 10 Kanak separatists in 1984. Tjibaou, who reacted to the ruling by declaring that his followers would have to abandon their stance of pacifism, and his deputy, Yeiwéné Yeiwéné, were indicted for 'incitement to violence'. In April 1988 four gendarmes were killed, and 27 held hostage in a cave on the island of Ouvéa, by supporters of the FLNKS. Two days later, Kanak separatists prevented about one-quarter of the Territory's polling stations from opening when local elections were held. The FLNKS boycotted the elections. Although 12 of the gendarmes taken hostage were subsequently released, six members of a French anti-terrorist squad were captured. French security forces immediately laid siege to the cave and, in the following month, made an assault upon it, leaving 19 Kanaks and two gendarmes dead. Following the siege, allegations that three Kanaks had been executed or left to die, after being arrested, led to an announcement by the new French Socialist Government that a judicial inquiry into the incident was to be opened.

At the elections to the French National Assembly in June 1988, both New Caledonian seats were retained by the RPCR. Michel Rocard, the new French Prime Minister, chaired negotiations in Paris, between Jacques Lafleur (leader of the RPCR) and Tjibaou, who agreed to transfer the administration of the Territory to Paris for 12 months. Under the provisions of the agreement (known as the Matignon Accord), the Territory was to be divided into three administrative Provinces prior to a territorial plebiscite on independence to be held in 1998. Only people resident in the Territory in 1988, and their direct descendants, would be allowed to vote in the plebiscite. The agreement also provided for a programme of economic development, training in public administration for Kanaks, and institutional reforms. The Matignon Accord was presented to the French electorate in a referendum, held on 6 November 1988, and approved by 80% of those voting (although an abstention rate of 63% of the electorate was recorded). The programme was approved by a 57% majority in New Caledonia, where the rate of abstention was 37%. In November, under the terms of the agreement, 51 separatists were released from prison, including 26 Kanaks implicated in the incident on Ouvéa.

In May 1989 the leaders of the FLNKS, Tjibaou and Yeiwéné, were murdered by separatist extremists, alleged to be associated with the Front Uni de Libération Kanak (FULK), a grouping which had until then formed part of the FLNKS, but which opposed the Matignon Accord on the grounds that it conceded too much to the European settlers. The assassinations were regarded as an attempt to disrupt the implementation of the Accord. Elections to the three Provincial Assemblies were nevertheless held, as scheduled, in June: the FLNKS won a majority of seats in the Province of the North and the Province of the Loyalty Islands, while the RPCR obtained a majority in the Province of the South, and also emerged as the dominant party in the Territorial Congress, with 27 of the 54 seats; the FLNKS secured 19 seats.

The year of direct rule by France ended, as agreed, on 14 July 1989, when the Territorial Congress and Provincial Assemblies assumed the administrative functions allocated to them in the Matignon Accord (see below under Government). In November the French National Assembly approved an amnesty (as stipulated in the Matignon Accord) for all who had been involved in politically-motivated violence in New Caledonia before August 1988, despite strong opposition from the right-wing French parties.

In April 1991 the LKS announced its intention to withdraw from the Matignon Accord, accusing the French Government, as well as several Kanak political leaders, of seeking to undermine Kanak culture and tradition. The RPCR's policy of encouraging the immigration of skilled workers from mainland France and other European countries continued to be a source of conflict between the conservative coalition and the FLNKS.

At elections for the Representative to the French Senate in September 1992, the RPCR's candidate, Simon Loueckhote, narrowly defeated Roch Wamytan, the Vice-President of the FLNKS.

Debate concerning the political future of the Territory continued in 1994. In October the RPCR leader, Jacques Lafleur, proposed that New Caledonia abandon the planned 1998 referendum on self-determination, in favour of a 30-year agreement with France, similar to the Matignon Accord, but with provision for greater autonomy in judicial matters. The UC, however, rejected the proposal and reiterated its demand for a gradual transfer of power from France to New Caledonia, culminating in a return to sovereignty in 1998.

French presidential elections took place in April/May 1995. During the second round of voting in the Territory, the socialist candidate, Lionel Jospin, received 25.9% of the total votes, while the candidate of the Gaullist Rassemblement pour la République (RPR), Jacques Chirac, won 74.1%. (Chirac was elected to the presidency with 52.6% of votes cast throughout the republic.)

At provincial elections in July 1995 the RPCR remained the most successful party, although its dominance was reduced considerably. The FLNKS remained in control of the Provinces of the North and the Loyalty Islands, while the RPCR retained a large majority in the Province of the South. The RPCR retained an overall majority in the Territorial Congress, while the FLNKS remained the second largest party. Considerable gains were made by a newly-formed party led by a Nouméa businessman, Une Nouvelle-Calédonie pour Tous (UNCT), which secured seven seats in the Territorial Congress and seven seats in the Provincial Government of the South. An estimated 67% of the electorate participated in the elections. However, a political crisis subsequently arose as a result of the UNCT's decision to align itself with the FLNKS, leaving the RPCR with a minority of official positions in the congressional committees. Lafleur would not accept a situation in which the UNCT appeared to be the dominant party in Congress, and Pierre Frogier, the RPCR's President of Congress, refused to convene a congressional sitting under such circumstances. The deadlock was broken only when the FLNKS released a statement in October, reiterating the importance of the relationship between the FLNKS and the RPCR as signatories of the Matignon Accord, and proposing the allocation of congressional positions on a proportional basis.

Negotiations between the French Government and delegations from the FLNKS and the RPCR were held in Paris in late 1995. It was agreed that further discussions would take place in early 1996, involving representatives from numerous interest groups in the Territory, to examine the possibility of achieving a consensus solution on the future of the islands. Thus, the major political groups in New Caledonia sought to achieve a consensus solution on the Territory's future, which could be presented to the electorate for approval in the 1998 referendum. It was widely believed that this was preferable to a simple 'for' or 'against' vote on independence, which would necessarily polarize the electorate and create a confrontational political climate.

Elections to the French National Assembly in May–June 1997 were boycotted by the pro-independence FLNKS and LKS, resulting in a relatively low participation rate among the electorate. Jacques Lafleur and Pierre Frogier, both candidates of the RPCR, were elected to represent New Caledonia. Intensive negotiations involving the RPCR, the FLNKS and the French Government took place throughout early 1996. The process, however, was disrupted by a dispute over the disclosure of confidential information regarding the talks to the French press (responsibility for which was later admitted by Jacques Lafleur) and the belief by pro-independence leaders that France had apparently reneged on its promise to consider all available options for the Territory's political future by discounting the possibility of outright independence. France's refusal to grant final approval for a large-scale nickel smelter project in the North Province (see Economic Affairs) until the achievement of consensus in the discussions on autonomy prompted accusations of blackmail from several sources within the Territory and fuelled suspicions that metropolitan France would seek to retain control of the islands' valuable mineral resources in any settlement on New Caledonia's future status. The issue proved to be a serious obstacle in the negotiations and resulted in the virtual cessation of discussions between the two sides during the remainder of 1996. The FLNKS argued that the smelter project should be administered by local interests, consistent with the process of reallocating responsibility for the economy from metropolitan France to the Territory as advocated in the Matignon Accord. Their demands were supported by widespread industrial action in the mining sector during late 1996.

In February 1997 the French Minister for Overseas Territories travelled to the Territory in an attempt to achieve an exchange agreement on nickel between the Société Minière du Sud-Pacifique (SMSP), controlled by the North Province, and the French-owned company, with numerous interests in the islands, Société Le Nickel (SLN). The minister failed to resolve the dispute during his visit; however, at the end of the month, in a complete reversal of its previous position, the French Government announced its decision not to compensate SLN for any losses incurred. The decision provoked strong criticism from SLN and Eramet, the French mining conglomerate, of which SLN is a subsidiary, and attracted protests from shareholders and employees of the company. During March large-scale demonstrations were held by the UC and the pro-independence trade union, USTKE, in support of the SMSP's acquisition of the smelter. Meanwhile, another trade union, USOENC (which represented a high proportion of SLN employees), organized a protest rally against the unequal exchange of mining sites. Frustrated at SLN's seemingly intransigent position in the negotiations, the FLNKS organized protests and blockades at all the company's major mining installations. Supporters of the pro-independence organization also restricted shipments of ore around the Territory. Consequently, four mines were forced to close, while a 25% reduction in working hours was imposed on 1,500 mine workers, prompting protests by SLN employees and demands from USOENC that the blockades be removed. In January 1998 Roch Wamytan urged the French Prime Minister, Lionel Jospin, to settle the dispute by the end of the month in order that official negotiations on the political future of the Territory, in preparation for the referendum, might begin. The position of the FLNKS had been somewhat undermined by the decision, in the previous month, of a breakaway group of pro-independence politicians (including prominent members of the UC, Parti de Libération Kanak (PALIKA), the UMP and the LKS) to begin negotiations with the RPCR concerning the dispute. These moderate supporters of independence formed the Fédération des Comités de Coordination des Indépendantistes (FCCI) in 1998. A draft agreement on the exchange of deposits was signed by SLN and the SMSP on 1 February, and in April a deal between the SMSP and a Canadian company for the establishment of the nickel smelter was concluded. If construction of the smelter had not begun by the end of 2005, control of the nickel deposits transferred to the SMSP was to revert to SLN. Meanwhile, the French Government agreed to pay compensation of some 1,000m. French francs to Eramet for the reduction in the company's reserves.

Following the signing of the nickel agreement (see above), tripartite talks on the constitutional future of New Caledonia resumed in Paris in late February 1998. Discussions between representatives of the French Government, the FLNKS and the RPCR continued in March, despite a temporary boycott of the talks by the RPCR delegation, which requested the inclusion of various other minor political groups at the negotiations, including the FCCI. On 21 April, following a final round of talks in Nouméa, an agreement was concluded by the three sides. The agreement, which became known as the Nouméa Accord, postponed the referendum on independence for a period of between 15 and 20 years but provided for a gradual transfer of powers to local institutions. The document also acknowledged the negative impact of many aspects of French colonization on the Territory and emphasized the need for greater recognition of the importance of the Kanak cultural identity in the political development of the islands. The Nouméa Accord was signed on 5 May.

On 6 July 1998 the French Parliament (the National Assembly and the Senate) voted in favour of adopting the proposed changes regarding the administration of New Caledonia, which were to be incorporated in an annex to the French Constitution. In the following month the French Minister for Overseas Territories returned to New Caledonia for discussion on draft legislation for the devolution process. In September a new political group, called the Comité Provisoire pour la Défense des Principes Républicains de la Nouvelle-Calédonie Française, was formed in opposition to the Nouméa Accord, with support from members of the Front National and other right-wing parties. The UNCT, which was dissatisfied with several aspects of the accord, also urged its supporters to vote against the agreement.

The Nouméa Accord was presented to the electorate of New Caledonia in a referendum on 8 November 1998, when it was decisively approved, with 71.9% of votes cast in favour of the agreement. The Province of the North registered the strongest vote in favour of the accord (95.5%), while the Province of the South recorded the most moderate level of approval (62.9%). In late December the French National Assembly unanimously approved draft legislation regarding the definitive adoption of the accord. The Senate similarly approved the legislation in February 1999. In March of that year, however, the French Constitutional Council declared its intention to allow any French person who had resided in New Caledonia for 10 years or more to vote in provincial elections. This decision was criticized by Roch Wamytan, leader of the FLNKS, as well as by politicians in the French National Assembly and Senate, who claimed that this was in breach of the Nouméa Accord, whereby only those residing in New Caledonia in 1998 would be permitted to vote in provincial elections. Pro-independence groups threatened to boycott the elections (to be held in May). In response to this, the French Government announced that the Accord would be honoured, claiming that the Constitutional Council had breached the Nouméa Accord, and stating that this contravention would be rectified. In June the French Council of Ministers announced that it had drafted legislation restricting eligibility for voting in provincial elections and in any future referendums on sovereignty, to those who had been eligible to vote in the November 1998 referendum on the Nouméa Accord, and to their children upon reaching the age of majority. This decision was condemned by the right-wing Front National, and by the leader of the RPCR.

At the general election held on 9 May 1999, no party gained an absolute majority. However, Lafleur's anti-independence RPCR won 24 of the 54 seats in the Territorial Congress, and formed a coalition with the recently-established FCCI and, on an informal level, with the Front National, thus creating an anti-independence block of 31 seats in the chamber. The pro-independence FLNKS won 18 seats. Simon Loueckhote was re-elected as President of the Territorial Congress in late May. Results of the elections in the Loyalty Island Province were officially challenged by the moderate independence parties, LKS and FCCI, as well as by the RPCR, following the issue by the electoral commissioner for the Province of a report claiming that a large number of irregularities had occurred. A new election was held in June 2000, at which a coalition of the RPCR, FCCI, LKS and FULK obtained 44.8% of votes and six seats. The FLNKS obtained 37.3% of votes and six seats, and PALIKA 17.8% of votes and two seats. The composition of the Territorial Congress therefore remained unchanged. Robert Xowie was re-elected as President of the Province.

On 28 May 1999 the Territorial Congress elected Jean Lèques as the first President of the Government of New Caledonia, under the increased autonomy terms of the Nouméa Accord. The new Government was elected on the basis of proportional representation and replaced the French High Commissioner as New Caledonia's executive authority. The election of Léopold Jorédié, leader of the FCCI, as Vice-President was denounced by the FLNKS, which argued that, as the second largest party in Congress and as joint negotiators in the Nouméa Accord, the post should have gone to its leader, Roch Wamytan. In the formation of the Government the RPCR-FCCI was awarded seven positions and the FLNKS four.

In October 1999 Wamytan threatened to withdraw from the Government, in protest at the lack of co-operation among parties. He claimed that sections of the Nouméa Accord requiring power to be distributed among the various political parties had not been observed (see above). In December Vice-President Léopold Jorédié received a one-year suspended prison sentence following accusations of misuse of public funds. Jorédié was charged with illegally obtaining grants totalling an estimated 5.5m. francs CFP, for the benefit of his son.

In July 2000 concern was expressed by the French Government over the implementation of the 'collegiality' clause in the Nouméa Accord, which provides for greater political co-operation among parties. Repeated threats by the FLNKS to withdraw from the Government because of its discontent with the RPCR's lack of power-sharing led to the establishment of an agreement between New Caledonia and the French State detailing the role of the two Governments in areas such as education and foreign policy; the role of the traditional chiefs in legal matters was also specified. In August Lafleur threatened to resign from his seat in the French National Assembly, following the upholding of a ruling convicting him of slander against Bruno Van Peteghem, an activist opposing construction plans for a complex near Nouméa. However, in early September Lafleur retracted his threat, following pleas by RPCR members.

In August 2000 the Government introduced a 'social pact', aimed at addressing social issues and ongoing industrial conflicts. It proposed an increase in the minimum wage and suggested local employment priorities, subject to ratification by employers' unions in September.

At the FLNK's annual conference, held in November 2000, Wamytan was re-elected President of the party (Wamytan was also narrowly re-elected leader of the UC); at the same time a new pro-independence party, the Groupe UC du Congrès, formed by a breakaway faction of the UC, was officially recognized by both the UC and the FLNKS.

In March 2001 the municipal elections confirmed the predominance of the RPCR in the south, when it took 39 of the 49 seats in Nouméa. However, in the country as a whole the RPCR controlled only 14 of the 33 municipalities in New Caledonia, against the 19 held by pro-independence parties, principally the UC, PALIKA, LKS and FLNKS. The FLNKS won a majority in the north and took all three communes in the Loyalty Islands. Jean Lèques resigned as President and was replaced by fellow RPCR politician, Pierre Frogier, in April. Déwé Gorodey of the FLNKS was elected Vice-President. The election to the two most senior posts took place after the Congress had elected an 11-member Government consisting of seven RPCR-FCCI coalition members, three from the FLNKS and one from the UC.

In October 2001 the French Council of State ruled that the 11th seat in the New Caledonian Government had been incorrectly allocated to the FLNKS following the local elections of April 2001. As a result, FCCI leader Raphaël Mapou replaced Aukusitino Manuohalalo of the FLNKS as Minister for Social Security and Health. The leader of the FLNKS, Roch Wamytan, threatened to resign from the Government in protest. In the same month, however, Wamytan was replaced as President of the UC by his deputy, Pascal Naouna; many members believed that Wamytan's dual role as President of both the UC and FLNKS was weakening the party. Then, in November, Wamytan lost the presidency of the FLNKS following a leadership struggle between its two main factions, the UC and PALIKA. The political bureau of the FLNKS was to lead the party until its internal disputes were settled. Wamytan was subsequently replaced as Minister for Customary Affairs and Relations with the Senate by Mapou, who was in turn replaced as Minister for Social Security and Health by Manuohalalo.

In June 2001, meanwhile, as a result of the failure to resolve industrial action over the dismissal of 12 employees from public works company Lefèbvre Pacifique, the Union Syndicale des Travailleurs Kanak et des Exploités (USTKE) extended its strike to 24-hour blockades of supermarkets, petrol stations, state radio and television companies, schools, the port and airport. In July 2001 a 100,000 francs CFP monthly minimum wage (as provided for in the 'social pact' brokered by Jacques Lafleur in September 2000) was implemented. Further strike action affected the tourist industry when, in December, USTKE launched a strike and occupation of the Château Royal complex, following Club Med's announcement of the Nouméa holiday resort's closure.

Meanwhile, a long-standing dispute over the ownership of a Wallisian settlement—Ave Maria, near Nouméa—had led to an outbreak of violence between Wallisian and Kanak communities in December 2001. The Kanak community in neighbouring Saint Louis demanded the departure of all Wallisians from Ave Maria by March. The French High Commissioner mediated at several meetings in January 2002 in an attempt to resolve the issue, leading to the Wallisian spokesman's suggestion that his community might be prepared to leave Ave Maria, provided it was offered an alternative 25 ha of land in which to resettle. Four working groups were established in April to rehouse Wallisians, to improve the area's public facilities, and to reintegrate youths who had abandoned the education system. In November the Kanak and Wallisian communities signed an accord, mediated by the High Commissioner, to end the violence, which had claimed three lives in total. About half of the 140 Wallisian families present in Saint Louis had left by the end of 2002; under the terms of the accord, the rest were to be resettled in 2003.

In the first round of the presidential election, held on 21 April 2002, Chirac obtained 48.4% of the vote on the islands, followed by Jospin, who won 22.4%, and eliminated nationally. In the second round, held on 5 May, Chirac overwhelmingly defeated Jean-Marie Le Pen of the extreme right-wing Front National, with 80.4% of the vote. Elections to the French National Assembly were held in June 2002. The UC and PALIKA could not agree upon their choice of President for the FLNKS. The UC therefore refused to take part in the elections and urged its supporters to abstain from the poll, thereby depriving the President of PALIKA, Paul Néaoutyine, of any chance of re-election to the National Assembly. Lafleur was thus re-elected as a deputy in the French legislature, winning 55.7% of the votes cast in the second round of polling; Frogier was also re-elected, with 55.7% of the vote; the rate of abstention was almost 60%. In December Lafleur announced his 'progressive retirement' from politics, although he gave no precise date.

Following two resignations in July 2002, a series of ministerial reorganizations took place. The Minister for Employment and Public Services resigned and was replaced by a fellow RPCR member, Georges Naturel. In late July Raphaël Mapou resigned, following his criticism of the tendering of mining and prospecting rights in the Southern Province to a Canadian mining company. He was replaced by Corinne Fuluhea of the RPCR. Shortly afterwards, her portfolio was altered to that of Professional Training. In November the sole UC member of the Government, Gerald Cortot, resigned, prompting the immediate dissolution of the Government, as stipulated in the Nouméa Accord. Later that month the size of the cabinet was reduced to 10 members, and the congress appointed a new administration, with Frogier reappointed as President; the cabinet contained seven members of the RPCR-FCCI coalition, two from the FLNKS and one from the UC. The FLNKS was scheduled to hold a congress to elect a new leader in May 2003.

Government

The French Government is represented in New Caledonia by its High Commissioner, and controls a number of important spheres of government, including external relations, defence, justice, finance, external trade and secondary education. In July 1989 administrative reforms were introduced, as stipulated in the Matignon Accord (which had been approved by national referendum in November 1988). New Caledonia was divided into three Provinces (North, South and Loyalty Islands), each governed by an assembly, which is elected on a proportional basis. The members of the three Provincial Assemblies together form the Territorial Congress. Members are subject to re-election every five years. The responsibilities of the Territorial Congress include New Caledonia's budget and fiscal affairs, infrastructure and primary education, while the responsibilities of the Provincial Assemblies include local economic development, land reform and cultural affairs. The Government of New Caledonia is elected by the Territorial Congress, and comprises between seven and 11 members. Under the terms of the Nouméa Accord (which was approved by a referendum in November 1998), it replaces the French High Commissioner as New Caledonia's executive authority. A gradual transfer of power from metropolitan France to local institutions was to be effected over a period of between 15 and 20 years under the terms of the Nouméa Accord.

In addition, New Caledonia elects two deputies to the French National Assembly in Paris and one representative to the French Senate on the basis of universal adult suffrage; one Economic and Social Councillor is also nominated. New Caledonia may also be represented at the European Parliament.

Defence

In August 2002 France was maintaining a force of 2,600 military personnel in New Caledonia, including a gendarmerie of about 750.

Economic Affairs

In 2000, according to World Bank estimates, New Caledonia's gross national income (GNI) at average 1998–2000 prices totalled US $3,203m., equivalent to $15,060 per head (or $21,880m. per head on an international purchasing-power parity basis). During 1990–2000 it was estimated that GNI per head increased, in real terms, at an average annual rate of 0.7%. Over the same period the population rose by an average annual rate of 2.4%. During 1990–2000 New Caledonia's gross domestic product (GDP) increased, in real terms, at an average annual rate of 1.6%. GDP declined by 3.2% in 1998, but increased by 0.9% in 1999 and by 2.1% in 2000.

Agriculture and fishing contributed only 1.9% of GDP in 1999, and 7.2% of the employed labour force were engaged in the sector in 1996. In 1997 only some 0.7% of total land area was used for arable purposes or permanent crops. Maize, yams, sweet potatoes and coconuts have traditionally been the principal crops. However, pumpkins (squash) became an important export crop for the Japanese market during the 1990s, with 2,200 metric tons exported in 2000 (compared with 500 tons in 1993). Lychees became a new, albeit as yet small, export in 2001; eight metric tons each were exported to Japan, New Zealand and French Polynesia. Livestock consists mainly of cattle and pigs. New Caledonia also began to export deer, principally to Thailand, in 1994. In 1998 an Australian company announced major investment in a chicken-farming project in the North Province, increasing the number of chickens from 1,000 in 1995 to 330,000 in 2000. The main fisheries products are tuna and shrimps (most of which are exported to Japan). A total of 1,651 metric tons of farmed shrimps were produced in 2001 (compared with 632 tons in 1993), and a giant clam project was undertaken in 1996. Fish and prawn exports increased in value by 413m. francs CFP between January and November 2001, compared with the corresponding period of the previous year.

Industry (comprising mining, manufacturing, construction and utilities) provided 19.6% of GDP in 1997, and employed 27.4% of the working population in 1995. Although mining employed only 3.2% of New Caledonia's working population in 1995, it constitutes the most important industrial sector. In 1999 mining and quarrying contributed an estimated 10% of GDP. New Caledonia possesses the world's largest known nickel deposits, accounting for about 30% of the world's known reserves, and is the world's largest producer of ferro-nickel. Sales of nickel accounted for 89.3% of export revenues in 1999 (of which 56.2% was ferro-nickel). In 1999 a Canadian company announced the construction of a pilot smelter at Goro, in the South Province. It was hoped that the plant would produce up to 27,000 tons of nickel per year by 2003. The project, which was to cost an estimated US $1,060m., envisaged the construction of a deep-water port, international airport, power station and associated infrastructure, and was expected to provide 2,000 jobs. However, work was suspended in late 2002, while the Canadian company sought more capital; operations were not expected to begin until 2005 at the earliest. In 1998 the nickel industry was adversely affected by the Asian financial crisis, which resulted in a dramatic decline in demand, a period of unrest among workers at the most severely affected mines and the consequent loss of some 300 jobs. Compared with the previous year, metallurgical production increased by 3.9% in 2001. The introduction of the single European currency, effected in January 2002, provided a boost to the nickel industry. (Both the one and two-euro coins used New Caledonian nickel.) In November 2001, however, in response to a decline in world nickel prices, the Société Minière du Sud Pacifique (SMSP) announced plans to reduce its mining activity by 50%, entailing the redundancy of 600 workers. Nevertheless, this did not affect the SMSP's joint project with a Canadian company: the construction of a new nickel-smelting plant in the North Province. Construction had yet to commence in early 2003; the plant was to employ 700 people and produce up to 54,000 tons of nickel a year.

The manufacturing sector, which provided 4.0% of GDP in 1997 and (together with electricity, gas and water) engaged 10.9% of the employed labour force in 1995, consists mainly of small and medium-sized enterprises, most of which are situated around the capital, Nouméa, producing building materials, furniture, salted fish, fruit juices and perishable foods.

Electrical energy is provided by thermal power stations (71.0% in 1999) and by hydroelectric plants. Solid fuels and mineral products accounted for 9.4% of total imports in 1998. In 1996 construction began on a plant producing wind-generated electricity near Nouméa, at a cost of US $7m., which provides some 4.5m. kWh of energy per year. In 2001 nine windmills were installed on Lifou, one of the Loyalty Islands, to deliver more than 800,000 kWh through the island's electricity network, as part of the Government's attempt to reduce expensive imports of diesel fuel. Plans were announced in early 2003 to install a further 31 windmills in the South Province.

Service industries together contributed 73.7% of GDP in 1999 and engaged 69.4% of the employed labour force in 1996. The tourism sector in New Caledonia, however, has failed to witness similar expansion to that experienced in many other Pacific islands. Tourist arrivals were seriously affected by political unrest and outbreaks of violence in the late 1980s between the Caldoches and Kanaks. Having increased from 99,735 in 1999 to 109,587 in 2000, the number of tourist arrivals declined to 100,515 in 2001; the figure rose to 103,933 in 2002. Receipts from tourism declined from US $140m. in 1997 to $112m. in 1998.

In 2000 New Caledonia recorded a visible trade deficit of some 42,490m. francs CFP, and there was a surplus of 25,242m. francs CFP, equivalent to 7.2% of that year's GDP, on the current account of the balance of payments (a deficit of 3,000m. francs CFP was registered in 1999). In 2001, however, the trade deficit increased to an estimated 64,700m. francs CFP. The principal imports in 1999 were mineral fuels, foodstuffs and machinery and transport equipment. France is the main trading partner, providing some 40.3% of imports 2001 and purchasing 26.1% of exports in 2001; other major trading partners in that year were Japan (which purchased 23.1% of exports), Taiwan (17.6% of exports), Australia and Singapore.

The budget for 1999 envisaged a surplus of 3,529m. francs CFP. Budgetary expenditure for 2002 was set at 86,400m. francs CFP. In 2001 budgetary aid from France totalled the equivalent of €755,317m., increasing to €777,965 in 2002. The annual rate of inflation in Nouméa averaged 2.0% in 1990–2000, and averaged 2.3% in 2001. Some 11.2% of the labour force were unemployed in 1999. In December 2001 there were 8,259 job-seekers, a rise of 10.1% compared with the corresponding month of the previous year. A total of 10,325 were registered as unemployed in June 2002.

New Caledonia forms part of the Franc Zone (see p. 237), is an associate member of the UN's Economic and Social Commission for Asia and the Pacific (ESCAP) and is a member, in its own right, of the Pacific Community (see p. 304). Following the adoption of the Nouméa Accord in 1998 (see Recent History), New Caledonia obtained observer status at the Pacific Islands Forum in 1999.

New Caledonia's economy is vulnerable to factors affecting the islands' important nickel industry, which included political unrest during the 1980s and fluctuations in international prices for the commodity in the 1990s. The Nouméa Accord, approved by referendum in November 1998 (see Recent History), aimed to improve the economic conditions of the Kanak population and to increase their participation in the market economy and in public administration. Despite previous attempts to redress the balance of New Caledonian society (most importantly in the Matignon Accord of 1988), the indigenous population remained largely excluded from New Caledonia's economic and political administration, and a considerable proportion continued to experience economic hardship in the late 1990s. In mid-1999 the RPCR leader, Jacques Lafleur, revealed proposals for the creation of an inter-provincial committee for economic development, which would allow the comparatively wealthy South Province to assist the economic development of the other Provinces. Moreover, it was hoped that the development of those sectors generally considered not to have reached their full potential (notably tourism, aquaculture, fishing and farm agriculture) would alleviate the economic uncertainty created by the need to reduce dependency on France. In an effort to encourage investment in New Caledonia, legislation to replace the system of tax deductions with one of tax credits was expected to be adopted in 2002. In the tourism sector, visitor arrivals declined by 8.4% in 2001 compared with the previous year. In 2003, furthermore, Air France planned to cease its operations in New Caledonia. The route to Tokyo, where Air France would provide connections to Paris, was to be taken over by Air Calédonie International (AirCalin), which was given a tax concession by the French Government on the cost of two new aircraft. In late 1999 a joint French and Australian research mission made an offshore discovery of what was believed to be the world's largest gas deposit, measuring an estimated 18,000 sq km. It was hoped that this indicated the presence of considerable petroleum reserves. Construction of facilities at two nickel mines was expected to commence in 2003–05, and it was thought that this would significantly increase nickel production. The effect of the decline in world nickel prices during 2001 was compounded by the downturn in the aviation industry that followed the terrorist attacks on the USA in September (aeronautical companies normally being significant consumers of special nickel alloys). Nickel prices, however, appeared to be recovering in mid-2002.

Education

Education is compulsory for 10 years between six and 16 years of age. Schools are operated by both the State and churches, under the supervision of three Departments of Education: the Provincial department responsible for primary level education, the New Caledonian department responsible for primary level inspection, and the State department responsible for secondary level education. The French Government finances the state secondary system. Primary education begins at six years of age, and lasts for five years; secondary education, beginning at 11 years of age, comprises a first cycle of four years and a second, three-year cycle. In 2000 there were 81 pre-primary schools, 204 primary schools and 72 secondary schools. In 1999 there were 19 technical and higher institutions (of which 11 were private). Some 400 students attend universities in France. In 1987 the French University of the Pacific (based in French Polynesia) was established, with a centre in Nouméa, and in 1999 it was divided into two universities. In 2000 the University of New Caledonia had 60 teachers and 1,600 students. Several other vocational tertiary education centres exist in New Caledonia. According to UNESCO, total public expenditure on education in 1993 was 1,652m. French francs.

Public Holidays

2003: 1 January (New Year's Day), 5 March (Missionary Day), 21 April (Easter Monday), 1 May (Labour Day), 8 May (Liberation Day), 29 May (Ascension Day), 9 June (Whit Monday), 14 July (Fall of the Bastille), 8 September (Internal Autonomy Day), 24 September (anniversary of possession by France), 1 November (All Saints' Day), 11 November (Armistice Day), 25 December (Christmas Day).

2004: 1 January (New Year's Day), 5 March (Missionary Day), 12 April (Easter Monday), 1 May (Labour Day), 8 May (Liberation Day), 20 May (Ascension Day), 30 May (Whit Monday), 14 July (Fall of the Bastille), 8 September (Internal Autonomy Day), 24 September (anniversary of possession by France), 1 November (All Saints' Day), 11 November (Armistice Day), 25 December (Christmas Day).

Weights and Measures

The metric system is in force.

Statistical Survey

Source (unless otherwise stated): Institut Territorial de la Statistique et des Etudes Economiques, BP 823, 98845 Nouméa; tel. 275481; fax 288148; internet www.itsee.nc.

AREA AND POPULATION

Area (sq km): New Caledonia island (Grande-Terre) 16,372; Loyalty Islands 1,981 (Lifou 1,207, Maré 642, Ouvéa 132); Isle of Pines 152; Belep Archipelago 70; Total 18,575 (7,172 sq miles).

Population: 164,173 (males 83,862, females 80,311) at census of 4 April 1989; 196,836 (males 100,762, females 96,074) at census of 16 April 1996; 215,904 (official estimate) at 1 January 2002. _Population by province_ (1996 census): Loyalty Islands 20,877, North Province 41,413, South Province 134,546.

Density (1 January 2002): 11.6 per sq km.

Ethnic Groups (census of 1996): Melanesians 86,788; French and other Europeans 67,151; Wallisians and Futunians (Polynesian) 17,763; Indonesians 5,003; Tahitians (Polynesian) 5,171; Others 14,960.

Principal Town (1 January 2002): Nouméa (capital), population 83,266.

Births, Marriages and Deaths (2001): Registered live births 4,326 (birth rate 20.2 per 1,000); Registered marriages 925 (marriage rate 4.3 per 1,000); Registered deaths 1,131 (death rate 5.3 per 1,000).

Expectation of Life (years at birth, 2001): Males 70.5; Females 76.1.

Employment (persons aged 14 years and over, 1995, provisional): Agriculture, hunting, forestry and fishing 2,489; Mining and quarrying 1,651; Manufacturing and Electricity, gas and water 5,583; Construction 6,824; Trade, restaurants and hotels 8,477; Transport, storage and communications 2,754; Financing, insurance, real estate and business services 5,676; Community, social and personal services 9,710; Activities not adequately defined 7,920; Total employed 51,260; Unemployed 7,410; Total labour force 58,670. Source: UN, _Statistical Yearbook for Asia and the Pacific. 1996_ (census results, excluding military conscripts): Agriculture 4,663; Industry 8,177; Construction 6,890; Services 44,647; Total employed 64,377; Unemployed 15,048. _1999_ Total employed 58,698; Unemployed 7,390; Total labour force 66,088 (Source: Institut d'Emission d'Outre-Mer, _Annual Report_).

AGRICULTURE, ETC.

Principal Crops (FAO estimates, '000 metric tons, 2001): Maize 2.5; Potatoes 1.6; Sweet potatoes 3.0; Cassava 2.8; Taro (Coco yam) 2.3; Yams 11.0; Coconuts 15.0; Vegetables 3.8; Bananas 1.2; Other fruits 3.1. Source: FAO.

Livestock (FAO estimates, '000 head, year ending September 2001): Horses 11.5; Cattle 123; Pigs 40; Sheep 0.5; Goats 1.5; Poultry 510. Source: FAO.

Livestock Products (FAO estimates, '000 metric tons, 2001): Beef and veal 4.0; Pig meat 1.4; Poultry meat 0.8; Cows' milk 3.6; Hen eggs 1.6; Cattle hides (fresh) 0.5. Source: FAO.

Forestry ('000 cubic metres, 1994): _Roundwood removal_: Sawlogs and veneer logs 2.8; Other industrial wood 2.0 (FAO estimate); Total 4.8. _Sawnwood production_: 3.3 (all broadleaved). _1995–2000_: Annual output as in 1994 (FAO estimates). Source: FAO.

Fishing (metric tons, live weight, 2000): Capture 3,250 (Albacore 895, Yellowfin tuna 250, Bigeye tuna 517, Sea cucumbers 500 (FAO estimate)); Aquaculture 1,754 (Shrimps and prawns 1,723); Total catch 5,004. Source: FAO, _Yearbook of Fishery Statistics_.

MINING

Production ('000 metric tons): Nickel ore (metal content) 110.1 in 1999; 123.5 in 2000; 117.6 in 2001. Source: US Geological Survey.

INDUSTRY

Production (2001): Ferro-nickel and nickel matte 58,973 metric tons (nickel content); Electric energy 1,729 million kWh.

Cement: 84,000 metric tons in 1997 (Source: UN, _Statistical Yearbook for Asia and the Pacific_).

FINANCE

Currency and Exchange Rates: see French Polynesia.

Territorial Budget (million francs CFP, 2001): _Revenue_: 81,337; _Expenditure_: 81,337. French government transfers 86,344.

Aid from France (US $ million): 336.6 in 1997; 336.3 in 1998; 314.9 in 1999. Source: UN, _Statistical Yearbook for Asia and the Pacific_.

Money Supply (million francs CFP at 31 December 2001): Currency in circulation 10,473; Demand deposits 94,525; Total money 104,998. Source: Institut d'Emission d'Outre-Mer.

Cost of Living (Consumer Price Index for Nouméa; base: December 1992 = 100): 111.4 in 1999; 113.1 in 2000; 115.7 in 2001.

Gross Domestic Product (million francs CFP at current prices): 347,303 in 2000. Source: _Bank of Hawaii, An Update on New Caledonia_.

Expenditure on the Gross Domestic Product (million francs CFP at current prices, 1992): Government final consumption expenditure 94,770; Private final consumption expenditure 159,514; Increase in stocks 416; Gross fixed capital formation 66,818; _Total domestic expenditure_ 321,518; Exports of goods and services 47,246; _Less_ Imports of goods and services 88,403; _Sub-total_ 280,361; _Statistical discrepancy_ 1,066; _GDP in purchasers' values_ 281,427. Source: UN, _National Accounts Statistics_.

Gross Domestic Product by Economic Activity (million francs CFP at current prices, 1997): Agriculture and food processing 12,835; Energy, mining and metallurgy 37,232; Other manufactures 13,815; Construction and public works 17,447; Transport and communication 23,415; Services and commerce 152,659; Salaries 91,857; Total 349,260. Source: _Bank of Hawaii, An Update on New Caledonia_.

Balance of Payments (million francs CFP, 2000): Trade balance –42,490; Services (net) –5,161; *Balance on goods and services* –47,651; Other income (net) 33,394; *Balance on goods, services and income* –14,257; Current transfers (net) 39,500; *Current balance* 25,242; Capital account (net) 179; Direct investment (net) –5,492; Portfolio investment (net) –15,367; Other capital (incl. charges in reserves) –4,738; Net errors and omissions 176. Source: Institut d'Emission d'Outre-Mer.

EXTERNAL TRADE

Principal Commodities (million francs CFP, 1999): *Imports*: Prepared foodstuffs, beverages, spirits and vinegar, tobacco and manufactured substitutes 18,233; Mineral products 10,579; Products of chemical or allied industries 8,860; Plastics, rubber and articles thereof 4,526; Paper-making material, paper and paperboard and articles thereof 3,115; Textiles and textile articles 3,967; Base metals and articles thereof 8,048; Machinery and mechanical appliances, electrical equipment, sound and television apparatus 22,617; Vehicles, aircraft, vessels and associated transport equipment 17,613; Total (incl. others) 112,808. *Exports*: Ferro-nickel 29,445; Nickel matte 8,764; Nickel ore 8,583; Prawns 1,868; Total (incl. others) 52,388. *2001:* Imports c.i.f. 124,400; Exports c.i.f. 59,700 (Source: Direction Régionale des Douanes).

Principal Trading Partners (million francs CFP, 2001): *Imports*: Australia 20,666.6; Belgium 1,659.9; China, People's Republic 2,977.9; France (metropolitan) 50,046.6; Germany 3,996.6; Italy 3,619.7; Japan 3,868.5; Korea, Republic 1,445.0; New Zealand 6,131.5; Singapore 7,551.4; Spain 2,485.9; United Kingdom 2,812.1; USA 4,910.6; Total (incl. others) 124,037.8. *Exports*: Australia 4,492.4; Belgium 1,236.2; Finland 1,422.2; France (metropolitan) 15,523.2; Italy 1,370.8; Japan 13,733.0; Korea, Republic 2,612.7; Spain 4,355.3; Taiwan 10,455.8; USA 1,446.4; Total (incl. others) 59,511.9. Source: Direction Régionale des Douanes.

TRANSPORT

Road Traffic (motor vehicles in use, 2001): Total 85,499.

Shipping (2001): Vessels entered 478; Goods unloaded 1,298,829 metric tons, Goods loaded 210,197 metric tons. *Merchant Fleet* (vessels registered, '000 grt, at 31 December 1992): 14.

Civil Aviation (La Tontouta airport, Nouméa, 2001): Passengers arriving 173,913, Passengers departing 172,854; Freight unloaded 3,661 metric tons, Freight loaded 1,401 metric tons.

TOURISM

Foreign Tourist Arrivals (arrivals by air): 109,587 in 2000; 100,515 in 2001; 103,933 in 2002.

Tourist Arrivals by Country of Residence (2000): Australia 18,012, France 30,702, French Polynesia 3,676, Japan 31,051, New Zealand 9,576, Vanuatu 2,606, Wallis and Futuna Islands 4,420; Total (incl. others) 109,587.

Receipts (US $ million): 140.0 in 1997; 111.8 in 1998. Source: partly World Tourism Organization, *Yearbook of Tourism Statistics*.

COMMUNICATIONS MEDIA

Radio Receivers (1997): 107,000 in use*.

Television Receivers (2000): 106,000 in use†.

Telephones (2000): 51,005 main lines in use†.

Facsimile Machines (1994): 2,200 in use‡.

Mobile Cellular Telephones (2000): 49,948 subscribers†.

Internet Users (estimate, 2000): 24,000†.

Daily Newspapers (1999): 1.
* Source: UNESCO, *Statistical Yearbook*.
† Source: International Telecommunication Union.
‡ Source: UN, *Statistical Yearbook*.

EDUCATION

Pre-primary (2000): 81 schools; 13,033 pupils.

Primary (2001): 289 schools; 1,837 teachers (incl. pre-primary); 36,996 pupils.

Secondary (2001): 64 schools; 2,371 teachers; 29,036 pupils.

Higher (2000): 55 teachers; 2,069 students.
Source: Vice-Rectorat de Nouvelle-Calédonie.

Adult Literacy Rate: Males 94.0%; Females 92.1% in 1989.

Directory

The Constitution

The constitutional system in New Caledonia is established under the Constitution of the Fifth French Republic and specific laws, the most recent of which were enacted in July 1989 in accordance with the terms agreed by the Matignon Accord. A referendum on the future of New Caledonia (expected to be conducted in 1998) was postponed for a period of between 15 and 20 years while a gradual transfer of power from metropolitan France to local institutions is effected under the terms of the Nouméa Accord, concluded in 1998. Under the terms of the Nouméa Accord, the islands are declared to be an Overseas Country of the French Republic, of which they remain an integral part. The High Commissioner is the representative of the State in the Territory and is appointed by the French Government. The High Commissioner is responsible for external relations, defence, law and order, finance and secondary education. New Caledonia is divided into three Provinces, of the South, the North and the Loyalty Islands. Each is governed by a Provincial Assembly, which is elected on a proportional basis and is responsible for local economic development, land reform and cultural affairs. Members of the Assemblies (40 for the South, 22 for the North and 14 for the Loyalty Islands) are subject to re-election every five years. A proportion of the members of the three Provincial Assemblies together form the Congress of New Caledonia (32 for the South, 15 for the North, and seven for the Loyalty Islands), which is responsible for the territorial budget and fiscal affairs, infrastructure and primary education. The Assemblies and the Congress each elect a President to lead them. The Government of New Caledonia is elected by the Congress, and comprises between seven and 11 members. Under the terms of the Nouméa Accord, it replaces the French High Commissioner as the Territory's executive authority. Provision is also made for the maintenance of Kanak tradition: there are eight custom regions, each with a Regional Consultative Custom Council. These eight Councils, with other appropriate authorities, are represented on the Customary Senate, which is composed of 16 members (two elected from each regional council for a six-year period); the Senate is consulted by the Congress and the Government. Local government is conducted by 33 communes. New Caledonia also elects two deputies to the National Assembly in Paris and one Senator, on the basis of universal adult suffrage. One Economic and Social Councillor is also nominated. New Caledonia may be represented in the European Parliament.

The Government

(April 2003)

STATE GOVERNMENT

High Commissioner: DANIEL CONSTANTIN (took office August 2002).
Secretary-General: ALAIN TRIOLLE.
Deputy Secretary-General: CAMILLE PUTOIS.

LOCAL GOVERNMENT

Secretary-General: PATRICK JAMIN.
Deputy Secretary-General: ARMAND LEDER.
Deputy Secretary-General: JULES HMALOKO.

COUNCIL OF MINISTERS

President: PIERRE FROGIER (RPCR).
Vice-President and Minister for Culture, Youth and Sports: DÉWÉ GORODEY (FLNKS).
Minister for Agriculture and Fishing: MAURICE PONGA (RPCR).
Minister for Education: LÉOPOLD JORÉDIÉ (FCCI).
Minister for Employment and Public Services: GEORGES NATUREL (RPCR).
Minister for Transport and Communications and Social Dialogue: PIERRE MARESCA (RPCR).
Minister for Economic Affairs, Relations with the Economic and Social Council and Relations with Congress: ALAIN LAZARE (RPCR).
Minister for Finance and the Budget, responsible for the Development of New Caledonia: HERVÉ CHATELAIN (RPCR).
Minister for Customary Affairs and Relations with the Senate and the Custom Consultative Council: ROCH WAMYTAN (FLNKS).
Minister for Professional Training: CORINNE FULUHEA (RPCR).

Minister for Infrastructure: Gérald Cortot (UC).

GOVERNMENT OFFICES

Office of the High Commissioner: Haut-commissariat de la République en Nouvelle-Calédonie, 1 ave Maréchal Foch, BP C5, 98848 Nouméa Cédex; tel. 266300; fax 272828; internet www.etat .nc.

New Caledonian Government: *Présidence du Gouvernement:* 8 route des Artifices, BP M2, 98849 Nouméa Cédex; *Congrès de la Nouvelle-Calédonie:* 1 blvd Vauban, BP 31, 98845 Nouméa Cédex; tel. 246565; fax 246550; tel. 273129; fax 277020; e-mail cellule .communication@gouv.nc; e-mail courrier@congres.nc.

Office of the Secretary-General of the Government of New Caledonia: Immeuble administratif Jacques Iekawe, 18 ave Paul Doumer, BP M2, 98844 Nouméa Cédex; tel. 256000; fax 286848; e-mail lmoprini@gouv.nc; internet www.gouv.nc.

Government of the Province of the Loyalty Islands: Gouvernement Provincial des Iles Loyauté, BP 50, 98820 Wé, Lifou, Loyalty Islands; tel. 455100; fax 455100; e-mail loyalty@loyalty.nc; internet www.loyalty.nc.

Government of the Province of the North: Gouvernement Provincial du Nord, BP 41, 98860 Koné, Grande-Terre; tel. 477100; fax 355475.

Government of the Province of the South: Hôtel de la Province Sud, 9 Route des Artifices Artilleries, Port Moselle, BP 4142, 98846 Nouméa Cédex; tel. 258000; fax 274900; internet www.province-sud .nc.

GOVERNMENT DEPARTMENTS

Department of Administrative Services and Computer Technology: 3 rue Gustave Flaubert, Baie de l'Orphelinat, BP 8231, 98807 Nouméa Cédex; tel. 275858; fax 281919; e-mail smai@gouv.nc; internet www.gouv.nc/smai.

Department of Agriculture, Forestry and Environment: 209 rue Anatole Bénébig, BP 180, 98845 Nouméa Cédex; tel. 232530; fax 232550; e-mail direction@dafe.nc.

Department of Civil Aviation: 179 rue Gervolino, BP H1, 98849 Nouméa Cédex; tel. 265200; fax 265202; e-mail brigitte.pasquialini@ aviation-civile.gouv.fr; internet www.dgac.fr.

Department of Culture: 75 rue Sébastopol, BP C5, Nouméa; tel. 242181; fax 242180; e-mail mac@hc.culture.nc; Dir Jean-Jacques Garnier.

Department of Education: Vice-Réctorat, 22 rue J. B. Dézarnaulds, BP G4, 98848 Nouméa Cédex; tel. 266100; fax 273048; internet www.ac-nouméa.nc.

Department of Employment: 12 rue de Verdun, BP 141, 98845 Nouméa Cédex; tel. 275572; fax 270494; e-mail dt@gouv.nc; internet www.gouv.nc/dtnc.

Department of Finance: 4 rue Monchovet, BP E4, 98848 Nouméa Cédex; tel. 279200; fax 272675; e-mail tg162.contact@cpfinances .gouv.fr; internet www.finances.gouv.fr.

Department of Human Resources and Civil Service: Nouméa.

Department of Infrastructure, Topography and Transport: 1 bis rue Unger, 1ère vallée du Tir, BP A2, 98848 Nouméa Cédex; tel. 280300; fax 281760; e-mail dittt@gouv.nc; internet www.gouv.nc/ditt.

Department of Maritime Affairs: 2 bis rue Russeil, BP 36, Nouméa Cédex; tel. 272626; fax 287286; e-mail affmar@gouv.nc; internet www.mer.gouv.fr.

Department of Mines and Energy: 1 ter, rue Edouard Unger, 1ère Vallée du Tir, BP 465, 98845 Nouméa Cédex; tel. 273944; fax 272345; e-mail mines@gouv.nc; internet www.gouv.nc/sme.

Department of Social Security and Health: 5 rue Général Galliéni, BP 3278, 98846 Nouméa Cédex; tel. 243700; fax 243702; e-mail dtass@territoire.nc; internet www.gouv.nc/dtass.

Department of Youth and Sports: 23 ave Jean Jaurès, BP810, 98845 Nouméa Cédex; tel. 252384; fax 254585; e-mail djsnc@gouv .nc; internet www.gouv.nc/djsnc; Dir Romain Marcet.

Legislature

ASSEMBLÉES PROVINCIALES

Members of the Provincial Assemblies are elected on a proportional basis for a five-year term. Each Provincial Assembly elects its President. A number of the members of the Provincial Assemblies sit together to make up the Territorial Congress. The Assembly of the Northern Province has 22 members (including 15 sitting for the Territorial Congress), the Loyalty Islands 14 members (including

seven for the Congress) and the Southern Province has 40 members (including 32 for the Congress).

Election, 9 May 1999 (results by province)

Party	North	South	Loyalty Islands
Rassemblement pour la Calédonie dans la République (RPCR)	4	25	2
Front de Libération Nationale Kanak Socialiste (FLNKS)	6	6	6
Union Nationale pour l'Indépendance (UNI—PALIKA)	8	—	—
Fédération des Comités de Coordination des Indépendantistes (FCCI)	4	—	2
Front National (FN)	—	5	—
Alliance pour la Calédonie (APLC)	—	4	—
Libération Kanak Socialiste (LKS)	—	—	2
Parti de Libération Kanak (PALIKA)	—	—	2
Total	22	40	14

Province of the North: President Paul Néaoutyine (UNI—PALIKA).

Province of the South: President Jacques Lafleur (RPCR).

Province of the Loyalty Islands: President Robert Xowie (FLNKS).

Note: following allegations of irregularities in the Loyalty Islands poll, a second election in that province was held on 25 June 2000, following which the distribution of seats remained unchanged.

CONGRÈS

A proportion of the members of the three Provincial Assemblies sit together, in Nouméa, as the Congress of New Caledonia. There are 54 members (out of a total of 76 sitting in the Provincial Assemblies).

President: Simon Loueckhote (RPCR).

Election, 9 May 1999 (results for the Territory as a whole)

Party	Votes	%	Seats
RPCR	30,774	38.80	24
FLNKS	13,824	17.43	12
UNI	4,831	6.09	5
FCCI	7,515	9.48	4
FN	5,374	6.78	4
APLC	4,830	6.09	3
LKS	2,046	2.58	1
PALIKA	1,335	1.68	1
Others	8,789	11.08	1
Total	79,321	100.00	54

PARLEMENT

Deputies to the French National Assembly: Jacques Lafleur (RPCR), Pierre Frogier (RPCR).

Representative to the French Senate: Simon Loueckhote (RPCR).

Political Organizations

Alliance pour la Calédonie (APLC): 40, rue de la République, BP 14534, 98803 Nouméa Cédex; tel. 273367; fax 273370; e-mail courier@alliance.nc; internet www.alliance.nc; Leader Didier Leroux.

Fédération des Comités de Coordination des Indépendantistes (FCCI): f. 1998 by breakaway group from FLNKS; Leaders Léopold Jorédié, Raphaël Mapou, François Burck.

Front Calédonien (FC): extreme right-wing; Leader M. Sarran.

Front de Libération Nationale Kanak Socialiste (FLNKS): Nouméa; tel. 272599; f. 1984 (following dissolution of Front Indépendantiste); pro-independence; Pres. (vacant); a grouping of the following parties:

Groupe UC du Congrès: Nouméa; f. 2000 by breakaway faction of the UC.

Parti de Libération Kanak (PALIKA): f. 1975; 5,000 mems; Leader Paul Néaoutyine.

Rassemblement Démocratique Océanien (RDO): Nouméa; f. 1994 by breakaway faction of UO; supports Kanak sovereignty; Pres. ALOISIO SAKO.

Union Calédonienne (UC): f. 1952; 11,000 mems; Pres. PASCAL NAOUNA; Sec.-Gen. DANIEL YEIWÉNÉ.

Union Nationale pour l'Indépendance (UNI): c/o Congrès de la Nouvelle-Calédonie; Leader PAUL NÉAOUTYINE.

Union Progressiste Mélanésienne (UPM): f. 1974 as the Union Progressiste Multiraciale; 2,300 mems; Pres. VICTOR TUTUGORO; Sec.-Gen. RENÉ POROU.

Front National (FN): BP 4198, Nouméa 98846; tel. 258068; fax 258064; e-mail sariman@province-sud.nc; extreme right-wing; Leader GUY GEORGE.

Génération Calédonienne: f. 1995; youth-based; aims to combat corruption in public life; Pres. JEAN RAYMOND POSTIC.

Libération Kanak Socialiste (LKS): Maré, Loyalty Islands; moderate, pro-independence; Leader NIDOÏSH NAISSELINE.

Rassemblement pour la Calédonie dans la République (RPCR): 19 ave du Maréchal Foch, BP 306, 98845 Nouméa; tel. 282620; fax 284033; f. 1977; affiliated to the metropolitan Rassemblement pour la République (RPR); in favour of retaining the status quo in New Caledonia; Leader JACQUES LAFLEUR; a coalition of the following parties:

Centre des Démocrates Sociaux (CDS): f. 1971; Leader JEAN LÈQUES.

Parti Républicain (PR): Leader PIERRE MARESCA.

Union Océanienne (UO): Nouméa; f. 1989 by breakaway faction of RPCR; represents people whose origin is in the French Overseas Territory of Wallis and Futuna; conservative; Leader MICHEL HEMA.

Other political organizations participating in the elections of May 1999 included: **Développer Ensemble pour Construire l'Avenir (DECA), Renouveau, Citoyens Ensemble, La Calédonie Autrement, Front Uni de Libération Kanak (FULK), Groupe Alliance Multiraciale (GAM)** and **Indépendance et Progrès.**

Judicial System

Court of Appeal: Palais de Justice, BP F4, 98848 Nouméa; tel. 279350; fax 269185; e-mail pp.ca-noumea@justice.fr; First Pres. GÉRARD FEY; Procurator-Gen. GÉRARD NÉDELLEC.

Court of the First Instance: 2 blvd Extérieur, BP F4, 98848 Nouméa; fax 276531; e-mail p.tpi-noumea@justice.fr; Pres. JEAN PRADAL; Procurator of the Republic ROBERT BLASER; There are two subsidiary courts, with resident magistrates, at Koné (Province of the North) and Wé (Province of the Loyalty Islands).

Customary Senate of New Caledonia: Conseil Consultatif Coutumier, 68 ave J. Cook, POB 1059, Nouville; tel. 242000; fax 249320; f. 1990; consulted by Local Assembly and French Govt on matters affecting land, Kanak tradition and identity; mems: 40 authorities from eight custom areas; Pres. BERGE KAWA; Vice-Pres. JOSEPH PIDJOT.

Religion

The majority of the population is Christian, with Roman Catholics comprising about 55% of the total in 1998. About 3% of the inhabitants, mainly Indonesians, are Muslims.

CHRISTIANITY

The Roman Catholic Church

The Territory comprises a single archdiocese, with an estimated 110,000 adherents in 1999. The Archbishop participates in the Catholic Bishops' Conference of the Pacific, based in Fiji.

Archbishop of Nouméa: Most Rev. MICHEL-MARIE-BERNARD CALVET, Archevêché, BP 3, 4 rue Mgr-Fraysse, 98845 Nouméa; tel. 265353; fax 265352; e-mail archeveche@ddec.nc.

The Anglican Communion

Within the Church of the Province of Melanesia, New Caledonia forms part of the diocese of Vanuatu (q.v.). The Archbishop of the Province is the Bishop of Central Melanesia (resident in Honiara, Solomon Islands).

Protestant Churches

Eglise évangélique en Nouvelle-Calédonie et aux Iles Loyauté: BP 277, Nouméa; f. 1960; Pres. Rev. SAILALI PASSA; Gen. Sec. Rev. TELL KASARHEROU.

Other churches active in the Territory include the Assembly of God, the Free Evangelical Church, the Presbyterian Church, the New Apostolic Church, the Pentecostal Evangelical Church and the Tahitian Evangelical Church.

The Press

L'Avenir Calédonien: 10 rue Gambetta, Nouméa; organ of the Union Calédonienne; Dir PAÏTA GABRIEL.

La Calédonie Agricole: BP 111, 98845 Nouméa Cédex; tel. 243160; fax 284587; every 2 months; official publ. of the Chambre d'Agriculture; Pres. ANDRÉ MAZURIER; Man. GEORGES ROUCOU; circ. 3,000.

Eglise de Nouvelle-Calédonie: BP 3, 98845 Nouméa; fax 265352; f. 1976; monthly; official publ. of the Roman Catholic Church; circ. 450.

Les Nouvelles Calédoniennes: 41–43 rue de Sébastopol, BP G5, 98848 Nouméa; tel. 272584; fax 281627; internet www .nouvelles-caledoniennes.nc; f. 1971; daily; Publr PHILIPPE HERSANT; Dir BRUNO FRANCESCHI; Editor MARC SPISSER; circ. 18,500.

Télé 7 Jours: route de Vélodome, BP 2080, 98846 Nouméa Cédex; tel. 284598; weekly.

NEWS AGENCY

Agence France-Presse (AFP): 15 rue Docteur Guégan, 98800 Nouméa; tel. 263033; fax 278699; Correspondent FRANCK MADOEUF.

Publishers

Editions d'Art Calédoniennes: 3 rue Guynemer, BP 1626, Nouméa; tel. 277633; fax 281526; art, reprints, travel.

Editions du Santal: 5 bis rue Emile-Trianon, 98846 Nouméa; tel. and fax 262533; e-mail santal@offratel.nc; history, art, travel, birth and wedding cards; Dir PAUL-JEAN STAHL.

Grain de Sable: BP 577, Nouméa; tel. 273057; fax 285707; e-mail lokisa@canl.nc; literature, travel.

Île de Lumière: BP 8401, Nouméa Sud; tel. 289858; history, politics.

Savannah Editions SARL: BP 3086, 98846 Nouméa; e-mail savannahmarc@hotmail.com; f. 1994; sports, travel, leisure.

Société d'Etudes Historiques de la Nouvelle-Calédonie: BP 63, 98845 Nouméa; tel. 767155.

Broadcasting and Communications

TELECOMMUNICATIONS

France Cables et Radio (FCR): Télécommunications extérieures de la Nouvelle-Calédonie, BP A1, 98848 Nouméa Cédex; tel. 266600; fax 266666; Dir PHILIPPE DUPUIS.

Offices des Postes et Télécommunications: Le Waruna, 2 rue Monchovet, Port Plaisance, 98841 Nouméa Cédex; tel. 268210; fax 262927; e-mail direction@opt.nc; Dir JEAN-YVES OLLIVAUD.

BROADCASTING

Radio

NRJ Nouvelle-Calédonie: 41–43 rue Sebastopol, BP G5, 98848 Nouméa; tel. 279446; fax 279447.

Radio Djiido: 29 rue du Maréchal Juin, BP 1671, 98803 Nouméa Cédex; tel. 253515; fax 272187; f. 1985; community station; broadcasts in French; pro-independence.

Radio Nouvelle Calédonie: Mont Coffin, BP 93, Nouméa Cédex; tel. 274327; fax 281252; f. 1942; fmrly Radiodiffusion Française d'Outre-mer (RFO); 24 hours of daily programmes in French; Dir ALAIN LE GARREC; Editor-in-Chief FRANCIS ORNY.

Radio Rythme Bleu: BP 578, Nouméa; tel. 254646; fax 284928; e-mail RRB@lagoon.nc; Dir CHRISTIAN PROST.

Television

RFO-Télé Nouvelle-Calédonie: Radio Télévision Française d'Outre Mer (RFO), Mont Coffin, BP 93, Nouméa; tel. 274327; fax 281252; f. 1965; transmits 10 hours daily; Dir ALAIN LE GARREC.

Canal Calédonie: 30 rue de la Somme, BP 1797, 98845 Nouméa; subscription service.

Canal Outre-mer (canal+): Nouméa; f. 1995; cable service.

Finance

(cap. = capital; res = reserves; dep. = deposits; m. = million;
brs = branches; amounts in CFP francs unless otherwise stated)

BANKING

Agence Française de Développement: 5 Rue Barleux, BP JI,
98849 Nouméa Cédex; tel. 282088; fax 282413.

Banque de Nouvelle-Calédonie: 25 ave de la Victoire, BP L3,
98849 Nouméa Cédex; tel. 257400; fax 274147; internet www.boh.nc;
f. 1974; adopted present name Jan. 2002; owned by Bank of Hawaii
(USA—94.5%) and Crédit Lyonnais (France—3%); cap. 3,617.7m.,
res 1,294.3m. dep. 45,661.2m. (Dec. 2001); Pres.and Chair DOMINIQUE
MONNERON; Gen. Man. GILLES THERRY; 7 brs.

Banque Calédonienne d'Investissement (BCI): BP K5, 54 ave
de la Victoire, 98849 Nouméa; tel. 256565; fax 274035; internet www
.bci.nc.

BNP Paribas Nouvelle-Calédonie (France): 37 ave Henri
Lafleur, BP K3, 98849 Nouméa Cédex; tel. 258400; fax 258459;
e-mail bnp.nc@bnpparibas.com; f. 1969 as Banque Nationale de
Paris; present name adopted in 2001; cap. 28.0m. euros, res 315.6m.
euros (Dec. 2001); Gen. Man. GÉRARD D'HERE; 10 brs.

Société Générale Calédonienne de Banque: 44 rue de l'Alma,
Siège et Agence Principale, 98848 Nouméa Cédex; tel. 256300; fax
276245; e-mail sgcb@canl.nc; f. 1981; cap. 1,068.4m., res 5,053.5m.,
dep. 81,547.6m. (Dec. 2001); Gen. Man. DOMINIQUE POIGNON; 12 brs.

Trade and Industry

DEVELOPMENT ORGANIZATIONS

New Caledonia Economic Development Agency (ADECAL):
15 rue Guynemer, BP 2384, 98846 Nouméa Cédex; tel. 249077; fax
249087; e-mail adecal@offratel.nc; internet www.adecal.nc/; f. 1995;
promotes investment within New Caledonia; Dir JEAN-MICHEL ARLIE.

Agence de Développement de la Culture Kanak: Centre Tjibaou, rue des Accords de Matignon BP 378, 98845 Nouméa Cédex;
tel. 414545; fax 414546; e-mail adck@adck.nc; internet www.adck.nc
.Pres; MARIE-CLAUDE TJIBAOU; Dir-Gen. OCTAVE TOGNA; Dir of Culture
EMMANUEL KASARHEROU.

**Agence de Développement Rural et d'Aménagement Foncier
(ADRAF):** 1 rue de la Somme, BP 4228, 98847 Nouméa Cédex; tel.
258600; fax 258604; e-mail dgadraf@offratel.nc; f. 1986, reorganized
1989; acquisition and redistribution of land; Chair. DANIEL CON-
STANTIN; Dir-Gen. LOUIS MAPOU.

Agence pour l'Emploi de Nouvelle Calédonie: 3 rue de la
Somme, BP 497, 98845 Nouméa Cédex; tel. 281082; fax 272079;
internet www.apenc.nc.

Conseil Economique et Social: 14 ave Georges Clemenceau, BP
4766, 98847 Nouméa Cédex; tel. 278517; fax 278509; e-mail ces@
gouv.nc; represents trade unions and other organizations that are
involved in the economic, social and cultural life of the Territory;
Pres. BERNARD PAUL; Gen. Sec. YOLAINE ELMOUR.

Institut Calédonien de Participation: Nouméa; f. 1989 to
finance development projects and encourage the Kanak population
to participate in the market economy.

CHAMBERS OF COMMERCE

Chambre d'Agriculture: 3 rue A. Desmazures, BP 111, 98845
Nouméa Cédex; tel. 243160; fax 284587; e-mail canc-gr@canl.nc; f.
1909; 33 mems; Pres. GEORGES ROHCOU.

Chambre de Commerce et d'Industrie: 15 rue de Verdun, BP
M3, 98849 Nouméa Cédex; tel. 243100; fax 243131; e-mail cci@cci.nc;
internet www.cci.nc; f. 1879; 29 mems; Pres. MICHEL QUINTARD; Gen.
Sec. MICHEL MERZEAU.

Chambre des Métiers: 10 ave James Cook, BP 4186, 98846
Nouméa Cédex; tel. 282337; fax 282729.

STATE-OWNED INDUSTRIES

Société Minière du Sud Pacifique (SMSP): Nouméa; 87% owned
by SOFINOR, 5% owned by SODIL; nickel-mining co; subsidiaries:
Compagnie Maritime Calédonienne (CMC) (stevedoring), Nouméa
Nickel, Nord Industrie Services, Nickel Mining Corporation (NMC),
Bienvenue, San 3; Man. Dir ANDRÉ DANG VAN NHA.

Société Le Nickel (SLN): Doniambo; tel. 245300; fax 275989; 60%
owned by the Eramet group, privatized in 1999; nickel mining,
processing and sales co; CEO YVES RAMBAUD; Man. Dir PHILIPPE
VECTEN.

EMPLOYERS' ORGANIZATION

MEDEF Nouvelle-Calédonie/Fédération Patronale: Immeuble
Jules Ferry, 1 rue de la Somme, BP 466, 98845 Nouméa Cédex; tel.
273525; fax 274037; e-mail medefnc@medef.nc; f. 1936; represents
the leading companies of New Caledonia in the Defence of professional interests, co-ordination, documentation and research in
socio-economic fields; Pres. OLIVIER RAZAVET; Sec.-Gen. FRANÇOIS PER-
ONNET.

TRADE UNIONS

Confédération des Travailleurs Calédoniens: Nouméa; Sec.-
Gen. R. JOYEUX; grouped with:

> **Fédération des Fonctionnaires:** Nouméa; Sec.-Gen. GILBERT
> NOUVEAU.

> **Syndicat Général des Collaborateurs des Industries de
> Nouvelle Calédonie:** Sec.-Gen. H. CHAMPIN.

**Union Syndicale des Travailleurs Kanak et des Exploités
(USTKE):** BP 4372, Nouméa; tel. 277210; fax 277687; Leader
LOUIS KOTRA UREGEÏ.

**Union des Syndicats des Ouvriers et Employés de Nouvelle-
Calédonie (USOENC):** BP 2534, Vallée du Tir, Nouméa; tel. and
fax 259640; e-mail c1vr@canl.nc; Sec.-Gen. DIDIER GUENANT-JEANSON.

Union Territoriale Force Ouvrière: 13 rue Jules Ferry, BP 4773,
98847 Nouméa; tel. 274950; fax 278202; e-mail utfonc98@ifrance
.com; internet www.ifrance.com.fo98000; f. 1982; Sec.-Gen. JEAN-
CLAUDE NÉGRE.

Transport

ROADS

In 1983 there was a total of 5,980 km of roads on New Caledonia
island; 766 km were bitumen-surfaced, 589 km unsealed, 1,618 km
stone-surfaced and 2,523 km tracks in 1980. The outer islands had a
total of 470 km of roads and tracks in 1980.

SHIPPING

Most traffic is through the port of Nouméa. Passenger and cargo
services, linking Nouméa to other towns and islands, are regular and
frequent. There are plans to develop Nepoui, in the Province of the
North, as a deep-water port and industrial centre.

Port Autonome de la Nouvelle-Calédonie: BP 14, 98845
Nouméa Cédex; tel. 255000; fax 275490; e-mail noumeaportnc@canl
.nc; Port Man. PHILIPPE LAFLEUR; Harbour Master EDMUND MARTIN.

Compagnie Wallisienne de Navigation: BP 1080, Nouméa; tel.
232910; fax 287388; e-mail amb.noumea@offratel.nc; Chair. ARMAND
BALLANDE; Man. Dir JEAN-YVES BOILEAU.

Somacal: BP 2099, 98846 Nouméa; tel. 273898; fax 259315.

CIVIL AVIATION

There is an international airport, Tontouta, 47 km from Nouméa,
and an internal network, centred on Magenta airport, which provides air services linking Nouméa to other towns and islands. Air
France operates a service four times a week between Nouméa and
Paris via Tokyo, Air Calédonie International (AirCalin) operates two
flights weekly from Nouméa to Osaka, two weekly flights to Sydney
and Brisbane, and one weekly flight to Auckland and Papeete
(French Polynesia) and AOM two flights weekly, from Paris to
Nouméa via Sydney. Other airlines providing services to the island
include Air New Zealand, Air Vanuatu and Qantas.

Air Calédonie: BP 212, Nouméa; tel. 250300; fax 254869; e-mail
commercial@air-caledonie.nc; internet www.air-caledonie.nc; f.
1954; services throughout New Caledonia; 283,593 passengers carried in 1999/2000; Pres. and CEO OLIVIER RAZAVET.

Air Calédonie International (Aircalin): 8 rue Frédéric Surleau,
BP 3736, 98846 Nouméa Cédex; tel. 265546; fax 272772; e-mail dg
.aci@canl.nc; internet www.aircalin.nc/aci.htm; f. 1983; 62% owned
by Territorial Govt; services to Sydney and Brisbane (Australia),
Auckland (New Zealand), Nadi (Fiji), Papeete (French Polynesia),
Wallis and Futuna Islands, Port Vila (Vanuatu) and Osaka and
Tokyo (Japan); Chair. CHARLES LAVOIX; CEO JEAN-MICHEL MASSON.

Tourism

An investment programme was begun in 1985 with the aim of developing and promoting tourism. A total of 2,388 hotel rooms were available in 1999. In that year there were 99,735 visitors to New Caledonia, of whom 31.1% came from Japan, 29.6% from France, 14.6% from Australia and 7.1% from New Zealand. Tourist arrivals declined from 109,587 in 2000 to 100,515 in 2001. The industry earned US $111.8m. in 1998.

New Caledonia Tourism South: Immeuble Nouméa-Centre, 20 rue Anatole France; BP 688, 98845 Nouméa Cédex; tel. 242080; fax 242070; e-mail info@nouvellecaledonie-sud.com; internet www .nouvellecaledonietourisme-sud.com; f. 2001; international promotion of tourism in the Southern Province of New Caledonia; Chair. JEAN-CLAUDE BRIAULT; Dir JEAN-MICHEL FOUTREIN.

GABON

Introductory Survey

Location, Climate, Language, Religion, Flag, Capital

The Gabonese Republic is an equatorial country on the west coast of Africa, with Equatorial Guinea and Cameroon to the north and the Congo to the south and east. The climate is tropical, with an average annual temperature of 26°C (79°F) and an average annual rainfall of 2,490 mm (98 ins). The official language is French, but Fang (in the north) and Bantu dialects (in the south) are also widely spoken. About 60% of the population are Christians, mainly Roman Catholics. Most of the remainder follow animist beliefs. The national flag (proportions 3 by 4) has three equal horizontal stripes, of green, yellow and blue. The capital is Libreville.

Recent History

Formerly a province of French Equatorial Africa, Gabon was granted internal autonomy in November 1958, and proceeded to full independence on 17 August 1960. Léon M'Ba, the new Republic's President, established Gabon as a one-party state. Following his death in November 1967, M'Ba was succeeded by the Vice-President, Albert-Bernard Bongo, who organized a new ruling party, the Parti démocratique gabonais (PDG). Gabon enjoyed political stability and rapid economic growth in the 1970s, underpinned by substantial foreign investment in the development and exploitation of its petroleum reserves. However, the social and economic problems that accompanied the subsequent decline in world petroleum prices led to the emergence in 1981 of a moderate opposition group, the Mouvement de redressement national (MORENA), which demanded the restoration of a multi-party system. Bongo maintained his commitment to a single-party framework, in which he undertook to allow democratic debate. MORENA responded by forming a government-in-exile in Paris, from which it unsuccessfully sought to put forward a candidate to challenge Bongo in the presidential election held in November 1986.

Following a period of preoccupation with internal divisions, MORENA resumed its campaign against the Government in early 1989. In May the Chairman of MORENA, Fr Paul M'Ba Abessole, visited Gabon and, after a meeting with Bongo, announced that he and many of his supporters would return to Gabon. In January 1990 representatives of MORENA announced that M'Ba Abessole had been dismissed from the leadership of the movement, following his declaration of support for the Government. M'Ba Abessole subsequently formed a breakaway faction, known as MORENA des bûcherons (renamed Rassemblement national des bûcherons in 1991 to avoid confusion with the rival MORENA—originels).

A number of arrests took place in October 1989, following an alleged conspiracy to overthrow the Government. It was claimed that the plot had been instigated by Pierre Mamboundou, the leader of the Union du peuple gabonais (UPG, an opposition movement based in Paris). In early 1990 a series of strikes and demonstrations reflected increasing public discontent with economic austerity measures. In February a 'special commission for democracy' (which had been established by the PDG) submitted a report condemning Gabon's single-party political system. Bongo subsequently announced that extensive political reforms were to be introduced and that the ruling party was to be replaced by a new organization, the Rassemblement social-démocrate gabonais (RSDG). However, strike action continued in a number of sectors, resulting in severe disruption.

In March 1990 the PDG announced that a multi-party system was to be introduced, under the supervision of the RSDG, at the end of a five-year transitional period. A national conference was convened in late March to determine the programme for the reforms. The conference (which was attended by representatives of more than 70 political organizations, as well as professional bodies and other special interest groups) rejected Bongo's proposals for a transitional period of political reform under the aegis of the RSDG, and demanded the immediate establishment of a multi-party system and the formation of a new government, which would hold office only until legislative elections could take place. Bongo acceded to the decisions of the conference, and in late April Casimir Oye Mba, the Governor of the Banque des états de l'Afrique centrale, was appointed Prime Minister of a transitional administration, which included several opposition members.

In May 1990 the Central Committee of the PDG and the legislature, the Assemblée nationale, approved constitutional changes that would facilitate the transition to a multi-party political system. The existing presidential mandate (effective until January 1994) was to be respected; thereafter, elections to the presidency would be contested by more than one candidate, and the tenure of office would be reduced to five years, renewable only once. At the same time, Bongo resigned as Secretary-General of the PDG, claiming that this role was now incompatible with his position as Head of State. In the same month, however, the death, in suspicious circumstances, of Joseph Rendjambe, the Secretary-General of the opposition Parti gabonais du progrès (PGP), provoked violent demonstrations in protest at Bongo's alleged complicity in the death. A national curfew was imposed in response to the increasing unrest, while French troops were briefly deployed in Gabon, to protect the interests of the 20,000 resident French nationals, and several hundred Europeans were evacuated. It was announced in early June that the French military reinforcements were to be withdrawn, and the national curfew was lifted in the following month. Port-Gentil, however, remained under a state of emergency until mid-August.

Legislative elections were scheduled for 16 and 23 September 1990. The first round of the elections was disrupted by violent protests by voters who claimed that the PDG was engaging in electoral fraud. Following further allegations of widespread electoral malpractices, results in 32 constituencies were declared invalid, although the election of 58 candidates (of whom 36 were members of the PDG) was confirmed. The interim Government subsequently conceded that electoral irregularities had taken place, and further voting was postponed until 21 and 28 October. A commission, representing both the PDG and opposition parties, was established to supervise polling. At the elections the PDG won an overall majority in the 120-member Assemblée nationale, with 62 seats, while opposition candidates secured 55 seats.

On 27 November 1990 a Government of National Unity, under Casimir Oye Mba, was formed. Sixteen posts were allocated to members of the PDG, while the remaining eight portfolios were distributed among members of five opposition parties. A new draft Constitution, which was promulgated on 22 December, endorsed reforms that had been included in the transitional Constitution, introduced in May. Further measures included the proposed establishment of an upper house, to be known as the Sénat, which was to control the balance and regulation of power. A Constitutional Council was to replace the administrative chamber of the Supreme Court, and a National Communications Council was to be formed to ensure the impartial treatment of information by the state media.

The final composition of the Assemblée nationale was determined in March 1991, when elections took place in five constituencies, where the results had been annulled, owing to alleged malpractice. Following the completion of the elections, the PDG held a total of 66 seats in the Assemblée nationale, while various opposition groups held 54 seats. The two most prominent opposition movements, the PGP and the Rassemblement national des bûcherons (RNB), held 19 and 17 seats respectively.

In May 1991 six opposition parties formed an alliance, known as the Co-ordination de l'opposition démocratique (COD), in protest at the delay in the implementation of the new Constitution. The COD also demanded the appointment of a new Prime Minister, the abolition of certain institutions under the terms of the Constitution, and the liberalization of the state-controlled media. Following a general strike, organized by the COD, Bongo announced the resignation of the Council of Ministers, and declared that he was prepared to implement fully the new Constitution. He also claimed that, in accordance with the Constitution, several institutions, including the High Court of Justice, had been dissolved, and that a Constitutional Court and a National Communications Council had been established. However, opposition parties within the COD refused to be represented in a new Government of National Unity, of which Oye Mba was appointed as Prime Minister. Later that month opposition deputies who had taken part in the boycott of the Assemblée nationale resumed parliamentary duties. On 22 June Oye Mba appointed a new coalition Government, in which 14 members of the previous Council of Ministers retained their portfolios. Members of MORENA–originels, the Union socialiste gabonaise (USG) and the Association pour le socialisme au Gabon (APSG) were also represented in the Government.

In February 1992 MORENA–originels, the USG and the Parti socialiste gabonais formed an alliance within the COD, known as the Forum africain pour la reconstruction (FAR). In the same month a general strike, which was organized by the RNB (without the support of other opposition groups), in an attempt to oblige the Government to comply with the demands presented by the COD, was only partially observed. Later in February the Government announced that a multi-party presidential election would take place in December 1993.

In mid-February 1992 a meeting of supporters of the RNB was violently suppressed by security forces. In the same month the university in Libreville was closed, and a ban on political gatherings and demonstrations was imposed, following protests by students against inadequate financing. Later in February the COD organized a one-day general strike in Port-Gentil (which was only partially observed), followed by a one-day campaign of civil disobedience, which suspended economic activity in Port-Gentil and Libreville. At the end of February the Government reopened the university, and ended the ban on political gatherings and demonstrations. In March, however, the COD instigated a further one-day campaign of civil disobedience in Libreville, following the violent suppression of a demonstration by teachers who were demanding improvements in salaries and working conditions. In April the PDG organized a pro-Government demonstration, in an attempt to gain public support.

In early July 1992 the Assemblée nationale adopted a new electoral code, despite protests by the FAR that the Government had failed to comply with the demands presented by the COD in October 1991. Later in July a motion of censure against the Government, proposed by opposition deputies in the Assemblée nationale in response to the postponement of local government elections, was defeated. The Council of Ministers was reshuffled in August, and in December three members of the PDG, including a former minister, were expelled from the party, after establishing a faction, known as the Cercle des libéraux réformateurs (CLR).

In November 1993 five political associations, the PDG, the USG, the APSG, the CLR and the Parti de l'unité du peuple gabonais, agreed to support Bongo's candidacy in the forthcoming presidential election, while eight opposition candidates established an informal alliance, known as the Convention des forces du changement. Later in the same month a number of demonstrations were staged by members of the opposition, in support of demands for the revision of the electoral register. Clashes between opposition and government supporters ensued, following opposition allegations that irregularities in the electoral register indicated deliberate malpractice on the part of the Government. In early December the Government agreed to revise the register in part, but rejected opposition demands that the election be postponed.

At the presidential election, which took place on 5 December 1993, Bongo was re-elected, winning 51.18% of votes cast, while M'Ba Abessole (the leader of the RNB) secured 26.51% of the votes. The official announcement of the results prompted rioting by opposition supporters, in which several foreign nationals were attacked (apparently as a result of dissatisfaction with international observers, who declared that no electoral irregularities had taken place). Five deaths were reported after security forces suppressed the unrest, and a national curfew and state of alert were subsequently imposed. M'Ba Abessole, however, claimed that he had won the election, and formed a Haut conseil de la République, later redesignated as the Haut conseil de la résistance (HCR), which included the majority of opposition presidential candidates, and a parallel government. Despite the reports by international observers that the elections had been conducted fairly, the opposition appealed to the Constitutional Court to annul the results, on the grounds that the Government had perpetrated electoral malpractice. In December Bongo condemned M'Ba Abessole's formation of a parallel administration, and invited the other candidates who

had contested the election to participate in a government of national consensus. As a result of the administrative confusion, local government elections, which were due to take place in late December, were postponed until March 1994. (In February 1994 they were further postponed, to August.)

In early January 1994 the USA criticized Bongo's administration for alleged infringement of human rights, after three opposition leaders, including two presidential candidates, were prevented from leaving the country. Later that month the Constitutional Court ruled against the appeal by the opposition and endorsed the election results. On 22 January Bongo was officially inaugurated as President. In mid-February the national curfew and the state of alert, which had been in force since December 1993, were repealed, but later that month were reimposed, after a general strike, in support of demands for an increase in salaries to compensate for a devaluation of the CFA franc in January, degenerated into violence. Security forces destroyed the transmitters of a radio station owned by the RNB (which had supported the strike), and attacked M'Ba Abessole's private residence, resulting in clashes with protesters. Strike action was suspended after four days, following negotiations between the Government and trade unions; nine people had been killed during that period, according to official figures (although the opposition claimed that a total of 38 had died).

In March 1994 Oye Mba resigned and dissolved the Council of Ministers. Later that month he was reappointed as Prime Minister, and, following the opposition's refusal to participate in a government of national unity, formed a 38-member administration, solely comprising representatives of the presidential majority (apart from one member of the PGP, who was expected to be expelled from that party). The size of the new Government, in view of the deterioration of the economy, prompted widespread criticism, and two of the newly appointed ministers subsequently refused to assume their allocated posts, apparently owing to disagreement regarding the composition of the portfolios. In the same month the Assemblée nationale approved a constitutional amendment that provided for the establishment of a Sénat (which the opposition had resisted) and repealed legislation prohibiting unsuccessful presidential candidates from participating in the Government within a period of 18 months. In June opposition parties agreed to a further postponement of the local government elections, to early 1995. In August opposition parties announced that they were prepared to participate in a coalition government, on condition that it was installed as a transitional organ pending legislative elections. In September negotiations between the Government and opposition took place in Paris, under the auspices of the Organization of African Unity (OAU, now the African Union, see p. 130), in order to resolve remaining differences concerning the results of the presidential election and the proposed formation of a government of national unity. In mid-September the RNB, which was attending the discussions, indicated that it would refuse to join a coalition government.

At the end of September 1994 an agreement was reached, as a result of the Paris meetings, whereby a transitional coalition government was to be installed, with local government elections scheduled to take place after a period of one year, followed by legislative elections six months later; the electoral code was to be revised and an independent electoral commission established, in an effort to ensure that the elections be conducted fairly. In early October Oye Mba resigned from office and dissolved the Council of Ministers. Shortly afterwards Bongo appointed Dr Paulin Obame-Nguema, a member of the PDG who had served in former administrations, as Prime Minister. Obame-Nguema subsequently formed a 27-member Council of Ministers, which included six opposition members. The composition of the new Government was, however, immediately criticized by the opposition, on the grounds that it was entitled to one-third of ministerial portfolios in proportion to the number of opposition deputies in the Assemblée nationale; the HCR announced that the opposition would boycott the new administration, which, it claimed, was in violation of the Paris accord. Four opposition members consequently refused to accept the portfolios allocated to them, although two of these finally agreed to join the Government. (The portfolios that remained vacant were later assigned to a further two opposition members.) In November associates of Bongo established an informal grouping, known as the Mouvement des amis de Bongo.

In January 1995 controversy emerged over the extent of the authority vested in the Assemblée nationale, after members of the HCR refused to participate in the drafting of the new electoral code until the Paris agreement was ratified. The Constitutional Court subsequently ruled that the Assemblée nationale was not empowered, under the terms of the Constitution, to ratify the agreement. In February, however, opposition deputies ended a boycott of the Assemblée nationale, following a further ruling by the Constitutional Court that the Assemblée nationale was entitled to act as a parliamentary body, pending the installation of a Sénat after the legislative elections in 1996, but that the constitutional provisions adopted under the terms of the Paris accord would require endorsement by referendum. In April Bongo announced that a referendum to endorse the constitutional amendments would take place in June. In the same month, in accordance with the Paris accord, the Cabinet approved legislation providing for the release of prisoners detained on charges involving state security. Later in April Gabon withdrew its ambassador in Paris, in protest at reports by the French media regarding Bongo's alleged involvement with prostitutes; a number of demonstrations in support of Bongo took place in Libreville. Government efforts to prohibit two pro-opposition newspapers, which had published French press reports considered to be critical of Bongo, were rejected by the National Communications Council. At the national referendum (which had been postponed until 24 July), the constitutional amendments were approved by 96.5% of votes cast, with 63% of the electorate participating. In September 1995, following dissent within the UPG, Sébastien Mamboundou Mouyama, the Minister of Social Affairs and National Solidarity, was elected party Chairman, replacing Pierre Mamboundou. However, the latter subsequently regained the leadership of the UPG. (Mamboundou Mouyama formed a new political party, the Mouvement alternatif, in August 1996.)

During early 1996 opposition parties criticized the Government for delaying the implementation of the electoral timetable contained in the Paris accord. At the beginning of May, following a meeting attended by all the officially recognized political parties, Bongo agreed to establish a National Electoral Commission to formulate a timetable for local, legislative and senatorial elections, in consultation with all the official parties. It was also decided that access to state-controlled media and election funding should be equitably divided. On 20 May 1996 the Assemblée nationale's mandate expired, and Obame-Nguema's Government resigned at the beginning of June, in accordance with the Paris accord. Bongo, however, rejected the resignation on the grounds that the Government should, before leaving office, organize the elections and finalize pending agreements with the IMF and the World Bank. At the beginning of October the National Electoral Commission adopted a timetable for legislative elections: the first round was to take place on 17 November, with a second round scheduled for 1 December. HCR representatives denounced the timetable, withdrew from the commission and demanded the postponement of the local and legislative elections. In mid-October Pierre-Claver Maganga Moussavou, the leader of the Parti social-démocrate (PSD), was forced to resign from the Government, following his condemnation of the electoral timetable. The Chairman of the HCR claimed that the 'dismissal' was a violation of the Paris accord. Later that month a minor reshuffle of the Council of Ministers was effected.

Organizational problems disrupted the local elections, which were held on 20 October 1996, having been postponed twice previously; according to reports, only 15% of the electorate participated. The PDG gained control of the majority of the municipalities, although the PGP secured victory in Port-Gentil, while the RNB was successful in the north of the country. Elections in Fougamou (where voting had not taken place) and Libreville (where the results had been invalidated) were eventually rescheduled for 24 November, although the RNB demanded the validation of the original results. On 24 November the RNB secured 62 of the 98 seats available in Libreville; M'Ba Abessole was subsequently elected mayor.

Legislative elections were rescheduled on several occasions, owing to the delay in the release of the local election results and the failure to revise electoral registers in time. The first round of the elections took place on 15 December 1996, without major incidents. Later that month it was reported that the PDG had obtained 47 of the 55 seats that were decided in the first round of voting. The opposition disputed the results, and there were demands for protest marches and a boycott of the second round of voting. The PDG secured a substantial majority of the seats decided in the second round, which was held on 29 December, winning 84 seats, while the RNB obtained seven, the PGP six

and independent candidates four, with the remaining 14 seats shared by the CLR, the UPG, the USG and others. Polling was unable to proceed for the five remaining seats, and results in a number of other constituencies were later annulled, owing to irregularities. (Following by-elections held in August 1997, during which five people were reportedly killed in violent incidents in north-east Gabon, the PDG held 88 seats, the PGP nine and the RNB five.) Guy Ndzouba Ndama was elected President of the new Assemblée nationale. Obame-Nguema was reappointed Prime Minister on 27 January, and a new Council of Ministers, dominated by members of the PDG, was announced on the following day. The PGP, the main opposition party represented in the Assemblée nationale, had refused to participate in the new Government.

Elections to the new Sénat took place on 26 January and 9 February 1997, with senators to be elected by members of municipal councils and departmental assemblies. The PDG won 53 of the Sénat's 91 seats, while the RNB secured 20 seats, the PGP four, the Alliance démocratique et républicaine (ADERE) three, the CLR one, and the RDP one, with independent candidates obtaining nine seats. The results for a number of seats were annulled, however, and in subsequent by-elections, held later that year, the PDG increased its representation to 58 seats, while the RNB held 20 seats and the PGP four.

On 18 April 1997, at a congress of deputies and senators, constitutional amendments which extended the presidential term to seven years, provided for the creation of the post of Vice-President and formally designated the Sénat as an upper chamber of a bicameral legislature were adopted, despite the protests of opposition leaders who objected to the creation of a vice-presidency and demanded that a referendum be held. The Vice-President was to deputize for the President as required, but was not to have any power of succession. In late May Didjob Divungui-di-N'Dingue, a senior member of the ADERE and a candidate in the 1993 presidential election, was appointed to the new post. Although officially part of the HCR, the ADERE had signed a number of local electoral agreements with other parties, including the PDG, prior to the legislative elections.

In September 1998 opposition parties withdrew their members from the National Electoral Commission in protest at alleged irregularities in the voter registration process for the forthcoming presidential election. In October President Bongo confirmed that he was to seek re-election; his candidature was formally accepted later that month, together with those of Kombila, M'Ba Abessole and Alain Egouang Nze for the RNB, Pierre Mamboundou for the HCR, Maganga Moussavou for the PSD, and two independents.

At the presidential election, which was held on 6 December 1998, Bongo was re-elected by 66.55% of votes cast, while Mamboundou received 16.54% of the votes and M'Ba Abessole secured 13.41%. The reported rate of participation was 53.8%. Opposition parties rejected the results, again alleging electoral malpractice, and called for fresh elections to be held. None the less, Bongo was inaugurated as President on 21 January 1999, and a new 42-member Council of Ministers, headed by Jean-François Ntoutoume Emane, was subsequently appointed. A minor reshuffle took place in February.

In early 1999 student demonstrations and strike action by civil servants severely disrupted health and education services, with some schools closed for up to three months. Industrial action by university teachers occurred in April and June 2000. In January 2001 post and telecommunications workers began a nation-wide strike in support of their demands for improved working conditions. The industrial action ended in early February when the Government agreed to the financial demands of the workers.

In December 1999 it was announced that Bongo had reduced the Council of Ministers in size from 42 to 31 members. In August 2000 four opposition parties, including the RNB (which subsequently changed its name to the Rassemblement pour le Gabon—RPG), formed a coalition, the Front des parties du changement, in preparation for legislative and local elections scheduled to be held in 2001. In January 2001 a minor cabinet reshuffle was effected after the Minister for Equipment and Construction, Zacharie Myboto, resigned, on the grounds that his position had become untenable, owing to an alleged campaign to discredit him because of his objections to democratic reforms. In August the Government requested a postponement of the local elections owing to financial difficulties; the Constitutional Court concurred, and they were delayed until April 2002. Despite a ruling by the Constitutional Court that they should take place no later than 30 September, local elections were subsequently postponed further, until 29 December.

Meanwhile, elections to the Assemblée nationale took place on 9 and 23 December 2001. Three opposition parties accused the Government of falsely inflating voter registration lists and boycotted the elections, while others called for the first round to be annulled, as a result of reputed irregularities and high abstention rates, reported to have reached some 80% in urban areas. In the event, the elections were postponed in three districts until 6 January 2002, owing to violent incidents, and voting was repeated on 20 January in a further two constituencies where candidates had received the same number of votes and in a third district where violence had marred the initial ballot. An outbreak of the Ebola virus (see below) resulted in the indefinite postponement of voting in the north-eastern district of Zadie. The PDG won 86 seats in the Assemblée, which was supplemented by 19 seats secured by independents with links to the PDG and other parties affiliated to the ruling party. Opposition parties obtained a total of 14 seats (the RPG eight, the PSD two and the UPG one).

A new, enlarged 39-member Council of Ministers, which included four opposition representatives, was appointed in late January 2002. Ntoutoume Emane was reappointed as Prime Minister, while M'Ba Abessole was named Minister of State for Human Rights and Missions. The new Government's priorities were stated to be poverty alleviation, social reintegration and the eradication of corruption. In the same month two universities were closed by the Government in an attempt to end industrial action by lecturers, who had been on strike since November 2001, in support of demands for salary increases and the payment of arrears.

During March and April 2002 the Constitutional Court annulled the results of voting in the December 2001 elections to the Assemblée nationale in 12 constituencies, including eight in which the PDG had been successful, owing to irregularities. On 26 May and 9 June by-elections took place in these 12 constituencies and in Zadie (where voting had been postponed); the PDG won 10 of the 13 seats contested, increasing its representation to 88 seats. Notably, two government ministers, the Minister of National Education, Daniel Ona Ondo, and the Minister-delegate for the Budget, Senturel Ngoma Madoungou, had their election to the Assemblée confirmed at the by-elections held in their constituencies.

Throughout late 2002 the ruling PDG formed a number of alliances with minor opposition parties. In November the Parti de l'unité du peuple gabonais and the Mouvement commun de développement agreed formally to join the PDG, and in the same month the Parti gabonais du centre indépandant resolved to support the 'presidential majority' in the local elections scheduled for December. Meanwhile, in September the forced closure of the *Gabaon* and *Misamu* weekly newspapers aroused international concern. In December expatriate teachers (which represent some 40% of teachers in Gabon's secondary schools, according to official figures) undertook strike action in support of their demands for the renewal of work permits and the payment of salary arrears.

In the local elections of 29 December 2002 the PDG achieved an apparent landslide victory once again, although success was marred by the apparent apathy of the electorate, with voter participation estimated at less than 20% in some areas. The opposition called for the results to be annulled, citing allegedly fraudulent adjustments carried out to the register of voters prior to the elections (some 73,000 persons were officially removed from the register in November 2002, bringing the total removed since the 2001 legislative elections to some 243,000). In late January 2003 Bongo reshuffled the Council of Ministers, promoting M'Ba Abessole to the post of Vice-Prime Minister, Minister of Agriculture, Livestock and Rural Development, in charge of Human Rights. Elections to the Senate took place on 9 February 2003; according to provisional results, the PDG won more than 60 of the upper chamber's 91 seats, followed by the RPG, which secured eight seats. In early April a further, minor reshuffle was effected.

President Bongo has pursued a policy of close co-operation with France in the fields of economic and foreign affairs. Relations became strained in March 1997, however, when allegations that Bongo had been a beneficiary in an international fraud emerged, during a French judicial investigation into the affairs of the petroleum company Elf-Aquitaine (which subsequently merged with Total and PetroFina to form Total-FinaElf). The Chairman of Elf-Gabon, André Tarallo, was temporarily detained, and overseas bank accounts, said to contain Gabonese government funds, were blocked. In response, Bongo cancelled a visit to France and reportedly threatened to impose economic sanctions on French oil interests in Gabon. In October 1999 a further judicial investigation into the affairs of Elf-Aquitaine, carried out by Swiss authorities, revealed that Tarallo had used bank accounts in that country secretly to transfer large sums of money to several African heads of state, among them Bongo. Bongo denied personally receiving direct payments from Elf and maintained that such 'bonus' payments were made only to the Gabonese Government. However, a report released in November, following a separate investigation by the US Congress into money 'laundering' and corruption among political figures, alleged that the US banking group Citibank had assisted Bongo in transferring 'political gifts', including some US $50m. contributed to his 1993 election campaign fund, which had been paid into 'offshore' accounts by Elf.

Bongo has often acted as an intermediary in regional disputes, chairing the OAU *ad hoc* committee seeking to resolve the border dispute between Chad and Libya, and encouraging dialogue between Angola and the USA. In 1997 he mediated in civil conflicts in Zaire (now the Democratic Republic of the Congo—DRC), the Central African Republic (CAR) and the Republic of the Congo. In July of that year the Government expressed concern at the large numbers of refugees arriving in Gabon and subsequently announced plans for repatriation. Throughout late 1998 Bongo participated in discussions with other central African leaders in an attempt to find a solution to the political and military crisis in the DRC, which had been invaded by Rwandan and Ugandan troops in August of that year. At a summit meeting held in Libreville in September, it was decided that Bongo would chair a monitoring and consultations committee on the conflict.

In July 1999 a summit meeting of central African heads of government took place in Libreville to discuss the problem of displaced people in the region. Bongo appealed for regional solidarity in addressing this issue, and proposed the formation of a new organization to assist the region's refugees. Later that month the Gabonese Government appealed for international assistance following a further influx of refugees from renewed fighting in the DRC. At the Gulf of Guinea summit held in Libreville in November the seven countries represented agreed to form the Commission du Golfe de Guinée, a consultation framework designed to promote co-operation and development among the member countries as well as to take measures towards the prevention and resolution of conflicts affecting those countries. In the same month Gabon established diplomatic relations with Libya. In December Bongo was designated as the official mediator in negotiations between the Government and militia groups in the Republic of the Congo, which subsequently led to the conclusion of a peace agreement.

In January 2000, under the framework of the Renforcement des capacités africaines de maintien de la paix (a French initiative designed to enhance the abilities of African countries to intervene in conflicts on their own continent), a military exercise involving personnel from eight countries from the central African region took place in Lambaréné, Gabon. Known as 'Gabon 2000', the exercise was orientated towards conflict resolution and was supported, with technical assistance, by eight industrialized nations, including France, the United Kingdom and the USA.

At a meeting of the Communauté économique et monétaire de l'Afrique centrale (CEMAC) in Libreville in early December 2001, Bongo was appointed to chair a commission, also comprising Presidents Idriss Deby and Denis Sassou-Nguesso of Chad and the Republic of the Congo, respectively, to find a lasting solution to instability in the CAR (q.v.). In October 2002 a CEMAC summit in Libreville sought to defuse tensions between the CAR and Chad, following outbreaks of violence on their common border. In November Gabonese soldiers arrived in the CAR as part of a CEMAC peace-keeping force; the Gabonese contingent totalled some 300 troops in January 2003. In February the Gabonese Government pledged 100m. francs CFA towards a planned national dialogue in the CAR, aimed at resolving the conflict in that country. In April Gabon confirmed its recognition of the new administration of Gen. François Bozize, following his return from exile in France and assumption of the CAR presidency.

In February 1996 the northern part of Gabon was quarantined in response to an outbreak of Ebola haemorrhagic fever, in which at least 13 people died, according to WHO. In April it was reported that the World Bank and the World Wide Fund for Nature were seeking to identify areas of equatorial forest for conservation, amid fears that increasing exploitation by logging companies would imperil the survival of indigenous plant and animal species. (In January 2003 the European Union—EU—and the USA donated US $6.5m. and $53m., respectively, towards forest conservation initiatives.) It was also feared that opening up the forest could lead to another outbreak of the Ebola virus, of which forest-dwelling fauna are believed to be carriers. In October 1996 a second outbreak claimed 14 lives in the north-east of the country, and by January 1997 a further 40 deaths had been reported. The Ebola virus re-emerged in the north-east of Gabon in December 2001, when 11 people were killed by the virus. The whole region was quarantined, but by early April 2002 the WHO had confirmed 65 cases. The EU donated $260,370 to Gabon to combat the Ebola virus. In early May it was announced that the outbreak had been contained, although the disease had claimed an estimated 53 lives.

In March 2003 relations with Equatorial Guinea became tense, following Gabon's occupation of the uninhabited island of Mbagne, which lies in potentially oil-rich waters north of Libreville, and south-west of the Equato-Guinean mainland. Both countries claimed sovereignty over the island.

Government

The Constitution of March 1991 provides for a multi-party system, and vests executive power in the President, who is directly elected by universal suffrage for a period of seven years. The President appoints the Prime Minister, who is Head of Government and who (in consultation with the President) appoints the Council of Ministers. Legislative pwer is vested in the Assemblée nationale, comprising 120 members, who are elected by direct universal suffrage for a term of five years, and the 91-member Sénat, which is elected by members of municipal councils and departmental assemblies for a term of six years. The independence of the judiciary is guaranteed by the Constitution. Gabon is divided into nine provinces, each under an appointed governor, and 37 prefectures.

Defence

At 1 August 2002 the army consisted of 3,200 men, the air force of 1,000 men, and the navy of an estimated 500 men. Paramilitary forces numbered 2,000. Military service is voluntary. France maintains a military detachment of 750 in Gabon. The defence budget for 2002 was estimated at 90,000m. francs CFA.

Economic Affairs

In 2001, according to estimates by the World Bank, Gabon's gross national product (GNI), measured at average 1999–2001 prices, was US $3,990m., equivalent to $3,160 per head (or $5,460 per head on an international purchasing-power parity basis). During 1990–2001, it was estimated, the population increased at an average annual rate of 2.8%, while gross domestic product (GDP) per head declined, in real terms, by an average of 0.4% per year. Overall GDP increased, in real terms, at an average annual rate of 2.4% in 1990–2001; growth in 2001 was 2.5%.

Agriculture (including forestry and fishing) contributed an estimated 7.6% of GDP in 2001. About 36.6% of the labour force were employed in the agricultural sector in that year. Cocoa, coffee, oil palm and rubber are cultivated for export. Gabon has yet to achieve self-sufficiency in staple crops: imports of foods accounted for 33.8% of the value of total imports in 1996. The principal subsistence crops are plantains, cassava and maize. The exploitation of Gabon's forests (which cover about 75% of the land area) is a principal economic activity. The forestry sector accounted for an estimated 2.8% of GDP in 2001, and engaged an estimated 15% of the working population in 1991. In 2000 okoumé timber accounted for an estimated 65% of all timber production. Although Gabon's territorial waters contain important fishing resources, their commercial exploitation is minimal. Agricultural GDP declined at an average annual rate of 0.3% in 1990–2001; however, growth in 2001 was 4.2%.

Industry (including mining, manufacturing, construction and power) contributed an estimated 56.6% of GDP in 2001. About 14.1% of the working population were employed in the sector in 1991. Industrial GDP increased at an average annual rate of 1.5% in 1990–2001; growth in 2001 was 2.0%.

Mining accounted for an estimated 47.9% of GDP in 2001 (with 46.2% contributed by the petroleum sector alone). In 2001 sales of petroleum and petroleum products provided an estimated 78.2% of export revenue. In January 2002 a new oilfield

was discovered in south-east Gabon, estimated to hold 20m.–50m. barrels of crude petroleum. Gabon is among the world's foremost producers and exporters of manganese (which contributed an estimated 4.5% of export earnings in 2001). Significant deposits of uranium have been exploited since the late 1950s at Mounana; however, with all reserves having been exhausted, operations ceased in early 1999. Major reserves of iron ore remain undeveloped, owing to the lack of appropriate transport facilities. Small amounts of gold are extracted, and the existence of many mineral deposits, including talc, barytes, phosphates, rare earths, titanium and cadmium, has also been confirmed. In 1999 it was expected that mining of substantial niobium (columbium) reserves at Mabounie would commence in the early 21st century. In 1995–2001, according to the IMF, mining GDP declined at an estimated average annual rate of 8.4%. The IMF estimated a decline of 5.4% in mining GDP in 2001.

The manufacturing sector contributed an estimated 5.6% of GDP in 2001. The principal activities are the refining of petroleum and the processing of other minerals, the preparation of timber and other agro-industrial processes. The chemicals industry is also significant. According to IMF estimates, manufacturing GDP increased at an average annual rate of 7.5% in 1995–2001; growth in 2001 was an estimated 5.0%.

In 1999 71.3% of electrical energy was provided by hydroelectric power, 17.8% by petroleum and 10.9% by natural gas. Imports of fuel and energy comprised an estimated 15.6% of the total value of merchandise imports in 2000.

Services engaged 18.8% of the economically active population in 1991 and provided an estimated 35.8% of GDP in 2001. The GDP of the services sector increased at an average annual rate of 3.8% in 1990–2001; growth in 2001 was 2.8%.

In 1999 Gabon recorded a visible trade surplus of US $1,588.3m., and there was a surplus of $390.4m. on the current account of the balance of payments. In 1999 the principal source of imports (50.2%) was France; other major sources were the USA and Italy. The principal market for exports in that year was the USA (50.6%); France was also an important purchaser. The principal exports in 2001 were petroleum and petroleum products, timber and manganese. The principal imports in 1996 were machinery and transport equipment, basic manufactures, food products and chemicals and related products.

In 2001 there was an estimated budgetary surplus of 214,000m. francs CFA (equivalent to 6.3% of GDP). Gabon's external debt totalled US $3,995m. at the end of 2000, of which $3,512m. was long-term public debt. In that year the cost of debt-servicing was equivalent to 15.0% of the value of exports of goods and services. In 1990–2001 the average annual rate of inflation was 3.8%. Consumer prices increased by 2.1% in 2001. The Government estimated about 20% of the labour force to be unemployed in 1996.

Gabon is a member of the Central African organs of the Franc Zone (see p. 239), and of the Communauté économique des états de l'Afrique centrale (CEEAC, see p. 339). In 1996 Gabon, which had been a member of the Organization of the Petroleum Exporting Countries (OPEC, see p. 298) since 1973, withdrew from the organization.

Gabon's potential for economic growth is based on its considerable mineral and forestry resources. Gabon's economic situation deteriorated substantially in 1998–99 as a result of falling petroleum prices and the negative impact of the Asian economic crisis on timber exports. Further strain was placed on the economy by the suspension of loans from the Agence française de développement, and from March 1999 Gabon had no IMF programme. The economy began to recover in 2000 as a result of higher petroleum prices and improved timber export revenues. In October the IMF approved an 18-month stand-by credit, worth some US $119m., in support of the Government's economic programme for 2000–01, and in December the 'Paris Club' of international creditors agreed to reschedule about $532m. of Gabon's debt. However, arrears of foreign debt continued to accumulate during 2001, as petroleum prices declined. The Government agreed to impose a strict austerity programme, as recommended by the IMF and the World Bank. The 2002 budget, which was adopted in October 2001, was based on an anticipated 6.7% decline in the price of a barrel of crude petroleum in 2002, but a significantly higher amount of manganese exports, which were forecast to rise by 22.6%, to 2.1m. metric tons. In 2002 a series of new contracts for the exploration of gold, diamonds and numerous industrial metals were awarded. In mid-2002 the Government concurred with predictions by the

World Bank that petroleum production in Gabon would decline by some 50%, in relation to 1996 levels, during the following five years. None the less, onshore production at the Nguino and Etame oilfields commenced in September 2002 (with capacity of some 6,000 and 16,000 b/d, respectively); petroleum production in 2002 was estimated at 300,000 b/d. Efforts to diversify the economy, to reduce dependency on export products, and to lower the level of public debt were priorities in 2002. It was hoped that this could be achieved through further development of the forestry, agriculture, fisheries and services sectors. Progress towards improving Gabon's negligible earnings from fisheries was achieved with the opening, in 2002, of a new fish-processing plant in Port-Gentil (financed by the Japanese Government, at a cost of some 4,480m. francs CFA), in addition to new initiatives to control overfishing. However, in spite of falling petroleum revenue, levels of government corruption were reported to be increasing in the early 2000s, and allegations of nepotism and misappropriation of state funds persisted.

Education

Education is officially compulsory for 10 years between six and 16 years of age. Primary and secondary education is provided by state and mission schools. Primary education begins at the age of six and lasts for six years. Secondary education, beginning at 12 years of age, lasts for up to seven years, comprising a first cycle of four years and a second of three years. In 1999/2000 enrolment at primary schools was equivalent to 151.5% of children in the appropriate age-group (151.9% of boys; 151.0% of girls), according to UNESCO estimates, while 1998/99 enrol-

ment at secondary schools was equivalent to 54.4% of children in the relevant age-group (58.3% of boys; 50.5% of girls).The Université Omar Bongo is based at Libreville and the Université des Sciences et des Techniques de Masuku at Franceville. In 1998 7,473 students were enrolled at institutions providing tertiary education. The 1994 budget allocated 78,850m. francs CFA (19% of total administrative spending) to expenditure on education.

Public Holidays

2003: 1 January (New Year's Day), 12 February* (Id al-Adha, feast of the Sacrifice), 12 March (Anniversary of Renovation, foundation of the Parti démocratique gabonais), 21 April (Easter Monday), 1 May (Labour Day), 14 May* (Mouloud, birth of Muhammad), 9 June (Whit Monday), 17 August (Anniversary of Independence), 1 November (All Saints' Day), 26 November* (Id al-Fitr, end of Ramadan), 25 December (Christmas).

2004: 1 January (New Year's Day), 2 February* (Id al-Adha, feast of the Sacrifice), 12 March (Anniversary of Renovation, foundation of the Parti démocratique gabonais), 12 April (Easter Monday), 1 May (Labour Day), 2 May* (Mouloud, birth of Muhammad), 31 May (Whit Monday), 17 August (Anniversary of Independence), 1 November (All Saints' Day), 14 November* (Id al-Fitr, end of Ramadan), 25 December (Christmas).

*These holidays are dependent on the Islamic lunar calendar and may vary by one or two days from the dates given.

Weights and Measures

The metric system is in official use.

Statistical Survey

Source (unless otherwise stated): Direction Générale de l'Economie, Ministère de la Planification, de l'Economie et de l'Administration Territoriale, Libreville.

Area and Population

AREA, POPULATION AND DENSITY

Area (sq km)	267,667*
Population (census results)	
8 October 1960–May 1961	448,564
31 July 1993	
Males	501,784
Females.	513,192
Total	1,014,976
Population (UN estimates at mid-year)†	
2000	1,230,000
2001	1,262,000
2002	1,293,000
Density (per sq km) at mid-2002	4.8

* 103,347 sq miles.

† Source: UN, *World Population Prospects: The 2000 Revision*.

REGIONS

(1993 census)

Region	Area (sq km)	Population	Density (per sq km)	Chief town
Estuaire . . .	20,740	463,187	22.3	Libreville
Haut-Ogooué .	36,547	104,301	2.9	Franceville
Moyen-Ogooué .	18,535	42,316	2.3	Lambaréné
N'Gounié . .	37,750	77,781	2.1	Mouila
Nyanga . . .	21,285	39,430	1.9	Tchibanga
Ogooué-Ivindo .	46,075	48,862	1.1	Makokou
Ogooué-Lolo .	25,380	43,915	1.7	Koula-Moutou
Ogooué-Maritime .	22,890	97,913	4.3	Port-Gentil
Woleu-N'Tem .	38,465	97,271	2.5	Oyem
Total. . . .	267,667	1,014,976	3.8	

PRINCIPAL TOWNS

(population at 1993 census)

Libreville (capital) .	419,596	Mouila.	16,307
Port-Gentil . .	79,225	Lambaréné . . .	15,033
Franceville . .	31,183	Tchibanga. . . .	14,054
Oyem . . .	22,404	Koulamoutou. . .	11,773
Moanda . . .	21,882	Makokou	9,849

Mid-2001 (UN estimate): Libreville (capital) 573,000 (Source: UN, *World Urbanization Prospects: The 2001 Revision*).

BIRTHS AND DEATHS

(UN estimates, annual averages)

	1985–90	1990–95	1995–2000
Birth rate (per 1,000) . . .	35.9	36.8	37.8
Death rate (per 1,000)	17.0	16.3	15.8

Source: UN, *World Population Prospects: The 2000 Revision*.

Expectation of life (WHO estimates, years at birth): 59.3 (males 58.0; females 60.5) in 2001 (Source: WHO, *World Health Report*).

ECONOMICALLY ACTIVE POPULATION

(estimates, '000 persons, 1991)

	Males	Females	Total
Agriculture, etc.	187	151	338
Industry	62	9	71
Services	69	26	95
Total labour force	318	186	504

Source: UN Economic Commission for Africa, *African Statistical Yearbook*.

Mid-2001 (estimates, '000 persons): Agriculture, etc. 207; Total 566 (Source: FAO).

Health and Welfare

KEY INDICATORS

Total fertility rate (children per woman, 2001)	5.4
Under-5 mortality rate (per 1,000 live births, 2001) . .	90
HIV/AIDS (% of persons aged 15–49, 1994)	4.16
Hospital beds (per 1,000 head, 1990)	3.19
Health expenditure (2000): US $ per head (PPP) . . .	171
Health expenditure (2000): % of GDP	3.0
Health expenditure (2000): public (% of total)	68.6
Access to water (% of persons, 2000).	70
Access to sanitation (% of persons, 2000)	21
Human Development Index (2000): ranking	117
Human Development Index (2000): value	0.637

For sources and definitions, see explanatory note on p. vi.

Agriculture

PRINCIPAL CROPS

('000 metric tons)

	1999	2000	2001*
Maize	25.4	25.9	26.0
Cassava (Manioc)	224	228	230
Taro (Coco Yam)*	58.5	59	59
Yams*	150	155	155
Sugar cane	152.1	236.5	235.0
Groundnuts (in shell) . . .	18.7	19.6	20.0
Oil palm fruit*	32	32	32
Vegetables*	34.5	35.0	35.0
Bananas*	11.5	12.0	12.0
Plantains	265	270	270
Other fruits*	12.0	12.0	12.0
Natural rubber*	11	11	11

* FAO estimates.

Source: FAO.

LIVESTOCK

(FAO estimates, '000 head, year ending September)

	1998	1999	2000
Cattle	34	35	36
Pigs	211	212	213
Sheep	191	195	198
Goats	89	90	91
Chickens	3,000	3,100	3,200
Rabbits	295	295	300

Figures for 2001 assumed to be unchanged from 2000.

Source: FAO.

LIVESTOCK PRODUCTS

(FAO estimates, '000 metric tons)

	1998	1999	2000
Beef and veal	1.1	1.1	1.1
Pig meat	3.1	3.1	3.1
Poultry meat	3.6	3.7	3.7
Rabbit meat	1.8	1.8	1.8
Game meat	20.5	21.0	21.0
Cows' milk	1.6	1.6	1.6
Hen eggs	1.9	2.0	2.0

Figures for 2001 assumed to be unchanged from 2000.

Source: FAO.

Forestry

ROUNDWOOD REMOVALS

('000 cubic metres)

	1999	2000	2001*
Sawlogs, veneer logs and logs for sleepers	2,338	2,584	2,584
Fuel wood*	511	515	518
Total	2,849	3,099	3,102

* FAO estimates.

Source: FAO.

SAWNWOOD PRODUCTION

('000 cubic metres, incl. railway sleepers)

	1999	2000	2001
Total	98	88	142

Source: FAO.

Fishing

('000 metric tons, live weight)

	1998	1999	2000
Capture	53.6	51.1	47.5
Tilapias	3.5	4.2	4.2
Other freshwater fishes . . .	3.5	5.8	5.7
Sea catfishes	1.3	1.4	0.9
Grunts, sweetlips, etc. . .	1.7	1.1	0.8
West African croakers . . .	4.7	3.4	2.3
Lesser African threadfin . .	3.5	2.8	2.5
Bonga shad	19.3	17.4	14.8
Sharks, rays, skates, etc.. . .	1.9	1.3	0.7
Southern pink shrimp . . .	2.3	0.1	0.1
Aquaculture	0.2	0.6	0.6
Total catch	53.8	51.7	48.1

Source: FAO, *Yearbook of Fishery Statistics*.

Mining

	1999	2000	2001
Crude petroleum ('000 barrels)*	125,000	118,625	110,000
Natural gas (million cu metres)* .	99	99	99
Manganese ore ('000 metric tons): gross weight	1,908	1,700	1,790
Manganese ore ('000 metric tons): metal content	881	804	n.a.
Uranium (metric tons)† ‡ . . .	347	—	—
Gold (kilograms)* † §	70	70	70

* Estimated production.

† Figures refer to the metal content of ores and concentrates.

‡ The Moanda uranium mine closed in 1999.

§ Excluding production smuggled out of the country (estimated at more than 400 kg annually in recent years).

Source (unless otherwise indicated): US Geological Survey.

Industry

PETROLEUM PRODUCTS
('000 metric tons)

	1996	1997	1998
Liquefied petroleum gas.	11	10	10
Motor spirit (petrol)	76	71	60
Kerosene	68	81	85*
Jet fuel	28	23	26*
Distillate fuel oils	165	230	213
Residual fuel oils.	308	285	298*
Bitumen (asphalt)	14	10	12*

* Provisional or estimated figure.

Source: UN, *Industrial Commodity Statistics Yearbook.*

SELECTED OTHER PRODUCTS
('000 metric tons, unless otherwise indicated)

	1999	2000	2001
Palm oil (crude)* †	6	6	6
Plywood ('000 cu metres)†	134	104	135
Veneer sheets ('000 cu metres) †	133	91	63
Cement* ‡	200	210	210

* Estimated production.
† Data from the FAO.
‡ Data from the US Geological Survey.

Beer ('000 hectolitres): 905 in 1993; 801 in 1994; 816 in 1995.

Soft drinks ('000 hectolitres): 390 in 1993; 351 in 1994; 416 in 1995.

Electric energy (million kWh): 1,213 in 1996; 1,257 in 1997; 1,277 in 1998 (estimate).

Source: UN, *Industrial Commodity Statistics Yearbook.*

Finance

CURRENCY AND EXCHANGE RATES

Monetary Units
100 centimes = 1 franc de la Coopération financière en Afrique centrale (CFA)

Sterling, Dollar and Euro Equivalents (31 December 2002)
£1 sterling = 1,008.17 francs CFA
US $1 = 625.50 francs CFA
€1 = 655.96 francs CFA
10,000 francs CFA = £9.919 = $15.987 = €15.245

Average Exchange Rate (francs CFA per US $)
2000	711.98
2001	733.04
2002	696.99

Note: An exchange rate of 1 French franc = 50 francs CFA, established in 1948, remained in force until January 1994, when the CFA franc was devalued by 50%, with the exchange rate adjusted to 1 French franc = 100 francs CFA. This relationship to French currency remained in effect with the introduction of the euro on 1 January 1999. From that date, accordingly, a fixed exchange rate of €1 = 655.957 francs CFA has been in operation.

BUDGET
('000 million francs CFA)

Revenue	1999	2000	2001*
Petroleum revenue	368.7	814.7	781.4
Profits tax	172.3	553.3	443.2
Royalties	165.8	223.3	180.2
Production-sharing and assets	7.7	6.5	88.5
Dividends	22.8	30.8	60.6
Other	n.a.	0.9	8.8
Non-petroleum revenue	445.0	392.9	408.8
Tax revenue	420.9	384.6	395.3
Direct taxes	91.6	81.9	99.0
Company taxes	53.7	55.7	67.8
Individual taxes	37.9	26.2	31.2
Indirect taxes	58.2	80.2	70.7
Value-added taxes	44.4	71.9	60.7
Taxes on goods and services	13.8	8.2	9.0
Taxes on refined petroleum products	2.0	3.8	2.3
Taxes on international trade and transactions	164.6	214.7	211.0
Import duties	146.7	186.1	184.1
Export duties	17.9	28.6	26.9
Other revenue	130.6	16.1	28.9
Total	813.7	1,207.6	1,190.1

Expenditure	1999	2000	2001*
Current expenditure	660.6	674.8	790.9
Wages and salaries	214.0	216.6	213.4
Other goods and services	124.2	128.2	135.5
Transfers and subsidies	126 5	117.8	139.2
Interest payments	195.9	212.0	302.8
Capital expenditure	118.9	105.1	118.3
Net lending	—	6.2	25.1
Sub-total	779.5	786.1	934.2
Adjustment for payment arrears	-3.3	276.2	42.0
Total (cash basis)	775.2	1,062.3	976.2

* Estimates.

Source: IMF, *Gabon: Selected Issues and Statistical Appendix* (May 2002).

INTERNATIONAL RESERVES
(US $ million at 31 December)

	2000	2001	2002
Gold*	3.50	3.57	4.40
IMF special drawing rights	0.07	0.06	0.00
Reserve position in IMF	0.19	0.23	0.24
Foreign exchange	189.83	9.57	139.40
Total	193.59	13.43	144.04

* Valued at market-related prices.

Source: IMF, *International Financial Statistics.*

MONEY SUPPLY
(million francs CFA at 31 December)

	2000	2001	2002
Currency outside banks	116,175	128,187	132,020
Demand deposits at commercial and development banks	203,510	203,735	214,267
Total money (incl. others)	320,455	332,224	346,692

Source: IMF, *International Financial Statistics.*

COST OF LIVING
(Consumer price index; base: 1990 = 100)

	1999	2000	2001
Food	132.0	132.7	139.3
All items (incl. others)	146.3	147.0	150.1

Source: UN, *Monthly Bulletin of Statistics.*

NATIONAL ACCOUNTS
('000 million francs CFA at current prices)

Expenditure on the Gross Domestic Product

	1999	2000	2001*
Government final consumption expenditure.	338.2	344.9	348.9
Private final consumption expenditure.	1,224.6	1,307.4	1,467.3
Gross fixed capital formation . .	687.3	790.3	842.9
Total domestic expenditure. .	2,250.1	2,442.6	2,659.1
Exports of goods and services . .	1,645.1	2,419.5	2,046.4
Less Imports of goods and services	1,055.6	1,285.2	1,318.0
GDP in purchasers' values . .	2,839.6	3,576.9	3,387.4

* Estimates.

Source: IMF, *Gabon: Selected Issues and Statistical Appendix* (May 2002).

Gross Domestic Product by Economic Activity

	1999	2000	2001*
Agriculture, livestock, hunting and fishing	137.4	141.2	147.0
Forestry	72.4	85.9	87.4
Petroleum exploitation and research.	1,049.8	1,716.1	1,429.3
Other mining	56.9	53.8	51.9
Manufacturing	159.8	162.2	173.5
Electricity and water . . .	32.9	33.6	35.0
Construction and public works. .	99.3	69.7	62.4
Trade	234.6	241.4	244.9
Transport	145.1	150.0	157.4
Financial services	18.6	19.1	19.6
Government services. . . .	294.9	297.9	300.3
Other services	346.7	359.1	384.6
GDP at factor cost. . . .	2,648.5	3,330.0	3,093.3
Import duties	191.1	246.9	294.1
GDP in purchasers' values . .	2,839.6	3,576.9	3,387.4

* Estimates.

Source: IMF, *Gabon: Selected Issues and Statistical Appendix* (May 2002).

BALANCE OF PAYMENTS
(US $ million)

	1997	1998	1999
Exports of goods f.o.b.	3,032.7	1,907.6	2,498.8
Imports of goods f.o.b.	−1,030.6	−1,163.2	−910.5
Trade balance	2,002.1	744.4	1,588.3
Exports of services	232.9	219.6	280.9
Imports of services	−952.7	−991.0	−867.0
Balance on goods and services	1,282.3	−27.0	1,002.2
Other income received . . .	39.0	57.5	84.2
Other income paid	−755.5	−572.5	−653.1
Balance on goods, services and income	565.8	−542.1	433.3
Current transfers received . . .	62.7	36.6	42.6
Current transfers paid	−97.1	−90.0	−85.6
Current balance	531.4	−595.5	390.4
Capital account (net)	5.8	1.8	5.4
Direct investment abroad . . .	−21.0	−33.2	−73.9
Direct investment from abroad. .	−311.3	146.6	−156.6
Portfolio investment assets . . .	260.1	19.2	22.4
Portfolio investment liabilities . .	−20.7	−0.2	−0.7
Other investment assets . . .	18.3	−220.7	−109.0
Other investment liabilities . . .	−551.6	−77.5	−369.1
Net errors and omissions . . .	−108.4	92.5	−106.7
Overall balance	−197.4	−667.0	−397.8

Source: IMF, *International Financial Statistics*.

External Trade

PRINCIPAL COMMODITIES

Imports c.i.f. (US $ million)*	1993	1994	1996
Food and live animals . .	131.5	105.8	145.7
Meat and meat preparations . .	34.8	32.0	37.8
Fresh, chilled or frozen meat .	31.5	28.9	32.8
Cereals and cereal preparations .	35.5	32.3	48.4
Mineral fuels, lubricants, etc. .	14.5	17.1	31.6
Refined petroleum products . .	14.2	16.8	27.4
Chemicals and related products	83.6	70.1	93.0
Medicinal and pharmaceutical products.	30.7	18.4	33.4
Medicaments (incl. veterinary) .	28.3	16.7	30.7
Basic manufactures . . .	123.8	112.1	150.2
Iron and steel.	30.9	27.3	37.3
Tubes, pipes and fittings . . .	23.7	19.7	24.3
Machinery and transport equipment.	316.4	314.3	351.9
Power-generating machinery and equipment	26.9	25.9	26.3
Machinery specialized for particular industries	21.0	46.4	36.9
Civil engineering and contractors' plant and equipment	12.1	30.9	23.2
General industrial machinery, equipment and parts	67.0	82.2	105.9
Pumps, centrifuges, etc. . . .	25.3	32.6	45.8
Electrical machinery, apparatus, etc.	59.0	46.4	65.6
Road vehicles and parts. . . .	68.7	57.6	84.2
Passenger motor cars (excl. buses).	30.8	18.6	29.4
Other transport equipment . . .	57.8	42.8	12.3
Ships, boats and floating structures	50.8	37.9	4.1
Miscellaneous manufactured articles.	77.9	62.3	89.1
Professional, scientific and controlling instruments, etc. .	21.3	16.9	29.8
Total (incl. others)	774.9	707.5	898.1

* Figures for 1995 are not available.

Source: UN, *International Trade Statistics Yearbook*.

Exports ('000 million francs CFA)	1999	2000	2001*
Petroleum and petroleum products	1,143.2	1,827.8	1,509.1
Manganese	88.3	85.8	86.7
Timber.	246.7	278.0	237.5
Total (incl. others)	1,540.0	2,285.3	1,929.2

* Estimates.

Source: IMF, *Gabon: Selected Issues and Statistical Appendix* (May 2002).

PRINCIPAL TRADING PARTNERS
(US $ million)

Imports c.i.f.*	1993	1994	1996
Belgium-Luxembourg	22.5	24.5	37.1
Cameroon	6.3	12.0	12.1
Côte d'Ivoire	6.3	7.6	13.7
France (incl. Monaco)	370.4	281.4	384.8
Germany	27.8	39.7	41.1
Italy	24.3	29.6	31.3
Japan	n.a.	n.a.	53.8
Morocco	10.1	4.5	6.6
Netherlands	36.0	35.1	40.8
Panama	—	11.3	—
SACU†.	3.5	4.5	9.3
Spain	11.2	11.4	21.0
Thailand	4.3	3.3	15.3
United Kingdom	29.4	45.1	42.8
USA	71.0	83.5	93.4
Total (incl. others)	774.9	707.5	898.1

Exports f.o.b.*	1993	1994	1996
Canada	52.3	—	—
Chile	81.6	22.6	17.5
China, People's Repub. .	29.4	54.5	136.2
France (incl. Monaco) . . .	505.6	361.6	239.8
Gibraltar	17.2	42.0	n.a.
Israel	9.9	19.8	34.5
Japan	n.a.	n.a.	66.1
Korea, Repub..	16.1	35.4	24.2
Morocco	14.5	76.2	16.8
Netherlands	2.9	89.0	30.7
Netherlands Antilles. . . .	n.a.	n.a.	121.4
Portugal	1.9	91.2	6.3
Singapore	17.1	40.6	2.0
Spain	32.9	92.5	36.8
Switzerland-Liechtenstein . .	10.8	9.8	34.7
United Kingdom	93.1	61.8	7.3
USA	1,388.2	1,192.9	2,015.3
Total (incl. others)	2,637.0	2,391.0	3,145.6

* Figures for 1995 are not available.
† Southern African Customs Union, comprising Botswana, Lesotho, Namibia, South Africa and Swaziland.

Source: UN, *International Trade Statistics Yearbook*.

Transport

RAILWAYS
(traffic)

	1998	1999	2000
Passengers carried ('000) . .	178	202	237
Freight carried ('000 metric tons) .	3,291	2,893	3,130

Source: IMF, *Gabon: Selected Issues and Statistical Appendix* (May 2002).

ROAD TRAFFIC
(estimates, motor vehicles in use)

	1994	1995	1996
Passenger cars	22,310	24,000	24,750
Lorries and vans	14,850	15,840	16,490

Source: IRF, *World Road Statistics*.

INTERNATIONAL SEA-BORNE SHIPPING
(freight traffic, '000 metric tons)

	1988	1989	1990
Goods loaded	8,890	10,739	12,828
Goods unloaded	610	213	212

Source: UN, *Monthly Bulletin of Statistics*.

CIVIL AVIATION
(traffic on scheduled services)

	1996	1997	1998
Kilometres flown (million) . . .	7	8	8
Passengers carried ('000) . . .	431	469	467
Passenger-kilometres (million) . .	728	826	829
Total ton-kilometres (million) . .	100	112	111

Source: UN, *Statistical Yearbook*.

Tourism

	1998	1999	2000
Tourist arrivals	195,323	177,834	155,432

Tourism receipts (US $ million): 8 in 1998; 11 in 1999; 7 in 2000.

Source: World Tourism Organization.

Communications Media

	1999	2000	2001
Television receivers ('000 in use)	300	400	n.a.
Telephones ('000 main lines in use)	38.0	39.0	39.0
Mobile cellular telephones ('000 subscribers).	8.9	120.0	120.0
Personal computers ('000 in use)	10	12	15
Internet users ('000)	3	15	15

1996: 2 daily newspapers (average circulation 33,000 copies).

1997: 501 facsimile machines in use

1999: 600,000 radio receivers in use.

Sources: UNESCO, *Statistical Yearbook*; UN, *Statistical Yearbook*; International Telecommunication Union.

Education

(1998/99)

	Institutions	Teachers	Pupils		
			Males	Females	Total
Pre-primary* . . .	9	37	465	485	950
Primary	1,175	6,022	133,524	131,720	265,244
Secondary:					
General	88†	3,078	42,308	37,974	80,282
Technical and vocational . .	11†		4,038	2,123	6,161
Tertiary	2*	585	4,806	2,667	7,473

* 1991/92 figure(s).
† 1996 figure.

Source: UNESCO Institute for Statistics.

Adult literacy rate (UNESCO estimates): 63.3% (males 73.7%; females 53.4%) in 1995 (Source: UNESCO, *Statistical Yearbook*).

Directory

The Constitution*

The Constitution of the Gabonese Republic was adopted on 14 March 1991. The main provisions are summarized below

PREAMBLE

Upholds the rights of the individual, liberty of conscience and of the person, religious freedom and freedom of education. Sovereignty is vested in the people, who exercise it through their representatives or by means of referendums. There is direct, universal and secret suffrage.

HEAD OF STATE*

The President is elected by direct universal suffrage for a five-year term, renewable only once. The President is Head of State and of the Armed Forces. The President may, after consultation with his ministers and leaders of the Assemblée nationale, order a referendum to be held. The President appoints the Prime Minister, who is Head of Government and who is accountable to the President. The President is the guarantor of national independence and territorial sovereignty.

EXECUTIVE POWER

Executive power is vested in the President and the Council of Ministers, who are appointed by the Prime Minister, in consultation with the President.

LEGISLATIVE POWER

The Assemblée nationale is elected by direct universal suffrage for a five-year term. It may be dissolved or prorogued for up to 18 months by the President, after consultation with the Council of Ministers and President of the Assemblée. The President may return a bill to the Assemblée for a second reading, when it must be passed by a majority of two-thirds of the members. If the President dissolves the Assemblée, elections must take place within 40 days.

The Constitution also provides for the establishment of an upper chamber (the Sénat), to control the balance and regulation of power.

POLITICAL ORGANIZATIONS

Article 2 of the Constitution states that 'Political parties and associations contribute to the expression of universal suffrage. They are formed and exercise their activities freely, within the limits delineated by the laws and regulations. They must respect the principles of democracy, national sovereignty, public order and national unity'.

JUDICIAL POWER

The President guarantees the independence of the judiciary and presides over the Conseil Supérieur de la Magistrature. Supreme judicial power is vested in the Supreme Court.
*A constitutional amendment, adopted by the legislature on 18 April 1997, extended the presidential term to seven years and provided for the creation of the post of Vice-President.

The Government

HEAD OF STATE

President: El Hadj OMAR (ALBERT-BERNARD) BONGO (took office 2 December 1967, elected 25 February 1973, re-elected December 1979, November 1986, December 1993 and December 1998).

Vice-President: DIDJOB DIVUNGUI-DI-N'DINGUE.

COUNCIL OF MINISTERS
(April 2003)

The Government comprises members of the Parti démocratique gabonais (PDG) and the Rassemblement pour le Gabon (RPG).

Prime Minister and Head of Government: JEAN-FRANÇOIS NTOU-TOUME EMANE (PDG).

Vice-Prime Minister, Minister of Territorial Administration: EMMANUEL ONDO-METHOGO (PDG).

Vice-Prime Minister, Minister of Towns: ANTOINE MBOUMBOU MIYAKOU (PDG).

Vice-Prime Minister, Minister of Agriculture, Livestock and Rural Development, in charge of Human Rights: Fr PAUL M'BA ABESSOLE (RPG).

Minister of State for Planning and Development: CASIMIR OYÉ MBA (PDG).

Minister of State for Foreign Affairs, Co-operation and Francophone Affairs: JEAN PING (PDG).

Minister of State for Economic Affairs, Finance, the Budget and Privatization: PAUL TOUNGUI (PDG).

Minister of State for Transport and Civil Aviation: PAULETTE MISSAMBO (PDG).

Minister of State for Trade, Industrial Development and Regional Integration: JEAN-RÉMY PENDY BOUYIKI (PDG).

Minister of State for Housing, Urbanization and Cadastral Services: JACQUES ADIAHÉNOT (PDG).

Minister of the Interior, Security and Decentralization: IDRISS NGARI (PDG).

Minister of Justice, Guardian of the Seals: HONORINE DOSSOU NAKI (PDG).

Minister of National Defence: ALI BONGO (PDG).

Minister of Mining, Energy and Water Resources: RICHARD ONOUVIET (PDG).

Minister of Public Affairs, Administrative Reform and Modernization of the State: PASCAL DÉSIRÉ MISSONGO (PDG).

Minister of Public Health: FAUSTIN BOUKOUBI (PDG).

Minister of Communications, Posts and Information Technology: MEHDI TEALE (PDG).

Minister of National Solidarity and Social Welfare: ANDRÉ MBA OMANE (PDG).

Minister of National Education: DANIEL ONA ONDO (PDG).

Minister of Water, Forestry, Fishing, Reafforestation and the Environment: EMILE DOUMBA (PDG).

Minister of Family Affairs, the Protection of Children and Women: ANGELIQUE NGOMA (PDG).

Ministry of Tourism and Crafts: JEAN MASSIMA (PDG).

Minister of Public Works, Equipment and Construction: EGIDE BOUNDONO-SIMANGOYE (PDG).

Minister of Higher Education, Research and Technology: VINCENT MOULENGUI BOUKOSS (RPG).

Minister in charge of Relations with Parliament, Government Spokesperson: RENÉ NDEMEZO OBIANG (PDG).

Minister of Small- and Medium-sized Enterprises: PAUL BIYOGHÉ-MBA (PDG).

Minister of Youth and Sports: ALFRED MABICKA (PDG).

Minister of the Merchant Navy and Ports: FÉLIX SIBY (PDG).

Minister of Professional Training and Social Reintegration: BARNABÉ NDAKI (PDG).

Minister of Culture, the Arts and Popular Education: PIERRE AMOUGHE MBA (RPG).

Minister of Labour and Employment: CLOTAIRE CHRISTIAN IVALA (PDG).

There were also nine Ministers-delegate.

MINISTRIES

Office of the Prime Minister: BP 546, Libreville; tel. 77-89-81.

Ministry of Agriculture, Livestock and Rural Development: BP 551, Libreville; tel. 72-09-60.

Ministry of Communications, Posts and Information Technology: Libreville.

Ministry of Culture, the Arts and Popular Education: BP 1007, Libreville; tel. 76-32-33; tel. 72-36-88.

Ministry of Economic Affairs, Finance, the Budget and Privatization: BP 165, Libreville; tel. 76-12-10; fax 76-59-74.

Ministry of Family Affairs, the Protection of Children and Women: BP 5684, Libreville; tel. 77-50-32.

Ministry of Foreign Affairs, Co-operation and Francophone Affairs: BP 2245, Libreville; tel. 73-94-65.

Ministry of Higher Education, Research and Technology: BP 2217, Libreville; tel. 72-41-08.

Ministry of Housing, Urbanization and Cadastral Services: BP 512, Libreville; tel. 77-31-02.

Ministry of Human Rights and Missions: Libreville.

Ministry of the Interior, Security and Decentralization: BP 2110, Libreville; tel. 72-00-75.

Ministry of Justice: BP 547, Libreville; tel. 74-66-28; fax 72-33-84.

Ministry of Labour and Employment: BP 4577, Libreville; tel. 74-32-18.

Ministry of the Merchant Navy and Ports: Libreville.

Ministry of Mining, Energy and Water Resources: BP 576, Libreville; tel. 77-22-39.

Ministry of National Defence: BP 13493, Libreville; tel. 77-86-94.

Ministry of National Education: BP 6, Libreville; tel. 76-13-01; fax 74-14-48.

Ministry of National Solidarity and Social Welfare: Libreville.

Ministry of Planning and Development: Libreville.

Ministry of Professional Training and Social Reintegration: Libreville.

Ministry of Public Affairs, Administrative Reform and Modernization of the State: BP 496, Libreville; tel. 76-38-86.

Ministry of Public Health: BP 50, Libreville; tel. 76-36-11.

Ministry of Public Works, Equipment and Construction: BP 49, Libreville; tel. 76-38-56; fax 74-80-92.

Ministry of Small- and Medium-sized Enterprises: BP 3096, Libreville; tel. 74-59-21.

Ministry of Territorial Administration: Libreville.

Ministry of Tourism and Crafts: BP 178, Libreville; tel. 76-34-62.

Ministry of Towns: Libreville.

Ministry of Trade, Industrial Development and Regional Integration: Libreville.

Ministry of Transport and Civil Aviation: BP 803, Libreville; tel. 74-71-96; fax 77-33-31.

Ministry of Water, Forestry, Fishing, Reafforestation and the Environment: BP 3974, Libreville; tel. 76-01-09; fax 76-61-83.

Ministry of Youth and Sports: BP 2150, Libreville; tel. 74-00-19; fax 74-65-89.

President and Legislature

PRESIDENT

Presidential Election, 6 December 1998

Candidate	% of votes
El Hadj Omar (Albert-Bernard) Bongo	66.55
Pierre Mamboundou	16.54
Fr Paul M'Ba Abessole	13.41
Pierre-André Kombila	1.54
Pierre-Claver Maganga Moussavou	0.99
Others	0.97
Total	**100.00**

ASSEMBLÉE NATIONALE

President: GUY NDZOUBA NDAMA.

Secretary-General: JEAN-BAPTISTE YAMA-LEGNONGO.

General Election, 9 and 23 December 2001

Party	Seats
Parti démocratique gabonais (PDG)	86
Independents	12
Rassemblement pour le Gabon (RPG)	8
Parti gabonais du progrès (PGP)	3
Parti social-démocrate (PSD)	2
Union du peuple gabonais (UPG)	1
Others	7
Total	**119***

*Including results of elections that were postponed until 6 and 20 January 2002, owing to violent incidents, and of elections that were repeated in two constituencies where candidates received the same number of votes. Voting was postponed indefinitely in the district of Zadie following an outbreak of Ebola fever. During March and April the Constitutional Court annulled the results of voting in a further 12 constituencies, owing to irregularities. On 26 May and 9 June by-elections took place in these 12 constituencies and in Zadie; the PDG won 10 of the 13 seats contested, increasing its overall representation to 88 seats.

SÉNAT

President: GEORGES RAWIRI.

Secretary-General: FÉLIX OWANSANGO DEACKEU.

Election, 26 January and 9 February 1997*

Party	Seats
Parti démocratique gabonais (PDG)	53
Rassemblement national des bûcherons (RNB)†	20
Independents	9
Parti gabonais du progrès (PGP)	4
Alliance démocratique et républicaine (ADERE)	3
Cercle des libéraux réformateurs (CLR)	1
Rassemblement pour la démocratie et le progrès (RDP)	1
Total	**91**

*Following the annulment of a number of results, the PDG gained a further five seats at by-elections held later in 1997.
†Renamed Rassemblement pour le Gabon (RPG) in October 2000.
Note: Elections to the Senate were held on 9 February 2003. According to provisional results, the PDG won more than 60 seats, and the RPG secured eight seats.

Political Organizations

Alliance démocratique et républicaine (ADERE): Pres. MBOUMBOU NGOMA; Sec.-Gen. DIDJOB DIVUNGUI-DI-N'DINGUE.

Alliance des républicains pour le développement (ARD): f. 2001; Pres. MARIE-AUGUSTINE HOUANGNI AMBOUROUE.

Association pour le socialisme au Gabon (APSG): Pres. V. MAPANGOU MOUCANI MOUETSA.

Cercle des libéraux réformateurs (CLR): f. 1993 by breakaway faction of the PDG; Leader JEAN-BONIFACE ASSELE.

Cercle pour le renouveau et le progrès (CRP).

Congrès pour la démocratie et la justice (CDJ): Pres. JULES BOURDES OGOULIGUENDE.

Convention des forces du changement: f. 1993 as an informal alliance of eight opposition presidential candidates.

Coordination de l'opposition démocratique (COD): f. 1991 as an alliance of eight principal opposition parties; Chair. SÉBASTIEN MAMBOUNDOU MOUYAMA.

Forum africain pour la reconstruction (FAR): f. 1992; a factional alliance within the COD; Leader Prof. LÉON MBOU-YEMBI; comprises three political parties.

> **Mouvement de redressement national (MORENA—originels):** f. 1981; in Paris, France; Leader PIERRE-ANDRÉ KOMBILA KOUMBA.

> **Parti socialiste gabonais (PSG):** f. 1991; Leader Prof. LÉON MBOYEBI.

> **Union socialiste gabonais (USG):** Leader Dr SERGE MBA BEKALE.

Forum centriste de socialisme africain: f. 2000; Leader ANDRÉ EYEGHE.

Front national (FN): f. 1991; Leader MARTIN EFAYONG.

Front des parties du changement (FPC): f. 2000 as an alliance of four opposition parties to contest the 2001 legislative elections.

Gabon Avenir: f. 1999; Leader SYLVESTRE OYOUOMI.

Mouvement alternatif: f. 1996; Leader SÉBASTIEN MAMBOUNDOU MOUYAMA.

Mouvement pour la démocratie, le développement et la réconciliation nationale (Modern): Libreville; f. 1996; Leader GASTON MOZOGO OVONO.

Parti démocratique gabonais (PDG): BP 268, Libreville; tel. 70-31-21; fax 70-31-46; f. 1968; sole legal party 1968–90; Leader OMAR BONGO; Sec.-Gen. SIMPLICE GUEDET MANZELA.

Parti gabonais du centre indépendant (PGCI): allied to the PDG; Leader JEAN-PIERRE LEMBOUMBA LEPANDOU.

Parti gabonais du progrès (PGP): f. 1990; Pres. PIERRE-LOUIS AGONDJO-OKAWÉ; Sec.-Gen. ANSELME NZOGHE.

Parti des libéraux démocrates (PLD): Leader MARC SATURNIN NAN NGUEMA.

Parti social-démocrate (PSD): f. 1991; Leader PIERRE-CLAVER MAGANGA MOUSSAVOU.

Rassemblement des démocrates (RD): f. 1993.

Rassemblement pour la démocratie et le progrès (RDP): Pres. PIERRE EMBONI.

Rassemblement pour le Gabon (RPG): f. 1990 as MORENA des bûcherons, renamed Rassemblement national des bûcherons in 1991, name changed as above in 2000; allied to the PDG; Leader Fr PAUL M'BA ABESSOLE; Sec.-Gen. Prof. VINCENT MOULENGUI BOUKOSSO.

Rassemblement des Gaullois: Libreville; f. 1994; registered 1998; 5,000 mems; Pres. MAX ANICET KOUMBA-MBADINGA.

Union pour la démocratie et le développement Mayumba (UDD).

Union démocratique et sociale (UDS): f. 1996; Leader HERVÉ ASSAMANET.

Union nationale pour la démocratie et le développement (UNDD): f. 1993; supports President Bongo.

Union du peuple gabonais (UPG): f. 1989 in Paris, France; Leader PIERRE MAMBOUNDOU; Sec.-Gen. DAVID BADINGA.

Diplomatic Representation

EMBASSIES IN GABON

Algeria: BP 4008, Libreville; tel. 73-23-18; fax 73-14-03; e-mail ambalgabon@tiggabon.com; Ambassador ABDELHAMID CHEBCHOUB.

Angola: BP 4884, Libreville; tel. 73-04-26; fax 73-76-24; Ambassador BERNARDO DOMBELE M'BALA.

Argentina: BP 4065, Libreville; tel. 74-05-49; Ambassador HUGO HURTUBEI.

Belgium: BP 4079, Libreville; tel. 73-29-92; fax 73-96-94; e-mail Libreville@diplobel.org; Ambassador IVO GOEMANS.

Bénin: BP 3851, Akebe, Libreville; tel. 73-76-82; fax 73-77-75; Ambassador TIMOTHÉE ADANLIN.

Brazil: BP 3899, Libreville; tel. 76-05-35; fax 74-03-43; e-mail emblibreville@inet.ga; Ambassador SERGIO SEABRA DE NORONAHA.

Cameroon: BP 14001, Libreville; tel. 73-28-00; Ambassador JEAN KOE NTONGA.

Canada: blvd Pasteur, BP 4037, Libreville; tel. 73-73-54; fax 73-73-88; e-mail lbvre@dfait-maeci.gc.ca; Ambassador LOUIS POISSON.

Central African Republic: Libreville; tel. 72-12-28; Ambassador FRANÇOIS DIALLO.

China, People's Republic: BP 3914, Libreville; tel. 74-32-07; fax 74-75-96; e-mail gzy@internetgabon.com; Ambassador TIANMIN GUO.

Congo, Democratic Republic: BP 2257, Libreville; tel. 74-32-53; Ambassador KABANGI KAUMBU BULA.

Congo, Republic: BP 269, Libreville; tel. 73-29-06; Ambassador PIERRE OBOU.

Côte d'Ivoire: BP 3861, Libreville; tel. 73-82-68; Ambassador GÉORGES GOHO BAH.

Egypt: BP 4240, Libreville; tel. 73-25-38; fax 73-25-19; Ambassador SIHAM SALEM RAHMY MOKHTAR.

Equatorial Guinea: BP 1462, Libreville; tel. 75-10-56; Ambassador CRISANTOS NDONGO ABA MESSIAN.

France: blvd de l'Indépendance, BP 2125, Libreville; tel. 76-10-56; fax 74-48-78; e-mail ambafran@inet.ga; internet www.chez.com/ambafrangabon; Ambassador PHILIPPE SELZ.

Germany: blvd de l'Indépendance, BP 299, Libreville; tel. 76-01-88; fax 72-40-12; e-mail amb-allegmagne@inet.ga; Ambassador BURKHARD RANFT.

Guinea: BP 4046, Libreville; tel. 73-85-09; Ambassador MOHAMED SAMPIL.

Holy See: blvd Monseigneur Bessieux, BP 1322, Libreville (Apostolic Nunciature); tel. 74-45-41; Apostolic Nuncio Most Rev. MARIO ROBERTO CASSARI (Titular Archbishop of Tronto).

Italy: Immeuble Personnaz et Gardin, rue de la Mairie, BP 2251, Libreville; tel. 74-28-92; fax 74-80-35; e-mail ambiasciata-italia@internetgabon.com; Ambassador LUDOVICO TASSONI ESTENSE DE CASTELVECCHIO.

Japan: BP 3341, Libreville; tel. 73-22-97; fax 73-60-60; Ambassador SADAMU FUJIWARA.

Korea, Republic: BP 2620, Libreville; tel. 73-40-00; fax 73-00-79; Ambassador OH SANG-SHIK.

Lebanon: BP 3341, Libreville; tel. 73-96-45; Ambassador CHARAMY HABIB AYOUB.

Mauritania: BP 3917, Libreville; tel. 74-31-65; Ambassador EL HADJ THIAM.

Morocco: BP 3983, Libreville; tel. 77-41-51; fax 77-41-50; Ambassador MOHAMED GHALI TAZI.

Nigeria: BP 1191, Libreville; tel. 73-22-03; Ambassador IGNATIUS HEKAIRE AJURU.

Russia: BP 3963, Libreville; tel. 72-48-69; fax 72-48-70; e-mail ambrusga@inet.ga; Ambassador USEVOLD SOUKHOV.

São Tomé and Príncipe: BP 489, Libreville; tel. 72-09-94; Ambassador URBINO JOSÉ GONHALVES BOTELÇO.

Senegal: BP 3856, Libreville; tel. 77-42-67; Ambassador IBRAHIM KABA.

Serbia and Montenegro: Libreville; tel. 73-30-05; Ambassador ČEDOMIR STRBAC.

South Africa: Immeuble les Arcades, 142 rue des Chavannes, BP 4063, Libreville; tel. 77-45-30; fax 77-45-36; Ambassador MONGEHI SAMUEL MONAISA.

Spain: Immeuble Diamant, blvd de l'Indépendance, BP 2105, Libreville; tel. 72-12-64; fax 74-88-73; Ambassador DOMINGO DE SILOS MANSO GARCÍA.

Togo: BP 14160, Libreville; tel. 73-29-04; Ambassador AHLONKO KOFFI AQUEREBURU.

Tunisia: BP 3844, Libreville; tel. 73-28-41; Ambassador EZZEDINE KERKENI.

USA: blvd de la Mer, BP 4000, Libreville; tel. 76-20-03; fax 74-55-07; e-mail CLOLIBREVILLE@state.gov; internet usembassy.state.gov/libreville; Ambassador KENNETH P. MOOREFIELD.

Judicial System

Supreme Court: BP 1043, Libreville; tel. 72-17-00; three chambers: judicial, administrative and accounts; Pres. BENJAMIN PAMBOU-KOMBILA.

Constitutional Court: Libreville; tel. 72-57-17; fax 72-55-96; Pres. MARIE MADELEINE MBORANTSUO.

Courts of Appeal: Libreville and Franceville.

Court of State Security: Libreville; 13 mems; Pres. FLORENTIN ANGO.

Conseil Supérieur de la Magistrature: Libreville; Pres. El Hadj OMAR BONGO (Vice-Pres., Pres. of the Supreme Court (*ex officio*)).

There are also Tribunaux de Première Instance (County Courts) at Libreville, Franceville, Port-Gentil, Lambaréné, Mouila, Oyem, Koula-Moutou, Makokou and Tchibanga.

Religion

About 60% of Gabon's population are Christians, mainly adherents of the Roman Catholic Church. About 40% are animists, and fewer than 1% are Muslims.

CHRISTIANITY

The Roman Catholic Church

Gabon comprises one archdiocese and three dioceses. At 31 December 2000 the estimated number of adherents in the country was equivalent to 52.8% of the total population.

Bishops' Conference

Conférence Episcopale du Gabon, BP 2146, Libreville; tel. 72-20-73. f. 1989; Pres. Most Rev. BASILE MVÉ ENGONE (Archbishop of Libreville).

Archbishop of Libreville: Most Rev. BASILE MVÉ ENGONE, Archevêché, Sainte-Marie, BP 2146, Libreville; tel. 72-20-73.

Protestant Churches

Christian and Missionary Alliance: active in the south of the country; 16,000 mems.

Eglise Evangélique du Gabon: BP 10080, Libreville; tel. 72-41-92; f. 1842; independent since 1961; 120,000 mems; Pres. Pastor SAMUEL NANG ESSONO; Sec. Rev. EMILE NTETOME.

The Evangelical Church of South Gabon and the Evangelical Pentecostal Church are also active in Gabon.

The Press

Afric'Sports: BP 3950, Libreville; tel. 76-24-74; monthly; sport; CEO SERGE ALFRED MPOUHO; Man. YVON PATRICE AUBIAN; circ. 5,000.

Le Bûcheron: BP 6424, Libreville; tel. 72-50-20; f. 1990; weekly; official publ. of the Rassemblement national des bûcherons; Editor DÉSIRÉ ENAME.

Bulletin Evangélique d'Information et de Presse: BP 80, Libreville; monthly; religious.

Bulletin Mensuel de Statistique de la République Gabonaise: BP 179, Libreville; monthly; publ. by Direction Générale de l'Economie.

La Cigale Enchantée: Libreville; bi-monthly; satirical.

L'Economiste Gabonais: BP 3906, Libreville; quarterly; publ. by the Centre gabonais du commerce extérieur.

Gabon d'Aujourd'hui: BP 750, Libreville; weekly; publ. of the Ministry of Culture, the Arts and Popular Education.

Gabon Libre: BP 6439, Libreville; tel. 72-42-22; weekly; Dir DZIME EKANG; Editor RENÉ NZOVI.

Gabon-Matin: BP 168, Libreville; daily; publ. by Agence Gabonaise de Presse; Man. HILARION VENDANY; circ. 18,000.

La Griffe: BP 4928, Libreville; tel. 74-73-45; f. 1990; weekly; independent; satirical; Editor-in-Chief RAPHAEL NTOUTOUME NKOGHE; Editor NDJOUMBA MOUSSOCK.

Journal Officiel de la République Gabonaise: BP 563, Libreville; f. 1959; fortnightly; Man. EMMANUEL OBAMÉ.

Ngondo: BP 168, Libreville; monthly; publ. by Agence Gabonaise de Presse.

Le Progressiste: blvd Léon-M'Ba, BP 7000, Libreville; tel. 74-54-01; f. 1990; Dir BENOÎT MOUITY NZAMBA; Editor JACQUES MOURENDE-TSIOBA.

La Relance: Libreville; tel. 70-31-66; weekly; publ. of the Parti démocratique gabonais; Pres. JACQUES ADIAHÉNOT; Dir RENÉ NDEMEZO'O OBIANG.

Le Réveil: BP 20386, Libreville; tel. and fax 73-17-21; weekly; Man. ALBERT YANGARI; Editor RENÉ NZOVI; circ. 8,000.

La Tribune des Affaires: BP 2234, Libreville; tel. 72-20-64; fax 74-12-20; monthly; publ. of the Chambre de Commerce, d'Agriculture, d'Industrie et des Mines du Gabon.

La Voix du Peuple: BP 4049, Libreville; tel. 76-20-45; f. 1991; Publisher Parti de l'unité du peuple gabonais; weekly; Editor-in-Chief JEAN KOUMBA; Editor MAURIC-BLAISE NDZADIENGA MAYILA; circ. 4,000.

Sept Jours: BP 213, Libreville; weekly.

L'Union: Sonapresse, BP 3849, Libreville; tel. 73-58-61; fax 73-58-62; f. 1974; 75% state-owned; daily; official govt publ; Man. Dir and Editor VINCENT MAVOUNGOU; circ. 20,000.

NEWS AGENCIES

Agence Gabonaise de Presse (AGP): BP 168, Libreville.

Association Professionnelle de la Presse Ecrite Gabonaise (APPEG): BP 3849, Libreville; e-mail wmestre@gabon-presse.org.

BERP International: BP 8483, Libreville; tel. 33-80-16; fax 77-58-81; e-mail BERP8483@hotmail.com; f. 1995; Dir ANTOINE LAWSON.

Foreign Bureau

Agence France-Presse (AFP): Immeuble Sogapal, Les Filaos, BP 788, Libreville; tel. 76-14-36; fax 72-45-31; e-mail afp-libreville@tiggabon.com; Dir JEAN-PIERRE REJETE.

Publishers

Gabonaise d'Imprimerie (GABIMP): BP 154, Libreville; tel. 70-22-55; fax 70-31-85; f. 1973; Dir BÉATRICE CAILLOT.

Multipress Gabon: blvd Léon-M'Ba, BP 3875, Libreville; tel. 73-22-33; f. 1973; Chair. PAUL BORY.

Société Imprimerie de l'Ogooué (SIMO): BP 342, Port-Gentil; f. 1977; Man. Dir URBAIN NICOUE.

Société Nationale de Presse et d'Edition (SONAPRESSE): BP 3849, Libreville; tel. 73-21-84; f. 1975; Pres. and Man. Dir JOSEPH RENDJAMBE.

Broadcasting and Communications

TELECOMMUNICATIONS

Société Gabonaise de Télécommunications (GABTEL): BP 4069, Libreville; tel. 70-24-24; fax 70-24-25; e-mail gabtel@inet.ga; f. 1989; provider of telecommunications, including satellite, systems; Dir-Gen. GEORGES BELON.

Société des Télécommunications Internationales Gabonaises (TIG): BP 2261, Libreville; tel. 78-77-56; fax 74-19-09; f. 1971; cap. 3,000m. francs CFA; 61% state-owned; planning and devt of international telecommunications systems; Man. Dir A. N'GOUMA MWYUMALA.

Celtel Gabon, Libertis and Telecel Gabon operate mobile telecommunication services in Gabon.

BROADCASTING

Radio

The national network, 'La Voix de la Rénovation', and a provincial network broadcast for 24 hours each day in French and local languages.

Africa No. 1: BP 1, Libreville; tel. 76-00-01; fax 74-21-33; e-mail africa1@inet.ga; internet www.africa1.com; f. 1980; 35% state-controlled; international commercial radio station; daily programmes in French and English; Pres. LOUIS BARTHÉLEMY MAPANGOU; Sec.-Gen. MICHEL KOUMBANGOYE.

Radiodiffusion-Télévision Gabonaise (RTG): BP 150, Libreville; tel. 73-20-25; f. 1959; state-controlled; Dir-Gen. JOHN JOSEPH MBOUROU; Dir of Radio GILLES TERENCE NZOGHE.

Radio Fréquence 3: f. 1996.

Radio Génération Nouvelle: f. 1996; Dir JEAN-BONIFACE ASSELE.

Radio Mandarine: f. 1995.

Radio Soleil: f. 1995; affiliated to Rassemblement national des bûcherons.

Radio Unité: f. 1996.

Television

Radiodiffusion-Télévision Gabonaise (RTG): BP 150, Libreville; tel. 73-21-52; fax 73-21-53; f. 1959; state-controlled; Dir-Gen. JOHN JOSEPH MBOUROU; Dir of Television JULES CÉSAR LEKOGHO.

Télé-Africa: Libreville; tel. 76-20-33; private channel; daily broadcasts in French.

Télédiffusion du Gabon: f. 1995.

Finance

(cap. = capital; res = reserves; dep. = deposits; m. = million; brs = branches; amounts in francs CFA)

BANKING

Central Bank

Banque des Etats de l'Afrique Centrale (BEAC): BP 112, Libreville; tel. 76-13-52; fax 74-45-63; e-mail beaclbv@beac.int; HQ in Yaoundé, Cameroon; f. 1973; bank of issue for mem. states of the Communauté économique et monétaire de l'Afrique centrale (CEMAC, fmrly Union douanière et économique de l'Afrique centrale), comprising Cameroon, the Central African Repub., Chad, the Repub. of the Congo, Equatorial Guinea and Gabon; res 177,417m., total assets 2,034,793m. (Dec. 2001); Gov. JEAN-FÉLIX MAMALEPOT; Dir in Gabon PHILIBERT ANDZEMBE; 3 brs in Gabon.

Commercial Banks

Banque Internationale pour le Commerce et l'Industrie du Gabon, SA (BICIG): ave du Colonel Parant, BP 2241, Libreville; tel. 76-26-13; fax 74-64-10; e-mail bicigdoi@inet.ga; f. 1973; 27.7% state-owned; cap. 12,000m., res 32,614m., dep. 205,508m. (Dec. 1999); Pres. ETIENNE GUY MOUVAGHA TCHIOBA; 9 brs.

Banque Internationale pour le Gabon: Immeuble Concorde, blvd de l'Indépendance, BP 106, Libreville; tel. 76-26-26; fax 76-20-53.

BGFIBANK: BP 2253, Libreville; tel. 76-23-26; fax 74-08-94; e-mail bgfi@internetgabon.com; internet www.bgfi.com; f. 1972 as Banque Gabonaise et Française Internationale (BGFI); name changed as above in March 2000; 10% state-owned; cap. 10,023.9m., res 11,143.1m., dep. 239,482.4m. (Dec. 2000); Chair. PATRICE OTHA; Dir-Gen. HENRI-CLAUDE OYIMA; 3 brs.

Citibank: BP 3940, Libreville; tel. 73-30-00; fax 73-37-86; total assets 41,350m. (Dec. 1998); Dir-Gen. NUHAD KALIM SALIBA.

Crédit Foncier du Gabon: blvd de l'Indépendance, BP 3905, Libreville; tel. 72-47-45; fax 76-08-70; 90% state-owned; under enforced administration since June 1996; Interim Admin. FABIEN OVONO-NGOUA.

Union Gabonaise de Banque, SA (UGB): ave du Colonel Parant, BP 315, Libreville; tel. 77-70-00; fax 76-46-16; e-mail andre.froissant@creditlyonnais.fr; internet ugb-interactif.com; f. 1962; 25% state-owned; 56.25% owned by Crédit Lyonnais (France); cap. 5,000m., res 5,993m., dep. 91,000m. (Dec. 2001); Chair. MARCEL DOUPAMBY-MATOKA; Gen. Man. ANDRÉ FROISSANT; 6 brs.

Development Banks

Banque Gabonaise de Développement (BGD): rue Alfred Marche, BP 5, Libreville; tel. 76-24-29; fax 74-26-99; e-mail bdg@internetgabon.com; internet www.bgd-gabon.com; f. 1960; 69% state-owned; cap. 5,200.0m., res 3,363.5m., dep. 9,387.2m. (Dec. 1999); Pres. NOËL MBOUMBOU NGOMA; Chair. PHILIBERT ANDZEMBE; Dir-Gen. CLAUDE AYO IGUENDHA.

Banque Gabonaise et Française Internationale Participations: blvd de l'Indépendance, BP 2253, Libreville; tel. 76-23-26; fax

74-08-94; e-mail bgfi@internetgabon.com; internet www.bgfi.com; f. 1997; cap. 1,500m. (Dec. 1999); Dir-Gen. HENRI-CLAUDE OYIMA.

Banque Nationale de Crédit Rural (BNCR): ave Bouet, BP 1120, Libreville; tel. 72-47-42; fax 74-05-07; f. 1986; 74% state-owned; cap. 1,350m., total assets 6,885m. (Dec. 1998); Pres. GÉRARD MEYO M'EMANE; Man. Dir GEORGES ISSEMBE.

Société Nationale d'Investissement du Gabon (SONADIG): BP 479, Libreville; tel. 72-09-22; fax 74-81-70; f. 1968; state-owned; cap. 500m. Pres. ANTOINE OYIEYE; Dir-Gen. NARCISSE MASSALA TSAMBA.

Financial Institution

Caisse Autonome d'Amortissement du Gabon: BP 912, Libreville; tel. 74-41-43; management of state funds; Dir-Gen. MAURICE EYAMBA TSIMAT.

INSURANCE

Agence Gabonaise d'Assurance et de Réassurance (AGAR): BP 1699, Libreville; tel. 74-02-22; fax 76-59-25; f. 1987; Dir-Gen. ANGE GOULOUMES.

Assurances Générales Gabonaises (AGG): ave du Colonel Parant, BP 2148, Libreville; tel. 76-09-73; fax 76-57-41; f. 1974; Dir-Gen. ALAIN WELLER.

Assureurs Conseils Franco-Africains du Gabon (ACFRA-GABON): BP 1116, Libreville; tel. 72-32-83; Chair. FRÉDÉRIC MARRON; Dir M. GARNIER.

Assureurs Conseils Gabonais-Faugère et Jutheau & Cie: Immeuble Shell-Gabon, rue de la Mairie, BP 2138, Libreville; tel. 72-04-36; fax 76-04-39; represents foreign insurance cos; Dir GÉRARD MILAN.

Groupement Gabonais d'Assurances et de Réassurances (GGAR): Libreville; tel. 74-28-72; f. 1985; Chair. RASSAGUIZA AKEREY; Dir-Gen. DENISE OMBAGHO.

Mutuelle Gabonaise d'Assurances: ave du Colonel Parant, BP 2225, Libreville; tel. 72-13-91; fax 76-47-49; Dir-Gen. M. VERON.

Omnium Gabonais d'Assurances et de Réassurances (OGAR): 546 blvd Triomphal Omar Bongo, BP 201, Libreville; tel. 76-15-96; fax 76-58-16; f. 1976; owned by Assurances Générales de France; general; Pres. MARCEL DOUPAMBY-MATOKA; Man. Dir EDOUARD VALENTIN.

Société Nationale Gabonaise d'Assurances et de Réassurances (SONAGAR): ave du Colonel Parant, BP 3082, Libreville; tel. 76-28-97; f. 1974; owned by l'Union des Assurances de Paris (France); Dir-Gen. JEAN-LOUIS MESSAN.

SOGERCO-Gabon: BP 2102, Libreville; tel. 76-09-34; f. 1975; general; Dir M. RABEAU.

L'Union des Assurances du Gabon (UAG): ave du Colonel Parant, BP 2141, Libreville; tel. 74-34-34; fax 74-14-53; f. 1976; Chair. ALBERT ALEWINA CHAVIOT; Dir EKOMIE AFENE.

Trade and Industry

GOVERNMENT AGENCY

Conseil Economique et Social de la République Gabonaise: BP 1075, Libreville; tel. 73-19-46; fax 73-19-44; comprises representatives from salaried workers, employers and Govt; commissions on economic, financial and social affairs and forestry and agriculture; Pres. LOUIS GASTON MAYILA.

DEVELOPMENT ORGANIZATIONS

Agence Française de Développement: BP 64, Libreville; tel. 74-33-74; fax 74-51-25; fmrly Caisse Française de Développement; Dir ANTOINE BAUX.

Agence Nationale de Promotion de la Petite et Moyenne Entreprise (PROMOGABON): BP 2111, Libreville; tel. 26-79-19; fax 74-89-59; e-mail promogabon@inet.ga; f. 1964; state-controlled; promotes and assists small- and medium-sized industries; Pres. SIMON BOULAMATARI; Man. Dir JEAN-FIDÈLE OTANDO.

Centre Gabonais de Commerce Extérieur (CGCE): BP 3906, Libreville; tel. 76-11-67; promotes foreign trade and investment in Gabon; Man. Dir MICHEL LESLIE TEALE.

Commerce et Développement (CODEV): BP 2142, Libreville; tel. 76-06-73; f. 1976; 95% state-owned; proposed transfer to private ownership announced 1986; import and distribution of capital goods and food products; Chair. and Man. Dir JÉRÔME NGOUA-BEKALE.

Mission Française de Coopération: BP 2105, Libreville; tel. 76-10-56; fax 74-55-33; administers bilateral aid from France; Dir JEAN-CLAUDE QUIRIN.

Office Gabonais d'Amélioration et de Production de Viande (OGAPROV): BP 245, Moanda; tel. 66-12-67; f. 1971; development of private cattle farming; manages ranch at Lekedi-Sud; Pres. PAUL KOUNDA KIKI; Dir-Gen. VINCENT ÉYI-NGUI.

Palmiers et Hévéas du Gabon (PALMEVEAS): BP 75, Libreville; f. 1956; state-owned; palm-oil development.

Société de Développement de l'Agriculture au Gabon (AGRO-GABON): BP 2248, Libreville; tel. 76-40-82; fax 76-44-72; f. 1976; 93% state-owned; scheduled to be privatized; Man. Dir ANDRÉ PAUL-APANDINA.

Société de Développement de l'Hévéaculture (HEVEGAB): BP 316, Libreville; tel. 72-08-29; fax 72-08-30; f. 1981; 99.9% state-owned; development of rubber plantations in the Mitzic, Bitam and Kango regions; Chair. FRANÇOIS OWONO-NGUEMA; Man. Dir RAYMOND NDONG-SIMA.

Société Gabonaise de Recherches et d'Exploitations Minières (SOGAREM): Libreville; state-owned; research and development of gold mining; Chair. ARSÈNE BOUNGUENZA; Man. Dir SERGE GASSITA.

Société Gabonaise de Recherches Pétrolières (GABOREP): BP 564, Libreville; tel. 75-06-40; fax 75-06-47; exploration and exploitation of hydrocarbons; Chair. HUBERT PERRODO; Man. Dir P. F. LECA.

Société Nationale de Développement des Cultures Industrielles (SONADECI): Libreville; tel. 76-33-97; f. 1978; state-owned; agricultural development; Chair. PAUL KOUNDA KIKI; Man. Dir GEORGES BEKALÉ.

CHAMBER OF COMMERCE

Chambre de Commerce, d'Agriculture, d'Industrie et des Mines du Gabon: BP 2234, Libreville; tel. 72-20-64; fax 74-64-77; f. 1935; regional offices at Port-Gentil and Franceville; Pres. JOACHIM BOUSSAMBA-MAPAGA; Sec.-Gen. DOMINIQUE MANDZA.

EMPLOYERS' ORGANIZATIONS

Confédération Patronale Gabonaise: BP 410, Libreville; tel. 76-02-43; fax 74-86-52; e-mail patronat.gabon@assala.net; f. 1959; represents industrial, mining, petroleum, public works, forestry, banking, insurance, commercial and shipping interests; Pres. J. C. BALOCHE; Sec.-Gen. ERIC MESSERSCHMITT.

Conseil National du Patronat Gabonais (CNPG): Libreville; Pres. RAHANDI CHAMBRIER; Sec.-Gen. THOMAS FRANCK EYA'A.

Syndicat des Entreprises Minières du Gabon (SYNDI-MINES): BP 260, Libreville; Pres. ANDRÉ BERRE; Sec.-Gen. SERGE GREGOIRE.

Syndicat des Importateurs Exportateurs du Gabon (SIMPEX): Libreville; Pres. ALBERT JEAN; Sec.-Gen. R. TYBERGHEIN.

Syndicat des Producteurs et Industriels du Bois du Gabon: BP 84, Libreville; tel. 72-26-11; fax 77-44-43; e-mail synfoga@inet.ga.

Syndicat Professionnel des Usines de Sciages et Placages du Gabon: Port-Gentil; f. 1956; Pres. PIERRE BERRY.

Union des Représentations Automobiles et Industrielles (URAI): BP 1743, Libreville; Pres. M. MARTINENT; Sec. R. TYBERGHEIN.

Union Nationale du Patronat Syndical des Transports Urbains, Routiers et Fluviaux du Gabon (UNAPASY-TRUFGA): BP 1025, Libreville; f. 1977; Pres. LAURENT BELLAL BIBANG-BI-EDZO; Sec.-Gen. AUGUSTIN KASSA-NZIGOU.

UTILITIES

Société d'Energie et d'Eau du Gabon (SEEG): BP 2082, Libreville; tel. 72-19-11; fax 76-11-34; f. 1950; 51% owned by Cie Générale des Eaux (France) and Electricity Supply Board International (Ireland); controls 35 electricity generation and distribution centres and 32 water production and distribution centres; Chair. of Bd FRANÇOIS OMBANDA.

TRADE UNIONS

Confédération Gabonaise des Syndicats Libres (CGSL): BP 8067, Libreville; tel. 77-37-82; fax 74-45-25; f. 1991; Sec.-Gen. FRANCIS MAYOMBO; 16,000 mems.

Confédération Syndicale Gabonaise (COSYGA): BP 14017, Libreville; f. 1969 by the Govt, as a specialized organ of the PDG, to organize and educate workers, to contribute to social peace and economic development, and to protect the rights of trade unions; Gen. Sec. MARTIN ALLINI.

Transport

RAILWAYS

The construction of the Transgabonais railway, which comprises a section running from Owendo (the port of Libreville) to Booué (340 km) and a second section from Booué to Franceville (357 km), was completed in 1986. By 1989 regular services were operating between Libreville and Franceville. Some 2.9m. metric tons of freight and 215,000 passengers were carried on the network in 1999. In 1998 the railways were transferred to private management.

ROADS

In 2000 there were an estimated 8,464 km of roads, including 2,093 km of main roads and 6,371 km of secondary roads; about 9.9% of the road network was paved.

INLAND WATERWAYS

The principal river is the Ogooué, navigable from Port-Gentil to Ndjolé (310 km) and serving the towns of Lambaréné, Ndjolé and Sindara.

Compagnie de Navigation Intérieure (CNI): BP 3982, Libreville; tel. 72-39-28; fax 74-04-11; f. 1978; scheduled to be privatized; responsible for inland waterway transport; agencies at Port-Gentil, Mayumba and Lambaréné; Chair. JEAN-PIERRE MENGWANG ME NGYEMA; Dir-Gen. JEAN LOUIS POUNAH-NDJIMBI.

SHIPPING

The principal deep-water ports are Port-Gentil, which handles mainly petroleum exports, and Owendo, 15 km from Libreville, which services mainly barge traffic. The main ports for timber are at Owendo, Mayumba and Nyanga, and there is a fishing port at Libreville. The construction of a deep-water port at Mayumba is planned. A new terminal for the export of minerals, at Owendo, was opened in 1988. In 2001 the merchant shipping fleet had a total displacement of 12,541 grt. In 1997 the Islamic Development Bank granted a loan of 11,000m. francs CFA for the rehabilitation of Gabon's ports.

Compagnie de Manutention et de Chalandage d'Owendo (COMACO): BP 2131, Libreville; tel. 70-26-35; f. 1974; Pres. GEORGES RAWIRI; Dir in Libreville M. RAYMOND.

Office des Ports et Rades du Gabon (OPRAG): BP 1051, Libreville; tel. 70-00-48; fax 70-37-35; f. 1974; scheduled to be privatized; national port authority; Pres. ALI BONGO; Dir-Gen. JEAN PIERRE OYIBA.

SAGA Gabon: BP 518, Port-Gentil; tel. 55-54-00; fax 55-21-71; Chair. G. COGNON; Man. Dir DANIEL FERNÁNDEZ.

Société Nationale d'Acconage et de Transit (SNAT): BP 3897, Libreville; tel. 70-04-04; fax 70-13-11; f. 1976; 51% state-owned; scheduled to be privatized; freight transport; Dir-Gen. GUSTAVE BONGO.

Société Nationale de Transports Maritimes (SONATRAM): BP 3841, Libreville; tel. 74-06-32; fax 74-59-67; f. 1976; relaunched 1995; 51% state-owned; river and ocean cargo transport; Man. Dir RAPHAEL MOARA WALLA.

Société du Port Minéralier d'Owendo: f. 1987; majority holding by Cie Minière de l'Ogooué; management of a terminal for minerals at Owendo.

SOCOPAO–Gabon: BP 4, Libreville; tel. 70-21-40; fax 70-02-76; f. 1983; freight transport and storage; Dir DANIEL BECQUERELLE.

CIVIL AVIATION

There are international airports at Libreville, Port-Gentil and Franceville, 65 other public and 50 private airfields linked mostly with the forestry and petroleum industries.

Air Affaires Gabon: BP 3962, Libreville; tel. 73-25-13; fax 73-49-98; f. 1975; domestic passenger chartered and scheduled flights; Chair. RAYMOND BELLANGER.

Air Service Gabon (ASG): BP 2232, Libreville; tel. 73-24-08; fax 73-60-69; f. 1965; charter flights; Chair. JEAN-LUC CHEVRIER; Gen. Man. FRANÇOIS LASCOMBES.

Compagnie Nationale Air Gabon: BP 2206, Libreville; tel. 73-00-27; fax 73-01-11; f. 1951 as Cie Aérienne Gabonaise; began operating international services in 1977, following Gabon's withdrawal from Air Afrique (see under Côte d'Ivoire); 80% state-owned; scheduled to be privatized; internal and international cargo and passenger services; Chair. EMMANUEL NZE BEKALE; Man. Dir DIEUDONNÉ MBOUBOU MOUDHOUMA.

Société de Gestion de l'Aéroport de Libreville (ADL): BP 363, Libreville; tel. 73-62-44; fax 73-61-28; e-mail adl@inet.ga; f. 1988; 26.5% state-owned; management of airport at Libreville; Pres. CHANTAL LIDJI BADINGA; Dir-Gen. PIERRE ANDRÉ COLLET.

Tourism

Tourist arrivals were estimated at 155,432 in 2000, and receipts from tourism totalled US $7m. in that year. The tourism sector is being extensively developed, with new hotels and associated projects and the promotion of national parks. In 1996 there were 74 hotels, with a total of 4,000 rooms.

Centre Gabonais de Promotion Touristique (GABONTOUR): BP 2085, Libreville; tel. 72-85-04; fax 72-85-03; e-mail gabontour@internetgabon.com; internet www.internetgabon.com/tourisme; f. 1988; Dir-Gen. JOSEPH ADJEMBIMANDE.

Office National Gabonais du Tourisme: BP 161, Libreville; tel. 72-21-82.

THE GAMBIA

Introductory Survey

Location, Climate, Language, Religion, Flag, Capital

The Republic of The Gambia is a narrow territory around the River Gambia on the west coast of Africa. Apart from a short coastline on the Atlantic Ocean, the country is a semi-enclave in Senegal. The climate is tropical, with a rainy season from July to September. Away from the river swamps most of the terrain is covered by savannah bush. Average temperatures in Banjul range from 23°C (73°F) in January to 27°C (81°F) in July, while temperatures inland can exceed 40°C (104°F). English is the official language, while the principal vernacular languages are Mandinka, Fula and Wolof. About 85% of the inhabitants are Muslims; most of the remainder are Christians, and there are a small number of animists. The national flag (proportions 2 by 3) has red, blue and green horizontal stripes, with two narrow white stripes bordering the central blue band. The capital is Banjul.

Recent History

Formerly administered with Sierra Leone, The Gambia became a separate British colony in 1888. Party politics rapidly gained momentum following the establishment of a universal adult franchise in 1960. Following legislative elections in May 1962, the leader of the People's Progressive Party (PPP), Dr (later Sir) Dawda Kairaba Jawara, became Premier. Full internal self-government followed in October 1963. On 18 February 1965 The Gambia became an independent country within the Commonwealth, with Jawara as Prime Minister. The country became a republic on 24 April 1970, whereupon Jawara took office as President. He was re-elected in 1972 and again in 1977, as a result of overwhelming PPP victories in legislative elections.

In July 1981 a coup was attempted while Jawara was visiting the United Kingdom. Left-wing rebels formed a National Revolutionary Council and proclaimed their civilian leader, Kukoi Samba Sanyang, as Head of State. Under the terms of a mutual defence pact, Senegalese troops assisted in suppressing the rebellion. About 1,000 people were arrested, and more than 60 people were subsequently sentenced to death, although no executions took place. A state of emergency remained in force until February 1985. All those convicted of involvement in the insurrection were released by early 1991.

The first presidential election by direct popular vote was held in May 1982. Jawara was re-elected, with 72% of the votes cast; he was opposed by the leader of the National Convention Party (NCP), Sheriff Mustapha Dibba (who remained in detention until June for his alleged involvement in the abortive coup). In the concurrent legislative elections the PPP won 27 of the 35 elective seats in the House of Representatives. At legislative elections in March 1987 the PPP took 31 of the 36 directly elected seats in the House of Representatives. In the presidential election Jawara was re-elected with 59% of the votes cast; Dibba received 27% of the votes, and Assan Musa Camara, a former Vice-President who had recently formed the Gambian People's Party (GPP), won 14%. Rumours of financial impropriety, corruption and the abuse of power at ministerial level persisted throughout the decade, with at least four government members dismissed between 1984 and 1990.

Plans were announced in August 1981 for a confederation of The Gambia and Senegal, to be called Senegambia. The confederal agreement came into effect in February 1982; a Confederal Council of Ministers, headed by President Abdou Diouf of Senegal (with President Jawara as his deputy), held its inaugural meeting in January 1983, as did a 60-member Confederal Assembly. Agreements followed on co-ordination of foreign policy, communications, defence and security, but Senegal was critical of Jawara's reluctance to proceed towards full economic and political integration. In August 1989 Diouf announced that Senegalese troops were to leave The Gambia, apparently in protest at a request by Jawara that The Gambia be accorded more power within the confederal structures. The confederation was dissolved in September, and a period of tension between the two countries followed: The Gambia alleged that the Senegalese authorities had introduced trade and travel restrictions, while Senegal accused The Gambia of harbouring rebels of the Mouvement des forces démocratiques de la Casamance (MFDC), an organization seeking independence for the Casamance region—which is virtually separated from the northern segment of Senegal by the enclave of The Gambia. In January 1991 the two countries signed an agreement of friendship and co-operation. However, relations were again strained in September 1993, when Senegal unilaterally closed the border, apparently in connection with anti-smuggling operations.

Despite an earlier announcement that he would not be seeking a sixth presidential mandate, Jawara was re-elected in April 1992, receiving 58% of the votes cast. Dibba took 22% of the votes cast. In elections to the House of Representatives the PPP retained a clear majority, with 25 elected members. The NCP secured six seats, the GPP two and independent candidates the remaining three.

On 22 July 1994 Jawara was deposed by a self-styled Armed Forces Provisional Ruling Council (AFPRC), a group of five young army officers led by Lt (later Col) Yahya Jammeh, in a bloodless coup. Jawara left The Gambia aboard a US navy vessel and later took up residence in the United Kingdom. The AFPRC suspended the Constitution and banned all political activity. The new regime undertook to eliminate corruption, pledging a return to civilian rule once this had been accomplished. Jammeh pronounced himself Head of State and appointed a mixed civilian and military Government. Purges of the armed forces and public institutions were implemented, and in November it was announced that 10 of Jawara's former ministers would be tried on charges of corruption.

The AFPRC's timetable for a transition to civilian rule, published in October 1994, envisaged a programme of reform culminating in the inauguration of new elected institutions in December 1998. The length of the transition period prompted criticism both internationally and domestically. In November the AFPRC announced that a coup attempt, involving military officers who reputedly wished to install an entirely military regime, had been foiled. Some 50 soldiers were reported to have been killed during the attempt and its suppression, and several arrests were made.

In late November 1994 Jammeh commissioned a National Consultative Committee (NCC) to make recommendations regarding a possible shortening of the period of transition to civilian rule. In January 1995 two members of the AFPRC (the Vice-President, Sana Sabally, and Sadibou Hydara, the Minister of the Interior), both of whom were said to be opposed to a curtailment of the transition period (the NCC proposed a return to civilian government in July 1996), were arrested, following an alleged attempt to seize power. In December Sabally was sentenced to nine years' imprisonment for plotting to overthrow Jammeh; Hydara was reported to have died of natural causes while in detention.

The death penalty, which had been abolished in April 1993, was restored by government decree in August 1995, reportedly in response to a recent increase in the murder rate. In October Capt. Ebou Jallow, the official spokesman of the AFPRC, sought asylum in Senegal, accusing Jammeh's regime of complicity in murder and arbitrary arrests. The AFPRC asserted that Jallow had embezzled government funds prior to his departure, and in January 1998 a Swiss court ordered the return of US $3m. that Jallow had transferred from the Central Bank of The Gambia to a personal bank account in Geneva.

In November 1995 a government decree conferring wide powers of arrest and detention on the Minister of the Interior was issued. In January 1996 Jawara was charged *in absentia* with embezzlement, following investigations into the alleged diversion of proceeds from the sale of petroleum donated by Nigeria. In subsequent months the confiscation was ordered of the assets in The Gambia of Jawara and 11 former government members. In July the Minister of Health and Social Welfare was arrested and charged with the misappropriation of state funds.

Although the AFPRC stated its commitment to freedom of expression, a ban on the publication of journals by political organizations was introduced shortly after the July 1994 coup. Subsequent periodic incidents of the arrest of, or fines against, journalists provoked considerable international concern, while several non-Gambian journalists were deported.

The draft of a report by a Constitutional Review Commission (established in April 1995) was published in March 1996. Despite demands by the European Union (EU) and the Commonwealth, as well as by individual countries that had previously been major donors to The Gambia, for an expedited return to civilian rule, the AFPRC continued to assert that it would adhere to its revised timetable. In April, however, it was announced that it would be impossible to complete the return to elected civilian government by July, and in May new dates were set for the constitutional referendum, and for presidential and legislative elections, which would now take place in August, September and December, respectively. Opponents of the AFPRC criticized provisions of the Constitution that, they alleged, had been formulated with the specific intention of facilitating Jammeh's election to the presidency (although the Head of State had frequently asserted that he would not seek election).

The constitutional referendum took place on 8 August 1996. The rate of participation was high (85.9%), and 70.4% of voters endorsed the new document. A presidential decree was issued in the following week reauthorizing party political activity. Shortly afterwards, however, a further decree (Decree 89) was promulgated, according to which all holders of executive office in the 30 years prior to July 1994 were to be prohibited from seeking public office, with the PPP, the NCP and the GPP barred from contesting the forthcoming presidential and parliamentary elections. Thus, the only parties from the Jawara era authorized to contest the elections were the People's Democratic Organization for Independence and Socialism (PDOIS) and the People's Democratic Party. The effective ban on the participation of all those associated with political life prior to the military takeover in the restoration of elected institutions was strongly criticized by the Commonwealth Ministerial Action Group on the Harare Declaration (CMAG, see p. 165), which had hitherto made a significant contribution to the transition process. At the same time the AFPRC announced that the presidential poll was to be postponed by two weeks, to 26 September 1996.

Jammeh formally announced his intention to contest the presidency in mid-August 1996. At the end of the month the establishment of a political party supporting Jammeh, the Alliance for Patriotic Reorientation and Construction (APRC), was reported. In early September Jammeh resigned from the army, in order to contest the presidency as a civilian, as required by the Constitution. The presidential election proceeded on 26 September. Three people were reportedly killed, and more than 30 injured, in violence shortly before the poll. According to official results, Jammeh secured the presidency, with 55.77% of the votes cast, ahead of Ousainou Darboe, the leader of the United Democratic Party (UDP), who received 35.84%. Darboe sought refuge for several days in the residence of the Senegalese ambassador. The rate of participation by voters was again high, especially in rural areas, although observers, including CMAG, expressed doubts as to the credibility of the election results. The dissolution of the AFPRC was announced the same day. Jammeh was inaugurated as President on 18 October. In November an unconditional amnesty was extended to more than 40 political detainees. Also in November an attack on an army camp at Farafenni, 100 km east of Banjul, resulted in the deaths of six people.

Legislative elections took place on 2 January 1997, after a postponement of three weeks. All the registered parties presented candidates for the 45 elective seats in the new National Assembly. The Gambian authorities, opposition groups and most international observers expressed broad satisfaction at the conduct of the poll. (The Commonwealth did not send observers, owing to the continued ban on former members of Jawara's administration from seeking public office.) As expected, the APRC won an overwhelming majority of seats, securing 33 elective seats (including five in which the party was unopposed). The UDP obtained seven elective seats, the National Reconciliation Party (NRP) two, and the PDOIS one; independent candidates won two seats. The overall rate of participation by voters was 73.2%. As Head of State, Jammeh was empowered by the Constitution to nominate four additional members of parliament, from whom the Speaker and Deputy Speaker would be chosen. The opening session of the National Assembly, on 16 January, accordingly elected Mustapha Wadda, previously Secretary-General of the APRC and Secretary at the Presidency, as

Speaker. This session denoted the full entry into force of the Constitution and thus the inauguration of the Second Republic.

Under the new Constitution, ministers of cabinet rank were designated Secretaries of State, and the Government was reorganized to this effect in March 1997. Isatou Njie-Saidy, Secretary of State for Health, Social Welfare and Women's Affairs, was appointed Vice-President. However, most of the responsibilities hitherto associated with this post were transferred to the Secretary of State for the Office of the President, a position now held by Edward Singhateh: although Singhateh had succeeded Sabally as AFPRC Vice-President in early 1995, he was, under the terms of the new Constitution, too young (at 27 years of age) to assume the office of Vice-President. In April 1997 civilian appointees, including Jawara's former head of police, replaced the remaining four military regional governors.

Supporters of the new regime attributed the electoral success of Jammeh and the APRC to the popularity within The Gambia of the ambitious infrastructural projects undertaken since July 1994, citing in particular the construction of more new schools and hospitals than had been built in 30 years by the Jawara administration, as well as a new airport terminal and modernized port facilities, a television station, and plans for a national university. However, Jammeh's critics condemned what they regarded as excessive expenditure on 'prestige' projects.

In February 1997 CMAG reiterated its earlier concerns regarding the implications of Decree 89, and in July again urged the immediate removal of the ban on political activities by those connected with the Jawara administration. In September, none the less, CMAG reported signs of progress in the democratization process.

In April 1997 the trial began (in camera) of five alleged mercenaries suspected of involvement in the November 1996 attack on the Farafenni barracks. The accused apparently confirmed reports that they had formed part of a 40-strong commando group, trained in Libya and led by Kukoi Samba Sanyang, which had fought for Charles Taylor's National Patriotic Front of Liberia during the early 1990s. Four of the accused were subsequently sentenced to death on charges of treason; the fifth defendant died in detention in May 1997. In October, however, the Supreme Court ruled that the convictions were unsustainable and ordered that the four be retried on conspiracy charges.

In February 1998 the director and a journalist of a private radio station, Citizen FM, were detained, and the Government ordered the closure of the station and an associated newspaper, *New Citizen*, citing the station's failure to comply with new tax requirements for independent broadcasters. Opponents of the closure noted that the station had recently broadcast information concerning the National Intelligence Agency (NIA). The director of Citizen FM, Baboucar Gaye, launched an appeal against the closure of the station and, following several adjournments, accused the Government of employing delaying tactics. Further concern about press freedom arose in May 1999, when the *Daily Observer*, the only remaining newspaper that openly criticized the Government, was purchased by a businessman closely associated with Jammeh; despite assurances of non-interference in editorial matters, staff who had criticized the Government were subsequently removed from their posts. In July *The Independent*, a recently launched newspaper, was ordered to suspend publication because of alleged irregularities in its registration. It was, however, claimed that the Government had ordered the suspension following the publication of an article that repeated accusations, made by the UDP, of widespread corruption in the Jammeh regime.

Meanwhile, opposition activists continued to allege harassment by the Government. In May 1998 nine people, including Lamine Wa Juwara of the UDP, were arrested in a raid on the mosque at Brikama. Juwara was involved in a lawsuit seeking compensation for alleged wrongful imprisonment for 20 months without charge following the 1994 coup. Darboe was also briefly imprisoned. In late July Juwara's claim for damages was rejected by the Supreme Court on the grounds that a clause in the Constitution granted immunity to the former AFPRC in connection with the transition period.

In January 1999 four cabinet members were dismissed, as was the Managing Director of the National Water and Electricity Company, amid allegations that financial mismanagement had occurred in certain government departments. In January 2000 allegations of government corruption emerged after the disclosure in legal proceedings in the United Kingdom that significant sums of money generated by the sale of crude petroleum had been paid into an anonymous Swiss bank account. The crude petroleum had been granted to The Gambia for trading purposes by the Nigerian Government between August 1996 and June 1998, reportedly in recognition of Jammeh's opposition in 1995 to the imposition of sanctions by the Commonwealth against Nigeria. Jammeh vigorously denied any involvement in the matter. In mid-January 2000 Jammeh effected a minor cabinet reshuffle.

On 15 January 2000 the security forces announced that they had forestalled an attempted military coup. It was reported that during efforts to arrest the conspirators a lieutenant in the State Guard had been killed and the Commander of the State Guard, Lt Landing Sanneh, the officer in charge of security at the presidential palace, had been wounded. Another member of the State Guard was killed on the following day, while attempting to evade arrest. In February 2001 Sanneh was acquitted of charges of treason, but was immediately rearrested; in September he was convicted by court martial of plotting to overthrow the Government and sentenced to 16 years' imprisonment with hard labour.

Meanwhile, in April 2000 the death of a student in firemen's barracks, reputedly following torture, and the alleged rape of a schoolgirl by a member of the security forces precipitated serious student unrest in Banjul, Brikama and Serrekunda. Police and fire stations were burned down, and some 14 people were killed and 30 injured during the disturbances; despite initial official denials, it later became apparent that the security forces had used live ammunition to quell the protests. In May Jammeh assured the UN Secretary-General, Kofi Annan, who was visiting The Gambia, that those responsible for the deaths would be brought to justice and announced that a commission of inquiry had been established to investigate the disturbances.

In May 2000, amid allegations of bribe-taking, the Secretary of State for Local Government, Lands and Religious Affairs was dismissed. Later that month five men were detained by the NIA in connection with an alleged plot to assassinate Jammeh and overthrow the APRC Government. After their arrest without trial was declared unconstitutional by the High Court, a total of seven men were subsequently charged with treason. The trial, which opened in December 2000, was adjourned several times during 2001 and early 2002, recommencing in February 2003. Meanwhile, in July 2000 the Supreme Court finally upheld Baboucar Gaye's appeal against the closure of Citizen FM in February 1998 and ordered that Gaye's confiscated broadcasting equipment be returned to him; the radio station was reopened later in the year.

In August 2000 the APRC suggested that it would not be possible to hold local government elections in November, as scheduled, as the National Assembly had yet to approve the local government act. A major cabinet reshuffle also took place in August. Notably, Edward Singhateh retained his position as Secretary of State for Presidential Affairs, gaining additional responsibility for works, communications and information.

In December 2000 Jammeh dismissed Anglican Bishop Solomon Tilewa Johnson from his position as Chairman of the Independent Electoral Commission (IEC), stating his incompetence for the post. Johnson's predecessor, Gabriel Roberts, was reappointed, despite allegations that he had been involved in fraudulent behaviour to benefit the APRC at the parliamentary and presidential elections of 1996 and 1997. The dismissal of Johnson, which the opposition described as unconstitutional, followed his instigation of a court case in response to the Government's failure to enact the local government act.

In January 2001 the commission of inquiry into the student unrest of April 2000 published its report. The Government rejected the commission's recommendation that the Secretary of State for the Interior, Ousman Badjie, and senior police officials should accept responsibility for the disturbances. Shortly afterwards Pap Cheyassin Secka was dismissed as Secretary of State for Justice and Attorney-General and replaced by Joseph Henry Joof. Secka's dismissal was widely welcomed by opposition members, who claimed that he had increased political interference in the judiciary, particularly regarding the findings of the commission of inquiry, and had facilitated Johnson's removal from the IEC.

In February 2001 Jammeh assured the Secretary-General of the Commonwealth, Don McKinnon, that Decree 89 would be repealed in the near future. Omar Jallow, a government minister under Jawara, announced that he had filed a lawsuit at the Court of Appeal challenging the validity of Decree 89, after the High Court had declared in 2000 that it lacked the authority to hear the case. In April widespread public dissent was reported, after the National Assembly passed legislation, proposed by Badjie, which effectively granted indemnity from prosecution to those (including Badjie himself) found responsible for the disturbances and killings that had occurred during the student protests of April 2000.

In May 2001 the National Assembly and the President approved a number of constitutional amendments, which were to be submitted to a referendum, to be held before the end of November. The opposition protested that the proposed changes, including the extension of the presidential term from five to seven years, the introduction of a presidential prerogative to appoint local chiefs, and the replacement of the permanent IEC with an *ad hoc* body, would further increase the powers of the President and precipitate acts of electoral fraud at the forthcoming parliamentary and presidential elections. In June 12 journalists at *The Daily Observer*, including the editor-in-chief, resigned, claiming that the APRC was seeking to determine its editorial line.

In late July 2001 Jammeh announced the abrogation of Decree 89, although several prominent individuals who had participated in pre-1994 administrations, including Jawara and Sabally, remained prohibited from seeking public office under separate legislation. None the less, the PPP, the NCP and the GPP were subsequently re-established. In August the UDP, the PPP and the GPP formed a coalition and announced that Darboe would be its presidential candidate in the forthcoming election. Opposition supporters and other observers claimed that the compilation of voters' lists had been accompanied by widespread fraud. In particular, concern was expressed that foreign citizens (notably Senegalese nationals of the Diola ethnic group) resident in The Gambia had been registered as eligible to vote, while the IEC maintained that, owing to a lack of funds, it would be impossible to extend the opportunity to vote to Gambian citizens resident abroad.

In August 2001 the Secretary of State for Foreign Affairs, Sedate Jobe, resigned, reportedly in connection with the recent expulsion from The Gambia of a British diplomat (see below). Blaise Baboucar Jagne, Secretary of State for Foreign Affairs in 1995–96, was reappointed to the post.

By mid-September 2001 five candidates had announced their intention to contest the presidential election, which was to be held in October. In addition to Darboe, the candidate of the opposition UDP-PPP-GPP coalition, Jammeh would be challenged by Dibba for the NCP, Hamat Bah for the NRP and Sidia Jatta for the PDOIS. In early October Jallow, the Chairman of the PPP, appeared in court on charges of assault, but was freed on bail. A number of violent incidents were reported during the week before the presidential election. In Serrekunda, a suburb of Banjul, members of the security forces fired shots in order to disperse a rally by supporters of Darboe, and one person was killed during clashes between opposition supporters and soldiers. The dead man was reportedly an unarmed opposition activist who had been shot by a police-officer, and an inquiry into the incident was launched by the Department of State for the Interior.

The presidential election was held, as scheduled, on 18 October 2001. Controversy was provoked by a reported relaxation in identification requirements for voters, and a turn-out of some 90% was recorded. Jammeh was re-elected to the presidency, with 52.84% of the votes cast, according to official results, ahead of Darboe, who won 32.59% of the votes. Bah secured 7.78%, followed by Dibba and Jatta, with 3.77% and 3.02% respectively. Although Darboe conceded defeat, members of the opposition subsequently disputed the legitimacy of the results, reiterating claims of incorrect practice in the distribution of voting credentials and in the counting of ballots. None the less, international observers, including representatives of the Commonwealth, described the poll as being largely free and fair.

Following the election, a number of eminent opposition figures were arrested. On 22 October 2001 a leading Gambian human rights activist, Lamin Sillah, was detained by the security forces, after he alleged, in a radio interview, that members of the opposition had been subject to harassment and sustained detention. Subsequent reports suggested that up to 60 opposition supporters had been arrested in the week after the election, and that the homes of prominent members of the UDP had been attacked, allegedly by members of the youth wing of the APRC. Following pressure from international human rights campaigners, Sillah was released. Baboucar Gaye was also arrested, and the radio station again closed, officially on the grounds that it had defaulted on tax payments. In early November Darboe announced his party's intention to take legal action to secure the release of UDP activists who remained in prison. Additionally, in late October it was reported that several senior civil servants who were believed to be sympathetic to opposition parties, including the director of the national radio and television stations and a number of military officers, had been dismissed after the election. The dismissals reflected the implementation of a pledge made by Jammeh, in his election campaign, that he would ensure the loyalty to the President of civil and military organizations. Meanwhile, in late October the IEC announced the postponement of the referendum on proposed constitutional changes, which had been scheduled for mid-November. In late December, at his inauguration, President Jammeh granted an unconditional amnesty to Jawara, guaranteeing the former President's security should he decide to return to The Gambia. In late March 2002 Jammeh effected a cabinet reshuffle.

In late December 2001 the UDP–PPP–GPP coalition announced that it would boycott legislative elections scheduled for mid-January 2002, as a result of the alleged addition of some 50,000 foreign citizens to electoral lists and the reputed transfer of voters between the electoral lists of different constituencies. Having denied these accusations, on 22 December 2001 the IEC announced that the APRC had secured 33 of the 48 elective seats in the enlarged National Assembly, in constituencies where the party was unopposed owing to the boycott. At the elections, which took place on 17 January 2002, the APRC won 12 of the 15 contested seats, giving the party an overall total of 45 elective seats; the PDOIS obtained two seats, and the NRP one. Electoral turn-out was reportedly low. An additional five members of parliament were appointed by President Jammeh, in accordance with the Constitution. Dibba, whose NCP had formed an alliance with the APRC prior to the elections, was appointed Speaker of the new National Assembly.

The long-delayed municipal elections, which were finally held on 25 April 2002, were boycotted by the UDP and the PDOIS; consequently, the APRC was unopposed in some 85 of the 113 local seats, and won a total of 99 seats, securing control of all seven regional authorities. The NRP was the only other political organization to gain representation in local government in the elections, winning five seats; the remaining nine seats were secured by independent candidates. In early May the National Assembly approved legislation that imposed stricter regulations over the print media, in accordance with which all journalists not working for the state-controlled media would be required to register with a National Media Commission. The law was condemned by the Gambia Press Union (GPU), which announced that it would not co-operate with the new Commission. (In November the GPU further declared that it would challenge the constitutionality of the Commission in court.) Concerns about press freedom in The Gambia were heightened in August, when the director and a journalist of *The Independent* were arrested, following the publication of an article alleging that the Vice-President had recently married, a claim that was denied. Meanwhile, in early June Jawara returned to The Gambia from exile in the United Kingdom; at the end of the month he was officially received by Jammeh at the presidential residence, and later tendered his resignation as leader of the PPP. In July legislation was adopted that allowed Jammeh to appoint up to 20 Secretaries of State to his Cabinet, instead of 15.

In August 2002 Juwara of the UDP alleged that the party's campaign funds had been diverted prior to the April elections to pay for Darboe's outstanding income-tax debts. The UDP expelled Juwara, accusing him of trying to challenge Darboe for the leadership, and in mid-October Juwara formed a new party, the National Democratic Action Movement (NDAM). In early November the leader of the youth wing of the UDP, Shyngle Nyassi, was arrested in connection with information from the NIA that allegedly implicated him in the sale of forged documents to Gambians seeking asylum abroad. Nyassi, however, claimed that his arrest was a response to his criticism of the Government's economic policies. Vocal conflict between the NDAM and the APRC was followed, in late November, by a call from Omar Jallow for Jammeh's resignation. Meanwhile, Nyassi was arrested again, along with Darboe and two other members of the UDP, in connection with the murder of an APRC supporter, Alieu Njie, in June 2000; their trial was to commence in April 2003. Also in November 2002, the opposition UDP–PPP–GPP coalition split, following the resignation of its Chairman, Assan Musa Camara, while President Jammeh dismissed a number of members of his Cabinet, accusing them of lacking

seriousness. Notably, Jammeh took over the agriculture portfolio himself, amid opposition doubts of his qualification for the position. In early 2003 it was reported that a crisis had emerged in the judicial system, owing to non-renewal of contracts and a number of resignations during the previous year; the Court of Appeal was left with only two judges, fewer than required for a quorum, the High Court had only three, and, after the dismissal of Hassan Jallow in July 2002, there were no judges in the Supreme Court.

After the 1994 coup The Gambia's traditional aid donors and trading partners suspended much co-operation, although vital aid projects generally continued. The Jammeh administration therefore sought new links: diplomatic relations with Libya, severed in 1980, were restored in November 1994, and numerous co-operation agreements ensued. Links with the Republic of China (Taiwan), ended in 1974, were re-established in July 1995, whereupon Taiwan became one of the Gambia's major sources of funding.

Despite the presence in Senegal of prominent opponents of his Government, Jammeh also sought to improve relations with that country, and in January 1996 the two countries signed an agreement aimed at increasing bilateral trade and at minimizing cross-border smuggling; a further trade agreement was concluded in April 1997. In June the two countries agreed to take joint measures to combat insecurity, illegal immigration, arms-trafficking and drugs-smuggling. In January 1998 the Government of Senegal welcomed an offer by Jammeh to mediate in the conflict in the southern province of Casamance: the separatist MFDC is chiefly composed of the Diola ethnic group, of which Jammeh is a member. In December 2000 the Gambian Government sent a delegation to participate in talks between the MFDC and the Senegalese Government. Conflict between the transport unions of Senegal and The Gambia over border duties led to the temporary closure of border-crossings with Senegal on several occasions during 2002.

In June 1998 Jammeh offered to mediate in the conflict between the Government and rebel forces in Guinea-Bissau (q.v.); the rebel leader, Brig. Ansumane Mané, was a Diola of Gambian extraction. In January 1999 The Gambia agreed to provide troops for an ECOMOG (see Economic Community of West African States, see p. 191) peace-keeping mission in Guinea-Bissau. After the defeat of government forces in Guinea-Bissau in May 1999, the Gambian authorities secured the safe passage of former President Vieira to The Gambia, from where he departed for Portugal. The killing of Mané in December 2000 was widely regarded as a serious set-back for Gambian foreign policy. In June 2002 relations with Guinea-Bissau were strained after President Kumba Yalá of Guinea-Bissau threatened to invade The Gambia, accusing Jammeh of involvement in a failed coup attempt in May and of support for the Casamance rebels. An exchange of visits by the foreign ministers of the two countries, followed by UN intervention in July, relieved the tension, however; relations had improved further by September, when Yalá visited Banjul.

In January 2001 the Gambian Government denied that it was implicated, as stated in a UN report, in the illicit trafficking of diamonds to benefit dissident groups in Angola and Sierra Leone.

Relations with the United Kingdom were strained in 2001, following the expulsion of the British Deputy High Commissioner, Bharat Joshi, from The Gambia in late August. The Gambian authorities alleged that the diplomat had interfered in the country's internal affairs, following his attendance at an opposition meeting, but emphasized the action had been taken against Joshi, and not the United Kingdom. However, in late September the Gambian Deputy High Commissioner in London was expelled from the United Kingdom, and further retaliatory measures were implemented against The Gambia. Relations were restored during 2002. In January 2002 the EU representative, George Marc-André, was declared *persona non grata* by the Gambian authorities and requested to leave the country.

Government

The Constitution of the Second Republic of The Gambia, which was approved in a national referendum on 8 August 1996, entered into full effect on 16 January 1997. Under its terms, the Head of State is the President of the Republic, who is directly elected by universal adult suffrage. No restriction is placed on the number of times a President may seek re-election. Legislative authority is vested in the National Assembly, comprising 48 members elected by direct suffrage and five members nominated by the President of the Republic. The President appoints government members, who are responsible both to the Head of State and to the National Assembly. The Gambia is divided into eight local government areas.

Defence

In August 2002 the Gambian National Army comprised 800 men (including a marine unit of about 70 and a presidential guard) in active service. Military service has been mainly voluntary; however, the Constitution of the Second Republic, which entered into full effect in January 1997, makes provision for compulsory service. The defence budget for 2002 was estimated at D45m.

Economic Affairs

In 2001, according to estimates by the World Bank, The Gambia's gross national income (GNI), measured at average 1999–2001 prices, was US $440m., equivalent to $330 per head (or $1,730 on an international purchasing-power parity basis). During 1990–2001, it was estimated, the population increased at an average annual rate of 3.4%, while gross domestic product (GDP) per head increased, in real terms, at an average of 0.2% per year. Overall GDP increased, in real terms, at an average annual rate of 3.6% in 1990–2001; growth in 2001 was 5.7%.

Agriculture (including forestry and fishing) contributed 37.6% of GDP in 2001. About 78.6% of the labour force were employed in the sector in that year. The dominant agricultural activity is the cultivation of groundnuts. Exports of groundnuts and related products accounted for an estimated 68.2% of domestic export earnings in 1999; however, a significant proportion of the crop is frequently smuggled for sale in Senegal, and the industry is also vulnerable to drought, which destroyed over 50% of the 2001/02 harvest. Cotton, citrus fruits, mangoes, avocados and sesame seed are also cultivated for export. The principal staple crops are rice, millet, sorghum and maize, although The Gambia remains heavily dependent on imports of rice and other basic foodstuffs. Fishing makes an important contribution both to the domestic food supply and to export earnings: exports of fish and fish products contributed an estimated 12.6% of the value of domestic exports in 1999. In mid-2001 the Government announced the construction of a major new fishing port in Banjul, which was to be completed by 2003, at a cost of US $10m. Agricultural GDP increased at an average annual rate of 3.3% in 1990–2001; growth in 2001 was 6.1%.

Industry (including manufacturing, construction, mining and power) contributed 12.7% of GDP in 2001. About 9.7% of the labour force were employed in the sector at the time of the 1993 census. Industrial GDP increased at an average annual rate of 2.0% in 1990–2001; growth in 2001 was 5.7%.

The Gambia has no economically viable mineral resources, although seismic surveys have indicated the existence of deposits of petroleum. Deposits of kaolin and salt are currently unexploited. Manufacturing contributed an estimated 5.2% of GDP in 2001, and employed about 6.3% of the labour force in 1993. The sector is dominated by agro-industrial activities, most importantly the processing of groundnuts and fish. Beverages and construction materials are also produced for the domestic market. Manufacturing GDP increased at an average annual rate of 1.8% in 1990–2001; growth in 2001 was 4.5%.

The Gambia is highly reliant on imported energy. Imports of fuel and energy comprised an estimated 5.4% of the value of total imports in 2000.

The services sector contributed 49.7% of GDP in 2001. The tourist industry is of particular significance as a generator of foreign exchange. Tourism contributed about 10% of annual GDP in the early 1990s, and employed about one-third of workers in the formal sector at that time. The international response to the 1994 coup and its aftermath had a severe impact on tourism to The Gambia, although the industry recovered strongly from 1996 onwards. The Jammeh administration has expressed its intention further to exploit the country's potential as a transit point for regional trade and also as a centre for regional finance and telecommunications. The GDP of the services sector increased at an average annual rate of 4.3% in 1990–2001; growth in 2001 was 4.9%.

In 2000 The Gambia recorded a visible trade deficit of US $65.00m., while there was a deficit of $19.11m. on the current account of the balance of payments. In 1999 the principal source of imports was Germany, which supplied an estimated 13.8% of total imports; other major sources were the United Kingdom, France, the People's Republic of China and Belgium. The two largest markets for exports in that year were Belgium (an estimated 7.7% of total exports) and the United Kingdom. The Gambia's principal domestic exports in 1999 were

groundnuts and related products, fish and fish products, and fruit and vegetables. The principal imports in that year were food and live animals, machinery and transport equipment, basic manufactures and mineral fuels and lubricants.

In 1999 there was an estimated overall budget deficit of D208.2m. (equivalent to 4.2% of that year's GDP). The Gambia's total external debt was US $470.8m. at the end of 2000, of which $425.2m. was long-term public debt. In that year the cost of debt-servicing was equivalent to 7.0% of the value of exports of goods and services. The average annual rate of inflation was 4.2% in 1990–2000; consumer prices increased by an average of 0.8% in 2000. The rate of unemployment was estimated at some 26% of the labour force in mid-1994.

The Gambia is a member of the Economic Community of West African States (ECOWAS, see p. 187), of the Gambia River Basin Development Organization (OMVG, see p. 340), of the African Groundnut Council (see p. 335), of the West Africa Rice Development Association (WARDA, see p. 338), and of the Permanent Inter-State Committee on Drought Control in the Sahel (CILSS, see p. 341).

The military coup of July 1994 caused considerable economic disruption to The Gambia. A return to growth from 1995 was, in large part, underpinned by the recovery in the tourism sector. The installation of elected civilian institutions in early 1997 prompted the international economic community to recommence full support, which had been partially suspended following the coup, and in mid-1998 the IMF approved a three-year Enhanced Structural Adjustment Facility (subsequently renamed the Poverty Reduction and Growth Facility, PRGF) in support of the Government's economic programme for 1998–2001. In December 2000 it was announced that The Gambia was to receive US $91m. in debt-service relief over 15 years under the Heavily Indebted Poor Countries initiative. The Gambia's overriding dependence on the largely unmodernized groundnut sector remains an obstacle to sustained growth, although the gradual introduction of reforms, which sought to improve relations between public- and private-sector interests, and between production and marketing interests, in the sector, commenced in 2000. Concern has also been expressed at the level of borrowing incurred by the Jammeh Government to finance its extensive infrastructural programme; the level of The Gambia's international indebtedness has risen sharply since 1995. In March 2002 the USA finally lifted economic sanctions imposed on the Gambia following the 1994 coup, and in September the US Agency for International Development, noting progress made towards democratization, confirmed that The Gambia would be eligible for funding under the US African Growth and Opportunity Act from 1 January 2003. A Poverty Reduction Strategy Paper was submitted to the IMF and the World Bank in May 2002, and in early July the IMF approved a further PRGF, for the period 2002–05, equivalent to some $27m. The Government aimed to achieve real GDP growth of 6% per year in 2002–04, and to reduce the fiscal deficit to 2.1% of GDP by 2005 by introducing measures to limit public spending.

Education

Primary education, beginning at seven years of age, is free but not compulsory and lasts for six years. Secondary education, from 13 years of age, comprises two cycles, each lasting three years. A revised education policy, to be implemented in 1998–2003, envisaged the merging of the first three-year cycle of secondary education with primary education to provide nine years of consolidated elementary education. In 1999/2000 total enrolment at primary schools included 69.8% of children in the relevant age-group (boys 74.6%; girls 64.9%), while secondary enrolment was equivalent to only 27.0% (boys 31.1%; girls 23.0%). The Jammeh administration has, since 1994, embarked on an ambitious project to improve educational facilities and levels of attendance and attainment. A particular aim has been to ameliorate access to schools for pupils in rural areas. Post-secondary education is available in teacher training, agriculture, health and technical subjects. Some 1,591 students were enrolled at tertiary establishments in 1994/95. The University of The Gambia, at Banjul, was officially opened in 2000. In 1977 The Gambia introduced Koranic studies at all stages of education, and many children attend Koranic schools (daara). In 1999 current expenditure by the central Government on education was an estimated D146.0m., equivalent to 22.9% of non-interest current spending.

Public Holidays

2003: 1 January (New Year's Day), 12 February* (Eid al-Kebir, Feast of the Sacrifice), 18 February (Independence Day), 18 April (Good Friday), 1 May (Workers' Day), 14 May* (Eid al-Moulid, Birth of the Prophet), 22 July (Anniversary of the Second Republic), 15 August (Assumption/St Mary's Day), 26 November* (Eid al-Fitr, end of Ramadan), 25 December (Christmas).

2004: 1 January (New Year's Day), 2 February* (Eid al-Kebir, Feast of the Sacrifice), 18 February (Independence Day), 9 April (Good Friday), 1 May (Workers' Day), 2 May* (Eid al-Moulid, Birth of the Prophet), 22 July (Anniversary of the Second Republic), 15 August (Assumption/St Mary's Day), 14 November* (Eid al-Fitr, end of Ramadan), 25 December (Christmas).

* These holidays are dependent on the Islamic lunar calendar and may vary by one or two days from the dates given.

Weights and Measures

Imperial weights and measures are used. Importers and traders also use the metric system.

Statistical Survey

Source (unless otherwise stated): Department of Information Services, 14 Daniel Goddard St, Banjul; tel. 225060; fax 227230.

Area and Population

AREA, POPULATION AND DENSITY

Area (sq km)	11,295*
Population (census results)	
15 April 1983	687,817
15 April 1993	
Males	519,950
Females	518,195
Total	1,038,145
Population (official estimate at mid-year)	
2000	1,393,000
Density (per sq km) at mid-2000	123.3

* 4,361 sq miles.

ETHNIC GROUPS

1993 census (percentages): Mandinka 39.60; Fula 18.83; Wolof 14.61; Jola 10.66; Serahule 8.92; Serere 2.77; Manjago 1.85; Bambara 0.84; Creole/Aku 0.69; Others 1.23.

PRINCIPAL TOWNS

(population at 1993 census)

Banjul (capital) . .	42,326	Lamin	10,668
Brikama . . .	41,761	Gunjur	9,983
Bakau . . .	28,882	Basse	9,265
Farafenni . .	20,956	Soma	7,988
Serrekunda . .	18,901	Bansang . . .	5,743
Sukuta . . .	16,667		

BIRTHS AND DEATHS

(UN estimates, annual averages)

	1985–90	1990–95	1995–2000
Birth rate (per 1,000) . . .	46.5	43.2	40.4
Death rate (per 1,000) . . .	21.5	19.9	18.5

Source: UN, *World Population Prospects: The 2000 Revision.*

Expectation of life (WHO estimates, years at birth): 58.5 (males 56.2; females 61.0) in 2001 (Source: WHO, *World Health Report*).

ECONOMICALLY ACTIVE POPULATION*

(persons aged 10 years and over, 1993 census)

	Males	Females	Total
Agriculture, hunting and forestry	82,886	92,806	175,692
Fishing	5,610	450	6,060
Mining and quarrying . . .	354	44	398
Manufacturing	18,729	2,953	21,682
Electricity, gas and water supply	1,774	84	1,858
Construction	9,530	149	9,679
Wholesale and retail trade; repair of motor vehicles, motorcycles and personal and household goods	33,281	15,460	48,741
Hotels and restaurants	3,814	2,173	5,987
Transport, storage and communications	13,421	782	14,203
Financial intermediation . . .	1,843	572	2,415
Other community, social and personal service activities . .	25,647	15,607	41,254
Activities not adequately defined .	10,421	6,991	17,412
Total labour force	207,310	138,071	345,381

* Figures exclude persons seeking work for the first time, but include other unemployed persons.

Mid-2001 (estimates in '000): Agriculture, etc. 540; Total 687 (Source: FAO).

Health and Welfare

KEY INDICATORS

Total fertility rate (children per woman, 2001)	4.9
Under-5 mortality rate (per 1,000 live births, 2001) . .	126
HIV/AIDS (% of persons aged 15–49, 2001)	1.60
Physicians (per 1,000 head, 2001)	0.14
Hospital beds (per 1,000 head, 2000)	1.00
Health expenditure (2000): US $ per head (PPP) . . .	46
Health expenditure (2000): % of GDP	4.1
Health expenditure (2000): public (% of total)	82.4
Access to water (% of persons, 2000)	62
Access to sanitation (% of persons, 2000)	37
Human Development Index (2000): ranking	160
Human Development Index (2000): value	0.405

For sources and definitions, see explanatory note on p. vi.

Agriculture

PRINCIPAL CROPS
('000 metric tons)

	1999	2000	2001
Rice (paddy)	31.7	34.1	19.2
Maize	20.4	22.0	29.0
Millet	80.9	94.6	105.0
Sorghum	18.0	25.0	33.4
Cassava (Manioc)*	6.0	7.5	7.5
Pulses*	4.0	5.5	5.5
Groundnuts (in shell)	123.0	138.0	151.1
Oil palm fruit*	35.0	35.0	35.0
Other vegetables*	8.0	9.0	9.0
Fruits (incl. mangoes)*	4.2	4.2	4.2

* FAO estimates.

Source: FAO.

LIVESTOCK
(FAO estimates, '000 head, year ending September)

	1999	2000	2001
Cattle	361	364	323
Goats	150	145	228
Sheep	111	106	129
Pigs*	14	14	8
Asses*	35	35	35
Horses*	17	17	17
Poultry*	730	780	586

* FAO estimates.

Source: FAO.

LIVESTOCK PRODUCTS
(FAO estimates, '000 metric tons)

	1999	2000	2001
Beef and veal	3.4	3.5	3.1
Goat meat	0.4	0.4	0.6
Mutton and lamb	0.3	0.3	0.4
Poultry meat	1.2	1.3	1.0
Game meat	1.0	1.0	1.0
Other meat	0.4	0.4	0.2
Cows' milk	7.6	7.6	7.6
Poultry eggs	0.7	0.7	0.7

Source: FAO.

Forestry

ROUNDWOOD REMOVALS
('000 cubic metres, excluding bark)

	1998	1999	2000
Sawlogs, veneer logs and logs for sleepers*†	106	106	106
Other industrial wood‡† . . .	7	7	7
Fuel wood	500	505	505
Total	613	618	618

* Assumed to be unchanged since 1994.
† FAO estimates.
‡ Assumed to be unchanged since 1993.
Source: FAO.

Fishing

('000 metric tons, live weight)

	1998	1999	2000
Capture	29.0	30.0	29.0
Tilapias	1.1	1.1	1.1*
Sea catfishes	0.5	0.5	0.7
Bonga shad	22.0	21.3*	20.1
Croakers and drums	0.9	1.1	1.3
Sharks, rays, skates	0.6	0.6	0.7
Aquaculture*	0.0	0.0	0.0
Total catch	29.0	29.0*	29.0

* FAO estimate(s).

Source: FAO, *Yearbook of Fishery Statistics*.

Mining

	1998	1999	2000
Clay (metric tons)*	1,200	1,200	1,200
Silica sand ('000 metric tons) . .	270	250*	250*

* Estimated production.

Source: US Geological Survey.

Industry

SELECTED PRODUCTS
('000 metric tons, unless otherwise stated)

	1997	1998	1999
Salted, dried or smoked fish . .	1.1	n.a.	n.a.
Palm oil—unrefined*	2.5	2.5	2.5
Groundnut oil*	19.5	12.5	33.3
Beer of millet	25.5	27.3	28.8
Electric energy (million kWh)† . .	93.6	122.2	126.2*

2000 ('000 metric tons): Palm oil (unrefined) 2.5*; Groundnut oil 28.4*; Beer of millet 39.4.

2001 ('000 metric tons): Palm oil (unrefined) 2.5*; Groundnut oil 26.1*; Beer of millet 43.9*.

* Estimate(s) or provisional figure(s).
† Data from the National Water and Electricity Company Ltd.

Source: mainly FAO.

Finance

CURRENCY AND EXCHANGE RATES

Monetary Units
100 butut = 1 dalasi (D)

Sterling, Dollar and Euro Equivalents (28 June 2002)
£1 sterling = 29.411 dalasi
US $1 = 19.135 dalasi
€1 = 19.087 dalasi
1,000 dalasi = £34.00 = $52.26 = €52.39

Average Exchange Rate (dalasi per US $)
1999	11.395
2000	12.788
2001	15.687

BUDGET
(million dalasi)

Revenue*	1997	1998†	1999‡
Tax revenue	714.7	751.1	773.7
Direct taxes	168.5	185.1	201.8
Taxes on personal incomes .	72.3	76.4	81.3
Taxes on corporate profits .	81.8	93.7	81.3
Indirect taxes	546.2	566.0	571.8
Domestic taxes on goods and services	71.5	65.3	77.3
Domestic sales tax . .	57.1	63.0	64.7
Taxes on international trade .	474.7	500.7	494.5
Customs duties . . .	119.7	145.1	183.0
Sales tax on imports . . .	146.4	149.9	158.6
Petroleum taxes	208.5	205.8	152.9
Duty	178.6	177.3	132.3
Sales tax	29.9	28.5	20.6
Other current revenue . .	84.8	80.4	105.0
Government services and charges	40.1	35.1	75.1
Interest, dividends and property	23.0	38.6	22.0
Central Bank profit	17.4	4.0	4.6
Total	**799.5**	**831.5**	**878.7**

Expenditure§	1997	1998†	1999‡
Current expenditure	794.6	799.8	887.0
Expenditure on goods and services	470.9	447.5	490.8
Wages and salaries . . .	269.3	282.9	301.7
Other goods and services . .	201.6	164.5	189.1
Interest payments	214.7	236.9	248.3
Internal	155.2	180.4	187.5
External	59.5	56.4	60.9
Subsidies and transfers . . .	109.0	115.4	129.8
Emergency relief	—	—	18.0
Capital expenditure¶	349.9	259.9	261.0
Total	**1,144.5**	**1,059.7**	**1,148.0**

* Excluding grants received (million dalasi): 53.0 in 1997; 88.5 in 1998; 65.8 in 1999.
† Estimates.
‡ Preliminary figures.
§ Excluding lending minus repayments (million dalasi): −20.9 in 1997; −31.2 in 1998; −29.8 in 1999.
¶ Including foreign-financed extrabudgetary expenditure (million dalasi): 60.6 in 1997; 0.0 in 1998; 0.0 in 1999.

Source: IMF, *The Gambia: Selected Issues* (August 2000).

INTERNATIONAL RESERVES
(US $ million at 31 December)

	2000	2001	2002
IMF special drawing rights . . .	0.23	0.02	0.02
Reserve position in IMF	1.93	1.87	2.02
Foreign exchange	107.27	104.13	n.a.
Total	**109.43**	**106.02**	**n.a.**

Source: IMF, *International Financial Statistics*.

MONEY SUPPLY
(million dalasi at 31 December)

	1999	2000	2001
Currency outside banks . . .	379.72	540.26	600.75
Demand deposits at commercial banks	336.32	443.27	524.66
Total money	**716.04**	**983.53**	**1,125.41**

Source: IMF, *International Financial Statistics*.

COST OF LIVING
(Consumer Price Index for Banjul and Kombo St Mary's; base: 1974 = 100)

	1997	1998	1999
Food	1,511.8	1,565.8	1,628.8
Fuel and light	2,145.8	1,854.9	2,076.0
Clothing*	937.5	981.8	999.9
Rent	1,409.6	1,431.3	1,428.6
All items (incl. others)	**1,441.5**	**1,457.3**	**1,512.9**

* Including household linen.

All items (Consumer Price Index; base: 1995 = 100): 109.1 in 1999; 110.0 in 2000 (Source: IMF, *International Financial Statistics*).

NATIONAL ACCOUNTS
(million dalasi at current prices)

Expenditure on the Gross Domestic Product

	1997*	1998*	1999†
Government final consumption expenditure	735.1	743.3	753.6
Private final consumption expenditure	3,146.2	3,399.4	3,758.9
Increase in stocks	717.7	819.8	880.5
Gross fixed capital formation .			
Total domestic expenditure .	**4,599.0**	**4,962.5**	**5,393.0**
Exports of goods and services .	1,884.8	2,263.1	2,353.0
Less Imports of goods and services	2,303.7	2,746.5	2,790.4
GDP in purchasers' values .	**4,180.1**	**4,479.1**	**4,955.6**
GDP at constant 1976/77 prices	**641.0**	**672.5**	**710.1**

Gross Domestic Product by Economic Activity

	1997*	1998*	1999†
Agriculture, hunting, forestry and fishing	1,074.8	1,228.1	1,466.5
Manufacturing	218.8	219.0	234.6
Electricity and water	59.8	70.0	82.0
Construction	205.3	218.2	236.2
Trade, restaurants and hotels .	587.3	647.4	735.0
Transport and communications .	636.7	656.8	717.6
Real estate and business services .	280.6	282.1	299.8
Government services	375.9	394.1	421.6
Other services‡	194.6	197.5	204.4
GDP at factor cost	**3,633.9**	**3,913.1**	**4,397.6**
Indirect taxes, *less* subsidies . .	546.2	566.0	558.0
GDP in purchasers' values .	**4,180.1**	**4,479.1**	**4,955.6**

* Estimates.
† Preliminary figures.
‡ Including banking and insurance, net of imputed bank service charges.

Source: IMF, *The Gambia: Selected Issues* (August 2000).

BALANCE OF PAYMENTS
(US $ million, year ending 30 June)

	1995	1996	1997
Exports of goods f.o.b.	122.96	118.75	119.61
Imports of goods f.o.b.	-162.53	-217.10	-207.09
Trade balance	-39.57	-98.35	-87.48
Exports of services	53.71	101.21	109.35
Imports of services	-69.25	-77.03	-74.67
Balance on goods and services .	-55.11	-74.17	-52.81
Other income received . . .	4.37	6.01	3.73
Other income paid	-9.58	-9.28	-11.30
Balance on goods, services and income	-60.32	-77.44	-60.38
Current transfers received . .	55.81	35.10	45.04
Current transfers paid . . .	-3.68	-5.35	-8.22
Current balance	-8.19	-47.70	-23.56
Capital account (net) . . .	—	8.52	5.74
Direct investment from abroad. .	7.78	10.80	11.98
Other investment assets . .	-3.66	5.62	10.28
Investment liabilities . . .	20.65	42.18	17.19
Net errors and omissions . .	-15.63	-4.94	-14.22
Overall balance	0.94	14.47	7.40

Source: IMF, *International Financial Statistics*.

1998 (US $ million): Exports 132.53; Imports 195.44; Trade balance -62.91; Services and factor income (net) 1.09; Current transfers (net) 61.18; Current account balance -0.64; Capital and financial account 12.78; Errors and omissions -2.51; Overall balance 9.63 (Source: African Development Bank).

1999 (US $ million): Exports 119.63; Imports 192.45; Trade balance -72.82; Services and factor income (net) 6.75; Current transfers (net) 51.56; Current account balance -14.50; Capital and financial account 13.09; Errors and omissions 6.12; Overall balance 4.71 (Source: African Development Bank).

2000 (US $ million): Exports 124.67; Imports 189.67; Trade balance -65.00; Services and factor income (net) 5.19; Current transfers (net) 40.70; Current account balance -19.11; Capital and financial account 20.67; Errors and omissions 0.00; Overall balance 1.56 (Source: African Development Bank).

External Trade

PRINCIPAL COMMODITIES
(million dalasi)

Imports c.i.f.	1997	1998	1999
Food and live animals	570.9	956.6	726.3
Beverages and tobacco . . .	48.9	74.4	83.1
Mineral fuels, lubricants, etc. . .	124.4	142.8	121.3
Animal and vegetable oils . .	62.8	98.7	66.8
Chemicals	170.0	131.2	116.1
Basic manufactures	160.0	241.1	253.9
Machinery and transport equipment	373.7	502.7	456.4
Miscellaneous manufactured articles	201.7	207.5	273.1
Total (incl. others)	1,773.8	2,426.4	2,206.9

Exports f.o.b.*	1997	1998	1999
Groundnuts and groundnut products	49.2	139.9	197.6
Fish and fish products . . .	44.2	33.6	36.6
Fruit and vegetables	11.5	25.9	19.2
Cotton products	9.6	6.7	2.4
Total (incl. others)	139.4	229.4	289.8

* Excluding re-exports (million dalasi) 11.0 in 1997; 50.2 in 1998; 23.2 in 1999.

2000: Exports f.o.b. (US $ million) Groundnuts (in shell) 7.4; Agricultural products total 9.6 (Source: FAO).

2001: Exports f.o.b. (US $ million) Groundnuts (in shell) 11.7; Groundnuts (shelled) 4.3 (FAO estimate); Groundnut oil 1.5; Agricultural products total 16.2 (Source: FAO).

PRINCIPAL TRADING PARTNERS
(million dalasi)

Imports c.i.f.	1997	1998	1999
Belgium	86.8	163.1	126.8
China, People's Repub. . . .	68.9	140.5	140.8
Côte d'Ivoire	104.3	145.2	89.8
France (incl. Monaco) . . .	167.3	220.6	148.3
Germany	148.0	179.6	305.3
Hong Kong	50.5	82.8	96.7
Italy	47.9	30.6	31.8
Japan	55.3	77.2	71.5
Netherlands	84.5	163.8	105.3
Senegal	42.8	38.1	50.0
Spain	67.8	87.1	38.1
Thailand	6.2	125.6	27.3
United Kingdom	261.2	338.5	235.1
USA	171.2	168.9	109.2
Total (incl. others)	1,773.8	2,426.4	2,206.9

Exports f.o.b.	1997	1998	1999
Belgium	7.3	16.8	24.2
China, People's Repub. . . .	2.6	6.9	1.4
France (incl. Monaco) . . .	27.5	153.9	2.3
Germany	3.5	20.6	10.1
Hong Kong	2.6	1.4	0.8
Japan	3.2	5.3	2.1
Netherlands	7.4	9.0	3.3
Senegal	5.3	7.3	5.9
Spain	29.2	8.9	7.7
United Kingdom	22.0	34.8	15.7
USA	6.5	1.4	3.0
Total (incl. others)	150.4	279.6	313.0

Transport

ROAD TRAFFIC
(estimates, motor vehicles in use)

	1995	1996	1997
Passenger cars	6,972	6,925	7,267
Lorries and vans	3,778	4,045	4,147

SHIPPING

Merchant Fleet
(registered at 31 December)

	1999	2000	2001
Number of vessels	8	8	8
Total displacement (grt) . . .	1,884	1,884	1,884

Source: Lloyd's Register-Fairplay, *World Fleet Statistics*.

International Sea-borne Freight Traffic
('000 metric tons)

	1996	1997	1998
Goods loaded	55.9	38.1	47.0
Goods unloaded	482.7	503.7	493.2

CIVIL AVIATION
(traffic on scheduled services)

	1992	1993	1994
Kilometres flown (million) . . .	1	1	1
Passengers carried ('000) . . .	19	19	19
Passenger-km (million) . . .	50	50	50
Total ton-km (million) . . .	5	5	5

Source: UN, *Statistical Yearbook*.

Tourism

FOREIGN VISITORS BY COUNTRY OF ORIGIN*

	1997	1998	1999
Austria	863	1,819	1,356
Belgium	3,795	3,703	3,015
Denmark	2,237	2,836	2,956
Germany	18,460	22,189	25,393
Netherlands	10,365	10,762	9,625
Sweden	5,478	5,574	5,556
United Kingdom	38,378	37,437	40,588
Total (incl. others)	84,751	91,106	96,126

* Air charter tourist arrivals.

Source: World Tourism Organization, *Yearbook of Tourism Statistics*.

Receipts from tourism (million dalasi): 326.1 in 1997; 511.8 in 1998 (Source: IMF, *The Gambia: Selected Issues*, August 2000).

Communications Media

	1999	2000	2001
Television receivers ('000 in use) .	4	4	n.a.
Telephones ('000 main lines in use)	29.2	33.3	35.0
Mobile cellular telephones ('000 subscribers)	5.3	5.6	43.0
Personal computers ('000 in use) .	10	15	17
Internet users ('000)	3	4	18

Source: International Telecommunication Union.

Radio receivers ('000 in use): 196 in 1997.

Facsimile machines (number in use, year ending 31 March): 1,149 in 1997/98.

Daily newspapers: 1 in 1996 (average circulation 2,000 copies).

Non-daily newspapers: 4 in 1996 (estimated average circulation 6,000 copies).

Book production: 14 titles in 1996 (10,000 copies).

Sources: UNESCO, *Statistical Yearbook*; UN, *Statistical Yearbook*.

Education

(1998/99, unless otherwise indicated)

	Institutions	Teachers	Students		
			Males	Females	Total
Pre-primary . .	264	408*	15,205	13,618	28,823
Primary . . .	332	4,578	81,360	69,043	150,403
Junior Secondary	75	1,338	20,142	14,018	34,160
Senior Secondary	27	598	8,102	4,507	12,609
Tertiary . . .	5	155	1,018*	573*	1,591*

* 1994/95 figure.

Source: Department of State for Education, Banjul.

Adult literacy rate (UNESCO estimates): 36.6% (males 44.0%; females 29.4%) in 2000 (Source: UN Development Programme, *Human Development Report*).

Directory

The Constitution

Following the *coup d'état* of July 1994, the 1970 Constitution was suspended and the presidency and legislature, as defined therein, dissolved. A Constitutional Review Commission was inaugurated in April 1995; the amended document was approved in a national referendum on 8 August. The new Constitution of the Second Republic of The Gambia entered into full effect on 16 January 1997.

Decrees issued during the transition period (1994–96) are deemed to have been approved by the National Assembly and remain in force so long as they do not contravene the provisions of the Constitution of the Second Republic.

The Constitution provides for the separation of the powers of the executive, legislative and judicial organs of state. The Head of State is the President of the Republic, who is directly elected by universal adult suffrage. No restriction is placed on the number of times a President may seek re-election. Legislative authority is vested in the National Assembly, comprising 48 members elected by direct universal suffrage and five members nominated by the President of the Republic. The Speaker and Deputy Speaker of the Assembly are elected, by the members of the legislature, from among the President's nominees. The Constitution upholds the principle of executive accountability to parliament. Thus, the Head of State appoints government members, but these are responsible both to the President and to the National Assembly. Ministers of cabinet rank take the title of Secretary of State. Committees of the Assembly have powers to inquire into the activities of ministers and of government departments, and into all matters of public importance.

In judicial affairs, the final court of appeal is the Supreme Court. Provision is made for a special criminal court to hear and determine all cases relating to the theft and misappropriation of public funds.

The Constitution provides for an Independent Electoral Commission, an Independent National Audit Office, an Office of the Ombudsman, a Lands Commission and a Public Service Commission, all of which are intended to ensure transparency, accountability and probity in public affairs.

The Constitution guarantees the rights of women, of children and of the disabled. Tribalism and other forms of sectarianism in politics are forbidden. Political activity may be suspended in the event of a state of national insecurity.

The Government

HEAD OF STATE

President: Col (retd) Alhaji YAHYA A. J. J. JAMMEH (proclaimed Head of State 26 July 1994; elected President 26 September 1996, re-elected 18 October 2001).

Vice-President: ISATOU NJIE-SAIDY.

THE CABINET
(April 2003)

President: Col (retd) Alhaji YAHYA A. J. J. JAMMEH.

Vice-President and Secretary of State for Women's Affairs: ISATOU NJIE-SAIDY.

Secretary of State for Works and Infrastructure: Capt. (retd) EDWARD DAVID SINGHATEH.

Secretary of State for Fisheries, Natural Resources and the Environment: SUSAN WAFFA-OGOO.

Secretary of State for Justice, Attorney-General: JOSEPH HENRY JOOF.

Secretary of State for Foreign Affairs: BLAISE BABOUCAR JAGNE.

Secretary of State for Finance and Economic Affairs: FAMARA L. JATTA.

Secretary of State for Health and Social Welfare: Alhaji YAN-KUBA GASSAMA.

Secretary of State for Local Government and Lands: MALAFI JARJU.

Secretary of State for the Interior and Religious Affairs: OUSMAN BADJIE.

Secretary of State for Education: ANN THERESE NDONG-JATTA.

Secretary of State for Tourism and Culture: Capt. (retd) YAN-KUBA TOURAY.

Secretary of State for Communication, Information and Technology: Alhaji BAKARY NJIE.

Secretary of State for Trade, Industry and Employment: MOMODOU S. SALLAH.

Secretary of State for Youth and Sports: SAMBA FAAL.

Secretary-General, Head of the Civil Service: ALIEU NGUM.

DEPARTMENTS OF STATE

Office of the President: PMB, State House, Banjul; tel. 227881; fax 227034; e-mail info@statehouse.gm; internet www.statehouse .gm.

Office of the Vice-President: State House, Banjul; tel. 227605; fax 224012; e-mail vicepresident@statehouse.gm.

Department of State for Communication, Information and Technology: Half-Die, Banjul; tel. 227668.

Department of State for Education: Willy Thorpe Bldg, Banjul; tel. 227236; fax 224180; internet www.edugambia.gm.

Department of State for Finance and Economic Affairs: The Quadrangle, POB 9686, Banjul; tel. 228291; fax 227954.

Department of State for Fisheries, Natural Resources and the Environment: 5 Marina Parade, Banjul; tel. 228702; fax 228628.

Department of State for Foreign Affairs: 4 Col Muammar Ghadaffi Ave, Banjul; tel. 225654; fax 223578.

Department of State for Health, Social Welfare and Women's Affairs: The Quadrangle, Banjul; tel. 227881; fax 223178; e-mail dpi@dosh.gm; internet www.dosh.gm.

Department of State for the Interior and Religious Affairs: ECOWAS Ave, Banjul; tel. 228511; fax 223063.

Department of State for Justice: Col Muammar Ghadaffi Ave, Banjul; tel. 228181; fax 225352.

Department of State for Local Government and Lands: The Quadrangle, Banjul; tel. 228291.

Department of State for Tourism and Culture: New Administrative Bldg, The Quadrangle, Banjul; tel. 227593; fax 227753; e-mail masterplan@gamtel.gm; internet www.linktogambia.com.

Department of State for Trade, Industry and Employment: Central Bank Bldg, Independence Drive, Banjul; tel. 228332; fax 229220.

Department of State for Works and Infrastructure: MID Rd, Kanifing, Banjul; tel. 227449; fax 226655.

Department of State for Youth and Sports: The Quadrangle, Banjul; tel. 225264; fax 225267; e-mail dosy-s@qanet.gm.

President and Legislature

PRESIDENT

Presidential Election, 18 October 2001

Candidate	Votes	% of votes
Yahya A. J. J. Jammeh (APRC) . . .	242,302	52.84
Ousainou N. Darboe (UDP-PPP-GPP Coalition)	149,448	32.59
Hamat N. K. Bah (NRP)	35,671	7.78
Sheriff Mustapha Dibba (NCP) . . .	17,271	3.77
Sidia Jatta (PDOIS)	13,841	3.02
Total	**458,533**	**100.00**

NATIONAL ASSEMBLY

Speaker: SHERIFF MUSTAPHA DIBBA.

General Election, 17 January 2002

Party	Seats
Alliance for Patriotic Reorientation and Construction (APRC)	45*
People's Democratic Organization for Independence and Socialism (PDOIS)	2
National Reconciliation Party (NRP)	1
Total	**48†**

* Including 33 seats taken in constituencies in which the party was unopposed.

† The President of the Republic is empowered by the Constitution to nominate five additional members of parliament. The total number of members of parliament is thus 53.

Political Organizations

Alliance for Patriotic Reorientation and Construction (APRC): 72 Tafsir Demba Ndow St, Banjul; tel. 222020; fax 222021; e-mail campaign@jammeh2001.org; internet www.jammeh2001.org; f. 1996; Chair. President YAHYA A. J. J. JAMMEH.

Gambia People's Party (GPP): Banjul; f. 1986; socialist; banned from contesting the 1996 presidential election and 1997 legislative elections; contested 2001 presidential election in coalition with the PPP and the UDP; boycotted 2002 legislative elections; Leader ASSAN MUSA CAMARA.

National Convention Party (NCP): 47 Antouman Faal St, Banjul; f. 1977; banned from contesting the 1996 presidential election and 1997 legislative elections; supported the APRC in 2002 legislative elections; Leader SHERIF MUSTAPHA DIBBA.

National Democratic Action Movement (NDAM): Banjul; f. 2002; Leader and Sec.-Gen. LAMIN WAA JUWARA.

National Reconciliation Party (NRP): Banjul; f. 1996; Leader HAMAT N. K. BAH.

People's Democratic Organization for Independence and Socialism (PDOIS): POB 2306, 1 Sambou St, Churchill, Srerekunda; tel. 393177; fax 466180; e-mail FOROYAA@qanet.gm; f. 1986; socialist; Leaders HALIFA SALLAH, SAM SARR, SIDIA JATTA.

People's Progressive Party (PPP): Ninth St East, Fajara M Section, Banjul; f. 1959; fmr ruling party in 1962–94; banned from contesting 1996 presidential election and 1997 legislative elections; contested 2001 presidential election in coalition with the GPP and the UDP; boycotted 2002 legislative elections; Chair. AMADOU OMAR JALLOW (acting).

United Democratic Party (UDP): 1A Rene Blain St, Banjul; tel. 201730; fax 224601; e-mail udpgambia@info.org; internet www .udpgambia.org; f. 1996; contested 2001 presidential election in coalition with the GPP and the PPP; boycotted 2002 legislative elections; Sec.-Gen. and Leader OUSAINOU N. DARBOE; Nat. Pres. Col (retd) SAM SILLAH.

Diplomatic Representation

EMBASSIES AND HIGH COMMISSIONS IN THE GAMBIA

China (Taiwan): 26 Radio Gambia St, Kanifing South, POB 916, Banjul; tel. 374046; fax 374055; Ambassador EDGAR LIN.

Guinea-Bissau: Banjul; tel. and fax 228134; Ambassador ABEL COELHO DE MENDONÇA.

Liberia: Garba-Jahumpa Rd, Bakau Newtown, POB 2982, Banjul; tel. 496775; fax 396629; Chargé d'affaires a.i. ERIC R. TOGBA.

Libya: Banjul; tel. 223213; fax 223214; Chargé d'affaires a.i. ABDUS-SALAM ABUZAID.

Nigeria: Garba Jahumpa Rd, Bakau Newtown, POB 630, Banjul; tel. 495803; fax 496456; High Commissioner AYUBA JACOB NGBAKO.

Senegal: Kairaba Ave, POB 385, Banjul; tel. 373752; fax 373750; Ambassador Gen. MOMODOU DIOP.

Sierra Leone: 67 Daniel Goddard St, POB 448, Banjul; tel. 228206; fax 229814; High Commissioner IBRAHIM MORIKEH FOFANA.

United Kingdom: 48 Atlantic Rd, Fajara, POB 507, Banjul; tel. 495133; fax 496134; e-mail bhcbanjul@gamtel.gm; High Commissioner ERIC JENKINSON.

USA: The White House, Kairaba Ave, Fajara, PMB 19, Banjul; tel. 391971; fax 392475; e-mail ambanjul@gamtel.gm; Ambassador JACKSON MCDONALD.

Judicial System

The judicial system of The Gambia is based on English Common Law and legislative enactments of the Republic's Parliament which include an Islamic Law Recognition Ordinance whereby an Islamic Court exercises jurisdiction in certain cases between, or exclusively affecting, Muslims.

The Constitution of the Second Republic guarantees the independence of the judiciary. The Supreme Court is defined as the final court of appeal. Provision is made for a special criminal court to hear and determine all cases relating to theft and misappropriation of public funds.

Supreme Court of The Gambia

Law Courts, Independence Drive, Banjul; tel. 227383; fax 228380. Consists of the Chief Justice and up to six other judges.

Chief Justice: MOHAMMED ARIF.

The **Banjul Magistrates Court**, the **Kanifing Magistrates Court** and the **Divisional Courts** are courts of summary jurisdiction presided over by a magistrate or in his absence by two or more lay justices of the peace. There are resident magistrates in all divisions. The magistrates have limited civil and criminal jurisdiction, and appeal from these courts lies with the Supreme Court. **Islamic Courts** have jurisdiction in matters between, or exclusively affecting, Muslim Gambians and relating to civil status, marriage, succession, donations, testaments and guardianship. The Courts administer Islamic *Shari'a* law. A cadi, or a cadi and two assessors, preside over and constitute an Islamic Court. Assessors of the Islamic Courts are Justices of the Peace of Islamic faith. **District Tribunals** have appellate jurisdiction in cases involving customs and traditions. Each court consists of three district tribunal members, one of whom is selected as president, and other court members from the area over which it has jurisdiction.

Attorney-General: JOSEPH HENRY JOOF.

Solicitor-General: RAYMOND SOCK.

Religion

About 85% of the population are Muslims. The remainder are mainly Christians, and there are a few animists, mostly of the Diola and Karoninka ethnic groups.

ISLAM

Banjul Central Mosque: King Fahd Bun Abdul Aziz Mosque, Box Bar Rd, POB 562, Banjul; tel. 228094; Imam Ratib Alhaji ABDOULIE M. JOBE; Dep. Imam Ratib Alhaji TAFSIR GAYE.

Supreme Islamic Council: Banjul; Chair. Alhaji BANDING DRAMMEH; Vice-Chair. Alhaji OUSMAN JAH.

CHRISTIANITY

The Christian Council of The Gambia: MDI Rd, Kanifing, POB 27, Banjul; tel. 392092; e-mail gchristianc@hotmail.com; f. 1966; seven mems (churches and other Christian bodies); Chair. Rt Rev. MICHAEL J. CLEARY (Roman Catholic Bishop of Banjul); Sec.-Gen. DANIEL ABLE-THOMAS.

The Anglican Communion

The diocese of The Gambia, which includes Senegal and Cape Verde, forms part of the Church of the Province of West Africa. The Archbishop of the Province is the Bishop of Koforidua, Ghana. There are about 1,500 adherents in The Gambia.

Bishop of The Gambia: Rt Rev. SOLOMON TILEWA JOHNSON, Bishopscourt, POB 51, Banjul; tel. 227405; fax 229495; e-mail anglican@qanet.gm.

The Roman Catholic Church

The Gambia comprises a single diocese (Banjul), directly responsible to the Holy See. At 31 December 2000 there were an estimated 30,500 adherents of the Roman Catholic Church in the country. The diocese administers a development organization (Caritas, The Gambia), and runs 63 schools and training centres. The Bishop of Banjul is a member of the Inter-territorial Catholic Bishops' Conference of The Gambia and Sierra Leone (based in Freetown, Sierra Leone).

Bishop of Banjul: Rt Rev. MICHAEL J. CLEARY, Bishop's House, POB 165, Banjul; tel. 393437; fax 390998; e-mail mcleary@gamtel.gm.

Protestant Churches

Abiding Word Ministries: POB 207, Serrekunda; tel. and fax 394035; e-mail ncwc.awm@commit.gm; f. 1988; Senior Pastor Rev. FRANCIS FORBES.

Methodist Church: POB 288, Banjul; tel. 227425; f. 1821; Chair. and Gen. Supt Rev. TITUS K. A. PRATT.

BAHÁ'Í FAITH

National Spiritual Assembly: POB 583, Banjul; tel. 229015; e-mail alsalihi@commit.gm.

The Press

All independent publications are required to register annually with the Government and to pay a registration fee.

The Daily Observer: POB 131, Banjul; tel. 496608; fax 496878; e-mail observer@qanet.gm; internet www.qanet.gm/Observer/observer.html; f. 1992; daily; independent; Man. Dir BUBACARR BALOEH; Editor-in-Chief PASCHAL EZE (acting).

Foroyaa (Freedom): 1 Sambou St, Churchill's Town, POB 2306, Serrekunda; tel. 393177; fax 393177; e-mail foroyaa@qanet.gm; internet www.gambian.com/foroyaa/foroyaa.htm; 2 a week; publ. by the PDOIS; Editors HALIFA SALLAH, SAM SARR, SIDIA JATTA.

The Gambia Daily: Dept of Information, 14 Daniel Goddard St, Banjul; tel. 225060; fax 227230; e-mail gamna@gamtel.gm; internet www.gambianews.com; f. 1994; govt organ; Dir of Information EBRUMA COLE; circ. 500.

The Gambian: Banjul; 3 a week; Editor NGAING THOMAS.

The Independent: next to A-Z Supermarket, Kairaba Ave, Banjul; e-mail independent@qanet.gm; internet www.qanet.gm/Independent/independent.html; f. 1999; 2 a week; independent; Dir Alhaji YORRO JALLOW; Editor-in-Chief DEMBA ALI JAWO (acting).

The Point: 2 Garba Jahumpa Rd, Fajara, Banjul; tel. 497441; fax 497442; e-mail point@qanet.gm; internet www.qanet.gm/point/point .html; f. 1991; 2 a week; Man. Editor DEYDA HYDARA; circ. 3,000.

The Toiler: 31 OAU Blvd, POB 698, Banjul; Editor PA MODOU FALL.

The Worker: 6 Albion Place, POB 508, Banjul; publ. by the Gambia Labour Union; Editor M. M. CEESAY.

NEWS AGENCY

Gambia News Agency (GAMNA): Dept of Information, 14 Daniel Goddard St, Banjul; tel. 225060; fax 227230; e-mail gamna@gamtel .gm; Dir EBRIMA COLE.

PRESS ASSOCIATION

Gambia Press Union: 10 Atlantic Rd, Fajara, POB 1440, Banjul; tel. 497945; fax 497946; e-mail gpu@qanet.gm; affiliated to West African Journalists' Association; Pres. DEMBA ALI JAWO.

Publishers

National Printing and Stationery Corpn: Banjul; state-owned.

Sunrise Publishers: POB 955, Banjul; tel. 393538; e-mail sunrise@ qanet.gm; regional history, politics and culture.

Broadcasting and Communications

TELECOMMUNICATIONS

Africell (Gambia): Banjul; f. 2001; provider of mobile cellular telecommunications.

Gambia Telecommunications Co Ltd (GAMTEL): Gamtel House, 3 Nelson Mandela St, POB 387, Banjul; tel. 229999; fax 228004; e-mail gen-info@gamtel.gm; internet www.gamtel.gm; f. 1984; state-owned; also operates mobile cellular telecommunications network, Gamcel; Man. Dir ABDOURAHMAN M'BOOB.

BROADCASTING

Radio

Citizen FM: Banjul; independent commercial broadcaster; broadcasts news and information in English, Wolof and Mandinka; rebroadcasts selected programmes from the British Broadcasting Corpn; operations suspended in Oct. 2001; Propr BABOUCAR GAYE; News Editor EBRIMA SILLAH.

Farafenni Community Radio: Farafenni; tel. 735527.

FM B Community Radio Station: Brikama; tel. 483000; FM broadcaster.

Gambia Radio and Television Services (GRTS): Kariaba Ave, POB 387, Banjul; tel. 373918; fax 374242; e-mail grts@qanet.gm; f. 1962; state-funded, non-commercial broadcaster; radio broadcasts in English, Mandinka, Wolof, Fula, Diola, Serer and Serahuli; Chair. BAKARY NJIE; Dir BORA MBOGE.

Radio 1 FM: 44 Kairaba Ave, POB 2700, Serrekunda; tel. 396076; fax 394911; e-mail george.radio1@qanet.gm; f. 1990; private station broadcasting FM music programmes to the Greater Banjul area; Dir GEORGE CHRISTENSEN.

Radio Gambia: Mile 7, Banjul; tel. 495101; fax 495923; e-mail semafye@hotmail.com.

Radio Syd: POB 279, Banjul; tel. 228170; fax 226490; e-mail radiosyd@gamtel.gm; f. 1970; medium-wave commercial station broadcasting mainly music; programmes in English, French, Wolof, Mandinka and Fula; also tourist information in Swedish; Dir CONSTANCE WADNER ENHÖRNING; Man. BENNY HOLGERSON.

Sud FM: Buckle St, POB 64, Banjul; tel. 222359; fax 222394; e-mail sudfm@gamtel.gm; Man. MAMADOU HOUSSABA BA.

West Coast Radio: Manjai Kunda, POB 2687, Serrekunda; tel. 460911; fax 461193; e-mail wcr@delphi.com; FM broadcaster.

The Gambia also receives broadcasts from Radio Democracy for Africa (f. 1998), a division of the Voice of America, and the British Broadcasting Corpn.

Television

Gambia Radio and Television Services (GRTS): see Radio; television broadcasts commenced 1995.

Finance

(cap. = capital; res = reserves; dep. = deposits; m. = million; brs = branches; amounts in dalasi)

BANKING

Central Bank

Central Bank of The Gambia: 1–2 ECOWAS Ave, Banjul; tel. 228103; fax 226969; e-mail centralbank.gambia@qanet.gm; f. 1971; bank of issue; monetary authority; cap. 1.0m., res 3.0m., dep. 993.6m. (Dec. 1998); Gov. MOMODOU CLERKE BAJO; Gen. Man. VALDEMAR R. JENSEN.

Other Banks

Arab-Gambian Islamic Bank: 7 ECOWAS Ave, POB 1415, Banjul; tel. 223773; fax 223770; e-mail agib@qanet.gm; internet www.agib.gm; f. 1996; 30.1% owned by Islamic Development Bank (Saudi Arabia); cap. 5.8m., total assets 58.8m. (Dec. 1999); Chair. Dr OMAR ZUHAIR HAFIZ; Man. Dir MAMOUR MALICK JAGNE; 1 br.

Continent Bank Ltd: Mamadi Manjang Highway, Kanifing, POB 142, Banjul; tel. 393000; fax 396666; e-mail continent.bank@gamtel.gm; internet www.gambianews.com/continentbank; f. 1990; cap. 3.6m., dep. 66.6m. (Dec. 1999); Man. Dir OMAR S. JAATA (acting); 2 brs.

First International Bank Ltd: 6 OAU Blvd, POB 1997, Banjul; tel. 202004; fax 202001; e-mail fib@gamtel.gm; f. 1999; 52.5% owned by Slok Nigeria Ltd; cap. 10.0m., dep. 21.9m. (Dec. 2001); Chair. Dr BABACAR NDIAYE; Man. Dir and CEO O. E. ONWUCHEKWA.

International Bank for Commerce and Industry (Gambia) Ltd: 11A Liberation Ave, POB 211, Banjul; tel. 218144; fax 229312; e-mail ibc@qanet.gm; f. 1968; owned by Banque Mauritanienne pour le Commerce et l'Industrie; cap. and res 16.5m., dep. 179.1m. (Dec. 1999); Chair. SIDI MOHAMED ABBASS; Man. Dir MORY GUEBA CISSÉ; 2 brs.

Standard Chartered Bank (Gambia) Ltd: 8 ECOWAS Ave, POB 259, Banjul; tel. 228681; fax 227714; e-mail alieu.njai@gm.standardchartered.com; internet www.standardchartered.com/gm/index.html; f. 1978; 75% owned by Standard Chartered Holdings BV, Amsterdam; cap. and res 65.9m., dep. 542.4m. (Dec. 1999); Man. Dir STANLEY TSIKIRAYI; 3 brs.

Trust Bank Ltd (TBL): 3–4 ECOWAS Ave, POB 1018, Banjul; tel. 225778; fax 225781; e-mail info@trustbank.gm; internet www.trustbank.gm; f. 1992; fmrly Meridien BIAO Bank Gambia Ltd; 30% owned by Data Bank, 25% by Social Security and Housing Finance Corpn, 10% by Boule & Co Ltd; cap. 27m., res 58.0m., total assets 538.4m. (Dec. 2000); Chair. KEN OFORI ATTA; Man. Dir PA MACOUMBA NJIE; 4 brs.

INSURANCE

Capital Insurance Co Ltd: 22 Anglesea St, POB 485, Banjul; tel. 228544; fax 229219; e-mail capinsur@gamtel.gm; f. 1985; Man. Dir JOSEPH C. FYE.

The Gambia National Insurance Co Ltd (GNIC): 19 Karaiba Ave, Fajara, KSMD, POB 750, Banjul; tel. 395725; fax 395716; e-mail info@gnic.gm; internet www.gnic.gm; f. 1974; privately owned; Chair. M. O. DRAMMEH; Man. Dir WILLIAM B. COKER; 3 brs.

Gamstar Insurance Co Ltd: 79 Daniel Goddard St, POB 1276, Banjul; tel. 226021; fax 229755; internet www.gamstarinsurance.net; f. 1991; Man. Dir BAI NDONGO FAAL.

Great Alliance Insurance Co: 10 Nelson Mandela St, POB 750, Banjul; tel. 227839; fax 229444; e-mail info@gaic.gm; internet www.gaic.gm; f. 1989; Man. Dir YABOR FORSTER.

Londongate Insurance: 1–3 Liberation Ave, POB 602, Banjul; tel. 201740; fax 201742; internet www.londongate.co.uk/gambia_profile.htm; e-mail izadi@londongate.gm; f. 1999; owned by Boule & Co Ltd.

Prime Insurance Co Ltd: 10c Nelson Mandela St, POB 277, Banjul; tel. 222476; e-mail prime@qanet.gm; f. 1997; Man. Dir PA ALASSAN JAGNE.

Senegambia Insurance Co Ltd (SIC): POB 880, Banjul; tel. 228866; fax 226820; f. 1983; Man. Dir B. CISSÉ; 6 brs.

Insurance Association

Insurance Association of The Gambia (IAG): Banjul.

Trade and Industry

GOVERNMENT AGENCIES

Gambia Divestiture Agency (GDA): 80 OAU Blvd, Banjul; tel. 202530; fax 202533; internet www.gda.gm; f. 2001; Man. Dir (vacant).

Indigenous Business Advisory Services: Serrekunda; tel. 496098.

National Environmental Agency (NEA): 5 Fitzgerald St, Banjul; tel. 228056; fax 229701.

National Investment Promotion Authority (NIPA): Independence Drive, Banjul; tel. 228332; fax 229220; f. 1994 to replace the National Investment Bd; CEO S. M. MBOGE.

National Trading Corpn of The Gambia Ltd (NTC): 1–3 Liberation Avenue, POB 61, Banjul; tel. 228323; fax 227790; f. 1973; transfer pending to private-sector ownership; Man. Dir CHARBEL N. L. ELHAJJ; 15 brs.

CHAMBER OF COMMERCE

Gambia Chamber of Commerce and Industry (GCCI): NTC Complex, ECOWAS Ave, POB 333, Banjul; tel. 227042; fax 229671; e-mail gcci@qanet.gm; internet www.gambiachamber.gm; f. 1967 by merger; Chief Exec. KEBBA T. N'JAI.

UTILITIES

National Water and Electricity Company: POB 609, Banjul; tel. 496430; fax 496751; f. 1996; in 1999 control was transferred to the Bassau Development Corporation, Côte d'Ivoire, under a 15-year contract; electricity and water supply, sewerage services; Chair. A. M. JENG; Man. Dir BABOUCAR M. JOBE.

NAWEC Ltd: POB 609, Banjul; tel. 497495; fax 228260; fmrly part of National Water and Electricity Company; distribution of electricity and water; subsidiary co Gampower Ltd; Chair. A. ALLEN (acting); Man. Dir B. BALDEN.

CO-OPERATIVES

Federation of Agricultural Co-operatives: Banjul.

The Gambia Co-operative Union (GCU): POB 505, Banjul; tel. 374788; fax 392582; f. 1959; co-operative for groundnut producers; Gen. Man. LAMIN WILLY JAMMEH; 110,000 mems.

TRADE UNIONS

Association of Gambia Sailors: c/o 31 OAU Blvd, POB 698, Banjul; tel. 223080; fax 227214.

Dock Workers' Union: Albert Market, POB 852, Banjul; tel. 229448; fax 225049.

Gambia Labour Union: 6 Albion Place, POB 508, Banjul; f. 1935; Pres. B. B. KEBBEH; Gen. Sec. MOHAMED CEESAY; 25,000 mems.

Gambia Workers' Confederation: 12 Clarkson St, POB 698, Banjul; tel. 223080; fax 227214; f. 1958 as The Gambia Workers' Union, present name adopted in 1985; Sec.-Gen. PA MOMODOU FAAL; 30,000 mems (2001).

The Gambia National Trades Union Congress (GNTUC): Trade Union House, 31 OAU Blvd, POB 698, Banjul; Sec.-Gen. EBRIMA GARBA CHAM.

Transport

Gambia Public Transport Corpn: Factory St, Kanifing Industrial Estate, POB 801, Banjul; tel. 392230; fax 392454; f. 1975; operates road transport and ferry services; Chair. SALIFU KUJABI.

RAILWAYS

There are no railways in The Gambia.

ROADS

In 1996 there were an estimated 2,700 km of roads in The Gambia, of which 850 km were main roads, and 520 km were secondary roads. In that year only about 35% of the road network was paved. Some roads are impassable in the rainy season. The expansion and upgrading of the road network is planned, as part of the Jammeh administration's programme to improve The Gambia's transport infrastructure. Among intended schemes is the construction of a motorway along the coast, with the aid of a loan of US $8.5m. from Kuwait. In early 1999 Taiwan agreed to provide $6m. for road construction programmes, and in early 2000 work began on the construction of a dual carriageway between Serrekunda-Mandina-Ba, supported by funds from the Islamic Development Fund and the Organization of the Petroleum Exporting Counties.

Gambia Public Transport Corpn (GPTC): POB 801, Kanifing; tel. 392230; fax 392454; provides bus services; state-owned; Man. Dir AMAT NJIE (acting).

SHIPPING

The River Gambia is well suited to navigation. A weekly river service is maintained between Banjul and Basse, 390 km above Banjul, and a ferry connects Banjul with Barra. Small ocean-going vessels can reach Kaur, 190 km above Banjul, throughout the year. Facilities at the port of Banjul were modernized and expanded during the mid-1990s, with the aim of enhancing The Gambia's potential as a transit point for regional trade. In 1999 three advanced storage warehouses were commissioned with total storage space of 8,550 sq m.

Gambia Ports Authority: 34 Liberation Ave, POB 617, Banjul; tel. 229940; fax 227268; e-mail info@gamport.gm; internet www .gamport.gm; f. 1972; Man. Dir ADAMA DEEN.

The Gambia River Transport Co Ltd: 61 Wellington St, POB 215, Banjul; tel. 227664; river transport of groundnuts and general cargo; Man. Dir. LAMIN JUWARA; 200 employees.

The Gambia Shipping Agencies Ltd: 2 Cotton St, POB 256, Banjul; tel. and fax 227518; e-mail gamship@gamship.gm; internet www.gamship.com; f. 1984; shipping agents and forwarders; Man. Dir STEN C. HEDEMANN; 30 employees.

Interstate Shipping Co (Gambia) Ltd: POB 437, Banjul; tel. 227644; fax 229347; transport and storage.

CIVIL AVIATION

Banjul International Airport, at Yundum, 27 km from the capital, handled some 275,000 passengers and 3,000 metric tons of cargo in 1992. Construction of a new terminal, at a cost of some US $10m., was completed in late 1996. Facilities at Yundum have been upgraded by the US National Aeronautics and Space Administration (NASA), to enable the airport to serve as an emergency landing site for space shuttle vehicles.

Gambia Civil Aviation Authority: Banjul National Airport, Yundum; tel. 472831; fax 472190.

Gambia International Airlines: 8 Hagan St, PMB, Banjul; tel. 472751; fax 472750; e-mail info@gia.gm; f. 1996; state-owned; sole handling agent at Banjul, sales agent; Chair. WILLIAM JAMMEH; Man. Dir LAMIN K. MANJANG.

Tourism

Tourists are attracted by The Gambia's beaches and also by its abundant birdlife. A major expansion of tourism facilities was carried out in the early 1990s. Although there was a dramatic decline in tourist arrivals in the mid-1990s (owing to the political instability), the tourism sector recovered well; some 96,126 tourists visited The Gambia in 1999. In 1998 estimated earnings from tourism were D511.8m. An annual 'Roots Festival' was inaugurated in 1996, with the aim of attracting African-American visitors to The Gambia.

The Gambia Hotels' Association: c/o The Bungalow Beach Hotel, POB 2637, Serrekunda; tel. 465288; fax 466180; Chair. ARDE SARGE.

The Gambia Tourist Authority: Kololi, POB 4085, Bakau; tel. 462491; fax 462487; e-mail dg@gta.gm; f. 2001; Dir-Gen. HABIB S. DRAMMEH.

GEORGIA

Introductory Survey

Location, Climate, Language, Religion, Flag, Capital

Georgia is situated in west and central Transcaucasia, on the southern foothills of the Greater Caucasus mountain range. There is a frontier with Turkey to the south-west and a western coastline on the Black Sea. The northern frontier with Russia follows the axis of the Greater Caucasus, and includes borders with the Russian republics of Dagestan, Chechnya, Ingushetiya, North Ossetia (Osetiya), Kabardino-Balkariya and Karachai-Cherkessiya. To the south lies Armenia, and to the south-east is Azerbaijan. Georgia includes two autonomous republics (Abkhazia and Ajaria) and the autonomous region of South Ossetia. (The status of Abkazia and South Ossetia remained in dispute.) The Black Sea coast and the Rion plains have a warm, humid, subtropical climate, with annual rainfall of more than 2,000 mm and average temperatures of 6°C (42°F) in January and 23°C (73° F) in July. Eastern Georgia has a more continental climate, with cold winters and hot, dry summers. The official language is Georgian (a member of the Caucasian language group), which is written in the Georgian script. Most of the population are adherents of Christianity; the principal denomination is the Georgian Orthodox Church. Islam is professed by Ajarians, Azerbaijanis, Kurds and some others. Most Ossetians in Georgia are Eastern Orthodox Christians, although their co-nationals in North Ossetia are mainly Sunni Muslims. There are also other Christian groups, and a small number of adherents of the Jewish faith (both European and Georgian Jews). The national flag (proportions 3 by 5) consists of a field of cornelian red, with a canton, divided into two equal horizontal stripes of black over white, in the upper hoist. The capital is Tbilisi.

Recent History

A powerful kingdom in medieval times, Georgia subsequently came under periods of foreign domination, and was annexed by the Russian Empire from the 19th century, until its collapse in 1917. An independent Georgian state was established on 26 May 1918; ruled by a Menshevik Socialist Government, it received recognition from the Bolshevik Government of Soviet Russia by treaty in May 1920. However, Georgia was invaded by Bolshevik troops in early 1921, and a Georgian Soviet Socialist Republic (SSR) was proclaimed on 25 February. In December 1922 it was absorbed into the Transcaucasian Soviet Federative Socialist Republic (TSFSR), which, on 22 December, became a founder member of the USSR. The Georgian SSR became a full union republic in 1936, when the TSFSR was disbanded.

During the 1930s Georgians suffered persecution under the Soviet leader, Stalin (Iosif V. Dzugashvili), himself an ethnic Georgian. The first victims had been opponents of Stalin during his time as a revolutionary leader in Georgia, but later the persecution became more indiscriminate. Most members of the Georgian leadership were dismissed after Stalin's death in 1953. There was a further purge in 1972, when Eduard Shevardnadze became First Secretary of the Communist Party of Georgia (CPG) and attempted to remove officials who had been accused of corruption. Despite Soviet policy, Georgians retained a strong national identity. Opposition to a perceived policy of 'russification' was demonstrated in 1956, when anti-Russian riots were suppressed by security forces, and in 1978, when there were mass protests against the weakened status of the Georgian language in the new Constitution. Shevardnadze remained leader of the CPG until July 1985, when he became Minister of Foreign Affairs in the Government of the USSR.

The increased freedom of expression that followed the election of Mikhail Gorbachev as the Soviet leader in 1985 allowed the formation of unofficial groups, which campaigned on linguistic, environmental and ethnic issues. Such groups were prominent in organizing demonstrations in November 1988 against russification in Georgia. In February 1989 Abkhazians renewed a campaign, begun in the 1970s, for secession of their autonomous republic (in north-western Georgia) from the Georgian SSR (see below). Counter-demonstrations were staged in the capital, Tbilisi, by Georgians demanding that Georgia's territorial integrity be preserved. On the night of 8–9 April 1989 Soviet security forces attacked demonstrators in Tbilisi, who were demanding that Abkhazia remain within the republic and advocating the restoration of Georgian independence, killing 16 people and injuring many more. Despite the subsequent resignation of state and party officials (including the First Secretary of the CPG, Dzhumber Patiashvili) and the announcement of an official investigation into the deaths, anti-Soviet sentiment and inter-ethnic conflict increased sharply in the republic. Public outrage over the killings and the increasing influence of unofficial groups forced the CPG to adapt its policies to retain some measure of popular support. In November the Georgian Supreme Soviet (legislature), which was dominated by CPG members, declared the supremacy of Georgian laws over all-Union (USSR) laws. In February 1990 the same body declared Georgia 'an annexed and occupied country', and in the following month the Georgian Constitution was amended, removing the CPG's monopoly on power. Pressure from newly established opposition parties forced the elections to the Georgian Supreme Soviet, which were scheduled for 25 March, to be postponed to allow a more liberal election law to be drafted. Legislation permitting full multi-party elections was finally adopted in August.

Attempts to create a united front for the independence movement were unsuccessful. In early 1990, however, many of the principal political parties united in the Round Table–Free Georgia coalition. This and other leading parties aimed to achieve independence by parliamentary means and were willing, in the mean time, to participate in elections to Soviet institutions such as the Georgian Supreme Soviet. Many of the more radical parties, however, united in the National Forum, headed by Giorgi Chanturia, which announced its intention to boycott the elections to the Supreme Soviet and, instead, elect a rival parliament, the National Congress. The announcement of elections to the Congress, to be held on 30 September (thus pre-empting the elections to the Supreme Soviet, scheduled for late October), caused increased tension. However, although the elections to the National Congress took place as scheduled, only 51% of the electorate participated, and many parties did not present candidates.

In the elections to the Supreme Soviet, held on 28 October and 11 November 1990, the Round Table–Free Georgia coalition, led by Zviad Gamsakhurdia, won 155 seats in the 250-seat chamber, and 64% of the votes cast. All 14 of the political parties and coalitions involved in the election campaign, including the CPG, were united in seeking Georgia's independence. The CPG won only 64 seats, while the remainder were won by the Georgian Popular Front (GPF), smaller coalitions and independents. The elections were boycotted by many non-ethnic Georgians, since parties limited to one area of the country were prevented from participating.

The new Supreme Soviet convened for the first time on 14 November 1990 and elected Gamsakhurdia as its Chairman. Two symbolic gestures of independence were adopted: the territory was, henceforth, to be called the Republic of Georgia and the white, black and cornelian-coloured flag of independent Georgia was officially adopted. Tengiz Sigua, also a member of the Round Table–Free Georgia coalition, was appointed Chairman of the Council of Ministers. The new Supreme Soviet adopted several controversial laws at its first session, declaring illegal the conscription of Georgians into the Soviet armed forces. Many young men were reported to have joined nationalist paramilitary groups or were ready to join the National Guard (a *de facto* republican army), which the Supreme Soviet established in January 1991.

The Georgian authorities officially boycotted the all-Union referendum on the future of the USSR, held in nine other Soviet republics, in March 1991, but polling stations were opened in the autonomous territories of South Ossetia and Abkhazia, and in local military barracks. In South Ossetia 43,950 people took part in the referendum; of these, only nine voted against the preservation of the USSR. In Abkhazia almost the entire non-Georgian population voted to preserve the Union. The Georgian leadership refused to participate in the negotiations on a new union treaty. Instead, on 31 March the Government conducted a referendum asking whether 'independence should be restored

on the basis of the act of independence of 26 May 1918'. Of those eligible to vote, 95% participated in the referendum, 93% of whom voted for independence. On 9 April 1991 the Georgian Supreme Soviet approved a decree formally restoring Georgia's independence. Georgia thus became the first republic to secede from the USSR. Direct elections to the newly established post of executive President, held in May, were won by Gamsakhurdia, who received 86.5% of the votes cast. Voting did not take place in South Ossetia or Abkhazia.

Although Gamsakhurdia received a high level of popular support, there was considerable opposition from other politicians to what was perceived as an authoritarian style of rule. His actions during the failed Soviet coup of August 1991 were also strongly criticized, and he initially refrained from publicly condemning the coup leaders. After the coup had collapsed, Gamsakhurdia's position became tenuous. Tengiz Kitovani, the leader of the National Guard (who had been dismissed by Gamsakhurdia on 19 August, when the Soviet coup attempt began), announced that 15,000 of his men had remained loyal to him and were no longer subordinate to the President. Kitovani was joined in opposition to Gamsakhurdia by Sigua, who had resigned as Chairman of the Council of Ministers in mid-August. In September 30 opposition parties united to demand the resignation of Gamsakhurdia and organized a series of anti-Government demonstrations. When opposition supporters occupied the television station in Tbilisi, several people were killed in clashes between Kitovani's troops and those forces loyal to Gamsakhurdia.

Throughout October 1991 demonstrations continued, but the strength of Gamsakhurdia's support among the rural and working-class population, his arrests of prominent opposition leaders and imposition of a state of emergency in Tbilisi, and his effective monopoly of the republican media all weakened the position of the opposition. In December armed conflict broke out, as the opposition resorted to force to oust the President. Kitovani and Jaba Ioseliani, the leader of the paramilitary *Mkhedrioni* (Horsemen) group were joined by other opposition figures and increasing numbers of former Gamsakhurdia supporters. The fighting was mostly confined to central Tbilisi, around the parliament buildings, where Gamsakhurdia was besieged. More than 100 people were believed to have been killed. Gamsakhurdia and some of his supporters fled Georgia on 6 January 1992 (eventually taking refuge in southern Russia). A few days previously the opposition had declared Gamsakhurdia deposed and formed a Military Council, led by Kitovani and Ioseliani, which appointed Tengiz Sigua as acting Chairman of the Council of Ministers. The office of President was abolished, and the functions of Head of State were to be exercised by the Chairman of the Supreme Soviet.

In mid-January 1992 Sigua began the formation of a new Government. An Interim Consultative Council, comprising representatives of all the major political groups (with the exception of the CPG, which had been disbanded in August 1991), was established, in an attempt to create stability. In early March 1992 Eduard Shevardnadze returned to Georgia, and a State Council was created to replace the Military Council in legislative and executive matters. The State Council, of which Shevardnadze was designated Chairman, comprised 50 members, drawn from all the major political organizations, and included Sigua, Ioseliani and Kitovani. Shevardnadze succeeded in reconciling the various factions of the State Council, as well as the leaders of the two principal military bodies, the National Guard and the *Mkhedrioni*. The loyalty of these forces was essential to Shevardnadze in suppressing repeated attempts by Gamsakhurdia and his supporters in early 1992 to re-establish control. Further civil unrest ensued, especially in the western strongholds (including Abkhazia) of Gamsakhurdia's supporters (or 'Zviadists'), and curfews were imposed in Tbilisi and other towns. By April government troops had re-established control in the rebellious areas. In July, however, one of Georgia's deputy premiers was taken hostage by 'Zviadists' in western Georgia. This was followed by the kidnapping of Roman Gventsadze, the Minister of Internal Affairs, and several other officials. In response, the State Council dispatched more than 3,000 National Guardsmen to Abkhazia, where the hostages were believed to be held, prompting armed resistance by Abkhazian militia. In mid-August three of the hostages, including Gventsadze, were released.

An election to the Supreme Council (as the Supreme Soviet was now known) was held on 11 October 1992, amid intensified hostilities in Abkhazia and the threat of disruptive actions by the 'Zviadists'. In the event, however, the election was conducted peacefully, although it was boycotted in South Ossetia, Mengrelia and parts of Abkhazia. An estimated 75% of the total electorate participated. Of the more than 30 parties and alliances contesting the election, none succeeded in gaining a significant representation in the 235-seat legislature. The largest number of seats (just 29) was won by the centrist Peace bloc, which mainly comprised former communists and intellectuals. Of greater consequence, however, was the direct election of the legislature's Chairman—effectively a presidential role—which was held simultaneously. Shevardnadze was the sole candidate for the post, winning more than 95% of the total votes cast, thus obtaining the legitimate popular mandate that he had hitherto lacked.

The Supreme Council convened for the first time in early November 1992 and adopted a decree on state power, whereby supreme executive authority was vested in Shevardnadze as the Council's Chairman (or Head of State), in conjunction with the Council of Ministers, while the Supreme Council remained the highest legislative body. Shevardnadze was also elected Commander-in-Chief of the Georgian armed forces and Sigua was re-elected Chairman of the Council of Ministers. One of the principal aims of the new Government was to create a unified army; an 11-member National Security and Defence Council was established for this purpose in early 1993. A comprehensive programme of economic reform was also initiated.

Almost immediately, Shevardnadze was confronted by opposition from within his own administration. In response to rumours that Kitovani was plotting to overthrow him, Shevardnadze suspended the National Security and Defence Council in May 1993, also dismissing Kitovani from his post as Minister of Defence. In August the entire Council of Ministers tendered its resignation, following the legislature's rejection of the proposed budget. In the following month Shevardnadze appointed a new Council of Ministers, which was headed by Otar Patsatsia, a former CPG official. Shevardnadze himself tendered his resignation as Head of State in mid-September, in response to accusations of dictatorial methods. However, crowds blockaded the parliament building, demanding his reinstatement, and the Supreme Council rejected Shevardnadze's resignation.

By late September 1993 Georgia appeared ungovernable: confronted by the growing political and economic crisis and military defeat in Abkhazia (see below), Shevardnadze's position was made more precarious by the reappearance of Gamsakhurdia and the 'Zviadists' in western Georgia. In early October the former President's forces captured the Black Sea port of Poti as well as the strategic town of Samtredia, blocking all rail traffic to Tbilisi. As the rebel forces advanced eastwards, Shevardnadze persuaded the Supreme Council to agree to Georgia's immediate membership of the Commonwealth of Independent States (CIS, see p. 172), established in December 1991 by 11 former Soviet republics. In late October 1993 Russian troops were dispatched to Georgia, and by early November the 'Zviadists' had been entirely routed from the republic. In early January 1994 it was reported that Gamsakhurdia had committed suicide, after having been surrounded by government troops in western Georgia.

Georgia's formal admittance to the CIS was delayed until early December 1993, when all of the member states finally granted their approval. Despite the restoration of some measure of stability in the republic, in November Shevardnadze extended the state of emergency (which had been declared in September) until early 1994. Shevardnadze also created his own party, the Citizens' Union of Georgia (CUG), from several existing parties. In February 1994 the *Mkhedrioni* group was transformed into a 'Rescue Corps', as part of the continuing process of creating a unified army.

Throughout 1994 Shevardnadze sought to curb the increasing level of organized crime in the republic; however, assassinations and other acts of political violence remained widespread, as rival paramilitary groups—often based on regional affiliations or loyalty to certain powerful figures—competed for influence. Shevardnadze's own administration was undermined by clan-based rivalries. Popular opposition to the regime escalated, and regular demonstrations against Shevardnadze were held. New opposition parties emerged: a National Liberation Front (NLF) was established by Sigua and Kitovani with the declared aim of restoring Georgia's territorial integrity (i.e. regaining Abkhazia); in June several small parties claiming to be successors to the CPG merged as the United Communist Party of Georgia

(UCPG). Nevertheless, in May more than 30 political and public organizations, including leading opposition parties (such as the GPF and Giorgi Chanturia's National Democratic Party of Georgia—NDPG) signed a declaration 'of national unity and accord' in an attempt to bring stability to Georgian politics. In December, however, the wave of political violence culminated in the assassination of Chanturia. In January 1995 Kitovani led an armed convoy of some 350 NLF supporters towards Abkhazia in an apparent attempt to 'liberate' the region. The convoy was halted and disarmed by government security forces; Kitovani was arrested and the NLF was banned. Attempts to curtail the criminal activities of the numerous politico-military groups operating in Georgia culminated in May, when the leading such group, Ioseliani's Rescue Corps, was ordered to surrender its arms.

In August 1995 the Supreme Council adopted Georgia's new Constitution, which had been prepared by a special constitutional commission. The document provided for a strong executive presidency and a 235-member unicameral Georgian Parliament. The Government was to be directly subordinate to the President, to whom it would act as an advisory body. The post of Prime Minister was abolished; the most senior position in the Government was henceforth to be that of the Minister of State, who was to co-ordinate the ministers' work and liaise with the President. The country (the official title of which was changed from the Republic of Georgia to Georgia) was described as 'united and undivided'; however, the territorial status of Abkhazia and South Ossetia was not defined. It was stated that, following the eventual conclusion of political settlements in those regions, the Georgian Parliament would be transformed into a bicameral body (comprising a Council of the Republic and a Senate, the latter representing the various territorial units of Georgia).

The Constitution was due to be signed at an official ceremony on 29 August 1995, but the signing was postponed until 17 October, following an assassination attempt on Shevardnadze. Igor Giorgadze, the Minister of State Security, was subsequently named by state prosecutors as the chief instigator of the plot, along with his deputy and a leading member of the Rescue Corps. The three men consequently fled abroad, and Shevardnadze announced the complete disbandment of the Rescue Corps.

A direct election to the restored post of President of Georgia was held on 5 November 1995, in which Shevardnadze won almost 75% of the votes cast. His closest rival (with only 19%) was Dzhumber Patiashvili. The election of the new Georgian Parliament was held simultaneously with the presidential election. A mixed system of voting was employed: 150 seats were to be filled by proportional representation, while the remaining 85 deputies were to be elected by majority vote in single-member constituencies. The election was boycotted in Abkhazia and in parts of South Ossetia. Only three parties contesting the 150 proportional seats succeeded in obtaining the 5% of the votes necessary for representation in the Parliament. Of these, Shevardnadze's CUG won the largest number of seats (90), followed by the NDPG (31) and the All-Georgian Union of Revival, chaired by Aslan Abashidze, the regional leader of Ajaria (25 seats). Only about one-half of the single-mandate seats were filled; however, following a further two rounds of voting, all 85 deputies were elected. This gave a total of 231 parliamentarians (representing 11 parties); the CUG held a total of 107 seats, but it was supported by many of the other parties that obtained representation. Approximately 64% of the registered electorate was believed to have participated in the legislative election.

The Georgian Parliament convened for the first time in late November 1995 and elected as its Chairman (Speaker) Zurab Zhvania, General Secretary of the CUG and a close associate of Shevardnadze. In early December Shevardnadze appointed Nikoloz Lekishvili, formerly Mayor of Tbilisi, as Minister of State. The remaining members of the Government were appointed later in the month. In January 1996, in accordance with the Constitution, a National Security Council was established as a consultative body dealing with issues relating to defence and security and the elimination of terrorism and corruption.

Meanwhile, in late 1995 criminal proceedings commenced in Tbilisi against Kitovani, in connection with the NLF's attempted raid on Abkhazia in early 1995 (see above). In May 1996 Ioseliani, the former leader of the *Mkhedrioni*, was convicted of complicity in the assassination attempt against Shevardnadze in August 1995 (he was released under a presidential amnesty in April 2000 and died in March 2003). In June 1996

supporters of former President Gamsakhurdia received lengthy prison sentences for their role in the civil war of 1993. Kitovani was convicted on charges of establishing an illegal armed formation in September 1996 and was sentenced to eight years' imprisonment. (He was released by presidential decree in May 1999.)

In July 1997 the Minister of State Security resigned, after the Ministry was discovered to have authorized the monitoring of journalists' telephone calls. Documentary evidence of corruption within the Ministries of Defence and of the Interior was also discovered, and a review of the state security system was announced. A Civil Code, second in importance only to the Constitution, was adopted in June, and capital punishment was formally abolished.

On 9 February 1998 President Shevardnadze survived a second attempt on his life. Investigations into the assassination attempt, which reportedly involved 20 'Zviadists', were completed in December, although the results were not made public. In March Guram Absandze, Minister of Finance under the Gamsakhurdia administration, was arrested in the Russian capital, Moscow, and returned to Georgia for trial. Absandze managed to escape from a maximum security prison in Tbilisi in October 1999, but he was recaptured, and subsequently sentenced to 17 years' imprisonment in August 2001 (although he was later pardoned). Further arrests were made in May 1999, following the discovery of a new plot to overthrow Shevardnadze. All those arrested were reported to have links with Igor Giorgadze, and the group included both existing and former state officials; one of the accused died in detention, and 10 others were sentenced to terms of imprisonment in November 2001.

Meanwhile, on 19 February 1998 four observers from the UN Observer Mission in Georgia (UNOMIG, see below) were briefly taken hostage in the western town of Zugdidi by Gamsakhurdia supporters. The leader of the kidnappers, Gocha Esebua (who was also suspected of involvement in the assassination attempt earlier in February), was killed in a gun battle with police in late March; there were violent scenes at his funeral, and five people were reportedly killed. In July most of the Government, including the Minister of State, Lekishvili, resigned, to permit the President to carry out a major ministerial reorganization. In the following month the former ambassador to Russia, Vazha Lortkipanidze, was appointed the new Minister of State. In October a two-day armed insurrection by rebel troops in western Georgia ended when the 'Zviadist' mutineers surrendered to government forces at Kutaisi. Following this incident and the subsequent escape of the rebel leaders, the Minister of State Security, Jemal Gakhokidze, resigned in late October.

In July 1999 Parliament approved a constitutional amendment, which increased the minimum requirement for parliamentary representation from 5% to 7% of the votes cast under the system of proportional representation. A number of blocs and alliances were formed following the announcement in August of a legislative election, to be held on 31 October. The most significant of these, chaired by Aslan Abashidze, was the Union for the Revival of Georgia, comprising the All-Georgian Union of Revival, the Socialist Party, the Union of Traditionalists, the People's Party and the 21st Century bloc. The election, held in two rounds, on 31 October and 14 November, was contested by 32 parties and blocs, with the participation of 68% of the electorate. Final results showed a resounding victory for the CUG, which obtained 130 seats (85 proportional and 45 constituency). The Union for the Revival of Georgia bloc and the Industry Will Save Georgia bloc secured 58 seats (51 proportional, 7 constituency) and 15 seats (14 proportional, 1 constituency), respectively. The mandate of the 12 Abkhazian deputies was extended. Despite opposition allegations of irregularities, observers from the Organization for Security and Co-operation in Europe (OSCE, see p. 283) declared the election lawful. The new Parliament re-elected Zhvania as Chairman. In late November Lortkipanidze was awarded presidential powers for the settlement of conflicts in Georgia. In the following month the responsibilities of the Minister of State were expanded further by the President, and Lortkipanidze was accorded powers similar to those of a prime minister.

In the presidential election of 9 April 2000, Shevardnadze demonstrated the strength of his position against the fragmented opposition, securing 79.8% of the votes cast, with only Dzhumber Patiashvili, the former First Secretary of the CPG, obtaining any other significant result, with 16.7% of the votes. The Ajarian leader, Aslan Abashidze, withdrew his candidacy just before the election. Electoral violations were noted by the

OSCE, but the Parliamentary Assembly of the Council of Europe, see p. 181 and the Central Election Committee reported no major infringements of voting procedure. On 11 May the Georgian Parliament endorsed the appointment of Gia Arsenishvili as the new Minister of State, and the cabinet was approved three days later.

In September 2001 Shevardnadze announced his resignation from the chairmanship of the CUG, in compliance with demands from both the opposition and from within the party; Shevardnadze had confirmed in the previous month that he would not seek to amend the Constitution to remove the stipulation preventing him from standing for a third presidential term in 2005. At the end of October 2001 public discontent cumulated in large-scale protests in Tbilisi, after Rustavi 2, an independent television station that had been critical of the Government, was raided by security officials during a live broadcast, in what was widely interpreted as an attack on media freedom. Suspicions of state interference in the actions of the media had already been roused, following the murder, in July, of a journalist for the station, who had been carrying out an investigation into official corruption. Zurab Zhvania, the parliamentary Chairman, urged both the Minister of State Security, Vakhtang Kutateladze, and the Minister of Internal Affairs, Kakha Targamadze, to resign, in order to avert further protests. However, the latter refused to comply with Zhvania's request, and the popular protests intensified, with demands for further resignations, including that of Shevardnadze. Consequently, on 1 November Shevardnadze announced the dismissal of the entire Government. The Procurator-General, Gia Meparishvili, subsequently resigned from his post, as did Zhvania, who stated that Shevardnadze no longer understood the needs of the public; he was replaced by Nino Burdzhanadze. A new Government was approved by Parliament in two stages, on 21 November and 5 December; Valerian Khaburdzhania was appointed as Minister of State Security and Koba Narchemashvili as Minister of Internal Affairs. In mid-December there were opposition protests over the appointment by the new Procurator-General, Nugzar Gabrichidze, of Burdzhanadze's husband, Badri Bitsadze, as his deputy; there were concerns that the appointment would obscure the distinction between the executive and legislative branches of government. On 21 December Avtandil Dzhorbenadze was appointed as Minister of State; he was succeeded as Minister of Labour, Health and Social Welfare by Amiran Gamkrelidze. In February 2002 Nugzar Sadzhaya, the Secretary of the National Security Council, died from apparently self-inflicted gun-shot wounds, one week after allegations emerged of his involvement in politically motivated assassinations; he was replaced by Tedo Japaridze.

In May 2002 the Minister of Finance, Zurab Nogaideli, and the Minister of Tax Revenue, Levan Dzneladze, were dismissed, after reportedly failing to meet budgetary targets. The Ministry of Tax Revenue was subsequently merged with the Ministry of Finance, headed by Mirian Gogiashvili. Meanwhile, following divisions within the CUG, in late May the Supreme Court ruled that the faction of the CUG that continued to support President Shevardnadze was the legitimate grouping, rather than an opposing 'reformist' faction, which had been established by Zhvania; in June Zhvania founded a new political party, the United Democrats. In early June municipal elections took place. The CUG suffered a serious reverse, failing to win any seats on Tbilisi City Council, and the New Rights Party, another party composed of disenchanted CUG members, won the largest number of seats nation-wide. In late June Dzhorbenadze was elected as the new Chairman of the CUG, although Shevardnadze retained an honorary role. The party was to be restructured, in advance of parliamentary elections, due to be held in late 2003. In late October 2002 the Minister of Construction and Urban Planning, Merab Adeishvili, was dismissed; he was replaced by Giorgi Isakadze. Also in late October the founding congress of a new opposition party took place. The party, the Union of National Concord and Justice, was led by Guram Absandze.

Meanwhile, a series of high-profile kidnappings took place in 2002–03, raising fears of increasing lawlessness. Notably, in early November 2002 a British banker, who had been taken hostage by armed men, disguised as police officers, near his home in Tbilisi, was released following a rescue operation, after being held captive in the Pankisi Gorge region for over four months. In December the father of a vice-president of the Russian petroleum company LUKoil was discovered dead, following his abduction 10 days earlier; three people were sub-

sequently arrested. In late March 2003 Zaza Dzhikia, a businessman and the son of the Governor of Samegrelo-Zemo Svaneti Oblast, Bondo Dzhikia, was released, having been taken hostage in Tbilisi five days previously.

Following his return to Georgia in March 1992, Shevardnadze struggled to resolve the inter-ethnic tensions in Georgia's autonomous territories, which had intensified following the election of Gamsakhurdia's nationalist Government in 1990, and which led to serious armed conflict in South Ossetia and Abkhazia. Ossetia, the original inhabitants of which are an East Iranian people, was divided into two parts under Stalin, North Ossetia falling under Russian jurisdiction and South Ossetia becoming an autonomous region of Georgia. At the census of 1979 ethnic Ossetians comprised 66% of the region's population. The long-standing Georgian animosity towards the Ossetians stems not only from ethnic differences, but also from the Ossetians' traditional pro-Russian stance. The current dispute began in 1989, when Ossetian demands for greater autonomy and eventual reunification with North Ossetia (which would entail secession from Georgia and integration into Russia) led to violent clashes between local Georgians and Ossetians. Troops of the Soviet Ministry of Internal Affairs were dispatched to South Ossetia in January 1990, but in September the South Ossetian Supreme Soviet (legislature) proclaimed South Ossetia's independence and state sovereignty within the USSR. This decision was declared unconstitutional by the Georgian Supreme Soviet, which in December formally abolished the region's autonomous status. Following renewed violence, the Georgian legislature declared a state of emergency in Tskhinvali, the South Ossetian capital.

In January 1991 Soviet President Gorbachev annulled both South Ossetia's declaration of independence and the Georgian Supreme Soviet's decision of December 1990. However, violence continued throughout 1991, with the resulting displacement of many thousands of refugees. There was a series of cease-fires, all of which were almost immediately violated. In December the South Ossetian Supreme Soviet declared both a state of emergency and a general mobilization, in response to the Georgian Government's dispatch of troops to the region. In the same month the South Ossetian legislature adopted a second declaration of the region's independence, as well as a resolution in favour of its integration into Russia. The resolutions were endorsed by South Ossetians at a referendum held in January 1992. While denouncing these developments, the new administration in Tbilisi (the Military Council) none the less declared its willingness to discuss the issue. However, hostilities continued between the rival factions, compounded by the intervention of Georgian government troops (which, by April, were attacking Tskhinvali). The situation was further complicated by the arrival of volunteer fighters from North Ossetia, in support of their South Ossetian neighbours.

In late June 1992 negotiations between Shevardnadze and President Yeltsin of Russia led to an agreement to secure a lasting cease-fire and a peaceful solution to the conflict (in which more than 400 Georgians and 1,000 Ossetians had been killed since 1989). Peace-keeping monitors (comprising Georgians, Ossetians and Russians) were deployed in South Ossetia during July, with the simultaneous withdrawal of all armed forces from the region. The return of refugees began in that month. However, although the cease-fire remained in force, no political settlement to the conflict was reached, and South Ossetia remained effectively a seceded territory; on 23 December 1993 it introduced a new Constitution. The lack of a formal settlement delayed the repatriation of refugees: in early 1994 some 11,000 South Ossetians remained in North Ossetia, while some 7,000 ethnic Georgians had yet to return to their homes. In July 1995 representatives from Georgia, Russia, North Ossetia and South Ossetia reopened talks on a political settlement, under the aegis of the OSCE. The South Ossetian leadership demanded recognition of the region's independence, rejecting proposals to grant South Ossetia the status of an autonomous republic within Georgia. However, significant progress was achieved in April 1996, when a memorandum 'on strengthening mutual trust and security measures' was initialled in Tskhinvali; it was signed in Moscow in the following month. Meetings were subsequently held between President Shevardnadze and Ludvig Chibirov, the Chairman of the South Ossetian legislature, to negotiate South Ossetia's political status. In September, however, the legislature of the separatist region approved an amendment to its Constitution to allow the introduction of a presidential government. Despite the Georgian leadership's declaration that the results of any election would be considered illegitimate, an election to the post of President of South Ossetia was held on 10 November, and was won by Chibirov.

Quadripartite negotiations were held at intervals throughout 1997, at which it was agreed that the policing role of peace-keeping forces deployed in South Ossetia was to be transferred to regional law-enforcement bodies. Talks held in Moscow in March confirmed the principle of Georgia's territorial integrity, while allowing a measure of self-determination for South Ossetia. In September, at a meeting between Shevardnadze and Chibirov, an agreement was signed on the return of refugees to South Ossetia, described as the main concern of the two sides. Legislative elections took place in South Ossetia in May 1999; the Communist Party secured about 39% of the votes cast. The elections were not recognized by the OSCE or by the Georgian authorities, who refused to fill the four seats (of 33) reserved for ethnic Georgian deputies. In April 2001 a referendum was held in South Ossetia, at which 69% of those who participated voted in favour of adopting amendments to the 1993 Constitution, which included the designation of both Georgian and Russian as official languages, in addition to Ossetian. The plebiscite was not recognized as legal by the Georgian Government, and it was boycotted by South Ossetia's ethnic Georgian population. In a presidential election held in South Ossetia in November–December 2001 a Russian-based businessman, Eduard Kokoyev, emerged as the victor, after a second round of voting, in which he secured 55% of the votes cast. Although Kokoyev declared himself to be willing to resume talks with the Georgian Government, he also expressed an interest in developing closer ties with Russia, particularly with North Ossetia. Kokeyev was inaugurated as the region's President on 18 December. In December 2002 Kokeyev took part in negotiations with Shevardnadze's special envoy for the conflict in South Ossetia, Vakhtang Rcheulishvili, although no formal agreement was reported.

The cease-fire that was declared in South Ossetia in mid-1992 coincided with a resurgence of violence in the Autonomous Republic of Abkhazia. As in South Ossetia, a movement for Abkhazian secession from Georgia had been revived in 1989. Abkhazians are a predominantly Muslim people and their region had enjoyed virtual sovereignty within Georgia during the 1920s. However, in 1930 Abkhazia was made an autonomous republic and, on Stalin's orders, large numbers of western Georgians were resettled in the region. As a result, by 1989 ethnic Abkhazians comprised only 18% of the area's population, and Georgians constituted the largest ethnic group (46%). The Georgian Government repeatedly rejected Abkhazian secessionist demands on these demographic grounds. The movement for Abkhazian independence was also fiercely resisted by the local Georgian population. In July 1989 there were violent clashes between ethnic Georgians and Abkhazians in Sukhumi, the republic's capital, resulting in 14 deaths. A state of emergency was imposed throughout Abkhazia, but troops did not succeed in preventing further inter-ethnic violence.

In August 1990 the Abkhazian Supreme Soviet voted to declare independence from Georgia. This declaration was pronounced invalid by the Georgian Supreme Soviet, and Georgians living in Abkhazia staged protests and began a rail blockade of Sukhumi. In late August Georgian deputies in the Abkhazian legislature succeeded in reversing the declaration of independence. Inter-ethnic unrest continued during late 1990 and in 1991. Following the overthrow of Zviad Gamsakhurdia, in January 1992, there was renewed unrest in Abkhazia, as large numbers of ethnic Georgians demonstrated in support of the former President. In July the Abkhazian legislature declared Abkhazia's sovereignty as the 'Republic of Abkhazia'.

A period of violent armed conflict began in August 1992, when the Georgian Government dispatched some 3,000 members of the National Guard to the secessionist republic. It was claimed that the troops had been sent to release senior officials who had been taken hostage by the 'Zviadists' and who were allegedly being held in Abkhazia (see above), but the covert reason for their deployment, it was believed, was to suppress the growing secessionist movement. Abkhazian militia launched a series of attacks against the Georgian troops, but failed to retain control of Sukhumi. The Chairman of the Abkhazian legislature and leader of the independence campaign, Vladislav Ardzinba, retreated north with his forces, establishing his base at Gudauta. The situation was complicated by the dispatch of Russian paratroopers to the region to protect Russian military bases.

Relations between Georgia and Russia became strained, following Georgian accusations that conservative elements within the Russian leadership and armed forces were supplying military equipment and personnel to Abkhazia. In October 1992 the Abkhazians launched a successful counter-offensive, regaining control of all of northern Abkhazia, and reportedly killing hundreds of its ethnic Georgian inhabitants; hostilities intensified in the first half of 1993. Peace talks were held at regular intervals, finally culminating in the signing of a provisional peace agreement, in July, by Georgian and Abkhazian leaders. The cease-fire held (albeit with minor violations) until mid-September, when the Abkhazians launched surprise attacks in parts of the region, capturing Sukhumi after 11 days of intense fighting. Shevardnadze, who had arrived in Sukhumi at the start of the offensive, was forced to flee by air, under heavy bombardment. By late September almost all Georgian forces had been expelled from Abkhazia, and the region was declared 'liberated'.

Several hundred people were believed to have been killed during the fighting, and more than 200,000 people fled Abkhazia. Many thousands of the refugees were subsequently stranded, in freezing conditions, in the mountainous border region separating Abkhazia and Georgia, where large numbers perished. The situation in Abkhazia following the rout of the Georgian forces was reported to be close to anarchy, with atrocities allegedly being perpetrated against remaining ethnic Georgians and other nationalities by Abkhazians. Nevertheless, in early December 1993 Georgian and Abkhazian officials signed an eight-point 'memorandum of understanding' at UN-sponsored talks in Geneva, Switzerland. A small number of UN military personnel, part of UNOMIG (see p. 67) were subsequently dispatched to Sukhumi in a peace-keeping capacity.

Outbreaks of violence continued in Abkhazia throughout 1994, despite the holding of peace talks (under UN and other auspices) at regular intervals. The fundamental disagreement between the Georgian and Abkhazian delegations concerned the future status of Abkhazia: Ardzinba demanded full independence (or confederal ties at the least) for Abkhazia, while the Georgian Government insisted on the preservation of Georgia's territorial integrity. However, hope for a peaceful solution was raised in May, by the declaration of a full cease-fire (only statements or memorandums had been issued up to this point). Under the accord, a contingent of some 2,500 CIS (mainly Russian) peace-keepers were deployed in June, joining the (augmented) UN observer force in Abkhazia. Nevertheless, the peace-keeping presence was unable to prevent renewed hostilities.

In November 1994 the Abkhazian legislature adopted a new Constitution, which declared the 'Republic of Abkhazia' to be a sovereign state. Ardzinba was elected to the new post of 'President'. The declaration of sovereignty was condemned by the Georgian Government, and the peace negotiations were subsequently suspended. Protests were also voiced by the USA, Russia and the UN Security Council, all of which reaffirmed their recognition of Georgia's territorial integrity. Peace talks were resumed in 1995, despite periodic outbreaks of violence in Abkhazia. In January 1996, at a summit meeting of CIS leaders in Moscow, it was agreed to implement Shevardnadze's request for economic sanctions to be imposed against Abkhazia until it consented to rejoin Georgia.

On 23 November 1996 an election to the secessionist Abkhazian legislature, the People's Assembly, was held. The UN and the OSCE severely criticized the holding of the election, and the Georgian authorities declared the election results to be invalid. President Shevardnadze organized a simultaneous plebiscite among refugees from Abkhazia; voters were asked whether they supported the holding of a parliamentary election in Abkhazia prior to the restoration of Georgia's territorial integrity and the repatriation of refugees, and it was reported that some 99% of refugees had taken part, of whom almost all had voted against the holding of the election.

The mandate of the CIS peace-keeping forces in Abkhazia was the focus of much controversy in 1997. Members of the Abkhazian faction in the Georgian Parliament staged a hunger strike in March, demanding the withdrawal of the CIS peace-keepers. None the less, at the CIS summit meeting later in that month the peace-keepers' mandate was extended. Violent clashes took place in the Kodori Gorge region of Abkhazia in July 1997. Peace talks sponsored by the UN were subsequently held in Geneva, but no formal conclusion was reached. The UN observers' mandate, which expired on 31 July, was renewed for a further six months, and was subsequently granted successive six-monthly extensions. Russian proposals for a settlement of the conflict, which provided for substantial autonomy for Abkhazia, while retaining Georgia's territorial integrity, were welcomed by Shevardnadze, but rejected by Ardzinba, who continued to demand equal status for Abkhazia within a confederation. In August 1997, for the first time since 1992, Ardzinba visited Georgia, together with the Russian Minister of Foreign Affairs, Yevgenii Primakov. Talks were held with Shevardnadze and a reaffirmation of both sides' commitment to a peaceful resolution of the conflict was made. Further talks were held in the following month.

At the CIS summit meeting held in October 1997, the mandate of the CIS peace-keepers was extended until 31 January 1998. Shevardnadze, although welcoming the decision, criticized the peace-keepers' failure to create the conditions necessary for the safe return of ethnic Georgian refugees. The refugees, and the Tbilisi-based official leadership of Abkhazia, continued to demand the withdrawal of the Russian-led forces, fearing an escalation of Russian military intervention in the republic. A partial lifting by Russia of the economic sanctions against Abkhazia was condemned by Shevardnadze. UN-sponsored talks were convened in mid-November 1997, at which it was agreed to establish a joint Co-ordinating Council, with the task of incorporating working groups to resolve the three main issues: a cessation of armed hostilities, the repatriation of refugees and the settlement of economic and social issues. Representatives of the parties to the conflict, as well as Russian, UN and European Union (EU, see p. 199) delegates were to participate in the council.

In March 1998 the Georgian Parliament declared the forthcoming local elections in Abkhazia invalid. In May tension escalated when there was a renewal of hostilities, following a move by Abkhazian troops to enter the neutral zone separating Abkhazia from Georgia, in order to force ethnic Georgians out of the district of Gali. The Georgian forces were put on full combat alert, and tens of thousands of ethnic Georgian refugees fled into Georgia. Following emergency peace talks, a cease-fire was agreed and came into force on 26 May. UN observers reported the following day that hostilities had ceased and Ardzinba imposed a three-month state of emergency in the area (which was extended in August). Peace negotiations were resumed in June; Georgia's key demand was the prompt and unconditional repatriation to Gali of some 35,000 ethnic Georgians who had been forced to flee the city by Abkhazian troops.

In September 1998 four observers from UNOMIG were injured when their vehicle was attacked by gunmen in Sukhumi. Abkhazia and Georgia blamed each other for the attack, and Ardzinba imposed a curfew on the region. Ensuing peace talks proved unsuccessful and hostilities continued. In January 1999, however, Ardzinba agreed to permit ethnic Georgian refugees to return to Gali from 1 March. Their return was hindered by a blockade of the road bridge connecting Georgia with Abkhazia, which had begun in mid-February, by refugees demanding, *inter alia*, that Georgia leave the CIS and that persecution of ethnic Georgian guerrillas be stopped. The Russian peace-keeping forces and UNOMIG were not permitted to pass, thus thwarting scheduled quadripartite talks on Abkhazia, due to be held in Gali. The protest ended in mid-March. In August the National Security Council voted to extend the mandate of the CIS peace-keepers.

On 3 October 1999 Ardzinba, the sole candidate, was re-elected President with 99% of the votes cast; the rate of participation was 87.7%. The election was declared illegal by international observers. In a referendum held simultaneously, 97% of the votes cast upheld the 1994 Constitution, proclaiming the region as an independent, democratic republic. Shortly afterwards the Abkhazian legislature unanimously passed the State Independence Act. None the less, Georgia remained determined to pursue peace talks. In July 2000 a UN-sponsored protocol on stabilization measures was signed by both Abkhazia and Georgia. However, violent incidents continued. Most prominently, a number of UN military observers were kidnapped in both June and December, and in August the leader of the Abkhazian opposition and human-rights consultant to the UN, Zurab Achba, was assassinated.

In mid-March 2001, at a summit meeting held in Yalta, Ukraine, under UN auspices, Abkhazia and Georgia signed an accord renouncing the use of force. However, hostilities resumed in Abkhazia in early October, when a UN helicopter was shot down over the Kodori Gorge, killing all nine of its passengers,

including UNOMIG's Deputy Chief Military Observer. The UN mission was subsequently suspended, and violence in the region intensified. Abkhazian officials blamed the attack on allied pro-Georgian guerrillas and dissidents from the separatist Russian republic of Chechnya; they also claimed that Georgian forces had launched earlier attacks on both Abkhazian villages and the Russian-led peace-keeping forces, in an attempt to regain control of the Kodori region, although these allegations were strongly denied by the Georgian Government. The Abkhazian authorities blamed Georgia for subsequent aerial attacks on villages in the Gorge; Georgia, in turn, attributed responsibility for the attacks to Russia, and made repeated allegations of violations of Georgian airspace by Russian aircraft in October–November. The Georgian Government despatched troops to the region in mid-October, ostensibly to protect the ethnic Georgian population there, in what was deemed by the UN to be a violation of the cease-fire agreement of 1994. The Abkhazian authorities also interpreted the deployment of Georgian troops in the region as an act of aggression, and were reported to have appealed to Russia to help prevent full-scale civil conflict. Russia, which pledged a policy of non-interference in Georgia's internal affairs, was subsequently reported to have implemented strengthened security measures along the Georgian–Russian border. In mid-October 2001 the Georgian Parliament voted to request the immediate withdrawal of the CIS peace-keeping force from Abkhazia, stating that it had failed to fulfil its mandate; however, President Shevardnadze argued against its removal, as no substitute force was forthcoming. Meanwhile, following negotiations between the Georgian and Abkhazian authorities, a protocol was signed by both sides on 17 January 2002, according to which Georgia agreed to withdraw the troops deployed in the Kodori Gorge; the two sides signed a further protocol on 2 April, and on 11 April the Georgian Ministry of Defence announced that the withdrawal of its military forces had taken place as agreed. However, in the same month Abkhazia suspended its participation in the UN-sponsored Co-ordinating Council. Meanwhile, UNOMIG resumed its activities on 1 February 2002, and recommenced patrols of the Kodori Gorge, together with the Russian-led peace-keeping forces, in late March, following the extension of their mandate. At a CIS summit meeting, held in Almaty at the beginning of March, Shevardnadze and the Russian President, Vladimir Putin, agreed to amend the mandate of the CIS peace-keeping forces, to satisfy Georgian demands that they withdraw to a more northerly position, undertake policing duties and include forces from countries other than Russia. Legislative elections, postponed from November 2001, which were held in Abkhazia on 2 March 2002, were deemed to be illegal by the Georgian Government, and were not recognized as valid by international organizations including the UN and the OSCE. The Abkhazian *de facto* premier, Anri Dzhergenia, was dismissed in December, and Gennadii Gagulia was appointed as his replacement. In April 2003 a new premier, Raul Khadzhimba, was appointed.

On 29 July 2002 the UN Security Council had adopted Resolution 1427, which called for the resumption of negotiations on Abkhazia's status within Georgia; however, no progress was made during the remainder of 2002. In late January 2003 the National Security Council ruled that Georgia would not approve a renewal of the CIS peace-keepers' mandate (which had expired at the end of December 2002) until, *inter alia*, the definition of the conflict zone was extended and a recently resumed railway link from the Russian Black Sea port of Sochi to Tbilisi, via Sukhumi, was halted; the Government objected to the operation of the train service prior to the repatriation of refugees displaced from Abhkazia in 1992–93. In late January 2003, at a summit meeting of the CIS, Shevardnadze and Putin held talks on the CIS peace-keeping forces, and it was subsequently reported that Putin had capitulated to demands for the temporary suspension of the railway link. On 30 January the UN Security Council adopted Resolution 1462, which, while welcoming the reduction in tension in the Kodori region, expressed regret at the lack of progress in reaching a political settlement on the status of Abkhazia, and warned that should an agreement on the extension of the CIS peace-keepers' mandate not be reached, the mandate of the unarmed UN monitors in Abkhazia would be reviewed. In early February Georgian and Russian officials held further inconclusive negotiations on the renewal of the mandate of the CIS peace-keeping forces, and in mid-February the US State Department issued a statement recommending the extension of the peace-keepers' mandate. Finally, on 17 February the National Security Council agreed to remove all objections to its renewal. In early March Shevardnadze and Putin held talks in Sochi, at which Putin expressed his support for a number of proposals, which sought to help resolve the Abkhaz conflict. On 7 March the Presidents issued a joint statement, according to which they agreed to expedite the repatriation of displaced persons to Abkhazia, prior to the resumption of the Sochi–Sukhumi–Tbilisi railway service and the renovation of the Inguri hydroelectric plant. In addition, they agreed to extend indefinitely the mandate of the CIS peace-keeping forces, until either Georgia or Abkhazia explicitly demanded its withdrawal.

The Autonomous Republic of Ajaria proved to be the least troubled of Georgia's three autonomous territories. Despite being of ethnic Georgian origin, the Ajars, whose autonomous status was the result of a Soviet-Turkish Treaty of Friendship (1921), retained a sense of separate identity, owing to their adherence to Islam. In recent years some Christian Georgians have considered the Muslim Ajars a threat to a unified Georgian nation. Tensions between Muslims and Christians increased in 1991, after the Georgian Supreme Soviet ruled as unconstitutional a law relating to elections to the Ajar Supreme Soviet, which restricted nominations for the forthcoming election to permanent residents of Ajaria. In April there were prolonged demonstrations in protest against proposals to abolish Ajar autonomy and against perceived 'christianization' of the Muslim population. Ajaria remained calm from the latter half of 1991, in an otherwise volatile region. In February 1993, however, there were reports of provocations against Russian troops in Ajaria by armed Ajar groups. In February 1995 there was reported to have been an assassination attempt against Aslan Abashidze, the Chairman of the Ajarian Supreme Council (regional leader), and against the commander of Russian military forces in Ajaria. Elections to the Supreme Council (legislature) of Ajaria were held in September 1996 and the majority of seats were won by the All-Georgian Union of Revival party. Abashidze was re-elected Chairman of the Council. In December the deployment of armoured vehicles, allegedly from Russian military units, on the streets of Batumi, the republic's capital, led to tension between the Georgian authorities and the leadership of Ajaria; Abashidze denied reports that a state of emergency had been declared, and announced that the military units were carrying out deployment exercises.

In October 1999 relations between Ajaria and Georgia deteriorated when Abashidze called Shevardnadze the 'father of terrorists'. In the same month, Ajaria refused to release prisoners who had been pardoned by Shevardnadze under an amnesty; criminal proceedings were subsequently instigated against the region. Abashidze was highly vocal in his criticism of the Georgian elections held in October and November, and in late November he relinquished his parliamentary mandate; his seat was allocated to a member of his party. In November 2001 Abashidze stood as the only candidate in a direct election to the new post of Head of the Republic, which replaced that of Chairman of the Ajarian Supreme Council; in the same month he was appointed as President Shevardnadze's personal representative for conflict resolution in Abkhazia. On 4 December Ajaria's new bicameral legislature, composed of the Council of the Republic and the Senate, held its inaugural session, following the implementation of amendments to the region's Constitution, which had been agreed in July.

Georgia was one of only four republics of the USSR not to join the CIS at its formation in December 1991. However, as civil and separatist conflicts threatened to destroy the country, Shevardnadze was forced to reverse official policy on the CIS, and in late 1993 the republic was admitted to that body, including its collective security system. In May 1999, however, Georgia failed to renew its adherence to the Collective Security Treaty, as it did not consider the system relevant to its problems. Georgia's relations with Russia were strained by developments in secessionist Abkhazia in 1992–93 and by Georgian accusations of Russian involvement. However, in February 1994 Georgia and Russia signed a 10-year treaty of friendship and co-operation. The treaty provided, *inter alia*, for the establishment of Russian military bases in Georgia to 'protect the security of the CIS'. Abkhazian and South Ossetian leaders opposed the treaty, claiming that Russian-Georgian military co-operation would lead to an escalation of tension in the region. Nationalist opposition forces in Georgia also opposed the strengthening of the republic's ties with Russia. In 1996 President Shevardnadze and the Georgian legislature threatened to close the military bases, unless Russia adopted a firmer stance against the separatists in South Ossetia and Abkhazia. In 1997–98 Russia continued to

participate in the search for a resolution of the Abkhaz conflict, although tension between Georgia and Russia increased over the issue of the CIS peace-keepers and the partial lifting of economic sanctions against Abkhazia (see above). Furthermore, Georgia criticized its exclusion by Russia and Ukraine from decisions pertaining to the division of the former Black Sea Fleet. In July 1998 Georgia assumed control of its maritime borders, following the withdrawal of Russian maritime patrols. A 150-km section of the state land border with Turkey was transferred from Russian to Georgian control in December. In May 2000 representatives of Bulgaria, Georgia, Romania, Russia, Turkey and Ukraine agreed to establish an international naval unit, Blackseafor.

The lifting of restrictions on the Russian–Abkhazian border in September 1999 angered Georgia, and further tension occurred later in the year, owing to the Russian–Chechen conflict. Georgia denied allegations that it was harbouring Chechen soldiers and selling arms to the breakaway republic. Shevardnadze consistently reiterated his refusal to comply with Russian requests for Russian and Georgian troops to patrol jointly the Georgian border with Dagestan and confirmed his opposition to the use of existing Russian bases to initiate attacks on Chechnya. In August, following an accidental bomb attack by Russia on the border with Chechnya, it was agreed that all Russian border guards deployed in Abkhazia and Ajaria would be withdrawn by the beginning of November. Furthermore, in November it was agreed that two of the four Russian military bases on Georgian territory would be withdrawn by mid-2001 (the bases were eventually closed in November of that year). Negotiations on the closure of the two remaining bases were ongoing in early 2003.

In 2000 there were violent disturbances in the Pankisi Gorge, close to the Chechen border, which was inhabited by both ethnic Chechens and Chechen refugees. There were repeated kidnappings; in August three International Committee of the Red Cross (ICRC, see p. 251) workers were taken hostage for a period of nine days. In December local people began to patrol the troubled zone themselves. Despite this, in the same month Shevardnadze reiterated Georgia's refusal to carry out joint operations in the area with Russian troops. Russia's decision to implement a full visa regime for Georgian citizens entering its territory from January 2001 caused further antagonism between the two countries, particularly since citizens of both Abkhazia and South Ossetia were to be exempt from the requirement. Russia claimed that it had introduced the regime as a temporary measure, to prevent the unrestricted movement of Chechen insurgents, but Georgia interpreted it as an attempt to undermine its territorial integrity, in retaliation for Georgia's unwillingness to assist Russia in the Chechen conflict.

In January 2002 Georgian security forces launched a campaign to reassert government authority and restore order to the Pankisi region, prompting speculation that the operation had been undertaken in an attempt to forestall direct military intervention by Russia. None the less, later that month local residents decided to form their own force to secure the release of hostages held in the Pankisi Gorge, and drew up a petition to demand the repatriation of the 7,000 Chechen refugees who were believed to be residing there. At the end of January Georgia's Deputy Minister of State Security was shot and killed in the Pankisi Gorge, and four policemen were taken hostage in the Gorge in February, prompting élite government security forces to be dispatched to the region; the hostages were released after three days. In the same month the US chargé d'affaires in Georgia announced that militants from the Islamist al-Qa'ida (Base) organization (linked to the Saudi-born fundamentalist, Osama bin Laden, held responsible by the USA for the large-scale terrorist attacks on the cities of New York and Washington, DC, of 11 September 2001) were believed to have infiltrated the Pankisi Gorge from Afghanistan, together with Chechen and other Islamist extremists, a claim that the Georgian authorities appeared unable to refute. At the end of February 2002 the USA announced that it was to implement a military-training programme in Georgia, in order to equip the armed forces for operations in the Pankisi Gorge; the Georgia Train and Equip programme was officially inaugurated in late May.

Relations between Georgia and Russia deteriorated in August 2002, and on 23 August Georgia accused Russia of perpetrating an act of aggression, and announced its preparedness to make use of 'all possible means' to repel subsequent attacks, when the aerial bombardment of the Pankisi Gorge by unmarked aircraft led to at least one death; Russia denied responsibility for the attack, although the incident was confirmed by OSCE observers. Some 1,000 government troops consequently entered the Gorge, in an attempt to impose control over the region. In mid-September Russian President Putin wrote to the UN Secretary-General, warning that unless the Georgian Government was prepared to take direct action to eliminate the Chechen rebels alleged to be operating from its territory, Russia would take unilateral action to counteract the perceived terrorist threat. In early October Georgia extradited five suspected Chechen militants to Russia, although this prompted demonstrations by Chechen refugees living in the Pankisi region, who feared that the suspects would be executed without trial. Relations with Russia subsequently improved when, on 6 October, at a CIS summit meeting held in Chișinău, Moldova, Presidents Shevardnadze and Putin reached an agreement, according to which the two countries were to resume joint patrols of their common border, and seek to resolve border issues by diplomatic means.

Georgia sought to develop its international relations from the mid-1990s. In April 1996, together with Armenia and Azerbaijan, it signed an agreement on partnership and co-operation with the EU, and in January 1999 it joined the Council of Europe. In October it was announced that Georgia planned to apply for membership of NATO by 2005, although in 2000 President Shevardnadze indicated that the country might eventually declare itself to have neutral status.

Government

Under the Constitution of August 1995, the President of Georgia is Head of State and the head of the executive, and also Commander-in-Chief of the Armed Forces. The President is directly elected for a five-year term (and may not hold office for more than two consecutive terms). The Government (headed by the Minister of State), is accountable to the President, to whom it acts as an advisory body. The supreme legislative body is the unicameral 235-member Georgian Parliament, which is directly elected for four years. (The Constitution provides for a future bicameral Parliament, comprising a Council of the Republic and a Senate, following the eventual restoration of Georgia's territorial integrity.) Georgia contains three autonomous territories: the Autonomous Republic of Ajaria, Abkhazia and South Ossetia. The status of the latter two remains disputed (see above). The rest of the country is divided into nine regions (oblasts), each headed by a state-appointed governor.

Defence

One of the principal objectives of the Government following independence in 1991 was to create a unified army from the various existing paramilitary and other groups. A National Security Council (headed by the President of Georgia) was established in early 1996 as a consultative body co-ordinating issues related to defence and security. In August 2002 the country's total armed forces numbered some 17,500: an army of 8,620, a navy of 1,830, an air force of 1,250, and some 5,800 in centrally controlled units. The Ministry of Internal Affairs controls a militia of 6,300 troops and a border guard of 5,400. There were also 4,000 Russian troops based in Georgia in 2001. Military service is for 18 months. In late 1993 Georgia joined the CIS and its collective security system; however, Georgia failed to renew its participation in the system upon its expiry in May 1999. In March 1994 Georgia joined NATO's (see p. 271) 'Partnership for Peace' programme of military co-operation. The 2002 budget allocated some 70m. lari to defence, representing a significant increase compared with the defence budget for 2001 (33.1m.).

Economic Affairs

In 2001, according to estimates by the World Bank, Georgia's gross national income (GNI), measured at average 1999–2001 prices, was US $3,097m., equivalent to $620 per head (or $2,860 per head on an international purchasing-power parity basis). During 1990–2001, it was estimated, the population decreased by an average of 0.8% per year, while gross domestic product (GDP) per head decreased, in real terms, by an annual average of 7.4%. Overall GDP decreased, in real terms, by an average of 8.2% annually during 1990–2001. Real GDP increased by 2.0% in 2000 and by 4.5% in 2001.

Agriculture contributed an estimated 20.6% of GDP in 2001, when the sector (including hunting, forestry and fishing) provided 52.7% of employment. Georgia's exceedingly favourable climate allows the cultivation of subtropical crops, such as tea and oranges. Other fruit (including wine grapes), flowers, tobacco and grain are also cultivated. The mountain pastures

are used for sheep- and goat-farming. In 1996 private agricultural production provided more than 85% of total output. Although the GDP of the agricultural sector declined dramatically from 1990, growth was recorded from 1995. During 1995–2000, according to the World Bank, agricultural GDP increased, in real terms, by an average of 1.4% per year. The real GDP of the sector increased by 3.0% in 1999 and by 3.5% in 2000.

Industry contributed 22.7% of GDP in 2001, and the sector (comprising mining, manufacturing, utilities and construction) provided 9.3% of employment. The most significant parts of the sector are the agro-processing and energy industries. According to the World Bank, industrial GDP decreased, in real terms, by an annual average of 5.4% in 1995–2000. However, industrial GDP increased by 2.0% each year in 1999 and 2000.

Mining and quarrying accounted for just 0.4% of employment in 2001. The principal minerals extracted are coal, petroleum and manganese ore, but reserves of high-grade manganese ore are largely depleted. There are also deposits of coal, copper, gold and silver. Substantial natural gas deposits were discovered in 1994–96.

According to the World Bank, the manufacturing sector contributed 7.5% of GDP in 2000, and it provided 5.5% of employment in 2001. Although the machinery and metal-working industries, traditionally the most important parts of the sector, were in decline in the late 1990s, manufacturing GDP increased, in real terms, by an average of 4.6% per year in 1995–2000. Real manufacturing GDP increased by 3.0% each year in 1999 and 2000.

Georgia has traditionally been highly dependent on imports of fuel and energy, in particular the import of crude petroleum from Russia. However, from 1993, when the prices of imported energy were raised to international market prices, there was a significant reduction in the amount of fuel imported, leading to widespread energy shortages; in mid-1996 the Georgian Government was negotiating with international organizations to construct some 200 hydroelectric power stations over the following 10 years. Hydroelectric power accounted for 80.1% of total electricity production in 1999, and natural gas accounted for 17.4% of production in that year. Imports of fuel and energy comprised an estimated 18.5% of total imports in 2002. In April 1999 a pipeline to transport petroleum to Supsa, on Georgia's Black Sea coast, from Baku, Azerbaijan, officially entered into service. There were also plans for the construction of a natural gas pipeline from Baku to Erzurum, Turkey, via Georgia, by 2005. In the mean time, Georgia obtained natural gas from Russia, via Armenia. However, Georgia hoped to become less dependent on Russia for its energy requirements, by developing its own energy resources.

The services sector contributed an estimated 56.8% of GDP in 2001, and engaged 38.0% of the employed labour force. Trade is the sector's most significant activity, although tourism expanded from the mid-1990s; the number of tourist arrivals increased by 45.8% in 1995–99. According to the World Bank, the GDP of the services sector decreased, in real terms, by an annual average of 8.6% in 1995–2000. However, real sectoral GDP increased by 1.7% in 1999 and by 5.5% in 2000.

In 2001 Georgia recorded a visible trade deficit of US $549.5m., while there was a deficit of $211.7m. on the current account of the balance of payments. In 2001 Turkey was the principal source of imports (accounting for 21.1% of the total), followed by Russia (18.3%); other major sources were Azerbaijan, Germany and Ukraine. The principal market for exports in that year was Russia (accounting for 28.5% of the total), while Turkey purchased 26.6% of exports; other important purchasers were Turkmenistan, the United Kingdom and Switzerland. The principal exports in 2002 were aircraft, iron and steel scrap, unwrought or semi-manufactured gold, and wine and related products. The principal imports in that year were petroleum products, crude petroleum and natural gas, medicines and sugar.

In 2000 there was a budgetary deficit of 242.7m. lari (equivalent to 4.1% of GDP). At the end of 2000 Georgia's total external debt was US $1,633m., of which $1,271m. was long-term public debt. The cost of debt-servicing in that year was equivalent to 9.6% of the value of exports of goods and services. The annual rate of inflation averaged 26.8% during 1994–2001. Consumer prices increased by 4.1% in 2000 and by 4.7% in 2001. In 2001 the rate of unemployment was 11.2%, according to International Labour Organization data.

In 1992 Georgia became a member of the IMF and the World Bank, as well as joining the European Bank for Reconstruction and Development (EBRD, see p. 193). Georgia is also a member of the Organization of the Black Sea Economic Co-operation (see p. 293). In June 2000 Georgia became a full member of the World Trade Organization (WTO, see p. 323).

The collapse of the USSR in 1991 and the outbreak of three armed conflicts in Georgia adversely affected the country's economy. Georgia became increasingly dependent on international aid, and the instability in the republic discouraged investment by foreign companies. However, with the return of relative political stability in 1994, the Government embarked on a programme of comprehensive stabilization. Although adverse domestic developments and the Russian financial crisis severely disrupted the Georgian economy in mid-1998, the currency had stabilized by mid-1999, and the opening of the Baku–Supsa petroleum pipeline in April of that year was expected to lead to increased revenue. However, tax revenues remained low, resulting in accumulating wages' and pensions' arrears. In January 2001 Georgia agreed to the so-called 'zero option' (already negotiated with many successor states), whereby Russia assumed responsibility for Georgia's share of the Soviet debt, in exchange for its renunciation of any claim to Soviet assets. The IMF duly resumed lending to Georgia, which had been suspended since July 1999, pledging US $141m. over a three-year period. The World Bank was to allocate a further $215m. towards structural reform, and in March 2001 the so-called 'Paris Club' of official creditors agreed to implement beneficial debt restructuring for Georgia. In February 2003 agreement was finally reached on the construction of the planned Baku–Tbilisi–Erzurum natural gas pipeline (see above), and construction work commenced in April on a pipeline to transport petroleum from Baku, via Tbilisi, to Ceyhan (Turkey); President Shevardnadze anticipated that the implementation of the project would attract more than 600m. lari in foreign investment during 2003–05. In early 2003 the World Bank reduced its agreed lending to Georgia, owing to the Government's failure to realize commitments regarding policy and anti-corruption measures. In March the IMF stated that it would withhold support for the further deferral of the country's Paris Club arrears, unless it recorded progress in revenue collection, the structural reorganization of the Government and reform of the energy sector (the Government had reduced electricity tariffs, contrary to international advice). The state budget for 2003 (finally adopted at the end of January) envisaged a budgetary deficit equivalent to some 3% of GDP, a 4.5% increase in GDP and an annual rate of inflation of around 5%.

Education

Education is officially compulsory for nine years, between the ages of six and 14. Primary education begins at six years of age and lasts for four years. Secondary education, beginning at the age of 10, lasts for a maximum of seven years, comprising a first cycle of five years and a second cycle of two years. Free secondary education is available for the highest-achieving 30% of primary-school pupils. In 1997 34% of children of the relevant age-group attended pre-primary schools. Primary enrolment in that year was equivalent to 88% of the relevant age group (89% for males, 88% for females), while the comparable ratio for secondary enrolment was 77% (78% males, 76% females). In the 1998/99 academic year there were 1,641 secondary day schools, with a total enrolment of 599,400 pupils. In 1994/95 75.4% of secondary-school pupils were taught in Georgian-language schools, while 3.9% were taught in Russian-language schools, 3.7% in Armenian-language schools, 6.1% in Azerbaijani-language schools and 9.6% in mixed Georgian- and Russian-language schools. In 1998/99 128,372 students were enrolled at institutions of higher education (including universities); enrolment was equivalent to 42% of the relevant age-group in 1996/97. Government expenditure on education amounted to a total of 99.5m. lari in 1998.

Public Holidays

2003: 1 January (New Year), 7 January (Christmas), 19 January (Epiphany), 13 March (Mother's Day), 26–28 April (Easter), 26 May (Independence Day), 28 August (St Mary's Day, Mariamoba), 14 October (Svetitskovloba), 23 November (St Giorgi's Day, Giorgoba).

2004: 1 January (New Year), 7 January (Christmas), 19 January (Epiphany), 13 March (Mother's Day), 10–12 April (Easter), 26 May (Independence Day), 28 August (St Mary's Day, Mariamoba), 14 October (Svetitskovloba), 23 November (St Giorgi's Day, Giorgoba).

Weights and Measures

The metric system is in force.

Statistical Survey

Source (unless otherwise indicated): State Department for Statistics, 380085 Tbilisi, K. Gamsakhurdia 4; tel. (32) 33-14-50; fax (32) 93-89-36; e-mail ngabunia@statistics.gov.ge; internet georgia-gateway.org/SDS.

Area and Population

AREA, POPULATION AND DENSITY

Area (sq km)	69,700*
Population (census results)†	
17 January 1979	4,993,182
12 January 1989	
Males	2,562,040
Females	2,838,801
Total	5,400,841
Population (UN estimates at mid-year)‡	
1999	5,282,000
2000	5,262,000
2001	5,239,000
Density (per sq km) at mid-2001	75.2

* 26,911 sq miles.

† Population is *de jure*. The *de facto* total at the 1989 census was 5,443,359.

‡ Source: UN, *World Population Prospects: The 2000 Revision*.

POPULATION BY NATIONALITY

(1989 census result)

	%
Georgian	68.8
Armenian	9.0
Russian	7.4
Azerbaijani	5.1
Ossetian	3.2
Greek	1.9
Abkhazian	1.7
Others	2.9
Total	100.0

PRINCIPAL TOWNS

(estimated population at 1 January 2002)

Tbilisi (capital) . .	1,103,500	Batumi	124,100
Kutaisi	215,700	Sukhumi	112,000*
Rustavi	138,200	Gori	66,500

* 1 January 1994.

Source: Thomas Brinkhoff, *City Population* (www.citypopulation.de).

BIRTHS, MARRIAGES AND DEATHS

	Registered live births		Registered marriages		Registered deaths	
	Number	Rate (per 1,000)	Number	Rate (per 1,000)	Number	Rate (per 1,000)
1993 . .	61,594	11.3	24,105	4.4	48,938	9.0
1994 . .	57,311	10.6	21,908	4.0	41,596	7.7
1995 . .	56,341	10.4	21,481	4.0	37,874	7.0
1996 . .	53,669	9.9	19,253	3.6	34,414	6.4
1997 . .	52,020	9.8	17,100*	3.2*.	37,679	7.1
1998* . .	57,300	10.8	15,343	2.9	41,600	7.9

* Provisional data.

Sources: mainly UN, *Demographic Yearbook*; Caucasus Health International Forum.

2000: Births 40,392 (number), 8.2 (rate); Deaths 41,320 (number), 8.4 (rate) (Source: UN, *Population and Vital Statistics Report*).

Expectation of life (WHO estimates, years at birth): 68.9 (males 65.4; females 72.4) in 2001 (Source: WHO, *World Health Report*).

EMPLOYMENT

(annual averages, '000 persons)*

	1999	2000	2001
Agriculture, hunting and forestry	903.2	910.4	989.9
Fishing	1.2	0.8	0.5
Mining and quarrying . . .	6.1	6.3	7.3
Manufacturing	111.5	103.9	102.4
Electricity, gas and water supply	21.0	29.1	29.2
Construction	24.9	32.0	35.3
Wholesale and retail trade; repair of motor vehicles and personal and household goods . . .	153.2	174.8	181.5
Hotels and restaurants . . .	15.4	15.0	16.0
Transport, storage and communications	68.5	71.9	83.1
Financial intermediation . .	10.9	9.0	10.2
Real estate, renting and business activities	40.3	37.7	38.7
Public administration and defence; compulsory social security . .	106.5	105.8	105.6
Education	138.5	114.2	138.7
Health and social work . . .	77.9	85.2	85.3
Other community, social and personal service activities . .	42.5	45.3	46.5
Private households with employed persons	6.9	3.2	4.1
Extra-territorial organizations and bodies	1.9	1.9	2.0
Activities not adequately defined	0.7	2.3	1.3
Total employed. . . .	1,731.5	1,748.8	1,877.6
Unemployed	277.5	212.2	235.6
Total labour force	2,009.1	1,961.2	2,113.0
Males	1,044.3	1,051.6	1,093.5
Females	964.8	909.6	1,019.5

* Figures exclude employment in the informal sector, estimated to total about 750,000 persons at the end of 1997.

Source: ILO.

Health and Welfare

KEY INDICATORS

Total fertility rate (children per woman, 2001).	1.4
Under-5 mortality rate (per 1,000 live births, 2001) . .	29
HIV/AIDS (% of persons aged 15–49, 2001)	<0.10
Physicians (per 1,000 head, 1998)	4.36
Hospital beds (per 1,000 head, 1996)	4.81
Health expenditure (2000): US $ per head (PPP) . .	199
Health expenditure (2000): % of GDP	7.1
Health expenditure (2000): public (% of total) . . .	10.5
Human Development Index (2000): ranking	81
Human Development Index (2000): value	0.748

For sources and definitions, see explanatory note on p. vi.

Agriculture

PRINCIPAL CROPS

('000 metric tons)

	1999	2000	2001
Wheat	226.1	89.4	306.0
Barley	50.8	30.1	98.4
Maize	490.5	295.9	288.6
Potatoes	443.3	302.0	415.0
Sugar beet*	23.1	23.0	23.0
Nuts*	50.9	44.7	36.2
Sunflower seed	40.5	2.6	3.0
Cabbages	102†	125	76.7†
Tomatoes†	210	155	202.6
Cucumbers and gherkins† . .	42.0	30.2	27.6
Dry onions†	45	31	33.2
Other vegetables†	18	13	9.9
Oranges	56.0	40.0	32.0†
Apples	98.2	83.0	66.2
Pears	40.5	34.2	27.5†
Sour cherries†	27.0	24.0	19.5
Peaches and nectarines . .	15.2	12.8	10.2†
Plums	22.6	19.1	15.4†
Grapes	220.0	210.0	180.0†
Watermelons	108.2	80.0	70.0*
Other fruit*	43.3	36.5	29.2
Tea (made)	60.3	24.0	30.0*
Tobacco (leaves)	1.9	1.9	2.1*

* FAO estimate(s).
† Unofficial figure(s).

Source: FAO.

LIVESTOCK

('000 head at 1 January)

	1999	2000	2001
Horses	34.1	35.2	38.5
Cattle	1,122	1,177	1,180
Buffaloes	33	35	33
Pigs	411	443	445
Sheep	553	540*	560*
Goats	80	88*	99*
Chickens	8,473	7,826	8,495
Turkeys†	405	400	405

* Unofficial figure.
† FAO estimates.

Source: FAO.

LIVESTOCK PRODUCTS

('000 metric tons)

	1999	2000	2001
Beef and veal	41.3	48.3	47.0
Mutton and lamb	6.9	8.9	7.6
Pig meat	40.8	36.9	34.7
Poultry meat	11.3	13.7	12.8
Cows' milk	660.3	618.9	690.4
Hen eggs*	21.7	20.7	21.9

* Unofficial figures.

Source: FAO.

Fishing

(metric tons, live weight)

	1998	1999	2000
Capture	3,001	1,680	2,450
Rainbow trout	—	80	100
Whiting	53	41	40*
European sprat	24	42	42*
European anchovy	2,346	1,264	2,080
Sharks, rays and skates	550	18	21
Aquaculture	96	83	86
Common carp	42	34	35
Total catch	**3,097**	**1,763**	**2,536**

* FAO estimates.

Source: FAO, *Yearbook of Fishery Statistics*.

Mining

('000 metric tons, unless otherwise indicated)

	1998	1999	2000
Coal	14.7	12.0	7.0
Crude petroleum	119.2	91.3	109.5
Natural gas (million cu m)	—	—	100.0
Manganese ore	50.0	47.9	59.1

Source: US Geological Survey.

Industry*

SELECTED PRODUCTS
('000 metric tons, unless otherwise indicated)

	1998	1999	2000
Refined sugar	—	20.0	35.3
Canned foodstuffs	1.9	6.6	4.6
Wine ('000 hectolitres)	218	194	182
Beer ('000 hectolitres)	74	126	235
Vodka and liqueurs ('000 hectolitres)	31	46	43
Soft drinks ('000 hectolitres)	290	220	290
Mineral water ('000 hectolitres)	291	245	362
Cigarettes (million)	600	1,300	300
Textile fabrics (million sq metres)	0.2	0.2	—
Mineral fertilizers	55.4	95.1	100.2
Synthetic ammonia	77.5	126.6	136.2
Motor spirit (petrol)	2.4	3.6	1.8
Distillate fuel oil (diesel fuel)	4.7	22.3	8.8
Building bricks (million)	13.1	7.7	4.7
Steel	56.4	7	—
Steel pipes	8.8	0.1	0.2
Electric energy (million kWh)	8,100	8,100	7,400

* Data for South Ossetia and Abkhazia are not included.

Finance

CURRENCY AND EXCHANGE RATES

Monetary Units
100 tetri = 1 lari

Sterling, Dollar and Euro Equivalents (31 December 2002)
£1 sterling = 3.369 lari
US $1 = 2.090 lari
€1 = 2.192 lari
100 lari = £29.69 = $47.85 = €45.62

Average Exchange Rate (lari per US $)
2000   1.9762
2001   2.0730
2002   2.1957

Note: On 25 September 1995 Georgia introduced the lari, replacing interim currency coupons at the rate of 1 lari = 1,000,000 coupons. From April 1993 the National Bank of Georgia had issued coupons in various denominations, to circulate alongside (and initially at par with) the Russian (formerly Soviet) rouble. From August 1993 coupons became Georgia's sole legal tender, but their value rapidly depreciated. The transfer from coupons to the lari lasted one week, and from 2 October 1995 the lari became the only permitted currency in Georgia.

BUDGET
(million lari)*

Revenue†	1998	1999	2000
Tax revenue	526.1	649.2	706.6
Taxes on income	87.8	104.8	108.2
Taxes on profits	50.5	55.6	79.7
Value-added tax	219.7	248.1	289.8
Customs duties	67.0	33.7	53.1
Other current revenue	97.1	42.8	45.6
Extrabudgetary revenue‡	117.5	133.1	144.8
Total	**740.8**	**825.1**	**897.1**

Expenditure§	1998	1999	2000
Current expenditure	997.3	1,132.5	1,094.2
Wages and salaries	176.7	190.8	180.1
Other goods and services‖	202.4	190.9	132.2
Subsidies and transfers	119.3	142.2	166.7
Interest payments	114.8	159.0	178.4
Extrabudgetary expenditure¶	212.5	211.7	203.7
Local government expenditure	171.7	237.9	233.1
Capital expenditure	65.5	48.7	30.2
Total	**1,062.8**	**1,181.2**	**1,124.4**

* Figures represent a consolidation of the State Budget (covering the central Government and local administrations) and extrabudgetary funds.

† Excluding grants received (million lari): 45.7 in 1998; 48.2 in 1999; 16.2 in 2000.

‡ Comprising the revenues of the Social Security Fund, the Employment Fund, the Privatization Fund and the Road Fund (established in October 1995).

§ Excluding net lending (million lari): 33.6 in 1998; 71.7 in 1999; 31.6 in 2000.

‖ Comprising other goods and services, other current expenditure and unclassified expenditure.

¶ Including the payment of pensions and unemployment benefit.

INTERNATIONAL RESERVES
(US $ million at 31 December)

	2000	2001	2002
IMF special drawing rights	3.27	3.96	2.89
Reserve position in the IMF	0.01	0.01	0.01
Foreign exchange	106.13	155.40	194.64
Total	**109.41**	**159.37**	**197.55**

Source: IMF, *International Financial Statistics*.

MONEY SUPPLY
(million lari at 31 December)

	2000	2001	2002
Currency outside banks . . .	315.18	348.85	390.79
Demand deposits	53.20	45.33	62.01
Total money (incl. others) . .	368.38	394.23	452.84

Source: IMF, *International Financial Statistics*.

COST OF LIVING
(Consumer price index for five cities; base: 1995 = 100)

	1999	2000	2001
Food, beverages and tobacco . .	171.4	173.7	185.2
Fuel and light	305.6	373.5	394.8
Clothing (incl. footwear) . . .	168.4	168.0	169.4
Rent	129.3	136.0	140.1
All items (incl. others)	184.3	191.7	200.7

Source: ILO.

NATIONAL ACCOUNTS

Gross Domestic Product
(million lari at current prices)

	1998	1999	2000
Government final consumption expenditure	556.6	581.2	504.7
Private final consumption expenditure	4,350.5	4,760.0	5,073.3
Increase in stocks	57.5	65.4	75.6
Gross fixed capital formation . .	561.2	1,024.9	944.6
Total domestic expenditure . .	5,525.8	6,431.5	6,598.2
Exports of goods and services . .	826.6	1,080.2	1,389.6
Less Imports of goods and services	1,863.6	2,159.6	2,397.1
Sub-total	4,488.8	5,352.3	5,590.6
Statistical discrepancy . . .	551.8	313.7	380.0
GDP in purchasers' values . .	5,040.6	5,666.0	5,970.6

Gross Domestic Product by Economic Activity
(% of total)

	1998	1999	2000
Agriculture, forestry and fishing	26.7	24.7	20.0
Industry*	12.3	13.0	14.0
Construction	4.6	3.7	3.8
Trade	10.4	11.5	12.7
Hotels and restaurants	1.9	2.4	2.4
Transport and communications . .	10.9	11.9	14.4
Financial intermediation . . .	1.2	1.6	1.7
General administration and defence	3.9	3.5	3.2
Education	2.8	3.3	3.6
Health	4.5	4.3	5.1
Other services	20.7	20.1	19.2
Total	100.0	100.0	100.0

* Principally mining, manufacturing, electricity, gas and water.

BALANCE OF PAYMENTS
(US $ million)

	1999	2000	2001
Exports of goods f.o.b.	329.5	459.0	496.1
Imports of goods f.o.b.	−863.4	−970.5	−1,045.6
Trade balance	−533.9	−511.5	−549.5
Exports of services	216.9	206.4	314.1
Imports of services	−224.0	−216.3	−236.9
Balance on goods and services .	−541.0	−521.4	−472.3
Other income received	211.4	178.6	97.7
Other income paid	−64.5	−61.1	−65.4
Balance on goods, services and income	−394.1	−403.9	−440.0
Current transfers received . . .	228.7	163.2	246.4
Current transfers paid	−33.0	−28.3	−18.1
Current balance	−198.4	−269.0	−211.7
Capital account (net)	−7.1	−4.8	−5.2
Direct investment abroad . . .	−1.0	0.5	0.1
Direct investment from abroad . .	82.3	131.1	109.8
Portfolio investment assets . . .	—	2.7	−0.1
Portfolio investment liabilities . .	6.2	—	—
Other investment assets . . .	9.3	−7.7	−24.6
Other investment liabilities . .	38.7	−33.8	124.5
Net errors and omissions . . .	55.7	187.4	34.9
Overall balance	−14.3	6.4	27.7

Source: IMF, *International Financial Statistics*.

External Trade

PRINCIPAL COMMODITIES
(US $ million)

Imports f.o.b.	2000	2001	2002
Crude petroleum and petroleum products . . .	71.9	87.7	87.3
Petroleum gases and other gaseous hydrocarbons . . .	48.6	47.1	45.6
Sugar	24.6	24.1	37.1
Cigars and cigarettes	29.4	18.7	18.1
Wheat	21.9	11.2	13.8
Flour	20.3	14.8	n.a.
Medicines	33.9	38.3	45.8
Automobiles	15.2	12.4	21.8
Total (incl. others)	650.7	678.7	720.0

Exports f.o.b.	2000	2001	2002
Iron and steel scrap	39.0	32.9	31.5
Ferro-alloys	13.6	17.5	14.5
Aluminium waste and scrap . .	12.9	15.4	n.a.
Gold (unwrought or semi-manufactured)	n.a.	12.5	28.5
Aircraft	7.1	35.7	44.5
Crude petroleum and natural gas	12.8	n.a.	n.a.
Petroleum products	6.4	n.a.	n.a.
Tea	6.1	n.a.	n.a.
Fertilizers	16.2	4.9	11.0
Nuts	19.3	9.8	n.a.
Copper ore	9.8	9.6	n.a.
Wine and related products . .	29.0	32.2	26.2
Mineral water	9.5	11.7	15.3
Electricity	7.2	11.1	n.a.
Total (incl. others)	329.9	320.0	325.0

PRINCIPAL TRADING PARTNERS
(US $ million)

Imports c.i.f.	2000	2001
Armenia	13.5	n.a.
Azerbaijan	55.4	73.2
Germany	50.2	69.1
Italy	17.3	25.5
Russia	91.9	91.3
Switzerland	22.7	14.0
Turkey	104.0	105.0
Ukraine	35.4	49.5
United Kingdom	23.0	25.1
USA	35.7	27.8
Total (incl. others)	449.0	498.2

Exports f.o.b.	2000	2001
Armenia	13.7	n.a.
Azerbaijan	21.3	10.6
Germany	34.3	7.9
Italy	12.4	8.6
Russia	69.6	73.5
Switzerland	13.4	15.6
Turkey	74.8	68.7
Turkmenistan	n.a.	28.9
Ukraine	11.0	11.7
United Kingdom	10.3	22.9
USA	7.3	9.5
Total (incl. others)	268.0	257.8

Source: partly National Bank of Georgia.

Transport

RAILWAYS
(traffic)

	1998	1999	2000
Passenger-km (million)	397	349	450
Freight net ton-km (million) . .	2,574	3,139	3,910

Source: UN, *Statistical Yearbook for Asia and the Pacific.*

ROAD TRAFFIC
('000 motor vehicles in use)

	1998*	1999	2000
Passenger cars	260.4	247.9	244.8
Buses	14.8	18.9	19.8
Lorries and vans	56.2	50.0	47.0

* Estimates.

Source: International Road Federation, *World Road Statistics.*

SHIPPING

Merchant Fleet
(registered at 31 December)

	1999	2000	2001
Number of vessels	104	118	201
Total displacement ('000 grt) . . .	132.2	118.6	276.6

Source: Lloyd's Register-Fairplay, *World Fleet Statistics.*

CIVIL AVIATION
(traffic on scheduled services)

	1997	1998	1999
Kilometres flown (million) . . .	3	5	5
Passengers carried ('000) . . .	110	175	159
Passenger-km (million) . . .	206	340	307
Total ton-km (million)	20	34	30

Source: UN, *Statistical Yearbook.*

Tourism

FOREIGN TOURIST ARRIVALS

Country of Residence	1998	1999	2000
CIS countries*	177,162	219,318	220,327
Turkey	102,160	100,955	84,170
USA	4,633	7,846	9,308
Total (incl. others)	317,063	383,817	387,258

* Comprising Armenia, Azerbaijan, Belarus, Kazakhstan, Kyrgyzstan, Moldova, Russia, Tajikistan, Turkmenistan, Ukraine and Uzbekistan.

Tourism receipts (US $ million): 423 in 1998; 400 in 1999.

Source: World Tourism Organization, *Yearbook of Tourism Statistics.*

Communications Media

	1995	1996	1997
Radio receivers ('000 in use) . . .	3,005	3,010	3,020
Television receivers ('000 in use) .	2,550	2,560	2,570
Telephones ('000 main lines in use) .	554.3	567.4	616.5
Facsimile machines (number in use) .	n.a.	500	n.a.
Mobile cellular telephones ('000 subscribers)	0.2	2.3	30.0
Internet users ('000)	0.6	2.0	3.0
Book production*: titles . . .	1,104	581	n.a.
Book production*: copies ('000) . .	1,627	834	n.a.
Newspapers (titles)	127	123	161

* Including pamphlets.

1998: Television receivers ('000 in use) 2,580; Telephones ('000 main lines in use) 628.8; Mobile cellular telephones ('000 subscribers) 60.0; Internet users ('000) 5.0; Newspapers (titles) 243, (annual circulation, '000) 15,900.

1999: Television receivers ('000 in use) 2,585; Telephones ('000 main lines in use) 671.5; Mobile cellular telephones ('000 subscribers) 102.5; Internet users ('000) 20.0; Book production (titles) 697.

2000: Television receivers ('000 in use) 2,590; Telephones ('000 main lines in use) 757.5; Mobile cellular telephones ('000 subscribers) 185.5; Internet users ('000) 23.0.

2001: Telephones ('000 main lines in use) 867.6; Mobile cellular telephones ('000 subscribers) 295.0; Internet users ('000) 25.0.

Sources: UN, *Statistical Yearbook*; UNESCO, *Statistical Yearbook*; and International Telecommunication Union.

Education

(1998/99)

	Institutions	Students
Pre-primary schools	1,241	74,200
General education: Day schools (primary)* . .	1,538	116,400
General education: Day schools (secondary) .	1,641	599,400
General education: Day schools (special) . . .	18	1,900
General education: Evening schools . .	40	4,800
State secondary specialized schools	83	32,406
Private secondary specialized schools . .	58	7,179
Vocational/technical schools	89	n.a.
State higher schools (incl. universities) . .	24	90,100
Private higher schools (incl. universities) . .	154	38,272

* Including primary schools covering part of the secondary syllabus.

Teachers (1998/99): Total in general day schools 71,700 (excl. teachers in special schools); Total in institutes of higher education 11,166.

Source: Georgia Development Gateway.

Adult literacy rate (UNESCO estimates): 99.5% (males 99.7%; females 99.4%) in 1995 (Source: UNESCO, *Statistical Yearbook*).

Directory

The Constitution

A new Constitution was approved by the Georgian legislature on 24 August 1995; it entered into force on 17 October. The Constitution replaced the Decree on State Power of November 1992 (which had functioned as an interim basic law). The following is a summary of the Constitution's main provisions:

GENERAL PROVISIONS

Georgia is an independent, united and undivided state, as confirmed by the referendum conducted throughout the entire territory of the country (including Abkhazia and South Ossetia) on 31 March 1991, and in accordance with the Act on the Restoration of the State Independence of Georgia of 9 April. The Georgian state is a democratic republic. Its territorial integrity and the inviolability of its state borders are confirmed by the republic's Constitution and laws.

All state power belongs to the people, who exercise this power through referendums, other forms of direct democracy, and through their elected representatives. The State recognizes and defends universally recognized human rights and freedoms. The official state language is Georgian; in Abkhazia both Georgian and Abkhazian are recognized as state languages. While the State recognizes the exceptional role played by the Georgian Orthodox Church in Georgian history, it declares the complete freedom of faith and religion as well as the independence of the Church from the State. The capital is Tbilisi.

FUNDAMENTAL HUMAN RIGHTS AND FREEDOMS

Georgian citizenship is acquired by birth and naturalization. A Georgian citizen may not concurrently be a citizen of another state. Every person is free by birth and equal before the law, irrespective of race, colour, language, sex, religion, political and other views, national, ethnic and social affiliation, origin and place of residence. Every person has the inviolable right to life, which is protected by law. No one may be subjected to torture or inhuman, cruel or humiliating treatment or punishment.

Freedom of speech, thought, conscience and faith are guaranteed. The mass media are free. Censorship is prohibited. The right to assemble publicly is guaranteed, as is the right to form public associations, including trade unions and political parties. Every citizen who has attained the age of 18 years has the right to participate in referendums and elections of state and local administrative bodies.

THE GEORGIAN PARLIAMENT

The Georgian Parliament is the supreme representative body, implementing legislation and determining the basis of the country's domestic and foreign policies. It controls the activities of the Government, within the limits prescribed by the Constitution, and has other powers of implementation.

Parliament is elected on the basis of universal, equal and direct suffrage by secret ballot, for a term of four years. It is composed of 235 members: 150 elected by proportional representation (with a minimum requirement of 7% of the votes cast to secure parliamentary representation) and 85 by majority vote in single-member constituencies. Any citizen who has attained the age of 25 years and has the right to vote may be elected a member of Parliament. The instigation of criminal proceedings against a member of Parliament, and his/her detention or arrest, are only permitted upon approval by Parliament. A member of Parliament may not hold any position in state service or engage in entrepreneurial activities.

Parliament elects a Chairman and Deputy Chairmen (including one Deputy Chairman each from deputies elected in Abkhazia and Ajaria), for the length of its term of office. Members of Parliament may unite to form parliamentary factions. A faction must have no fewer than 10 members.

Following the creation of the appropriate conditions throughout the territory of Georgia and the formation of bodies of local self-government, the Georgian Parliament will be composed of two chambers: the Council of the Republic and the Senate. The Council of the Republic will be composed of deputies elected according to the proportional system. The Senate will be composed of deputies elected in Abkhazia, Ajaria and other territorial units of Georgia, and five members appointed by the President of Georgia.

THE PRESIDENT OF GEORGIA AND THE GOVERNMENT

The President of Georgia is Head of State and the head of executive power. The President directs and implements domestic and foreign policy, ensures the unity and territorial integrity of the country, and supervises the activities of state bodies in accordance with the Constitution. The President is the supreme representative of Georgia in foreign relations. He/she is elected on the basis of universal, equal and direct suffrage by secret ballot, for a period of five years. The President may not be elected for more than two consecutive terms. Any citizen of Georgia who has the right to vote and who has attained the age of 35 years and lived in Georgia for no less than 15 years, is eligible to be elected President.

The President of Georgia concludes international treaties and agreements and conducts negotiations with foreign states; with the consent of Parliament, appoints and dismisses Georgian ambassadors and other diplomatic representatives; receives the credentials of ambassadors and other diplomatic representatives of foreign states and international organizations; with the consent of Parliament, appoints members of the Government and Ministers; is empowered to remove Ministers from their posts; submits to Parliament the draft state budget, after agreeing upon its basic content with parliamentary committees; in the event of an armed attack on Georgia, declares a state of war, and concludes peace; during war or mass disorders, when the country's territorial integrity is threatened, or in the event of a *coup d'état* or an armed uprising, an ecological catastrophe or epidemic, or in other instances when the bodies of state power cannot implement their constitutional powers normally, declares a state of emergency; with the consent of Parliament, has the right to halt the activities of representative bodies of self-government or territorial units (if their activities create a threat to the sovereignty and territorial integrity of the country) as well as to halt state bodies in the exercise of their constitutional powers; signs and promulgates laws; decides questions of citizenship and the granting of political asylum; grants pardons; schedules elections to Parliament and other representative bodies; has the right to revoke acts of subordinate executive bodies; is the Commander-in-Chief of the Armed Forces; and appoints members of the National Security Council, chairs its meetings, and appoints and dismisses military commanders.

The President enjoys immunity. During his/her period in office, he/she may not be arrested, and no criminal proceedings may be instigated against him/her. In the event that the President violates the Constitution, betrays the State or commits other crimes, Parliament may remove him/her from office (with the approval of the Constitutional Court or the Supreme Court).

Members of the Government are accountable to the President. They do not have the right to hold other posts (except party posts), to engage in entrepreneurial activities or to receive a wage or any other permanent remuneration for any other activities. Members of the Government may be removed from their posts by an edict of the President or by Parliament. Ministries perform state management in specific spheres of state and public life. Each Ministry is headed by a Minister, who independently adopts decisions on questions within his/her sphere of jurisdiction.

JUDICIAL POWER

Judicial power is independent and is implemented only by the courts. Judges are independent in their activities and are subordinate only to the Constitution and the law. Court proceedings are held in public (except for certain specified instances). The decision of the court is delivered in public. Judges enjoy immunity. It is prohibited to instigate criminal proceedings against a judge or to detain or arrest him/her, without the consent of the Chairman of the Supreme Court.

The Constitutional Court is the legal body of constitutional control. It is composed of nine judges, three of whom are appointed by the President, three elected by Parliament, and three appointed by the Supreme Court. The term of office of members of the Constitutional Court is 10 years.

The Supreme Court supervises legal proceedings in general courts according to the established judicial procedure and, as the court of first instance, examines cases determined by law. On the recommendation of the President of Georgia, the Chairman and judges of the Supreme Court are elected by Parliament for a period of at least 10 years.

The Procurator's Office is an institution of judicial power, which carries out criminal prosecution, supervises the preliminary investigation and the execution of a punishment, and supports the state prosecution. On the recommendation of the President of Georgia, the Procurator-General is appointed by Parliament for a term of five years. Lower-ranking procurators are appointed by the Procurator-General.

DEFENCE OF THE STATE

Georgia has armed forces to protect the independence, sovereignty and territorial integrity of the country, and also to fulfil international obligations. The President of Georgia approves the structure of the armed forces and Parliament ratifies their numerical strength, on the recommendation of the National Security Council. The National Security Council, which is headed by the President of Georgia, carries out military organizational development and the defence of the country.

The Government

HEAD OF STATE

President of Georgia: EDUARD SHEVARDNADZE (elected by direct popular vote 5 November 1995; re-elected 9 April 2000).

GOVERNMENT
(April 2003)

Minister of State and Head of the State Chancellery: AVTANDIL DZHORBENADZE.

Minister of Agriculture and Produce: DAVIT KIRVALIDZE.

Minister of Culture: SESILI GOGIBERIDZE.

Minister of Defence: Gen. DAVIT TEVZADZE.

Minister of Economics, Industry and Trade: GIORGI GACHECHILADZE.

Minister of Education: ALEKSANDZRE KARTOZIA.

Minister of Environmental Protection and Natural Resources: NINO CHKHOBADZE.

Minister of Finance: MIRIAN GOGIASHVILI.

Minister of Foreign Affairs: IRAKLI MENAGHARISHVILI.

Minister of Fuel and Energy: DAVIT MIRTSKHULAVA.

Minister of Labour, Health and Social Welfare: AMIRAN GAMKRELIDZE.

Minister of Internal Affairs: KOBA NARCHEMASHVILI.

Minister of Justice: ROLAND GILIGASHVILI.

Minister of Refugees and Resettlement: VALERIAN VASHAKIDZE.

Minister of State Property Management: SOLOMON PAVLIASHVILI.

Minister of State Security: VALERIAN KHABURDZHANIA.

Minister of Transport and Communications: Dr MERAB ADEISHVILI.

Minister of Construction and Urban Planning: GIORGI ISAKADZE.

Minister of Emergency Affairs: MALKHAZ KAKABADZE.

MINISTRIES

Office of the President: 300002 Tbilisi, Rustaveli 29; tel. (32) 99-74-75; fax (32) 99-96-30; e-mail office@presidpress.gov.ge.

Office of the Government: 380018 Tbilisi, Ingorovka 7; tel. (32) 93-59-07; fax (32) 98-23-54.

Ministry of Agriculture and Produce: 380023 Tbilisi, Kostava 41; tel. (32) 99-02-72; fax (32) 99-94-44.

Ministry of Construction and Urban Planning: 380060 Tbilisi, Vazha Pshavela 16; tel. (32) 37-42-76; fax (32) 22-05-41.

Ministry of Culture: 380008 Tbilisi, Rustaveli 37; tel. (32) 93-22-55; fax (32) 99-90-37; e-mail info@mc.gov.ge; internet www.mc.gov.ge.

Ministry of Defence: 380007 Tbilisi, Universitetis 2A; tel. (32) 98-39-30; fax (32) 98-39-29.

Ministry of Economics, Industry and Trade: 380008 Tbilisi, Chanturia 12; tel. (32) 93-33-61; fax (32) 93-15-35.

Ministry of Education: 380002 Tbilisi, Uznadze 52; tel. (32) 95-88-86; fax (32) 77-00-73; internet www.parliament.ge/education.

Ministry of Emergency Affairs: Tbilisi.

Ministry of Environmental Protection and Natural Resources: 380015 Tbilisi, Kostava 68A; tel. (32) 23-06-64; fax (32) 94-34-20; e-mail irisi@gmep.kneta.ge; internet www.parliament.ge/governance/gov/enviro/parliament/ministry.htm.

Ministry of Finance: 380062 Tbilisi, Abashidze 70; tel. (32) 22-68-05; fax (32) 93-19-22; e-mail minister@mof.ge; internet www.mof.ge.

Ministry of Foreign Affairs: 380018 Tbilisi, 9 April 4; tel. (32) 98-93-77; fax (32) 99-72-48; internet www.mfa.gov.ge.

Ministry of Fuel and Energy: 380007 Tbilisi, Lermontov 10; tel. (32) 99-60-98; fax (32) 93-35-42.

Ministry of Labour, Health and Social Welfare: 380060 Tbilisi, K. Gamsakhurdia 30; tel. (32) 38-70-71; fax (32) 37-00-86.

Ministry of Internal Affairs: 380014 Tbilisi, Didikheivani 10; tel. (32) 99-62-96; fax (32) 98-65-32.

Ministry of Justice: 380008 Tbilisi, Griboedov 19; tel. (32) 93-27-21; fax (32) 93-02-25.

Ministry of Refugees and Resettlement: 380008 Tbilisi, Dadiani 30; tel. (32) 94-16-11; fax (32) 92-14-27.

Ministry of State Property Management: 380062 Tbilisi, Chavchavadze 64; tel. (32) 29-48-75; fax (32) 22-52-09; internet web.sanet.ge/mospm.

Ministry of State Security: 380018 Tbilisi, 9 April 4; tel. (32) 92-23-15; fax (32) 93-27-91.

Ministry of Transport and Communications: 380060 Tbilisi, Rustaveli 12; tel. (32) 93-28-46; fax (32) 77-00-17; e-mail mtc@iberiapac.ge; internet www.mtc.gov.ge.

President and Legislature

PRESIDENT

Presidential Election, 9 April 2000

Candidates	Votes	%
Eduard Shevardnadze	1,870,311	79.82
Dzhumber Patiashvili	390,486	16.66
Kartlos Gharibashvili	7,863	0.34
Avtandil Joglidze	5,942	0.25
Vazha Zhghenti	3,363	0.14
Tengiz Asanidze	2,793	0.12
Total*	2,343,176	100.00

* Including 62,418 spoilt voting papers (2.66% of the total).

GEORGIAN PARLIAMENT

Sakartvelos Parlamenti

380028 Tbilisi, Rustaveli 8; tel. (32) 93-61-70; fax (32) 99-93-86; internet www.parliament.ge.

Chairman: NINO BURDZHANADZE.

Deputy Chairmen: GIORGI TSERETELI, ROSTOM DZHAPARIDZE, VAKHTANG KOLBAYA, VAKHTANG RCHEULISHVILI, ELDAR SHENGELAIA, MERAB SAMADASHVILI.

General Election, 31 October and 14 November 1999

Parties and blocs	Party lists		Single-member constituency seats	Total seats
	% of votes*	Seats		
Citizens' Union of Georgia	41.9	85	45	130
Union for the Revival of Georgia bloc	25.7	51	7	58
Industry Will Save Georgia bloc	7.8	14	1	15
Georgian Labour Party	6.7	0	2	2
Abkhazian deputies†	—	—	12	12
Independent candidates	—	—	17	17
Total (incl. others)	100.0	150	84	234‡

* In order to win seats, parties needed to obtain at least 7% of the total votes cast.

† Owing to the electoral boycott in the secessionist region of Abkhazia, the mandates of 12 deputies from Abkhazia (elected to the legislature in 1992) were renewed.

‡ One of the single-member constituency seats remained unfilled. According to the Constitution of August 1995, the unicameral Georgian Parliament would be transformed into a bicameral body following the eventual restoration of Georgia's territorial integrity. The future Parliament would comprise a Council of the Republic and a Senate (the latter representing the various territorial units of the country).

Political Organizations

More than 40 parties and alliances contested the legislative election of 31 October 1999. The following are among the most prominent parties in Georgia:

Agrarian Party of Georgia: Tbilisi; f. 1994; Chair. ROIN LIPARTELIANI.

All Georgian Union of Revival: Batumi, Gogebashvili 7; tel. (222) 76-500; f. 1992; 200,000 mems; Chair. ASLAN ABASHIDZE.

Christian Democratic Union of Georgia: 380060 Tbilisi, Kazbegi 19; tel. (32) 37-25-34; fax (32) 37-47-44; f. 1990; centre-right; Leader GIORGI KOBAKHIDZE.

Citizens' Union of Georgia (CUG) (SMK): Tbilisi, Chavchavadze 55; tel. (32) 99-94-79; fax (32) 93-15-84; e-mail cug@access.sanet.ge; f. 1993; 300,000 mems; Chair. AVTANDIL DZHORBENADZE; Exec. Sec. GELA KVARATSKELIA.

Communist Party of Georgia: Tbilisi; tel. (32) 53-25-17; f. 1992; Chair. IVANE TSIKLAURI.

Conservative Party of Georgia: Tbilisi, Sabaduri 32; tel. (32) 72-44-73; f. 1995; legal successor to the Liberal–Conservative Party; separated from the Monarchist Party; Chair. GIORGI KARTOZIA.

Georgian Labour Party: Tbilisi, Javakhishvili 48; tel. (32) 94-39-22; fax (32) 96-60-46; f. 1997; main aim is the social protection of the population; Chair. SHALVA NATELASHVILI; 64,000 mems.

Georgian People's Party: Tbilisi; f. 1996 by dissident members of the National Democratic Party of Georgia.

Georgian Social Democratic Party: 380018 Tbilisi, 9 April 2; tel. (32) 99-95-50; fax (32) 98-73-89; f. 1893; ruling party 1918–21; re-established 1990; Chair. Prof. JEMAL KAKHNIASHVILI.

Georgian Social-Realistic Party: f. 1999; centrist party aimed at building united democratic Georgian state; Chair. Dr GURAM BEROZASHVILI.

Georgian Union of Reformers and Agrarians: Tbilisi; f. 1999; merger of Reformers' Union of Georgia and the Agrarian Union.

Industry Will Save Georgia: Tbilisi, Marjvena Sanapiro 7; tel. (32) 94-09-81; f. 1999; opposition alliance; Chair. GIORGI TOPADZE.

Liberal Democratic Party: Tbilisi; Chair. MIKHEIL NANEISHVILI.

Mtsvanta Partia (Green Party of Georgia): 380012 Tbilisi, Davit Aghmashenebeli 182; tel. (32) 95-20-33; fax (32) 35-16-74; e-mail party@access.sanet.ge; f. 1990; Chair. GIORGI GACHECHILADZE.

National Democratic Party of Georgia: 380008 Tbilisi, Rustaveli 21; tel. (32) 98-35-36; fax (32) 93-19-78; e-mail ndpfc@parliament.ge; f. 1981; centre-right; Leader IRINA SHARISHVILI-CHANTURIA.

National Independence Party: 380007 Tbilisi, Machabeli 8; tel. (32) 98-27-70; f. 1988; Chair. IRAKLI TSERETELI.

National Movement: 380018 Tbilisi, Vukol Beridze 9; tel. (32) 93-89-69; fax (32) 92-12-31; f. 2001; Co-Chair. MIKHEIL SAAKASHVILI, REVAZ SHAVISHVILI, LEVAN BERDZENISHVILI.

Nationalist Party: Tbilisi; tel. (32) 95-14-85; f. 1993; Chair. ZAZA VASHAKMADZE.

New Rights Party: 380014 Tbilisi, Bevreti 3; tel. (32) 92-03-18; fax (32) 92-38-58; e-mail newrights@kheta.ge; internet newrights.org.ge; f. 2000 as the New Faction by former members of the Citizens' Union of Georgia; name changed as above in 2001; won majority of seats in the municipal elections held in June 2002; Chair. LEVAN GACHECHILADZE.

Party for Liberation of Abkhazia: Tbilisi; advocates the restoration of the jurisdiction of Georgia and constitutional order in Abkhazia; f. 1998; Chair. TAMAZ NADAREISHVILI.

People's Patriotic Union of Georgia: Tbilisi; left-wing alliance; Chair. IGOR GIORGADZE.

People's Party—Didgori: Tbilisi, Uznadze 56; tel. (32) 96-03-69; fax (32) 93-57-98; e-mail pppess@parliament.ge; f. 1996; Chair. MAMUKA GIORGIADZE.

Republican Party of Georgia: Tbilisi, Antoneli 31/2; tel. and fax (32) 93-25-36; e-mail cdc@access.sanet.ge; f. 1995; absorbed Georgian Popular Front (f. 1989); Chair. IVLIANE KHAINDRAVA.

Rightist Alternative Alliance: Tbilisi; f. 2000; alliance between the Union of Georgian Traditionalists and the Liberal Economic Party.

Round Table—Free Georgia: Tbilisi, Dgebuadze 4; tel. (32) 95-48-20; f. 1990; opposition party uniting supporters of former President Zviad Gamsakhurdia; Chair. SOSO DZHADZHANIDZE.

Socialist Party of Georgia: Tbilisi, Leselidze 41; tel. (32) 98-33-67; fax (32) 93-27-09; e-mail spg@geo-plus.net; f. 1995; Chair. VAKHTANG RCHEULISHVILI.

Union for the Revival of Georgia: Batumi, Ninoshvili 5; tel. (222) 76-500; fax (222) 76-510; principal opposition alliance including parties loyal to the former President, Zviad Gamsakhurdia (the All-Georgian Union of Revival, the Socialist Party of Georgia, the Union of Traditionalists, the People's Party and the 21st Century bloc); Chair. ASLAN ABASHIDZE.

Union of Georgian Realists: f. 1997; aims to achieve political and economic stability in a united Georgia.

Union of Georgian Traditionalists: Tbilisi, Arsena 10; f. 1990; Chair. AKAKI ASATIANI.

Union of National Concord and Justice: Tbilisi; f. 2002; Leader GURAM ABSANDZE.

United Communist Party of Georgia: Tbilisi; tel. (32) 38-41-65; f. 1994; 87,000 mems (2000); First Sec. PANTELEIMON GIORGADZE.

United Democrats: Tbilisi, Marshal Gelovani 4A; tel. (32) 95-98-23; f. 2002; radical centrist; formed from the reformist faction of CUG; Chair. ZURAB ZHVANIA.

Unity Alliance (Ertoba): Tbilisi; f. 2001; social-democratic; Co-Chair. DZHUMBER PATIASHVILI, ALEXANDER CHACHIA.

Diplomatic Representation

EMBASSIES IN GEORGIA

Armenia: 380002 Tbilisi, Tetelashvili 4; tel. (32) 95-94-43; fax (32) 99-01-26; Ambassador GEORGE KHOSROEV.

Azerbaijan: 380079 Tbilisi, Mukhadze 4; tel. and fax (32) 23-40-37; Ambassador HAJAN HAJIYEV.

China, People's Republic: 380008 Tbilisi, Barnov 52; POB 224; tel. (32) 99-80-11; fax (32) 93-12-76; e-mail gzj@access.sanet.ge; Ambassador XU JIANGUO.

Czech Republic: 380054 Tbilisi, Tsereteli 57; tel. (32) 95-44-37; fax (32) 95-40-92; e-mail tbilisi@embassy.mzv.cz; Ambassador JIŘI NEKVASIL.

France: 380008 Tbilisi, Gogebashvili 15; tel. (32) 93-42-10; fax (32) 95-33-75; internet www.multimania.com/ambafce/index.htm; Ambassador MIREILLE MUSSO.

Germany: 380012 Tbilisi, Davit Aghmashenebeli 166; tel. (32) 95-09-36; fax (32) 95-89-10; e-mail deut.bot.tbilissi@access.sanet.ge; Ambassador UWE SCHRAMM.

Greece: 380079 Tbilisi, Arakishvili 5; tel. and fax (32) 93-89-81; fax (32) 00-10-39; e-mail grembgeo@access.sanet.ge; Ambassador CONSTANTINA MAVROSKELIDOU.

Holy See: 380086 Tbilisi, Dzhgenti 40, Nutsubidze Plateau II; tel. (32) 94-13-05; fax (32) 29-39-44; e-mail nuntius@access.sanet.ge; Apostolic Nuncio Most Rev. CLAUDIO GUGEROTTI (Titular Archbishop of Ravello).

Iran: 380060 Tbilisi, Zovreti 16; tel. (32) 98-69-90; fax (32) 98-69-93; Ambassador HOSSEIN AMIAN TUSIMI.

Israel: 380012 Tbilisi, Davit Aghmashenebeli 61; tel. (32) 96-02-13; fax (32) 95-17-09; Ambassador EHUD EITAM.

Italy: 380008 Tbilisi, Chitadze 3A; tel. (32) 99-64-18; fax (32) 99-64-15; e-mail ambita.tbilisi@access.sanet.ge; Ambassador MICHELANGELO PIPAN.

Korea, Republic: Tbilisi; Ambassador YI CHONG-PIN.

Poland: Tbilisi, Zubalashvili 19; tel. (32) 92-03-98; fax (32) 92-03-97; Chargé d'affaires MAREK MARTINEK.

Romania: Tbilisi, Lvov 7; tel. (32) 25-00-98; fax (32) 25-00-97; e-mail ambasada@caucasus.net; Ambassador CONSTANTIN GIRBEA.

Russia: 380002 Tbilisi, Tsinamdzgvrishvili 90; tel. (32) 95-59-11; fax (32) 95-52-33; Ambassador VLADIMIR CHKHIKVISHVILI.

Turkey: 380002 Tbilisi, Davit Aghmashenebeli 61; tel. (32) 95-20-14; fax (32) 95-18-10; e-mail tiblisbe@mfa.gov.tr; Ambassador DICLE KOPUZ.

Ukraine: 380060 Tbilisi, Oniashvili 75; tel. (32) 98-93-62; fax (32) 23-71-45; e-mail emb_ge@mfa.gov.ua; internet www.uaembingeorgia.gov.ua; Ambassador STEFAN VOLKOVETSKII.

United Kingdom: 380003 Tbilisi, Sheraton Palace Hotel; tel. (32) 95-54-97; fax (32) 00-10-65; e-mail british.embassy@caucasus.net; internet www.britishembassy.org.ge; Ambassador DEBORAH BARNES-JONES.

USA: 380026 Tbilisi, Atoneli 25; tel. (32) 98-99-67; fax (32) 93-37-59; internet web.sanet.ge/usembassy; Ambassador RICHARD MILES.

Judicial System

Constitutional Court: Tbilisi, Rustaveli 29; e-mail court@const
.gov.ge; internet www.constcourt.gov.ge; Chair. DZHONI KHETSURIANI.

Supreme Court

380010 Tbilisi, Zubalashvilebi 32; tel. (32) 99-65-46; fax (32) 99-01-
64; e-mail reception@supremecourt.ge.

Chair. LADO CHANTURIA.

Procurator-General: NUGZAR GABRICHIDZE.

First Deputy Procurator-General: BADRI BITSADZE.

Council of Justice: Tbilisi, Davit Aghmashenebeli 80; tel. and fax
(32) 95-86-77; e-mail justice@caucasus.net; f. 1997; 12-member
council that co-ordinates the appointment of judges and their activities; four mems nominated by the President, four by Parliament and
four by the Supreme Court; Exec. Sec. ZURAB ABASHIDZE.

Religion

CHRISTIANITY

The Georgian Orthodox Church

The Georgian Orthodox Church is divided into 27 dioceses, and
includes not only Georgian parishes, but also several Russian, Greek
and Armenian Orthodox communities, which are under the jurisdiction of the Primate of the Georgian Orthodox Church. There are
40 monasteries and convents, two theological academies and four
seminaries.

Patriarchate: 380005 Tbilisi, King Erekle II Sq. 1; tel. (32) 99-03-
78; fax (32) 98-71-14; e-mail ecclesia@access.sanet.ge; internet www
.orthodox-patriarchate-of-georgia.org.ge; Catholicos-Patriarch of All
Georgia ILIA II.

The Roman Catholic Church

The Apostolic Administrator of the Caucasus is the Apostolic Nuncio
to Georgia, Armenia and Azerbaijan, who is resident in Tbilisi (see
Diplomatic Representation).

ISLAM

There are Islamic communities among the Ajarians, Abkhazians,
Azerbaijanis, Kurds and some Ossetians. The country falls under
the jurisdiction of the Muslim Board of Transcaucasia, based in
Baku (Azerbaijan).

The Press

Department of the Press: 380008 Tbilisi, Jorjiashvili 12; tel. (32)
98-70-08; govt regulatory body; Dir V. RTSKHILADZE.

PRINCIPAL NEWSPAPERS

In 1998 243 newspaper titles were printed, with a total annual
circulation of 15.9m. Those listed below appear in Georgian, except
where otherwise stated.

Akhalgazrda Iverieli (Young Iberian): Tbilisi, Kostava 14; tel. (32)
93-31-49; 3 a week; organ of the Georgian Parliament; Editor MERAB
BALARJISHVILI.

Akhali Taoba (New Generation): Tbilisi, Davit Aghmashenebeli
89/24; tel. (32) 95-25-89; fax (32) 94-06-91; e-mail akhtao@geo.net.ge;
internet www.opentext.org.ge/akhalitaoba; f. 1993; in Georgian;
Editor SOSO GONIASHVILI.

Dilis Gazeti (Morning Newspaper): Tbilisi, Marjanishvili 5; tel. (32)
96-91-88; fax (32) 96-91-81; e-mail dilgazet@access.sanet.ge;
internet www.opentext.ge/dilisgazeti; Editor MANANA KARTOZIA.

Droni (Times): Tbilisi, Kostava 14; tel. (32) 99-56-54; e-mail
newspdroni@usa.net; internet www.opentext.org.ge/droni/; 2 a
week; Editor-in-Chief SOSO SIMONISHVILI.

Eri (Nation): Tbilisi; weekly; organ of the Georgian Parliament;
Editor A. SILAGADZE.

Ertoba: Tbilisi; f. 1918; weekly; organ of the Georgian Social Democratic Party.

Georgian Messenger: Tbilisi, Chavchavadze 55; tel. and fax (32)
22-76-21; e-mail gtze@messenger.com.ge; internet www.messenger
.com.ge; f. 1919; daily; in English; Editor-in-Chief ZAZA GACHECHI-
LADZE.

Georgian Times: Tbilisi, Gorgasali 37; tel. (32) 93-10-25; fax (32)
99-60-97; e-mail times@gtze.com.ge; internet www.georgiantimes

.ge; f. 1993; weekly; in English, Georgian and Russian; Editor-in-
Chief ZVIAD POCHKHUA; circ. 2,000.

Iberia Spektri (Iberian Spectrum): Tbilisi, Machabeli 11; tel. (32)
98-73-87; fax (32) 98-73-88; internet www.opentext.org.ge/
iberia-spectri/; Editor IRAKLI GOTSIRIDZE.

Literaturuli Sakartvelo (Literary Georgia): Tbilisi, Gudiashvili
Sq. 2; tel. (32) 99-84-04; internet www.opentext.org.ge/
literaturulisakartvelo/; weekly; organ of the Union of Writers of
Georgia; Editor TAMAZ TSIVTSIVADZE.

Mamuli (Native Land): Tbilisi; fortnightly; organ of the Rustaveli
Society; Editor T. CHANTURIA.

Respublika (Republic): 380096 Tbilisi, Kostava 14; tel. and fax (32)
93-43-91; f. 1990; weekly; independent; Editor J. NINUA; circ. 40,000.

Rezonansi: Tbilisi, Davit Aghmashenebeli 89–24; tel. (32) 95-69-38;
fax (32) 96-92-60; e-mail n1001@geo.net.ge; internet www
.resonancedaily.com.ge; f. 1992; daily; Editor-in-Chief LASHA
TUGUSHI; circ. 10,000.

Sakartvelo (Georgia): 380096 Tbilisi, Kostava 14; tel. (32) 99-92-26;
internet www.opentext.org.ge/sakartvelo/; 5 a week; organ of the
Georgian Parliament; Editor SERGO DZHANASHIA.

Shvidi Dghe (Seven Days): Tbilisi, Krilov 5; tel. (32) 94-35-52; fax
(32) 95-40-76; e-mail dge7@caucasus.net; internet www.opentext
.org.ge_7dge; f. 1991; weekly; Dir GELA GURGENIDZE; Editor KOBA
AKHALBEDASHVILI; circ. 3,000.

Svobodnaya Gruziya (Free Georgia): Tbilisi, Rustaveli 42; tel. (32)
93-13-54; fax (32) 93-17-06; e-mail new@caucasus.net; internet www
.svobodnaya-gruzia.com; f. 1922 as Zanya Vostoka, name changed as
above in 1991; socio-political; in Russian; Editor-in-Chief TATO
LASCHISHVILI; circ. 5,000.

Tavisupali Sakartvelo (Free Georgia): 380008 Tbilisi, POB W227;
tel. (32) 95-48-20; weekly; organ of Round Table—Free Georgia
party.

Tbilisi Times: 380007 Tbilisi, Kostava 20; tel. (32) 98-76-13; fax
(32) 99-63-24; e-mail david@tbilisitimes.com; internet www
.tbilisitimes.com; in English and Georgian; independent, non-profit;
Dirs DAVID DZIDZIKASHVILI, SHAVLEG SHAVERDASHVILI.

Vestnik Gruzii (Georgian Herald): Tbilisi; 5 a week; organ of the
Georgian Parliament; in Russian; Editor V. KESHELAVA.

Weekly Post: 380002 Tbilisi, POB 85; tel. and fax (32) 94-07-07;
e-mail weekpost@iberiapac.ge; f. 1991; Editor BESIK KHARANAULI.

PRINCIPAL PERIODICALS

Alashara: 394981 Sukhumi, Govt House, kor. 1; tel. (122) 2-35-40;
organ of the Abkhazian Writers' Organization of the Union of
Writers of Georgia; in Abkhazian.

Dila (Morning): 380096 Tbilisi, Kostava 14; tel. (32) 93-41-30; f.
1904; fortnightly; illustrated; for 5–12 year-olds; Editor-in-Chief
DODO TSIVTSIVADZE; circ. 4,500.

Drosha (Banner): Tbilisi; f. 1923; monthly; politics and fiction;
Editor O. KINKLADZE.

Fidiyag: Tskhinvali; tel. (344) 2-22-65; organ of the South Ossetian
Writers' Organization of the Union of Writers of Georgia; in Ossetian.

Khelovneba (Art): Tbilisi; f. 1953, fmrly Sabchota Khelovneba
(Soviet Art); monthly; journal of the Ministry of Culture; Editor N.
GURABANIDZE.

Kritika (Criticism): 380008 Tbilisi, Rustaveli 42; tel. (32) 93-22-85;
f. 1972; every 2 months; publ. by Merani Publishing House; journal
of the Union of Writers of Georgia; literature, miscellaneous; Editor
V. KHARCHILAVA.

Kurieri: Tbilisi, Kostava 14; tel. (32) 99-00-49; Editor IRAKLI TSINT-
SADZE.

Literaturnaya Gruziya (Literary Georgia): 380008 Tbilisi, Kostava 5; tel. (32) 99-06-59; fax (32) 22-47-37; e-mail abzianidze@
hotmail.com; f. 1957; quarterly journal; politics, art and fiction; in
Russian; Editor Prof. ZAZA ABZIANIDZE.

Metsniereba da Tekhnika (Science and Technology): 380060 Tbilisi; f. 1949; monthly; publ. by the Metsniereba Publishing House;
journal of the Georgian Academy of Sciences; popular; Editor Z.
TSILOSANI.

Mnatobi (Luminary): 380008 Tbilisi, Rustaveli 28; tel. (32) 99-51-
56; f. 1924; monthly; journal of the Union of Writers of Georgia;
fiction, poetry and arts; Editor T. CHILADZE.

Nakaduli (Stream): Tbilisi, Kostava 14; tel. (32) 93-31-81; f. 1926;
fmrly *Pioneri*; monthly; journal of the Ministry of Education; illustrated; for 10–15-year-olds; Editor MANANA GELASHVILI; circ. 5,000.

Niangi (Crocodile): 380096 Tbilisi, Kostava 14; f. 1923; fortnightly; satirical; Editor Z. BOLKVADZE.

Politika (Politics): Tbilisi; theoretical, political, social sciences; Editor M. GOGUADZE.

Sakartvelos Kali (Georgian Woman): 380096 Tbilisi, Kostava 14; tel. (32) 99-98-71; f. 1957; popular, socio-political and literary; Editor-in-Chief NARGIZA MGELADZE; circ. 3,000.

Sakartvelos Metsnierebata Akedemiis Matsne (Herald of the Georgian Academy of Sciences, Biological Series): Tbilisi; f. 1975; 6 a year; in Georgian, English and Russian; Editor-in-Chief VAZHA OKUJAVA.

Sakartvelos Metsnierebata Akedemiis Matsne (Herald of the Georgian Academy of Sciences, Chemical Series): Tbilisi; f. 1975; quarterly; in Georgian, English and Russian; Editor-in-Chief TEI-MURAZ ANDRONIKASHVILI.

Sakartvelos Metsnierebata Akademiis Moambe (Bulletin of Georgian Academy of Sciences): 380008 Tbilisi, Rustaveli 52; tel. (32) 99-75-93; fax (32) 99-88-23; e-mail bulletin@presid.achet.ge; f. 1940; 6 a year; in Georgian and English; Editor-in-Chief ALBERT TAVKHELIDZE.

Sarke: Tbilisi, Chubinashvili 50; tel. (32) 96-75-43; Editor MEDEA SANAIA.

Saunje (Treasure): 380007 Tbilisi, Dadiani 2; tel. (32) 72-47-31; f. 1974; 6 a year; organ of the Union of Writers of Georgia; foreign literature in translation; Editor S. NISHNIANIDZE.

Tsiskari (Dawn): 380007 Tbilisi, Khidis 1/29; tel. (32) 99-85-81; f. 1957; monthly; organ of the Union of Writers of Georgia; fiction; Editor ZAUR KALANDIA.

NEWS AGENCIES

Black Sea Press: Tbilisi, Rustaveli 42; tel. (32) 98-94-69; fax (32) 93-17-49; Dir DAVIT IMEDASHVILI.

Iberia: Tbilisi, Marjanishvili 5; tel. (32) 93-64-22; Dir KAKHA GAGLOSHVILI.

Iprinda: Tbilisi, Rustaveli 19; tel. (32) 99-03-77; fax (32) 98-73-65; Dir KETEVAN BOKHUA.

Kontakt: Tbilisi, Kostava 68; tel. (32) 36-04-79; fax (32) 22-18-45; Dir DIMITRI KIKVADZE.

Prime News Agency: Tbilisi, Kutateladze 5; tel. (32) 92-32-12; fax (32) 92-32-02; e-mail pna@pna.com.ge; internet www.prime-news .com.ge; f. 1997 after dissolution of BGI news agency.

Sakinform: 380008 Tbilisi, Rustaveli 42; tel. (32) 93-19-20; fax (32) 99-92-00; e-mail gha@Iberiapac.ge; internet www.sakinform.ge; f. 1921; state information agency; Dir KAKHA IMNADZE.

Sarke Information Agency: 380002 Tbilisi, Davit Aghmashene-beli 63; tel. (32) 95-06-59; fax (32) 95-08-37; e-mail info@sarke.com; internet www.sarke.com; f. 1992; economic and business news from Georgia and the Caucasus; Dir VALERIAN KHUKHUNASHVILI; Editor-in-Chief VICTORIA GUJELASHVILI.

JOURNALISTS' ASSOCIATION

Independent Association of Georgian Journalists: 380002 Tbilisi, Marjanishvili 5, Rm 230; tel. and fax (32) 95-68-50; e-mail iagj@gol.ge; internet www.iagj.gol.ge; f. 2000; Pres. ZVIAD POCHKHUA.

Journalists' Federation of Georgia: 380005 Tbilisi, Erekles 6; tel. (32) 98-24-47; Chair. AKAKI SIKHARULIDZE.

Publishers

Ganatleba (Education): 380064 Tbilisi, Chubinashvili 50; tel. (32) 95-50-97; f. 1957; educational, literature; Dir L. KHUNDADZE.

Georgian National Universal Encyclopaedia: Tbilisi, Tsereteli 1; Editor-in-Chief A. SAKVARELIDZE.

Khelovneba (Art): 380002 Tbilisi, Davit Aghmashenebeli 179; f. 1947; Dir N. DZHASHI.

Merani (Writer): 380008 Tbilisi, Rustaveli 42; tel. (32) 99-64-92; fax (32) 93-46-75; e-mail hmerani@iberiapac.ge; f. 1921; fiction; Dir G. GVERDTSITELI.

Metsniereba (Sciences): 380060 Tbilisi, Gamrekeli 19; tel. and fax (32) 37-22-97; e-mail publicat@gw.acnet.ge; f. 1941; Industrial-Publishing Corpn of the Georgian Academy of Sciences; Dir DAVID KOLOTAURI; Editor CISANA KARTOZIA.

Nakaduli (Stream): 380094 Tbilisi, Gamsakhurdia 28; tel. (32) 38-69-12; f. 1938; books for children and youth; Dir BAKUR SULAKAURI.

Publishing House of Tbilisi State University: 380079 Tbilisi, Chavchavadze 14; f. 1933; scientific and educational literature; Editor V. GAMKRELIDZE.

Sakartvelo (Georgia): 380002 Tbilisi, Marjanishvili 5; tel. (32) 95-42-01; f. 1921; fmrly *Sabchota Sakartvelo* (Soviet Georgia); political, scientific and fiction; Dir DZHANSUL GVINJILIA.

Broadcasting and Communications

TELECOMMUNICATIONS

National Regulatory Authority: Tbilisi; Chair. VAKHTANG ABA-SHIDZE.

Telecom Georgia: 380058 Tbilisi, Rustaveli 31; tel. (32) 99-91-97; fax (32) 00-11-11; e-mail isonishvili@telecom.ge; f. 1994; provides telecommunications services; 51% state-owned, 30% owned by International Telecell Inc. (USA), 19% owned by Bulcom (Cyprus); Pres. G. KHMALADZE; Dir N. KAKHELI.

BROADCASTING

State Department of Television and Radio: Tbilisi, Kostava 68; tel. (32) 36-81-66; e-mail gtvr@iberiapac.ge; Chair. (vacant).

Television

Ajaria TV: 384500 Batumi, Memed Abashidze 41; tel. (222) 74-370; fax (222) 74-371; e-mail ajaratv@ajaratv.com; internet www.ajaratv .com; Chief Exec. TAMAZ BAKURIDZE; Dir VAKHTANG TODUA.

Channel 7: Tbilisi; tel. (32) 94-31-65; fax (32) 33-12-33; e-mail channel@macrocom.ge; internet www.macrocom.com.ge; f. 2000; cable television, 15 channels.

Georgian Television: 380071 Tbilisi, Kostava 68; tel. and fax (32) 29-42-54; e-mail foraf@access.sanet.ge; internet www.geotvr.ge; f. 1956; two stations; relays from Russian television.

Rustavi 2: 380077 Tbilisi, Vazha-Pshavela 45; tel. (32) 32-22-71; fax (32) 25-00-31; e-mail tv@rustavi2.com; internet www.rustavi2.com; f. 1994; independent; Gen. Dir NIKA TABATADZE.

Radio

Georgian Radio: 380071 Tbilisi, Kostava 68; tel. (32) 36-83-62; fax (32) 36-86-65; f. 1956; govt-controlled; broadcasts in Georgian and Russian, with regional services for Abkhazia, Ajaria and South Ossetia; foreign service in English and German; two stations; Dir VAKHTANG NANITASHVILI.

Finance

(cap. = capital; res = reserves; dep. = deposits; m. = million; brs = branches; amounts in lari, unless otherwise indicated)

BANKING

In August 1991 the Georgian Supreme Soviet adopted legislation which nationalized all branches of all-Union (USSR) banks in Georgia. Georgian branches of the USSR State Bank (Gosbank) were transferred to the National Bank of Georgia.

In 1995 more than 50% of the commercial banks in Georgia (then numbering almost 230) were closed down, as many banks did not satisify general legal provisions and only five properly complied with the paid-in captial requirement. The remaining banks were to be audited by the National Bank to verify their commercial viability. In April 1995 three of the five specialized state commercial banks (consisting of the domestic branches of the specialized banks of the former USSR) merged to form the United Georgian Bank. In 1996 the authorized capital requirement was raised to 5m. lari. At March 2003 there were 27 commercial banks operating in Georgia.

Central Bank

National Bank of Georgia: 380005 Tbilisi, Leonidze 3–5; tel. (32) 99-65-05; fax (32) 99-93-46; e-mail nbg@access.sunet.ge; internet www.nbg.gov.ge; f. 1991; cap. 1.3m., res 25.1m., dep. 185.3m., total assets 1,612m. (Dec. 2001); Pres. and Chair. of Bd IRAKLI MANAGADZE; 9 brs.

Other Banks

Agro-Business Bank: Tbilisi, Budapeshti 10; tel. (32) 25-08-20; fax (32) 93-28-80; internet www.abg.com.ge; f. 2000; cap. 6.9m., dep. 4.1m. (Dec. 2001); wholly owned by the European Commission; Chair. MIKHEIL MGALOBLISHVILI; 61 brs.

Bank of Georgia: 380005 Tbilisi, Pushkin 3; tel. (32) 44-41-05; fax (32) 44-41-82; e-mail welcome@bog.ge; internet www.bog.ge; f. 1991 as Zhilsotsbank—Social Development Bank, one of five specialized state commercial banks; renamed as above 1994; universal joint-stock commercial bank; cap. 44.9m., dep. 98.7m. (Dec. 2002); Pres. VLADIMER PATEISHVILI; Gen. Dir ELGUJA SILAGADZE; 25 brs.

Cartu Bank JSC: 380062 Tbilisi, Chavchavadze 39A; tel. (32) 23-00-21; fax (32) 23-03-83; e-mail cartubank@cartubank.ge; internet www.cartubank.ge; f. 1996 name changed as above Sept. 1998; cap. 12.5m., res 1.9m., dep. 3.7m. (Dec. 2000); Pres. GURAM CHAGELISHVILI; Chair. of Bd G. CHRDILELI; 4 brs.

Cavcasioni: 380062 Tbilisi, Chubinishvili 41; tel. (32) 95-14-44; fax (32) 95-93-93; e-mail caucasioni@iberiapac.ge; f. 1992; cap. 3.0m., res 0.1m., dep. 0.4m. (Dec. 1999); Pres. BESO MAGRADZE; Chair. ZAZIA PANKVELASHVILI.

Georgian Capital Bank: 384517 Batumi, Gogebashvili 60; tel. (222) 7-65-82; fax (222) 7-60-01; e-mail inter@gmb-batumi.com; f. 1993; cap. 3.6m., res 0.3m., dep. 13m. (Dec. 1998); Chair. NUGZAR MIKELADZE; 4 brs.

Georgian Post Bank: 380064 Tbilisi, Tsinamdzghvrili 95; tel. (32) 96-24-05; fax (32) 95-72-23; e-mail gps@iberiapac.ge.

Intellectbank: 380064 Tbilisi, Davit Aghmashenebeli 127; tel. (32) 23-70-83; fax (32) 95-09-31; e-mail intellect@iberiapac.ge; internet www.intellectbank.net; f. 1993; equity 5.8m., dep. 27.1m. (Dec. 1999); Pres. KAKHA GIUASHVILI; Gen. Dir VLADIMER CHANISHVILI; 14 brs.

TBC Bank: 380079 Tbilisi, Chavchavadze 11; tel. (32) 22-06-61; fax (32) 22-04-06; e-mail info@tbcbank.com.ge; internet www.tbcbank.com.ge; f. 1992; cap. 5.0m., res 24.9m., dep. 134.4m. (2002); Pres. VAKHTANG BUTSKHRIKIDZE; 9 brs.

TbilCreditBank: 380008 Tbilisi, Rustaveli 27; tel. (32) 98-60-10; fax (32) 98-27-83; e-mail tbilcred@caucasus.net; internet www.tbilcreditbank.com; f. 1994; cap. 5.5m., dep. 7m. (Dec. 1999); Chair. and Chief Exec. DAVIT BUADZE.

Tbiluniversalbank Ltd: 380071 Tbilisi, Kostava 70; tel. (32) 99-82-92; fax (32) 98-61-68; e-mail info@tub.ge; internet www.tbiluniversalbank.com; f. 1994 as Superbank; name changed as above 1995; cap. 5.0m., dep. 11.2m. (Dec. 2002); Chair. of Dirs TARIEL GVALIA; Chair. of Supervisory Bd NIKOLOZ TEVZADZE; 3 brs.

United Georgian Bank: 380002 Tbilisi, Uznadze 37; tel. (32) 95-60-85; fax (32) 99-91-39; e-mail admin@ugb.com.ge; internet www.ugb.com.ge; f. 1995 by merger of three specialized state commercial banks; cap. 21.0m., res 3.2m., dep. 72.9m. (2002); Chair. of Supervisory Bd IVANE CHKARTISHVILI; Gen. Dir IRAKLI KOVZANADZE; 18 brs.

STOCK EXCHANGE

Georgian Stock Exchange: 380062 Tbilisi, Chavchavadze 74A; tel. (32) 22-07-18; fax (32) 25-18-76; e-mail info@gse.ge; internet www.gse.ge; f. 1999; Chair. of Supervisory Bd GEORGE LOLADZE; Gen. Dir VAKHTANG SVANADZE.

CURRENCY EXCHANGE

Tbilisi Interbank Currency Exchange (TICEX): 380005 Tbilisi, Galaktion Tabidze 4; tel. (32) 92-34-43; fax (32) 92-23-01; Gen. Dir DAVIT KLDIASHVILI.

Trade and Industry

GOVERNMENT AGENCIES

Georgian Investment Centre: 380077 Tbilisi, Kazbegi 42; tel. (32) 23-41-34; fax (32) 92-18-40; e-mail gic@access.sanet.ge; internet www.gic.ge; f. 1996 to promote foreign and domestic investment; Dir SABA SARISHVILI.

State Property Management Agency: Tbilisi; f. 1992; responsible for divestment of state-owned enterprises.

INSURANCE

Aldagi Insurance Co: 380062 Tbilisi, Chavchavadze 62; tel. (32) 29-49-07; fax (32) 29-49-05; e-mail aldagi@aldagi.com.ge; internet www.aldagi.com.ge; f. 1990; Chair. GURAM ASSATHIANY; Gen. Dir TENGIZ MEZURNISHVILI.

Anglo-Georgian Insurance Co (AGIC): 380030 Tbilisi, I. Abashidze 29; tel. (32) 25-03-51; fax (32) 25-03-50; e-mail post@agic.com.ge; internet www.agic.com.ge; f. 1998 as a joint-stock co; all types of insurance; Gen. Dir FRANCIS MATHEW.

Central Insurance Co: 380019 Tbilisi, Tsereteli 126; tel. (32) 98-87-18; Gen. Dir NIKOLAI A. DVALADZE.

Georgian Pension and Insurance Holding Co: Tbilisi, Chavchavadze 1, Bldg 5; tel. (32) 92-01-20; internet www.gpih.ge; Gen. Dir PAATA GADZADZE.

Georgian International Insurance Ltd: Tbilisi; tel. (32) 983-94-80; fax (32) 98-94-79; f. 1993; Pres. V. KIZIKURASHVILI; Dir IGOR KARPOVICH.

CHAMBER OF COMMERCE

Georgian Chamber of Commerce and Industry: 380079 Tbilisi, Chavchavadze 11; tel. (32) 23-00-45; fax (32) 23-57-60; e-mail gcci@access.sanet.ge; internet www.gcci.org.ge; f. 1963; brs in Sukhumi and Batumi; Chair. GURAM D. AKHVLEDIANI.

TRADE ASSOCIATION

Georgian Import Export (Geoimpex): 380008 Tbilisi, Giorgiashvili 12; tel. (32) 99-70-90; fax (32) 98-25-41; Gen. Dir T. A. GOGOBERIDZE.

UTILITIES

Electricity

AES Telasi: 380054 Tbilisi, Vani 3; tel. (32) 25-52-11; fax (32) 77-99-78; internet www.AES-TELASI.com; privatized in 1999; 75% owned by AES Silk Road BV, a subsidiary of AES Corpn (USA); Dir MICHAEL SCHOLEY.

Department of Power Supply: Tbilisi, V. Vekua 1; tel. (32) 98-05-65; attached to the Ministry of Fuel and Energy.

Sakenergo: 380005 Tbilisi, V. Vekua 1; tel. (32) 98-98-14; fax (32) 98-31-97; formerly state-owned energy supplier; in 1996 restructured into three cos (generation, transmission and distribution); transformation into joint-stock cos in progress in 1997; Gen. Dir VAZHA METREVELI.

Sakenergogeneratsia: 380005 Tbilisi, V. Vekua 1; tel. and fax (32) 98-98-13; state power-generating co; Gen. Dir G. BADURASHVILI.

Gas

International Gas Corpn of Georgia: joint-stock co; Chair. ALEKSANDR GOTSIRIDZE.

Tbilgazi Ltd: 380007 Tbilisi, Mitsskevichi 18; tel. (32) 38-76-25; fax (32) 37-56-51; gas production co; Chair. TSAAVA VACHTANGI.

Saktransgasmretsvi: 380077 Tbilisi, Delisi III 22; tel. (32) 93-22-04; fax (32) 99-66-83; e-mail transgas@access.sanet.ge; f. 1962; state-owned; operates main gas pipelines; Chair. of Bd IVANE ZAZASHVILI.

Water

Tbilisi Water Utility: Tbilisi; scheduled for privatization.

TRADE UNIONS

Amalgamation of Trade Unions of Georgia (GTUA): 380122 Tbilisi, Shartava 7; tel. (32) 38-29-95; fax (32) 22-46-63; e-mail gtua@geo.net.ge; f. 1995 as Confederation of Trade Unions of Georgia, name changed as above in 2000; comprises branch unions with a total membership of approx. 800,000; Chair. IRAKLI TUGUSHI.

Free Trade Union of Journalists: Tbilisi, Vazha Pshavela pr. 43; f. 2000; over 100 mems; Chair. BEZHAN MESKHI.

Transport

RAILWAYS

In 1997 Georgia's rail network (including the sections within the secessionist republic of Abkhazia) totalled approximately 1,600 km. However, some 500 km of track was reported to be in a poor state of repair, as a result of which the capacity of some sections of the network had decreased by more than 75% since 1990. The main rail links are with Russia, along the Black Sea coast, with Azerbaijan, with Armenia and with Iran. The Georgian–Armenian railway continues into eastern Turkey. Civil conflict in the mid-1990s disrupted sections of the railway network. The separatist war in Abkhazia resulted in the severance of Georgia's rail connection with Russia. However, services to the Russian capital, Moscow, resumed in mid-1997, following a four-year interruption. In mid-1998 it was announced that the European Bank for Reconstruction and Development was to assist with the refurbishment of the railways.

The first section of the Tbilisi Metro was opened in 1966; by 1999 the system comprised two lines with 20 stations, totalling 23 km in length, and three extensions, totalling 15 km, were under construction.

Georgian Railways Ltd: 380012 Tbilisi, Tamara Mepe 15; tel. (32) 94-20-60; fax (32) 95-25-27; e-mail a.chkhaidze@georail.org.ge; internet www.railway.ge; f. 1872, following the dissolution of the former Soviet Railways, became a ltd co in 1998; Chair. AKAKI CHKHAIDZE.

Tbilisi Metropolitena: 380012 Tbilisi, Pl. Vokzalnaya 2; tel. (32) 95-15-78; fax (32) 93-41-86; e-mail almer@iberiapac.ge; f. 1966; Gen. Man. GURAM GABUNIA.

ROADS

In 2000 the total length of roads in use was an estimated 20,362 km (including 15,562 km of secondary roads). In the same year 93.5% of roads were paved. Under a presidential decree issued in 1996, a plan to modernize and develop the road system in Georgia was to be implemented.

SHIPPING

There are international shipping services with Black Sea and Mediterranean ports. The main ports are at Batumi, Poti and Sukhumi.

Shipowning Company

Georgian Shipping Company: 384517 Batumi, Gogebashvili 60; tel. (222) 14-02-312; fax (222) 73-91-114; Pres. Capt. B. VARSHANIDZE.

Port Authorities

Port of Batumi: 384500 Batumi, Gogebashvili 20; tel. (222) 76-261; fax (222) 76-830; e-mail bsport@batumi.net; internet www.batport.batumi.net; operates cargo port; Gen. Dir DZHAMBUL NINIDZE; 1,413 employees.

Port of Poti: 384694 Poti, David Agmashenebeli 52; tel. (393) 20-660; fax (393) 20-688; e-mail ptp@iberiapac.ge; internet www.potiport.com; operation of cargo port; Gen. Dir DZHEMAL INAISHVILI.

CIVIL AVIATION

Air Georgia: 380062 Tbilisi, I. Chavchavadze 49A; tel. (32) 29-40-53; fax (32) 23-34-23; e-mail airgeo@caucasus.net; internet www.airgeorgia.com; national and international transport of passengers and freight; Dir ELGOUDZHA DVALI.

Iveria: Tbilisi; f. 1998 as a joint-stock co following merger.

Orbi (Georgian Airlines): 380058 Tbilisi, Tbilisi Airport; tel. (32) 98-73-28; fax (32) 49-51-51; successor to the former Aeroflot division in Georgia; charter and scheduled services to destinations in the CIS and the Middle East; Chief Exec. VASILI S. DZHAMILBAZISHVILI.

Sukhumi United Aviation Detachment (Taifun—Adjal Avia): 384962 Sukhumi, Babushara Airport; tel. (122) 22021; domestic scheduled and chartered flights; Commdr ZAUR K. KHAINDRAVA.

Tourism

Prior to the disintegration of the USSR, Georgia attracted some 1.5m. tourists annually (mainly from other parts of the USSR), owing to its location on the Black Sea and its favourable climate. However, following the outbreak of civil conflict in the early 1990s in South Ossetia and Abkhazia, there was an almost complete cessation in tourism. Efforts to regenerate the sector were made in the late 1990s, with the historic buildings of Tbilisi and the surrounding area one of the primary attractions. The ski resort at Gudauri also remained popular with foreign tourists in the winter months. Other attractions included the mineral spas in the Borzhomi Gorge, and Mount Kazbek. In 1999 receipts from tourism totalled US $400m. and, according to the World Tourism Organization, there were 387,258 tourist arrivals in 2000, compared with 383,817 in 1999. However, instability in the country in the early 2000s appeared likely to be of detriment to tourist revenues.

Department of Tourism: 380074 Tbilisi, Chavchavadze 80; tel. (32) 22-61-25; fax (32) 29-40-52; Chair. KONSTANTINE SALIA.

GERMANY
Introductory Survey

Location, Climate, Language, Religion, Flag, Capital

The Federal Republic of Germany, which was formally established in October 1990 upon the unification of the Federal Republic of Germany (FRG, West Germany) and the German Democratic Republic (GDR, East Germany), lies in the heart of Europe. Its neighbours to the west are the Netherlands, Belgium, Luxembourg and France, to the south Switzerland and Austria, to the east the Czech Republic and Poland, and to the north Denmark. The climate is temperate, with an annual average temperature of 9°C (48°F), although there are considerable variations between the North German lowlands and the Bavarian Alps. The language is German. There is a small Sorbian-speaking minority (numbering about 100,000 people). About 33% of the population are Protestants and a further 33% are Roman Catholics. The national flag (proportions 3 by 5) consists of three equal horizontal stripes, of black, red and gold. The capital is Berlin.

Recent History

Following the defeat of the Nazi regime and the ending of the Second World War in 1945, Germany was divided, according to the Berlin Agreement, into US, Soviet, British and French occupation zones. Berlin was similarly divided. The former German territories east of the Oder and Neisse rivers, with the city of Danzig (now Gdańsk), became part of Poland, while the northern part of East Prussia, around Königsberg (now Kaliningrad), was transferred to the USSR. After the failure of negotiations to establish a unified German administration, the US, French and British zones were integrated economically in 1948. In May 1949 a provisional Constitution, the Grundgesetz (Basic Law), came into effect in the three zones (except in Saarland—see below), and federal elections were held in August. On 21 September 1949 a new German state, the Federal Republic of Germany (FRG), was established in the three Western zones. The FRG was governed from Bonn in Nordrhein-Westfalen. (Saarland was not incorporated into the FRG until 1957.) In October 1949 Soviet-occupied Eastern Germany declared itself the German Democratic Republic (GDR), with the Soviet zone of Berlin as its capital. This left the remainder of Berlin (West Berlin) as an enclave of the FRG within the territory of the GDR.

The FRG and GDR developed sharply divergent political and economic systems. The leaders of the GDR created a socialist state, based on the Soviet model. As early as 1945 large agricultural estates in eastern Germany were nationalized, followed in 1946 by major industrial concerns. Exclusive political control was exercised by the Sozialistische Einheitspartei Deutschlands (SED, Socialist Unity Party of Germany), which had been formed in April 1946 by the merger of the Communist Party of Germany and the branch of the Sozialdemokratische Partei Deutschlands (SPD, Social Democratic Party of Germany) in the Soviet zone. Other political parties in eastern Germany were under the strict control of the SED, and no political activity independent of the ruling party was permitted. In 1950 Walter Ulbricht was appointed Secretary-General (later restyled First Secretary) of the SED.

The transfer, as war reparations, of foodstuffs, livestock and industrial equipment to the USSR from eastern Germany had a devastating effect on the area's economy in the immediate post-war period. In June 1953 increasing political repression and severe food shortages led to uprisings and strikes, which were suppressed by Soviet troops. The continued failure of the GDR to match the remarkable economic recovery of the FRG prompted a growing number of refugees to cross from the GDR to the FRG (between 1949 and 1961 an estimated 2.5m. GDR citizens moved permanently to the FRG). Emigration was accelerated by the enforced collectivization of many farms in 1960, and in August 1961 the GDR authorities hastily constructed a guarded wall between East and West Berlin.

In May 1971 Ulbricht was succeeded as First Secretary of the SED by Erich Honecker. Ulbricht remained Chairman of the Council of State (Head of State), a post that he had held since 1960, until his death in August 1973. He was initially succeeded in this office by Willi Stoph, but in October 1976 Stoph returned to his previous post as Chairman of the Council of Ministers, and Honecker became Chairman of the Council of State. Under Honecker, despite some liberalization of relations with the FRG, there was little relaxation of repressive domestic policies. Honecker strongly opposed the political and economic reforms that began in the USSR and some other Eastern European countries in the mid-1980s.

The 1949 elections in the FRG resulted in victory for the conservative Christlich-Demokratische Union Deutschlands (CDU, Christian Democratic Union of Germany), together with its sister party in Bavaria, the Christlich-Soziale Union (CSU, Christian Social Union). The SPD was the largest opposition party. Dr Konrad Adenauer, the leader of the CDU, was elected Federal Chancellor by the Bundestag (Federal Assembly); Theodor Heuss became the first President of the Republic. Under Adenauer's chancellorship (which lasted until 1963) and the direction of Dr Ludwig Erhard, his Minister of Economics (and successor as Chancellor), the FRG rebuilt itself rapidly to become one of the most affluent and economically dynamic states in Europe, as well as an important strategic ally of other Western European states and the USA. The Paris Agreement of 1954 gave full sovereign status to the FRG from 5 May 1955, and also granted it membership of NATO (see p. 271).

The CDU/CSU held power in coalition with the SPD from 1966 to 1969, under the chancellorship of Dr Kurt Kiesinger, but lost support at the 1969 general election, allowing the SPD to form a coalition Government with the Freie Demokratische Partei (FDP, Free Democratic Party), under the chancellorship of Willy Brandt, the SPD leader. Following elections in November 1972, the SPD became, for the first time, the largest party in the Bundestag. In May 1974, however, Brandt resigned as Chancellor, after the discovery that his personal assistant had been a clandestine agent of the GDR. He was succeeded by Helmut Schmidt of the SPD, hitherto the Minister of Finance. A deteriorating economic situation was accompanied by a decline in the popularity of the Government and increasing tension between the coalition partners. In the general election of October 1976 the SPD lost its position as largest party in the Bundestag, but the SPD-FDP coalition retained a slender majority.

At the general election of October 1980 the SPD-FDP coalition secured a 45-seat majority in the Bundestag. However, over the next two years the coalition became increasingly unstable, with the partners divided on issues of nuclear power, defence and economic policy. In September 1982 the coalition finally collapsed when the two parties failed to agree on budgetary measures. In October the FDP formed a Government with the CDU/CSU, under the chancellorship of Dr Helmut Kohl, the leader of the CDU. This new partnership was consolidated by the results of the general election of March 1983, when the CDU/CSU substantially increased its share of the votes cast, obtaining 48.8% of the total, compared with 38.8% for the SPD, now led by Hans-Jochen Vogel. An environmentalist party, Die Grünen (The Greens), gained representation in the Bundestag for the first time. In July 1984 Prof. Karl Carstens, who had held the post of Federal President since 1979, was succeeded by Dr Richard von Weizsäcker, also of the CDU. The CDU/CSU-FDP coalition retained power after the general election of January 1987, although with a reduced majority; Kohl was reappointed Chancellor by the Bundestag.

During the period 1949–69 the FRG, under the CDU/CSU, remained largely isolated from Eastern Europe, owing to the FRG Government's refusal to recognize the GDR as an independent state or to maintain diplomatic relations with any other states that recognized the GDR. When Willy Brandt of the SPD became Chancellor in 1969, he adopted a more conciliatory approach to relations with Eastern Europe and, in particular, towards the GDR, a policy which came to be known as Ostpolitik. In 1970 formal discussions were conducted between representatives of the GDR and the FRG for the first time, and there was a significant increase in diplomatic contacts between the FRG and the other countries of Eastern Europe. In 1970 treaties were signed with the USSR and Poland, in which the FRG formally renounced claims to the eastern territories of the Third

Reich and recognized the 'Oder–Neisse Line' as the border between Germany (actually the GDR) and Poland. Further negotiations between the GDR and the FRG, following a quadripartite agreement on West Berlin in September 1971, clarified access rights to West Berlin and also allowed West Berliners to visit the GDR. In December 1972 the two German states signed a 'Basic Treaty', agreeing to develop normal, neighbourly relations with each other, to settle all differences without resort to force, and to respect each other's independence. The Treaty permitted both the FRG and the GDR to join the UN in September 1973, and allowed many Western countries to establish diplomatic relations with the GDR, although both German states continued to deny formal diplomatic recognition to each other.

In December 1981 the first official meeting took place between the two countries' leaders for 11 years, when Chancellor Schmidt of the FRG travelled to the GDR for discussions with Honecker. Inter-German relations deteriorated following the deployment, in late 1983, of US nuclear missiles in the FRG, and the subsequent siting of additional Soviet missiles in the GDR. Nevertheless, official contacts were maintained, and Honecker made his first visit to the FRG in September 1987.

Relations between the two German states were dramatically affected by political upheavals that occurred in the GDR in late 1989 and 1990. In the latter half of 1989 many thousands of disaffected GDR citizens emigrated illegally to the FRG, via Czechoslovakia, Poland and Hungary. The exodus was accelerated by the Hungarian Government's decision, in September 1989, to permit citizens of the GDR to leave Hungary without exit visas. Meanwhile, there was a growth in popular dissent within the GDR, led by Neues Forum (New Forum), an independent citizens' action group which had been established to encourage discussion of democratic reforms, justice and environmental issues.

In early October 1989, following official celebrations to commemorate the 40th anniversary of the foundation of the GDR, anti-Government demonstrations erupted in East Berlin and other large towns. Eventually, as the demonstrations attracted increasing popular support, intervention by the police ceased. (It was later reported that the SED Politburo had voted narrowly against the use of the armed forces to suppress the civil unrest.) In mid-October, as the political situation became more unsettled, Honecker resigned as General Secretary of the SED, Chairman of the Council of State and Chairman of the National Defence Council, ostensibly for reasons of ill health. He was replaced in all these posts by Egon Krenz, a senior member of the SED Politburo. Krenz immediately offered concessions to the opposition, initiating a dialogue with the members of Neues Forum (which was legalized in early November) and with church leaders. There was also a noticeable liberalization of the media, and an amnesty was announced for all persons who had been detained during the recent demonstrations and for those imprisoned for attempting to leave the country illegally. However, large demonstrations, to demand further reforms, continued in many towns throughout the GDR.

On 7 November 1989, in a further attempt to placate the demonstrators, the entire membership of the GDR Council of Ministers (including the Chairman, Willi Stoph) resigned. On the following day the SED Politburo also resigned. On 9 November restrictions on foreign travel for GDR citizens were ended, and all border crossings to the FRG were opened. During the weekend of 10–11 November an estimated 2m. GDR citizens crossed into West Berlin, and the GDR authorities began to dismantle sections of the wall dividing the city. Dr Hans Modrow, a leading member of the SED who was regarded as an advocate of greater reforms, was appointed Chairman of a new Council of Ministers. The new Government pledged to introduce comprehensive political and economic reforms and to hold free elections in 1990.

In early December 1989 the Volkskammer (the GDR's legislature) voted to remove provisions in the Constitution that protected the SED's status as the single ruling party. However, the mass demonstrations continued, prompted by revelations of corruption and personal enrichment by the former leadership and of abuses of power by the state security service (Staatssicherheitsdienst, known colloquially as the Stasi, which was subsequently disbanded). A special commission was established to investigate such charges, and former senior officials, including Honecker and Stoph, were expelled from the SED and placed under house arrest, pending legal proceedings. As the political situation became increasingly unstable, the entire

membership of the SED Politburo and Central Committee, including Krenz, resigned, and both bodies, together with the post of General Secretary, were abolished. Shortly afterwards, Krenz also resigned as Chairman of the Council of State; he was replaced by Dr Manfred Gerlach, the Chairman of the Liberal-Demokratische Partei Deutschlands (LDPD, Liberal Democratic Party of Germany). Dr Gregor Gysi, a prominent defence lawyer who was sympathetic to the opposition, was elected to the new post of Chairman of the SED (restyled the Partei des Demokratischen Sozialismus—PDS, Party of Democratic Socialism, in February 1990).

In December 1989 and January 1990 all-party talks took place in the GDR, resulting in the formation, in early February, of a new administration, designated the Government of National Responsibility (still led by Modrow), to remain in office until elections were held. The GDR's first free legislative elections took place on 18 March 1990, with the participation of 93% of those eligible to vote. The East German CDU obtained 40.8% of the total votes cast, while the newly re-established East German SPD and the PDS secured 21.8% and 16.4% respectively. In April a coalition Government was formed, headed by Lothar de Maizière, leader of the Eastern CDU. Five parties were represented in the new Government: the CDU, the SPD, the Liga der Freien Demokraten (League of Free Democrats) and two smaller parties—the Deutsche Soziale Union (German Social Union) and Demokratische Aufschwung (Democratic Departure). The PDS was not invited to join the coalition.

As a result of the changes within the GDR and the subsequent free contact between Germans of east and west, the issue of possible unification of the two German states inevitably emerged. In November 1989 Chancellor Kohl proposed a plan for the eventual unification of the two countries by means of an interim confederal arrangement. In December Kohl made his first visit to the GDR, where he held discussions with the East German leadership. The two sides agreed to develop contacts at all levels and to establish joint economic, cultural and environmental commissions. However the GDR Government initially insisted that the GDR remain a sovereign, independent state. Nevertheless, in February 1990, in response to growing popular support among GDR citizens for unification, Modrow publicly advocated the establishment of a united Germany. Shortly afterwards, Kohl and Modrow met in Bonn, where they agreed to establish a joint commission to achieve full economic and monetary union between the GDR and the FRG. The new coalition Government of the GDR, formed in April 1990, pledged its determination to achieve German unification in the near future. In mid-May the legislatures of the GDR and the FRG approved the Treaty Between the FRG and the GDR Establishing a Monetary, Economic and Social Union; the Treaty came into effect on 1 July. Later in July the Volkskammer approved the re-establishment on GDR territory of the five Länder (states)—Brandenburg, Mecklenburg-Vorpommern (Mecklenburg-Western Pomerania), Sachsen (Saxony), Sachsen-Anhalt (Saxony-Anhalt) and Thüringen (Thuringia)—which had been abolished by the GDR Government in 1952 in favour of 14 Berzirke (districts). On 31 August 1990 the Treaty Between the FRG and the GDR on the Establishment of German Unity was signed in East Berlin by representatives of the two Governments. The treaty stipulated, *inter alia*, that the newly-restored Länder would accede to the FRG on 3 October 1990, and that the 23 boroughs of East and West Berlin would jointly form the Land (state) of Berlin.

Owing to the complex international status of the FRG and the GDR and the two countries' membership of opposing military alliances (respectively, NATO and the now-defunct Warsaw Pact), the process of German unification also included negotiations with other countries. In February 1990 representatives of 23 NATO and Warsaw Pact countries agreed to establish the so-called 'two-plus-four' talks (the FRG and the GDR, plus the four countries that had occupied Germany after the Second World War—France, the USSR, the United Kingdom and the USA) to discuss the external aspects of German unification. In June both German legislatures approved a resolution recognizing the inviolability of Poland's post-1945 borders, stressing that the eastern border of a future united Germany would remain along the Oder–Neisse line. In July, at bilateral talks in the USSR with Chancellor Kohl, the Soviet leader, Mikhail Gorbachev, agreed that a united Germany would be free to join whichever military alliance it wished, thus permitting Germany to remain a full member of NATO. The USSR also pledged to withdraw its armed forces (estimated at 370,000 in 1990) from GDR territory within four years, and it was agreed that a united Germany would reduce the strength of its armed forces to 370,000 within the same period. This agreement ensured a successful result to the 'two-plus-four' talks, which were concluded in September in Moscow, where the Treaty on the Final Settlement with Respect to Germany was signed. In late September the GDR withdrew from the Warsaw Pact.

On 1 October 1990 representatives of the four countries that had occupied Germany after the Second World War met in New York to sign a document in which Germany's full sovereignty was recognized. Finally, on 3 October, the two German states were formally unified. On the following day, at a session of the Bundestag (which had been expanded to permit the representation of former deputies of the GDR Volkskammer), five prominent politicians from the former GDR were sworn in as Ministers without Portfolio in the Federal Government.

Prior to unification, the CDU, the SPD and the FDP of the GDR had merged with their respective counterparts in the FRG to form three single parties. At state elections in the newly-acceded Länder, held in mid-October 1990, the CDU obtained an average of 41% of the total votes cast and won control of four Land legislatures, while the SPD received an average of 27% of the total votes cast and gained a majority only in Brandenburg. This surge of support for Chancellor Kohl and the CDU was confirmed by the results of elections to the Bundestag in early December (the first all-German elections since 1933). The CDU (together with the CSU) won 43.8% of the total votes cast, and thus secured a total of 319 seats in the 662-member Bundestag. The SPD achieved its poorest result in a general election since 1957, receiving 33.5% of the votes cast and winning 239 seats in the legislature (a result attributed, in large part, to the party's cautious stance on unification). The FDP won 11% of the total votes cast, and consequently 79 seats in the Bundestag, its most successful result in legislative elections since 1961. Unexpectedly, the West German Grünen lost the 42 seats that they had previously held in the legislature, having failed to obtain the necessary 5% of the votes cast in the area formerly constituting the FRG. However, as a result of a special clause in the electoral law (adopted in October 1990, and valid only for the legislative elections of December 1990), which permitted representation in the Bundestag for parties of the former GDR that received at least 5% of the total votes cast in former GDR territory, the party's eastern German counterpart, in coalition with Bündnis 90 (Alliance 90), secured eight seats in the legislature. Under the same ruling, the PDS won 17 seats in the Bundestag (having received almost 10% of the total votes cast in the area formerly constituting the GDR).

Dr Kohl was formally re-elected to the post of Federal Chancellor in mid-January 1991, immediately after the formation of the new Federal Government. This comprised 20 members, but included only three politicians from the former GDR. The FDP's representation was increased from four to five ministers, reflecting the party's success in the recent legislative elections.

Investigations into the abuse of power by the administration of the former GDR, conducted during the early 1990s, prompted the dismissal or resignation from government posts of several former SED politicians. In January 1991 the German authorities temporarily suspended efforts to arrest Honecker on charges of manslaughter (for complicity in the deaths of people who had been killed while attempting to escape from the GDR), owing to the severe ill health of the former GDR leader. In March it was announced that Honecker had been transferred, without the permission of the German authorities, to the USSR, and in December he took refuge in the Chilean embassy in Moscow.

One of the most serious problems confronting the Government immediately following unification was that of escalating unemployment in eastern Germany, as a result of the introduction of market-orientated reforms which were intended to integrate the economic system of the former GDR with that of the rest of the country. A substantial increase in the crime rate in eastern Germany was also recorded. A further disturbing social issue, particularly in the eastern Länder, was the resurgence of extreme right-wing and neo-Nazi groups. Moreover, there were also fears of a resurgence of political violence, following a series of terrorist acts culminating in the assassination, in April 1991, of Detlev Rohwedder, the executive head of the Treuhandanstalt (the trustee agency that had been established in March 1990 to supervise the privatization of state-owned enterprises in the former GDR). Responsibility for this and other attacks was claimed by the Rote Armee Fraktion (RAF, Red Army Faction),

a terrorist organization that had been active in the FRG during the 1970s. (The RAF eventually disbanded in 1998.)

Increasing popular discontent with the Government's post-unification policies was reflected in successive victories for the SPD in Land elections in the first half of 1991, causing the SPD to regain its majority in the Bundesrat, which it had lost to the CDU/CSU-FDP coalition in October 1990. In June 1991 the Bundestag voted in favour of Berlin as the future seat of the legislature and of government; it was envisaged that the transfer of organs of government from Bonn to Berlin would be completed by 2000.

At the beginning of January 1992 some 2m. Stasi files were opened to public scrutiny. In February Erich Mielke, the former head of the Stasi, was brought to trial on charges of murder, and in September Markus Wolf, the former head of East Germany's intelligence service, was charged with espionage, treason and corruption; both were subsequently found guilty and each was sentenced to six years' imprisonment. Meanwhile, Honecker returned to Germany from Russia in July 1992. He was brought to trial in November, together with five other defendants (among them Mielke and Stoph), on charges of manslaughter and embezzlement. In April 1993, however, the charges against Honecker were suspended. (The former East German leader, who was terminally ill, had been allowed to leave for Chile in January of that year; he died in May 1994.) Stoph was also released on grounds of ill health. In May 1993 Hans Modrow was found guilty of electoral fraud at communal elections that had taken place in the former GDR in 1989; Modrow was subsequently sentenced to nine months' imprisonment (suspended).

The issue of asylum-seekers dominated domestic politics during the early 1990s. At Land elections in April 1992, both the CDU and the SPD lost considerable support to right-wing extremist parties. In June the Bundestag approved controversial legislation which aimed to accelerate the processing of applications by refugees and introduced stricter rules for the granting of asylum. A six-week limit was imposed on the time that could be devoted to the consideration of each case, during which period applicants would be required to stay in special camps. Extreme nationalistic sentiment in some quarters led to an escalation in brutal attacks against asylum seekers and foreign workers during the early 1990s. In August 1992 neo-Nazi youths attacked refugee centres in more than 15 towns and bombed a memorial to the Holocaust (the Nazis' extermination of an estimated 6m. Jews) in Berlin. Sporadic attacks continued throughout Germany (though mainly in the east) in September and October. Several neo-Nazi vandals were arrested, but there was criticism of the lenient sentences imposed on those convicted. The murder in November of three Turkish immigrants in an arson attack in Mölln, Schleswig-Holstein, prompted the Government to ban several right-wing groups that were believed to have been responsible for co-ordinating attacks on foreigners. In December the main political parties reached agreement on the terms of a constitutional amendment to the law of asylum, and the new provisions, empowering immigration officials to refuse entry to economic migrants while still facilitating the granting of asylum to persons who were deemed to be political refugees, were approved by the Bundestag and the Bundesrat in May 1993. The Ministry of the Interior estimated that a record total of 438,191 people had sought asylum in Germany during 1992. By 1998, however, mainly as a result of the 1993 legislation, the number of applications had fallen to 98,644. During May 1993 the deaths of five Turkish women in an arson attack near Köln precipitated protest demonstrations throughout Germany and widespread condemnation in the international media. In May 1994 the Bundesrat approved measures to impose stricter penalties on perpetrators of right-wing violence and on those who denied the existence of the Holocaust; further strong measures against nationalist extremists were adopted in September.

The CDU/CSU-FDP coalition was re-elected at a general election held in October 1994; its majority in the Bundestag (enlarged to 672 seats) was, however, sharply reduced, from 134 to 10 seats. The CDU (with the CSU) won 41.4% of the votes cast and 294 seats, the SPD 36.4% of the votes cast and 252 seats, Bündnis 90/Die Grünen 7.3% of the votes cast and 50 seats, the FDP (which had lost representation at several Land parliament elections during 1994) 6.9% of the votes cast and 47 seats, and the PDS 4.4% of the votes cast and 30 seats. (The PDS secured 17.7% of the votes cast in the eastern Länder.) The right-wing extremist organizations did not attract strong support. In early November the ruling coalition negotiated a new political programme, with the creation of jobs a priority. Shortly afterwards Dr Kohl was formally re-elected as the Federal Chancellor, by a narrow margin of five votes.

In May 1995 the Federal Constitutional Court ruled that alleged former East German spies should not be prosecuted by Federal courts regarding crimes that were committed against the Federal Republic on behalf of the former GDR prior to unification; consequently in October the 1992 conviction of Markus Wolf on espionage charges was overturned. In November 1996 the Federal Constitutional Court ruled that the legal principles of the FRG regarding human rights could be retroactively applied to actions carried out within the former GDR. Thus, in January 1997 Wolf was charged with abduction, coercion and assault. In August Egon Krenz and two other former senior SED members, Günther Schabowski and Günther Kleiber, were found guilty of the manslaughter and attempted manslaughter of people who had sought to flee the former GDR; all three were sentenced to terms of imprisonment. The convictions were upheld in November 1999, following unsuccessful appeals. Krenz's conviction was again upheld in 2001, following an unsuccessful appeal to the European Court of Human Rights. Schabowski and Kleiber were pardoned in September 2000 and were released on the eve of the 10th anniversary of German reunification in early October.

The activities of extreme right-wing organizations increased significantly in 1997, and during the latter half of the year a series of incidents was reported that suggested the infiltration of some sections of the armed forces by neo-Nazi interests. In late April 1998 the extreme right-wing and openly xenophobic Deutsche Volksunion (DVU, German People's Union) won unprecedented support at an election to the Land parliament for the economically depressed Sachsen-Anhalt region of eastern Germany, securing 12.9% of the votes cast.

Tensions within the CDU/CSU–FDP coalition became apparent in 1997, mainly concerning the desirability and means of meeting the so-called 'convergence criteria' for participation in European economic and monetary union (EMU) by 1999. Record levels of unemployment continued to cause concern, as well as an unexpectedly large deficit on the 1997 budget. In January 1998 three economists and a professor of law initiated a challenge at the Federal Constitutional Court to Germany's proposed participation in EMU, on the grounds that it would contravene the Government's constitutional duty to pursue sound monetary policy. However, in early April the Court ruled that the issue of a common European currency was outside its jurisdiction and was, rather, the responsibility of the Government. In late April, despite evidence of widespread opposition to the new currency, the Bundestag voted strongly in favour of Germany's participation in EMU.

At the general election held in late September 1998 the CDU/CSU–FDP coalition was decisively defeated by the SPD, which won 298 of the total seats in the Bundestag (reduced to 669). The CDU took 198 seats, both the CSU and Bündnis 90/Die Grünen secured 47, the FDP 43 and the PDS 36. Neither the right-wing Republikaner nor the DVU gained representation in the federal legislature. Following the election, Kohl resigned as Chairman of the CDU; he was replaced by the party's parliamentary leader, Dr Wolfgang Schäuble. Meanwhile, the SPD and Bündnis 90/Die Grünen swiftly negotiated a coalition pact, which was formally approved by both parties at conferences in late October. Shortly afterwards Gerhard Schröder of the SPD (formerly the Minister President of Niedersachsen) was elected Federal Chancellor by a large majority of Bundestag members; the following day a new Federal Government was announced, which included three ministers representing Bündnis 90/Die Grünen. The most prominent of these was the new Federal Vice-Chancellor and Minister of Foreign Affairs, Joseph (Joschka) Fischer, who was formerly the parliamentary leader of the ecological parties. Oskar Lafontaine, the Chairman of the SPD, was appointed Minister of Finance, charged with the responsibility for guiding Germany into EMU. The SPD–Bündnis 90/Die Grünen coalition held a 21-seat majority in the Bundestag.

In early November 1998 Schröder delivered his first major policy statement, placing high priority on reducing the rising level of unemployment; measures were also planned to expedite the economic reconstruction of the eastern Länder, to reform the pension system, to impose an 'ecological' tax on energy consumption and gradually to curtail the country's nuclear energy programme. It soon became apparent, however, that the two coalition partners envisaged very different time-scales for the abandonment of atomic power. While the SPD favoured the phased closure of the 19 national nuclear power plants over a minimum period of 25 years, the ecological parties aimed to act far more swiftly. In mid-December Schröder overruled his Bündnis 90/Die Grünen Minister of the Environment, Nature Conservation and Nuclear Safety, Jürgen Trittin, when Trittin unilaterally attempted both to cancel contracts with British and French companies for the reprocessing of German nuclear waste and to dismiss the chiefs of the national atomic power safety commissions.

In early March 1999 Lafontaine resigned as Minister of Finance, apparently in protest at an evident lack of support for his economic policies and management from within both the business community and the Government; he also vacated his seat in the Bundestag and the chairmanship of the SPD. Hans Eichel of the SPD, hitherto the Minister-President of Hesse, was appointed as the new Minister of Finance. In the following month Schröder was elected to the post of Chairman of the SPD. In early May the Government approved legislation which enabled people born in Germany of resident foreign parents to hold both German citizenship (hitherto denied them) and the nationality of one parent until adulthood, whereupon they would be required to relinquish one. This represented a significant departure from previous ethnically-orientated citizenship legislation, and was intended to encourage the social assimilation of Germany's foreign population (numbering some 7m. in 1999). The opposition CDU had strongly opposed an initial proposal to grant a full right of dual nationality.

At the beginning of June 1999 Dr Roman Herzog of the CDU was replaced as Federal President by Prof. Dr Johannes Rau of the SPD, formerly Minister-President of Nordrhein-Westfalen. During mid-1999 most organs of government moved from Bonn to Berlin (the capital and henceforth permanent seat of government). Both the Bündnis 90/Die Grünen alliance (which was becoming increasingly polarized between idealist and more pragmatic elements) and the SPD (which was popularly regarded as having betrayed its avowed commitment to social justice following the announcement in June of a package of economic austerity measures designed to redress the decelerating economic growth rate and to appease the alienated business sector) performed poorly at several elections to Land legislatures during the second half of 1999; by late 1999 the ruling coalition had control of less than two-fifths of votes in the Bundesrat (Federal Council). Nevertheless, in early December Schröder was re-elected to the post of Chairman of the SPD, by a higher margin of support than that achieved at the April party election.

During November 1999 the opposition CDU became embroiled in a scandal concerning the discovery of a system of secret bank accounts, which had been used to deposit undisclosed donations to the party throughout the 1990s. (In accordance with the Grundgesetz, all substantial funding of political parties must be declared.) Allegations subsequently emerged that the CDU leadership had covertly (and possibly with the knowledge of former French President François Mitterrand) accepted a large bribe from the then state-owned French oil company, Elf Aquitaine, in connection with its purchase in 1992 of an eastern German oil refinery. It was also alleged that, in 1998, the CDU had granted an export licence to an arms exporting interest in return for an undeclared party donation. The former Chancellor, Kohl, admitted knowledge of some secret party funding, but repeatedly refused to name any sources; in late December 1999 he became the subject of a criminal investigation. Kohl resigned his honorary chairmanship of the CDU following an ultimatum from party members to clarify his role in the scandal or risk suspension from his honorary position. The incumbent CDU leadership was also implicated in the scandal, including the party Chairman, Dr Schäuble, who had been a close ally of Kohl under the previous administration. Schäuble was, however, confirmed by the party as its Chairman in January 2000, despite his offer of resignation, following his belated confession earlier in the month that in 1994 he had accepted a donation of DM 100,000 in cash from an arms dealer, Karlheinz Schreiber, who was implicated in the funding scandal. (In August 2000 a court ruled that Schreiber should stand trial on charges of tax evasion, bribery and conspiracy to defraud in connection with the German Government's sale of tanks to Saudi Arabia during the Gulf War.) Schäuble established a CDU independent inquiry into the funding scandal in January 2000, which subsequently revealed that funding irregularities had persisted for decades in German politics. The inquiry established that during the 1970s between US $15m. and $20m. was paid in cash to the main political parties by the German intelligence agency to support developing democracies in Spain and Portugal. Throughout January 2000 further revelations emerged, including the secretion of more than DM 13m. in illegal foreign accounts by the Hesse regional branch of the CDU. The Minister-President of Hesse, Roland Koch, however, retained the support of both his party and its regional coalition partner, the FDP. In September Koch also won a vote of confidence in the state legislature following fresh media accusations that he had benefited from large corporate donations in the late 1990s. In February 2000 the CDU was fined DM 41m. for irregularities in the Hesse accounts for 1998. The following day Schäuble resigned as Chairman of the CDU, accepting responsibility for mishandling the funding scandal. In March a formal investigation was launched into suspected illegal party financing by the former head of the Chancellery under Schröder, Bodo Hombach; the SPD had not previously been implicated in the party funding scandals. In November 2001 federal prosecutors abandoned their investigation of Schäuble, thus enabling him to contend the forthcoming national elections. By January 2002, however, another funding scandal had emerged when the Bundestag and state prosecutors launched preliminary investigations into allegations that the CSU had improperly obtained funds from federal authorities by incorrectly classifying its income.

Meanwhile, following the withdrawal from contention in March 2000 of the former Minister of Defence, Volke Rühe (owing to the party's poor performance under his leadership in the state legislative election in Schleswig-Holstein in late February), the CDU's Secretary-General, Angela Merkel, was elected Chairman at the party congress in April. Merkel, who had secured significant support as a result of her determination to expose the CDU's financial irregularities, was considered more liberal than her predecessors. In March excerpts from transcripts of telephone conversations of the CDU treasurer under Kohl, Uwe Lüthje, and other CDU officials, which had been illegally recorded by the Stasi, appeared to indicate that Kohl had been aware of the irregular party funding earlier than he had previously admitted. Following a campaign by Kohl, the leaders of the principal parties agreed in May to forbid the use of the transcripts by the parliamentary committee investigating financial irregularities in the CDU, and, in July 2001, Kohl secured a court ruling banning the publication of the transcripts. However, in May 2000 the state prosecutor concluded that there were sufficient grounds for the criminal prosecution of Kohl on charges of fraud and bribery (although as an incumbent member of the legislature Kohl was immune from prosecution). In his testimony in June to the parliamentary committee Kohl continued to admit accepting illegal secret contributions to party funds, but refuted allegations that such donations had influenced government policy decisions (including the sale of an East German oil refinery to Elf Aquitaine). Kohl's credibility was diminished still further that month when a report was published revealing that two-thirds of chancellery records relating to the period in question had been destroyed following Kohl's defeat in the 1998 general election. The files were however, discovered in July in the archives of the Konrad Adenauer Foundation, a right-wing policy unit.

In September 2000 Kohl resumed his seat in the legislature for the first time since December 1999. He declined an invitation to the 10th anniversary celebration of unification in October 2000 on the grounds that, despite his central role in achieving German unification, he had not been invited to speak. In December another fine, of DM 7.7m., was imposed on the CDU by the Speaker of the Bundestag, Wolfgang Thierce, as a consequence of illegal fund-raising. Kohl had transferred DM 8m. (largely raised through donations) to the CDU in June to contribute to the payment of fines. The CDU's appeal against the previous fine, of DM 41m., was upheld by a court in January 2001, although Thierce announced his intention to appeal against the ruling. In February Kohl accepted the proposal of the state prosecutor that he should pay a fine of DM 300,000 in exchange for the abandonment of the criminal investigation into his acceptance of illegal contributions to the CDU in the 1990s; this arrangement subsequently gained judicial approval. The parliamentary inquiry continued, however, as did Kohl's refusal to name the illegal contributors to his party.

In December 1999 the German Government agreed to pay a substantial sum in compensation to people who had worked as forced labourers for German companies or been deprived of their assets under the Nazi regime; it was hoped that this would forestall a growing number of lawsuits taken out against German industrial interests and banks by survivors of the Holocaust. Chancellor Schröder announced that the Government would raise DM 5,000m. towards the proposed DM 10,000m. fund; the other DM 5,000m. was to be raised by Germany's largest banks and companies. The Government's share was to be financed by state privatizations and contributions from the Länder. The USA agreed to contribute US $10m. as a gesture of solidarity. In March 2000 Schröder announced an improved agreement, which resolved differences between categories of victims and added a further DM 200m. to the compensation fund. The extra money was to derive from interest income and from a separate settlement between Swiss banks and Holocaust victims. The larger German insurers declined to contribute to the fund being raised by industry because of potentially overlapping claims from separate negotiations involving many leading European insurers. The compensation agreement was eventually signed in July, and, following the resolution of legal difficulties, payments finally began in May 2001. In June, however, one of the fund's trustees, Lothar Evers, launched legal proceedings against bankers and 'unknown insiders' on suspicion of fraud and breach of trust. State prosecutors were to investigate claims of currency losses of up to DM 200m. after money for Polish victims was exchanged into złotys. A representative of victims in the USA also filed a mismanagement lawsuit against the fund's administrators.

In June 2000, following months of negotiations between the Government and the nuclear industry, Schröder announced that an agreement had been concluded to decommission the country's 19 nuclear power plants (which accounted for almost one-third of power requirements) without compensation by 2021. Under the accord, the reprocessing of nuclear fuel would end by 2005 (although the transportation of spent fuel for reprocessing elsewhere could continue under certain conditions). Despite some reservations on the part of a significant number of members of Bündnis 90/Die Grünen who had favoured an immediate cessation of nuclear power generation, the agreement was endorsed at a party conference later that month. Rioting erupted over three days in March 2001 as thousands of anti-nuclear protesters attempted to halt a consignment of 85 metric tons of nuclear waste being transported by train and lorry from France to a storage site at a disused salt-mine in Gorleben in Lower Saxony. Around 20,000 riot police and other security units were deployed to remove the activists, some of whom had chained and cemented themselves to the rail track; about 600 protesters were arrested. The police action constituted the largest police deployment in Germany's post-war history. In September the Federal Government approved a bill regulating the phasing out of nuclear power, under which the first plant would close in 2003; by mid-March 2002, however, the legislation had yet to be approved by the Bundestag.

In August 2000, in response to growing fears concerning the escalation of neo-Nazi violence against immigrants, the Government announced a series of measures to combat racist attacks, including the establishment of a panel to investigate a potential ban on the extremist right-wing party, the Nationaldemokratische Partei Deutschlands (NPD, National Democratic Party). Despite some opposition to the plan, on the grounds that it was unconstitutional and would afford neo-Nazis an undesirably high level of publicity, in early October the Federal Minister of the Interior formally proposed the ban, which subsequently received the support of 14 of the 16 Länder. The application to the Constitutional Court to ban the NPD on the grounds that it was anti-Semitic, racist and supported violence was approved by the Bundesrat in November and by the Bundestag in December. In January 2002, however, the Court postponed hearing the case when it emerged that one of the senior NPD activists whose statements were to be used in evidence against the party was an informant for the Bundesamt für Verfassungsschutz (BfV, Office for the Protection of the Constitution); the Court dismissed the case in March 2003. Meanwhile, in the latter half of 2000 Schröder demanded stricter application of existing legislation and tougher sentencing from the courts when dealing with right-wing extremists. In August the Government approved the expenditure of DM 75m. over three years to support local youth initiatives committed to fighting racism, anti-Semitism and xenophobia, and in January 2001 the Minister of Justice, Herta Däubler-Gmelin, announced that her Ministry would provide DM 10m. to compensate the victims of far-right violence, threats or insults.

In January 2001 a series of photographs emerged which appeared to show the Minister of Foreign Affairs assaulting a police-officer during a demonstration in Frankfurt in 1973. Fischer had never hidden his leftist militant past, but claimed he was a firm advocate of peaceful protest. He admitted to having fought unarmed against the police, but only after intense provocation, and flatly denied ever having used weapons. Fischer gave evidence later that month as a character witness in the trial of a former international militant activist, Hans Joachim Klein, when he again asserted that he had never favoured armed struggle. A criminal investigation into allegations of perjury by Fischer in the Klein trial was opened in February following claims by a former member of the extremist RAF that she had lived in Fischer's house during 1973; the investigation was abandoned in April when prosecutors concluded that Fischer had never knowingly had contact with members of the RAF.

In January 2001 the Minister of Health, Andrea Fischer, and the Minister of Food, Agriculture and Forestry, Karl-Heinz Funke, resigned amid growing national alarm at the spread of bovine spongiform encephalopathy (BSE) in cattle and accusations that they had ignored the risks posed by infected beef, which was linked to a new strain of Creutzfeldt-Jakob disease, a fatal degenerative illness affecting humans. Despite the crisis that had afflicted the agricultural sector in the United Kingdom, Funke had initially insisted that special anti-BSE measures were inappropriate in Germany. Such measures were, however, introduced in November 2000 following the confirmation of the first two cases of BSE in German cattle. By the end of January 2001 confirmed cases of BSE in German cattle had increased to 20. In response to public fears about BSE, Schröder created a new Ministry of Consumer Protection, Food and Agriculture, to which he appointed Renate Künast of Bündnis 90/Die Grünen. In February the Government introduced new legislation intended to combat the spread of BSE. The legislation gave the Ministry of Consumer Protection, Food and Agriculture the right to issue rulings on matters such as cattle feed and culling procedures without requiring the approval of the Bundestag. The Ministry was also authorized to order slaughterhouses to proceed with the culling of BSE-infected animals—many farmers had complained of difficulty in finding abattoirs that were prepared to accept infected animals. The penalty for using meat-based cattle feed, hitherto the imposition of fines, was increased to a maximum of five years' imprisonment.

In late September 2001, following the attacks in the USA by suspected Islamist extremists, the Federal Government abolished the so-called 'religious privilege', thus removing legal protection for and allowing the banning of any religious organizations suspected of promoting terrorism. In early December police raided the premises of 20 militant Islamist groups throughout Germany, some of which were suspected of having links with the al-Qa'ida (Base) organization (an Islamist extremist group led by the Saudi-born militant Osama bin Laden, which was widely believed to have organized the attacks in the USA in September). Public concern was heightened by the fact that there was evidence that at least three of the presumed perpetrators of the US atrocities had recently lived in Hamburg and other German cities. Plans to introduce more liberal immigration laws were abandoned, and further new legislation was introduced to increase national security, including the extension of existing anti-terrorism legislation, which had hitherto only covered terrorist acts in Germany, to apply, in addition, to such acts committed in other countries. Measures to block funding channels for militant activists allowed the police access to bank account details of alleged terrorists. Further steps to control money-laundering were introduced, including the foundation of a centralized Financial Intelligence Unit, and the burden of proof regarding the authenticity of suspicious funds was moved from the banks and police to the client. Controls on employees with access to high-security areas of airports were made more stringent. All of these measures were to be funded by an immediate increase in tax on cigarettes and insurance policies.

In August 2002 five armed members of a group entitled the Democratic Iraqi Opposition of Germany occupied the Iraqi embassy in Berlin for five hours, demanding the overthrow of the Iraqi President, Saddam Hussain. German special forces stormed the building and ended the occupation peacefully. Also in August, a Moroccan national, Mounir El Motassadeq, was charged with offences under anti-terrorism legislation relating to the suicide attacks of 11 September 2001 in the USA; prosecutors claimed that El Motasseq had been involved in financing the attacks. He stood trial in Hamburg, was convicted as an accessory to 3,066 murders, and was sentenced to 15 years'

imprisonment. In early September German police arrested a Turkish national and his US-German fiancée in their home, near the headquarters of the US army in Europe, in Heidelberg. The couple were in possession of equipment and chemicals that could potentially have been used to manufacture explosives, as well as bomb-making manuals and a picture of Osama bin Laden. It was believed that the couple had been planning an attack to mark the anniversary of the 11 September 2001 attacks. Later that month the German authorities banned 16 Islamist groups linked to the Cologne-based 'Kalifatsstaat' ('Caliphate State'), an extremist Islamist group dedicated to the overthrow of Turkey's secular Government which had been banned, together with 20 related associations, in December 2001.

In July 2002 Schröder dismissed the Minister of Defence, Rudolf Scharping, when it emerged that Scharping had received payments from a lobbyist; Peter Struck was appointed to replace him.

At the general election held on 22 September 2002 the SPD received 38.52% of the votes cast, winning 251 seats in the Bundestag. The CDU received 29.52% of the votes cast and won 190 seats, the CSU 8.99% (58 seats), the Grünen 8.56% (55 seats), the FDP 7.37% (47 seats) and the PDS 3.99% (two seats). The SPD-Bündnis 90/Die Grünen coalition remained in government. The SPD's position was, however, severely weakened and the Government's popularity suffered as a result of financial austerity measures adopted in an attempt to ward off economic recession. Legislative elections were held in two Länder, Niedersachsen and Hesse, in February 2003, at which the SPD suffered emphatic defeats at the hands of the CDU, which strengthened its majority in the Bundesrat to such an extent that it was able to block government legislation.

On 27 January 2003 (the 58th anniversary of the liberation of the concentration camp Auschwitz) the Government signed an agreement establishing a formal partnership with the Jewish population in Germany, according the Jewish faith the same legal status as the Protestant and Roman Catholic churches in Germany.

The orientation of Germany's foreign policy after unification broadly followed that of the pre-1990 FRG. The united Germany remained committed to a leading role in the European Community (EC—now European Union, EU), of which the FRG was a founding member, and NATO, while placing greater emphasis on defence co-operation with France. The country was also strongly committed to close relations with Eastern Europe, in particular with the USSR and, subsequently, its successor states. Relations between the FRG and the USSR had improved significantly during the 1980s, culminating in the signing, in September 1990, of a Treaty on Good-Neighbourliness, Partnership and Co-operation. In April 1992 Germany and Russia agreed to a mutual cancellation of debts, and in December of the same year the two countries concluded an agreement whereby the Russian Government would grant autonomy to the 2.5m. ethnic Germans in the Volga region of Russia. In September 1996 the Land interior ministers agreed that the Länder could begin deporting some of the 320,000 refugees from Bosnia and Herzegovina who had been given temporary refuge in Germany. In October the German Government signed an agreement with the Federal Republic of Yugoslavia (FRY—now Serbia and Montenegro), providing for the return of about 135,000 Yugoslav refugees to the FRY over a three-year period (from the beginning of December). In January 1997, following more than a year of complex diplomatic negotiations, Dr Kohl and the Prime Minister of the Czech Republic, Václav Klaus, signed a joint declaration regretting past wrongs committed on both sides before, during and after the Second World War.

Following the Iraqi invasion and annexation of Kuwait in August 1990, the German Government expressed support for the deployment of US-led allied forces in the region of the Persian (Arabian) Gulf, and contributed substantial amounts of financial and technical aid to the effort to liberate Kuwait, although there were mass demonstrations against the allied action in many parts of Germany. Despite criticism from certain countries participating in the alliance, Germany did not contribute troops to the allied force, in accordance with a provision in the Grundgesetz that was widely interpreted as prohibiting intervention outside the area of NATO operations. In July 1992, however, the Government announced that it was to send a naval destroyer and reconnaissance aircraft to the Adriatic Sea to participate in the UN force monitoring the observance of UN sanctions on the FRY. This deployment was subsequently approved by the Bundestag. In April 1993 the Constitutional Court ruled that German forces could join the UN operation to enforce an air exclusion zone over Bosnia and Herzegovina. Germany dispatched troops to assist the UN relief effort in Somalia in mid-1993. In May 1994 the Constitutional Court declared the participation of German military units in collective international defence and security operations, with the approval of the Bundestag in each instance, to be compatible with the Grundgesetz. In March 1997, while supervising the evacuation from Albania of citizens of western European states, German troops opened fire on hostile forces for the first time since 1945. From March to early June 1999 Germany participated in the ongoing NATO military offensive against the FRY, despite misgivings from left-wing elements within the ruling SPD-Bündnis 90/Die Grünen coalition.

In May 1992 Germany and France reached agreement on the establishment of a combined defence corps, which, they envisaged, would provide the basis for a pan-European military force under the aegis of Western European Union (WEU, see p. 318). The so-called Eurocorps became operational in November 1995. In December 2000 the heads of government of the EU (except Denmark) endorsed the plan for a European Rapid Reaction Force (RRF), which had been adopted by EU ministers in November (although NATO was to remain central to European defence). The RRF's first commander was to be a German, Lt-Gen. Rainer Schuwirth; Germany had pledged the largest number of troops (13,500) for a deployed RRF.

In early September 2001 German troops were dispatched to participate in a NATO peace-keeping mission in the former Yugoslav republic of Macedonia, despite opposition to the deployment by members of Bündnis 90/Die Grünen. In the aftermath of the terrorist attacks in the USA on 11 September, Schröder pledged 'unlimited solidarity' to the US administration, and announced plans to send 3,900 troops to take part in the US-led military action in Afghanistan. These plans were strongly opposed by the majority of members of Bündnis 90/Die Grünen, although Schröder enjoyed the support of the Green Minister of Foreign Affairs, Joseph Fischer. Opposition to the proposed deployment of German troops in Afghanistan increased to such an extent that by early November the governing coalition appeared close to collapse. Schröder embarked on the high-risk strategy of linking the parliamentary vote on the troop deployment to a vote of confidence in his Government; the Chancellor won the confidence vote, which was held on 16 November, albeit by a narrow majority. In November 2002 the Bundestag voted to extend the deployment of troops in Afghanistan by a further year.

In late 2002 and early 2003 the Franco-German *entente* was renewed, largely owing to the two countries' shared opposition to the US-led military action in Iraq. In February Germany and France, together with Belgium, vetoed proposals to deploy NATO troops in Turkey; they later ended their vetoes on the condition that the troops be deployed only to defend Turkey, and not to attack Iraq.

In December 1992 the Bundestag ratified the Treaty on European Union, which had been approved by EC Heads of Government at Maastricht in December 1991. At the same time the lower house approved an amendment to the Grundgesetz (negotiated in May 1992 with the Länder), whereby the state assemblies would be accorded greater involvement in the determination of German policy within the EC. The Bundesrat ratified the Maastricht Treaty later in December 1992. In April 1998 the Bundestag approved Germany's participation in EMU, which took effect in January 1999. In conjunction with other EU member states, Germany suspended normal diplomatic relations with neighbouring (and fellow EU member) Austria in early February 2000, following the formation in that country of a coalition Government that included the far right-wing Freiheitlichen (Freedom Party); sanctions were lifted in September.

Government

Germany is composed of 16 Länder (states), each Land having its own constitution, legislature and government.

The country has a parliamentary regime, with a bicameral legislature. The Upper House is the Bundesrat (Federal Council), with 69 seats. Each Land has between three and six seats, depending on the size of its population. The term of office of Bundesrat members varies in accordance with Land election dates. The Lower House, and the country's main legislative organ, is the Bundestag (Federal Assembly), with 669 deputies, who are elected for four years by universal adult suffrage (using a mixed system of proportional representation and direct voting).

Executive authority rests with the Federal Government, led by the Federal Chancellor, who is elected by an absolute majority of the Bundestag and appoints the other Ministers. The Federal President is elected by a Federal Convention (Bundesversammlung), which meets only for this purpose and consists of the Bundestag and an equal number of members elected by Land parliaments. The President is a constitutional Head of State with little influence on government.

Each Land has its own legislative assembly, with the right to enact laws except on matters that are the exclusive right of the Federal Government, such as defence, foreign affairs and finance. Education, police, culture and environmental protection are in the control of the Länder. Local responsibility for the execution of Federal and Land laws is undertaken by the Gemeinden (communities).

Defence

Germany is a member of the North Atlantic Treaty Organization (NATO, see p. 271). In January 2001 the Government announced that the armed forces were to be reduced from 310,000 to 280,000, with the number of conscripts being lowered from 130,000 to 80,000 through the reduction of military service from 10 months to nine months. In August 2002 Germany's armed forces totalled some 296,000, including 107,000 conscripts. The strength of the army stood at 203,200, including 89,500 conscripts. The navy numbered 25,500 (including 5,000 conscripts), and there were 67,300 in the air force (16,100 conscripts). The defence budget for 2002 totalled €24,400m.

At German unification, the National People's Army of the former GDR was dissolved, and 50,000 of its members were incorporated into the German Bundeswehr (armed forces). In accordance with a Soviet-German agreement, concluded in September 1990, the USSR withdrew its 370,000 troops from the territory of the former GDR during 1990–94, while Germany significantly reduced the total strength of its armed forces during the 1990s. In August 2002 the USA, the United Kingdom and France had approximately 89,050 troops stationed in Germany, while Belgium and the Netherlands maintained, respectively, forces of 2,000 and 2,600 men.

Economic Affairs

In 2001, according to estimates by the World Bank, Germany's gross national income (GNI), measured at average 1999–2001 prices, was US $1,947,951m., equivalent to $23,700 per head (or $25,530 per head on an international purchasing-power parity basis). During 1990–2001, it was estimated, the population increased by an average of 0.3% per year, while Germany's gross domestic product (GDP) per head grew, in real terms, by an average of 1.3% annually. Overall GDP expanded, in real terms, at an average annual rate of 1.6% in 1990–2001; growth was 3.0% in 2000 and 0.6% in 2001.

Agriculture (including hunting, forestry and fishing) engaged 2.7% of the employed labour force in 2000, and provided 1.2% of Germany's GDP in that year. The principal crops are potatoes, sugar beet, barley and wheat. Wine production is also important in western Germany. Agricultural GDP increased, in real terms, at an average annual rate of 1.3% in 1990–2000; it expanded by 2.4% in 1999 and by 2.0% in 2000.

Industry (including mining, power, manufacturing and construction) engaged 33.1% of the employed labour force and contributed 30.1% of GDP in 2000. Industrial GDP increased at an average annual rate of just 0.3% in 1990–2000; it declined by 0.3% in 1999, but expanded by 3.3% in 2000.

The mining sector engaged 0.4% of the employed labour force in 2000 and contributed 0.3% of GDP in 1999. The principal mining activities are the extraction of lignite (low-grade brown coal), hard coal and salts.

The manufacturing sector provided 23.1% of GDP in 2000; in that year manufacturing engaged 23.3% of the employed labour force. Measured by value of output, the principal branches of manufacturing in 1999 were transport equipment (accounting for 18.3% of the total), non-electric machinery (11.8%), chemical products (10.0%) and food products (9.7%). Passenger motor cars remain an important export. During the 1990s companies specializing in microelectronics and biotechnology performed well in both eastern and western Germany. Real manufacturing GDP remained largely unchanged in 1991–1999; it increased by 1.5% in 1998, and by 0.4% in 1999.

Of the total energy produced in 1999, coal accounted for 52.9% (27.7% was hard coal and 25.1% was lignite, or brown coal, which is primarily used in the eastern Länder), nuclear power accounted for 29.2%, and natural gas for 11.2%. In 2000 the Government announced plans to abandon the use of nuclear power by 2021. In 2000 imports of mineral fuels accounted for an estimated 8.7% of Germany's total imports.

Services engaged 64.2% of the employed labour force and contributed 68.8% of GDP in 2000. The GDP of the services sector increased, in real terms, at an annual average rate of 2.4% in 1990–2000: it grew by 2.2% in 1999 and by 3.4% in 2000.

In 2001 Germany recorded a visible trade surplus of US $88,512m., and there was a surplus of $2,442m. on the current account of the balance of payments. More than one-half of Germany's total trade in 2000 was conducted with other countries of the European Union (EU, see p. 199). France is the most significant individual trading partner, supplying 9.9% of imports and purchasing 11.1% of exports in 2001. Other principal sources of imports in that year were the Netherlands (8.9%), the USA (8.7%) and the United Kingdom (7.3%); the other major purchasers of exports were the USA (10.7%), the United Kingdom (8.4%) and Italy (7.5%). The principal imports in 2001 were machinery and transport equipment (accounting for 37.5% of the total, with road vehicles and parts comprising 8.7%), basic manufactures (12.6%), miscellaneous manufactured articles (12.2%), and chemicals and related products (10.0%). The principal exports were machinery and transport equipment (accounting for 52.0% of the total, with road vehicles and parts comprising 18.0%), basic manufactures (13.5%), chemicals and related products (12.7%), and miscellaneous manufactured articles (9.3%).

The budgetary deficit for 2001 totalled €49,632m. (equivalent to 2.4% of GDP). Annual inflation averaged 2.2% during 1990–2000. Consumer prices rose by an annual average of 1.9% in 2000 and 2.5% in 2001. Some 7.9% of the labour force were unemployed in April 2000.

Germany is a member of the EU and of the Organisation for Economic Co-operation and Development (OECD, see p. 277).

From the mid-1990s austerity measures were introduced in Germany in an attempt to reduce the budgetary deficit (which had expanded rapidly, owing to the costs of reunification) prior to the third stage of European economic and monetary union (EMU). Euro notes and coins entered circulation from 1 January 2002, and became Germany's sole currency (replacing the Deutsche Mark) at the end of February. GDP growth in 2001, preliminarily assessed at 0.6%, was the lowest in all but one year since reunification (GDP had actually declined in 1993), with GDP failing to expand for two consecutive quarters. A less favourable international market for Germany's export-orientated industrial base exemplified the difficulties confronting other EU members: many of Germany's large industrial firms were reporting disappointing results, especially in the period immediately following the suicide attacks on the USA in September 2001. The construction sector had shed 150,000 jobs over the year, and a further 90,000 were expected to be lost in 2002. During 2002 collapsing stock prices, record bankruptcies and mass unemployment, combined with the delayed costs of reunification and a long-term deceleration in the growth of productivity, led to stagnation in the German economy, which grew by only 0.2% over the year. The causes of this long-term decline in productivity were varied and partly still unknown. Some problems were, however, evident: the banking sector, in particular, was operating at a level of productivity only 20% of what it could achieve with proper efficiencies. Other sectors suffered from low productivity because they were shielded from competition, owing largely to German society's wariness of consolidation, restructuring and out-sourcing. A shortfall in tax revenue for 2002 of some €15,400m. led to Germany's budget deficit reaching 3.8% of GDP, constituting an embarrassing breach of the EU's Stability and Growth Pact; furthermore, analysts predicted that Germany would again breach the Pact's 3% limit

in 2003, if only by a small margin. Output was expected to contract again during 2003, pushing Germany into a 'double-dip' recession, and the Government reduced its growth forecast from 1.5% to just 1.0%. It was feared that tax increases and reductions in budgetary expenditure, announced by the Government in the hope of reducing the budgetary deficit, would decrease consumer confidence and corporate investment, thereby prolonging the country's economic slowdown. Most analysts considered the prospect of a reduction in European Central Bank interest rates as 'too little too late'; what the economy instead needed was significant structural reform. In March 2003 the Government proposed legislation under which welfare benefits would be reduced, labour-market rules relaxed and a loan of €15,000m. made to the building sector and local authorities. However, by that time the Government's popularity had suffered to such an extent that the opposition CDU had obtained a majority in the Bundesrat large enough to block the planned tax increases, making the immediate future for the German economy uncertain.

Education

The Basic Law assigns the control of important sectors of the education system to the governments of the Länder. These do, however, co-operate quite closely to ensure a large degree of conformity in the system. Compulsory schooling begins at six years of age and continues for nine years (in some Länder for 10). Until the age of 18, all young people who do not continue to attend a full-time school must attend a part-time vocational school (Berufsschule). Primary education lasts four years (six years in some Länder) and is provided free of charge. Attendance at the Grundschule (elementary school) is obligatory for all children, after which their education continues at one of four types of secondary school. Approximately one-third of this age-group attend the Hauptschule (general school) for five or six years, after which they may enter employment, but continue their education part-time for three years at a vocational school. Alternatively, pupils may attend the Realschule (intermediate school) for up to nine years, the Gymnasium (grammar school) for nine years (for eight years in some Länder), or the Gesamtschule (comprehensive school, not available in all parts of the country) for up to nine years. The Abitur (grammar school leaving certificate) is a necessary prerequisite for university education.

In 1997 total expenditure on education by the Federal Government, the Länder Governments and the municipalities amounted to DM 172,600m. (9.2% of total public expenditure).

Public Holidays

2003: 1 January (New Year's Day), 6 January (Epiphany)*, 18 April (Good Friday), 21 April (Easter Monday), 1 May (Labour Day), 29 May (Ascension Day), 9 June (Whit Monday), 19 June (Corpus Christi)*, 15 August (Assumption)*, 3 October (Day of Unity), 31 October (Reformation Day)*, 1 November (All Saints' Day)*, 25–26 December (Christmas), 31 December (New Year's Eve).

2004: 1 January (New Year's Day), 6 January (Epiphany)*, 9 April (Good Friday), 12 April (Easter Monday), 1 May (Labour Day), 20 May (Ascension Day), 31 May (Whit Monday), 10 June (Corpus Christi)*, 15 August (Assumption)*, 3 October (Day of Unity), 31 October (Reformation Day)*, 1 November (All Saints' Day)*, 25–26 December (Christmas), 31 December (New Year's Eve).

* Religious holidays observed in certain Länder only.

In Sachsen (Saxony) only, *Buss und Bettag* (Repentence Day) is celebrated on the first Wednesday on or after 16 November each year: 19 November in 2003; 17 November in 2004.

Weights and Measures

The metric system is in force.

Statistical Survey

Source (unless otherwise indicated): Statistisches Bundesamt, 65180 Wiesbaden; tel. (611) 752405; fax (611) 753330; e-mail info@statistik-bund.de; internet www.statistik-bund.de.

Area and Population

AREA, POPULATION AND DENSITY

Area (sq km)*	357,022
Population (official estimates at 31 December)	
1998	82,037,011
1999	82,163,475
2000	82,259,540†
Density (per sq km) at 31 December 2000	230.4

* 137,846 sq miles.

† Of the total (rounded to the nearest 100), 40,156,500 were males and 42,103,000 females.

STATES

	Area (sq ('000) km)	Population ('000) at 31 Dec. 2000	Density (per sq km)	Capital
Baden-Württemberg	35,751	10,524	294	Stuttgart
Bayern (Bavaria)	70,548	12,230	173	München
Berlin	892	3,382	3,793	Berlin
Brandenburg	29,477	2,602	88	Potsdam
Bremen	404	660	1,633	Bremen
Hamburg	755	1,715	2,271	Hamburg
Hessen (Hesse)	21,114	6,068	287	Wiesbaden
Mecklenburg-Vorpommern (Mecklenburg-Western Pomerania)	23,173	1,776	77	Schwerin
Niedersachsen (Lower Saxony)	47,616	7,926	166	Hannover
Nordrhein-Westfalen (North Rhine-Westphalia)	34,081	18,010	528	Düsseldorf
Rheinland-Pfalz (Rhineland-Palatinate)	19,847	4,035	203	Mainz
Saarland	2,569	1,069	416	Saarbrücken
Sachsen (Saxony)	18,413	4,426	240	Dresden
Sachsen-Anhalt (Saxony-Anhalt)	20,446	2,615	128	Magdeburg
Schleswig-Holstein	15,763	2,790	177	Kiel
Thüringen (Thuringia)	16,172	2,431	150	Erfurt
Total	357,022	82,260	230	—

PRINCIPAL TOWNS
(estimated population at 31 December 2000)

Berlin (capital)	3,382,200	Gelsenkirchen	278,700
Hamburg	1,715,400	Karlsruhe	278,600
München (Munich)	1,210,200	Wiesbaden	270,100
Köln (Cologne)	962,900	Münster	265,600
Frankfurt am Main	646,600	Mönchengladbach	263,000
Essen	595,200	Chemnitz	259,200
Dortmund	589,000	Augsburg	255,000
Stuttgart	583,900	Halle an der Saale*	247,700
Düsseldorf	569,400	Braunschweig (Brunswick)	245,800
Bremen	539,400	Aachen (Aix-la-Chapelle)	244,400
Hannover (Hanover)	515,000	Krefeld	239,900
Duisburg	514,900	Kiel	232,600
Leipzig	493,200	Magdeburg	231,500
Nürnberg (Nuremberg)	488,400	Oberhausen	222,200
Dresden	477,800	Lübeck	213,400
Bochum	391,100	Freiburg im Breisgau	205,100
Wuppertal	366,400	Hagen	203,200
Bielefeld	321,800	Erfurt	200,600
Mannheim	306,700	Rostock	200,500
Bonn	302,200	Kassel	194,800

* Including Halle-Neustadt.

BIRTHS, MARRIAGES AND DEATHS

	Registered live births Number	Rate (per 1,000)	Registered marriages Number	Rate (per 1,000)	Registered deaths Number	Rate (per 1,000)
1993	798,447	9.8	442,605	5.5	897,270	11.1
1994	769,603	9.5	440,244	5.4	884,661	10.9
1995	765,221	9.4	430,534	5.3	884,588	10.8
1996	796,013	9.7	427,297	5.2	882,843	10.8
1997	812,173	9.9	422,776	5.2	860,389	10.5
1998	785,034	9.6	417,420	5.1	852,382	10.4
1999	770,744	9.4	430,674	5.2	846,330	10.3
2000	766,999	9.3	418,550	5.1	838,797	10.2

Expectation of life (WHO estimates, years at birth): 78.2 (males 75.1; females 81.1) in 2001 (Source: WHO, *World Health Report*).

IMMIGRATION AND EMIGRATION

	1998	1999	2000*
Immigrant arrivals	802,456	874,023	841,158
Emigrant departures	755,358	672,048	674,038

* Provisional figures.

ECONOMICALLY ACTIVE POPULATION
(sample surveys, '000 persons aged 15 years and over, at April)

	1998	1999	2000*
Agriculture, hunting and forestry	1,016	1,020	982
Fishing	8	6	6
Mining and quarrying	182	161	152
Manufacturing	8,461	8,532	8,542
Electricity, gas and water	305	311	290
Construction	3,183	3,146	3,118
Wholesale and retail trade; repair of motor vehicles, motorcycles and personal and household goods	5,154	5,208	5,190
Hotels and restaurants	1,130	1,188	1,219
Transport, storage and communications	1,920	1,953	2,008
Financial intermediation	1,273	1,291	1,333
Real estate, renting and business activities	2,581	2,738	2,923
Public administration and defence; compulsory social security	3,174	3,178	3,103
Education	1,927	1,948	1,928
Health and social work	3,534	3,665	3,696
Other community, social and personal service activities	1,826	1,879	1,944
Private households with employed persons	150	141	137
Extra-territorial organizations and bodies	36	37	33
Total employed	35,860	36,402	36,604
Unemployed	3,849	3,503	3,127
Total labour force	39,709	39,905	39,731
Males	22,583	22,564	22,371
Females	17,126	17,341	17,360

* At May.

Source: ILO.

Health and Welfare

KEY INDICATORS

Total fertility rate (children per woman, 2001)	1.3
Under-five mortality rate (per 1,000 live births, 2001) . . .	5
HIV/AIDS (% of persons aged 15–49, 2001)	0.10
Physicians (per 1,000 head, 1998)	3.50
Hospital beds (per 1,000 head, 1998)	9.3
Health expenditure (2000): US $ per head (PPP)	2,754
Health expenditure (2000): % of GDP	10.6
Health expenditure (2000): public (% of total)	75.1
Human Development Index (2000): ranking	17
Human Development Index (2000): value	0.925

For sources and definitions, see explanatory note on p. vi.

Agriculture

PRINCIPAL CROPS
('000 metric tons)

	1999	2000	2001
Wheat	19,615	21,622	22,838
Barley	13,301	12,106	13,495
Maize	3,257	3,324	3,505
Rye	4,329	4,154	5,132
Oats	1,339	1,087	1,151
Mixed grain	2,611	2,979	3,589
Potatoes	11,569	13,193	11,503
Sugar beet*	27,569	27,870	24,730
Dry broad beans	96	62	81
Sunflower seed†	84	64	62
Rapeseed	4,285	3,586	4,160
Cabbages	786	750	692
Cauliflowers	157	138	131
Cucumbers and gherkins . .	194	208	210
Dry onions	262	317	287
Green beans	44	47	48
Carrots	380	432	444
Grapes†	1,659‡	1,360‡	1,350§
Apples‖	1,036	1,131	922
Pears‖	54	65	47
Cherries‖	75	80	69
Plums‖	55	60	41
Strawberries‖	109	104	110
Currants†	155	158	148

* Deliveries to sugar factories.
† Source: FAO.
‡ Unofficial figure.
§ FAO estimate.
‖ Marketed production only.

LIVESTOCK
('000 head at December)

	1999	2000	2001
Horses	475.8	476.0*	506.2
Cattle†	14,657.9	14,567.7	14,226.6
Pigs†	26,001.5	25,766.8	25,957.8
Sheep*	2,280	2,150	2,140
Goats*	125	135	140
Chickens	107,659	110,000*	109,993
Geese	402	400*	408
Ducks	1,927	1,900*	2,185
Turkeys	8,315	8,800*	9,471

* Source: FAO; year ending September.
† At November.

LIVESTOCK PRODUCTS
('000 metric tons)

	1999	2000	2001
Beef and veal	1,374	1,303	1,361
Mutton and lamb	44	48	46
Pig meat	4,103	3,982	4,074
Poultry meat	748	801	862
Cows' milk	28,334	28,331	28,191
Goats' milk	22	22	22
Butter	427	425	420
Cheese	1,563	1,656	1,773
Hen eggs	882	900	890
Honey	20	20	18
Wool: greasy*	15	15	15
Wool: scoured*	7	7	7
Cattle hides*	162	152	152

* FAO estimates.

Source: FAO.

Forestry

ROUNDWOOD REMOVALS
('000 cubic metres, excluding bark)

	1999	2000	2001
Sawlogs, veneer logs and logs for sleepers	23,404	36,537	22,456
Pulpwood	10,289	9,882	n.a.
Other industrial wood . . .	1,370	4,433	3,393
Fuel wood	2,571	2,622	1,287
Total	37,634	53,710	39,483

Source: FAO.

SAWNWOOD PRODUCTION
('000 cubic metres, including railway sleepers)

	1999	2000	2001
Coniferous (softwood) . . .	14,537	15,020	14,902
Broadleaved (hardwood) . . .	1,559	1,320	1,287
Total	16,096	16,340	16,189

Source: FAO.

Fishing

('000 metric tons, live weight)

	1998	1999	2000
Capture	266.6	238.9	205.7
Freshwater fishes . . .	20.6	20.6	20.4
Atlantic cod	23.1	22.0	18.4
Saithe (Pollock) . . .	13.6	13.3	12.4
Blue whiting (Poutassou) . .	18.0	3.1	12.7
Atlantic redfishes . . .	20.3	18.4	14.3
Atlantic horse mackerel . .	34.4	24.4	16.8
Atlantic herring . . .	47.0	50.9	47.0
Sardinellas	17.4	24.2	—
Atlantic mackerel . . .	21.5	20.0	23.0
Common shrimp . . .	14.8	17.5	17.4
Aquaculture	67.0	73.6	60.0
Common carp	10.7	10.5	10.5
Rainbow trout	25.0	25.0	25.0
Blue mussel	31.2	37.9	24.1
Total catch	333.6	312.5	265.6

Note: Figures exclude aquatic mammals, recorded by number rather than by weight. The number of harbour porpoises caught was: 5 in 1998; 3 in 1999; 5 in 2000.

Source: FAO, *Yearbook of Fishery Statistics*.

Mining

('000 metric tons, unless otherwise indicated)

	1999	2000	2001
Hard coal	39,523	33,612	27,361
Brown coal	161,228	167,623	175,301
Crude petroleum	2,739	3,123	3,365
Natural gas (petajoules)*	626.5	591.6	604.6
Salt (unrefined)	8,405	6,566	6,537

* Source: UN, *Monthly Bulletin of Statistics*.

Industry

SELECTED PRODUCTS

('000 metric tons, unless otherwise indicated)

	1999	2000	2001
Margarine	595	546	538
Flour	4,118	4,164	4,383
Refined sugar	4,247	4,305	3,792
Beer ('000 hl)	107,479	106,877	106,372
Cigarettes (million)	204,631	206,770	213,793
Cotton yarn (pure and mixed)	80	89	89
Woven cotton fabrics ('000 sq metres)	403,404	423,968	414,320
Carpets and rugs ('000 sq metres)	159,474	n.a.	n.a.
Newsprint	1,750	2,006	2,090
Brown-coal briquettes	2,072	1,810	1,740
Pig-iron*	27,932	30,846	n.a.
Crude steel*	42,056	46,376	n.a.
Motor spirit (petrol)	25,557	25,863	24,779
Diesel oil†	44,123	45,122	45,079
Cement	38,099	n.a.	n.a.
Sulphuric acid	1,720	1,578	1,594
Nitrogenous fertilizers (N)	1,152	1,274	1,079
Artificial resins and plastics	12,658	13,631	13,531
Synthetic rubber	598	598	583
Soap	n.a.	136	n.a.
Aluminium (unwrought):			
primary	412	469	458
secondary	455	499	542
Refined lead (unwrought)	265	284	268
Refined zinc (unwrought)	347	319	313
Refined copper	550	545	544
Passenger cars and minibuses ('000)	5,418	5,248	5,487
Bicycles ('000)	2,801	2,973	2,673
Clocks, watches and non-electronic time-measuring instruments ('000)	n.a.	15,144	12,500
Footwear ('000 pairs)‡	31,480	27,907	26,911
Electricity (million kWh)	551,400	564,450	n.a.

* Source: US Geological Survey.
† Including light heating oil.
‡ Excluding rubber and plastic footwear.

Finance

CURRENCY AND EXCHANGE RATES

Monetary Units
 100 cent = 1 euro (€)

Sterling and Dollar Equivalents (31 December 2002)
 £1 sterling = 1.5370 euros
 US $1 = 0.9536 euros
 100 euros = £65.06 = $104.87

Average Exchange Rate (euros per US $)
 2000 1.0854
 2001 1.1175
 2002 1.0626

Note: The national currency was formerly the Deutsche Mark (DM). From the introduction of the euro, with German participation, on 1 January 1999, a fixed exchange rate of €1 = 1.95583 DM was in operation. Euro notes and coins were introduced on 1 January 2002. The euro and local currency circulated alongside each other until 28 February, after which the euro became the sole legal tender. Some of the figures in this Survey are still in terms of Deutsche Marks.

BUDGET

(million DM)*

Revenue	1999	2000	2001†
Current receipts	1,742,783	1,762,470	888,412
Taxes and similar revenue	1,585,221	1,617,885	810,930
Income from economic activity	43,850	34,461	21,287
Interest	10,200	11,197	7,860
Allocations and grants for current purposes	434,759	442,071	238,112
Other receipts	75,817	73,036	30,094
Less Deductible payments on the same level	407,064	416,180	219,870
Capital receipts	72,067	147,691	34,060
Sale of property	40,417	126,704	17,152
Loans and grants for investment	51,632	49,984	24,823
Repayment of loans	24,052	14,184	12,101
Public sector borrowing	1,232	1,268	575
Less Deductible payments on the same level	45,266	44,449	20,965
Total	1,814,850	1,910,161	922,472

Expenditure	1999	2000	2001†
Current expenditure	1,686,068	1,700,537	886,140
Personnel expenses	350,994	351,900	181,033
Goods and services	409,300	419,255	215,501
Interest	137,602	132,810	66,870
Allocations and grants for current purposes	1,195,508	1,212,752	642,605
Less Deductible payments on the same level	407,064	416,180	219,870
Capital expenditure	173,313	173,300	85,964
Construction	61,903	61,272	30,415
Purchase of property	20,669	20,199	10,666
Allocations and grants for investment	103,921	103,804	48,247
Loans	24,655	24,328	9,960
Sale of shares	5,371	6,214	6,919
Repayment expenses in the public sector	2,059	1,932	724
Less Deductible payments on the same level	45,266	44,449	20,965
Total	1,859,381	1,873,837	972,104

* Figures represent a consolidation of the accounts of all public authorities, including the Federal Government and Land administrations.
† Figures for 2001 are in million euros.

INTERNATIONAL RESERVES

(US $ million at 31 December)*

	2000	2001	2002
Gold†	30,606	30,728	37,972
IMF special drawing rights	1,763	1,793	1,980
Reserve position in IMF	5,460	5,901	6,695
Foreign exchange	49,667	43,615	42,495
Total	87,496	82,037	89,142

* Data on gold and foreign exchange holdings exclude deposits made with the European Monetary Institute (now the European Central Bank).
† National valuation.

Source: IMF, *International Financial Statistics*.

MONEY SUPPLY

(million euros at 31 December)

	2000	2001	2002
Currency issued	142,152	82,835	112,162*
Demand deposits at banking institutions	448,682	533,668	582,500

* Currency put into circulation by the Deutsche Bundesbank was 141,300 million euros.

Source: IMF, *International Financial Statistics*.

COST OF LIVING

(Consumer Price Index for All Private Households; base: 1995 = 100)

	1999	2000	2001
Food	101.7	101.2	105.8
Clothes and shoes	101.8	102.0	102.7
Rent	107.4	110.9	114.2
Energy			
Furniture, domestic appliances and other household expenses	102.1	102.1	103.0
Transport	107.6	113.6	117.2
Communications	88.2	84.5	82.3
Health	110.6	111.0	112.3
Entertainment and culture	103.4	104.5	106.2
All items	104.9	106.9	109.6

NATIONAL ACCOUNTS

(provisional, million euros at current prices)

National Income and Product

	1999	2000	2001
Compensation of employees	1,065,090	1,097,660	1,116,550
Operating surplus	411,370	415,790	422,990
Domestic factor incomes	1,476,460	1,513,450	1,539,540
Consumption of fixed capital	291,550	302,530	312,210
Gross domestic product at factor cost	1,768,010	1,815,980	1,851,750
Indirect taxes	241,400	244,380	246,280
Less Subsidies	35,110	34,860	35,030
GDP in purchasers' values	1,974,300	2,205,500	2,063,000
Factor income from abroad	89,790	112,640	129,640
Less Factor income paid abroad	102,080	120,280	128,070
Gross national product	1,962,010	2,017,860	2,054,570
Less Consumption of fixed capital	291,550	302,530	312,210
National income in market prices	1,670,460	1,715,330	1,742,360
Other current transfers from abroad	9,600	10,090	9,640
Less Other current transfers paid abroad	29,400	29,670	29,510
National disposable income	1,650,660	1,695,750	1,722,490

Expenditure on the Gross Domestic Product

	1999	2000	2001
Government final consumption expenditure	378,400	384,470	393,170
Private final consumption expenditure	1,149,560	1,182,830	1,218,110
Increase in stocks	3,490	12,140	−5,170
Gross fixed capital formation	426,040	438,000	417,810
Total domestic expenditure	1,957,490	2,017,530	2,023,920
Exports of goods and services	586,570	683,270	721,400
Less Imports of goods and services	569,760	675,300	682,320
GDP in purchasers' values	1,974,300	2,025,500	2,063,000
GDP at constant 1995 prices	1,911,100	1,968,500	1,979,600

Gross Domestic Product by Economic Activity

	1999	2000	2001
Agriculture, hunting and forestry Fishing	21,700	22,000	23,250
Mining and quarrying Electricity, gas and water supply	43,040	40,000	41,770
Manufacturing	410,050	439,320	442,000
Construction	100,640	95,920	90,960
Wholesale and retail trade; repair of motor vehicles, motorcycles and personal and household goods	191,300	197,020	200,350
Hotels and restaurants	23,930	24,540	25,370
Transport, storage and communications	106,620	111,490	116,990
Financial intermediation Real estate, renting and business activities*	546,690	560,470	575,370
Public administration and defence; compulsory social security Education Health and social work Other community, social and personal service activities Private households with employed persons	394,350	397,260	404,540
Sub-total	1,838,320	1,886,030	1,920,600
Less Imputed bank service charges	66,070	66,840	67,000
GDP at basic prices	1,772,250	1,819,190	1,853,600
Taxes on products	212,610	216,980	219,910
Less subsidies on products	10,560	10,670	10,510
GDP in purchasers' values	1,974,300	2,025,500	2,063,000

* Including imputed rents of owner-occupied dwellings.

BALANCE OF PAYMENTS

(US $ million)

	1999	2000	2001
Exports of goods f.o.b.	542,726	549,841	569,951
Imports of goods f.o.b.	−472,692	−492,331	−481,439
Trade balance	70,035	57,510	88,512
Exports of services	86,927	85,571	87,502
Imports of services	−139,146	−135,480	−138,480
Balance on goods and services	17,815	7,601	37,533
Other income received	86,126	99,897	105,341
Other income paid	−95,707	−102,988	−116,609
Balance on goods, services and income	8,234	4,510	26,265
Current transfers received	16,959	15,771	15,153
Current transfers paid	−44,261	−40,671	−38,977
Current balance	−19,069	−20,390	2,442
Capital account (net)	−156	6,191	−834
Direct investment abroad	−109,419	−53,002	−42,745
Direct investment from abroad	54,585	207,715	31,526
Portfolio investment assets	−190,321	−195,956	−115,257
Portfolio investment liabilities	176,307	39,341	114,189
Financial derivatives liabilities	−1,672	−3,914	5,923
Other investment assets	−70,847	−79,681	−87,062
Other investment liabilities	111,119	121,209	67,144
Net errors and omissions	35,359	−26,735	19,209
Overall balance	−14,115	−5,222	−5,466

Source: IMF, *International Financial Statistics*.

DEVELOPMENT AID

(public and private development aid to developing countries and multilateral agencies, million euros)

	1998	1999	2000
Public development co-operation .	5,020	5,177	5,458
Bilateral	3,140	3,076	2,915
Multilateral	1,880	2,101	2,543
Other public transactions . .	−289	−168	−495
Bilateral	−33	−40	−495
Multilateral	−256	−128	—
Private development aid . . .	874	931	918
Other private transactions . . .	14,577	12,838	7,596
Bilateral	13,384	13,070	9,423
Multilateral	1,194	−232	−1,827
Total	20,183	18,777	13,477

External Trade

(Note: Figures include trade in second-hand ships, and stores and bunkers for foreign ships and aircraft. Imports exclude military supplies under the off-shore procurement programme and exports exclude war reparations and restitutions, except exports resulting from the Israel Reparations Agreement)

PRINCIPAL COMMODITIES

(distribution by SITC, million euros)

Imports c.i.f.	1999	2000	2001
Food and live animals . .	29,500	30,972	29,916
Crude materials (inedible) except fuels	15,279	18,903	16,968
Mineral fuels, lubricants, etc. .	25,648	47,641	46,869
Petroleum, petroleum products, etc.	18,374	35,479	31,700
Chemicals and related products	43,902	51,637	54,963
Basic manufactures . . .	62,212	74,383	69,064
Machinery and transport equipment.	173,025	210,618	206,202
Power-generating machinery and equipment	14,373	18,638	18,507
General industrial machinery, equipment and parts . . .	15,762	18,434	18,309
Office machines and automatic data-processing equipment . .	26,652	32,096	29,456
Telecommunications and sound equipment	13,032	18,187	19,179
Other electrical machinery, apparatus and appliances .	32,574	44,491	41,106
Road vehicles (incl. air-cushion vehicles) and parts* . . .	45,067	47,189	47,984
Other transport equipment . .	14,291	18,393	18,957
Miscellaneous manufactured articles.	61,546	69,839	66,884
Articles of apparel and clothing accessories (excl. footwear) .	20,140	21,854	20,839
Total (incl. others)†	444,797	538,343	550,273

Exports f.o.b.	1999	2000	2001
Food and live animals . . .	18,812	21,696	21,313
Chemicals and related products	66,604	77,854	80,815
Basic manufactures	73,460	87,229	86,077
Metal manufactures	15,451	17,680	17,885
Machinery and transport equipment. . . .	265,108	314,875	331,166
Power-generating machinery and equipment	17,274	20,619	22,587
Machinery specialized for particular industries	26,508	30,509	31,042
General industrial machinery and equipment	34,492	39,121	40,574
Office machines and automatic data-processing equipment . .	13,583	18,653	16,748
Telecommunications and sound equipment	13,768	18,565	19,474
Electrical machinery, apparatus and appliances	40,562	52,028	50,622
Road vehicles (incl. air-cushion vehicles) and parts* . . .	92,320	105,659	114,950
Other transport equipment . . .	17,414	20,322	24,827
Miscellaneous manufactured articles.	51,540	58,794	59,482
Total (incl. others)†	510,008	597,481	637,333

* Excluding tyres, engines and electrical parts.

† Including monetary gold. Also included are returns and replacements, not allocated to their appropriate headings.

PRINCIPAL TRADING PARTNERS*

(million euros, including gold)

Imports c.i.f.	1999	2000	2001†
Austria.	18,288.0	20,498.2	20,754.9
Belgium	21,652.8	24,612.3	28,446.2
China, People's Republic . .	13,794.5	18,554.9	19,740.0
Czech Republic	10,157.6	12,877.5	14,510.8
Denmark	7,442.6	8,880.7	9,108.1
Finland	4,675.3	5,881.6	6,357.3
France	45,559.1	50,863.2	51,670.6
Hungary	8,962.2	10,634.0	11,973.3
Ireland.	11,355.7	10,749.3	16,627.3
Italy	33,106.8	35,778.2	35,676.7
Japan	21,778.6	26,848.4	22,599.5
Korea, Republic	4,108.8	5,883.0	4,663.2
Netherlands	36,088.8	44,739.7	46,280.1
Norway	6,970.8	10,602.8	11,485.8
Poland	9,218.6	11,939.7	13,503.2
Portugal	4,770.4	5,469.4	5,468.1
Russia	8,376.9	14,700.7	14,521.0
Spain	14,666.5	16,087.8	15,617.9
Sweden	8,305.4	10,202.3	9,116.2
Switzerland	17,070.2	18,797.9	19,793.4
Taiwan.	5,541.5	7,628.6	6,490.1
Turkey.	5,664.1	6,202.1	6,547.3
United Kingdom	30,757.3	36,924.5	38,204.4
USA	36,790.1	47,124.2	45,453.7
Total (incl. others)	444,796.6	538,342.7	550,273.0

Exports f.o.b.	1999	2000	2001†
Austria	28,295.0	32,436.7	32,644.5
Belgium	26,812.0	30,105.1	31,358.8
China, People's Republic . . .	6,948.9	9,459.1	12,064.3
Czech Republic	10,037.6	12,797.3	14,937.8
Denmark	8,758.3	9,605.7	10,344.3
Finland	5,811.8	7,005.4	6,766.7
France	58,577.7	67,418.4	70,672.2
Hungary	8,481.8	10,299.6	10,519.7
Italy	38,335.5	45,011.7	47,515.8
Japan	10,367.0	13,195.7	13,072.5
Netherlands	34,354.9	38,994.1	39,296.7
Poland	12,338.5	14,512.5	15,277.9
Portugal	5,877.8	6,254.9	6,405.6
Russia	5,075.3	6,660.0	10,257.6
Spain	22,684.1	26,732.5	28,388.4
Sweden	11,657.1	13,525.0	12,932.3
Switzerland	22,807.8	25,596.1	27,611.2
Turkey	5,877.7	8,340.9	6,006.3
United Kingdom	43,124.2	49,377.1	53,271.4
USA	51,425.4	61,764.6	67,306.9
Total (incl. others)	520,007.7	597,480.5	637,332.7

* Imports by country of production; exports by country of consumption. The distribution by countries excludes stores and bunkers for ships and aircraft (million DM): Imports 1,051.6 in 1999, 1,442.1 in 2000; Exports 2,275.8 in 1999, 3,277.8 in 2000.
† Provisional figures.

Transport

FEDERAL RAILWAYS
(traffic)

	1999	2000	2001
Passengers (million) . . .	1,963	2,002	2,001
Passenger-km (million) . . .	73,587	75,080	75,314
Freight net ton-km (million) . .	71,356	76,032	74,260

ROAD TRAFFIC
('000 licensed vehicles at 1 January)

	2000	2001	2002
Passenger cars	42,423.3	43,772.3	44,383.3
Lorries	2,491.1	2,610.9	2,649.1
Buses	84.9	86.7	86.5
Motorcycles	3,1783.5	3,410.5	3,557.4
Trailers	4,749.7	4,960.2	5,105.3

SHIPPING

Inland Waterways

	1999	2000	2001
Freight ton-km (million) . . .	62,692	66,466	64,818

Merchant Fleet
(registered at 31 December)

	1999	2000	2001
Number of vessels	1,028	994	906
Displacement ('000 grt) . . .	6,513.8	6,552.2	6,300.2

Source: Lloyd's Register-Fairplay, *World Fleet Statistics*.

Sea-borne Traffic

	1997	1998	1999
Vessels entered ('000 net registered tons):*			
Domestic (coastwise)	19,785	43,667	21,213
International	260,553	263,470	269,637
Vessels cleared ('000 net registered tons):*			
Domestic	19,664	67,036	20,529
International	235,110	237,071	246,887
Freight unloaded ('000 metric tons):†			
International	136,249	140,846	137,759
Freight loaded ('000 metric tons):†			
International	69,058	69,098	73,858
Total domestic freight ('000 metric tons)	8,011	7,444	10,005

* Loaded vessels only.
† Including transhipments.

CIVIL AVIATION
(traffic on scheduled services)

	1997	1998	1999
Kilometres flown (million) . . .	704	736	788
Passengers carried ('000) . . .	45,805	49,417	54,247
Passenger-km (million) . . .	86,189	90,393	104,602
Total ton-km (million) . . .	14,822	15,301	16,950

Source: UN, *Statistical Yearbook*.

Tourism

FOREIGN TOURIST ARRIVALS
('000)*

Country of Residence	1999	2000	2001
Austria	723.5	782.3	790.8
Belgium and Luxembourg . . .	723.4	780.8	743.9
Denmark	653.3	667.3	640.6
France	824.1	857.6	818.4
Italy	998.6	1,017.6	988.6
Japan	818.0	914.2	778.8
Netherlands	1,923.1	2,059.5	2,053.5
Poland	311.1	339.6	334.7
Spain	399.2	435.0	411.9
Sweden	684.3	761.1	711.1
Switzerland	954.9	1,056.5	1,057.1
United Kingdom	1,598.8	1,864.3	1,664.8
USA	2,016.5	2,407.6	1,916.8
Total (incl. others)	16,137.1	18,002.3	16,886.6

* Figures refer to arrivals at registered accommodation establishments.

Tourism receipts (million euros): 17,240 in 1999; 19,130 in 2000; 19,216 in 2001.

Communications Media

	1999	2000	2001
Television receivers ('000 in use) .	47,660	48,170	n.a.
Telephones ('000 main lines in use)	48,500	49,400	52,280
Mobile cellular telephones ('000 subscribers).	23,470	48,145	56,245
Personal computers ('000 in use) .	24,400	27,640	n.a.
Internet users ('000).	14,400	24,000	30,000

Source: International Telecommunication Union.

Facsimile machines ('000 in use, 1998): 6,000.

Radio receivers ('000 in use, 1997): 77,800.

Book production (titles*, 1996): 71,515.

Daily newspapers (1996): 375, average circulation ('000 copies) 25,500.

Non-daily newspapers (1996): 36, average circulation ('000 copies) 6,600.
* Including pamphlets.

Sources: UNESCO, *Statistical Yearbook*; UN, *Statistical Yearbook*.

Education

(1999)

	Teachers	Students
Pre-primary .	5,090	67,400
Primary .	168,194	3,532,700
Secondary:		
first stage .	317,899	5,267,100
second stage .	61,945	765,900
special .	57,696*	415,400
Higher:		
Non-university institutions	17,882†	443,200
Universities and equivalent institutions . .	138,881†	1,330,800

* Excluding Thuringia.
† Full-time staff only.

Source: Ministry of Education and Research, Berlin.

Directory

The Constitution

The Basic Law (Grundgesetz), which came into force in the British, French and US Zones of Occupation in Germany (excluding Saarland) on 23 May 1949, was intended as a provisional Constitution to serve until a permanent one for Germany as a whole could be adopted. (Saarland was incorporated into the Federal Republic of Germany in 1957.) The Parliamentary Council which framed the Basic Law intended to continue the tradition of the Constitution of 1848–49, and to preserve some continuity with subsequent German constitutions (with Bismarck's Constitution of 1871, and with the Weimar Constitution of 1919), while avoiding the mistakes of the past.

With the accession of the five newly re-established eastern Länder and East Berlin to the Federal Republic on 3 October 1990, the Basic Law became the Constitution of the entire German nation.

The Basic Law has 182 articles, divided into 14 sections, and is introduced by a short preamble.

I. BASIC RIGHTS

The opening articles of the Constitution guarantee the dignity of man, the free development of his personality, the equality of all persons before the law, and freedom of faith and conscience. Men and women shall have equal rights, and no one shall suffer discrimination because of sex, descent, race, language, homeland and origin, faith or religion or political opinion.

No one may be compelled against his conscience to perform war service as a combatant (Article 4). All Germans have the right to assemble peacefully and unarmed and to form associations and societies. Everyone has the right freely to express and to disseminate his opinion through speech, writing or pictures. Freedom of the press and freedom of reporting by radio and motion pictures are guaranteed (Article 5). Censorship is not permitted.

The State shall protect marriage and the family, property and the right of inheritance. The care and upbringing of children is the natural right of parents. Illegitimate children shall be given the same conditions for their development and their position in society as legitimate children. Schools are under the supervision of the State. Religion forms part of the curriculum in the State schools, but parents have the right to decide whether the child shall receive religious instruction (Article 7).

A citizen's dwelling is inviolable; house searches may be made only by Court Order. No German may be deprived of his citizenship if he would thereby become stateless. The politically persecuted enjoy the right of asylum (Article 16).

II. THE FEDERATION AND THE LÄNDER

Article 20 describes the Federal Republic (Bundesrepublik Deutschland) as a democratic and social federal state. The colours of the Federal Republic are black-red-gold, the same as those of the Weimar Republic. Each Land within the Federal Republic has its own Constitution, which must, however, conform to the principles laid down in the Basic Law. All Länder, districts and parishes must have a representative assembly resulting from universal, direct, free, equal and secret elections (Article 28). The exercise of governmental powers is the concern of the Länder, in so far as the Basic Law does not otherwise prescribe. Where there is incompatibility, Federal Law overrides Land Law (Article 31). Every German has in each Land the same civil rights and duties.

Political parties may be freely formed in all the states of the Federal Republic, but their internal organization must conform to democratic principles, and they must publicly account for the sources of their funds. Parties that seek to impair or abolish the free and democratic basic order or to jeopardize the existence of the Federal Republic of Germany are unconstitutional (Article 21). So are activities tending to disturb the peaceful relations between nations, and, especially, preparations for aggressive war, but the Federation may join a system of mutual collective security in order to preserve peace (Articles 26 and 24). The rules of International Law shall form part of Federal Law and take precedence over it and create rights and duties directly for the inhabitants of the Federal territory (Article 25).

The territorial organization of the Federation may be restructured by Federal Law, subject to regional plebiscites and with due regard to regional, historical and cultural ties, economic expediency and the requirements of regional policy and planning.

III. THE BUNDESTAG

The Federal Assembly (Bundestag) is the Lower House. Its members are elected by the people in universal, free, equal, direct and secret elections, for a term of four years*. Any person who has reached the age of 18 is eligible to vote and any person who has reached the age of 18 is eligible for election (Article 38). A deputy may be arrested for a punishable offence only with the permission of the Bundestag, unless he be apprehended in the act or during the following day.

The Bundestag elects its President and draws up its Standing Orders. Most decisions of the House require a majority vote. Its meetings are public, but the public may be excluded by the decision of a two-thirds' majority. Upon the motion of one-quarter of its members the Bundestag is obliged to set up an investigation committee.

* The elections of 1949 were conducted on the basis of direct election, with some elements of proportional representation. In January 1953 the draft of a new electoral law was completed by the Federal Government and was approved shortly before the dissolution. The new law represents a compromise between direct election and proportional representation, and is designed to prevent the excessive proliferation of parties in the Bundestag.

IV. THE BUNDESRAT

The Federal Council (Bundesrat) is the Upper House, through which the Länder participate in the legislation and the administration of the Federation, and in matters relating to the European Union (EU). The Bundesrat consists of members of the Land governments, which appoint and recall them (Article 51). Each Land has at least three votes; Länder with more than two million inhabitants have four, and those with more than six million inhabitants have five. Länder with more than seven million inhabitants have six votes. The votes of each Land may only be given as a block vote. The Bundesrat elects its President for one year. Its decisions are taken by simple majority vote. Meetings are public, but the public may be excluded. The members of the Federal Government have the right, and, on demand, the obligation, to participate in the debates of the Bundesrat.

V. THE FEDERAL PRESIDENT

The Federal President (Bundespräsident) is elected by the Federal Convention (Bundesversammlung), consisting of the members of the Bundestag and an equal number of members elected by the Land Parliaments (Article 54). Every German eligible to vote in elections for the Bundestag and over 40 years of age is eligible for election. The candidate who obtains an absolute majority of votes is elected, but if such majority is not achieved by any candidate in two ballots, whoever receives most votes in a further ballot becomes President. The President's term of office is five years. Immediate re-election is permitted only once. The Federal President must not be a member of the Government or of any legislative body or hold any salaried office. Orders and instructions of the President require the counter-signature of the Federal Chancellor or competent Minister, except for the appointment or dismissal of the Chancellor or the dissolution of the Bundestag.

The President represents the Federation in its international relations and accredits and receives envoys. The Bundestag or the Bundesrat may impeach the President before the Federal Constitutional Court on account of wilful violation of the Basic Law or of any other Federal Law (Article 61).

VI. THE FEDERAL GOVERNMENT

The Federal Government (Bundesregierung) consists of the Federal Chancellor (Bundeskanzler) and the Federal Ministers (Bundesminister). The Chancellor is elected by an absolute majority of the Bundestag on the proposal of the Federal President (Article 63). Ministers are appointed and dismissed by the President upon the proposal of the Chancellor. Neither he nor his Ministers may hold any other salaried office. The Chancellor determines general policy and assumes responsibility for it, but within these limits each Minister directs his department individually and on his own responsibility. The Bundestag may express its lack of confidence in the Chancellor only by electing a successor with the majority of its members; the President must then appoint the person elected (Article 67). If a motion of the Chancellor for a vote of confidence does not obtain the support of the majority of the Bundestag, the President may, upon the proposal of the Chancellor, dissolve the House within 21 days, unless it elects another Chancellor within this time (Article 68).

VII. THE LEGISLATION OF THE FEDERATION

The right of legislation lies with the Länder in so far as the Basic Law does not specifically accord legislative powers to the Federation. Distinction is made between fields within the exclusive legislative powers of the Federation and fields within concurrent legislative powers. In the field of concurrent legislation the Länder may legislate so long and so far as the Federation makes no use of its legislative right. The Federation has this right only in matters relating to the creation of equal living conditions throughout the country and in cases where the preservation of legal and economic unity is perceived to be in the national interest. Exclusive legislation of the Federation is strictly limited to such matters as foreign affairs, Federal finance, citizenship, migration, currency, copyrights, customs, railways, waterways, shipping and post and telecommunications. In most other fields, as enumerated (Article 74), concurrent legislation exists.

The legislative organ of the Federation is the Bundestag, to which Bills are introduced by the Government, by members of the Bundestag or by the Bundesrat (Article 76). After their adoption they must be submitted to the Bundesrat, which may demand, within three weeks, that a committee of members of both houses be convened to consider the Bill (Article 77). In so far as its express approval is not needed, the Bundesrat may veto a law within two weeks. This veto can be overruled by the Bundestag, with the approval of a majority of its members. When the Bill requires the consent of the Bundesrat, such an overruling may not take place.

An amendment of the Basic Law requires a majority of two-thirds in both houses, but an amendment affecting the division of the Federation into Länder and the basic principles contained in Articles 1 and 20 is inadmissible (Article 79).

VIII. THE EXECUTION OF FEDERAL LAWS AND THE FEDERAL ADMINISTRATION

The Länder execute Federal Laws as matters of their own concern in so far as the Basic Law does not otherwise determine. In doing so, they regulate the establishment of the authorities and the administrative procedure, but the Federal Government exercises supervision in order to ensure that the Länder execute Federal Laws in an appropriate manner.

In order to avert imminent danger to the existence of the democratic order, a Land may call in the police forces of other Länder; and if the Land in which the danger is imminent is itself not willing or able to fight the danger, the Federal Government may place the police in the Land, or the police forces in other Länder, under its instructions (Article 91).

IX. THE ADMINISTRATION OF JUSTICE

Judicial authority is vested in independent judges, who are subject only to the law and who may not be dismissed or transferred against their will (Article 97).

Justice is exercised by the Federal Constitutional Court, by the Superior Federal Courts and by the Courts of the Länder. The Federal Constitutional Court decides on the interpretation of the Basic Law in cases of doubt, on the compatibility of Federal Law or Land Law with the Basic Law, and on disputes between the Federation and the Länder or between different Länder. Superior Federal Courts are responsible for the spheres of ordinary, administrative, fiscal, labour and social jurisdiction. If a Superior Federal Court intends to judge a point of law in contradiction to a previous decision of another Superior Federal Court, it must refer the matter to a special senate of the Superior Courts. Extraordinary courts are inadmissible.

The freedom of the individual may be restricted only on the basis of a law. No one may be prevented from appearing before his lawful judge (Article 101). Detained persons may be subjected neither to physical nor to mental ill-treatment. The police may hold no one in custody longer than the end of the day following the arrest without the decision of a court. Any person temporarily detained must be brought before a judge who must either issue a warrant of arrest or set him free, at the latest on the following day. A person enjoying the confidence of the detainee must be notified forthwith of any continued duration of a deprivation of liberty. An act may be punished only if it was punishable by law before the act was committed, and no one may be punished more than once for the same criminal act. A criminal act may not be punished by sentence of death.

X. FINANCE

The Federation has the exclusive power to legislate only on customs and fiscal monopolies; on most other taxes, especially on income, property and inheritance, it has concurrent power to legislate with the Länder (see VII above).

Customs, fiscal monopolies, excise taxes (with the exception of the beer tax) and levies within the framework of the EU are administered by Federal finance authorities, and the revenues thereof accrue to the Federation. The remaining taxes are administered, as a rule, by the Länder and the Gemeinden (communities) to which they accrue. Income tax, corporation tax and value-added tax are shared taxes, accruing jointly to the Federation and the Länder (after deduction of a proportion of income tax for the municipalities; Article 106). The Federation and the Länder shall be self-supporting and independent of each other in their fiscal administration (Article 109). In order to ensure the working efficiency of the Länder with low revenues and to equalize their differing burdens of expenditure, there exists a system of revenue-sharing among the Länder; in addition, the Federation may make grants, out of its own funds, to the poorer Länder. All revenues and expenditures of the Federation must be estimated for each fiscal year and included in the budget, which must be established by law before the beginning of the fiscal year. Decisions of the Bundestag or the Bundesrat that increase the budget expenditure proposed by the Federal Government require its approval (Article 113).

XI. TRANSITIONAL AND CONCLUDING PROVISIONS

Articles 116–146 regulate a number of unrelated matters of detail, such as the relationship between the old Reich and the Federation. Article 143 contains divergences from the Basic Law, with regard to the newly-acceded Länder, as stipulated in the Unification Treaty.

The Government

HEAD OF STATE

Federal President: Prof. Dr JOHANNES RAU (inaugurated 1 July 1999).

THE FEDERAL GOVERNMENT
(April 2003)

A coalition of the Sozialdemokratische Partei Deutschlands (Social Democratic Party—SPD) and Bündnis 90/Die Grünen (Alliance 90/Greens).

Federal Chancellor: GERHARD SCHRÖDER (SPD).

Federal Vice-Chancellor and Minister of Foreign Affairs: JOSEPH (JOSCHKA) FISCHER (Bündnis 90/Die Grünen).

Minister of the Interior: OTTO SCHILY (SPD).

Minister of Justice: BRIGITTE ZYPRIES (SPD).

Minister of Finance: HANS EICHEL (SPD).

Minister of Economics and Labour: WOLFGANG CLEMENT (Independent).

Minister of Consumer Protection, Food and Agriculture: RENATE KÜNAST (Bündnis 90/Die Grünen).

Minister of Defence: PETER STRUCK (SPD).

Minister of Family Affairs, Senior Citizens, Women and Youth: RENATE SCHMIDT (SPD).

Minister of Health and Social Security: ULLA SCHMIDT (SPD).

Minister of Transport, Building and Housing: MANFRED STOLPE (SPD).

Minister of the Environment, Nature Conservation and Nuclear Safety: JÜRGEN TRITTIN (Bündnis 90/Die Grünen).

Minister of Education and Research: EDELGARD BULMAHN (SPD).

Minister of Economic Co-operation and Development: HEIDE-MARIE WIECZOREK-ZEUL (SPD).

MINISTRIES

Office of the Federal President: Schloss Bellevue, 11010 Berlin; tel. (30) 20000; e-mail poststelle@bpra.bund.de; internet www .bundespraesident.de.

Federal Chancellery: Willy-Brandt Str. 1, 10557 Berlin; tel. (30) 40000; fax (30) 40002357; e-mail bundeskanzler@bundeskanzler.de; internet www.bundeskanzler.de.

Press and Information Office of the Federal Government: Dorotheenstr. 84, 10117 Berlin; tel. (1888) 2720; fax (1888) 2722555; e-mail posteingang@bpa.bund.de; internet www.government.de.

Ministry of Consumer Protection, Food and Agriculture: Postfach 42, 10177 Berlin; Wilhelmstr. 54, 10121 Berlin; tel. (30) 20060; fax (30) 20064262; e-mail internet@bml.bund.de; internet www.bml.de.

Ministry of Defence: Stauffenbergstr. 18, 10785 Berlin; tel. (30) 200400; fax (30) 20048333; e-mail poststelle@bmvg.bund400.de; internet www.bundeswehr.de.

Ministry of Economic Co-operation and Development: Stresemannstr. 94, Europahaus, 10963 Berlin; tel. (30) 25030; fax (30) 25034847; e-mail poststelle@bmz.bund.de; internet www.bmz.de.

Ministry of Economics and Labour: Scharnhorststr. 34–37, 10115 Berlin; tel. (1888) 6150; fax (1888) 6157010; e-mail info@bmwi .bund.de; internet www.bmwi.de.

Ministry of Education and Research: Hannoversche Str. 30, 10115 Berlin; tel. (1888) 570; fax (1888) 575270; e-mail bmbf@bmbf .bund.de; internet www.bmbf.de.

Ministry of the Environment, Nature Conservation and Nuclear Safety: Alexanderpl. 6, 10178 Berlin; tel. (1888) 3050; fax (1888) 3052044; e-mail service@bmu.de; internet www.bmu.de.

Ministry of Family Affairs, Senior Citizens, Women and Youth: Taubenstr. 42/43, 10117 Berlin; tel. (30) 206550; fax (30) 206551145; e-mail info@bmfsfj.bund.de; internet www.bmfsfj.de.

Ministry of Finance: Wilhelmstr. 97, 10117 Berlin; tel. (30) 22420; fax (30) 22423260; e-mail poststelle@bmf.bund.de; internet www .bundesfinanzministerium.de.

Ministry of Foreign Affairs: Werderscher Markt 1, 10117 Berlin; tel. (1888) 170; fax (1888) 173402; e-mail poststelle@ auswaertiges-amt.de; internet www.auswaertiges-amt.de.

Ministry of Health and Social Security: Postfach 080163, 10117 Berlin; Mohrenstr. 62, 10001 Berlin; tel. (30) 206400; fax (30) 206404974; e-mail info@bmg.bund.de; internet www.bmgesundheit .de.

Ministry of the Interior: Alt-Moabit 101D, 10559 Berlin; tel. (1888) 6810; fax (1888) 6812926; e-mail poststelle@bmi.bund.de; internet www.bmi.bund.de.

Ministry of Justice: Mohrenstr. 37, 10117 Berlin; tel. (30) 202570; fax (30) 20259525; e-mail poststelle@bmj.bund.de; internet www .bmj.bund.de.

Ministry of Transport, Building and Housing: Invalidenstr. 44, 10115 Berlin; tel. (30) 20080; fax (30) 20081920; e-mail buergerinfo@ bmvbw.bund.de; internet www.bmvbw.de.

Legislature

BUNDESTAG
(Federal Assembly)

Pl. der Republik 1, 11011 Berlin; tel. (30) 2270; internet www .bundestag.de.

President: WOLFGANG THIERSE (SPD).

Vice-Presidents: ANKE FUCHS (SP), DRUDOLF SEITERS (CSU), Dr ANTJE VOLLMER (Bündnis 90/Die Grünen), Dr HERMANN OTTO SOLMS (FDP), PETRA BLÄSS (PDS).

General Election, 22 September 2002

Parties and Groups	Votes*	%	Seats
Sozialdemokratische Partei Deutschlands (SPD)	18,488,668	38.52	251
Christlich-Demokratische Union Deutschlands (CDU)	14,167,561	29.52	190
Christlich-Soziale Union Deutschlands (CSU)	4,315,080	8.99	58
Bündnis 90/Die Grünen	4,110,355	8.56	55
Freie Demokratische Partei (FDP)	3,538,815	7.37	47
Partei des Demokratischen Sozialismus (PDS)	1,916,702	3.99	2
Others	1,459,299	3.04	—
Total	47,996,480	100.00	603

* Figures refer to valid second votes (i.e. for state party lists). The total number of valid first votes (for individual candidates) was 47,841,724.

BUNDESRAT
(Federal Council)

President: Prof. Dr WOLFGANG BÖHMER (CDU).

The Bundesrat has 69 members. Each Land (state) has three, four, five or six votes, depending on the size of its population, and may send as many members to the sessions as it has votes. The head of government of each Land is automatically a member of the Bundesrat. Members of the Federal Government attend the sessions, which are held every two to three weeks.

Länder	Seats
Nordrhein-Westfalen (North Rhine-Westphalia)	6
Bayern (Bavaria)	6
Baden-Württemberg	6
Niedersachsen (Lower Saxony)	6
Hessen (Hesse)	4
Sachsen (Saxony)	5
Rheinland-Pfalz (Rhineland-Palatinate)	4
Berlin	4
Sachsen-Anhalt (Saxony-Anhalt)	4
Thüringen (Thuringia)	4
Brandenburg	4
Schleswig-Holstein	4
Mecklenburg-Vorpommern (Mecklenburg-Western Pomerania)	3
Hamburg	3
Saarland	3
Bremen	3
Total	69

The Land Governments

The 16 Länder of Germany are autonomous but not sovereign states, enjoying a high degree of self-government and extensive legislative powers. Thirteen of the Länder have a Landesregierung (Government) and a Landtag (Assembly). The equivalent of the Landesregierung in Berlin, Bremen and Hamburg is the Senate. The equivalent of the Landtag is the House of Representatives in Berlin and the City Council in Bremen and Hamburg.

BADEN-WÜRTTEMBERG

The Constitution was adopted by the Assembly in Stuttgart on 11 November 1953 and came into force on 19 November. The Minister-President, who is elected by the Assembly, appoints and dismisses Ministers. The Government, which is responsible to the Assembly, is currently formed by a coalition of the CDU and the FDP/DVP.

Minister-President: ERWIN TEUFEL (CDU).

Landtag von Baden-Württemberg: Haus des Landtags, Konrad-Adenauer-Str. 3, 70173 Stuttgart; tel. (711) 20630; fax (711) 2063299; e-mail post@landtag-bw.de; internet www.landtag-bw.de. The composition of the Assembly, as the result of elections held on 25 March 2001, is as follows:

President of Assembly: PETER STRAUB (CDU).

Party	Seats
Christlich-Demokratische Union Deutschlands (CDU)	63
Sozialdemokratische Partei Deutschlands (SPD) . .	45
Bündnis 90/Die Grünen	10
Freie Demokratische Partei/Demokratische Volkspartei (FDP/DVP)	10

The Land is divided into four administrative districts: Stuttgart, Karlsruhe, Tübingen and Freiburg.

BAYERN (BAVARIA)

The Constitution of Bayern provides for a bicameral Assembly and a Constitutional Court. Provision is also made for referendums. The Minister-President, who is elected by the Assembly for four years, appoints the Ministers and Secretaries of State with the consent of the Assembly. The Government is currently formed from the majority party (CSU).

Minister-President: Dr EDMUND STOIBER (CSU).

Bayerischer Landtag: Landtagsamt, Maximilaneum, 81627 München; tel. (89) 41260; fax (89) 41261392; e-mail poststelle@bayern.landtag.de; internet www.bayern.landtag.de. The composition of the Assembly, as a result of elections held on 13 September 1998, is as follows:

President of Assembly: JOHANN BÖHM (CSU).

Party	Seats
Christlich-Soziale Union Deutschlands (CSU) . . .	121
Sozialdemocratische Partei Deutschlands (SPD) . .	67
Bündnis 90/Die Grünen	13
Independent.	3

The Senate, or second chamber, consists of 60 members, divided into 10 groups representing professional interests, e.g. agriculture, industry, trade, the professions and religious communities. Every two years one-third of the Senate is newly elected. In February 1998 a majority of voters who participated in a Land referendum on the future of the Senate favoured its abolition.

President of the Senate: HERIBERT THALLMAIR (CSU).

Bayern is divided into seven districts: Mittelfranken, Oberfranken, Unterfranken, Schwaben, Niederbayern, Oberpfalz and Oberbayern.

BERLIN

The House of Representatives (Abgeordnetenhaus) is the legislative body. The executive agency is the Senate, which is composed of the Governing Mayor (Regierender Bürgermeister) and up to 10 Senators, from among whom the deputy mayor is elected. The Governing Major and the senators are elected by a majority of the House of Representatives. The Senate is responsible to the House of Representatives and dependent on its confidence. The Senate is currently composed of a coalition of the SPD and Bündnis 90/Die Grünen.

Regierender Bürgermeister: KLAUS WOWEREIT (SPD).

Abgeordnetenhaus von Berlin: Niederkirchnerstr. 3–5, 10117 Berlin; tel. (30) 23252325; e-mail verwaltung@parlament-berlin.de; internet www.parlament-berlin.de. The composition of the House of Representatives, as the result of elections held on 21 October 2001, is as follows:

President of House of Representatives: WALTER MOMPER (SPD).

Party	Seats
Sozialdemocratische Partei Deutschlands (SPD) . .	44
Christlich-Demokratische Union Deutschlands (CDU)	35
Partie des Demokratischen Sozialismus (PDS) . . .	33
Freie Demokratische Partei (FDP)	15
Bündnis 90/Die Grünen	14

BRANDENBURG

The Government is currently formed from a coalition of the SPD and the CDU.

Minister-President: MATTHIAS PLATZECK (SPD).

Landtag Brandenburg: Postfach 601064, 14410 Potsdam; Am Havelblick 8, 14473 Potsdam; tel. (331) 9660; fax (331) 9661210; e-mail poststelle@landtag.brandenburg.de; internet www.landtag.brandenburg.de. The composition of the Assembly, as a result of elections held on 5 September 1999, is as follows:

President of Assembly: Dr HERBERT KNOBLICH (SPD).

Party	Seats
Sozialdemocratische Partei Deutschlands (SPD) . .	37
Christlich-Demokratische Union Deutschlands (CDU)	25
Partei des Demokratischen Sozialismus (PDS) . . .	22
Deutsche Volksunion (DVU)	5

BREMEN

The Constitution of the Free Hanseatic City of Bremen was sanctioned by referendum of the people on 12 October 1947. The main constitutional organs are the City Council (legislature), the Senate (government) and the Constitutional Court. The Senate is the executive organ elected by the Council for the duration of its own tenure of office. The Senate elects from its own ranks two Mayors (Bürgermeister), one of whom becomes President of the Senate. Decisions of the Council are subject to the delaying veto of the Senate. The Senate is currently formed from a coalition of the SPD and the CDU.

First Bürgermeister and President of the Senate: Dr HENNING SCHERF (SPD).

Bremische Bürgerschaft: Am Markt 20, 28195 Bremen; tel. (421) 3614555; fax (421) 36112492; e-mail geschaeftsstelle@buergerschaft.bremen.de; internet www.bremische-buergerschaft.de. The election of 6 June 1999 resulted in the following composition:

President of the City Council: CHRISTIAN WEBER (CDU).

Party	Seats
Sozialdemocratische Partei Deutschlands (SPD) . .	47
Christlich-Demokratische Union Deutschlands (CDU)	42
Bündnis 90/Die Grünen	10
Deutsche Volksunion (DVU)	1

HAMBURG

The Constitution of the Free and Hanseatic City of Hamburg was adopted in June 1952. The City Council (legislature) elects the members of the Senate (government), which in turn elects the President and the President's deputy from its own ranks. The President remains in office for one year, but may stand for re-election. The Senate is currently formed by a coalition of the CDU, the FDP and the Schill-Partei.

President of Senate and First Bürgermeister: OLE VON BEUST (CDU).

Bürgerschaft der Freien und Hansestadt Hamburg: Rathaus, Rathausmarkt 1, 20095 Hamburg; tel. (40) 428312408; fax (40) 428312558; e-mail oeffentlichkeitsservice@blc.hamburg.de; internet www.hamburg.de/buergerschaft.

The City Council was elected on 23 September 2001, and is composed as follows:

President: Dr DOROTHEE STAPELFELDT (SPD).

Party	Seats
Sozialdemocratische Partei Deutschlands (SPD) . .	46
Christlich-Demokratische Union Deutschlands (CDU)	33
Partei Rechtsstaatlicher Offensive	25
Die Grünen/Grüne Alternative Liste (GAL)	11
Freie Demokratische Partei (FDP)	6

HESSEN (HESSE)

The Constitution of this Land dates from 1 December 1946. The Minister-President is elected by the Assembly, and appoints and dismisses Ministers with its consent. The Assembly can force the resignation of the Government by a vote of no confidence. The Government is currently formed from a coalition of the CDU and FDP.

Minister-President: ROLAND KOCH (CDU).

Hessischer Landtag: Schlosspl.1–3, 65183 Wiesbaden; tel. (611) 3500; fax (611) 350434; e-mail poststelle@ltg.hessen.de; internet www.landtag.hessen.de.

The Assembly, elected on 2 February 2003, is composed as follows:

President of Assembly: KLAUS PETER MÖLLER (CDU).

Party	Seats
Christlich-Demokratische Union Deutschlands (CDU)	56
Sozialdemokratische Partei Deutschlands (SPD)	33
Bündnis 90/Die Grünen	12
Freie Demokratische Partei (FDP)	9

Hessen is divided into three governmental districts: Kassel, Giessen and Darmstadt.

MECKLENBURG-VORPOMMERN (MECKLENBURG-WESTERN POMERANIA)

The Constitution was adopted by the Assembly on 14 May 1993. The Government is currently formed from a coalition of the SPD and the PDS.

Minister-President: HARALD RINGSTORFF (SPD).

Landtag Mecklenburg-Vorpommern: Schloss, Lennéstr. 1, 19053 Schwerin; tel. (385) 5250; fax (385) 5252141; e-mail poststelle@landtag-mv.de; internet www.landtag-mv.de.

The composition of the Assembly, as a result of elections held on 22 September 2002, is as follows:

President of Assembly: SYLVIA BRETSCHNEIDER (SPD).

Party	Seats
Sozialdemokratische Partei Deutschlands (SPD)	33
Christlich-Demokratische Union Deutschlands (CDU)	25
Partei des Demokratischen Sozialismus (PDS)	13

NIEDERSACHSEN (LOWER SAXONY)

The Constitution was adopted by the Assembly on 19 May 1993 and came into force on 1 June. The Government is currently formed from a coalition of the CDU and the FDP.

Minister-President: CHRISTIAN WULFF.

Landtag Niedersachsen: Hinrich-Wilhelm-Kopf-Pl. 1, 30159 Hannover; tel. (511) 30300; fax (511) 30302806; e-mail pressestelle@lt.niedersachsen.de; internet www.landtag-niedersachsen.de.

As a result of elections held on 2 February 2003, the Assembly is composed as follows:

President of Assembly: JÜRGEN GANSÄUER (CDU).

Party	Seats
Christlich-Demokratische Union Deutschlands (CDU)	91
Sozialdemokratische Partei Deutschlands (SPD)	63
Freie Demokratische Partei (FDP)	15
Bündnis 90/Die Grünen	14

Niedersachsen is divided into four governmental districts: Braunschweig, Hannover, Lüneburg and Weser-Ems.

NORDRHEIN-WESTFALEN (NORTH RHINE-WESTPHALIA)

The present Constitution was adopted by the Assembly on 6 June 1950, and was endorsed by the electorate in the elections held on 18 June. The Government is presided over by the Minister-President, who appoints Ministers. It is currently formed from a coalition of the SPD and Bündnis 90/Die Grünen.

Minister-President: PEER STEINBRÜCK (SPD).

Landtag von Nordrhein-Westfalen: Postfach 101143, 40002 Düsseldorf; Pl. des Landtags 1, 40221 Düsseldorf; tel. (211) 8840; fax (211) 8842258; e-mail email@landtag.nrw.de; internet www.landtag.nrw.de.

The Assembly, elected on 14 May 2000, is composed as follows:

President of Assembly: ULRICH SCHMIDT (SPD).

Party	Seats
Sozialdemokratische Partei Deutschlands (SPD)	102
Christlich-Demokratische Union Deutschlands (CDU)	88
Freie Demokratische Partei (FDP)	24
Bündnis 90/Die Grünen	15

The Land is divided into five governmental districts: Düsseldorf, Münster, Arnsberg, Detmold and Köln.

RHEINLAND-PFALZ (RHINELAND-PALATINATE)

The three chief agencies of the Constitution of this Land are the Assembly, the Government and the Constitutional Court. The Minister-President is elected by the Assembly, with whose consent he/she appoints and dismisses Ministers. The Government, which is dependent on the confidence of the Assembly, is currently composed of a coalition of the SPD and the FDP.

Minister-President: KURT BECK (SPD).

Landtag Rheinland-Pfalz: Postfach 3040, 55020 Mainz; Deutschhauspl. 12, 55116 Mainz; tel. (6131) 2080; fax (6131) 2082447; e-mail praesident@landtag.rlp.de; internet www.landtag.rlp.de.

The members of the Assembly are elected according to a system of proportional representation. Its composition, as the result of elections held on 25 March 2001, is as follows:

President of Assembly: CHRISTOPH GRIMM (SPD).

Party	Seats
Sozialdemokratische Partei Deutschlands (SPD)	49
Christlich-Demokratische Union Deutschlands (CDU)	38
Freie Demokratische Partei (FDP)	8
Bündnis 90/Die Grünen	6

Rheinland-Pfalz is divided into three districts: Koblenz, Rheinhessen-Pfalz (Rheinhessen-Palatinate) and Trier.

SAARLAND

Under the Constitution which came into force on 1 January 1957, Saarland was politically integrated into the FRG as a Land. It was economically integrated into the FRG in July 1959. The Minister-President is elected by the Assembly. The Government is currently formed from a coalition of the CDU and the SPD.

Minister-President: PETER MÜLLER (CDU).

Landtag des Saarlandes: Postfach 101833, 66018 Saarbrücken; e-mail postmaster@lds.uni-sb.de; internet www.landtag-saar.de.

The composition of the Assembly, as a result of elections held on 5 September 1999, is as follows:

President of the Assembly: HANS LEY (CDU).

Party	Seats
Christlich-Demokratische Union Deutschlands (CDU)	26
Sozialdemokratische Partei Deutschlands (SPD)	25

SACHSEN (SAXONY)

The Government is formed by the majority party (CDU).

Minister-President: Prof. Dr GEORG MILBRADT (CDU).

Sächsischer Landtag: Postfach 120905, 01008 Dresden; Bernhard-von-Lindenau Pl. 1, 01067 Dresden; tel. (351) 49350; fax (351) 4935900; e-mail info@landtag.sachsen.de; internet www.sachsen.de/de/bf/landtag.

The composition of the Assembly, as a result of elections held on 19 September 1999, is as below:

President of Assembly: ERICH ILTGEN (CDU).

Party	Seats
Christlich-Demokratische Union Deutschlands (CDU)	76
Partei des Demokratischen Sozialismus (PDS)	30
Sozialdemokratische Partei Deutschlands (SPD)	14

SACHSEN-ANHALT (SAXONY-ANHALT)

The Government is currently formed by the majority party (CDU).

Minister-President: Prof. Dr WOLFGANG BÖHMER (CDU).

Landtag von Sachsen-Anhalt: Dompl. 6–9, 39104 Magdeburg; tel. (391) 5600; fax (391) 5601123; e-mail landtag@lt.lsa-net.de; internet www.landtag.sachsen-anhalt.de.

The composition of the Assembly, as a result of elections held on 21 April 2002, is as follows:

President of Assembly: Prof. Dr ADOLF SPOTKA (CDU).

Party	Seats
Christlich-Demokratische Union Deutschlands (CDU)	48
Sozialdemokratische Partei Deutschlands (SPD)	25
Partei des Demokratischen Sozialismus (PDS)	25
Deutsche Volksunion (DVU)	17

Sachsen-Anhalt is divided into three governmental districts: Magdeburg, Halle and Dessau.

SCHLESWIG-HOLSTEIN

The Provisional Constitution was adopted by the Assembly on 13 December 1949. The Government consists of the Minister-President and the Ministers appointed by the Minister-President. The Government is currently formed from a coalition of the SPD and Bündnis 90/Die Grünen.

Minister-President: HEIDE SIMONIS (SPD).

Landtag Schleswig-Holstein: Düsternbrooker Weg 70, 24105 Kiel; tel. (431) 9881120; fax (431) 9881119; e-mail joachim.koehler@landtag.ltsh.de; internet www.sh-landtag.de.

The composition of the Assembly, as the result of elections held on 27 February 2000, is as follows:

President of Assembly: HEINZ-WERNER ARENS (SPD).

Party	Seats
Sozialdemokratische Partei Deutschlands (SPD) . .	41
Christlich-Demokratische Union Deutschlands (CDU)	33
Freie Demokratische Partei (FDP)	7
Bündnis 90/Die Grünen	5
Südschleswigscher Wählerverband*	3

*Represents the Danish minority in Schleswig-Holstein.

THÜRINGEN (THURINGIA)

The Assembly Government is currently led by the CDU.

Minister-President: Dr BERNHARD VOGEL (CDU).

Thüringer Landtag: Postfach 941, 99096 Erfurt; tel. (361) 37700; fax (361) 3772016; e-mail pressestelle@landtag.thueringen.de; internet www.landtag.thueringen.de.

The composition of the Assembly, as a result of elections held on 12 September 1999, is as follows:

President of Assembly: CHRISTINE LIEBERKNECHT (CDU).

Party	Seats
Christlich-Demokratische Union Deutschlands (CDU)	49
Partei des Demokratischen Sozialismus (PDS) . .	21
Sozialdemokratische Partei Deutschlands (SPD) . .	18

Political Organizations

Bündnis 90/Die Grünen (Alliance 90/Greens): Pl. vor dem Neuen Tor 1, 10115 Berlin; tel. (30) 284420; fax (30) 28442210; e-mail info@gruene.de; internet www.gruene.de; f. 1993 by merger of Bündnis 90 (f. 1990, as an electoral political asscn of citizens' movements of the former GDR) and Die Grünen (f. 1980, largely comprised of the membership of the Grüne Aktion Zukunft, the Grüne Liste, Umweltschutz and the Aktionsgemeinschaft Unabhängiger Deutscher, also including groups of widely varying political views); essentially left-wing party programme includes ecological issues, democratization of society at all levels, social justice, comprehensive disarmament; Chair. ANGELIKA BEER, REINHARD BÜTIKOFER; Parliamentary Leaders KATRIN GÖRING-ECKARDT, KRISTA SAGER; Sec.-Gen. STEFFI LEMKE.

Christlich-Demokratische Union Deutschlands (in Bavaria: Christlich-Soziale Union Deutschlands) (CDU/CSU) (Christian Democratic and Christian Social Union):

CDU: Konrad-Adenauer-Haus, Klingelhöferstr. 8, 10785 Berlin; tel. (30) 220700; fax (30) 22070111; e-mail post@cdu.de; internet www.cdu.de; f. 1945; became a federal party in 1950; advocates united action between Catholics and Protestants for rebuilding German life on a Christian-Democratic basis, while guaranteeing private property and the freedom of the individual, and for a 'free and equal Germany in a free, politically united and socially just Europe'; other objectives are to guarantee close ties with allies within NATO and the principle of self-determination; in Oct. 1990 incorporated the CDU of the former GDR; c. 630,173 mems (April 2000); Chair. Dr ANGELA MERKEL; Sec.-Gen. LAURENZ MEYER; Parliamentary Leader Dr ANGELA MERKEL.

CSU: Nymphenburger Str. 64, 80335 München; tel. (89) 12430; fax (89) 1243220; e-mail landesleitung@csu-bayern.de; internet www.csu.de; f. 1946; Christian Social party, aiming for a free-market economy 'in the service of man's economic and intellectual freedom'; also combines national consciousness with support for a united Europe; 181,000 mems; Chair. Dr EDMUND STOIBER; Sec.-Gen. Dr THOMAS GOPPEL.

Deutsche Kommunistische Partei (DKP) (German Communist Party): Hoffnungstr. 18, 45127 Essen; tel. (201) 225148; fax (201) 202467; e-mail dkp.pv@t-online-de; internet www.dkp.de; 7,000 mems (1998); Chair. HEINZ STEHR.

Deutsche Volksunion (DVU) (German People's Union): Postfach 600464, 81204 München; tel. (89) 896085; fax (89) 8341534; internet www.dvu.net; f. 1987; extreme right-wing.

Freie Demokratische Partei (FDP) (Free Democratic Party): Reinhardtstr. 14, 10117 Berlin; tel. (30) 2849580; fax (30) 28495822; e-mail tdh@fdp.de; internet www.fdp.de; f. 1948; represents democratic and social liberalism and makes the individual the focal point of the State and its laws and economy; in Aug. 1990 incorporated the three liberal parties of the former GDR—the Association of Free Democrats, the German Forum Party and the FDP; publishes *Die Liberale Depesche*; c. 62,720 mems (Dec. 2000); Chair. Dr GUIDO WESTERWELLE; Dep. Chair. RAINER BRÜDERLE, Dr WALTER DÖRING; Chair. in Bundestag Dr WOLFGANG GERHARDT; Sec.-Gen. CORNELIA PIEPER.

Freie Demokratische Partei/Demokratische Volkspartei (FDP/DVP): Konrad Adenauer-Str. 12, 70173 Stuttgart; tel. (711) 2063627; fax (711) 2063610; e-mail post@fdp.landtag-bw.de; internet www.fdp-dvp-fraktion.de; f. 1948; Chair ERNST PFISTER.

Nationaldemokratische Partei Deutschlands (NPD) (National Democratic Party of Germany): Postfach 840157, 12531 Berlin; tel. (30) 650110; fax (30) 65011142; e-mail npdbgst@aol.com; internet www.npd.net; f. 1964; right-wing; 15,000 mems; youth organization Junge Nationaldemokraten (JN), 6,000 mems; Chair. UDO VOIGT.

Neues Forum (New Forum): Rosa-Luxemburg-Str. 19, 10178 Berlin; tel. (30) 2479404; fax (30) 2477261; e-mail info@neuesforum.de; internet www.neuesforum.de; f. 1989 as a citizens' action group; played prominent role in democratic movement in former GDR; Leaders KAROLIN SCHUBERT, MATTHIAS BÜCHNER, MICHAEL BONEHR.

Partei des Demokratischen Sozialismus (PDS) (Party of Democratic Socialism): Kleine Alexanderstr. 28, 10178 Berlin; tel. (30) 240090; fax (30) 24009425; e-mail redaktion@pds-online.de; internet www.pds-online.de; successor to the Sozialistische Einheitspartei Deutschlands (SED—Socialist Unity Party, f. 1946 as a result of the unification of the Social Democratic Party and the Communist Party in Eastern Germany), which had been the dominant political force in the GDR until late 1989; adopted present name Feb. 1990; has renounced Stalinism, opposes fascism, right-wing extremism and xenophobia, advocates a socially- and ecologically-orientated market economy with public, collective and private ownership of the means of production, supports international disarmament and peaceful solutions to international conflicts; 77,000 mems (Dec. 2002); Chair. GABRIELLE ZIMMER; Hon. Chair. Dr HANS MODROW.

Die Republikaner (REP) (Republican Party): Postfach 870210, 13162 Berlin; tel. (30) 79098310; fax (30) 79098315; e-mail republikaner-bgs@t-online.de; internet www.rep.de; f. 1983; conservative right wing; c. 15,000 mems; Chair. Dr ROLF SCHLIERER.

Sozialdemokratische Partei Deutschlands (SPD) (Social Democratic Party of Germany): Wilhelmstr. 141, 10963 Berlin; tel. (30) 259910; fax (30) 410; e-mail parteivorstand@spd.de; internet www.spd.de; f. 1863; maintains that a vital democracy can be built only on the basis of social justice; advocates for the economy as much competition as possible, as much planning as necessary to protect the individual from uncontrolled economic interests; favours a positive attitude to national defence, while supporting controlled disarmament; rejects any political ties with Communism; in September 1990 incorporated the SPD of the former GDR; 693,894 mems (Dec. 2002); Chair. GERHARD SCHRÖDER; Gen. Sec. OLAF SCHOLZ.

There are also numerous other small parties, none of them represented in the Bundestag, covering all shades of the political spectrum and various regional interests.

Diplomatic Representation

EMBASSIES IN GERMANY

Afghanistan: Liebfrauenweg 1A, 53125 Bonn; tel. (228) 251927; fax (228) 255310; Chargé d'affaires AMANULLAH JAYHOON.

Albania: Friedrichstr. 231, 10969 Berlin; tel. (30) 2593050; fax (30) 25930599; e-mail albanische.botschaft@microcall.de; Ambassador BASHKIM ZENELI.

Algeria: Görschstr. 45–46, 13187 Berlin; tel. (30) 4816170; fax (30) 4863137; Ambassador MOHAMMED HANECHE.

Angola: Wallstr. 58, 10179 Berlin; tel. (30) 2408970; fax (30) 24089712; e-mail botschaft@botschaftangola.de; internet www.botschaftangola.de; Ambassador ALBERTO DO CARMO BENTO RIBEIRO.

Argentina: Dorotheenstr. 89, 10117 Berlin; tel. (30) 2266890; fax (30) 2291400; e-mail info@argentinische-botschaft.de; internet www.argentinische-botschaft.de; Ambassador ENRIQUE J. A. CANDIOTI.

Armenia: Hillmannstr. 5, 13467 Berlin; tel. (30) 4050910; fax (30) 40509125; e-mail armemb@t-online.de; Ambassador Dr ASHOT VOSKANIAN.

Australia: Wallstr. 76–79, 10179 Berlin; tel. (30) 8800880; fax (30) 880088310; e-mail info@australian-embassy.de; internet www .australian-embassy.de; Ambassador PAMELA FAYLE.

Austria: Stauffenbergstr. 1, 10785 Berlin; tel. (30) 202870; fax (30) 2290569; e-mail berlin-de@bmaa.gv.at; internet www .oesterreichische-botschaft.de; Ambassador Dr MARKUS LUTTEROTTI.

Azerbaijan: Axel-Springer-Str. 54A, 10117 Berlin; tel. (30) 2062946; fax (30) 20629482; e-mail azerbembgermany@aol.com; Ambassador HUSEYNAGA SADIGOV.

Bahrain: Klingelhöfer Str. 7, 10785 Berlin; tel. (30) 86877777; fax (30) 86877788; Ambassador ADEL SATER.

Bangladesh: Dovestr. 1, 10587 Berlin; tel. (30) 3989750; fax (30) 39897510; e-mail bdootbn@aol.com; Ambassador ASHFAQUR RAHMAN.

Belarus: Am Treptower Park, 12345 Berlin; tel. (30) 5363590; fax (30) 53635923; Ambassador VLADIMIR SKVORTSOV.

Belgium: Jägerstr. 52–53, 10117 Berlin; tel. (30) 206420; fax (30) 20642200; e-mail berlin@diplobel.org; internet www.diplobel.org/ deutschland; Ambassador LODE WILLEMS.

Benin: Postfach 200254, 53179 Bonn; Rüdigerstr. 10, 53132 Bonn; tel. (228) 943870; fax (228) 857192; Ambassador ISSA KPARA.

Bolivia: Wichmannstr. 6, 10787 Berlin; tel. (30) 2639150; fax (30) 26391515; e-mail embajada.bolivia@berlin.de; internet www.bolivia .de; Ambassador Dr ERNESTO FERNANDO SCHILLING KRIETE.

Bosnia and Herzegovina: Bürgerstr. 12, 53173 Bonn; Ambassador ANTON BALKOVIĆ.

Brazil: Wallstr. 57, 10179 Berlin; tel. (30) 726280; fax (30) 72628320; e-mail brasil@brasemberlim.de; Ambassador ROBERTO PINTO FERREIRA MAMERI ABDENUR.

Brunei: Kronenstr. 55–58, 10117 Berlin; tel. (30) 2060760; Ambassador MAHADI BIN Haji WASLI.

Bulgaria: Mauerstr. 11, 10117 Berlin; tel. (30) 2010922; fax (30) 2086838; e-mail info@botschaft-bulgarien.de; internet www .botschaft-bulgarien.de; Ambassador NIKOLAI APOSTOLOFF.

Burkina Faso: Karolingerpl. 10–11, 14052 Berlin; tel. (30) 30105990; fax (30) 301059920; e-mail embassy_burkina_faso@ t-online.de; Ambassador XAVIER NIODOGO.

Burundi: Berliner Str. 36, 10715 Berlin; tel. (30) 86399028; fax (30) 86391085; e-mail embassyberlin@burundi.de; Ambassador TÉRENCE NSANZE.

Cambodia: Benjamin-Vogelsdorf-Str., 13187 Berlin; Ambassador KHEK LERANG.

Cameroon: Rheinallee 76, 53173 Bonn; tel. (228) 356038; fax (228) 359058; e-mail botschaftkamerun@yahoo.fr; Ambassador JEAN MELAGA.

Canada: Friedrichstr. 95, 10117 Berlin; tel. (30) 203120; fax (30) 20312590; internet www.kanada-info.de; Ambassador MARIE BERNARD-MEUNIER.

Cape Verde: Dorotheenstr. 43, 10117 Berlin; tel. (30) 20450955; fax (30) 20450966; e-mail info@embassy-capeverde.de; internet www .embassy-capeverde.de; Ambassador OLIVIO MELÍCIO PIRES.

Central African Republic: Rheinaustr. 120, 53225 Bonn; tel. (228) 233564; Ambassador MARTIN-GÉRARD TEBITO.

Chad: Basteistr. 80, 53173 Bonn; tel. (228) 356026; fax (228) 355887; Ambassador MAHAMAT ABDELRASSOUL.

Chile: Kronprinzenstr. 20, 53173 Bonn; tel. (228) 955840; fax (228) 9558440; e-mail echilede@t-online.de; Ambassador RICARDO HORMAZÁBAL SÁNCHEZ.

China, People's Republic: Kurfürstenallee 12, 53177 Bonn; tel. (228) 955970; fax (228) 361635; Ambassador MA CHANRONG.

Colombia: Kurfürstenstr. 84, 10787 Berlin; tel. (30) 2639610; fax (30) 26396125; e-mail emcol@t-online.de; Ambassador HERNÁN BELTZ-PERALTA.

Congo, Democratic Republic: Im Meisengarten 133; 53179 Bonn; tel. (228) 858160; fax (228) 9349237; Ambassador LHELO BOLOTO.

Congo, Republic: Rheinallee 45, 53173 Bonn; tel. and fax (228) 358355; e-mail botschaft.kongobrz@t-online.de; Chargé d'affaires a.i. SERGE MICHEL ODZOCKI.

Costa Rica: Langenbachstr. 19, 53113 Bonn; tel. (228) 540040; fax (228) 549053; e-mail 100730.1020@compuserve.com; Ambassador Prof. Dr RAFAEL ANGEL HERRA.

Côte d'Ivoire: Königstr. 93, 53115 Bonn; tel. (228) 212098; fax (228) 217313; e-mail ambic@t-online.de; Ambassador FLORENT AMIN ATSE.

Croatia: Ahornstr. 4, 10787 Berlin; tel. (30) 21915514; fax (30) 23628965; e-mail info@kroatische-botschaft.de; Chargé d'affaires SLAVKO NOVOKMET.

Cuba: Stavanger Str. 20, 10439 Berlin; tel. (30) 91611810; fax (30) 9164553; e-mail embacuba-berlin@t-online.de; internet www .botschaft-kuba.de; Ambassador MARCELINO MEDINA GONZALEZ.

Cyprus: Wallstr. 27, 10179 Berlin; tel. (30) 3086830; fax (30) 27591454; e-mail cyprusembassy@t-online.de; Ambassador Dr CHRISTOS N. PSILOGENIS.

Czech Republic: Wilhelmstr. 44, 10117 Berlin; tel. (30) 226380; fax (30) 2294033; e-mail embassy.mzv.cz; internet www.mfa.cz/ berlin; Ambassador BORIS LAZAR.

Denmark: Rauchstr. 1, 10785 Berlin; tel. (30) 50502000; fax (30) 50502050; e-mail beramb@um.dk; internet www.daenemark.org; Ambassador GUNNAR ORTMANN.

Dominican Republic: Burgstr. 87, 53177 Bonn; tel. (228) 364956; fax (228) 352576; Ambassador Prof. Dr VINICIO ALFONSO TOBAL UREÑA.

Ecuador: Kaiser-Friedrich-Str. 90, 10585 Berlin; tel. (30) 2386217; fax (30) 34787126; e-mail mecuadoral@t-online.de; internet www .embecuador.de; Ambassador Dr WERNER MOELLER FREILE.

Egypt: Kronprinzenstr. 2, 53173 Bonn; tel. (228) 956830; fax (228) 364304; Ambassador MAHMOUD AHMED FATHY MOUBARAK.

El Salvador: Joachim-Karnatz-Allee 47, 10557 Berlin; tel. (30) 2064660; fax (30) 22488244; e-mail embasalva@t-online.de; internet www.botschaft-elsalvador.de; Ambassador EDGARDO SUÁREZ MALLAGRAY.

Eritrea: Stavangerstr. 18, 10439 Berlin; tel. (30) 4467460; fax (30) 44674621; e-mail er.embassy@freenet.de; Ambassador ZEMEDE TEKLE.

Estonia: Hildebrandtstr. 5, 10785 Berlin; tel. (30) 25460600; fax (30) 25460601; e-mail embassy.berlin@mfa.ee; internet www.estemb.de; Ambassador Dr RIINA KIONKA.

Ethiopia: Boothstr. 20A, 12207 Berlin; tel. (30) 772060; fax (30) 7720624; Ambassador HIRKY AMANUEL.

Finland: Rauchstr. 1, 10787 Berlin; tel. (30) 505030; fax (30) 5050333; e-mail ber.sanomat@formin.fi; internet www.finland.de; Ambassador LEIF FAGERNÄS.

France: Kochstr. 6/7, 10969 Berlin; tel. (30) 2063900; fax (30) 20639010; Ambassador CLAUDE MARTIN.

Gabon: Kronprinzenstr. 52, 53173 Bonn; tel. (228) 365844; fax (228) 359195; Ambassador PAUL BUNDUKU LATHA.

Georgia: Am Kurpark 6, 53177 Bonn; tel. (228) 957510; fax (228) 9575120; Ambassador Dr KONSTANTIN GABASHVILI.

Ghana: Rheinallee 58, 53173 Bonn; tel. (228) 367960; fax (228) 363498; Ambassador ROWLAND ISSIFU ALHASSAN.

Greece: Jägerstr. 54/55, 10117 Berlin; tel. (30) 206260; fax (30) 20626444; internet www.griechenland-botschaft.de; Ambassador DIMITRIOS KYPREOS.

Guatemala: Joachim-Karnatz-Allee 47, 10557 Berlin; tel. (30) 2064363; fax (30) 20643659; internet www.guatemala.travel.com.gt; Ambassador FRANCISCO VILLAGRÁN DE LEÓN.

Guinea: Rochusweg 50, 53129 Bonn; tel. (228) 231098; fax (228) 231097; Ambassador NAMANKOUMBA KOUYATE.

Haiti: Meinekestr. 5, 10719 Berlin; tel. (30) 88554134; fax (30) 88554135; e-mail haibot@aol.com; Ambassador Dr ALRICH NICOLAS.

Holy See: Postfach 610218, 10923 Berlin; Lilienthalstr. 3A, 10965 Berlin; tel. (30) 616240; fax (30) 61624300; e-mail apostoliche_nuntiatur@t-online.de; Apostolic Nuncio Mgr GIOVANNI LAJOLO.

Honduras: Cuxhavenerstr. 14, 10555 Berlin; tel. (30) 39743710; fax (30) 39749712; e-mail informacion@embahonduras.de; Ambassador ROBERT FLORES BERMUDEZ.

Hungary: Unter den Linden 76, 10117 Berlin; tel. (30) 203100; fax (30) 2291314; e-mail nktitkarsag@hungarische-botschaft.de; Ambassador GERGELY PRÓHLE.

Iceland: Rauchstr. 1, 10787 Berlin; tel. (30) 50504000; fax (30) 50504300; e-mail icemb.berlin@utn.stjr.is; internet www .botschaft-island.de; Ambassador JON EGILL EGILSSON.

India: Tiergartenstr. 17, 10785 Berlin; tel. (30) 257950; fax (30) 25795102; e-mail info@indianembassy.de; internet www .indianembassy.de; Ambassador SHRI T. C. A. RANGACHARI.

Indonesia: Bernkasteler Str. 2, 53175 Bonn; tel. (228) 382990; fax (228) 311393; Ambassador IZHAR IBRAHIM.

Iran: Podbielskiallee 65–67, 14195 Berlin; tel. (30) 843530; fax (30) 54353535; e-mail iran.botschaft@t-online.de; internet www .iranbotschaft.de; Ambassador SEYD SHAMSEDDIN KHAREGHANI.

Iraq: Annaberger Str. 289, 53175 Bonn; Chargé d'affaires SHAMIL A. MOHAMMED.

Ireland: Friedrichstr. 200, 10117 Berlin; tel. (30) 220720; fax (30) 22072299; e-mail info@irish-embassy.de; Ambassador NOEL FAHEY.

Israel: Auguste-Victoria-Str. 74–76, 14193 Berlin; tel. (30) 89045500; fax (30) 89045309; e-mail botschaft@israel.de; Ambassador SHIMON STEIN.

Italy: Dessauerstr. 28–29, 10963 Berlin; tel. (30) 254400; fax (30) 25440116; e-mail ambitalia.segr@t-online.de; Ambassador SILVIO FAGIOLO.

Jamaica: Schmargendorfer Str. 32, 12159 Berlin; tel. (30) 8599450; fax (30) 85994540; e-mail info@jamaican-embassy-berlin.de; Ambassador MARCIA GILBERT-ROBERTS.

Japan: Hiroshimastr. 6, 10785 Berlin; tel. (30) 210940; fax (30) 21094222; e-mail info@embjapan.de; internet www.embjapan.de; Ambassador YUSHU TAKASHIMA.

Jordan: Heerstr. 201, 13585 Berlin; tel. (30) 3699600; fax (30) 36996011; Ambassador FAROUK KASRAWI.

Kazakhstan: Nordendstr. 14/15, 13156 Berlin; tel. (30) 470070; fax (30) 47007125; Ambassador VYACHESLAV GIZZATOV.

Kenya: Markgrafenstr. 63, 10969 Berlin; tel. (30) 2592660; fax (30) 25926650; Ambassador FROST EDWIN OTIENO JOSIAH.

Korea, Democratic People's Republic: Glinkastr. 5–7, 10117 Berlin; tel. (30) 2293189; fax (30) 2293191; Ambassador HYON BO PAK.

Korea, Republic: Schöneberger Ufer 89/91, 10785 Berlin; tel. (30) 260650; fax (30) 2606551; Ambassador KICHOO LEE.

Kuwait: Griegstr. 5–7, 14193 Berlin; tel. (30) 8973000; fax (30) 89730010; e-mail kuwaitembassyberlin@hotmail.com; Ambassador FAISAL RASHED AL-GHAIS.

Kyrgyzstan: Otto-Suhr-Allee 146, 10585 Berlin; tel. (30) 34781338; fax (30) 34781362; e-mail 101477.1160@compuserve.com; Ambassador Dr APAS DSCHMAGULOV.

Laos: Bismarckallee 2A, 14193 Berlin; tel. (30) 89060647; fax (30) 89060648; Chargé d'affaires a.i. KHOUANTA PHALIVONG.

Latvia: Reinerzstr. 40–41, 14193 Berlin; tel. (30) 8260020; fax (30) 82600233; Ambassador Dr MĀRTIŅŠ VIRJIS.

Lebanon: Berliner Str. 127, 13187 Berlin; tel. (30) 4749860; fax (30) 47487858; Ambassador MOHAMAD ISSA.

Lesotho: Godesberger Allee 50, 53175 Bonn; tel. (228) 308430; fax (228) 3084322; e-mail lesoembger@aol.com; Ambassador LEBOHANG NTS'INYI.

Liberia: Mainzerstr. 259, 53179 Bonn; tel. (228) 340822; Ambassador RUFUS WEBSTER SIMPSON.

Libya: Beethovenallee 12A, 53173 Bonn; tel. (228) 820090; fax (228) 364260; Secretary of the People's Committee MOHAMMED AL BARANI.

Lithuania: Katharinenstr. 9, 10711 Berlin; tel. (30) 890681; fax (30) 890681; e-mail botschaftlitauen@t-online.de; Ambassador Prof. Dr VAIDIEVUTIS GERALAVIČIUS.

Luxembourg: Klingelhöfer Str. 7, 10785 Berlin; tel. (30) 2639570; fax (30) 26395727; e-mail berlin.amb@mae.etat.lu; Ambassador Dr JULIEN ALEX.

Macedonia, former Yugoslav republic: Koenigsallee 2–4, 14193 Berlin; tel. (30) 8906950; fax (30) 89541194; e-mail amba.berlin@t-online.de; Ambassador Dr GORAN RAFAJLOVSKI.

Madagascar: Rolandstr. 48, 53179 Bonn; tel. (228) 953590; fax (228) 334628; e-mail madagaskar-botschaft@t-online.de; internet www.botschaft-madagaskar.de; Ambassador DENIS ANDRIAMANDROSO.

Malawi: Mainzer Str. 124, 53179 Bonn; tel. (228) 943350; fax (228) 9433537; e-mail malawibonn@aol.com; Ambassador Rev Dr S. S. NCOZANA.

Malaysia: Kurfürstendamm 50, 10707 Berlin; tel. (30) 8857490; fax (30) 88729028; Ambassador Dato' ABDUL KADIR MOHAMED DEEN.

Mali: Basteistr. 86, 53173 Bonn; tel. (228) 357048; fax (228) 361922; Ambassador OUSMANE DEMBÉLÉ.

Malta: Klingelhöfer Str. 7, 10785 Berlin; tel. (30) 2639110; fax (30) 26391123; e-mail maltaembgrm@ndh.net; Ambassador WILLIAM C. SPITERI.

Mauritania: Bonnerstr. 48, 53173 Bonn; tel. (228) 364024; fax (228) 361788; Ambassador HAMOUD OULD ELY.

Mexico: Klingelhöfer Str. 3, 10785 Berlin; tel. (30) 2693230; fax (30) 269323700; e-mail emb@embamexale.de; internet www.embamex.de; Ambassador PATRICIA ESPINOSA.

Moldova: Gotlandstr. 16, 10439 Berlin; tel. (30) 44652970; fax (30) 44652972; e-mail botschaft_moldova_berlin@compuserve.com; Ambassador NICOLAE TABACARU.

Monaco: Klingelhöfer Str. 7, 01785 Berlin; tel. (30) 2639033; fax (30) 2690344; e-mail ambassademonaco@aol.com; Ambassador RAINIER IMPERTI.

Mongolia: Gotlandstr. 12, 10439 Berlin; tel. (30) 4469320; fax (30) 4469321; e-mail mongolbot@aol.com; Ambassador DENDEV TERBISHDAGVA.

Morocco: Niederwallstr. 39, 10117 Berlin; tel. (30) 2061240; fax (30) 20612420; e-mail morokko-botschaft@t-online.de; Ambassador Dr ABDELADIM LHAFI.

Mozambique: Adenauerallee 46A, 53113 Bonn; tel. (228) 263921; fax (228) 213920; e-mail emoza@ad.com; Ambassador MANUEL TOMÁS LUBISSE.

Myanmar: Zimmerstr. 56, 10117 Berlin; tel. (30) 2061570; fax (30) 20615720; e-mail emb.my.berlin@t-online.de; Ambassador U NYUNT MAUNG SHEIN.

Namibia: Wichmannstr. 5, 10787 Berlin; tel. (30) 2540950; fax (30) 25409555; e-mail namibiaberlin@aol.com; Ambassador HINYANGERWA PIUS ASHEEKE.

Nepal: Guerickestr. 27, 10587 Berlin; tel. (30) 34359920; fax (30) 34359906; e-mail rneberlin@t-online.de; internet www.nepalembassy-germany.com; Ambassador BALRAM SINGH MALLA.

Netherlands: Friedrichstr. 95, 10117 Berlin; tel. (30) 209560; fax (30) 20956441; e-mail nlgovbln@bln.nlamb.de; internet www.niederlandeweb.de; Ambassador Dr NIKOLAOS VAN DAM.

New Zealand: Friedrichstr. 60, 10117 Berlin; tel. (30) 206210; fax (30) 20621114; e-mail nzemb@t-online.de; internet www.nzembassy.com/germany; Ambassador W. A. COCHRANE.

Nicaragua: Konstantinstr. 41, 53179 Bonn; tel. (228) 362505; fax 354001; Ambassador SUYAPA INDIANA PADILLA TERCERO.

Niger: Dürenstr. 9, 53173 Bonn; tel. (228) 3502782; fax (228) 3502768; Ambassador AMADOU TOURÉ.

Nigeria: Platannanstr. 98A, 13156 Berlin; tel. (30) 4772300; fax (30) 4772555; e-mail nigeriaembassy@yahoo.com; Ambassador E. P. ECHERUO.

Norway: Rauchstr. 1, 10787 Berlin; tel. (30) 505050; fax (30) 505055; e-mail emb.berlin@mfa.no; internet www.norwegen.org; Ambassador MORTEN WETLAND.

Oman: Lindenallee 11, 53173 Bonn; tel. (228) 357031; fax (228) 357045; Ambassador AHMED M. AL-HINAI.

Pakistan: Schaperstr. 29, 10719 Berlin; Ambassador ASIF EZDI.

Panama: Joachim-Karnatz-Allee 45, 10557 Berlin; Ambassador ENRIQUE THAYER.

Papua New Guinea: Moltkestr. 44–46, 53173 Bonn; e-mail 106555.326@compuserve.com; Chargé d'affaires PETER RAKA.

Paraguay: Hardenbergstr. 12, 10623 Berlin; tel. (30) 3199860; fax (30) 31998617; e-mail embapyde@t-online.de; Ambassador JOSÉ MARTÍNEZ LEZCENO.

Peru: Mohrenstr. 42, 10117 Berlin; tel. (30) 2064103; fax (30) 20641051; e-mail eprfa@aol.com; internet members.aol.com/perusipan; Chargé d'affaires a.i. HUBERT WIELAND CONROY.

Philippines: Uhlandstr. 97, 10715 Berlin; tel. (30) 8649500; fax (30) 8732551; e-mail berlinpe@t-online.de; Ambassador JOSÉ A. ZAIDE.

Poland: Lassenstr. 19–21, 14193 Berlin; tel. (30) 223130; fax (30) 2213155; e-mail info@botschaft-polen.de; internet www.botschaft-polen.de; Ambassador Dr JERZY KRANZ.

Portugal: Zimmerstr. 56, 10117 Berlin; tel. (30) 590063500; fax (30) 590063600; e-mail mail@botschaftportugal.de; Ambassador Dr JOÃO DE VALLERA.

Qatar: Postfach 48, 53132 Bonn; Brunnenallee 6, 53117 Bonn; tel. (228) 957520; fax (228) 9575255; e-mail qatarbonn@compuserve.com; Ambassador SALEH MOHAMED SALEH AL-NESEF.

Russia: Unter den Linden 63–65, 10117 Berlin; tel. (30) 2291110; fax (30) 2299397; e-mail posolstvo@russische-botschaft.de; internet www.russische-botschaft.de; Ambassador SERGEI BORISOVICH KRYLOV.

Rwanda: Beethovenallee 72, 53173 Bonn; tel. (228) 3670236; fax (228) 351922; e-mail ambrwabonn@aol.com; internet www.rwanda-botschaft.de; Ambassador LAUREN NGIRABANZI.

Saudi Arabia: Kurfürstendamm 63, 10787 Berlin; Ambassador ABBAS FAIG GHAZZAWI.

Senegal: Argelanderstr. 3, 53115 Bonn; tel. (228) 218008; fax (228) 217815; Ambassador Gen. PAUL BADJI.

Sierra Leone: Rheinallee 20, 53173 Bonn; tel. (228) 352001; fax (228) 364269; e-mail uwurie@aol.com; Ambassador UMARU BUNDU WURIE.

Singapore: Friedrichstr. 200, 10117 Berlin; tel. (30) 2263430; fax (30) 22634355; e-mail info@singapore-embassy.de; Ambassador Prof. WALTER WOON.

Slovakia: Pariser Str. 44, 10707 Berlin; tel. (30) 8892620; fax (30) 88926222; e-mail presse@botschaft-slowakei.de; internet www .botschaft-slowakei.de; Ambassador JÁN FOLTÍN.

Slovenia: Hausvogteipl. 3–4, 10117 Berlin; tel. (30) 2061450; fax (30) 20614570; e-mail vbn@mzz-dkp.gov.si; Ambassador IVO VAJGL.

South Africa: Friedrichstr. 60, 10117 Berlin; tel. (30) 220730; fax (30) 22073190; e-mail botschaft@suedafrika.org; internet www .suedafrika.org; Ambassador Prof. Dr SIBUSISO M. E. BENGU.

Spain: Schöneberger Ufer 89–91, 10785 Berlin; tel. (30) 2540070; fax (30) 25799557; e-mail botschaft.spanien@t-online.de; internet www.spanischebotschaft.de; Ambassador JOSÉ PEDRO SEBASTIÁN DE ERICE.

Sri Lanka: Niklas Str. 19, 14163 Berlin; tel. (30) 80909749; fax (30) 80909761; e-mail info@srilanka-botschaft.de; internet www .srilanka-botschaft.de; Ambassador C. D. CASIE CHETTY.

Sudan: Kurfürstendamm 151, 10709 Berlin; tel. (30) 8906980; fax (30) 89409693; e-mail post@sudan-embassy.de; internet www .sudan-embassy.de; Ambassador AHMED GAAFAR ABDELKARIM.

Sweden: Rauchstr. 1, 10787 Berlin; tel. (30) 505060; fax (30) 50506789; e-mail ambassaden.berlin@foreign.ministry.se; internet www.schweden.org; Ambassador CARL THAM.

Switzerland: Otto-von-Bismarck-Allee 4A, 10557 Berlin; tel. (30) 3904000; fax (30) 3911030; e-mail vertretung@ber.rep.admin.ch; internet www.botschaft-schweiz.de; Ambassador Dr WERNER BAUMANN.

Syria: Andreas-Hermes-Str. 5, 53175 Bonn; tel. (228) 819920; fax (228) 8199299; Ambassador WALID HEZBOR.

Tajikistan: Otto-Suhr-Allee 84, 10585 Berlin; tel. (30) 3479300; fax (30) 34793029; Ambassador NURALI SAIDOV.

Tanzania: Theaterpl. 26, 53177 Bonn; tel. (228) 358051; fax (228) 358226; Ambassador ANDREW M. DARAJA.

Thailand: Lepsiusstr. 64–66, 12163 Berlin; tel. (30) 794810; fax (30) 79481511; Ambassador SURAPONG JAYANAMA.

Togo: Beethovenallee 13, 53173 Bonn; tel. (228) 9028918; fax (228) 9675463; e-mail info@togo.de; internet www.togo.de; Chargé d'affaires a.i. GABIN KOUEVI ANANOK.

Tunisia: Lindenallee 16, 14050 Berlin; tel. (30) 30820673; fax (30) 30820683; Ambassador ANOUAR BERRAIES.

Turkey: Rungestr. 9, 10179 Berlin; tel. (30) 275850; fax (30) 27590915; e-mail turk.em.berlin@t-online.de; internet www .turkischebotschaft.de; Ambassador OSMAN KORUTÜRK.

Turkmenistan: Langobardenallee 14, 14052 Berlin; tel. (30) 30102452; fax (30) 30102453; e-mail botschaft-turkmenistan@ t-online.de; Ambassador DORTKULI AYDOGDYEV.

Ukraine: Albrechtstr. 26, 10117 Berlin; tel. (30) 288870; fax (30) 28887163; e-mail ukremb@t-online.de; internet www .botschaft-ukraine.de; Ambassador Dr ANATOLIY PONOMARENKO.

United Arab Emirates: Katharine-Heinrith-Ufer 1, 10787 Berlin; tel. (228) 267070; fax (228) 2670714; Ambassador ALI MOHAMMAD AL-ZAROUNI.

United Kingdom: Wilhelmstr. 70, 10117 Berlin; tel. (30) 204570; fax (30) 20457574; e-mail presse@fco.mail.gov.uk; internet www .britischebotschaft.de; Ambassador Sir PAUL LEVER.

USA: Neustädtische Kirche 4/5, 10117 Berlin; tel. (30) 83052805; fax (30) 20453644; internet www.usembassy.de; Ambassador JOHN CHRISTIAN KORNBLUM.

Uruguay: Budapester Str. 39, 10787 Berlin; tel. (30) 2639016; fax (30) 26390170; e-mail urubrande@t-online.de; Ambassador Dr ZULMA GUELMAN.

Uzbekistan: Mauerstr. 83–84, 10117 Berlin; tel. (30) 22487457; fax (30) 22679963; Ambassador Dr VLADIMIR IMAMOVICH NOROV.

Venezuela: Grosse Weinmeisterstr. 53, 14469 Potsdam; e-mail info@botschaft-venezuela.de; Chargé d'affaires a.i. ANNA FRANCESCA CAZZADERE DE MONTEIRO.

Viet Nam: Elsenstr. 3, 12435 Berlin; tel. (30) 53630108; fax (30) 53630200; e-mail sqvnberlin@t-online.de; Ambassador Dr NGUYEN BA SON.

Yemen: Rheinbabenallee 18, 14199 Berlin; tel. (30) 8973050; fax (30) 89730562; e-mail info@botschaft-jemen.de; internet www .botschaft-jemen.de; Ambassador MOHY A. AL-DHABBI.

Zambia: Axel-Springer Str. 54A; tel. (30) 2062940; fax (30) 20629419; Ambassador Lt-Gen. G. SIBAMBA (Rtd).

Zimbabwe: Kommandantenstr. 80, 10117 Berlin; tel. (30) 2062263; fax (30) 20455062; Ambassador GIFT PUNUNGWE.

Judicial System

Justice is administered in accordance with the federal structure through the courts of the Federation and the Länder, as well as the Federal Constitutional Court and the Constitutional Courts of the Länder. Judges are independent and responsible to the law. They are not removable except by the decision of a court. One-half of the judges of the Federal Constitutional Court are elected by the Bundestag and the other half by the Bundesrat. A committee for the selection of judges participates in the appointment of judges of the Superior Federal Courts.

FEDERAL CONSTITUTIONAL COURT

Bundesverfassungsgericht
(Federal Constitutional Court)

Postfach 1771, 76006 Karlsruhe; Schlossbezirk 3, 76131 Karlsruhe; tel. (721) 91010; fax (721) 9101382; e-mail bverfg@ bundesverfassungsgericht.de; internet www .bundesverfassungsgericht.de.

President: Prof. Dr HANS-JÜRGEN PAPIER.

Vice-President: Prof. Dr WINFRIED HASSEMER.

Director: Dr ELKE LUISE BARNSTEDT.

Judges of the First Senate: RENATE JAEGER, Dr EVELYN HAAS, Dr DIETER HÖMIG, Prof. Dr UDO STEINER, Dr CHRISTINE HOHMANN-DENNHARDT, Dr HOFFMANN-RIEM, Prof. Dr BRUN-OTTO BRYDE.

Judges of the Second Senate: BERTOLD SOMMER, Dr HANS-JOACHIM JENTSCH, Prof. Dr WINFRIED HASSEMER, Dr SIEGFRIED BROSS, Prof. Dr LERKE OSTERLOH, Prof. Dr DI FABIO, RUDOLF MELLINGHOFF.

SUPERIOR FEDERAL COURTS

Bundesarbeitsgericht

Hugo-Preuss-Pl. 1, 99084 Erfurt; tel. (361) 26360; fax (261) 26362000; internet www.bundesarbeitsgericht.de.

President: Prof. Dr HELLMUT WISSMANN.

Vice-President: Dr KARL HEINZ PEIFER.

Bundesgerichtshof
(Federal Court of Justice)

Herrenstr. 45A, 76133 Karlsruhe; tel. (721) 1590; fax (721) 159830; e-mail eingangsstelle@bgh.bund.de; internet www .bundesgerichtshof.de.

President: Prof. Dr HIRSCH.

Vice-President: Dr BURKHARD JÄHNKE.

Presidents of the Senate: Prof. Dr WILLI ERDMANN, Dr VOLKER RÖHRICHT, Dr EBERHARD RINNE, WILLFRIED TERNO, Dr JOACHIM WENZEL, Dr GERDA MÜLLER, Prof. Dr EIKE ULLMANN, Dr KATHARINA DEPPERT, Dr GERHART KREFT, GERD NOBBE, Dr HAHNE, Dr GERHARD SCHÄFER, Prof. Dr KLAUS TOLKSDORF, Dr INGEBORG TEPPERWIEN, MONIKA HARMS.

Federal Solicitor-General: KAY NEHM.

Federal Prosecutors: REINER SCHULTE, VOLKHARD WACHE, Dr HANS-JOACHIM KURTH.

Bundessozialgericht

Graf-Bernadotte-Pl. 5, 34119 Kassel; tel. (501) 31071; fax (501) 3107475; e-mail presse@bsg.bund.de; internet www .bundessozialgericht.de.

President: MATTHIAS VON WULFFEN.

Vice-President: Dr INGEBORG WOLFF.

Bundesverwaltungsgericht
(Federal Administrative Court)

Postfach 100854, 04008 Leipzig; Simonspl. 1, 04107 Leipzig; tel. (341) 20070; fax (341) 20081000; internet www.bverwg.de.

President: Dr EVERHARDT FRANSSEN.

Vice-President: ECKHART HIEN.

Presidents of the Senate: ERICH BERMEL, WERNER MEYER, Dr NORBERT NIEHUES, FRIEDRICH SEEBASS, Dr GÜNTER GAENTZSCH, Dr HORST SÄCKER, Prof. Dr HANS-JOACHIM DRIEHAUS, Dr JOACHIM MAIWALD, Dr NIKOLAUS VOGELGESANG, Dr OSWIN MÜLLER.

Bundesfinanzhof
(Federal Financial Court)
Postfach 860240, 81629 München; Ismaninger Str. 109, 81675 München; tel. (89) 92310; fax (89) 9231201; e-mail bundesfinanzhof@bfh
.bund.de; internet www.bundesfinanzhof.de.

President: Dr IRIS EBLING.

Vice-President: WOLFGANG SPINDLER.

Presidents of the Senate: Prof. Dr FRANZ WASSERMEYER, Dr GERHARD MÖSSLANG, HEIDE BOEKER, CHRISTIAN HERDEN, Dr WILFRIED WAGNER, Prof. Dr WALTER DRENSECK, Dr WERNER HEIN, Dr HANS JOACHIM HERRMANN, Dr GEORG GRUBE.

Religion

CHRISTIANITY

Arbeitsgemeinschaft Christlicher Kirchen in Deutschland (Council of Christian Churches in Germany): Postfach 900617, 60446 Frankfurt a.M. Ludolfusstr. 2–4, 60487 Frankfurt a.M. tel. (69) 2470270; fax (69) 24702730; e-mail info@ack-oec.de; internet www.oekumene-ack.de; 23 affiliated Churches, including the Roman Catholic Church and the Orthodox Church in Germany.

The Roman Catholic Church

Germany comprises seven archdioceses and 20 dioceses. At 31 December 1999 there were an estimated 27,001,233 adherents (about 33% of the population).

Bishops' Conference
Deutsche Bischofskonferenz, Postfach 2962, 53019 Bonn; Bonner Talweg 177, 53129 Bonn; tel. (228) 103290; fax (228) 103299; e-mail sekretariat@dbk.de.

Pres. Cardinal Dr KARL LEHMANN (Bishop of Mainz); Sec. Pater Dr HANS LANGENDÖRFER.

Archbishop of Bamberg: (vacant), Postfach 120153, 96049 Bamberg; Dompl. 3, 96033 Bamberg; tel. (951) 5020; fax (951) 502212.

Archbishop of Berlin: Cardinal GEORG MAXIMILIAN STERZINSKY, Wundtstr. 48–50, 14057 Berlin; tel. (030) 326840; fax (030) 32684276.

Archbishop of Freiburg im Breisgau: (vacant), Herrenstr. 35, 79098 Freiburg i. Br. tel. (761) 21881; fax (761) 2188230; e-mail erzbischof@ordinariat-freiburg.de; internet www
.erzbistum-freiburg.de.

Archbishop of Hamburg: Dr LUDWIG AVERKAMP, Postfach 101925, 20013 Hamburg; Danzigerstr. 52A, 20099 Hamburg; tel. (40) 248770; fax (40) 24877233; e-mail egv@erzbistum-hamburg.de; internet www.erzbistum-hamburg.de.

Archbishop of Köln: Cardinal Dr JOACHIM MEISNER, Generalvikariat, Marzellenstr. 32, 50668 Köln; tel. (221) 16420; fax (221) 1642700.

Archbishop of München and Freising: Cardinal Dr FRIEDRICH WETTER, Postfach 330360, 80079 München; Rochhusstr. 5–7, 80063 München; tel. (89) 21370; fax (89) 21371585.

Archbishop of Paderborn: Cardinal Dr JOHANNES JOACHIM DEGENHARDT, Erzbischöfliches Generalvikariat, Dompl. 3, 33098 Paderborn; tel. (5251) 1250; fax (5251) 125470.

Commissariat of German Bishops—Catholic Office: Postfach 040060, 10063 Berlin; Hannoversche Str. 5, 10115 Berlin; tel. (30) 288780; fax (30) 28878108; e-mail post@kath-buero.de; represents the German Conference of Bishops before the Federal Govt on political issues; Leader Prälat Dr KARL JÜSTEN.

Central Committee of German Catholics: Hochkreuzallee 246, 53175 Bonn; tel. (228) 382970; fax (228) 3829744; e-mail info@zdk.de; internet www.zdk.de; f. 1868; summarizes the activities of Catholic laymen and lay-organizations in Germany; Pres. Prof. Dr HANS JOACHIM MEYER; Gen. Sec. Dr STEFAN VESPER.

Evangelical (Protestant) Churches
About 33% of the population are members of the Evangelical Churches.

Evangelische Kirche in Deutschland (EKD) (Evangelical Church in Germany): Herrenhäuser Str. 12, 30419 Hannover; tel. (511) 27960; fax (511) 2796707; e-mail presse@ekd.de; internet www
.ekd.de; The governing bodies of the EKD are its Synod of 120 clergy and lay members which meets at regular intervals, the Conference of member churches, and the Council, composed of 15 elected members; the EKD has an ecclesiastical secretariat of its own (the Evangelical Church Office), including a special office for foreign relations; Chair. of the Council Präses MANFRED KOCK; Pres. of the Office VALENTIN SCHMIDT.

Synod of the EKD: Herrenhäuser Str. 12, 30419 Hannover; tel. (511) 2796114; fax (511) 2796707; e-mail synode@ekd.de; Pres. Dr JÜRGEN SCHMUDE.

Deutscher Evangelischer Kirchentag (German Evangelical Church Assembly): Postfach 1555, 36005 Fulda; Magdeburgerstr. 59, 36037 Fulda; tel. (661) 969500; fax (661) 9695090; e-mail fulda@kirchentag.de; internet www.kirchentag.de; Pres. Dr ELISABETH RAISER; Gen. Sec. FRIEDERIKE WOLDT.

Churches and Federations within the EKD:

Arnoldshainer Konferenz: Jebensstr. 3, 10623 Berlin; tel. (30) 310010; fax (30) 31001200; e-mail postfache@eku-online.de; internet www.eku-kirche.de; f. 1967; a loose federation of the church governments of one Lutheran, two Reformed Territorial and all United Churches, aiming at greater co-operation between them; Chair. of Council Landesbischof Dr ULRICH FISCHER.

Evangelische Kirche der Union (EKU) (Evangelical Church of the Union): Chancellery, Jebensstr. 3, 10623 Berlin; tel. (30) 310010; fax (30) 31001200; e-mail postfach@eku-online.de; internet www
.eku-online.de; composed of Lutheran and Reformed elements; includes the Evangelical Churches of Anhalt, Berlin-Brandenburg, Silesian Oberlausitz, Pomerania, the Rhineland, Saxony and Westphalia; Chair. of Synod Vizepräses NIKOLAUS SCHNEIDER; Chair. of Council Präses MANFRED SORG; Pres. of Administration Dr WILHELM HÜFFMEIER.

Reformierter Bund (Reformed Alliance): Vogelsangstr. 20, 42109 Wuppertal; tel. (202) 755111; fax (202) 754202; e-mail reformierter
.bund@wtal.de; f. 1884; unites the Reformed Territorial Churches and Congregations of Germany (with an estimated 2m. mems). The central body of the Reformed League is the 'Moderamen', the elected representation of the various Reformed Churches and Congregations; Moderator Rev. PETER BUKOWSKI; Gen. Sec. Rev. HERMANN SCHAEFER.

Vereinigte Evangelisch-Lutherische Kirche Deutschlands (VELKD) (The United Evangelical-Lutheran Church of Germany): Postfach 510409, 30634 Hannover; Richard-Wagner-Str. 26, 30177 Hannover; tel. (511) 62611; fax (511) 6261511; e-mail zentrale@velkd.de; internet www.velkd.de; f. 1948; 11m. mems; unites all but three of the Lutheran territorial Churches within the Evangelical Church in Germany; Presiding Bishop Bischof Dr HANS CHRISTIAN KNUTH (Schleswig).

Affiliated to the EKD:

†**Bremen Evangelical Church:** Postfach 106929, Franziuseck 2–4, 28199 Bremen; tel. (421) 55970; Pres. BRIGITTE BOEHME.

Bund Evangelisch-Reformierter Kirchen (Association of Evangelical Reformed Churches): Wieblingenweg 6, 38112 Braunschweig; tel. (531) 312640; e-mail dresler-krommingen@gmx.de; Chair. Präses SABINE DRESSLER-KROMMINGA.

†**Church of Lippe:** Leopoldstr. 27, 32756 Detmold; tel. (5231) 97660; fax (5231) 976850; e-mail oeff@lippische-landeskirche.de; internet www.lippische-landeskirche.de; Landessuperintendent GERRIT NOLTENSMEIER.

†**Evangelical Church in Baden:** Postfach 2269, 76010 Karlsruhe; Blumenstr. 1, 76133 Karlsruhe; tel. (721) 91750; fax (721) 9175550; e-mail info@ekiba.de; internet www.ekiba.de; Landesbischof Dr ULRICH FISCHER.

†**Evangelical Church in Berlin-Brandenburg:** Georgenkirchstr. 69/70, 10249 Berlin; tel. (30) 2434400; fax (30) 24344500; e-mail info@bb-evangelisch.de; internet www.bb-evangelisch.de; Bischof Prof. Dr WOLFGANG HUBER.

†**Evangelical Church in Hessen and Nassau:** Pauluspl. 1, 64276 Darmstadt; tel. (6151) 405284; fax (6151) 405441; Pres. Prof. Dr PETER STEINACKER.

†**Evangelical Church in the Rhineland:** Postfach 300339, 40403 Düsseldorf; Hans-Böckler-Str. 7, 40476 Düsseldorf; tel. (211) 45620; fax (211) 4562490; e-mail pressestelle@ekir.de; internet www.ekir
.de; Pres. MANFRED KOCK.

†**Evangelical Church of Kurhessen-Waldeck:** Postfach 410260, 34141 Kassel-Wilhelmshöhe; Wilhelmshöher Allee 330, 34131 Kassel; tel. (561) 93780; fax (561) 9378400; e-mail landeskirchenamt@ekkw.de; internet www.ekkw.de; Bischof Dr MARTIN HEIN.

†**Evangelical Church of the Palatinate:** Dompl. 5, 67346 Speyer; tel. (6232) 6670; fax (6232) 667228; e-mail kirchenpraesident@evkirchepfalz.de; internet www.evpfalz.de; Pres. EBERHARD CHERDRON.

†**Evangelical Church of Westfalen:** Altstädter Kirchpl. 5, 33602 Bielefeld; tel. (521) 5940; fax (521) 594129; e-mail

landeskirchenamt@lka.ekvw.de; internet www.ekvw.de; Präses MANFRED SORG.

*Evangelical-Lutheran Church in Bayern: Meiserstr. 11–13, 80333 München; tel. (89) 55950; fax (89) 5595444; e-mail poep@elkb .de; internet www.bayern-evangelisch.de; Landesbischof Dr JOHANNES FRIEDRICH.

Evangelical-Lutheran Church in Braunschweig: Dietrich-Bonhoeffer-Str. 1, 38300 Wolfenbüttel; tel. (5331) 8020; fax (5331) 802707; e-mail info@luth-braunschweig.de; internet www .luth-braunschweig.de; Landesbischof Dr FRIEDRICH WEBER.

Evangelical-Lutheran Church in Oldenburg: Philosophenweg 1, 26121 Oldenburg; tel. (441) 77010; fax (441) 7701299; e-mail presse@ev-kirche-ol.de; internet www.ev-kirche-oldenburg.de; Bischof PETER KRUG.

Evangelical-Lutheran Church in Thuringia: Dr-Moritz-Mitzenheim Str. 2A, 99817 Eisenach; tel. (3691) 67899; e-mail landeslandeskirchenamt@elkth.de; internet www .ev-kirche-thueringen.de; Landesbischof ROLAND HOFFMANN.

*Evangelical-Lutheran Church of Hannover: Haarstr. 6, 30169 Hannover; tel. (511) 5635830; fax (511) 56358311; e-mail landesbischoefin@evlka.de; internet www.evlka.de; Landesbischöfin Dr MARGOT KÄSSMANN.

Evangelical-Lutheran Church of Mecklenburg: Münzstr. 8, 19010 Schwerin; tel. (385) 51850; fax (385) 5185170; e-mail okr@ ellm.de; internet www.kirche-mv.de; Landesbischof HERMANN BESTE.

*Evangelical-Lutheran Church of North Elbe: Bischof Dr HANS CHRISTIAN KNUTH (Plessenstr. 5a, 24837 Schleswig; tel. (4621) 22056; fax (4621) 22194); Bischof BÖRBEL VON WARLENBERG-POFLER (Bädenstr. 3–5, 23564 Lübeck; tel. (451) 790201); Bishop MARIA JEPSEN (20457 Hamburg, Neue Burg 1; tel. (40) 373050); Pres. of North Elbian Church Administration Bischöfin BÄRBEL WARTENBERG-POTTER.

Evangelical-Lutheran Church of Saxony: Postfach 120552, 01006 Dresden; Lukasstr. 6, 01069 Dresden; tel. (351) 46920; fax (351) 4692109; e-mail kirche@evlks.de; internet www.evlks.de; Landesbischof VOLKER KRESS.

*Evangelical-Lutheran Church of Schaumburg-Lippe: Herderstr. 27, 31675 Bückeburg; tel. (5722) 9600; e-mail lka-bueckeburg@t-online.de; Landesbischof JÜRGEN JOHANNESDOTTER.

Evangelical-Reformed Church: Saarstr. 6, 26789 Leer; tel. (491) 91980; fax (491) 9198251; e-mail info@reformiert.de; internet www .reformiert.de; Moderator GARRELT DUIN; Synod Clerks Rev. WALTER HERRENBRÜCK, ERNST-JOACHIM PAGENSTECHER.

†Evangelical-Lutheran Church in Württemberg: Postfach 101342, Gänsheidestr. 4, 70184 Stuttgart; tel. (711) 21490; fax (711) 2149236; e-mail landesbischof@elk.wue.de; internet www.elk-wue .de; Landesbischof Dr GERHARD MAIER.

Herrnhuter Brüdergemeine or Europäisch-Festländische Brüder-Unität (Moravian Church): Badwasen 6, 73087 Bad Boll; tel. (7164) 94210; fax (7164) 942199; f. 1457; there are 25 congregations in Germany, Switzerland, Denmark, Sweden, Estonia and the Netherlands, with approx. 30,000 mems; Chair. Rev. HANS-BEAT MOTEL.

* Member of the VELKD.

† member of the EKU.

Other Evangelical (Protestant) Churches

Arbeitsgemeinschaft Mennonitischer Gemeinden in Deutschland (Asscn of Mennonite Congregations in Germany): Ringstr. 3, 67677 Enkenbach-Alsenborn; tel. (6303) 3883; fax (6303) 983739; e-mail rwrc.funck@t-online.de; internet www.mennoniten .de; f. 1886; re-organized 1990; Chair. WERNER FUNCK.

Bund Evangelisch-Freikirchlicher Gemeinden (Union of Evangelical Free Church Congregations; Baptists): Friedberger Str. 101, 61350 Bad Homburg v.d.H. tel. (6172) 80040; fax (6172) 800436; e-mail befg@baptisten.org; internet www.baptisten.org; f. 1849; Pres. SIEFRIED GROSSMANN; Vice-Pres. Dr RAIMUND UTSCH.

Bund Freier evangelischer Gemeinden (Covenant of Free Evangelical Churches in Germany): Postfach 4005, 58426 Witten; Goltenkamp 4, 58452 Witten; tel. (2302) 9370; fax (2302) 93799; e-mail bund@feg.de; internet www.feg.de; f. 1854; Pres. PETER STRAUCH; Administrator KLAUS KANWISCHER; 33,000 mems.

Evangelisch-altreformierte Kirche von Niedersachsen (Evangelical Reformed Church of Lower Saxony): Ehm-Schipper-Weg 2, 26736 Krummhörn-Campen; tel. (4927) 329; fax (4927) 912969; e-mail gerdschrader@compuserve.de; Sec. Rev. GERHARD SCHRADER.

Evangelisch-methodistische Kirche (United Methodist Church): Wilhelm-Leuschner-Str. 8, 60329 Frankfurt a.M. tel. (69) 2425210; fax (69) 24252129; e-mail kirchenkanzlei@emk.de; f. 1968; Bishop Dr WALTER KLAIBER.

Gemeinschaft der Siebenten-Tags-Adventisten (Seventh-Day Adventist Church): Postfach 4260, 73745 Ostfildern; Senefelderstr. 15, 73760 Ostfildern; tel. (711) 448190; fax (711) 4481960; e-mail sdv .zentrale@adventisten.de.

Heilsarmee in Deutschland (Salvation Army in Germany): Salierring 23–27, 50677 Köln; tel. (221) 208190; fax (221) 2081951; e-mail nhq@ger.salvationarmy.org; internet www.heilsarmee.de; f. 1886; Leader Commdr WERNER FREI.

Mülheimer Verband Freikirchlich-Evangelischer Gemeinden (Pentecostal Church): Habenhauser Dorfstr. 27, 28279 Bremen; tel. (421) 8399130; fax (421) 8399136; e-mail mv-bremen@t-online .de; f. 1913.

Selbständige Evangelisch-Lutherische Kirche (Independent Evangelical-Lutheran Church): Schopenhauerstr. 7, 30625 Hannover; tel. (511) 557808; fax (511) 551588; e-mail selk@selk.de; internet www.selk.de; f. 1972; Bishop Dr DIETHARDT ROTH; Exec. Sec. Rev. MICHAEL SCHÄTZEL.

Other Christian Churches

Alt-Katholische Kirche (Old Catholic Church): Gregor-Mendel-Str. 28, 53115 Bonn; tel. (228) 232285; fax (228) 238314; e-mail info@ alt-katholisch.de; internet www.alt-katholisch.de; seceded from the Roman Catholic Church as a protest against the declaration of Papal infallibility in 1870; belongs to the Utrecht Union of Old Catholic Churches; in full communion with the Anglican Communion; Pres. Bischof JOACHIM VOBBE (Bonn); 28,000 mems.

Apostelamt Jesu Christi: Madlower Hauptstr. 38, 03050 Cottbus; tel. (355) 541227; Pres. WALDEMAR ROHDE.

Armenisch-Apostolische Orthodoxe Kirche in Deutschland: Allensteiner Str. 5, 50735 Köln; tel. (221) 7126223; fax (221) 7126267; e-mail armenischediozese@hotmail.com; Archbishop KAREKIN BEKDJIAN.

Griechisch-Orthodoxe Metropolie von Deutschland (Greek Orthodox Metropoly of Germany): Postfach 300555, 53185 Bonn; Dietrich-Bonhoeffer-Str. 2, 53227 Bonn; tel. (228) 462041; fax (228) 464989; internet www.orthodoxie.net.

Religiöse Gesellschaft der Freunde (Quäker) (Society of Friends): Planckstr. 20, 10117 Berlin; tel. (30) 2082284; fax (30) 2082284; f. 1925; 311 mems.

Russische Orthodoxe Kirche—Berliner Diözese (Russian Orthodox Church): Postfach 17, 10267 Berlin; Wildensteiner Str. 10, 10318 Berlin; tel. (30) 50379488; fax (30) 5098153; e-mail red .stimme@snafu.de; Archbishop FEOFAN.

ISLAM

There are an estimated 2.6m. Muslims in Germany.

JUDAISM

The membership of Jewish synagogues in Germany numbered some 74,289 in 1998.

Zentralrat der Juden in Deutschland (Central Council of Jews in Germany): Tucholskystr. 9, Leo-Baeck-Haus, 10117 Berlin; tel. (30) 2844560; fax (30) 28445613; e-mail info@zentralratdjuden.de; internet www.zentralratdjuden.de; Pres. Bd of Dirs PAUL SPIEGEL; Exec. Dir STEPHAN J. KRAMER.

Jüdische Gemeinde zu Berlin (Jewish Community in Berlin): Fasanenstr. 79–80, 10623 Berlin; e-mail vorstand@jg-berlin.org; Pres. Dr ALEXANDER BRENNER.

The Press

The German Press Council was founded in 1956 as a self-regulatory body, and is composed of publishers and journalists. It formulates guide-lines and investigates complaints against the press.

In 1968 a government commission stipulated various limits on the proportions of circulation that any one publishing group should be allowed to control: (1) 40% of the total circulation of newspapers or 40% of the total circulation of magazines; (2) 20% of the total circulation of newspapers and magazines together; (3) 15% of the circulation in one field if the proportion owned in the other field is 40%.

Deutscher Presserat (German Press Council): Postfach 7160, 53071 Bonn; tel. (228) 985720; fax (228) 9857299; e-mail info@ presserat.de; internet www.presserat.de; Dir LUTZ TILLMANNS.

The principal newspaper publishing groups are:

Axel Springer Verlag AG: Axel-Springer-Str. 65, 10888 Berlin; Axel-Springer-Pl. 1, 20355 Hamburg; tel. (30) 25910; fax (30) 251606; tel. (40) 34700; fax (40) 345811; internet www.asv.de; f. 1946; the largest newspaper publishing group in continental

Europe; includes five major dailies *Die Welt, Hamburger Abendblatt, Bild, Berliner Morgenpost, BZ,* three Sunday papers *Welt am Sonntag, Bild am Sonntag, BZ am Sonntag,* and radio, television, women's and family magazines; Chair. AUGUST A. FISCHER.

Gruner + Jahr AG & Co Druck- und Verlagshaus: Am Vossbarg, 25524 Itzehoe; and Am Baumwall 11, 20459 Hamburg; tel. (4821) 7771; fax (4821) 777449; tel. (40) 37030; fax (40) 3703600; internet www.co.guj.de; owns, amongst others, *Stern, Brigitte, Capital, Eltern, Schöner Wohnen, Hamburger Morgenpost; Financial Times Deutschland,* a jt venture with *Financial Times* (UK) was launched in Feb. 2000.

Süddeutscher-Verlag GmbH: Sendlingerstr. 80, 80331 München; tel. (89) 21830; fax (89) 2183787; internet www.sueddeutsche.de; f. 1945; owns *Süddeutsche Zeitung,* special interest periodicals.

JahreszeitenVerlag GmbH: Possmoorweg 5, 22301 Hamburg; tel. (40) 27170; fax (40) 27172056; f. 1948; owns, amongst others, the periodicals *Für Sie* and *Petra*; Pres. THOMAS GANSKE.

Heinrich-Bauer-Verlag: Postfach 4660, 20077 Hamburg; Burchardstr. 11, 20095 Hamburg; and Charles-de-Gaulle-Str. 8, 81737 München; tel. (40) 30190; fax (40) 30191043; tel. (89) 678600; fax (89) 6702033; internet www.bauerverlag.de; owns 108 popular illustrated magazines, including *Bravo* (München), *Neue Revue* (Hamburg), *Maxi, Neue Post, TV Horen + Sehen* and *TV Movie*; Pres. HEINRICH BAUER.

Verlag Aenne Burda GmbH & Co KG: Am Kesterdamm 1, 77652 Offenburg; tel. (781) 840; fax (781) 843291; internet www.burda.de; f. 1908; publs incl. *Burda Modemagazin, Bild + Funk, Focus, Freundin, Meine Familie & ich* and *Schweriner Volkszeitung*; 10 Mans.

PRINCIPAL DAILIES

Aachen

Aachener Nachrichten: Postfach 110, 52002 Aaachen; Dresdner Str. 3, 52068 Aachen; tel. (241) 51010; fax (241) 5101399; internet www.an-online.de; f. 1872; circ. 67,000.

Aachener Zeitung: Postfach 500110, 52085 Aachen; Dresdner Str. 3, 52068 Aachen; tel. (241) 51010; fax (241) 5101399; internet www.aachener-zeitung.de; f. 1946; Editor-in-Chief BERND MATHIEU; circ. 106,000.

Ansbach

Fränkische Landeszeitung: Postfach 1362, 91504 Ansbach; Nürnberger Str. 9–17, 91522 Ansbach; tel. (981) 95000; fax (981) 13961; Editors-in-Chief GERHARD EGETEMAYER, PETER M. SZYMANOWSKI; circ. 50,000.

Aschaffenburg

Main-Echo: Postfach 548, 63736 Aschaffenburg; Weichertstr. 20, 63739 Aschaffenburg a.M. tel. (6021) 3960; fax (6021) 396499; e-mail redaktionssekretariat@main-echo.de; internet www.main-echo.de; Editors HELMUT WEISS, Dr HELMUT TEUFEL; circ. 93,000.

Augsburg

Augsburger Allgemeine: Curt-Frenzel-Str. 2, 86167 Augsburg; tel. (821) 7770; fax (821) 7772067; e-mail chefredaktion@augsburger-allgemeiner.de; internet www.augsburger-allgemeine.de; daily (Mon. to Sat.); Editors-in-Chief RAINER BONHORST, WALTER ROLLER, KLAUS-DIETER DÜSTER; circ. 370,000.

Baden-Baden

Badisches Tagblatt: Postfach 120, 76481 Baden-Baden; Stefanienstr. 1–3, 76530 Baden-Baden; tel. (7221) 215241; fax (7221) 215240; Editors-in-Chief HARALD BESINGER, VOLKER-BODO ZANGER; circ. 41,000.

Bamberg

Fränkischer Tag: Gutenbergstr. 1, 96050 Bamberg; tel. (951) 1880; fax (951) 188118; internet www.fraenkischer-tag.de; Publr Dr HELMUTH JUNGBAUER; circ. 75,800.

Bautzen

Serbske Nowiny: Tuchmacher Str. 27, 02625 Bautzen; tel. (3591) 577232; e-mail serbske-nowiny@t-online.de; evening; Sorbian language paper; Editor BENEDIKT DYRLICH; circ. 1,500.

Berlin

Berliner Kurier: Karl-Liebknecht-Str. 29, 10178 Berlin; tel. (30) 23279; fax (30) 23275606; e-mail berliner-kurier@berlinonline.de; internet www.Berlinonline.de; f. 1990; evening; publ. by Gruner + Jahr AG; Editor CAROLINE METHNER; circ. 149,795.

Berliner Morgenpost: Axel-Springer-Str. 65, 10888 Berlin; tel. (30) 25910; fax (30) 2516071; e-mail redaktion@morgenpost.de; internet www.berliner-morgenpost.de; f. 1898; publ. by Axel Springer Verlag AG; Editor-in-Chief Dr WOLFRAM WEIMER; circ. 184,100.

Berliner Zeitung: Karl-Liebknecht-Str. 29, 10178 Berlin; tel. (2) 23279; fax (30) 23275581; e-mail berliner-zeitung@berlinonline.de; internet www.berliner-zeitung.de; f. 1945; morning (except Sunday); publ. by Gruner + Jahr AG; Editor Dr UWE VORKÖTTER; circ. 193,493.

BZ (Berliner Zeitung): Axel-Springer-Str. 65, 10888 Berlin; tel. (30) 25910; fax (30) 2510928; internet www.bz-berlin.de; f. 1877; publ. by Axel Springer Verlag AG; Editor WOLFGANG KRYSZOHN; circ. 313,500.

Junge Welt: Berlin; tel. (30) 22330; fax (30) 1302865; internet www.jungewelt.de; f. 1947; morning; Editor JENS KÖNIG; circ. 158,000.

Neues Deutschland: Alt-Stralau 1–2, 10245 Berlin; tel. (30) 293905; fax (30) 29390600; internet www.nd-online.de; f. 1946; morning; independent; Editor WOLFGANG SPICKERMANN; circ. 58,476.

Der Tagesspiegel: Postfach 304330, 10723 Berlin; Potsdamer Str. 87, 10785 Berlin; tel. (30) 260090; fax (30) 26009332; e-mail info@tagesspiegel.de; internet www.tagesspiegel.de; f. 1945; circ. 151,000.

Die Welt: Axel-Springer-Str. 65, 10888 Berlin; tel. (30) 25910; fax (30) 251606; internet www.welt.de; f. 1946; publ. by Axel Springer Verlag AG; Editor Dr THOMAS LÖFFELHOLZ; circ. 216,800.

Bielefeld

Neue Westfälische: Postfach 100225, 33502 Bielefeld; Niederstr. 21–27, 33602 Bielefeld; tel. (521) 5550; fax (521) 555520; internet www.nw-news.de; f. 1967; circ. 219,850.

Westfalen-Blatt: Postfach 8740, 33531 Bielefeld; Südbrackstr. 14–18, 33611 Bielefeld; tel. (521) 5850; fax (521) 585370; internet www.westfalen-blatt.de; f. 1946; Editor CARL-W. BUSSE; circ. 147,400.

Bonn

General-Anzeiger: Justus-von-Liebig-Str. 15, 53121 Bonn; tel. (228) 66880; fax (228) 6688170; internet www.general-anzeiger-bonn.de; f. 1725; independent; Publrs HERMANN NEUSSER, HERMANN NEUSSER, Jr, MARTIN NEUSSER; Editor Dr HELMUT HERLES; circ. 90,000.

Braunschweig

Braunschweiger Zeitung: Postfach 3263, 38022 Braunschweig; Hamburger Str. 277, 38114 Braunschweig; tel. (531) 39000; fax (531) 3900610; internet www.newsclick.de; circ. 170,400.

Bremen

Bremer Nachrichten: Postfach 107801, 28078 Bremen; Martinistr. 43, 28195 Bremen; tel. (421) 36710; fax (421) 3379233; f. 1743; Publr HERBERT C. ORDEMANN; Editor DIETRICH IDE; circ. 30,000.

Weser-Kurier: Postfach 107801, 28078 Bremen; Martinistr. 43, 28195 Bremen; tel. (421) 36710; fax (421) 3379233; internet www.weser-kurier.de; f. 1945; Publr HERBERT C. ORDEMANN; Editor VOLKER WEISE; circ. 160,000.

Bremerhaven

Nordsee-Zeitung: Postfach 27512, 27512 Bremerhaven; Hafenstr. 140, 27576 Bremerhaven 1; tel. (471) 5970; fax (471) 597567; internet www.nordsee-zeitung.de; Chief Editor JÖRG JUNG; circ. 77,500.

Chemnitz

Freie Presse: Postfach 261, Brückenstr. 15, 09111 Chemnitz; tel. (371) 6560; fax (371) 643042; internet www.freiepresse.de; f. 1963; morning; Editor DIETER SOIKA; circ. 461,900.

Cottbus

Lausitzer Rundschau: Postfach 100279, 03002 Cottbus; Str. der Jugend 54, 03050 Cottbus; tel. (355) 4810; fax (355) 481245; internet www.lr-online.de; independent; morning; Chief Officers FRANK LÜDECKE, B. LISKE; circ. 160,000.

Darmstadt

Darmstädter Echo: Postfach 100155, 64276 Darmstadt; Holzhofallee 25–31, 64295 Darmstadt; tel. (6151) 3871; fax (6151) 387448; internet www.echo-online.de; f. 1945; Publrs Dr HANS-PETER BACH, HORST BACH; Editor-in-Chief ROLAND HOF; circ. 87,300.

Dortmund

Ruhr-Nachrichten: Postfach 105051, Westenhellweg 86–88, 44047 Dortmund; internet www.westline.de; f. 1949; Editor FLORIAN LENSING-WOLFF; circ. 215,400.

Westfälische Rundschau: Postfach 105067, 44047 Dortmund; Brüderweg 9; Dortmund 44135; tel. (201) 8040; fax (201) 8042841; internet www.westfaelische-rundschau.de; Editor FRANK BÜNTE; circ. 250,000.

Dresden

Dresdner Morgenpost: Ostra-Allee, 01067 Dresden; tel. (51) 4864; fax (51) 4951116; circ. 126,700.

Dresdner Neueste Nachrichten/Union: Hauptstr. 21, 01097 Dresden; tel. (351) 8075210; fax (351) 8075212; morning; Editor-in-Chief DIRK BIRGEL; circ. 39,000.

Sächsische Zeitung: Haus der Presse, Ostra-Allee 20, 01067 Dresden; tel. (351) 48640; fax (351) 48642354; e-mail redaktion@ sz-online.de; internet www.sz-online.de; f. 1946; morning; publ. by Gruner + Jahr AG; Editor-in-Chief PETER CHRIST; circ. 397,700.

Düsseldorf

Düsseldorf Express: Postfach 1132, 40002 Düsseldorf; Königsallee 27, 40212 Düsseldorf; tel. (211) 13930; fax (211) 324835.

Handelsblatt: Postfach 102741, 40018 Düsseldorf; Kasernenstr. 67, 40213 Düsseldorf; tel. (211) 8870; fax (211) 329954; e-mail handelsblatt@rhb.de; internet www.handelsblatt.de; 5 a week; Publr DIETER VON HOLTZBRINCK; circ. 156,473.

Rheinische Post: Zülpicherstr. 10, 40549 Düsseldorf; tel. (211) 5050; fax (211) 5052575; internet www.rp-online.de; f. 1946; Editor ULRICH REITZ; circ. 349,200.

Westdeutsche Zeitung: Postfach 101132, 40002 Düsseldorf; Königsallee 27, 40212 Düsseldorf; tel. (211) 83820; fax (211) 83822392; e-mail wzn@wz-newsline.de; internet www.wz-newsline .de; Editor-in-Chief MICHAEL HARTMANN; Publr Dr M. GIRARDET; circ. 176,800.

Erfurt

Thüringer Allgemeine: Gottstedter Landstr. 6, 99092 Erfurt; tel. (361) 2274; fax (361) 2275144; e-mail redaktion@ thueringer-allgemeine.de; internet www.thueringer-allgemeine.de; f. 1946; morning; Editor-in-Chief SERGEJ LOCHTHOFEN; circ. 330,000.

Essen

Neue Ruhr Zeitung: Friedrichstr. 34–38, 45128 Essen; tel. (201) 8042605; fax (201) 8042121; Editor-in-Chief Dr RICHARD KIESSLER; circ. 215,000.

Westdeutsche Allgemeine Zeitung: Friedrichstr. 34–38, 45128 Essen; tel. (201) 8040; fax (201) 8042841; Editor RALF LEHMANN; circ. 650,000.

Flensburg

Flensburger Tageblatt: Postfach 1553, 25804 Flensburg; Nikolaistr. 7, 24937 Flensburg; tel. (461) 8080; fax (461) 8082121.

Frankfurt am Main

Frankfurter Allgemeine Zeitung: Hellerhofstr. 2–4, 60327 Frankfurt a.M. tel. (69) 75910; fax (69) 75911743; internet www.faz .net; f. 1949; Editors DIETER ECKART, BERTHOLD KOHLER, Dr GÜNTHER NONNENMACHER, Dr FRANK SCHIRRMACHER, HOLGER STELTZNER; circ. 400,000.

Frankfurter Neue Presse: Postfach 100801, 60008 Frankfurt a.M. Frankenallee 71–81, 60327 Frankfurt a.M. tel. (69) 75010; fax (69) 75014330; internet www.fnp.de; independent; Editor GERHARD MUMME; circ. 110,440.

Frankfurter Rundschau: Grosse Eschenheimer Str. 16–18; 60313 Frankfurt a.M. tel. (69) 21991; fax (69) 21993666; internet www .fr-aktuell.de; Editors Dr WOLFGANG STORZ, STEPHEN HEBEL, JUERGEN METKEMEYER; circ. 189,000.

Frankfurt an der Oder

Märkische Oderzeitung: Postfach 178, 15201 Frankfurt a.d. Oder; Kellenspring 6, 15230 Frankfurt a.d. Oder; tel. (335) 55300; fax (335) 23214; morning; Editor HEINZ KURTZBACH; circ. 150,633.

Freiburg im Breisgau

Badische Zeitung: Pressehaus, Basler Str. 88, 79115 Freiburg i. Br. tel. (761) 4960; fax (761) 4965008; e-mail redaktion@ badische-zeitung.de; internet www.badische-zeitung.de; f. 1946; Editor THOMAS HAUSER; circ. 171,990.

Gera

Ostthüringer Zeitung: De-Smit-Str. 18, 6500 Gera; tel. (70) 6120; fax (70) 51233; morning; Editor-in-Chief ULLRICH ERZIGKEIT; circ. 237,537.

Göttingen

Göttinger Tageblatt: Postfach 1953, 37009 Göttingen; Dransfelder Str. 1, 37079 Göttingen; tel. (551) 9011; fax (551) 901229; e-mail info@goettinger.tageblatt.de; internet www .goettinger-tageblatt.de; f. 1889; Man. Dirs HERBERT FLECKEN, GÜNTER GRIFFELS; Editor-in-Chief BERNO HILDER; circ. 50,200.

Hagen

Westfalenpost: Schürmannstr. 4, 58097 Hagen; tel. (2331) 9170; fax (2331) 9174263; e-mail westfalenpost@cityweb.de; f. 1946; Chief Editor BODO ZAPP; circ. 160,000.

Halle

Haller Kreisblatt: Postfach 1452, 33779 Halle; Gutenbergstr. 2, 33790 Halle.

Hamburg

Bild: Axel-Springer-Pl. 1, 20355 Hamburg; tel. (40) 34700; fax (40) 345811; internet www.bild.de; f. 1952; publ. by Axel Springer Verlag AG; Chief Editor KAI DICKMANN; circ. 4,412,200.

Hamburger Abendblatt: Axel-Springer-Pl. 1, 20355 Hamburg; tel. (40) 34700; fax (40) 345811; internet www.abendblatt.de; publ. by Axel Springer Verlag AG; Editor-in-Chief KLAUS KRUSE; circ. 315,600.

Hamburger Morgenpost: Griegstr. 75, 22763 Hamburg; tel. (40) 8830303; fax (40) 88303237; e-mail iamedien@www.mopo.de; internet www.mopo.de; publ. by Gruner + Jahr AG; circ. 140,700.

Hannover

Hannoversche Allgemeine Zeitung: Bemeroder Str. 58, 30148 Hannover, 30559 Hannover; tel. (511) 5180; fax (511) 527328; internet www.niedersachsen.com; circ. 269,600.

Neue Presse: Postfach 149, 30001 Hannover; Bemeroder Str. 58, 30559 Hannover; tel. (511) 51010; fax (511) 524554.

Heidelberg

Rhein-Neckar-Zeitung: Postfach 104560, 69035 Heidelberg; Hauptstr. 23, 69117 Heidelberg; tel. (6221) 5191; fax (6221) 519217; e-mail rnz-kontakt@rnz.de; internet www.rnz.de; f. 1945; morning; Publrs Dr LUDWIG KNORR, WINFRIED KNORR, Dr RUPRECHT SCHULZE; circ. 102,500.

Heilbronn

Heilbronner Stimme: Allee 2, 74072 Heilbronn; tel. (7131) 6150; fax (7131) 615200; e-mail gl@stimme.de; internet www.stimme.de; f. 1946; Editor-in-Chief Dr WOLFGANG BOK; circ. 102,500.

Hof-Saale

Frankenpost: Postfach 1320, 95012 Hof-Saale; Poststr. 9–11, 95028 Hof-Saale; tel. (9281) 8160; fax (9281) 816283; e-mail fp-redaktion@frankenpost.de; internet www.frankenpost.de; publ. by Frankenpost Verlag GmbH; Editor-in-Chief MALTE BUSCHBECK; circ 85,000.

Ingolstadt

Donaukurier: Postfach 100259, 85002 Ingolstadt; Stauffenbergstr. 2A, 85051 Ingolstadt; tel. (841) 96660; fax (841) 9666255; e-mail redaktion@donaukurier.de; internet www.donaukurier.de; f. 1872; Publr ELIN REISSMÜLLER; circ. 84,700.

Kassel

Hessische/Niedersächsische Allgemeine: Postfach 101009, 34010 Kassel; Frankfurter Str. 168, 34121 Kassel; tel. (561) 20300; fax (561) 2032116; internet www.hna.de; f. 1959; independent; circ. 189,200.

Kempten

Allgäuer Zeitung: Postfach 3155, 87440 Kempten; Heisinger Str. 14, 87437 Kempten; tel. (831) 2060; fax (831) 206379; internet www .all-in.de; f. 1968; Publrs GEORG FÜRST VON WALDBURG-ZEIL, GÜNTER HOLLAND; circ. 117,900.

Kiel

Kieler Nachrichten: Postfach 1111, 24100 Kiel; Fleethörn 1–7, 24103 Kiel; tel. (431) 9030; fax (431) 903935; internet www.kn.online .de; publ. by Axel Springer Verlag; Chief Editor JÜRGEN HEINEMANN; circ. 113,400.

Koblenz

Rhein-Zeitung: Postfach 1540, August-Horch-Str. 28, 56070 Koblenz; tel. (261) 89200; fax (261) 892476; internet www .rhein-zeitung.de; Editor MARTIN LOHMANN; circ. 246,100.

Köln

Express: Postfach 100410, 50450 Köln; Breite Str. 70, 50667 Köln; tel. (221) 2240; fax (211) 2242524; internet www.express.de; f. 1964; Publr ALFRED NEVEN DUMONT; circ. 370,000.

Kölner Stadt-Anzeiger: Amsterdamer Str. 192, 50735 Köln; tel. (221) 2240; fax (221) 2242524; internet www.ksta.de; f. 1876; Publr ALFRED NEVEN DUMONT; Editor FRANZ SOMMERFELD; circ. 294,400.

Kölnische Rundschau: Postfach 102145, 50461 Köln; Stolkgasse 25–45, 50667 Köln; tel. (221) 16320; fax (221) 1632491; e-mail jost .springensguth@kr-redaktion.de; internet www.rundschau-online .de; f. 1946; Publr HELMUT HEINEN; Editor-in-Chief JOST SPRING-ENSGUTH; circ. 155,100.

Konstanz

Südkurier: Postfach 102001, Presse- und Druckzentrum, 78420 Konstanz; Max-Stromeyer-Str. 178, 78467 Konstanz; tel. (7531) 9990; fax (7531) 991485; e-mail redaktion@suedkurier.de; internet www.skol.de; f. 1945; circ. 148,990.

Leipzig

Leipziger Volkszeitung: Peterssteinweg 19, 04107 Leipzig; tel. (341) 21811; fax (341) 310992; internet www.lvz-online.de; f. 1894; morning; publ. by Axel Springer Verlag AG; circ. 264,000.

Leutkirch im Allgäu

Schwäbische Zeitung: Postfach 1145, 88291 Leutkirch im Allgäu; Rudolf-Roth-Str. 18, 88299 Leutkirch im Allgäu; tel. (7561) 800; fax (7561) 80134; e-mail redaktion@schwaebische-zeitung.de; internet www.schwaebische-zeitung.de; f. 1945; Editor JOACHIM UMBACH; circ. 196,000.

Lübeck

Lübecker Nachrichten: Herrenholz 10–12, 23556 Lübeck; tel. (451) 1440; fax (451) 1441022; internet www.ln-online.de; f. 1945; publ. by Axel Springer Verlag AG; Chief Editor THOMAS LUBOWSKI; circ. 115,900.

Ludwigshafen

Die Rheinpfalz: Postfach 211147, 67011 Ludwigshafen; Amtsstr. 5–11, 67059 Ludwigshafen; tel. (621) 590201; fax (621) 5902336; Dir Dr THOMAS SCHAUB; circ. 249,410.

Magdeburg

Magdeburger Volksstimme: Bahnhofstr. 17, 39104 Magdeburg; tel. (391) 59990; fax (391) 388400; f. 1890; morning; publ. by Magdeburger Verlags- und Druckhaus GmbH; Editor-in-Chief Dr HEINZ-GEORG OETTE; circ. 316,900.

Mainz

Allgemeine Zeitung: Postfach 3120, 55021 Mainz; Erich-Dombrowski-Str. 2, 55127 Mainz; tel. (6131) 1440; fax (6131) 144504; internet www.main-rheiner.de; publ. by Rhein-Main-Presse; circ. 134,000.

Mannheim

Mannheimer Morgen: Postfach 102164, 68021 Mannheim; Dudenstr. 12–26, 68167 Mannheim; tel. (621) 39201; fax (621) 3921376; e-mail redaktion@mamo.de; internet www.morgenweb.de; f. 1946; Publr R. VON SCHILLING; Chief Editor HORST ROTH; circ. 177,419.

München

Abendzeitung: Sendlingerstr. 10, 80331 München; tel. (89) 23770; fax (89) 2377478; internet www.abendzeitung.de; f. 1948; Dir CHRISTOPH MATTES; Editor-in-Chief KURT RÖTTGEN; circ. 165,074.

Münchner Merkur: Paul-Heyse-Str. 2–4, 80336 München; tel. (89) 53060; fax (89) 53068651; internet www.merkur-online.de; Publr Dr DIRK IPPEN; Editor ERNST HEBEKER; circ. 283,000.

Süddeutsche Zeitung: Sendlingerstr. 8, 80331 München; tel. (89) 21830; fax (89) 2183787; internet www.sueddeutsche.de; f. 1945; publ. by Süddeutscher-Verlag GmbH; Editors-in-Chief HANS-WERNER KILZ, Dr GERNOT SITTNER; circ. 427,644.

TZ: Paul-Heyse-Str. 2–4, 80336 München; tel. (89) 53060; fax (89) 5306552; e-mail sekretariat@tz-online.de; f. 1968; Editor KARL SCHERMANN; circ. 152,000.

Münster

Münstersche Zeitung: Postfach 5560, 48030 Münster; Neubrück-enstr. 8–11, 48143 Münster; tel. (251) 5920; fax (251) 592212; e-mail mz-redaktion@westline.de; internet www.westline.de; f. 1871; independent; Editor Dr GREGOR BOTHE; circ. 46,860.

Westfälische Nachrichten: Soester Str. 13, 48155 Münster; tel. (251) 6900; fax (251) 690105; internet www.wnonline.de; Chief Editor Dr NORBERT TIEMANN; circ. 125,900.

Neubrandenburg

Nordkurier: Flurstr. 2, 17034 Neubrandenburg; tel. (395) 45750; fax (395) 4575694; internet www.nordkurier.de; circ. 340,000.

Nürnberg

Nürnberger Nachrichten: Marienstr. 9–11, 90402 Nürnberg; tel. (911) 2160; fax (911) 2162326; internet www.nn-online.de; f. 1945; Editor FELIX HARTLIEB; circ. 344,000.

Oberndorf-Neckar

Schwarzwälder Bote: Postfach 1380, 78722 Oberndorf-Neckar; Kirchtorstr. 14, 78727 Oberndorf-Neckar; tel. (7423) 780; fax (7423) 7873; internet www.swol.de; circ. 104,300.

Oelde

Die Glocke: Engelbert-Holterdorf-Str. 4–6, 59302 Oelde; tel. (2522) 730; fax (2522) 73216; f. 1880; Editors FRIED GEHRING, ENGELBERT HOLTERDORF; circ. 65,500.

Offenbach

Offenbach Post: Postfach 100263, 63002 Offenbach; Waldstr. 226, 63071 Offenbach; tel. (69) 850080; fax (69) 85008198; internet www .op-online.de; f. 1947; Publr UDO BINTZ; circ. 53,200.

Oldenburg

Nordwest-Zeitung: Postfach 2527, 26015 Oldenburg; Peterstr. 28–34, 26121 Oldenburg; tel. (441) 998801; fax (441) 99882029; internet www.nwz-online.de; publ. by Nordwest-Zeitung Verlagsgesellschaft mbH & Co KG; Editor ROLF SEELHEIM; circ. 130,000.

Osnabrück

Neue Osnabrücker Zeitung: Postfach 4260, 49032 Osnabrück; Breiter Gang 10–16 and Grosse Str. 17–19, 49074 Osnabrück; tel. (541) 3250; fax (541) 325275; e-mail redaktion@neue-oz.de; internet www.neue-oz.de; f. 1967; Editors-in-Chief EWALD GELDING, Dr JÜRGEN WERMSER; circ. 179,700.

Passau

Passauer Neue Presse: Medienstr. 5, 94036 Passau; tel. (851) 8020; fax (851) 802256; internet www.pnp.de; f. 1946; circ. 162,900.

Potsdam

Märkische Allgemeine: Postfach 601153, 14411 Potsdam; Friedrich-Engels-Str. 24, 14473 Potsdam; tel. (331) 28400; fax (331) 2840310; e-mail chefredaktion@mazonline.de; internet www .maerkischeallgemeine.de; f. 1990; morning; independent; Chief Editor Dr KLAUS ROST; circ. 190,000.

Regensburg

Mittelbayerische Zeitung: Margaretenstr. 4, 93047 Regensburg; tel. (941) 207270; fax (941) 207307; e-mail gf@mz.donau.de; internet www.donau.de; f. 1945; Editors PETER ESSER, THOMAS ESSER; circ. 136,012.

Rostock

Ostsee-Zeitung: Richard-Wagner-Str. 1A, 18055 Rostock; tel. (81) 3650; fax (81) 365244; internet www.ostsee-zeitung.de; f. 1952; publ. by Axel Springer Verlag AG; Editor GERD SPILKER; circ. 214,300.

Saarbrücken

Saarbrücker Zeitung: Gutenbergstr. 11–23, 66117 Saarbrücken; tel. (681) 5020; fax (681) 5022500; internet www.sz-newsline.de; f. 1761; Editor RUDOLPH BERNHARD; circ. 183,500.

Schwerin

Schweriner Volkszeitung: Gutenbergstr. 1, 19061 Schwerin; tel. (385) 63780; fax (385) 3975140; internet www.svz.de; f. 1946; Editor CHRISTOPH HAMM; circ. 144,800.

Straubing

Straubinger Tagblatt: Ludwigspl. 30, 94315 Straubing; tel. (9421) 940115; fax (9421) 940155; e-mail service@idowa.de; internet www .idowa.de; f. 1860; morning; Chief Editor Dr HERMANN BALLE; circ. 140,000.

Stuttgart

Stuttgarter Nachrichten: Postfach 104452, 70039 Stuttgart; Plieninger Str. 150, 70567 Stuttgart; tel. (711) 72050; fax (711) 7205747; internet www.stuttgarter-nachrichten.de; f. 1946; Editor-in-Chief JÜRGEN OFFENBACH; circ. 270,000.

Stuttgarter Zeitung: Postfach 106032, 70049 Stuttgart; Plieninger Str. 150, 70567 Stuttgart; tel. (711) 72050; fax (711) 7205516; internet www.stuttgarter-zeitung.de; f. 1945; Chief Editor PETER CHRIST; circ. 151,600.

Trier

Trierischer Volksfreund: Postfach 3770, 54227 Trier; Hanns-Martin-Schleyer-Str. 8, 54294 Trier; tel. (651) 71990; fax (651) 7199990; e-mail redaktion@intrinet.de; internet www.intrinet.de; Chief Editor WALTER W. WEBER; circ. 100,000.

Ulm

Südwest Presse: Frauenstr. 77, 89073 Ulm; tel. (731) 1560; fax (731) 156308; internet www.suedwest-presse.de; circ. 107,800.

Weiden

Der Neue Tag: Postfach 1340, 92603 Weiden; Weigelstr. 16, 92637 Weiden; tel. (961) 850; fax (961) 44499; Editor-in-Chief HANS KLEMM; circ. 87,400.

Weimar

Thüringische Landeszeitung: Marienstr. 14, 99423 Weimar; tel. (3643) 206411; fax (3643) 206413; f. 1945; morning; Editor HANS HOFFMEISTER; circ. 62,000.

Wetzlar

Wetzlarer Neue Zeitung: Elsa-Brandström-Str. 18, 35578 Wetzlar; tel. (6441) 9590; fax (6441) 71684; f. 1945; Editor WULF EIGENDORF; circ. 75,000.

Wiesbaden

Wiesbadener Kurier: Postfach 6029, 65050 Wiesbaden; Langgasse 21, 65183 Wiesbaden; tel. (611) 3550; fax (611) 355377; internet www.main-rheiner-de; Chief Editors MATTHIAS FRIEDRICH, FRIEDRICH ROEINGH; circ. 86,700.

Würzburg

Main-Post: Berner Str. 2, 97084 Würzburg; tel. (931) 60010; fax (931) 6001242; internet www.mainpost.de; f. 1883; independent; Publrs MANFRED WINTERBACH, DAVID BRANDSTÄTTER, KNUT MÜLLER; Editor-in-Chief MICHAEL REINHARD; circ. 153,300.

SUNDAY AND WEEKLY PAPERS

Bayernkurier: Nymphenburger Str. 64, 80636 München; tel. (89) 120041; e-mail redaktion@bayernkurier.de; internet www .bayernkurier.de; weekly; organ of the CSU; Chief Editor PETER SCHMALZ; circ. 81,000.

Bild am Sonntag: Axel-Springer-Pl. 1, 20350 Hamburg; tel. (40) 34700; fax (40) 345811; f. 1956; Sunday; publ. by Axel Springer Verlag AG; Chief Editor CLAUS STRUNZ; circ. 2,647,629.

BZ am Sonntag: Axel-Springer-Str. 65, 10888 Berlin; tel. (30) 25910; fax (30) 2510928; f. 1992; publ. by Axel Springer Verlag AG; circ. 157,714.

Frankfurter Allgemeine Sonntagszeitung: Hellerhofstr. 2–4, 60327 Frankfurt a.M. tel. (69) 75910; fax (69) 75911773; e-mail sonntagszeitung@faz.de; internet www.faz.de; Sunday; Publrs DIETER ECKART, BERTHOLD KOHLER, GÜNTHER NONNENMACHER, FRANK SCHIRRMACHER, HOLGER STELTZNER; circ. 267,700 (2002).

Rheinischer Merkur: Postfach 201164, 53141 Bonn; Godesberger Allee 91, 53175 Bonn; tel. (228) 8840; fax (228) 884299; e-mail anzeigen@merkur.de; internet www.merkur.de; f. 1946; weekly; circ. 106,000.

Sonntag aktuell: Plienigerstr. 150, 70567 Stuttgart; tel. (711) 72050; fax (711) 7205930; Sunday; circ. 869,500.

Welt am Sonntag: Axel-Springer-Str. 65, 10888 Berlin; tel. (30) 259100; e-mail wams.leser@asv.de; internet www.welt.de; Sunday; publ. by Axel Springer Verlag AG; Editor Dr THOMAS GARMS; circ. 465,347.

Die Zeit: Speersort 1, Pressehaus, 20095 Hamburg; tel. (40) 32800; fax (40) 327111; internet www.zeit.de; f. 1946; weekly; Editors-in-Chief Dr JOSEF JOFFE, Dr MICHAEL NAUMANN; circ. 455,000.

SELECTED PERIODICALS

Agriculture

Agrar Praxis: Ernst-Mey-Str. 8, 7022 Leinfelden-Echterdingen; tel. (711) 7594423; f. 1882; monthly; Editor-in-Chief KLAUS NIEHÖRSTER; circ. 60,250.

Bauernzeitung: Postfach 310448, 10634 Berlin; Wilhelmsaue 37, 10713 Berlin; e-mail bauernzeitung@bauernverlag.de; internet www.bauernzeitung.de; f. 1960; agricultural weekly; Editor RALF STEPHAN; circ. 34,000.

Bayerisches Landwirtschaftliches Wochenblatt: Postfach 200523, 80005 München; Bayerstr. 57, 80335 München; tel. (89) 53098901; fax (89) 5328537; e-mail blw@dlv.de; internet www .wochenblatt-dlv.de; f. 1810; weekly; organ of the Bayerischer Bauernverband; Editor-in-Chief JOHANNES URBAN; circ. 108,000.

Eisenbahn-Landwirt: Essen; tel. (201) 670525; f. 1918; monthly; Dir HANS HÜSKEN; circ. 120,000.

Das Landvolk: Warmbüchenstr. 3, 30159 Hannover; fax (511) 3670468; fortnightly; issued by Landbuch-Verlag GmbH; Chief Editor GÜNTHER MARTIN BEINE; circ. 98,000.

Landpost: Wollgrasweg 31, 70599 Stuttgart; tel. (711) 451275; fax (711) 456603; e-mail raiser@vdaw.de; internet www.vdaw.de; f. 1945; weekly; agriculture and gardening; Editor ERICH REICH; circ. 31,000.

Art, Drama, Architecture and Music

Art. Das Kunstmagazin: Am Baumwall 11, 20459 Hamburg; tel. (40) 37030; fax (40) 37035618; e-mail kunst@art-magazin.de; internet www.art-magazin.de; monthly; publ. by Gruner + Jahr AG; circ. 70,000.

Intelligente Architektur: Fasanenweg 18, 70771 Leinfelden-Echterdingen; tel. (711) 7591286; fax (711) 7591410; e-mail ait-red@ ait-online.de; internet www.ait-online.de; f. 1890; monthly; Editor Dr D. DANNER; circ. 16,000.

Theater der Zeit: Klosterstr. 68–70, 10179 Berlin; tel. (30) 24722414; fax (30) 24722415; e-mail tdz@mail.blinx.de; internet www.theaterderzeit.de; f. 1946; monthly; theatre, drama, opera, musical, children's theatre, puppet theatre, ballet; Editor (vacant); circ. 8,000.

Theater heute: Reinhardtstr. 29, 10117 Berlin; tel. (30) 25449510; fax (30) 25449512; e-mail redaktion@theaterheute.de; internet www .theaterheute.de; f. 1960; monthly; Editors BARBARA BURCKHARDT, EVA BEKRENDT, Dr MICHAEL MERSCHMEIER, Dr FRANZ WILLE.

Economics, Finance and Industry

Absatzwirtschaft: Postfach 101102, 40002 Düsseldorf; Kasernenstr. 67, 40213 Düsseldorf; tel. (211) 8871422; fax (211) 8871420; e-mail absatzwirtschaft@vhb.de; internet www.absatzwirtschaft.de; f. 1958; monthly; marketing; Dir UWE HOCH; Editor FRIEDHELM PÄLIKE; circ. 23,000.

Atw—Internationale Zeitschrift für Kernenergie: Postfach 101102, 40002 Düsseldorf; tel. (211) 8871442; fax (211) 8871440; e-mail w.liebholz@vhb.de; f. 1956; monthly; technical, scientific and economic aspects of nuclear engineering and technology; Editors Dr W.-M. LIEBHOLZ, E. PASCHE; circ. 4,500.

Der Betrieb: Postfach 101102, 40002 Düsseldorf; Kasernenstr. 67, 40123 Düsseldorf; tel. (211) 8871451; fax (211) 8871450; e-mail der-betrieb@vhb.de; weekly; business administration, revenue law, labour and social legislation; circ. 36,000.

Capital: Gruner + Jahr AG, 50927 Köln; tel. (221) 490800; fax (221) 4908285; e-mail capital@capital.de; internet www.capital.de; f. 1962; six a year; business magazine; circ. 219,000.

Creditreform: Postfach 1102, Kasernenstr. 67, 40002 Düsseldorf; tel. (211) 8871461; fax (211) 8871463; f. 1879; Editor KLAUS-WERNER ERNST; circ. 124,870.

Finanzwirtschaft: Am Friedrichshain 22, 10400 Berlin; tel. (30) 42151237; fax (30) 42151300; 12 a year; public-sector finance and economics; circ. 4,818.

Getränketechnik, Zeitschrift für das technische Management: Nürnberg; tel. (911) 23830; fax (911) 204956; six a year; trade journal for the brewing and beverage industries; circ. 8,518.

H&V Journal Handelsvermittlung und Vertrieb: Mainzer-Land-Str. 251, 60326 Frankfurt a.M. Siegel-Verlag Otto Müller GmbH; tel. (69) 75890950; fax (69) 75890960; e-mail hv-journal@ svffm.de; internet www.svffm.de; f. 1949; monthly; Editor Dr ANDREAS PAFFHAUSEN; circ. 17,000.

Industrie-Anzeiger: Postfach 100252, 70746 Leinfelden-Echterdingen; tel. (711) 7594452; e-mail ia.redaktion@konradin.de; internet www.industrienet.de; f. 1879; weekly; Editor-in-Chief Dr R. LANGBEIN; circ. 50,000.

Management International Review: Abraham-Lincoln-Str. 46, 65189 Wiesbaden; tel. (611) 7878230; fax (611) 7878411; quarterly; English; publ. by Gabler Verlag; Editor Prof. Dr K. MACHARZINA (Stuttgart-Hohenheim).

VDI Nachrichten: Postfach 101054, Heinrichstr. 24, 40001 Düsseldorf; tel. (211) 61880; fax (211) 6188306; e-mail redaktion@vdi-nachrichten.com; internet www.vdi-nachrichten.com; f. 1946; weekly; technology and economics; circ. 165,000.

Versicherungswirtschaft: Klosestr. 22, 76137 Karlsruhe; tel. (721) 35090; fax (721) 31833; e-mail rehnert@vvw.de; internet www .vvw.de; f. 1946; fortnightly; Editors KARL-HEINZ REHNERT, HUBERT CLEMENS; circ. 12,000.

Wirtschaftswoche: Kasernenstr. 67, 40213 Düsseldorf; tel. (211) 8770; fax (211) 887972114; e-mail wiwo@vhb.de; internet www.wiwo .de; weekly; business; Publrs Dr HEIK AFHELDT, Dr RENATE MERKLEIN; Editor STEFAN BARON; circ. 163,000.

Education and Youth

Bravo: Charles-de-Gaulle-Str. 8, 81737 München; tel. (89) 6786700; fax (89) 6702033; weekly; for young people; circ. 1,659,360.

Computer Bild: Axel-Springer-Pl. 1, 20350 Hamburg; tel. (40) 34724300; fax (40) 34724683; e-mail redaktion@computerbild.de; internet www.computerbild.de; f. 1996; publ. by Axel Springer Verlag AG; circ. 947,807.

Deutsche Lehrerzeitung: Berlin; tel. (2) 23809414; fax (2) 20183645; f. 1954; weekly for teachers; Editor RAINER WINKEL; circ. 22,000.

Erziehung und Wissenschaft: Goldammerweg 16, 45134 Essen; tel. (201) 843000; fax (201) 472590; e-mail info@stamm.de; internet www.stamm.de; f. 1948; monthly; Editor-in-Chief STEFFEN WELZEL; circ. 259,185.

Geographische Rundschau: Georg-Westermann-Allee 66, 38104 Braunschweig; tel. (531) 708385; fax (531) 708329; e-mail gr@ westermann.de; internet www.geographischerunschau.de; f. 1949; monthly; Man. Editor REINER JUENGST; circ. 12,000.

PÄDAGOGIK: Werderstr. 10, 69469 Weinheim; tel. (6201) 6007349; fax (6201) 6007354; f. 1949; monthly; Editor Prof. Dr J. BASTIAN; circ. 13,000.

Praxis Deutsch: Postfach 100150, 30917 Seelze; tel. (511) 40004139; fax (511) 40004219; e-mail redaktion.pd@friedrich-verlag .de; six a year; German language and literature; circ. 25,000.

Law

Deutsche Richterzeitung: Seufertstr. 27, 53173 Bonn; fax (228) 334723; f. 1909; monthly; circ. 11,000.

Juristenzeitung: Postfach 2040, 72010 Tübingen; Wilhelmstr. 18, 72074 Tübingen; tel. (7071) 92352; fax (7071) 92367; e-mail jz@mohr .de; f. 1944; fortnightly; Editor HEIDE SCHAPKA; circ. 6,000.

Juristische Rundschau: Postfach 303421, 10728 Berlin; Lützowstr. 33, 10785 Berlin; tel. (30) 2600123; fax (30) 26005329; e-mail wdg-info@degruyter.de; internet www.degruyter.de; f. 1922; monthly; Editors-in-Chief Prof. Dr DIRK OLZEN, Prof. Dr HERBERT TRÖNDLE.

Neue Juristische Wochenschrift: Bretsozenstr. 7B, 60325 Frankfurt a.M. tel. (69) 7560910; fax (69) 75609149; f. 1947; weekly; Editor-in-Chief R. A. MARTIN W. KEEFF; circ. 55,000.

Rabels Zeitschrift für ausländisches und internationales Privatrecht: Mittelweg 187, 20148 Hamburg; tel. (40) 41900263; fax (40) 41900288; f. 1927; quarterly; Editors JÜGEN BASEDOW, KLAUS J. HOPT, HEIN KÖTZ.

Versicherungsrecht: Klosestr. 22, 76137 Karlsruhe; tel. (721) 35090; fax (721) 31833; e-mail redaktion-versr@vvw.de; internet www.vvw.de; f. 1950; three a month; Editors Prof. Dr EGON LORENZ, KARL-HEINZ REHNERT; circ. 6,700.

Zeitschrift für die gesamte Strafrechtswissenschaft: Postfach 303421, 10728 Berlin; Lützowstr. 33, 10785 Berlin; tel. (30) 26005123; fax (30) 26005329; e-mail wdg-info@degruyter.de; internet www.degruyter.de; f. 1881; quarterly; Editor-in-Chief Prof. Dr HANS JOACHIM HIRSCH.

Politics, Literature, Current Affairs

Akzente: Vilshofener Str. 10, 81679 München; tel. (89) 998300; fax (89) 99830460; e-mail zeller@hanser.de; internet www.hanser.de; f. 1954; Editor MICHAEL KRÜGER.

Buch Aktuell: Postfach 101852/62, 44018 Dortmund; Königswall 21, 44137 Dortmund; tel. (231) 90560; fax (231) 9056110; e-mail post@harenberg.de; internet www.harenberg.de; three a year; Editor BODO HARENBERG; circ. 630,000.

Focus: Arabellastr. 23, 81925 München; tel. (89) 92500; fax (89) 92502026; e-mail anzeigen@focus.de; internet www.focus.de; f. 1993; weekly; political, general; publ. by Burda GmbH & Co KG; circ. 764,000.

Gegenwartskunde: Postfach 300551, 51334 Leverkusen (Opladen); tel. (2171) 49070; fax (2171) 490711; e-mail lesbudpubl@ aol.com; internet www.leske-budrich.de; quarterly; economics, politics, education; publ. by Leske Verlag + Budrich GmbH; Editors S. REINHARDT, H.-H. HARTWICH, B. SCHÄFERS, R. STURM.

Internationale Politik: Rauchstr. 18, 10787 Berlin; tel. (30) 25423146; fax (30) 25423167; e-mail ip@dgap.org; f. 1946; monthly; journal of the German Society for Foreign Affairs; publ. by W. Bertelsmann Verlag GmbH & Co KG, Bielefeld; Editor Prof. Dr WERNER WEIDENFELD; Exec. Editor Dr ANGELIKA VOLLE; circ. 4,800.

Literarische Welt: Axel-Springer-Str. 65, 10888 Berlin; tel. (30) 25912916; fax (30) 25912939; e-mail feuilleton@welt.de; f. 1971; weekly; literary supplement of *Die Welt*.

Merian Jahreszeiten Verlag: Harvestehuder Weg 42, 20149 Hamburg; tel. (40) 44188240; fax (40) 44188310; e-mail redaktion@ merian.de; internet www.merian.de; f. 1948; monthly; every issue deals with a country or a city; Chief Editor ANDREAS HALLASCHKA; circ. 150,000.

Merkur (Deutsche Zeitschrift für europäisches Denken): München; tel. (89) 29163111; fax (89) 29163114; internet www .merkur.de; f. 1947; monthly; literary, political; Editors KARL HEINZ BOHRER, KURT SCHEEL; circ. 6,000.

Neue Deutsche Literatur: Neue Promenade 6, 10178 Berlin; tel. (30) 28394238; fax (30) 28394100; e-mail ndl@aufbau-verlag.de; f. 1953; six a year; review of literature; Editor JÜRGEN ENGLER.

Neue Gesellschaft—Frankfurter Hefte: Hiroshimastr. 17, 10785 Berlin; tel. (30) 2693581720; fax (30) 26935855; e-mail norbert .seitz@fes.de; f. 1946; monthly; cultural, political; Editors HOLGER BÖRNER, KLAUS HARPPRECHT, JOHANNES RAU, CAROLA STERN, HANS-JOCHEN VOGEL; circ. 6,000.

Neue Rundschau: Hedderichstr. 114, 60596 Frankfurt; tel. (69) 60620; fax (69) 6062319; e-mail neuerundschau@s-fischer.de; f. 1890; quarterly; literature and essays; Editors HANS-JÜRGEN BALME, JÖRG BONG, HELMUT MAYER; circ. 3,000.

Sozialdemokrat Magazin: Am Michaelshof 8, 5300 Bonn 2; tel. (228) 361011; publ. by Vorwärts Verlag GmbH; circ. 834,599.

Der Spiegel: Brandstwiete 19/Ost-West-Str. 23, 20457 Hamburg; tel. (40) 30070; fax (40) 30072247; e-mail spiegel@spiegel.de; internet www.spiegel.de; f. 1947; weekly; political, general; Publr RUDOLF AUGSTEIN; Editor-in-Chief STEFAN AUST; circ. 1,050,000.

Universitas: Postfach 101061, 70009 Stuttgart; Birkenwaldstr. 44, 70191 Stuttgart; tel. (711) 25820; fax (711) 2582290; e-mail universitas@hirzel.de; internet www.hirzel.de/universitas; f. 1946; monthly; scientific, literary and philosophical; Editors Dr CHRISTIAN ROTTA, DIRK KATZSCHMANN; circ. 4,500.

VdK-Zeitung: Wurzerstr. 4A, 53175 Bonn; tel. (228) 820930; fax (228) 8209343; e-mail info@vdk.de; internet www.vdk.de; f. 1950; monthly; publ. by Sozialverband VdK Deutschland eV; Editors ULRICH LASCHET, SABINE KOHLS, MICHAEL PAUSDER, TANJA SCHÄFER, THOMAS A. SEEHUBER; circ. 1,000,000.

VdK-Zeitung, Bayern: Schellingstr. 31, 80799 München; tel. (89) 2117127; fax (89) 2117280; e-mail info@vdk.de; internet www .vdk-bayern.de; f. 1948; monthly; publ. by Sozialverband VdK Deutschland eV; Editor ALBRECHT ENGEL; circ. 1,100,000.

Popular

Anna: Arabellastr. 23, 81925 München; tel. (89) 92502772; fax (89) 92502745; f. 1974; publ. by Burda GmbH & Co KG; knitting and needlecrafts; Editor AENNE BURDA.

Auto Bild: Brieffach 3910, 20350 Hamburg; tel. (40) 34700; fax (40) 34727176; e-mail redaktion@autobild.de; internet www.autobild.de; f. 1986; publ. by Axel Springer Verlag AG; circ. 837,013.

Das Beste Readers Digest: Postfach 106020, 70049 Stuttgart; Augustenstr. 1, 70178 Stuttgart; tel. (711) 66020; fax (711) 6602547; e-mail verlag@dasbeste.de; internet www.dasbeste.de; magazines, general, serialized and condensed books, music and video programmes; Man. Dir WERNER NEUNZIG; circ. 1,100,000.

Bild der Frau: Axel-Springer-Pl. 1, 20355 Hamburg; tel. (40) 34700; f. 1983; publ. by Axel Springer Verlag AG; circ. 1,858,711.

Bild + Funk: München; tel. (89) 92502772; fax (89) 92502745; internet www.burda.de; publ. by Burda GmbH & Co KG; radio and television weekly; Editor GÜNTER VAN WAASEN; circ. 1,040,829.

Brigitte: Am Baumwell 11, 20459 Hamburg; tel. (40) 37030; fax (40) 37035679; internet www.brigitte.de; fortnightly; women's magazine; publ. by Gruner + Jahr AG; circ. 1,000,000.

Bunte: Arabellastr. 23, 81925 München; tel. (89) 92500; fax (89) 92503427; internet www.bunte.de; f. 1948; weekly family illustrated; publ. by Bunte Entertainment Verlag GmbH; circ. 780,238.

Burda Modemagazin: Am Destendamm 1, 77652 Offenburg; tel. (781) 840; fax (781) 843291; e-mail burdamoden@vab.burda.com; internet www.burdadamode.com; f. 1949; monthly; fashion, beauty; publ. by Verlag Aenne Burda GmbH & Co KG; circ. 1,000,000.

Deutschland: Postfach 10081, 60008 Frankfurt a.M. Frankenallee 71–81, 60327 Frankfurt a.M. tel. (69) 75010; fax (69) 75094361; e-mail vertrieb.deutschland@thein-main.net; internet www .magazine-deutschland.de; six a year; edns in German, Chinese, English, French, Hebrew, Hungarian, Japanese, Polish, Portuguese, Russian, Spanish, Turkish, Ukrainian; circ. 450,000.

Elle: Arabellastr. 23, 81925 München; tel. (89) 92500; fax (89) 92503332; e-mail elle@elle.burda.com; internet www.elle.de; monthly; publ. by ELLE Verlag GmbH.

Eltern: Weihenstephanerstr. 7, 81673 München; tel. (89) 41520; fax (89) 4152666; f. 1966; monthly; for parents; publ. by Gruner + Jahr AG; Editor ANDREA KETTERER; circ. 400,000.

Eulenspiegel: Gubener Str. 47, 10243 Berlin; tel. (30) 29346311; fax (30) 29346322; e-mail redaktion@eulenspiegel-zeitschrift.de; internet www.eulenspiegel-zeitschrift.de; f. 1946; political satirical and humorous monthly; Editors JÜRGEN NOWAK, HARTMUT BERLIN; circ. 120,000.

Familie & Co: Axel-Springer-Pl. 1, 20350 Hamburg; tel. (40) 34700; fax (40) 34727431; e-mail redaktion@familie.de; internet www .familie.de; f. 1996; monthly; publ. by Axel Springer Verlag AG; circ. 240,951.

FF: Mauerstr. 86–88, 10117 Berlin; tel. (30) 231010; fax (30) 23101265; weekly; Editor ALFRED WAGNER; circ. 610,000.

Frau aktuell: Adlerstr. 22, Düsseldorf; tel. (211) 36660; fax (211) 3666231; e-mail frauaktuell@waso.de; f. 1965; Editor INGRID THEIS; circ. 450,000.

Frau im Spiegel: Griegstr. 75, 22763 Hamburg; tel. (40) 8830305; fax (40) 88303486; women's magazine; circ. 690,861.

Freundin: Arabellastr. 23, 81925 München; tel. (89) 92500; fax (89) 92503991; e-mail freundin@burda.com; internet www.freundin.com; f. 1948; fortnightly; for young women; publ. by Burda GmbH & Co KG; Chief Editor ULRIKE SCHLÜTER; circ. 660,070.

Funk Uhr: Axel-Springer-Pl. 1, 20355 Hamburg; tel. (40) 34726315; fax (40) 726977; f. 1952; radio and television weekly; publ. by Axel Springer Verlag AG; Editor IMRE KUSZTRICH; circ. 1,305,749.

Für Dich: Karl-Liebknecht-Str. 29, 10178 Berlin; tel. (2) 2440; fax (2) 2443327; f. 1962; women's weekly; Editors Dr HANS EGGERT, PETER PANKAU; circ. 350,000.

Für Sie: Possmoorweg 5, 22301 Hamburg; tel. (40) 27172300; fax (40) 27172048; e-mail anzeigen@fuer-sie.de; internet www.fuer-sie .de; fortnightly; women's magazine; circ. 572,159.

Gong: Innere Cramer-Klett-Str. 6, 90403 Nürnberg; fax (911) 5325197; internet www.gonginfo.de; f. 1948; radio and TV weekly; Editor RAINER STILLER.

Guter Rat!: Mollstr. 1, 10178 Berlin; tel. (30) 23876600; fax (30) 23876395; e-mail redaktion@guter-rat.de; f. 1945; monthly; consumer magazine; Editor-in-Chief WERNER ZEDLER; circ. 260,000.

Hörzu: Postfach 4110, Axel-Springer-Pl. 1, 20355 Hamburg; tel. (40) 34700; fax (40) 34722628; f. 1946; radio and television; publ. by Axel Springer Verlag AG; Editor MICHAEL HOHMANN; circ. 2,300,000.

Journal für: Axel-Springer-Pl. 1, 20355 Hamburg; tel. (40) 34700; fax (40) 34727023; e-mail chefredaktion.jfdf@asv.de; f. 1978; fortnightly; women's magazine; publ. by Axel Springer Verlag AG; circ. 480,000.

Kicker-Sportmagazin: Badstr. 4–6, 90402 Nürnberg; tel. (911) 2160; e-mail info@kicker.de; internet www.kicker.de; f. 1920; two a week; illustrated sports magazine; publ. by Olympia Verlag; Man. Dir DIETRICH PUSCHMANN; circ. 270,711 (Monday), 236,677 (Thursday) (2002).

Marie Claire: Weihenstephaner Str. 7, 81673 München; tel. (89) 415200; fax (89) 4152636; e-mail marie.claire@muc.guj.de; publ. by Gruner + Jahr AG; Editor-in-chief HANS-HERMANN SPRADO; circ. 163,388.

Meine Familie & ich: Arabellastr. 23, 81925 München; tel. (89) 92500; fax (89) 92503030; publ. by Burda GmbH & Co KG; circ. 620,000.

Neue Post: Postfach 2427, Burchardstr. 11, 20095 Hamburg; weekly; circ. 1,728,750.

Neue Revue: Postfach 2411, Ost-West-Str. 20, 20077 Hamburg; tel. (40) 30190; fax (40) 30194401; e-mail neue-revue@hbv.de; f. 1946; illustrated weekly; Editor-in-Chief PETER BARTEL; circ. 1,121,184.

Petra: Jahreszeiten Verlag, Possmoorweg 1, 22301 Hamburg; tel. (40) 27173009; fax (40) 27173020; e-mail redaktion@petra.de; internet www.petra.de; monthly; circ. 331,725.

Praline: Hammerbrookstr. 5, 20097 Hamburg; fax (40) 24870190; weekly; women's magazine; circ. 569,300.

Schöner Wohnen: Am Baumwall 11, 20459 Hamburg; tel. (40) 37032701; monthly; homes and gardens; publ. by Gruner + Jahr AG; Editor ANGELIKA JAHR; circ. 327,000.

7 Tage: Postfach 100450, 76485 Baden-Baden; Stadelhofer Str. 14, 76530 Baden-Baden; tel. (7221) 3501391; fax (7221) 3501399; f. 1843; weekly; Chief Editor KARIN KARSTEN; circ. 480,000.

Sport Bild: Axel-Springer-Pl. 1, 20350 Hamburg; tel. (40) 34724250; fax (40) 34724382; e-mail sportbild@asv.de; internet www .sportbild.de; f. 1988; weekly; publ. by Axel Springer Verlag AG; circ. 522,717.

Stern: 20444 Hamburg; tel. (40) 37030; fax (40) 37035631; e-mail info@stern.de; internet www.stern.de; illustrated weekly; publ. by Gruner + Jahr AG; Editors-in-Chief THOMAS OSTERKORN, ANDREAS PETZOLD; circ. 1,102,075.

TV Hören + Sehen: Burchardstr. 11, 20095 Hamburg; tel. (40) 30194001; fax (40) 30194081; f. 1962; weekly; Chief Editor MARION HORN; circ. 2,936,670.

TVneu: Axel-Springer-Pl. 1, 20355 Hamburg; tel. (40) 34700; fax (40) 345811; publ. by Axel Springer Verlag AG; circ. 917,293.

Wochenend: Burchardstr. 11, 20095 Hamburg; tel. (40) 30190; fax (40) 30194081; f. 1948; weekly; Editor GERD ROHLOF; circ. 668,278.

Religion and Philosophy

Christ in der Gegenwart: Hermann-Herder-Str. 4, 79104 Freiburg i. Br. tel. (761) 2717276; fax (761) 2717518; e-mail cig@herder .de; f. 1948; weekly; Editor JOHANNES RÖSER; circ. 36,000.

Der Dom: Karl-Schurz-Str. 26, 33100 Paderborn; tel. (5251) 1530; fax (5251) 153104; e-mail karl.wegner@bonifatius.de; internet www .derdom.org; f. 1946; weekly; Catholic; publ. by Bonifatius GmbH, Druck-Buch-Verlag; circ. 65,000.

Europa Magazin: Postfach 104864, Landhausstr. 82, 70190 Stuttgart; tel. (711) 285500; fax (711) 2855083; e-mail verlag@ europamagazin.de; f. 1949; six a year; publ. by Verlag Axel B. Trunkel.

Evangelischer Digest: Postfach 104864, Landhausstr. 82, 70190 Stuttgart; tel. (711) 285500; fax (711) 2855083; e-mail verlag@ trunkel.de; internet www.trunkel.de; f. 1958; monthly; publ. by Verlag Axel B. Trunkel; circ. 9,300.

Katholischer Digest: Postfach 104864, Landhausstr. 82, 70190 Stuttgart; tel. (711) 285500; fax (711) 2855083; e-mail verlag@ trunkel.de; internet www.trunkel.de; f. 1949; monthly; publ. by Verlag Axel B. Trunkel; circ. 28,900.

Katholisches Sonntagsblatt: Senefelderstr. 12, 73760 Ostfildern; tel. (711) 44060; fax (711) 4406101; e-mail ks@schwabenverlag.de; internet www.schwabenverlag.de; f. 1848; weekly; publ. by Schwabenverlag AG; circ. 71,500.

Katholische Sonntagszeitung für Deutschland—Die Christliche Familie: Ruhrtalstr. 52–60, 45239 Essen; tel. (201) 8492411; f. 1885; weekly; Publr Dr DIRK HERMANN VOSS; Chief Editor CORNELIA SCHAFFOLD.

Die Kirche: Berlin; tel. (30) 28303922; fax (30) 2829321; f. 1945; Protestant weekly; Editors-in-Chief GERHARD THOMAS, LUTZ BORGMANN; circ. 35,000.

Kirche und Leben: Postfach 4320, 48024 Münster; Breul 27, 48143 Münster; tel. (251) 48390; fax (251) 4839122; e-mail k-und-l@ muenster.de; internet www.kirche-und-leben.muenster.de; f. 1945; weekly; Catholic; Chief Editor Dr HANS-JOSEF JOEST; circ. 160,000.

Kirchenzeitung für das Erzbistum Köln: Postfach 102041, 50460 Köln; Ursulapl. 1, 50668 Köln; tel. (221) 1619131; fax (221) 1619216; weekly; Chief Editor Mgr ERICH LÄUFER; circ. 120,000.

Philosophisches Jahrbuch: Ludwig-Maximilians-Universität, Geschwister-Scholl-Pl. 1, 80539 München; f. 1893; two a year.

Der Sonntagsbrief: Postfach 104864, Landhausstr. 82, 70190 Stuttgart; tel. (711) 285500; fax (711) 2855083; e-mail verlag@

trunkel.de; internet www.trunkel.de; f. 1974; monthly; publ. by Verlag Axel B. Trunkel; circ. 36,000.

Standpunkt: Berlin; tel. (2) 6350915; f. 1973; Protestant monthly; circ. 3,000.

Der Weg: Postfach 102253, 40013 Düsseldorf; tel. (211) 915110; e-mail wegredaktion@wegredaktion.de; weekly; Protestant; Editor ANDREAS KRZOK; circ. 50,000.

Weltbild: 86131 Augsburg; tel. (821) 70048350; fax (821) 70048349; f. 2001; fortnightly; Catholic; Editor ALBERT HERCHENBACH; circ. 270,000.

Science and Medicine

Angewandte Chemie: Postfach 101161, 69451 Weinheim; tel. (6201) 606315; fax (6201) 602328; e-mail angewandte@wiley-vch.de; f. 1888; fortnightly; circ. 4,000; international edition in English, f. 1962; circ. 3,000.

Ärztliche Praxis: Gräfelfing; tel. (89) 898170; fax (89) 89817120; two a week; Editor WOLFRAM HAASE; circ. 60,000.

Berichte der Bunsen-Gesellschaft für physikalische Chemie: VCH Verlagsgesellschaft mbH, Postfach 101161, Pappelallee 3, 69451 Weinheim/Bergstr. tel. (6201) 6060; f. 1894; monthly; Editors R. AHLRICHS, W. FREYLAND, M. KAPPES, P. C. SCHMIDT; circ. 2,300.

Chemie-Ingenieur-Technik: Postfach 101161, 69451 Weinheim; tel. (6201) 606520; fax (6201) 606500; e-mail cit@wiley-vch.de; f. 1928; monthly; Editor B. BOECK; circ. 7,807.

Der Chirurg: Kirschnerstr. 1 (INF 110), 69120 Heidelberg; tel. (6221) 402813; fax (6221) 402014; f. 1928; monthly; Editor Prof. Dr Ch. HERFARTH; circ. 7,650.

Deutsche Apotheker Zeitung: Postfach 101061, 70009 Stuttgart; Birkenwaldstr. 44, 70191 Stuttgart; tel. (711) 2582238; fax (711) 2582291; e-mail daz@deutscher-apotheker-verlag.de; internet www .deutscher-apotheker-verlag.de; f. 1861; weekly; Editor PETER DITZEL; circ. 34,000.

Deutsche Medizinische Wochenschrift: Rüdigerstr. 14, 70469 Stuttgart; tel. (711) 8931232; fax (711) 8931235; e-mail dmw@ thieme.de; internet www.thieme.de/dmw; f. 1875; weekly; Editor-in-Chief M. MIDDEKE; circ. 30,000.

Deutsche Zahnärztliche Zeitschrift: Deutscher Ärzte-Verlag, Dieselstr. 2, 50859 Köln; tel. (2234) 7011242; fax (2234) 7011515; e-mail dey@aerzteverlag.de; internet www.zahnheilkunde.de; f. 1945; monthly; dental medicine; Editors Prof. Dr GEURTSEN, Prof. Dr TH. KERSCHBAUM, Dr G. MASCHINSKI; circ. 5,300.

Elektro Automation: Ernst-Mey-Str. 8, 70771 Leinfelden-Echterdingen; tel. (711) 7594279; fax (711) 7594221; e-mail ea.redaktion@ konradin.de; internet www.ea-online.de; f. 1948; monthly; Editor-in-Chief STEFAN ZIEGLER; circ. 21,100.

Europa Chemie: Frankfurt a.M. tel. (69) 25561516; fax (69) 239564; e-mail europa-chemie@metronet.de; f. 1949; three a month; industrial chemistry, the environment and economics; Editor-in-Chief Dr G. SCHRIMPF; circ. 2,800.

Geologische Rundschau: Geologische Vereinigung e.V., Vulkanstr. 23, 56743 Mendig; tel. (2652) 989360; fax (2652) 989361; e-mail geol.ver@t-online.de; internet www.g-v.de; f. 1910; six a year; general, geological; Pres. Prof. Dr D. BERNOULLI; circ. 2,000.

Handchirurgie, Mikrochirurgie, Plastische Chirurgie: Postfach 300504, 70445 Stuttgart; Rüdigerstr. 14, 70469 Stuttgart; tel. (711) 89310; fax (711) 8931453; 6 a year; Editors Prof. Dr D. BUCK-GRAMCKO, Prof. Dr W. SCHNEIDER.

Journal of Neurology: Steinkopff Verlag, Poststr. 9, 64293 Darmstadt; tel. (6151) 828990; fax (6151) 8289940; e-mail tschech .steinkopff@springer.de; internet www.steinkopff.springer.de; f. 1891; official journal of the European Neurological Society; Editors-in-Chief T. BRANDT, D. H. MILLER.

Kosmos: Postfach 106012, Neckarstr. 121, 7000 Stuttgart 10; tel. (711) 26310; fax (711) 2631107; f. 1904; monthly; popular nature journal; Editor Dr RAINER KÖTHE; circ. 80,000.

Mund-, Kiefer- und Gesichtschirurgie: Glückstr. 11, 91054 Erlangen; tel. (9131) 8533601; fax (9131) 8536228; e-mail friedrich .neukam@mkg.imed.uni-erlangen.de; internet www.mkg .uni-erlangen.de; seven a year; oral and maxillofacial surgery and oral pathology; Editor Prof. Dr FRIEDRICH W. NEUKAM.

Medizinische Klinik: München; tel. (89) 532920; fax (89) 53292100; e-mail verlag@urban-vogel.de; internet www.urban-vogel .de; f. 1904; monthly; Editor Prof. Dr J. KÖBBERLING; circ. 10,000.

Nachrichten aus der Chemie: Postfach 900440, 60444 Frankfurt a.M. tel. (69) 7917462; fax (69) 7917463; e-mail nachrichten@gdch .de; internet www.gdch.de/nch; f. 1953; monthly; journal of the German Chemical Society; Editor-in-Chief Dr ERNST GUGGOLZ; circ. 30,000.

Naturwissenschaftliche Rundschau: Postfach 101061, 70009 Stuttgart; Birkenwaldstr. 44, 70191 Stuttgart; tel. (711) 2582295; fax (711) 2582283; e-mail nr@wissenschaftliche-verlagsgesellschaft .de; f. 1948; monthly; scientific; Editor KLAUS REHFELD; circ. 5,000.

Planta Medica: Postfach 301120, 70451 Stuttgart, Georg Thieme Verlag, Rüdigerstr. 14, 70469 Stuttgart; tel. (711) 89310; fax (711) 8931298; e-mail leser.service@thieme.de; f. 1952; 12 a year; journal of the Society of Medicinal Plant Research; Editor Prof. Dr ADOLF NAHRSTEDT.

Rfe: Am Friedrichshain 22, 10407 Berlin; tel. (30) 42151313; fax (30) 42151208; f. 1952; monthly; technology and marketing of consumer goods electronics, multimedia, audio, video, broadcasting, TV; circ. 30,000.

Zahnärztliche Praxis: München-Gräfelfing; tel. (89) 898170; fax (89) 853799; monthly; circ. 16,500.

Zeitschrift für Allgemeinmedizin: Postfach 300504, 70445 Stuttgart; Steiermärker Str. 3–5, 70469 Stuttgart; tel. (711) 89310; fax (711) 8931706; e-mail sabine.merkens@medizinverlage.de; f. 1924; fortnightly; general and family medicine; publ. by Hippokrates Verlag in MVS, Medizinverlage Stuttgart, GmbH & Co KG; Editors Dr W. MAHRINGER, Dr U. MARSCH-ZIEGLER, Prof. Dr M. KOCHEN, Prof. Dr H.-H. ABHOLZ, Dr W. NIEBLING; circ. 4,000.

Zeitschrift für Klinische Psychologie, Psychiatrie u. Psychotherapie: Postfach 2540, Jühenpl. am Rathaus, 33055 Paderborn; f. 1952; quarterly; Editor Prof. Dr F. PETERMANN.

Zeitschrift für Metallkunde: Heisenbergstr. 5, 70569 Stuttgart; tel. (711) 6893520; fax (711) 6893522; f. 1911; monthly; materials research; Editors G. PETZOW, M. RÜHLE, P. P. SCHEPP.

Zeitschrift für Zahnärztliche Implantologie: Deutscher Zahnärzte-Verlag, Dieselstr. 2, 50859 Köln; tel. (2234) 7011242; fax (2234) 7011515; e-mail dey@aerzteverlag.de; internet www .zahnheilkunde.de; f. 1984; quarterly; dental medicine; Editors Prof. Dr V. STRUNZ, Prof. Dr H. SPIEKERMANN, Prof. Dr W. WAGNER; circ. 1,700.

Zentralblatt für Neurochirurgie: Friedrich-Wilhelms Universität, Sigmund-Freud-Str. 25, 53127 Bonn; tel. (228) 2876521; fax (228) 2876573; f. 1936; four a year; neuro-surgery, spine surgery, traumatology; Editor Prof. Dr J. SCHRAMM; circ. 1,200.

NEWS AGENCIES

DDP Nachrichtenagentur GmbH: Friedrichstr. 108, 10117 Berlin; tel. (30) 2312210; fax (30) 23122170; e-mail redaktion@ddp .de; internet www.ddp.de; f. 1946; fmrly official news agency of the GDR; maintains 32 branch offices in Germany; provides a daily news service and features in German; Man. Dirs LUTZ SCHUMACHER, ALEXANDER ROP.

Deutsche Presse-Agentur GmbH (dpa): Mittelweg 38, 20148 Hamburg; tel. (40) 41130; fax (40) 41132219; e-mail info@dpa.de; f. 1949; supplies all the daily newspapers, broadcasting stations and more than 1,000 further subscribers throughout Germany with its national and regional text, photo, audio, graphics and online services. English, Spanish, Arabic and German language news is also transmitted via direct satellite and the internet to press agencies, newspapers, radio and television stations, online services and non-media clients in more than 100 countries; Dir-Gen. Dr WALTER RICHTBERG; Editor-in-Chief Dr WILM HERLYN.

VWD: Niederurseler Allee 8–10, 65760 Eschborn; tel. (6196) 4050; fax (6196) 405303; e-mail feedback@vwd.de; internet www.vwd.de; f. 1849; economic and financial news; Man. Dirs MICHAEL FRANK, SPENCER BOSSE.

Foreign Bureaux

Agence France-Presse (AFP): Friedrichstr. 108–109, 10117 Berlin; tel. (30) 30876110; fax (30) 30876270; e-mail post@afp.de; internet www.afp.de; Mans N. C. WORTMANN, P. FEUILLY.

Agencia EFE (Spain): Heussallee 2–10, Pressehaus II/12–14, 53113 Bonn; tel. (228) 214058; fax (228) 224147; Bureau Chief GUILLERMO DÍAZ.

Agenzia Nazionale Stampa Associata (ANSA) (Italy): Berlin; tel. (30) 726262500; fax (30) 726262525; Bureau Chief FLAMINIA BUSSOTTI.

Associated Press GmbH (AP) (USA): Moselstr. 27, Frankfurt a.M; tel. (69) 272300; fax (69) 251289; also in Hamburg, Stuttgart, Berlin, München; Man. STEPHEN H. MILLER.

Česká tisková kancelář (ČTK) (Czech Republic): Heussallee 2–10, Pressehaus I/207, 53113 Bonn; tel. (228) 215811; fax 214189; f. 1918; Correspondent FRANTIŠEK VACLAVIK.

Informatsionnoye Telegrafnoye Agentstvo Rossii-Telegrafnoye Agentstvo Suverennykh Stran (ITAR-TASS) (Russia):

Heussallee 2–10, Pressehaus I/133, 53113 Bonn; tel. (228) 215665; fax (228) 210627.

Inter Press Service (IPS) (Italy): Tulpenfeld 7, 53113 Bonn; tel. (228) 9145710; fax (228) 261205; Bureau Chief Ramesh Jaura.

Jiji Tsushin (Japan): Mittelweg 38, 20148 Hamburg; tel. (40) 445553; fax (40) 456849.

Kyodo Tsushin (Japan): Bonn; tel. (228) 225543; fax (228) 222198; Chief Correspondent Kakuya Ogata.

Magyar Távirati Iroda (MTI) (Hungary): Heussallee 2–10, Pressehaus I/202, 53113 Bonn; tel. (228) 210820; fax (228) 210821; Correspondent László Dorogman.

Reuters (UK): Friedrich-Ebert-Anlage 49, 60327 Frankfurt a.M. tel. (69) 75651000; fax (69) 75651515; internet www.reuters.de.

United Press International (UPI) (USA): Bonn; tel. (228) 263787; Bureau Man. and Chief Correspondent Peter G. Bild.

Xinhua (New China) News Agency (People's Republic of China): Lyngsbergstr. 33, 5300 Bonn 2; tel. (228) 331845; fax (228) 331247; Chief Correspondent Hu Xudong.

RIA—Novosti (Russia) is also represented.

PRESS AND JOURNALISTS' ASSOCIATIONS

Bundesverband Deutscher Zeitungsverleger eV (German Newspaper Publishers' Association): Markgrafenstr. 15, 10969 Berlin; tel. (30) 7262980; fax (30) 726298299; e-mail bdzv@bdzv.de; internet www.bdzv.de; 11 affiliated Land Asscns; Pres. Helmut Heinen; Chief Sec. Dr Volker Schulze.

Deutscher Journalisten-Verband (German Journalists' Association): Bennauerstr. 60, 53115 Bonn; tel. (228) 201720; fax (228) 2017233; e-mail djv@djv.de; internet www.djv.de; Chair. Prof. Dr Sigfried Weischenberg; Man. Dir Hubert Engeroff; 16 Land Asscns.

Verband Deutscher Zeitschriftenverleger eV (Association of German Periodical Publishers): Markgrafenstr. 15, 10969 Berlin; tel. (30) 726298101; fax (30) 7262898103; e-mail info@vdz.de; internet www.vdz.de; seven affiliated Land Asscns; Pres. Dr Hubert Burda; Man. Dir Wolfgang Fürstner.

Verein der Ausländischen Presse (VAP) (Foreign Press Association): Heussallee 2–10, Pressehaus I/35, 53113 Bonn; tel. (228) 210885; fax (228) 219672; f. 1951; Chair. Ahmet Külahci.

Publishers

The following is a selection of the most prominent German publishing firms:

ADAC Verlag GmbH: Am Westpark 8, 81373 München; tel. (89) 76760; fax (89) 76764621; e-mail clare.billig@zentrale.adac.de; internet www.adac.de; f. 1958; guidebooks, legal brochures, maps, magazines ADAC-Motorwelt, Deutsches Autorecht; Man. Dir Manfred M. Angele.

Ariston Verlag GmbH & Co KG: München; tel. (89) 7241034; fax (89) 7241718; f. 1964; medicine, psychology; Man. Dir Frank Auerbach.

Aufbau-Verlag GmbH: Neue Promenade 6, 10178 Berlin; tel. (30) 283940; fax (30) 28394100; e-mail info@aufbau-verlag.de; f. 1945; fiction, non-fiction, classical literature; Dirs Peter Dempewolf, René Strien.

J. P. Bachem Verlag GmbH: Ursulapl. 1, 50668 Köln; tel. (221) 16190; fax (221) 1619159; f. 1818; economics, social science, religion; Dirs Dr Clemens J. B. Sandmann, Lambert Bachem.

Bauverlag GmbH: Am Klingenweg 4A, 65396 Walluf; tel. (61213) 7000; fax (61213) 700122; f. 1929; civil engineering, architecture, environment, energy, etc. Dirs Otto Gmeiner, Reiner Grochowski.

Verlag C. H. Beck oHg: Postfach 400340, 80703 München, Wilhelmstr. 9, 80801 München; tel. (89) 381890; fax (89) 38189398; e-mail info@beck.de; internet www.beck.de; f. 1763; law, science, theology, archaeology, philosophy, philology, history, politics, art, literature; Dirs Dr Hans Dieter Beck, Wolfgang Beck.

Bertelsmann Buch AG: Neumarkterstr. 18, 81673 München; tel. (89) 43720; fax (89) 43722938; f. 1994; general, reference; Chair. Frank Wössner.

Bibliographisches Institut und F. A. Brockhaus GmbH: Postfach 100311, 68167 Dudenstr. 6, 68003 Mannheim; tel. (621) 390101; fax (621) 3901391; f. 1805; encyclopaedias, dictionaries, travel, natural sciences, memoirs, archaeology; Dirs Hubertus Brockhaus, Claus Greuner, Dr Michael Wegner.

BLV Verlagsgesellschaft mbH: Lothstr. 29, 80797 München; tel. (89) 127050; fax (89) 12705354; e-mail blv-verlag@t-online.de; internet www.blv.de; f. 1946; gardening, nature, sports, fitness;

equestrian, hunting, fishing, travel, food and drink, agriculture; Man. Dirs Hartwig Schneider (books), Hans-Peter Kliemann (magazines).

Breitkopf & Härtel: Postfach 1707, Walkmühlstr. 52, 65195 Wiesbaden; tel. (611) 450080; fax (611) 4500859; e-mail info@breitkopf.com; internet www.breitkopf.com; f. 1719; music and music books; Dirs Lieselotte Sievers, Gottfried Möckel.

Brönner Verlag GmbH: Stuttgarter Str. 18–24, 6000 Frankfurt a.M. tel. (69) 26000; fax (69) 2600223; art; Dirs Klaus Breidenstein, Hans-Jürgen Breidenstein.

Verlag Bruckmann München: Innsbrucker Ring 15, 81673 München; tel. (89) 1306990; fax (89) 13069930; f. 1858; travel guides, illustrated travel books, video cassettes; Man. Dir Dr Jörg D. Stiebner.

Bund-Verlag GmbH: Postfach 900168, 60441 Frankfurt; Theodor-Heuss-Allee 90–98, 60486 Frankfurt; tel. (69) 7950100; fax (69) 79501010; e-mail kontakt@bund-verlag.de; internet www.bund-verlag.de; f. 1947; legal studies and commentaries, economics, politics, etc. Man. Dirs Christian Poulsen, Norbert Schaepe.

Verlag Georg D. W. Callwey GmbH & Co: Streitfeldstr. 35, 81673 München; tel. (89) 4360050; fax (89) 436005113; e-mail buch@callwey.de; internet www.callwey.de; f. 1884; architecture, painting, gardens, art restoration, crafts, do-it-yourself; Man. Dir Detlef Kotte.

Carlsen Verlag GmbH: Postfach 500380, 22703 Hamburg; Völckersstr. 14–20, 22765 Hamburg; tel. (40) 398040; fax (40) 39804390; e-mail info@carlsen.de; internet www.carlsen.de; f. 1953; children's and comic books; Dirs Klaus Humann, Klaus Kämpfe-Burghardt.

Cornelsen Verlag GmbH & Co: Mecklenburgische Str. 53, 14197 Berlin; tel. (30) 897850; fax (30) 89786299; e-mail c-mail@cornelsen.de; internet www.cornelsen.de; f. 1946; school textbooks, educational software; Man. Dirs Hans-Jörg Düllemann, Alfred Grüner, Wolf-Rüdger Feldmann, Martin Hüppe, Dr Hans Weymar.

Delius Klasing Verlag: Siekerwall 21, 33602 Bielefeld; tel. (521) 5590; fax (521) 559113; e-mail info@delius-klasing.de; internet www.delius-klasing.de; f. 1911; yachting, motor boats, surfing, mountain biking, race biking, basketball, motor cars; Dir Konrad Delius.

Deutsche Verlags-Anstalt GmbH: Postfach 106012, 70049 Stuttgart; Neckarstr. 121, 70190 Stuttgart; tel. (711) 26310; fax (711) 2631292; e-mail info@dva.de; f. 1831; general; CEO Jürgen Horbach.

Deutscher Taschenbuch Verlag GmbH & Co KG (DTV): Postfach 400422, 80704 München; Friedrichstr. 1A, 80801 München; tel. (89) 381670; fax (89) 346428; e-mail verlag@dtv.de; internet www.dtv.de; f. 1961; general fiction, history, music, reference, children, natural and social science, medicine, textbooks; Man. Dirs Wolfgang Balk, Markus Angst.

Verlag Moritz Diesterweg: Hedderichstr. 108–110, 60596 Frankfurt a.M. tel. (69) 420810; fax (69) 42081200; internet www.diesterweg.de; f. 1860; text books, languages, social sciences, sciences, pedagogics; Dirs Ralf Meier, Ulrich Pokern.

Droemersche Verlagsanstalt Th. Knaur Nachf GmbH & Co: Rauchstr. 9–11, 81679 München; tel. (89) 92710; fax (89) 9271168; f. 1901; general literature, non-fiction, art books, paperbacks; Man. Dirs Dr Peter Schaper, Günther Fetzer.

DuMont Monte GmbH & Co KG: Amsterdamer Str. 192, 50735 Köln; tel. (221) 2241831; fax (221) 2241878; e-mail montevertrieb@dumontverlag.de; internet www.dumontverlag.de; f. 1956; art, garden, cookery, calendars; Publr Helena Bommetsheim.

Econ Verlagsgruppe: Postfach 151329, Goethestr. 43, 80336 München; fax (89) 5148229; e-mail michael.then@verlag.goethestr.com; general fiction and non-fiction, business and computing books; Publr Christian Strasser; Editor-in-Chief Margit Ketterle.

Egmont Pestalozzi Verlag GmbH: Schleissheimer Str. 267, 80809 München; tel. (89) 358116; fax (89) 35811869; internet www.pestalozzi-verlag.de; f. 1844; children's books; Man. Dirs Rehné Herzig, Frank Knau.

Egmont vgs verlagsgesellschaft mbH: Gertrudenstr. 30–36, 50667 Köln; tel. (221) 208110; fax (221) 2081166; e-mail info@vgs.de; internet www.vgs.de; f. 1970; fiction, hobbies, natural sciences, culture, popular culture, TV, history; Dirs Dr Michael Schweins, Bernward Malaka.

Eichborn Verlag: Kaiserstr. 66, 60329 Frankfurt a.M. 1; tel. (69) 2560030; fax (69) 25600330; f. 1980; literature non-fiction, historical science, humour, cartoons; Man. Dir Dr Matthias Kierzek.

Europaverlag: München; tel. (89) 9827790; fax (89) 98277950; e-mail info@europaverlag.de; fiction, non-fiction, poetry, biography and current events; Dirs Gisela Anna Stümpel, Wolfgang Weidmann.

Falk-Verlag GmbH: Hamburg; tel. (40) 725990; fax (40) 72599200; f. 1945; maps, guidebooks, phrasebooks; Man. Dir Dr HELGE LINTZ-HÖFT.

Falken-Verlag GmbH: Schöne Aussicht 21, 65527 Niedernhausen; tel. (6127) 7020; fax (6127) 702133; internet www.falken.de; f. 1923; health, cooking, management, business; Man. Dir Dr HANS-ULRICH VON FREYBERG.

S. Fischer Verlag GmbH: Postfach 700355, 60553 Frankfurt a.M. Hedderichstr. 114, 60596 Frankfurt a.M. tel. (69) 60620; fax (69) 6062319; e-mail info@s-fischer.de; internet www.s-fischer.de; f. 1886; general, paperbacks; Publr MONIKA SCHOELLER; Man. Dirs LOTHAR KLEINER.

Franzis' Verlag GmbH: Gruber Str. 46, 85586 Poing; tel. (8121) 950; fax (8121) 951696; internet www.franzis.de; f. 1924; Gen. Man. Dr RÜDIGER HENNIGS.

Gräfe und Unzer Verlag GmbH: Grillparzer Str. 12, 81675 München; tel. (89) 419810; fax (89) 41981113; internet www .graefe-und-unzer.de; f. 1722; cookery, health, nature, travel, business; Man. Dirs Dr STEFAN HOYER, GEORG KESSLER, GÜNTER KOPIETZ.

Walter de Gruyter GmbH & Co KG Verlag: Postfach 303421, 10728 Berlin; Genthiner Str. 13, 10785 Berlin; tel. (30) 260050; fax (30) 26005251; internet www.degruyter.de; f. 1919; humanities and theology, law, science, medicine, mathematics, economics, general; Man. Dirs REINHOLD TOKAR, Dr HANS-ROBERT CRAM.

Hallwag Verlag GmbH: 73760 Ostfildern; tel. (711) 449840; fax (711) 44984-60; maps, travel guides, wine, other reference.

Carl Hanser Verlag: Kolbergerstr. 22, 81679 München; tel. (89) 998300; fax (89) 984809; e-mail info@hanser.at; internet www .hanser.de; f. 1928; modern literature, plastics, technology, chemistry, science, economics, computers, children's books; Man. Dirs WOLFGANG BEISLER, STEPHAN D. JOSS, MICHAEL KRÜGER.

Harenberg Kommunikation Verlags- und Mediengesellschaft mbH & Co KG: Postfach 101852, 44018 Dortmund; Königswall 21, 44137 Dortmund; tel. (231) 90560; fax (231) 9056110; e-mail post@harenberg.de; internet www.harenberg.de; f. 1973; almanacs, encyclopaedias, calendars, periodicals; Man. Dir BODO HARENBERG.

Rudolf Haufe Verlag GmbH & Co KG: Hindenburgstr. 64, 79102 Freiburg i. Br. tel. (761) 36830; fax (761) 3683195; e-mail online@ haufe.de; internet haufe.de; f. 1934; business, law, taxation, information management, finance, social science; Man. Dirs UWE RENALD MÜLLER, MARTIN LAQUA, HELMUTH HOPFNER.

Verlag Herder GmbH & Co KG: Hermann-Herder-Str. 4; 79104 Freiburg i. Br. tel. (761) 27170; fax (761) 2717520; e-mail info@ herder.de; internet www.herder.de; f. 1801; religion, philosophy, psychology, history, education, art, encyclopaedias, children's books, gift books, periodicals; Proprs Dr HERMANN HERDER, MANUEL GREGOR HERDER.

Wilhelm Heyne Verlag: Paul-Heyse-Str. 28, 80336 München; tel. (89) 51480; fax (89) 51482229; e-mail verlag@heyne.de; internet www.heyne.de; f. 1934; fiction, biography, history, cinema, etc. Publr ULRICH GENZLER.

Hoffmann und Campe Verlag: Postfach 1304445, 20139 Hamburg; Harvestehuderweg 42, 20149 Hamburg; tel. (40) 441880; fax (40) 44188202; e-mail claudia.fischer@hoca.de; internet www .hoffmann-und-campe.de; f. 1781; biography, fiction, history, economics, science; Man. Dirs Dr RAINER MORITZ, UWE MARSEN.

Dr Alfred Hüthig Verlag GmbH: Im Weiher 10, 6900 Heidelberg; tel. (6221) 4890; fax (6221) 489279; f. 1925; chemistry, chemical engineering, metallurgy, dentistry, etc.

Axel Juncker-Verlag: Postfach 401120, 80711 München; Miesvan-der-Rohe-Str. 1, 80807 München; tel. (89) 360960; fax (89) 36096222; e-mail redaktion@axel-juncker.de; internet www .langenscheidt.de; f. 1902; dictionaries, language courses, reference; Man. Dirs KARL ERNST TIELEBIER-LANGENSCHEIDT, ANDREAS LANGEN-SCHEIDT.

S. Karger GmbH: Lörracherstr. 16A, 79115 Freiburg; tel. (761) 452070; fax (761) 4520714; f. 1890; medicine, psychology, natural science; Man. Dir S. KARGER.

Gustav Kiepenheuer Verlag: Gerichtsweg 28, 04103 Leipzig; tel. (341) 9954600; fax (341) 9954620; internet www.aufbau-verlag.de; f. 1910; fiction, non-fiction, cultural history; Chief Editor BIRGIT PETER.

Verlag Kiepenheuer & Witsch & Co: Rondorferstr. 5, 50968 Köln 51; tel. (221) 376850; fax (221) 388595; e-mail umolitor@kiwi-koeln .de; internet www.kiwi-koeln.de; f. 1948; general fiction, biography, history, sociology, politics; Man. Dir Dr REINHOLD NEVEN DU MONT.

Ernst Klett Verlag GmbH: Postfach 106016, 70049 Stuttgart; Rotebühlstr. 77, 70178 Stuttgart; tel. (711) 66720; fax (711) 6672800; internet www.klett.de; f. 1844; secondary school and university textbooks (especially German as a foreign language), dictionaries,

atlases, teaching aids; Dirs MICHAEL KLETT, ROLAND KLETT, Dr THOMAS KLETT.

Verlag W. Kohlhammer GmbH: Hessbrühlstr. 69, 70565 Stuttgart; tel. (711) 78630; fax (711) 7863263; f. 1866; periodicals, general textbooks; Man. Dirs Dr JÜRGEN GUTBROD, HANS-JOACHIM NAGEL.

Kösel-Verlag GmbH & Co: Flüggenstr. 2, 80639 München; tel. (89) 178010; fax (89) 17801111; e-mail info@koesel.de; internet www .koesel.de; f. 1593; philosophy, religion, psychology, esoteric, family and education; Dir Dr CHRISTOPH WILD.

Kreuz Verlag GmbH: Postfach 800669; Breitwiesenstr. 30, 70565 Stuttgart; tel. (711) 788030; fax (711) 7880310; f. 1983; theology, psychology, pedagogics; Man. Dir Dr SABINE SCHUBERT.

Verlag der Kunst GmbH: Rosa-Menzer-Str. 12, 01309 Dresden; tel. (351) 3100052; fax (351) 3105245; e-mail verlag-der-kunst.dd@ t-online.de; internet www.txt.de/vdk; f. 1952; art books and reproductions; Dir ROGER N. GREENE.

Peter Lang GmbH—Europäischer Verlag der Wissenschaften: Postfach 940225, 60460 Frankfurt a.M. Eschborner Landstr. 42–50, 60489 Frankfurt a.M. tel. (69) 7807050; fax (69) 78075500; e-mail zentrale.Frankfurt@peterlang.com; internet www .peterlang.de; sociology, politics, communications, linguistics, science of law, literature, theology, economics.

Langenscheidt-Verlag: Postfach 401120, 80711 München; Miesvan-der-Rohe Str. 1, 80807 München; tel. (89) 360960; fax (89) 36096222; e-mail mail@langenscheidt.de; internet www .langenscheidt.de; f. 1856; foreign languages, German for foreigners, dictionaries, textbooks, language guides, records, cassettes, video cassettes, software, electronic dictionaries; Man. Dirs KARL ERNST TIELEBIER-LANGENSCHEIDT, ANDREAS LANGENSCHEIDT.

Gustav Lübbe Verlag GmbH: Scheidtbachstr. 23–25, 51469 Bergisch Gladbach; tel. (2202) 1210; internet www.luebbe.de; f. 1964; general fiction and non-fiction, biography, history, etc. Man. Dirs PETER MOLDEN, KARLHEINZ JUNGBECK.

Hermann Luchterhand Verlag GmbH: Postfach 2352, 56513 Neuwied; Heddesdorfer Str. 31, 56564 Neuwied; tel. (2631) 8010; fax (2631) 801204; e-mail info@luchterhand.de; internet www .luchterhand.de; f. 1924; insurance, law, taxation, labour; Man. Dir J. LUCZAK.

Mairs Geographischer Verlag: Postfach 3151, Marco-Polo-Zentrum, 7302 Ostfildern 4; tel. (711) 45020; fax (711) 4502310; f. 1848; road maps, atlases, tourist guides; Man. Dir Dr VOLKMAR MAIR.

J. B. Metzler Verlag: Postfach 103241, Kernerstr. 43, 70028 Stuttgart; tel. (711) 229020; fax (711) 2290290; internet www .metzlerverlag.de; f. 1682; literature, music, pedagogics, linguis tics, history, economics, commerce, textbooks; Dir Dr BERND LUTZ.

Verlag Moderne Industrie AG & Co KG: Justus-von-Liebig-Str. 1, 86895 Landsberg; tel. (8191) 1250; fax (8191) 125211; f. 1952; management, investment, technical; Man. Dir JOHANNES SEVKET GÖZALAN.

Morgenbuch Verlag GmbH: Berlin; tel. (2) 6504151; f. 1958; belles-lettres, politics; Dir Dr WOLFGANG TENZLER.

Verlagsgesellschaft Rudolf Müller GmbH & Co KG: Stolberger Str. 84, 50933 Köln; tel. (221) 54970; fax (221) 5497326; e-mail gf@ rudolf-mueller.de; internet www.rudolf-mueller.de; f. 1840; architecture, construction, engineering, education; Publrs Dr CHRISTOPH MÜLLER, RUDOLF M. BLESER.

Verlag Friedrich Oetinger: Poppenbütteler Chaussee 53, 22397 Hamburg; tel. (40) 60790902; fax (40) 6072326; e-mail oetlinger@ vsg-hamburg.de; juvenile, illustrated books; Man. Dirs SILKE WEITENDORF, THOMAS HUGGLE.

Oldenbourg Verlage: Rosenheimerstr. 145, 81671 München; tel. (89) 450510; fax (89) 45051333; internet www.oldenbourg.de; f. 1858; technology, science, history, textbooks, mathematics, economics, dictionaries, periodicals; Dirs Dr D. HOHM, WOLFGANG DICK, JOHANNES OLDENBOURG.

Omnis Verlag GmbH: Berlin; tel. (30) 85962838; fax (30) 85962840; e-mail info@omnis-verlag.de; art, children's, belleslettres, history.

Pabel-Moewig Verlag KG: Karlsruher Str. 31, 76437 Rastatt; tel. (7222) 130; fax (7222) 13301; Gen. Man. GERHARD STEDTFELD.

Verlag Paul Parey: Hamburg; tel. (40) 339690; fax (40) 33969198; internet www.parey.de; f. 1848; biology, botany, zoology, ethnology, veterinary science, laboratory animals science, food technology and control, agriculture, starch research and technology, brewing and distilling, forestry, horticulture, phytomedicine, plant and environment protection, water management, hunting, fishing, dogs, equitation; technical and scientific journals; Dirs Dr FRIEDRICH GEORGI, Dr RUDOLF GEORGI.

Manfred Pawlak Grossantiquariat und Verlagsgesellschaft mbH: Mielkprülerstr. 31, 82211 Herrsching; tel. (8152) 37070; fax (8152) 370748; f. 1949; history, art, general interest; Dir ULRIKE PAWLAK.

Piper Verlag GmbH: Postfach 430861, Georgenstr. 4, 80799 München; tel. (89) 3818010; fax (89) 338704; e-mail info@piper.de; internet www.piper.de; f. 1904; literature, philosophy, theology, psychology, natural sciences, political and social sciences, history, biographies, music; Dir VIKTOR NIEMANN.

Quell Verlag: Postfach 897, Furtbachstr. 12A, 7000 Stuttgart 1; tel. (711) 601000; f. 1830; Protestant literature; Dirs Dr WOLFGANG REISTER, WALTER WALDBAUER.

Ravensburger Buchverlag Otto Maier GmbH: Postfach 1860, Marktstr. 22–26, 88188 Ravensburg, 88212 Ravensburg; tel. (751) 860; fax (751) 861289; e-mail info@ravensburger.de; internet www.ravensburger.de; f. 1883; Man. Dirs Dr DETLEV LUX, HANSJÖRG SCHIRMER.

Philipp Reclam jun. Verlag GmbH: Siemensstr. 32, 71254 Ditzingen bei Stuttgart; tel. (7156) 1630; fax (7156) 163197; e-mail werbung@reclam.de; internet www.reclam.de; f. 1828; literature, literary criticism, fiction, history of culture and literature, philosophy and religion, biography, fine arts, music; Partner FRANK RAINER MAX.

Rowohlt Taschenbuch Verlag GmbH: Hamburgerstr. 17, 21465 Reinbek bei Hamburg; tel. (40) 72721; fax (40) 7272319; internet www.rowohlt.de; f. 1908/1953; science, fiction, translations of international literature; Dirs Dr HELMUT DÄHNE, NICOLAUS HANSEN.

K. G. Saur Verlag GmbH: Postfach 70 16 20, 81316 München; Ortlerstr. 8, 81373 München; tel. (89) 769020; fax (89) 76902150; e-mail info@saur.de; internet www.saur.de; f. 1949; library science, reference, dictionaries, journals. Microfiches, CD-ROMs, online databases; 3 brs in Leipzig, Osnabrück and Zürich; subsidiary of the Gale Group, Div of Thomson Learning Int.

Schattauer GmbH: Postfach 104543, 70040 Stuttgart; Hoelderlinstr. 3, 70174 Stuttgart; tel. (711) 229870; fax (711) 2298750; e-mail info@schattauer.de; internet www.schattauer.de; f. 1949; medicine and related sciences; Publr DIETER BERGEMANN.

Verlag Dr Otto Schmidt KG: Unter den Ulmen 96–98, 50968 Köln; tel. (221) 9373801; fax (221) 93738943; f. 1905; university textbooks, jurisprudence, tax law; Man. Dir K. P. WINTERS.

Egmont Franz Schneider Verlag GmbH: Schleissheimer Str. 267, 80809 München; tel. (89) 358116; fax (89) 35811755; e-mail postmaster@schneiderbuch.de; internet www.schneiderbuch.de; f. 1913; children's books; Editor-in-Chief UTE FREUDENBERGER.

Schroedel Schulbuchverlag GmbH: Hildesheimer Str. 202–206, 30519 Hannover; tel. (511) 83880; fax (511) 8388343; f. 1982; school textbooks and educational software; Man. Dirs THOMAS BAUMANN, Dr WERNER KUGEL.

Springer-Verlag GmbH & Co KG: Heidelberger Pl. 3, 14197 Berlin; tel. (30) 827870; fax (30) 8214091; f. 1842; medicine, biology, mathematics, physics, chemistry, psychology, engineering, geosciences, philosophy, law, economics; Proprs Prof Dr DIETRICH GÖTZE, RÜDIGER GEBAUER, Dr ULRICH VEST, Dr HANS-DIETER HAENEL.

Stamm Verlag: Fuggerstr. 7, 51149 Köln; e-mail info@stam.de; internet www.stam.de; reference.

Stollfuss Verlag Bonn GmbH & Co KG: Dechenstr. 7, 53115 Bonn; tel. (228) 7240; fax (228) 659723; reference, fiscal law, economics, investment, etc. Man. Dir WOLFGANG STOLLFUSS.

Suhrkamp Verlag GmbH & Co: Postfach 101945, 60019 Frankfurt a.M. Suhrkamp Haus, Lindenstr. 29–35, 60325 Frankfurt a.M. tel. (69) 756010; fax (69) 75601522; e-mail geschaftsleitung@suhrkamp.de; internet www.suhrkamp.de; f. 1950; modern German and foreign literature, philosophy, poetry; Dir (vacant).

Sybex Verlag GmbH: emil-Hoffmann-Str. 1, 50996 Köln; tel. (2236) 3999700; fax (2236) 3999229; e-mail sybex@sybex.de; internet www.sybex.de; f. 1981; computer books and software; Man. Dirs HANS NOLDEN, GERHARD PROLLIUS, ANJA SCHRIEVER.

Georg Thieme Verlag: Postfach 301120; 70451 Stuttgart; Rüdigerstr. 14, 70469 Stuttgart; tel. (711) 89310; fax (711) 8931298; e-mail info@thieme.com; internet www.thieme.com; f. 1886; medicine and natural science; Man. Dirs Dr GÜNTHER HAUFF, ALBRECHT HAUFF.

Thienemann Verlag GmbH: Blumenstr. 36, 70182 Stuttgart; tel. (711) 210550; fax (711) 2105539; e-mail info@thienemann.de; internet www.thienemann.de; f. 1849; picture books, children's books, juveniles; Dir KLAUS WILLBERG.

Transpress Verlagsgesellschaft mbH: Borkumstr. 2, 13181 Berlin; tel. (30) 47805151; fax (30) 47805160; f. 1990; specialized literature on transport and marketing; Man. Dr HARALD BÖTTCHER.

Verlag Eugen Ulmer GmbH & Co: Postfach 700561, 70574 Stuttgart; tel. (711) 45070; fax (711) 4507120; e-mail info@ulmer.de; f. 1868; agriculture, horticulture, science, periodicals; Dir ROLAND ULMER.

Verlag Ullstein GmbH: Charlottenstr. 13, 10969 Berlin; tel. (30) 25913570; fax (30) 25913523; f. 1894; literature, art, music, theatre, contemporary history, biography; Pres. Dr JÜRGEN RICHTER.

Ullstein Heyne List GmbH & Co KG: Paul-Heyse-Str. 28, 80336 München; tel. (89) 51480; fax (89) 51482229; f. 1894; general fiction, history, music, art, philosophy, religion, psychology; Editorial Dir CHRISTIAN STRASSER.

Urban & Fischer Verlag GmbH & Co KG: Postfach 100537, 07705 Jena; Löbdergraben 14A, 07745 Jena; tel. (3641) 6263; fax (3641) 626500; e-mail journals@urbanfischer.de; internet www.urbanfischer.de/journals; f. 1878; biological science, medical science; Dir BERND ROLLE.

Urban & Schwarzenberg GmbH: Karlstr. 45, 80333 München; tel. (89) 53830; fax (89) 5383221; f. 1866; medicine, natural sciences; Man. Dir MICHAEL URBAN.

Verlagsgruppe Weltbild GmbH: Steinerne Furt 67–72, 86167 Augsburg; tel. (821) 70040; fax (821) 70042790; internet www.weltbild.com; f. 1949; religion, philosophy, fashion, heraldry, nature and environment, culture, history, photography, literature, health, travel.

Georg Westermann Verlag GmbH: Postfach 3320, Georg-Westermann-Allee 66, 38023 Braunschweig; tel. (531) 7080; fax (531) 796569; f. 1838; non-fiction, paperbacks, periodicals; Dir Dr HANS-DIETER MÖLLER.

Wiley-VCH Verlag GmbH & Co KGaA: Boschstr. 12, 69469 Weinheim; tel. (6201) 6060; fax (6201) 606328; e-mail service@wiley-vch.de; internet www.wiley-vch.de; f. 1921; natural sciences, especially chemistry, chemical engineering, civil engineering, architecture, biotechnology, materials science, life sciences, information technology and physics, scientific software, business, management, computer science, finance and accounting; Man. Dir Dr MANFRED ANTONI.

Verlag Klaus Wingefeld: Lindenstr. 12, 71686 Remseck; fax (7146) 871881; e-mail kinderbuchverlag@t-online.de.

PRINCIPAL ASSOCIATION OF BOOK PUBLISHERS AND BOOKSELLERS

Börsenverein des Deutschen Buchhandels eV (German Publishers and Booksellers Association): Postfach 100442, 60004 Frankfurt a.M. Grosser Hirschgraben 17–21, 60311 Frankfurt a.M. tel. (69) 13060; fax (69) 1306201; e-mail info@boev.de; internet www.boersenverein.de; f. 1825; Chair. DIETER SCHORMANN; Man. Dir Dr HARALD HEKER.

Broadcasting and Communications

TELECOMMUNICATIONS

Debitel AG: 70545 Stuttgart; e-mail presse@de.debitel.com; internet www.debitel.com; owned by Swisscom AG.

Deutsche Telekom AG: Postfach 2000, 53105 Bonn; tel. (228) 1810; fax (228) 18171915; internet www.telekom.de; f. 1989; partially privatized 1995 with further privatization pending; 31% state-owned, 12% owned by Kreditanstalt für Wiederaufbau, 57% owned by private shareholders; fmr monopoly over national telecommunications network removed Jan. 1998; demerger from T-Mobil pending during 2002; Chair. Supervisory Bd Dr HANS-DIETRICH WINKHAUS; Chair. Bd of Management Prof. Dr HELMUT SIHLER; CEO KAI-UWE RICKE.

E-plus Mobilfunk GmbH: Postfach 300307, 40403 Düsseldorf; E-Plus-Pl. 1, 40468 Düsseldorf; tel. (211) 4480; fax (211) 4482222; internet www.eplus.de; f. 1995; Chair. Supervisory Bd ALAIN D. BANDLE.

Mannesmann Mobilfunk GmbH: Am Seestern 1, 40547 Düsseldorf; tel. (211) 5330; fax (211) 5332200; internet www.d2mannesmann.de; operates D2 mobile telephone network; subsidiary of Mannesmann AG, Telecommunications Division (takeover by Vodafone-AirTouch PLC, UK, pending); Chair. JÜRGEN VON KUCZKOWSKI.

Mannesmann o-tel-o GmbH: Deutz-Mulheimer-Str. 111, 51063 Köln; tel. (221) 8080; fax (221) 8087566; internet www.o-tel-o.de; operates fixed line telephone network; subsidiary of Mannesmann AG, Telecommunications Division (takeover by Vodafone-AirTouch PLC, UK, pending).

Mannesmann Arcor AG: Kölnerstr. 5, 65760 Eschborn; fax (69) 21694444; e-mail arcor@arcor.net; internet www.arcor.de; operates fixed line telephone network; subsidiary of Mannesmann AG, Telecommunications Division (takeover by Vodafone-AirTouch PLC, UK, pending).

MobilCom AG: Postfach 520, 24753 Rendsburg; Hollerstr. 126, 24782 Rendsburg; internet www.mobilcom.de; f. 1991; Chair. GERHARD SCHMID.

T-Mobil: internet www.t-mobil.de; f. 1992; subsidiary of Deutsche Telekom AG; f. 1992; operates T-D1 mobile telephone network.

Viag Interkom: internet www.viaginterkom.de; f. 1995; Chair. MAXIMILIAN ARDELT.

Associations

Deutscher Multimedia Verband (dmmv): Kaistr. 14, 40221 Düsseldorf; tel. (211) 6004560; fax (211) 60045633; e-mail info@dmmv.de; internet www.dmmv.de; 1,300 mems (Feb. 2001).

Verband Privater Rundfunk und Telekommunikation eV (VPRT) (Assocation of Commercial Broadcasting and Telecommunications Cos): Stromstr. 1, 10555 Berlin; tel. (30) 398800; fax (30) 39880148; e-mail vprt@vprt.de; internet www.vprt.de; 160 mems (Jan. 2002).

Regulatory Authority

Regulierungsbehörde für Telekommunikation und Post (RegTP): Tulpenfeld 4, 53113 Bonn; tel. (228) 140; fax (228) 148872; e-mail poststelle@regtp.de; internet www.regtp.de; f. 1997 as a regulatory body responsible for supervising the liberalization (commencing in Jan. 1998) of the post and telecommunications sector; Pres. MATTHIAS KURTH.

BROADCASTING

Radio

Regional public radio stations are co-ordinated by the ARD (see below). There are also numerous regional commercial radio stations.

Public Stations

Arbeitsgemeinschaft der öffentlich-rechtlichen Rundfunkanstalten der Bundesrepublik Deutschland (ARD) (Association of Public Law Broadcasting Organizations): Bertramstr. 8, 60320 Frankfurt a.M. tel. (69) 590607; fax (69) 1552075; e-mail info@ard.de; internet www.ard.de; f. 1950; Chair. Prof. JOBST PLOG; the co-ordinating body of Germany's public service radio and television organizations; each of the following radio stations broadcasts 3–5 channels:

Bayerischer Rundfunk: Rundfunkpl. 1, 80300 München; tel. (89) 590001; fax (89) 59002375; internet www.bronline.de; Dir-Gen. Prof. ALBERT SCHARF; Broadcasting Council Prof. Dr WILHELM WIMMER; Chair. Admin. Bd JOHANN BÖHM.

Radio Bremen: Bürgermeister-Spitta-Allee 45, 28329 Bremen; tel. (421) 2460; fax (421) 2461010; internet www.radiobremen.de; f. 1945; radio and television; Dir-Gen. Dr HEINZ GLÄSSGEN.

Deutsche Welle: Kurt-Schumacher-Str 3, 53113 Bonn; tel. (221) 3892500; fax (221) 3892510; e-mail info@dw-world.de; internet www.dw-world.de; f. 1953; German short-wave radio and satellite television service; broadcasts daily in 31 languages for Europe and overseas; Dir-Gen. ERIK BETTERMANN.

DeutschlandRadio: Hans Rosenthal Pl., 10825 Berlin; tel. (30) 85030; internet www.deutschlandradio.de; Dir-Gen. ERNST ELLITZ.

Hessischer Rundfunk: Bertramstr. 8, 60320 Frankfurt a.M. tel. (69) 1551; fax (69) 1552900; internet www.hr-online.de; Dir-Gen. Dr HELMUT REITZE.

Mitteldeutscher Rundfunk: Kanstr. 71–73, 04275 Leipzig; tel. (341) 3000; fax (341) 3005544; internet www.mdr.de; f. 1992; Dir-Gen. Prof. Dr UDO REITER.

Norddeutscher Rundfunk: Rothenbaumchaussee 132, 20149 Hamburg; tel. (40) 41560; fax (40) 447602; internet www.ndr.de; f. 1956; Dir-Gen. JOBST PLOG.

Ostdeutscher Rundfunk Brandenburg: Marlene-Dietrich-Allee 20, 14482 Potsdam; tel. (331) 7310; fax (331) 7213571; e-mail kom@orb.de; internet www.orb.de; Dir-Gen. Prof. HANSJÜRGEN ROSENBAUER.

Saarländischer Rundfunk: Funkhaus Halberg, 66100 Saarbrücken; tel. (681) 6020; fax (681) 6023874; internet www.sr-online.de; f. 1952; Dir-Gen. FRITZ RAFF.

Sender Freies Berlin: Masurenallee 8–14, 14057 Berlin; tel. (30) 30310; fax (30) 3015062; e-mail info@sfb.de; internet www.sfb.de; Dir-Gen. Dr HORST SCHÄTTLE; Chair. Broadcasting Council MARIANNE BRINCKMEIER; Dir of Radio JENS WENDLAND; Dir of TV BARBARA GROTH.

Süddeutscher Rundfunk: Postfach 106040, 70049 Stuttgart; Neckarstr. 230, 70190 Stuttgart; tel. (711) 9290; fax (711) 9292600; internet www.sdr.de; f. 1924; Dir-Gen. HERMANN FÜNFGELD.

Südwestrundfunk: Neckarstr. 230, 70150 Stuttgart; tel. (49) 9290; fax (49) 9292600; internet www.swr.de; Dir-Gen. PETER VOSS.

WDR (Westdeutscher Rundfunk): Appellhofpl. 1, 50667 Köln; tel. (221) 2200; fax (221) 2204800; internet www.wdr.de; Dir-Gen. FRITZ PLEITGEN.

Commercial Radio

Verband Privater Rundfunk und Telekommunikation eV (VPRT): see under Telecommunications; represents privately-owned radio stations.

Television

There are three public-service television channels. The autonomous regional broadcasting organizations combine to provide material for the First Programme which is produced by ARD. The Second Programme (Zweites Deutsches Fernsehen/ZDF) is completely separate and is controlled by a public corporation of all the Länder. It is partly financed by advertising. The Third Programme (also produced by ARD) provides a cultural and educational service in the evenings only with contributions from several of the regional bodies. Commercial television channels also operate.

Public Stations

ARD: Programmdirektion Deutsches Fernsehen: Arnulfstr. 42, 80335 München; tel. (89) 590001; fax (89) 59003249; Chair. INGO DAHRENDORF; co-ordinates the following regional public-service television organizations: Bayerischer Rundfunk Fernsehen, Hessischer Rundfunk Fernsehen, MDR Fernsehen, NDR Fernsehen, ORB Fernsehen, Radio Bremen Fernsehen, Saarländischer Rundfunk Fernsehen, SDR Fernsehen, SFB Fernsehen, SNF Fernsehen, WDR Fernsehen.

Zweites Deutsches Fernsehen (ZDF): 55100 Mainz; tel. (6131) 701; fax (6131) 702157; e-mail info@zdf.de; internet www.zdf.de; f. 1961 by the Länder Govts as a second television channel; 104 main transmitters; Dir-Gen. MARKUS SCHÄCHTER.

Commercial Television

Verband Privater Rundfunk und Telekommunication eV (VPRT): see under Telecommunications; represents privately-owned satellite, cable and digital television cos.

Finance

(cap. = capital; res = reserves; dep. = deposits; m. = million; brs = branches; amounts in Deutsche Marks (DM) or euros (€))

The Deutsche Bundesbank, the central bank of Germany, consists of the central administration in Frankfurt am Main (considered to be the financial capital of the country) and 9 main offices (Landeszentralbanken) with 140 branches. In carrying out its functions as determined by law the Bundesbank is independent of the Federal Government, but is required to support the Government's general economic policy. As a member of the European System of Central Banks (ESCB), the Bundesbank implements the single monetary policy determined by the Governing Council of the European Central Bank (ECB).

All credit institutions other than the Bundesbank are subject to governmental supervision through the Federal Banking Supervisory Office (Bundesaufsichtsamt für das Kreditwesen) in Berlin. Banks outside the central banking system are divided into three groups: private commercial banks, credit institutions incorporated under public law and co-operative credit institutions. All these commercial banks are 'universal banks', conducting all kinds of customary banking business. There is no division of activities. As well as the commercial banks there are a number of specialist banks, such as private or public mortgage banks.

The group of private commercial banks includes all banks incorporated as a company limited by shares (Aktiengesellschaft—AG, Kommanditgesellschaft auf Aktien—KGaA) or as a private limited company (Gesellschaft mit beschränkter Haftung—GmbH) and those which are known as 'regional banks' because they do not usually function throughout Germany; and those banks which are established as sole proprietorships or partnerships and mostly have no branches outside their home town. The main business of all private commercial banks is short-term lending. The private bankers fulfil the most varied tasks within the banking system.

The public law credit institutions are the savings banks (Sparkassen) and the Landesbank-Girozentralen. The latter act as central banks and clearing houses on a national level for the savings banks. Laws governing the savings banks limit them to certain sectors—credits, investments and money transfers—and they concentrate on the areas of home financing, municipal investments and the trades. In December 1998 there were 594 savings banks and 13 Landesbank-Girozentralen in Germany.

The head institution of the co-operative system is the DZ BANK Deutsche Zentrale-Genossenschaftsbank AG. In December 1998 there were three regional co-operative central banks and 2,256 local co-operative banks.

In 1990 there was a total of 4,700 banks in Germany; by 2000 this number had decreased to 2,900.

BANKS

The Central Banking System

Germany participates in the ESCB, which consists of the ECB and the national central banks of all 15 European Union (EU) member states. Stage III of European Monetary Union (EMU), the launch of the euro, commenced (with 11 initial participants) on 1 January 1999. Euro banknotes and coins were issued on 1 January 2002; the Deutsche Mark remained legal tender until 28 February 2002.

Deutsche Bundesbank: Postfach 100602, 60006 Frankfurt a.M. Wilhelm-Epstein-Str. 14, 60431 Frankfurt a.M. tel. (69) 95661; fax (69) 5601071; e-mail presse-information@bundesbank.de; internet www.bundesbank.de; f. 1957; aims, in conjunction with the other members of the ESCB, to maintain price stability in the euro area. The Bundesbank, *inter alia*, holds and maintains foreign reserves of the Federal Republic of Germany, arranges for the execution of domestic and cross-border payments, contributes to the stability of payment and clearing systems and is involved in surveillance of credit and financial services institutions. The Bundesbank (which has nine regional offices—Hauptverwaltungen) is the principal bank of the Federal Länder Govts, carrying accounts for public authorities, executing payments and assisting with borrowing on the capital market. The Bundesbank has reserve positions in, and claims on, the IMF and the ECB. The Governing Board determines the Bundesbank's business policy; members of the Federal Govt may take part in the deliberations of the Council but may not vote; Pres. ERNST WELTEKE; Vice-Pres. Dr JÜRGEN STARK.

Hauptverwaltung Berlin: Steinpl. 2, 10623 Berlin; tel. (30) 34750; fax (30) 34751990; e-mail volkswirtschaft.hv-berlin@bundesbank.de; internet www.bundesbank.de/hv/bbb; Pres. Bd of Management ULRICH PREUSS.

Hauptverwaltung Düsseldorf: Berliner Allee 14, 40212 Düsseldorf; tel. (211) 8740; e-mail lzb-nrw@t-online.de; internet www.bundesbank.de/lzb-nrw; Pres. EBERHARD HEINKE.

Hauptverwaltung Frankfurt: Taunusanlage 5, 60329 Frankfurt a.M. tel. (69) 23880; fax (69) 23882130; e-mail presse-information@lzb-hessen.bundesbank.de; internet www.bundesbank.de/lzb-h; Pres. Dr HANS RECKERS; Vice-Pres. JÖRGEN HETTINGER.

Hauptverwaltung Hamburg: Ost-West-Str. 73, 20459 Hamburg; tel. (40) 37070; fax (40) 37072205; e-mail lzb-hms-pressestelle@t-online.de; Pres. Bd of Management Prof. Dr ROLF EGGERT.

Hauptverwaltung Hannover: 30159 Hannover; tel. (511) 30332231; fax (511) 30332260; Pres. Bd of Management GEORG KUTTER.

Hauptverwaltung Leipzig: Postfach 901121, 04358 Leipzig; tel. (341) 8600; fax (341) 8602389; e-mail zentrale.mailstelle@lzb-sth.bundesbank.de; internet www.bundesbank.de/lzb-sth.

Hauptverwaltung Mainz: Hegelstr. 65, 52122 Mainz; tel. (6131) 3770; fax (6131) 377750; e-mail volkswirtschaft@lzb-rs.bundesbank.de; internet www.bundesbank.de/lzb-rs; Pres. HELMUT RITTGEN.

Hauptverwaltung München: Ludwigstr. 13, 80539 München; tel. (89) 28895; fax (89) 28893598; e-mail post@lzb-bayern.bundesbank.de; internet www.bundesbank.de/lzb-bayern; Pres. Bd of Management Prof. Dr FRANZ-CHRISTOPH ZEITLER.

Hauptverwaltung Stuttgart: Marstallstr. 3, 70173 Stuttgart; tel. (711) 9440; fax (711) 9441903; e-mail hv-stuttgart@bundesbank.de; internet www.bundesbank.de; Pres. Bd of Management WILHELM ERGENZINGER.

Private Commercial Banks

In December 1998 328 private commercial banks were operating in Germany. The most prominent of these are listed below:

Baden-Württembergische Bank AG: Postfach 106014, 70049 Stuttgart; Kleiner Schlosspl. 11, 70173 Stuttgart; tel. (711) 1800; fax (711) 1801712; e-mail info@bw-bank.de; internet www.bw-bank.de; f. 1977 by merger of Badische Bank, Handelsbank Heilbronn and Württembergische Bank; cap. €92m., res €607m., dep. €22,536m. (Dec. 2000); Chair. GERHARD STRATTHAUS; 53 brs.

Bankgesellschaft Berlin AG: Alexanderpl. 2, 10178 Berlin; tel. (30) 245500; fax (30) 24566333; e-mail ir@bankgesellschaft.de; internet www.bankgesellschaft.de; f. 1994; cap. €558m., res €3,524m., dep. €189,503m. (Dec. 2000); majority stake held by Berlin Land Govt; Chair. Supervisory Bd ERUST-OTTO SANDVOSS; Chair. Bd of Management HAUS-JÖRG VETTER.

Bayerische Hypo- und Vereinsbank AG (HypoVereinsbank): Postfach 100101, 80333 München; Am Tucherpark 16, 80538 München; tel. (89) 3780; fax (89) 378113422; e-mail info@hypovereinsbank.de; internet www.hypovereinsbank.de; f. 1998 by merger of Bayerische Hypotheken- und Wechsel Bank AG (f. 1835) and Bayerische Vereinsbank AG (f. 1869); cap. €1,607m., res €17,532m., dep. €616,509m. (Dec. 2000); Chair. Supervisory Bd Dr KURT VIERMETZ; Chair. Bd of Management Dr ALBRECHT SCHMIDT; 1,426 brs.

Berliner Volksbank eG: Budapester Str. 35, 10787 Berlin; tel. (30) 30630; fax (30) 30631550; e-mail international.division@berliner-volksbank.de; internet www.berliner-volksbank.de; f. 1860; cap. DM 572m., res DM 477m., dep. DM 18,072m. (Dec. 2000); Chair. Prof. Dr DIETMAR WINJE.

Citibank AG: Postfach 110333, 60038 Frankfurt a.M. Neue Mainzer Str. 75, 60311 Frankfurt a.M. tel. (69) 13660; fax (69) 13661113; internet www.citigroup.com; f. 1976; cap. DM 426m., res DM 404m., res DM 224m., dep. DM 8,892m. (Dec. 2000); Chair. Supervisory Bd Prof. K. PETER MAILÄNDER; Chair. Bd of Management Dr THOMAS F. HUERTAS; 2 brs.

Citibank Privatkunden AG: Postfach 101818, 40009 Düsseldorf; Kasernenstr. 10, 40213 Düsseldorf; tel. (211) 89840; fax (211) 8984222; internet www.citibank.de; f. 1926 as KKB Bank KGaA; present name adopted 1991; cap. DM 156m., res. DM 907m., dep. DM 15,576m. (Dec. 1999); Man. WILLY P. SOCQUET; 300 brs.

Commerzbank AG: Kaiserpl., 60311 Frankfurt a.M. tel. (69) 13620; fax (69) 285389; e-mail ir@commerzbank.de; internet www.commerzbank.de; f. 1870; cap. €1,386m., res €10,595m., dep. €391,141m. (Dec. 2000); Chair. Supervisory Bd Dr MARTIN KOHLHAUSSEN; Chair. Bd of Management KLAUS-PETER MÜLLER; 964 brs.

Deutsche Bank AG: Taunusanlage 12, 60325 Frankfurt a.M. tel. (69) 91000; fax (69) 91033422; e-mail db.presse@db.com; internet www.deutsche-bank.de; f. 1870; cap. €1,591m., res €15,983m., dep. €604,885m. (Dec. 2001); Chair. Supervisory Bd ROLF E. BREUER; Chair. Bd of Management JOSEF ACKERMANN; 133 brs.

Dresdner Bank AG: Jürgen-Ponto-Pl. 1, 60329 Frankfurt a.M. tel. (69) 2630; fax (69) 634004; e-mail investor.relations@dresdener-bank.com; internet www.dresdner-bank.de; f. 1872; cap. €1,354m., res €9,885m. (Dec. 2000); Chair. Supervisory Bd Dr HENNING SCHULTE-NOELLE; Chair. Bd of Management BERND FAHRHOLZ; more than 1,400 brs.

Dresdner Bank Lateinamerika AG: Postfach 301246, 20305 Hamburg; Neuer Jungfernstieg 16, 20354 Hamburg; tel. (40) 35950; fax (40) 35953314; e-mail public-relations@dbla.com; internet www.dbla.com; f. 1906; fmrly Deutsch-Südamerikanische Bank AG; cap. €100m., res €336m., dep. €9,795m. (Dec. 2000); Chair. Supervisory Bd HEINRICH LINZ; Chair. Bd of Management WOLFGANG DAMBMANN.

HSBC Trinkaus & Burkhardt KGaA: Postfach 101108, 40002 Düsseldorf; Königsallee 21–23, 40212 Düsseldorf; tel. (211) 9100; fax (211) 910616; f. 1785; current name adopted 1999; cap. €70m., res €575m., dep. €7,917m. (Dec. 2001); Chair. and Man. Dir Dr SIEGHARDT ROMETSCH; 6 brs.

ING BHF-Bank AG: Bockenheimer Landstr. 10, 60323 Frankfurt a.M. tel. (69) 7180; fax (69) 7182296; e-mail kontakt@bhf.ing.com; internet www.ing-bhf-bank.com; f. 1856; cap. €215m., res €2,463m., dep. €46,976m. (Sep. 2002); Man. Dir SYTSE ADRIAAN ANDRINGA.

J. P. Morgan AG: Grüneburgweg 2, 60322 Frankfurt a.M. tel. (69) 71581; fax (69) 71582209; f. 1947; cap. €59m., res €83m., dep. €4,711m. (Dec. 1999); Chair. RAINER GEBBE.

Merck Finck & Co: Pacellistr. 16, 80333 München; tel. (89) 21040; fax (89) 299814; e-mail info@merckfinck.de; internet www.merckfinck.de; f. 1870; cap. €153m., res €9m., dep. €1,780m. (Dec. 2001); Partners GERD SCHMITZ-MORKRAMER, UTZ-DIETER BOLSTORFF, ANDREW LAWSON.

Oldenburgische Landesbank AG: Postfach 2605, 26016 Oldenburg; Stau 15–17, 26122 Oldenburg; tel. (441) 2210; fax (441) 210310; e-mail olb@olb.de; internet www.olb.de; f. 1868; cap. €60m., res €306m., dep. €7,645m. (Dec. 2001); Spokesman Bd of Management H.-D. GELLER.

Oppenheim (Sal) Jr & Cie KGaA: Postfach 102743, 50467 Köln; Unter Sachsenhausen 4; 50667 Köln; tel. (221) 14501; fax (221) 1451512; e-mail info@oppenheim.de; internet www.oppenheim.de; f.

1789; cap. €200m., res €481m., dep. €6,658m. (Dec. 2002); Chair. MATTHIAS GRAF VON KROCKOW; 16 brs.

SchmidtBank GmbH & Co KGaA: Postfach 1629, 95015 Hof; Ernst-Reuter-Str. 119, 95030 Hof; tel. (9281) 6010; fax (9281) 601427; e-mail bankrelations@schmidtbank.de; internet www .schmidtbank.de; f. 1828; cap. DM 417m., res DM 89m., dep. DM 10,667m. (Dec. 2000); Chair. Dr PAUL WIEANDT; 125 brs.

SEB AG: Mainzer Landstr. 16, 60325 Frankfurt a.M. tel. (69) 2580; fax (69) 2587578; e-mail info@seb.de; internet www.seb.de; f. 1958 as BfG—Bank AG, adopted current name 2000; cap. €775m., res €428m., dep. €23,314m. (Dec. 2000); Chair. LARS LUNDQUIST; 177 brs.

Skandinaviska Enskilda Banken AG: Postfach 101957, 60019 Frankfurt a.M. Rahmhofstr. 2–4, 60313 Frankfurt a.M. tel. (69) 290210; fax (69) 284191; f. 1975; 100% owned by SEB AG; cap. DM 81m., res DM 69m., dep. DM 2,027m. (Dec. 1999); Chair. ZAID PEDERSEN; Man. Dirs WOLFGANG AZGELANDER, LARS TÖRNQUIST; 2 brs.

UBS Warburg AG: Stephanstr. 14–16, 60313 Frankfurt a.M. tel. (69) 13690; fax (69) 13691366; internet www.ubswarburg.com; f. 1998 as Warburg Dillon Read AG by merger of Schweizerischer Bankverein (Deutschland) and Union Bank of Switzerland (Deutschland) AG; present name adopted 2000; cap. €125m., res €166m., dep. €22,160m. (Dec. 2000); Man. Dirs PETER AARTS, Dr RICHARD JAEKEL, STEFAN WINTER.

Vereins- und Westbank AG: Alter Wall 22, 20457 Hamburg; tel. (40) 369201; fax (40) 36922870; internet www.vuw.de; f. 1974 by merger; cap. €174m., res €426m., dep. €18,023m. (Dec. 2001); Man. Dirs HARALD BOBERG, FRANK DIEGEL, ROLF KIRCHFELD, Dr ULRICH MEINCKE, Dr STEPHAN SCHÜLLER; 190 brs.

Weberbank Pirvatbankiers KGaA: Postfach 110580, 10835 Berlin; Hohenzollerndamm 134, 14199 Berlin; tel. (30) 897980; fax (30) 89798900; internet www.weberbank.de; f. 1949 as Weberbank Berliner Industriebank, current name adopted 2001; cap. €52m., res €126m., dep. €4,946m. (Dec. 2001); Partners Dr ANDREAS BÖDECKER, Dr CHRISTIAN GRÜN, CORNELIUS KOCH, MICHAEL GRAF STRASOLDO; 3 brs.

Westfalenbank AG: Postfach 102710, 44727 Bochum; Huestr. 21–25, 44787 Bochum; tel. (234) 6160; fax (234) 6164400; e-mail info@ westfalenbank.de; internet www.westfalenbank.de; f. 1921; cap. DM 99m., res DM 175m., dep. DM 4,659m. (Dec. 2001); Chair. DIETMAR P. BINKOWSKA.

Public-Law Credit Institutions

Together with the private banks, the banks incorporated under public law (savings banks—Sparkassen—and their central clearing houses—Landesbank-Girozentralen) play a major role within the German banking system. In 1998 there were 594 savings banks and 13 central clearing houses. In July 2001 the Government signed an agreement with the EU to end state guarantees for the Landesbanken over four years.

Bayerische Landesbank Girozentrale: Brienner Str. 18, 80333 München; tel. (89) 217101; fax (89) 217123579; e-mail kontakt@blb .de; internet www.bayernlb.de; f. 1972; cap. €3,719m., res €3,858m., dep. €274,716m. (Dec. 2000); Chair. Bd of Management WERNER SCHMIDT.

Bremer Landesbank Kreditanstalt Oldenburg: Domshof 26, 28195 Bremen; tel. (421) 3320; fax (421) 3322625; e-mail kontakt@ bremerlandesbank.de; internet www.bremerlandesbank.de; f. 1983; cap. €748m., res €311m., dep. €31,968m. (Dec. 2001); Chair. Dr PETER HASSKAMP.

DGZ DekaBank Deutsche Kommunalbank: Postfach 120320, 10593 Berlin; Bismarckstr. 101, 10625 Berlin; tel. (30) 3159670; fax (30) 31596730; e-mail service@deka.de; internet www.deka.de; f. 1999; through merger of Deutsche Girozentrale-Deutsche Kommunalbank and Dekabank GmbH; issues Pfandbriefe (bonds); cap. €587m., res €549m., dep. €73,348m. (Dec. 2000); Chair. Bd of Management AXEL WEBER.

Hamburgische Landesbank-Girozentrale: Gerhart-Hauptmann- Pl. 50, 20095 Hamburg; tel. (40) 33330; fax (40) 33332707; e-mail info@hamburglb.de; internet www.hamburglb.de; f. 1938; cap. €1,914m., res €861m., dep. €79,446m. (Dec. 2001); Chair. ALEXANDER STUHLMANN; 4 brs.

Landesbank Baden-Württemberg: Postfach 106049, 70049 Stuttgart; tel. (711) 1270; fax (711) 1273278; e-mail kontakt@lbbw .de; internet www.lbbw.de; f. 1999; by merger of Landesgirokasse, L-Bank Landeskreditbank Baden-Württemberg and Südwestdeutsche Landesbank Girozentrale; cap. €2,204m., res €3,522m., dep. €275,381m. (Dec. 2000); Chair. Bd of Management HANS DIETMAR SAUER.

Landesbank Berlin Girozentrale: Bundesallee 171, 10889 Berlin-Wilmersdorf; tel. (30) 869801; fax (30) 86983074; e-mail information@lbb.de; internet www.lbb.de; f. 1818; cap. €844m., res €1,413m., dep. €91,351m. (Dec. 2000); Chair. Bd of Management NORBERT PAWLOWSKI; 178 brs.

Landesbank Hessen-Thüringen Girozentrale: Main Tower, Neue Mainzer Str. 52–58, 60297 Frankfurt a.M. tel. (69) 913201; fax (69) 291517; internet www.helaba.de; cap. €1,945m., res €1,123m., dep. €113,670m. (Dec. 2000); Chair. Dr GÜNTHER MERL.

Landesbank Saar Girozentrale: Ursulinenstr. 2, 66111 Saarbrücken; tel. (681) 38301; fax (681) 3831295; e-mail saarlb@aol.com; internet www.saarlb.de; f. 1941; cap. €168m., res €105m., dep. €13,076m. (Dec. 2000); Pres. Dr MAX HÄRING; Chair. KARL HEINZ TRAUTMANN.

Landesbank Schleswig-Holstein Girozentrale: Martendsdamm 6, 24103 Kiel; tel. (431) 90001; fax (431) 9002446; e-mail info@ lb-kiel.de; internet www.lb-kiel.de; f. 1917; cap. €1,009m., res €2,612m., dep. €117,371m. (Dec. 2000); Chair. Dr DIETRICH RÜMKER.

LRP Landesbank Rheinland-Pfalz Girozentrale: Grosse Bleiche 54–56, 55098 Mainz; tel. (6131) 1301; fax (6131) 132724; e-mail lrp@lrp.de; internet www.lrp.de; f. 1958; cap. €496m., res €572m., dep. €57,302m. (Dec. 2000); Chair. and CEO Dr KLAUS G. ADAM.

Norddeutsche Landesbank Girozentrale (NORD/LB): Georgspl. 1, 30159 Hannover; tel. (511) 3610; fax (511) 3612502; internet www.nordlb.de; f. 1970; by merger of several north German banks; cap. €1,218m., res €2,298m., dep. €120,958m. (Dec. 2000); Chair. Dr MANFRED BODIN; 172 brs.

Westdeutsche Landesbank Girozentrale: Herzogstr. 15, 40217 Düsseldorf; tel. (211) 82601; fax (211) 8266119; e-mail presse@ westlb.de; internet www.westlb.de; f. 1969; cap. €1,184m., res €7,678m., dep. €362,498m. (Dec. 2000); Chair. Dr JÜRGEN SENGERA.

Central Bank of Co-operative Banking System

DZ BANK (Deutsche Zentrale-Genossenschaftsbank AG): Am Pl. der Republik, 60265 Frankfurt a.M. tel. (69) 744701; fax (69) 74471685; internet www.dzbank.de; f. 1949; cap. €1,469m., res €1,513m., dep. €251,049m. (Dec. 2000); Chair. Supervisory Bd CHRISTOPHER PLEISTER; Chair. Bd of Management Dr ULRICH BRIXNER; 46 brs.

DZ BANK is a specialist wholesale bank and is the central institution in the German co-operative banking sector, which comprises 2,248 local co-operative banks, three regional central banks and a number of specialist financial institutions.

Specialist Banks

Although Germany is considered the model country for universal banking, banks that specialize in certain types of business are also extremely important. In December 1998 there were 51 specialist banks. A selection of the most prominent among these is given below:

Allgemeine HypothekenBank Rheinboden AG: Postfach 170162, 60075 Frankfurt a.M. Bockenheimer Landstr. 25, 60325 Frankfurt a.M. tel. (69) 71790; fax (69) 7179100; e-mail info@ahbr .com; internet www.ahbr.com; f. 1962 as Allgemeine Hypotheken Bank AG, present name adopted 2001; cap. €101m., res €876m., dep. €87,521m. (Dec. 2001); Chair. HORST ALEXANDER SPITZKOPF; 8 brs.

Berlin-Hannoversche Hypothekenbank AG: Budapester Str. 1, 10787 Berlin; tel. (30) 259990; fax (30) 25999131; e-mail kommunikation@berlinhyp.de; internet www.berlinhyp.de; f. 1996 by merger; cap. €74m., res €594m., dep. €43,597m. (Dec. 2000); Chair. Supervisory Bd Dr WOLFGANG RUPFF; Chair. Bd of Management KLAUS LANDOWSKY.

DePfa Deutsche Pfandbriefbank AG: Postfach 2169, 65011 Wiesbaden; Paulinenstr. 15, 65189 Wiesbaden; tel. (611) 3480; fax (611) 3482549; e-mail tsai-chin.kou@depfa.com; internet www.depfa .com; f. 1922; cap. €107m., res €1,430m., dep. €165,931m. (Dec. 2001); Chair. Supervisory Bd Dr JÜRGEN WESTPHAL.

Deutsche Hypothekenbank AG: Georgspl. 8, 30159 Hannover; tel. (511) 30450; fax (511) 3045459; e-mail mail@deutsche-hypo.de; internet www.deutsche-hypo.de; f. 1872; cap. €23m., res €247m., dep. €22,245m. (Dec. 2000); Chair. Supervisory Bd LOUIS GRAF VON ZECH; 7 brs.

Deutsche Postbank AG: Friedrich-Ebert-Allee 114–126, 53113 Bonn; tel. (228) 9200; fax (228) 9202818; internet www.postbank.de; f. 1990; cap. €409m., res €4,090m., dep. €79,815m. (Dec. 2000); 100% owned by Deutsche Post AG; Chair. Prof. Dr WULF VON SCHIMMELMANN.

Eurohypo AG: Taunusanlage 9, 60329 Frankfurt a.M. tel. (180) 3497600; fax (180) 3497688888; e-mail mailbox.eurohypo@db.com; internet www.eurohypo.com; f. 2002 by merger of Deutsche Hyp (f. 1862), Europhypo (f. 1862) and Rheinhyp (f.1871); res €350m., dep. €227,900m., total assets €237,200m. (Jan 2002); Chair. Management Bd Dr KARSTEN VON KÖLLER; Chair. Supervisory Bd Dr JOACHIM VON HARBOU; 16 brs.

HVB Real Estate Bank AG: Von-der-Tann-Str. 2, 80539 München; tel. (89) 28800; fax (89) 288010226; internet www.hvbrealestate.de; f. 2001; by merger of Bayerische Handelsbank AG, Süddeutsche Bodencreditbank AG and Nürnberger Hypothekenbank AG; cap. €133m., res €995m., dep. €73,737m. (Dec. 2001).

IKB Deutsche Industriebank AG: Postfach 101118, 40002 Düsseldorf; Willhelm-Bötzkes-Str.1, 40474 Düsseldorf; tel. (211) 82210; fax (211) 82212559; internet www.ikb.de; f. 1949; cap. €225m., res €844m., dep. €29,043m. (March 2001); Gen. Mans Dr MARKUS GUTTHOFF, CLAUS MOMBURG, J. NEUPEL, S. ORTSEIFEN, G.-J. V. PUTTKAMER, Dr A. V. TIPPELSKIRCH.

KfW (Kreditanstalt für Wiederaufbau): Postfach 111141, 60046 Frankfurt a.M. Palmengartenstr. 5–9, 60325 Frankfurt a.M. tel. (69) 74310; fax (69) 74312944; e-mail info@kfw.de; internet www.kfw.de; f. 1948; cap. €511m., res €5,429m., dep. €200,812m. (Dec. 2000); Chair. Bd of Management HANS W. REICH.

Münchener Hypothekenbank eG: Nussbaumstr. 12, 80336 München; tel. (89) 53870; fax (89) 5387900; e-mail mhbinof@ muenchener-hyp.de; internet www.muenchener-hyp.de; f. 1896; cap. €209m., res €209m., dep. €28,599m. (Dec. 2001); Chair. Prof. Dr WILLIBALD J. FOLZ.

Bankers' Organizations

Bundesverband deutscher Banken (Association of German Banks): Postfach 040307, 10062 Berlin; Burgstr. 28, 10178 Berlin; e-mail bdb@bdb.de; internet www.bdb.de; f. 1951; Gen. Man. MANFRED WEBER.

Bundesverband der Deutschen Volksbanken und Raiffeisenbanken eV (BVR) (Association of German Co-operative Banks and Agricultural Credit Co-operatives): Schellingstr. 4, 10785 Berlin; e-mail poststelle@bvr.de; internet www.bvr.de; f. 1972; Pres. Dr CHRISTOPHER PLEISTER; 1,500 mems.

Bundesverband Öffentlicher Banken Deutschlands eV (Association of German Public-Sector Banks): Lennéstr. 11, 10785 Berlin; tel. (30) 81920; fax (30) 8192222; e-mail postmaster@voeb.de; internet www.voeb.de.

Deutscher Sparkassen- und Giroverband eV (German Savings Banks Association): Postfach 1429, Simrockstr. 4, 53113 Bonn; tel. (228) 2040; fax (228) 204250; e-mail postmaster@dsgv.de; internet www.dsgv.de; Pres. Dr DIETRICH H. HOPPENSTEDT.

STOCK EXCHANGES

Frankfurt am Main: Deutsche Börse AG, Börsenplatz 4, 60313 Frankfurt a.M. tel. (69) 21010; fax (69) 29977580; internet www.exchange.de; f. 1585 as Frankfurter Wertpapierbörse; also operates Neuer Markt (f. 1997) listing high growth cos; 269 mems; Chair. Supervisory Bd ROLF-ERNST BREUER; Chair. of Bd of Management Dr WERNER G. SEIFERT.

Berlin: Berliner Wertpapierbörse, Fasanenstr. 85, 10623 Berlin; tel. (30) 3110910; fax (30) 31109179; internet www.berlinerboerse .de; f. 1685; 109 mems; Pres. HANS LEUKERS.

Bremen: Bremer Wertpapierbörse, Postfach 100726, 28007 Bremen; Kohlhökerstr. 29, 28203 Bremen; tel. (421) 277440; fax (421) 2774490; e-mail info@boerse-bremer.de; internet www.boerser-bremer.de; 67 mems; Pres. HORST-GÜNTER LUCKE; Man. AXEL H. SCHUBERT.

Düsseldorf: Börse Düsseldorf AG; Ernst-Schneider-Pl. 1, 40212 Düsseldorf; e-mail kontakt@boerse-duesseldorf.de; internet www .boerse-duesseldorf.de; tel. (211) 13890; fax (211) 133287; f. 1935; 125 mem. firms; Pres. HAROLD HORAUF; Gen. Mans Dr DETLEF IRMEN, DIRK ELBERSKIRCH.

München: Bayerische Börse AG, Lenbachpl. 2A, 80333 München; tel. (89) 5490450; fax (89) 54904531; e-mail info@bayerische-boerse .de; internet www.bayerische-boerse.de; 145 mems; Chair. Supervisory Bd Dr ALBRECHT SCHMIDT; Chair, Bd of Management Dr NORBERT JUCHEM.

North Germany (Hamburg and Hannover): Börsen AG, Schauenburgerstr. 49, 20095 Hamburg, Rathenaustr. 2; 30159 Hannover; tel. (40) 3613020; fax (40) 36130223; tel. (511) 327661; fax (511) 324915; f. 1999; by merger of Hanseatische Wertpapierbörse Hamburg and Niedersächsische Börse zu Hannover; 109 and 81 mems, respectively; Pres. (Hamburg) UDO BANDOW; Chair. Pres. Rechtsanwalt (Hannover) FRIEDRICH KERSTING.

Stuttgart: Baden-Württembergische Wertpapierbörse, Königstr. 28, 70173 Stuttgart; tel. (711) 2229850; fax (711) 2268119; f. 1861; 141 mems; Pres. ROLF LIMBACH; Man. Dir Dr PETER LUDWIG.

INSURANCE

German law specifies that property and accident insurance may not be jointly underwritten with life, sickness, legal protection or credit insurance by the same company. Insurers are therefore obliged to establish separate companies to cover the different classes of insurance. In December 1997 there were 2,004 insurance companies (excluding reinsurance companies, of which there were 35 in 1997/98). A selection of the most prominent is given below.

Aachener und Münchener Lebensversicherung AG: Robert-Schuman-Str. 51, 52066 Aachen; tel. (241) 600101; fax (241) 60015138; internet www.aachenerundmuenchener.de; f. 1868; Chair. Dr WOLFGANG KASKE; Gen. Man. Dr MICHAEL KALKA.

Albingia Versicherungs-AG: Ballindamm 39, 20095 Hamburg; tel. (40) 30220; fax (40) 30222585; e-mail infoa@albingia.de; internet www.albingia.de; f. 1901; Chair. Dr K. ASCHER; Gen. Man. V. BREMKAMP.

Allianz AG: Königinstr. 28, 80802 München; tel. (89) 38000; fax (89) 349941; internet www.allianz.com; f. 1890; Chair. Supervisory Bd Dr KLAUS LIESEN; Chair. Bd of Mans Dr HENNING SCHULTE-NOELLE.

Allianz Lebensversicherungs-AG: Reinsburgstr. 19, 70178 Stuttgart; tel. (711) 6630; fax (711) 6632654; internet www.allianz .de; f. 1922; Chair. Supervisory Bd Dr H. SCHULTE-NOELLE; Chair. Bd of Mans Dr G. RUPPRECHT.

Allianz Versicherungs AG: Elsa-Brandström-Str. 10–12, 80802 München; tel. (89) 38000; fax (89) 349941; e-mail medienzentrale@ allianz.de; f. 1985; Chair. Dr H. SCHULTE-NOELLE; Gen. Man. Dr R. HAGEMANN.

AXA Colonia Krankenversicherung AG: 50592 Köln; tel. (221) 148125; fax (221) 14832602; f. 1962; Chair. CLAAS KLEYBOLDT; Gen. Man. Dr CARL HERMANN SCHLEIFFER.

AXA Lebensversicherung AG: Gereonstr. 71, 50670 Köln; tel. (1803) 556622; fax (221) 14822750; e-mail service@axa.de; internet www.axa.de; f. 1853; Chair Supervisory Bd CLAAS KLEYBOLDT; Chair. Bd of Management Dr CLAUS-MICHAEL DILL.

AXA Versicherung AG: Colonia-Allee 10–20, 50670 Köln; tel. (1803) 556622; fax (221) 14822740; e-mail service@axa.de; internet www.axa.de; f. 1839 as Colonia Kölnischer Freier Versicherung AG, present name adopted 2001; Chair. Supervisory Bd CLAAS KLEYBOLDT; Chair. Bd of Management Dr CLAUS-MICHAEL DILL.

Continentale Krankenversicherung AG: Postfach 105032, 44047 Dortmund; tel. (231) 9190; fax (231) 9191799; f. 1926; Chair. F. LENSING-WOLFF; Gen. Man. Dr H. HOFFMANN.

DBV-Winterthur Lebensversicherung AG: Frankfurter Str. 50, 65178 Wiesbaden; tel. (611) 3630; fax (611) 3636565; e-mail info@ dbv-winterthur.de; f. 1872; Chair. T. SCHULTE; Man. Dir H. FALK.

Debeka Krankenversicherungsverein AG: Ferdinand-Sauerbruch-Str. 18, 56058 Koblenz; tel. (261) 4980; fax (261) 41402; f. 1905; Chair. P. KUREPKAT; Gen. Man. P. GREISLER.

Deutsche Krankenversicherung AG: Postfach 100865, 50448 Köln; Aachener Str. 300, 50933 Köln; tel. (221) 5780; fax (221) 5783694; internet www.dkv.com; f. 1927; Chair. Dr HANS-JÜRGEN SCHINZLER; Gen. Man. Dr J. BOETIUS.

Deutscher Herold Lebensversicherungs-AG: Postfach 1448, 53004 Bonn; tel. (228) 26801; fax (228) 2683692; f. 1921; Chair. W. SOBOTA; Gen. Man. H. D. RITTERBEX.

Frankfurter Versicherungs-AG: Theodor-Stern-Kai 1, 60596 Frankfurt a.M. tel. (69) 71260; fax (69) 712684455; internet www .frankfurter-alliance.de; f. 1929; Chair. Dr R. HAGEMANN; Gen. Man. Dr KARL LUDWIG FRHR VON FREYBERG.

Gerling-Konzern Allgemeine Versicherungs-AG: Postfach 100808, 50448 Köln; tel. (221) 1441; fax (221) 1443319; internet www.gerling.com; f. 1918; Chair. Supervisory Bd Dr J. ZECH; Chair. Bd of Management B. JANSKI.

Gothaer Versicherungsbank Versicherungsverein AG: Arnoldipl. 1, 50598 Köln; tel. (221) 30800; fax (221) 308103; internet www .gothaer.de; f. 1820; Chair. Supervisory Bd Dr KLAUS MURMANN; Chair. Bd Management Dr WOLFGANG PEINER.

Haftpflicht-Unterstützungs-Kasse kraftfahrender Beamter Deutschlands a.G. in Coburg (HUK-COBURG): Bahnhofspl., 96444 Coburg; tel. (9561) 960; fax (9561) 963636; e-mail info@ huk-cobwg.de; internet www.huk.de; f. 1933; CEO ROLF-PETER HOENEN.

HDI Haftpflichtverband der Deutschen Industrie Versicherungsverein a.G.: Postfach 510360, 30633 Hannover; tel. (511) 6450; fax (511) 6454545; internet www.hdi.de; f. 1903; Chair. Dr H.-J. FONK; Gen. Man. W.-D. BAUMGARTL.

Hamburg-Mannheimer Versicherungs-AG: Überseering 45, 22297 Hamburg; tel. (40) 63760; fax (40) 63762885; e-mail prr@ hamburg-mannheimer.de; internet www.hamburg-mannheimer.de; merger with Victoria Versicherung AG pending; f. 1899; Chair. Dr EDGAR JAMMOTT; Gen. Man. Dr GÖTZ WRICKE.

IDUNA Vereinigte Lebensversicherung AG für Handwerk, Handel und Gewerbe: Neue Rabenstr. 15–19, 20354 Hamburg;

tel. (40) 41240; e-mail info@signal-iduna.de; internet www
.signal-iduna.de; f. 1914; Chair. Supervisory Bd G. KURTZ; Gen. Man.
REINHOLD SCHULTE.

LVM-Versicherungen: Kolde-Ring 21, 48126 Münster; tel. (251)
7020; fax (251) 7021099; e-mail info@lvm.de; internet www.lvm.de;
f. 1896; Chair. JOCHEN BORCHERT; Gen. Man. G. KETTLER.

SIGNAL Krankenversicherung aG: Joseph-Scherer-Str. 3,
44139 Dortmund; tel. (231) 1350; fax (231) 1354638; e-mail info@
signal-iduna.de; internet www.signal-iduna.de; f. 1907; Chair.
Supervisory Bd G. KUTZ; Gen. Man. REINHOLD SCHULTE.

Vereinte Krankenversicherung AG: Fritz-Schäffer-Str. 9, 81737
München; tel. (89) 67850; fax (89) 67856523; e-mail service-center@
vereinte.de; internet www.vereinte.de; f. 1925; Chair. Dr ULRICH
RUMM.

Victoria Versicherung AG: Victoriapl. 1–2, 40198 Düsseldorf; tel.
(221) 4770; fax (211) 4772222; e-mail info@victoria.de; internet www
.victoria.de; merger with Hamburg-Mannheimer Versicherungs-AG
pending; f. 1904; Chair. Dr E. JANNOTT; Gen. Man. HORST DÖRING.

Victoria Lebensversicherung AG: Victoriapl. 1–2, 40198 Düsseldorf; tel. (211) 4770; fax (211) 4772222; e-mail info@victoria.de;
internet www.victoria.de; merger with Hamburg-Mannheimer Versicherungs-AG pending; f. 1929; Chair. Dr E. JANNOTT; Gen. Man.
MICHAEL ROSENBERG.

Volksfürsorge Deutsche Lebensversicherung AG: Postfach
106420, 20043 Hamburg; tel. (40) 28650; fax (40) 28653369; f. 1913;
Chair. Dr WOLFGANG KASKE; Gen. Man. Dr H. JÄGER.

**Württembergische AG Versicherungs-Beteiligungsgesell-
schaft:** Gutenbergstr. 30, 70176 Stuttgart; tel. (711) 6620; fax (711)
6622520; e-mail keu@wuerttembergische.de; internet www
.wuerttembergische.de; f. 1828; Chair. Supervisory Bd Dr G.
BÜCHNER; Chair. Bd of Management G. MEHL.

Reinsurance

Deutsche Rückversicherung AG: Düsseldorf; tel. (211) 455401;
fax (211) 4554199; f. 1951; Chair. Dr G. SCHMIDT; Gen. Man. JÜRGEN
REHMANN.

**DARAG Deutsche Versicherungs- und Rückversicherungs-
AG:** Postfach 10, 13062 Berlin; Gustav-Adolf-Str. 130, 13086 Berlin;
tel. (30) 477080; fax (30) 47708100; f. 1957; re-formed 1990; fire and
non-life, technical, cargo transport, marine hull, liability, aviation
insurance and reinsurance; Chair. KLAUS-DIETER LÄSSKER; Gen. Man.
Dr INGO WELTHER.

ERC-Aachener Rückversicherungs-Gesellschaft AG: Postfach
25, 52001 Aachen; tel. (241) 93690; fax (241) 9369205; f. 1853; Chair.
Supervisory Bd KAJ AHLMANN; Chair. Management Bd BERNHARD C.
FINK.

ERC Frankona Rückversicherungs-AG: Postfach 860380, 81630
München; Maria-Theresia-Str. 35, 81675 München; tel. (89) 92280;
fax (89) 9228395; f. 1886; Chair. DAVID L. CALHOUN; Gen. Man.
BERNARD C. FINK.

Gerling-Konzern Globale Rückversicherungs-AG: Hohenzol-
lernring 72, 50672 Köln; tel. (221) 1441; fax (221) 1443718; internet
www.ggre.com; f. 1954; Chair. NORBERT STROHSCHEIN.

Hamburger Internationale Rückversicherung AG: Postfach
1161, 25452 Rellingen; Halstenbekerweg 96A, 25462 Rellingen; tel.
(4101) 4710; fax (4101) 471298; f. 1965; Chair. IVOR KIVERSTEIN; Gen.
Man. R. SOLL.

Hannover Rückversicherungs-AG: Postfach 610369, 30603
Hannover; Karl-Wiechert-Allee 50, 30625 Hannover; tel. (511)
56040; fax (511) 56041188; e-mail info@hannover-re.com; internet
www.hannover-re.com; f. 1966; Chair. Supervisory Bd W. BAUM-
GARTL; Chair. Management Bd W. ZELLER.

Kölnische Rückversicherungs-Gesellschaft AG: Postfach
102244, 50668 Köln; Theodor-Heuss-Ring 11, 50462 Köln; tel. (221)
97380; fax (221) 9738494; e-mail contact@gcr.com; internet www.gcr
.com; f. 1846; Chair. Dr PETER LÜTKE-BORNEFELD.

Münchener Rückversicherungs-Gesellschaft AG: Königinstr.
107, 80802 München; tel. (89) 38910; fax (89) 399056; e-mail info@
munichre.com; internet www.munichre.com; f. 1880; all classes of
reinsurance; Chair. ULRICH HARTMANN; Gen. Man. Dr HANS-JÜRGEN
SCHINZLER.

R + V Versicherung-AG Reinsurance: Sonnenberger Str. 44,
65193 Wiesbaden; tel. (611) 533940; fax (611) 529610; f. 1935; all
classes of reinsurance; Chair. W. GRÜGER; Gen. Man. Dr J. FÖRTERER.

Swiss Re Germany AG: Dieselstr. 11, 85774 Unterföhring bei
München; tel. (89) 38440; fax (89) 38442279; e-mail info.srmuc@
swissre.com; internet www.swissre.com; Chair. Dr B. GAS; Gen.
Man. M. LIES.

Principal Insurance Association

Gesamtverband der Deutschen Versicherungswirtschaft eV:
Friedrichstr. 191, 10117 Berlin; tel. (30) 20205000; fax (30)
20206000; e-mail berlin@gdv.org; internet www.gdv.de; f. 1948;
affiliating three mem. asscn and 441 mem. cos; Pres. and CEO Dr
BERND MICHAELS (Düsseldorf).

Trade and Industry

GOVERNMENT AGENCIES

Bundesagentur für Aussenwirtschaft (German Office for Foreign Trade): Postfach 100522, 50445 Köln; Agrippastr. 87–93, 50676
Köln; tel. (221) 20570; fax (221) 2057212; e-mail info@bfai.de;
internet www.bfai.de.

**Bundesverband des Deutschen Gross- und Aussenhandels
eV:** Bonn; tel. (228) 260040; fax (228) 2600455; f. 1949; Dir-Gen. Dr
PETER SPARY; 77 mem. asscns.

Hauptverband des Deutschen Einzelhandels eV: Köln; tel.
(221) 9365502; fax (221) 93655719; e-mail hde@einzelhandel.de;
internet www.einzelhandel.de; f. 1947; Chair. HERMANN FRANZEN;
Exec. Dir HOLGER WENZEL.

Industrial Investment Council (IIC): Charlottenstr. 57, 10104
Berlin; tel. (30) 20945660; fax (30) 20945666; e-mail info@iic.de;
internet www.iic.de; promotes investment in eastern Germany;
Chair. HORST DIETZ.

Zentralverband Gewerblicher Verbundgruppen: Vorgebirgsstr. 43, 53119 Bonn; tel. (228) 985840; fax (228) 9858410; f.
1992; six dirs; c. 400 mems.

CHAMBERS OF COMMERCE

Deutscher Industrie- und Handelstag (Association of German
Chambers of Industry and Commerce): Adenauerallee 148, 53113
Bonn; tel. (228) 1040; fax (228) 104158; Pres. HANS PETER STIHL; Sec.-
Gen. Dr FRANZ SCHOSER; affiliates 83 Chambers of Industry and
Commerce.

There are Chambers of Industry and Commerce in all the principal
towns and also 14 regional associations including:

**Arbeitsgemeinschaft Hessischer Industrie- und Handels-
kammern:** Börsenpl. 4, 60313 Frankfurt a.M. tel. (69) 21971384;
fax   (69)   21971497;   internet   www
.arbeitsgemeinschaft-hessischer-ihks.de; Chair. Dr WOLF KLINZ;
Sec.-Gen. Dr WOLFGANG LINDSTAEDT; 11 mems.

**Arbeitsgemeinschaft der Industrie- und Handelskammern in
Mecklenburg-Vorpommern:** Schlossstr. 17, 19053 Schwerin; tel.
(385) 51030; fax (385) 5103136; e-mail info@schwerin.ihk.de; Pres.
HANSHEINRICH LIESBERG; Man. Dir. KLAUS-MICHAEL ROTHE.

**Arbeitsgemeinschaft der Industrie- und Handelskammern
Rheinland-Pfalz:** Herzogenbuscher Str. 12, 54292 Trier; tel. (651)
9777101; fax (651) 9777105; e-mail lamberty@trier.ihk.de; Sec.
WOLFGANG NATUS; four mems.

**Arbeitsgemeinschaft der Industrie- und Handelskammern in
Sachsen:** Str. der Nationen 25, 0911 Chemnitz; tel. (371) 69000; fax
(371) 643018.

**Arbeitsgemeinschaft   Norddeutscher   Industrie- und
Handelskammern:** Adolphspl. 1, 20457 Hamburg; tel. (40) 366382;
Vice-Pres. Dr MARTIN WILLICH; Sec. Dr UWE CHRISTIANSEN.

**Arbeitsgemeinschaft der Thuringer Industrie- und Handels-
kammern:** Weimarische Str. 45, 99099 Erfurt; tel. (361) 34840; fax
(361) 3485972; f. 1991; Pres. NIELS LUND CHRESTENSEN.

**Baden-Württembergischer   Industrie- und   Handelskam-
mertag:** Jägerstr. 40, 70174 Stuttgart; tel. (711) 22550060; fax (711)
22550077; e-mail info@baden-wuerttemberg.ihk.de; internet www
.bw.ihk.de; Chair. TILL CASPER.

Bayerischer Industrie- und Handelskammertag: Max-Joseph-
Str. 2, 80333 München; tel. (89) 51160; fax (89) 5116306; Pres. Dr
CLAUS HIPP; Sec.-Gen. Dr REINHARD DÖRFLER; 10 mems.

IHK-Vereinigung Schleswig-Holstein: Fackenburger Allee 2,
23554 Lübeck; tel. (451) 60060; fax (451) 6006999; e-mail ihk@
luebeck.ihk.de; Chair. HANS GEORG RIECKMANN; Sec.-Gen. UNDINE
STRICKER-BERGHOFF.

Industrie- und Handelskammer Magdeburg: Postfach 1840,
Alter Markt 8, 39104 Magdeburg; tel. (391) 56930; fax (391)
5693193; e-mail internet@magdeburg.ihk.de; internet www
.magdeburg.ihk.de; f. 1825; Pres. Dr KLAUS HIECKMANN.

Industrie- und Handelskammern Potsdam: Breite Str. 2A–C,
14467 Potsdam; tel. (331) 2786251; fax (331) 2786190; e-mail

ullmann@potsdam.ihk.de; internet www.Potsdam.ihk24.de; f. 1990; Pres. Dr VICTOR STIMMING; CEO PETER EGENTER.

Niedersächsischer Industrie- und Handelskammertag (NIHK): Postfach 3029, 30030 Hannover; Schiffgraben 49, 30175 Hannover; tel. (511) 3107289; fax (511) 3107383; e-mail nihk@hannover.ihk.de; f. 1899; Pres. Prof. Dr KLAUS E. GOEHRMANN; Man. Dir Dr WILFRIED PREWO; 7 mems.

Vereinigung der Industrie- und Handelskammern in Nordrhein-Westfalen: Postfach 240120, 40090 Düsseldorf; tel. (211) 367020; fax (211) 3670221; CEO HANS GEORG CRONE-ERDMANN; Pres. Dr JÖRG MITTELSTEN SCHEID; 16 mems.

INDUSTRIAL AND TRADE ASSOCIATIONS

Bundesverband der Deutschen Industrie eV (Federation of German Industry): Breite Str. 29, 10178 Berlin; tel. (30) 20281566; fax (30) 20282566; e-mail presse@bdi-online.de; Pres. Dr MICHAEL ROGOWSKI; Dir-Gen. Dr LUDOLF VON WARTENBERG; mems include some of the following asscns:

Arbeitsgemeinschaft Keramische Industrie eV (Ceramics): Postfach 1624, 95090 Selb; Schillerstr. 17, 95100 Selb; tel. (987) 8080; fax (987) 70492; Pres. WENDELIN VON BOCH; Man. PETER FRISCH-HOLZ.

Bundesverband Baustoffe—Steine und Erden eV (Building): Postfach 610486, 10928 Berlin; Kochstr. 66, 10969 Berlin; tel. (30) 72619990; fax (30) 726199912; e-mail info@bvbaustoffe.de; internet www.baustoffindustrie.de; f. 1948; Pres. Dr JÜRGEN LOSE; Chief Dir Dr WOLFGANG MACK.

Bundesverband Bekleidungsindustrie eV (Clothing): Postfach 100955, 50449 Köln; Mevissenstr. 15, 50668 Köln; tel. (221) 7744110; fax (221) 7744118; e-mail bbi@bbi-online.de; internet www.bbi-online.de; Pres. PAUL DANKBAR; Dirs-Gen. BERND KEMPER, FRIED-HELM N. SARTORIS.

Bundesverband der Deutschen Entsorgungswirtschaft (BDE) (Waste Disposal and Recycling): Tempelhofer Ufer 37, 10963 Berlin; tel. (30) 59003350; fax (30) 590033599; e-mail info@bde-berlin.de; internet www.bde-berlin.de; Pres. BERNARD KEMPER; Dir-Gen. FRANK-RAINER BILLIGMANN.

Bundesverband der Deutschen Luft- und Raumfahrtindustrie eV (BDLI) (German Aerospace Industries Asscn): Friedrichstr. 152, 10117 Berlin; tel. (30) 2061400; fax (30) 20614090; e-mail info@bdli.de; internet www.bdli.de; f. 1952; Pres. RAINER HERTRICH; Man. Dir Dr HANS EBERHARD BIRKE.

Bundesverband Druck und Medien eV (Printing and Media): Postfach 1869, 65008 Wiesbaden; Biebricher Allee 79, 65187 Wiesbaden; tel. (611) 8030; fax (611) 803113; e-mail info@bvdm-online.de; f. 1947; Pres. MANFRED ADRIAN; Man. Dir THOMAS MAYER; 12 mem. asscns.

Bundesverband Glasindustrie eV (Glass): Postfach 101753, 40008 Düsseldorf; Am Bonneshof 5, 40474 Düsseldorf; tel. (211) 4796134; fax (211) 9513751; e-mail info@bvglas.de; internet www.bvglas.de; Chair. Dr LEOPOLD VON HEIMENDAHL; 5 mem. asscns.

Bundesverband Schmuck, Uhren, Silberwaren und Verwandte Industrien eV: Zerrenstr. 32, 75172 Pforzheim; tel. (7231) 33041; fax (7231) 355887; e-mail info@bv-schmuck-uhren.de; internet www.bv-schmuck-uhren.de; Pres. LOTHAR KELLER; Man. Dir Dr ALFRED SCHNEIDER.

Bundesvereinigung der Deutschen Ernährungsindustrie eV (Food): Godesberger Allee 142–148, 53175 Bonn; tel. (228) 308290; fax (228) 3082999; e-mail bve@bve-online.de; internet www.bve-online.de; f. 1949; Chair. Dr PETER TRAUMANN; Chief Gen. Man. Prof. Dr MATTHIAS HORST.

Deutscher Giessereiverband (Foundries): Postfach 10 19 61, 40100 Düsseldorf; Sohnstr. 70, 40237 Düsseldorf; tel. (211) 68710; fax (211) 6871333; e-mail info@dgv.de; internet www.dgv.de; Pres. Dr ARNOLD KAWLATH; Man. Dir Dr KLAUS URBAT.

Deutscher Hotel- und Gaststättenverband eV (DEHOGA): Am Weidendamm 1A, 10117 Berlin; tel. (30) 7262520; fax (30) 72625242; f. 1949; Pres. ERNST FISCHER; Gen. Sec. CHRISTIAN EHLERS; over 85,000 mems.

Gemeinschaftsausschuss der Deutschen gewerblichen Wirtschaft (Joint Committee for German Industry and Commerce): Köln; tel. (221) 370800; fax (221) 3708730; f. 1950; a discussion forum for the principal industrial and commercial orgs; Pres. Dr TYLL NECKER; 16 mem. orgs.

Gesamtverband kunststoffverarbeitende Industrie eV (GKV) (Plastics): Am Hauptbahnhof 12, 60329 Frankfurt a.M. tel. (69) 271050; fax (69) 232799; e-mail tenhagen-gkv@t-online.de; internet www.gkv.de; f. 1950; Chair. GÜNTER SCHWANK; Sec.-Gen. JOACHIM DEN HAGEN; 750 mems.

Gesamtverband der deutschen Text- und Modeindustrie eV (Textiles and Clothing): Postfach 5340, 65728 Eschborn; Frankfurter Str. 10–14, 65760 Eschborn; tel. (6196) 9660; fax (6196) 42170; internet www.textil-online.de; f. 1948; Dir-Gen. Dr WOLF R. BAUMANN.

Hauptverband der Deutschen Bauindustrie eV (Building): Wiesbaden; tel. (611) 7720; fax (611) 772240; f. 1948; Pres. Dr OTHMAR FRANZ; Dir-Gen. MICHAEL KNIPPER; 23 mem. asscns.

Hauptverband der Deutschen Holz und Kunststoffe verarbeitenden Industrie und verwandter Industriezweige eV (HDH) (Woodwork): Flutgraben 2, 53604 Bad-Honnef; tel. (2224) 93770; fax (2224) 937777; e-mail info@hdh-ev.de; internet www.hdh-ev.de; f. 1948; Pres. HELMUT LÜBKE; Man. Dir DIRK-UWE KLAAS; 24 mem. asscns.

Hauptverband der Papier, Pappe und Kunststoffe verarbeitenden Industrie eV (HPV) (Paper, Board and Plastic): Strubbergstr. 70, 60489 Frankfurt a.M. tel. (69) 9782810; fax (69) 97828130; e-mail info@hpv-ev.org; internet www.hpv-ev.org; f. 1948; 10 regional groups, 20 production groups; Pres. LUTZ BOEDER; Dir-Gen. THOMAS BECK; 1,300 mems.

Kaliverein eV (Potash): Postfach 410554, 34067 Kassel; Wilhelmshöher Allee 239, 34121 Kassel; tel. (561) 318270; fax (561) 3182716; e-mail kaliverein@k-plus-s.com; internet www.kaliverein.de; f. 1905; Pres. Dr RALF BETHKE; Man. Dir Dr ARNE BROCKHOFF.

Mineralölwirtschaftsverband eV (Petroleum): Steindamm 55, 20099 Hamburg; tel. (40) 248490; fax (40) 24849-253; e-mail mwv@mwv.de; internet www.mwv.de; f. 1946; Chair. WILHELM BONSE-GEUKING; Man. Dir Dr PETER SCHLÜTER.

SPECTARIS—Deutscher Industrieverband für optische, medizinische und mechatronische Technologien eV (German Industrial Asscn for Optical, Medical and Mechatronical Technologies): Kirchweg 2, 50858 Köln; tel. (221) 9486280; fax (221) 94862880; e-mail info@spectaris.de; internet www.spectaris.de; f. 1949; Chair. Prof. Dr UTZ CLAASSEN; Dir SVEN BEHRENS.

Verband der Automobilindustrie eV (Motor Cars): Postfach 170563, 60079 Frankfurt a.M. Westendstr. 61, 60325 Frankfurt a.M. tel. (69) 975070; fax (69) 97507261; e-mail info@vda.de; internet www.vda.de; Pres. Prof. Dr BERND GOTTSCHALK.

Verband der Chemischen Industrie eV (Chemical Industry): Karlstr. 21, 60329 Frankfurt a.M. tel. (69) 25560; fax (69) 2556-1471; e-mail vci@vci.de; internet www.chemische-industrie.de; f. 1877; Pres. Prof. Dr WILLHELM SIMSON; Dir-Gen. Dr WILFRIED SAHM; 1,500 mems.

Verband der Cigarettenindustrie (Cigarettes): Königswinterer Str. 550, 53227 Bonn; tel. (228) 449060; fax (228) 442582; e-mail vdc@vdc.bonn.de; Chair. THIERRY PATERNOT; Dir-Gen. Dr ERNST BRÜCKNER.

Verband Deutscher Maschinen- und Anlagenbau eV (VDMA) (German Engineering Federation): Postfach 710864, 60498 Frankfurt a.M. Lyoner Str. 18, 60528 Frankfurt a.M. tel. (69) 66030; fax (69) 66031511; e-mail puoe@vdma.org; internet www.vdma.org; f. 1892; Pres. EBERHARD REUTHER; Gen. Man. Dr HANNES HESSE.

Verband Deutscher Papierfabriken eV (Paper): Adenauerallee 55, 53113 Bonn; tel. (228) 267050; fax (228) 2670562; Pres. HANS-MICHAEL GELLENKAMP; Dir-Gen. KLAUS WINDHAGEN.

Verband für Schiffbau und Meerestechnik eV (Shipbuilding): An der Alster 1, 20099 Hamburg; tel. (40) 2801520; fax (40) 28015230; e-mail info@vsm.de; internet www.vsm.de; Gen. Dir Dr WERNER SCHÖTTELNDREYER; Man. Dirs VOLKHARD MEIER, Dr MATHIAS MÜNCHAU.

Verein der Zuckerindustrie (Sugar): Am Hofgarten 8, 53113 Bonn; tel. (228) 22850; fax (228) 2285100; e-mail wvz-vdz@zuckerverbaende.de; internet www.zuckerverbaende.de; f. 1850; Chair. Dr KLAUS KORN; Dir-Gen. Dr DIETER LANGENDORF.

Wirtschaftsverband der Deutschen Kautschukindustrie eV (WDK) (Rubber): Zeppelinallee 69, 60487 Frankfurt a.M. tel. (69) 79360; fax (69) 7936165; e-mail info@wdk.de; internet www.wdk.de; f. 1894; Pres. PAUL EBERHARD-KRUG; Gen. Man. FRITZ KATZENSTEINER; 87 mems.

Wirtschaftsverband Erdöl- und Erdgasgewinnung eV (Association of Crude Oil and Gas Producers): Brühlstr. 9, 30169 Hannover; tel. (511) 121720; fax (511) 1217210; e-mail info@erdoel-erdgas.de; internet www.erdoel-erdgas.de; f. 1945; Pres. WULF HAGEMANN; Gen. Man. JOSEF SCHMID.

Wirtschaftsverband Stahlbau und Energietechnik (SET) (Steel and Energy): Postfach 320420, 40419 Düsseldorf; Sternstr. 36, 40479 Düsseldorf; tel. (211) 4987092; fax (211) 4987036; e-mail set@set-online.de; internet www.set-online.de; Chair. KLAUS DIETER RENNERT; Dir-Gen. R. MAASS.

WSM—Wirtschaftsverband Stahl- und Metallverarbeitung eV (Steel and Metal-Processing Industry): Postfach 105121, 40858 Ratingen; An der Pönt 48, 40885 Ratingen; tel. (2102) 1860; fax (2102) 186169; internet www.wsm-net.de; Pres. JÜRGEN R. THUMANN; Dir-Gen. Dr ANDREAS MOEHLENKAMP.

Centralvereinigung Deutscher Wirtschaftsverbände für Handelsvermittlung und Vertrieb: Am Weidendamm 1A, 10117 Berlin; tel. (30) 72625600; fax (30) 72625699; e-mail centralvereinigung@cdh.de; internet www.cdh.de; f. 1902; Pres. HORST PLATZ; Gen. Sec. Dr ANDREAS PAFFHAUSEN; 18,000 mems.

Wirtschaftsvereinigung Bergbau eV (Mining): Postfach 120736, 10597 Berlin; Am Schillertheater 4, 10625 Berlin; tel. (30) 3151820; e-mail wvb.berlin@t-online.de; internet www.wv-bergbau.de; Pres. Dr VOLKER SCHÄFER; Gen. Man. Dr HEINZ-NORBERT SCHÄCHTER; 15 mem. asscns.

WirtschaftsVereinigung Metalle (Metal): Postfach 105463, 40045 Düsseldorf; Am Bonneshof 5, 40474 Düsseldorf; tel. (211) 47960; fax (211) 4796400; e-mail postmaster@ne-metalnet.de; internet www.ne-metalnet.de; Pres. Dr WERNER MARNETTE; Dir-Gen. MARTIN KNEER.

Wirtschaftsvereinigung Stahl (Steel): Postfach 105464, 40045 Düsseldorf; Sohnstr. 65, 40237 Düsseldorf; tel. (211) 67070; fax (211) 6707310; e-mail wvstahl@wvstahl.de; internet www.stahl-online.de; Pres. Prof. Dr DIETER AMELING; Dir ALBRECHT KORMANN.

Wirtschaftsvereinigung Ziehereien und Kaltwalzwerke eV (Metal): Drahthaus, Kaiserswerther Str. 137, 40474 Düsseldorf; tel. (211) 4564246; fax (211) 432154; Chair. JÜRGEN R. THUMANN; Gen. Man. GÜNTER MÜLLER.

Zentralverband des Deutschen Handwerks: Mohrenstr. 20/21, 10117 Berlin; tel. (30) 206190; fax (30) 20619460; e-mail info@zdh .de; internet www.zdh.de; f. 1949; Pres. DIETER PHILPP; Gen. Sec. HANNS-EBERHARD SCHLEYER; 56 mem. chambers, 52 asscns.

Zentralverband Elektrotechnik- und Elektronikindustrie eV (ZVEI) (Electrical and Electronic Equipment): Postfach 701261, 60591 Frankfurt a.M. Stresemannallee 19, 60596 Frankfurt a.M. tel. (69) 63020; fax (69) 6302317; e-mail zvei@zvei.org; internet www .zvei.org; f. 1918; Chair. DIETMAR HARTING; Dirs Dr HORST GERLACH, GOTTHARD GRASS; 1,400 mems.

EMPLOYERS' ORGANIZATIONS

Bundesvereinigung der Deutschen Arbeitgeberverbände (BDA) (Confederation of German Employers' Associations): im Haus des Deutschen Wirtschaft, 11054 Berlin; tel. (30) 20330; fax (30) 20331055; e-mail info@bda-online.de; internet www.bda-online .de; f. 1904; represents the professional and regional interests of German employers in the social policy field, affiliates 14 regional asscns, and 54 branch asscns, of which some are listed under industrial asscns; Pres. Dr DIETER HUNDT; Dirs Dr REINHARD GÖHNER, JÜRGEN HUSMANN, DIETMAR HEISE.

Affiliated associations:

Arbeitgeberkreis Gesamttextil im Gesamtverband der Textilindustrie in der Bundesrepublik Deutschland eV (General Textile Employers' Organization): Frankfurter Str. 10–14, 65760 Eschborn; tel. (6196) 9660; fax (6196) 42170; internet www.textil-online.de; Chair. HARTMUT BIELEFELD; Dir Dr KLAUS SCHMIDT; 9 mem. asscns.

Arbeitgeberverband der Cigarettenindustrie (Employers' Association of Cigarette Manufacturers): Harvestehuder Weg 88, 20149 Hamburg; tel. (40) 445739; fax (40) 443039; f. 1949; Pres. SIEGFRIED HANKE; Dir LUTZ SANNIG.

Arbeitgeberverband der Deutschen Binnenschiffahrt eV (Employers' Association of German Inland Waterway Transport): Dammstr. 15–17, 47119 Duisburg; tel. (203) 8000631; fax (203) 8000628; e-mail vbw-eubinsch@t-online.de; Pres. Dr WOLFGANG HÖNEMANN; Dir G. DÜTEMEYER.

Arbeitgeberverband der Deutschen Glasindustrie eV (German Glass Industry Employers' Association): Postfach 200219, 80002 München; Max-Joseph-Str. 5, 80333 München; tel. (89) 55178400; fax (89) 55178444; e-mail info@avglas.de; internet www.avglas.de; Pres. PETER WEINMANN; Gen. Man. GERNOT STEIN-BACHER.

Arbeitgeberverband der Deutschen Kautschukindustrie (ADK) eV (German Rubber Industry Employers' Association): Schiffgraben 36, 30175 Hannover; tel. (511) 85050; fax (511) 8505201; e-mail agv-hannover@vmn.de; internet www.adk-ev.de; Pres. JÜRGEN KREBAUM; Gen. Man. DIETRICH KRÖNCKE.

Arbeitgeberverband Deutscher Eisenbahnen eV (German Railway Employers' Association): Volksgartenstr. 54A, 50677 Köln; tel. (221) 9318450; fax (221) 93184588; Pres. Dr HANS-PETER SCHIFF; Dir Dr HANS-PETER ACKMANN.

Arbeitgeberverband des Privaten Bankgewerbes eV (Private Banking Employers' Association): Burgstr. 28, 10178 Berlin; tel. (30) 590011270; f. 1954; 149 mems; Pres. Dr TESSEN VON HEYDERBRECK; Dir GERD BENRATH.

Arbeitgeberverband der Versicherungsunternehmen in Deutschland (Employers' Association of Insurance Companies): Postfach 860120, 81628 München; Arabellastr. 29, 81925 München; tel. (89) 9220010; fax (89) 92200150; e-mail agvvers@ agv-vers.de; internet www.agv-vers.de; f. 1950; Pres. HANS SCHREIBER; Dir-Gen. Dr JÖRG MÜLLER-STEIN.

Bundesarbeitgeberverband Chemie eV (Federation of Employers' Associations in the Chemical Industry): Postfach 1280, 65002 Wiesbaden; Abraham-Lincoln-Str. 24, 65189 Wiesbaden; tel. (611) 778810; fax (611) 7788123; e-mail info@bavc.de; internet www.bavc.de; Pres. Dr RÜDIGER ERCKEL; Dir HANS PAUL FREY; 11 mem. asscns.

Bundesvereinigung der Arbeitgeber im Bundesverband Bekleidungsindustrie eV (Confederation of Employers of the Clothing Industry): Postfach 100955, 50449 Köln; Mevissenstr. 15, 50668 Köln; tel. (221) 7744110; fax (221) 7744118; e-mail bbi@ bbi-online.de; internet www.bbi-online.de; Pres. WILFRIED BRANDES; Dir BERND KEMPER; 18 mem. asscns.

Gesamtverband der Deutschen Land- und Forstwirtschaftlichen Arbeitgeberverbände eV (Federation of Agricultural and Forestry Employers' Associations): Godesberger Allee 142–148, 53175 Bonn; tel. (228) 8198249; fax (228) 8198204; e-mail glfa@bauernverband.net; Pres. LOTHAR LEMPE; Sec. BURKHARD MÖLLER.

Gesamtverband der metallindustriellen Arbeitgeberverbände eV (Federation of the Metal Trades Employers' Associations): Volksgartenstr. 54A, 50677 Köln; tel. (221) 33990; fax (221) 3399233; e-mail info@gesamtmetall.de; Pres. Dr WERNER STUMPFE; 15 mem. asscns.

Vereinigung der Arbeitgeberverbände der Deutschen Papierindustrie eV (Federation of Employers' Associations of the German Paper Industry): Adenauerallee 55, 53113 Bonn; tel. (228) 2672810; fax (228) 215270; e-mail vap-papier@t-online.de; Pres. REINHOLD O. SCHADLER; Dir PETER KARTHÄUSER; 8 mem. asscns.

Vereinigung der Arbeitgeberverbände energie- und versorgungswirtschaftlicher Unternehmungen (Employers' Federation of Energy and Power Supply Enterprises): Kurt Schumacher-Str. 24, 30159 Hannover; tel. (511) 911090; fax (511) 9110940; f. 1962; Pres. Dr ACHIM MIDDELSCHULTE; Dir HERMANN D. STRÖHMBERG; 6 mem. asscns.

Regional employers' associations:

Landesvereinigung Baden-Württembergischer Arbeitgeberverbände eV: Postfach 700501, 70574 Stuttgart; Löffelstr. 22–24, 70597 Stuttgart; tel. (711) 76820; fax (711) 7651675; e-mail info@suedwestmetall.de; internet www.agv-bw.de.de; Pres. Dr DIETER HUNDT; Dir Dr ULRICH BROCKER; 44 mem. asscns.

Vereinigung der Bayerischen Wirtschaft (Federation of Employers' Associations in Bavaria): Postfach 202061, 80020 München; Max-Joseph-Str. 5, 80333 München; tel. (89) 55178100; fax (89) 55178111; e-mail info@vbw-bayern.de; internet www.vbw-bayern.de; Pres. RANDOLF RODENSTOCK; Gen. Man STEPHAN GÖTZL; 76 mem. asscns.

Vereinigung der Unternehmensverbände in Berlin und Brandenburg eV (Federation of Employers' Associations in Berlin and Brandenburg): Am Schillertheater 2, 10625 Berlin; tel. (30) 310050; fax (30) 31005166; e-mail uvb@uvb-online.de; internet www.uvb-online.de; Pres. GERD VON BRANDENSTEIN; Dir Dr HARTMANN KLEINER; 62 mem. asscns.

Die Unternehmensverbände im Lande Bremen eV (Federation of Employers' Associations in the Land of Bremen): Postfach 100727, 28007 Bremen; Schillerstr. 10, 28195 Bremen; tel. (421) 368020; fax (421) 3680249; Pres. Dr MANFRED AHLSDORFF; Dir EBERHARD SCHODDE; 15 mem. asscns.

UVNord—Vereinigung der Unternehmensverbände in Hamburg und Schleswig-Holstein eV (Federation of Employers' Associations in Hamburg and Schleswig-Holstein): Postfach 601969, 22219 Hamburg; Kapstadtring 10, 22297 Hamburg; tel. (40) 63785100; fax (40) 63785075; e-mail meineke@uvnord.de; internet www.uvnord.de; Pres. Prof. Dr HANS HEINRICH DRIFTMANN; Dir JÜRGEN MEINEKE; 53 mem. asscns.

Vereinigung der Hessischen Unternehmerverbände eV (Hessian Federation of Enterprise Associations): Postfach 500561, 60394 Frankfurt a.M. Emil-von-Behring-Str. 4, 60439 Frankfurt a.M. tel. (69) 958080; fax (69) 95808126; e-mail info@ vhu.de; internet www.vhu.de; f. 1947; Pres. Prof. DIETER WEIDEMANN; Dir and Sec. VOLKER FASBENDER; 50 mem. asscns.

Vereinigung der Unternehmensverbände für Mecklenburg-Vorpommern eV (Federation of Employers' Associations of Mecklenburg-West Pomerania): Eckdrift 93, 19061 Schwerin; tel. (385) 6356100; fax (385) 6356151; e-mail info@vumv.de; internet www.vumv.de; Pres. KLAUS HERING; Dir Dr THOMAS KLISCHAN; 28 mem. asscns.

Unternehmensverbände Niedersachsen eV (Federation of Employers' Associations in Lower Saxony): Schiffgraben 36, 30175 Hannover; tel. (511) 8505243; fax (511) 8505268; e-mail uvn@uvn-online.de; internet www.uvn-online.de; f. 1951; Pres. GOETZ VON ENGELBRECHTEN; Dir Dr VOLKER MÜLLER; 67 mem. asscns.

Landesvereinigung der Arbeitgeberverbände Nordrhein-Westfalen eV (North Rhine-Westphalia Federation of Employers' Associations): Postfach 300643, 40406 Düsseldorf; Uerdingerstr. 58–62, 40474 Düsseldorf; tel. (211) 45730; fax (211) 4573206; e-mail arbeitgebernrw@arbeitgebernrw.de; internet www.arbeitgebernrw.de; Pres. Dr JOCHEN F. KIRCHHOFF; Dir Dr HANSJÖRG DÖPP; 92 mem. asscns.

Landesvereinigung Unternehmerverbände Rheinland-Pfalz eV (LVU) (Federation of Employers' Associations in the Rhineland Palatinate): Postfach 2966, 55019 Mainz; Hindenburgstr. 32, 55118 Mainz; tel. (6131) 55750; fax (6131) 557539; e-mail contact@lvu.de; internet www.lvu.de; f. 1963; Pres. Dr GERHARD F. BRAUN; Gen. Man WERNER SIMON; 27 mem. asscns.

Vereinigung der Saarländischen Unternehmensverbände (Federation of Employers' Associations in Saarland): Postfach 650433, 66143 Saarbrücken; Harthweg 15, 66119 Saarbrücken; tel. (681) 954340; fax (681) 9543474; e-mail kontakt@vsu.de; internet www.vsu.de; Pres. Dr WALTER KOCH; Dir Dr HEIKO JÜTTE; 16 mem. asscns.

Vereinigung der Sächsischen Wirtschaft eV (VSW) (Federation of Employers' Associations in Saxony): Postfach 300200, 01131 Dresden; Washingtonstr. 16/16A, 01139 Dresden; tel. (351) 255930; fax (351) 2559378; e-mail info@wirtschaftsverbaende-sachsen.de; internet www.wirtschaftsverbaende-sachsen.de; Pres. WOLFGANG HEINZE; Gen. Man. Dr ANDREAS WINKLER; 40 mem. asscns.

Landesvereinigung der Arbeitgeber-und-Wirtschaftsverbände Sachsen-Anhalt eV (Provincial Federation of Employers' and Managers' Associations of Saxony-Anhalt): Hegelstr. 39, 39104 Magdeburg; tel. (391) 5982250; fax (391) 5982259; e-mail info@lvsa.org; internet www.lvsa.org; Pres. Dr HELGE FÄNGER; Gen. Man. KLAUS LIEDKE; 31 mem. asscns.

Verband der Wirtschaft Thüringens eV (Association of Thuringian Management): Postfach 100753, 99007 Erfurt; Lossiusstr. 1, 99094 Erfurt; tel. (361) 67590; fax (361) 6759222; e-mail info@vwt.de; internet www.vet.de; Pres. WALTER BOTSCHATZKI; Dir LOTAR SCHMIDT; 37 mem. asscns.

UTILITIES

Electricity

Bewag AG: 12432 Berlin; tel. (30) 26711077; fax (30) 26714667; e-mail bewag@bewag.com; internet www.bewag.de; f. 1884; supplies Berlin; promotes development of urban utilization of renewable energy resources.

E.ON Energie AG: Brienner Str. 40, 80333 München; tel. (800) 2030408; fax (800) 3888883; e-mail info@eon-energie.de; internet www.eon-energie.de; f. 2000; by merger of Bayernwerk AG and Preussenelektra AG; Jt Chairs of Bd ULRICH HARTMANN, Prof. Dr WILHELM SIMSON.

Energie Baden-Württemberg (EnBW): Durlacher Allee 93; tel. (800) 999; e-mail info@enbw.com; internet www.enbw.com.

Hamburgische Electrizitäts-Werke AG (HEW): Überseering 12, 22297 Hamburg; tel. (40) 63960; fax (40) 63862770; e-mail hew@hew.de; internet www.hew.de; 73% owned by regional Govt; supplies Hamburg region.

RWE Energie AG: Postfach 103165, 45031 Essen; Kruppstr. 5, 45128 Essen; tel. (201) 1851; fax (201) 1854313; internet www.rweenergie.de; acquired Thames Water Utilities Ltd (UK) in 2000 and American Water Works Asscn (USA) in 2001; Pres. DIETMAR KUHNT; CEO MANFRED REMMEL.

VDEW—Verband der Elektrizitätswirtschaft eV: Stresemannallee 23, 60596 Frankfurt a.M. tel. (69) 63041; fax (69) 6304289; e-mail vdew-info@vdew.net; internet www.strom.de; asscn of electricity supply cos; Dir-Gen. Dr EBERHARD MELLER.

Vereinigte Elektrizitätswerke Westfalen AG (VEW): Postfach 105056, 44047 Dortmund; Rheinlanddamm 24, 44139 Dortmund; tel. (231) 4381; e-mail info@vew.de; internet www.vew.de; partly state-owned; serves North Rhine-Westphalia.

Vereinigte Energiewerke AG (VEAG): Chaussestr. 23, 10115 Berlin; tel. (30) 51512521; fax (30) 51502220; e-mail info@veag.de; internet www.veag.de; serves eastern Germany.

Gas

Bundesverband der Deutschen Gas- und Wasserwirtschaft eV (BGW): Berlin; tel. (30) 280410; internet www.bgw.de; asscn of gas and water cos.

GASAG Berliner Gaswerke AG: 10703 Berlin; tel. (30) 78720; fax (30) 78723044; e-mail service@gasag.de; internet www.gasag.de; Chair. Supervisory Bd Dr KARL KAUERMANN.

Gasversorgung Süddeutschland GmbH (GVS): Stuttgart; internet www.gvs-erdgas.de; f. 1961; Chair. Supervisory Bd GERHARD WIDDER.

Ruhrgas AG: Huttropstr. 60, 45138 Essen; tel. (201) 18400; fax (201) 1843766; e-mail info@ruhrgas.com; internet www.ruhrgas.de; f. 1926; Chair. Dr BURCKHARD BERGMANN.

Vereinigte Elektrizitätswerke Westfalen AG (VEW): Postfach 105056, 44047 Dortmund; Rheinlanddamm 24, 44139 Dortmund; tel. (231) 4381; e-mail info@vew.de; internet www.vew.de; partly state-owned; supplies gas (and electricity see above) to North Rhine-Westphalia.

TRADE UNIONS

Following German unification in October 1990, the trade unions of the former GDR were absorbed into the member unions of the DGB (see below).

Deutscher Gewerkschaftsbund (DGB): Henriette-Herz-Pl. 2, 10178 Berlin; tel. (30) 240600; fax (30) 24060471; e-mail ulrike.wheeler@bundesvorstand.dgb.de; internet www.dgb.de; f. 1949; Pres. MICHAEL SOMMER; Vice-Pres. URSULA ENGELEN-KEFER.

The following unions, with a total of 8,310,783 members (December 1998), are affiliated to the DGB:

Industriegewerkschaft Bauen-Agrar-Umwelt (Building and Construction Trade): Olof-Palme-Str. 19, 60439 Frankfurt a.M. tel. (69) 957370; fax (69) 95737800; e-mail presse@igbau.de; internet www.igbau.de; Pres. KLAUS WIESEHÜGEL; 539,744 mems (Dec. 2000).

Industriegewerkschaft Bergbau, Chemie, Energie (IG BCE) (Mining, Chemical and Energy): Postfach 3047, 30030 Hannover; Königsworther Pl. 6, 30167 Hannover; tel. (511) 76310; fax (511) 7631713; e-mail abt.internationales.europa@igbce.de; internet www.igbce.de; Pres. HUBERTUS SCHMOLDT; 837,000 mems. (Dec. 2002).

Gewerkschaft der Eisenbahner Deutschlands (Railwaymen): Weilburger Str. 24; 60326 Frankfurt a.M. tel. (69) 7536204; fax (69) 7536223; e-mail gdad.hansen@t-online.de; Pres. NORBERT HANSEN; 352,161 mems (Dec. 1998).

Gewerkschaft Erziehung und Wissenschaft (Education and Sciences): Reifenberger Str. 21, 60489 Frankfurt a.M. tel. (69) 789730; fax (69) 78973201; e-mail info@gew.de; internet www.gew.de; Pres. Dr EVA-MARIA STANGE; 268,520 mems (Aug. 2001).

Gewerkschaft Leder (Leather): Willi-Bleicher-Str. 20, 70174 Stuttgart; tel. (711) 295555; fax (711) 293345; Pres. WERNER DICK; 25,000 mems (Dec. 1994).

IG Metall—die Gewerkschaft in Produktion und Dienstleistung der Bereiche Metall-Elektro, Textil-Bekleidung, Holz-Kunststoff (Metal Workers' Union): Lyoner Str. 32, 60528 Frankfurt a.M. tel. (69) 66930; fax (69) 66932843; e-mail presse.igm@igmetall.de; internet www.igmetall.de; Chair. KLAUS ZWICKEL; 2.7m. mems (1999).

Gewerkschaft Nahrung-Genuss-Gaststätten (Food, Delicacies and Catering): Haubachstr. 76, 22765 Hamburg; tel. (40) 380130; fax (40) 3892637; e-mail hauptverwaltung@ngg.net; internet www.ngg.net; f. 1949; Pres. FRANZ-JOSEF MÖLLENBERG; 250,000 mems (Jan. 2002).

Gewerkschaft der Polizei (Police Union): Stromstr. 4, 10555 Berlin; tel. (30) 399921111; fax (30) 39921211; e-mail buero-vorstand@gdp-online.de; f. 1950; Chair. KONRAD FREIBERG; Sec. W. DICKE; 193,578 mems (Dec. 1998).

Vereinte Dienstleistungsgewerkschaft—Ver.di (United Services Union): Potsdamer Pl. 10, 10785 Berlin; tel. (30) 69560; internet www.verdi.de; f. 2001 by a merger of Gewerkschaft Handel, Banken und Versicherungen, Industriegewerkschaft Medien, Gewerkschaft Öffentliche Dienste, Transport und Verkehr, Deutsche Postgewerkschaft and Deutsche Angestellten-Gewerkschaft; Chair. FRANK BSIRSKE; 3m. mems (2001).

The following is the largest union outside the DGB:

DBB—Beamtenbund und Tarifunion (Civil Servants' Federation and Tariff Union): Friedrichstr. 169–170, 10117 Berlin; tel. (30) 408140; fax (30) 40814999; e-mail post@dbb.de; internet www .dbb.de; f. 1918; Pres. ERHARD GEYER; 1.3m. mems (2001).

Transport

RAILWAYS

In 1999 the total length of track in Germany was 80,447 km, of which 46,373 km was electrified. In June 2001 new inter-city express rail links were opened on the Berlin–Hamburg, Munich–Zurich and Nuremberg–Dresden routes.

Deutsche Bahn AG (German Railways): Potsdamer Pl. 2, 10785 Berlin; tel. (30) 29761131; fax (30) 29761919; e-mail medienbetreuung@bku.db.de; internet www.bahn.de; f. 1994; following merger of Deutsche Bundesbahn and Deutsche Reichsbahn; state-owned (transfer to private-sector ownership pending); Chair. HARTMUT MEHDORN.

Metropolitan Railways

Berliner Verkehrsbetriebe (BVG) (Berlin Transport Authority): Anstalt des öffentlichen Rechts, 10783 Berlin; Potsdamer Str. 188, 10729 Berlin; Postfach 303131, 10773 Berlin; tel. (30) 2560; fax (30) 25649256; e-mail info@bvg.de; internet www.bvg.de; f. 1929; operates approx. 143.3 km of underground railway; also runs tram and bus services; Chair. ANDREAS GRAF VON ARNIM.

Münchner Verkehrsgesellschaft mbH (MVG): Emmy-Noether-Str. 2, 80287 München; tel. (89) 21910; fax (89) 21912405; e-mail info@swm.de; internet www.mvg-mobil.de; underground (85 km), tramway (71 km), omnibus (412 km); Man. HERBERT KÖNIG.

Association

Verband Deutscher Verkehrsunternehmen (VDV) (Association of German Transport Undertakings): Kamekestr. 37–39, 50672 Köln; tel. (221) 579790; fax (221) 514272; e-mail info@vdv.de; internet www.vdv.de; f. 1895; public transport, freight transport by rail; publishes *Der Nahverkehr* (10 a year) and *Bus + Bahn* (monthly); Pres. Dr DIETER LUDWIG; Exec. Dir Prof Dr ADOLF MÜLLER-HELLMANN.

ROADS

In 1999 there were 11,515 km of motorway, 41,321 km of other main roads and 177,899 km of secondary roads. A new 200–km motorway connecting Lübeck, via Rostock, to Stettin (in Poland) was due to be completed in 2005, at an expected cost of DM 3,700m.

INLAND WATERWAYS

There are 7,467 km of navigable inland waterways, including the Main–Danube Canal, linking the North Sea and the Black Sea, which was opened in 1992. Inland shipping accounts for about 20% of total freight traffic.

Associations

Bundesverband der Deutschen Binnenschiffahrt eV (BDB): Dammstr. 15–17, 47119 Duisburg; tel. (203) 8000661; fax (203) 8000621; e-mail infobdb@binnenschiff.de; internet www .binnenschiff.de; f. 1948; central Inland Waterway Association to further the interests of operating firms; Pres. HEINZ HOFMANN; 6 Mans.

Bundesverband Öffentlicher Binnenhäfen eV: Hammer Landstr. 3, 41460 Neuss; tel. (2131) 21624; fax (2131) 908282; e-mail boeb@binnenhafen.de; internet www.binnenhafen.de; Chair. ERICH STAAKE.

Bundesverband der Selbstständigen Abteilung Binnenschiffahrt eV (BDS): August-Bier-Str. 18, 53129 Bonn; tel. (228) 746337; fax (228) 746569; e-mail infobds@binnenschiff.de; Man. Dir ANDREA BECKSCHÄFER.

Deutsche Binnenreederei Binnenschiffahrt Spedition Logistik GmbH: Alt Stralau 55–58, 10245 Berlin; tel. (30) 293760; fax (30) 29376201; e-mail dbr@binnenreederei.de; internet www .binnenreederei.de; f. 1949; Dir-Gen. HANS-WILHELM DÜNNER.

Hafenschiffahrtsverband Hamburg eV: Mattenwiete 2, 20457 Hamburg; tel. (40) 3789090; fax (40) 37890970.

Verein für europäische Binnenschiffahrt und Wasser-strassen eV (VBW): Dammstr. 15–17, 47119 Duisburg; tel. (203) 8000627; fax (203) 8000628; e-mail vbw-eubinsch@t-online.de; internet www.vbw-ev.de; f. 1877; represents all brs of the inland waterways; Pres. Prof. D. SCHRÖDER; Dir G. DÜTEMEYER.

SHIPPING

The principal seaports for freight are Bremen, Hamburg, Rostock-Überseehafen and Wilhelmshaven. Some important shipping companies are:

Argo Reederei Richard Adler & Söhne: Postfach 107529, 28075 Bremen; Am Wall 187–189, 28195 Bremen; tel. (421) 363070; fax (421) 321575; e-mail argo@argo-adler.de; internet www.argo-adler .de; f. 1896; shipowners; Propr MAX ADLER.

Aug. Bolten, Wm. Miller's Nachfolger GmbH & Co: Mattentwiete 8, 20457 Hamburg; tel. (40) 36010; fax (40) 3601423; e-mail info@aug-bolten.de; internet www.aug-bolten.de; tramp; Man. Dir DIETER OSTENDORF.

Bugsier- Reederei- und Bergungs-Gesellschaft mbH & Co: Postfach 112273, 20422 Hamburg; Johannisbollwerk 10, 20459 Hamburg; tel. (40) 311110; fax (40) 313693; e-mail info@bugsier.de; internet www.bugsier.de; salvage, towage, tugs, ocean-going heavy lift cranes, submersible pontoons, harbour tugs; Man. Dirs B. J. SCHUCHMANN, J. W. SCHUCHMANN, A. HUETTMANN.

Christian F. Ahrenkiel GmbH & Co: Postfach 10 02 20, 20001 Hamburg; An der Alster 45, 20099 Hamburg; tel. (40) 248380; fax (40) 24838346; e-mail info@ahrenkiel.net; internet www.ahrenkiel .net; f. 1950; shipowners, operators and managers.

DAL Deutsche Afrika-Linien GmbH & Co: Palmaille 45, 22767 Hamburg; tel. (40) 380160; fax (40) 38016663; Europe and South Africa; Man. Dirs Dr E. VON RANTZAU, H. VON RANTZAU.

Deutsche Seereederei—Rostock GmbH: Lange Str. 1A, 18055 Rostock; tel. (381) 4580; fax (381) 4582215; container ships, general cargo ships, bulk carriers, cargo trailer ships, railway ferries, special tankers.

Döhle, Peter, Schiffahrts GmbH & Co KG: Postfach 500440, 22767 Hamburg; Palmaille 33, 22767 Hamburg; tel. (40) 381080; fax (40) 38108255; internet www.doehle.de; Man. Dir JOCHEN DÖHLE; shipbrokers, chartering agent, shipowners.

Egon Oldendorff: Willy-Brandt-Allee 6, 235544 Lübeck; tel. (451) 15000; fax (451) 73522; internet www.oldendorff.com; Pres. H. OLDENDORFF; Dirs J. HAGEMANN, P. TWISS, T. WEBER, K. WILKENS.

Ernst Russ GmbH: Alsterufer 10, 20354 Hamburg; tel. (40) 414070; fax (40) 41407111; f. 1893; world-wide.

F. Laeisz Schiffahrtsgesellschaft mbH & Co KG: Postfach 111111, 20411 Hamburg; Trostbrücke 1, 20457 Hamburg; tel. (40) 368080; fax (40) 364876; e-mail info@laeiszline.de; internet www .laeisz.de; f. 1983; Dirs NikolausW. SCHÜES, Nikolaus H. SCHÜES, HERBERT JUNIEL.

Fisser & v. Doornum GmbH & Co: Postfach 130365, Feldbrunnenstr. 43, 20148 Hamburg; tel. (40) 441860; fax (40) 4108050; f. 1879; tramp; Man. Dirs CHRISTIAN FISSER, Dr MICHAEL FISSER.

Hamburg Südamerikanische Dampfschiffahrts-Gesellschaft KG: Ost-West-Str. 59–61, 20457 Hamburg; tel. (40) 37050; fax (40) 37052400; e-mail central@hsdgham.hamburg-sued.com; internet www.hamburg-sued.com; f. 1871; world-wide service.

Hapag-Lloyd AG: Ballindamm 25, 20095 Hamburg; tel. (40) 30010; fax (40) 336432; e-mail info@hapag-lloyd.de; internet www .hapag-lloyd.com; f. 1970; North, Central and South America, Middle East, Asia, Australasia; Chair. MICHAEL BEHRENDT.

John T. Essberger GmbH & Co: Postfach 500429, Palmaille 49, 22767 Hamburg; tel. (40) 380160; fax (40) 38016579; f. 1924; Man. Dirs Dr E. VON RANTZAU, H. VON RANTZAU.

Oldenburg-Portugiesische Dampfschiffs-Rhederei GmbH & Co KG: Postfach 110869, 20408 Hamburg; Kajen 10, 20459 Hamburg; tel. (40) 361580; fax (40) 364131; e-mail info@opdr.de; internet www.opdr.de; f. 1882; Gibraltar, Spain, Portugal, Madeira, North Africa, Canary Islands; Man. Dirs G. KEMPF, J. BERGMANN.

Rhein-, Maas und See-Schiffahrtskontor GmbH: Krausstr. 1A, 47119 Duisburg; tel. (203) 8040; fax (203) 804-330; e-mail rms-team@rheinmaas.de; internet www.rheinmaas.de; f. 1948.

Sloman Neptun Schiffahrts-AG: Postfach 101469, 28014 Bremen; Langenstr. 44, 28195 Bremen; tel. (421) 17630; fax (421) 1763321; e-mail info@sloman-neptun.com; f. 1873; Scandinavia, North-western Europe, Mediterranean, North Africa; gas carriers; agencies, stevedoring; Mans SVEN-MICHAEL EDYE, DIRK LOHMANN.

Walther Möller & Co: Thedestr. 2, 22767 Hamburg; tel. (40) 3803910; fax (40) 38039199; e-mail chartering@wmco.de; internet www.wmco.de.

Shipping Organizations

Verband Deutscher Küstenschiffseigner (German Coastal Shipowners' Association): Hamburg-Altona; tel. (40) 313435; fax (40) 315925; f. 1896; Pres. PETER TH. HAUSEN; Man. KLAUS KÖSTER.

Verband Deutscher Reeder eV (German Shipowners' Association): Postfach 305580, 20317 Hamburg; Esplanade 6, 20354 Hamburg; tel. (40) 350970; fax (40) 35097211; e-mail vdr@reederverband.de; internet www.reederverband.de; Pres. FRANK LEONHARDT; Man. Dir Dr BERND KRÖGER.

Zentralverband der Deutschen Seehafenbetriebe eV (Federal Association of German Seaport Operators): Am Sandtorkai 2, 20457 Hamburg; tel. (40) 366203; fax (40) 366377; e-mail info@zds-seehaefen.de; f. 1932; Chair. PETER DIETRICH; 246 mems.

CIVIL AVIATION

There are three international airports in the Berlin region and further international airports at Köln-Bonn, Dresden, Düsseldorf, Frankfurt, Hamburg, Hannover, Leipzig, München and Stuttgart. Plans were under way in 2000 for the construction of a major new international airport to serve Berlin.

Aero Lloyd Flugreisen Luftverkehrs-KG: Postfach 2029, Lessingstr. 7–9, 61440 Oberursel; tel. (6171) 62501; fax (6171) 625109; f. 1981; charter services; Gen. Mans Dr W. SCHNEIDER, WOLFGANG JOHN.

Deutsche Lufthansa AG: Von-Gablenz-Str. 2–6, 50679 Köln; tel. (221) 8260; fax (221) 8263818; f. 1953; extensive world-wide network; Chair. Supervisory Bd Dr KLAUS SCHELDE; Chair. Exec. Bd JÜRGEN WEBER.

Germania Fluggesellschaft mbH: Flughafen Berlin Tegel, Gebäude Z3, 13405 Berlin; tel. (30) 41012836; fax (30) 41013500; e-mail info@germaniaairline.de; internet www.germania-flug.de; f. 1978; charter and scheduled flights; Man. Dr HINRICH BISCHOFF.

Hapag-Lloyd Flug-GmbH: Postfach 420240, Flughafenstr. 10, 30855 Langenhagen; tel. (511) 97270; fax (511) 9727739; e-mail info@hlag.de; internet www.hapag-lloyd.de; f. 1972; charter and scheduled passenger services; Exec. Chair. MICHAEL BEHRENDT.

LTU Lufttransport-Unternehmen GmbH: Flughafen, Halle 8, 40474 Düsseldorf; tel. (211) 9418888; fax (211) 9418881; f. 1955; charter and scheduled services; Man. Dir PETER HASLEBACHER.

Lufthansa Cargo AG: Langer Kornweg 34, 65441 Kelsterbach; tel. (6107) 777615; fax (6107) 777888; f. 1993; wholly-owned subsidiary of Lufthansa; freight-charter world-wide; Man. Dirs WALTER GEHL, JEAN-PETER JANSEN, STEFAN LAUER.

Lufthansa CityLine GmbH: Flughafen Köln/Bonn, Heinrich-Steinmann-Str., 51147 Köln; tel. (2203) 5960; fax (2203) 596801; e-mail unternehmenskommunikation@dlh.de; internet www.lufthansacityline.com; scheduled services; Man. Dirs KARL-HEINZ KÖPFLE, Dr THOMAS DRÄGER.

Thomas Cook: Am Grunen Weg 3, 65440 Kelsterbach; tel. (6107) 9390; fax (6107) 939440; internet www.condor.com; f. 1955 as Condor Flugdienst GmbH, current name adopted 2003; 90% owned by Thomas Cook AG, 10% owned by Lufthansa; charter airline; Man. Dirs MANFRED SCHWABENBAUER, CLAUS DIETER WEHR.

Tourism

Germany's tourist attractions include spas, summer and winter resorts, mountains, medieval towns and castles, and above all a variety of fascinating cities. The North and Baltic Sea coasts, the Rhine Valley, the Black Forest, the mountains of Thuringia, the Erzgebirge and Bavaria are the most popular areas. In 1998 there were 54,247 hotels and guesthouses in Germany, with 2,404,688 beds available for tourists. The total number of foreign visitors was about 16.9m. in 2001, compared with around 18.0m. in 2000.

Deutsche Zentrale für Tourismus eV (DZT) (German National Tourist Board): Beethovenstr. 69, 60325 Frankfurt a.M. tel. (69) 974640; fax (69) 751903; e-mail info@d-z-t.com; internet www.germany-tourism.de; f. 1948; CEO URSULA SCHÖRCHER.

GHANA

Introductory Survey

Location, Climate, Language, Religion, Flag, Capital

The Republic of Ghana lies on the west coast of Africa, with Côte d'Ivoire to the west and Togo to the east. It is bordered by Burkina Faso to the north. The climate is tropical, with temperatures generally between 21°C and 32°C (70°–90°F) and average annual rainfall of 2,000 mm (80 ins) on the coast, decreasing inland. English is the official language, but there are 10 major national languages (each with more than 250,000 speakers), the most widely spoken being Akan, Ewe, Mole-Dagomba and Ga. Many of the inhabitants follow traditional beliefs and customs. Christians comprise an estimated 69% of the population. The national flag (proportions 2 by 3) has three equal horizontal stripes, of red, yellow and green, with a five-pointed black star in the centre of the yellow stripe. The capital is Accra.

Recent History

Ghana was formed as the result of a UN-supervised plebiscite in May 1956, when the British-administered section of Togoland, a UN Trust Territory, voted to join the Gold Coast, a British colony, in an independent state. Ghana was duly granted independence, within the Commonwealth, on 6 March 1957, becoming the first British dependency in sub-Saharan Africa to achieve independence under majority rule. Dr Kwame Nkrumah, the Prime Minister of the former Gold Coast since 1952, became Prime Minister of the new state. Ghana became a republic on 1 July 1960, with Nkrumah as President. In 1964 the Convention People's Party, led by Nkrumah, was declared the sole authorized party.

In February 1966 Nkrumah, whose repressive policies and financial mismanagement had caused increasing resentment, was deposed in a military coup, whose leaders established a governing National Liberation Council, led by Gen. Joseph Ankrah. In April 1969 Ankrah was replaced by Brig. (later Lt-Gen.) Akwasi Afrifa, and a new Constitution was introduced. Power was returned in October to an elected civilian Government, led by Dr Kofi Busia. However, in reaction to increasing economic and political difficulties, the army again seized power in January 1972, under the leadership of Lt-Col (later Gen.) Ignatius Acheampong. Some improvement in Ghana's economic situation was achieved by the military, which announced in 1977 that it intended to relinquish power following a general election to be held in 1979. These plans, however, were forestalled in July 1978 by Acheampong's deputy, Lt-Gen. Frederick Akuffo, who assumed power in a bloodless coup. Tensions within the army became evident in May 1979, when junior military officers staged an unsuccessful coup attempt. The alleged leader of the conspirators, Flight-Lt Jerry Rawlings, was imprisoned, but was subsequently released by other officers. On 4 June he and his associates successfully seized power, amid popular acclaim, established the Armed Forces Revolutionary Council (AFRC), led by Rawlings, and introduced measures to eradicate corruption. Acheampong and Akuffo were among nine senior officers who were convicted on charges of corruption and executed.

The AFRC indicated that its assumption of power was temporary, and the elections took place in June 1979, as scheduled, although the return to civilian rule was postponed until September. The People's National Party, led by Dr Hilla Limann, emerged with the largest number of parliamentary seats and formed a coalition Government with support from the smaller United National Convention. Dr Limann took office as President in September. However, dissatisfaction with measures taken by the Government to improve the economy provoked widespread civil unrest.

On 31 December 1981 Rawlings seized power for a second time, and established a governing Provisional National Defence Council (PNDC), with himself as Chairman. The Council of State was abolished, the Constitution suspended, the legislature dissolved and political parties banned. In 1982 city and district councils were replaced by People's Defence Committees (PDC), which were designed to allow popular participation in local government. In 1984 the PDC were redesignated as Committees for the Defence of the Revolution (CDR).

The PNDC's policies initially received strong support, but discontent with the regime and with the apparent ineffectiveness of its economic policies was reflected by a series of coup attempts; between 1984 and 1987 some 34 people were executed for their alleged involvement in plots to overthrow the Government. In July 1987 the PNDC announced that elections for district assemblies, scheduled for mid-1987, were to be postponed until late 1988, and that the ban on political parties was to remain. In April 1988 there was an extensive government reshuffle. Elections for the district assemblies were held between December 1988 and February 1989. Although one-third of the 7,278 members of the district assemblies were appointed by the PNDC, the establishment of the assemblies was envisaged as the first stage in the development of a new political system of national democratic administration.

On 24 September 1989 a coup attempt was staged, led by a close associate of Rawlings, Maj. Courage Quashigah. Shortly afterwards the Commander of the Armed Forces was dismissed, and Rawlings assumed personal control of the armed forces until June 1990. In October 1989 five senior members of the security forces, including Quashigah, were arrested on charges of conspiring to assassinate Rawlings. The predominance of the Ewe ethnic group in government positions and other important posts was initially considered to be the cause of the revolt, although a board of inquiry into the allegations of treason concluded that most of the conspirators were motivated by personal grievances and ambition. In January 1990 five more arrests were made in connection with the coup attempt. In August the human rights organization Amnesty International criticized the continued detention of Quashigah and six other members of the security forces, claiming that they were imprisoned for political dissension.

In July 1990, in response to pressure from Western aid donors to introduce further democratic reforms, the PNDC announced that a National Commission for Democracy (NCD) would organize a series of regional debates to consider Ghana's political and economic future. (Ten such debates took place between July and October 1992.) In August the newly formed Movement for Freedom and Justice (MFJ) criticized the NCD, claiming that it was too closely associated with the PNDC, and also demanded the abolition of legislation prohibiting political associations, the release of all political prisoners, the cessation of press censorship and the holding of a national referendum on the restoration of a multi-party system. In September the MFJ accused the PNDC of intimidation, after its inaugural meeting was suppressed by security forces. In October the PNDC pledged to accept the conclusions of any national consensus on future democracy in the country.

In December 1990 Rawlings announced proposals for the introduction of a constitution by the end of 1991; the PNDC was to consider recommendations presented by the NCD, and subsequently to convene a consultative body to determine constitutional reform. However, the MFJ, the Christian Council of Ghana and the Ghana Bar Association objected to the proposals, on the grounds that no definite schedule for political reform had been presented, and that no criteria had been established for the composition of the consultative body.

In March 1991 the NCD presented a report on the democratic process, which recommended the election of an executive President for a fixed term, the establishment of a legislature and the creation of the post of Prime Minister. In May the PNDC endorsed the restoration of a multi-party system and approved the NCD's recommendations, although it was emphasized that the formation of political associations remained prohibited. Later in May the Government announced the establishment of a 260-member Consultative Assembly, which was to present a draft constitution to the PNDC by the end of 1991. The Government appointed a nine-member committee of constitutional experts, who were to submit recommendations for a draft constitution to the Consultative Assembly by the end of July.

In June 1991 the Government reiterated denials that a number of political prisoners were detained in Ghana. In the same month the PNDC announced an amnesty for political exiles, which did not, however, include persons who were implicated in acts of subversion against the Government. In August the committee of constitutional experts submitted a series of recommendations for reform, which included the establishment of a parliament and a council of state. It was proposed that the President, who would also be Commander-in-Chief of the Armed Forces, would be elected by universal suffrage for a four-year term of office, while the leader of the party that commanded a majority in the legislature would be appointed as Prime Minister. However, the subsequent review of the draft Constitution by the Consultative Assembly was impeded by opposition demands for a boycott, on the grounds that the number of government representatives in the Assembly was too high. Later in August Rawlings announced that presidential and legislative elections were to take place in late 1992.

In December 1991 the Government established an Interim National Electoral Commission (INEC), which was to be responsible for the demarcation of electoral regions and the supervision of elections and referendums. In January 1992 the Government extended the allocated period for the review of the draft Constitution to the end of March. In March Rawlings announced a programme for transition to a multi-party system, which was to be completed on 7 January 1993. Later in March 1992 the Government granted an amnesty to 17 prisoners who had been convicted of subversion, including Quashigah.

At the end of March 1992 the Consultative Assembly approved the majority of the constitutional recommendations that had been submitted to the PNDC. However, the proposed creation of the post of Prime Minister was rejected by the Assembly; executive power was to be vested in the President, who would appoint a Vice-President. Opposition groups subsequently objected to a provision in the draft Constitution that members of the Government be exempt from prosecution for human rights violations allegedly committed during the PNDC's rule. At a national referendum on 28 April, however, the draft Constitution was approved by 92% of votes cast, with 43.7% of the electorate voting.

On 18 May 1992 the Government introduced legislation permitting the formation of political associations; political parties were henceforth required to apply to the INEC for legal recognition, although emergent parties were not permitted to use names or slogans associated with 21 former political organizations that remained proscribed, and individual monetary contributions to political parties were restricted. Later in May the High Court rejected an application for an injunction against the legislation by opposition leaders, who claimed that it was biased in favour of the PNDC.

In June 1992 a number of political associations were established, many of which were identified with supporters of former President Nkrumah; six opposition movements, including the People's National Convention (PNC), led by ex-President Limann, were subsequently granted legal recognition. In the same month a coalition of pro-Government organizations, the National Democratic Congress (NDC), was formed to contest the forthcoming elections on behalf of the PNDC. However, an existing alliance of Rawlings' supporters, the Eagle Club, refused to join the NDC, and created its own political organization, the Eagle Party (later known as the EGLE—Every Ghanaian Living Everywhere—Party). In July Rawlings rejected the EGLE Party's nomination as its candidate for the presidential election. In August the Government promulgated a new electoral code, which included a provision that in the event that no presidential candidate received more than 50% of votes cast the two candidates with the highest number of votes would contest a second round within 21 days. In September Rawlings officially retired from the air force (although he retained the post of Commander-in-Chief of the Armed Forces in his capacity as Head of State), in accordance with the new Constitution, and accepted a nomination to contest the presidential election as a candidate of the NDC. The NDC, the EGLE Party and the National Convention Party (NCP) subsequently formed a pro-Government electoral coalition, known as the Progressive Alliance.

Rawlings was elected President on 3 November 1992, securing 58.3% of the votes cast. The four opposition parties that had presented candidates, the PNC, the New Patriotic Party (NPP), the National Independence Party (NIP) and the People's Heritage Party (PHP), claimed that there had been widespread electoral malpractice, although international observers maintained that, despite isolated irregularities, the election had been conducted fairly. Later in November these four parties withdrew

from the forthcoming legislative elections (scheduled for 8 December), in protest at the Government's refusal to comply with their demands for the compilation of a new electoral register and the investigation of alleged misconduct during the presidential election. As a result, the legislative elections were postponed until 22 December, and subsequently by a further week, and the nomination of new candidates permitted. In December the opposition claimed that many of its members had left Ghana, as a result of widespread intimidation by the Government. In the legislative elections, which took place on 29 December, the NDC secured 189 of the 200 seats in the Parliament, while the NCP obtained eight seats, the EGLE Party one seat and independent candidates the remaining two. According to official figures, however, only 29% of the electorate voted in the elections.

On 7 January 1993 Rawlings was sworn in as President of what was designated the Fourth Republic, the PNDC was dissolved and the new Parliament was inaugurated. Later in January the NPP, the PNC, the NIP and the PHP formed an alliance, known as the Inter-party Co-ordinating Committee, and announced that they were to act as an official opposition to the Government, despite their lack of representation in the Parliament. At the end of January Rawlings began to submit nominations for members of the Council of Ministers and the Council of State for approval by the Parliament. However, he announced that members of the existing Government were to remain in office in an interim capacity, pending the appointment of a Council of Ministers and other officials. The opposition subsequently criticized the delay in the formation of a new government and protested that the new Constitution did not permit members of the former PNDC to remain in office. In March the nomination of a number of ministers was approved by the Parliament. Later that month legislation was promulgated to exempt from prosecution perpetrators of offences that had been committed under the auspices of the former PNDC Government.

In April 1993 elections took place for the regional seats in the Council of State. In May a 17-member Council of Ministers, which included several ministers who had served in the former PNDC administration, was inaugurated. In July the Supreme Court upheld a motion by the NPP that certain existing legislation was in contravention of the Constitution. In August the NPP announced that it was prepared to recognize the legitimacy of the Government. In November a 20-member National Security Council, chaired by the Vice-President, Kow Nkensen Arkaah, was inaugurated. In December the PHP, the NIP and a faction of the PNC, all of which comprised supporters of ex-President Nkrumah, merged to form a new organization, known as the People's Convention Party (PCP).

In February 1994 long-standing hostility between the Konkomba ethnic group and the land-owning Nanumba intensified into clashes in the Northern Region in which some 500 people were killed, following demands by the Konkomba for traditional status that would entitle them to own land. The Government subsequently dispatched troops and imposed a state of emergency in seven districts. None the less, skirmishes continued in the region, and subsequently involved several other ethnic groups. Some 6,000 Konkomba were reported to have fled to Togo. In March and May 1994 minor government reorganizations were effected. Meanwhile, elections to the District Assemblies took place in March, except in those districts subject to the state of emergency. In April the Government instigated negotiations between representatives of the various groups involved in the conflict in the Northern Region. In the same month the authorities claimed that reported threats to kill Quashigah (the instigator of the coup attempt in 1989) and editors of two privately owned newspapers were part of a conspiracy to destabilize the Government. Meanwhile, the state of emergency in the Northern Region (where a total of 1,000 people had been killed, and a further 150,000 displaced) was extended for one month. In early June, however, the factions involved in the hostilities signed a peace agreement that provided for the imposition of an immediate cease-fire. The Government subsequently announced that troops were to be permanently stationed in the Northern Region in order to prevent further conflict, and established a negotiating team that was to attempt to resolve the inter-ethnic differences. In early August the Government announced that order had been restored in the Northern Region and repealed the state of emergency.

In March 1995 the Government imposed a curfew in the Northern Region following renewed ethnic violence, in which about 100 people were killed. In April a joint commission, comprising prominent members of the Konkomba and Nanumba, was established, in an effort to resolve the conflict. Meanwhile, the imposition, in February, of value-added tax (VAT) prompted widespread protests, while civil servants threatened to initiate strike action; a series of demonstrations culminated in May, when five people were killed in clashes between government supporters and protesters. (The Government subsequently agreed to suspend VAT, although it was reintroduced, at a lower rate, in 1999.) Later in May the National Executive Committee of the NCP decided to withdraw the party from the government coalition, claiming that the NDC had dominated the alliance. However, Arkaah, a member of the NCP, announced that he was to retain the office of Vice-President (despite rumours of ill-feeling between Arkaah and the President, which had been prevalent for several months), as his mandate remained valid. In July the long-serving Minister of Finance, Kwesi Botchwey, resigned, apparently in response to the failure to introduce VAT; a minor reorganization of the Council of Ministers ensued. At a by-election in the same month, a joint candidate of the PNC, NPP, NCP and PCP secured the vacant seat. In October the Chairman of the NCP resigned, following dissent within the party. In November the Commission on Human Rights and Administrative Justice commenced investigations into allegations of corruption on the part of government ministers and civil servants.

In early 1996 opposition parties demanded the resignation of Rawlings, following an incident in which the President allegedly assaulted Arkaah. Rawlings reshuffled his Council of Ministers in March. In April presidential and parliamentary elections were scheduled for December. A consolidation of the opposition parties took place prior to the deadline for the nomination of candidates in September. In May Kwame Pianim, prospective presidential candidate for the NPP, was disqualified from the elections on the grounds of his conviction for treason in 1982. In the same month the Popular Party for Democracy and Development (PPDD) merged with the PCP and declared its support for unity with the NPP. In June Thomas Appiah resigned for personal reasons as Chairman of the NCP and Vice-Chairman of the PCP. In July the NCP announced that it had removed Arkaah as its leader, following his selection as presidential candidate by the PCP. In August the NPP and the PCP formed an electoral coalition, the Great Alliance; it was subsequently announced that John Kufuor, of the NPP, was to be the Great Alliance's presidential candidate, with Arkaah as the candidate for the vice-presidency. The NCP stated that it would support the NDC in the forthcoming elections, while the PNC announced its intention to contest the elections alone, with Edward Mahama as its presidential candidate. In September the NDC nominated Rawlings as its presidential candidate. By 18 September, the official deadline for the nomination of candidates, only the Great Alliance, the Progressive Alliance (the NDC, the EGLE party and the Democratic People's Party—DPP) and the PNC had succeeded in having their nomination papers accepted. In October the NCP, which, according to the Electoral Commission (EC), had not presented the appropriate papers, declared its intention to take legal action against the Commission. In late October at least 20 people were wounded in clashes between NDC and NPP militants in Tamale and Kibi. In November a network of independent Domestic Election Observers was created to oversee the December elections. The resignation of the Minister of the Interior in October was followed, in November, by the resignations of the Minister of Trade and Industry and a presidential aide, following corruption allegations.

In the presidential election, which took place on 7 December 1996, Rawlings was re-elected, with 57.2% of the votes cast, while Kufuor secured 39.8%. In the parliamentary elections the NDC's representation was reduced to 133 seats, while the NPP won 60 seats, the PCP five and the PNC one seat. Voting was postponed in one constituency, owing to a legal dispute concerning the eligibility of candidates. (The seat was subsequently won by the NPP in a by-election in June 1997.) Despite opposition claims of malpractice, international observers declared that the elections had been conducted fairly, and an electoral turnout of 76.8% was reported. At the end of December the PCP announced that the Great Alliance had broken down. On 7 January 1997 Rawlings was sworn in as President.

The appointment of a new Council of Ministers led to a protracted dispute between the NDC and the opposition, prompting a series of parliamentary boycotts by the NPP, which insisted that all ministerial appointees be approved by the

parliamentary appointments committee prior to assuming their duties. In February 1997 opposition parties sought a ruling from the Supreme Court to prevent Kwame Peprah, the reappointed Minister of Finance, from presenting the budget. Owing to the NDC's parliamentary majority, however, procedures were approved to allow those ministers who had been retained from the previous Government to avoid the vetting process. The majority of ministerial appointments had been made by April, although a number of posts were not filled until June. In early June the Supreme Court ruled that all presidential nominees for ministerial positions had to be approved by Parliament, even if they had served in the previous Government. Following the ruling, the NPP withdrew from the chamber on several occasions when ministers attempted to address Parliament. The Government subsequently announced that it was prepared to submit all ministers to vetting procedures.

In September 1997 it was reported that three people had been killed, and more than 1,000 displaced, in the Brong-Ahafo Region, following inter-ethnic skirmishes, which had been prompted by a dispute over land-ownership. In January 1998 four people were killed, and 26 injured, in an outbreak of violence between opposing Muslim factions in the region; 57 people were subsequently arrested. In September 1998 108 people were arrested in Kumasi, in the Ashanti Region, following violent clashes between rival Muslim sects.

Following further accusations of government corruption, Rawlings dismissed a Minister of State in February 1998, after a committee of inquiry discovered lapses of propriety regarding a sea defence project. In August the NCP and the PCP merged to form the Convention Party. An earlier attempt by the party to register as the Convention People's Party (CPP) had been rejected on the grounds that the use of the name of a proscribed party was unconstitutional. (This decision was reversed in 2000, however, when the Convention Party was permitted to adopt the name and logo of Nkrumah's former party.) In October 1998 the NPP nominated Kufuor to stand again as its presidential candidate, in elections due to be held in 2000. At an NDC congress in December 1998 the position of 'Life Chairman' of the party was created for Rawlings, who confirmed that he would comply with the terms of the Constitution and not stand for a third term as President. In April 1999 Rawlings announced that the incumbent Vice-President, John Evans Atta Mills, was to contest the election on behalf of the NDC. In June, owing to dissatisfaction within the NDC at the changes carried out at the party congress and at Rawlings' pronouncement regarding his successor, a group of party members broke away to form a new political organization, the National Reform Party (NRP). Rawlings carried out three government reshuffles in late 1999 and early 2000. In April 2000 Rawlings granted amnesty to some 1,000 prisoners, including two former army officers convicted of participating in subversive activities in the 1980s. At the end of April Mills was elected unopposed as the NDC presidential candidate for the forthcoming election.

In August 2000 it was announced that the presidential and parliamentary elections would take place on 7 December. Seven parties had submitted presidential candidates by the closure of nominations in mid-September. In addition to Mills and Kufuor, the candidates included Mahama, for the PNC, and George Hagan, for the CPP. The EGLE Party and the DPP announced their support for Mills.

Isolated outbreaks of violence occurred between supporters of the NPP and the NDC in early November 2000, prompting traditional chiefs to organize a 'peace conference' later that month. The conference, which was attended by representatives of all the political parties contesting the elections, accused politicians of making inflammatory statements, but was criticized by opposition groups for failing to apportion sufficient blame on the President. The leadership of the NDC and the NPP subsequently urged their supporters to desist from acts of violence. In early December the Supreme Court reversed an EC decision that only those with new photographic identity cards would be allowed to vote in the forthcoming elections, ruling that old forms of identification, bearing thumbprints, would also be accepted. Opposition parties criticized the ruling; the NPP claimed that it would enable the NDC to manipulate the electoral process. The EC had earlier admitted that the electoral register included some 1.5m. non-existent voters. Meanwhile, the former campaign manager of the NPP, who had defected from the party in November, alleged that it was intending to instigate electoral fraud.

An estimated 62% of the electorate voted in the elections on 7 December 2000 (although, as a result of the inaccurate voters' register, it was claimed that the real rate of participation could have been as high as 80%). Observers from the Organization of African Unity (now the African Union, see p. 130) subsequently declared the elections to have been held in an orderly and fair manner. In Bawku, in the Upper East Region, at least 10 people died in inter-ethnic clashes largely unrelated to the elections. In the elections to the 200-seat Parliament the NPP won 100 seats, while the NDC obtained 92 seats, the PNC three, the CPP one, and independent candidates four. The NPP thus became the largest parliamentary party for the first time, gaining an unprecedented degree of support in rural areas. In the presidential election Kufuor won 48.2% of the valid votes cast, and Mills secured 44.5%; a second round of voting, between Kufuor and Mills, was scheduled for 28 December.

In late December 2000 there were reports of isolated violent incidents of a politically motivated nature across Ghana. Although the second round of the presidential election proceeded largely without incident on 28 December, minor disruptions to voting were reported; it was also reported that an NPP deputy had been stabbed in Accra by uniformed men, who had also fired on two of his supporters. Kufuor was elected to the presidency, with 56.9% of the valid votes cast. Mills conceded defeat on 30 December, and Rawlings congratulated Kufuor on his victory. The NPP attributed its victory to discontent with corruption in the former administration and its reluctance to implement economic and structural reforms.

On 7 January 2001 Kufuor was inaugurated as President; on the following day it was announced that Rawlings had accepted a goodwill ambassadorial post at the UN for one year. President Kufuor announced the appointment of 11 ministers on 11 January, including his brother, Kwame Addo Kufuor, as Minister of Defence. On 22 January Kufuor completed the formation of his new Council of Ministers, naming a further 12 ministers and four ministers of state. The Government notably included one member from each of the CPP, the NRP and the PNC. However, the NDC criticized as unconstitutional Kufuor's decision to allow his ministerial nominees to exercise executive authority prior to their approval by Parliament and announced that the case would be brought before the Supreme Court.

The stated priority of the new Government was the creation of wealth, which was to be encouraged by greater promotion of the private sector and through the eradication of corruption within government and in the parastatal sector. To this effect, Vice-President Alhaji Aliu Mahama announced that a code of conduct for ministers and government appointees, to be prepared in conjunction with civil society organizations, would be implemented. Additionally, Kufuor rejected symbols of the Rawlings era, including the throne used by the outgoing President, and announced that the presidential jet, which Rawlings had purchased in 1999, was to be sold. In February 2001 it was announced that members of the military were to be forbidden from celebrating the anniversaries of the coups staged by Rawlings in 1979 and 1981, and that their participation in quasi-political organizations was also to be prohibited. In addition, Kufuor ordered the suspension of the heads of six public-sector financial institutions, to facilitate an investigation into allegations of embezzlement.

Also in February 2001 Kufuor announced that a National Reconciliation Commission (NRC) was to be established to investigate allegations of human rights abuses and other violations committed by state representatives. According to proposed legislation, the NRC, which would operate for a period of one year (with a provision permitting its operation to be extended by a further six months), would be charged with investigating three periods of military rule and unconstitutional government since independence: 24 February 1966–21 August 1969, 13 January 1972–23 September 1979 and 31 December 1981–6 January 1983.

The new Government's attempts to improve the financial situation of the country proved controversial. In February 2001 the Government announced that the price of petroleum was to be gradually doubled in order to reduce the state debt, although wages were also to be increased, to reduce the impact of the rise, in an attempt to minimize public discontent. Further disquiet was provoked, in March, by the announcement that Ghana was to seek assistance under the Heavily Indebted Poor Countries initiative of the IMF and the World Bank. The Minister of Youth and Sports, Mallam Ali Yussif Issah, the sole ministerial representative of the PNC in the Government, resigned in mid-March

after allegedly losing a suitcase containing US $46,000 intended as a bonus for the national football team; in July Issah was sentenced to four years' imprisonment for theft and fraudulently causing the loss of state resources.

In August 2001 Kufuor called for a national debate on the introduction of state funding for political parties, with the intention of strengthening participation in the democratic process. In September Harona Esseku, who had served in the 1969–72 Government, was appointed as the new Chairman of the NPP. Kufuor effected a minor ministerial reshuffle in October. In December violent clashes between members of the Mamprusi and Kusasi ethnic groups in Bawku reportedly resulted in some 50 deaths. A curfew was imposed in the town, and in mid-December a delegation of ministers and military officials visited the region and announced the establishment of a commission of inquiry into the dispute.

In early December 2001 a former Deputy Minister of Finance in the Rawlings Government, Victor Selormey, was sentenced to eight years' imprisonment and fined 20m. cedis, after being convicted of defrauding the Ghanaian Government of US $1.3m., in conjunction with a US associate. At the end of the month the remains of three former military Heads of State, Akuffo, Afrifa and Acheampong, and five other senior officers who were executed in the 1979 coup were exhumed and reburied, in response to a request to the President by the widows of the dead men. Despite protests by the NDC, which had sought to ensure that the mandate of the proposed NRC would incorporate the entire period from independence until January 1993, in mid-January 2002 Kufuor endorsed the legislation on the creation of the Commission, following its approval by Parliament. In March the Supreme Court ruled that 'fast-track' courts, such as those that had convicted Issah and Selormey, were unconstitutional, thus nullifying their previous decisions. This was widely regarded as a victory for the opposition, which had claimed that the 'fast-track' system had targetted members of the former Rawlings administration.

In late March 2002 the Minister of the Interior and the Minister for the Northern Region both resigned, following the deaths of some 40 people during inter-ethnic clashes in the north of Ghana, which had been prompted by the abduction and murder of Ya-na Yakuba Andani, king of the Dagomba, in Yendi. A state of emergency was declared in the region, and a commission of inquiry was established, headed by traditional leaders. In mid-May Lt-Gen. Joshua Hamidu, the National Security Adviser, resigned after allegations of his involvement in the murder were investigated by the commission. Also in May, Kufuor officially launched the NRC, although it did not commence work until September. In April, meanwhile, the election of Dr Obed Asamoah as the new Chairman of the NDC created divisions within the party between supporters of Asamoah and Rawlings.

During August 2002 Rawlings accused the Kufuor Government of incompetence, urging 'positive defiance' from the Ghanaian people; he was subsequently summoned for questioning by the Bureau of National Investigations. In September a number of accusations of financial impropriety were made against Rawlings and former associates. In November, following the arrest of three NDC parliamentarians on charges of fraud and the reckless loss of state revenues, the NDC boycotted the Parliament in protest; this followed an earlier boycott over a controversial US $1,000m. development loan, which the NDC claimed had been obtained by the Government without due diligence.

In December 2002 Mills was nominated as the NDC's candidate for the presidential election due in 2004, defeating Botchwey, the former Minister of Finance. In January 2003 the NPP endorsed Kufuor as its presidential candidate. Meanwhile, the CPP, the NRP and the Great Consolidated People's Party were considering a merger prior to the elections. In late March Kufuor effected a major government reshuffle.

Following a military coup in Burkina Faso in October 1987, which was condemned by the Ghanaian Government, links between the two countries were temporarily strained, but improved following meetings between Rawlings and Capt. Blaise Compaoré, the Burkinabè leader, in early 1988. In December 1989, however, Ghana was accused by Burkina Faso of involvement in an attempt to overthrow the Burkinabè Government. In January 1990 120 Ghanaians were deported from Burkina Faso without official explanation. In March 1998 Ghana and Burkina Faso agreed to establish a joint commission to manage water resources. Tensions had previously arisen over

Burkinabè plans to build hydroelectric dams on a major tributary of the Volta river. Further agreements on co-operation were signed in August during a visit to Ghana by Compaoré.

In 1986 relations between Ghana and Togo became strained, following subversive activity by Ghanaian dissidents based in Togo, and an attempted coup in Togo, which was allegedly initiated from Ghanaian territory. The border between the two countries was closed for several months from October. Between December 1988 and January 1989 more than 130 Ghanaians were deported from Togo, where they were alleged to be residing illegally. In October 1991 the Governments of Ghana and Togo signed a bilateral agreement on the free movement of goods and persons. In October 1992, however, Ghana denied claims that it was implicated in subversive activity by Togolese dissidents based in Ghana. In November Rawlings formally protested to the Togolese Government, after five Ghanaians were killed by Togolese security forces on the border between the two countries.

In March 1993 the Rawlings administration denied allegations, made by the Togolese Government, of Ghanaian complicity in an armed attack on the residence of Togo's President, Gen. Gnassingbé Eyadéma. In January 1994 relations with Togo deteriorated further, following an attempt to overthrow the Togolese Government, which the Togolese authorities claimed had been staged by armed dissidents based in Ghana. The Ghanaian Chargé d'affaires in Togo was arrested, and Togolese forces killed 12 Ghanaians and attacked a customs post and several villages near the border. Ghana, however, denied any involvement in the coup attempt, and threatened to retaliate against further acts of aggression. In May allegations by the Togolese Government that Ghana was responsible for bomb attacks in Togo, owing to a lack of border security, led to further tension between the two nations. Later that year, however, relations between the two countries improved, and in November full diplomatic links were formally restored. In December Togo's border with Ghana (which had been closed in January 1994) was reopened. In August 1995 the Togolese Government denied involvement in the assassination of a political opponent who had taken refuge in Ghana. In February 1996 the Parliaments of Ghana and Togo established friendship groups. By the end of 1996 some 48,000 Togolese refugees were estimated to have received payment for voluntary repatriation. Eyadéma and Rawlings met in Accra in May 1998, and in August a joint operation was mounted to arrest a group of armed men from Ghana who had attacked military posts in Togo. In August 1999, following recent Togolese incursions into Ghanaian territory and airspace, delegations from the two countries met in Ghana for negotiations. In September the Ghanaian Government proposed that the Ghana–Togo border demarcation commission resume its work. In January 2001 President Kufuor's first state visit, following his inauguration, was to Togo, provoking criticism from pro-democracy protesters, who noted that the visit coincided with celebrations to mark the 34th anniversary of the coup that brought Eyadéma to power. Kufuor stated that his Government would be vigilant in preventing attacks on Togo from Ghanaian territory. In October 2002 the Togolese Minister of Foreign Affairs and Co-operation, Koffi Panou, denied allegations of an assassination plot against former President Rawlings.

Ghana enjoys a reputation as a peace-keeper in the region, and in 2002 was the fifth largest contributor to UN peace-keeping missions world-wide. During the conflict in Liberia (q.v.), which commenced in December 1989, Ghana contributed troops to the Monitoring Group (ECOMOG) of the Economic Community of West African States (ECOWAS, see p. 187). As Chairman of the ECOWAS Conference of Heads of State and Government, Rawlings mediated prolonged negotiations between the warring Liberian factions in the mid-1990s, and by mid-1997 some 17,000 Liberian refugees had arrived in Ghana. In August Rawlings was the first foreign leader to visit Liberia following its return to civilian rule. In January 1999 Ghanaian ECOMOG troops began to leave Liberia.

In June 1997 Ghana, Côte d'Ivoire, Guinea and Nigeria formed the 'committee of four', which was established by ECOWAS to monitor the situation in Sierra Leone, following the staging of a military coup in the previous month; troops were dispatched to participate in a peace-keeping force. It was reported in February 1998 that Ghana had opposed the use of force by the Nigerian contingent of this peace-keeping unit to overthrow the military government in Sierra Leone. Following the reinstatement of the democratically elected Government in

March, ECOMOG units remained in the country and continued to launch attacks against rebel forces, which still retained control of a number of areas. In August 2002 it was estimated that 928 Ghanaian troops were stationed in Sierra Leone.

The Kufuor administration has sought to increase Ghanaian involvement in conflict resolution within west and central Africa. In November 2001 some 401 Ghanaian troops were dispatched to participate in peace-keeping duties in the Democratic Republic of the Congo, under the auspices of the UN Mission in the Democratic Republic of the Congo (MONUC, see p. 66); they completed their final withdrawal in October 2002. After the outbreak of an armed rebellion in Côte d'Ivoire (q.v.) in September 2002, Ghana denied accusations by the Ivorian rebels that it had intervened in support of President Laurent. At the end of September an emergency ECOWAS summit on the conflict was convened in Accra. In late October Ghana pledged to provide troops to a proposed ECOWAS peace-keeping force for Côte d'Ivoire; the first contingent of the 266 Ghanaian soldiers to be contributed was deployed in February 2003. In March 2003 further talks between Gbagbo and the rebel groups took place in Accra.

Government

Under the terms of the Constitution, which was approved by national referendum on 28 April 1992, Ghana has a multi-party political system. Executive power is vested in the President, who is the Head of State and Commander-in-Chief of the Armed Forces. The President is elected by direct universal suffrage for a maximum of two four-year terms of office. Legislative power is vested in a 200-member unicameral Parliament, which is elected by direct universal suffrage for a four-year term. The President appoints a Vice-President, and nominates a Council of Ministers, subject to approval by the Parliament. The Constitution also provides for a 25-member Council of State, principally comprising regional representatives and presidential nominees, and a 20-member National Security Council, chaired by the Vice-President, which act as advisory bodies to the President.

Ghana has 10 regions, each headed by a Regional Minister, who is assisted by a regional co-ordinating council. The regions constitute 110 administrative districts, each with a District Assembly, which is headed by a District Chief Executive. Regional colleges, which comprise representatives selected by the District Assemblies and by regional Houses of Chiefs, elect a number of representatives to the Council of State.

Defence

At 1 August 2002 Ghana had total armed forces of 7,000 (army 5,000, navy 1,000 and air force 1,000). The defence budget for 2002 was estimated at 328,000m. cedis.

Economic Affairs

In 2001, according to estimates by the World Bank, Ghana's gross national income (GNI), measured at average 1999–2001 prices, was US $5,731m., equivalent to $290 per head (or $1,980 on an international purchasing-power parity basis). During 1990–2001, it was estimated, the population increased at an average annual rate of 2.4%, while gross domestic product (GDP) per head increased, in real terms, by an average of 1.8% per year. Overall GDP increased at an average annual rate of 4.3% in 1990–2001; growth in 2001 was 4.0%.

Agriculture (including forestry and fishing) contributed 35.9% of GDP in 2001. An estimated 56.6% of the labour force were employed in the sector in that year. The principal cash crops are cocoa beans (Ghana being one of the world's leading producers, and exports of which accounted for 31.6% of total exports in 1999, although their contribution declined to 15.8% in 2000), coffee, bananas, cassava, oil palm, coconuts, limes, kola nuts and shea-nuts (karité nuts). Timber production is also important, with the forestry sector accounting for 3.8% of GDP in 1997, and cork and wood, and manufactures thereof, contributing 9.0% of total export earnings in 2000. Fishing satisfies more than three-quarters of domestic requirements. During 1990–2001, according to the World Bank, agricultural GDP increased at an average annual rate of 3.3%; growth in 2001 was 3.7%.

Industry (including mining, manufacturing, construction and power) contributed 25.2% of GDP in 2001, and employed 12.8% of the working population in 1984. According to the World Bank, industrial GDP increased at an average annual rate of 2.8% in 1990–2001; growth in 2001 was 4.0%.

Mining contributed 5.7% of GDP in 1997, and employed 0.5% of the working population in 1984. Gold and diamonds are the major minerals exported, although Ghana also exploits large reserves of bauxite and manganese ore. According to IMF figures, the GDP of the mining sector increased by an average of 5.1% per year in 1993–97 and by 5.6% in 1997.

Manufacturing contributed 9.2% of GDP in 2001, and employed 10.9% of the working population in 1984. The most important sectors are food processing, textiles, vehicles, cement, paper, chemicals and petroleum. According to the World Bank, manufacturing GDP declined at an average annual rate of 1.9% in 1990–2001; growth in 2001 was 7.7%.

According to figures published by the World Bank, some 76.4% of Ghana's production of electricity was from hydro-electric power in 1999, with the Akosombo and Kpong plants being the major sources, while the remaining 23.6% was derived from petroleum. Low rainfall resulted in a severe energy crisis in 1998, prompting the Government to accelerate plans for the further development of thermal power. In August 1999 the Governments of Ghana, Benin, Togo and Nigeria agreed jointly to finance the West African Gas Pipeline, which was to supply natural gas from Nigeria to the three recipient countries. The project was scheduled to be completed in 2005. Imports of fuel comprised 21.4% of the total value of merchandise imports in 2000. Electricity is exported to Benin and Togo.

The services sector contributed 38.9% of GDP in 2001, and engaged 26.1% of the working population in 1984. According to the World Bank, the GDP of the services sector increased at an average annual rate of 5.7% in 1990–2001; growth in 2001 was 4.3%.

In 2000 Ghana recorded a visible trade deficit of US $842.9m., and there was a deficit of $412.6m. on the current account of the balance of payments. In 2000 the principal source of imports was Nigeria (10.9%); other major sources were the United Kingdom, the USA and Germany. Switzerland was the principal market for exports (taking 23.5% of the total) in that year; other important purchasers were the United Kingdom, the Netherlands and the USA. The principal exports in 2000 were gold (which accounted for 36.7% of total export earnings), cocoa beans and timber and timber products. The principal imports in 2000 were machinery and transport equipment, petroleum products, basic manufactures, and food and live animals.

According to provisional figures, Ghana's overall budget deficit for 2000 was 2,140,000m. cedis (equivalent to 7.9% of GDP). Ghana's external debt totalled US $6,657m. at the end of 2000, of which $5,529m. was long-term public debt. In the same year the cost of debt-servicing was equivalent to 19.3% of exports of goods and services. In 1990–2001 the average annual rate of inflation was 26.7%. Consumer prices increased by 32.9% in 2001. In 1995 some 41,000 people were registered as unemployed in Ghana.

Ghana is a member of the Economic Community of West African States (ECOWAS, see p. 187), of the International Cocoa Organization (ICCO, see p. 336), and of the International Coffee Organization (ICO, see p. 336).

Although Ghana's economy has made steady progress since the transfer to civilian rule in 1992, it remains vulnerable to unfavourable weather conditions and to fluctuations in international commodity prices. In May 1999 the IMF approved a three-year Enhanced Structural Adjustment Facility (subsequently renamed the Poverty Reduction and Growth Facility—PRGF), equivalent to US $209.4m., in support of the Government's economic reform programme. Economic concerns, following a sustained fall in prices of gold and cocoa during 1999–2000, were widely regarded as being a major factor in ensuring the election to the presidency, in December 2000, of John Kufuor, who was perceived to be a proponent of greater economic reform, particularly closer monitoring of public expenditure. The price of petroleum and electricity and water tariffs were significantly increased during 2001, and by the end of the year the state-owned water and electricity companies were reportedly able to cover their operating costs. Two loans, issued by the IMF under the PRGF arrangements in August 2000 and June 2001, were deemed during 2001 to have been based on inaccurate financial information provided by Ghana. In February 2002, by which time the first non-compliant loan had been repaid, the IMF granted a waiver with regard to the immediate repayment of the second loan, stating that the Ghanaian authorities had demonstrated their commitment to improving transparency and auditing. Also in February it was announced that Ghana was to receive a total of some $3,700m. in debt-service relief from its creditors over a period of 20 years, under the Heavily Indebted Poor Countries initiative of the IMF and the World Bank. It was forecast that this would allowe Ghana to reduce debt-servicing payments from an annual average of $350m. in 1997–2000 to an annual average of $230m. in 2002–2004. In May 2002 international donors, co-ordinated by the World Bank, agreed to provide $1,000m. to fill the Government's financing gap for 2002. A poor global cocoa harvest in 2001, together with concerns regarding the effect of civil unrest on production in Côte d'Ivoire, led the international market price for cocoa to rise dramatically; as a result, an estimated 60,000 metric tons of cocoa were smuggled into Côte d'Ivoire during 2002 to avoid the Ghana Cocoa Board (COCOBOD) purchasing monopoly. A production shortfall prompted fears in July 2002 that stock would have to be purchased back from Côte d'Ivoire, and in October COCOBOD raised prices by 37% in an effort to curtail further smuggling. In November 2002 Ghana withdrew, under pressure from development partners, from further negotiations on a controversial loan of $1,000m. from the International Financial Consortium.

Education

Education is officially compulsory for eight years between the ages of six and 14. Primary education begins at the age of six and lasts for six years. Secondary education, beginning at the age of 12, lasts for a further seven years, comprising a first cycle lasting four years and a second cycle of three years. Following four years of junior secondary education, pupils are examined to determine admission to senior secondary school courses, or to technical and vocational courses. In 1998/99 primary enrolment included 50.5% of children in the relevant age-group (boys 51.2%; girls 49.7%), while the comparable ratio for secondary enrolment in that year was 26.1% (boys 29.0%; girls 23.2%). Some 82,346 students were enrolled in higher education in 1996/97, with 23,126 students attending the country's five universities. By 1998/99 there were seven universities in Ghana, and other tertiary institutions included 38 teacher-training colleges, eight polytechnics and 61 technical colleges. Expenditure on education by the central Government in 1998 was 608,000m. cedis (18.2% of total spending).

Public Holidays

2003: 1 January (New Year's Day), 12 February* (Eid-al-Adha, Feast of the Sacrifice), 6 March (Independence Day), 18–21 April (Easter), 1 May (Labour Day), 1 July (Republic Day), 26 November* (Eid-al-Fitr, end of Ramadan), 6 December (National Farmers' Day), 25–26 December (Christmas).

2004: 1 January (New Year's Day), 2 February* (Eid-al-Adha, Feast of the Sacrifice), 6 March (Independence Day), 9–12 April (Easter), 1 May (Labour Day), 1 July (Republic Day), 14 November (Eid-al-Fitr*, end of Ramadan), 6 December (National Farmers' Day), 25–26 December (Christmas).

*These holidays are dependent on the Islamic lunar calendar and may vary by one or two days from the dates given.

Weights and Measures

The metric system is in force.

Statistical Survey

Source (except where otherwise stated): Ghana Statistical Service, POB GP1350, Accra; e-mail csps@ncs.gom.gh.

Area and Population

AREA, POPULATION AND DENSITY

Area (sq km)	238,537*
Population (census results)	
11 March 1984	12,296,081
26 March 2000	
Males	9,320,794
Females.	9,524,471
Total	18,845,265
Density (per sq km) at 2000 census	79.0

* 92,100 sq miles.

POPULATION BY REGION

(2000 census)

Region	Population	Capital
Ashanti	3,600,358	Kumasi
Brong-Ahafo.	1,798,058	Sunyani
Central	1,593,888	Cape Coast
Eastern	2,101,650	Koforidua
Greater Accra	2,903,753	Accra
Northern.	1,805,428	Tamale
Upper East	919,549	Bolgatanga
Upper West	575,579	Wa
Volta	1,630,254	Ho
Western	1,916,748	Takoradi
Total.	18,845,265	

PRINCIPAL TOWNS

(population at 1984 census)

Accra (capital) . .	867,459	Takoradi	61,484
Kumasi	376,249	Cape Coast . . .	57,224
Tamale	135,952	Sekondi	31,916
Tema	131,528		

Mid-2000 (UN projection, including suburbs, among them Tema and Tema New Town): Accra 1,976,000 (Source: UN, *World Urbanization Prospects: The 1999 Revision*).

BIRTHS AND DEATHS

(UN estimates, annual averages)

	1985–90	1990–95	1995–2000
Birth rate (per 1,000)	41.1	37.4	34.0
Death rate (per 1,000)	12.0	11.2	10.8

Source: UN, *World Population Prospects: The 2000 Revision*.

Expectation of life (WHO estimates, years at birth): 57.4 (males 55.8; females 58.9) in 2001 (Source: WHO, *World Health Report*).

ECONOMICALLY ACTIVE POPULATION
(1984 census)

	Males	Females	Total
Agriculture, hunting, forestry and fishing	1,750,024	1,560,943	3,310,967
Mining and quarrying	24,906	1,922	26,828
Manufacturing	198,430	389,988	588,418
Electricity, gas and water . . .	14,033	1,404	15,437
Construction	60,692	3,994	64,686
Trade, restaurants and hotels . .	111,540	680,607	792,147
Transport, storage and communications	117,806	5,000	122,806
Financing, insurance, real estate and business services . . .	19,933	7,542	27,475
Community, social and personal services	339,665	134,051	473,716
Total employed.	2,637,029	2,785,451	5,422,480
Unemployed	87,452	70,172	157,624
Total labour force	2,724,481	2,855,623	5,580,104

Source: ILO, *Yearbook of Labour Statistics*.

Mid-2001 (estimates in '000): Agriculture, etc. 5,534; Total 9,771 (Source: FAO).

Health and Welfare

KEY INDICATORS

Total fertility rate (children per woman, 2001).	4.3
Under-5 mortality rate (per 1,000 live births, 2001) . . .	100
HIV/AIDS (% of persons aged 15–49, 2001)	3.00
Physicians (per 1,000 head, 1996)	0.06
Hospital beds (per 1,000 head, 1997)	1.46
Health expenditure (2000): US $ per head (PPP) . . .	51
Health expenditure (2000): % of GDP	4.2
Health expenditure (2000): public (% of total)	53.5
Access to water (% of persons, 2000).	64
Access to sanitation (% of persons, 2000)	63
Human Development Index (2000): ranking	129
Human Development Index (2000): value	0.548

For sources and definitions, see explanatory note on p. vi.

Agriculture

PRINCIPAL CROPS

('000 metric tons)

	1999	2000	2001
Rice (paddy)	209.8	248.7	274.6
Maize	1,014.5	1,012.7	938.0
Millet	159.8	169.4	134.4
Sorghum	302.0	279.8	279.7
Sweet potatoes*	90.0	90.0	90.0
Cassava (Manioc)	7,845.4	8,107.0	8,965.8
Taro (Coco Yam)	1,707.4	1,625.0	1,687.5
Yams	3,249.0	3,363.0	3,546.7
Sugar cane*	140.0	140.0	140.0
Groundnuts (in shell)	193.0†	200.0	258.0
Coconuts*	305.0	315.0	315.0
Copra*	12.0	10.8	10.8
Oil palm fruit	1,031.9	1,050.0*	1,050.0*
Karité nuts (Shea nuts)*	52.0	65.0	65.0
Tomatoes	215.0*	200.0	200.0*
Chillies and green peppers*	270.0	270.0	270.0
Dry onions*	38.5	38.5	38.5
Green beans*	17.0	20.0	20.0
Okra	150.0*	100.0	100.0*
Bananas	15.0*	10.0	10.0*
Plantains	2,046.2	1,932.0	1,932.0*
Oranges	270.0*	300.0	300.0*
Lemons and limes*	30.0	30.0	30.0*
Pineapples	35.0*	60.0	60.0*
Other fruit*	53.1	53.2	51.0*
Cottonseed*	20.0	22.0	44.0
Pimento and allspice*	22.0	22.0	22.0*
Cocoa beans	397.7†	436.6	410.0†
Natural rubber	10.1†	13.2†	13.2*

* FAO estimate(s).
† Unofficial figure.

Source: FAO.

LIVESTOCK

('000 head, year ending September)

	1999	2000	2001
Horses*	3	3	3
Asses*	14	15	15
Cattle	1,288	1,302	1,302*
Pigs	332	324	324*
Sheep	2,658	2,743	2,743*
Goats	2,931	3,077	3,100*
Poultry	18,810	20,472	20,472*

* FAO estimate(s).

Source: FAO.

LIVESTOCK PRODUCTS

(FAO estimates '000 metric tons)

	1998	1999	2000
Beef and veal	20.7	21.3	24.4
Mutton and lamb	6.5	6.7	9.5
Goat meat	6.5	6.9	10.2
Pig meat	10.8	10.1	10.9
Poultry meat	16.0	17.1	19.5
Game meat	57	57	57
Other meat	33	33	33
Cows' milk	33.1	33.4	33.8
Hen eggs	18.6	19.9	21.7
Cattle hides	2.6	2.7	2.8

Figures for 2001 assumed to be unchanged from 2000.

Source: FAO.

Forestry

ROUNDWOOD REMOVALS

('000 cubic metres, excl. bark)

	1998	1999	2000
Sawlogs, veneer logs and logs for sleepers	1,138	1,102	998
Other industrial wood*	89	89	89
Fuel wood†	20,678	20,678	20,678
Total	21,905	21,869	21,765

* FAO estimates (output assumed to be unchanged since 1995).
† FAO estimates (output assumed to be unchanged since 1994).

Source: FAO.

SAWNWOOD PRODUCTION

('000 cubic metres, incl. railway sleepers)

	1998	1999	2000
Total (all broadleaved)	590	454	243

Source: FAO.

Fishing

('000 metric tons, live weight)

	1998	1999	2000
Capture	442.8	492.8	452.1
Freshwater fishes	74.5	74.5	74.5
Bigeye grunt	12.1	12.7	10.0
Jack and horse mackerels	16.6	11.9	2.8
Round sardinella	56.0	57.2	102.0
Madeiran sardinella	15.5	12.1	15.0
Other sardinellas	33.3	19.7	18.4
European anchovy	44.6	32.1	83.5
Skipjack tuna	34.2	43.5	30.0
Yellowfin tuna	17.8	28.3	17.0
Chub mackerel	30.2	15.5	29.6
Sharks, rays, skates	43.4	115.9	22.2
Aquaculture	0.4*	0.4*	0.5
Total catch	443.2	493.2	452.1

* FAO estimate.

Source: FAO, *Yearbook of Fishery Statistics*.

Mining

('000 metric tons, unless otherwise indicated)

	1998	1999	2000
Crude petroleum ('000 barrels)	2,190	2,190	2,200
Bauxite	442	355	504
Manganese ore: gross weight	537	639	896
Manganese ore: metal content*	172	204	287
Silver (kilograms)†	3,630	3,950	3,630
Gold (kilograms)‡	72,541	79,946	72,080
Salt (unrefined)*	50	50	50
Diamonds ('000 carats)§	809	680	920*

* Estimated production.
† Estimated silver content of exported doré.
‡ Gold content of ores and concentrates, excluding smuggled or undocumented output.
§ Of the total, the estimated production of gemstones (in '000 carats) was: 649 in 1998; 544 in 1999; 736 in 2000.

Source: US Geological Survey.

2001: Bauxite ('000 metric tons) 678.4; Manganese ('000 metric tons) 1,076; Gold ('000 ounces) 2,381.3; Diamonds ('000 carats) 1,090.1 (Source: Ghana Minerals Commission).

2002: Bauxite ('000 metric tons) 647.2; Manganese ('000 metric tons) 1,135.5; Gold ('000 ounces) 2,235.1; Silver ('000 ounces) 51.7; Diamonds ('000 carats) 940.6 (Source: Ghana Minerals Commission).

Industry

SELECTED PRODUCTS
('000 metric tons, unless otherwise indicated)

	1997	1998	1999
Groundnut oil.	19.7	28.2	25.4
Coconut oil	7.0	7.5	7.0
Palm oil	92.0	111.4	110.0*
Palm kernel oil	10.1	10.7	10.2
Beer of barley†	75.0	95.0	110.0
Beer of millet	60.1	72.2	66.8
Beer of sorghum	279.4	326.2	253.8
Motor gasoline (petrol)	200	205†	n.a.
Kerosene†	101	103†	n.a.
Diesel and gas oil	270	272†	n.a.
Cement	1,700†	1,630	1,870
Aluminium (unwrought)‡	151.6§	56.1§	114.0¶
Electric energy (million kWh)†	6,652	6,662	n.a.

2000 ('000 metric tons): Groundnut oil 26.3; Coconut oil 6.2; Palm oil 108*; Palm kernel oil 10.4; Beer of barley 110†; Beer of millet 71.0; Beer of sorghum 235.0

2001 (FAO estimates, '000 metric tons): Groundnut oil 34.4; Coconut oil 6.5; Palm oil 10; Palm kernel oil 10.5; Beer of barley 80.0; Beer of millet 56.0; Beer of sorghum 237.5; Butter of karité nuts 17.8.

* Unofficial figure.
† Provisional or estimated figure(s).
‡ Primary metal only.
§ Data from *World Metal Statistics* (London).
¶ Data from US Geological Survey.

Sources: FAO; UN, *Industrial Commodity Statistics Yearbook*.

Finance

CURRENCY AND EXCHANGE RATES

Monetary Units
100 pesewas = 1 new cedi

Sterling, Dollar and Euro Equivalents (31 December 2002)
£1 sterling = 13,601.69 cedis
US $1 = 8,438.82 cedis
€1 = 8,849.79 cedis
100,000 cedis = £7.352 = $11.850 = €11.298

Average Exchange Rate (cedis per US $)
2000   5,455.06
2001   7,170.76
2002   7,932.70

GENERAL BUDGET
('000 million new cedis)

Revenue*	1999	2000	2001†
Tax revenue	3,056	4,415	6,045
Direct taxes	918	1,409	1,978
Company tax.	446	697	836
Indirect taxes	1,353	2,018	2,711
Sales tax and value-added tax on domestic goods	323	385	581
Sales tax and value-added tax on imports.	469	887	1,259
Petroleum tax	394	532	599
Trade taxes.	785	987	1,356
Import duties	531	808	1,076
Cocoa export duty	254	179	280
Non-tax revenue	310	396	315
Total	3,366	4,811	6,360

Expenditure	1999	2000	2001†
Recurrent expenditure	3,382	5,034	6,806
Wages and salaries	1,161	1,423	2,059
Goods and services	485	700	576
Subventions	287	445	666
Transfers	298	432	509
Interest payments.	1,150	2,033	2,997
Domestic (accrual)	872	1,446	2,298
External (accrual)	278	587	699
Capital expenditure	2,007	2,491	3,139
Domestic	851	1,145	1,036
External	1,157	1,346	2,103
Total	5,389	7,525	9,945

* Excluding grants received ('000 million new cedis): 343 in 1999; 574 in 2000; 1,700 in 2001. Also excluded are the proceeds from the divestiture of state-owned enterprises ('000 million new cedis): 53 in 1999; 323 in 2000; 120 in 2001.
† Projections.

Source: IMF, *Ghana: Fourth Review Under the Poverty Reduction and Growth Facility, Requests for Waiver of Performance Criteria and for Extension of the Commitment Period—Staff Report; Staff Statement; News Brief on the Executive Board Discussion; and Statement by the Executive Director for Ghana* (March 2002).

INTERNATIONAL RESERVES
(US $ million at 31 December)

	2000	2001	2002
Gold*	79.3	78.9	n.a.
IMF special drawing rights.	0.5	4.0	3.7
Foreign exchange.	231.5	294.2	n.a.
Total	311.3	377.1	n.a.

* National valuation.

Source: IMF, *International Financial Statistics*.

MONEY SUPPLY
('000 million new cedis at 31 December)

	1999	2000	2001
Currency outside banks.	1,585.9	2,637.6	3,089.0
Deposits of non-financial public enterprises.	54.6	23.8	4.4
Demand deposits at deposit money banks	892.1	791.7	1,930.3
Total money (incl. others).	2,490.2	3,441.5	5,035.0

Source: IMF, *International Financial Statistics*.

COST OF LIVING
(Consumer Price Index; base: 1990 = 100)

	1999	2000	2001
Food (incl. beverages)	663.1	741.4	913.6
All items	810.0	1,013.7	1,347.4

Source: UN, *Monthly Bulletin of Statistics*.

NATIONAL ACCOUNTS
('000 million new cedis at current prices)

National Income and Product

	1995	1996	1997
GDP in purchasers' values	7,752.6	11,339.2	14,113.4
Net factor income from abroad.	−155.1	−220.0	−273.9
Gross national product	7,597.5	11,119.2	13,839.5
Less Consumption of fixed capital.	514.0	800.8	996.7
National income in market prices	7,083.5	10,318.4	12,842.8

Source: IMF, *International Financial Statistics*.

Expenditure on the Gross Domestic Product
(preliminary figures)

	1996	1997	1998
Government final consumption expenditure	1,366	1,744	1,786
Private final consumption expenditure	8,443	11,869	13,386
Increase in stocks	102	127	190
Gross fixed capital formation .	2,332	3,278	4,076
Total domestic expenditure .	12,243	17,018	19,438
Exports of goods and services . .	3,641	4,574	5,927
Less Imports of goods and services	4,545	7,478	8,070
GDP in purchasers' values . .	11,339	14,113	17,296
GDP at constant 1993 prices	4,351	4,534	4,747

Source: IMF, *Ghana: Statistical Appendix* (January 2000).

Gross Domestic Product by Economic Activity

	1996	1997	1998
Agriculture and livestock . . .	2,750	3,193	3,900
Cocoa	690	656	853
Forestry and logging	297	477	614
Fishing	680	724	863
Mining and quarrying	536	720	894
Manufacturing	979	1,278	1,555
Electricity, water and gas . . .	302	426	448
Construction	857	1,200	1,474
Transport, storage and communications	423	580	717
Wholesale and retail trade . .	655	917	1,138
Finance, real estate and business services	430	587	731
Public administration, defence and other government services .	1,122	1,377	1,711
Other community, social and personal services	249	342	423
Private non-profit services . .	97	133	164
GDP at factor cost	10,067	12,608	15,482
Indirect taxes, *less* subsidies . .	1,272	1,505	1,814
GDP in purchasers' values .	11,339	14,113	17,296

Source: IMF, *Ghana: Statistical Appendix* (January 2000).

BALANCE OF PAYMENTS
(US $ million)

	1998	1999	2000
Exports of goods f.o.b.	2,090.8	2,005.5	1,898.4
Imports of goods f.o.b.	−2,896.5	−3,228.1	−2,741.3
Trade balance	−805.7	−1,226.6	−842.9
Exports of services	438.6	467.8	504.3
Imports of services	−673.6	−665.9	−597.3
Balance on goods and services .	−1,040.7	−1,420.7	−935.9
Other income received . . .	26.7	15.0	15.6
Other income paid	−163.0	−146.8	−123.2
Balance on goods, services and income	−1,177.0	−1,552.5	−1,043.5
Current transfers received . . .	751.0	637.8	649.3
Current transfers paid	−17.1	−17.8	−18.4
Current balance	−443.1	−932.5	−412.6
Capital account (net)	−1.0	−1.0	—
Direct investment from abroad . .	55.7	62.6	110.3
Other investment assets . . .	88.1	183.1	41.0
Other investment liabilities . .	306.1	308.8	114.5
Net errors and omissions . . .	102.1	289.4	−111.7
Overall balance	107.9	−89.6	−258.5

Source: IMF, *International Financial Statistics*.

External Trade

PRINCIPAL COMMODITIES
(distribution by SITC, US $ million)

Imports c.i.f.	1998	1999	2000
Food and live animals . . .	282.6	328.3	319.9
Fish, crustaceans and molluscs, and preparations thereof . .	103.5	105.2	80.1
Fish, fresh, chilled or frozen . .	96.4	97.3	75.7
Fish, frozen, excluding fillets .	86.7	94.3	70.1
Cereals and cereal preparations .	92.9	101.6	115.3
Crude materials (inedible), except fuels	97.2	96.7	140.7
Mineral fuels, lubricants, etc. .	535.0	532.6	629.2
Petroleum, petroleum products, etc.	490.7	466.1	579.4
Crude petroleum and oils obtained from bituminous materials	171.7	252.1	315.1
Petroleum products, refined . .	303.2	187.0	238.0
Chemicals and related products	279.4	309.1	282.0
Basic manufactures	382.3	388.5	433.4
Non-metallic mineral manufactures	81.3	85.9	94.1
Iron and steel	87.9	91.5	73.9
Machinery and transport equipment	1,134.1	1,131.9	890.1
Power-generating machinery and equipment	137.7	67.4	65.3
Machinery specialized for particular industries	193.8	147.5	107.2
General industrial machinery and equipment, and parts thereof .	150.7	161.3	141.7
Telecommunications, sound recording and reproducing equipment	47.5	99.0	62.2
Other electric machinery, apparatus and appliances, and parts thereof	118.9	118.9	124.8
Road vehicles and parts* . . .	448.7	493.3	340.1
Passenger motor vehicles (excluding buses)	122.3	268.8	179.0
Motor vehicles for the transport of goods or materials . . .	218.4	144.7	106.5
Miscellaneous manufactured articles	140.8	168.4	153.9
Total (incl. others)	2,911.3	3,003.8	2933.2

* Data on parts exclude tyres, engines and electrical parts.

Exports f.o.b.	1998	1999	2000
Food and live animals	628.5	636.4	483.3
Fish, crustaceans and molluscs, and preparations thereof	69.2	72.2	75.7
Fish, prepared or preserved	51.2	54.3	57.1
Vegetables and fruit	25.8	98.0	87.3
Fruit and nuts, fresh, dried	17.4	90.5	32.6
Fruit, fresh or dried	10.5	81.6	12.4
Pineapples, fresh or dried	9.3	80.5	11.1
Coffee, tea, cocoa, spices and manufactures thereof	521.7	458.2	313.3
Cocoa	512.5	450.5	305.4
Cocoa beans, raw, roasted	447.5	400.6	258.6
Cocoa butter and paste	64.9	49.4	45.3
Cocoa butter (fat or oil)	50.1	39.7	29.9
Crude materials (inedible) except fuels	162.2	165.9	165.1
Cork and wood	100.1	110.8	94.2
Wood, non-coniferous species, sawn, planed, tongued, grooved, etc.	97.9	107.1	82.3
Wood, non-coniferous species, sawn lengthwise, sliced or peeled	95.2	104.5	61.3
Mineral fuels, lubricants, etc.	37.8	56.1	81.8
Basic manufactures	154.9	226.4	239.1
Cork and wood manufactures (excl. furniture)	105.1	93.8	56.6
Veneers, plywood, 'improved' wood and other wood, worked	101.2	57.5	51.3
Wood sawn lengthwise, veneer sheets, etc., up to 5 mm in thickness	96.5	40.9	38.1
Aluminium and aluminium alloys, unwrought	23.8	54.6	146.9
Machinery and transport equipment	8.4	38.1	19.3
Gold, non-monetary, unwrought or semi-manufactured	120.4	100.6	612.7
Total (incl. others)	1,158.0	1,269.7	1670.9

Source: UN, *International Trade Statistics Yearbook*.

PRINCIPAL TRADING PARTNERS
(US $ million)

Imports c.i.f.	1998	1999	2000
Australia	42.0	40.3	38.0
Belgium	124.7*	202.6	144.0
Brazil	36.7	40.9	53.2
Canada	54.4	55.8	57.8
China, People's Repub.	65.6	96.8	93.3
Côte d'Ivoire	69.4	77.2	68.6
France (incl. Monaco)	93.5	87.9	93.5
Germany	237.9	222.7	207.5
Hong Kong	21.6	35.2	23.5
India	43.2	52.3	49.5
Israel	47.3	5.6	3.3
Italy (incl. San Marino)	127.4	112.8	147.4
Japan	123.0	84.4	53.1
Korea, Democratic People's Republic	4.1	5.3	68.0
Korea, Republic	97.3	136.3	0.0
Malaysia	10.7	30.4	n.a.
Nigeria	115.7	240.5	320.6
Netherlands	150.0	209.8	186.2
SACU†	104.4	104.1	n.a.
South Africa	—	—	98.2
Spain	123.2	84.0	141.2
Sweden	45.5	35.3	34.1
Switzerland-Liechtenstein	45.7	24.4	30.2
Thailand	22.3	31.4	36.5
Togo	29.2	36.0	50.3
United Kingdom	348.8	307.8	268.4
USA	313.5	261.3	219.3
Total (incl. others)	2,911.3	3,003.8	2,933.2

Exports f.o.b.	1998	1999	2000
Bahamas	0.1	0.9	19.5
Belgium	60.1*	46.7	31.8
Benin	1.7	13.5	11.0
Burkina Faso	7.3	62.3	6.3
China, People's Republic	2.0	3.3	27.7
Cyprus	0.7	2.7	25.1
France (incl. Monaco)	66.6	50.1	41.8
The Gambia	0.2	18.3	0.5
Germany	87.4	57.3	89.7
Ireland	26.9	9.6	14.1
Italy (incl. San Marino)	59.5	81.2	49.0
Japan	49.5	50.4	24.0
Netherlands	184.3	179.2	186.9
Niger	7.4	18.1	10.8
Nigeria	8.5	6.8	27.0
Russia	19.0	4.4	7.8
SACU†	40.2	41.2	—
South Africa	—	—	29.8
Spain	87.3	35.7	22.3
Switzerland-Liechtenstein	43.2	37.7	392.6
Togo	27.0	44.9	63.8
Trinidad and Tobago	0.0	33.4	0.0
Turkey	11.7	11.3	18.5
United Kingdom	219.5	288.0	315.0
USA	54.4	69.2	98.1
Total (incl. others)	1,158.0	1,269.7	1,670.9

* Including Luxembourg.
† Southern African Customs Union, comprising Botswana, Lesotho, Namibia, South Africa and Swaziland.

Source: UN, *International Trade Statistics Yearbook*.

Transport

RAILWAYS
(traffic)

	1996
Passengers carried ('000)	2,100
Freight carried ('000 metric tons)	857
Passenger-km (million)	208
Net ton-km (million)	152.8

Source: *Railway Directory*.

ROAD TRAFFIC
('000 motor vehicles in use at 31 December)

	1994	1995*	1996*
Passenger cars	90.0	90.0	90.0
Lorries and vans	44.7	45.0	45.0

* Estimates.

Source: International Road Federation, *World Road Statistics*.

SHIPPING

Merchant Fleet
(registered at 31 December)

	1999	2000	2001
Number of vessels	205	210	212
Total displacement ('000 grt)	117.5	118.7	123.1

Source: Lloyd's Register-Fairplay, *World Fleet Statistics*.

International Sea-borne Freight Traffic
(estimates, '000 metric tons)

	1991	1992	1993
Goods loaded	2,083	2,279	2,424
Goods unloaded	2,866	2,876	2,904

Source: UN Economic Commission for Africa, *African Statistical Yearbook*.

CIVIL AVIATION
(traffic on scheduled services)

	1996	1997	1998
Kilometres flown (million) . . .	6	6	6
Passengers carried ('000) . . .	197	211	210
Passenger-km (million)	655	702	705
Total ton-km (million)	91	99	97

Source: UN, *Statistical Yearbook*.

Tourism

ARRIVALS BY NATIONALITY

	1997	1998	1999
Côte d'Ivoire	15,646	16,729	17,916
France	11,759	12,573	13,466
Germany	15,702	16,788	17,980
Liberia.	8,534	9,124	9,772
Netherlands	7,878	8,423	9,021
Nigeria.	44,667	47,757	51,147
Togo	9,739	10,413	11,152
United Kingdom	28,177	30,126	32,264
USA	21,465	22,950	24,580
Total (incl. others)*	325,433	347,949	372,651

* Includes Ghanaian nationals resident abroad: 88,585 in 1997; 94,713 in 1998; 101,437 in 1999.

Source: World Tourism Organization, *Yearbook of Tourism Statistics*.

Receipts from tourism (US $ million): 266 in 1997; 284 in 1998; 342 in 1999.

Communications Media

	1999	2000	2001
Television receivers ('000 in use)	2,266	2,390	n.a.
Telephones ('000 main lines in use)	158.6	237.2	242.1
Mobile cellular telephones ('000 subscribers).	70.0	130.0	193.8
Personal computers ('000 in use)	50	60	70
Internet users ('000)	20.0	30.0	40.5

Source: International Telecommunication Union.

Radio receivers ('000 in use): 4,400 in 1997.

Facsimile machines (number in use, estimate): 5,000 in 1995.

Daily newspapers: 4 titles in 1996 (average circulation 250,000).

Sources: UNESCO, *Statistical Yearbook*; UN, *Statistical Yearbook*.

Education

(1996/97, unless otherwise indicated)

	Institu-tions	Teachers	Students		
			Males	Females	Total
Primary . . .	13,014	71,330	1,245,036	1,088,311	2,333,347
Junior secondary .	5,880	40,417	413,686	324,362	738,048
Senior secondary .	504	11,458	118,948	75,837	194,785
Technical institutes . .	61	n.a.	n.a.	n.a.	23,642
Teacher training .	38	1,001*	n.a.	n.a.	20,399
Polytechnics . .	8	n.a.	n.a.	n.a.	15,179
Universities . .	5	700*†	n.a.	n.a.	23,126

* 1989/90 figure.
† Excluding the University of Ghana.

1998/99: *Primary* 13,115 institutions; *Junior secondary* 6,394 institutions; *Senior secondary* 512 institutions; *Teacher training* 38 institutions; *Technical institutes* 61 institutions; *Polytechnics* 8 institutions; *Universities* 7 institutions.

Source: mainly Ministry of Education, Accra.

Adult literacy rate (UNESCO estimates): 71.5% (males 80.3%; females 62.9%) in 2000 (Source: UN Development Programme, *Human Development Report*).

Directory

The Constitution

Under the terms of the Constitution of the Fourth Republic, which was approved by national referendum on 28 April 1992, Ghana has a multi-party political system. Executive power is vested in the President, who is Head of State and Commander-in-Chief of the Armed Forces. The President is elected by universal adult suffrage for a term of four years, and appoints a Vice-President. The duration of the President's tenure of office is limited to two four-year terms. It is also stipulated that, in the event that no presidential candidate receives more than 50% of votes cast, a new election between the two candidates with the highest number of votes is to take place within 21 days. Legislative power is vested in a 200-member unicameral Parliament, which is elected by direct adult suffrage for a four-year term. The Council of Ministers is appointed by the President, subject to approval by the Parliament. The Constitution also provides for a 25-member Council of State, principally comprising presidential nominees and regional representatives, and a 20-member National Security Council (chaired by the Vice-President), both of which act as advisory bodies to the President.

The Government

HEAD OF STATE

President and Commander-in-Chief of the Armed Forces: JOHN AGYEKUM KUFUOR (inaugurated 7 January 2001).

Vice-President: Alhaji ALIU MAHAMA.

COUNCIL OF MINISTERS
(April 2003)

A coalition of the New Patriotic Party (NPP), the Convention People's Party (CPP) and the National Reform Party (NRP).

Senior Minister, responsible for Public-Sector Reform and the National Institutional Renewal Programme: JOSEPH HENRY MENSAH (NPP).

Minister of Finance and Economic Planning: YAW OSAFO MAAFO (NPP).

Minister of Defence: KWAME ADDO KUFUOR (NPP).

Minister of Foreign Affairs: NANA ADDO DANKWA AKUFO ADDO (NPP).

Attorney-General, Minister of Justice: PAPA OWUSU ANKOMAH (NPP).

Minister of Trade, Industry and Special Presidential Initiatives: ALAN KYEREMANTENG (Ind.).

Minister of the Interior: HACKMAN OWUSU-AGYEMANG (NPP).

Minister of Local Government and Rural Development: KWADJO ADJEI DARKO (NPP).

Minister of Education, Youth and Sports: KWADWO BAAH-WIREDU (NPP).

Minister of Primary, Secondary and Girl-Child Education: CHRISTINE CHURCHER (NPP).

Minister of Food and Agriculture: Maj. (retd) Courage Quarshigah (NPP).

Minister of Roads, Highways and Transport: Dr Richard Winfred Anane (NPP).

Minister of Health: Dr Kwaku Afriyie (NPP).

Minister of Communications and Technology: Albert Kan-Dapaah (NPP).

Minister of Lands and Forestry: Prof. Dominic Fobih (NPP).

Minister of Mines: Cecilia Bannerman (NRP).

Minister of Manpower, Development and Employment: Yaw Barimah (NPP).

Minister of Works and Housing: Alhaji Mustapha Ali Idris (NPP).

Minister of Energy: Dr Paa Kwesi Nduom (CPP).

Minister of Tourism and the Modernization of the Capital City: Jake Obetsebi-Lamptey (NPP).

Minister of Science and the Environment: Prof. Kasim Kasanga (Ind.).

Minister of Women's and Children's Affairs: Gladys Asmah (NPP).

Minister of Private-Sector Development: Kwamena Bartels (NPP).

Minister of Parliamentary Affairs: Felix Owusu-Agyapong (NPP).

Minister of Ports, Harbours and Railways: Prof. Christopher Ameyaw-Akumfi (NPP).

Minister of Regional Co-operation and the New Partnership for Africa's Development: Dr Kofi Konadu Apraku (NPP).

Minister of Information: Nana Akomea (NPP).

Minister of Presidential Affairs: Alhaji Moctar Musa Bamba (NPP).

There are also three Ministers of State and some 20 Deputy Ministers.

REGIONAL MINISTERS
(April 2003)

Ashanti: Sampson Kwaku Boafo.

Brong Ahafo: Nana Kwadwo Seini.

Central: Isaac Edumadze.

Eastern: Dr S. K. Osafo Mensah.

Greater Accra: Sheikh I. C. Quaye.

Northern: Ernest Akofuor Debrah.

Upper East: Mohamed Salifu.

Upper West: Mogtari Sahanun.

Volta: Kwasi Owusa-Yeboah.

Western: Joseph Boahen Aidoo.

MINISTRIES

All ministries are based in Accra.

Office of the President: POB 1627, Osu, Accra; tel. 665415.

Ministry of Communications and Technology: POB M41, Accra; tel. (21) 228011; fax (21) 229786.

Ministry of Defence: Burma Camp, Accra; tel. (21) 777611; fax (21) 773951.

Ministry of Education, Youth and Sports: POB M45, Accra; tel. (21) 665421; fax (21) 664067; internet www.ghana.edu.gh.

Ministry of Energy: POB M212, Accra; tel. (21) 667151; fax (21) 668262.

Ministry of Finance and Economic Planning: POB M40, Accra; tel. (21) 665441; fax (21) 667069; internet www.finance.gov.gh.

Ministry of Food and Agriculture: POB M37, Accra; tel. (21) 665421; fax (21) 663250; e-mail mofa@africaonline.com.gh.

Ministry of Foreign Affairs: POB M53, Accra; tel. (21) 664951; fax (21) 665363.

Ministry of Health: POB M44, Accra; tel. (21) 662014; fax (21) 666808.

Ministry of the Interior: POB M42, Accra; tel. (21) 665421; fax (21) 667450.

Ministry of Justice: POB M60, Accra; tel. (21) 665051; fax (21) 662497.

Ministry of Lands and Forestry: POB M212, Accra; tel. (21) 665421; fax (21) 666801.

Ministry of Local Government and Rural Development: POB M50, Accra; tel. (21) 664763; fax (21) 661015.

Ministry of Manpower, Development and Employment: POB M84, Accra; tel. (21) 665349; fax (21) 662683; e-mail manpower@idngh.com.

Ministry of Mines: Private Mail Bag, Ministries Post Office, Accra; tel. (21) 672337; fax (21) 666801.

Ministry of Parliamentary Affairs: Parliament House, Accra; tel. 664716.

Ministry of Roads, Highways and Transport: POB M57, Accra; tel. (21) 668314.

Ministry of Science and the Environment: POB 232, Accra; tel. (21) 666049; fax (21) 666828.

Ministry of Tourism and the Modernization of the Capital City: POB 4386, Accra; tel. (21) 666701; fax (21) 666182; e-mail motgov@hotmail.com; internet www.ghanatourism.gov.gh.

Ministry of Trade, Industry and Special Presidential Initiatives: POB M47, Accra; tel. (21) 665421; fax (21) 664115; e-mail gatewayl@ghana.com.

Ministry of Women's and Children's Affairs: POB M232, Accra; tel. (21) 662626; fax (21) 666828; e-mail barnes@africaonline.com.gh.

Ministry of Works and Housing: POB M43, Accra; tel. (21) 666850; fax (21) 663268; e-mail mwh@ighmail.com.

President and Legislature

PRESIDENT

Presidential Election, First Ballot, 7 December 2000

Candidate	Votes	% of votes
John Agyekum Kufuor (NPP)	3,131,739	48.17
John Evans Atta Mills (NDC)	2,895,575	44.54
Edward Mahama (PNC)	189,659	2.92
George Hagan (CPP)	115,641	1.78
Augustus (Goosie) Tanoh (NRP)	78,629	1.21
Dan Lartey (GCPP)	67,504	1.04
Charles Wereko-Brobby (UGM)	22,123	0.34
Total	6,500,870	100.00

Second Ballot, 28 December 2000

Candidate	Votes	% of votes
John Agyekum Kufuor (NPP)	3,631,263	56.90
John Evans Atta Mills (NDC)	2,750,124	43.10
Total	6,381,387	100.00

PARLIAMENT

Speaker: Peter Ala Adjetey.

Legislative Elections, 7 December 2000

Party	% of votes	Seats
New Patriotic Party (NPP)	45.0	100
National Democratic Congress (NDC)	41.2	92
People's National Convention (PNC)	3.4	3
Convention People's Party (CPP)	1.3	1
Independents	n.a.	4
Total	100.0	200

COUNCIL OF STATE

Chairman: Prof. Alex Kwapong.

Political Organizations

Convention People's Party (CPP): 60 Mango Tree Ave, Asylum Down, POB 10939, Accra-North; tel. (21) 227763; f. 1998 as Convention Party by merger of the National Convention Party; f. 1992; and the People's Convention Party; f. 1993; present name adopted in 2000; Nkrumahist; Chair. Dr Abubakar Alhassan; Sec.-Gen. Dr Nii Noi.

EGLE (Every Ghanaian Living Everywhere) Party: Kokomlemle, POB 1859, Accra; tel. (21) 231873; f. 1992 as the Eagle Party; Chair. Owuraku Amofa; Sec.-Gen. Sam Pee Yalley.

Great Consolidated People's Party (GCPP): Citadel House, POB 3077, Accra; tel. (21) 331034; f. 1996; Nkrumahist; Chair. Dan Lartey; Sec.-Gen. John Amekah.

National Democratic Congress (NDC): 641/4 Ringway Close, Kokomlemle, POB 5825, Accra-North; tel. (21) 224905; internet www.ndc.org.gh; f. 1992; party of fmr Pres. Jerry Rawlings; Chair. Dr Obed Asamoah; Sec.-Gen. Alhaji Huudu Yahaya.

National Reform Party (NRP): 31 Mango Tree Ave, Asylum Down, POB 19403, Accra-North; tel. (21) 228578; f. 1999 by a breakaway group from the NDC; Chair. Peter Gameli Kpordugbe; Sec.-Gen. Kyeretwie Opoku.

New Patriotic Party (NPP): C912/2 Duade St, Kokomlemle, POB 3456, Accra-North; tel. (21) 227951; fax (21) 224418; e-mail npp@africanonline.com.gh; internet www.nppghana.org; f. 1992 by supporters of the fmr Prime Minister, Kofi Busia, and J. B. Danquah; Chair. Harona Esseku; Sec.-Gen. Dan Botwe.

People's National Convention (PNC): Kokomlemle, near Sadisco, POB 7795, Accra; tel. (21) 236389; f. 1992; Nkrumahist; Chair. Dr John F. Edwin; Sec.-Gen. Scotts Pwamang.

United Ghana Movement (UGM): 1 North Ridge Cres., Accra; tel. (21) 225581; fax (21) 231390; e-mail info@ugmghana.org; f. 1996 by a breakaway group from the NPP; Chair. Nii Armah Tagoe; Sec.-Gen. Eric Dutenya Kwabla.

Diplomatic Representation

EMBASSIES AND HIGH COMMISSIONS IN GHANA

Algeria: 22 Josif Broz Tito Ave, POB 2747, Cantonments, Accra; tel. (21) 776719; fax (21) 776828; e-mail embdzacc@africaonline.com.gh; Ambassador Hassane Rabehi.

Benin: 19 Volta St, Second Close, Airport Residential Area, POB 7871, Accra; tel. (21) 774860; fax (21) 774889; Ambassador Pierre Sadeler.

Brazil: Millenium Heights Bldg, 14 Liberation Link, POB CT3859, Airport Commercial Area, Accra; tel. (21) 774908; fax (21) 778566; e-mail brasemb@ighmail.com; Ambassador Paulo Américo V. Wolowski.

Bulgaria: 3 Kakramadu Rd, East Cantonments, POB 3193, Accra; tel. (21) 772404; fax (21) 774231; e-mail bulembgh@ghana.com; Chargé d'affaires George Mitev.

Burkina Faso: 772/3, Asylum Down, off Farrar Ave, POB 651, Accra; tel. (21) 221988; fax (21) 221936; e-mail ambafaso@ghana.com; Ambassador Marc Oubkiri Yao.

Canada: 42 Independence Ave, POB 1639, Accra; tel. (21) 228555; fax (21) 773792; e-mail accra@dfait-maeci.gc.ca; internet www.dfait-maeci.gc.ca/accra; High Commissioner Jean-Pierre Bolduc.

China, People's Republic: 6 Agostino Neto Rd, Airport Residential Area, POB 3356, Accra; tel. (21) 777073; fax (21) 774527; e-mail chinaemb@ghana.com; Ambassador Lu Yongshou.

Côte d'Ivoire: 9 18th Lane, off Cantonments Rd, POB 3445, Christiansborg, Accra; tel. (21) 774611; fax (21) 773516; Ambassador Amon Tanoe Emmanuel.

Cuba: 20 Amilcar Cabral Rd, Airport Residential Area, POB 9163 Airport, Accra; tel. (21) 775868; Ambassador Juan Carretero.

Czech Republic: C260/5, Kanda High Rd No. 2, POB 5226, Accra-North; tel. (21) 223540; fax (21) 225337; e-mail accraczemb@ighmail.com; Ambassador Jindřich Junek.

Denmark: 67 Dr Isert Rd, 8th Ave Extension, North Ridge, POB C596, Accra; tel. (21) 253473; fax (21) 228061; e-mail accamb@accamb.um.dk; Ambassador Ole Blicher-Olsen.

Egypt: 27 Noi Fetreke St, Roman Ridge, POB 2508, Accra; tel. and fax (21) 776795; Ambassador Abdel Moheim Ahmed Talaat.

Ethiopia: 6 Adiembra Rd, East Cantonments, POB 1646, Accra; tel. (21) 775928; fax (21) 776807; e-mail ethioemb@ghana.com; Ambassador Abdi Dolal.

France: 12th Rd, off Liberation Ave, POB 187, Accra; tel. (21) 774480; fax (21) 778321; e-mail ambaccra@africaonline.com.gh; Ambassador Jean-Michel Berrit.

Germany: 6 Ridge St, North Ridge, POB 1757, Accra; tel. (21) 221311; fax (21) 221347; e-mail geremb@wwwplus.com; internet www.accra.diplo.de; Ambassador Dr Harald Löschner.

Guinea: 11 Osu Badu St, Dzorwulu, POB 5497, Accra-North; tel. (21) 777921; fax (21) 760961; Ambassador Dore Diale Drus.

Holy See: 8 Drake Ave, Airport Residential Area, POB 9675, Accra; tel. (21) 777759; fax (21) 774019; Apostolic Nuncio Most Rev. George Kocherry (Titular Archbishop of Othona).

India: 12 Mankata Ave, Airport Residential Area, POB 3040, Accra; tel. (21) 775601; fax (21) 772176; e-mail indiahc@ghana.com; High Commissioner Arun Kumar Banerjee.

Iran: 12 Sir Arku Korsah St, Roman Ridge, POB 12673, Accra-North; tel. and fax (21) 777043; Ambassador Majid Izmark.

Italy: Jawaharlal Nehru Rd, POB 140, Accra; tel. (21) 775621; fax (21) 777056; e-mail ambital@africaonline.com.gh; Ambassador Giancarlo Izzo.

Japan: 8 Tito Ave, off Jawaharlal Nehru Ave, POB 1637, Accra; tel. (21) 775615; fax (21) 762553; Ambassador Hiromu Nitta.

Korea, Democratic People's Republic: 139 Nortei Ababio Loop, Ambassadorial Estate, Roman Ridge, POB 13874, Accra; tel. (21) 777825; Ambassador (vacant).

Korea, Republic: 3 Abokobi Rd, East Cantonment, POB GP13700, Accra-North; tel. (21) 776157; fax (21) 772313; e-mail koreaadm@africaonline.gh; Ambassador Chung Eiu-Min.

Lebanon: F864/1 off Cantonments Rd, Osu, POB 562, Accra; tel. (21) 776727; fax (21) 764290; e-mail lebanon@its.com.gh; Ambassador Charbel Aoun.

Liberia: 10 West Cantonments, off Jawaharlal Nehru Rd, POB 895, Accra; tel. (21) 775641; Ambassador W. Elwood Greaves.

Libya: 14 Sixth St, Airport Residential Area, POB 9665, Accra; tel. (21) 774820; Secretary of People's Bureau Dr Fatima Magame.

Mali: Agostino Neto Rd, Airport Residential Area, POB 1121, Accra; tel. (21) 666423; Ambassador Muphtah Ag Hairy.

Netherlands: 89 Liberation Rd, Thomas Sankara Circle, POB CT1647, Accra; tel. (21) 773644; fax (21) 773655; e-mail acc@minbuza.nl; internet www.ambaccra.nl; Ambassador Arie van der Wiel.

Niger: E104/3 Independence Ave, POB 2685, Accra; tel. and fax (21) 229011; Ambassador Abdoulkarimou Seini.

Nigeria: 5 Tito Ave, POB 1548, Accra; tel. (21) 776158; fax (21) 774395; e-mail nighicom@africaonline.com.gh; High Commissioner Sam Nnamdi Okechukwo.

Pakistan: 11 Ring Rd East, Danquah Circle, POB 1114, Accra; tel. (21) 776059; High Commissioner Zafir Hilaly.

Russia: F856/1, Ring Rd East, POB 1634, Accra; tel. (21) 775611; fax (21) 772699; e-mail russia@ghana.com; internet www.ghana.mid.ru; Ambassador Valery Orlov.

Saudi Arabia: 10 Noi Fetreke St, Roman Ridge, Airport Residential Area, POB 670, Accra; tel. (21) 774311; fax (21) 773424; e-mail ghemb@mofa.gov.sa; Chargé d'affaires a.i. Anwar Abdul Fattah Abdrabbuh.

South Africa: 10 Klotey Cres., Labone North, POB 298, Accra; tel. (21) 762380; fax (21) 762381; e-mail sahcgh@africaonline.com.gh; High Commissioner Dr M. M. Phologane.

Spain: Drake Ave Extension, Airport Residential Area, POB 1218, Accra; tel. (21) 774004; fax (21) 776217; e-mail embespgh@mail.mae.es; Ambassador Fernando Corral.

Switzerland: Kanda Highway/Ridge Rd, North Ridge, POB 359, Accra; tel. (21) 228125; fax (21) 223583; e-mail vertretung@acc.rep.admin.ch; internet www.eda.admin.ch/accra; Ambassador Georg Zubler.

Togo: Togo House, near Cantonments Circle, POB C120, Accra; tel. (21) 777950; fax (21) 777961; Ambassador Assiongbor Folivi.

United Kingdom: Osu Link, off Gamel Abdul Nasser Ave, POB 296, Accra; tel. (21) 7010650; fax (21) 7010655; e-mail high.commission.accra@fco.gov.uk; High Commissioner Rod Pullen.

USA: Ring Road East, POB 194, Accra; tel. (21) 775347; fax (21) 776008; e-mail usembassy@state.gov/ghana; Ambassador Mary Carlin Yates.

Judicial System

The civil law in force in Ghana is based on the Common Law, doctrines of equity and general statutes which were in force in England in 1874, as modified by subsequent Ordinances. Ghanaian customary law is, however, the basis of most personal, domestic and contractual relationships. Criminal Law is based on the Criminal Procedure Code, 1960, derived from English Criminal Law, and since amended. The Superior Court of Judicature comprises a Supreme Court, a Court of Appeal, a High Court and a Regional Tribunal; Inferior Courts include Circuit Courts, Circuit Tribunals, Community Tribunals and such other Courts as may be designated by law. In 2001 'fast-track' court procedures were established to accelerate the delivery of justice. However, in March 2002 the Supreme Court ruled that the 'fast-track' courts were unconstitutional; the Attorney-General subsequently applied for a judicial review of the ruling.

Supreme Court

Consists of the Chief Justice and not fewer than nine other Justices. It is the final court of appeal in Ghana and has jurisdiction in matters relating to the enforcement or interpretation of the Constitution.

Chief Justice: EDWARD K. WIREDU.

Court of Appeal: Consists of the Chief Justice and not fewer than five Judges of the Court of Appeal. It has jurisdiction to hear and determine appeals from any judgment, decree or order of the High Court.

High Court: Comprises the Chief Justice and not fewer than 12 Justices of the High Court. It exercises original jurisdiction in all matters, civil and criminal, other than those for offences involving treason. Trial by jury is practised in criminal cases in Ghana and the Criminal Procedure Code, 1960, provides that all trials on indictment shall be by a jury or with the aid of Assessors.

Circuit Courts: Exercise original jurisdiction in civil matters where the amount involved does not exceed C100,000. They also have jurisdiction with regard to the guardianship and custody of infants, and original jurisdiction in all criminal cases, except offences where the maximum punishment is death or the offence of treason. They have appellate jurisdiction from decisions of any District Court situated within their respective circuits.

District Courts: To each magisterial district is assigned at least one District Magistrate who has original jurisdiction to try civil suits in which the amount involved does not exceed C50,000. District Magistrates also have jurisdiction to deal with all criminal cases, except first-degree felonies, and commit cases of a more serious nature to either the Circuit Court or the High Court. A Grade I District Court can impose a fine not exceeding C1,000 and sentences of imprisonment of up to two years and a Grade II District Court may impose a fine not exceeding C500 and a sentence of imprisonment of up to 12 months. A District Court has no appellate jurisdiction, except in rent matters under the Rent Act.

Juvenile Courts: Jurisdiction in cases involving persons under 17 years of age, except where the juvenile is charged jointly with an adult. The Courts comprise a Chairman, who must be either the District Magistrate or a lawyer, and not fewer than two other members appointed by the Chief Justice in consultation with the Judicial Council. The Juvenile Courts can make orders as to the protection and supervision of a neglected child and can negotiate with parents to secure the good behaviour of a child.

National Public Tribunal: Considers appeals from the Regional Public Tribunals. Its decisions are final and are not subject to any further appeal. The Tribunal consists of at least three members and not more than five, one of whom acts as Chairman.

Regional Public Tribunals: Hears criminal cases relating to prices, rent or exchange control, theft, fraud, forgery, corruption or any offence which may be referred to them by the Provisional National Defence Council.

Special Military Tribunal: Hears criminal cases involving members of the armed forces. It consists of between five and seven members.

Attorney-General: NANA AKUFFO ADDO.

Religion

According to the 2000 census, 69% of the population were Christians and 15.6% Muslims, while 6.9% followed indigenous beliefs.

CHRISTIANITY

Christian Council of Ghana: POB 919, Accra; tel. (21) 776678; fax (21) 776725; f. 1929; advisory body comprising 14 mem. churches (2001); Gen. Sec. Rev. ROBERT ABOAGYE-MENSAH.

The Anglican Communion

Anglicans in Ghana are adherents of the Church of the Province of West Africa, comprising 12 dioceses, of which seven are in Ghana.

Archbishop of the Province of West Africa and Bishop of Koforidua: Most Rev. ROBERT GARSHONG ALLOTEY OKINE, POB 980, Koforidua; tel. (81) 2329; fax (21) 669125; e-mail archbishopwa@yahoo.com.

Bishop of Accra: Rt Rev. JUSTICE OFEI AKROFI, Bishopscourt, POB 8, Accra; tel. (21) 662292; fax (21) 669125; e-mail cpwa@ghana.com.

Bishop of Cape Coast: Rt Rev. KOBINA ADDUAH QUASHIE, Bishopscourt, POB A233, Adisadel Estates, Cape Coast; tel. (42) 32502; fax (42) 32637.

Bishop of Kumasi: Rt Rev. DANIEL YINKAH SARFO, Bishop's Office, St Cyprian's Ave, POB 144, Kumasi; tel. and fax (51) 24117; e-mail kumangli@africaonline.com.gh.

Bishop of Sekondi: Rt Rev. ANDREW KWAKU FUACHIE OKOH, POB 85, Sekondi; tel. (21) 669125.

Bishop of Sunyani: Rt Rev. THOMAS AMPAH BRIENT, Bishop's House, POB 23, Sunyani; tel. (61) 213; fax (61) 7203; e-mail deegyab@ighmail.com.

Bishop of Tamale: Rt Rev. EMMANUEL ARONGO, POB 110, Tamale NR; tel. (71) 22906; fax (71) 22849.

The Roman Catholic Church

Ghana comprises three archdioceses and 15 dioceses. At 31 December 2000 there were 2,242,118 adherents in the country, equivalent to 10.4.% of the total population.

Ghana Bishops' Conference

National Catholic Secretariat, POB 9712, Airport, Accra; tel. (21) 500491; fax (21) 500493; e-mail dscncs@africaonline.com.gh. f. 1960; Pres. Most Rev. PETER K. APPIAH-TURKSON (Archbishop of Cape Coast).

Archbishop of Accra: Most Rev. DOMINIC KODWO ANDOH, Chancery Office, POB 247, Accra; tel. (21) 222728; fax (21) 231619.

Archbishop of Cape Coast: Most Rev. PETER KODWO APPIAH-TURKSON, Archbishop's House, POB 112, Cape Coast; tel. (42) 32593; fax (42) 33473; e-mail archcape@ghana.com.

Archbishop of Tamale: Most Rev. GREGORY EBO KPIEBAYA, Gumbehini Rd, POB 42, Tamale; tel. and fax (71) 22425; e-mail tambio@africaonline.com.gh.

Other Christian Churches

African Methodist Episcopal Zion Church: POB MP522, Mamprobi, Accra; tel. (21) 669200; e-mail amezion@africaonline.com.gh; f. 1898; Pres. Rt Rev. WARREN M. BROWN.

Christian Methodist Episcopal Church: POB 3906, Accra; Pres. Rev. YENN BATA.

Church of Pentecost: POB 2194, Accra; tel. (21) 777911; fax (21) 774721; e-mail cophq@ghana.com; internet www.thechurchofpentecost.com; Chair. Apostle M.K. NTUMY; 1,021,856 mems (July 2002).

Evangelical-Lutheran Church of Ghana: POB KN197, Kaneshie; tel. (21) 223487; fax (21) 220947; e-mail elcga@africaonline.com.gh; Pres. Rt Rev. Dr PAUL KOFI FYNN; 26,000 mems.

Evangelical-Presbyterian Church of Ghana: 19 Main St, Tesano, PMB, Accra-North; tel. (21) 220381; fax (21) 233173; f. 1847; Moderator Rev. JAPHET YAO LEDO; 295,000 mems.

Ghana Baptist Convention: POB 1979, Kumasi; tel. (51) 5215; f. 1963; Pres. Rev. FRED DEEGBE; Sec. Rev. FRANK ADAMS; 63,200 mems.

Ghana Mennonite Church: POB 5485, Accra; fax (21) 220589; f. 1957; Moderator Rev. MICHAEL BADASU; Sec. ISAAC K. QUARTEY; 4,800 mems.

Ghana Union Conference of Seventh-day Adventists: POB GP1016, Accra; tel. (21) 223720; fax (21) 227024; e-mail gucsda@ghana.com; f. 1943; Pres. Pastor P. O. MENSAH; Sec. Pastor SETH A. LARMIE.

Methodist Church of Ghana: E252/2, Liberia Rd, POB 403, Accra; tel. (21) 228120; fax (21) 227008; e-mail mcghqs@africaonline.com.gh; Pres. Rt Rev. Dr SAMUEL ASANTE ANTWI; Sec. Rev. MACLEAN AGYIRI KUMI; 341,000 mems.

Presbyterian Church of Ghana: POB 106, Accra; tel. (21) 662511; fax (21) 665594; f. 1828; Moderator Rt Rev. ANTHONY ANTWI BEEKO; Sec. Rev. Dr D. N. A. KPOBI; 422,500 mems.

The African Methodist Episcopal Church, the F'Eden Church and the Religious Society of Friends (Quakers) are also active in Ghana.

ISLAM

In 2000 some 15.6% of the population of Ghana were Muslims, with a particularly large concentration in the Northern Region. The majority are Malikees.

Coalition of Muslim Organizations: Accra.

Ghana Muslim Representative Council: Accra.

Chief Imam: Sheikh USMAN NUHU SHARABUTU.

BAHÁ'Í FAITH

National Spiritual Assembly: BP 7098, Accra-North; tel. (21) 222127; e-mail bahaigh@ghana.com.

The Press

DAILY NEWSPAPERS

Daily Graphic: Graphic Rd, POB 742, Accra; tel. (21) 228911; fax (21) 669886; e-mail info@graphicghana.com; internet www .graphicghana.com; f. 1950; state-owned; Editor Elvis D. Aryeh; circ. 100,000.

Daily Guide: Accra; internet www.dailyguidenews.com; privately owned.

The Ghanaian Times: New Times Corpn, Ring Rd West, POB 2638, Accra; tel. (21) 228282; fax (21) 229398; e-mail newtimes@ ghana.com; f. 1958; state-owned; Editor Robert Bentil (acting); circ. 45,000.

PERIODICALS

Bi-Weekly

Network Herald: NBS Multimedia, Private Mail Bag, OSU, Accra; tel. (21) 701184; fax (21) 762173; e-mail herald@ghana.com; internet www.networkherald.gh; f. 2001; Editor Mawuko Zormelo.

Weekly

Bombshell: Crossfire Publications, POB 376, Sakumono, Accra; tel. (21) 234750; fax (21) 233172; Editor Ben Asamoah.

Business and Financial Times: POB CT16, Cantonments, Accra; tel. and fax (21) 223334; e-mail editor@financialtimesghana.com; internet www.financialtimesghana.com; f. 1989; Editor John Hanson; circ. 20,000.

Champion: POB 6828, Accra-North; tel. (21) 229079; Man. Dir Mark D. N. Addy; Editor Frank Caxton Williams; circ. 300,000.

Christian Chronicle: Accra; Editor George Naykene.

The Crusading Guide: POB 8523, Accra-North; tel. (21) 763339; fax (21) 761541; Editor Kweku Baako Jr.

The Democrat: Democrat Publications, POB 13605, Accra; tel. (21) 76804; Editor L. K. Nyaho.

The Dispatch: 1 Dade Walk, North Labone, POB C1945, Cantonments, Accra; tel. (21) 763339; e-mail ephson@usa.net; Editor Ben Ephson.

Echo: POB 5288, Accra; f. 1968; Sun. Man. Editor M. K. Frimpong; circ. 40,000.

Entertaining Eye: Kad Publications, POB 125, Darkuman-Accra; Editor Nana Kwakye Yiadom; circ. 40,000.

Evening Digest: News Media Ltd, POB 7082, Accra; tel. (21) 221071; Editor P. K. Anantitetteh.

Experience: POB 5084, Accra-North; Editor Alfred Yaw Poku; circ. 50,000.

Free Press: Tommy Thompson Books Ltd, POB 6492, Accra; tel. (21) 225994; independent; Editor Eben Quarcoo.

Ghana Life: Ghana Life Publications, POB 11337, Accra; tel. (21) 229835; Editor Nikki Boa-Amponsem.

Ghana Palaver: Palaver Publications, POB 15744, Accra-North; internet www.ghana-palaver.com; tel. (21) 232495; f. 1994; Editor Bruce Quansah.

Ghanaian Chronicle: General Portfolio Ltd, PMB, Accra-North; tel. (21) 227789; fax (21) 775895; e-mail chronicle@africaonline.com .gh; internet www.ghanaian-chronicle.com; Editor Ebo Quansah; circ. 60,000.

Ghanaian Dawn: Dawn Publications, POB 721, Mamprobi, Accra; Editor Mabel Lindsay.

The Ghanaian Voice: Newstop Publications, POB 514, Mamprobi, Accra; tel. (21) 226943; e-mail voice@aspcc.africaonline.co.gh; Editor Dan K. Ansah; circ. 100,000.

The Gossip: Gossip Publications, POB 5355, Accra-North; Editor C. A. Acheampong.

Graphic Showbiz: Graphic Rd, POB 742, Accra; tel. (21) 684001; fax (21) 684025; e-mail showbiz@graphic.com.gh; internet www .graphic.com; state-owned; Editor Nanabanyin Dadson.

Graphic Sports: Graphic Rd, POB 742, Accra; tel. (21) 228911; e-mail graphic@ghana.com; state-owned; Editor Joe Aggrey; circ. 60,000.

The Guide: Western Publications Ltd, POB 8253, Accra-North; tel. (21) 232760; Editor Kweku Baako Jnr.

The Heritage: POB AC503, Arts Center, Accra; tel. (21) 258820; fax (21) 258823; e-mail heritage@africaonline.gh; internet www .theheritagenews.com; Chair. Stephen Owusu; Editor Nii Noi Vanderpuye (acting).

High Street Journal: POB 7974, Accra-North; tel. (12) 239835; fax (12) 239837; e-mail hsjaccra@ghana.com; Editor Sheikh Abutiate.

The Independent: Clear Type Press Bldg Complex, off Graphic Rd, POB 4031, Accra; tel. and fax (12) 661091; internet www .independent-gh.com; f. 1989; Editor Kabral Blay Amihere.

The Mirror: Graphic Rd, POB 742, Accra; tel. (21) 228911; fax (21) 669886; f. 1953; state-owned; Sat. Editor E. N. V. Provencal; circ. 90,000.

The New Ghanaian: Tudu Publishing House, POB 751, Tamale; tel. (71) 22579; Editor Razak El-Alawa.

New Nation: POB 6828, Accra-North; Editor S. N. Sasraku; circ. 300,000.

Public Agenda: P. A. Communications, POB 5564, Accra-North; tel. (21) 238821; fax (21) 231687; e-mail isodec@ghana.com; f. 1994; Editor Yao Graham; circ. 12,000.

Sporting News: POB 5481, Accra-North; f. 1967; Man. Editor J. Oppong-Agyare.

The Standard: Standard Newspapers & Magazines Ltd, POB 765, Accra; tel. (21) 220165; Roman Catholic; Editor Isaac Fritz Andoh; circ. 10,000.

Statesman: Kinesic Communications, POB 846, Accra; tel. and fax (21) 233242; official publ. of the New Patriotic Party; Editor Harunna Attah.

The Weekend: Newstop Publications, POB 514, Mamprobi, Accra; tel. and fax (21) 226943; Editor Emmanuel Yartey; circ. 40,000.

Weekly Events: Clear Type Image Ltd, 29 Olympic Street (Enterprise House), Kokomlemle, POB 7634, Accra-North; tel. (21) 223085; Editor Joris Jordan Dodoo.

Weekly Insight: Militant Publications Ltd, POB K272, Accra New Town, Accra; tel. (21) 660148; fax (21) 774338; e-mail insight93@ yahoo.com; f. 1993; independent; English; Editor Kwesi Pratt Jr.

Weekly Spectator: New Times Corpn, Ring Road West, POB 2638, Accra; tel. (21) 228282; fax (21) 229398; state-owned; f. 1963; Sun. Editor Willie Donkor; circ. 165,000.

Other

Africa Flamingo: Airport Emporium Ltd, POB 9194, Accra; monthly; Editor Felix Amanfu; circ. 50,000.

African Observer: POB 1171, Kaneshie, Accra; tel. (21) 231459; bimonthly; Editor Steve Mallory.

African Woman: Ring Rd West, POB 1496, Accra; monthly.

AGI Newsletter: c/o Asscn of Ghana Industries, POB 8624, Accra-North; tel. (21) 777283; e-mail agi@ighmail.com; f. 1974; quarterly; Editor (vacant); circ. 1,500.

AGOO: 6 Kofi Oku Rd, Rose Cottage, Palladium, POB 1291, Accra; tel. (21) 668252; fax (21) 669575; e-mail info@agoomagazine; internet www.agoomagazine.com; monthly; lifestyle magazine; Publr Kojo Bonsu.

Akwansosem: Ghana Information Services, POB 745, Accra; tel. (21) 228011; quarterly; in Akuapim Twi, Asanti Twi and Fante; Editor Kathleen Ofosu-Appiah.

Armed Forces News: General Headquarters, Directorate of Public Relations, Burma Camp, Accra; tel. (21) 776111; f. 1966; quarterly; Editor Adotey Ankrah-Hoffman; circ. 4,000.

Boxing and Football Illustrated: POB 8392, Accra; f. 1976; monthly; Editor Nana O. Ampomah; circ. 10,000.

Business and Financial Concord: Sammy Tech Consult Enterprise, POB 5677, Accra-North; tel. (21) 232446; fortnightly; Editor Kwabena Richardson.

Chit Chat: POB 7043, Accra; monthly; Editor Rosemond Adu.

Christian Messenger: Presbyterian Book Depot Bldg, POB 3075, Accra; tel. and fax (21) 662415; f. 1883; English-language; every two weeks; also **The Presbyterian** (in Twi and Ga); quarterly; Editor G. B. K. Owusu; circ. 40,000.

Drum: POB 1197, Accra; monthly; general interest.

Ghana Journal of Science: Ghana Science Asscn, POB 7, Legon; tel. (21) 500253; monthly; Editor Dr A. K. Ahafia.

Ghana Official News Bulletin: Information Services Dept, POB 745, Accra; English; political, economic, investment and cultural affairs.

Ghana Review International: POB 14307, Accra; tel. (21) 234056; fax (21) 237970; e-mail accra@ghanareview.com; internet www .ghanareview.com; monthly; general interest; Publr NANA OTUO ACHEAMPONG; Man. Editor (Ghana Office) EFAM AWO DOVI; circ. 100,000 (internationally).

Ideal Woman (Obaa Sima): POB 5737, Accra; tel. (21) 221399; f. 1971; fortnightly; Editor KATE ABBAM.

Insight and Opinion: POB 5446, Accra; quarterly; Editorial Sec. W. B. OHENE.

Legon Observer: POB 11, Legon; fax (21) 774338; f. 1966; publ. by Legon Society on National Affairs; fortnightly; Chair. J. A. DADSON; Editor EBOW DANIEL.

Police News: Police HQ, Accra; monthly; Editor S. S. APPIAH; circ. 20,000.

The Post: Ghana Information Services, POB 745, Accra; tel. (21) 228011; f. 1980; monthly; current affairs and analysis; circ. 25,000.

Radio and TV Times: Ghana Broadcasting Corpn, Broadcasting House, POB 1633, Accra; tel. (21) 221161; f. 1960; quarterly; Editor SAM THOMPSON; circ. 5,000.

The Scope: POB 8162, Tema; monthly; Editor EMMANUEL DOE ZIORKLUI; circ. 10,000.

Students World: POB M18, Accra; tel. (21) 774248; fax (21) 778715; e-mail aframpub@ighmail.com; f. 1974; monthly; educational; Man. Editor ERIC OFEI; circ. 10,000.

The Teacher: Ghana National Asscn of Teachers, POB 209, Accra; tel. (21) 221515; fax (21) 226286; f. 1931; quarterly; circ. 30,000.

Truth and Life: Gift Publications, POB 11337, Accra-North; monthly; Editor Pastor KOBENA CHARM.

Uneek: POB 230, Achimota, Accra; tel. (21) 543853; fax (21) 231355; e-mail info@uneekmagazine.com; internet www.uneekmagazine .com; f. 1998; monthly; leisure, culture; CEO and Editor FRANCIS ADAMS.

The Watchman: Watchman Gospel Ministry, POB GP 4521, Accra; tel. (21) 502011; fax (21)507428; e-mail sonlife@africaonline.com.gh; fortnightly; Pres. and CEO DIVINE P. KUMAH; Chair. Dr E. K. OPUNI.

NEWS AGENCY

Ghana News Agency: POB 2118, Accra; tel. (21) 665136; fax 669841; e-mail ghnews@ncs.com.gh; f. 1957; Gen. Man. SAM B. QUAICOE; 10 regional offices and 110 district offices.

PRESS ASSOCIATION

Ghana Journalists Association: POB 4636, Accra; tel. (21) 234692; fax (21) 234694; e-mail info@ghanamedia.com; internet www.ghanamedia.com/gja; Pres. GIFTY AFFENYI-DADZIE.

Publishers

Advent Press: POB 0102, Osu, Accra; tel. (21) 777861; f. 1937; Gen. Man. EMMANUEL C. TETTEH.

Adwinsa Publications (Ghana) Ltd: Advance Press Bldg, 3rd Floor, School Rd, POB 92, Legoh Accra; tel. (21) 221654; f. 1977; general, educational; Man. Dir KWABENA AMPONSAH.

Afram Publications: POB M18, Accra; tel. (21) 412561; e-mail aframpub@punchgh.com; f. 1974; textbooks and general; Man. Dir ERIC OFEI.

Africa Christian Press: POB 30, Achimota; tel. (21) 244147; fax (21) 220271; e-mail acpbooks@ghana.com; f. 1964; religious, fiction, theology, children's, leadership; Gen. Man. RICHARD A. B. CRABBE.

Allgoodbooks Ltd: POB AN10416, Accra-North; tel. (21) 664294; fax (21) 665629; e-mail allgoodbooks@hotmail.com; f. 1968; children's; Man. Dir MARY ASIRIFI.

Asempa Publishers: POB GP919, Accra; tel. (21) 233084; fax (21) 235140; e-mail asempa@ghana.com; f. 1970; religion, social issues, African music, fiction, children's; Gen. Man. Rev. EMMANUEL B. BORTEY.

Assembly Press Ltd-Ghana Publishing Corpn: POB 124, Accra; tel. (21) 664338; fax (21) 664330; e-mail asspcom@africaonline.com .gh; internet www.africaonline.com.gh/Assembly; f. 1965; state-owned; textbooks and general fiction and non-fiction; Man. Dir F. K. NYARKO.

Baafour and Co: POB K189, Accra New Town; f. 1978; general; Man. B. KESE-AMANKWAA.

Benibengor Book Agency: POB 40, Aboso; fiction, biography, children's and paperbacks; Man. Dir J. BENIBENGOR BLAY.

Black Mask Ltd: Accra; tel. (21) 234577; f. 1979; textbooks, plays, novels, handicrafts; Man. Dir YAW OWUSU ASANTE.

Editorial and Publishing Services: POB 5743, Accra; general, reference; Man. Dir M. DANQUAH.

Educational Press and Manufacturers Ltd: POB 9184, Airport-Accra; tel. (21) 220395; f. 1975; textbooks, children's; Man. G. K. KODUA.

Encyclopaedia Africana Project: POB 2797, Accra; tel. (21) 776939; fax (21) 779228; e-mail eap@africaonline.com.gh; internet www.endarkenment.com/eap; f. 1962; reference; Dir GRACE BANSA.

Frank Publishing Ltd: POB MB414, Accra; tel. (21) 240711; f. 1976; secondary school textbooks; Man. Dir FRANCIS K. DZOKOTO.

Ghana Universities Press: POB GP4219, Accra; tel. (21) 513383; fax (21) 501930; f. 1962; scholarly, academic and general; CEO Dr K. M. GANU.

Golden Wings Publications: 26 Mantse Kwao St, POB 1337, Accra; educational and children's; Man. Editor GREGORY ANKRAH.

Miracle Bookhouse: POB 7487, Accra-North; tel. (21) 226684; f. 1977; general; Man. J. APPIAH-BERKO.

Moxon Paperbacks: POB M160, Accra; tel. (21) 761175; fax (21) 777971; f. 1967; travel and guide books, fiction and poetry, Africana, telephone directory; Man. Dir JAMES MOXON.

Sam-Woode Ltd: A.979/15 Dansoman High Street, POB 12719, Accra-North; tel. (21) 305287; fax (021) 310482; e-mail samwoode@ ghana.com; educational and children's; Chair. KWESI SAM-WOODE.

Sedco Publishing Ltd: Sedco House, 5 Tabon St, North Ridge, POB 2051, Accra; tel. (21) 221332; fax (21) 220107; e-mail sedco@ africaonline.com.gh; f. 1975; educational; Chair. COURAGE K. SEGBAWU; Man. Dir FRANK SEGBAWU.

Sheffield Publishing Co: Accra; tel. (21) 667480; fax (21) 665960; f. 1970; religion, politics, economics, science, fiction; Publr RONALD MENSAH.

Tema Press: Tema Industrial Area, Accra; state-owned; privatization pending in 2002; educational books.

Unimax Macmillan Ltd: 42 Ring Rd South Industrial Area, POB 10722, Accra-North; tel. (21) 227443; fax (21) 225215; e-mail info@ unimacmillan.com; internet www.unimacmillan.com; representative of Macmillan UK; atlases, educational and children's; Man. Dir EDWARD ADDO.

Waterville Publishing House: POB 195, Accra; tel. (21) 663124; f. 1963; general fiction and non-fiction, textbooks, paperbacks, Africana; Man. Dir H. W. O. OKAI.

Woeli Publishing Services: POB NT601, Accra New Town; tel. and fax (21) 229294; f. 1984; children's, fiction, academic; Dir W. A. DEKUTSEY.

PUBLISHERS' ASSOCIATIONS

Ghana Book Development Council: POB M430, Accra; tel. (21) 229178; f. 1975; govt-financed agency; promotes and co-ordinates writing, production and distribution of books; Exec. Dir D. A. NIMAKO.

Ghana Book Publishers' Association (GBPA): POB LT471, Laterbiokorshie, Accra; tel. (21) 229178; fax (21) 220271; e-mail acpbooks@ghana.com; Exec. Sec. STEPHEN BROBBEY.

Private Newspaper Publishers' Association of Ghana (PRINPAG): POB 125, Darkuman, Accra; Chair. NANA KOFI KOOMSON; Gen. Sec. K. AGYEMANG DUAH.

Broadcasting and Communications

TELECOMMUNICATIONS

ACG Telesystems (Westel) Ghana Ltd: Dr Isert Rd, 7th Ave Ext., Ridge PMB, Accra-North; tel. (21) 232308; fax (21) 232309; e-mail btaylor@acg.com.gh; f. 1997; owned jointly by Ghana National Petroleum Corpn and Western Wireless Corpn USA; Man. Dir WILLIAM TAYLOR.

Ghana Telecom: Telecom House, nr Kwame Nkrumah Circle, Accra-North; tel. (21) 221001; fax (21) 227965; e-mail ghanatel@ncs .com.gh; internet www.ghanatel.net; f. 1995; 30% transferred to private ownership in 1997; Dir-Gen. Brig. HENRY KWAME ANYIDOHO; Man. Dir ADNAN ROFIEE.

Mobitel: 1 Dzorwulu Crescent, Airport West, Private Mail Bag, KIA, Accra; tel. (21) 701088; fax (21) 223128; e-mail info@ mobitelghana.com; internet www.mobitelnet.com; f. 1990; mobile cellular telephone services; Man. Dir SOBAN PASHA.

Spacefon: Auto Parts Bldg, Graphic Rd, South Industrial Area, Accra; tel. (21) 300000; fax (021) 231974; internet www.spacefon .com; f. 1996; mobile cellular telephone services.

BROADCASTING

There are internal radio broadcasts in English, Akan, Dagbani, Ewe, Ga, Hausa and Nzema, and an external service in English and French. There are three transmitting stations, with a number of relay stations. The Ghana Broadcasting Corporation operates two national networks, Radio 1 and Radio 2, which broadcast from Accra, and four regional FM stations. In 2002 there were also 15 independent commercial and community FM stations. There are eight main colour television transmitters.

Ghana Broadcasting Corpn: Broadcasting House, POB 1633, Accra; tel. (21) 221161; fax (21) 221157; e-mail gbc@ghana.com; internet www.gbc.com.gh; f. 1935; Dir-Gen. Dr KOFI FRIMPONG; Dir of TV Prof. MARK DUODU; Dir of Radio YAW OWUSU-ADDO.

Joy FM: 355 Faanofa St, Kokomlemle, POB 17202, Accra; tel. (21) 233558; fax (21) 224405; e-mail joyfm@ncs.com.gh; internet www .myjoyonline.com; f. 1995; news, information and music broadcasts; Dir KWESI TWUM.

Metro TV: Metro House, 59 Josiah Tongirar St, Labone, Accra; POB C1609, Cantonments, Accra; tel. (21) 765701; fax (21) 765702; e-mail webdesign@metrotv.com.gh; internet www.metrotv.com.gh.

Radio Ada: POB KA9482, Accra; tel. (968) 3713; fax (21) 500032; e-mail radioada@ghana.com; f. 1998; community broadcasts in Dangme; Dirs ALEX QUARMYNE, WILMA QUARMYNE.

Radio Gold FM: POB 17298, Accra; tel. (22) 300281; fax (22) 300284; e-mail radiogold@africaonline.com.gh; internet www .africaonline.com.gh/RadioGold; Man. Dir BAFFOE BONNIE.

Spirit FM: Starcom Broadcasting Services Ltd., 45 Water Rd, Kanda Highway, North Ridge, POB CT3850, Cantonments, Accra; tel. (21) 225716; fax (21) 221983; internet www.starcomcorporate .com; Christian broadcasts in Greater Accra.

TV3: 12th Road, Kanda, opp. French embassy, Accra; tel. (21) 228679; fax (21) 763450; e-mail cbo@tv3.com.gh; internet www.tv3 .com.gh; f. 1997; private television station; progamming in English and local languages; Man. Dir MUSNI BINMOHAMAD.

Finance

(cap. = capital; res = reserves; dep. = deposits; m. = million; brs = branches; amounts in cedis)

BANKING

The commercial banking sector comprised nine commercial banks, four development banks and four merchant banks in 1998. There were also 130 rural banks and several non-banking financial institutions.

Central Bank

Bank of Ghana: Cedi House, Liberia Rd, POB 2674, Accra; tel. (21) 666902; fax (21) 662996; e-mail secretary@bog.gov.gh; internet www .bog.gov.gh; f. 1957; bank of issue; cap. 100,000m., res 250,329m., dep. 1,244,614m. (Dec. 2000); Gov. PAUL ACQUAH.

Commercial and Development Banks

Agricultural Development Bank: Cedi House, Liberia Rd, POB 4191, Accra; tel. (21) 662758; fax (21) 662846; e-mail adbweb@ africaonline.com.gh; internet www.adbghana.com; f. 1965; 51.8% state-owned, 48.2% owned by Bank of Ghana; credit facilities for farmers and commercial banking; cap. and res 390,064.5m., dep. 968,713.0m. (Dec. 2002); Chair. PAUL S. M. KORANTENG; Man. Dir SAMMY A. WELBECK; 32 brs.

Ghana Commercial Bank Ltd: POB 134, Accra; tel. (21) 664914; fax (21) 662168; e-mail gcbmail@gcb.com.gh; internet www.gcb.com .gh; f. 1953; 46.8% state-owned; cap. 20,000m., res 3,898m., dep. 1,720,419m. (Dec. 2001); Chair. K. G. OSEI BONSU (acting); Man. Dir MATILDA OBENG-ANSONG (acting); 130 brs.

Leasafric Ghana Ltd: 7 Main St, Tesano, POB C74, Accra; tel. (21) 240140; fax (21) 228375; e-mail leasafric@africaonline.com.gh; cap. 1,218m, total assets 11,913m. (Dec. 1999); Chair. JOHN KOBINA RICHARDSON; Man. Dir SETH K. DEI.

National Investment Bank Ltd (NIB): 37 Kwame Nkrumah Ave, POB 3726, Accra; tel. (21) 240001; fax (21) 240030; e-mail info@ nib-ghana.com; f. 1963; 86.4% state-owned; provides long-term investment capital, jt venture promotion, consortium finance man. and commercial banking services; cap. 3,259.7m., total assets 168,754m. (Dec. 1998); Chair. NICHOLAS AKPEBU; Man. Dir SIMPSON E. S. KULEKE; 11 brs.

NTHC Ltd: Martco House, Okai Mensah Link, off Kwame Nkrumah Ave, POB 9563, Airport, Accra; tel. (21) 238492; fax (21) 229975; e-mail nthc@ghana.com; internet www.nthcghana.com; fmrly National Trust Holding Co. Ltd; f. 1976 to provide stockbrokerage services, asset management and financial advisory services; cap. 9,000m. (2001); Chair. BENJAMIN ADU-AMANKWA; Man. Dir Dr A. W. Q. BARNOR.

Prudential Bank Ltd: PMB, GPO, Accra; tel. (21) 226322; fax (21) 226803; e-mail prudential@ghana.com; f. 1996; cap. 1,500m., total assets 47,381m. (Dec. 1998); Chair. JOHN SACKAH ADDO; Man. Dir STEPHEN SEKYERE-ABANKWA.

SSB Bank Ltd: POB 13119, Accra; tel. (21) 221726; fax (21) 220713; e-mail enquiries@ssb.com.gh; internet www.ssb.com.gh; f. 1976; as Social Security Bank; 50.7% owned by Société Générale, France; cap. 6,735m., dep. 765,453m., total assets 1,365,630m. (Dec. 2001); Chair. FRANCIS EMMANUEL YAO ATTIPOE; Man. Dir PRYCE KOYO THOMPSON; 38 brs.

The Trust Bank Ltd: 68 Kwame Nkrumah Ave, POB 1862, Accra; tel. (21) 240049; fax (21) 240059; e-mail trust@ghana.com; internet www.ttbgh.net; f. 1996; 35% owned by Banque Belgolaise (Belgium), 33% owned by the Social Security and National Insurance Trust; cap. 10,000m., res 13,260m., dep. 185,302m. (Dec. 2000); Chair. ALEX AWUKU; Man. Dir JEAN-MARIE MARQUEBREUCQ; 6 brs.

Merchant Banks

CAL Merchant Bank Ltd: 45 Independence Ave, POB 14596, Accra; tel. (21) 221056; fax (21) 231104; e-mail calbank@calbank-gh .com; internet www.calbank-gh.com; f. 1989; cap. 6,578m., res 40,319m., dep. 207,346m. (Dec. 2001); Chair. GEORGE VICTOR OKOH; Man. Dir FRANK BRAKO ADU, Jr.

Ecobank Ghana Ltd (EBG): 19 Seventh Ave, Ridge West, PMB-GPO, Accra; tel. (21) 228812; fax (21) 231934; e-mail ecobankgh@ ecobank.com; f. 1989; 93.7% owned by Ecobank Transnational Inc (Togo, operating under the auspices of the Economic Community of West African States); cap. 18,200m., res 84,289m., dep. 1,125,859m. (Dec. 2001); Chair. EDWARD PATRICK LARBI GYAMPOH; Man. Dir ALBERT KOBINA ESSEIN; 5 brs.

First Atlantic Merchant Bank Ltd: Atlantic Place, 1 Seventh Ave, Ridge West, POB C1620, Cantonments, Accra; tel. (21) 231433; fax (21) 231399; e-mail info@firstatlanticbank.com.gh; internet www .firstatlanticbank.com.gh; f. 1994; cap. 2,657m., res 19,574m., dep. 152,312m. (Dec. 2001); Chair. PHILIP OWUSU; Man. Dir JUDE ARTHUR.

Merchant Bank (Ghana) Ltd: Merban House, 44 Kwame Nkrumah Ave, POB 401, Accra; tel. (21) 666331; fax (21) 667305; e-mail merban_services@merbangh.com; internet www.merbankgh .com; f. 1972; cap. 5,000m., res 56,476m., dep. 442,267m. (Dec. 2001); Chair. Dr JOHN KOBINA RICHARDSON; Man. Dir CHRIS N. N. NARTEY; 5 brs.

Foreign Banks

Barclays Bank of Ghana Ltd (UK): Barclays House, High St, POB 2949, Accra; tel. (21) 664901; fax (21) 667420; e-mail barclays .ghana@barclays.com; internet www.africa.barclays.com/ghana .htm; f. 1971; 10% state-owned; cap. 1,000m., res 315,502m., dep. 1,819,836m. (Dec. 2000); Chair. NANA WEREKO AMPEM II; Man. Dir K. QUANSAH; 26 brs.

International Commerical Bank (Ghana) Ltd: Independence Ave, Makola Shopping Mall, POB 20057, Accra; tel. (21) 666190; fax (21) 666221; e-mail icb@icbank-gh.com; dep. 17,637m., total assets 34,176m. (Dec. 1999); Chair. JOSEPHINE SIVARETNAM; CEO GEORGE KOSHY.

Stanbic Bank Ghana: POB CT2344, Cantonments, Accra; tel. (21) 250071; fax (21) 234685; e-mail stanbic@ghana.com; internet www .stanbic.com.gh; f. 1999; subsidiary of the Standard Bank of South Africa Ltd; cap. 15,602m., total assets 14,363m. (Dec. 1999); Chair. JOHN LEGGET; Man. Dir JAMES P STANDING; 1 br.

Standard Chartered Bank Ghana Ltd (UK): High St, POB 768, Accra; tel. (21) 664591; fax (21) 667751; e-mail dzaney@scb.ghana .nhs.compuserve.com; internet www.standardchartered.com/gh/ index.html; f. 1896 as Bank of British West Africa; cap. 40,405m., res 240,797m., dep. 1,636,143m. (Dec. 2001); Chair. PETER SULLIVAN; CEO VISHNU MOHAN; 28 brs.

STOCK EXCHANGE

Ghana Stock Exchange (GSE): Cedi House, 5th Floor, Liberia Rd, POB 1849, Accra; tel. (21) 669908; fax (21) 669913; e-mail stockex@ ghana.com; internet www.gse.com.gh; f. 1990; 52 mems; Chair. NORBERT KUDJAWU; CEO YEBOA AMOAH.

INSURANCE

Donewell Insurance Co Ltd: POB 2136, Accra; tel. (21) 760483; fax (21) 760484; e-mail donewell@africaonline.com.gh; internet www .ghanaclassifieds.com/donewell; f. 1992; Chair. JOHN S. ADDO.

Enterprise Insurance Co Ltd: POB 50, Accra; tel. (21) 666848; fax (21) 666186; e-mail eicltd@africaonline.com.gh; f. 1972; Chair. TREVOR TREFGARNE; Man. Dir GEORGE OTOO.

Ghana Union Assurance Co Ltd: POB 1322, Accra; tel. (21) 780625; fax (21) 780647; e-mail gua@ghana.com; f. 1973; insurance underwriting; Man. Dir KWADWO DUKU.

Great African Insurance Co Ltd: POB 12349, Accra North; tel. (21) 227459; fax (21) 228905; f. 1980; Man. Dir KWASI AKOTO.

Metropolitan Insurance Co Ghana Ltd: POB GP20084, Accra; tel. (21) 225296; fax (21) 237872; e-mail met@africaonline.com.gh; internet www.met-insurance.com; f. 1994; Chair. P. K. THOMPSON; CEO D. A. MENSAH.

State Insurance Corpn of Ghana Ltd: POB 2363, Accra; tel. (21) 666961; fax (21) 662205; e-mail sic.info@ighmail.com; f. 1962; state-owned; privatization pending; all classes of insurance; Chair. LARRY ADJETEY; Man. Dir EBENEZER ALLOTEY.

Social Security and National Insurance Trust: Pension House, POB M149, Accra; tel. (21) 667742; fax (21) 662226; f. 1972; covers over 650,000 contributors; Dir-Gen. ERIC ADJEI.

Vanguard Assurance Co Ltd: POB 1869, Accra; tel. (21) 666485; fax (21) 668610; e-mail vanguard@ghana.com; internet www .vanguardassurance.com; f. 1974; general accident, marine, motor and life insurance; Chair. NANA AWUAH-DARKO APEM; 7 brs.

Several foreign insurance companies operate in Ghana.

Trade and Industry

GOVERNMENT AGENCIES

Divestiture Implementation Committee: F35/5 Ring Road East, Labone, POB CT102, Cantonments, Accra; tel. (21) 772049; fax (21) 773126; e-mail dic@ncs.com.gh; internet www.ghana.com.gh/dic; f. 1988; Chair. C. O. NYANOR; Exec. Sec. BENSON POKU-ADJEI.

Food Production Corpn: POB 1853, Accra; f. 1971; state corpn providing employment for youth in large-scale farming enterprises; controls 76,900 ha of land (16,200 ha under cultivation); operates 87 food farms on a co-operative and self-supporting basis, and rears poultry and livestock.

Ghana Export Promotion Council (GEPC): POB M146, Accra; tel. (21) 228813; fax (21) 668263; e-mail gepc@ghana.com; internet www.exportghana.org; f. 1974; Exec. Sec. EDWARD BOATENG.

Ghana Food Distribution Corpn: POB 4245, Accra; tel. (21) 228428; fax (21) 225352; f. 1970; buys, stores, preserves, distributes and retails foodstuffs through 10 regional centres; Man. Dir JIMMY EDWARD.

Ghana Free Zones Board: POB M626, Accra; tel. (21) 780532; fax (21) 780534; e-mail freezone@africaonline.com.gh; internet www .ghanaclassifieds.com/gfzb; f. 1996; approves establishment of cos in export processing zones; Dir ANDY APPIAH-KUBI (acting).

Ghana Heavy Equipment Ltd: Accra; fmrly subsidiary of Ghana National Trading Corpn; organizes exports, imports and production of heavy equipment; Chair. KOFI ASARE DARKWA POKU.

Ghana Industrial Holding Corpn (GIHOC): POB 2784, Accra; tel. (21) 664998; f. 1967; controls and manages state enterprises, including steel, paper, bricks, paint, electronics, metals, canneries, distilleries and boat-building factories; also has three subsidiary cos and four jt ventures; dissolution approved by law in 1993; Chair. J. E. K. MOSES; Man. Dir J. K. WILLIAMS.

Ghana Investment Promotion Centre (GIPC): POB M193, Accra; tel. (21) 665125; fax (21) 663801; e-mail gipc@ghana.com; internet www.gipc.org.gh; f. 1981; negotiates new investments, approves projects, registers foreign capital and decides extent of govt participation; Chair. P. V. OBENG.

Ghana Minerals Commission: 9 Switchback Rd Residential Area, Cantonments, POB M248, Accra; tel. (21) 772783; fax (21) 773324; e-mail mincom@mincomgh.org; internet www.mincomgh.org; f. 1986 to regulate and promote Ghana's mineral industry; CEO BENJAMIN NII AYI ARYEE.

Ghana Standards Board: c/o POB MB245, Accra; tel. (21) 500065; fax (21) 500092; e-mail gsbnep@ghana.com; f. 1967; establishes and promulgates standards; promotes standardization, industrial efficiency and development and industrial welfare, health and safety; operates certification mark scheme; 403 mems; Chair. Prof. EMMANUEL KENNETH AGYEI; Exec. Dir A. D. NTIFORD.

Ghana Trade and Investment Gateway Project (GHATIG): POB M47, Accra; tel. 663439; fax 665423; e-mail gateway1@ghana .com; promotes private investment and trade, infrastructural development of free trade zones and export processing zones.

National Board for Small-scale Industries: Ministry of Trade, Industry and Special Presidential Initiatives, POB M85, Accra; f. 1985; promotes small and medium-scale industrial and commercial enterprises by providing credit, advisory services and training.

DEVELOPMENT ORGANIZATION

Agence Française de Développement (AFD): 8th Rangoon Close, POB 9592, Airport, Accra; tel. (21) 778757; fax (21) 778755; e-mail afd@ncs.com.gh; internet www.afd.fr; f. 1985; fmrly Caisse Française de Développement; Dir LAURENT DURIEZ.

CHAMBER OF COMMERCE

Ghana National Chamber of Commerce: POB 2325, Accra; tel. (21) 662427; fax (21) 662210; e-mail gncc@ncs.com.gh; f. 1961; promotes and protects industry and commerce, organizes trade fairs; 2,500 individual mems and 8 mem. chambers; Pres. ATO AMPIAH; CEO SAL D. AMEGAVIE.

INDUSTRIAL AND TRADE ASSOCIATIONS

Best Fibres Development Board: POB 1992, Kumasi; f. 1970; promotes the commercial cultivation of best fibres and their processing, handling and grading.

Federation of Associations of Ghanaian Exporters (FAGE): POB M124, Accra; tel. (21) 232554; fax (21) 232726; e-mail fage@ ighmail.com; internet www.ghana-exporter.org; non-governmental, not-for-profit organization for exporters of non-traditional exports; over 2,500 mems.

Ghana Cocoa Board (COCOBOD): Cocoa House, Kwame Nkrumah Ave, POB 933, Accra; tel. (21) 221212; fax (21) 667104; e-mail cocobod@africaonline.com.gh; internet www.cocobod.org; f. 1985; monopoly purchaser of cocoa until 1993; responsible for purchase, grading and export of cocoa, coffee and shea nuts; also encourages production and scientific research aimed at improving quality and yield of these crops; controls all exports of cocoa; CEO KWAME SARPONG.

Ghana Timber Export Development Division (GTEDD): POB 515, Takoradi; tel. (31) 22921; fax (31) 23339; e-mail gtedb@ghana .com; internet www.trada.org.uk/ghana/news/index.html; f. 1985; promotes the development of the timber industry and the sale and export of timber; Chair. JOHN ASMAH; Exec. Dir DOUGLAS ASAMAMY.

Grains and Legumes Development Board: POB 4000, Kumasi; tel. (51) 4231; e-mail gldb@africaonline.com.gh; f. 1970; state-controlled; produces, processes and stores seeds and seedlings, and manages national seed security stocks.

EMPLOYERS' ORGANIZATION

Ghana Employers' Association: State Enterprises Commission Bldg, POB 2616, Accra; tel. (21) 678455; fax (21) 678405; e-mail geadmin@ghanaemployers.org; internet www.ghanaemployers.org; f. 1959; 300 mems (2002); Pres. ATO AMPIAH; Vice-Pres. Dr CHARLES MENSAH.

Affiliated Bodies

Association of Ghana Industries: Trade Fair Centre, POB AN8624, Accra-North; tel. (21) 779793; fax (21) 773143; e-mail agi@ agi.org.gh; internet www.agi.org.gh; f. 1957; Pres. Prince KOFI KLUDJESON; Exec. Dir ANDREW E. QUAYSON; 500 mems.

Ghana Booksellers' Association: POB 10367, Accra-North; tel. (21) 773002; fax (21) 773242; e-mail minerva@ghana.com; Pres. FERD J. REIMMER; Gen. Sec. ADAMS. AHIMAH.

Ghana Chamber of Mines: Minerals House 10, Sixth St, Airport Residential Area, POB 991, Accra; tel. (21) 760652; fax (21) 760653; e-mail chamber@ghanachamines.com; internet www .ghanachamines.com; f. 1928; Pres. JAMES K. ANAMAN; CEO JOYCE WEREKO-BROBBY.

Ghana Electrical Contractors' Association: POB 1858, Accra.

Ghana National Association of Teachers: POB 209, Accra; tel. (21) 221515; fax (21) 226286; f. 1931; Pres. G. N. NAASO; Gen. Sec. PAUL OSEI-MENSAH.

Ghana National Contractors' Association: c/o J. T. Osei and Co, POB M11, Accra.

Ghana Timber Association (GTA): POB 1020, Kumasi; tel. and fax (51) 25153; f. 1952; promotes, protects and develops timber industry; Chair. TETTEH NANOR.

UTILITIES

Regulatory Body

Public Utilities Regulatory Commission: POB CT3095, Cantonments, Accra; tel. (21) 244181; fax (21) 224188; e-mail purcsec@ghana.com; internet www.purc.com.gh; f. 1997.

Electricity

Electricity Co of Ghana (ECG): Electro-Volta House, POB 521, Accra; tel. (21) 664941; fax (21) 666262; e-mail ecgho@gh.com; privatization proposed in 2002; Chair. KWAME SAARAH MENSAH; Man. Dir Chief MUSA B. ADAM.

Volta River Authority: Electro-Volta House, POB M77, Accra; tel. (21) 664941; fax (21) 662610; e-mail orgsrv@accra.vra.com; f. 1961; controls the generation and distribution of electricity; CEO CHARLES WEREKO-BROBBY.

Water

Ghana Water Co Ltd (GWCL): POB M194, Accra; tel. (21) 666781; fax (21) 663552; e-mail gwsc@africaonline.com.gh; f. 1965 to provide, distribute and conserve water supplies for public, domestic and industrial use, and to establish, operate and control sewerage systems; Chair. C. W. SACKEYFIO; Man. Dir CHARLES ADJEI.

CO-OPERATIVES

In 1998 there were 11,154 registered co-operative societies, grouped into four sectors: industrial, financial, agricultural and service.

Department of Co-operatives: POB M150, Accra; tel. (21) 666212; fax (21) 772789; f. 1944; govt-supervised body, responsible for registration, auditing and supervision of co-operative socs; Registrar R. BUACHIE-APHRAM.

Ghana Co-operatives Council Ltd (GACOCO): POB 4034, Accra; tel. (21) 232195; f. 1951; co-ordinates activities of all co-operative socs and plays advocacy role for co-operative movement; comprises 11 active nat. asscns and two central organizations; Sec.-Gen. ALBERT AGYEMAN PREMPEH.

The five national associations and two central organizations include the Ghana Co-operative Marketing Asscn Ltd, the Ghana Co-operative Credit Unions Asscn Ltd, the Ghana Co-operative Distillers and Retailers Asscn Ltd, and the Ghana Co-operative Poultry Farmers Asscn Ltd.

TRADE UNIONS

Ghana Federation of Labour: POB 209, Accra; tel. (27) 552433; Sec.-Gen. ABRAHAM KOOMSON; 10,540 mems.

Trades Union Congress (Ghana) (TUC): Hall of Trade Unions, POB 701, Accra; tel. (21) 662568; fax (21) 667161; e-mail tuc@ighmail.com; f. 1945; 17 affiliated unions; Chair. ALEX K. BONNEY; Sec.-Gen. KWASI ADU-AMANKWAH.

Transport

RAILWAYS

Ghana has a railway network of 1,300 km, which connects Accra, Kumasi and Takoradi.

Ghana Railways Corpn: POB 251, Takoradi; tel. (31) 22181; fax (31) 23797; f. 1901; responsible for the operation and maintenance of all railways; Man. Dir M. K. ARTHUR.

ROADS

In 1996 Ghana had an estimated total road network of 37,800 km, including 30 km of motorways, 5,230 km of main roads, and 9,620 km of secondary roads; some 24.1% of the road network was paved. A five-year Road Sector Expenditure Programme, costing US $259m., commenced in 1995. Construction work on 36 bridges nation-wide, funded by the Japanese Government, was due to commence during 2003.

Ghana Highway Authority: POB 1641, Accra; tel. (21) 666591; fax (21) 665571; f. 1974 to plan, develop, administer and maintain trunk roads and related facilities; CEO B. L. T. SAKIBU.

Vanef STC: POB 7384, 1 Adjuma Cres., Ring Rd West Industrial Area, Accra; tel. (21) 221912; fax (21) 221945; e-mail stc@ghana.com; internet www.vanef-stc.com; f. 1965; fmrly State Transport Company, transferred to private-sector ownership in 2000; regional and international coach services; CEO JAMES OWUSU BONSU.

SHIPPING

The two main ports are Tema (near Accra) and Takoradi, both of which are linked with Kumasi by rail. A project to upgrade facilities at both ports, at a cost of US $365m., was to commence in 1998. In 1996 some 6.7m. metric tons of goods were handled at the two ports.

Ghana Ports and Harbour Authority: POB 150, Tema; tel. (22) 202631; fax (22) 202812; e-mail ghpa@ghana.com; holding co for the ports of Tema and Takoradi; Dir Gen. BEN OWUSU MENSAH.

Alpha (West Africa) Line Ltd: POB 451, Tema; operates regular cargo services to West Africa, the UK, the USA, the Far East and northern Europe; shipping agents; Man. Dir AHMED EDGAR COLLINGWOOD WILLIAMS.

Black Star Line Ltd: 4th Lane, Kuku Hill Osu, POB 248, Accra; tel. (21) 2888; fax (21) 2889; f. 1957; state-owned; transfer to private sector pending; operates passenger and cargo services to Europe, the United Kingdom, Canada, the USA, the Mediterranean and West Africa; shipping agents; Chair. MAGNUS ADDICO; Man. Dir Capt. V. N. ATTUQUAYEFIO.

Bunktrad Shipping and Trading Ltd: 4th Floor, Trust Towers, POB 14801, Accra; tel. (21) 238401; fax (21) 236121; e-mail bunktrad@africaonline.com.gh; charters tankers; Dir SAM SACKLEY.

Holland West-Afrika Lijn NV: POB 269, Accra; cargo services to and from North America and the Far East; shipping agents.

Liner Agencies and Trading (Ghana) Ltd: POB 214, Tema; tel. (22) 202987; fax (22) 202989; e-mail enquiries@liner-agencies.com; international freight services; shipping agents; Dir J. OSSEI-YAW.

Maersk Sealand Ghana: Obourwe Bldg, Torman Rd, Fishing Harbour Area, POB 8800, Community 7, Tema; tel. (22) 206740; fax (22) 202048; e-mail tmamkt@maersk.com; internet www.maersksealand.com/Ghana; f. 2001; owned by Maersk (Denmark); offices in Tema, Takoradi and Kumasi; Man. Dir PETER SMIDT-NIELSEN.

Remco Shipping Lines Ltd: POB 3898, Accra; tel. (21) 224609.

Scanship (Ghana) Ltd: CFAO Bldg, High St, POB 1705, Accra; tel. (21) 664314; shipping agents.

Association

Ghana Shippers' Council: Enterprise House, 5th Floor, High St, POB 1321, Accra; tel. (21) 666915; fax (21) 668768; e-mail scouncil@shippers-gh.com; internet www.ghanashipperscouncil.org; f. 1974; represents interests of 28,000 registered Ghanaian shippers; also provides cargo-handling and allied services; Chief Exec. KOFI MBIAH.

CIVIL AVIATION

The main international airport is at Kotoka (Accra). There are also airports at Kumasi, Takoradi, Sunyani and Tamale. The construction of a dedicated freight terminal at Kotoka Airport was completed in 1994. In 2000 592,276 passengers and 46,085 metric tons of freight passed through Kotoka Airport.

Ghana Civil Aviation Authority (GCAA): PMB, Kotoka International Airport, Accra; tel. (21) 776171; fax (21) 773293; e-mail centre-gcaa@ighmail.com; internet www.gcaa.com.gh; f. 1986; Chair. S. AKUFFO; Dir-Gen. Capt. JOE A. BOACHIE.

Gemini Airlines Ltd (Aero Gem Cargo): America House, POB 7238, Accra-North; tel. (21) 665785; fax (21) 771921; e-mail aerogemcargo@hotmail.com; f. 1974; operates weekly cargo flight between Accra and London; Gen. Man. P. OKINE.

Ghana Airways Ltd.: Ghana Airways House, Ghana Airways Avenue, POB 1636, Accra; tel. (21) 773321; fax (21) 772738; e-mail ghanaairways@ighmail.com; f. 1958; state-owned; operates regional services and international routes to West African, Asian and European destinations, and to the USA and South Africa; CEO SAM E. JONAH; Man. Dir MARWAN TRABOULSI.

Tourism

Ghana's attractions include fine beaches, game reserves, traditional festivals, and old trading forts and castles. In 1996 a 15-year Integrated National Tourism Development Plan was initiated, under which annual tourist arrivals were targeted to exceed 1m. by 2020. In 1999 372,651 tourists visited Ghana, with revenue from tourism totalling US $342m.

Ghana Tourist Board: POB GP3106, Accra-North; tel. (21) 238330; fax (21) 244611; e-mail gtb@africaonline.com.gh; internet www.ghanatourism.com; f. 1968; Exec. Dir MARTIN MIREKU (acting).

Ghana Association of Tourist and Travel Agencies: Ramia House, Kojo Thompson Rd, POB 7140, Accra; tel. (21) 228933; Pres. JOSEPH K. ANKUMAH; Sec. JOHNNIE MOREAUX.

Ghana Tourist Development Co Ltd: POB 8710, Accra; tel. (21) 776109; fax (21) 772093; f. 1974; develops tourist infrastructure, incl. hotels, restaurants and casinos; operates duty-free shops; Man. Dir ALFRED KOMLADZEI.

GREECE

Introductory Survey

Location, Climate, Language, Religion, Flag, Capital

The Hellenic Republic lies in south-eastern Europe. The country consists mainly of a mountainous peninsula between the Mediterranean Sea and the Aegean Sea, bounded to the north by Albania, the former Yugoslav republic of Macedonia and Bulgaria, and to the east by Turkey. To the south, east and west of the mainland lie numerous Greek islands, of which the largest is Crete. The climate is Mediterranean, with mild winters and hot summers. The average temperature in the capital is 28°C (82°C) in July and 9°C (48°C) in January. The language is Greek, of which there are two forms—the formal language (katharevoussa) and the language commonly spoken and taught in schools (demotiki). Almost all of the inhabitants profess Christianity, and the Greek Orthodox Church, to which about 97% of the population adhere, is the established religion. The national flag (proportions 2 by 3) displays nine equal horizontal stripes of blue and white, with a white cross throughout a square canton of blue at the upper hoist. The capital is Athens.

Recent History

The liberation of Greece from the German occupation (1941–44) was followed by a civil war, which lasted until 1949. The communist forces were defeated, and the constitutional monarchy re-established. King Konstantinos (Constantine) acceded to the throne on the death of his father, King Paul, in 1964. A succession of weak governments and conflicts between the King and his ministers, and an alleged conspiracy involving military personnel, culminated in a coup, led by right-wing army officers, in April 1967. An attempted counter-coup, led by the King, failed, and he went into exile. Col Georgios Papadopoulos emerged as the dominant personality in the new regime, becoming Prime Minister in December 1967 and Regent in March 1972. The regime produced nominally democratic constitutional proposals, but all political activity was banned and its opponents were expelled from all positions of power or influence.

Following an abortive naval mutiny, Greece was declared a republic in June 1973; Papadopoulos was appointed President in July. Martial law was ended, and a civilian Cabinet was appointed in preparation for a general election. However, a student uprising in Athens in November was violently suppressed by the army, and Papadopoulos was overthrown by another military coup. Lt-Gen. Phaidon Ghizikis was appointed President, and a mainly civilian Cabinet, led by Adamantios Androutsopoulos, was installed, but effective power lay with a small group of officers and the military police under Brig.-Gen. Demetrios Ioannides. As a result of the failure of the military junta's attempt to overthrow President Makarios of Cyprus, and its inability to prevent the Turkish invasion of the island (see the chapter on Cyprus) in July 1974, the Androutsopoulos Cabinet collapsed in July 1974. President Ghizikis summoned from exile a former Prime Minister, Konstantinos Karamanlis, who was invited to form a civilian Government of National Salvation. Martial law was ended, the press was released from state control and political parties, including the communists, were allowed to operate freely. A general election in November resulted in a decisive victory for Karamanlis's New Democracy Party (Nea Dimokratia—ND), which won 220 of the 300 parliamentary seats. A referendum in December rejected proposals for a return to constitutional monarchy, and in June 1975 a new republican Constitution, providing for a parliamentary democracy, was promulgated. In the same month Prof. Konstantinos Tsatsos, a former cabinet minister, was elected President by the Vouli (Parliament).

In the general election of November 1977 ND was re-elected with a reduced majority. In May 1980 Karamanlis was elected President; Georgios Rallis subsequently assumed the leadership of ND and was appointed Prime Minister. Rallis encountered considerable opposition from the increasingly popular Panhellenic Socialist Movement (Panhellinion Socialistikon Kinema—PASOK). In the general election of October 1981 PASOK secured an absolute majority in the Vouli. The PASOK leader, Andreas Papandreou, became Prime Minister of the first socialist Government in Greek history, which was initially committed to withdrawal from the European Community (EC, now the European Union—EU, see p. 199), to the removal of US military bases from Greek territory and to the implementation of an extensive programme of domestic reform.

In March 1985 Papandreou unexpectedly withdrew support for President Karamanlis's candidacy for a further five-year term in office. The Prime Minister planned to amend the 1975 Constitution to relieve the President of all executive power and render the Head of State's functions largely ceremonial. Karamanlis resigned in protest, and the Vouli elected Christos Sartzetakis, a judge, as President, in a vote that was widely considered to be unconstitutional. A general election was held in June 1985 to enable the Government to secure support for the proposed constitutional changes. PASOK was returned to power, winning 161 seats in the 300-member Vouli; ND secured 126 seats. In October the Government introduced a stringent programme of economic austerity, provoking widespread industrial unrest, which continued throughout 1986. In March 1986, despite considerable opposition from ND, the Vouli approved a series of constitutional amendments limiting the influence of the President, whose executive powers were transferred to the legislature.

In May 1987, in response to numerous accusations made by ND of mismanagement and corruption on the part of the Government, Papandreou sought and won a parliamentary vote of confidence in his Government. Opposition to the Government's economic austerity programme had continued in 1987 and in November Papandreou was forced to modify the programme. Despite strikes by teachers and doctors in June 1988, a parliamentary motion expressing 'no confidence' in the Government was defeated. However, the Government suffered a serious reverse in November, when several leading members of the Cabinet were implicated in a major financial scandal involving alleged embezzlement from the Bank of Crete, and were forced to resign.

In January 1989 the Greek Left Party (Elliniki Aristera—EAR), led by Leonidas Kyrkos, formed an electoral alliance with the 'Exterior' faction of the Communist Party of Greece (Kommunistiko Komma Ellados—KKE), under the leadership of Charilaos Florakis, to create the Coalition of the Left and Progress (Synaspismos), commonly referred to as the Left Coalition. At a general election in June, ND won the largest proportion of the votes cast, but failed to attain an overall majority in the Vouli. Following the failure of both ND and PASOK to reach an agreement with the Left Coalition to form a coalition government, President Sartzetakis empowered the Left Coalition to seek a coalition agreement. The Left Coalition unexpectedly agreed to form an interim administration with ND, on the condition that the ND leader, Konstantinos Mitsotakis, renounced his claim to the premiership. Accordingly, Tzannis Tzannetakis, an ND deputy for Athens, was appointed Prime Minister in a new Cabinet, which included two communist ministers. The unprecedented conservative-communist coalition announced its intention to govern for only three months, during which time it would aim to implement a katharsis (campaign of purification) of Greek politics. Accordingly, the administration resigned in early October, having initiated investigations into the involvement of officials of the former socialist Government, including Papandreou, in a number of scandals involving banking, armaments and financial transactions. The President of the Supreme Court, Yannis Grivas, was subsequently appointed Prime Minister in an interim Cabinet composed of non-political personalities, which was to oversee the year's second general election. However, the result of the election, conducted in November, was again inconclusive (ND won 46% of the total votes cast, PASOK 41% and the Left Coalition 11%). The political crisis was temporarily resolved in mid-November, when the three parties agreed to form a coalition that would administer the country pending the results of a further poll, to be conducted in April 1990. Xenofon Zolotas, a former Governor of the Bank of Greece, was appointed Prime Minister to lead the interim Cabinet. However, following a dispute over military promotions in February 1990, the Government collapsed, and the same non-political individuals who had overseen the November 1989 election were reinstated to govern until the new general election. Attempts by the Vouli in February and March 1990 to elect a head of state by the required majority were unsuccessful, owing largely to a decision taken by ND representatives to abstain from voting, following the refusal of their candidate, Karamanlis, to take part in the election. A general election, conducted in April, finally resolved the parliamentary impasse; ND secured 150 seats in the Vouli. Following the announcement of the results, Mitsotakis secured the support of Konstantinos Stefanopoulos, the leader (and the one elected parliamentary representative) of the Party of Democratic Renewal (Komma Dimokratikis Ananeosis—DIANA), thereby enabling him to form the first single-party Government since 1981. In May 1990 Karamanlis took office as President for a five-year term, following his election by 153 of the 300 members of the Vouli. Stefanopoulos formally rejoined ND in June.

The failure of the interim administrations to reach a consensus on comprehensive economic programmes, and the unpopularity of austerity measures introduced by the new Government, led to widespread industrial unrest. Throughout 1990 appeals by trade unions for general strikes were regularly supported by more than 1m. workers, seriously disrupting public services and industry. Despite apparent public dissatisfaction with many policies instigated by the new administration, ND was successful in municipal elections held in October. In November reforms to the electoral law, providing for a modified form of proportional representation, in which political parties wishing to appoint representatives to the Vouli would require a minimum of 3% of the national vote in a general election, were finally ratified. Left-wing parties vehemently criticized the new electoral system, which also incorporated procedural disincentives to the formation of political alliances to contest elections, as unconstitutional.

In March 1991 Andreas Papandreou and three of his former ministers were tried on charges of complicity in large-scale embezzlement from the Bank of Crete during their terms of office. Papandreou, who asserted that his indictment had been politically motivated, was tried *in absentia*; in January 1992 he was acquitted of all charges, while two of the former ministers received minor sentences (the third had died during the trial).

In August 1991 Mitsotakis effected a comprehensive reorganization of the Cabinet (including the removal of his daughter from the post of Under-Secretary to the Prime Minister), in response to public criticism of family involvement in politics. In April 1992 the Prime Minister successfully sought a vote of confidence from the Vouli, following the dismissal of the Minister of Foreign Affairs, Antonis Samaras, and Mitsotakis's assumption of the portfolio, in order to co-ordinate personally the Greek response to attempts by the former Yugoslav republic of Macedonia (FYRM) to achieve international recognition as the independent Republic of Macedonia (see below). As part of a cabinet reorganization effected in August (which included the controversial reappointment of the Prime Minister's daughter to her previous post), Michalis Papakonstantinou, a staunch defender of national territorial integrity, was allocated the foreign affairs portfolio. Ministerial disaffection with what was perceived as Mitsotakis's moderate stance regarding the FYRM, and with the Government's policy of economic austerity, increased in late 1992, but was curtailed somewhat following the Prime Minister's dismissal and reorganization of the entire Cabinet in early December. Industrial unrest continued throughout 1992 and 1993, in response to privatization plans and further austerity measures.

In September 1993 two ND deputies resigned, in response to an appeal for support by Political Spring (Politiki Anixi—POLAN), a centre-right party that had been established in July by Antonis Samaras. The consequent loss of Mitsotakis's one-seat majority in the Vouli obliged him to offer the Government's resignation and to call an early general election. At the election, conducted in October, PASOK obtained 46.9% of the total votes cast and 170 of the 300 parliamentary seats, while ND received 39.3% of the votes and 111 seats, and POLAN secured 4.9% of the votes and 10 seats. At the end of October Mitsotakis resigned as leader of ND.

Papandreou's victory in the general election provoked immediate concern among members of the EU, owing to the anti-European attitude the PASOK leader had adopted during his previous tenure of office; however, Papandreou gave assurances of his commitment to European integration. In May 1994 Papan-

dreou, contrary to his post-election commitment to revoke the privatization programme, announced his intention to generate revenue through the sale of a minority share in the state telecommunications company. (The privatization of the company was not initiated until March 1996, with an offer of 8% of the company's equity.) Following a reduction in electoral support for PASOK in elections to the European Parliament in June, Papandreou undertook a reorganization of the Cabinet.

In March 1995 Stefanopoulos was elected President by 181 of the 300 members of the Vouli, having failed to secure the required two-thirds' majority in two earlier rounds of voting; jointly favoured by PASOK and POLAN, he took office on 10 March. From mid-1995 tensions within the governing PASOK became increasingly evident. In August a deputy was expelled from the party following his public criticism of the political influence of Papandreou's wife, Dimitra Liani-Papandreou, who had been appointed Chief of Staff in October 1993. In September 1995 the Minister of Industry, Energy and Technology and of Commerce, Konstantinos Simitis, resigned, citing interference in his policies by senior PASOK officials. Simitis, together with Theodhoros Pangalos, who had resigned from the party's executive committee earlier in the month, Vasiliki (Vasso) Papandreou, a former EU Commissioner, and Paraskevas Avgerinos, a former Minister of EU Affairs, constituted a group of 'dissident' PASOK deputies (referred to as the Group of Four) who urged the resignation of Papandreou, in view of his failing health, and further reforms to modernize the party. In November Papandreou was admitted to hospital suffering from pneumonia; Apostolos-Athanassios (Akis) Tsohatzopoulos (a close associate of Papandreou), who had joined the Cabinet in September and was replaced as Secretary-General of PASOK in October, assumed his prime ministerial duties. Papandreou's condition remained critical throughout December, and in January 1996 the opposition parties expressed their concern at the power vacuum resulting from Papandreou's confinement, although a parliamentary motion of 'no confidence' in the Government was defeated. On 15 January Papandreou submitted his resignation as Prime Minister, although he remained leader of PASOK. Three days later Simitis was elected to the premiership, having won the support of 86 of the 167 members of the PASOK parliamentary party (compared with 75 by his nearest opponent, Tsohatzopoulos) in a second round of voting. Simitis awarded Pangalos the foreign affairs portfolio, but retained Tsohatzopoulos and Gerasimos Arsenis (another supporter of Papandreou who had also contested the leadership election) in the Cabinet in an attempt to unite the party. However, pro-European ministers who supported Simitis's desire for economic reform replaced the majority of Papandreou's former associates.

Almost immediately after assuming the premiership in January 1996, Simitis was confronted by a sharp escalation in hostilities with Turkey (see below). Following his acceptance of a US-brokered compromise to defuse the situation, Simitis was vigorously condemned by all opposition parties. In February the Prime Minister dismissed the Chief of the General Staff of the armed forces, Adm. Christos Lyberis, owing to the latter's disclosure of government deliberations concerning the use of military force against Turkey during the Aegean crisis.

Following the death of Papandreou in June 1996, Simitis was elected leader of PASOK at a party congress, with 53.5% of the votes cast, defeating his closest rival, Tsohatzopoulos, who represented the populist faction of the party. None the less, in August Simitis announced that an early general election was to be held (not due by law until October 1997), in order to obtain a firm mandate for his Government to pursue the reforms needed to achieve European economic and monetary union (EMU) targets, and for the Government's implementation of its proposed foreign affairs policies. In the poll, which was held on 22 September 1996, PASOK won 162 of the 300 parliamentary seats, with 41.5% of the votes cast, securing victory over ND which, having conducted a populist campaign, took 108 seats (38.2%). Support for POLAN declined substantially, and the party lost all 10 of the seats gained at the previous election. Key ministers in the new PASOK administration were retained from the outgoing Cabinet, in particular to ensure continuity in foreign policy and management of the economy. Following ND's electoral defeat, Miltiades Evert resigned as party leader, but was re-elected to the position the following month. In March 1997 Konstantinos Karamanlis (a nephew of his namesake, the former President and ND party leader) was elected leader of ND, despite his lack of experience in government.

Meanwhile, labour unrest continued in late 1996 and early 1997, and a general strike took place in November 1996, observed by 3m. workers, to protest against new austerity measures. Despite increasing criticism from former supporters, who accused him of abandoning PASOK's commitment to protecting low-income workers, Simitis continued to implement unpopular austerity policies in accordance with his commitment to meeting the 'convergence' criteria of EMU. A further general strike, in protest at pay and conditions, was widely observed in October 1997. In December Simitis expelled three deputies from PASOK's parliamentary group for voting against budget proposals for 1998, which were subsequently passed by a considerable margin by the Vouli.

Meanwhile, in June 1997 the Supreme Court upheld legislation (adopted by the PASOK administration in April 1994) to renationalize property owned by the exiled monarch, King Konstantinos, and to remove his family's citizenship. In April 1998 the King presented his case to the European Court of Human Rights, which ruled in November 2000 that the Court had violated the King's rights.

Industrial action continued to cause disruption in 1998. Two weeks of strikes took place early in the year, culminating in a rally in Athens in early February. In May a widely observed general strike was organized in protest at privatization plans and the implementation of further austerity measures. The response to the strikes, in particular the use of riot police, caused divisions within the Government; however, at the end of June, after six weeks, the strike ended and the privatization programme was approved. Following a defeat sustained by PASOK at the local elections, held in October, a minor cabinet reorganization was effected. In late November, in response to criticism of its austerity programme, the Government sought and won a parliamentary vote of confidence; Simitis had threatened to expel PASOK deputies from the party if they failed to support the motion.

In February 1999 it emerged that Abdullah Ocalan, the leader of the proscribed Kurdistan Workers' Party (Partiya Karkeren Kurdistan—PKK), accused by Turkey of a number of terrorist charges, had been given refuge at the Greek embassy in Kenya before being captured by the Turkish authorities. Kenya officially denounced Greece for allowing Ocalan to enter the country without informing the Kenyan authorities. Kurdish groups demonstrated at Greek embassies across Europe, and the Ministers of the Interior, Public Administration and Decentralization, of Foreign Affairs and of Public Order resigned, prompting a cabinet reorganization. Vasiliki (Vasso) Papandreou, formerly Minister of Development, was appointed Minister of the Interior, Public Administration and Decentralization, and Georgios Papandreou (the son of the late Andreas Papandreou) replaced Theodoros Pangalos as Minister of Foreign Affairs.

Industrial action continued in 1999. In January student demonstrations, in protest at an educational reform law, escalated into riots in Athens, and in July the appointment of a new management team at Olympic Airways led to stoppages over fears of widespread redundancies. At the beginning of February 2000 Prime Minister Simitis announced that an early general election was to be held on 9 April. On 9 February Stefanopoulos was re-elected President by 269 of the 300 members of the Vouli, defeating his sole opponent, Leonidas Kyrkos of the Left Coalition; Stefanopoulos was the first incumbent President of Greece to be re-elected to the post. In the April general election PASOK, again led by Simitis, was returned to office, winning 43.8% of the votes cast and 158 parliamentary seats, thus narrowly defeating ND, which obtained 42.7% of the votes and 125 seats. The KKE won 5.2% of the ballot and 11 seats, and the Coalition of the Left and Progress secured 3.2% and six seats. On 12 April Simitis formed a new Government, the principal portfolios remaining with their previous incumbents.

In September 2000 some 80 people were killed when a ferry sank off the island of Paros, giving rise to concerns about maritime safety regulations in the coastal-shipping industry. In November Simitis dismissed Theodoros Pangalos, who had returned to the Cabinet as Minister of Culture in April, after Pangalos expressed criticism of government policies, including a draft bill on labour-market reform. Pangalos was replaced by Evangelos Venizelos. In December the Greek General Confederation of Labour staged a 24-hour strike in protest at the planned labour reform.

In March 2001 problems encountered following the opening of a new international airport in Athens contributed to anxiety about the country's preparedness for the Olympic Games, due to be held in the capital in 2004. Additional concerns were raised over the state of the railway infrastructure, progress made towards the construction of sporting venues and accommodation for use during the Games, and the extensive recent terrorist activity in Greece (see below). In April 2001 widespread support for public protests, including a general strike, resulted from government plans to raise the retirement age and reform pension funds; little progress had been made towards resolving the issue by the time the budget for 2002 was announced in October 2001. Meanwhile, in May the first papal visit in over 1,000 years had taken place; in the course of his visit Pope John Paul II had attempted to assuage Orthodox sensitivities, apologizing for past Roman Catholic transgressions.

In October 2001 Simitis reshuffled the Cabinet, following his re-election as party leader at a PASOK congress held earlier in the month. The Prime Minister's main party rival, Tsohatzopoulos, was transferred to the post of Minister of Development; he was replaced as Minister of National Defence by Ioannis Papantoniou, formerly Minister of the Economy and Finance. Other significant changes included the appointment of Dimitris Reppas, hitherto Minister of Press and Media, as Minister of Labour and Social Affairs, and that of Nikos Christodoulakis, who had previously held the development portfolio, as Minister of the Economy and Finance.

In mid-January 2002 a daily newspaper published a report linking some 124 PASOK members of the Vouli to terrorist groups operating in the 1970s and 1980s. The report, based on a Greek intelligence document produced in 1988, also accused Andreas Papandreou and three former ministers of having undergone training in Palestinian-run camps in Lebanon in the late 1970s. PASOK officials denied the accusations.

Meanwhile, in late January 2002 farmers began to blockade the main highway linking Athens and Thessaloníki, demanding higher cotton subsidies and compensation for massive crop damage, caused by severe weather conditions. In early April farmers staged renewed blockades, after having failed to reach agreement with the Government. Later that month public-sector workers held a one-day strike to protest against government plans to reform the largest state pension fund. Strikes by public workers continued throughout May, and led, at the end of the month, to the closure of airports, ports and public offices. A further strike took place in mid-June. In September consumer groups organized a widely observed, one-day boycott of shops and retailers, in protest against the price increases that had followed the adoption of the euro as the national currency at the beginning of the year. Another one-day strike was organized by airport and public-sector workers in early December, bringing further disruption to the country.

In late October 2002 Dora Bakoyanni, a former Minister of Culture and the daughter of former Prime Minister Mitsotakis, was elected Mayor of Athens, with almost 60% of the votes cast; Bakoyanni, a member of ND, had been supported by the conservative opposition. At the same time, conservative forces registered strong gains in local and regional elections. In December Bakoyanni narrowly escaped assassination when a gunman opened fire on her car; although Bakoyanni's husband had been assassinated in 1989 by a member of the dissident organization November 17 (see below), there was no apparent link to that organization.

Throughout the 1990s numerous attacks against 'capitalist' (and particularly US) military and commercial targets in Greece were carried out by dissident groups, in particular the extremist left-wing November 17 Revolutionary Organization (active since 1975) and the Revolutionary People's Struggle (ELA). In July 1992 November 17 claimed responsibility for an attempt to assassinate the Minister of Finance, in which a member of the public died, and in December an ND deputy was shot and injured by the same group, in protest against alleged corruption within the Government, and against recent economic initiatives. In 1994 further attacks targeted foreign companies, and in July the November 17 group claimed responsibility for the assassination of a Turkish diplomat. A series of measures to combat terrorism was announced by the Government in September, following a bomb attack on a police vehicle. In February 1996 an attempted attack on the US embassy in Athens was believed by police to have been co-ordinated by November 17 activists. In May 1997 three November 17 insurgents shot and killed a shipowner in Piraeus, and in December a bomb was discovered outside the office of the Minister of Development; a similar device was placed outside the offices of a Canadian gold-mining company. In January 1998 the police arrested more than 15 suspected members of the Fighting Guerrilla Faction, a left-wing group believed to be responsible for a number of bombings, including an attack on the offices of Alitalia, the Italian airline, in 1997. In January and February 1998 there were several explosions at the offices of US companies in Greece; these were thought to be related to US action in Iraq (see the chapter on Iraq), although an anti-tank rocket attack on a US bank was attributed to November 17. During May an incendiary attack was carried out at the office of the Minister of Press and Mass Media and an explosive device was found at the office of the Minister of Transport and Communications; there were also explosions at the Ionian and Popular Bank of Greece and Olympic Airways. Dissident activities continued into the early 2000s. In June 2000 the British defence attaché, Brig. Stephen Saunders, was assassinated by the November 17 group, which claimed that Saunders had helped to co-ordinate the NATO bombing of the Serbian province of Kosovo and Metohija, Yugoslavia, in 1999 (which had been strongly opposed in Greece—see below). Saunders' murder led to international concern that Greece was failing to co-operate fully with international anti-terrorist efforts, although in July 2000 a series of anti-terrorist initiatives was agreed between Greece and the United Kingdom. In November, however, the ELA claimed responsibility for four bomb attacks in Athens and in January 2001 a member of the Vouli was injured in Piraeus in an attack that was attributed to November 17. In June the Vouli approved widespread changes to criminal legislation in an attempt to improve Greece's widely criticized record on combating dissident activity. The amendments, which introduced non-jury criminal trials, a limited right to appeal and broader police powers of surveillance, and which permitted the non-consensual DNA testing of suspects, provoked strong objections from legal associations and civil liberties groups. However, in July Greece's failure adequately to tackle crime was emphasized by the resignation of the Chief of Police, Lt-Gen. Ioannis Georgakopoulos, following the escape of a prominent criminal during a police raid. Six of the country's highest-ranking police officers were subsequently either dismissed or demoted. Following the large-scale terrorist attacks on the US cities of New York and Washington, DC, of 11 September, counter-insurgency activities and the need to undertake measures to combat effectively the November 17 organization gained even greater political significance.

In 2002 the Government made significant progress in combating dissident activity, when during July the authorities apprehended 14 suspected members of November 17. The first to be arrested was Savvas Xiros (representing the first-ever arrest of an alleged member of the organization), who had been injured in a bomb explosion, and the police were subsequently able to arrest the suspected leader of November 17, Alexandros Giotopoulos, and two of Xiros' brothers, one of whom reportedly confessed to the assassination in 2000 of Brig. Stephen Saunders. Shortly afterwards the Government announced that November 17 had been dismantled; the organization was thought to have been responsible for a total of 23 murders since its inception. In September 2002 Dimitris Koufodinas, believed to be the second-highest-ranking member of November 17, surrendered to police in Athens. By January 2003 a total of 19 suspected members of November 17 had been apprehended; in February the police arrested four suspected members of ELA. Meanwhile, in January it had been reported that a number of Greece's wealthiest individuals had paid large sums of money to November 17, in order to be kept off its list of targets.

The trials of Giotopoulos, Koufodinas and several other alleged members of November 17 commenced in early March 2003. The two principal defendants were accused of over 1,000 criminal acts, including murder, terrorism and bank robbery, although, by law, they were unable to be charged with acts perpetrated more than 20 years previously. Giotopoulos and Koufodinas denied the charges, although Koufodinas admitted holding a political role in the organization. The trials were expected to last for several months and involve hundreds of witnesses, including many from the political establishment.

In the mean time, in 2001 the Greek central bank had increased measures to counter money 'laundering', amid international concern about the role of Greek banks in handling funds of the former Yugoslav President, Slobodan Milošević (who had been indicted by the International Criminal Tribunal for the former Yugoslavia—see chapter on Serbia and Montenegro), and his associates; in September the Ministry of Justice began an inquiry to examine more than 250 accounts held at Athens-based banks by companies linked to Milošević. In February 2002 the Government agreed, at the request of the Tribunal, to permit further investigation of the accounts. In November 2001, meanwhile, the arrest, on espionage charges, of 14 British and Dutch visitors, threatened to damage relations with the United Kingdom and the Netherlands. Some observers subsequently suggested that their release in December, pending trial, had resulted from political pressure, and there were concerns that the independence of the Greek judicial system had been compromised. In late April 2002 those apprehended (who described themselves as aircraft enthusiasts) were convicted, and awarded sentences ranging from one to three years' imprisonment. However, in November an appeals court overturned the convictions. A number of those pardoned were seeking compensation from the Greek authorities in early 2003.

Greece became a full member of the EC (now EU) in January 1981, having signed the treaty of accession in 1979. Although originally critical of Greece's membership, the PASOK Government confined itself to seeking modification of the terms of accession, in order to take into account the underdeveloped Greek economy, and gave qualified assent to concessions proposed by the EC in 1983. In July 1992 the Vouli voted overwhelmingly to ratify the Treaty on European Union. In January 2003 Greece assumed the rotating presidency of the EU for a six-month period. The country sought to focus attention on the adjacent Balkans region and to continue work to facilitate the planned accession of 10 new members (including Cyprus) in 2004. Greece also used its presidency to urge a peaceful solution to the US-led campaign (supported by a number of European countries) to remove the regime of Saddam Hussain in Iraq.

Relations with Turkey have been characterized by long-standing disputes concerning Cyprus (q.v.) and sovereignty over the continental shelf beneath the Aegean Sea. The difficulties in relations with Turkey were exacerbated by the unilateral declaration of an 'independent' Turkish-Cypriot state in Cyprus in November 1983 (the 'Turkish Republic of Northern Cyprus'—'TRNC'), together with various minor sovereignty disputes over islands in the Aegean Sea, which led to Greece's withdrawal from military exercises of the North Atlantic Treaty Organization (NATO) in August 1984 and to a boycott of manoeuvres in subsequent years. In March 1987 a disagreement between Greece and Turkey over petroleum-prospecting rights in disputed areas of the Aegean Sea almost resulted in military conflict. In January 1988, however, the Greek and Turkish Prime Ministers, meeting in Davos, Switzerland, agreed that the two countries' premiers should meet annually in order to improve bilateral relations (the Davos meeting was the first formal contact between Greek and Turkish Heads of Government for 10 years), and that joint committees should be established to negotiate peaceful solutions to disputes.

In 1994, however, the issue of the demarcation of territorial waters in the Aegean Sea re-emerged as a major source of tension. Greece's right to extend its territorial waters from six to 12 nautical miles, as enshrined in the international Convention on the Law of the Sea (see International Seabed Authority, see p. 254), was strongly condemned by Turkey, which feared the loss of shipping access, via the Aegean Sea, to international waters. The dispute intensified prior to the scheduled entry into force of the Convention, in mid-November, with both countries conducting concurrent military exercises in the Aegean. In early 1995 the Greek Government obstructed an agreement to establish a customs union between Turkey and the EU until, in March, it secured a defined agreement from the EU regarding a timetable for accession negotiations with Cyprus. The concern surrounding the international Convention on the Law of the Sea re-emerged in June, when the Vouli ratified the treaty; Turkey conducted further military exercises in the region. In early 1996 tensions were exacerbated by conflicting claims of sovereignty over Imia (Kardak), a group of uninhabited islands in the Aegean Sea. By late January Greek and Turkish military vessels were patrolling the islands and attempts were made to raise the respective national flags on the territory. The situation was defused when the new PASOK administration complied with a petition by the US Government to withdraw all military vessels and troops from the area and to remove the national flags.

In February 1996 Greek opposition delayed the implementation of a financial protocol of the EU-Turkey customs union; Greece claimed that Turkey's aggressive action in the Aegean violated the terms of the customs-union agreement. Although the Greek Prime Minister, Konstantinos Simitis, resolved to pursue a more constructive foreign-policy stance towards Turkey, a series of incidents throughout 1996 involving alleged violations of Greek airspace by Turkish aircraft and confrontations between Greek and Turkish patrol vessels in the Aegean precluded any improvement in relations. In July Greece finally withdrew its opposition to Turkey's participation in an EU-Mediterranean assistance programme, in response to a joint statement by EU Heads of Government urging an end to Turkey's 'hostile policy' towards Greece; however, the block on funds from the customs-union agreement remained in effect. In August, following an escalation in intercommunal tension in Cyprus, the Greek armed forces were placed on full alert. In November Greece announced an extensive programme to modernize the Greek military infrastructure, which, it insisted, was necessary to counter the perceived threat of military action by Turkey, yet which contributed to international concern at the escalating militarization of the region.

In April 1997 the Greek Deputy Minister of Foreign Affairs met his Turkish counterpart in Malta, under EU auspices, and it was agreed to establish two committees of independent experts who would communicate through the EU to explore ways of improving relations between the two countries. At a NATO summit in Madrid, Spain, in July Simitis and the Turkish President, Süleyman Demirel, held direct talks (the first such meeting for three years), which led to an agreement, known as the Madrid Declaration, in which they pledged not to use violence or the threat of violence in resolving the countries' bilateral disputes. However, relations remained strained, particularly concerning Greek support of Cyprus's application for membership of the EU; Turkey threatened annexation of the 'TRNC' should Cyprus be admitted to the organization. Further tension was caused by frequent alleged violations of Greek airspace by Turkish military aircraft, in particular the reported harassment of an aircraft carrying the Greek Minister of Defence from Cyprus to Greece, following joint military exercises with Greek Cypriot forces. In November, however, Simitis held a meeting with the Turkish Prime Minister, Mesut Yılmaz, at which it was agreed to explore confidence-building measures. Turkey, however, continued to advocate dialogue on all issues, whereas Greece reaffirmed its commitment to a gradual approach, insisting that Turkey accept international arbitration for disputes over sovereignty in the Aegean as a prerequisite both to official talks and to the lifting of Greece's veto on EU financial aid to Turkey. In November Greece threatened to oppose Turkey's participation in a planned EU enlargement conference in London, unless Turkey abandoned its attempts to prevent EU accession talks with Cyprus, which were due to begin in 1998, and threatened to veto the admission to the EU of other applicant countries if Cyprus were rejected. At a NATO summit in early December 1997 an agreement was signed, under which Greece and Turkey would share control of military flights in the Aegean under NATO's new military command structure (although this agreement had yet to be endorsed by the political leaders of each country). Later that month, however, Turkey resumed its violations of Greek airspace over the Aegean.

As Cyprus began accession talks with the EU in March 1998, Greece reiterated its intention to veto the admission of other countries if Cyprus were not included, and its refusal to lift its veto on EU financial aid to Turkey. In June the NATO Secretary-General, Javier Solana, announced that Greece and Turkey had agreed to continue talks regarding confidence-building measures and to activate a 1988 agreement providing for a flight moratorium over the Aegean in July and August. In an attempt to improve relations with Turkey, in August Greece attempted to persuade Cyprus to cancel its proposed purchase of an anti-aircraft missile system. Turkey later welcomed the decision, taken at the end of December, not to deploy the missile system in Cyprus; despite Turkey's insistence that it was not a suitable alternative location, missiles were deployed on Crete in March 1999.

In July 1999 talks were held in New York between the Greek and Turkish Ministers of Foreign Affairs. Around the same time, however, Greece alleged that two Turkish military aircraft had intercepted a Greek aircraft carrying the Minister of Transport to Cyprus and had forced it briefly to alter course. Relations between the two countries improved in late August when Greece offered both financial and material assistance to Turkey, following a severe earthquake in the north-west of that country; Greece also announced its intention to lift its veto on EU financial aid to Turkey. Turkey reciprocated Greece's provision of emergency assistance when an earthquake struck Athens in early September. Later that month the Mayor of İstanbul visited

Athens, where he held talks with the city's Mayor, and in November it was announced that jointly operated train services were to be introduced between Greece and Turkey. At an EU summit, held in Helsinki, Finland, in December, a diplomatic impasse was finally ended when Greece formally lifted its objections to Turkey's membership of the EU, although the conditions for its accession depended on the resolution of both the Cyprus issue and of its dispute with Greece in the Aegean. The notable improvement in relations between Greece and Turkey was evident in late January 2000 when the Greek Minister of Foreign Affairs, Georgios Papandreou, visited Ankara for talks with his Turkish counterpart, İsmail Cem, and the Turkish Prime Minister, in the first official visit by a Greek Minister of Foreign Affairs to Turkey since 1962. During negotiations a number of agreements on matters such as investment, crime and tourism, were signed by the two sides. In early February 2000 the *rapprochement* between Greece and Turkey continued with an official visit to Athens by the Turkish Minister of Foreign Affairs, during which further co-operation agreements (primarily relating to economic affairs) were signed. In October 2000, however, Greece withdrew from a joint NATO military exercise in the Aegean Sea, after it accused Turkey of preventing Greek airplanes from flying over the disputed islands of Limnos and Ikaria.

Despite this reverse, in April 2001 both Greece and Turkey announced significant reductions in their weapons-procurement programmes. In June, in a further gesture of reconciliation, Papandreou and Cem discussed the possibility of allowing Turkish nationals to visit Greek islands in the Aegean for day trips without the need for visas. In November Greece and Turkey signed an agreement that allowed the former country to repatriate illegal Turkish immigrants. The Greek Government believed that as many as 750,000 illegal immigrants had entered the country from Turkey since 1998. None the less, the issue of Cyprus continued to overshadow bilateral relations and in May Cem announced there would be 'no limits' to Turkey's response were Cyprus to be admitted to full membership of the EU before a political settlement had been reached. In February 2002, however, the Greek and Turkish foreign ministers recommenced talks, following the resumption of negotiations between the Greek- and Turkish-Cypriot sides over the issue of Cyprus.

In late March 2002 Greece and Turkey signed an agreement to build a 285-km natural gas pipeline, which would eventually allow Turkey to supply Greece with 500,000 cu m of gas per day. Subsequently, in April, the two countries sent a joint delegation of their respective Ministers of Foreign Affairs to Israel, as a symbolic measure, in an attempt to promote a solution to the ongoing Israeli–Palestinian conflict. In September a series of meetings took place between Greek and Turkish officials and government ministers, and in October Papandreou offered his support for the scheduling of EU accession negotiations with Turkey. During late 2002 and early 2003 the Greek- and Turkish-Cypriot leaders made significant progress towards reaching a final peace agreement on Cyprus, which would permit the entire island to accede to the EU in May 2004; however, the subsequent collapse of the peace plan in March 2003 (see Cyprus chapter) meant that only the Greek-Cypriot part of Cyprus would accede to the EU in the following year, and threatened Greece's much-improved relations with Turkey.

In August 1985 Greece and Albania reopened their borders, which had remained closed since 1940, and Greece formally annulled claims to North Epirus (southern Albania), where there is a sizeable Greek minority. In August 1987 the Greek Government put a formal end to a legal vestige of the Second World War by proclaiming that it no longer considered Greece to be at war with Albania. In April 1988 relations between Greece and Albania improved significantly when the two countries signed an agreement to promote trade between their border provinces. During the early 1990s, however, bilateral relations were severely strained by persisting concerns relating to the treatment of ethnic Greeks residing in Albania (numbering an estimated 300,000), the illegal immigration of several thousand Albanians seeking work opportunities or political asylum in Greece and the efforts of the Greek Government to secure their return. In March 1996 President Stefanopoulos signed a treaty of friendship and co-operation with Albania's President, Sali Berisha. Several issues appeared to have been resolved, with Albania agreeing to provide Greek-language education in schools serving the ethnic Greek population and Greece declaring its willingness to issue temporary work permits for at least 150,000 seasonal workers from Albania.

Following a revolt in southern Albania in March 1997, the Greek Government obtained guarantees from Albania for the security of the ethnic Greek population and negotiated with rebel leaders to ensure stability. Greece contributed 700 men to a multinational force led by Italy, which was established with a mandate to facilitate the distribution of humanitarian aid. Albanian banditry became a security problem in June and July, especially on the island of Corfu, where naval frigates clashed with Albanian pirates. In August Greece agreed to legitimize the status of tens of thousands of illegal Albanian immigrants by granting them temporary work permits in exchange for assistance from Albania in combating cross-border crime. During April 1998 the two countries signed a military-training accord; plans were later announced for joint military exercises and Greece pledged to provide military reconstruction aid to Albania. In August the establishment was announced of a free border zone between the two countries to take effect in 2000; citizens of either country living in this area were to be given special entry documents for both Greece and Albania. A new border crossing was opened between Greece and Albania in May 1999. By 2002 there were an estimated 350,000–600,000 Albanians living in Greece, mainly concentrated in Athens and Thessaloníki. However, the stabilization of the political situation in Albania meant that the influx of Albanians into Greece had decreased considerably in recent years. None the less, Greece was expected to put forward proposals to the EU, which would allow people from Albania and the former Yugoslavia greater freedom of movement and make it easier for them to obtain seasonal or temporary employment in the EU.

Attempts after 1991 by the FYRM to achieve international recognition as an independent state were strenuously opposed by the Greek Government, which insisted that 'Macedonia' was a purely geographical term (delineating an area that included a large part of northern Greece) and expressed fears that the adoption of such a name could imply ambitions on the Greek province of Macedonia and might foster a false claim to future territorial expansion. In early 1993 the Greek administration withdrew its former objection to the use of the word 'Macedonia', and its derivatives, as part of a fuller name for the new republic. At the end of March the Greek Government accepted a UN proposal that the title 'the former Yugoslav republic of Macedonia' should be used temporarily and agreed to hold direct talks with the FYRM to consider confidence-building measures. In late 1993 the newly elected PASOK Government strongly criticized recognition of the FYRM by several EU members and, despite assurances that it would adopt a more conciliatory attitude, in February 1994 the Government condemned a decision by the USA (the final member of the UN Security Council to do so) to recognize the FYRM. At an emergency meeting in mid-February, the Cabinet agreed to prevent any movement of goods, other than humanitarian aid, into the FYRM via the northern Greek port of Thessaloníki. The initiative was widely criticized by the international community as effectively constituting an illegal trade embargo, and the EU ministers responsible for foreign affairs urged Greece to revoke the measures, which, it was determined, violated EU law. Intensive negotiations with the Greek authorities failed to resolve the issue and in mid-April the European Commission commenced legal proceedings against Greece at the Court of Justice of the European Communities. In April 1995 a preliminary opinion of the Court determined that the embargo was not in breach of Greece's obligations under the Treaty of Rome. In September the ministers responsible for foreign affairs of Greece and the FYRM, meeting in New York, under UN auspices, signed an interim accord to normalize relations between the two countries, which included recognition of the existing international border. Under the terms of the agreement, Greece was to grant access to the port facilities at Thessaloníki and to remove all obstructions to the cross-border movement of people and goods following a period of 30 days, during which the FYRM was to approve a new state flag (removing the symbolic Vergina sun). The measures were successfully implemented by mid-October; a few days later agreement was concluded on the establishment of liaison offices in the two countries' capitals. Negotiations were to be pursued regarding the issue of a permanent name for the FYRM, which would be acceptable to both sides. In March 1997 the Greek Minister of Foreign Affairs visited the FYRM for the first time since its independence from Yugoslavia. In the first half of 2001 armed insurrection by ethnic Albanian militants of the self-syled National Liberation Army in the FYRM (q.v.) caused alarm in Greece, and there was international concern that

Greek armed forces would intervene in any full-scale civil conflict in the FYRM. However, following the deployment of a NATO force in June and the signature of a peace agreement in August, stability began to be restored to the republic. Meanwhile, in 1999 work had commenced on the construction of a pipeline to carry petroleum from the FYRM's capital, Skopje, to Thessaloníki. The 214-km pipeline was inaugurated in early July 2002, at a ceremony attended by the Prime Minister of the FYRM, Ljubčo Georgievski, and the Greek Minister of Development, Akis Tsohatzopoulos.

During the conflict in the former Yugoslavia, Greece pursued an active involvement in efforts to promote a peaceful political settlement in the region. In contrast to most of its European partners, Greece maintained close relations with the Yugoslav Government and advocated the removal of the UN-imposed trade embargo against Serbia and Montenegro. Greece's stance, which was shared notably by Bulgaria and Russia, contributed to a strengthening of relations between these countries. In late 1998 Greece advocated a diplomatic solution to the ethnic conflict in the Yugoslav province of Kosovo and Metohija, and in March 1999 declared that it would not participate in the newly launched NATO air offensive against Serb targets, which continued until June. Insurgent activity, in protest at the NATO bombardment, increased in Greece during 1999; in April a bomb in an Athens hotel resulted in one person being killed and another seriously injured. In May rocket attacks, attributed to the November 17 Revolutionary Organization, were launched on the residences of the Dutch and German ambassadors to Greece and on three foreign banks in Athens. The murder of the British defence attaché, Brig. Stephen Saunders in June 2000 was also attributed to November 17, which cited his alleged involvement in the co-ordination of the NATO action (see above). Public opinion in Greece was, in general, strongly opposed to the NATO bombardment and a planned three-day visit by US President Bill Clinton in November was reduced to a 24-hour visit, following a series of protests (including two bombing incidents). During Clinton's stay demonstrations escalated into riots in Athens, and around the same time Greece unexpectedly withdrew from a proposed anti-terrorism pact with the USA.

In July 2000 Germany and Greece became involved in a diplomatic dispute, after a Greek court took steps to expropriate German assets to compensate the families of victims of Nazi war crimes. The court's action followed a demand by the Greek Supreme Court in April that Germany pay DM 55m. in compensation to residents of the village of Distomo, in central Greece, where Nazi occupiers killed over 200 people in June 1944. Germany filed a caveat in response to the court's decision, effectively delaying proceedings until October 2001. Despite this, however, German property in prominent sites in Athens was impounded in September, although court officials prevented the property from being sold. In September 2002 Greece's highest court, the Special Supreme Tribunal, ruled against some 60,000 Nazi victims who were seeking compensation from Germany for atrocities committed during the Nazi occupation. Germany maintained that it had settled all compensation claims in the 1960s.

Government

Under the Constitution of June 1975, the President is Head of State and is elected by the Vouli (Parliament) for a five-year term. The President appoints the Prime Minister and, upon his recommendation, the other members of the Cabinet. In March 1986 the Vouli approved a series of constitutional amendments, divesting the President of his executive powers and transferring them to the legislature (see The Constitution). The unicameral Vouli has 300 members, directly elected by universal adult suffrage for four years. Greece comprises 13 regions, including Greater Athens, and is divided into 54 administrative divisions.

Defence

Greece returned to the military structure of NATO in 1980, after an absence of six years. Military service is compulsory for all men between 18 and 40 years of age, and lasts for up to 19 months. In 1978 women were given the right to volunteer for military service of 30–50 days' basic training and for specialized training. In 1998 a law was passed providing for the conscription of women (for four days a year) to assist in the defence of the border regions. At 1 August 2002 the armed forces numbered 177,600, of whom 98,321 were conscripts, and included an army of 114,000 (with a national guard of 34,000), a navy of 19,000 and an air force of 33,000; in addition, there was a coast guard and customs force of 4,000. The USA occupied two military bases in Greece, with a total of 290 troops stationed there in August 2002. In 2000 Greece committed 3,500 troops to the proposed joint EU rapid reaction force, which was to be ready for deployment by 2003. In 2003 reforms were being introduced, which would reduce the size of the armed forces to 90,000 by 2005. The duration of compulsory military service was to be reduced to 12 months, and many units were to be disbanded. According to budget estimates for 2002, €3,400m. was allocated to defence in that year.

Economic Affairs

In 2001, according to estimates by the World Bank, Greece's gross national income (GNI), measured at average 1999–2001 prices, was US $124,553m., equivalent to $11,780 per head (or $17,860 per head on an international purchasing-power parity basis). During 1990–2001, it was estimated, the population increased at an average annual rate of 0.4%, while gross domestic product (GDP) per head increased, in real terms, at an average annual rate of 2.1%. Overall GDP increased, in real terms, at an average annual rate of 2.4% in 1990–2001. According to the IMF, real GDP increased by 4.3% in 2000 and by 4.1% in 2001.

Agriculture (including hunting, forestry and fishing) contributed some 7.7% of GDP in 1999 and engaged 16.0% of the employed labour force in 2001. The principal cash crops are fruit and vegetables (which, together, accounted for 9.1% of total export earnings in 2000), cereals, sugar beet and tobacco. Real agricultural GDP increased at an average annual rate of 1.6% in 1990–99; the GDP of the agricultural sector increased by 2.6% in 1998 and by 1.4% in 1999.

Industry (including mining, manufacturing, power and construction) provided 22.8% of GDP in 1999 and engaged 22.8% of the employed labour force in 2001. During 1990–99 industrial GDP increased at an average annual rate of 1.2%, in real terms; sectoral GDP increased by 4.5% in 1999 and by 6.5% in 2000. Following the International Olympic Committee's—IOC (see p. 246) announcement, in 1997, that the 2004 Olympic Games would be held in Athens, public expenditure on infrastructure projects stimulated growth in the construction industry; the GDP of the sector recorded an increase of 6.1%, in real terms, in 1998.

Mining and quarrying contributed 0.5% of GDP in 1999 and engaged 0.5% of the employed labour force in 2001. Mineral fuels and lubricants, iron and steel, and aluminium and aluminium alloys are the major mineral/metal exports. Lignite, magnesite, silver ore and marble are also mined. In addition, Greece has small reserves of uranium and natural gas.

Manufacturing provided 11.7% of GDP in 1999 and engaged 14.2% of the employed labour force in 2001. The most important branches in 1995, measured by output in factor values, were food products (accounting for 20.1% of the total), metals and metal products (12.3%), textiles and clothing (11.0%), petroleum refining (10.5%) and chemicals (9.5%). The GDP of the manufacturing sector increased, in real terms, by an annual average of 0.6% in 1990–98; production increased by 1.3% in 1998 and by 1.5% in 1999.

Energy is derived principally from lignite, which accounted for 65.6% of production in 1999, and petroleum, which accounted for 16.5%. Greece is exploiting an offshore petroleum deposit in the north-eastern Aegean Sea. Hydroelectric and solar power resources are also being developed. Mineral fuels represented 13.5% of the total value of imports in 2000.

The services sector contributed 69.5% of GDP in 1999 and engaged 61.2% of the employed labour force in 2001. Tourism is an important source of foreign exchange. In 2000 visitor arrivals totalled 12.5m. and receipts from the tourist sector amounted to US $9,221m., compared with $6,188m. in 1998. During 1990–99 GDP from the services sector increased, in real terms, at an average annual rate of 2.4%; sectoral GDP increased by 3.3% in 1998 and by 2.4% in 1999.

In 2001 Greece recorded a visible trade deficit of US $19,087m., and there was a deficit of $9,400m. on the current account of the balance of payments. In 2000 the principal source of imports (12.9%) was Italy, closely followed by Germany (12.8%); other major sources were France (including Monaco), the Netherlands, the United Kingdom and Japan. The principal market for exports in 2000 was Germany (12.3%); other major purchasers were Italy, the United Kingdom and the USA. The principal exports in 2000 were basic manufactures (in particular, non-ferrous metals), miscellaneous manufactured articles (especially clothing and accessories), mineral fuels and lubricants, food and live animals, and machinery and transport

equipment. The principal imports were machinery and transport equipment (most notably road vehicles and parts), basic manufactures, mineral fuels and lubricants (mainly petroleum and petroleum products), chemicals and miscellaneous manufactured articles.

In 2000 there was a budgetary deficit of 1,692,000m. drachmae (equivalent to 4.1% of GDP), according to provisional figures. Greece's total public external debt was 8,330,000m. drachmae at the end of 1997. In 1999 the cost of debt-servicing was equivalent to 9% of GDP. In 1990–2001 the average annual rate of inflation was 8.7%; consumer prices increased by 3.2% in 2000, by 3.4% in 2001 and by 3.6% in 2002. According to official figures, some 10.2% of the labour force were unemployed in 2001; however, it was predicted that the rate of unemployment would decrease to around 9% by the end of 2004, owing to continued economic growth and structural changes in the employment market.

Greece is a member of the EU, the Organisation for Economic Co-operation and Development (OECD, see p. 277) and the Organization of the Black Sea Economic Co-operation (see p. 293).

The priority of the Simitis Government was to ensure the admittance of Greece to full EU economic and monetary union (EMU) by 2001. The projected budgetary deficit for 1999 met the target for EMU entry and in February–March 2000 a rate of inflation of 2% was recorded, thereby qualifying Greece for full EMU membership from 1 January 2001. Greece thus became the 12th member country in the so-called 'euro-zone', and the common European currency, the euro, duly replaced the drachma as the country's legal tender from 1 January 2002. Although Greece did not satisfy the requirement stipulated in the Maastricht Treaty that the ratio of government debt to GDP be less than 60%, the Government aimed to achieve this objective by the end of the decade. Greece's public-sector debt was equivalent to some 98.9% of GDP in 2001, and it was projected to represent 95.2% of GDP in 2002, owing to increased privatization revenues and, subject to EU approval, receipts from structural aid. Growth in GDP of 3.7% was anticipated in 2003. The predicted growth was primarily expected to be generated by construction activity relating to the forthcoming Olympic Games and by the anticipated package of EU structural aid. Meanwhile, it was hoped that the country's improved relations with Turkey would allow a reduction in defence expenditure, and it was expected that construction of the proposed Ankara (Turkey)–Kotomini (Greece) pipeline, agreed in March 2002, would be of benefit to the Greek economy. The stabilization of the countries of the former Yugoslavia and the Balkans also provided Greece with an opportunity to expand its commercial influence in the region. However, the planned admission to the EU of several Central and Eastern European countries in 2004 was likely to result in a decline in EU transfers to Greece, as funds would be diverted to new members. In addition, the Greek economy faced challenges from the ongoing privatization programme, and popular opposition to certain aspects of it, as well as Greece's overdependency on trade with Italy and Germany, both of which were experiencing reduced growth in the early 2000s.

Education

Education is available free of charge at all levels, and is officially compulsory for all children between the ages of six and 15 years. Primary education begins at the age of six and lasts for six years. Secondary education, beginning at the age of 12, is generally for six years, divided into two equal cycles. The vernacular language (demotiki) has replaced the formal version (katharevoussa) in secondary education. In 1998 primary enrolment included 95% of children in the relevant age-group, and the comparable ratio at secondary schools was 86%. In 1996 enrolment in tertiary education was equivalent to some 47% of the relevant age-group. In 2000/01 some 240,336 students were enrolled in institutions of higher education. In 2000, according to provisional data, budgetary expenditure on education was 1,440,000m. drachmae (representing 9.3% of total expenditure).

Public Holidays

2003: 1 January (New Year's Day), 6 January (Epiphany), 10 March (Clean Monday), 25 March (Independence Day), 25–28 April (Greek Orthodox Easter), 1 May (Labour Day), 16 June (Whit Monday), 15 August (Assumption of the Virgin Mary), 28 October ('Ochi' Day, anniversary of Greek defiance of Italy's 1940 ultimatum), 25–26 December (Christmas).

2004: 1 January (New Year's Day), 6 January (Epiphany), 23 February (Clean Monday), 25 March (Independence Day), 9–12 April (Greek Orthodox Easter), 1 May (Labour Day), 31 May (Whit Monday), 15 August (Assumption of the Virgin Mary), 28 October ('Ochi' Day, anniversary of Greek defiance of Italy's 1940 ultimatum), 25–26 December (Christmas).

Weights and Measures

The metric system is in force.

Statistical Survey

Source (unless otherwise stated): National Statistical Service of Greece, Odos Lykourgou 14–16, 101 66 Athens; tel. (1) 03289530; fax (1) 03241102; e-mail info@statistics.gr; internet www.statistics.gr.

Area and Population

AREA, POPULATION AND DENSITY

Area (sq km)	131,957*
Population (census results)†	
17 March 1991	10,259,900
March 2001	
Males	5,426,446
Females.	5,537,574
Total	10,964,020
Density (per sq km) at March 2001	83.1

* 50,949 sq miles.

† Including armed forces stationed abroad, but excluding foreign forces stationed in Greece.

PRINCIPAL TOWNS

(population at 1991 census)

Athinai (Athens, the capital). . .	772,072	Iráklion	116,178
		Larissa	113,090
Thessaloníki (Salonika) . . .	383,967	Volos	77,192
		Kavala. . . .	58,025
Piraeus	182,671	Serres	50,390
Patras	153,344	Canea	50,077

BIRTHS, MARRIAGES AND DEATHS

	Registered live births		Registered marriages		Registered deaths	
	Number	Rate (per 1,000)	Number	Rate (per 1,000)	Number	Rate (per 1,000)
1992 . .	104,081	10.1	48,631	4.7	98,231	9.5
1993 . .	101,799	9.8	62,195	6.0	97,419	9.4
1994 . .	103,763	9.9	56,813	5.4	97,807	9.4
1995 . .	101,495	9.7	63,987	6.1	100,158	9.6
1996 . .	100,718	9.6	45,408	4.3	100,740	9.6
1997 . .	102,038	9.7	60,535	5.8	99,738	9.5
1998 . .	100,894	9.6	55,489	5.5	102,668	9.8
1999 . .	100,643	9.6	61,165	5.8	103,304	9.8

2000 (provisional): Registered live births 117,140; Registered deaths 105,439 (Source: UN, *Demographic Yearbook* and *Vital Statistics and Population Report*).

Expectation of life (WHO estimates, years at birth): 78.1 (males 75.5; females 80.8) in 2001 (Source: WHO, *World Health Report*).

ECONOMICALLY ACTIVE POPULATION

(sample surveys, '000 persons aged 15 years and over, April–June)*

	1999	2000	2001
Agriculture, hunting and forestry .	657.4	659.5	615.7
Fishing	11.7	11.2	11.3
Mining and quarrying	18.6	16.5	17.8
Manufacturing	568.8	557.0	557.4
Electricity, gas and water supply .	40.9	38.1	34.3
Construction	273.3	276.6	284.8
Wholesale and retail trade; repair of motor vehicles, motorcycles and personal and household goods	673.8	677.9	673.2
Hotels and restaurants . . .	252.8	252.7	255.0
Transport, storage and communications	248.2	251.4	250.0
Financial intermediation . . .	93.7	107.7	108.0
Real estate, renting and business activities	199.0	195.5	213.0
Public administration and defence; compulsory social security . .	277.5	293.1	290.3
Education	244.2	242.1	251.1
Health and social work . . .	186.3	183.7	177.8
Other community, social and personal service activities . .	141.1	128.4	126.8
Private households with employed persons	51.5	54.7	51.1
Extra-territorial organizations and bodies	1.0	0.2	n.a.
Total employed	3,939.8	3,946.3	3,917.5
Unemployed	523.4	491.1	444.7
Total labour force	4,463.2	4,437.4	4,362.2
Males	2,668.3	2,650.7	2,606.6
Females	1,794.9	1,786.7	1,755.7

* Including members of the regular armed forces, but excluding persons on compulsory military service.

Source: ILO.

Health and Welfare

KEY INDICATORS

Total fertility rate (children per woman, 2001)	1.3
Under-5 mortality rate (per 1,000 live births, 2001) . . .	5
HIV/AIDS (% of persons aged 15–49, 2001)	0.17
Physicians (per 1,000 head, 1995)	3.92
Hospital beds (per 1,000 head, 1997)	5
Health expenditure (2000): US $ per head (PPP) . . .	1,390
Health expenditure (2000): % of GDP	8.3
Health expenditure (2000): public (% of total)	55.5
Human Development Index (2000): ranking	24
Human Development Index (2000): value	0.885

For sources and definitions, see explanatory note on p. vi.

Agriculture

PRINCIPAL CROPS
('000 metric tons)

	1999	2000	2001
Wheat	2,064.0	2,183.4	2,084.4
Rice (paddy)	161.4	147.5	150.5
Barley	320.0	302.9	274.1
Maize	1,949.9	2,037.5	2,034.8
Rye	35.8	32.0	33.1
Oats	85.9	86.4	81.5
Potatoes	866.7	883.3	936.7
Sugar beet	2,388.8	3,033.2	2,882.4
Dry beans	25.0	23.6	23.0
Other pulses*	3.5	3.5	3.5
Almonds	46.3	47.2	55.3
Olives	2,196.6	2,273.8	2,249.4
Sunflower seed	55.5	35.0	22.8
Cabbages	203.0	200.0	200.0
Tomatoes	2,098.4	2,057.2	1,819.9
Cucumbers and gherkins	152.6	160.9	160.0*
Aubergines	75.0	76.0	75.0*
Chillies and green peppers	102.3	103.7	100.0*
Dry onions	193.0	189.5	208.0
Watermelons	684.7	662.8	644.2
Cantaloupes and other melons	160.0	164.1	165.0*
Grapes	1,200.0*	1,200.0*	1,200.0*
Apples	318.2	285.0	243.2
Pears	74.0	96.5	85.3
Peaches and nectarines	884.2	920.3	927.1
Oranges	1,117.8	1,068.4	1,022.3
Tangerines, mandarins, clementines and satsumas	92.6	84.0	107.5
Lemons and limes	182.0	172.8	174.3
Apricots	85.3	82.0	68.5
Tobacco (leaves)	139.8	136.6	136.5
Cotton (lint)†	384.0	443.0	455.6

* FAO estimate(s).
† Unofficial figures.

Source: FAO.

LIVESTOCK
('000 head, year ending 30 September)

	1999	2000	2001
Horses	31	33*	33*
Mules	35	35*	35*
Asses	73	72*	72*
Cattle	583	590	585†
Pigs	933	906	936
Sheep	8,930	8,732	9,269
Goats	5,520	5,293	5,180
Chickens	28,453	28,500*	28,000*

* FAO estimate.
† Unofficial figure.

Source: FAO.

LIVESTOCK PRODUCTS
('000 metric tons)

	1999	2000	2001
Beef and veal	66.6	65.7	59.9
Mutton and lamb*	79.5	77.5	78.0
Goat meat*	47.0	47.5	44.1
Pig meat	138.3	143.1	136.6
Horse meat†	2.7	2.7	2.7
Poultry meat	153.4	154.2	154.2†
Other meat†	7.0	7.0	7.0
Cows' milk	777.0	789.0*	815.0*
Sheep's milk	654.0	700.0*	670.0*
Goats' milk*	450.0	450.0	435.0
Cheese	242.4	233.3	233.7
Butter	4.4	3.6	2.8
Poultry eggs	119.1	116.6	106.4
Honey	14.2	13.7	14.0
Wool: greasy	9.8	9.5	9.6†
Wool: scoured	5.7	5.8	5.8†
Cattle hides†	12.7	12.5	12.6
Sheepskins†	16.8	16.8	16.8
Goatskins†	10.2	10.1	9.5

* Unofficial figure(s).
† FAO estimate(s).

Source: FAO.

Forestry

ROUNDWOOD REMOVALS
('000 cubic metres, excl. bark)

	1998	1999	2000
Sawlogs, veneer logs and logs for sleepers	360	696	683
Pulpwood	135	115	113
Fuel wood	1,197	1,403	1,375
Total	1,692	2,214	2,171

Source: FAO.

2001 (FAO estimates): Production assumed to be unchanged from 2000.

SAWNWOOD PRODUCTION
('000 cubic metres, incl. railway sleepers)

	1998	1999	2000
Coniferous (softwood)	85	87	85
Broadleaved (hardwood)	52	53	52
Total	137	140	137

Source: FAO.

2001 (FAO estimates): Production assumed to be unchanged from 2000.

Fishing

('000 metric tons, live weight)

	1998	1999	2000
Capture	108.6	118.8	99.3
Freshwater fishes	3.7	2.8	2.9
Mediterranean horse mackerel	4.4	3.5	3.9
European pilchard (sardine)	17.7	15.2	16.0
European anchovy	17.1	16.5	9.9
Mediterranean mussel	6.4	15.9	0.5
Aquaculture	59.9	79.3	79.9
Barramundi (giant sea perch)	18.5	23.9	26.7
Dorada	22.0	32.8	38.5
Mediterranean mussel	14.5	16.9	9.8
Total catch	188.2	216.0	179.2

Note: Figures exclude aquatic plants and aquatic mammals.

Source: FAO, *Yearbook of Fishery Statistics*.

Mining

('000 metric tons, unless otherwise indicated)

	1999	2000	2001*
Lignite	61,861	65,000*	60,000
Crude petroleum ('000 barrels)	1,200*	2,093	2,000
Iron ore*†	600	575	575
Bauxite	1,883	1,991	1,990
Zinc concentrates	19.6	16.9	20.0
Lead concentrates	22.0	18.2	27.7
Silver ore (metric tons)†	45.8	37.1	36.0
Magnesite	495	500*	500
Salt (unrefined)	176	180	180
Bentonite	1,050	1,150*	1,150
Kaolin*	65	65	65
Gypsum	687	750*	700
Marble ('000 cu m)	178	200*	200
Natural gas ('000 barrels)*	350	350	350

* Estimate(s).

† Figures refer to the metal content of ores and concentrates.

Source: US Geological Survey.

Industry

SELECTED PRODUCTS

('000 metric tons, unless otherwise indicated)

	1996	1997	1998
Edible fats	44	n.a.	n.a.
Olive oil (crude)	433	457	435
Raw sugar	288	396	220
Wine ('000 hectolitres)	1,783	1,455	1,456
Beer ('000 hectolitres)	3,766	3,950	3,886
Cigarettes (million)	38,268	36,909	21,427
Cotton yarn	223.9	222.4	109.7
Woven cotton fabrics—pure and mixed (metric tons)	n.a.	n.a.	6,000
Wool yarn (metric tons)	13,900	12,800	4,900
Woven woollen fabrics—pure and mixed (metric tons)	1,322	1,670	792
Yarn of artificial material (metric tons)	9,500	n.a.	11,400
Fabrics of artificial fibres (metric tons)	11,513	n.a.	n.a.
Footwear—excl. rubber and plastic ('000 pairs)	6,769	6,202	5,716
Rubber and plastic footwear ('000 pairs)	3,294	n.a.	n.a.
Paper and paperboard	340	n.a.	n.a.
Sulphuric acid	1,544	1,655	814
Hydrochloric acid (21° Bé)	90.6	66.7	53.1
Nitric acid (54% or 36.3° Bé)	462	n.a.	n.a.
Polyvinyl chloride	94.8	105.9	108.3
Liquefied petroleum gas	555	561	650*
Naphthas	977	970	932*
Motor spirit (petrol)	3,383	3,607	3,671*
Jet fuels	1,942	1,949	1,934*
Distillate fuel oils	4,760	5,144	5,544*
Residual fuel oils	7,424	7,149	6,959*
Cement	13,391	13,660	14,207
Crude steel (incl. alloys)	852	1,020	1,104
Aluminium (unwrought)	141.3	132.0	160.6
Electric energy (million kWh)	42,123	43,743	46,363*

* Estimate(s).

1999 ('000 metric tons): Olive oil (crude) 436; Raw sugar 252; Crude steel (incl. alloys) 960; Aluminium (unwrought) 160.8.

Source: mainly UN, *Industrial Commodity Statistics Yearbook*.

Finance

CURRENCY AND EXCHANGE RATES

Monetary Units

100 cent = 1 euro (€)

Sterling, Dollar and Euro Equivalents (31 December 2002)

£1 sterling = 1.537 euros

US $1 = 0.9536 euros

100 euros = £65.06 = $104.87

Average Exchange Rate (euros per US $)

2000	1.0854
2001	1.1175
2002	1.0626

Note: The national currency was formerly the drachma. Greece became a member of the euro area on 1 January 2001, after which a fixed exchange rate of €1 = 340.75 drachmae was in operation. Euro notes and coins were introduced on 1 January 2002. The euro and local currency circulated alongside each other until 28 February, after which the euro became the sole legal tender. Some of the figures in this Survey are still in terms of drachmae.

BUDGET

('000 million drachmae)*

Revenue	1998	1999	2000†
Ordinary budget	9,498.4	10,592.9	11,650.0
Tax revenue	8,839.7	9,897.3	10,890.2
Direct taxes	3,591.3	4,043.5	4,527.0
Personal income tax	1,587.0	1,825.3	1,780.0
Corporate income tax	1,018.3	1,136.7	1,550.0
Indirect taxes	5,248.2	5,853.8	6,363.2
Consumption taxes	1,856.1	1,909.0	1,895.0
Transaction taxes	3,251.0	3,778.6	4,276.0
Value-added tax	2,723.3	2,987.5	3,380.0
Stamp duty	292.5	288.9	301.0
Non-tax revenue	658.7	695.6	759.8
Capital receipts	378.2	400.9	442.0
Investment budget	914.0	1,010.0	1,200.0
Receipts from European Union	891.0	977.0	1,130.0
SAGAP‡	793.0	806.0	895.0
Total	11,205.4	12,408.9	13,745.0

Expenditure	1998	1999†	2000†
Defence	1,018	1,053	1,186
Education	1,217	1,402	1,440
Health, social welfare and insurance	2,229	2,194	2,424
Agriculture	1,242	1,256	1,416
Interest payments§	3,024	3,123	3,165
Other purposes	4,602	5,304	5,779
Total §	13,331	14,332	15,410
Ordinary budget	10,661	11,276	11,995
Investment budget	1,877	2,250	2,520
SAGAP‡	793	806	895

* Figures refer to the budgetary transactions of the central Government, excluding the operations of social security funds and public entities (such as hospitals, educational institutions and government agencies) with individual budgets.

† Provisional.

‡ Special Account for Guarantees of Agricultural Products.

§ Excluding capitalized interest ('000 million drachmae): 27 in 1998.

Source: IMF, *Greece: Selected Issues and Statistical Appendix* (April 2001).

INTERNATIONAL RESERVES

(US $ million at 31 December)*

	2000	2001	2002
Gold†	753.2	1,090.0	1,349.0
IMF special drawing rights	12.0	9.7	15.1
Reserve position in IMF	296.8	357.3	438.4
Foreign exchange	13,115.5	4,787.0	7,629.0
Total	14,177.5	6,243.0	9,431.5

* Figures exclude deposits made with the European Monetary Institute.

† Gold reserves are valued at market-related prices.

Source: IMF, *International Financial Statistics*.

MONEY SUPPLY
('000 million drachmae at 31 December)

	2000	2001*	2002*
Currency in circulation . . .	3,097.3	8,708	9,208†
Demand deposits at banking institutions	4,348.3	15,930	15,106
Total money	7,445.5	24,720	24,314

* Figures in terms of million euros.

† Currency put into circulation by the Bank of Greece was 9,984 million euros.

Source: IMF, *International Financial Statistics*.

COST OF LIVING
(Consumer Price Index; base: 1990 = 100)

	1999	2000	2001
Food	211.6	215.6	226.6
Fuel and light	153.6	173.8	174.1
Clothing	228.6	233.4	241.2
Rent	318.4	330.8	343.9
All items (incl. others) . . .	234.9	242.4	250.7

Source: ILO.

NATIONAL ACCOUNTS
(million drachmae at current prices)

Expenditure on the Gross Domestic Product*

	1999	2000	2001
Government final consumption expenditure	5,819,900	6,408,400	7,049,200
Private final consumption expenditure	27,156,900	28,893,500	30,790,300
Increase in stocks	−106,600	17,500	−198,900
Gross fixed capital formation .	8,346,600	9,377,600	10,420,500
Total domestic expenditure	41,216,800	44,697,000	47,997,300
Exports of goods and services .	7,893,200	10,343,400	11,235,700
Less Imports of goods and services	10,720,900	13,633,700	14,748,700
GDP in purchasers' values .	38,389,100	41,406,700	44,483,700
GDP at constant 1995 prices	30,885,800	32,217,200	33,538,100

* Figures are rounded to the nearest 100 million drachmae.

Source: IMF, *International Financial Statistics*.

Gross Domestic Product by Economic Activity*

	1997	1998	1999
Agriculture, hunting, forestry and fishing	2,553,841	2,643,877	2,644,665
Mining and quarrying	192,147	198,190	186,686
Manufacturing	3,695,617	3,795,714	4,022,654
Electricity, gas and water . . .	607,820	712,796	802,368
Construction	2,188,204	2,460,781	2,865,626
Wholesale and retail trade . . .	4,364,847	4,742,332	4,963,192
Hotels and restaurants	2,112,042	2,381,895	2,464,202
Transport, storage and communication	1,894,198	2,108,467	2,206,029
Financial intermediation† . . .	1,335,175	1,445,873	1,604,264
Real estate, renting and business activities	5,160,676	5,535,197	5,711,787
Public administration and defence	2,100,650	2,243,620	2,355,400
Education	1,447,970	1,580,841	1,661,407
Health and social work	1,604,949	1,797,003	1,947,327
Other services	830,097	902,041	953,757
Private households with employed persons	81,393	87,358	96,277
Sub-total	30,169,626	32,635,985	34,485,641
Less Financial intermediation services indirectly measured	894,085	987,199	1,083,532
Gross value added in basic prices	29,275,541	31,648,786	33,402,109
Indirect taxes, *less* subsidies .	3,828,299	4,223,715	4,745,110
GDP in market prices . . .	33,103,840	35,872,501	38,147,219

* Figures are provisional.

† Including imputed rents of owner-occupied dwellings.

BALANCE OF PAYMENTS
(US $ million)

	1999	2000	2001*
Exports of goods f.o.b.	8,544.7	10,201.5	10,615
Imports of goods f.o.b.	−26,495.6	−30,440.4	−29,702
Trade balance	−17,950.9	−20,238.9	−19,087
Exports of services	16,505.8	19,238.9	19,456
Imports of services	−9,250.7	−11,286.4	−11,589
Balance on goods and services	−10,695.8	−12,286.4	−11,220
Other income received	2,576.5	2,807.2	1,885
Other income paid	−3,248.1	−3,692.1	−3,652
Balance on goods, services and income	−11,367.4	−13,171.3	−12,987
Current transfers received . . .	4,956.5	4,115.8	4,592
Current transfers paid	−884.0	−764.2	−1,005
Current balance	−7,294.9	−9,819.7	−9,400
Capital account (net)	2,211.2	2,112.3	2,153
Direct investment abroad . . .	−542.3	−2,098.5	−611
Direct investment from abroad .	567.3	1,083.4	1,585
Portfolio investment assets . .	−857.5	−1,183.9	−474
Portfolio investment liabilities . .	6,754.4	9,261.7	9,012
Financial derivatives liabilities	418.6	348.3	74
Other investment assets . .	−2,913.0	6,970.0	−1,539
Other investment liabilities . .	4,050.0	−3,551.0	−7,511
Net errors and omissions . . .	41.6	−549.8	1,011
Overall balance	2,435.5	2,572.8	−5,699

* Figures are rounded to the nearest million US dollars.

Source: IMF, *International Financial Statistics*.

External Trade

PRINCIPAL COMMODITIES
(US $ million)

Imports c.i.f.	1998	1999	2000
Food and live animals . . .	3,302.0	2,852.9	2,727.4
Meat and meat preparations . .	856.7	721.3	685.0
Crude materials (inedible) except fuels	883.9	673.5	707.0
Mineral fuels, lubricants, etc. .	2,229.4	1,541.6	4,013.2
Petroleum, petroleum products, etc.	2,062.8	1,407.5	3,739.9
Crude petroleum oils, etc. . .	1,705.3	944.8	3,015.0
Chemicals and related products	3,643.1	3,235.3	3,414.9
Medicinal and pharmaceutical products	1,080.3	1,060.2	1,133.2
Medicaments (incl. veterinary medicaments)	890.5	910.4	974.7
Basic manufactures	5,217.6	4,262.9	4,566.0
Textile yarn, fabrics, etc. . .	1,143.2	942.0	859.2
Iron and steel	894.3	672.8	838.9
Machinery and transport equipment	10,479.6	9,954.4	10,195.6
Machinery specialized for particular industries . . .	1,033.2	882.4	676.4
General industrial machinery equipment and parts . . .	1,198.5	1,198.4	1,177.8
Telecommunications and sound equipment	1,278.3	1,120.8	1,293.4
Other electrical machinery apparatus, etc.	1,263.0	1,045.2	1,101.4
Road vehicles and parts* . . .	2,641.6	3,076.2	2,841.6
Passenger motor cars (excl. buses)	1,570.2	1,926.6	1,886.1
Other transport equipment* . .	1,936.0	1,495.2	1,820.8
Ships, boats and floating structures	1,132.1	674.8	1,568.3
Miscellaneous manufactured articles	3,616.6	3,254.9	3,386.4
Clothing and accessories (excl. footwear)	1,054.7	931.1	1,005.3
Total (incl. others)	30,266.7	26,570.2	29,816.0

* Excluding tyres, engines and electrical parts.

Exports f.o.b.	1998	1999	2000
Food and live animals	2,000.9	1,676.5	1,596.3
Vegetables and fruit	1,295.2	1,018.7	999.2
Fresh or dried fruit and nuts (excl. oil nuts)	492.8	428.5	417.5
Preserved fruit and fruit preparations	349.8	253.0	292.7
Beverages and tobacco	596.5	615.3	513.5
Tobacco and manufactures	447.2	494.3	393.6
Unmanufactured tobacco (incl. refuse)	333.6	357.5	264.0
Crude materials (inedible) except fuels	573.5	607.5	594.8
Textile fibres and waste	263.2	353.0	313.1
Cotton	253.1	345.5	305.0
Raw cotton (excl. linters)	230.4	328.8	289.4
Mineral fuels, lubricants, etc.	736.5	1,024.6	1,611.8
Petroleum, petroleum products, etc.	707.3	995.8	1,527.7
Refined petroleum products	605.2	851.5	1,373.6
Animal and vegetable oils, fats and waxes	357.7	476.0	247.0
Fixed vegetable oils and fats	353.9	470.5	243.4
Soft fixed vegetable oils	352.2	469.7	241.8
Olive oil	315.1	451.0	226.5
Chemicals and related products	666.4	693.8	837.9
Basic manufactures	2,301.5	1,910.6	1,965.7
Textile yarn, fabrics, etc.	536.9	411.2	406.7
Non-metallic mineral manufactures	410.4	319.8	328.4
Lime, cement, etc.	303.8	244.5	246.3
Non-ferrous metals	615.1	581.1	640.0
Aluminium	457.5	430.3	455.3
Worked aluminium and aluminium alloys	351.7	327.1	367.9
Machinery and transport equipment	1,173.8	1,024.7	1,314.9
Electrical machinery, apparatus etc.	319.5	291.0	328.6
Miscellaneous manufactured articles	2,293.8	1,947.6	1,937.1
Clothing and accessories (excl. footwear)	1,820.7	1,504.9	1,405.3
Total (incl. others)	10,867.8	10,149.8	10,964.5

Source: UN, *International Trade Statistics Yearbook*.

PRINCIPAL TRADING PARTNERS
(US $ million)*

Imports c.i.f.	1998	1999	2000
Austria	299.2	249.2	249.4
Belgium-Luxembourg	1,036.4	n.a.	n.a.
Bulgaria	394.9	351.1	398.8
China, People's Republic	591.8	545.8	699.4
Denmark	425.1	337.9	305.1
Egypt	400.8	188.9	142.9
Finland	349.9	351.3	452.3
France (incl. Monaco)	2,595.4	2,289.8	2,153.4
Germany	4,505.4	3,896.9	3,812.9
Iran	616.4	394.1	1,166.1
Italy	4,824.0	4,007.1	3,855.6
Japan	992.0	1,144.3	1,179.0
Korea, Republic	949.0	732.2	1,110.8
Netherlands	1,874.7	1,655.7	1,734.8
Russia	494.1	504.4	1,094.5
Saudi Arabia	462.4	290.1	949.1
Spain	1,071.4	914.1	1,018.0
Sweden	607.6	490.0	550.0
Switzerland	478.2	513.1	413.3
Turkey	369.7	366.5	396.1
United Kingdom	1,926.8	1,602.6	1,482.5
USA	1,397.9	1,473.2	1,022.5
Total (incl. others)	30,266.7	26,570.2	29,816.0

Exports f.o.b.	1998	1999	2000
Albania	194.4	222.1	248.8
Austria	129.5	105.6	91.6
Belgium-Luxembourg	176.1	n.a.	n.a.
Bulgaria	442.5	447.4	450.5
Cyprus	416.7	414.8	509.4
Egypt	114.8	86.9	109.7
France (incl. Monaco)	504.8	410.4	374.1
Germany	1,994.1	1,552.9	1,345.7
Israel	124.4	115.8	185.6
Italy	1,293.2	1,278.5	1,011.1
Lebanon	114.0	104.7	145.3
Macedonia, former Yugoslav republic	269.3	428.3	470.8
Malta	104.9	112.1	136.4
Netherlands	329.8	291.7	316.8
Romania	203.0	212.7	384.3
Russia	269.1	245.7	249.2
Spain	276.5	317.9	334.7
Sweden	147.6	113.9	136.1
Turkey	346.1	335.3	550.3
Ukraine	84.6	44.6	42.1
United Kingdom	756.2	635.9	691.8
USA	516.1	594.4	638.2
Yugoslavia	187.2	112.7	131.4
Total (incl. others)	10,867.8	10,149.8	10,964.5

* Imports by country of first consignment; exports by country of consumption.

Source: UN, *International Trade Statistics Yearbook*.

Transport

RAILWAYS
(estimated traffic)

	1996	1997	1998
Passenger-kilometres (million)	1,752	1,783	1,559
Net ton-kilometres (million)	350	330	399

ROAD TRAFFIC
(motor vehicles in use at 31 December)

	1998*	1999*	2000
Passenger cars	2,675,676	2,928,881	3,195,065
Buses and coaches	26,320	26,769	27,037
Lorries and vans	987,357	1,023,987	1,057,422
Motorcycles and mopeds	2,138,987	2,332,231	2,438,930

* Estimate(s).

Source: International Road Federation, *World Road Statistics*.

SHIPPING

Merchant fleet
(registered at 31 December)

	1999	2000	2001
Number of vessels	1,491	1,529	1,529
Total displacement ('000 grt)	24,833.3	26,401.7	2,678.2

Source: Lloyd's Register-Fairplay, *World Fleet Statistics*.

Freight traffic

	1994	1995	1996
Vessels entered ('000 net reg. tons)	68,785	73,059	87,867
Goods loaded ('000 metric tons)*	21,087	21,940	21,356
Goods unloaded ('000 metric tons)*	33,048	38,573	38,549

* International sea-borne shipping.

CIVIL AVIATION
(domestic and foreign flights of Olympic Airways)

	1996	1997	1998
Kilometres flown ('000) . . .	65,847	68,415	67,606
Passenger-kilometres ('000). . .	8,533,168	9,260,651	8,561,153
Freight ton-kilometres ('000) . .	118,738	129,100	112,615
Mail ton-kilometres ('000) . . .	12,669	14,662	20,265

Tourism

TOURISTS BY COUNTRY OF ORIGIN
(foreign citizens, excl. cruise passengers)

Country	1997	1998	1999
Austria.	388,118	450,195	501,602
Belgium-Luxembourg	229,310	273,674	332,913
Denmark	344,261	292,532	336,248
France	426,678	486,201	545,981
Germany	1,994,670	2,136,515	2,450,137
Italy	533,303	659,688	745,915
Netherlands	464,144	548,339	616,807
Sweden	472,481	467,617	468,793
Switzerland	295,731	289,387	308,138
United Kingdom	1,711,942	2,044,243	2,433,033
USA	240,555	219,362	229,314
Yugoslavia (former)	198,999	201,633	103,077
Total (incl. others)	10,070,325	10,916,046	12,164,088

2000: 12,500,000 tourist arrivals.

Receipts (US $ million): 6,188 in 1998; 8,783 in 1999; 9,221 in 2000.

Source: World Tourism Organization, *Yearbook of Tourism Statistics*.

Communications Media

	1999	2000	2001
Telephone ('000 main lines in use)	5,610.9	5,659.3	5,607.7
Mobile cellular telephones ('000 subscribers).	3,904.0	5,932.0	7,962.0
Personal computers ('000 in use)	750.0	750.0	860.0
Internet users ('000)	705.8	1,000.0	1,400.0

Radio receivers ('000 in use): 4,481 in 1997.

Television receivers ('000 in use): 2,357 in 1997.

Facsimile machines ('000 in use, estimate): 40,000 in 1996.

Daily newspapers (1997): Number 122; Average circulation ('000 copies) 1,389.

Books (titles published): 4,225 in 1996.

Sources: UN, *Statistical Yearbook*, UNESCO, *Statistical Yearbook*, and International Telecommunication Union.

Education

(2000/01)

	Institutions	Teachers	Students
Pre-primary.	5,675	n.a.	144,657
Primary	6,212	48,852	641,368
Secondary: General	3,217	54,719	604,412
Secondary: Technical, vocational and ecclesiastical	669	15,270	157,217
Higher: Universities	18	10,149	148,772
Higher: Technical, vocational and ecclesiastical	74	8,902	91,564

Adult literacy rate (UNESCO estimates): 97.2% (males 98.5%; females 96.0%) in 2000 (Source: UN Development Programme, *Human Development Report*).

Directory

The Constitution

A new Constitution for the Hellenic Republic came into force on 11 June 1975. The main provisions of this Constitution, as subsequently amended, are summarized below.

Greece shall be a parliamentary democracy with a President as Head of State. All powers are derived from the people and exist for the benefit of the people. The established religion is that of The Eastern Orthodox Church of Christ.

EXECUTIVE AND LEGISLATIVE

The President

In March 1986 a series of amendments to the Constitution was approved by a majority vote of Parliament, which relieved the President of his executive power and transferred such power to the legislature, thus confining the Head of State to a largely ceremonial role.

The President is elected by Parliament for a period of five years. The re-election of the same person shall be permitted only once. The President represents the State in relations with other nations, is Supreme Commander of the armed forces and may declare war and conclude treaties. The President shall appoint the Prime Minister and, on the Prime Minister's recommendation, the other members of the Government. The President shall convoke Parliament once every year and in extraordinary session whenever he deems it reasonable. In exceptional circumstances the President may preside over the Cabinet, convene the Council of the Republic, and suspend Parliament for a period not exceeding 30 days. In accordance with the amendment of March 1986, the President was deprived of the right to dismiss the Prime Minister, his power to call a referendum was limited, and the right to declare a state of emergency was transferred to Parliament. The President can now dissolve Parliament only if the resignation of two Governments in quick succession demonstrates the absence of political stability. If no party has a majority in Parliament, the President must offer an opportunity to form a government to the leader of each of the four biggest parties in turn, strictly following the order of their parliamentary strengths. If no party leader is able to form a government, the President may try to assemble an all-party government; failing that, the President must appoint a caretaker cabinet, led by a senior judge, to hold office until a fresh election takes place. The Constitution continues to reserve a substantial moderating role for the President, however, in that he retains the right to object to legislation and may request Parliament to reconsider it or to approve it with an enlarged majority.

The Government

The Government consists of the Cabinet which comprises the Prime Minister and Ministers. The Government determines and directs the general policy of the State in accordance with the Constitution and the laws. The Cabinet must enjoy the confidence of Parliament and may be removed by a vote of no confidence. The Prime Minister is to be the leader of the party with an absolute majority in Parliament, or, if no such party exists, the leader of the party with a relative majority.

The Council of the Republic

The Council of the Republic shall be composed of all former democratic Presidents, the Prime Minister, the leader of the Opposition and the parliamentary Prime Ministers of governments which have enjoyed the confidence of Parliament, presided over by the President. It shall meet when the largest parties are unable to form a government with the confidence of Parliament and may empower the President to appoint a Prime Minister who may or may not be a member of Parliament. The Council may also authorize the President to dissolve Parliament.

Parliament

Parliament is to be unicameral and composed of not fewer than 200 and not more than 300 deputies elected by direct, universal and secret ballot for a term of four years. Parliament shall elect its own President, or Speaker. It must meet once a year for a regular session of at least five months. Bills passed by Parliament must be ratified by the President and the President's veto can be nullified by an absolute majority of the total number of deputies. Parliament may impeach the President by a motion signed by one-third and passed by two-thirds of the total number of deputies. Parliament is also empowered to impeach present or former members of the Government. In these cases the defendant shall be brought before an *ad hoc* tribunal presided over by the President of the Supreme Court and composed of 12 judges. Certain legislative work, as specified in the Constitution, must be passed by Parliament in plenum, and Parliament cannot make a decision without an absolute majority of the members present, which under no circumstances shall be less than one-quarter of the total number of deputies. The Constitution provides for certain legislative powers to be exercised by not more than two Parliamentary Departments. Parliament may revise the Constitution in accordance with the procedure laid down in the Constitution.

THE JUDICIAL AUTHORITY

Justice is to be administered by courts of regular judges, who enjoy personal and functional independence. The President, after consultations with a judicial council, shall appoint the judges for life. The judges are subject only to the Constitution and the laws. Courts are divided into administrative, civil and penal and shall be organized by virtue of special laws. They must not apply laws which are contrary to the Constitution. The final jurisdiction in matters of judicial review rests with a Special Supreme Tribunal.

Certain laws, passed before the implementation of this Constitution and deemed not contrary to it, are to remain in force. Other specified laws, even if contrary to the Constitution, are to remain in force until repealed by further legislation.

INDIVIDUAL AND SPECIAL RIGHTS

All citizens are equal under the Constitution and before the law, having the same rights and obligations. No titles of nobility or distinction are to be conferred or recognized. All persons are to enjoy full protection of life, honour and freedom, irrespective of nationality, race, creed or political allegiance. Retrospective legislation is prohibited and no citizen may be punished without due process of law. Freedom of speech, of the Press, of association and of religion are guaranteed under the Constitution. All persons have the right to a free education, which the state has the duty to provide. Work is a right and all workers, irrespective of sex or other distinction, are entitled to equal remuneration for rendering services of equal value. The right of peaceful assembly, the right of a person to property and the freedom to form political parties are guaranteed under the Constitution. The exercise of the right to vote by all citizens over 18 years of age is obligatory. No person may exercise his rights and liberties contrary to the Constitution.

MOUNT ATHOS

The district of Mount Athos shall, in accordance with its ancient privileged status, be a self-governing part of the Greek State and its sovereignty shall remain unaffected.

The Government

HEAD OF STATE

President: KONSTANTINOS STEFANOPOULOS (took office 10 March 1995; re-elected 9 February 2000).

THE CABINET
(April 2003)

Prime Minister: KONSTANTINOS (COSTAS) SIMITIS.

Minister of State: STEFANOS MANIKAS.

Minister of the Economy and Finance: NIKOLAOS CHRISTODOU-LAKIS.

Minister of Foreign Affairs: GEORGIOS PAPANDREOU.

Minister of National Defence: IOANNIS PAPANTONIOU.

Minister of the Interior, Public Administration and Decentralization: KONSTANTINOS SKANDALIDIS.

Minister of Development: APOSTOLOS-ATHANASSIOS (AKIS) TSOHATZO-POULOS.

Minister of the Environment, Physical Planning and Public Works: VASILIKI (VASSO) PAPANDREOU.

Minister of Education and Religious Affairs: PETROS EPHTHI-MIOU.

Minister of Labour and Social Affairs: DIMITRIS REPPAS.

Minister of Health and Welfare: COSTAS STEFANIS.

Minister of Agriculture: GEORGIOS DRYS.

Minister of Justice: PHILIPPOS PETSALNIKOS.

Minister of Culture: EVANGELOS VENIZELOS.

Minister of Transport and Communications: CHRISTOS VERELIS.

Minister of Public Order: MIKHAIL KHRISOKHOIDHIS.

Minister of Merchant Marine: GEORGIOS ANOMERITIS.

Minister of Press and Mass Media: CHRISTOS PROTOPAPAS.

Minister of Macedonia and Thrace: GEORGIOS PASCHALIDIS.

Minister of the Aegean: NIKOS SIFOUNAKIS.

MINISTRIES

Office of the President: Odos Vas. Georgiou 7, 106 74 Athens; tel. (21) 07283111; fax (21) 07248938.

Office of the Prime Minister: Maximos Mansion, Herodou Atticou 19, 106 74 Athens; tel. (21) 03385242; fax (21) 07241776; e-mail mail@primeminister.gr; internet www.primeminister.gr.

Ministry of the Aegean: Filellinon 9, 105 57 Athens; tel. (21) 03311714; fax (21) 03227544; e-mail athens1@ypai.gr; internet www.ypai.gr.

Ministry of Agriculture: Odos Acharnon 2–6, 104 32 Athens; tel. (21) 02124000; fax (21) 05240475; e-mail webmaster@minagric.gr; internet www.minagric.gr.

Ministry of Culture: Odos Bouboulinas 20, 106 82 Athens; tel. (21) 08201637; fax (21) 08201373; e-mail w3admin@culture.gr; internet www.culture.gr.

Ministry of Development: Odos Mihalakopoulou 80, 101 92 Athens; tel. (21) 07482770; fax (21) 07788279; internet www.ypan.gr.

Ministry of the Economy and Finance: Odos Nikis 5–7, 101 80 Athens; tel. (21) 03332000; internet www.ypetho.gr.

Ministry of Education and Religious Affairs: Odos Metropoleos 15, 105 57 Athens; tel. (21) 03230461; fax (21) 03248264; e-mail edu_ref@ypepth.gr; internet www.ypepth.gr.

Ministry of the Environment, Physical Planning and Public Works: Odos Amaliados 17, 115 23 Athens; tel. (21) 06415700; fax (21) 06432589; e-mail minister@minenv.gr; internet www.minenv.gr.

Ministry of Foreign Affairs: Odos Akadimias 1, 106 71 Athens; tel. (21) 03681000; fax (21) 03624195; e-mail mfa@mfa.gr; internet www.mfa.gr.

Ministry of Health and Welfare: Odos Aristotelous 17, 104 33 Athens; tel. (21) 05232820; fax (21) 05231707; e-mail info@ypyp.gr; internet www.ypyp.gr.

Ministry of the Interior, Public Administration and Decentralization: Odos Stadiou 27, 101 83 Athens; tel. (21) 03223521; fax (21) 03240631; e-mail kominatos@ypes.gr; internet www.ypes.gr.

Ministry of Justice: Odos Mesogeion 96, 115 27 Athens; tel. (21) 07711019; fax (21) 07759879; e-mail minjust@otenet.gr; internet www.ministryofjustice.gr.

Ministry of Labour and Social Affairs: Odos Pireos 40, 104 37 Athens; tel. (21) 05295000; fax (21) 05249805; e-mail postmaster@www.labor-ministry.gr; internet www.labor-ministry.gr.

Ministry of Macedonia and Thrace: Administration Bldg, 541 23 Thessaloníki; tel. (231) 0264321; fax (231) 0263332; e-mail webmaster@mathra.gr; internet www.mathra.gr.

Ministry of Merchant Marine: Odos Gregoriou Lambraki 150, Piraeus; tel. (21) 04121211; fax (21) 04134286; e-mail yen@yen.gr; internet www.yen.gr.

Ministry of National Defence: Mesogion Pentagono, Athens; tel. (21) 06555911; fax (21) 06443832; e-mail epyetha@mod.gr; internet www.mod.gr.

Ministry of Press and Mass Media: Odos Zalokosta 10, 101 63 Athens; tel. (21) 03630911; fax (21) 03609682; e-mail press01@otenet.gr; internet www.minpress.gr.

Ministry of Public Order: P. Khanellopoulou 4, 101 77 Athens; tel. (21) 06977000; fax (21) 06921675; e-mail ydt@otenet.gr; internet www.ydt.gr.

Ministry of Transport and Communications: Odos Xenofontos 13, 101 91 Athens; tel. (21) 03251211; fax (21) 03239039; e-mail yme@otenet.gr; internet www.yme.gr.

Legislature

VOULI

Parliament

Parliament Bldg, Syntagma Sq., 101 80 Athens; tel. (21) 03288434; fax (21) 03310013; e-mail infopar@parliament.gr; internet www .parliament.gr.

President of the Vouli: APOSTOLOS KAKLAMANIS.

General Election, 9 April 2000

Parties	Seats	% of votes
Panhellenic Socialist Movement (PASOK)	158	43.8
New Democracy (ND)	125	42.7
Communist Party (KKE)	11	5.2
Coalition of the Left and Progress . . .	6	3.2
Democratic Social Movement (DHKKI). .	—	2.7
Others	—	2.4
Total	**300**	**100.0**

Political Organizations

Coalition of the Left and Progress (Synaspismos): Pl. Elefthrias 1, 105 53 Athens; tel. (21) 03378400; fax (21) 03217003; e-mail intrelations@syn.gr; internet www.syn.gr; f. 1989 as an alliance of the nine political groups comprising the Greek Left Party and the Communist Party of Greece ('of the Exterior'); in 1991 the conservative faction of the Communist Party withdrew from the alliance; however, the Coalition continued to command considerable support from the large reformist faction of the KKE; transformed into a single party in 1992; Pres. NIKOS KONSTANTOPOULOS.

Communist Party of Greece (KKE) (Kommunistiko Komma Ellados): Leoforos Irakliou 145, Perissos, 142 31 Athens; tel. (21) 02592111; fax (21) 02592286; e-mail cpg@kke.gr; internet www.kke .gr; f. 1918; banned 1947, reappeared 1974; Gen. Sec. ALEKA PAPARIGA.

Democratic Social Movement (DIKKI): Odos Halkokondili 9, 106 77 Athens; tel. (21) 03801712; fax (21) 03839047; e-mail dikki@ otenet.gr; internet www.dikki.gr; f. 1995; leftist party; opposes further integration with the EU; Leader DIMITRIS TSOVOLAS.

Democratic Socialist Party (KODISO): Odos Mavromichali 9, 106 79 Athens; tel. (21) 03602716; fax (21) 03625901; f. 1979 by former EDIK deputies; favours membership of the EU and political wing of NATO, decentralization and a mixed economy; Pres. CH. PROTOPAPAS.

Greek National Political Union (EPEN): Athens; tel. (21) 03643760; fax (21) 08943100; f. 1984; right-wing; Leader CHRYS-SANTHOS DIMITRIADIS.

Hellenic Liberal Party: Athens; tel. (21) 03606111; f. 1910; aims to revive political heritage of fmr Prime Minister, Eleftherios Venizelos; 6,500 mems; Pres. NIKITAS VENIZELOS.

Liberal Party: Athens; f. 1999; Founder STEFANOS MANOS.

New Democracy Party (ND) (Nea Dimokratia): Odos Rigillis 18, 106 74 Athens; tel. (21) 07290071; fax (21) 07214327; e-mail valinak@otenet.gr; internet www.neadimokratia.gr; f. 1974 by Konstantinos Karamanlis; a broadly-based centre-right party which advocates social reform in the framework of a liberal economy; supports European integration and enlargement; led and completed Greece's accession into the EU; Pres. Dr KONSTANTINOS AL. KARAMANLIS; Dir-Gen. IOANNIS VARTHOLOMEOS.

Panhellenic Socialist Movement (PASOK) (Panellinion Socialistikon Kinima): Odos Charilaou Trikoupi 50, Athens; tel. (21) 03232049; e-mail pasok@pasok.gr; internet www.pasok.gr; f. 1974; incorporates Democratic Defence and Panhellenic Liberation Movement resistance organizations; supports social welfare, decentralization and self-management, aims at a Mediterranean socialist development through international co-operation; 500 local organizations, 30,000 mems; Leader KONSTANTINOS (COSTAS) SIMITIS; Sec.-Gen. COSTAS LALIOTIS.

Political Spring (POLAN) (Politiki Anixi): Patision 67, 104 34 Athens; tel. (21) 08228301; fax (21) 08210531; e-mail anixi@otenet .gr; internet www.politikianixi.gr; f. 1993; centre-right; Leader ANTONIS C. SAMARAS.

Union of Democratic Centre Party (EDIK) (Enossi Dimokratikou Kentrou): Odos Charilaou Trikoupi 18, 106 79 Athens; tel. (21) 03609711; fax (21) 03612792; e-mail edik@edik.gr; internet www .edik.gr; f. 1974; democratic socialist party, merging Centre Union (f. 1961 by Georgios Papandreou) and New Political Forces (f. 1974 by

Prof. Ioannis Pesmazoglou and Prof. G. A. Mangakis); favours a united Europe; Chair. Prof. NEOKLIS SARRIS.

Other parties include the People's Militant Unity Party (f. 1985 by PASOK splinter group), the Progressive Party (f. 1979, right-wing), the (Maoist) Revolutionary Communist Party of Greece (EKKE), the Panhellenic Unaligned Party of Equality (PAKI, f. 1988; Leader KHARALAMBOS ALOMA TAMONTSIDES), Olympianism Party (pacifist, Leader GIORGIOS ZOE), and the left-wing United Socialist Alliance of Greece (ESPE, f. 1984).

Dissident organizations include the left-wing November 17 Revolutionary Organization (f. 1975; opposed to Western capitalism and the continuing existence of US military bases in Greece), the 1 May Revolutionary Organization, the Revolutionary People's Struggle (ELA), People's Revolutionary Solidarity, the Anti-State Struggle group, the Christos Tsoutsouvis Revolutionary Organization, the Revolutionary Praxis, Fighting Guerilla Faction and Autonomous Cells of Rebel Action.

Diplomatic Representation

EMBASSIES IN GREECE

Albania: Odos Karachristou 1, Kolonaki, 115 21 Athens; tel. (21) 07234412; fax (21) 07231972; Ambassador BASHKIM ZENELI.

Algeria: Leoforos Vassileos Konstantinou 14, 116 35 Athens; tel. (21) 07564191; fax (21) 07018681; e-mail ambdzath@otenet.gr; Ambassador KAMEL HOUHOU.

Argentina: Leoforos Vassilissis Sofias 59, Athens; tel. (21) 07224753; fax (21) 07227568; e-mail egrecmrs@compulink.gr; internet www.europanas.com/Argentina-Grecia-en.htm; Ambassador JORGE DE BELAUSTEGUI.

Armenia: Leoforos Sygrou 159, 171 21 Athens; tel. and fax (21) 09345727; e-mail armenia@hol.gr; Ambassador VAHRAN KAZGOIAN.

Australia: Odos Dimitriou Soutsou 37/Odos Tsoha 24, 115 21 Athens; tel. (21) 06447303; e-mail ausembgr@hol.gr; internet www .ausemb.gr; Ambassador ROSS BURNS.

Austria: Leoforos Alexandras 26, 106 83 Athens; tel. (21) 08257230; fax (21) 08219823; e-mail austria@ath.forthnet.gr; Ambassador Dr RENÉ POLLITZER.

Belgium: Odos Sekeri 3, 106 71 Athens; tel. (21) 03617886; fax (21) 03604289; e-mail athens@diplobel.org; Ambassador CLAUDE RIJMENANS.

Bosnia and Herzegovina: Hatzikosta 3, 115 21 Athens; tel. (21) 06411375; fax (21) 06423154.

Brazil: Plateia Philikis Etairias 14, 106 73 Athens; tel. (21) 07213039; Ambassador ALCIDES DA COSTA GUIMARÃES FILHO.

Bulgaria: Odos Stratigou Kallari 33A, Palaio Psychiko, 154 52 Athens; tel. (21) 06478105; fax (21) 06478130; Ambassador BRANIMIR PETROV.

Canada: Odos Ioannou Ghennadiou 4, 115 21 Athens; tel. (21) 07254011; fax (21) 07273460; e-mail athns@dfait-maeci.gc.ca; Ambassador DEREK R. T. FRASER.

Chile: Leoforos Vasilissis Sofias 25, 106 74 Athens; tel. (21) 07252574; fax (21) 07252536; e-mail embachilegr@ath.forthnet.gr; internet www.europanas.com/Chile-Grecia-en.htm; Ambassador MARCIA COVARRUBIAS.

China, People's Republic: Odos Krinon 2A, Paleo Psychiko, 154 52 Athens; tel. (21) 06723282; fax (21) 06723819; Ambassador TANG ZHENQI.

Colombia: Vrasida 3, 115 28 Athens; tel. (21) 07236848; fax (21) 07246270; Ambassador ENRIQUE GAVIRIA-LIEVANO.

Congo, Democratic Republic: Athens; tel. (21) 06847013; Ambassador BOMOLO LOKOKA.

Croatia: Tzavela 4, Neo Psychiko, 154 51 Athens; tel. (21) 06777059; fax (21) 06711208; e-mail croatemb@hol.gr; Ambassador DANIEL BUČAN.

Cuba: Odos Sofokleou 5, Filothei, 152 37 Athens; tel. (21) 06842807; fax (21) 06849590; Ambassador ANA MARÍA GONZÁLEZ SUÁREZ.

Cyprus: Odos Herodotou 16, 106 75 Athens; tel. (21) 07232727; fax (21) 07231927; e-mail cyempkl@hol.gr; Ambassador KHARALAMBOS CHRISTOFOROU.

Czech Republic: Odos Georgiou Seferis 6, Palaio Psychiko, 154 52 Athens; tel. (21) 06713755; fax (21) 06710675; e-mail athens@ embassy.mzv.cz; Ambassador VLADIMÍR ZAVÁZAL.

Denmark: Leoforos Vassilissis Sofias 11, 106 71 Athens; tel. (21) 03608315; fax (21) 03636163; e-mail athamb@athamb.um.dk; Ambassador HANS GRUNNET.

Egypt: Leoforos Vassilissis Sofias 3, 106 71 Athens; tel. (21) 03618612; fax (21) 03603538; e-mail emthens@hol.gr; Ambassador Dr MAGDA SHAHIN.

Estonia: Patriarchou Ioakeim 48, 106 76 Athens; tel. (21) 07229803; fax (21) 07229804; e-mail estemb@otenet.gr; Chargé d'affaires a.i. KATRIN KANARIK.

Finland: Odos Eratosthenous 1, 181 23 Athens; tel. (21) 07010444; fax (21) 07515064; e-mail sanomat.ate@formin.fi; Ambassador OLE NORRBACK (designate).

France: Leoforos Vassilissis Sofias 7, 106 71 Athens; tel. (21) 03391000; fax (21) 03391009; e-mail ambafran@hol.gr; internet www.ambafrance-gr.org; Ambassador JEAN-MAURICE RIPERT.

Georgia: Odos Agiou Dimitriou 24, 154 52 Paleo Psihio, Athens; tel. (21) 06716737; fax (21) 06716722; e-mail embassygeo@hol.gr; Ambassador ZVIAD CHUMBURIDZE.

Germany: Odos Karaoli and Dimitriou 3, 106 75 Athens; tel. (21) 07285111; fax (21) 07251205; e-mail info@germanembassy.gr; internet www.germanembassy.gr; Ambassador ALBERT SPIEGEL.

Holy See: POB 65075, Odos Mavili 2, Palaio Psychiko, 154 52 Athens; tel. (21) 06722728; fax (21) 06742849; e-mail nunate@mail .otenet.gr; Apostolic Nuncio Most Rev. PAUL FOUAD TABET (Titular Archbishop of Sinna).

Honduras: Leoforos Kifissias 74, 115 26 Athens; tel. (21) 06982021; fax (21) 06982080; e-mail hondugre@otenet.gr; Chargé d'affaires a.i. TEODOLINDA BANEGAS DE MAKRIS.

Hungary: Odos Kalvou 16, Palaio Psychiko, 154 52 Athens; tel. (21) 06725337; fax (21) 06740890; e-mail huembath@otenet.gr; Ambassador MÁRIA SZÉKELY.

India: Odos Kleanthous 3, 106 74 Athens; tel. (21) 07216227; fax (21) 07211252; e-mail indembassy@ath.forthnet.gr; Ambassador AFTAB SETH.

Indonesia: Odos Papanastasidu 55, Palaio Psychiko, 154 52 Athens; tel. (21) 06712737; fax (21) 06756955; Ambassador FRANCISCO LOPEZ DA CRUZ.

Iran: Odos Kalari 16, Palaio Psychiko, Athens; tel. (21) 06471436; Ambassador MAHDI KHANDAGH ABADI.

Iraq: Odos Mazaraki 4, Palaio Psychiko, Athens; tel. (21) 06715012; Ambassador FAROUKH AL-FIDYAN.

Ireland: Leoforos Vassileos 7, Konstantinou, Athens; tel. (21) 07232771; fax (21) 07240217; Ambassador MARGARET HENNESSY.

Israel: Odos Marathonodromou 1, Palaio Psychiko, 154 52 Athens; tel. (21) 06719530; fax (21) 06479510; Ambassador DAVID SASSON.

Italy: Odos Sekeri 2, 106 74 Athens; tel. (21) 03617260; fax (21) 03617330; e-mail ambaten@hol.gr; Ambassador AGOSTINO MATHIS.

Japan: 21st Floor, Athens A Tower, Leoforos Messoghion 2–4, Pirgas Athinon, 115 27 Athens; tel. (21) 07758101; fax (21) 07758206; Ambassador TOSHIO MOCHIZUKI.

Jordan: Odos Panagi Zervou 30, Palaio Psychiko, 154 10 Athens; tel. (21) 06474161; fax (21) 06470578; Ambassador AMJAD MAJALI.

Korea, Republic: Odos Eratosthenous 1, 116 35 Athens; tel. (21) 07012122; Ambassador TAE KYU HAN.

Kuwait: Odos Marathonodromou 27, Palaio Psychiko, 154 52 Athens; tel. (21) 06473593; fax (21) 06875875; Ambassador ALI FAHED AZ-ZAID.

Latvia: Odos Irodotou 9, Kolonaki, 106 74 Athens; tel. (21) 07294483; fax (21) 07294479; e-mail latvia@otenet.gr; Ambassador MARTINS LACIS.

Lebanon: 6, Odos Maritou 25, Palaio Psychiko, 154 52 Athens; tel. (21) 06755873; fax (21) 06755612; e-mail grlibemb@otenet.gr; Ambassador WILLIAM HABIB.

Libya: Odos Vironos 13, Palaio Psychiko, 154 52 Athens; tel. (21) 06472120; Secretary of the People's Bureau AYAD M. TAYARI.

Malta: Leoforos Vassilissis Sofias 63, 115 21 Athens; tel. (21) 07258153; fax (21) 07258152.

Mexico: Plateia Philikis Etairias 14, 106 73 Athens; tel. (21) 07294780; fax (21) 07294783; e-mail embgrecia@sre.gob.mx; Chargé d'affaires a.i. LUIS ALBERTO BARRERO-STAHL.

Morocco: Odos Mousson 14, Palaio Psychiko, 154 52 Athens; tel. (21) 06744209; fax (21) 06749480; Ambassador LOFTI AOUAD.

Netherlands: Leoforos Vassileos Konstantinou 5–7, 106 74 Athens; tel. (21) 07239701; fax (21) 07248900; e-mail ath@minbuza.gr; internet www.dutchembassy.gr/; Ambassador P. R. BROUWER.

New Zealand: Leoforos Kifissias 268, 152 32 Halandri, Athens; tel. (21) 06874700; fax (21) 06874444; e-mail costas.cotsilinis@gr .pwcglobal.com; Ambassador PETER BENNETT.

Nicaragua: Leoforos Syggrou 206, Athens; tel. (21) 09585064.

Nigeria: Odos Iakinthon 50, Palaio Psychiko, Athens; tel. (21) 06718007; fax (21) 06718008; Ambassador FRANKLIN NCHITA OGBUEWU.

Norway: Leoforos Vassilissis Sofias 23, 106 74 Athens; tel. (21) 07246173; fax (21) 07244989; e-mail norwemba@netplan.gr; Ambassador JAN WESSEL HEGG.

Pakistan: Odos Loukianou 6, Kolonaki, 106 75 Athens; tel. (21) 07290122; fax (21) 07257641; e-mail info@pak-embassy.gr; internet www.pak-embassy.gr; Ambassador JAVED HAFIZ.

Panama: Akti Miaoyli 23, Athens; tel. (21) 04133180.

Paraguay: Odos Alopekis 2, 106 75 Athens; tel. (21) 07210669; internet www.europanas.com/Paraguay-Grecia-en.htm.

Peru: Semitelou 2, 115 28, Athens; tel. (21) 07792761; fax (21) 07792905; e-mail lepruate@compulink.gr; Ambassador BERTHA VEGA PÉREZ.

Philippines: Xenophodos 9, Athens; tel. (21) 03241615; Ambassador LOURDES G. MORALES.

Poland: Odos Chryssanthemon 22, Palaio Psychiko, 154 52 Athens; tel. (21) 06778260; fax (21) 06718394; e-mail atenyamb@internet.gr; internet www.poland-embassy.gr; Ambassador GRZEGORZ DZIEMIDOWICZ.

Portugal: Leoforos Vassilissis Sofias 23, 106 74 Athens; tel. (21) 07290096; fax (21) 07245122; e-mail embportg@otenet.gr; Ambassador ANTÓNIO SYDER SANTIAGO.

Romania: Odos Emmanuel Benaki 7, Palaio Psychiko, Athens; tel. (21) 06728875; fax (21) 06728883; e-mail roumaniaembassy@ath .forthnet.gr; Ambassador CAIUS TRÀIAN DRAGOMIR.

Russia: Odos Nikiforou Litra 28, Palaio Psychiko, 154 52 Athens; tel. (21) 06725235; fax (21) 06479708; Ambassador MIKHAIL BOCHARNIKOV.

Saudi Arabia: Odos Marathonodromou 71, Palaio Psychiko, 154 52 Athens; tel. (21) 06716911; Ambassador Sheikh ABDULLAH ABDULRAHMAN AL-MALHOOQ.

Serbia and Montenegro: Leoforos Vassilissis Sofias 106, Athens; tel. (21) 07774344; Ambassador DRAGMIR VUČIĆEVIĆ.

Slovakia: Odos Georgiou Seferis 4, Palaio Psychiko, 154 52 Athens; tel. (21) 06776757; fax (21) 06776760; e-mail zuateny@compulink.gr; Ambassador JAROSLAV CHLEBO.

South Africa: Leoforos Kifissias 60, 151 25 Athens; tel. (21) 06106645; fax (21) 06106640; e-mail embassy@southafrica.gr; internet www.southafrica.gr; Ambassador JANNIE MOMBERG.

Spain: Odos D. Areapagitou 21, 117 42 Athens; tel. (21) 09213123; fax (21) 09214264; e-mail emb-esp@otenet.gr; Ambassador JAVIER JIMÉNEZ-UGARTE.

Sweden: Leoforos Vassileos Konstantinou 7, 106 74 Athens; tel. (21) 07290421; fax (21) 07229953; e-mail ambassaden.athens@foreign .ministry.se; Ambassador BJÖRN ELMÉR.

Switzerland: Odos Iassiou 2, 115 21 Athens; tel. (21) 07230364; fax (21) 07299471; e-mail vertretung@ath.rep.admin.ch; Ambassador MARIA LUISA CARONI.

Syria: Odos Marathonodromou 79, Palaio Psychiko, Athens; tel. (21) 06725577; Ambassador SHAHIN FARAH.

Thailand: Odos Taigetou 23, Palaio Psychiko, 154 52 Athens; tel. (21) 06717969; fax (21) 06479508; Ambassador SUKHUM RASMIDATTA.

Tunisia: Odos Anthéon 2, Palaio Psychiko, 154 52 Athens; tel. (21) 06717590; fax (21) 06713432; e-mail tunisie@otenet.gr; Ambassador MUHAMMAD BACHROUCH.

Turkey: Odos Vassileos Gheorghiou B 8, 106 74 Athens; tel. (21) 07245915; fax (21) 07229597; e-mail turkembgr@hol.gr; Ambassador YIGIT ALPOGAN.

Ukraine: Odos Stefanu Delta 2–4, 152 37 Athens; tel. (21) 06718957; fax (21) 06855363; e-mail ukrembas@otenet.gr.

United Kingdom: Odos Ploutarchou 1, 106 75 Athens; tel. (21) 07272600; fax (21) 07272734; e-mail britania@hol.gr; internet www .british-embassy.gr; Ambassador DAVID MADDEN.

USA: Leoforos Vassilissis Sofias 91, 106 60 Athens; tel. (21) 07212951; fax (21) 07226724; e-mail usembassy@usembassy.gr; internet www.usembassy.gr; Ambassador THOMAS J. MILLER.

Uruguay: Odos Likavitou I G, 106 72 Athens; tel. (21) 03613549; Ambassador ULYSSES PEREIRA REVERBEL.

Venezuela: Leoforos Vassilissis, Sophias 112, Athens; tel. (21) 07708769; Ambassador OLGA LUCILA CARMONA.

Judicial System

The Constitution of 1975 provided for the establishment of a Special Supreme Tribunal. Other provisions in the Constitution provided for a reorganization of parts of the judicial system to be accomplished through legislation.

SUPREME ADMINISTRATIVE COURTS

Special Supreme Tribunal: Odos Patision 30, Athens; has final jurisdiction in matters of constitutionality.

Council of State

Odos Panepistimiou 47, 105 64 Athens; tel. (21) 03223830; fax (21) 03231154.

has appellate powers over acts of the administration and final rulings of administrative courts; has power to rule upon matters of judicial review of laws.

President: Vassilis Botopoulos.

SUPREME JUDICIAL COURT

Supreme Civil and Penal Court

Leoforos Alexandros 121, 115 22 Athens; tel. (21) 06411506; fax (21) 06433799; e-mail areios@otenet.gr.

Supreme court in the State, having also appellate powers; consists of six sections, four Civil and two Penal, and adjudicates in quorum.

President: Stephanos Mathias.

COURTS OF APPEAL

There are 12 Courts of Appeal with jurisdiction in cases of Civil and Penal Law of second degree, and, in exceptional penal cases, of first degree.

COURTS OF FIRST INSTANCE

There are 59 Courts of First Instance with jurisdiction in cases of first degree, and in exceptional cases, of second degree. They function both as Courts of First Instance and as Criminal Courts. For serious crimes the Criminal Courts function with a jury.

In towns where Courts of First Instance sit there are also Juvenile Courts. Commercial Tribunals do not function in Greece, and all commercial cases are tried by ordinary courts of law. There are, however, Tax Courts in some towns.

OTHER COURTS

There are 360 Courts of the Justice of Peace throughout the country. There are 48 Magistrates' Courts (or simple Police Courts).

In all the above courts, except those of the Justice of Peace, there are District Attorneys. In Courts of the Justice of Peace the duties of District Attorney are performed by the Public Prosecutor.

Religion

CHRISTIANITY

The Eastern Orthodox Church

The Orthodox Church of Greece

Odos Ioannou Gennadiou 14, 115 21 Athens; tel. (21) 07218381.

f. 1850; 78 dioceses, 8,335 priests, 84 bishops, 9,025,000 adherents (1985)

The Greek branch of the Holy Eastern Orthodox Church is the officially established religion of the country, to which nearly 97% of the population profess adherence. The administrative body of the Church is the Holy Synod of 12 members, elected by the bishops of the Hierarchy.

Primate of Greece: Archbishop of Athens Christodoulos.

Within the Greek State there is also the semi-autonomous Church of Crete, composed of seven Metropolitans and the Holy Archbishopric of Crete. The Church is administered by a Synod consisting of the seven Metropolitans under the Presidency of the Archbishop; it is under the spiritual jurisdiction of the Ecumenical Patriarchate of Constantinople (based in İstanbul, Turkey), which also maintains a degree of administrative control.

Archbishop of Crete: Archbishop Timotheos (whose See is in Heraklion).

There are also four Metropolitan Sees of the Dodecanese, which are spiritually and administratively dependent on the Ecumenical Patriarchate and, finally, the peninsula of Athos, which constitutes the region of the Holy Mountain (Mount Athos) and comprises 20 monasteries. These are dependent on the Ecumenical Patriarchate

of Constantinople, but are autonomous and are safeguarded constitutionally.

The Roman Catholic Church

Latin Rite

Greece comprises four archdioceses (including two directly responsible to the Holy See), four dioceses and one Apostolic Vicariate. At 31 December 2000 there were an estimated 52,063 adherents in the country.

Bishop's Conference: Conferentia Episcopalis Graeciae, Odos Homirou 9, 106 72 Athens; tel. (21) 03624311; fax (21) 03618632; f. 1967; Pres. Most Rev. Nikolaos Fóskolos (Archbishop of Athens).

Archdiocese of Athens: Archbishopric, Odos Homirou 9, 106 72 Athens; tel. (21) 03624311; fax (21) 03618632; Archbishop Most Rev. Nikolaos Fóskolos.

Archdiocese of Rhodes: Archbishopric, Odos I. Dragoumi 5A, 851 00 Rhodes; tel. (2241) 021845; fax (2241) 026688; Apostolic Administrator Most Rev. Nikolaos Fóskolos (Archbishop of Athens).

Metropolitan Archdiocese of Corfu, Zante and Cefalonia: Archbishopric, Montzenikhov 3, 491 00 Kerkyra; tel. and fax (2661) 030277; Archbishop Mgr Antonios Varthalitis.

Metropolitan Archdiocese of Naxos, Andros, Tinos and Mykonos: Archbishopric, 842 00 Tinos; tel. (2283) 022382; fax (2283) 024769; e-mail karcntam@thn.forthnet.gr; also responsible for the suffragan diocese of Chios; Archbishop Mgr Nikolaos Printesis.

Apostolic Vicariate of Salonika (Thessaloníki): Leoforos Vassilissis Olgas 120B, 546 45 Thessaloníki; tel. (231) 0835780; Apostolic Administrator Archbishop Mgr of Corfu Antonios Varthalitis.

Byzantine Rite

Apostolic Exarchate for the Byzantine Rite in Greece: Odos Akarnon 246, 112 53 Athens; tel. (21) 08670170; fax (21) 08677039; e-mail grcathex@hol.gr; 2 parishes (Athens and Jannitsa, Macedonia); 7 secular priests, 2,300 adherents (31 Dec. 1999); Exarch Apostolic Mgr Anarghyros Printesis (Titular Bishop of Gratianopolis).

Armenian Rite

Exarchate for the Armenian Catholics in Greece: Odos René Piot 2, 117 44 Athens; tel. (21) 09014089; fax (21) 09012109; 550 adherents (31 Dec. 1999); Exarch Archpriest Nichan Karakeheyan.

Protestant Church

Greek Evangelical Church (Reformed): Odos Markon Botsari 24, 117 41 Athens; tel. (21) 09222684; e-mail info@gec.gr; internet www.gec.gr; f. 1858; comprises 30 organized churches; 5,000 adherents (1996); Moderator Rev. Meletis Meletiadis.

ISLAM

The law provides as religious head of the Muslims a Chief Mufti; the Muslims in Greece possess a number of mosques and schools.

JUDAISM

The Jewish population of Greece, estimated in 1943 at 75,000 people, was severely reduced as a result of the German occupation. In 1994 there were about 5,000 Jews in Greece.

Central Board of the Jewish Communities of Greece: Odos Voulis 36, 105 57 Athens; tel. (21) 03244315; fax (21) 03313852; e-mail info@kis.gr; internet www.kis.gr; f. 1945; officially recognized representative body of the communities of Greece; Pres. Moses Konstantinis.

Jewish Community of Athens: Odos Melidoni 8, 105 53 Athens; tel. (21) 03252823; fax (21) 03220761; e-mail isrkath@hellasnet.gr; Rabbi Jacob D. Arar.

Jewish Community of Larissa: Odos Kentavrou 27, Larissa; tel. (241) 0220762; Rabbi Elie Sabetai.

Jewish Community of Thessaloníki: Odos Tsimiski 24, 546 24 Thessaloníki; tel. (231) 0275701; e-mail jct1@compulink.gr; internet www.jct.gr; Pres. David Saltiel; Rabbi Uri Buskilla.

The Press

PRINCIPAL DAILY NEWSPAPERS

Morning papers are not published on Mondays, nor afternoon papers on Sundays. Afternoon papers are more popular than morning ones. In 1997 there were 122 daily newspaper titles.

Athens

Acropolis: Leoforos Ionias 166, 111 44 Athens; tel. and fax (21) 02114594; f. 1881; morning; Independent-Conservative; Acropolis Publications SA; Publr G. LEVIDES; Dir MARNIS SKOUNDRIDAKIS; circ. 50,819.

Apogevmatini (The Afternoon): Odos Phidiou 12, 106 78 Athens; tel. (21) 06430011; fax (21) 03609876; f. 1956; independent; Publr GEORGIOS HATZIKONSTANTINOU; Editor P. KARAYANNIS; circ. 67,257.

Athens Daily Post: Odos Stadiou 57, Athens; tel. (21) 03249504; f. 1952; morning; English; Owner G. SKOURAS.

Athens News: Odos Christou Lada 3, 102 37 Athens; tel. (21) 03333161; fax (21) 03231384; e-mail athnews@dolnet.gr; internet athensnews.dolnet.gr; f. 1952; morning; English; Publr CHRISTOS D. LAMBRAKIS; circ. 6,500.

Athlitiki Icho (Athletics Echo): Odos Aristonos 5-7, 104 41 Athens; tel. (21) 05232201; fax (21) 05232433; f. 1945; morning; Editor K. GEORGALAS; circ. 40,000.

Avgi (Dawn): Odos Ag. Konstantiou 12, 104 31 Athens; tel. (21) 05231831; fax (21) 05231830; e-mail editors@telephos.gr; internet www.avgi.org/nea-avgi/main_page.asp; f. 1952; morning; independent newspaper of the left; Dir and Editor L. VOUTSAS; circ. 5,400.

Avriani (Tomorrow): Odos Dimitros 11, 177 78 Athens; tel. (21) 03424090; fax (21) 03452190; f. 1980; evening; Publr GEORGE KOURIS; circ. 51,317.

Dimokratikos Logos (Democratic Speech): Odos Dimitros 11, 177 78 Athens; tel. (21) 03424023; fax (21) 03452190; f. 1986; morning; Dir and Editor KOSTAS GERONIKOLOS; circ. 7,183.

Eleftheri Ora: Odos Akademias 32, 106 72 Athens; tel. (21) 03621868; fax (21) 03603258; f. 1981; evening; Editor G. MIHALO-POULOS; circ. 1,026.

Eleftheros Typos (Free Press): Iroos Matsi, Ano Kalamaki, Athens; tel. (21) 09942431; f. 1983; evening; Dir and Editor CH. PASALARIS; circ. 167,186.

Eleftherotypia (Press Freedom): Odos Minoou 10–16, 117 43 Athens; tel. (21) 09296001; fax (21) 09028311; internet www.enet.gr/online/online_p1.jsp; f. 1974; evening; Publr CHR. TEGOPOULOS; Dir S. FYNDANIDIS; circ. 115,000.

Estia (Vesta): Odos Anthimou Gazi 7, 105 61 Athens; tel. (21) 03230650; fax (21) 03243071; e-mail estianews@otenet.gr; f. 1894; afternoon; Publr and Editor KOINONIA ASTIKOU DIKAIOU; circ. 60,000.

Ethnos (Nation): Odos Benaki 152, Metamorfosi Chalandriou, 152 35 Athens; tel. (21) 06580640; fax (21) 06396515; internet www .ethnos.gr; f. 1981; evening; Publr GEORGE BOBOLAS; Dir TH. KALOUDIS; circ. 84,735.

Express: Odos Halandriou 39, Paradissos Amaroussiou, 151 25 Athens; tel. (21) 06850200; fax (21) 06852202; internet www.kapatel .gr/express; f. 1963; morning; financial; Publr Hellenews Publications; Editor D. G. KALOFOLIAS; circ. 28,000.

Filathlos: Odos Dimitros 11, 177 78 Athens; tel. (21) 03424090; f. 1982; morning; Dir NICK KARAGIANNIDIS; Publr and Editor G. A. KOURIS; circ. 40,000.

Imerissia (Daily): Odos Benaki & Ag. Nektariou, Metamorfosi Chalandriou, 152 35 Athens; tel. (21) 06061729; fax (21) 06016563; e-mail imerissia@pegasus.gr; internet www.pegasus.gr; f. 1947; morning; Publr PETROS ANTONIADIS; Man. Editor ANONIS DALIPIS; circ. 26,000.

Kathimerini (Every Day): Ethnarchou Makariou 185–47 & Odos Falireos 2, Athens; tel. (21) 04808000; fax (21) 04808202; e-mail kathi-editor@ekathimerini.com; internet www.kathimerini.gr; f. 1919; morning; Conservative; Editor THEMISTODIS ALAFOUZOS; circ. 34,085.

Kerdos (Profit): Leoforos Kifissias 178, Halandri, 152 31 Athens; tel. (21) 06747881; fax (21) 06747893; e-mail mail@kerdos.gr; internet www.kerdos.gr; f. 1985; morning; Publr and Man. Editor VASILIS VALAMVANOS; circ. 18,000.

Messimvrini (Midday): El Venizelou 10, 106 71 Athens; tel. (21) 03646019; fax (21) 03636125; f. 1980; evening; Publr and Dir PANOS LOUKAKOS; circ. 17,451.

Naftemporiki (Daily Journal): Odos Lenorman 205, 104 42 Athens; tel. (21) 05198000; fax (21) 05146013; internet www.naftemporiki .gr; f. 1924; morning; non-political journal of finance, commerce and shipping; Dir M. ATHANASSIADIS; circ. 35,000.

Ora Gia Spor (Time for Sport): Athens; tel. (21) 09251200; fax (21) 09226167; f. 1991; sport; Editor EVANGELOS SEMBOS.

Rizospastis (Radical): Odos Irakliou 145, Perissos, 142 31 Athens; tel. (21) 02522002; fax (21) 02529480; internet www.rizospastis.gr/wwwengine; f. 1974; morning; pro-Soviet communist; Dir T. TSIGAS; Editor G. TRIKALINOS; circ. 28,740.

Ta Nea (News): Odos Christou Lada 3, 102 37 Athens; tel. (21) 03250611; fax (21) 03228797; internet ta-nea.dolnet.gr; f. 1944; liberal; evening; Dir L. KARAPANAYIOTIS; Editor CHRISTOS LAMBRAKIS; circ. 135,000.

Vradyni (Evening Press): Athens; tel. (21) 05231001; f. 1923; evening; right-wing; Gen. Man. H. ATHANASIADOU; circ. 71,914.

Patras

Peloponnesos: Maizonos 206, 262 22 Patras; tel. (261) 0312530; fax (261) 0312535; f. 1886; independent conservative; Publr and Editor S. DOUKAS; circ. 7,000.

Thessaloníki

Ellinikos Vorras (Greek North): Odos Grammou-Vitsi 19, 551 34 Thessaloníki; tel. (231) 0416621; f. 1935; morning; Publr TESSA LEVANTIS; Dir N. MERGIOS; circ. 14,467.

Thessaloníki: Odos Monastiriou 85, 546 27 Thessaloníki; tel. (231) 0521621; f. 1963; evening; Propr Publishing Co of Northern Greece SA; Dir LAZAROS HADJINAKOS; Editor KATERINA VELLIDI; circ. 36,040.

SELECTED PERIODICALS

Agora (Market): Leoforos Kifissias 178, Halandri, 151 31 Athens; tel. (21) 06473384; fax (21) 06477893; f. 1987; fortnightly; politics, finance; Dir ANT. KEFALAS; circ. 20,000.

Aktines: Odos Karytsi 14, 105 61 Athens; tel. (21) 03235023; f. 1938; monthly; current affairs, science, philosophy, arts; aims to promote a Christian civilization; Publr Christian Union; circ. 10,000.

Athèmes: Athens; monthly; French; cultural; Chief Editor EMMA-NUEL ADELY; circ. 5,000.

The Athenian: Athens; tel. (21) 03222802; fax (21) 03223052; e-mail the-athenian@hol.gr; internet www.hol.gr; f. 1974; monthly; English; Publr KONSTANTINOS GEROU; Editor JOANNA STAVROPOULOS; circ. 14,000.

Auto Express: Odos Halandriou 39, Halandri, 152 32 Athens; tel. (21) 06816906; fax (21) 06825858; Dir D. KALOFOLIAS; circ. 18,828.

Computer Gia Olous (Computers for All): Leoforos Syngrou 44, 117 42 Kallithea, Athens; tel. (21) 09238672; fax (21) 09216847; monthly; Editor GEORGE CHRISTOPOULOS.

Deltion Diikiseos Epichiriseon Euro-Unial (Business Administration Bulletin Euro-Unial): Odos Rhigillis 26, 106 74 Athens; tel. (21) 07235736; fax (21) 07240000; e-mail busadmibul@otenet.gr; monthly; Editor I. PAPAMICHALAKIS; circ. 26,000.

Demosiografiki (Journalism): Procopiou 7–9, 171 24 Athens; tel. (21) 09731338; e-mail harrynic@yahoo.com; f. 1987; quarterly; Dir JOHN MENOÚNOS; circ. 4,000.

Ekonomicos Tachydromos (Financial Courier): Odos Christou Lada 3, 102 37 Athens; tel. (21) 03333630; fax (21) 03238740; e-mail oikonomikos@dolnet.gr; f. 1926; weekly; illustrated magazine; Man. Editor NIKOS NIKOLAOU; circ. 23,000.

Elle: Odos Kleisthenous 213, 153 44 Athens; tel. (21) 06062531; fax (21) 06062648; e-mail magelle@compulink.gr; f. 1988; monthly; women's magazine; Editor FLORA TZIMAKA; circ. 57,120 (1997).

Epiloghi: Odos Stadiou 4, 105 64 Athens; tel. (21) 03238427; fax (21) 03235160; e-mail epilogi@mail.hol.gr; f. 1962; weekly; economics; Editor GEORGE MALOUHOS.

Greece's Weekly for Business and Finance: Athens; tel. (21) 07707280; weekly; English; finance; Dir V. KORONAKIS.

Gynaika (Women): Odos Fragoklissias 7, Marousi, 151 25 Athens; tel. (21) 06199149; fax (21) 06104707; f. 1950; monthly; fashion, beauty, cookery, social problems, news; Publr CHRISTOS TERZOPOULOS; circ. 45,000.

Hellenews: Odos Halandriou 39, Marousi, 151 25 Athens; tel. (21) 06199400; fax (21) 06199421; e-mail alexm@express.kapatel.gr; weekly; English; finance and business; Publr Hellenews Publications; Editor J. M. GERMANOS.

Idaniko Spiti (Ideal Home): Odos St Nectarios, 152 35 Athens; tel. (1) 06061777; fax (1) 06011044; e-mail pa@pegasus.gr; internet www .idanikospiti.gr; f. 1990; monthly; interior decoration; Editor PETROS ANTONIADIS; circ. 60,000 (2002).

Klik: Odos Fragoklisias 7, 151 25 Athens; tel. (21) 06897945; fax (21) 06899153; internet www.klik.gr; f. 1987; monthly; popular music, media and fashion; Editor PETROS COSTOPOULOS.

Marie Claire: Odos Stadiou 24, 105 64 Athens; tel. (21) 03333654; fax (21) 03227770; e-mail marieclaire@dolnet.gr; monthly; women's magazine.

Men: Odos Fragoklisias 7, 151 25 Athens; tel. (21) 06826680; fax (21) 06824730; internet www.men.gr/index.htm; six a year; men's fashion and general interest.

Oikonomiki Viomichaniki Epitheorissis (Industrial Review): Odos Zalokosta 4, 106 71 Athens; tel. (21) 03626360; fax (21) 03626388; e-mail editor@oikonomiki.gr; internet www.oikonomiki .gr; f. 1934; monthly; industrial and economic review; Publr A. C. VOVOLINI-LASKARIDIS; Editor D. KARAMANOS; circ. 25,000.

48 Ores (48 Hours): Leoforos Alexandras 19, 114 73 Athens; tel. (21) 06430313; fax (21) 06461361; weekly; Dir and Editor SP. KARATZAFERIS; circ. 9,127.

Pantheon: Odos Christou Lada 3, 102 37 Athens; tel. (21) 03230221; fax (21) 03228797; every two weeks; Publr and Dir N. THEOFANIDES; circ. 23,041.

Politika Themata: Odos Ypsilantou 25, 106 75 Athens; tel. (21) 07218421; weekly; Publr J. CHORN; Dir C. KYRKOS; circ. 2,544.

Pontiki (Mouse): Odos Massalias 10, 106 81 Athens; tel. (21) 03609531; weekly; humour; Dir and Editor K. PAPAIOANNOU.

Ptisi (Flight and Space): Odos Helioupoleos 2–4, 172 37 Athens; tel. (21) 09792500; fax (21) 09792528; e-mail tpress@techlink.gr; internet www.techlink.gr; f. 1975; monthly; Editor COSTAS CAVATHAS; circ. 68,000 (1997).

Radiotileorassi (Radio-TV): Odos Mourouzi 16, 106 74 Athens; tel. (21) 07224811; weekly; circ. 134,626.

Technika Chronika (Technical Times): Odos Karageorgi Servias 4, 105 62 Athens; tel. (21) 03234751; f. 1952; monthly; general edition on technical and economic subjects; Editor D. ROKOS; circ. 12,000.

Tilerama: Odos Voukourestiou 18, 106 71 Athens; tel. (21) 03607160; fax (21) 03607032; f. 1977; weekly; radio and television; circ. 189,406.

To Vima (Tribune): Odos Christou Lada 3, 102 37 Athens; tel. (21) 03333103; fax (21) 03239097; f. 1922; weekly; liberal; Dir and Editor STAVROS R. PSYCHARIS; circ. 250,000.

La Tribune héllenique: Athens; every two months; French; politics, economics; Dir THEODORE BENAKIS; circ. 3,000.

NEWS AGENCIES

Athens News Agency (ANA): Odos Tsoha 36, 115 21 Athens; tel. (21) 06400560; fax (21) 06400581; e-mail ape@ana.gr; internet www .ana.gr; f. 1895; correspondents in leading capitals of the world and towns throughout Greece; Man. Dir NIKOLAS VOULELIS; Gen. Dir ANDREAS CHRISTODOULIDES.

Foreign Bureaux

Agence France-Presse (AFP): Athens; tel. (21) 03633388; Bureau Chief JEAN-PIERRE ALTIER.

Agencia EFE: Athens; tel. (21) 03635826; Bureau Chief D. MARÍA-LUISA RUBIO; Correspondent JUAN JOSÉ FERNÁNDEZ ELORRIAGA.

Agenzia Nazionale Stampa Associata (ANSA): Odos Kanari 9, 106 71 Athens; tel. (21) 03605285; fax (21) 03635367; Correspondent FRANCESCO INDRACCOLO.

Associated Press (AP): Leoforos Amalias 52, 105 52 Athens; tel. (21) 03310802; fax (21) 03310804.

Deutsche Presse-Agentur (dpa): Miniati 1, 116 36 Athens; tel. (21) 09247774; fax (21) 09222185; Correspondent HILDEGARD HÜLSENBECK.

Dow Jones Newswire: Leoforos Amalias 52, 105 58 Athens; tel. (21) 07248496; fax (21) 03313180.

Informatsionnoye Telegrafnoye Agentstvo Rossii—Telegrafnoye Agentstvo Suverennykh Stran (ITAR—TASS): Odos Gizi 39, Palaio Psychiko, 15 452 Athens; tel. and fax (21) 06713069; Bureau Chief VLADIMIR V. MALYSHEV.

Reuters Hellas SA: 7th Floor, Kolokotroni 1/Leoforos Stadiou, 105 62 Athens; tel. (21) 03647610; fax (21) 03604490; Man. Dir WILLIAM CAIRLEY.

Rossiiskoye Informatsionnoye Agentstvo—Novosti (RIA—Novosti): Odos Irodotou 9, 138 Athens; tel. (21) 07291016; Bureau Chief BORIS KOROLYOV; Correspondent J. KURIZIN.

Xinhua (New China) News Agency: Odos Amarilidos 19, Palaio Psychiko, Athens; tel. (21) 06724997; Bureau Chief XIE CHENGHAO.

PRESS ASSOCIATIONS

Enosis Antapokriton Xenou Tipou (Foreign Press Association of Greece): Odos Akademias 23, 106 71 Athens; tel. (21) 03637318; fax (21) 03605035.

Enosis Syntakton Imerission Ephimeridon Athinon (Journalists' Union of Athens Daily Newspapers): Odos Akademias 20, 106 71 Athens; tel. (21) 03632601; fax (21) 03632608; f. 1914; Pres.

DIMITRIOS MATHIOPOULOS; Gen. Sec. MANOLIS MATHIOUDAKIS; 1,400 mems.

Enosis Syntakton Periodikou Tipou (Journalists' Union of the Periodical Press): Odos Valaoritou 9, 106 71 Athens; tel. (21) 03633427; fax (21) 03638627; e-mail espt@otenet.gr; internet www .magazinepress.gr; Pres. ATHENESE PAPANDROPOULOS; 650 mems.

Publishers

Agkyra Publications: Leoforos Kifisou 85, Egaleo, 122 41 Athens; tel. (21) 03455276; fax (21) 03474732; f. 1890; general; Man. Dir DIMITRIOS PAPADIMITRIOU.

Akritas: Odos Efessou 24, 171 21 Athens; tel. (21) 09334554; fax (21) 09311436; e-mail akritaspublications@ath.forthnet.gr; f. 1979; history, spirituality, children's books.

D. I. Arsenidis & Co: Odos Akademias 57, 106 79 Athens; tel. (21) 03629538; fax (21) 03618707; biography, literature, children's books, history, philosophy, social sciences; Man. Dir JOHN ARSENIDIS.

Boukoumanis Editions: Odos Mavromichali 1, 106 79 Athens; tel. (21) 03618502; fax (21) 03630669; f. 1967; history, politics, sociology, psychology, belles-lettres, educational, arts, children's books, ecology; Man. ELIAS BOUKOUMANIS.

Dorikos Publishing House: Odos Charalabou Sotiriou 9–11, 114 72 Athens; tel. (21) 06454726; fax (21) 03301866; f. 1958; literature, fiction, history, politics; Editor ROUSSOS VRANAS.

Ekdotike Athenon SA: Odos Academias 34, 106 72 Athens; tel. (21) 03608911; fax (21) 03606157; e-mail ekdath@aias.gr; f. 1961; history, archaeology, art; Pres. GEORGE A. CHRISTOPOULOS.

G. C. Eleftheroudakis SA: Odos Panepistimiou 17, 105 64 Athens; tel. (21) 03314180; fax (21) 03239821; e-mail elebooks@netor.gr; f. 1915; general, technical and scientific; Man. Dir VIRGINIA ELEFTHEROUDAKI-GREGOU.

Exandas Publrs: Odos Didotou 57, 106 81 Athens; tel. (21) 03804885; fax (21) 03813065; e-mail info@exandasbooks.gr; internet www.exandasbooks.gr; f. 1974; fiction, literature, social sciences; Pres. MAGDA N. KOTZIA.

Govostis Publishing SA: Zoodohou Pigis 21, 106 81 Athens; tel. (21) 03815433; fax (21) 03816661; e-mail cotsos@compulink.gr; f. 1926; arts, fiction, politics; Pres. COSTAS GOVOSTIS.

Denise Harvey: Katounia, 340 05 Limni, Evia; tel. and fax (2227) 031154; e-mail denise@teledomenet.gr; f. 1972; modern Greek literature and poetry, belles-lettres, theology, translations, selected general list (English and Greek); Man. Dir DENISE HARVEY.

Hestia-I.D. Kollaros & Co SA: Odos Solonos 60, 106 72 Athens; tel. (21) 03615077; fax (21) 03606759; f. 1885; literature, history, politics, architecture, philosophy, travel, religion, psychology, textbooks, general; Gen. Dir MARINA KARAITIDIS.

Kastaniotis Editions SA: Odos Zalogou 11, 106 78 Athens; tel. (21) 03301208; fax (21) 03822530; e-mail info@kastaniotis.com; internet www.kastaniotis.com; f. 1969; fiction and non-fiction, including arts, social sciences and psychology, children's books; Man. Dir ATHANASIOS KASTANIOTIS.

Kritiki Publishing: Odos Koletti 25, 106 77 Athens; tel. (21) 03803730; fax (21) 03803740; e-mail biblia@kritiki.gr; internet www .kritiki.gr; f. 1987; economics, politics, literature, philosophy, business/management, popular science; Pres. THEMIS MINOGLOU.

Kronos: Odos Egnatia 33, 546 26 Thessaloníki; tel. (231) 0532077; fax (231) 0538158; Dir TH. GIOTAS.

Lambrakis Press SA: Odos Christou Lada 3, 102 37 Athens; tel. (21) 03333555; fax (21) 03228797; internet www.dolnet.gr; newspapers and magazines; 18 titles.

Livani Publishing Org.: Odos Solonos 98, 106 80 Athens; tel. (21) 03610589; fax (21) 03617791; e-mail glykeria@livanis.gr; general; Publr A. A. LIVANI.

Minoas SA: Odos Posseidonos 1, 141 21 N. Iraklio, Athens; tel. (21) 02711222; fax (21) 02711056; e-mail info@minoas.gr; internet www .minoas.gr; f. 1952; fiction, art, history; Man. Dir IOANNIS KONSTANTAROPOULOS.

Odos Panos: Odos Didotou 39, 106 08 Athens; tel. and fax (21) 03616782; internet www.odospanos-cigaret.gr; poetry, drama, biography.

Papazissis Publishers: Nikitara 2, 106 78 Athens; tel. (21) 03822496; fax (21) 03809150; e-mail papazisi@otenet.gr; internet www.papzisi.gr; f. 1929; economics, politics, law, history, school books; Man. Dir VICTOR PAPAZISSIS.

Patakis Publications: Odos Valtetsiou 14, 106 80 Athens; tel. (21) 03638362; fax (21) 03628950; art, reference, literature, educational, philosophy, psychology, sociology, religion, music, children's books, educational toys, CD-Rom and audiobooks; Pres. STEFANOS PATAKIS.

Pontiki Publications SA: Odos Massalias 10, 106 80 Athens; tel. (21) 03609531; fax (21) 03645406; f. 1979; govt, history, political science; Man. Dir KOSTAS TABANIS.

John Sideris: Odos Stadiou 44, 105 64 Athens; tel. (21) 03229638; fax (21) 03245052; f. 1898; school textbooks, general; Man. J. SIDERIS.

J. G. Vassiliou: Odos Hippokratous 15, 106 79 Athens; tel. (21) 03623382; fax (21) 03623580; f. 1913; fiction, history, philosophy, dictionaries and children's books; Pres. J. VASSILIOU.

Government Publishing House

Government Printing House: Odos Kapodistriou 34, 104 32 Athens; tel. (21) 05248320.

PUBLISHERS' FEDERATIONS

Hellenic Federation of Publishers and Booksellers: Odos Themistokleus 73, 106 83 Athens; tel. (21) 03300924; fax (21) 03301617; e-mail poev@otenet.gr; f. 1961; Pres. GEORGE DARDANOS; Gen. Sec. TITOS MYLONOPOULOS.

Publishers' and Booksellers' Association of Athens: Odos Themistokleus 73, 106 83 Athens; tel. (21) 03303268; fax (21) 03823222; e-mail seva@otenet.gr; Pres. ELENI KANAKI; Sec. STELIOS ELLINIADIS.

Broadcasting and Communications

TELECOMMUNICATIONS

National Telecommunications Commission (NTC): Leoforos Kifissias 60, 151 25 Athens; tel. (21) 06805040; fax (21) 06805049; e-mail info@eet.gr; internet www.eet.gr; regulatory body; Chair. EMMANOUIL GIACOUMAKIS.

Organismos Telepikoinonion tis Elladas SA (OTE) (Hellenic Telecommunications Organization): Leoforos Kifissias 99, 151 24 Maroussi, Athens; tel. (21) 08827015; fax (21) 06115825; e-mail ote@ote.gr; internet www.ote.gr; f. 1949; owned 42% by the Government, 58% by public shareholders; 6m. lines in service; Chair. and Chief Exec. NIKOS MANASSIS.

COSMOTE: Leoforos Kifissias 44, 151 25 Athens; tel. (21) 06177700; fax (21) 06177594; e-mail customercare@cosmote.gr; internet www.cosmote.gr; 59% owned by OTE, 18%-owned by Telenor (Norway), 7% owned by WR Com (based in Cyprus); the remaining 16% of shares were offered for tender in Oct. 2000; mobile services; Man. Dir NIKOS MANASSIS.

Maritel: Odos Egaleo 8, 185 45 Piraeus; tel. (21) 04599500; fax (21) 04599600; e-mail maritel@maritel.gr; internet www.maritel.gr; OTE subsidiary; marine telecommunications; Chair. THEODOROS VENIAMIS; Man. Dir MICHALIS MICHAELIDES.

Panafon Hellenic Telecom SA: Leoforos Messoghion 2, 115 27 Athens; tel. (21) 07483601; e-mail webmaster@panafon.gr; internet www.panafon.gr; 55%-owned by Vodafone Europe Holdings BV (United Kingdom); mobile telecommunications; Chair. JULIAN HORN-SMITH; Chief Exec. GEORGE KORONIAS.

Telestet Hellas SA: Leoforos Alex. Papagoy 8, 157 71 Athens; tel. (21) 07772033; e-mail po@telestet.gr; internet www.telestet.gr; 75%-owned by STET International; mobile network; Man. Dir GIACINTO CICCHESE.

RADIO

Elliniki Radiophonia Tileorassi (ERT, SA) (Greek Radio-Television): Leoforos Messoghion 432, 153 42 Athens; tel. (21) 06066835; fax (21) 06009325; e-mail pxristofylakou@ert.gr; state-controlled since 1938; Chair. and Man. Dir PANAGHIOTIS PANAGHIOTOU.

Elliniki Radiophonia (ERA) (Greek Radio): POB 60019, Leoforos Messoghion 432, 153 42 Aghia Paraskevi, Athens; tel. (1) 06066815; fax (1) 06009425; e-mail ijanetakos@ert.gr; Dir IOANNIS TZANNETAKOS.

Macedonia Radio Station: Odos Angelaki 2, 546 21 Thessaloníki; tel. (231) 0299400; fax (231) 0299451; e-mail info@ert3.gr; internet www.ert3.gr.

TELEVISION

A television network of 17 transmitters is in operation. The State's monopoly of television broadcasting ended in 1990, and by 1998 there were 17 private broadcasters.

State stations

Elliniki Radiophonia Tileorassi (ERT, SA) (Greek Radio-Television): see Radio.

Elliniki Tileorassi 1 (ET1) (Greek Television 1): Leoforos Messoghion 136, 115 27 Athens; tel. (21) 07758824; fax (21) 07797776; e-mail kalavanos@ert.gr; internet www.ert.gr/et1; Dir-Gen. KONSTANTINOS ALAVANOS.

ET2: Leoforos Messoghion 136, 115 25 Athens; tel. (21) 07701911; fax (21) 07797776; Dir-Gen. PANAYOTIS PANAYOTOU.

ET3: Aggelaki 2, 546 21 Thessaloníki; tel. (231) 0299610; fax (231) 0299655; e-mail pr@ert3.gr; internet www.ert.gr/et3; Dir-Gen. DEMETRIS KATSANTONIS.

Private stations

Antenna TV: Leoforos Kifissias 10–12, 151 25 Maroussi, Athens; tel. (21) 0688600; fax (21) 06834349; e-mail webmaster@antenna.gr; internet www.antenna.gr; Chair. M. X. KYRIAKOU.

Channel Seven-X: Leoforos Kifissias 64, 151 25 Maroussi, Athens; tel. (21) 06897600; fax (21) 06897608.

City Channel: Leoforos Kastoni 14, 41223 Larissa; tel. (241) 232839; fax (241) 232013.

Mega Channel: Leoforos Messoghion 117, 115 26 Athens; tel. (21) 06903000; fax (21) 06983600; e-mail ngeorgiou@megatv.com; internet www.megatv.com; f. 1989; Man. Dir ELIAS TSIGAS.

Neo Kanali SA: Pireos 9—11, 105 52 Athens; tel. (21) 05238230; fax (21) 05247325.

Serres TV: Nigritis 27, 62124 Serres.

Skai TV: Phalereos & Ethnarchou 2, Macaroiu, N. Phaliro.

Star Channel: Dimitras 37, 1178 Tayros, Athens; tel. (21) 03450626; fax (21) 03452190.

Tele City: Praxitelous 58, 17674 Athens; tel. (21) 09429222; fax (21) 09413589.

Teletora: Lycabetous 17, 10672 Athens; tel. (21) 03617285; fax (21) 03638712.

Traki TV: Central Square, 67100 Xanthi; tel. (2541) 020670; fax (2541) 027368.

TRT: Odos Zachou 5, 38333 Volos; tel. (2421) 0288013; fax (2421) 036888.

TV Macedonia: Nea Egnatia 222, 54642 Thessaloníki; tel. (231) 0850512; fax (231) 0850513.

TV Plus: Athens; tel. (21) 09028707; fax (21) 09028310.

TV-100: Odos Aggelaki 16, 54621 Thessaloníki; tel. (231) 0265828; fax (231) 0267532.

Finance

(cap. = capital; p.u. = paid up; res = reserves; dep. = deposits; dre = drachmae; m. = million; br. = branch)

BANKING

Central Bank

Bank of Greece: Leoforos E. Venizelos 21, 102 50 Athens; tel. (21) 03201111; fax (21) 03232239; e-mail secretariat@bankofgreece.gr; internet www.bankofgreece.gr; f. 1927; state bank of issue; cap. dre 16,686.5m., res dre 226,687.2m., dep. dre 8,027,697.7m. (Dec. 1999); Gov. NIKOS GARGANOS; 27 brs.

Commercial Banks

Agricultural Bank of Greece SA: Odos Panepistimiou 23, 105 64 Athens; tel. (21) 03230521; fax (21) 03234386; e-mail ategt@ate.gr; internet www.ate.gr; f. 1929; 83.31% owned by State; mainly provides banking services to rural and semi-rural regions; cap. €1,746.0m., res €100.4m., dep. €10,742.26m. (Dec. 2000); Pres. PETROS LAMBROU; 440 brs.

Alpha Bank AE: Stadiou 40, 102 52 Athens; tel. (21) 03260000; fax (21) 03265438; e-mail secretariat@alpha.gr; internet www.alpha.gr; f. 1879, renamed 2000; cap. dre 253,714.5m., res dre 265,303.2m., dep. dre 6,793,088.2m. (Dec. 2000); Chair. and Gen. Man. IOANNIS S. COSTOPOULOS; 214 brs.

Aspis Bank: Odos Othonosm Syntagma, 105 57 Athens; tel. (21) 03364000; fax (21) 03221409; internet www.aspisbank.gr; f. 1992; cap. dre 15,200.0m., res dre 58,760.0m., dep. dre 149,399.9m. (Dec. 1999); Pres., Chair. and Man. Dir KONSTANTINOS KARATZAS.

Bank of Attica SA: Odos Omirou 23, 106 72 Athens; tel. (21) 03646910; fax (21) 03646115; e-mail attiki3@netor.gr; internet www .vergina.compulink.gr/attica; f. 1925; affiliated to the Commercial Bank of Greece; cap. dre 4,742.1m., res dre 44,838.0m., dep. dre 357,962.3m. (Dec. 2000); Chair. SOULIS-CHRISTOS APOSTOLOPOULOS; 50 brs.

Commercial Bank of Greece SA: Odos Sophokleous 11, 102 35 Athens; tel. (21) 03310606; fax (21) 03254484; e-mail pubrel@ combank.gr; internet www.combank.gr; f. 1907; cap. dre 145,588.5m., res dre 540,670.5m., dep. dre 5,205,005.5m. (Dec. 2001); Chair. and CEO IOANNIS STOURNARAS; Vice-Chair. and Gen. Man. GEORGE MICHELIS; 370 brs.

EFG Eurobank Ergasias SA: Odos Othonos 8, 105 57 Athens; tel. (21) 03337000; fax (21) 03233866; internet www.eurobank.gr; f. 1990 as Euromerchant Bank SA (Eurobank), renamed EFG Eurobank in 1997, and as above in 2000; merged with Bank of Athens and Bank of Crete in 1999, and with Ergobank in 2000; cap. dre 246,308m., res dre 394,247m., dep. dre 4,784,013m. (Dec. 2000); Pres. X. NIKITAS; CEO NIKOLAS NANOPOULOS; 330 brs.

Egnatia Bank SA: Odos Danaidon 4, 546 26 Thessaloníki; tel. (231) 0598600; fax (231) 0598675; e-mail pr@egnatiabank.gr; internet www.egnatiabank.gr; f. 1991; merged with Bank of Central Greece in 1999; cap. dre 38,139.6m., res dre 40,280.7m., dep. dre 499,885.0m. (Dec. 2000); Pres. VASSILLIS THEOCHARAKIS; Man. Dir and Gen. Man. VASSILLIS KELTSOPOULOS; 60 brs.

General Bank of Greece SA: Odos Panepistimiou 9, 102 29 Athens; tel. (21) 03327000; fax (21) 03222271; f. 1937 as Bank of the Army Share Fund, renamed General Hellenic Bank in 1966, and as above in 1998; cap. dre 16,972.1m., res dre 24,348.3m., dep. dre 527,077.9m. (Dec. 1999); Chair. JOHN MANOS; Gen. Man. JOHN MOURGELAS; 94 brs.

Investment Bank of Greece SA: Leoforos Syngrou 80–88, 117 41 Kallithea, Athens; tel. (21) 09281840; fax (21) 09246410; f. 2000; total assets dre 40,109.8m. (Feb. 2001); Pres. ANASTASIOS TZAVELLAS; Man. Dir DIMITRIS S. PAPADOPOULOS.

Laiki Bank Hellas SA: Odos Panepistimiou 16, 106 72 Athens; tel. (21) 03550000; fax (21) 03243141; f. 1992 as European Popular Bank, renamed as above in 2000; cap. dre 15,250m., res dre 13,421.8m., dep. dre 259,735.6m. (Dec. 1999); Chair. KIKIS LAZARIDES; Dep. Gen. Man. CHRISTOS STYLANIDES; 22 brs.

National Bank of Greece SA (NBG): Odos Aeolou 86, 102 32 Athens; tel. (21) 03441000; fax (21) 03346550; internet www.nbg.gr; f. 1841; state-controlled, but operates independently of the Government; cap. dre 340,085.2m., res dre 516,576.2m., dep. dre 13,216,800.6m. (Dec. 2000); Gov. THEODOROS B. KARATZAS; 595 brs.

Piraeus Bank SA: Leoforos Amalias 20, 105 57 Athens; tel. (21) 03335000; fax (21) 03335080; internet www.piraeusbank.gr; f. 1916; merged with Macedonia Thrace Bank and Xiosbank in June 2000; cap. dre 148,760.8m., res dre 254,984.2m., dep. dre 1,032,304.1m. (Dec. 1999); Chair. M. SALLAS; Vice-Chair. I. GEORGANAS; 200 brs.

Piraeus Prime Bank SA: Leoforos Vassilissis Sofias 75, 115 21 Athens; tel. (21) 07250323; fax (21) 07210134; e-mail ppb@ppb.gr; f. 1981 as Banque Franco-Hellenique de Commerce International et Maritime SA, renamed Credit Lyonnais Grèce 1994 and as above 1998; cap. dre 20,000m., res dre 3,858.9m., dep. dre 71,049.9m. (Dec. 1999); Pres. and Chair. MICHAEL SALLAS; Gen. Man. LEONIDAS METAXAS; 1 br.

Telesis Investment Bank SA: Odos Fragoklissias 5, 151 25 Maroussi, Athens; tel. (21) 06196960; fax (21) 06199191; e-mail telesisbk@telesis.gr; f. 1990 as Dorian Bank, renamed as above in 2000; cap. dre 41,720.0m., res dre 40,870.6m., dep. dre 98,849.2m. (Dec. 1999); Chair. MARINA EFRAIMOGLU; 4 brs.

Development Banks

Hellenic Industrial Development Bank SA: Leoforos Syngrou 87, 117 45 Kallithea, Athens; tel. (21) 09242900; fax (21) 09241513; e-mail news@etba.gr; internet www.etba.gr/etba/etbag.html; f. 1964; state-owned limited liability banking company; the major Greek institution in the field of industrial investment; cap. dre 245,890.0m., res dre 44,424.3m., dep. dre 502,897.6m. (Dec. 1996); Chair. and Gov. GEORGE KASMAS; 11 brs.

National Investment Bank for Industrial Development SA: Leoforos Amalias 12–14, 105 57 Athens; tel. (21) 03242651; fax (21) 03296211; e-mail public@eteba.gr; internet www.eteba.gr; f. 1963; cap. dre 8,971.8m., res dre 44,572.4m., dep. dre 447,259.0m. (Dec. 1999); long-term loans, equity participation, promotion of co-operation between Greek and foreign enterprises; Chair. THEODORE KARATZAS; Man. Dir DEMETRIOS GOUMAS; 1 br.

STOCK EXCHANGE

Athens Stock Exchange: Odos Sophokleous 10, 105 59 Athens; tel. (21) 03211301; fax (21) 03213938; e-mail webmaster@ase.gr; internet www.ase.gr; f. 1876; Pres. PANAYOTIS ALEXAKIS; Vice-Pres. THEODOROS PANTOLAKIS.

PRINCIPAL INSURANCE COMPANIES

Agrotiki Hellenic Insurance Co: Leoforos Syngrou 163, 171 21 Kallithea, Athens; tel. (21) 9379100; fax (21) 09358924; e-mail info@ agroins.com; internet www.agroins.com; Gen. Man. TR. LISIMACHOU.

Alpha Asfalistiki Insurance: Leoforos Kifissias 44, 151 25 Maroussi, Athens; tel. (21) 06905500; fax (21) 06913941; e-mail info@ alpha-insurance.gr; internet www.alpha-insurance.gr; f. 1940; Chair. PHOTIS P. COSTOPOULOS; Man. Dir D. PALEOLOGOS; Gen. Man. JOHN L. GALANOPOULOS.

Aspis Pronia General Insurance SA: Leoforos Kifissias 62, 151 25 Maroussi, Athens; tel. (21) 06198960; fax (21) 06198974; e-mail info@aspis.gr; internet www.aspis.gr; f. 1941; Pres. and Chief Exec. PAUL PSOMIADES.

Atlantiki Enosis: Odos Messoghion 71, 115 26 Athens; tel. (21) 07799211; fax (21) 07794446; f. 1970; Gen. Man. N. LAPATAS.

Commercial Value SA: Leoforos Kifissias 250–254, 152 31 Athens; tel. (21) 06742411; fax (21) 06741826; e-mail united@atheneos.com; internet www.commercialvalue.gr; f. 2002 by merger; fmrly United Insurance Co SA; Pres. D. DASKALOPOULOS; Man. Dir P. ATHENEOS.

Dynamis SA: Leoforos Syngrou 106, 117 41 Kallithea, Athens; tel. (21) 09227255; fax (21) 09237768; e-mail genka@asfgenka.gr; f. 1977; Man. Dir NIKOLAS STAMATOPOULOS.

Egnatia Co: Leoforos Syngrou 240, 176 72 Kallithea; tel. (21) 09577802; fax (21) 09579348; Rep. P. MIGAS.

Emporiki Life: Odos Korai 6, 105 64 Athens; tel. (21) 03282346; fax (21) 03282441; e-mail mzanatta@emporikilife.gr; f. 1940; Chair. DIMITRIS FRANGETIS; Exec. Dir MICHAEL ZANATTA.

Ethniki Hellenic General Insurance Co SA: Odos Karageorgi Servias 8, 102 10 Athens; tel. (21) 03299000; fax (21) 03236101; e-mail ethniki@ethniki-asfalistiki.gr; internet www .ethniki-asfalistiki.gr; f. 1891; Gen. Man. C. PHILIPOU.

Galaxias Insurance Co: Leoforos Syngrou 40–42, 117 42 Kallithea, Athens; tel. (21) 09241082; fax (21) 09241698; f. 1967; Gen. Man. I. TSOUPRAS.

Gothaer Hellas SA: Odos Michalakopoulou 174, 115 27 Athens; tel. (21) 07750801; fax (21) 07757094; Gen. Man. S. GALANIS.

Hellas Insurance Co SA: Leoforos Kifissias 119, 151 24 Marousi, Athens; tel. (21) 08127600; fax (21) 08027189; e-mail nick.nardis@ aig.com; internet www.aig-greece.gr; f. 1973; Gen. Man. N. NARDIS.

Hellenic Reliance General Insurances SA: Leoforos Kifissias 304, 152 32 Halandri, Athens; tel. (21) 06843733; fax (21) 06843734; f. 1990; Man. Dir S. F. TRIANTAFYLLAKIS.

Hellenobretanniki General Insurances SA: Leoforos Messogion 2–4, 115 27 Athens; tel. (21) 07755301; fax (21) 07714768; f. 1988.

Helvetia General Insurance Co: Leoforos Kifissias 124, 115 26 Athens; tel. (21) 06980840; fax (21) 06923446; f. 1943; Gen. Man. J. DELENDAS.

Horizon General Insurance Co SA: Leoforos Amalias 26A, 105 57 Athens; tel. (21) 03227932; fax (21) 03225540; e-mail horizon@hol.gr; f. 1965; Gen. Mans THEODORE ACHIS, CHR. ACHIS.

Hydrogios: Odos Solonos 137, 176 75 Athens; tel. (21) 09477200; fax (21) 09477222; Gen. Man. A. KASKARELIS.

Ikonomiki: Odos Kapodistriou 38, 104 32 Athens; tel. (21) 05243374; fax (21) 05234962; f. 1968; Gen. Man. D. NIKOLAIDIS.

Imperial Hellas SA: Leoforos Syngrou 253, 171 22 N. Smirni, Athens; tel. (21) 09426352; fax (21) 09426202; e-mail imperiasf@hol .gr; internet www.imperial.gr; f. 1971; Gen. Man. G. TZANIS.

Interamerican Hellenic Life Insurance Co SA: Interamerican Plaza, Leoforos Kifissias 117, 151 80 Maroussi, Athens; tel. (21) 06191111; fax (21) 06191877; e-mail moissism@interamerican.gr; internet www.interamerican.gr; f. 1971; 79.38% owned by Eureko, a Netherlands-based insurance group; Pres. and Man. Dir DIMITRI KONTOMINAS.

Interamerican Health Assistance Insurance Co SA: Interamerican Plaza, Leoforos Kifissias 117, 151 80 Maroussi, Athens; tel. (21) 06191111; fax (21) 06191886; e-mail health@ interamerican.gr; internet www.interamerican.gr; Man. Dir A. PAPAGIANNOPOULOS.

Interamerican Property and Casualty Insurance Co SA: Interamerican Plaza, Leoforos Kifissias 117, 151 80 Maroussi, Athens; tel. (21) 06191111; fax (21) 06191872; e-mail custserv@

interamerican.gr; internet www.interamerican.gr; f. 1974; Man. Dir C. BERTSIAS.

Interamerican Road Assistance Insurance Co SA: Leoforos Syngrou 350, 176 74 Kallithea, Athens; tel. (21) 09304080; fax (21) 09304083; e-mail intauto@compulink.gr; internet www .interamerican.gr; Man. Dir G. SOUVAGIS.

Kykladiki Insurance Co SA: Leoforos Syngrou 80–88, 117 41 Kallithea, Athens; tel. (21) 09247664; fax (21) 09247344; f. 1919; Gen. Man. PAN. KATSIKOSTAS.

Victoria General Insurance Co SA: Odos Tsimiski 21, 546 22 Thessaloníki; tel. (231) 0371100; fax (231) 0371392; e-mail victoria@ victoria.gr; internet www.victoria.gr; f. 1972; Man. Dir G. ANDONIADIS.

Phoenix-General Insurance Co of Greece SA: Odos Omirou 2, 105 64 Athens; tel. (21) 03295111; fax (21) 03239135; e-mail phoenix@phoenix.gr; internet www.phoenix.gr; f. 1928; general insurance; Rep. G. KOTSALOS.

Poseidon SA: Odos Karaiskou 163, 185 35 Piraeus; tel. (21) 04522685; fax (21) 04184337; e-mail poseidon@otenet.gr; f. 1972; Gen. Man. THANOS J. MELAKOPIDES.

Sideris Insurance Co SA: Odos Lekka 3–5, 105 63 Athens; tel. (21) 03224484; e-mail siderisa@acci.gr; fax (21) 03231066; Dir G. SIDERIS.

Syneteristiki General Insurance Co: Leoforos Syngrou 367, 175 64 Kallithea, Athens; tel. (21) 09491280; fax (21) 09403148; e-mail syne-ins@hol.gr; Gen. Man. D. ZORBAS.

A large number of foreign insurance companies also operate in Greece.

Insurance Association

Association of Insurance Companies: Odos Xenophontos 10, 105 57 Athens; tel. (21) 03334100; fax (21) 03334149; e-mail info@eaee .gr; internet www.eaee.gr; 114 mems, of which 32 are foreign insurance companies operating in Greece; Gen. Man. MARGARITA ANTONAKI.

Trade and Industry

GOVERNMENT AGENCY

Organismos Anasinkrotiseos Epicheiriseon (Industrial Reconstruction Organization): Athens; f. 1982; reconstruction and sale of Greek businesses under state receivership.

CHAMBERS OF COMMERCE

Athens Chamber of Commerce and Industry: Odos Akademias 7, 106 71 Athens; tel. (21) 03625342; fax (21) 03618810; e-mail info@ acci.gr; internet www.acci.gr; f. 1919; Pres. JOHN KOCPRALOS; Sec.-Gen. DRACOULIS FOUNDOUKAKOS; 70,000 mems.

Athens Chamber of Small and Medium-sized Industries: Odos Akademias 18, 106 71 Athens; tel. (21) 03680700; fax (21) 03614726; e-mail info@acsmi.gr; internet www.acsmi.gr; f. 1940; Pres. G. KYRIOPOULOS; Sec.-Gen. ATH. PAVLOU; c. 60,000 mems.

Handicraft Chamber of Piraeus: Odos Karaiscou 111, 185 32 Piraeus; tel. (21) 04110443; fax (21) 04179495; e-mail info@bep.gr; internet www.bep.gr; f. 1925; Pres. KONSTANTINOS MOSCHOLIOS; Sec.-Gen. PANTELIS ANTONIADIS; 18,500 mems.

Piraeus Chamber of Commerce and Industry: Odos Loudovikou 1, 185 31 Piraeus; tel. (21) 4177241; fax (21) 4178680; f. 1919; Pres. GEORGE KASSIMATIS; Sec.-Gen. KONSTANTINOS SARANTOPOULOS.

Thessaloníki Chamber of Commerce and Industry: Odos Tsimiski 29, 546 24 Thessaloníki; tel. (231) 0224438; fax (231) 0230237; f. 1919; Pres. PANTELIS KONSTANTINIDIS; Sec.-Gen. EMMANUEL VLACHOYANNIS; 14,500 mems.

INDUSTRIAL AND TRADE ASSOCIATIONS

Federation of Greek Industries (SEV): Odos Xenophontos 5, 105 57 Athens; tel. (21) 03237325; fax (21) 03222929; e-mail main@fgi .org.gr; internet www.fgi.org.gr; f. 1907; Chair. ELEFTHERIOS ANTONAKOPOULOS; 950 mems.

Federation of Industries of Northern Greece: Morihovou 1, 7th Floor, 546 35 Thessaloníki; tel. (231) 0539817; fax (231) 0546244; e-mail secretariat@sbbe.gr; internet www.sbbe.gr; f. 1915; Pres. SIMEONIDIS DIMITRIOS.

Hellenic Cotton Board: Leoforos Syngrou 150, 176 71 Kallithea, Athens; tel. (21) 09225011; fax (21) 09249656; f. 1931; state organization; Pres. P. K. MYLONAS.

Hellenic Organization of Small and Medium-sized Industries and Handicrafts (EOMMEX): Odos Xenias 16, 115 28 Athens; tel.

(21) 07491100; fax (21) 07491146; e-mail w3master@eommex.gr; internet www.eommex.gr; Pres. GEORGE FRANTZESKAKIS.

UTILITIES

Electricity

Public Power Corpn (DEH): Odos Xalkokondyli 30, 104 32 Athens; tel. (21) 05230301; fax (21) 05238445; e-mail info@dei.gr; internet www.dei.gr; f. 1950; 84% state-owned, generating capacity 11,158 MW (June 2001); generation, transmission and distribution of electricity in Greece; Chair. G. BIRDIMIRIS; Gen. Man. A. PAPATHANASIOU.

Gas

Public Gas Corpn (DEPA): Leoforos Messoghian 207, 115 25 Athens; tel. (21) 06793500; fax (21) 06749504; e-mail info@depa.gr; internet www.depa.gr; f. 1988; 35% owned by Hellenic Petroleum SA, 65% state-owned; scheduled for privatization in 2002; began gas imports 1997, initially for industrial use; Man. Dir ARISTEIDIS VAKIRLIS.

Water

In 1980 a law was passed under which Municipal Enterprises for Water Supply and Sewerage (DEYA) were created to manage drinking water and sewerage throughout Greece. Since then some 90 DEYA have been established.

The Hellenic Union of Municipal Enterprises for Water Supply and Sewerage (EDEYA): Odos Anthimou Gaza 3, 4122 22 Larissa; internet www.edeya.gr; f. 1989; 67 mems; co-ordinates activities of DEYA and represents them to the Government.

TRADE UNIONS

There are about 5,000 registered trade unions, grouped together in 82 federations and 86 workers' centres, which are affiliated to the Greek General Confederation of Labour.

Greek General Confederation of Labour (GSEE): Odos Patission 69, Athens; tel. (21) 08834611; fax (21) 08229802; e-mail info@ gsee.gr; internet www.gsee.gr; f. 1918; Pres. CHRISTOS PROTOPAPAS; Gen. Sec. IOANNIS THEONAS; 700,000 mems.

Pan-Hellenic Federation of Seamen's Unions (PNO): Livanos Bldg, Akti Miaouli 47–49, 185 36 Piraeus; tel. (21) 04292960; fax (21) 04293040; f. 1920; confederation of 14 marine unions; Pres. IOANNIS CHELAS; Gen. Sec. JOHN HALAS.

Transport

RAILWAYS

A five-year programme to upgrade the Greek rail network was initiated in 1996, supported by 350m. drachmae from EU structural funds. The major undertaking was to electrify the 500-km Athens–Thessaloníki line and to extend services to the Bulgarian border. Construction of a 26.3-km electrified extension to the Athens–Piraeus line, in order to provide a three-line urban railway system for Athens, designated Metro Line 1, was completed in 2000. Metro Lines 2 and 3, each measuring some 9 km, were scheduled to open prior to the holding of the Olympic Games in 2004.

Attiko Metro SA: Mesogion Ave 191–93, 115 25 Athens; tel. (21) 06792399; fax (21) 06726126; e-mail info@ametro.gr; internet www .ametro.gr; f. 1999; planning, design, construction and operation of Metro Lines 2 and 3; Chair. IOANNIS CHRISSIKOPOULOS.

Ilektriki Sidirodromi Athinon–Pireos (ISAP) (Athens–Piraeus Electric Railways): Odos Athinas 67, 105 52 Athens; tel. (21) 03248311; fax (21) 03223935; internet www.isap.gr; state-owned; 25.6 km of electrified track; Chair. JOHN MANIATIS; Man. Dir GERASSIMO K. DRAGONAS.

Organismos Sidirodromon Ellados (OSE) (Hellenic Railways Organization Ltd): Odos Karolou 1–3, 104 37 Athens; tel. (21) 05248395; fax (21) 05243290; internet www.ose.gr; f. 1971; state railways; total length of track: 2,511 km; Chair. CHR. PAPAGEORGIOU; Dir-Gen. A. LAZARIS.

ROADS

In 1999 there were an estimated 117,000 km of roads in Greece. Of this total, an estimated 9,100 km were main roads, and 470 km were motorways. Major new roads under construction in early 2002 included a 65-km ring road for Athens, and the 680-km Egnatia highway, extending from the Adriatic coast to the Turkish border, which was scheduled for completion in 2003.

INLAND WATERWAYS
There are no navigable rivers in Greece.

Corinth Canal: built 1893; over six km long, links the Corinthian and Saronic Gulfs; shortens the journey from the Adriatic to the Piraeus by 325 km; spanned by three single-span bridges, two for road and one for rail; can be used by ships of a maximum draught of 22 ft and width of 60 ft; managed since June 2001 by Sea Containers Group (United Kingdom).

SHIPPING
In 2001 the Greek merchant fleet totalled 1,529 vessels amounting to 28,678,240 grt. Greece controls one of the largest merchant fleets in the world. The principal ports are Piraeus, Patras and Thessaloníki.

Union of Greek Shipowners: Akti Miaouli 85, 185 38 Piraeus; f. 1916; Pres. JOHN GOUMAS.

Port Authorities

Port of Patras: Patras Port Authority, Central Port Office, Patras; tel. (261) 0341002; fax (261) 0327136; Harbour Master Capt. NIKOLAS RAFAILOVITS.

Piraeus Port Authority: Piraeus Port Authority, Akti Miaouli 10, 185 35 Piraeus; tel. (21) 04520911; fax (21) 04286843; e-mail olpdsx@otenet.gr; internet www.olp.gr; Pres. SOTIRIS THEOFANIS; Man. Dir HARILAOS PSARAFTIS; Harbour Master Capt. EMMANUEL PELOPONNESIOS.

Port of Thessaloníki: Thessaloníki Port Authority, POB 10467, 541 10 Thessaloníki; tel. (231) 0593911; fax (231) 0510500; e-mail secretariat@thpa.gr; internet www.thpa.gr; Chief Exec. SOTIRIS I. THEOFANIS.

Among the largest shipping companies are:

Anangel Shipping Enterprises SA: Leoforos Syngrou 354, 176 74 Kallithea, Athens; tel. (21) 09467200; fax (21) 09408820; e-mail mail@anangel.gr; internet www.anangel.gr; Man. Dir J. PLATSIDAKIS.

Attika Shipping Co: Odos Voucourestion 16, 10671 Athens; tel. (21) 03609631; fax (21) 03601439; Dir G. PRIOVOLOS.

Bilinder Marine Corpn SA: Odos Igias 1–3 and Akti Themistokleos, 185 36 Piraeus; tel. (21) 04287300; fax (21) 04287355; Gen. Man. V. ARMOGENI.

Ceres Hellenic Shipping Enterprises Ltd: Akti Miaouli 69, 185 37 Piraeus; tel. (21) 04591000; fax (21) 04283552; e-mail chse@ceres.gr; internet www.ceres.gr; Dir NICK FISTES.

Chandris (Hellas) Inc: POB 80067, Akti Miaouli 95, 185 38 Piraeus; tel. (21) 04290300; fax (21) 04290256; e-mail chandris@19080845.multimessage.com; Man. Dirs A. C. PIPERAS, M. G. SKORDIAS.

Costamare Shipping Co SA: Odos Zephyrou 60 and Leoforos Syngrou, 175 64 Kallithea, Athens; tel. (21) 09390000; fax (21) 09409051; Pres. Capt. V. C. KONSTANTAKOPOULOS; Man. Dir Capt. G. SARDIS.

European Navigation Inc: Odos Artemissiou 2 and Fleming Sq., 166 75 Athens; tel. (21) 08981581; fax (21) 08946777; Dir P. KARNESSIS.

Glafki (Hellas) Maritime Co: Odos Mitropoleos 3, 105 57 Athens; tel. (21) 03244991; fax (21) 03228944; Dirs M. FRAGOULIS, G. PANAGIOTOU.

Golden Union Shipping Co SA: Odos Aegales 8, 185 45 Piraeus; tel. (21) 04329900; fax (21) 04627933; Man. Dir THEODORE VENIAMIS.

M. Koutlakis and Co Ltd: Makras Stoas 5, 185 31 Piraeus; tel. (21) 04129428; fax (21) 04178755; Dir M. KOUTLAKIS.

Laskaridis Shipping Co Ltd: Odos Chimaras 5, 151 25 Maroussi, Athens; tel. (21) 06899090; fax (21) 06806762; e-mail athens@laskship.cc.cwmail.com; Man. Dirs P. C. LASKARIDIS, A. C. LASKARIDIS.

Marmaras Navigation Ltd: Odos Filellinon 4–6, Okeanion Bldg, 185 36 Piraeus; tel. (21) 04294226; fax (21) 04294304; Dir D. DIAMANTIDES.

Minoan Lines Shipping SA: Odos 25 August 17, 712 02 Iraklion; tel. (281) 330301; fax (281) 330308; internet www.minoan.gr; Pres. KONSTANTINOS KLIRONOMAS.

Naftomar Shipping and Trading Co Ltd: Leoforos Alkyonidon 243, 166 73 Voula; tel. (21) 09670220; fax (21) 09670237; e-mail naftomar@naftomar.gr; Man. Dir RIAD ZEIN.

Strintzis Lines Maritime S.A.: Odos Akti Possidonos 26, 185 31 Piraeus; tel. (21) 04225000; fax (21) 04225265; internet www.strintzis.gr; Man. Dir G. STRINTZIS.

Thenamaris (Ships Management) Inc: Odos Athinas 16, Kavouri, 166 71 Athens; tel. (21) 08969111; fax (21) 08969653; e-mail sg.gd@thenamaris.gr; Dir K. MARTINOS.

Tsakos Shipping and Trading SA: Leoforos Syngrou 367, Faliro, 175 64 Kallithea, Athens; tel. (21) 09380700; fax (21) 09480710; Dirs P. N. TSAKOS, E. SAROGLOU.

United Shipping and Trading Co of Greece SA: Odos Iassonos 6, 185 37 Piraeus; tel. (21) 04283660; fax (21) 04283630; Dir CH. TSAKOS.

Varnima Corporation International SA: Odos Irodou Attikou 12A, 151 24 Maroussi, Athens; tel. (21) 08093000; fax (21) 08093222; e-mail john_k@attglobal.net; Gen. Man. S. V. SPANOUDAKIS.

CIVIL AVIATION
There are international airports at Athens, Thessaloníki, Alexandroupolis, Corfu, Lesbos, Andravida, Rhodes, Kos and Heraklion/Crete, and 24 domestic airports (of which 13 are authorized to receive international flights). A new international airport called Eleftherios Venizelos, at Spata, some 25 km east of Athens, was opened in March 2001. The airport was expected to have a handling capacity of 16m. passengers per year.

Cronus Airlines: Leoforos Vauliogmenis 500, 174 56 Alimos; tel. (21) 09956400; fax (21) 09956405; e-mail info@cronus.gr; internet www.cronus.gr; f. 1995; charter services to the United Kingdom, East Africa and Middle East; Chair. IOANNIS TH. MANETAS.

Olympic Airways SA: Leoforos Syngrou 96–100, 117 41 Kallithea, Athens; tel. (21) 09269111; fax (21) 09267154; e-mail olyair10@otenet.gr; internet www.olympic-airways.gr; f. 1957; state-owned, privatization plans collapsed in early 2002; domestic services linking principal cities and islands in Greece, and international services to Singapore, Thailand, South Africa and the USA, and throughout Europe and the Middle East; Chair. and Chief Exec. DIONYSIOS KALOFONOS.

Olympic Aviation: Leoforos Syngrou 96–100, 117 41 Kallithea, Athens; tel. (1) 09269111; fax (1) 09884059; wholly owned subsidiary of Olympic Airways; independent operator of scheduled domestic and regional services; Chair. STERGIOS PAPASIS; Chief Exec. PETROS STEFANOU.

Tourism

The sunny climate, the natural beauty of the country and its great history and traditions attract tourists to Greece. There are numerous islands and many sites of archaeological interest. The number of tourists visiting Greece increased from 1m. in 1968 to 12.5m. in 2000. Receipts from tourism, which totalled US $120m. in 1968, reached $9,221m. in 2000. More visitors were expected to be attracted to Greece in 2004, when the country was to host the Olympic Games.

Ellinikos Organismos Tourismou (EOT) (Greek National Tourist Organization): Odos Amerikis 2B, 105 64 Athens; tel. (21) 03223111; fax (21) 03252895; e-mail info@gnto.gr; internet www.gnto.gr; Pres. IOANNIS STEFANIDES; Vice-Pres. IOANNIS ROUBATIS.

GRENADA

Introductory Survey

Location, Climate, Language, Religion, Flag, Capital

Grenada, a mountainous, heavily-forested island, is the most southerly of the Windward Islands, in the West Indies. The country also includes some of the small islands known as the Grenadines, which lie to the north-east of Grenada. The most important of these are the low-lying island of Carriacou and its neighbour, Petit Martinique. The climate is semi-tropical, with an average annual temperature of 28°C (82°F) in the lowlands. Annual rainfall averages about 1,500 mm (60 ins) in the coastal area and 3,800 mm to 5,100 mm (150–200 ins) in mountain areas. Most of the rainfall occurs between June and December. The majority of the population speak English, although a French patois is sometimes spoken. According to the census of 1991, 82% of Grenada's population were of African descent, while 13% were of mixed ethnic origins. Most of the population profess Christianity, and the main denominations are Roman Catholicism (to which 53% of the population adhered at the time of the 1991 census) and Anglicanism (about 14% of the population). The national flag (proportions 1 by 2) consists of a diagonally-quartered rectangle (yellow in the upper and lower segments, green in the right and left ones) surrounded by a red border bearing six five-pointed yellow stars (three at the upper edge of the flag, and three at the lower edge). There is a red disc, containing a large five-pointed yellow star, in the centre, and a representation of a nutmeg (in yellow and red) on the green segment near the hoist. The capital is St George's.

Recent History

Grenada was initially colonized by the French but was captured by the British in 1762. The Treaty of Versailles recognized British control in 1783. Grenada continued as a British colony until 1958, when it joined the Federation of the West Indies, remaining a member until the dissolution of the Federation in 1962. Full internal self-government and statehood in association with the United Kingdom were achieved in March 1967. During this period, the political life of Grenada was dominated by Herbert Blaize, the leader of the Grenada National Party (GNP), and Eric Gairy, a local trade union leader, who in 1950 founded the Grenada United Labour Party (GULP), with the support of an associated trade union. Gairy became Premier after the elections of 1967 and again after those of 1972, which he contested chiefly on the issue of total independence. Grenada became independent, within the Commonwealth, on 7 February 1974, with Gairy as Prime Minister. Domestic opposition to Gairy was expressed in public unrest, and the formation by the three opposition parties—the GNP, the United People's Party and the New Jewel Movement (NJM)—of the People's Alliance, which contested the 1976 general elections and reduced GULP's majority in the Lower House.

The opposition regarded the rule of Sir Eric Gairy, as he became in June 1977, as increasingly autocratic and corrupt, and on 13 March 1979 he was replaced in a bloodless coup by the leader of the left-wing NJM, Maurice Bishop. The new People's Revolutionary Government (PRG) suspended the 1974 Constitution and announced the imminent formation of a People's Consultative Assembly to draft a new constitution. Meanwhile, Grenada remained a monarchy, with the British Queen as Head of State, represented in Grenada by a Governor-General. During 1980–81 there was an increase in repression, against a background of mounting anti-Government violence and the PRG's fears of an invasion by US forces.

By mid-1982 relations with the USA, the United Kingdom and the more conservative members of the Caribbean Community and Common Market (CARICOM, see p. 155) were becoming increasingly strained: elections had not been arranged, restrictions against the privately-owned press had been imposed, many detainees were still awaiting trial, and Grenada was aligning more closely with Cuba and the USSR. Cuba was contributing funds and construction workers for the airport at Point Salines, a project which further strengthened the US Government's conviction that Grenada was to become a centre for Soviet manoeuvres in the area.

In March 1983 the armed forces were put on alert, in response to renewed fears that the USA was planning to invade. (The USA strenuously denied any such plans.) In June Bishop sought to improve relations with the USA, and announced the appointment of a commission to draft a new constitution. The more left-wing members of the PRG denounced this attempt at conciliation as an ideological betrayal. A power struggle developed between Bishop and his deputy, Bernard Coard, the Minister of Finance and Planning. In October Bishop was placed under house arrest, allegedly for his refusal to share power with Coard. The commander of the People's Revolutionary Army (PRA), Gen. Austin Hudson, subsequently announced that Bishop had been expelled from the NJM. On 19 October thousands of Bishop's supporters stormed the house, freed Bishop, and demonstrated outside the PRA headquarters. PRA forces responded by firing into the crowd. Later in the day, Bishop, three of his ministers and two trade unionists were executed by the PRA. The Government was replaced by a 16-member Revolutionary Military Council (RMC), led by Gen. Austin and supported by Coard and one other minister. The remaining NJM ministers were arrested and imprisoned, and a total curfew was imposed.

Regional and international outrage at the assassination of Bishop, in addition to fears of a US military intervention, were so intense that after four days the RMC relaxed the curfew, reopened the airport and promised a swift return to civilian rule. However, the Organisation of Eastern Caribbean States (OECS, see p. 341) resolved to intervene in an attempt to restore democratic order, and asked for assistance from the USA, which readily complied. (It is unclear whether the decision to intervene preceded or followed a request for help to the OECS by the Grenadian Governor-General, Sir Paul Scoon.) On 25 October 1983 some 1,900 US military personnel invaded the island, accompanied by 300 troops from Jamaica, Barbados and member countries of the OECS. Fighting continued for some days, and the USA gradually increased its troop strength, with further reinforcements waiting off shore with a US naval task force. The RMC's forces were defeated, while Coard, Austin and others who had been involved in the coup were detained.

On 9 November 1983 Scoon appointed a non-political interim Council to assume responsibility for the government of the country until elections could be held. Nicholas Brathwaite, a former Commonwealth official, was appointed Chairman of this Council in December. The 1974 Constitution was reinstated (although the country did not rejoin the East Caribbean Supreme Court), and an electoral commission was created. By mid-December the USA had withdrawn all its forces except 300 support troops who were to assist the 430 members of Caribbean forces remaining on the island. A 550-member police force, trained by the USA and the United Kingdom, was established, including a paramilitary body that was to be the new defence contingent.

Several political parties that had operated clandestinely or from exile during the rule of the PRG re-emerged and announced their intention of contesting the elections for a new House of Representatives. Sir Eric Gairy returned to Grenada in January 1984 to lead GULP, but stated that he would not stand as a candidate himself. In May three former NJM ministers formed the Maurice Bishop Patriotic Movement (MBPM) to contest the elections. A number of centrist parties emerged or re-emerged, including Blaize's GNP. Fears that a divided opposition would allow GULP to win a majority of seats in the new House resulted in an agreement by several of these organizations, in August 1984, to form the New National Party (NNP), led by Blaize.

At the general election held in December 1984 the NNP achieved a convincing victory by winning 14 of the 15 seats in the House of Representatives, with 59% of the popular votes. Both GULP (which won 36% of the votes cast) and the MBPM claimed that the poll had been fraudulent, and the one successful GULP candidate, Marcel Peters, initially refused to take his seat in protest. He subsequently accepted the seat, but was expelled from the party and formed the Grenada Democratic Labour Party (GDLP). Blaize became Prime Minister. US and

Caribbean troops remained in Grenada, at Blaize's request, until September 1985.

The trial of 19 detainees (including Coard, his wife, Phyllis, and Gen. Austin), accused of murder and conspiracy against Bishop and six of his associates, opened in November 1984. However, repeated adjournments postponed the trial of 18 of the detainees until April 1986. One of the detainees agreed to give evidence for the State in return for a pardon. Eventually, the jury returned verdicts on 196 charges of murder and conspiracy to murder in December. Fourteen of the defendants were sentenced to death, three received prison sentences of between 30 and 45 years, and one was acquitted.

Internal differences gradually led to the disintegration of the NNP. In 1986 its parliamentary strength was reduced to 12 seats, following the resignation of two members who subsequently formed the Democratic Labour Congress (DLC). Three more government members resigned in April 1987, and joined forces with the DLC and the GDLP in July to form a united opposition, with six seats in the House of Representatives. In October they formally launched a new party, the National Democratic Congress (NDC), led by George Brizan, who had earlier been appointed parliamentary opposition leader. In January 1989 Brizan resigned as leader of the NDC in order to allow the election of Nicholas Brathwaite (head of the interim Government of 1983–84) to that post.

During 1988–89 the actions of the Blaize Government, under provisions of the controversial Emergency Powers Act of 1987, gave rise to concerns both within the opposition and among regional neighbours. Deportation orders and bans were enforced by the administration against prominent left-wing politicians and journalists from the region, and a variety of books and journals were proscribed.

Meanwhile, a deterioration in Blaize's health coincided with a growing challenge to his administration from within the NNP during 1988. In January 1989 Blaize was replaced as party leader by his cabinet colleague, Dr Keith Mitchell, although he remained Prime Minister. In July, however, following allegations of corruption by the NDC, Blaize announced the dismissal of Mitchell and the Chairman of the NNP, accusing them of violating the principles of cabinet government. Amid uncertainty as to whether the Blaize faction had formed a separate party, two more members of the Government resigned, thus reducing support for the Blaize Government to only five of the 15 members of the House of Representatives. Blaize did not officially announce the formation of a new party, the National Party (TNP), until late August, by which time he had advised the acting Governor-General to prorogue Parliament. (The Government thereby avoided being defeated in a motion of 'no confidence', the immediate dissolution of Parliament and the prospect of an early general election.) The term of the Parliament was due to expire at the end of December, and a general election had to be held within three months. However, Blaize died in mid-December, and the Governor-General appointed Ben Jones, Blaize's former deputy and the new leader of TNP, as Prime Minister. At the general election, held in March 1990, no party achieved an absolute majority in the House of Representatives. The NDC won seven of the 15 seats, GULP won four, while TNP and the NNP won only two each. The NDC achieved a working majority in Parliament when one of GULP's successful candidates announced his defection to the NDC. Brathwaite subsequently became Prime Minister and appointed a new Cabinet.

In July 1991 the Court of Appeal upheld the original verdicts that had been imposed in 1986 on the defendants in the Bishop murder trial, and further pleas for clemency were rejected. Preparations for the imminent hanging of the 14, however, provoked international outrage, and in August Brathwaite announced that the death sentences were to be commuted to terms of life imprisonment. His decision (which was contrary to prevailing public opinion on Grenada) was considered to have been influenced by intense pressure from politicians and human rights organizations, together with the potential detrimental effect on the country's important tourist industry.

Brathwaite resigned as leader of the NDC in September 1994 and was succeeded by George Brizan. In February 1995 Brathwaite resigned as Prime Minister, and was succeeded by Brizan. At the general election held in June, the NNP secured eight of the 15 seats in the House of Representatives, while the NDC's representation was reduced to five seats. The remaining two seats were secured by GULP. Dr Keith Mitchell, leader of the NNP, became Prime Minister and appointed a Cabinet. The NNP subsequently undertook negotiations with GULP in an attempt to strengthen its single-seat majority and to secure the two-thirds' majority required to amend the Constitution. In July Francis Alexis resigned as deputy leader of the NDC, alleging that an NDC member of Parliament had been unfairly treated by the party prior to the election. In November he and three other former NDC members announced the formation of a new opposition group, the Democratic Labour Party (DLP).

The appointment in August 1996 of Daniel (later Sir Daniel) Williams to the post of Governor-General provoked considerable controversy because of Williams' connections with the NNP (he had been deputy leader of the party during the 1980s) and his previous role as a cabinet minister in the Government of Herbert Blaize. Opposition members staged a walk-out at his inauguration ceremony, a protest that led to Brizan, the Leader of the Opposition, being suspended from the House of Representatives for one month.

In May 1997 GULP joined with the NDC, TNP, the DLP and the MBPM to announce a strategy of co-operation in opposing the Government on major national issues, accusing Mitchell of a lack of consultation and of 'growing dictatorship'. In the previous month an opposition motion of 'no confidence' in the Government had been rejected by the House of Representatives. At the end of June the establishment was announced of an eighth political party, the Grenada Progressive Party, led by Prescott Williams.

In March 1997 the Government's Mercy Committee rejected a request made by the Conference of Churches of Grenada for the release, on the grounds of their deteriorating physical and mental health, of Phyllis Coard and another of those serving terms of life imprisonment for the murder of Maurice Bishop. None the less, the Committee gave assurances that the detainees' medical requirements would receive attention, and that conditions at the prison where they were being held would be improved. Also in March Mitchell announced plans for the establishment of a national commission to investigate the 1979–83 revolutionary period.

Sir Eric Gairy, the founder and leader of GULP, died in August 1997. A lengthy power struggle within the party ensued, but a convention to elect Gairy's successor was eventually held in April/May 1998. In a controversial vote, Herbert Preudhomme (a former Deputy Prime Minister) narrowly defeated his opponent, who subsequently launched a protest against alleged electoral fraud.

In January 1998 Mitchell announced a cabinet reorganization and the creation of a new ministry, of Carriacou and Petit Martinique affairs, to be headed by Elvin Nimrod. In September the NDC and GULP announced that they had begun a working dialogue to seek to unseat the Government. In late November the Minister of Foreign Affairs, Raphael Fletcher, resigned from the Government and NNP in order to join GULP, citing his 'growing disenchantment and disagreement' with Mitchell. His resignation resulted in the dissolution of Parliament in early December; a general election was called for January 1999, although constitutionally it was not due until mid-2000. The DLP and GULP agreed to contest the election together in an informal alliance known as United Labour.

At the general election held on 18 January 1999 (in which 56.5% of the electorate voted), the NNP achieved a comprehensive victory, receiving 62.2% of total votes cast and obtaining all of the 15 seats in the House of Representatives. The NDC won 24.9% of the votes, while the United Labour alliance received only 11.6%. Keith Mitchell retained his position as Prime Minister and appointed a new Cabinet. Several ministers retained their portfolios, while Mitchell himself replaced Fletcher as Minister of Foreign Affairs. The NNP's return to power constituted the first time in the country's history that a political party had been given two successive terms in government. In its electoral campaign the party had highlighted its recent successes in maintaining strong economic growth and reducing unemployment.

In late September and early October 1999 two leading journalists were arrested on separate charges of alleged criminal libel. One of the detainees was the editor of *Grenada Today*, George Worme, who had published a letter accusing Mitchell of having bribed voters during the last election campaign. Opposition parties, human rights organizations and media associations claimed that the Government was seeking to intimidate independent journalists. In November 2000 the Grenada High Court ruled that the charge brought against Worme was unconstitutional, since it violated his right to free expression.

Also in early October 1999 Bernard Coard, the former Deputy Prime Minister serving a term of life imprisonment with 16 others for the 1983 murder of Prime Minister Maurice Bishop and a number of his associates (see above), issued a statement in which he accepted full responsibility for the crimes; it was, however, unclear as to whether he was speaking on behalf of all 17 prisoners. In February 2002 it was announced that three former soldiers jailed in 1986 for Bishop's murder and that of seven others during the 1983 coup attempt were to be released. A High Court Judge deemed it unconstitutional for them to serve multiple sentences for manslaughter to run consecutively.

In June 2000 Mitchell dismissed Baptiste from the Government, after Baptiste was reported to have openly criticized Mitchell's running of the country. Mitchell reportedly offered Baptiste the opportunity to remain as an NNP member of Parliament, or to join the opposition. Baptiste opted for the latter and became the sole opposition member in the House of Representatives (he subsequently became a member of GULP).

In September 2000 three diplomats from the People's Republic of China, including the ambassador to Trinidad and Tobago, were deported after they were accused of making statements that 'constituted interference in the internal affairs of Grenada'. The delegation were staying on the island for three days as guests of the Grenada-China Friendship Society, a non-political organization recently formed by Baptiste, which aimed to promote closer links between the two countries. From 1983 Grenada has maintained diplomatic relations with the Republic of China (Taiwan) instead of the People's Republic of China.

In January 2001 the Minister of Foreign Affairs, Mark Isaac, was dismissed, reportedly following his decision to re-establish diplomatic relations with Libya without first gaining cabinet approval. Elvin Nimrod succeeded him. In March Raymond Anthony replaced Lawrence Joseph as Attorney-General and was also appointed Minister of Legal Affairs, a portfolio hitherto held by Nimrod. Joseph was appointed Minister of Labour and Local Government. At the same time, Nimrod was given the international trade portfolio. In January 2002 there was a further reorganization of cabinet portfolios.

In January 2001 Michael Baptiste formed a new opposition party, the United Labour Congress (ULC). Later in the year the ULC merged with GULP and at the party's convention in December Baptiste was elected opposition leader. In February 2003 Gloria Payne-Banfield succeeded Baptiste as GULP leader, in preparation for legislative elections, scheduled to be held by January 2004.

In October 2001 the World Bank approved US $10m. in loan and credit support to Grenada to strengthen its response to, and preparedness for, natural disasters; the funds were also intended to finance road reconstruction and flood control programmes.

In November 2001 the Grenada Trade Union Council threatened to call its members out on strike if the Government did not abandon plans to make changes to labour laws. The proposed legislation, which included proposals to make illegal certain types of industrial action, followed labour unrest in April and May 2000. Opposition parties also condemned the proposed legislation.

In February 2003 GULP elected a civil servant, Gloria Payne-Banfield, as its new leader. Michael Baptiste remained the opposition leader.

As a member of the OECS, Grenada has been involved in discussions concerning the possible formation of a political union. In 1988 Grenada, Dominica, Saint Lucia and Saint Vincent and the Grenadines decided to proceed with their own plans for a political union. In 1990 it was agreed that a Windward Islands Regional Constituent Assembly (RCA) would be convened to discuss the economic and political feasibilities of creating a federation. In late 1992 members of Grenada's House of Representatives fully endorsed a continuation of progress towards political unity. In 1995 the newly-elected Mitchell Government expressed its commitment to increased political and economic integration between the four countries.

In May 1996 Grenada signed two treaties with the USA, relating to mutual legal assistance and extradition, as part of a regional campaign to combat drugs-trafficking. Improved relations with Cuba, which had been severely strained since 1983, resulted in offers of assistance with education, health and agriculture in Grenada in early 1997. In August 1998 President Fidel Castro Ruz of Cuba visited Grenada at Mitchell's invitation, provoking protest from GULP and the DLP, which demanded the release of political prisoners from Cuban jails and the implementation by Cuba of certain human rights agreements. Diplomatic relations between Grenada and Cuba (which had been suspended in 1983) were restored in December 1999, and in January 2003 a new hospital was opened in St George's, partly financed by the Cuban Government. In 2000 Grenada also restored diplomatic relations with Libya (suspended in 1983) and established diplomatic relations with Belarus. In 2001 Libya granted Grenada, along with other eastern Caribbean islands, access to a US $2,000m. development fund. It was also reported, in September, that Libya had agreed to purchase the entire output of Grenada's bananas and would provide the island with a set of grants and loans worth US $4m., as well as cancelling a US $6m. loan for the construction of Grenada's international airport in 1981.

In late 2001 Canada announced that Grenadians travelling to Canada would require visas. This reflected growing international concern over Grenada's Economic Citizenship Programme, under which passports were sold to non-citizens. Following the terrorist attacks in the USA in September 2001, Grenada came under increased pressure to abandon the Programme. The Government initially refused to bow to international pressure, but, in December 2002, it announced the closure of the Programme.

Government

Grenada has dominion status within the Commonwealth. The British monarch is Head of State and is represented locally by a Governor-General. The Cabinet, led by the Prime Minister, holds executive power. Parliament comprises the Senate, made up of 13 Senators appointed by the Governor-General on the advice of the Prime Minister and the Leader of the Opposition, and the 15-member House of Representatives, elected by universal adult suffrage. The Cabinet is responsible to Parliament.

Defence

A regional security unit was formed in 1983, modelled on the British police force and trained by British officers. A paramilitary element, known as the Special Service Unit and trained by US advisers, acts as the defence contingent and participates in the Regional Security System, a defence pact with other East Caribbean states.

Economic Affairs

In 2001, according to estimates by the World Bank, Grenada's gross national income (GNI), measured at average 1999–2001 prices, was US $368m., equivalent to US $3,720 per head (or US $6,720 per head on an international purchasing-power parity basis). In 1990–2001 Grenada's population increased at an average rate of 0.5% per year, while gross domestic product (GDP) per head increased, in real terms, by an average of 2.3% per year. Overall GDP increased, in real terms, at an average annual rate of 2.8% in 1990–2001. According to the IMF, real GDP decreased by 3.3% in 2001.

According to preliminary figures, agriculture (including hunting, forestry and fishing) contributed 6.9% of GDP in 2002. The sector engaged 13.8% of the employed labour force in 1998. Grenada, known as the Spice Island of the Caribbean, is the one of the world's largest producers of nutmeg (Indonesia produces some 75% of the world's total). In 2000, according to preliminary IMF data, sales of nutmeg and mace (the pungent red membrane around the nut) accounted for 23.1% of Grenada's domestic export earnings. The other principal cash crops are cocoa and bananas. Exports of bananas were suspended in early 1997 by the Windward Islands Banana Development and Exporting Company (WIBDECO) because of poor quality, but were permitted to resume in late 1998, following a rehabilitation programme. Nevertheless, exports of bananas were still greatly reduced in 1999–2002. Livestock production, for domestic consumption, is important on Carriacou. There are extensive timber reserves on the island of Grenada; forestry development is strictly controlled and involves a programme of re-afforestation. Exports of fish contributed an estimated 7.3% of domestic export earnings in 2002. Agricultural GDP decreased at an average annual rate of 0.1% in 1998–2002. The sector decreased by 3.2% in 2001 and by an estimated 4.2% in 2002.

Industry (mining, manufacturing, construction and utilities) provided 20.7% of GDP in 2002, according to preliminary figures, and engaged 23.9% of the employed labour force in 1998. The mining sector accounted for only 0.2% of employment in 1998 and 0.8% of GDP in 2002. Manufacturing, which contributed 6.8% of GDP in 2002 and employed 7.4% of the working population in 1998, consists mainly of the processing of agricultural products and of cottage industries producing garments and spice-based items. A nutmeg oil distillation plant commenced production in 1995, and exports of the oil earned some EC $2m. in that year. From the late 1990s the electronic component sector gained in significance. Exports from this sector accounted for nearly two-fifths (39.2%) of domestic merchandise exports in 2002. Rum, soft drinks, paints and varnishes, household paper products and the tyre-retreading industries are also important. Manufacturing GDP increased by an average of 5.0% per year in 1998–2002. The sector's GDP decreased by 7.6% in 2001, before increasing by an estimated 3.0% in 2002. Overall, industrial GDP increased by an annual average of 4.4% in 1998–2002. The GDP of the industrial sector decreased by 9.2% in 2001, but increased by an estimated 0.3% in 2002.

Grenada is dependent upon imports for its energy requirements, and in 2002 fuel accounted for an estimated 9.9% of the total cost of imports.

The services sector contributed 72.4% of GDP in 2002, when hotels and restaurants accounted for some 8.3% of GDP. Tourism receipts totalled around US $83.5m. in 2001. From the mid-1980s until the late 1990s Grenada's tourist industry experienced a rapid expansion. However, total visitor arrivals declined by 16.5% in 2000, to 316,500, and by a further 12.3% in 2001, to an estimated 277,600. The decrease was mainly owing to a massive fall in cruise-ship arrivals (26.6% in 2000 and 18.2% in 2001). Stop-over arrivals, however, remained relatively stable in both years. Of total stop-over visitors (excluding non-resident Grenadians) in 2001, 29.7% were from the USA, 26.3% from the United Kingdom and 25.4% from Caribbean countries. The GDP of the services sector increased at an average annual rate of 3.9% in 1998–2002.

In 2001 Grenada recorded a visible trade deficit of US $133.2m. and there was a deficit of US $85.1m. on the current account of the balance of payments. In 2002 the principal source of imports was the USA, accounting for 45.8% of the total, according to preliminary figures. The USA is also the principal market for exports, taking 38.9% of the total in the same year. The principal exports are electronic components and nutmeg. The principal imports in 2002 were machinery and transport equipment, basic manufactures and foodstuffs. The trade deficit is partly offset by earnings from tourism, capital receipts and remittances from Grenadians working abroad.

In 2001 there was an overall budgetary deficit of EC $92.2m. (equivalent to 8.6% of GDP). Grenada's total external debt was US $206.7m. at the end of 2000, of which US $180.9m. was long-term public debt. In 2000 the cost of debt-servicing was equivalent to 4.6% of the value of exports of goods and services. The average annual rate of inflation was 2.6% in 1990–99; consumer prices increased by by 2.2% in 2000, by 3.2% in 2001 and by an estimated 3.0% in 2002. According to IMF estimates, 12.2% of the labour force were unemployed at the end of 2002. Grenada receives some EC $21m. per year in remittances from more than 100,000 Grenadians living abroad, especially in Canada, the USA and the United Kingdom.

Grenada is a member of CARICOM (see p. 155). It is also a member of the Economic Commission for Latin America and the Caribbean (ECLAC, see p. 31), the Organization of American States (OAS, see p. 288), the Organisation of Eastern Caribbean States (OECS, see p. 341) and is a signatory of the Cotonou Agreement (see p. 234), the successor arrangement to the Lomé Conventions between the African, Caribbean and Pacific (ACP) countries and the European Union. Grenada is a member of the Eastern Caribbean Securities Exchange (based in Saint Christopher and Nevis).

Grenada's economy remains largely dependent upon agriculture, which is vulnerable to adverse weather conditions and infestation by pests. In 1990 the economy's susceptibility to the fluctuations in international commodity prices was demonstrated following the breakdown of Grenada's cartel agreement with Indonesia (signed in 1987). The two countries subsequently concluded several informal agreements in an attempt to stabilize the world nutmeg market through closer co-operation. From 1997 a decline in production of nutmeg in Indonesia resulted in higher prices on the external market, stimulating a significant increase in Grenada's output. In 1999 export earnings from nutmeg increased to US $14.9m. (compared with US $8.7m. in 1998). However, this figure had decreased to US $12.8m. by 2002, according to preliminary figures. The need for further economic diversification has recently been underscored by the loss, from 2006, of preferential access to European markets for banana producers of the ACP countries.

In the late 1990s the Government attempted to diversify the economy partly through the expansion of the 'offshore' financial sector. Since the introduction of legislation in 1997, some 900 'offshore' financial companies (including 21 banks) have been registered in Grenada; in September 1999 the creation of a regulatory body, the International Business and Finance Corporation, was announced. In January 2000, moreover, the Government established the Grenada International Financial Services Authority (GIFSA) to regulate the international financial services sector. In the same year, following Grenada's inclusion on international money-laundering and 'tax havens' blacklists and the collapse (and subsequent government takeover) of an 'offshore' bank, the Government introduced measures to strengthen the GIFSA. These included: redoubling efforts to combat money-laundering and drugs-trafficking; the establishment of a bank supervision department to ensure that all financial institutions operated within the norms of the sector; and a review of all existing legislation governing the financial services sector to comply with the requirements of the Organisation for Economic Co-operation and Development (OECD) by March 2001. As part of this effort, in this month the Government revoked the licences of 17 'offshore' banks and, in June, withdrew a further six licences. As a result of these efforts, and after making a commitment to move towards the exchange of information in tax investigations by 2005, in March 2002 Grenada was removed from the OECD list. The country was also removed from the FATF list in February 2003, following improvements to the supervisory capacity of the Financial Intelligence Unit, the police force and GIFSA.

The most promising sector of the economy was tourism, from which revenue more than doubled between 1990 and 1999. However, revenue from the sector fell in 2001, and the terrorist attacks in the USA in September of that year were expected to have a negative effect on the industry in 2002. In late 2002 the Government announced plans to invest EC $15m. in tourism in 2003, in a bid to stimulate the sector. Growth in tourism during the 1990s, in turn, stimulated the construction sector, the GDP of which expanded by an annual average of 12.4% in 1996–2000; however, the sector registered a contraction of 14.5% in 2001, and there was a further estimated contraction of 6.1% in 2001. Some 95% of taxpayers were effectively exempted from personal income tax obligations after April 1996, when the Government raised significantly the income threshold for liability for this tax. In 2001 the IMF again urged the Grenadian Government to tighten fiscal policy in order to improve the state of public finances (which continue to suffer from sizeable internal and external debts), warning that otherwise the high economic growth of recent years would become unsustainable. In particular, the IMF called for the removal of discretionary tax concessions. Reduced government revenue and increased salary costs resulted in an increase in the fiscal deficit from 3.1% in 2000 to 6.8% of GDP in 2001, financed mainly through local commercial borrowing and an accumulation of arrears. The deficit was expected to widen further, to the equivalent of 9.0% of GDP in 2002. The economic contraction of 2001 was a result of an international downturn in tourism, lower international prices for nutmeg, reduced production of some other crops, and production cutbacks in a local electronics plant. A further contraction in GDP of 0.5% was forecast for 2002.

Education

Education is free and compulsory for children between the ages of five and 16 years. Primary education begins at five years of age and lasts for seven years. Secondary education, beginning at the age of 12, lasts for a further five years. In 1996 a total of 23,449 children received public primary education in 57 schools. There were 20 public secondary schools in 2002, with 7,445 pupils registered, in 1996. Technical Centres have been established in St Patrick's, St David's and St John's, and the Grenada National College, the Mirabeau Agricultural School and the Teachers' Training College have been incorporated into the Technical and Vocational Institute in St George's. The Extra-Mural Department of the University of the West Indies has a branch in St George's. A School of Medicine has been established at St George's University (SGU), where a School of Arts and Sciences was also founded in 1997, while there is a School of Fishing at Victoria. Total budgetary expenditure on education was EC $52.5m. in 2001 (equivalent to 12.5% of total expenditure).

Public Holidays

2003: 1 January (New Year's Day), 7 February (Independence Day), 18 April (Good Friday), 21 April (Easter Monday), 5 May (Labour Day), 9 June (Whit Monday), 19 June (Corpus Christi), 4–5 August (Emancipation Holidays), 11–12 August (Carnival), 25 October (Thanksgiving Day), 25–26 December (Christmas).

2004: 1 January (New Year's Day), 7 February (Independence Day), 9 April (Good Friday), 12 April (Easter Monday), 1 May (Labour Day), 31 May (Whit Monday), 10 June (Corpus Christi), 2–3 August (Emancipation Holidays), 9–10 August (Carnival), 25 October (Thanksgiving Day), 25–26 December (Christmas).

Weights and Measures

The metric system is in use.

Statistical Survey

Source (unless otherwise stated): Central Statistical Office, Ministry of Finance, Trade, Industry and Planning; Financial Complex, The Carenage, St George's; tel. 440-2731; fax 440-4115; e-mail director@economicaffairs.grenada.gd; internet economicaffairs.grenada.gd.

AREA AND POPULATION

Area: 344.5 sq km (133.0 sq miles).

Population: 94,806 (males 46,637; females 48,169) at census of 12 May 1991 (excluding 537 persons in institutions and 33 persons in the foreign service); 100,895 at census of 25 May 2001 (preliminary).

Density (May 2001): 292.9 per sq km.

Principal Town: St George's (capital), population 3,908 (2001 census, preliminary).

Births and Deaths (registrations, 2001, provisional): Live births 1,899 (birth rate 18.8 per 1,000); Deaths 727 (death rate 7.2 per 1,000).

Expectation of Life (WHO estimates, years at birth): 67.2 (males 65.8; females 68.7) in 2001. Source: WHO, *World Health Report*.

Employment (employees only, 1998): Agriculture, hunting, forestry and fishing 4,794; Mining and quarrying 58; Manufacturing 2,579; Electricity, gas and water 505; Construction 5,163; Wholesale and retail trade 6,324; Restaurants and hotels 1,974; Transport, storage and communications 2,043; Financing, insurance and real estate 1,312; Public administration, defence and social security 1,879; Community services 3,904; Other services 2,933; Activities not adequately defined 1,321; Total employed 34,789 (males 20,733; females 14,056).

HEALTH AND WELFARE

Key Indicators

Total Fertility Rate (children per woman, 2001): 3.5.

Under-5 Mortality Rate (per 1,000 live births, 2001): 25.

Physicians (per 1,000 head, 1997): 0.50.

Hospital Beds (per 1,000 head, 1996): 5.27.

Health Expenditure (2000): US $ per head (PPP): 212.

Health Expenditure (2000): % of GDP: 4.8.

Health Expenditure (2000): public (% of total): 70.1.

Access to Water (% of persons, 2000): 94.

Access to Sanitation (% of persons, 2000): 97.

Human Development Index (2000): value: 0.747. For sources and definitions, see explanatory note on p. vi.

AGRICULTURE, ETC.

Principal Crops (FAO estimates, '000 metric tons, 2001): Roots and tubers 4.1; Sugar cane 6.8; Pigeon peas 0.6; Coconuts 6.8; Vegetables 2.6; Bananas 4.1; Plantains 0.7; Oranges 0.9; Grapefruit and pomelos 2.0; Apples 0.5; Plums 0.7; Mangoes 1.9; Avocados 1.8; Other fruits 4.5; Cocoa beans 1.0; Nutmeg, mace and cardamons 2.1. Source: FAO.

Livestock (FAO estimates, '000 head, year ending September 2001): Cattle 4.4; Pigs 5.8; Sheep 13.1; Goats 7.1; Asses 0.7. Source: FAO.

Livestock Products (FAO estimates, '000 metric tons, 2001): Poultry meat 0.6; Cows' milk 0.5; Hen eggs 0.9. Source: FAO.

Fishing (metric tons, live weight, 2000): Capture 1,696 (Red hind 67, Blackfin tuna 163, Yellowfin tuna 402, Atlantic sailfish 164, Atlantic blue marlin 86, Swordfish 84, Bigeye scad 137, Common dolphinfish 167, Barracudas 57); Aquaculture 4; Total catch 1,700. Source: FAO, *Yearbook of Fishery Statistics*.

INDUSTRY

Production (1994): Rum 3,000 hectolitres; Beer 24,000 hectolitres; Wheat flour 4,000 metric tons (1996); Cigarettes 15m.; Electricity 108 million kWh (1997). Source: mainly UN, *Industrial Commodity Statistics Yearbook*.

FINANCE

Currency and Exchange Rates: 100 cents = 1 Eastern Caribbean dollar (EC $). *Sterling, US Dollar and Euro Equivalents* (31 December 2002): £1 sterling = EC $4.352; US $1 = EC $2.700; €1 = EC $2.831; EC $100 = £22.98 = US $37.04 = €35.32. *Exchange Rate:* Fixed at US $1 = EC $2.70 since July 1976.

Budget (EC $ million 2001): *Revenue:* Tax revenue 254.5 (Taxes on income and profits 57.2, Taxes on property 10.1, Taxes on domestic goods and services 44.9, Taxes on international trade and transactions 142.3); Other current revenue 28.2; Capital revenue 0.5; Total 283.2, excluding grants received (45.2). *Expenditure:* Current expenditure 258.0 (Personal emoluments 127.6, Goods and services 35.4, Lease payments 17.3, Interest payments 27.9, Transfers and subsidies 49.8); Capital expenditure 162.6; Total 420.6. Source: IMF, *Grenada: Statistical Appendix* (February 2003).

International Reserves (US $ million at 31 December 2002): IMF special drawing rights 0.00; Foreign exchange 87.84; Total 87.84. Source: IMF, *International Financial Statistics*.

Money Supply (EC $ million at 31 December 2002): Currency outside banks 75.15; Demand deposits at deposit money banks 176.75; Total money (incl. others) 252.34. Source: IMF, *International Financial Statistics*.

Cost of Living (Consumer Price Index; base: 1987 = 100): 140.5 in 2000; 145.0 in 2001; 149.4 in 2002 (preliminary figure). Source: IMF, *Grenada: Statistical Appendix* (February 2003).

Expenditure on the Gross Domestic Product (preliminary, EC $ million at current prices, 2001): Government final consumption expenditure 183.85; Private final consumption expenditure 668.99; Gross fixed capital formation 344.18; *Total domestic expenditure* 1,197.02; Exports of goods and services 631.64; *less* Imports of goods and services 753.59; *GDP in purchasers' values* 1,075.05.

Gross Domestic Product by Economic Activity (preliminary, EC $ million at current prices, 2002): Agriculture, hunting, forestry and fishing 68.5; Mining and quarrying 7.9; Manufacturing 67.5; Electricity and water 52.9; Construction 77.2; Wholesale and retail trade 89.5; Restaurants and hotels 82.5; Transport and communications 216.4; Finance and insurance 101.3; Real estate 33.3; Government services 162.6; Other services 33.0; *Sub-total* 992.6; *Less* Imputed bank service charge 84.1; *GDP at factor cost* 908.5. Source: IMF, *Grenada: Statistical Appendix* (February 2003).

Balance of Payments (US $ million, 2001): Exports of goods f.o.b. 63.60; Imports of goods f.o.b. −196.83; *Trade balance* −133.23; Exports of services 133.53; Imports of services −71.32; *Balance on goods and services* −71.02; Other income received 3.73; Other income paid −39.43; *Balance on goods, services and income* −106.72; Current transfers received 31.02; Current transfers paid −9.36; *Current balance* −85.05; Capital account (net) 41.98; Direct investment from abroad 48.85; Portfolio investment assets −0.42; Portfolio investment liabilities 0.70; Other investment assets −5.30; Other investment liabilities 6.89; Net errors and omissions 11.97; *Overall balance* 5.84. Source: IMF, *International Financial Statistics*.

EXTERNAL TRADE

Principal Commodities (preliminary, US $ million, 2002): *Imports:* Food 38.7; Fuel 23.0; Chemicals 25.9; Basic manufactures 39.1; Machinery and transport equipment 63.9; Miscellaneous manufactured articles 30.1; Total (incl. others) 233.2 (excl. unrecorded imports). *Exports:* Nutmeg 12.8; Fish 4.4; Flour 5.0; Electronic components 23.4; Total (incl. others) 59.7 (excl. re-exports 4.7). Source: IMF, *Grenada: Statistical Appendix* (February 2003).

Principal Trading Partners (US $ million, 1999): *Imports c.i.f.:* Argentina 0.8; Barbados 5.6; Canada 7.1; Guyana 2.1; Honduras 2.3; Japan 11.0; Netherlands 2.0; Trinidad and Tobago 43.2; United Kingdom 16.2; USA 84.5; Venezuela 2.3; Total (incl. others) 202.2. *Exports f.o.b.:* Antigua and Barbuda 1.1; Barbados 1.9; Canada 1.0; Dominica 1.4; Dominican Republic 1.2; France 2.0; French West Indies 2.9; Germany 4.0; Italy 0.4; Jamaica 1.1; Netherlands 7.2; Saint Christopher and Nevis 0.4; Saint Lucia 2.5; Saint Vincent and the Grenadines 0.9; Trinidad and Tobago 0.8; United Kingdom 1.4; USA 6.8; Total (incl. others) 36.3. Source: UN, *International Trade Statistics Yearbook. 2002* (preliminary, EC $ million): Imports c.i.f. 572.1 (CARICOM 146.1; EU 71.5; USA 262.1); Exports f.o.b. 161.1 (CARICOM 35.8; EU 55.6; USA 62.7). Source: IMF, *Grenada: Statistical Appendix* (February 2003).

TRANSPORT

Road Traffic ('000 motor vehicles in use, 2000): Passenger cars 15.5; Commercial vehicles 3.9. Source: UN, *Statistical Yearbook*.

Shipping: *Merchant Fleet* (registered at 31 December 2001) 6 vessels (total displacement 1,009 grt) (Source: Lloyd's Register-Fairplay, *World Fleet Statistics). International Sea-borne Freight Traffic* (estimates, '000 metric tons, 1995): Goods loaded 21.3; Goods unloaded 193.0. *Ship Arrivals* (1991): 1,254. *Fishing vessels* (registered, 1987): 635.

Civil Aviation (aircraft arrivals, 1995): 11,310.

TOURISM

Visitor Arrivals ('000): 379.0 (107.0 stop-overs, 245.5 cruise-ship passengers, 8.2 excursionists) in 1999; 316.5 (110.8 stop-overs, 180.3 cruise-ship passengers, 7.4 excursionists) in 2000; 277.6 (108.4 stop-overs, 147.4 cruise-ship passengers, 6.8 excursionists) in 2001 (preliminary). Source: IMF, *Grenada: Statistical Appendix* (February 2003).

Receipts from Tourism (US $ million): 88.2 in 1999; 92.6 in 2000; 83.5 in 2001 (preliminary). Source: IMF, *Grenada: Statistical Appendix* (February 2003).

COMMUNICATIONS MEDIA

Radio Receivers (1997): 57,000 in use*.

Television Receivers (1999): 35,000 in use*.

Telephones (2001): 32,800 main lines in use‡.

Facsimile Machines (1996): 270 in use†.

Mobile Cellular Telephones (2001): 6,400 subscribers‡.

Personal Computers (2001): 13,000 in use‡.

Internet Users (2001): 5,200‡.

Non-Daily Newspapers (1996): 4; circulation 14,000*.

* Source: UNESCO, *Statistical Yearbook*.
† Source: UN, *Statistical Yearbook*.
‡ Source: International Telecommunication Union.

EDUCATION

Pre-primary (1994): 74 schools; 158 teachers; 3,499 pupils.

Primary (1995): 57 schools; 849 teachers; 23,449 pupils (1996)*.

Secondary (1995): 20 schools (2002); 381 teachers; 7,445 pupils (1996)*.

Higher (excluding figures for the Grenada Teachers' Training College, 1993): 66 teachers; 651 students.
* Source: Caribbean Development Bank, *Social and Economic Indicators 2001*.

Adult Literacy Rate: 94.4 in 2000 (Source: Secretariat of the Organisation of Eastern Caribbean States).

Directory

The Constitution

The 1974 independence Constitution was suspended in March 1979, following the coup, and almost entirely restored between November 1983, after the overthrow of the Revolutionary Military Council, and the elections of December 1984. The main provisions of this Constitution are summarized below:

The Head of State is the British monarch, represented in Grenada by an appointed Governor-General. Legislative power is vested in the bicameral Parliament, comprising a Senate and a House of Representatives. The Senate consists of 13 Senators, seven of whom are appointed on the advice of the Prime Minister, three on the advice of the Leader of the Opposition and three on the advice of the Prime Minister after he has consulted interests which he considers Senators should be selected to represent. The Constitution does not specify the number of members of the House of Representatives, but the country consists of 15 single-member constituencies, for which representatives are elected for up to five years, on the basis of universal adult suffrage.

The Cabinet consists of a Prime Minister, who must be a member of the House of Representatives, and such other ministers as the Governor-General may appoint on the advice of the Prime Minister.

There is a Supreme Court and, in certain cases, a further appeal lies to Her Majesty in Council.

The Government

Head of State: HM Queen ELIZABETH II (succeeded to the throne 6 February 1952).

Governor-General: Sir DANIEL WILLIAMS (appointed 8 August 1996).

THE CABINET
(April 2003)

Prime Minister and Minister of National Security and Information: Dr KEITH CLAUDIUS MITCHELL.

Minister of Finance, Trade, Industry and Planning: ANTHONY BOATSWAIN.

Minister of Foreign Affairs and International Trade, and of Carriacou and Petit Martinique Affairs, and of Legal Affairs: Sen. ELVIN NIMROD.

Minister of Health and the Environment: CLARICE MODESTE-CURWEN.

Minister of Education: AUGUSTINE JOHN.

Minister of Youth, Sports and Community Development: ADRIAN MITCHELL.

Minister of Agriculture, Lands, Forestry and Fisheries: CLARIS CHARLES.

Minister of Tourism, Civil Aviation, Social Security, Gender and Family Affairs, and Culture: BRENDA HOOD.

Minister of Housing, Social Services and Co-operatives: CUTHBERT BRIAN McQUEEN.

Minister of Communications, Works and Public Utilities: Sen. GREGORY BOWEN.

Minister of Transport: OLIVER ARCHIBALD.

Minister of Implementation: JOSLYN WHITEMAN.

Minister of Labour and Local Government: Sen. LAWRENCE JOSEPH.

Attorney-General and Minister of Legal Affairs: Sen. RAYMOND ANTHONY.

MINISTRIES

Office of the Governor-General: Government House, St George's; tel. 440-2401; fax 440-6688.

Office of the Prime Minister: Ministerial Complex, 6th Floor, St George's; tel. 440-2255; fax 440-4116; e-mail gndpm@caribsurf.com.

Ministry of Agriculture, Lands, Forestry and Fisheries: Ministerial Complex, 2nd and 3rd Floors, St George's; tel. 440-2708; fax 440-4191; e-mail grenfish@caribsurf.com.

Ministry of Carriacou and Petit Martinique Affairs: Beauséjour, Carriacou; tel. 443-6026; fax 443-6040.

Ministry of Communications, Works and Public Utilities: Ministerial Complex, 4th Floor, St George's; tel. 440-2181; fax 440-4122; e-mail ministerworks@caribsurf.com.

Ministry of Education: Ministerial Complex, Botanical Gardens, St George's; tel. 440-2166; fax 440-6650; e-mail mail@mined.edu.gd.

Ministry of Finance, Trade, Industry and Planning: Financial Complex, The Carenage, St George's; tel. 440-2731; fax 440-4115; e-mail director@economicaffairs.grenada.gd; internet economicaffairs.grenada.gd.

Ministry of Foreign Affairs and International Trade: Ministerial Complex, 4th Floor, Botanical Gardens, St George's; tel. 440-2640; fax 440-4184; e-mail faffgnd@caribsurf.com.

Ministry of Health and the Environment: Ministerial Complex, 1st and 2nd Floors, Botanical Gardens, St George's; tel. 440-2649; fax 440-4127; e-mail minhealthgrenada@caribsurf.com.

Ministry of Housing, Social Services, Culture and Co-operatives: Ministerial Complex, 1st and 2nd Floors, Botanical Gardens, St George's; tel. 440-6917; fax 440-6924; e-mail mhousing@hotmail.com.

Ministry of Implementation: Ministerial Complex, 6th Floor, St George's; tel. 440-2255; fax 440-4116; e-mail gndpm@caribsurf.com.

Ministry of Information: Ministerial Complex, 6th Floor, Botanical Gardens, St George's; tel. 440-2255; fax 440-4116.

Ministry of Labour and Local Government: Ministerial Complex, 3rd Floor, St George's; tel. 440-2532; fax 440-4923.

Ministry of Legal Affairs: Church St, St George's; tel. 440-2050; fax 440-6630; e-mail legalaffairs@caribsurf.com.

Ministry of National Security: Ministerial Complex, Botanical Gardens, St George's; tel. 440-2255.

Ministry of Tourism, Civil Aviation, Social Security, Gender and Family Affairs: Ministerial Complex, 4th Floor, Botanical Gardens, St George's; tel. 440-0366; fax 440-0443; e-mail mot@caribsurf.com; internet www.spiceisle.com.users.mot.

Ministry of Transport: Young St, St George's.

Ministry of Youth, Sports and Community Development: Ministerial Complex, 2nd Floor, Botanical Gardens, St George's; tel. 440-6917; fax 440-6924; e-mail yscm@caribsurf.com.

Legislature

PARLIAMENT

Houses of Parliament: Church St, St George's; tel. 440-2090; fax 440-4138.

Senate

President: Sen. Dr JOHN WATTS.

There are 13 appointed members.

House of Representatives

Speaker: GEORGE McGUIRE.

General Election, 18 January 1999

	Votes	%	Seats
New National Party (NNP)	25,897	62.2	15*
National Democratic Congress (NDC)	10,399	24.9	—
United Labour†	4,853	11.6	—
Others	455	1.1	—
Total	41,604	100.0	15

* In June 2000 the NNP's parliamentary representation was reduced to 14 seats after one of its deputies, Michael Baptiste, joined the opposition. As a consequence, United Labour gained one seat in the House of Representatives.

† Informal electoral alliance composed of the Grenada United Labour Party (GULP) and the Democratic Labour Party (DLP).

Political Organizations

Grenada United Labour Party (GULP): St George's; f. 1950; merged with United Labour Congress in 2001; right-wing; Pres. WILFRED HAYES; Leader GLORIA PAYNE-BANFIELD.

Maurice Bishop Patriotic Movement (MBPM): St George's; f. 1984 by former members of the New Jewel Movement; socialist; Leader TERRENCE MARRYSHOW.

National Democratic Congress (NDC): St George's; f. 1987 by former members of the NNP and merger of Democratic Labour Congress and Grenada Democratic Labour Party; centrist; Leader TILLMAN THOMAS; Dep. Leader GEORGE PRIME.

The National Party (TNP): St George's; f. 1989 by Prime Minister Herbert Blaize and his supporters, following a split in the New National Party; Chair. GEORGE McGUIRE; Leader BEN JONES.

New National Party (NNP): St George's; f. 1984 following merger of Grenada Democratic Movement, Grenada National Party and National Democratic Party; centrist; Chair. LAWRENCE JOSEPH; Leader Dr KEITH MITCHELL; Dep. Leader GREGORY BOWEN.

People's Labour Movement (DLP): St George's; f. 1995 by former members of the NDC; formerly known as the Democratic Labour Party; Leader Dr FRANCIS ALEXIS; Pres. Dr TERRANCE MARRYSHOW.

United Republican Party (URP): St George's; f. 1993 by Grenadians residing in New York, USA; Leader ANTONIO LANGDON.

Diplomatic Representation

EMBASSIES AND HIGH COMMISSION IN GRENADA

Belgium: St George's; Ambassador BOUDOIUM VANDERHULST.

China (Taiwan): L'Anse aux Epines, St George's; tel. 440-3054; fax 440-4177; e-mail rocemgnd@caribsurf.com; Ambassador ALLAN LII-SHANG JIANG.

Cuba: L'Anse aux Epines, St George's; tel. 444-1884; fax 444-1877; e-mail embacubagrenada@caribsurf.com; Ambassador HUMBERTO RIVERO ROSARIO.

United Kingdom: British High Commission, Netherland Bldg, Grand Anse, St George's; tel. 440-3536; fax 440-4939; e-mail bhcgrenada@caribsurf.com; High Commissioner resident in Barbados.

USA: POB 54, St George's; tel. 444-1173; fax 444-4820; e-mail usembgd@caribsurf.com; internet www.spiceisle.com/homepages/usembgd/embinfo; Ambassador resident in Barbados.

Venezuela: Upper Lucas St, POB 201, St George's; tel. 440-1721; fax 440-6657; e-mail embavengda@caribsurf.com; Ambassador EDNA FIGUERA CEDEÑO.

Judicial System

Justice is administered by the West Indies Associated States Supreme Court, composed of a High Court of Justice and a Court of Appeal. The Itinerant Court of Appeal consists of three judges and sits three times a year; it hears appeals from the High Court and the Magistrates' Court. The Magistrates' Court administers summary jurisdiction.

In 1988 the OECS excluded the possibility of Grenada's readmittance to the East Caribbean court system until after the conclusion of appeals by the defendants in the Maurice Bishop murder trial (see Recent History). Following the conclusion of the case in 1991,

Parliament voted to rejoin the system, thus also restoring the right of appeal to the Privy Council in the United Kingdom.

Attorney-General: Sen. RAYMOND ANTHONY.

Puisne Judges: DENYS BARROW, KENNETH BENJAMIN, LYLE K. ST PAUL.

Registrar of the Supreme Court: ROBERT BRANCH.

President of the Court of Appeal: C. M. DENNIS BYRON.

Office of the Attorney-General: Church St, St George's; tel. 440-2050; fax 440-6630; e-mail legalaffairs@caribsurf.com.

Religion

CHRISTIANITY

The Roman Catholic Church

Grenada comprises a single diocese, suffragan to the archdiocese of Castries (Saint Lucia). The Bishop participates in the Antilles Episcopal Conference (based in Port of Spain, Trinidad and Tobago). At 31 December 2001 there were an estimated 55,825 adherents in the diocese.

Bishop of St George's in Grenada: Rev. VINCENT DARIUS, Bishop's House, Morne Jaloux, POB 375, St George's; tel. 443-5299; fax 443-5758; e-mail bissac@caribsurf.com.

The Anglican Communion

Anglicans in Grenada are adherents of the Church in the Province of the West Indies, and represented 14% of the population at the time of the 1991 census. The country forms part of the diocese of the Windward Islands (the Bishop, the Rt Rev. SEHON GOODRIDGE, resides in Kingstown, Saint Vincent).

Other Christian Churches

The Presbyterian, Methodist, Plymouth Brethren, Baptist, Salvation Army, Jehovah's Witness, Pentecostal (7.2% of the population in 1991) and Seventh-day Adventist (8.5%) faiths are also represented.

The Press

NEWSPAPERS

Barnacle: Frequente Industrial Park, St George's; tel. 440-5151; monthly; Editor IAN GEORGE.

The Grenada Informer: Market Hill, POB 622, St George's; tel. 440-1530; fax 440-4119; e-mail movanget@caribsurf.com; f. 1985; weekly; Editor CARLA BRIGGS; circ. 6,000.

Grenada Today: St John's St, POB 142, St George's; tel. 440-4401; internet www.belgrafix.com/gtoday98.htm; weekly; Editor GEORGE WORME.

The Grenadian Voice: 10 Melville St, POB 633, St George's; tel. 440-1498; fax 440-4117; e-mail gvoice@caribsurf.com; internet www.grenadianvoice.com; weekly; Editor LESLIE PIERRE; circ. 3,000.

Government Gazette: St George's; weekly; official.

PRESS ASSOCIATION

Press Association of Grenada: St George's; f. 1986; Pres. LESLIE PIERRE.

Inter Press Service (IPS) (Italy) is also represented.

Publisher

Anansi Publications: Hillsborough St, St George's; tel. 440-0800; e-mail aclouden@caribsurf.com.

Broadcasting and Communications

TELECOMMUNICATIONS

Regulatory Authority

Eastern Caribbean Telecommunications Authority: Castries, Saint Lucia; f. 2000 to regulate telecommunications in Grenada, Dominica, Saint Christopher and Nevis, Saint Lucia and Saint Vincent and the Grenadines.

National Telecommunications Regulatory Commission: POB 854, St George's; tel. 435-6872; fax 435-2132; e-mail gntrc@

caribsurf.com; internet www.spiceisle.com/gnrtc; Chair. LINUS SPENCER THOMAS.

Major Service Providers

In April 2001 the Government agreed to liberalize the telecommunications sector by the end of 2003. The monopoly of the sector hitherto enjoyed by Cable & Wireless was ended.

Cable and Wireless Grenada Ltd: POB 119, The Carenage, St George's; tel. 440-1000; fax 440-4134; e-mail gndinfo@caribsurf.com; internet www.candw.gd; f. 1989; until 1998 known as Grenada Telecommunications Ltd (Grentel); 30% govt-owned; CEO ERRALD MILLER; Gen. Man. CARLYLE ROBERTS.

Grenada Postal Corporation: Burns Point, St George's; tel. 440-2526; fax 440-4271; e-mail gpc@caribsurf.com; internet gndonline.com; Chair. GORDON ROBINSON; Man. LEO ROBERTS.

BROADCASTING

Grenada Broadcasting Network (GBN): Observatory Rd, POB 535, St George's; tel. 440-2446; fax 440-4180; e-mail gbn@caribsurf.com; internet www2.spiceisle.com; f. 1972; 60% privately-owned, 40% govt-owned; Chair. KEN GORDON; Man. Dir RICHARD PURCELL.

Radio

Grenada Broadcasting Network (Radio): (see Broadcasting).

The Harbour Light of the Windwards: Carriacou; tel. and fax 443-7628; e-mail hbrlight@caribsurf.com; Station Man. RANDY CORNELIUS; Chief Engineer JOHN MCPHERSON.

Spice Capitol Radio FM 90: Springs, St George's; tel. 440-0162.

Television

Television programmes from Trinidad and from Barbados can be received on the island.

Grenada Broadcasting Network (Television): (see Broadcasting).

Finance

(cap. = capital; res = reserves; dep. = deposits; amounts in Eastern Caribbean dollars)

The Eastern Caribbean Central Bank (see p. 343), based in Saint Christopher, is the central issuing and monetary authority for Grenada.

Eastern Caribbean Central Bank—Grenada Office: Monckton St, St George's; tel. 440-3016; fax 440-6721.

BANKING

Regulatory Authority

Grenada International Financial Services Authority: Bldg 5, Financial Complex, The Carenage, St George's; tel. 440-6575; fax 440-4780; e-mail gifsa@caribsurf.com; internet gifsa-grenada.com; f. 1999; Chair. RICHARDSON ANDREWS; Deputy Chair. TIMOTHY ANTOINE.

Commercial Banks

Grenada Co-operative Bank Ltd: 8 Church St, POB 135, St George's; tel. 440-2111; fax 440-6600; e-mail co-opbank@caribsurf.com; f. 1932; Man. Dir and Sec. G. V. STEELE; brs in St Andrew's and St Patrick's.

Grenada Development Bank: POB 734, Melville St, St George's; tel. 440-2382; fax 440-6610; e-mail gdbbank@caribsurf.com; f. 1976 following merger; Chair. ARNOLD CRUICKSHANK; Man. CAMPBELL BLENMAN.

National Commercial Bank of Grenada Ltd: NCB House, POB 857, Grand Anse, St George's; tel. 444-2265; fax 444-5500; e-mail ncbgnd@caribsurf.com; internet www.ncbgrenada.com; f. 1979; 51% owned by Republic Bank Ltd, Port of Spain; cap. 15.0m., res 8.1m., dep. 333.1m. (Sept. 1999); Chair. RONALD HARFORD; Man. Dir DANIEL ROBERTS; 9 brs.

Foreign Banks

Bank of Nova Scotia (Canada): Granby and Halifax Sts, POB 194, St George's; tel. 440-3274; fax 440-4173; Man. B. ROBINSON; 3 brs.

Caribbean Commercial Bank (Trinidad and Tobago): St George's; 1 br.

FirstCaribbean International Bank Ltd: Church St, St George's; tel. 440–3232; f. 2003; 87.5% owned by Barclays Bank PLC (United Kingdom) and Canadian Imperial Bank of Commerce; CEO CHARLES PINK; Exec. Dir SHARON BROWN; 4 brs.

RBTT Bank Grenada Ltd: Corner of Cross and Halifax Sts, POB 4, St George's; tel. 440-3521; fax 440-4153; e-mail gbcltd@caribsurf .com; f. 1983; 10% govt-owned; cap. 7.4m., res 8.8m., dep. 256.6m. (Dec. 2000); Chair. BRUCE AANENSEN; Man. Dir MAXIM PAZOS; 4 brs.

STOCK EXCHANGE

Eastern Caribbean Securities Exchange: based in Basseterre, Saint Christopher and Nevis; e-mail info@ecseonline.com; internet www.ecseonline.com; f. 2001; regional securities market designed to facilitate the buying and selling of financial products for the eight member territories—Anguilla, Antigua and Barbuda, Dominica, Grenada, Montserrat, Saint Christopher and Nevis, Saint Lucia and Saint Vincent and the Grenadines; Gen. Man. BALJIT VOHRA.

INSURANCE

Several foreign insurance companies operate in Grenada and the other islands of the group. Principal locally-owned companies include the following:

Grenada Insurance and Finance Co Ltd: Young St, POB 139, St George's; tel. 440-3004.

Grenada Motor and General Insurance Co Ltd: Scott St, St George's; tel. 440-3379.

Grenadian General Insurance Co Ltd: Corner of Young and Scott Sts, POB 47, St George's; tel. 440-2434; fax 440-6618.

Trade and Industry

CHAMBERS OF COMMERCE

Grenada Chamber of Industry and Commerce, Inc: DeCaul Bldg, Mt Gay, POB 129, St George's; tel. 440-2937; fax 440-6627; e-mail gcic@caribsurf.com; internet www.spiceisle.com/homepages/ gcic; f. 1921; incorporated 1947; 170 mems; Pres. CHRISTOPHER DE ALLIE; Exec. Dir CHRISTOPHER DERIGGS.

Grenada Manufacturing Council: POB 129, St George's; tel. 440-2937; fax 440-6627; e-mail gcic@caribsurf.com; f. 1991 to replace Grenada Manufacturers' Asscn; Chair. CHRISTOPHER DEALLIE.

INDUSTRIAL AND TRADE ASSOCIATIONS

Grenada Cocoa Association: Scott St, St George's; tel. 440-2234; fax 440-1470; f. 1987 following merger; changed from co-operative to shareholding structure in late 1996; Chair. REGINALD BUCKMIRE; Man. ANDREW HASTICK.

Grenada Co-operative Banana Society: Scott St, St George's; tel. 440-2486; fax 440-4199; e-mail gbcs@caribsurf.com; f. 1955; a statutory body to control production and marketing of bananas; Exec. Chair. DANIEL LEWIS; Gen. Man. JOHN MARK (acting).

Grenada Co-operative Nutmeg Association: Lagoon Rd, POB 160, St George's; tel. 440-2117; fax 440-6602; e-mail gcna.nutmeg@ caribsurf.com; internet www.grenadanutmeg.com; f. 1947; processes and markets all the nutmeg and mace grown on the island; to include the production of nutmeg oil; Chair. RAMSEY RUSH; Gen. Man. TERENCE MOORE.

Grenada Industrial Development Corporation: Frequente Industrial Park, Frequente, St George's; tel. 444-1035; fax 444-4828; e-mail gidc@caribsurf.com; internet www.grenadaworld.com; f. 1985; Chair. R. ANTHONY JOSEPH; Man. SONIA RODEN.

Marketing and National Importing Board: Young St, St George's; tel. 440-1791; fax 440-4152; e-mail mnib.com@caribsurf.com; f. 1974; govt-owned; imports basic food items, incl. sugar, rice and milk; Chair. RICHARDSON ANDREWS; Gen. Man. FITZROY JAMES.

EMPLOYERS' ORGANIZATION

Grenada Employers' Federation: Mt Gay, POB 129, St George's; tel. 440-1832; 60 mems.

There are several marketing and trading co-operatives, mainly in the agricultural sector.

UTILITIES

Public Utilities Commission: St George's.

Electricity

Grenada Electricity Services Ltd (Grenlec): Halifax St, POB 381, St George's; tel. 440-2097; fax 440-4106; e-mail grenlec@ caribsurf.com; internet www.carilec.org/grenlec; generation and distribution; 90% privately-owned, 10% govt-owned; Chair. G. ROBERT BLANCHARD Jr; Gen. Man. VERNON LAWRENCE.

Water

National Water and Sewerage Authority: The Carenage, POB 392, St George's; tel. 440-2155; fax 440-4107; f. 1969; Chair. MICHAEL PIERRE; Man. ALLEN McQUIRE.

TRADE UNIONS

Grenada Trade Union Council (GTUC): Green St, POB 411, St George's; tel. 440-3733; fax 440-3733; e-mail gtuc@caribsurf.com; Pres. DEREK ALLARD; Gen. Sec. RAY ROBERTS.

Bank and General Workers' Union (BGWU): Bain's Alley, St George's; tel. 440-3563; fax 440-0778; e-mail bgwu@caribsurf.com; Pres. DEREK ALLARD; Gen. Sec. JUSTIN CAMPBELL.

Commercial and Industrial Workers' Union: Bain's Alley, POB 191, St George's; tel. 440-3423; fax 440-3423; Pres. ELLIOT BISHOP; Gen. Sec. BARBARA FRASER; 492 mems.

Grenada Manual, Maritime and Intellectual Workers' Union (GMMIWU): c/o Birchgrove, St Andrew's; tel. 442-7724; fax 442-7724; Pres. BERT LaTOUCHE; Gen. Sec. OSCAR WILLIAMS.

Grenada Union of Teachers (GUT): Marine Villa, POB 452, St George's; tel. 440-2992; fax 440-9019; f. 1913; Pres. MARVIN ANDALL; Gen. Sec. ELAINE McQUEEN; 1,300 mems.

Media Workers' Association of Grenada (MWAG): St George's; f. 1999; Pres. LEW SMITH.

Public Workers' Union (PWU): Tanteen, POB 420, St George's; tel. 440-2203; fax 440-6615; e-mail pwu-cpsa@caribsurf.com; f. 1931; Pres. LAURETTE CLARKSON; Gen. Sec. SHIRLEY MODESTE.

Seamen and Waterfront Workers' Union: Ottway House, POB 154, St George's; tel. 440-2573; fax 440-7199; e-mail swwu@caribsurf .com; f. 1952; Pres. ALBERT JULIEN; Gen. Sec. LYLE SAMUEL; 350 mems.

Technical and Allied Workers' Union (TAWU): Green St, POB 405, St George's; tel. 440-2231; fax 440-5878; f. 1958; Pres.-Gen. Sen. CHESTER HUMPHREY; Gen. Sec. ANDRÉ LEWIS.

Transport

RAILWAYS

There are no railways in Grenada.

ROADS

In 1999 there were approximately 1,040 km (646 miles) of roads, of which 61.3% were paved. Public transport is provided by small private operators, with a system covering the entire country.

SHIPPING

The main port is St George's, with accommodation for two ocean-going vessels of up to 500 ft. A number of shipping lines call at St George's. Grenville, on Grenada, and Hillsborough, on Carriacou, are used mostly by small craft.

Grenada Ports Authority: POB 494, The Carenage, St George's; tel. 440-7678; fax 440-3418; e-mail grenport@caribsurf.com; internet www.grenadaports.com; Chair. WALTER ST JOHN; Gen. Man. AMBROSE PHILLIP.

CIVIL AVIATION

The Point Salines International Airport, 10 km (6 miles) from St George's, was opened in October 1984, and has scheduled flights to most East Caribbean destinations, including Venezuela, and to the United Kingdom and North America. Work on an EC $30m.-project to renovate and expand the airport began in early 2000. There is an airfield at Pearls, 30 km (18 miles) from St George's, and Lauriston Airport, on the island of Carriacou, offers regular scheduled services to Grenada, Saint Vincent and Palm Island (Grenadines of Saint Vincent).

Grenada is a shareholder in the regional airline, LIAT (see under Antigua and Barbuda).

Grenada Airports Authority: Point Salines Int. Airport, POB 385, St George's; tel. 444-4101; fax 444-4838; e-mail gaa@caribsurf .com; f. 1985; Chair. MICHAEL McINTYRE; CEO GEORGE LEID; Gen. Man. DONALD McPHAIL.

Airlines of Carriacou: Point Salines International Airport, POB 805, St Georges; tel. 444-1475; fax 444-2898; e-mail cayar@caribsurf .com; internet www.travelgrenada.com/aircarriacou.htm; f. 1992; national airline, operates in association with LIAT; Man. Dir ARTHUR W. BAIN.

Tourism

Grenada has the attractions of both white sandy beaches and a scenic, mountainous interior with an extensive rain forest. There are also sites of historical interest, and the capital, St George's, is a noted beauty spot. In 2001 there were an estimated 277,600 visitor arrivals, of which 147,400 were cruise-ship passengers, and tourism earned an estimated some US $83.5m. There were approximately 1,670 hotel rooms in 1996. In 1997 a joint venture between the Government of Grenada and the Caribbean Development Bank to upgrade and market some 50 unprofitable hotels was implemented. In addition, the Ministry of Tourism, in conjunction with the Board of Tourism and the Hotel Association, announced a 10-year development plan to increase hotel capacity to 2,500 rooms.

Grenada Board of Tourism: Burns Point, POB 293, St George's; tel. 440-2279; fax 440-6637; e-mail gbt@caribsurf.com; internet www.grenadagrenadines.com; f. 1991; Chair. RICHARD STRACHAN; Dir WILLIAM JOSEPH.

Grenada Hotel and Tourism Association Ltd: POB 440, St George's; tel. 444-1353; fax 444-4847; e-mail grenhota@caribsurf.com; internet www.grenadahotelsinfo.com; f. 1961; Pres. LAWRENCE LAMBERT; Dirs SHEREE ANN ADAMS, IAN DABREO, ROYSTON HOPKIN, RUSS FIELDEN, LEO GARBUTT, JOE GAYLORD, LENWORTH GORDON, ANN BAYNE GRIFFITH, ESTHER NOEL.

GUATEMALA

Introductory Survey

Location, Climate, Language, Religion, Flag, Capital

The Republic of Guatemala lies in the Central American isthmus, bounded to the north and west by Mexico, with Honduras and Belize to the east and El Salvador to the south. It has a long coastline on the Pacific Ocean and a narrow outlet to the Caribbean Sea. The climate is tropical in the lowlands, with an average temperature of 28°C (83°F), and more temperate in the central highland area, with an average temperature of 20°C (68°F). The official language is Spanish, but more than 20 indigenous languages are also spoken. Almost all of the inhabitants profess Christianity: the majority are Roman Catholics, while about 10% are Protestants. The national flag (proportions 5 by 8) has three equal vertical stripes, of blue, white and blue, with the national coat of arms (depicting a quetzal, the 'bird of freedom', and a scroll, superimposed on crossed rifles and sabres, encircled by a wreath) in the centre of the white stripe. The capital is Guatemala City.

Recent History

Under Spanish colonial rule, Guatemala was part of the Viceroyalty of New Spain. Independence was obtained from Spain in 1821, from Mexico in 1824 and from the Federation of Central American States in 1838. Subsequent attempts to revive the Federation failed and, under a series of dictators, there was relative stability, tempered by periods of disruption. A programme of social reform was begun by Juan José Arévalo (President in 1944–50) and his successor, Col Jacobo Arbenz Guzmán, whose policy of land reform evoked strong opposition from landowners. In 1954 President Arbenz was overthrown in a coup led by Col Carlos Castillo Armas, who invaded the country with US assistance. Castillo became President but was assassinated in July 1957. The next elected President, Gen. Miguel Ydigoras Fuentes, took office in March 1958 and ruled until he was deposed in March 1963 by a military coup, led by Col Enrique Peralta Azurdia. He assumed full powers as Chief of Government, suspended the Constitution and dissolved the legislature. A Constituent Assembly, elected in 1964, introduced a new Constitution in 1965. Dr Julio César Méndez Montenegro was elected President in 1966, and in 1970 the candidate of the Movimiento de Liberación Nacional (MLN), Col (later Gen.) Carlos Araña Osorio, was elected President. Despite charges of fraud in the elections of March 1974, Gen. Kjell Laugerud García of the MLN took office as President in July.

President Laugerud sought to discourage extreme right-wing violence and claimed some success, although it was estimated that 50,000–60,000 people were killed in political violence between 1970 and 1979. In March 1978 Gen. Fernando Romeo Lucas García was elected President. The guerrilla movement increased in strength in 1980–1981, while the Government was accused of the murder and torture of civilians and, particularly, persecution of the country's indigenous Indian inhabitants, who comprise 60% of the population.

In the presidential elections of March 1982, from which the left-wing parties were absent, the Government's candidate, Gen. Angel Aníbal Guevara, was declared the winner; however, the elections were denounced as fraudulent by the other presidential candidates. Guevara was prevented from taking office in July by a coup on 23 March, in which a group of young right-wing military officers installed Gen. José Efraín Ríos Montt (a candidate in the 1974 presidential elections) as leader of a three-man junta. Congress was closed, and the Constitution and political parties suspended. In June Gen. Ríos Montt dissolved the junta and assumed the presidency. He attempted to fight corruption, reorganized the judicial system and disbanded the secret police. The number of violent deaths diminished. However, after initially gaining the support of the national university, the Roman Catholic Church and the labour unions and hoping to enter into dialogue with the guerrillas, who refused to respond to an amnesty declaration in June, Ríos Montt declared a state of siege, and imposed censorship of the press, in July. In addition, the war against the guerrillas intensified, and a civil defence force of Indians was established. The efficiency and ruthlessness of the army increased. Whole villages were burnt, and many inhabitants killed, in order to deter the Indians from supporting the guerrillas. Ríos Montt's increasingly corporatist policies alienated all groups, and his fragile hold on power was threatened in 1982 by several attempted coups, which he managed to forestall.

The US Administration was eager to renew sales of armaments and the provision of economic and military aid to Guatemala, which had been suspended in 1977 as a result of serious violations of human rights. In January 1983 the US Government, satisfied that there had been a significant decrease in such violations during Ríos Montt's presidency, announced the resumption of arms sales to Guatemala. However, independent reports claimed that the situation had deteriorated, and revealed that 2,600 people had been killed during the first six months of Ríos Montt's rule. In March the army was implicated in the massacre of 300 Indian peasants at Nahulá, and there was a resurgence in the activity of both left- and right-wing 'death squads'. The President declared a 30-day amnesty for guerrillas and political exiles, and lifted the state of siege. Furthermore, he announced the creation of an electoral tribunal to oversee a proposed transfer from military rule to civilian government. In April the army launched a new offensive, which made significant gains against the guerrillas. The Government's pacification programme comprised three phases of aid programmes, combined with the saturation of the countryside by anti-guerrilla units. The 'guns and beans' policy provided food and medicine in exchange for recruitment to the Patrullas de Autodefensa Civil (PAC), a pro-Government peasant militia. (By 1985 these self-defence patrols numbered 900,000 men.) The 'roofs, bread and work' phase involved the development of 'model villages', and the 'Aid Programme for Areas in Conflict' was an ambitious rural development scheme.

By mid-1983 opposition to the President was widespread. On 8 August Gen. Oscar Humberto Mejía Victores, the Minister of Defence, led a successful coup against President Ríos Montt. The new President announced the abolition of the secret tribunals and ended press censorship. A 90-day amnesty for guerrillas was announced in October and subsequently extended throughout 1984. Urban and rural terrorism continued to escalate, however, and in November 1983 the Government was accused of directing a campaign of kidnappings against the Roman Catholic Church. Following the murder in northern Guatemala of six US aid workers, the USA suspended US $50m. in aid to Guatemala in 1984. Israel continued to supply weapons to Guatemala, and Israeli military advisers were reported to be active in the country. In accordance with the President's assurance of electoral reform, elections for a Constituent Assembly were held in July 1984, at which the centre groups, including the newly formed Unión del Centro Nacional (UCN), obtained the greatest number of votes. Under the system of proportional representation, however, the right-wing coalition of the MLN and the Central Auténtica Nacionalista (CAN) together obtained a majority of seats in the Assembly.

Guatemala's new Constitution was promulgated in May 1985. Elections for the presidency, the Congreso Nacional (National Congress) and 331 mayoralties were scheduled to be held in November. Prior to the elections, there was a substantial increase in rebel activity and political assassinations by 'death squads'. Furthermore, in September violent protests, led by students and trade unionists, erupted in reaction to a series of price increases.

Eight candidates participated in the presidential election in November 1985, but the main contest was between Jorge Carpio Nicolle, the candidate of the UCN, and Mario Vinicio Cerezo Arévalo, the candidate of the Partido Democracia Cristiana Guatemalteca (PDCG). As neither of the leading candidates obtained the requisite majority, a second round of voting was held in December, when Cerezo secured 68% of the votes cast. The PDCG formed the majority party in the new Congreso Nacional and won the largest proportion of mayoralties. Cerezo was believed to enjoy the support of the US Administration, which increased its allocation of economic aid and resumed military aid to Guatemala, in support of the new civilian Government.

Immediately prior to the transfer of power in January 1986, the outgoing military Government decreed a general amnesty to encompass those suspected of involvement in abuses of human rights since March 1982. In the following month, however, in an attempt to curb the continuing violence and to improve the country's poor record for the observance of human rights, the notorious Department of Technical Investigations was dissolved and replaced by a new criminal investigations unit. Violence continued unabated, however, with 700 killings reported in the first six months of 1986. Cerezo claimed that not all murders were politically motivated, while his relations with the armed forces remained precarious. Meanwhile, a grouping of relatives of victims of repression, the Grupo de Apoyo Mutuo (GAM) attracted increasing support, and in August about 3,000 demonstrators took part in a protest to demand information on the fate of the thousands of *desaparecidos* ('disappeared'). In April 1987 the creation of a government commission to investigate disappearances was announced. Nevertheless, by mid-1988 there were frequent reports of torture and killings by right-wing 'death squads' as discontent with the Government's liberal policies increased. In September 1989 the Consejo Nacional de Desplazados de Guatemala (CONDEG) was created to represent the 1m. refugees who had fled their homes since 1980. According to the UN Commission for Human Rights almost 3,000 complaints of human rights abuses were lodged in 1989.

In August 1987 a peace plan for the region was signed in Guatemala City by the Presidents of Costa Rica, El Salvador, Guatemala, Honduras and Nicaragua. Although the plan was principally concerned with the conflicts in Nicaragua and El Salvador, it also referred to the long-standing guerrilla war in Guatemala. Subsequently, a Commission of National Reconciliation (CNR) was formed in compliance with the terms of the accord. In October representatives of the Guatemalan Government and the main guerrilla grouping, the Unidad Revolucionaria Nacional Guatemalteca (URNG), met in Spain to discuss the question of peace in Guatemala. The negotiations ended without agreement. Right-wing pressure on the Government, and an attempted coup in May 1988, forced Cerezo to postpone further negotiations with the URNG. After another coup plot was discovered in July, Cerezo rejected the URNG's proposal for a truce.

During 1989 guerrilla activity by groups from both the right and the left intensified. Many political figures and labour leaders fled the country after receiving death threats from paramilitary groups. In January a new leftist group emerged, the Comando Urbano Revolucionario, which joined the URNG guerrillas. Meanwhile, Cerezo refused to negotiate with the URNG for as long as its members remained armed. In September the URNG made further proposals for negotiations, following the signing of the Tela Agreement (the Central American peace plan accord), but these were rejected. A major counter-insurgency operation was launched by the Government in December. In the same month, Cerezo accused the ruling party in El Salvador of supplying weapons to the right-wing death squads of Guatemala.

In May 1989 another coup attempt was foiled without bloodshed. During August and September a secret right-wing military organization perpetrated a series of terrorist attacks in an attempt to destabilize the Government. At the same time, the ruling party was undergoing a political crisis, following its internal presidential primary elections in August. The PDCG's choice of presidential candidate had been split between Alfonso Cabrera Hidalgo, the party's Secretary-General and former Minister of Foreign Affairs, and René de León Schlotter, the leader of the party's left wing and Minister of Urban and Rural Development. The most likely compromise candidate, Danilo Barillas, had been assassinated a short while before the selection procedure, allegedly by the extreme right, which, by provoking disunity within the PDCG, hoped to give an advantage to its own candidates. The former military ruler, Gen. José Efraín Ríos Montt, also presented his candidacy for the presidential election that was to take place one year later. He was supported by the moderate Partido Institucional Democrático (PID) and the Frente de Unidad Nacional (FUN) and secured considerable public support. However, in October 1990 his candidacy was declared invalid on constitutional grounds (under the Constitution, anyone taking part in, or benefiting from, a military coup was disqualified from participating in elections).

In August 1989 Cerezo and his Mexican counterpart held a meeting, aimed at resolving the refugee problem and at establishing collaboration against drugs-trafficking in the region. As Mexico had begun implementing measures to combat the problem of drugs-trafficking within its borders, with some success, Guatemala was consequently developing as a new centre for heroin production and cocaine transhipments from Central America to the USA. Local efforts to confront the problem were largely ineffective, and a US $1m. programme dedicated mainly to the aerial spraying of poppy fields, financed by the USA, was hampered by ground-level retaliatory attacks.

Despite Cerezo's promise to restrict the unlawful activities of the armed forces and right-wing death squads, the number of politically-motivated assassinations and 'disappearances' escalated in 1990. In March the US ambassador was recalled, in protest at the President's continued failure to curb the growing incidence of human rights violations. In the same month the URNG and the CNR began discussions in Norway with a view to resolving the problem of reincorporating the armed movements into the country's political process. In June representatives of the CNR and of nine political parties, including the ruling PDCG, met for further talks with the URNG in Spain. As a result of these negotiations, the URNG pledged not to disrupt the presidential and legislative elections scheduled for November, and agreed to participate in a constituent assembly to reform the Constitution.

In the presidential election of November 1990 none of the presidential candidates obtained an absolute majority in the first round, leading to a second ballot on 6 January 1991 between the two leading candidates, Jorge Serrano Elías of the Movimiento de Acción Solidaria (MAS) and Jorge Carpio Nicolle of the UCN. Serrano, a former member of the 1982 Ríos Montt Government, who secured the support of right-wing opinion, received 68% of the votes cast. The MAS failed to secure a majority in the legislative elections, however, and in an effort to offset the imbalance in Congress, Serrano invited members of the Plan por el Adelantamiento Nacional (PAN) and the Partido Socialista Democrático (PSD) to participate in the formation of a coalition Government.

In April 1991 a fresh round of direct talks between the URNG and the Government was begun in Mexico City. The initial meeting resulted in an agreement on negotiating procedures and an agenda for further talks. However, in an attempt to destabilize the Government's efforts at national reconciliation, members of the state security forces, believed to be acting independently of their superiors, launched a campaign of violence, directing death threats against leaders of trade unions and human rights organizations, and murdering a PSD politician. These actions indicated a clear division within the military between those favouring a negotiated settlement and those regarding the talks merely as a political platform for the rebels. In late 1991 the ombudsman, Ramiro de León Carpio, secured the resignation of the Director of the National Police, Col. Mario Enrique Paíz Bolanos, who was alleged to be responsible for the use of torture. Further peace talks at the end of the year failed to produce any agreement.

Negotiations between the Government and the URNG, which took place in Mexico City in August 1992, led to concessions by the Government, which agreed to curb the expansion of the PAC. These self-defence patrols played a major role in the army's counter-insurgency campaign and were widely accused of human rights violations. The URNG, which maintained that *campesinos* (peasants) were forcibly enlisted into the PAC, included in its conditions for a peace agreement the immediate dissolution of the patrols. In November the Government accepted renewed proposals by the URNG for the establishment of a commission on past human rights violations, but only on the pre-condition that the rebels sign a definitive peace accord. In January 1993 Serrano announced his commitment to the negotiation and signing of a peace agreement with the URNG within 90 days. In the event that an agreement was not reached, Serrano pledged that a cease-fire would be implemented at the end of that period, provided that the URNG demonstrate its commitment to the peace process. In response, the URNG called for a 50% reduction in the size of the armed forces, and repeated demands for the immediate dissolution of the PAC and the dismissal of military officials implicated in human rights violations. The Government rejected these proposals. Talks stalled in March, owing principally to government demands that the URNG disarm as a precondition to the implementation of procedures for the international verification of human rights in

Guatemala. Negotiations were suspended in May, owing to the prevailing constitutional crisis (see below).

In June 1993 the URNG announced a unilateral cease-fire as a gesture of goodwill to the incoming President Ramiro de León Carpio. Government proposals announced in July, which aimed to involve all sectors of society in a Permanent Forum for Peace addressing social, economic and human rights problems independently of simultaneous cease-fire negotiations with the URNG, were rejected by the rebels. In August, in a concession to the URNG, de León announced the reform of the Estado Mayor Presidencial, a military body widely accused of human rights offences. However, in the following month the army announced that it would be resuming military operations against the rebels, which had been suspended in June. In October the Government presented a revised peace plan to the UN, providing for the creation of a Permanent Forum for Peace and renewed cease-fire negotiations with a view to an eventual amnesty for the URNG; the plan was, however, rejected by the rebels. Preliminary talks were finally resumed in Mexico in January 1994.

In May 1992 fears of a possible military coup were raised by a series of bombings and bomb threats in the capital. The campaign was widely recognized as the activity of right-wing elements of the military and the private sector, which aimed to force the Government to abandon its plans to implement tax reforms and to cease negotiations with the URNG. In July the Minister of the Interior, Fernando Hurtado Prem, was forced to resign amidst allegations of police brutality. The decision followed the violent dispersal by anti-riot police of some 500 *campesinos* who had gathered outside the Palacio Nacional to demand the resolution of a land dispute.

In May 1993 unrest at economic austerity measures escalated as public confidence in the Government declined. In that month a rally attended by some 10,000 people was staged in the capital to demand Serrano's resignation. With the MAS no longer able to effect a constructive alliance in Congress and the country's stability in jeopardy, on 25 May Serrano, with the support of the military, suspended parts of the Constitution and dissolved Congress and the Supreme Court. A ban was imposed on the media and Serrano announced that he would rule by decree pending the drafting of a new constitution by a constituent assembly, which was to be elected within 60 days. In addition to civil unrest, Serrano cited widespread corruption (which, he alleged, permeated all state institutions) as the motive for his actions. The constitutional coup provoked almost unanimous international condemnation, with the USA immediately suspending in excess of US $30m. in aid. Such pressure, in addition to overwhelming domestic opposition, led the military to reappraise its position and, opting to effect a return to constitutional rule, it forced the resignation of Serrano, who relinquished his post on 1 June and subsequently fled to El Salvador. He was later granted political asylum in Panama. The Minister of National Defence, Gen. José Domingo García Samayoa, assumed control of the country, pending the election of a new president. An attempt by Vice-President Gustavo Adolfo Espina Salguero to assume the presidency was prevented by a legislative boycott of his ratification. He was later ruled ineligible for the post by the Constitutional Court.

On 3 June 1993 the entire Cabinet, excluding García and the Minister of the Interior, Francisco Perdomo Sandoval, resigned. On the same day the Attorney-General presented charges, including those of violation of the Constitution, abuse of authority and embezzlement, against Serrano, Espina and Perdomo, all of whom were reported to have left the country. On 5 June, following an order by the Constitutional Court, Congress reconvened and conducted elections for a new president. The Instancia Nacional de Consenso (INC), a broad coalition of political parties, business leaders and trade unions which had been instrumental in removing Serrano from office, proposed three candidates, of whom Ramiro de León Carpio, the former human rights ombudsman, was elected President in an uncontested second round of voting. The USA subsequently restored its aid programme to Guatemala.

In August 1993, as an initial measure in a campaign to eradicate corruption from state institutions and restore dwindling public confidence in his Government, de León requested the voluntary resignation of Congress and the Supreme Court. The request caused a serious division in the legislature, which separated into two main factions, the Gran Grupo Parlamentario (GGP), which included some 70 members of the MAS, UCN, PAN and the Frente Republicano Guatemalteco (FRG) and supported the dismissal of 16 deputies identified by the INC

as corrupt, and a group of 38 deputies, including members of the PDCG and independents, who supported the voluntary resignation of all 116 deputies. In September, following the suspension of a congressional session by the President of Congress, Fernando Lobo Dubón (a member of the PDCG), the GGP defied the decision and elected a new President of Congress. Although Lobo was temporarily reinstated by the Constitutional Court, the GGP threatened to boycott any further sessions convened by him. In order to resolve the impasse, de León requested the Supreme Electoral Tribunal to put the issue to a referendum. However, in early November the Constitutional Court upheld a Supreme Court injunction of the previous month, suspending the referendum.

In mid-November 1993, a compromise was reached between the Government and the legislature, involving a series of constitutional reforms which were summarily approved by Congress in order to be put to a referendum on 30 January 1994. The reforms were subsequently approved by the referendum, although fewer than 20% of the electorate participated in the voting, reflecting popular concern that more extensive reforms were necessary. The reforms took effect in early April, and fresh legislative elections were to be held in mid-August. The new Congress, which was to serve until 14 January 1996, was to appoint the members of a new, enlarged Supreme Court. Other reforms included a reduction in the terms of office of the President, legislature and municipal authorities (from five to four years), and of the Supreme Court justices (from six to five years), and a reduction in the number of seats in Congress. In April 1994 a climate of escalating violence and instability, characterized by attacks on legislators and foreign citizens, and by the assassination of the President of the Constitutional Court, prompted de León to place the army in charge of internal security.

In January 1994 preliminary talks between the Government and the URNG resulted in an agreement on the resumption of formal peace negotiations, to be based on the agenda agreed in Mexico in April 1991. In March agreement was reached on a timetable aimed at achieving a definitive peace agreement by the end of the year. In addition, a general human rights agreement was signed, providing guarantees, including a government commitment to eliminate illegal security corps, strengthen national human rights institutions and cease obligatory military recruitment. Agreement was also reached on the establishment of a UN human rights mission to verify the implementation of the accord. Further talks in Oslo, Norway, resulted in the signing, in June, of agreements on the resettlement of people displaced by the civil war (estimated to number some 1m.), and on the establishment of a Comisión para el Esclarecimiento Histórico (CEH—Commission for Historical Clarification) to investigate human rights violations committed during the 33-year conflict. The role of the CEH, the creation of which was strongly opposed by the security forces, would be to report on past violations, but would not extend to initiating legal proceedings against offenders.

In August 1994 the URNG withdrew from the peace negotiations and accused the Government of failing to observe the human rights provisions agreed in March. Talks resumed in November, but remained deadlocked until February 1995, when a new timetable for negotiations, achieved with UN mediation, was announced. The new agenda, which was formally agreed by the Government and the URNG in March, provided for a cease-fire agreement by June and the signing of a definitive peace accord in August. In March the issue of the identity and rights of indigenous peoples was finally resolved. The principal remaining issues to be discussed included agrarian and other socio-economic reform, the role of the armed forces, the resettlement of displaced people and the incorporation of URNG guerrillas into civilian life. However, talks continued beyond the agreed deadline, and throughout 1995, without agreement on the substantive issues. In September, in an attempt to lend impetus to the peace process, the Government announced the demobilization of the approximately 24,000-strong paramilitary force, the Comisionados Militares. However, in the following month a military patrol killed 11 people in an attack on a resettlement area for refugees returning from Mexico at Xamán in the department of Alta Verapaz. The incident prompted the resignation of the Minister of National Defence.

At the legislative election held in August 1994 only some 20% of the electorate exercised their vote, again reflecting widespread scepticism at the extent to which the reforms instigated by de León would serve to rid Guatemalan institutions of corruption. Of the 80 seats in the new legislature (reduced from 116), the FRG secured 32, the PAN 24, the PDCG 13, the UCN seven, the MLN three and the Unión Democrática (UD) one. Despite winning the greatest number of seats, the FRG, led by Gen. (retd) José Efraín Ríos Montt, was excluded from the 12-member congressional directorate by an alliance of the PAN, PDCG, MLN and UD. However, in December the PDCG transferred its allegiance to the FRG and Ríos Montt was subsequently elected President of Congress. His inauguration in January 1995 provoked demonstrations by human rights organizations, which considered him responsible for the deaths of as many as 15,000 civilians as a result of counter-insurgency operations conducted during his period as *de facto* ruler in 1982–83.

In September 1994 the UN General Assembly formally announced the establishment of the Human Rights Verification Mission in Guatemala (MINUGUA), as envisaged in the March 1994 agreement between the Government and the URNG. The mission, which was to comprise 220 human rights observers, 60 police and 10 military officers, began arriving in November.

In March 1995 Guatemala's record on human rights came under particular scrutiny. At the beginning of the month the USA announced that it had suspended all remaining military aid to the country, in protest at the Government's failure to investigate cases involving the murder or disappearance of US citizens in Guatemala. In the same month MINUGUA issued its first report. The document drew attention to human rights abuses perpetrated by the security forces and the PAC, and the Government's failure to investigate such incidents was once again condemned.

In June 1995 Ríos Montt formally requested registration as a candidate in the forthcoming presidential election, despite the constitutional provision precluding the candidacy of anyone who had previously come to power by means of a coup, as Ríos Montt had done in 1982. In August the Supreme Electoral Tribunal confirmed that he was not eligible to stand for election and in the same month the Supreme Court ruled that he should be temporarily suspended from his position as President of Congress to answer charges of abuse of authority and violation of the Constitution. The charges concerned an attempt by Ríos Montt and several other FRG deputies to impeach the magistrates of the Supreme Electoral Tribunal without first securing congressional approval.

The presidential and legislative elections on 12 November 1995 were notable for the return to the electoral process, for the first time for more than 40 years, of the left wing, which was represented by the Frente Democrático Nueva Guatemala (FDNG). In addition, the URNG, which had boycotted all previous elections, declared a unilateral cease-fire to coincide with the electoral campaign and urged people to exercise their vote. As no candidate received the necessary 50% of the votes to win the presidential election outright, the two leading candidates, Alvaro Enrique Arzú Irigoyen of the PAN and Alfonso Portillo of the FRG, contested a second round of voting on 7 January 1996, at which Arzú secured a narrow victory. At the legislative election the PAN secured 43 of the total of 80 seats in Congress, the FRG won 21, the Alianza Nacional (AN) nine, the FDNG six, and the MLN obtained the remaining seat.

Shortly after assuming office in January 1996, Arzú implemented a comprehensive reorganization of the military high command, replacing those officers who were not in favour of a negotiated peace settlement. In late February Arzú met the high command of the URNG in Mexico City, the first direct meeting between a Guatemalan President and the rebels since the early 1970s. In March Congress ratified the International Labour Organization's Convention on the rights of indigenous peoples. However, the document, which had been before Congress since 1992 and had encountered strong opposition from landed interests, had been amended by Congress, prompting protests by Indian organizations. On 20 March the URNG announced an indefinite unilateral cease-fire. Arzú responded immediately by ordering the armed forces to suspend counter-insurgency operations.

On 6 May 1996 the Government and the URNG signed an agreement on agrarian and socio-economic issues. The accord, which aimed to address the problem of widespread poverty by establishing a more efficient and equitable agrarian structure, provided for the introduction of a new agrarian bank (which would supply funds for *campesinos* to purchase property), the establishment of a land registry to define ownership and the introduction of a land tax. The Government also undertook to

double expenditure on health and education over the next four years. In response, the URNG suspended its 'war-tax' (protection money extorted from landowners and businesses). In that month Congress approved legislation limiting the right of public-sector employees to strike. A demonstration by trade unions in protest at the legislation was dispersed by the security forces. In the following month Congress adopted legislation that made members of the armed forces accountable to civilian courts for all but strictly military crimes.

In September 1996 the Government and the URNG signed an agreement in Mexico City on the strengthening of civilian power and the role of the armed forces. Under the terms of the accord, all military and intelligence services were to be placed under the authority of the Government. The police force was to be reorganized, with the creation of a new National Civilian Police force (Policía Nacional Civil), which would replace the existing units from mid-1997. The armed forces were to be reduced in size by one-third and were to relinquish responsibility for internal security. Also confirmed in the accord was the abolition of the PAC. By early December the demobilization of the PAC, estimated to number some 202,000 members, was officially concluded. Later that month a general amnesty law was approved by Congress. Whilst the law did not exonerate former combatants for human rights violations, the rebels expressed concern that the amnesty was too extensive and that atrocities committed by the armed forces would go unpunished. Human rights groups announced plans to take legal action to have the law annulled.

On 29 December 1996 the Government and the URNG signed the definitive peace treaty in Guatemala City, bringing to an end some 36 years of civil war, during which an estimated 140,000 people had died. The demobilization of URNG guerrillas, estimated to number some 3,250, was to be supervised by MINUGUA. Earlier in the year the URNG had established a 44-member political council to prepare for the reconstitution of the organization as a broad-based political party. Demobilization was completed in May 1997.

In March 1997 Congress approved legislation providing for the privatization of state-owned companies, prompting widespread protest by trade unionists. In late March the UN General Assembly renewed the mandate of MINUGUA for a further year to monitor the implementation of the peace treaty. In June the URNG registered as a political party in formation and elected a transitional leadership committee to conduct the transformation of the movement. Elections to a provisional executive committee were held in August.

In February 1998, in an effort to curb rising violent crime, the Government began the deployment of an additional 10,000 troops and police throughout the country. In April the UN Human Rights Commission removed Guatemala from the list of countries under its observation. The decision did not affect the operations of MINUGUA, which continued to monitor the fulfilment of the peace accords. In June MINUGUA released a report detailing the rising incidence of crime in Guatemala and criticizing the Government's failure to control the activities of paramilitary vigilante groups and the apparent inability of the justice system to deal with cases of serious crime.

In April 1998 the auxiliary bishop of the metropolitan diocese of Guatemala City, Juan José Gerardi Conedera, was murdered. Gerardi had been a founder of the Roman Catholic Church's Oficina de Derechos Humanos del Arzobispado (ODHA—Archbishopric's Human Rights Office), and a prominent critic of the armed forces. Days before his death Gerardi had presented a report by the ODHA documenting human rights abuses committed during the civil conflict, of which army personnel were found responsible for some 80%. Although two civilian suspects were subsequently detained in connection with Gerardi's murder, the Church and human rights groups expressed the widely-held belief that the real perpetrators had been members of the armed forces. In July, in what the Church and human rights groups interpreted as a further attempt to conceal the truth, a priest, Mario Orantes Nájera (who had been the first to discover Gerardi's body), was arrested. He was formally charged with Gerardi's murder in October. In November, in a report commissioned by the Church, former chief prosecutor Acisclo Valladares Molina asserted that the murder revealed all the signs of an extra-judicial execution. In February 1999 the presiding judge in the case, Henry Monroy, ordered the release of Orantes on grounds of insufficient evidence. However, in March Monroy withdrew from the case after allegedly receiving threats against his life. In October the state prosecutor investigating the murder, Celvin Galindo, also resigned after receiving death threats. Galindo, who went into exile in the USA, subsequently questioned the ability and political will of the Government to resolve the case, in view of the alleged military involvement in the murder. The case finally went to trial in 2001 and on 8 June former intelligence chief Col (retd) Disrael Lima Estrada, his son, Capt. Byron Lima Oliva, and a former member of the presidential guard, José Obdulio Villanueva, were convicted of Bishop Gerardi's murder; Orantes was convicted of conspiring in his death. In early August the Chief Public Prosecutor, Leopoldo Zeissig, was forced to flee the country after also receiving death threats. However, in October 2002 a Court of Appeal overturned the convictions and ordered a retrial, after accepting the defence's argument that there had been irregularities in the testimony of a key witness.

In August 1999, in what was widely regarded as a test case for the judicial system, 25 members of the armed forces convicted of the massacre in 1995 of 11 civilians in Xamán, Alta Verapaz, received minimum sentences of five years' imprisonment. The case was the first in which military personnel accused of killing civilians had been tried by a civilian court and the decision, which provoked public outrage, served greatly to undermine confidence in the courts' ability to administer justice in the remaining 625 cases of massacres attributed to the security forces. By contrast, in late 1998 death sentences had been passed on three members of the PAC found guilty of participating in massacres of civilians. In December 1999 MINUGUA issued a report stating that commitments made by the Arzú administration under the 1996 peace treaty to reduce the influence of the military remained unfulfilled. It asserted that, contrary to the treaty, the armed forces had increased its presence in some rural areas, and that the Government had failed to order the dissolution of the presidential guard, which was to have been replaced by a unit under civilian control. In late 2000 the UN Secretary-General, Kofi Annan, recommended that MINUGUA's mandate be renewed for a further year. According to MINUGUA, the number of extra-judicial executions doubled between 1996 and 2000 and in the latter year the incidence of death threats increased significantly.

In February 1999 the CEH published its final report, in which it attributed more than 93% of human rights violations committed during the civil conflict to the armed forces and state paramilitaries. It announced that 200,000 people had been killed or had 'disappeared' between 1962 and 1996, the majority of them Mayan Indians. It described counter-insurgency operations during the period 1981–83 as 'genocide' against the Mayan people. It also concluded that the USA had financed and trained Guatemalan forces responsible for atrocities. The report recommended that compensation be provided for the families of victims, that prosecutions be brought against those suspected of crimes against humanity and that a purge of the armed forces be implemented. It proposed that a special commission be established to study the conduct of the army and security forces during the armed conflict. In response, the Government described the Commission's findings as 'controversial', and did not express any intention of pursuing its recommendations.

In late 1999 the Guatemalan Nobel Peace Prize winner, Rigoberta Menchú, filed a case in Spain against former generals Ríos Montt, Lucas García and Mejía Victores, and other military officers, for the crimes of genocide, state terrorism and torture. However, in December 2000 the Spanish National High Court ruled that it was not competent to investigate the case. Menchú was to launch an appeal against the ruling. In August 2000 the Government accepted responsibility for 44 cases of human rights violations being investigated by the Inter-American Commission on Human Rights and, in early 2001, paid compensation for those deaths involving street children. Also in December, the Commission also ruled that the military was responsible for the torture and murder of guerrilla leader Efraín Bamaca Velásquez. In March 2002 the Government was ordered to make indemnity payments amounting to US $500,000 to Bamaca's family. At the end of 2000 the ODHA filed a case against Ríos Montt for human rights violations during his regime. On 6 June 2001 11 indigenous communities filed genocide charges against Ríos Montt and other senior officers in his command, for his role in a series of massacres by the army during his rule. It remained to be seen if the case would make any progress through even the initial phases of investigation.

The URNG formally registered as a political party in December 1998. The application followed the approval by Congress in October of constitutional reforms provided for in the

1996 peace accords. The reforms, which concerned the rights of indigenous peoples, the role of the armed forces and the police, and the strengthening of the courts, were to be ratified in a referendum. At the referendum, conducted on 16 May 1999, 55.6% of participating voters rejected the constitutional amendments. However, the turn-out was extremely low, with only 18.6% of the 4m. registered voters taking part, and observers attributed the result to a lack of information and to mistrust of the political establishment by the electorate rather than to the rejection of the peace accords themselves. The Government, for its part, pledged that the peace process would not be affected by the result. At presidential and legislative elections, conducted on 7 November, the voter turn-out, at some 40%, was greatly improved. As no candidate received the necessary 50% of the votes to win the presidential election outright, the two leading candidates, Alfonso Antonio Portillo Cabrera of the FRG and Oscar Berger Perdomo of the PAN, contested a second round of voting on 26 December, in which Portillo secured victory with 68.3% of the votes cast. Of the 113 seats in the legislature (enlarged from 80 seats) the FRG secured an outright majority with 63 seats, while the PAN won 37, the Alianza Nueva Nación nine, the PDCG two, and the Partido Liberal Progresista and La Organización Verde each obtained one seat.

The new Government of President Portillo, which took office on 14 January 2000, immediately undertook the promises demilitarization of the upper echelons of government, and announced that one of its priorities was the narrowing of the fiscal deficit. A Governability Pact was unveiled, intended to build consensus between the representatives of the state and the country's political and social leaderships. Local levels of government were to promote debate among civil society organizations on six issues: citizen security, justice, demilitarization and human rights; decentralization, rural development and the environment; education; political reform and civil-society participation; integral human development; and the Fiscal Pact, a long-term public-expenditure strategy. On 18 December President Portillo created a Ministry of the Environment, headed by Haroldo Quej Chen. Chen was later replaced by Sergio Lavarreda.

In June 2000 a political crisis ensued after it was revealed that illegal modifications had been made to legislation setting the tax on alcoholic beverages after it had been approved by Congress. The Supreme Court appointed a judge to investigate those believed to be responsible: 23 FRG deputies and the President of Congress, Ríos Montt. On 5 March 2001 the parliamentary immunity of those accused was removed by the Supreme Court and Ríos Montt temporarily resigned the congressional presidency, while five of the 23 deputies were ordered to give up their seats. However, the following day the Supreme Court exonerated the members of all charges, ruling that there was no case to answer (although it was subsequently announced that a government inquiry into Ríos Montt's role in the affair was to be held).

Kidnappings and other violent crimes increased in 2001. Human rights organizations denounced attacks against their members, which appeared to be politically motivated. In the first half of the year these included the murder of US nun, Ann Ford, who had worked on human rights projects in the El Quiché region, and the attempted kidnap of an Amnesty International worker, Barbara Bocek.

Disputes between the Government and the Congreso Nacional resulted in virtual paralysis in policy-making throughout 2001. In mid-March two deputies defected from the FRG to join the Unidad Nacional de Esperanza, a coalition established by the former presidential candidate Alvaro Colom Caballero, thus reducing the FRG's legislative majority to 61. On 2 March the Minister of Public Finance, Manuel Maza Castellanos, resigned following allegations of mishandling of public funds. His resignation prompted a reorganization of cabinet portfolios; a further reshuffle took place in the following month. In June the Minister of Communications, Transport and Public Works, Luis Rabbe, was dismissed following the identification of irregularities within the ministry. On 24 August Arnoldo Noriega resigned as leader of the URNG, owing to internal disputes; Alba Estela Maldonado was elected to succeed him.

Following the rejection in the Congreso Nacional of various efforts to increase tax collection, in July 2001 the FRG finally approved legislation to increase value-added tax (VAT) from 10% to 12%, from August. Business groups led a one-day national strike was held in protest, and further demonstrations occurred during the following week. Subsequently, the Vice-

President, Francisco Reyes López, was accused of using government offices to fabricate propaganda against the leading businessman in the campaign against the VAT increase, Jorge Briz. Seven people supporting the accusation were forced to leave the country after receiving death threats.

In November 2001 Brig.-Gen. (retd) Eduardo Arévalo Lacs, hitherto the Minister of National Defence, was appointed Minister of the Interior, replacing Byron Barrientes (who was subsequently charged with the embezzlement of government funds). Gen. Lacs' appointment to the interior ministry was met with protests by civil society and human rights groups, which claimed that his appointment contravened the peace agreements. There were further protests in January 2002 when Gen. Lacs dismissed the director of the police force, Ennio Rivera Cardona, and replaced him with a former head of the disbanded national police, Luis Arturo Paniagua, who had been accused of human rights abuses. President Portillo's announcement, in the same month, of the establishment of a human rights team to monitor the security forces did little to allay the objections. Furthermore, in February, at a meeting of international donors in Washington, DC, USA, the Government was criticized for its lack of progress in implementing the terms of the peace accords.

In late February 2002 the President of the central bank, Lizardo Sosa López, was kidnapped by an unknown group; however, he was released unharmed at the end of the month, in exchange for an undisclosed amount of money. A presidential spokesman reported that Gen. Lacs had intervened to release Sosa. However, the Government subsequently denied any involvement in the case.

In March 2002 a congressional commission was formed to investigate claims made by a Panamanian newspaper that President Portillo, Vice-President Reyes and other prominent government officials had established bank accounts in Panama for the purpose of money-laundering. Shortly after the investigation began, three of the six commissioners resigned, questioning the objectivity of commission. The Attorney-General, Carlos García, and the Auditor-General's Office also began separate investigations. The allegations provoked mass protests in Guatemala City by trade-union members and socialist and religious groups, who demanded the President's resignation. The former President and human rights ombudsman, Ramiro Léon de Carpio, resigned his seat in Congress in protest at government corruption and 10 other FRG deputies threatened to do the same. At the end of the month the Auditor-General's Office closed its investigation into the allegations, declaring that evidence used to support the claims had been fabricated. However, the other investigations continued and in May the congressional commission concluded in its report that there was enough evidence to support a full inquiry. Following an exchange of information with Panamanian authorities in June, however, the case collapsed, owing to a lack of evidence. President Portillo welcomed the result and claimed that he had been the victim of powerful business interests who objected to his reformist policies.

Meanwhile, violent attacks against public figures continued in 2002. In mid-March, days after he had given a speech at the anti-Portillo demonstrations, the leader of the opposition group Partido Patriótico, Jorge Rosal Zea, was shot and killed. In late April an employee of a human rights organization was murdered in Guatemala City. A report published by the Human Rights Office of the Guatemalan Archbishopric in mid-June concluded that the state was unable to ensure that laws were observed.

There were several ministerial changes in 2002. In mid-May the Minister of Agriculture, Livestock and Food, Jorge Rolando Escoto Marroquín, resigned. He was replaced by Edin Raymundo Barrientos. In early July the controversial Minister of Interior, Gen. Lacs, resigned. He cited personal reason for his departure, but during his brief tenure in office he had encountered criticism for his failure to combat corruption in the police force. Furthermore, several officials had been accused of human rights violations in an anti-drugs-trafficking operation in the north of the country. Lacs was succeeded by José Adolfo Reyes. Then, in late August, President Portillo dismissed the Minister of National Defence, Gen. Alvaro Mendez Estrada; he was replaced by Gen. Robin Moran Munoz, hitherto National Defence Chief of Staff and a civil war veteran. Finally, in December the Minister of Foreign Affairs, Gabriel Orellana, resigned; he was replaced by Edgar Armando Gutiérrez Girón.

In June 2002 a group of foreign tourists were taken hostage in the ruins of the ancient Mayan town Tikal by some 2,000 paramilitaries who claimed that they still had not received payment from the Government for their role in the civil war. The tourists were freed two days later when the Government agreed to compensate the paramilitaries. The move was criticized by human rights organizations who alleged that the Government had yet to pay reparations to the paramilitaries' victims. In July, in an attempt to improve the image of the Government's policy on human rights and in response to a plea from the head of the Roman Catholic Church, Pope John Paul II, who visited Guatemala in the same month, President Portillo announced that he would not authorize the execution of any prisoners during the remainder of his term in office. He also proposed legislation abolishing capital punishment. However, the proposal was immediately rejected by a parliamentary committee.

In August 2002 some 30,000 *campesinos* occupied farms and blocked major roads across the country, preventing access to ports and border crossings to Mexico, Honduras and El Salvador. The protest was organized by the Coordinadora Nacional de Organizaciones Campesinas (CNOC—National Co-ordinating Committee of Peasant Organizations) in support of land reform.

In September 2002 the trial began of two former colonels and one former general accused of ordering the murder of anthropologist Myrna Mack in 1990. The prosecution maintained that the killing had been carried out in reaction to a report produced by Mack implicating the Government in violent anti-insurgency campaigns against Mayan Indians during the civil war. In early October Col (retd) Juan Valencia Osorio was convicted of ordering the murder; he was sentenced to 30 years' imprisonment. The two other accused, Gen. (retd.) Edgar Godoy and Col (retd) Juan Guillermo Oliva were cleared of charges of complicity. The trial was only the second in which former members of the military élite had been tried for war crimes and was interpreted as an encouraging sign that the state was increasingly willing to act in curbing the power of the military.

An increase in extra-judicial executions in 2002 prompted MINUGUA to warn, in late September, that the rule of law was jeopardized in several regions of the country. Furthermore, in the following month, the US Assistant Secretary of State for the Western Hemisphere, Otto Reich, expressed his concern at levels of corruption, drugs-trafficking and continuing human rights abuses in Guatemala. The Government reacted angrily to what it percieved to be unwarranted intervention into domestic affairs by the USA and recalled its Ambassador to Washington in protest. Nevertheless, President Portillo subsequently announced a number of reforms to the security forces, including the dissolution of the Departmento de Operaciones Antinarcoticos (DNOA—Department of Anti-Narcotics Operations) and the creation of a new unit, Unidades Moviles Operativas, to combat drugs-trafficking and terrorism. Units of the armed forces were also deployed on the streets to support the work of the police. In February 2003, however, the USA added Guatemala to the list of nations it considered unco-operative in combating drugs-trafficking. The country also remained on the Financial Action Task Force on Money Laundering's (FATF—based in Paris) 'blacklist'.

Presidential elections were scheduled to be held in November 2003. In November 2002 the opposition PAN again selected Oscar Berger Perdomo to be its candidate. It was considered likely that former President Ríos Montt would be selected as the FRG's nominee, particularly as his candidature had received the support of President Portillo. However, constitutionally he was barred from standing for presidential office, having come to power through through unconstitutional means in 1982.

Until the return to civilian government in 1986, Guatemala remained steadfast in its claims to the neighbouring territory of Belize, a former British dependency. In protest at the United Kingdom's decision to grant independence to Belize, in accordance with a UN General Assembly resolution of November 1980, Guatemala severed diplomatic relations with the United Kingdom. However, Guatemala's new Constitution, which took effect in January 1986, did not include Belize in its delineation of Guatemalan territory. In December full diplomatic relations were resumed. The removal of economic sanctions and trade restrictions from Belize in late 1986 opened the way to Guatemalan investment in that territory and to the possibility of joint development projects.

In May 1988, following discussions in Miami, USA, between representatives of Guatemala, Belize and the United Kingdom, it was agreed to establish a permanent Joint Commission to formulate a draft treaty to resolve Guatemala's claims to Belize. In October the Commission announced the establishment of three subcommissions, to be responsible for drafting the treaty; the delimitation of the border; and the creation of a joint development zone, with the co-operation of the United Kingdom and the European Community (EC, now European Union—EU). Approval of the treaty was to be decided by referendums, to be held in both Guatemala and Belize.

In September 1991 Guatemala and Belize signed an accord under the terms of which Belize pledged to legislate to reduce its maritime boundaries and to allow Guatemala access to the Caribbean Sea and use of its port facilities. In return, President Serrano officially announced his country's recognition of Belize as an independent state and established diplomatic relations. The Belizean legislature approved the Maritime Areas Bill in January 1992. Serrano's decision to recognize Belize, made without consulting Congress and without holding a referendum, provoked protests from the opposition, who claimed that Serrano's actions were unconstitutional. In November 1992 Guatemala's Constitutional Court rejected a request by opposition deputies to declare Serrano's actions unconstitutional. In an address to the nation, Serrano subsequently confirmed that Guatemala maintained its territorial claim on Belize. At the end of November Congress voted to ratify Serrano's decision to recognize Belize.

In April 1993 Guatemala and Belize signed a non-aggression pact, affirming their intent to refrain from the threat or use of force against each other, and preventing either country from being used as a base for aggression against the other. In September the United Kingdom announced that the British garrison, which had been stationed in Belize since the mid-1970s, was to be withdrawn by October 1994.

In March 1994, Guatemala formally reaffirmed its territorial claim to Belize, prompting the Belizean Government to seek talks with the British Government regarding assistance with national defence. Concern was also expressed by the Standing Committee of Ministers of Foreign Affairs of the Caribbean Community and Common Market (CARICOM, see p. 155), which reaffirmed its support for Belizean sovereignty. In September 1996 the Ministers of Foreign Affairs of Guatemala and Belize conducted preliminary talks in New York, USA, concerning a resumption of negotiations on the territorial dispute. In August 1997 President Arzú ordered an increased military presence on the border with Belize following reports of incursions by Belizean troops into Guatemalan territory.

In November 1998 a joint Guatemalan–Belizean commission was established to deal with immigration and cross-border traffic. In August 2000 a panel of negotiators was established at the headquarters of the Organization of American States (OAS, see p. 288) in Washington, DC, to supervise the process of bilateral negotiations. In November the two countries agreed to initiate joint patrols of the unofficial common border. However, during 2000 and 2001 there were various alleged incursions of Belizean soldiers into the proximity zone between the two countries.

In February 2001 the Pan-American Institute of Geography and History in Mexico City issued a report determining the position of the 'adjacency line' between Belize and Guatemala, which was subsequently accepted by both countries. Negotiations in 2001 focused on the issue of Guatemalans living in the disputed area, who, according to Belize, were being used by Guatemala to assert sovereignty over the territory; an agreement was later reached to relocate the families. In December the OAS appointed a special envoy to investigate the deaths, in the previous month, of three Guatemalans in the disputed area. In May 2002 the Belizean Government formally compensated the families of those killed.

In June 2002 the Minister of Foreign Affairs, Gabriel Orellana Rojas, and his Belizean counterpart, Assad Shoman, met for OAS-mediated discussions on the issue. Relations with Belize subsequently appeared to improve when, in July, the President of Belize, Said Musa, attended a ceremony in Guatemala City marking the twinning of the city with the Belizean capital, Belmopan. In late July, during a tour of Central America, Pope John Paul II urged the two countries to find a solution to the border dispute. A high-ranking member of the papal delegation, Cardinal Angelo Sodano, mediated in talks between Orellana and Shoman. Further negotiations in August under OAS auspices yielded some success; in early September proposals were outlined for a solution to the dispute. These included the provision that Guatemala would recognize Belize's land boundary as set out in the Treaty of 1859, and the creation of a model settlement for peasants and landless farmers in the area.

Guatemalan farmers occupying land within the Belize border were to have priority rights of residency to this settlement. These was also provision for a Free Trade Agreement between the two countries and a Development Trust Fund, managed by the Inter-American Development Bank, to fund poverty-alleviation schemes in the border region. In addition, Guatemala would receive an Exclusive Economic Zone in the Gulf of Honduras, amounting to 2,000 sq miles of marine territory, contributed by both Belize and Honduras, although those countries were to retain fishing rights and 50% of any mineral resources discovered in the sea-bed. A commission, comprising representatives from Belize, Guatemala and Honduras, would oversee the establishment and management of an Ecological Marine Park in the coastal areas and a separate Tripartite Regional Fisheries Management Commission would manage fishing in the Gulf of Honduras. The details of the agreeement were concluded on 30 September and the two countries were to hold simultaneous public referendums by the end of November. However, the fatal shooting of a Guatemalan on the Belizean side of the border in early October prompted the Congreso Nacional unanimously to approve a resolution recommending that President Portillo establish temporary military outposts on the border. The Belizean Government subsequently extended the deadline for the holding of the referendums. Following further conciliatory discussions, in February 2003 the foreign ministers of both countries signed a co-operation agreement pending a final settlement of the dispute.

Government

Guatemala is a republic comprising 22 departments. Under the 1986 Constitution (revised in 1994), legislative power is vested in the unicameral Congreso Nacional (National Congress), with 113 members elected for four years by universal adult suffrage. Of the total seats, 91 are filled by departmental representation and 22 according to national listing. Executive power is held by the President (also directly elected for four years), assisted by a Vice-President and an appointed Cabinet.

Defence

In August 2002 the armed forces totalled an estimated 31,400, of whom 29,200 were in the army (including 23,000 conscripts), 1,500 in the navy (including 650 marines) and 700 in the air force. In addition, there were paramilitary forces of 19,000. Military service is by selective conscription for 30 months. In September 1996, as part of the ongoing peace process, the Government signed an agreement with the rebel URNG whereby the armed forces were to be placed under the control of the Government. Under the terms of the accord, the armed forces were reduced in number by one-third in 1997. This reduction included the disbanding of the Policía Militar Ambulante (Mobile Military Police), which was completed in late 1997. The accord also provided for the abolition of the Patrullas de Autodefensa Civil (PAC), which were demobilized in late 1996. In September 2002 President Portillo announced plans to reduce the armed forces by 20%. Defence expenditure in 2001 was put at US $190m.

Economic Affairs

In 2001, according to estimates by the World Bank, Guatemala's gross national income (GNI), measured at average 1999–2001 prices, was US $19,559m., equivalent to $1,670 per head (or $3,850 per head on an international purchasing-power parity basis). During 1990–2001, it was estimated, the population increased by an average of 2.8% per year, while gross domestic product (GDP) per head increased, in real terms, by an average of 1.2% per year. Overall GDP increased, in real terms, at an average annual rate of 3.9% in 1990–2001; growth in 2001 was 2.1%.

Agriculture, including hunting, forestry and fishing, contributed an estimated 22.6% of GDP in 2001. In 2002 an estimated 38.7% of the active labour force were employed in this sector. The principal cash crops are coffee (which accounted for 24.4% of export earnings in 2000), sugar cane and bananas. Exports of shrimps are also significant. In recent years the country has successfully expanded production of less traditional crops, such as mangoes, berries and green beans. The drought and subsequent food crisis of May–August 2001 resulted in the destruction of crops in many areas of the country, although it was hoped that the second crop of the year would be successful. In September 2001 the Government announced an aid programme of 'soft' loans and refinancing credits for the coffee sector; the programme was to include an advertising campaign to encourage domestic coffee sales. However, coffee exports were estimated to have fallen by 38% in 2002, compared with the harvest of 2001, owing to a regional crisis in the coffee industry. During 1990–2001 agricultural GDP increased, in real terms, by an estimated average of 2.7% per year. Growth in agricultural GDP was an estimated 0.1% in 2001.

Industry, including mining, manufacturing, construction and power, contributed an estimated 19.9% of GDP in 2000. This sector employed an estimated 20.0% of the working population in 2002. Industrial GDP increased by an estimated average of 3.9% per year in 1990–2001. Growth in industrial GDP was an estimated 1.6% in 2001.

Mining contributed an estimated 0.5% of GDP in 2000 and employed an estimated 0.2% of the working population in 2002. The most important mineral export is petroleum, although this accounted for only 0.1% of total export earnings in 2000. In addition, copper, antimony, lead, zinc and tungsten are mined on a small scale. There are also deposits of nickel, gold and silver. Mining GDP decreased by 2.0% in 1999, and by a further 8.3% in 2000.

Guatemala's industrial sector is the largest in Central America. Manufacturing contributed an estimated 13.1% of GDP in 2001 and employed an estimated 13.6% of the working population in 2000. The main branches of manufacturing, measured by gross value of output, are food-processing, textiles, plastic products, paper and paper products, pharmaceuticals and industrial chemicals. Manufacturing GDP increased by an average of 2.6% per year in 1990–2001. Growth in manufacturing GDP was an estimated 1.6% in 2001. Guatemala's clothing assembly, or *maquila*, manufacturing sector expanded in the late 1990s and employed some 80,000 workers in 1998. However, in 2001, owing to the introduction of a business tax and the economic slowdown in the USA towards the end of the year, the sector contracted; 38 *maquila* factories closed, while a further 229 were threatened with closure.

Energy is derived principally from hydroelectric power and, to a lesser extent, mineral fuels. Hydroelectric power was responsible for 51.3% of total electricity production in 1999, and petroleum provided 43.3% of electric energy in the same year. Guatemala is a marginal producer of petroleum and, in 2001, produced an estimated 8.9m. barrels. Petroleum reserves were estimated at 526m. barrels in January 2000. Reserves of natural gas were put at some 109,000m. cu ft in the same year. Imports of petroleum and petroleum products comprised 11.0% of the value of total imports in 2000. In late 1998 80% of the capital of the state-owned Empresa Eléctrica de Guatemala was sold to foreign investors for US $520m. At the same time, the Instituto Nacional de Electrificación was sold for $100m. In late 2001 Guatemala and Mexico reached agreement, under the 'Plan Puebla–Panamá' (see below), on a project to link their electricity grids. It was hoped that the project would improve regional power infrastructure and attract investment in the sector.

In 2001 the services sector contributed an estimated 57.7% of GDP and, in 2002, it employed an estimated 37.5% of the working population. The GDP of the services sector increased by an average of 4.5% per year in 1990–2001; growth in the sector was an estimated 2.7% in 2001.

In 2001 Guatemala recorded a visible trade deficit of US $2,277.5m., and there was a deficit of $1,237.9m. on the current account of the balance of payments. In 2001 the principal source of imports (35.0%) was the USA; other major suppliers were Mexico, Japan and El Salvador. The USA was also the principal market for exports (taking 26.7% of exports in that year); other significant purchasers were El Salvador, Honduras, Costa Rica and Nicaragua. The main exports in 2000 were coffee, vegetables and fruit, and chemical products. The principal imports were machinery and transport equipment, basic manufactures, chemicals and mineral fuels and lubricants.

In 2001 there was a budgetary deficit of 638.7m. quetzales, equivalent to some 0.4% of GDP. At the end of 2000 Guatemala's total external debt stood at US $4,622m. of which US $3,287m. was long-term public debt, in that year equivalent to 9.4% of GDP. In that year the cost of debt-servicing totalled $438m. In 1990–2000 the average annual rate of inflation was 11.5%. Consumer prices increased by an average of 5.2% in 1999 and by 6.0% in 2000. Annual inflation reached 8.9% in 2001, mainly owing to the increase in value-added tax (VAT, see below). An estimated 7.5% of the labour force were unemployed in 1999.

Guatemala is a member of the Central American Common Market (CACM, see p. 160). In 2000 Guatemala, El Salvador and Honduras signed a free-trade agreement with Mexico, which promised greater market access and increased bilateral trade. In May 2001 the Central American countries, including Guatemala, reached an agreement with Mexico to establish a series of joint transport, industry and tourism projects intended to integrate the region, called the 'Plan Puebla–Panamá'.

In 1991 the Government adopted a structural adjustment programme in order to address the serious fiscal imbalances and external debt problems that had characterized the previous decade. The resultant economic recovery enabled the Government to resume relations with international credit agencies and to clear debt arrears. However, low tax revenue was a major problem, forcing the Government to borrow heavily, keeping interest rates high, discouraging investment and impeding growth. In 1995 the legislature approved a series of reforms to the tax system, which, in turn, facilitated a new stand-by agreement with the IMF. The signing of the peace accord in December 1996, which signalled the end of the civil conflict, improved Guatemala's economic prospects significantly. It was envisaged that expenditure of US $2,500m. would be required to implement the accord. In January 1997 international donors pledged $1,900m. in loans and donations towards the Government's reconstruction programme. However, the funding was contingent upon the Government significantly increasing tax revenues. Significant increases were expected following the creation of an independent tax superintendency in 1998. However, as a result of the destruction caused by 'Hurricane Mitch' in November 1998, the curtailment of external credit from banks owing to instability in the international financial markets, and declining international prices for Guatemala's principal exports of coffee and sugar, economic growth slowed significantly in 1999. The incoming Government of Alfonso Portillo introduced a Fiscal Pact. The agreement, signed in May 2000 by government and opposition representatives and business and community leaders, comprised eight distinct areas: fiscal balance of payments, state revenue, tax administration, public spending, public debt, public property, supervision and control mechanisms, and fiscal decentralization. The agreement was criticized in various sectors, which claimed that participant groups in the process were given little or no time to discuss in depth any proposals. One of the Pact's principal aims was to increase tax revenue to 12% of GDP by 2002, either through an increased rate of VAT or more effective collection of VAT. In July 2001 legislation to increase VAT to 12% was controversially approved and, in spite of a constitutional challenge, the VAT increase was introduced in August.

In December 2000 legislation was approved to allow the circulation of the US dollar and other convertible currencies, for use in a wide range of transactions, from 1 May 2001. However, in May a constitutional challenge to the law was made, which arguing that it violated the constitutional requirement that the Central Bank remain in exclusive control of foreign exchange. In June the Financial Action Task Force on Money Laundering (FATF) added Guatemala to their 'blacklist' of countries targeted for international scrutiny regarding potential money-laundering activities within the banking sector. The country remained on the list in February 2003. In February 2002, at a meeting in Washington, DC, international donors pledged a further US $1,300m. in loans and grants to aid Guatemala's post-war reconstruction programmes, less than the Government had been hoping for. The Portillo administration's lack of progress in implementing the peace accords was considered the main reason for the shortfall in funding. The funding was also contingent on the Government improving public finances and accelerating the implementation of the peace accords. The aid was to be directed towards the judicial, health and education sectors.

In June 2002 the Government formulated the 2002–04 Economic Action Plan, which aimed to develop the private sector and attract foreign investment. A state-funded agency was established to encourage foreign investment and a series of privatization and public works programmes were created. Tax incentives were also introduced for private sector companies who invested in projects to improve the country's infrastructure. In late September Congress approved a budget which envisaged increased government spending in 2003. Opposition parties claimed that the budget was overly ambitious and suspected that surplus funds would be diverted to the campaign for the November 2003 elections. The following month the approval, by a narrow congressional majority, for the issue of US $700m. of bonds on the European markets caused further concern. While the central bank maintained that the proceeds would be used to stabilize the economy, the Government announced that the money would fund improvements in health and education and the demobilization of 20% of the army. Opposition parties and business leaders interpreted this as further evidence of government plans to introduce expensive voter-pleasing initiatives and began legal challenges to the scheme. The IMF similarly criticized the sale and suggested any further government expenditure should be funded by an increase in taxation. In January 2003 President Portillo introduced, by decree, tax rises on numerous goods, including fuel and wheat. The decree was successfully challenged in the Constitutional Court by the country's major chamber of commerce, the Comité Coordinador de Asociaciones Agrícolas, Comerciales, Industriales y Financieras. However, the President reinstated the decree, stating that the measures would benefit the poor. In March 2003 the Government used US $26m. of the proceeds from the bond issue to enable the state-owned bank, Crédito Hipotecario Nacional, to take over the failed Banco del Nor-Oriente. Opposition groups claimed that the take-over contravened recent legislation requiring the liquidation of failed banks. Police issued a warrant for the arrest of one of the bank's founders, Angelo Bruno Stragá Juárez, a close friend of the President.

While exports were estimated to have decreased overall in 2002, trade with Mexico increased by 22%, following the implementation of the free trade agreement concluded in 2000. Negotiations on the establishment of a Central American Free Trade Agreement with the USA were also under way in 2003. In 2002 Guatemala also received remittances of more than US $950m. from citizens working abroad, approximately double the amount received in the previous year. It was hoped that the increase would help to decrease the deficit on the current account in 2003. The economy was estimated to have grown by 2.2% in 2002 and was forecast to expand by 2.5% in 2003.

Education

Elementary education is free and, in urban areas, compulsory between seven and 14 years of age. Primary education begins at the age of seven and lasts for six years. Secondary education, beginning at 13 years of age, lasts for up to six years, comprising two cycles of three years each. In 1999 there were 9,607 preprimary schools, 17,905 primary schools and 3,118 secondary schools. In 1997 enrolment at primary schools was equivalent to 73.8% of children in the relevant age-group (males 77.4%; females 70.2%). The comparable figure for secondary education in that year was 34.9% (males 38.1%; females 31.7%). There are five universities. In 1981 a 'national literacy crusade' was launched by the Government. In 1999 enrolment in primary, secondary and tertiary education was equivalent to 49% of the relevant age groups. In 1997 budgetary expenditure on education was an estimated 1,670.5m. quetzales (15.3% of total spending).

Public Holidays

2003: 1 January (New Year's Day), 6 January (Epiphany), 18–21 April (Easter), 1 May (Labour Day), 30 June (Anniversary of the Revolution), 15 August (Assumption, Guatemala City only), 15 September (Independence Day), 12 October (Columbus Day), 20 October (Revolution Day), 1 November (All Saints' Day), 24–25 December (Christmas), 31 December (New Year's Eve).

2004: 1 January (New Year's Day), 6 January (Epiphany), 9–12 April (Easter), 1 May (Labour Day), 30 June (Anniversary of the Revolution), 16 August (Assumption, Guatemala City only), 15 September (Independence Day), 12 October (Columbus Day), 20 October (Revolution Day), 1 November (All Saints' Day), 24–25 December (Christmas), 31 December (New Year's Eve).

Weights and Measures

The metric system is in official use.

Statistical Survey

Sources (unless otherwise stated): Banco de Guatemala, 7a Avda 22-01, Zona 1, Apdo 365, Guatemala City; tel. 230-6222; fax 253-4035; internet www .banguat.gob.gt ; Instituto Nacional de Estadística, Edif. América 4°, 8a Calle 9-55, Zona 1, Guatemala City; tel. 232-6136; fax 232-4790; e-mail info-ine@ ine.gob.gt; internet www.segeplan.gob.gt/ine.

Area and Population

AREA, POPULATION AND DENSITY

Area (sq km)	
Land	108,429
Inland water	460
Total	108,889*
Population (census results)†	
26 March 1981	
Males	3,015,826
Females	3,038,401
Total	6,054,227
17 April 1994	8,322,051
Population (official estimates at mid-year)	
1999	11,088,372
2000	11,385,334
2001	11,681,268
Density (per sq km) at mid-2001	107.3

* 42,042 sq miles.

† Excluding adjustments for underenumeration, estimated to have been 13.7% in 1981.

DEPARTMENTS

(estimated population at mid-2001)

Alta Verapaz	848,146	Petén	346,771
Baja Verapaz	207,775	Quetzaltenango	694,584
Chimaltenango	437,623	Quiché	602,384
Chiquimula	320,982	Retalhuleu	245,882
El Progreso	146,279	Sacatepéquez	267,877
Escuintla	489,225	San Marcos	863,173
Guatemala	2,654,195	Santa Rosa	325,496
Huehuetenango	906,024	Solola	316,646
Izabal	340,527	Suchitepéquez	411,626
Jalapa	277,493	Totonicapán	369,348
Jutiapa	391,277	Zacapa	217,935

PRINCIPAL TOWNS

(estimated population at mid-2001)

Guatemala City	1,022,000	Quetzaltenango	152,228
Mixco	452,131	San Juan	
		Sacatepéquez	142,445
Villa Nueva	390,329	Jalapa	118,943
San Pedro Carcha	165,972	Escuintla	114,626
Cobán	165,687	Totonicapán	105,092

BIRTHS, MARRIAGES AND DEATHS

	Registered live births		Registered marriages		Registered deaths	
	Number	Rate (per 1,000)	Number	Rate (per 1,000)	Number	Rate (per 1,000)
1993	370,138	36.9	45,736	4.6	64,515	6.4
1994	381,497	37.0	48,356	4.7	74,761	7.2
1995	371,091	34.9	49,701	4.7	65,159	6.1
1996	377,723	34.6	47,428	4.3	60,618	5.5
1997	387,862	36.9	51,908	4.9	67,691	6.4
1998	400,133	27.0	52,499	4.9	69,847	6.5
1999	409,034	27.1	62,034	5.6	65,139	5.9
2000	425,410	26.8	58,305	5.1	67,300	5.9

Expectation of life (WHO estimates, years at birth): 69.5 (males 66.3; females 72.7) in 2001 (Source: WHO, *World Health Report*).

ECONOMICALLY ACTIVE POPULATION
(official estimates for May–June 2002)

	Males	Females	Total
Agriculture, forestry, hunting and fishing	1,535,598	308,667	1,844,265
Mining and quarrying	11,279	—	11,279
Industry	327,119	389,514	716,633
Construction	207,765	5,242	213,007
Electricity, gas, water and sanitary services	10,892	1,781	12,673
Commerce	511,305	539,194	1,050,499
Transport, storage and communications	92,581	11,336	103,917
Financial services	17,684	13,829	31,513
Community and personal services	218,841	382,990	601,831
Activities not adequately described	131,806	51,961	183,767
Total	**3,064,870**	**1,704,514**	**4,769,384**

Health and Welfare

KEY INDICATORS

Total fertility rate (children per woman, 2001)	4.6
Under-5 mortality rate (per 1,000 live births, 2001)	58
HIV/AIDS (% of persons aged 15–49, 1994)	1.38
Physicians (per 1,000 head, 1997)	0.93
Hospital beds (per 1,000 head, 1996)	0.98
Health expenditure (2000): US $ per head (PPP)	192
Health expenditure (2000): % of GDP	4.7
Health expenditure (2000): public (% of total)	47.9
Access to water (% of persons, 2000)	92
Access to sanitation (% of persons, 2000)	85
Human Development Index (2000): ranking	120
Human Development Index (2000): value	0.631

For sources and definitions, see explanatory note on p. vi.

Agriculture

PRINCIPAL CROPS
('000 metric tons)

	1999	2000	2001
Maize	1,024.9	1,053.6	1,091.5
Sugar cane	16,350.0*	16,552.4	16,934.9
Pulses*	122.9	126.6	129.2
Oil palm fruit*	291.0	291.7	295.0
Tomatoes	166.5	172.4*	175.0
Cantaloupes and other melons	151.3	186.3*	188.2
Other fresh vegetables*	444.1	462.2	319.3
Bananas	732.5	841.0*	789.3
Lemons and limes	127.1	128.3*	130.8
Watermelons	124.7	126.1	126.6*
Cantaloupes and other melons	151.3	186.3	188.2
Mangoes	176.0	179.4	183.0
Other fresh fruit*	352.7	366.0	429.8
Coffee (green)†	293.5	312.0	275.7

* FAO estimate(s).
† Unofficial figures.

Source: FAO.

LIVESTOCK
('000 head, year ending September)

	1999	2000	2001
Horses*	119	120	120
Asses*	10	10	10
Mules*	39	39	38
Cattle*	2,500	2,600	2,500
Sheep*	551	551	552
Pigs	1,376	1,424	1,450*
Goats	111	111	112*
Chickens*	33,000	34,000	35,000

* FAO estimate(s).

Source: FAO.

LIVESTOCK PRODUCTS
('000 metric tons)

	1999	2000	2001
Beef and veal	62	62*	62*
Pig meat	23.9	24.5*	25*
Chicken meat	137	140	144†
Other meat*	5.2	5.3	5.3
Cows' milk	258.3*	259.6*	270†
Cheese*	11.1	11.1	11.1
Butter*	0.6	0.6	0.6
Hen eggs*	109	109	109
Honey	1.5	1.4	1.6†
Hides and skins*	8.9	8.8	8.8

* FAO estimate(s).
† Unofficial figure.

Source: FAO.

Forestry

ROUNDWOOD REMOVALS
('000 cubic metres, excl. bark)

	1999	2000	2001
Sawlogs, veneer logs and logs for sleepers*	504	464	464
Other industrial wood	2	3	3
Fuel wood*	14,203	14,540	14,870
Total	**14,709**	**15,007**	**15,337**

* FAO estimates.

Source: FAO.

SAWNWOOD PRODUCTION
('000 cubic metres, incl. railway sleepers)

	1999	2000	2001
Coniferous (softwood)	195	180	180
Broadleaved (hardwood)	40	40	40*
Total	**235**	**220**	**220**

* FAO estimate.

Fishing

('000 metric tons, live weight)

	1998	1999	2000
Capture	10.8	11.0	40.7
Freshwater fishes	6.5	7.0	7.3
Skipjack tuna	—	—	12.9
Yellowfin tuna	—	—	4.7
Bigeye tuna	—	—	12.8
Other marine fishes	0.9	0.9	0.7
Penaeus shrimps	2.0	1.4	1.2
Pacific seabobs	1.3	1.6	0.4
Aquaculture	3.1	4.9	4.0
Tilapias	1.6	3.3	2.3
Penaeus shrimps	1.4	1.4	1.5
Total catch	**13.9**	**15.9**	**44.7**

Source: FAO, *Yearbook of Fishery Statistics*.

Mining

SELECTED PRODUCTS

('000 metric tons, unless otherwise indicated)

	1996	1997	1998
Crude petroleum	729	975	1,272*
Antimony ore (metric tons)	880	822	440†
Limestone	1,280	1,300	10,061
Sand, silica and quartz	67	81	50†
Gravel and crushed stone	1,387	1,045	1,197

* Estimate.
† Source: US Geological Survey.

Source: UN, *Industrial Commodity Statistics Yearbook*.

1999 (estimates): Limestone 4.4m. metric tons; Sand and gravel 1,085,000 cu m; Silica sand 46,249 cu m; Crushed stone 50,000 metric tons.

2000 (estimates): Limestone 4.5m. metric tons; Sand and gravel 1,663,000 cu m; Silica sand 69,374 cu m; Crushed stone 50,000 metric tons.

Sources: US Geological Survey and Ministry of Energy and Mines.

Industry

SELECTED PRODUCTS

('000 metric tons, unless otherwise indicated)

	1998	1999	2000
Cement	1,330	1,885	1,901
Sugar	580	899	785
Cigarettes (million)	4,184	4,376	4,262

Electricity: 4,132 million kWh in 1997.

Finance

CURRENCY AND EXCHANGE RATES

Monetary Units
100 centavos = 1 quetzal

Sterling, Dollar and Euro Equivalents (31 December 2002)
£1 sterling = 12.583 quetzales
US $1 = 7.807 quetzales
€1 = 8.197 quetzales
1,000 quetzales = £79.47 = $128.09 = €122.14

Average Exchange Rate (quetzales per US dollar)
2000   7.7632
2001   7.8586
2002   7.8216

Note: In December 2000 legislation was approved to allow the circulation of the US dollar and other convertible currencies, for use in a wide range of transactions, from 1 May 2001.

BUDGET
(million quetzales)

Revenue*	1999	2000	2001
Current revenue	14,683.2	16,039.4	17,639.6
Taxation	13,863.1	15,071.6	15,966.2
Taxes on income, profits and capital gains	2,896.5	3,688.7	4,139.8
Corporate	1,495.8	2,004.3	2,059.7
Domestic taxes on goods and services	8,885.6	9,376.1	9,679.2
Sales, turnover or value-added taxes	6,241.0	7,037.9	6,983.1
Excises	1,829.6	1,797.0	2,177.3
Taxes on international trade and transactions	1,817.5	1,807.3	1,979.9
Customs duties	1,814.1	1,805.8	1,979.0
Other current revenue	820.2	967.8	1,673.4
Entrepreneurial and property income	179.9	314.3	897.4
Administrative fees, non-industrial and incidental sales	300.8	264.2	295.0
Contributions to government employee pension and welfare funds within government	302.6	356.7	414.2
Capital revenue	0.3	0.2	2.5
Total	13,967.1	15,205.8	17,656.2

Expenditure†	1999	2000	2001
Current expenditure	12,631.4	14,680.7	17,226.0
Expenditure on goods and services	9,511.5	10,822.7	12,802.5
Interest payments	1,528.6	1,672.7	2,111.2
Subsidies and other current transfers	1,591.2	2,185.3	2,312.3
Transfers to non profit-making institutions and households	1,243.0	1,900.2	2,063.5
Capital expenditure	3,546.5	3,336.8	3,601.8
Acquisition of fixed capital assets	2,143.9	1,838.9	1,654.7
Capital transfers	1,402.5	1,497.9	1,947.0
Domestic transfers	1,305.4	1,222.2	1,711.0
To other levels of national government	1,297.3	1,217.9	1,705.8
Adjustment	195.9	203.2	207.4
Total	16,373.7	18,220.8	21,035.2

* Excluding grants received (million quetzales): 188.2 in 1999; 348.5 in 2000; 565.7 in 2001.

† Excluding lending minus repayments (million quetzales): 1,585.5 in 1999; −974.6 in 2000; −2,174.5 in 2001.

Source: IMF, *Government Finance Statistics Yearbook*.

INTERNATIONAL RESERVES
(US $ million at 31 December)

	2000	2001	2002
Gold*	9.1	9.2	9.1
IMF special drawing rights	9.8	8.5	8.2
Foreign exchange	1,736.6	2,283.7	2,290.9
Total	1,746.4	2,292.2	2,299.1

* Valued at US $42.22 per troy ounce.

Source: IMF, *International Financial Statistics*.

MONEY SUPPLY
(million quetzales at 31 December)

	2000	2001	2002
Currency outside banks	7,298.2	8,360.7	8,733.2
Demand deposits at deposit money banks	11,271.5	12,512.2	13,930.4
Total money (incl. others)	18,832.2	21,059.0	22,839.5

Source: IMF, *International Financial Statistics*.

COST OF LIVING
(Consumer Price Index; base: 1990 = 100)

	1998	1999	2000
Food	255.7	261.3	272.6
Clothing	200.1	207.0	213.6
Rent	255.0	278.0	292.9
All items (incl. others)	266.4	280.2	297.0

Source: ILO.

NATIONAL ACCOUNTS

Expenditure on the Gross Domestic Product
(million quetzales at current prices)

	1999	2000	2001
Government final consumption expenditure	8,552	10,458	12,501
Private final consumption expenditure	114,554	124,568	136,867
Increase in stocks	−728	2,517	1,556
Gross fixed capital formation	24,205	24,109	25,656
Total domestic expenditure.	146,583	161,652	176,580
Exports of goods and services	25,711	30,147	29,998
Less Imports of goods and services	37,008	43,352	45,156
GDP in purchasers' values	135,287	148,447	161,421

Source: IMF, *International Financial Statistics.*

Gross Domestic Product by Economic Activity
(million quetzales at constant 1958 prices)

	1998	1999	2000
Agriculture, hunting, forestry and fishing	1,105.3	1,128.6	1,155.9
Mining and quarrying	29.4	28.8	26.4
Manufacturing	639.8	656.0	669.4
Electricity, gas and water	161.8	179.6	210.9
Construction	112.0	120.8	100.6
Trade, restaurants and hotels	1,162.8	1,199.9	1,239.7
Transport, storage and communications	426.2	455.1	486.4
Finance, insurance and real estate	244.9	257.7	265.1
Ownership of dwellings	217.2	225.6	232.6
General government services	347.3	365.8	382.7
Other community, social and personal services	268.8	279.1	290.2
Total	4,715.5	4,896.9	5,059.7

Source: UN, *Statistical Yearbook for Latin America and the Caribbean.*

BALANCE OF PAYMENTS
(US $ million)

	1999	2000	2001
Exports of goods f.o.b.	2,780.6	3,085.1	2,864.6
Imports of goods f.o.b.	−4,225.7	−4,742.0	−5,142.1
Trade balance	−1,445.1	−1,656.9	−2,277.5
Exports of services	699.5	777.0	1.031
Imports of services	−790.7	−825.4	−898.0
Balance on goods and services	−1,536.3	−1,705.3	−2,144.5
Other income received	76.2	214.4	317.5
Other income paid	−280.7	−424	−407.6
Balance on goods, services and income	−1,740.8	−1,914.9	−2,234.6
Current transfers received	754.4	908.2	1,031.8
Current transfers paid	−39.5	−42.9	−35.1
Current balance	−1,025.9	−1,049.6	1,237.9
Capital account (net)	68.4	85.5	93.3
Direct investment from abroad	154.6	229.9	455.5
Portfolio investment assets	−26.0	−36.3	−44.9
Portfolio investment liabilities	136.5	78.9	−175.4
Other investment assets	199.9	213.2	156.7
Other investment liabilities	172.5	1,035	778.1
Net errors and omissions	195.0	86.1	98.1
Overall balance	−125.0	642.7	474.3

Source: IMF, *International Financial Statistics.*

External Trade

PRINCIPAL COMMODITIES
(US $ million)

Imports c.i.f.	1998	1999	2000
Food and live animals	422.7	466.5	494.7
Cereals and cereal preparations	104.9	149.5	150.4
Mineral fuels, lubricants, etc.	385.7	448.6	622.1
Petroleum, petroleum products etc.	343.6	403.1	535.8
Crude petroleum oils, etc.	90.9	117.0	169.8
Refined petroleum products	244.4	277.7	356.3
Other fuel oils	121.6	137.5	174.4
Chemicals and related products	756.8	743.3	780.0
Medicinal and pharmaceutical products	161.8	177.4	185.2
Medicaments (incl. veterinary medicaments)	128.6	146.2	152.4
Artificial resins, plastic materials etc.	146.7	153.6	169.8
Products of polymerizations, etc.	127.4	131.8	146.5
Basic manufactures	898.5	754.8	826.7
Paper, paperboards and manufactures	204.0	194.7	230.9
Paper and paperboard	130.5	129.5	150.7
Iron and steel	252.9	164.3	174.4
Machinery and transport equipment	1,600.1	1,612.1	1,583.7
Power-generating machinery and equipment	118.5	177.9	157.4
Machinery specialized for particular industries	219.7	170.5	150.0
Telecommunications and sound equipment	160.7	254.7	282.6
Road vehicles and parts	590.3	495.7	499.6
Passenger motor cars (excl. buses)	252.4	198.6	213.5
Motor vehicles for the transport of goods	185.7	172.7	158.3
Miscellaneous manufactured articles	365.5	345.4	376.2
Total (incl. others)	4,650.8	4,554.3	4,882.4

Exports f.o.b.	1998	1999	2000
Food and live animals	1,463.8	1,322.0	1,406.3
Cereals and cereal preparations	67.8	79.7	74.7
Vegetables and fruit	317.2	299.9	353.5
Fresh or dried fruit and nuts (excl. oil nuts)	237.4	192.9	243.3
Bananas and plantains	194.6	144.6	178.1
Sugar, sugar preparations and honey	336.7	205.9	203.7
Sugar and honey	332.3	201.0	197.6
Raw beet and cane sugars	316.6	195.2	190.8
Coffee, tea, cocoa and spices	625.6	621.6	657.5
Coffee (incl. husks and skins) and substitutes containing coffee	586.8	561.9	575.4
Crude materials (inedible) except fuels	122.1	129.2	162.3
Mineral fuels, lubricants, etc.	61.7	86.2	162.4
Crude petroleum oils, etc.	58.3	80.9	159.3
Chemicals and related products	292.6	322.5	308.8
Medicinal and pharmaceutical products	85.3	85.0	85.2
Medicaments (incl. veterinary)	81.7	81.3	82.0
Essential oils, perfume materials and cleansing preparations	100.4	109.7	110.4
Basic manufactures	321.7	276.8	301.4
Miscellaneous manufactured articles	174.9	191.4	204.5
Total (incl. others)	2,581.7	2,458.2	2,699.4

PRINCIPAL TRADING PARTNERS
(US $ million)

Imports c.i.f.	1999	2000	2001
Aruba	56.4	—	—
Brazil	57.9	67.3	84.2
Canada	118.9	124.7	140.6
Costa Rica	141.4	200.9	232.2
El Salvador	201.9	313.8	385.0
Germany	121.5	126.2	158.9
Honduras	78.9	84.1	129.3
Italy	48.7	55.7	56.8
Japan	181.6	166.6	289.7
Korea, Republic	38.5	69.2	77.0
Mexico	498.0	576.0	594.5
Panama	146.0	162.0	69.5
Spain	63.8	69.3	83.6
USA	1,805.7	2,071.2	1,964.6
Venezuela	205.6	275.8	271.8
Total (incl. others)	4,559.9	5,171.4	5,606.6

Exports f.o.b.	1999	2000	2001
Belgium*	24.9	34.8	11.9
Canada	35.0	63.1	42.7
Costa Rica	121.2	126.8	156.3
El Salvador	278.6	341.1	477.1
Germany	99.4	107.8	58.2
Honduras	192.2	233.1	295.3
Japan	58.0	62.5	42.3
Korea, Republic	31.9	28.6	94.0
Mexico	97.3	120.1	79.0
Netherlands	41.1	30.7	15.8
Nicaragua	93.1	114.3	130.6
Panama	77.1	54.7	43.3
Russian Federation	13.0	20.7	31.3
USA	837.6	971.2	643.1
Total (incl. others)	2,460.4	2,699.0	2,412.6

* Includes figures for Luxembourg.

Transport

RAILWAYS
(traffic)

	1994	1995	1996
Passenger-km (million)	991	0	0
Freight ton-km (million)	25,295	14,242	836

Source: UN, *Statistical Yearbook*.

ROAD TRAFFIC
(motor vehicles in use at 31 December)

	1997	1998	1999
Passenger cars	470,016	508,868	578,733
Buses and coaches	9,843	10,250	11,017
Lorries and vans	34,220	37,057	42,219
Motorcycles and mopeds	111,358	117,536	129,664

Source: IRF, *World Road Statistics*.

SHIPPING

Merchant Fleet
(registered at 31 December)

	1999	2000	2001
Number of vessels	6	9	8
Total displacement ('000 grt)	0.9	4.7	4.6

Source: Lloyd's Register-Fairplay, *World Fleet Statistics*.

International Sea-borne Freight Traffic
('000 metric tons)

	1992	1993	1994
Goods loaded	2,176	1,818	2,096
Goods unloaded	3,201	3,025	3,822

CIVIL AVIATION
(traffic on scheduled services)

	1996	1997	1998
Kilometres flown (million)	6	5	7
Passengers carried ('000)	300	508	794
Passenger-km (million)	530	368	480
Total ton-km (million)	71	77	50

Source: UN, *Statistical Yearbook*.

Tourism

TOURIST ARRIVALS BY COUNTRY OF ORIGIN

	1999	2000	2001
Canada	19,149	15,915	17,277
Costa Rica	25,556	21,851	28,974
El Salvador	272,747	289,970	214,114
France	14,584	13,965	15,312
Germany	18,069	20,045	20,985
Honduras	59,545	51,545	59,224
Italy	17,225	16,241	18,358
Mexico	54,901	53,576	61,326
Nicaragua	30,497	16,207	15,882
Spain	18,289	18,144	24,190
USA	182,597	186,784	193,285
Total (incl. others)	822,695	826,240	835,492

Tourism receipts (US $ million): 570 in 1999; 535 in 2000; 493 in 2001.

Communications Media

	1999	2000	2001
Telephones ('000 main lines in use)	611	650	756
Mobile cellular telephones ('000 subscribers)	338	697	1,134
Personal computers ('000 in use)	110	n.a.	100
Internet users ('000)	65	n.a.	200

Source: International Telecommunication Union.

Radio receivers ('000 in use): 835 in 1997.

Television receivers ('000 in use): 680 in 1999 (Source: UN, *Statistical Yearbook*).

Daily newspapers (number): 7 in 1996.

Facsimile machines (number in use): 10,000 in 1996.

Education
(1999)

	Institutions	Teachers	Students
Pre-primary	9,607	11,813	308,240
Primary	17,905	47,811	1,825,088
Secondary	3,118	20,543	305,818
Tertiary	1,462	13,105	146,291

Adult literacy rate (UNESCO estimates): 68.6% (males 76.1%; females 61.2%) in 2000 (Source: UN Development Programme, *Human Development Report*).

Directory

The Constitution*

In December 1984 the Constituent Assembly drafted a new Constitution (based on that of 1965), which was approved in May 1985 and came into effect in January 1986. A series of amendments to the Constitution were approved by referendum in January 1994 and came into effect in April 1994. The Constitution's main provisions are summarized below:

Guatemala has a republican representative democratic system of government and power is exercised equally by the legislative, executive and judicial bodies. The official language is Spanish. Suffrage is universal and secret, obligatory for those who can read and write and optional for those who are illiterate. The free formation and growth of political parties whose aims are democratic is guaranteed. There is no discrimination on grounds of race, colour, sex, religion, birth, economic or social position or political opinions.

The State will give protection to capital and private enterprise in order to develop sources of labour and stimulate creative activity.

Monopolies are forbidden and the State will limit any enterprise which might prejudice the development of the community. The right to social security is recognized and it shall be on a national, unitary, obligatory basis.

Constitutional guarantees may be suspended in certain circumstances for up to 30 days (unlimited in the case of war).

CONGRESS

Legislative power rests with Congress, which is made up of 113 deputies, 91 of whom are elected according to departmental representation. The remaining 22 deputies are elected by national listing. Congress meets on 15 January each year and ordinary sessions last four months; extraordinary sessions can be called by the Permanent Commission or the Executive. All Congressional decisions must be taken by absolute majority of the members, except in special cases laid down by law. Deputies are elected for four years; they may be re-elected after a lapse of one session, but only once. Congress is responsible for all matters concerning the President and Vice-President and their execution of their offices; for all electoral matters; for all matters concerning the laws of the Republic; for approving the budget and decreeing taxes; for declaring war; for conferring honours, both civil and military; for fixing the coinage and the system of weights and measures; for approving, by two-thirds' majority, any international treaty or agreement affecting the law, sovereignty, financial status or security of the country.

PRESIDENT

The President is elected by universal suffrage, by absolute majority for a non-extendable period of four years. Re-election or prolongation of the presidential term of office are punishable by law. The President is responsible for national defence and security, fulfilling the Constitution, leading the armed forces, taking any necessary steps in time of national emergency, passing and executing laws, international policy, nominating and removing Ministers, officials and diplomats, co-ordinating the actions of Ministers of State. The Vice-President's duties include presiding over Congress and taking part in the discussions of the Council of Ministers.

ARMY

The Guatemalan Army is intended to maintain national independence, sovereignty and honour, territorial integrity and peace within the Republic. It is an indivisible, apolitical, non-deliberating body and is made up of land, sea and air forces.

LOCAL ADMINISTRATIVE DIVISIONS

For the purposes of administration the territory of the Republic is divided into 22 Departments and these into 330 Municipalities, but this division can be modified by Congress to suit interests and general development of the Nation without loss of municipal autonomy. Municipal authorities are elected every four years.

JUDICIARY

Justice is exercised exclusively by the Supreme Court of Justice and other tribunals. Administration of Justice is obligatory, free and independent of the other functions of State. The President of the Judiciary, judges and other officials are elected by Congress for five years. The Supreme Court of Justice is made up of 13 judges. The President of the Judiciary is also President of the Supreme Court. The Supreme Court nominates all other judges. Under the Supreme Court come the Court of Appeal, the Administrative Disputes Tribunal, the Tribunal of Second Instance of Accounts, Jurisdiction

Conflicts, First Instance and Military, the Extraordinary Tribunal of Protection. There is a Court of Constitutionality presided over by the President of the Supreme Court.

* Under the terms of an accord, signed with the URNG in September 1996, concerning civilian power and the role of the armed forces, the Government undertook to revise the Constitution to relieve the armed forces of responsibility for internal security. This role was assumed by a new National Civilian Police force from mid-1997.

The Government

HEAD OF STATE

President: ALFONSO ANTONIO PORTILLO CABRERA (took office 14 January 2000).

Vice-President: JUAN FRANCISCO REYES LÓPEZ.

CABINET
(April 2003)

Minister of Foreign Affairs: EDGAR ARMANDO GUTIÉRREZ GIRÓN.

Minister of the Interior: JOSÉ ADOLFO REYES.

Minister of National Defence: Gen. ROBIN MORAN MUNOZ.

Minister of Public Finance: EDUARDO WEYMANN FUENTES.

Minister of Economy: PATRICIA RAMIREZ CEBERG.

Minister of Public Health and Social Welfare: MARIO BOLAÑOS.

Minister of Communications, Infrastructure and Public Housing: FLORA MARINA ESCOBAR GORDILLO DE RAMOS.

Minister of Agriculture, Livestock and Food: CARLOS SETT.

Minister of Education: MARIO ROLANDO TORRES.

Minister of Employment and Social Security: VICTOR HUGO GODOY.

Minister of Energy and Mines: RAÚL EDMUNDO ARCHILA SERRANO.

Minister of Culture and Sport: OTILIA LUX DE COTÍ.

Minister of the Environment: SERGIO LAVARREDA.

MINISTRIES

Ministry of Agriculture, Livestock and Food: Edif. Monja Blanca, 7 Avda 12-90, Zona 13, Guatemala City; tel. 362-4764; fax 332-8302; e-mail magadest@intelnet.net.gt; internet www.maga.gob.gt.

Ministry of Communications, Infrastructure and Public Housing: Edif. Antiguo Cocesna, 8a Avda y 15 Calle, Zona 13, Guatemala City; tel. 362-6051; fax 362-6059; e-mail relpublicas@micivi.gob.gt; internet www.micivi.gob.gt.

Ministry of Culture and Sport: 12 Avda 11-65, Zona 1, Guatemala City; tel. 253-0543; fax 253-0540; internet www.minculturadeportes.gob.gt.

Ministry of Economy: 8a Avda 10-43, Zona 1, Guatemala City; tel. 238-3330; fax 238-2413; e-mail nhernandez@mail.mineco.gob.gt; internet www.mineco.gob.gt.

Ministry of Education: Palacio Nacional, 6a Calle 1-87, Zona 10, Guatemala City; tel. 360-0911; fax 361-0350; e-mail informatica@mineduc.gob.gt; internet www.mineduc.gob.gt.

Ministry of Employment and Social Security: Edif. NASA, 14 Calle 5-49, Zona 1, Guatemala City; tel. 230-1361; fax 251-3559; internet www.mintrabajo.gob.gt.

Ministry of Energy and Mines: Diagonal 17, 29–78, Zona 11, Guatemala City; tel. 477-0743; fax 476-3175; e-mail informatica@mem.gob.gt; internet www.mem.gob.gt.

Ministry of the Environment: Edif. Plaza Robi 3°, 5a Calle 4-31, Zona 1, 01001 Guatemala; tel. 230-1719; fax 220-3784.

Ministry of Foreign Affairs: 2a Avda La Reforma 4-47, Zona 10, Guatemala City; tel. 331-8410; fax 331-8510; e-mail webmaster@minex.gob.gt; internet www.minex.gob.gt.

Ministry of the Interior: 6a Avda 4-64, Zona 4, 3°, Guatemala City; tel. 362-0238; fax 362-0239.

Ministry of National Defence: Antigua Escuela Politécnica, Avda La Reforma 1-45, Zona 10, Guatemala City; tel. 360-9890; fax 360-9909; internet www.mindef.mil.gt.

Ministry of Public Finance: Centro Cívico, 8a Avda y 21 Calle, Zona 1, Guatemala City; tel. 251-1380; fax 251-0987; internet www .minfin.gob.gt.

Ministry of Public Health and Social Welfare: Escuela de Enfermería, 3°, 6a Avda 3-45, Zona 1, Guatemala City; tel. 475-2121; fax 475-2168; internet www.mspas.gob.gt.

President and Legislature

PRESIDENT

Election, 7 November 1999

	% of votes cast
Alfonso Antonio Portillo Cabrera (FRG)	47.8
Oscar Berger Perdomo (PAN)	30.3
Alvaro Colom Caballeros (ANN)	12.3
Acisclo Valladares Molina (PLP)	3.1
Juan Francisco Bianchi Castillo (ARDE)	2.1
Ana Catalina Soberanis Reyes (FDNG)	1.3
José Enrique Asturias Rudeke (LOV)	1.1
Danilo Julián Roca Barillas (UCN)	1.0
Total (incl. others)	100.0

Since none of the candidates achieved the required 50% of the votes necessary to win outright, a second round of voting was held on 26 December 1999. At this election Alfonso Antonio Portillo Cabrera (FRG) received 68.3% of the valid votes cast, while Oscar Berger Perdomo (PAN) won the remaining 31.7%.

CONGRESO NACIONAL

President: Gen. (retd) JOSÉ EFRAÍN RÍOS MONTT.

Vice-Presidents: CÉSAR LEONEL SOTO ARANGO, ZURY MAYTÉ RÍOS-MONTT SOSA DE LÓPEZ-VILLATORO, LUIS ALFONSO ROSALES MARROQUÍN.

Election, 7 November 1999

	Seats
Frente Republicano Guatemalteco (FRG)	63
Partido de Avanzada Nacional (PAN)	37
Alianza Nueva Nación (ANN)	9
Partido Democracia Cristiana Guatemalteca (PDCG)	2
Partido Liberal Progresista (PLP)	1
La Organización Verde (LOV)	1
Total	113

Political Organizations

Acción Reconciliadora Democrática (ARDE): 4a Avda 14-53, Zona 1, Guatemala City; tel. 232-0591; fax 251-4076; centre-right; Sec.-Gen. HERLINDO ALVAREZ DEL CID.

Alianza Democrática: 6 Avda 15-41, Zona 1, Guatemala City; tel. 591-4158; f. 1992; centre party; Leader LEOPOLDO URRUTIA.

Alianza Nueva Nación (ANN): electoral alliance comprising:

Desarrollo Integral Auténtico (DIA): 12a Calle 'A' 2-18, Zona 1, Guatemala City; tel. and fax 232-8044; e-mail morlain@guate .net; left-wing party; Sec.-Gen. JORGE LUIS ORTEGA TORRES.

Unidad de Izquierda Democrática (UNID): Guatemala City; left-wing party.

Unidad Revolucionaria Nacional Guatemalteca (URNG): see below.

Alianza Popular Cinco (AP5): 6a Avda 3-23, Zona 1, Guatemala City; tel. 231-6022; Sec.-Gen. MAX ORLANDO MOLINA NARCISO.

Central Auténtica Nacionalista (CAN): 15a Avda 4-31, Zona 1, Guatemala City; tel. 251-2992; f. 1980; from the CAO (Central Arañista Organizado); Leader HÉCTOR MAYORA DAWE; Sec.-Gen. JORGE ROBERTO ARANA ESPAÑA.

Comité Guatemalteca de Unidad Patriota (CGUP): f. 1982; opposition coalition consisting of:

Frente Democrático Contra la Represión (FDCR): Leader RAFAEL GARCÍA.

Frente Popular 31 de Enero (FP-31): f. 1980; left-wing amalgamation of student, peasant and trade union groups.

Frente de Avance Nacional (FAN): 3a Calle 'A' 1-66, Zona 10, Guatemala City; tel. 231-8036; right-wing group; Sec.-Gen. FEDERICO ABUNDIO MALDONADO GULARTE.

Frente Cívico Democrático (FCD): Guatemala City; Leader JORGE GONZÁLEZ DEL VALLE.

Frente Demócrata Guatemalteco: Leader CLEMENTE MARROQUÍN ROJAS.

Frente Democrático Nueva Guatemala (FDNG): left-wing faction of Partido Revolucionario; Pres. JORGE GONZÁLEZ DEL VALLE; Sec.-Gen. RAFAEL ARRIAGA.

Frente Republicano Guatemalteco (FRG): 3a Calle 5-50, Zona 1, Guatemala City; tel. 238-0826; internet www.frg.com.gt; f. 1988; right-wing group; Leader Gen. (retd) JOSÉ EFRAÍN RÍOS MONTT.

Frente de Unidad Nacional (FUN): 6a Avda 5-18, Zona 12, Guatemala City; tel. 271-4048; f. 1971; nationalist group; Leader GABRIEL GIRÓN ORTIZ.

Fuerza Demócrata Popular: 11a Calle 4-13, Zona 1, Guatemala City; tel. 251-5496; f. 1983; democratic popular force; Sec.-Gen. Lic. FRANCISCO REYES IXCAMEY.

Fuerza Nueva: Leader CARLOS RAFAEL SOTO.

La Organización Verde (LOV): 5a Calle 'A' 0-64, Zona 3, Guatemala City; tel. 230-3946; suspended in 2000; Sec.-Gen. MARCOS EMILIO RECINOS ALVAREZ; electoral coalition comprising:

Unidad Social Demócrata.

Unión Democrática (UD): Of. E, 3°, Vista Hermosa II, 1a Calle 18-83, Zona 15, 01015 Guatemala City; tel. 369-7074; fax 369-3062; e-mail chea@infovia.com.gt; internet www.ud.org.gt; f. 1983; Sec.-Gen. RODOLFO ERNESTO PAIZ ANDRADE.

Movimiento de los Descamisados (MD): Avda J. R. Barrios L. 896 Sta Luisa, Zona 6, Guatemala City; Sec.-Gen. ENRIQUE MORALES PÉREZ.

Movimiento Humanista de Integración Demócrata: Guatemala City; f. 1983; Leader VICTORIANO ALVAREZ.

Movimiento de Liberación Nacional (MLN): Of. 10A, Condiminio Reforma, Avda Reforma 10-00, Zona 9, Guatemala City; tel. 331-1093; fax 331-6865; e-mail mln@wepa.com.gt; internet www .wepa.com.gt/mln; f. 1960; extreme right-wing; 95,000 mems; Leader Lic. MARIO AUGUSTO SANDÓVAL ALARCÓN; Sec.-Gen. ULYSSES CHARLES DENT WEISSENBERG.

Movimiento 20 de Octubre: Leader MARCO ANTONIO VILLAMAR CONTRERAS.

Pantinamit: f. 1977; represents interests of Indian population; Leader FERNANDO TEZAHUIC TOHÓN.

Partido de Avanzada Nacional (PAN): 7a Avda 10-38, Zona 9, Guatemala City; tel. 334-1702; fax 331-9906; internet www.pan.org .gt; Leader ALVARO ENRIQUE ARZÚ IRIGOYEN; Sec.-Gen. LEONEL ELISEO LÓPEZ RODAS.

Partido de la Democracia Cristiana de Guatemalteca (PDCG): Avda Elena 20-66, Zona 3, Guatemala City; tel. 238-4988; fax 337-0966; f. 1955; 130,000 mems; suspended in 2000; Sec.-Gen. MARCO VINICIO CEREZO AREVALO.

Partido Demócrata Guatemalteco (PDG): Guatemala City; Sec.-Gen. JORGE ANTONIO REYNA CASTILLO.

Partido Institucional Democrático (PID): Guatemala City; f. 1965; 60,000 mems; moderate conservative; Sec.-Gen. OSCAR HUMBERTO RIVAS GARCÍA; Dir DONALDO ALVAREZ RUIZ.

Partido Libertador Progresista (PLP): 5a Calle 5-44, Zona 1, Guatemala City; tel. 232-5548; e-mail plp@intelnet.net.gt; f. 1990; suspended in 2000; Sec.-Gen. ACISCLO VALLADARES MOLINA.

Partido Patriótico: Guatemala City; f. 2001; populist, military, opposition party; Pres. OTTO PEREZ MOLINA.

Partido Petenero: Guatemala City; f. 1983; defends regional interests of El Petén.

Partido Progresista (PP): 1a Calle 6-77, Zona 2, Guatemala City; Sec.-Gen. JOSÉ RAMÓN FERNÁNDEZ GONZÁLEZ.

Partido Reformador Guatemalteco (PREG): 3a Calle 9-59, Zona 1, Guatemala City; tel. 22-8759; Sec.-Gen. MIGUEL ANGEL MONTEPEQUE CONTRERAS.

Partido Revolucionario de los Trabajadores Centro-americanos (PRTC): Guatemala City.

Partido Social Cristiano (PSC): P. Savoy, Of. 113, 8°, 8a Calle 9-41, Zona 1, Guatemala City; tel. 274-0577; f. 1983; Sec.-Gen. ALFONSO ALONZO BARILLAS.

Partido Socialista Democrático (PSD): Guatemala City; f. 1978; Sec.-Gen. SERGIO ALEJANDRO PÉREZ CRUZ.

Partido de Unificación Anticomunista (PUA): Guatemala City; right-wing party; Leader LEONEL SISNIEGA OTERO.

Unidad Nacional de Esperanza (UNE): Guatemala City; f. 2001 following a split within the PAN; Founder and Pres. ALVARO COLOM CABALLERO.

Unidad Nacionalista Organizada (UNO): Calzada Aguilar Batres 17-14, Zona 11, Guatemala City; Sec.-Gen. MARIO ROBERTO ARMANDO PONCIANO CASTILLO.

Unión del Centro Nacional (UCN): Guatemala City; tel. 253-6211; fax 253-4038; f. 1984; centre party; Sec.-Gen. EDMOND MULET.

Union Nacional (UN): 18 Calle 14-82, Zona 13, Guatemala City; tel. 362-7127; fax 362-7139; e-mail union_nacional2004@hotmail .com; f. 1997; Sec.-Gen. JORGE CANALE NANNE.

Unión Reformista Social (URS): 5a Calle 'A' 0-64, Zona 3, Guatemala City; Sec.-Gen. MARCOS EMILIO RECINOS ALVAREZ.

In February 1982 the principal guerrilla groups unified to form the **Unidad Revolucionaria Nacional Guatemalteca (URNG) (Guatemalan National Revolutionary Unity)** ; Avda Simeón Cañas 8-01, Zona 2, Guatemala City; tel. 288-4440; fax 254-0572; e-mail prensaurng@guate.nethas links with the PSD; Sec.-Gen. (vacant). The political wing of the URNG was the **Representación Unitariade la Oposición Guatemalteca (RUOG)** At the end of 1996 the URNG consisted of:

Ejército Guerrillero de los Pobres (EGP): f. 1972; draws main support from Indians of western highlands; works closely with the **Comité de Unidad Campesina (CUC)** (Committee of Peasant Unity) and radical Catholic groups; mems 4,000 armed, 12,000 unarmed.

Fuerzas Armadas Rebeldes (FAR): formed early 1960s; originally military commission of CGTG; associated with the CNT and CONUS trade unions; based in Guatemala City, Chimaltenango and El Petén; Commdr JORGE ISMAEL SOTO GARCÍA ('Pablo Monsanto').

Organización del Pueblo en Armas (ORPA): f. 1979; military group active in San Marcos province; originally part of FAR; Commdr RODRIGO ASTURIAS ('Gaspar Ilom').

Partido Guatemalteco del Trabajo (PGT): communist party; divided into three armed factions: PGT-Camarilla (began actively participating in war in 1981); PGT-Núcleo de Conducción y Dirección; PGT-Comisión Nuclear; Gen. Sec. RICARDO ROSALES ('Carlos González').

In December 1996 the Government and the URNG signed a definitive peace treaty, bringing the 36-year conflict to an end. The demobilization of the URNG guerrillas began in March 1997 and was completed by early May. In June the URNG registered as a political party in formation. In August the movement held elections to a provisional executive committee. The URNG applied for formal recognition as a political party in October 1998 and was formally registered in December. In May 1999 the URNG formed an alliance, the Alianza Nueva Nación, with the FDNG (which later withdrew from the alliance), the UNID and the DIA in order to contest the legislative elections of November 1999.

Diplomatic Representation

EMBASSIES IN GUATEMALA

Argentina: 2a Avda 11-04, Zona 10, Apdo 112 y 256-A, Guatemala City; tel. 332-6419; fax 332-1654; e-mail embargen@intelnet.net.gt; internet www.comtech.net.gt/argentina; Chargé d'affaires a.i. HORACIO LUIS M. LAZZARI MATHIEU.

Austria: Edif. Plaza Marítima, 4°, 6a Avda 20-25, Zona 10, Guatemala City; tel. 368-1134; fax 333-6180; e-mail austriabot@intelnet .net.gt; Ambassador GABRIEL KRAMARICS.

Belize: Edif. El Reformador, Suite 803, 8°, Avda de la Reforma 1-50, Zona 9, Guatemala City; tel. 334-5531; fax 334-5536; e-mail embelguat@guate.net; internet www.embajadadebelize.org; Ambassador MOISES CAL.

Brazil: 18a Calle 2-22, Zona 14, Apdo 196-A, Guatemala City; tel. 337-0949; fax 337-3475; e-mail braembx@intelnet.net.gt; Ambassador GUILDA MARIA RAMOS GUIMARAES.

Canada: Edif. Edyma Plaza, 8°, 13a Calle 8-44, Zona 10, Apdo 400, Guatemala City; tel. 333-6102; fax 333-6189; e-mail gtmla@ dfait-maeci.gc.ca; internet www.dfait-maeci.gc.ca/guatemala/; Ambassador JAMES LAMBERT.

Chile: 14 Calle 15-21, Zona 13, Guatemala City; tel. 334-8273; fax 334-8276; e-mail embaguatechile@adsl.cl; Ambassador JORGE MOLINA VALDIVIESO.

China (Taiwan): 4a Avda 'A' 13–25, Zona 9, Apdo 1646, Guatemala City; tel. 339-0711; fax 332-2668; e-mail echina@intelnet.net.gt; Ambassador FRANCISCO L. Y. HWANG (designate).

Colombia: Edif. Gemini 10, 12a Calle, 1a Avda, Zona 10, Guatemala City; tel. 335-3602; fax 335-3603; e-mail embajada.col@gold .guate.net; Ambassador HERNANDEZ RÁMIREZ JARAMILLO.

Costa Rica: Edif. Galerías Reforma, 3°, Of. 604, Avda de la Reforma 8-60, Zona 9, Guatemala City; tel. 331-9604; fax 332-1522; e-mail embarica@intelnet.net.gt; Ambassador YOLANDA INGIANNA-MAINIERI.

Cuba: Avda las Americas 20-72, Zona 13, Guatemala City; tel. 332-4066; fax 332-5525; Ambassador ANGEL LORENZO ABASCAL IGLESIAS.

Dominican Republic: Edif. Géminis 10, Suite 804, Torre Sur, 12 Calle 1-25, Zona 10, Guatemala City; tel. 338-2170; fax 338-2171; Ambassador MAGDA MEJÍA-RICART GUZMÁN.

Ecuador: 4 Avda 12-04, Zona 14, Guatemala City; tel. 337-2994; fax 368-1831; e-mail embecuad@guate.net; Ambassador MAURICIO PEREZ MARTINEZ.

Egypt: Edif. Cobella, 5°, 5 Avda 10-84, Zona 14, Apdo 502, Guatemala City; tel. 333-6296; fax 368-2808; e-mail egyptemb@quetzal .net; Ambassador MOHAMED HADI MOUSTAFA EL TONSI.

El Salvador: 5a Avda 8-15, Zona 9, Guatemala City; tel. 360-7660; fax 334-2069; e-mail emsalva@pronet.net.gt; Ambassador HUGO ROBERTO CARILLO CORLETO.

France: Edif. Marbella, 11°, 16a Calle 4-53, Zona 10, Apdo 1252, Guatemala City; tel. 337-4080; fax 337-3180; e-mail diplo@ ambafrance.org.gt; internet www.ambafrance.org.gt; Ambassador GILLES VIDAL.

Germany: Edif. Plaza Marítima, 2°, 20 Calle 6-20, Zona 10, Guatemala City; tel. 337-0028; fax 333-6906; e-mail embalemana@intelnet .net.gt; Ambassador WALTER EICKHOFF.

Holy See: 10a Calle 4-47, Zona 9, Apdo 22, Guatemala City (Apostolic Nunciature); tel. 332-4274; fax 334-1918; e-mail nuntius@c.net .gt; Apostolic Nuncio Most Rev. RAMIRO MOLINER INGLÉS (Titular Archbishop of Sarda).

Honduras: Edif. Géminis 10, 12°, Torre Sur, 12 Calle 1-25, Of. 1211-1206B, Zona 10, Guatemala City; tel. 335-3281; fax 335-2851; e-mail embhon@infovia.com.gt; Ambassador ELSA PALAU DE FERNÁNDEZ.

Israel: 13a Avda 14-07, Zona 10, Guatemala City; tel. 333-4624; fax 333-6950; e-mail isrembgu@guaweb.net; Ambassador YAACOV PARAN.

Italy: 5a Avda 8-59, Zona 14, Guatemala City; tel. 337-4557; fax 337-0795; e-mail ambaguat@intelnet.net.gt; Ambassador PIETRO PORCARELLI.

Japan: Edif. Torre Internacional, 10°, Avda de la Reforma 16-85, Zona 10, Guatemala City; tel. 367-2244; fax 367-2245; e-mail embjpninfo@micro.com.gt; Ambassador KAGEFUMI UENO.

Korea, Republic: Edif. El Reformador, 7°, Avda de la Reforma 1-50, Zona 9, Apdo 1649, Guatemala City; tel. 334-5480; fax 334-5481; e-mail korembsy@intelnet.net.gt; Ambassador YOUNG-HEE HAHN.

Malta: 12 Calle 2-04, Edif. Plaza del Sol, Zona 9, Guatemala City; tel. 339-4349; fax 331-2979; Ambassador MAX HEURTEMATTE.

Mexico: 15 Calle 3-20, Centro Ejecutivo, 7°, Zona 10, Guatemala City; tel. 333-7254; fax 333-7615; e-mail embamexguat@itelgua.com; Ambassador CARMEN MORENO TOSCANO.

Nicaragua: 10a Avda 14-72, Zona 10, Guatemala City; tel. 368-0785; fax 337-4264; e-mail embanic-guat@intco.com.gt; Ambassador FRANCISCO JAVIER RAMOS SÁNCHEZ.

Norway: Edif. Murano Center 15°, Of. 1501, 14 Calle 3-51, Zona 10, Apdo 1764, Guatemala City; tel. 366-5908; fax 366-5928; e-mail ambgua@norad.no; Ambassador RALF O. BERG.

Panama: 10 Avda 18-53, La Cañada, Apdo 929A, Zona 14, Guatemala City; tel. 368-2805; fax 337-2446; Ambassador JOSÉ ORLANDO CALVO VELÁZQUEZ.

Peru: 2a Avda 9-67, Zona 9, Guatemala City; tel. 331-8558; fax 334-3744; e-mail leprugua@concyt.gob.gt; Ambassador ALFREDO ARECCO SABLICH.

Spain: 6a Calle 6-48, Zona 9, Guatemala City; tel. 379-3530; fax 379-3533; e-mail embaespa@terra.com.gt; Ambassador RAMON GANDARIAS ALONSO DE CELIS.

Sweden: 8a Avda 15-07, Zona 10, Guatemala City; tel. 333-6536; fax 333-7607; e-mail swedish-emb@gua.gbm.net; Ambassador MARIA LEISSNER.

Switzerland: Edif. Torre Internacional, 14°, 16 Calle 0-55, Zona 10, Apdo 1426, Guatemala City; tel. 367-5520; fax 367-5811; e-mail swissemgua@c.net.gt; Ambassador CHRISTIAN HAUSWIRTH.

United Kingdom: Edif. Torre Internacional, 11°, Avda de la Reforma, 16 Calle, Zona 10, Guatemala City; tel. 367-5425; fax 367-

5430; e-mail embasy@infovia.com.gt; Ambassador RICHARD DOUGLAS LAVERS.

USA: Avda de la Reforma 7-01, Zona 10, Guatemala City; tel. 331-1541; fax 331-8885; internet www.usembassy.state.gov/guatemala; Ambassador JOHN R. HAMILTON.

Uruguay: Edif. Plaza Marítima, 3°, Of. 341, 6a Avda 20-25, Zona 10, Guatemala City; tel. 368-0810; fax 333-7553; e-mail uruguate@ guate.net; Ambassador CARLOS ALBÉRICO VILLAR RIVERO.

Venezuela: Edif. Atlantis, Of. 601, 13 Calle 3-40, Zona 10, Apdo 152, Guatemala City; tel. 366-9832; fax 366-9838; e-mail embavene@ concyt.gob.gt; Ambassador MIRIAM PRADO BRICEÑO.

Judicial System

Corte Suprema
Centro Cívico, 21 Calle 7-70, Zona 1, Guatemala City.
The members of the Supreme Court are appointed by the Congress.

President of the Supreme Court: CARLOS ALFONSO ALVAREZ-LOBOS VILLATORO.

Members: J. R. QUESADA FERNÁNDEZ, H. A. DE LEÓN VELASCO, O. MARROQUÍN GUERRA, A. CARRILLO CASTILLO, A. RAMÍREZ DE ARIAS, H. L. MAUL FIGUEROA, M. LUCERO SIBLEY, E. D. BARREDA, V. N. GUTIÉRREZ VARGAS, G. A. HURTADO FLORES, H. R. PINEDA SÁNCHEZ.

Civil Courts of Appeal
10 courts, five in Guatemala City, two in Quezaltenango, one each in Jalapa, Zacapa and Antigua. The two Labour Courts of Appeal are in Guatemala City.

Judges of the First Instance: Seven civil and 10 penal in Guatemala City, two civil each in Quezaltenango, Escuintla, Jutiapa and San Marcos, one civil in each of the 18 remaining Departments of the Republic.

Religion

Almost all of the inhabitants profess Christianity, with a majority belonging to the Roman Catholic Church. In recent years the Protestant Churches have attracted a growing number of converts.

CHRISTIANITY

The Roman Catholic Church
For ecclesiastical purposes, Guatemala comprises two archdioceses, 10 dioceses and the Apostolic Vicariates of El Petén and Izabal. At 31 December 2000 adherents represented about 76.0% of the total population.

Bishops' Conference
Conferencia Episcopal de Guatemala, Secretariado General del Episcopado, Km 15, Calzada Roosevelt 4-54, Zona 7, Mixco, Apdo 1698, Guatemala City; tel. 433-1831; fax 433-1834; e-mail ceg@ quetzal.net; internet www.iglesiacatolica.org.gt.
f. 1973; Pres. RODOLFO QUEZADA TORUÑO (Archbishop of Guatemala City).

Archbishop of Guatemala City: RODOLFO QUEZADA TORUÑO, Arzobispado, 7a Avda 6-21, Zona 1, Apdo 723, Guatemala City; tel. 232-9707; fax 238-0004; e-mail quezadat@intelnet.net.gt.

Archbishop of Los Altos, Quezaltenango—Totonicapán: VÍCTOR HUGO MARTÍNEZ CONTRERAS, Arzobispado, 11a Avda 6-27, Zona 1, Apdo 11, 09001 Quezaltenango; tel. 761-2840; fax 761-6049.

The Anglican Communion
Guatemala comprises one of the five dioceses of the Iglesia Anglicana de la Región Central de América.

Bishop of Guatemala: Rt Rev. ARMANDO GUERRA SORIA, Avda Castellana 40-06, Zona 8, Apdo 58-A, Guatemala City; tel. 272-0852; fax 472-0764; e-mail diocesis@infovia.com.gt; diocese founded 1967.

Protestant Churches
The Baptist Church: Convention of Baptist Churches of Guatemala, 12a Calle 9-54, Zona 1, Apdo 322, Guatemala City; tel. 22-4227; f. 1946; Pres. Lic. JOSÉ MARROQUÍN R.

Church of Jesus Christ of Latter-day Saints: 12a Calle 3-37, Zona 9, Guatemala City; 17 bishoprics, 9 chapels; Regional Rep. GUILLERMO ENRIQUE RITTSCHER.

Congregación Luterana La Epifanía (Evangelical Lutheran Congregation La Epifanía): 2a Avda 15-31, Zona 10, Apdo 651, 01010

Guatemala City; tel. 368-0301; fax 366-4968; e-mail egeb@guate.net; Pres. Rev. ECKHARD GEBSER; 350 mems.

Lutheran Church: Consejo Nacional de Iglesias Luteranas, Apdo 1111, Guatemala City; tel. 22-3401; 3,077 mems; Pres. Rev. DAVID RODRÍGUEZ U.

Presbyterian Church: Iglesia Evangélica Presbiteriana Central, 6a Avda 'A' 4-68, Zona 1, Apdo 655, Guatemala City; tel. 232-0791; fax 232-2832; f. 1882; 36,000 mems; Pastor Rev. JOSÉ RAMIRO BOLAÑOS RIVERA.

Union Church: Guatemala City; tel. 331-6904; fax 362-3961; e-mail unionchurch@guate.net; f. 1943; Pastor W. KARL SMITH.

BAHÁ'Í FAITH

National Spiritual Assembly of the Bahá'ís: 3a Calle 4-54, Zona 1, Guatemala City; tel. 232-9673; fax 232-9673; e-mail aenguate@ emailgua.com; mems resident in 464 localities; Sec. MARVIN E. ALVARADO E.

The Press

PRINCIPAL DAILIES

Al Día: Avda de la Reforma 6-64, Zona 9, Guatemala City; tel. 339-0870; fax 339-1276; f. 1996; Pres. LIONEL TORIELLO NÁJERA; Dir GERARDO JIMÉNEZ ARDÓN.

Diario de Centroamérica: 18a Calle 6-72, Zona 1, Guatemala City; tel. 22-4418; internet www.dca.gob.gt; f. 1880; morning; official; Dir LUIS MENDIZÁBAL; circ. 15,000.

La Hora: 9a Calle 'A' 1-56, Zona 1, Apdo 1593, Guatemala City; tel. 250-0447; fax 251-7084; e-mail lahora@lahora.com.gt; internet www .lahora.com.gt; f. 1920; evening; independent; Dir ÓSCAR MARROQUÍN ROJAS; circ. 18,000.

Impacto: 9a Calle 'A' 1-56, Apdo 1593, Guatemala City; tel. 22-6864; fax 251-7084; daily.

La Nación: 1a Avda 11-12, Guatemala City.

El Periódico: 15a Avda 24-51, Zona 13, Guatemala City; tel. 362-0242; fax 332-9761; e-mail periodic@gold.guate.net; f. 1996; morning; independent; Pres. JOSÉ RUBÉN ZAMORA; Editors JUAN LUIS FONT, SYLVIA GEREDA; circ. 50,000.

Prensa Libre: 13a Calle 9-31, Zona 1, Apdo 2063, Guatemala City; tel. 230-5096; fax 251-8768; e-mail webmaster@prensalibre.com.gt; internet www.prensalibre.com; f. 1951; morning; independent; Gen. Man. EDGAR CONTRERAS MOLINA; Editor GONZALO MARROQUÍN GODOY; circ. 120,000.

Siglo Veintiuno: 7a Avda 11-63, Zona 9, Guatemala City; tel. 360-6704; fax 331-9145; e-mail buzon21@sigloxxi.com; internet www .sigloxxi.com; f. 1990; morning; Pres. LIONEL TORIELLO NÁJERA; circ. 65,000.

La Tarde: 14a Avda 4-33, Guatemala City.

PERIODICALS

AGA: 9a Calle 3-43, Zona 1, Guatemala City; monthly; agricultural.

Crónica Semanal: Guatemala City; tel. 235-2155; fax 235-2360; f. 1988; weekly; politics, economics, culture; Publr FRANCISCO PÉREZ.

Gerencia: La Asociación de Gerentes de Guatemala, Edif. Aseguradora General, 7°, 10a Calle 3-17, Guatemala City; tel. 231-1644; fax 231-1646; e-mail agg@guate.net; internet www.nortropic.com/ gerencia; f. 1967; monthly; official organ of the Association of Guatemalan Managers; Editor MARGARITA SOLOGUREN.

El Industrial: 6a Ruta 9-21, Zona 4, Guatemala City; monthly; official organ of the Chamber of Industry.

Inforpress Centroamericana: Guatemala City; fax 232-9034; e-mail inforpre@guate.net; internet www.inforpressca.com/ inforpress; f. 1972; weekly; Spanish; regional political and economic news and analysis; Dir ARIEL DE LEÓN.

Panorama Internacional: 13a Calle 8-44, Zona 9, Apdo 611-A, Guatemala City; tel. 233-6367; fax 233-6203; weekly; politics, economics, culture.

PRESS ASSOCIATIONS

Asociación de Periodistas de Guatemala (APG): 14a Calle 3-29, Zona 1, Guatemala City; tel. 232-1813; fax 238-2781; e-mail apg@ terra.com.gt; f. 1947; Pres. SALVADOR BONINI; Sec. MARIO DOMÍNGUEZ VALIENTE.

Cámara Guatemalteca de Periodismo (CGP): Guatemala City; Pres. EDUARDO DÍAZ REINA.

Círculo Nacional de Prensa (CNP): Guatemala City; Pres. Israel Tobar Alvarado.

NEWS AGENCIES

Inforpress Centroamericana: Guatemala City; tel. and fax 221-0301; e-mail inforpre@guate.net; internet www.inforpressca.com/CAR; f. 1972; independent news agency; publishes two weekly news bulletins, in English and Spanish.

Foreign Bureaux

ACAN-EFE (Central America): Edif. El Centro, 8°, Of. 8-21, 9a Calle y 7a Avda, Zona 1, Of. Guatemala City; tel. 251-9454; fax 251-9484; Man. Ana Carolina Alpírez A.

Agenzia Nazionale Stampa Associata (ANSA) (Italy): Torre Norte, Edif. Géminis 10, Of. 805, 12a Calle 1-25, Zona 10, Guatemala City; tel. 235-3039; Chief Alfonso Anzueto López.

Deutsche Presse-Agentur (dpa) (Germany): 5a Calle 4-30, Zona 1, Apdo 2333, Guatemala City; tel. 251-7505; fax 251-7505; Correspondent Julio César Anzueto.

Inter Press Service (IPS) (Italy): Edif. El Centro, 3°, Of. 13, 7a Avda 8-56, Zona 1, Guatemala City; tel. 253-8837; fax 251-4736; Correspondent George Rodríguez-Oteiza.

United Press International (UPI) (USA): Guatemala City; tel. and fax 251-4258; Correspondent Amafredo Castellanos.

Publishers

Ediciones América: 12a Avda 14-55ʙ, Zone 1, Guatemala City; tel. 251-4556; internet www.edicionesb-america.com/guatemala; Man. Dir Rafael Escobar Argüello.

Ediciones Gama: 5a Avda 14-46, Zone 1, Guatemala City; tel. 234-2331; Man. Dir Sara Monzón de Echeverría.

Ediciones Legales 'Commercio e Industria': 12a Avda 14-78, Zone 1, Guatemala City; tel. 253-5725; Man. Dir Luis Emilio Barrios.

Editorial del Ministerio de Educación: 15a Avda 3-22, Zona 1, Guatemala City.

Editorial Nueva Narrativa: Edif. El Patio, Of. 106, 7a Avda 7-07, Zona 4, Guatemala City; Man. Dir Max Araújo A.

Editorial Oscar de León Palacios: 6a Calle 'A' 10-12, Zone 11, Guatemala City; tel. 272-1636; educational texts; Man. Dir Oscar de León Castillo.

Editorial Palo de Hormigo: O Calle 16-40, Zone 15, Col. El Maestro, Guatemala City; tel. 369-2080; fax 369-8858; e-mail juanfercif@hotmail.com; f. 1990; Man. Dir Juan Fernando Cifuentes.

Editorial Universitaria: Edif. de la Editorial Universitaria, Universidad de San Carlos de Guatemala, Ciudad Universitaria, Zona 12, Guatemala City; tel. and fax 476-9628; literature, social sciences, health, pure and technical sciences, humanities, secondary and university educational textbooks, Editor Raúl Figueroa Sarti.

F & G Editores: 30 Avda 'B' 4-50, Zona 7, Jardines de Tikal I, Guatemala City; fax 474-0214; e-mail fgeditor@guate.net; internet www.fygeditores.com; f. 1990 as Figueroa y Gallardo, changed name in 1993; law, literature and social sciences; Editor Raúl Figueroa Sarti.

Piedra Santa: 5a Calle 7-55, Zona 1, Guatemala City; tel. 220-1524; fax 232-9053; f. 1947; children's literature, text books; Man. Dir Irene Piedra Santa.

Seminario de Integración Social Guatemalteco: 11a Calle 4-31, Zona 1, Guatemala City; tel. 22-9754; f. 1956; sociology, anthropology, social sciences, educational textbooks.

Broadcasting and Communications

TELECOMMUNICATIONS

Regulatory Authority

Superintendencia de Telecomunicaciones de Guatemala: Edif. Murano Center, 16°, 14a Calle 3-51, Zona 10, Guatemala City; tel. 366-5880; fax 366-5890; e-mail supertel@sit.gob.gt; internet www.sit.gob.gt; Superintendent José Romeo Orellana.

Major Service Providers

BellSouth Guatemala: Edif. Torre Empresarial 10°, 7a Avda 3-33, Zona 9, Guatemala City; tel. 385-6000; fax 385-6162; internet www.bellsouth.com.gt; f. 2000; provides mobile telecommunications services in Guatemala.

Empresa Guatemalteca de Telecomunicaciones (Guatel): Guatemala City; internet www.guatel.com.gt; 95% share transferred to private ownership in 1998; Dir Alfredo Guzmán.

Other service providers include: FT & T (Telered), Cablenet, Universal de Telecomunicaciones, Comunicaciones Celulares, Telefónica Centroamérica Guatemala, Servicios de Comunicaciones Personales Inalámbricas, A-tel Communications, Telecomunicaciones de Guatemala, Cybernet de Centroamérica, Teléfonos del Norte, Americatel Guatemala, Desarrollo Integral, BNA, TTI, Optel, Concert Global Networks.

BROADCASTING

Dirección General de Radiodifusión y Televisión Nacional: Edif. Tipografía Nacional, 3°, 18 de Septiembre 6-72, Zona 1, Guatemala City; tel. 253-2539; f. 1931; government supervisory body; Dir-Gen. Enrique Alberto Hernández Escobar.

Radio

In early 2002 the Government announced plans to sell 14 radio broadcasting frequencies. There are currently five government and six educational stations, including:

La Voz de Guatemala: 18a Calle 6-72, Zona 1, Guatemala City; tel. 253-2539; government station; Dir Arturo Soto Echeverría.

Radio Cultural TGN: 4a Avda 30-09, Zona 3, Apdo 601, Guatemala City; tel. 471-4378; fax 440-0260; e-mail tgna@guate.net; internet www.pacogarcia.com/radiocultural.htm; f. 1950; religious and cultural station; programmes in Spanish and English, Cakchiquel and Kekchí; Dir Esteban Sywulka; Man. Anthony Wayne Berger.

There are some 80 commercial stations, of which the most important are:

Emisoras Unidas de Guatemala: 4a Calle 6-84, Zona 13, Guatemala City; tel. 440-5133; fax 440-5159; e-mail rboileau@tikal.net.gt; internet www.emisorasunidas.com; f. 1964; Pres. Jorge Edgardo Archila Marroquín; Vice-Pres. Rolando Archila Marroquín.

Radio Cinco Sesenta: 14a Calle 4-73, Zona 11, Guatemala City; Dir Edna Castillo Obregón.

Radio Continental: Guatemala City; Dir Roberto Vizcaíno R.

Radio Nuevo Mundo: 6a Avda 10-45, Zona 1, Apdo 281, Guatemala City; fax 232-2036; f. 1947; Man. Alfredo González Gamarra.

Radio Panamericana: 1a Avda 35-48, Zona 7, Guatemala City; Dir Jaime J. Paniagua.

La Voz de las Américas: Guatemala City; Dir Augusto López S.

Television

In September 2001 the Government announced that two new television broadcasting licences, for VHF television channels five and nine, would be granted, in order to prevent a monopoly of ownership in the television industry.

Canal 5—Televisión Cultural y Educativa, SA: 4a Calle 18-38, Zona 1, Guatemala City; tel. 238-1781; fax 232-7003; f. 1980; cultural and educational programmes; Dir Alfredo Herrera Cabrera.

Radio-Televisión Guatemala, SA: 30a Avda 3-40, Zona 11, Apdo 1367, Guatemala City; tel. 594-6320; fax 294-7492; internet www.canal3.com.gt; f. 1956; commercial station; operates channels 3 and 10; Pres. Lic. Max Kestler Farnés; Vice-Pres. J. F. Villanueva.

Teleonce: 20a Calle 5-02, Zona 10, Guatemala City; tel. 368-2532; fax 368-2221; e-mail jcof@infovia.com.gt; internet canal11y13.homestead.com/20CALLE.html; f. 1968; commercial; Gen. Dir Juan Carlos Ortiz.

Televisiete, SA: 30a Avda 3-40, Zona 11, Apdo 1242, Guatemala City; tel. 594-5320; fax 369-1393; internet www.canal7.com.gt; f. 1988; commercial station channel 7; Dir Abdón Rodríguez Zea.

Trecevisión, SA: 20a Calle 5-02, Zona 10, Guatemala City; tel. 368-2532; e-mail jcof@infovia.com.gt; internet canal11y13.homestead.com/20CALLE.html; commercial; Dir Ing. Pedro Melgar R; Gen. Man. Gilda Valladares Ortiz.

Finance

(cap. = capital; p.u. = paid up; res = reserves; dep. = deposits; m. = million; brs = branches; amounts in quetzales)

BANKING

Superintendencia de Bancos: 9a Avda 22-00, Zona 1, Apdo 2306, Guatemala City; tel. 232-0001; fax 232-5301; e-mail info@sib.gob.gt; internet www.sib.gob.gt; f. 1946; Superintendent Douglas O. Borja Vielman.

Central Bank

Banco de Guatemala: 7a Avda 22-01, Zona 1, Apdo 365, Guatemala City; tel. 230-6222; fax 253-4035; e-mail webmaster@banguat .gob.gt; internet www.banguat.gob.gt; f. 1946; cap. 41,049.4, res 94.8m., dep. 23,941.5m. (Dec. 2001); Pres. LIZARDO ARTURO SOSA LÓPEZ; Man. EDWIN HAROLDO MATUL RUANO.

State Commercial Bank

Crédito Hipotecario Nacional de Guatemala: 7a Avda 22-77, Zona 1, Apdo 242, Guatemala City; tel. 230-6562; fax 238-0744; e-mail jpedchn@infovia.com.gt; internet www.chn.net.gt; f. 1930; government-owned; Pres. FABIÁN PIRA ARRIVILLAGA; Gen. Man. SERGIO DURINI CÁRDENAS; 35 agencies.

Private Commercial Banks

Banco Agromercantil de Guatemala, SA: 7a Avda 7-30, Zona 9, 01009 Guatemala City; tel. 338-6565; fax 339-4192; e-mail agromercantil@bam.com.gt; internet www.agromercantil.com.gt .com; f. 2000 as Banco Central de Guatemala; changed name to Banco Agrícola Mercantil in 1948; name changed as above in 2000, following merger with Banco del Agro; Gen. Man. RAFAEL VIEJO RODRÍGUEZ; 77 brs.

Banco de América Central, SA: Local 6-12, 1°, 7a Avda 6-26, Zona 9, Guatemala City; tel. 360-9440; fax 362-7342.

Banco Americano, SA: 11 Calle 7-44, Zona 9, 01009 Guatemala City; tel. 332-4330; fax 332-4320; e-mail grufin@infovia.com.gt.

Banco de Antigua, SA: 5a Avda 12-35, Zona 9, Guatemala City; tel. 361-2102; fax 361-2102.

Banco del Café, SA: Avda de la Reforma 9-30, Zona 9, Apdo 831, Guatemala City; tel. 361-3645; fax 331-1480; e-mail mercadeo@ bancafe.com.gt; internet www.bancafe.com.gt; f. 1978; total assets 6.63m. (1999); merged with Multibanco in 2000; Pres. EDUARDO MANUEL GONZÁLEZ RIVERA; Gen. Man. JUAN GERARDO PONCIANO GÓMEZ.

Banco de Comercio: Edif. Centro Operativo, 6a Avda 8-00, Zona 9, Guatemala City; tel. 339-0504; fax 339-0555; internet www .bancomercio.com.gt; f. 1991; 33 brs.

Banco Corporativo, SA: 6a Avda 4-38, Zona 9, 01009 Guatemala City; tel. 334-3468; fax 334-3763; e-mail corpo@guate.net.

Banco Cuscatlan de Guatemala, SA: Edif. Céntrica Plaza, 15 Calle 1-04, Zona 10, 01010 Guatemala City; tel. 366-2828; fax 366-2818.

Banco del Ejército, SA: 7a Avda 3-73, Zona 9, Apdo 1797, 01009 Guatemala City; tel. 362-7042; fax 362-7102; e-mail banejer@ banejer.net.gt; internet www.banejer.com.gt; f. 1972; cap. 72.2m., res 22.2m., dep. 735.9m. (Dec. 1997); absorbed by Crédito Hipotecario Nacional in Nov. 2002; Pres. Col GUIDO FERNANDO ABDALA PEÑAGOS; 14 brs.

Banco de Exportación, SA (BANEX): Avda de la Reforma 11-49, Zona 10, Guatemala City; tel. 331-9861; fax 332-2879; e-mail infbanex@banex.net.gt; internet www.banex.net.gt; f. 1985; cap. 353.3m., res 48.1m., dep. 1,212.0m. (Dec. 2001); Pres. ALEJANDRO BOTRÁN; Man. ROBERTO ORTEGA HERRERA; 15 brs.

Banco Industrial, SA (BAINSA): Edif. Centro Financiero, Torre 1, 7a Avda 5-10, Zona 4, Apdo 744, Guatemala City; tel. 234-5111; fax 331-9437; e-mail soporbia@pronet.net.gt; internet www.bi.com.gt; f. 1964 to promote industrial development; total assets 7.91m. (1999); Pres. JUAN MIGUEL TORREBIARTE LANTZENDORFFER; Gen. Man. Lic. DIEGO PULIDO ARAGÓN.

Banco Inmobiliario, SA: 7a Avda 11-59, Zona 9, Apdo 1181, Guatemala City; tel. 334-0303; fax 332-1419; e-mail info@bancoinmob .com.gt; internet www.bcoinmob.com.gt; f. 1958; cap. 77.6m., res 0.4m., dep. 738.6m. (Dec. 2002); Pres. ADEL ABED ANTÓN TURJUMAN PORTILLO; 38 brs.

Banco Internacional, SA: Torre Internacional, Avda Reforma 15-85, Zona 10, Apdo 2588, Guatemala City; tel. 366-6666; fax 366-6743; e-mail binter60@gua.gbm.net; internet www.bcointer.com/gt; f. 1976; cap. 50.0m., res 15.4m., dep. 822.6m. (Dec. 1997); Pres. JUAN RUIZ SKINNER-KLÉE; Gen. Man. JOSÉ MANUEL REQUEJO SÁNCHEZ; 29 brs.

Banco Privado para el Desarrollo, SA: 7a Avda 8-46, Zona 9, Guatemala City; tel. 361-7777; fax 361-7217.

Banco del Quetzal, SA: Edif. Plaza El Roble, 7a Ave 6-26, Zona 9, Apdo 1001-A, 01009 Guatemala City; tel. 331-8333; fax 332-6937; e-mail bager@infovia.com.gt; f. 1984; cap. 37.4m., dep. 342.7m. (July 1994); Pres. Lic. MARIO ROBERTO LEAL PIVARAL; Gen. Man. ALFONSO VILLA DEVOTO.

Banco Reformador, SA: 7a Avda 7-24, Zona 9, 01009 Guatemala City; tel. 362-0888; fax 362-0108; cap. 1,720m. merged with Banco de la Construcción in 2000; 60 brs; Pres. ROLANDO LUCERO.

Banco SCI: Edif. SCI Centre, Avda La Reforma 9-76, Zona 9, 01009 Guatemala City; tel. 331-7515; fax 331-2262; e-mail atencion@sci .net.gt; internet www.sci.com.gt; f. 1967.

Banco de los Trabajadores: Avda Reforma 6-20, Zona 9, 01001 Guatemala City; tel. 385-3000; fax 251-8902; f. 1966; deals with loans for establishing and improving small industries as well as normal banking business; Pres. Lic. CÉSAR AMILCAR BÁRCENAS; Gen. Man. Lic. OSCAR H. ANDRADE ELIZONDO.

Banco Uno: Edif. Unicentro, 1°, Blvd Los Próceres, 18 Calle 5-56, Zona 10, Guatemala City; tel. 366-1777; fax 366-1818; e-mail bancouno@gua.pibnet.com; internet www.bancouno.com.gt.

G & T Continental: 7a Avda 1-86, Zona 4, Guatemala City; and Plaza Continental, 6a Avda 9-08, Zona 9, Guatemala City; tel. 331-2333; fax 332-9083; tel. 331-2333; fax 339-2091; e-mail gfc@email .continet.com.gt; internet www.gytcontinental.com.gt; f. 2000 following merger of Banco Continental and Banco Granai y Townson; total assets 11.4m. (2000); 130 brs.

Vivibanco, SA: 6a Avda 12-98, Zona 9, 01009 Guatemala City; tel. 332-6818; fax 339-4321.

State Development Bank

Banco Nacional de Desarrollo Agrícola (BANDESA): 9a Calle 9-47, Zona 1, Apdo 350, Guatemala City; tel. 253-5222; fax 253-7927; f. 1971; agricultural development bank; Pres. Minister of Agriculture, Livestock and Food; Gen. Man. GUSTAVO ADOLFO LEAL CASTELLANOS.

Finance Corporations

Corporación Financiera Nacional (CORFINA): 11a Avda 3-14, Zona 1, Guatemala City; tel. 253-4550; fax 22-5805; f. 1973; provides assistance for the development of industry, mining and tourism; Pres. Lic. SERGIO A. GONZÁLEZ NAVAS; Gen. Man. Lic. MARIO ARMANDO MARTÍNEZ ZAMORA.

Financiera Guatemalteca, SA (FIGSA): 1a Avda 11-50, Zona 10, Apdo 2460, Guatemala City; tel. 361-2667; fax 331-0873; e-mail figsa@figsa.com; internet www.figsa.com; f. 1962; investment agency; Pres. CARLOS GONZÁLEZ BARRIOS; Gen. Man. Ing. ROBERTO FERNÁNDEZ BOTRÁN.

Financiera Industrial, SA (FISA): Centro Financiero, Torre 2, 7a Avda 5-10, Zona 4, Apdo 744, Guatemala City; tel. 232-1750; fax 231-1773; f. 1981; cap. 3m., res 6.2m. (Aug. 1991); Pres. CARLOS ARÍAS MASSELLI; Gen. Man. Lic. ELDER F. CALDERÓN REYES.

Financiera de Inversión, SA: 11a Calle 7-44, Zona 9, Guatemala City; tel. 332-4020; fax 332-4320; f. 1981; investment agency; cap. 15.0m. (June 1997); Pres. Lic. MARIO AUGUSTO PORRAS GONZÁLEZ; Gen. Man. Lic. JOSÉ ROLANDO PORRAS GONZÁLEZ.

Foreign Bank

Lloyds TSB Group PLC (United Kingdom): Edif. Gran Vía, 6a Avda 9-51, Zona 9, Guatemala City; tel. 332-7580; fax 332-7641; f. 1959; cap. 18.7m., dep. 79.5m. (2000); Man. N. M. A. HUBBARD; 10 brs.

Banking Association

Asociación Bancaria de Guatemala: Diagonal 6, 10-01 Zona 10, Centro Gerencial Las Margaritas, Torre 2, 5°, Of. 502, Guatemala City; tel. 336-6080; fax 336-6094; internet www.abg.org.gt; f. 1961; represents all state and private banks; Pres. Lic. LUIS LARA GROJEC.

STOCK EXCHANGE

Bolsa de Valores Nacional SA Guatemala: 7 Avda 5-10, Zona 4, Centro Financiero, Torre II, 2°, Guatemala City; tel. 331-7181; fax 332-1721; e-mail bvn@bvnsa.com.gt; internet www.bvnsa.com.gt; f. 1987; the exchange is commonly owned (one share per associate) and trades stocks from private companies, government bonds, letters of credit and other securities.

INSURANCE

National Companies

Aseguradora General, SA: 10a Calle 3-70, Zona 10, Guatemala City; tel. 332-5933; fax 334-2093; e-mail generaliguate@generali .com.gt; f. 1968; Pres. JUAN O. NIEMANN; Man. ENRIQUE NEUTZE A.

Aseguradora Guatemalteca, SA: Edif. Torre Azul, 10°, 4a Calle 7-53, Zona 9, Guatemala City; tel. 361-0206; fax 361-1093; e-mail aseguate@guate.net; f. 1978; Pres. Gen. CARLOS E. PINEDA CARRANZA; Man. CÉSAR A. RUANO SANDOVAL.

Cía de Seguros Generales Granai & Townson, SA: 2a Ruta, 2-39, Zona 4, Guatemala City; tel. 334-1361; fax 332-2993; f. 1947; Pres. ERNESTO TOWNSON R; Exec. Man. MARIO GRANAI FERNÁNDEZ.

Cía de Seguros Panamericana, SA: Avda de la Reforma 9-00, Edif. Plaza Panamericana, Zona 9, Guatemala City; tel. 232-5922; fax 231-5026; f. 1968; Pres. FRANK PURVIS; Gen. Man. Lic. SALVADOR ORTEGA.

Cía de Seguros El Roble, SA: Torre 2, 7a Avda 5-10, Zona 4, Guatemala City; tel. 332-1702; fax 332-1629; f. 1973; Pres. FEDERICO KÖNG VIELMAN; Man. Ing. RICARDO ERALES CÓBAR.

Comercial Aseguradora Suizo-Americana, SA: 7a Avda 7-07, Zona 9, Apdo 132, Guatemala City; tel. 334-1661; fax 331-5495; e-mail seguros@grupocasa.com.gt; internet www.grupocasa.com.gt; f. 1946; Pres. WILLIAM BICKFORD B; Gen. Man. DAVID H. LEMUS PIVARAL.

Departamento de Seguros y Previsión del Crédito Hipotecario Nacional: 7a Avda 22-77, Zona 1, Centro Cívico, Guatemala City; tel. 250-0271; fax 253-8584; f. 1935; Pres. FABIÁN PIRA; Man. SERGIO DURINI.

Empresa Guatemalteca Cigna de Seguros, SA: Edif. Plaza Marítima, 10°, 6a Avda 20-25, Zona 10, Guatemala City; tel. 337-2285; fax 337-0121; e-mail cigna@starnet.com.gt; f. 1951; Gen. Man. Lic. RICARDO ESTRADA DARDÓN.

La Seguridad de Centroamérica, SA: 7a Avda 12-23, Edif. Etísa, 3°, Plazuela España, Zona 9, Guatemala City; tel. 361-3050; fax 361-3026; e-mail aglasec@gua.net; f. 1967; Pres. EDGARDO WAGNER D; Vice-Pres. RICARDO CAU MARTÍNEZ.

Seguros Alianza, SA: 7a Avda 12-23, Edif. Etísa, 6°, Plazuela España, Zona 9, Guatemala City; tel. 331-5475; fax 331-0023; e-mail segualia@infovia.com.gt; f. 1968; Pres. LUIS FERNANDO SAMAYOA; Gen. Man. DAVID LEMUS PIVARAL.

Seguros de Occidente, SA: 7a Calle 'A' 7-14, Zona 9, Guatemala City; tel. 331-1222; fax 334-2787; e-mail seguros@occidente.com.gt; internet www.occidente.com.gt; f. 1979; Pres. Lic. PEDRO AGUIRRE; Gen. Man. CARLOS LAINFIESTA.

Seguros Universales, SA: 4a Calle 7-73, Zona 9, Apdo 1479, Guatemala City; tel. 334-0733; fax 332-3372; e-mail seguros@universales.net; f. 1962; Manager PEDRO NOLASCO SICILIA.

Insurance Association

Asociación Guatemalteca de Instituciones de Seguros (AGIS): Edif. Torre Profesional I, Of. 703, 4°, 6a Avda 0-60, Zona 4, Guatemala City; tel. 335-2140; fax 335-2357; e-mail agis@intelnet.net.gt; internet www.agis.centroamerica.com; f. 1953; 12 mems; Pres. ENRIQUE NUETZE A; Man. Lic. FERNANDO RODRÍGUEZ TREJO.

Trade and Industry

DEVELOPMENT ORGANIZATIONS

Comisión Nacional Petrolera: Diagonal 17, 29-78, Zona 11, Guatemala City; tel. 276-0680; fax 276-3175; f. 1983; awards petroleum exploration licences.

Consejo Nacional de Planificación Económica: 9a Calle 10-44, Zona 1, Guatemala City; tel. 251-4549; fax 253-3127; e-mail mrayo@ns.concyt.gob.gt; f. 1954; prepares and supervises the implementation of the national economic development plan; Sec.-Gen. MARIANO RAYO MUÑOZ.

Corporación Financiera Nacional (CORFINA): see under Finance (Finance Corporations).

Empresa Nacional de Fomento y Desarrollo Económico de El Petén (FYDEP): Guatemala City; tel. 231-6834; f. 1959; attached to the Presidency; economic development agency for the Department of El Petén; Dir FRANCISCO ANGEL CASTELLANOS GÓNGORA.

Instituto de Fomento de Hipotecas Aseguradas (FHA): Edif. Aristos Reforma, 2°, Avda Reforma 7-62, Zona 9, Guatemala City; tel. 362-9434; fax 362-9492; e-mail promocion@fha.com.gt; internet www.fha.com.gt; f. 1961; insured mortgage institution for the promotion of house construction; Pres. Lic. HOMERO AUGUSTO GONZÁLEZ BARILLAS; Man. Lic. JOSÉ SALVADOR SAMAYOA AGUILAR.

Instituto Nacional de Administración Pública (INAP): 5a Avda 12-65, Zona 9, Apto 2753, Guatemala City; tel. 26-6339; f. 1964; provides technical experts to assist all branches of the Government in administrative reform programmes; provides in-service training for local and central government staff; has research programmes in administration, sociology, politics and economics; provides postgraduate education in public administration; Gen. Man. Dr ARIEL RIVERA IRÍAS.

Instituto Nacional de Transformación Agraria (INTA): 14a Calle 7-14, Zona 1, Guatemala City; tel. 28-0975; f. 1962 to carry out agrarian reform; current programme includes development of the 'Faja Transversal del Norte'; Pres. Ing. NERY ORLANDO SAMAYOA; Vice-

Pres Ing. SERGIO FRANCISCO MORALES-JUÁREZ, ROBERTO EDMUNDO QUIÑÓNEZ LÓPEZ.

CHAMBERS OF COMMERCE AND INDUSTRY

Comité Coordinador de Asociaciones Agrícolas, Comerciales, Industriales y Financieras (CACIF): Edif. Cámara de Industria de Guatemala, 6a Ruta 9-21, Zona 4, Guatemala City; tel. 231-0651; co-ordinates work on problems and organization of free enterprise; mems: 6 chambers; Pres. JORGE BRIZ; Sec.-Gen. RAFAEL POLA.

Cámara de Comercio de Guatemala: 10a Calle 3-80, Zona 1, Guatemala City; tel. 28-2681; fax 251-4197; internet www.tradepoint.org.gt/redtp/camaras/camcom; f. 1894; Gen. Man. EDGARDO RUIZ.

Cámara de Industria de Guatemala: 6a Ruta 9-21, 12°, Zona 4, Apdo 214, Guatemala City; tel. 334-0850; fax 334-1090; internet www.tradepoint.org.gt/redtp/camaras/camind; f. 1958; Pres. JUAN JOSÉ URRUELA KONG; Gen. Man. CARLOS PERALTA.

INDUSTRIAL AND TRADE ASSOCIATIONS

Asociación de Agricultores Productores de Aceites Esenciales: Guatemala City; tel. 234-7255; f. 1948; essential oils producers' asscn; 40 mems; Pres. FRANCISCO RALDA; Gen. Man. CARLOS FLORES PAGAZA.

Asociación de Azucareros de Guatemala (ASAZGUA): Edif. Tívoli Plaza, 6a Calle 6-38, Zona 9, Guatemala City; fax 231-8191; f. 1957; sugar producers' asscn; 19 mems; Gen. Man. Lic. ARMANDO BOESCHE.

Asociación de Exportadores de Café: 11a Calle 5-66, 3°, Zona 9, Guatemala City; coffee exporters' asscn; 37 mems; Pres. EDUARDO GONZÁLEZ RIVERA.

Asociación General de Agricultores: 9a Calle 3-43, Zona 1, Guatemala City; f. 1920; general farmers' asscn; 350 mems; Pres. DAVID ORDÓÑEZ; Man. PEDRO ARRIVILLAGA RADA.

Asociación Nacional de Avicultores (ANAVI): Edif. Galerías Reforma, Torre 2, 9°, Of. 904, Avda de la Reforma 8-60, Zona 9, Guatemala City; tel. 231-1381; fax 234-7576; f. 1964; national asscn of poultry farmers; 60 mems; Pres. Lic. FERNANDO ROJAS; Dir Dr MARIO A. MOTTA GONZÁLEZ.

Asociación Nacional de Fabricantes de Alcoholes y Licores (ANFAL): Guatemala City; tel. 292-0430; f. 1947; distillers' asscn; Pres. FELIPE BOTRÁN MERINO; Man. Lic. JUAN GUILLERMO BORJA MOGOLLÓN.

Asociación Nacional del Café—Anacafé: Edif. Etisa, Plazuela España, Zona 9, Guatemala City; tel. 236-7180; fax 234-7023; e-mail sellodepureza@anacafe.org; internet www.anacafe.org; f. 1960; national coffee asscn; Pres. WILLIAM STIXRUD.

Cámara del Agro: 15a Calle 'A' 7-65, Zona 9, Guatemala City; tel. 26-1473; f. 1973; Man. CÉSAR BUSTAMANTE ARAÚZ.

Consejo Nacional del Algodón: 11a Calle 6-49, Zona 9, Guatemala City; tel. 234-8390; fax 234-8393; f. 1964; consultative body for cultivation and classification of cotton; 119 mems; Pres. ROBERTO MARTÍNEZ R; Man. ALFREDO GIL SPILLARI.

Gremial de Huleros de Guatemala: Guatemala City; tel. 231-4917; f. 1970; rubber producers' guild; 125 mems; Pres. JOSÉ LUIS RALDA; Man. Lic. CÉSAR SOTO.

UTILITIES

Electricity

Empresa Eléctrica de Guatemala, SA: 6a Avda 8-14, Zona 1, Guatemala City; tel. 230-4040; fax 253-1746; e-mail consultas@eegsa.net; internet www.eegsa.com; f. 1972; state electricity producer; 80% share transferred to private ownership in 1998; Pres. RICARDO CASTILLO SINIBALDI.

Instituto Nacional de Electrificación (INDE): Edif. La Torre, 7a Avda 2-29, Zona 9, Guatemala City; tel. (2) 34-5711; fax (2) 34-5811; e-mail gerencia.general@inde.gob.gt; internet www.inde.gob.gt; f. 1959; former state agency for the generation and distribution of hydroelectric power; principal electricity producer; privatized in 1998; Gen. Man JORGE JUÁREZ.

CO-OPERATIVES

Instituto Nacional de Cooperativas (INACOP): 4a Calle 4-37, Zona 9, 01001 Guatemala City; tel. 234-1097; fax 234-7536; technical and financial assistance in planning and devt of co-operatives; Man. CÉSAR AUGUSTO MASSELLA BARRERA.

TRADE UNIONS

Frente Nacional Sindical (FNS) (National Trade Union Front): Guatemala City; f. 1968 to achieve united action in labour matters; affiliated are two confederations and 11 federations, which represent 97% of the country's trade unions and whose General Secretaries form the governing council of the FNS. The affiliated organizations include:

Comité Nacional de Unidad Sindical Guatemalteca (CONUS): Guatemala City; Leader MIGUEL ANGEL SOLÍS; Sec.-Gen. GERÓNIMO LÓPEZ DÍAZ.

Confederación General de Sindicatos (General Trade Union Confederation): 18a Calle 5-50, Zona 1, Apdo 959, Guatemala City.

Confederación Nacional de Trabajadores (National Workers' Confederation): Guatemala City; Sec.-Gen. MIGUEL ANGEL ALBI-ZÚREZ.

Consejo Sindical de Guatemala (Guatemalan Trade Union Council): Guatemala City; f. 1955; admitted to ICFTU and ORIT; Gen. Sec. JAIME V. MONGE DONIS; 30,000 mems in 105 affiliated unions.

Federación Autónoma Sindical Guatemalteca (Guatemalan Autonomous Trade Union Federation): Guatemala City; Gen. Sec. MIGUEL ANGEL SOLÍS.

Federación de Obreros Textiles (Textile Workers' Federation): Edif. Briz, Of. 503, 6a Avda 14-33, Zona 1, Guatemala City; f. 1957; Sec.-Gen. FACUNDO PINEDA.

Federación de Trabajadores de Guatemala (FTG) (Guatemalan Workers' Federation): 5a Calle 4-33, Zona 1, Guatemala City; tel. 22-6515; Promoter ADRIAN RAMÍREZ.

A number of unions exist without a national centre, including the Union of Chicle and Wood Workers, the Union of Coca-Cola Workers and the Union of Workers of the Enterprise of the United Fruit Company.

Central General de Trabajadores de Guatemala (CGTG): 3a Avda 12-22, Zona 1, Guatemala City; tel. 232-9234; fax 251-3212; e-mail cgtg@guate.net; f. 1987; Sec.-Gen. JOSÉ E. PINZÓN SALAZAR.

Central Nacional de Trabajadores (CNT): Guatemala City; f. 1972; cover all sections of commerce, industry and agriculture including the public sector; clandestine since June 1980; Sec.-Gen. JULIO CELSO DE LEÓN; 23,735 mems.

Unidad de Acción Sindical y Popular (UASP): 10 Avda 'A' 5-40, Zona 1, Guatemala City; f. 1988; broad coalition of leading labour and peasant organizations; includes:

Comité de la Unidad Campesina (CUC) (Committee of Peasants' Unity): 31 Avda 'A' 14-46, Zona 7, Ciudad de Plata, Guatemala City; tel. and fax 594-9754.

Confederación de Unidad Sindical de Trabajadores de Guatemala (CUSG): 5a Calle 4-33, Zona 1, Guatemala City; tel. 22-6515; f. 1983; Sec.-Gen. FRANCISCO ALFARO MIJANGOS.

Federación Nacional de Sindicatos de Trabajadores del Estado de Guatemala (FENASTEG): 10 Avda 5-40, Zona 1, Guatemala City; tel. and fax 232-2772; Sec. ARMANDO SÁNCHEZ.

Sindicato de Trabajadores de la Educación Guatemaltecos (STEG).

Sindicato de Trabajadores de la Industria de la Electricidad (STINDE).

Sindicato de Trabajadores del Instituto Guatemalteco de Seguro Social (STIGSS).

Unidad Sindical de Trabajadores de Guatemala (UNSITRAGUA): 10 Avda 5-40, Zona 1, Guatemala City; tel. and fax 238-2272; e-mail unsitragua@pronet.net.gt; Sec. Gen. SERGIO GUZMÁN.

Transport

RAILWAYS

In 1998 there were 1,390 km of railway track in Guatemala, of which some 102 km were plantation lines.

Ferrocarriles de Guatemala (FEGUA): 18 Calle 9-03, Zona 1, Guatemala City; tel. 232-7720; fax 238-3039; e-mail fegua@quetzalnet.com; internet www.quetzalnet.com/quetzalnet/fegua; f. 1968; 50-year concession to rehabilitate and operate railway awarded in 1997 to the US Railroad Devt Corpn; 782 km from Puerto Barrios and Santo Tomás de Castilla on the Atlantic coast to Tecún Umán on the Mexican border, via Zacapa, Guatemala City and Santa María. Branch lines: Santa María–San José; Las Cruces–Champerico. From Zacapa another line branches southward to Anguiatú, on the border with El Salvador; owns the ports of Barrios (Atlantic) and San José (Pacific); first 65-km section, Guatemala City—El Chile, and a further 300-km section, extending to Barrios, reopened in 1999; Interventor ANDRÉS PORRAS.

ROADS

In 1999 there were an estimated 14,021 km of roads, of which 3,081 km were paved. The Guatemalan section of the Pan-American highway is 518.7 km long and totally asphalted. In 2002 plans were discussed for the construction of a highway between Huehuetenango and Izabal under the 'Plan Puebla–Panamá' at an estimated cost of US $292m. The highway would take five years to complete.

SHIPPING

Guatemala's major ports are Puerto Barrios and Santo Tomás de Castilla, on the Gulf of Mexico, San José and Champerico on the Pacific Ocean, and Puerto Quetzal, which was redeveloped in the late 1990s. In June 2002 the Government announced plans for the expansion of shipping facilities at Puerto Quetzal and Santo Tomás de Castilla in the near future.

Armadora Marítima Guatemalteca, SA: 14a Calle 8-14, Edif. Armagua, 5°, Zona 1, Apdo 1008, Guatemala City; tel. 230-4686; fax 253-7464; cargo services; Pres. and Gen. Man. L. R. CORONADO CONDE.

Empresa Portuaria 'Quetzal': Edif. Torre Azul, 1°, 4a Calle 7-53, Zona 9, Guatemala City; tel. 334-7101; fax 334-8172; e-mail pquetzal@terra.com.gt; internet www.puerto-quetzal.com; port and shipping co; Man. LEONEL MONTEJO.

Empresa Portuaria Nacional Santo Tomás de Castilla: Guatemala City; tel. 232-3685; fax 232-6894; internet www.empornac.gob.gt; Man. ENRIQUE SALAZAR.

Flota Mercante Gran Centroamericana, SA: Guatemala City; tel. 231-6666; f. 1959; services from Europe (in association with WITASS), Gulf of Mexico, US Atlantic and East Coast Central American ports; Pres. R. S. HERRERÍAS; Gen. Man. J. E. A. MORALES.

Líneas Marítimas de Guatemala, SA: Edif. Plaza Marítima, 8°, 6a Avda 20-25, Zona 10, Guatemala City; tel. 237-0166; cargo services; Pres. J. R. MATHEAU ESCOBAR; Gen. Man. F. HERRERÍAS.

Several foreign lines link Guatemala with Europe, the Far East and North America.

CIVIL AVIATION

There are two international airports, 'La Aurora' in Guatemala City and at Santa Elena Petén. In June 2002 the Government announced plans for the potential construction of a new international airport outside Guatemala City and for the renovation and modernization of the airport at Santa Elena Petén.

Aerolíneas de Guatemala (AVIATECA): Avda Hincapié 12-22, Aeropuerto 'La Aurora', Zona 13, Guatemala City; tel. 331-0375; fax 334-7846; internet www.grupotaca; f. 1945; internal services and external services to the USA, Mexico, and within Central America; transferred to private ownership in 1989; Pres. Ing. JULIO OBOLS GOMES; Gen. Man. ENRIQUE BELTRONERA.

Aeroquetzal: Guatemala City; tel. 231-8282; fax 232-1491; scheduled domestic passenger and cargo services, and external services to Mexico.

Aerovías: Guatemala City; tel. 232-5686; fax 234-7470; operates scheduled and charter cargo services; Pres. FERNANDO ALFONSO CASTILLO R; Vice-Pres. NELSON C. PUENTE.

Aviones Comerciales de Guatemala (Avcom): Avda Hincapié, Aeropuerto 'La Aurora', Zona 13, Guatemala City; tel. 231-5821; fax 232-4946; domestic charter passenger services.

Tourism

As a result of violence in the country, the annual total of tourist arrivals declined from 504,000 in 1979, when tourist receipts were US $201m., to 192,000 in 1984 (receipts $56.6m.). After 1985, however, the number of arrivals recovered and were recorded as some 835,492 in 2001, when receipts were an estimated $493m.

Instituto Guatemalteco de Turismo (INGUAT) (Guatemala Tourist Commission): Centro Cívico, 7a Avda 1-17, Zona 4, Guatemala City; tel. 331-1333; fax 331-4416; e-mail inguat@guate.net; internet www.guatemala.travel.com.gt; f. 1967; policy and planning council: 11 mems representing the public and private sectors; Pres. ALEJANDRO BOTRÁN; Dir MARIANO BELTRANENA FALLA.

Asociación Guatemalteca de Agentes de Viajes (AGAV) (Guatemalan Association of Travel Agents): 6a Avda 8-41, Zona 9, Apdo 2735, Guatemala City; tel. 231-0320; Pres. MARÍA DEL CARMEN FERNÁNDEZ O.

GUINEA

Introductory Survey

Location, Climate, Language, Religion, Flag, Capital

The Republic of Guinea lies on the west coast of Africa, with Sierra Leone and Liberia to the south, Senegal and Guinea-Bissau to the north, and Mali and Côte d'Ivoire inland to the east. The climate on the coastal strip is hot and moist, with temperatures ranging from about 32°C (90°F) in the dry season to about 23°C (73°F) in the wet season (May–October). The interior is higher and cooler. The official language is French, but Soussou, Manika and six other national languages are widely spoken. Most of the inhabitants are Muslims, but some follow traditional animist beliefs. Around 2% are Roman Catholics. The national flag (proportions 2 by 3) consists of three equal vertical stripes, of red, yellow and green. The capital is Conakry.

Recent History

The Republic of Guinea (formerly French Guinea, part of French West Africa) became independent on 2 October 1958, after 95% of voters rejected the Constitution of the Fifth Republic under which the French colonies became self-governing within the French Community. The new state was the object of punitive reprisals by the outgoing French authorities: all aid was withdrawn, and the administrative infrastructure destroyed. The Parti démocratique de Guinée—Rassemblement démocratique africain (PDG—RDA) became the basis for the construction of new institutions. Its leader, Ahmed Sekou Touré, became President, and the PDG—RDA the sole political party.

Sekou Touré, formerly a prominent trade unionist, pursued vigorous policies of socialist revolution. Opposition was ruthlessly crushed, and Sekou Touré perpetuated rumours of a 'permanent conspiracy' by foreign powers to overthrow his regime. Notably, an abortive invasion by Portuguese troops and Guinean exiles in 1970 prompted the execution of many of those convicted of involvement. By 1983 almost 2m. Guineans were estimated to have fled the country.

All private trade was forbidden in 1975, and an 'economic police' established. In August 1977 demonstrations by women in Conakry, in protest against the abolition of the traditional market and the abuse of power by the 'economic police', provoked rioting in other towns, as a result of which three state governors were killed. Sekou Touré subsequently disbanded the 'economic police', and allowed limited private trading to recommence in July 1979. In November 1978 it was announced that the functions of the PDG—RDA and the State were to be merged, and the country was renamed the People's Revolutionary Republic of Guinea. There was, none the less, a general move away from rigid Marxism and a decline in relations with the USSR, as Guinea sought a political and economic *rapprochement* with its African neighbours, with France and with other Western powers.

At legislative elections in January 1980 voters endorsed the PDG—RDA's list of 210 candidates for a new Assemblée nationale (to replace the former Assemblée législative). In May 1982 Sekou Touré was returned unopposed to the presidency for a fourth seven-year term of office, reportedly receiving 100% of the votes cast.

In January 1984 a plot to overthrow the Government was disclosed; thousands of Guineans were reportedly detained, accused of complicity in the affair. In March Sekou Touré died while undergoing surgery in the USA. On 3 April, before a successor had been chosen by the ruling party, the armed forces seized power in a bloodless coup. A Comité militaire de redressement national (CMRN) was appointed, headed by Col (later Gen.) Lansana Conté, and Col Diarra Traoré became Prime Minister. The PDG—RDA and the legislature were dissolved, and the Constitution was suspended. The CMRN pledged to restore democracy and to respect human rights; some 250 political prisoners were released, and a relaxation of press restrictions was announced. In May the 'Second Republic of Guinea' was proclaimed. By mid-1984 an estimated 200,000 Guinean exiles had returned to the country.

Trials of former associates of Sekou Touré, most of whom had been detained since the coup, began in November 1984. In December President Conté assumed the posts of Head of Government and Minister of Defence; the post of Prime Minister was abolished, and Traoré was demoted to a lesser post. In July 1985 Traoré attempted to seize power while Conté was out of the country. Troops loyal to Conté suppressed the revolt, and Traoré was arrested, along with more than 200 suspected sympathizers. In May 1987 it was announced that 58 people, including nine former government ministers, had been sentenced to death in secret trials for crimes committed under Sekou Touré or following the 1985 coup attempt. The announcement did little to allay international suspicions that many detainees had been executed in the aftermath of the abortive coup, and in December 1987 Conté admitted that Traoré had died in the hours following his arrest. In January 1988 an amnesty was announced for 67 political prisoners, including Sekou Touré's widow and son.

In October 1985 Conté began to implement radical economic reforms, demanded by the World Bank and IMF. In December the Council of Ministers was reorganized to include a majority of civilians. In late 1989 Conté announced that, following a national referendum on a proposed new constitution, a joint civilian and military Comité transitoire de redressement national (CTRN) would replace the CMRN. After a transitional period of not more than five years, civilian rule would be established, with an executive and legislature directly elected within a two-party system. The draft Constitution of what was designated the Third Republic was reportedly endorsed by 98.7% of the 97.4% of the electorate who voted in a referendum on 23 December 1990; the 36-member CTRN was inaugurated in February 1991 under Conté's chairmanship.

In November 1990, meanwhile, Conté appealed to political exiles to return to Guinea. Alpha Condé, the leader of the Rassemblement populaire guinéen (RPG—an unofficial political organization whose activities the authorities had suppressed), returned to Guinea in May 1991, after a long period of exile. Three arrests were made when security forces dispersed a meeting of Condé's supporters, and a ban was subsequently imposed on unauthorized meetings and demonstrations. Condé was subsequently granted political asylum in Senegal.

In October 1991 Conté announced that a law authorizing the registration of an unlimited number of political parties would come into effect in April 1992, and that legislative elections would be held before the end of 1992. The Constitution was promulgated on 23 December 1991, and in January 1992 Conté ceded the presidency of the CTRN (whose membership was, at the same time, reduced to 15), in conformity with the constitutional separation of executive and legislative powers. In February most military officers and all those who had returned from exile after the 1984 coup (known as *Guinéens de l'extérieur*) were removed from the Council of Ministers.

In April 1992 17 political parties, including the RPG, were legalized; Condé returned to Guinea in June. It was subsequently rumoured that the pro-Conté Parti pour l'unité et le progrès (PUP), established by prominent *Guinéens de l'extérieur*, was benefiting from state funds. In December the Government postponed indefinitely the legislative elections, which had been scheduled for the end of that month. Subsequent indications that the parliamentary elections would not take place until after a presidential election caused resentment among the opposition, which had hoped to present a single candidate (from the party that had performed best in the legislative elections) for the presidency.

In October 1993 the Supreme Court approved eight candidates for the presidential election, scheduled for 5 December. Among Conté's main rivals were Condé, Mamadou Boye Bâ of the Union pour la nouvelle République (UNR) and Siradiou Diallo of the Parti pour le renouveau et le progrès (PRP); the election was subsequently postponed until 19 December. At least four deaths were recorded in pre-election violence, and there were six deaths in Conakry, as voting proceeded. The official rate of participation by voters was 78.5%. Preliminary results indicated that Conté had secured an absolute majority of the votes cast, obviating the need for a second round of voting. Opposition claims that the result had been manipulated in favour of Conté intensified when the Supreme Court annulled the outcome of voting in the Kankan and Siguiri prefectures (in both of which Condé had won more than 95% of the votes). According to official results, Conté was elected with 51.7% of the votes cast; Condé took 19.6% of the votes, Bâ 13.4% and Diallo 11.9%.

Conté, who had resigned from the army in order to contest the election as a civilian, was inaugurated as President on 29 January 1994. His stated priorities included the strengthening of national security and the promotion of economic growth. A major restructuring of the Council of Ministers was implemented in August. In February 1995 Conté readopted his military title.

At the delayed legislative elections, which were held on 11 June 1995, some 846 candidates, from 21 parties, contested the 114 seats in the Assemblée nationale. As preliminary results indicated that the PUP had won an overwhelming majority in the legislature, the so-called 'radical' opposition (the RPG, the PRP and the UNR) announced their intention to boycott the assembly, protesting that voting had been conducted fraudulently. According to the final results, which were verified by the Supreme Court in July (whereupon the Assemblée nationale officially superseded the CTRN), the PUP won 71 seats—having taken 30 of the 38 single-member constituencies and 41 of the 76 seats allocated by a system of national proportional representation. Of the eight other parties to win representation, the RPG secured 19 seats, while the PRP and the UNR each won nine seats. Some 63% of the registered electorate were reported to have voted. At municipal elections in late June the PUP won control of 20 of the country's 36 municipalities. In July the RPG, the PRP and the UNR joined with nine other organizations in a Coordination de l'opposition démocratique (Codem), which indicated its willingness to enter into a dialogue with the authorities. El Hadj Boubacar Biro Diallo, of the PUP, was elected as the Speaker of the Assemblée nationale, which was officially inaugurated on 30 August.

In February 1996 Conté was reportedly seized as he attempted to flee the presidential palace during a mutiny by disaffected elements of the military, and was held by rebels for some 15 hours until he made concessions including a doubling of salaries and immunity from prosecution for those involved in the uprising. The Minister of Defence, Col Abdourahmane Diallo, was dismissed, and Conté assumed personal responsibility for defence. It was estimated that about 50 people were killed and at least 100 injured, as up to 2,000 rebels, apparently including members of the Presidential Guard, clashed with forces loyal to Conté.

In February 1996 Codem withdrew from a parliamentary commission investigating the circumstances surrounding the coup attempt, in protest at Conté's allusions to opposition links with anti-Government elements within the military. The initial recommendations of the commission included a complete separation of the political and military elements in national life. In March it was announced that eight members of the military, including four senior officers, had been charged with undermining state security in connection with the coup attempt.

Conté instigated a number of administrative reforms during 1996. The armed forces Chief of Staff and the military Governor of Conakry, both of whom had been regarded as close associates of the President, were replaced in April. In July Conté announced the appointment of a non-partisan economist, Sydia Touré, as Prime Minister, the first time that position had existed under the Third Republic. A comprehensive reorganization of the Government included the division of the Ministry of the Interior into two separate departments (one responsible for territorial administration and decentralization, the other for security).

In June 1997 it was announced that a State Security Court was to be established to deal with matters of exceptional jurisdiction, and that its first task would be to try the alleged leaders of the 1996 mutiny, including Cmmdr Joseph Gbago Zoumanigui, a former member of the CMRN, and allegedly a main conspirator, who was believed to have fled Guinea. The establishment of the court provoked strong criticism both by the opposition parties and the Guinean lawyers' association, which expressed particular concern that there was no constitutional provision for such a court, that its members were to be personally appointed by Conté, and that the mutiny trial was to be held in camera. A ministerial reorganization was effected in October 1997. Notably, Dorank Assifat Diassény, hitherto Minister of Territorial Administration and Decentralization, was transferred to the higher education and scientific research portfolio,

but shortly afterwards was appointed Minister of National Defence (thereby becoming the first civilian to hold this post since the 1984 *coup d'état*).

Some 96 defendants were brought before the State Security Court in February 1998, to answer charges related to the attempted coup of 1996, although hearings were immediately adjourned. Hearings resumed in March, but were again adjourned, following reports that defence lawyers were refusing to represent their clients, whose rights were, they alleged, being infringed. The Court reconvened in September; 38 of the accused received custodial sentences ranging from seven months to 15 years, some with hard labour (Zoumanigui was sentenced *in absentia*), while 51 defendants were acquitted.

In March 1998 Bâ and two other UNR deputies were arrested, following the deaths of nine people as a result of violence in Conakry. The brief detention, in April, of two RPG deputies who had attended a political rally in eastern Guinea further exacerbated tensions, and Codem-affiliated deputies boycotted the opening ceremony of the new session of the Assemblée nationale. Bâ was released in June, and in September his two UNR colleagues resumed their seats in the legislature, having been released from custody. In October Boubacar Biro Diallo was suspended from the PUP, after he denounced the alleged torture of detainees; he subsequently left the party.

Meanwhile, Codem denounced proposals for the establishment of an Haut conseil aux affaires électorales (HCE), which was to act in conjunction with the Ministry of the Interior and Decentralization in preparing and supervising the forthcoming presidential election. The 68-member HCE was to comprise representatives of the parliamentary majority, as well as opposition delegates, ministerial representatives and members of civil society. The opposition again alleged that the PUP was abusing the state apparatus in support of Conté, and that a ban on public demonstrations would disadvantage other candidates. Conté was challenged by four candidates, including Bâ, representing the Union pour le progrès et le renouveau (UPR, formed in 1998 by a merger of the UNR and the PRP), and Alpha Condé (who had been outside Guinea since April 1997, owing to fears for his safety), for the RPG. Despite violent incidents during the election campaign, voting proceeded as scheduled on 14 December 1998. However, the arrest of Condé two days after the poll, near the border with Côte d'Ivoire, on the grounds that he was seeking to leave the country illegally and was plotting against the state, provoked further violence, in which at least 12 people were reported to have been killed. In late December Condé was formally charged with having recruited mercenaries with the aim of overthrowing the Conté regime. Meanwhile, opposition representatives denounced the conduct of the election as fraudulent and withdrew from the HCE. The official results confirmed a decisive victory for Conté, with 56.11% of the valid votes cast; Bâ won 24.62% and Condé 16.58%. The rate of participation by registered voters was 71.4%.

At his inauguration, on 30 January 1999, Conté emphasized that his administration would ensure the defence of individual freedoms and security, and gave an undertaking that all abuses, including those committed by the security forces, would be severely punished. In March Lamine Sidimé, hitherto Chief Justice of the Supreme Court, was appointed Prime Minister of a new Government. An apparent purge of the military high command, in mid-March, included the removal from office of former Chief of Staff Col Oumar Sanko; 18 officers were dismissed, accused of high treason, and 13 retired early, on the grounds of what were termed 'serious faults' arising from the 1996 mutiny. Local government elections were postponed in June.

Opposition groups and human rights organizations campaigned throughout 1999 and 2000 for the release of Alpha Condé and other activists detained at the time of the 1998 presidential election. Condé's defence counsel withdrew from the case in February 1999, citing serious violations of the rule of law and exercise of legal practice on the part of the authorities. Lawyers complained in particular of being denied free access to their client, who was being held in solitary confinement, and that a French defence lawyer had been denied entry to Guinea. The lawyers resumed their defence in April. In July it was announced that Condé's trial would begin in September; however, a decree published in August stating that the RPG leader would be tried by the State Security Court provoked further controversy. Moreover, it was reported that Condé would not be allowed foreign lawyers. In the event, Condé's trial was further delayed, and his lawyers protested that neither the defence nor the prosecution had received any documentation relating to the trial. Meanwhile, in March 1999 13 RPG officials were sentenced to four months' imprisonment, convicted of disturbing public order, but were released at the President's behest; 15 others were sentenced *in absentia* to five years' detention.

In January 2000 a major government reshuffle was announced. In February members of the Assemblée nationale, including PUP deputies, urged the President to release Condé, noting that Condé possessed parliamentary immunity from prosecution. In mid-April the trial of Condé and his 47 co-defendants began, on charges that included plotting to kill President Conté, hiring mercenaries and threatening state security. However, following the rejection of their appeal that the trial be abandoned, the defence lawyers withdrew from the case, and a further postponement ensued. The case reopened in early May, but was again postponed, as the defendants rejected the defence lawyers appointed by the court. At the reopening of the trial in late May Condé refused to speak; the case was adjourned until August to allow the defence to prepare their case.

Conté effected a further ministerial reshuffle in June 2000. Notably, the Ministry of Security was abolished and incorporated into the Ministry of Territorial Administration and Decentralization. Eight parties presented candidates in the delayed local elections, which were held on 25 June. Legislative elections, which had been scheduled for the same date, were postponed. Prior to the announcement of the results a series of clashes between the security forces and UPR members resulted in at least five deaths. The PUP and its allies secured control of 33 of the 38 constituencies.

In September 2000 Condé was sentenced to five years' imprisonment, while seven other defendants were given custodial sentences of between 18 months and three years; 40 other defendants were acquitted. Two days prior to the conclusion of the trial, President Conté had accused Condé of having instigated fighting on Guinea's borders with Sierra Leone and Liberia.

In early September 2000 an armed rebellion in the forest region of south-east Guinea reportedly resulted in at least 40 deaths. Instability subsequently intensified in regions near the borders with Sierra Leone and Liberia, with incidences of cross-border attacks on Guinean civilians and the military becoming increasingly common. An attack on Macenta, near the Liberian border, in mid-September led to 35 deaths, according to official figures, including that of an official of the UN High Commissioner for Refugees (UNHCR). Fighting between armed groups and Guinean soldiers was reported to have led to some 360 deaths between early September and mid-October. The Government attributed the upsurge in violence to forces supported by the Governments of Liberia and Burkina Faso, and to members of the Sierra Leonean rebel group, the Revolutionary United Front (RUF, see Sierra Leone chapter), in alliance with Guinean dissidents. In October 2000 a previously unknown organization, the Rassemblement des forces démocratiques de Guinée, claimed responsibility for the armed attacks, which, it stated, were an attempt to overthrow President Conté. Following an attack on the town of Forécariah, the local Governor expelled some 32,000 refugees from the region, many of whom were subject to further attacks, particularly following a speech made by Conté, in which he accused refugees from Sierra Leone and Liberia of forming alliances with rebel groups seeking to destabilize Guinea.

Meanwhile, the Assemblée nationale failed to reconvene, as planned, on 25 September 2000. The Government announced that the delayed legislative elections would be held on 26 November. However, Codem declared that it would not participate in elections until national security had been re-established, and in November Conté issued a decree postponing the legislative elections indefinitely. In December the human rights organization Amnesty International issued a report in which it demanded the immediate and unconditional release of Condé and 47 other detainees in Guinea. The report also questioned the independence of the State Security Court.

In November 2000 an attack on two villages in Kindia prefecture was attributed to forces associated with the RUF. Later that month a series of cross-border attacks in Guéckédou prefecture were reportedly conducted by former members of a faction of a dissolved Liberian dissident group, the United Liberation Movement of Liberia for Democracy (ULIMO), ULIMO—K (see chapter on Liberia), which President Conté had previously supported. In December rebel attacks on Guéckédou

and Kissidougou, near to the 'Parrot's Beak' area of Guinea, which borders on both Sierra Leone and Liberia, led to more than 230 deaths, and the almost complete destruction of the city of Guéckédou. The Government estimated that some 94,000 people had been displaced as a result of fighting in the region, and aid agencies withdrew from south-east Guinea later in the month, as a result of the heightened instability.

In early January 2001 Conté assumed personal control of defence; Diasseny, hitherto Minister at the Presidency, in charge of National Defence, was, however, retained as a cabinet member, receiving the title of Minister, Special Adviser at the Presidency. In mid-January a number of opposition parties met with the PUP and its allies in a national political dialogue initiated by Conté, although Codem declared that the release of Condé was a precondition to further discussions.

As rebel attacks continued, reports that Guinean planes had launched minor air offensives on rebel-held border areas of Sierra Leone emerged in mid-January 2001. In late January and early February more than 130 deaths were reported in a series of attacks around Macenta. Allegations persisted that an unofficial alliance between former ULIMO—K rebels and Guinean government forces had broken down, with the result that ULIMO—K forces were now attacking Guinean military and civilian targets. Renewed clashes around Guéckédou delayed, and ultimately prevented, the proposed deployment by the Economic Community of West African States (ECOWAS, see p. 187) of an ECOMOG force, which had been intended to monitor stability and border security in the region from mid-February. A rebel attack on Nongoa, a garrison town close to the 'Parrot's Beak' region, in March, forced an estimated 10,000 people to disperse northwards. Meanwhile, in February the death penalty, which had been suspended in 1984, was officially restored, and four of five defendants sentenced to death in 1995 were executed by firing squad (the fifth had died in detention).

Alpha Condé and two of his co-defendants were unexpectedly released from prison in mid-May 2001, following the granting of a presidential pardon. Condé, none the less, was prohibited from participating in political activities for a period of unspecified duration. In mid-June President Conté announced his intention to hold a referendum on proposed constitutional amendments that would remove the restriction on the number of terms of office the President could serve and allow candidates aged over 70 years to contest the presidency. (These changes would enable Conté to contest a third term of office.) Additionally, Conté sought to increase the presidential mandate from five years to seven, to take effect from the presidential election of 2003. It remained unclear whether the referendum would itself meet constitutional requirements, as it sought to validate a presidential decree without any reference to the legislature; international donors to Guinea, including the USA and the European Union (EU), urged Guinea to abide by democratic standards and to uphold the provisions of its Constitution.

In June 2001 N'Faly Kaba, the leader of a hitherto unknown rebel group, the Union des forces pour une Guinée nouvelle (UFGN), announced that his organization was leading the continuing rebellion in the south of Guinea, claiming responsibility for several attacks earlier in the year. Kaba stated that the group comprised close associates of former Prime Minister Diarra Traoré and those involved in the failed coup of July 1985, and that Zoumanigui was co-ordinating the rebellion. In September 2001 Kaba announced that, following the failure of secret negotiations with the Guinean authorities, the UFGN would resume armed struggle to overthrow Conté. At the end of that month, however, Kaba was arrested in Côte d'Ivoire, as he attempted to enter that country illegally from Guinea; Kaba denied any involvement in armed insurgency.

Meanwhile, in late June 2001, in response to a court ruling, gendarmes enforced the closure of the headquarters of the Union des forces républicaines (UFR), the party led by former Prime Minister Sydia Touré, who had recently formed a group to oppose Conté's proposed constitutional amendments, the Mouvement contre le référendum et pour l'alternance démocratique (Morad). At the end of September Condé resumed his functions as a parliamentary deputy. Morad also announced its intention to prevent the conduct of the overdue legislative elections, which were scheduled to take place on 27 December. Condé's status remained a subject of controversy: the Speaker of the Assemblée nationale, Boubacar Biro Diallo, refuted allegations, made in October by the Minister of Justice, Abou Camara, that Condé's return to parliament was illegal, on the grounds that his conviction had not been quashed, while opposition deputies contended that, as Condé had never officially been deprived of his parliamentary immunity, his arrest and detention had been unlawful.

The constitutional referendum took place on 11 November 2001, following violent clashes between security forces and those opposed to the referendum earlier in the month. According to official results, 98.4% of those who voted approved the amendments, and 87.2% of the registered electorate participated. Opposition members disputed the results, alleging that less than 20% of the electorate had voted. The presidential term of office was thus extended from five years to seven, with effect from the presidential election due in 2003, and the constitutional provision restricting the President to two terms of office was rescinded. Moreover, the President was to be permitted to appoint local government officials, who were hitherto elected. In mid-November Codem announced its boycott of the forthcoming legislative elections; however, at the end of the month these elections were again postponed indefinitely.

Despite the overwhelming official result in favour of the amendments, opposition to the referendum was expressed very strongly, in particular by Boubacar Biro Diallo (who remained Speaker of the reconvened Assemblée nationale, whose mandate had, officially, expired in July 2000) and by Jean-Marie Doré, the leader of the Union pour le progrès de la Guinée (UPG), both of whom deplored the lack of involvement of the legislature in deciding such a major constitutional change.

In mid-April 2002 President Conté issued a decree, scheduling the repeatedly postponed elections to the Assemblée nationale for 30 June; a further presidential decree, issued later in April, established a Conseil national electoral, to be responsible for the supervision of the electoral process. However, concern was expressed that the short period between the establishment of the Conseil and the holding of elections would be insufficient to ensure transparency in the conduct of the polls, and the EU subsequently withheld funding towards the elections. In late May four opposition parties, which had announced their intention to boycott the legislative elections, including the RPG and the UFR, announced the formation of a political alliance, the Front de l'alternance démocratique (FRAD). Notably, Boubacar Biro Diallo, who was not affiliated to any party, and Bâ, the honorary President of the UPR, pledged allegiance to the FRAD, and a split in the UPR became increasingly apparent between those, led by Siradiou Diallo, the President of the party, who sought to engage with the electoral process, and those, led by Bâ, who rejected any such engagement. In all, some 20 opposition parties announced that they were to boycott the elections. In early June Conté appointed François Lonseny Fall, previously the representative of Guinea to the UN, as Minister at the Presidency, responsible for Foreign Affairs.

The elections to the Assemblée nationale were held on 30 June 2002, as scheduled. A turn-out of 71.6% was recorded, according to official figures. The PUP increased its majority in the legislature, winning all 38 single-member constituency seats (in all of which the party was unopposed) and 47 of the 76 seats allocated by proportional representation, giving it a total of 85 seats. Other pro-presidential parties secured five seats, while the UPR became the second largest party in the Assemblée, with 20 seats, and the UPG won three seats. Opposition parties, both those of the FRAD and those that contested the elections, alleged that fraudulent practice had been widespread in the conduct of the elections, and the US ambassador to Guinea expressed concern at apparent irregularities in the poll. During July several opposition parties, including the UPG and the UPR, demanded that fresh elections be held; the UPG also announced that its three deputies were to boycott parliament, although the results of the elections were confirmed by the Supreme Court at the end of that month. In late September the Secretary-General of the PUP, Aboubacar Somparé, was elected as Speaker of the Assemblée nationale.

In mid-October 2002 Bâ was elected as President of a new party, the Union des forces démocratiques de Guinée (UFDG), which largely comprised the faction of the UPR that had boycotted the elections to the Assemblée nationale. The UFDG was affiliated to the FRAD, which announced its intention of nominating a common opposition candidate at the presidential election scheduled to be held in December 2003. At the end of December 2002 the FRAD issued a statement in which it denounced both the constitutional referendum held in November 2001 and the recent elections to the Assemblée nationale as illegitimate.

Meanwhile, following a period of several weeks during which President Conté seldom appeared in public (with his premature return from a state visit to Saudi Arabia and the cancellation of a state visit to Japan particularly notable), rumours circulated regarding the President's health. In mid-December 2002 Conté made an unexpected public appearance, having reportedly returned from abroad, and announced what was termed a minor government reshuffle; a Secretary of State for Security was appointed, and other reforms were made to the security apparatus. At the end of December it was confirmed that Conté was receiving medical treatment in Morocco. None the less, it was announced in mid-January 2003 that Conté was to contest the forthcoming presidential election, as the candidate of a grouping known as the Coordination de la mouvance présidentielle.

In August 1990 Guinean armed forces were deployed along the border with Liberia, following a series of violent incursions by deserters from the Liberian army. Guinean army units also participated in the ECOMOG cease-fire monitoring group, deployed in Liberia in that month (see ECOWAS). In April 1991 it was announced that a Guinean contingent was to be dispatched to Sierra Leone to assist that country in repelling violations of its territory by Charles Taylor's National Patriotic Front of Liberia. In October 1992 the Guinean Government admitted that Liberian forces were being trained in Guinea; it was stated that those receiving instruction were to constitute the first Liberian government forces following an eventual restoration of peace in that country.

Following the *coup d'état* in Sierra Leone in April 1992, ex-President Maj.-Gen. Joseph Momoh was granted asylum in Guinea. His successor, Capt. Valentine Strasser, also took refuge in Guinea after he was deposed in January 1996. Close co-operation was developed with the new regime of President Ahmed Tejan Kabbah from March 1996. Kabbah, in turn, fled to Guinea in May 1997, following the seizure of power in Sierra Leone by forces led by Maj. Johnny Paul Koroma. Some 1,500 Guinean troops were dispatched in support of the Nigerian-led ECOMOG force in Sierra Leone. Guinea joined other members of the international community in condemning the subversion of constitutional order in Sierra Leone, and became a member of the 'Committee of Four' (with Côte d'Ivoire, Ghana and Nigeria) charged with ensuring the implementation of decisions and recommendations pertaining to the situation in Sierra Leone, prior to Kabbah's reinstatement, in March 1998, as President of Sierra Leone.

The Liberian Government formally protested to Guinea in April 1999, in response to what it termed an invasion from Guinea of the border town of Voinjama, in Lofa County, by a rebel group, which had been repelled by the Liberian armed forces. The Guinean Government denied the accusations. In August the Liberian Government declared a state of emergency, again claiming that an invasion force had entered Liberia from Guinea, and the border between the two countries was closed. Guinea again denied involvement and urged international observers to visit the border area to verify that incursions were not originating from Guinea. In late August ECOWAS ministers responsible for foreign affairs agreed to establish a commission in an effort to resolve the issue of border insecurity in this region. In September Guinea protested to the Organization of African Unity (now the African Union, see p. 130), the UN and ECOWAS, after 28 people were allegedly killed in attacks by Liberian troops on villages in the Macenta region. None the less, at an extraordinary summit meeting of ECOWAS leaders in mid-September, Presidents Conté and Taylor made pledges of good neighbourliness and non-aggression. The summit condemned the attacks, without apportioning blame. The functions of the Mano River Union (MRU, see p. 341) were to be reactivated, with its members—Guinea, Liberia and Sierra Leone—directed to exchange information on suspected perpetrators of subversive activities, and to establish a joint committee on border security.

Liberia reopened the border with Guinea in February 2000, and in April the ministers responsible for security of the MRU states agreed to allow reciprocal inspections of border areas; a meeting between military officials from the three countries took place in May. None the less, in July the Liberian Government reported renewed fighting in the Lofa region, following an attack by rebel groups allegedly based in Guinea. The Liberian Government, which dispatched reinforcements to the area, threatened to attack the bases of the rebel groups in Guinea and accused the Guinean authorities of complicity with the rebels, although Guinea again denied any involvement in the attacks.

Relations between Guinea and Liberia deteriorated as tensions in the border region intensified from September 2000 (see above). In that month the Liberian consul-general was declared *persona non grata* by the Guinean Government, while Liberia accused the Guinean authorities of impeding the evacuatation of Liberian nationals from the unstable border regions of Guinea. In early October tripartite discussions were held between Guinea, Liberia and Sierra Leone.

In December 2000 ECOWAS announced that a regional peace-keeping force would be deployed along Guinea's borders with Liberia and Sierra Leone for a period of six months from February 2001. However, the establishment of the force (which was opposed by Conté) was subsequently postponed indefinitely, and in the event was not deployed.

In January 2001 Liberia accused the Guinean Government of having supported the recent shelling of towns in its Foya district and recalled its ambassador from Conakry. Also in January Liberia announced that it would deploy an infantry battalion at the border with Guinea, in response to Guinea's announcement that it would strengthen its military presence in border regions. In late January the Liberian Government protested to ECOWAS and the UN following an attack on its embassy in Conakry. In February Taylor reiterated allegations, initially made in the previous month, that Guinea permitted dissidents to launch cross-border attacks on Foya and Kolahun in northern Liberia. The Liberian Government accused Guinea of launching further air and artillery attacks on Voinjama in late February, while a US-based group, Human Rights Watch, claimed that Guinean shellfire had killed at least 41 civilians in Sierra Leone since September 2000. Conté boycotted an ECOWAS conference in Abuja, Nigeria, in April 2001, which had been organized to discuss the conflict in the countries of the MRU, in protest at Taylor's attendance: Liberia had recently expelled the ambassadors of Guinea and Sierra Leone and also sealed its borders with the two countries. In mid-May Guinean forces fired artillery shells at RUF-held positions in northern Sierra Leone, as a UN-supported disarmament process commenced in that country. As the peace process in Sierra Leone advanced in mid-2001, violent unrest in Guinea also abated. In June Kabbah and Conté met in Kambia, in northern Sierra Leone, to discuss regional tensions; following the discussions it was announced that the commercial highway between Conakry and Freetown, closed since 1998, was to reopen.

In August 2001 the Liberian authorities withdrew all restrictions imposed on the Guinean and Sierra Leonean diplomatic presence in the Liberian capital, Monrovia, and the ambassadors of the two countries resumed their duties. In August and September the foreign ministers of Guinea, Liberia and Sierra Leone held three meetings, one in each of the countries, which aimed to advance progress towards peace in the region. At the end of September Taylor announced that Liberia was to reopen its borders with Guinea and Sierra Leone.

In February 2002, as violence by rebel groups in Liberia escalated and extended to the outskirts of Monrovia, the Guinean authorities denied allegations, made by Taylor (and subsequently reiterated by Guinean opposition leader Jean-Marie Doré), that Guinea supported rebels of the Liberians United for Reconciliation and Democracy (see chapter on Liberia). In late February Taylor, Conté and Kabbah participated in a summit in Rabat, Morocco to discuss the cross-border insurgencies affecting the three countries. Following further meetings by ministers from the three countries, in Freetown, Sierra Leone, and in Conakry, and a conference attended by civil society organizations from the three countries held in Conakry in March, agreement was reached on a number of measures intended to ensure border security and to combat insurgency; in particular joint defence and security troops were to be deployed along the common borders to facilitate the return of refugees and to monitor the movement of small arms in the region. In mid-April it was reported that Guinea had begun to deploy troops along its border with Liberia in compliance with this initiative. In December Guinea withdrew its troops from the Yenga region of Sierra Leone, where they had been located since late 2000, and conceded that the territory occupied was Sierra Leonean

The protracted conflicts in Liberia and Sierra Leone have resulted in the presence in Guinea of large numbers of refugees —variously estimated to number 5%–15% of the total population. UNHCR assessed the total number of refugees in Guinea at 427,205 at the beginning of 2001, although by the end of the

year the number of refugees had decreased, according to provisional figures, to 178,444, as stability returned to the region.

Relations with both the Government of France and with private French interests strengthened considerably in the 1990s: official assistance from, and trade with, France is of great importance to the Guinean economy, as is French participation in the mining sector and in newly privatized organizations. However, in the early 2000s military assistance from France to Guinea was reduced and, to some extent, supplanted by support from other sources: Guinea signed a pact of military co-operation with Russia in 2001, and received military aid from the People's Republic of China in 2002, while in mid-2002 the US military participated in the training of Guinean troops.

Government

Under the terms of the Constitution promulgated on 23 December 1991, and amended in April 1992, the President of the Republic, who is Head of State, is elected for five years by universal adult suffrage, in the context of a multi-party political system. A constitutional amendment, approved by referendum on 11 November 2001, extended the presidential mandate to seven years, effective from the presidential election due in 2003. The 114-member Assemblée nationale, which holds legislative power, is elected by universal suffrage for a five-year term. The President of the Republic is also Head of Government, and in this capacity appoints the other members of the Council of Ministers.

Local administration is based on eight administrative entities —the city of Conakry and seven administrative regions—each under the authority of an appointed Governor; the country is sub-divided into 33 prefectures. Conakry, which comprises a separate administrative unit, is divided into five communes.

Defence

In August 2002 Guinea's active armed forces totalled 9,700, comprising an army of 8,500, a navy of 400 and an air force of 800. Paramilitary forces comprised a Republican Guard of 1,600 and a 1,000-strong gendarmerie, as well as a reserve 'people's militia' of 7,000. Military service is compulsory (conscripts were estimated at some 7,500 in 2001) and lasts for two years. The defence budget for 2002 was estimated at 85,000m. FG.

Economic Affairs

In 2001, according to estimates by the World Bank, Guinea's gross national income (GNI), measured at average 1999–2001 prices, was US $3,043m., equivalent to $400 per head (or $1,980 on an international purchasing-power parity basis). During 1990–2001, it was estimated, the population increased at an average annual rate of 2.5%, while gross domestic product (GDP) per head increased, in real terms, by an average of 1.2% per year. Overall GDP increased, in real terms, at an average annual rate of 3.7% in 1990–2001; growth in 2001 was 2.9%.

Agriculture (including hunting, forestry and fishing) contributed an estimated 24.8% of GDP in 2001. About 83.5% of the labour force were employed in the agricultural sector in that year. The principal cash crops are fruits, oil palm, groundnuts and coffee. Important staple crops include cassava, rice and other cereals and vegetables. The attainment of self-sufficiency in rice and other basic foodstuffs remains a priority. The food supply is supplemented by the rearing of cattle and other livestock. The Government has made efforts towards the commercial exploitation of Guinea's forest resources (forests cover about two-thirds of the country's land area) and substantial fishing stocks. During 1990–2001 agricultural GDP increased at an average annual rate of 3.7%. Agricultural GDP declined by 2.6% in 2000, in part as a result of civil unrest in the south of the country, but increased by 2.4% in 2001.

Industry (including mining, manufacturing, construction and power) contributed an estimated 38.4% of GDP in 2001. An estimated 1.9% of the employed labour force were engaged in the industrial sector in 1990. Industrial GDP increased at an average annual rate of 4.3% in 1990–2001; growth in 2001 was 5.8%.

Measured at constant 1996 prices, mining contributed 17.1% of GDP in 1999. Only 0.7% of the employed labour force were engaged in the sector at the time of the 1983 census. Guinea is the world's foremost exporter of bauxite and the second largest producer of bauxite ore, possessing between one-quarter and one-third of known reserves of the mineral. In 2000 exports of aluminium ore and concentrates and aluminium hydroxide together provided 62.6% of export earnings. Gold and diamonds are also mined: in 2000 gold contributed 18.4% of export earn-

GUINEA

Introductory Survey

ings; in 1999, the most recent year for which figures were available, diamonds contributed 7.5% of export revenue. The eventual exploitation of valuable reserves of high-grade iron ore at Mt Nimba, near the border with Liberia, is envisaged, although political instability in the region from 1999 has resulted in delays in developing exploitation of these reserves. The expansion of the gold mine at Siguiri by the Société Ashanti Goldfields de Guinée, the country's principal gold-mine operator, was expected to be completed by mid-2004. Of Guinea's other known mineral deposits, only granite is exploitable on a commercial scale. The GDP of the mining sector increased at an average annual rate of 5.8% in 1994–99; growth in 1999 was 3.2%.

The manufacturing sector remains largely undeveloped, contributing only an estimated 4.5% of GDP in 2001. In 1983 only 0.6% of the employed labour force were engaged in the manufacturing sector. Other than the country's one alumina smelter, most industrial companies are involved in import-substitution, including the processing of agricultural products and the manufacture of construction materials. Manufacturing GDP increased at an average annual rate of 4.6% in 1990–2001; growth in 2001 was 5.5%.

Electricity generation is, at present, insufficient to meet demand, and power failures outside the mining and industrial sectors (in which the largest operators generate their own power supplies) have been frequent. However, Guinea possesses considerable hydroelectric potential. The 75-MW Garafiri dam project was inaugurated in 1999, and a further major scheme, at Kaléta, was scheduled for completion in the early 2000s. In the mean time, some 600,000 metric tons of hydrocarbons are imported annually, and in 2000 imports of fuel accounted for 24.9% of the value of total merchandise imports. In October 2001 it was announced that the Nigerian National Petroleum Corpn was to begin supplying petroleum products to Guinea

The services sector contributed an estimated 36.8% of GDP in 2001. During 1990–2001 the sector's GDP increased at an average annual rate of 3.0%; growth in 2001 was 0.3%.

In 2001 Guinea recorded a visible trade surplus of US $169.2m., while there was a deficit of $102.4m. on the current account of the balance of payments. The principal suppliers of imports in 2000 were Côte d'Ivoire (which supplied 21.4% of the total), France, the USA and Beligum-Luxembourg. The principal markets for exports in that year were France (which took 33.0% of exports), the USA, Spain and Germany. Ukraine and Russia are notable markets for Guinean bauxite. The principal exports in 2000 were aluminium ore and concentrate, gold, miscellaneous manufactured articles and aluminium hydroxide. The principal imports included refined petroleum products, machinery and transport equipment, food and live animals, and basic manufactures.

In 2000 Guinea's overall budget deficit was estimated at 135,100m. FG, equivalent to 2.5% of GDP. The country's total external debt was US $3,388m. at the end of 2000, of which $2,940m. was long-term public debt. In that year the cost of debt-servicing was equivalent to 15.3% of the value of exports of goods and services. Annual inflation averaged 7.3% in 1990–2000; consumer prices increased by an average of 6.9% in 2000.

Guinea is a member of the Economic Community of West African States (ECOWAS, see p. 187), of the Gambia River Basin Development Organization (OMVG, see p. 340), of the International Coffee Organization (see p. 336), of the West Africa Rice Development Association (WARDA, see p. 338) and of the Mano River Union (see p. 341).

Guinea's potential for the attainment of wealth is substantial, owing to its valuable mineral deposits, water resources and generally favourable climate; however, the economy remains over-dependent on revenue from bauxite reserves and on external assistance, the country's infrastructure is inadequate and its manufacturing base narrow. Since 1985 economic liberalization measures have been undertaken, and by the late 1990s success had been achieved in reducing the rate of inflation, foreign-exchange reserves had increased, as had private invest-

ment in the economy, while considerable GDP growth had been achieved. In January 1997 the IMF approved a three-year loan, equivalent to US $101m., under the Enhanced Structural Adjustment Facility (subsequently renamed the Poverty Reduction and Growth Facility—PRGF). Budget revenue was lower than envisaged in 2000, partly owing to a decline in traditional exports, and GDP growth in that year was considerably lower than forecast. Insecurity in neighbouring Liberia and Sierra Leone during the 1990s also had a detrimental effect on Guinea's economy; in late 2000 the Government stated that unrest in the border regions with Sierra Leone and Liberia had cost Guinea some US $15m.–$18m. annually since 1989. Instability in the southern regions of Guinea in 2000–01 adversely affected agriculture output, although national security improved later in 2001. Conversely, the onset of unrest in Côte d'Ivoire in September 2002 appeared to have some positive economic consequences for Guinea, at least in the short term: in particular, the loss of government control over large areas of the north of Côte d'Ivoire resulted in a notable increase in international trade, particularly from Mali, routed through the port of Conakry, as access to the larger Ivorian port at Abidjan became increasingly uncertain. However, up to one-half of the 230,000 Guinean citizens resident in Côte d'Ivoire in 1998, a large proportion of whom were cocoa farmers, and an important source of revenue for Guinea, were reported to have returned to their homeland by early 2003. In December 2000 the IMF and the World Bank announced that Guinea would be a recipient of some $880m. in debt relief as part of the Heavily Indebted Poor Countries initiative. In May 2001 the IMF approved a further three-year PRGF arrangement for Guinea, worth $82m. over three years; the programme aimed to generate annual GDP growth of 6.5% by 2004, while other measures, adopted as part of a Poverty Reduction Strategy Paper, sought to reduce poverty over the longer term, and to improve levels of healthcare and education.

Education

Education is provided free of charge at every level in state institutions. Primary education, which begins at seven years of age and lasts for six years, is officially compulsory. In 1999/2000, however, enrolment at primary schools included only 49.0% of children in the relevant age-group (boys 56.4%; girls 41.4%). Secondary education, from the age of 13, lasts for seven years, comprising a first cycle (collège) of four years and a second (lycée) of three years. According to UNESCO estimates, enrolment at secondary schools in 1998/99 included only 11.9% of children in the appropriate age-group (boys 17.1%; girls 6.5%). There are universities at Conakry and Kankan, and other tertiary institutions at Manéyah, Boké and Faranah. Independent schools, which had been banned for 23 years under the Sekou Touré regime, were legalized in 1984. Budget estimates for 1999 allocated 62,300m. FG to education (equivalent to 8.1% of total budgetary expenditure).

Public Holidays

2003: 1 January (New Year's Day), 21 April (Easter Monday), 1 May (Labour Day), 14 May* (Mouloud, birth of Muhammad), 27 August (Anniversary of Women's Revolt), 28 September (Referendum Day), 2 October (Republic Day), 1 November (All Saints' Day), 22 November (Day of 1970 Invasion), 26 November* (Id al-Fitr, end of Ramadan), 25 December (Christmas).

2004: 1 January (New Year's Day), 12 April (Easter Monday), 1 May (Labour Day), 2 May* (Mouloud, birth of Muhammad), 27 August (Anniversary of Women's Revolt), 28 September (Referendum Day), 2 October (Republic Day), 1 November (All Saints' Day), 14 November* (Id al-Fitr, end of Ramadan), 22 November (Day of 1970 Invasion), 25 December (Christmas).

*These holidays are determined by the Islamic lunar calendar and may vary by one or two days from the dates given.

Weights and Measures

The metric system is in force.

Statistical Survey

Source (unless otherwise stated): Direction Nationale de la Statistique, BP 221, Conakry; tel. 44-21-48.

Area and Population

AREA, POPULATION AND DENSITY

Area (sq km)	245,857*
Population (census results)	
4–17 February 1983	4,533,240†
31 December 1996‡	
Males	3,497,551
Females	3,658,855
Total	7,156,406
Population (official estimates at mid-year)	
1998	7,607,000
1999	7,842,800
Density (per sq km) at mid-1999	31.9

* 94,926 sq miles.
† Excluding adjustment for underenumeration.
‡ Including refugees from Liberia and Sierra Leone (estimated at 640,000).

ETHNIC GROUPS

1995 (percentages): Peul 38.7; Malinké 23.3; Soussou 11.1; Kissi 5.9; Kpellé 4.5; Others 16.5 (Source: La Francophonie).

PRINCIPAL TOWNS

(population at 1996 census)

Conakry (capital)	1,092,936	Kankan	100,192
N'Zérékoré . . .	107,329		

BIRTHS AND DEATHS

(UN estimates, annual averages)

	1985–90	1990–95	1995–2000
Birth rate (per 1,000)	46.8	44.0	45.7
Death rate (per 1,000)	21.3	19.0	18.2

Source: UN, *World Population Prospects: The 2000 Revision.*

Expectation of life (WHO estimates, years at birth): 51.9 (males 50.1; females 53.8) in 2001 (Source: WHO, *World Health Report*).

ECONOMICALLY ACTIVE POPULATION

(ILO estimates, '000 persons at mid-1990)

	Males	Females	Total
Agriculture, hunting, forestry and fishing. . . .	1,338	1,336	2,674
Industry	40	18	58
Manufacturing	13	6	18
Services	234	101	335
Total labour force	1,612	1,455	3,067

Source: ILO.

1996 census: Total employed labour force 3,278,834.

Mid-2001 ('000 persons): Agriculture, etc. 3,426; Total labour force 4,104 (Source: FAO).

Health and Welfare

KEY INDICATORS

Total fertility rate (children per woman, 2001)	6.0
Under-5 mortality rate (per 1,000 live births, 2001) . . .	160
HIV/AIDS (% of persons aged 15–49, 1994).	1.54
Physicians (per 1,000 head, 1995)	0.13
Hospital beds (per 1,000 head, 1990)	0.55
Health expenditure (2000): US $ per head (PPP) . . .	56
Health expenditure (2000): % of GDP	3.4
Health expenditure (2000): public (% of total)	57.1
Access to water (% of persons, 2000).	48
Access to sanitation (% of persons, 2000)	58
Human Development Index (2000): ranking	159
Human Development Index (2000): value	0.414

For sources and definitions, see explanatory note on p. vi.

Agriculture

PRINCIPAL CROPS

('000 metric tons)

	1999	2000	2001*
Rice (paddy)	750	870	870
Maize	92.0	95.0	95.0
Fonio	95.0	123.0	123.0
Sweet potatoes*	134.9	135.0	135.0
Cassava (Manioc)	900.0	1,000.0	1,000.0
Taro (Coco Yam)	28.0	28.0	28.0
Yams*	88.0	88.0	88.0
Sugar cane*	270	270	270
Pulses*	60	55	55
Groundnuts (in shell)	190.0	210.0	210.0
Coconuts*	18	18	18
Oil palm fruit*	830	830	830
Vegetables*	476	476	476
Bananas*	150	150	150
Plantains*	429	430	430
Citrus fruit*	215	210	210
Mangoes*	83	83	83
Pineapples*	71.9	71.5	71.5
Other fruit*	45.5	45.0	45.0
Cotton (lint)	21.0*	29.6†	29.6
Cottonseed	20.0*	25.0	25.0
Coffee (Green)*	20.9	20.5	20.5

* FAO estimate(s).
† Unofficial figure.

Source: FAO.

LIVESTOCK

('000 head, year ending September)

	1999	2000	2001*
Cattle	2,368	2,679	2,679
Sheep	687	892	892
Goats	948	1,012	1,012
Pigs	84	98	97
Horses*	3	3	3
Asses*	2	2	2
Poultry	11,184	11,855	11,855

* FAO estimates.

Source: FAO.

LIVESTOCK PRODUCTS
(FAO estimates, '000 metric tons)

	1999	2000	2001
Beef and veal	20.7	23.3	23.3
Poultry meat	3.2	3.4	3.4
Mutton and lamb	2.0	2.6	2.6
Goat meat	3.6	3.9	3.9
Other meat	6.4	6.8	6.8
Cows' milk	62.0	72.2	72.2
Goats' milk	5.7	6.0	6.0
Poultry eggs	11.8	12.2	12.2
Cattle hides	3.4	3.9	3.9

Source: FAO.

Forestry

ROUNDWOOD REMOVALS
(FAO estimates, '000 cubic metres, excl. bark)

	1999	2000	2001
Sawlogs, veneer logs and logs for sleepers	138	138	138
Other industrial wood	513	513	513
Fuel wood	11,576	11,444	11,490
Total	12,227	12,095	12,141

Source: FAO.

SAWNWOOD PRODUCTION
('000 cubic metres, incl. railway sleepers)

	1998	1999	2000
Total (all broadleaved)	26	26*	26*

* FAO estimate.
Figures for 2001 assumed to be unchanged from 2000.
Source: FAO.

Fishing

('000 metric tons, live weight)

	1998	1999	2000
Freshwater fishes	4.0	4.0	4.0
Sea catfishes	2.6	2.4	4.6
Bobo croaker	2.8	2.1	4.0
West African croakers	2.6	1.8	3.4
Porgies and seabreams	3.0	3.3	1.8
Sardinellas	6.3	8.9	13.3
Bonga shad	27.9	33.8	29.0
Jack and horse mackerels	7.1	0.5	6.1
Total catch (incl. others)	69.8	87.3	91.5

Source: FAO, *Yearbook of Fishery Statistics*.

Mining

(estimates, '000 metric tons, unless otherwise indicated)

	1998	1999	2000
Bauxite*	15,000	15,000	15,000
Gold (kilograms)†	11,700	13,300	13,300
Salt (unrefined)	n.a.	15	15
Diamonds ('000 carats)†‡	400	550	450

* Dried equivalent of crude ore.
† Including artisanal production.
‡ Of the total, the estimated production of gemstones (in '000 carats) was: 300 in 1998; 410 in 1999.
Source: US Geological Survey.

Industry

SELECTED PRODUCTS
('000 metric tons, unless otherwise indicated)

	1999	2000	2001
Palm oil (unrefined)*†	50	50	50
Beer of barley*†	10.3	11.5	7.8
Raw sugar*	25‡	25‡	25†
Alumina (calcined equivalent)§	500	n.a.	n.a.

Salted, dried or smoked fish ('000 metric tons): 10.8*in 1997.

Electric energy (million kWh): 545.0 in 1998.

* Data from FAO.
† Estimates.
‡ Unofficial figures.
§ Data from the US Geological Survey.
Source: FAO; UN, *Industrial Commodity Statistics Yearbook*.

Finance

CURRENCY AND EXCHANGE RATES

Monetary Units
100 centimes = 1 franc guinéen (FG or Guinean franc)

Sterling, Dollar and Euro Equivalents (31 October 2002)
£1 sterling = 3,070.2 Guinean francs
US $1 = 1,968.1 Guinean francs
€1 = 1,941.3 Guinean francs
10,000 Guinean francs = £3.257 = $5.081 = €5.151

Average Exchange Rate (Guinean francs per US $)
2000   1,746.9
2001   1,950.6
2002   1,975.8

BUDGET
('000 million Guinean francs)

Revenue*	1998	1999†	2000†
Mining-sector revenue	126.4	117.3	146.4
Special tax on mining products	116.7	109.6	n.a.
Other revenue	370.4	399.9	448.2
Tax revenue	337.4	367.1	394.3
Taxes on income and profits	48.1	57.7	58.3
Personal	26.1	29.0	n.a.
Corporate	9.5	13.3	n.a.
Taxes on domestic production and trade	217.4	228.6	216.8
Value-added tax (VAT)	96.4	102.7	n.a.
Excise surcharge	8.5	9.5	n.a.
Petroleum excise tax	66.3	70.7	n.a.
Taxes on international trade	71.9	80.8	119.1
Import duties	67.8	76.7	n.a.
Total	496.7	517.2	594.6

Expenditure‡	1998	1999†	2000†
Current expenditure	387.7	429.5	504.0
Wages and salaries	181.2	194.7	206.2
Other goods and services	89.4	89.6	110.4
Subsidies and transfers	53.0	70.7	97.6
Interest payments	64.1	74.5	89.8
Public investment programme	250.4	343.9	386.6
Domestically financed	41.4	48.9	41.6
Externally financed	209.0	295.0	345.0
Restructuring of banking system	13.6	—	—
Sub-total	651.7	773.4	890.6
Adjustment for payments arrears	66.9	3.4	-38.0
Total (cash basis)	718.6	776.8	852.6

* Excluding grants received ('000 million Guinean francs): 127.8 in 1998; 111.1 in 1999; 125.3 in 2000.
† Estimates.
‡ Excluding lending minus repayments ('000 million Guinean francs): 3.9 in 1998; 0.2 in 1999; 2.4 in 2000.

Sources: IMF, *Guinea: Statistical Appendix* (January 2001) and *Guinea: Request for a Three-Year Arrangement Under the Poverty Reduction and Growth Facility—Staff Report and Press Release on the Executive Board Discussion* (March 2002).

INTERNATIONAL RESERVES

(US $ million at 31 December)

	2000	2001	2002
IMF special drawing rights	0.25	0.80	1.66
Reserve position in IMF	0.10	0.09	0.10
Foreign exchange	147.56	199.34	169.64
Total	147.91	200.23	171.40

Source: IMF, *International Financial Statistics*.

MONEY SUPPLY

(million Guinean francs at 31 December)

	2000	2001	2002
Currency outside banks	288,468	310,063	349,781
Demand deposits at commercial banks	177,997	226,047	300,520
Total (incl. others)	499,885	559,993	681,228

Source: IMF, *International Financial Statistics*.

COST OF LIVING

(Consumer Price Index for Conakry; base: 1990 = 100)

	1998	1999	2000
Food	185.4	195.4	203.2
Fuel and light	179.4	188.6	205.5
Clothing	146.3	148.3	154.4
Housing	164.4	170.0	176.3
All items (incl. others)	181.9	190.0	203.1

Source: ILO, *Yearbook of Labour Statistics*.

NATIONAL ACCOUNTS

Expenditure on the Gross Domestic Product

('000 million Guinean francs at current prices)

	1997	1998	1999
Government final consumption expenditure	255.6	270.6	284.3
Private final consumption expenditure	3,001.4	3,326.9	3,694.2
Increase in stocks	57.0	59.0	45.0
Gross fixed capital formation	921.5	871.2	1,020.2
Total domestic expenditure	4,235.5	4,527.7	5,043.7
Exports of goods and services	844.1	1,019.7	1,028.6
Less Imports of goods and services	936.4	1,113.4	1,241.0
GDP in purchasers' values	4,143.3	4,434.0	4,831.3
GDP at constant 1996 prices	4,086.5	4,271.6	4,412.9

Gross Domestic Product by Economic Activity

('000 million Guinean francs at constant 1996 prices)

	1997	1998	1999
Agriculture, hunting, forestry and fishing	824.1	866.8	914.4
Mining and quarrying	679.5	703.3	725.8
Manufacturing	149.9	157.7	168.0
Electricity, gas and water	23.0	25.0	26.5
Construction	351.2	375.1	407.4
Trade	1,096.4	1,149.0	1,190.4
Transport	239.3	257.3	266.3
Administration	234.9	230.2	172.4
Other services	326.0	344.5	361.4
GDP at factor cost	3,924.4	4,109.0	4,232.6
Indirect taxes	162.2	162.7	180.3
GDP in purchasers' values	4,086.5	4,271.6	4,412.9

Source: IMF, *Guinea: Statistical Appendix* (January 2001).

BALANCE OF PAYMENTS

(US $ million)

	1999	2000	2001
Exports of goods f.o.b.	635.7	666.4	731.0
Imports of goods f.o.b.	−581.8	−587.1	−561.8
Trade balance	53.9	79.3	169.2
Exports of services	113.1	68.0	102.8
Imports of services	−364.6	−284.9	−319.1
Balance on goods and services	−197.6	−137.6	−47.1
Other income received	24.7	23.5	11.4
Other income paid	−106.9	−101.1	−113.7
Balance on goods, services and income	−279.8	−215.2	−149.4
Current transfers received	80.0	88.6	91.5
Current transfers paid	−15.1	−28.5	−44.5
Current balance	−214.9	−155.1	−102.4
Direct investment from abroad	63.4	9.9	1.6
Portfolio investment assets	−20.0	8.7	4.6
Other investment assets	0.1	−17.0	11.6
Other investment liabilities	73.0	6.7	−30.0
Net errors and omissions	22.4	82.1	−1.9
Overall balance	−76.0	−64.7	−116.5

Source: IMF, *International Financial Statistics*.

External Trade

PRINCIPAL COMMODITIES
(US $ million)

Imports c.i.f.	1996	1997	2000*
Food and live animals	118.3	113.4	110.0
Cereals and cereal preparations	70.4	71.7	55.9
Rice	55.5	41.4	28.8
Rice, semi-milled or wholly milled	51.1	40.5	28.8
Rice, semi-milled or milled (unbroken)	48.9	31.6	17.0
Beverages and tobacco	14.7	23.3	26.3
Tobacco and tobacco manufactures	9.5	20.6	23.6
Tobacco, manufactured	4.8	17.3	23.1
Cigarettes	3.9	13.6	23.0
Mineral fuels, lubricants, etc.	171.9	63.9	152.8
Petroleum, petroleum products, etc.	171.9	63.7	152.6
Petroleum products, refined	169.8	62.5	151.6
Motor spirit, incl. aviation spirit	63.4	19.6	—
Gas oils	77.7	26.0	—
Chemicals and related products	38.6	43.6	51.6
Medicinal and pharmaceutical products	13.8	15.0	23.3
Medicaments (incl. veterinary medicaments)	12.9	14.0	21.6
Medicaments (incl. veterinary medicaments) containing other substances	12.1	13.2	21.5
Basic manufactures	96.8	100.3	81.5
Non-metallic mineral manufactures	17.0	19.1	19.0
Iron and steel	17.7	18.9	19.3
Manufactures of metals	16.3	22.2	10.0
Machinery and transport equipment	153.3	219.6	116.2
Power-generating machinery and equipment	17.0	22.4	6.3
Machinery specialized for particular industries	11.6	20.7	8.8
General industrial machinery, equipment and parts	31.6	33.8	22.8
Telecommunications, sound recording and reproducing equipment	10.4	65.3	4.5
Telecommunication equipment, parts and accessories	8.9	64.0	3.8
Television, radio-broadcasting, transmitters, etc.	0.4	58.6	0.9
Electric machinery, apparatus and parts	29.6	23.0	13.7
Road vehicles	40.9	44.9	53.1
Passenger motor vehicles (excl. buses)	20.6	29.2	26.3
Miscellaneous manufactured articles	33.3	35.6	51.0
Total (incl. others)	647.7	619.7	612.4

Exports f.o.b.	1996	1997	2000*
Food and live animals	25.3	44.1	11.9
Coffee, tea, cocoa, spices and manufactures thereof	16.6	35.8	7.8
Coffee, not roasted; coffee husks and skins	11.6	31.3	6.6
Crude materials (inedible) except fuels	492.0	412.5	283.5
Cork and wood	n.a.	0.2	6.8
Wood, simply worked, and railway sleepers of wood	n.a.	0.2	6.4
Wood, non-coniferous species, sawn lengthwise, sliced or peeled	n.a.	0.2	5.9
Raw cotton, excl. linters, not carded or combed	6.9	2.8	5.6
Aluminium ore and concentrate	484.4	409.3	269.9
Mineral fuels, lubricants, etc.	4.2	8.7	0.2
Peat, not agglomerated	—	7.4	—
Chemicals and related products	91.6	66.1	56.9
Aluminium hydroxide	89.5	65.9	56.9
Basic manufactures	37.1	49.7	5.4
Diamonds (non-industrial), not mounted or set	34.4	48.9	—
Diamonds, rough, unsorted	34.4	47.3	—
Machinery and transport equipment	41.5	14.1	4.7
Machinery specialized for particular industries	32.4	4.0	0.2
Civil engineering, contractors' plant and equipment and parts	30.1	3.5	0.1
Construction and mining machinery	27.5	2.8	n.a.
Bulldozers, angledozers and levellers, self-propelled	25.5	1.1	n.a.
Road vehicles	7.3	2.7	n.a.
Miscellaneous manufactured articles	0.7	55.4	61.9
Measuring, checking, analysis, controlling instruments and parts	0.2	55.1	0.2
Gold, non-monetary, unwrought or semi-manufactured	15.2	31.2	96.3
Total (incl. others)	709.2	684.5	522.4

* Data for 1998 and 1999 was unavailable.

Source: UN, *International Trade Statistics Yearbook*.

1999 ('000 million Guinean francs): Imports 766.0 (Mineral fuels, etc 62.2, Cereals 64.0, Mechanical machines and parts 92.9, Electric machines 50.6, Road vehicles 57.4) ; Exports 748.7 (Coffee 11.1, Bauxite 410.0; Alumina 118.8, Diamonds 56.4, Gold 117.7).

PRINCIPAL TRADING PARTNERS
(US $ million)*

Imports c.i.f.	1996	1997	2000*
Australia	0.5	4.8	7.2
Belgium-Luxembourg	57.2	50.8	47.4†
Brazil	11.8	3.5	2.7
Canada	8.1	2.9	1.4
China, People's Republic	14.7	16.5	28.4
Côte d'Ivoire	113.7	47.1	130.9
Cyprus	—	—	9.6
Denmark	6.6	2.0	4.1
France (incl. Monaco)	122.0	137.9	121.2
Gabon	14.4	3.1	7.3
Germany	10.1	10.2	19.2
Hong Kong	14.7	9.7	6.1
India	27.0	5.8	11.4
Italy	24.7	22.6	21.0
Japan	31.2	35.6	34.2
Netherlands	21.7	14.7	14.3
Nigeria	10.6	3.3	1.7
Pakistan	11.5	14.4	4.1
Senegal	10.4	7.0	4.0
Southern African Customs Union‡	0.9	14.0	—
United Kingdom	12.6	77.4	9.2
USA	46.9	47.0	48.4
Viet Nam	7.9	20.5	3.2
Total (incl. others)	647.7	619.7	612.4

Exports f.o.b.		1996	1997	2000*
Belgium-Luxembourg	. . . .	27.1	45.7	n.a.
Cameroon .	. . . .	18.4	21.4	9.6
Canada	. . . .	47.6	20.4	17.2
Finland	. . . .	7.2	12.5	—
France (incl. Monaco)	. . .	54.9	84.6	172.6
Germany .	. . .	26.1	21.1	32.1
Hungary	. . .	—	—	5.8
Ireland.	. . . .	64.1	63.6	47.5
Italy	. . . .	32.7	19.9	0.4
Malta .	. . .	—	1.8	6.3
Morocco .	. . .	1.6	2.8	7.3
Norway .	. . .	14.5	14.6	—
Russia .	. . .	45.6	12.2	21.6
Senegal .	. . .	26.3	4.0	0.1
Seychelles .	. . .	—	0.2	5.8
Spain .	. . . .	67.5	101.5	50.1
Sudan .	. . .	—	—	6.5
Switzerland-Liechtenstein .	.	8.2	4.2	26.5
Ukraine	. . .	0.8	0.7	15.5
United Kingdom .	. . .	18.7	80.7	17.4
USA	. . . .	205.1	141.9	66.7
Total (incl. others)	. . .	709.2	684.5	522.4

* Data for 1998 and 1999 was unavailable.
† Excluding trade with Luxembourg.
‡ Comprising Botswana, Lesotho, Namibia, South Africa and Swaziland.
Source: UN, *International Trade Statistics Yearbook*.

Transport

RAILWAYS
(estimated traffic)

	1991	1992	1993
Freight ton-km (million) . . .	660	680	710

Source: UN Economic Commission for Africa, *African Statistical Yearbook*.

ROAD TRAFFIC
(estimates, '000, motor vehicles in use)

	1994	1995	1996
Passenger cars	13.2	13.7	14.1
Lorries and vans	18.0	19.4	21.0

Source: IRF, *World Road Statistics*.

SHIPPING

Merchant Fleet
(registered at 31 December)

	1999	2000	2001
Number of vessels . . .	31	33	33
Total displacement ('000 grt) . .	10.7	11.3	11.4

Source: Lloyd's Register-Fairplay, *World Fleet Statistics*.

International Sea-borne Freight Traffic
(Port of Conakry, '000 metric tons)

	1997	1998	1999
Goods loaded	2,130	2,194	2,089
Goods unloaded	1,610	1,680	1,850

CIVIL AVIATION
(traffic on scheduled services)

	1997	1998	1999
Kilometres flown (million) . . .	1	1	1
Passengers carried ('000) . . .	36	36	59
Passenger-km (million) . . .	55	55	94
Total ton-km (million) . . .	6	6	10

Source: UN, *Statistical Yearbook*.

Tourism

FOREIGN VISITOR ARRIVALS*

Country of origin		1998	1999	2000
Argentina .	. . .	n.a.	1,165	10
Belgium	. . .	1,386	1,651	1,438
Canada	. . .	n.a.	849	1,006
Côte d'Ivoire .	. . .	n.a.	1,327	2,081
France .	. . .	4,550	4,982	7,333
Germany .	. . .	846	716	949
Italy	. . .	1,850	686	811
Lebanon .	. . .	1,765	325	165
Liberia .	. . .	n.a.	708	254
Mali .	. . .	n.a.	612	1,118
Senegal .	. . .	n.a.	1,265	2,651
Sierra Leone .	. . .	n.a.	1,693	2,948
United Kingdom .	. . .	1,080	960	1,316
USA .	. . .	n.a.	1,423	2,532
Total (incl. others)	. . .	23,000	27,345	32,598

* Air arrivals at Conakry airport.

Receipts from tourism (US $ million): 1 in 1998; 7 in 1999; 12 (estimate) in 2000.

Source: World Tourism Organization, *Yearbook of Tourism Statistics*; World Bank.

Communications Media

	1999	2000	2001
Television receivers ('000 in use) . .	343	351	n.a.
Telephones ('000 main lines in use) .	46.2	62.4	25.5
Facsimile machines (estimated number in use) . .	3,186	n.a.	n.a.
Mobile cellular telephones ('000 subscribers) . .	25.2	42.1	55.7
Personal computers ('000 in use) . .	27	29	32
Internet users ('000)	5	8	15

Source: International Telecommunication Union.

Radio receivers ('000 in use): 380 in 1999 (Source: UNESCO, *Statistical Yearbook*).

Non-daily newspapers: 1 title in 1996 (average circulation 20,000) (Source: UNESCO, *Statistical Yearbook*).

Education

(1997/98, unless otherwise indicated)

			Students		
	Institutions	Teachers	Males	Females	Total
Pre-primary . .	202*	594	n.a.	n.a.	30,857
Primary . . .	3,723	17,340†	425,644	249,088	790,497†
Secondary‡ . .	358	5,356	122,598	43,336	165,934
Tertiary* . .	n.a.	307	780	1,098	1,878

* 1996/97 figure(s).
† 1999/2000 figure.
‡ 1998/99 figures.

Adult literacy rate (UNESCO estimates): 35.9% (males 50.0%; females 22.0%) in 1995.

Sources: International Development Association, IMF, *Guinea: Poverty Reduction Strategy Paper—Joint Staff Assessment* (July 2001) and UNESCO, *Statistical Yearbook*.

Directory

The Constitution

The Constitution (*Loi fondamentale*) of the Third Republic of Guinea was adopted in a national referendum on 23 December 1990 and promulgated on 23 December 1991. An 'organic law' of 3 April 1992, providing for the immediate establishment of an unlimited number of political parties, countermanded the Constitution's provision for the eventual establishment of a two-party political system. There was to be a five-year period of transition, overseen by a Comité transitoire de redressement national (CTRN), to civilian rule, at the end of which executive and legislative authority would be vested in organs of state elected by universal adult suffrage in the context of a multi-party political system. The CTRN was dissolved following the legislative elections of June 1995. Amendments to provisions concerning the President were approved by referendum in November 2001.

The Constitution defines the clear separation of the powers of the executive, the legislature and the judiciary. The President of the Republic, who is Head of State, must be elected by an absolute majority of the votes cast, and a second round of voting is held should no candidate obtain such a majority at a first round. The duration of the presidential mandate is seven years, with effect from the election due in 2003, and elections are by universal adult suffrage. Any candidate for the presidency must be more than 40 years old, must not be a serving member of the armed forces, and must be proposed by a political party. There are no restrictions on the number of terms of office the President may serve. The President is Head of Government, and is empowered to appoint ministers and to delegate certain functions. The legislature is the 114-member Assemblée nationale. One-third of the Assemblée's members are elected as representatives of single-member constituencies, the remainder being appointed from national lists, according to a system of proportional representation. The legislature is elected, by universal suffrage, with a five-year mandate.

The Government

HEAD OF STATE

President: Gen. LANSANA CONTÉ (took office 4 April 1984; elected 19 December 1993; re-elected 14 December 1998).

COUNCIL OF MINISTERS
(April 2003)

President of the Republic and President of the Council of Ministers: Gen. LANSANA CONTÉ.

Prime Minister: LAMINE SIDIMÉ.

Adviser to the Presidency of the Republic, in charge of Relations with the Republican Institutions: El Hadj THIERNO MAMADOU CELLOU DIALLO.

Minister at the Presidency, in charge of Foreign Affairs: FRANÇOIS LONCENY FALL.

Minister, Special Adviser at the Presidency: DORANK ASSIFAT DIASSÉNY.

Minister of Justice, Keeper of the Seals: ABOU CAMARA.

Minister of Territorial Administration, Decentralization and Security: MOUSSA SOLANO.

Minister of the Economy and Finance: CHEICK AMADOU CAMARA.

Minister of Planning: NIANKOYE FASSOU SAGNO.

Minister of Trade, Industry and Small- and Medium-sized Enterprises: MARIAMA DÉO BALDE.

Minister of Mines, Geology and the Environment: ALPHA MADY SOUMAH.

Minister of Agriculture and Livestock: JEAN PAUL SARR.

Minister of Fishing and Aquaculture: OUMAR KOUYATÉ.

Minister of Water and Energy: MORY KABA.

Minister of Public Works and Transport: CELLOU DALEIN DIALLO.

Minister of Town Planning and Housing: BLAISE FOROMO.

Minister of Communications: MAMADY CONDÉ.

Minister of Pre-university and Civil Education: KALEMA GINAVOGUI.

Minister of Technical Education and Professional Training: IBRAHIMA SOUMAH.

Minister of Higher Education and Scientific Research: EUGÈNE CAMARA.

Minister of Public Health: Dr MAMADOU SALIOU DIALLO.

Minister of Youth, Sports and Culture: ABDEL KADER SANGARÉ.

Minister of Tourism, Hotels and Handicrafts: SYLLA KOUMBA DIAKITÉ.

Minister of Employment and the Civil Service: LAMINE KAMARA.

Minister of Social Affairs, Women's Promotion and Children's Affairs: MARIAMA ARIBOT.

Minister, Secretary-General of the Presidency: El Hadj FODÉ BANGOURA.

Secretary of State for Security: MOUSSA SAMPIL.

Secretary-General of the Government: El Hadj OUSMANE SANOKO.

MINISTRIES

Office of the Prime Minister: Cité des Nations, BP 5141, Conakry; tel. 41-52-83; fax 41-52-82.

Ministry of Agriculture and Livestock: Face Cité du Port, BP 576, Conakry; tel. 41-11-81; fax 41-11-69.

Ministry of Communications: Boulbinet près de l'ORTG, BP 617, Conakry; tel. 41-50-01; fax 41-47-97; e-mail com@sutelgui.net.gn.

Ministry of the Economy and Finance: face au collège Boulbinet, BP 221, Conakry; tel. 45-17-95; fax 41-30-59.

Ministry of Employment and the Civil Service: près de la Cathédrale Sainte-Marie, Conakry; tel. 41-16-09.

Ministry of Fishing and Aquaculture: face à la Cité du Port, BP 307, Conakry; tel. 41-35-23; fax 41-35-28.

Ministry of Foreign Affairs: face au Port, ex-Primature, BP 2519, Conakry; tel. 41-33-42; fax 41-16-21.

Ministry of Higher Education and Scientific Research: face à la Cathédrale Sainte-Marie, BP 964, Conakry; tel. 41-19-01; fax 41-20-12.

Ministry of Justice: face Immeuble 'La Paternelle', Conakry; tel. 45-29-06.

Ministry of Mines, Geology and the Environment: BP 295, Conakry; tel. 41-38-33; fax 41-49-13.

Ministry of Planning: Conakry.

Ministry of Pre-university and Civil Education: BP 2201, Conakry; tel. 41-19-05.

Ministry of Public Health: BP 585, Conakry; tel. 41-20-32; fax 41-41-38.

Ministry of Public Works and Transport: BP 715, Conakry; tel. 41-36-39; fax 41-35-77.

Ministry of Social Affairs, Women's Promotion and Children's Affairs: Corniche-Ouest, face au Terminal Conteneurs du Port de Conakry, BP 527, Conakry; tel. 41-20-15; fax 41-46-60.

Ministry of Technical Education and Professional Training: face aux Jardins du 2 Octobre, BP 2201, Conakry; tel. 41-44-84; fax 41-33-54.

Ministry of Territorial Administration, Decentralization and Security: près de la Gendarmerie Nationale, BP 3495, Conakry; tel. 41-44-15; fax 45-45-07.

Ministry of Tourism, Hotels and Handicrafts: Conakry; tel. 41-49-94.

Ministry of Town Planning and Housing: blvd du Commerce, BP 846, Conakry; tel. 41-32-00; fax 41-46-88.

Ministry of Trade, Industry and Small- and Medium-sized Enterprises: BP 468, Conakry; tel. 44-26-06; fax 44-49-90.

Ministry of Water and Energy: Conakry.

Ministry of Youth, Sports and Culture: ave du Port Secrétariat, BP 262, Conakry; tel. 41-10-88; fax 41-19-26.

President and Legislature

PRESIDENT

Election, 14 December 1998

Candidate		Votes	% of votes
Lansana Conté (PUP)	. . . . .	1,455,007	56.11
Mamadou Boye Bâ (UPR)	. . . .	638,563	24.62
Alpha Condé(RPG)	. . . . .	429,934	16.58
Jean-Marie Doré (UPG)	. . . .	44,476	1.72
Charles-Pascal Tolno (PPG)	. . .	24,771	0.95
Total	. . . .	2,593,021	100.00

ASSEMBLÉE NATIONALE

Assemblée nationale: Palais du Peuple, BP 414, Conakry; tel. 45-21-56; fax 45-17-00; e-mail s.general@assemblee.gov.gn; internet www.assemblee.gov.gn.

Speaker: ABOUBACAR SOMPARÉ.

General election, 30 June 2002

Party	% of votes	Seats
Parti de l'unité et du progrès (PUP) . . .	61.57	85
Union pour le progrès et le renouveau (UPR)	26.63	20
Union pour le progrès de la Guinée (UPG) .	4.11	3
Parti démocratique de Guinée— Rassemblement démocratique africain (PDG—RDA)	3.40	3
Alliance nationale pour le progrès (ANP) .	1.98	2
Parti pour l'unité et le développement (PUD)	0.69	1
Others	1.61	—
Total	100.00	114*

*Comprising 76 seats allocated by proportional representation from national party lists and 38 seats filled by voting in single-member constituencies, all of which were won by the PUP.

Advisory Council

Economic and Social Council: Immeuble FAWAZ, Corniche Sud, Coléaah, Matam, BP 2947, Conakry; tel. 45-21-35; fax 45-31-24; f. 1997; 45 mems; Pres. MICHEL KAMANO; Sec.-Gen. MAMADOU BOBO CAMARA.

Political Organizations

There were 46 officially registered parties in mid-2000. Of those active in early 2003, the following were the most important

Alliance nationale pour le progrès (ANP): Conakry; opposes Govt of Pres. Conté; Leader Dr SAGNO MOUSSA.

Front de l'alternance démocratique (FRAD): Conakry; f. 2002; opposes Govt of Pres. Conté; boycotted legislative elections in 2002; Pres. MAMADOU BOYE BÂ; affiliated parties include:

> **Parti démocratique africain (PDA):** Conakry; Pres. MARCEL CROS.

> **Parti Dyama:** Conakry; Leader MOHAMED MANSOUR KABA.

> **Rassemblement populaire guinéen (RPG):** Conakry; e-mail alphaconde@multimania.com; internet lerpgguinee.efrance-pro.com/parti.asp; socialist; Leaders ALPHA CONDÉ, AHMED TIDIANE CISSÉ.

> **Union des forces démocratiques (UFD):** Conakry; Pres. ALFA IBRAHIM SOW.

> **Union des forces démocratiques de Guinée (UFDG):** Conakry; f. 2002 by faction of UPR (q.v.) in protest at that party's participation in elections to Assemblée nationale; Pres. MAMADOU BOYE BÂ; Sec.-Gen. AMADOU OURY BAH.

> **Union des forces républicaines (UFR):** Conakry; e-mail ufrguinee@yahoo.fr; internet www.ufrguinee.org; f. 1992; social-democratic; Pres. SIDYA TOURÉ; Sec.-Gen. BAKARY ZOUMANIGUI.

Parti démocratique de Guinée—Rassemblement démocratique africain (PDG—RDA): Conakry; f. 1946; revived 1992; supports Govt of Pres. Conté; Leader El Hadj ISMAËL MOHAMED GASSIM GHUISSEIN.

Parti écologiste de Guinée (PEG—Les Verts): BP 3018, Quartier Boulbinet, 5e blvd, angle 2e ave, Commune de Kaloum, Conakry; tel. 44-37-01; supports Govt of Pres. Conté; Leader OUMAR SYLLA.

Parti du peuple de Guinée (PPG): BP 1147, Conakry; socialist; opposes Govt of Pres. Conté; Leader CHARLES-PASCAL TOLNO.

Parti pour l'unité et le développement (PUD): Conakry; opposed to Govt of Pres. Conté; Leader BARRY MAMADOU BHOYE.

Parti de l'unité et du progrès (PUP): Camayenne, Conakry; Pres. Gen. LANSANA CONTÉ; Sec.-Gen. El Hadj Dr SÉKOU KONATÉ (acting).

Union pour le progrès de la Guinée (UPG): Conakry; opposes Govt of Pres. Conté; Leader JEAN-MARIE DORÉ.

Union pour le progrès et le renouveau (UPR): Conakry; f. 1998 by merger of the Parti pour le renouveau et le progrès and the Union pour la nouvelle République; opposes Govt of Pres. Conté; Pres. SIRADIOU DIALLO.

Note: In January 2003 supporters of Pres. Conté announced the formation of a grouping, the **Coordination de la mouvance présidentielle**, to support the candidacy of Conté at the presidential election scheduled to be held in December of that year.

Diplomatic Representation

EMBASSIES IN GUINEA

Algeria: Commune de Kaloum, face Etat Major de la Gendarmerie Nationale, BP 1004, Conakry; tel. 44-15-03; fax 41-15-08.

Canada: BP 99, Conakry; tel. 46-23-95; fax 46-42-35; e-mail cnaky@dfait-maeci.gc.ca; Ambassador DENIS BRIAND.

China, People's Republic: Quartier Donka, Cité Ministérielle, Commune de Dixinn, BP 714, Conakry; tel. 41-48-35; fax 46-22-99; e-mail amb-chine1@eti-bull.net; Ambassador GONG YUANXING.

Congo, Democratic Republic: Quartier Almamya, ave de la Gare, Commune du Kaloum, BP 880, Conakry; tel. 45-15-01.

Côte d'Ivoire: blvd du Commerce, BP 5228, Conakry; tel. 45-10-82; fax 45-10-79; Ambassador JEANNOT ZORO BI BAH.

Cuba: Corniche-Nord, Coronthie, Commune du Kaloum, BP 71, Conakry; tel. 44-42-68; fax 41-50-76; Ambassador LUIS DELGADO PÉREZ.

Egypt: Corniche-Sud, BP 389, Conakry; tel. and fax 41-23-94; e-mail ambassadeegypte.conakry@eti-bull.net; Ambassador NOFAL ES-SAYED.

France: Immeuble Chavanel, blvd du Commerce, BP 570, Conakry; tel. 41-16-05; fax 41-27-08; e-mail amb.fr.conakry@eti-bull.net; Ambassador DENIS BAUER.

Germany: 2e blvd, Kaloum, BP 540, Conakry; tel. 41-15-06; fax 45-22-17; e-mail amball@sotelgui.net.gn; Ambassador REINHARD BUCHHOLZ.

Ghana: Immeuble Ex-Urbaine et la Seine, BP 732, Conakry; tel. 44-15-10; Ambassador Alhaji SHAIBU MUSAH SHARIF.

Guinea-Bissau: Quartier Bellevue, Commune de Dixinn, BP 298, Conakry; Ambassador MALAM CAMARA.

Holy See: La Minière, BP 2016, Conakry; tel. 46-36-71; fax 42-28-14; e-mail nonce@biasy.net; Apostolic Nuncio Most Rev. ALBERTO BOTTARI DE CASTELLO (Titular Archbishop of Foraziana).

Iran: Commune de Dixinn, BP 310, Conakry; tel. 41-15-98; Ambassador JAVAD ROWSHAN ZAMIR QOROQI.

Japan: Lanseboundji, Corniche Sud, Commune de Matam, BP 895, Conakry; tel. 41-36-07; fax 41-25-75; Ambassador KEIICHI KITABAN.

Korea, Democratic People's Republic: BP 723, Conakry; Ambassador KIM KYONG SIN.

Liberia: Cité Ministérielle, Donka, Commune de Dixinn, BP 18, Conakry; tel. 42-26-71; Chargé d'affaires SIAKA FAHNBULLEH.

Libya: Commune de Kaloum, BP 1183, Conakry; tel. 41-41-72; Ambassador B. AHMED.

Malaysia: Conakry; Ambassador Dato' SAW CHING HONG.

Mali: La Minière, Commune de Dixinn, BP 299, Conakry; tel. 41-15-39; Ambassador HAMADOUN IBRAHIMA ISSABRÉ.

Morocco: Cité des Nations, Villa 12, Commune du Kaloum, BP 193, Conakry; tel. 41-36-86; fax 41-38-16; Ambassador JAOUAD EL-HIMDI.

Nigeria: Corniche Sud, Quartier de Matam, BP 54, Conakry; tel. 41-43-75; Ambassador PETER N. OYEDELE.

Russia: Matam-Port, km 9, BP 329, Conakry; tel. 46-37-25; fax 41-27-77; e-mail ambrus-gui@mirinet.net.gn; Ambassador IGOR G. IVASHCHENKO.

Saudi Arabia: Quartier Camayenne, Commune de Dixinn, BP 611, Conakry; tel. 46-24-87; fax 46-58-84; e-mail gnemb@mofa.gov.sa; Chargé d'affaires ABDULLAH NASSER AL CHARIF.

Senegal: BP 842, Conakry; tel. and fax 44-44-13; Ambassador MAKHILY GASSAMA.

Serbia and Montenegro: BP 1154, Conakry; tel. 46-42-65; e-mail ambyugui@leland-gn.org; Ambassador DANILO MILIĆ.

Sierra Leone: Quartier Bellevue, face aux cases présidentielles, Commune de Dixinn, BP 625, Conakry; tel. 44-50-08; Ambassador Commdr MOHAMED DIABY.

Togo: ave de la République, Immeuble Kaloum, Commune du Kaloum, BP 3633, Conakry; tel. 41-47-72.

Ukraine: Commune de Calum, Corniche Nord, Quartier Camayenne, BP 1350, Conakry; tel. 45-37-56; fax 45-37-95; e-mail ambgv@sotelgui.net.gn; Ambassador IVAN D. SHEVCHENKO.

USA: rue KA 038, BP 603, Conakry; tel. 41-15-20; fax 41-15-22; e-mail amemconakry.adm@eti-bull.net; internet usembassy.state.gov/conakry; Ambassador REUBEN BARRIE WALKLEY.

Judicial System

The Constitution of the Third Republic embodies the principle of the independence of the judiciary, and delineates the competences of each component of the judicial system, including the Higher Magistrates' Council, the Supreme Court, the High Court of Justice and the Magistrature.

Supreme Court

Corniche-Sud, Camayenne, Conakry; tel. 41-11-67.

Pres. ALPHONSE ABOLY.

Director of Public Prosecutions: ANTOINE IBRAHIM DIALLO.

Note: A State Security Court was established in June 1997, with exceptional jurisdiction to try, 'in times of peace and war', crimes against the internal and external security of the State. Members of the court are appointed by the President of the Republic. There is no constitutional provision for the existence of such a tribunal.

President of the State Security Court: Commdr SAMA PANNIVAL BANGOURA.

Religion

It is estimated that 85% of the population are Muslims and 8% Christians, while 7% follow animist beliefs.

ISLAM

Ligue Islamique Nationale: BP 386, Conakry; tel. 41-23-33; f. 1988; Sec.-Gen. El Hadj AHMED TIDIANE TRAORÉ.

CHRISTIANITY

The Roman Catholic Church

Guinea comprises one archdiocese and two dioceses. At 31 December 2000 there were an estimated 133,641 Roman Catholics in Guinea, comprising about 2.0% of the total population.

Bishops' Conference

Conférence Episcopale de la Guinée, BP 1006 bis, Conakry; tel. and fax 41-32-70; e-mail dhewara@eti.met.gn.

Pres. (vacant).

Archbishop of Conakry: (vacant), Archevêché, BP 2016, Conakry; tel. 41-32-70; fax 44-20-80; e-mail dhewara@eti.met.gn.

The Anglican Communion

Anglicans in Guinea are adherents of the Church of the Province of West Africa, comprising 12 dioceses. The diocese of Guinea and Guinea-Bissau (as the diocese of Guinea) was established in 1985 as the first French-speaking diocese in the Province. The Archbishop of the Province is the Bishop of Koforidua, Ghana.

Bishop of Guinea: Rt Rev. ALBERT D. GÓMEZ, Cathédrale Toussaint, BP 105, Conakry; tel. 45-13-23.

BAHÁ'Í FAITH

Assemblée spirituelle nationale: BP 2010, Conakry 1; e-mail kouchek@sotelgui.net.gn.

The Press

REGULATORY AUTHORITY

National Council of Communication: en face Primature, BP 2955, Conakry; tel. 46-15-05; fax 41-23-85; f. 1991; regulates the operations of the press, and of radio and television; regulates political access to the media; nine mems; two meetings each week; Pres. EMILE TOMPAPA.

NEWSPAPERS AND PERIODICALS

In early 2003 there were more than 200 periodicals and newspapers officially registered with the Conseil National de la Communication, although only around 60 were believed to be in operation at that time.

Le Démocrate: Conakry; tel. 41-57-62; fax 41-43-19; weekly.

Le Diplomate: BP 2427, Conakry; tel. and fax 41-23-85; f. 2002; Dir SANOU KERFALLAH CISSÉ.

L'Evénement de Guinée: BP 796, Conakry; tel. 44-33-91; monthly; independent; f. 1993; Dir BOUBACAR SANKARELA DIALLO.

Fonike: BP 341, Conakry; sport and general; Dir IBRAHIMA KALIL DIARE.

La Guinée Actuelle: Sans Fils, près Le Makity, BP 3618, Conakry; tel. 69-36-20.

Le Guinéen: Conakry; f. 2002; Dir JEAN-MARIE MORGAN.

Horoya (Liberty): Coléah, BP 191, Conakry; tel. 41-34-75; fax 45-10-16; e-mail horoya@leland-gn.org; govt daily; Dir OUSMANE CAMARA.

L'Indépendant: route du Palais du Peuple, BP 2427, Conakry; tel. 41-57-62; fax 41-43-19; e-mail indepdt@mirinet.net.gn; weekly; also *L'Indépendant Plus*; Publr ABOUBACAR SYLLA; Editor-in-Chief SALIOU SAMB.

Journal Officiel de Guinée: BP 156, Conakry; fortnightly; organ of the Govt.

La Lance: route du Palais du Peuple, BP 2427, Conakry; tel. and fax 41-23-85; e-mail la-lance@mirinet.net.gn; internet lynx.afribone.net.gn/lce; weekly; general information; Dir SOULEYMANE E. DIALLO.

Le Lynx: Immeuble Baldé Zaïre Sandervalia, BP 4968, Conakry; tel. 41-23-85; fax 45-36-96; e-mail le-lynx@mirinet.net.gn; internet lynx.afribone.net.gn; f. 1992; weekly; satirical; Editor SOULEYMANE E. DIALLO.

La Nouvelle Tribune: blvd Diallo Tally entre 5e et 6e avenue, BP 6698, Conakry; tel. 54-69-79; e-mail abdcond@yahoo.fr; weekly, Tuesdays; general; Dir of Publication ABDOULAYE CONDÉ.

L'Observateur: Immeuble Baldé, Conakry; tel. 40-05-24; independent; Dir EL-BÉCHIR DIALLO.

L'Oeil du Peuple: Conakry; weekly; independent; Dir of Publishing ISMAËL BANGOURA.

Sanakou: Labé, Foutah Djallon, Moyenne-Guinée; tel. 51-13-19; e-mail sanakoulabe@yahoo.fr; internet www.afrikeguinee.com/afriqueguinee/sanakou; f. 2000; monthly; general news; Publr IDRISSA SAMPIRING DIALLO; Editor-in-Chief YAMOUSSA SOUMAH; circ. 1,000.

Le Scribe: 124 rue MO-268, BP 1305, Conakry; tel. 22-75-87; e-mail lescribe@mirinet.net.gn; f. 1997; evangelical Christian magazine; Dir JOSEPH SOURO CAMARA; Editor-in-Chief PIERRE CAMARA.

Le Soleil: BP 3576, Conakry; tel. 67-17-73; e-mail soleil2000gn@yahoo.fr.

3-P Plus (Parole-Plume-Papier) Magazine: 7e ave Bis Almamyah, BP 5122, Conakry; tel. 45-22-32; fax 45-29-31; e-mail 3p-plus@mirinet.net.gn; internet www.mirinet.net.gn/3p_plus; journal of arts and letters; supplements *Le Cahier de l'Economie*, *Mag-Plus: Le Magazine de la Culture*; monthly; Pres. MOHAMED SALIFOU KEÏTA; Editor-in-Chief NAMAN CAMARA.

NEWS AGENCY

Agence Guinéenne de Presse: BP 1535, Conakry; tel. 46-54-14; f. 1960; Man. Dir MOHAMED CONDÉ.

PRESS ASSOCIATION

Association Guinéenne des Editeurs de la Presse Indépendante (AGEPI): Conakry; f. 1991; an asscn of independent newspaper publishers; Chair. BOUBACAR SANKARELA DIALLO.

Publishers

Les Classiques Guinéens—SOGUIDIP: 545 rue KA020, Boulbinet; tel. 41-31-19; fax 41-47-40; e-mail cheick.soguidip@mirinet .net.gn; f. 1999; history, politics; Dir Cheick ABDOUL KABA.

Editions du Ministère de l'Education Nationale: Direction nationale de la recherche scientifique, BP 561, Conakry; tel. 44-19-50; f. 1959; general and educational; Dir Prof. KANTÉ KABINÉ.

Editions Gandall (Knowledge): BP 542, Conakry; tel. and fax 46-35-07; e-mail gandall@mirinet.net.gn; internet www .editionsgandall.com; f. 1992; fiction and non-fiction, poetry and school books in Pular and French; Dir MAMADOU ALIOU SOW.

Société Africaine d'Edition et de Communication (SEAC): Belle-Vue, Commune de Dixinn, BP 6826, Conakry; tel. 29-71-41; e-mail dtniane@biasy.com; social sciences, reference, literary fiction.

Broadcasting and Communications

TELECOMMUNICATIONS

Regulatory Bodies

Direction Nationale des Postes et Télécommunications: BP 5000, Conakry; tel. 41-13-31; fax 45-31-16; e-mail koly@leland-gn .org; f. 1997; regulates transport, postal and telecommunications services; Dir. KOLY CAMARA.

Comité National de Coordination des Télécommunications (CNCT): BP 5000, Conakry; tel. 41-40-79; fax 45-31-16; Exec. Sec. SEKOU BANGOURA.

Service Providers

Intercel: Quartier Coleah Larseboundji, près du pont du 8 Novembre, Immeuble le Golfe, BP 965, Conakry; tel. 45-57-44; fax 40-92-92; e-mail info@gn.intercel.net; mobile cellular telephone operator; fmrly Telecel Guinée; Dir FRANÇOIS DICK.

Société des Télécommunications de Guinée (SOTELGUI): 4e blvd, BP 2066, Conakry; tel. 41-12-12; fax 45-02-01; e-mail marzuki@sotelgui.net.gn; internet www.sotelgui.net.gn; f. 1993; privatized 1995; 60% owned by Telkom Malaysia; 40% state-owned; also provides mobile cellular services (as Lagui); 51,020 subscribers (1998); Dir El Hadj MARZUKI ABDULLAH.

Spacetel Guinée SA (Mobilis Guinée): BP 835, Conakry; tel. and fax 12-66-00-11; e-mail aboukhalil@spacetelguinee.com; f. 1994; mobile cellular telephone operator; operates with a range of 50km around Conakry; 5,000 subscribers (1998); Chair. ABOU KHALIL.

BROADCASTING

Regulatory Authority

Conseil National de la Communication (CNC): see above.

Radio

Radiodiffusion-Télévision Guinéenne (RTG): BP 391, Conakry; tel. 44-22-05; fax 44-39-98; broadcasts in French, English, Créole-English, Portuguese, Arabic and local languages; Dir-Gen. AISSATOU BELLA DIALLO; Dir of Radio ISSA CONDÉ.

Radio Rurale de Guinée: BP 391, Conakry; tel. 2-11-09; fax 41-47-97; e-mail ruralgui@mirinet.net.gn; network of rural radio stations.

Television

Radiodiffusion-Télévision Guinéenne (RTG): see Radio; transmissions in French and local languages; one channel; f. 1977.

Finance

(cap. = capital; res = reserves; m. = million; brs = branches; amounts in Guinean francs)

BANKING

Central Bank

Banque Centrale de la République de Guinée (BCRG): 12 blvd du Commerce, BP 692, Conakry; tel. 41-26-51; fax 41-48-98; e-mail gouv-bcrg@eti-bull.net; f. 1960; bank of issue; Gov. IBRAHIMA CHÉRIF BAH; Dep. Gov. FODÉ SOUMAH.

Commercial Banks

Banque Internationale pour le Commerce et l'Industrie de la Guinée (BICI—GUI): ave de la République, BP 1484, Conakry; tel. 41-45-15; fax 41-39-62; e-mail rsancho.bicigui@eti-bull.net; f. 1985; 51% state-owned; cap. and res 15,830m., total assets 197,815m. (Dec. 1998); affiliated to BNP Paribas (France); Pres. IBRAHIMA SOUMAH; Man. Dir BERNARD DELEUZE; 11 brs.

Banque Populaire Maroco-Guinéenne (BPMG): Immeuble BPMG, blvd du Commerce, Kaloum, BP 4400, Conakry 01; tel. 41-36-93; fax 41-32-61; f. 1991; 55% owned by Crédit Populaire du Maroc, 45% state-owned; cap. 24.7m., res 5.2m., dep. 20.5m. (Dec. 2002); Pres. EMMANUEL GNAN; Dir-Gen. IRAQI HOUSSAINI AHMED; 3 brs.

Ecobank Guinée: Immeuble Al Iman, ave de la République, BP 5687, Conakry; tel. 45-58-77; fax 45-42-41; e-mail ecobankgn@ ecobank.com; f. 1999; wholly owned by Ecobank Transnational Inc. (Togo—operating under the auspices of the Economic Community of West African States); cap. and res 1,839m., total assets 24,721m. (Dec. 1999); Pres. SANGARE N'FALY; Man. Dir KUMLAN ADJARHO OWEH.

First American Bank of Guinea: blvd du Commerce, angle 9ème Ave, BP 4540, Conakry; tel. 41-34-32; fax 41-35-29; f. 1994; jt-owned by Mitan Capital Ltd, Grand Cayman and El Hadj Haidara Abdourahmane Chérif, Mali.

International Commercial Bank: 4e ave Boulbinet, Bâtiment 346, BP 3547, Conakry; tel. 41-25-89; fax 41-25-92; f. 1997; total assets 19.6m. (Dec. 1999); Pres. JOSÉPHINE PREMLA; Man. Dir HAMZA BIN ALIAS.

Société Générale de Banques en Guinée (SGBG): Immeuble Boffa, Cité du Chemin de Fer, BP 1514, Conakry; tel. 41-17-41; fax 41-25-65; e-mail sgbg@biasy.net; internet www.sgbg.net.gn; f. 1985; 42% owned by Société Générale (France); cap. 20m., total assets 144,680m. (Dec. 2000); Pres. ROGER SERVONNET; Man. Dir JEAN-CLAUDE ROBERT.

Union Internationale de Banques en Guinée (UIBG): 6e ave de la République, angle 5e blvd, BP 324, Conakry; tel. 41-43-09; fax 41-42-77; e-mail de@uibg.com.gn; f. 1988; 68.3% owned by Crédit Lyonnais Global Banking (France); cap. and res 3,612m., total assets 44,384m. (Dec. 1999); Pres. ALPHA AMADOU DIALLO; Dir-Gen. ROLAND ANTHOINE-MILHOMME.

Islamic Bank

Banque Islamique de Guinée: Immeuble Nafaya, ave de la République, BP 1247, Conakry; tel. 41-50-86; fax 41-50-71; e-mail bigmiconakry@eti-bull.net; f. 1983; 68.5% owned by Dar al-Maal al-Islami (DMI Trust); cap. 8,500m., total assets 21,550m. (Dec. 2000); Pres. ADERRAOUF BENESSAIAH; Man. Dir ABDELMAJID BENJELLOUN.

INSURANCE

Société Guinéenne d'Assurance Mutuelle (SOGAM): BP 4340, Conakry; tel. 44-50-58; fax 41-25-57; f. 1990; Chair. Dr M. K. BAH; Man. Dir P. I. NDAO.

Société Nouvelle d'Assurance de Guinée (SONAG): BP 3363, Conakry; tel. 41 49 77; fax 41-43-03.

Union Guinéenne d'Assurances et de Réassurances (UGAR): Place des Martyrs, BP 179, Conakry; tel. 41-48-41; fax 41-17-11; e-mail ugar@ugar.com.gn; f. 1989; 40% owned by AXA (France), 35% state-owned; cap. 2,000m. Man. Dir RAPHAËL Y. TOURÉ.

Trade and Industry

GOVERNMENT AGENCIES

Centre de Promotion et de Développement Miniers (CPDM): BP 295, Conakry; tel. 41-15-44; fax 41-49-13; e-mail cpdm@mirinet .net.gn; f. 1995; promotes investment and co-ordinates devt strategy in mining sector; Dir MOCIRÉ SYLLA.

Entreprise Nationale Import-Export (IMPORTEX): BP 152, Conakry; tel. 44-28-13; state-owned import and export agency; Dir MAMADOU BOBO DIENG.

Office de Promotion des Investissements Privés-Guichet Unique (OPIP): Conakry; tel. 41-49-85; fax 41-39-90; e-mail dg@ opip.org.gn; internet www.mirinet.net.gn/opip; f. 1992; promotes private investment; Dir-Gen. DIANKA KOEVOGUI.

DEVELOPMENT ORGANIZATIONS

Agence Française de Développement (AFD): 5e ave, BP 283, Conakry; tel. 41-25-69; fax 41-28-74; e-mail afd@mirinet.net.gn; internet www.afd.fr; Dir in Guinea YVES BOUDOT.

Association Française des Volontaires du Progrès (AFVP): BP 570, Conakry; tel. 46-14-78; fax 46-20-71; e-mail afvp-gui@biasy .net; internet www.afvp.org; f. 1987; development and research projects; Nat. Delegate EMMANUEL POILANE.

Mission Française de Coopération et d'Action Culturelle: BP 373, Conakry; tel. 41-23-45; fax 41-43-56; administers bilateral aid; Dir in Guinea ANDRÉ BAILLEUL.

CHAMBERS OF COMMERCE

Chambre de Commerce, d'Industrie et d'Agriculture de Guinée: BP 545, Conakry; tel. 45-45-16; fax 45-45-17; f. 1985; Pres. Capt. THIANA DIALLO; Sec.-Gen. MOHAMED SAID FOFANA; 70 mems.

Chambre Economique de Guinée: BP 609, Conakry.

TRADE AND EMPLOYERS' ASSOCIATIONS

Association des Commerçants de Guinée: BP 2468, Conakry; tel. 41-30-37; fax 45-31-66; Sec.-Gen. OUMAR CAMARA.

Association des Femmes Entrepreneurs de Guinée (AFEG): BP 790, Conakry; fax 41-32-06.

Conseil du Patronat Guinéen: Dixinn Bora, BP 6403, Conakry; tel. and fax 41-24-70; e-mail msylla@leland-gn.org; f. 1992; Pres. El Hadj MAMADOU SYLLA.

Fédération Patronale de l'Agriculture et de l'Elevage (FEPAE): BP 5684, Conakry; tel. 22-95-56; fax 41-54-36; Pres. MAMDOU SYLLA; Sec.-Gen. MAMADY CAMARA.

Groupement des Importateurs Guinéens (GIG): BP 970, Conakry; tel. 42-18-18; fax 42-19-19; Pres. FERNAND BANGOURA.

UTILITIES

Electricity

Barrage Hydroélectrique de Garafiri: BP 1770, Conakry; tel. 41-50-91; inaugurated 1999.

Electricité de Guinée (EDG): BP 1463, Conakry; tel. 45-18-56; fax 45-18-53; e-mail di.sogel@biasy.net; f. 2001 to replace Société Guinéenne d'Electricité; majority state-owned; production, transport and distribution of electricity; Dir-Gen. KABINÉ CAMARA.

Entreprise Nationale d'Electricité de Guinée (ENELGUI): BP 322, Conakry; tel. 41-42-43; fax 44-17-51; production of electricity; Man. Dir BOKARY SYLLA.

Water

Service National d'Aménagement des Points d'Eau (SNAPE): BP 2064, Conakry; tel. 41-18-93; fax 41-50-58; e-mail snape@mirinet .net.gn; supplies water in rural areas.

Société Nationale des Eaux de Guinée (SONEG): BP 150, Conakry; tel. 45-44-77; e-mail oaubot@seg.org.gn; f. 1988; national water co; Dir-Gen. Dr OUSMANE ARIBOT; Sec.-Gen. MAMADOU DIOP.

TRADE UNIONS

Confédération Nationale des Travailleurs de Guinée (CNTG): Bourse du Travail, Corniche Sud 004, BP 237, Conakry; tel. and fax 41-50-44; f. 1984; Sec.-Gen. MOHAMED SAMBA KÉBÉ.

Organisation Nationale des Syndicats Libres de Guinée (ONSLG): BP 559, Conakry; tel. 41-52-17; fax 43-02-83; 27,000 mems (1996).

Union Syndicale des Travailleurs de Guinée (USTG): BP 1514, Conakry; tel. 41-25-65; fax 41-25-58; 26,000 mems (1996).

Transport

RAILWAYS

There are 1,086 km of railways in Guinea, including 662 km of 1-m gauge track from Conakry to Kankan in the east of the country, crossing the Niger at Kouroussa. The contract for the first phase of the upgrading of this line was awarded to a Slovak company in early 1997. Three lines for the transport of bauxite link Sangaredi with the port of Kamsar in the west, via Boké, and Conakry with Kindia and Fria, a total of 383 km.

Office National des Chemins de Fer de Guinée (ONCFG): BP 589, Conakry; tel. 44-46-13; fax 41-35-77; f. 1905; Man. Dir MOREL MARGUERITE CAMARA.

Chemin de Fer de Boké: BP 523, Boké; operations commenced 1973.

Chemin de Fer Conakry–Fria: BP 334, Conakry; operations commenced 1960; Gen. Man. A. CAMARA.

Chemin de Fer de la Société des Bauxites de Kindia: BP 613, Conakry; tel. 41-38-28; operations commenced 1974; Gen. Man. K. KEITA.

ROADS

The road network comprised 21,215 km of roads (of which 1,959 km were paved) in 1999. An 895-km cross-country road links Conakry to Bamako, in Mali, and the main highway connecting Dakar (Senegal) to Abidjan (Côte d'Ivoire) also crosses Guinea. The road linking Conakry to Freetown (Sierra Leone) forms part of the Trans West African Highway, extending from Morocco to Nigeria.

La Guinéenne-Marocaine des Transports (GUIMAT): Conakry; f. 1989; owned jtly by Govt of Guinea and Hakkam (Morocco); operates national and regional transport services.

Société Générale des Transports de Guinée (SOGETRAG): Conakry; f. 1985; 63% state-owned; bus operator.

SHIPPING

Conakry and Kamsar are the international seaports. Conakry handled 3.9m. metric tons of foreign trade in 1999, while in 1994 some 12m. tons of bauxite were transported to Kamsar for shipment.

Getma Guinea SA: Cité du Chemin de Fer, BP 1648, Conakry; tel. 41-32-05; fax 41-42-73; e-mail contact@getma.com; internet www .getma.com; f. 1978; fmrly Société Guinéenne d'Entreprises de Transports Maritimes et Aeriens; marine transportation; Chair. JEAN-JACQUES GRENIER.

Port Autonome de Conakry (PAC): BP 805, Conakry; tel. 41-27-28; fax 41-26-04; e-mail pac@eti-bull.net; internet www.eti-bull.net/ pac; haulage, porterage; Gen. Man. ALIOU DIALLO.

Société Navale Guinéenne (SNG): BP 522, Conakry; tel. 44-29-55; fax 41-39-70; f. 1968; state-owned; shipping agents; Dir-Gen. NOUNKÉ KEITA.

SOAEM: BP 3177, Conakry; tel. 41-25-90; fax 41-20-25; e-mail soaem.gn@mirinet.net.gn.

SOTRAMAR: Kamsar; e-mail sotramar@sotramar.com; f. 1971; exports bauxite from mines at Boké through port of Kamsar.

Transmar: 33 blvd du Commerce, Kaloum, BP 3917, Conakry; tel. 43-05-41; fax 43-05-42; e-mail transmar@eti.net.gn; shipping, stevedoring, inland transport.

CIVIL AVIATION

There is an international airport at Conakry-Gbessia, and smaller airfields at Labé, Kankan and Faranah. Facilities at Conakry have been upgraded, at a cost of US $42.6m.; the airport handled some 300,000 passengers in 1999.

Air Guinée Express: 6 ave de la République, BP 12, Conakry; tel. 44-46-02; fax 41-29-07; e-mail air-guinee@mirinet.net.gn; f. 2002 to replace Air Guinée (f. 1960); regional and internal services; Dir-Gen. ANTOINE CROS.

Guinée Air Service: Aéroport Conakry-Gbessia; tel. 41-27-61.

Guinée Inter Air: Aéroport Conakry-Gbessia; tel. 41-37-08.

Société de Gestion et d'Exploitation de l'Aéroport de Conakry (SOGEAC): BP 3126, Conakry; tel. 46-48-03; f. 1987; manages Conakry-Gbessia international airport; 51% state-owned.

Tourism

Some 32,598 tourists visited Guinea in 2000; receipts from tourism in that year totalled an estimated US $12m.

Office National du Tourisme: Immeuble al-Iman, 6e ave de la République, BP 1275, Conakry; tel. 45-51-63; fax 45-51-64; e-mail ontour@leland-gn.org; internet www.mirinet.net.gn/ont; f. 1997; Dir-Gen. IBRAHIM A. DIALLO.

GUINEA-BISSAU

Introductory Survey

Location, Climate, Language, Religion, Flag, Capital

The Republic of Guinea-Bissau lies on the west coast of Africa, with Senegal to the north and Guinea to the east and south. The climate is tropical, although maritime and Sahelian influences are felt. The average temperature is 20°C (68°F). The official language is Portuguese, of which the locally spoken form is Creole (Crioulo). There are 19 local languages, of which the most widely spoken are Balanta-Kentohe, Pulaar (Fula), Mandjak, Mandinka and Papel. The principal religious beliefs are animism and Islam. There is a small minority of Roman Catholics and other Christian groups. The national flag (proportions 1 by 2) has two equal horizontal stripes, of yellow over light green, and a red vertical stripe, with a five-pointed black star at its centre, at the hoist. The capital is Bissau.

Recent History

Portuguese Guinea (Guiné) was colonized by Portugal in the 15th century. Nationalist activism began to emerge in the 1950s. Armed insurgency commenced in the early 1960s, and by 1972 the Partido Africano da Independência da Guiné e Cabo Verde (PAIGC) was in control of two-thirds of the country. The independence of the Republic of Guinea-Bissau was unilaterally proclaimed in September 1973, with Luís Cabral (the brother of the founder of the PAIGC, Amílcar Cabral) as President of the State Council. Hostilities ceased following the military coup in Portugal in April 1974, and on 10 September Portugal recognized the independence of Guinea-Bissau under the leadership of Luís Cabral.

The PAIGC regime introduced measures to establish a single-party socialist state. At elections in December 1976 and January 1977 voters chose regional councils from which a new National People's Assembly (Assembléia Nacional Popular) was later selected. In 1978 the Chief State Commissioner, Francisco Mendes, died; he was succeeded by Commander João Vieira, hitherto State Commissioner for the Armed Forces and President of the Assembléia Nacional Popular.

The PAIGC initially supervised both Cape Verde and Guinea-Bissau, the Constitutions of each remaining separate but with a view to eventual unification. These arrangements were terminated in November 1980, when President Cabral was deposed in a coup organized by Vieira, who was installed as Chairman of the Council of the Revolution. Diplomatic relations between Guinea-Bissau and Cape Verde were restored after the release of Cabral from detention in 1982. In May 1982 President Vieira removed several left-wing ministers from the Government and appointed Vítor Saúde Maria, Vice-Chairman of the Council of the Revolution and former Minister of Foreign Affairs, as Prime Minister.

In 1983 Vieira established a commission to examine plans for the revision of the Constitution and the electoral code. In March 1984 Vieira dismissed Saúde Maria from the premiership. Although his removal from office was attributed to his alleged involvement in a coup plot, it appeared that the principal reason for Saúde Maria's dismissal was his opposition to the proposed constitutional changes, which would accord more power to the President. In late March Vieira formally assumed the role of Head of Government, and elections to regional councils took place. In May the Assembléia Nacional Popular, which had been dissolved following the 1980 coup, was re-established, and the Council of the Revolution was replaced by a 15-member Council of State (Conselho de Estado), selected from among the members of the Assembléia. Vieira was subsequently elected as President of the Conselho de Estado and Head of State. The Assembléia immediately ratified the new Constitution, and formally abolished the position of Prime Minister.

A campaign against corruption, initiated by Vieira in August 1985, apparently provoked a military coup attempt in November, led by Col Paulo Correia, the First Vice-President of the Conselho de Estado, and other senior army officers. Correia was subsequently executed.

In November 1986 the PAIGC endorsed proposals for the liberalization of the economy and re-elected Vieira as party Secretary-General for a further four years. In February 1987

Vieira appointed Dr Vasco Cabral, hitherto Minister of Justice, as Permanent Secretary of the Central Committee of the PAIGC, in an attempt to reinforce party support for the programme of economic liberalization.

In early 1989 it was announced that the PAIGC had established a six-member national commission to revise the Constitution. Regional elections took place in early June, at which 95.8% of those who voted endorsed the single PAIGC list. In mid-June the Regional Councils, in turn, elected the Assembléia Nacional Popular, which subsequently elected the Conselho de Estado, of which Vieira was re-elected President.

In December 1990 the Central Committee of the PAIGC agreed to the adoption of a multi-party system, following a period of transition, and the holding of a presidential election in 1993. In May 1991 a series of constitutional amendments ending one-party rule were approved by the Assembléia Nacional Popular, terminating the political monopoly of the PAIGC. In addition, all links between the PAIGC and the armed forces were severed, and the introduction of a free-market economy was guaranteed. New legislation in October accorded greater freedom to the press and permitted the formation of new trade unions. In November the Frente Democrática (FD) became the first opposition party to obtain official registration.

In December 1991 a major government reshuffle took place, in which the office of Prime Minister was restored. Carlos Correia was appointed to the post. In late 1991 and early 1992 three further opposition parties obtained legal status: the Resistência da Guiné-Bissau—Movimento Bah-Fatah (RGB—MB), led by Domingos Fernandes Gomes; the Frente Democrática Social (FDS), led by Rafael Barbosa; and the Partido Unido Social Democrático (PUSD), led by Vítor Saúde Maria. Following a split in the FDS, a further party, the Partido para a Renovação Social (PRS), was established in January 1992 by the former Vice-Chairman of the FDS, Kumba Yalá. In the same month four opposition parties—the PUSD, FDS, RGB—MB and the Partido da Convergência Democrática (PCD), led by Victor Mandinga—agreed on the establishment of a 'democratic forum', whose demands included the dissolution of the political police, the creation of an electoral commission and an all-party consultation on the setting of election dates. In March 1992 some 30,000 people attended an opposition demonstration in Bissau, the first such mass-meeting to be permitted by the Government. The demonstrators were protesting against alleged government corruption and violations of human rights by the security forces. In the same month it was announced that presidential and legislative elections would take place in November and December, respectively.

In May 1992 a dissident group, known as the 'Group of 121', broke away from the PAIGC to form the Partido de Renovação e Desenvolvimento (PRD). The PRD advocated the establishment of a transitional government, pending elections, and the disbanding of the political police. In mid-May the leader of the RGB—MB, Domingos Fernandes Gomes, returned from exile in Portugal and, with the leaders of the FD, PCD, FDS and the PUSD, met Vieira to discuss further democratic reform.

In July 1992, following threats by the 'democratic forum' that it would form a parallel government and boycott elections if the PAIGC did not seek consensus with the opposition on electoral issues, the Government agreed to establish a multi-party national transition commission to organize and oversee the democratic process. In late July the leader of the Frente da Luta para a Libertação da Guiné, François Kankoila Mendy, returned from The Gambia after a 40-year exile. Two further opposition parties—the Partido Democrático do Progresso (PDP), led by Amine Michel Saad, and the Movimento para a Unidade e a Democracia (MUDE), led by Filinto Vaz Martins—were legalized in August. In November 1992 the Government announced the postponement of presidential and legislative elections until March 1993.

Legislation preparing for the transition to a multi-party democracy was approved by the Assembléia Nacional Popular in February 1993, and in the following month a commission was appointed to supervise the forthcoming elections. However, reports in March of a coup attempt against the Government threatened to disrupt the transition to democracy. Initial reports indicated that Maj. Robalo de Pina, commander of the Forças de Intervenção Rápida (an élite guard responsible for presidential security), had been assassinated in what appeared to be an army rebellion, provoked by disaffection at poor standards of pay and living conditions. Some 50 people were arrested, including the leader of the PRD, João da Costa. Opposition politicians claimed that the incident had been contrived by the Government in an effort to discredit the opposition. Da Costa and nine other PRD detainees were released in June pending trial, but were forbidden to engage in political activity. In May, following a further split in the FDS, a new political party, the Partido da Convenção Nacional (PCN), was formed. In July Vieira announced that multi-party presidential and legislative elections would be held in March 1994. In August 1993 da Costa was rearrested for allegedly violating the conditions of his parole, prompting renewed accusations by opposition politicians that the Government's actions were politically motivated. Following a threatened boycott of the National Electoral Commission by the opposition, da Costa was conditionally released. He was subsequently tried, but was acquitted in February 1994.

One week before the designated date of the elections, Vieira announced their postponement, owing to financial and technical difficulties. In May 1994 it was announced that the elections would be held in July. In early May six opposition parties, the FD, FDS, MUDE, PDP, PRD and the Liga Guineense de Protecção Ecológica (LIPE), formed a coalition, the União para a Mudança (UM). The elections took place on 3 July, although voting was extended for two days, owing to logistical problems. The PAIGC secured a clear majority in the Assembléia Nacional Popular, winning 62 of the 100 seats, while in the presidential election Vieira obtained 46.3% of the votes, and his nearest rival, Kumba Yalá of the PRS, secured 21.9% of the votes. As no candidate had obtained an absolute majority, the two leading candidates contested a second round of polling on 7 August. Despite receiving the combined support of all the opposition parties, Yalá was narrowly defeated, securing 48.0% of the votes, compared with Vieira's 52.0%. Yalá contested the results, accusing the PAIGC of electoral fraud and claiming that the state security police had conducted a campaign of intimidation against opposition supporters. Yalá's claims were, however, rejected, and on 20 August he accepted the results of the election, while affirming that the PRS would not participate in the new Government. International observers later declared the elections to have been free and fair. Vieira was inaugurated as President on 29 September and appointed Manuel Saturnino da Costa (the Secretary-General of the PAIGC) as Prime Minister in late October. The Council of Ministers was appointed in November, comprising solely members of the PAIGC.

In April 1995 the FD, FDS, MUDE, PDP and the PRD reconstituted the UM coalition and elected João da Costa as President and Amine Saad as Secretary-General. The LIPE, which had two representatives in the legislature and was a member of the original UM coalition, did not join the new organization, which was granted legal status in November. In August legal status was granted to a new party, the Partido Social Democrático (PSD), which was formed by dissidents from the RGB—MB.

Guinea-Bissau attained membership of the Union économique et monétaire ouest-africaine (see p. 238) in March 1997 and entered the Franc Zone in April. The national currency was replaced, over a three-month transitional period, by the franc CFA, and the Banque centrale des états de l'Afrique de l'ouest assumed the central banking functions of the Banco Central da Guiné-Bissau.

In May 1997, in order to address what Vieira described as a serious political crisis that was undermining the functioning of the State, da Costa was dismissed. Carlos Correia was subsequently appointed Prime Minister, and a new 14-member Council of Ministers was inaugurated in June. On 11 October Correia was dismissed, bringing to an end an institutional crisis that had lasted since his inauguration as Prime Minister in June. The legislative process had been obstructed by opposition deputies who claimed that, by omitting to consult those parties represented in the legislature on Correia's appointment, Vieira had acted unconstitutionally. In October the Supreme Court ruled that Vieira had indeed contravened the Constitution. Following consultations with party leaders, Vieira reappointed Correia on 13 October, with the full support of the main opposition parties.

In March 1998, following protest by opposition parties at delays in the organization of legislative elections, an independent national elections commission was established. The elections were due to be held in July. In April a new political party, the União Nacional para a Democracia e o Progresso (UNDP), led by former Minister of the Interior Abubacar Baldé, was established. In the same month Brig. Ansumane Mané, who had recently been dismissed as Chief of Staff of the Armed Forces, publicly accused the Minister of Defence and a group of officers of the armed forces of involvement in arms-trafficking to separatists from the Senegalese region of Casamance, a practice which, he maintained, was long-established and continued with the acquiescence of Vieira. Vieira was re-elected President of the PAIGC in May, while Paulo Medina was elected to the new post of Permanent Secretary; the post of Secretary-General was abolished.

In June 1998 rebel troops, led by Mané, seized control of the Bra military barracks in the capital, as well as other strategic locations in the city, including the international airport. Mané subsequently formed a 'military junta for the consolidation of democracy, peace and justice' and demanded the resignation of Vieira and his administration. With the support of Senegalese and Guinean soldiers, troops loyal to the Government attempted unsuccessfully to regain control of rebel-held areas of the city, and heavy fighting ensued. Over the following days more than 3,000 foreign nationals were evacuated from the capital to Senegal. An estimated further 200,000 residents of Bissau fled the city, prompting fears of a humanitarian disaster, with the hostilities preventing aid organizations from distributing emergency food and medical supplies to the refugees. Fighting continued into July, with many members of the Guinea-Bissau armed forces reportedly defecting to the side of the rebels.

On 26 July 1998, following mediation by a delegation from the lusophone commonwealth body, the Comunidade dos Países de Língua Portuguesa (CPLP, see below), the Government and the rebels agreed to implement a truce. On 25 August representatives of the Government and the rebels met, under the auspices of the CPLP and the Economic Community of West African States (ECOWAS, see p. 187), on Sal island, Cape Verde, where agreement was reached to transform the existing truce into a cease-fire. The accord provided for the reopening of the international airport and for the deployment of international forces to maintain and supervise the cease-fire. In September talks between the Government and the rebels resumed in Abidjan, Côte d'Ivoire. However, the rebels' demand that all Senegalese and Guinean forces be withdrawn from the country as a prerequisite to a definitive peace agreement was rejected by the Government. The rebels, in turn, rejected a proposal for the establishment by Senegal of a buffer zone within Guinea-Bissau territory along the border with Casamance. In October the rebels agreed to a government proposal for the creation of a demilitarized zone separating the opposing forces in the capital. However, before the proposal could be formally endorsed, the cease-fire collapsed, as fighting erupted in the capital and several other towns. On 20 October the Government imposed a nation-wide curfew, and on the following day Vieira declared a unilateral cease-fire. By that time almost all of the government troops had joined forces with the rebels, who were thought to control some 99% of the country. On 23 October Brig. Mané agreed to conform to a 48-hour truce to allow Vieira to clarify his proposals for a negotiated peace settlement, and agreement was subsequently reached for direct talks to be held in Banjul, The Gambia. At the talks, which took place on 29 October, the rebels confirmed that they would not seek Vieira's resignation. Further talks, held under the aegis of ECOWAS, in Abuja, Nigeria, resulted in the signing of a peace accord on 1 November. Under the terms of the accord, the two sides reaffirmed the cease-fire of 25 August, and resolved that the withdrawal of Senegalese and Guinean troops from Guinea-Bissau be conducted simultaneously with the deployment of an ECOMOG (ECOWAS Cease-fire Monitoring Group) interposition force, which would guarantee security on the border with Senegal. It was also agreed that a government of national unity would be established, to include representatives of the rebel junta, and that presidential and legislative elections would be held no later than March 1999. In November 1998 agreement was reached on the composition of a Joint Executive Commission to implement the peace accord. On 3 December Francisco José Fadul was appointed Prime Minister, and later that month Vieira and Mané reached agreement on the allocation of portfolios to the two sides.

In January 1999 Fadul announced that presidential and legislative elections would not take place in March, as envisaged in the Abuja accord, and would not be conducted until the end of the year. Also in January agreement was reached between the Government, the rebel military junta and ECOWAS on the strength of the ECOMOG interposition force, which was to comprise some 710 troops. Agreement was also reached on a timetable for the withdrawal of Senegalese and Guinean troops from the country. However, at the end of January hostilities resumed in the capital. On 9 February talks between the Government and the rebels produced agreement on a cease-fire and provided for the immediate withdrawal of Senegalese and Guinean troops. On 20 February the new Government of National Unity was announced. The disarmament of rebel troops and those loyal to the President, as provided for under the Abuja accord, began in early March. The withdrawal of Senegalese and Guinean troops was completed that month, following an extension of the deadline, from 28 February to 16 March, owing to logistical problems. In April a report was released by the Assembléia Nacional Popular exonerating Mané of charges of trafficking arms to the Casamance rebels. While the report, which had been due for release in June 1998 when hostilities began, called for the reinstatement of Mané as Chief of Staff of the Armed Forces, it revealed that Vieira's presidential guard had been heavily implicated in the arms-trafficking.

In early May 1999 Vieira announced that presidential and legislative elections would take place on 28 December. However, on 7 May, to widespread condemnation by the international community, Vieira was overthrown by the rebel military junta. Fighting had erupted in Bissau on the previous day when rebel troops seized stockpiles of weapons that had been at Bissau airport since the disarmament of the rival forces in March. The rebels, who claimed that their actions had been prompted by Vieira's refusal to allow his presidential guard to be disarmed, surrounded the presidential palace and forced its surrender. Vieira subsequently took refuge at the Portuguese embassy, where on 10 May he signed an unconditional surrender. The President of the Assembléia Nacional Popular, Malam Bacai Sanhá, was appointed acting President of the Republic pending a presidential election. The Government of National Unity remained in office. At a meeting of the ruling bodies of the PAIGC that month, Vieira was replaced as party President in an interim capacity by Manuel Saturnino da Costa. At a meeting in late May of representatives of the Government, the military junta and the political parties, agreement was reached that Vieira should stand trial for his involvement in arms-trafficking to the Casamance separatists and for political and economic crimes relating to his terms in office. Vieira agreed to stand trial, but only after receiving medical treatment abroad, after which, he pledged, he would return to Guinea-Bissau. At a meeting of ECOWAS foreign ministers held in Togo that month Vieira's overthrow was condemned, and demands were made for him to be permitted to leave Guinea-Bissau. It was also decided that ECOMOG forces would be withdrawn from the country, and the last troops left in early June. That month Vieira went into exile in Portugal where he was offered political asylum. Also in June Sanhá announced that presidential and legislative elections would take place by 28 November. In July constitutional amendments were introduced limiting the tenure of presidential office to two terms and abolishing the death penalty. It was also stipulated that the country's principal offices of state could only be held by Guinea-Bissau nationals born of Guinea-Bissau parents.

In September 1999 an extraordinary congress of the PAIGC voted to expel Vieira from the party. Also expelled were the former Prime Minister Carlos Correia and five ministers from his administration, while the incumbent Minister of Defence and Freedom Fighters, Francisco Benante, was appointed President of the party. In October a mass grave was discovered containing the bodies of 22 people thought to have been executed during the Vieira regime. An earlier such discovery, of 14 bodies, had been made in the previous month. Later in October the Attorney-General, Amine Michel Saad, announced that he had sufficient evidence to prosecute Vieira for crimes against humanity and expressed his intention to seek Vieira's extradition from Portugal.

Presidential and legislative elections took place on 28 November 1999, with voting extended for a further day owing to logistical problems. Of the 102 seats in the enlarged legislature, the PRS secured 38, the RGB—MB 28, the PAIGC 24, Aliança Democrática (AD, an alliance of the FD and the PCD) four, the

UM three, the PSD three, and the FDS and the UNDP one each. As no candidate received the necessary 50% of the votes to win the presidential election outright, the leading candidates, Kumba Yalá of the PRS and Malam Bacai Sanhá of the PAIGC, contested a second round of voting on 16 January 2000, at which Yalá secured victory with 72% of the votes cast. Yalá assumed power on 17 February and installed a new Council of Ministers, which included members of several former opposition parties, later that month. Caetano N'Tchama of the PRS was appointed Prime Minister. The election was subsequently judged by international observers to have been 'free and fair'. In April Fernando Correia was appointed Minister of Defence to replace Lt-Col Veríssimo Correia Seabra. In May it was reported that tensions were increasing between Yalá and certain elements in the army, who viewed Gen. Ansumane Mané as the rightful leader of the country, on the grounds that it was he who had ousted Vieira from power. The refusal of Lamine Sanhá, the commander of the national navy, to resign, following his dismissal by Yalá (Sanhá had allegedly received bribes in return for the release of a Korean fishing boat that had entered Guinea-Bissau's waters illegally) further exacerbated tensions. However, Sanhá subsequently agreed to stand down, following an agreement by Yalá to co-operate and communicate further with the military. Also in that month a new political party, the Aliança Socialista da Guiné-Bissau (ASG) was formed, under the leadership of the former President of the national Human Rights League, Fernando Gomes.

In September 2000 four government ministers (all members of the RGB—MB) were dismissed by N'Tchama, apparently as a result of a disagreement with the PRS over the terms of the coalition agreement. However, later that month, following negotiations between the two parties, the ministers were reinstated in order to prevent a crisis within the coalition, as no party was able to command a majority. In October Yalá appointed a State Council, comprising members of all parliamentary political parties, which was to have an advisory role.

Demonstrations organized by the PAIGC, in support of demands for the resignation of the coalition Government, took place in Bissau in November 2000. In late November Mané declared himself Commander-in-Chief of the armed forces, following renewed violence in Bissau, instigated by soldiers loyal to Mané. However, government troops quickly suppressed the insurgency, and a number of opposition leaders were arrested. Mané fled the capital, and was subsequently shot dead by the security forces. Trials of those involved commenced in May 2002.

In January 2001 the Minister for Education, Science and Technology, João José Silva Monteiro, and the Minister for War Veterans, Iancuba Indjai, were dismissed. A minor government reshuffle later that month was prompted by the resignation, in protest at the earlier dismissals, of a number of RGB—MB ministers, who claimed that they had not been consulted by N'Tchama, in violation of the coalition agreement. The RGB—MB subsequently withdrew from the coalition Government (formed with the PRS) as a gesture of solidarity with the ministers. In mid-March Yalá dismissed N'Tchama in an attempt to increase stability in the minority Government; the former Deputy Prime Minister and Minister of Foreign Affairs, Faustino Fudut Imbali, was appointed in his place and subsequently formed a new broad-based Government, which included a number of members of opposition parties (despite the appointments not being endorsed by the respective political parties). None the less, despite opposition from many of its members, the PAIGC agreed to support the new minority Government. In response, opposition parties established the United Opposition Platform and proposed a motion of 'no confidence' in the Government in early April; however the vote was suspended for two weeks, to allow Imbali to form a new Government, more agreeable to the opposition. In May the Government's programme was accepted by the Assembléia Nacional Popular, with the support of the PAIGC. Nevertheless, in August renewed calls for the Government's resignation were prompted by revelations that an estimated US $15m. in state funds had inexplicably disappeared (see Economic Affairs). Later that month the Minister of Internal Administration, António Artur Sanhá, was dismissed following his involvement in a personal scandal that had led to a number of demonstrations in the capital, Bissau. Sanhá was replaced by Almara Nhassé, hitherto Minister of Agriculture and Forestry.

In September 2001 Yalá was accused of acting unconstitutionally in replacing three Supreme Court judges with justices who had been dismissed by President Vieira in 1993. Later in September a strike was staged by judges in protest at Yalá's actions. Meanwhile, Yalá's decision, in August, to expel the leaders of an Islamic group, Ahmadiyya, from the country, on the grounds that the movement was threatening Guinea-Bissau's political stability, was subsequently overturned by a court. In October rumours of a military *coup d'état* were denied by the Government and by the Chief of Staff of the Armed Forces, Brig.-Gen. Verissimo Seabra. Later that month, however, a motion of 'no confidence' in Yalá was approved by the Assembléia Nacional Popular; the vote had been instigated by opposition parties in response to what they considered to be increasingly unconstitutional actions by the President. Yalá then threatened to suspend the Assembléia for a 10-year period. At the same time, former Prime Minister Fadul established a new political party, the Partido para a Democracia e a Cidadania, which he hoped would assist in decentralizing power in Guinea-Bissau. In late November, following her dismissal from office by Yalá, the former Minister of Foreign Affairs, Antonieta Rosa Gomes, accused the President of fostering political instability. A demonstration against Yalá in Bissau, attended by some 10,000 people, followed further demands for the President's resignation by a coalition of 10 opposition parties.

In early December 2001 the Government stated that it had prevented a military *coup d'état*, and arrested the Deputy Chief of Staff of the Armed Forces and a former navy head. The Government alleged that those involved had intended to kill a number of military officers and civilians, including the President and the Chief of Staff of the Armed Forces; the opposition-dominated Assembléia Nacional Popular contested this, however, demanding that evidence be produced. Yalá subsequently dismissed Prime Minister Imbali, citing a lack of transparency in government and failure to address the country's social and economic difficulties. Imbali was replaced by Almara Nhassé, a member of the PRS and hitherto Minister of Internal Administration. Nhassé immediately formed a new Government, composed solely of members of the ruling coalition, and pledged to develop the agricultural, energy, tourism and social sectors. Later that month Nhassé was elected President of the PRS, in place of Yalá.

In early February 2002 the leader of the opposition ASG, Fernando Gomes, was arrested, following accusations that he had misappropriated some US $44,000 in donations during his time as President of the national Human Rights League. The current Vice-President of the League was also apprehended. The arrests were criticized by the ASG, as well as by the human rights organization Amnesty International, on the grounds that they were politically motivated. Gomes was released later that month, while the Human Rights League dismissed its current President and Vice-President in late March for their alleged involvement in the embezzlement scandal. Meanwhile, in early March Yalá replaced the late Mario Lopes with António Man as President of the Supreme Court in an action deemed unconstitutional by opposition parties, as the appointment should have been made internally. In mid-April a new party, the Partido de Solidariedade e Trabalho, was established, led by Iancuba Indjai, the former President of the UM. A minor government reshuffle followed in late April, and in late May the Minister of Internal Administration, Marcelino Cabral, was dismissed and replaced by Rui Sanhá. Also in May, former Prime Minister Imbali was accused by Yalá of involvement in the embezzlement of €2.2m. of public funds while in office; he was detained for questioning in July, but later released at Yalá's request.

In May 2002 Yalá announced that some 24 people had been arrested following an attempted coup. The President threatened to invade The Gambia, which he accused of having supported the leaders of the unsuccessful coup, prompting a diplomatic crisis (see below). In mid-June Yalá declared an amnesty for those involved in the alleged coups of December 2001 and May 2002. At the RGB—MB conference in July, Helder Vaz was elected President of the party, despite internal splits and the conference being declared illegal by the Ministry of Internal Administration. Meanwhile, after filing a case against Nhassé for abuse of power, the Attorney General, Caetano N'Tchama, was dismissed in mid-August; the President and Deputy President of the Supreme Court were also arrested, in connection with the misappropriation of funds. Artur Sanhá, then Minister of Fisheries and the Sea, rejected the post of Supreme Court President and was dismissed from his ministerial position. Yalá's actions were subsequently deemed unconstitutional and also provoked conflict with Nhassé, who claimed not to have been consulted over Sanhá's dismissal. Tensions were relieved

somewhat by a meeting between the President and Prime Minister in late August.

During September 2002 Yalá dismissed Rui Sanhá as Minister of Internal Administration; he was replaced in mid-October by António Man, erstwhile President of the Supreme Court. At the end of September Mandinga, the leader of the PCD, reported an assassination attempt, following his criticism of the Government; the Government denied such an attempt had occurred. In October the RGB—MB held a congress in Bissau, despite its prohibition by the Ministry of Internal Administration, which resulted in the imposition of a travel ban on the party. The developing political uncertainty in the country intensified in mid-November, when Yalá dissolved the Assembléia Nacional Popular and dismissed the Government, citing its incompetence in coping with the economic crisis. Legislative elections were scheduled initially for February 2003, although later delayed. Mario Pires was appointed as Prime Minister, to head a transitional Government, which was dominated by the PRS. In early December 2002 a student protest in Bissau in support of state teachers, who had closed all public schools since the beginning of the academic year in October demanding the payment of salary arrears and bonuses, was dispersed by the security forces.

Further government changes were effected in December 2002 and January 2003: Augusto Ussumane So replaced Rui Duarte de Barros as Minister of the Economy and Finance, and Filomena Tipote was replaced as Minister for Public Administration and Labour by Yalá's political advisor, Tibna Sambé Na Wana. During February five members of the PAIGC, including former Prime Minister Carlos Correia, were arrested without charge, provoking opposition outrage; they were subsequently released at Yalá's request. Meanwhile, the closure of the private radio station Rádio Bombolom and of the local offices of the Portuguese station Radiodifusão Portuguesa/Africa (RTP/Africa), and the dismissal of the news editor of the state-run Radiodifusão Nacional, aroused concerns regarding the freedom of the media prior to the elections. Several political coalitions opposing the PRS were formed in late 2002 and early 2003 in preparation for the legislative elections, which had been postponed until 20 April. In December 2002 the PSD, the LIPE, the Partido da Renovação e Progresso and the Partido Socialista Guineense created the União Eleitoral. In February 2003 the Plataforma Unida 'Mufunesa Larga Guiné' was formed by the AD (comprising the FD and the PCD), the FDS, the Frente da Luta para a Libertação da Guiné and the Grupo de Democratas Independentes, which had been established by Vaz and other former members of the RGB—MB, following a court decision to award the leadership of that party to Salvador Tchongo. In March Fadul returned to the country after a two-year exile to lead the PUSD. In late March Yalá announced that the elections were to be further delayed, until 6 July. In mid-April Man was dismissed as Minister of Internal Administration. This was followed in early May by the dismissal and unexplained arrest of the Minister of Defence, Marcelino Cabral, and the Minister of the Presidency of the Council of Ministers, José de Piña. Cabral was replaced by Tipote, although tension arose when military chiefs failed to attend her inauguration.

Relations with Portugal deteriorated in October 1987, when six Portuguese vessels were seized for alleged illegal fishing in Guinea-Bissau's territorial waters. Portugal retaliated by suspending non-medical aid, but revoked its decision in November, after the vessels were released. A few days later, however, the head of security at the embassy of Guinea-Bissau in Lisbon requested political asylum and disclosed the presence of explosive devices in the embassy, allegedly intended for use against members of the RGB—MB (see above). These allegations were vehemently denied by the Government of Guinea-Bissau. A visit by the Portuguese Prime Minister, Aníbal Cavaco Silva, in 1989 signified an improvement in relations between the two countries. In July 1996 Vieira made an official visit to Portugal, during which agreement was reached on improved bilateral relations. In the same month Guinea-Bissau was among the five lusophone African nations which, along with Brazil and Portugal, officially established the CPLP, a lusophone grouping intended to benefit each member state by means of joint co-operation in technical, cultural and social matters. In March 2003 relations deteriorated following the closure of RTP/Africa's offices in Guinea-Bissau (see above).

In 1989 a dispute arose between Guinea-Bissau and Senegal over the demarcation of maritime borders. Guinea-Bissau began proceedings against Senegal in the International Court of Justice (ICJ) after rejecting an international arbitration tribunal's ruling in favour of Senegal. Guinea-Bissau requested direct negotiations with Senegal, and enlisted the aid of President Mubarak of Egypt, then the President of the Organization of African Unity (now the African Union), and President Soares of Portugal as mediators. Guinea-Bissau and Senegal came close to armed conflict in May 1990, following a Senegalese military incursion into Guinea-Bissau territory. In November 1991 the ICJ ruled that a 1960 agreement regarding the demarcation of maritime borders between Guinea-Bissau and Senegal remained valid. In December 1992, in retaliation for the deaths of two Senegalese soldiers at the hands of Casamance separatists, the Senegalese air force and infantry bombarded alleged Casamance separatist bases in the São Domingos area of Guinea-Bissau. In response, the Government of Guinea-Bissau protested to the Senegalese authorities against the violation of Guinea-Bissau's borders and air space and denied Senegalese claims that it was providing support for the rebels. The Senegalese Government offered assurances that there would be no repetition of the incident. In March, in an apparent attempt to convince Senegal that it did not support the rebels, the Government handed over Abbé Augustin Diamacouné Senghor, one of the exiled leaders of the Casamance separatists, to the Senegalese authorities. In October 1993 the Presidents of Guinea-Bissau and Senegal signed an agreement in Dakar, providing for the joint management and exploitation of the countries' maritime zones. Petroleum resources were to be divided, with Senegal receiving an 85% share and Guinea-Bissau the remaining 15%. Fishing resources were to be divided according to the determination of a joint management agency. The agreement was renewable after a period of 20 years. In December 1995 the legislature authorized the ratification of the October 1993 accord. In the previous month the ICJ announced that Guinea-Bissau had halted all proceedings regarding the border dispute with Senegal.

In February 1995 the Senegalese air force bombarded a village in Guinea-Bissau, close to the border with Senegal. Despite an acknowledgement by the Senegalese authorities that the bombing had occurred as a result of an error, the Senegalese armed forces conducted a similar attack later in the same month. In March, in an attempt to achieve a *rapprochement*, President Abdou Diouf of Senegal visited Guinea-Bissau to provide a personal apology for the two recent incidents and to offer a commitment that Senegal would respect Guinea-Bissau's sovereignty. In September, following a meeting at Gabú, in Guinea-Bissau, between representatives of both Governments, agreement was reached on strengthening co-operation and establishing regular dialogue concerning security on the countries' joint border. However, a further attack by the Senegalese air force in October prompted the Guinea-Bissau legislature to form a commission of inquiry to investigate such border incidents. In November Prime Minister da Costa paid a three-day visit to Senegal, aimed at strengthening co-operation between the two countries. In June 1996 a meeting held at Kolda, in Senegal, between ministerial delegations from Guinea-Bissau and Senegal resulted in renewed commitments to improved collaboration on security.

In April 2000 there were renewed reports of incidents on the border between Senegal and Guinea-Bissau, in which five people were alleged to have been killed; however, the Senegalese Government denied accusations that its troops had entered Guinea-Bissau, and in May requested assistance from Guinea-Bissau to resolve the Casamance conflict. Also in that month, calls by the Senegalese President, Abdoulaye Wade, for the presence of UN military observers along the border between the two countries, were rejected by Yalá. However, in July Yalá agreed to provide assistance to Senegal, in the hope of finding a rapid solution to the separatist conflict in that country. On 5 August an agreement was signed by Yalá and Wade ordering the immediate reopening of the border between the two countries; moreover, the agreement provided for the establishment of a joint military force to patrol the border area. It was also agreed that a joint commission would be set up to 'identify and return' cattle and other goods allegedly stolen by Guinea-Bissau citizens in the area. In July 2001 Senegal and Guinea-Bissau issued a joint statement reaffirming their commitment to the agreement reached in August of the previous year. In March 2002 Alexandre Djibas, the leader of a Casamance rebel faction, was arrested and deported to Senegal, following assurances that he would be released. Also during March, 124 Senegalese fishermen were arrested for fishing in Guinea-Bissau's territorial waters. Improved security arrangements along the Casamance border were confirmed at a meeting in July, following a decline in border incidents.

Relations between Guinea-Bissau and The Gambia were severely strained in June 2002, when President Yalá accused the Government of The Gambia of harbouring and training Casamance rebels and former associates of Gen. Mané, the leader of the coup of 1998 and attempted coup of 2000. With specific reference to the alleged attempted coup of May 2002, Yalá threatened invasion of The Gambia if support for the rebels continued; President Jammeh of The Gambia denied any such support was being provided. A visit to The Gambia by Guinea-Bissau's then Minister of Foreign Affairs, Filomena Tipote, in mid-June eased tensions somewhat, and was followed by UN intervention in July, which recommended the reactivation of a joint commision of the two countries. An improvement in relations was signalled by a visit by Yalá to The Gambia in September.

Following the rebel uprising against President Laurent Gbagbo of Côte d'Ivoire in September 2002, Guinea-Bissau committed troops to an ECOWAS peace-keeping force to monitor the cease-fire signed in October.

Government

Under the terms of the 1984 Constitution (revised in 1991, 1996 and 1999), Guinea-Bissau is a multi-party state, although the formation of parties on a tribal or geographical basis is prohibited. Legislative power is vested in the Assembléia Nacional Popular, which comprises 102 members, elected by universal adult suffrage for a term of four years. Following the dissolution of the Assembléia Nacional Popular by President Yalá in November 2002, legislative elections were scheduled for 6 July 2003. Executive power is vested in the President of the Republic, who is Head of State and who governs with the assistance of an appointed Council of Ministers, led by the Prime Minister. The President is elected by universal adult suffrage for a term of five years.

Defence

In August 2002 the armed forces officially totalled an estimated 9,250 men (army 6,800, navy 350, air force 100 and paramilitary gendarmerie 2,000). However, unofficial numbers were believed to be much higher, as forces were swollen by veterans and civilian volunteers following the rebellion that removed President Vieira in 1999. During July and August 2002 a project to demobilize some 4,000 men was overseen by Portugal. Expenditure on defence in 2001 was budgeted at an estimated US $3m.

Economic Affairs

In 2001, according to estimates by the World Bank, Guinea-Bissau's gross national income (GNI), measured at average 1999–2001 prices, was US $202m., equivalent to $160 per head (or $710 on an international purchasing-power parity basis). During 1990–2001, it was estimated, the population increased at an average annual rate of 2.4% per year, while gross domestic product (GDP) per head decreased, in real terms, by an average of 1.0% per year. Overall GDP increased, in real terms, at an average annual rate of 1.4% in 1990–2001; growth in 2001 was 0.2%.

Agriculture (including forestry and fishing) contributed an estimated 56.1% of GDP in 2001, according to preliminary figures, and employed an estimated 82.5% of the labour force in that year. The main cash crops are cashew nuts (which contributed 95.6% of total export earnings in 2001) and cotton. Other crops produced include rice, roots and tubers, groundnuts, maize, millet and sorghum. Livestock and timber production are also important. The fishing industry developed rapidly during the 1990s, and earnings from fishing exports and the sale of fishing licences are a significant source of government revenue (revenue from fishing licences was 7,430m. francs CFA in 2001, equivalent to 26.0% of total revenue). According to the World Bank, agricultural GDP increased, in real terms, by an average of 3.3% per year in 1990–2001; growth in 2001 was 1.4%.

Industry (including mining, manufacturing, construction and power) employed an estimated 4.1% of the economically active population at mid-1994 and provided an estimated 12.7% of GDP in 2001, according to preliminary figures. According to the World Bank, industrial GDP decreased, in real terms, by an average of 1.9% per year in 1990–2001; however, growth of 5.0% was recorded in 2001.

The mining sector is underdeveloped, although Guinea-Bissau possesses reserves of bauxite, phosphates, diamonds and gold. Drilling of three offshore petroleum wells began in

November 1989. A Canadian company was scheduled to commence production of phosphate rock at Farim, in the north of the country, in 2003.

The sole branches of the manufacturing sector are food-processing, brewing and timber- and cotton-processing, while there are plans to develop fish-processing. Manufacturing, mining and power contributed an estimated 10.3% of GDP in 2001, according to preliminary figures. According to the World Bank, manufacturing GDP decreased, in real terms, by an average of 1.9% per year in 1990–2001; however, growth of 8.3% was recorded in 2001.

Energy is derived principally from thermal and hydroelectric power. Imports of petroleum and petroleum products comprised 6.2% of the value of total imports in 2001. Energy production since 1999 has been insufficient to supply demand in Bissau, mainly owing to fuel shortages caused by government-set low prices, and to equipment failures caused by poor maintenance. As a result, most energy is currently supplied by private generators.

Services employed an estimated 19.4% of the economically active population at mid-1994 and provided an estimated 31.2% of GDP in 2001, according to preliminary figures. According to the World Bank, the combined GDP of the service sectors increased, in real terms, at an average rate of 1.1% per year in 1990–2001; growth in 2001 was 9.3%.

In 2001 Guinea-Bissau recorded a trade deficit of US $32.6m., and there was a deficit of $37.8m. on the current account of the balance of payments. In 2001 the principal source of imports was Portugal (29.9%); other major suppliers were Senegal and the People's Republic of China. In that year India was the principal market for exports (85.6%). The principal export in 2001 was cashew nuts. The principal imports in that year were food and live animals, transport equipment, electrical equipment and machinery, and passenger vehicles.

In 2001 there was an estimated budgetary deficit of 14,600m. francs CFA, equivalent to 10.0% of GDP. Guinea-Bissau's total external debt was US $941.5m. at the end of 2000, of which $818.3m. was long-term public debt. In that year the cost of debt-servicing was equivalent to 8.6% of the total value of exports of goods and services. In 1990–2001 the average annual rate of inflation was 29.8%. Consumer prices increased by an average of 3.4% in 2001.

Guinea-Bissau is a member of the Economic Community of West African States (ECOWAS, see p. 187) and of the West African organs of the Franc Zone (see p. 238).

Guinea-Bissau is one of the world's poorest countries. Its economy is largely dependent on the traditional rural sector, which employs the vast majority of the labour force and produces primarily for subsistence. Since the late 1980s Guinea-Bissau has evolved from a rigidly controlled command economy into a largely free-market economy. The economy remains very dependent on foreign financing, which accounts for a significant part of budget revenue. The economy was seriously threatened by the military uprising of June 1998. The extensive destruction of public buildings and private business premises imposed a heavy burden on the country's underdeveloped infrastructure, necessitating appeals for humanitarian aid. Following the overthrow of President Vieira in May 1999, the Government urged the international community to continue with economic aid. In December 2000 the IMF and the World Bank's International Development Association awarded some US $790m. in debt-service relief as part of the enhanced Heavily Indebted Poor Countries initiative. Moreover, a three-year Poverty Reduction and Growth Facility, worth some $18m., was awarded by the IMF in support of the Government's 2000–03 programme of economic reform. The programme's principal objectives included improved access to social services and education, greater fiscal transparency, a decrease in the rate of inflation, the demobilization of the military and the reform of the civil service. However, in May 2001, as the Government appeared to be struggling to achieve its objectives, the IMF and the World Bank indicated their intention to suspend the aid programme for a period of four months, pending an investigation into the disappearance of $15m. in donor assistance, which the Government was unable to explain. Although Guinea-Bissau was still able to resort to bilateral aid, the suspension represented a significant set-back, as 80% of the 2001 budget was to be financed by foreign aid. The results of the investigation, published in November, indicated the presence of non-justifiable government expenditure, valued at some 10,500m. francs CFA. Meanwhile, a programme of privatization, which had been interrupted by the military conflict, resumed in May. With support from the World Bank, more than 24 public and parastatal companies in the sectors of telecommunications, tourism, fishing, and port and airport management were to be divested by 2006. An IMF/World Bank mission in November 2001, at the end of a three-month short-term macreconomic programme, found some signs of economic improvement, but a final assessment, in March 2002, indicated that the Government had failed to meet fiscal targets. Furthermore, the 2002 budget was not approved until July of that year, with government spending hitherto effected by decree. A decision to increase public-sector wages from September 2002 was criticized by the IMF, despite the Government's earlier commitment, in June, to cut 3,000 civil service jobs. The banking sector had been seriously threatened by the political upheavals since 1998, and during early 2002 several banks in Guinea-Bissau ceased operations.

Education

Education is officially compulsory only for the period of primary schooling, which begins at seven years of age and lasts for six years. Secondary education, beginning at the age of 13, lasts for up to five years (a first cycle of three years and a second of two years). In 1988 the total enrolment at primary and secondary schools was equivalent to 38% of the school-age population (males 49%; females 27%). In 1999/2000 enrolment at primary schools included 53.6% of children in the relevant age-group (males 62.6%; females 44.5%). In that year enrolment at secondary schools was equivalent to 20.4% of children in the relevant age-group (males 26.4%; females 14.4%). Expenditure on education by the central Government in 1989 was 5,051m. pesos (2.7% of total spending). In 1997 the International Development Association approved a credit of US $14.3m. for a project to expand and upgrade the education system. In January 1991 President Vieira announced plans for the establishment of the country's first university, which was due to open in Bissau in October 2003. Some 200 students completed their studies in Havana, Cuba, in 2002, while a further 186 had scholarships to study in Paris, France, and Dakar, Senegal.

Public Holidays

2003: 1 January (New Year), 20 January (Death of Amílcar Cabral), 12 February* (Tabaski, Feast of the Sacrifice), 8 March (International Women's Day), 1 May (Labour Day), 3 August (Anniversary of the Killing of Pidjiguiti), 24 September (National Day), 14 November (Anniversary of the Movement of Readjustment), 26 November* (Korité, end of Ramadan), 25 December (Christmas Day).

2004: 1 January (New Year), 20 January (Death of Amílcar Cabral), 2 February* (Tabaski, Feast of the Sacrifice), 8 March (International Women's Day), 3 May (for Labour Day), 3 August (Anniversary of the Killing of Pidjiguiti), 24 September (National Day), 14 November* (Korité, end of Ramadan, and Anniversary of the Movement of Readjustment), 25 December (Christmas Day).

*Religious holidays, which are dependent on the Islamic lunar calendar, may differ by one or two days from the dates shown.

Weights and Measures

The metric system is used.

Statistical Survey

Area and Population

AREA, POPULATION AND DENSITY

Area (sq km)	36,125*
Population (census results)	
16–30 April 1979.	753,313
1 December 1991	
Males	476,210
Females.	507,157
Total	983,367
Population (UN estimates at mid-year)†	
1998	1,149,000
1999	1,173,000
2000	1,190,000
Density (per sq km) at mid-2000	32.9

* 13,948 sq miles.

† Source: UN, *World Population Prospects: The 2000 Revision.*

ETHNIC GROUPS

1996 (percentages): Balanta 30; Fulani 20; Mandjak 14; Mandinka 12; Papel 7; Other 16 (Source: CPLP).

POPULATION BY REGION
(1991 census)

Bafatá. . . .	143,377	Gabú	134,971
Biombo . . .	60,420	Oio	156,084
Bissau . . .	197,610	Quinara . . .	44,793
Bolama/Bijagos . .	26,691	Tombali . . .	72,441
Cacheu . . .	146,980	**Total** . . .	983,367

PRINCIPAL TOWNS
(population at 1979 census)

Bissau (capital) . .	109,214		
Bafatá	13,429	Catió	5,170
Gabú*	7,803	Cantchungo† . .	4,965
Mansôa . . .	5,390	Farim	4,468

* Formerly Nova Lamego.

† Formerly Teixeira Pinto.

Mid-2001 (UN estimate, including suburbs): Bissau 292,000 (Source: UN, *World Urbanization Prospects: The 2001 Revision*).

BIRTHS AND DEATHS

	1998	1999	2000
Birth rate (per 1,000) . .	44.8	44.7	44.7
Death rate (per 1,000) . . .	20.2	20.0	19.7

Source: African Development Bank.

Expectation of life (WHO estimates, years at birth, 2001): 59.3 (males 45.9; females 48.7) in 2001 (Source: WHO, *World Health Report*).

ECONOMICALLY ACTIVE POPULATION
('000 persons at mid-1994)

	Males	Females	Total
Agriculture, etc.	195	175	370
Industry	15	5	20
Services	80	14	94
Total	290	194	484

Source: UN Economic Commission for Africa, *African Statistical Yearbook.*

Mid-2001 (estimates in '000): Agriculture, etc. 462; Total labour force 560 (Source: FAO).

Health and Welfare

KEY INDICATORS

Total fertility rate (children per woman, 2001)	6.0
Under-5 mortality rate (per 1,000 live births, 2001) . .	211
HIV/AIDS (% of persons aged 15–49, 2001).	2.81
Physicians (per 1,000 head, 1996)	0.17
Hospital beds (per 1,000 head, 1990)	1.48
Health expenditure (2000): US $ per head (PPP) . . .	28
Health expenditure (2000): % of GDP	3.9
Health expenditure (2000): public (% of total) . . .	65.4
Access to water (% of persons, 2000).	49
Access to sanitation (% of persons, 2000)	47
Human Development Index (2000): ranking	167
Human Development Index (2000): value	0.349

For sources and definitions, see explanatory note on p. vi.

Agriculture

PRINCIPAL CROPS
('000 metric tons)

	1999	2000	2001
Rice (paddy)	80	104†	100*
Maize	27	26	26*
Millet	12	21†	21*
Sorghum	15	11	15*
Cassava*	32	32	34
Other roots and tubers* . . .	65	65	65
Sugar cane*	6	6	6
Cashew nuts	73	80*	80*
Groundnuts (in shell)* . . .	19	19	19
Coconuts*	46	46	46
Oil palm fruit*	80	80	80
Vegetables*	25	25	25
Plantains*.	38	38	38
Oranges*	5	5	5
Other fruits*	30.5	30.5	30.5

* FAO estimate(s).

† Unofficial figure.

Source: FAO.

LIVESTOCK
(FAO estimates, '000 head, year ending September)

	1999	2000	2001
Cattle	530	530	515
Pigs	345	345	350
Sheep	285	285	285
Goats	325	325	325

Source: FAO.

LIVESTOCK PRODUCTS
(FAO estimates, '000 metric tons)

	1999	2000	2001
Beef and veal	4.4	4.5	4.5
Pig meat	10.6	10.6	10.8
Cows' milk	13.3	13.3	13.3
Goats' milk	2.9	2.9	2.9

Source: FAO.

Forestry

ROUNDWOOD REMOVALS
('000 cubic metres, excluding bark)

	1997	1998	1999
Sawlogs, veneer logs and logs for sleepers*	40	40	40
Other industrial wood	124	127	130
Fuel wood†	422	422	422
Total	586	589	592

* Assumed to be unchanged since 1971.
† Assumed to be unchanged since 1979.

2000–2001: Production as in 1999 (FAO estimates).

Source: FAO.

SAWNWOOD PRODUCTION
('000 cubic metres, including railway sleepers)

	1997	1998	1999
Total*	16	16	16

* Assumed to be unchanged since 1971.

2000–2001: Production as in 1999 (FAO estimate).

Source: FAO.

Fishing

(FAO estimates, metric tons, live weight)

	1997	1998	1999
Freshwater fishes	250	200	200
Meagre	500	430	350
Croakers and drums	1,040	850	650
Mullets	3,200	2,650	2,200
Natantian decapods	1,100	900	800
Total catch (incl. others)	7,250	6,000	5,000

2000: figures assumed to be unchanged from 1999.

Source: FAO, *Yearbook of Fishery Statistics*.

Industry

SELECTED PRODUCTS
('000 metric tons, unless otherwise indicated)

	1999	2000	2001*
Hulled rice	62.7	65.8	69.1
Groundnuts (processed)	6.2	6.5	6.8
Bakery products	6.3	6.9	7.6
Frozen fish	1.5	1.6	1.7
Dry and smoked fish	3.3	3.5	3.6
Vegetable oils (million litres)	3.2	3.4	3.6
Beverages (million litres)	3.1	3.3	3.5
Distilled liquor (million litres)	1.0	1.1	1.1
Dairy products (million litres)	1.0	1.1	1.1
Wood products	4.2	4.4	4.7
Soap	2.4	2.5	2.6
Electric energy (million kWh)	15.5	20.8	20.0

* Preliminary.

Source: IMF, *Guinea-Bissau: Statistical Appendix* (July 2002).

Finance

CURRENCY AND EXCHANGE RATES

Monetary Units
100 centimes = 1 franc de la Communauté financière africaine (CFA)

Sterling, Dollar and Euro Equivalents (31 December 2002)
£1 sterling = 1,008.17 francs CFA
US $1 = 625.50 francs CFA
€1 = 655.96 francs CFA
10,000 francs CFA = £9.919 = $15.987 = €15.245

Average Exchange Rate (francs CFA per US $)
2000   731.35
2001   735.12
2002   644.35

Note: An exchange rate of 1 French franc = 50 francs CFA, established in 1948, remained in force until January 1994, when the CFA franc was devalued by 50%, with the exchange rate adjusted to 1 French franc = 100 francs CFA. This relationship to French currency remained in effect with the introduction of the euro on 1 January 1999. From that date, accordingly, a fixed exchange rate of €1 = 655.957 francs CFA has been in operation. Following Guinea-Bissau's admission in March 1997 to the Union économique et monétaire ouest-africaine, the country entered the Franc Zone on 17 April. As a result, the Guinea peso was replaced by the CFA franc, although the peso remained legal tender until 31 July. The new currency was introduced at an exchange rate of 1 franc CFA = 65 Guinea pesos. At 31 March 1997 the exchange rate in relation to US currency was $1 = 36,793.3 Guinea pesos.

BUDGET
(million francs CFA)

Revenue*	1999	2000	2001
Tax revenue	12,820	17,543	14,724
Income taxes	1,796	3,132	2,731
Business profits	687	1,739	1,325
Individuals	1,102	1,383	1,379
Consumption taxes	1,292	1,439	1,453
General sales tax	2,367	3,959	3,487
Taxes on international trade and transactions	7,018	8,304	6,467
Import duties	2,444	3,702	2,409
Export duties	3,248	4,166	3,807
Port service charges	1,326	436	251
Non-tax revenue	11,070	11,976	13,806
Entrepreneurial and property income	336	395	1,949
Fees and duties	8,661	8,336	7,885
Fishing licences	8,404	7,625	7,430
Total	23,890	29,519	28,530

Expenditure	1999	2000	2001
Current expenditure	28,488	51,800	41,513
Wages and salaries	6,918	10,499	11,270
Goods and services	8,000	10,865	6,675
Transfers	4,769	5,268	6,844
Scheduled external interest payments	8,800	8,800	12,226
Capital expenditure	14,900	15,807	21,648
Total	43,388	67,607	63,162

* Excluding grants received ('000 million francs CFA): 6.0 in 1999; 21.7 in 2000; 19.0 in 2001.

Source: IMF, *Guinea-Bissau: Statistical Appendix* (July 2002).

CENTRAL BANK RESERVES
(US $ million at 31 December)

	2000	2001	2002
IMF special drawing rights	0.04	0.20	0.40
Foreign exchange	66.69	69.28	102.31
Total	66.73	69.47	102.71

Source: IMF, *International Financial Statistics*.

MONEY SUPPLY
(million francs CFA at 31 December)

	2000	2001	2002
Currency outside banks . . .	44,245	53,054	70,223
Demand deposits at deposit money banks	19,985	16,261	14,623
Total money (incl. others) . . .	64,524	69,535	85,074

Source: IMF, *International Financial Statistics*.

COST OF LIVING
(Consumer Price Index; base: 1995 = 100)

	1999	2000	2001
Food, beverages and tobacco . .	237.7	258.2	266.9

Source: IMF, *International Financial Statistics*.

NATIONAL ACCOUNTS

Expenditure on the Gross Domestic Product
(US $ million at current prices)

	1998	1999	2000
Government final consumption expenditure	19.15	24.20	30.06
Private final consumption expenditure	204.02	202.65	204.31
Increase in stocks . . . }	26.50	37.83	38.14
Gross fixed capital formation . }			
Total domestic expenditure .	249.67	264.68	272.51
Exports of goods and services .	29.82	55.75	68.44
Less Imports of goods and services	73.94	96.06	125.48
GDP in purchasers' values .	205.56	224.36	215.47

Source: African Development Bank.

Gross Domestic Product by Economic Activity
(million francs CFA at current prices, estimates)

	1999	2000	2001*
Agriculture, hunting, forestry and fishing	82,165	88,015	80,413
Mining and quarrying . . . }			
Manufacturing . . . . . }	13,984	14,979	14,824
Electricity, gas and water . . }			
Construction	2,799	3,427	3,426
Trade, restaurants and hotels .	21,147	23,332	24,275
Transport, storage and communications	5,177	5,545	5,825
Finance, insurance, real estate, etc . . . . }			
Community, social and personal services (excl. government) . }	592	579	538
Government services	9,914	13,835	14,158
GDP at factor cost	135,778	149,711	143,458
Indirect taxes	2,444	3,702	2,409
GDP at market prices† . . .	138,223	153,413	145,867

* Preliminary.
† Based on unrounded data.

Source: IMF, *Guinea-Bissau: Statistical Appendix* (July 2002).

BALANCE OF PAYMENTS
(US $ million)

	1999	2000	2001
Exports of goods f.o.b.	51.2	62.1	47.2
Imports of goods f.o.b.	−65.6	−85.6	−79.8
Trade balance	−14.4	−23.5	−32.6
Exports of services	4.6	6.4	7.3
Imports of services	−30.5	−40.1	−35.8
Balance on goods and services	−40.3	−57.3	−61.1
Other income paid	−14.3	−12.3	−16.0
Balance on goods, services and income	−54.6	−69.6	−77.1
Official current transfers (net) . .	23.0	32.8	23.1
Private current transfers (net) . .	4.6	8.3	16.2
Current balance	−27.0	−28.4	−37.8
Capital account (net)	20.0	15.7	24.1
Financial account (net)	−28.3	21.4	−20.8
Net errors and omissions . . .	−15.5	20.0	−3.9
Overall balance	−34.6	8.7	−34.5

Source: IMF, *Guinea-Bissau: Statistical Appendix* (July 2002).

External Trade

PRINCIPAL COMMODITIES
(US $ million)

Imports c.i.f.	1999	2000	2001
Food and live animals	24.0	21.5	18.1
Rice	17.7	7.0	6.4
Beverages and tobacco . . .	2.0	6.0	5.3
Other consumer goods . . .	3.5	4.7	4.2
Petroleum and petroleum products	7.9	4.7	6.0
Diesel fuel and gasoline . . .	7.1	4.4	4.7
Construction materials	0.4	6.5	5.0
Transport equipment	5.9	9.4	12.8
Passenger vehicles	1.6	5.2	6.9
Freight vehicles	1.9	3.4	4.5
Vehicle parts	2.6	0.9	1.2
Electrical equipment and machinery	2.9	5.4	7.4
Total (incl. others)	82.0	103.8	96.7

Exports f.o.b.	1999	2000	2001
Cashew nuts	48.6	59.8	45.1
Total (incl. others)	51.2	62.1	47.2

Source: IMF, *Guinea-Bissau: Statistical Appendix* (July 2002).

PRINCIPAL TRADING PARTNERS
(percentage of trade)

Imports	1999	2000	2001
Cape Verde	2.9	1.3	0.1
China, People's Repub.	12.9	7.4	10.9
France	2.3	4.7	4.7
Germany	3.0	3.1	2.4
Italy	0.6	1.2	1.1
Japan	8.1	7.2	5.6
Netherlands	6.7	10.6	6.6
Portugal	24.0	34.0	29.9
Senegal	18.2	12.0	27.4
Spain	1.0	1.7	0.8
USA	1.1	0.3	1.2

Exports	1999	2000	2001
France	0.0	0.0	1.7
India	85.2	85.9	85.6
Netherlands	0.0	2.4	0.0
Nigeria	0.0	1.4	0.0
Portugal	0.1	0.9	3.8
Senegal	0.1	0.0	2.5
Spain	1.7	0.0	0.1

Source: IMF, *Guinea-Bissau: Statistical Appendix* (July 2002).

Transport

ROAD TRAFFIC
(motor vehicles in use, estimates)

	1994	1995	1996
Passenger cars	5,940	6,300	7,120
Commercial vehicles	4,650	4,900	5,640

Source: International Road Federation, *World Road Statistics*.

SHIPPING
Merchant Fleet
(registered at 31 December)

	1999	2000	2001
Number of vessels	24	25	24
Total displacement (grt). . . .	6,350	6,685	6,459

Source: Lloyd's Register-Fairplay, *World Fleet Statistics*.

International Sea-Borne Freight Traffic
(UN estimates, '000 metric tons)

	1991	1992	1993
Goods loaded	40	45	46
Goods unloaded	272	277	283

Source: UN Economic Commission for Africa, *African Statistical Yearbook*.

CIVIL AVIATION
(traffic on scheduled services)

	1996	1997	1998
Kilometres flown (million) . . .	1	0	0
Passengers carried ('000) . .	21	21	20
Passenger-km (million)	10	10	10
Total ton-km (million)	1	1	1

Source: UN, *Statistical Yearbook*.

Communications Media

	1999	2000	2001
Telephones ('000 main lines in use)	6.1	11.1	12.0
Facsimile machines (number in use)	550	550	n.a.
Internet users ('000)	1.5	3.0	4.0

Radio receivers ('000 in use): 49 in 1997.

Daily newspapers: 1 (average circulation 6,000 copies) in 1996.

Sources: UNESCO, *Statistical Yearbook*; UN, *Statistical Yearbook*; International Telecommunication Union.

Education

(1999)

	Institutions	Teachers	Students Males	Students Females	Students Total
Pre-primary . . .	54	194	2,027	2,132	4,159
Primary	759	4,306	89,401	60,129	149,530
Secondary: general .	n.a.	1,913	16,109	8,925	25,034
Secondary: technical and vocational . . .	n.a.		208	72	280
Tertiary	n.a.	n.a.	n.a.	n.a.	463

* UNESCO estimate.

Source: UNESCO Institute for Statistics.

Adult literacy rate (UNESCO estimates): 38.5% (males 54.4%; females 23.2%) in 2000 (Source: UN Development Programme, *Human Development Report*).

Directory

The Constitution

A new Constitution for the Republic of Guinea-Bissau was approved by the Assembléia Nacional Popular on 16 May 1984 and amended in May 1991, November 1996 and July 1999 (see below). The main provisions of the 1984 Constitution were:

Guinea-Bissau is an anti-colonialist and anti-imperialist Republic and a State of revolutionary national democracy, based on the people's participation in undertaking, controlling and directing public activities. The Partido Africano da Independência da Guiné e Cabo Verde (PAIGC) shall be the leading political force in society and in the State. The PAIGC shall define the general bases for policy in all fields.

The economy of Guinea-Bissau shall be organized on the principles of state direction and planning. The State shall control the country's foreign trade.

The representative bodies in the country are the Assembléia Nacional Popular and the regional councils. Other state bodies draw their powers from these. The members of the regional councils shall be directly elected. Members of the councils must be more than 18 years of age. The Assembléia Nacional Popular shall have 150 members, who are to be elected by the regional councils from among their own members. All members of the Assembléia Nacional Popular must be over 21 years of age.

The Assembléia Nacional Popular shall elect a 15-member Council of State (Conselho de Estado), to which its powers are delegated between sessions of the Assembléia. The Assembléia also elects the President of the Conselho de Estado, who is also automatically Head of the Government and Commander-in-Chief of the Armed Forces. The Conselho de Estado will later elect two Vice-Presidents and a Secretary. The President and Vice-Presidents of the Conselho de Estado form part of the Government, as do Ministers, Secretaries of State and the Governor of the National Bank.

The Constitution can be revised at any time by the Assembléia Nacional Popular on the initiative of the deputies themselves, or of the Conselho de Estado or the Government.

Note: Constitutional amendments providing for the operation of a multi-party political system were approved unanimously by the Assembléia Nacional Popular in May 1991. The amendments stipulated that new parties seeking registration must obtain a minimum of 2,000 signatures, with at least 100 signatures from each of the nine provinces. (These provisions were adjusted in August to 1,000 and 50 signatures, respectively.) In addition, the amendments provided for the Assembléia Nacional Popular (reduced to 100 members) to be elected by universal adult suffrage, for the termination of official links between the PAIGC and the armed forces, and for the operation of a free-market economy. Multi-party elections took place in July 1994.

In November 1996 the legislature approved a constitutional amendment providing for Guinea-Bissau to seek membership of the Union économique et monétaire ouest-africaine and of the Franc Zone.

In July 1999 constitutional amendments were introduced limiting the tenure of presidential office to two terms and abolishing the death penalty. It was also stipulated that the country's principal offices of state could only be held by Guinea-Bissau nationals born of Guinea-Bissau parents.

The Government

HEAD OF STATE

President of the Republic and Commander-in-Chief of the Armed Forces: KUMBA YALÁ (assumed power 17 February 2000).

COUNCIL OF MINISTERS
(May 2003)

Prime Minister: MARIO PIRES.

Minister of Internal Administration: FERNANDO LANDIM.

Minister of Defence: FILOMENA MASCARENHAS TIPOTE.

Minister of the Presidency of the Council of Ministers: (vacant).

Minister of Foreign Affairs and International Co-operation: JOÃOZINHO VIEIRA.

Minister of Justice: VESÀ GOMES NA LUAK.

Minister of the Economy and Finance: AUGUSTO USSUMANE SO.

Minister of Agriculture, Forestry and Livestock: DANIEL SULEIMANE EMBALO.

Minister of Public Administration and Labour: TIBNA SAMBÉ NA WANA.

Minister of Education: FILOMENA LOPES.

Minister of Public Health: ANTÓNIO SERIFO EMBALO.

Minister of Trade, Industry, Tourism and Handicrafts: BOTCHÉ CANDÉ.

Minister of Social Infrastructure: DIONISIO CABI.

There are, in addition, six Secretaries of State.

MINISTRIES

Office of the Prime Minister: Avda Unidade Africana, CP 137, Bissau; tel. 211308; fax 201671.

Ministry of Agriculture, Forestry and Livestock: Avda Amílcar Cabral, CP 102, Bissau; tel. 202251; fax 201157.

Ministry of Defence: Amura, Bissau; tel. 213297.

Ministry of the Economy and Finance: CP 67, Avda 3 de Agosto, Bissau; tel. 215193; fax 214586.

Ministry of Education: Rua Areolino Cruz, Bissau; tel. 202244.

Ministry of Foreign Affairs and International Co-operation: Rua Gen. Omar Torrijo, Bissau; tel. 202752; fax 202378.

Ministry of Internal Administration: Avda Unidade Africana, Bissau; tel. 201527.

Ministry of Justice: Avda Amílcar Cabral, CP 17, Bissau; tel. 202187.

Ministry of the Presidency of the Council of Ministers: Bissau.

Ministry of Public Administration and Labour: Bissau.

Ministry of Public Health: CP 50, Bissau; tel. 201107; fax 201701.

Ministry of Social Infrastructure: CP 14, Bissau; tel. 202466; fax 201137.

Ministry of Trade, Industry, Tourism and Handicrafts: Avda 3 de Agosto, CP 67, Bissau; tel. 202172; fax 202171.

President and Legislature

PRESIDENT

Presidential Election, First Ballot, 28 November 1999

Candidate	% of votes
Kumba Yalá (PRS)	38.8
Malam Bacai Sanhá (PAIGC)	23.4
Faustino Fudut Imbali (PUSD/RGB—MB)	8.2
Fernando Gomes (Independent)	7.0
João Tatis Sá (Independent)	6.5
Abubacar Baldé (UNDP)	5.4
Total (incl. others)	100.0

Second Ballot, 16 January 2000

Candidate	% of votes
Kumba Yalá (PRS)	72.0
Malam Bacai Sanhá (PAIGC)	28.0
Total	100.0

ASSEMBLÉIA NACIONAL POPULAR

General Election, 28 November 1999

Party	Seats
Partido para a Renovação Social (PRS)	38
Resistência da Guiné-Bissau—Movimento Bah-Fatah (RGB—MB)	28
Partido Africano da Independência da Guiné e Cabo Verde (PAIGC)	24
Aliança Democrática (AD)	4
União para a Mudança (UM)	3
Partido Social Democrático (PSD)	3
Frente Democrática Social (FDS)	1
União Nacional para a Democracia e o Progresso (UNDP)	1
Total (incl. others)	102

Political Organizations

Aliança Socialista da Guiné-Bissau (ASG): Bissau; f. 2000; Leader FERNANDO GOMES.

Foro Cívico da Guiné/Social Democracia (FCG/SD): Bissau; Leader ANTONIETA ROSA GOMES.

Movimento Democrático da Guiné-Bissau: Bissau; f. 2002; Leader SILVESTRE ALVES.

Partido Africano da Independência da Guiné e Cabo Verde (PAIGC): CP 106, Bissau; f. 1956; fmrly the ruling party in both Guinea-Bissau and Cape Verde; although Cape Verde withdrew from the PAIGC following the coup in Guinea-Bissau in Nov. 1980, Guinea-Bissau has retained the party name and initials; Leader FRANCISCO BENANTE.

Partido Democrático Guineense (PDG): Lisbon, Portugal; f. 2002; Leader MANUEL CÁ.

Partido para o Desenvolvimento e a Cidadania (PDC): Lisbon, Portugal; f. 2001; banned from contesting 2003 legislative elections; Leader FRANCISCO JOSÉ FADUL.

Partido para a Renovação Social (PRS): c/o Assembléia Nacional Popular, Bissau; f. 1992 by four mems of the Frente Democrática Social; officially registered in Oct. 1992; Pres. ALMARA NHASSÉ.

Partido de Solidariedade e Trabalho (PST): Bissau; f. 2002; Leader IANCUBA INDJAI.

Partido da Unidade Nacional (PUN): Bissau; f. 2002; Leader IDRISSA DJALO.

Partido Unido Social Democrático (PUSD): Bissau; f. 1991; officially registered in Jan. 1992; Leader FRANCISCO JOSÉ FADUL.

Plataforma Unida 'Mufunesa Larga Guiné': f. 2003 as coalition to contest legislative elections; comprises the following parties:

> **Aliança Democrática (AD):** c/o Assembléia Nacional Popular, Bissau; Leader VICTOR MANDINGA.

> > **Frente Democrática (FD):** Bissau; f. 1991; officially registered in Nov. 1991; Pres. CANJURA INJAI; Sec.-Gen. MARCELINO BATISTA.

> > **Partido da Convergência Democrática (PCD):** Bissau; Leader VICTOR MANDINGA.

> **Frente Democrática Social (FDS):** c/o Assembléia Nacional Popular, Bissau; f. 1991; legalized in Dec. 1991; Leader RAFAEL BARBOSA.

> **Frente da Luta para a Libertação da Guiné (FLING):** Bissau; f. 1962 as an external opposition movement; legally registered in May 1992; Leader KATENGUL MENDY.

> **Grupo de Democratas Independentes (GDI):** Bissau; f. 2003 by fmr mems of the RGB—MB; Leader HELDER VAZ.

Resistência da Guiné-Bissau—Movimento Bah-Fatah (RGB—MB): c/o Assembléia Nacional Popular, Bissau; f. 1986 in Lisbon, Portugal, as Resistência da Guiné-Bissau—Movimento Bafatá; adopted present name prior to official registration in Dec. 1991; maintains offices in Paris (France), Dakar (Senegal) and Praia (Cape Verde); President SALVADOR TCHONGO.

União Eleitoral (UE): f. 2002 as coalition to contest legislative elections of 2003; comprises the following parties:

> **Liga Guineense de Protecção Ecológica (LIPE):** Bairro Missirá 102, CP 1290, Bissau; tel. and fax 252309; f. 1991; ecology party; Pres. Alhaje BUBACAR DJALÓ.

Partido da Renovação e Progresso (PRP): Bissau; Leader MAMADÚ URI DJALÓ.

Partido Social Democrático (PSD): c/o Assembléia Nacional Popular, Bissau; f. 1995 by breakaway faction of RGB—MB; Leader JOAQUIM BALDÉ; Sec.-Gen. GASPAR FERNANDES.

Partido Socialista Guineense (PSG): Bissau; Leader CIRÍLO VIEIRA.

União para a Mudança (UM): c/o Assembléia Nacional Popular, Bissau; f. 1994 as coalition to contest presidential and legislative elections, re-formed April 1995; comprises the following parties:

Movimento para a Unidade e a Democracia (MUDE): Bissau; officially registered in Aug. 1992; Leader FILINTO VAZ MARTINS.

Partido Democrático do Progresso (PDP): Bissau; f. 1991; officially registered in Aug. 1992; Pres. of Nat. Council AMINE MICHEL SAAD.

Partido de Renovação e Desenvolvimento (PRD): Bissau; f. 1992 as the 'Group of 121' by PAIGC dissidents; officially registered in Oct. 1992; Leaders MANUEL RAMBOUT BARCELOS, AGNELO REGALA.

União Nacional para a Democracia e o Progresso (UNDP): c/o Assembléia Nacional Popular, Bissau; f. 1998; Leader ABUBACAR BALDÉ.

Diplomatic Representation

EMBASSIES IN GUINEA-BISSAU

Brazil: Rua São Tomé, Bissau; tel. 201327; fax 201317; Ambassador LUIZ FERNANDO NAZARETH.

China, People's Republic: Avda Francisco João Mendes, Bissau; tel. 203637; fax 203590; e-mail Chinemba@sol.gtelecom.gw; Ambassador GAO KEXIANG.

Cuba: Rua Joaquim N'Com 1, Bissau; tel. 213579; Ambassador DIOSDADO FERNÁNDEZ GONZÁLEZ.

Egypt: Avda Omar Torrijos, Rua 15, CP 72, Bissau; tel. 213642; Ambassador MOHAMED REDA FARAHAT.

France: Avda 14 de Novembro, Bairro de Penha, CP 195, 1011 Bissau; tel. 201312; fax 201285; Ambassador BERNARD LE TOURNEAU.

Guinea: Rua 14, no. 9, CP 396, Bissau; tel. 212681; Ambassador MOHAMED LAMINÉ FODÉ.

Libya: Rua 16, CP 362, Bissau; tel. 212006; Representative DOKALI ALI MUSTAFA.

Portugal: Avda Cidade de Lisboa, Apdo 76, 1021 Bissau; tel. 201261; fax 201269; e-mail emb.port.bissau@sol.gtelecom.gw; Ambassador JORGE JACOB DE CARVALHO.

Russia: Avda 14 de Novembro, CP 308, Bissau; tel. 251036; fax 251028; Ambassador MIKHAIL S. VOLKOV.

Senegal: Avda Omar Torrijos 43A, Bissau; tel. 211561; Ambassador MAMADOU NIANG.

Judicial System

The Supreme Court is the final court of appeal in criminal and civil cases and consists of nine judges appointed by the President. Nine Regional Courts serve as the final court of appeal for the 24 Sectoral Courts, and deal with felony cases and major civil cases. The Sectoral Courts hear minor civil cases.

President of the Supreme Court: MAMADU AMIRO DJALÓ.

Religion

According to the 1991 census, 45.9% of the population are Muslims, 39.7% are animists and 14.4% are Christians, mainly Roman Catholics.

CHRISTIANITY

The Roman Catholic Church

Guinea-Bissau comprises a single diocese, directly responsible to the Holy See. The Bishop participates in the Episcopal Conference of Senegal, Mauritania, Cape Verde and Guinea-Bissau, currently based in Senegal. At 31 December 2000 there were an estimated 136,000 adherents in the country.

Bishop of Bissau: JOSÉ CÂMNATE NA BISSIGN, CP 20, Avda 14 de Novembro, 1001 Bissau Codex; tel. 251057; fax 251058.

The Anglican Communion

Anglicans in Guinea-Bissau are adherents of the Church of the Province of West Africa, comprising 12 dioceses.

Bishop of Guinea and Guinea-Bissau: Rt Rev. ALBERT GÓMEZ, Cathédrale Toussaint, BP 105, Conakry, Guinea.

The Press

Baguerra: Bissau; owned by the Partido da Convergência Democrática.

Banobero: Rua José Carlos Schwarz, CP 760, Bissau; tel. 230702; fax 230705; e-mail banobero@netscape.net; weekly; Dir FERNANDO JORGE PEREIRA.

Correio-Bissau: Bissau; weekly; f. 1992; Editor-in-Chief JOÃO DE BARROS; circ. 9,000.

Diário de Bissau: Rua Vitorino Costa 29, Bissau; tel. 203049; three a week.

Fraskera: Bairro da Ajuda, 1ª fase, CP 698, Bissau; tel. 253060; fax 253070.

Gazeta de Notícias: Avda dos Combatentes da Liberdade, Bissau; tel. 222881.

Journal Nô Pintcha: Avda do Brasil, CP 154, Bissau; tel. 213713; Dir Sra CABRAL; circ. 6,000.

Voz de Bissau: Rua Eduardo Mondlane, Apdo 155, Bissau; tel. 202546.

Wandan: Rua António M'Bana, 6, CP 760, Bissau; tel. 201789.

NEWS AGENCY

Agência Noticiosa da Guiné-Bissau (ANG): Avda Domingos Ramos, CP 248, Bissau; tel. 212151; fax 202155.

Broadcasting and Communications

TELECOMMUNICATIONS

Guiné-Telecom: Bissau; 49% state-owned.

RADIO AND TELEVISION

An experimental television service began transmissions in 1989. Regional radio stations were to be established at Bafatá, Cantchungo and Catió in 1990. In 1990 Radio Freedom, which broadcast on behalf of the PAIGC during Portuguese rule and had ceased operations in 1974, resumed transmissions.

Radiodifusão Nacional da República da Guiné-Bissau: Avda Domingos Ramos, Praça dos Martires de Pindjiguiti, CP 191, Bissau; tel. 212426; fax 253070; e-mail rdn@eguitel.com; internet www .guine-bissau.net/guine_net/rdn; govt-owned; broadcasts in Portuguese on short-wave, MW and FM; Dir-Gen. ALFREDO ANTÓNIO SAMI.

Rádiotelevisão Nacional da Guiné-Bissau (RTGB): Bairro de Luanda, CP 178, Bissau; tel. 221920; fax 221941.

Rádio Bafatá: CP 57, Bafatá; tel. 411185.

Rádio Bombolom: Bairro Cupelon, CP 877, Bissau; tel. 201095; f. 1996; licence suspended Feb. 2003; independent; Dir AGNELO REGALA.

Rádio Mavegro: Rua Eduardo Mondlane, CP 100, Bissau; tel. 201216; fax 201265.

Rádio Pindjiguiti: Bairro da Ajuda, 1ª fase, CP 698; tel. 253070; f. 1995; independent.

Finance

(cap. = capital; res = reserves; m. = million; brs = branches; amounts in francs CFA unless otherwise indicated)

BANKING

Central Bank

Banque Centrale des Etats de l'Afrique de l'Ouest (BCEAO): Avda Amílcar Cabral 124, CP 38, Bissau; tel. 215548; fax 201305; HQ in Dakar, Senegal; f. 1955; bank of issue for the mem. states of the Union économique et monétaire ouest-africaine (UEMOA, comprising Benin, Burkina Faso, Côte d'Ivoire, Guinea-Bissau, Mali, Niger, Senegal and Togo); cap. and res 850,500m., total assets 5,157,700m. (Dec. 2001); Gov. CHARLES KONAN BANNY; Dir in Guinea-Bissau LUÍS CÂNDIDO LOPES RIBEIRO.

Other Banks

Banco da África Ocidental, SARL: Rua Guerra Mendes, CP 18A/18C, 1360 Bissau; tel. 203418; fax 203412; e-mail bao@sol .gtelecom.gw; f. 2000; Chair. Dr GONÇALO SEQUEIRA BRAGA; Dir VITOR GUILHERME DE MATOS FILIPE.

Banco Internacional da Guiné-Bissau, SARL (BIGB): Avda Amilcar Cabral, CP 74, Bissau; tel. 213662; fax 201377; Chair. AVITO J. DA SILVA.

Caixa de Crédito da Guiné: Bissau; govt savings and loan institution.

Caixa Económica Postal: Avda Amílcar Cabral, Bissau; tel. 212999; postal savings institution.

STOCK EXCHANGE

In 1998 a regional stock exchange, the Bourse Régionale des Valeurs Mobilières, was established in Abidjan, Côte d'Ivoire, to serve the member states of the UEMOA.

INSURANCE

Instituto Nacional de Seguros e Previdência Social: CP 62, Bissau; tel. and fax 201665; state-owned; Gen. Man. A. MONDES.

Trade and Industry

CHAMBER OF COMMERCE

Câmara de Comércio, Industria e Agricultura da Guiné-Bissau: Sede Provisória, Rua Guerra Mendes 20, CP 88, Bissau; tel. and fax 201602; f. 1987; Pres. CANJURA INJAI.

INDUSTRIAL AND TRADE ASSOCIATIONS

Associação Industrial da Guiné-Bissau: Rua Vitorino Costa 46, 1° andar, CP 48, Bissau; tel. and fax 204025.

Direcção de Promoção do Investimento Privado (DPIP): Rua 12 de Setembro, Bissau Velho, CP 1276, Bissau; tel. 205156; fax 203181; e-mail dpip@mail.bissau.net.

Procajú: Bissau; internet www.steelecom/cashew; private-sector association of cashew producers.

UTILITIES

Electricity and Water

Empresa de Electricidade e Águas da Guiné-Bissau (EAGB): Apdo 6, EAGB E.P., Bissau; tel. 215191; fax 202716; operated under contract by private management co.

Gas

Empresa Nacional de Importação e Distribuição de Gás Butano: CP 269, Bissau; state gas distributor.

TRADE UNION

União Nacional dos Trabalhadores da Guiné (UNTG): 13 Avda Ovai di Vievra, CP 98, Bissau; tel. 212094; Pres. DEFEJADO LIMA DA COSTA; Sec.-Gen. MÁRIO MENDES CORREIA.

Legislation permitting the formation of other trade unions was approved by the Assembléia Nacional Popular in 1991.

Transport

RAILWAYS

There are no railways in Guinea-Bissau. In March 1998 Guinea-Bissau and Portugal signed an agreement providing for the construction of a railway linking Guinea-Bissau with Guinea.

ROADS

In 1999, according to International Road Federation estimates, there were about 4,400 km of roads, of which 453 km were paved. A major road rehabilitation scheme is proceeding, and an international road, linking Guinea-Bissau with The Gambia and Senegal, is planned.

SHIPPING

Under a major port modernization project, the main port at Bissau was to be renovated and expanded, and four river ports were to be upgraded to enable barges to load and unload at low tide. The total cost of the project was estimated at US $47.4m., and finance was provided by the World Bank and Arab funds.

Empresa Nacional de Agências e Transportes Marítimos: Rua Guerva Mendes 4–4A, CP 244, Bissau; tel. 212675; fax 213023; state shipping agency; Dir-Gen. M. LOPES.

CIVIL AVIATION

There is an international airport at Bissau, which there are plans to expand, and 10 smaller airports serving the interior.

Transportes Aéreos da Guiné-Bissau (TAGB): Aeroporto Osvaldo Vieira, CP 111, Bissau; tel. 201277; fax 251536; f. 1977; domestic services and flights to France, Portugal, the Canary Islands (Spain), Guinea and Senegal; Dir Capt. EDUARDO PINTO LOPES.

Air Bissau: CP 111, Bissau; tel. 251063; fax 251008.

Tourism

Central de Informação e Turismo: CP 294, Bissau; state tourism and information service.

Direcção Geral do Turismo: CP 1024, Bissau; tel. 202195; fax 204441.

GUYANA

Introductory Survey

Location, Climate, Language, Religion, Flag, Capital

The Co-operative Republic of Guyana lies on the north coast of South America, between Venezuela to the west and Suriname to the east, with Brazil to the south. The narrow coastal belt has a moderate climate with two wet seasons, from April to August and from November to January, alternating with two dry seasons. Inland, there are tropical forests and savannah, and the dry season lasts from September to May. The average annual temperature is 27°C (80°F), with average rainfall of 1,520 mm (60 ins) per year inland, rising to between 2,030 mm (80 ins) and 2,540 mm (100 ins) on the coast. English is the official language but Hindi, Urdu and Amerindian dialects are also spoken. The principal religions are Christianity (which is professed by about 50% of the population), Hinduism (about 33%) and Islam (less than 10%). The national flag (proportions 3 by 5 when flown on land, but 1 by 2 at sea) is green, with a white-bordered yellow triangle (apex at the edge of the fly) on which is superimposed a black-bordered red triangle (apex in the centre). The capital is Georgetown.

Recent History

Guyana was formerly British Guiana, a colony of the United Kingdom, formed in 1831 from territories finally ceded to Britain by the Dutch in 1814. A new Constitution, providing for universal adult suffrage, was introduced in 1953. The elections of April 1953 were won by the left-wing People's Progressive Party (PPP), led by Dr Cheddi Bharat Jagan. In October, however, the British Government, claiming that a communist dictatorship was threatened, suspended the Constitution. An interim administration was appointed. The PPP split in 1955, and in 1957 some former members founded a new party, the People's National Congress (PNC), under the leadership of Forbes Burnham. The PNC drew its support mainly from the African-descended population, while PPP support came largely from the (Asian-descended) 'East' Indian community.

A revised Constitution was introduced in December 1956 and fresh elections were held in August 1957. The PPP won and Dr Jagan became Chief Minister. Another Constitution, providing for internal self-government, was adopted in July 1961. The PPP won the elections in August and Dr Jagan was appointed premier in September. In the elections of December 1964, held under the system of proportional representation that had been introduced in the previous year, the PPP won the largest number of seats in the Legislative Assembly, but not a majority. A coalition Government was formed by the PNC and The United Force (TUF), with Burnham as Prime Minister. This coalition led the colony to independence, as Guyana, on 26 May 1966.

The PNC won elections in 1968 and in 1973, although the results of the latter, and every poll thenceforth until the defeat of the PNC in 1992, were disputed by the opposition parties. Guyana became a co-operative republic on 23 February 1970, and Arthur Chung was elected non-executive President in March. In 1976 the PPP, which had boycotted the National Assembly since 1973, offered the Government its 'critical support'. Following a referendum in July 1978 that gave the Assembly power to amend the Constitution, elections to the Assembly were postponed for 15 months. The legislature assumed the role of a constituent assembly, established in November 1978, to draft a new constitution. In October 1979 elections were postponed for a further year. In October 1980 Forbes Burnham declared himself executive President of Guyana, and a new Constitution was promulgated.

Internal opposition to the PNC Government had increased after the assassination in June 1980 of Dr Walter Rodney, leader of the Working People's Alliance (WPA). The Government was widely believed to have been involved in the incident; an official inquest into Rodney's death was finally ordered in November 1987, but in 1988 it produced a verdict, rejected by the opposition, of death by misadventure. All opposition parties except the PPP and TUF urged their supporters to boycott the December 1980 elections to the National Assembly. The PNC, under Burnham, received 77.7% of the votes, according to official results, and won 41 of the 53 elective seats, although allegations of substantial electoral malpractice were made, both within the country and by international observers. None the less, Burnham was formally inaugurated as President in January 1981.

In 1981 arrests and trials of opposition leaders continued, and in 1982 the Government's relations with human rights groups, and especially the Christian churches, deteriorated further. Editors of opposition newspapers were threatened, political violence increased, and the Government was accused of interference in the legal process. Industrial unrest and public discontent continued in 1983, as Guyana's worsening economic situation increased opposition to the Government, and led to growing disaffection within the trade union movement and the PNC. There were more strikes in 1984, and in December Burnham announced some concessions, including a rise in the daily minimum wage (virtually the only increase since 1979).

Burnham died in August 1985 and was succeeded as President by Desmond Hoyte, hitherto the First Vice-President and Prime Minister. President Hoyte's former posts were assumed by Hamilton Green, previously the First Deputy Prime Minister. At a general election in December the PNC won 78% of the votes and 42 of the elective seats in the National Assembly. Hoyte was declared President-elect. Opposition groups, including the PPP and WPA, denounced the poll as fraudulent. In January 1986 five of the six opposition parties formed the Patriotic Coalition for Democracy (PCD).

During 1988 the opposition expressed fears about the independence of the judiciary. The opposition also claimed that the Government's continued recourse to the laws of libel against its critics was an abuse of the legal system. Social unrest and industrial disruption in 1988 continued to hamper government efforts to reform the economy, while the Government's hold on power was further compromised, following a division within the trade union movement. Seven unions withdrew from the Trades Union Congress (TUC) in September, alleging that elections for TUC officials were weighted in favour of PNC-approved candidates. The seven independent unions formed a separate congress, the Federation of Independent Trade Unions in Guyana (FITUG), in October. However, the Government refused to negotiate with the FITUG, accusing it of being politically motivated. Furthermore, the severity of austerity measures contained in the budget of March 1989, which included a devaluation of the currency, prompted a six-week strike in the sugar and bauxite industries.

Outside the formal opposition of the political parties, the Government also experienced pressure from members of the Guyana Human Rights Association, business leaders and prominent religious figures. This culminated, in January 1990, in the formation of a movement for legal and constitutional change, Guyanese Action for Reform and Democracy (Guard), which initiated a series of mass protests, urging the Government to accelerate the process of democratic reform. To counter this civic movement, the PNC began mobilizing its own newly-established Committees to Re-elect the President (Creeps). Guard accused the Creeps of orchestrating violent clashes at Guard's rallies, and of fomenting racial unrest in the country in an attempt to regain support from the Afro-Guyanese population.

In October 1990 the former US President Jimmy Carter visited President Hoyte to discuss matters related to electoral reform. It was agreed that a new electoral register would be compiled. However, the date of the forthcoming general election was postponed, following the approval of legislation by the PNC in January 1991, extending the term of office of the National Assembly by two months after its official dissolution date of 2 February 1991. In March a further two-month extension of the legislative term provoked the resignation of TUF and PPP members from the National Assembly (in addition to the WPA members, who had resigned a month earlier). Similar extensions followed in May and July, owing to alleged continuing problems relating to electoral reforms. The National Assembly was finally dissolved in late September. The publication of the revised electoral register in that month, however, revealed widespread inaccuracies, including the omission of an estimated 100,000 eligible voters. In November several opposition parties announced a boycott of the general election, which had been rescheduled for mid-December. However, on 28 November Hoyte declared a state of emergency in order to legitimize a further postponement of the election (which, according to the Constitution, was due to take place by 28 December). Legislation restoring the opposition seats in the National Assembly followed, and the Assembly was reconvened. In mid-December the state of emergency was extended until June 1992. A further revised electoral register was published in that month, and was finally approved by the Elections Commission in August. The election took place on 5 October and resulted in a narrow victory for the PPP in alliance with the CIVIC movement (a social and political movement of businessmen and professionals), which secured 32 of the 65 elective seats in the National Assembly (53.5% of the votes), while the PNC secured 31 (42.3% of the votes). The result, which signified an end to the PNC's 28-year period in government, provoked riots by the mainly Afro-Guyanese PNC supporters in Georgetown, in which two people were killed. International observers were, however, satisfied that the elections had been fairly conducted, and on 9 October Dr Cheddi Bharat Jagan took office as President. On the following day Jagan appointed Samuel Hinds, an industrialist who was not a member of the PPP, as Prime Minister.

Following a joint conference in September 1993, the unions belonging to the TUC and the FITUG agreed to reunify as the TUC. In May 1994 a strike, organized by four public-sector unions in support of demands for pay increases, was ended after 10 days when the Government agreed to a 35% increase in the minimum wage.

At municipal and local government elections held in August 1994, the first to be contested since 1970, the PPP/CIVIC alliance secured control of 49 of the 71 localities concerned. However, the important post of mayor of Georgetown was won by former PPP member Hamilton Green, representing Good and Green Georgetown, a party founded specifically to contest the election in the capital.

In December 1994 the National Assembly approved a proposal, drafted by the PPP, for the creation of a select parliamentary committee to review the Constitution, with a view to adopting reforms prior to the next general election, due in 1997. However, the PNC, whose support would be required to gain the two-thirds' majority necessary for constitutional amendments, voted against the proposal, favouring instead the appointment of a constituent assembly.

In August 1995 a serious environmental incident resulted in the temporary closure of Omai Gold Mines Ltd (OGML). The company, which began production in the Omai District of Essequibo province in 1993, was responsible for an increase of some 400% in Guyana's gold production in subsequent years and was Guyana's largest foreign investor. However, in August 1995 a breach in a tailings pond (a reservoir where residue from the gold extraction process is stored) resulted in the spillage of some 3.5m. cu m of cyanide-tainted water, of which a large volume flowed into the Omai river, a tributary of the Essequibo river. Environmental warnings were issued to residents of the Essequibo region, and the National Assembly approved a resolution to close the mine for an indefinite period pending an inquiry into the incident. In January 1996 a government-appointed commission of inquiry recommended that OGML be permitted to resume operations subject to the prior implementation of certain environmental safeguards. OGML resumed operations in the following month.

In February 1996, amid growing public concern at an increase in criminal violence, Guyana resumed judicial executions with the hanging of a convicted murderer. The execution, the first for more than five years, provoked protest from human rights organizations.

In March 1997, following the death of Dr Cheddi Bharat Jagan, Prime Minister Hinds succeeded to the presidency, in accordance with the provisions of the Constitution. Hinds subsequently appointed Janet Jagan, the widow of the former President, to the post of Prime Minister. In September the PPP/CIVIC alliance formally adopted Jagan as its presidential candidate for the forthcoming general election.

At the general election of 15 December 1997 delays in the verification of votes prompted protest by PNC supporters who accused the Government of electoral fraud, and 11 protesters were injured during clashes with the security forces. With some 90% of the votes counted, the Chairman of the Elections Commission, Doudnauth Singh, declared that Jagan had established an unassailable lead, and on 19 December she was inaugurated

as President. Singh's actions were strongly criticized as being premature by opposition parties, and the PNC expressed its intention to appeal to the High Court to have Jagan's appointment annulled. In the following days PNC supporters began a series of public demonstrations in protest at the alleged electoral fraud and at Jagan's appointment. On 31 December the final election results were declared. With two legislative seats remaining to be decided by the National Congress of Local Democratic Organs (see The Constitution), the PPP/CIVIC alliance secured 34 seats, the PNC won 26, and TUF, the Alliance for Guyana and the Guyana Democratic Party each obtained one seat. (In February 1998 the remaining two seats were declared to have been won by the PPP/CIVIC alliance.)

In January 1998, in the light of continued unrest being fomented by opposition supporters, the Government accepted a proposal by private-sector leaders for an international audit of the election to be conducted. The PNC, however, rejected the proposal and demanded instead the holding of fresh elections. In mid-January, in rejection of an appeal by the PNC, the Chief Justice ruled that it was beyond the jurisdiction of the High Court to prohibit Jagan from exercising her presidential functions pending a judicial review of the election. The ruling provoked serious disturbances in Georgetown, which, in turn, prompted the Government to introduce a one-month ban on public assemblies and demonstrations in the capital. Nevertheless, public protests by PNC supporters continued in defiance of the ban, resulting in confrontation with the security forces. However, in mid-January, following mediation by a three-member Caribbean Community and Common Market (CARICOM, see p. 155) commission, headed by a former Minister of Foreign Affairs of Barbados, Sir Henry Forde, it was announced that an agreement (the Herdmanston Agreement) had been signed by Jagan and PNC leader Desmond Hoyte, which provided for the organization of fresh elections within 36 months and the creation of a constitutional commission to make recommendations on constitutional reform, subsequently to be submitted to a national referendum and a National Assembly vote. The agreement also made provision for an independent audit of the December election, and in February the PPP/CIVIC alliance and the PNC agreed on the legal procedures necessary for the audit, which was to be conducted by a CARICOM electoral team, to be authorized. Meanwhile, although the PNC had submitted the names of 22 deputies who would represent the party in an emergency, the PNC continued to boycott the National Assembly. In early June the CARICOM commission upheld the published results of the December poll, declaring that there had been only minor procedural irregularities. While both the PPP and the PNC were bound to abide by the findings of the commission (under the terms of the Herdmanston Agreement), Hoyte continued publicly to question the legitimacy of the Jagan administration. Later in the month, mounting political frustration, arising from the National Assembly's informing the PNC that its deputies had effectively forfeited their legislative seats (having failed to attend six consecutive sittings), erupted onto the streets of Georgetown. PNC supporters congregated in the capital, where violent demonstrations against the Government escalated into riots that were dispersed by the security forces with rubber bullets and tear gas. However, renewed CARICOM mediation between the PPP and the PNC, at the CARICOM annual summit in Saint Lucia in early July, produced fresh commitments from both sides to restore peaceful political dialogue, renew discussions on constitutional reform and reinstate full legislative participation. Legislation designed to enable the PNC deputies to recover their seats in the legislature was subsequently formulated by both sides, and the PNC (with the exception of Hoyte—who continued to deny the legitimacy of Jagan's authority) rejoined the National Assembly on 14 July.

In August 1998 the National Assembly announced a 14-member select committee on constitutional reform, entrusted with establishing the terms of reference and composition of a national reform commission. The select committee comprised eight members of the PPP/CIVIC alliance, four from the PNC and one each from the TUF and the AFG. In January 1999 the 20-member Constitutional Reform Commission was created, comprising representatives of the country's principal political parties and community groups. The Commission had until the end of July 1999 to formulate recommendations for constitutional reform.

In April 1999 the Constitutional Reform Commission began public consultations. The PPP/CIVIC alliance submitted proposals suggesting that the country should be renamed the Republic of Guyana, and that the President should be limited to two consecutive terms of office. The PPP/CIVIC also proposed the deletion of the clause in the Constitution whereby the President is empowered to dissolve the National Assembly should he/she be censured by the Assembly. These proposals were subsequently adopted in the report published by the Commission in July. The Commission further proposed that the President should no longer have the power to dismiss a public officer in the public interest, and the President and Cabinet should be collectively responsible to the National Assembly and should resign if defeated in a vote of 'no confidence'.

In late April 1999 the Guyana Public Service Union (GPSU) called a general strike after the Government had offered a pay rise of between 3% and 4.5% in response to the union's demand for an increase of at least 40%. Other public-sector unions later joined the GPSU in taking industrial action, and much of the country was paralysed. Tension was exacerbated following the serving of legal summonses to three prominent union leaders for having organized protest marches in defiance of a government ban, while in mid-May the police opened fire (with pellet guns) on an allegedly violent crowd of strikers, injuring 17 people. After 56 days of industrial action, an agreement was finally reached between the unions and the authorities in late June, which granted public-sector workers an interim pay rise of 4.6% prior to the full settlement of their claim by an arbitration tribunal. Many members of the GPSU were reported to be dissatisfied with the agreement, and the headquarters of the union were subsequently attacked, while the Minister for Public Service, George Fung-On, was assaulted in his car. In September the arbitration tribunal awarded public-sector workers an increase of 31.6% in 1999 and 26.7% in 2000. The Government, however, announced that it would only be bound by the tribunal's findings if it could be proved that the tribunal had followed the correct procedures, and it also warned the unions that the cost of the pay rises might necessitate redundancies.

In early August 1999 President Jagan announced her retirement on the grounds of ill health. Jagan was replaced as President by the erstwhile Minister of Finance, Bharrat Jagdeo. The appointment of Jagdeo, whose relative youth (he was 35 years of age at the time of his appointment), reported willingness to reach across the political divide, and strong background in economics all contributed to his popularity, was widely welcomed in Guyana and by the international community. Jagdeo, who announced that he was to continue the largely market-orientated policies of the Jagan administration, reappointed Samuel Hinds as Prime Minister (Hinds had earlier resigned in accordance with the requirements of the Constitution), and announced that there was to be no cabinet reorganization in the immediate future. There was, however, controversy at the absence of Hoyte and other PNC representatives from the President's inauguration ceremony; Hoyte, who had refused to recognize Jagan as President, was reported to have declined to recognize any successor nominated by her. In late November Saisnarine Kowlessar, the head of the University of Guyana's Department of Management, was appointed Minister in the Office of the President with responsibility for Finance, a portfolio previously held by the President. The President also appointed Geoffrey Da Silva as the new Minister of Trade, Industry and Tourism, replacing Michael Shree Chan, who had retired on the grounds of ill health.

In December 1999 the National Assembly approved the establishment of a committee to supervise the revision of the Constitution prior to the legislative elections scheduled for mid-January 2001. Two 'task forces' were also established by the National Assembly; one was to deal with electoral reform and the other was to establish an Ethnic Relations Commission. In June 2000 a political consensus was reached on the proposed electoral reform. In the following month, the National Assembly approved legislation making the electoral reform task force a permanent institution (to be known as the Guyana Elections Commission—GECOM). In August legislation allowing for the creation of the Ethnic Relations Commission was passed (although it was not officially established until December). In October the legislature unanimously approved a constitutional amendment establishing a mixed system of proportional representation combining regional constituencies and national candidate lists. Also approved was the abolition of the Supreme Congress of the People of Guyana and the National Congress of Local Democratic Organs. On the same day Winslow Martin Zephyr was elected as the new Speaker of the National

Assembly, following the death earlier in the month of Derek Jagan.

However, on 17 November 2000 GECOM announced that the elections that, according to the Herdmanston Agreement, were to be held on 17 January 2001, were to be postponed, owing to delays in the enactment of the proposed reform. A dispute had arisen between the Government and the PNC over the number of parliamentary seats that were to be allocated by region. (In early December a new election date of 19 March 2001 was announced.) GECOM proposed that an all-party committee would be established to decide who was to rule the country in January–March. The PPP/CIVIC alliance immediately declared its intention to continue to govern until March, while the opposition insisted that the Government should resign on 17 January and that an interim coalition Government should be formed. However, in December an all-party committee decided that the PPP/CIVIC was to remain in office, but was to limit its powers. In the same month the National Assembly approved a constitutional amendment removing the President's immunity from prosecution and limiting his power to appoint only four ministers from outside the National Assembly.

The general and regional elections of 19 March 2001 were preceded by demonstrations over the late distribution of voter identification cards (despite the announcement, in mid-February, that voters would be allowed to use other forms of identification). The elections, which were contested by 11 political parties, were overseen by an international delegation led by former US President Jimmy Carter. The PPP/CIVIC secured 53.0% of the votes cast. The party also obtained a majority in the National Assembly, with 34 seats; while the PNC (which contested the elections as the PNC/Reform) won 27 seats, the Guyana Action Party, in alliance with the WPA, won two seats, while Rise, Organize and Rebuild Guyana Movement and TUF each secured one seat. Some 89.9% of the registered electorate participated. International observers declared the elections to be generally free and fair, and on 23 March Jagdeo was officially declared President-elect. However, the PNC/Reform alleged that there had been a number of breaches of electoral procedure and successfully obtained a High Court injunction postponing the presidential inauguration. Three people were injured in the subsequent violent demonstrations. In late March the Chief Justice refused a further request to stay the proceedings, and ordered an immediate declaration of the official results. On 31 March Bharrat Jagdeo was sworn in as President. A new Cabinet was announced in early April, with additional ministers announced over the next few months. Further protests greeted the reappointment of PPP member Roger Luncheon as head of the civil service.

In an attempt to reduce the intensity of the continuing violence, on 25 April 2001 Jagdeo and Hoyte announced confidence-building measures and the establishment of joint committees to examine and report on critical issues, including land distribution and housing, and the bauxite industry. (In March they had also issued a joint statement pledging to co-operate in the drafting of a new constitution.) In May the Government announced the depoliticization of the social service: a Ministry of Public Service Management was to be created, separate from the Office of the President.

In June 2001 the National Assembly approved legislation making the appointment of the Chancellor of Justice and Chief of Justice the joint responsibility of the President and the leader of the opposition. On 4 September Dr Steve Surujbally was appointed Chairman of the Elections Commission; the Commission was preparing for local elections, which had been last held in 1994. In October a report commissioned by the British Foreign and Commonwealth Office suggested a series of improvements to Guyana's judicial system, including the appointment of more judges and magistrates, and an increase in government finance.

In early 2002 human rights organizations criticized the actions of the police force and of its the recently-appointed head, Floyd McDonald, after a number of civilians were shot and killed by police officers in separate incidents throughout the country.

On 15 March 2002 opposition parties walked out of a debate on the 2002 budget, in protest at the delay in the implementation of the recommendations of the various joint committees. The PNC/Reform and the PPP announced that they would pursue a policy of active non-co-operation with the Government. A period of social unrest ensued, accompanied by a high incidence of violent crime. The disorder culminated on 3 July in an attack by opposition protestors on the presidential offices during a meeting of CARICOM heads of government. The security forces opened fire on the protestors, killing two and wounding 15. The protesters had been participating in a demonstration organized by the recently formed People's Solidarity Movement. While condemning the violence, the PNC/Reform leadership announced their support for the demonstrators' grievances of racial discrimination and police brutality. Later in the month the leaders of the opposing parties began a series of consultations with representatives from the Church, trade unions, private sector companies and the judiciary, in an effort to ascertain their ideas of how shared governance could function in Guyana.

In August 2002 President Jagdeo announced plans for the creation of an additional special police force to combat the rising crime rate. In the same month, Hoyte was re-elected leader of the PNC/Reform. However, the social unrest continued, prompting businesses in Georgetown to close for two days in early October. In late September the National Assembly approved stricter laws for prosecuting crime; however, further anti-terrorism legislation, proposed by the Minister of Legal Affairs, Doodnauth Singh, was criticized by senior members of the judiciary as well as human rights groups, who feared a contravention of basic civil liberties guaranteed by the Constitution.

In December 2002 Hoyte died unexpectedly after suffering a heart attack. Robert Corbin was subsequently elected as the new leader of the PNC/Reform in early February 2003. He pledged a policy of 'constructive engagement' with the PPP. Following negotiations between party leaders, agreement was reached on a number of issues, including local government reform, opposition representation on state bodies, as well on media legislation and an inquiry into the conduct of the police force. As a result, in May the PNC/Reform ended its boycott of the National Assembly.

Guyana has border disputes with its neighbours, Venezuela and Suriname, although relations with Brazil have continued to improve through trade and military agreements. Suriname restored diplomatic representation in Guyana in 1979 and bilateral meetings were resumed at the end of the year. In 1983 relations improved further as a result of increased trade links between the countries. In late 1998 it was announced that a joint border commission, created to negotiate the settlement of a territorial dispute between Suriname and Guyana, was to be revived, after a two-year suspension. The two countries were also expected to conclude an agreement on fishing rights. However, in May 2000 Suriname formally claimed that Guyana had violated its territorial integrity by granting a concession to the Canadian-based company, CGX Energy Inc, to explore for petroleum and gas. Negotiations to settle the dispute opened in Kingston, Jamaica, on 14 July 2001. However, the talks ended four days later without any agreement between the two countries. At the end of January 2002 the Presidents of the two countries met to discuss the possibility of a production-sharing agreement. However, relations deteriorated when, in June, the Surinamese navy forcibly ejected a rig that had been authorized by Guyana to drill in waters disputed by the two countries. In late October a further meeting of the joint border commission was held in Suriname.

In 1962 Venezuela renewed its claim to 130,000 sq km (50,000 sq miles) of land west of the Essequibo river (nearly two-thirds of Guyanese territory). The area was accorded to Guyana in 1899, on the decision of an international tribunal, but Venezuela based its claim on a papal bull of 1493, referring to Spanish colonial possessions. The Port of Spain Protocol of 1970 put the issue in abeyance until 1982. Guyana and Venezuela referred the dispute to the UN in 1983, and, after a series of UN efforts and a visit to Venezuela by President Hoyte, the two countries agreed to a mutually acceptable intermediary, suggested by the UN Secretary-General, in August 1989. In March 1999 Guyana and Venezuela established a joint commission, the High Level Binational Commission, which was intended to expedite the resolution of the territorial dispute and to promote mutual co-operation. However, in September the Venezuelan Government alleged that the Guyanese authorities had granted concessions to petroleum companies within the disputed areas, and in October President Chávez of Venezuela, speaking on the 100th anniversary of the international tribunal's decision, announced his Government's intention to reopen its claim to the territory. Reports of Venezuelan troop movements near the border area caused alarm in Guyana, but were described by the Venezuelan authorities as part of a campaign against drugs-traffickers. In December an agreement was reached between the

two countries on co-operation in the fisheries sector. Early in 2000 Guyana signed an agreement with the US-based Beal Aerospace Corpn to build the world's first private satellite-launching facility in the disputed territory of Essequibo. However, following objections by Venezuela and financial difficulties, the company abandoned the project. Nevertheless, in January 2001 Venezuela announced an oil exploration project in the same disputed zone. Later in the year the Venezuelan Government allegedly refused to grant Guyana entry to the Caracas energy accord for special oil concessions, as it had other Caribbean nations, owing to the border dispute. However, Guyana was later invited to join the accord.

Throughout the 1990s Guyana became more closely integrated with CARICOM (see p. 155), and CARICOM played an active role in attempts to achieve a peace agreement between the PPP and PNC in the late 1990s. In 2000 President Jagdeo led negotiations on entry into the World Trade Organization (see p. 323). In September 2001 construction began in Georgetown on the new CARICOM headquarters. At the third Summit of the Americas, held in Québec City, Canada, in April 2001, President Jagdeo reiterated the need for a fund to assist Caribbean nations in the transition to free trade.

Government

Under the 1980 Constitution, legislative power is held by the unicameral National Assembly, with 65 members: 53 elected for five years by universal adult suffrage, on the basis of proportional representation, and 12 regional representatives. In the elections of March 2001 the regional constituency lists were combined with the national candidate lists. Executive power is held by the President, who leads the majority party in the Assembly and holds office for its duration. The President appoints and heads a Cabinet, which includes the Prime Minister, and may include Ministers who are not elected members of the Assembly. The Cabinet is collectively responsible to the National Assembly. Guyana comprises 10 regions, each having a regional democratic council that returns a representative to the National Assembly.

Defence

In August 2002 the Combined Guyana Defence Force consisted of some 1,600 men (of whom 1,400 were in the army, 100 were in the air force and some 100 in the navy). One-third of the combined forces are civilian personnel. A paramilitary force, the People's Militia, totalled 1,500. Defence expenditure was budgeted at an estimated $ G1,020m. for 2002.

Economic Affairs

In 2001, according to estimates by the World Bank, Guyana's gross national income (GNI), measured at average 1999–2001 prices, was US $641m., equivalent to $840 per head (or $3,750 per head on an international purchasing-power parity basis). During 1990–2001, it was estimated, the population increased at an average annual rate of 0.4%,while gross domestic product (GDP) per head increased, in real terms, by an average of 4.1% per year. Overall GDP increased, in real terms, at an average annual rate of 4.6% in 1990–2001; growth in 2001 was 1.5%.

Agriculture (including forestry and fishing) provided an estimated 41.2% of GDP in 2001 and employed an estimated 17.5% of the economically active population in mid-2000. The principal cash crops are sugar cane (sugar providing an estimated 27.6% of the value of total domestic exports in 2000) and rice (10.5% in 2000). The sugar industry alone accounted for an estimated 16.0% of GDP in 2001, and, it was estimated, employed about 24,000 people at peak season in 2000. Sugar production levels in 1999 were the highest since 1978. However, at the beginning of the 21st century the sugar industry was threatened by the disappearing preferential markets and the increasing cost of employment. Despite this, preliminary figures indicated an increase of 12% in sugar exports in 2002. In June the Government announced a major restructuring of the state sugar company, Guysuco (Guyana Sugar Corpn Inc), including the construction of a new refinery at Berbice. Vegetables and fruit are cultivated for the local market, and livestock-rearing is being developed. Fishing (particularly for shrimp) is also important, and accounted for an estimated 6.7% of GDP in 2000. In the late 1990s the Government initiated a project to develop a sustainable fishing industry. Agricultural production increased at an average annual rate of 5.2% during 1990–2001. Agricultural GDP declined, in real terms, by 1.0% in 2000, but increased by 3.5% in 2001.

Timber resources in Guyana are extensive and under-developed. In 2000 the forestry sector contributed an estimated 2.1% of GDP. According to FAO estimates, some 77% of the country's total land area consisted of forest and woodland in 1994. In 2000 timber shipments provided an estimated 8.3% of total domestic exports, compared with 7.4% in the previous year. Although foreign investment in Guyana's largely undeveloped interior continues to be encouraged by the Government, there is much popular concern at the extent of the exploitation of the rainforest. The forestry sector increased at an average annual rate of 10.3% in 1990–2000. In 1999 the sector increased by 13.0%, but in 2000 it declined by 16.4%.

Industry (including mining, manufacturing and construction) provided an estimated 23.4% of GDP in 2001 and engaged 20.4% of the employed labour force in 1992. Industrial GDP increased at an average annual rate of 6.6% in 1990–2001. Industrial GDP decreased, in real terms, by 2.0% in 2000, but increased by 0.5% in 2001.

Mining contributed an estimated 15.4% of GDP in 2001, and employed 4.8% of the total working population in 1980. Bauxite, which is used for the manufacture of aluminium, is one of Guyana's most valuable exports, and accounted for an estimated 15.5% of total domestic exports in 2000. However, owing to high production costs and unfavourable investment conditions, in January 2002 the US-based aluminium company Alcoa withdrew from the Aroaima bauxite and aluminium mine, selling its share to the Guyana Government. Preliminary results indicated that bauxite production had decreased by 17% in the first four months of 2002. In September the Government merged the Bermine and Aroaima bauxite companies, in an effort to improve the performance of the sector. The registered production of gold (accounting for an estimated 24.4% of domestic exports in 2000) increased considerably during the late 1980s and 1990s, reaching a peak in production in 1998. However, owing to high production costs and poor ore quality, productivity declined in 1999 and 2000, although gold exports increased significantly in the later year. In 2000 the gold industry was estimated to directly employ some 32,000 people. There are also significant diamond resources and some petroleum reserves. In 2000 Mazaruni Granite Products Ltd initiated a US $34m. development and modernization programme of granite production. The GDP of the mining sector was estimated to have increased by an average of 7.1% per year in 1990–2000. The sector's GDP decreased, in real terms, by 8.4% in 1999, but increased by 5.9% in 2000. In 2000 a seven-year programme was initiated to develop and regenerate one of the principal bauxite mining towns, Linden, through the promotion of non-bauxite enterprises.

Manufacturing (including power) accounted for an estimated 3.5% of GDP in 2001 and, according to the 1980 census, employed 14.4% of the total working population. The main activities are the processing of bauxite, sugar, rice and timber. Manufacturing GDP increased at an average annual rate of 7.7% in 1990–2001. Manufacturing GDP decreased by an estimated 13.6% in 2000, but increased by 3.5% in 2001.

Energy requirements are almost entirely met by imported hydrocarbon fuels. In 2000, according to preliminary figures, fuels and lubricants constituted 20.7% of the total value of imports (mainly from Venezuela and Trinidad and Tobago). Despite the border dispute, in early 2001 Venezuela granted Guyana, along with a number of other Caribbean nations, entry to the Caracas energy accord for special petroleum concessions. In November 2002 Venezuela agreed to supply oil at a discount of 25%, providing that the price on world markets remained above US $30 per barrel. Construction began in mid-2002 on the 100 MW Amaila Falls hydroelectric power project, while further hydroelectric projects were in the planning stage. However, the project failed to gain the support of the state power company, Guyana Power and Light Inc. and construction was halted in early 2003. In June 2002 the Inter-American Development Bank (IDB) approved a loan for $27.4m. to fund the extension of electricity lines to the coastal regions.

The services sector contributed an estimated 35.4% of GDP in 2001 and engaged 43.2% of the employed labour force in 1980. The GDP of the services sector increased by an average of 3.0% per year in 1990–2001. Services GDP increased, in real terms, by an estimated 0.6% in 2001.

In 2001 Guyana recorded a visible trade deficit of US $93.6m. and a deficit of $129.0m. on the current account of the balance of payments. In 1998 the principal source of imports was the USA (26.6%). Trinidad and Tobago and the United Kingdom are other important suppliers of imports. In 1998 Canada was the principal market for exports (26.9% of total exports); the United Kingdom, Trinidad and Tobago and the Netherlands are also significant recipients. The principal exports are sugar, gold, bauxite and rice, and the principal imports are capital goods and consumer goods.

In 1999 the overall budget deficit was an estimated $ G2,791m. (equivalent to 2.6% of GDP). According to World Bank estimates, by the end of 2000 Guyana's external debt totalled US $1,455m. of which US $1,213m. was long-term public debt. The cost of debt-servicing in 2000 was US $116m. Urban consumer prices increased by 6.2% in 2000 and by 2.6% in 2001. An estimated 11.7% of the labour force were unemployed in 1992.

Guyana is a founder member of CARICOM (see p. 155). It is also a member of the UN Economic Commission for Latin America and the Caribbean (ECLAC, see p. 31) and of the International Sugar Organization (see p. 337).

In 1988, in response to serious economic decline, the Government introduced an extensive recovery programme of adjustment measures and structural reforms. Funds were made available under two Enhanced Structural Adjustment Facilities (ESAF), approved by the IMF in 1990 and in 1994. In 1996 negotiations with the 'Paris Club' of creditor nations and Trinidad and Tobago resulted in the cancellation of 67% of Guyana's bilateral debt with five creditor nations (a total reduction of US $395m.). In 1998, however, Guyana was severely affected by a substantial period of drought, and, as a consequence, real GDP declined by 1.5% in this year, while the rate of inflation increased to 4.6%. In July 1998 the Government secured a new three-year ESAF with the IMF, and in May 1999 the IMF and the World Bank declared that Guyana had become eligible for some $410m. in nominal debt-service relief under the Initiative for Heavily Indebted Poor Countries (HIPC). It was hoped that the estimated 24% reduction in the external debt burden would permit increased budgetary spending on education and social welfare. However, following industrial action by public-sector workers in mid-1999 (see Recent History), the Government was obliged to grant salary increases of 26.6%, effective from January 2000, thereby reducing the funds available for development expenditure; the decision was criticized by the IMF. In November 2000 Guyana became eligible for additional debt relief under the enhanced HIPC initiative. Upon successful completion of a series of pre-arranged conditions, including economic growth and attacking poverty, Guyana was to qualify for additional debt relief totalling $590m. In August 2001 Guyana and Brazil signed the Partial Scope Agreement, whereby import duties on a range of products and the 25% levy on ocean freight imports would be waived. In late 2001 the Bank of Guyana initiated discussions with the Caribbean Financial Task Force (CFTF) on the creation of a special unit to ensure that Guyana's financial system was clean and transparent; Guyana intended to join the CFTF in 2002.

The political impasse between the Government and PNC/Reform and the high crime rate hindered efforts to attract foreign investment to Guyana in 2002. Neverthelesss, in the 2002 budget, the Jagdeo administration reiterated its aims to reduce poverty and further to industrialize the economy. In September the IMF made a US $73m. three-year credit available to the Government for a poverty reduction scheme. In recognition of Guyana's success in making progress towards structural reform and maintaining economic stability, in November the IMF also approved a $64m. debt relief programme under the HIPC initiative.

Education

Education is officially compulsory, and is provided free of charge, for eight years between six and 14 years of age. Primary education begins at six years of age and lasts for at least six years. Secondary education, beginning at 12 years of age, lasts for up to five years, comprising a first cycle of three years and a second cycle of two years. Gross primary enrolment in 1998/1999 was equivalent to an estimated 97.5% of children in the relevant age-group (boys 100.0%; girls 94.3%). Gross secondary enrolment in 1997 was equivalent to an estimated 74.9% of children in the relevant age-group (boys 73.4%; girls 76.4%). There are also 14 technical, vocational, special and higher educational institutions. These include the University of Guyana in Georgetown and a teacher training college. Expenditure on education by the central Government in 1996 was estimated at $ G4,590m., and represented 10.0% of total government expenditure in that year. In 2002 the IDB approved a loan of US $30m. to assit with the modernisation of basic education in Guyana.

Public Holidays

2003: 1 January (New Year's Day), 12 February (Id al-Adha, feast of the Sacrifice*), 23 February (Mashramani, Republic Day), 18 April (Good Friday), 21 April (Easter Monday), 1 May (Labour Day), 5 May (Indian Heritage Day), 14 May (Yum an-Nabi, birth of the Prophet*), 7 July (Caribbean Day), 4 August (Freedom Day), 26 November (Id al-Fitr, end of Ramadan*), 25–26 December (Christmas).

2004: 1 January (New Year's Day), 2 February (Id al-Adha, feast of the Sacrifice*), 23 February (Mashramani, Republic Day), 9

April (Good Friday), 12 April (Easter Monday), 1 May (Labour Day), 2 May (Yum an-Nabi, birth of the Prophet*), 5 May (Indian Heritage Day), 5 July (Caribbean Day), 2 August (Freedom Day), 14 November (Id al-Fitr, end of Ramadan*), 25–26 December (Christmas).

*These holidays are dependent on the Islamic lunar calendar and may vary by one or two days from the dates given.

In addition, the Hindu festivals of Holi Phagwah (usually in March) and Divali (October or November) are celebrated. These festivals are dependent on sightings of the moon and their precise date is not known until two months before they take place.

Weights and Measures

The metric system has been introduced.

Statistical Survey

Source (unless otherwise stated): Bank of Guyana, 1 Church St and Ave of the Republic, POB 1003, Georgetown; tel. 226-3261; fax 227-2965; e-mail communications@bankofguyana.org.gy; internet www.bankofguyana.org.gy.

AREA AND POPULATION

Area: 214,969 sq km (83,000 sq miles).

Population: 758,619 (males 375,481, females 382,778) at census of 12 May 1980; 701,704 (males 344,928, females 356,776) at census of 12 May 1991; 763,000 in 2001 (UN estimate at mid-year).

Density (2001): 3.5 per sq km.

Ethnic Groups (official estimates, 1999): 'East' Indians 51%, Africans 41%, Portuguese and Chinese 2%, Amerindians 6%, Others less than 1.

Regions (estimated population, 1986): Barima–Waini 18,500; Pomeroon–Supenaam 42,000; Essequibo Islands–West Demerara 102,800; Demerara–Mahaica 310,800; Mahaica–Berbice 55,600; East Berbice–Corentyne 149,000; Cuyuni–Mazaruni 17,900; Potaro–Siparuni 5,700; Upper Takutu–Upper Essequibo 15,300; Upper Demerara–Berbice 38,600.

Principal Towns (official estimates): Georgetown (capital) 151,679; Linden 28,560; New Amsterdam 18,460; Corriverton 13,429. Source: Government Information Agency.

Births and Deaths (official estimates): Birth rate 21.8 per 1,000 in 1995–2000, 17.9 per 1,000 in 2000; Crude death rate 7.4 per 1,000 in 1995–2000, 8.4 per 1,000 in 2000.

Expectation of Life (WHO estimates, years at birth): 64.0 (males 61.3; females 64.0) in 2001. Source: WHO, *World Health Report*.

Economically Active Population (persons between 15 and 65 years of age, 1980 census): Agriculture, forestry and fishing 48,603; Mining and quarrying 9,389; Manufacturing 27,939; Electricity, gas and water 2,772; Construction 6,574; Trade, restaurants and hotels 14,690; Transport, storage and communications 9,160; Financing, insurance, real estate and business services 2,878; Community, social and personal services 57,416; Activities not adequately defined 15,260; Total employed 194,681 (males 153,645; females 41,036); Unemployed 44,650 (males 26,439, females 18,211); Total labour force 239,331 (males 180,084, females 59,247). *Mid-2000* (estimates): Agriculture, etc. 56,000; Total labour force 320,000 (Source: FAO).

HEALTH AND WELFARE

Key Indicators

Total Fertility Rate (children per woman, 2001): 2.4.

Under-5 Mortality Rate (per 1,000 live births, 2001): 72.

HIV/AIDS (% of persons aged 15–49, 2001): 2.70.

Physicians (per 1,000 head, 1997): 0.18.

Hospital Beds (per 1,000 head, 1996): 3.87.

Health Expenditure (2000): US $ per head (PPP): 197.

Health Expenditure (2000): % of GDP: 5.1.

Health Expenditure (2000): public (% of total): 82.7.

Access to Water (% of persons, 2000): 94.

Access to Sanitation (% of persons, 2000): 87.

Human Development Index (2000): ranking: 103.

Human Development Index (2000): value: 0.708.
For sources and definitions, see explanatory note on p. vi.

AGRICULTURE, ETC.

Principal Crops (FAO estimates, '000 metric tons, 2000): Rice (paddy) 540; Cassava (Manioc) 28; Roots and tubers 16; Sugar cane 3,000; Coconuts 75; Vegetables 10; Bananas 13; Plantains 18; Other fruit 20. Source: FAO.

Livestock (FAO estimates, '000 head, year ending September 2001): Horses 2; Asses 1; Mules 0.2; Cattle 220; Sheep 130; Pigs 20; Goats 79; Chickens 12,500. Source: FAO.

Livestock Products (FAO estimates, '000 metric tons, 2001): Beef and veal 2; Mutton and lamb 1; Sheep and goat meat 1; Pig meat 1; Chicken meat 12; Cows' milk 30; Hen eggs 2. Source: FAO.

Forestry ('000 cubic metres, 2001): Roundwood removals: Sawlogs, veneer logs and logs for sleepers 173, Other industrial wood 19, Fuel wood 876 (FAO estimate); Total 1,068; Sawnwood production: Total 30. Source: FAO.

Fishing ('000 metric tons, live weight, 2000): Capture 48.8 (Marine fishes 27.7, Atlantic seabob 16.7); Aquaculture 0.6; Total catch 54.2. Source: FAO, *Yearbook of Fishery Statistics*.

MINING

Production (preliminary figures, 2001): Bauxite 1,985,000 metric tons; Gold 14,183 kilograms. Source: US Geological Survey.

INDUSTRY

Selected Products (preliminary figures, 1996, unless otherwise indicated): Raw sugar 284,477 metric tons (2001); Rum 237,000 hectolitres; Beer 112,000 hectolitres; Cigarettes 400.2m.; Electric energy 830m. kWh (1998). Sources: mainly UN, *Industrial Commodity Statistics Yearbook*; IMF, *Guyana: Statistical Appendix* (February 1998).

FINANCE

Currency and Exchange Rates: 100 cents = 1 Guyana dollar ($ G). Sterling, *US Dollar and Euro Equivalents* (31 December 2002): £1 sterling = $ G309.06; US $1 = $ G191.75; €1 = $ G201.09; $ G1,000 = £3.236 = US $5.215 = €4.973. *Average Exchange Rate:* ($ G per US $): 182.4 in 2000; 187.3 in 2001; 190.7 in 2002.

Budget (estimates, $ G million, 1999): *Revenue:* Tax revenue 33,647 (Income tax 13,618, Property tax 607, Consumption tax 12,297, Taxes on international trade 4,590, Other tax 2,535); Other current revenue 2,388; Total 36,033, excl. grants received (5,320). *Expenditure:* Current expenditure 32,922 (Personnel emoluments 11,821, Other goods and services 6,215, Interest 9,455, Transfers 5,430); Capital expenditure 11,222; Total (incl. lending minus repayments) 44,144. Source: IMF, *Guyana: Statistical Annex* (January 2001).

International Reserves (US $ million at 31 December 2002): IMF special drawing rights 4.66, Foreign exchange 279.8; Total 284.47. Source: IMF, *International Financial Statistics*.

Money Supply ($ G million at 31 December 2001): Currency outside banks 15,138.3, Demand deposits at commercial banks 10,944.6; Total money (including also private-sector deposits at the Bank of Guyana 26,089.4. Source: IMF, *International Financial Statistics*.

Cost of Living (Urban Consumer Price Index; base: 1995 = 100): 124.7 in 1999; 132.4 in 2000; 135.9 in 2001. Source: IMF, *International Financial Statistics*.

Expenditure on the Gross Domestic Product (estimates, $ G million at current prices, 1998): Government final consumption expenditure 19,114; Private final consumption expenditure 70,843; Gross fixed capital formation 31,144; *Total domestic expenditure* 121,101; Exports of goods and services 103,920; *Less* Imports of goods and services, 116,557; *GDP in purchasers' values* 108,465. Source: IMF, *Guyana: Recent Economic Developments* (June 1999).

Gross Domestic Product by Economic Activity (estimates, $ G million at current factor cost, 2001): Agriculture (incl. forestry and fishing) 43,300; Mining and quarrying 16,156; Manufacturing (incl. power) 3,681; Construction 4,771; Distribution 4,268; Transport and communication 7,138; Rented dwellings 3,848; Financial services 3,387; Other services 1,570; Government 16,976; GDP at factor cost 105,095; Indirect taxes, less subsidies 18,570; GDP at market prices 123,665.

Balance of Payments (US $ million, 2001): Exports of goods f.o.b. 490.3; Imports of goods f.o.b. −583.9; *Trade balance* −93.6; Exports of services (net) −20.4; *Balance on goods and services* −114; Other income received (net) −58.6; *Balance on goods, services and income* −115.3; Current transfers received (net) 44.0; *Current balance* −129.0; Capital transfer 30.8; Government long-term capital (net) 39.4; Private long-term capital (net) 56.0; Short-term capital (net) −10.9; Net errors and omissions 4.9; *Overall balance* −8.4.

EXTERNAL TRADE

Principal Commodities (preliminary figures, US $ million, 2000): *Imports c.i.f.:* Capital goods 131.6; Consumer goods 164.4; Fuel and lubricants 121.0; Other intermediate goods 168.2; Total (incl. others) 585.8. *Exports f.o.b.:* Bauxite 76.3; Sugar 118.8; Rice 51.8; Gold 120.3; Shrimps 50.1; Timber 40.9; Total (incl. others, excl. re-exports) 492.9.

Principal Trading Partners (estimates, US $ million, 1998): *Imports:* Cuba 17; Netherlands 12; Trinidad and Tobago 121; United Kingdom 43; USA 160; Total (incl. others) 601. *Exports:* Canada 141; Netherlands 13; Trinidad and Tobago 14; United Kingdom 108; Total (incl. others) 525.

TRANSPORT

Road Traffic ('000 vehicles in use, 1998): Passenger cars 9.5; Commercial vehicles 3.2. Source: UN, *Statistical Yearbook*.

Shipping (international sea-borne freight traffic, estimates in '000 metric tons, 1990): Goods loaded 1,730; Goods unloaded 673 (Source: UN, *Monthly Bulletin of Statistics*). *Merchant Fleet* (at 31 December 2001): Vessels 59; Displacement 15,169 grt (Source: Lloyd's Register-Fairplay, *World Fleet Statistics*).

Civil Aviation (traffic on scheduled services, 1999): Kilometres flown (million) 2; passengers carried ('000) 70; passenger-km (million) 277; total ton-km (million) 28. Source: UN, *Statistical Yearbook*.

TOURISM

Tourist Arrivals ('000): 65.8 in 1998; 74.9 in 1999; 105.0 in 2000.

Tourist Receipts (US $ million): 39 in 1997; 60 in 1998; 52 in 1999. Sources: Caribbean Development Bank, *Social and Economic Indicators 2001*, and World Bank, *World Development Indicators*.

COMMUNICATIONS MEDIA

Radio Receivers (1999): 400,000 in use*.

Television Receivers (2000): 70,000 in use*.

Telephones (2000): 68,400 main lines in use†.

Facsimile Machines (1990): 195 in use†.

Mobile Cellular Telephones (2001): 39,500 subscribers†.

Personal Computers (2001): 23,000 in use‡.

Internet Users (2001): 95,000‡.

Daily Newspapers (1998): 2; estimated circulation (1996) 42,000*.

Non-daily Newspapers (1988): 6 (estimate); estimated circulation 84,000*.

Book Production (school textbooks, 1996): 1 title.

* Source: UNESCO, *Statistical Yearbook*.
† Source: UN, *Statistical Yearbook*.
‡ Source: International Telecommunication Union.

EDUCATION

Pre-primary (1999/2000): Institutions 320; Teachers 2,218; Students 36,995.

Primary (1999/2000): Institutions 423; Teachers 3,951; Students 105,800.

General Secondary (1999/2000): Institutions 70; Teachers 1,972; Students 36,055.

Special Education (1997/98): Institutions 6; Teachers 28; Students 585.

Technical and Vocational (1997/98): Institutions 6; Teachers 168; Students 3,307.

Teacher Training (1997/98): Institutions 1; Teachers 70; Students 1,235.

University (1997/98): Institutions 1; Teachers 383; Students 4,671.

Private Education (1997/98): Institutions 5; Teachers 138; Students 1,590.
Source: Ministry of Education.

Adult Literacy Rate (UNESCO estimates): 98.5% (males 98.9%; females 98.1%) in 2000 (Source: UN Development Programme, *Human Development Report*).

Directory

The Constitution*

Guyana became a republic, within the Commonwealth, on 23 February 1970. A new Constitution was promulgated on 6 October 1980, and amended in 2000 and 2001. Its main provisions are summarized below:

The Constitution declares the Co-operative Republic of Guyana to be an indivisible, secular, democratic sovereign state in the course of transition from capitalism to socialism. The bases of the political, economic and social system are political and economic independence, involvement of citizens and socio-economic groups, such as co-operatives and trade unions, in the decision-making processes of the State and in management, social ownership of the means of production, national economic planning and co-operativism as the principle of socialist transformation. Personal property, inheritance, the right to work, with equal pay for men and women engaged in equal work, free medical attention, free education and social benefits for old age and disability are guaranteed. Additional rights include equality before the law, the right to strike and to demonstrate peacefully, the right of indigenous peoples to the protection and preservation of their culture, and a variety of gender and work-related rights. Individual political rights are subject to the principles of national sovereignty and democracy, and freedom of expression to the State's duty to ensure fairness and balance in the dissemination of information to the public. Relations with other countries are guided by respect for human rights, territorial integrity and non-intervention.

THE PRESIDENT

The President is the supreme executive authority, Head of State and Commander-in-Chief of the armed forces, elected for a term of office, usually of five years' duration, with no limit on re-election. The successful presidential candidate is the nominee of the party with the largest number of votes in the legislative elections. The President may prorogue or dissolve the National Assembly (in the case of dissolution, fresh elections must be held immediately) and has discretionary powers to postpone elections for up to one year at a time for up to five years. The President may be removed from office on medical grounds, or for violation of the Constitution (with a two-thirds' majority vote of the Assembly), or for gross misconduct (with a three-quarters' majority vote of the Assembly if allegations are upheld by a tribunal).

The President appoints a First Vice-President and Prime Minister who must be an elected member of the National Assembly, and a Cabinet of Ministers, which may include non-elected members and is collectively responsible to the legislature. The President also appoints a Leader of the Opposition, who is the elected member of the Assembly deemed by the President most able to command the support of the opposition.

THE LEGISLATURE

The legislative body is a unicameral National Assembly of 65 members; 53 members are elected by universal adult suffrage in a system of proportional representation, 10 members are elected by the 10

Regional Democratic Councils and two members are elected by the National Congress of Local Democratic Organs. The Assembly passes bills, which are then presented to the President, and may pass constitutional amendments.

LOCAL GOVERNMENT

Guyana is divided into 10 Regions, each having a Regional Democratic Council elected for a term of up to five years and four months, although it may be prematurely dissolved by the President. Local councillors elect from among themselves deputies to the National Congress of Democratic Organs. This Congress and the National Assembly together form the Supreme Congress of the People of Guyana, a deliberative body which may be summoned, dissolved or prorogued by the President and is automatically dissolved along with the National Assembly.

OTHER PROVISIONS

Impartial commissions exist for the judiciary, the public service and the police service. An Ombudsman is appointed, after consultation between the President and the Leader of the Opposition, to hold office for four years.

* In October 2000 several amendments to the Constitution were approved by the National Assembly. These included the introduction of a mixed system of proportional representation, combining regional constituencies and national candidate lists, and the abolition of the Supreme Congress of the People of Guyana and of the National Congress of Local Democratic Organs. In January 2001 the High Court ruled that the 1997 election of the legislature was null and void. However, it granted temporary validity to legislation passed after December 1997. In December 2000 the National Assembly approved a constitutional amendment removing a President's immunity from prosecution and limiting the presidential power to appoint ministers from outside the National Assembly to a maximum of four, and two parliamentary secretaries.

The Government

HEAD OF STATE

President: BHARRAT JAGDEO (sworn in 11 August 1999; re-elected 19 March 2001).

CABINET
(April 2003)

Prime Minister: SAMUEL A. HINDS.

Minister of Parliamentary Affairs in the Office of the President: PANDIT REEPU DAMAN PERSAUD.

Minister of Home Affairs: RONALD GAJRAJ.

Minister of Foreign Affairs: Dr RUDY INSANALLY.

Minister of Foreign Trade in the Ministry of Foreign Affairs: CLEMENT ROHEE.

Minister of Finance: SAISNARINE KOWLESSAR.

Minister of Agriculture: NAVIN CHANDARPAL.

Minister of Fisheries, Crops and Livestock: SATYADEOW SAWH.

Minister of Legal Affairs and Attorney-General: DOODNAUTH SINGH.

Minister of Information: PREM MISIR.

Minister of Education: Dr HENRY JEFFREY.

Minister of Health: Dr LESLIE RAMSAMMY.

Minister of Housing and Water: SHAIK BAKSH.

Minister of Labour, Human Services and Social Security: Dr DALE BISNAUTH.

Minister of Tourism, Industry and Commerce: MANZOOR NADIR.

Minister of Amerindian Affairs: CAROLYN RODRIGUES.

Minister of Local Government and Regional Development: HARRIPERSAUD NOKTA.

Minister of Public Service Management: JENNIFER WESTFORD.

Minister of Transport, Communication and Hydraulics: CARL ANTHONY XAVIER.

Minister of Culture, Youth and Sports: GAIL TEIXIERA.

Secretary to the Cabinet: Dr ROGER LUNCHEON.

MINISTRIES

Office of the President: New Garden St and South Rd, Georgetown; tel. 225-1330; fax 226-3395.

Office of the Prime Minister: Wights Lane, Georgetown; tel. 227-3101; fax 226-7563.

Office of Amerindian Affairs: New Garden St, Georgetown; tel. 226-5167.

Ministry of Agriculture: POB 1001, Regent and Vlissingen Rds, Georgetown; tel. 227-5527; fax 227-3638; e-mail guyagri@hotmail.com; internet www.sdnp.org.gy/minagri.

Ministry of Culture, Youth and Sports: 71 Main St, North Cummingsburg, Georgetown; tel. 226-0142; fax 226-5067.

Ministry of Education: 21 Brickdam, Stabroek, POB 1014, Georgetown; tel. 223-7900; fax 225-8511; internet www.sdnp.org.gy/minedu.

Ministry of Finance: Main and Urquhart Sts, Georgetown; tel. 227-1114; fax 226-1284.

Ministry of Fisheries, Crops and Livestock: Regent and Vlissengen Rds, Georgetown; tel. 225-8310; fax 227-2978; e-mail minfcl@sdnp.org.gy; internet www.sdnp.org.gy/minagri.

Ministry of Foreign Affairs: Takuba Lodge, 254 South Rd and New Garden St, Georgetown; tel. 226-1607; fax 225-9192; e-mail minfor@sdnp.org.gy; internet www.sdnp.org.gy/minfor.

Ministry of Health: Brickdam, Stabroek, Georgetown; tel. 226-1560; fax 225-6958; e-mail moh@sdnp.org.gy; internet www.sdnp.org.gy/moh.

Ministry of Home Affairs: 6 Brickdam, Stabroek, Georgetown; tel. 225-7270; fax 226-2740.

Ministry of Housing and Water: Homestretch Ave, Durban Park, Georgetown; tel. 225-7192.

Ministry of Information: Area B, Homestretch Ave, Durban Park, Georgetown; tel. 227-1101; fax 226-4003; e-mail gis@sdnp.org.gy; internet www.sdnp.org.gy/mininfo.

Ministry of Labour, Human Services and Social Security: 1 Water and Cornhill Sts, Stabroek, Georgetown; tel. 225-0655; fax 227-1308; e-mail nrdocgd@sdnp.org.gy; internet www.sdnp.org.gy/mohss.

Ministry of Legal Affairs and Office of the Attorney-General: 95 Carmichael St, Georgetown; tel. 225-3607; fax 225-0732.

Ministry of Local Government and Regional Development: De Winkle Bldgs, Fort St, Kingston, Georgetown; tel. 225-8621.

Ministry of Public Service Management: 64 Waterloo St, North Cummingsburg; tel. 227-2365; fax 225-6954.

Ministry of Tourism, Industry and Commerce: 229 South Rd, Lacytown, Georgetown; tel. 226-2505; fax 225-4370; e-mail ministry@mintic.gov.gy; internet www.sdnp.org.gy/mtti.

Ministry of Transport, Communication and Hydraulics: Battery Rd, Kingston, Georgetown; tel. 225-9350.

President and Legislature

NATIONAL ASSEMBLY

Speaker: WINSLOW MARTIN ZEPHYR.

Deputy Speaker: CLARISSA RIEHL.

Election, 19 March 2001

Party	No. of seats		
	Regional	National	Total
People's Progressive Party/ CIVIC (PPP/CIVIC) . . .	11	23	34
People's National Congress/ Reform (PNC/Reform) . . .	13	14	27
Guyana Action Party/Working People's Alliance (GAP/WPA)	1	1	2
Rise, Organize and Rebuild Guyana Movement (ROAR) .	—	1	1
The United Force (TUF) . . .	—	1	1
Total	**25**	**40**	**65**

Under Guyana's system of proportional representation, the nominated candidate of the party receiving the most number of votes was elected to the presidency. Thus, on 23 March 2000 the candidate of the PPP/CIVIC alliance, Bharrat Jagdeo, was declared President-elect, defeating Hugh Desmond Hoyte of the PNC/Reform alliance. Jagdeo was inaugurated as President on 31 March.

Political Organizations

CIVIC: New Garden St, Georgetown; social/political movement of businessmen and professionals; allied to PPP; Leader SAMUEL ARCHIBALD ANTHONY HINDS.

Guyana Action Party (GAP): Georgetown; allied to WPA; Leader PAUL HARDY.

Guyana Democratic Party (GDP): Georgetown; f. 1996; Leaders ASGAR ALLY, NANDA K. GOPAUL.

Guyana Labour Party (GLP): Georgetown; f. 1992 by members of Guyanese Action for Reform and Democracy.

Guyana National Congress (GNC): Georgetown.

Guyana People's Party (GPP): Georgetown; f. 1996; Leader MAX MOHAMED.

Guyana Republican Party (GRP): Paprika East Bank, Essequibo; f. 1985; right-wing; Leader LESLIE PRINCE (resident in the USA).

Guyana's Alliance for Progress: 199 Charlotte Street, Georgetown; tel. 227-8845; e-mail guyanasalliance@yahoo.com; internet guyanese.webjump.com.

Horizon and Star (HAS): Georgetown.

Justice For All Party (JFAP): 73 Robb and Wellington Sts, Lacytown, Georgetown; tel. 226-5462; fax 227-3050; e-mail sharma@guyana.net.gy; internet www.jfa-gy.com; Leader CHANDRANARINE SHARMA.

National Democratic Front (NDF): Georgetown; Leader JOSEPH BACCHUS.

National Front Alliance: Georgetown.

National Independence Party: Georgetown; Leader SAPHIER HUSSIEN.

National Republican Party (NRP): Georgetown; f. 1990; after a split with URP; right-wing; Leader ROBERT GANGADEEN.

Patriotic Coalition for Democracy (PCD): Georgetown; f. 1986 by five opposition parties; the PCD campaigns for an end to alleged electoral malpractices; principal offices, including the chair of the collective leadership, rotate among the parties; now comprises the following three parties:

Democratic Labour Movement (DLM): 34 Robb and King Sts, 4th Floor, Lacytown, POB 10930, Georgetown; f. 1983; democratic-nationalist; Pres. PAUL NEHRU TENNASSEE.

People's Democratic Movement (PDM): Stabroek House, 10 Croal St, Georgetown; tel. 226-4707; fax 226-3002; f. 1973; centrist; Leader LLEWELLYN JOHN.

People's Progressive Party (PPP): Freedom House, 41 Robb St, Lacytown, Georgetown; tel. 227-2095; fax 227-2096; e-mail ppp@guyana.net.gy; internet www.pppcivic.org; f. 1950; Marxist-Leninist; allied to CIVIC; Leader JANET JAGAN; Gen. Sec. DONALD RAMOTAR.

People's National Congress/Reform (PNC/Reform): Congress Place, Sophia, POB 10330, Georgetown; tel. 225-7852; fax 225-6055; e-mail pnc@guyana-pnc.org; internet www.guyana-pnc.org; f. 1955 after a split with the PPP; Reform wing established in 2000; PNC Leader ROBERT CORBIN; Reform Leader STANLEY MING; Reform Chair. JEROME KHAN.

People's Republic Party: POB 10162, Georgetown; e-mail info@peoplesrepublicparty.com; internet www.mins.net/prp; Chair HARRY DAS.

People's Solidarity Movement: Georgetown; f. 2002; Afro-Guyanese opposition grouping.

People's Unity Party of Guyana (PUP): POB 10-1223, Georgetown; e-mail peter@ramsaroop.com; internet www.peoplesunityparty.com; f. 1999; Leader PETER R. RAMSAROOP.

Rise, Organize and Rebuild Guyana Movement (ROAR): 186 Parafield, Leonora, West Coast Demerara, POB 101409, Georgetown; tel. 068-2452; e-mail guyroar@hotmail.com; internet www.jaiag.com; f. 1999.

The United Force (TUF): 95 Robb and New Garden Sts, Bourda, Georgetown; tel. 226-2596; fax 225-2973; e-mail manzoornadir@yahoo.com; internet tuf.homestead.com/index.htm; f. 1960; right-wing; advocates rapid industrialization through govt partnership and private capital; Leader MANZOOR NADIR.

United People's Party: 77 Winter Place, Brickdam, Georgetown; tel. 227-5217; fax 227-5166; e-mail unitedguyana@yahoo.com; internet upp.webjump.com.

United Republican Party (URP): Georgetown; f. 1985; right-wing; advocates federal govt; Leader Dr LESLIE RAMSAMMY.

United Workers' Party (UWP): Georgetown; f. 1991; Leader WINSTON PAYNE.

Working People's Alliance (WPA): Walter Rodney House, Lot 80, Croal St, Stabroek, Georgetown; tel. 225-6624; internet www.saxakali.com/wpa; originally popular pressure group, became political party 1979; independent Marxist; allied to GAP; Collective Leadership EUSI KWAYANA, Dr CLIVE THOMAS, Dr RUPERT ROOPNARINE, WAZIR MOHAMED.

Diplomatic Representation

EMBASSIES AND HIGH COMMISSIONS IN GUYANA

Brazil: 308 Church St, Queenstown, POB 10489, Georgetown; tel. 225-7970; fax 226-9063; e-mail bragetown@solutions2000.net; Ambassador NEY DO PRADO DIEGUEZ.

Canada: High and Young Sts, POB 10880, Georgetown; tel. 227-2081; fax 225-8380; e-mail grgtn@dfait-maecl.gc.ca; High Commissioner SERGE MARCOUX.

China, People's Republic: Botanic Gardens, Mandella Ave, Georgetown; tel. 227-1651; fax 225-9228; Ambassador SONG TAO.

Cuba: 40 High St, Kingston, Georgetown; tel. 226-6732; Ambassador JOSÉ MANUEL INCLAN EMBADE.

India: Bank of Baroda Bldg, 10 Ave of the Republic, POB 101148, Georgetown; tel. 226-3996; fax 225-7012; High Commissioner Dr PRAKASH V. JOSHI.

Russia: 3 Public Rd, Kitty, Georgetown; tel. 226-9773; fax 227-2975; Ambassador IGOR NIKOLAEVICH PROKOPYEV.

Suriname: 304 Church St, POB 10508, Georgetown; tel. 226-7844; Ambassador MANORMA SOEKNANDAN.

United Kingdom: 44 Main St, POB 10849, Georgetown; tel. 226-5881; fax 225-3555; e-mail consular@georgetown.mail.fco.gov.uk; internet www.britain-un-guyana.org; High Commissioner STEPHEN HISCOCK.

USA: Duke and Young Sts, Kingston, Georgetown; tel. 225-4900; fax 225-8497; Ambassador RONALD GODDARD.

Venezuela: 296 Thomas St, South Cummingsburg, Georgetown; tel. 226-1543; fax 225-3241; e-mail embveguy@guyana.net.gy; Ambassador JEAN-FRANÇOIS PULVENIS.

Judicial System

The Judicature of Guyana comprises the Supreme Court of Judicature, which consists of the Court of Appeal and the High Court (both of which are superior courts of record), and a number of Courts of Summary Jurisdiction.

The Court of Appeal, which came into operation in 1966, consists of the Chancellor as President, the Chief Justice, and such number of Justices of Appeal as may be prescribed by the National Assembly.

The High Court of the Supreme Court consists of the Chief Justice as President of the Court and Puisne Judges. Its jurisdiction is both original and appellate. It has criminal jurisdiction in matters brought before it on indictment. A person convicted by the Court has a right of appeal to the Guyana Court of Appeal. The High Court of the Supreme Court has unlimited jurisdiction in civil matters and exclusive jurisdiction in probate, divorce and admiralty and certain other matters. Under certain circumstances, appeal in civil matters lies either to the Full Court of the High Court of the Supreme Court, which is composed of not less than two judges, or to the Guyana Court of Appeal.

A magistrate has jurisdiction to determine claims where the amount involved does not exceed a certain sum of money, specified by law. Appeal lies to the Full Court.

Chancellor of Justice: DESIRÉE BERNARD.

Chief Justice: CARL SINGH.

High Court Justices: NANDRAM KISSOON, CLAUDETTE SINGH.

Attorney-General: DOODNAUTH SINGH.

Religion

CHRISTIANITY

Guyana Council of Churches: 26 Durban St, Lodge, Georgetown; tel. 225-3020; e-mail bishopedghill@hotmail.com; f. 1967 by merger of the Christian Social Council (f. 1937) and the Evangelical Council

(f. 1960); 15 mem. churches, 1 assoc. mem. Chair. Bishop JUAN A. EDGHILL; Sec. Rev. KEITH HALEY.

The Anglican Communion

Anglicans in Guyana are adherents of the Church in the Province of the West Indies, comprising eight dioceses. The Archbishop of the Province is the Bishop of the North Eastern Caribbean and Aruba, resident in St John's, Antigua. The diocese of Guyana also includes French Guiana and Suriname. In 1986 the estimated membership in the country was 125,000.

Bishop of Guyana: Rt Rev. RANDOLPH OSWALD GEORGE, Austin House, 49 High St, Georgetown 1; tel. 226-4183; fax 226-3353.

The Baptist Church

The Baptist Convention of Guyana: POB 10149, Georgetown; tel. 226-0428; Chair. Rev. ALFRED JULIEN.

The Lutheran Church

The Lutheran Church in Guyana: Lutheran Courts, POB 88, New Amsterdam; tel. (3) 3425; fax (3) 6479; e-mail lcg@guyana.net .gy; f. 1947; 11,000 mems; Pres. Rev. ROY K. THAKURDYAL.

The Roman Catholic Church

Guyana comprises the single diocese of Georgetown, suffragan to the archdiocese of Port of Spain, Trinidad and Tobago. At 31 December 2000 adherents of the Roman Catholic Church comprised about 12% of the total population. The Bishop participates in the Antilles Episcopal Conference Secretariat, currently based in Port of Spain, Trinidad.

Bishop of Georgetown: G. BENEDICT SINGH, Bishop's House, 27 Brickdam, POB 10720, Stabroek, Georgetown; tel. 226-4469; fax 225-8519; e-mail rcbishop@networksgy.com.

Other Christian Churches

Other denominations active in Guyana include the African Methodist Episcopal Church, the African Methodist Episcopal Zion Church, the Church of God, the Church of the Nazarene, the Ethiopian Orthodox Church, the Guyana Baptist Mission, the Guyana Congregational Union, the Guyana Presbyterian Church, the Hallelujah Church, the Methodist Church in the Caribbean and the Americas, the Moravian Church and the Presbytery of Guyana.

BAHÁ'Í FAITH

National Spiritual Assembly: 220 Charlotte St, Bourda, Georgetown; tel. and fax 226-5952; e-mail nsaguy@sdnp.org.gy; internet www.sdnp.org.gy/bahai; incorporated in 1976; 68 communities in 1998.

HINDUISM

Hindu Religious Centre: Georgetown; tel. 225-7443; f. 1934; Hindus account for about one-third of the population; Pres. RAMRAJ JAGNANDAN; Gen. Sec. CHRISHNA PERSAUD.

ISLAM

The Central Islamic Organization of Guyana (CIOG): M.Y.O. Bldg, Woolford Ave, Thomas Lands, POB 10245, Georgetown; tel. 225-8654; fax 225-2475; e-mail ciog@sdnp.org.gy; internet www.ciog .gy; Pres. Alhaji FAZEEL M. FEROUZ; Gen. Sec. MUJTABA NASIR.

Guyana United Sad'r Islamic Anjuman: 157 Alexander St, Kitty, POB 10715, Georgetown; tel. 226-9620; f. 1936; 120,000 mems; Pres. Haji A. H. RAHAMAN; Sec. YACOOB HUSSAIN.

The Press

DAILIES

Guyana Chronicle: 2A Lama Ave, Bel Air Park, POB 11, Georgetown; tel. 226-3243; fax 227-5208; e-mail khan@guyana.net.gy; internet www.guyanachronicle.com; f. 1881; govt-owned; also produces weekly *Sunday Chronicle* (tel. 226-3243); Editor-in-Chief SHARIEF KHAN; circ. 23,000 (weekdays), 43,000 (Sundays).

Stabroek News: 46–47 Robb St, Lacytown, Georgetown; tel. 225-7473; fax 225-4637; e-mail stabroeknews@stabroeknews.com; internet www.stabroeknews.com; f. 1986; also produces weekly *Sunday Stabroek*; liberal independent; Editor-in-Chief DAVID DE CAIRES; Editor ANAND PERSAUD; circ. 20,000 (weekdays), 33,000 (Sundays).

WEEKLIES AND PERIODICALS

The Catholic Standard: 293 Oronoque St, Queenstown, POB 10720, Georgetown; tel. 226-1540; f. 1905; weekly; Editor COLIN SMITH; circ. 10,000.

Diocesan Magazine: 144 Almond and Oronoque Sts, Queenstown, Georgetown; quarterly.

Guyana Business: 156 Waterloo St, POB 10110, Georgetown; tel. 225-6451; f. 1889; organ of the Georgetown Chamber of Commerce and Industry; quarterly; Editor C. D. KIRTON.

Guyana Review: 143 Oronoque St, POB 10386, Georgetown; tel. 226-3139; fax 227-3465; e-mail guyrev@networksgy.com; internet www.guyanareview.com; f. 1993; monthly.

Guynews: Georgetown; monthly.

Kaieteur News: 24 Saffon St, Charlestown; tel. 225-8452; fax 225-8473; f. 1994; independent weekly; Editor W. HENRY SKERRETT; circ. 30,000.

Mirror: Lot 8, Industrial Estate, Ruimveldt, Greater Georgetown; tel. 226-2471; fax 226-2472; e-mail ngmirror@guyana.net.gy; internet www.mirrornewsonline.com; owned by the New Guyana Co Ltd; Sundays; Editor ROBERT PERSAUD; circ. 25,000.

New Nation: Congress Place, Sophia, Georgetown; tel. 226-7891; f. 1955; organ of the People's National Congress; weekly; Editor FRANCIS WILLIAMS; circ. 26,000.

The Official Gazette of Guyana: Guyana National Printers Ltd, Lot 1, Public Road, La Penitence; weekly; circ. 450.

Thunder: Georgetown; f. 1950; organ of the People's Progressive Party; quarterly; Editor RALPH RAMKARRAN; circ. 5,000.

NEWS AGENCIES

Guyana Information Services: Office of the President, New Garden St and South Rd, Georgetown; tel. 226-3389; fax 226-4003; f. 1993; Dir MILTON DREPAUL.

Foreign Bureaux

Xinhua (New China) News Agency (People's Republic of China): 52 Brickdam, Stabroek, Georgetown; tel. 226-9965.

Associated Press (USA) and Informatsionnoye Telegrafnoye Agentstvo Rossii-Telegrafnoye Agentstvo Suverennykh Stran (ITAR—TASS) (Russia) are also represented.

Publishers

Guyana Free Press: POB 10386, Georgetown; tel. 226-3139; fax 227-3465; e-mail guyrev@networksgy.com; books and learned journals.

Guyana National Printers Ltd: 1 Public Rd, La Penitence, POB 10256, Greater Georgetown; tel. 225-3623; e-mail gnpl@guyana.net .gy; f. 1939; govt-owned printers and publishers; privatization pending; Chair. DESMOND N. MOHAMED.

Guyana Publications Inc: 46/47 Robb St, Lacytown, Georgetown; tel. 225-7473; fax 225-4637; e-mail stabroeknews.com; internet www .stabroeknews.com.

Broadcasting and Communications

TELECOMMUNICATIONS

The telecommunications sector was to be restructured and opened up to competition in 2002.

Caribbean Wireless Telecom (CWT): Georgetown; f. 1999; mobile cellular telephone service; CEO EARL SINGH.

Guyana Telephones and Telegraph Company (GT & T): 79 Brickdam, POB 10628, Georgetown; tel. 226-7840; fax 226-2457; internet www.gtt.co.gy; f. 1991; formerly state-owned Guyana Telecommunications Corpn; 80% ownership by Atlantic Tele-Network (USA); Gen. Man. SONITA JAGAN; Chair. CORNELIUS PRIOR.

BROADCASTING

Radio

Guyana Broadcasting Corporation (GBC): Broadcasting House, 44 High St, POB 10760, Georgetown; tel. 225-8734; fax 225-8756; e-mail gbd.-gm@guyana.net.gy; f. 1979; operates channels GBC 1 (Coastal Service) and GBC 2 (National Service); Voice of Guyana; Gen. Man. DESMOND MOHAMED (acting).

Television

In May 2001 the Government implemented the regulation of all broadcast frequencies. All television broadcast operations were required to be fully licensed by 31 July. By December 15 of the 18 television stations in Guyana had acquired licences. Two private stations relay US satellite television programmes.

Guyana Television: 68 Hadfield St, Georgetown; tel. 226-0116; fax 226-2253; e-mail mgootsarran@hotmail.com; f. 1993; fmrly Guyana Television Corporation; govt-owned; limited service; Gen. Man. MARTIN GOOTSARRAN.

Finance

(dep. = deposits; m. = million; brs = branches; amounts in Guyana dollars)

BANKING

Central Bank

Bank of Guyana: 1 Church St and Ave of the Republic, POB 1003, Georgetown; tel. 226-3250; fax 227-2965; e-mail boglib@guyana.net .gy; internet www.bankofguyana.org.gy; f. 1965; cap. 1,000m., res 11,121m., dep. 97,852m. (Dec. 2000); central bank of issue; acts as regulatory authority for the banking sector; Gov. DOLLY S. SINGH; Man. LAWRENCE T. WILLIAMS.

Commercial Banks

Demerara Bank Ltd: 230 Camp and South Sts, Georgetown; tel. 225-0610; fax 225-0601; e-mail banking@demerarabank.com; internet www.demerarabank.com; f. 1994; cap. 450m., res 103m., dep. 8,223m. (Sept. 2000); Chair. YESU PERSAUD; Man. AHMED M. KHAN.

Guyana Americas Merchant Bank (GBTI): GTBI Bldg, 138 Regent St, Lacytown, Georgetown; tel. 223-5193; fax 223-5195; e-mail gambi@networksgy.com; f. 2001; merchant bank.

Guyana Bank for Trade and Industry Ltd: 47–48 Water St, POB 10280, Georgetown; tel. 226-8430; fax 227-1612; e-mail banking@ gbtibank.com; internet www.gbtibank.com; f. 1987 to absorb the operations of Barclays Bank; cap. 800m., dep. 19,398m., res 507m. (Dec. 2000); CEO R. K. SHARMA; 6 brs.

Guyana National Co-operative Bank: 1 Lombard and Cornhill Sts, Georgetown; tel. 225-7810; fax 226-0231; e-mail gncbgm@ guyana.net.gy; f. 1970; merged with Guyana Co-operative Agricultural and Industrial Development Bank in 1995; sale to National Bank of Industry and Commerce expected to be completed by late 2003. Gen. Man. JOHN FLANAGAN; 9 brs.

National Bank of Industry and Commerce (NBIC): 38–40 Water St, POB 10440, Georgetown; tel. 226-4091; fax 227-2921; 51% govt-owned; 17.5% owned by National Insurance Scheme; Man. Dir CONRAD PLUMMER; 5 brs.

Foreign Banks

Bank of Baroda (India): 10 Ave of the Republic, POB 10768, Georgetown; tel. 226-4005; fax 225-1691; e-mail bobinc@guyana .notgguy; f. 1908; Chief Man. P. SAVID.

Bank of Nova Scotia (Canada): 104 Carmichael St, POB 10631; Georgetown; tel. 225-9222; fax 225-9309; e-mail bns.guyana@ scotiabank.com; Man. FARRIED SULLIMAN; 5 brs.

Citizens' Bank Guyana Inc (Jamaica): 201 Camp and Charlotte Sts, Lacytown, Georgetown; tel. 226-1705; fax 227-1719; e-mail citizens@guyana.net.gy; internet citizens-carib.com/guyana.htm; f. 1994; Chair. DENNIS LALOR.

INSURANCE

Demerara Mutual Life Assurance Society Ltd: Demerara Life Bldg, 61–62 Robb St and Ave of the Republic, POB 10409, Georgetown; tel. 225-8991–3; fax 225-58995; e-mail demlife@networksgy .com; f. 1891; Chair. RICHARD B. FIELDS; Gen. Man. KEITH N. CHOLMONDELEY.

Diamond Fire and General Insurance Inc: High St, Kingston, Georgetown; tel. 223-9771; fax 223-9770; e-mail diamondins@ solutions2000.net; f. 2000; privately owned; cap. $G 100m.

Guyana Co-operative Insurance Service: 46 Main St, Georgetown; tel. 225-9153; f. 1976; 67% share offered for private ownership in 1996; Chair. G. A. LEE; Gen. Man. PAT BENDER.

Guyana and Trinidad Mutual Life Insurance Co Ltd: Lots 27–29, Robb and Hincks Sts, Georgetown; tel. 225-7910; fax 225-9397; e-mail gtmgroup@gtm_gy.com; f. 1925; Chair. HAROLD B. DAVIS; Man.

Dir R. E. CHEONG; affiliated company: Guyana and Trinidad Mutual Fire Insurance Co Ltd.

Hand-in-Hand Mutual Fire and Life Group: 1–4 Ave of the Republic, POB 10188, Georgetown; tel. 225-0462; fax 225-7519; f. 1865; fire and life insurance; Chair. J. A. CHIN; Gen. Man. K. A. EVELYN.

Insurance Association

Insurance Association of Guyana: 54 Robb St, Bourda, POB 10741, Georgetown; tel. 226-3514; f. 1968.

Trade and Industry

GOVERNMENT AGENCIES

Environmental Protection Agency, Guyana: IAST Campus, University of Guyana, Georgetown; tel. 022-5785; fax 022-2442; e-mail epa@sdnp.org.gy; f. 1988 as Guyana Agency for the Environment, renamed 1996; formulates, implements and monitors policies on the environment; Dir Dr WALTER CHIN.

Guyana Energy Agency (GEA): Georgetown; e-mail ecgea@sdnp .org.gy; f. 1998 as successor to Guyana National Energy Authority.

Guyana Marketing Corporation: 87 Robb and Alexander Sts, Georgetown; tel. 226-8255; fax 227-4114; e-mail newgmc@ networksgy.com; Chair. GEOFREY DA SILVA; Gen. Man. ROXANNE GREENIDGE.

Guyana Office for Investment (Go-Invest): 190 Camp and Church Sts, Georgetown; tel. 225-0658; fax 225-0655; e-mail goinvest@sdnp.org.gy; internet www.goinvest.gov.gy; f. 1994; Chair. BHARRAT JAGDEO; CEO GEOFFREY DA SILVA.

Guyana Public Communications Agency: Georgetown; tel. 227-2025; f. 1989; Exec. Chair. KESTER ALVES.

DEVELOPMENT ORGANIZATIONS

State Planning Commission: 229 South St, Lacytown, Georgetown; tel. 226-8093; fax 227-2499; Chief Planning Officer CLYDE ROOPCHAND.

Institute of Private Enterprise Development (IPED): Georgetown; f. 1986 to help establish small businesses; total loans provided $G771m. and total jobs created 9,021 (1999); Chair. YESU PERSAUD.

CHAMBER OF COMMERCE

Georgetown Chamber of Commerce and Industry: 156 Waterloo St, Cummingsburg, POB 10110, Georgetown; tel. 225-5846; fax 226-3519; f. 1889; 122 mems; Pres. JOHN S. DE FREITAS; Chief Exec. G. C. FUNG-ON.

INDUSTRIAL AND TRADE ASSOCIATIONS

Bauxite Industry Development Company Ltd: 71 Main St, Georgetown; tel. 225-7780; fax 226-7413; f. 1976; Chair. J. I. F. BLACKMAN.

Guyana Rice Development Board: 117 Cowan St, Georgetown; tel. 225-8717; fax 225-6486; e-mail grdb@gol.net.gy; internet www .cra.cc/grdb; f. 1994 to assume operations of Guyana Rice Export Board and Guyana Rice Grading Centre; Chair. and CEO CHARLES KENNARD.

Livestock Development Co Ltd: 58 High St, Georgetown; tel. 226-1601.

EMPLOYERS' ORGANIZATIONS

Consultative Association of Guyanese Industry Ltd: 157 Waterloo St, POB 10730, Georgetown; tel. 226-4603; fax 227-0725; e-mail pscentre@guyana.net.gy; f. 1962; 193 mems, 3 mem. asscns, 159 assoc. mems; Pres. YESU PERSAUD.

Forest Products Association of Guyana: 157 Waterloo St, Georgetown; tel. 226-9848; f. 1944; 47 mems; Pres. L. J. P. WILLEMS; Exec. Officer WARREN PHOENIX.

Guyana Manufacturers' Association Ltd: 62 Main St, Cummingsburg, Georgetown; tel. 227-4295; fax 227-0670; f. 1967; 190 members; Pres. KIM KISSOON; Exec. Sec. TREVOR SHARPLES.

Guyana Rice Producers' Association: Lot 104, Regent St, Lacytown, Georgetown; tel. 226-4411; f. 1946; *c.* 35,000 families; Pres. BUDRAM MAHADEO.

UTILITIES

Electricity

Guyana Power and Light Inc: 40 Main St, POB 10390, Georgetown; tel. 225-4618; fax 227-1978; e-mail jlynn@networksgy.com; f. 1999; fmrly Guyana Electricity Corpn; 50% state-owned; 50% owned by Americas and Caribbean Power (ACP) Ltd; Chair. ADAM HEDAYAT; CEO JOHN LYNN.

Water

Guyana Water Authority (GUYWA): Georgetown; e-mail ceoguywa@guyananet.com; to be succeeded by Guyana Water in 2002; CEO KARAN SINGH.

CO-OPERATIVE SOCIETIES

Chief Co-operatives Development Officer: Ministry of Human Services, Social Security and Labour, 1 Water and Cornhill Sts, Stabroek, Georgetown; tel. 225-8644; fax 225-3477; f. 1948; L. MILLER.

In October 1996 there were 1,324 registered co-operative societies, mainly savings clubs and agricultural credit societies, with a total membership of 95,950.

TRADE UNIONS

Trades Union Congress (TUC): Critchlow Labour College, Woolford Ave, Non-pareil Park, Georgetown; tel. 226-1493; fax 227-0254; f. 1940; national trade union body; 16 affiliated unions; merged with the Federation of Independent Trade Unions in Guyana in 1993; Pres. NORRIS WITTER; Gen. Sec. LINCOLN LEWIS.

Amalgamated Transport and General Workers' Union: 46 Urquhart St, Georgetown; tel. 226-6243; fax 225-6602; Pres. RICHARD SAMUELS; Gen. Sec. VICTOR JOHNSON.

Association of Masters and Mistresses: c/o Critchlow Labour College, Georgetown; tel. (2) 68968; Pres. GANESH SINGH; Gen. Sec. T. ANSON SANCHO.

Clerical and Commercial Workers' Union (CCWU): Clerico House, 140 Quamina St, South Cummingsburg, POB 101045, Georgetown; tel. 225-2827; fax 227-2618; Pres. ROY HUGHES; Gen. Sec. GRANTLEY L. CULBARD.

General Workers' Union: Norton St, Kingston, Georgetown; tel. 226-4879; f. 1954; terminated affiliation to People's National Congress in 1989; Pres. NORRIS WITTER; Gen. Sec. PANCHAN SINGH; 3,000 mems.

Guyana Bauxite and General Workers' Union: 180 Charlotte St, Georgetown; tel. (2) 54654; Pres. CHARLES SAMPSON; Gen. Sec. LEROY ALLEN.

Guyana Labour Union: 198 Camp St, Cummingsburg, Georgetown; tel. 227-1196; fax 225-0820; Pres. SAMUEL WALKER; Gen. Sec. CARVILLE DUNCAN; 6,000 mems.

Guyana Local Government Officers' Union: c/o Abbatoir, Georgetown; tel. 227-2131; Pres. ANDREW GARNETT; Gen. Sec. SANDRA HOOPER.

Guyana Mining, Metal and General Workers' Union: 56 Wismar St, Linden, Demerara River; tel. (4) 6822; Pres. ERIC TELLO; Gen. Sec. LESLIE GONSALVES; 5,800 mems.

Guyana Postal and Telecommunication Workers' Union: 310 East St, Georgetown; tel. 226-5255; fax 225-1633; Pres. MAUREEN WALCOTT-FORTUNE; Gen. Sec. PAUL SANDIFORD.

Guyana Teachers' Union: Woolford Ave, POB 738, Georgetown; tel. 226-3183; fax 227-0403; Pres. LANCELOT BAPTISTE; Gen. Sec. SHIRLEY HOOPER.

National Mining and General Workers Union: 10 Church St, New Amsterdam, Berbice; tel. (3) 3496; Pres. CYRIL CONWAY; Gen. Sec. MARILYN GRIFFITH.

National Union of Public Service Employees: 4 Fort St, Kingston, Georgetown; tel. 227-1491; Pres. ROBERT JOHNSON; Gen. Sec. PATRICK QUINTYNE.

Printing Industry and Allied Workers' Union: Georgetown; tel. 226-8968; Gen. Sec. LESLIE REECE.

Public Employees' Union: Regent St, Georgetown; Pres. REUBEN KHAN.

Union of Agricultural and Allied Workers (UAAW): 10 Hadfield St, Werk-en-Rust, Georgetown; tel. 226-7434; Pres. JEAN SMITH; Gen. Sec. SEELO BAICHAN.

University of Guyana Workers' Union: POB 841, Turkeyen, Georgetown; tel. 223-5869; supports Working People's Alliance; Pres. Dr CLIVE THOMAS; Gen. Sec. A. ESOOP.

Guyana Agricultural and General Workers' Union (GAWU): 59 High St and Wight's Lane, Kingston, Georgetown; tel. 227-2091; fax 227-2093; e-mail gawu@networksgy.com; Pres. KOMAL CHAND; Gen. Sec. SEEPAUL NARINE; 20,000 mems.

Guyana Public Service Union (GPSU): 160 Regent Rd and New Garden St, Georgetown; tel. 225-0518; fax 226-5322; Pres. PATRICK YARDE; Gen. Sec. LAWRENCE MENTIS; 11,600 mems.

National Association of Agricultural, Commercial and Industrial Employees (NAACIE): 64 High St, Kingston, Georgetown; tel. 227-2301; f. 1946; Pres. ALBERT PERSAUD; Gen. Sec. KAISREE TAKECHANDRA; *c.* 2,000 mems.

Transport

RAILWAY

There are no public railways in Guyana.

Linmine Railway: Mackenzie, Linden; tel. (4) 2279; fax (4) 6795; bauxite transport; 15 km of line, Coomara to Linden; Superintendent O. BARNWELL.

ROADS

The coastal strip has a well-developed road system. In 1999 there were an estimated 7,970 km (4,859 miles) of paved and good-weather roads and trails. In August 2001 construction began on a bridge across the Takutu river, linking Guyana to Brazil. In the following month a European Union-funded road improvement programme between Crabwood Creek and the Guyana–Suriname Ferry Terminal was completed; the project was intended to help integrate the region. The US $40m. rehabilitation of the Mahaica–Rosignol road was to begin in 2002, partly funded by the Inter-American Development Bank. Construction of a bridge over the Berbice river also was to begin in early 2002.

SHIPPING

Guyana's principal ports are at Georgetown and New Amsterdam. The port at Linden serves for the transportation of bauxite products. A ferry service is operated between Guyana and Suriname. Communications with the interior are chiefly by river, although access is hindered by rapids and falls. There are 1,077 km (607 miles) of navigable rivers. The main rivers are the Mazaruni, the Potaro, the Essequibo, the Demerara and the Berbice. In 2000 the Brazilian Government announced that it was to finance the construction of both a deep-water port and a river bridge.

Transport and Harbours Department: Battery Rd, Kingston, Georgetown; tel. 225-9350; e-mail t&hd@solutions2000.net; Gen. Man. IVOR B. ENGLISH; Harbour Master STEPHEN THOMAS.

Shipping Association of Guyana Inc: 5–9 Lombard St, Georgetown; tel. 226-1448; fax 225-0849; e-mail gnsc@futurenetgynet.com; f. 1952; Pres. CLINTON WILLIAMS; Sec. and Man. W. V. BRIDGEMOHAN; members:

Guyana National Industrial Company Inc: 2–9 Lombard St, Charlestown, POB 10520, Georgetown; tel. 225-8428; fax 225-8526; metal foundry, ship building and repair, agents for a number of international transport cos; Man. Dir and CEO CLAUDE SAUL.

Guyana National Shipping Corporation Ltd: 5–9 Lombard St, La Penitence, POB 10988, Georgetown; tel. 226-1732; fax 225-3815; e-mail gnsc@guyana.net.gy; internet www.gnsc.com; govt-owned; Exec. Chair. DESMOND MOHAMED; Man. Dir M. F. BASCOM.

John Fernandes Ltd: 24 Water St, POB 10211, Georgetown; tel. 225-6294; fax 226-1881; e-mail chris@jf-ltd.com; ship agents, pier operators and stevedore contractors; Man. Dir C. J. FERNANDES.

CIVIL AVIATION

The main airport is Timehri International, 42 km (26 miles) from Georgetown. In 1998 there were some 94 airstrips. In June 2001 the national carrier, the Guyana Airways Corpn (GAC—known as Guyana Airways 2000 from June 1999, following the sale of a 51% stake in the company to a consortium of local businesses), suspended operations. This terminated an agreement signed in 1996, consolidating the air links between Guyana and Suriname.

Eldorado Airlines: Georgetown.

Roraima Airways: 101 Cummings St, Bourda, Georgetown; tel. 225-9648; fax 225-9646; e-mail ral@roraimaairways.com; internet www.roraimaairways.com; f. 1992; Owner GERALD GOUVEIA.

Tourism

Despite the beautiful scenery in the interior of the country, Guyana has limited tourist facilities, and began encouraging tourism only in the late 1980s. During the 1990s Guyana began to develop its considerable potential as an eco-tourism destination. However, tourist arrivals declined towards the end of the decade. The total number of visitors to Guyana in 2000 was 105,000. Tourism receipts totalled US $52m. in 1999.

Tourism and Hospitality Association of Guyana: 157 Waterloo Street, Georgetown; tel. 225-0807; fax 225-0817; e-mail thag@networksgy.com; internet www.exploreguyana.com; f. 1992; Exec. Dir INDIRA ANANDJIT.

HAITI

Introductory Survey

Location, Climate, Language, Religion, Flag, Capital

The Republic of Haiti occupies the western part of the Caribbean island of Hispaniola (the Dominican Republic occupies the remaining two-thirds) and some smaller offshore islands. Cuba, to the west, is less than 80 km away. The climate is tropical but the mountains and fresh sea winds mitigate the heat. Temperatures vary little with the seasons, and the annual average in Port-au-Prince is about 27°C (80°F). The rainy season is from May to November. The official languages are French and Creole. About 70% of the population belong to the Roman Catholic Church, the country's official religion, and other Christian churches are also represented. The folk religion is voodoo, a fusion of beliefs originating in West Africa involving communication with the spirit-world through the medium of trance. The national flag (proportions variable) has two equal vertical stripes, of dark blue and red. The state flag (proportions 3 by 5) has, in addition, a white rectangular panel, containing the national coat of arms (a palm tree, surmounted by a Cap of Liberty and flanked by flags and cannons), in the centre. The capital is Port-au-Prince.

Recent History

Haiti was first colonized in 1659 by the French, who named the territory Saint-Domingue. French sovereignty was formally recognized by Spain in 1697. Following a period of internal unrest, a successful uprising, begun in 1794 by African-descended slaves, culminated in 1804 with the establishment of Haiti as an independent state, ruled by Jean-Jacques Dessalines, who proclaimed himself Emperor. Hostility between the negro population and the mulattos continued throughout the 19th century until, after increasing economic instability, the USA intervened militarily and supervised the government of the country from 1915 to 1934. Mulatto interests retained political ascendancy until 1946, when a negro President, Dumarsais Estimé, was installed following a military coup. Following the overthrow of two further administrations, Dr François Duvalier, a country physician, was elected President in 1957.

The Duvalier administration soon became a dictatorship, maintaining its authority by means of a notorious private army, popularly called the Tontons Macoutes (Creole for 'Bogeymen'), who used extortion and intimidation to crush all possible opposition to the President's rule. In 1964 Duvalier became President-for-Life, and at his death in April 1971 he was succeeded by his 19-year-old son and designated successor Jean-Claude Duvalier.

At elections held in February 1979 for the 58-seat National Assembly, 57 seats were won by the official government party, the Parti de l'Unité Nationale. The first municipal elections for 25 years, which took place in 1983, were overshadowed by allegations of electoral fraud and Duvalier's obstruction of opposition parties. No opposition candidates were permitted to contest the elections for the National Assembly held in February 1984.

In April 1985 Duvalier announced a programme of constitutional reforms, including the eventual appointment of a Prime Minister and the formation of political parties, subject to certain limiting conditions. In September Roger Lafontant, the minister most closely identified with the Government's acts of repression, was dismissed. However, protests organized by the Roman Catholic Church and other religious groups gained momentum, and further measures to curb continued disorder were adopted in January 1986. The university and schools were closed indefinitely, and radio stations were forbidden to report on current events. Duvalier imposed a state of siege and declared martial law.

In February 1986, following intensified public protests, Duvalier and his family fled from Haiti to exile in France, leaving a five-member National Council of Government (Conseil National Gouvernemental—CNG), led by the Chief of Staff of the army, Gen. Henri Namphy, to succeed him. The interim military-civilian Council appointed a new Cabinet. The National Assembly was dissolved, and the Constitution was suspended. Later in the month, the Tontons Macoutes were disbanded.

Prisoners from Haiti's largest gaol were freed under a general amnesty. However, renewed rioting occurred to protest against the inclusion in the new Government of known supporters of the former dictatorship. In March 1986 there was a cabinet reshuffle. The new, three-member, CNG comprised Gen. Namphy, Col (later Brig.-Gen.) Williams Régala and Jacques François.

In April 1986 Gen. Namphy announced a proposed timetable for elections to restore constitutional government by February 1988. The first of these elections, to select 41 people (from 101 candidates) who would form part of the 61-member Constituent Assembly that was to revise the Constitution, took place in October 1986. However, the level of participation at the election was only about 5%.

The new Constitution was approved by 99.8% of voters in a referendum held on 29 March 1987. An estimated 50% of the electorate voted. An independent Provisional Electoral Council (Conseil Electoral Provisoire—CEP) was appointed to supervise the presidential and legislative elections, which were scheduled for 29 November.

On 29 November 1987 the elections were cancelled three hours after voting had begun, owing to renewed violence and killings, for which former members of the Tontons Macoutes were believed to be responsible. The Government dissolved the CEP and took control of the electoral process. In December a new CEP was appointed by the Government, and elections were rescheduled for 17 January 1988. Leslie Manigat of the Rassemblement des Démocrates Nationalistes et Progressistes (RDNP), with 50.3% of the total votes cast, was declared the winner of the presidential election. Legislative and municipal elections were held concurrently. Opposition leaders alleged that there had been extensive fraud and malpractice.

The Manigat Government took office in February 1988, but was overthrown by disaffected members of the army in June. Gen. Namphy, whom Manigat had attempted to replace as army Chief of Staff, assumed the presidency and appointed a Cabinet comprising members of the armed forces. The Constitution of 1987 was abrogated, and Duvalier's supporters returned to prominence, as did the Tontons Macoutes.

On 18 September 1988 Gen. Namphy was ousted in a coup, led by Brig.-Gen. Prosper Avril (who became President), who advocated the introduction of radical reforms. In November an independent electoral body, the Collège Electoral d'Haïti (CEDA), was established to supervise future elections, to draft an electoral law and to ensure proper registration of voters.

In March 1989 President Avril partially restored the Constitution of 1987 and restated his intention to hold democratic elections. In the following month the Government survived two coup attempts by the Leopard Corps, the country's élite anti-subversion squadron, and the Dessalines battalion, based in Port-au-Prince. Both battalions were subsequently disbanded.

In early January 1990, during the President's absence abroad on official business, the Rassemblement National, a broadly-based opposition coalition including conservative and left-wing political organizations, initiated a series of strikes and demonstrations to protest against the Government's economic policies. On 20 January, following his return to Haiti, Avril imposed a 30-day state of siege and a series of restrictions on political activity; however, these lasted only a few days. At the same time it was announced that all political prisoners had been released.

Avril resigned as President in March 1990, in response to sustained popular and political opposition, together with diplomatic pressure from the USA. Before entering temporary exile in the USA, Avril ceded power to the Chief of the General Staff, Gen. Hérard Abraham, who subsequently transferred authority to Ertha Pascal-Trouillot, a member of the Supreme Court. As President of a civilian interim Government, Pascal-Trouillot shared power with a 19-member Council of State, whose principal function was to assist in preparations for the elections that were to be held later in the year. In May a new CEP was established. In September the CEP announced the postponement, until mid-December, of the elections, owing to a delay in the arrival of necessary funds and materials from donor countries.

The presidential and legislative elections took place on 16 December 1990. Fr Jean-Bertrand Aristide, a left-wing Roman Catholic priest representing the Front National pour le Changement et la Démocratie (FNCD), won an overwhelming victory in the presidential election, securing some 67% of the votes cast. His closest rival was Marc Bazin, the candidate of the centre-right Mouvement pour l'Instauration de la Démocratie en Haïti (MIDH), who obtained about 14% of the poll. However, the results of the concurrent first round of legislative voting were less decisive. Aristide's FNCD won five of the 27 seats in the Senate, and 18 (of 83) seats in the Chamber of Deputies, while the Alliance Nationale pour la Démocratie et le Progrès (ANDP) secured 16 seats in the lower house. Seven other seats in the Chamber of Deputies were distributed among other political parties.

In January 1991, one month before Aristide was due to be sworn in as President, a group of army officers, led by Roger Lafontant, seized control of the presidential palace, and forced Pascal-Trouillot to announce her resignation. However, the army remained loyal to the Government and arrested Lafontant and his associates. A low turn-out in the second round of legislative voting, on 20 January 1991, was attributed to popular unease as a result of the recent coup attempt. The most successful party, the FNCD, won a further nine seats in the Chamber of Deputies, and an additional eight in the Senate, thereby failing to secure an overall majority in the two legislative chambers.

Aristide was inaugurated as President on 7 February 1991. The new Head of State subsequently initiated proceedings to secure the extradition from France of ex-President Duvalier to face charges that included embezzlement, abuse of power and murder. Aristide also undertook the reform of the armed forces (in July Gen. (later Lt-Gen.) Raoul Cédras replaced Gen. Hérard Abraham as Commander-in-Chief). In February the new President nominated one of his close associates, René García Préval, as Prime Minister.

In April 1991 Ertha Pascal-Trouillot was arrested on charges of complicity in the attempted coup three months previously. She was initially released, pending the completion of investigations, and in September left the country. In July Roger Lafontant was found guilty of organizing the attempted coup and sentenced to life imprisonment.

On 30 September 1991 a military junta, led by Gen. Cédras, overthrew the Government. Following diplomatic intervention by the USA, France and Venezuela, Aristide was allowed to go into exile. The coup received international condemnation, and an almost immediate economic embargo was imposed on Haiti by the Organization of American States (OAS, see p. 288). Many hundreds of people were reported to have been killed during the coup, including the imprisoned Lafontant. On 7 October military units assembled 29 members of the legislature and coerced them into approving the appointment of Joseph Nerette as interim President, and several days later a new Cabinet was announced. The OAS, however, continued to recognize Aristide as the legitimate President.

During the following months the OAS attempted to negotiate a settlement. However, the two sides remained deadlocked over the conditions for Aristide's return, the main obstacles being Aristide's insistence that Cédras be imprisoned or exiled, and the legislature's demands for an immediate repeal of the OAS embargo and a general amnesty. In February 1992, following OAS-supervised talks in Washington, DC, between Aristide and members of a Haitian legislative delegation, an agreement was signed providing for the installation of René Théodore, leader of the Mouvement pour la Reconstruction Nationale, as Prime Minister. He was to govern in close consultation with the exiled Aristide and facilitate his return. Aristide undertook to respect all decisions taken by the legislature since the coup of September 1991, and agreed to a general amnesty for the police and armed forces. The economic embargo imposed by the OAS was to be revoked on ratification of the agreement by the legislature. However, in mid-March 1992 politicians opposed to the accord were reportedly coerced into withdrawing from a joint session of the Senate and the Chamber of Deputies, leaving it inquorate. In late March, following an appeal by interim President Nerette, the Supreme Court declared the agreement null and void, on the grounds that it violated the Constitution by endangering the country's sovereignty. In response, the OAS increased economic sanctions against Haiti.

In May 1992, following a tripartite summit meeting involving the legislature, the Government and the armed forces, an agreement providing for a 'consensus government' was ratified by the Senate. The agreement envisaged the appointment of a new Prime Minister and a multi-party government of national consensus to seek a solution to the political crisis and negotiate an end to the economic embargo. In June the legislature, in the absence of the FNCD (which boycotted the sessions) approved the nomination of Marc Bazin, of the MIDH, to be Prime Minister. Under the terms of the tripartite agreement, the presidency was left vacant, ostensibly to allow for Aristide's return, although commentators suggested that this was purely a political manoeuvre by the military-backed Government and that such an eventuality was unlikely. A Cabinet, comprising members of most major parties (with the significant exception of the FNCD), was installed, with the army retaining control of the interior and defence. The appointment of the new Government provoked world-wide condemnation.

In July 1992 a 10-member 'presidential commission', headed by Fr Antoine Adrien, was appointed by Aristide to hold negotiations with what he termed the 'real forces' in Haiti, referring to the armed forces and the wealthy élite. In September the Government agreed to allow the presence of an 18-member OAS commission in Haiti to help to guarantee human rights, reduce violence and assess progress towards a resolution of the prevailing political crisis. In February 1993 a further agreement was reached with the OAS and the UN on sending another international civil commission comprising some 200 representatives.

In April 1993 the joint envoy of the UN and the OAS, Dante Caputo, visited Haiti to present a series of proposals for the restoration of democratic rule in Haiti. These provided for the resignation of the military high command in return for a full amnesty for those involved in the coup of 1991, and for the establishment of a government of consensus and the eventual reinstatement of Aristide. A sum of US $1,000m. in economic aid was to become available once democracy was restored. However, the proposals were rejected by Cédras.

In early June 1993 the USA imposed sanctions against Haiti. Shortly afterwards Bazin resigned as Prime Minister. His position was believed to have become untenable following the refusal of several cabinet ministers to respect his demand for their resignation, and the withdrawal of the support in the legislature of the Parti National Progressiste Révolutionnaire (PANPRA)—which deprived the Government of a parliamentary majority. In late June, following the imposition of a world-wide petroleum and arms embargo by the UN Security Council, Cédras agreed to attend talks with Aristide on Governor's Island, New York, under the auspices of the UN and the OAS. On 3 July the so-called Governor's Island peace accord was signed, delineating a 10-point agenda for Aristide's reinstatement. Under the terms of the accord the embargo was to be revoked following the installation of a new Prime Minister (to be appointed by Aristide), Cédras would retire and a new Commander-in-Chief of the armed forces would be appointed by Aristide, who would return to Haiti by 30 October. The accord was approved by Haiti's main political parties, and a six-month political 'truce' was agreed to facilitate the transition. Legislation providing for a series of political and institutional reforms, as required under the terms of the accord, was to be enacted, including provision for the transfer of the police force to civilian control.

In August 1993 the legislature ratified the appointment by Aristide of Robert Malval as Prime Minister. The UN Security Council subsequently suspended its petroleum and arms embargo. In September a concerted campaign of political violence and intimidation by police auxiliaries, known as 'attachés', threatened to undermine the Governor's Island accord. Demands made by Malval that the attachés be disbanded were ignored by the chief of police, Col Joseph Michel François. With the upsurge of a Duvalierist tendency, largely embodied by the attachés, a new political party, the Front Revolutionnaire pour l'Avancement et le Progrès d'Haïti (FRAPH), was founded in opposition to any attempt to reinstate Aristide. In late September the UN Security Council approved a resolution providing for the immediate deployment of a lightly-armed United Nations Mission In Haiti (UNMIH, renamed United Nations Support Mission in Haiti in June 1996, United Nations Transition Mission in Haiti in July 1997, and United Nations Civilian Police Mission in Haiti (MIPONUH) in November 1997). A new unarmed mission, the International Civilian Support Mission in Haiti, superseded MIPONUH in March 2000, comprising 150 members, to advise in the creation of a new police force and the modernization of the army. The new mission's mandate ended on 6 February 2001.

In October 1993, in violation of the Governor's Island accord, Cédras and François refused to resign their posts, asserting that the terms of the amnesty offered by Aristide were not sufficiently broad. In that month the campaign of political violence by the attachés escalated. A US vessel transporting members of the UNMIH was prevented from docking at Port-au-Prince, and its arrival prompted violent demonstrations of defiance by the attachés. Several days later the Minister of Justice, Guy Malary, was assassinated. In response, the US Government ordered six warships into Haitian territorial waters to enforce the reimposed UN embargo. As a result of the instability, the UN/OAS international civil commission and other foreign government personnel were evacuated to the Dominican Republic.

In December 1993 Malval officially resigned as Prime Minister. In discussions with the US Government held earlier in the month, Malval announced a new initiative for a National Salvation Conference, involving multi-sector negotiations (to include the military) on a return to democratic rule. However, Aristide rejected the proposals, proposing instead a National Reconciliation Conference, excluding the military, which took place in Miami, USA, in mid-January 1994. Following the military regime's failure to meet the revised UN deadline of 15 January to comply with the terms of the Governor's Island accord, in late January the USA unilaterally imposed further sanctions denying officers of the military regime access to assets held in the USA and cancelling their travel visas. In that month members of the UN/OAS international civil commission began to return to Haiti.

In February 1994 a 13-member faction of the Senate—including eight members elected in January 1993 in partial legislative elections condemned as illegal by the USA and UN and widely regarded as an attempt by the military regime to legitimize its rule—appointed Bernard Sansaricq as President of the Senate. However, the incumbent President of the Senate, Firmin Jean-Louis, did not relinquish his position and continued to be recognized by the international community. In the same month Aristide twice rejected peace plans drafted by the USA, demanding instead the implementation of the Governor's Island accord.

In April 1994 the US Government abandoned its attempts to effect a compromise solution to the crisis in Haiti in favour of the implementation of more rigorous economic sanctions with a view to forcing the military regime to relinquish power. On 6 May the UN Security Council approved a resolution introducing sanctions banning all international trade with Haiti, excluding food and medicine, reducing air links with the country and preventing members of the regime from gaining access to assets held outside Haiti.

In early 1994 the 13-member faction of the Senate led by Bernard Sansaricq declared the presidency of the Republic vacant, invoking Article 149 of the Constitution, which provides that, in case of prolonged absence by the Head of State, the position may be assumed by the President of the Court of Cassation. In May, with the support of the armed forces, the 13 Senators and 30 members of the Chamber of Deputies—not a sufficient number to form a quorum—appointed the President of the Court of Cassation, Emile Jonassaint, provisional President of the Republic. He subsequently appointed a new Cabinet. The appointment of the Jonassaint administration was denounced as illegal by the international community and by the outgoing acting Prime Minister, Robert Malval. In the following month, the USA increased sanctions against Haiti. Jonassaint's appointment also revealed a division within the three-man junta at the head of the military regime—namely Cédras, François and the Chief of Staff of the army, Brig.-Gen. Philippe Biamby. François reportedly opposed the move and did not attend the inauguration ceremony.

In July 1994 the Haitian junta issued an order providing for the expulsion of the UN/OAS international civil commission. The order was immediately condemned by the UN Security Council. On 31 July the UN Security Council passed a resolution authorizing 'all necessary means' to remove the military regime from power. The terms of the resolution also provided for a UN peace-keeping force to be deployed once stability had been achieved, to remain in Haiti until February 1996, when Aristide's presidential term expired. In August the UN officially abandoned efforts to effect a peaceful solution to the crisis in Haiti. In the same month leaders of the Caribbean Community

and Common Market (CARICOM, see p. 155) agreed to support a US-led military invasion.

On 19 September 1994 a nominally multinational force comprised almost entirely of US troops began a peaceful occupation of Haiti. The occupation followed the diplomatic efforts of a mission led by former US President Jimmy Carter, which resulted in a compromise agreement, thus narrowly avoiding a full-scale invasion. Under the terms of the agreement, the Haitian security forces were to co-operate with the multilateral force in effecting a transition to civilian rule. All sanctions were to be lifted and the military junta granted 'early and honourable retirement' following legislative approval of a general amnesty law, or by 15 October at the latest (the date when Aristide was to return from exile to resume his presidency). The agreement did not, however, require the junta's departure from Haiti, nor did it address the reform of the security forces. In late September the legislature began a joint session to discuss the draft amnesty law. Those legislators elected illegally in January 1993 were replaced by legislators returning from exile in the USA. Following the occupation, acts of violence by the Haitian police against supporters of Aristide led to a modification of the rules of operation of the multinational force, allowing for intervention to curb the violence. In late September the USA announced the suspension of its unilateral sanctions, although the Haitian military's assets in the USA remained frozen. A few days later the UN Security Council approved a resolution ending all sanctions against Haiti with effect from the day after the return of Aristide.

In early October 1994 Aristide signed a decree authorizing legislation, approved by the legislature that month, for the amnesty of those involved in the coup of September 1991. Cédras and Biamby promptly went into exile in Panama, whilst François was reported to have already fled to the Dominican Republic, where he was granted asylum. Later that month the USA formally ended its freeze on the assets of the Haitian military regime, estimated to be worth some US $79m. On 12 October Robert Malval resumed office as interim Prime Minister following the resignation of the Jonassaint administration. Aristide returned to Haiti on 15 October to resume his presidency and on 25 October appointed Smarck Michel as premier. He also appointed Gen. Jean-Claude Duperval provisional Commander-in-Chief of the armed forces and Gen. Bernardin Poisson Chief of Staff of the army.

A new Cabinet, comprising mainly members of the pro-Aristide Organisation Politique Lavalas (OPL), was inaugurated on 8 November 1994. In mid-November Gen. Poisson succeeded Gen. Duperval as Commander-in-Chief of the armed forces. Later that month the legislature approved the separation of the police from the army.

In December 1994 the formation of a new CEP, responsible for organizing and supervising the forthcoming legislative, local and municipal elections, was completed. However, owing to procedural delays the elections were thought unlikely to be held until mid-1995, leaving a period of legislative inactivity, between the end of the current legislative term, ending in January 1995, and the inauguration of a new legislature, at a time when reform would be vital to the successful transition to peaceful civilian rule. In mid-December 1994 Aristide authorized the creation of a national commission of truth and justice to investigate past human rights violations, and ordered the reduction of the armed forces to 1,500 (from an estimated combined army and police force of 7,000–7,500). In the following month two commissions were established for the restructuring of the armed forces and the new civilian police force.

In January 1995 US military commanders certified that the situation in Haiti was sufficiently stable to enable the transfer of authority to the UN. On 30 January the UN Security Council adopted a resolution authorizing the deployment of a UN force of 6,000 troops and 900 civil police to succeed the incumbent multinational force. The UN force, entitled (like that deployed in 1993) the United Nations Mission in Haiti (UNMIH), was to be led by a US commander and include some 2,400 US troops. It was to be responsible for reducing the strength of the army and training both the army and the 4,000-strong (subsequently increased to 6,000) civilian police force, as well as maintaining the 'secure and stable' environment.

On 31 March 1995, against a background of increasing violence and criticism at the inadequacy of the interim police force, authority was officially transferred from the multinational force to the UNMIH. The security situation deteriorated further in April, revealing widespread discontent at high prices, unemployment and the planned privatization of state enterprises. In late April Aristide announced that, following the election of the new legislature, he would seek a constitutional amendment providing for the abolition of the armed forces. (The armed forces were subsequently disbanded, although the constitutional amendment providing for their official abolition could not be approved until the end of the new legislative term.)

The first round of legislative, local and municipal elections (including elections to 18 of the 27 seats in the Senate, all 83 seats in the Chamber of Deputies, 125 mayorships and 555 local councils) were held on 25 June 1995. Owing to administrative failures and isolated incidents of violence and intimidation, voting continued into the following day. Despite the extension, thousands of intending voters were unable to participate, and a further, complementary poll was to be scheduled. The widespread irregularities prompted several opposition parties to demand the annulment of the elections and the dissolution of the CEP, which many perceived as too closely associated with the OPL, the party with majority representation in the Government. The official election results, which were released in mid-July, indicated that all of the 21 seats so far decided had been won by the Plateforme Politique Lavalas (PPL), a three-party electoral alliance comprising the OPL, the Mouvement pour l'Organisation du Pays and the Pati Louvri Baryè. The results were rejected by the majority of opposition parties, which announced a boycott of the electoral process. Continued criticism of the CEP by the opposition led to the resignation of the President of the CEP, Anselme Rémy, in late July.

In early August 1995 the FNCD, MIDH and PANPRA withdrew their respective representatives from the Government, in protest at the absence of a resolution to the electoral dispute. The Minister of Culture, Jean-Claude Bajeux, of the Congrès National des Movements Démocratiques (KONAKOM) resisted his party's demand that he resign, and remained the sole opposition member in the Cabinet. On 13 August, following successive postponements, the complementary elections, for voters who had been denied the opportunity to vote on 25 June, were conducted in 21 districts. A further 17 seats were decided, all of which were won by the PPL. In late August the US Government presented a plan aimed at resolving the electoral dispute. However, its proposals, which included the annulment of the first round elections in many areas, were rejected by the CEP. The second round of voting was held on 17 September, despite the boycott that was maintained by the main opposition parties, and resulted in further large gains for the PPL, which won 17 of the 18 contested seats in the 27-member Senate and 68 seats in the 83-member Chamber of Deputies. The remaining contested seats were won mainly by independent candidates.

In October 1995 Michel resigned as Prime Minister, and was succeeded by the Minister of Foreign Affairs, Claudette Werleigh. She indicated that the new administration intended to retain control of strategic state enterprises, which Michel had planned to sell, and would seek a national debate on the issue of privatization.

In November 1995, despite extensive popular support for Aristide to continue in office for a further three years (to compensate for those years spent in exile), the President confirmed that he would leave office in February 1996. At a presidential election held on 17 December 1995, which was boycotted by all the main opposition parties except KONAKOM, the candidate endorsed by Aristide, René Préval (Prime Minister between February and September 1991), was elected with some 87.9% of the votes cast. He was inaugurated as President on 7 February 1996, and later that month the legislature approved the appointment of Rosny Smarth as Prime Minister. A new Cabinet was sworn in on 6 March.

The months following the inauguration of the Smarth administration were marked by a high incidence of violence in the capital. In mid-August 1996, against a background of unrest and general hostility towards government economic policy, in particular plans for the privatization of state enterprises, a series of armed attacks were conducted against public buildings, including the parliament building and the central police headquarters. The attacks followed the arrest that month, at the headquarters of the right-wing Mobilisation pour le Développement National (MDN), of some 20 former officers of the armed forces who were accused of plotting against the Government. In August two leading members of the MDN were murdered by unidentified gunmen. Opposition politicians accused the Government of responsibility for the killings, and evidence emerged implicating members of the presidential guard in the murders.

In mid-September, on the advice of the US Government, Préval dismissed the head of the presidential guard and initiated a reorganization of the unit.

In November 1996, as a result of diverging interests within the PPL, Aristide officially established a new political party, La Fanmi Lavalas (FL), which, it was anticipated, would promote his candidacy for the next presidential election. Aristide had openly expressed his opposition to Préval's adoption of economic policies proposed by the IMF, notably the privatization of state enterprises. Unrest continued, and in mid-January 1997 a general strike, in support of demands for the resignation of the Smarth administration and the reversal of the planned divestment of state enterprises, received considerable support.

On 6 April 1997 partial legislative elections were held for nine of the 27 seats in the Senate and two seats in the Chamber of Deputies, as well as elections to local councils. The elections were boycotted by many opposition parties, and less than 5% of the electorate participated in the poll. Of the legislative seats contested only two, in the Senate, were decided, both of which were secured by candidates of the FL. The OPL, the majority party in the governing coalition, alleged that members of the CEP had manipulated the election results in favour of Aristide's party, and demanded the resignation of the CEP and the conduct of a fresh ballot. OAS observers of the poll supported the claims of electoral irregularities, and, following strong international pressure the CEP postponed the second round of the elections, scheduled for 25 May, until mid-June (they were subsequently postponed indefinitely). The OPL had announced that it would boycott the second round elections.

In the light of mounting popular opposition, on 9 June 1997 Smarth resigned from office, although he remained Prime Minister in a caretaker capacity pending the appointment of a replacement. Smarth criticized the CEP for failing to annul the results of the April elections and thus perpetuating the electoral impasse. In the following month Préval nominated Ericq Pierre as Smarth's replacement, but his nomination was rejected by the Chamber of Deputies. In September supporters of Aristide announced the formation of a new 25-member Anti-Neoliberal Bloc in the lower house. In the light of Préval's failure to nominate a candidate for Prime Minister who was acceptable to the legislature, on 20 October Smarth announced that he was to cease his role as caretaker Prime Minister and recommended that his Cabinet resign. Several ministers complied with this request and in late October Préval redesignated their portfolios to remaining cabinet members.

In November 1997, in an effort to resolve the political crisis, Préval nominated Hervé Y. Denis, an economist and former Minister of Information, Culture and Co-ordination in the Government of Robert Malval, as Prime Minister. In addition, Préval announced the establishment of an electoral commission, comprising three independent legal experts, to resolve the electoral deadlock, and the resignation of six of the nine members of the CEP. The OPL, however, continued to demand the annulment of the April elections and the replacement of the entire CEP. In January 1998 the legislature formally announced its decision to reject the nomination of Denis. The FL subsequently rejected a proposal by the OPL for the creation of a body to mediate in the legislature and thus facilitate the appointment of a new Prime Minister.

In March 1998, following negotiations with the Anti-Neoliberal Bloc, the OPL (renamed the Organisation du Peuple en Lutte in February) withdrew its demands for the annulment of the April 1997 elections as a precondition for the approval of a new Prime Minister, and proposed three candidates. However, Préval subsequently renominated Denis: his candidacy was rejected by the legislature for a second time in April. In July Préval finally agreed to replace the CEP. Préval subsequently received the support of the OPL for the nomination of the incumbent Minister of National Education, Jacques Edouard Alexis, for Prime Minister. Conversely, the Anti-Neoliberal Bloc opposed the nomination of Alexis, who, it maintained, favoured the structural adjustment policies advocated by the IMF. In August the FL announced that it had formally gone into opposition to the Préval administration.

In November 1998 the Senate voted to extend the legislature's current term to October 1999; under electoral legislation adopted in 1995, the term of office of legislators elected in that year's delayed vote had been shortened by one year in order to restore the constitutional timetable of elections, and was thus due to end in January 1999. In December 1998 Alexis was finally declared eligible to assume the office of Prime Minister, subject to his nomination being approved by the legislature (which did not occur until November 2000). The decision had been delayed by a report by the state auditing board, subsequently declared inaccurate, which found irregularities in Alexis' tenure as Minister of National Education. On 11 January 1999 Préval announced that he would no longer recognize the legislature, rejecting the Senate's earlier decision to extend its mandate, and declared that he would install a new government by presidential decree. In mid-January Préval withdrew parliamentary funding, prompting the legislature to seek a Supreme Court ruling on the constitutionality of the 1995 electoral law. Préval also entered into consultations with opposition parties in an effort to reach agreement on the composition of a new CEP. In February the Supreme Court postponed indefinitely a decision concerning the electoral law.

On 25 March 1999 Préval appointed by decree a new Cabinet headed by Alexis and including representatives of five small opposition parties that had negotiated an agreement with the President to end the political impasse. The OPL, which had ceased negotiations following the murder, in early March, of one of its leaders, was not included in the new administration. The party, which alleged that the killing had been perpetrated by supporters of Aristide, also stated that it would boycott any elections organized by the new CEP, which was appointed in that month. In May the Supreme Court refused to rule on the legality of Préval's decision to end the funding of the outgoing parliament. The OPL subsequently announced that it had accepted that the parliamentary term had ended and that it would participate in the forthcoming elections. In June the CEP announced that it would disregard the results of the flawed partial legislative elections of April 1997, and presented draft electoral legislation that envisaged the holding of legislative elections in November and December 1999. Préval criticized the CEP's decision concerning the 1997 elections, but in July 1999 he signed a decree annulling them. A new electoral law set 28 November as a provisional date for the first round of legislative and local elections; however, the elections were subsequently postponed, for logistical and financial reasons, on several occasions, prompting violent protests in the capital.

On 21 May 2000 the first round of legislative and municipal elections was held; an estimated 60% of the electorate participated. Opposition parties alleged that the results had been manipulated in favour of the FL, claims supported by OAS observers, and demanded the annulment of the election and the conduct of a fresh ballot. The CEP rejected these claims, but in mid-June the CEP President, Léon Manus, fled to the Dominican Republic, claiming that he had received death threats following his refusal to validate the first-round results. His flight prompted demonstrations by Aristide supporters, demanding the publication of the results. According to official first-round results, the FL won 16 of the 19 contested seats in the Senate, and 26 of the 83 seats in the lower house. The results were criticized as inaccurate by the UN, the OAS and numerous foreign governments. Nevertheless, a second round of voting went ahead on 9 July (postponed from 25 June). Opposition protests and a boycott by the 15-party opposition coalition, the Convergence Démocratique (CD) resulted in a low voter turn-out (an estimated 10%) and a high incidence of violence, with 10 separate bombs killing two people. According to official results, the FL won 72 seats in the Chamber of Deputies and 18 of the 19 seats contested in the 27-seat upper house (the Pati Louvri Baryè won one seat). The party also secured control of some 80% of the local councils. In September Préval announced that elections to the presidency and to renew the remaining eight senate seats would be held in November. The CD immediately announced its intention to boycott the elections.

In mid-October 2000 it was revealed that an attempt by members of the police force to overthrow the Government had been uncovered. The seven police officers accused of planning the coup fled to the Dominican Republic, and were subsequently granted asylum in Ecuador. The Government reacted by dismissing several senior police officers. In November a court sentenced Gen. Cédras and 36 other senior army officers to life imprisonment with hard labour, *in absentia*, for their role in the murders of 15 people in the shanty town of Raboteau in May 1994.

At the presidential election of 26 November 2000, Aristide was elected with some 91.7% of the votes cast; the remaining six candidates all won less than 2.0% of the ballot. According to official estimates some 60.5% of the electorate voted, although opposition leaders claimed a far lower participation. The only

official observer mission, from CARICOM, estimated a 30% voter turn-out. In concurrently-held partial legislative elections, the FL also won the remaining eight seats in the Senate, and the one remaining seat in the Chamber of Deputies.

An eight-member Transition Committee was established in December 2000 to oversee the smooth transfer of power to Aristide, who was to take office on 7 February 2001. However, on 7 December the CD announced the formation of an alternative, provisional Government, known as the Front Alternatif, with the intention of holding fresh elections within two years. The announcement provoked widespread violent demonstrations by Aristide supporters. In early February 2001 the CD further announced that this Front Alternatif was to be headed by Gérard Gourgue. Discussions between the President-elect and opposition leaders ended without agreement. On 15 February seven of the Senators controversially awarded seats in the May 2000 election resigned. Two days after his inauguration, President Aristide named Jean-Marie Chérestal, a former Minister of Finance, as Prime Minister, and in early March a new Cabinet was appointed. The CD responded by calling for a month of anti-Government protests. In the same month, in an attempt to end the political impasse, Aristide appointed a new nine-member CEP to investigate the results of the disputed May 2000 elections. The CD was not represented on the Council. In March it was announced that legislative elections would be held one year early, in November 2002, in order to satisfy international and opposition criticism and to restore the flow of foreign aid, suspended since May 2000. (As well as an end to the political crisis and a strengthening of the democratic process, the resumption of aid was also dependent on Haiti implementing anti-drugs-trafficking measures and improving its human rights record.) Three days later violent protests broke out in Port-au-Prince, in which three people died and dozens were injured. Government supporters attempted to burn down the CD's headquarters and demanded the arrest of Gourgue. Violence continued over the following months and a number of opposition party members were arrested on treason and terrorism charges. In July, following further OAS mediation, the Government confirmed that legislative and local elections would be held in 2002, although a timetable remained to be agreed; an accord was also reached on the composition of the new CEP. The CEP would additionally organize an election to the seven Senate seats vacated in February.

Political violence continued throughout 2001. In late July an attempted *coup d'état*, responsibility for which was attributed to former members of the armed forces, resulted in the deaths of six policemen. In October the FL announced the resumption of OAS-mediated talks with the opposition, but these again ended unsuccessfully. In early November three people were killed during violent demonstrations in the La Saline district of Port-au-Prince and one week later the CD organized a widely-observed national strike in protest at the deteriorating economic situation. Then, on 18 December, an armed group, allegedly composed of former members of the armed forces, attacked the presidential palace. At least four people were killed in the coup attempt, which prompted further outbreaks of violence as hundreds of government supporters attacked the homes and offices of opposition leaders in retaliation. The Government announced that former police chief Guy Philippe was wanted in connection with the palace attack; he subsequently fled the country. The opposition claimed that the coup attempt had been staged by the Government in order to justify further repression, and demanded that a UN mission be deployed to monitor the situation. In July 2002 an OAS Commission of Inquiry reported that no attempted coup had taken place and chastised the Government for its reluctance to punish those of its supporters who engaged in violence against the opposition.

In 2001 the investigation into the death of radio journalist Jean Léopold Dominique, who had been murdered in April 2000, was obstructed by death threats and pressure from supporters of the principal suspect in the case, FL Senator and former police chief, Dany Toussaint. In June Claudy Gassant, the judge supervising the investigation, resigned, complaining of insufficient protection against death threats. He subsequently left the country. The investigation was stalled until July 2002, when a new investigating magistrate, Bernard Saint Vil, was appointed.

On 23 January 2002, against a background of continuing political and economic turmoil, Prime Minister Chérestal resigned his post, following allegations of corruption, and criticism over his inability to resolve the crisis. There was further controversy in the following month when 13 opposition activists, including eight CD members, were arrested and charged with operating a kidnapping organization. The CD claimed that the arrests were politically motivated and that the charges had been fabricated. In February Marc Andre Dirogene, an FL representative in the Chamber of Deputies, was assassinated in Port-au-Prince by unidentified gunmen. On 15 March Aristide appointed Senate speaker and prominent FL member, Yvon Neptune, as Prime Minister. Neptune subsequently reshuffled his Cabinet, removing several ministers who had attracted controversy; he signalled his commitment to encouraging dialogue to end the political stalemate by appointing Marc Bazin as Minister without Portfolio with specific responsibility for negotiations with the opposition. In June Aristide met with opposition leaders for the first time in two years, but the talks achieved little progress. Further OAS-mediated dialogue in the following month also failed to make any significant headway. Meanwhile, Haiti's accession to full membership of CARICOM in July increased international pressure on Aristide to bring about an end to political instability in the country and allow new elections to take place. In August violent demonstrations occurred in the northern city of Gonaïves when the political activist Amiot Metayer escaped from prison, together with over 100 other inmates. Metayer was one of several Government supporters imprisoned for damaging the homes of opposition members following the attack on the presidential palace in December 2001. In September Calixte Delatour was allocated the justice portfolio following the resignation of Jean-Baptiste Brown.

In late 2002 the ongoing political unrest in the country intensified as the November deadline for the creation of a new electoral council passed unfulfilled. On 17 November some 15,000 people in Cap-Haïtien participated in the largest anti-Government rally held in the country since the re-election of President Aristide in 2000. Himmler Rebu, a former armed forces colonel who had led an unsuccessful coup attempt in 1989, called on the protesters to rise up against the repressive Aristide regime. Shortly afterwards students protested in Petit-Goave against a rumoured rise in examination fees; subsequent clashes with the police resulted in the deaths of four people. In the aftermath of the violence the Minister of National Education, Myrtho Célestin Saurel, resigned. Meanwhile, on 22 November supporters of Aristide rioted in Port-au-Prince to protest against the anti-Government rallies. President Aristide refused to resign, stating that he believed the crisis could best be resolved through the formation of an electoral council and the holding of new elections. While the opposition continued to refuse to nominate representatives to an electoral council, five of the nation's civil groups chose representatives in November, having initially refused to do so until the Government demonstrated its commitment to guaranteeing public safety. In early December a general strike led by the opposition was joined by members of Haiti's private sector and, shortly afterwards, the headquarters of the MDN in Port-au-Prince were set alight by arsonists. There was also a reported attempt to assassinate FL Senator Dany Toussaint. During an address to his supporters in Les Cayes, President Aristide accused the opposition of attempting to orchestrate a coup. Meanwhile, opposition parties united in calling for the resignation of Aristide. The demonstrations continued throughout December and into 2003.

International relations, although improved after 1971, continued to be strained because of Haiti's unpopular political regimes and government corruption. Relations between Haiti and its neighbour on the island of Hispaniola, the Dominican Republic, have traditionally been tense because of the use of the border area by anti-Government guerrillas, smugglers and illegal emigrants, resulting in the periodic closure of the border. In March 1996, following an official visit to the Dominican Republic by Préval, the first by a Haitian President since 1935, a joint communiqué was issued establishing a bilateral commission to promote improved co-operation between the two countries. In June 1998, following an official visit to Haiti by the President of the Dominican Republic, Leonel Fernández Reyna, agreement was reached to establish joint border patrols to combat the traffic of drugs and other contraband between the two countries. In November 1999 Préval submitted a formal protest to the Dominican Republic following a spate of summary deportations of Haitians from the neighbouring country; according to human rights observers, some 8,000 Haitians were forcibly repatriated in the first three weeks of that month. Following a direct meeting between representatives of the two Governments, a

protocol was signed in early December limiting the repatriations. Relations between the two countries were strained in November 2000 following the Dominican Republic's refusal to extradite the police officers accused of planning a coup against the Préval Government in the previous month (see above). The number of Haitians entering the Dominican Republic increased in 2001, owing to the deteriorating economic situation in the country as a result of the continuing suspension of foreign aid. At the end of the year bilateral relations were strained further when the Dominican Republic refused to extradite former Haitian police chief Guy Philippe, who was suspected of plotting the December attack on the presidential palace (see above). In January 2002 President Aristide paid his first official visit to the Dominican Republic and held talks with President Mejía, during which agreements were signed on economic co-operation and border and immigration issues.

Following the coup of 30 September 1991, the USA came under international criticism for its forced repatriation of Haitian refugees fleeing the repressive military regime. In November, following an appeal by the Haitian Refugee Center in Miami, USA, a US federal judge in Florida ordered a temporary halt to the repatriation. However, at the end of January 1992 the US Supreme Court annulled the federal judge's ruling, and repatriation resumed. While a small percentage of refugees were considered for political asylum, the US Government insisted that the majority were economic refugees and therefore not eligible for asylum. In May President George Bush issued an executive order providing for refugees who were intercepted at sea by the US coastguard to be repatriated immediately without any evaluation being made of their right to asylum. The decision, which was condemned by human rights groups, was overturned in July by an appeals court in New York. However, in August the US Supreme Court suspended the appeals court decision, and the executive order stood pending a definitive ruling by the Supreme Court itself. In June 1993 the US Supreme Court ruled to uphold the executive order of May 1992, continued under the Clinton Administration. In May 1994, following concerted pressure from US groups, including a 40-strong black caucus in the US Congress, the US Government reversed its policy regarding Haitian refugees, agreeing to resume hearings for all asylum applications—to be conducted at screening centres established later on the British dependent territory of the island of Grand Turk and off the shore of Jamaica. The new policy prompted a renewed exodus of thousands of refugees forcing a further change of US policy in July under which refugees granted asylum were henceforth to be held indefinitely in 'safe havens' outside the USA. In early 2002 Haiti was 'decertified' by the USA for its failure to combat drugs-trafficking. In October of that year around 200 Haitian illegal immigrants arrived in Florida, prompting the launch of a campaign by Haitian-American leaders to encourage US businesses to invest in Haiti in an attempt to halt the flow of those emigrating for economic reasons. In the same month the US Federal Bureau of Investigation (FBI) issued indictments for drugs-trafficking offences to 19 people in New York with alleged links to the Haitian Government and police force.

Government

The Constitution, approved by referendum in March 1987, provided for a bicameral legislature, comprising a 77-member Chamber of Deputies (later enlarged to 83 members) and a 27-member Senate. The Chamber of Deputies was elected for a term of four years, while the Senate was elected for a term of six years with one-third renewed every two years. Both houses were elected by universal adult suffrage. Executive power was held by the President, who was elected by universal adult suffrage for a five-year term and could not stand for immediate re-election. The President selected a Prime Minister from the political party commanding a majority in the legislature. The Prime Minister chose a Cabinet in consultation with the President. However, the Constitution was interrupted by successive coups, in June and September 1988 and September 1991. A return to constitutional rule was finally effected in October 1994, following the intervention of a US-led multinational force and the reinstatement of the exiled President Aristide.

There are nine Départements, subdivided into arrondissements and communes.

Defence

In November 1994, following the return to civilian rule, measures providing for the separation of the armed forces from the police force were approved by the legislature. In December

President Aristide ordered the reduction of the armed forces to 1,500. In that month two commissions were established for the restructuring of the armed forces and the formation of a new 4,000-strong civilian police force (later enlarged to 6,000). In 1995 the armed forces were effectively dissolved, although officially they remained in existence pending an amendment to the Constitution providing for their abolition. In August 2002 the civilian police force numbered an estimated 5,300. There was also a coast guard of 30. The security budget for 2001 was an estimated US $41m.

Economic Affairs

In 2001, according to estimates by the World Bank, Haiti's gross national income (GNI), measured at average 1999–2001 prices, was US $3,887m., equivalent to $480 per head (or $1,450 per head on an international purchasing-power parity basis). In 1990–2001 the population increased at an average annual rate of 2.1%, while gross domestic product (GDP) per head decreased, in real terms, by an average of 2.7% per year. Haiti's overall GDP decreased, in real terms, at an average annual rate of 0.7% in 1990–2001; real GDP increased by 1.1% in 1999/2000, but decreased by 1.6% in 2000/01.

Agriculture (including hunting, forestry and fishing) contributed an estimated 27.4% of GDP in 2000/01, measured at constant 1986/87 prices. About 61.7% of the total labour force were engaged in agricultural activities in mid-2001. The principal cash crop is coffee (which accounted for 4.1% of export earnings in 1999/2000). The export of oils for cosmetics and pharmaceuticals is also important. The main food crops are sugar, bananas, maize, sweet potatoes and rice. However, in recent years falling quality and cheaper imports of sugar cane forced closure of all the country's major sugar factories, although one of them, at Darbonne, near Léogane, reopened in January 2001. During 1990–2000, according to the World Bank, the real GDP of the agricultural sector decreased at an average annual rate of 1.8%; agricultural GDP decreased by an estimated 3.6% in 1999/2000, but increased by an estimated 0.6% in 2000/01.

Industry (including mining, manufacturing, construction and power) contributed 15.9% of GDP at constant prices in 2000/01. About 8.8% of the employed labour force were engaged in the sector in 1990. According to the World Bank, industrial GDP declined at an average annual rate of 0.9% in 1990–2000; it increased by 3.3% in 1999/2000, but decreased by an estimated 1.3% in 2000/01.

Mining contributed 0.1% of GDP at constant prices in 2000/01. About 1% of the employed labour force were engaged in extractive activities in 1990. Marble, limestone and calcareous clay are mined. There are also unexploited copper, silver and gold deposits.

Manufacturing contributed 7.9% of GDP at constant prices in 2000/01. Some 35,000 people were engaged in the sector in mid-2000. The most important branches in 1996, measured by value added, were food products, textiles (including apparel, leather and fur products and footwear), chemicals (including rubber and plastic products) and tobacco. Manufacturing GDP decreased by an average of 11.8% per year in 1989–99; manufacturing GDP decreased by 0.1% in 1999/2000, but increased by an estimated 0.2% in 2000/01.

Energy is derived principally from local timber and charcoal. In 1999 38.4% of the country's public electricity came from hydroelectric power, while 61.6% of electricity came from petroleum. Severe shortfalls of electricity in 2000–01 led the Government to contract a Dominican and a US-Haitian company to add 70 MW to the national supply, increasing it by one-third. Imports of fuel products accounted for 17.1% of the value of imports in 1999/2000.

The services sector contributed 56.6% of GDP at constant prices in 2000/01 and engaged 22.8% of the employed labour force in 1990. According to the World Bank, the GDP of the services sector increased by an average of 0.1% per year in 1990–2000. It increased by 3.9% in 1999/2000, but decreased by an estimated 0.2% in 2000/01.

In 2000/01 Haiti recorded a visible trade deficit of US $399.3m., and there was a deficit of $53.5m. on the current account of the balance of payments. In 1998 the principal source of imports (60%) was the USA; the USA was also the principal market for exports (87%) in that year. Other significant trading partners were France, Canada, Japan and the Dominican Republic. The principal exports in 1999/2000 were manufactured articles (30.7%) and coffee (4.1%). The principal imports in that year were food and live animals (22.7%), manufactured goods and mineral fuels. In 2000 smuggling was estimated to have accounted for two-thirds of Haiti's imports.

In the financial year ending 30 September 2001 there was a budgetary deficit of 1,887.0m. gourdes (equivalent to 2.2% of GDP). At the end of 2000 Haiti's total external debt was US $1,169m., of which $1,040m. was long-term public debt. In that year the cost of debt-servicing was equivalent to 8.0% of the total value of exports of goods and services. The annual rate of inflation averaged 13.9% in 1995–2002. Consumer prices increased by an average of 14.2% in 2001 and by 9.9% in 2002. Some 60% of the labour force were estimated to be unemployed in 2001. Remittances from Haitians living abroad were equivalent to 17% of GDP in 2000.

Haiti is a member of the International Coffee Organization (see p. 336) and the Latin American Economic System (SELA, see p. 340). In July 2002 Haiti became a full member of the Caribbean Community and Common Market (CARICOM, see p. 155). Haiti is also a signatory of the European Union's (EU) Cotonou Agreement (see p. 234) (which replaced the Lomé Convention from June 2000), although from 2000 the disbursement of funds under this accord were suspended while the political crisis continued (see Recent History).

In terms of average income, Haiti is the poorest country in the Western hemisphere, and there is extreme inequality of wealth. The suspension of all non-humanitarian aid and the imposition of successive, and increasingly severe, economic sanctions by the international community, following the military coup of September 1991, had devastating effects on the Haitian economy, serving to exacerbate the extreme poverty endured by the majority of the population. Following the return to civilian rule in late 1994, sanctions were ended and preparations made for the release of aid and new loans. At a meeting of donor nations in Paris in January 1995 measures were agreed for the implementation of an Emergency Economic Recovery Programme, subject to the conclusion of a stand-by agreement with the IMF. However, structural adjustment measures stipulated by the IMF, notably the divestment of public enterprises and the rationalization of the civil service, were not approved by the legislature until late 1996. The IMF subsequently approved a three-year credit of US $131m. under an Enhanced Structural Adjustment Facility (ESAF), which, in turn, facilitated access to further multilateral development aid totalling in excess of $1,000m. However, owing to a parliamentary crisis (see Recent History) the majority of the reforms were not implemented, thus obstructing the disbursement of development aid. By the time of the expiry of the ESAF in October 1999 the bulk of the IMF financing had not been drawn. Furthermore, in November the Alexis administration, which was inaugurated in March of that year, revealed that international agencies had almost entirely failed to honour promises to finance its $311m. short-term economic action plan, initiated in May. Economic growth slowed further from 2000 onwards, exacerbated by the ongoing political impasse, which continued to impede investment and private-sector confidence, as well as the implementation of the necessary structural adjustments that would allow economic development. The main source of growth was the continued expansion of exports, principally from the textile sector. However, it was the continuing suspension of international aid to Haiti that was the main reason for the deteriorating economy. In January 2000 the EU suspended payment of almost $350m. in aid to Haiti, and the Inter-American Development Bank was withholding $220m. in loans. Furthermore, in September 2001 loan facilities were suspended by the World Bank after Haiti failed to meet loan repayments for the sixth consecutive month. Although humanitarian funds (estimated at $55m. in 2002) continued to be disbursed, the international community made it clear that confidence in Haiti's democratic process had to be restored before financial aid could be resumed. In September 2002 the Permanent Council of the OAS approved a resolution formally requesting that the international community resume financial aid to Haiti in order to avert a humanitarian crisis; it was hoped that up to $500m. of suspended aid and loans would be released upon the Government's fulfilment of certain conditions. From October 2002 the currency experienced significant devaluation, in part owing to rumours (which were subsequently denied) that the Government intended to convert balances held in dollar bank accounts into gourdes at rates lower than market prices. In December the Inter-American Development Bank announced the disbursement of a $950,000 loan intended to fund a programme to improve the Government's efficiency in its management of public policy. In an attempt to encourage foreign investment the Government approved a new law offering several incentives, including a 15-year 'tax holiday', to foreign businesses prepared to invest in the country. Popular protests in late 2002 continued into 2003, contributing to a further deterioration of the country's economic situation.

Education

Education is provided by the State, by the Roman Catholic Church and by other religious organizations, but many schools charge for tuition, books or uniforms. Teaching is based on the French model, and French is used as the language of instruction. Primary education, which normally begins at six years of age and lasts for six years, is officially compulsory. Secondary education usually begins at 12 years of age and lasts for a further six years, comprising two cycles of three years each. In 1997 primary enrolment included only 19.4% of children in the relevant age-group (18.9% of boys; 19.9% of girls). Enrolment at secondary schools in 1997 was equivalent to only 34.2% of children in the relevant age-group (35.2% of boys; 33.2% of girls). In 1999 combined enrolment in primary, secondary and tertiary education was 52%. Higher education is provided by 18 vocational training centres and 42 domestic science schools, and by the Université d'Etat d'Haïti, which has faculties of law, medicine, dentistry, science, agronomy, pharmacy, economic science, veterinary medicine and ethnology. Government expenditure on education in 1990 was 216m. gourdes, equivalent to 20.0% of total government expenditure.

Public Holidays

2003: 1 January (Independence Day), 2 January (Heroes of Independence), 3 March (Shrove Monday, half-day), 4 March (Shrove Tuesday), 14 April (Pan-American Day), 18 April (Good Friday), 1 May (Labour Day), 18 May (Flag Day), 22 May (National Sovereignty), 15 August (Assumption), 24 October (United Nations Day), 2 November (All Souls' Day, half-day), 18 November (Army Day and Commemoration of the Battle of Vertières), 5 December (Discovery Day), 25 December (Christmas Day).

2004: 1 January (Independence Day), 2 January (Heroes of Independence), 23 February (Shrove Monday, half-day), 24 February (Shrove Tuesday), 9 April (Good Friday), 14 April (Pan-American Day), 1 May (Labour Day), 18 May (Flag Day), 22 May (National Sovereignty), 15 August (Assumption), 24 October (United Nations Day), 2 November (All Souls' Day, half-day), 18 November (Army Day and Commemoration of the Battle of Vertières), 5 December (Discovery Day), 25 December (Christmas Day).

Weights and Measures

Officially the metric system is in force but many US measures are also used.

Statistical Survey

Sources (unless otherwise stated): Banque de la République d'Haïti, angle rue du Magasin d'État et rue des Miracles, BP 1570, Port-au-Prince; tel. 299-1000; fax 299-1145; e-mail webmaster@brh.net; internet www.brh.net; Ministère des Finances, Port-au-Prince.

Area and Population

AREA, POPULATION AND DENSITY

Area (sq km)	27,750*
Population (census results)†	
31 August 1971	4,329,991
30 August 1982	
Males	2,448,370
Females	2,605,422
Total	5,053,792
Population (official estimates at mid-year)‡	
1999	6,774,081
2000	7,180,294
2001	8,132,000§
Density (per sq km) at mid-2001	293.0

* 10,714 sq miles.
† Excluding adjustment for underenumeration.
‡ Provisional figures.
§ Population is *de jure*.

DEPARTMENTS

(population estimates, 2000)

Artibonite. . . .	1,013,779	North-West . . .	420,971
Central	490,790	South	653,398
Grande-Anse . .	641,399	South-East . . .	457,013
North	759,318	West	2,494,862
North-East . . .	248,764	**Total**	7,180,294

PRINCIPAL TOWNS

(estimated population at mid-1997)

Port-au-Prince					
(capital). . . .	917,112	Pétionville . . .	76,155
Carrefour	306,074	Gonaïves	63,690
Delmas	257,247	Saint-Marc . . .	49,128
Cap-Haïtien . . .	107,026	Les Cayes	48,838

Source: Thomas Brinkhoff, *City Population* (internet www.citypopulation.de).

Mid-2001 (UN estimate, incl. suburbs): Port-au-Prince 1,838 (Source: UN, *World Urbanization Prospects: The 2001 Revision*).

BIRTHS AND DEATHS

(World Bank estimates)

	1998	1999	2000
Crude birth rate (per 1,000) . .	31	n.a.	32
Crude death rate (per 1,000) . .	13	n.a.	13

Source: World Bank, *World Development Indicators*.

Expectation of life (WHO estimates, years at birth): 50.0 (males 45.6; females 54.7) in 2001 (Source: WHO, *World Health Report*).

ECONOMICALLY ACTIVE POPULATION

(official estimates, persons aged 10 years and over, mid-1990)

	Males	Females	Total
Agriculture, hunting, forestry and fishing	1,077,191	458,253	1,535,444
Mining and quarrying	11,959	12,053	24,012
Manufacturing	83,180	68,207	151,387
Electricity, gas and water . . .	1,643	934	2,577
Construction	23,584	4,417	28,001
Trade, restaurants and hotels . .	81,632	271,338	352,970
Transport, storage and communications	17,856	2,835	20,691
Financing, insurance, real estate and business services . .	3,468	1,589	5,057
Community, social and personal services	81,897	73,450	155,347
Activities not adequately defined .	33,695	30,280	63,975
Total employed	1,416,105	923,356	2,339,461
Unemployed	191,333	148,346	339,679
Total labour force	1,607,438	1,071,702	2,679,140

Source: ILO, *Yearbook of Labour Statistics*.

Mid-2001 (estimates in '000): Agriculture, etc. 2,210; Total labour force 3,582 (Source: FAO).

Health and Welfare

KEY INDICATORS

Total fertility rate (children per woman, 2001)	4.1
Under-5 mortality rate (per 1,000 live births, 2000)	125
HIV/AIDS (% of persons aged 15–49, 2001)	6.10
Physicians (per 1,000 head, 1992)	0.08
Hospital beds (per 1,000 head, 1996)	0.71
Health expenditure (2000): US $ per head (PPP)	54
Health expenditure (2000): % of GDP	4.9
Health expenditure (2000): public (% of total)	49.3
Access to water (% of persons, 2000)	46
Access to sanitation (% of persons, 2000)	28
Human Development Index (2000): ranking	146
Human Development Index (2000): value	0.471

For sources and definitions, see explanatory note on p. vi.

Agriculture

PRINCIPAL CROPS

('000 metric tons)

	1999*	2000	2001
Rice (paddy)	100	130	103
Maize	250	202.5	180
Sorghum	100	98	80
Sweet potatoes	172	180	174
Cassava (Manioc)	325	337.7	332
Yams	195	200	197
Other roots and tubers*	53	51.6	52
Sugar cane	1,000	800	1,008
Fresh vegetables*	217.9	225.9	198.9
Bananas	290	322.5	290
Plaintains*	290	290	280
Mangoes	225	250	250
Other fruit*	166.5	174.4	148.8

* FAO estimate(s).

Source: FAO.

LIVESTOCK

('000 head, year ending September)

	1999*	2000	2001*
Horses*	490	500	501
Mules*	80	82	82
Asses*	210	215	215
Cattle	1,300	1,430	1,440
Pigs	800	1,000	1,001
Sheep	138	152	152
Goats	1,619	1,942	1,942
Poultry*	5,390	5,390	5,905

* FAO estimate(s).

Source: FAO.

LIVESTOCK PRODUCTS

('000 metric tons)

	1999*	2000	2001*
Beef and veal	31.0	40.3	40.5
Goat meat	5.4	6.5	6.5
Pig meat	26.9	28.0	29.0
Horse meat*	5.4	5.5	5.6
Poultry meat*	7.6	8.3	8.4
Cows' milk	37.5	41.3	42.0
Goats' milk*	20.0	24.0	24.4
Hen eggs	3.8	4.1	4.2
Cattle hides*	4.8	5.8	5.8

* FAO estimates.

Source: FAO.

Forestry

ROUNDWOOD REMOVALS

(FAO estimates, '000 cubic metres, excl. bark)

	1999	2000	2001
Sawlogs, veneer logs and logs for sleepers*	224	224	224
Other industrial wood*	15	15	15
Fuel wood	1,955	1,964	1,971
Total	2,193	2,203	2,210

* Output assumed to be unchanged since 1971.

Source: FAO.

SAWNWOOD PRODUCTION

('000 cubic metres, incl. railway sleepers)

	1969	1970	1971
Coniferous (softwood)	5	8	8
Broadleaved (hardwood)	10	5	6
Total	14	13	14

1972–2001: Annual production as in 1971 (FAO estimates).

Source: FAO.

Fishing

(FAO estimates, metric tons, live weight)

	1998	1999	2000
Freshwater fishes	500	500	500
Marine fishes	4,000	3,800	3,800
Caribbean spiny lobster	200	200	200
Natantian decapods	150	150	150
Stromboid conchs	350	300	300
Total catch (incl. others)	5,259	5,000	5,000

Source: FAO, *Yearbook of Fishery Statistics*.

Industry

SELECTED PRODUCTS

(metric tons, unless otherwise indicated, year ending 30 September)

	1999/2000
Edible oils	38,839.6
Butter	2,972.2
Margarine	2,387.4
Cornflour	104,542.6
Soap	30,069.9
Detergent	4,506.1
Beer ('000 cases of 24 bottles)	784.5
Beverages ('000 cases of 24 bottles)	1,807.7
Rum ('000 750ml bottles)	2,009.5
Electric energy (million kWh)	697.6

Finance

CURRENCY AND EXCHANGE RATES

Monetary Units
100 centimes = 1 gourde

Sterling, Dollar and Euro Equivalents (31 December 2002)
£1 sterling = 60.619 gourdes
US $1 = 37.609 gourdes
€1 = 39.441 gourdes
1,000 gourdes = £16.497 = $26.589 = €25.354

Average Exchange Rate (gourdes per US $)
2000   21.171
2001   24.429
2002   29.250

Note: The official rate of exchange was maintained at US $1 = 5 gourdes until September 1991, when the central bank ceased all operations at the official rate, thereby unifying the exchange system at the 'floating' free market rate.

BUDGET
(million gourdes, year ending 30 September)

Revenue	1999	2000	2001
Current receipts	6,084	6,256	6,509
Internal receipts	4,779	4,605	4,504
Customs	1,306	1,651	1,772
Transfers from public enterprises	207	16	0
Total	6,292	6,272	6,509

Expenditure	1999	2000	2001
Current expenditure	5,310	5,795	7,150
Wages and salaries	2,926	3,243	3,387
Operations	1,735	1,794	2,678
Interest on public debt	616	628	767
External debt	339	323	436
Internal debt	276	305	331
Other current expenditure	−293	−161	−51
Capital expenditure	1,488	2,063	1,578
Total *	6,827	7,850	8,728

* Including net lending (million gourdes): 30 in 1999; −9 in 2000; 0 in 2001.

Source: IMF, *Haiti: Selected Issues* (February 2002).

INTERNATIONAL RESERVES
(US $ million at 31 December)*

	2000	2001	2002
IMF special drawing rights	0.1	0.5	0.5
Reserve position in IMF	0.1	0.1	0.1
Foreign exchange	183.0	141.0	65.8
Total	183.2	141.6	66.4

* Excluding gold (valued at market-related prices, US $ million): 6.6 in 1989.

Source: IMF, *International Financial Statistics*.

MONEY SUPPLY
(million gourdes at 31 December)*

	2000	2001	2002
Currency outside banks	5,807.2	6,584.3	8,687.5
Demand deposits at commercial banks	3,251.2	3,749.2	4,396.1
Total money (incl. others)	9,220.2	10,610.2	13,503.5

* Beginning in September 1997, data are based on an improved sectorization of the accounts.

Source: IMF, *International Financial Statistics*.

COST OF LIVING
(Consumer Price Index, year ending 30 September; base: 1997 = 100)

	1999	2000	2001
Food	111.8	122.7	141.7
Clothing and footwear	134.9	166.4	—
Rent	133.1	156.2	—
All items	120.2	136.9	156.1

Source: ILO.

All items (base 1995 = 100): 249.3 in 2002 (Source: IMF, *International Financial Statistics*).

NATIONAL ACCOUNTS
(million gourdes, year ending 30 September)

Expenditure on the Gross Domestic Product
(at current prices)

	1999/2000	2000/01	2001/02
Final consumption expenditure	72,446	82,353	90,433
Gross capital formation	21,208	22,106	23,528
Total domestic expenditure	93,654	104,459	113,961
Exports of goods and services	9,849	10,208	11,582
Less Imports of goods and services	25,923	29,225	33,379
GDP in purchasers' values	77,580	85,442	92,164
GDP at constant 1987 prices	13,138	12,991	12,874

Source: IMF, *International Financial Statistics*.

Gross Domestic Product by Economic Activity
(at constant 1986/87 prices)

	1998/99	1999/2000*	2000/01†
Agriculture, hunting, forestry and fishing	3,553	3,424	3,446
Mining and quarrying	14	14	14
Manufacturing	987	986	988
Electricity, gas and water	90	87	49
Construction	870	939	948
Trade, restaurants and hotels	3,251	3,403	3,424
Transport, storage and communication	665	725	751
Business services	1,501	1,566	1,552
Other services	1,444	1,433	1,385
Sub-total	12,375	12,577	12,557
Less Imputed bank service charge	343	459	494
Total	12,032	12,119	12,061
Import duties	992	1,020	920
GDP in purchasers' values	13,025	13,138	12,981

* Provisional figures.
† Estimates.

BALANCE OF PAYMENTS
(US $ million, year ending 30 September)

	1999	2000*	2001*
Exports of goods f.o.b.	339.4	0	293.5
Imports of goods f.o.b.	−936.8	−1,014.4	−692.8
Trade balance	−597.4	−1,014.4	−399.3
Exports of services	188.6	172.5	144.5
Imports of services	−231.8	−262.1	−96.1
Balance on goods and services	−640.7	−1,104.0	−788.8
Other income paid	−12.7	−9.2	−8.2
Balance on goods, services and income	−872.5	−1,113.2	−797.0
Current transfers received	673.7	712.4	743.6
Current balance	20.4	−400.8	−53.5
Direct investment from abroad	30.0	13.3	4.4
Other investments	51.1	−25.3	43.1
Net errors and omissions	−80.1	367.2	7.2
Overall balance	21.4	−45.7	1.2

* Preliminary figures.

External Trade

PRINCIPAL COMMODITIES
(US $ million, year ending 30 September)

Imports c.i.f.	1998	1999	2000
Food and others*	307.9	361.6	308.9
Mineral fuels, lubricants, etc.	80.8	83.2	186.6
Machinery and transport equipment	142.1	164.9	171.5
Manufactured goods	223.2	257.2	289.1
Total (incl. others)	883.9	1,010.6	1,090.7

* Including beverages, oils and fats, and pharmaceutical products.

Exports f.o.b.	1998	1999	2000
Agricultural exports	40.7	37.7	32.4
Coffee	21.8	18.0	13.5
Light manufactures*	244.9	295.5	281.3
Domestic inputs	33.7	30.4	23.6
Imported inputs	211.2	265.1	257.7
Total (incl. others)	299.4	348.7	327.1

* Includes valuation and classification adjustments made by Banque de la République d'Haiti.

Source: IMF, *Haiti: Selected Issues* (February 2002).

PRINCIPAL TRADING PARTNERS
(US $ million, year ending 30 September)*

Imports c.i.f.		1989/90	1990/91	1991/92
Belgium	. . . . . .	3.4	3.7	2.9
Canada	. . . . .	22.0	31.9	15.2
France	. . . . .	24.5	32.4	17.2
Germany, Federal Republic	.	14.6	19.2	10.0
Japan	. . . . .	23.6	31.2	17.7
Netherlands	. . . .	11.2	13.9	8.7
United Kingdom	. . . .	5.6	6.7	4.2
USA	. . . . .	153.1	203.2	126.7
Total (incl. others)	. . . .	332.2	400.5	277.2

Exports f.o.b.†		1989/90	1990/91	1991/92
Belgium	. . . . . .	15.9	19.5	6.0
Canada	. . . . .	4.5	4.7	2.3
France	. . . . .	17.4	21.6	6.1
Germany, Federal Republic	.	5.4	6.6	2.4
Italy	. . . . .	16.5	20.7	8.7
Japan	. . . . .	2.4	2.9	0.9
Netherlands	. . . .	3.4	4.3	1.4
United Kingdom	. . . .	2.3	2.3	0.7
USA	. . . . .	78.3	96.3	39.7
Total (incl. others)	. . . .	163.7	198.7	74.7

* Provisional.
† Excluding re-exports.

Source: Administration Générale des Douanes.

Transport

ROAD TRAFFIC
('000 motor vehicles in use)

	1994	1995	1996
Passenger cars	30.0	49.0	59.0
Commercial vehicles . . .	30.0	29.0	35.0

1999 ('000 motor vehicles in use): Passenger cars 93.0; Commercial vehicles 61.6.

Source: UN, *Statistical Yearbook*.

SHIPPING
Merchant Fleet
(registered at 31 December)

	1999	2000	2001
Number of vessels . . .	4	4	4
Total displacement ('000 grt) . .	1.2	1.2	1.2

Source: Lloyd's Register-Fairplay, *World Fleet Statistics*.

International Sea-borne Freight Traffic
('000 metric tons)

	1988	1989	1990
Goods loaded	164	165	170
Goods unloaded	684	659	704

Source: UN, *Monthly Bulletin of Statistics*.

CIVIL AVIATION (international flights, 1995): Passengers arriving 367,900; Passengers departing 368,330.

Tourism

TOURIST ARRIVALS BY COUNTRY OF ORIGIN

	1998	1999	2000
Canada	. . . . .	15,489	15,955	14,752
Dominican Republic	. . . .	7,905	6,769	7,034
France	. . . . .	6,984	6,318	6,420
Jamaica	. . . . .	n.a.	3,069	3,531
USA	. . . . .	93,978	92,543	92,921
Total (incl. others)	. . . .	146,837	143,362	140,492

Receipts from tourism (US $ million): 80 in 1997; 58 in 1998; 57 in 1999.

Sources: World Tourism Organization, *Yearbook of Tourism Statistics* and World Bank, *World Development Indicators*.

Communications Media

	1999	2000	2001
Telephones ('000 main lines in use)	70.0	72.5	80.0
Mobile cellular telephones ('000 subscribers)	25.0	n.a.	91.5
Personal computers ('000 in use) .	2.0	n.a.	n.a.
Internet users ('000)	6.0	6.0*	30.0

* Estimate.

Source: International Telecommunication Union.

Radio receivers ('000 in use): 415 in 1997.

Television receivers ('000 in use): 42 in 1999.

Daily newspapers: 4 in 1996 (total circulation 20,000 copies).

Book production: 340 titles published in 1995.

Sources: UNESCO, *Statistical Yearbook*, UN, *Statistical Yearbook*.

Education

(1994/95)

	Institutions	Teachers	Students
Pre-primary	. . . . .	n.a.	n.a.	230,391*
Primary	. . . .	10,071	30,205	1,110,398
Secondary	. . . .	1,038	15,275	195,418
Tertiary	. . . .	n.a.	654*	6,288*

* 1990/91 figure.

Adult literacy rate (UNESCO estimates): 49.8% (males 52.0%; females 47.8%) in 2000 (Source: UN Development Programme, *Human Development Report*).

Directory

The Constitution

The Constitution of the Republic of Haiti, which was approved by the electorate in a referendum held in March 1987, provided for a system of power-sharing between a President (who may not serve two consecutive five-year terms), a Prime Minister, a bicameral legislature (comprising a chamber of deputies elected for four years and a senate whose members serve six-year terms, one-third of whom are elected every two years) and regional assemblies. The army and the police were no longer to be a combined force. The death penalty was abolished. Official status was given to the Creole language spoken by Haitians and to the folk religion, voodoo (vaudou). The Constitution was suspended after a military *coup d'état* in June 1988. It was restored when the military ruler, Brig.-Gen. Prosper Avril, fled in March 1990 and an interim President was appointed, pending a presidential election in December 1990. Fr Jean-Bertrand Aristide was elected President, but was deposed in September 1991 by a military coup. In October a new President and Government were installed by the army. In June 1992 the presidency was declared to be vacant, but in May 1994 a pro-military faction of the Senate declared the head of the Supreme Court, Émile Jonassaint, provisional President. Following US mediation, US forces (officially an international peace-keeping force) arrived on the island on 19 September. Lt-Gen. Raoul Cédras, the Commander-in-Chief of the armed forces, resigned on 10 October, and Jonassaint resigned the following day. On 15 October President Aristide returned to Haiti, to begin the restoration of constitutional government. He declared the army dissolved in April 1995. The constitutional amendment formally abolishing it was due to be passed by the legislature elected in May and July 2000.

The Government

HEAD OF STATE

President: JEAN-BERTRAND ARISTIDE (assumed office on 7 February 2001).

CABINET
(April 2003)

Prime Minister: YVON NEPTUNE.

Minister of Agriculture and Natural Resources: SÉBASTIEN HILAIRE.

Minister of Culture and Communications: LILAS DESQUIRON.

Minister of Economy and Finance: GUSTAVE FAUBERT.

Minister of the Environment: WEBSTER PIERRE.

Minister of Foreign Affairs and Religion: JOSEPH PHILIPPE ANTONIO.

Minister for Haitians Residing Abroad: LESLIE VOLTAIRE.

Minister of Health: HENRI-CLAUDE VOLTAIRE.

Minister of the Interior: JOCELERME PRIVERT.

Minister of Justice: CALIXTE DELATOUR.

Minister of National Education: MARIE-CARMELLE AUSTIN.

Minister of Planning and External Co-operation: PAUL DURET.

Minister of Public Works: HARRY CLINTON.

Minister of Social Affairs: EUDES SAINT-PREUX CRAAN.

Minister of Tourism: MARTINE DEVERSON.

Minister of Trade and Industry: LESLIE GOUTHIER.

Minister of Women's Affairs and Rights: GINETTE LUBIN.

Minister without Portfolio (in charge of Negotiations with the Opposition): MARC BAZIN.

Secretary of State for Communication: MARIO DUPUY.

Secretary of State for Literacy: MARYSE GUITEAU.

Secretary of State for Public Security: GÉRARD DUBREUIL.

Secretary of State for Youth, Sports and Civic Service: HERMANN NAU.

Secretary of State for Finance: (vacant).

Secretary of State for Social Affairs: PIERRE RICHARD PIERRE.

MINISTRIES

Office of the President: Palais National, Champ de Mars, Port-au-Prince; tel. 222-3024.

Office of the Prime Minister: Villa d'Accueil, Delmas 60, Musseau, Port-au-Prince; tel. 245-0007; fax 245-1624.

Ministry of Agriculture and Natural Resources: route Nationale 1, Damien, Port-au-Prince; tel. 222-3596.

Ministry of Culture and Communications: 4 rue Nagny, Port-au-Prince; tel. 221-1716; e-mail dg1@haiticulture.org.

Ministry of Economy and Finance: Palais des Ministères, Port-au-Prince; tel. 222-0724.

Ministry of the Environment: Haut Turgeau 181, Port-au-Prince; tel. 245-7572; fax 245-7360; e-mail dgmde@rehred-haiti.net; internet www.rehred-haiti.net.

Ministry of Foreign Affairs and Religion: blvd Harry S Truman, Cité de l'Exposition, Port-au-Prince; tel. 222-8482; fax 223-1668.

Ministry for Haitians Residing Abroad: 87 ave Jean-Paul II, Turgeau, Port-au-Prince; tel. 244-4321; fax 245-3400; internet haiti2004lakay.com; f. 1995.

Ministry of Health: Palais de Ministères, Port-au-Prince; tel. 222-1583; fax 222-4066.

Ministry of the Interior: Palais des Ministères, Port-au-Prince; tel. 222-6490; fax 223-5742.

Ministry of Justice: ave Charles Sumner 19, Port-au-Prince; tel. 245-1626.

Ministry of National Education: rue Dr Audain, Port-au-Prince; tel. 222-1036; fax 223-7887.

Ministry of Planning and External Co-operation: Palais des Ministères, Port-au-Prince; tel. 222-4148; fax 223-4193.

Ministry of Public Works: Palais des Ministères, BP 2002, Port-au-Prince; tel. 222-2164; fax 223-4586.

Ministry of Social Affairs: rue de la Révolution 16, Port-au-Prince; tel. 222-1244.

Ministry of Tourism: Port-au-Prince; tel. 223-0723; e-mail feedback-ht@intermediahaiti.com; internet www.haititourisme.com.

Ministry of Trade and Industry: rue Légitime 26, Champ-de-Mars, Port-au-Prince; tel. 222-1628; fax 223-8402.

Ministry of Women's Affairs and Rights: Champ de Mars, Port-au-Prince; tel. 222-1479.

President and Legislature

PRESIDENT

Presidential Election, 26 November 2000

Candidates	% of votes
Jean-Bertrand Aristide (FL)	91.7
Jean-Arnold Dumas	2.0
Evan Nicolas	1.6
Serge Sylvain	1.3
Calixte Dorisca	1.3
Jacques Philippe Dorce	1.1
Paul Arthur Fleurival	1.0
Total (incl. others)	100.0

LEGISLATURE

Sénat
(Senate)

President: FOUREL CELESTIN.

Elections, 21 May, 9 July and 26 November 2000

	Seats
La Fanmi Lavalas (FL)	26*
Pati Louvri Baryè (PLB)	1
Total	27

*In June 2001 seven FL senators resigned their seats.

Chambre des Députés
(Chamber of Deputies)

President: YVES CRYSTALLIN.

Elections, 21 May, 9 July and 26 November 2000

	Seats
La Fanmi Lavalas (FL)	73
Mouvement Chrétien pour Batir une Nouvelle Haïti (MOCHRENA)	3
Espace de Concertation	2
Pati Louvri Baryè (PLB)	2
Koordinasyon Resistans Grandans (KOREGA-ESCANP)	1
Organisation du Peuple en Lutte (OPL)	1
Independent	1
Total	83

Political Organizations

Alliance pour l'Avancement d'Haïti (ALAH): BP 13350, Station de Delmas, Port-au-Prince; tel. 245-0446; fax 257-4804; e-mail reynoldgeorges@yahoo.com; Leader REYNOLD GEORGES.

L'Alternative pour le Changement (AC): Port-au-Prince; f. 2000; Leader GÉRARD BLOT.

Congrès National des Mouvements Démocratiques (KONAKOM): f. 1987; social democratic; Leader VICTOR BENOÎT.

Convergence Démocratique (CD): f. 2000; coalition of 15 anti-Lavalas parties; Leaders SERGE GILLES, EVANS PAUL, MICHA GAILLARD.

Espace de Concertation: f. 1999; centre-left coalition; Leader EVANS PAUL.

La Fanmi Lavalas: f. 1996; formed a coalition with the MOP, the OPL and the PLB; Leader JEAN-BERTRAND ARISTIDE.

Jeunesse Pouvoir Populaire (JPP): f. 1997; Leader RENÉ CIVIL.

Konfederasyon Inite Demokratik (KID): f. 1986; Leader EVANS PAUL.

Koordinasyon Resistans Grandans (KOREGA-ESCANP): e-mail crb@maf.org; regionally based; radical left; Leader Fr JOACHIM SAMEDI.

Mobilisation pour le Développement National (MDN): c/o CHISS, 33 rue Bonne Foi, BP 2497, Port-au-Prince; tel. 222-3829; e-mail info@mdnhaiti.org; internet www.mdnhaiti.org; f. 1986; Pres. HUBERT DE RONCERAY; Sec.-Gen. MAX CARRE.

Mouvement Chrétien pour Batir une Nouvelle Haïti (MOCHRENA): f. 1991; Leader LUC MÉSADIEU.

Mouvement Démocratique pour la Libération d'Haïti (MODELH): Leader FRANÇOIS LATORTUE.

Mouvement pour l'Instauration de la Démocratie en Haïti (MIDH): 114 av Jean Paul II, Port-au-Prince; tel. 245-8377; f. 1986; centre-right; Pres. MARC BAZIN.

Mouvement pour l'Organisation du Pays (MOP): f. 1946; centre party; Leader JEAN MOLIÈRE.

Mouvement Patriotique pour le Sauvetage National (MPSN): f. 1998; right-wing coalition; Leader HUBERT DE RONCERAY.

Mouvement pour la Reconstruction Nationale (MRN): f. 1991; Leader RENÉ THÉODORE.

Organisation du Peuple en Lutte (OPL): f. 1991 as Organisation Politique Lavalas; name changed as above 1998; Leaders GÉRARD PIERRE-CHARLES, SAUVEUR PIERRE-ÉTIENNE.

Parti Agricole et Industrie National (PAIN): Leader LOUIS DEJOIE.

Parti des Démocrates Haïtiens (PADEMH): Leader JEAN-JACQUES CLARK PARENT.

Parti Démocratique et Chrétien d'Haïti (PDCH): f. 1979; Christian Democrat party; Leader JOACHIN PIERRE.

Parti pour un Développement Alternatif (PADH): Leader GÉRARD DALVIUS.

Parti National Progressiste Révolutionnaire (PANPRA): f. 1989; social-democratic; Leader SERGE GILLES.

Parti Populaire National: f. 1999; Leader BEN DUPUY.

Parti Social Chrétien d'Haïti (PSCH): Leader GRÉGOIRE EUGÈNE.

Pati Louvri Baryè (PLB): f. 1992; Leader RENAUD BERNARDIN.

Rassemblement des Démocrates Chrétiens (RDC): Leader EDDY VOLEL.

Rassemblement des Démocrates Nationalistes et Progressistes (RDNP): f. 1979; centre party; Sec.-Gen. LESLIE FRANÇOIS MANIGAT.

Union Démocrates Patriotiques (UDP): Leader ROCKFELLER GUERRE.

Diplomatic Representation

EMBASSIES IN HAITI

Argentina: 4 impasse Dumain, Montana Pétionville, BP 1755, Port-au-Prince; tel. 257-1635; fax 256-6414; e-mail embarghaiti@hainet.net; Chargé d'affaires a.i. MARIO JOSÉ PINO.

Bahamas: Port-au-Prince; Ambassador FRANKLIN O'BRIEN ROLLE.

Brazil: 168 Place Boyer, Pétionville, BP 6140, Port-au-Prince; tel. 256-9662; fax 256-0900; e-mail embpap@haitiworld.com; Ambassador ANTÓNIO FERREIRA DA ROCHA.

Canada: 18 route de Delmas, BP 826, Port-au-Prince; tel. 298-3050; fax 298-3801; e-mail pmce@dfait-maeci.gc.ca; internet www.port-au-prince.gc.ca; Ambassador KENNETH MURRAY COOK.

Chile: 2 rue Coutilien, Musseau, Port-au-Prince; tel. 256-7960; fax 257-0623; e-mail echileht@acn2.net; Ambassador ISMAEL LLONA MOUAT.

China (Taiwan): 16 rue Léon Nau, Pétionville, BP 655, Port-au-Prince; tel. 257-2899; fax 256-8067; e-mail ambrdc@acn2.net; Ambassador HSIN-PING HSIEH.

Colombia: Rue Serin, Delmas 71, Complexe Lafayette No 1, 6120, Port-au-Prince; tel. 249-8630; fax 249-6625; e-mail epuerto@minrelext.gov.co; Ambassador EDUARDO CASAS ACOSTA.

Cuba: 18 rue Marion, Peguy Ville, POB 15702, Port-au-Prince; tel. 256-3812; fax 257-8566; e-mail ecuhaiti@hainet.net; Ambassador ROLANDO GÓMEZ GONZÁLEZ.

Dominican Republic: rue Panaméricaine 121, BP 56, Pétionville, Port-au-Prince; tel. 257-0383; fax 257-9215; Ambassador ALBERTO EMILIO DESPRADEL CABRAL.

Ecuador: BP 2531, Port-au-Prince; tel. 222-4576; Chargé d'affaires ADOLFO ALVAREZ.

France: 51 place des Héros de l'Indépendance, BP 1312, Port-au-Prince; tel. 222-0951; fax 223-9858; internet www.ambafrance-ht.org; Ambassador YVES GAUDEUL.

Germany: 2 impasse Claudinette, Bois Moquette, Pétionville, BP 1147, Port-au-Prince; tel. 257-7280; fax 257-4131; e-mail germanem@haitelonline.com; Ambassador Dr GORDON KRICKE.

Holy See: rue Louis Pouget, Morne Calvaire, BP 326, Port-au-Prince; tel. 257-6308; fax 257-3411; e-mail nonciature@haitiworld.com; Apostolic Nuncio Most Rev. LUIGI BONAZZI (Titular Archbishop of Atella).

Japan: Villa Bella Vista 2, impasse Tulipe, Desprez, Port-au-Prince; tel. 245-3333; fax 245-8834; Chargé d'affaires a.i. KANJI KITAZAWA.

Mexico: Delmas 60, 2, BP 327, Port-au-Prince; tel. 257-8100; fax 256-6528; e-mail embmxhai@yahoo.com; Ambassador ANACELIA PÉREZ DE MEYER.

Spain: 54 rue Pacot, State Liles, BP 386, Port-au-Prince; tel. 245-4410; fax 245-3901; e-mail ampespht@mail.mae.es; Ambassador RAFAEL MATOS GONZÁLEZ DE CAREAGA.

USA: 5 blvd Harry S Truman, BP 1761, Port-au-Prince; tel. 223-5511; fax 223-5515; Ambassador JAMES FOLEY (designate).

Venezuela: blvd Harry S Truman, Cité de l'Exposition, BP 2158, Port-au-Prince; tel. 222-0973; e-mail venhtamb@compa.net; Ambassador MARCO REQUENA.

Judicial System

Law is based on the French Napoleonic Code, substantially modified during the presidency of François Duvalier.

Courts of Appeal and Civil Courts sit at Port-au-Prince and the three provincial capitals: Gonaïves, Cap Haïtien and Port de Paix. In principle each commune has a Magistrates' Court. Judges of the Supreme Court and Courts of Appeal are appointed by the President.

Supreme Court

Port-au-Prince; tel. 222-3212; internet www.haiti.org/courcass.htm.

Pres. CLAUSEL DÉBROSSE; Vice-Pres. PRADEL PÉAN.

Citizens' Rights Defender: NECKER DESSABLES.

Religion

Roman Catholicism and the folk religion voodoo (vaudou) are the official religions. There are various Protestant and other denominations.

CHRISTIANITY

The Roman Catholic Church

For ecclesiastical purposes, Haiti comprises two archdioceses and seven dioceses. At 31 December 2000 adherents represented some 94.3% of the population.

Bishops' Conference

Conférence Episcopale de Haïti, angle rues Piquant et Lamarre, BP 1572, Port-au-Prince; tel. 222-5194; fax 223-5318; e-mail ceh56@hotmail.com.

f. 1977; Pres. Rt Rev. HUBERT CONSTANT (Bishop of Fort-Liberté).

Archbishop of Cap-Haïtien: Most Rev. FRANÇOIS GAYOT, Archevêché, rue 19–20 H, BP 22, Cap-Haïtien; tel. 262-1278; fax 262-0593.

Archbishop of Port-au-Prince: Most Rev. FRANÇOIS-WOLFF LIGONDÉ, Archevêché, rue Dr Aubry, BP 538, Port-au-Prince; tel. 222-2043; e-mail archeveche.pap@globalsud.com.

The Anglican Communion

Anglicans in Haiti fall under the jurisdiction of a missionary diocese of Province II of the Episcopal Church in the USA.

Bishop of Haiti: Rt Rev. JEAN ZACHE DURACIN, Eglise Episcopale d'Haïti, BP 1309, Port-au-Prince; fax 257-3412; e-mail epihaiti@globalsud.net.

Protestant Churches

Baptist Convention: BP 20, Cap-Haïtien; tel. 262-0567; e-mail conventionbaptiste@yahoo.com; f. 1964; Pres. Rev. GÉDÉON EUGÈNE.

Lutheran Church: Petite Place Cuzeau, BP 13147, Delmas, Port-au-Prince; tel. 246-3179; f. 1975; Minister BEN BICHOTTE.

Other denominations active in Haiti include Methodists and the Church of God 'Eben-Ezer'.

The Press

DAILIES

Le Matin: 88 rue du Quai, BP 367, Port-au-Prince; tel. 222-2040; f. 1908; French; independent; circ. 5,000.

Le Nouvelliste: 198 rue du Centre, BP 1316, Port-au-Prince; tel. 223-2114; fax 223-2313; f. 1898; evening; French; independent; circ. 6,000.

PERIODICALS

Haïti en Marche: 8 ruelle Cheriez, Port-au-Prince; tel. 245-1910; fax 513-5688; internet www.haitienmarche.com; weekly; Editor MARCUS GARCIA.

Haïti Progrès: 11 rue Capois, Port-au-Prince; tel. 222-6513; internet www.haiti-progres.com; weekly; Dir BEN DUPUY.

Haïti Observateur: 98 ave John Brown, Port-au-Prince; tel. 228-0782; weekly; Editor LÉO JOSEPH.

Le Messager du Nord-Ouest: Port de Paix; weekly.

Le Moniteur: BP 214 bis, Port-au-Prince; tel. 222-1744; 2 a week; French; the official gazette; circ. 2,000.

Optique: French Institute, BP 1316, Port-au-Prince; monthly; arts.

Le Septentrion: Cap-Haïtien; weekly; independent; Editor NELSON BELL; circ. 2,000.

NEWS AGENCIES

Agence Haïtienne de Presse (AHP): 6 rue Fernand, Port-au-Prince; tel. 245-7222; fax 245-5836; e-mail ahp@haitiworld.com; internet www.ahphaiti.org; Dir-Gen. VENEL REMARAIS.

Foreign Bureaux

Agence France-Presse (AFP): 72 rue Pavée, BP 62, Port-au-Prince; tel. 222-3469; fax 222-3759; Bureau Chief DOMINIQUE LEVANTI.

Agencia EFE (Spain): Port-au-Prince; tel. 255-9517; Correspondent HEROLD JEAN-FRANÇOIS.

Associated Press (AP) (USA): BP 2443, Port-au-Prince; tel. 257-4240; Correspondent MIKE NORTON.

Inter Press Service (Italy): 16 rue Malval, Turgeau, Port-au-Prince, HT6113; tel. 260-5512; fax 260-5513; e-mail ipshaiti@mediacom-ht.com; Correspondent IVES-MARIE CHANEL.

Prensa Latina (Cuba): Port-au-Prince; tel. 246-5149; internet www.prensa-latina.org; Correspondent JACQUELÍN TELEMAQUE.

Reuters (United Kingdom): Port-au-Prince; Correspondent MICHAEL DEIBERT.

Publishers

Editions des Antilles: route de l'Aéroport, Port-au-Prince.

Editions Caraïbes S.A.: 57 rue Pavée, BP 2013, Port-au-Prince; tel. 222-0032; Man. PIERRE J. ELIE.

Editions du Soleil: BP 2471, rue du Centre, Port-au-Prince; tel. 222-3147; education.

L'Imprimeur Deux: Le Nouvelliste, 198 rue du Centre, Port-au-Prince.

Maison Henri Deschamps—Les Entreprises Deschamps Frisch, SA: 25 rue Dr Martelly Seïde, BP 164, Port-au-Prince; tel. 223-2215; fax 223-4976; e-mail entreprisesdeschamps@globelsud.net; f. 1898; education and literature; Man. Dir JACQUES DESCHAMPS, Jr; CEO PETER J. FRISCH.

Natal: Imprimerie, rue Barbancourt, Port-au-Prince; Dir ROBERT MALVAL.

Théodore: Imprimerie, rue Dantes Destouches, Port-au-Prince.

Broadcasting and Communications

TELECOMMUNICATIONS

Conseil National des Télécommunications (CONATEL): 16 ave Marie Jeanne, Cité de l'Exposition, BP 2002, Port-au-Prince; tel. 222-0300; fax 222-0579; f. 1969; govt communications licensing authority; Dir-Gen. JEAN ARY CÉANT.

Télécommunications d'Haïti (Téléco): blvd Jean-Jacques Dessalines, BP 814, Port-au-Prince; tel. 245-2200; fax 223-0002; e-mail info@haititeleco.com; internet www.haititeleco.com; Dir-Gen. (vacant).

BROADCASTING

Radio

Radio Antilles International: 175 rue du Centre, BP 2335, Port-au-Prince; tel. 223-0696; f. 1984; independent; Dir-Gen. JACQUES SAMPEUR.

Radio Cacique: 5 Bellevue, BP 1480, Port-au-Prince; tel. 245-2326; f. 1961; independent; Dir JEAN-CLAUDE CARRIÉ.

Radio Caraïbes: 19 rue Chavannes, Port-au-Prince; tel. 223-0644; f. 1973; independent.

Radio Galaxie: 17 rue Pavée, Port-au-Prince; independent; Dir YVES JEAN-BART.

Radio Haïti Inter: Delmas 66A, 522, en face de Delmas 91, BP 737, Port-au-Prince; tel. 257-3111; f. 1935; independent; Dir MICHÈLE MONTAS.

Radio Lakansyèl: 285 route de Delmas, Port-au-Prince; tel. 246-2020; independent; Dir ALEX SAINT-SURIN.

Radio Lumière: Côte-Plage 16, BP 1050, Port-au-Prince; f. 1959; tel. 234-0330; f. 1959; Protestant; independent.

Radio Magic Stéreo: 346 route de Delmas, Port-au-Prince; tel. 245-5404; independent; Dir FRITZ JOASSIN.

Radio Metropole: 8 Delmas 52, BP 62, Port-au-Prince; tel. 246-2626; fax 246-3130; f. 1970; independent; Dir-Gen. RICHARD WIDMAIER.

Radio Nationale d'Haïti: 174 rue du Magasin de l'Etat, BP 1143, Port-au-Prince; tel. 223-5712; fax 223-5911; govt-operated; Dir-Gen. MICHEL FAVARD.

Radio Plus: 85 rue Pavée, BP 1174, Port-au-Prince; tel. 222-1588; independent; Dir LIONEL BÉNJAMIN.

Radio Port-au-Prince: Stade Sylvio Cator, BP 863, Port-au-Prince; f. 1979; independent; Dir GEORGE L. HÉRARD.

Radio Signal FM: 127 rue Louverture, Pétionville, BP 391, Port-au-Prince; tel. 298-4370; fax 298-4372; e-mail signalfm@netcourrier.com; f. 1991; independent; Dir-Gen. ANNE-MARIE ISSA.

Radio Soleil: BP 1362, Archevêché de Port-au-Prince; tel. 222-3062; fax 222-3516; f. 1978; Catholic; independent; educational; broadcasts in Creole and French; Dir Fr ARNOUX CHÉRY.

Radio Solidarité: Port-au-Prince; Dir VENEL REMARAIS.

Radio Superstar: 38 rue Safran, Delmas 68, Port-au-Prince; tel. 257-7219; independent; Dir ALBERT CHANCY.

Radio Tropic FM: 6 ave John Brown, Port-au-Prince; tel. 223-6565; independent; Dir GUY JEAN.

Radio Vision 2000: Port-au-Prince; internet www.radiovision2000.com; Dir LÉOPOLD BERLANGER.

Television

PVS Antenne 16: 137 rue Monseigneur Guilloux, Port-au-Prince; tel. and fax 222-1277; f. 1988; independent; Dir-Gen. RAYNALD DELERME.

Télé Haïti: blvd Harry S Truman, BP 1126, Port-au-Prince; tel. 222-3887; fax 222-9140; f. 1959; independent; pay-cable station with 33 channels; in French, Spanish and English; Dir MARIE CHRISTINE MOURRAL BLANC.

Télévision Nationale d'Haïti: Delmas 33, BP 13400, Port-au-Prince; tel. 246-2952; fax 246-0693; e-mail info@haiticulture.net; internet www.haiticulture.net/tnh/index.htm; f. 1979; govt-owned; cultural; 4 channels in Creole, French and Spanish; administered by four-mem. board; Dir RAYNALD LOUIS.

Trans-America: ruelle Roger, Gonaïves; tel. 74-0113; f. 1990; independent; Dir-Gen. HÉBERT PELISSIER.

TVA: rue Liberté, Gonaïves; independent; cable station with three channels; Dir-Gen. GÉRARD LUC JEAN-BAPTISTE.

Finance

(cap. = capital; m. = million; res = reserves; dep. = deposits; amounts in gourdes; brs = branches)

BANKING

Central Bank

Banque de la République d'Haïti: angle rues du Magasin de l'Etat et des Miracles, BP 1570, Port-au-Prince; tel. 299-1069; fax 222-2607; e-mail brh_adm@brh.net; internet www.brh.net; f. 1911 as Banque Nationale de la République d'Haiti; name changed as above in 1979; bank of issue; cap. 50m., res 4,084.0m., dep. 9,986.4m. (Sept. 2001); Pres. VENEL JOSEPH; Dir-Gen. REGINALD MONDESIR.

Commercial Banks

Banque Industrielle et Commerciale d'Haïti: 158 rue Dr Aubry, Port-au-Prince; tel. 299-6800.

Banque Nationale de Crédit: angle rues du Quai et des Miracles, BP 1320, Port-au-Prince; tel. 299-4081; fax 222-3331; f. 1979; cap. 25m., dep. 729.9m. (Sept. 1989); Pres. EDOUARD RACINE; Gen. Man. SOCRATE L. DEVIME.

Banque Populaire Haïtienne: angle rues des Miracles et du Centre, Port-au-Prince; tel. 299-6000; fax 222-4389; e-mail bphdg@brh.net; f. 1955; state-owned; cap. and res 22m., dep. 614m. (31 Dec. 2001); 3 brs; Dir-Gen. REGINALD MONDÉSIR; Gen Man. RODNEE DESCHINEAU.

Banque de Promotion Commerciale et Industrielle SA (PRO-MOBANK): 113 rue Faubert, Pétionville; tel. 299-8000; fax 299-8132; e-mail marketing@mail.promobank.net; f. 1974 as B.N.P. Haïti, name changed as above 1994; cap. 60.4m., res 16.4m., dep. 1,183.4m. (Dec. 1998); Pres. RONALD GEORGES; Gen. Man. JEAN PERRE.

Banque de l'Union Haïtienne: angle rues du Quai et Bonne Foi, BP 275, Port-au-Prince; tel. 299-8513; fax 223-2852; e-mail buh@buhsa.com; f. 1973; cap. 30.1m., res 6.2m., dep. 1,296.7m. (Sept. 1997); Pres. OSWALD J. BRANDT II; 11 brs.

Capital Bank: 149-151 rue des Miracles, BP 2464, Port-au-Prince; tel. 299-6500; fax 299-6519; e-mail capitalbank@brh.net; fmrly Banque de Crédit Immobilier, SA; Pres. BERNARD ROY; Gen. Man. LILIANE C. DOMINIQUE.

Sogebank, SA (Société Générale Haïtienne de Banque, SA): route de Delmas BP 1315, Delmas; tel. 229-5230; fax 229-5022; f. 1986; cap. 79.5m. Pres. JEAN CLAUDE NADAL; Dir-Gen. CHARLES CLERMONT; 7 brs.

Sogebel (Société Générale Haïtienne de Banque d'Espargne et de Logement): route de l'Aéroport, BP 2409, Delmas; tel. 229-5353; fax 229-5352; f. 1988; cap. 15.1m., dep. 249.9m. Gen. Man. CLAUDE PIERRE-LOUIS; 2 brs.

Unibank: 94 place Geffard, BP 46, Port-au-Prince; tel. 299-2300; fax 229-2332; e-mail info@unibank.net; f. 1993; cap. 100m., res 17.5m., dep. 3,366m. (Sept. 1999); Pres. F. CARL BRAUN; Dir-Gen. FRANCK HELMCKE; 20 brs.

Foreign Banks

Bank of Nova Scotia (Canada): 360 blvd J. J. Dessalines, BP 686, Port-au-Prince; tel. 299-3000; fax 229-3204; Man. CHESTER A. S. HINKSON; 3 brs.

Citibank, NA (USA): 242 route de Delmas, BP 1688, Port-au-Prince; tel. 246-2600; fax 246-0985; Vice-Pres. GLADYS M. COUPET.

Société Caribéenne de Banque, SA: 37 rue Pavée, BP 80, Port-au-Prince; tel. 299-7000; fax 299-7036; e-mail socabankcard@usa.net.

Development Bank

Banque Haïtienne de Développement: 220 ave Lamartinière, Port-au-Prince; tel. 244-3636; fax 244-3737; Dir-Gen. YVES LEREBOURS.

INSURANCE

National Companies

L'Atout Assurance, SA: 77 rue Lamarre, Port-au-Prince; tel. 223-9378; Dir JEAN EVEILLARD.

Compagnie d'Assurances d'Haïti, SA (CAH): étage Dynamic Entreprise, route de l'Aéroport, BP 1489, Port-au-Prince; tel. 246-0700; fax 246-0236; f. 1978; Pres. PHILIPPE R. ARMAND.

Excelsior Assurance, SA: rue 6, no 24, Port-au-Prince; tel. 245-8881; fax 245-8598; Dir-Gen. EMMANUEL SANON.

Générale d'Assurance, SA: Champ de Mars, Port-au-Prince; tel. 222-5465; fax 222-6502; f. 1985; Dir-Gen. ROLAND ACRA.

Haïti Sécurité Assurance, SA: 16 rue des Miracles, BP 1754, Port-au-Prince; tel. 223-2118; Dir-Gen. WILLIAM PHIPPS.

International Assurance, SA (INASSA): angle rues des Miracles et Pétion, Port-au-Prince; tel. 222-1058; Dir-Gen. RAOUL MÉROVÉ-PIERRE.

Multi Assurances, SA: route de l'Aéroport, Port-au-Prince; tel. 246-0700; fax 246-0236; Dir-Gen. PHILIPPE ARMAND.

National Assurance, SA (NASSA): 25 rue Ferdinand Canapé-Vert, Port-au-Prince, HT6115; tel. 245-9800; fax 245-9701; e-mail nassa@nassagroup.com; Dir-Gen. FRITZ DUPUY.

Office National d'Assurance Vieillesse (ONA): Champ de Mars, Port-au-Prince; tel. 222-1655; Dir-Gen. MARGARETH LAMUR.

Société de Commercialisation d'Assurance, SA (SOCOMAS): autoroute de Delmas, BP 636, Port-au-Prince; tel. 249-3090; Dir-Gen. JEAN DIDIER GARDÈRE.

Foreign Companies

Les Assurances Léger, SA (France): 40 rue Lamarre, BP 2120, Port-au-Prince; tel. 222-3451; fax 223-8634; Pres. GÉRARD N. LÉGER.

Cabinet d'Assurances Fritz de Catalogne (USA): angle rues du Peuple et des Miracles, BP 1644, Port-au-Prince; tel. 222-6695; fax 223-0827; Dir FRITZ DE CATALOGNE.

Capital Life Insurance Company Ltd (Bahamas): angle rues du Peuple et des Miracles, BP 1644, Port-au-Prince; tel. 222-6695; fax 223-0827; Agent FRITZ DE CATALOGNE.

Groupement Français d'Assurances (France): Port-au-Prince; Agent ALBERT A. DUFORT.

National Western Life Insurance (USA): 13 rue Pie XII, Cité de l'Exposition, Port-au-Prince; tel. 223-0734; Agent VORBE BARRAU DUPUY.

Insurance Association

Association des Assureurs d'Haïti: c/o Les Assurances Léger, SA, 40 rue Lamarre, BP 2120, Port-au-Prince; tel. 223-2137; fax 223-8634; Dir GÉRARD N. LÉGER.

Trade and Industry

GOVERNMENT AGENCY

Centre de Promotion des Investissements et des Exportations Haïtiennes (PROMINEX): Port-au-Prince; Pres. CLAUDE LEVY.

DEVELOPMENT ORGANIZATIONS

Fonds de Développement Industriel (FDI): Immeuble PROMO-BANK, 4 étage, ave John Brown et rue Lamarre, BP 2597, Port-au-Prince; tel. 222-7852; fax 222-8301; f. 1981; Dir ROOSEVELT SAINT-DIC.

Société Financière Haïtienne de Développement, SA (SOFIHDES): 11 blvd Harry S Truman, BP 1399, Port-au-Prince; tel. 222-8904; fax 222-8997; f. 1983; industrial and agro-industrial project financing, accounting, data processing, management consultancy; cap. 7.5m. (1989); Dir-Gen. FAUBERT GUSTAVE; 1 br.

CHAMBERS OF COMMERCE

Chambre de Commerce et d'Industrie d'Haïti (CCIH): blvd Harry S Truman, Cité de l'Exposition, BP 982, Port-au-Prince; tel. 223-0786; fax 222-0281; e-mail ccih@compa.net; internet www.intervision2000.com/iv2-trop/index.html; f. 1895; Exec. Dir MAURICE LAFORTUNE.

Chambre de Commerce et d'Industrie Haïtiano-Américaine (HAMCHAM): First National City Bank, route de Delmas, BP 13486, Delmas, Port-au-Prince; tel. 246-2600; fax 246-0985; f. 1979; Pres. GLADYS COUPET.

Chambre de Commerce et d'Industrie des Professions du Nord: BP 244, Cap-Haïtien; tel. 262-2360; fax 262-2895.

Chambre Franco-Haïtienne de Commerce et d'Industrie (CFHCI): Le Plaza Holiday Inn, rue Capois, Champ de Mars, Port-au-Prince; tel. 223-8404; fax 223-8131; f. 1987; Pres. PATRICK VICTOR; Sec. AXAN ABELLARD.

INDUSTRIAL AND TRADE ORGANIZATIONS

Association des Industries d'Haïti (ADIH): 199 route de Delmas, entre Delmas 31 et 33, étage Galerie 128, BP 2568, Port-au-

Prince; tel. 246-4509; fax 246-2211; f. 1980; Pres. RICHARD COLES; Exec. Dir MARLÈNE SAM.

Association Nationale des Distributeurs de Produits Pétroliers (ANADIPP): Centre Commercial Dubois, route de Delmas, Bureau 401, Port-au-Prince; tel. 246-1414; fax 245-0698; f. 1979; Pres. MAURICE LAFORTUNE.

Association Nationale des Importateurs et Distributeurs de Produits Pharmaceutiques (ANIDPP): c/o Maison Nadal, rue du Fort Per, Port-au-Prince; tel. 222-1418; fax 222-4767; Pres. BERNARD CRAAN.

Association des Producteurs Agricoles (APA): BP 1318, Port-au-Prince; tel. 246-1848; fax 246-0356; f. 1985; Pres. REYNOLD BONNEFIL.

Association des Producteurs Nationaux (APRONA): c/o Mosaïques Gardère, ave Hailé Sélassié, Port-au-Prince; tel. and fax 511-8611; e-mail frantzgardere@hotmail.com; Pres. FRANTZ GARDÈRE.

Association des Exportateurs de Café (ASDEC): c/o USMAN, ave Somoza/Delmas, BP B-65, Port-au-Prince; tel. 222-2627; fax 222-1394; Pres. FRITZ BRANDT.

UTILITIES

Electricity

Electricité d'Haïti: rue Dante Destouches, Port-au-Prince; tel. 222-4600; state energy utility company; Dir ROSEMOND PRADEL.

Péligre Hydroelectric Plant: Artibonite Valley.

Saut-Mathurine Hydroelectric Plant: Les Cayes.

TRADE UNIONS

Association des Journalistes Haïtiens (AJH): Sec.-Gen. GUYLER C. DELVA.

Centrale Autonome des Travailleurs Haïtiens (CATH): 93 rue des Casernes, Port-au-Prince; tel. 222-4506; f. 1980; Sec.-Gen. FIGNOLE SAINT-CYR.

Centrale des Travailleurs Haïtiens (CTH): f. 1989; Sec.-Gen. JEAN-CLAUDE LEBRUN.

Confédération Ouvriers Travailleurs Haïtiens (KOTA): 155 rue des Césars, Port-au-Prince.

Confédération Nationale des Educateurs Haïtiens (CNEH): rue Berne 21, Port-au-Prince; tel. 245-1552; fax 245-9536; f. 1986.

Fédération Haïtienne de Syndicats Chrétiens (FHSC): BP 416, Port-au-Prince; Pres. LÉONVIL LEBLANC.

Fédération des Ouvriers Syndiqués (FOS): angle rues Dr Aubry et des Miracles 115, BP 371, Port-au-Prince; tel. 222-0035; f. 1984; Pres. JOSEPH J. SÉNAT.

Organisation Générale Indépendante des Travailleurs et Travailleuses d'Haïti (OGITH): 121, 2-3 étage, angle route Delmas et Delmas 11, Port-au-Prince; tel. 249-0575; e-mail pnumas@yahoo.fr; f. 1988; Gen. Sec. PATRICK NUMAS.

Syndicat des Employés de l'EDH (SEEH): c/o EDH, rue Joseph Janvier, Port-au-Prince; tel. 222-3367.

Union Nationale des Ouvriers d'Haïti (UNOH): Delmas 11, 121 bis, Cité de l'Exposition, BP 3337, Port-au-Prince; f. 1951; Pres. MARCEL VINCENT; Sec.-Gen. FRITZNER ST VIL; 3,000 mems from 8 affiliated unions.

A number of unions are non-affiliated and without a national centre, including those organized on a company basis.

Transport

RAILWAYS

The railway service, for the transportation of sugar cane, closed during the early 1990s.

ROADS

In 1999, according to International Road Federation estimates, there were 4,160 km (2,585 miles) of roads, of which 24.3% was paved.

SHIPPING

Many European and American shipping lines call at Haiti. The two principal ports are Port-au-Prince and Cap-Haïtien. There are also 12 minor ports.

Autorité Portuaire Nationale: blvd La Saline, BP 616, Port-au-Prince; tel. 222-1942; fax 223-2440; e-mail jjulio@mail.com; f. 1978; Dir-Gen. JULIO JULIEN.

CIVIL AVIATION

The international airport, situated 8 km (5 miles) outside Port-au-Prince, is the country's principal airport, and is served by many international airlines linking Haiti with the USA and other Caribbean islands. There is an airport at Cap-Haïtien, and smaller airfields at Jacmel, Jérémie, Les Cayes and Port-de-Paix.

Air Haïti: Aéroport International, Port-au-Prince; tel. 246-3311; f. 1969; began cargo charter operations 1970; scheduled cargo and mail services from Port-au-Prince to Cap-Haïtien, San Juan (Puerto Rico), Santo Domingo (Dominican Republic), Miami and New York (USA).

Caribintair: Aéroport International, Port-au-Prince; tel. 246-0778; scheduled domestic service and charter flights to Santo Domingo (Dominican Republic) and other Caribbean destinations.

Haiti Air Freight, SA: Aéroport International, BP 170, Port-au-Prince; tel. 246-2572; fax 246-0848; cargo carrier operating scheduled and charter services from Port-au-Prince and Cap-Haïtien to Miami (USA) and Puerto Rico.

Haiti International Airlines: Delmas 65, Rue Zamor 2, Port-au-Prince; tel. 434-7201; f. 1996; scheduled passenger and cargo services between Port-au Prince to Miami and New York (USA); Pres. and Chair. KHAN RAHMAN.

Tourism

Tourism was formerly Haiti's second largest source of foreign exchange. However, as a result of political instability, the number of cruise ships visiting Haiti declined considerably, causing a sharp decline in the number of tourist arrivals. With the restoration of democracy in late 1994, the development of the tourism industry was identified as a priority by the Government. In 2000 stop-over tourists totalled 140,492, while cruise-ship excursionists numbered 246,221 in 1998. Receipts from tourism in 1999 totalled US $57m.

Secrétariat d'Etat au Tourisme: 8 rue Légitime, Champ de Mars, Port-au-Prince; tel. 221-5960; fax 222-8659; e-mail info@ haititourisme.org; internet www.haititourisme.org; Minister of Tourism MARTINE DEVERSON.

Association Haïtienne des Agences de Voyages: Port-au-Prince; tel. 222-8855; fax 222-2054.

Association Touristique d'Haïti: rue Lamarre, Choucoune Plaza, Pétionville, BP 2562, Port-au-Prince; tel. 257-4647; fax 257-4134; Pres. DOMINIQUE CARVONIS; Exec. Dir GILIANE CÉSAR JOUBERT.

HONDURAS

Introductory Survey

Location, Climate, Language, Religion, Flag, Capital

The Republic of Honduras lies in the middle of the Central American isthmus. It has a long northern coastline on the Caribbean Sea and a narrow southern outlet to the Pacific Ocean. Its neighbours are Guatemala to the west, El Salvador to the south-west and Nicaragua to the south-east. The climate ranges from temperate in the mountainous regions to tropical in the coastal plains: temperatures in the interior range from 15°C (59°F) to 24°C (75°F), while temperatures in the coastal plains average about 30°C (86°F). There are two rainy seasons in upland areas, May–July and September–October. The national language is Spanish. Almost all of the inhabitants profess Christianity, and the overwhelming majority are adherents of the Roman Catholic Church. The national flag (proportions 1 by 2) has three horizontal stripes, of blue, white and blue, with five blue five-pointed stars, arranged in a diagonal cross, in the centre of the white stripe. The capital is Tegucigalpa.

Recent History

Honduras was ruled by Spain from the 16th century until 1821 and became a sovereign state in 1838. From 1939 the country was ruled as a dictatorship by Gen. Tiburcio Carías Andino, leader of the Partido Nacional (PN), who had been President since 1933. In 1949 Carías was succeeded as President by Juan Manuel Gálvez, also of the PN. In 1954 the leader of the Partido Liberal (PL), Dr José Ramón Villeda Morales, was elected President, but was immediately deposed by Julio Lozano Díaz, himself overthrown by a military Junta in 1956. The Junta organized elections in 1957, when the PL secured a majority in Congress and Villeda was re-elected President. He was overthrown in 1963 by Col (later Gen.) Oswaldo López Arellano, the Minister of Defence, who, following elections held on the basis of a new Constitution, was appointed President in June 1965.

A presidential election in March 1971 was won by Dr Ramón Ernesto Cruz Uclés, the PN candidate. In December 1972, however, Cruz was deposed in a bloodless coup, led by former President López. In March 1974, at the instigation of the Consejo Superior de las Fuerzas Armadas (Supreme Council of the Armed Forces), President López was replaced as Commander-in-Chief of the Armed Forces by Col (later Gen.) Juan Melgar Castro, who was appointed President in April 1975. President Melgar was forced to resign by the Consejo Superior de las Fuerzas Armadas in August 1978, and was replaced by a military Junta. The Commander-in-Chief of the Armed Forces, Gen. Policarpo Paz García, assumed the role of Head of State, and the Junta promised that elections would take place.

Military rule was ended officially when, in April 1980, elections to a Constituent Assembly were held. The PL won 52% of the votes but was unable to assume power. Gen. Paz was appointed interim President for one year. At a general election in November 1981 the PL, led by Dr Roberto Suazo Córdova, secured an absolute majority in the Asamblea Nacional (National Assembly). Suazo was sworn in as President in January 1982. However, real power lay in the hands of Col (later Gen.) Gustavo Alvarez Martínez, who was appointed Head of the Armed Forces in the same month. In November Gen. Alvarez became Commander-in-Chief of the Armed Forces, having brought about an amendment to the Constitution in that month, whereby the posts of President and Commander-in-Chief of the Armed Forces, which had been merged under the rule of the military Junta, were separated. During 1982 and 1983 Gen. Alvarez suppressed increasing political unrest by authorizing the arrests of trade union activists and left-wing sympathizers; 'death squads' were allegedly also used to eliminate 'subversive' elements of the population. In March 1984 Gen. Alvarez was deposed as Commander-in-Chief of the Armed Forces by a group of army officers.

At the November 1985 presidential election the leading candidate of the PN, Rafael Leonardo Callejas Romero, obtained 42% of the individual votes cast, but the leading candidate of the PL, José Simeón Azcona del Hoyo (who had obtained only 27% of the individual votes cast), was declared the winner because, in accordance with a new electoral law, the combined votes of the PL's candidates secured the requisite majority of 51% of the total votes cast.

In February 1988 a report by the human rights organization Amnesty International gave evidence of an increase in violations of human rights by the armed forces and by right-wing 'death squads'. In August of that year, and again in 1989, the Inter-American Court of Human Rights (an organ of the Organization of American States—OAS, see p. 288) found the Honduran Government guilty of the 'disappearances' of Honduran citizens between 1981 and 1984, and ordered that compensation be paid to the families involved. In January 1989 Gen. Alvarez was killed by left-wing guerrillas in Tegucigalpa. The PL secured a majority of seats in the Asamblea Nacional at legislative elections held in November, while Callejas of the PN won the concurrent presidential election, receiving 51% of the votes cast. Callejas assumed office in January 1990. The new administration promptly adopted economic austerity measures, which provoked widespread social unrest.

In May 1991 units of the armed forces were implicated in the massacre of nine farmers during a dispute over land ownership. In the following month Amnesty International published a report alleging the mistreatment, torture and killing of detainees by members of the Honduran security forces, and the International Confederation of Free Trade Unions accused the security forces of complicity in the assassinations of several trade union organizers during 1990 and early 1991. In January 1992 the Government announced the creation of a special commission to investigate numerous accusations of corruption against government officials.

In March 1993, in response to increasing pressure by human rights organizations and criticism by the State Department of the USA, the Government established a special commission to investigate allegations of human rights violations by the armed forces and to evaluate the need for a reform of the security forces and the judiciary. In its report, the commission recommended the replacement of the armed forces' much-criticized secret counter-intelligence organization, the División Nacional de Investigaciones (DNI), with a body under civilian control. Other recommendations included the establishment of a fully independent Public Ministry office headed by a democratically-elected Attorney-General.

At presidential and legislative elections in November 1993 Carlos Roberto Reina Idiaquez, the candidate of the PL, was elected President, winning 52% of the votes cast. The PL also obtained a clear majority in the Asamblea Nacional, with 71 seats, while the PN secured 55 seats and the Partido Innovación y Unidad—Social Democracia (PINU) won the remaining two seats. Legislation replacing the DNI with a new ministry, the Dirección de Investigación Criminal (DIC), was approved in December 1993. On taking office in January 1994 Reina, a former President of the Inter-American Court of Human Rights, expressed his commitment to the reform of the judicial system and the armed forces, reducing the latter's size and sphere of influence. In that month, following the release by the National Commission for the Protection of Human Rights of a report incriminating the armed forces in the disappearance of 184 people in the previous decade, the head of the Commission, Leo Valladares Lanza, demanded the resignation of the Commander-in-Chief of the Armed Forces, Gen. Luis Alonso Discua Elvir. At the time of the disappearances Discua had been the Commander of Battalion 3-16, the army intelligence unit widely regarded as responsible for the murder of left-wing political activists. As a result of the report, the Supreme Court ordered an investigation of the allegations.

In April 1994 an apparent attempt to assassinate Reina was thwarted when one of three Nicaraguan hired assassins revealed the plot to the Honduran authorities. The Nicaraguans reportedly had been offered US $400,000 by a Honduran, Luis Hernández Sosa, to conduct the killing. Reina dismissed suggestions of a political motive for the attempt, attributing it instead to the work of criminals opposed to his efforts to suppress drugs-trafficking in Honduras. In that month demonstrations were organized in the capital in protest at the deterioration of living standards caused by the Government's economic austerity policies. Demonstrations also occurred in the department of Copán where peasant organizations blocked the Pan-American Highway in support of demands for Reina to honour election commitments to reduce the severity of the economic policies of the previous administration.

In May 1994 the Asamblea Nacional approved a constitutional reform abolishing compulsory military service (the amendment was ratified in April 1995). Also approved was the transfer of the police from military to civilian control. In that month measures initiated by the Callejas administration for the establishment of a Public Ministry were officially completed. The new ministry was to be supervised by the DIC, which was inaugurated in January 1995. The DNI was officially disbanded in June 1994.

In July 1994, following protracted demonstrations in the capital, 4,000 members of indigenous organizations occupied the Asamblea Nacional building and succeeded in securing an agreement with the Government granting rights and social assistance to the country's indigenous community, including the creation of the first indigenous municipality in Yamaranguila, Intibucá. The following months were characterized by growing social and political tension, including several bomb attacks. Concern was raised by human rights organizations that the climate of instability was being fomented by the armed forces in an attempt to stem the rapid diminution of its powers. In August however, Reina conceded the temporary reintroduction of compulsory conscription in order to fill some 7,000 vacancies which the armed forces complained were impairing military efficiency. In the same month Reina ordered an investigation into charges of corruption and drugs-trafficking in the air force. Widespread concern at the possibility that growing tension between the Government and the armed forces might result in a military coup prompted Gen. Discua to issue a statement denying any such intentions and reaffirming military support for the civilian authorities. In mid-August an increase in the incidence of crime and violent demonstrations resulting from the accumulating effect of austerity measures, a worsening energy crisis and food shortages, forced the Government to declare a state of national emergency and to deploy the armed forces to maintain order.

In November 1994 public-sector unions organized strikes in protest at low pay, poor working conditions and the Government's failure to honour earlier pay agreements. The disputes were resolved, however, following government promises of concessions. In late November corruption charges were filed by the public prosecutor's office against former President Callejas and 12 of his former ministers.

In July 1995 sustained protests by members of indigenous organizations, in support of demands that the Government honour its commitments of July 1994 to the indigenous community, culminated in a 2,000-strong demonstration in the capital. The protests resulted in renewed pledges by the Government to provide social assistance and grant land titles to the indigenous population. In September the PL, PN, PINU and Partido Demócrata Cristiano de Honduras (PDCH) established the Consejo Nacional de Convergencia (National Convergence Council) in order to seek a consensus on political, social and economic issues.

In July 1995, in an unprecedented development in the Government's efforts to investigate past human rights violations, a civilian court issued indictments against 10 senior officers of the security services who had been involved in the activities of Battalion 3-16 during the 1980s. The charges concerned the kidnapping, torture and attempted murder in 1982 of six left-wing students. However, the officers refused to appear in court, invoking an amnesty granted in 1991 which, they claimed, afforded them immunity from prosecution. In October a warrant was issued for the arrest of several of the officers, who promptly went into hiding. In January 1996 the Supreme Court ruled that the officers were not entitled to protection under the 1991 amnesty law, overturning an earlier decision by the Court of Appeal. Information concerning the activities of Battalion 3-16, which had been financed and trained by the US Central Intelligence Agency, was sought from the US Government by Valladares to support the prosecution of this and other human rights cases.

In January 1996 Col. Mario Raúl Hung Pacheco succeeded Gen. Discua as Commander-in-Chief of the Armed Forces, and was subsequently promoted to the rank of General. In the following month, in an apparent demonstration of his control over the military high command, Reina ignored the nominations for a new Minister of National Defence and Public Security proposed by Gen. Hung, appointing his own candidate instead. In the following month a grenade was thrown into the grounds of the presidential residence, prompting speculation that the armed forces had been responsible for the attack.

In July 1996 the Human Rights Defence Committee (Codeh) claimed that the extra-judicial execution of five former military intelligence agents had occurred in recent months, and alleged that the killings were the responsibility of military officers who were attempting to prevent evidence of human rights violations from coming to light. Later that month four officers of the armed forces were arrested for allegedly conspiring to overthrow the Commander-in-Chief of the Armed Forces. Gen. Hung, however, dismissed the incident, claiming that it merely reflected the discontent within the ranks at low pay and reductions in the defence budget.

In October 1996 a bomb exploded, without causing injury, at the parliament building in the capital. A further device was defused outside the headquarters of the PL. Responsibility for the attacks was claimed later that month by a previously unknown organization describing itself as 'Hambre' (Hunger), which claimed to be acting in response to recent rises in fuel prices. However, the President of Codeh, Ramón Custodio, expressed the popular suspicion that the attacks had been perpetrated by the armed forces in an attempt to pressurize the civilian authorities into reversing the decline in military influence in the country. In mid-October Custodio's home in San Pedro Sula was the target of a grenade attack. A further such attack was conducted in early November on a central court building in Tegucigalpa, resulting in one fatality. In response, the Government deployed some 3,000 troops to patrol the capital and San Pedro Sula. An organization known as 'Justa C.' claimed responsibility for the attack and issued death threats to several judges involved in the investigation of cases concerning official corruption and human rights abuses by the armed forces.

In February 1997 demonstrations by thousands of public-sector employees, who were protesting in support of demands for salary increases, culminated in violent clashes between demonstrators and the security forces. The Government subsequently signed a social pact with labour leaders, which included commitments to increased social spending and price controls on basic goods. In May, following the killing of two ethnic minority leaders in the previous month, more than 3,000 members of the indigenous community conducted a march from the western departments of Copán and Ocotepeque to the capital to protest outside the presidential palace. As a result, Reina signed an agreement to conduct a full investigation into the killings and to accelerate the distribution of some 7,000 ha of land to the indigenous community. However, the killing of a further two ethnic minority leaders later that month led to accusations by human rights groups that attempts were being made to eliminate minority autonomous organizations. In March 2000 four leaders of the Chortí people were shot and killed by a land-owner's private security guards.

At the general election held on 30 November 1997 Carlos Roberto Flores Facussé, the candidate of the ruling PL, was elected President, winning 52.7% of the votes cast; Alba Nora Gúnera de Melgar, the PN candidate, took 42.7% of the votes. The PL also obtained a majority in the Asamblea Nacional, with 67 seats, while the PN secured 55 seats, the PINU won three, the PDCH two and the left-wing Partido de Unificación Democrática (PUD) obtained the remaining seat. In December Flores announced his intention to conduct a restructuring of the armed forces. He was inaugurated on 27 January 1998.

In May 1998 control of the police force was transferred from the military to the civilian authorities. The Fuerza de Seguridad Pública, which had been under military control since 1963 and was widely suspected of perpetrating human rights abuses, was replaced by a new force, the Policía Nacional. Nevertheless, reports of human rights abuses continued.

In November 1998, in the wake of the devastation caused by 'Hurricane Mitch', which struck the country in late October, causing losses estimated at US $5,000m., Flores declared a state of emergency and imposed a curfew in order to combat widespread looting. At least 6,600 people were estimated to have died, with a further 8,052 people reported missing, as a result of the storms, which left some 2.13m. homeless and caused widespread damage to the country's infrastructure, as well as destroying principal export crops.

In January 1999 the Asamblea Nacional ratified a constitutional amendment abolishing the post of Commander-in-Chief of the Armed Forces and transferring its responsibilities to the Minister of National Defence and Public Security. The military's ruling body, the Consejo Superior de las Fuerzas Armadas, was also disbanded. In July, acting on intelligence reports of a plot by senior-ranking military officers to overthrow the Government, Flores implemented a number of changes to the military high command. Notably, the Head of the Joint Chiefs of Staff, Col Eugenio Romero Eucedo, who was suspected of being one of the principal instigators of the coup plot, was replaced by the head of the presidential guard, Col Daniel López Carballo, who was considered to be loyal to the presidency. The plot itself was believed to have been prompted by resentment in the officer corps at the determination of the Minister of National Defence, Edgardo Dumas Rodríguez, to exert civilian control over the armed forces, and in particular at his plans to investigate military expenditure and supervise the armed forces' extensive business activities.

In mid-December 2000 the PL confirmed that its nominee in the presidential election that was scheduled to be held in November 2001 would be Rafael Piñeda Ponce, the President of the Asamblea Nacional. Luis Cosenza was initially chosen to be the PN's presidential candidate. However, as expected, in early March 2001 he was replaced by his ally, Ricardo Maduro Joest, after a dispute over Maduro's nationality (he was born in Panama) had been resolved.

The failure of the harvest in eight provinces following two months of severe drought prompted the Government to declare a state of emergency in July 2001. UN agents distributed aid from the World Food Programme to the 12,000 families affected. In August the Government engaged a UN Special Rapporteur on extra-judicial, summary and arbitrary executions, Asama Jahangir, to investigate the alleged organized murder of street children in recent years. Jahangir concluded that since 1998, some 800 children had been killed by youth gangs and members of the police and private security forces. The Minister of Public Security, Gautama Fonseca Zuniga, subsequently announced an inquiry into police involvement in the killings. In the same month, in response to increasing conflict between the youth gangs, President Flores ordered the deployment of 3,000 army troops and armed police on to the streets of Tegucigalpa, San Pedro Sula and El Progreso. In response to pressure from human rights organizations, in March 2003 the Government announced that a special commission would be established to investigate the murders of street children. The Permanent Commission on Physical and Moral Integrity of Children would comprise of church leaders and government officials.

Legislative and presidential elections were scheduled for 25 November 2001. In May the Asamblea Nacional approved legislation enabling the considerable number of Honduran nationals resident in the USA to vote in the presidential election, although they continued to be excluded from the legislative ballot. Five candidates contested the presidential election; the PN candidate, Ricardo Maduro Joest, emerged victorious, with 52.21% of valid votes cast, compared to 44.26% secured by the PL nominee, Rafael Piñeda Ponce. The third-placed candidate, Olban Valladares of the PINU, attracted only 1.45% of the valid votes. The PN also gained a majority in the Asamblea Nacional, winning 61 seats. The number of PL deputies was reduced to 55, while the remaining 12 seats were distributed among the PUD (five seats), the PINU (four seats) and the PDCH (three seats). Observers from the OAS reported no serious irregularities, although a PN legislative candidate was assassinated in Tegucigalpa the day before the election; three PL party workers were later arrested.

Maduro assumed the presidency on 27 January 2002 and a new Government was installed, which included Guillermo Pérez-Cadalso Arias as Minister of Foreign Affairs and Jorge Ramón Hernández Alcerro as Minister of the Interior and Justice. The new President immediately began an offensive on against crime, sending 10,000 troops to patrol the streets of Tegucigalpa, San Pedro Sula, La Ceiba and Choluteca. He announced that the armed forces would play a greater role in the anti-crime effort, a declaration that was met with opposition domestically and internationally. He affirmed his intention to reorganize the police force and to reform the criminal justice system, in order to reduce corruption. Another stated priority of Maduro was tax reform and a reduction in government expenditure, in an attempt to secure debt relief from the IMF. This aim was met with hostility by opposition parties, who argued that proposals to levy taxes on a broader range of basic goods and services would exacerbate poverty levels in the country. They

suggested that public money should instead be invested in measures to alleviate deprivation.

Nevertheless, in May 2002 the fiscal reform bill was approved in the Asamblea Nacional; a number of PL deputies walked out of the debate in protest. In June the PDCH and one defector from the PUD formed a coalition agreement with the Government, thereby giving it a majority in the Asamblea Nacional, allowing the budget to be approved. In the same month, teachers began a strike in protest at their wages and working conditions. The Minister of Public Education, Carlos Avila Molina, reacted by reducing the striking teachers' wages. A pay deal offered in August was rejected. Later in August, coffee growers demonstrated in Tegucigalpa against the Government's alleged failure to make available a US $20m. loan granted by the Republic of China (Taiwan) to help stimulate the coffee sector. The demonstration escalated into violence and some 500 protesters were arrested.

Honduras experienced rising crime throughout 2002, despite the increased security measures introduced by President Maduro. Most of the victims were business men and women, prompting many to flee the country. In November a bomb was detonated outside the presidential residence; no-one was injured. In the same month, the Government announced a new housing initiative, which controversially involved borrowing funds from public-sector pensions. The programme placed further strain on relations between the Government and public-sector workers. Teachers, together with employees of the state water company who objected to plans to transfer responsibility for water services from the state to the municipalities, held an anti-Government demonstration in Tegucigalpa. The protest, which lasted two days, resulted in violent clashes between those protesting and the police, which left 20 injured. Industrial unrest persisted into 2003; in March medical staff at public hospitals began intermittent strikes to demand higher salaries. Public-sector discontent was likely to continue throughout the year as the Government reduced public expenditure in order to secure IMF funding (see Economic Affairs, below).

From the early 1980s former members of the Nicaraguan National Guard, regarded by the left-wing Sandinista Government of Nicaragua as counter-revolutionaries ('Contras'), established bases in Honduras, from which they conducted raids across the border between the two countries, allegedly with support from the Honduran armed forces. In 1983, when Honduran foreign policy was controlled by the pro-US Gen. Alvarez (the Commander-in-Chief of the Armed Forces), US involvement in Honduras increased substantially. In February 1983 the USA and Honduras initiated 'Big Pine', a series of joint military manoeuvres on Honduran territory which enabled the USA to construct permanent military installations in Honduras. In return for considerable military assistance from the USA, the Honduran Government permitted US military aid to be supplied to the Contras based in Honduras.

Following the overthrow of Gen. Alvarez in 1984, public opposition to the US military presence in Honduras increased, causing a temporary deterioration in relations between Honduras and the USA. In 1985 the USA declined to enter into a security pact with Honduras, but confirmed that it would take 'appropriate' measures to defend Honduras against any Communist aggression. In August of that year the Honduran Government announced that it would prevent the US Government from supplying further military aid to the Contras through Honduras. However, following a visit by President Azcona to the USA in 1986, the supply of aid was believed to have resumed. Relations with Nicaragua deteriorated sharply in 1986, when Honduran troops were mobilized in an attempt to curb alleged border incursions by Nicaraguan government forces. In December, however, following revelations that the USA had secretly sold weapons to the Government of Iran and that the proceeds had been used to finance the activities of the Contra rebels, President Azcona requested the departure of the Contras from Honduras.

In August 1987 Honduras, Costa Rica, El Salvador, Guatemala and Nicaragua signed a Central American peace plan, known as the 'Esquipulas agreement', the crucial provisions of which were the implementation of simultaneous cease-fires in Nicaragua and El Salvador, a halt to foreign assistance to rebel groups, democratic reform in Nicaragua, a ban on the use of foreign territory as a base for attack, and the establishment of national reconciliation commissions in each of the Central American nations. However, the commitment of the Honduran Government to the accord appeared to be only partial. Claiming that it no longer permitted the Nicaraguan Contras to maintain bases on its territory, the Honduran Government opposed a clause in the agreement providing for the establishment of a committee to monitor the dismantling of Contra bases in Honduras.

In March 1988 several thousand US troops were temporarily deployed in Honduras, in response to an incursion into Honduran territory by the Nicaraguan army. Further violations of the border between Honduras and Nicaragua occurred during that year, as Nicaraguan troops forced at least 12,000 Contra rebels, based in the border area, into Honduras. In November President Azcona declared his opposition to the presence of the Contras in his country. In the following month the International Court of Justice (ICJ) announced it would consider an application, submitted by the Nicaraguan Government in 1986, in which Nicaragua contended that Honduras had breached international law by allowing the Contras to operate from its territory. In response, the Honduran Government threatened to withdraw support from the Esquipulas agreement.

In February 1989, at summit meeting of the five Central American Presidents in El Salvador, an agreement was reached whereby the Contra forces encamped in Honduras would demobilize, while President Ortega of Nicaragua guaranteed that free and fair elections would take place in his country by February 1990. At a further summit meeting, held in August at Tela, Honduras, the conditions for the demobilization of the Contras were expanded. The Honduran Government agreed to the establishment by the UN and the OAS of an international commission to oversee the voluntary repatriation or removal to a third country of the rebel forces by December 1989; in return, the Nicaraguan Government agreed to abandon the action that it had initiated against Honduras at the ICJ. The rebel units officially disbanded and left Honduras in June 1990.

In June 1995 Honduras and Nicaragua signed an accord providing for the visible demarcation of each country's territorial waters in the Gulf of Fonseca, and the establishment of a joint naval patrol to police the area. The agreement followed frequent disputes concerning fishing rights in the Gulf, which occurred as a consequence of inefficient demarcation. Despite the agreement, however, conflict continued, and the demarcation process did not begin until May 1998. In early 2000 there was an exchange of gunfire between Honduran and Nicaraguan patrol boats in the Gulf (where jurisdiction was shared with El Salvador).

In December 1999 a further dispute arose with Nicaragua, prompting it to sever commercial ties with, and impose import taxes on, Honduras, in direct contravention of Central American free-trade undertakings. The dispute stemmed from the Caribbean Sea Maritime Limits Treaty, which Honduras had signed with Colombia in 1986 and had finally ratified in late November 1999, thereby formally recognizing a frontier with Colombia, the demarcation of which granted Colombia territorial rights to areas of the Caribbean historically claimed by Nicaragua. In February 2000, following OAS mediation, the two countries agreed to establish a maritime exclusion zone in the disputed area. In the following month, representatives of Honduras and Nicaragua met in Washington, DC, where they signed an accord on joint patrols in the Caribbean, pending a ruling by the ICJ, and on combined operations in the Gulf of Fonseca. Agreement was also reached on the withdrawal of forces from the land border area. However, in February 2001 the Nicaraguan defence minister accused Honduras of violating the March 2000 accords by carrying out military exercises in the area. Following further talks under OAS auspices, in June the foreign ministers of the two countries agreed to allow monitors into the disputed area to verify troop deployment. In August 2001, however, the Nicaraguan authorities again accused Honduras of moving troops and military equipment into the area, with the intention of launching an attack on their country. The Government denied the accusations. In July 2002 the situation further deteriorated when the Nicaraguan Government announced plans to sell oil-drilling rights in the disputed area. Nicaragua also reported that Honduras had again increased the number of armed forces in the border region; the Honduran Government maintained that the troops were deployed as part of a campaign to stop the spread of dengue fever in the area. In August Honduras threatened to impose tariffs on all Nicaraguan goods in protest. The following month Nicaragua announced that it had received several bids and intended to proceed with the sale of drilling rights. However, in March 2003, the Nicaraguan Asamblea Nacional voted to suspend import taxes on Honduran goods,

imposed in 1999. The ICJ was not expected to rule on the dispute until 2004.

A long-standing dispute between Honduras and El Salvador, regarding the demarcation of the two countries' common border and rival claims to three islands in the Gulf of Fonseca, caused hostilities to break out between the two countries in 1969. Although armed conflict soon subsided, the Honduran and Salvadorean Governments did not sign a peace treaty until 1980. In 1982 the Honduran armed forces were engaged against guerrilla forces in El Salvador, indicating an improvement in Honduran–Salvadorean relations. Honduran troops were also reportedly responsible for the deaths of several hundred Salvadorean refugees in Honduras during that year. In 1986, however, the Governments of Honduras and El Salvador agreed that their conflicting territorial claims should be examined by the ICJ. In September 1992 the ICJ awarded Honduras sovereignty over some two-thirds of the disputed mainland territory and over one of the disputed islands in the Gulf of Fonseca. However, in subsequent years disputes continued to arise concerning the legal rights of those people resident in the reallocated territory, particularly with regard to land ownership. Following protracted negotiation, a convention governing the acquired rights and nationality of those people was finally signed by the Presidents of both countries in January 1998. An agreement was also signed providing for the demarcation of the countries' common border to be undertaken within one year. By September 2000 232.5 km of the 374 km border had been demarcated. In August 2001 the Government unexpectedly expelled two members of the El Salvadorean military from the country, accusing them of obtaining highly-sensitive documents relating to national security matters.

In November 1991 the Presidents of Honduras and El Salvador signed an agreement to establish a free-trade zone on their common border, and subsequently to seek economic union. In May 1992 the Governments of Honduras, El Salvador and Guatemala agreed to promote trade and investment between the three countries. A further agreement, concluded by Honduras, El Salvador and Guatemala in October of that year, provided for the eventual establishment of a Central American political federation.

In January 2002 Honduras restored diplomatic relations with Cuba, suspended since the 1959 revolution that brought Fidel Castro Rúz to power. Relations between the two countries had gradually improved thereafter, and Cuba supplied doctors and medical aid to Honduras following the devastation caused by Hurricane Mitch in 1998. Increased economic activity between the two countries prompted the Honduran Government to open an interests section in the Cuban capital in late 2001. In December 2001 the Government also concluded an agreement with the United Kingdom defining the maritime border between Honduras and the Cayman Islands.

Government

Under the provisions of the Constitution approved by the Asamblea Nacional in 1982, the President is elected by a simple majority of the voters. The President holds executive power and has a single four-year mandate. Legislative power is vested in the Asamblea Nacional (National Assembly), with 128 members elected by universal adult suffrage for a term of four years. The country is divided into 18 local Departments.

Defence

Military service is voluntary. Active service lasts eight months, with subsequent reserve training. In August 2002 the armed forces totalled 8,300 men, of whom 5,500 were in the army, 1,000 in the navy and 1,800 in the air force. Paramilitary forces numbered 6,000 men. In 2002 government expenditure on defence was budgeted at 1,884m. lempiras. In 2001 annual assistance from the USA had been reduced to US $0.5m. (from $20.2m. in 1990), although it was increased to $0.6m. in 2002. In 2002 some 356 US troops were based in Honduras.

Economic Affairs

In 2000, according to estimates by the World Bank, Honduras' gross national income (GNI), measured at average 1999–2001 prices, was US $5,992m., equivalent to $900 per head (or $2,450 per head on an international purchasing-power parity basis). During 1990–2001, it was estimated, the population increased at an average annual rate of 2.8%, while gross domestic product (GDP) per head increased, in real terms, by an average of 1.9% per year. Overall GDP increased, in real terms, at an average annual rate of 3.1% in 1990–2001; growth in 2001 was 2.6%.

Agriculture (including hunting, forestry and fishing) contributed an estimated 14.1% of GDP in 2001 and employed 31.7% of the total labour force in mid-2000. The principal cash crop is traditionally coffee, although owing to high production costs and low prices on the world markets, coffee exports contributed only 12.3% of all export earnings in 2001, compared with 24.8% in 2000. Banana production decreased during the 1990s and, following the destruction of more than 70% of the total crop as a result of 'Hurricane Mitch', bananas contributed only an estimated 3.0% of all export earnings in 1999. Furthermore, in June 2000 one of the principal banana corporations, Chiquita Brands, announced a substantial reduction in its operations in the country following hurricane damage and a downturn in the market. In spite of these set-backs, by 2001 earnings from banana exports had risen to 15% of total export earnings. The main subsistence crops include maize, plantains, beans, rice, sugar cane and citrus fruit. Exports of shellfish make a significant contribution to foreign earnings (supplying 15.6% of total export earnings in 2001). Agricultural GDP increased at an average annual rate of 1.9% during 1990–2000; the sector increased by 9.5% in 2000, but decreased by 0.1% in 2001.

Industry (including mining, manufacturing, construction and power) contributed an estimated 31.4% of GDP in 2001 and employed 22.0% of the economically active population in 1999. Industrial GDP increased at an average annual rate of 4.0% during 1990–2000; it increased by 5.2% in 2000 and by 1.6% in 2001.

Mining contributed an estimated 1.8% of GDP in 2001 and employed 0.2% of the economically active population in 1999. Lead and zinc are the major mineral exports. Gold, silver, copper and low-grade iron ore are also mined. In addition, small quantities of petroleum derivatives are exported. Until the end of the 1990s, when new funding was announced, the gold, silver and other mineral deposits had remained unexplored. The GDP of the mining sector increased by an average of 5.4% per year in 1991–2000; it increased by 1.7% in 2000, but decreased by 3.3% in 2001.

Manufacturing contributed an estimated 20.3% of GDP in 2001 and employed 16.4% of the economically active population in 1999. The most important branches, measured by gross value of output, were food products, beverages (including beer), cigarettes, apparel and wood products. In 2000 the successful *maquiladora* (assembly plant) sector employed some 100,000 local workers. Manufacturing GDP increased at an average annual rate of 3.8% during 1990–2000, by 5.5% in 2000 and by 5.2% in 2001.

Energy is derived principally from hydroelectric power, which accounted for some 62.6% of electricity production in 1999. Petroleum accounted for a further 32.3% of electrical energy output. Imports of mineral fuels and lubricants accounted for an estimated 13.4% of the value of total imports in 2001. Fuel wood remains a prime source of domestic energy. In 2001 the US company, AES Corporation, announced plans to construct a US $650m. natural gas plant that would supply some 800 MW of electricity to Honduras and other countries in the region. The plant was to be completed by 2003. In May 2002 a cable connecting the electricity distribution networks of Honduras and El Salvador was activated; the connection process was completed in September.

The services sector contributed an estimated 54.5% of GDP in 2001 and engaged 42.9% of the working population in 1999. The GDP of the services sector increased by an average of 3.7% per year in 1990–2000; the sector increased by 5.0% in 2000 and by 5.3% in 2001.

In 2001 Honduras recorded a visible trade deficit of US $876.5m., while there was a deficit of $669.8m. on the current account of the balance of payments. Workers' remittances from abroad totalled about $409m. in 2000. In 2001 the principal source of imports (46.2%) was the USA; other major suppliers were Guatemala, El Salvador and Mexico. The USA was also the principal market for exports (38.4%) in that year; other significant purchasers were El Salvador, Guatemala and Belgium. The principal exports in 2001 were shellfish and bananas. The principal imports in 2001 were machinery and electrical equipment, chemicals and related products, and mineral products.

In 1999 there was a budgetary deficit of 3,576m. lempiras (equivalent to 4.7% of GDP in that year). Honduras' external debt totalled US $5,487m. at the end of 2000, of which $4,897m. was long-term public debt. In that year the cost of debt-servicing

represented 19.3% of the value of exports of goods and services. The annual rate of inflation averaged 16.9% in 1990–2001. Consumer prices increased by an annual average of 9.6% in 2001. Some 4.2% of the labour force were unemployed in that same year; however, it was estimated that more than 35% of the work-force were underemployed.

Honduras is a member of the Central American Common Market (CACM, see p. 160). In 2003 negotiations towards a Central American Free Trade Agreement with the USA were under way.

In terms of average income, Honduras is among the poorest nations in the Western hemisphere, with some 79% of the population living below the poverty line. In October 1998 the Honduran economy was devastated by the effects of 'Hurricane Mitch'. Much of the country's infrastructure was destroyed, and as many as 2.13m. people left homeless. Losses in agricultural production were estimated at US $200m. for 1998, rising to more than $500m. for 1999, while the total cost to the economy of the hurricane damage was estimated at $5,000m. In May 1999 the Consultative Group for Honduras of international financial agencies and donor countries agreed to provide $2,800m. for the reconstruction process. In March the IMF approved a three-year Enhanced Structural Adjustment Facility (ESAF) totalling $215m. in support of the Government's economic programme for 1999–2001. In the following month the 'Paris Club' of creditor governments agreed to suspend Honduras' bilateral debt-service payments for a period of three years, and offered a 67% reduction in its debt of $1,170m. on the condition that it complied with the terms of the ESAF. These included commitments by the Government to reduce public expenditure, rationalize state bureaucracy, and sustain its privatization programme. The successful implementation of these measures also facilitated further debt relief under the 'Heavily Indebted Poor Countries' (HIPC) initiative of the World Bank, to which Honduras was admitted in December 1999. In July 2000 the IMF and the World Bank announced that the country's debt service payments would be reduced by $900m. over 20 years. However, in December the IMF suspended a $22m. disbursement to the Honduran Government owing to the lack of progress in its privatization programme. In 2000 the economy grew by 5.2%, in part owing to the continuing growth in the *maquiladora* sector and investment in the post-hurricane reconstruction programme. Growth slowed to 2.6% in 2001, however, mainly owing to low international prices for bananas and coffee exports and the effects of the drought. The rising crime rate and tax incentives offered by Nicaragua were also reported to be responsible for the closure of several *maquiladora* plants and branches of international firms in Honduras in 2001.

The Government of Ricardo Maduro Joest, which took office in January 2002, pledged to maintain an austere economic policy and to reduce violent crime in an attempt to attract foreign investment and qualify for further IMF funding. Honduras was scheduled to resume debt-rescheduling payments to the Paris Club of creditors at the end of 2002, although the new Government was successful in its request that payments be suspended for a further year. However, in order to secure further financial assistance, including qualification for a new HIPC initiative worth some $960m. over the next 15 years, the Government had to convince the IMF of its intention to reduce the fiscal deficit. To this end, in early 2002 President Maduro declared his intention to proceed with the much-delayed privatization of the state telecommunications company, Hondutel, and of the national energy company, ENEE (Empresa Nacional de Energía Eléctrica). The first stage of the privatization of ENEE was completed by the end of 2002; however, the sale of Hondutel was further delayed and in November the Government announced plans to sell a 25% stake in the telecommunications company by 2005. The Government also introduced a number of new taxes, principally on government services introduced measures to eliminate tax evasion, and announced a series of reforms intended to reduce public-sector expenditure, prompting discontent among public workers throughout 2001. A visiting IMF delegation in October praised the Government's reduction in public-sector spending, but indicated that tax evasion remained a problem, as well as the high fiscal deficit. In December the IMF announced that a new funding agreement would be delayed until March 2003. Maduro subsequently announced that the rate of taxation on high incomes would be increased and that public-sector salaries would be 'frozen', although he resisted pressure to reduce wages. Nevertheless, the measures were met with further hostility from workers and it remained unclear if the moves would succeed in reducing the fiscal deficit enough to satisfy the IMF. Although the Government had predicted that the economy would grow by as much as 5.0%, overall growth in 2002 was estimated to be only 1.9%, owing to low commodity prices and the economic problems of the country's major trading partners.

Education

Primary education, beginning at seven years of age and lasting for six years, is officially compulsory and is provided free of charge. Secondary education, which is not compulsory, begins at the age of 13 and lasts for up to five years, comprising a first cycle of three years and a second of two years. On completion of the compulsory period of primary education, every person is required to teach at least two illiterate adults to read and write. In 1998 the enrolment at primary schools included 87.5% of children in the relevant age-group (males 86.4%; females 88.6%), while enrolment at secondary schools in that year was equivalent to only 36.0% of children in the appropriate age-group (males 34.1%; females 37.9%). There are seven universities, including the Autonomous National University in Tegucigalpa. For 1995 the education budget was 1,353m. lempiras

(16.5% of total government expenditure). In December 2000 the Inter-American Development Bank (IDB) approved a US $29.6m. loan to expand and reform the education system. In December 2002 the World Bank announced a grant of US $90m. to fund schemes to enable more children to attend secondary school.

Public Holidays

2003: 1 January (New Year's Day), 14 April (Pan-American Day/Bastilla's Day), 18–21 April (Easter), 1 May (Labour Day), 15 September (Independence Day), 3 October (Morazán Day), 21 October (Army Day), 25 December (Christmas).

2004: 1 January (New Year's Day), 8–11 April (Easter), 14 April (Pan-American Day/Bastilla's Day), 1 May (Labour Day), 15 September (Independence Day), 3 October (Morazán Day), 12 October (Discovery Day), 21 October (Army Day), 25 December (Christmas).

Weights and Measures

The metric system is in force, although some old Spanish measures are used, including: 25 libras = 1 arroba; 4 arrobas = 1 quintal (46 kg).

Statistical Survey

Sources (unless otherwise stated): Department of Economic Studies, Banco Central de Honduras—BANTRAL, 6a y 7a Avda, 1a Calle, Apdo 3165, Tegucigalpa; tel. 237-2270; fax 238-0376; Dirección General de Estadística y Censo, Blvd Suyapa, Col. Florencia Sur, Ed. Gómez, Apdo 9412, Tegucipgalpa; e-mail info@ine.online.hn; internet www.ine-hn.org.

Area and Population

AREA, POPULATION AND DENSITY

Area (sq km)	112,492*
Population (census results)†	
29 May 1988	4,614,377
1 August 2001	
Males	3,230,958
Females	3,304,386
Total	6,535,344
Population (official estimates at mid-year)	
1998	6,179,700
1999	6,385,000
2000	6,597,100
Density (per sq km) at mid-2001	58.1

* 43,433 sq miles.

† Excluding adjustments for underenumeration, estimated to have been 10% at the 1974 census.

PRINCIPAL TOWNS

(estimated population, '000 at mid-2001)

Tegucigalpa . . .	1,089.2	Siguatepeque . . .	53.7
San Pedro Sula . .	490.6	Puerto Cortés . .	36.0
El Progreso . . .	115.0	Juticalpa . . .	34.8
La Ceiba	111.2	Santa Rosa de	
Choluteca	101.6	Copán . . .	28.6
Comayagua . . .	77.4	Tela	26.6
Danlí	68.8	Olanchito . . .	23.9

BIRTHS AND DEATHS

(World Bank estimates, annual averages)

	1998	1999	2000
Birth rate (per 1,000)	32	31	31
Death rate (per 1,000)	6	5	6

Expectation of life (WHO estimates, years at birth): 67.3 (males 64.4; females 70.3) in 2001 (Source: WHO, *World Health Report*).

ECONOMICALLY ACTIVE POPULATION

('000 persons aged 10 years and over)

	1997	1998	1999
Agriculture, hunting, forestry and fishing	772.7	738.4	806.1
Mining and quarrying . . .	3.1	4.5	3.8
Manufacturing	361.7	368.3	376.9
Electricity, gas and water . . .	6.7	7.0	8.2
Construction	88.3	110.7	117.8
Trade, restaurants and hotels . .	393.8	440.0	489.1
Transport, storage and communications	46.8	54.6	56.0
Financing, insurance, real estate and business services . . .	41.4	52.5	49.9
Community, social and personal services	374.1	359.1	391.1
Total employed	2,088.5	2,134.9	2,299.0
Unemployed	69.4	87.7	89.3
Total labour force	2,157.9	2,222.6	2,388.3

Source: ILO, *Yearbook of Labour Statistics*.

Mid-2000 (estimates in '000): Agriculture, etc. 762; Total labour force 2,405 (Source: FAO).

May 2001: Total employed 2,334,596; Total unemployed 103,402; Total labour force 2,437,998.

Health and Welfare

KEY INDICATORS

Total fertility rate (children per woman, 2001) . . .	3.9
Under-5 mortality rate (per 1,000 live births, 2001) . . .	38
HIV/AIDS (% of persons aged 15–49, 2001)	1.60
Physicians (per 1,000 head, 1997)	0.83
Hospital beds (per 1,000 head, 1996)	1.06
Health expenditure (2000): US $ per head (PPP) . . .	165
Health expenditure (2000): % of GDP	6.8
Health expenditure (2000): public (% of total)	63.1
Access to water (% of persons, 2000)	90
Access to sanitation (% of persons, 2000)	77
Human Development Index (2000): ranking	116
Human Development Index (2000): value	0.638

For sources and definitions, see explanatory note on p. vi.

Agriculture

PRINCIPAL CROPS
('000 metric tons)

	1999	2000	2001
Maize	477.5	533.6	516.1
Sorghum	71.3	64.7	74.7
Sugar cane	3,755.8	3,974.0	4,117.0
Dry beans	53.4	85.0	59.2
Oil palm fruit	609.4	618.6	668.8
Cabbages	37.8	38.0*	37.5*
Tomatoes	43.2	46.4	49.8
Cantaloupes and other melons	76.8	88.7	80.0*
Other vegetables*	102.5	102.3	100.0
Bananas	452.6	469.0	515.8
Plantains	250.0	245.0*	240.0*
Oranges	126.2	120.0	120.0*
Pineapples	70.0	71.0	70.0*
Other fruit*	73.6	71.9	66.8
Coffee (green)	157.4	193.3	205.5

* FAO estimate(s).

Source: FAO.

LIVESTOCK
('000 head, year ending September)

	1999	2000	2001
Cattle	1,715	1,780	1,715
Sheep*	14	14	14
Goats*	30	31	32
Pigs*	473	470473	480
Horses*	178	179	180
Mules*	70	70	70
Asses*	23	23	23
Chickens*	16,800	17,300	18,000

* FAO estimates.

Source: FAO.

LIVESTOCK PRODUCTS
('000 metric tons)

	1999	2000	2001
Beef and veal	55	55	55
Pig meat	9.3	9.5	9.7
Chicken meat	68.8	75.6	80.3
Cows' milk	562.7	571.1	593.8
Cheese	8.8	9.0*	9.0*
Butter*	4.3	4.4	4.4
Hen eggs*	41.8	41.2	43.4
Cattle hides*	9.4	9.5	9.5

* FAO estimate(s).

Source: FAO.

Forestry

ROUNDWOOD REMOVALS
('000 cubic metres, excl. bark)

	1999	2000	2001
Sawlogs, veneer logs and logs for sleepers	853	756	832
Other industrial wood	3	—	—
Fuel wood*	8,694	8,732	8,720
Total	9,550	9,488	9,552

* FAO estimates.

Source: FAO.

SAWNWOOD PRODUCTION
('000 cubic metres, incl. railway sleepers)

	1999	2000	2001
Coniferous (softwood)	404	437	412
Broadleaved (hardwood)	15	7	5
Total	419	444	417

Source: FAO.

Fishing

('000 metric tons, live weight)

	1998	1999	2000
Capture	8.3*	9.0	15.3
Yellowfin tuna	1.4	1.3	4.2
Porgies, seabreams	0.2	0.7	0.1
Caribbean spiny lobster	0.3	0.6	3.2
Penaeus shrimps	1.8	1.0	4.2
Stromboid conchs	0.5*	—	0.8
Cuttlefish, bobtail squids	0.9	1.1	0.7
Octopuses, etc.	0.1	0.6	—
Aquaculture*	8.1	8.2	8.5
Penaeus shrimps*	8.0	8.0	8.5
Total catch *	16.4	17.2	23.8

* FAO estimate(s).

Source: FAO, *Yearbook of Fishery Statistics*.

Mining

(metal content)

	1998	1999	2000
Lead ('000 metric tons)	6	5	4
Zinc ('000 metric tons)	41	41	36
Silver (metric tons)	60	54	51

Industry

SELECTED PRODUCTS

	1999	2000	2001
Raw sugar ('000 quintales)	4,893	7,307	7,609
Cement ('000 bags of 42.5 kg)	28,493	29,507	30,999
Cigarettes ('000 packets of 20)	229,303	282,771	299,220
Beer ('000 12 oz bottles)	271,354	255,804	244,968
Soft drinks ('000 12 oz bottles)	1,182,248	1,321,317	1,357,559
Wheat flour ('000 quintales)	2,394	2,502	2,483
Fabric ('000 yards)	79,449	98,931	119,010
Alcoholic drinks ('000 litres)	6,063	7,165	8,162
Vegetable oil and butter ('000 lb)	80,428	93,483	93,103

Finance

CURRENCY AND EXCHANGE RATES

Monetary Units
100 centavos = 1 lempira

Sterling, Dollar and Euro Equivalents (31 December 2002)
£1 sterling = 27.277 lempiras
US $1 = 16.923 lempiras
€1 = 17.747 lempiras
1,000 lempiras = £36.66 = $59.09 = €56.35

Average Exchange Rate (lempiras per US $)
2000   14.8392
2001   15.4737
2002   16.4334

BUDGET
(million lempiras)

Revenue	1997	1998	1999*
Current revenue	10,374.4	13,214.2	14,621.5
Taxes	8,652.1	11,973.0	13,538.1
Direct taxes . . .	2,512.3	3,377.4	2,891.6
Income tax . . .	2,293.3	3,110.2	2,646.7
Property tax . . .	219.0	267.2	244.9
Indirect taxes . . .	6,138.0	8,593.4	10,643.9
Exports. . . .	88.3	72.3	7.9
Imports . . .	2,067.8	2,043.2	1,977.1
Non-tax revenue . . .	1,422.1	943.4	741.7
Transfers	300.2	297.8	341.7
Other revenue (incl. capital revenue).	3.4	3.2	0.0
Total	10,377.8	13,217.4	14,621.5

Expenditure	1997	1998	1999*
Current expenditure	10,072.2	11,182.3	12,359.0
Consumption expenditure . .	5,421.8	6,692.5	8,177.5
Interest	2,697.8	2,314.3	1,700.4
Internal debt. . . .	1,090.9	647.8	562.0
External debt . . .	1,606.9	1,666.5	1,138.4
Transfers	1,952.6	2,175.5	2,481.1
Capital expenditure	2,912.8	3,569.2	5,601.1
Real investment . . .	1,661.2	1,811.9	2,294.1
Transfers	1,243.2	1,730.0	3,306.6
Net lending	740.9	540.0	237.6
Total	13,725.9	15,291.5	18,197.7

* Estimates.

CENTRAL BANK RESERVES
(US $ million at 31 December)

	2000	2001	2002
Gold*	5.99	6.05	7.11
IMF special drawing rights . .	0.10	0.32	0.47
Foreign exchange . . .	1,301.70	1,404.40	1,511.80
Reserve position in IMF . .	11.24	10.84	11.73
Total	1,319.03	1,453.29	1,531.11

* National valuation.

Source: IMF, *International Financial Statistics*.

MONEY SUPPLY
(million lempiras at 31 December)

	2000	2001	2002
Currency outside banks . .	4,727	5,166	5,549
Demand deposits at commercial banks	6,180	6,344	7,668
Total money (incl. others) . .	11,954	12,388	14,234

Source: IMF, *International Financial Statistics*.

COST OF LIVING
(Consumer Price Index; base: 1990 = 100)

	1997	1998	1999
Food	419.7	468.9	505.9
Fuel and power	382.0	374.0	340.0
Clothing and footwear . . .	363.5	420.0	474.7
Rent	326.2	362.3	401.4
All items	378.4	430.2	480.4

2000: Food 531.2; Clothing and footwear 499.8; All items 509.2.

2001: Food 577.2; Clothing and footwear 543.5; All items 558.2.

Source: ILO.

NATIONAL ACCOUNTS
(million lempiras at current prices)

Expenditure on the Gross Domestic Product

	1999	2000	2001
Government final consumption expenditure . . .	8,726	11,218	13,687
Private final consumption expenditure	53,226	62,310	71,923
Increase in stocks	3,687	3,995	5,977
Gross fixed capital formation . .	22,987	23,336	24,231
Total domestic expenditure. .	88,626	100,859	115,818
Exports of goods and services . .	31,627	36,803	37,309
Less Imports of goods and services	43,157	49,362	54,083
GDP in purchasers' values .	77,096	88,300	99,044
GDP at constant 1978 prices .	6,750	7,104	7,287

Source: IMF, *International Financial Statistics*.

Gross Domestic Product by Economic Activity

	1999	2000	2001
Agriculture, hunting, forestry and fishing	10,501	11,493	12,213
Mining and quarrying . . .	1,325	1,497	1,587
Manufacturing	12,916	15,207	17,540
Electricity, gas and water . .	3,208	3,655	3,728
Construction	3,863	4,157	4,261
Wholesale and retail trade, restaurants and hotels . . .	8,365	9,633	10,918
Transport, storage and communications	3,423	4,232	5,061
Finance, insurance and real estate	7,155	8,328	9,404
Owner-occupied dwellings . .	3,990	4,579	5,201
Public administration and defence	3,875	4,590	5,667
Other services	7,261	8,938	10,806
GDP at factor cost . . .	65,882	76,309	86,386
Indirect taxes, *less* subsidies .	11,214	11,599	12,426
GDP in purchasers' values .	77,096	87,908	98,812

BALANCE OF PAYMENTS
(US $ million)

	1999	2000	2001
Exports of goods f.o.b. . . .	1,756.3	2,001.2	1,930.9
Imports of goods f.o.b. . . .	−2,509.6	−2,669.6	−2,807.4
Trade balance	−753.3	−668.4	−876.5
Exports of services	474.1	478.8	480.8
Imports of services	−502.4	−622.9	−653.4
Balance on goods and services.	−781.6	−812.5	−1,049.1
Other income received . . .	80.5	110.1	88.0
Other income paid	−235.7	−256.8	−235.2
Balance on goods, services and income	−936.8	−959.2	1,196.3
Current transfers received . .	354.6	447.4	573.7
Current transfers paid . . .	−42.4	−44.9	−47.2
Current balance	−624.6	−556.7	−669.8
Capital account (net) . . .	110.9	98.9	95.0
Direct investment from abroad. .	237.3	282.0	195.0
Portfolio investment assets . .	−72.4	−115.4	−46.7
Financial derivatives liabilities .	−16.1	−1.2	n.a.
Other investment assets . .	−132.2	−157.3	−68.8
Other investment liabilities . .	186.8	−37.6	75.4
Net errors and omissions . .	122.0	129.7	87.7
Overall balance	−188.3	−357.4	−323.2

Source: IMF, *International Financial Statistics*.

External Trade

PRINCIPAL COMMODITIES
(US $ million, preliminary figures)

Imports c.i.f.	1999	2000	2001
Live animals and meat products .	71.5	94.1	92.7
Vegetables and fruit . . .	134.4	145.0	142.7
Mineral fuels and lubricants . .	256.4	383.6	401.6
Chemicals and related products .	351.7	390.2	432.5
Plastic and manufactures . .	147.4	165.7	183.8
Paper, paperboard and manufactures	120.9	145.9	163.3
Textile yarn, fabrics and manufactures	85.9	80.9	60.1
Metal and manufactures . .	245.2	201.6	262.7
Food products.	260.1	263.1	290.6
Machinery and electrical appliances	519.3	465.6	478.1
Transport equipment . . .	279.1	299.1	286.0
Total (incl. others)	2,676.1	2,854.7	2,997.4

Exports f.o.b.	1999	2000	2001
Bananas	38.1	124.2	196.6
Coffee	256.1	339.4	161.3
Lead and zinc	53.9	50.8	35.8
Shellfish	189.3	191.7	204.8
Melons	47.0	37.6	40.0
Soaps and detergents . . .	38.7	45.7	50.6
Timber	27.5	33.5	30.8
Cigars and cigarettes . . .	55.4	59.7	57.6
Total (incl. others)	1,164.4	1,369.8	1,310.9

PRINCIPAL TRADING PARTNERS
(US $ million, preliminary figures)

Imports c.i.f.	1999	2000	2001
Brazil	30.9	29.6	31.1
Colombia	28.0	34.5	36.2
Costa Rica	97.8	100.9	107.7
El Salvador	180.4	225.1	236.4
Germany	46.4	35.9	37.7
Guatemala	224.7	233.1	240.0
Japan	107.2	113.2	118.9
Mexico	136.6	141.0	148.1
Netherlands	27.6	10.7	11.2
Nicaragua	38.0	37.3	40.3
Spain	30.6	29.9	31.4
USA	1,193.3	1,318.8	1,385.8
Venezuela	29.3	63.1	66.3
Total (incl. others)	2,676.1	2,854.7	2,997.4

Exports f.o.b.	1999	2000	2001
Belgium	48.2	78.1	73.6
Costa Rica	27.3	30.3	31.6
El Salvador	83.3	119.9	123.6
France	12.1	12.8	12.1
Germany	42.9	74.9	70.7
Guatemala	72.9	83.5	90.2
Italy	24.8	20.4	19.3
Japan	55.6	42.4	40.0
Netherlands	16.1	21.7	20.5
Nicaragua	73.7	30.8	23.1
Spain	38.4	15.9	15.0
United Kingdom	12.6	38.6	36.4
USA	457.4	534.1	503.8
Total (incl. others)	1,164.4	1,369.8	1,310.9

Transport

ROAD TRAFFIC
(motor vehicles in use)

	1997	1998	1999
Passenger cars	268,142	306,426	326,541
Buses and coaches	15,329	16,930	18,419
Lorries and vans	33,279	37,242	40,903
Motorcycles and bicycles . . .	74,437	82,794	90,890

Source: IRF, *World Road Statistics*.

SHIPPING

Merchant Fleet
(registered at 31 December)

	1999	2000	2001
Number of vessels	1,511	1,407	1,183
Total displacement ('000 grt) . .	1,219.6	1,111.0	966.5

Source: Lloyd's Register-Fairplay, *World Fleet Statistics*.

International Sea-borne Freight Traffic
('000 metric tons)

	1988	1989	1990
Goods loaded	1,328	1,333	1,316
Goods unloaded	1,151	1,222	1,002

Source: UN, *Monthly Bulletin of Statistics*.

CIVIL AVIATION
(traffic on scheduled services)

	1993	1994	1995
Kilometres flown (million) . . .	4	5	5
Passengers carried ('000) . . .	409	449	474
Passenger-km (million)	362	323	341
Total ton-km (million)	50	42	33

Source: UN, *Statistical Yearbook*.

Tourism

VISITOR ARRIVALS BY COUNTRY OF ORIGIN

	1998	1999	2000
Canada	8,025	7,648	8,732
Costa Rica	12,665	13,654	15,755
El Salvador	32,534	54,496	79,365
Guatemala	30,393	40,159	66,924
Mexico	10,185	11,057	10,902
Nicaragua	39,285	38,915	64,350
USA	127,303	144,487	150,531
Total (incl. others)	321,149	370,847	470,727

Receipts from tourism (US $ million): 164 in 1998; 165 in 1999; 240 in 2000.

Arrivals ('000): 371 in 1999; 480 in 2000.

Sources: World Tourism Organization, *Yearbook of Tourism Statistics*; World Bank, *World Development Indicators*.

Communications Media

	1999	2000	2001
Telephones ('000 main lines in use)	297.2	298.7	309.7
Mobile cellular telephones ('000 subscribers)	78.6	155.3	237.6
Personal computers ('000 in use)	60	60*	80
Internet users ('000)	20	40	40*

* Estimate.

Radio receivers ('000 in use): 2,450 in 1997.

Television receivers ('000 in use): 620 in 2000.

Daily newspapers: 6 in 1997.

Weekly newspapers: 3 in 1997.

Sources: International Telecommunication Union; UN, *Statistical Yearbook*; UNESCO, *Statistical Yearbook*.

Education

(2001)

	Institutions	Teachers	Students
Pre-primary	2,890	3,973	125,202
Primary	9,746	32,568	1,109,242
Secondary	1,000	15,647	195,072
University level*	10	5,088	76,573

* 1998 figures.

Adult literacy rate (UNESCO estimates): 74.6% (males 74.7%; females 74.5%) in 2000 (Source: UN Development Programme, *Human Development Report*).

Directory

The Constitution

Following the elections of April 1980, the 1965 Constitution was revised. The new Constitution was approved by the National Assembly in November 1982, and amended in 1995. The following are some of its main provisions:

Honduras is constituted as a democratic Republic. All Hondurans over 18 years of age are citizens.

THE SUFFRAGE AND POLITICAL PARTIES

The vote is direct and secret. Any political party that proclaims or practises doctrines contrary to the democratic spirit is forbidden. A National Electoral Council will be set up at the end of each presidential term. Its general function will be to supervise all elections and to register political parties. A proportional system of voting will be adopted for the election of Municipal Corporations.

INDIVIDUAL RIGHTS AND GUARANTEES

The right to life is declared inviolable; the death penalty is abolished. The Constitution recognizes the right of habeas corpus and arrests may be made only by judicial order. Remand for interrogation may not last more than six days, and no-one may be held incommunicado for more than 24 hours. The Constitution recognizes the rights of free expression of thought and opinion, the free circulation of information, of peaceful, unarmed association, of free movement within and out of the country, of political asylum and of religious and educational freedom. Civil marriage and divorce are recognized.

WORKERS' WELFARE

All have a right to work. Day work shall not exceed eight hours per day or 44 hours per week; night work shall not exceed six hours per night or 36 hours per week. Equal pay shall be given for equal work. The legality of trade unions and the right to strike are recognized.

EDUCATION

The State is responsible for education, which shall be free, lay, and, in the primary stage, compulsory. Private education is liable to inspection and regulation by the State.

LEGISLATIVE POWER

Deputies are obliged to vote, for or against, on any measure at the discussion of which they are present. The National Assembly has power to grant amnesties to political prisoners; approve or disapprove of the actions of the Executive; declare part or the whole of the Republic subject to a state of siege; declare war; approve or withhold approval of treaties; withhold approval of the accounts of public expenditure when these exceed the sums fixed in the budget; decree, interpret, repeal and amend laws, and pass legislation fixing the rate of exchange or stabilizing the national currency. The National Assembly may suspend certain guarantees in all or part of the Republic for 60 days in the case of grave danger from civil or foreign war, epidemics or any other calamity. Deputies are elected in the proportion of one deputy and one substitute for every 35,000 inhabitants, or fraction over 15,000. Congress may amend the basis in the light of increasing population.

EXECUTIVE POWER

Executive power is exercised by the President of the Republic, who is elected for four years by a simple majority of the people. No President may serve more than one term.

JUDICIAL POWER

The Judiciary consists of the Supreme Court, the Courts of Appeal and various lesser tribunals. The nine judges and seven substitute judges of the Supreme Court are elected by the National Assembly for a period of four years. The Supreme Court is empowered to declare laws unconstitutional.

THE ARMED FORCES

The Armed Forces are declared by the Constitution to be essentially professional and non-political. The President exercises direct authority over the military.

LOCAL ADMINISTRATION

The country is divided into 18 Departments for purposes of local administration, and these are subdivided into 290 autonomous Municipalities; the functions of local offices shall be only economic and administrative.

The Government

HEAD OF STATE

President: RICARDO MADURO JOEST (assumed office 27 January 2002).

Vice-President: VICENTE WILLIAMS AGASSE.

CABINET
(April 2003)

Minister of the Interior and Justice: JORGE RAMÓN HERNÁNDEZ ALCERRO.

Minister in the Office of the President: LUIS COSENZA JIMÉNEZ.

Minister of Foreign Affairs: GUILLERMO PÉREZ-CADALSO ARIAS.

Minister of Industry and Commerce: JULIETTE HANDAL DE CASTILLO.

Minister of Finance: JOSÉ ARTURO ALVARADO SÁNCHEZ.

Minister of National Defence: FEDERICO BREVÉ TRAVIESO.

Minister of Public Security: JUAN ANGEL ARIAS.

Minister of Labour and Social Welfare: GERMÁN LEITZELAR.

Minister of Health: ELÍAS LIZARDO.

Minister of Public Education: CARLOS AVILA MOLINA.

Minister of Public Works, Transport and Housing: JORGE CARRANZA.

Minister of Culture, Art and Sports: MIREYA BATRES.

Minister of Agriculture and Livestock: MARIANO JIMÉNEZ TALAVERA.

Minister of Natural Resources and Environment: PATRICIA PANTING GALO.

Minister of Tourism: THIERRY DE PIERREFEU.

MINISTRIES

Office of the President: Palacio José Cecilio del Valle, Blvd Juan Pablo II, Tegucigalpa; tel. 232-6282; fax 231-0097.

Ministry of Agriculture and Livestock: Tegucigalpa.

Ministry of Culture, Art and Sports: Avda La Paz, Apdo 3287, Tegucigalpa; tel. 236-9643; fax 236-9532; e-mail editc@sdnhon.org.hn; internet www.secad.gob.hn.

Ministry of Finance: 5a Avda, 3a Calle, Tegucigalpa; tel. 222-1278; fax 238-2309; e-mail joaralva@sispu.hn.

Ministry of Foreign Affairs: Centro Cívico Gubernamental, Antigua Casa Presidencial, Blvd Kuwait, Contiguo a la Corte Suprema de Justicia, Tegucigalpa; tel. 234-1962; fax 234-1484; internet www.sre.hn.

Ministry of Health: 4a Avda, 3a Calle, Tegucigalpa; tel. 22-1386; fax 238-4141; internet www.paho-who.hn/ssalud.htm.

Ministry of Industry and Commerce: Edif. Salame, 5a Avda, 4a Calle, Tegucigalpa; tel. 238-2025; fax 237-2836.

Ministry of the Interior and Justice: Palacio de los Ministerios, 2°, Tegucigalpa; tel. 237-1130; fax 237-1121; e-mail dgaatm@sdnhon.org.hn.

Ministry of Labour and Social Welfare: Edif. Olympus (STSS), Col. Puerta del Sol, Contiguo a SETCO, Intersección Bulevares Villa Olímpica, La Hacienda, Tegucigalpa; tel. 235-3455; fax 235-3456.

Ministry of National Defence and Public Security: 5a Avda, 4a Calle, Tegucigalpa; tel. 22-8560; fax 238-0238.

Ministry of Natural Resources and Environment: 100 m al sur del Estadio Nacional, Apdo 1389, Tegucigalpa; tel. 239-4296; fax 232-6250; e-mail jcuerva@serna.gob.hn; internet www.serna.gob.hn.

Ministry of Public Education: 1a Avda, 2a y 3a Calle 201, Comayagüela, Tegucigalpa; tel. 22-8517; fax 237-4312.

Ministry of Public Security: Tegucigalpa.

Ministry of Public Works, Transport and Housing: Barrio La Bolsa, Comayagüela, Tegucigalpa; tel. 233-7690; fax 25-2227.

Ministry of Tourism: Edif. Salame, 5a Avda, 4a Calle, Tegucigalpa; tel. 238-2025; fax 237-2836.

President and Legislature

PRESIDENT

Election, 25 November 2001

Candidate	Votes cast	% of votes
Ricardo Maduro Joest (PN)	1,137,734	52.21
Rafael Piñeda Ponce (PL)	964,590	44.26
Olban F. Valladares (PINU)	31,666	1.45
Matías Funes (PUD)	24,102	1.11
Marco Orlando Iriarte (PDCH)	21,089	0.97
Total*	2,179,181	100.00

* Excluding 23,927 blank ballots, 81,959 spoilt votes and 1,163,213 abstentions.

ASAMBLEA NACIONAL

President: PORFIRIO LOBO SOSA.

General Election, 25 November 2001

	Seats
Partido Nacional (PN)	61
Partido Liberal (PL)	55
Partido de Unificación Democrática (PUD)	5
Partido Innovación y Unidad—	
Social Democracia (PINU)	4
Partido Demócrata Cristiano de Honduras (PDCH) . . .	3
Total	128

Political Organizations

Asociación para el Progreso de Honduras (APROH): right-wing grouping of business interests and members of the armed forces; Vice-Pres. MIGUEL FACUSSÉ; Sec. OSWALDO RAMOS SOTO.

Francisco Morazán Frente Constitucional (FMFC): f. 1988; composed of labour, social, political and other organizations.

Frente Patriótico Hondureño (FPH): left-wing alliance comprising:

Partido de Acción Socialista de Honduras (PASOH): Leaders MARIO VIRGILIO CARAS, ROGELIO MARTÍNEZ REINA.

Partido Comunista de Honduras—Marxista-Leninista (PCH—ML): f. 1954; gained legal status 1981; linked with DNU; Leader RIGOBERTO PADILLA RUSH.

Partido Demócrata Cristiano de Honduras (PDCH): internet www.pdch.hn; legally recognized in 1980; Pres. Dr HERNÁN CORRALES PADILLA; Vice-Pres. VICENTE WILLIAMS.

Partido Innovación y Unidad—Social Democracia (PINU): 29 Avda de Comayagüela 912, Apdo 105, Tegucigalpa; tel. 237-1357; fax 237-4245; f. 1970; legally recognized in 1978; Leader OLBAN F. VALLADARES.

Partido Liberal (PL): Col. Miramonte atrás del supermercado La Colonia, No 1, Tegucigalpa; tel. 232-0520; fax 232-0797; f. 1891; factions within the party include the Alianza Liberal del Pueblo, the Movimiento Florista (Leader Carlos Roberto Flores Facussé), and the Movimiento Liberal Democrático Revolucionario (Pres. Jorge Arturo Reina); Pres. CARLOS ROBERTO FLORES FACUSSÉ; Sec.-Gen. ROBERTO MICHELETTI BAIN.

Partido Nacional (PN): Paseo el Obelisco, Comayagüela, Tegucigalpa; tel. 237-7310; fax 237-7365; f. 1902; traditional right-wing party; internal opposition tendencies include Movimiento Democratizador Nacionalista (MODENA), Movimiento de Unidad y Cambio (MUC), Movimiento Nacional de Reivindicación Callejista (MON-ARCA) and Tendencia Nacionalista de Trabajo; Pres. CARLOS URBIZO; Sec. MARIO AGUILAR GONZÁLEZ.

Partido de Unificación Democrática (PUD): f. 1993; left-wing coalition comprising Partido Revolucionario Hondureño, Partido Renovación Patriótica, Partido para la Transformación de Honduras and Partido Morazanista.

Pueblo Unido en Bloque por Honduras (PuebloH): Tegucigalpa; f. 1999; Leader RAMÓN CUSTODIO.

Unión Revolucionaria del Pueblo (URP): f. 1980 following split in Communist Party; peasant support.

The Dirección Nacional Unificada—Movimiento Revolucionario Hondureño (DNU—MRH) comprises the following guerrilla groups:

Fuerzas Populares Revolucionarias (FRP) Lorenzo Zelaya.

Frente Morazanista para la Liberación de Honduras (FMLH). Froylan Turcios.

Movimiento Popular de Liberación Cinchonero (MPLC).

Movimiento de Unidad Revolucionaria (MUR).

Partido Revolucionario de los Trabajadores Centroamericanos de Honduras (PRTCH).

Other guerrilla forces include the **Alianza por Acción Anticomunista (AAA)** and the **Frente Popular de Liberación, Nueve de Mayo (FPL).**

Diplomatic Representation

EMBASSIES IN HONDURAS

Argentina: Avda José María Medina 417, Col. Rubén Darío, Apdo 3208, Tegucigalpa; tel. 232-3376; fax 231-0376; e-mail emarho@hondudata.com; Ambassador JUAN ANGEL PEÑA.

Brazil: Col. La Reforma, Calle La Salle 1309, Apdo 341, Tegucigalpa; tel. 236-5867; fax 236-5873; e-mail brastegu@hondudata.com; Chargé d'affaires a.i. SERGIO ELIAS COURY.

Canada: Centro Financiero BANEXPO, 3°, Bulevar San Juan Bosco, Colonia Payaqui; tel. 238-1456; fax 237-0822; e-mail tglpamicro@x400.gc.ca; Ambassador LOUISE LÉGER.

Chile: Edif. Interamericana frente Los Castaños, Blvd Morazán, Apdo 222, Tegucigalpa; tel. 232-4095; fax 232-8853; e-mail echilehn@cablecolor.hn; Ambassador GERMÁN CARRASCO.

China (Taiwan): Col. Palmira, Avda República de Panamá 2043, Tegucigalpa; tel. 239-5837; fax 232-7645; e-mail hnd@mofa.gov.tw; Ambassador CHING-YEN CHANG.

Colombia: Edif. Palmira, 4°, Col. Palmira, Apdo 468, Tegucigalpa; tel. 232-9709; fax 232-8133; e-mail emcolhon@multivisionhn.net; Ambassador GERMÁN RAMÍREZ BULLA.

Costa Rica: Residencial El Triángulo, 1 Calle, Lomas del Guijarro, Apdo 512, Tegucigalpa; tel. 232-1768; fax 232-1876; e-mail embacori@honduras.quik.com; Ambassador EDGAR GARCÍA MIRANDA.

Cuba: Avda Palmeras, Colonia Florencia Sur, Tegucigalpa; tel. 239-0610; fax 235-7624; Ambassador JACINTO PABLOS MUÑOZ.

Dominican Republic: Calle Principal frente al Banco Continental, Col. Miramontes, Tegucigalpa; tel. 239-0130; fax 239-1594; e-mail embadom@compunet.hn; Ambassador ELADIO KNIPPING VICTORIA.

Ecuador: Col. Palmira, Avda Juan Lindo 122, Apdo 358, Tegucigalpa; tel. 236-5980; fax 236-6929; e-mail mecuahon@hondutel .hn; Chargé d'affaires a.i. Dr MARCELO FABIAN HURTADO LOMAS.

El Salvador: Col. San Carlos, Calzada República del Uruguay 219, Apdo 1936, Tegucigalpa; tel. 239-0901; fax 236-9403; e-mail embasal@worksitsnet.net; Ambassador SIGIFREDO OCHOA PÉREZ.

France: Col. Palmira, Avda Juan Lindo, Callejón Batres 337, Apdo 3441, Tegucigalpa; tel. 236-6800; fax 236-8051; e-mail ambafrance@ cablecolor.hn; Ambassador MICHEL AVIGNON.

Germany: Edif. Paysen, 3°, Blvd Morazán, Apdo 3145, Tegucigalpa; tel. 232-3161; fax 239-9018; e-mail embalema@netsys.hn; Ambassador Dr THOMAS BRUNS.

Guatemala: Col. Las Minitas, Calle Arturo López Rodezno 2421, Tegucigalpa; tel. 232-5018; fax 232-8469; e-mail embaguahon3@ cablecolor.hn; Ambassador ERWIN FERNANDO GUZMÁN OVALLE.

Holy See: Palacio de la Nunciatura Apostólica, Col. Palmira, Avda Santa Sede 412, Apdo 324, Tegucigalpa; tel. 236-6613; fax 232-8280; e-mail nunciatureateg@hondudata.com; Apostolic Nuncio Most Rev. GEORGE PANIKULAM (Titular Archbishop of Arpaia).

Italy: Col. Reforma, Avda Principal 2602, Apdo 317, Tegucigalpa; tel. 236-6810; fax 236-5659; e-mail ambtegus@cablecolor.hn; Ambassador ESTEFANO MARÍA CACCIGUERRA RANGHIERI.

Japan: Col. San Carlos, 3a y 4a Calles, contiguo estacionamiento Supermercado Sucasa, Apdo 125-C, Tegucigalpa; tel. 236-6828; fax 236-6100; Ambassador MASAMI TAKEMOTO.

Mexico: Col. Palmira, Avda República de México 2402, Apdo 769, Tegucigalpa; tel. 232-4039; fax 232-4719; e-mail embamexhond@ cablecolor.hn; Ambassador WALTERIO ASTIÉ BURGOS.

Nicaragua: Col. Tepeyac, Bloque M-1, Avda Choluteca 1130, Apdo 392, Tegucigalpa; tel. 232-7224; fax 231-1412; e-mail embanic@ hondudata.com; Ambassador Dr DOMINGO SALINAS ALVARADO.

Panama: Edif. Palmira, 2°, Col. Palmira, Apdo 397, Tegucigalpa; tel. 239-5508; fax 232-8147; e-mail ephon@hondudata.com; Ambassador IRIS ONEIDA VEGA RAMOS.

Peru: Col. La Reforma, Calle Principal 2618, Tegucigalpa; tel. 221-0596; fax 236-6070; e-mail embaperu@netsys.hn; Chargé d'affaires a.i. CARLOS ALBERTO YRIGOYEN FORNO.

Spain: Col. Matamoros, Calle Santander 801, Apdo 3223, Tegucigalpa; tel. 236-6875; fax 236-8682; e-mail embesphn@hondutel .hn; Ambassador JAVIER NAGORE SAN MARTÍN.

Sweden: Paseo República de Argentina, Casa 354, Col. Palmira, Apdo 4390; Tegucigalpa; tel. 221-0951; fax 221 3533; Ambassador VICTOR SAÚL SIERRA COREA.

United Kingdom: Edif. Financiero BANEXPO, 3°, Blvd San Juan Bosco, Col. Payaqui, Apdo 290, Tegucigalpa; tel. 232-0612; fax 232-5480; e-mail british.embassy.tegucigalpa@fco.gov.uk; Ambassador KAY COOMBS.

USA: Avda La Paz, Apdo 3453, Tegucigalpa; tel. 232-3120; fax 232-0027; Ambassador LARRY PALMER.

Venezuela: Col. Rubén Darío, entre Avda Las Minitas y Avda Rubén Darío 2321, Apdo 775, Tegucigalpa; tel. 232-1879; fax 232-1016; e-mail emvenezue@hondutel.hn; Ambassador MARÍA SALAZAR SANABRIA.

Judicial System

Justice is administered by the Supreme Court (which has nine judges), five Courts of Appeal, and departmental courts (which have their own local jurisdiction).

Tegucigalpa has two Courts of Appeal which have jurisdiction (1) in the department of Francisco Morazán, and (2) in the departments of Choluteca Valle, El Paraíso and Olancho.

The Appeal Court of San Pedro Sula has jurisdiction in the department of Cortés; that of Comayagua has jurisdiction in the departments of Comayagua, La Paz and Intibucá; and that of Santa Bárbara in the departments of Santa Bárbara, Lempira and Copán.

Supreme Court: Edif. Palacio de Justicia, contiguo Col. Miraflores, Centro Cívico Gubernamental, Tegucigalpa; tel. 233-9208; fax 233-6784.

President of the Supreme Court of Justice: OSCAR ARMANDO AVILA.

Attorney-General: (vacant).

Religion

The majority of the population are Roman Catholics; the Constitution guarantees toleration to all forms of religious belief.

CHRISTIANITY

The Roman Catholic Church

Honduras comprises one archdiocese and six dioceses. At 31 December 2000 some 81.3% of the population were adherents.

Bishops' Conference

Conferencia Episcopal de Honduras, Los Laureles, Comayagüela, Apdo 3121, Tegucigalpa; tel. 229-1111; fax 229-1144; e-mail ceh@ unicah.org.hn.

f. 1929; Pres. Cardinal OSCAR ANDRÉS RODRÍGUEZ MARADIAGA (Archbishop of Tegucigalpa).

Archbishop of Tegucigalpa: Cardinal OSCAR ANDRÉS RODRÍGUEZ MARADIAGA, Arzobispado, 3a y 2a Avda 1113, Apdo 106, Tegucigalpa; tel. 237-0353; fax 222-2337.

The Anglican Communion

Honduras comprises a single missionary diocese, in Province IX of the Episcopal Church in the USA.

Bishop of Honduras: Rt Rev. LEOPOLD FRADE, Apdo 586, San Pedro Sula; tel. 556-6155; fax 556-6467; e-mail episcopal@mayanet.hn.

The Baptist Church

Baptist Convention of Honduras: Apdo 2176, Tegucigalpa; tel. and fax 236-6717; e-mail conibah@sigmanet.hn; Pres. Pastor ALEXIS SALVADOR VIDES.

Other Churches

Iglesia Cristiana Luterana de Honduras (Christian Lutheran Church of Honduras): Apdo 2861, Tegucigalpa; tel. and fax 225-4464; fax 225-4893; e-mail iclh@mayanet.hn; Pres. Rev. J. GUILLERMO FLORES V; 1,000 mems.

BAHÁ'Í FAITH

National Spiritual Assembly: Sendero de los Naranjos 2801, Col. Castaños, Apdo 273, Tegucigalpa; tel. 232-6124; fax 231-1343; e-mail bahaihon@globenet.hn; mems resident in 667 localities.

The Press

DAILIES

El Faro Porteño: Puerto Cortés.

La Gaceta: Tegucigalpa; f. 1830; morning; official govt paper; Dir MARCIAL LAGOS; circ. 3,000.

El Heraldo: Avda los Próceres, Frente Instituto del Tórax, Barrio San Felipe, Apdo 1938, Tegucigalpa; tel. 236-6000; fax 21-0778; f. 1979; morning; independent; Dir JOSÉ FRANCISCO MORALES CÁLIX; circ. 45,000.

El Nuevo Día: 3a Avda, 11–12 Calles, San Pedro Sula; tel. 52-4298; fax 57-9457; e-mail elndia@hondutel.hn; f. 1994; morning; independent; Pres. ABRAHAM ANDONIE; Editor ARMANDO CERRATO; circ. 20,000.

El Periódico: Carretera al Batallón, Tegucigalpa; tel. 234-3086; fax 234-3090; f. 1993; morning; Pres. EMIN ABUFELE; Editor OSCAR ARMANDO MARTÍNEZ.

La Prensa: 3a Avda, 6a–7a Calles No 34, Apdo 143, San Pedro Sula; tel. 53-3101; fax 53-0778; e-mail laprensa@simon.intertel.hn; internet www.laprensahn.com; f. 1964; morning; independent; Exec. Dir NELSON EDGARDO FERNÁNDEZ; Editor NELSON GARCÍA; circ. 62,000.

El Tiempo: Altos del Centro Comercial Miramontes, Col. Miramontes, Tegucigalpa; tel. 231-0418; internet www.tiempo.hn; f. 1970; liberal; Editor MANUEL GAMERO; circ. 42,000.

El Tiempo: 1a Calle, 5a Avda 102, Santa Anita, Apdo 450, San Pedro Sula; tel. 53-3388; fax 53-4590; e-mail tiempo@simon.intertel

.hn; internet www.tiempo.hn; f. 1960; morning; left-of-centre; Pres. JAIME ROSENTHAL OLIVA; Editor MANUEL GAMERO; circ. 35,000.

La Tribuna: Col. Santa Bárbara, Comayagüela, Apdo 1501, Tegucigalpa; tel. 233-1138; fax 233-1188; e-mail tribuna@david.intertel .hn; internet www.latribuna.hn; f. 1977; morning; independent; Dir ADÁN ELVIR FLORES; Pres. JOSÉ DANIEL VILLEDA; circ. 45,000.

PERIODICALS

Cambio Empresarial: Apdo 1111, Tegucigalpa; tel. 237-2853; fax 237-0480; monthly; economic, political, social; Editor JOAQUÍN MEDINA OVIEDO.

El Comercio: Cámara de Comercio e Industrias de Tegucigalpa, Blvd Centroamérica, Apdo 3444, Tegucigalpa; tel. 232-4200; fax 232-0759; f. 1970; monthly; commercial and industrial news; Dir-Gen. Lic. HÉCTOR MANUEL ORDÓÑEZ.

Cultura para Todos: San Pedro Sula; monthly.

Espectador: San Pedro Sula; weekly.

Extra: Tegucigalpa; tel. 237-2533; f. 1965; monthly; independent; current affairs; Editor VICENTE MACHADO VALLE.

Hablemos Claro: Edif. Abriendo Brecha, Blvd Suyapa, Tegucigalpa; tel. 232-8058; fax 239-7008; e-mail abrecha@hondutel.hn; f. 1990; weekly; Editor RODRIGO WONG ARÉVALO; circ. 15,000.

Hibueras: Apdo 955, Tegucigalpa; Dir RAÚL LANZA VALERIANO.

Presente: Tegucigalpa; monthly.

Revista Ideas: Tegucigalpa; 6 a year; women's interest.

Revista Prisma: Tegucigalpa; quarterly; cultural; Editor MARÍA LUISA CASTELLANOS.

Sucesos: Tegucigalpa; monthly.

Tribuna Sindical: Tegucigalpa; monthly.

PRESS ASSOCIATION

Asociación de Prensa Hondureña: Apdo 59C, Tegucigalpa; tel. 237-8107; fax 237-8102; f. 1930; Pres. GUILLERMO PAGÁN SOLORZANO.

FOREIGN NEWS AGENCIES

Agence France-Presse (AFP) (France): Tegucigalpa; Correspondent WINSTON CÁLIX.

Agencia EFE (Spain): Edif. Jiménez Castro, 5°, Of. 505, Tegucigalpa; tel. 22-0493; Bureau Chief ARMANDO ENRIQUE CERRATO CORTÉS.

Agenzia Nazionale Stampa Associata (ANSA) (Italy): Edif. La Plazuela, Barrio La Plazuela, Tegucigalpa; tel. 237-7701; Correspondent RAÚL MONCADA.

Deutsche Presse-Agentur (dpa) (Germany): Edif. Jiménez Castro, Of. 203, 4a Calle y 5a Avda, No 405, Apdo 3522, Tegucigalpa; tel. 237-8570; Correspondent WILFREDO GARCÍA CASTRO.

Inter Press Service (IPS) (Italy): Apdo 228, Tegucigalpa; tel. 232-5342; Correspondent JUAN RAMÓN DURÁN.

Reuters (United Kingdom): Edif. Palmira, frente Honduras Maya, 5°, Col. Palmira, Tegucigalpa; tel. 231-5329.

Publishers

Compañía Editora Nacional, SA: 5a Calle Oriente, No 410, Tegucigalpa.

Editora Cultural: 6a Avda Norte, 7a Calle, Comayagüela, Tegucigalpa.

Editorial Nuevo Continente: Tegucigalpa; tel. 22-5073; Dir LETICIA SILVA DE OYUELA.

Editorial Paulino Valladares, Carlota Vda de Valladares: 5a Avda, 5a y 6a Calle, Tegucigalpa.

Guaymuras: Apdo 1843, Tegucigalpa; tel. 237-5433; fax 237-4931; e-mail editorial@sigmanet.hn; f. 1980; Dir ISOLDA ARITA MELZER; Admin. ROSENDO ANTÚNEZ.

Industria Editorial Lypsa: Apdo 167-C, Tegucigalpa; tel. 22-9775; Man. JOSÉ BENNATON.

Universidad Nacional Autónoma de Honduras: Blvd Suyapa, Tegucigalpa; tel. 231-4601; fax 231-4601; f. 1847.

Broadcasting and Communications

TELECOMMUNICATIONS

Comisión Nacional de Telecomunicaciones (Conatel): Apdo 15012, Tegucigalpa; tel. 221-3500; fax 221-0578; e-mail nhernandez@conatel.hn; Pres. NORMAN ROY HERNÁNDEZ D; Exec. Sec. WALTER DAVID SANDOVAL.

Empresa Hondureña de Telecomunicaciones (Hondutel): Apdo 1794, Tegucigalpa; tel. 237-9802; fax 237-1111; scheduled for partial privatization by 2005; Gen. Man. ALSONSO VALENZUELA.

BROADCASTING

Radio

Radio América: Col. Alameda, frente a la Droguería Mandofer, Apdo 259, Tegucigalpa; tel. 232-8338; fax 232-1009; commercial station; f. 1948; 13 relay stations; Pres. MANUEL ANDONIE FERNÁNDEZ; Gen. Man. BERNARDINO RIVERA.

Radio Capital: Col. Al Prado, 1a calle, Tegucigalpa; tel. 233-6576.

Radio Caribe: Barrio La Isla, La Ceiba, Atlantida; tel. 242-0082.

Radio Catolica La Dimension: 12 Avda, Tegucigalpa; tel. 242-0082.

Radio Centro: Col. Florencia, Tegucigalpa; tel. 232-5178.

Radio Club Honduras: Salida Chamelecon, San Pedro Sula; tel. 252-3173.

Radio Cultura: Col. Lara, 2–3 Avda, 3a. calle, Tegucigalpa; tel. 221-1290.

Radio Nacional de Honduras: Zona El Olvido, Apdo 403, Tegucigalpa; tel. 238-5478; fax 237-9721; f. 1976; official station, operated by the Govt; Dir ROY ARTHURS LEYLOR.

Radio Tegucigalpa: Edif. Landa Blanca, Calle La Fuente, Tegucigalpa; tel. 238-3880; f. 1982; Dir NERY ARTEAGA; Gen. Man. ANTONIO CONDE MAZARIEGOS.

La Voz de Centroamérica: 9a Calle, 10a Avda 64, Apdo 120, San Pedro Sula; tel. 52-7660; fax 57-3257; f. 1955; commercial station; Gen. Man. NOEMI SIKAFFY.

La Voz de Honduras: Blvd Suyapa, Apdo 642, Tegucigalpa; commercial station; 23 relay stations; Gen. Man. NOEMI VALLADARES.

Television

Centroamericana de Televisión, Canal 7 y 4: Edif. Televicentro, Blvd Suyapa, Apdo 734, Tegucigalpa; tel. 239-2081; fax 232-0097; f. 1959; Pres. JOSÉ RAFAEL FERRARI; Gen. Man. RAFAEL ENRIQUE VILLEDA.

Compañía Televisora Hondureña, SA: Blvd Suyapa, Apdo 734, Tegucigalpa; tel. 232-7835; fax 232-0097; f. 1959; main station Channel 5; nine relay stations; Gen. Man. JOSÉ RAFAEL FERRARI.

Corporación Centroamericana de Comunicaciones, SA de CV: 9a Calle, 10aAvda 64, Barrio Guamilito, Apdo 120, San Pedro Sula; tel. 557-5033; fax 557-3257; e-mail info@vicatv.hn; internet www.vicatv.hn; f. 1986; Pres. BLANCA SIKAFFY.

Voz y Imagen de Centro América: 9a Calle, 10aAvda 64, Barrio Guamilito, Apdo 120, San Pedro Sula; tel. 52-7660; fax 57-3257; Channels 9, 2 and 13; Pres. BLANCA SIKAFFY.

Telesistema Hondureño, SA, Canal 3: Edif. Televicentro, Blvd Suyapa, Apdo 734, Tegucigalpa; tel. 237-7064; fax 232-5019; f. 1967; Pres. MANUEL VILLEDA TOLEDO; Gen. Man. RAFAEL ENRIQUE VILLEDA.

Telesistema Hondureño, Canal 7: Col. Tara, Apdo 208, San Pedro Sula; tel. 53-1229; fax 57-6343; f. 1967; Pres. MANUEL VILLEDA TOLEDO; Dir JOSÉ RAFAEL FERRARI.

Trecevisión: Apdo 393, Tegucigalpa; subscriber TV; one relay station in San Pedro Sula; Gen. Man. F. PON AGUILAR.

Finance

(cap. = capital; res = reserves; dep. = deposits; m. = million; brs = branches; amounts in lempiras unless otherwise stated)

BANKING

Central Bank

Banco Central de Honduras (BANTRAL): Avda Juan Ramón Molina, 7a Avda y 1a Calle, Apdo 3165, Tegucigalpa; tel. 237-2270; fax 237-1876; internet www.bch.hn; f. 1950; bank of issue; cap. 63.7m., res 373.5m., dep. 4,762.2m. (Dec. 1992); Pres. MARÍA ELENA MONDRAGÓN; 4 brs.

Commercial Banks

Banco Atlántida, SA (BANCATLAN): Plaza Bancatlán, Blvd Centroamérica, Apdo 3164, Tegucigalpa; tel. 232-1050; fax 232-6120; e-mail webmaster@bancatlan.hn; internet www.bancatlan.hn; f. 1913; cap. 750.0m., res 130.8m., dep. 7,722.2m. (Dec. 2002); Exec. Pres. GUILLERMO BUESO; Exec. Vice-Pres GUSTAVO OVIEDO, GABRIELA NÚÑEZ DE REYES, ILDOIRA G. DE BONILLA; 17 brs.

Banco del Comercio, SA (BANCOMER): 6a Avda, Calle SO 1-2, Apdo 160, San Pedro Sula; tel. 54-3600; Pres. RODOLFO CÓRDOBA PINEDA; 4 brs.

Banco Continental, SA (BANCON): Edif. Continental, 3a Avda 7, entre 2a y 3a Calle, Apdo 390, San Pedro Sula; tel. 239-2288; fax 239-0388; f. 1974; cap. 100m., res 14.3m., dep. 304.5m. (Dec. 1994); Pres. JAIME ROSENTHAL OLIVA; 6 brs.

Banco de las Fuerzas Armadas, SA (BANFFAA): Centro Comercial Los Castaños, Blvd Morazán, Apdo 877, Tegucigalpa; tel. 232-0164; fax 231-3825; e-mail webmaster@banffaa.hn; internet www.banffaa.hn; f. 1979; cap. 10m., res 33.2m., dep. 428.1m. (Dec. 1992); Pres. LUIS ALFONSO DISCUA ELVIR; Gen. Man. CARLOS RIVERA XATRUCH; 15 brs.

Banco Futuro: Edif. La Plazuela, 3a y 4a Calle, 4a Avda 1205, Tegucigalpa; tel. 237-4000; fax 237-1835; internet www.futuro.hn.

Banco Grupo El Ahorro Hondureño (BGA): Intersección Blvd Suyapa y Blvd Juan Pablo Segundo, Apdo 0344, Tegucigalpa; tel. 232-0909; fax 228-2876; e-mail bga@bancobga.com; internet www.bancobga.com; f. 2000; following a merger of Banco del Ahorro Hondureño and Banco La Capitalizadora Hondureña; cap. 656m., dep. 7,379m.; 125 brs.

Banco de Honduras, SA: Blvd Suyapa, Col. Loma Linda Sur, Tegucigalpa; tel. 232-6122; fax 232-6167; f. 1889; total assets 15,106m. (1999); Gen. Man. PATRICIA FERRO; 3 brs.

Banco Mercantil, SA: Blvd Suyapa, frente a Emisoras Unidas, Apdo 116, Tegucigalpa; tel. 232-0006; fax 232-3137; internet www.bamernet.hn; Pres. JOSÉ LAMAS; Gen. Man. JACOBO ATALA.

Banco de Occidente, SA (BANCOCCI): 6a Avda, Calle 2-3, Apdo 3284, Tegucigalpa; tel. 237-0310; fax 237-0486; e-mail boccipan@pty.com; f. 1951; cap. and res 69m., dep. 606m. (June 1994); Pres. and Gen. Man. JORGE BUESO ARIAS; Vice-Pres. EMILIO MEDINA R; 6 brs.

Banco Sogerin, SA: 8a Avda, 1a Calle, Apdo 440, San Pedro Sula; tel. 550-3888; fax 550-2001; e-mail sogelba@hondutel.hn; f. 1969; in Nov. 2002 it was reported that the Govt had intervened in the operations of Banco Sogerin; cap. and res 150.8m., dep. 857.9m. (Dec. 2000); Pres. and Gen. Man. EDMOND BOGRÁN ACOSTA; 31 brs.

Banco de los Trabajadores, SA (BANCOTRAB): 3a Avda, 13a Calle, Paseo El Obelisco, Comayagüela, Apdo 3246, Tegucigalpa; tel. 237-8723; f. 1967; cap. and res US $6.6m., dep. $43.1m. (Dec. 1992); Pres. ROLANDO DEL CID VELÁSQUEZ; 13 brs.

Development Banks

Banco Centroamericano de Integración Económica: Edif. Sede BCIE, Blvd Suyapa, Apdo 772, Tegucigalpa; tel. 228-2182; fax 228-2183; internet www.bcie.org; f. 1960 to finance the economic development of the Central American Common Market and its mem. countries; mems Costa Rica, El Salvador, Guatemala, Honduras, Nicaragua; cap. and res US $1,005.7m. (June 1999); Exec. Pres. ALEJANDRO ARÉVALO.

Banco Financiera Centroamericana, SA (FICENSA): Edif. La Interamericana, Blvd Morazán, Apdo 1432, Tegucigalpa; tel. 238-1661; fax 238-1630; f. 1974; private org. providing finance for industry, commerce and transport; total assets 11,023m. (1999); Pres. OSWALDO LÓPEZ ARELLANO; Gen. Man. ROQUE RIVERA RIBAS.

Banco Hondureño del Café, SA (BANHCAFE): Calle República de Costa Rica, Blvd Juan Pablo II, Col. Lomas del Mayab, Apdo 583, Tegucigalpa; tel. 232-8370; fax 232-8671; e-mail bcafeinf@hondutel.hn; f. 1981 to help finance coffee production; owned principally by private coffee producers; cap. 63.1m., res 110.3m., dep. 1,174.8m. (Dec. 2000); Pres. RAMÓN DAVID RIVERA; Gen. Man. RENÉ ARDÓN MATUTE; 50 brs.

Banco Municipal Autónomo (BANMA): 6a Avda, 6a Calle, Tegucigalpa; tel. 22-5963; fax 237-5187; f. 1963; Pres. JUSTO PASTOR CALDERÓN; 2 brs.

Banco Nacional de Desarrollo Agrícola (BANADESA): 4a Avda y 5a Avda, 13a y 14a Calles, Apdo 212, Tegucigalpa; tel. 237-2201; fax 237-5187; f. 1980; govt development bank (transfer to private ownership pending); loans to agricultural sector; cap. 34.5m., res 42.7m., dep. 126.9m. (March 1993); Pres. GUSTAVO A. ZELAYA CHÁVEZ; 34 brs.

Financiera Nacional de la Vivienda (FINAVI): Apdo 1194, Tegucigalpa; f. 1975; housing development bank; Exec. Pres. Lic. ELMAR LIZARDO.

Foreign Bank

Lloyds TSB Bank PLC (United Kingdom): Centro Comercial El Dorado, Blvd Morazán, Apdo 3136, Tegucigalpa; tel. 236-6864; fax 236-9211; e-mail lloydstsb@lloydstsb.hn; Man. PAUL McEVOY.

Banking Associations

Asociación Hondureña de Instituciones Bancarias (AHIBA): Blvd Suyapa entre Edif. que fue de Canón y Agencias Panamericanas, Apdo 1344, Tegucigalpa; tel. 235-6770; fax 239-0191; e-mail ahiba@ahiba.hn; f. 1956; 21 mem. banks; Exec. Dir. CAMILO ATALA F.

Comisión Nacional de Bancos y Seguros (CNBS): Edif. Anexo Banco Central de Honduras, Comayagüela, Tegucigalpa; tel. 238-0580; fax 237-6232; internet www.bch.hn/frames/; Pres. ANA CRISTINA MEJÍA DE PEREIRA.

STOCK EXCHANGE

Bolsa Hondureña de Valores: Edif. Martínez Valenzuela, 1°, 2a Calle, 3a Avda, San Pedro Sula; tel. 553-4410; fax 553-4480; e-mail bhvsps@bhv.hn2.com; Gen. Man. MARCO TULIO LÓPEZ PEREIRA.

INSURANCE

American Home Assurance Co: Edif. Los Castaños, 4°, Blvd Morazán, Apdo 3220, Tegucigalpa; tel. 232-3938; fax 232-8169; f. 1958; Mans LEONARDO MOREIRA, EDGAR WAGNER.

Aseguradora Hondureña, SA: Edif. El Planetario, 4°, Col. Lomas de Guijarro Sur, Calle Madrid, Avda Paris, Apdo 312, Tegucigalpa; tel. 232-2729; fax 231-0982; e-mail gerencia@asegurahon.hn; f. 1954; Pres. JOSÉ MARÍA AGURCIA; Gen. Man. GERARDO CORRALES.

Compañía de Seguros El Ahorro Hondureño, SA: Edif. Trinidad, Avda Colón, Apdo 3643, Tegucigalpa; tel. 237-8219; fax 237-4780; e-mail elahorro@seguroselahorro.hn; f. 1917; Pres. JORGE A. ALVARADO.

Interamericana de Seguros, SA: Col. Los Castaños, Apdo 593, Tegucigalpa; tel. 232-7614; fax 232-7762; f. 1957; Pres. CAMILO ATALA FARAJ; Gen. Man. LUIS ATALA FARAJ.

Pan American Life Insurance Co (PALIC): Edif. PALIC, Avda República de Chile 804, Tegucigalpa; tel. 220-5757; fax 232-3907; e-mail palic@david.intertel.hn; f. 1944; Gen. Man. ALBERTO AGURCIA.

Previsión y Seguros, SA: Edif. Maya, Col. Palmira, Apdo 770, Tegucigalpa; tel. 231-2127; fax 232-5215; f. 1982; Pres. Gen. HÉCTOR CASTRO CABUS; Gen. Man. P. M. ARTURO BOQUÍN OSEJO.

Seguros Atlántida: Edif. Sonisa, Costado Este Plaza Bancatlán, Tegucigalpa; tel. 232-4014; fax 232-3688; e-mail morellana@bancatlan.hn; f. 1986; Pres. GUILLERMO BUESO; Gen. Man. JUAN MIGUEL ORELLANA.

Seguros Continental, SA: 3A Avda 2 y 3, 7a Calle, Apdo 320, San Pedro Sula; tel. 550-0880; fax 550-2750; f. 1968; Pres. JAIME ROSENTHAL OLIVA; Gen. Man. MARIO R. SOLÍS.

Seguros Crefisa: Edif. Ficensa, 1°, Blvd Morazán, Apdo 3774, Tegucigalpa; tel. 238-1750; fax 238-1714; e-mail ggerencia@crefisa.hn; internet www.crefisa.hn; f. 1993; Pres. OSWALDO LÓPEZ ARELLANO; Gen. Man. MARIO BATRES PIÑEDA.

Insurance Association

Cámara Hondureña de Aseguradores (CAHDA): Edif. Los Jarros, Blvd Morazán, Local 313, Apdo 3290, Tegucigalpa; tel. 239-0342; fax 232-6020; e-mail cahda@gbm.hn; f. 1974; Man. JOSÉ LUIS MONCADA RODRÍGUEZ.

Trade and Industry

GOVERNMENT AGENCIES

Fondo Hondureño de Inversión Social (FHIS): Tegucigalpa; internet www.fhis.hn; social investment fund; Dir LEONI YUWAI.

Fondo Social de la Vivienda (FOSOVI): Col. Florencia, Tegucigalpa; tel. 239-1605; social fund for housing, urbanization and devt; Gen. Man. MARIO MARTÍ.

Secretaria Técnica del Consejo Superior de Planificación Económica (CONSUPLANE): Edif. Bancatlán, 3°, Apdo 1327, Comayagüela, Tegucigalpa; tel. 22-8738; f. 1965; national planning office; Exec. Sec. FRANCISCO FIGUEROA ZÚÑIGA.

DEVELOPMENT ORGANIZATIONS

Consejo Hondureño de la Empresa Privada (COHEP): Edif. COHEP contiguo a Plaza Visión, Calle Yoro, Col. Tepeyac, Apdo 3240, Tegucigalpa; tel. 235-3336; fax 235-3344; e-mail presidencia@

cohep.com; f. 1968; comprises 23 private enterprises; Pres. Dr JULI-ETTE HANDAL DE CASTILLO.

Corporación Financiera de Olancho: f. 1977 to co-ordinate and manage all financial aspects of the Olancho forests project; Pres. RAFAEL CALDERÓN LÓPEZ.

Corporación Hondureña de Desarrollo Forestal (COH-DEFOR): Salida Carretera del Norte, Zona El Carrizal, Comayagüela, Apdo 1378, Tegucigalpa; tel. 22-8810; fax 22-2653; f. 1974; semi-autonomous org. exercising control and man. of the forestry industry; transfer of all sawmills to private ownership was proceeding in 1991; Gen. Man. PORFIRIO LOBO S.

Dirección General de Minas e Hidrocarburos (General Directorate of Mines and Hydrocarbons): Blvd Miraflores, Apdo 981, Tegucigalpa; tel. 232-7848; fax 232-7848; Dir-Gen. MIGUEL VILLEDA VILLELA.

Instituto Hondureño del Café (IHCAFE): Apdo 40-C, Tegucigalpa; tel. 237-3131; f. 1970; coffee devt programme; Gen. Man. FERNANDO D. MONTES M.

Instituto Hondureño de Mercadeo Agrícola (IHMA): Apdo 727, Tegucigalpa; tel. 235-3193; fax 235-5719; f. 1978; agricultural devt agency; Gen. Man. TULIO ROLANDO GIRÓN ROMERO.

Instituto Nacional Agrario (INA): Col. La Almeda, 4a Avda, entre 10a y 11a Calles, No 1009, Apdo 3391, Tegucigalpa; tel. 232-8400; fax 232-8398; agricultural devt programmes; Exec. Dir ERASMO PORTILLO FERNÁNDEZ.

CHAMBERS OF COMMERCE

Cámara de Comercio e Industrias de Cortés: 17a Avda, 10a y 12a Calle, Apdo 14, San Pedro Sula; tel. 53-0761; f. 1931; 812 mems; Pres. ROBERTO REYES SILVA; Dir LUIS FERNANDO RIVERA.

Cámara de Comercio e Industrias de Tegucigalpa: Blvd Centroamérica, Apdo 3444, Tegucigalpa; tel. 232-4200; fax 232-0759; e-mail camara@ccit.hn; internet www.ccit.hn; Pres. ANTONIO TAVEL OTERO.

Federación de Cámaras de Comercio e Industrias de Honduras (FEDECAMARA): Edif. Castañito, 2°, 6a Avda, Col. los Castaños, Apdo 3393, Tegucigalpa; tel. 232-1870; fax 232-6083; e-mail fedecamara@sigmanet.hn; internet www.sieh.org; f. 1948; 1,200 mems; Pres. Ing. JAVIER CHACÓN; Exec. Dir JUAN MANUEL MOYA.

Fundación para la Inversión y Desarrollo de Exportaciones (FIDE) (Foundation for Investment and Export Development): Condominio Loma, 4°, Col. Lomas del Guijarro, POB 2029, Tegucigalpa; tel. 235-3471; fax 235-3484; internet www.hondurasinfo.hn; f. 1984; private, non-profit agency; Pres. NORMAN GARCÍA.

INDUSTRIAL AND TRADE ASSOCIATIONS

Asociación de Bananeros Independientes (ANBI) (National Association of Independent Banana Producers): San Pedro Sula; tel. 22-7336; f. 1964; 62 mems; Pres. Ing. JORGE ALBERTO ALVARADO; Sec. CECILIO TRIMINIO TURCIOS.

Asociación Hondureña de Productores de Café (Coffee Producers' Association): 10a Avda, 6a Calle, Apdo 959, Tegucigalpa.

Asociación Nacional de Exportadores de Honduras (ANEXHON) (National Association of Exporters): Tegucigalpa; comprises 104 private enterprises; Pres. Dr RICHARD ZABLAH.

Asociación Nacional de Industriales (ANDI) (National Association of Manufacturers): Blvd Los Próceres 505, Apdo 20-C, Tegucigalpa; Pres. HÉCTOR BULNES; Exec. Sec. DORCAS DE GONZALES.

Asociación Nacional de Pequeños Industriales (ANPI) (National Association of Small Industries): Apdo 730, Tegucigalpa; Pres. JUAN RAFAEL CRUZ.

Federación Nacional de Agricultores y Ganaderos de Honduras (FENAGH) (Farmers and Livestock Breeders' Association): Tegucigalpa; tel. 231-1392; Pres. ROBERTO GALLARDO LARDIZÁBAL.

Federación Nacional de Cooperativas Cañeras (Fenacocal) (National Federation of Sugar Cane Co-operatives): Tegucigalpa.

UTILITIES

Electricity

Empresa Nacional de Energía Eléctrica (ENEE) (National Electrical Energy Co): 2a ave, 9 y 10 Calles, Comayagüela, Tegucigalpa; tel. 238-5977; fax 237-9881; e-mail eneege@enee.hn; internet www.enee.hn; f. 1957; state-owned electricity co; scheduled for privatization; Pres. GILBERTO RAMOS DUBÓN; Man. ÁNGELO BOTAZZI.

TRADE UNIONS

Asociación Nacional de Empleados Públicos de Honduras (ANDEPH) (National Association of Public Employees of Honduras): Barrio Los Dolores, Avda Paulino Valladares, frente Panadería Italiana, atrás Iglesia Los Dolores, Tegucigalpa; tel. 237-4393; Pres. FAUSTO MOLINA CASTRO.

Confederación de Trabajadores de Honduras (CTH) (Workers' Confederation of Honduras): Edif. Beige, 2 , Avda Juan Ramón Molina, Barrio El Olvido, Apdo 720, Tegucigalpa; tel. 238-7859; fax 237-4243; f. 1964; affiliated to CTCA, ORIT, CIOSL, FIAET and ICFTU; Pres. WILFREDO GALEAS ANGEL MEZA; Sec.-Gen. REINA DINORA ANTÚNEZ; 200,000 mems; comprises the following federations:

Federación Central de Sindicatos Libres de Honduras (FECESITLIH) (Honduran Federation of Free Trade Unions): antiguo Edif. EUKZKADI, 3era Avda 3 y 4, Calles 336, Comayagüela, Tegucigalpa; tel. 237-3955; affiliated to CTH, ORIT, CIOSL; Pres. ROSA ALTAGRACIA FUENTES.

Federación Sindical de Trabajadores Nacionales de Honduras (FESITRANH) (Honduran Federation of Farmworkers): 10a Avda, 11a Calle, Barrio Los Andes, San Pedro Sula, Apdo 245, Cortés; tel. 57-2539; f. 1957; affiliated to CTH; Pres. MAURO FRANCISCO GONZÁLES.

Sindicato Nacional de Motoristas de Equipo Pesado de Honduras (SINAMEQUIPH) (National Union of HGV Drivers): Avda Juan Ramón Molina, Barrio El Olvido, Tegucigalpa; tel. 237-4415; affiliated to CTH, IFF; Pres. ERASMO FLORES.

Central General de Trabajadores de Honduras (CGTH) (General Confederation of Labour of Honduras): Barrio La Granja, antiguo Local CONADI, Comayagüela, Apdo 1236, Tegucigalpa; tel. 225-2509; attached to Partido Demócrata Cristiano; Sec.-Gen. FELICITO ÁVILA ORDÓÑEZ.

Federación Auténtica Sindical de Honduras (FASH): Barrio La Granja, antiguo Local CONADI, Apdo 1236, Comayagüela, Tegucigalpa; tel. 225-2509; affiliated to CGT, CCT, CLAT, CMT; Sec.-Gen. JOSÉ HUMBERTO LARA ENAMORANDO.

Federación Sindical del Sur (FESISUR): Barrio La Ceiba, una cuadra al norte del Instituto Santa María Goretti, Apdo 256, Choluteca; tel. 882-0328; affiliated to CGT, CLAT, CMT; Pres. REINA DE ORDÓÑEZ.

Federación de Trabajadores del Sur (FETRASUR) (Federation of Southern Workers): Choluteca.

Federación Unitaria de Trabajadores de Honduras (FUTH): Barrio La Granja, contiguo Banco Atlántida, Casa 3047, frente a mercadito la granja, Apdo 1663, Comayagüela, Tegucigalpa; tel. 225-1010; f. 1981; linked to left-wing electoral alliance Frente Patriótico Hondureño; Pres. JUAN ALBERTO BARAHONA MEJÍA; 45,000 mems.

Frente de Unidad Nacional Campesino de Honduras (FUNA-CAMH): f. 1980; group of farming co-operatives and six main peasant unions as follows:

Asociación Nacional de Campesinos Hondureños (ANACH) (National Association of Honduran Farmworkers): Edif. Chávez Mejía, 2°, Calle Juan Ramón Molina, Barrio El Olvido Tegucigalpa; tel. 238-0558; f. 1962; affiliated to CTH, ORIT, CIOSL; Pres. BENEDICTO CÁRCAMO MEJÍA; 80,000 mems.

Federación de Cooperativas Agropecuarias de la Reforma Agraria de Honduras (FECORAH): Casa 2223, antiguo Local de COAPALMA, Col. Rubén Darío, Tegucigalpa; tel. 232-0547; fax 225-2525; Pres. Ing. WILTON SALINAS.

Frente Nacional de Campesinos Independientes de Honduras.

Unión Nacional de Campesinos (UNC) (National Union of Farmworkers): antiguo Local CONADI, Barrio La Granja, Comayagüela, Tegucigalpa; tel. 225-1005; linked to CLAT; Sec.-Gen. RANDOLFO VELÁSQUEZ BARAHONA; c. 25,000 mems.

Unión Nacional de Campesinos Auténticos de Honduras (UNCAH).

Unión Nacional de Cooperativas Populares de Honduras (UNACOOPH).

Transport

RAILWAYS

The railway network is confined to the north of the country and most lines are used for fruit cargo.

Ferrocarril Nacional de Honduras (National Railway of Honduras): 1a Avda entre 1a y 2a Calle, Apdo 496, San Pedro Sula; tel.

and fax 552-8001; f. 1870; govt-owned; 595 km of track; Gen. Man. M. A. QUINTANILLA.

Tela Railroad Co: La Lima; tel. 56-2037; Pres. RONALD F. WALKER; Gen. Man. FREDDY KOCH.

Vaccaro Railway: La Ceiba; tel. 43-0511; fax 43-0091; fmrly operated by Standard Fruit Co.

ROADS

In 1999 there were an estimated 13,603 km of roads in Honduras, of which 20.4 km were paved. Some routes have been constructed by the Instituto Hondureño del Café and COHDEFOR in order to facilitate access to coffee plantations and forestry development areas. In November 2000 the World Bank approved a US $66.5m. loan to repair roads and bridges damaged or destroyed by 'Hurricane Mitch' in 1998. In March 2003 the Central American Bank for Economic Integration approved funding, worth $22.5m., for the construction of a highway from Puerto Cortés to the Guatemalan border.

Dirección General de Caminos: Barrio La Bolsa, Comayagüela, Tegucigalpa; tel. 225-1703; fax 225-2469; f. 1915; Dir KATHYA M. PASTOR; highways board.

SHIPPING

The principal port is Puerto Cortés on the Caribbean coast, which is the largest and best-equipped port in Central America. Other ports include Tela, La Ceiba, Trujillo/Castilla, Roatán, Amapala and San Lorenzo; all are operated by the Empresa Nacional Portuaria. There are several minor shipping companies. A number of foreign shipping lines call at Honduran ports.

Empresa Nacional Portuaria (National Port Authority): Apdo 18, Puerto Cortés; tel. 55-0192; fax 55-0968; f. 1965; has jurisdiction over all ports in Honduras; a network of paved roads connects Puerto Cortés and San Lorenzo with the main cities of Honduras, and with the principal cities of Central America; Gen. Man. ROBERTO VALENZUELA SIMÓN.

CIVIL AVIATION

Local airlines in Honduras compensate for the deficiencies of road and rail transport, linking together small towns and inaccessible districts. There are four international airports: Golosón airport in La Ceiba, Ramón Villeda Morales airport in San Pedro Sula, Toncontín airport in Tegucigalpa, and Juan Manuel Gálvaz airport in Roatán. In 2001 it was announced that San Francisco Airport, USA, was to invest some US $150m. in the four airports over two years. In 2000 plans for a new airport inside the Copán Ruinas archaeological park, 400 km west of Tegucigalpa, were announced.

Isleña Airlines: Avda San Isidro, frente al Parque Central, Apdo 402, La Ceiba; tel. 43-2683; fax 43-2632; e-mail islena@caribe.hn; internet www.caribe.hn; domestic service and service to Guatemala, Nicaragua and the Cayman Islands; Pres. and CEO ARTURO ALVARADO WOOD.

Líneas Aéreas Nacionales, SA (LANSA): La Ceiba; f. 2001; scheduled international services and flights within Central America.

Sol Air: Tegucigalpa; f. 2002; daily flights to Miami, FL, USA from Tegucigalpa and San Pedro Sula.

Tourism

Tourists are attracted by the Mayan ruins, the fishing and boating facilities in Trujillo Bay and Lake Yojoa, near San Pedro Sula, and the beaches on the northern coast. There is an increasing eco-tourism industry. In May 2001 the tomb of a Mayan king was discovered near to the Copán Ruinas archaeological park; it was expected to become an important tourist attraction. Honduras received around 470,727 tourists in 2000, when tourism receipts totalled US $240m.

Instituto Hondureño de Turismo: Edif. Europa, 5°, Col. San Carlos, Apdo 3261, Tegucigalpa; tel. 222-2124; fax 222-6621; e-mail tourismo@iht.hn; internet www.letsgohonduras.hn; f. 1972; dept of the Secretaría de Cultura y Turismo; Dir-Gen. RICARDO MARTÍNEZ.

HUNGARY

Introductory Survey

Location, Climate, Language, Religion, Flag, Capital

The Republic of Hungary (known as the Hungarian People's Republic between August 1949 and October 1989) lies in Eastern Europe, bounded to the north by Slovakia, to the east by Ukraine and Romania, to the south by the Serbian province of Vojvodina (Serbia and Montenegro) and Croatia, and to the west by Slovenia and Austria. Its climate is continental, with long, dry summers and severe winters. Temperatures in Budapest are generally between −3°C (27°F) and 28°C (82°F). The language is Hungarian (Magyar). There is a large Romany community (numbering between 500,000 and 700,000 people), and also Croat, German, Romanian, Serbian, Slovak, Slovene and Jewish minorities. Most of the inhabitants profess Christianity, and the largest single religious denomination is the Roman Catholic Church, representing about 62% of the population. Other Christian groups are the Calvinists (20%), the Lutheran Church (5%) and the Hungarian Orthodox Church. The national flag (proportions 2 by 3) consists of three equal horizontal stripes, of red, white and green. The capital is Budapest.

Recent History

Although Hungary co-operated with Nazi Germany before the Second World War and obtained additional territory when Czechoslovakia was partitioned in 1938 and 1939, when it sought to break the alliance in 1944 the country was occupied by German forces. In January 1945 Hungary was liberated by Soviet troops and signed an armistice, restoring the pre-1938 frontiers. It became a republic in February 1946. Meanwhile, land distribution, instituted in 1945, continued. Nationalization measures began in December 1946, despite opposition from the Roman Catholic Church. In the 1947 elections the communists became the largest single party, with 22.7% of the votes. The communists merged with the Social Democrats to form the Hungarian Workers' Party in June 1948. A People's Republic was established in August 1949.

As First Secretary of the Workers' Party, Mátyás Rákosi became the leading political figure, and opposition was removed by means of purges and political trials. Rákosi became Prime Minister in 1952, but after the death of the Soviet leader Stalin (Iosif V. Dzhugashvili) one year later, he was replaced by the more moderate Imre Nagy, and a short period of liberalization followed. Rákosi, however, remained as First Secretary, and in 1955 forced Nagy's resignation. András Hegedüs, sponsored by Rákosi, was appointed Prime Minister. Dissension between the Rákosi and Nagy factions increased in 1956; in July Rákosi was forced to resign but was replaced by a close associate, Ernő Gerő.

The consequent discontent provoked demonstrations against communist domination, and in October 1956 fighting broke out. Nagy was reinstated as Prime Minister, renounced membership of the Warsaw Pact (the defence grouping of the Soviet bloc) and promised other controversial reforms. In November Soviet troops, stationed in Hungary under the 1947 peace treaty, intervened, and the uprising was suppressed. A new Soviet-supported Government, led by János Kádár, was installed. Some 20,000 participants in the uprising were arrested, of whom 2,000 were subsequently executed, including Nagy and four associates. Many opponents of the regime were deported to the USSR. Kádár, who was appointed the leader of the renamed Hungarian Socialist Workers' Party (HSWP), held the premiership until January 1958, and from September 1961 to July 1965.

In march 1985 a HSWP Congress re-elected Kádár leader of the party, with the new title of General Secretary of the Central Committee. The Congress reaffirmed the party's commitment to economic reforms, which had been introduced in 1968. The legislative election in June 1985 was the first to give voters a wider choice of candidates under the system of mandatory multiple nominations. In June 1987 Pál Losonczi was replaced in the largely ceremonial post of President of the Presidential Council by Károly Németh, a leading member of the HSWP. Károly Grósz, a member of the Politburo, was appointed Chairman of the Council of Ministers.

At a special ideological conference of the HSWP, held in May 1988, Kádár was replaced as General Secretary of the Central Committee by Károly Grósz, and promoted to the newly created and purely ceremonial post of HSWP President; he lost his membership of the Politburo. About one-third of the members of the Central Committee (in particular, conservative associates of Kádár) were replaced by younger politicians. The new Politburo included Rezső Nyers, who had been largely responsible for the economic reforms initiated in 1968, but who had been removed from the Politburo in 1975. Grósz declared his commitment to radical economic and political change, although he excluded the immediate possibility of a multi-party political system. In June 1988 Dr Brunó Ferenc Straub, who was not a member of the HSWP, was elected to the post of President of the Presidential Council, in succession to Károly Németh. In November Miklós Németh, a prominent member of the HSWP, replaced Grósz as Chairman of the Council of Ministers.

Following Grósz's appointment as leader of the HSWP, there was a relaxation of censorship laws and independent political groups were formally established. In January 1989 the right to strike was fully legalized. In the same month the National Assembly enacted two laws guaranteeing the right to demonstrate and to form associations and political parties independent of the HSWP. In February the HSWP agreed to abandon the clause in the Constitution upholding the party's leading role in society. In the following month an estimated 100,000 people took part in a peaceful anti-Government demonstration in Budapest, in support of demands for democracy, free elections, the withdrawal of Soviet troops, and an official commemoration of the 1956 uprising and of the execution of Imre Nagy in 1958.

During 1989 there was increasing evidence of dissension within the HSWP between conservative and reformist members. (At least 100,000 members had tendered their resignation between late 1987 and early 1989.) In April the Politburo was replaced by a smaller body. In the following month the Council of Ministers declared its independence from the HSWP; Kádár was relieved of his post as President of the HSWP and of his membership of the Central Committee of the party, officially for health reasons. In June a radical restructuring of the HSWP was effected, following increasing dissatisfaction among members with Grósz's leadership: although Grósz remained as General Secretary of the party, the newly elected Chairman, Rezső Nyers, effectively emerged as the party's leading figure.

In June 1989 discussions were initiated between the HSWP and representatives of opposition groups regarding the holding of multi-party elections, changes to the presidential structure, amendments to the Constitution and economic reforms. Evidence of the opposition's increasing strength was provided at a provincial by-election in July, when a joint candidate of the centre-right Hungarian Democratic Forum (HDF), the liberal Alliance of Free Democrats (AFD) and the Federation of Young Democrats (FYD) became the first opposition deputy since 1947 to win representation in the legislature. Four of five further by-elections were won by opposition candidates in July–September.

At an HSWP Congress in October 1989, delegates voted to reconstitute the party as the Hungarian Socialist Party (HSP), with Nyers as Chairman. The HSP initially failed to attract a large membership, however, and in December HSWP activists declared that their party had not been dissolved, and that it retained a membership of around 80,000. Gyula Thürmer was elected the HSWP President.

On 23 October 1989 (the anniversary of the 1956 uprising) the Republic of Hungary was proclaimed. In preparation the National Assembly approved fundamental amendments to the Constitution, including the removal of the clause guaranteeing one-party rule. A new electoral law was approved, and the Presidential Council was replaced by the post of President of the Republic. Mátyás Szűrös, the President of the National Assembly (Speaker), was named President of the Republic, on an interim basis.

Hungary's first free multi-party elections since 1945 were held, in two rounds, on 25 March and 8 April 1990. The elections were held under a mixed system of proportional and direct representation and were contested by a total of 28 parties and groups. The HDF received the largest proportion of the total votes cast (42.7%) and 165 of the 386 seats in the National Assembly. The Independent Smallholders' Party (ISP, which advocated the restoration to its original owners of land collectivized after 1947) and the Christian Democratic People's Party (CDPP), both of which contested the second round of the election in alliance with the HDF, secured 43 and 21 seats, respectively. The AFD obtained the second largest proportion of the votes (23.8%), winning 92 seats in the Assembly. The FYD, which was closely aligned with the AFD, obtained 21 seats. The HSP, with 8.5% of the votes, secured 33 seats in the legislature. The HSWP failed to secure the 4% of the votes required for representation.

A coalition Government was formed in May 1990, comprising members of the HDF (which held the majority of posts), together with members of the ISP, the CDPP and three independents. József Antall, the Chairman of the HDF, had earlier been elected to chair the new Council of Ministers. Among the declared aims of the new Government was membership of the European Community (now European Union—EU, see p. 199) and a full transition to a Western-style market economy. In August Árpád Göncz, a writer and member of the AFD, was elected President of the Republic by a substantial majority of the legislature. In May Gyula Horn, the Minister of Foreign Affairs in the outgoing Government, had replaced Nyers as leader of the HSP.

At elections in September and October 1990, designed to replace the Soviet-style council system with a system of multi-party self-governing local bodies, a coalition of the AFD and the FYD won control of Budapest and many other cities, while in rural areas independent candidates obtained a majority of the votes. The governing coalition's poor result was attributed, in large part, to its failure to redress the recent sharp increase in the rates of inflation and unemployment.

In mid-1991 the National Assembly approved legislation to compensate the former owners of land and property that had been expropriated between 1939 and 1989. In May the National Assembly approved legislation to provide compensation for persons killed, imprisoned or deported, or whose property had been expropriated, for political reasons during the period 1939–89. Further legislation was approved in early 1993 allowing for prosecutions in connection with crimes committed under the communist regime.

In February 1992 the Chairman of the ISP, József Torgyán, announced that his party was to withdraw from the government coalition, in protest at what he claimed to be a lack of political influence. However, most of the ISP's deputies in the National Assembly refused to withdraw their support for the Government, thus causing a rift in the party. In April as many as 20,000 people were reported to have attended an anti-Government demonstration organized by Torgyán in Budapest. The split in the party was formalized in June, when members who remained loyal to Antall suspended Torgyán as their Chairman, and elected László Horváth to chair what subsequently became the United Historic Smallholders' Party.

In September 1992 some 50,000 people demonstrated in Budapest against extreme right-wing figures, including the Vice-Chairman of the HDF, István Csurka; the Government's failure to censure Csurka prompted widespread criticism. At an HDF congress in January 1993 Antall avoided a threatened revolt by accepting the election of six right-wing extremists to the party's presidium. In May Lajos Für resigned from his position as Secretary-General of the HDF, claiming that he had not been able to maintain the unity of the party, which was divided between supporters of Csurka and centrists led by Antall. In July, however, Csurka was expelled from the HDF for his increasingly unacceptable views. (He subsequently founded the Hungarian Justice and Life Party—HJLP.) Antall died in December; he was succeeded as Prime Minister by Dr Péter Boross, an independent and hitherto the Minister of the Interior, who had acted as premier while Antall was receiving medical treatment. In February 1994 Für was elected Chairman of the HDF.

Legislative elections, which took place on 8 and 29 May 1994, resulted in a clear parliamentary majority for the HSP, which received 33.0% of the votes cast for regional party lists and won 209 of the National Assembly's 386 seats. The AFD won 19.8% of the votes and 70 seats, while the HDF won only 11.7% of the votes and 37 seats. The Independent Smallholders' and Peasants' Party (ISPP—formerly the ISP), the CDPP and the FYD won, respectively, 26, 22 and 20 seats. Csurka's HJLP attracted only 1.6% of the votes in the first round and did not proceed to the second. Horn announced that the HSP would be willing to

form a government with the AFD, and the two parties signed a coalition agreement (whereby the HSP was to control the majority of posts in the Council of Ministers, while the AFD would have the right to veto government decisions) in late June. With 279 seats in the National Assembly, the coalition held the two-thirds' majority necessary to institute constitutional reforms. Horn was invested as Prime Minister in July. At municipal elections in December the HSP won 32.3% of the votes and the AFD 15.7%.

Meanwhile, controversy over alleged government interference in branches of the mass media had arisen in mid-1992. During 1992–93 many senior media figures had resigned or been dismissed, and in October 1993 some 10,000 people had demonstrated in Budapest to demand press freedom. In June 1994 129 Hungarian Radio employees, who had been dismissed in March, ostensibly for economic reasons, were reinstated; their dismissal had prompted further mass demonstrations and widespread accusations that the Government sought to use the state radio service for propaganda purposes, since many of those dismissed were known for their anti-Government views. In July, however, the directors of Hungarian Radio and Hungarian Television were dismissed, having been accused of favouring the former HDF administration. In October the Constitutional Court declared government interference in the media to be unlawful.

In January 1995 László Bekesi, the HSP Minister of Finance, resigned, following disagreements with Horn regarding economic reform; the Director of the State Property Agency was dismissed in the same month, owing to alleged mismanagement. In late February Dr Lajos Bokros of the HSP was designated Minister of Finance, and Horn appointed Tamás Suchman, also of the HSP, to the newly created post of Minister for Privatization, under the jurisdiction of the Ministry of Finance. A new president of the central bank was also appointed. Economic austerity measures, adopted in March, prompted strong domestic criticism, and the ministers responsible for public health and for national security (both members of the HSP) resigned shortly after the programme was announced. In May the National Assembly approved legislation that was designed to accelerate the privatization process. On 19 June Göncz was re-elected President of the Republic by the National Assembly. At the end of June the Constitutional Court ruled that elements of the austerity programme announced (specifically those relating to welfare provisions) were unconstitutional. Accordingly, in late July the National Assembly approved new adjustments, including increases in fuel prices and reductions in government expenditure, in an attempt to mitigate losses arising from the judgment. The economic programme continued to cause dissent within the Government, and the HSP Minister of Labour tendered her resignation in October, in protest at the social consequences. In late November, following a ruling by the Constitutional Court against the validity of further provisions of the austerity programme, Bokros submitted his resignation, although this was rejected by Horn. In mid-February 1996, however, Bokros again tendered his resignation (which was accepted). A banker, Péter Medgyessy, who had been Chairman of the Planning and Economic Committee in the administration of Miklós Németh, was appointed the new Minister of Finance.

Division was reported in the HDF in early March 1996, following the election of Sándor Lezsák to the party leadership. Denouncing what it regarded as an increasingly nationalistic tendency in the party, a faction led by Iván Szabó (who had been Minister of Finance in the HDF Government) formed a new organization, the Hungarian Democratic People's Party. In August Imre Dunai resigned from the post of Minister of Industry and Trade, ostensibly on grounds of ill health; it was reported that he had opposed the proposed increases in fuel prices. Dunai was replaced by Tamás Suchman (who retained responsibility for the privatization portfolio). In January 1997 the Government finally increased fuel prices, although by far less than originally envisaged. Meanwhile, in October 1996 the Government removed the directors of the Hungarian Privatization and State Holding Company (ÁPV Rt—formed in 1995 by the amalgamation of the State Property Agency and State Holding Company), after it emerged that they had endorsed payments that contravened the body's internal regulations. Horn subsequently announced the dismissal of Suchman from the Government.

In September 1997 Horn rejected demands that he resign from office by a committee that had been established to investigate the past of senior politicians; the committee claimed that Horn had served with a paramilitary force that had restored communist power following the 1956 rebellion, and that he had suppressed political opposition through the security services. Meanwhile, following a NATO summit meeting, which took place in Madrid, Spain, in July 1997, Hungary was invited to enter into discussions regarding its application for membership of the Organization. A national referendum on the country's entry into NATO was conducted on 16 November, at which its accession was approved by 85.3% of the votes cast, with the participation of 49% of the electorate. In December the HDF established an electoral alliance with the Federation of Young Democrats—Hungarian Civic Party (FYD—HCP, which had been reconstituted from the FYD) and the Hungarian Christian Democratic Federation, a newly formed association of break-away members of the CDPP.

The first round of the legislative election, which was contested by 26 parties, took place on 10 May 1998: the HSP secured 32.3% of the votes cast, the FYD—HCP won 28.2% of the votes, and the ISPP 13.8%. Following a second round of voting on 24 May, however, the FYD—HCP, with 147 seats, obtained the highest representation in the National Assembly; the HSP received 134 seats, the ISPP 48, the HDF 18 and the HJLP 14. The defeat of the HSP was widely attributed to discontent with social and economic conditions, and the increasing rate of crime. At the inaugural session of the new legislature in June, a member of the FYD—HCP, János Áder, was elected President of the National Assembly. In the same month, following inter-party negotiations, the FYD—HCP signed an agreement with the HDF and the ISPP, providing for the formation of a new coalition government. In early July the Chairman of the FYD—HCP, Viktor Orbán, was elected to the office of Prime Minister by the National Assembly, which subsequently approved the installation of a new Council of Ministers, comprising 11 representatives of the FYD—HCP, four of the ISPP (later renamed the Independent Smallholders' and Civic Party—ISCP), one of the HDF and one of the Hungarian Christian Democratic Federation. The new Government presented a programme for the reduction of crime and the improvement of social and economic conditions.

In September 1998, following the resignation of Horn from the leadership of the HSP, in response to the party's electoral defeat, a former minister, László Kovács, was elected Chairman. Local government elections were conducted in October: it was reported that the three government coalition parties had received 39.6% of the votes cast, while the HSP and AFD won 35.1% of the votes. In December the HSP and AFD deputies boycotted the legislature, in protest at government proposals for the appointment of new management boards of the state media supervisory bodies. In February 1999 the National Assembly approved Hungary's membership of NATO, and the country formally joined the Organization in the following month. In December Orbán implemented a minor government reorganization. At an FYD—HCP congress in January 2000, László Kövér, hitherto the Minister without Portfolio responsible for National Security, replaced Orbán as leader of the party; he was to resign from the Council of Ministers later that year.

In the presidential election, held on 5 June 2000, Ferenc Mádl, the sole candidate, obtained 251 votes out of the possible 386 in the first round of voting. As he had failed to obtain the requisite two-thirds' majority, a second round of voting was held on 6 June. However, this ballot, too, proved inconclusive and a final round of voting was held on the same day. Mádl took office on 4 August.

In December 2000 Mihály Varga was nominated to succeed Zsigmond Járai as Minister of Finance from March 2001, when Járai was to become Governor of the National Bank. In January a power struggle within the leadership of the ISCP resulted in the expulsion of a deputy, László Csucs, from the National Assembly and the dismissal of the Chairman of the party's Budapest branch. Csucs and four disaffected deputies subsequently attempted to remove József Torgyán from the leadership of the ISCP while he was on an official visit overseas. Upon his return, the four deputies resigned from the ISCP, thereby reducing the party's representation in the National Assembly to 43. In February Torgyán resigned his position as Minister of Agriculture and Regional Development, owing to his implication in a corruption scandal at his ministry. András Vonza was appointed to succeed him in March. In May, at its party convention in Budapest, the ISCP's parliamentary faction voted to elect Zsolt Lányi as its leader, and subsequently voted to expel Torgyán; simultaneously, however, Torgyán was returned as Chairman of the ISCP at a party convention in Cegléd. The

procedural committee of the National Assembly subsequently ruled that Torgyán should, thereafter, hold the status of an independent deputy in the legislature. (Torgyán was finally removed from the chairmanship of the ISCP in May 2002, and expelled from the party in November.)

In June 2001 the National Assembly passed the 'status' law on Hungarians in neighbouring states. The law, which came into force at the beginning of January 2002, granted ethnic Hungarians living in adjacent countries education, employment and medical rights in Hungary (although not permanent residence), thereby prompting protests from Romania and Slovakia (see below) that the law discriminated against their non-ethnic Hungarian populations, and constituted a violation of sovereignty. The law was regarded by the opposition as a populist measure in advance of the parliamentary elections, which were scheduled to be held in April 2002.

In September 2001 the governing FYD—HCP and HDF signed a co-operation agreement for the forthcoming legislative elections; in December a number of ISCP deputies (including the Minister of the Environment, Béla Turi-Kovács) agreed to participate in the election in co-operation with the FYD—HCP and the HDF. The legislative elections were held, as scheduled, on 7 and 21 April 2002. Although the FYD—HCP-HDF alliance won 48.7% of the total votes cast (188 seats), a left-wing coalition of the HSP (46.1% of the votes and 178 seats) and the AFD (5.2% of the votes and 20 seats) secured an overall majority in the National Assembly. Péter Medgyessy of the HSP was sworn in as Prime Minister on 27 May; the Council of Ministers comprised eight further members of the HSP, four members of the AFD and three independents. The new Government consisted of 14 ministries, following the merger of the Ministries of Economic Affairs and of Transport and Water Management, the abolition of the Ministry of Social and Family Affairs, and the creation of two new ministries of Labour and Employment and of Information Technology and Communications; the Minister without Portfolio attached to the Office of the Prime Minister was awarded substantial additional areas of responsibility.

In June 2002 media allegations prompted the new Prime Minister to reveal that he had served as a counter-intelligence agent at the Ministry of Finance in 1977–82. Medgyessy insisted that he had worked to protect sensitive economic information from the KGB (the Soviet secret service), in order to negotiate Hungarian membership of the IMF, and the Government announced plans for legislation that would grant improved access to secret service records; the AFD (which had originally been founded by anti-communist dissidents in 1988) subsequently retracted its threat to withdraw from the governing coalition. In July two parliamentary commissions were established to investigate both the past role of Medgyessy and the alleged links of other post-communist government officials with the Soviet-era security service. Meanwhile, in early July the leader of the FYD—HCP, Zoltán Pokorni, who had led demands for Medgyessy's resignation, had relinquished his own party and parliamentary posts, after his father's role as a communist informer was revealed. It subsequently emerged that several members of the FYD—HCP (which had emphasized its anti-communist past during campaigning for the legislative election) had counter-intelligence associations, thereby severely damaging the party's reputation. Controversy increased in August, when two senior conservative figures, President Mádl and the Governor of the National Bank, Zsigmond Járai, reportedly refused to allow information pertaining to their own counter-intelligence histories to be made public. Local elections took place on 20 October, in which the governing coalition consolidated its position; the results of the elections confirmed the FYD—HCP's diminishing popularity.

In mid-December 2002 the National Assembly voted to adopt a number of constitutional amendments, which were required in order to enable the country to become a full member of the EU. In a national referendum, held on 12 April 2003, some 84% of participants voted in support of Hungarian membership of the EU. Meanwhile, in mid-February the Minister without Portfolio attached to the Prime Minister's office, Elemér Kiss, became the first minister to resign from the HSP-AFD Government, owing to allegations of corruption. He was replaced by Péter Kiss, hitherto the Minister of Labour and Employment; Sándor Burány took the labour and employment portfolio. However, Medgyessy's failure to consult the minority AFD before reorganizing the Council of Ministers temporarily led to tensions within the governing coalition.

There has been considerable activism within Hungary by the country's ethnic minorities for the protection of their rights. In July 1993 the National Assembly adopted legislation guaranteeing the cultural, civil and political rights of 12 minority groups and prohibiting all forms of ethnic discrimination. Following the approval of this legislation, minority-rights activists launched a new campaign to change Hungary's electoral law, with the aim of securing the direct representation of ethnic groups in the legislature. In the 1994 municipal elections, ethnic minorities were able to elect their own local ethnic authorities, with consultative roles on cultural and educational issues affecting the community. In February 1995 Hungary signed the Council of Europe (see p. 181) Convention on the Protection of National Minorities. In April the Roma of Hungary elected their own governing body, the National Autonomous Authority of the Romany Minority (the first such body in the former Eastern bloc), which was empowered to administer funds and deliberate issues affecting the Roma; none the less, an increase in overt nationalism among the parties of the right became an issue of considerable concern in the 1990s. In the elections held in April 1995 and in January 1999 all of the Authority's 53 seats were won by the Lungo Drom Alliance, led by Florian Farkas. Further elections to the National Autonomous Authority, which took place in January 2003, were declared invalid, and new elections were held on 1 March. The left-wing Democratic Roma Coalition secured 49 of the 53 seats available, in the first defeat for the Lungo Drom Alliance.

In August 1996 Hungary and Romania finalized a bilateral treaty (which was formally signed in September), guaranteeing the inviolability of the joint border between the two countries and the rights of ethnic minorities. In February 1997 the Ministers of Defence of Hungary and Romania signed a co-operation agreement, providing for the protection and exchange of military secrets between the two countries, and the establishment of a joint military unit, which would be deployed in peace-keeping operations. In May President Göncz made an official visit to Romania (the first by a Hungarian Head of State). In January 2000 an environmental disaster in Romania, caused by a cyanide spill at the Baia Mare gold mine, poisoned the Tisza river, which flows through Hungary, prompting tensions between the two countries. The mine subsequently accepted full responsibility for the disaster and compensation was to be awarded.

In early August 2001 a meeting between Viktor Orbán and Prime Minister Adrian Năstase of Romania failed to resolve the tensions arising from Hungary's decision to introduce the 'status' law on Hungarians beyond the borders (see above) from January 2002. (There were some 1,434,377 ethnic Hungarians in Romania in 2002.) However, a memorandum of understanding was signed by the two Prime Ministers in late December 2001, which extended the short-term employment rights offered to ethnic Hungarians under the terms of the law to all Romanian citizens. In October 2002 President Mádl made a state visit to Romania.

Apart from issues arising from the presence of a large ethnic Hungarian minority in Slovakia (numbering almost 520,528 in 2001), relations between Hungary and Slovakia have been strained by a dispute over the Gabčíkovo-Nagymaros hydroelectric project (a joint Hungarian-Czechoslovak scheme initiated in 1977), involving the diversion of a 222-km stretch of the River Danube and the construction of a twin-dam system. In November 1989 the Hungarian Government announced that it was abandoning the scheme, following pressure from environmentalists. Czechoslovakia decided, in July 1991, to proceed unilaterally with the project; the resumption of work, in February 1992, prompted the Hungarian Government to abrogate the 1977 treaty with effect from May 1992. In April 1993 it was agreed to refer the case to the International Court of Justice (ICJ) and to operate a temporary water-management scheme in the mean time.

In March 1995 (despite protests by nationalists within Hungary against concessions made by the Government) Horn and his Slovak counterpart, Vladimír Mečiar, signed a Treaty of Friendship and Co-operation in which the two countries undertook to guarantee the rights of ethnic minorities and recognized the inviolability of their joint border. The Treaty finally came into effect in May 1996, following its ratification by the Slovak President. In August 1997 discussions between Horn and Mečiar resulted in an agreement that a joint committee be established to monitor the standard of human rights of ethnic Hungarians resident in Slovakia and the Slovak community in Hungary; however, there was subsequent dissent over the composition of the proposed committee. In September relations between Hungary and Slovakia became strained, after Horn rejected a suggestion by Mečiar that a voluntary repatriation programme for the respective ethnic communities in the two countries be initiated. Later in September the ICJ concluded proceedings regarding the dispute over the Gabčíkovo-Nagymaros hydroelectric project, ruling that both countries had contravened international law: Hungary had breached the terms of the agreement by withdrawing from the project, and the former Czechoslovakia had continued work without the permission of the Hungarian Government. Both Hungary and Slovakia were required to pay compensation for damages incurred, and to resume negotiations regarding the further implementation of the agreement. Hungarian and Slovak delegations were subsequently established to conduct discussions on the ruling of the ICJ. In December 1999 Hungary submitted a document to the Slovak Government, in which it renounced any claim to a share of the hydroelectric energy produced by the dam project, but requested an increase in the flow of common water along the Danube, in order to maintain the ecological balance. In February 2001 Slovakia accepted that it had no legal means to compel Hungary to proceed with the project, but stated that it would seek compensation from the Hungarian Government. The entry into force of the Hungarian 'status' law (see above) in January 2002 threatened to damage relations with Slovakia, although that country had in place a similar law, which granted privileges to the Slovakian diaspora. In February the Slovak parliament voted to reject the Hungarian law, claiming that it abrogated the treaty of May 1996. Meanwhile, relations with Slovakia and the Czech Republic became strained in February 2002, after Prime Minister Orbán made a statement urging that the withdrawal of the Beneš Decrees, which had provided for, in particular, the expulsion of ethnic Germans from Czechoslovakia after the Second World War, be a prerequisite for the accession of those countries to the EU. The Prime Ministers of Slovakia and the Czech Republic subsequently refused to attend a summit meeting of the four countries of the Visegrad Group (established by the Czech Republic, Hungary, Poland and Slovakia, following the collapse of communist rule, to promote economic, defence and other co-operation in the region), which had been scheduled to take place in March. In early March 2003 the Council of Europe drafted a resolution urging the Hungarian Government to amend the status law. Also in early March, however, Hungary agreed to suspend the application of the law in Slovakia, pending the approval by the National Assembly of a draft amendment stipulating that the legislation was not to apply in EU member countries (Slovakia was expected to accede to the EU in 2004, along with Hungary—see below).

In November 1990 Hungary was the first Eastern European country to become a member of the Council of Europe. Hungary's associate membership of the EU came into effect on 1 February 1994, and in April of that year Hungary became the first post-communist state to apply for full EU membership; in December 2002 Hungary was one of 10 countries formally invited to join the EU in May 2004, although it was not expected to adopt the common European currency, the euro, until 2007. In March 1996 Hungary was admitted to the Organisation for Economic Co-operation and Development (OECD, see p. 277). From December 1995 US troops belonging to the NATO-controlled Implementation Force in Bosnia and Herzegovina (IFOR) were stationed at an air base at Taszar, in south-western Hungary; a second base was subsequently established at the southern town of Pécs. In May 1996 the Government indicated that it would be willing for US troops to remain in Hungary, following the withdrawal of peace-keeping forces from Bosnia and Herzegovina. Hungary contributed some 450 troops to IFOR in 1996, and continued to support its replacement Stabilization Force (SFOR, see p. 274). Hungary was formally admitted to NATO in March 1999 (see above), although it was subsequently subject to some criticism for failing to fulfil its financial commitments. During the NATO bombardment of Yugoslavia (which commenced in late March 1999—see chapter on Serbia and Montenegro) the Government allowed NATO forces to use Hungarian military bases and airspace. The base at Taszar was also used by the USA in early 2003 for the training of Iraqi opposition forces in relation to the US-led campaign to bring about 'regime change' in Iraq (see the chapters on the USA and Iraq).

Government

Legislative power is held by the unicameral National Assembly (Országgyűlés), comprising 386 members, who are elected for four years by universal adult suffrage under a mixed system of proportional and direct representation. The President of the Republic (Head of State) is elected by the National Assembly for a term of five years. The President, who is also Commander-in-Chief of the Armed Forces, may be re-elected for a second term. The Council of Ministers, the highest organ of state administration, is elected by the Assembly on the recommendation of the President. For local administrative purposes Hungary is divided into 19 counties (*megyei*) and the capital city (with 22 districts). A 53-member National Autonomous Authority of the Romany Minority, first elected in April 1995, is empowered to administer funds disbursed by the central Government.

Defence

Military service begins at the age of 18 years. The period of military service was reduced from one year to nine months in November 1997, and further reduced to six months in June 2001, with effect from March 2002. Compulsory military service was scheduled to be abolished in 2005. The total regular forces in August 2002 numbered 33,400 (including 22,900 conscripts): army 23,600, air force 7,700 and centrally controlled personnel 2,100. Paramilitary forces comprised 12,000 border guards, as well as 2,000 members of the internal security forces. In March 1999 Hungary became a member of NATO. Government expenditure on defence in 2000 was 142,600m. forint (representing 2.7% of total expenditure). Defence expenditure amounted to some 265,000m. in 2001, in line with NATO recommendations that Hungary increase its spending on defence to the equivalent of 2% of GDP by 2006.

Economic Affairs

In 2001, according to estimates by the World Bank, Hungary's gross national income (GNI), measured at average 1999–2001 prices, was US $48,924m., equivalent to $4,800 per head (or $12,570 per head on an international purchasing-power parity basis). During 1990–2001, it was estimated, the population decreased at an average annual rate of 0.2%, while gross domestic product (GDP) per head increased, in real terms, by an average of 1.2% per year. Hungary's overall GDP increased, in real terms, at an average annual rate of 1.0% during 1990–2001; real GDP grew by 5.2% in 2000 and by 3.8% in 2001.

Agriculture (including forestry and fishing) contributed an estimated 4.1% of GDP in 2000 and 6.2% of the employed labour force were engaged in the sector in 2001. The principal crops are wheat, maize, sugar beet, barley and potatoes. Viticulture is also important. During 1990–2000, according to the World Bank, real agricultural GDP declined at an average annual rate of 3.3%. The GDP of the sector increased by 0.9% in 1999, but declined by 3.5% in 2000.

Industry (including mining, manufacturing, construction, and power) contributed an estimated 33.8% of GDP in 2000, and engaged 34.2% of the employed labour force in 2001. According to preliminary government figures, 52% of total industrial production was exported in 2002; industrial exports increased by 8.7% in 2001 and by 5.7% in 2002. In 2002 the output of construction increased by 20% compared with the previous year, owing to state-financed infrastructural investment. The World Bank estimated that real industrial GDP increased at an average annual rate of 2.5% in 1990–2000. Industrial GDP increased by 7.2% in 1999 and by 9.2% in 2000.

Mining and quarrying accounted for only 0.3% of GDP in 2000, and engaged 0.3% of the employed labour force in 2001. Hungary's most important mineral resources are lignite (brown coal) and natural gas. Petroleum, bauxite and hard coal are also exploited. During 1990–98 the output of the mining sector declined at an average annual rate of 11.1%. Production fell by 8.4% in 1997 and by 20.4% in 1998.

The manufacturing sector contributed an estimated 25.2% of GDP in 2000, and engaged 24.8% of the employed labour force in 2001. In 1995 the principal branches of the sector, in terms of their contribution to gross production, were food products (accounting for 22.6% of the total), machinery and electrical equipment (13.2%), metals and metal products (11.9%) and chemicals (10.6%). Manufacturing GDP increased, in real terms, at an average annual rate of 7.6% in 1991–2000. Manufacturing GDP increased by 8.0% in 1999 and by 11.0% in 2000.

In 1999 37.9% of Hungary's electricity production was generated by nuclear power, 25.9% was generated by coal, 21.1% by natural gas and 14.3% by petroleum. Fuel imports represented 8.4% of the value of total merchandise imports in 2000.

The services sector has a significant role in the Hungarian economy, contributing an estimated 62.1% of GDP in 2000, and engaging 59.6% of the employed labour force in 2001. According to the World Bank, the GDP of the services sector increased, in real terms, at an average rate of 1.0% per year in 1990–2000. The GDP of the services sector increased by 3.2% in 1999 and by 2.9% in 2000.

In 2001 Hungary recorded a visible trade deficit of US $2,018m., and there was a deficit of $1,097m. on the current account of the balance of payments. In 2001 the principal source of imports was Germany (accounting for 24.9% of the total); other major sources were Italy, Austria and Russia. Germany was also the principal market for exports in that year (35.6%); other important purchasers were Austria, Italy and France. The principal exports in 2000 were machinery and transport equipment, basic manufactures, miscellaneous manufactured articles (most notably clothing and accessories), chemical products, and food and live animals. The main imports in that year were machinery and transport equipment (most notably electrical machinery and apparatus), basic manufactures, miscellaneous manufactured articles, chemical products and mineral fuels.

Hungary's overall budgetary deficit in 2000 was an estimated 464,700m. forint (equivalent to 4.2% of GDP). The country's total external debt at the end of 2000 was estimated to be US $29,415m., of which $14,251m. was long-term public debt. In that year the cost of debt-servicing was equivalent to 24.4% of the value of exports of goods and services. The annual rate of inflation averaged 13.0% in 1990–2001; consumer prices increased by 9.2% in 2001 and by 5.3% in 2002. The average rate of unemployment was 5.8% in 2002.

Hungary is a member (as a 'Country of Operations') of the European Bank for Reconstruction and Development (EBRD, see p. 193). Hungary became an associate member of the EU in February 1994, and subsequently applied for full EU membership. In March 1996 Hungary was admitted to OECD. Hungary was expected to accede to the EU in May 2004.

In 1990 the Hungarian Government pledged to effect a full transition to a Western-style market economy, although a liberalization programme was accompanied by economic hardship. In 1994 the Government announced a series of devaluations of the forint, a widening and acceleration of the privatization programme, and reductions in expenditure on social security and welfare. By the late 1990s the Government's fiscal policy had resulted in a decline in both the public-sector deficit and the rate of inflation. In December 1999 it was announced that, as a result of the success in achieving economic stabilization, Hungary would be one of the first of the applicant nations to be admitted to the EU; in December 2002 it was invited to become a full member in May 2004. Despite the global economic downturn, Hungary maintained growth in 2001–02. Although the rate of GDP growth decelerated slightly in 2002, to 3.3%, according to preliminary figures, that figure compared favourably with other regional economies, and consumer-price inflation was reduced. However, the current-account deficit increased dramatically in 2002, primarily owing to a decline in the export of services, particularly in the tourism sector. The budgetary deficit also increased in 2002, to represent some 9% of GDP; the budget for 2003 aimed to reduce the deficit to the equivalent of 4.5% of GDP. None the less, in early 2003 the IMF warned Hungary that it must reduce fiscal spending or anticipate the introduction of economic austerity measures if it was to fulfil the economic criteria for EU accession; the Fund also recommended that salaries be maintained at their existing levels (following pledges of increases in 2002). In mid-2002 Hungary had been removed from the Financial Action Task Force's list of countries identified as havens for 'money-laundering' (the processing of illegally obtained funds into legitimate accounts). However, the rate of foreign investment slowed in that year, and it was expected to decline further in 2003 owing to increased production costs, resulting from higher salaries, inflationary pressures and the increasing strength of the country's currency.

Education

Children under the age of three years attend crèches (bölcsődék), and those between the ages of three and six years attend kindergartens (óvodák). Education is compulsory between the ages of six and 16 years. Primary education begins at six years of age, with the basic school (általános iskola), and continues until the age of 14. In 2000 primary enrolment included 98% of children in the relevant age-group, while the comparable ratio for secondary education was 97%. In southern Hungary bilingual schools have been established to promote the languages of the national minorities. The majority of children continue with their education after 16 years of age. The most popular types of secondary school are the grammar school (gimnázium) and the secondary vocational school (szakközépiskola). The gimnázium provides a four-year course of mainly academic studies, although some vocational training does feature on the curriculum. The szakközépiskola offers full vocational training together with a general education, emphasis being laid on practical work. Apprentice training schools (szakmunkásképző intézetek) are attached to factories, agricultural co-operatives, etc., and lead to full trade qualifications. Further educational reform is being directed at revising the curricula and the method of assessing pupils. In 1999–2000 the system of higher education underwent a major transformation, as a result of which, from 1 January 2000, there were 30 state-run universities and colleges, 26 church universities and colleges and six colleges run by various foundations. In 2000 an estimated 25% of the relevant age-group continued into tertiary education. Expenditure on education in 2000 was some 256,200m. forint (equivalent to 4.8% of total government expenditure). In 2003 the Government allocated more than 1,000m. forint in grants to support Romany students pursuing higher education.

Public Holidays

2003: 1 January (New Year's Day), 15 March (Anniversary of 1848 uprising against Austrian rule), 21 April (Easter Monday), 1 May (Labour Day), 9 June (Whit Monday), 15 August (Assumption), 20 August (Constitution Day), 23 October (Day of the Proclamation of the Republic), 1 November (All Saints' Day), 25–26 December (Christmas).

2004: 1 January (New Year's Day), 15 March (Anniversary of 1848 uprising against Austrian rule), 12 April (Easter Monday), 1 May (Labour Day), 31 May (Whit Monday), 15 August (Assumption), 20 August (Constitution Day), 23 October (Day of the Proclamation of the Republic), 1 November (All Saints' Day), 25–26 December (Christmas).

Weights and Measures

The metric system is in force.

Statistical Survey

Source (unless otherwise stated): Központi Statisztikai Hivatal (Hungarian Central Statistical Office), 1525 Budapest, Keleti Károly u. 5–7; tel. (1) 345-6136; fax (1) 345-6378; e-mail erzsebet.veto@office.ksh.hu; internet www.ksh.hu.

Area and Population

AREA, POPULATION AND DENSITY

Area (sq km)	93,030*
Population (census results)	
1 January 1990	10,374,823
1 February 2001	
Males	4,863,610
Females	5,333,509
Total	10,197,119
Population (official estimates at 30 December)†	
2001	10,175,000
2002	10,152,000
Density (per sq km) at 30 December 2002	109.2

* 35,919 sq miles.

† Figures are rounded.

Languages (1990 census): Magyar (Hungarian) 98.5%; German 0.4%; Slovak 0.1%; Romany 0.5%; Croatian 0.2%; Romanian 0.1%.

ADMINISTRATIVE DIVISIONS

(2001 census)

	Area (sq km)	Population	Density (per sq km)	County Town (with population)*
Counties:				
Bács-Kiskun . .	8,445	546,753	64.7	Kecskemét (105,464)
Baranya . .	4,430	408,019	92.1	Pécs (158,607)
Békés	5,631	397,074	70.5	Békéscsaba (63,958)
Borsod-Abaúj-Zemplén .	7,247	745,154	102.8	Miskolc (173,629)
Csongrád . .	4,263	433,388	101.7	Szeged (159,133)
Fejér	4,359	434,547	99.7	Székesfehérvár (105,293)
Győr-Moson-Sopron . .	4,089	434,956	106.4	Győr (127,275)
Hajdú-Bihar .	6,211	553,043	89.0	Debrecen (205,032)
Heves	3,637	325,673	89.5	Eger (57,891)
Jász- Nagykun-Szolnok . .	5,582	415,819	74.5	Szolnok (76,875)
Komárom-Esztergom . .	2,265	316,780	139.9	Tatabánya (72,054)
Nógrád . . .	2,544	220,576	86.7	Salgótarján (44,404)
Pest	6,393	1,080,759	169.1	Budapest†(1,838,753)
Somogy . .	6,036	335,463	55.6	Kaposvár (66,826)
Szabolcs-Szatmár-Bereg .	5,937	582,795	98.2	Nyíregyháza (112,882)
Tolna	3,703	250,062	67.5	Szekszárd (35,358)
Vas	3,337	268,653	80.5	Szombathely (82,074)
Veszprém . .	4,613	374,346	81.2	Veszprém (62,631)
Zala	3,784	298,056	78.8	Zalaegerszeg (61,033)
Capital City				
Budapest† . .	525	1,775,203	3,381.3	—
Total	93,030	10,197,119	109.6	—

* At 1 January 1999.

† Budapest has separate County status. The area and population of the city are not included in the larger County (Pest) which it administers.

PRINCIPAL TOWNS

(population at 1 January 2002)

Budapest (capital) .	1,739,569		Nyíregyháza . . .	117,002
Debrecen . . .	206,564		Kecskemét . . .	107,267
Miskolc	182,408		Székesfehérvár . .	104,059
Szeged	163,699		Szombathely . . .	81,228*
Pécs	159,794		Szolnok	75,962*
Győr	129,287		Tatabánya . . .	71,701*

* 1 January 2000.

Source: Statistics Finland.

BIRTHS, MARRIAGES AND DEATHS

	Registered live births		Registered marriages		Registered deaths	
	Number	Rate (per 1,000)	Number	Rate (per 1,000)	Number	Rate (per 1,000)
1994	115,598	11.3	54,114	5.3	146,889	14.3
1995	112,054	11.0	53,463	5.2	145,431	14.2
1996	105,272	10.3	48,930	4.8	143,130	14.0
1997	100,350	9.9	46,905	4.6	139,434	13.7
1998	97,301	9.6	44,915	4.4	140,870	13.9
1999	94,645	9.4	45,465	4.5	143,210	14.2
2000	97,597	9.6	48,110	4.7	135,601	13.3
2001	97,047	9.5	43,583	4.3	132,183	13.0
2002*	96,800	9.5	46,000	4.5	132,700	13.1

* Preliminary data, figures are rounded.

Expectation of Life (WHO estimates, years at birth): 71.7 (males 67.3; females 76.1) in 2001 (Source: WHO, *World Health Report*).

ECONOMICALLY ACTIVE POPULATION
(labour force surveys, '000 persons aged 15 years to 74 years)

	1999	2000	2001
Agriculture, hunting, forestry and fishing	270.4	251.7	239.4
Mining and quarrying	24.4	19.2	13.0
Manufacturing	928.9	931.3	955.8
Electricity, gas and water supply	89.8	80.1	79.5
Construction	253.0	267.8	272.7
Wholesale and retail trade; repair of motor vehicles, motorcycles and personal and household goods	517.5	540.9	548.4
Hotels and restaurants	133.2	133.3	143.0
Transport, storage and communications	308.3	311.8	310.9
Financial intermediation	80.9	83.7	78.9
Real estate, renting and business activities	183.9	204.6	219.6
Public administration and defence; compulsory social security	301.9	299.0	289.6
Education	306.9	317.8	309.8
Health and social work	239.2	241.7	234.9
Other community, social and personal service activities	169.8	162.7	160.3
Private household with employed persons	2.0	1.9	2.5
Extra-territorial organizations and bodies	1.4	1.6	1.2
Total employed *	3,811.4	3,849.1	3,859.5
Unemployed	284.7	262.5	232.9
Total labour force	4,096.2	4,111.6	4,092.4
Males	2,273.8	2,281.9	2,273.3
Females	1,822.4	1,829.7	1,819.1

Source: ILO.
* Excluding persons on child-care leave.

2002 (labour force surveys, '000 persons aged 15 years to 74 years): Total employed (excl. persons on child-care leave) 3,870.6; Unemployed 238.8; Total labour force 4,109.4.

Health and Welfare

KEY INDICATORS

Total fertility rate (children per woman, 2001)	1.3
Under-5 mortality rate (per 1,000 live births, 2001)	9
HIV/AIDS (% of persons aged 15–49, 2001)	0.06
Physicians (per 1,000 head, 1998)	3.57
Hospital beds (per 1,000 head, 1999)	8.2
Health expenditure (2000): US $ per head (PPP)	846
Health expenditure (2000): % of GDP	6.8
Health expenditure (2000): public (% of total)	75.7
Access to water (% of persons, 2000)	99
Access to sanitation (% of persons, 2000)	99
Human Development Index (2000): ranking	35
Human Development Index (2000): value	0.835

For sources and definitions, see explanatory note on p. vi.

Agriculture

PRINCIPAL CROPS
('000 metric tons)

	1999	2000	2001
Wheat	2,639.1	3,692.5	5,196.8
Barley	1,042.1	900.5	1,299.1
Maize	7,149.3	4,984.3	7,857.7
Rye	80.3	86.5	121.1
Oats	180.4	97.5	149.7
Triticale (wheat-rye hybrid)	253.8	235.6	393.9
Potatoes	1,198.7	863.5	908.4
Sugar beet	2,933.5	1,976.2	2,903.0
Dry beans	107.9	47.6	n.a.
Soybeans (Soya beans)	77.5	30.8	41.5
Sunflower seed	792.9	483.6	632.3
Rapeseed	327.9	179.3	205.1
Cabbages	192.1	130.1	161.3
Tomatoes	301.5	203.4	235.8
Cucumbers and gherkins	125.8	102.7	98.6
Chillies and green peppers	171.2	134.2	134.8
Dry onions	149.5	114.7	174.3
Green peas	163.0	153.3	283.1
Carrots	117.2	89.3	99.3
Green corn	255.7	291.2	415.6
Other vegetables*	386.9	160.6	315.5
Peaches and nectarines	71.0	64.1	56.7
Plums	97.8	91.3	89.8
Grapes	570.3	684.0	811.4
Watermelons	124.9	133.4	130.2
Pimento	33.1	40.0	59.7
Apples	444.5	694.6	605.4
Tobacco (leaves)	15.7	10.5	8.9

* Unofficial figures.

Source: FAO.

LIVESTOCK
('000 head, year ending September)

	1999	2000	2001
Cattle	873	857	805
Pigs	5,479	5,335	4,834
Sheep	909	934	1,129
Goats	149	87	90
Horses	70	70*	75
Chickens	30,557	25,890	30,716
Ducks	2,378	2,269	1,480
Geese	1,074	1,226	1,470
Turkeys	1,986	1,859	3,300

* FAO estimate.

Source: FAO.

LIVESTOCK PRODUCTS
('000 metric tons)

	1999	2000	2001
Beef and veal	51.0	49.4†	47.0*
Mutton and lamb	3.6	2.8*	3.5*
Pig meat	625.9	622.0	587.0†
Poultry meat	399.4	461.4	495.1
Rabbit meat	9.1†	8.8†	9.0*
Cows' milk	2,106.6	2,145.0	2,142.9
Sheep's milk	31.0	33.3	41.5
Goats' milk	4.2	10.8	11.2
Butter	16.6	12.0	13.6
Cheese	91.8	95.6	108.4
Hen eggs	177.2	176.2	182.1
Other poultry eggs	3.4	3.2	3.5
Honey	16.0	15.2	11.3
Wool: greasy	3.4	3.4	3.9
Wool: scoured	1.3†	1.3†	2.3
Cattle hides (fresh)*	3.1	3.0	3.2†

* FAO estimate(s).
† Unofficial figure.

Source: FAO.

Forestry

ROUNDWOOD REMOVALS
('000 cu metres, excl. bark)

	1999*	2000	2001
Sawlogs, veneer logs and logs for sleepers	1,445	1,380	1,430
Pulpwood	515	612	594
Other industrial wood	1,340	1,314	1,468
Fuel wood	2,475	2,597	2,319
Total	5,775	5,903	5,811

* Unofficial figures.

Source: FAO.

SAWNWOOD PRODUCTION
('000 cu metres, incl. railway sleepers)

	1999	2000	2001
Coniferous (softwood)	98	77	75
Broadleaved (hardwood)	210	214	144
Total	308	291	219

Source: FAO.

Fishing

(metric tons, live weight)

	1998	1999	2000
Capture	7,265	7,514	7,101
Common carp	3,373	3,279	3,212
Silver carp	731	676	365
Other cyprinids	1,895	1,666	1,710
Aquaculture	10,222	11,947	12,886
Common carp	7,069	8,158	8,656
Silver carp	1,943	1,882	1,640
Total catch	17,487	19,461	19,987

Source: FAO, *Yearbook of Fishery Statistics*.

Mining

('000 metric tons, unless otherwise indicated)

	1997	1998	1999
Hard coal	924	877	738
Brown coal	6,552	6,004	6,110
Lignite	8,089	7,610	7,696
Crude petroleum	1,360	1,258	1,243
Bauxite	743	909	935
Natural gas (million cu metres)	4,689	4,340	3,693

2000 ('000 metric tons): Bauxite 1,047 (Source: US Geological Survey).

Industry

SELECTED PRODUCTS
('000 metric tons, unless otherwise indicated)

	1997	1998	1999
Crude steel	1,819	1,940	1,920
Cement	2,811	2,999	2,980
Nitrogenous fertilizers*	262.1	224.9	188.0
Refined sugar	487.2	439.4	438.3
Buses (number)	1,951	1,232	706
Leather footwear ('000 pairs)	11,868	11,649	12,639
Electric power (million kWh)	35,305	37,023	36,968
Television receivers ('000)†	963	1,703	2,521
Radio receivers ('000)	528	2,328	2,700

* Production in terms of nitrogen.

† Including video monitors and video projectors.

Finance

CURRENCY AND EXCHANGE RATES

Monetary Units
100 fillér = 1 forint

Sterling, Dollar and Euro Equivalents (31 December 2002)
£1 sterling = 362.91 forint
US $1 = 225.16 forint
€1 = 236.12 forint
1,000 forint = £2.755 = $4.441 = €4.235

Average Exchange Rate (forint per US dollar)
2000   282.179
2001   286.490
2002   257.887

BUDGET
('000 million forint)*

Revenue†	1998	1999	2000
Tax revenue	3,221.8	3,857.1	4,227.3
Taxes on income, profits and capital gains	694.8	840.6	988.4
Individual	477.5	578.1	695.7
Corporate	217.3	262.5	292.7
Social security contributions	1,069.0	1,323.9	1,288.0
Domestic taxes on goods and services	1,241.2	1,460.9	1,710.6
General sales, turnover or value-added taxes	796.9	941.8	1,153.7
Excises	320.6	463.7	505.9
Import duties	131.6	141.1	137.7
Other current revenue	438.1	522.1	508.8
Entrepreneurial and property income	150.4	174.6	164.2
Administrative fees and charges, non-industrial and incidental sales	168.5	154.7	207.7
Capital revenue	26.3	23.3	26.5
Total	3,686.2	4,402.5	4,762.6

Expenditure‡	1998	1999	2000
General public services	237.6	240.3	387.3
Defence	102.1	102.1	142.6
Public order and safety	169.6	169.6	198.2
Education	381.2	381.2	256.2
Health	265.4	265.3	321.6
Social security and welfare	1,331.1	1,331.4	1,703.3
Housing and community amenities	68.9	68.9	81.8
Recreational, cultural and religious affairs and services	79.5	79.5	99.5
Economic affairs and services	558.3	449.4	717.5
Agriculture, forestry, fishing and hunting	157.0	157.0	178.5
Transport and communications	184.6	112.0	242.0
Other purposes	1,329.7	1,802.3	1,375.6
Interest payments	779.0	843.9	788.0
Total	4,523.2	4,890.1	5,283.6
Current	4,111.2	4,476.2	4,631.3
Capital	412.0	413.9	652.3

* Figures refer to the consolidated operations of the central Government, comprising the State Budget, the Pension Fund, the Health Insurance Fund and six extrabudgetary funds.

† Excluding grants received ('000 million forint): 78.6 in 1998; –33.9 in 1999; 19.4 in 2000.

‡ Excluding lending minus repayments ('000 million forint): –106.2 in 1998; –98.0 in 1999; –36.9 in 2000.

Source: partly IMF, *Government Finance Statistics Yearbook*.

INTERNATIONAL RESERVES
(US $ million at 31 December)

	2000	2001	2002
Gold*	28	28	35
IMF special drawing rights	12	21	33
Reserve position in IMF	263	405	595
Foreign exchange	10,915	10,302	9,721
Total	11,218	10,755	10,384

* National valuation.

Source: IMF, *International Financial Statistics*.

MONEY SUPPLY
('000 million forint at 31 December)

	2000	2001	2002
Currency outside banks . . .	883.9	1,037.6	1,181.8
Demand deposits at commercial and savings banks	1,494.3	1,738.3	2,121.0
Total money (incl. others) . .	2,378.4	2,775.9	3,302.9

Source: IMF, *International Financial Statistics.*

COST OF LIVING
(Consumer Price Index; base: 1990 = 100)

	1999	2000	2001
Food	493.7	539.1	613.5
Fuel and light	1,160.0	1,265.6	1,396.0
Clothing and footwear . . .	497.7	526.6	554.5
Rent	510.6	592.8	695.9
All items (incl. others) . . .	569.5	625.3	682.8

Source: ILO.

NATIONAL ACCOUNTS
('000 million forint at current prices)

Expenditure on the Gross Domestic Product

	1999	2000	2001
Government final consumption expenditure	1,156.7	1,293.7	1,636.5
Private final consumption expenditure*	7,272.1	8,297.0	9,502.7
Increase in stocks* . . .	523.4	909.4	571.0
Gross fixed capital formation . .	2,724.5	3,179.9	3,484.7
Total domestic expenditure . .	11,676.7	13,680.0	15,194.9
Exports of goods and services .	6,038.3	8,053.5	8,995.8
Less Imports of goods and services	−6,321.6	−8,582.7	−9,314.2
GDP in purchasers' values . .	11,393.5	13,150.8	14,876.4
GDP at constant 1995 prices . .	10,508.2	11,053.8	11,475.6

* Includes non-profit institutions serving households.

Source: IMF, *International Financial Statistics.*

Gross Domestic Product by Economic Activity

	1998	1999	2000
Agriculture, hunting, forestry and fishing	4,915.1	4,835.2	4,723.1
Mining and quarrying . . .	281.3	284.1	308.8
Manufacturing	21,353.2	23,402.4	28,763.3
Electricity, gas and water supply .	3,418.7	3,891.9	4,303.2
Construction	4,058.0	4,638.3	5,199.9
Wholesale and retail trade; repair of motor vehicles, motorcycles and personal and household goods	10,286.0	10,975.1	12,270.2
Hotels and restaurants . . .	1,581.0	1,781.2	2,012.9
Transport, storage and communications	8,751.2	10,184.0	10,962.7
Financial intermediation . .	3,676.8	3,944.6	4,550.8
Real estate, renting and business activities	1,3,323.8	16,039.3	18,885.6
Public administration and defence; compulsory social security . .	6,387.3	7,234.2	8,167.3
Education	4,110.6	4,779.5	5,352.8
Health and social work . . .	3,931.2	4,461.0	5,218.8
Other community, social and personal service activities . .	2,660.4	3,279.6	3,424.3
Sub-total	88,734.6	99,730.3	114,143.8
Less Financial intermediation services indirectly measured . .	2,450.8	2,838.1	3,012.7
Gross value added in basic prices	91,185.4	102,568.4	117,155.7
Taxes *less* subsidies on products .	14,590.5	17,042.8	19,621.0
GDP in market prices . . .	105,775.9	136,654.0	136,776.7

UN: *National Accounts Statistics.*

BALANCE OF PAYMENTS
(US $ million)

	1999	2000	2001
Exports of goods f.o.b.	21,848	25,747	28,071
Imports of goods f.o.b.	−24,037	−27,506	−30,089
Trade balance	−2,189	−1,760	−2,018
Exports of services	5,649	6,251	7,707
Imports of services	−4,263	−4,476	−5,544
Balance on goods and services	−803	15	146
Other income received . . .	775	942	1,111
Other income paid	−2,417	−2,516	−2,599
Balance on goods, services and income	−2,446	−1,559	−1,342
Current transfers received . . .	582	520	589
Current transfers paid	−243	−289	−344
Current balance	−2,106	−1,328	−1,097
Capital account (net)	29	270	317
Direct investment abroad . . .	−252	−532	−337
Direct investment from abroad . .	1,977	1,646	2,440
Portfolio investment assets . . .	−75	−309	−149
Portfolio investment liabilities . .	2,065	−187	1,526
Financial derivatives assets . .	852	753	579
Financial derivatives liabilities .	−889	−692	−457
Other investment assets . . .	−1,170	−1,014	−3,430
Other investment liabilities . .	2,197	2,555	446
Net errors and omissions . . .	−282	−109	79
Overall balance	2,335	1,052	−84

Source: IMF, *International Financial Statistics.*

External Trade

Note: Beginning in 1997, Hungary's customs territory includes the country's industrial free zones.

PRINCIPAL COMMODITIES
(distribution by SITC, million forint)

Imports c.i.f.	1998	1999	2000
Food and live animals . .	183,608	176,710	228,688
Mineral fuels, lubricants, etc.	361,302	406,814	759,982
Petroleum, petroleum products, etc.	161,338	213,229	400,907
Gas (natural and manufactured) .	159,902	145,290	293,329
Chemicals and related products	565,446	633,457	800,169
Basic manufactures . . .	1,056,034	1,179,487	1,499,000
Textile yarn, fabrics, etc. . .	250,717	271,797	304,477
Machinery and transport equipment	2,566,694	3,334,386	4,666,921
Power-generating machinery and equipment	355,915	403,973	509,379
Machinery specialized for particular industries . . .	179,789	204,644	239,950
General industrial machinery equipment and parts . . .	320,716	411,089	480,545
Office machines and automatic data-processing machines . .	319,846	443,359	640,189
Telecommunications and sound equipment	336,457	406,616	588,020
Other electrical machinery apparatus, etc.	600,755	820,947	1,448,297
Road vehicles and parts (excl. tyres, engines and electrical parts) . .	385,384	572,179	665,365
Miscellaneous manufactured articles	593,037	740,751	890,388
Total (incl. others)	5,511,511	6,645,562	9,064,022

Exports f.o.b.	1998	1999	2000
Food and live animals	470,124	437,320	517,196
Chemicals and related products	346,986	365,629	527,262
Basic manufactures	613,358	680,487	853,605
Machinery and transport equipment	2,564,268	3,401,417	4,765,001
Power-generating machinery and equipment	601,241	689,036	795,897
Office machines and automatic data-processing machines	522,323	794,017	1,102,489
Telecommunications and sound equipment	371,889	471,385	857,673
Other electrical machinery apparatus, etc.	533,377	654,676	941,702
Road vehicles and parts (excl. tyres, engines and electrical parts)	302,915	535,343	697,584
Miscellaneous manufactured articles	649,656	768,553	915,262
Clothing and accessories (excl. footwear)	273,871	311,368	345,223
Total (incl. others)	4,934,502	5,938,525	7,942,804

PRINCIPAL TRADING PARTNERS
(US $ million)*

Imports c.i.f.	1999	2000	2001
Austria	2,502.7	2,366.0	2,487.8
Belgium and Luxembourg	752.9	751.8	791.6
China, People's Republic	610.2	n.a.	n.a.
Czech Republic	529.6	646.2	714.8
Finland	317.6	372.7	353.6
France	1,313.2	1,400.5	1,578.5
Germany	8,188.8	8,213.0	8,393.1
Italy	2,158.8	2,407.2	2,647.4
Japan	1,148.2	n.a.	n.a.
Korea, Republic	355.5	n.a.	n.a.
Netherlands	703.3	708.4	699.4
Poland	587.0	605.2	777.0
Romania	n.a.	328.6	362.0
Russia	1,631.1	2,588.6	2,369.3
Singapore	399.9	n.a.	n.a.
Slovakia	474.7	574.9	602.6
Spain	468.6	572.8	616.6
Sweden	317.9	368.8	348.3
Switzerland and Liechtenstein	426.0	n.a.	n.a.
United Kingdom	853.0	1,017.1	992.7
USA	504.1	569.1	n.a.
Total (incl. others)	28,008.2	32,079.5	33,681.9

Exports f.o.b.	1999	2000	2001
Austria	2,399.4	2,442.5	2,416.8
Belgium and Luxembourg	760.0	886.6	1,014.3
Czech Republic	370.0	465.3	553.4
France	1,123.1	1,470.2	1,817.8
Germany	9,600.1	10,471.3	10,859.5
Ireland	250.6	250.7	329.5
Italy	1,476.9	1,654.4	1,905.2
Netherlands	1,296.5	1,522.4	1,402.2
Poland	519.4	605.2	609.4
Romania	467.6	574.2	764.2
Russia	356.2	455.4	472.3
Slovakia	279.0	288.5	411.5
Slovenia	266.9	279.7	308.4
Spain	406.6	522.5	629.4
Switzerland and Liechtenstein	304.3	n.a.	n.a.
United Kingdom	1,119.8	1,156.3	1,314.4
USA	1,892.6	2,715.2	n.a.
Total (incl. others)	25,012.5	28,091.9	30,497.8

* Imports by country of origin; exports by country of destination.
Source: partly Ministry of Economic Affairs, Budapest.

Transport

RAILWAYS
(traffic)

	1998	1999	2000
Passengers carried (million)	157.0	156.8	156.4
Passenger-kilometres (million)	8,884	9,514	9,789
Net ton-kilometres (million)	8,150	7,734	7,842

2001: 7,731 net ton-kilometres (million).

ROAD TRAFFIC
(motor vehicles in use at 31 December)

	1997	1998	1999
Passenger cars	2,297,115	2,365,000	2,400,000
Buses and coaches	18,616	19,386	19,100
Lorries and vans	315,242	325,300	324,000
Motorcycles and mopeds	137,983	137,983	137,000

Source: IRF, *World Road Statistics*.

2001: Public road motor vehicle stock ('000) 2,974.

SHIPPING

Merchant Fleet
(registered at 31 December)

	1997	1998	1999
Number of vessels	6	2	1
Total displacement ('000 grt)	26.7	15.3	11.9

Source: Lloyd's Register-Fairplay, *World Fleet Statistics*.

Inland Waterways
(traffic)

	1998	1999	2000
Freight carried ('000 metric tons)	2,108	2,074	2,390
Freight ton-km (million)	2,482	1,644	1,561

CIVIL AVIATION
(traffic)

	1998	1999	2000
Passengers carried	2,188,000	2,352,000	2,476,000
Passenger-km ('000)	3,038,000	3,513,000	3,539,000
Cargo carried: metric tons	15,000	16,000	31,000
Cargo ton-km	42,100,000	55,500,000	68,000,000

Tourism

TOURISTS BY COUNTRY OF ORIGIN
('000 arrivals, including visitors in transit)

	1998	1999	2000
Austria	5,996	5,532	5,139
Bulgaria	332	354	395
Czech Republic and Slovakia	5,847	4,619	4,273
Germany	3,852	3,206	2,949
Poland	540	460	643
Romania	4,197	3,581	4,661
Russia	147	106	125
Total (incl. others)	33,624	28,803	31,141

2001: 30,679,000 arrivals.

2002: 31,739,000 arrivals.

Tourist receipts (US $ million): 2,504 in 1998; 2,203 in 1999; 3,434 in 2000.

Communications Media

	1998	1999	2000
Radio receivers ('000 in use) . .	7,245	7,231	n.a.
Television receivers ('000 in use) .	4,377	4,519	4,451
Telephones ('000 main lines in use)	3,423.0	3,725.8	3,479.0
Facsimile machines ('000 in use) .	180	n.a.	n.a.
Mobile cellular telephones ('000 subscribers).	1,070.2	1,628.2	3,000.4
Personal computers ('000 in use) .	400	750	870
Internet users ('000).	660	600	715
Book production: titles	10,626	9,731	8,986
Book production:copies	47,046	44,652	35,246
Daily newspapers	33	n.a.	n.a.
Average daily circulation . . .	1,846,000	n.a.	n.a.

2001: Telephones ('000 main lines in use) 3,260; Mobile cellular telephones ('000 subscribers) 4,968; Personal computers ('000 in use) 1,000; Internet users ('000) 1,480; Book production (titles) 8,837, (copies) 32,615.

Sources: partly UNESCO, *Statistical Yearbook*, and International Telecommunication Union.

Education

(1999/2000, estimates, unless otherwise indicated)

	Institutions	Teachers	Students		
			Males	Females	Total
Pre-primary . .	4,643	31,409	188,565	177,139	365,704
Primary . . .	3,696	82,829	491,101	469,500	960,601
Secondary: general. . .	1,533	14,155	57,641	87,569	145,210
Secondary: teacher training* . .	n.a.	n.a.	159	1,045	1,104
Secondary: vocational . .	990	26,512	195,268	162,035	357,303
Higher: universities etc.	30	12,804	53,520†	52,761†	88,479
Higher: other .	59	8,338	23,167†	33,716†	83,037

* Estimated figures for full-time teacher training.
† 1998/99 figure.

Adult literacy rate (UNESCO estimates): 99.3% (males 99.7%; females 99.5%) in 2000 (Source: UN Development Programme, *Human Development Report*).

Directory

The Constitution

A new Constitution was introduced on 18 August 1949, and the Hungarian People's Republic was established two days later. The Constitution was amended in April 1972 and December 1983. Further, radical amendments were made in October 1989. Shortly afterwards, the Republic of Hungary was proclaimed.

The following is a summary of the main provisions of the Constitution, as amended in October 1989.

GENERAL PROVISIONS

The Republic of Hungary is an independent, democratic constitutional state in which the values of civil democracy and democratic socialism prevail in equal measures. All power belongs to the people, which they exercise directly and through the elected representatives of popular sovereignty.

Political parties may, under observance of the Constitution, be freely formed and may freely operate in Hungary. Parties may not directly exercise public power. No party has the right to guide any state body. Trade unions and other organizations for the representation of interests safeguard and represent the interests of employees, members of co-operatives and entrepreneurs.

The State safeguards the people's freedom, the independence and territorial integrity of the country as well as the frontiers thereof, as established by international treaties. The Republic of Hungary rejects war as a means of settling disputes between nations and refrains from applying force against the independence or territorial integrity of other states, and from threats of violence.

The Hungarian legal system adopts the universally accepted rules of international law. The order of legislation is regulated by an Act of constitutional force.

The economy of Hungary is a market economy, availing itself also of the advantages of planning, with public and private ownership enjoying equal right and protection. Hungary recognizes and supports the right of undertaking and free competition, limitable only by an Act of constitutional force. State-owned enterprises and organs pursuing economic activities manage their affairs independently, in accordance with the mode and responsibility as provided by law.

The Republic of Hungary protects the institutions of marriage and the family. It provides for the indigent through extensive social measures, and recognizes and enforces the right of each citizen to a healthy environment.

GOVERNMENT

National Assembly

The highest organ of state authority in the Republic of Hungary is the National Assembly, which exercises all the rights deriving from the sovereignty of the people and determines the organization, direction and conditions of government. The National Assembly enacts the Constitution and laws, determines the state budget, decides the socio-economic plan, elects the President of the Republic and the Council of Ministers, directs the activities of ministries, decides upon declaring war and concluding peace and exercises the prerogative of amnesty.

The National Assembly is elected for a term of four years and members enjoy immunity from arrest and prosecution without parliamentary consent. It meets at least twice a year and is convened by the President of the Republic or by a written demand of the Council of Ministers or of one-fifth of the Assembly's members. It elects a President, Deputy Presidents and Recorders from among its own members, and it lays down its own rules of procedure and agenda. As a general rule, the sessions of the National Assembly are held in public.

The National Assembly has the right of legislation which can be initiated by the President of the Republic, the Council of Ministers or any committee or member of the National Assembly. Decisions are valid only if at least half of the members are present, and they require a simple majority. Constitutional changes require a two-thirds majority. Acts of the National Assembly are signed by the President of the Republic.

The National Assembly may pronounce its dissolution before the expiry of its term, and in the event of an emergency may prolong its mandate or may be reconvened after dissolution. A new National Assembly must be elected within three months of dissolution and convened within one month of polling day.

Members of the National Assembly are elected on the basis of universal, equal and direct suffrage by secret ballot, and they are accountable to their constituents, who may recall them. All citizens of 18 years and over have the right to vote, with the exception of those who are unsound of mind, and those who are deprived of their civil rights by a court of law.

President of the Republic

The President of the Republic is the Head of State of Hungary. He/she embodies the unity of the nation and supervises the democratic operation of the mechanism of State. The President is also the Commander-in-Chief of the Armed Forces. The President is elected by the National Assembly for a period of five years, and may be re-elected for a second term. Any citizen of Hungary qualified to vote, who has reached 35 years of age before the day of election, may be elected President.

The President may issue the writ for general or local elections, convene the National Assembly, initiate legislation, hold plebiscites, direct local government, conclude international treaties, appoint diplomatic representatives, ratify international treaties, appoint higher civil servants and officers of the armed forces, award orders and titles, and exercise the prerogative of mercy.

Council of Ministers

The highest organ of state administration is the Council of Ministers, responsible to the National Assembly and consisting of the Prime Minister and other Ministers who are elected by the National Assembly on the recommendation of the President of the Republic. The Council of Ministers directs the work of the ministries (listed in a special enactment) and ensures the enforcement of laws and the fulfilment of economic plans; it may issue decrees and annul or modify measures taken by any central or local organ of government.

Local Administration

The local organs of state power are the county, town, borough and town precinct councils, whose members are elected for a term of four years by the voters in each area. Local councils direct economic, social and cultural activities in their area, prepare local economic plans and budgets and supervise their fulfilment, enforce laws, supervise subordinate organs, maintain public order, protect public property and individual rights, and direct local economic enterprises. They may issue regulations and annul or modify those of subordinate councils. Local Councils are administered by an Executive Committee elected by and responsible to them.

JUDICATURE

Justice is administered by the Supreme Court of the Republic of Hungary, county and district courts. The Supreme Court exercises the right of supervising in principle the judicial activities and practice of all other courts.

All judicial offices are filled by election; Supreme Court, county and district court judges are all elected for an indefinite period; the President of the Supreme Court is elected by the National Assembly. All court hearings are public unless otherwise prescribed by law, and those accused are guaranteed the right of defence. An accused person must be considered innocent until proved guilty.

Public Prosecutor

The function of the Chief Public Prosecutor is to supervise the observance of the law. He is elected by the National Assembly, to whom he is responsible. The organization of public prosecution is under the control of the Chief Public Prosecutor, who appoints the public prosecutors.

RIGHTS AND DUTIES OF CITIZENS

The Republic of Hungary guarantees for its citizens the right to work and to remuneration, the right of rest and recreation, the right to care in old age, sickness or disability, the right to education, and equality before the law; women enjoy equal rights with men. Discrimination on grounds of sex, religion or nationality is a punishable offence. The State also ensures freedom of conscience, religious worship, speech, the press and assembly. The right of workers to organize themselves is stressed. The freedom of the individual, and the privacy of the home and of correspondence are inviolable. Freedom for creative work in the sciences and the arts is guaranteed.

The basic freedoms of all workers are guaranteed and foreign citizens enjoy the right of asylum.

Military service (with or without arms) and the defence of their country are the duties of all citizens.

The Government

HEAD OF STATE

President of the Republic: FERENC MÁDL (elected 6 June 2000; took office 4 August 2000).

COUNCIL OF MINISTERS
(May 2003)

A coalition of the Hungarian Socialist Party (HSP) and the Alliance of Free Democrats (AFD).

Prime Minister: PÉTER MEDGYESSY (HSP).

Minister of Foreign Affairs: LÁZSLÓ KOVÁCS (HSP).

Minister of Defence: FERENC JUHÁSZ (HSP).

Minister of Finance: CSABA LÁSZLÓ (Ind.).

Minister of Economy and Transport: ISTVÁN CSILLAG (AFD).

Minister of Home Affairs: MÓNIKA LAMPERTH (HSP).

Minister of Agriculture and Rural Development: IMRE NÉMETH (HSP).

Minister of Health, Social and Family Affairs: JUDIT CSEHÁK (HSP).

Minister of Justice: PÉTER BÁRÁNDY (Ind.).

Minister of Labour and Employment: SÁNDOR BURÁNY (HSP).

Minister of Environmental Protection and Water Management: MIKLOS PERSANYI (AFD).

Minister of Information Technology and Telecommunications: KÁLMÁN KOVÁCS (AFD).

Minister of Cultural Heritage: ISTVÁN HILLER (HSP).

Minister of Education: BÁLINT MAGYAR (AFD).

Minister of Children, Youth and Sports: FERENC GYURCSANY (HSP).

Minister without Portfolio (attached to the Office of the Prime Minister): PÉTER KISS (HSP).

Minister without Portfolio (responsible for the Co-ordination of EU Integration): ENDRE JUHASZ.

Minister without Portfolio (responsible for Equal Opportunities): KATALIN LEVAL.

MINISTRIES

Office of the President: 1055 Budapest, Kossuth Lajos tér 3–5; tel. (1) 441-4103.

Office of the Prime Minister: 1055 Budapest, Kossuth Lajos tér 1–3; tel. (1) 441-4000; fax (1) 268-3050; internet www.kancellaria .gov.hu.

Ministry of Agriculture and Rural Development: 1055 Budapest, Kossuth Lajos tér 11; tel. (1) 301-4000; fax (1) 301-0408; internet www.fvm.hu.

Ministry of Children, Youth and Sports: 1054 Budapest, Hold u. 1; tel. (1) 311-9080; fax (1) 269-0188; internet www.ism.hu/start .htm.

Ministry of Defence: 1055 Budapest, Balaton u. 7–11; tel. (1) 236-5111; fax (1) 311-0182; internet www.honvedelem.hu.

Ministry of Economy and Transport: 1055 Budapest, Honvéd u. 13–15; tel. (1) 302-2355; fax (1) 374-2700; internet www.gm.hu.

Ministry of Education: 1055 Budapest, Szalay u. 10–14; tel. (1) 302-0600; fax (1) 302-2002; internet www.om.hu.

Ministry of Environmental Protection and Water Management: 1011 Budapest, POB 351, Fő u. 44–50; tel. (1) 457-3300; fax (1) 201-2846; e-mail kozonsir@mail.ktm.hu; internet www.ktm.hu.

Ministry of Finance: 1051 Budapest, József Nádor tér 2–4; tel. (1) 318-2066; fax (1) 318-2570; internet www.p-m.hu.

Ministry of Foreign Affairs: 1027 Budapest, Bem rkp. 47; tel. (1) 458-1000; fax (1) 212-5981; internet www.mfa.gov.hu.

Ministry of Health, Social and Family Affairs: Budapest; internet www.eum.hu.

Ministry of Home Affairs: 1051 Budapest, József Attila u. 2–4; tel. (1) 331-3700; fax (1) 118-2870; internet www.b-m.hu.

Ministry of Justice: 1055 Budapest, Kossuth Lajos tér 4; tel. (1) 441-3003; internet www.im.hu.

Ministry of Information Technology and Telecommunications: Budapest.

Ministry of Labour and Employment: Budapest.

Ministry of Cultural Heritage: 1077 Budapest, Wesselényi u. 20–22; tel. (1) 484-7100; fax (1) 484-7172; internet www.nkom.hu.

Legislature

ORSZÁGGYÜLÉS
(National Assembly)

National Assembly
1055 Budapest, Kossuth Lajos tér 1–3; 1357 Budapest, POB 2; tel. (1) 441-4000; fax (1) 441-5000; internet www.mkogy.hu.

President of the National Assembly: KATALIN SZILI.

Deputy Presidents: IBOLYA DAVID, LÁSZLÓ MANOUR, PÉTER HARRACH, JÓZSEF SZAJER, FERENC WEKLER.

General election, 7 and 21 April 2002

Parties	% of votes	Seats
Federation of Young Democrats—Hungarian Civic Party-Hungarian Democratic Forum (FYD—HCP-HDF)	48.70	188
Hungarian Socialist Party (HSP)	46.11	178
Alliance of Free Democrats (AFD)	5.18	20
Total	100.00	386

Political Organizations

Agrarian Association (Agrarszövetség): Budapest; Chair. TAMÁS NAGY.

Alliance of Free Democrats (AFD) (Szabad Demokraták Szövetsége—SzDSz): 1143 Budapest, Gizella u. 36; tel. (1) 223-2050; fax (1) 221-0579; e-mail zsolt.udvarvolgyi@szdsz.hu; internet www .szdsz.hu; f. 1988; 19,000 mems (2000); Chair. GÁBOR KUNCZE.

Centrum Party: Budapest; tel. (1) 301-5040; fax (1) 301-5048; e-mail centruminfo@axelero.hu; internet www.centrum-part.hu; f. 2001; electoral coalition of the Hungarian Democratic People's Party, the Christian Democratic People's Party, the Third Side for Hungary Association (HOME) and the Green Democrats Party; Chair. MIHÁLY KUPA.

Christian Democratic People's Party (CDPP) (Kereszténydemokrata Néppárt—KDNP): 1126 Budapest, Nagy Jenő u. 5; tel. (1) 175-0333; fax (1) 155-5772; e-mail kulugy@kdnp.hu; internet www .kdnp.hu; re-formed 1989; formed an electoral alliance, the Centrum Party (q.v.), to contest the 2002 legislative election; Chair. TIDAVAR BARTÓK.

Democratic Roma Coalition: ethnic Roma party; left-wing.

Entrepreneurs' Party: Budapest; was to support the Centrum Party in the 2002 legislative election; Chair. JÓSZEF TACAKS.

Federation of Young Democrats—Hungarian Civic Party (FYD—HCP) (Magyar Polgári Párt—FIDESZ): 1062 Budapest, Lendvay u. 28; tel. (1) 269-5353; fax (1) 269-5343; e-mail sajto@fidesz .parlament.hu; internet www.fidesz.hu; f. 1988 as the Federation of Young Democrats; renamed April 1995; formed an alliance with the Hungarian Democratic Forum to contest the general election of 2002; 10,000 mems; Leader JANOS ADER.

Green Party of Hungary: Budapest; f. 1989; Chair. ZOLTÁN MEDVECZKY.

Hungarian Christian Democratic Federation (MKDSZ): f. 1997 by breakaway members of the Christian Democratic People's Party; allied to the Federation of Young Democrats—Hungarian Civic Party; Chair. LÁSZLÓ SURJAN.

Hungarian Civic Co-operation Association (Magyar Polgari Egyuettmuekoedes Egyesuelet): Budapest; f. 1996; Chair. GYÖRGY GRANASZTOI; Gen. Sec. ZOLTÁN VESZELOVSZKI.

Hungarian Democratic Forum (HDF) (Magyar Demokrata Fórum—MDF): 1026 Budapest, Szilágyi Erszébet fasor 73; 1539 Budapest, POB 579; tel. (1) 212-2828; fax (1) 225-2290; internet www.mdf.hu; f. 1987; centre-right; formed an alliance with the Federation of Young Democrats—Hungarian Civic Party to contest the general election of 2002; 25,000 mems (2001); Chair. Dr IBOLYA DÁVID.

Hungarian Democratic People's Party (HDPP) (Magyar Demokrata Néppárt—MDN): Budapest; f. 1996 by former mems of the Hungarian Democratic Forum; moderate; formed an electoral alliance, the Centrum Party (q.v.), to contest the 2002 legislative election; Chair. ERZSÉBET PUSZTAI.

Hungarian Justice and Life Party (HJLP) (Magyar Igazság és Élet Párt—MIEP): 1085 Budapest, Rökk Szilárd u. 19; tel. and fax (1) 3171-2692; internet www.miep.hu; f. 1993; Chair. ISTVÁN CSURKA.

Hungarian Social Democratic Party (HSDP) (Magyarországi Szocialdemokrata Párt—MSzDP): Budapest; tel. and fax (1) 342-3547; f. 1890; absorbed by Communist Party in 1948; revived 1988; affiliated with the Social Democratic Youth Movement; 3,000 mems (Dec. 1997); Chair. MÁTYÁS SZŰRÖS.

Hungarian Socialist Party (HSP) (Magyar Szocialista Párt—MSzP): 1081 Budapest, Köztársaság tér 26; tel. (1) 210-0046; fax (1) 210-0081; internet www.mszp.hu; f. 1989 to replace the Hungarian Socialist Workers' Party; 40,000 mems (Dec. 1999); Chair. LÁSZLÓ KOVÁCS.

Hungarian Workers' Party (HWP) (Magyar Munkáspárt—MMP): 1082 Budapest, Baross u. 61; tel. (1) 334-2721; fax (1) 313-5423; e-mail mpzoo@matavnet.hu; internet www.munkaspart.hu; f. 1956 as Hungarian Socialist Workers' Party; dissolved and replaced by Hungarian Socialist Party (see above) in 1989; re-formed in 1989 as Hungarian Socialist Workers' Party, name changed as above 1992; approx. 30,000 mems (Oct. 1992); Pres. Dr GYULA THÜRMER.

Independent Smallholders' and Civic Party (ISCP) (Független Kisgazda-, Földmunkás- és Polgári Párt—FKgP): 1056 Budapest, Belgrád rkp. 24; tel. and fax (1) 3181824; internet www.fkgp.hu; f. 1988 as the Independent Smallholders' Party, name subsequently changed to the Independent Smallholders' and Peasants' Party; 60,000 mems; Chair. Dr MIKLOS RETI.

Lungo Drom Alliance: 5000 Szolnok, Szapáry u. 19; tel. (56) 420-110; ethnic Roma party; right-wing; Leader FLORIAN FARKAS.

New Left Alliance: Budapest; f. 2001; formed from eight left-wing organizations; agreed to form an electoral coalition with the Romany Co-operation Party of Hungary to contest the 2002 general election; Pres. LÁSZLÓ SCHILLER.

Peace Party of Hungarian Gypsies (Magyar Ciganyok Bekepartja): Budapest; f. 1993; Leader ALBERT HORVÁTH.

Smallholder Alliance—Party of the Smallholder Federation: Budapest; f. 2002 by former mems of the ISCP; conservative; Chair. SANDOR CSEH.

United Historic Smallholders' Party (UHSP) (Egyesült Kisgazdapárt—Történelmi Tagozat—EKgP–TT): Budapest; f. 1992 as the 'Historical Section' of the Independent Smallholders' Party (now the ISCP); renamed 1993; Gen. Sec. ANTAL BELAFI.

Diplomatic Representation

EMBASSIES IN HUNGARY

Albania: 1026 Budapest, Gábor Áron u. 55; tel. (1) 326-8905; fax (1) 326-8904; Ambassador ISUF BASHKURTI.

Algeria: 1121 Budapest, Zugligeti u. 27; tel. (1) 200-6860; fax (1) 200-6781; Ambassador BACHIR ROUIS.

Argentina: 1023 Budapest, Vérhalom u. 12–16, II, 3A; tel. (1) 326-0492; fax (1) 326-0494; Ambassador GUILLERMO JORGE MCGOUGH.

Australia: 1126 Budapest, Királyhágó tér 8–9; tel. (1) 457-9777; fax (1) 201-9792; e-mail ausembbp@mail.datanet.hu; internet www .australia.hu; Ambassador LEO CRUISE.

Austria: 1068 Budapest, Benczúr u. 16; tel. (1) 351-6700; fax (1) 352-8795; e-mail budapest@austroamb.hu; Ambassador Dr ERICH KUSSBACH.

Belgium: 1015 Budapest, Toldy Ferenc u. 13; tel. (1) 201-1571; fax (1) 375-1566; e-mail ambabel.budapest@mail.datanet.hu; Ambassador MICHEL CARLIER.

Belarus: 1126 Budapest, Agárdi u. 3B; tel. (1) 214-0553; fax (1) 214-0554; e-mail hungary@belembassy.org; Ambassador ANDREI YEUDACHENKA.

Bosnia and Herzegovina: 1026 Budapest, Pasaréti u. 48; tel. (1) 212-0106; fax (1) 212-0109.

Brazil: 1062 Budapest, Délibáb u. 30; tel. (1) 351-0060; fax (1) 351-0066; e-mail hunbrem@ind.eunet.hu; Ambassador LUCIANO OZORIO ROSA.

Bulgaria: 1062 Budapest, Andrássy u. 115; tel. (1) 322-0824; fax (1) 322-5215; e-mail bgembhu@ibm.net; Ambassador CHRISTO HALATCHEV.

Cambodia: Budapest; tel. (1) 155-1128; fax (1) 155-1128; Ambassador UNG SEAN.

Canada: 1121 Budapest, Budakeszi u. 32; tel. (1) 392-3360; fax (1) 392-3390; internet www.kanada.hu; Ambassador RONALD R. HALPIN (desig.).

Chile: 1023 Budapest, Vérhalom u. 12–16, III, 35; tel. (1) 212-0061; fax (1) 212-0059; e-mail echilehu@pronet.hu; internet www.chile.hu; Ambassador CELSO ENRIQUE MORENO LAVAL.

China, People's Republic: 1068 Budapest, Benczúr u. 17; tel. (1) 332-4872; fax 322-9067; e-mail knnk@mail.matav.hu; Ambassador ZHAO XIDI.

Colombia: 1025 Budapest, Józsefhegyi u. 28-30 G-6; tel. (1) 325-7617; fax (1) 325-7618; e-mail embajada.budapest@colombia.hu; Ambassador BELARMINO PINILLA.

Costa Rica: Budapest; tel. (1) 1851-431; Ambassador JORGE EDOARDO VILLAFRANCA NÚÑEZ.

Croatia: 1065 Budapest, Munkácsy Mihály u. 15; tel. (1) 269-5657; fax (1) 354-1319; e-mail hrvhu1@mail.euroweb.hu; Ambassador Dr STANKO NICK.

Cuba: 1025 Budapest, Józsefhegyi u. 28–30, II, 6u. tel. (1) 200-8916; fax (1) 200-8045; e-mail embacuba.bud@mail.matav.hu; Ambassador CARLOS TREJO SOSA.

Cyprus: 1051 Budapest, Dorottya u. 3, III, 2–3u. tel. (1) 266-1330; fax (1) 266-0538.

Czech Republic: 1064 Budapest, Rózsa u. 61; tel. (1) 351-0539; fax (1) 351-9189; e-mail budapest@embassy.mzv.cz; Ambassador RUDOLF JINDRÁK.

Denmark: 1122 Budapest, Határőr u. 37; tel. (1) 355-7320; fax (1) 375-3803; Ambassador CLAUS JUUL NEILSON.

Ecuador: 1021 Budapest, Budakeszi u. 55D, P8, V/1; tel. (1) 200-8918; fax (1) 200-8682; e-mail mecuahun@hu.inter.net; Ambassador RAÚL MANTILLA-LARREA.

Egypt: 1016 Budapest, Bérc u. 16; tel. (1) 381-0475; fax (1) 381-0571; e-mail ambegp@pronet.hu; internet ceg.uiuc.edu/~haggag/embassy.html; Ambassador MUHAMMAD ELSAYED ABBAS.

Estonia: 1062 Budapest, Lendvay u. 12, Fsz. 3; tel. (1) 312-4725; fax (1) 302-6527; e-mail lluht@estemb.hu; Ambassador TOIVO TASA.

Finland: 1118 Budapest, Kelenhegyi u. 16A; tel. (1) 279-2500; fax (1) 385-0843; e-mail sanomat.bud@formin.fi; Ambassador PEKKA KUJASALO.

France: 1062 Budapest, Lendvay u. 27; tel. (1) 332-4980; fax (1) 311-8291; e-mail ambasfn-presse@matavnet.hu; internet www.ambafrance.hu; Ambassador DOMINIQUE DE COMBLES DE NAYVES.

Germany: 1014 Budapest, Úri u. 64–66u. tel. and fax (1) 488-3505; e-mail info@deutschebotschaft-budapest.hu; internet www.deutschebotschaft-budapest.hu; Ambassador WILFRIED GRUBER.

Greece: 1063 Budapest, Szegfű u. 3; tel. (1) 413-2600; fax (1) 342-1934; e-mail greekemb@mail.matav.hu; Ambassador NIKOLAOS KALANTZIANOS.

Holy See: 1126 Budapest, Gyimes u. 1–3; tel. (1) 355-8979; fax (1) 355-6987; e-mail nuntbud@communio.hcbc.hu; Apostolic Nuncio Most Rev. KARL-JOSEF RAUBER (Titular Archbishop of Iubaltiana).

India: 1025 Budapest, Búzavirág u. 14; tel. (1) 325-7742; fax (1) 325-7745; e-mail chancery@indemb.datanet.hu; internet www.indianembassy.hu; Ambassador LAKSHMI PURI.

Indonesia: 1068 Budapest, Városligeti fasor 26; tel. (1) 342-8508; fax (1) 322-8669; e-mail kbribud@mail.datanet.hu; internet www.indonesia.hu; Ambassador HASSAN ABDULDJALIL.

Iran: 1143 Budapest, Stefánia u. 97; tel. (1) 460-9260; fax (1) 460-9430; e-mail embiran@pronet.hu; Ambassador Dr MORTEZA SAFFARI NATANZI.

Iraq: 1146 Budapest, Hermina u. 7; tel. (1) 384-5071; fax (1) 384-5072; Ambassador JAHEED RABAH AHMEED.

Ireland: 1944 Budapest, Bank Center Gránit Torony, VII; tel. (1) 302-9600; fax (1) 302-9599; e-mail iremb@elender.hu; Ambassador JIM FLAVIN.

Israel: 1026 Budapest, Fullánk u. 8; tel. (1) 200-0781; fax (1) 200-0783; e-mail budapest@israel.org; Ambassador JUDITH VARNAI SHORER.

Italy: 1143 Budapest, Stefánia u. 95; tel. (1) 343-6065; fax (1) 343-6058; e-mail ambital@pronet.hu; internet www.ambitalia.hu; Ambassador GIOVAN BATTISTA VERDERAME.

Japan: 1125 Budapest, Zalai u. 7; tel. (1) 275-1275; fax (1) 275-1281; internet www.japan-embassy.hu; Ambassador YOSHITOMO TANAKA.

Kazakhstan: 1025 Budapest, II ker., Kapy u. 59; tel. (1) 275-1300; fax (1) 275-2092; e-mail kazak@euroweb.hu; Ambassador SAGYNBEK TURSUNOV.

Korea, Republic: 1062 Budapest, Andrássy u. 109; tel. (1) 351-1179; fax (1) 351-1182; e-mail koremb@mail.matav.hu; Ambassador DEA WON SUH.

Lebanon: 1112 Budapest, Sasadi u. 160; tel. (1) 249-0900; fax (1) 249-0901.

Libya: 1143 Budapest, Stefánia u. 111; tel. (1) 343-6076; fax (1) 343-1583; Head of People's Bureau OMAR MUFTAH DALLAL.

Macedonia, former Yugoslav republic: 1022 Budapest, Felső Zölmádli u. 120; tel. and fax (1) 315-1921.

Malaysia: 1022 Budapest, Tapolcsányi u. 18; tel. (1) 326-8312; fax (1) 326-8413; e-mail wbdpest@mail.matav.hu.

Mexico: 1023 Budapest, Vérhalom u. 12–16, III, 31–33; tel. (1) 326-0447; fax (1) 326-0485; Ambassador JOSÉ LUIS MARTÍNEZ Y H.

Moldova: 1111 Budapest, Budafoki u. 9–11; tel. (1) 209-1191; fax (1) 209-1195.

Mongolia: 1022 Budapest II, k. Bogár u. 14/C; tel. (1) 212-4579; fax (1) 212-5731; e-mail mnk@mail.matavnet.hu; Ambassador DERGELDALIYN DZAMBADZANCAN.

Morocco: 1026 Budapest, Törökvész Lejtő 12A; tel. (1) 200-7855; fax (1) 275-1437; e-mail sifamabudap@attglobal.net; Ambassador SAAD BADDOU.

Netherlands: 1022 Budapest, Füge u. 5–7, 2 District; 1388 Budapest, POB 56; tel. (1) 336-6300; fax (1) 326-5978; e-mail nlbdpez@nextra.hu; internet www.netherlandsembassy.hu; Ambassador F. P. R. VAN NOUHUYS.

New Zealand: Budapest; tel. (1) 131-2144; fax (1) 131-0593; Chargé d'affaires TAMÁS TAKATSY.

Nigeria: 1022 Budapest, Árvácska u. 6; tel. (1) 212-2021; fax (1) 212-2025; e-mail nigeria@matavnet.hu; internet www.nigerianembassy.hu; Ambassador: Chief ABAYOMI AKINTOLA.

Norway: 1015 Budapest, Ostrom u. 13, POB 32; tel. (1) 212-9400; fax (1) 212-9410; e-mail norwegian.embassy@pronet.hu; internet www.norvegia.hu; Ambassador JAN G. JØLLE.

Pakistan: 1125 Budapest, Adonis u. 3A; tel. (1) 355-8017; fax (1) 375-1402; e-mail pakemb@mail.matav.hu.

Panama: 1118 Budapest, Iglói u. 6/B2; tel. and fax (1) 466-9817; e-mail embpanbu@freemail.c3.hu.

Peru: 1025 Budapest, Józsefhegyi u. 28–30, F/2; tel. (1) 335-4019; fax (1) 355-1019; e-mail leprubda@mail.datanet.hu; Ambassador BERTHA VEGA PÉREZ.

Philippines: 1026 Budapest, Gábor Áron u. 58; tel. (1) 200-5523; fax (1) 200-5528; e-mail phbuda@mail.datanet.hu; Ambassador ALEJANDRO DEL ROSARIO.

Poland: 1068 Budapest, Városligeti fasor 16; tel. (1) 342-5566; fax (1) 351-1722; e-mail amb.bud@ind.eunet.hu; Ambassador GRZEGORZ LUBCZYK.

Portugal: 1024 Budapest, Romer Flóris u. 58; tel. (1) 316-2645; fax (1) 316-2642; e-mail embport@mail.matav.hu; Ambassador JOÃO CARLOS BESSA PINTO VERSTEEG.

Romania: 1146 Budapest, Thököly u. 72; tel. (1) 352-0271; fax (1) 343-6035; e-mail roembbud@mail.datanet.hu; Ambassador CALIN FABIAN.

Russia: 1062 Budapest, Bajza u. 35; tel. (1) 302-5230; fax (1) 353-4164; Ambassador VALERY MUSATOV.

Serbia and Montenegro: 1068 Budapest, Dózsa György u. 92B; tel. (1) 322-9838; fax (1) 322-1438; e-mail ambjubo@mail.datanet.hu; Chargé d'affaires BRANISAL NOVAKOVIĆ.

Slovakia: 1143 Budapest, Stefánia u. 22-24; tel. (1) 460-9010; fax (1) 460-9020; e-mail slovakem@matavnet.hu; Chargé d'affaires JURAJ PALACKA.

Slovenia: 1025 Budapest, Cseppkö u. 68; tel. (1) 438-5600; fax (1) 325-9187; Ambassador IDA MOČIVNIK.

South Africa: 1026 Budapest, Gárdonyi Géza út. 17; tel. (1) 392-0999; fax (1) 200-7277; e-mail saemb@elender.hu; internet www.sa-embassy.hu; Ambassador DRIES VENTER.

Spain: 1067 Budapest, Eötvös u. 11B; tel. (1) 342-9992; fax (1) 351-0572; Ambassador FERNANDO PERPIÑÁ-ROBERT.

Sweden: 1146 Budapest, Ajtósi Dürer sor 27A; tel. (1) 460-6020; fax (1) 460-6021; e-mail ambassaden.budapest@foreign.ministry.se; Ambassador STEFFAN CARLSSON.

Switzerland: 1143 Budapest, Stefánia u. 107; tel. (1) 460-7040; fax (1) 343-9492; e-mail vertretung@bud.rep.admin.ch; internet www.swissembassy.hu; Ambassador RUDOLF WEIERSMUELLER.

Syria: 1026 Budapest, Harangvirág u. 3; tel. (1) 200-8046; fax (1) 200-8048; Ambassador (vacant).

Thailand: 1025 Budapest, Verecke u. 79; tel. (1) 438-4020; fax (1) 438-4023; e-mail thaiemba@mail.datanet.hu; Ambassador CHALERMPOM AKE-URU.

Tunisia: 1021 Budapest, Budakeszi u. 55D; tel. (1) 200-8929; fax (1) 200-8931; e-mail ambtunb@mail.matav.hu; Chargé d'affaires ABDELWAHEB BOUZOUITA.

Turkey: 1062 Budapest, Andrássy u. 123; tel. (1) 344-5025; fax (1) 344-5143; e-mail budapest@turkisembassy.hu; Ambassador BEDRETTIN TUNABAS.

Ukraine: 1143 Budapest, Stefania u. 77; tel. (1) 422-4122; fax (1) 220-9873; e-mail ukran.kovetseg@mail.datanet.hu; Ambassador Dr VASYL V. DURDYNETS.

United Kingdom: 1051 Budapest, Harmincad u. 6; tel. (1) 266-2888; fax (1) 266-0907; e-mail info@britemb.hu; internet www.britishembassy.hu; Ambassador JOHN NICHOLS (desig.).

USA: 1054 Budapest, Szabadság tér 12; tel. (1) 475-4400; fax (1) 475-4764; internet www.usis.hu; Ambassador NANCY GOODMAN BRINKER.

Uruguay: 1023 Budapest 2, Vérhalom u. 12–16, I, 3; tel. and fax (1) 326-0459; e-mail urupest@euroweb.hu; Ambassador HOMERO DIEGO MARTÍNEZ LAWLOR.

Venezuela: 1023 Budapest, Vérhalom u. 12–16, I, 14; tel. (1) 326-0460; fax (1) 326-0450; e-mail venhu@ibm.net; Ambassador JORGE A. GONZÁLEZ.

Viet Nam: 1068 Budapest 2, Benczúr u. 18; tel. (1) 342-5583; fax (1) 325-8798; Ambassador DAO THI TAM.

Yemen: 1025 Budapest, Józsefhegyi u. 28-30, D/6; tel. (1) 212-3991; fax (1) 212-3883; e-mail al-yemen.al-saida@matavnet.hu; Ambassador (vacant).

Judicial System

The system of court procedure in Hungary is based on an Act that came into effect in 1953 and has since been updated frequently. The system of jurisdiction is based on the local courts (district courts in Budapest, city courts in other cities), labour courts, county courts (or the Metropolitan Court) and the Supreme Court. In the legal remedy system of two instances, appeals against the decisions of city and district courts can be lodged with the competent county court and the Metropolitan Court of Budapest respectively. Against the judgment of first instance of the latter, appeal is to be lodged with the Supreme Court. The Chief Public Prosecutor and the President of the Supreme Court have the right to submit a protest on legal grounds against the final judgment of any court.

By virtue of the 1973 Act, effective from 1974 and modified in 1979, the procedure in criminal cases is differentiated for criminal offences and for criminal acts. In the first instance, criminal cases are tried, depending on their character, by a professional judge; where justified by the magnitude of the criminal act, by a council composed of three members, a professional judge and two lay assessors, while in major cases the court consists of five members, two professional judges and three lay assessors. In the Supreme Court, second instance cases are tried only by professional judges. The President of the Supreme Court is elected by the National Assembly. Judges are appointed by the President of the Republic for an indefinite period. Assessors are elected by the local municipal councils.

In the interest of ensuring legality and a uniform application of the law, the Supreme Court exercises a principled guidance over the jurisdiction of courts. In the Republic of Hungary judges are independent and subject only to the Law and other legal regulations.

The Minister of Justice supervises the general activities of courts. the Chief Public Prosecutor is elected by the National Assembly. The Chief Public Prosecutor and the Prosecutor's Office provide for the consistent prosecution of all acts violating or endangering the legal order of society, the safety and independence of the state, and for the protection of citizens.

The Prosecutors of the independent prosecuting organization exert supervision over the legality of investigations and the implementation of punishments, and assist with specific means in ensuring that legal regulations should be observed by state, economic and other organs and citizens, and they support the legality of court procedures and decisions.

President of the Supreme Court: ZOLTÁN LOMNICI.

Chief Public Prosecutor: PÉTER POLT.

Constitutional Court: 1015 Budapest, Donáti u. 35-45; tel. (1) 488-3100; fax (1) 212-1170; internet www.mkab.hu; Pres. Dr JÁNOS NÉMETH.

Religion

CHRISTIANITY

Ecumenical Council of Churches in Hungary (Magyarországi Egyházak Ökumenikus Tanácsa): 1026 Budapest, Bimbó u. 127; tel. (1) 394-4847; fax (1) 394-1210; e-mail oikoumene@lutheran.hu; internet oikoumene.lutheran.hu; f. 1943; member churches: Baptist, Bulgarian Orthodox, Evangelical Lutheran, Hungarian Orthodox, Methodist, Reformed Church, Romanian Orthodox and Serbian Orthodox; Pres. Bishop Dr MIHÁLY MÁRKUS; Gen. Sec. Dr TIBOR GÖRÖG.

The Roman Catholic Church

Hungary comprises four archdioceses, nine dioceses (including one for Catholics of the Byzantine rite) and one territorial abbacy (directly responsible to the Holy See). At 31 December 2000 the Church had 6,226,089 adherents in Hungary.

Bishops' Conference: Magyar Katolikus Püspöki Konferencia, 1071 Budapest, Városligeti fasor 45; tel. (1) 342-6959; fax (1) 342-6957; e-mail pkt@katolikus.hu; f. 1969; Pres. Dr ISTVÁN SEREGÉLY (Archbishop of Eger).

Latin Rite

Archbishop of Eger: Dr ISTVÁN SEREGÉLY, 3301 Eger, Széchenyi u. 1, POB 80; tel. (36) 313-259; fax (36) 320-508; e-mail egersek@ektf.hu.

Archbishop of Esztergom-Budapest: Cardinal Dr PÉTER ERDŐ (Primate of Hungary), 1014 Budapest, Uri u. 62; tel. (1) 202-5611; fax (1) 202-5458.

Archbishop of Kalocsa-Kecskemét: Dr BALÁZS BÁBEL, 6301 Kalocsa, POB 29, Szentháromság tér 1; tel. (78) 462-166; fax (78) 462-130; e-mail kalocsa@hcbc.hu.

Archbishop of Veszprém: Dr GYULA MÁRFI, 8200 Veszprém, Vár u. 16-18; tel. (88) 426-088; fax (88) 426-287; e-mail veszprem@communio.hcbc.hu.

Byzantine Rite

Bishop of Hajdúdorog: SZILÁRD KERESZTES, 4401 Nyiregyháza, Bethlen u. 5, POB 60; tel. (42) 317-397; fax (42) 314-734; 253,000 adherents (Dec. 1999); the Bishop is also Apostolic Administrator of the Apostolic Exarchate of Miskolc, with an estimated 25,000 Catholics of the Byzantine rite (Dec. 1999).

Protestant Churches

Baptist Union of Hungary (Magyarországi Baptista Egyház): 1068 Budapest, Benczur u. 31; tel. (1) 343-0618; fax (1) 352-9707; e-mail baptist.convention@mail.datanet.hu; f. 1846; 11,500 mems; Pres. Rev. KÁLMÁN MÉSZÁROS; Gen.-Sec. Rev. KORNÉL MÉSZÁROS.

Evangelical Lutheran Church in Hungary (Magyarországi Evangélikus Egyház): 1085 Budapest, Üllöi u. 24; tel. (1) 317-5567; fax (1) 317-0872; e-mail orszagos@lutheran.hu; 430,000 mems (1992); Presiding Bishop IMRE SZEBIK; Dir KÁROLY HAFENSCHER.

Hungarian Methodist Church (Magyarországi Metodista Egyház): 1032 Budapest, Kiscelli u. 73; tel. (1) 250-1536; fax (1) 250-1849; e-mail kiscelli@axelero.hu; Superintendent ISTVÁN CSERNÁK.

Reformed Church in Hungary—Presbyterian (Magyarországi Református Egyház): 1146 Budapest, Abonyi u. 21; tel. (1) 343-7870; e-mail rch@mail.elender.hu; 2m. mems (1987); 1,306 churches; Pres. of Gen. Synod Bishop Dr GUSZTÁV BÖLCSKEI.

Unitarian Church in Hungary (Magyarországi Unitárius Egyház): 1055 Budapest V, Nagy Ignác u. 4; tel. (1) 111-2801; Bishop Rev. MARTIN BENCZE.

The Eastern Orthodox Church

Hungarian Orthodox Church (Magyar Orthodox Egyház): 1052 Budapest, Petőfi tér 2.1.2. tel. (1) 318-4813; Archbishop PAVEL PONOMARJOV.

Romanian Orthodox Church in Hungary (Magyarországi Román Ortodox Egyház): 5700 Gyula, Sz. Miklos park 2; tel. and fax (66) 361-281; f. 1997; monastic community; Bishop SOFRONIE DRINCEC.

Serbian Orthodox Diocese (Szerb Görögkeleti Egyházmegye): 2000 Szentendre, POB 22; Bishop Dr DANILO KRISTIC.

The Russian (6,000 mems) and Bulgarian Orthodox Churches are also represented.

BUDDHISM

Hungarian Buddhist Mission (Magyarországi Buddhista Misszió): 1386 Budapest, Postafiók 952; tel. (36) 138-52098; e-mail amm@dakiniland.net; internet www.dharma.hu; Rep. Dr LAJOS PRESSING.

Hungarian Zen Buddhist Community (Magyarországi Csan Buddhista Közösség): Budapest; Leader FÁRAD LOTFI.

ISLAM

There are about 3,000 Muslims in Hungary.

Hungarian Islamic Community (Magyar Iszlám Közösség): Budapest; tel. (1) 177-7602; Leader Dr BALÁZS MIHÁLFFY.

JUDAISM

The Jewish community in Hungary is estimated to number between 100,000 and 120,000 people. Some 80% of Hungary's Jewish community resides in Budapest.

Federation of Jewish Communities in Hungary (Magyarországi Zsidó Hitközségek Szövetsége): 1075 Budapest, Sip u. 12, Budapesti Zsidó Hitközség (Jewish Community of Budapest); tel. (1) 342-1335; fax (1) 342-1790; e-mail bzsh@mail.matav.hu; 80,000 mems; 40 active synagogues; Orthodox and Conservative; Pres. ANDRAS HEISLER; Chief Rabbi of Hungary Dr PÉTER KARDOS.

The Press

In 1998 there were 33 dailies, with an average daily circulation of 1,846,000. Budapest dailies circulate nationally. The most popular are: *Népszabadság, Nemzeti Sport* and *Népszava*. *Népszabadság*, the most important daily, was formerly the central organ of the Hungarian Socialist Workers' Party, but is now independent. Most daily newspapers were partially foreign-owned.

PRINCIPAL DAILIES

Békéscsaba

Békés Megyei Hírlap (Békés County News): 5601 Békéscsaba, Munkácsy u. 4; tel. (66) 446-242; fax (66) 441-020; internet www .bmhirlap.hu; f. 1945; Editor-in-Chief ZOLTÁN ÁRPÁSI; circ. 49,000.

Budapest

Blikk: Budapest; f. 1994; colour tabloid.

Magyar Hirlap (Hungarian Journal): 1087 Budapest, Kerepesi u. 29B; tel. (1) 210-0050; fax (1) 210-3737; internet www.magyarhirlap .hu; f. 1968; 100% foreign-owned; Editor-in-Chief MÁTYÁS VINCE; circ. 75,000.

Magyar Nemzet (Hungarian Nation): Budapest; tel. (1) 141-4320; internet www.magyarnemzet.com; 45% foreign-owned; Editor-in-Chief GÁBOR LISZKAY; circ. 100,000.

Mai Nap (Today): 1145 Budapest, Szugló u. 14; tel. (1) 470-1382; fax (1) 470-1351; e-mail info@mainap.hu; f. 1988; Editor-in-Chief FERENC KÖSZEGI; circ.100,000.

Metro: 1106 Budapest, Fehér u. 10, 21-es épület; tel. (1) 431-6464; fax (1) 431-6465; e-mail szerk@metro.hu; internet www.metro.hu; Editor IZBÉKI GÁBOR.

NAPI Gazdaság (World Economy): 1135 Budapest, Csata u. 32; tel. (1) 350-4349; fax (1) 350-1117; e-mail napi@mail.eleuder.hu; internet www.napi.hu; Editor-in-Chief ADÁM DANKÓ; circ. 16,000.

Nemzeti Sport (National Sport): 1141 Budapest, Szugló u. 83-85; tel. (1) 460-2600; fax (1) 460-2612; Editor-in-Chief TAMÁS SZEKERES; circ. 140,000.

Népszabadság (People's Freedom): 1960 Budapest, Bécsi u. 122-124; tel. (1) 436-4500; fax (1) 387-8699; e-mail eotvosp@ nepszabadsag.hu; internet www.nepszabadsag.hu; f. 1942; independent; Editor-in-Chief PÁL EÖTVÖS; circ. 200,000.

Népszava (Voice of the People): 1022 Budapest, Törökvész u. 30A; tel. (1) 202-7788; fax (1) 202-7798; e-mail online@nepszava.hu; internet www.nepszava.hu; f. 1873; Editor ANDRÁS KERESZTY; circ. 120,000.

Pest Megyei Hirlap (Pest County Journal): Budapest; tel. (1) 138-2399; Editor-in-Chief Dr ANDRÁS BÁRD; circ. 43,000.

Pesti Hirlap (Pest Journal): 1051 Budapest, Október 6 u. 8; tel. (1) 117-6162; fax (1) 117-6029; f. 1993; Editor-in-Chief ANDRÁS BENCSIK; circ. 50,000.

Üzlet (Business): Budapest; tel. (1) 111-8260; Editor-in-Chief IVÁN ÉRSEK.

Debrecen

Hajdú-Bihari Napló (Hajdú-Bihar Diary): 4024 Debrecen, Dósa nádor tér 10; tel. (52) 413-395; fax (52) 412-326; e-mail naplo@iscomp .hu; internet www.naplo.hu; f. 1944; Editor-in-Chief ZSOLT PORCSIN; circ. 60,000.

Dunaújváros

A Hirlap (The Journal): 2400 Dunaújváros, Városháza tér 1; tel. (25) 16-010; Editor-in-Chief CSABA D. KISS.

Eger

Heves Megyei Hirlap (Heves County Journal): 3301 Eger, Barkóczy u. 7; tel. (36) 13-644; e-mail hmhirlap@axels.hu; internet www .agria.hu/hmhirlap; Editor-in-Chief LEVENTE KAPOSI; circ. 33,000.

Győr

Kisalföld: 9021 Győr, Újlak u. 4/a; tel. (96) 504-444; fax (96) 504-414; e-mail kisalfoldmail.matav.hu; internet www.kisalfold.hu; Editor-in-Chief NYERGES CSABA.

Kaposvár

Somogyi Hirlap (Somogy Journal): 7401 Kaposvár, Latinca Sándor u. 2A; tel. (82) 11-644; internet www.somogyihirlap.hu; Editor-in-Chief Dr IMRE KERCZA; circ. 59,000.

Kecskemét

Petőfi Népe: 6000 Kecskemét, Szabadság tér 1A; tel. (76) 481-391; internet www.petofinepe.hu; Editor-in-Chief Dr DÁNIEL LOVAS; circ. 60,000.

Miskolc

Déli Hirlap (Midday Journal): 3527 Miskolc, Bajcsy-Zsilinszky u. 15; tel. (46) 42-694; Editor-in-Chief DEZSŐ BEKES; circ. 20,000.

Észak-Magyarország (Northern Hungary): 3527 Miskolc, Bajcsy-Zsilinszky u. 15; tel. (46) 341-888; internet www.eszak.hu/eszako.2; Editor-in-Chief LÁSZLÓ GÖRÖMBÖLYI; circ. 45,000.

Nyíregyháza

Kelet-Magyarország (Eastern Hungary): 4401 Nyíregyháza, Zrínyi u. 3–5; tel. (42) 11-277; Editor-in-Chief Dr SÁNDOR ANGYAL; circ. 80,000.

Pécs

Új Dunántúli Napló: 7601 Pécs, Hunyadi u. 11; tel. (72) 15-000; internet 195.184.19.151/index.php3; Editor-in-Chief JENŐ LOMBOSI; circ. 84,000.

Salgótarján

Új Nógrád (New Nógrád): 3100 Salgótarján, Palócz Imre tér 4; tel. (32) 10-589; Editor-in-Chief LÁSZLÓ SULYOK; circ. 23,000.

Szeged

Délvilág (Southern World): 6740 Szeged, Tanácsköztársaság u. 10; tel. (62) 14-911; internet www.delvilag.hu; Editor-in-Chief ISTVÁN NIKOLÉNYI; circ. 20,000.

Délmagyarország (Southern Hungary): 6740 Szeged, Stefánia 10; tel. (62) 481-281; internet www.delmagyar.szeged.hu; Editor-in-Chief IMRE DLUSZTUS; circ. 70,000.

Székesfehérvár

Fejér Megyei Hirlap (Fejér County Journal): 8003 Székesfehérvár, Honvéd u. 8; tel. (22) 12-450; Editor-in-Chief JÁNOS Á. SZABÓ; circ. 52,000.

Szekszárd

Tolna Megyei Népújság (Tolna News): 7100 Szekszárd, Liszt Ferenc tér 3; tel. (74) 16-211; Editor-in-Chief GYÖRGYNÉ KAMARÁS; circ. 32,000.

Szolnok

Új Néplap (New People's Paper): 5001 Szolnok, Kossuth tér 1, I. Irodaház; tel. (56) 42-211; internet www.ujneplap.hu; Editor-in-Chief JÓZSEF HAJNAL; circ. 46,000.

Szombathely

Vas Népe (Vas People): 9700 Szombathely, Berzsenyi tér 2; tel. (94) 12-393; Editor-in-Chief SÁNDOR LENGYEL; circ. 65,000.

Tatabánya

24 Óra (24 Hours): 2800 Tatabánya, Fö tér 4; tel. (34) 514-012; fax (34) 514-011; e-mail szerk.kom@axels.hu; internet www.24ora.hu; Editor-in-Chief FERENC SZTRAPÁK; circ. 23,000.

Veszprém

Napló (Diary): 8201 Veszprém, Szabadság tér 15; tel. (80) 27-444; Editor-in-Chief ELEMÉR BALOGH; circ. 58,000.

Zalaegerszeg

Zalai Hirlap (Zala Journal): 8901 Zalaegerszeg, Ady Endre u. 62; tel. (92) 12-575; Editor-in-Chief JÓZSEF TARSOLY; circ. 71,000.

WEEKLIES

Élet és Irodalom (Life and Literature): 1089 Budapest, Rezsö tér 15; tel. (1) 210-2157; fax (1) 269-9241; e-mail es@es.hu; internet www.es.hu; f. 1957; literary and political; Editor ZOLTÁN KOVÁCS; circ. 16,000.

Élet és Tudomány (Life and Science): 1088 Budapest, Bródy Sándor u 16; tel. and fax (1) 138-2472; f. 1946; popular science; Editor-in-Chief Dr HERCZEG JÁNOS; circ. 20,000.

Evangélikus Élet (Evangelical Life): 1085 Budapest, Üllői u. 24; tel. and fax (1) 117-1108; f. 1933; Evangelical–Lutheran Church newspaper; Editor MIHÁLY TÓTH-SZÖLLŐS; circ. 12,000.

Heti Világgazdaság (World Economy Weekly): 1124 Budapest, Németvölgy u. 62-64; tel. (1) 3555-411; fax (1) 3555-693; internet www.hvg.hu; f. 1979; Editor-in-Chief IVÁN LIPOVECZ; circ. 141,000.

Képes Újság (Illustrated News): 1085 Budapest, Gyulai Pál u. 14; tel. (1) 113-7660; f. 1960; Editor MIHÁLY KOVÁCS; circ. 400,000.

Ludas Matyi: Budapest; tel. (1) 133-5718; satirical; Editor JÓZSEF ÁRKUS; circ. 352,000.

L'udové Noviny (People's News): 1065 Budapest, Nagymező u. 49; tel. (1) 131-9184; in Slovak, for Slovaks in Hungary; Editor PÁL KONDÁCS; circ. 1,700.

Magyar Mezőgazdaság (Hungarian Agriculture): 1355 Budapest, Kossuth Lajos tér 11; tel. (1) 112-2433; f. 1946; Editor-in-Chief Dr KÁROLY FEHÉR; circ. 24,000.

Magyar Nők Lapja (Hungarian Women's Journal): 1022 Budapest, Törökvész u. 30A; tel. (1) 212-4020; fax (1) 326-8264; e-mail noklapja@noklapja.ekh.hu; f. 1949; Editor-in-Chief LILI ZÉTÉNYI; circ. 550,000.

Magyarország (Hungary): Budapest; tel. (1) 138-4644; f. 1964; news magazine; Editor DÉNES GYAPAY; circ. 200,000.

Narodne Novine (People's News): 1396 Budapest, POB 495; tel. (1) 112-4869; f. 1945 for Yugoslavs in Hungary; in Serbo-Croat and Slovene; Chief Editor MARKO MARKOVIĆ; circ. 2,800.

Neue Zeitung (New Paper): 1391 Budapest, Lendvay u. 22, POB 224; tel. (1) 302-6877; e-mail neueztg@mail.elender.hu; f. 1957 for Germans in Hungary; Editor JOHANN SCHUTH; circ. 4,500.

Rádió és Televízióújság (Radio and TV News): 1801 Budapest; tel. (1) 138-8114; fax (1) 138-7349; f. 1924; Editor MÁRTA BÓDAY; circ. 300,000.

Reform: Budapest; tel. and fax (1) 122-4240; f. 1988; popular tabloid; 50% foreign-owned; Editor PÉTER TŐKE; circ. 300,000.

Reformátusok Lapja: 1395 Budapest, POB 424; tel. (1) 117-6809; fax (1) 117-8386; f. 1957; Reformed Church paper for the laity; Editor-in-Chief and Publr ATTILA P. KOMLÓS; circ. 30,000.

Szabad Föld (Free Earth): 1087 Budapest, Könyves Kálmán krt 76; tel. and fax (1) 133-6794; f. 1945; Editor GYULA ECK; circ. 720,000.

Szövetkezet (Co-operative): 1054 Budapest, Szabadság tér 14; tel. (1) 131-3132; National Council of Hungarian Consumer Co-operative Societies; Editor-in-Chief ATTILA KOVÁCS; circ. 85,000.

Tallózó: 1133 Budapest, Visegrádi u. 110-112; tel. and fax (1) 149-8707; f. 1989; news digest; Editor-in-Chief GYÖRGY ANDAI; circ. 35,000.

Tőzsde Kurir (Hungarian Stock Market Courier): Budapest; tel. (1) 122-3273; fax (1) 142-8356; business; Editor-in-Chief ISTVÁN GÁBOR BENEDEK.

Új Ember (New Man): 1053 Budapest, Kossuth Lajos u. 1; tel. (1) 117-3661; fax (1) 117-3471; f. 1945; religious weekly; Editor LÁSZLÓ RÓNAY; circ. 70,000.

OTHER PERIODICALS
(Published monthly unless otherwise indicated)

Állami Gazdaság (State Farming): General Direction of State Farming, Budapest; tel. (1) 112-4617; fax (1) 111-4877; f. 1946; Editor P. GÖRGÉNYI.

Beszeloe (The Speaker): 1364 Budapest, POB 143; tel. and fax (1) 302-1271; e-mail beszelo@mailc3.hu; culture and criticism; Editor-in-Chief ILONA KISS.

Business Partner Hungary: 1081 Budapest, Csokonai u. 3; tel. (1) 303-9586; fax (1) 303-9582; e-mail nemeth@kopdat.hu; internet www.kopdat.hu; f. 1986; every two months; English and German; economic journal published by Economic, Research Marketing and Computing Co Ltd (KOPINT-DATORG); Head of Dept ILONA NÉMETH.

Egyházi Krónika (Church Chronicle): 1052 Budapest, Petőfi tér 2.1.2; tel. and fax (1) 318-4813; f. 1952; every 2 months; Eastern Orthodox Church journal; Editor Archpriest Dr FERIZ BERKI.

Elektrotechnika (Electrical Engineering): 1055 Budapest, Kossuth Lajos tér 6–8; tel. (1) 353-0117; fax (1) 353-4069; e-mail lernyei.mee@mtesz.hu; f. 1908; organ of Electrotechnical Association; Editor Dr JÁNOS BENCZE; circ. 6,500.

Élelmezési Ipar (Food Industry): 1372 Budapest, POB 433; tel. (1) 214-6691; fax (1) 214-6692; e-mail mail.mete@mtesz.hu; internet www.mtesz.hu; f. 1947; Scientific Society for Food Industry; Editor Dr ISTVÁN TÓTH-ZSIGA.

Energia és Atomtechnika (Energy and Nuclear Technology): 1055 Budapest, Kossuth Lajos tér 6–8; tel. (1) 153-2751; fax (1) 156-1215; f. 1947; every two months; Scientific Society for Energy Economy; Editor-in-Chief Dr G. BŐKI.

Energiagazdálkodás (Energy Economy): 1055 Budapest, Kossuth Lajos tér 6; tel. (1) 153-2751; fax (1) 153-3894; Scientific Society for Energetics; Editor Dr ANDOR ANESINI.

Ezermester (The Handyman): Budapest; tel. (1) 132-1987; f. 1957; do-it-yourself magazine; Editor JÓZSEF PERÉNYI; circ. 50,000.

Gép (Machinery): 1027 Budapest, Fő u. 68; tel. (1) 135-4175; fax (1) 153-0818; f. 1949; Scientific Society of Mechanical Engineering; Editor Dr KORNÉL LEHOFER.

Hungarian Business Herald: Budapest; tel. and fax (1) 186-6143; f. 1970; quarterly review published in English and German by the Ministry of Industry and Trade; Editor-in-Chief Dr GERD BIRÓ; circ. 4,000.

Hungarian Travel Magazine: Budapest, Múzeum u. 11; tel. (1) 138-4643; quarterly in English and German; illustrated journal of the Tourist Board for visitors to Hungary; Man. Editor JÚLIA SZ. NAGY.

Ipar-Gazdaság (Industrial Economy): 1371 Budapest, POB 433; tel. (1) 202-1083; f. 1948; Editor Dr TAMÁS MÉSZÁROS; circ. 4,000.

Jogtudományi Közlöny (Law Gazette): 1535 Budapest, POB 773; 1015 Budapest, Donáti u. 35-45; tel. (1) 355-0330; fax (1) 355-0441; e-mail jogtud@mkab.hu; f. 1866; legal and administrative sciences; Editor-in-Chief Dr IMRE VÖRÖS; circ. 1,000.

Kortárs (Contemporary): 1426 Budapest, POB 108; tel. (1) 342-1168; e-mail kortars@elender.hu; internet www.elender.hu/kortars; f. 1957; literary gazette; Editor-in-Chief IMRE KIS PINTÉR; circ. 5,000.

Közgazdasági Szemle (Economic Review): 1112 Budapest, Budaörsi u. 43–45; tel. (1) 315-3165; fax (1) 315-3166; internet www.kozgazdasagiszemle.hu; f. 1954; published by Cttee for Economic Sciences of Hungarian Academy of Sciences; Editor KATALIN SZABÓ; circ. 3,000.

Made in Hungary: 1426 Budapest, POB 3; economics and business magazine published in English by Hungarian News Agency (MTI); Editor GYÖRGY BLASITS.

Magyar Hirek (Hungarian News): Budapest; tel. (1) 122-5616; fax (1) 122-2421; every 2 weeks; illustrated magazine primarily for Hungarians living abroad; Editor GYÖRGY HALÁSZ; circ. 70,000.

Magyar Jog (Hungarian Law): 1054 Budapest, Szemere u. 10; tel. (1) 311-4880; fax (1) 311-4013; f. 1953; law; Editor-in-Chief Dr JÁNOS NÉMETH; circ. 2,200.

Magyar Közlöny (Official Gazette): Budapest; tel. (1) 112-1236; Editor Dr ELEMÉR KISS; circ. 90,000.

Magyar Tudomány (Hungarian Science): Hungarian Academy of Sciences, 1051 Budapest, Nádor u. 7; tel. and fax (1) 317-9524; e-mail matud@hefka.iif.hu; internet www.matud.hu; f. 1846; monthly; multidisciplinary science review; Editors VILMOS CSÁNYI, ZSUZSA SZENTGYÖRGYI.

Pedagógusok Lapja (Teachers' Review): 1068 Budapest, Városligeti fasor 10; tel. (1) 322-8464; e-mail psz-seh@mail.matav.hu; internet www.deltasoft.hu/pszseh; f. 1945; published by the Hungarian Union of Teachers; Editor-in-Chief ÁROK ANTAL; circ. 10,000.

Református Egyház (Reformed Church): 1146 Budapest, Abonyi u. 21; tel. (1) 343-7870; f. 1949; official journal of the Hungarian Reformed Church; Editor-in-Chief LAJOS TÓTH; circ. 1,300.

Statisztikai Szemle (Statistical Review): 1525 Budapest, POB 51; tel. (1) 487-4343; fax (1) 487-4344; e-mail statszemle@ksh.gov.hu; internet www.ksh.hu/statszml; f. 1923; Editor-in-Chief Dr LÁSZLÓ HUNYADI; circ. 800.

Technika (Technology): 1027 Budapest, Fö u. 68; tel. (1) 201-7083; fax (1) 201-8564; f. 1957; official journal of the Hungarian Academy of Engineering; monthly in Hungarian, annually in English, German and Russian; Editor-in-Chief MARGIT WELLEK; circ. 15,000.

Turizmus (Tourism): 1088 Budapest, Múzeum u. 11; tel. (1) 266-5853; fax (1) 338-4293; e-mail turizmus@mail.matav.hu; Editor ZSOLT SZEBENI; circ. 8,000.

Új Élet (New Life): 1075 Budapest, Síp u. 12; tel. (1) 322-2829; every 2 weeks; for Hungarian Jews; Editor Dr PÉTER KARDOS; circ. 5,000.

Új Technika (New Technology): Budapest; tel. (1) 155-7122; f. 1967; popular industrial quarterly; circ. 35,000.

Vigilia: 1364 Budapest, POB 48; tel. (1) 317-7246; fax (1) 317-7682; e-mail vigilia@hcbc.hu; internet www.hcbc.hu/vigilia; f. 1935; Catholic; Editor LÁSZLÓ LUKÁCS; circ. 4,000.

NEWS AGENCIES

HT Press News Agency: 1149 Budapest, Angol u. 22; tel. and fax (1) 363-1472.

Hungarian News Agency Co (Magyar Távirati Iroda Rt—MTI): 1016 Budapest, Naphegy tér 8; tel. (1) 375-6722; fax (1) 375-3973; internet www.mti.hu; f. 1880; 19 brs in Hungary; 14 bureaux abroad; Pres. MATYAS VINCE.

Foreign Bureaux

Agence France-Presse (AFP): 1016 Budapest, Naphegy u. 29; tel. (1) 356-8416; fax (1) 201-9161; e-mail afpbud@elender.hu; Correspondent ESZTER SZÁMADÓ.

Agenzia Nazionale Stampa Associata (ANSA) (Italy): 1054 Budapest, Vadász u. 31; tel. (1) 332-3555; fax (1) 332-3556; Bureau Chief GAETANO ALIMENTI.

Associated Press (AP) (USA): Budapest; tel. (1) 156-9129; Correspondent ALEX BANDY.

Informatsionnoye Telegrafnoye Agentstvo Rossii—Telegrafnoye Agentstvo Suverennykh Stran (ITAR—TASS) (Russia): 1023 Budapest, Vérhalom u. 12–16; Correspondent YEVGENII POPOV.

Reuters (United Kingdom): 1088 Budapest, Rákóczi u. 1–3, East-West Business Centre; tel. (1) 266-2410; fax (1) 266-2030; internet www.reuters.hu; Chief Correspondent MITYA NEW.

Rossiyskoye Informatsionnoye Agentstvo—Novosti (RIA—Novosti) (Russia): Budapest; tel. (1) 132-0594; fax (1) 142-3325; Bureau Chief A. POPOV.

Tlačová agentúra Slovenskej republiky (TASR) (Slovakia): Budapest; tel. and fax (1) 135-1843; Bureau Chief PETER KLENKO.

Xinhua (New China) News Agency (People's Republic of China): Budapest; tel. (1) 176-7548; fax (1) 176-2571; Chief Correspondent ZHOU DONGYAO.

PRESS ASSOCIATIONS

Hungarian Newspaper Publishers' Association: 1034 Budapest, Bécsi ùt 122-124; tel. (1) 368-8674; fax (1) 388-6707; e-mail mle.peto@mail.matav.hu; f. 1990; Gen. Sec. JÁNOS PETŐ; 40 mems.

National Association of Hungarian Journalists (Magyar Újságírók Országos Szövetsége—MÚOSZ): 1062 Budapest, Andrássy u. 101; tel. (1) 322-1699; fax (1) 322-1881; f. 1896; Gen. Sec. GÁBOR BENCSIK; 7,000 mems.

Publishers

PRINCIPAL PUBLISHING HOUSES

Akadémiai Kiadó: 1117 Budapest, Prielle Kornélia u. 4; tel. (1) 464-8200; fax (1) 464-8201; e-mail custservice@akkrt.hu; internet www.akkrt.hu; f. 1828; humanities, social, natural and technical sciences, dictionaries, textbooks and periodicals; Hungarian and English; Man. Dir BUCSI SZABÓ ZSOLT.

Corvina Kiadó Kft.: 1051 Budapest, Vörösmarty tér 1; tel. (1) 318-4347; fax (1) 318-4410; e-mail corvina@mail.matav.hu; f. 1955; Hungarian works translated into foreign languages, art and educational books, fiction and non-fiction, tourist guides, cookery books and musicology; Man. Dir ISTVÁN BART.

EMB Music Publisher Ltd: Budapest, V. Vörösmarty t. 1; tel. (1) 483-3100; fax (1) 483-3101; e-mail musicpubl@emb.hu; internet www.emb.hu; f. 1950; music publishing and books on musical subjects; Dir ISTVÁN HOMOLYA.

Európa Könyvkiadó: 1055 Budapest, Kossuth Lajos tér 13–15; tel. (1) 131-2700; fax (1) 131-4162; f. 1945; world literature translated into Hungarian; Man. LEVENTE OSZTOVITS.

Gondolat Könyvkiadó Vállalat: Budapest; tel. (1) 138-3358; fax (1) 138-4540; f. 1957; popular scientific publications on natural and social sciences, art, encyclopaedic handbooks; Dir GYÖRGY FEHÉR.

Helikon Kiadó: 1053 Budapest, Papnövelde u. 8; tel. (1) 117-4865; fax (1) 117-4865; bibliophile books; Dir KATALIN BERGER.

Képzőművészeti Kiadó: Budapest; tel. (1) 251-1527; fax (1) 251-1527; fine arts; Man. Dr ZOLTÁN KEMENCZEI.

Kossuth Kiadó Rt.: 1043 Budapest, Csányi László u. 36; tel. (1) 370-0607; fax (1) 370-0602; e-mail rt@kossuted.hu; f. 1944; social sciences, educational and philosophy publications, information technology books; Man. ANDRÁS SÁNDOR KOCSIS.

Közgazdasági és Jogi Könyvkiadó Rt: Budapest; tel. (1) 112-6430; fax (1) 111-3210; f. 1955; business, economics, law, sociology, psychology, tax, politics, education, dictionaries; Man. Dir DAVID G. YOUNG.

Magvető Könyvkiadó: 1806 Budapest, POB 123; tel. (1) 235-5032; e-mail magveto@lira.hu; f. 1955; literature; Dir GÉZA MORCSÁNYI.

Medicina Könyvkiadó Rt: 1054 Budapest, Zoltan u. 8; tel. (1) 112-2650; fax (1) 112-2450; f. 1957; books on medicine, sport, tourism; Dir BORBÁLA FARKASVÖLGYI.

Mezőgazda Kiadó: 1165 Budapest, Koronafürt u. 44; tel. (1) 407-6575; fax (1) 407-7571; ecology, natural sciences, environmental protection, food industry; Man. Dr LAJOS LELKES.

Móra Ferenc Ifjúsági Kiadó Rt.: 1134 Budapest, Váci u. 19; tel. (1) 320-4740; fax (1) 320-5382; e-mail mora_kiado@elender.hu; f. 1950; youth and children's books; Man. Dr JÁNOS CS. TÓTH.

Műszaki Könyvkiadó: 1033 Budapest III, Szentendre u. 89–93; tel. (1) 437-2405; fax (1) 437-2404; e-mail lakatosz@muszakikiado.hu; internet www.muszakikiado.hu; f. 1955; scientific and technical, vocational and general text books; Man. SÁNDOR BÉRCZI.

Nemzeti Tankönyvkiadó Rt. (National Textbook Publishing House): 1143 Budapest, Szobránc u. 6-8; tel. (1) 460-1800; fax (1) 460-1869; e-mail public@ntk.hu; internet www.ntk.hu; f. 1949; school and university textbooks, pedagogical literature and language books; Gen. Man. JÓZSEF PÁLFI.

Népszava Lapés Könyvkiadó Vállalat: Budapest; tel. (1) 122-4810; National Confederation of Hungarian Trade Unions; Man. Dr JENŐ KISS.

Statiqum Kiadó és Nyomda Kft: 1033 Budapest, Kaszásdülő u. 2; tel. (1) 250-0311; fax (1) 168-8635; f. 1991; publications on statistics, system-management and computer science; Dir BENEDEK BELECZ.

Szépirodalmi Könyvkiadó: Budapest; tel. (1) 122-1285; f. 1950; modern and classical Magyar literature; Man. SÁNDOR Z. SZALAI.

Zrinyi Kiadó: 1087 Budapest, Kerepesi u. 29B; tel. (1) 133-9165; military literature; Man. MÁTÉ ESZES.

PUBLISHERS' ASSOCIATION

Hungarian Publishers' and Booksellers' Association (Magyar Könyvkiadók és Könyvterjesztők Egyesülése): Budapest; tel. (1) 343-2540; fax (1) 343-2541; e-mail mkke@mkke.hu; f. 1795; most leading Hungarian publishers are members of the Association; Pres. ISTVÁN BART; Sec.-Gen. PÉTER ZENTAI.

WRITERS' UNION

Association of Hungarian Writers (Magyar Írószövetség): 1062 Budapest, Bajza u. 18; tel. (1) 322-8840; f. 1945; Pres. BÉLA POMOGÁTS.

Broadcasting and Communications

TELECOMMUNICATIONS

Matáv Hungarian Telecommunications Co: 1541 Budapest, Krisztina krt 6–8; tel. (1) 458-0000; fax (1) 458-7176; e-mail investor.relations@ln.matav.hu; internet www.matav.hu; f. 1991; 60% owned by Deutsche Telekom AG (Germany); telecommunications service provider; Chief Exec. ELEK STRAUB; 16,034 employees.

Pannon GSM Rt: 2040 Budaörs, Baross u. 165; tel. (1) 464-6000; fax (1) 464-6100; internet www.pgsm.hu; f. 1993; 100% owned by Telenor (Norway); mobile telecommunications; Chair. KLAUS HOLGAARD RASMUSSEN (desig.).

Westel Rt: 1117 Budapest, Kaposvár u. 5-7; tel. (1) 265-9210; fax (1) 204-4128; e-mail customer_service@westel.hu; internet www.westel.hu; mobile telecommunications and internet service provider; Chief Exec. ANDRÁS SUGÁR.

BROADCASTING

Hungarian National Radio and Television Board (Országos Rádió és Televízió Testület—ORTT): 1088 Budapest, Reviczky u. 5; tel. (1) 429–8600; fax (1) 267–2612; e-mail ehorvath@ortt.hu; internet www.ortt.hu; Dir ISTVÁN HAJDU.

RADIO

Hungarian Radio (Magyar Rádió): 1800 Budapest, Bródy Sándor u. 5–7; tel. (1) 328-8388; fax (1) 328-7004; internet www.radio.hu; f. 1924; stations: Radio Kossuth, Radio Petőfi, Radio Bartók (mainly classical music); 8 regional studios; external broadcasts in English, German, Hungarian, Romanian, Russian, Slovak and Serbo-Croat; Pres. ISTVÁN SZIJARTO (acting).

Antenna Hungária Magyar Msorszóró És, Rádióhírközlési Rt: 1119 Budapest, Petzvál József u 31–33; tel. (1) 203-6060; fax (1) 203-6093; internet www.ahrt.hu; f. 1989; radio and television broadcasting; Chief Exec. ISTVÁN MÁTÉ; 1,290 employees.

Radio C: 1086 Budapest, Teleki tér. 7; tel. (1) 459-0095; fax (1) 459-0094; internet www.radioc.hu; f. 2001; Roma radio station; news and cultural programming suspended in April 2003 owing to lack of funds; Man. GYÖRGY KERENYI.

Radio Danubius: f. 1986; privatized 1998; broadcasts news, music and information in Hungarian 24 hours a day; transmitting stations in Budapest, Lake Balaton region, Sopron, Szeged and Debrecen; Dir JÓZSEF LÁSZLÓ.

TELEVISION

Hungarian Television (Magyar Televízió): 1810 Budapest, Szabadság tér 17; tel. (1) 353-3200; fax (1) 373-4133; e-mail mtvintrel@intrel.mtv.hu; internet www.mtv.hu; f. 1957; first channel, MTV 1, terrestrial, broadcasts 19 hours a day and the second channel, MTV 2, satellite, 24 hours a day, colour transmissions; 100 high-capacity relay stations; Pres. IMRE RAGÁTS (acting).

Antenna Hungária Magyar Msorszóró És, Rádióhírközlési Rt: 1119 Budapest, Petzvál József u 31–33; tel. (1) 203-6060; fax (1) 203-6093; internet www.ahrt.hu; f. 1989; radio and television broadcasting; Chief Exec. ISTVÁN MÁTÉ; 1,290 employees.

Finance

(cap. = capital; res = reserves; dep. = deposits; m. = million; amounts in forint unless otherwise stated)

Under economic reforms, introduced in 1987, three banks were established to assume the commercial banking activities of the National Bank of Hungary: the Hungarian Credit Bank, the Commercial and Credit Bank and the Budapest Bank. The already existing Hungarian Foreign Trade Bank and the National Savings and Commercial Bank also became fully chartered financial institutions. At the end of 1998 28 of Hungary's 36 commercial banks were foreign- or jointly-owned, and there were an additional seven specialized financial institutions. There were also 241 savings co-operatives. By 2001 there were a total of 42 commercial banks in operation in Hungary.

Responsibility for bank supervision is divided between the National Bank of Hungary and the State Banking Supervision Agency. Under legislation introduced in January 1997, the supervisory responsibilities of the National Bank were restricted to areas relating to the operation of monetary policy and the foreign-exchange system.

BANKING

Central Bank

National Bank of Hungary (Magyar Nemzeti Bank): 1850 Budapest, Szabadság tér 8–9; tel. (1) 269-4760; fax (1) 332-3913; internet www.mnb.hu; f. 1924; bank of issue; conducts international transactions; supervises banking system; cap. 10,000m., res 30,862m., dep. 2,202,879m. (Dec. 2001); Pres. ZSIGMOND JÁRAI; 23 brs.

Commercial Banks

Bank of Hungarian Savings Co-operatives Ltd (Magyar Takarékszövetkezeti Bank Rt): 1122 Budapest, Pethényi köz 10; 1525 Budapest, POB 775; tel. (1) 202-3777; fax (1) 355-9082; e-mail info@tbank.hu; internet www.takarekbank.hu; f. 1989; cap. 2,040.8m., res 3,517.1m., dep. 104,465.4m. (Dec. 2000); Pres. PETER DIECKMANN; Gen. Man. PÉTER CSICSÁKY.

BNP Paribas Bank (Hungaria) RT: 1055 Budapest, Honvéd u. 20; tel. (1) 374-6300; fax (1) 269-3967; e-mail info.hu@bnpparibas.com; f. 1991; wholly owned by BNP Paribas (France); cap. 3,500m., res 2,329m., dep. 58,153m. (Dec. 1999); Chair. JACQUES DE LAROSIÈRE; Gen. Man. LÁSZLÓ HAÁS.

Budapest Bank RT: 11138 Budapest, POB 1852, Váci u. 202; tel. (1) 328-1700; fax (1) 269-2417; e-mail info@bbrt.hu; internet www.budapestbank.hu; f. 1987; cap. 19,350m., res 5,768m., dep. 270,902m. (Dec. 2000); 99.25% owned by GE Capital International Financing Corpn (USA); Chief Exec. RICHARD PELLY; 56 brs.

Central-European International Bank Ltd (CIB): 1537 Budapest, Medve u. 4–14, POB 394; tel. (1) 212-1330; fax (1) 212-4200; e-mail cib@cib.hu; internet www.cib.hu; f. 1979; 100% owned by IntesaBci Holding International SA (Luxembourg); merged with CIB Hungária Bank Rt in 1998; cap. 23,500m., res 15,800m., dep. 545,873m. (Dec. 2001); Chair. Dr GYÖRGY SURÁNYI; Dir-Gen. and Chief Exec. ADÁM FARKAS.

Citibank RT: 1051 Budapest, Szabadság tér 7, Bank Center, Citibank Tower; 1367 Budapest, POB 123; tel. (1) 374-5000; fax (1) 374-5100; internet www.citibank.hu; f. 1986; merged with Europai Kereskedelmi Bank RT in 1999; cap. 13,005m., res 3,997m., dep. 241,252m. (Dec. 2001); Chief Exec. and Gen. Man. MARK T. ROBINSON.

Commerzbank (Budapest) RT: 1054 Budapest, Széchenyi rkp. 8; 1254 Budapest, POB 1070; tel. (1) 374-8100; fax (1) 269-4530; e-mail commerzbank@commerzbank.hu; internet www.commerzbank.hu; f. 1993; cap. 2,466.9m., res 6,206.0m., dep. 110, 208.3m. (Dec. 1999); Pres. and Chair. of Sup. Bd ANDREAS DE MAIZIÈRE; Chair., Chief Exec. and Man. Dir MARTIN FISCHEDICK.

Erste Bank Hungary RT: 1054 Budapest, Hold u. 16; tel. (1) 373-2400; fax (1) 373-2499; internet www.erstebank.hu; f. 1987 as Mezobank RT; present name adopted 1998; cap. 11,210m., res 1,392m., dep. 244,280m. (Dec. 2001); Chair. REINHARD ORTNER; Chief Exec. PÉTER KISBENEDEK; 72 brs.

General Banking and Trust Co. Ltd (Altalános Értékforgalmi Bank RT): 1055 Budapest, Markó u. 9; tel. (1) 269-1473; fax (1) 269-

1442; e-mail esebok@gbt.hu; internet www.gbt.hu; f. 1922; 25.5% owned by Gazprombank (Russia); cap. US $76.9m., res –$19.3m., dep. $916.3m. (Dec. 2001); Chair. and Chief Exec. MEGDET RAKHIMKULOV; 11 brs.

Hungarian Development Bank (MFB) Ltd (Magyar Fejlesztési Bank RT): 1051 Budapest, Nádor u. 31; tel. (1) 428-1400; fax (1) 428-1490; e-mail bank@mfb.hu; internet www.mfb.hu; f. 1991 as an investment company; authorized as a bank 1993; cap. 72,270m. (Dec. 2001), res 22,358.6m., dep. 93,388.0m. (Dec. 2000); Chair. of Bd GYÖRGY ZDEBORSKY.

Hungarian Foreign Trade Bank Ltd (Magyar Külkereskedelmi Bank RT): 1056 Budapest, V. Váci u. 38; tel. (1) 269-0922; fax (1) 269-0959; e-mail exterbank@mkb.hu; internet www.mkb.hu; f. 1950; commercial banking; 89.3% owned by Bayerische Landesbank (Germany); cap. 11,520m., res 69,326m., dep. 786,106m. (Dec. 2001); Chair. and Chief Exec. TAMÁS ERDEI; 29 brs.

HVB Bank Hungary RT: 1054 Budapest, Akadémia u. 17; 1363 Budapest, POB 58; tel. (1) 369-0812; fax (1) 353-4959; internet www.hvb.hu; f. 2001 by merger of Bank Austria Creditanstalt Hungary RT and Hypovereinsbank Hungary RT; 100% owned by Bank Austria Creditanstalt AG; cap. 24,118m., res 12,089m., dep. 451,919m. (Dec. 2001); Chief Exec. Dr MATTHIAS KUNSCH.

ING Bank RT: 1061 Budapest, Andrássy u. 9; tel. (1) 235-8700; fax (1) 322-2288; internet www.ing.hu; f. 1992 as NMB Bank; present name adopted 1996; 100% owned by ING Bank NV (Netherlands); cap. 15,758m., res 5,281m., dep. 134,648m. (Dec. 1999); Man. Dir RANDOLPH S. KOPPA.

Inter-Európa Bank RT: 1054 Budapest, Szabadság tér 15, POB 65; tel. (1) 373-6000; fax (1) 269-2526; e-mail ieb@ieb.hu; internet www.ieb.hu; f. 1981 as INTERINVEST; cap. 6,934m., res 2,498m., dep. 115,519m. (Dec. 2001); Chair. FERENC BARTHA; Man. Dir EZIO SALVAI; 20 brs.

Kereskedelmi és Hitelbank RT (K&H Bank RT): 1051 Budapest, Vigadó tér 1; tel. (1) 328-9000; fax (1) 328-9696; e-mail khbinfo@khb.hu; internet www.khb.hu; f. 1987; merged with Kvantum Investment Bank in 1998, merged with ABN Amro (Magyar) Bank RT in 2001; 59.1% owned by KBC Bank NV (Belgium), 40.2% owned by ABN Amro Bank NV (Netherlands); cap. 34,089m., dep. 444,565m. (Dec. 2001); Chair. Dr ISTVÁN SZALKAI; Chief Exec. TIBOR E. REJTÖ; 176 brs.

Konzumbank RT: 1054 Budapest, Tüköry u. 4, POB 300; tel. (1) 374-7300; fax (1) 374-7355; e-mail info@konzumbank.hu; internet www.konzumbank.hu; f. 1986; 85.7% owned by Hungarian Development Bank (MFB) Ltd; cap. 5,231m., res –735m., dep. 74,084m. (Dec. 2001); Chair. GYULA GAÁL; Chief Exec. TIBOR FERENCI.

National Savings and Commercial Bank Ltd—OTP Bank (Országos Takarékpénztár és Kereskedelmi Bank RT): 1051 Budapest, Nádor u. 16; tel. (1) 353-1444; fax (1) 312-6858; e-mail otpbank@otpbank.hu; internet www.otpbank.hu; f. 1949; savings deposits, credits, foreign transactions; privatized in 1996; cap. 28,000m., res 98,335m., dep. 1,709,380m. (Dec. 2000); Chair. and Chief Exec. Dr SÁNDOR CSÁNYI; 424 brs.

Postbank and Savings Bank Corporation—Postabank (Postabank és Takarékpénztár RTt): 1132 Budapest, Váci u. 48; tel. (1) 318-0855; fax (1) 317-1369; e-mail info@postabank.hu; internet www.postabank.hu; f. 1988; 96.8% owned by Hungarian Post; cap. 20,021m., res 20,467m., dep. 272,597m. (Dec. 2000); Chair. JÚLIA KIRÁLY; Chief Exec. BÉLA SINGLOVICS; 71 brs.

Raiffeisen Bank RT: 1054 Budapest, Akademia u. 6, POB 173; tel. (1) 484-4400; fax (1) 484-4444; e-mail info@raiffeisen.hu; internet www.raiffeisen.hu; f. 1986 as Unicbank RT; present name adopted 1999; 96.8% owned by Raiffeisen Group (Austria); cap. 21,891m., res 9,688m., dep. 293,219m. (Dec. 2001); Pres. Dr HERBERT STEPIC; Man. Dir Dr PÉTER FELCSUTI; 41 brs.

Westdeutsche Landesbank (Hungaria) RT: 1075 Budapest, Madách Imre ut. 13–14; tel. (1) 268-1680; fax (1) 268-1933; e-mail public@westlb.hu; internet www.westlb.de; f. 1985; present name adopted 1993; cap. 4,485.8m., res 2,487.7m., dep. 79,353.3m. (Dec. 2001); Chair. and Dir-Gen. JÜRGEN PHILIPPER; Dir-Gen. GEZA EGYED.

Specialized Financial Institutions

Hungarian Export-Import Bank Ltd—EXIMBANK (Magyar Export-Import Bank RT): 1065 Budapest, Nagymezö u. 46-48; tel. (1) 374-9100; fax (1) 269-4476; e-mail eximh@eximbank.hu; internet www.eximbank.hu; cap. 10,100m., res 1,789m., dep. 100,598m. (Dec. 2001); Chief Exec. Dr FRIGYES BÁNKI.

Merkantil Bank Ltd: 1051 Budapest, József Attila u. 24; tel. (1) 429-7600; fax (1) 429-7601; e-mail molnar.andrasne@mail.merkantil.hu; internet www.merkantil.hu; f. 1988; affiliated to National Savings and Commercial Bank Ltd—OTP Bank; automobile financing transactions; cap. 1,100m. Chair. and Chief Exec. ADÁM KOLOSSVÁRY.

Opel Bank Hungary RT: 1027 Budapest, Kapás u. 11-15; tel. (1) 457-9110; Gen. Man. JARI ARJAVALTA.

Porsche Bank Hungaria RT.: 1139 Budapest, Váci ut. 85; tel. (1) 465-4700; fax (1) 465-4775; e-mail info@porschebank.hu; internet www.porschebank.hu; Pres. PÁL ANTALL.

Rákóczi Regional Development Bank Ltd (Rákóczi Regionális Fejlesztési Bank RT): 3530 Miskolc, Mindszent tér 1; tel. (46) 510-300; fax (46) 510-396; e-mail central@rakoczibank.hu; f. 1992; Gen. Man. KORNÉL KOSZTICZA.

Other Financial Institution

Central Corporation of Banking Companies (Pénzintézeti Központ): 1093 Budapest, Lónyay u. 38; tel. (1) 117-1255; fax (1) 215-9963; f. 1916; banking, property, rights and interests, deposits, securities, and foreign exchange management; cap. 11,127m., res 3,548m., dep. 12,289m; Chair. and Chief Exec. PÉTER KIRÁLY; 3 brs.

STOCK EXCHANGE

Budapest Stock Exchange (Budapesti Értéktőzsde): 1052 Budapest, Deák Ferenc u. 5; tel. (1) 429-6700; fax (1) 429-6800; e-mail info@bse.hu; internet www.bse.hu; Pres. GYÖRGY JAKITSKY.

COMMODITY EXCHANGE

Budapest Commodity Exchange (Budapesti Árutőzsde): 1134 Budapest, Róbert Károly krt 61–65; tel. (1) 465-6979; fax (1) 465-6981; e-mail bce@bce-bat.com; internet www.bce-bat.com; Chair. ATTILA KOVÁCS.

INSURANCE

In July 1986 the state insurance enterprise was divided into two companies, one of which retained the name of the former Állami Biztosító. By 1995 13 insurance companies had been established.

AB-AEGON Általános Biztosító RT: 1091 Budapest, u. Üllői 1; tel. (1) 218-1866; fax (1) 217-7065; f. 1949 as Állami Biztosító, reorganized 1986, present name since 1992; handles pensions, life and property insurance, insurance of agricultural plants, co-operatives, foreign insurance, etc; Gen. Man. Dr GÁBOR KEPECS.

Garancia Insurance Company (Garancia Biztosító RT): 1054 Budapest, Vadász u. 12; tel. (1) 269-2533; fax (1) 269-2549; f. 1988; cap. 4,050m; Gen. Man. and Chief Exec. Dr ZOLTÁN NAGY; 25 brs.

Hungária Insurance Company (Hungária Biztosító RT): 1054 Budapest, Bajcsy u. 52; tel. (1) 301-6565; fax (1) 301-6100; f. 1986; handles international insurance, industrial and commercial insurance and motor-car, marine, life, household, accident and liability insurance; cap. 4,266m; Chair. and Chief Exec. Dr MIHÁLY PATAI.

QBE Atlasz Insurance Company (QBE Atlasz Biztosító RT): 1143 Budapest, Stefánia ùt 51; tel. (1) 460-1400; fax (1) 460-1499; e-mail qbe-atlasz@atlasz.hu; internet www.qbeatlasz.hu; f. 1988; cap. 1,000m; Gen. Man. DORON GROSSMAN.

Trade and Industry

GOVERNMENT AGENCY

Hungarian Privatization and State Holding Company (ÁPV Rt): 1133 Budapest, Pozsonyi u. 56; tel. (1) 237-4400; fax (1) 237-4100; e-mail apvrt@apvrt.hu; internet www.apvrt.hu; f. 1995; by merger of the State Property Agency and the State Holding Company; Chair. CSABA FARAGÓ.

NATIONAL CHAMBERS OF COMMERCE AND AGRICULTURE

Hungarian Chamber of Agriculture (Magyar Agrárkamara): 1119 Budapest, Etele ut. 57; tel. (1) 371-5517; fax (1) 371-5510; e-mail agota@kozpont.agrarkamara.hu; internet www.agrarkamara.hu; Pres. MIKLÓS CSIKAI.

Hungarian Chamber of Commerce and Industry (Magyar Kereskedelmi és Iparkamara): 1372 Budapest V, POB 452; tel. (1) 474-5141; fax (1) 250-5138; e-mail mkik@mkik.hu; f. 1850; central organization of the 23 Hungarian county chambers of commerce and industry; based on a system of voluntary membership; over 46,000 mems. Pres. Dr LÁSZLÓ PARRAGH; Sec.-Gen. PÉTER DUNAI.

REGIONAL CHAMBERS OF COMMERCE

Bács-Kiskun County Chamber of Commerce: 6000 Kecskemét, Árpád krt 4, POB 228; tel. (76) 501-500; fax (76) 501-538; e-mail bkmkik@mail.datanet.hu; internet www.iparkamara.hu; f. 1994; Chair. JÓZSEF GAÁL; Sec. LÁSZLÓ LEITNER.

Békés County Chamber of Commerce and Industry: 5600 Békéscsaba, Penza ltp. 5; tel. (66) 451-775; fax (66) 324-976; e-mail bmkik@elender.hu; internet www.bmkik.ini.hu; Chair. TAMÁS HÓDSÁGI; Sec. ZSOLT TÓTH.

Borsod-Abaúj-Zemplén County Chamber of Commerce and Industry (Borsod-Abaúj-Zemplén Kereskedelmi és Iparkamara): 3525 Miskolc, Szentpáli u. 1; tel. (46) 328-539; fax (46) 328-722; e-mail bokik@mail.bokik.hu; internet www.bokik.hu; f. 1990; membership of 1,100 cos; Pres. TAMÁS BIHALL; Sec. ANNA BAÁN-SZILÁGYI.

Budapest Chamber of Industry and Commerce (Budapesti Kereskedelmi és Iparkamara): 1016 Budapest, Krisztina krt 99; tel. (1) 488-2173; fax (1) 488-2180; e-mail nemzetkozi@bkik.hu; internet www.bkik.hu; f. 1850; Chair. LÁSZLÓ KOJI; Sec.-Gen. CSABA BAZSC.

Csongrád County Chamber of Commerce and Industry: 6721 Szeged, Tisza L. krt 2–4; tel. (62) 423-451; fax (62) 426-149; e-mail csmkik@tiszanet.hu; internet www.tiszanet.hu/kamara; Chair. ISTVÁN SZERI; Sec. LAJOS HORVÁTH.

Fejér County Chamber of Commerce and Industry (Fejér Megyei Kereskedelmi és Iparkamara): 8000 Székesfehérvár, Petőfi u. 5; tel. (22) 327-627; fax (22) 510-312; Chair. JENŐ RADETZKY; Sec.-Gen. Dr MIKLÓS SISKA.

Győr-Moson-Sopron County Chamber of Commerce and Industry: 9001 Győr, Király u. 20; tel. (96) 318-485; fax (96) 319-650; Chair. PÉTER JANCSÓ; Dir JÓZSEF VÁPÁR.

Hajdú-Bihar County Chamber of Commerce and Industry: 4025 Debrecen, Petőfi tér 10; tel. (52) 500-721; fax (52) 500-720; Chair. FERENC MIKLÓSSY; Sec. Dr EVA SKULTÉTI.

Heves County Chamber of Commerce and Industry: 3300 Eger, Telekessy u. 2; tel. (36) 429-612; fax (36) 312-989; Chair. LEVENTE NAGY; Sec.-Gen. GÁBOR FÜLÖP.

Jász-Nagykun-Szolnok County Chamber of Commerce and Industry: 5000 Szolnok, Verseghy Park 8; tel. (56) 510-610; fax (56) 370-005; e-mail kamara@jnszmkik.hu; internet www.jnszmkik.hu; Chair. Dr ANDRÁS SZIRÁKI; Sec. Dr IMRE KERÉKGYÁRTÓ.

Komárom-Esztergom County Chamber of Commerce and Industry: 2800 Tatabánya, Előd vezér u. 17; tel. and fax (34) 316-259; Chair. Dr ISTVÁN HORVÁTH; Sec. ZOLTÁN BÁTOR.

Nógrád County Chamber of Commerce and Industry: 3100 Salgótarján, Alkotmàny u. 9A; tel. (32) 520-860; fax (32) 520-862; e-mail nklk@nklk.hu; internet www.ccinograd.com; Chair. FODOR ERZSÉBET KOVÁCS; Sec. Dr ERZSÉBET KURUCZ.

Pécs-Baranya County Chamber of Commerce and Industry: 7625 Pécs, Dr Majorossy I. u. 36; tel. (72) 211-592; fax (72) 211-604; Chair. GYULA HIGI; Sec. TAMÁS SÍKFÓI.

Pest County Chamber of Commerce and Industry (Pest Megyei Kereskedelmi és Iparkamara): 1056 Budapest, Vàci u. 40; tel. (1) 317-7666; fax (1) 317-7755; e-mail titkarsag@pmkik.hu; internet www.pmkik.hu; Chair. Dr ZOLTÁN VERECZKEY; Sec.-Gen. Dr LAJOS KUPCSOK.

Somogy Chamber of Commerce and Industry (Somogyi Kereskedelmi és Iparkamara): 7400 Kaposvár, Anna u. 6; tel. (82) 501-000; fax (82) 501-046; e-mail skik@skik.hu; internet www.skik.hu; Chair. JÓZSEF VARGA; Dep. Pres. LAJOS HORVÁTH.

Szabolcs-Szatmár-Bereg County Chamber of Commerce and Industry: 4400 Nyíregyháza, Szarvas u. 1–3; tel. (42) 416-074; fax (42) 311-750; Chair. Dr JÁNOS VERES; Sec. Dr IMRE JAKAB.

Tolna County Chamber of Commerce and Industry: 7100 Szekszárd, Arany J. u. 23–25; tel. (74) 411-661; fax (74) 411-456; e-mail rostasrostas@tmkik.hu; Chair. Dr KÁLMÁN BERTHA; Sec. ILONA ROSTAS.

Vas County Chamber of Commerce and Industry (Vas Megyei Kereskedelmi és Iparkamara): 9700 Szombathely, Honvéd tér 2; tel. (94) 312-356; fax (94) 316-936; e-mail vmkik@vmkik.hu; internet www.vmkik.hu; Chair. VINCE KOVÁCS; Sec.-Gen. SÁNDOR KISS.

Veszprém County Chamber of Commerce and Industry: 8200 Veszprém, Budapest u. 3; tel. (88) 429-008; fax (88) 412-150; e-mail vkik@veszpremikamara.hu; internet www.veszpremikamara.com; Chair. KÁROLY HENGER; Dir TAMÁS CSABAI.

Zala County Chamber of Commerce and Industry (Zalai Kereskedelmi és Iparkamara): 8900 Zalaegerszeg, Petőfi u. 24; tel. (92) 550-510; fax (92) 550-525; e-mail zmkik@zmkik.hu; Chair. IMRE FARKAS; Sec.-Gen. ISTVÁN TÓTH.

INDUSTRIAL AND TRADE ASSOCIATIONS

HUNICOOP Foreign Trade Company Ltd for Industrial Co-operation: 1367 Budapest 5, POB 111; tel. (1) 267-1477; fax (1) 267-1482; agency for foreign companies in Hungary, export and import.

Interco-operation Co Ltd for Trade Promotion: 1085 Budapest, POB 136; tel. (1) 118-9966; fax (1) 118-2161; establishment and carrying out of co-operation agreements, representation of foreign companies, brands, marketing and distribution, joint ventures and import-export deals.

Hungarian Industrial Association (Magyar Iparszövetség—OKISz): 1146 Budapest, Thököly u. 58–60; tel. (1) 343-5570; fax (1) 343-5521; e-mail okisz@okiszinfo.hu; internet www.okiszinfo.hu; safeguards interests of over 2,000 member enterprises (all private); Pres. LÁSZLÓ HÖRÖMPÖLY.

National Co-operative Council (Országos Szövetkezeti Tanács——OSzT): 1054 Budapest, Szabadság tér 14; tel. (1) 312-7467; fax (1) 311-3647; f. 1968; Pres. TAMÁS FARKAS; Sec. Dr JÓZSEF PÁL.

National Federation of Agricultural Co-operators and Producers (Mezőgazdasági Szövetkezők és Termelők Országos Szövetsege——MOSZ): 1054 Budapest, Akadémia u. 1–3; tel. and fax (1) 353-2552; e-mail mosz@mail.tvnet.hu; internet www.msztorz.hu; f. 1990; frmly Termelő szövetkezetek Országos Tanácsa TOT (National Council of Agricultural Co-operatives); Pres. TAMÁS NAGY; Sec.-Gen. GÁBOR HORVÁTH; est. 1,300 mem. orgs.

National Federation of Consumer Co-operatives (Általános Fogyasztási Szövetkezetek Országos Szövetsége——ÁFEOSz): 1054 Budapest, Szabadság tér 14; tel. (1) 153-4222; fax (1) 111-3647; safeguards interests of Hungarian consumer co-operative societies; organizes co-operative wholesale activities; Pres. Dr PÁL BARTUS; 800,000 mems.

UTILITIES

Hungarian Energy Office: 1081 Budapest, Köztársaság tér 7; tel. (1) 317-4089; fax (1) 317-1330; e-mail hivatal.energia@eh.ikm.x400gw.itb.hu; f. 1994; regulation and supervision of activities performed by gas and electricity companies, price regulation and protection of consumer interest; Pres. GYÖRGY HATVANI.

Electricity

AES-Tisza Erőmű Kft (AES-Tisza Power Plant Company): 3581 Tiszaújváros Pf 53; tel. (49) 547-333; fax (49) 341-756; internet www.aes.hu; f. 1992; re-founded 1999; owned by AES Corpn (USA); electricity generation and merchandising; Chair. ALLAN B. DWYER; 544 employees.

Budapest Electricity Plc (Budapesti Elektromos Művek Rt, ELMÜ Rt): 1132 Budapest, Váci u. 72–74; tel. (1) 238-1000; fax (1) 238-2822; e-mail elmu@elmu.hu; internet www.elmu.hu; f. 1949; transmission and distribution of electricity; Chair. of Supervisory Bd Dr KLAUS BUSSFELD; 3,371 employees.

Dédász Rt (South Transdanubian Electricity Distribution): 7626 Pécs, Rákóczi, u. 73B; tel. (72) 441-022; fax (72) 445-633; internet www.dedasz.hu; Chair. ZOLTÁN PALUSKA.

Démász Rt (South Hungarian Power Supply Plc): 6720 Szeged, Klauzál tér 9; tel. (62) 476-576; fax (62) 482-500; internet www.demasz.hu; f. 1951; distributes electricity to South-Eastern Hungary; Chair. of Bd Dr DANIEL DUMONT; 1,864 employees.

Dunamenti Power Plant Rt: 2440 Százhalombatta, Erőmű u. 2; tel. (23) 354-161; fax (23) 354-381; electricity generation; Chair. TIBOR KUHL.

Édász Rt (North-Transdanubian Electricity Supply Co): 9027 Győr, Kandó Kálmán u. 11–13; tel. (96) 521-000; fax (96) 521-888; e-mail webmaster@edasz.hu; internet www.edasz.hu; f. 1951; generates and supplies electricity; Chair. BÉLA KÜNSZLER; 2,272 employees.

Émász Rt (North Hungarian Electricity Supply Co Ltd): 3525 Miskolc, Dózsa Gy, u. 13; tel. (46) 411-875; fax (46) 411-871; internet www.emasz.hu.

Hungarian Power Companies Ltd (Magyar Villamos Müvek Rt——MVM Rt): 1255 Budapest, POB 77; 1011 Budapest, Vám u. 5–7; tel. (1) 224-6200; fax (1) 202-1246; e-mail mvm@mvm.hu; internet www.mvm.hu; Hungarian national electricity wholesaler and power-system controller; all 6 distributors and 6 (of 8) power-plant companies privatized in 1995–97; Chair. GYULA LENGYEL.

Mátrai Erőmű Részvénytársaság (Mátra Power Plant Rt): 3272 Visonta, Erőmű u. 11; tel. (37) 328-001; fax (37) 328-036; internet www.mert.hu; electricity generation; Chair. JÓSZEF VALASKA; 3,645 employees.

National Power Grid Company Ltd: 1054 Budapest, Szabadsajto u. 5.

Paks Nuclear Plant Ltd (Paksi Atomeromu v Pav): 7031 Paks, POB 71; tel. (75) 508-833; fax (75) 506-662; internet www.npp.hu; f. 1992; electrical energy production; Plant Man. SÁNDOR NAGY; 2,800 employees.

Tiszántúli Áramszolgáltató Részvénytársaság—Titász (East Hungarian Electricity Supply Co): 4024 Debrecen, Kossuth Lajos u. 4; tel. (52) 410-011; fax (52) 414-031; internet www.titasz.hu; Chair. FRANZ ERÉNYI.

Vértesi Erőmű Részvénytársaság (Vértes Power Plant Rt): 2840 Oroszlány, Pf. 23; tel. (34) 360-255; fax (34) 360-882; e-mail vert@vert.hu; internet www.vert.hu; electricity and heat generation; Chair. KÁROLY TAKÁCS; 5,438 employees.

Gas

Budapest Gas Works (Fögáz) Rt: 1081 Budapest, Köztársaság tér 20; tel. (1) 477-1111; fax (1) 477-1277; internet www.fogaz.hu; f. 1856; gas distribution; Chair. DEZSŐ VASANITS.

Degaz—Delalfoldi Gázszolgáltató Rézvénytársaság: 6724 Szeged, Pulcz u. 44; tel. (62) 472-572; fax (63) 324-943; e-mail ugyfel@degas.hu; internet www.degas.hu; public gas supply and services; 1,327 employees.

Hungarian Oil and Gas Company Ltd (MOL) (Magyar Olaj és Gázipari Rt): 1117 Budapest, Október huszonharmadika u. 18; tel. (1) 209-0000; fax (1) 209-0005; e-mail webmaster@mol.hu; internet www.mol.hu; f. 1991; by merger of part of the National Oil and Gas Trust and a technical development co; privatized in 1995, with the state retaining a 25% stake; petroleum and gas exploration, processing, transportation and distribution; 12,000 employees; Chair. and Chief Exec. ZSOLT HERNÁDI.

Tigáz—Tiszántúli Gázszolgáltató Részvénytársaság: 4200 Hajdúszoboszló, Rákóczi u. 184; tel. (52) 558-100; fax (52) 361-149; e-mail titkarsaga@tigaz.hu; internet www.hungas.hu/tagok/tigaz.html; f. 1950; 40% owned by Italgas Gruppo (Italy); gas distribution; Chair. MARINO BIAGIO; 3,324 employees.

TRADE UNIONS

Since 1988, and particularly after the restructuring of the former Central Council of Hungarian Trade Unions (SzOT) as the National Confederation of Hungarian Trade Unions (MSzOSz) in 1990, several new union federations have been created. Several unions are affiliated to more than one federation, and others are completely independent. In May 2000 a trade-unions co-operation council was established.

Trade Union Federations

Association of Hungarian Free Trade Unions (Magyar Szabad Szakszervezetek Szövetsége): Budapest; f. 1994; 200,000 mems.

Autonomous Trade Union Confederation (Autonóm Szakszervezetek Svövetsége): 1068 Budapest, Benczúr u. 45; tel. (1) 342-1776; Pres. LAJOS FŐCZE.

Democratic Confederation of Free Trade Unions (Független Szakszervezetek Demokratikus Ligája—FSzDL): 1068 Budapest, Benczúr u. 41; tel. (1) 321-5262; fax (1) 321-5405; e-mail info@liganet.hu; f. 1988; Pres. ISTVÁN GASKÓ; 98,000 mems.

Principal affiliated unions include:

> **Democratic Trade Union of Scientific Workers** (Tudományos Dolgozók Demokratikus Szakszervezete——TDDSz): 1068 Budapest, Városligeti fasor 38; tel. (1) 142-8438; f. 1988; Chair. PÁL FORGACS.

Federation of Unions of Intellectual Workers (Értelmiségi Szakszervezeti Tömörülés——ÉSzT): 1068 Budapest, Városligeti fasor 10; tel. (1) 122-8456; Pres. Dr LÁSZLÓ KIS; Gen. Sec. Dr GÁBOR BÁNK.

Forum for the Co-operation of Trade Unions (Szakszervezetek Együttmûködési Fóruma—SzEF): 1068 Budapest VIII, Puskin u. 4; tel. (1) 138-2651; fax (1) 118-7360; f. 1990; Pres. Dr ENDRE SZABÓ.

Principal affiliated unions include:

> **Federation of Hungarian Public Service Employees' Unions** (Közszolgálati Szakszervezetek Szövetsége): 1081 Budapest, Kiss Jozsef u. 8 II em; tel. (1) 313-5436; fax (1) 133-7223; f. 1945; Pres. PÉTER MICHALKO; Vice-Pres. Dr JUDIT BÁRDOS, Dr CSILLA NOVÁK.

National Confederation of Hungarian Trade Unions (Magyar Szakszervezetek Országos Szövetsége——MSzOSz): Budapest; tel. (1) 352-1815; fax (1) 342-1799; f. 1898; reorganized 1990; Pres. Dr LÁSZLO SÁNDOR; Dep. Pres. FERENC RABI; 405,000 mems in 41 mem. orgs.

Principal affiliated unions include:

> **Commercial Employees' Trade Union** (Kereskedelmi Alkalmazottak Szakszervezete): 1066 Budapest, Jókai u. 6; tel. (1) 331-8970; fax (1) 332-3382; e-mail saling@axelero.hu; f. 1900; Pres. Dr JÓZSEF SÁLING; 80,000 mems.

> **Federation of Hungarian Metalworkers' Unions** (Vasass Szakszervezeti Szövetség): 1086 Budapest, Magdolna u. 5–7; tel. (1) 210-0130; fax (1) 210-01167; e-mail vasasszaksz@mail.datanet.hu; f. 1877; Pres. KÁROLY SZŐKE; 53,000 mems.

Federation of Agricultural, Forestry and Water Supply Workers' Unions (Mezőgazdasági, Erdészeti és Vizügyi Dolgozók Szakszervezeti Szövetsége——MEDOSZ): 1066 Budapest, Jókai u. 2; tel. (1) 301-9050; fax (1) 331-4568; e-mail medosz.net@matavnet.hu; f. 1906; Gen. Sec. Dr ANDRÁS BERECZKY; 16,086 mems.

Federation of Chemical Workers' Unions of Hungary, Confederation Founding Section (Magyar Vegyipari Dolgozók Szakszervezeti Szövetsége, össz-szövetségi alapító tagozata): Budapest; tel. (1) 342-1778; fax (1) 342-9975; Gen. Sec. GYÖRGY PASZTERNÁK; 12,000 mems.

Federation of Communal Service Workers' Unions (Kommunális Dalgozók Szakszervezete): 1068 Budapest, Benczur u. 43; tel. (1) 111-6950; Gen. Sec. ZSOLT PÉK; 28,000 mems.

Federation of Hungarian Artworkers' Unions (Müvészeti Szakszervezetek Szövetsége): 1068 Budapest, Városligeti fasor 38; tel. (1) 342-8927; fax (1) 342-8372; e-mail eji@mail.datanet.hu; f. 1957; Pres. LÁSZLÓ GYIMESI; 32,000 mems.

Federation of Local Industry and Municipal Workers' Unions (Helyiipari és Városgazdasági Dolgozók Szövetségének): 1068 Budapest, Benczúr u. 43; tel. (1) 311-6950; f. 1952; Pres. JÓZSEFNÉ SVEVER; Gen. Sec. PÁL BAKÁNYI; 281,073 mems.

Federation of Municipal Industries and Service Workers' Unions (Települési Ipari és Szolgáltatási Dolgozók Szakszervezete): 1068 Budapest, Benczur u. 43; tel. (1) 111-6950; Gen. Sec. ZOLTÁN SZIKSZAI; 20,000 mems.

Federation of Postal and Telecommunications Workers' Unions (Postai és Hirközlési Dolgozók Szakszervezeti Szövetsége): 1146 Budapest, Cházár András u. 13; tel. (1) 142-8777; fax (1) 121-4018; f. 1945; Pres. ENIKŐ HESZKY-GRICSER; 69,900 mems.

Federation of Transport Workers' Unions (Közlekedési Dolgozók Szakszervezeteinek Szövetségé): 1081 Budapest, Köztársaság tér 3; tel. (1) 113-9046; f. 1898; Pres. ISTVÁN TRENKA; 8,000 mems.

Hungarian Federation of Food Industry Workers' Unions (Magyar Élelmezésipari Dolgozók Szakszervezeteinek Szövetsége): 1068 Budapest, Városligeti fasor 44; tel. (1) 122-5880; fax (1) 142-8568; f. 1905; Pres. GYULA SÓKI; Gen. Sec. BÉLA VANEK; 226,243 mems.

Hungarian Graphical Workers' Union (Nyomdaipari Dolgozók Szakszervezete): 1085 Budapest, Kölcsey u. 2; tel. (1) 266-0065; fax (1) 266-0028; f. 1862; Pres. ANDRÁS BÁRSONY; Vice-Pres JÁNOS ACZÉL, EMIL SZELEI; 17,000 mems.

Hungarian Union of Teachers (Magyar Pedagógusok Szakszervezete): 1068 Budapest, Városligeti fasor 10; tel. (1) 122-8456; fax (1) 142-8122; f. 1945; Gen. Sec. ISTVÁNNÉ SZÖLLŐSI; 200,000 mems.

Hungarian Union of Textile Workers (Magyar Textilipari Dolgozók Szakszervezete): 1068 Budapest, Rippl-Rónai u. 2; tel. (1) 428-196; fax (1) 122-5414; f. 1905; Pres. (vacant); Gen. Sec. TAMÁS KELETI; 70,241 mems.

Union of Health Service Workers (Egészségügyben Dolgozók Szakszervezeteinek Szövetsége): 1051 Budapest, Nádor u. 32, POB 36; tel. (1) 110-645; f. 1945; Pres. Dr ZOLTÁN SZABÓ; Gen. Sec. Dr PÁLNÉ KÁLLAY; 280,536 mems.

Union of Leather Industry Workers (Bőripari Dolgozók Szakszervezete): 1062 Budapest, Bajza u. 24; tel. (1) 342-9970; f. 1868; Gen. Sec. TAMÁS LAJTOS; 12,000 mems.

Union of Clothing Workers (Ruházatipari Dolgozók Szakszervezete): 1077 Budapest, Almássy tér 2; tel. (1) 342-3702; fax (1) 122-6717; f. 1892; Gen. Sec. TAMÁS WITTICH; 22,000 mems.

Workers Unions of Mining and Energy (Bánya—és Energiaipari Dolgozók Szakszervezete): 1068 Budapest, Városligeti fasor 46–48; tel. (1) 322-1226; fax (1) 342-1942; e-mail bdsz@banyasz.hu; f. 1913; Pres. FERENC RABI; Vice-Pres. Dr JÁNOS HORN; 80,000 mems.

Transport

RAILWAYS

In 2001 the rail network in Hungary amounted to a length of 7,897 km. Some 156.4m. passengers were carried in 2000. There is an underground railway in Budapest, which had a network of three lines, totalling 33 km in 2002; a fourth line was also planned. Since 1996 PHARE, the European Union's programme for the economic reconstruction of Eastern Europe, has financed a number of modernization projects of the rail network. In 2000 the EU pledged an annual contribution of almost €50m. to fund vital railway and road infrastructure projects.

Budapest Transport Company (BKV) Rt: 1072 Budapest, Akácfa u. 15; tel. (1) 461-6500; fax (1) 461-6557; internet www.bkv.hu; operates metro system, suburban railway network, trams, trolley buses, and conventional buses; served 1,428m. passengers in 2000; Chair. BOTOND ABA; 12,681 employees.

Hungarian State Railways Ltd (Magyar Államvasutak—MÁV): 1940 Budapest, Andrássy u. 73–75; tel. (1) 322-0660; fax (1) 342-8596; internet www.mav.hu; f. 1868; transformed into joint-stock co in 1993; total network 7,785 km, including 2,628 km of electrified lines (2000); Chief Exec. ZOLTÁN MÁNDOKI; Gen. Dir MÁRTON KUKELY; 55,046 employess.

Railway of Győr–Sopron–Ebenfurth (Győr–Sopron–Ebenfurti-Vasút—GySEV/ROeEE): 1011 Budapest, Szilágyi Dezső tér 1; internet www.gysev.hu; Hungarian-Austrian-owned railway; 162 km in Hungary, 65 km in Austria, all electrified; transport of passengers and goods; Dir-Gen. Dr LÁSZLÓ FEHÉRVÁRI.

ROADS

In 2001 there were 448 km of motorways and 30,322 km of national public roads. There are extensive long-distance bus services. Road passenger and freight transport is provided by the state-owned Volán companies and by individual operators. There were plans to extend the road from Budapest to Vienna, Austria; however, owing to the lack of funds, this and a 10-year plan to extend connections to Croatia, Romania and Ukraine, were delayed. The European Union's annual contribution of almost €50m., from 2000, was to fund vital projects. In 2003 a road development programme was approved, for the construction of 420 km of roads, including 326 km of motorways and 94 km of high-speed roads by the beginning of 2007, at a cost of 1,100m. forint (the programme was to be partly funded by loans from the European Bank for Reconstruction and Development and the European Investment Bank). The central budget for 2003 allocated 79,400m. forint for road development.

Hungarocamion: 1442 Budapest, POB 108; tel. (1) 257-3600; fax (1) 256-6755; international road freight transport company; 17 offices in Europe and the Middle East; fleet of 1,100 units for general and specialized cargo; Gen. Man. GABRIELLA SZAKÁL; 3,800 employees.

Centre of Volán Enterprises (Volán Vállalatok Központja): 1391 Budapest, Erzsébet krt 96, POB 221; tel. (1) 112-4290; centre of 25 Volán enterprises for inland and international road freight and passenger transport, forwarding, tourism; fleet of 17,000 lorries, incl. special tankers for fuel, refrigerators, trailers, 8,000 buses for regular passenger transport; 3 affiliates, offices and joint-ventures in Europe; Head ELEMER SASLICS.

SHIPPING AND INLAND WATERWAYS

At the end of 1994 the Hungarian river merchant fleet comprised 199 vessels, with a capacity totalling 223,718 dwt, but by the end of 2000 no vessels were registered.

Hungarian Shipping Co (MAHART—Magyar Hajózási Rt): 1366 Budapest, POB 58; 1052 Budapest, Apáozai Čs. J, u. 11; tel. (1) 484-6421; fax (1) 484-6422; e-mail freeport@mahart.hu; internet www.freeport.hu; f. 1895; transportation of goods on the Rhine–Main–Danube waterway; carries passenger traffic on the Danube; operates port activities at Budapest Csepel National and Free Port (port agency service, loading, storage, handling goods); management of multi-modal and combined transport (cargo booking, oversized goods, chartering); ship-building and ship-repair services; Dir-Gen. Capt. LÁSZLÓ SOMLÓVÁRI.

MAFRACHT International Shipping, Forwarding and Agency Ltd Co: 1364 Budapest 4, POB 105; tel. (1) 266-1208; fax (1) 266-1329; shipping agency.

CIVIL AVIATION

The Ferihegy international airport is 16 km from the centre of Budapest. Ferihegy-2 opened in 1985. In 1999 a new passenger terminal opened. Balatonkiliti airport, near Siófok in western Hungary, reopened to international traffic in 1989. Public internal air services resumed in 1993, after an interval of 20 years, between Budapest and Nyíregyháza, Debrecen, Szeged, Pécs, Szombathely and Győr.

Air Traffic and Airport Administration (Légiforgalmi és Repülőtéri Igazgatóság): 1675 Budapest, POB 53; tel. (1) 291-8722; fax (1) 157-6982; f. 1973; controls civil air traffic and operates Ferihegy and Siófok Airports; Dir-Gen. TAMÁS ERDEI.

General Directorate of Civil Aviation (Légügyi Főigazgatóság): Budapest; tel. (1) 342-2544; fax (1) 322-2848; controls civil aviation; Dir-Gen. ÖDÖN SKONDA.

Hungarian Airlines (Magyar Légiközlekedési Részvénytársaság—MALÉV Rt): 1051 Budapest, Roosevelt tér 2, POB 122; tel. (1) 235-3535; fax (1) 266-2685; internet www.malev.hu; f. 1946; regular services from Budapest to Europe, North Africa, North America,

Asia and the Middle East; Pres. Ferenc Szarvas; Chief Exec. Ferenc Kovács.

LinAir Hungarian Regional Airlines: 1675 Budapest, POB 53; tel. (1) 296-7092; fax (1) 296-7891; e-mail info@linair.hu; internet www.linair.hu; f. 1994; regional carrier; Man. Dir Tamás Kovács.

Tourism

Tourism has developed rapidly and is an important source of foreign exchange. Lake Balaton is the main holiday centre for boating, bathing and fishing. Hungary's cities have great historical and recreational attractions, and the annual Budapest Spring Festival is held in March. Budapest has numerous swimming pools watered by thermal springs, which are equipped with modern physiotherapy facilities. Revenue from tourism in 2000 totalled US 3434m. com-

pared with \$2,203m. in 1999. There were 31.7m. foreign visitors in 2002.

Association of Hungarian Travel Agencies: 1364 Budapest, POB 267; tel. and fax (1) 318-4977; e-mail muisz@mail.selectrade .hu; internet www.miwo.hu/partner/muisz; f. 1973; Pres. Gabriella Molnár; Gen.-Sec. Csabo Csók.

Hungarian Travel Agency (Idegenforgalmi, Beszerzési, Utazási és Szállitási Rt—IBUSZ): 1364 Budapest, Ferenciek tér 5; tel. (1) 118-6866; fax (1) 117-7723; f. 1902; has 118 brs throughout Hungary; Gen. Man. Dr Erika Szemenkár.

Tourinform: 1052 Budapest, Sütő u. 2; tel. (1) 317-9800; fax (1) 317-9656; e-mail tourinform@mail.hungarytourism.hu; internet www .hungarytourism.hu.

Tourism Office of Budapest: 1364 Budapest, POB 215; tel. (1) 266-0479; fax (1) 266-7477; e-mail info@budapestinfo.hu; internet www.budapestinfo.hu; Dir László Fekete.

ICELAND

Introductory Survey

Location, Climate, Language, Religion, Flag, Capital

The Republic of Iceland comprises one large island and numerous smaller ones, situated near the Arctic Circle in the North Atlantic Ocean. The main island lies about 300 km (190 miles) south-east of Greenland, about 1,000 km (620 miles) west of Norway and about 800 km (500 miles) north of Scotland. The Gulf Stream keeps Iceland warmer than might be expected, with average temperatures ranging from 10°C (50°F) in the summer to 1°C (34°F) in winter. Icelandic is the official language. Almost all of the inhabitants profess Christianity: the Evangelical Lutheran Church is the established church and embraces about 87% of the population. The civil flag (proportions 18 by 25) displays a red cross, bordered with white, on a blue background, the upright of the cross being towards the hoist; the state flag (proportions 9 by 16) bears the same design, but has a truncated triangular area cut from the fly. The capital is Reykjavík.

Recent History

Iceland became independent on 17 June 1944, when the Convention that linked it with Denmark, under the Danish crown, was terminated. Iceland became a founder member of the Nordic Council (see p. 266) in 1952, and has belonged to both the North Atlantic Treaty Organization (NATO, see p. 271) and the Council of Europe, see p. 181 since 1949. Membership of the European Free Trade Association (EFTA, see p. 195) was formalized in 1970.

From 1959 to 1971 Iceland was governed by a coalition of the Independence Party (IP) and the Social Democratic Party (SDP). Following the general election of June 1971, Ólafur Jóhannesson, the leader of the Progressive Party (PP), formed a coalition Government with the left-wing People's Alliance (PA) and the Union of Liberals and Leftists. At the general election held in June 1974 voters favoured right-wing parties, and in August the IP and the PP formed a coalition Government, led by the leader of the IP, Geir Hallgrímsson. Failure adequately to address economic difficulties resulted in a decline in the coalition's popularity, however, and prompted the Government's resignation in June 1978, following extensive election gains by the PA and the SDP. Disagreements over economic measures, and over the PA's advocacy of Icelandic withdrawal from NATO, led to two months of negotiations before a new government could be formed. In September Jóhannesson formed a coalition of the PP with the PA and the SDP, but this Government, after addressing immediate economic necessities, resigned in October 1979, when the SDP withdrew from the coalition. An interim administration was formed by Benedikt Gröndal, the leader of the SDP. The results of a general election, held in December, were inconclusive, and in February 1980 Gunnar Thoroddsen of the IP formed a coalition Government with the PA and the PP.

In June 1980 Vigdís Finnbogadóttir, a non-political candidate who was favoured by left-wing groups because of her opposition to the US military airbase at Keflavík, achieved a narrow victory in the election for the mainly ceremonial office of President. She took office on 1 August 1980, becoming the world's first popularly-elected female Head of State. The coalition Government lost its majority in the Lower House of the Althingi/Alþingi (parliament) in September 1982, and a general election took place in April 1983. The IP received the largest share (38.7%) of the votes cast, but two new parties, the Social Democratic Alliance (SDA) and the Women's List (WL), together won almost 13% of the votes cast. A centre-right coalition was formed by the IP and the PP, with Steingrímur Hermannsson (the leader of the PP and former Minister of Fisheries and Communications) as Prime Minister. In May 1985 the Althingi unanimously approved a resolution declaring the country a 'nuclear-free zone', i.e. banning the entry of nuclear weapons.

A general election for an enlarged, 63-seat Althingi was held in April 1987. Both parties of the outgoing coalition suffered losses: the IP's representation decreased from 24 to 18 seats, and the PP lost one of its 14 seats. The right-wing Citizens' Party (CP, which had been formed only one month earlier by Albert Guðmundsson, following his resignation from the Ministry of Energy and Industry and from the IP) won seven seats. Ten seats were won by the SDP, which included former members of the SDA (disbanded in 1986). A coalition of the IP, the PP and the SDP was formally constituted in July 1987. Thorsteinn Pálsson, the leader of the IP since November 1983 and the Minister of Finance in the outgoing Cabinet, was appointed Prime Minister.

In June 1988 President Finnbogadóttir (who had begun a second term in office, unopposed, in August 1984) was elected for a third term, receiving more than 90% of the votes cast. This was the first occasion on which an incumbent President seeking re-election had been challenged. In August 1992 the President began a fourth term of office, her candidacy being unopposed.

In September 1988 the SDP and the PP withdrew from the Pálsson Government, following disagreements over economic policy. Later that month, the leader of the PP, Steingrímur Hermannsson, became Prime Minister in a centre-left coalition with the SDP and the PA. The new Government committed itself to a series of devaluations of the króna, and introduced austerity measures, with the aim of lowering the rate of inflation and stimulating the fishing industry.

Following the resignation of Guðmundsson from the leadership of the CP in January 1989, relations between this party and the left improved, and in September a new Government, based on a coalition agreement between the PP, the SDP, the PA, the CP and the Association for Equality and Social Justice, was formed. Hermannsson, who remained as Prime Minister, affirmed that the new Government would not change its policies, emphasizing the need to reduce inflation and to stimulate economic growth, as well as reiterating an earlier declaration of the Althingi that no nuclear weapons would be located in Iceland.

In March 1991 Davíð Oddsson, the mayor of Reykjavík, successfully challenged Pálsson for the leadership of the IP. At a general election in April the IP emerged as the largest single party, securing 26 seats (with 38.6% of the votes cast), mostly at the expense of the CP. Although the incumbent coalition would have retained an overall majority of seats, the SDP decided to withdraw from the coalition, chiefly as a result of the failure to reach agreement on Iceland's position in the discussions between EFTA and the European Community (EC—now European Union—EU, see p. 199), with regard to the creation of a European Economic Area (EEA, see p. 195). A new coalition Government was formed in late April by the IP and the SDP, with Oddsson as Prime Minister; the new administration promised economic liberalization and a strengthening of links with the USA and Europe (although no application for membership of the EC was envisaged), but was faced with a deteriorating economic situation.

In 1991 Iceland's Constitution was amended, ending the system whereby the Althingi was divided into an Upper House (one-third of the members) and a Lower House.

Although the IP secured the largest number of seats (25, with 37% of the votes cast) at a general election in April 1995, the SDP obtained only seven seats, three fewer than in the previous election. Later in the month a new coalition Government was formed, comprising the IP and the PP, with Oddsson continuing as Prime Minister, and Halldór Ásgrímsson, the leader of the PP, being named Minister of Foreign Affairs. Since both parties in the coalition opposed the Common Fisheries Policy of the EU, it was considered unlikely that Iceland would apply for full membership of the EU in the near future.

Following the decision by Finnbogadóttir not to seek re-election as President in 1996, the principal candidates were Ólafur Ragnar Grímsson, a former leader of the PA (who had previously opposed Iceland's membership of NATO), Pétur Hafstein, a justice in the Supreme Court, and Guðrún Agnarsdóttir of the WL. In the election, held on 29 June 1996, Grímsson secured 41% of the votes cast, while Hafstein won 29% and Agnarsdóttir gained 26%. Grímsson duly took office as President in August. He began a second term of office in August 2000, his candidacy being unopposed.

At a general election held on 8 May 1999 the IP obtained the largest share of the votes cast (40.7%) and won 26 seats, thereby remaining the party with the largest representation in the Althingi. An electoral grouping entitled The Alliance, which was composed of the PA, the SDP, the People's Movement and the WL, received 26.8% of the votes and won 17 seats, while the PP won 18.4% (12 seats). Two new parties also secured seats in the Althingi: the Left-Green Movement, established by three former PA deputies, obtained 9.1% of the votes cast (six seats), while the Liberal Party, founded by the former IP minister Sverrir Hermannsson, won 4.2% (two seats). A new coalition Government, which, once again, comprised the IP and the PP, and which continued to be led by Oddsson, took office at the end of the month.

In February 2003 the mayor of Reykjavik, Ingibjorg Solrún Gísladóttir, resigned in order to pursue her candidacy for the post of Prime Minister in the general election, which was scheduled for 10 May. Gísladóttir, who had been elected for a third term as mayor in May 2002, was selected as prime minsterial candidate by the The Alliance, although Össur Skarphéðinsson remained the party leader. Oddsson, who was re-elected as leader of the IP at the end of March 2003, was also seeking re-election as Prime Minister.

At the general election, held on 10 May 2003, the IP remained the largest party in the Althingi, winning 33.7% of the votes cast and securing 22 seats. By mid-May a government had yet to be appointed, butit was expected that the IP would renew its coalition with the PP, which had won 17.7% of the votes cast and 12 seats. The Alliance won 31.7% of the votes cast and 20 seats, the Left-Green Movement 8.8% and 5 seats and the Liberal Party 7.4% and 4 seats. Owing to the system of electoral lists—whereby representatives are chosen according to their position on the party list—Solrún Gísladóttir did not receive a seat in the Althingi; there was, ,however, speculation that Margrét Frimanssdóttir (deputy leader of the Alliance) might forfeit her seat in favour of Gísladóttir. Owing to a reorganization of the constituencies, Christian Palsson, a former member of the IP, did not gain a place on the party list. He therefore decided to contest the election as an indepedent, and formed the Framboð óháðra i Suðurkjördæmi. A second new party, Nýtt Afl, was formed by a cross-party grouping of once-prominent politicians who were dissatisfied both with the fishing quotas and a lack of openness in Icelandic society. Neither new party managed to gain representation in the Althingi.

In March 2003 Japan Tobacco International launched legal proceedings against the Icelandic Government, claiming that legislation recently introduced under which tobacco could no longer be advertised on television or displayed in shops breached EEA laws.

The importance of fishing to Iceland's economy, and fears of excessive exploitation of the fishing grounds near Iceland by foreign fleets, caused the Icelandic Government to extend its territorial waters to 12 nautical miles (22 km) in 1964 and to 50 nautical miles (93 km) in 1972. British opposition to these extensions resulted in two 'cod wars'. In October 1975 Iceland unilaterally introduced a fishing limit of 200 nautical miles (370 km), both as a conservation measure and to protect Icelandic interests. The 1973 agreement on fishing limits between Iceland and the United Kingdom expired in November 1975, and failure to reach a new agreement led to the third and most serious 'cod war'. Casualties occurred, and in February 1976 Iceland temporarily severed diplomatic relations with the United Kingdom, the first diplomatic break between two NATO countries. In June the two countries reached an agreement, and in December the British trawler fleet withdrew from Icelandic waters. In June 1979 Iceland declared its exclusive rights to the 200-mile fishing zone. Following negotiations between the EC and EFTA on the creation of the EEA, an agreement was reached (in October 1991) allowing tariff-free access to the EC for 97% of Iceland's fisheries products by 1997, while Iceland was to allow EC vessels to catch 3,000 metric tons of fish per year in its waters, in return for some access to EC waters. The EEA agreement was ratified by the Althingi in January 1993 and entered into force in January 1994.

In August 1993 a dispute developed between Iceland and Norway over fishing rights in an area of the Barents Sea fished by Iceland, over which Norway claimed jurisdiction. The dispute continued throughout 1994, and in June the Norwegian coastguards cut the nets of Icelandic trawlers fishing for cod in the disputed region. Iceland's case was weakened in January 1995, when Canada officially recognized Norway's sovereign rights over the disputed area (a fisheries protection zone extending 200 km around the Svalbard archipelago). A similar dispute arose in August 1996 between Iceland and Denmark over fishing rights in an area of the Atlantic Ocean between Iceland and Greenland (a self-governing province of Denmark). The Danish Government claimed that an agreement had been concluded in 1988 to allow fishing boats that were in possession of a licence issued in Greenland to operate in the area. Iceland, however, denied the existence of such an agreement, and announced that Danish boats would not be permitted to fish in the disputed area.

Iceland strongly criticized the moratorium on commercial whaling, imposed (for conservation purposes) by the International Whaling Commission (IWC, see p. 332) in 1986, and continued to catch limited numbers of whales for scientific purposes until 1989, when it halted whaling, following appeals by environmental organizations for an international boycott of Icelandic products. In 1991 Iceland announced its withdrawal from the IWC (with effect from June 1992), claiming that certain species of whales were not only too plentiful to be in danger of extinction, but were also threatening Iceland's stocks of cod and other fish. In 1994 a report, commissioned by the Government, recommended that limited hunting be resumed in the future. In March 1999 the Althingi voted to end the self-imposed 10-year ban on whaling and requested the Government to implement the ruling, urging a resumption of hunting as soon as possible. Iceland's application to rejoin the IWC, with an unprecedented exemption that would allow it to disregard the moratorium on commercial whaling, was rejected in July 2001. It was, however, granted permission to attend discussions as an observer without voting rights. Its bid for full membership was rejected again in May 2002 but in October Iceland was readmitted, when the Government undertook not to allow the resumption of commercial whaling until at least 2006 and after that not to resume commercial whaling while negotiations on a revised management plan were achieving progress. In March 2003 Iceland announced its intention to submit plans to the IWC to resume whaling for scientific research purposes. From the 1990s whale watching emerged as a tourist attraction; it attracted some 59,000 tourists in 2001.

In April 2002 President Ólafur Ragnar Grímsson became the first Icelandic Head of State to visit Russia. Grímsson met with President Putin, among others, to discuss political, economic, and cultural co-operation; trade was expected to increase between the two countries as a result of the meeting.

Government

According to the Constitution, executive power is vested in the President (elected for four years by universal adult suffrage) and the Cabinet, consisting of the Prime Minister and other ministers appointed by the President. In practice, however, the President performs only nominally the functions ascribed in the Constitution to this office, and it is the Cabinet alone that holds real executive power. Legislative power is held jointly by the President and the unicameral Althingi (parliament), with 63 members elected by universal suffrage for four years (subject to dissolution by the President), using a system of proportional representation in eight multi-member constituencies. The Cabinet is responsible to the Althingi. For the purposes of local government Iceland is divided into 122 municipalities; in 2003 the municipalities were undergoing a process of amalgamation which was expected to continue over the next few years.

Defence

Apart from a 120-strong coastguard, Iceland has no defence forces of its own, but it is a member of NATO (see p. 271). There are units of US forces at Keflavík airbase, which is used for observation of the North Atlantic Ocean, under a bilateral agreement made in 1951 between Iceland and the USA. The airfield at Keflavík is a base for the US airborne early warning system. In August 2002 a total of 1,478 US military personnel (navy 960, air force 470, marines 48) were stationed in Iceland, together with a 16-strong naval contingent from the Netherlands.

Economic Affairs

In 2001, according to estimates by the World Bank, Iceland's gross national income (GNI), measured at 1999–2001 prices, was US $8,201m., equivalent to $28,880 per head (or $29,830 per head on an international purchasing-power parity basis). During 1990–2001, it was estimated, the population increased at an average annual rate of 1.0%, while gross domestic product (GDP) per head increased, in real terms, by an average of 1.6% per year. Iceland's overall GDP increased, in real terms, at an average annual rate of 2.6% during 1990–2001; GDP increased by 5.0% in 2000 and by 3.0% in 2001.

Agriculture (including fishing) contributed some 9.4% of GDP in 1997; 7.8% of the employed labour force were engaged in the agricultural sector in 2001. The principal agricultural products are dairy produce and lamb, although these provided less than 1% of export earnings in 1997. Marine products accounted for 63.3% of total export earnings in 2000. A cod quota system is in place to avoid the depletion of fish stocks through over-fishing as happened in previous years. During 1990–99 agricultural GDP (including fishing) declined at an average annual rate of 1.6%; agricultural GDP (excluding fishing) increased at an average annual rate of 1.1% over the same period, while the GDP of the fishing sector declined by 2.3% per year. Agricultural GDP (excluding fishing) increased, in real terms, by 3.2% in 1998 and by 3.9% in 1999; the GDP of the fishing sector declined by 8.0% in 1998 and by 1.6% in 1999.

Industry (including mining, manufacturing, construction and power) contributed 28.2% of GDP in 1997. In 2001 22.7% of the employed labour force were engaged in the industrial sector. Mining activity is negligible. During 1990–98 industrial GDP increased at an average annual rate of 2.2%; industrial GDP increased by 5.8% in 1997 and by 8.2% in 1998.

Manufacturing contributed 16.7% of GDP in 1997, and employed 14.6% of the labour force in 2001. The most important sectors, measured by gross value of output (excluding fish processing, which dominates the sector), are the production of aluminium, diatomite, fertilizer, cement and ferro-silicon. In March 2003 the Althingi approved proposals to construct a new aluminium smelter in the Eastern Highlands, despite considerable popular opposition on environmental grounds. The proposals included the damming of two rivers to create a reservoir of 22 sq km above Vatnajokull (Europe's biggest glacier), in order to produce hydroelectric power for the smelter. Fish processing contributed 4.9% of GDP in 1997; however, the GDP of the fish-processing sector declined by 5.3% in 1998 and by 1.1% in 1999. Manufacturing GDP (including fish processing) increased, in real terms, at an average annual rate of 2.4% in 1990–99; it increased by 4.1% in 1998 and by 4.9% in 1999.

Iceland is potentially rich in hydroelectric and geothermal power, but both energy sources are significantly underexploited. Hydroelectric power has promoted the development of the aluminium industry, while geothermal energy provides nearly all the country's heating and hot water. In 1999 hydroelectric power provided 84.1% of the country's electricity; petroleum provided only 0.1% in the same year. Fuel imports comprised 9.4% of the value of merchandise imports in 2000. In 2001 Iceland announced its intention to develop the world's first economy free of carbon dioxide emissions by using hydrogen or methanol-powered fuel cells. Hydrogen-fuelled buses were expected to start operating in Reykjavík in 2003. In December 2001 the Government approved plans for the construction of a new hydroelectric power plant in Karahnjukar, in the east of the country.

Services contributed 62.4% of GDP in 1997 and employed 69.5% of the labour force in 2001. GDP from services increased, in real terms, at an annual average rate of 2.9% during 1990–98; it grew by 6.1% in 1997 and by 5.3% in 1998. The tourism sector is becoming an increasingly significant source of revenue; the number of foreign visitors totalled 302,913 in 2000; receipts from tourism totalled 37,720m. krónur in 2001.

In 2000 Iceland recorded a visible trade deficit of US $474m. and there was a deficit of $848m. on the current account of the balance of payments. In 2001 the principal sources of imports were Germany (providing 12.2% of the total), the USA (11.1%), Denmark (8.6%) and Norway (7.8%); the principal market for exports was the United Kingdom (accounting for 18.2% of the total), followed by Germany (14.9%) Netherlands (10.9%) and the USA (10.3%). In 1999 EU member countries provided 60.0% of Iceland's merchandise imports and took 64.2% of exports. The principal imports in 2000 were machinery and transport equipment, manufactured goods and road vehicles. The principal exports in the same year were marine products (including animal feeds), manufactured goods and aluminium.

In 2001 there was a budgetary deficit of 16,866m. krónur, equivalent to 2.2% of GDP. Iceland's net external debt was equivalent to 56.3% of GDP at the end of 1998; the cost of debt-servicing was equivalent to an estimated 21.0% of export earnings in the same year. The annual rate of inflation averaged 3.5% in 1990–2001; consumer prices increased by 6.4% in 2001 and by 5.2% in 2002. The unemployment rate averaged 1.4% in 2001.

Iceland is a member of the Nordic Council (see p. 266), the Nordic Council of Ministers (see p. 267), the European Free Trade Association (EFTA, see p. 195) and the Organisation for Economic Co-operation and Development (OECD, see p. 277). Although Iceland is not a member of the European Union (EU, see p. 199), it joined the EU's Schengen Agreement along with Denmark, Finland and Sweden (all EU members) by virtue of its membership in the Nordic passport union (Norway also joined).

During the late 1990s the Icelandic economy expanded rapidly, partly as a result of the recovery of the fishing industry but largely owing to the diversification of the economy through extensive deregulation and restructuring (begun in the early 1990s). The tourism sector has expanded rapidly, while significant biotechnology and information technology industries have also been developed. The financial sector has benefited from the liberalization of capital flows and a series of privatizations. Although economic growth slowed during 2000 (partly as a result of the decrease in fishing quotas, owing to lower stock estimates, thus easing inflationary pressures, the announcement of lower stock estimates in mid-2000 led to the rapid depreciation of the currency and the temporary closure of the interbank foreign exchange market; interest rates were raised to protect the króna from further decline, leaving little flexibility to control inflation. Continuing strong consumer confidence also led to a large deficit on the current account of the balance of payments, owing to increased purchases of imported consumer goods. However, the Government presided over a budgetary surplus equivalent to 3% of GDP in 2000, much of which was allocated to reduce public indebtedness and to improve pension provision—Iceland expected to be free of public debt by 2004. In January 2002 the rising unemployment rate was countered by a reduction in the cost of health services and a 'freeze' on tax increases in order to reduce the rate of inflation. Moreover, a number of food taxes were reduced, and the tax on profits was lowered from 30% to 15% in an attempt to persuade Icelandic businesses that were registered off shore to return to the country. The strength of the króna also allowed the Government to reduce fuel prices in early 2002. Plans to develop hydrogen or methanol-powered fuel cells, especially for the fishing fleet (which currently uses diesel engines), offered the economy a potential solution to its exaggerated exposure to fluctuations in the price of petroleum. The outlook for the medium-term was mixed: the Central Bank forecast negligible GDP growth for 2002 and growth of 1.5% in 2003, yet unemployment was falling and the privatization programme was progressing. Moreover, controversial proposals to build a large aluminium smelting plant and associated hydroelectric power plants in the Eastern Highlands were approved by the Althingi in March 2003; the smelting plant (which was scheduled to be completed in 2007) was expected to double the amount of aluminium exported from Iceland. Iceland has benefited greatly from its membership of the European Economic Area (see p. 195), but is reluctant to join the EU, owing to the potentially adverse effects of the Common Fisheries Policy on the Icelandic fishing industry. However, the Government is likely to come under increased pressure in the future to establish some form of link with the European single currency, the euro, to protect certain industries, notably tourism, from the effects of currency fluctuations.

Education

Education is compulsory and free for 10 years between six and 16 years of age (primary and lower secondary levels). Upper secondary education begins at 16 years of age and usually lasts for four years. In 2000 90% of 16-year-olds were continuing their education at a secondary school. Iceland has eight institutions providing tertiary-level education, including two non-university institutions. Expenditure on education by all levels of government in 1999 was 36,598m. krónur, representing 5.9% of total public expenditure. Local communities finance compulsory education.

Public Holidays

2003: 1 January (New Year's Day), 17 April (Maundy Thursday), 18 April (Good Friday), 21 April (Easter Monday), 24 April (First Day of Summer), 1 May (Labour Day), 29 May (Ascension Day), 9 June (Whit Monday), 17 June (National Day), 4 August (Bank Holiday), 24–26 December (Christmas), 31 December (New Year's Eve).

2004: 1 January (New Year's Day), 8 April (Maundy Thursday), 9 April (Good Friday), 12 April (Easter Monday), 22 April (First Day of Summer), 1 May (Labour Day), 20 May (Ascension Day), 31 May (Whit Monday), 17 June (National Day), 2 August (Bank Holiday), 24–26 December (Christmas), 31 December (New Year's Eve).

Weights and Measures

The metric system is in force.

Statistical Survey

Sources (unless otherwise stated): Statistics Iceland, Borgartúni 20A, 150 Reykjavík; tel. 5281000; fax 5281099; e-mail statice@statice.is; internet www.statice.is; Seðlabanki Íslands (Central Bank of Iceland), Kalkofnsvegur 1, 150 Reykjavík; tel. 5699600; internet www.sedlabanki.is.

AREA AND POPULATION

Area: 103,000 sq km (39,769 sq miles).

Population: 204,578 at census of 1 December 1970; 286,250 (males 143,290; females 142,960) at 1 December 2001.

Density (per sq km): 2.7 (2001).

Principal Towns (population at 1 December 2001): Reykjavík (capital) 112,268; Kópavogur 24,229; Hafnarfjörður 20,223; Akureyri 15,632.

Births, Marriages and Deaths (year ending 1 December 2001): Live births 4,091 (birth rate 14.3 per 1,000); Marriages 1,484 (marriage rate 5.2 per 1,000); Deaths 1,725 (death rate 6.0 per 1,000).

Expectation of Life (years at birth, WHO estimates): 79.8 (males 78.2; females 81.3) in 2001. Source: WHO, *World Health Report*.

Employment (2001): Agriculture and fishing 12,400; Manufacturing 23,200; Electricity and water supply 1,500; Construction 11,400; Trade, restaurants and hotels 29,500; Transport, storage and communications 10,100; Finance, real estate and business services 20,000; Public administration, education, health services and other services not specified 50,900; Total 159,000.

HEALTH AND WELFARE

Key Indicators

Total Fertility Rate (children per woman, 2001): 1.9.

Under-5 Mortality Rate (per 1,000 live births, 2001): 4.

HIV/AIDS (% of persons aged 15–49, 2001): 0.15.

Physicians (per 1,000 head, 2001): 3.46.

Hospital Beds (per 1,000 head, 2001): 7.8.

Health Expenditure (2000): US $ per head (PPP): 2,626.

Health Expenditure (2000): % of GDP: 8.9.

Health Expenditure (2000): public (% of total): 84.4.

Human Development Index (2000): ranking: 7.

Human Development Index (2000): value: 0.936.

For sources and definitions, see explanatory note on p. vi.

AGRICULTURE, ETC.

Principal Crops (metric tons, 2001): Cereals 4,337; Potatoes 11,366; Cabbages 503; Tomatoes 964; Cucumbers 1,049; Turnips 730.

Livestock (2001): Cattle 70,168; Sheep 473,535; Horses 73,809; Pigs 4,561; Hens 128,241; Other poultry 28,733.

Livestock Products (metric tons, 2001): Mutton and lamb 8,616; Beef and veal 3,683; Pig meat 5,284; Milk ('000 litres, processed) 106,149; Wool (unwashed) 675; Sheepskins 2,030*; Eggs 2,750. * FAO estimate. Source: partly FAO.

Fishing (metric tons, live weight, 2001): Atlantic cod 240,002; Saithe 31,941; Haddock 39,825; Atlantic redfishes 92,527; Capelin 918,417; Atlantic herring 178,950; Shrimp 30,790; Total (incl. others) 1,986,584.

INDUSTRY

Selected Products ('000 metric tons, unless otherwise indicated, 2001): Frozen fish 247.1 (demersal catch); Salted, dried or smoked fish 123.4; Cement 143.7 (2000); Ferro-silicon 103.4 (2000); Aluminium (unwrought) 224.4 (2000); Electric energy 8,028 million kWh.

FINANCE

Currency and Exchange Rates: 100 aurar (singular: eyrir) = 1 new Icelandic króna (plural: krónur). *Sterling, Dollar and Euro Equivalents* (31 December 2002): £1 sterling = 129.88 krónur; US $1 = 80.58 krónur; €1 = 84.50 krónur; 1,000 krónur = £7.699 = $12.410 = €11.834. *Average Exchange Rate* (krónur per US $): 78.616 in 2000; 97.425 in 2001; 91.662 in 2002.

Budget (million krónur, 1997): *Revenue:* Tax revenue 132,415 (Taxes on income, profits and capital gains 32,745, Social security contributions 14,353, Taxes on property 6,895, Domestic taxes on goods and services 76,035); Other current revenue 21,211 (Entrepreneurial and property income 9,435, Administrative fees and charges, non-industrial and incidental sales 6,866); Capital revenue 1,574; Total 136,369. *Expenditure:* General public services 8,846; Public order and safety 6,875; Education 15,526; Health 36,916; Social security and welfare 36,064; Housing and community amenities 1,081; Recreational, cultural and religious affairs and services 4,592; Economic affairs and services 25,097 (Agriculture, forestry, fishing and hunting 8,915, Transport and communications 11,597); Other purposes 17,993 (Interest payments 15,606); Total 152,990 (current 141,904, capital 11,087—excluding lending minus repayments 347). Note: Figures refer to consolidated operations of the central Government, comprising budgetary accounts and social security funds (Source: IMF, *Government Finance Statistics Yearbook*). *1998* (million krónur): Total revenue 220,800; Total expenditure 218,000. *1999* (estimates, million krónur): Total revenue 225,900; Total expenditure 243,800. *2000* (estimates, million krónur): Total revenue 276,300; Total expenditure 256,400Note: Figures for 1998–2000 refer to transactions of the public sector (including local government units). Source: Central Bank of Iceland.

International Reserves (US $ million at 31 December 2002): IMF special drawing rights 0.1; Reserve position in IMF 25.3; Foreign exchange 414.7; Total 440.0. Figures exclude gold, which was valued at US $5.0m. in 2002. Source: IMF, *International Financial Statistics*.

Money Supply (provisional, million krónur at 31 December 2002): Currency outside banks 7,666; Demand deposits at commercial and savings banks 75,934; Total money 83,600. Source: IMF, *International Financial Statistics*.

Cost of Living (consumer price index for Reykjavík; average of monthly figures; base: May 1988 = 100): 183.3 in 1998; 189.6 in 1999; 199.1 in 2000.

Gross Domestic Product in Purchasers' Values (million krónur at current prices): 606,558 in 1999; 658,284 in 2000; 744,190 in 2001.

Expenditure on the Gross Domestic Product (million krónur at current prices, 2001): Government final consumption expenditure 175,519; Private final consumption expenditure 408,413; Increase in stocks –2,084; Gross fixed capital formation 166,190; *Total domestic expenditure* 748,038; Exports of goods and services 303,444; *Less* Imports of goods and services 307,292; *Gross domestic product* 744,190.

GDP by Economic Activity (million krónur at current prices, 1997): Agriculture 8,351; Fishing 33,748; Manufacturing 74,828; Electricity and water supply 18,278; Construction 33,684; Trade, restaurants and hotels 55,635; Transport, storage and communications 34,975; Finance, insurance, real estate and business services 88,381; Other private services 21,420; Government services 63,212; Private non-profit institutions serving households 16,318; *Sub-total* 448,828; Statistical discrepancies 14,460; *Less* Imputed bank service charges 21,837; *GDP at factor cost* 441,451; Indirect taxes 93,504; *Less* Subsidies 10,276; *GDP in purchasers' values* 524,679.

Balance of Payments (US $ million, 2000): Exports of goods f.o.b. 1,902, Imports of goods f.o.b. –2,376, *Trade balance* –474; Exports of services 1,049, Imports of services –1,164, *Balance on goods and services* –589; Other income received 154, Other income paid –403, *Balance on goods, services and income* –839; Current transfers received 6, Current transfers paid –16, *Current balance* –848; Capital account (net) –3, Direct investment abroad –368, Direct investment from abroad 145, Portfolio investment assets –668, Portfolio investment liabilities 1,142, Financial derivatives assets 15, Financial derivatives liabilities –16, Other investment assets –174, Other investment liabilities 684, Net errors and omissions –71, *Overall balance* –69. Source: IMF, *International Financial Statistics*.

EXTERNAL TRADE

Principal Commodities (distribution by SITC, million krónur, 2001): *Imports c.i.f.:* Food and live animals 18,275.7 (Crude materials, inedible 14,056.6 (aluminium ores and concentrates, incl. alumina 9,467.5); Mineral fuels and lubricants 19,673.2 (petroleum products, refined 17,626.6); Chemicals and related products 22,651.3 (medicinal and pharmaceutical products 6,371.0); Basic manufactures 31,563.3 (metal products 9,601.9); Machinery and transport equipment 74,985.0 (general industrial machinery and equipment 8,559.3; office machines and computers 7,821.1; telecommunications equipment, etc. 7,329.3; Other electrical machinery, apparatus and appliances 14,321.5; Road vehicles 13,068.5, of which motor cars 8,013.9; Other transport equipment 14,284.1, of which aircraft and associated equipment 7,342.0, ships, boats and floating structures 6,940.5); Miscellaneous manufactured articles 35,044.7 (apparel and clothing accessories 8,260.7); Total (incl. others) 220,874.0. *Exports f.o.b.:* Food and live animals 120,989.9 (fish, crustaceans, molluscs and preparations thereof 106,730.0, of which fish, fresh, chilled or frozen 61,991.4; fish, dried, salted or smoked 28,675.6; marine products, prepared or preserved 13,250.2); Animal feeds (excl. unmilled cereals) 13,127.2; Basic manufactures 47,736.4 (aluminium 39,380.1); Machinery and transport equipment 9,568.5; Total (incl. others) 196,582.2.

Principal Trading Partners (million krónur, country of consignment, 2001): *Imports c.i.f.:* Australia 6,212.2; Belgium 4,120.9; China, People's Republic 6,352.4; Denmark 19,077.6; Finland 3,724.2; France 6,982.6; Germany 26,908.8; Ireland 2,487.0; Italy 6,802.9; Japan 7,297.6; Netherlands 14,554.4; Norway 17,234.6; ; Russia 3,551.2; Spain 4,341.8; Sweden 12,757.4; Switzerland 3,039.3; United Kingdom 16,609.6; USA 24,505.6; Total (incl. others) 220,874.0. *Exports f.o.b.:* Belgium 2,798.9; Canada 2,115.8; Denmark (incl. Faroe Islands) 10,867.9; France 7,687.9; Germany 29,292.2; Italy 2,517.1; Japan 6,838.6; Netherlands 21,442.1; Norway 10,384.3; Spain 10,538.6; Sweden 2,084.7; Switzerland 6,400.0; United Kingdom 35,839.1; USA 20,329.9; Total (incl. others) 196,582.2.

TRANSPORT

Road Traffic (registered motor vehicles at 1 January 2002): Passenger cars 161,576; Buses and coaches 1,711; Goods vehicles 19,990; Motorcycles 1,752.

Shipping: *Merchant fleet* (registered vessels, 1 January 2002): Fishing vessels 959 (displacement 188,526 grt); Passenger ships, tankers and other vessels 176 (displacement 44,156 grt). *International freight traffic* ('000 metric tons, 1994): Goods loaded 1,162; Goods unloaded 1,733.

Civil Aviation (scheduled external Icelandic traffic, '000, 1996): Kilometres flown 22,526, Passenger-kilometres 2,801,000, Cargo ton-kilometres 52,655, Mail ton-kilometres 1,987.

TOURISM

Foreign Visitors by Country of Origin (2000): Denmark 28,456, Finland 9,359, France 14,955, Germany 32,664, Italy 8,147, Netherlands 10,259, Norway 24,280, Sweden 29,488, United Kingdom 45,106, USA 53,637; Total (incl. others) 302,913.

Receipts from Tourists (million krónur): 27,498 in 1999, 30,459 in 2000; 37,720 in 2001.

COMMUNICATIONS MEDIA

Radio Receivers (2002): 94,840 licensed.

Television Receivers (2002): 91,952 licensed.

Telephones (2001): 190,600 main lines in use*.

Facsimile Machines (1993): 4,100 in use (Source: UN, *Statistical Yearbook*).

Mobile Cellular Telephones (subscribers, 2001): 235,400*.

Personal Computers ('000 in use, 2001): 120*.

Internet Users ('000, 2001): 195*.

Books (production, 1999): 1,866 titles (incl. new editions).

Daily Newspapers (2001): 3 (combined circulation 100,000 copies per issue).

* Source: International Telecommunication Union.

EDUCATION

Institutions (2001): Pre-primary 261; Primary and secondary (lower level) 193; Secondary (higher level) 36; Tertiary (universities and colleges) 11.

Teachers (incl. part-time, 2001): Pre-primary 3,575; Primary and secondary (lower level) 4,490; Secondary (higher level) 1,516 (2000); Tertiary 1,517 (2000).

Students (2001): Pre-primary 15,578; Primary 31,502; Secondary (lower level) 12,635; Secondary (higher level) 20,740; Tertiary 11,964.

Directory

The Constitution

The Constitution came into force on 17 June 1944, when Iceland became an independent Republic. The main provisions of the Constitution, including subsequent amendments, are summarized below:

GOVERNMENT

Legislative power is vested jointly in the President of the Republic and the Althingi (Alþingi). Executive power is vested in the President. The authority vested in the President shall be exercised through the Cabinet. The President appoints the Ministers to the Cabinet under the auspices of the Prime Minister, or the Prime Minister-elect when a new Cabinet is being assembled. The President may be dismissed only if a resolution supported by three-quarters of the Alþingi is approved by a plebiscite.

The President is elected for four years by universal suffrage. All those qualified to vote who have reached the age of 35 years are eligible for the Presidency.

The Alþingi is composed of 63 Members, elected by the people by secret ballot on the basis of proportional representation, for four years, in eight multi-member constituences. The franchise for general elections to the Alþingi is universal above the age of 18. Every national having the right to vote and an unblemished reputation is eligible to be elected to the Alþingi, except for the Justices of the Supreme Court. Seats that fall vacant between legislative elections are filled by substitutes elected at the same time as titular Members.

The Alþingi is convened by the President for a regular session every year on 1 October and continues in session until the same date next year, unless the election period of its Members has elapsed earlier or it has been dissolved. The President may adjourn meetings of the Alþingi, but not for more than two weeks not more than once a year. The President may dissolve the Alþingi. Elections must then be held within two months and the Alþingi must reassemble within eight months. Sessions are held in one chamber and its meetings are public. The Alþingi elects a Speaker, who presides over its proceedings.

Legislative bills are either submitted to the Alþingi by the President through his/her Ministers or by individual Members of the Alþingi. Bills must be given three readings in the Alþingi and be approved by a simple majority before they are submitted to the President. If the President disapproves a bill it nevertheless becomes valid, but must be submitted to a plebiscite.

Each Member of the Alþingi has the right to request, subject to the permission of the Alþingi, information from a Minister or an answer, orally or in writing, regarding a public matter, by tabling a question or requesting a report. Ministers are responsible to the Alþingi and may be impeached by that body, in which case they are tried by the Court of Impeachment.

LOCAL GOVERNMENT

Iceland is divided into 122 municipalities, which have definite geographical boundaries and cover the entire island. These municipalities are currently undergoing a process of amalgamation, which is expected to continue over the next few years. In each municipality there is a municipal council, elected every four years. All citizens over the age of 18 years are eligible to vote. In larger municipalities councillors are elected by proportional representation and frequently on party political lines. In the smallest rural areas councillors are usually elected on an individual basis. Municipal councils are enacted to set their own property rates and local income taxes, within certain limits determined by law. A municipal executive council (elected every year) is in charge of the chief administration, including municipal finances, budgeting, personnel and legal matters. Executive councils may also take charge of infrastructural investments and public works.

The Government

HEAD OF STATE

President: ÓLAFUR RAGNAR GRÍMSSON (took office 1 August 1996; began a second term in August 2000).

THE CABINET*
(April 2003)

A coalition of the Independence Party (IP) and the Progressive Party (PP).

Prime Minister and Minister of the Statistical Bureau of Iceland: DAVÍÐ ODDSSON (IP).

Minister of Foreign Affairs and External Trade: HALLDÓR ÁSGRÍMSSON (PP).

Minister of Finance: GEIR H. HAARDE (IP).

Minister of Fisheries: ÁRNI M. MATHIESEN (IP).

Minister of Justice and Ecclesiastical Affairs: SÓLVEIG PÉTURSDÓTTIR (IP).

Minister of Agriculture: GUÐNÍ ÁGÚSTSSON (PP).

Minister of the Environment and Nordic Co-operation: SIV FRIDLEIFSDÓTTIR (PP).

Minister of Industry and Commerce: VALGERUR SVERRISDÓTTIR (PP).

Minister of Education, Science and Culture: TÓMAS INGI OLRICH (IP).

Minister of Social Affairs: PÁLL PÉTURSSON (PP).

Minister of Communications: STURLA BÖÐVARSSON (IP).

Minister of Health and Social Security: JÓN KRISTJÁNSSON (PP).

* A general election was held on 10 May 2003. As of mid-May, a new government had yet to be appointed.

MINISTRIES

Office of the President: Stadastaður, Soleyjargata 1, 150 Reykjavík; tel. 5404400; fax 5624802; e-mail forseti@forseti.is.

Prime Minister's Office: Stjórnarráðshúsinu v/Lækjargötu, 150 Reykjavík; tel. 5458400; fax 5624014; e-mail postur@for.stjr.is; internet www.stjr.is/for.

Ministry of Agriculture: Sölvhólsgata 7, 150 Reykjavík; tel. 5459750; fax 5521160; e-mail postur@lan.stjr.is; internet www.stjr.is/lan.

Ministry of Communications: Hafnarhúsinu við Tryggvagötu, 150 Reykjavík; tel. 5609630; fax 5621702; e-mail postur@sam.stjr.is.

Ministry of Education, Science and Culture: Sölvhólsgata 4, 150 Reykjavík; tel. 5459500; fax 5623068; e-mail postur@mrn.stjr.is; internet www.menntamalaraduneyti.is.

Ministry of the Environment: Vonarstræti 4, 150 Reykjavík; tel. 5458600; fax 5624566; e-mail postur@environment.is; internet www.environment.is.

Ministry of Finance: Arnarhváli, 150 Reykjavík; tel. 5459200; fax 5628280; e-mail postur@fjr.stjr.is; internet www.government.is/fjr.

Ministry of Fisheries: Skúlagötu 4, 150 Reykjavík; tel. 5609670; fax 5621853; e-mail sjavar@hafro.is; internet www.stjr.is/sjr.

Ministry of Foreign Affairs: Raudarárstíg 25, 150 Reykjavík; tel. 5459900; fax 5622373; e-mail external@utn.stjr.is; internet www.mfa.is.

Ministry of Health and Social Security: Laugavegi 116, 150 Reykjavík; tel. 5609700; fax 5519165; e-mail postur@htr.stjr.is; internet www.stjr.is/htr.

Ministry of Industry and Commerce: Arnarhváli, 150 Reykjavík; tel. 5609070; fax 5621289; e-mail postur@ivr.stjr.is; internet www.stjr.is/ivr.

Ministry of Justice and Ecclesiastical Affairs: Arnarhváli, 150 Reykjavík; tel. 5459000; fax 5525127; e-mail postur@dkm.stjr.is; internet www.stjr.is/dkm.

Ministry of Social Affairs: Hafnarhúsinu við Tryggvagötu, 150 Reykjavík; tel. 5458100; fax 5524804; e-mail postur@fel.stjr.is; internet felagsmalaraduneyti.is.

President and Legislature

PRESIDENT

Presidential Election, 29 June 1996*

	Number of votes cast	% of votes
Ólafur Ragnar Grímsson	68,370	40.9
Pétur K. Hafstein	48,863	29.2
Guðrún Agnarsdóttir	43,578	26.0
Ástthór Magnússon	4,422	2.6

* In 2000 Ólafur Ragnar Grimsson was unopposed as a presidential candidate and the Althingi awarded him another term without holding the scheduled election.

ALTHINGI
(Alþingi)

Alþingi

v/Austurvöll, 150 Reykjavík; tel. 5630500; fax 5630520; e-mail parlsec@althingi.is; internet www.althingi.is.

Speaker of the Alþingi: HALLDÓR BLÖNDAL.

Secretary-General (Clerk) of the Alþingi: FRIDRIK ÓLAFSSON.

General Election, 10 May 2003*

	Number of votes	% of votes	Seats
Sjálfstæðisflokkurinn (Independence Party)	61,707	33.7	22
Samfylkingin (The Alliance)†	56,700	31.0	20
Framsóknarflokkurin (Progressive Party)	32,484	17.7	12
Vinstrihreyfing—grænt framboð (Left-Green Movement)	16,129	8.8	5
Frjáslindi flokkurin (Liberal Party)	13,523	7.4	4
Nýtt Afl	1,791	1.0	—
Framboð óháðra i Suðurkjördæmi	844	0.5	—
Total	169,655	100.0	63

* Preliminary results.
† Samfylkingin comprises Alþýðubandalagið (the People's Alliance), Alþýðuflokkurinn (the Social Democratic Party), Þjóðvaki—hreyfing fólksins (the People's Movement) and Samtók um kvennalista (the Women's List).
Note: A general election was scheduled for 10 May 2003.

Political Organizations

Framsóknarflokkurinn (Progressive Party—PP): Hverfisgata 33, POB 453, 121 Reykjavík; tel. 5404300; fax 5404301; e-mail framsokn@framsokn.is; internet www.framsokn.is; f. 1916 with a programme of social liberalism and co-operation; Chair. HALLDÓR ÁSGRÍMSSON; Vice-Chair. GUÐNI ÁGÚSTSSON; Parliamentary Leader KRISTINN H. GUNNARSSON; Sec.-Gen. ARNI MAGNÚSSON.

Frjálslindi flokkurinn (Liberal Party): c/o v/Austurvöll, 150 Reykjavík; tel. 5630500; fax 5630520; f. by Sverrir Hermannsson, former member of the IP and former cabinet minister; Leader SVERRIR HERMANNSSON.

Samfylkingin (The Alliance): Austurstræti 14, 101 Reykjavík; tel. 5511600; e-mail samfylking@samfylking.is; internet www.samfylking.is; f. 1999 by merger of Alþýðubandalagið (People's Alliance—PA, f. 1956), Alþýðuflokkurinn (Social Democratic Party—SDP, f. 1916), Samtök um kvennalista (Women's List—WL, f. 1983) and Þjóðvaki—hreyfing fólksins (Awakening of the Nation—

People's Movement, f. 1994); Chair. Össur Skarphédinsson; Vice-Chair. Margrét Frímannsdóttir; Parliamentary Leader Bryndís Hlödversdóttir.

Sjálfstæðisflokkurinn (Independence Party—IP): Háaleitisbraut 1, 105 Reykjavík; tel. 5151700; fax 5151717; e-mail xd@xd.is; internet www.xd.is; f. 1929 by an amalgamation of the Conservative and Liberal Parties; advocates social reform within the framework of private enterprise and the furtherance of national and individual independence; Leader Davíð Oddsson; Dep. Leader Geir H. Haarde; Parliamentary Leader Sigríður Anna Þórðardóttir.

Vinstrihreyfingin—grænt framboð (Left-Green Movement): Hafnarstræti 20, POB 175, 121 Reykjavík; tel. 5528872; e-mail vg@vg.is; internet www.vg.is; f. 1999 by dissident members of the PA, the Women's List, the Greens and independent left-wingers; Leader Steingrímur J. Sigfússon; Parliamentary Leader Ögmundur Jónasson.

Two new parties, **Nýtt Afl** and **Framboð óháðra i Suðurkjördæmi**, were formed to contest the 2003 general election.

Diplomatic Representation

EMBASSIES IN ICELAND

Canada: Túngata 14, 101 Reykjavík; tel. 5335550; fax 5335551; e-mail embassy.canada@mmedia.is; Ambassador Gerald R. Skinner.

China, People's Republic: Víðimelur 29, 107 Reykjavík; tel. 5526751; fax 5626110; internet www.china-embassy.is; Ambassador Jia Zhengyun.

Denmark: Hverfisgata 29, 101 Reykjavík; tel. 5750300; fax 5750310; e-mail rekamb@rekamb.um.dk; Ambassador Flemming Mørch.

Finland: Túngata 30, 101 Reykjavík; tel. 5100100; fax 5623880; e-mail finamb@li.is; Ambassador Timo H. Koponen.

France: Túngata 22, 101 Reykjavík; tel. 5517621; fax 5628177; e-mail amb.fran@itn.is; internet www.ambafrance.is; Ambassador Louis Bardollet.

Germany: Laufásvegur 31, POB 400, 121 Reykjavík; tel. 5301100; fax 5301101; e-mail germanembassy@islandia.is; Ambassador Dr Hendrik Dane.

Japan: Hotel Saga, Hagatorgi, 107 Reykjavík; tel. 5108600; fax 5108605; Chargé d'affaires a.i. Minoru Okazaki.

Norway: Fjólugata 17, 101 Reykjavík; tel. 5200700; fax 5529553; e-mail emb.Reykjavik@mfa.no; internet www.noregur.is; Ambassador Kjell H. Halvorsen.

Russia: Garðastræti 33, 101 Reykjavík; tel. 5515156; fax 5620633; e-mail russemb@itn.is; Ambassador Anatolii S. Zaytsev.

Sweden: Lagmuli 7, POB 8136, 128 Reykjavík; tel. 5201230; fax 5201235; e-mail sveamb@itn.is; Ambassador Herman af Trolle.

United Kingdom: Laufásvegur 31, 101 Reykjavík; POB 460, 121 Reykjavík; tel. 5505100; fax 5505105; e-mail britemb@centrum.is; Ambassador John Howard Culver.

USA: Laufásvegur 21, 101 Reykjavík; tel. 5629100; fax 5629139; Ambassador Barbara J. Griffiths.

Judicial System

All cases are heard in Ordinary Courts except those specifically within the jurisdiction of Special Courts. The Ordinary Courts include both a lower division of urban and rural district courts presided over by the district magistrates, and the Supreme Court.

Justices of the Supreme Court are appointed by the President and cannot be dismissed except by the decision of a court. The Justices elect the Chief Justice for a period of two years.

Supreme Court
Dómhúsið v. Arnarhól, 150 Reykjavík; tel. 5103030; fax 5623995; e-mail haestirettur@haestirettur.is; internet www.haestirettur.is.

Chief Justice: Guðrun Erlendsdóttir.

Justices: Árni Kolbeinsson, Garðar Gíslason, Gunnlaugur Clæssen, Haraldur Henrysson, Hrafn Bragason, Ingibjörg Benediktsdóttir, Markús Sigurbjörnsson, Pétur Kr. Hafstein.

Religion

CHRISTIANITY

Protestant Churches

Þjóðkirkja Íslands (Evangelical Lutheran Church of Iceland): Biskupsstofa, Laugavegur 31, 150 Reykjavík; tel. 5351500; fax 5513284; e-mail kirkjan@kirkjan.is; internet www.kirkjan.is; the national Church, endowed by the State; about 87% of the population are members; Iceland forms one diocese, with two suffragan sees; 280 parishes and 150 pastors; Bishop Karl Sigurbjörnsson.

Fríkirkjan í Reykjavík (The Congregational Church in Reykjavík): POB 1671, 121 Reykjavík; tel. 5527270; fax 5527287; e-mail hjorturm@frikirkian.is; f. 1899; Free Lutheran denomination; 5,500 mems; Head Hjortur M. Johannsson.

Óhádi söfnuðurinn (Independent Congregation): Reykjavík; Free Lutheran denomination; 1,100 mems; Head Rev. Petur Thorarinsson.

Seventh-day Adventists: Suðurhlið 36, 105 Reykjavík; tel. 5887800; fax 5887808; e-mail sda@mmedia.is; internet www.sda.is.

The Roman Catholic Church
Iceland comprises a single diocese, directly responsible to the Holy See. At 31 December 2000 there were an estimated 4,307 adherents in the country (about 1.5% of the total population).

Bishop of Reykjavík: Most Rev. Dr Jóhannes M. Gijsen, Biskupsstofa, POB 490, Hávallagata 14, 121 Rekyjavík; tel. 5525388; fax 5623878; e-mail catholica@vortex.is.

The Press

PRINCIPAL DAILIES

Althýdubladið (The Labour Journal): Hverfisgata 8–10, 101 Reykjavík; tel. 5625566; fax 5629244; f. 1919; organ of the Social Democratic Party; Editor Hrafn Jökulsson; circ. 4,000.

DV (Dagbladið-Vísir): Útgáfufélagið DV ehf, Skaftahlíð 24, POB 5480, 105 Reykjavík; tel. 5505000; fax 5505020; e-mail ritstjorn@dv.is; internet www.strik.is/dv; f. 1981; independent; Editor Oli Björn Kárason; circ. 35,000.

Dagur-Tíminn: Strandgata 31, POB 58, 600 Akureyri; tel. 4606100; fax 4627639; f. 1918; restructured 1996; organ of the Progressive Party; Editor Stefán Jón Hafstein.

Morgunbladið (Morning News): Kringlan 1, POB 3040, 103 Reykjavík; tel. 5691100; fax 5691181; e-mail mbl@mbl.is; internet www.mbl.is; f. 1913; independent; Editor-in-Chief Styrmir Gunnarsson; circ. 55,000.

WEEKLIES

Austri: Tjarnarbraut 19, POB 173, 700 Egilsstaðir; tel. 4711984; e-mail austri@eldhorn.is; local newspaper; f. 1979; Editor Jón Kristjánsson; circ. 2,000.

Einherji: Siglufjorður; organ of the Progressive Party.

Fiskifréttir: Seljavegur 2, 101 Reykjavík; tel. 5155500; fax 5155599; e-mail fiskifrettir@frodi.is; f. 1983; weekly; for the fishing industry; Editor Guðjón Einarsson; circ. 6,000.

Íslendingur-Ísafold (Icelander-Icecountry): Kaupangi v/Mýrarveg, 600 Akureyri; tel. 4621500; f. 1915 for North and East Iceland; Editor Stefán Sigtryggsson.

Séð & Heyrt: Seljavegur 2, 101 Reykjavík; tel. 5155652; fax 5155599; e-mail bjarni@frodi.is; showbusiness and celebrities; Editors Bjarni Brynjolfsson, Kristjan Thorvaldsson; circ. 23,000.

Siglfirðingur: Siglufjorður; organ of the Independence Party.

Skagabladið: Skólabraut 21, 300 Akranesi; tel. 4314222; fax 4314122; f. 1984; local newspaper; Editor Sigurður Sverrisson; circ. 1,500.

Suðurnesjafréttir: Hafnargötu 28, 230 Keflavík; tel. 4213800; fax 4213802; f. 1992; local newspaper; Editors Emil Páll Jónsson, Halldór Levi Björnsson; circ. 6,500.

Sunnlenska Fréttabladið: Austurvegi 1, 800 Selfoss; tel. 4823074; fax 4823084; f. 1991; local newspaper; Editor Bjarni Harðarson; circ. 6,300.

Vikan: Seljavegur 8, 101 Reykjavík; tel. 5155500; fax 5155592; e-mail johanna@frodi.is; Editors Johanna Hardardottir, Hrund Hauksdóttir; circ 13,000–17,000.

Vikublaðið (The Weekly Paper): Reykjavík; tel. 5528655; fax 5517599; f. 1992; organ of People's Alliance; Editor FRIÐRIK THÓR GUÐMUNDSSON; circ. 3,000–4,000.

Víkurblaðið: Heðinsbraut 1, 640 Húsavík; tel. 4641780; fax 4641399; f. 1979; local newspaper; Editor JÓHANNES SIGURJÓNSSON; circ. 1,300.

Víkurfréttir: Grundarvegur 23, 260 Reykjanesbær; tel. 4214717; fax 4212777; e-mail pket@vf.is; internet www.vf.is; f. 1983; local newspaper; Editor PÁLL KETILSSON; circ. 6,500.

OTHER PERIODICALS

Atlantica: Borgartún 23, 105 Reykjavík; tel. 5127517; fax 5618646; e-mail heimur@heimur.is; internet www.heimur.is; 6 a year; in-flight magazine of Icelandair; Editor JON KALDAL.

AVS (Arkitektur, verktækni og skipulag): Garðastræti 17, 101 Reykjavík; tel. 5616577; fax 5616571; e-mail skipark@skipark.is; f. 1979; 4 a year; architecture, design, planning and environment; Editor GESTUR ÓLAFSSON; circ. 6,000.

Bændablaðið: POB 7080, 127 Reykjavík; tel. 5630300; fax 5623058; e-mail ath@bi.bondi.is; f. 1995; fortnightly; organ of the Icelandic farmers' union; Editor ÁSKELL THÓRISSON; circ. 6,400.

Bíllinn: Reykjavík; tel. 5526090; fax 5529490; f. 1982; 3–4 a year; cars and motoring equipment; Editor LEÓ M. JÓNSSON; circ. 4,000.

Bleikt og Blátt: Seljavegur 2, 101 Reykjavík; tel. 5155500; fax 5155599; e-mail bogb@frodi.is; f. 1989; 6 a year; sex education, communication between men and women; Editor HRUND HAUKS-DÓTTIR; circ. 11,000.

Eiðfaxi: Dugguvogur 10, POB 8133, 128 Reykjavík; tel. 5882525; fax 5882528; e-mail eidfaxi@eidfaxi.is; internet www.eidfaxi.is; f. 1977; monthly; horse-breeding and horsemanship; Man. Dir GYÐA GERÐARSDÓTTIR; Editors JENS EINARSSON, HULDA G. GEIRSDÓTTIR; circ. 7,000.

Fjármálatíðindi: Kalkofnsvegur 1, 150 Reykjavík; tel. 5699600; fax 5699608; e-mail sedlabanki@sedlabanki.is; internet www.sedlabanki.is; 2 a year; economic journal published by the Central Bank; circ. 1,600.

Freyr, búnaðarblað: Baendahöllin við Hagatorg, 107 Reykjavík; tel. 5630300; fax 5623058; e-mail me@bondi.is; internet www.bondi.is; monthly; agriculture; Editors ÁSKELL THORISSON, MATTHIAS EGGERTSSON; circ. 1,600.

Frjáls Verslun (Free Trade): Borgartún 23, 105 Reykjavík; tel. 5617575; fax 5618646; f. 1939; 10 a year; business magazine; Editor JÓN G. HAUKSSON; circ. 6,000–9,000.

Gestgjafinn: Héðinshúsið, Seljavegur 2, 101 Reykjavík; tel. 5155506; fax 5155599; e-mail gestgjafinn@frodi.is; f. 1981; 12 a year; food and wine; Editor SÓLVEIG BALDURSDÓTTIR; circ. 13,000–16,000.

Hagtíðindi (Monthly Statistics): Statistics Iceland, Borgartún 20A, 150 Reykjavík; tel. 5281000; fax 5281098; e-mail statice@statice.is; internet www.statice.is; f. 1916; monthly; Dir-Gen. HALLGRIMUR SNOR-RASON; circ. 800.

Hár og Fegurð (Hair and Beauty Magazine): Skúlagata 54, 105 Reykjavík; tel. and fax 5628141; e-mail pmelsted@vortex.is; internet www.vortex.is/fashion; f. 1980; 3 a year; hair, beauty, fashion; Editor PÉTUR MELSTEÐ.

Heilbrigðismál: Skógarhlíð 8, 105 Reykjavík; tel. 5621414; fax 5621417; f. 1949; quarterly; public health; Editor JÓNAS RAGNARSSON; circ. 6,000.

Heima Er Bezt: Suðurlandsbraut 14, 108 Reykjavík; tel. 5155210; fax 5155201; e-mail heb@athjgli.is; f. 1951; monthly; literary; Editor GUÐJÓN BALDVINSSON; circ. 3,000.

Heimsmynd: Reykjavík; tel. 5622020; fax 5622029; f. 1986; 10 a year; general interest; Editor KARL BIRGISSON; circ. 8,000.

Hús og Híbýli: Seljavegur 2, 101 Reykjavík; tel. 5155500; fax 5155599; e-mail hogh@frodi.is; f. 1978; 12 a year; architecture, family and homes; Editor LÓA ALDÍSARDÓTTIR; circ. 13,000–16,000.

Húsfreyjan (The Housewife): Túngata 14, 101 Reykjavík; tel. 5517044; f. 1950; quarterly; the organ of the Federation of Icelandic Women's Societies; Editor HRAFNHILDUR VALGARÐS; circ. 4,000.

Iceland Business: Borgartún 23, 105 Reykjavík; tel. 5127517; fax 5618646; e-mail icelandreview@icelandreview.com; internet www.icelandreview.com; f. 1994; 3 a year; in English; Editor JON KALDAL.

Iceland Review: Borgartún 23 105 Reykjavík; tel. 5127517; fax 5618646; e-mail icelandreview@icelandreview.com; internet www.icelandreview.com; f. 1963; quarterly, in English; general; Editor JON KALDAL.

Innflutningur (Import): Reykjavík; tel. 5813411; fax 5680211; f. 1991; 3–4 a year; Editor SÓLVEIG BALDURSDÓTTIR; circ. 5,000.

Lisin að lifa: Reykjavík; tel. 5882111; fax 5882114; e-mail feb@islandia.is; f. 1986; 4 a year; for elderly people; Editor SU BJÖRGUINS; circ. 13,000–15,000.

Mannlíf: Seljavegur 2, 101 Reykjavík; tel. 5155500; fax 5155599; e-mail mannlif@frodi.is; f. 1984; 10 a year; general interest; Editor GERDUR KRISTNÝ GUÐJÖNSDÓTTIR; circ. 16,000.

Myndbönd mánaðarins (Videos of the Month): Reykjavík; tel. 5811280; fax 5811286; f. 1993; monthly; Editor GUÐBERGUR ÍSLEIFSSON; circ. 26,000.

Ný menntamál: Reykjavík; tel. 5531117; e-mail hannes@ismennt.is; f. 1983; quarterly; educational issues; Editor HANNES ÍSBERG; circ. 6,500.

NýttLíf: Seljavegur 2, 101 Reykjavík; tel. 5155660; fax 5155599; e-mail nyttlif@frodi.is; f. 1978; 11 a year; fashion; Editor GULLVEIG SÆMUNDSDÓTTIR; circ. 13,000–17,000.

Peningamál: Kalkofnsvegur 1, 150 Reykjavik; tel. 5699600; fax 5699608; e-mail publish@centbk.is; internet www.sedlabanki.is; f. 1999; quarterly bulletin published by the Central Bank; circ. 1,600.

Sjávarfréttir: Seljavegur 2, 101 Reykjavík; tel. 5155500; fax 5155599; e-mail fiskifrettir@frodi.is; f. 1973; yearly; ship registry, statistics on Icelandic fisheries; Editor GUÐJÓN EINARSSON; circ. 5,500.

Skutull (Harpoon): Fjarðarstræti 2, 400 Isafjörður; tel. 4563948; fax 4565148; e-mail stapi@simnet.is; f. 1923; monthly; organ of the Social Democratic Party; Editor GÍSLI HJARTARSON.

Stúdentablaðið: Stúdentaheimilinu v/Hringbraut, 101 Reykjavík; tel. 5700850; fax 5700855; e-mail shi@hi.is; internet www.shi.hi.is; f. 1924; 8 issues during the academic year; students' interests; Editor SIGTRYGGUR MAGNASON; circ. 7,500.

Sveitastjórnarmál: Háaleitisbraut 11, 128 Reykjavík; tel. 5813711; fax 5687866; f. 1941; 24 a year; publ. by the Asscn of Icelandic Municipalities; Editor UNNAR STEFÁNSSON; circ. 3,400.

Uppeldi: Síðumúli 27, 108 Reykjavík; tel. 5709500; fax 5709501; f. 1988; quarterly; children, parenting and family matters; Editor KRISTÍN ELFA GUÐNADÓTTIR; Dir STEFANÍA JÓNSDÓTTIR; circ. 7,000.

Úrval (Digest): Thverholt 11, 105 Reykjavík; tel. 5505000; fax 5505999; f. 1942; bi-monthly; Editor SIGURÐUR HREIÐARSSON; circ. 6,500.

Veiðimaðurinn (Hunter): Hédinshúsið, Seljavegur 2, 101 Reykjavík; tel. 5155500; fax 5155599; e-mail frodi@frodi.is; f. 1984; 3 a year; fishing and hunting; Editor GYLFI PALSSON; circ. 5,000–7,000.

Vera: ægisgötu 4, 101 Reykjavík; tel. 5526310; fax 5527560; e-mail vera@vera.is; internet www.vera.is; f. 1982; 6 a year; feminist issues; Editor ELÍSABET THORGEIRSDÓTTIR.

Vikan: Seljavegur 2, 101 Reykjavík; tel. 5155500; fax 5155599; f. 1938; 50 a year; family; Editor ÉLÍN ALBERTSDÓTTIR; circ. 17,000.

Víkingur (Seaman): Borgartún 18, 105 Reykjavík; 10 a year; Editor SIGURJÓN VALDIMARSSON.

Vinnan (Work): Grensásvegur 16A, 108 Reykjavík; tel. 5813044; fax 5680093; e-mail arnar@gsi.is; 6 a year; f. 1943; publ. by Icelandic Federation of Labour; Editor Dr GUÐMUNDUR ARNASON; circ. 5,000.

Ægir: Skerpla, Suðurlandsbraut 10, Reykjavík; tel. 5681225; fax 5681224; f. 1905; published by the Fisheries Association of Iceland in co-operation with Athygli ehf Publishing; monthly; Editors BJARNI KR. GRÍMSSON, JÓHANN ÓLAFUR HALLDÓRSSON; circ. 2,500.

Æskan og ABC (The Youth and ABC): Eiríksgötu 5, 101 Reykjavík; tel. 5510248; fax 5510248; f. 1897; 9 a year; children's magazine; Editor KARL HELGASON.

NEWS AGENCIES

Foreign Bureaux

Agence France-Presse (AFP): Garðastræti 13, 101 Reykjavík; tel. 5510586; Correspondent GÉRARD LEMARQUIS.

United Press International (UPI) (USA): Reykjavík; tel. 5539816; Correspondent BERNARD SCUDDER.

Publishers

Æskan: Stangarhyl 4, 110 Reykjavík; tel. 5305400; fax 5305401; e-mail karl@aeskan.is; internet www.aeskan.is; general, children's books, magazines; Dir KARL HELGASON.

Bifröst: Skjaldborg/Birtingur, bokaklubbur, c/o Reynir Johannsson, Grensasvegi 14, 128 Reykjavík; tel. 5882400; fax 5888994; e-mail skjaldborg@skjaldborg.is; f. 1988; spiritual, self-help, new age; Dir BJORN EIRIKSSON.

Bjartur & Salka: Bræðraborgarstig 9, 101 Reykjavík; tel. 5621828; fax 5628360; e-mail snar@itn.is; f. 1989; contemporary fiction; Dir SNÆBJÖRN ARNGRÍMSSON.

Bókaútgáfan Bjartur: Bræðraborgarstígur 9, 101 Reykjavík; tel. 5621826; fax 5628360; f. 1989; contemporary fiction; Man. Dir SNÆBJÖRN ARNGRÍMSSON.

Bókaútgáfan Björk: Birkivöllum 30, 800 Selfoss; tel. 4821394; fax 4823894; f. 1941; children's; Dir ERLENDUR DANIELSSON.

Bókaútgáfan Hólar: Byggðavegi 101B, 600 Akureyri; tel. 4622515; fax 5871180; f. 1995; general; Dir JÓN HJALTASON.

Edda–Media and Publishing: Suðurlandsbraut 12, 108 Reykjavík; tel. 5222000; fax 5222026; e-mail edda@edda.is; internet www.edda.is; Gen. Dir HALLDÓR GUÐMUNDSSON.

Almenna bókafélagið: Suðurlandsbraut 12, 108 Reykjavík; tel. 5503000; fax 5503033; general; Publ. Dir BJARNI ÞORSTEINSSON.

Forlagið: Suðurlandsbraut 12, 108 Reykjavík; tel. 5222000; fax 5222022; e-mail forlagid@edda.is; f. 1984; general; Publ. Dir KRISTJÁN B. JONASSON.

Iceland Review, bókadeild: Suðurlandsbraut 12, 108 Reykjavík; tel. 5222000; fax 5222026; e-mail edda@edda.si; internet www.edda.is; Dir HALLDÓR GUÐMUNDSSON.

Mál og menning: Laugavegi 18, 101 Reykjavík; tel. 5152500; fax 5152505; e-mail info@mm.is; internet www.mm.is; f. 1937; Dir HALLDÓR GUÐMUNDSSON.

Vaka-Helgafell: Síðumúli 6, 108 Reykjavík; tel. 5503000; fax 5503033; e-mail vaka@vaka.is; f. 1942; general, fiction, non-fiction; Dir PÉTUR MÁR ÓLAFSSON.

Fjölvi—Vasa: Njorvasundi 15A, 104 Reykjavík; tel. 5688433; fax 5688142; e-mail fjolvi@mmedia.is; f. 1966; general; Dir ÞORSTEINN THORARENSEN.

Frjáls fjölmiðlun: Þverholt 11, POB 5380, 105 Reykjavík; tel. 5505000; fax 5505999; f. 1981; fiction in translation, romance; Gen. Man. EYJÓLFUR SVEINSSON.

Fróði Publishing House: Seljavegi 2, 101 Reykjavík; tel. 5155500; fax 5155599; e-mail frodi@frodi.is; internet www.frodi.is; Dir MAGNÚS HREGGVIÐSSON.

Fróði Ltd: Seljavegi 2, 101 Reykjavík; tel. 5155500; fax 5155599; e-mail frodi@frodi.is; internet www.frodi.is; f. 1989; general, magazines; Dir MAGNÚS HREGGVIÐSSON.

Iðunn: Seljavegi 2, 101 Reykjavík; tel. 5155500; fax 5155579; e-mail idunn@idunn.is; internet www.frodi.is; f. 1945; general; Dir. JÓN KARLSSON.

Háskólaútgáfan (University of Iceland Press): Háskóli Íslands v/Suðurgötu, 101 Reykjavík; tel. 5254003; fax 5255255; e-mail hu@hi.is; f. 1988; non-fiction, science, culture, history; Man. Dir JÖRUNDUR GUÐMUNDSSON.

Hið íslenska bókmenntafélag: Síðumúli 21, 108 Reykjavík; tel. 5889060; fax 5889095; e-mail hib@islandia.is; internet www.hib.is; f. 1816; general; Pres. SIGURÐUR LÍNDAL; Dir SVERRIR KRISTINSSON.

Hið íslenska Fornritafélag: Síðumúli 21, 108 Reykjavík; tel. 5889060; fax 5889095; e-mail hib@islandia.is; internet www.hib.is; f. 1928; Pres. J. NORDAL.

Hörpuútgáfan: Stekkjarholti 8–10, POB 25, 300 Akranes; tel. 4312860; fax 4313309; e-mail bragi@horpuutgafan.is; f. 1960; fiction, general; Dir BRAGI ÞORÐARSON.

Islendingasagnaútgáfan—Muninn: POB 488, 222 Hafnarfjörður; tel. 8985868; fax 5655868; e-mail muninn@isl.is; f. 1945; poetry, fiction, children's, general non-fiction; Dir BENEDIKT KRISTJÁNSSON.

Krydd í tilveruna: Bakkasel 10, 109 Reykjavík; tel. 5575444; fax 5575466; f. 1989; mainly cookery; Dir ANTON ÖRN KJAERNSTED.

Leiðarljós: Sólbrekku, Hellum, 355 Snæfellsbær; tel. 4356810; fax 4356801; e-mail leidar@centrum.is; f. 1995; self-help, spiritual, non-fiction; Dir GUÐRÚN BERGMANN.

Mál og mynd: Bræðraborgarstig 9, 101 Reykjavík; tel. 5528866; fax 5528870; e-mail malogmynd@centum.is; non-fiction; Dir ÍVAR GISSURARSON.

Námsgagnastofnun (National Centre for Educational Materials): Laugavegí 166, 105 Reykjavík; tel. 5528088; fax 5624137; e-mail simi@nams.is; f. 1979; Dir INGIBJÖRG ÁSGEIRSDÓTTIR.

Nýja bókafélagið: Kringlunni 7, 108 Reykjavík; tel. 5111777; fax 5111770; e-mail jakobf@simnet.is; f. 1999; general; Dir JAKOB F. ÁSGEIRSSON.

Ormstunga: Ránargötu 20, 101 Reykjavík; tel. 5610055; fax 5524650; e-mail books@ormstunga.is; internet www.ormstunga.is; f. 1992; Icelandic and foreign fiction and non-fiction; Dir GÍSLI MÁR GÍSLASON.

PP Forlag: Ármúla 29, 108 Reykjavík; tel. 5687054; fax 5687053; e-mail pilot@mi.is; internet www.ppforlag.com; f. 1997; general; Dir SIGRÚN HALLDÓRSDÓTTIR.

Reykholt: Reykjavík; tel. 5888821; fax 5888380; f. 1987; general; Dir REYNIR JÓHANNSSON.

Samhjálp: Hverfisgötu 42, 101 Reykjavík; tel. 5611000; fax 5610050; e-mail samhjalp@samhjalp.is; internet www.samhjalp.is; religious, pentecostal; Dir HEIDAR GUÐNASON.

Setberg: Freyjugötu 14, POB 619, 101 Reykjavík; tel. 5517667; fax 5526640; f. 1950; fiction, cookery, juvenile, picture books, activity books and children's books; Dir ARNBJÖRN KRISTINSSON.

Skálholtsútgáfan: Laugavegi 31, 101 Reykjavík; tel. 5521090; fax 5621595; e-mail kirkbok@ismennt.is; f. 1981; non-fiction, Christian church; Man. Dir EDDA MÖLLER.

Skjaldborg Ltd: Grensásvegi 14, POB 8427, 108 Reykjavík; tel. 5882400; fax 5888994; e-mail skjaldborg@skjaldborg.is; general; Dir BJÖRN EIRÍKSSON.

Sögufélagið: Fischersundi 3, 101 Reykjavík; tel. 5514620; f. 1902; non-fiction, history; Dir RAGNHEIÐUR ÞORLÁKSDÓTTIR.

Stofnun Arna Magnussonar: Arnagarður v/ Suðurgotu, 101 Reykjavík; tel. 5254010; fax 5254035; e-mail rosat@hi.is; internet www .am.hi.is; f. 1972; non-fiction; Dir VÉSTEINN ÓLASON.

Þjóðsaga: Kringlunni 7, 108 Reykjavík; tel. 5111777; fax 5111770; e-mail pbk@hansa.is; non-fiction; Dir PÁLL BRAGI KRISTJÁNSSON.

PUBLISHERS' ASSOCIATION

Félag íslenskra bókaútgefenda (Icelandic Publishers' Asscn): Barónsstíg 5, 101 Reykjavík; tel. 5118020; fax 5115020; e-mail baekur@mmedia.is; internet www.bokautgafa.is; f. 1889; Pres. SIGURDUR SVAVARSSON; Man. BENEDIKT KRISTJANSSON.

Broadcasting and Communications

TELECOMMUNICATIONS

The local telecommunications market was deregulated, in accordance with European rules, on 1 January 1998.

Post and Telecom Administration: Smiðjuvegur 68–70, 200 Kópavogur; tel. 5101500; fax 5101509; e-mail pta@pta.is; internet www.pta.is.

Hallo!–Frjáls fjarskipti ehf: Skúlagötu 19, 101 Reyakjvík; tel. 5350500; fax 5525051; e-mail hallo@hallo.is; internet www.hallo.is; provides mobile telecommunications; Gen. Man. INGVAR GARÐARSSON.

Iceland Telecom Ltd: Austurvöllur, 150 Reykjavík; tel. 5506000; fax 5506009; e-mail siminn@siminn.is; internet www.siminn.is; f. 1998; operation of telecommunications; also operation of Skyggnir, earth station for satellite telecommunications; partially privatized 2001; Pres. and CEO THORARINN V. THORARINSSON.

Íslandssími: Borgartún 30, 105 Reykjavík; f. 1999; provides mobile telecommunications; specializes in corporate, fixed line and internet operations; CEO EYTHOR ARNALDS.

Lina.Net ehf: Skúlagötu 19, 101 Reykjavík; tel. 5951200; fax 5951299; e-mail linanet@lina.net; internet www.lina.net; f. 1999; provides mobile telecommunications; Man. Dir ERIKUR BRAGASON.

Nordial á Islandi hf: Reykjavík; tel. 6931315; provides international service.

Tal hf: Síðumúli 28, 108 Reykjavík; tel. 5706000; fax 5706001; e-mail tal@tal.is; internet www.tal.is; mobile telephone operator; controlled 30% of mobile calls in 2000; CEO OSKAR MAGNUSSON.

BROADCASTING

Ríkisútvarpið (Icelandic National Broadcasting Service): Broadcasting Centre, Efstaleiti 1, 150 Reykjavík; tel. 5153000; fax 5153010; e-mail isradio@ruv.is; internet www.ruv.is; f. 1930; Dir-Gen. MARKÚS ÖRN ANTONSSON; Chair. of Programme Board GUNNLAUGUR SÆVAR GUNNLAUGSSON.

Radio

Ríkisútvarpið: Radio Division, Efstaleiti 1, 150 Reykjavík; tel. 5153000; fax 5153010; f. 1930; Dir of Radio DORA INGVADOTTIR; Programme 1 has two long-wave, three medium-wave and 77 FM transmitters broadcasting 127 hours a week; Programme 2 has 67 FM transmitters broadcasting 168 hours a week.

Akraneskaupstaður: Stillholt 16–18, 300 Akranes; broadcasts only in Akranes; Dir BJÖRN LÁRUSSON.

Almiðlun ehf: Trönuhraun 6, 220 Hafnarfjörður; tel. 5651766; fax 5651796; broadcasts in Hafnarfjörður and Reykjavík area; Dir HALLDÓR ÁRNI SVEINSSON.

Bjarni Jónasson: Brekkugata 1, 900 Vestmannaeyjar; tel. 4811534; fax 4813475; broadcasts only in Vestmannaeyjar; Dir BJARNI JÓNASSON.

Búðarhreppur: Hafnargata 12, 750 Fáskrúðsfjörður; broadcasts only in Fáskrúðsfjörður.

Evrópsk Fjölmiðlun: Hlaðbae 11, 110 Reykjavík; tel. 5676111; Dir ERÍKUR SIGURBJÖRNSSON.

Fínn Miðill hf: Aðalstræti 6, 101 Reykjavík; tel. 5116500; fax 5116501.

Fjölbrautarskóli Norðurlands vestra: 550 Sauðárkrókur; broadcasts only in Sauðárkrókur.

Hallbjörn Hjartarson: Brimnesi, 545 Skagaströnd; tel. 4522960; e-mail hjh@li.is; broadcasts in Skaga-strönd, Blönduós and Sauðárkrókur; Dir HALLBJÖRN HJARTARSON.

Íslenska Útvarpsfélagið hf (Icelandic Broadcasting Corporation): Lyngháls 5, 110 Reykjavík; tel. 5156000; fax 5156860; f. 1986; privately-owned; Pres. SIGURÐUR G. GUÐJÓHNSSON.

Bylgjan: Lyngháls 5, 110 Reykjavík; tel. 5156300; fax 5156830.

Kristilega útvarpsstöðin Lindin: Krókháls 4A, 110 Reykjavík; tel. 5671030; e-mail lindin@lindin.is; Dir MICHAEL E. FITZGERALD.

Norðurljós (Northern Lights Communications): Lyngháls 5, 110 Reykjavík; tel. 5156000; fax 5156860; f. 1986; privately-owned; Pres. SIGURÐUR G. GUÐJÓHNSSON.

Útvarp Vestmannaeyjar: Brekkugata 1, 900 Vestmannaeyjar; tel. 4811534; fax 4813475; broadcasts only in Vestmannaeyjar; Dir BJARNI JÓNASSON.

Útvarpsklúbburinn Sköpun: Reykjavík; Dir SVERRIR JÚLÍUSSON.

Vila–Árna Útvarp: Skipholt 6, 355 Ólafsvík; tel. 4361334; fax 4361379; Dir VILHELM ARNASON.

Television

Ríkisútvarpið—Sjónvarp (Icelandic National Broadcasting Service—Television): Efstaleiti 1, 150 Reykjavík; tel. 5153000; fax 5153010; e-mail tvnews@ruv.is; internet www.ruv.is; f. 1966; covers 99% of the population; broadcasts daily, total 70 hours a week; Dir-Gen. MARKÚS ÖRN ANTONSSON; Man. Dir BJARNI GUÐMUNDSSON.

Aksjón ehf: Strandgötu 31, 600 Akureyri; tel. 4611050; fax 4612356; e-mail aksjon@nett.is; broadcasts only in Akureyri; Dir GÍSLI GUNNLAUGSSON.

Almiðlun ehf: Trönuhraun 6, 220 Hafnarfjörður; tel. 5651766; fax 5651796; broadcasts only in Hafnarfjörður; Dir HALLDÓR ÁRNI SVEINSSON.

Fjölsýn: Strandvegur 47, 900 Vestmannaeyjar; tel. 4811300; fax 4812643; e-mail sigit@eyjar.is; broadcasts only in Vesstmannaeyjar; Dir OMAR GUÐMUNDSSON.

Íslenska Útvarpsfélagið hf (Icelandic Broadcasting Corporation): Lyngháls 5, 110 Reykjavík; tel. 5156000; fax 5156860; f. 1986; privately-owned 'pay-TV' station; Pres. HREGGVIÐUR JÓNSSON.

Íslenska Sjónvarpsfélagið hf: Skipholti 19, 105 Reykjavík.

Kristniboðskirkjan: Grensásvegur 8, 108 Reykjavík; tel. 5683131; fax 5683741; broadcasts only in the Reykjavík area; religious; Dir EIRÍKUR SIGURBJÖRNSSON.

Stöð 3: Krokhals 6, 112 Reykjavík; tel. 5335600; fax 5335699; f. 1996; Dir MAGNÚS KRISTJÁNSSON.

Sunnlensk fjömiðlun hf: Eyrarvegur 2, 800 Selfoss; tel. 4823840; fax 4833758; broadcasts only in Selfoss; Dir EINAR SIGURÐSSON.

Villa Video: Skipholt 6, 335 Ólafsvík; tel. 4361563; fax 4361379; broadcasts only in Ólafsvík; Dir VILHELM ÁRNASON.

The US Navy operates a radio station (24 hours a day), and a cable television service (80 hours a week), on the NATO base at Keflavík.

Finance

(cap. = capital; res = reserves; dep. = deposits; m. = million; kr = krónur; brs = branches)

BANKING

Iceland's banking and finance system has undergone substantial transformation. In 1989–90 the number of commercial banks was reduced from seven to three, by amalgamating four banks to form Íslandsbanki as the only remaining major commercial bank in private ownership. A further restructuring of the banking sector commenced in 2000 with the merger of Íslandsbanki with the recently privatized investment bank, FBA. By early 2003 the Icelandic Government had withdrawn completely from the country's commercial banking sector having sold its controlling stakes in the second and third largest retail banks, Bunarðarbanki Íslands and Landsbanki Íslands. Furhter consolidation of the banking sector was expected. The 27 savings banks operate a commercial bank, Icebank, which functions as a central banking institution. In January 1995 full liberalization of foreign exchange regulations on the movement of capital was realized.

Central Bank

Seðlabanki Íslands (Central Bank of Iceland): Kalkofnsvegur 1, 150 Reykjavík; tel. 5699600; fax 5699605; e-mail sedlabanki@sedlabanki.is; internet www.sedlabanki.is; f. 1961; cap. and res 21,602m. kr, total assets 102,076m. kr (Dec. 2000); Chair. of Bd of Govs BIRGIR ÍSLEIFUR GUNNARSSON.

Principal Banks

Búnaðarbanki Íslands (Agricultural Bank of Iceland): Austurstræti 5, 155 Reykjavík; tel. 5256000; fax 5256189; e-mail webmaster@bi.is; internet www.bi.is; f. 1929; independent bank, incorporated and partially transferred to the private sector in 1998; cap. 4,222m. kr, res 2,657m. kr, dep. 81,752m. kr (Dec. 2000); Chair. MAGNÚS GUNNARSSON; CEOs ARNI TOMASSON, SOLON R. SIGURÐSSON; 36 brs.

Icebank Ltd (Sparisjóðabanki Íslands hf): Rauðarárstígur 27, POB 5220, 125 Reykjavík; tel. 5404000; fax 5404001; e-mail icebank@icebank.is; internet www.icebank.is; f. 1986; central bank of the 27 Icelandic savings banks and wholly owned by them; cap. 604m. kr, res 371m. kr, dep. 42,400m. kr (Dec. 2000); Chair. GEIRMUNDUR KRISTINSSON; Man. Dir SIGURÐUR HAFSTEIN; 54 brs.

Íslandsbanki hf: Kirkjusandur, 155 Reykjavík; tel. 4404000; fax 4404001; e-mail isb@isb.is; internet www.isb.is; f. 2000 by merger of Íslandsbanki hf (f. 1990) and FBA; cap. 20,400m. kr, res 7,383m. kr, dep. 83,000m. kr (Dec. 2001); CEOs BJARNI ÁRMANNSSON, VALUR VALSSON; Chair. KRISTJÁN RAGNARSSON; 29 brs.

Kaupþing banki hf: Ármúli 13, 108 Reykjavík; tel. 5151500; fax 5151509. e-mail radgjof@kaupthing.is; internet www.kaupthing.is; f. 1982; cap. 1,626m. kr, res 4,603m. kr, dep. 62,366m. kr (Dec. 2001); Chair. SIGURDUR EINARSSON; CEO HREIDAR MÁR.

Landsbanki Íslands hf (National Bank of Iceland Ltd): Austurstræti 11, 155 Reykjavík; tel. 5606600; fax 5606000; internet www.landsbanki.is; f. 1885; incorporated and partially transferred to the private sector in 1988; cap. 6,846m. kr, res 2,654m. kr, dep. 212,007m. kr (Dec. 2000); Chair. Bd Dir HELGI S. GUÐMUNDSSON; Group Man. Dir and CEO HALLDÓR J. KRISTJANSSON; 54 brs.

STOCK EXCHANGE

Iceland Stock Exchange: Laugaveg 182, 105 Reykjavík; tel. 5252800; fax 5252888; e-mail icex@icex.is; internet www.icex.is; f. 1985; Pres. and CEO THORDUR FRIDJONSSON; Chair. BJARNI ARMANNSSON.

INSURANCE

Tryggingastofnun Ríkisins (State Social-Security Institution): Laugavegi 114, 150 Reykjavík; tel. 5604400; fax 5624535; f. 1936; Man. Dir KARL STEINAR GUÐNASON; Chair. of Tryggingaráð (Social-Security Bd) BOLLI HÉÐINSSON.

Private Insurance Companies

Alþjóða líftryggingarfélagið hf: Lágmúla 5, 108 Reykjavík; tel. 5401400; fax 5401401; e-mail alif@alif.is; internet www.alif.is; f. 1966; life insurance.

Íslandstrygging hf: Sætúni 8, 105 Reykjavík; tel. 5141000; fax 5141001; f. 2002; Gen. Man. EINAR BALDVINSSON.

Íslensk Endurtrygging hf (Icelandic Reinsurance Co Ltd): Suðurlandsbraut 6, 108 Reykjavík; tel. 5331200; fax 5331201; f. 1939; Gen. Man. BJARNI THORDARSON.

Líftryggingamiðstöin hf: Aðalstræti 6–8, 101 Reykjavík; tel. 5152000; fax 5152020; f. 2002; Gen. Man. GUNNAR FELIXSON.

Líftryggingafélag Íslands hf: Ármúla 3, 108 Reykjavík; tel. 5605060; fax 5605100; internet www.lif.is.

Sameinaða líftryggingarfélagið hf: Sigtún 42, POB 5180, 125 Reykjavík; tel. 5695400; fax 5815455.

Sjóvá-Almennar tryggingar hf (Marine-General Insurance Co): Kringlan 5, POB 3200, 103 Reykjavík; tel. 5692500; fax 5813718; f. 1988; all branches except life; Chair. BENEDIKT SVEINSSON; Gen. Mans EINAR SVEINSSON, ÓLAFUR B. THORS.

Trygging hf: Aðalstræti 6, 101 Reykjavík; tel. 5152000; fax 5152020.

Tryggingamiðstöðin hf: Aðalstræti 6, 101 Reykjavík; tel. 5152000; fax 5152020; internet www.tmhf.is.

Vátryggingafélag Íslands hf: Ármúla 3, 108 Reykjavík; tel. 5605060; fax 5605100; e-mail info@vis.is; internet www.vis.is; f. 1989; Chair. KJARTAN GUNNARSSON; Man. Dir FINNUR INGÓLFSSON.

Vélbátaábyrgðarfélagið Grótta: Síðumúla 29, 108 Reykjavík; tel. 5536800; fax 5536812.

Viðlagatrygging Íslands: Laugavegi 162, 105 Reykjavík; tel. 5529677; fax 5629675.

Vörður—Vátryggingafélag: Skipagötu 9, 600 Akureyri; tel. 4648000; fax 4648001; e-mail oli@vordur.is.

Supervisory Authority

Fjármálaeftirlitið—Financial Supervisory Authority (FME): Suðurlandsbraut 32, 108 Reykjavík; tel. 5252700; fax 5252727; e-mail fme@fme.is; internet www.fme.is; f. 1999; by merger of Insurance Supervisory Authority and Bank Inspectorate of the Central Bank of Iceland; Man. Dir PÁLL GUNNAR PÁLSSON.

Trade and Industry

GOVERNMENT AGENCIES

Orkustofnun (National Energy Authority): Grensásvegi 9, 108 Reykjavík; tel. 5696000; fax 5688896; e-mail os@os.is; internet www.os.is; f. 1967; advises the Minister of Industry and Commerce on matters concerning energy; studies Icelandic energy resources and energy uses; Dir-Gen. THORKELL HELGASON.

Trade Council of Iceland: POB 1000, 121 Reykjavík; tel. 5114000; fax 5114040; e-mail icetrade@icetrade.is; internet www.icetrade.is; provides information on Icelandic exporters and products; Man. Dir JÓN ÁSBERGSSON.

CHAMBER OF COMMERCE

Verslunarráð Íslands (Iceland Chamber of Commerce): Hús verslunarinnar, 103 Reykjavík; tel. 5107100; fax 5686564; e-mail mottaka@chamber.is; internet www.chamber.is; f. 1917; Chair. BOGI PALSSON; Gen. Sec. VILHJÁLMUR EGILSSON; 370 mems.

INDUSTRIAL AND TRADE ASSOCIATIONS

Fiskifélag Íslands (Fisheries Association): Skipholt 17, 10 Reykjavík; tel. 5510500; fax 5527969; e-mail fi@fiskifelag.is; internet www.fiskifelag.is; f. 1911; conducts technical and economic research and services for fishing vessels and for fishing industry; Man. PETUR BJARNASON.

Landssamband Íslenskra Útvegsmanna (Icelandic Fishing Vessel Owners' Federation): Borgartúni 35, 105 Reykjavík; tel. 5910300; fax 5910301; e-mail fridrik@liu.is; internet www.liu.is; f. 1939; Chair. K. RAGNARSSON; Man. FRIÐRIK JÓN ARNGRÍMSSON.

SÍF Ltd (Union of Icelandic Fish Producers Ltd): Fornubuðir 5, POB 20, 222 Hafnarfjörður; tel. 5508000; fax 5508001; e-mail sif@sif.is; internet www.sif.is; f. 1932; exporting salted fish, seafood and fish products; Gen. Man. GUNNAR ÖRN KRISTJÁNSSON.

EMPLOYERS' ORGANIZATIONS

Samtök atvinnulífsins (Confederation of Icelandic Employers): Garðastræti 41, POB 520, 121 Reykjavík; tel. 5115000; fax 5115050; e-mail jonina.gissurardottir@sa.is; f. 1934; Chair. FINNUR GEIRSSON; Man. Dir ARI EDWALD.

Samtök Iðnaðarins (Federation of Icelandic Industries—FII): Borgartúni 35, POB 1450, 121 Reykjavík; tel. 5910100; fax 5910101; e-mail mottaka@si.is; internet www.si.is; f. 1993 by merger of Federation of Icelandic Industries (f. 1933), Federation of Icelandic Crafts and Industries (f. 1932) and four other employers' organizations; Chair. VILMUNDUR JOSEFSSON; Gen. Man SVEINN HANNESSON; 2,500 mems.

UTILITIES

Electricity

Hitaveita Suðurnesja (Suðurnes Regional Heating Corpn): Brekkustíg 36, POB 225, 260 Nardvík; f. 1974; produces and distributes hot-water heating and electricity for the Suðurnes region.

Landsvirkjun (National Power Company): Háaleitisbraut 68, 103 Reykjavík; tel. 5159000; fax 5159007; e-mail landsvirkjun@lv.is; internet www.landsvirkjun.is; f. 1965; generates, transmits, sells and distributes electric power wholesale to public distribution systems and industrial enterprises; Chair. JOHANNES GEIR SIGURGEIRSSON; Man. Dir FRIDRIK SOPHUSSON.

Orkubú Vestfjarda (Vestfjords Power Company): Stakkanesi 1, 400 Isafjördur; f. 1977; produces, distributes and sells electrical energy in the Vestfjords area.

Rafmagnsveitur Ríkisins (RARIK) (Iceland State Electricity): Rauðarárstíg 10, 105 Reykjavík; tel. 5605500; fax 5605600; internet www.rarik.is; f. 1947; produces, procures, distributes and sells electrical energy; also provides consultancy services.

TRADE UNIONS

Althýðusamband Íslands (ASÍ) (Icelandic Federation of Labour): Grensásvegi 16A, 128 Reykjavík; tel. 5813044; fax 5680093; e-mail asi@asi.is; internet www.asi.is; f. 1916; affiliated to ICFTU, the European Trade Union Confederation and the Council of Nordic Trade Unions; Chair. GRÉTAR THORSTEINSSON; Gen. Sec. GYLFI ARNBJÖRNSSON; 65,000 mems.

Menningar- og Fræðslusamband Althýðu (MFA) (Workers' Educational Association): Grensásveg 16A, 108 Reykjavík; tel. 5331818; fax 5331819; e-mail ieg@asi.is; internet www.asi.is; Chair. HAUKUR HARDARSON; Gen. Sec. INGIBJORG E. GUÐMUNDSDOTTIR.

Bandalag Starfsmanna Ríkis og Bæja (BSRB) (Municipal and Government Employees' Association): Grettisgötu 89, 105 Reykjavík; tel. 5626688; fax 5629106; e-mail bsrb@tv.is; f. 1942; Chair. ÖGMUNDUR JÓNASSON; 17,506 mems.

Blaðamannafélag Íslands (Union of Icelandic Journalists): Síðumúla 23, Reykjavík; tel. 5539155; fax 5539177; e-mail bi@press.is; internet www.press.is; f. 1897; Chair. HJÁLMAR JÓNSSON; 550 mems.

Transport

RAILWAYS

There are no railways in Iceland.

ROADS

Much of the interior is uninhabited and the main road follows the coastline. Regular motor coach services link the main settlements. At 31 December 2001 Iceland had 12,998 km of roads, of which 4,310 km were main roads. Approximately 75% of the main roads are paved.

Bifreiðastöð Íslands hf (BSÍ) (Iceland Motor Coach Service): Umferðarmiðstöðinni, Vatnsmýrarveg 10, 101 Reykjavík; tel. 5522300; fax 5529973; f. 1936; 45 scheduled bus lines throughout Iceland; also operates sightseeing tours and excursions; Chair. ÓSKAR SIGURJÓNSSON; Man. Dir GUNNAR SVEINSSON.

SHIPPING

Heavy freight is carried by coastal shipping. The principal seaport for international shipping is Reykjavík.

Port Authority

Port of Reykjavík: Harbour Bldg, Tryggvagötu 17, POB 382, 121 Reykjavík; tel. 5528900; fax 5258990; e-mail hofnin@rhofn.rvk.is; internet www.portofreykjavik.is; Dir HANNES VALDIMARSSON.

Principal Companies

Eimskip (Iceland Steamship Co Ltd): Pósthússtræti 2, POB 220, 101 Reykjavík; tel. 5257000; fax 5257009; e-mail info@eimskip.com; internet www.eimskip.com; f. 1914 as Eimskipafélag Íslands; transportation and logistics services incl. ground operation, warehousing, coastal service, trucking and intermodal transportation between Iceland and the United Kingdom, Scandinavia, the rest of Europe, the USA and Canada; Man. Dir INGIMUNDUR SIGURPÁLSSON.

Nesskip hf: POB 175, 172 Seltjarnarnes; tel. 5625055; fax 5612052; e-mail nesskip@nesskip.is; internet www.nesskip.is; f. 1974; bulk cargo shipping services to the USA, Canada, Russia, Scandinavia, the Baltic countries and other parts of Europe; agency and chartering for vessels in all Icelandic ports; Chair. E. SVEINSSON; Man. Dir G. ÁSGEIRSSON.

Samskip hf: Holtabakki v/Holtaveg, 104 Reykjavík; tel. 5698300; fax 5698327; e-mail samskip@samskip.is; internet www.samskip.is; services to Europe, the USA, and the Far East; Dir ÓLAFUR ÓLAFSSON.

CIVIL AVIATION

Air transport is particularly important to Iceland and is used both for the transport of people and to transport agricultural produce from remote districts. More than 90% of passenger traffic between Iceland and other countries is by air. There are regular air services between Reykjavík and outlying townships. There is an international airport at Keflavík, 47 km from Reykjavík.

Air Atlanta Icelandic: Atlanta House, POB 80, 270 Mosfellsbaer; tel. 5157700; fax 5157716; e-mail admin@atlanta.is; internet www .atlanta.is; f. 1986; charter international flights; Chair. ARNGRIMUR JOHANNSSON.

Air Iceland: Reykjavík Airport, 101 Reykjavík; tel. 5703000; fax 5703001; e-mail jonkarl@airiceland.is; internet www.airiceland.is; f. 1959; scheduled, regional flights; 96%-owned by Icelandair; Chair. SIGURDUR HELGASON; Gen. Man. JÓN KARL ÓLAFSSON.

Iceland Express ehf: Suðurlandsbraut 24, 108 Reykjavík; tel. 5500650; fax 5500601; e-mail info@icelandexpress.is; internet www .icelandexpress.com; f. 2002; daily scheduled flights between Iceland, Denmark and the United Kingdom; Chair. SIGURDUR I. HALL-DÓRSSON; Man. Dir JÓHANNES GEORGSSON.

Icelandair (Flugleiðir hf): Reykjavík Airport, 101 Reykjavík; tel. 5050300; fax 5050350; e-mail pr@icelandair.is; internet www .icelandair.net; f. 1973 as the holding company for the two principal

Icelandic airlines, Flugfélag Íslands (f. 1937) and Loftleiðir (f. 1944); in 1979 all licences, permits and authorizations previously held by Flugfélag Íslands and Loftleiðir were transferred to it; network centred in Reykjavík, to nine domestic airfields, and scheduled external services to more than 20 international destinations in northern Europe and the USA; Pres. and CEO SIGURÐUR HELGASON.

Tourism

Iceland's main attraction for tourists lies in the rugged beauty of the interior, with its geysers and thermal springs. In 2000 there were 302,913 tourist arrivals, an increase of more than 40,000 visitors compared with 1998.

Iceland Tourist Board: Lækjargata 3, 101 Reykjavík; tel. 5355500; fax 5355501; e-mail info@icetourist.is; internet www .icetourist.is; Gen. Man. MAGNÚS ODDSSON.

INDIA

Introductory Survey

Location, Climate, Language, Religion, Flag, Capital

The Republic of India forms a natural sub-continent, with the Himalaya mountain range to the north. Two sections of the Indian Ocean—the Arabian Sea and the Bay of Bengal—lie to the west and east, respectively. India's neighbours are Tibet (the Xizang Autonomous Region of the People's Republic of China), Bhutan and Nepal to the north, Pakistan to the north-west and Myanmar (formerly Burma) to the north-east, while Bangladesh is surrounded by Indian territory except for a short frontier with Myanmar in the east. Near India's southern tip, across the Palk Strait, is Sri Lanka. India's climate ranges from temperate to tropical, with an average summer temperature on the plains of approximately 27°C (85°F). Annual rainfall varies widely, but the summer monsoon brings heavy rain over much of the country in June and July. The official language is Hindi, spoken by about 30% of the population. English is used as an associate language for many official purposes. The Indian Constitution also recognizes 17 regional languages, of which the most widely spoken are Telugu, Bengali, Marathi, Tamil, Urdu and Gujarati. In addition, many other local languages are used. According to the 1991 census, about 82% of the population are Hindus and 11% Muslims. There are also Christians, Sikhs, Buddhists, Jains and other minorities. The national flag (proportions 2 by 3) has three equal horizontal stripes, of saffron, white and green, with the Dharma Chakra (Wheel of the Law), in blue, in the centre of the white stripe. The capital is New Delhi.

Recent History

After a prolonged struggle against British colonial rule, India became independent, within the Commonwealth, on 15 August 1947. The United Kingdom's Indian Empire was partitioned, broadly on a religious basis, between India and Pakistan. The principal nationalist movement that had opposed British rule was the Indian National Congress (later known as the Congress Party). At independence the Congress leader, Jawaharlal Nehru, became India's first Prime Minister. Sectarian violence, the movement of 12m. refugees, the integration of the former princely states into the Indian federal structure and a territorial dispute with Pakistan over Kashmir presented major problems to the new Government.

India became independent as a dominion, with the British monarch as Head of State, represented by an appointed Governor-General. In November 1949, however, the Constituent Assembly approved a republican Constitution, providing for a president (with mainly ceremonial functions) as head of state. Accordingly, India became a republic on 26 January 1950, although remaining a member of the Commonwealth. France transferred sovereignty of Chandernagore to India in May 1950, and ceded its four remaining Indian settlements in 1954.

The lack of effective opposition to Congress policies expedited industrialization and social reform. In December 1961 Indian forces overran the Portuguese territories of Goa, Daman and Diu, which were immediately annexed by India. Border disputes with the People's Republic of China escalated into a brief military conflict in 1962. Nehru died in May 1964 and was succeeded by Lal Bahadur Shastri. India and Pakistan fought a second war over Kashmir in 1965. Following mediation by the USSR, Shastri and President Ayub Khan of Pakistan signed a joint declaration, aimed at a peaceful settlement of the Kashmir dispute, on 10 January 1966. Shastri died on the following day, however, and Nehru's daughter, Indira Gandhi, became Prime Minister.

Following the presidential election of August 1969, when two factions of Congress supported different candidates, the success of Indira Gandhi's candidate split the party. The Organization (Opposition) Congress, led by Morarji Desai, emerged in November, but at the next general election to the lower house of the legislature, the Lok Sabha (House of the People), held in March 1971, Indira Gandhi's wing of Congress won 350 of the 515 elective seats.

Border incidents led to a 12-day war with Pakistan in December 1971. The Indian army rapidly occupied East Pakistan, which India recognized as the independent state of Bangladesh. Indira Gandhi and President Zulfikar Ali Bhutto of Pakistan held a summit conference at Shimla in June–July 1972, when the two leaders agreed that their respective forces should respect the cease-fire line in Kashmir, and that India and Pakistan should resolve their differences through bilateral negotiations or other peaceful means. In 1975 the former protectorate of Sikkim became the 22nd state of the Indian Union, leading to tensions in India's relations with Nepal.

A general election to the Lok Sabha was held in March 1977, when the number of elective seats was increased to 542. The election resulted in victory for the Janata (People's) Party, chaired by Morarji Desai, who became Prime Minister. The Janata Party and an allied party, the Congress for Democracy, together won 298 of the 540 seats where polling took place. Congress obtained 153 seats. In January 1978 Indira Gandhi became leader of a new breakaway political group, the Congress (Indira) Party, known as Congress (I).

In 1979 the Government's ineffectual approach to domestic problems provoked a wave of defections by Lok Sabha members of the Janata Party. Many joined Raj Narain, who formed a new party, the Lok Dal, the policies of which were based on secularism. Congress (I) lost its position as official opposition party after defections from its ranks to the then official Congress Party by members who objected to Indira Gandhi's perceived authoritarianism. The resignation of Desai's Government in July was followed by the departure from the Janata Party of Charan Singh, who became the leader of the Lok Dal and, shortly afterwards, Prime Minister in a coalition with both Congress parties. When Congress (I) withdrew its support, Singh's 24-day administration collapsed, and Parliament was dissolved. A general election to the Lok Sabha was held in January 1980. Congress (I) received 42.7% of the total votes and won an overwhelming majority (352) of the elective seats. The Janata Party won only 31 seats, while the Lok Dal secured 41 seats. Indira Gandhi was reinstated as Prime Minister. Presidential rule was imposed in nine states, hitherto governed by opposition parties, in February. At elections to state assemblies in June, Congress (I) won majorities in eight of them.

By-elections in June 1981 for the Lok Sabha and state assemblies were notable because of the overwhelming victory that Rajiv Gandhi, the Prime Minister's son, obtained in the former constituency of his late brother (killed in an air crash in 1980) and because of the failure of the fragmented Janata Party to win any seats. In February 1983 Rajiv Gandhi became a General Secretary of Congress (I).

Indira Gandhi's Government faced serious problems, as inter-communal disturbances in several states (particularly Assam and Meghalaya) continued in 1982–83, with violent protests against the presence of Bengali immigrants. Election defeats in Andhra Pradesh, Karnataka and Tripura represented a series of set-backs for Indira Gandhi. Disturbances occurred in Jammu and Kashmir during local elections in 1983 and 1984. Alleged police corruption and the resurgence of caste violence (notably in Bihar and Gujarat) caused further problems for the Government.

There was also unrest in the Sikh community of Punjab, despite the election to the Indian presidency in July 1982 of Giani Zail Singh, the first Sikh to hold the position. Demands were made for greater religious recognition, for the settlement of grievances over land and water rights, and over the sharing of the state capital at Chandigarh with Haryana; in addition, a minority called for the creation of a separate Sikh state ('Khalistan'). In October 1983 the state was brought under presidential rule. However, the violence continued, and followers of an extremist Sikh leader, Jarnail Singh Bhindranwale, established a terrorist stronghold inside the Golden Temple (the Sikh holy shrine) at Amritsar. The Government sent in troops to dislodge the terrorists and the assault resulted in the death of Bhindranwale and hundreds of his supporters, and serious damage to sacred buildings. A curfew was imposed, and army personnel blockaded Amritsar.

In October 1984 Indira Gandhi was assassinated by militant Sikh members of her personal guard. Her son, Rajiv Gandhi, was immediately sworn in as Prime Minister, despite his lack of ministerial experience. The widespread communal violence that erupted throughout India, resulting in more than 2,000 deaths, was curbed by prompt government action. Congress (I) achieved a decisive victory in elections to the Lok Sabha in December. Including the results of the January 1985 polling, the party received 49.2% of the total votes and won 403 of the 513 contested seats.

In February 1986 there were mass demonstrations and strikes throughout India in protest at government-imposed increases in the prices of basic commodities. The opposition parties united against Rajiv Gandhi's policies, and Congress (I) suffered considerable reversals in the indirect elections to the upper house of the legislature, the Rajya Sabha (Council of States) in March. In April Rajiv Gandhi attempted to purge Congress (I) of critics calling themselves 'Indira Gandhi loyalists', and, in a major government reorganization, he appointed Sikhs to two senior positions. The Prime Minister survived an assassination attempt by three Sikhs in October.

In June 1986 Laldenga, the leader of the Mizo National Front (MNF), signed a peace agreement with Rajiv Gandhi, thus ending Mizoram's 25 years of rebellion. The accord granted Mizoram limited autonomy in the drafting of local laws, independent trade with neighbouring foreign countries and a general amnesty for all Mizo rebels. Laldenga led an interim coalition government until February 1987, when the MNF won an absolute majority at elections to the state assembly. In that month Mizoram and Arunachal Pradesh were officially admitted as the 23rd and 24th states of India, and in May the Union Territory of Goa became India's 25th state.

During 1987 Congress (I) experienced serious political setbacks. It sustained defeats in a number of state elections, and political tensions were intensified by an open dispute between the Prime Minister and the outgoing President, Giani Zail Singh. Public concern was aroused by various accusations of corruption and financial irregularities made against senior figures in the ruling party. Notable among these scandals was the 'Bofors affair', in which large payments were allegedly made to Indian agents by a Swedish company in connection with its sales of munitions to the Indian Government. The Prime Minister denied any involvement, and a committee of inquiry subsequently exonerated him of any impropriety. Several ministers resigned from the Government, among them the Minister of Defence, Vishwanath Pratap (V. P.) Singh, who was also, with three other senior politicians, expelled from Congress (I) in July for 'anti-party activities'. V.P. Singh soon emerged as the leader of the Congress (I) dissidents, and in October formed a new political group, the Jan Morcha (People's Front), advocating more radical social change.

In 1988 a more confrontational style was adopted by the central administration towards non-Congress (I) state governments, and presidential rule was imposed in states suffering political instability. The opposition forces attained a degree of unity when four major centrist parties, the Indian National Congress (S), the Jan Morcha, the Janata Party and the Lok Dal, and three major regional parties formed a coalition National Front (Rashtriya Morcha), to oppose Congress (I) at the next election. Three of the four centrist parties formed a new political grouping, the Janata Dal (People's Party), which was to work in collaboration with the National Front. V.P. Singh, who was widely regarded as Rajiv Gandhi's closest rival, was elected President of the Janata Dal.

At the general election to the Lok Sabha held in November 1989, Congress (I) lost its overall majority. Of the 525 contested seats, it won 193, the Janata Dal and its electoral allies in the National Front won 141 and three, respectively, and the right-wing Hindu nationalist Bharatiya Janata Party (BJP) won 88. In early December, after the National Front had been promised the support of the communist parties and the BJP, V.P. Singh was sworn in as the new Prime Minister. He appointed Devi Lal, the populist Chief Minister of Haryana and President of Lok Dal (B), as Deputy Prime Minister, and a Kashmiri Muslim, Mufti Mohammed Sayeed, as Minister of Home Affairs. This latter appointment was widely seen as a gesture of reconciliation to the country's Muslims and as reaffirmation of the Government's secular stance. A few weeks later V.P. Singh's Government won a vote of confidence in the Lok Sabha, despite the abstention of all the Congress (I) members. In January 1990 the Government ordered the mass resignation of all the state Governors; the President then appointed new ones. In February elections were held to 10 state assemblies, all formerly controlled by Congress

(I). Congress (I) lost power in eight of the 10 assemblies and there was a notable increase in support for the BJP.

In July 1990 Devi Lal was dismissed from his post as Deputy Prime Minister, for nepotism, disloyalty and for making unsubstantiated accusations of corruption against ministerial colleagues. In August there were violent demonstrations in many northern Indian states against the Government's populist decision to implement the recommendations of the 10-year-old Mandal Commission and to raise the quota of government and public-sector jobs reserved for deprived sections of the population. In October the Supreme Court directed the Government to halt temporarily the implementation of the quota scheme, in an attempt to curb the caste violence.

In October 1990 the BJP withdrew its support for the National Front, following the arrest of its President, Lal Krishna Advani, as he led a controversial procession of Hindu devotees to the holy town of Ayodhya, in Uttar Pradesh, to begin the construction of a Hindu temple on the site of a disused ancient mosque. V.P. Singh accused the BJP leader of deliberately inciting inter-communal hatred by exhorting Hindu extremists to join him in illegally tearing down the mosque. Paramilitary troops were sent to Ayodhya, and thousands of Hindu activists were arrested, in an attempt to prevent a Muslim–Hindu confrontation. However, following repeated clashes between police and crowds, Hindu extremists stormed and slightly damaged the mosque and laid siege to it for several days.

In November 1990 one of the Prime Minister's leading rivals in the Janata Dal, Chandra Shekhar (with the support of Devi Lal), formed his own dissident faction, known as the Janata Dal (Socialist) or Janata Dal (S) (which merged with the Janata Party in April 1991 to become the Samajwadi Party). The Lok Sabha convened for a special session, at which the Government overwhelmingly lost a vote of confidence. V.P. Singh immediately resigned, and the President invited Rajiv Gandhi, as leader of the party holding the largest number of seats in the Lok Sabha, to form a new government. Rajiv Gandhi refused the offer, in favour of Chandra Shekhar. Although the strength of the Janata Dal (S) in the Lok Sabha comprised only about 60 deputies, Congress (I) had earlier offered it unconditional parliamentary support. On 10 November 1990 Chandra Shekhar was sworn in as Prime Minister. Devi Lal became Deputy Prime Minister and President of the Janata Dal (S). Shekhar won a vote of confidence in the Lok Sabha and a new Council of Ministers was appointed. Although Shekhar succeeded in initiating talks between the two sides in the Ayodhya dispute, violence between Hindus and Muslims in- creased throughout India in December.

In January 1991 the Prime Minister imposed direct rule in Tamil Nadu, claiming that this was necessitated by the increased activity of Sri Lankan Tamil militants in the state, which had led to the breakdown of law and order. In the resultant riots more than 1,000 arrests were made. The Government suffered a further set-back in February. Five members of the Council of Ministers were forced to resign when they lost their seats in the Lok Sabha for violating India's anti-defection laws: they had left the Janata Dal to join the Janata Dal (S). The fragility of the parliamentary alliance between the Janata Dal (S) and Congress (I) became apparent in March, when the Congress (I) deputies boycotted Parliament, following the revelation that Rajiv Gandhi's house had been kept under police surveillance. In an unexpected counter-move, Chandra Shekhar resigned, but accepted the President's request that he remain as head of an interim Government until the holding of a fresh general election.

As the general election, which was scheduled to take place over three days in late May 1991, approached, it seemed likely that no party would win an outright majority and that the political stalemate would continue. On 21 May, however, after the first day's polling had taken place, Rajiv Gandhi was assassinated, by members of the Tamil separatist group, the Liberation Tigers of Tamil Eelam (LTTE), while campaigning in Tamil Nadu. Consequently, the remaining elections were postponed until mid-June. The final result gave Congress (I) 227 of the 511 seats contested, the BJP, which almost doubled its share of the vote compared with its performance in the 1989 general election, won 119 seats, and the Janata Dal, the popularity of which had considerably declined, gained only 55 seats. P.V. Narasimha Rao, who had been elected as acting President of Congress (which had gradually shed its (I) suffix) following Rajiv Gandhi's assassination, assumed the premiership and appointed a new Council of Ministers. The new Government's main priority on assuming power was to attempt to solve the country's severe economic crisis, caused by an enormous foreign debt, high inflation, a large deficit on the current account of the balance of payments, and an extreme shortage of foreign exchange reserves. The new Minister of Finance, Dr Manmohan Singh (an experienced economist and former Governor of the Reserve Bank of India), launched a far-reaching programme of economic liberalization and reform, including the dismantling of bureaucratic regulations and the encouragement of private and foreign investment. In late September the Government announced the adoption of the recommendations of the Mandal Commission that 27% of government jobs and institutional places be reserved for certain lower castes, in addition to the 22.5% already reserved for 'untouchable' castes and tribal people. (In November 1992 the Supreme Court ruled that non-Hindus, such as Christians and Sikhs, who were socially disadvantaged were also entitled to job reservations.)

After a brief reconciliatory period in the latter half of 1991, Narasimha Rao's Government began to be faced with problems, both from opposition agitation and from within its own ranks. In January 1992 the BJP increased communal tension between Hindus and Muslims by hoisting the national flag on Republic Day in Srinagar, the capital of Kashmir (see below). In mid-1992 efforts were also made by the BJP to use the contentious issue of the Ayodhya site (the Ram Janmabhoomi/Babri Masjid—Hindu temple/Muslim mosque—dispute, see above) to embarrass the Government. In May a major financial scandal involving the Bombay Stock Exchange was uncovered. It was alleged that several members of the Council of Ministers were amongst the beneficiaries, allegations that prompted the resignation of the Minister of State for Commerce. In July, however, the Congress candidate, Dr Shankar Dayal Sharma, was elected, with no serious opposition, to the presidency.

Following the collapse of talks in November 1992 between the Vishwa Hindu Parishad (VHP) (World Hindu Council) and the All India Babri Masjid Action Committee regarding the Ayodhya dispute, the VHP and the BJP appealed for volunteers to begin the construction of a Hindu temple on the site of the existing mosque in early December. As thousands of Hindu militants assembled in Ayodhya, thousands of paramilitary troops were dispatched to the town in an attempt to avert any violence. Despite the armed presence, however, the temple/mosque complex was stormed by the Hindu volunteers, who proceeded to tear down the remains of the ancient mosque. This highly inflammatory action provoked widespread communal violence throughout India (Bombay, or Mumbai as it was later renamed, being one of the worst-affected areas), which resulted in more than 1,200 deaths, and prompted world-wide condemnation, notably from the neighbouring Islamic states of Pakistan and Bangladesh, where violent anti-Hindu demonstrations were subsequently held. The central Government also strongly condemned the desecration and demolition of the holy building and pledged to rebuild it. The leaders of the BJP, including L. K. Advani and the party's President, Dr Murli Manohar Joshi, and the leaders of the VHP were arrested, the BJP Chief Minister of Uttar Pradesh resigned, the state legislature was dissolved and Uttar Pradesh was placed under President's rule. The security forces took full control of Ayodhya, including the disputed complex, meeting with little resistance. The Government banned five communal organizations, including the VHP and two Muslim groups, on the grounds that they promoted disharmony among different religious communities. Throughout India stringent measures were taken by the security forces to suppress the Hindu/Muslim violence, which lasted for about one week. In mid-December the Government established a commission of inquiry into the events leading to the demolition of the mosque at Ayodhya. In an attempt to avert any further acts of Hindu militancy, the central Government dismissed the BJP administrations in Madhya Pradesh, Rajasthan and Himachal Pradesh and placed these three states under presidential rule. Narasimha Rao's various actions were given implicit approval later that month when a motion of 'no confidence' presented by the BJP against the Government was soundly defeated. In late December the Government announced plans to acquire all the disputed areas in Ayodhya. The acquired land would be made available to two trusts, which would be responsible for the construction of a new Hindu temple and a new mosque and for the planned development of the site.

There was a resurgence in Hindu/Muslim violence in India's commercial centre, Mumbai, and in Ahmedabad in January 1993, however, necessitating the imposition of curfews and the dispatch of thousands of extra paramilitary troops to curb the serious unrest. In an apparent attempt to restore public confidence in the Government, Narasimha Rao carried out an extensive reshuffle of the Council of Ministers in mid-January. Despite a government ban on communal rallies, thousands of Hindu militants attempted to converge on the centre of New Delhi to attend a mass rally organized by the BJP in late February. In an effort to prevent the proposed rally taking place, thousands of BJP activists were arrested throughout India and the crowds that did gather in the capital were dispersed by the security forces using batons and tear gas. In March there were a number of bomb explosions in Mumbai, resulting in some 250 casualties. Notorious criminals Dawood Ibrahim and Abu Salem, who fled India after the explosions, were suspected of organizing the bomb attacks in retaliation for the nation-wide communal riots provoked by the destruction of the mosque in Ayodhya (see above).

In July 1993 Narasimha Rao narrowly survived a vote of 'no confidence', which was proposed in the Lok Sabha by virtually all the opposition parties. The following month the Prime Minister suffered a blow to his political prestige when the Government was forced to abandon two proposed bills (aimed at the BJP, in particular), which would have banned political parties from using religious appeals in campaigns. However, in November in the state assembly elections in the four northern states where BJP state administrations had been dismissed by the central Government in December 1992 following the Ayodhya crisis, the BJP regained power in only one state, Rajasthan, while Congress obtained outright majorities in Himachal Pradesh and Madhya Pradesh. These results appeared to highlight a definite decline in the popularity of the BJP. In December 1993 Congress's political standing was strengthened when a small faction of the Janata Dal led by Ajit Singh merged with the ruling party, thus giving the latter a parliamentary majority.

The following year, 1994, was, for the most part, a period of relative political stability. The extensive economic reforms continued to show positive results and Narasimha Rao's premiership appeared fairly secure, with the opposition suffering from fragmentation (particularly the Janata Dal) and with no serious challenges from within Congress itself. In mid-1994, however, the opposition deputies boycotted parliamentary proceedings for three weeks in protest at what they regarded as lack of effective action following an official inquiry into the 1992 securities scandal in order to understate the involvement of Congress ministers. The popularity and strength of the ruling Congress appeared to have declined considerably by the end of 1994, when the party suffered crushing defeats in elections to the state assemblies in Andhra Pradesh and Karnataka (former strongholds of Congress); it was also defeated in state elections in Sikkim. In late December the Government's image was enhanced to some extent when three ministers were finally forced to resign over their alleged roles in corruption scandals (the Prime Minister had earlier been reluctant to dismiss them). Shortly afterwards, the Minister for Human Resource Development, Arjun Singh, who was widely viewed as Narasimha Rao's main rival within Congress, resigned from his post, citing his dissatisfaction and frustration at the Government's perceived incompetence regarding corruption, the Bombay Stock Exchange scandal, the Ayodhya crisis and the investigation into Rajiv Gandhi's assassination. In January 1995, with important state elections rapidly approaching, Narasimha Rao attempted to quell increasing dissent within his Government and party by suspending Arjun Singh from the working committee of Congress for 'anti-party activities'; in the following month the rebel politician was expelled from the party. In May Singh, together with Narain Dutt Tewari, recruited dissident members of Congress in many states and formed a new breakaway party, known as the All India Indira Congress (Tewari); the party merged with Congress, however, in December 1996.

Congress enjoyed mixed results in the state elections held in February/March 1995. In an apparent attempt to bolster his political standing, Narasimha Rao reshuffled and enlarged the Council of Ministers in mid-September. In January 1996, however, accusations of corruption came to the fore in Indian politics when the Central Bureau of Investigation charged seven leading politicians, including L.K. Advani of the BJP, Devi Lal and Arjun Singh, and sought the prosecution of three Union ministers (who subsequently resigned) for allegedly accepting large bribes from a Delhi-based industrialist, Surendra Jain. The sheer scale of the scandal (known as the Hawala—illegal money transfer—case), in terms of the sums involved and the number of people implicated, led to widespread public disillusionment with politicians in general. At the end of January another high-ranking political figure, the President of the Janata Dal, S. R. Bommai, was implicated in the scandal; Bommai subsequently resigned from his post. In February Congress's hopes of retaining power in the forthcoming general election appeared increasingly fragile when three more ministers resigned from the Council of Ministers after their names had been linked to the Hawala case. Meanwhile, the Prime Minister was connected to the prosecution, on charges of cheating and criminal conspiracy, of a flamboyant faith healer and 'godman', Chandraswami, who had been consulted by generations of political leaders, including Narasimha Rao himself.

The results of the general election, which was held over three days at the end of April and early May 1996, gave no party or group an overall majority. The largest party in terms of seats was the BJP, which won 160 seats, and with the support of the Shiv Sena and other smaller allies could count on an overall legislative strength of 194 seats. Congress secured 136 seats. The National Front (comprising the Janata Dal and its allies) and Left Front (representing the two major communist parties) together obtained 179 seats, with the remainder won by minor parties and independents. On 15 May, as soon as the electoral position was clear, the President asked the BJP under its new parliamentary leader, Atal Bihari Vajpayee, to form the new Government and to prove its majority support within two weeks. Given the antagonism felt towards the BJP by the majority of other political parties, the latter task proved impossible, and Vajpayee resigned on 28 May in anticipation of his Government's inevitable defeat in a parliamentary vote of confidence. In the mean time, the National and Left Fronts had merged to form an informal coalition known as the United Front (UF), which comprised a total of 13 parties, with the Janata Dal, the Samajwadi Party, the two communist parties and the regional Dravida Munnetra Kazhagam (DMK) and Telugu Desam as its major components. With Congress prepared to lend external support, the UF was able to form a Government at the end of May. A former Chief Minister of Karnataka, H. D. Deve Gowda, was selected to lead the UF and the new Government.

In September 1996 Narasimha Rao resigned from the leadership of Congress after he was ordered to stand trial for his alleged involvement in the Chandraswami case; the party presidency was assumed by the veteran politician, Sitaram Kesri. Later that month separate charges of forgery and criminal conspiracy (dating back to the former Prime Minister's tenure of the external affairs ministry in the 1980s) were made against the beleaguered Narasimha Rao; he resigned in December 1996 as Congress's parliamentary leader and was replaced in the following month by Kesri.

At the end of March 1997 Deve Gowda was faced with a serious political crisis when Congress threatened to withdraw its parliamentary support for the UF Government. On 11 April the Prime Minister resigned following the defeat of the UF administration in a vote of confidence (by 158 votes to 292). A few days later Inder Kumar Gujral, the Minister of External Affairs in the outgoing Government, was chosen by the UF to replace Deve Gowda as leader of the coalition. On 22 April Gujral was sworn in as Prime Minister and appointed a new Council of Ministers. In May Sonia Gandhi, the widow of the former Prime Minister Rajiv Gandhi, joined Congress as a 'primary member', and in the following month Kesri was re-elected President of the party in Congress's first contested leadership poll since 1977. In June 1997 the ruling coalition was faced with another high-level corruption case when the President of the Janata Dal and Chief Minister of Bihar, Laloo Prasad Yadav, was forced to resign from his posts prior to his arrest on several counts of conspiracy in a corruption scandal involving the supply of animal fodder for non-existent livestock. Yadav subsequently formed a breakaway faction of his party, known as the Rashtriya Janata Dal, and Sharad Yadav was elected as the new President of the Janata Dal. In July Kocheril Raman Narayanan was elected, almost unanimously, as India's new President; this appointment was particularly notable in that Narayanan was the first Indian President to originate from a Dalit (or 'untouchable') background. In September former Prime Minister Narasimha Rao was charged in a Delhi court with corruption and criminal conspiracy. In the same month a five-year investigation into the destruction of the mosque at Ayodhya in 1992 led to charges of criminal conspiracy and incitement to riot being filed against senior BJP and religious leaders,

including L. K. Advani and the leader of Shiv Sena, Balashaheb 'Bal' Thackeray.

The UF Government looked increasingly insecure in late November 1997 when Congress threatened to withdraw its parliamentary support unless the Tamil Nadu-based DMK, which was alleged to be indirectly implicated in the 1991 assassination of Rajiv Gandhi, was expelled from the coalition. Prime Minister Gujral rejected Congress's demand, and was consequently forced to resign on 28 November when Congress withdrew its support for the Government, as earlier threatened. This constituted the third government collapse in less than two years. In early December President Narayanan dissolved the Lok Sabha following the inability of both Congress and the BJP to form an alternative coalition government. It was announced that Gujral would retain the premiership in an acting capacity pending the holding of a fresh general election in early 1998.

During December 1997 Congress suffered a series of internal splits and defections in at least six states. In an apparent attempt to halt the fragmentation of the ailing party, in late December Sonia Gandhi agreed to campaign on behalf of Congress in the run-up to the general election. After a low-key start Sonia Gandhi gained in confidence and popularity during the campaign and attracted ever-larger crowds; she steadfastly refused, however, to stand for actual parliamentary office. Sonia Gandhi's deceased husband was, once again, in the forefront of political news at the end of January 1998, when 26 Tamil militants implicated in the murder of Rajiv Gandhi were sentenced to death by a court in Chennai (Madras). (In May 1999, however, the Supreme Court in New Delhi acquitted 19 defendants and commuted the sentences of three others.)

In the general election, which was held in February/March 1998, the BJP and its regional allies established themselves as the pre-eminent force in Indian politics. The BJP emerged as the largest party, with 182 of the 545 seats in the Lok Sabha, but failed to win an overall majority. Congress secured 142 seats, and shortly after the election Sonia Gandhi replaced Kesri as the party's President. On 19 March President Narayanan appointed the parliamentary leader of the BJP, Atal Bihari Vajpayee (who had briefly held the premiership in mid-1996), as Prime Minister and asked him to form a stable coalition government and to seek a legislative vote of confidence within the next 10 days. This he did (by 274 votes to 261) on 28 March, with the support of the All-India Anna Dravida Munnetra Kazhagam (AIADMK), the Telugu Desam (which eventually left the UF) and a number of other minor groups. None the less, it was apparent from the very outset that Vajpayee's 14-party coalition Government had a fragile hold on power and that the Prime Minister would be required to use both skill and tact to retain his position.

In May 1998 the Government shocked both India and the rest of the world by ordering the carrying out of a series of underground nuclear test explosions. This provocative action was at first greeted with massive popular enthusiasm, but Pakistan's retaliatory tests and a rapid realization of the negative international consequences (particularly the imposition of economic sanctions by the USA) soon led to a more measured domestic assessment.

In early July 1998, in the face of strong opposition from several groups, the Government was forced to defer a parliamentary bill proposing the reservation of one-third of seats in the Lok Sabha and in state legislatures for women (male deputies again prevented the introduction of the Women's Reservation Bill in December).

In November 1998 Congress showed a strong revival in its popularity at the expense of the BJP when it removed the ruling party from power in state elections to Rajasthan and Delhi (both traditionally BJP strongholds) and unexpectedly retained its majority in the elections to the legislature in Madhya Pradesh. Congress's resurgence was variously ascribed to Sonia Gandhi's rising popularity, a reaction to the BJP's inefficiency and public anger at the soaring prices of basic commodities (notably onions, India's most basic staple after rice).

In early December 1998 tens of thousands of Christians throughout India held a day of protest against alleged Hindu persecution, which, they claimed, had escalated considerably since the assumption of power by the BJP in March. Later in the month widespread disruption was caused by a one-day nationwide strike called by various trade unions in protest against the Government's economic policies. At the end of December a fresh outbreak of violence against Christians by Hindu zealots was reported in Gujarat; further incidents were reported in January 1999.

In early April 1999 Prime Minister Vajpayee rejected demands by the BJP's troublesome coalition partner the AIADMK (whose controversial leader, Jayalalitha Jayaram, was faced with ongoing investigations into corruption allegations) to reinstate the Chief of Staff of the Navy and to dismiss the Minister of Defence, George Fernandes; the following day the two AIADMK ministers resigned from the Government. The President resolved the resultant political stalemate by forcing Vajpayee to seek a parliamentary vote of confidence. The Government narrowly lost the motion (by 270 votes to 269) and the President then invited Sonia Gandhi to assemble a new coalition. Following her failure to do so, the Lok Sabha was dissolved on 26 April and fresh elections were called. Vajpayee and his Government remained in power, in an acting capacity, pending the holding of the polls.

In May 1999 Congress's erstwhile parliamentary leader, Sharad Pawar, who had earlier publicly criticized Sonia Gandhi's foreign (Italian) origins, announced the formation of a breakaway party, entitled the Nationalist Congress Party (NCP); the NCP absorbed the Indian National Congress (S) in the following month. The outbreak of hostilities between Indian and Pakistani troops in the Kargil area of Kashmir in mid-1999 (see below) had a very positive effect on the nationalist BJP's standing and, in particular, on that of Vajpayee, who, as acting Prime Minister, was widely perceived to have responded with dignity, firmness and commendable restraint in the face of Pakistani provocation. The fact that India, in effect, emerged victorious from the Kargil crisis (in forcing a Pakistani retreat) had a major impact on the public's perception of the acting Government.

The BJP contested the general election, held in September–October 1999, at the head of a 24-member alliance, known as the National Democratic Alliance (NDA), which comprised numerous and diverse minor regional and national parties with little shared ideology. The NDA won an outright majority in the Lok Sabha, with 299 of the 545 seats, while Congress and its electoral allies obtained 134 seats. Although Sonia Gandhi won both of the seats that she herself contested in Karnataka and Uttar Pradesh, her lack of political experience, her weak grasp of Hindi and her foreign birth all contributed to Congress's worst electoral defeat since India's independence. Following his appointment as leader of the NDA, Vajpayee was sworn in as Prime Minister for a third term at the head of a large coalition Government.

Shortly after its return to power, the BJP-led administration was faced with widespread problems caused by a devastating cyclone, which struck the eastern state of Orissa at the end of October 1999, leaving more than 10,000 people dead and up to 1.5m. people homeless. A massive and costly relief programme was launched and large amounts of foreign aid were urgently requested. The authorities were much criticized, however, for their slow response to the tragedy, and in December the Chief Minister of Orissa resigned amid continuing criticism of his administration's handling of the aftermath of the cyclone.

Despite protests organized by Hindu fundamentalists and threats of sabotage, the head of the Roman Catholic Church, Pope John Paul II, carried out a peaceful state visit of India, amid tight security, in early November 1999. During the pontiff's meetings with senior Indian politicians, he broached the subject of the recent upsurge in anti-Christian persecution and called for greater religious tolerance (while asserting the freedom to proselytize).

The induction of four additional ministers into the Government in late November 1999 (including the creation of a Ministry of Information Technology, reflecting the growing importance of this sector to the Indian economy) appeared to contradict the Minister of Finance's publicly-stated resolve to reduce administrative costs. In late December the Government again attempted unsuccessfully to introduce the Women's Reservation Bill in the Lok Sabha; the lower house descended into chaos when opposition deputies staged a rowdy demonstration against the controversial legislation. (A further attempt to introduce the legislation in December 2000 was also unsuccessful.)

In February and March 2000 state elections were held. Overall, regional parties fared better than Congress and the BJP. In mid-November Sonia Gandhi was re-elected President of Congress. Meanwhile, at the end of May a government reorganization took place. In late August the Minister of Power, Ranjaram Kumaramangalam, died. A month later the Council

of Ministers was partially reorganized and its membership was expanded to 76 members. The Council of Ministers was reorganized again in November.

In mid-May 2000 the Government introduced three items of legislation in the Lok Sabha to establish the states of Chhattisgarh, Jharkhand and Uttaranchal, and amended versions were finally passed by the Lok Sabha and Rajya Sabha in August. The three new states came into being in November.

In July 2000 a threat to arrest the leader of the Shiv Sena, Bal Thackeray, for his alleged role in the 1992–93 communal riots, led to violent conflict on the streets. Although Thackeray was duly arrested, a Mumbai court dismissed the charges on account of the fact that the case was concerned with relatively old events which fell outside the country's statute of limitations. Vajpayee forced the Minister of Law, Justice and Company Affairs, Ram Jethmalani, to resign after he opposed the Supreme Court. In October the former Prime Minister, P. V. Narasimha Rao, was convicted of corruption. He was sentenced to three years' imprisonment and was fined Rs. 100,000. (In March 2002, however, his conviction was overturned by the High Court in New Delhi.) In October 2000 the former Chief Minister of Tamil Nadu, Jayalalitha, was convicted of corruption and sentenced to three years' imprisonment, and the Central Bureau of Investigation filed charges against three Indian businessmen, the Hinduja brothers, for allegedly accepting bribes in the 'Bofors' affair (see above).

In June 2000 violent attacks against Christians resumed. In an attempt to show that the Government was taking the problem seriously, Vajpayee met a delegation of bishops to discuss the renewed violence. Nevertheless, in July Indian Christians protested across South India, demanding protection against the attacks. In October the leader of the fundamentalist Hindu group Rashtriya Swayamsevak Sangh (RSS—National Volunteer Organization) urged the Government to replace 'foreign' churches with a national church and to expel all Christian missionaries. The RSS campaign caused embarrassment for the Government, in particular Vajpayee, who requested the newly appointed BJP President, Bangaru Laxman, to declare that the views of the RSS did not represent those of the BJP.

In early December 2000 communal tension between Hindus and Muslims increased, following Vajpayee's statement that the construction of the Ram Janmabhoomi, the Hindu temple, in Ayodhya was an expression of 'national sentiment that has yet to be realized' and part of the 'unfinished agenda' of his Government. Although the Prime Minister later attempted to diminish his remarks, declaring that he did not support the destruction of the Muslim Babri Masjid mosque, the opposition demanded an immediate apology and forced the abrupt adjournment of the Lok Sabha and Rajya Sabha. Opposition members also called for the resignation of three ministers, including L. K. Advani, who were expected to face charges issued by the Central Bureau of Investigation in a case relating to the demolition of the Babri Masjid. Vajpayee rejected the demand, confirming that the Government would abide by the judgment of the Supreme Court with regard to the three ministers. In February 2001 an Indian high court ruled that nearly 40 people could be brought to trial in connection with the destruction of the mosque in Ayodhya, and that senior BJP leaders would not be among the defendants, owing to certain technicalities. In January plans for a negotiated settlement over the religious site in Ayodhya suffered a set-back when the All India Babri Masjid Action Committee ruled out negotiations with the VHP. VHP leaders convened a religious parliament, the Dharma Sansad, at the Maha Kumbh Mela (the largest ever Hindu gathering) in January–February. The Dharma Sansad stated that all obstacles impeding the construction of the temple should be removed by the relevant organizations by mid-March 2002.

The 2001 national census, compiled during February, was believed to be the largest demographic study ever undertaken. The preliminary results of the census, announced in March, confirmed that the total population of India had exceeded 1,000m. (1,027,015,247) for the first time.

A new series of political and financial scandals exposed continuing corruption at the highest levels of government and commerce, and further undermined popular confidence in the BJP and its moral posturing. In March 2001 an internet news service, tehelka.com, revealed videotaped evidence of senior NDA politicians and army officials accepting bribes from tehelka.com employees posing as facilitators seeking to secure a bogus defence contract. Among those exposed in this way were the President of the BJP, Bangaru Laxman, and the leader of the Samata Party, Jaya Jaitly. Both resigned from their posts following the revelations, as did the Minister of Defence, George Fernandes, who had been implicated in the scandal by Jaitly's use of his official residence as location for the illicit transaction. (Prime Minister Vajpayee narrowly avoided involvement through implication himself.) The Minister of Railways, Mamata Banerjee of the All India Trinamool Congress, took this opportunity to resign from her cabinet post and withdrew her party from the ruling coalition. Some days later the defence portfolio was assigned to Minister of External Affairs Jaswant Singh, while the railways portfolio was subsequently awarded to the Minister of Agriculture, Nitish Kumar. Although Vajpayee agreed to appoint a commission of inquiry into the affair, his reluctance to agree to the establishment of a joint parliamentary committee to investigate the scandal resulted in (largely successful) opposition attempts to stall proceedings in the lower house during April. Meanwhile, in early March a national financial crisis had been narrowly averted when stocks and shares across the country fluctuated wildly following the resignation of the president of the Bombay Stock Exchange after he was implicated in an investigation by the national stock market regulator into allegations of widespread share price manipulation and insider trading. Moreover, in July the chairman of India's largest investment fund (Unit Trust of India—UTI) was arrested on charges of financial misappropriation. Once again Vajpayee was alleged to have been loosely connected to the affair.

Elections to four state assemblies and one union territory assembly, conducted in May 2001, resulted in major gains for Congress and its electoral allies (in Kerala and Assam) and significant reversals for the parties of the NDA coalition (most notably in Tamil Nadu where the Secular Front, led by the regional AIADMK, trounced the incumbent DMK—a member of the NDA—by a margin of 160 seats). Mounting political crises in the states of Manipur and Tamil Nadu in May and June (see below) and inconclusive direct negotiations between Vajpayee and President Musharraf of Pakistan in July (see below), all contributed to increasing disillusionment within the NDA. At the end of July Vajpayee offered to resign, exasperated by the factional tensions within the coalition, but was persuaded to retract the offer on the following day, after an expression of consolidated NDA support for his leadership. At the end of August the All India Trinamool Congress and the Pattali Makkal Katchi (which had withdrawn from the NDA in February owing to regional party divisions) rejoined the governing coalition. At the beginning of September Vajpayee expanded and reorganized the Council of Ministers, and in October George Fernandes (now the leader of the Samata Party) was reappointed Minister of Defence.

In the aftermath of the devastating terrorist attacks on the US mainland on 11 September 2001, for which the USA held the al-Qa'ida (Base) organization of Osama bin Laden responsible, the Indian Government sought to emphasize its own uncompromising response to the activities of illegal organizations. In late September national security forces clashed with members of the outlawed Students' Islamic Movement of India (SIMI—which was alleged to be linked to both al-Qa'ida and the militant Hizbul Mujahideen, see below) in Lucknow, Uttar Pradesh. Three SIMI supporters were killed during the altercation, after which some 240 SIMI activists were arrested across the country, together with the organization's president. In late October the Government promulgated the Prevention of Terrorism Ordinance 2001 (POTO), which replaced anti-terrorism legislation dating from 1987. The Government claimed that the new act, which broadened the definitions of terrorist activity and the preventative and retaliatory powers of the Government (to the evident discomfort of the opposition), was necessary to accommodate the recommendations and resolutions of the UN and the international community since 11 September, and to address the recent increase in domestic terrorist activity in India. The new ordinance proscribed indefinitely 23 organizations engaged in principally separatist activities. Meanwhile, the Indian Government was increasingly frustrated by the conciliatory overtures made to the Pakistani Government by the USA in pursuit of full Pakistani co-operation with its activities in neighbouring Afghanistan.

A series of audacious terrorist attacks perpetrated by Kashmiri separatists and suspected Islamist militants severely tested the resolve of the Government in late 2001 and early 2002 (see below), resulting in an unexpected consolidation of popular and political support for the coalition. Some opponents, however, suggested that the Government's uncompromising approach to foreign policy in particular (which had brought the country to the brink of renewed military conflict with Pakistan in December 2001, see below) amounted to little more than irresponsible 'sabre rattling' designed to attract nationalist support ahead of crucial state elections scheduled for early 2002.

In mid-October 2000 the Supreme Court approved the continuation of work on the controversial Sardar Sarovar dam, on the Narmada River in Gujarat. Construction stopped in 1994, when environmental activists, representing the tens of thousands of people whom the dam would displace, lodged a case against the authorities. The World Bank had withdrawn its funding, citing environmental concerns, in 1993. Campaigners against the project claimed that the authorities had failed to provide an acceptable rehabilitation and resettlement programme. In January 2001 a devastating earthquake occurred in Gujarat, the epicentre being in the coastal town of Bhuj. More than 30,000 people were killed and over 1m. people were made homeless. The central Government and the Government of Gujarat were criticized for their tardy reaction to the disaster, a delay that reportedly led to greater loss of life.

In January 2002 Prime Minister Vajpayee resumed efforts to resolve the dispute over a religious site in Ayodhya, Uttar Pradesh. The All India Babri Masjid Action Committee, however, refused to enter negotiations with the uncompromising VHP. In early February the BJP declared in its manifesto for state elections in Uttar Pradesh that it would abide by a court decision or a negotiated settlement between the Hindu and Muslim groups over the disputed site. The BJP had traditionally enjoyed close links with the VHP, but national politics required the governing party to distance itself from the militant Hindu group. As the deadline set by a religious parliament, the Dharma Sansad, to begin building the temple in mid-March approached (see above), hundreds of Hindu activists assembled in Ayodhya to take part in the illegal construction. Despite warnings by the Government that it would enforce the law, a senior VHP leader announced in late February that the movement of building material to the site would begin on 15 March. In late February communal violence broke out in Gujarat after a train carrying members of the VHP returning from Ayodhya was attacked by a suspected group of Muslims in the town of Godhra. The attack, in which 60 Hindu activists were killed, provoked a cycle of communal violence throughout Gujarat that lasted for several weeks and resulted in the deaths of up to 2,000 people, most of whom were Muslims. The Indian army was drafted in to quell the riots. Opposition members demanded the resignation of the Minister of Home Affairs, L. K. Advani, and the Chief Minister of Gujarat, Narendra Modi, for failing to control the riots, amid claims that the Government deliberately prevented the police from controlling the Hindu activists. In late April the European Union's report on the situation in Gujarat, which corroborated a number of other reports published in the same month, concluded that the riots and killings had been, contrary to the official account, not in reaction to the attack on a train carrying Hindu activists, but in fact an organized massacre of Muslims and that the security forces had been under orders not to intervene. Modi eventually resigned and recommended the dissolution of the state assembly in mid-July; he was requested to continue as leader of an interim administration until state elections were held in December. Meanwhile, in mid-March security forces prevented Hindu nationalists from defying a court order and entering the disputed religious site in Ayodhya. In March 2003 the Allahabad High Court ordered the Archaeological Survey of India to carry out an excavation at the disputed site to ascertain whether a Hindu temple existed beneath the Babri mosque. Meanwhile, the VHP continued its campaign to build a temple at the site.

In the mean time, assembly elections in the states of Manipur, Punjab, Uttaranchal and Uttar Pradesh took place in late February 2002. The BJP fared badly in all four elections. Congress enjoyed victory in Punjab and Uttaranchal; Manipur and Uttar Pradesh were left with hung assemblies. Congress formed a coalition government in Manipur in March; Uttar Pradesh was placed under presidential rule until the BJP and Bahujan Samaj Party reached a power-sharing agreement in early May. At the end of April the Minister of Coal and Mines resigned and withdrew his Lok Jan Shakti party from the NDA in protest against the Government's handling of the situation in Gujarat. Meanwhile, in late March a constitutional review commission, chaired by former Chief Justice M. N. Venkatachaliah, submitted a report of its two-year review of the country's Constitution. The report recommended about 250 changes in the laws relating to political parties, elections, fundamental rights and judicial and executive accountability. The report, however, did not address the issue on whether a person of foreign origin should hold a constitutional post, a question particularly relevant to Italian-born Sonia Gandhi's position. In mid-May the Lok Sabha elected unopposed Manohar Joshi as its speaker, replacing Mohan Chandra Balayogi, who died in March. At the end of June, the Minister of Home Affairs, L. K. Advani, was assigned the additional portfolio of Deputy Prime Minister, prompting speculation that Advani had been nominated as Vajpayee's eventual successor. In early July a government reorganization took place in which Jaswant Singh and Yashwant Sinha, the Ministers of Foreign Affairs and Finance, respectively, exchanged portfolios. At the same time Venkaiah Naidu was designated President of the BJP, replacing Jana Krishnamurthy, who was appointed Minister of Law and Justice. Later that month a presidential election was held. The Government's candidate, Aavul Pakkiri Jainulabidin Abdul Kalam, a South Indian Muslim who was closely involved in the development of the country's missile and nuclear programme, convincingly won the election. In August the more orthodox Bhairon Singh Shekhawat was elected as Vice-President (his predecessor died two weeks before the scheduled election date). In late August Vajpayee replaced Suresh Prabhu, the widely respected Minister of Power and member of Shiv Sena, with Anant Gangareem Geete, another member of Shiv Sena. Vajpayee had been reportedly under pressure from the leader of Shiv Sena, Bal Thackeray, to carry out the ministerial change, prompting a debate over the Prime Minister's authority with regard to selecting his Council of Ministers. Thackeray had accused Prabhu of not doing enough to serve the financial interests of the militant Hindu party.

In mid-August 2002 the Election Commission rejected interim Chief Minister Narendra Modi's request to conduct early elections to the Gujarat state assembly in October, stating that the situation was not stable enough: many people were still displaced after the riots and communal tensions prevailed in the region. In September Modi launched a controversial 4,800–km Hindu nationalist *gaurav rath yatra* (pride march) around the state of Gujarat in an attempt to garner support for the BJP. Although the Election Commission banned Modi from using the incident in Godhra as an election tool, the symbol of a burning train was displayed on election posters across the state. Communal tensions in the region rose in response to Modi's Hindu nationalist and overtly anti-Muslim election campaign. The elections to the Gujarat state assembly took place on 12 December. The BJP won 51% of the vote, securing 126 of the 182 seats in the state legislature. Congress, criticized for selecting only five Muslim candidates and for attempting to attract the Hindu nationalist vote (albeit at a lesser level than the BJP), despite being a secular party, won only 51 seats. Modi returned to power as Chief Minister. Meanwhile, in late September two armed assailants forced entry into a Hindu temple in Gujarat and shot dead 29 worshippers and injured 74 people; three commandos were also killed. The gunmen were shot dead by security forces, ending a night-long siege of the temple. It was believed that the perpetrators, reportedly members of a relatively unknown militant Islamist group called Tehrik-i-Kasas (Movement of Revenge), carried out the attack in retaliation for the deaths of Gujarati Muslims in the riots earlier in the year. The Indian Government accused the Pakistani Government of orchestrating the attack, an allegation strongly rejected by the latter.

In late January 2003 Vajpayee carried out an extensive government reorganization, promoting several principal economic reformers to senior cabinet positions in an attempt to boost the economic liberalization programme. The most significant move was Arun Jaitley's reinstatement as the Minister of Law and Justice, with the additional charge of the ministry of commerce and industry. The Minister of Disinvestment, Arun Shourie, was also awarded the ministry of communications and information technology. The transfer of senior ministers to leading roles within the BJP was regarded as a move to strengthen the party ahead of state elections scheduled for February and the general election due to take place in 2004. In the weeks leading up to the state elections in Himachal Pradesh, Meghalaya, Nagaland and Tripura, Hindu activists representing the BJP and VHP focused on inciting Hindu nationalist sentiment in an attempt to reproduce the victory achieved in Gujarat two months previously. However, the BJP fared badly in all four elections, held on 26 February, losing power in Himachal Pradesh to Congress. Congress formed a coalition government in Meghalaya and lost power in Nagaland to the Democratic Alliance of Nagaland. The Communist Party of India (Marxist) retained power in Tripura.

In the mean time, in early January 2003 the Government announced that it had established a Nuclear Command Authority to manage India's nuclear weapons, giving sole authority to launch a nuclear strike to the Prime Minister and his advisers. The Government also stated that it would forego its 'no first use' policy on nuclear weapons if India were the target of a major attack using chemical or biological weapons. A number of bomb explosions occurred in Mumbai in December 2002–January 2003, killing at least two people and injuring almost 90. No group claimed responsibility.

Regional issues continue to play an important role in Indian political affairs. In 1986 the Gurkhas (of Nepalese stock) in West Bengal launched a campaign for a separate autonomous homeland in the Darjeeling region and the recognition of Nepali as an official language. The violent separatist campaign, led by the Gurkha National Liberation Front (GNLF), was prompted by the eviction of about 10,000 Nepalis from the state of Meghalaya, where the native residents feared that they were becoming outnumbered by immigrants. When violent disturbances and a general strike were organized by the GNLF in June 1987, the central Government agreed to hold tripartite talks with the GNLF's leader, Subhas Ghising, and the Chief Minister of West Bengal. The Prime Minister rejected the GNLF's demand for an autonomous Gurkha state, but Ghising agreed to the establishment of a semi-autonomous Darjeeling Hill Development Council. Under the formal peace agreement, the GNLF was to cease all agitation and to surrender weapons, while the state government was to release all GNLF detainees. The Government agreed to grant Indian citizenship to all Gurkhas born or domiciled in India. Elections to the Darjeeling Hill Development Council were held in November. The GNLF won 26 of the 28 elective seats (the 14 remaining members of the Council were to be nominated) and Ghising was elected Chairman of the Council. However, the GNLF continued to demand the establishment of a fully autonomous Gurkha state. In 1992 a constitutional amendment providing for the recognition of Nepali as an official language was adopted.

In December 1985 an election for the state assembly in Assam was won by the Asom Gana Parishad (AGP) (Assam People's Council), a newly formed regional party. This followed the signing, in August, of an agreement between the central Government and two groups of Hindu activists, concluded after five years of sectarian violence, which limited the voting rights of immigrants (mainly Bangladeshis) to Assam. When the accord was announced, Bangladesh stated that it would not take back Bengali immigrants from Assam and denied that it had allowed illegal refugees to cross its borders into Assam. Another disaffected Indian tribal group, the Bodos of Assam, demanded a separate state of Bodoland within India. In February 1989 the Bodos, under the leadership of the All Bodo Students' Union (ABSU), intensified their separatist campaign by organizing strikes, bombings and violent demonstrations. The central Government dispatched armed forces to the state. In August the ABSU agreed to hold peace talks with the state government and central government officials. The ABSU agreed to suspend its violent activities, while the Assam government agreed to suspend emergency security measures. The situation became more complicated in 1989, when a militant Maoist group, the United Liberation Front of Assam (ULFA), re-emerged. The ULFA demanded the outright secession of the whole of Assam from India. In 1990 the ULFA claimed responsibility for about 90 assassinations, abductions and bombings. In November, when the violence began to disrupt the state's tea industry, the central Government placed Assam under direct rule, dispatched troops to the state and outlawed the ULFA. By late December the unrest seemed to have been substantially quelled. In the state elections in 1991 the AGP was defeated, and a Congress (I)— which later became known simply as Congress—ministry took power. In September, following the breakdown of prolonged talks with the ULFA, the Government launched a new offensive against the ULFA guerrillas and declared the entire state a disturbed area. The ULFA suffered a serious set-back in mid-1992 when a large number of its leading members surrendered to the authorities. Meanwhile, following the suspension of violence by the ABSU, the Bodo Security Force (BSF) assumed the leading role in the violent campaign for a separate state of Bodoland. The separatist campaign was intensified in 1992 with indiscriminate killings, abductions, bomb explosions and large-scale extortion. The BSF was outlawed by the central Government in November. At a tripartite meeting attended by the Minister of State for Home Affairs, the Chief Minister of Assam and the President of the ABSU in Guwahati in February 1993, a memorandum was signed providing for the establishment of a 40-member Bodoland Autonomous Council, which would be responsible for the socio-economic and cultural affairs of the Bodo people. However, attacks leading to substantial loss of life were made by Bodo and ULFA activists in the second half of the 1990s both on the security forces and on non-tribal groups in the area. In March 2000 the Government and Bodo militants agreed to a cease-fire. Peace negotiations were under way, and in September the cease-fire was extended by one year. However, violence between the state government and the ULFA continued. In February 2002 it was reported that the Assam state assembly had passed a resolution granting a degree of autonomy to the Bodo people through the creation of a territorial council for the Bodos of four western districts of the state. Elsewhere in north-eastern India, violence, both intertribal (particularly against ethnic Bengali settlers) and anti-Government, continued during this period in Tripura, Bihar, Mizoram, Manipur and Nagaland.

In June 2001 a decision by the union Government to extend the duration of a cease-fire arrangement with Nagaland separatists, which encompassed territories beyond the state borders, provoked condemnation and concerns about the expansionist ambitions of the rebels in the neighbouring states of Manipur, Assam and Arunachal Pradesh, where there were known to be bases of the National Socialist Council of Nagaland—Isak Muivah (NSCN—IM), a rebel organization that had openly advocated the creation of a 'greater Nagaland'. In Manipur, where the collapse of the governing Samata-led coalition had led to the imposition of President's rule in the previous month, there was consolidated political opposition to the move and fierce popular objection, prompting the dispatch of national para-military forces to the region to restore order. In late July the national Government agreed to restrict the cease-fire arrangement to the state of Nagaland, angering local political groups in that state. In November 2002 the central Government lifted its ban on the NSCN–IM and agreed to hold unconditional negotiations on the political status of Nagaland. The move allowed the leaders of the separatist group to travel to India for the first time in 37 years. At the end of talks in January 2003 the Naga leaders declared that the separatist insurgency had ended and both sides declared their commitment to continuing the peace process until a permanent peace settlement was reached. The issue of a 'greater Nagaland', however, was avoided. In state elections in February, Congress lost power to the Democratic Alliance of Nagaland.

In September 1985 there was a temporary improvement in the unstable situation in Punjab when an election for the state assembly was held, following an agreement between the central Government and the main Sikh party, the Shiromani Akali Dal (SAD). The election was peaceful and resulted in a victory for the SAD, which assumed power after two years of presidential rule. Part of the 1985 agreement was the proposed transfer of Chandigarh, since 1966 the joint capital of Punjab and Haryana, to Punjab alone. In return, Haryana was to benefit from the completion of the Sutlej-Yamuna canal, to bring irrigation water from Punjab to the dry south of the state, and the transfer of several Hindi-speaking border villages from Punjab to Haryana. Four commissions were established to organize the transfer, but all failed, and the transfer subsequently appeared to have been suspended indefinitely. In January 1986 Sikh extremists re-established a stronghold inside the Golden Temple complex at Amritsar and Hindu–Sikh violence continued throughout the year. In mid-1986 the extremists separated from the ruling moderate SAD (Longowal) and formed several militant factions. In 1987 Rajiv Gandhi reimposed President's rule in Punjab. Despite the resumption of discussions between the Government and the moderate Sikh leaders, the violence continued. In November 1991 more than 50,000 extra troops were deployed in Punjab (bringing the total number of army, paramilitary and police forces in the state to about 200,000) as part of an intensification of operations against Sikh separatists in the run-up to the state elections and parliamentary by-elections, which were held in mid-February 1992. Congress won 12 of the 13 parliamentary seats in Punjab and gained an overall majority in the state legislature. The elections, which brought to an end five years of presidential rule, were, however, boycotted by the

leading factions of the SAD and attracted an extremely low turn-out. The Congress state government that was formed under the leadership of Beant Singh, therefore, lacked any real credibility. Despite the continuing violence between the separatists and the security forces, the large turn-out in the municipal elections in September (the first in 13 years) afforded some hope that normality was returning to Punjab. Local council elections, held in January 1993 (the first in 10 years), also attracted a substantial turn-out. The security situation improved steadily in the course of 1993 and political activity revived. In late August 1995, however, violence erupted in Punjab again when Beant Singh was killed in a car-bomb exploded by suspected Sikh extremists in Chandigarh. This seemed to have been an isolated act of terrorism. The national elections in April/May 1996 were conducted smoothly in the Punjab, and gave the mainstream SAD a convincing victory in the state's parliamentary constituencies. The incumbent Congress administration was routed by an SAD/BJP electoral alliance in state elections held in February 1997; in contrast to the 1992 state elections, turn-out was high. In both the 1998 and 1999 parliamentary elections the SAD again established an electoral alliance with the BJP, and was awarded representation in Vajpayee's consecutive administrations.

At state elections conducted in May 2001 the AIADMK returned to power in Tamil Nadu. Despite receiving a three-year prison sentence following her conviction on corruption charges in October 2000, AIADMK leader Jayalalitha was sworn in as Chief Minister (an office she had previously held in 1991–96) with the proviso that she secure the right to appeal against her convictions within six months in order to remain in office. In September the Supreme Court overturned her appointment as Chief Minister. In December, however, the Chennai High Court acquitted Jayalalitha of corruption charges enabling her to contest a by-election in Tamil Nadu in late February 2002. Following her victory, Jayalalitha was elected leader of the AIADMK legislative group and, subsequently, replaced her colleague as Chief Minister of Tamil Nadu.

In 1986 India and Bangladesh signed an agreement on measures to prevent 'cross-border terrorism'. In 1988 the two countries established a joint working committee to examine methods of averting the annual devastating floods in the Ganges delta. In 1992 the Indian Government, under the provisions of an accord signed with Bangladesh in 1974, formally leased the Tin Bigha Corridor (a small strip of land covering an area of only 1.5 ha) to Bangladesh for 999 years. India maintained sovereignty over the Corridor, but the lease gave Bangladesh access to its enclaves of Dahagram and Angarpota. The transfer of the Corridor occasioned protests from right-wing quarters in India, who also made an issue over the presence in Delhi and other cities of illegal immigrants from Bangladesh and claimed that the Bangladesh Government had done little to protect its Hindu minority. In December 1996 India signed an 'historic' treaty with Bangladesh, which was to be in force for 30 years, regarding the sharing of the Ganges waters. The worst fighting between the two countries since 1976 took place in April 2001 on the Bangladeshi border with the Indian state of Meghalaya. Some 16 members of the Indian Border Security Forces and three members of the Bangladesh Rifles were killed. The situation was brought under control, and the two sides entered border negotiations in June as a result of which two joint working groups were established to review the undemarcated section of the border. Relations between India and Bangladesh deteriorated in November 2002 as a result of accusations by India's Deputy Prime Minister and Minister of Home Affairs, Lal Krishna Advani, that al-Qa'ida had increased its activities in Bangladesh since the BNP-led coalition's assumption of power in October 2001. Advani also claimed that Bangladesh was covertly assisting al-Qa'ida and Pakistan's Inter-Services Intelligence Agency, and was providing refuge for Indian separatist groups. The Bangladeshi Government strongly denied the allegations. In January 2003 the Indian Government announced plans to deport, for reasons of security, some 16m. Bangladeshis who it claimed were working and living in India illegally. The Bangladeshi Government rejected the claim as groundless.

Relations between India and Nepal deteriorated in 1989, when India decided not to renew two bilateral treaties determining trade and transit, insisting that a common treaty covering both issues be negotiated. Nepal refused, stressing the importance of keeping the treaties separate on the grounds that Indo-Nepalese trade issues are negotiable, whereas the right of transit is a recognized right of land-locked countries. India responded by closing most of the transit points through which Nepal's trade is conducted. The dispute was aggravated by Nepal's acquisition of Chinese-made military equipment, which, according to India, violated the Treaty of Peace and Friendship of 1950. However, in June 1990 India and Nepal signed an agreement restoring trade relations and reopening the transit points. Chandra Shekhar visited Kathmandu in February 1991 (the first official visit to Nepal by an Indian Prime Minister since 1977), shortly after it was announced that the first free elections in Nepal were to be held in May. In June 1997 the Indian Prime Minister, Inder Kumar Gujral, made a visit to Nepal and announced the opening of a transit route through north-east India between Nepal and Bangladesh. Gujral and the Nepalese Prime Minister, Lokendra Bahadur Chand, also agreed that there should be a review of the 1950 treaty between the two countries.

Relations with Pakistan had deteriorated in the late 1970s and early 1980s, owing to Pakistan's potential capability for the development of nuclear weapons and as a result of major US deliveries of armaments to Pakistan. The Indian Government believed that such deliveries would upset the balance of power in the region and precipitate an 'arms race'. Pakistan's President, Gen. Mohammad Zia ul-Haq, visited India in 1985, when he and Rajiv Gandhi announced their mutual commitment not to attack each other's nuclear installations and to negotiate the sovereignty of the disputed Siachen glacier region in Kashmir. Pakistan continued to demand a settlement of the Kashmir problem in accordance with earlier UN resolutions, prescribing a plebiscite under the auspices of the UN in the two parts of the state, now divided between India and Pakistan. India argued that the problem should be settled in accordance with the Shimla agreement of 1972, which required that all Indo-Pakistani disputes be resolved through bilateral negotiations. The Indian decision to construct a barrage on the River Jhelum in Jammu and Kashmir, in an alleged violation of the 1960 Indus Water Treaty, also created concern in Pakistan. In December 1988 Rajiv Gandhi visited Islamabad for discussions with Pakistan's Prime Minister, Benazir Bhutto. The resulting agreements included a formal pledge not to attack each other's nuclear installations. Relations reached a crisis in late 1989, when the outlawed Jammu and Kashmir Liberation Front (JKLF) and several other militant Muslim groups intensified their campaigns of civil unrest, strikes and terrorism, demanding an independent Kashmir or unification with Pakistan. The Indian Government dispatched troops to the region and placed the entire Srinagar valley under curfew. Pakistan denied India's claim that the militants were trained and armed in Pakistan-held Kashmir (known as Azad Kashmir). In January 1990 Jammu and Kashmir was placed under Governor's rule, and in July under President's rule. Tension was eased in December, following discussions between the Ministers of External Affairs of both countries. Violence between the Indian security forces and the militant groups, however, continued during 1991–92. Throughout 1993 and in early 1994, the Government's approach to the Kashmir crisis was a combination of a tough military policy and generally fruitless attempts to engage in dialogue. In December 1994 Pakistan was successful in securing the passage of a resolution condemning reported human rights abuses by Indian security forces in Kashmir at a summit meeting of the Organization of the Islamic Conference (OIC, see p. 295). (In the same month Pakistan's decision to close down its consulate in Mumbai, amid claims of Indian support for acts of terrorism in Karachi, provided a further indication of the growing rift between the two countries.) By 1996 the total death toll resulting from the conflict in Jammu and Kashmir, including civilians, security force personnel and militants, was estimated at up to 20,000. The situation in Kashmir improved somewhat, however, when elections for the national parliamentary seats were held in the troubled state shortly after the general election in April/May 1996. There was a reasonably high turn-out, although there were widespread complaints that the security forces had pressurized voters into going to the polling stations. Following the successful holding of elections to the Lok Sabha, state elections were conducted in Jammu and Kashmir in September (the first to be held since 1987) and attracted a turn-out of more than 50%, despite being boycotted by the majority of the separatist groups and being dismissed as a sham by the Pakistani Government. The moderate Jammu and Kashmir National Conference, led by Dr Farooq Abdullah, won the majority of seats in the state assembly, and, on assuming power, immediately offered to instigate talks with the separatist leaders.

Meanwhile, in June 1994 the Indian army had begun to deploy a new missile, named the Prithvi, which had the capacity to reach most of Pakistan. While the 'arms race' between the two countries continued, with claims on both sides concerning the other's missile programmes, talks (which had been suspended since 1994) were resumed in March 1997, both at official and at ministerial level. Tension increased in September when a large-scale outbreak of artillery exchanges along the Line of Control (LoC) resulted in about 40 civilian deaths. After a hiatus of more than one year (during which time both countries carried out controversial nuclear test explosions—see above), Indo-Pakistani talks at foreign secretary level regarding Kashmir and other issues were resumed in Islamabad in October 1998. In February 1999 relations appeared to improve considerably when Prime Minister Vajpayee made an historic bus journey (inaugurating the first passenger bus service between India and Pakistan) over the border to Lahore. Following his welcome by the Pakistani Prime Minister, Mohammad Nawaz Sharif, the two leaders held a summit meeting (the first to be conducted in Pakistan for 10 years), at which they signed the Lahore Declaration, which, with its pledges regarding peace and nuclear security, sought to allay world-wide fears of a nuclear 'flash-point' in South Asia, and committed the two sides to working towards better relations and to implementing a range of confidence-building measures. The contentious subject of Jammu and Kashmir was, however, largely avoided.

Despite the apparent *rapprochement* between India and Pakistan, in April 1999 both countries carried out separate tests on their latest missiles, which were capable of carrying nuclear warheads. In early May the situation deteriorated drastically when the Indian army discovered that Islamist guerrilla groups, reinforced by regular Pakistani troops had occupied strategic positions on the Indian side of the LoC in the Kargil area of Kashmir. Air-strikes launched by the Indian air force at the end of the month failed to dislodge the so-called 'infiltrators', and the army was forced to wage an expensive and lengthy campaign, during which more than 480 Indian soldiers were killed and two Indian military aircraft were shot down. In mid-July, however, Indian military dominance combined with US diplomatic pressure led to a Pakistani withdrawal. In August there was renewed tension when India shot down a Pakistani naval reconnaissance aircraft near Pakistan's border with Gujarat, killing all 16 personnel on board; Pakistan retaliated the following day by opening fire on Indian military aircraft in the same area.

In October/November 1999 there was a notable increase in terrorist incidents in Kashmir, and Indian and Pakistani forces were reported to have resumed skirmishes across the LoC. Relations between the two countries worsened in early November after the success of Vajpayee in promoting an official condemnation of the new Pakistani military regime by the Commonwealth heads of government, following the military coup in Pakistan in mid-October, led by Gen. Pervez Musharraf. In December the Indian Government stated that it would not resume dialogue with Pakistan until the latter halted 'cross-border terrorism'.

In late December 1999 the Kashmir conflict came to international attention when a group of five Islamist fundamentalists hijacked an Indian Airlines aircraft and held its 155 passengers captive at Qandahar airport in southern Afghanistan for one week. The hijackers, who killed one of the hostages, demanded a large ransom payment and the release of 36 militant Muslim supporters of the Kashmiri separatist movement who were being held in Indian prisons. Under increasing domestic pressure to prioritize the safety of the hostages, the Indian Government agreed to release three of the prisoners in exchange for the safe return of the captive passengers and crew. Despite Indian accusations of complicity, the Pakistani Government denied any links with the hijackers. In early January 2000 Prime Minister Vajpayee stated that India would 'work towards getting Pakistan declared a terrorist state'.

In April 2000 there were indications that the Indian Government was willing to re-establish dialogue with Kashmiri militants. Leaders of the All-Party Hurriyat Conference, an organization that to an extent, acted as the political voice for some of the militant groups, were released in April and May. In July one of the main militant groups, the Hizbul Mujahideen, declared a three-month cease-fire. The gesture obtained a quick and positive response from the Indian Government: the Indian Army suspended all offensive operations against the Kashmiri militants for the first time in 11 years. Other militant groups, however, denounced the cessation of hostilities as a betrayal and continued their violent campaign, in an attempt to disrupt the peace process. The Hizbul Mujahideen ended the cease-fire at the beginning of August because the Indian Government opposed a tripartite discussion including representatives of Pakistan. As a result, Pakistan appeared rather moderate and India somewhat intransigent. Vajpayee accused Pakistan of orchestrating the events, of encouraging divisions among militant leaders and of turning the Kashmir issue into a pan-Islamic movement.

Following the collapse of the cease-fire, violence in the region intensified. In November the Chief Minister of Jammu and Kashmir, Dr Farooq Abdullah, announced the instigation of a judicial inquiry into the killing of 36 unarmed Sikhs in March and the killing of five alleged militants a few days later by Indian security forces. In the same month the Indian Government declared the suspension of combat operations against Kashmiri militants during the Muslim holy month of Ramadan. The unilateral cease-fire began at the end of November (and was subsequently extended, at intervals, until the end of May); Indian security forces were authorized to retaliate if fired upon. The majority of national parties and foreign governments supported the cessation of hostilities, although the Pakistani authorities described the cease-fire as 'meaningless' without simultaneous constructive dialogue. The All-Party Hurriyat Conference welcomed the development and offered to enter negotiations with Pakistani authorities in order to prepare for tripartite discussions. The Hizbul Mujahideen and other militant groups, however, rejected the offer and continued their campaign of violence, extending their activities as far as the Red Fort in Old Delhi, where three people were shot dead in December. In the same month Pakistan extended an invitation to the All-Party Hurriyat Conference to participate in joint preparations for the establishment of tripartite negotiations. Although Abdul Ghani Lone, a leading member of the All-Party Hurriyat Conference, was permitted to make a private visit to Islamabad in November, passport applications for a delegation of leaders were subsequently refused. In mid-January 2001 the Indian high commissioner to Pakistan visited Gen. Musharraf. This meeting signified the first high-level contact since the military coup in Pakistan in 1999. The two officials urged an early resumption of negotiations on the Kashmir question. At the end of May the Government announced the end of its unilateral cease-fire; more than 1,000 people were estimated to have been killed in violence related to the crisis in the region since the cease-fire was first announced in November 2000.

Relations with Pakistan appeared to improve following the earthquake in Gujarat in January 2001, when Pakistan offered humanitarian relief to India and the leaders of the two countries thus established contact. In May Vajpayee issued an unexpected invitation to Gen. Musharraf to attend bilateral negotiations in Agra in July. However, hopes for a significant breakthrough on the issue of Kashmir were frustrated by the failure of the two leaders to agree to a joint declaration at the conclusion of the dialogue; the divergent views of the two sides on the priority issue in the dispute (cross-border terrorism according to India, and Kashmiri self-determination in the opinion of Pakistan) appeared to be more firmly entrenched than ever. Violence increased in the region following the disappointment engendered by the meeting, and in August the Indian Government extended its official 'disturbed area' designation (invoking the 1990 Armed Forces—Special Powers—Act) to cover all districts of the provinces of Jammu and Kashmir (only Ladakh was unaffected). Tension with Pakistan was heightened considerably following a guerrilla-style attack on the state assembly building in Srinagar on 1 October. An estimated 38 people (including two of the four assailants) were killed and around 70 were wounded in the attack and in the subsequent confrontation with security forces. The Indian Government attributed responsibility for the attack to the Pakistan-based Jaish-e-Mohammed and Lashkar-e-Taiba groups. Tensions were exacerbated later in the month when Gen. Musharraf rejected official Indian requests to ban the activities of the organization in Pakistan, although he did publicly condemn the attack. Skirmishes between Indian and Pakistani security forces along the LoC threatened to erupt into open conflict later in the month.

On 13 December 2001 five armed assailants gained access to the grounds of the union parliament in New Delhi and attempted to launch an apparent suicide attack on the parliament building, where some 300 MPs had congregated for a routine session. Although no parliamentary deputies were hurt in the attack, nine people (including a number of policemen,

some security officials and a groundsman) were killed and some 25 were injured in the botched assault; the five assailants were also killed in the attack. The Indian authorities again attributed responsibility for the attack to the Jaish-e-Mohammed and Lashkar-e-Taiba groups, and suggested that the five assailants appeared to be of Pakistani origin. Pakistan, which had been among the many countries to express immediate condemnation of the attack (which was popularly described as an assault on democracy), now demanded to see concrete proof to support the allegations made by the Indian Government, while the US Government urged the Indian authorities to exercise restraint in their response. Tensions between India and Pakistan continued to mount when Mohammed Afzal, a member of Jaish-e-Mohammed arrested in Kashmir on suspicion of complicity in the incident, admitted his involvement and alleged publicly that Pakistani security and intelligence agencies had provided support to those directly responsible for the attack. India recalled its high commissioner from Islamabad and announced that overground transport services between the two countries would be suspended from 1 January 2002. As positions were reinforced with troops and weapons (including missiles) on both sides of the LoC, there was considerable international concern that such brinkmanship might propel the two countries (each with nuclear capabilities) into renewed armed conflict. Mindful of the potential detriment to security at Pakistan's border with Afghanistan that could result from escalated conflict in Kashmir, the USA applied increased pressure on the beleaguered Pakistani Government (already facing vociferous domestic opposition to its accommodation of US activities in Afghanistan) to adopt a more conciliatory attitude towards India's security concerns, and in late December the Pakistani authorities followed the US Government's lead in 'freezing' the assets of the two groups held responsible for the attack on India. The leaders of the two groups were later detained by the Pakistani authorities (who arrested some 80 suspected militants in the last week of December 2001), but, despite an evident satisfaction at this development, the Indian Government continued to dismiss much of the Pakistani response as superficial and demanded that the two leaders be extradited (together with 20 other named Pakistan-based militants) to stand trial in India. However, in December 2002 Pakistan freed one of the leaders, Maulana Masood Azhar, from house arrest. Later that month a special court established under POTO (see above) convicted three Kashmiri Muslims—Mohammed Afzal, Shaukat Hussain and S. A. R. Geelani—of organizing the attack on the union parliament and sentenced them to death. Two of the accused were reportedly members of Jaish-e-Mohammed; the third was a member of the JKLF. Navjot Sandhu, the wife of Shaukat Hussain, was sentenced to five years' imprisonment on charges of criminal conspiracy.

It had been hoped that tensions between the two countries might be diffused by renewed dialogue between Vajpayee and Musharraf at a summit meeting of the South Asian Association for Regional Co-operation convened in Nepal in the first week of January 2002, but contacts between the two men were minimal, and troops on both sides of the LoC continued to exchange gunfire in the days following the conference. However, on 12 January Musharraf yielded to relentless international pressure by publicly condemning the activities of militant extremists based in Pakistan and announcing the introduction of a broad range of measures to combat terrorist activity and religious zealotry, including the proscription of five extremist organizations (among them the Jaish-e-Mohammed and the Lashkar-e-Taiba). Within two days the Pakistani authorities claimed to have closed almost 500 offices used by the five organizations and to have arrested some 1,400 suspected activists, prompting considerable international praise for the initiative. An armed attack by four suspected Islamist militants on a US cultural centre in Kolkata (Calcutta) on 22 January, in which five Indian policemen were killed and more than 20 were injured, placed relations between the two countries under renewed strain when the Indian authorities attempted to link the unidentified assailants (who escaped after the attack) to the Pakistani intelligence services. However, it was hoped that reports published in late January which indicated that the number of terrorist incidents in Jammu and Kashmir had halved since the introduction of Pakistan's new counter-insurgency measures earlier in the month would help foster a more substantial improvement in future relations between the two countries. Tensions between the two countries rose again, following a suspected Islamist militant attack on an army camp in Jammu and Kashmir in mid-May, in which 34 people were killed, including 19 civilians.

India identified the gunmen as Pakistani nationals and a few days later requested the withdrawal of Pakistan's high commissioner to India. The two countries appeared to be on the brink of war again as positions were reinforced with troops and weapons on both sides of the LoC. Exchanges of gunfire across the LoC intensified. India declared that it would be prepared to go to war after the monsoon season ended (in September) if its neighbour refused to halt 'cross-border terrorism'. Musharraf denied that Pakistan was aiding incursions into Jammu and Kashmir and would not rule out first use of nuclear weapons. Indo-Pakistani relations deteriorated further following the assassination of Abdul Ghani Lone, the leader of the All-Party Hurriyat Conference on 21 May, by suspected Islamist militants. As a result of international efforts to ease tensions between the two neighbours, in June India withdrew five naval ships from patrol of the coast of Pakistan and allowed Pakistani civilian aircraft to enter its airspace, in response to Pakistani pledges to halt cross-border infiltration. In mid-October the Minister of Defence stated that India would withdraw a large number of troops from the international border with Pakistan; the number of troops along the LoC would remain unchanged, however. Pakistan responded by withdrawing a portion of its troops.

Meanwhile, the crisis between India and Pakistan and the related militant activity within Kashmir adversely affected the Indian Government's relations with the All-Party Hurriyat Conference. A number of attacks by suspected Islamist militants were carried out in Jammu and Kashmir in July and August 2002. In mid-July the Chief Minister of Jammu and Kashmir announced that scientific tests had shown that five men killed by Indian security forces in March 2000 had been local civilians and not, as maintained at the time, militants responsible for the murder of 36 unarmed Sikhs (see above). In early August 2002 it was announced that state elections would be held in Jammu and Kashmir in four phases, from mid-September. The All-Party Hurriyat Conference declared that it would boycott the election, regarding it as meaningless unless a referendum on independence was held first. In September the state Minister of Law and Parliamentary Affairs of Jammu and Kashmir was assassinated by suspected militant Islamists intent on disrupting the election campaign and poll. Violence continued throughout the election period; in mid-September Kashmiri separatists attempted to assassinate the state Minister of Tourism. The first two phases of the election took place on 16 and 24 September. The union Government hailed the 47% turn-out at the first phase as a triumph for democracy, although there were reports that Indian security forces had used coercion to ensure voter attendance in some instances. In the second phase, voter turn-out declined marginally to 42%. The All-Party Hurriyat Conference successfully urged many voters to boycott the election and hold a strike: only 11% of the electorate in Srinagar participated in the election; conversely, the turn-out in rural constitutencies near Srinagar and Jammu was higher than average. The third and fourth rounds were held on 1 and 8 October; overall, voter turn-out reached 44%. The election resulted in the surprising defeat of the Jammu and Kashmir National Conference. No single party had won an outright majority, however: the Jammu and Kashmir National Conference secured 28 seats, Congress won 20 seats and the regional People's Democratic Party (PDP) won 16 seats. The All-Party Hurriyat Conference rejected the result and demanded that a plebiscite be established; the Pakistani Government dismissed the election as a 'sham' and 'farcical'. Violence overshadowed the polls: at least 730 people had reportedly been killed since the announcement of the elections. Congress and the PDP were invited to form a coalition government; however, the national Government had to assume direct control over Jammu and Kashmir after the two parties were unable to come to a power-sharing arrangement by 17 October, the expiry date of the outgoing assembly. Eventually, in late October Congress and the PDP reached a compromise: it was agreed that PDP leader Mufti Mohammed Sayeed would be Chief Minister for the first three years, followed by local Congress president Ghulam Nabi Azad for the next three years. The coalition government was inaugurated in early November. Kashmiri separatists dismissed Sayeed's policy of reconciliation by continuing their violent campaign. Nevertheless, as promised at the end of October, Sayeed authorized the release of several political prisoners charged with 'non-serious' crimes. The release of Yasin Malik, the leader of the JKLF detained under the POTO in March, was the most significant. The state Government also pledged to disband the Special Operations Group of the police, which had been accused in the past of serious human rights

violations. In late November suspected Islamist militants attacked two Hindu temples in Jammu, resulting in the deaths of 14 people. The Indian authorities attributed responsibility for the attack to the Lashkar-e-Taiba group. In December a legislator of the PDP was assassinated.

Indo-Pakistani relations deteriorated in early 2003. Tensions were exacerbated by India's latest set of 'routine' ballistic-missile tests, the violence in Kashmir and India's new military agreement with Russia (see below). In late January India ordered four officials at Pakistan's high commission in New Delhi to leave the country within 48 hours for 'indulging in activities incompatible with their official status', a euphemism for spying. Pakistan reacted by expelling four officials at the Indian high commission in Islamabad. In early February India expelled Pakistan's acting high commissioner, Jalil Abbas Jilani, accusing him of funding Kashmiri separatist groups. Four other Pakistani officials were charged with spying and expelled. Pakistan retaliated by giving India's acting high commissioner, Sudhir Vyas, and four colleagues 48 hours to leave, for allegedly spying. India declared that it would not hold negotiations with Pakistan until the latter ceased 'cross-border terrorism'. In late April, during a visit to Jammu and Kashmir, Vajpayee offered to enter negotiations with Pakistan, provided that the latter closed down its alleged militants' training camps. A subsequent telephone conversation between Vajpayee and the Pakistani Prime Minister in early May resulted in an agreement to restore diplomatic relations and civil aviation links, and to begin peace negotiations.

Since 1983 India's relations with Sri Lanka have been dominated by conflicts between the island's Sinhalese and Tamil communities, in which India has sought to arbitrate. In July 1987 Rajiv Gandhi and the Sri Lankan President, Junius Jayewardene, signed an accord aimed at settling the conflict. An Indian Peace-Keeping Force (IPKF) was dispatched to Sri Lanka but encountered considerable resistance from the Tamil separatist guerrillas. Following the gradual implementation of the peace accord, the IPKF troops completed their withdrawal in March 1990. Violence flared up again, however, and the flow of Sri Lankan refugees into Tamil Nadu increased considerably. By late 1991 the number of Sri Lankans living in refugee camps in the southern Indian state was estimated at more than 200,000. The assassination of Rajiv Gandhi in May 1991, by members of the LTTE, completed India's disenchantment with the latter organization. Measures were subsequently taken by the state government in Tamil Nadu to suppress LTTE activity within the state, and also to begin the process of repatriating refugees. The repatriation programme (allegedly conducted on a voluntary basis) proved a slow and difficult process. In May 1992 the LTTE was officially banned in India. In December 1998 the Indian Prime Minister and Sri Lankan President signed a bilateral free-trade agreement, which finally came into effect in March 2000.

During 1981 there was an improvement in India's relations with the People's Republic of China. Both countries agreed to attempt to find an early solution to their Himalayan border dispute and to seek to normalize relations, and a number of working groups were subsequently established. In February 1991 a major breakthrough occurred when a draft protocol for 1991/92, including the proposed resumption of border trade between the two countries for the first time in three decades, was signed. All six border posts had been closed since the brief border war in 1962. In December 1991 the Chinese Prime Minister, Li Peng, made an official visit to India (the first such visit to India by a Chinese Prime Minister for 31 years), during which a memorandum on the resumption of bilateral border trade was signed. Bilateral border trade was actually resumed between India and China in July 1992. In December 1994 it was announced that India and China had agreed to hold joint military exercises in 1995 along the border in the Himalayan region of Ladakh. Sino-Indian relations were further strengthened as a result of a three-day visit to India conducted by the Chinese President, Jiang Zemin, in November 1996 (the first visit by a Chinese Head of State to India). Despite the gradual improvement in relations, however, India has frequently indicated that it is unhappy with the nuclear asymmetry between the two countries and with what it perceives as China's willingness to transfer missiles and missile technology to Pakistan. Sino-Indian relations deteriorated following India's 1998 nuclear tests, partly because China believed that India was using a fabricated threat from China to justify its actions. In June 1999 the Indian Minister of External Affairs visited Beijing to restore

Sino-Indian dialogue. In 2000 relations improved. During border negotiations in November, India and China exchanged detailed maps of the middle sector of the Line of Actual Control: a significant step towards resolving differences. In January 2001 a senior Chinese official, Li Peng, visited India in an effort further to improve bilateral relations.

In February 2001 the Indian Government granted political asylum to Ugyen Trinley Dorje, one of three claimants to the title of 17th Karmapa Lama (head of the Karma Kagyu Buddhist sect), who had fled to India from Chinese-ruled Tibet in December 1999.

Prior to its disintegration in December 1991, the USSR was a major contributor of economic and military assistance to India. In early 1992 both Russia and Ukraine agreed to maintain arms supplies to India, and in February an Indo-Russian trade and payments protocol was signed. The President of Russia, Boris Yeltsin, made an official visit to India in 1993, during which he signed an Indo-Russian Treaty of Friendship and Co-operation. In October 1996 India and Russia signed a defence co-operation agreement (later extended to 2010), and in December India signed a US $1,800m. contract to purchase 40 fighter aircraft from Russia. In June 1998 Russia defied a G-8 ban on exporting nuclear technology to India by agreeing to supply the latter with two nuclear reactors. In November 1999 India and Russia signed a defence agreement regarding their joint manufacture of military aircraft and submarines. In October 2000 the newly elected Russian President, Vladimir Putin, visited India. The two countries signed a declaration of 'strategic partnership', which involved co-operation on defence, economic matters and international terrorism issues. India signed a contract to purchase 50 Sukhoi-30 fighter aircraft from Russia, with a licence to manufacture around 150 more. The agreement, reportedly worth more than $3,000m., was finalized in December. In February 2001 India agreed to buy 310 T-90 Russian tanks, at an estimated cost of $700m. In June the two countries successfully conducted tests of a new, jointly developed supersonic cruise missile; the PJ-10 was thought to be unique in the world. In November it was announced that Russia had been awarded a contract to build a nuclear power plant in Tamil Nadu. At the Conference on Interaction and Confidence-Building Measures in Asia in June 2002 at Almaty, Kazakhstan, Putin attempted to act as a mediator between India and Pakistan, without success. In January 2003 India signed an agreement with Russia to lease four Tu22 long-range nuclear bombers and two nuclear-capable submarines and to pay for the restoration of a Russian aircraft carrier. The contract would significantly improve India's ability to deliver its nuclear warheads.

Following the collapse of the USSR, a long-time ally of India, in December 1991, the Indian Government sought to strengthen its ties with the USA. In January 1992 discussions were held between Indian and US officials regarding military co-operation and ambitious joint defence projects. However, the USA remains concerned about the risks of nuclear proliferation in the South Asia region as a whole, and has yet to achieve a mutual understanding with India on this issue (India has repeatedly refused to sign the Nuclear Non-Proliferation Treaty—NPT). In addition, despite India's recent adoption of a programme of economic liberalization, conflicts over trade and related issues have arisen between the USA and India. During a visit to India by the US Secretary of Defense in January 1995, a 'landmark' agreement on defence and security co-operation was signed by the two countries.

In mid-1996, in a move that provoked widespread international condemnation, India decided not to be party to the Comprehensive Test Ban Treaty (CTBT), which it had earlier supported, so long as the existing nuclear powers were unwilling to commit themselves to a strict timetable for full nuclear disarmament. In May 1998 India's controversial decision to explode five nuclear test devices and to claim thereby its new status as a nuclear-weapons state, led to a rapid escalation in the 'arms race' with Pakistan (which responded with its own series of nuclear tests). The USA, with limited support from other countries, subsequently imposed economic sanctions on both India and Pakistan until such time as they had signed the NPT and the CTBT and taken steps to reverse their nuclear programmes. Immediately after the tests, India announced a self-imposed moratorium on further testing and launched itself into intense diplomatic activity. During 1998–99 the USA lifted some of the sanctions imposed on India and Pakistan, whilst reiterating its requests that the two countries sign the CTBT and exercise restraint in their respective missile programmes to ensure peace

in South Asia. The US President, Bill Clinton, made an official six-day state visit to India in March 2000 (the first by a US President since 1978). President Clinton appeared to endorse India's opinion that the Kashmir issue was a local matter and did not directly concern the international community. In September Vajpayee visited the USA. He continued to assert that consensus among Indian ministers had to be reached before a decision on the CTBT could be made. In mid-January 2001 India successfully test-fired its Agni-II intermediate ballistic missile for the second time. Vajpayee declared that the test was necessary for India's national security; however, the move was criticized by Pakistan, Japan and the United Kingdom and caused concern in China. In late September 2001 US President George W. Bush announced an end to the military and economic sanctions imposed against India and Pakistan in 1998. The decision followed the renewal of high-level military contacts between the USA and India in April and May and Pakistan's co-operation with US counter-terrorism initiatives against neighbouring Afghanistan in the aftermath of the terrorist attacks carried out on US mainland targets on 11 September. During a visit to India in November, US Secretary of Defense Donald Rumsfeld discussed further defence co-operation possibilities with the Indian authorities and announced that the US Government was prepared to resume the sale of specific defence materials to India.

Government

India is a federal republic. Legislative power is vested in Parliament, consisting of the President and two Houses. The Council of States (Rajya Sabha) has 245 members, most of whom are indirectly elected by the state assemblies for six years (one-third retiring every two years), the remainder being nominated by the President for six years. The House of the People (Lok Sabha) has 543 elected members, serving for five years (subject to dissolution). A small number of members of the Lok Sabha may be nominated by the President to represent the Anglo-Indian community, while the 543 members are directly elected by universal adult suffrage in single-member constituencies. The President is a constitutional Head of State, elected for five years by an electoral college comprising elected members of both Houses of Parliament and the state legislatures. The President exercises executive power on the advice of the Council of Ministers, which is responsible to Parliament. The President appoints the Prime Minister and, on the latter's recommendation, other ministers.

India contains 28 self-governing states, each with a Governor (appointed by the President for five years), a legislature (elected for five years) and a Council of Ministers headed by the Chief Minister. Bihar, Jammu and Kashmir, Karnataka, Maharashtra and Uttar Pradesh have bicameral legislatures, the other 23 state legislatures being unicameral. Each state has its own legislative, executive and judicial machinery, corresponding to that of the Indian Union. In the event of the failure of constitutional government in a state, presidential rule can be imposed by the Union. There are also six Union Territories and one National Capital Territory, administered by Lieutenant-Governors or Administrators, all of whom are appointed by the President. The Territories of Delhi and Pondicherry also have elected chief ministers and state assemblies.

Defence

At 1 August 2002 the total strength of India's armed forces was 1,298,000: an army of 1,100,000, a navy of 53,000 and an air force of 145,000. Active paramilitary forces totalled 1,089,700 men, including the 174,000-strong Border Security Force (based mainly in the troubled state of Jammu and Kashmir). Military service is voluntary, but, under the amended Constitution, it is the fundamental duty of every citizen to perform national service when called upon. The proposed defence budget for 2003/04 was estimated at Rs 769,325.9m. (equivalent to 17.5% of total expenditure).

Economic Affairs

In 2001, according to estimates by the World Bank, India's gross national income (GNI), measured at average 1999–2001 prices, was US $474,323m., equivalent to $460 per head (or $2,450 per head on an international purchasing-power parity basis). During 1990–2001, it was estimated, the population increased at an average annual rate of 1.8%, while gross domestic product (GDP) per head increased, in real terms, by an average of 3.5% in 1990–2001. Overall GDP increased, in real terms, at an average annual rate of 5.4% in 1990–2001; growth reached 4.0%

in 2000/01 and 5.4% in 2001/02. In 2002/03 economic growth was expected to be 4.5%.

Agriculture (including forestry and fishing) contributed an estimated 24.5% of GDP in 2001. About 59.2% of the economically active population were employed in agriculture in 2001. The principal cash crops are cotton (cotton fabrics and yarn accounted for 7.9% of total export earnings in 2000/01), tea, rice, spices and cashew nuts. Coffee and jute production are also important. The average annual growth rate in the output of the agricultural sector was 2.5% in 1990–2001. According to estimates by the Asian Development Bank (ADB), agricultural GDP contracted by 0.2% in 2000/01 and grew by 5.7% in 2001/02.

Industry (including mining, manufacturing, power and construction) contributed an estimated 27.1% of GDP in 2001. According to World Bank estimates, about 12.9% of the working population were employed in the industrial sector in 1995. Industrial GDP increased at an average annual rate of 5.6% in 1990–2001. According to the ADB, the rate of growth of the GDP of the industrial sector reached 6.3% in 2000/01, but declined to 3.3% in 2001/02.

Mining contributed an estimated 2.2% of GDP in 2001/02, and employed 0.6% of the working population in 1991. Iron ore and cut diamonds are the major mineral exports. Coal, limestone, zinc and lead are also mined. In 1999 India was the third largest coal producer in the world after the People's Republic of China and the USA. According to the ADB, mining GDP increased by an average annual rate of 4.1% during 1994/95–2000/01.

Manufacturing contributed an estimated 15.9% of GDP in 2001, and employed 10.0% of the working population in 1991. The GDP of the manufacturing sector increased at an average annual rate of 5.8% during 1990–2001. According to the ADB manufacturing GDP rose by 6.8% in 1999/2000 and by 5.6% in 2000/01. In 1998 the most important branches, measured by gross value of output, were food products (accounting for 16.8% of the total), iron and steel (11.1%), textiles (9.6%) and industrial chemicals (8.5%).

In late 1998 India had a total generating capacity of 81,000 MW. In 1999 thermal plants accounted for an estimated 81.8% of total power generation and hydroelectric plants (often dependent on monsoons) for 15.4%; the remaining 2.5% was contributed principally by nuclear power. Imports of mineral fuels, lubricants, etc. comprised 22.2% of the cost of total imports in 1999/2000.

The services sector, which is dominated by the rapidly expanding data-processing business, the growing number of business call centres and the tourism industry, contributed an estimated 48.4% of GDP in 2001, and engaged 20.5% of the economically active population in 1991. The GDP of the services sector increased by an average of 7.3% per year in 1990–2001; according to the ADB, the rate of growth reached 4.8% in 2000/01 and 6.5% in 2001/02.

In 2000 India recorded a trade deficit of US $12,193m., and there was a deficit of $4,198m. on the current account of the balance of payments. In 2001/02 the principal source of imports (an estimated 6.1%) and the principal market for exports (an estimated 19.4%) was the USA. Other major trading partners were Japan, the United Kingdom, Belgium, Hong Kong, the United Arab Emirates and Germany. The principal exports in 2001/02 were ready-made garments, pearls, precious and semi-precious stones and cotton. The principal imports were mineral fuels and lubricants, pearls, precious and semi-precious stones and machinery and mechanical appliances.

In the financial year ending 31 March 2004 there was a projected budgetary deficit of Rs 1,536,370m., equivalent to 5.6% of GDP. In 2000, according to the UN, India's total official development assistance stood at US $1,487.2m. (of which $775.3m. was in the form of grants and $711.9m. was in the form of loans). India's total external debt was $100,367m. at the end of 2000, of which $96,903m. was long-term public debt. In that year the cost of debt-servicing was equivalent to 12.8% of earnings from the exports of goods and services. The average annual rate of inflation was an estimated 8.5% in 1990–2001; consumer prices rose by by 4.0% in 2000 and by 3.7% in 2001. In rural India the number of people wholly unemployed comprise about 6% of the potential labour force for adult males, but the proportion is around 23% when account is taken of underemployment.

India is a member of the Asian Development Bank (ADB, see p. 143), of the UN's Economic and Social Commission for Asia and the Pacific, of the South Asian Association for Regional Co-operation (SAARC, see p. 310) and of the Colombo Plan (see p. 339).

The process of wide-ranging economic reform initiated in 1991, including trade and investment liberalization, industrial deregulation, disinvestment by the Government in public enterprises and their gradual privatization, financial and tax reforms, etc., has continued despite several changes in government. By 2000 a variety of sectors—including power, coal, telecommunications, postal services, transport (with the exception of the railways) and insurance—had been opened up to private (domestic and foreign) investment. The 2001/02 budget envisaged an expansion of the divestment programme; however, political and popular opposition to the programme persisted, and further progress was mired in financial scandals and procedural obstacles in the Lok Sabha later in the year. Nevertheless, by the end of 2001/02 the Government had partially transferred a number of companies, including the telecommunications monopoly Videsh Sanchar Nigam Ltd (VSNL) and Indian Tourism Development, to the private sector. Restrictions on foreign participation in a number of sectors (including the pharmaceuticals industry) were eased or lifted to encourage greater foreign investment, although confidence in the initiative was somewhat undermined, later in the year, by the collapse of the US energy corporation, Enron, the largest foreign investor in India. In 2002/03 the Government negotiated the sale of stakes in Hindustan Zinc and car manufacturer Maruti Udyog. In late 2002 ministers ended months of infighting by reaching a compromise to sell a stake in Hindustan Petroleum Corpn Ltd to a strategic investor and a portion on Bharat Petroleum Corpn Ltd to the public through a share offering. It was hoped that this agreement would revive other ongoing privatization deals, such as the sale of National Aluminium Co. Despite the global economic slowdown and an unexpected monsoon failure, the economy in 2002/03 improved in the areas of exports, industrial production, foreign-exchange reserves, foreign investment and inflation. In 2001/02 India recorded a current-account surplus for the first time in 23 years. The surplus was estimated to have increased in 2002/03. However, attempts to address India's unwieldy fiscal deficit (traditionally fuelled by the country's modest tax base and cumbersome local government apparatus) have been largely frustrated by the repeated stalling of the divestment programme and the costs associated with natural disasters and volatile foreign relations and internal security concerns, and the deficit remains a major cause of concern to potential foreign investors and international donors. The 2003/04 union budget envisaged a fiscal deficit equivalent to 5.6% of GDP, and GDP growth of about 6.0% (compared with the annual average target of 8% contained in the Tenth Five-Year Plan, 2002–07). Value-added tax was to be introduced at state level from the beginning of 2003/04, eventually to replace the central sales tax. The late 1990s witnessed India's rapid emergence as a 'software superpower'; in 2000 software exports constituted the country's single largest export item, earning, according to the National Association of Software and Service Companies (Nasscom), an estimated US $3,900m. in 1999/2000. Despite the global economic slowdown, software exports were forecast to expand by 30% in 2002/03, to reach $7,000m. The rapidly expanding industry presented increasing employment opportunities. Nevertheless, concern grew over the high number of qualified information technology professionals leaving the country for better-paid work elsewhere. In the early 2000s business call centres had become the fastest growing industry in India, expanding by 70% in 2002 and providing $1,470m. in revenue in the same year. An increasing number of multinational companies were moving their call centre operations to India, largely owing to cheaper labour costs and low long-distance telephone charges. Nasscom forecast that the revenue from call centres would reach $24,000m. by 2008.

Education

Education is primarily the responsibility of the individual state governments. Elementary education for children between the ages of six and 14 years is theoretically compulsory in all states except Nagaland and Himachal Pradesh. There are facilities for free primary education (lower and upper stages) in all the states. Enrolment at the first level of education in 1996 was equivalent to 101% of children aged six to 10 years (110% of boys; 90% of girls). Secondary enrolment in 1996 was equivalent to 49% of those aged 11 to 17 (59% of boys; 39% of girls). India had a total of 231 universities and institutions with university status in 1999/2000, and some 11,381 university and affiliated colleges. University enrolment was 7.73m. in 2000/01. Budgetary expenditure on education and literacy for 2003/04 was forecast at 98,611.8m. rupees (2.2% of total spending).

Public Holidays

The public holidays observed in India vary locally. The dates given below apply to Delhi. As religious feasts depend on astronomical observations, holidays are usually declared at the beginning of the year in which they will be observed. It is not possible, therefore, to indicate more than the month in which some of the following holidays will occur.

2003: 1 January (New Year's Day), 26 January (Republic Day), 12 February (Id ul-Zuha, Feast of the Sacrifice), 5 March (Muharram, Islamic New Year), 18 March (Holi), 15 April (Mahavir Jayanti), 18 April (Good Friday), 21 April (Easter Monday), 14 May (Birth of the Prophet), 16 May (Buddha Purnima), 15 August (Independence Day), 20 August (Janmashtami), 2 October (Mahatma Gandhi's Birthday), 5 October (Dussehra), 25 October (Diwali), 9 November (Guru Nanak Jayanti), 26 November (Id al-Fitr, end of Ramadan), 25–26 December (Christmas).

2004: 1 January (New Year's Day), 26 January (Republic Day), 2 February (Id ul-Zuha, Feast of the Sacrifice), 22 February (Muharram, Islamic New Year), 6 March (Holi), 3 April (Mahavir Jayanti), 9 April (Good Friday), 12 April (Easter Monday), 2 May (Birth of the Prophet), 4 May (Buddha Purnima), 15 August (Independence Day), 6 September (Janmashtami), 2 October (Mahatma Gandhi's birthday), 22 October (Dussehra), 12 November (Diwali), 14 November (Id al-Fitr, end of Ramadan), 26 November (Guru Nanak Jayanti), 25–26 December (Christmas).

Weights and Measures

The metric system has been officially introduced. The imperial system is also still in use, as are traditional Indian weights and measures, including:

1 tola = 11.66 grams;
1 seer = 933.1 grams;
1 maund = 37.32 kg;
1 lakh = (1,00,000) = 100,000;
1 crore = (1,00,00,000) = 10,000,000.

Statistical Survey

Source (unless otherwise stated): Central Statistical Organization, Ministry of Statistics and Programme Implementation, Sardar Patel Bhavan, Patel Chowk, New Delhi 110 001; tel. (11) 23732150; fax (11) 23342384; e-mail moscc@bol.net.in; internet mospi.nic.in.

Area and Population

AREA, POPULATION AND DENSITY*

Area (sq km)	3,166,414†
Population (census results)	
1 March 1991‡ §	846,302,688
1 March 2001‖ ¶	
Males	531,277,078
Females.	495,738,169
Total	1,027,015,247
Population (official estimates at mid-year)[1]	
1999	986,611,000
2000	1,002,142,000
2001	1,017,544,000
Density (per sq km) at March 2001 . .	324

* Including Sikkim (incorporated into India on 26 April 1975) and the Indian-held part of Jammu and Kashmir.

† 1,222,559 sq miles.

‡ Excluding adjustment for underenumeration, estimated at 1.5%.

§ Including estimate for the Indian-held part of Jammu and Kashmir.

‖ Provisional results.

¶ Including estimates for certain areas in the states of Gujarat and Himachal Pradesh where the census could not be conducted, owing to recent natural disasters.

[1] Not adjusted to take account of the 2001 census results.

Source: Registrar General of India.

STATES AND TERRITORIES
(population at 2001 census)

	Area (sq km)	Population (provisional)	Density (per sq km)	Capital
States				
Andhra Pradesh	275,069	75,727,541	275	Hyderabad
Arunachal Pradesh[1]	83,743	1,091,117	13	Itanagar
Assam . . .	78,438	26,638,407	340	Dispur
Bihar* . . .	94,163	82,878,796	880	Patna
Chhattisgarh .	135,191	20,795,956	154	Raipur
Goa[5] . .	3,702	1,343,998	363	Panaji
Gujarat . . .	196,022	50,596,992	258	Gandhinagar
Haryana . . .	44,212	21,082,989	477	Chandigarh[2]
Himachal Pradesh .	55,673	6,077,248	109	Shimla
Jammu and Kashmir[3] . .	101,387	10,069,917	99	Srinagar
Jharkhand . .	79,714	26,909,428	338	Ranchi
Karnataka . .	191,791	52,733,958	275	Bangalore
Kerala . . .	38,863	31,838,619	819	Thiruvananthapuram (Trivandrum)
Madhya Pradesh*	308,245	60,385,118	196	Bhopal
Maharashtra .	307,713	96,752,247	314	Mumbai (Bombay)
Manipur . . .	22,327	2,388,634	107	Imphal
Meghalaya . .	22,429	2,306,069	103	Shillong
Mizoram[4] . .	21,081	891,058	42	Aizawl
Nagaland . .	16,579	1,988,636	120	Kohima
Orissa . . .	155,707	36,706,920	236	Bhubaneswar
Punjab . . .	50,362	24,289,296	482	Chandigarh[2]
Rajasthan . .	342,239	56,473,122	165	Jaipur
Sikkim . . .	7,096	540,493	76	Gangtok
Tamil Nadu . .	130,058	62,110,839	478	Chennai (Madras)
Tripura . . .	10,486	3,191,168	304	Agartala
Uttaranchal* .	53,483	8,479,562	159	Dehradun
Uttar Pradesh* .	240,928	166,052,859	689	Lucknow
West Bengal .	88,752	80,221,171	904	Kolkata (Calcutta)
Territories				
Andaman and Nicobar Islands .	8,249	356,265	43	Port Blair
Chandigarh[2]. .	114	900,914	7,902	Chandigarh
Dadra and Nagar Haveli	491	220,451	449	Silvassa
Daman and Diu[5]	112	158,059	1,411	Daman
Delhi . . .	1,483	13,782,976	9,294	Delhi
Lakshadweep .	32	60,595	1,894	Kavaratti
Pondicherry . .	480	973,829	2,029	Pondicherry

* Chhattisgarh, Jharkhand and Uttaranchal (formerly parts of Madhya Pradesh, Bihar and Uttar Pradesh respectively) were granted statehood in November 2000; figures for area and population have been adjusted accordingly.
[1] Arunachal Pradesh was granted statehood in February 1987.
[2] Chandigarh forms a separate Union Territory, not within Haryana or Punjab. As part of a scheme for a transfer of territory between the two states, Chandigarh was due to be incorporated into Punjab on 26 January 1986, but the transfer was postponed.
[3] Figures refer only to the Indian-held part of the territory.
[4] Mizoram was granted statehood in February 1987.
[5] Goa was granted statehood in May 1987. Daman and Diu remain a Union Territory.

Source: *Census of India*, 2001.

PRINCIPAL TOWNS
(provisional population at 2001 census*)

Greater Mumbai (Bombay)	11,914,398	Ranchi	846,454
Delhi	9,817,439	Jodhpur	846,408
Kolkata (Calcutta)	4,580,544	Gwalior	826,919
Bangalore	4,292,223	Vijayawada (Vijayavada)	825,436
Chennai (Madras)	4,216,268	Chandigarh	808,796
Ahmedabad	3,515,361	Guwahati	808,021
Hyderabad	3,449,878	Hubli-Dharwar	786,018
Pune (Poona)	2,540,069	Tiruchirapalli	746,062
Kanpur (Cawnpore)	2,532,138	Thiruvananthapuram (Trivandrum)	744,739
Surat	2,433,787	Mysore	742,261
Jaipur (Jeypore)	2,324,319	Jalandhar	701,223
Lucknow	2,207,340	Bareilly	699,839
Nagpur	2,051,320	Kota	695,899
Indore	1,597,441	Salem	693,236
Bhopal	1,433,875	Aligarh	667,732
Ludhiana	1,395,053	Bhubaneswar	647,302
Patna	1,376,950	Moradabad	641,240
Vadodara (Baroda)	1,306,035	Gorakhpur	624,570
Thane (Thana)	1,261,517	Raipur	605,131
Agra	1,259,979	Kochi (Cochin)	596,473
Kalyan	1,193,266	Jamshedpur	570,349
Varanasi (Banaras)	1,100,748	Bhilai Nagar	553,837
Nashik	1,076,967	Amravati	549,370
Meerut	1,074,229	Cuttack	535,139
Faridabad Complex	1,054,981	Bikaner	529,007
Haora (Howrah)	1,008,704	Warangal	528,570
Pimpri-Chinchwad	1,006,417	Guntur	514,707
Allahabad	990,298	Bhavnagar	510,958
Amritsar	975,695	Durgapur	492,996
Visakhapatnam (Vizag)	969,608	Ajmer	485,197
Ghaziabad	968,521	Kolhapur	485,183
Rajkot	966,642	Ulhasnagar	472,943
Jabalpur (Jubbulpore)	951,469	Saharanpur	452,925
Coimbatore	923,085	Jamnagar	447,734
Madurai	922,913	Bhatpara	441,957
Srinagar	894,940	Kozhikode (Calicut)	436,527
Solapur	873,037	Ujjain	429,933
Aurangabad	872,667	Bokaro Steel City	394,173
		Jhansi	383,248
		Rajahmundry	313,347

* Figures refer to the city proper in each case.

Capital: New Delhi, provisional population 294,783 at 2001 census.

Provisional population of principal urban agglomerations at 2001 census: Greater Mumbai (Bombay) 16,368,084; Kolkata (Calcutta) 13,216,546; Delhi 12,791,458; Chennai (Madras) 6,424,624; Bangalore 5,686,844; Hyderabad 5,533,640; Ahmedabad 4,519,278; Pune (Poona) 3,755,525; Surat 2,811,466; Kanpur 2,690,486; Jaipur (Jeypore) 2,324,319; Lucknow 2,266,933; Nagpur 2,122,965; Patna 1,707,429; Indore 1,639,044; Vadodara (Baroda) 1,492,398; Bhopal 1,454,830; Coimbatore 1,446,034; Ludhiana 1,395,053; Kochi (Cochin) 1,355,406; Visakhapatnam (Vizag) 1,329,472; Agra 1,321,410; Varanasi (Banaras) 1,211,749; Madurai 1,194,665; Meerut 1,167,399; Nashik 1,152,048; Jabalpur (Jubbulpore) 1,117,200; Jamshedpur 1,101,804; Asansol 1,090,171; Dhanbad 1,064,357; Faridabad 1,054,981; Allahabad 1,049,579; Amritsar 1,011,327; Vijayawada (Vijayavada) 1,011,152; Rajkot 1,002,160.

BIRTHS AND DEATHS
(estimates, based on Sample Registration Scheme)

	1998	1999	2000
Birth rate (per 1,000)	26.5	26.0	25.8
Death rate (per 1,000)	8.5	8.6	8.5

Expectation of life (WHO estimates, years at birth): 60.8 (males 60.0; females 64.4) in 2001 (Source: WHO, *World Health Report*).

ECONOMICALLY ACTIVE POPULATION
(persons aged five years and over, 1991 census, excluding Jammu and Kashmir)

	Males	Females	Total
Agriculture, hunting, forestry and fishing	139,361,719	51,979,110	191,340,829
Mining and quarrying	1,536,919	214,356	1,751,275
Manufacturing	23,969,433	4,702,046	28,671,479
Construction	5,122,468	420,737	5,543,205
Trade and commerce	19,862,725	1,433,612	21,296,337
Transport, storage and communications	7,810,126	207,620	8,017,746
Other services	23,995,194	5,316,428	29,311,622
Total employed	221,658,584	64,273,909	285,932,493
Marginal workers	2,705,223	25,493,654	28,198,877
Total labour force	224,363,807	89,767,563	314,131,370

Unemployment (work applicants at 31 December, '000 persons aged 14 years and over): 40,371 (males 30,438; females 9,933) in 1999; 41,344 (males 30,887; females 10,457) in 2000; 41,996 (males 31,111; females 10,885) in 2001 (Source: ILO).

2001 census (provisional): Main workers 313,173,394 (males 240,520,672, females 72,652,722); Marginal workers 89,338,796 (males 34,943,064, females 54,395,732); Total 402,512,190 (males 275,463,736, females 127,048,454).

Health and Welfare

KEY INDICATORS

Total fertility rate (children per woman, 2001)	3.1
Under-5 mortality rate (per 1,000 live births, 2001)	93
HIV/AIDS (% of persons aged 15–49, 2001)	0.79
Physicians (per 1,000 head, 1999)	0.52
Hospital beds (per 1,000 head, 1999)	0.92
Health expenditure (2000): US $ per head (PPP)	71.0
Health expenditure (2000): % of GDP	4.9
Health expenditure (2000): public (% of total)	17.8
Access to water (% of persons, 2000)	88
Access to sanitation (% of persons, 2000)	31
Human Development Index (2000): ranking	124
Human Development Index (2000): value	0.577

For sources and definitions, see explanatory note on p. vi.

Agriculture

PRINCIPAL CROPS

('000 metric tons, year ending 30 June)

	1998/99	1999/2000	2000/01
Rice (milled)	86,080	89,680	84,870
Sorghum (Jowar)	8,410	8,690	7,720
Cat-tail millet (Bajra)	6,950	5,780	7,060
Maize	11,150	11,510	12,070
Finger millet (Ragi)	2,610	2,290	2,740
Small millets	670	620	600
Wheat	71,290	76,370	68,760
Barley	1,540	1,450	1,430
Total cereals	188,700	196,390	185,250
Chick-peas (Gram)	6,800	5,120	3,520
Pigeon-peas (Tur)	2,710	2,690	2,260
Dry beans, dry peas, lentils and other pulses	5,700	5,600	4,890
Total food grains	203,910	209,800	195,920
Groundnuts (in shell)	8,980	5,250	6,220
Sesame seed	530	480	590
Rapeseed and mustard	5,660	5,790	4,210
Linseed	270	240	190
Castor beans	840	770	870
Total edible oil seeds (incl. others)	24,750	20,710	18,400
Cotton lint*	12,290	11,530	9,650
Jute†	8,840	9,420	9,250
Kenaf (Mesta)†	970	1,130	1,230
Tea (made)	850	816	827
Sugar cane: production gur	28,870	29,930	29,920
Sugar cane: production cane	288,720	299,320	299,210
Tobacco (leaves)	700	609	600
Potatoes	22,490	24,700	22,100

* Production in '000 bales of 170 kg each.
† Production in '000 bales of 180 kg each.

2001/02 (provisional figures): Rice 90,750; Wheat 73,530; Pulses 13,790; Total food grains 211,170; Total edible oil seeds 21,160; Cotton lint 11,300; Jute 9,370; Sugar cane 289,410.

Sources: Directorate of Economics and Statistics, Ministry of Agriculture and Ministry of Commerce (for tea).

LIVESTOCK

('000 head, year ending September)

	1999	2000	2001
Cattle*	214,877	218,800	219,642
Sheep	57,600*	57,900*	58,200†
Goats	122,530*	123,000*	123,500†
Pigs†	16,500	17,000	17,500
Horses†	800	800	800
Asses†	1,000	1,000	1,000
Mules†	200	200	200
Buffaloes*	92,090	93,772	94,132
Camels†	1,030	1,030	1,030
Chickens†	388,000	399,000	413,400

* Unofficial figure(s).
† FAO estimate(s).

Source: FAO.

LIVESTOCK PRODUCTS

('000 metric tons)

	1999	2000	2001
Beef and veal*	1,421.4	1,442.0	1,462.6
Buffalo meat*	1,410.4	1,421.4	1,426.9
Mutton and lamb*	228.0	229.2	230.4
Goat meat*	466	467	469
Pig meat*	560.0	577.5	595.0
Poultry meat*	558.9	575.1	595.4
Cows' milk†	32,800	34,000	35,000
Buffaloes' milk†	43,000	44,600	45,800
Goats' milk†	3,120	3,240	3,320
Butter†	296	330	500
Ghee†	1,464	1,630	1,750
Hen eggs†	1,732.5	1,783.0	1,905.8
Wool: greasy	46.5	47.6	47.6*
Wool: scoured	31.2†	31.9†	31.9*
Cattle and buffalo hides (fresh)*	954	971	976
Sheepskins (fresh)*	51.8	52.1	52.4
Goatskins (fresh)*	127.8	128.3	128.9

* FAO estimate(s).
† Unofficial figure(s).

Source: FAO.

Forestry

ROUNDWOOD REMOVALS

('000 cubic metres, excl. bark)

	1998	1999	2000
Sawlogs, veneer logs and logs for sleepers*†	18,350	18,350	18,350
Pulpwood	450	817	397
Other industrial wood	118	134	107
Fuel wood*‡	277,380	277,380	277,380
Total	296,298	296,681	296,234

* FAO estimates.
† Output assumed to be unchanged since 1985.
‡ Output assumed to be unchanged since 1996.

Source: FAO.

SAWNWOOD PRODUCTION

('000 cubic metres, incl. railway sleepers)

	1998	1999	2000
Coniferous sawnwood	1,200	1,200	1,100
Broadleaved sawnwood	7,200	7,200	6,800
Total	8,400	8,400	7,900

Source: FAO.

Fishing

('000 metric tons, live weight)

	1998	1999	2000
Capture	3,373.5	3,472.2	3,594.4
Bombay-duck (Bummalo)	179.9	181.8	169.0
Croakers and drums	275.2	317.8	285.9
Indian oil-sardine (sardinella)	173.4	147.7	168.3
Indian mackerel	184.4	179.4	170.7
Aquaculture	1,902.2	2,120.3	2,095.1
Roho labeo	468.0	515.6	567.4
Mrigal carp	426.2	469.7	516.9
Catla	450.4	496.3	546.2
Total catch	5,275.7	5,592.5	5,689.5

Source: FAO, *Yearbook of Fishery Statistics*.

Mining

('000 metric tons, unless otherwise indicated)

	1999/2000	2000/01	2001/02*
Coal	304,103	333,696	327,644
Lignite	22,124	22,947	23,503
Iron ore†	77,604	80,762	83,367
Manganese ore†	1,586	1,595	1,553
Bauxite	7,054	7,993	8,585
Chalk (Fireclay)	407	441	368
Kaolin (China clay)	816	871	808
Dolomite	2,842	3,078	3,088
Gypsum	3,247	2,644	2,888
Limestone	128,762	127,202	129,771
Crude petroleum	31,949	32,426	32,037
Sea salt‡	15,585	13,584	18,496
Chromium ore†	1,738	1,972	1,811
Phosphorite	1,192	1,351	1,057
Kyanite	6	5	4
Magnesite	326	318	280
Steatite	557	596	549
Copper ore†	3,085	3,498	3,497
Lead concentrates†	63	54	52
Zinc concentrates†	360	366	399
Mica—crude (metric tons)	1,807	1,154	1,266
Gold (kilograms)	2,586	2,615	2,759
Diamonds (carats)	40,956	57,407	81,448
Natural gas (million cu m)§	26,885	27,860	27,863

* Provisional figures.

† Figures refer to gross weight. The estimated metal content is: Iron 63%; Manganese 40%; Chromium 30%; Copper 1.2%; Lead 70%; Zinc 60%.

‡ Unofficial figures.

§ Figures refer to gas utilized.

Source: Indian Bureau of Mines.

Industry

SELECTED PRODUCTS

('000 metric tons, unless otherwise indicated)

	1999/2000	2000/01	2001/02
Refined sugar*	17,470	19,250	18,496
Cotton cloth (million sq metres)	18,989	19,718	19,440
Jute manufactures	1,591	1,625	1,400
Paper and paper board	3,459	3,090	4,930
Soda ash	1,515	1,631	1,541
Fertilizers	14,286	14,770	16,964
Petroleum products	79,900	96,600	n.a.
Cement	100,400	99,500	106,491
Pig-iron (saleable)	3,184	3,063	3,836
Finished steel	27,200	29,300	n.a.
Aluminium (metric tons)	497,900	620,400	549,310
Diesel engines—stationary (number)	348,300	306,000	n.a.
Sewing machines (number)	59,800	48,800	76,982
Television receivers (number)	2,561,600	2,335,100	1,990,400
Electric fans (number)	5,800,000	8,080,000	8,940,000
Passenger cars and multipurpose vehicles (number)	699,200	632,200	573,146
Commercial vehicles (number)	173,469	152,000	146,314
Motorcycles, mopeds and scooters (number)	3,722,000	3,755,000	4,324,631
Bicycles (number)	13,733,000	14,974,000	12,925,600

* Figures relate to crop year (beginning November) and are in respect of cane sugar only.

Finance

CURRENCY AND EXCHANGE RATES

Monetary Units

100 paise (singular: paisa) = 1 Indian rupee

Sterling, Dollar and Euro Equivalents (31 December 2002)

£1 sterling = 77.41 rupees

US $1 = 48.03 rupees

€1 = 50.37 rupees

1,000 Indian rupees = £12.92 = $20.482 = €19.85

Average Exchange Rate (rupees per US $)

2000   44.942

2001   47.186

2002   48.610

UNION BUDGET

(million rupees, rounded, year ending 31 March)

Revenue	2001/02*	2002/03†	2003/04‡
Tax revenue (net)	1,336,620	1,641,770	1,841,690
Customs receipts	402,683	455,000	493,500
Union excise duties	725,554	873,830	967,910
Corporation tax	366,091	447,000	514,990
Other taxes on income	320,041	373,000	440,700
Other taxes and duties	56,233	70,349	98,172
Less States' share of tax revenue	528,415	561,412	637,577
Less Surcharge transferred to National Calamity Contingency Fund	5,566	16,000	36,000
Other current revenue	677,868	727,590	697,660
Interest receipts (net)	355,154	405,710	391,596
Dividends and profits	172,891	201,939	178,611
Receipts of Union Territories	5,210	5,234	5,462
External grants	17,516	9,818	14,610
Other receipts (net)	127,097	104,890	107,377
Recoveries of loans (net)	164,035	182,508	180,231
Disinvestment of equity in public-sector enterprises	36,460	33,600	132,000
Total	2,214,983	2,585,468	2,851,581

Expenditure	2001/02*	2002/03†	2003/04‡
Central Ministries/Departments	3,198,147	3,563,790	3,880,059
Agriculture and Co-operation	22,172	20,670	25,683
Fertilizers	135,434	123,116	131,427
Defence	650,825	668,822	769,326
Economic Affairs	1,253,963	1,356,162	1,496,140
Food and Public Distribution	177,581	243,563	280,628
Home Affairs	104,104	116,422	121,391
Education and Literacy	80,203	90,365	98,612
Rural Development	105,841	151,951	102,893
Road Transport and Highways	72,418	70,209	80,313
State Plans	397,105	443,560	474,584
Union Territories	29,276	32,782	33,308
Total	3,624,528	4,040,133	4,387,951
Current§	3,016,111	3,416,482	3,662,267
Capital	608,418	623,651	725,683

* Provisional figures.

† Revised estimates.

‡ Forecasts.

§ Including interest payments (million rupees): 1,074,602 in 2001/02; 1,156,634 in 2002/03; 1,232,231 in 2003/04.

Source: Government of India, Union Budget 2003/04.

INTERNATIONAL RESERVES

(US $ million at 31 December)

	2000	2001	2002
Gold*	2,252	2,329	2,712
IMF special drawing rights	2	5	7
Reserve position in IMF	637	614	665
Foreign exchange	37,264	45,251	66,994
Total	40,154	48,199	70,377

* National valuation (9,153 rupees per ounce in 2000; 9,756 rupees per ounce in 2001; 11,325 rupees per ounce in 2002).

Source: IMF, *International Financial Statistics*.

MONEY SUPPLY

(million rupees, last Friday of year ending 31 March)

	1999/2000	2000/01	2001/02
Currency with the public . . .	1,890,820	2,095,500	2,414,000
Demand deposits with banks . .	1,496,810	1,662,700	1,782,840
Other deposits with Reserve Bank	30,330	36,290	28,500
Total money	3,417,960	3,794,490	4,225,340

Source: Reserve Bank of India.

COST OF LIVING

(Consumer Price Index for Industrial Workers; base: 1990 = 100)

	1999	2000	2001
Food (incl. beverages) . . .	232.5	236.6	241.9
Fuel and light	205.6	241.7	263.9
Clothing (incl. footwear). . .	199.3	207.9	210.5
Rent	236.3	250.5	273.6
All items (incl. others) . . .	228.0	237.1	246.2

Source: ILO.

NATIONAL ACCOUNTS

('000 million rupees at current prices, year ending 31 March)

National Income and Product

	1998/99	1999/2000	2000/01
Domestic factor incomes* . . .	14,494.2	15,732.1	16,974.0
Consumption of fixed capital . .	1,666.1	1,824.3	1,984.4
Gross domestic product at factor cost	16,160.3	17,556.4	18,958.4
Indirect taxes . . . . . }			
Less Subsidies . . . . . }	1,422.4	1,740.0	1,921.5
GDP in purchasers' values .	17,582.8	19,296.4	20,879.9
Factor income from abroad . . }			
Less Factor income paid abroad }	−149.7	−154.3	−174.1
Gross national product . .	17,433.1	19,142.1	20,705.7
Less Consumption of fixed capital	1,666.1	1,824.3	1,984.4
National income in market prices	15,767.0	17,317.8	18,721.3
Other current transfers from abroad	434.9	532.8	587.6
Less Other current transfers paid abroad.	2.5	1.5	3.4
National disposable income .	16,199.4	17,849.2	19,305.4

* Compensation of employees and the operating surplus of enterprises.

Expenditure on the Gross Domestic Product

	1998/99	1999/2000	2000/01*
Government final consumption expenditure.	2,117.7	2,481.3	2,759.0
Private final consumption expenditure.	11,359.3	12,614.5	13,395.9
Increase in stocks	−11.9	322.2	212.2
Gross fixed capital formation . .	3,732.1	4,169.4	4,569.8
Total domestic expenditure. .	17,197.2	19,587.4	20,936.9
Exports of goods and services . .	1,952.8	2,277.0	2,901.8
Less Imports of goods and services	2,247.4	2,657.0	3,060.9
Statistical discrepancy . . .	680.2	89.1	102.1
GDP in purchasers' values . .	17,582.8	19,296.4	20,879.9

* Estimates.

Gross Domestic Product by Economic Activity

(at current factor cost)

	1998/99	1999/2000	2000/01*
Agriculture	1,232.4	4,214.0	4,300.9
Forestry and logging. . . .	185.7	189.6	195.4
Fishing	180.8	201.9	223.5
Mining and quarrying . . .	351.1	405.2	446.5
Manufacturing	2,517.9	2,668.9	2,997.5
Electricity, gas and water supply	424.8	438.9	495.3
Construction	919.2	1,054.4	1,164.3
Trade, hotels and restaurants . .	2,247.3	2,415.4	2,612.9
Transport, storage and communications	1,113.1	1,241.9	1,383.3
Banking and insurance . . .	958.1	1,190.8	1,165.5
Real estate and business services .	857.6	1,014.9	1,201.0
Public administration and defence	992.9	1,153.0	1,246.2
Other services	1,179.3	1,367.6	1,526.1
Total	16,160.3	17,556.4	18,958.4

* Provisional estimates.

BALANCE OF PAYMENTS

(US $ million)

	1998	1999	2000
Exports of goods f.o.b. . . .	34,076	36,877	43,132
Imports of goods f.o.b. . . .	−44,828	−45,556	−55,325
Trade balance	−10,752	−8,679	−12,193
Exports of services	11,691	14,509	18,331
Imports of services	−14,540	−17,271	−19,913
Balance on goods and services .	−13,601	−11,441	−13,775
Other income received . . .	1,806	1,919	2,280
Other income paid	−5,443	−5,629	−6,156
Balance on goods, services and income	−17,238	−15,151	−17,651
Current transfers received . . .	10,402	11,958	13,504
Current transfers paid	−67	−35	−51
Current balance	−6,903	−3,228	−4,198
Direct investment abroad . . .	−48	−79	−335
Direct investment from abroad. .	2,635	2,169	2,315
Portfolio investment liabilities . .	−601	2,317	1,619
Other investment assets . . .	−3,239	−450	−1,136
Other investment liabilities . .	9,837	5,623	7,152
Net errors and omissions . . .	1,390	313	670
Overall balance	3,071	6,664	6,087

Source: IMF, *International Financial Statistics*.

OFFICIAL DEVELOPMENT ASSISTANCE

(US $ million)

	1998	1999	2000
Bilateral donors	896.4	826.7	638.7
Multilateral donors	713.2	664.6	848.5
Total	1,609.6	1,491.3	1,487.2
Grants	802.6	772.2	775.3
Loans	807.0	719.1	711.9
Per caput assistance (US $) . .	1.7	1.5	1.5

Source: UN, *Statistical Yearbook for Asia and the Pacific*.

External Trade

PRINCIPAL COMMODITIES
(million rupees, year ending 31 March)

Imports c.i.f.	1999/2000	2000/01	2001/02
Animal and vegetable oil, fats and waxes	84,693	64,671	70,800
Mineral fuels, mineral oils and products of their distillation . .	621,833	801,539	752,185
Organic chemicals	75,640	73,080	87,951
Natural or cultured pearls, precious and semi-precious stones, precious metals and articles thereof; imitation jewellery; coin	443,802	443,476	445,992
Nuclear reactors, boilers, machinery, mechanical appliances and parts thereof. .	168,059	193,557	202,652
Electrical machinery and equipment and parts thereof; sound and television apparatus .	99,229	122,326	151,747
Total (incl. others)	2,155,284	2,308,728	2,451,997

Exports f.o.b.	1999/2000	2000/01	2001/02
Fish, crustaceans and molluscs	50,436	62,878	58,072
Mineral fuels, mineral oils and products of their distillation . .	3,938	88,216	104,109
Organic chemicals	59,321	79,023	76,739
Cotton	94,608	110,019	95,100
Natural or cultured pearls, precious and semi-precious stones, precious metals and articles thereof; imitation jewellery; coin	328,620	339,321	350,056
Nuclear reactors, boilers, machinery, mechanical appliances and parts thereof. .	43,118	65,251	74,910
Total (incl. others)	1,595,618	2,035,710	2,090,180

Source: Ministry of Commerce and Industry.

PRINCIPAL TRADING PARTNERS
(million rupees, year ending 31 March)

Imports c.i.f.	1999/2000	2000/01	2001/02
Australia	46,875	48,551	62,290
Belgium	159,520	131,116	131,773
Canada	16,488	18,140	25,250
China, People's Republic . . .	55,591	68,626	97,119
France	30,845	29,275	40,264
Germany	79,775	80,386	96,724
Hong Kong	35,442	38,928	34,761
Indonesia	41,326	41,584	49,448
Iran	47,209	9,650	13,536
Israel	25,217	19,758	20,400
Italy	31,804	33,056	33,612
Japan	109,883	84,159	102,368
Korea, Republic	47,857	40,831	54,434
Kuwait	56,796	5,147	3,514
Malaysia	84,473	53,761	54,060
Nigeria	126,895	2,914	4,155
Russia	27,004	23,649	25,539
Saudi Arabia	104,832	28,375	22,128
Singapore	50,279	66,878	62,194
South Africa	87,347	46,685	68,719
Switzerland	112,566	144,369	136,912
United Arab Emirates	86,806	30,105	43,642
United Kingdom	117,109	144,725	122,244
USA	154,274	137,739	150,211
Total (incl. others). . . .	2,155,284	2,308,728	2,451,997

Exports f.o.b.	1999/2000	2000/01	2001/02
Australia	17,475	18,542	19,936
Bangladesh	27,573	42,717	47,796
Belgium	59,264	67,181	66,321
Canada	25,058	29,991	27,891
China, People's Republic . . .	23,358	37,978	45,400
Egypt	10,257	16,331	22,069
France	38,884	46,599	45,069
Germany	75,329	87,146	85,290
Hong Kong	108,803	120,646	112,856
Indonesia	14,108	18,262	25,454
Israel	21,653	21,576	20,413
Italy	48,522	59,790	57,542
Japan	73,032	81,980	72,036
Korea, Republic	20,651	20,593	22,481
Malaysia	19,373	27,783	36,899
Netherlands	38,383	40,207	41,201
Nigeria	12,727	17,573	26,857
Russia	41,076	40,614	38,067
Saudi Arabia	32,174	37,595	39,414
Singapore	29,150	40,070	46,371
Spain	23,744	30,437	32,297
Sri Lanka	21,635	29,245	30,088
Thailand.	19,482	24,218	30,195
United Arab Emirates. . . .	90,250	118,666	118,838
United Kingdom	88,173	105,015	103,056
USA	363,804	425,099	406,018
Total (incl. others).	1,595,618	2,035,710	2,090,180

Source: Ministry of Commerce and Industry.

Transport

RAILWAYS
(million, year ending 31 March)

	1999/2000	2000/01	2001/02
Passengers	4,585	4,833	5,145
Passenger-km.	430,666	457,022	497,651
Freight (metric tons)	478.2	504.2	492.5
Freight (metric ton-km)	308,039	315,516	331,800

Source: Railway Board, Ministry of Railways.

ROAD TRAFFIC
('000 motor vehicles in use at 31 March)

	1998	1999	2000*
Private cars, jeeps and taxis . .	5,138	5,556	6,042
Buses and coaches	538	540	559
Goods vehicles	2,536	2,554	2,681
Motorcycles and scooters . . .	28,642	31,328	33,913
Others	4,514	4,897	5,198
Total	41,368	44,875	48,393

* Provisional figures.

Source: Transport Research Division, Ministry of Surface Transport.

SHIPPING

Merchant Fleet
(registered at 31 December)

	1999	2000	2001
Vessels.	971	987	1,018
Displacement ('000 grt)	6,914.8	6,662.1	6,688.2

Source: Lloyd's Register-Fairplay, *World Fleet Statistics*.

International Sea-borne Traffic
(year ending 31 March)

	1998/99	1999/2000	2000/01
Vessels ('000 nrt)*:			
Entered	48,512	60,850	55,466
Cleared	39,031	41,187	38,043
Freight ('000 metric tons)†:			
Loaded	101,247	110,301	135,331
Unloaded	186,797	225,049	233,007

* Excluding minor and intermediate ports.
† Including bunkers.

Sources: Transport Research Division, Ministry of Surface Transport;
Directorate General of Commercial Intelligence and Statistics.

CIVIL AVIATION
(traffic)

	1999/2000	2000/01	2001/02
Kilometres flown ('000)	193,417	202,955	221,521
Passenger-km ('000)	24,623,528	26,215,657	24,787,619
Freight ton-km ('000)	532,611	548,994	505,227
Mail ton-km ('000)	33,838	33,241	34,773

Source: Directorate General of Civil Aviation.

Tourism

FOREIGN VISITORS BY COUNTRY OF ORIGIN*

	1999	2000	2001
Australia	73,041	53,995	52,691
Canada	82,892	84,013	88,600
CIS	34,620	35,988	24,831
France	85,891	100,022	102,434
Germany	85,033	83,881	80,011
Italy	50,677	50,419	41,351
Japan	79,373	98,159	80,634
Malaysia	52,613	60,513	57,869
Netherlands	48,826	46,370	42,368
Singapore	53,310	46,612	42,824
Sri Lanka	120,072	129,193	112,813
United Kingdom	345,085	432,624	405,472
USA	251,925	348,292	329,147
Total (incl. others)	2,024,131	2,180,039	2,053,208

* Figures exclude nationals of Bangladesh and Pakistan. Including these,
the total was 2,481,928 in 1999, 2,649,378 in 2000 and 2,537,282 in 2001.

Source: Ministry of Tourism.

Receipts from tourism (million rupees): 129,510 in 1999; 142,380 in
2000; 143,440 in 2001.

Communications Media

	1998	1999	2000
Television receivers ('000 in use) .	70,000	75,000	79,000
Telephones ('000 main lines in use)	21,593.7	26,511.3	32,436.1
Mobile cellular telephones ('000 in use)	1,195.4	1,195.4	3,577.1
Personal computers ('000 in use)	2,700	3,300	4,600
Internet users ('000)	1,400	2,800	5,000
Daily newspapers	4,890	5,157	5,364
Non-daily newspapers and other periodicals	n.a.	41,161	43,781

1997: Radio receivers ('000 in use) 116,000; Facsimile machines ('000 in
use, year ending 31 March) 100.

2001: Telephones ('000 main lines in use) 34,732.1; Mobile cellular telephones ('000 in use) 5,725.2; Internet users ('000) 7,000.

Sources: International Telecommunication Union; UN, *Statistical Yearbook*; Register of Newspapers for India; Ministry of Information and
Broadcasting.

Education

(2000/01*)

	Institutions	Teachers	Students
Primary	638,738	1,896,791	113,826,978
Middle	206,269	1,326,652	42,810,005
Secondary (high school) . . .	87,675	1,005,845	18,992,698
Higher secondary (new pattern)	33,741	755,798	7,429,219
Intermediate/pre-degree/junior college	4,631		2,422,072

* Provisional figures.

Source: Planning, Monitoring and Statistics Division, Ministry of Human
Resource Development.

Adult literacy rate (UNESCO estimates): 57.2% (males 68.4%; females
45.4%) in 2000 (Source: UN Human Development Programme, *Human
Development Report*).

Directory

The Constitution

The Constitution of India, adopted by the Constituent Assembly on
26 November 1949, was inaugurated on 26 January 1950. The
Preamble declares that the People of India solemnly resolve to
constitute a Sovereign Democratic Republic and to secure to all its
citizens justice, liberty, equality and fraternity. There are 397
articles and nine schedules, which form a comprehensive document.

UNION OF STATES

The Union of India comprises 28 states, six Union Territories and
one National Capital Territory. There are provisions for the formation and admission of new states.

The Constitution confers citizenship on a threefold basis of birth,
descent, and residence. Provisions are made for refugees who have
migrated from Pakistan and for persons of Indian origin residing
abroad.

FUNDAMENTAL RIGHTS AND DIRECTIVE PRINCIPLES

The rights of the citizen contained in Part III of the Constitution are
declared fundamental and enforceable in law. 'Untouchability' is
abolished and its practice in any form is a punishable offence. The
Directive Principles of State Policy provide a code intended to ensure
promotion of the economic, social and educational welfare of the
State in future legislation.

THE PRESIDENT

The President is the head of the Union, exercising all executive
powers on the advice of the Council of Ministers responsible to
Parliament. He is elected by an electoral college consisting of elected
members of both Houses of Parliament and the Legislatures of the
States. The President holds office for a term of five years and is
eligible for re-election. He may be impeached for violation of the
Constitution. The Vice-President is the ex officio Chairman of the
Rajya Sabha and is elected by a joint sitting of both Houses of
Parliament.

THE PARLIAMENT

The Parliament of the Union consists of the President and two
Houses: the Rajya Sabha (Council of States) and the Lok Sabha
(House of the People). The Rajya Sabha consists of 245 members, of
whom a number are nominated by the President. One-third of its

members retire every two years. Elections are indirect, each state's legislative quota being elected by the members of the state's legislative assembly. The Lok Sabha has 543 members elected by adult franchise; not more than 13 represent the Union Territories and National Capital Territory. Two members are nominated by the President to represent the Anglo-Indian community.

GOVERNMENT OF THE STATES

The governmental machinery of states closely resembles that of the Union. Each of these states has a governor at its head appointed by the President for a term of five years to exercise executive power on the advice of a council of ministers. The states' legislatures consist of the Governor and either one house (legislative assembly) or two houses (legislative assembly and legislative council). The term of the assembly is five years, but the council is not subject to dissolution.

LANGUAGE

The Constitution provides that the official language of the Union shall be Hindi. (The English language will continue to be an associate language for many official purposes.)

LEGISLATION—FEDERAL SYSTEM

The Constitution provides that bills, other than money bills, can be introduced in either House. To become law, they must be passed by both Houses and receive the assent of the President. In financial affairs, the authority of the Lower House is final. The various subjects of legislation are enumerated on three lists in the seventh schedule of the Constitution: the Union List, containing nearly 100 entries, including external affairs, defence, communications and atomic energy; the State List, containing 65 entries, including local government, police, public health, education; and the Concurrent List, with over 40 entries, including criminal law, marriage and divorce, labour welfare. The Constitution vests residuary authority in the Centre. All matters not enumerated in the Concurrent or State Lists will be deemed to be included in the Union List, and in the event of conflict between Union and State Law on any subject enumerated in the Concurrent List the Union Law will prevail. In time of emergency Parliament may even exercise powers otherwise exclusively vested in the states. Under Article 356, 'If the President on receipt of a report from the government of a state or otherwise is satisfied that a situation has arisen in which the Government of the state cannot be carried on in accordance with the provisions of this Constitution, the President may by Proclamation: (a) assume to himself all or any of the functions of the government of the state and all or any of the powers of the governor or any body or authority in the state other than the Legislature of the state; (b) declare that the powers of the Legislature of the state shall be exercisable by or under the authority of Parliament; (c) make such incidental provisions as appear to the President to be necessary': provided that none of the powers of a High Court be assumed by the President or suspended in any way. Unless such a Proclamation is approved by both Houses of Parliament, it ceases to operate after two months. A Proclamation so approved ceases to operate after six months, unless renewed by Parliament. Its renewal cannot be extended beyond a total period of three years. An independent judiciary exists to define and interpret the Constitution and to resolve constitutional disputes arising between states, or between a state and the Government of India.

OTHER PROVISIONS

Other Provisions of the Constitution deal with the administration of tribal areas, relations between the Union and states, inter-state trade and finance.

AMENDMENTS

The Constitution is flexible in character, and a simple process of amendment has been adopted. For amendment of provisions concerning the Supreme Courts and the High Courts, the distribution of legislative powers between the Union and the states, the representation of the states in Parliament, etc., the amendment must be passed by both Houses of Parliament and must further be ratified by the legislatures of not less than half the states. In other cases no reference to the state legislatures is necessary.

Numerous amendments were adopted in August 1975, following the declaration of a state of emergency in June. The Constitution (39th Amendment) Bill laid down that the President's reasons for proclaiming an emergency may not be challenged in any court. Under the Constitution (40th Amendment) Bill, 38 existing laws may not be challenged before any court on the ground of violation of fundamental rights. Thus detainees under the Maintenance of Internal Security Act could not be told the grounds of their detention and were forbidden bail and any claim to liberty through natural or common law. The Constitution (41st Amendment) Bill provided that the President, Prime Minister and state Governors should be immune from criminal prosecution for life and from civil prosecution during their term of office.

In November 1976 a 59-clause Constitution (42nd Amendment) Bill was approved by Parliament and came into force in January 1977. Some of the provisions of the Bill are that the Indian Democratic Republic shall be named a 'Democratic Secular and Socialist Republic'; that the President 'shall act in accordance with' the advice given to him by the Prime Minister and the Council of Ministers, and, acting at the Prime Minister's direction, shall be empowered for two years to amend the Constitution by executive order, in any way beneficial to the enforcement of the whole; that the term of the Lok Sabha and of the State Assemblies shall be extended from five to six years; that there shall be no limitation on the constituent power of Parliament to amend the Constitution, and that India's Supreme Court shall be barred from hearing petitions challenging constitutional amendments; that strikes shall be forbidden in the public services and the Union Government have the power to deploy police or other forces under its own superintendence and control in any state. Directive Principles are given precedence over Fundamental Rights: 10 basic duties of citizens are listed, including the duty to 'defend the country and render national service when called upon to do so'.

The Janata Party Government, which came into power in March 1977, promised to amend the Constitution during the year, so as to 'restore the balance between the people and Parliament, Parliament and the judiciary, the judiciary and the executive, the states and the centre, and the citizen and the Government that the founding fathers of the Constitution had worked out'. The Constitution (43rd Amendment) Bill, passed by Parliament in December 1977, the Constitution (44th Amendment) Bill, passed by Parliament in December 1977 and later redesignated the 43rd Amendment, and the Constitution (45th Amendment) Bill, passed by Parliament in December 1978 and later redesignated the 44th Amendment, reversed most of the changes enacted by the Constitution (42nd Amendment) Bill. The 44th Amendment is particularly detailed on emergency provisions: An emergency may not be proclaimed unless 'the security of India or any part of its territory was threatened by war or external aggression or by armed rebellion.' Its introduction must be approved by a two-thirds majority of Parliament within a month, and after six months the emergency may be continued only with the approval of Parliament. Among the provisions left unchanged after these Bills were a section subordinating Fundamental Rights to Directive Principles and a clause empowering the central Government to deploy armed forces under its control in any state without the state government's consent. In May 1980 the Indian Supreme Court repealed sections 4 and 55 of the 42nd Amendment Act, thus curtailing Parliament's power to enforce directive principles and to amend the Constitution. The death penalty was declared constitutionally valid.

The 53rd Amendment to the Constitution, approved by Parliament in August 1986, granted statehood to the Union Territory of Mizoram; the 55th Amendment, approved in December 1986, granted statehood to the Union Territory of Arunachal Pradesh; and the 57th Amendment, approved in May 1987, granted statehood to the Union Territory of Goa (Daman and Diu remain, however, as a Union Territory). The 59th Amendment, approved in March 1988, empowered the Government to impose a state of emergency in Punjab, on the grounds of internal disturbances. In December 1988 the minimum voting age was lowered from 21 to 18 years. The 71st Amendment, approved in August 1992, gave official language status to Nepali, Konkani and Manipuri. In August 2000 legislation to permit the establishment of three new states, Chhattisgarh, Jharkhand and Uttaranchal, was approved by Parliament. The 93rd amendment, approved in May 2002, ensured free and compulsory education for children from the age of six to 14.

THE PANCHAYAT RAJ SCHEME

This scheme is designed to decentralize the powers of the Union and State Governments. It is based on the Panchayat (Village Council) and the Gram Sabha (Village Parliament) and envisages the gradual transference of local government from state to local authority. Revenue and internal security will remain state responsibilities at present. By 1978 the scheme had been introduced in all the states except Meghalaya, Nagaland and 23 out of 31 districts in Bihar. The Panchayat operated in all the Union Territories except Lakshadweep, Mizoram (which became India's 23rd state in February 1987) and Pondicherry. The 72nd Amendment, approved in late 1992, provided for direct elections to the Panchayats, members of which were to have a tenure of five years.

The Government

President: Aavul Pakkiri Jainulabidin Abdul Kalam (sworn in 25 July 2002).

Vice-President: Bhairon Singh Shekhawat (sworn in 19 August 2002).

COUNCIL OF MINISTERS
(April 2003)

A coalition of the Bharatiya Janata Party (BJP), the Biju Janata Dal (BJD), the Dravida Munnetra Kazhagam (DMK), the Shiv Sena (SS), the Shiromani Akali Dal (SAD), Jammu and Kashmir National Conference, the Marumalarchi Dravida Munnetra Kazhagam (MDMK), the Janata Dal (United) (JD—U), the Samata Party (SP), the Rashtriya Lok Dal (RLD), the All India Trinamool Congress, the Pattali Makkal Katchi and Independents (Ind.).

Prime Minister*: ATAL BIHARI VAJPAYEE (BJP).

Deputy Prime Minister and Minister of Home Affairs, and of Personnel, Public Grievances and Pensions: LAL KRISHNA ADVANI (BJP).

Minister of External Affairs: YASHWANT SINHA (BJP).

Minister of Finance and Company Affairs: JASWANT SINGH (BJP).

Minister of Defence: GEORGE FERNANDES (SP).

Minister of Health and Family Welfare and of Parliamentary Affairs: SUSHMA SWARAJ (BJP).

Minister of Tourism and Culture: JAGMOHAN (BJP).

Minister of Agriculture: AJIT SINGH (RLD).

Minister of Environment and Forests: T. R. BAALU (DMK).

Minister of Urban Development and Poverty Alleviation: ANANTH KUMAR (BJP).

Minister of Labour: SAHIB SINGH VERMA (BJP).

Minister of Human Resource Development, of Ocean Development and of Science and Technology: Dr MURLI MANOHAR JOSHI (BJP).

Minister of Small-scale Industries and of Development of the North-Eastern Region: Dr C. P. THAKUR (BJP).

Minister of Law and Justice and of Commerce and Industry: ARUN JAITLEY (BJP).

Minister of Power: ANANT GANGARAM GEETE (SS).

Minister of Communications and Information Technology and of Disinvestment: ARUN SHOURIE (BJP).

Minister of Petroleum and Natural Gas: RAM NAIK (BJP).

Minister of Tribal Affairs: JUEL ORAM (BJP).

Minister of Social Justice and Empowerment: Dr SATYA NARAYAN JATIYA (BJP).

Minister of Shipping: SHATRUGHAN SINHA (BJP).

Minister of Rural Development: SHANTA KUMAR (BJP).

Minister of Chemicals and Fertilizers: SUKHDEV SINGH DHINDSA (SAD).

Minister of Textiles: KASHIRAM RANA (BJP).

Minister of Consumer Affairs, and Food and Public Distribution: SHARAD YADAV (JD—U).

Minister of Civil Aviation: SYED SHAHNAWAZ HUSSAIN (BJP).

Minister of Water Resources: ARJUN CHARAN SETHI (BJP).

Minister of Youth Affairs and Sports: VIKRAM VERMA (BJP).

Minister of Railways: NITISH KUMAR (SP).

Minister of Coal: KARIYA MUNDA (BJP).

Minister of Heavy Industries and Public Enterprises: BALASAHEB VIKHE PATIL (SS).

Minister without portfolio: MURASOLI MARAN (DMK).

Ministers of State with Independent Charge

Minister of State for Road Transport and Highways: Maj.-Gen. B. C. KHANDURI (BJP).

Minister of State for Mines: RAMESH BAIS (BJP).

Minister of State for Non-Conventional Energy Sources: M. KANNAPAN (MDMK).

Minister of State for Steel: B. K. TRIPATHY (BJD).

Minister of State for Information and Broadcasting: RAVI SHANKAR PRASAD (BJP).

Minister of State for Food-Processing Industries: N. T. SHANMUGHAM (PMK).

Minister of State for Agro and Rural Industries: SANGH PRIYA GAUTAM (BJP).

There are, in addition, 41 Ministers of State without independent charge.

* The Prime Minister is also in charge of ministries and departments not allotted to others.

MINISTRIES

President's Office: Rashtrapati Bhavan, New Delhi 110 004; tel. (11) 23015321; fax (11) 23017290; internet www.goidirectory.nic.in.

Vice-President's Office: 6 Maulana Azad Rd, New Delhi 110 011; tel. (11) 23016344; fax (11) 23018124.

Prime Minister's Office: South Block, New Delhi 110 011; tel. (11) 23013040; fax (11) 23016857; internet www.pmindia.nic.in.

Ministry of Agriculture: Krishi Bhavan, Dr Rajendra Prasad Rd, New Delhi 110 001; tel. (11) 23382651; fax (11) 23386004.

Ministry of Atomic Energy: South Block, New Delhi 110 011; tel. (11) 23011773; fax (11) 23013843.

Ministry of Chemicals and Fertilizers: Shastri Bhavan, New Delhi 110 001; tel. (11) 23387892; fax (11) 23386222.

Ministry of Civil Aviation: Rajiv Gandhi Bhavan, Safdarjung Airport, New Delhi 110 023; tel. (11) 24610358; fax (11) 24610354; e-mail web@civilav.delhi.nic.in; internet www.civilaviation.nic.in.

Ministry of Coal and Mines: Shram Shakti Bhavan, Rafi Marg, New Delhi 110 001; tel. (11) 23384777; fax (11) 23387738; e-mail secy.moc@sb.nic.in; internet www.coal.nic.in.

Ministry of Commerce and Industry: Udyog Bhavan, New Delhi 110 011; tel. (11) 23016664; fax (11) 23014335; internet www .commin.nic.in.

Ministry of Communications and Information Technology: Sanchar Bhavan, 20 Asoka Rd, New Delhi 110 001; tel. (11) 23719898; fax (11) 23782344; e-mail ddgir@sancharnet.in; internet www.moc.gov.in.

Ministry of Consumer Affairs, Food and Public Distribution: Krishi Bhavan, New Delhi 110 001; tel. (11) 23384882; fax (11) 23388302; internet www.fcamin.nic.in.

Ministry of Defence: South Block, New Delhi 110 011; tel. (11) 23012380; internet www.mod.nic.in.

Ministry of Disinvestment: Public Enterprises Bhavan, Block 14, CGO Complex, Lodi Rd, New Delhi 110 003; tel. (11) 24368040; fax (11) 24368043.

Ministry of Electronics: Electronics Niketan, 6 CGO Complex, New Delhi 110 003; tel. (11) 24364041; fax (11) 24363134.

Ministry of Environment and Forests: Paryavaran Bhavan, CGO Complex Phase II, Lodi Rd, New Delhi 110 003; tel. (11) 24360721; fax (11) 24360678; e-mail secy@menf.delhi.nic.in; internet www.envfor.nic.in.

Ministry of External Affairs: South Block, New Delhi 110 011; tel. (11) 23012318; fax (11) 23010700; internet www.meadev.inc.in.

Ministry of Finance and Company Affairs: North Block, New Delhi 110 001; tel. (11) 23092611; fax (11) 23012477; e-mail jsdea@ finance.delhi.nic.in; internet www.finmin.nic.in.

Ministry of Food-Processing Industries: Panchsheel Bhavan, Khelgaon Marg, New Delhi 110 049; tel. (11) 26493225; fax (11) 26493228.

Ministry of Health and Family Welfare: Nirman Bhavan, New Delhi 110 011; tel. (11) 23018863; fax (11) 23014252; e-mail secyhlth@mohfw.delhi.nic.in; internet www.mohfw.nic.in.

Ministry of Heavy Industries and Public Enterprises: Udyog Bhavan, New Delhi 110 011; tel. (11) 23012433; fax (11) 23011770.

Ministry of Home Affairs: North Block, New Delhi 110 001; tel. (11) 23092989; fax (11) 23095750; e-mail mhaweb@mhant.delhi.nic .in; internet www.mha.nic.in.

Ministry of Human Resource Development: Shastri Bhavan, New Delhi 110 001; tel. (11) 23386995; fax (11) 23384093.

Ministry of Information and Broadcasting: Shastri Bhavan, New Delhi 110 001; tel. (11) 23382639; fax (11) 23383513; internet www.mib.nic.in.

Ministry of Labour: Shram Shakti Bhavan, Rafi Marg, New Delhi 110 001; tel. (11) 23710265; fax (11) 23711708; e-mail labour@lisd .delhi.nic.in; internet www.labour.nic.in.

Ministry of Law and Justice: Shastri Bhavan, Dr Rajendra Prasad Rd, New Delhi 110 001; tel. (11) 23384777; fax (11) 23387259; e-mail lawmin@caselaw.delhi.nic.in; internet www.nic .in/lawmin/.

Ministry of Non-Conventional Energy Sources: Block 14, CGO Complex, Lodi Rd, New Delhi 110 003; tel. (11) 24361481; fax (11) 24361298; e-mail secymnes@ren02.nic.in; internet www.mnes.nic .in.

Ministry of Ocean Development: Block 12, CGO Complex, Lodi Rd, New Delhi 110 003; tel. (11) 24360874; fax (11) 24360779.

Ministry of Parliamentary Affairs: Parliament House, New Delhi 110 001; tel. (11) 23017663; fax (11) 23017726; e-mail parlmin@sansad.nic.in; internet www.mpa.nic.in.

Ministry of Personnel, Public Grievances and Pensions: North Block, New Delhi 110 001; tel. (11) 23094848; fax (11) 23092432; e-mail pgweb@arpg.delhi.nic.in; internet www.persmin.nic.in.

Ministry of Petroleum and Natural Gas: Shastri Bhavan, New Delhi 110 001; tel. (11) 23383501; fax (11) 23384787; e-mail dspdi.png@sb.nic.in; internet www.petroleum.nic.in.

Ministry of Power: Shram Shakti Bhavan, New Delhi 110 001; tel. (11) 23710271; fax (11) 23717519; internet www.powermin.nic.in.

Ministry of Railways: Rail Bhavan, Raisina Rd, New Delhi 110 001; tel. (11) 23384010; fax (11) 23384481; e-mail crb@del2.vsnl.net.in; internet www.indianrailway.com.

Ministry of Road Transport and Highways: Parivahan Bhavan, 1 Sansad Marg, New Delhi 110 001; tel. (11) 23714104; fax (11) 23714324; internet www.nic.in/most.

Ministry of Rural Development: Krishi Bhavan, New Delhi 110 001; tel. (11) 3384467; fax (11) 3782502; e-mail arunbhat@rural.delhi.nic.in; internet www.rural.nic.in.

Ministry of Science and Technology: Technology Bhavan, New Mehrauli Rd, New Delhi 110 016; tel. (11) 26511439; fax (11) 26863847; internet www.mst.nic.in.

Ministry of Small-scale Industries and Agro and Rural Industries: Udyog Bhavan, New Delhi, 110 011; tel. (11) 23012107; internet www.ssi.nic.in.

Ministry of Social Justice and Empowerment: Shastri Bhavan, Dr Rajendra Prasad Rd, New Delhi 110 001; tel. (11) 23382683; fax (11) 23384918; e-mail secywel@sb.nic.in; internet www.socialjustice.nic.in.

Ministry of Statistics and Programme Implementation: Sardar Patel Bhavan, Patel Chowk, New Delhi 110 001; tel. (11) 23742150; fax (11) 23742067; e-mail moscc@bol.net.in; internet mospi.nic.in.

Ministry of Steel: Udyog Bhavan, New Delhi 110 011; tel. (11) 23015489; fax (11) 23013236; e-mail dvs@ub.nic.in; internet www.nic.in/steel.

Ministry of Textiles: Udyog Bhavan, New Delhi 110 011; tel. (11) 23011769; fax (11) 23013711; e-mail textiles@ub.delhi.nic.in; internet www.texmin.nic.in.

Ministry of Tourism and Culture: Transport Bhavan, Parliament St, New Delhi 110 001; tel. (11) 23711792; fax (11) 23710518.

Ministry of Tribal Affairs: Rm 212.D, Shastri Bhavan, New Delhi; tel. (11) 23381652; e-mail dirtdb.wel@sb.nic.in; internet www.tribal.nic.in.

Ministry of Urban Development and Poverty Alleviation: Nirman Bhavan, New Delhi 110 011; tel. (11) 23019377; fax (11) 23014459; e-mail secyurban@alpha.nic.in; internet www.urbanindia.nic.in.

Ministry of Water Resources: Shram Shakti Bhavan, Rafi Marg, New Delhi 110 001; tel. (11) 23710305; fax (11) 23710253; internet www.wrmin.nic.in.

Ministry of Youth Affairs and Sports: Shastri Bhavan, Dr Rajendra Prasad Rd, New Delhi 110 001; tel. (11) 23382897; fax (11) 23387418; internet www.yas.nic.in.

Legislature

PARLIAMENT

Rajya Sabha
(Council of States)

Most of the members of the Rajya Sabha are indirectly elected by the State Assemblies for six years, with one-third retiring every two years. The remaining members are nominated by the President.

Chairman: BHAIRON SINGH SHEKHAWAT.

Deputy Chairman: NAJMA HEPPTULLAH.

Distribution of Seats, January 2003

Party	Seats
Congress*	61
Janata Dal	2
Communist Party of India—Marxist	13
Telugu Desam	13
Bharatiya Janata Party	45
Samajwadi Party	11
Rashtriya Janata Dal	8
Dravida Munnetra Kazhagam	8
Shiromani Akali Dal	4
Biju Janata Dal	4
Tamil Maanila Congress	2
Nationalist Congress Party	3
Samata Party	2
Muslim League	2
All-India Anna Dravida Munnetra Kazhagam	9
Communist Party of India	5
Jammu and Kashmir National Conference	1
Shiv Sena	5
Bahujan Samaj Party	5
Revolutionary Socialist Party	3
Indian National Lok Dal	4
Independents and others	24
Nominated	11
Total	**245**

* Formerly known as the Congress (Indira) Party, or Congress (I); name gradually changed to the Congress Party in the early to mid-1990s.

Lok Sabha
(House of the People)

Speaker: MANOHAR JOSHI.

General Election, 5, 11, 18 and 25 September and 3 October 1999

Party	Seats
National Democratic Alliance	299
Bharatiya Janata Party	182
Dravida Munnetra Kazhagam	12
Marumalarchi Dravida Munnetra Kazhagam	4
Pattali Makkal Katchi	5
Janata Dal (United)	20
Shiv Sena	15
Shiromani Akali Dal	2
Indian National League	4
Himachal Vikash Congress	1
Telugu Desam	29
Biju Janata Dal	10
All India Trinamool Congress	8
Sikkim Democratic Front	1
Manipur State Congress Party	1
Jammu and Kashmir National Conference	4
M.G.R. Anna D.M. Kazhagam	1
Congress and allies	134
Congress	112
Rashtriya Janata Dal	7
All-India Anna Dravida Munnetra Kazhagam	10
Muslim League Kerala State Committee	2
Rashtriya Lok Dal	2
Kerala Congress (M)	1
Bahujan Samaj Party	14
Communist Party of India	4
Communist Party of India—Marxist	32
Samajwadi Party	26
Nationalist Congress Party	7
Revolutionary Socialist Party	3
Asom Gana Parishad	1
Peasants' and Workers' Party of India	1
Janata Dal (Secular)	1
Independents and others	20
Nominated	2*
Vacant	1
Total	**545**

* Nominated by the President to represent the Anglo-Indian community.

State Governments

(April 2003)

ANDHRA PRADESH
(Capital—Hyderabad)

Governor: SURJIT SINGH BARNALA.

Chief Minister: N. CHANDRABABU NAIDU (Telugu Desam).

Legislative Assembly: 294 seats (Telugu Desam 180, Congress 90, Communist—CPI—M 2, Bharatiya Janata Party 12, independents and others 9, vacant 1).

ARUNACHAL PRADESH
(Capital—Itanagar)

Governor: ARVIND DAVE.

Chief Minister: MUKUT MITHI (Congress).

Legislative Assembly: 60 seats (Congress 53, Nationalist Congress Party 4, Arunachal Congress 1, independents 2).

ASSAM
(Capital—Dispur)

Governor: Lt-Gen. (retd) S. K. SINHA.

Chief Minister: TARUN GOGOI (Congress).

Legislative Assembly: 126 seats (Congress 70, Asom Gana Parishad 21, Bharatiya Janata Party 8, Nationalist Congress Party 3, All-India Trinamool Congress 1, independents and others 23).

BIHAR
(Capital—Patna)

Governor: VINOD CHANDRA PANDE.

Chief Minister: RABRI DEVI (Rashtriya Janata Dal).

Legislative Assembly: 243 seats (Rashtriya Janata Dal 114, Bharatiya Janata Party 35, Congress 12, Samata Party 29, Janata Dal—United 18, Bahujan Samaj Party 5, Communist—CPI 6, Communist—CPI—M 2, Communist—Marxist-Leninist (Liberation) 6, independents and others 16).

Legislative Council: 96 seats.

CHHATTISGARH
(Capital—Raipur)

Governor: DINESH NANDAN SAHAYA.

Chief Minister: AJIT JOGI (Congress).

Legislative Assembly: 90 seats (Congress 62, Bharatiya Janata Party 23, Bahujan Samaj Party 3, others 2).

GOA
(Capital—Panaji)

Governor: KIDAR NATH SAHANI.

Chief Minister: MANOHAR PARRIKAR (Bharatiya Janata Party).

Legislative Assembly: 40 seats (Bharatiya Janata Party 17, Congress 16, United Goans Democratic Party 3, Maharashtrawadi Gomantak Party 2, others 2).

GUJARAT
(Capital—Gandhinagar)

Governor: SUNDAR SINGH BHANDARI.

Chief Minister: NARENDRA MODI (Bharatiya Janata Party).

Legislative Assembly: 182 seats (Bharatiya Janata Party 127, Congress 51, Janata Dal—United 2, independents 2).

HARYANA
(Capital—Chandigarh)

Governor: BABU PARMANAND.

Chief Minister: OM PRAKASH CHAUTALA (Indian National Lok Dal).

Legislative Assembly: 90 seats (Congress 21, Indian National Lok Dal 46, Haryana Vikas Party 2, Bharatiya Janata Party 6, National Congress Party 1, Republican Party of India 1, Bahujan Samaj Party 1, independents and others 12).

HIMACHAL PRADESH
(Capital—Shimla)

Governor: SURAJ BHAN.

Chief Minister: VIRBHADRA SINGH (Congress).

JAMMU AND KASHMIR
(Capitals—(Summer) Srinagar, (Winter) Jammu)

Governor: GIRISH CHANDRA SAXENA.

Chief Minister: MUFTI MOHAMMED SAYEED (People's Democratic Party).

Legislative Assembly: 87 seats (Jammu and Kashmir National Conference 28, Congress 21, People's Democratic Party 15, Panther's Party 4, Communist Party of India—CPI—M 2, independents and others 17).

Legislative Council: 36 seats.

JHARKHAND
(Capital—Ranchi)

Governor: M. RAMA JOIS.

Chief Minister: BABULAL MARANDI (Bharatiya Janata Party).

Legislative Assembly: 81 seats (Bharatiya Janata Party 32, Congress 11, Jharkhand Mukti Morcha 12, Rashtriya Janata Dal 9, Samata Party 4, Janata Dal—United 4, others 9).

KARNATAKA
(Capital—Bangalore)

Governor: T. N. CHATURVEDI.

Chief Minister: SOMANAHALLI MALLIAM KRISHNA (Congress).

Legislative Assembly: 224 seats (Congress 132, Bharatiya Janata Party 44, Janata Dal—Secular 19, Janata Dal—United 9, independents and others 20).

Legislative Council: 75 seats.

KERALA
(Capital—Thiruvananthapuram)

Governor: SIKANDER BAKHT.

Chief Minister: A. K. ANTHONY (Congress).

Legislative Assembly: 140 seats (Congress 63, Communist—CPI—M 23, Muslim League 16, Kerala Congress (M) 9, Communist—CPI 7, Janata Dal—Secular 3, Nationalist Congress Party 2, Kerala Congress 2, Kerala Congress (Joseph) 2, Revolutionary Socialist Party 2, independents and others 11).

MADHYA PRADESH
(Capital—Bhopal)

Governor: Dr BHAI MAHAVIR.

Chief Minister: DIGVIJAY SINGH (Congress).

Legislative Assembly: 230 seats (Congress 126, Bharatiya Janata Party 80, Bahujan Samaj Party 9, Samajwadi Party 4, independents and others 11).

MAHARASHTRA
(Capital—Mumbai)

Governor: MOHAMMAD FAZAL.

Chief Minister: SUSHIL KUMAR SHINDE (Congress).

Legislative Assembly: 288 seats (Congress 75, Shiv Sena 69, Nationalist Congress Party 58, Bharatiya Janata Party 56, Janata Dal—Secular 2, Peasants' and Workers' Party 5, Bharatiya Bahujan Mahasangh 3, Communist—CPI—M 2, Samajwadi Party 2, independents and others 16).

Legislative Council: 78 seats.

MANIPUR
(Capital—Imphal)

Governor: VED PRAKASH MARWAH.

Chief Minister: OKRAM IBOBI SINGH (Congress).

Legislative Assembly: 60 seats (Congress 20, Federal Party of Manipur 13, Manipur State Congress Party 7, Communist—CPI 5, Bharatiya Janata Party 4, Nationalist Congress Party 3, Samata Party 3, Manipur People's Party 2, others 3).

MEGHALAYA
(Capital—Shillong)

Governor: M. M. JACOB.

Chief Minister: D. D. LEPANG (Congress).

Legislative Assembly: 60 seats (Congress 22, Nationalist Congress Party 14, United Democratic Party 9, Bharatiya Janata Party 2, Meghalaya Democratic Party 4, Khun Hynniewtrep National Awakening Party 2, independents 5, vacant 2).

MIZORAM
(Capital—Aizawl)

Governor: AMOLAK RATTAN KOHLI.

Chief Minister: ZORAMTHANGA (Mizo National Front).

Legislative Assembly: 40 seats (Mizo National Front 21, Congress 6, Mizo People's Conference 12, others 1).

NAGALAND
(Capital—Kohima)

Governor: SHYAMAL DUTTA.

Chief Minister: NEIPHU RIO (Democratic Alliance of Nagaland).

Legislative Assembly: 60 seats (Congress 21, Nagaland People's Front 19, Bharatiya Janata Party 7, National Democratic Movement 4, Janata Dal—U 2, Samata Party 1, independents 4, vacant 2).

ORISSA
(Capital—Bhubaneswar)

Governor: M. M. RAJENDRAN.

Chief Minister: NAVEEN PATNAIK (Biju Janata Dal).

Legislative Assembly: 147 seats (Biju Janata Dal 68, Bharatiya Janata Party 38, Congress 26, Jharkhand Mukti Morcha 3, Communist—CPI 1, Communist—CPI—M 1, Janata Dal—Secular 1, All India Trinamool Congress 1, independents 8).

PUNJAB
(Capital—Chandigarh)

Governor: Lt-Gen. (retd) J. F. R. JACOB.

Chief Minister: AMARINDER SINGH (Congress).

Legislative Assembly: 117 seats (Congress 63, Shiromani Akali Dal 41, Bharatiya Janata Party 3, independents and others 10).

RAJASTHAN
(Capital—Jaipur)

Governor: ANSHUMAN SINGH.

Chief Minister: ASHOK GEHLOT (Congress).

Legislative Assembly: 200 seats (Congress 150, Bharatiya Janata Party 36, Janata Dal 3, Communist—CPI—M 1, Bahujan Samaj Party 2, independents and others 8).

SIKKIM
(Capital—Gangtok)

Governor: V. RAMA RAO.

Chief Minister: PAWAN KUMAR CHAMLING (Sikkim Democratic Front).

Legislative Assembly: 32 seats (Sikkim Democratic Front 25, Sikkim Sangram Parishad 7).

TAMIL NADU
(Capital—Chennai)

Governor: P. S. RAMAMOHAN RAO.

Chief Minister: JAYARAM JAYALALITHA (All-India Anna Dravida Munnetra Kazhagam).

Legislative Assembly: 234 seats (All-India Anna Dravida Munnetra Kazhagam 132, Dravida Munnetra Kazhagam 27, Tamil Maanila Congress 23, Pattali Makkal Katchi 20, Congress 7, Communist—CPI—M 6, Communist—CPI 5, Bharatiya Janata Party 4, All India Forward Bloc 1, independents and others 9).

TRIPURA
(Capital—Agartala)

Governor: Lt-Gen. (retd) K. M. SETH.

Chief Minister: MANIK SARKAR (Communist—CPI—M).

Legislative Assembly: 60 seats (Communist—CPI—M 37, Congress 12, Revolutionary Socialist Party 2, Communist—CPI 1, independents 7, vacant 1).

UTTARANCHAL
(Capital—Dehradun)

Governor: SUDARSHAN AGARWAL.

Chief Minister: NARAIN DUTT TIWARI (Congress).

Legislative Assembly: 70 seats (Congress 36, Bharatiya Janata Party 19, Bahujan Samaj Party 7, independents and others 8).

UTTAR PRADESH
(Capital—Lucknow)

Governor: VISHNU KANT SHASTRI.

Chief Minister: Ms MAYAWATI (Bahujan Samaj Party).

Legislative Assembly: 403 seats (Samajwadi Party 143, Bahujan Samaj Party 99, Bharatiya Janata Party 88, Congress 25, Rashtriya Lok Dal 14, Rashtriya Kranti Party 4, Communist—CPI—M 2, Janata Dal—United 2, independents and others 26).

Legislative Council: 108 seats.

WEST BENGAL
(Capital—Kolkata)

Governor: VIREN J. SHAH.

Chief Minister: BUDDHADEV BHATTACHARYA (Communist—CPI—M).

Legislative Assembly: 294 seats (Communist—CPI—M 143, All India Trinamool Congress 60, Congress 26, All India Forward Bloc 25, Revolutionary Socialist Party 17, Communist—CPI 7, independents and others 16).

UNION TERRITORIES

Andaman and Nicobar Islands (Headquarters—Port Blair): Lt-Gov. NAGENDRA NATH JHA.

Chandigarh (Headquarters—Chandigarh): Administrator Lt. Gen (retd) J. F. R. JACOB.

Chandigarh was to be incorporated into Punjab state on 26 January 1986, but the transfer was postponed indefinitely.

Dadra and Nagar Haveli (Headquarters—Silvassa): Administrator O. P. KELKAR.

Daman and Diu (Headquarters—Daman): Administrator O. P. KELKAR.

Lakshadweep (Headquarters—Kavaratti): Administrator K. S. MEHRA.

Pondicherry (Capital—Pondicherry): Lt-Gov. K. R. MALKANI; Chief Minister N. RANGASAMY (Congress).

Assembly: 30 seats (Congress 13, DMK 12, AIADMK 3, Tamil Maanila Congress 2).

NATIONAL CAPITAL TERRITORY

Delhi (Headquarters—Delhi): Lt-Gov. VIJAY KUMAR KAPOOR; Chief Minister SHEILA DIXIT (Congress).

Assembly: 70 seats (Congress 52, Bharatiya Janata Party 15, Janata Dal 1, independents 2).

Political Organizations

MAJOR NATIONAL POLITICAL ORGANIZATIONS

All India Congress Committee: 24 Akbar Rd, New Delhi 110 011; tel. (11) 23019080; fax (11) 23017047; internet www.indiancongress .org; f. 1978 as Indian National Congress (I), as a breakaway group under Indira Gandhi; name of party gradually changed to Indian National Congress or Congress Party in the early to mid-1990s; merged with Tamil Maanila Congress in 2002; Pres. SONIA GANDHI; Gen. Secs MOHSINA KIDWAI, KAMAL NATH, MUKUL WASNIK, MOTILAL VORA, OSCAR FERNANDES, VYLAR RAVI; 35m. mems (1998).

Bahujan Samaj Party (Majority Society Party): c/o Lok Sabha, New Delhi; promotes the rights of the *Harijans*('Untouchables') of India; Leader KANSHI RAM; Gen. Sec. Ms MAYAWATI.

Bharatiya Janata Party (BJP) (Indian People's Party): 11 Ashok Rd, New Delhi 110 001; tel. (11) 23382234; fax (11) 23782163; e-mail bjpco@del3.vsnl.net.in; internet www.bjp.org; f. 1980 as a breakaway group from Janata Party; radical right-wing Hindu party; Pres. K. M. VENKAIAH NAIDU; Gen. Secs RAJNATH SINGH, PRAMOD MAHAJAN, MUKHTAR ABBAS NAQVI, SANJAY JOSHI, ANITA ARYA; 10.5m. mems.

Communist Party of India (CPI): Ajoy Bhavan, Kotla Marg, New Delhi 110 002; tel. (11) 23235546; fax (11) 23235543; e-mail cpi@vsnl .com; internet www.cpofindia.org; f. 1925; advocates the establishment of a socialist society led by the working class, and ultimately of a communist society; nine-mem. central secretariat; Gen. Sec. ARDHENDU BHUSHAN BARDHAN; 555,010 mems (2000).

Communist Party of India—Marxist (CPI—M): A. K. Gopalan Bhavan, 27–29 Bhai Vir Singh Marg, New Delhi 110 001; tel. (11)

23344918; fax (11) 23747483; e-mail cpim@vsnl.com; internet www
.cpim.org; f. 1964 as breakaway group from the CPI; maintained an
independent position; managed by a central committee of 77 mems
and a politburo of 17 mems; Leaders BUDDHADEV BHATTACHARYA, JYOTI
BASU, E. K. NAYANAR, PRAKASH KARAT, SITARAM YECHURY, SOMNATH
CHATTERJEE; Gen. Sec. HARKISHAN SINGH SURJEET; 814,408 mems
(2002).

Janata Dal (People's Party): 7 Jantar Mantar Rd, New Delhi 110
001; tel. (11) 23368833; fax (11) 23368138; f. 1988 as a merger of
parties within the Rashtriya Morcha; advocates non-alignment, the
eradication of poverty, unemployment and wide disparities in
wealth, and the protection of minorities; 136-mem. National Executive; Pres. SHARAD YADAV; Sec.-Gen. Dr BAPU KALDATE; split into two
factions in July 1999—Janata Dal (United), headed by Sharad
Yadav, and Janata Dal (Secular), headed by H. D. Deve Gowda.

Nationalist Congress Party (NCP): 10 Dr Bishambhar Das Marg,
New Delhi 110001; tel. (11) 23359218; fax (11) 23352112; f. 1999 as
breakaway faction of Congress; Pres. SHARAD PAWAR; Gen. Secs TARIQ
ANWAR, P. A. SANGMA, T. B. PEETHAMBARAN, Dr JAGANNATH MISHRA.

MAJOR REGIONAL POLITICAL ORGANIZATIONS

Akhil Bharat Hindu Mahasabha: Hindu Mahasabha Bhavan,
Mandir Marg, New Delhi 110 001; tel. (11) 23342087; fax (11)
23363105; f. 1915; seeks the establishment of a democratic Hindu
state; Pres. DINESH CHANDRA TYAGI; Gen. Sec. Dr MADANLAL GOYAL;
525,000 mems.

All-India Anna Dravida Munnetra Kazhagam (AIADMK) (All-
India Anna Dravidian Progressive Asscn): Lloyd's Rd, Chennai 600
004; f. 1972; breakaway group from the DMK; Chair. (vacant); Gen.
Sec. JAYARAM JAYALALITHA.

All India Forward Bloc: 28 Gurudwara Rakabganj Rd, New Delhi
110 001; tel. and fax (11) 23714131; e-mail dbiswas@sansad.nic.in; f.
1940 by Netaji Subhash Chandra Bose; socialist aims, including
nationalization of major industries, land reform and redistribution,
and the establishment of a union of socialist republics through
revolution; Gen. Sec. DEBABRATA BISWAS; 900,000 mems (1999).

All India Trinamool Congress: 125-D, Parliament House, New
Delhi 110 001; tel. (11) 23034355; internet www.trinamool.org;
Leader MAMATA BANERJEE.

Asom Gana Parishad (AGP) (Assam People's Council): Golaghat,
Assam; f. 1985; draws support from the All-Assam Gana Sangram
Parishad and the All-Assam Students' Union (Pres. Keshab
Mahanta; Gen. Sec. Atul Bora); advocates the unity of India in
diversity and a united Assam; Pres. BRINDABAN GOSWAMI; a break-
away faction formed a new central exec. committee under Pulakesh
Barua in April 1991.

Dravida Munnetra Kazhagam (DMK): Anna Arivalayam, Tey-
nampet, Chennai 600 018; f. 1949; aims at full autonomy for states
(primarily Tamil Nadu) within the Union, to establish regional
languages as state languages and English as the official language
pending the recognition of regional languages as official languages of
the Union; Pres. MUTHUVEL KARUNANIDHI; Gen. Sec. K. ANBAZHAGAN;
more than 4m. mems.

Indian National Lok Dal: c/o Rajya Sabha, New Delhi.

Jammu and Kashmir National Conference (JKNC): Mujahid
Manzil, Srinagar 190 002; tel. (194) 271500; fmrly All Jammu and
Kashmir National Conference; f. 1931; renamed 1939, reactivated
1975; state-based party campaigning for internal autonomy and
responsible self-govt; Pres. OMAR ABDULLAH; Gen. Sec. SHEIKH NAZIR
AHMAD; 1m. mems.

Jharkhand Mukti Morcha: c/o Rajya Sabha, New Delhi.

Pattali Makkal Katchi: Chennai; Leader Dr RAMADAS.

Peasants' and Workers' Party of India: Mahatma Phule Rd,
Naigaum, Mumbai 400 014; f. 1949; Marxist; seeks to nationalize all
basic industries, to promote industrialization, and to establish a
unitary state with provincial boundaries drawn on a linguistic basis;
Gen. Sec. DAJIBA DESAI; c. 10,000 mems.

Rashtriya Loktantrik Morcha (National Democratic Front): New
Delhi; f. 1998; Convenor MULAYAM SINGH YADAV; includes:

Rashtriya Janata Dal (RJD) (National People's Party): New
Delhi; f. 1997 as a breakaway group from Janata Dal; Leader
LALOO PRASAD YADAV.

Samajwadi Party (Socialist Party): New Delhi; f. 1991 by the
merger of the Janata Dal (S) and the Janata Party; Pres. MULAYAM
SINGH YADAV; Gen. Sec. AMAR SINGH.

Republican Party of India (RPI): Ensa Hutments, I Block, Azad
Maidan, Fort, Mumbai 400 001; tel. (22) 22621888; main aim is to
realize the aims and objects set out in the preamble to the 1950
Constitution; Pres. PRAKASH RAO AMBEDKAR; Gen. Sec. RAMDAS ATHA-
VALE; 100,000 mems.

Revolutionary Socialist Party: c/o Lok Sabha, New Delhi.

Samata Party: 220 VP House, Rafi Marg, New Delhi 110 001; tel.
(11) 23352280; fax (11) 23350349; f. 1994; Pres. GEORGE FERNANDES.

Shiromani Akali Dal: Baradan Shri Darbar Sahib, Amritsar; f.
1920; merged with Congress Party 1958–62; Sikh party composed of
several factions both moderate and militant; seeks the establishment of an autonomous Sikh state of 'Khalistan'; Pres. (Shiromani
Akali Dal—Badal) PRAKASH SINGH BADAL; Sec.-Gen. (Shiromani Akali
Dal—Badal) GURDEV SINGH DHINDSA.

Shiv Sena: Shiv Sena Bhavan, Ram Ganesh Gadkari Chowk,
Dadar, Mumbai 400 028; tel. (22) 24309128; e-mail senabhavan@
shivsena.org; internet www.shivsena.org; f. 1966; militant Hindu
group; Pres. BALASHAHEB 'BAL' THACKERAY.

Telugu Desam (Telugu Nation): 3-5-910, Himayatnagar, Hydera-
bad 500 029; tel. (842) 2237290; f. 1982; state-based party (Andhra
Pradesh); campaigns against rural poverty and social prejudice;
Pres. N. CHANDRABABU NAIDU; 8m. mems.

Diplomatic Representation

EMBASSIES AND HIGH COMMISSIONS IN INDIA

Afghanistan: 5/50F Shanti Path, Chanakyapuri, New Delhi 110
021; tel. (11) 26883602; fax (11) 26875439; e-mail mizanafghan@
yahoo.com; Ambassador MASOOD KHALILI.

Algeria: E-6/5 Vasant Vihar, New Delhi 110 057; tel. (11) 26146706;
fax (11) 26147033; e-mail abdbelar@yahoo.fr; Ambassador
ABDELKRIM BELARBI.

Angola: C-17, Malcha Marg, Chanakyapuri, New Delhi 110 021; tel.
(11) 26110701; fax (11) 26113512; e-mail xietuang@del2.vsnl.net.in;
internet www.angolaembassyindia.com; Ambassador ANA MARIA
TELES CARREIRA.

Argentina: B-2, Anand Niketan, New Delhi 110 021; tel. (11)
24104836; fax (11) 24104761; e-mail eindi@mantraonline.com;
Ambassador GERARDO BIRITOS.

Armenia: E-1/20, Vasant Vihar, New Delhi 110 057; tel. (11)
26147328; fax (11) 26147329; e-mail armemb@vsnl.com; Ambassador ARMEN BAIBOURTIAN.

Australia: 1/50-G Shanti Path, Chanakyapuri, New Delhi 110 021;
tel. (11) 26888223; fax (11) 26885199; internet www.ausgovindia
.com; High Commissioner PENNY WENSLEY.

Austria: EP–13 Chandragupta Marg, Chanakyapuri, New Delhi
110 021; tel. (11) 26889050; fax (11) 26886929; e-mail new-delhi-ob@
bmaa.gv.at; Ambassador Dr JUTTA STEFAN-BASTL.

Bangladesh: 56 Ring Rd, Lajpat Nagar-III, New Delhi 110 024; tel.
(11) 26834065; fax (11) 26839237; e-mail bdoot.del@smy.sprintrpg
.ems.vsnl.net.in; High Commissioner TUFAIL KARIM HAIDER.

Belarus: 163 Jor Bagh, New Delhi 110 003; tel. (11) 24694518; fax
(11) 24697029; e-mail india@belembassy.org; Ambassador ULADZIMIR
A. SAKALOVSKY.

Belgium: 50N, Shanti Path, Chanakyapuri, New Delhi 110 021; tel.
(11) 26889851; fax (11) 26885821; e-mail ambabel@del2.vsnl.net.in;
Ambassador GUY TROUVEROY.

Bhutan: Chandragupta Marg, Chanakyapuri, New Delhi 110 021;
tel. (11) 26889807; fax (11) 26876710; e-mail bhutan@vsnl.com;
Ambassador: Lyonpo DAGO TSHERING.

Bosnia and Herzegovina: C—7/9 Vasant Vihar, New Delhi 110
057; tel. (11) 26147415; fax (11) 26143042; Ambassador ZELJKO
JANJETOVIĆ.

Brazil: 8 Aurangzeb Rd, New Delhi 110 011; tel. (11) 23017301; fax
(11) 23793684; e-mail brasindi@vsnl.com; Ambassador VERA BAR-
ROUIN MACHADO.

Brunei: A-42 Vasant Marg, Vasant Vihar, New Delhi 110 057; tel.
(11) 26148340; fax (11) 26142101; e-mail suhtaindb@del3.vsnl.net
.in; High Commissioner Dato' PADUKA Haji ABDUL GHAFAR BIN Haji
ISMAIL.

Bulgaria: 16/17 Chandragupta Marg, Chanakyapuri, New Delhi
110 021; tel. (11) 26115550; fax (11) 26876190; e-mail bulemb@
mantraonline.com; internet www.bulgariaembindia.com; Chargé
d'affaires BORISLAV KOSTOV SUGAREV.

Burkina Faso: C-12, Anand Niketan, New Delhi 110 016; tel. (11)
24671678; fax (11) 24671745; e-mail emburnd@bol.net.in; Chargé
d'affaires GANDA MOISE ZARE.

Cambodia: N-14 Panchsheel Park, New Delhi 110 017; tel. (11)
26495092; fax (11) 26495093; e-mail camboemb@del2.vsnl.net.in;
Ambassador CHEANG ENG NGUON.

Canada: Shanti Path, Chanakyapuri, New Delhi 110 021; tel. (11) 26876500; fax (11) 26876579; e-mail domcan.delhi@delhi01.x400.gc.ca; High Commissioner PETER S. SUTHERLAND.

Chile: 146 Jorbagh, New Delhi 110 003; tel. (11) 24617123; fax (11) 24617102; e-mail embchile@vsnl.com; Ambassador MANUEL CÁRDENAS.

China, People's Republic: 50D Shanti Path, Chanakyapuri, New Delhi 110 021; tel. (11) 26112345; fax (11) 26881250; e-mail chinaemb@del3.vsnl.net.in; internet www.chinaembassy-india.com; Ambassador HUA JUN-DUO.

Colombia: 82D Malcha Marg, Chanakyapuri, New Delhi 110 021; tel. (11) 26110773; fax (11) 26112486; Ambassador MARÍA CLARA BETANCUR.

Congo, Democratic Republic: B-39 Soami Nagar, New Delhi 110 017; tel. (11) 26222796; fax (11) 26227226; Ambassador KITENGE NKUMBI KASONGO.

Croatia: A-15 West End, New Delhi 110 021; tel. (11) 26876871; fax (11) 26876873; e-mail croemnd@del1.vsnl.net.in; Chargé d'affaires JELICA KRISTO.

Cuba: 4 Munirka Marg, New Delhi 110 057; tel. (11) 26143849; fax (11) 26143806; e-mail embcuind@ndf.vsnl.net.in; Ambassador JOSÉ ELOY VALDES.

Cyprus: 106 Jor Bagh, New Delhi 110 003; tel. (11) 24697503; fax (11) 24628828; e-mail cyprus@del3.vsnl.net.in; internet www.cyprushcdelhi.com; High Commissioner ANDREAS G. SKARPARIS.

Czech Republic: 50M Niti Marg, Chanakyapuri, New Delhi 110 021; tel. (11) 26110205; fax (11) 26886221; e-mail newdelhi@embassy.mzv.cz; Ambassador JAROMÍR NOVOTNÝ.

Denmark: 11 Aurangzeb Rd, New Delhi 110 011; tel. (11) 23010900; fax (11) 23792019; e-mail denmark@vsnl.com; internet www.denmarkindia.com; Ambassador MICHAEL STERNBERG.

Egypt: 1/50M Niti Marg, Chanakyapuri, New Delhi 110 021; tel. (11) 26114096; fax (11) 26885355; e-mail egypt@del2.vsnl.net.in; Ambassador KHEIRELDIN ABDEL-LATIF MOHAMMED.

Ethiopia: 7/50G Satya Marg, Chanakyapuri, New Delhi 110 021; tel. (11) 26119513; fax (11) 26875731; e-mail delethem@bol.net.in; Ambassador Dr TEKETEL FORSSIDO.

Finland: E–3 Nyaya Marg, Chanakyapuri, New Delhi 110 021; tel. (11) 26115258; fax (11) 26886713; e-mail sanomat.NDE@formin.fi; internet www.finembindia.com; Ambassador GLEN LINDHOLM.

France: 2/50E Shanti Path, Chanakyapuri, New Delhi 110 021; tel. (11) 26118790; fax (11) 26872305; e-mail mef-delhi@tresor-dree.org; internet www.france-in-india.org; Ambassador FRANÇOIS GOLDBLATT.

Germany: 6 Block 50G, Shanti Path, Chanakyapuri, New Delhi 110 021; tel. (11) 26871831; fax (11) 26873117; e-mail germany@vsnl.com; internet www.germanembassy-india.org; Ambassador HEIMO RICHTER.

Ghana: 50-N Satya Marg, Chanakyapuri, New Delhi 110 021; tel. (11) 26883298; fax (11) 26883202; e-mail ghstarin@vsnl.net.in; High Commissioner Prof. MIKE OQUAYE.

Greece: 32 Dr S. Radhakrishnan Marg, Chanakyapuri, New Delhi 110 021; tel. (11) 26880700; fax (11) 26888010; e-mail hellemb@id.eth.net; internet www.greeceinindia.com; Ambassador EFSTATHIOS LOZOS.

Holy See: 50C Niti Marg, Chanakyapuri, New Delhi 110 021 (Apostolic Nunciature); tel. (11) 26889184; fax (11) 26874286; e-mail nuntius@bol.net.in; Pro-Nuncio Most Rev. PEDRO LÓPEZ QUINTANA (Titular Archbishop of Diocletiana).

Hungary: Plot 2, 50M Niti Marg, Chanakyapuri, New Delhi 110 021; tel. (11) 26114737; fax (11) 26886742; e-mail huembdel@giasdl01.vsnl.net.in; Ambassador LÁSZLÓ FODOR.

Indonesia: 50A Chanakyapuri, New Delhi 110 021; tel. (11) 26114100; fax (11) 26885460; e-mail iembassy@giasdl01.vsnl.net.in; Ambassador ZAKARIA SOEMIN TAATMADJA.

Iran: 5 Barakhamba Road, New Delhi 110 001; tel. (11) 23329600; fax (11) 23325493; e-mail iranemin@vsnl.com; Ambassador: Mir MAHMOUD-MOUSSAVI KHAMENEH.

Iraq: E-1/24, Vasant Vihar, New Delhi 110 057; tel. (11) 26149085; fax (11) 26149016; Chargé d'affaires ADDAY AL-SAKAB.

Ireland: 230 Jor Bagh, New Delhi 110 003; tel. (11) 24626733; fax (11) 24697053; e-mail ireland@ndf.vsnl.net.in; Ambassador PHILIP MCDONOGH.

Israel: 3 Aurangzeb Rd, New Delhi 110 011; tel. (11) 23013238; fax (11) 23014298; e-mail israelem@vsnl.com; Ambassador DAVID APHEK.

Italy: 50E Chandragupta Marg, Chanakyapuri, New Delhi 110 021; tel. (11) 26114355; fax (11) 26873889; e-mail italemb@del3.vsnl.net.in; internet www.italembdelhi.com; Ambassador BENEDETTO AMARI.

Japan: Plots 4–5, 50G Shanti Path, Chanakyapuri, New Delhi 110 021; tel. (11) 26876581; fax (11) 26885587; Ambassador AKIRA HAYASHI.

Jordan: 30 Golf Links, New Delhi 110 003; tel. (11) 24653318; fax (11) 24653353; e-mail jordemb@ndf.vsnl.net.in; Ambassador NABIL TALHOUNI.

Kazakhstan: 4 Olof Palme Marg, Vasant Vihar, New Delhi 110 057; tel. (11) 26144779; fax (11) 26144778; e-mail embaskaz@giasdl01.vsnl.net.in; Ambassador ASKAR O. SHAKIROV.

Kenya: 34 Paschimi Marg, New Delhi 110 057; tel. (11) 26146537; fax (11) 26146550; e-mail kenpedel@ndf.vsnl.net.in; High Commissioner L. O. AMAYO.

Korea, Democratic People's Republic: D-14 Maharani Bagh, New Delhi 110 065; tel. (11) 26829644; fax (11) 26829645; Ambassador JANG KWANG SON.

Korea, Republic: 9 Chandragupta Marg, Chanakyapuri, POB 5416, New Delhi 110 021; tel. (11) 26885412; fax (11) 26884840; e-mail embkorea@vsnl.com; Ambassador KWON SOON-TAE.

Kuwait: 5A Shanti Path, Chanakyapuri, New Delhi 110 021; tel. (11) 24100791; fax (11) 26873516; Ambassador ABDULLAH AHMED AL-MURAD.

Kyrgyzstan: C-93 Anand Niketan, New Delhi 110 021; tel. (11) 24108008; fax (11) 24108009; e-mail kyrghyz@netscape.net; Ambassador BAKTYBEK BESHIMOV.

Laos: A-104/7 Parmanand Estate, Maharani Bagh, New Delhi 110 065; tel. (11) 26933319; fax (11) 26323048; e-mail amlaodl@ndb.vsnl.net.in; Ambassador KHAMPASONG DOUANGSITHI.

Lebanon: 26–B Sardar Patel Marg, Chanakyapuri, New Delhi 110 021; tel. (11) 26111919; fax (11) 26111415; e-mail lebemb@vsnl.net.in; Ambassador Dr JEAN DANIEL.

Libya: 22 Golf Links, New Delhi 110 003; tel. (11) 24697717; fax (11) 24633005; e-mail libya@bol.net.in; Sec. of People's Bureau NURI EL-FITURI AL-MADANI.

Luxembourg: 730 Gadaipur Rd, Branch Post Office, Gadaipur, New Delhi 110 030; tel. (11) 26156663; fax (11) 26801971; e-mail paulsteinmetz@internet.lu; Ambassador PAUL STEINMETZ.

Malaysia: 50M Satya Marg, Chanakyapuri, New Delhi 110 021; tel. (11) 26111291; fax (11) 26881538; e-mail miondelhi@del2.vsnl.net.in; High Commissioner Dato' S. K. CHOO.

Mauritius: 41 Jesus and Mary Marg, Chanakyapuri, New Delhi 110 021; tel. (11) 24102161; fax (11) 24102194; e-mail mhcnd@bol.net.in; High Commissioner D. SEEWOO.

Mexico: 26–D Sardar Patel Marg, New Delhi 110 021; tel. (11) 24107182; fax (11) 24107185; e-mail embamexindia@mantraonline.com; internet www.embamexindia.org; Ambassador JULIO FAESLER CARLISLE.

Mongolia: 34 Archbishop Makarios Marg, New Delhi 110 003; tel. (11) 24631728; fax (11) 24633240; e-mail embassy.mongolia@gems.vsnl.net.in; Ambassador OIDOVYN NYAMDAVAA.

Morocco: 33 Archbishop Makarios Marg, New Delhi 110 003; tel. (11) 24636920; fax (11) 24636925; e-mail sifamand@giasdl01.vsnl.net.in; internet www.moroccoembindia.com; Ambassador MOHAMED LOUAFA.

Mozambique: B-3/24, Vasant Vihar, New Delhi 110 057; tel. (11) 26156663; fax (11) 26156665; e-mail salvaro64@hotmail.com; High Commissioner CARLOS A. DO ROSARIO.

Myanmar: 3/50F Nyaya Marg, Chanakyapuri, New Delhi 110 021; tel. (11) 26889007; fax (11) 26877942; e-mail myandeli@nda.vsnl.net.in; Ambassador U KYAW THU.

Namibia: A-2/6 Vasant Vihar, New Delhi 110 057; tel. (11) 26144772; fax (11) 26146120; e-mail nhcdelhi@del2.vsnl.net.in; High Commissioner Maj-Gen. CHARLES NAMOLOH.

Nepal: Barakhamba Rd, New Delhi 110 001; tel. (11) 23329218; fax (11) 23326857; e-mail ramjanki@del2.vsnl.net.in; Ambassador Dr BHEKH B. THAPA.

Netherlands: 6/50F Shanti Path, Chanakyapuri, New Delhi 110 021; tel. (11) 26884951; fax (11) 26884956; e-mail nde@minbuza.nl; internet www.holland-in-india.org; Ambassador P. F. C. KOCH.

New Zealand: 50N Nyaya Marg, Chanakyapuri, New Delhi 110 021; tel. (11) 26883170; fax (11) 26883165; e-mail nzhc@ndf.vsnl.net.in; High Commissioner CAROLINE J. MCDONALD.

Nigeria: 21 Olof Palme Marg, Vasant Vihar, New Delhi 110 057; tel. (11) 26146221; fax (11) 26146617; e-mail nhcnd@ndre.vsnl.net.in; internet www.nigeriadelhi.com; High Commissioner KABIRU AHMED.

Norway: 50C Shanti Path, Chanakyapuri, New Delhi 110 021; tel. (11) 26873532; fax (11) 26873814; e-mail noramb@vsnl.com; Ambassador TRULS HANEVOLD.

Oman: EP-10/11, Chandragupta Marg, Chankyapuri, New Delhi 110 021; tel. (11) 26885622; fax (11) 26885621; e-mail omandelhi@vsnl.com; Ambassador KHALIFA BIN ALI BIN ESSA AL-HARTHY.

Pakistan: 2/50G Shanti Path, Chanakyapuri, New Delhi 110 021; tel. (11) 24676004; fax (11) 26872339; e-mail pakhc@nda.vsnl.net.in; Chargé d'affaires MUNAWAR SAEED BHATTI.

Panama: C-321, Defence Colony, New Delhi 110 024; tel. (11) 24642518; fax (11) 24642350; e-mail panaind@bol.net.in; Ambassador ALEJANDRO A. GARRIDO.

Peru: G-15 Maharani Bagh, New Delhi 110 065; tel. (11) 26312610; fax (11) 26312557; e-mail info@embaperuindia.com; internet www.embaperuindia.com.

Philippines: 50N Nyaya Marg, Chanakyapuri, New Delhi 110 021; tel. (11) 26889091; fax (11) 26889054; e-mail phndelhi@del2.vsnl.net.in; Ambassador JOSÉ P. DEL ROSARIO, Jr.

Poland: 50M Shanti Path, Chanakyapuri, New Delhi 110 021; tel. (11) 26889211; fax (11) 26871914; e-mail gorski@del2.vsnl.net.in; internet www.poltradeindia.org; Ambassador Dr KRZYSZTOF MAJKA.

Portugal: 8 Olof Palme Marg, Vasant Vihar, New Delhi 110 057; tel. (11) 26142215; fax (11) 26141343; e-mail embportin@del3.vsnl.net.in; internet www.embportindia.com; Ambassador JOAQUIM JOSÉ L. F. MARQUES CURTO.

Qatar: G-5 Anand Niketan, New Delhi 110 021; tel. (11) 26117988; fax (11) 26886080; Ambassador YOUSEF H. AL-SAI.

Romania: A-52 Vasant Marg, Vasant Vihar, New Delhi 110 057; tel. (11) 26140447; fax (11) 26140611; e-mail emrond@hotmail.com; Ambassador PETRU PETRA.

Russia: Shanti Path, Chanakyapuri, New Delhi 110 021; tel. (11) 26873799; fax (11) 26876823; e-mail indrusem@del2.vsnl.net.in; Ambassador ALEKSANDR KADAKIN.

Rwanda: 41 Paschimi Marg, New Delhi 110 057; tel. (11) 28661604; fax (11) 28661605; e-mail rwanda@spectranet.com; Chargé d'affaires CHARLOTTE MUKANKUSI.

Saudi Arabia: D-12, New Delhi South Extension Part II, New Delhi 110 049; tel. (11) 26252470; fax (11) 26254444; Ambassador SALEH M. AL-GHAMDI.

Senegal: C-6/11, Vasant Vihar, New Delhi 110 057; tel. (11) 26147687; fax (11) 24103743; Ambassador AHMED EL MANSOUR DIOP.

Serbia and Montenegro: 3/50G Niti Marg, Chanakyapuri, New Delhi 110 021; tel. (11) 26873661; fax (11) 26885535; e-mail zvezda@del2.vsnl.net.in; Ambassador ZARKO MILOŠEVIĆ.

Singapore: E-6 Chandragupta Marg, Chanakyapuri, New Delhi 110 021; tel. (11) 26885659; fax (11) 26886798; e-mail singhnd@giasdl.vsnl.net.in; High Commissioner CHAK MUM SEE.

Slovakia: 50M Niti Marg, Chanakyapuri, New Delhi 110 021; tel. (11) 26889071; fax (11) 26877941; e-mail skdelhi@giasdl01.vsnl.net.in; Ambassador LADISLAV VOLKO.

Slovenia: E–94, 2nd Floor, Malcha Marg, Chanakyapuri, New Delhi 110 021; tel. (11) 26879237; fax (11) 26879236; e-mail vnd@mzz-dkp.sigov.si; Ambassador (vacant).

Somalia: A-17, Defence Colony, New Delhi 110 024; tel. (11) 24619559; Ambassador MOHAMED OSMAN OMAR.

South Africa: B-18 Vasant Marg, Vasant Vihar, New Delhi 110 057; tel. (11) 26149411; fax (11) 26143605; e-mail highcommissioner@sahc-india.com; internet www.sahc-india.com; High Commissioner M. E. NKOANA MASHABANE.

Spain: 16 Sunder Nagar, New Delhi 110 003; tel. (11) 24359004; fax (11) 24359040; Ambassador DON ALBERTO ESCUDERO.

Sri Lanka: 27 Kautilya Marg, Chanakyapuri, New Delhi 110 021; tel. (11) 23010201; fax (11) 23793604; e-mail lankacom@del2.vsnl.net.in; High Commissioner MANGALA MOONESINGHE.

Sudan: Plot No. 3, Shanti Path, Chanakyapuri, New Delhi 110 021; tel. (11) 26873785; fax (11) 26883758; e-mail sudandel@del3.vsnl.net.in; Ambassador A. ABDALHALEEM MOHAMMED.

Sweden: Nyaya Marg, Chanakyapuri, New Delhi 110 021; tel. (11) 24197100; fax (11) 26885401; e-mail embassy.new.delhi@sida.se; Ambassador JOHAN NORDENFELT.

Switzerland: Nyaya Marg, Chanakyapuri, New Delhi 110 021; tel. (11) 26878872; fax (11) 26873093; e-mail swienidel@vsnl.com; Ambassador Dr WALTER B. GYGER.

Syria: D-5/8, Vasant Vihar, New Delhi 110 057; tel. (11) 26140233; fax (11) 26143107; Ambassador MOHSEN AL-KHAYER.

Tanzania: 10/1 Sarv Priya Vihar, New Delhi 110 016; tel. (11) 26853046; fax (11) 26968408; High Commissioner EVA LILIAN NZARO.

Thailand: 56N Nyaya Marg, Chanakyapuri, New Delhi 110 021; tel. (11) 26118103; fax (11) 26872029; e-mail thaiemb@nda.vsnl.net.in; Ambassador BANDHIT SOTIPALALIT.

Trinidad and Tobago: 131 Jor Bagh, New Delhi 110 003; tel. (11) 24618186; fax (11) 24624581; e-mail hcreptt@giasdl01.vsnl.net.in; High Commissioner TEDWIN HERBERT (acting).

Tunisia: 23 Paschimi Marg, Vasant Vihar, New Delhi 110 057; tel. (11) 26145346; fax (11) 26145301; e-mail embtun@nde.vsnl.net.in; Ambassador ELYES KASRI.

Turkey: 50N Nyaya Marg, Chanakyapuri, New Delhi 110 021; tel. (11) 26889054; fax (11) 26881409; e-mail tembdelhi@mantraonline.com; Ambassador HASAN GOGUS.

Turkmenistan: 1/13 Shanti Niketan, New Delhi 110 021; tel. (11) 26118409; fax (11) 26118332; e-mail turkmind@del3.vsnl.net.in; Ambassador ASHIR ATAEV.

Uganda: B-3/26 Vasant Vihar, New Delhi 110 057; tel. (11) 26144413; fax (11) 26144405; e-mail ughcom@ndb.vsnl.net.in; High Commissioner JULIET BETTY K. KAJUMBA (acting).

Ukraine: 46 Paschimi Marg, Vasant Vihar, New Delhi 110 057; tel. (11) 26146041; fax (11) 26146043; e-mail embassy@bol.net.in; internet www.ukraineembassyindia.com; Ambassador OLEH Y. SEMENETS.

United Arab Emirates: EP–12 Chandragupt Marg, New Delhi 110 021; tel. (11) 26872937; fax (11) 26873272; e-mail embassyabudhabi@bol.net.in; Ambassador SAEED M. AL-SHAMSI.

United Kingdom: Shanti Path, Chanakyapuri, New Delhi 110 021; tel. (11) 26872161; fax (11) 26872882; e-mail bhcndcom@del3.vsnl.net.in; internet www.ukinindia.com; High Commissioner Sir ROBERTSON YOUNG.

USA: Shanti Path, Chanakyapuri, New Delhi 110 021; tel. (11) 24198000; fax (11) 24190060; e-mail newdelhi@pd.state.gov; Ambassador ROBERT D. BLACKWILL.

Uruguay: A 16/2 Vasant Vihar, New Delhi 110 057; tel. (11) 26151991; fax (11) 26144306; e-mail uruind@del3.vsnl.net.in; Ambassador ENRIQUE ANCHORDOQUI.

Uzbekistan: EP-40 Dr S. Radhakrishnan Marg, Chanakyapuri, New Delhi 110 021; tel. (11) 24670774; fax (11) 24670773; e-mail uzembind@vsnl.com; Ambassador Dr IBRAHIM MAVLANOV.

Venezuela: N-114 Panchshila Park, New Delhi 110 017; tel. (11) 26496913; fax (11) 26491686; e-mail embavene@del2.vsnl.net.in; Ambassador WALTER MÁRQUEZ.

Viet Nam: 17 Kautilya Marg, Chanakyapuri, New Delhi 110 021; tel. (11) 23012123; fax (11) 23017714; e-mail sqdelhi@del3.vsnl.net.in; Ambassador TRAN TRONG KHANH.

Yemen: J-16, Hauz Khas, New Delhi 110 016; tel. (11) 26602481; fax (11) 26602483; e-mail yemenemb@del3.vsnl.net.in; Ambassador Dr MOHAMED SAAD ALI.

Zambia: C-79 Anand Niketan, New Delhi 110 021; tel. (11) 24101289; fax (11) 24101520; e-mail zambiand@nde.vsnl.net.in; High Commissioner Prof. MOSES MUSONDA.

Zimbabwe: F-63 Poorvi Marg, Vasant Vihar, New Delhi 110 057; tel. (11) 26140430; fax (11) 26154316; e-mail zimdelhi@vsnl.net; High Commissioner LUCIA MUVINGI.

Judicial System

THE SUPREME COURT

The Supreme Court, consisting of a Chief Justice and not more than 25 judges appointed by the President, exercises exclusive jurisdiction in any dispute between the Union and the states (although there are certain restrictions where an acceding state is involved). It has appellate jurisdiction over any judgment, decree or order of the High Court where that Court certifies that either a substantial question of law or the interpretation of the Constitution is involved. The Supreme Court can enforce fundamental rights and issue writs covering habeas corpus, mandamus, prohibition, quo warranto and certiorari. The Supreme Court is a court of record and has the power to punish for its contempt.

Provision is made for the appointment by the Chief Justice of India of judges of High Courts as ad hoc judges at sittings of the Supreme Court for specified periods, and for the attendance of retired judges at sittings of the Supreme Court. The Supreme Court has advisory jurisdiction in respect of questions which may be referred to it by the President for opinion. The Supreme Court is also empowered to hear appeals against a sentence of death passed by a State High Court in reversal of an order of acquittal by a lower court, and in a case in which a High Court has granted a certificate of fitness.

The Supreme Court also hears appeals which are certified by High Courts to be fit for appeal, subject to rules made by the Court. Parliament may, by law, confer on the Supreme Court any further powers of appeal.

The judges hold office until the age of 65 years.

Supreme Court: New Delhi; tel. (11) 23388942; fax (11) 23383792; internet www.caselaw.delhi.nic.in@bssc-cl.

Chief Justice of India: VISHESHWAR NATH KHARE.

Judges of the Supreme Court: BRIJESH KUMAR, S. RAJENDRA BABU, ASHOK BHAN, P. VENKATARAMA REDDY, SYED SHAH MOHAMMED QUADRI, DORAISWAMY RAJU, Y. K. SABHARWAL, HOTOI KHETOHO SEMA, BISHWANATH AGARWAL, RUMA PAL, S. N. VARIAVA, SHIVRAJ V. PATIL, K. G. BALAK-RISHNAN, MANHARLAL BHIKHALAL SHAH, B. N. SRIKRISHNA, A. R. LAKSH-MANAN, RAMESH CHANDRA LAHOTI, SANTOSH HEGDE, S. B. SINHA, GOVIND PRASAD MATHER, ARIJIT PASSAYAT, BISHESHWAR PRASAD SINGH, ARUN KUMAR.

Attorney-General: SOLI J. SORABJEE.

HIGH COURTS

The High Courts are the Courts of Appeal from the lower courts, and their decisions are final except in cases where appeal lies to the Supreme Court.

LOWER COURTS

Provision is made in the Code of Criminal Procedure for the constitution of lower criminal courts called Courts of Session and Courts of Magistrates. The Courts of Session are competent to try all persons duly committed for trial, and inflict any punishment authorized by the law. The President and the local government concerned exercise the prerogative of mercy.

The constitution of inferior civil courts is determined by regulations within each state.

Religion

BUDDHISM

The Buddhists in Ladakh (Jammu and Kashmir) are followers of the Dalai Lama. Head Lama of Ladakh: Kaushak Sakula, Dalgate, Srinagar, Kashmir. In 1991 there were 6.3m. Buddhists in India, representing 0.80% of the population.

Mahabodhi Society of India: 4-A, Bankim Chatterjee St, Kolkata 700 073; tel. and fax (33) 22415214; 11 centres in India, five centres world-wide; Pres. KALASURI M. WIPULASARA MAHA THERO; Gen. Sec. Dr D. REWATHA THERO.

HINDUISM

In 1991 there were 672.6m. Hindus in India, representing 82.4% of the population.

International Society for Krishna Consciousness: Sri Mayapur Chandrodaya Mandir, Sri Mayapur Dham, District Nadia; tel. (3472) 245233; f. 1966; 300 centres world-wide.

Rashtriya Swayamsevak Sangh (RSS) (National Volunteer Organization): Dr Hedgewar Bhawan, Mahal, Nagpur 440 002; tel. (712) 2720150; fax (712) 2721589; e-mail vishwa@rss.org; internet www.rss.org; f. 1925, banned in December 1992–June 1993 for its role in the destruction of the Babri mosque in Ayodhya; 30,000 *shakhas* (spiritual centres), 50,000 working centres; Pres. K. S. SUDARSHAN; Gen. Sec. MOHAN BHAGWAT.

Sarvadeshik Arya Pratinidhi Sabha: Asaf Ali Rd, Near Ram Lila Maidan, New Delhi 110 002; tel. (11) 23274771; e-mail vedicgod@nda.vsnl.net.in; internet www.whereisgod.com; f. 1875 by Maharshi Dayanand Saraswati; Pres. DEV RATNA ARYA; Sec. VED BRAT SHARMA.

Vishwa Hindu Parishad (VHP) (World Hindu Council): Sankat Mochan Ashram, Ramakrishna Puram VI, New Delhi 110 022; tel. (11) 26178992; fax (11) 26195527; e-mail asmita@ndc.vsnl.net.in; internet www.vhp.org; f. 1964, banned in December 1992–June 2003 for its role in the destruction of the Babri mosque in Ayodhya; Pres. VISHNU HARI DALMIA; Gen. Sec. Dr PRAVEEN TOGADIA.

ISLAM

Muslims are divided into two main sects, Shi'as and Sunnis. Most of the Indian Muslims are Sunnis. At the 1991 census Islam had 95.2m. adherents (11.2% of the population).

Jamiat Ulama-i-Hind (The Assembly of Muslim Religious Leaders of India): 1 Bahadur Shah Zafar Marg, New Delhi 110 002; tel. (11) 23311455; fax (11) 23316173; e-mail info@jamiatulamahind.org; internet www.jamiatulamahind.org; f. 1919; Pres. ASAD MADANI; Gen. Sec. Maulana MAHMOOD MADANI.

SIKHISM

In 1991 there were 16.3m. Sikhs (comprising 2.0% of the population), the majority living in the Punjab.

Sikh Gurdwara Prabandhak Committee: Darbar Sahab, Amritsar 143 001; tel. (183) 2553956; fax (183) 2553919; e-mail sgpc@vsnl.com; internet www.sgpc.net; f. 1925; highest authority in Sikhism; Pres. Prof. KIRPAL SINGH BADUNGAR; Gen. Sec. HARDALBIR S. SHAH; Jathedar Shri Akal Takht Saheb JOGINDER SINGH VEDANTI.

OTHER INDIAN FAITHS

Jainism: 3.4m. adherents (1991 census), 0.4% of the population.

Zoroastrians: More than 120,000 Parsis practise the Zoroastrian religion.

CHRISTIANITY

According to the 1991 census, Christians represented 2.3% of the population in India.

National Council of Churches in India: Christian Council Lodge, Civil Lines, POB 205, Nagpur 440 001; tel. (712) 2531312; fax (712) 2520554; e-mail nccindia@nagpur.dot.net.in; internet www.nccindia.org; f. 1914; mems: 26 reformed and three orthodox churches, 18 regional Christian councils, 14 All-India ecumenical orgs and seven related agencies; represents c. 10m. mems; Pres. Most Rev. GEEVARGHESE MAR COORILOS; Gen. Sec. Rev. Dr IPE JOSEPH.

Orthodox Churches

Malankara Orthodox Syrian Church: Devalokam, Kottayam 686 038; tel. (481) 2578500; fax (481) 2570569; c. 2.5m. mems (1995); 22 bishops, 21 dioceses, 1,340 parishes; Catholicos of the East and Malankara Metropolitan HH BASELIUS MARTHOMA MATHEWS II; Asscn Sec. A. K. THOMAS.

Mar Thoma Syrian Church of Malabar: Mar Thoma Sabha Office, Poolatheen, Tiruvalla 689 101; tel. (473) 2630313; fax (473) 2630327; e-mail marthoma@vsnl.com; c. 1m. mems (2001); Metropolitan Most Rev. Dr PHILIPOSE MAR CHRYSOSTOM MAR THOMA; Sec. Rev. Dr P. G. PHILIP.

The Malankara Jacobite Syrian Orthodox Church is also represented.

Protestant Churches

Church of North India (CNI): CNI Bhavan, 16 Pandit Pant Marg, New Delhi 110 001; tel. (11) 23716513; fax (11) 23716901; e-mail gscni@ndb.vsnl.net.in; internet www.cnisynod.org; f. 1970 by merger of the Church of India (fmrly known as the Church of India, Pakistan, Burma and Ceylon), the Council of the Baptist Churches in Northern India, the Methodist Church (British and Australasian Conferences), the United Church of Northern India (a union of Presbyterians and Congregationalists, f. 1924), the Church of the Brethren in India, and the Disciples of Christ; comprises 26 dioceses; c. 1.2m. mems (1999); Moderator Most Rev. Z. JAMES TEROM (Bishop of Chota Nagpur); Gen. Sec. Dr VIDYA SAGAR LALL.

Church of South India (CSI): CSI Centre, 5 Whites Rd, Chennai 600 014; tel. (44) 28521566; fax (44) 28524121; e-mail csi@vsnl.com; internet www.csisynod.org; f. 1947 by merger of the Weslyan Methodist Church in South India, the South India United Church (itself a union of churches in the Congregational and Presbyterian/Reformed traditions) and the four southern dioceses of the (Anglican) Church of India; comprises 21 dioceses (incl. one in Sri Lanka); c. 2.8m. mems (2000); Moderator Most Rev. K. J. SAMUEL (Bishop of East Kerala); Gen. Sec. Rev. G. DYVASIRVADAM.

Methodist Church in India: Methodist Centre, 21 YMCA Rd, Mumbai 400 008; tel. and fax (22) 23094316; e-mail gensecmci@vsnl.com; f. 1856 as the Methodist Church in Southern Asia; 600,000 mems (1998); Gen. Sec. Rev. TARANATH S. SAGAR.

Samavesam of Telugu Baptist Churches: C. A. M. Compound, Nellore 524 003; tel. (861) 2355732; fax (861) 2441647; f. 1962; comprises 856 independent Baptist churches; 578,295 mems (1995); Gen. Sec. Rev. T. NATHANIEL.

United Evangelical Lutheran Churches in India: 94 Purasawalkam High Rd, Kilpauk, Chennai 600 010; tel. (44) 25325659; fax (44) 26421870; e-mail gurukul@giasmdo1.vsnl.net.in; internet www.gltc.edu; f. 1975; 10 constituent denominations: Andhra Evangelical Lutheran Church, Arcot Lutheran Church, Evangelical Lutheran Church in Madhya Pradesh, Gossner Evangelical Lutheran Church in Chotanagpur and Assam, India Evangelical Lutheran Church, Jeypore Evangelical Lutheran Church, Northern Evangelical Lutheran Church, South Andhra Lutheran Church, Good Samaritan Evangelical Lutheran Church and Tamil Evangelical Lutheran Church; c. 1.3m. mems; Pres. Bishop JOHN FRANKLIN; Exec. Sec. Dr K. RAJARATNAM.

Other denominations active in the country include the Assembly of the Presbyterian Church in North East India, the Bengal-Orissa-Bihar Baptist Convention (6,000 mems), the Chaldean Syrian Church of the East, the Convention of the Baptist Churches of Northern Circars, the Council of Baptist Churches of North East

India, the Council of Baptist Churches of Northern India, the Hindustani Convent Church and the Mennonite Church in India.

The Roman Catholic Church

India comprises 25 archdioceses and 120 dioceses. These include four archdioceses and 25 dioceses of the the Syro-Malabar rite, and one archdiocese and five dioceses of the Syro-Malankara rite. The archdiocese of Goa and Daman is also the seat of the Patriarch of the East Indies. The remaining archdioceses are metropolitan sees. In December 2000 there were an estimated 16.7m. adherents of the Roman Catholic faith in the country.

Catholic Bishops' Conference of India (CBCI): CBCI Centre, 1 Ashok Place, Goledakkhana, New Delhi 110 001; tel. (11) 23344470; fax (11) 23364615; e-mail cbci@vsnl.com; internet www.cbcisite.com; f. 1944; Pres. Most Rev. CYRIL MAR BASELIOS MALANCHARUVIL (Archbishop of Thiruvananthapuram); Sec.-Gen. Most Rev. PERCIVAL JOSEPH FERNANDEZ (Auxiliary Bishop of Bombay (Mumbai).

Latin Rite

Conference of Catholic Bishops of India (CCBI)
CCBI Secretariat, Divya Deepti Sadan, 2nd Floor, 9–10 Bhai Vir Singh Marg, POB 680, New Delhi 110 001; tel. (11) 23364222; fax (11) 23364343; e-mail cbci@vsnl.com; internet www.cbcisite.com. f. 1994; Pres. Most Rev. TELESPHORO P. TOPPO (Archbishop of Ranchi).

Patriarch of the East Indies: Most Rev. RAUL NICOLAU GONSALVES (Archbishop of Goa and Daman), Paço Patriarcal, POB 216, Altinho, Panaji, Goa 403 001; tel. (832) 2223353; fax (832) 2224139; e-mail archbp@goatelecom.com.

Archbishop of Agra: Most Rev. Dr OSWALD GRACIAS, Cathedral House, Wazirpura Rd, Agra 282 003; tel. (562) 2351318; fax (562) 2353939; e-mail abpossie@sancharnet.in.

Archbishop of Bangalore: Most Rev. IGNATIUS PAUL PINTO, Archbishop's House, 75 Miller's Rd, Bangalore 560 046; tel. (80) 23330438; fax (80) 23330838; e-mail bgarchdi@bgl.vsnl.net.in.

Archbishop of Bhopal: Most Rev. PASCHAL TOPNO, Archbishop's House, 33 Ahmedabad Palace Rd, Bhopal 462 001; tel. (755) 2540829; fax (755) 2544737; e-mail adbhopal@vsnl.com; internet cbci.org/bhopal.htm.

Archbishop of Bombay (Mumbai): Cardinal IVAN DIAS, Archbishop's House, 21 Nathalal Parekh Marg, Fort, Mumbai 400 001; tel. (22) 22021093; fax (22) 22853872; e-mail bombaydiocese@vsnl.com; internet www.archbom.org.

Archbishop of Calcutta (Kolkata): Most Rev. LUCAS SIRKAR, Archbishop's House, 32 Park St, Kolkata 700 016; tel. and fax (33) 22807015; e-mail bls@cal2.vsnl.net.in.

Archbishop of Cuttack-Bhubaneswar: Most Rev. RAPHAEL CHEENATH, Archbishop's House, Satya Nagar, Bhubaneswar 751 007; tel. (674) 2502234; fax (674) 2501817; e-mail crcdc@mail.com.

Archbishop of Delhi: Most Rev. VINCENT M. CONCESSAO, Archbishop's House, 1 Ashok Place, Goledakkhana, New Delhi 110 001; tel. (11) 23343457; fax (11) 23746575; e-mail archbish@vsnl.com.

Archbishop of Guwahati: Most Rev. THOMAS MENAMPARAMPIL, Archbishop's House, POB 100, Guwahati 781 001; tel. (361) 2547664; fax (361) 2520588; e-mail bishop@gw1.dot.net.in; internet www.peacetoall.com.

Archbishop of Hyderabad: Most Rev. MARAMPUDI JOJI, Archbishop's House, Sardar Patel Rd, Secunderabad 500 003; tel. (40) 27805545; fax (40) 27718089; e-mail abphydmjoji@rediffmail.com.

Archbishop of Imphal: Most Rev. JOSEPH MITTATHANY, Archbishop's House, POB 35, Imphal 795 001; tel. (385) 2421292; fax (385) 2421293; e-mail jmittathany@hotmail.com.

Archbishop of Madras (Chennai) and Mylapore: Most Rev. JAMES MASILAMONY ARUL DAS, Archbishop's House, 21 San Thome High Rd, Chennai 600 004; tel. (44) 24941102; fax (44) 24941999; e-mail archmsml@vsnl.com.

Archbishop of Madurai: Most Rev. MARIANUS AROKIASAMY, Archbishop's House, K. Pudur, Madurai 625 007; tel. (452) 2566198; fax (452) 2566630; e-mail anupro@eth.net; internet www.maduraiarchdiocese.org.

Archbishop of Nagpur: Most Rev. ABRAHAM VIRUTHAKULANGARA, Archbishop's House, 25 Kamptee Rd, Mohan Nagar, Nagpur 440 001; tel. (712) 2533239; fax (712) 2527906; e-mail abpabrah@nagpur.dot.net.in.

Archbishop of Patna: Most Rev. BENEDICT JOHN OSTA, Archbishop's House, Bankipore, Patna 800 004; tel. (612) 2673811; fax (612) 2664816; e-mail archbishop@satyam.net.in.

Archbishop of Pondicherry and Cuddalore: Most Rev. Dr S. MICHAEL AUGUSTINE, Archbishop's House, Cathedral St, POB 193, Pondicherry 605 001; tel. (413) 2334748; fax (413) 2339911; e-mail abppondi@satyam.net.in; internet www.pondyarchdiocese.org.in.

Archbishop of Ranchi: Most Rev. TELESPHORE P. TOPPO, Archbishop's House, Purulia Rd, POB 5, Ranchi 834 001; tel. (651) 2204728; fax (651) 2304844; e-mail telestoppo@rediffmail.com.

Archbishop of Shillong: Most Rev. DOMINIC JALA, Archbishop's House, Shillong 793 003; tel. (364) 2223355; fax (364) 2211306; e-mail jala@dte.vsnl.net.in.

Archbishop of Verapoly: Most Rev. DANIEL ACHARUPARAMBIL, Latin Archbishop's House, POB 2581, Kochi 682 031; tel. (484) 2372892; fax (484) 2360911; e-mail vpoly@vsnl.com; internet www.verapolyarchdiocese.org.

Archbishop of Visakhapatnam: Most Rev. MARIADAS KAGITHAPU, Archbishop's House, Maharanipeta, Visakhapatnam 530 002; tel. (891) 2706428; fax (891) 2704404; e-mail kmariadas@satyam.net.in.

Syro-Malabar Rite

Major Archbishop of Ernakulam-Angamaly: Cardinal MAR VARKEY VITHAYATHIL, Major Archbishop's House, Ernakulam, POB 10, Kochi 682 031; tel. (484) 2352629; fax (484) 2366028; e-mail abperang@md3.vsnl.net.in; internet www.ernakulamarchdiocese.org.

Archbishop of Changanacherry: Most Rev. JOSEPH MAR POWATHIL, Archbishop's House, POB 20, Changanacherry 686 101; tel. (481) 2420040; fax (481) 2422540; e-mail abpchry@md2.vsnl.net.in; internet www.archdiocesechanganacherry.org.

Archbishop of Tellicherry: Most Rev. GEORGE VALIAMATTAM, Archbishop's House, POB 70, Tellicherry 670 101; tel. (490) 341058; fax (49) 34142; e-mail diocese@eth.net.

Archbishop of Trichur: Most Rev. JACOB THOOMKUZHY, Archbishop's House, Trichur 680 005; tel. (487) 333325; fax (487) 338204; e-mail carbit@md4.vsnl.net.in; internet archdioceseoftrichur.org.

Syro-Malankara Rite

Archbishop of Thiruvananthapuram: Most Rev. CYRIL MAR BASELIOS MALANCHARUVIL, Archbishop's House, Pattom, Thiruvananthapuram 695 004; tel. (471) 2541643; fax (471) 2541635; e-mail archbp03@md3.vsnl.net.in; internet www.malankara.net.

BAHÁ'Í FAITH

National Spiritual Assembly: Bahá'í House, 6 Canning Rd, POB 19, New Delhi 110 001; tel. (11) 23389326; fax (11) 23782178; e-mail nsaindia@bahaindia.org; internet www.bahaindia.org; c. 2m. mems; Sec.-Gen. Prof. ANIL SARWAL.

The Press

Freedom of the Press was guaranteed under the 1950 Constitution. In 1979 a Press Council was established (its predecessor was abolished in 1975), the function of which was to uphold the freedom of the press and maintain and improve journalistic standards.

The growth of a thriving press has been inhibited by cultural barriers caused by religious, social and linguistic differences. Consequently the English-language press, with its appeal to the educated middle-class urban readership throughout the states, has retained its dominance. The English-language metropolitan dailies are some of the widest circulating and most influential newspapers. The main Indian language dailies, by paying attention to rural affairs, cater for the increasingly literate non-anglophone provincial population. Most Indian-language papers have a relatively small circulation.

The majority of publications in India are under individual ownership (77% in 1999), and they claim a large part of the total circulation (60% in 1999). The most powerful groups, owned by joint stock companies, publish most of the large English dailies and frequently have considerable private commercial and industrial holdings. Four of the major groups are as follows:

Times of India Group: controlled by family of the late ASHOK JAIN; dailies: *The Times of India* (published in 11 regional centres), *Economic Times*, the Hindi *Navbharat Times* and *Sandhya Times*, the Marathi *Maharashtra Times* (Mumbai); periodicals: the English fortnightly *Femina* and monthly *Filmfare*.

Indian Express Group: controlled by the family of the late RAMNATH GOENKA; publishes nine dailies including the *Indian Express*, the Marathi *Lokasatta*, the Tamil *Dinamani*, the Telugu *Andhra Prabha*, the Kannada *Kannada Prabha* and the English *Financial Express*; six periodicals including the English weeklies the

Indian Express(Sunday edition), *Screen*, the Telugu *Andhra Prabha Illustrated Weekly* and the Tamil *Dinamani Kadir*(weekly).

Hindustan Times Group: controlled by the K. K. BIRLA family; dailies: the *Hindustan Times* (published from 10 regional centres), *Pradeep* (Patna) and the Hindi *Hindustan* (Delhi, Lucknow, Patna and Ranchi); periodicals: the weekly *Overseas Hindustan Times* and the Hindi monthly *Nandan* and *Kadambini* (New Delhi).

Ananda Bazar Patrika Group: controlled by AVEEK SARKAR and family; dailies: the *Ananda Bazar Patrika* (Kolkata) and the English *The Telegraph* (Guwahati, Kolkata and Siliguri); periodicals include: *Business World*, Bengali weekly *Anandamela*, Bengali fortnightly *Desh*, Bengali monthly *Anandalok* and the Bengali monthly *Sananda*.

PRINCIPAL DAILIES

Delhi (incl. New Delhi)

The Asian Age: D-27, South Extension Part II, New Delhi 110 049; tel. (11) 26250573; fax (11) 26251179; internet www.asianage.com; f. 1994; morning; English; also publ. from Ahmedabad, Bangalore, Guwahati, Kolkata, Mumbai and London; Editor-in-Chief M. J. AKBAR.

Business Standard: Pratap Bhavan, 5 Bahadur Shah Zafar Marg, New Delhi 110 002; tel. (11) 23720202; fax (11) 23720201; e-mail editor@business-standard.com; internet www.business-standard.com; morning; English; also publ. from Kolkata, Ahmedabad, Bangalore, Chennai, Hyderabad and Mumbai; Editor T. N. NINAN; combined circ. 56,000.

Daily Milap: 8A Bahadur Shah Zafar Marg, New Delhi 110 002; tel. (11) 23317651; fax (11) 23319166; e-mail info@milap.com; internet www.milap.com; f. 1923; Urdu; nationalist; Man. Editor PUNAM SURI; Chief Editor NAVIN SURI; circ. 31,250.

Daily Pratap: Pratap Bhawan, 5 Bahadur Shah Zafar Marg, New Delhi 110 002; tel. (11) 23318572; fax (11) 23730544; e-mail dailypratap@hotmail.com; f. 1919; Urdu; Editor K. NARENDRA; circ. 26,700.

Delhi Mid Day: World Trade Tower, Barakhamba Lane, New Delhi 110 001; tel. (11) 23414224; fax (11) 23412491; e-mail dmd01@rediffmail.com; f. 1989; Editor SANJAY KAPOOR.

The Economic Times: 7 Bahadur Shah Zafar Marg, New Delhi 110 002; tel. (11) 23302000; fax (11) 23323346; internet www.economictimes.com; f. 1961; English; also publ. from Kolkata, Ahmedabad, Bangalore, Hyderabad, Chennai and Mumbai; Editor (Delhi) ARINDAM SENGUPTA; combined circ. 435,300, circ. (Delhi) 123,400.

Financial Express: Bahadur Shah Zafar Marg, New Delhi 110 002; tel. (11) 23702100; fax (11) 23702164; e-mail editor@financialexpress.com; internet www.financialexpress.com; f. 1961; morning; English; also publ. from Ahmedabad (in Gujarati), Mumbai, Bangalore, Kolkata and Chennai; Chief Editor SANJAYA BARU; combined circ. 50,000.

The Hindu: INS Bldg, Rafi Marg, New Delhi 110 001; tel. (11) 23715426; fax (11) 23718158; f. 1878; morning; English; also publ. from eight other regional centres; Editor N. RAVI; combined circ. 885,100.

Hindustan: 18/20 Kasturba Gandhi Marg, New Delhi 110 001; tel. (11) 23361234; fax (11) 23704645; f. 1936; morning; Hindi; also publ. from Lucknow, Muzaffarpur, Ranchi, Bhagalpur, Varanasi and Patna; Editor CHANDRA PRAKASH GUPTA; combined circ. 673,100.

The Hindustan Times: 18/20 Kasturba Gandhi Marg, New Delhi 110 001; tel. (11) 23704612; fax (11) 23704589; internet www.hindustantimes.com; f. 1923; morning; English; also publ. from nine regional centres; Editor VIR SANGHVI; combined circ. 1,032,000.

Indian Express: Bahadur Shah Zafar Marg, New Delhi 110 002; tel. (11) 26511015; fax (11) 26511615; internet www.indianexpress.com; f. 1953; English; also publ. from seven other towns; Man. Editor VIVEK GOENKA; Editor-in-Chief SHEKHAR GUPTA; combined circ. 688,878, circ. (New Delhi, Jammu and Chandigarh) 138,100.

Janasatta: 9/10 Bahadur Shah Zafar Marg, New Delhi 110 002; tel. (11) 23702100; fax (11) 23702141; f. 1983; Hindi; also publ. from Kolkata; Editor-in-Chief PRABHASH JOSHI; Exec. Editor OM THANVI.

National Herald: Herald House 5A, Bahadur Shah Zafar Marg, New Delhi 110 002; tel. (11) 23315950; fax (11) 23313458; f. 1938; English; nationalist; Editor T. V. VENKITACHALAM; circ. 33,000.

Navbharat Times: 7 Bahadur Shah Zafar Marg, New Delhi 110 002; tel. (11) 23492041; fax (11) 23492168; f. 1947; Hindi; also publ. from Mumbai; Editor MADHUSUDAN ANAND; combined circ. 466,200, circ. (Delhi) 299,900.

The Pioneer: Link House, 3 Bahadur Shah Zafar Marg, New Delhi 110 002; tel. (11) 23755271; fax (11) 23755275; e-mail pioneer@del2.vsnl.net.in; internet www.dailypioneer.com; f. 1865; also publ. from Lucknow; Editor CHANDAN MITRA; combined circ. 154,000, circ. (Delhi) 78,000.

Punjab Kesari: Romesh Bhavan, 2 Printing Press Complex, nr Wazirpur DTC Depot, Ring Rd, Delhi 110 035; tel. (11) 27194459; fax (11) 27194470; e-mail ashwanik@nda.vsnl.net.in; Hindi; also publ. from Jalandhar and Ambala; Editor ASHWINI KUMAR; circ. 363,300 (Delhi), combined circ. 843,100.

Rashtriya Sahara: Amba Deep, Kasturba Gandhi Marg, New Delhi 110 001; tel. (11) 23755316; fax (11) 23755317; morning; Hindi; also publ. from Lucknow and Gorakhpur; Resident Editor NISHIT JOSHI; circ. 120,100 (New Delhi), 84,100 (Lucknow), 32,700 (Gorakhpur).

Sandhya Times: 7 Bahadur Shah Zafar Marg, New Delhi 110 002; tel. (11) 23492162; fax (11) 23492047; f. 1979; Hindi; evening; Editor SAT SONI; circ. 53,100.

The Statesman: Statesman House, 148 Barakhamba Rd, New Delhi 110 001; tel. (11) 23315911; fax (11) 23315295; e-mail thestatesman@vsnl.com; internet www.thestatesman.net; f. 1875; English; also publ. from Bhubaneswar, Kolkata and Siliguri; Editor-in-Chief C. R. IRANI; combined circ. 154,100.

The Times of India: 7 Bahadur Shah Zafar Marg, New Delhi 110 002; tel. (11) 23492049; fax (11) 23351606; internet www.timesofindia.com; f. 1838; English; also publ. from 10 other towns; Exec. Editor SHEKHAR BHATIA; combined circ. 2,131,400.

Andhra Pradesh

Hyderabad

Deccan Chronicle: 36 Sarojini Devi Rd, Hyderabad 500 003; tel. (40) 27803930; fax (40) 27805256; f. 1938; English; also published from Anantapur, Karimnagar, Rajahmundry, Vijayawada and Visakhapatnam; Editor-in-Chief M. J. AKBAR; Editor A. T. JAYANTI; circ. 407,600.

Eenadu: Somajiguda, Hyderabad 500 082; tel. (40) 23318181; fax (40) 23318555; e-mail eenadu@hd2.vsnl.net.in; internet www.eenadu.net; f. 1974; Telugu; also publ. from 23 other towns; Chief Editor RAMOJI RAO; combined circ. 1,100,000.

Newstime: 6-3-570 Somajiguda, Hyderabad 500 082; tel. (40) 23318181; fax (40) 23318555; f. 1984; also publ. from Vijaywada and Visakhapatnam; Editor RAMOJI RAO; circ. 60,000.

Rahnuma-e-Deccan: 12-2-837/A/3, Asif Nagar, Hyderabad 500 028; tel. (40) 23534943; fax (40) 23534945; e-mail rahnumadeccan@email.com; f. 1949; morning; Urdu; independent; Chief Editor SYED VICARUDDIN; circ. 25,000.

Siasat Daily: Jawaharlal Nehru Rd, Hyderabad 500 001; tel. (40) 24744109; fax (40) 24603188; e-mail editor@siasat.com; internet www.siasat.com; f. 1949; morning; Urdu; Editor ZAHID ALI KHAN; circ. 44,700.

Vijayawada

Andhra Jyoti: Andhra Jyoti Bldg, POB 712, Vijayawada 520 010; tel. (866) 2474532; f. 1960; Telugu; also publ. from Hyderabad, Visakhapatnam and Tirupati; Editor NANDURI RAMAMOHAN RAO; combined circ. 78,600.

Andhra Prabha: 16-1-28, Kolandareddy Rd, Poornanandampet, Vijayawada 520 003; tel. (866) 2571351; internet www.andhraprabha.com; f. 1935; Telugu; also publ. from Bangalore, Hyderabad, Chennai and Visakhapatnam; Editor V. V. DEEKSHITULU; combined circ. 24,500.

New Indian Express: 16-1-28, Kolandareddy Rd, Poornanandampet, Vijayawada 520 003; tel. (866) 2571351; English; also publ. from Bangalore, Belgaum, Kochi, Kozhikode, Thiruvananthapuram, Madurai, Chennai, Hyderabad, Visakhapatnam, Coimbatore and Bhubaneswar; Man. Editor MANOJ KUMAR SONTHALIA; Editor (Andhra Pradesh) P. S. SUNDARAM; combined circ. 251,900.

Assam

Guwahati

Amar Asom: G. S. Rd, Ulubari, Guwahati 781 007; tel. (361) 2544356; fax (361) 2540664; e-mail glpl@sancharnet.in; f. 1997; Assamese; Editor HOMEN BORGOHAIN; circ. 76,400.

Asomiya Pratidin: Maniram Dewan Rd, Guwahati 781 003; tel. (361) 2540420; fax (361) 2524634; e-mail protidin@gw1.vsnl.net.in; morning; Assamese; also published from Dibrugarh; circ. 103,700.

Assam Tribune: Tribune Bldgs, Maniram Dewan Rd, Chandmari, Guwahati 781 003; tel. (361) 661357; fax (361) 666398; e-mail webmaster@assamtribune.com; internet www.assamtribune.com; f. 1939; English; Man. Dir and Editor P. G. BARUAH; circ. 53,500.

Dainik Agradoot: Agradoot Bhavan, Dispur, Guwahati 781 006; tel. (361) 2261923; fax (361) 2260655; e-mail agradoot@sify.com; internet www.dainikagradoot.com; f. 1995; Assamese; Editor K. S. DEKA; circ. 74,500.

Dainik Assam: Tribune Bldgs, Maniram Dewan Rd, Chandmari, Guwahati 781 003; tel. (361) 2541360; fax (361) 2516356; e-mail webmaster@assamtribune.com; internet www.assamtribune.com; f. 1965; Assamese; Editor ANIL BARUAH; circ. 16,700.

The North East Daily: Maniram Dewan Rd, Chandmari, Guwahati 781 003; tel. (361) 2524594; fax (361) 2524634; e-mail protidin@gw1.vsnl.net.in; Assamese; circ. 34,891.

Jorhat

Dainik Janambhumi: Nehru Park Rd, Jorhat 785 001; tel. (376) 23320033; fax (376) 23321713; e-mail clarionl@sancharnet.in; f. 1972; Assamese; also published from Guwahati; Editor DEVA KR. BORAH; circ. 26,400.

Bihar

Patna

Aryavarta: Mazharul Haque Path, Patna 800 001; tel. (612) 2230716; fax (612) 2222350; e-mail aryavart@dte.vsnl.net.in; morning; Hindi; Editor BHAKTISHWAR JHA.

Hindustan Times: Buddha Marg, Patna 800 001; tel. (612) 2223434; fax (612) 2226120; f. 1918; morning; English; also publ. from nine regional centres; Editor VIR SANGHVI; combined circ. 1,032,000.

Indian Nation: Mazharul Haque Path, Patna 800 001; tel. (612) 2237780; fax (612) 2222350; e-mail aryavart@dte.vsnl.net.in; morning; English; Editor BHAKTISHWAR JHA.

The Times of India: Times House, Fraser Rd, Patna 800 001; tel. (612) 2226301; fax (612) 2233525; also publ. from New Delhi, Mumbai, Ahmedabad, Bangalore and Lucknow; Exec. Editor SHEKHAR BHATIA; combined circ. 2,131,400.

Chhattisgarh

Raipur

Dainik Bhaskar: Press Complex, Rajbandha Mandan, G. E. Rd, Raipur 492 001; tel. (771) 2535277; fax (771) 2535255; Hindi; morning; Editor R. C. AGRAWAL; circ. 94,800.

Deshbandhu: Deshbandhu Complex, Ramsagarpara Layout, Raipur 492 001; tel. (771) 2534911; fax (771) 2534955; e-mail deshbanr@bom6.vsnl.net.in; internet www.dailydeshbandhu.com; Hindi; also publ. from Jabalpur, Satna, Bilaspur and Bhopal; Chief Editor LALIT SURJAN; circ. 53,600 (Raipur), 19,300 (Satna), 24,240 (Bhopal), 19,637 (Jabalpur), 27,300 (Bilaspur).

Nava Bharat: Nava Bharat Bhavan Press Complex, G. E. Rd, Raipur 492 001; tel. (771) 2535544; fax (771) 2534936; Hindi; also publ. from Bilaspur; Editor PRAKASH MAHESHWARI; circ. 178,000.

Goa

Panaji

Gomantak: Gomantak Bhavan, St Inez, Panaji, Goa 403 001; tel. (832) 2422700; fax (832) 2422701; f. 1962; morning; Marathi and English edns; Editor LAXMAN T. JOSHI; circ. 16,500 (Marathi), 4,900 (English).

Navhind Times: Navhind Bhavan, Rua Ismail Gracias, POB 161, Panaji, Goa 403 001; tel. (832) 2225685; fax (832) 2224258; e-mail navhind@goa1.dot.net.in; internet www.navhindtimes.com; f. 1963; morning; English; Editor ARUN SINHA; circ. 32,900.

Gujarat

Ahmedabad

Gujarat Samachar: Gujarat Samachar Bhavan, Khanpur, Ahmedabad 380 001; tel. (79) 25504010; fax (79) 25502000; f. 1930; morning; Gujarati; also publ. from Surat, Rajkot, Vadodara, Mumbai, London and New York; Editor SHANTIBHAI SHAH; combined circ. 1,040,619.

Indian Express: 5th Floor, Sanidhya Bldg, Ashram Rd, Ahmedabad 380 009; tel. (79) 26583023; fax (79) 26575826; e-mail praman@express2.indexp.co.in; f. 1968; English; also publ. in 10 other towns; Man. Editor VIVEK GOENKA; Chief Editor SHEKHAR GUPTA; circ. (Ahmedabad and Vadodara) 28,200.

Lokasatta—Janasatta: Mirzapur Rd, POB 188, Ahmedabad 380 001; tel. (79) 25507307; fax (79) 25507708; f. 1953; morning; Gujarati; also publ. from Rajkot and Vadodara; Man. Editor VIVEK GOENKA; combined circ. 23,700.

Sandesh: Sandesh Bhavan, Lad Society Rd, Ahmedabad 380 054; tel. (79) 26765480; fax (79) 26754796; e-mail advt@sandesh.com; internet www.sandesh.com; f. 1923; Gujarati; also publ. from Bhavnagar, Vadodara, Rajkot and Surat; Editor FALGUNBHAI C. PATEL; combined circ. 756,700.

The Times of India: 139 Ashram Rd, POB 4046, Ahmedabad 380 009; tel. (79) 26582151; fax (79) 26583758; f. 1968; English; also publ. from Mumbai, Delhi, Bangalore, Patna and Lucknow; Resident Editor KINGSHUK NAG; circ. (Ahmedabad) 112,700.

Western Times: 'Western House', Marutinandan Complex, Madalpur, Ellisbridge, Ahmedabad 380 006; tel. (79) 26576738; fax (79) 26577421; e-mail western@icenet.net; f. 1967; English and Gujarati edns; also publ. (in Gujarati) from eight other towns; Man. Editor NIKUNJ PATEL; Editor RAMU PATEL; circ. (Ahmedabad) 30,490 (English), 42,540 (Gujarati).

Bhuj

Kutchmitra: Kutchmitra Bhavan, nr Indirabai Park, Bhuj 370 001; tel. (2832) 252090; fax (2832) 250271; e-mail kutchmitra@rediffmail.com; f. 1947; Propr Saurashtra Trust; Editor SURESH G. SHAH; circ. 39,400.

Rajkot

Jai Hind: Jai Hind Press Bldg, Babubhai Shah Marg, POB 59, Rajkot 360 001; tel. (281) 2440511; fax (281) 2448677; e-mail jaihind@satyam.net.in; f. 1948; morning and evening (in Rajkot as *Sanj Samachar*; Gujarati; also publ. from Ahmedabad; Editor Y. N. SHAH; combined circ. 107,300.

Phulchhab: Phulchhab Bhavan, Phulchhab Chowk, Rajkot 360 001; tel. (281) 2444611; fax (281) 2448751; f. 1950; morning; Gujarati; Propr Saurashtra Trust; Editor DINESH RAJA; circ. 84,500.

Surat

Gujaratmitra and Gujaratdarpan: Gujaratmitra Bhavan, nr Old Civil Hospital, Sonifalia, Surat 395 003; tel. (261) 23478703; fax (261) 23478700; e-mail gujaratmitra@satyam.net.in; f. 1863; morning; Gujarati; Editor B. P. RESHAMWALA; circ. 90,023.

Jammu and Kashmir

Jammu

Daily Excelsior: Excelsior House, Excelsior Lane, Janipura, Jammu Tawi 180 007; tel. (191) 2537055; fax (191) 2537831; e-mail editor@dailyexcelsior.com; internet www.dailyexcelsior.com; f. 1965; English; Editor S. D. ROHMETRA.

Kashmir Times: Residency Rd, Jammu 180 001; tel. (191) 2543676; fax (191) 2542028; e-mail kashmirtimes@vsnl.com; internet www.kashmirtimes.com; f. 1955; morning; English and Hindi; Editor PRABODH JAMWAL.

Srinagar

Greater Kashmir: 6 Pratap Park, Residency Rd, Srinagar 190 001; tel. (194) 2474339; fax (194) 2477782; e-mail editor@greaterkashmir.com; internet www.greaterkashmir.com; f. 1993; English; Chief Editor FAYAZ AHMED KALOO.

Jharkhand

Ranchi

Aj: Main Rd, Ranchi 834 001; tel. (651) 2311416; fax (651) 2306224; Hindi; morning; also publ. from eight other cities; Editor SHARDUL V. GUPTA; circ. 58,700; combined circ. 903,692.

Hindustan: Circular Court, Circular Rd, Ranchi 834 001; tel. (651) 2205811; Hindi; morning; also publ. from Patna, Delhi, Bhagalpur, Lucknow, Varanasi and Muzaffarpur; Editor CHANDRA PRAKASH; combined circ. 673,100.

Ranchi Express: 55 Baralal St, Ranchi 834 001; tel. (651) 2206320; fax (651) 2203466; e-mail rexpress@dte.vsnl.net.in; internet www.ranchiexpress.com; f. 1963; Hindi; morning; Editor AJAY MAROO; circ. 71,100.

Karnataka

Bangalore

Deccan Herald: 75 Mahatma Gandhi Rd, Bangalore 560 001; tel. (80) 25588999; fax (80) 25586443; e-mail ads@deccanherald.co.in; internet www.deccanherald.com; f. 1948; morning; English; also publ. from Hubli-Dharwar, Mangalore and Gulbarga; Editor-in-Chief K. N. SHANTH KUMAR; combined circ. 147,500.

Kannada Prabha: Express Bldgs, 1 Queen's Rd, Bangalore 560 001; tel. (80) 22866893; fax (80) 22866617; e-mail bexpress@bgl.vsnl.net.in; internet www.kannadaprabha.com; f. 1967; morning; Kannada; also publ. from Belgaum and Shimoga; Editor Y. N. Krishna-murthy; circ. 70,200.

New Indian Express: 1 Queen's Rd, Bangalore 560 001; tel. (80) 22256998; fax (80) 22256617; f. 1965; English; also publ. from Kochi, Hyderabad, Chennai, Madurai, Vijayawada and Vizianagaram; Man. Editor Manoj Kumar Sonthalia; combined circ. 251,900.

Prajavani: 75 Mahatma Gandhi Rd, Bangalore 560 001; tel. (80) 25588999; fax (80) 25586443; e-mail ads@deccanherald.co.in; internet www.prajavani.net; f. 1948; morning; Kannada; also publ. from Hubli-Dharwar and Gulbarga; Editor-in-Chief K. N. Shanth Kumar; combined circ. 302,300.

Hubli-Dharwar

Samyukta Karnataka: Koppikar Rd, Hubli 580 020; tel. (836) 2364303; fax (836) 2362760; e-mail info@samyuktakarnataka.com; internet www.samyuktakarnataka.com; f. 1933; Kannada; also publ. from Bangalore and Gulburga; Man. Editor K. Shama Rao; combined circ. 140,200.

Manipal

Udayavani: Udayavani Bldg, Press Corner, Manipal 576 119; tel. (8252) 2570845; fax (8252) 2570848; e-mail udayavani@manipalpress.com; internet www.udayavani.com; f. 1970; Kannada; also publ. from Manipal-Udupi and Mumbai; Editor T. Satish U. Pai; circ. 166,400.

Kerala

Kottayam

Deepika: POB 7, Kottayam 686 001; tel. (481) 2566706; fax (481) 2567947; e-mail deepika@md2.vsnl.net.in; internet www.deepika.com; f. 1887; Malayalam; independent; also publ. from Kannur, Kochi, Thiruvananthapuram and Thrissur; Man. Dir Jose T. Pattara; combined circ. 180,000.

Malayala Manorama: K. K. Rd, POB 26, Kottayam 686 001; tel. (481) 2563646; fax (481) 2562479; e-mail editor@malayalamanorama.com; internet www.manoramaonline.com; f. 1890; also publ. from 11 other regional centres; morning; Malayalam; Man. Dir and Editor Mammen Mathew; Chief Editor K. M. Mathew; combined circ. 1,214,134.

Kozhikode

Deshabhimani: 11/127 Convent Rd, Kozhikode 673 032; tel. (495) 2365286; fax (495) 2365883; f. 1946; morning; Malayalam; publ. by the CPI—M; also publ. from Kochi, Kottayam, Thrissur and Thiruvananthapuram; Chief Editor S. Ramachandran Pillai; combined circ. 178,200.

Mathrubhumi: Mathrubhumi Bldgs, K. P. Kesava Menon Rd, POB 46, Kozhikode 673 001; tel. (495) 2366655; fax (495) 2366656; e-mail mathrelt@md2.vsnl.net.in; internet www.mathrubhumi.com; f. 1923; Malayalam; also publ. from Thiruvananthapuram, Kannur, Thrissur, Kollam, Malappuram, Kottayam, Kochi, Bangalore, Chennai and Mumbai; Editor R. Gopalakrishnan; combined circ. 828,800.

Thiruvananthapuram

Kerala Kaumudi: POB 77, Pettah, Thiruvananthapuram 695 024; tel. (471) 2461010; fax (471) 2461985; e-mail editor@ekaumudi.com; internet www.keralakaumudi.com; f. 1911; Malayalam; also publ. from Kollam, Alappuzha, Kochi, Kannur and Kozhikode; Editor-in-Chief M. S. Mani; combined circ. 140,100.

Madhya Pradesh

Bhopal

Dainik Bhaskar: 6 Dwarka Sadan, Habibganj Rd, Bhopal 462 011; tel. (755) 2551601; fax (755) 2575190; e-mail mp@bhaskarit.com; f. 1958; morning; Hindi; also publ. from 14 other regional centres; Chief Editor R. C. Agarwal; combined circ. 1,570,300.

Indore

Naidunia: 60/1 Babu Labhchand Chhajlani Marg, Indore 452 009; tel. (731) 2763111; fax (731) 2763120; e-mail editor@naidunia.com; internet www.naidunia.com; f. 1947; morning; Hindi; Editor Abhay Chhajlani; circ. 134,012.

Maharashtra

Kolhapur

Pudhari: 2318, 'C' Ward, Kolhapur 416 002; tel. (231) 222251; fax (231) 222256; f. 1974; Marathi; Editor P. G. Jadhav; circ. 200,600.

Mumbai

Afternoon Despatch and Courier: 6 Nanabhai Lane, Fort, Mumbai 400 001; tel. (22) 22871616; fax (22) 22870371; e-mail aftnet@bom2.vsnl.net.in; internet www.afternoondc.com; evening; English; Editor Behram Contractor; circ. 65,800.

The Economic Times: Times of India Bldg, Dr Dadabhai Naoroji Rd, Mumbai 400 001; tel. (22) 22620271; fax (22) 22620144; e-mail etbom@timesgroup.com; internet www.economictimes.com; f. 1961; also publ. from New Delhi, Kolkata, Ahmedabad, Hyderabad, Chennai and Bangalore; English; Exec. Editor Jaideep Bose; combined circ. 435,300, circ. (Mumbai) 148,500.

Financial Express: Express Towers, Nariman Point, Mumbai 400 021; tel. (22) 22022627; fax (22) 22022139; e-mail iemumbai@express.indexp.co.in; internet www.financialexpress.com; f. 1961; morning; English; also publ. from New Delhi, Bangalore, Kolkata, Coimbatore, Kochi, Ahmedabad (Gujarati) and Chennai; Man. Editor Vivek Goenka; Chief Editor Sanjaya Baru; combined circ. (English) 30,800.

The Free Press Journal: Free Press House, 215 Free Press Journal Rd, Nariman Point, Mumbai 400 021; tel. (22) 22874566; fax (22) 22874688; e-mail freepress@bom2.vsnl.net.in; f. 1930; English; also publ. from Indore; Man. Editor G. L. Lakhotia; combined circ. 87,000.

Indian Express: Express Towers, Nariman Point, Mumbai 400 021; tel. (22) 22022627; fax (22) 22022139; f. 1940; English; also publ. from Pune and Nagpur; Man. Editor Vivek Goenka; Chief Editor Shekhar Gupta; combined circ. 191,900.

Inquilab: 156 D. J. Dadajee Rd, Tardeo, Mumbai 400 034; tel. (22) 24942586; fax (22) 24936571; e-mail azizk@mid-day.mailserve.net; internet www.inquilab.com; f. 1938; morning; Urdu; Editor Fuzail Jafferey; circ. 36,400.

Janmabhoomi: Janmabhoomi Bhavan, Janmabhoomi Marg, Fort, POB 62, Mumbai 400 001; tel. (22) 22870831; fax (22) 22874097; e-mail bhoomi@bom3.vsnl.net.in; f. 1934; evening; Gujarati; Propr Saurashtra Trust; Editor Kundan Vyas; circ. 55,395.

Lokasatta: Express Towers, Nariman Point, Mumbai 400 021; tel. (22) 22022627; fax (22) 22022139; internet www.loksatta.com; f. 1948; morning (incl. Sunday); Marathi; also publ. from Pune, Nagpur and Ahmednagar; Editor Dr Aroon Tikekar; combined circ. 369,400.

Maharashtra Times: Dr Dadabhai Naoroji Rd, POB 213, Mumbai 400 001; tel. (22) 22620271; fax (22) 22620144; f. 1962; Marathi; Editor Kumar Ketkar; circ. 197,300.

Mid-Day: 64 Sitaram Mills Compound, N. M. Joshi Marg, Lower Parel, Mumbai 400 011; tel. (22) 23054545; fax (22) 23054861; e-mail mid-day@giasbm01.vsnl.net.in; internet www.mid-day.com; f. 1979; daily and Sunday; English; Editor Ayaz Memon; circ. 124,700.

Mumbai Samachar: Red House, Syed Abdulla Brelvi Rd, Fort, Mumbai 400 001; tel. (22) 22045531; fax (22) 22046642; f. 1822; morning and Sunday; Gujarati; political, social and commercial; Editor Pinky Dalal; circ. 113,900.

Navakal: 13 Shenviwadi, Khadilkar Rd, Girgaun, Mumbai 400 004; tel. (22) 23860978; fax (22) 23860989; f. 1923; Marathi; Editor N. Y. Khadilkar; circ. 169,800.

Navbharat Times: Dr Dadabhai Naoroji Rd, Mumbai 400 001; tel. (22) 22620382; fax (22) 22620144; f. 1950; Hindi; also publ. from New Delhi, Jaipur, Patna and Lucknow; circ. (Mumbai) 166,300.

Navshakti: Free Press House, 215 Nariman Point, Mumbai 400 021; tel. (22) 22874566; fax (22) 22874688; f. 1932; Marathi; Editor D. B. Joshi; circ. 65,000.

Sakal: Sakal Bhavan, Plot No. 42-B, Sector No. 11, CBD Belapur, Navi Mumbai 400 614; tel. (22) 27574327; fax (22) 27574280; e-mail sakal@vsnl.in; f. 1970; daily; Marathi; also publ. from Pune, Aurangabad, Nasik, Kolhapur and Solapur; Editor Anil Mohan Takalkar; combined circ. 519,300.

The Times of India: The Times of India Bldg, Dr Dadabhai Naoroji Rd, Mumbai 400 001; tel. (22) 22620271; fax (22) 22620144; e-mail toieditorial@timesgroup.com; internet www.timesofindia.com; f. 1838; morning; English; also publ. from 10 regional centres; Exec. Editor Shekhar Bhatia; circ. (Mumbai) 530,500, combined circ. 2,131,400.

Nagpur

Hitavada: Wardha Rd, Nagpur 440 012; tel. (712) 2523155; fax (712) 2535093; e-mail hitavada@nagpur.dot.net.in; f. 1911; morning; English; also publ. from Raipur and Jabalpur; Man. Editor Banwarilal Purohit; Editor V. Phanshikar; circ. 54,900.

Lokmat: Lokmat Bhavan, Wardha Rd, Nagpur 440 012; tel. (712) 2523527; fax (712) 2526923; also publ. from Jalgaon, Akola, Pune and Nasik; Marathi; **Lokmat Samachar** (Hindi) publ. from

Nagpur, Akola and Aurangabad; **Lokmat Times** (English) publ. from Nagpur and Aurangabad; Editor VIJAY DARDA; combined circ. (Marathi) 454,100, (Hindi) 62,300.

Nava Bharat: Nava Bharat Bhavan, Cotton Market, Nagpur 440 018; tel. (712) 2726677; fax (712) 2723444; f. 1938; morning; Hindi; also publ. from 10 other cities; Editor-in-Chief R. G. MAHESWARI; combined circ. 645,900.

Tarun Bharat: 28 Farmland, Ramdaspeth, Nagpur 440 010; tel. (712) 2525052; fax (712) 2531758; e-mail ibharat@nagpur.dot.net.in; internet www.tarunbharat.com; f. 1941; Marathi; independent; also publ. from Belgaum; Chief Editor MAHESH MATHRE; circ. (Nagpur) 55,600, combined circ. 166,300.

Pune

Kesari: 568 Narayan Peth, Pune 411 030; tel. (20) 24459250; fax (20) 24451677; f. 1881; Marathi; also publ. from Solapur, Chiplun, Ahmednagar and Sangli; Editor ARVIND VYANKATESH GOKHALE; circ. (Pune) 44,300.

Sakal: 595 Budhwar Peth, Pune 411 002; tel. (20) 24455500; fax (20) 24450583; e-mail sakal@giaspn01.vsnl.net.in; internet www.esakal .com; f. 1932; daily; Marathi; also publ. from 10 other regional centres; Editor ANANT DIXIT; Man. Dir and Man. Editor PRATAP PAWAR; combined circ. 519,300.

Orissa

Bhubaneswar

Dharitri: B-26, Industrial Estate, Bhubaneswar 751 010; tel. (674) 2580101; fax (674) 2580795; e-mail dharitri@mail.com; internet www.dharitri.com; evening and morning; Oriya; Editor TATHAGATA SATPATHY; circ. 163,600.

Pragativadi: 178-B, Mancheswar Industrial Estate, Bhubaneswar 751 010; tel. (674) 2580298; fax (674) 2582636; e-mail pragativadi@ yahoo.com; Exec. Editor SAMAHIT BAL; circ. 123,000.

Cuttack

Prajatantra: Prajatantra Bldgs, Behari Baug, Cuttack 753 002; tel. (671) 2603071; fax (671) 2603063; f. 1947; Oriya; Editor BHARTRUHARI MAHTAB; circ. 119,300.

Samaj: Gopabandhu Bhavan, Buxibazar, Cuttack 753 001; tel. (671) 2301598; fax (671) 2301384; e-mail samaj@hotmail.com; f. 1919; Oriya; also publ. from Sambalpur; Editor MANORAMA MAHAPATRA; circ. 154,800.

Punjab

Chandigarh

The Tribune: Sector 29C, Chandigarh 160 020; tel. (172) 2655065; fax (172) 2655054; e-mail tribunet@ch1.dot.net.in; internet www .tribuneindia.com; f. 1881; (English edn), f. 1978 (Hindi and Punjabi edns); Editor (all edns) HARI JAISINGH; Editor (Hindi edn) VIJAY SAIGHAL; Editor (Punjabi edn) G. S. BHULLAR; circ. 229,000 (English), 48,300 (Hindi), 72,500 (Punjabi).

Jalandhar

Ajit: Ajit Bhavan, Nehru Garden Rd, Jalandhar 144 001; tel. (181) 22800960; f. 1955; Punjabi; Man. Editor S. BARJINDER SINGH; circ. 230,900.

Hind Samachar: Civil Lines, Jalandhar 144 001; tel. (181) 2280104; fax (181) 2280113; f. 1948; morning; Urdu; also publ. from Ambala Cantt; Editor-in-Chief VIJAY KUMAR CHOPRA; Jt Editor AVINASH CHOPRA; combined circ. 43,042.

Jag Bani: Civil Lines, Jalandhar 144 001; tel. (181) 2280104; fax (181) 2280113; f. 1978; morning; Punjabi; Editor-in-Chief VIJAY KUMAR CHOPRA; Jt Editor AVINASH CHOPRA; circ. 208,255.

Punjab Kesari: Civil Lines, Jalandhar 144 001; tel. (181) 2280104; fax (181) 2280113; f. 1965; morning; Hindi; also publ. from Delhi and Ambala; Editor-in-Chief VIJAY KUMAR CHOPRA; Jt Editor AVINASH CHOPRA; combined circ. 843,101.

Rajasthan

Jaipur

Rajasthan Patrika: Kesargarh, Jawahar Lal Nehru Marg, Jaipur 302 004; tel. (141) 2561582; fax (141) 2566011; e-mail info@ rajasthanpatrika.com; internet www.rajasthan_patrika.com; f. 1956; Hindi edn also publ. from eight other towns; Chief Editor GULAB KOTHARI; combined circ. (Hindi) 597,100.

Rashtradoot: M.I. Rd, POB 30, Jaipur 302 001; tel. (141) 2372634; fax (141) 2373513; f. 1951; Hindi; also publ. from Kota, Udaipur, Ajmer and Bikaner; CEO SOMESH SHARMA; Chief Editor RAJESH

SHARMA; circ. 368,482 (Jaipur), 76,763 (Kota), 45,250 (Bikaner), 38,023 (Udaipur), 27,514 (Ajmer).

Tamil Nadu

Chennai (Madras)

Daily Thanthi: 46 E.V.K. Sampath Rd, POB 467, Chennai 600 007; tel. (44) 25387731; fax (44) 25381720; f. 1949; Tamil; also publ. from Bangalore, Coimbatore, Cuddalore, Erode, Madurai, Nagercoil, Salem, Tiruchi, Tirunelveli, Pondicherry and Vellore; Gen. Man. D. RAJIAH; Editor R. THIRUVADI; combined circ. 608,600.

Dinakaran: 106/107 Kutchery Rd, Mylapore, POB 358, Chennai 600 004; tel. (44) 24941006; fax (44) 24933597; e-mail dinakaran@ dinakaran.com; internet www.dinakaran.com; f. 1977; Tamil; also publ. from Madurai, Tiruchirapalli, Vellore, Tirunelveli, Salem and Coimbatore; Man. Dir K. KUMARAN; Editor D. PAULRAJ; combined circ. 351,872.

Dinamalar: 8, Casa Major Rd, Egmore, Chennai 600 008; tel. (44) 28267106; fax (44) 28259926; e-mail malar@md3.vsnl.net.in; internet www.dinamalar.com; f. 1951; Tamil; also publ. from nine other towns; Editor R. KRISHNAMOORTHY; combined circ. 489,200.

Dinamani: Express Estates, Mount Rd, Chennai 600 002; tel. (44) 8520751; fax (44) 8524500; e-mail express@giasmd01.vsnl.net.in; internet www.dinamani.com; f. 1934; morning; Tamil; also publ. from Madurai, Coimbatore and Bangalore; Editor T. SAMBANDAM; combined circ. 158,300.

Financial Express: Vasanthi Medical Center, 30/20 Pycrofts Garden Rd, Chennai 600 006; tel. (44) 28231112; fax (44) 28231489; internet www.financialexpress.com; f. 1961; morning; English; also publ. from Mumbai, Ahmedabad (in Gujarati), Bangalore, Kochi, Kolkata and New Delhi; Man. Editor VIVEK GOENKA; combined circ. 32,594.

The Hindu: Kasturi Bldgs, 859/860 Anna Salai, Chennai 600 002; tel. (44) 28413344; fax (44) 28415325; e-mail wsvcs@thehindu.co.in; internet www.hinduonnet.com; f. 1878; morning; English; independent; also publ. from 10 other regional centres; Publr S. RANGARAJAN; Editor N. RAVI; combined circ. 925,000.

The Hindu Business Line: Kasturi Bldgs, 859/860 Anna Salai, Chennai 600 002; tel. (44) 28589060; fax (44) 28545703; e-mail bleditor@thehindu.co.in; internet www.hindubusinessline.com; f. 1994; morning; English; also publ. from 10 other regional centres; Publr S. RANGARAJAN; Editor N. RAM; combined circ. 42,500.

Murasoli: 93 Kodambakkam High Rd, Chennai 600 034; tel. (44) 28270044; fax (44) 28217515; f. 1960; organ of the DMK; Tamil; Editor S. SELVAM; circ. 54,000.

New Indian Express: Club House Rd, Chennai 600 002; tel. (44) 28461260; fax (44) 28461829; e-mail newexpress@vsnl.com; internet www.newindpress.com; f. 1932 as Indian Express; morning; English; also publ. from 11 other cities; Chair. and Man. Dir MANOJ KUMAR SONTHALIA; combined circ. 251,900.

Tripura

Agartala

Dainik Sambad: 11 Jagannath Bari Rd, POB 2, Agartala 799 001; tel. (381) 2326676; fax (381) 2324845; e-mail dainik2@sanchar.net .in; f. 1966; Bengali; morning; Editor BHUPENDRA CHANDRA DATTA BHAUMIK; circ. 44,500.

Uttaranchal

Dehradun

Amar Ujala: Shed 2, Patel Nagar Industrial Estate, Dehradun 248 003; tel. (135) 2720378; fax (135) 2721776; internet www.amarujala .com; Hindi; morning; also publ. from 10 other cities; Editor AJAY K. AGRAWAL; combined circ. 637,500.

Uttar Pradesh

Agra

Amar Ujala: Sikandra Rd, Agra 282 007; tel. (562) 2321600; fax (562) 2322181; e-mail amarujal@nde.vsnl.net.in; internet www .amarujala.com; f. 1948; Hindi; also publ. from Bareilly, Allahabad, Jhansi, Kanpur, Moradabad, Chandigarh and Meerut; Editor AJAY K. AGRAWAL; combined circ. 629,400.

Allahabad

Amrita Prabhat: 10 Tashkent Marg, Allahabad 211 001; tel. (532) 2600654; fax (532) 2605394; f. 1977; Hindi; CEO S. S. BAGGA; circ. 44,000.

Northern India Patrika: 10 Edmonstone Rd, Allahabad 211 001; tel. (532) 2600654; fax (532) 2605394; f. 1959; English; CEO S. S. BAGGA; circ. 46,000.

Kanpur

Dainik Jagran: Jagran Bldg, 2 Sarvodaya Nagar, Kanpur 208 005; tel. (512) 2216161; fax (512) 2218791; e-mail kanpur@knp.jagran .com; internet www.jagran.com; f. 1942; Hindi; also publ. from 15 other cities; Editor SANJAY GUPTA; combined circ. 1,499,600.

Lucknow

National Herald: Lucknow; f. 1938; Lucknow, 1968 Delhi; English; Editor-in-Chief D. V. VENKITACHALAM.

The Pioneer: Sahara Shopping Centre, Faizabad Rd, Lucknow 226 016; tel. (522) 2346444; fax (522) 2345582; f. 1865; English; also publ. from New Delhi; Editor CHANDAN MITRA; combined circ. 136,000.

Swatantra Bharat: 1st Floor, Suraj Deep Complex, 1 Jopling Rd, Lucknow 226 001; tel. (522) 2204306; fax (522) 2208701; e-mail sbharats@satyam.net.in; f. 1947; Hindi; also publ. from Kanpur; Editor K. K. SRIVASTAVA; circ. 80,700 (Lucknow), 65,157 (Kanpur).

Varanasi

Aj: Aj Bhavan, Sant Kabir Rd, Kabirchaura, Varanasi 221 001; tel. (542) 2393981; fax (542) 2393989; f. 1920; Hindi; also publ. from Gorakhpur, Patna, Allahabad, Ranchi, Agra, Bareilly, Lucknow, Jamshedpur, Dhanbad and Kanpur; Editor SHARDUL VIKRAM GUPTA; combined circ. 908,700.

West Bengal

Kolkata (Calcutta)

Aajkaal: 96 Raja Rammohan Sarani, Kolkata 700 009; tel. (33) 23509803; fax (33) 23500877; e-mail aajkaal@cal.vsnl.net.in; f. 1981; morning; Bengali; Chief Editor PRATAP K. ROY; circ. 137,000.

Ananda Bazar Patrika: 6 Prafulla Sarkar St, Kolkata 700 001; tel. (33) 22374880; fax (33) 22253241; internet www.anandabazar.com; f. 1922; morning; Bengali; also publ. from Siliguri; Editor AVEEK SARKAR; circ. 873,600.

Bartaman: 76A Acharya J.C. Bose Rd, Kolkata 700 014; tel. (33) 22443907; fax (33) 22441215; f. 1984; also publ. from Siliguri; Editor BARUN SENGUPTA; circ. 464,200.

Business Standard: 4/1 Red Cross Place, Kolkata 700 001; tel. (33) 22101314; fax (33) 22101599; f. 1975; morning; also publ. from New Delhi, Ahmedabad, Hyderabad, Bangalore, Chennai and Mumbai; English; Editor T. N. NINAN; combined circ. 56,000.

The Economic Times: 105/7A, S. N. Banerjee Rd, Kolkata 700 014; tel. (33) 22444243; fax (33) 22453018; English; also publ. from Ahmedabad, Delhi, Bangalore, Chennai, Hyderabad and Mumbai; circ. (Kolkata) 52,400.

Financial Express: 83 B. K. Pal Ave, Kolkata 700 005; morning; English; also publ. from Mumbai, Ahmedabad, Bangalore, Coimbatore, Kochi, Chennai and New Delhi; Man. Editor VIVEK GOENKA; combined circ. 30,800.

Ganashakti: 74A A. J. C. Bose Rd, Kolkata 700 016; tel. (33) 22458950; fax (33) 22448090; e-mail mail@ganashakti.co.in; internet www.ganashakti.com; f. 1967; morning; Bengali; also publ. from Siliguri; Editor DIPEN GHOSH; circ. 132,500.

Sambad Pratidin: 20 Prafulla Sarkar St, Kolkata 700 072; tel. (33) 22253707; fax (33) 22252536; e-mail pratidin@cal2.vsnl.net.in; internet www.sangbadpratidin.com; morning; Bengali; Editor SWAPAN SADHAN BASU; circ. 274,900.

Sandhya Aajkaal: 96 Raja Rammohan Sarani, Kolkata 700 009; tel. (33) 23509803; fax (33) 23500877; evening; Bengali; Chief Editor PRATAP K. ROY; circ. 21,600.

Sanmarg: 160C Chittaranjan Ave, Kolkata 700 007; tel. (33) 22414800; fax (33) 22415087; e-mail sanmarg@vsnl.com; f. 1948; Hindi; Editor RAMAWATAR GUPTA; circ. 104,600.

The Statesman: Statesman House, 4 Chowringhee Sq., Kolkata 700 001; tel. (33) 22257070; fax (33) 22250118; f. 1875; morning; English; independent; also publ. from New Delhi and Siliguri; Editor-in-Chief C. R. IRANI; combined circ. 154,100.

The Telegraph: 6 Prafulla Sarkar St, Kolkata 700 001; tel. (33) 22374880; fax (33) 22253240; e-mail thetelegraphindia@newscom .com; f. 1982; English; also publ. from Guwahati and Jamshedpur; Editor AVEEK SARKAR; circ. 288,800.

Uttar Banga Sambad: 7 Old Court House St, Kolkata 700 001; tel. (33) 22207618; fax (33) 22206663; f. 1980; Bengali; Editor S. C. TALUKDAR; circ. 111,400.

Vishwamitra: 74 Lenin Sarani, Kolkata 700 013; tel. (33) 22441139; fax (33) 22446393; e-mail vismtra@cal2.vsnl.net.in; f. 1915; morning; Hindi; commercial; Editor PRAKASH CHANDRA AGRAWALLA; combined circ. 91,006.

SELECTED PERIODICALS

Delhi and New Delhi

Alive: Delhi Press Bldg, E-3, Jhandewala Estate, Rani Jhansi Rd, New Delhi 110 055; tel. (11) 23529557; fax (11) 23625020; e-mail advertising@delhipressgroup.com; f. 1940; monthly; English; political and cultural; Editor PARESH NATH; circ. 8,000.

Bal Bharati: Patiala House, Publications Division, Ministry of Information and Broadcasting, New Delhi; tel. (11) 2387038; f. 1948; monthly; Hindi; for children; Editor SHIV KUMAR; circ. 30,000.

Biswin Sadi: B-1, Nizamuddin West, New Delhi 110 013; tel. (11) 24626556; f. 1937; monthly; Urdu; Editor Z. REHMAN NAYYAR; circ. 32,000.

Business Today: F-26 Connaught Place, New Delhi 110 001; tel. (11) 23315801; fax (11) 23318385; e-mail btoday@giasdl01.vsnl.net .in; internet www.business-today.com; fortnightly; English; Editor SANJAY NARAYAN; circ. 120,200.

Catholic India: CBCI Centre, 1 Ashok Place, Goldakkhana, New Delhi 110 001; tel. (11) 23344470; fax (11) 23364615; e-mail cbci@ vsnl.com; internet www.cbcisite.com; quarterly.

Champak: Delhi Press Bldg, E-3, Jhandewala Estate, Rani Jhansi Rd, New Delhi 110 055; tel. (11) 23529557; fax (11) 23625020; f. 1969; fortnightly (Hindi, English, Gujarati and Marathi edns); monthly (Kannada edn); children; Editor PARESH NATH; combined circ. 146,000.

Children's World: Nehru House, 4 Bahadur Shah Zafar Marg, New Delhi 110 002; tel. (11) 23316970; fax (11) 23721090; e-mail cbtnd@ vsnl.com; internet www.childrensbooktrust.com; f. 1968; monthly; English; Editor NAVIN MENON; circ. 25,000.

Competition Refresher: 2767, Bright House, Daryaganj, New Delhi 110 002; tel. (11) 23282226; fax (11) 23269227; e-mail psbright@ndf.vsnl.net.in; internet www.brightcareers.com; f. 1984; monthly; English; Chief Editor, Publr and Man. Dir PRITAM SINGH BRIGHT; circ. 175,000.

Competition Success Review: 604 Prabhat Kiran Bldg, Rajendra Place, Delhi 110 008; tel. (11) 25712898; fax (11) 25754647; monthly; English; f. 1964; Editor S. K. SACHDEVA; circ. 248,500.

Computers Today: Marina Arcade, G-59 Connaught Circus, New Delhi 110 001; tel. (11) 23736233; fax (11) 23725506; e-mail ctoday@ india-today.com; f. 1984; Editor J. SRIHARI RAJU; circ. 46,300.

Cricket Samrat: L–1, Kanchan House, Najafgarh Rd, Commercial Complex, nr Milan Cinema, New Delhi 110 015; tel. (11) 25191175; fax (11) 25469581; f. 1978; monthly; Hindi; Editor ANAND DEWAN; circ. 61,600.

Employment News: Government of India, East Block IV, Level 5, R. K. Puram, New Delhi 110 066; tel. (11) 26193316; fax (11) 26193012; e-mail empnews@bol.net.in; f. 1976; weekly; Hindi, Urdu and English edns; Gen. Man. and Chief Editor P. BHATNAGAR; Editor RANJANA DEV SARMAH; combined circ. 550,000.

Filmi Duniya: 16 Darya Ganj, New Delhi 110 002; tel. (11) 23278087; fax (11) 23279341; f. 1958; monthly; Hindi; Chief Editor NARENDRA KUMAR; circ. 132,100.

Filmi Kaliyan: 4675-B/21 Ansari Rd, New Delhi 110 002; tel. (11) 23272080; f. 1969; monthly; Hindi; cinema; Editor-in-Chief V. S. DEWAN; circ. 82,400.

Global Travel Express: 26F Rajiv Gandhi Chowk (Connaught Place), New Delhi 110 001; tel. (11) 23312329; fax (11) 24621633; e-mail nri@ndf.vsnl.net.in; f. 1993; monthly; English; travel and tourism; Chief Editor HARBHAJAN SINGH; Editor GURINDER SINGH; circ. 28,499.

Grih Shobha: Delhi Press Bldg, E-3 Jhandewala Estate, Rani Jhansi Rd, New Delhi 110 055; tel. (11) 23529557; fax (11) 23625020; e-mail grihshobha@delhipressgroup.com; f. 1979; monthly; Tamil, Kannada, Marathi, Hindi and Gujarati edns; women's interests; Editor PARESH NATH; circ. 92,000 (Kannada), 65,000 (Gujarati), 140,000 (Marathi), 335,000 (Hindi), 19,000 (Tamil), 15,000 (Telugu).

India Perspectives: Room 149B, 'A' Wing, Shastri Bhavan, New Delhi 110 001; tel. (11) 23389471; f. 1988; Editor BHARAT BHUSHAN.

India Today: F 14/15, Connaught Place, New Delhi 110 001; tel. (11) 23315801; fax (11) 23316180; e-mail letters.editor@intoday.com; internet www.india-today.com; f. 1975; English, Tamil, Telugu, Malayalam and Hindi; weekly; Editor PRABHU CHAWLA; Editor-in-Chief AROON PURIE; circ. 460,700 (English), 352,200 (Hindi), 60,200 (Tamil), 41,700 (Malayalam), 61,000 (Telugu).

Indian Railways: 411 Rail Bhavan, Raisina Rd, New Delhi 110 001; tel. (11) 23383540; fax (11) 23384481; f. 1956; monthly; English; publ. by the Ministry of Railways (Railway Board); Editor S. K. SINGH; circ. 12,000.

Journal of Industry and Trade: Ministry of Commerce, Delhi 110 011; tel. (11) 23016664; f. 1952; monthly; English; Man. Dir A. C. BANERJEE; circ. 2,000.

Junior Science Refresher: 2769, Bright House, Daryaganj, New Delhi 110 002; tel. (11) 23282226; fax (11) 23269227; e-mail psbright@ndf.vsnl.net.in; internet www.brightcareers.com; f. 1987; monthly; English; Chief Editor, Publr and Man. Dir PRITAM SINGH BRIGHT; circ. 118,000.

Kadambini: Hindustan Times House, Kasturba Gandhi Marg, New Delhi 110 001; tel. (11) 23704581; fax (11) 23704600; e-mail rajendrawasthy@hindustantimes.com; f. 1960; monthly; Hindi; Editor RAJENDRA AWASTHY; circ. 90,000.

Krishak Samachar: Bharat Krishak Samaj, Dr Panjabrao Deshmukh Krishak Bhavan, A-1 Nizamuddin West, New Delhi 110 013; tel. (11) 24619508; e-mail ffi@mantraonline.com; f. 1957; monthly; English and Hindi edns; agriculture; Editor Dr KRISHAN BIR CHAUDHARY; circ. (English) 6,000, (Hindi) 17,000.

Kurukshetra: Ministry of Rural Development, Room No. 655/661, 'A' Wing, Nirman Bhavan, New Delhi 110 011; tel. (11) 23015014; fax (11) 23386879; monthly; English; rural development; Editor P. V. RAO; circ. 14,000.

Mainstream: 145/1D Shahpur Jat, 1st Floor, nr Asiad Village, New Delhi 110 049; tel. (11) 26497188; fax (11) 26569352; English; weekly; politics and current affairs; Editor SUMIT CHAKRAVARTTY.

Mayapuri: A-5, Mayapuri Phase 1, New Delhi 110 064; tel. (11) 25138596; fax (11) 25133120; e-mail mayapuri@hotmail.com; f. 1974; weekly; Hindi; cinema; Editor A. P. BAJAJ; circ. 146,144.

Mukta: Delhi Press Bldg, E-3 Jhandewala Estate, Rani Jhansi Rd, New Delhi 110 055; tel. (11) 23529557; fax (11) 23625020; e-mail advertising@delhipressgroup.com; f. 1979; monthly; Hindi; youth; Editor PARESH NATH; circ. 13,000.

Nandan: Hindustan Times House, Kasturba Gandhi Marg, New Delhi 110 001; tel. (11) 23704562; fax (11) 23704600; e-mail jbharti@hindustantimes.com; f. 1963; monthly; Hindi; Editor JAI PRAKASH BHARTI; circ. 63,600.

New Age: 15 Kotla Rd, Delhi 110 055; tel. (11) 23230762; fax (11) 23235543; e-mail cpindia@del2.vsnl.net.in; f. 1953; main organ of the Communist Party of India; weekly; English; Editor SHAMEEM FAIZEE; circ. 215,000.

Organiser: Sanskriti Bhavan, D. B. Gupta Rd, Jhandewalan, New Delhi 110 055; tel. (11) 23526097; fax (11) 23516635; e-mail chari_s@vsnl.com; internet www.organiser.org; f. 1947; weekly; English; Editor SESHADRI CHARI; circ. 44,100.

Outlook: AB-10 Safdarjung Enclave, New Delhi 110 029; tel. (11) 26191421; fax (11) 26191420; e-mail outlook@outlookindia.com; internet www.outlookindia.com; f. 1995; weekly; Editor-in-Chief VINOD MEHTA; circ. 252,400.

Panchjanya: Sanskriti Bhavan, Deshbandhu Gupta Marg, Jhandewala, New Delhi 110 055; tel. (11) 23514244; fax (11) 23558613; e-mail panch@nde.vsnl.net.in; f. 1947; weekly; Hindi; general interest; nationalist; Chair. S. N. BANSAL; Editor TARUN VIJAY; circ. 59,300.

Punjabi Digest: 209 Hemkunt House, 6 Rajendra Place, POB 2549, New Delhi 110 008; tel. (11) 25715225; fax (11) 25761023; f. 1971; literary monthly; Gurmukhi; Chief Editor Sardar S. B. SINGH; circ. 84,200.

Sainik Samachar: Block L-1, Church Rd, New Delhi 110 001; tel. (11) 23019668; f. 1909; pictorial fortnightly for India's armed forces; English, Hindi, Urdu, Tamil, Punjabi, Telugu, Marathi, Kannada, Gorkhali, Malayalam, Bengali, Assamese and Oriya edns; Editor P. K. PATTAYANAK; circ. 20,000.

Saras Salil: Delhi Press Bldg, E-3, Jhandewala Estate, Rani Jhansi Rd, New Delhi 110 055; tel. (11) 23529557; fax (11) 23625020; f. 1993; fortnightly; Hindi, Marathi, Gujarati; Editor PARESH NATH; circ. 1,150,000 (Hindi), 12,000 (Marathi), 25,000 (Gujarati).

Sarita: Delhi Press Bldg, E-3, Jhandewala Estate, Rani Jhansi Rd, New Delhi 110 055; tel. (11) 23529557; fax (11) 23525020; e-mail advertising@delhipressgroup.com; f. 1945; fortnightly; Hindi; family magazine; Editor PARESH NATH; circ. 120,000.

Shama: 13/14 Asaf Ali Rd, New Delhi 110 002; tel. (11) 23232674; fax (11) 23235167; f. 1939; monthly; Urdu; art and literature; Editors M. YUNUS DEHLVI, IDREES DEHLVI, ILYAS DEHLVI; circ. 58,000.

Suman Saurabh: Delhi Press Bldg, E-3 Jhandewala Estate, Rani Jhansi Rd, New Delhi 110 055; tel. (11) 23529557; fax (11) 23625020; f. 1983; monthly; Hindi; youth; Editor PARESH NATH; circ. 37,000.

Sushama: 13/14 Asaf Ali Rd, New Delhi 110 002; tel. (11) 23232674; fax (11) 23235167; f. 1959; monthly; Hindi; art and literature; Editors IDREES DEHLVI, ILYAS DEHLVI, YUNUS DEHLVI; circ. 30,000.

Vigyan Pragati: PID Bldg, Dr K. S. Krishnan Marg, New Delhi 110 012; tel. (11) 25785647; fax (11) 25731353; f. 1952; monthly; Hindi; popular science; Editor DEEKSHA BIST; circ. 100,000.

Woman's Era: Delhi Press Bldg, E-3, Jhandewala Estate, Rani Jhansi Rd, New Delhi 110 055; tel. (11) 23529557; fax (11) 23625020; f. 1973; fortnightly; English; women's interests; Editor PARESH NATH; circ. 76,500.

Yojana: Yojana Bhavan, Sansad Marg, New Delhi 110 001; tel. (11) 23710473; e-mail yojana@techpilgrim.com; f. 1957; monthly; English, Tamil, Bengali, Marathi, Gujarati, Assamese, Malayalam, Telugu, Kannada, Punjabi, Urdu, Oriya and Hindi edns; Chief Editor SUBHASH SETIA; circ. 72,000.

Andhra Pradesh

Hyderabad

Andhra Prabha Illustrated Weekly: 591 Lower Tank Bund Rd, Express Centre, Domalaguda, Hyderabad 500 029; tel. (40) 2233586; f. 1952; weekly; Telugu; Editor POTTURI VENKATESWARA RAO; circ. 21,800.

Secunderabad

Andhra Bhoomi Sachitra Vara Patrika: 36 Sarojini Devi Rd, Secunderabad 500 003; tel. (842) 27802346; fax (842) 27805256; f. 1977; weekly; Telugu; Editor T. VENKATRAM REDDY; circ. 40,100.

Vijayawada

Andhra Jyoti Sachitra Vara Patrika: Vijayawada 520 010; tel. (866) 2474532; f. 1967; weekly; Telugu; Editor PURANAM SUBRAMANYA SARMA; circ. 59,000.

Bala Jyoti: Labbipet, Vijayawada 520 010; tel. (866) 2474532; f. 1980; monthly; Telugu; Assoc. Editor A. SASIKANT SATAKARNI; circ. 12,500.

Jyoti Chitra: Andhra Jyoti Bldgs, Vijayawada 520 010; tel. (866) 2474532; f. 1977; weekly; Telugu; Editor T. KUTUMBA RAO; circ. 20,100.

Swati Saparivara Patrika: Anil Bldgs, Suryaraopet, POB 339, Vijayawada 520 002; tel. (866) 2431862; fax (866) 2430433; e-mail vjwswati@sancharnet.in; f. 1984; weekly; Telugu; Editor VEMURI BALARAM; circ. 263,400.

Vanita Jyoti: Labbipet, POB 712, Vijayawada 520 010; tel. (866) 2474532; f. 1978; monthly; Telugu; Asst Editor J. SATYANARAYANA; circ. 13,100.

Assam

Guwahati

Agradoot: Agradoot Bhavan, Dispur, Guwahati 781 006; tel. (361) 2261923; fax (361) 2260655; e-mail agradoot@sify.com; f. 1971; bi-weekly; Assamese; Editor K. S. DEKA; circ. 45,000.

Asam Bani: Tribune Bldg, Guwahati 781 003; tel. (361) 2661356; fax (361) 2660594; e-mail dileepchandan@yahoo.com; internet www.assamtribune.com; f. 1955; weekly; Assamese; Editor DILEEP CHANDAN; circ. 14,000.

Sadin: Maniram Dewan Rd, Chandmari, Guwahati 781 003; tel. (361) 2524594; fax (361) 2524634; e-mail protidin@gw1.vsnl.net.in; weekly; Assamese; circ. 44,700.

Bihar

Patna

Anand Digest: Govind Mitra Rd, Patna 800 004; tel. (612) 2656557; fax (612) 2225192; f. 1981; monthly; Hindi; family magazine; Editor Dr S. S. SINGH; circ. 44,500.

Balak: Govind Mitra Rd, POB 5, Patna 800 004; tel. (612) 2650341; f. 1926; monthly; Hindi; children's; Editor S. R. SARAN; circ. 32,000.

Gujarat

Ahmedabad

Akhand Anand: Anand Bhavan, Relief Rd, POB 123, Ahmedabad 380 001; tel. (79) 2357482; f. 1947; monthly; Gujarati; Pres. ANAND AMIN; Editor Dr DILAVARSINH JADEJA; circ. 10,000.

Chitralok: Gujarat Samachar Bhavan, Khanpur, POB 254, Ahmedabad 380 001; tel. (79) 25504010; fax (79) 25502000; f. 1952; weekly; Gujarati; films; Man. Editor SHREYANS S. SHAH; circ. 20,000.

Sakhi: Sakhi Publications, Jai Hind Press Bldg, nr Gujarat Chamber, Ashram Rd, Navrangpura, Ahmedabad 380 009; tel. (79) 26581734; fax (79) 26587681; f. 1984; fortnightly; Gujarati; women's; Man. Editor NITA Y. SHAH; Editor Y. N. SHAH; circ. 10,000.

Shree: Gujarat Samachar Bhavan, Khanpur, Ahmedabad 380 001; tel. (79) 25504010; fax (79) 25502000; f. 1964; weekly; Gujarati; women's; Editor SMRUTIBEN SHAH; circ. 20,000.

Stree: Sandesh Bhavan, Lad Society Rd, Ahmedabad 380 054; tel. (79) 26765480; fax (79) 26753587; e-mail stree@sandesh.com; internet www.sandesh.com; f. 1962; weekly; Gujarati; Jt Editors RITABEN PATEL, LILABEN PATEL; circ. 42,170.

Zagmag: Gujarat Samachar Bhavan, Khanpur, Ahmedabad 380 001; tel. (79) 222821; f. 1952; weekly; Gujarati; for children; Editor BAHUBALI S. SHAH; circ. 38,000.

Rajkot

Amruta: Jai Hind Publications, Jai Hind Press Bldg, Babubhai Shah Marg, Rajkot 360 001; tel. (281) 2440513; fax (281) 2448677; e-mail info@jaihinddaily.com; f. 1967; weekly; Gujarati; films; Editor Y. N. SHAH; circ. 12,500.

Niranjan: Jai Hind Publications, Jai Hind Press Bldg, Babubhai Shah Marg, Rajkot 360 001; tel. (281) 2440517; fax (281) 2448677; e-mail info@jaihinddaily.com; f. 1972; fortnightly; Gujarati; children's; Editor N. R. SHAH; circ. 10,500.

Parmarth: Jai Hind Publications, Jai Hind Press Bldg, Babubhai Shah Marg, Rajkot 360 001; tel. (281) 2440511; fax (281) 2448677; e-mail info@jaihinddaily.com; monthly; Gujarati; philosophy and religion; Editor Y. N. SHAH; circ. 8,000.

Phulwadi: Jai Hind Publications, Jai Hind Press Bldg, Babubhai Shah Marg, Rajkot 360 001; tel. (281) 2440513; fax (281) 2448677; e-mail info@jaihinddaily.com; f. 1967; weekly; Gujarati; for children; Editor Y. N. SHAH; circ. 10,000.

Karnataka

Bangalore

Mayura: 75 Mahatma Gandhi Rd, Bangalore 560 001; tel. (80) 25588999; fax (80) 25587179; e-mail ads@deccanherald.co.in; f. 1968; monthly; Kannada; Editor-in-Chief K. N. SHANTH KUMAR; circ. 35,400.

Sudha: 75 Mahatma Gandhi Rd, Bangalore 560 001; tel. (80) 25588999; fax (80) 25587179; e-mail ads@deccanherald.co.in; f. 1965; weekly; Kannada; Editor-in-Chief K. N. HARI KUMAR; circ. 77,000.

Manipal

Taranga: Udayavani Bldg, Press Corner, Manipal 576 119; tel. (825) 570845; fax (825) 570563; e-mail taranga@manipalpress.com; internet www.udayavani.com; f. 1983; weekly; Kannada; Editor-in-Chief SANDHYA S. PAI; circ. 105,000.

Kerala

Kochi

The Week: Malayala Manorama Buildings, POB 4278, Kochi 682 036; tel. (484) 2316285; fax (484) 2315745; e-mail editor@theweek .com; internet www.the_week.com; f. 1982; weekly; English; current affairs; Chief Editor MAMMEN MATHEW; Editor PHILIP MATHEW; circ. 177,531.

Kottayam

Balarama: MM Publications Ltd, POB 226, Erayilkadavu, Kottayam 686 001; tel. (481) 2563721; fax (481) 2564393; e-mail vanbal@satyam.net.in; f. 1972; children's weekly; Malayalam; Chief Editor BINA MATHEW; Senior Man. V. SAJEEV GEORGE; circ. 245,080.

Malayala Manorama: K. K. Rd, POB 26, Kottayam 686 001; tel. (481) 2563646; fax (481) 2562479; e-mail editor@ malayalamanorama.com; internet www.malayalamanorama.com; f. 1937; weekly; Malayalam; also publ. from Kozhikode; Man. Dir and Editor MAMMEN MATHEW; Chief Editor MAMMEN VARGHESE; combined circ. 896,793.

Vanitha: MM Publications Ltd, POB 226, Erayilkadavu, Kottayam 686 001; tel. (481) 2563721; fax (481) 2564393; e-mail vanbal@ satyam.net.in; f. 1975; women's fortnightly; Malayalam; Chief Editor K. M. MATHEW; Senior Man. V. SAJEEV GEORGE; circ. 435,105.

Kozhikode

Arogya Masika: Mathrubhumi Bldgs, K. P. Kesava Menon Rd, Kozhikode 673 001; tel. (495) 2765381; fax (495) 2760138; e-mail arogyamasika@mat1.mathrubhumi.co.in; monthly; Malayalam; health; Man. Editor P. V. CHANDRAN; circ. 145,500.

Chitrabhumi: Mathrubhumi Bldgs, K. P. Kesava Menon Rd, Kozhikode 673 001; tel. (495) 2366655; fax (495) 2366656; weekly; Malayalam; films; Editor K. K. SREEDHARAN NAIR; circ. 34,500.

Grihalakshmi: Mathrubhumi Bldgs, K. P. Kesava Menon Rd, POB 46, Kozhikode 673 001; tel. (495) 2366655; fax (495) 2366656; e-mail mathrclt@md2.vsnl.net.in; internet www.mathrubhumi.com; f. 1979; monthly; Malayalam; women's; Editor K. K. SREEDHARAN NAIR; circ. 170,300.

Mathrubhumi Illustrated Weekly: Mathrubhumi Bldgs, K. P. Kesava Menon Rd, POB 46, Kozhikode 673 001; tel. (495) 2366655; fax (495) 2356656; f. 1923; weekly; Malayalam; Editor K. K. SREEDHARAN NAIR; circ. 64,000.

Sports Masika: Mathrubhumi Bldgs, K. P. Kesava Menon Rd, Kozhikode 673 001; tel. (495) 366655; fax (495) 366656; monthly; Malayalam; sport; Editor K. K. SREEDHARAN NAIR; circ. 77,400.

Quilon

Karala Sabdam: Thevally, Quilon 691 009; tel. (474) 272403; fax (474) 2740710; f. 1962; weekly; Malayalam; Man. Editor B. A. RAJAKRISHNAN; circ. 66,600.

Thiruvananthapuram

Kalakaumudi: Kaumudi Bldgs, Pettah, Thiruvananthapuram 695 024; tel. (471) 2443531; fax (471) 2442895; e-mail kalakaumudi@ vsnl.com; f. 1975; weekly; Malayalam; Chief Editor M. S. MANI; Gen. Man. ABRAHAM EAPEN; circ. 73,000.

Vellinakshatram: Kaumudi Bldgs, Pettah, Thiruvananthapuram 695 024; tel. (471) 2443531; fax (471) 2442895; e-mail kalakaumudi@ vsnl.com; internet www.vellinakshatram.com; f. 1987; film weekly; Malayalam; Editor PRASAD LAKSHMANAN; Man. Editor SUKUMARAN MANI; circ. 55,000.

Madhya Pradesh

Bhopal

Krishak Jagat: 14 Indira Press Complex, M. P. Nagar, POB 37, Bhopal 462 011; tel. (755) 2768452; fax (755) 2760449; e-mail krishjag@sanchar.net.in; internet www.krishakjagatindia.com; f. 1946; weekly; Hindi; agriculture; Chief Editor VIJAY KUMAR BONDRIYA; Editor SUNIL GANGRADE; circ. 100,000.

Maharashtra

Mumbai

Abhiyaan: Abhiyaan Press and Publications Ltd, 4A/B, Government Industrial Estate, Charkop, Kandivli (W), Mumbai 400 067; tel. (22) 28687515; fax (22) 28680991; f. 1986; weekly; Gujarati; Dir DILIP PATEL; Editor VINOD PANDYA; circ. 77,100.

Arogya Sanjeevani: C-14 Royal Industrial Estate, 5-B Naigaum Cross Rd, Wadala, Mumbai 400 031; tel. (22) 24138723; fax (22) 24133610; e-mail woman@bol.net.in; f. 1990; quarterly; Hindi; Editor SAROJ SHUKLA; circ. 62,907.

Auto India: Nirmal, Nariman Point, Mumbai 400 021; tel. (22) 22883946; fax (22) 22883940; e-mail editor@auto-india.com; f. 1994; monthly; Editor RAJ WARRIOR; circ. 46,900.

Bhavan's Journal: Bharatiya Vidya Bhavan, Mumbai 400 007; tel. (22) 23634462; fax (22) 23630058; f. 1954; fortnightly; English; literary; Man. Editor J. H. DAVE; Editor S. RAMAKRISHNAN; circ. 25,000.

Bombay Samachar: Red House, Sayed Abdulla Brelvi Rd, Mumbai 400 001; tel. (22) 22045531; fax (22) 22046642; e-mail samachar@ vsnl.com; f. 1822; weekly; Gujarati; Editor P. D. DALAL (acting); circ. 121,940.

Business India: Nirmal, 14th Floor, Nariman Point, Mumbai 400 021; tel. (22) 22883943; fax (22) 22883940; f. 1978; fortnightly; English; Publr ASHOK ADVANI; circ. 82,100.

Business World: 25–28 Atlanta, 2nd Floor, Nariman Point, Mumbai 400 021; tel. (22) 22851352; fax (22) 22870310; f. 1980; weekly; English; Editor AVEEK SARKAR; circ. 89,500.

Chitralekha: 62 Vaju Kotak Marg, Fort, Mumbai 400 001; tel. (22) 22614730; fax (22) 22615895; e-mail advertise@chitralekha.com; f. 1950; (Gujarati), f. 1989 (Marathi); weekly; Gujarati and Marathi; Editors BHARAT SHELANI, GYANESH MAHARAO; circ. 238,400 (Gujarati), 92,200 (Marathi).

Cine Blitz Film Monthly: 17/17H Cawasji Patel St, Fort, Mumbai 400 001; tel. (22) 22044143; fax (22) 22047984; f. 1974; English; Editor RITA K. MEHTA; circ. 184,100.

Debonair: Maurya Publications (Pvt) Ltd, 20/21, Juhu Centaur Hotel, Juhu Tara Rd, POB 18292, Mumbai 400 049; tel. (22) 26116632; fax (22) 26152677; e-mail maurya@debonairindia.com; f. 1972; monthly; English; Publr CHAITANYA PRABHU; CEO JOSEPH MASCARENHAS; circ. 110,000.

Economic and Political Weekly: Hitkari House, 284 Shahid Bhagatsingh Rd, Mumbai 400 001; tel. (22) 22696073; fax (22) 22696072; e-mail epw@vsnl.com; internet www.epw.org.in; f. 1966; English; Editor KRISHNA RAJ; circ. 132,800.

Femina: Times of India Bldg, Dr Dadabhai Naoroji Rd, Mumbai 400 001; tel. and fax (22) 22731385; e-mail femina@timesgroup.com; internet www.feminaindia.com; f. 1959; fortnightly; English; Editor SATHYA SARAN; circ. 113,800.

Filmfare: Times of India Bldg, Dr Dadabhai Naoroji Rd, Mumbai 400 001; tel. (22) 22731187; fax (22) 22731401; internet www.filmfare.com; f. 1952; monthly; English; Exec. Editor SHASHI BALIGA; circ. 156,400.

G: 62 Vaju Kotak Marg, Fort, Mumbai 400 001; tel. (22) 22614730; fax (22) 22615395; e-mail advertise@chitralekha.com; internet www.chitralekha.com; f. 1989; monthly; English; Editor BHARAT KAPADIA; circ. 61,437.

Gentleman: B-201, Teritex Business Service Centre, Saki Vihar, Mumbai 400 072; tel. (22) 28571490; fax (22) 28572447; e-mail gentleman@vsnl.com; f. 1980; monthly; English; Editor PREMNATH NAIR (acting).

Indian PEN: Theosophy Hall, 40 New Marine Lines, Mumbai 400 020; tel. (22) 22032175; e-mail ambika.sirkar@gems.vsnl.net.in; f. 1934; quarterly; organ of Indian Centre of the International PEN; Editor RANJIT HOSKOTE.

Janmabhoomi-Pravasi: Janmabhoomi Bhavan, Janmabhoomi Marg, Fort, POB 62, Mumbai 400 001; tel. (22) 22870831; fax (22) 22874097; e-mail bhoomi@bom3.vsnl.net.in; f. 1939; weekly; Gujarati; Propr Saurashtra Trust; Editor KUNDAN VYAS; circ. 94,100.

JEE: 62 Vaju Kotak Marg, Fort, Mumbai 400 001; tel. (22) 22614730; fax (22) 22615395; e-mail advertise@chitralekha.com; fortnightly; Gujarati and Marathi; Editor MADHURI KOTAK; circ. 92,160 (Gujarati), 30,150 (Marathi).

Meri Saheli: C-14 Royal Industrial Estate, 5-B Naigaum Cross Rd, Wadala, Mumbai 400 031; tel. (22) 24182797; fax (22) 24133610; e-mail woman@bol.net.in; f. 1987; monthly; Hindi; Editor HEMA MALINI; circ. 302,000.

Movie: Mahalaxmi Chambers, 5th Floor, 22 Bhulabhai Desai Rd, Mumbai 400 026; tel. (22) 24935636; fax (22) 24938406; f. 1981; monthly; English; Editor DINESH RAHEJA; circ. 70,700.

New Woman: C-14 Royal Industrial Estate, 5-B Naigaum Cross Rd, Wadala, Mumbai 400 031; tel. (22) 24138723; fax (22) 24133610; e-mail woman@bol.net.in; f. 1996; monthly; English; Editor HEMA MALINI; circ. 77,070.

Onlooker: Free Press House, 215 Free Press Journal Marg, Nariman Point, Mumbai 400 021; tel. (22) 22874566; f. 1939; fortnightly; English; news magazine; Exec. Editor K. SRINIVASAN; circ. 61,000.

Reader's Digest: Orient House, Adi Marzban Path, Ballard Estate, Mumbai 400 001; tel. (22) 22617291; fax (22) 22613347; f. 1954; monthly; English; Publr and Editor ASHOK MAHADEVAN; circ. 389,378.

Savvy: Magna Publishing Co Ltd, Magna House, 100/E Old Prabhadevi Rd, Prabhadevi, Mumbai 400 025; tel. (22) 24362270; fax (22) 24306523; e-mail savvy@magnamags.com; internet www.magnamags.com; f. 1984; monthly; English; Editor SAIRA MENEZES; circ. 99,500.

Screen: Express Tower, Nariman Point, Mumbai 400 021; tel. (22) 22022627; fax (22) 22022139; e-mail iemumbai@expressindia.co.in; f. 1951; film weekly; English; Editor BHAVNA SOMAYA; circ. 90,000.

Society: Magna Publishing Co Ltd, Magna House, 100/E Old Prabhadevi Rd, Prabhadevi, Mumbai 400 025; tel. (22) 24362270; fax (22) 24306523; e-mail magnapub@vsnl.com; internet www.magnamags.com; f. 1979; monthly; English; Editor LALITHA GOPALAN; circ. 67,200.

Stardust: Magna Publishing Co Ltd, Magna House, 100/E Old Prabhadevi Rd, Prabhadevi, Mumbai 400 025; tel. (22) 24362270; fax (22) 24306523; e-mail magnapub@vsnl.com; internet www.stardustindia.com; f. 1985; monthly; English; Editor ASHWIN VARDE; circ. 308,000.

Vyapar: Janmabhoomi Bhavan, Janmabhoomi Marg, POB 62, Fort, Mumbai 400 001; tel. (22) 22870831; fax (22) 22874097; e-mail rajeshbhayani@hotmail.com; f. 1949; (Gujarati), 1987 (Hindi); Gujarati (2 a week) and Hindi (weekly); commerce; Propr Saurashtra Trust; Editor RAJESH M. BHAYANI; circ. 27,900 (Gujarati), 12,800 (Hindi).

Nagpur

All India Reporter: AIR Ltd, Congress Nagar, POB 209, Nagpur 440 012; tel. (712) 2534321; fax (712) 2526283; e-mail air@allindiareporter.com; internet www.allindiareporter.com; f. 1914; weekly and monthly; English; law journals; Chief Editor V. R. MANOHAR; circ. 55,500.

Rajasthan

Jaipur

Balhans: Kesargarh, Jawahar Lal Nehru Marg, Jaipur 302 004; tel. (141) 2561582; fax (141) 2566011; e-mail info@rajasthanpatrika.com; internet www.rajasthanpatrika.com; fortnightly; Hindi; circ. 31,800.

Itwari Patrika: Kesargarh, Jawahar Lal Nehru Marg, Jaipur 302 004; tel. (141) 2561582; fax (141) 2566011; weekly; Hindi; circ. 12,000.

Rashtradoot Saptahik: HO, M.I. Rd, POB 30, Jaipur 302 001; tel. (141) 2372634; fax (141) 2373513; f. 1983; Hindi; also publ. from Kota and Bikaner; Chief Editor and Man. Editor RAJESH SHARMA; CEO SOMESH SHARMA; combined circ. 167,500.

Tamil Nadu

Chennai (Madras)

Ambulimama: 82 Defence Officers Colony, Ekkatuthangal, Chennai 600 097; tel. (44) 22313637; e-mail chandamama@vsnl.com; f. 1947; children's monthly; Tamil; Editor B. VISWANATHA REDDI; circ. 65,000.

Ambuli Ammavan: 82 Defence Officers Colony, Ekkatuthangal, Chennai 600 097; tel. (44) 22313637; e-mail chandamama@vsnl.com; f. 1970; children's monthly; Malayalam; Editor B. VISWANATHA REDDI; circ. 12,000.

Ananda Vikatan: 757 Anna Salai, Chennai 600 002; tel. (44) 28524054; fax (44) 28523819; e-mail editor@vikatan.com; internet www.vikatan.com; f. 1924; weekly; Tamil; Editor and Man. Dir S. BALASUBRAMANIAN; circ. 316,000.

Aval Vikatan: 757 Anna Salai, Chennai 600 002; tel. (44) 28524054; fax (44) 28523819; e-mail editor@vikatan.com; internet www.vikatan.com; f. 1998; fortnightly; Tamil; Editor B. SRINIVASAN; circ. 100,000.

Chandamama: 82 Defence Officers Colony, Ekkatuthangal, Chennai 600 097; tel. (44) 22313637; e-mail chandamama@vsnl.com; f. 1947; children's monthly; Hindi, Gujarati, Telugu, Kannada, English, Sanskrit, Bengali, Assamese; Editor B. VISWANATHA REDDI; combined circ. 420,000.

Chandoba: 82 Defence Officers Colony, Ekkatuthangal, Chennai 600 097; tel. (44) 22313637; e-mail chandamama@vsnl.com; f. 1952; children's monthly; Marathi; Editor B. VISWANATHA REDDI; circ. 93,000.

Chutti Vikatan: 757 Anna Salai, Chennai 600 002; tel. (44) 28524054; fax (44) 28523819; e-mail editor@vikatan.com; internet www.chuttivikatan.com; f. 1999; monthly; Tamil; Editor B. SRINIVASAN; Man. Dir S. BALASUBRAMANIAN; circ. 100,000.

Devi: 727 Anna Salai, Chennai 600 006; tel. (44) 28521428; f. 1979; weekly; Tamil; Editor B. RAMACHANDRA ADITYAN; circ. 84,600.

Dinamani Kadir: Express Estate, Mount Rd, Chennai 600 002; tel. (44) 28520751; fax (44) 28524500; weekly; Editor G. KASTURI RANGAN (acting); circ. 55,000.

Frontline: Kasturi Bldgs, 859/860 Anna Salai, Chennai 600 002; tel. (44) 28545435; fax (44) 28515205; e-mail frontline@thehindu.co.in; internet www.flonnet.com; f. 1984; fortnightly; English; current affairs; Publr S. RANGARAJAN; Editor N. RAM; circ. 67,225.

Hindu International Edition: 859/860 Anna Salai, Chennai 600 002; tel. (44) 28413344; fax (44) 28415325; f. 1975; weekly; English; Editor N. RAVI; circ. 3,000.

Jahnamamu (Oriya): 82 Defence Officers Colony, Ekkatuthangal, Chennai 600 097; tel. (44) 22313637; e-mail chandamama@vsnl.com; f. 1972; children's monthly; Editor B. VISWANATHA REDDI; circ. 111,000.

Junior Vikatan: 757 Anna Salai, Chennai 600 002; tel. (44) 28524054; fax (44) 28523819; e-mail editor@vikatan.com; internet www.vikatan.com; f. 1983; 2 times a week; Tamil; Editor and Man. Dir S. BALASUBRAMANIAN; circ. 185,900.

Kalai Magal: POB 604, Chennai 600 004; tel. (44) 24983099; f. 1932; monthly; Tamil; literary and cultural; Editor R. NARAYANASWAMY; circ. 10,200.

Kalki: 47 Jawaharlal Nehru Rd, Ekkatuthangal, Chennai 600 097; tel. (44) 22345621; e-mail kalkiweekly@vsnl.com; internet www.kalkiweekly.com; f. 1941; weekly; Tamil; literary and cultural; Editor SEETHA RAVI; circ. 45,000.

Kumudam: 151 Purasawalkam High Rd, Chennai 600 010; tel. (44) 26422146; fax (44) 26425041; e-mail kumudam@giasmd01.vsnl.net.in; f. 1947; weekly; Tamil; Editor Dr S. A. P. JAWAHAR PALANIAPPAN; circ. 340,400.

Kungumam: 93A Kodambakkam High Rd, Chennai 600 034; tel. (44) 28268177; f. 1978; weekly; Tamil; Editor PARASAKTHI; circ. 63,700.

Malaimathi: Chennai; f. 1958; weekly; Tamil; Editor P. S. ELANGO; circ. 48,100.

Muththaram: 93A Kogambakkam High Rd, Chennai 600 034; tel. (44) 2476306; f. 1980; weekly; Tamil; Editor PARASAKTHI; circ. 18,000.

Rani Muthu: 1091 Periyar E.V.R. High Rd, Chennai 600 007; tel. (44) 25324771; e-mail raniweekly@vsnl.net; f. 1969; fortnightly; Tamil; Editor A. M. SAMY; circ. 61,700.

Rani Weekly: 1091 Periyar E.V.R. High Rd, Chennai 600 007; tel. (44) 25324771; e-mail raniweekly@vsnl.net; f. 1962; Tamil; Editor A. M. SAMY; circ. 165,300.

Sportstar: Kasturi Bldgs, 859/860 Anna Salai, Chennai 600 002; tel. (44) 28413344; fax (44) 28415325; e-mail wsvcs@thehindu.co.in; internet www.tssonnet.com; f. 1978; weekly; English; Publr S. RANGARAJAN; Editor N. RAM; circ. 56,000.

Thuglak: 46 Greenways Rd, Chennai 600 028; tel. (44) 4936913; fax (44) 4936915; f. 1970; weekly; Tamil; Editor CHO S. RAMASWAMY; circ. 128,300.

Uttar Pradesh

Allahabad

Nutan Kahaniyan: 15 Sheo Charan Lal Rd, Allahabad 211 003; tel. (532) 2400612; f. 1975; Hindi; monthly; Chief Editor K. K. BHARGAVA; circ. 167,500.

West Bengal

Kolkata (Calcutta)

All India Appointment Gazette: 7 Old Court House St, Kolkata 700 001; tel. (33) 22206663; fax (33) 22296548; f. 1973; 2 a week; English; Editor S. C. TALUKDAR; circ. 158,900.

Anandalok: 6 Prafulla Sarkar St, Kolkata 700 001; tel. (33) 22374880; fax (33) 22253240; f. 1975; fortnightly; Bengali; film; Editor DULENDRA BHOWMIK; circ. 50,800.

Anandamela: 6 Prafulla Sarkar St, Kolkata 700 001; tel. (33) 22216600; fax (33) 22253240; f. 1975; weekly; Bengali; juvenile; Editor DEBASHIS BANDOPADHYAY; circ. 34,800.

Contemporary Tea Time: 1/2 Old Court House Corner, POB 14, Kolkata 700 001; tel. (33) 22200099; fax (33) 22435753; e-mail calcutta@ctl.co.in; internet www.ctl.co.in; f. 1988; quarterly; English; tea industry; Exec. Editor GITA NARAYANI; circ. 5,000.

Desh: 6 Prafulla Sarkar St, Kolkata 700 001; tel. (33) 22374880; fax (33) 22253240; f. 1933; fortnightly; Bengali; literary; Editor AVEEK SARKAR; circ. 62,100.

Khela: 96 Raja Rammohan Sarani, Kolkata 700 009; tel. (33) 23509803; f. 1981; weekly; Bengali; sports; Editor ASOKE DASGUPTA; circ. 9,500.

Naba Kallol: 11 Jhamapookur Lane, Kolkata 700 009; tel. (33) 23504294; e-mail devsahityer@caltiger.com; f. 1960; monthly; Bengali; Editor P. K. MAZUMDAR; circ. 25,700.

Prabuddha Bharata (Awakened India): 5 Dehi Entally Rd, Kolkata 700 014; tel. (33) 22440898; fax (33) 22450050; e-mail advaita@vsnl.com; internet www.advaitaonline.com; f. 1896; monthly; art, culture, religion and philosophy; Publr SWAMI BODHASARANANDA; circ. 7,500.

Sananda: 6 Prafulla Sarkar St, Kolkata 700 001; tel. (33) 22374880; fax (33) 22253241; f. 1986; monthly; Bengali; Editor APARNA SEN; circ. 121,400.

Saptahik Bartaman: 76A J. C. Bose Rd, Kolkata 700 014; tel. (33) 22448208; fax (33) 22441215; f. 1988; weekly; Bengali; Editor BARUN SENGUPTA; circ. 113,000.

Statesman: Statesman House, 4 Chowringhee Sq., Kolkata 700 001; tel. (33) 22257070; fax (33) 22250118; f. 1875; overseas weekly; English; Editor-in-Chief C. R. IRANI.

Suktara: 11 Jhamapooker Lane, Kolkata 700 009; tel. (33) 23504294; e-mail devsahityer@caltiger.com; f. 1948; monthly; Bengali; juvenile; Editor M. MAJUMDAR; circ. 37,300.

NEWS AGENCIES

Press Trust of India Ltd: 4 Parliament St, New Delhi 110 001; tel. (11) 23717642; fax (11) 23718714; f. 1947; re-established 1978; Chair. VINEET JAIN; Gen. Man. M. K. RAZDAN.

United News of India (UNI): 9 Rafi Marg, New Delhi 110 001; tel. (11) 23711700; fax (11) 23716211; e-mail uninet@del2.vsnl.net.in; f. 1961; Indian language news in Hindi and Urdu; English wire service; World TV News Service (UNISCAN); photograph service;

graphics service; special services covering banking and business; brs in 90 centres in India; Chair. MAHENDRA MOHAN GUPTA; Gen. Man. and Chief Editor VIRENDER MOHAN.

Foreign Bureaux

Agence France-Presse (AFP): 56 Janpath, 3rd Floor, New Delhi 110 001; tel. (11) 23738700; fax (11) 23311105; e-mail afpdelhi@afp.com; Bureau Chief RÉNÉ SLAMA.

Agencia EFE (Spain): 72 Jor Bagh, New Delhi 110 003; tel. (11) 24618092; fax (11) 24615013; Correspondent ISABEL CALLEJA SOLERA.

Agenzia Nazionale Stampa Associata (ANSA) (Italy): C-179 Defence Colony, New Delhi 110 024; tel. (11) 24615004; fax (11) 24640190; e-mail natale@giasdl01.vsnl.net.in; Bureau Chief BENIAMINO NATALE.

Associated Press (AP) (USA): 6B Jor Bagh Lane, New Delhi 110 003; tel. (11) 24698682; fax (11) 24616870; e-mail bbrown@ap.org; Bureau Chief BETH DUFF BROWN.

Deutsche Presse-Agentur (dpa) (Germany): 39 Golf Links, New Delhi 110 003; tel. (11) 24617792; fax (11) 24635772; e-mail dpadelhi@vsnl.com; Chief Rep. JÜRGEN HEIN.

Informatsionnoye Telegrafnoye Agentstvo Rossii—Telegrafnoye Agentstvo Suverennykh Stran (ITAR—TASS) (Russia): 3 Vasant Vihar, New Delhi 110 057; tel. (11) 26142351; fax (11) 26146292; Bureau Chief STANISLAV BYCHKOV.

Inter Press Service (IPS) (Italy): 49 (F.F.) Defence Colony Market, New Delhi 110 024; tel. (11) 24634154; fax (11) 24624725; Correspondent ANN NINAN.

Islamic Republic News Agency (IRNA) (Iran): SF-204, Jor Bagh, New Delhi 110 003; tel. (11) 24632009; fax (11) 24643369; e-mail irna@del2.vsnl.net.in; Bureau Chief RAMEZANALI YOUSEFI.

Kyodo News Service (Japan): 308 World Trade Centre, Babar Rd, New Delhi 110 001; tel. (11) 23411954; fax (11) 23414756; Bureau Chief KAZUMASA KOIKE.

Reuters (UK): 1 Kautilya Marg, Chanakyapuri, New Delhi 110 021; tel. (11) 23012024; fax (11) 23014043; e-mail delhi.newsroom@reuters.com; Bureau Chief MYRA MACDONALD.

United Press International (UPI) (USA): 706, Sector 7B, Chandigarh 160 019; tel. (172) 2794017; fax (172) 2790591; e-mail hsnanda@glide.net.in; Bureau Chief HARBAKSH SINGH NANDA.

Xinhua (New China) News Agency (People's Republic of China): B-3/60, Safdarjung Enclave, New Delhi 110 029; tel. (11) 26101886; fax (11) 26878879; Chief ZHOU XIAOZHENG.

The following agencies are also represented: Associated Press of Pakistan, A. P. Dow Jones, Bloomberg Business News, Depthnews, Knight-Ridder Financial News, Middle East News Agency and Viet Nam News Agency.

CO-ORDINATING BODIES

Press Information Bureau: Shastri Bhavan, Dr Rajendra Prasad Rd, New Delhi 110 001; tel. (11) 23383643; fax (11) 23383169; e-mail pio@hub.nic.in; internet www.pib.nic.in; f. 1946 to co-ordinate press affairs for the govt; represents newspaper managements, journalists, news agencies, parliament; has power to examine journalists under oath and may censor objectionable material; Prin. Information Officer SAHAB SINGH.

Registrar of Newspapers for India: Ministry of Information and Broadcasting, West Block 8, Wing 2, Ramakrishna Puram, New Delhi 110 066; tel. (11) 26018788; f. 1956 as a statutory body to collect press statistics; maintains a register of all Indian newspapers; Registrar G. D. BELIYA.

PRESS ASSOCIATIONS

All-India Newspaper Editors' Conference: 36–37 Northend Complex, Rama Krishna Ashram Marg, New Delhi 110 001; tel. (11) 23364519; fax (11) 23317499; f. 1940; c. 400 mems; Pres. VISHWA BANDHU GUPTA; Sec.-Gen. RAMU PATEL.

All India Small and Medium Newspapers' Federation: 26-F Rajiv Gandhi Chowk (Connaught Place), New Delhi 110 001; tel. (11) 23326000; e-mail nri@ndf.vsnl.net.in; c. 9,000 mems; Pres. HARBHAJAN SINGH; Gen. Secs B. C. GUPTA, B. M. SHARMA.

The Foreign Correspondents' Club of South Asia: AB-19 Mathura Rd, opposite Pragati Maidan Gate 3, New Delhi 110 001; tel. (11) 23388535; fax (11) 23385517; e-mail fcc@fccsouthasia.org; internet www.fccsouthasia.com; f. 1992; 425 mems; Pres. S. VENKATANARAYAN; Man. KIRAN KAPUR.

Indian Federation of Working Journalists: A-4/199 Basant Lane, Nr Railway Central Hospital, New Delhi 110 001; tel. (11) 23348894; fax (11) 23348871; f. 1950; 27,000 mems; Pres. K. VIKRAM RAO; Sec.-Gen. PARMANAND PANDEY.

Indian Journalists' Association: New Delhi; Pres. VIJAY DUTT; Gen. Sec. A. K. DHAR.

Indian Languages Newspapers' Asscn: Janmabhoomi Bhavan, Janmabhoomi Marg, POB 10029, Fort, Mumbai 400 001; tel. (22) 22870537; f. 1941; 320 mems; Pres. VIJAY KUMAR BONDRIYA; Hon. Gen. Secs PRADEEP G. DESHPANDE, KRISHNA SHEWDIKAR, LALIT SHRIMAL.

Indian Newspaper Society: INS Bldg, Rafi Marg, New Delhi 110 001; tel. (11) 23715401; fax (11) 23723800; e-mail indnews@nde.vsnl.net.in; f. 1939; 688 mems; Pres. PRATAP PAWAR; Sec.-Gen. P. K. LAHIRI.

National Union of Journalists (India): 7 Jantar Mantar Rd, 2nd Floor, New Delhi 110 001; tel. (11) 23368610; fax (11) 23369664; e-mail nujindia@ndf.vsnl.in; internet www.education.vsnl.com/nujindia; f. 1972; 12,000 mems; Pres. SHYAM KHOSLA; Sec.-Gen. P. K. ROY.

Press Club of India: 1 Raisina Rd, New Delhi 110 001; tel. 23719844; f. 1948; 4,500 mems; Pres. PRAKASH PATRA; Sec.-Gen. SANJEEV ACHARYA.

Press Council of India: Faridkot House, Ground Floor, Copernicus Marg, New Delhi 110 001; tel. (11) 23381681; established under an Act of Parliament to preserve the freedom of the press and maintain and improve the standards of newspapers and news agencies in India; 28 mems; Chair. Justice JAICHANDRA REDDY; Sec. REVA KHETRAPAL.

Press Institute of India: Sapru House Annexe, Barakhamba Rd, New Delhi 110 001; tel. (11) 23318066; fax (11) 23311975; e-mail pii@ndf.vsnl.net.in; internet www.piigrassroots.org; f. 1963; 29 mem. newspapers and other orgs; Chair. PHILIP MATHEWS; Dir AJIT BHATTACHARJEA.

Publishers

Delhi and New Delhi

Affiliated East-West Press (Pvt) Ltd: G-1/16 Ansari Rd, Daryaganj, New Delhi 110 002; tel. (11) 23264180; fax (11) 23260538; e-mail affiliat@vsnl.com; internet www.aewpress.com; textbooks and reference books; also represents scientific societies; Dirs SUNNY MALIK, KAMAL MALIK.

Allied Publishers (Pvt) Ltd: 13/14 Asaf Ali Rd, New Delhi 110 002; tel. (11) 23233002; fax (11) 23235967; e-mail aplnd@del2.vsnl.net.in; academic and general; Man. Dir S. M. SACHDEV.

Amerind Publishing Co (Pvt) Ltd: Oxford Bldg, N-56 Connaught Circus, New Delhi 110 001; tel. (11) 23314957; fax (11) 23322639; f. 1970; offices at Kolkata, Mumbai and New York; scientific and technical; Dirs MOHAN PRIMLANI, GULAB PRIMLANI.

Arnold Heinman Publishers (India) Pvt Ltd: New Delhi; f. 1969 as Arnold Publishers (India) Pvt Ltd; literature and general; Man. Dir G. A. VAZIRANI.

Atma Ram and Sons: 1376 Kashmere Gate, POB 1429, Delhi 110 006; tel. (11) 23973082; f. 1909; scientific, technical, humanities, medical; Man. Dir S. PURI; Dir Y. PURI.

B.I. Publications Pvt Ltd: 13 Daryaganj, New Delhi 110 002; tel. (11) 23274443; fax (11) 23261290; e-mail bidel@ndb.vsnl.net.in; f. 1959; academic, general and professional; Man. Dir K. S. MANI.

S. Chand and Co Ltd: 7361 Ram Nagar, Qutab Rd, near New Delhi Railway Station, New Delhi 110 055; tel. (11) 23672080; fax (11) 23677446; e-mail schand@vsnl.com; internet www.schandgroup.com; f. 1917; educational and general in English and Hindi; also book exports and imports; Man. Dir RAVINDRA KUMAR GUPTA.

Children's Book House: A-4 Ring Rd, South Extension Part I, POB 3854, New Delhi 110 049; tel. (11) 24636030; fax (11) 24636011; e-mail neeta@giasdl01.vsnl.net.in; internet www.neetaprakashan.com; f. 1952; educational and general; Dir R. S. GUPTA.

Children's Book Trust: Nehru House, 4 Bahadur Shah Zafar Marg, New Delhi 110 002; tel. (11) 23316970; fax (11) 23721090; e-mail cbtnd@vsnl.com; internet www.childrensbooktrust.com; f. 1957; children's books in English and other Indian languages; Editor C. G. R. KURUP; Gen. Man. RAVI SHANKAR.

Concept Publishing Co: A/15-16, Commercial Block, Mohan Garden, New Delhi 110 059; tel. (11) 25351460; fax (11) 25357103; e-mail publishing@conceptpub.com; f. 1975; geography, rural and urban development, education, sociology, economics, anthropology, agriculture, religion, history, law, philosophy, information sciences, ecology; Man. Dir ASHOK KUMAR MITTAL; Man. Editor NITIN MITTAL.

Frank Bros and Co (Publishers) Ltd: 4675A Ansari Rd, 21 Daryaganj, New Delhi 110 002; tel. (11) 23263393; fax (11) 23269032; e-mail fbros@ndb.vsnl.net.in; f. 1930; children's and educational books; Chair. R. C. GOVIL.

Global Business Press: GT Rd, 18–19 Dilshad Garden, Delhi 110 095; tel. (11) 22297792; fax (11) 22282332; business, management and computers; Dir SHEKHAR MALHOTRA.

Heritage Publishers: 32 Prakash Apartments, 5 Ansari Rd, Daryaganj, New Delhi 110 002; tel. (11) 23266258; fax (11) 23263050; e-mail heritage@nda.vsnl.net.in; f. 1973; social sciences, art and architecture, technical, medical, scientific; Propr and Dir B. R. CHAWLA.

Hind Pocket Books (Pvt) Ltd: 18–19 Dilshad Garden, Delhi 110 095; tel. (11) 22297792; fax (11) 22282332; e-mail gbp@del2.vsnl.net.in; f. 1958; fiction and non-fiction paperbacks in English, Hindi, Punjabi, Malayalam and Urdu; Chair DINANATH MALHOTRA; Exec. Dir SHEKHAR MALHOTRA.

Hindustan Publishing Corpn (India): 4805/24 Bharat Ram Rd, Daryaganj, New Delhi 110 002; tel. (11) 23254401; fax (11) 26193511; e-mail hpc@hpc.cc; internet www.hpc.cc; archaeology, pure and applied sciences, geology, sociology, anthropology, economics; Man. Partner P. C. KUMAR.

Kali for Women: B1/8 Hauz Khas, New Delhi 110 016; tel. (11) 26964497; fax (11) 26864497; e-mail kaliw@del2.vsnl.net.in; women's studies, social sciences, humanities, general non-fiction, fiction, etc. Heads of Organization URVASHI BUTALIA, RITU MENON.

Lalit Kala Akademi: Rabindra Bhavan, New Delhi 110 001; tel. (11) 23387241; fax (11) 23782485; e-mail lka@lalitkala.org.in; internet www.lalitkala.org.in; books on Indian art; Exec. Editor SHARDA GUPTA.

Lancers Books: POB 4236, New Delhi 110 048; tel. (11) 26241617; fax (11) 26992063; e-mail lanbooks@aol.com; f. 1977; politics (with special emphasis on north-east India), defence; Propr S. KUMAR.

Madhuban Educational Books: 576 Masjid Rd, Jangpura, New Delhi 110 014; tel. (11) 24314605; fax (11) 24310879; e-mail madhuban@vikaspublishing.com; f. 1969; school books, children's books; Chair. and Man. Dir CHANDER M. CHAWLA.

Motilal Banarsidass Publishers (Pvt) Ltd: 41 U.A. Bungalow Rd, Jawahar Nagar, Delhi 110 007; tel. (11) 23911985; fax (11) 23930689; e-mail mlbd@vsnl.com; internet www.mlbdbooks.com; f. 1903; religion, philosophy, astrology, yoga, linguistic, in English and Sanskrit; Man. Dir N. P. JAIN; 7 brs.

Munshiram Manoharlal Publishers Pvt Ltd: 54 Rani Jhansi Rd, POB 5715, New Delhi 110 055; tel. (11) 23671668; fax (11) 23612745; e-mail mrml@mantraonline.com; internet www.mrmlbooks.com; f. 1952; Indian art, architecture, archaeology, religion, music, law, medicine, dance, dictionaries, travel, history, politics, numismatics, Buddhism, philosophy, sociology, etc. Publishing Dir DEVENDRA JAIN; Dir ASHOK JAIN.

National Book Trust: A-5 Green Park, New Delhi 110 016; tel. (11) 26564020; fax (11) 26851795; e-mail nbtindia@ndb.vsnl.net.in; f. 1957; autonomous organization established by the Ministry of Human Resources Development to produce and encourage the production of good literary works; Chair. Dr SITAKANT MAHAPATRA; Dir NIRMAL KANTHI BHATACHARJEE.

National Council of Educational Research and Training (NCERT): Sri Aurobindo Marg, New Delhi 110 016; tel. (11) 26562708; fax (11) 26851070; e-mail dirc@glasdlo1.vsnl.net.in; f. 1961; school textbooks, teachers' guides, research monographs, journals, etc. CEO PURAN DHAND.

Neeta Prakashan: A-4 Ring Rd, South Extension Part I, POB 3853, New Delhi 110 049; tel. (11) 24636010; fax (11) 24636011; e-mail neeta@giasdl01.vsnl.net.in; internet www.neetaprakashan.com; f. 1960; educational, children's, general; Dir RAKESH GUPTA.

New Age International Pvt Ltd: 4835/24 Ansari Rd, Daryaganj, New Delhi 110 002; tel. (11) 23278348; fax (11) 23267437; e-mail del.nail@axcess.net.in; f. 1966; science, engineering, technology, management, humanities, social science; Dir K. K. GUPTA.

Oxford and IBH Publishing Co (Pvt) Ltd: 66 Janpath, New Delhi 110 001; tel. (11) 23324578; fax (11) 23710090; e-mail oxford@vsnl.com; f. 1964; science, technology and reference in English; Dir VIJAY PRIMLANI; Man. Dir MOHAN PRIMLANI.

Oxford University Press: YMCA Library Bldg, 1st Floor, Jai Singh Rd, POB 43, New Delhi 110 001; tel. (11) 23747124; fax (11) 23360897; e-mail mk@oupin.com; f. 1912; educational, scientific, medical, general and reference; Man. Dir MANZAR KHAN.

Penguin Books India (Pvt) Ltd: 11 Community Centre, Panchsheel Park, New Delhi 110 017; tel. (11) 26494401; fax (11) 26494403; e-mail penguin@del2.vsnl.net.in; f. 1987; Indian literature and general non-fiction in English; Chair. PETER FIELD; CEO and Publr DAVID DAVIDAR.

People's Publishing House (Pvt) Ltd: 5E Rani Jhansi Rd, New Delhi 110 055; tel. (11) 27524701; f. 1947; Marxism, Leninism, peasant movt; Dir SHAMEEM FAIZEE.

Pitambar Publishing Co Pvt Ltd: 888 East Park Rd, Karol Bagh, New Delhi 110 005; tel. (11) 23670067; fax (11) 23676058; e-mail pitambar@bol.net.in; internet www.pitambar.com; academic, children's books, textbooks and general; Man. Dir ANAND BHUSHAN; 5 brs.

Prentice-Hall of India (Pvt) Ltd: M-97 Connaught Circus, New Delhi 110 001; tel. (11) 22143344; fax (11) 23717179; e-mail phi@phindia.com; internet www.phindia.com; f. 1963; university-level text and reference books; Man. Dir A. K. GHOSH.

Pustak Mahal: 10B Netaji Subhas Marg, Daryaganj, New Delhi 110 002; tel. (11) 23272783; fax (11) 23260518; e-mail pustakmahal@vsnl.com; children's, general, computers, religious, encyclopaedia; Man. Dir RAM AVTAR GUPTA.

Rajkamal Prakashan (Pvt) Ltd: 1B Netaji Subhas Marg, New Delhi 110 002; tel. (11) 23274463; fax (11) 23251803; e-mail rajkamalprakashan@email.com; f. 1946; Hindi; literary; also literary journal and monthly trade journal; Man. Dir ASHOK MAHESH-WARI.

Rajpal and Sons: 1590 Madrasa Rd, Kashmere Gate, Delhi 110 006; tel. (11) 23865483; fax (11) 23867791; e-mail orienpbk@ndb.vsnl.net.in; f. 1891; humanities, social sciences, art, juvenile; Hindi; Chair VISHWANATH MALHOTRA.

RIS (Research and Information System) for the Non-Aligned and Other Developing Countries: Zone IV-B, Fourth Floor, India Habitat Centre, Lodhi Rd, New Delhi 110 003; tel. (11) 24682176; fax (11) 24682173; e-mail risnodec@del2.vsnl.net.in; internet www.ris.org.in; f. 1983; current and economic affairs involving non-aligned and developing countries; Dir-Gen. Dr V. R. PANCHAMUKHI.

Rupa & Co: 7/16 Ansari Rd, Daryaganj, POB 7017, New Delhi 110 002; tel. (11) 23278586; fax (11) 23277294; e-mail del.rupaco@axcess.net.in; internet www.rupaandco.com; f. 1936; Chief Exec. R. K. MEHRA.

Sage Publications India Pvt Ltd: B-42, Panchsheel Enclave, New Delhi 110 017; tel. and fax (11) 26491290; e-mail sageind@nda.vsnl.net.in; internet www.indiasage.com; f. 1981; social science, development studies, business and management studies; Man. Dir TEJESHWAR SINGH.

Sahitya Akademi: Rabindra Bhavan, 35 Ferozeshah Rd, New Delhi 110 001; tel. (11) 23386626; fax (11) 23382428; e-mail secy@ndb.vsnl.net.in; internet www.sahitya-akademi.org; f. 1956; bibliographies, translations, monographs, encyclopaedias, literary classics, etc. Pres. RAMAKANTA RATH; Sec. Dr K. SATCHIDANANDAN.

Scholar Publishing House (P) Ltd: 85 Model Basti, New Delhi 110 005; tel. (11) 23541299; fax (11) 23676565; e-mail scholar@vsnl.com; internet www.scholargroup.com; f. 1968; educational; Man. Dir RAJESH RANADE.

Shiksha Bharati: 1590 Madrasa Rd, Kashmere Gate, Delhi 110 006; tel. (11) 23869812; fax (11) 23867791; e-mail orientpbk@vsnl.com; f. 1955; textbooks, creative literature, popular science and juvenile in Hindi and English; Editor MEERA JOHRI.

Sterling Publishers (Pvt) Ltd: A-59 Okhla Industrial Area, Phase II, New Delhi 110 020; tel. (11) 26387070; fax (11) 26383788; e-mail ghai@nde.vsnl.net.in; internet www.sterlingpublishers.com; f. 1965; academic books on the humanities and social sciences, children's books, computer books, management books, paperbacks; Chair. and Man. Dir S. K. GHAI; Gen. Man. A. J. SEHGAL.

Tata McGraw-Hill Publishing Co Ltd: 7 West Patel Nagar, New Delhi 110 008; tel. (11) 25819304; fax (11) 25819302; e-mail info_india@mcgraw-hill.com; internet www.tatamcgrawhill.com; f. 1970; engineering, computers, sciences, medicine, management, humanities, social sciences; Chair. Dr F. A. MEHTA; Man. Dir Dr N. SUBRAHMANYAM.

Vikas Publishing House (Pvt) Ltd: 576 Masjid Rd, Jangpura, New Delhi 110 014; tel. (11) 24314605; fax (11) 24310879; e-mail helpline@vikaspublishing.com; f. 1969; computers, management, commerce, sciences, engineering, textbooks; Chair. and Man. Dir CHANDER M. CHAWLA.

A. H. Wheeler & Co Ltd: 411 Surya Kiran Bldg, 19 K. G. Marg, New Delhi 110 001; tel. (11) 23312629; fax (11) 23357798; e-mail wheelerpub@mantraonline.com; f. 1958; textbooks, reference books, computer science and information technology, electronics, management, telecommunications, social sciences, etc. Exec. Pres. ALOK BANERJEE.

Chennai (Madras)

Higginbothams Ltd: 814 Anna Salai, POB 311, Chennai 600 002; tel. (44) 28520640; fax (44) 28528101; e-mail higginbothams@vsnl.com; f. 1844; general; Dir S. CHANDRASEKHAR.

B. G. Paul and Co: 4 Francis Joseph St, Chennai; f. 1923; general, educational and oriental; Man. K. NILAKANTAN.

T. R. Publications Pvt Ltd: PMG Complex, 2nd Floor, 57 South Usman Rd, T. Nagar, Chennai 600 017; tel. (44) 24340765; fax (44) 24348837; e-mail trgeetha@giasmd01.vsnl.net.in; internet www.trpubs.com; Chief Exec. S. GEETHA.

Kolkata (Calcutta)

Academic Publishers: 12/1A Bankim Chatterjee St, POB 12341, Kolkata 700 073; tel. (33) 22414857; fax (33) 22413702; e-mail acabooks@cal.vsnl.net.in; f. 1958; textbooks, management, medical, technical; Man. Partner B. K. DHUR.

Advaita Ashrama: 5 Dehi Entally Rd, Kolkata 700 014; tel. (33) 22164000; fax (33) 22450050; e-mail advaita@vsnl.com; internet www.advaitaonline.com; f. 1899; religion, philosophy, spiritualism, Vedanta; publication centre of Ramakrishna Math and Ramakrishna Mission; Publication Man. Swami MUMUKSHANANDA.

Allied Book Agency: 18A Shyama Charan De St, Kolkata 700 073; general and academic; Dir B. SARKAR.

Ananda Publishers (Pvt) Ltd: 45 Beniatola Lane, Kolkata 700 009; tel. (33) 22414352; fax (33) 22193856; e-mail ananda@cal3.vsnl.net.in; internet www.anandapub.com; literature, general; Dir A. SARKAR; Man. Dir S. MITRA.

Assam Review Publishing Co: 27A Waterloo St, 1st Floor, Kolkata 700 069; tel. (33) 22482251; fax (33) 22482251; f. 1926; publrs of *The Assam Review and Tea News* (monthly) and *The Assam Directory and Tea Areas Handbook* (annually); Chief Exec. GOBIN-DALAL BANERJEE.

Dey's Publishing: 13 Bankim Chatterjee St, Kolkata 700 073; tel. (33) 22412330; fax (33) 22192041; academic books, religion, philosophy, general; Dir SUDHANGSHU KUMAR DEY.

Dey Sahitya Kutir: 21 Jhamapukur Lane, Kolkata 700 009; tel. (33) 22417406; children's, general; Dir PRABIR KUMAR MAJUMDAR.

Eastern Law House (Pvt) Ltd: 54 Ganesh Chunder Ave, Kolkata 700 013; tel. (33) 2374989; fax (33) 2150491; e-mail elh@cal.vsnl.net.in; f. 1918; legal, commercial and accountancy; Dir ASOK DE; br. in New Delhi.

Firma KLM Private Ltd: 257B B. B. Ganguly St, Kolkata 700 012; tel. (33) 22374391; fax (33) 22217294; e-mail fklm@satyam.net.in; internet www.firmaklm.com; f. 1950; Indology, scholarly in English, Bengali, Sanskrit and Hindi, alternative medicine; Man. Dir S. MUKHERJI.

Intertrade Publications (India) (Pvt) Ltd: 55 Gariahat Rd, POB 10210, Kolkata 700 019; f. 1954; economics, medicine, law, history and trade directories; Man. Dir Dr K. K. ROY.

A. Mukherjee and Co (Pvt) Ltd: 2 Bankim Chatterjee St, Kolkata 700 073; tel. (33) 22417406; fax (33) 27448172; f. 1934; educational and general in Bengali and English; Man. Dir RAJEEV NEOGI.

Naya Prokash: 206 Bidhan Sarani, POB 11468, Kolkata 700 006; tel. (33) 22414709; fax (33) 25382897; e-mail npsales@cal2.vsnl.net.in; f. 1960; agriculture, horticulture, Indology, history, political science; Man. Dir P. S. BASU.

Punthi Pustak: 136/4B Bidhan Sarani, Kolkata 700 004; religion, history, philosophy; Propr S. K. BHATTACHARYA.

Renaissance Publishers (Pvt) Ltd: 15 Bankim Chatterjee St, Kolkata 700 012; f. 1949; politics, philosophy, history; Man. Dir J. C. GOSWAMI.

Saraswati Library: 206 Bidhan Sarani, Kolkata 700 006; f. 1914; history, philosophy, religion, literature; Man. Partner B. BHATTA-CHARJEE.

M. C. Sarkar and Sons (Pvt) Ltd: 14 Bankim Chatterjee St, Kolkata 700 073; f. 1910; reference; Dirs SUPRIYA SARKAR, SAMIT SARKAR.

Visva-Bharati: 6 Acharya Jagadish Bose Rd, Kolkata 700 017; tel. (33) 22479868; f. 1923; literature; Dir ASHOKE MUKHOPADHYAY.

Mumbai

Bharatiya Vidya Bhavan: Munshi Sadan, Kulapati K. M. Munshi Marg, Mumbai 400 007; tel. (22) 23631261; fax (22) 23630058; e-mail brbhavan@bom7.vsnl.net.in; internet www.bhavans.info; f. 1938; art, literature, culture, education, philosophy, religion, history of India; various periodicals in English, Hindi, Sanskrit and other Indian languages; Pres. R. VENKATARAMAN; Dir-Gen. S. RAMAKRISHNAN.

Himalaya Publishing House: 'Ramdoot', Dr Bhalerao Marg (Kelewadi), Girgaon, Mumbai 400 004; tel. (22) 23860170; fax (22) 23877178; e-mail himpub@vsnl.net.in; f. 1976; textbooks and research work; Dir MEENA PANDEY; CEO D. P. PANDEY.

India Book House (Pvt) Ltd: 412 Tulsiani Chambers, Nariman Point, Mumbai 400 021; tel. (22) 22840165; fax (22) 22835099; e-mail info@ibhworld.com; Man. Dir DEEPAK MIRCHANDANI.

International Book House (Pvt) Ltd: Indian Mercantile Mansions (Extension), Madame Cama Rd, Mumbai 400 039; tel. (22) 22021634; fax (22) 22851109; e-mail ibh@vsnl.com; internet www.intbh.com; f. 1941; general, educational, scientific, technical, engineering, social sciences, humanities and law; Man. Dir S. K. Gupta; Exec. Dir Sanjeev Gupta.

Jaico Publishing House: 127 Mahatma Gandhi Rd, opposite Mumbai University, Mumbai 400 023; tel. (22) 22676702; fax (22) 22656412; e-mail jaicopub@vsnl.com; f. 1947; general paperbacks, management, computer and engineering books, etc. imports scientific, medical, technical and educational books; Man. Dir Ashwin J. Shah.

Popular Prakashan (Pvt) Ltd: 35c Pandit Madan Mohan Malaviya Marg, Tardeo, Popular Press Bldg, opp. Crossroads, Mumbai 400 034; tel. (22) 24941656; fax (22) 24945294; e-mail popularprakashan@vsnl.com; f. 1968; sociology, biographies, religion, philosophy, fiction, arts, music, current affairs, medicine, history, politics and administration in English and Marathi; Man. Dir R. G. Bhatkal.

Somaiya Publications (Pvt) Ltd: 172 Mumbai Marathi Granthasangrahalaya Marg, Dadar, Mumbai 400 014; tel. (22) 24130230; fax (22) 22047297; e-mail somaiyabooks@rediffmail.com; internet www.somaiya.com; f. 1967; economics, sociology, history, politics, mathematics, sciences, language, literature, education, psychology, religion, philosophy, logic; Chair. Dr S. K. Somaiya.

Taraporevala, Sons and Co (Pvt) Ltd D.B.: 210 Dr Dadabhai Naoroji Rd, Fort, Mumbai 400 001; tel. (22) 22071433; f. 1864; Indian art, culture, history, sociology, scientific, technical and general in English; Chief Exec. R. J. Taraporevala.

N. M. Tripathi (Pvt) Ltd: 164 Shamaldas Gandhi Marg, Mumbai 400 002; tel. (22) 22013651; f. 1888; general in English and Gujarati; Chair. A. S. Pandya; Man. Dir Kartik R. Tripathi.

Other Towns

Bharat Bharati Prakashan & Co: Western Kutchery Rd, Meerut 250 001; tel. 2663698; f. 1952; textbooks; Man. Dir Surendra Agarwal.

Bharati Bhawan: Thakurbari Rd, Kadamkuan, Patna 800 003; tel. (612) 2671356; fax (612) 2670010; e-mail bbpdpat@giascl01.vsnl.com; f. 1942; educational and juvenile; Man. Partner Tarit Kumar Bose.

Bishen Singh Mahendra Pal Singh: 23a New Connaught Place, POB 137, Dehradun 248 001; tel. (135) 2655748; fax (135) 2650107; e-mail bsmps@del2.vsnl.net.in; internet www.bishensinghbooks.com; f. 1957; botany, forestry, agriculture; Dirs Gajendra Singh Gahlot, Abhimanyu Gahlot.

Catholic Press: Ranchi 834 001; f. 1928; books and periodicals; Dir William Tigga.

Chugh Publications: 2 Strachey Rd, POB 101, Allahabad; tel. (532) 2623063; sociology, economics, history, general; Propr Ramesh Kumar Chugh.

Geetha Book House: K. R. Circle, Mysore 570 001; tel. (821) 233589; f. 1959; general; Dirs M. Gopala Krishna, M. Gururaja Rao.

Kalyani Publishers: 1/1 Rajinder Nagar, Civil Lines, Ludhiana, Punjab 141 008; tel. (161) 2745756; fax (161) 2745872; textbooks; Dir Usha Raj Kumar.

Kitabistan: 30 Chak, Allahabad 211 003; tel. (532) 2653219; f. 1932; general, agriculture, govt publs in English, Hindi, Urdu, Farsi and Arabic; Partners A. U. Khan, Sultan Zaman.

Krishna Prakashan Media (P) Ltd: (Unit) Goel Publishing House, 11 Shivaji Rd, Meerut 250 001; tel. (121) 2642946; fax (121) 2645855; textbooks; Man. Dir Satyendra Kumar Rastogi; Dir Anita Rastogi.

The Law Book Co (Pvt) Ltd: 18b Sardar Patel Marg, Civil Lines, POB 1004, Allahabad 211 001; tel. (532) 2624905; fax (532) 2420852; e-mail bagga1@nae.vsnl.net.in; f. 1929; legal texts in English; Dir Anil Bagga; Man. Dir L. R. Bagga.

Macmillan India Ltd: 315/316 Raheja Chambers, 12 Museum Rd, Bangalore 560 001; tel. (80) 25594120; fax (80) 25588713; e-mail chandra291@vsnl.com; internet www.macmillanindia.com; school and university books in English; general; Pres. and Man. Dir Rajiv Beri; Dir (Technical) Debashish Banerjee.

Navajivan Publishing House: PO Navajivan, Ahmedabad 380 014; tel. (79) 27540635; f. 1919; Gandhiana and related social science; in English, Hindi and Gujarati; Man. Trustee Jitendra Desai; Sales Man. Kapil Rawal.

Nem Chand and Bros: Civil Lines, Roorkee 247 667; tel. (1332) 72258; fax (1332) 73258; f. 1951; engineering textbooks and journals.

Orient Longman (Pvt) Ltd: 3-6-752 Himayat Nagar, Hyderabad 500 029; tel. (40) 2765049; fax (40) 2765046; e-mail orlongco@hd2.dot.net.in; f. 1948; educational, technical, general and children's in English and almost all Indian languages; Chair. Shanta Rameshwar Rao; Dirs Dr Nandini Rao, J. Krishnadev Rao.

Pilgrims Publishing: Pilgrims Book House, B27/98-A-8 Nawabganj Rd, Durga Kund, Varanasi 221 001; tel. (542) 2314060; fax (542) 2314059; e-mail pilgrims@satyam.net.in; internet www.pilgrimsbooks.com; f. 1986; first edition and reprint books on Nepal, Tibet, India and the Himalayas; Senior Editor Christopher N. Burchett.

Publication Bureau: Panjab University, Chandigarh 160 014; tel. (172) 2541782; f. 1948; textbooks, academic and general; Man. H. R. Grover.

Publication Bureau: Punjabi University, Patiala 147 002; tel. (175) 22826650; university-level text and reference books; Head of Bureau S. Sukhdial Singh.

Ram Prasad and Sons: Hospital Rd, Agra 282 003; tel. (562) 2367904; fax (562) 2360906; e-mail ea_08@yahoo.com; f. 1905; agricultural, arts, history, commerce, education, general, pure and applied science, economics, sociology; Dirs R. N, B. N, Y. N, Ravi Agarwal; Man. S. N. Agarwal; br. in Bhopal.

Government Publishing House

Publications Division: Ministry of Information and Broadcasting, Govt of India, Patiala House, New Delhi 110 001; tel. (11) 23386879; fax (11) 23386879; e-mail pubdiv1@bol.net.in; internet www.nic.in/indiapublications; f. 1941; culture, art, literature, planning and development, general; also 21 periodicals in English and several Indian languages; Dir P. S. Bhatnagar.

PUBLISHERS' ASSOCIATIONS

Bombay Booksellers' and Publishers' Association: No. 25, 6th Floor, Bldg No. 3, Navjivan Commercial Premises Co-op Society Ltd, Dr Bhadkamkar Marg, Mumbai 400 008; tel. (22) 23088691; f. 1961; 400 mems; Pres. K. M. Varghese; Gen. Sec. B. S. Fernandes.

Delhi State Booksellers' and Publishers' Association: 3026/7H Shiv Chowk, (South Patel Nagar) Ranjit Nagar, New Delhi 110 008; tel. (11) 25772748; fax (11) 25786769; e-mail rpnbooks@indiatimes.com; f. 1943; 400 mems; Pres. Dr S. K. Bhatia; Sec. Ranbir Singh.

Federation of Educational Publishers in India: 19 Rani Jhansi Rd, New Delhi 110 055; tel. (11) 3522607; fax (11) 3636103; f. 1987; 14 affiliated asscns; 168 mems; 24 associated mems; Pres. R. K. Gupta; Sec.-Gen. Kamal Arora.

Federation of Indian Publishers: Federation House, 18/1-C Institutional Area, nr JNU, New Delhi 110 067; tel. (11) 26964847; fax (11) 26864054; e-mail fipl@satyam.net.in; internet www.federationofindianpublishers.com; 18 affiliated asscns; 190 mems; Pres. Debajyoti Datta; Hon. Gen. Sec. Narendra Kumar.

Akhil Bharatiya Hindi Prakashak Sangh: A-2/1, Krishan Nagar, Delhi 110 051; tel. (11) 22219398; f. 1954; 400 mems; Pres. Inder Sengar; Gen. Sec. Arun Kumar Sharma.

All Assam Publishers' and Booksellers' Association: College Hostel Rd, Panbazar, Guwahati 780 001; tel. (361) 2634790; fax (361) 2513886; Pres. Nabin Baruah; Sec. J. N. Dutta Baruah.

All India Urdu Publications' and Booksellers' Association: 3243 Kuchatarachand, Daryaganj, New Delhi 110 002; tel. (11) 23257189; fax (11) 23265420; e-mail aakif@del3.vsnl.net.in; internet www.aakif.com; f. 1988; 150 mems; Pres. Dr Khaliq Anjum; Gen. Sec. S. M. Zafar Ali.

All Kerala Publishers' and Booksellers' Association: D. C. B. Complex, POB 214, Kottayam 686 001; Pres. N. E. Balakrishnan Marar.

Booksellers' and Publishers' Association of South India: 8, II Floor, Sun Plaza, G. N. Chetty Rd, Chennai 600 006; 158 mems; Pres. S. Chandrasekar; Sec. Ravi Chopra.

Gujarati Sahitya Prakashak Vikreta Mandal: Navajivan Trust, P.O. Navajivan, Ahmedabad 380 014; tel. (79) 27540635; 125 mems; Pres. Jitendra Desai; Sec. K. N. Madrasi.

Karnataka Publishers' Association: 53 Shamsingh Complex, Gandhi Bazar Main Rd, Bangalore 560 004; tel. (80) 2601638; Pres. S. V. Srinivasa Rao.

Orissa Publishers' and Booksellers' Association: Binodbihari, Cuttack 753 002; tel. (671) 2612855; f. 1973–74; 280 mems; Pres. Pitambar Mishra; Sec. Bhikari Charan Mohapatra.

Paschimbanga Prakasak Sabha: 206 Bidhan Sarani, Kolkata 700 006; tel. (33) 23504534; fax (33) 22413852; Pres. Bibhas Bhattacharjee; Gen. Sec. T. Saha.

Publishers' Association of West Bengal: 6-B, Ramanath Mazumder St, Kolkata 700 009; tel. (33) 2325580; 164 mems; Pres. MOHIT KUMAR BASU; Gen. Sec. SHANKARI BHUSAN NAYAK.

Publishers' and Booksellers' Association of Bengal: 93 Mahatma Gandhi Rd, Kolkata 700 007; tel. (33) 22411993; f. 1912; 4,500 mems; Pres. PRASOON BASU; Gen. Sec. CHITTA SINGHA ROY.

Punjabi Publishers' Association: Satnam Singh, Singh Brothers, Bazar Mai Sewan, Amritsar 143 006; tel. (183) 245787; Sec. SATNAM SINGH.

Vijayawada Publishers' Association: 27-1-68, Karl Marx Rd, Vijayawada 520 002; tel. (866) 2433353; fax (866) 2426348; 41 mems; Pres. DUPATI VIJAY KUMAR; Sec. U. N. YOGI.

Federation of Publishers' and Booksellers' Associations in India: 2nd Floor, 84 Daryaganj, New Delhi 110 002; tel. (11) 23272845; fax (11) 23281227; 16 affiliated asscns; 550 mems; Pres. SUKUMAR DAS; Sec. K. P. R. NAIR.

Publishers' and Booksellers' Guild: Guild House, 2B Jhamapukur Lane, Kolkata 700 009; tel. (33) 23544417; fax (33) 23604566; e-mail guild@cal2.vsnl.net.in; internet www.kolkatabookfaironline.com; f. 1975; 37 mems; organizes annual Kolkata Book Fair; Pres. JAYANT MANAKTALA; Sec. KALYAN SHAH.

Broadcasting and Communications

TELECOMMUNICATIONS

Telecom Regulatory Authority of India (TRAI): 16th Floor, Jawahar Vyapar Bhavan 1, Tolstoy Marg, New Delhi 110 001; tel. (11) 23357815; fax (11) 23738708; e-mail trai@del2.vsnl.net.in; internet www.trai.gov.in; f. 1998; Chair. S. S. SODHI; Vice-Chair. BAL KRISHAN ZUTSHI.

Bharti Telenet Ltd: Indore; f. 1998; India's first privately owned telephone network; Exec. Dir BHAGWAN KHURANA.

Ericsson: POB 10912, New Delhi 110 066.

ITI (Indian Telephone Industries) Ltd: 45/1 Magrath Rd, Bangalore 560 025; tel. (80) 25366116; fax (80) 25593188; internet www.itiltd-india.com; f. 1948; mfrs of all types of telecommunication equipment, incl. telephones, automatic exchanges and long-distance transmission equipment; also produces optical fibre equipment and microwave equipment; will manufacture all ground communication equipment for the 22 earth stations of the Indian National Satellite; in conjunction with the Post and Telegraph Department, a newly designed 2,000-line exchange has been completed; Chair. and Man. Dir LAKSHMI G. MENON.

Mahanagar Telephone Nigam Ltd (MTNL): Jeevan Bharati Tower, 124 Connaught Circus, New Delhi 110 001; tel. (11) 23742212; fax (11) 23314243; e-mail cmd@bol.net.in; internet www.mtnl.net.in; f. 1986; 66% state-owned; owns and operates telephone networks in Mumbai and Delhi; Chair. and Man. Dir NARINDER SHARMA.

Videsh Sanchar Nigam Ltd (VSNL): Lok Manya Videsh Sanchar Bhawan, Kasinath Dhuru Marg, Prabhadevi, Mumbai 400 028; tel. (22) 24322959; fax (22) 24365689; e-mail helpdesk@giaspn01.vsnl.net.in; internet www.vsnl.com; f. 1986; 26% state-owned; 45% owned by the Tata Group; Chair. RATAN N. TATA; Man. Dir S. K. GUPTA.

BROADCASTING

Prasar Bharati (Broadcasting Corpn of India): New Delhi; autonomous body; oversees operations of state-owned radio and television services; f. 1997; Chair. M. V. KAMATH; Chief Exec. K. S. SARMA.

Radio

All India Radio (AIR): Akashvani Bhavan, Parliament St, New Delhi 110 001; tel. (11) 23715411; fax (11) 23714061; broadcasting is controlled by the Ministry of Information and Broadcasting and is primarily govt-financed; operates a network of 208 stations and 332 transmitters (grouped into four zones— north, south, east and west), covering 98.8% of the population and over 90% of the total area of the country; Dir-Gen. T. R. MALAKAR.

The News Services Division of AIR, centralized in New Delhi, is one of the largest news organizations in the world. It has 45 regional news units, which broadcast 316 bulletins daily in 24 languages and 38 dialects. Eighty four bulletins in 19 languages are broadcast in the Home Services, 139 regional bulletins in 64 languages and dialects, and 64 bulletins in 25 languages in the External Services.

Television

Doordarshan India (Television India): Mandi House, Doordarshan Bhavan, Copernicus Marg, New Delhi 110 001; tel. (11) 23385958; fax (11) 23386507; f. 1976; broadcasting is controlled by the Ministry of Information and Broadcasting and is govt-financed; programmes: 280 hours weekly; 5 All-India channels, 11 regional language satellite channels, 5 state networks and 1 international channel; Dir-Gen. Dr S. Y. QURESHI.

In January 2002 74.8% of the country's area and 87.9% of the population were covered by the TV network. There were 1,231 transmitters in operation in that month. By 2000 51 programme production centres and nine relay centres had been established.

Finance

(cap. = capital; p.u. = paid up; res = reserves; dep. = deposits; m. = million; brs = branches; amounts in rupees)

BANKING

State Banks

Reserve Bank of India: Central Office Bldg, Shahid Bhagat Singh Rd, POB 10007, Mumbai 400 001; tel. (22) 22661602; fax (22) 22658269; e-mail rbiprd@giasbm01.vsnl.net.in; internet www.rbi.org.in; f. 1934; nationalized 1949; sole bank of issue; cap. 50m., res 65,000m., dep. 851,630m. (Sept. 2002); Gov. Dr BIMAL JALAN; Dep. Govs Dr RAKESH MOHAN, VEPA KAMESAN, G. P MUNIAPPAN; 4 offices and 14 brs.

State Bank of India: Corporate Centre, Madame Cama Rd, POB 10121, Mumbai 400 021; tel. (22) 22022426; fax (22) 22851391; e-mail sbiid@boms.vsnl.net.in; internet www.sbi.co.in; f. 1955; cap. p.u. 5,263m., res and surplus 146,980.8m., dep. 2,705,601.4m. (March 2002); 7 associates, 7 domestic subsidiaries/affiliates, 3 foreign subsidiaries, 4 jt ventures abroad; Chair. A. K. PURWAR; Man. Dirs A. K. BATRA, P. N. VENKATACHALAM; 9,085 brs (incl. 51 overseas brs and rep. offices in 31 countries).

State-owned Commercial Banks

Fourteen of India's major commercial banks were nationalized in 1969 and a further six in 1980. They are managed by 15-mem. boards of directors (two directors to be appointed by the central Government, one employee director, one representing employees who are not workmen, one representing depositors, three representing farmers, workers, artisans, etc., five representing persons with special knowledge or experience, one Reserve Bank of India official and one Government of India official). The Department of Banking of the Ministry of Finance controls all banking operations.

There were 65,931 branches of public-sector and other commercial banks in June 2001.

Aggregate deposits of all scheduled commercial banks amounted to Rs 12,397,730m. in September 2002.

Allahabad Bank: 2 Netaji Subhas Rd, Kolkata 700 001; tel. (33) 22208668; fax (33) 22488323; e-mail albfd@giascl01.vsnl.net.in; internet www.allahabadbank.com/; f. 1865; nationalized 1969; cap. p.u. 2,467m., res 7,338m., dep. 226,660m. (March 2002); Chair. and Man. Dir Dr B. SAMAL; 1,915 brs.

Andhra Bank: Andhra Bank Bldgs, Saifabad, 5-9-11 Secretariat Rd, Hyderabad 500 004; tel. (40) 23230001; fax (40) 23211050; e-mail dit@andhrabank.co.in; internet www.andhrabankindia.com; f. 1923; nationalized 1980; cap. p.u. 4,500m., res 4,339m., dep. 184,908m. (March 2002); Chair. and Man. Dir B. VASANTHAN; 980 brs and 87 extension counters.

Bank of Baroda: Baroda Corporate Centre, C-26, G-Block, Bandra-Kurla complex, Bandra East, Mumbai 400 054; tel. (22) 22615065; fax (22) 22610341; e-mail secbob@bol.net.in; internet www.bankofbaroda.com/; f. 1908; nationalized 1969; merged with Benares State Bank in 2002; cap. 2,943.3m., res 35,334.2m., dep. 618,045m. (March 2002); Chair. and Man. Dir P. S. SHENOY; 2,641 brs in India, 38 brs overseas.

Bank of India: Express Towers, Nariman Point, POB 234, Mumbai 400 021; tel. (22) 22023020; fax (22) 22024701; e-mail cmdboi@bom5.vsnl.net.in; internet www.bankofindia.com; f. 1906; nationalized 1969; cap. 4,880.8m., res and surplus 21,637.2m., dep. 608,330m. (March 2002); Chair. and Man. Dir K. V. KRISHNAMURTHY; 2,528 brs in India, 19 brs overseas.

Bank of Maharashtra: 'Lokmangal', 1501 Shivajinagar, Pune 411 005; tel. (20) 25532731; fax (20) 25533246; e-mail bomcocmd@vsnl.com; internet www.maharashtrabank.com; f. 1935; nationalized 1969; cap. 3,305.1m., res 3,672m., dep. 191,306.3m. (March 2002); Chair. and Man. Dir S. C. BASU; 1,179 brs.

Canara Bank: 112 Jayachamarajendra Rd, POB 6648, Bangalore 560 002; tel. (80) 22221581; fax (80) 22222704; e-mail canbank@blr .vsnl.net.in; internet www.canbankindia.com; f. 1906; nationalized 1969; cap. 5,778.7m., res 28,936.3m., dep. 640,300.1m. (March 2002); Chair. and Man. Dir R. V. SHASTRI; 2,348 brs in India, 1 br. overseas.

Central Bank of India: Chandermukhi, Nariman Point, Mumbai 400 021; tel. (22) 22026428; fax (22) 22044336; e-mail cbicpp@b01 .net.in; internet www.centralbankofindia.com; f. 1911; nationalized 1969; cap. 11,241.4m., res and surplus 8,726m., dep. 471,373.8m. (March 2002); Chair. and Man. Dir Dr DALBIR SINGH; 3,115 brs.

Corporation Bank: Mangaladevi Temple Rd, POB 88, Mangalore 575 001; tel. (824) 2426416; fax (824) 2444617; e-mail corpho@ corpbank.com; internet www.corpbank.com; f. 1906; nationalized 1980; cap. 1,434.4m., res 19,603.8m., dep. 189,240m. (March 2002); Chair. and Man. Dir K. CHERIAN VARGHESE; Exec. Dir P. K. GUPTA; 652 brs.

Dena Bank: Maker Towers 'E', 7th–10th Floor, Cuffe Parade, Colaba, POB 6058, Mumbai 400 005; tel. (22) 22189151; fax (22) 22189046; e-mail dena@giasbom01.vsnl.net.in; internet www .denabank.com; f. 1938 as Devkaran Nanjee Banking Co Ltd; nationalized 1969; cap. 2,068.2m., res and surplus 6,213.7m., dep. 153,546.9m. (March 2002); Chair. and Man. Dir A. G. JOSHI; 1,134 brs.

Indian Bank: 31 Rajaji Salai, POB 1866, Chennai 600 001; tel. (44) 25233231; fax (44) 25231278; e-mail indianbank@vsnl.com; internet www.indian-bank.com; f. 1907; nationalized 1969; cap. 38,039.6m., res 3,812.5m., dep. 240,388m. (March 2002); Chair. and Man. Dir RANJANA KUMAR; Exec. Dir M. B. N. RAO; 1,424 brs.

Indian Overseas Bank: 762 Anna Salai, POB 3765, Chennai 600 002; tel. (44) 28524212; fax (44) 28523595; e-mail iobmail@vsnl.com; internet www.iob.com; f. 1937; nationalized 1969; cap. 4,448m., res 3,172.2m., dep. 309,460m. (March 2002); Chair. and Man. Dir S. C. GUPTA; Exec. Dir R. NATARAJAN; 1,438 brs.

Oriental Bank of Commerce: Harsha Bhavan, E Block, Connaught Place, POB 329, New Delhi 110 001; tel. (11) 23323444; fax (11) 23321514; e-mail bdncmd@obcindia.com; internet www .obcindia.com; f. 1943; nationalized 1980; cap. 1,925.4m., res 14,271.9m., dep. 284,884m. (March 2002); Chair. and Man. Dir B. D. NARANG; 533 brs.

Punjab and Sind Bank: 21 Bank House, Rajendra Place, New Delhi 110 008; tel. (11) 25768831; fax (11) 25751765; internet www .punjabandsindbank.com; f. 1908; nationalized 1980; cap. 2,430.6m., res 1,307.4m., dep. 94,966m. (March 1999); Chair. and Man. Dir N. S. GUJRAL; Exec. Dir M. S. KAPUR; 811 brs.

Punjab National Bank: 7 Bhikaiji Cama Place, Africa Ave, New Delhi 110 066; tel. (11) 26102303; fax (11) 26196456; e-mail pnbmasd@nde.vsnl.net.in; internet www.pnbindia.com; f. 1895; nationalized 1969; merged with New Bank of India in 1993; cap. 2,122.4m., res 26,658m., dep. 641,234.8m. (March 2002); Chair. and Man. Dir S. S. KOHLI; Exec. Dir K. R. CHABRIA; 4,268 brs.

Syndicate Bank: POB 1, Manipal 576 119; tel. (8252) 2571181; fax (825) 2570266; e-mail idcb@syndicatebank.com; internet www .syndicatebank.com; f. 1925 as Canara Industrial and Banking Syndicate Ltd; name changed as above 1964; nationalized 1969; cap. 4,719.4m., res 7,467.0m., dep. 285,480m. (March 2002); Chair. and Man. Dir MICHAEL BASTIAN; 1,948 brs.

UCO Bank: 10 Biplabi Trailokya Maharaj Sarani (Brabourne Rd), POB 2455, Kolkata 700 001; tel. (33) 22254120; fax (33) 22253986; e-mail ucobank@vsnl.net; internet www.ucobank.com; f. 1943 as United Commercial Bank Ltd; nationalized 1969; name changed as above 1985; cap. 22,645.2m., res 4,969.5m., dep. 268,487.7m. (March 2002); Chair. and Man. Dir V. P. SHETTY; Exec. Dir M. M. VAISH; 1,797 brs.

Union Bank of India: Union Bank Bhavan, 239 Vidhan Bhavan Marg, Nariman Point, Mumbai 400 021; tel. (22) 22023060; fax (22) 22025238; e-mail ubihoc@vsnl.net.in; internet www .unionbankofindia.com; f. 1919; nationalized 1969; cap. 3,380m., res 17,690m., dep. 397,939m. (March 2002); Chair. and Man. Dir V. LEELADHAR; 2,023 brs.

United Bank of India: 16 Old Court House St, Kolkata 700 001; tel. (33) 2487471; fax (33) 2485852; e-mail utbihoc@giascl01.vsnl.net .in; internet www.unitedbankofindia.com; f. 1950; nationalized 1969; cap. 18,108.7m., res 1,583.2m., dep. 196,106.6m. (March 2002); Chair. and Man. Dir MADHUKAR; Exec. Dir G. R. SUNDARAVADIVEL; 1,316 brs.

Vijaya Bank: 41/2 Mahatma Gandhi Rd, Bangalore 560 001; tel. (80) 25584066; fax (80) 25598040; e-mail vijbank@bgl.vsnl.net.in; internet www.vijayabank.com; f. 1931; nationalized 1980; cap. 3,335.2m., res 3,295.1m., dep. 146,810m. (March 2002); Chair. and Man. Dir M. S. KAPUR; 842 brs.

Principal Private Banks

The Bank of Rajasthan Ltd: C-3 Sardar Patel Marg, Jaipur 302 001; tel. (141) 2381222; fax (141) 2381123; e-mail borit@jp1.dot.net .in; internet www.bankofrajasthan.com; f. 1943; cap. p.u. 1,003.7m., res 1,104.8m., dep. 39,599.8m. (March 2002); Chair. PRAVIN KUMAR TAYAL; Man. Dir K. M. BHATTACHARYA; 307 brs.

Bharat Overseas Bank Ltd: Habeeb Towers, 196 Anna Salai, Chennai 600 002; tel. (44) 28525686; fax (44) 28524700; e-mail bobl@ md3.vsnl.net.in; internet www.boblonline.com; f. 1973; cap. 157.5m., res 1,072.8m., dep. 18,232.6m. (March 2002); Chair. G. KRISHNAMURTHY; Gen. Man. G. CHANDRAN; 77 brs.

Bombay Mercantile Co-operative Bank Ltd: 78 Mohammed Ali Rd, Mumbai 400 003; tel. (22) 23425961; fax (22) 23433385; e-mail bmcb@bom5.vsnl.net.in; f. 1939; cap. 126m., res 1,696.6m., dep. 27,756.3m. (March 2000); Chair. A. R. KIDWAI; Man. Dir A. Q. SIDDIQUI; 53 brs.

The Catholic Syrian Bank Ltd: St Mary's College Rd, POB 502, Trichur 680 020; tel. (487) 2333020; fax (487) 2333435; e-mail csbho@md2.vsnl.net.in; internet www.casybank.com; f. 1920; cap. 99.9m., res 401.8m., dep. 31,910m. (March 2002); Chair. and CEO N. R. ACHAN; Gen. Man. JOHN J. ALAPATT; 284 brs.

Centurion Bank Ltd: 1201 Raheja Centre, Free Press Journal Marg, Nariman Point, Mumbai 400 021; tel. (22) 22047234; fax (22) 22845860; e-mail cblho@bom3.vsnl.net.in; internet www .centurionbank.com; f. 1995; cap. 1,524.7m., res 215.9m., dep. 47,048.3m. (March 2000); Chair. and Man. Dir V. JANAKIRAMAN.

City Union Bank Ltd: 149 TSR (Big) St, Kumbakonam 612 001; tel. (435) 2432322; fax (435) 2431746; e-mail cub@vsnl.com; internet www.cityunion.com; f. 1904; cap. 240.0m., res 797.4m., dep. 19,737m. (March 2002); Chair. V. NARYANAN; Chief Gen. Man. K. VENKATARAMAN; 114 brs.

The Federal Bank Ltd: Federal Towers, POB 103, Alwaye 683 101; tel. (484) 2623620; fax (484) 2621687; e-mail nrihelp@federalbank.co .in; internet www.federal-bank.com; f. 1931; cap. 217.2m., res and surplus 4,186.6m., dep. 88,650m. (March 2002); Chair. K. P. PADMAKUMAR; 410 brs.

Global Trust Bank Ltd: 303-48-3 Sardar Patel Rd, Secunderabad 500 003; tel. (40) 27819333; fax (40) 27815879; e-mail ask@ globaltrustbank.com; internet www.globaltrustbank.com; f. 1994; cap. p.u. 1,214m., res 2,729.6m., dep. 77,342.3m. (March 2001); Man. Dir SUDHAKAR GANDE; Exec. Dir SRIDHAR SUBASRI; 96 brs.

ICICI Bank: ICICI Towers, 4th Floor, South Tower, Bandra–Kurla Complex, Bandra (East), Mumbai 400 051; tel. (22) 26531414; fax (22) 26531167; e-mail sinorhn@icicibank.com; internet www .icicibank.com; f. 1994; cap. 2,203.6m., res and surplus 10,922.6m., dep. 163,782m. (March 2001); Man. Dir and CEO H. N. SINOR; 389 brs.

IndusInd Bank Ltd: IndusInd House, 425 Dadasaheb Bhadkamkar Marg, Lamington Rd, nr Opera House, Mumbai 400 004; tel. (22) 23859901; fax (22) 23859913; e-mail glob@indusind.com; internet www.indusind.com; f. 1994; cap. 1,590.2m., res 4,029.0m., dep. 84,001.2m. (March 2002); Chair. R. J. SAHANEY; Man. Dir BHASKAR GHOSE; 77 brs.

ING Vysya Bank Ltd: 72 St Marks Rd, Bangalore 560 001; tel. (80) 22272021; fax (80) 22272220; e-mail ibdbby.vbl@gnbom.global.net .in; internet www.vysbank.com; f. 1930; cap. 226.2m., res 6,301.2m., dep. 80,680m. (March 2002); Chair. G. MALLIKARJUNA RAO; Man. Dir BART HILLEMANS; 484 brs.

Jammu and Kashmir Bank Ltd: Corporate Headquarters, M. A. Rd, Srinagar 190 001; tel. (194) 2481930; fax (194) 2481923; e-mail jkbcosgr@jkbmail.com; internet www.jkbank.org; f. 1938; cap. p.u. 481.1m., res 8,889.2m., dep 129,111.1m. (March 2002); Chair. and CEO M. Y. KHAN; 440 brs.

The Karnataka Bank Ltd: POB 716, Kodialbail, Mangalore 575 003; tel. (824) 2440751; fax (824) 2441212; e-mail info@ktkbank.com; internet www.thekarnatakabankltd.com; f. 1924; cap. 135m., dep. 70,015m. (March 2002); Chair. and CEO Mr ANANTHAKRISHNA; 357 brs.

The Karur Vysya Bank Ltd: Erode Rd, POB 21, Karur 639 002; tel. (4324) 232520; fax (4324) 230202; e-mail kvbid@giasmd01.vsnl .net.in; f. 1916; cap. 60.0m., res 3,227.8m., dep. 41,800.6m. (March 2002); Chair. P. T. KUPPUSWAMY; Sr Gen. Man. V. DEVARAJAN; 213 brs.

Lakshmi Vilas Bank Ltd: Kathaparai, Salem Rd, POB 2, Karur 639 006; tel. (4324) 2320057; fax (4324) 2320068; e-mail lvbho.cppd@ gecsl.com; internet www.lakshmivilasbankltd.com; f. 1926; cap. 115.1m., res 1,529.1m., dep. 22,776.4m. (March 2001); Chair. A. KRISHNAMOORTHY; 211 brs.

The Sangli Bank Ltd: Rajwada Chowk, POB 158, Sangli 416 416; tel. (233) 2623611; fax (233) 2620666; e-mail san_sanbank@

sancharnet.in; f. 1916; cap. p.u. 60.2m., dep. 7,303.6m. (March 1995); Chair. and CEO A. R. BORDE; Gen. Man. S. R. GODBOLE; 178 brs.

The South Indian Bank Ltd: SIB House, Mission Quarters, Thrissur 680 001, Kerala; tel. (487) 2420020; fax (487) 2442021; e-mail head@southindianbank.com; internet www.southindianbank .com; f. 1929; cap. 357.4m., res 2,388.6m., dep. 59,197m. (March 2002); Chair. and CEO A. SETHUMADHAVAN; 380 brs.

Tamilnad Mercantile Bank Ltd: 57 Victoria Extension Rd, Tuticorin 628 002; tel. (461) 2321932; fax (461) 2322994; f. 1921 as Nadar Bank, name changed as above 1962; cap. 2.8m., res 2,764.3m., dep. 31,980.7m. (March 2001); Chair. R. NATARAJAN; 163 brs.

The United Western Bank Ltd: 172/4 Raviwar Peth, Shivaji Circle, POB 2, Satara 415 001; tel. (2162) 220517; fax (2162) 223374; internet www.uwbankindia.com; f. 1936; cap. 298.9m., res and surplus 1,967.7m., dep. 43,488.4m. (March 2000); Chair. and Chief Exec. SATISH MARATHE; Gen. Man. V. G. PALKAR; 227 brs.

Foreign Banks

ABN AMRO Bank NV (Netherlands): 14 Veer Nariman Rd, POB 97, Mumbai 400 023; tel. (22) 22042331; CEO ROMESH SOBTI; 11 brs.

Abu Dhabi Commercial Bank (UAE): Rehmat Manzil, 75-B Veer Nariman Rd, Mumbai 400 020; tel. (22) 22830235; fax (22) 22870686; Chief Exec. KHALIFA MOHAMMAD HUSSEIN; 1 br.

American Express Bank Ltd (USA): 7th Floor, Maker Chambers IV, 211 Nariman Point, Mumbai 400 021; tel. (22) 22833293; fax (22) 22872968; Country Head STEVE MARTIN; 4 brs.

Banca Nazionale del Lavoro Spa (Italy): 61 Maker Chambers VI, Nariman Point, Mumbai 400 021; tel. (22) 22047763; fax (22) 22023482; Rep. L. S. AGARWAL.

Bank Muscat SAOG (Oman): 29 Infantry Rd, Bangalore 560 001; tel. (80) 22867755; fax (80) 22862214; e-mail bmiimgt@bgl.vsnl.net .in; CEO SAMIT GHOSH; 1 br.

Bank of America NA (USA): Express Towers, POB 10080, Nariman Point, Mumbai 400 021; tel. (22) 22852882; fax (22) 22029016; Country Man. VISHWAVIR AHUJA; 3 brs.

Bank of Bahrain and Kuwait BSC: Jolly Maker Chambers II, Ground Floor, POB 11692, 225 Nariman Point, Mumbai 400 021; tel. (22) 22823698; fax (22) 22044458; Gen. Man. and CEO K. S. KRISHNA-KUMAR; 2 brs.

Bank of Ceylon: 1090 Poonamallee High Rd, Chennai 600 084; tel. (44) 26420972; fax (44) 25325590; e-mail ceybank@md3.vsnl.net.in; internet www.bocindia.com; Asst Vice-Pres. B. KARTHIK; Country Man. N. V. MOORTHY.

Bank of Nova Scotia (Canada): Mittal Tower B, Nariman Point, Mumbai 400 021; tel. (22) 22832822; fax (22) 22873125; Sr Vice-Pres. and CEO (India) DOUGLAS H. STEWART; Vice-Pres. and Man. BHASKAR DESAI; 4 brs.

Bank of Tokyo-Mitsubishi Ltd (Japan): Jeevan Prakash, Sir P. Mehta Rd, Mumbai 400 001; tel. (22) 22660564; fax (22) 22661787; Regional Rep. for India and Gen. Man. KUNIHIKO NISHIHARA; 4 brs.

Barclays Bank PLC (UK): 21–23 Maker Chambers VI, 2nd Floor, Nariman Point, Mumbai 400 021; tel. (22) 22044353; fax (22) 22043238; CEO AJAY SONDHI; 2 brs.

BNP Paribas (France): French Bank Bldg, 62 Homji St, Fort, Mumbai 400 001; tel. (22) 22660822; fax (22) 22679709; e-mail Mumbai1.admin@asia.bnpparibas.com; internet www.bnpparibas .co.in; cap. Rs 352m., res Rs 1,700m., dep. Rs 16,300m. (2002); Chief Exec. and Country Man. JONATHAN LYON; 8 brs.

Chinatrust Commercial Bank (Taiwan): 21-A Janpath, New Delhi 110 001; tel. (11) 3356001; fax (11) 3731815; e-mail ctcbindd@ ndf.vsnl.net.in; internet www.chinatrustindia.com; Gen. Man. and CEO ALTON C. C. WANG; 1 br.

Citibank, NA (USA): Sakhar Bhavan, 230 Backbay Reclamation, Nariman Point, Mumbai 400 021; tel. (22) 22025499; internet www .citibank.com/india; CEO SANJAY NAYAR; 16 brs.

Commerzbank AG (Germany): Free Press House, 215 Free Press Journal Rd, Nariman Point, Mumbai 400 021; tel. (22) 22885510; fax (22) 22885524; Gen. Mans G. SHEKHAR, PETER KENYON-MUIR; 2 brs.

Crédit Agricole Indosuez (France): Ramon House, 169 Backbay Reclamation, Mumbai 400 020; tel. (22) 22045104; fax (22) 22049108; Sr Country Officer ALAIN BUTZBACH; Gen. Man. NIRENDU MAZUMDAR.

Crédit Lyonnais (France): Apeejay House, 3rd Floor, 3 Dinshaw Vachha Rd, Mumbai 400 020; tel. (22) 22330300; fax (22) 22351888; Chief Exec. and Country Man. JEAN-YVES LE PAULMIER; 4 brs.

Deutsche Bank AG (Germany): DB House, Hazarimal Somani Marg, Fort, POB 1142, Mumbai 400 001; tel. (22) 22074720; fax (22) 22075047; Chief Country Officer DOUGLAS NEILSON; 5 brs.

Development Bank of Singapore Ltd: Free Press House, 14th Floor, Nariman Point, Mumbai 400 021; tel. (22) 22388888; fax (22) 22388899; internet www.dbs.com; 1 br.

Dresdner Bank (Germany): Hoechst House, Nariman Point, Mumbai 400 021; tel. (22) 22850009; 2 brs.

Fuji Bank Ltd (Japan): Maker Chambers III, 1st Floor, Jamnalal Bajaj Rd, Nariman Point, Mumbai 400 021; tel. (22) 22886638; fax (22) 22886640; CEO (India) and Gen. Man. TATSUJI TAMAKA; 1 br.

Hongkong and Shanghai Banking Corpn Ltd (Hong Kong): 52–60 Mahatma Gandhi Rd, POB 128, Mumbai 400 001; tel. (22) 22674921; fax (22) 22658309; internet www.hongkongbank.com; CEO and Country Head NIALL S. K. BOOKER; 30 brs.

ING Bank (Netherlands): Hoechst House, 7th Floor, 193 Backbay Reclamation, Nariman Point, Mumbai 400 005; tel. (22) 22029876; fax (22) 22046134; e-mail atul.sahasrabuddhe@asia.ing.com; Country Head ATUL SAHASRABUDDHE; 2 brs.

JP Morgan Chase Manhattan Bank: Mafatlal Centre, 9/F, Nariman Point, Mumbai 400 021; tel. (22) 22855666; fax (22) 22027772; Man. Dir and Sr Country Officer (India and South Asia) DOMINIC PRICE; 1 br.

Mashreq Bank PSC (United Arab Emirates): Air-India Bldg, Nariman Point, Mumbai 400 021; tel. (22) 22026096; fax (22) 22831278; CEO SUNEIL KUCCHAL.

Oman International Bank SAOG (Oman): 201 Raheja Centre, Free Press Journal Marg, Nariman Point, Mumbai 400 021; tel. (22) 22324848; fax (22) 22875626; e-mail oibind@bom3.vsnl.net.in; Country Man. G. PATTIBIRAMAN; 2 brs.

Société Générale (France): Maker Chambers IV, Bajaj Marg, Nariman Point, POB 11635, Mumbai 400 021; tel. (22) 22870909; fax (22) 22045459; e-mail sg.mumbai@sgib.com; CEO PAUL H. RUSCH; 4 brs.

Sonali Bank (Bangladesh): 'Apeejay House', 15 Park St, Kolkata 700 016; tel. (33) 22147998; Dep. Gen. Man. SIRAJUDDIN AHMED; 1 br.

Standard Chartered Grindlays Bank (UK): New Excelsior Bldg, 4th Floor, A. K. Naik Marg, POB 1806, Mumbai 400 001; tel. (22) 22075409; fax (22) 22072550; e-mail vkrishn@scbindia.mhs .compuserve.com; Chief Exec. CHRIS LOW; 61 brs.

State Bank of Mauritius Ltd: 101, Raheja Centre, 1st Floor, Free Press Journal Marg, Nariman Point, Mumbai 400 021; tel. (22) 22842965; fax (22) 22842966; Gen. Man. and CEO P. THONDRAYEN; 2 brs.

Sumitomo Bank (Japan): 15/F Jolly Maker Chamber No. 2, 225 Nariman Point, Mumbai 400 021; tel. (22) 22880025; fax (22) 22880026; CEO and Gen. Man. KOZO OTSUBO.

UFJ Bank Ltd (Japan): Mercantile House, Upper Ground Floor, 15 Kasturba Gandhi Marg, New Delhi 110 001; tel. (11) 23318008; fax (11) 23315162; f. 1933 as Sanwa Bank, name changed to above following merger with Tokai Bank in Jan. 2002; Gen. Man. NOBUO OJI.

Banking Organizations

Indian Banks' Association: Stadium House, 6th Floor, Block 3, Veer Nariman Rd, Churchgate, Mumbai 400 020; tel. (22) 22844999; fax (22) 22835638; e-mail ibastadium@vsnl.net; internet www.iba .org.in; 156 mems; Chair. Dr DALBIR SINGH; Sec. K. C. CHOWDHARY.

Indian Institute of Bankers: 'The Arcade', World Trade Centre, 2nd Floor, East Wing, Cuffe Parade, Mumbai 400 005; tel. (22) 22187003; fax (22) 22185147; e-mail iibgen@bom5.vsnl.net.in; internet www.iib.org.in; f. 1928; 343,202 mems; Pres. V. LEELADHAR; Chief Sec. R. H. SARMA.

National Institute of Bank Management: NIBM Post Office, Kondhwe Khurd, Pune 411 048; tel. (20) 26833080; fax (20) 26834478; e-mail director@nibm.ernet.in; internet www.nibmindia .com; f. 1969; Dir Dr ASISH SAHA.

DEVELOPMENT FINANCE ORGANIZATIONS

Agricultural Finance Corporation Ltd: Dhanraj Mahal, 1st Floor, Chhatrapati Shivaji Maharaj Marg, Mumbai 400 001; tel. (22) 22028924; fax (22) 22028966; e-mail afcl@vsnl.com; internet www .afcindia.com; f. 1968 by a consortium of 45 public- and private-sector commercial banks including development finance institutions to help increase the flow of investment and credit into agriculture and rural development projects; provides project consultancy services to commercial banks, Union and State govts, public-sector corpns, the World Bank, the ADB, FAO, the International Fund for Agricultural Development and other institutions and to individuals; undertakes techno-economic and investment surveys in agriculture and agro-industries etc. publishes quarterly journal *Financing Agriculture*; 3 regional offices and 9 br. offices; cap. p.u. 150m., res and surplus 20.5m. (March 2001); Chair. Dr. JAGDISH KAPOOR; Man. Dir A. M. ALAM.

Export-Import Bank of India: Centre 1, Floor 21, World Trade Centre, Cuffe Parade, Mumbai 400 005; tel. (22) 22185272; fax (22) 22182572; e-mail eximind@vsnl.com; internet www.eximbankindia .com; f. 1982; cap. 6,499.9m., res 12,026.4m., dep. 2,797.2m. (March 2002); offices in Bangalore, Chennai, Kolkata, New Delhi, Pune, Ahmedabad, Johannesburg, Budapest, Rome, Singapore and Washington, DC; Man. Dir T. C. VENKAT SUBRAMANIAN; Exec. Dir R. M. V. RAMAN.

Housing Development Finance Corpn Ltd (HDFC): Ramon House, 169 Backbay Reclamation, Mumbai 400 020; tel. (22) 22820282; fax (22) 22046758; e-mail info@hdfcindia.com; internet www.hdfcindia.com; provides loans to individuals and corporate bodies; Chair. DEEPAK S. PAREKH; Man. Dir KEKI M. MISTRY; 118 brs (incl. one overseas br).

Industrial Development Bank of India (IDBI): IDBI Tower, WTC Complex, Cuffe Parade, Colaba, Mumbai 400 005; tel. (22) 22189117; fax (22) 22180930; internet www.idbi.com; f. 1964; reorg. 1976; 72.1% govt-owned; India's premier financial institution for providing direct finance, refinance of industrial loans and bills, finance to large- and medium-sized industries, and for extending financial services, such as merchant banking and forex services, to the corporate sector; 5 zonal offices and 38 br. offices; cap. 6,528m., res 84,738m., dep. 410,828.9m. (March 2001); Chair. and Man. Dir P. P. VORA.

Small Industries Development Bank of India: 10/10 Madan Mohan Malviya Marg, Lucknow 226 001; tel. (522) 2209517; fax (522) 2209514; e-mail snairan@sidbi.com; internet www.sidbi .com; f. 1990; wholly owned subsidiary of Industrial Development Bank of India; promotes, finances and develops small-scale industries; cap. p.u. 4,500m., res 24,240m. (March 2000); Chair. P. B. NIMBALKAR; 39 offices.

Industrial Finance Corpn of India Ltd: IFCI Tower, 61 Nehru Place, New Delhi 110 019; tel. (11) 26487444; fax (11) 26488471; e-mail ifci@giasd01.vsnl.net.in; internet www.ifciltd.com; f. 1948 to provide medium- and long-term finance to cos and co-operative socs in India, engaged in manufacture, preservation or processing of goods, shipping, mining, hotels and power generation and distribution; promotes industrialization of less developed areas, and sponsors training in management techniques and development banking; cap. p.u. 10,679.5m., res 4,976.7m. (March 2002); Chair. and Man. Dir V. P. SINGH; 13 regional offices and 4 other offices.

Industrial Investment Bank of India: 19 Netaji Subhas Rd, Kolkata 700 001; tel. (33) 22209941; fax (33) 22208049; e-mail iibiho@vsnl.com; internet www.iibiltd.com; Chair. and Man. Dir Dr B. SAMAL (acting).

National Bank for Agriculture and Rural Development: Plot no. C-24, G Block, Bandra-Kurla Complex, Bangra (E), Mumbai 400 051; tel. (22) 26530000; fax (22) 26530002; e-mail nabpro@bom7.vsnl .net.in; internet www.nabard.org; f. 1982 to provide credit for agricultural and rural development through commercial, co-operative and regional rural banks; cap. p.u. 20,000m., res 29,479m. (March 2000); held 50% each by the cen. Govt and the Reserve Bank; Chair. Y. C. NANDA; Man. Dir M. V. S. CHALAPATI RAO; 17 regional offices, 10 sub-offices and 5 training establishments.

STOCK EXCHANGES

There are 24 stock exchanges (with a total of more than 9,985 listed companies) in India, including:

National Stock Exchange of India Ltd: Exchange Plaza, Bandra Kurla Complex, Bandra (East), Mumbai 400 051; tel. (22) 26598100; fax (22) 26598120; e-mail cc_nse@nse.co.in; internet www.nseindia .com; f. 1994; Chair. P. P. VORA; Man. Dir RAVI NARAIN.

Ahmedabad Share and Stock Brokers' Association: Kamdhenu Complex, opposite Sahajanand College, Panjarapole, Ambawadi, Ahmedabad 380 015; tel. (79) 26307971; fax (79) 26308877; e-mail ase@satyam.net.in; f. 1894; 299 mems; Pres. ATUL M. CHOKSHI; Exec. Dir RAJIV DESAI.

Bangalore Stock Exchange Ltd: 51 Stock Exchange Towers, 1st Corss, J. C. Rd, Bangalore 560 027; tel. (812) 22995234; fax (80) 22995242; e-mail edbgse@blr.vsnl.net.in; 234 mems; Pres. JAGDISH V. AHUJA; Exec. Dir K. KAMALA.

Bombay Stock Exchange: Phiroze Jeejeebhoy Towers, 25th Floor, Dalal St, Fort, Mumbai 400 001; tel. (22) 22655861; fax (22) 22655720; e-mail webmaster@bseindia.com; internet www.bseindia .com; f. 1875; 638 mems; Pres. DEENA MEHTA; Exec. Dir. and CEO MANOJ VAISH; Sec. A. A. TIRODKAR.

Calcutta Stock Exchange Association Ltd: 7 Lyons Range, Kolkata 700 001; tel. (33) 22206928; fax (33) 22104486; e-mail secretary@cse.india.com; internet www.cse-india.com; f. 1908; 917 mems; Pres. SUPRIYA GUPTA; Sec. P. K. RAY.

Delhi Stock Exchange Association Ltd: DSE House, 3/1 Asaf Ali Rd, New Delhi 110 002; tel. (11) 23292417; fax (11) 23292181; e-mail dse@vsnl.com; f. 1947; 379 mems; Pres. VIJAY BHUSAN; Exec. Dir P. K. SINGHAL.

Ludhiana Stock Exchange Association Ltd: Feroze Gandhi Market, Ludhiana 141 001; tel. (161) 2412316; fax (161) 2404748; e-mail lse@satyam.net.in; f. 1981; 301 mems; Chair. DINA RATH SHARMA; Gen. Man. H. S. SIDHU.

Madras Stock Exchange Ltd: Exchange Bldg, 11 Second Line Beach, POB 183, Chennai 600 001; tel. (44) 25221085; fax (44) 25244897; e-mail mseed@md3.vsnl.net.in; f. 1760; 171 mems; Pres. D. N. DAS; Exec. Dir P. J. MATHEW.

Mangalore Stock Exchange: Rama Bhavan Complex, 4th Floor, Kodialbail, Mangalore 575 003; tel. (824) 2440581; fax (824) 2440736; 146 mems; Pres. RAMESH RAI; Exec. Dir UMESH P. MASKERI.

Thiruvananthapuram Stock Exchange: Thiruvananthapuram; Dir JOSE JOHN.

Uttar Pradesh Stock Exchange Association Ltd: 14/113 Civil Lines, Kanpur 208 001; tel. (512) 2293174; fax (512) 2293175; e-mail upse@lw1.vsnl.net.in; 520 mems; Pres. R. K. AGARWAL; Exec. Dir Dr J. N. GUPTA.

The other recognized stock exchanges are: Hyderabad, Madhya Pradesh (Indore), Kochi, Pune, Guwahati, Jaipur, Bhubaneswar (Orissa), Coimbatore, Saurashtra, Meerut, Vadodara and Magadh (Patna).

INSURANCE

In January 1973 all Indian and foreign insurance companies were nationalized. The general insurance business in India is now transacted by only four companies, subsidiaries of the General Insurance Corpn of India, formed under the 1972 General Insurance Business Nationalisation Act. The Insurance Regulatory Development Authority Bill, approved by the legislature in December 1999, established a regulatory authority for the insurance sector and henceforth permitted up to 26% investment by foreign companies in new domestic, private-sector insurance companies.

General Insurance Corpn of India (GIC): 'Suraksha', 170 J. Tata Rd, Churchgate, Mumbai 400 020; tel. (22) 22833046; fax (22) 22855423; e-mail swift@gicofindia.com; internet www.gicofindia .com; f. 1973 by the reorg. of 107 private non-life insurance cos (incl. brs of foreign cos operating in the country) as the four subsidiaries listed below; Chair. P. C. GHOSH; Man. Dir P. B. RAMANUJAN.

National Insurance Co Ltd: 3 Middleton St, Kolkata 700 071; tel. (33) 22472130; fax (33) 22402369; e-mail hourgent@ nationalinsuranceindia.com; internet www .nationalinsuranceindia.com; Chair. and Man. Dir M. S. WADHWA; 19 regional offices, 254 divisional offices and 690 branch offices.

New India Assurance Co Ltd: New India Assurance Bldg, 87 Mahatma Gandhi Rd, Fort, Mumbai 400 001; tel. (22) 22674617; fax (22) 22652811; e-mail cmd@niacl.com; internet www.niacl .com; f. 1919; 26 regional offices, 393 divisional offices, 703 branch offices and 37 overseas offices; Chair. and Man. Dir R. BERI.

The Oriental Insurance Co Ltd: Oriental House, A-25/27 Asaf Ali Rd, New Delhi 110 002; tel. (11) 23279221; fax (11) 23263175; e-mail slmohan@oriental.nic.in; internet www.orientalinsurance .nic.in; Chair. and Man. Dir S. L. MOHAN.

United India Insurance Co Ltd: 24 Whites Rd, Chennai 600 014; tel. (44) 28520161; fax (44) 28525280; e-mail knb@united.nic .in; internet www.united.nic.in; Chair. and Man. Dir V. JAGANNATHAN.

Life Insurance Corpn of India (LIC): 'Yogakshema', Jeevan Bima Marg, Mumbai 400 021; tel. (22) 2021383; fax (22) 2020274; e-mail s.mathur@licindia.com; internet www.licindia.com; f. 1956; controls all life insurance business; Chair. S. B. MATHUR; Man. Dirs R. K. VASHISHTHA, R. N. BHARADWAJ; 100 divisional offices, 2,048 brs and three overseas offices.

Trade and Industry

GOVERNMENT AGENCIES AND DEVELOPMENT ORGANIZATIONS

Coal India Ltd: 10 Netaji Subhas Rd, Kolkata 700 001; tel. (33) 22488099; fax (33) 22483373; internet www.coalindia.nic.in; cen. govt holding with eight subsidiaries; responsible for almost total (more than 90%) exploration for, planning and production of coal mines; owns 498 coal mines throughout India; marketing of coal and its products; cap. p.u. Rs 72,205.4m., res and surplus Rs 15,985m., sales Rs 7,832m. (March 2001); Chair. and Man. Dir N. K. SHARMA; 660,000 employees (1995).

Cotton Corpn of India Ltd: Plot No. 3A, Sector No. 10, CBD Belapur, Navi Mumbai 400 614; tel. (22) 27579217; fax (22) 27576030; e-mail ccimum@bom7.vsnl.net.in; internet www.cotcorp .com; f. 1970 as an agency in the public sector for the purchase, sale and distribution of home-produced cotton and imported cotton staple fibre; exports long staple cotton; cap. p.u. Rs 250m., res and surplus Rs 2,046.8m., sales Rs 6,810m. (March 2001); Chair. and Man. Dir VISHWA NATH.

Export Credit Guarantee Corpn of India Ltd: Express Towers, 10th Floor, Nariman Point, Mumbai 400 021; tel. (22) 22044519; fax (22) 22829968; e-mail ecgcres@bom2.vsnl.net.in; internet www .ecgcindia.com; f. 1957 to insure for risks involved in exports on credit terms and to supplement credit facilities by issuing guarantees, etc. cap. Rs 4,400m., res Rs 3,629m. (March 2000); Chair. and Man. Dir P. M. A. HAKEEM; 29 brs.

Fertilizer Corpn of India Ltd: 'Madhuban', 55 Nehru Place, New Delhi 110 019; tel. (11) 26444971; fax (11) 26416694; e-mail fci@fci .hub.nic.in; internet www.fert-india.com; f. 1961; fertilizer factories at Sindri (Jharkand), Gorakhpur (Uttar Pradesh), Talcher (Orissa) and Ramagundam (Andhra Pradesh), producing nitrogenous and some industrial products; cap. Rs 7,467.4m., sales Rs 7,832m. (March 2001); Chair. and Man. Dir Dr SUDHIR KRISHNA.

Food Corpn of India: 16–20 Barakhamba Lane, New Delhi 110 001; tel. (11) 23413871; fax (11) 23413231; f. 1965 to undertake trading in food grains on a commercial scale but within the framework of an overall govt policy; to provide farmers an assured price for their produce; to supply food grains to the consumer at reasonable prices; also purchases, stores, distributes and sells food grains and other foodstuffs and arranges imports and handling of food grains and fertilizers at the ports; distributes sugar in a number of states and has set up rice mills; cap. p.u. Rs 22,945m., sales Rs 214,210m. (March 2001); Chair. A. M. GOKHALE; Man. Dir NARESH CHATURVEDI; 65,131 employees.

Handicrafts and Handlooms Exports Corpn of India Ltd: 5th Floor, Jawahar Vyapar Bhavan Annexe, 1 Tolstoy Marg, New Delhi 110 001; tel. (11) 23701086; fax (11) 23701051; e-mail hhecnd@ndc .vsnl.net.in; internet www.hhecworld.com; f. 1958; govt undertaking dealing in export of handicrafts, handloom goods, ready-to-wear clothes, carpets, jute, leather and precious jewellery, and import of bullion and raw silk; promotes exports and trade development; cap. p.u. Rs 118.2m., res and surplus Rs 89.5m. (March 2001); Chair. and Man. Dir K. K. SINHA.

Housing and Urban Development Corpn Ltd: HUDCO Bhavan, India Habitat Centre, Lodhi Rd, New Delhi 110 003; tel. (11) 24648160; fax (11) 24625308; internet www.hudcoindia.com; f. 1970 to finance and undertake housing and urban development programmes including the establishment of new or satellite towns and building material industries; cap. p.u. Rs 11,780m., res and surplus Rs 7,626.5m., sales 18,764m. (March 2001); 21 brs; Chair. and Man. Dir PANKAJ JAIN; Sec. GOPAL KRISHAN.

India Trade Promotion Organisation (ITPO): Pragati Bhavan, Pragati Maidan, Lal Bahadur Shastri Marg, New Delhi 110 001; tel. (11) 23371540; fax (11) 23378901; e-mail itpo@giasdl10.vsnl.net.in; internet www.indiatradepromotion.org; f. 1992 following merger; promotes selective development of exports of high quality products; arranges investment in export-orientated ventures undertaken by India with foreign collaboration; organizes trade fairs; operates Trade Information Centre; cap. p.u. Rs 2.5m., res and surplus Rs 2,102.1m. (March 2001); regional offices in Bangalore, Mumbai, Kolkata and Chennai, and international offices in Frankfurt, New York, Moscow, São Paulo and Tokyo; Chair. and Man. Dir J. VASU-DEVAN; Exec. Dir K. T. CHACKO.

Jute Corpn of India Ltd: 15-N, Nellie Sengupta Sarani, 7th Floor, Kolkata 700 087; tel. (33) 22166770; fax (33) 22166771; e-mail jutecorp@vsnl.net.in; f. 1971; objects: (i) to undertake price support operations in respect of raw jute; (ii) to ensure remunerative prices to producers through efficient marketing; (iii) to operate a buffer stock to stabilize raw jute prices; (iv) to handle the import and export of raw jute; (v) to promote the export of jute goods; cap. p.u. Rs 50m., sales Rs 786.3m. (March 2001); Chair. and Man. Dir A. K. KHASTAGIR.

Minerals and Metals Trading Corpn of India Ltd (MMTC): Scope Complex, Core-1, 7 Institutional Areas, Lodi Rd, New Delhi 110 003; tel. (11) 24362200; fax (11) 24360724; e-mail cpmr@ mmtclimited.com; internet www.mmtclimited.com; f. 1963; export of iron and manganese ore, ferro-manganese, finished stainless steel products, engineering, agricultural and marine products, textiles, leather items, chemicals and pharmaceuticals, mica, coal and other minor minerals; import of steel, non-ferrous metals, rough diamonds, fertilizers, etc. for supply to industrial units in the country; cap. p.u. Rs 500m., res Rs 5,361.8m., sales Rs 53,383.7m. (March 2001); 9 regional offices and 16 sub-regional offices in India; foreign offices in Japan, the Republic of Korea, Jordan and Romania; Chair. and Man. Dir SHIV DAYAL KAPOOR; 3,246 employees.

National Co-operative Development Corpn: 4 Siri Institutional Area, Hauz Khas, New Delhi 110 016; tel. (11) 26569246; fax (11) 26962370; e-mail editor@ncdc.delhi.nic.in; internet www.ncdc.nic .in; f. 1963 to plan, promote and finance country-wide programmes through co-operative societies for the production, processing, marketing, storage, export and import of agricultural produce, foodstuffs and notified commodities; also programmes for the development of poultry, dairy, fish products, coir, handlooms, distribution of consumer articles in rural areas and minor forest produce in the co-operative sector; 15 regional directorates; Pres. AJIT SINGH; Man. Dir DINESH RAI.

National Industrial Development Corpn Ltd: Chanakya Bhavan, Africa Ave, New Delhi 110 021; tel. (11) 24670153; fax (11) 26876166; e-mail nidc123@del2.vsnl.net.in; internet www .exploreindia.com/nidc; f. 1954; consultative engineering, management and infrastructure services to cen. and state govts, public and private sector enterprises, the UN and overseas investors; cap. p.u. Rs 187m. (March 2001); Chair. and Man. Dir PRANAB GHOSH.

National Mineral Development Corpn Ltd: Khanij Bhavan, 10-3-311/A Castle Hills, Masab Tank, POB 1352, Hyderabad 500 028; tel. (40) 23538713; fax (40) 23538711; e-mail nmdchyd@hdl.vsnl.net .in; internet www.nmdc-india.com; f. 1958; cen. govt undertaking; to exploit minerals (excluding coal, atomic minerals, lignite, petroleum and natural gas) in public sector; may buy, take on lease or otherwise acquire mines for prospecting, development and exploitation; iron ore mines at Bailadila-11C, Bailadila-14 and Bailadila-5 in Madhya Pradesh, and at Donimalai in Karnataka State; new 5m. metric ton iron ore mine under construction at Bailadila-10/11A; diamond mines at Panna in Madhya Pradesh; research and development laboratories and consultancy services covering all aspects of mineral exploitation at Hyderabad; investigates mineral projects; cap. p.u. Rs 1,321.6m., res and surplus Rs 8,188.6m. (March 2000); Chair. and Man. Dir P. R. TRIPATHI.

National Productivity Council: Utpadakta Bhavan, Lodi Rd, New Delhi 110 003; tel. (11) 24690331; fax (11) 24615002; e-mail npc@ren02.nic.in; internet www.npcindia.org; f. 1958 to increase productivity and to improve quality by improved techniques which aim at efficient and proper utilization of available resources; autonomous body representing national orgs of employers and labour, govt ministries, professional orgs, local productivity councils, small-scale industries and other interests; 12 regional directorates, 2 regional offices; 75 mems; Chair. V. GOVINDARAJAN; Dir-Gen. A. K. GOSWAMI.

National Research Development Corpn: 20–22 Zamroodpur Community Centre, Kailash Colony Extension, New Delhi 110 048; tel. (11) 26417821; fax (11) 26460506; e-mail nrdc@giasd101.vsnl.net .in; internet www.nrdcindia.com; f. 1953 to stimulate development and commercial exploitation of new inventions with financial and technical aid; finances development projects to set up demonstration units in collaboration with industry; exports technology; cap. p.u. Rs 44.2m., res and surplus Rs 45.3m. (March 2001); Man. Dir N. K. SHARMA.

National Seeds Corpn Ltd: Beej Bhavan, Pusa, New Delhi 110 012; tel. (11) 25852379; fax (11) 25766462; e-mail nsc@vsnl.com; f. 1963 to improve and develop the seed industry; cap. p.u. Rs 206.2m., res and surplus Rs 207.4m., sales Rs 642.3m. (March 2001); Chair. and Man. Dir KUMAR BHATIA.

The National Small Industries Corpn Ltd: NSIC Bhavan, Okhla Industrial Estate, New Delhi 110 020; tel. (11) 26926275; fax (11) 26926820; e-mail cmd@nsicindia.com; internet www.nsicindia.com; f. 1955 to aid, advise, finance and promote the interests of small industries; establishes and supplies machinery for small industries in other developing countries on turn-key basis; cap. p.u. Rs 1,679.9m. (March 2001); all shares held by the Govt; Chair. and Man. Dir RAJIV BHATNAGAR.

PEC Ltd: 'Hansalaya', 15 Barakhamba Rd, New Delhi 110 001; tel. (11) 23313619; fax (11) 23314797; e-mail pec@pecltd.org; internet www.pecltd.org; f. 1971; export of engineering, industrial and railway equipment; undertakes turn-key and other projects and management consultancy abroad; countertrade, trading in agro-commodities, construction materials (steel, cement, clinkers, etc.) and fertilizers; cap. p.u. Rs 15m., res and surplus Rs 209.7m. (March 2001); Chair. and Man. Dir A. K. SRIVASTAVA.

Rehabilitation Industries Corpn Ltd: 25 Mirza Ghalib St, Kolkata 700 016; tel. (33) 22441185; fax (33) 22451055; f. 1959 to create employment opportunities through multi-product industries, ranging from consumer goods to engineering products and services, for refugees from Bangladesh and migrants from Pakistan, repatriates from Myanmar and Sri Lanka, and other immigrants of Indian extraction; cap. p.u. Rs 47.6m. (March 2000); Chair. and Man. Dir ASHOK BASU.

State Farms Corpn of India Ltd: Farm Bhavan, 14–15 Nehru Place, New Delhi 110 019; tel. (11) 26446903; fax (11) 26226898; e-mail sfci@vsnl.net; f. 1969 to administer the central state farms;

activities include the production of quality seeds of high-yielding varieties of wheat, paddy, maize, bajra and jowar; advises on soil conservation, reclamation and development of waste and forest land; consultancy services on farm mechanization; auth. cap. Rs 241.9m., res and surplus Rs 385.6m. (March 2001); Chair. BHASKAR BARUA; Man. Dir ASHISH BAHUGUNA.

State Trading Corpn of India Ltd: Jawahar Vyapar Bhavan, Tolstoy Marg, New Delhi 110 001; tel. (11) 23701100; fax (11) 23701123; e-mail stcindia@vsnl.net; internet www.stcindia.com; f. 1956; govt undertaking dealing in exports and imports; cap. p.u. Rs 300m., res and surplus Rs 3,219.6m. (March 2002); 10 regional brs, 5 sub-brs and 1 office overseas; Chair. and Man. Dir Dr ARVIND PANDALAI; 1,069 employees (2002).

Steel Authority of India Ltd (SAIL): Ispat Bhavan, Lodi Rd, POB 3049, New Delhi 110 003; tel. (11) 24367481; fax (11) 24367015; e-mail sail.co@vsnl.co; internet www.sail.co.in; f. 1973 to provide co-ordinated development of the steel industry in the public sector; integrated steel plants at Bhilai, Bokaro, Durgapur, Rourkela; alloys steel plants at Durgapur and Salem; subsidiaries: Visvesvaraya Iron and Steel Ltd (Karnataka), Indian Iron and Steel Co (West Bengal) and Maharashtra Elektrosmelt Ltd; combined crude steel capacity is 12.5m. metric tons annually; equity cap. Rs 41,304m., res and surplus Rs 11,599.7m., sales Rs 140,645.2m. (March 2002); Chair. and Man. Dir V. S. JAIN; 160,000 employees (2000).

Tea Board of India: 14 B. T. M. Sarani (Brabourne Rd), POB 2172, Kolkata 700 001; tel. (33) 2251411; fax (33) 22251417; provides financial assistance to tea research stations; sponsors and finances independent research projects in universities and tech. institutions to supplement the work of tea research establishments; also promotes tea production and export; Chair. NABA KRISHNA DAS.

CHAMBERS OF COMMERCE

Associated Chambers of Commerce and Industry of India (ASSOCHAM): 147B, Gautam Nagar, Gulmohar Enclave, New Delhi 110 049; tel. (11) 26512477; fax (11) 26512154; e-mail assocham@sansad.nic.in; internet www.assocham.org; f. 1920; a central org. of 350 chambers of commerce and industry and industrial asscns representing more than 100,000 cos throughout India; 6 promoter chambers, 125 ordinary mems, 40 patron mems and 500 corporate associates; Pres. R. K. SOMANY; Sec.-Gen. JAYANT BHUYAN.

Federation of Indian Chambers of Commerce and Industry (FICCI): Federation House, Tansen Marg, New Delhi 110 001; tel. (11) 23738760; fax (11) 23320714; e-mail ficci.bisnet@gems.vsnl.net .in; internet www.bisnetindia.com; f. 1927; 432 ordinary mems, 50 corporate mems, 1,216 assoc. mems; Pres. A. C. MUTHIAH; Sec.-Gen. Dr AMIT MITRA.

ICC India: Federation House, Tansen Marg, New Delhi 110 001; tel. (11) 23738760; fax (11) 23320714; e-mail iccindia@del2.vsnl.net .in; internet www.iccindiaonline.org; f. 1929; 53 org. mems, 481 assoc. mems, 8 patron mems, 118 cttee mems; Pres. ARUNACHALAM VELLAYAN; Exec. Dir M. K. SANGHI.

Associated Chambers of Commerce and Industry of Uttar Pradesh: 2/122 Vishal Khand, Gomti Nagar, Lucknow 226 016; tel. (522) 2301956; fax (522) 2301958; e-mail asochmup@lw1.vsnl.net.in; internet www.assochamup.org; 475 mems; Pres. IRSHAD MIRZA; Sec.-Gen. R. K. JAIN.

Bengal Chamber of Commerce and Industry: 6 Netaji Subhas Rd, Kolkata 700 001; tel. (33) 22203733; fax (33) 22201289; e-mail bencham@cal3.vsnl.net.in; f. 1853; 210 mems; Pres. S. K. DHALL; Sec. PRADIP DAS GUPTA.

Bengal National Chamber of Commerce and Industry: 23 R. N. Mukherjee Rd, Kolkata 700 001; tel. (33) 22482951; fax (33) 22487058; e-mail bncci@bncci.com; internet www.bncci.com; f. 1887; 500 mems, 35 affiliated industrial and trading asscns; Pres. S. R. SAHA; Sec. D. P. NAG.

Bharat Chamber of Commerce: 9 Park Mansions, 2nd Floor, 57-A Park Street, Kolkata, 700 016; tel. (33) 22299591; fax (33) 22294947; e-mail bcc@cal2.vsnl.net.in; f. 1900; c. 500 mems; Pres. N. R. GOENKA; Sec. K. SARMA.

Bihar Chamber of Commerce: Khem Chand Chaudhary Marg, POB 71, Patna 800 001; tel. (612) 2670535; fax (612) 2689505; e-mail secgen@dte.vsnl.net.in; f. 1926; 600 ordinary mems, 125 org. mems, 10 life mems; Pres. O. P. SAH; Sec.-Gen. RAJA BABU GUPTA.

Bombay Chamber of Commerce and Industry: Mackinnon Mackenzie Bldg, 4 Shoorji Vallabhdas Rd, Ballard Estate, POB 473, Mumbai 400 001; tel. (22) 22614681; fax (22) 22621213; e-mail bcci@ bombaychamber.com; internet www.bombaychamber.com; f. 1836; 824 ordinary mems, 526 assoc. mems, 75 hon. mems; Pres. K. RAMACHANDRAN; Exec. Dir L. A. D'SOUZA.

Calcutta Chamber of Commerce: 18H Park St, Stephen Court, Kolkata 700 071; tel. (33) 22290758; fax (33) 22298961; e-mail calchamb@cal3.vsnl.net.in; 450 mems; Pres. P. D. TULSYAN; Sec.-Gen. KEWAL K. SAREEN.

Chamber of Commerce and Industry (Regd): O.B 31, Rail Head Complex, Jammu 180 012; tel. (191) 2472266; fax (191) 2472255; 1,069 mems; Pres. RAM SAHAI; Sec.-Gen. RAJENDRA MOTIAL.

Cochin Chamber of Commerce and Industry: Bristow Rd, Willingdon Island, POB 503, Kochi 682 003; tel. (484) 2668349; fax (484) 2668651; e-mail chamber@md2.vsnl.net.in; internet www .cochinchamber.com; f. 1857; 176 mems; Pres. V. R. NAIR; Sec. EAPEN KALAPURAKAL.

Federation of Andhra Pradesh Chambers of Commerce and Industry: 11-6-841, Red Hills, POB 14, Hyderabad 500 004; tel. (40) 23393658; fax (40) 23395083; e-mail info@fapcci.org; internet www .fapcci.org; f. 1917; 2,510 mems; Pres. O. P. TIBREWALA; Sec. G. HEMLATA.

Federation of Karnataka Chambers of Commerce and Industry: Kempegowda Rd, Bangalore 560 009; tel. (80) 22262355; fax (80) 22251826; e-mail fkcci@mantraonline.com; internet www .fkcci.net; f. 1916; 2,030 mems; Pres. K. N. JAYALINGAPPA; Sec. C. MANOHAR.

Federation of Madhya Pradesh Chambers of Commerce and Industry: Udyog Bhavan, 129A Malviya Nagar, Bhopal 462 003; tel. (755) 2573612; fax (755) 2551451; e-mail fmcci@bom6.vsnl.net.in; f. 1975; 500 ordinary mems, 58 asscn mems; Pres. RANJIT VITHALDAS; Sec.-Gen. PRAFULLA MAHESHWARI.

Goa Chamber of Commerce and Industry: Goa Chamber Bldg, Rua de Ormuz, POB 59, Panaji 403 001; tel. (832) 2224223; fax (832) 2223420; e-mail gcci@goatelecom.com; internet www.goachamber .org; f. 1908; 450 mems; Pres. NITIN KUNKOLIENKAR; Sec. Air Cmmdre (retd) P. K. PINTO.

Gujarat Chamber of Commerce and Industry: Shri Ambica Mills, Gujarat Chamber Bldg, Ashram Rd, POB 4045, Ahmedabad 380 009; tel. (79) 26582301; fax (79) 26587992; e-mail bis@ gujaratchamber.org; internet www.gujaratchamber.org; f. 1949; 7,713 mems; Pres. MAHENDRA A. SHAH; Sec.-Gen. S. C. SHAH.

Indian Chamber of Commerce: India Exchange, 4 India Exchange Place, India Exchange Bldg, Kolkata 700 001; tel. (33) 22203243; fax (33) 22213377; e-mail info@indianchamber.org; internet www.indianchamber.org; f. 1925; 300 ordinary mems, 42 assoc. mems, 20 corporate group mems, 17 affiliated asscns; Pres. VIKRAM THAPARO; Sec.-Gen. NAZEEB ARIF.

Indian Chamber of Commerce and Industry: Four Square House, 49 Community Centre, New Friends Colony, New Delhi 110 065; tel. (11) 26836468; fax (11) 26840775; e-mail iccind@yahoo.com .in; Pres. LALIT K. MODI; Hon. Sec. R. P. SWAMI.

Indian Merchants' Chamber: IMC Bldg, IMC Marg, Churchgate, Mumbai 400 020; tel. (22) 22046633; fax (22) 22048508; e-mail imc@ imcnet.org; internet www.imcnet.org; f. 1907; 185 asscn mems, 2,700 mem. firms; Pres. SURESH KOTAK; Sec. P. N. MOGRE.

Karnataka Chamber of Commerce and Industry: Karnataka Chamber Bldg, J. C. Nagar, Hubli 580 020; tel. (836) 2218234; fax (836) 2360933; e-mail kccihble@sify.com; internet www.kccihubli .org; f. 1928; 2,500 mems; Pres. MADAN B. DESAI; Hon. Sec. MOHAN TENGINKAI.

Madhya Pradesh Chamber of Commerce and Industry: Chamber Bhavan, Sanatan Dharam Mandir Marg, Gwalior 474 009; tel. (751) 2332916; fax (751) 2323844; f. 1906; 1,705 mems; Pres. GOVIND DAS AGARWAL; Sec. DEEPAK AGARWAL.

Madras Chamber of Commerce and Industry: Karumuttu Centre, 634 Anna Salai, Chennai 600 035; tel. (44) 24349452; fax (44) 24349164; e-mail mascham@md3.vsnl.net.in; internet www .mascham.com; f. 1836; 287 mem. firms, 48 assoc., 16 affiliated, 11 honorary, 3 others; Pres. K. V. SHETTY; Sec. R. SUBRAMANIAN.

Maharashtra Chamber of Commerce and Industry: Oricon House, 6th Floor, 12 K. Dubhash Marg, Fort, Mumbai 400 001; tel. (22) 22855859; fax (22) 22855861; e-mail maharashtrachamber@ vsnl.com; f. 1927; 1,954 mems; Pres. A. R. ANANDPARA; Sec.-Gen. S. P. RAJE.

Mahratta Chamber of Commerce, Industries and Agriculture: Tilak Rd, POB 525, Pune 411 002; tel. (20) 24440371; fax (20) 24447902; e-mail mccipune@vsnl.com; internet www.mcciapune .com; f. 1934; 1,256 mems; Pres. ATUL C. KIRLOSKAR; Dir.-Gen. D. K. ABHYANKAR.

Merchants' Chamber of Commerce: 15B Hemanta Basu Sarani, Kolkata 700 001; tel. (33) 22483123; fax (33) 22488657; e-mail mercham@cal.vsnl.net.in; internet www.mercham.org; f. 1901; 600 mems; Pres. SUSHIL DHANDHANIA; Dir-Gen. R. K. SEN.

Merchants' Chamber of Uttar Pradesh: 14/76 Civil Lines, Kanpur 208 001; tel. (512) 2531306; fax (512) 2547292; e-mail mercham@vsnl.net.in; internet merchantschamber-up.com; f. 1932; 180 mems; Pres. S. N. GUPTA; Sec. P. N. DIXIT.

North India Chamber of Commerce and Industry: 9 Gandhi Rd, Dehra Dun; tel. (935) 223479; f. 1967; 105 ordinary mems, 29 asscn mems, 7 mem. firms, 91 assoc. mems; Pres. DEV PANDHI; Hon. Sec. ASHOK K. NARANG.

Oriental Chamber of Commerce: 6A Dr Rajendra Prasad Sarani (Clive Row), Kolkata 700 001; tel. (33) 22202120; fax (33) 22203609; e-mail orientchamb@vsnl.net; f. 1932; 245 ordinary mems, 3 assoc. mems; Pres. SAMAR MOHAN SAHA; Sec. KAZI ABU ZOBER.

PHD Chamber of Commerce and Industry: PHD House, Thapar Floor, 4/2 Siri Institutional Area, opp. Asian Games Village, POB 130, New Delhi 110 016; tel. (11) 26863801; fax (11) 26568392; e-mail phdcci@del2.vsnl.net.in; internet www.phdcci.org; f. 1905; 1,630 mems, 115 asscn mems; Pres. P. K. JAIN; Sec.-Gen. Dr B. P. DHAKA.

Rajasthan Chamber of Commerce and Industry: Rajasthan Chamber Bhavan, M.I. Rd, Jaipur 302 003; tel. (141) 2565163; fax (141) 2561419; e-mail rajcham@jpl.vsnl.net.in; internet www.rajchamber.com; 575 mems; Pres. S. K. MANSINGHKA; Hon. Sec.-Gen. Dr K. L. JAIN.

Southern India Chamber of Commerce and Industry: Indian Chamber Bldgs, 6 Esplanade, POB 1208, Chennai 600 108; tel. (44) 25342228; fax (44) 25341876; e-mail sicci@md3.vsnl.net.in; f. 1909; 1,000 mems; Pres. R. MUTHU; Sec. J. PRASAD DAVIDS.

Upper India Chamber of Commerce: 113/47, Swaroop Nagar, POB 63, Kanpur 208 002; tel. (512) 2543905; fax (512) 2210684; f. 1888; 82 mems; Pres. DILIP BHARGAVA; Sec. S. P. SRIVASTAVA.

Utkal Chamber of Commerce and Industry Ltd: Barabati Stadium, Cuttack 753 005; tel. (671) 2301211; fax (671) 2302059; f. 1964; 208 mems; Pres. P. K. DAS; Sec. DEBABRATA DAS.

Uttar Pradesh Chamber of Commerce: 15/197 Civil Lines, Kanpur 208 001; tel. 2211696; f. 1914; 200 mems; Pres. Dr B. K. MODI; Sec. AFTAB SAMI.

INDUSTRIAL AND TRADE ASSOCIATIONS

Ahmedabad Textile Mills' Association: Ashram Rd, Navrangpura, POB 4056, Ahmedabad 380 009; tel. (79) 26582273; fax (79) 26588574; f. 1891; 21 mems; Pres. CHINTON N. PARIKH; Sec.-Gen. ABHINAVA SHUKLA.

All India Federation of Master Printers: A-370, 2nd Floor, Defence Colony, New Delhi 110 024; tel. (11) 24601570; fax (11) 24624808; e-mail aifmp@vsnl.com; f. 1953; 50 affiliates, 800 mems; Pres. S. R. SHARMA; Hon. Gen. Sec. MANOJ B. MEHTA.

All India Manufacturers' Organization (AIMO): Jeevan Sahakar, 4th Floor, Sir P.M. Rd, Fort, Mumbai 400 001; tel. (22) 22661016; fax (22) 22660838; f. 1941; 800 mems; Pres. KAMALKUMAR R. DUJODWALA; Hon. Gen. Sec. SURESH DEORA.

All India Plastics Manufacturers' Association: AIPMA House, A-52, St No. 1, MIDC, Andheri (East), Mumbai 400 093; tel. (22) 28217324; fax (22) 28216390; e-mail aipma@bom2.vsnl.net.in; internet www.aipma.org; f. 1947; 1,800 mems; Chair. MOHAN K. JAIN; Hon. Sec. AJAY DESAI.

All India Shippers' Council: Federation House, Tansen Marg, New Delhi 110 001; tel. (11) 23738760; fax (11) 23320714; f. 1967; 40 mems; Chair. RAMU S. DEORA; Sec. M. Y. REDDY.

Association of Man-made Fibre Industry of India: Resham Bhavan, 78 Veer Nariman Rd, Mumbai 400 020; tel. (22) 22040009; fax (22) 22049172; f. 1954; 7 mems; Pres. P. S. SHARMA; Sec. S. K. MARATHE.

Automotive Component Manufacturers' Association of India: 6th Floor, The Capital Court, Olof Parme Marg, Munirka, New Delhi 110 067; tel. (11) 26160315; fax (11) 26160317; e-mail acma@vsnl.com; internet www.acmainfo.com; 413 mems; Pres. DEEP KAPURIA; Exec. Dir VISHNU MATHUR.

Automotive Tyre Manufacturers' Association: PHD House, opp. Asian Games Village, Siri Fort Institutional Area, New Delhi 110 016; tel. (11) 26851187; fax (11) 26864799; e-mail atma@nda.vsnl.net.in; internet www.atmaindia.net.in; 11 mems; Chair. RAGHUPATI SINGHANIA; Dir-Gen. D. RAVINDRAN.

Bharat Krishak Samaj (Farmers' Forum, India): Dr Panjabrao Deshmukh Krishak Bhavan, A-1 Nizamuddin West, New Delhi 110 013; tel. (11) 24619508; fax (11) 24619509; e-mail ffi@mantraonline.com; f. 1954; national farmers' org. 5m. ordinary mems, 70,000 life mems; Chair. Dr BAL RAM JAKHAR; Exec. Chair./Gen. Sec. Dr KRISHAN BIR CHAUDHARY.

Bombay Metal Exchange Ltd: 88/90, Gulalwadi, Kika St, 1st Floor, Mumbai 400 004; tel. (22) 22421964; fax (22) 22422640; e-mail bme@bom8.vsnl.net.in; promotes trade and industry in non-ferrous metals; 460 mems; Pres. ASHOK G. BAFNA; Sec. T. S. B. IYER.

Bombay Shroffs Association: 233 Shaikh Memon St, Mumbai 400 002; tel. (22) 23425588; f. 1910; 350 mems; Pres. KISHORE J. SHAH; Hon. Secs RAJNIKANT O. DHARIA, PRANLAL R. SHETH.

Calcutta Flour Mills Association: 25/B Shakespeare Sarani, Kolkata 700 017; tel. (33) 22476723; fax (33) 22475944; e-mail swaika@vsnl.com; f. 1932; 28 mems; Chair. NAVNEET SWAIKA; Hon. Sec. RAVI BHAGAT.

Calcutta Tea Traders' Association: 6 Netaji Subhas Rd, Kolkata 700 001; tel. (33) 22201574; fax (33) 22201289; e-mail ctta@cal3.vsnl.net.in; f. 1886; 1,490 mems; Chair. K. N. DESAI; Sec. J. KALYANA SUNDARAM.

Cement Manufacturers' Association: Vishnu Kiran Chambers, 2142-47 Gurudwara Rd, Karol Bagh, New Delhi 110 005; tel. (11) 25763206; fax (11) 25738476; e-mail cmand@vsnl.com; internet cmaindia.org; 54 mems; 125 major cement plants; Pres. B. L. JAIN; Sec.-Gen. A. V. SRINIVASAN.

Confederation of Indian Industry (CII): 23 Institutional Area, Lodi Rd, New Delhi 110 003; tel. (11) 24629994; fax (11) 24626149; e-mail cii@ciionline.org; internet www.ciionline.org; f. 1974; 3,800 mem. cos; Pres. ASHOK SOOTA; Dir-Gen. TARUN DAS.

Consumer Electronics and Television Manufacturers' Association (CETMA): J-13, Jangpura Extension, New Delhi 110 014; tel. (11) 24327777; fax (11) 24321616; e-mail cetmadel@ndb.vsnl.net.in; 76 mems; Pres. RAJEEV KARWAL; Sec.-Gen. SURESH KHANNA.

East India Cotton Association: Cotton Exchange Bldg, 9th Floor, 175 Kalbadevi Rd, Marwari Bazar, Mumbai 400 002; tel. (22) 22014876; fax (22) 22015578; e-mail eica@bom8.vsnl.net.in; f. 1921; 417 mems; Pres. K. F. JHUNJHUNWALA; Gen. Sec. HEMANT MULKY.

Electronic Component Industries Association (ELCINA): ELCINA House, 422 Okhla Industrial Estate, New Delhi 110 020; tel. (11) 26928053; fax (11) 26923440; e-mail elcina@del2.vsnl.net.in; internet www.elcina.com; f. 1967; 255 mems; Pres. SANJIB NARAYAN; Sec.-Gen. SOMNATH CHATTERJEE.

Federation of Automobile Dealers Associations: 805 Surya Kiran, 19 Kasturba Gandhi Marg, New Delhi 110 001; tel. (11) 23320046; fax (11) 23320093; e-mail fadadelhi@vsnl.net; internet www.fadaweb.com; f. 1964; Pres. AJIT KUMAR CHORDIA; Sec.-Gen. GULSHAN AHUJA; 1,130 mems.

Federation of Gujarat Industries: Sidcup Tower, 4th Floor, nr Marble Arch, Race Course, Vadodara 390 007; tel. (265) 2311101; fax (265) 2339054; e-mail info@federationofgujarat.org; internet www.federationofgujarat.org; f. 1918; 350 mems; Pres. SHIVINDER SINGH CHAWLA; Sec. Dr PARESH RAVAL.

Federation of Hotel and Restaurant Associations of India: B-82 Himalaya House, 23 K. G. Marg, New Delhi 110 001; tel. (11) 23323770; fax (11) 23322645; e-mail fhrai@vsnl.com; internet www.fhrai.com; f. 1955; 2,674 mems; Pres. B. K. GUPTA; Sec.-Gen. SHYAM SURI.

Federation of Indian Export Organisations: PHD House, 3rd Floor, Siri Institutional Area, Hauz Khas, New Delhi 110 016; tel. (11) 26851310; fax (11) 26863087; e-mail fieo@nda.vsnl.net.in; internet www.fieo.com; f. 1965; 5,900 mems; Pres. M. RAFEEQUE AHMED; Dir-Gen. RANJIT LALL.

The Fertiliser Association of India: 10 Shaheed Jit Singh Marg, New Delhi 110 067; tel. (11) 26517305; fax (11) 26960052; e-mail fai@vsnl.com; internet www.fertindia.com; f. 1955; 1,625 mems; Chair. P. S. GAHLAUT; Dir-Gen. VIREN KAUSHIK.

Grain, Rice and Oilseeds Merchants' Association: 14-C, Groma House, 2nd Floor, Sector 19, Vashi, Navi Mumbai 400 703; tel. (22) 27897454; fax (22) 27897458; e-mail groma@vsnl.com; internet www.groma.org; f. 1899; 1,200 mems; Pres. HIRJI NANJI KENIA.

Indian Drug Manufacturers' Association: 102B Poonam Chambers, Dr A. B. Rd, Worli, Mumbai 400 018; tel. (22) 24944624; fax (22) 24950723; e-mail idma@giasbm01.vsnl.net.in; 600 mems; Pres. N. H. ISRANI; Sec.-Gen. I. A. ALVA.

Indian Electrical and Electronics Manufacturers' Association (IEEMA): 501 Kakad Chambers, 132 Dr Annie Besant Rd, Worli, Mumbai 400 018; tel. (22) 24936528; fax (22) 24932705; e-mail mumbai@ieema.org; internet www.ieema.org; f. 1948; 400 mems; Pres. R. N. MUKHIJA; Sec.-Gen. SUNIL P. MORE.

Indian Jute Mills Association: Royal Exchange, 6 Netaji Subhas Rd, Kolkata 700 001; tel. (33) 22209918; fax (33) 22205643; e-mail ijma@cal2.vsnl.net.in; sponsors and operates export promotion, research and product development; regulates labour relations; 40 mems; Chair. G. M. SINGHVI; Sec. SARIT RAY.

Indian Leather Products Association: Suite 6, Chatterjee International Centre, 14th Floor, 33-A, Jawaharlal Nehru Rd, Kolkata

700 071; tel. (33) 22267102; fax (33) 22468339; e-mail ilpa@cal2.vsnl .net.in; 120 mems; Pres. M. V. KULKARNI; Exec. Dir Dr P. K. DEY.

Indian Machine Tool Manufacturers' Association: 17 Nangal Raya Commercial Complex, New Delhi 110 046; tel. (11) 25592814; fax (11) 25599882; e-mail imtma@del2.vsnl.net.in; internet www .imtma.org; 400 mems; Pres. V. S. GOINDI; Sec. A. MUKHERJEE.

Indian Mining Association: 6 Netaji Subhas Rd, Kolkata 700 001; tel. (33) 22203733; f. 1892; 50 mems; Sec. K. MUKERJEE.

Indian Mining Federation: 135 Biplabi Rash Behari Basu Rd, 2nd Floor, Kolkata 700 001; tel. (33) 22428975; f. 1913; 40 mems; Chair. V. K. ARORA; Sec. S. K. GHOSE.

Indian Motion Picture Producers' Association: IMPPA House, Dr Ambedkar Rd, Bandra (West), Mumbai 400 050; tel. (22) 26486344; fax (22) 26480757; f. 1938; 2,000 mems; Pres. SMITA THACKERAY; Sec. DINKAR CHOWDHARY.

Indian National Shipowners' Association: 22 Maker Tower, F, Cuffe Parade, Mumbai 400 005; tel. (22) 22182103; fax (22) 22182104; e-mail insaf@insa.org.in; internet www.insa.org.in; f. 1929; 29 mems; Pres. P. K. SRIVASTAVA; Sec.-Gen. S. S. KULKARNI.

Indian Oilseeds & Produce Exporters' Association (IOPEA): 78/79 Bajaj Bhavan, Nariman Point, Mumbai 400 021; tel. (22) 22023225; fax (22) 22029236; e-mail iopea@bom3.vsnl.net.in; internet www.iopea.org; f. 1956; 350 mems; Chair. KISHOR BHEDA; Sec. A. N. SUBRAMANIAN.

Indian Refractory Makers' Association: 5 Lala Lajpat Rai Sarani, 4th Floor, Kolkata 700 020; tel. (33) 22810868; fax (33) 22814357; e-mail irma@giascl01.vsnl.net.in; internet www .irmaindia.org; 85 mems; Chair. C. D. KAMATH; Exec. Dir P. DAS GUPTA.

Indian Soap and Toiletries Makers' Association: 614 Raheja Centre, Free Press Journal Marg, Mumbai 400 021; tel. (22) 22824115; fax (22) 22853649; e-mail istma@bom3.vsnl.net.in; 38 mems; Pres. M. K. SHARMA; Sec.-Gen. R. HARIHARAN.

Indian Sugar Mills Association: Ansal Plaza, C–Block, 2nd Floor, Andrews Ganj, New Delhi 110 049; tel. (11) 26262294; fax (11) 26263231; e-mail sugarmil@nda.vsnl.net.in; f. 1932; 174 mems; Pres. ASHOK GOEL; Dir-Gen. S. L. JAIN.

Indian Tea Association: Royal Exchange, 6 Netaji Subhas Rd, Kolkata 700 001; tel. (33) 22102474; fax (33) 22434301; e-mail ita@ cal2.vsnl.net.in; internet www.indiatea.org; f. 1881; 63 mem. cos; 453 tea estates; Chair. BHARAT BAJORIA; Sec.-Gen. D. CHAKRABARTI.

Indian Woollen Mills' Federation: Churchgate Chambers, 7th Floor, 5 New Marine Lines, Mumbai 400 020; tel. (22) 22624372; fax (22) 22624675; e-mail iwmf@bom3.vsnl.net.in; f. 1963; 50 mems; Chair. V. K. BHARTIA; Sec.-Gen. A. C. CHAUDHURY.

Industries and Commerce Association: ICO Association Rd, POB 70, Dhanbad 826 001; tel. (326) 2303147; fax (326) 2303787; f. 1933; 70 mems; Pres. B. N. SINGH; Sec. K. R. CHAKRAVARTY.

Jute Balers' Association: 12 India Exchange Place, Kolkata 700 001; tel. (33) 22201491; f. 1909; 300 mems; Chair. NIRMAL KUMAR BHUTORIA; Sec. SUJIT CHOUDHURY.

Maharashtra Motor Parts Dealers' Association: 13 Kala Bhavan, 3 Mathew Rd, Mumbai 400 004; tel. (22) 23614468; 375 mems; Pres. J. C. UNADKAT; Sec. J. R. CHANDAWALLA.

Millowners' Association, Mumbai: Elphinstone Bldg, 10 Veer Nariman Rd, Fort, POB 95, Mumbai 400 001; tel. (22) 22040411; fax (22) 2832611; f. 1875; 23 mem. cos; Chair. NANDAN S. DAMANI; Sec.-Gen. V. Y. TAMHANE.

Mumbai Motor Merchants' Association Ltd: 304 Sukh Sagar, N. S. Patkar Marg, Mumbai 400 007; tel. (22) 28112769; 409 mems; Pres. S. TARLOCHAN SINGH ANAND; Gen. Sec. S. BHUPINDER SINGH SETHI.

Mumbai Textile Merchants' Mahajan: 250 Sheikh Memon St, Mumbai 400 002; tel. (22) 22065750; fax (22) 22000311; f. 1881; 1,900 mems; Pres. SURENDRA TULSIDAS SAVAI; Hon. Secs DHIRAJ S. KOTHARI, RAJESH B. PATEL.

National Association of Software and Service Companies (NASSCOM): International Youth Centre, Uma Shankar Dixit Marg, Chanakyapuri, New Delhi 110 021; tel. (11) 23010199; fax (11) 23015452; e-mail nasscom@nasscom.org; internet www.nasscom .org; more than 650 mems; Pres. KIRAN KARNIK.

Organisation of Pharmaceutical Producers of India (OPPI): Peninsular Chambers, Ground Floor, Ganpatrao Kadam Marg, Lower Parel, Mumbai 400 013; tel. (22) 24918123; fax (22) 24915168; e-mail indiaoppi@vsnl.com; internet www.indiaoppi.com; 60 ordinary mems, 7 associate mems, 3 affiliate mems; Pres. RANJIT SHAHANI; Dir-Gen. Dr AJIT DANGI.

Society of Indian Automobile Manufacturers: Core 4B, 5th Floor, India Habitat Centre, Lodhi Rd, New Delhi 110 003; tel. (11)

24647810; fax (11) 24648222; e-mail siamsoc@bol.net.in; f. 1960; 35 mems; Pres. R. SESHASAYEE; Exec. Dir RAJAT NANDI.

Southern India Mills' Association: 44 Racecourse, Coimbatore 641 018; tel. (422) 2211391; fax (422) 2217160; e-mail simacbe@vsnl .com; f. 1933; 303 mems; Chair. V. S. VELAYUTHAM; Sec. P. R. SUBRAMANIAN.

Surgical Manufacturers and Traders' Association: 60 Darya Ganj, New Delhi 110 002; tel. (11) 23271027; fax (11) 23258576; e-mail raviawasthi@hotmail.com; Pres. RAKESH SAWHNEY; Sec. RAVI AWASTHI.

Synthetic and Art Silk Mills' Association Ltd: 3rd Floor, Sasmira Bldg, Sasmira Marg, Worli, Mumbai 400 025; tel. (22) 24945372; fax (22) 24938350; e-mail sasma_100@pacific.net.in; f. 1939; 150 mems; Chair. V. S. CHALKE; Gen. Sec. K. A. SAMUEL.

Telecom Equipment Manufacturers' Association of India (TEMA): PHD House, 4th Floor, R. K. Dalmia Wing, opp. Asian Games Village, New Delhi 110 016; tel. (11) 26859621; fax (11) 26859620; e-mail tema@vsnl.com; internet www.tematelecom.org; Pres. N. K. GOYAL; Exec. Dir. S. K. KHANNA.

Travel Agents' Association of India: 2D Lawrence and Mayo House, 276 Dr D. N. Rd, Mumbai 400 001; tel. (22) 22074022; fax (22) 22074559; e-mail travels@bom2.vsnl.net.in; 1,700 mems; Pres. JEHANGIR KATGARA; Hon. Sec.-Gen. BHAGWAN KANUGA.

United Planters' Association of Southern India (UPASI): Glenview, POB 11, Coonoor 643 101; tel. (423) 230270; fax (423) 232030; e-mail upasi@vsnl.com; f. 1893; 950 mems; Pres. P. S. WALLIA; Sec.-Gen. ULLAS MENON.

EMPLOYERS' ORGANIZATIONS

Council of Indian Employers: Federation House, Tansen Marg, New Delhi 110 001; tel. (11) 23316121; fax (11) 23320714; f. 1956; comprises:

All India Organisation of Employers (AIOE): Federation House, Tansen Marg, New Delhi 110 001; tel. (11) 23316121; fax (11) 23320714; f. 1932; 196 mems (incl. 158 associate mems); Pres. ASHWIN DANI; Sec.-Gen. Dr AMIT MITRA.

Employers' Federation of India (EFI): Army and Navy Bldg, 148 Mahatma Gandhi Rd, Mumbai 400 001; tel. (22) 22844232; fax (22) 22843028; e-mail efisolar@vsnl.com; f. 1933; 28 asscn mems, 182 ordinary mems, 18 hon. mems; Pres. Dr RAM S. TARNEJA; Sec.-Gen. SHARAD S. PATIL.

Standing Conference of Public Enterprises (SCOPE): SCOPE Complex, 1st Floor, Core No. 8, 7 Lodi Rd, New Delhi 110 003; tel. (11) 24360101; fax (11) 24361371; e-mail scope@niesco .delhi.nic.in; internet www.niesco.delhi.nic.in; f. 1973; representative body of all central public enterprises in India; advises the Govt and public enterprises on matters of major policy and co-ordination; trade enquiries, regarding imports and exports of commodities, carried out on behalf of mems; 197 mems; Chair. SUBIR RAHA; Sec.-Gen. Dr S. M. DEWAN.

Employers' Association of Northern India: 14/113 Civil Lines, POB 344, Kanpur 208 001; tel. (512) 2210513; f. 1937; 190 mems; Chair. RAJIV KEHR; Sec.-Gen. P. DUBEY.

Employers' Federation of Southern India: Karumuttu Centre, 1st Floor, 634 Anna Salai, Chennai 600 035; tel. (44) 24349452; fax (44) 24349164; e-mail efsi@vsnl.net; f. 1920; 520 mems; Pres. R. VISWANATHAN; Sec. T. M. JAWAHARLAL.

UTILITIES

Electricity

Central Electricity Authority (CEA): Sewa Bhavan, R. K. Puram, New Delhi 110 066; tel. (11) 26108476; fax (11) 26105619; e-mail cea-edp@hub.nic.in; internet www.cea.nic.in; responsible for technical co-ordination and supervision of electricity programmes; advises Ministry of Power on all technical, financial and economic issues; Chair. H. L. BAJAJ.

Bombay Suburban Electric Supply Ltd: 6th Floor, Nagin Mahal, 82 Veer Nariman Rd, Mumbai 400 020; tel. (22) 22043287; fax (22) 22041280; internet www.bses.com; f. 1929; has monopoly in supply of electricity to Mumbai; Chair. ANIL AMBANI; Man. Dir S. S. DUA.

Calcutta Electricity Supply Corpn Ltd (CESC): CESC House, Chouringhee Sq., Kolkata 700 001; tel. (33) 22256040; fax (33) 22256334; f. 1978; generation and supply of electricity; Chair. R. P. GOENKA; Man. Dir SUMANTRA BANERJEE.

Damodar Valley Corpn: DVC Towers, VIP Rd, Kolkata 700 054; tel. (33) 23551935; fax (33) 23551937; e-mail dvchq@wb.nic.in; f. 1948 to administer the first multipurpose river valley project in India, the Damodar Valley Project, which aims at unified development of irrigation, flood control and power generation in West Bengal and Jharkhand; operates nine power stations, incl. thermal, hydel and gas turbine; power generating capacity 2,761.5 MW (1999); Chair. J. C. JETLI.

Dabhol Power Co: Dabhol; 65% owned by Enron (USA), 15% owned by the Maharashtra State Electricity Board (MSEB), 10% owned by Bechtel Enterprises Inc. (USA) and 10% owned by General Electric Co (USA); administered a two-phase project to establish plants with a power-generating capacity of 2,184 MW; first phase completed in 1999, second phase near completion in 2001; supplied electricity to the MSEB on a build-own-operate basis; production suspended in May 2001, following financial disagreements between Enron and the MSEB; sale of Enron's share of company under way in mid-2003; Man. Dir MOHAN GURUNATH.

Essar Power Ltd: Essar House, Mahalaxmi, Mumbai 400 034; tel. (22) 24950606; fax (22) 24950607; e-mail snpuia@essar.com; Chair. S. N. RUIA.

National Hydroelectric Power Corporation: Sector 33, Faridabad 121 003; e-mail yprasad@nhpc.nic.in; internet www .nhpcindia.com; f. 1975; Chair and Man. Dir YOGENDRA PRASAD.

National Thermal Power Corporation Ltd: Core-7, SCOPE Complex, Lodi Rd, New Delhi 110 003; tel. (11) 24360100; fax (11) 24361018; e-mail pr@ntpcn.ernet.in; internet www.ntpc.net; f. 1975; operates 11 coal-fired and five gas-fired power stations throughout India; Chair. and Man. Dir C. P. JAIN; 24,000 employees.

Noida Power Co Ltd: Commercial Complex, H Block, Alpha Sector II, Greater Noida, Uttar Pradesh 201 308; tel. (95120) 4326559; fax (95120) 4326448; f. 1922; distribution of electricity; Chair. and Man. Dir USHA CHATRATH; CEO P. NEOGI.

Nuclear Power Corporation of India Ltd: Commerce Center-1, World Trade Centre, Cuffe Parade, Mumbai 400 005; tel. (22) 22182171; fax (22) 22180109; internet www.npcil.org; Chair. and Man. Dir V. K. CHATURVEDI.

Power Grid Corporation of India Ltd: B-9, Qutab Institutional Area, Katwaria Sarai, New Delhi 110 016; tel. (11) 26560121; fax (11) 26560039; internet www.powergridindia.com; f. 1989; responsible for formation of national power grid; Chair. and Man. Dir R. P. SINGH.

Tata Power Co Ltd: Bombay House, 24 Homi Mody St, Mumbai 400 001; tel. (22) 22048331; fax (22) 22040505; internet www .tatapower.com; generation, transmission and distribution of electrical energy; Chair. RATAN N. TATA; Man. Dir FIRDOSE VANDREWALA.

Thana Electric Supply Co Ltd: Asian Bldg, 1st Floor, 17 Ramji Kamani Marg, Ballard Estate, Mumbai 400 001; tel. (22) 22615444; fax (22) 22611069; e-mail thanaele@bom2.vsnl.net.in; f. 1927; Man. Dir SURESH S. MEMMADY.

Gas

Gas Authority of India Ltd: 16 Bhikaji Cama Place, R. K. Puram, Delhi 110 066; tel. (11) 26172580; fax (11) 26185941; e-mail pbanerjee@gail.com.in; internet www.nic.in/gail; f. 1984; 80% state-owned; transports, processes and markets natural gas; constructing gas-based petrochemical complex; Chair. and Man. Dir PROSHANTO BANERJEE; 1,513 employees.

Water

Brihanmumbai Municipal Corporation (Hydraulic Engineers' Department): Municipal Corporation Offices, Ground Floor, Annex Bldg, Mahapalika Marg, Mumbai 400 001; tel. (22) 22620025; fax (22) 22700532; Head Eng. S. N. TURKAR.

Calcutta Municipal Corporation (Water Supply Department): 5 S. N. Banerjee Rd, Kolkata 700 013; tel. (33) 22444518; fax (33) 22442578; f. 1870; Chief Municipal Eng. DIBYENDU ROY CHOWDHURY.

Chennai Metropolitan Water Supply and Sewerage Board: No. 1 Pumping Station Rd, Chintadripet, Chennai 600 002; tel. (44) 28525717; f. 1978; Chair. and Man. Dir SANTHA SHEELA NAIR.

Delhi Jal Board: Varunalaya Phase II, Karol Bagh, New Delhi 110 005; tel. and fax (11) 23678380; e-mail prodjb@bol.net.in; internet www.delhijalboard.com; as Delhi Water Supply and Sewage Disposal Undertaking, reconstituted as above in 1998; part of the Delhi Municipal Corporation; f. 1957; production and distribution of potable water and treatment and disposal of waste water in Delhi; Chair. SHEILA DIXIT.

TRADE UNIONS

Indian National Trade Union Congress (INTUC): 4 Bhai Veer Singh Marg, New Delhi 110 001; tel. (11) 23747767; fax (11) 23364244; e-mail intuchq@del3.vsnl.net.in; f. 1947; 4,411 affiliated unions with a total membership of 7,937,436; affiliated to ICFTU; 32 state brs and 29 nat. feds; Pres. G. SANJEEVA REDDY; Gen. Sec. RAJENDRA PRASAD SINGH.

Indian National Cement Workers' Federation: Mazdoor Karyalaya, Congress House, Mumbai 400 004; tel. (22) 23871809; fax (22) 23870981; 49,000 mems; 38 affiliated unions; Pres. H. N. TRIVEDI; Gen. Sec. N. NANJAPPAN.

Indian National Chemical Workers' Federation: Tel Rasayan Bhavan, Tilak Rd, Dadar, Mumbai 400 014; tel. (22) 24121742; fax (22) 24130950; 35,000 mems; Pres. RAJA KULKARNI; Gen. Sec. R. D. BHARADWAJ.

Indian National Electricity Workers' Federation: 392 Sector 21-B, Faridabad 121 001; tel. (129) 2215089; fax (129) 2215868; e-mail inef@ndf.vsnl.net.in; f. 1950; 187,641 mems; 146 affiliated unions; Pres. D. P. PATHAK; Gen. Sec. S. L. PASSEY.

Indian National Metal Workers' Federation: D–81, Sector 18, Rourkela 769 003; tel. (661) 24646611; Pres. G. SANJEEVA REDDY; Gen. Sec. M. D. N. PANICKER.

Indian National Mineworkers' Federation: Imperial House, CJ-66 Salt Lake, Kolkata 700 091; tel. (33) 23345586; fax (33) 23372158; e-mail imme@vsnl.com; f. 1949; 351,454 mems in 139 affiliated unions; Pres. RAJENDRA P. SINGH; Gen. Sec. S. Q. ZAMA.

Indian National Paper Mill Workers' Federation: 6/B, LIGH, Barkatpura, Hyderabad 500 027; tel. (40) 27564706; Pres. G. SANJEEVA REDDY; Gen. Sec. R. CHANDRASEKHARAN.

Indian National Port and Dock Workers' Federation: 15 Coal Dock Rd, Kolkata 700 043; tel. (33) 22455929; f. 1954; 18 affiliated unions; 81,000 mems; Pres. JANAKI MUKHERJEE; Gen. Sec. G. KALAN.

Indian National Sugar Mills Workers' Federation: A-176, Darulsafa Marg, Lucknow 226 001; tel. (522) 2247638; 100 affiliated unions; 40,000 mems; Pres. ASHOK KUMAR SINGH; Gen. Sec. P. K. SHARMA.

Indian National Textile Workers' Federation: 27 Burjorji Bharucha Marg, Mumbai 400 023; tel. (22) 22671577; f. 1948; 400 affiliated unions; 363,790 mems; Pres. SACHIN AHIR; Gen. Sec. P. L. SUBHAIAH.

Indian National Transport Workers' Federation: Bus Mazdoor Karyalaya, L/1, Hathital Colony, Jabalpur 482 001; tel. (761) 2429210; 303 affiliated unions; 371,726 mems; Pres. G. SANJEEVA REDDY; Gen. Sec. K. S. VERMA.

National Federation of Petroleum Workers: Tel Rasayan Bhavan, Tilak Rd, Dadar, Mumbai 400 014; tel. (22) 24181742; fax (22) 24130950; f. 1959; 22,340 mems; Pres. RAJA KULKARNI; Gen. Sec. S. N. SURVE.

Bharatiya Mazdoor Sangh: Ram Naresh Bhavan, Tilak Gali, Pahar Ganj, New Delhi 110 055; tel. (11) 23562654; fax (11) 23582648; e-mail 40@bms.org.in; f. 1955; 4,600 affiliated unions with a total membership of 6.6m. 27 state brs; 30 nat. feds; Pres. HASMUKH DAVE; Gen. Sec. UDAY RAO PATWARDHAN.

Centre of Indian Trade Unions: BTR Bhavan, 13-A Rouse Ave, New Delhi 110 002; tel. (11) 23221306; fax (11) 23221284; e-mail citu@vsnl.com; f. 1970; 3,250,000 mems; 24 state and union territory brs; 3,900 affiliated unions, 10 nat. federations; Pres. E. BALANANDAN; Gen. Sec. M. K. PANDHE.

Assam Chah Karmachari Sangha: POB 13, Dibrugarh 786 001; tel. 20870; 13,553 mems; 20 brs; Pres. G. C. SARMAH; Gen. Sec. A. K. BHATTACHARYA.

All-India Trade Union Congress (AITUC): 24 Canning Lane, New Delhi 110 001; tel. (11) 23387320; fax (11) 23386427; e-mail aitucong@bol.net.in; f. 1920; affiliated to WFTU; 3m. mems, 3,000 affiliated unions; 26 state brs, 10 national federations; Pres. J. CHITHARANJAN; Gen. Sec. GURUDAS DASGUPTA.

Major affiliated unions:

Annamalai Plantation Workers' Union: Valparai, Via Pollachi, Tamil Nadu; over 21,000 mems.

Zilla Cha Bagan Workers' Union: Mal, Jalpaiguri, West Bengal; 15,000 mems; Pres. NEHAR MUKHERJEE; Gen. Sec. BIMAL DAS GUPTA.

United Trades Union Congress (UTUC): 249 Bepin Behari Ganguly St, Kolkata 700 012; tel. (33) 2275609; f. 1949; 584,523 mems from 413 affiliated unions; 10 state brs and 6 nat. feds; Pres. P. C. JOHN; Gen. Sec. S. R. SEN GUPTA.

Major affiliated unions:

All India Farm Labour Union: Patna; c. 35,000 mems; Pres. MAHENDRA SINGH TIKAIT.

Bengal Provincial Chatkal Mazdoor Union: Kolkata; textile workers; 28,330 mems.

Hind Mazdoor Sabha (HMS): 'Shrama-Sadhana', 57 D. V. Pradhan Rd, Hindu Colony, Dadar (East), Mumbai 400 014; tel. (22) 24144336; fax (22) 24102759; e-mail mki@vsnl.com; f. 1948; affiliated to ICFTU; 4.8m. mems from 2,800 affiliated unions; 20 state councils; 18 nat. industrial feds; Pres. PRABHU NARAYAN SINGH; Gen. Sec. UMRAOMAL PUROHIT.

Major affiliated unions:

Colliery Mazdoor Congress (Coalminers' Union): Pres. MADHU DANDAVATE; Gen. Sec. JAYANTA PODDER.

Mumbai Port Trust Dock and General Employees' Union: Pres. Dr SHANTI PATEL; Gen. Sec. S. K. SHETYE.

South Central Railway Mazdoor Union: 7C Railway Bldg, Accounts Office Compound, Secunderabad 500 371; tel. (40) 27821351; fax (40) 27821351; e-mail scrmu@hotmail.com; internet www.scrmu.org; f. 1966; 88,900 mems; Pres. C. SANKARA RAO; Gen. Sec. N. SUNDARESAN; 135 brs.

Transport and Dock Workers' Union: Gen. Sec. MANOHAR KOTWAL.

West Bengal Cha Mazdoor Sabha: Cha Shramik Bhavan, Jalpaiguri 735 101, West Bengal; tel. (3561) 231140; fax (3561) 230349; f. 1947; 55,000 mems; Pres. Prof. SUSHIL ROY; Gen. Sec. SAMIR ROY.

Western Railway Employees' Union: Pres. JAGDISH AJMERA; Gen. Sec. UMRAOMAL PUROHIT.

Confederation of Central Government Employees and Workers: 4B/6 Ganga Ram Hospital Marg, New Delhi 110 060; tel. (11) 22587804; 1.2m. mems; Pres. S. MADHUSUDAN; Sec.-Gen. S. K. VYAS.

Affiliated union:

National Federation of Post, Telephone and Telegraph Employees (NFPTTE): New Delhi 110 001; f. 1954; 221,880 mems (est.); Pres. R. G. SHARMA; Gen. Sec. O. P. GUPTA.

All India Bank Employees' Association (AIBEA): 3B Lall Bazar St, 1st Floor, Kolkata 700 001; tel. (33) 22489371; fax (33) 22486072; e-mail aibea@cal2.vsnl.net.in; internet bankunionaibea.org; 32 state units, 710 affiliated unions, 525,000 mems; Pres. SURESH D. DHOPESWARKAR; Gen. Sec. TARAKESWAR CHAKRABORTI.

All India Defence Employees' Federation (AIDEF): Survey No. 81, Elphinstone Rd, Khadki, Pune 411 003; tel. (20) 25818761; 358 affiliated unions; 200,000 mems; Pres. T. I. MADHAVAN; Gen. Secs S. BHATTACHARYA, C. SRIKUMAR.

All India Port and Dock Workers' Federation: 9 Second Line Beach, Chennai 600 001; tel. (44) 25224222; fax (44) 25225983; f. 1948; 100,000 mems in 34 affiliated unions; Pres. S. R. KULKARNI; Gen. Sec. S. C. C. ANTHONY PILLAI.

All India Railwaymen's Federation (AIRF): 4 State Entry Rd, New Delhi 110 055; tel. (11) 23343493; fax (11) 23363167; e-mail airf@ndb.vsnl.net.in; f. 1924; 1,138,023 mems (2001); 19 affiliated unions; Pres. UMRAOMAL PUROHIT; Gen. Sec. J. P. CHAUBEY.

National Federation of Indian Railwaymen (NFIR): 3 Chelmsford Rd, New Delhi 110 055; tel. (11) 23343305; fax (11) 23744013; e-mail nfir@satyam.net.in; f. 1952; 19 affiliated unions; 916,629 mems (2000); Pres. MAHENDRA PRATAP; Gen. Sec. M. RAGHAVAIAH.

Transport

RAILWAYS

India's railway system is the largest in Asia and the fourth largest in the world. In 2000 the total length of Indian railways exceeded 63,028 route-km. The network carried 12m. passengers and more than 1m. metric tons of freight traffic per day. The Government exercises direct or indirect control over all railways through the Railway Board. India's largest railway construction project of the 20th century, the 760-km Konkan railway line (which took seven years and almost US $1,000m. to build), was officially opened in January 1998.

A 16.45-km underground railway, which carries more than 1m. people daily, was completed in Kolkata in 1995. The first phase of a partially underground new metro system in New Delhi was scheduled for completion in 2005; the final phase was expected to be completed in 2010.

Ministry of Railways (Railway Board): Rail Bhavan, Raisina Rd, New Delhi 110 001; tel. (11) 23384010; fax (11) 23384481; e-mail crb@del2.vsnl.net.in; internet www.indianrailways.com; Chair. I. I. M. S. RANA.

Zonal Railways

The railways are grouped into 15 zones

Central: Chhatrapati Shivaji Terminus (Victoria Terminus), Mumbai 400 001; tel. (22) 22621230; fax (22) 22624555; e-mail gmcr@bom2.vsnl.net.in; internet www.cr-mumbai.com; Gen. Man. S. P. S. JAIN.

East Central: Hajipur; tel. (6224) 274728; fax (6224) 274738; f. 1996; Officer on Special Duty K. K. AGARWAL.

East Coast: Bhubaneswar 751 023; tel. (674) 300773; fax (674) 440753; e-mail bishtbms@hotmail.com; internet webind.com/eastcoastrailway; f. 1996; Officer on Special Duty SURENDER JAIN.

Eastern: 17 Netaji Subhas Rd, Kolkata 700 001; tel. (33) 22207596; fax (33) 22480370; Gen. Man. S. C. SENGUPTA.

North Central: Allahabad; tel. (532) 2624530; fax (532) 2624841; e-mail secyncr@hotmail.com; f. 1996; Gen Man. I. P. S. ANAND.

North Eastern: Gorakhpur 273 012; tel. (551) 2201041; fax (551) 2201842; e-mail gmner@nda.vsnl.net.in; Gen. Man. OM PRAKASH.

North Western: Jaipur; tel. (141) 2222695; fax (141) 2222936; Gen. Man. RAKESH MOHAN AGRAWAL.

Northeast Frontier: Maligaon, Guwahati 781 011; tel. (361) 2570422; fax (361) 2571124; f. 1958; Gen. Man. VIPIN NANDA.

Northern: Baroda House, Kasturba Gandhi Marg, New Delhi 110 001; tel. (11) 23387227; fax (11) 23384503; e-mail nragm@vsnl.com; Gen. Man. R. K. SINGH.

South Central: Rm 312, 3rd Floor, Rail Nilayam, Secunderabad 500 071; tel. (40) 27822874; fax (40) 2825316; internet www.scrailway.gov.in; Gen. Man. S. M. SINGLA.

South Eastern: 11 Garden Reach Rd, Kolkata 700 043; tel. (33) 24397876; fax (33) 24397826; e-mail gm@ser.railnet.gov.in; internet www.serailway.com; Gen. Man. V. N. GARG.

South Western: Bangalore; tel. (80) 22205773; fax (80) 22282787; f. 1996; Officer on Special Duty V. VIJAYALAKSHMI.

Southern: Park Town, Chennai 600 003; tel. (44) 25353157; fax (44) 25351439; internet www.srailway.com; Gen. Man. V. ANAND.

West Central: Jabalpur; tel. (761) 2627444; fax (761) 2328133; e-mail osdwcr@yahoo.com; f. 1996; Officer on Special Duty V. K. BHARGAV.

Western: Churchgate, Mumbai 400 020; tel. (22) 22005670; fax (22) 22017631; internet www.westernrailwayindia.com; Gen. Man. V. D. GUPTA.

ROADS

In December 2001 there were an estimated 3.15m. km of roads in India, 58,112 km of which were national highways. About 50% of the total road network was paved. In January 1999 the Government launched the ambitious 500,000m. rupee National Highways Development project, which included plans to build an east–west corridor linking Silchar with Porbandar and a north–south corridor linking Kashmir with Kanyakumari, as well as a circuit of roads linking the four main cities of Mumbai, Chennai, Kolkata and New Delhi.

Ministry of Road Transport (and Highways): Transport Bhavan, 1 Parliament St, New Delhi 110 001; tel. (11) 23715159; responsible for the construction and maintenance of India's system of national highways, with a total length of 58,112 km in 2001, connecting the state capitals and major ports and linking with the highway systems of neighbouring countries. This system includes 172 national highways which constitute the main trunk roads of the country.

Border Roads Development Board: f. 1960 to accelerate the economic development of the north and north-eastern border areas; it has constructed 29,229 km and improved 34,306 km of roads, and maintains about 16,872 km in the border areas.

National Highways Authority of India: G-5&6, Sector 10, Dwarka, New Delhi 110 045; tel. (11) 25074100; fax (11) 25080360; e-mail nhai@vsnl.com; internet www.nhai.org; f. 1995; planning, designing, construction and maintenance of national highways; under Ministry of Road Transport; Chair. S. NAUTIYAL.

INLAND WATERWAYS

About 14,500 km of rivers are navigable by power-driven craft, and 3,700 km by large country boats. Services are mainly on the Ganga and Brahmaputra and their tributaries, the Godavari, the Mahanadi, the Narmada, the Tapti and the Krishna.

Central Inland Water Transport Corpn Ltd: 4 Fairlie Place, Kolkata 700 001; tel. (33) 22202321; fax (33) 22436164; e-mail ciwtc@cal3.vsnl.net.in; internet www.ciwtc.com; f. 1967; inland water transport services in Bangladesh and the east and north-east Indian states; also shipbuilding and repairing, general engineering, lightering of ships and barge services; Chair. and Man. Dir S. C. DUA.

SHIPPING

In March 2002 India was 14th on the list of principal merchant fleets of the world. In mid-2001 the fleet had 515 ships, with a total displacement of 7.07m. grt. There were some 102 shipping companies operating in India in January 2000. The major ports are Chennai, Haldia, Jawaharlal Nehru (at Nhava Sheva near Mumbai), Kandla, Kochi, Kolkata, Mormugao, Mumbai, New Mangalore, Paradip (Paradeep), Tuticorin and Visakha (Visakhapatnam).

Chennai (Madras)

South India Shipping Corpn Ltd: Chennai; Chair. J. H. Tarapore; Man. Dir F. G. Dastur.

Kolkata (Calcutta)

India Steamship Co Ltd: India Steamship House, 21 Hemanta Basu Sarani, POB 2090, Kolkata 700 001; tel. (33) 22481171; fax (33) 22488133; e-mail india.steamship@gems.vsnl.net.in; f. 1928; cargo services; Chair. K. K. Birla; Man. Dir Ashok Kak; br in Delhi.

Surrendra Overseas Ltd: Apeejay House, 15 Park St, Kolkata 700 016; tel. (33) 22172372; fax (33) 22179596; e-mail solcal@apeejaygroup.com; internet www.apeejaygroup.com; shipowners; Chair. Jit Paul.

Mumbai (Bombay)

Century Shipping Ltd: Mumbai; tel. (22) 22022734; fax (22) 22027274; Chair. B. K. Birla; Pres. N. M. Jain.

Chowgule & Co (Pvt) Ltd: Bakhtawar, 3rd Floor, Nariman Point, POB 11596, Mumbai 400 021; tel. (22) 22026822; fax (22) 22024845; f. 1963; Chair. Vishwasrao Dattaji Chowgule; Man. Dir Shivajirao Dattaji Chowgule.

Essar Shipping Ltd: Essar House, 11 Keshavrao Khadye Marg, Mahalaxmi, Mumbai 400 034; tel. (22) 24950606; fax (22) 24950607; e-mail snruia@essar.com; f. 1975; Chair. S. N. Ruia; Man. Dir Sanjay Mehta.

The Great Eastern Shipping Co Ltd: Ocean House, 134/A Dr Annie Besant Rd, Worli, Mumbai 400 018; tel. (22) 24922100; fax (22) 24925900; internet www.greatship.com; f. 1948; cargo services; Exec. Chair. K. M. Sheth; Man. Dir Bharat Sheth; br in New Delhi.

Shipping Corpn of India Ltd: Shipping House, 245 Madame Cama Rd, Mumbai 400 021; tel. (22) 22026666; fax (22) 22026905; e-mail mail@sci.co.in; internet www.shipindia.com; f. 1961 as a govt undertaking; Chair. and Man. Dir P. K. Srivastava; brs in Kolkata, New Delhi, Chennai and Mumbai.

Tolani Shipping Co Ltd: 10A Bakhtawar, Nariman Point, Mumbai 400 021; tel. (22) 22026878; fax (22) 22870697; e-mail ops@tolanigroup.com; Chair. and Man. Dir Dr N. P. Tolani.

Varun Shipping Co Ltd: 3rd Floor, Laxmi Bldg, 6 Shoorji Vallabhdas Marg, Ballard Estate, Mumbai 400 001; tel. (22) 22658114; fax (22) 22621723; f. 1971; Chair. and Man. Dir Arun Mehta.

CIVIL AVIATION

There are five main international airports and 90 domestic airports and 27 civil enclaves. By mid-1998 nine airports (in Mumbai, Delhi, Chennai, Kolkata, Hyderabad, Ahmedabad, Goa, Bangalore and Thiruvananthapuram) had been identified for expansion/upgrading. The process of long-term leasing of Mumbai, Delhi, Chennai, Kolkata airports was under way in 2002 and was scheduled for completion in 2003.

Airports Authority of India: Rajiv Gandhi Bhavan, Safdarjung Airport, New Delhi 110 003; tel. (11) 24632950; fax (11) 24632990; e-mail aaichmn@vsnl.com; internet www.airportsindia.org.in; manages the international and domestic airports; Chair. S. K. Narula.

Air-India: Air-India Bldg, 218 Backbay Reclamation, Nariman Point, Mumbai 400 021; tel. (22) 22024142; fax (22) 22023686; e-mail hqpsai@bom3.vsnl.net.in; internet www.airindia.com; f. 1932 as Tata Airlines; renamed Air-India in 1946; in 1953 became a state corpn responsible for international flights; services to 46 online stations (incl. 2 cargo stations) and 84 offline offices throughout the world; Chair. K. Roy Paul; Man. Dir J. N. Gogoi.

Alliance Air-Airline Allied Services: 1st Floor, Domestic Arrival Terminal, Indira Gandhi International Airport, Palam, New Delhi 110 037; tel. (11) 25672729; fax (11) 25672006; e-mail aaslmd@del2.net.in; internet www.allianceair-india.com/; f. 1996; 100% owned by Indian Airlines; scheduled passenger services to regional destinations; Man. Dir Manek Paes.

Archana Airways: 41A Friends Colony (East), Mathura Rd, New Delhi 110 065; tel. (11) 26842001; fax (11) 26847762; f. 1991;

commenced operations 1993; scheduled and charter passenger services to domestic destinations; Dir/Chair. A. K. Bhartiya; Man. Dir N. K. Bhartiya.

Blue Dart Express: 88–89 Old International Terminal, Meenambakkam Airport, Chennai 600027; tel. (44) 22334995; fax (44) 22349067; e-mail bdal@md2.vsnl.net.in; internet www.bluedart.com; f. 1983 as Blue Dart Courier Services; name changed as above in 1990; air express transport co; Chair. Tushar K. Jani; Chief Exec. Niteen Gupte.

Continental Aviation: E-4/130 Arera Colony, Bhopal 462 016; tel. (755) 2566625; fax (755) 2563447; domestic passenger services; Gen. Man. Sam Verma.

Elbee Airlines: SM House, 11 Sahakar House, Vile Parla East, Mumbai 400 057; tel. (22) 28237006; fax (22) 28227201; e-mail elbeebom@bom4.vsnl.net.in; internet www.elbeenet.com/elbeeair.htm; f. 1994; scheduled and charter cargo services to domestic destinations; Chief Exec. Ashis Nain.

Gujarat Airways Ltd: 1st Floor, Sapana Shopping Centre, 20 Vishwas Colony, Alkapuri, Vadodara 390 005; tel. (265) 2330864; fax (265) 2339628; e-mail info@gujaratairways.com; internet www.gujaratairways.com; f. 1994; commenced operations 1995; scheduled services to domestic destinations; Chair. G. N. Patel; Man. Dir R. C. Sharma.

Indian Airlines: Airlines House, 113 Gurudwara Rakabganj Rd, New Delhi 110 001; tel. (11) 23716236; fax (11) 23711730; e-mail cmdial@vsnl.com; internet www.indianairlines.com; f. 1953; state corpn responsible for regional and domestic flights; services to 63 cities throughout India and to 16 destinations in the Middle East and the Far East; Chair. and Man. Dir Sunil Arora.

Jagson Airlines: 12E Vandana Bldg, 11 Tolstoy Marg, New Delhi 110 001; tel. (11) 23721594; fax (11) 23324693; e-mail jagson@id.eth.net; f. 1991; scheduled and charter passenger services to domestic destinations; Chair. Jagdish Gupta; Man. Dir Pradeep Gupta.

Jet Airways (India) Ltd: S. M. Centre, 1st Floor, Andheri-Kurla Rd, Andheri (East), Mumbai 400 059; tel. (22) 28505080; fax (22) 28505631; internet www.jetairways.com; f. 1992; commenced operations 1993; private co; scheduled passenger services to domestic and regional destinations; Chair. and Man. Dir Naresh Goyal; Exec. Dir Saroj K. Datta.

NEPC Airlines: 36 Wallajah Rd, Chennai 600 002; f. 1994; private co; passenger services to domestic destinations; Chair. and Man. Dir Ravi Prakash Khemka.

Sahara Airlines: Dr Gopaldas Bhawan, 3rd Floor, 28 Barakhamba Rd, New Delhi 110 001; tel. (11) 23326851; fax (11) 2375510; e-mail ukbose@saharaairline.com; internet www.saharaairline.com; f. 1991 as Sahara India Airlines; commenced operations 1993; private co; scheduled passenger and cargo services to domestic destinations; Chair. Subrata R. Sahara; CEO U. K. Bose.

TransBharat Aviation Ltd: 201 Laxmi Bhavan, 72 Nehru Place, Delhi 110 019; tel. (11) 26419600; fax (11) 23313353; f. 1990; commenced operations 1991; charter services throughout India.

UP Airways Ltd: Roopali House, A-2 Defence Colony, New Delhi 110 024; tel. (11) 24646290; fax (11) 24646292; e-mail sgsimpex@del3.vsnl.net.in; private co; charter services to domestic destinations; Chair. and Man. Dir Subhash Gulati; Chief Exec. Capt. H. S. Bedi.

Tourism

The tourist attractions of India include its scenery, its historic forts, palaces and temples, and its rich variety of wild life. Tourist infrastructure has recently been expanded by the provision of more luxury hotels and improved means of transport. In 2001 there were about 2.54m. foreign visitors to India, and revenue from tourism totalled an estimated 143,440m. rupees.

Ministry of Tourism: Transport Bhavan, Parliament St, New Delhi 110 001; tel. (11) 23711792; fax (11) 23710518; formulates and administers govt policy for promotion of tourism; plans the organization and development of tourist facilities; operates tourist information offices in India and overseas; Dir-Gen. V. K. Duggal.

India Tourism Development Corpn Ltd: SCOPE Complex, Core 8, 6th Floor, 7 Lodi Rd, New Delhi 110 003; tel. (11) 24360303; fax (11) 24362353; e-mail itdcscope@usa.net; internet www.theashokgroup.com; f. 1966; operates Ashok Group of hotels (largest hotel chain owner), resort accommodation, tourist transport services, duty-free shops and a travel agency and provides consultancy and management services; Chair. and Man. Dir Amitabh Kaul.

INDONESIA

Introductory Survey

Location, Climate, Language, Religion, Flag, Capital

The Republic of Indonesia consists of a group of about 18,108 islands (including rocks, reefs, sandbanks, etc.), lying between the mainland of South-East Asia and Australia. The archipelago is the largest in the world, and it stretches from the Malay peninsula to New Guinea. The principal islands are Java, Sumatra, Kalimantan (comprising more than two-thirds of the island of Borneo), Sulawesi (Celebes), Papua (formerly Irian Jaya, comprising the western part of the island of New Guinea), Maluku (the Moluccas) and West Timor (comprising part of the island of Timor). Indonesia's only land frontiers are with Papua New Guinea, to the east of Papua, with the Malaysian states of Sarawak and Sabah, which occupy northern Borneo, and with Timor-Leste (formerly East Timor), to the east of West Timor. The climate is tropical, with an average annual temperature of 26°C (79°F) and heavy rainfall during most seasons. Rainfall averages 706 mm (28 ins) annually in Indonesia, although there are large variations throughout the archipelago; the heaviest annual rainfall (2,286 mm or 90 ins) is along the equatorial rain belt, which passes through Sumatra, Borneo and Sulawesi. The official language is Bahasa Indonesia (a form of Malay); there are an estimated 583 other languages and dialects spoken in the archipelago, including Javanese, Sundanese, Arabic and Chinese. An estimated 88% of the inhabitants profess adherence to Islam. About 10% of the population are Christians, while most of the remainder are either Hindus or Buddhists. The national flag (proportions 2 by 3) has two equal horizontal stripes, of red and white. The capital is Jakarta, on the island of Java.

Recent History

Indonesia was formerly the Netherlands East Indies (except for the former Portuguese colony of Timor-Leste, see below). Dutch occupation began in the 17th century and gradually extended over the whole archipelago. Nationalist opposition to colonial rule began in the early 20th century. During the Second World War the territory was occupied by Japanese forces from March 1942. On 17 August 1945, three days after the Japanese surrender, a group of nationalists proclaimed the independence of Indonesia. The first President of the self-proclaimed republic was Dr Sukarno, a leader of the nationalist movement since the 1920s. The declaration of independence was not recognized by the Netherlands, which attempted to restore its pre-war control of the islands. After four years of intermittent warfare and negotiations between the Dutch authorities and the nationalists, agreement was reached on a formal transfer of power. On 27 December 1949 the United States of Indonesia became legally independent, with Sukarno continuing as President. Initially, the country had a federal Constitution which gave limited self-government to the 16 constituent regions. In August 1950, however, the federation was dissolved, and the country became the unitary Republic of Indonesia. The 1949 independence agreement excluded West New Guinea (subsequently Irian Jaya and known as Papua from 1 January 2002), which remained under Dutch control until October 1962; following a brief period of UN administration, however, it was transferred to Indonesia in May 1963.

Sukarno followed a policy of extreme nationalism, and his regime became increasingly dictatorial. His foreign policy was sympathetic to the People's Republic of China but, under his rule, Indonesia also played a leading role in the Non-aligned Movement (see p. 350). Inflation and widespread corruption eventually provoked opposition to Sukarno's regime; in September–October 1965 there was an abortive military coup, in which the Partai Komunis Indonesia (PKI—Indonesian Communist Party) was strongly implicated. A mass slaughter of alleged PKI members and supporters ensued. In March 1966 Sukarno was forced to transfer emergency executive powers to military commanders, led by Gen. Suharto, Chief of Staff of the Army, who outlawed the PKI. In February 1967 Sukarno transferred full power to Suharto. In March the Majelis Permusyawaratan Rakyat (MPR—People's Consultative Assembly) removed Sukarno from office and named Suharto acting President. He became Prime Minister in October 1967 and, following his election by the MPR, he was inaugurated as President in March 1968. In July 1971, in the first general election since 1955, the government-sponsored Sekretariat Bersama Golongan Karya (Joint Secretariat of Functional Groups), known as Golkar, won a majority of seats in the Dewan Perwakilan Rakyat (DPR—House of Representatives). Suharto was re-elected to the presidency in March 1973.

Under Suharto's 'New Order', real power passed from the legislature and the Cabinet to a small group of army officers and to the Operation Command for the Restoration of Order and Security (Kopkamtib), the internal security organization. Left-wing movements were suppressed, and a liberal economic policy adopted. A general election in May 1977 gave Golkar a majority in the legislature, and Suharto was re-elected President (unopposed) in March 1978. Despite criticism of the Government, Golkar won an increased majority in the elections in May 1982. In March 1983 Suharto was re-elected, again unopposed, as President.

During 1984 Suharto's attempt to introduce legislation requiring all political, social and religious organizations to adopt *pancasila*, the five-point state philosophy (belief in a supreme being; humanitarianism; national unity; democracy by consensus; social justice), as their only ideology encountered opposition. Serious rioting and a series of bombings and arson attempts in and around Jakarta were allegedly instigated by Muslim opponents of the proposed legislation, and many Muslims were tried and sentenced to long terms of imprisonment. A law concerning mass organizations was enacted in June 1985, and all the political parties had accepted *pancasila* by July. At the April 1987 general election, despite persistent international allegations of corruption and of abuses of human rights, particularly in East Timor (see below), Golkar won 299 of the 500 seats in the DPR. Moreover, for the first time, the party achieved an overall majority of seats in each of Indonesia's 27 provinces.

In February 1988 new legislation reaffirmed the 'dual (i.e. military and socio-economic) function' of the Indonesian Armed Forces (ABRI). In March Suharto was again re-elected unopposed as President. At the subsequent vice-presidential election, in a departure from previous procedure, Suharto did not recommend a candidate, but encouraged the MPR to choose one. However, Lt-Gen. (retd) Sudharmono, the Chairman of Golkar, and Dr Jailani Naro, the leader of the Partai Persatuan Pembangunan (PPP—United Development Party), were both nominated for the post, and Gen. Suharto was obliged to indicate his preference for Sudharmono before Naro withdrew his candidacy and Sudharmono was elected unopposed. ABRI disapproved of Sudharmono's appointment as, under his chairmanship of Golkar, there had been a shift away from military dominance in the grouping and he was suspected of having left-wing sympathies. In October Sudharmono resigned as Chairman of Golkar and was replaced by Gen. (retd) Wahono, who was acceptable both to ABRI and the developing bureaucratic élite.

In early 1989 tension arising from land disputes produced social unrest in three areas of Java and on the island of Sumbawa (east of Bali and Lombok), in Nusa Tenggara. The first student demonstrations since 1978 were held to protest against the Government's expropriation of land without sufficient indemnification for those subject to relocation. The armed forces did not attempt to suppress the student protests. Meanwhile, speculation over Suharto's successor had begun. In May 1989, however, Suharto warned officials to dismiss the topic of the succession and in September, when the Partai Demokrasi Indonesia (PDI—Indonesian Democratic Party) announced that it would support his candidacy, it appeared likely that he would seek election for a sixth term. In August 1990 a group of 58 prominent Indonesians issued a public demand to Suharto to retire from the presidency at the end of his current term of office and to permit greater democracy in Indonesia.

During 1991, in response to the growing demand for political *keterbukaan* (openness), several new organizations were formed to promote freedom of expression and other democratic values. As labour unrest grew, arrests and the alleged intimidation of political activists were instrumental in curbing expressions of dissent. In an attempt to control student unrest, political campaigns were banned on university campuses. In September Suharto removed several of the most outspoken members of Golkar from the list of candidates to contest the legislative elections, scheduled to take place on 9 June 1992.

The Government had, for some time, been seeking to win the support of the Muslim electorate in preparation for the presidential elections in 1993. In 1989 Suharto promoted legislation whereby decisions by Islamic courts no longer required confirmation by civil courts, and in December 1990 the President opened the symposium of the newly formed Association of Indonesian Muslim Intellectuals (ICMI), an organization which united a broad spectrum of Islamic interests. In 1991 Suharto made his first pilgrimage to Mecca, acceded to Islamic demands for certain educational reforms and supported the establishment of an Islamic bank. ABRI was opposed to the establishment of ICMI because it regarded the polarization of politics by religion as a threat to stability. During 1990 the nature of ABRI's dual function had been queried from within the armed forces, with some support evinced for a reduction of its political role. However, pressure from ABRI was widely believed to have led to Suharto's gestures towards democratization.

During the strictly monitored four-week campaign period leading to elections for the DPR, for local government bodies and for district councils, political parties were prohibited from addressing religious issues, the question of the dominant role of the ethnic Chinese community in the economy, or any subject that might present a threat to national unity. The opposition parties did, however, exploit the increasing public resentment about the rapidly expanding businesses of Suharto's children (some of whom had been awarded monopoly rights). The Forum for the Purification of People's Sovereignty (formed in 1991) urged the voters to boycott the elections, in an effort to elicit reforms from the Government.

On 9 June 1992 90.4% of the electorate participated in the election to the DPR, which resulted in a further victory for Golkar (although its share of the votes declined to 68%, compared with 73% in 1987). Golkar secured 282 of the 400 elective seats, while 62 seats were won by the PPP (a gain of one seat compared with 1987) and 56 seats (compared with 40) by the PDI, which had mobilized almost 3m. supporters at a rally in Jakarta in the week prior to the election.

In October 1992 Suharto accepted nominations by Golkar, the PPP, the PDI and ABRI for a sixth term of office as President. His victory in the presidential election, due to take place in March 1993, was thus assured. Attention then focused on the vice-presidency. Owing to the increasing public debate over ABRI's active involvement in political affairs and, in particular, concern over whether the appointment of 100 members of ABRI to the DPR remained justifiable, it was deemed important that ABRI consolidate its position through the election to the vice-presidency of its own principal candidate, Sutrisno. Suharto, however, was rumoured to support the prospective candidacy of the Minister of State for Research and Technology, Prof. Dr Ir Bucharuddin Jusuf (B. J.) Habibie, an influential Muslim leader and the then Chairman of ICMI. Other prominent contenders included Gen. Rudini (the Minister of Home Affairs) and Maj.-Gen. Wismoyo Arismunandar (the Commander of the Strategic Reserve Command—Kostrad—and Suharto's brother-in-law). In a manifestation of greater political openness, the merits of the prospective candidates were discussed in the local press. Sutrisno was subsequently endorsed as a vice-presidential candidate by the PDI, the PPP, ABRI and, finally, Golkar. At a meeting of the MPR on 10 and 11 March Suharto and Sutrisno were duly elected to the posts of President and Vice-President respectively.

Suharto's new 41-member Cabinet, which was announced in mid-March 1993, comprised 22 new appointees. ABRI representation was reduced from 11 to eight members, and the influential Rudini and Murdani were excluded. Those primarily responsible for the country's economic policy since 1988, Prof. Dr Johannes B. Sumarlin, Adrianus Mooy and Radius Prawiro (all western-educated Christians) were replaced, leaving only three Christians in the Cabinet; several members of ICMI were included in the new list, thus advancing the faction led by Habibie, who was unpopular with ABRI. Suharto announced that the new Government would pursue the aim of greater democracy and openness. In mid-1993 Suharto revoked a travel ban on all dissidents and established a National Council on Human Rights.

In October 1993 at the party Congress the Minister of Information, Harmoko, became the first civilian to be elected to the chairmanship of Golkar. In an unprecedented move, Suharto had openly endorsed Harmoko's candidacy; it was widely speculated that this was to prevent ABRI from supporting its own candidate and effectively denying the President a choice. Also at the Congress, Suharto's family entered active national politics; his son, Bambang Trihatmodjo, and daughter, Siti Hardijanti Rukmana (known as Mbak Tutut), who had both been appointed to the MPR in 1992, were elected to positions of responsibility within Golkar.

In July 1993 the incumbent Chairman of the PDI, Soerjadi, was re-elected to the post at a fractious party Congress. The Government invalidated the election of Soerjadi, who had incurred Suharto's displeasure by campaigning during the June 1992 elections for a limited presidential term of office, and appointed a 23-member 'caretaker board' pending new elections. An extraordinary Congress of the PDI ended inconclusively in early December owing to the unexpected candidacy for the chairmanship of Megawati Sukarnoputri, the daughter of former President Sukarno. Despite government pressure to elect Budi Hardjono, a senior party official, Megawati received overwhelming support from the participants of the Congress. The 'caretaker board' prevented a vote from taking place and the PDI delegates were dispersed at midnight as the government-issued licence to hold a congress expired. The Government then ordered the holding of a new PDI Congress, at which Megawati was elected Chairman.

In June 1993 the USA imposed a deadline of February 1994 for Indonesia to improve workers' rights or lose trade privileges under the Generalized System of Preferences. In an attempt to avoid sanctions, the Government adopted reforms to the only officially recognized trade union, the Serikat Pekerja Seluruh Indonesia (All Indonesia Workers' Union), introduced a substantial increase in the minimum wage and revoked the controversial 1986 Labour Law, which allowed the intervention of the armed forces in labour disputes. Workers subsequently went on strike, accusing employers of failing to pay the new minimum wage and demanding improved working conditions. In February 1994 the independent Serikat Buruh Sejahtera Indonesia (SBSI —Indonesian Prosperous Labour Union), which had had its application for registration formally rejected in June 1993, appealed for a one-hour national work stoppage. Two days prior to the strike the General Secretary of the SBSI, Muchtar Pakpahan, was arrested and charged with inciting hatred against the Government (he was released in the following month). In April 1994 riots broke out in Medan, Sumatra, over workers' demands for improved factory conditions and the implementation of the new minimum wage, and rapidly degenerated into attacks on Chinese property and business executives. The attacks on Chinese companies reflected a widely-held perception that the ethnic Chinese had benefited disproportionately from the country's rapid economic growth. Three members of the SBSI surrendered to the authorities in May and admitted to having organized the protest. Further strikes broke out later in the month in other parts of north Sumatra. In August Pakpahan was rearrested. He was given a three-year prison sentence in November for inciting labour unrest (which was later extended to four years). By that time, it was estimated that the majority of factories had complied with the provision of the new minimum wage.

In January 1995 it was announced by the armed forces that 300 members of the PDI were to be investigated for links to the 1965 coup attempt, following allegations that many members had relatives or contacts in the banned PKI. This apparent attempt to discredit the opposition grouping was followed in May by a ban on the presence of Megawati at the commemoration, in June, of the 25th anniversary of the death of her father, Sukarno, ostensibly because it might provoke outbreaks of violence.

Throughout 1995 the Indonesian authorities attempted to ascribe social unrest to communist subversion, asserting that a communist revival remained a threat to national security. In September the Chief of Staff of the Armed Forces named several prominent dissidents, including Muchtar Pakpahan (whose conviction for incitement had been overturned by the Supreme Court in that month), as members of 'formless organizations' which, he claimed, had infiltrated pressure groups to promote the resurgence of communism. In November 300 people were arrested in Java as subversives, who were allegedly using the tactics of the PKI.

In July 1995, in response to widespread condemnation of Indonesia's human rights violations, Suharto announced that three prisoners detained for their complicity in the 1965 coup attempt would be released to coincide with the 50th anniversary of independence in August. The administration also subsequently announced that the code ET (which stood for *Eks Tahanan Politik*—former political prisoner) was to be removed from identity papers following the anniversary. The measure affected about 1.3m. citizens, most of whom had been arrested following the 1965 coup attempt, but released without trial; ET status had subjected them to certain restrictions (for example, in employment) and to widespread discrimination. The Government also revoked legislation requiring a permit for political gatherings, although the security forces still had to be notified. This display of liberality was, however, tempered by a new campaign against press freedom and political dissent.

In October 1995 30 members of an extreme right-wing group, the Islamic State of Indonesia, were arrested in western Java for attempting to overthrow 'the unitary state of Indonesia'. There were fears that Suharto's apparent attempt to balance the influence of the armed forces with an emphasis on Islam would create religious disharmony. Critics blamed the ICMI-sponsored newspaper *Republika* and its magazine *Ummat* for fomenting religious passions, leading to outbreaks of violence. Social unrest was also caused, however, by a disparity in living standards; in January 1996 in Bandung, West Java, thousands took part in demonstrations against the disproportionately wealthy ethnic Chinese.

In December 1995 Suharto implemented an unprecedented mid-term cabinet reorganization, in which Prof. Dr Satrio Budiardjo Yudono was dismissed and the Ministry of Trade, over which he had presided, was merged with the Ministry of Industry. This dismissal of one of Habibie's protégés, the day before Habibie's re-election to the chairmanship of the increasingly powerful ICMI, was widely interpreted as a signal from Suharto for Habibie to restrain his political ambitions. The accusations of financial irregularities and nepotism levelled against the Minister of Communications, Haryanto Dhanutirto (also a close associate of Habibie), were similarly interpreted.

In early 1996 there were limited moves to create greater political freedom. In January the Government abolished permit requirements for political meetings (police permission was still necessary for public gatherings and demonstrations). In March a group of political activists established an Independent Election Monitoring Committee, which was immediately declared unconstitutional by the Government. In April the Government restored voting rights to 1,157,820 people who had been associated with the PKI, leaving a further 20,706 still ineligible to vote. The Government's increasing concern over potential opposition to Golkar in the 1997 elections, however, resulted in a return to more authoritarian practices. In May 1996 Sri Bintang Pamungkas, an outspoken member of the PPP expelled from the DPR in March 1995, received a custodial sentence of 34 months for insulting Suharto; he remained free, however, pending an appeal. In the same month Pamungkas formed a new political organization, the Partai Uni Demokrasi Indonesia (PUDI—United Democratic Party of Indonesia), which ABRI and the Government refused to recognize. In December the High Court upheld the verdict against Pamungkas, who subsequently appealed to the Supreme Court.

In June 1996 the Government responded to the increasing popularity of Megawati's leadership of the PDI, and consequent potential threat to Golkar: government supporters within the PDI organized a party congress in the northern Sumatran town of Medan, which removed Megawati as leader of the party, and installed a former Chairman, Soerjadi. PDI members loyal to Megawati (who contested the legitimacy of the congress) organized demonstrations in her support throughout the country during July, and occupied the PDI headquarters in Jakarta. At the end of July members of Soerjadi's PDI faction and the armed forces acted to remove Megawati and her supporters forcibly from the PDI headquarters, prompting mass rioting in Jakarta. Violent clashes ensued between protesters and the security forces, in which five people were killed. Following the riots, the Government declared the minor, Marxist-influenced Partai Rakyat Demokrasi (PRD) to be responsible for the disturbances, and renewed its campaign against communism, claiming that the PRD was the PKI's successor. In September the Government disbanded the PRD, declaring it to be a proscribed organization.

In an attempt to inhibit opposition efforts in the 1997 legislative elections, Suharto, in October 1996, ordered ABRI to suppress all political dissent. The Government's continued lack of commitment to its stated policy of political openness was demonstrated when, in November, it declared that it would take action against non-governmental organizations which violated Indonesian law and the *pancasila* ideology. In December the DPR ratified legislation granting the Government extensive powers to revoke the broadcasting permits of private television and radio stations. In the same month a government decree banned mass rallies during the 1997 election campaign. In February 1997 the Government announced that all election campaign speeches, including those broadcast on television and radio, were to be vetted to ensure their adherence to the *pancasila*.

Repressive measures against Megawati's faction of the PDI continued; in September 1996 the Government declared Megawati's new party headquarters in eastern Jakarta to be illegal and it was closed by the military. Candidates nominated by Megawati's faction for the 1997 parliamentary elections were omitted from the final list of candidates in January 1997. In April thousands of supporters of Megawati rallied outside the DPR to demand the right to contest the general election. In March Pamungkas was arrested for promoting a boycott of the legislative elections and two PUDI officials were also detained.

Prior to the general election, which was held on 29 May 1997, the Government permitted a campaign period of 25 days during which no two parties were permitted to campaign simultaneously in the same region. Despite this, there was extensive localized pre-election violence. In the worst incident 125 people were killed when a shopping centre was set alight during clashes between supporters of Golkar and the PPP in the provincial capital of Kalimantan, Banjarmasin; more than 150 others were killed in various other incidents across the country. Following the election, riots in Madura, as a result of PPP claims that ballots had not been counted, resulted in an unprecedented repeat of voting at 86 polling stations on 4 June. The final results of the election, which continued to attract allegations of fraud, revealed that Golkar had secured 74.3% of the vote (compared with 68.1% in 1992) giving it control of 325 seats, the PPP had won 89 seats, while Soerjadi's PDI had secured only 11 seats (compared with 56 in 1992).

Social unrest, which had been widespread in 1996, continued throughout 1997, as a result of religious tension, income disparity between social and ethnic groups and the repercussions of the transmigration programme initiated in 1971. The worst violence began in West Kalimantan in December 1996 as indigenous Dayak tribesmen massacred hundreds of Madurese transmigrants following an attack by Muslim youths on local schoolgirls. Despite a peace agreement in February 1997, fighting continued into March and thousands were displaced.

In August 1997 the two principal Muslim leaders, Abdurrahman Wahid and Amien Rais, the leader of the second largest Islamic grouping, Muhammadiyah, were excluded from the list of 500 civilian and military appointees to the MPR. Amien Rais had been forced to resign from a board of experts in ICMI in February for publicly criticizing the controversial Freeport mine in Irian Jaya (now Papua, see below).

Following a massive decline in the value of the Indonesian currency between August and October 1997, Suharto was forced to accept a rescue programme from the IMF to restore confidence in the country's economy. However, Suharto subsequently failed to implement reforms required by the IMF that he feared would provoke social and political unrest and adversely affect his family and friends, who had long benefited from control of lucrative monopolies and tariff protection of their businesses. In December widespread rumours of Suharto's ill health provoked a further crisis of confidence in the Indonesian economy. At the end of the month an unprecedented gathering of Muslim leaders and intellectuals took place, including members of ICMI; the participants rejected Suharto's leadership and rallied around Amien Rais, who had already offered himself as a presidential candidate. Wahid, although absent from the meeting, subsequently joined Amien Rais and Megawati (who had entered an informal alliance) in calling for Suharto's resignation. Megawati also, in a largely symbolic gesture since the President had to be a nominee of a party represented in the MPR, presented herself as a presidential candidate. In January 1998 Suharto delivered an unrealistic budget, which failed to comply with IMF stipulations. A further rapid decline of the currency and massive price increases of staple foodstuffs ensued, causing incidents of rioting. Following meetings with foreign leaders and IMF representatives, Suharto was forced to announce a second budget. Despite opposition to his candidacy, Suharto declared his acceptance of Golkar's nomination for the presidency (announced in October), thus assuring his victory in the forthcoming presidential election. He indicated that of the 13 contenders for the vice-presidency he would support Habibie's candidacy, despite the minister's unpopularity with ABRI

At the presidential election held on 10 March 1998 Suharto was re-elected unopposed. He then endorsed the nomination of Habibie as the new Vice-President, and on 14 March Suharto announced the appointment of a new, 36-member Cabinet, which included a number of members of his immediate circle of friends and family. (Prior to his re-election, Suharto had also appointed his son-in-law, Lt-Gen. Prabowo Subianto, as Commander of Kostrad.) Suharto's appointment of such a Cabinet defied the recommendations of the IMF. Student protests in support of calls for the President's resignation and for fundamental political and economic reforms increased, and on 5 May riots erupted in Jakarta, precipitated by the announcement of a 70% increase in the price of fuel. During the following days violence and unrest spread throughout the archipelago. On 12 May six students were shot dead by military snipers during a student protest at Trisakti University in Jakarta, and violence in the city reached a peak on 14 May. It was initially estimated that during 12–15 May 500 people were killed in the capital, while a further 700 perished elsewhere; however, a report published by Indonesia's leading human rights group in early June stated that at least 1,188 people had died in Jakarta alone. Thousands of buildings and vehicles were also destroyed, and a number of those who died were looters trapped inside burning buildings. Indonesia's ethnic-Chinese minority was the particular target for much of the violence that occurred in May: an uncertain number of Chinese were murdered, numerous Chinese women were raped, and Chinese homes and businesses were looted and burned. On 21 May, following sustained popular and political pressure to step down (including an unprecedented demand for his resignation by Harmoko on 18 May, and the resignation of the 14 economic ministers in the Cabinet), Suharto announced his resignation as President. Vice-President Habibie was sworn in immediately as Suharto's successor, and subsequently appointed a new 'reform Cabinet', which, however, included a number of ministers from the previous administration. The new President also announced the release of a number of political prisoners (including Muchtar Pakpahan and Sri Bintang Pamungkas), encouraged government departments to sever ties with enterprises owned by Suharto's family, and supported Gen. Wiranto in his dismissal of Suharto's son-in-law, Lt.-Gen. Prabowo, from his position in Kostrad (it was subsequently announced that Prabowo had been formally dismissed from the army following an investigation into his conduct as Commander of the unit, and was also to face a court martial). Habibie also announced that elections would be held in 1999; new political parties began to be formed in anticipation of fresh electoral laws. On 1 June 1998 an investigation into the assets of former President Suharto and other government officials was announced, and later the same month Habibie expelled 41 members of the MPR, including several close associates of Suharto, on account of alleged corruption, nepotism and collusion. (Seven members of Suharto's family were ousted from their seats in the MPR the following month.) Despite such moves, Habibie was considered by many to be under the control of Suharto, and there were repeated demands from student groups and other opposition organizations for Habibie to relinquish the presidency and for a transitional government to be installed.

Discontent and rioting continued across the archipelago throughout the latter half of 1998, fuelled by dissatisfaction at the pace of change under the new administration and by severe food shortages, as well as by increasing tension among different ethnic and religious groups. A four-day special session of the MPR was convened in Jakarta on 10 November, and on 13 November at least 16 people were killed and more than 400 injured when students and civilians clashed with soldiers outside the building where the MPR session was being held; the violence was the worst since the riots in May. Further riots occurred in Jakarta on 22 November, in which at least another 14 people died during clashes between Muslims and Catholics; churches and Christian schools were also attacked.

In November 1998 a report was published containing the findings of a panel appointed by the Government to investigate the riots in May. The panel found that elements of the military had acted as provocateurs during the riots (with particular suspicion falling on a unit led by Lt-Gen. Prabowo), concluding that the riots had been 'created as part of a political struggle at the level of the élite', and recommended that further investigations be carried out into the causes of the violent unrest. In December former President Suharto faced questioning at the Higher Prosecutor's Office over allegations of corruption; two former cabinet ministers, including Suharto's close associate, Mohammad (Bob) Hasan, were also summoned for questioning.

In December 1998 it was announced that a legislative election would be held on 7 June 1999; it was further announced that the MPR (including 200 additional delegates) would convene on 29 August to elect a new President. In early December 1998 a large demonstration was held in Jakarta by supporters of Megawati. In January 1999 a number of changes to the electoral laws were announced in advance of the forthcoming election: in accordance with a new electoral system combining both district and proportional voting, seats in the DPR were to be allocated proportionally, but only parties fielding candidates in a substantial number of districts would be permitted to contest the election. It was further announced that civil servants were no longer to be obliged to support Golkar, that the number of seats in the DPR allocated to the military was to be reduced from 75 to 38 and that the membership of the MPR was to be reduced from 1,000 to 700 (500 of whom would comprise the members of the DPR while, of the remainder, 135 were to be elected by the provincial assemblies and 65 appointed by the Komite Pemilihan Umum—General Election Committee).

Violent unrest continued across the archipelago throughout January and February 1999: at least 159 people were killed during clashes between Muslims and Christians on the island of Ambon, in the province of Maluku, while a number of others died in outbreaks of violence elsewhere. Although the campaigning for the forthcoming legislative election dominated the political agenda during the first half of 1999, the Habibie Government continued to pursue an extensive programme of reform during this period. Amongst new laws passed were several that benefited the provinces, including one providing for the election of district heads (*bupati*) by the district assemblies. In April the Subversion Law, introduced under the Suharto administration in 1963 and previously applied in the suppression of political dissidents, was repealed by the MPR (although some of the prohibitions covered by the law were retained). In May a presidential decree was announced in which Habibie removed a ban on the use and teaching of the Mandarin Chinese language and also outlawed discrimination on the grounds of ethnic origin. Two significant changes also took place in the armed forces in the first half of 1999: following a reshuffle of military personnel in January, in April the police force—part of the Indonesian military since 1962—was formally separated from the armed forces (although it remained under the control of the Ministry of Defence); and the armed forces resumed their revolutionary-era name, Tentara Nasional Indonesia (TNI—the Indonesian National Defence Forces), in place of the Suharto-era name, ABRI (the Armed Forces of the Republic of Indonesia). The Government remained under considerable public pressure, however, to investigate the accumulation of wealth by the Suharto family. Concerns also remained that the former President continued to exercise undue political influence.

President Habibie was nominated as the sole presidential candidate of the Golkar party on 14 May 1999, despite concerns expressed by some elements of the party regarding Habibie's close association with former President Suharto. On 18 May the three leading opposition parties—Megawati's Partai Demokrasi Indonesia Perjuangan (PDI—P, Indonesian Democratic Struggle Party), Abdurrahman Wahid's Partai Kebangkitan Bangsa (PKB, National Awakening Party), and Amien Rais's Partai Amanat Nasional (PAN, National Mandate Party)—agreed to form an informal electoral alliance against Golkar; however, the alliance exhibited instability from an early stage. The election campaign was formally opened on 19 May, and proceeded with only minimal incidents of violent disruption, with 48 parties competing for a share of the vote. The election was held as scheduled on 7 June; approximately 118m. people voted (a turn-out of 91%). As expected, Megawati's PDI—P led the polls, winning 34% of the votes cast (154 seats); the second largest share of the vote was unexpectedly won by Golkar, which secured 20% of votes cast (120 seats), performing poorly in the cities but achieving a strong result in the outer islands. Abdurrahman Wahid's PKB secured 59 seats, while Amien Rais's PAN won just 7% of the vote (35 seats). Some 14 other smaller parties also won seats in the MPR, with a combined share of the vote totalling about 7%. Despite allegations of irregularities in the election process, the results were finally endorsed by President Habibie on 3 August. In the context of the election results, Megawati and Habibie emerged initially as the main candidates for the presidency, which was originally scheduled to be decided in November. On 20 October, however, following the rejection of his presidential record by the MPR in a secret ballot, Habibie withdrew his candidacy just hours before the rescheduled vote was due to be held. Expectations that Megawati would be elected President increased immediately; however, Megawati failed to win the contest, receiving 313 votes compared with the 373 secured by Abdurrahman Wahid, the only other serious candidate, who had received the endorsement of a number of Islamic parties as well as the support of the Golkar party, following the withdrawal of Habibie. The announcement of Wahid's victory provoked outrage among Megawati's supporters, and violent protests ensued in Jakarta and elsewhere on Java, as well as on the island of Bali. On 21 October the MPR voted to appoint Megawati as Vice-President. The new Cabinet was announced on 26 October, and reflected the conciliatory and inclusive approach of the new President: it included both Islamist and nationalist representatives, as well as representatives of non-Javanese groups (reportedly including Acehnese, Bugis, Irianese (Papuan), Batak, Sumatran and Balinese minorities), and an ethnic Chinese was appointed as chief economic minister. Gen. Wiranto, who was appointed Co-ordinating Minister for Political Affairs and Security, was replaced as Minister of Defence by the former Minister of Education and Culture, Yuwono Sudarsono, the first civilian to hold the post. Wiranto was replaced as Commander-in-Chief of the TNI by Adm. Widodo Adi Sutjipto.

In October 1999 the newly appointed Attorney-General, Marzuki Darusman, announced that the investigation into the allegations of corruption made against former President Suharto—which had been closed under the Habibie Government on the alleged grounds of lack of evidence—was to be reopened. The apparent commitment of the new administration to addressing the issue of corruption was further emphasized in November, when Wahid urged the investigation of three government ministers. One of the ministers reportedly implicated, the Co-ordinating Minister for People's Welfare and the Eradication of Poverty and leader of the PPP, Hamzah Haz, resigned from the Cabinet in late November.

In the months following Wahid's election to the presidency, further violent unrest took place across the archipelago. Particularly serious ethnic violence continued on the island of Ambon in Maluku province where, according to official estimates in December 1999, more than 750 people had died and many thousands more had fled the region, since the renewal of violent clashes between Muslims and Christians in the region in January of that year. (Aid agencies, however, estimated the total number of dead to be much higher.) In mid-December President Wahid and Vice-President Megawati (who was subject to harsh criticism for her failure to address the crisis, despite having been charged by Wahid with special responsibility for Maluku) visited the region and urged an end to the conflict. Later the same month hundreds more troops were sent to Ambon to supplement the 2,500 already deployed in Maluku, following a further escalation of the violence and the occurrence of dozens more deaths. Although the predominantly Muslim northern districts of Maluku were formally separated as the new province of North Maluku in late 1999, this failed to dispel the tension, and in December violence flared on other islands in the region, with at least 265 people reported killed in clashes between Christians and Muslims on the island of Halmahera at the end of the month.

On 31 January 2000 Indonesia's National Human Rights Commission released a report containing the results of its investigation into the role of the Indonesian armed forces in human rights abuses in the former Indonesian province of Timor-Leste (see below). Thirty-three military officers, including the former Commander-in-Chief of the armed forces, Gen. Wiranto, were implicated. In response to the Commission's conclusions, President Wahid demanded Wiranto's resignation from his post of Co-ordinating Minister for Political Affairs and Security; Wiranto, however, openly defied Wahid's demands. In mid-February Wahid suspended Wiranto from his position; Wiranto was to maintain his ministerial rank, although his portfolio was allocated to the Minister of Home Affairs, Gen. (retd) Suryadi Sudirja, pending further investigation. Wiranto resigned in mid-May. In January, meanwhile, a reorganization took place within the TNI, in which officers loyal to Wiranto

were apparently removed from positions of influence. A second reorganization of senior military personnel was announced in February, in which Maj.-Gen. Agus Wirahadikusumah, who was reportedly committed to Wahid's policy of disengaging the military from Indonesian politics, was appointed as the head of Kostrad. In August doubts concerning the commitment of the Indonesian Government to the trial of military personnel suspected of involvement in gross human rights violations in Timor-Leste were provoked when the MPR introduced a constitutional amendment that excluded military personnel from prosecution for crimes committed prior to the enactment of the relevant legislation. Many international observers feared that this would seriously threaten the possibility of the prosecution of members of the Indonesian military believed responsible for recent human rights abuses in the territory. These doubts were compounded in early September, when Gen. Wiranto's name was not included on a list, announced by the Attorney-General's office, of 19 suspects.

In late April 2000 President Wahid dismissed from the Cabinet the Minister of State for Investment and Development of State Enterprises, Laksamana Sukardi of the PDI—P, and the Minister of Trade and Industry, Yusuf Kalla of the pro-Habibie wing of Golkar; Wahid subsequently suggested that both Ministers were guilty of corruption. In July Wahid faced fierce criticism from the DPR when he refused to explain the reasons for his dismissal of the two Ministers. Meanwhile, general misgivings about Wahid's style of government also increased during 2000. In August Wahid announced that he was to delegate the daily administration of the Government to Vice-President Megawati, although the President was to retain overall control. It was speculated by many observers that Wahid's announcement had been intended to safeguard his own position during the 12-day session of the MPR held on 7–18 August, in the context of widespread dissatisfaction with the President's record among the members of the legislative body. The announcement of the apparent power-sharing arrangement appeared to placate the MPR Amendments to the Constitution passed by the MPR in August, however, included articles defining explicitly the authority of the DPR, particularly in relation to the body's questioning and investigating of government activities; legislation was also passed to extend military representation in the MPR until 2009, four years after the date at which the military had been scheduled to lose its remaining 38 seats in the chamber. On 23 August President Wahid announced the formation of a new 26-member Cabinet. The incoming Cabinet included considerably fewer representatives of Megawati's PDI—P, reportedly resulting in serious tensions between the President and the Vice-President. Two of the most influential cabinet posts were allocated to Wahid loyalists: Susilo Bambang Yudhoyono was appointed Co-ordinating Minister for Political Affairs, Security and Social Welfare, while Rizal Ramli was designated Co-ordinating Minister for the Economy, Finance and Industry, replacing Kwik Kian Gie, who had resigned in advance of the reorganization.

In August 2000 former President Suharto was formally charged with corruption arising from his 30 years in power; however, in late September all corruption charges against him were dismissed after an independent team of doctors declared that the former President was mentally and physically unfit to stand trial, thereby provoking violent protests on the streets of Jakarta. (In December 2001, after some vacillation, the Supreme Court stated that it would not pursue the charges, owing to the former President's continued ill health. However, the Government's plans formally to abandon the case against him met with mounting criticism from early 2002.) In mid-September 2000, meanwhile, President Wahid announced that he had ordered the arrest of Suharto's youngest son, Hutomo Mandala Putra, in connection with a series of bomb threats and explosions in Jakarta in August and September in which supporters of Suharto and his family were suspected of involvement. In one attack in mid-September at least 15 people were killed when a bomb exploded at the Jakarta Stock Exchange. In late September Hutomo Mandala Putra was sentenced to 18 months' imprisonment after being convicted on an unrelated charge of fraudulent activity; however, he subsequently evaded arrest and went into hiding.

In July 2001 Justice Syafiuddin Kartasasmita, the judge who had upheld the sentence passed on Hutomo Mandala Putra, was shot by unidentified killers. In August two suspects confessed to the murder, but admitted in custody that Suharto's son had financed them and supplied the weapons used in the attack.

Meanwhile, two men were convicted of the bombing of the Jakarta Stock Exchange and sentenced to 20 years' imprisonment each. In October the corruption charge on which Hutomo Mandala Putra had initially been convicted was rejected by the Supreme Court. However, he remained in hiding owing to his suspected involvement in several other cases. In late November police finally arrested the fugitive, and in December the Supreme Court announced that Hutomo Mandala Putra would serve at least 11 months in prison for evading arrest, despite the fact that his original conviction had been overturned. During police questioning Suharto's son claimed that in October 2000 he had given a sum of money to two men close to President Wahid on the understanding that this would secure for him a presidential pardon. (Wahid denied all knowledge of this when questioned early in 2002.) In March 2002, following the conclusion of the police investigation, Hutomo Mandala Putra was charged with murder, illegal possession of weapons and fleeing from justice; his trial began in the same month. In May one of his lawyers was detained by police owing to allegations that witnesses had been bribed to lie during the trial. Meanwhile, the two men reported to have assassinated Justice Syafiuddin were found guilty of murder and sentenced to life imprisonment. A third man was sentenced to a four-year prison term in a separate trial for his involvement in planning the assassination. In July Hutomo Mandala Putra was found guilty of murder and sentenced to a 15-year prison term; he later announced that he did not intend to appeal against the verdict.

In September 2000 the DPR appointed a committee to investigate two financial scandals with which President Wahid had been linked. The first of the two scandals involved the irregular diversion of US $4.1m. from the funds of the Badan Urusan Logistic (BULOG—the National Logistics Agency), whilst the second concerned a donation of $2m. made by Sultan Hassanal Bolkiah of Brunei. Although, initially, there appeared to be no compelling evidence implicating Wahid in these scandals, the President's refusal to be questioned on either matter provoked intense frustration among legislators. The commission reported the findings of its investigation into President Wahid's involvement in late January 2001, concluding that Wahid 'could be suspected of playing a role' in the theft of BULOG funds by his personal masseur and that the President had been deliberately inconsistent in his explanations of how the donation from Sultan Hassanal Bolkiah (originally intended for social welfare) had been spent; however, the commission failed to present conclusive evidence that Wahid had personally benefited from either situation. Following the presentation of the committee's report, thousands of protesters demanding the resignation of the President clashed with police in violent demonstrations in Jakarta. In early February the DPR voted by 393 votes to four for the formal censure of Wahid over his alleged involvement in the scandals. According to Indonesian law, Wahid was given three months to respond to the motion of censure and to explain his actions to the DPR. If, three months after the original memorandum of censure, the members of the DPR should remain unsatisfied by the President's response, a further warning could be issued after which Wahid would be given 30 days to act before a vote could be held to remove him from office. Following the issue of the original memorandum of censure, however, the President continued to deny any wrongdoing, and dismissed the course of action taken by the DPR as being based on an interpretation of events rather than on the facts of the case. He also stated his intention to complete his term of presidential office. Tens of thousands of pro-Wahid demonstrators took to the streets in Surabaya and elsewhere in East Java (President Wahid's home province), and protesters set fire to the regional offices of Golkar, which had supported the vote to censure Wahid. Later in the same month Wahid offered himself for questioning by police investigating the two scandals.

In March 2001 more than 12,000 students held a demonstration in Jakarta to demand the President's resignation. In view of Wahid's unsatisfactory reply to his first censure, on 30 April the DPR voted overwhelmingly to issue a second censure and requested that the MPR convene a special session to begin impeachment proceedings. In May the Attorney-General commented that there was no evidence of the President's involvement in the corruption scandals over which he was being accused. Violent pro-Wahid demonstrations took place in East Java. However, on 30 May the DPR voted by a huge majority to instruct the MPR to begin an impeachment hearing on 1 August. In response, on 1 June the President reorganized his Cabinet, dismissing the Co-ordinating Minister for Political Affairs,

Security and Social Welfare, Susilo Bambang Yudhoyono. The Chief of Police, Gen. Surojo Bimantoro, was suspended after efforts to dismiss him were thwarted. A few days later the President initiated a further reallocation of ministerial portfolios, leading to the replacement of the Minister of Finance and State Enterprises Development, Prijadi Prapto Subardjo. On 9 July the President threatened to declare a state of emergency on 20 July if no compromise had been reached. The next day he reshuffled the Cabinet again and on 20 July he appointed a new Chief of Police without the support of the legislature and moved the deadline for the termination of impeachment efforts to 31 July. A special session of the MPR was convened the next day to which the President was summoned to give an account of his 21 months in power. President Wahid declared the session illegal and refused to attend. The next day he suspended the legislature, declaring a state of civil emergency, and urged that new elections be held in one year's time. However, the military refused to support the declaration, and the MPR declared that the President did not have the constitutional authority to dissolve it.

On 23 July 2001 President Abdurrahman Wahid was deposed as President following an immediate impeachment hearing. He was replaced by Vice-President Megawati Sukarnoputri, in a peaceful transition of power. On 26 July legislators elected the leader of the PPP, Hamzah Haz, to act as President Megawati's deputy. On 9 August the new President announced the composition of her first Cabinet. Of its 32 members, only four were ex-military men, in sharp contrast to previous practice. Most of the principal posts went to non-political professionals, including the appointment of Dorodjatun Kuntjoro-Jakti as Co-ordinating Minister for the Economy, Finance and Industry. Susilo Bambang Yudhoyono was reinstated as Co-ordinating Minister for Political Affairs, Security and Social Welfare.

In October 2001 President Megawati gave her assent to a prosecution request to question the Speaker of the DPR, Akbar Tandjung, over the alleged misappropriation of an estimated US $4m. of BULOG funds to finance the Golkar party election campaign in 1999. When questioned, Tandjung admitted that he had handled the money on the orders of then-President Habibie, but had passed it on to an Islamic charity to fund food supplies for the poor. However, Attorney-General Muhammad Abdul Rachman claimed that investigations showed that such contributions had never taken place. In December 2001 state prosecutors questioned former President Habibie in connection with the scandal, and in January 2002 Akbar Tandjung was formally declared to be a suspect, prompting fears of another political crisis. In March 2002 approximately 1,500 protesters gathered outside the DPR building to demand Tandjung's resignation and the establishment of an independent inquiry into the allegations that had been made against him; his trial on charges of corruption began one week later. In June Tandjung took the stand for the first time during his trial and denied any wrongdoing. However, in September he was convicted of the charges against him and sentenced to a three-year prison term; despite the failure of his first appeal, in early 2003 he remained at liberty and retained his post as Speaker pending a further appeal to the Supreme Court. Meanwhile, in March 2002 the Governor of Bank Indonesia, Dr Syahril Sabirin, was sentenced to three years in prison following his conviction for the theft of bank funds to finance the election campaign of former President Habibie. In August, however, his conviction was overturned by a court of appeal.

In August 2002 a series of constitutional amendments was passed following the annual session of the MPR. These provided for the direct election of both the President and Vice-President at the next national poll, scheduled to be held in 2004, and for the abolition of all seats held by non-elected representatives, effectively terminating military involvement in the legislature five years earlier than originally intended. The legislation also provided for a bicameral legislature through the creation of the Dewan Perwakilan Daerah (DPD—House of Representatives of the Regions) which, together with the DPR, would form the MPR. A total of 14 amendments received legislative assent; these constituted the 'Fourth Amendment' to the Constitution. However, a proposal for the introduction of Islamic *shari'a* law, endorsed by Vice-President Hamzah Haz and the PPP, was rejected.

In 2002 one of the most serious challenges facing the Indonesian Government was the alleged threat posed by terrorist activity, at both a domestic and regional level. In October the Government's response to this threat came under particularly close scrutiny when two bombs exploded in the tourist resort of Kuta, on the island of Bali. One of these explosions, which occurred outside a night-club, resulted in the deaths of more than 200 people, many of whom were tourists, mainly Australians. In its first admission that Islamist fundamentalists were operative within Indonesia, the Government initially attributed the attack to the international terrorist network al-Qa'ida, which it believed to have been working in collaboration with local terrorists. The DPR authorized two emergency decrees, bringing into effect several previously delayed anti-terrorism measures, including a law permitting suspects to be detained for up to seven days without charge. Two weeks after the bombings the Muslim cleric Abu Bakar Bashir, commander of the Majelis Mujahidin Indonesia (MMI—Indonesian Mujahideen Council) and alleged to be the spiritual head of the regional Islamist terrorist organization Jemaah Islamiah, was detained for questioning in relation to the attacks. (He had been questioned by police in January of that year over alleged links to al-Qa'ida but had been released without charge.) In the mean time the USA and the UN announced that they had designated Jemaah Islamiah a terrorist entity and 'frozen' its financial assets. The police made several further arrests as the investigation into the bombings proceeded and in November one of the suspects, known as Amrozi, confessed to his involvement and to having strong links to Jemaah Islamiah, as well as implicating several others in the attack. Later in the same month Imam Samudra was arrested on suspicion of having organized the attacks. He confessed to being a member of Jemaah Islamiah and to having planned earlier attacks, including the bombing of churches across the archipelago in December 2000 (see below), together with the operational leader of the organization, Riduan Isamuddin, also known as Hambali. In December Ali Gufron, also known as Mukhlas, who apparently had succeeded Hambali as operational leader, was also arrested and confessed to having helped to plan the Bali attack. The total number of suspects detained in connection with the bombings in Bali had reached an estimated 30 by the end of January 2003. The trials of those involved began in May. Meanwhile, Abu Bakar Bashir was charged with treason and involvement in several bombings carried out on churches in late 2000 (see below).

In January 2003 rises in fuel and electricity tariffs precipitated widespread protests across the archipelago, many of which had to be dispersed by police. The price rises were imposed as part of a series of economic reforms which had recently received IMF approval. In response to the continuing protests, the Government was forced to postpone increases in telephone tariffs and, shortly afterwards, reversed some fuel price rises.

One of the principal challenges facing the Wahid and Sukarnoputri Governments from 2000 was the escalation of communal violence across the archipelago, together with separatist tensions in individual regions such as Aceh and Papua (known as Irian Jaya until January 2002—see below). In 2000 some of the worst such violence again occurred in the provinces of Maluku and North Maluku, arising from an ongoing conflict between the region's Christian and Muslim populations. By mid-2000 more than 4,000 people were reported to have been killed and some 300,000 displaced. In June President Wahid declared a state of civil emergency in the provinces of Maluku and North Maluku. Later the same month, it was announced that around 1,400 of the 10,200 members of the armed forces in the region were to be replaced because they had become involved in the conflict, and in the case of at least one outbreak of serious violence it was reported that evidence had emerged of the military's collusion with elements of the militant Muslim paramilitary organization, Laskar Jihad, which had travelled to the region to participate in the campaign of violence, thus supporting the view of many observers that the Indonesian military was allowing Muslim attacks on Christians to take place. In December 18 people were reported to have been killed and more than 80 others injured in a series of bombings of Christian churches in nine towns and cities across Indonesia, including Jakarta, on Christmas Eve. No group claimed responsibility for the explosions, which were condemned by President Wahid. (In June 2002 an Iraqi citizen, Omar al-Faruq, who claimed to be the South-East Asian representative of the international terrorist network al-Qa'ida, was arrested and allegedly confessed to having participated in carrying out the bombings. Following the bombings in Bali, a senior operative of Jemaah Islamiah also confessed to involvement in the attacks.) In February 2001 violence also broke out in the province of Central Kalimantan,

where fierce resentment of Madurese transmigrants remained rife among the indigenous Dayak tribespeople. At least 428 Madurese were murdered by native Dayaks, and many of the victims were beheaded in accordance with traditional Dayak practices; many thousands more fled their homes. The failure of the armed forces to control the violence—the legacy of a resettlement programme begun under the Suharto Government in the 1970s—and to protect Madurese refugees in their care led to further allegations of the military's complicity in ethnic violence. In December 2001 the deaths of an estimated seven people, following an explosion on a boat carrying mainly Christian passengers, precipitated riots by Christian protesters in the city of Ambon in Maluku. The Christian community blamed Muslim extremists for the attack. Later in the same month gunmen killed nine Christians and wounded two others travelling on a ferry, as the disturbances continued.

In February 2002, following negotiations between the warring Muslim and Christian factions in Maluku and North Maluku, a peace treaty—the 'Malino II Agreement'—was signed in an attempt to bring an end to the violence endemic in the region. The agreement urged the expulsion of external groups such as Laskar Jihad from the area; it was criticized by at least one militant group, which claimed that the delegates sent to negotiate terms did not adequately represent its views. Shortly after the treaty was signed a series of bombs exploded in the city of Ambon; the Government condemned the attacks but insisted that they did not signify the failure of the peace agreement. In early April a further bombing took place in Ambon and the residence of the Governor was set alight. Another outbreak of violence occurred in the same month, following which Alex Manuputty, the leader of the Christian separatist organization the Maluku Sovereignty Front, was arrested and charged with treason for planning to raise a flag to commemorate the 52nd anniversary of the proclamation of the South Maluku Republic. On 25 April the Maluku Sovereignty Front raised flags in Ambon in remembrance of the anniversary, provoking Muslims in the area and prompting the leader of Laskar Jihad, Ja'far Umar Thalib, to urge all Muslims in the region to renew their war against the Christian community. Shortly afterwards violence broke out again in Ambon, resulting in the deaths of 14 Christians. In May Ja'far Umar Thalib was arrested for allegedly inciting the violence that led to the massacre of the Christians. Thalib was visited by the Vice-President, Hamzah Haz, during his detention, prompting widespread criticism and allegations that the Vice-President was attempting to win the political support of militant Muslims. In the same month the Co-ordinating Minister for Political Affairs, Security and Social Welfare, Susilo Bambang Yudhoyono, announced that the Government intended to expel many armed Muslim militants from Maluku and North Maluku and bring about the dissolution of the Maluku Sovereignty Front. In July 2002 two explosions in a Christian area of Ambon injured more than 50 people. In August the trial of Alex Manuputty and another Christian leader, Samuel Waileruny, for subversion began; meanwhile, Laskar Jihad leader Ja'far Umar Thalib also went on trial on charges of inciting hatred and rebellion and of defaming the President and Vice-President. In the following month an explosion at a sports stadium in Ambon resulted in the deaths of four people; furthermore, three Muslim women were killed on the island of Saparua, Maluku, and a van containing Christians was burnt by a Muslim mob. In October, following the bombings suspected to have been carried out by the Islamist separatist organization Jemaah Islamiah on the island of Bali, Laskar Jihad disbanded and left the region; Ja'far Umar Thalib claimed that the decision had been taken owing to the group's increasing political involvement and denied that it had any connection to events in Bali. In the same month 14 members of the Maluku Sovereignty Front were sentenced to terms of imprisonment for raising separatist flags in the province in April. In late January 2003 Alex Manuputty and Samuel Waileruny were found guilty of subversion and sentenced *in absentia* to three-year prison terms. Ja'far Umar Thalib was, however, acquitted of the charges against him.

In late 2001 violence also broke out in the province of Sulawesi, where ongoing religious tensions had caused approximately 1,000 deaths in the previous two years. In the first week of December at least seven people were killed and thousands left homeless following clashes between armed Muslim groups and Christians. The violence was believed to have been precipitated by the recent arrival of members of Laskar Jihad on the island. More than 2,000 police and troop reinforcements were sent to the area in an attempt to bring the situation under control, and the Chief Minister for Political Affairs, Security and Social Welfare also visited the region. The head of the National Intelligence Agency, Lt-Gen. Hendropriyono, stated that members of al-Qa'ida, the international terrorist network led by Osama bin Laden, had also been involved in the fighting. The statement was made in response to Western pressure on the Government to act against groups with links to al-Qa'ida following the terrorist attacks on the USA in September 2001. In late December, following two days of talks, a peace deal was concluded between the parties involved which, it was hoped, would bring an end to the fighting. However, explosions at four churches in the provincial capital, Palu, during New Year celebrations, highlighted the continuing political instability in the province. Sporadic violence continued to occur in Sulawesi throughout 2002. In June a bomb exploded on a passenger bus travelling towards Poso, Central Sulawesi, killing four people in the worst outbreak of violence to have occurred in the region since the signing of the peace agreement in the previous year. In December the Government announced that it intended to maintain the existing level of troops in the area, determined for one year under the terms of the peace agreement, for a further six months. In the same month two bombs exploded in Makassar, the capital of South Sulawesi, resulting in the deaths of three people.

On 1 January 2001 new legislation took effect devolving increased financial and administrative control to Indonesia's regional governments. (The central Government was, meanwhile, to retain control over justice, defence, foreign affairs and monetary policy.) The day after the introduction of the new legislation, the Minister of State for State Administrative Reforms, Ryaas Rasyid, resigned from his post, reportedly because of his frustration at the inadequacy of the Government's preparations for the implementation of the new decentralization policy, which was intended to defuse separatist tensions across the archipelago; he was later replaced by Feisal Tamin.

During 1974, meanwhile, several parties emerged within the small Portuguese colony of East Timor (which changed its name to Timor-Leste following its accession to independence on 20 May 2002), with aims ranging from full independence to integration with Indonesia or Australia. Indonesia, which had never presented a claim to East Timor, initially showed little interest in the territory. In 1975 Portuguese forces withdrew from the colony, and the territory's capital, Dili, was occupied by the forces of the left-wing Frente Revolucionária do Timor Leste Independente (Fretilin), which advocated independence for East Timor. To prevent Fretilin from gaining full control of the territory, Indonesian troops intervened and established a provincial government. (In December 2001 the declassification of US state papers relating to the Indonesian occupation revealed that the US Government had endorsed the invasion in the belief that it would curb the spread of communism in the region.) In July 1976 East Timor was declared the 27th province of Indonesia. Human rights organizations subsequently claimed that as many as 200,000 people, from a total population of 650,000, might have been killed by the Indonesian armed forces during the annexation. The Indonesian Government, however, ignored widespread international condemnation of the invasion. The UN meanwhile continued officially to recognize Portugal as the administrative power in East Timor. In February 1983 the UN Commission on Human Rights adopted a resolution affirming East Timor's right to independence and self-determination. In November 1990 the Indonesian Government rejected proposals by the military commander of Fretilin, José Alexandre (Xanana) Gusmão, for unconditional peace negotiations aimed at ending the armed struggle in East Timor. In August 1992 the UN General Assembly adopted its first resolution condemning Indonesia's violations of human rights in East Timor.

The downfall of President Suharto in May 1998 and the subsequent accession to the presidency of Habibie raised hopes, both internationally and within East Timor itself, that independence for the territory might be granted in the near future. In August it was announced that Indonesia and Portugal had agreed to hold discussions on the possibility of 'wide-ranging' autonomy for East Timor. In January 1999, however, the Indonesian Government unexpectedly announced that, if the East Timorese were to vote to reject Indonesia's proposals for autonomy, it would consider granting independence to the province. Although the Government was initially opposed to a referendum on the issue of independence for East Timor, it signed an agreement with Portugal on 5 May, giving its assent to a process

of 'popular consultation' to take the form of a UN-supervised poll to determine the territory's future status. The referendum proceeded on 30 August, and resulted in an overwhelming rejection by 78.5% of voters of the Indonesian Government's proposals for autonomy and in an endorsement of independence for East Timor. Following the announcement of the result of the referendum, which led to a rapid deterioration in the security situation in East Timor, in late September Indonesia and Portugal reiterated their agreement for the transfer of authority in East Timor to the UN. Also in late September the Indonesian armed forces formally relinquished responsibility for security in the territory to the UN peace-keeping force, the International Force for East Timor (Interfet); the last Indonesian troops left East Timor in late October. On 19 October the result of the referendum was ratified by the Indonesian MPR, thus permitting East Timor's accession to independence to proceed. (See the chapter on Timor-Leste.) In September 2000 Indonesia faced outrage from the UN and the international community following the murder of three UN aid workers by pro-Jakarta militias in West Timor. The Indonesian Government came under strong criticism for its failure to control the militia groups, which were believed by many to be receiving the support of the Indonesian military. Indonesia subsequently refused to co-operate with a planned UN investigation into the killings.

In September 2001 Câncio Lopes de Carvalho, one of the leaders of the militias created to disrupt East Timor's referendum on independence two years previously, stated that he was ready to name those responsible for the violence. In October Gen. Johny Lumintang was found guilty of involvement in human rights abuses in the area in a civil action brought in a US federal court and ordered to pay compensation to six East Timorese. In December 2001 10 members of a pro-Indonesia militia became the first individuals to be convicted of crimes against humanity in connection with the violence that had surrounded East Timor's vote for independence in 1999. However, the Indonesian Government continued to obstruct efforts to bring all those culpable to justice, blocking attempts to extradite an 11th man, a special forces officer, to face trial.

In January 2002, after some delay and in response to increasing criticism from the UN and much of Europe, the Government established a special court in Jakarta to try those suspected of contravening human rights, in East Timor and elsewhere. In February 17 pro-Jakarta militiamen and Indonesian soldiers were indicted by international prosecutors for alleged crimes against humanity in East Timor in 1999. Seven people, including the former Governor of East Timor, Abílio Soares, the chief of police, Brig.-Gen. Timbul Silaen, and the former district head, Herman Sedyono, were formally charged with crimes against humanity. Their cases were the first to be submitted to the newly established human rights tribunal in Jakarta; the trials began in March. In April former chief of the armed forces Gen. Wiranto, who had evaded prosecution, testified at the trial of Brig.-Gen. Timbul Silaen, alleging that the Indonesian armed forces had been assigned a 'mission impossible' in East Timor. In June the trial of militia leader Eurico Guterres, head of the youth wing of President Megawati's PDI—P, began in Jakarta. In August Abílio Soares was found guilty of two charges of 'gross rights violations' for his failure to prevent violence involving those subordinate to him and sentenced to a three-year prison term. The next day the human rights tribunal acquitted Brig.-Gen. Timbul Silaen of charges of failing to control his subordinates; five other police and army officers were also found not guilty. The verdicts provoked widespread international condemnation and led to calls for the UN to establish an international tribunal on Timor-Leste. In November 2002 the tribunal found Eurico Guterres guilty of crimes against humanity; he received a 10-year prison sentence. However, a further four defendants were acquitted by the tribunal, prompting renewed criticism from human rights activists and legal experts, who claimed that the court was deliberately sparing Indonesian police and military officers; both those convicted thus far were ethnic East Timorese civilians. In late December Lt-Col Soejarwo, Indonesia's military commander in Dili in 1999, became the first Indonesian officer to be found guilty of the charges against him; he was sentenced to a five-year prison term. However, international criticism was reinforced when another Indonesian army officer was acquitted of the charges against him in the same month. In February 2003 the UN indicted Gen. Wiranto, Abílio Soares and six other Indonesian generals for crimes committed in East Timor; the

Indonesian Government continued to refuse to hand over any of those indicted for trial.

In the mid-1970s dissent re-emerged in Aceh, which, at the end of the war of independence, had held the status of a full province of the Republic of Indonesia but which had subsequently had this status removed before being made a special territory (Daerah Istimewa) with considerable autonomy in religious and educational affairs. The dissent was provoked by the exploitation by the central Government of Aceh's natural resources and the subsequent lack of benefits from these operations received by the region itself. A sense of the erosion of Aceh's autonomy was heightened by the migration and transmigration of other Indonesians into the region and by the increasing power of the central Government, and in 1976 the Gerakan Aceh Merdeka (GAM—Free Aceh Movement) was formed by Hasan di Tiro, who declared independence in 1977. This small rebellion was swiftly suppressed by the armed forces; however, Tiro later established a government-in-exile in Sweden.

In 1989 opposition to the central Government rose again, this time led by the National Liberation Front Aceh Sumatra. The region was made a 'military operations zone' in 1990, thus allowing the armed forces far greater freedom to counter the uprising. By mid-1991 the rebellion had been largely suppressed; however, it was estimated that about 1,000 Acehnese had been killed in the process, as a result of the use of excessive and indiscriminate force by the military. The number of deaths continued to rise in subsequent years, and in 1993 Amnesty International estimated that about 2,000 Acehnese had been killed since 1989, with hundreds of others having 'disappeared'.

Aceh's status as a 'military operations zone' was revoked in June 1998, following the downfall of President Suharto in May, and an apology for past military excesses was made by Gen. Wiranto. The subsequent intended withdrawal of Indonesian troops from the province was suspended, however, following rioting in Aceh in September. Decentralization measures introduced by President Habibie failed to defuse resentment in the province, and public opinion in Aceh became increasingly sympathetic towards the notion of independence. Violence continued to escalate in the province throughout 1999. The discovery of several mass graves of people killed by the armed forces during security operations further exacerbated tension in the province. Violence continued to escalate following the legislative elections of 9 June as GAM guerrillas intensified their campaign for independence for Aceh.

In early November 1999, following the rejection by legislators in the provincial assembly of demands for the holding of a referendum on self-determination for Aceh, a provincial government building in western Aceh was set on fire during a demonstration by 5,000 protesters. While much of the ongoing widespread violence in the province was attributed to the separatist movement, it was believed by observers that some unrest was initiated by so-called 'provocateurs' acting to destabilize the province and undermine the separatist movement. In November the newly appointed President of Indonesia, Abdurrahman Wahid, confirmed an unexpected statement that the holding of a referendum in Aceh was a possibility. In late November, however, Wahid made it clear that the suggested poll would not include the option of independence, but would instead offer Aceh a broad degree of autonomy. Wahid's proposals angered the TNI, which, in the wake of the vote in favour of independence in East Timor in August, reportedly feared that, unless brought under control, the separatist movement in Aceh could potentially incite rebellion across the archipelago and contribute to national disintegration. The offer of increased autonomy, rather than independence, also failed to satisfy Acehnese separatists, and violence continued throughout the province. In May 2000 the Indonesian Government and Acehnese rebel negotiators agreed upon a cease-fire, which took effect from 2 June and was subsequently extended for an indefinite period. Violence continued throughout the province, however, and it was estimated by Acehnese human rights groups that more than 1,000 civilians had died in clashes between the Indonesian military and Acehnese rebels during 2000. In December thousands of Acehnese protesters rallied peacefully in Banda Aceh, demanding independence for the province. However, it was reported that at least 34 (and possibly as many as 200, according to human rights groups) unarmed civilians had been killed in the days preceding the rally as the result of military action to target Acehnese en route to the demonstration. On the day after the protest, Acehnese separatists withdrew from peace talks

with the Indonesian Government, stating that they would resume negotiations only when the military ceased killing Acehnese civilians. In January 2001 peace talks between the Indonesian Government and Acehnese separatists recommenced.

In March 2001, following talks between GAM and the security forces, 'peace zones' were established in two Aceh districts. These proved to be of limited effectiveness, however, and in April President Wahid signed a decree authorizing the security forces to assist the military in restoring law and order in the province by targeting armed separatist organizations. This brought an end to the uneasy truce prevailing in the region. In July one of President Megawati's first official actions was to sign into law a special autonomy plan for Aceh intended to assuage separatism. However, while generous in its scope, the legislation was criticized for failing to address the problems posed by the continued military presence in the area. Critics' concerns were borne out when an estimated 30 civilians were massacred on an Aceh palm oil plantation in August 2001. According to GAM, the military was responsible, having carried out the attack as retribution for a previous assault on a military post that had left several soldiers dead. In a speech commemorating the 56th anniversary of Indonesia's independence, President Megawati apologized to the troubled provinces of Aceh and Irian Jaya (now Papua) for the perpetration of years of human rights abuses. In September President Megawati visited the region in an attempt to defuse the tensions there; her visit was met with indifference by many regional groups. On 4 December 2001 Acehnese separatists marked the 25th anniversary of their struggle for independence. Security forces tore down over 100 separatist flags, and there were reports of some clashes between GAM members and the military.

Violence continued in Aceh throughout 2002. In January a strike called by GAM to protest against alleged brutality by the security forces was marred by explosions and gunfire. Shortly afterwards the commander of GAM, Abdullah Syafei, was killed during a gun battle with security forces on Sumatra; six other GAM members also died. In February talks took place between GAM and government representatives in Geneva, Switzerland, despite an earlier declaration by GAM that it intended to boycott negotiations while mourning the death of Syafei. The talks were adjourned with a statement confirming the right of the people of Aceh to rule themselves peacefully. However, on the same day renewed fighting occurred in the province, prompting the Government to resume a separate military command for Aceh, a move denounced by both GAM and human rights groups as an ill-advised attempt to resolve the region's problems using military means. In the following month fighting between separatists and government troops in the province resulted in the deaths of at least 23 people. In May, following further talks in Geneva, the Government and GAM agreed to work towards a cease-fire, signing an agreement which was to act as a mandate for future negotiations. However, the violence continued, with a GAM commander alleging later in the same month that the armed forces had killed 43 civilians in North Aceh in the preceding 10 days alone. In June 2002 Taslim Jalil, a member of the DPR from Aceh, was shot dead by unidentified gunmen; shortly afterwards Nasri Zamzam, a regional representative of the PPP, was also killed. Later in the same month GAM guerrillas ambushed a patrol of soldiers from the Kopassus special forces regiment at Banda Aceh airport, in North Sumatra, resulting in six deaths; GAM was also responsible for the reported murder of five workers and abduction of a further eight from an oil palm plantation in East Aceh. At the end of the month GAM issued a statement in support of the ongoing peace negotiations taking place in Geneva and in July it released 18 hostages whom it had been holding since the previous month, including nine crewmen who had been kidnapped while servicing the offshore petroleum industry near North Aceh. Meanwhile, following a trip to Aceh, the Co-ordinating Minister for Political Affairs, Security and Social Welfare, Susilo Bambang Yudhoyono, declared his support for the regional military commander's request to increase the military presence in the area if GAM did not accept the conditions that had been outlined following the talks that had been held in May and stated that he intended to request the declaration of a state of civil emergency in the province. Aceh's Legal Aid Institute reportedly claimed that, during the first six months of 2002, 771 people had been killed as a result of the conflict in the region. In September a British and a US woman were arrested and charged with having violated their visas while travelling in Aceh; they were believed to have made contact with GAM and stood trial over the allegations in November. In December both women were found guilty of the charges against them and sentenced to short prison terms; they were released in early 2003, having served most of their sentences while in custody.

In early November 2002 GAM announced that it was willing to sign a short-term peace accord with the Government to bring to an end the armed conflict ongoing in the region. However, it later stated that it wished to sign the truce at the end of the Islamic religious festival of Ramadan, which fell on 6 December. On 5 November GAM announced a unilateral truce during the period of Ramadan, but the truce broke down almost immediately as five people died during an exchange of gunfire in North Aceh. Meanwhile, in the largest military operation to have been carried out in the province for some time, government troops besieged a suspected GAM base in the industrial centre of Lhokseumawe. On 9 December Government and GAM representatives finally signed a peace agreement in Geneva. As well as establishing an immediate cease-fire, the deal provided for free elections (to be held in 2004), which would establish an autonomous, although not independent, government. The new provincial government would retain 70% of all fuel revenues. In return all rebels in the province would disarm in designated areas. Following the signing of the peace accord international peace monitors arrived in the region to observe the disarmament process and ensure adherence to the terms of the agreement.

In May 1977 there was a rebellion in the province of Irian Jaya (now known as Papua), annexed to Indonesia in 1963 (see above). The rebellion was said to have been organized by the Organisasi Papua Merdeka (OPM—Free Papua Movement), which seeks unification with Papua New Guinea. Fighting continued until December 1979, when Indonesia and Papua New Guinea finalized a new border administrative agreement. Frequent border incidents followed, however, and in early 1984 fighting broke out in Jayapura, the capital of Irian Jaya. As a result, about 10,000 refugees fled over the border into Papua New Guinea. In October 1984 Indonesia and Papua New Guinea signed a five-year agreement establishing a joint border security committee; by the end of 1985 Indonesians were continuing to cross into Papua New Guinea, but a limited number of repatriations took place in 1986. There was also concern among native Irian Jayans (who are of Melanesian origin) at the introduction of large numbers of Javanese into the province, under the Government's transmigration scheme. This was interpreted as an attempt to reduce the Melanesians to a minority and thus to stifle opposition. In 1986 it was announced that the Government intended to resettle 65m. people over a 20-year period, in spite of protests from human rights and conservation groups that the scheme would cause ecological damage and interfere with the rights of the native Irian Jayans. Relations with Papua New Guinea improved when the Prime Minister, Paias Wingti, visited Suharto in January 1988. However, a series of cross-border raids by the Indonesian armed forces in October and November, in an attempt to capture Melanesian separatists operating on the border, led to renewed tension between the two countries. In October 1990 the Governments of Indonesia and Papua New Guinea renewed the basic accord on border arrangements, which included an agreement on the formation of a joint defence committee and a formal commitment to share border intelligence. In early September 1992 the two countries agreed to facilitate the passage of border trade, and in the following month an Indonesian consulate was established in Vanimo.

In March 1991 the leader of the OPM, Melkianus Salossa (who had been arrested in Papua New Guinea in May 1990 and deported to Indonesia), was sentenced to life imprisonment. In May 1992 Indonesian troops crossed into Papua New Guinea to destroy an OPM camp at Wutung, prior to the legislative elections in Indonesia in June. In October 1993 clashes were reported in Irian Jaya between government troops and separatist rebels; the armed forces were alleged to have killed 73 inhabitants of a neighbouring village. In late February 1994 it was reported that the OPM had proposed entering into peace talks with the Indonesian Government.

In April 1995 the Australian Council for Overseas Aid (ACFOA) alleged that 37 Irian Jayans had been killed by security forces near the Freeport copper and gold mine between June 1994 and February 1995. In August the ACFOA's claims were reiterated by non-governmental organizations, which lodged a complaint with the National Commission on Human Rights in Jakarta about summary executions, arbitrary deten-

tions and torture in the province between mid-1994 and mid-1995. In November 1995 four members of ABRI were arrested in an investigation into the killing in May of 11 unarmed civilians at a prayer meeting. Also in November the Overseas Private Investment Corporation (a US government agency) cancelled political risk insurance valued at US $100m. for Freeport (a subsidiary of a US enterprise), citing environmental concerns. Freeport's perceived responsibility for the situation in Irian Jaya arose from its role as civil administrator in the area of the mine and also because the indigenous inhabitants' campaigns against Freeport's indiscriminate exploitation of natural resources in the area often resulted in their being killed by security forces as suspected members of the OPM.

In December 1995 clashes between Indonesian forces and the OPM intensified, forcing hundreds of refugees to cross into Papua New Guinea. Four people were killed in riots in Jayapura in March 1996. Riots near the Grasberg mine in the same month were the result of problems similar to those experienced by residents in the Freeport area (relating principally to the lack of any benefit from the mining project to the local community and to the potential impact of the project on the local environment). There were also tensions among the local Irianese, Indonesians from other provinces and commercial operators. In April Freeport agreed to allocate 1% of revenue over a period of 10 years to community development programmes for tribal groups living around the mine, and to tighten environmental safeguards.

In July 1998, following the resignation of President Suharto in May and his subsequent replacement by President Habibie, troops clashed with pro-independence demonstrators in Jayapura. Two people were reported to have been killed in the violence, and a further five were reportedly killed during an outbreak of violence on the island of Biak in July. In early October the Government revoked the status of Irian Jaya as a 'military operations zone' following the conclusion of a cease-fire agreement with the OPM in late September; however, the move was not followed by the withdrawal of troops from the region. In February 1999 Irian Jayan tribal leaders raised the issue of independence for the province at a meeting with President Habibie. (A referendum on self-determination for the province had been promised by the Indonesian Government prior to the territory's annexation in 1963; however, whilst a vote was eventually held in 1969, only tribal chiefs selected by Jakarta were allowed to participate and the result was widely discredited.) The independence movement in the province continued to strengthen throughout 1999, and was encouraged by the achievements of the East Timorese independence movement (see above). In early December independence demonstrations took place throughout Irian Jaya. Later the same month a delegation from the DPR visited the province and announced that the administration of the newly-elected President Abdurrahman Wahid had agreed to the popular demand that the province's name be changed from Irian Jaya to West Papua, although it was emphasized that this decision should not be construed as implying the Government's approval of any moves towards the province's secession from Indonesia. (It was subsequently reported, however, that the proposed change had failed to receive the requisite approval of the Indonesian legislature.)

In late May–early June 2000 the Papuan People's Congress was held in Jayapura. The Congress concluded with the adoption of a five-point resolution reinstating a declaration of independence for West Papua originally made in 1961, before the province's annexation to Indonesia. The declaration was, however, immediately rebuffed by the Indonesian Government. In early October between 30 and 40 people were killed and many others injured in clashes between police and West Papuan separatists in the town of Wamena when police attempted to remove a Morning Star independence flag being flown by the separatists. Although President Wahid had previously decreed that the flying of the Morning Star flag was allowed, provided that the flag was flown alongside, and slightly lower than, the Indonesian flag, following the violence the Government introduced a ban on the flying of the flag. In November and early December the Indonesian military took severe action against separatists; seven people were shot dead by the armed forces in an outbreak of violence in the town of Merauke, and dozens of separatist sympathizers, including the pro-independence leader, Theys Eluay, were arrested. On 1 December pro-independence supporters rallied in the province to mark the 39th anniversary of the first unilateral declaration of West

Papua's independence. The rallies were largely peaceful, but in the town of Fakfak two demonstrators were shot dead by police.

In March 2001 five West Papuan separatist leaders, including Theys Eluay, the leader of the Presidium Dewan Papua (PDP—Papua Presidium Council), were released on bail to await trial on charges of treason. In October the DPR gave its assent to legislation giving greater autonomy to the province, in an effort to defuse the separatist tensions that had given rise to more than 40 years of sporadic violence. As well as giving Irian Jaya more autonomy and a larger share of tax revenues, the legislation also proposed that the region be officially known as Papua and made provision for a bicameral Papua Peoples' Council, intended to safeguard indigenous interests. However, the separatist PDP swiftly rejected the deal as it failed to grant Irian Jaya complete independence. In November 2001 Theys Eluay was found dead in his car. He was believed to have been assassinated; some military involvement was suspected. In late December hundreds of students occupied the parliament building in Jayapura to demand a referendum on independence and to express their anger at the authorities' failure to find the killer of Theys Eluay. The protest came days before the autonomy reforms came into force on 1 January 2002, when the province officially became known as Papua.

In March 2002 it was reported that three soldiers from the Kopassus special forces regiment had been detained in connection with the murder of Theys Eluay. In the following month a further three Kopassus soldiers were arrested, although not formally charged, following the conclusion of the investigation, which had been conducted by a specially-appointed commission. In June Yafet Yelemaken, another member of the PDP, was found dead in suspicious circumstances, having attended a function protected by Kopassus forces on the preceding evening. In late August two US citizens and an Indonesian were killed following an ambush near the Freeport mine; while the Government immediately attributed the attack to the OPM, there was speculation that it could have been carried out by the military in an attempt to discredit local insurgents. On the following day government troops killed a man suspected of involvement in the ambush. In November it was alleged by police that Kopassus soldiers were suspected of involvement in the attack. On 1 December approximately 700 people attended a rally to commemorate the anniversary of the province's failed bid for independence. In January 2003 the trial began of four of seven Kopassus soldiers charged with the murder of Theys Eluay. In April they were convicted of the charges against them. Meanwhile, the central Government gave its approval to an initiative that would lead to the division of Papua into three smaller provinces. The proposal angered local leaders, who claimed that such action would threaten the region's autonomy.

Under Suharto, Indonesia's foreign policy was one of non-alignment, although the country maintained close relations with the West. As a member of the Association of South East Asian Nations (ASEAN), Indonesia supported the organization's opposition to Viet Nam's military presence in Cambodia and played a prominent role in attempts to find a political solution to the situation in Cambodia (q.v.). The Indonesian Minister of Foreign Affairs and his French counterpart were appointed Co-Chairmen of the Paris International Conference on Cambodia, which first met in August 1989. In 1997, following Second Prime Minister Hun Sen's assumption of sole power in Cambodia, Indonesia led ASEAN attempts to resolve the crisis.

In July 1985 Indonesia and the People's Republic of China signed a memorandum of understanding on the resumption of direct trade links, which had been suspended since 1967. In April 1988 the Indonesian Government indicated its readiness to re-establish full diplomatic relations with China, subject to an assurance that the latter would not seek to interfere in Indonesia's internal affairs; previously, Suharto had insisted that China acknowledge its alleged complicity in the 1965 attempted coup. Diplomatic relations were finally restored in August 1990, following an Indonesian undertaking to settle financial debts incurred with China by the Sukarno regime. In November Suharto visited China and Viet Nam (the first Indonesian leader to do so since 1964 and 1975 respectively). Suharto subsequently announced that former Indonesian communists living in exile would be permitted to return home, although they risked imprisonment. In 1995 China extended claims to territorial waters within Indonesia's exclusive economic zone, consequently threatening Indonesia's natural gas resources, in particular those situated in the region of the Natuna Islands. An extensive Indonesian military exercise in September 1996, which concluded at the Natuna Islands, was perceived as a demonstration of the archipelago's strength to China.

Bilateral relations between Indonesia and China suffered a reverse in 1998 following the violence perpetrated against ethnic Chinese Indonesians at the time of the fall of Suharto in May. China issued a strong diplomatic protest at the violence, and gave prominent coverage in the state-controlled media to reports of the rapes, arson and murders. Following his accession to the presidency, President Habibie publicly expressed his sympathy for the plight of the ethnic Chinese victims of violence. Subsequently, in May 1999, as part of an ongoing programme of general reform, Habibie lifted a ban that had existed on the use and teaching of the Mandarin Chinese language within Indonesia. In early December the newly-appointed President of Indonesia, Abdurrahman Wahid, made an official visit to China; Wahid was believed by observers to attach considerable importance to the improvement of relations with China. In November 2001 new President Megawati held discussions with the Chinese Prime Minister, Zhu Rongji, during his visit to the region to strengthen economic ties.

In December 1989 Indonesia and Australia concluded a temporary agreement providing for joint exploration for petroleum and gas in the Timor Gap, which had been a disputed area since 1978. However, no permanent sea boundary was approved. The validity of the Timor Gap agreement was challenged by Portugal, which instituted proceedings at the International Court of Justice (ICJ), on the grounds that the agreement infringed Portuguese sovereignty and interests; however, in June 1995 the ICJ rejected the case on the grounds that it would affect a country that was not represented, as Indonesia did not recognize the ICJ's jurisdiction. In June 1993 the East Timorese resistance began proceedings in the High Court of Australia to overturn legislation confirming the Timor Gap agreement on the grounds that Australia was bound by international law, which did not recognize Indonesia's annexation of East Timor. In April 1990 Indonesia and Australia restored defence co-operation links, following a four-year disruption. In September 1994 Vice-President Sutrisno became the first high-ranking Indonesian official to visit Australia since Suharto's last visit in 1975.

In July 1995 Indonesia withdrew the nomination of Lt-Gen. Herman Mantiri, a former Chief of the General Staff, as ambassador to Australia, owing to widespread protests there concerning his defence of the actions of the Indonesian armed forces in the 1991 Dili massacre. Relations with Australia were also strained by Australia's decision to allow 18 East Timorese refugees to remain in the country following their arrival by boat in May (although they were not granted political asylum), by several incidents involving the burning of the Indonesian flag in Australian cities in protest at Indonesia's occupation of East Timor, and by Australia's decision to investigate claims of new evidence about the killing of six Australia-based journalists during the annexation of East Timor in 1975. The Indonesian Government claimed that the journalists had died in cross-fire, while eyewitnesses stated that they had been executed by Indonesian troops. In June 1996 an Australian government report concluded that the journalists had been killed by the Indonesian army. A report published by the International Commission of Jurists, a human rights organization based in Switzerland, in 1998 concluded that Indonesian troops had killed the journalists in order to conceal Indonesia's invasion of East Timor, and in October of that year it was announced that Australia was to reopen a judicial inquiry into the killings. In late 2000 newly-declassified documents provided conclusive evidence that Australian officials had been aware of Indonesia's plans to invade East Timor. Meanwhile, in December 1995 Indonesia signed a treaty with Australia to enhance defence links, committing the two countries to consultation in the event of a threat to security. In October 1996 the Australia-Indonesia Development Area was created to develop economic links between the two countries and in March 1997 Indonesia and Australia signed a treaty defining permanent maritime boundaries between the two countries, whilst retaining the Timor Gap agreement. (Indonesia later ceased to be a party to the Timor Gap agreement when it relinquished control of the territory in October 1999.)

Following the downfall of Suharto in May 1998, relations between Indonesia and Australia continued to be affected by the issue of East Timor. In January 1999 the Indonesian Government expressed its 'deep regret' at Australia's announcement earlier the same month that it was to change its policy on East Timor and actively promote 'self-determination' in the territory. Following the vote in favour of independence held in East Timor in August 1999, Australia committed 4,500 peace-keeping troops to the International Force for East Timor (Interfet), which was formed by the UN to restore order in the territory following the violence perpetrated by pro-Jakarta militias after the announcement of the result of the poll. A military co-operation agreement between Indonesia and Australia, which had been signed four years previously, was reported in October to have been cancelled as a result of the Indonesian Government's displeasure at Australia's leading involvement in the peace-keeping operation. In 2000 relations between Indonesia and Australia continued to be strained. In November the Australian ambassador to Indonesia, John McCarthy, was physically attacked by a pro-Jakarta mob in Makassar, Sulawesi. The Australian Government accepted the Indonesian Government's apology for the incident.

Relations with Australia appeared to be improving in 2001. In June, following several postponements, President Wahid paid an official visit to Australia, the first by an Indonesian head of state for 26 years. The Australian Prime Minister, John Howard, became the first foreign leader to make an official visit to Indonesia following President Megawati's assumption of power when he arrived in Jakarta in August. However, later in the same month relations were strained once again when a cargo ship carrying hundreds of mainly Afghan asylum-seekers became stranded in the international waters between the two countries. Neither country agreed to accept responsibility for the refugees. In early September the Australian Minister for Foreign Affairs, Alexander Downer, arrived in Jakarta for talks with Indonesian Ministers on the problems raised by illegal trafficking of immigrants. In October the pressing nature of the immigrant issue was highlighted when more than 350 refugees, believed to be heading for Australia, drowned when their boat sank off the Indonesian coast. In the same month a missing boat carrying approximately 170 Iraqi and Afghan asylum seekers was found on the Indonesian island of Wera. In November the Minister of Foreign Affairs, Hassan Wirayuda, visited Canberra for further discussions on the issue, and the two countries agreed to work together to address the problem. Australia co-hosted a regional conference on people-smuggling in February 2002 in an attempt to find a solution. Earlier in the same month John Howard visited the country again. Both the Speaker of the DPR, Akbar Tandjung, and the Speaker of the MPR, Amien Rais, cancelled scheduled meetings with him and during his stay students protested in response to allegations that Australia was providing funding for separatist groups in Aceh and Papua. Howard denied such charges, claiming that he fully supported Indonesia's territorial integrity, and signed an agreement with President Megawati concerning counter-terrorism measures. Shortly afterwards Australia participated in a trilateral dialogue with Indonesia and East Timor regarding future co-operation issues; the talks were the first ever to be attended by the three countries. In May, following an initiative proposed during Prime Minister Howard's visit, the inaugural Australia-Indonesia dialogue was held in Bogor; Minister of Foreign Affairs Hasan Wirajuda met with his Australian counterpart, Alexander Downer, to discuss bilateral co-operation issues.

In October 2002 relations with Australia were seriously affected by the bomb attacks on the island of Bali, a popular destination for Australian tourists, which resulted in the deaths of almost 90 Australian citizens. While the Australian Government immediately offered its support and assistance to Indonesia in the aftermath of the attacks, as well as participating in the police investigation, a subsequent series of raids on the homes of Indonesian Muslims resident in Australia prompted Vice-President Hamzah Haz to warn that such an offensive could damage bilateral relations. In late November 2002 the Australian Prime Minister, John Howard, threatened Australia's relationship with several South-East Asian countries, including Indonesia, when he stated that Australia was prepared to launch pre-emptive attacks against perceived terrorist threats in other Asian countries. Gen. Endriartono Sutatro, commander-in-chief of the armed forces, commented that such a strike would be interpreted as an act of aggression by the Indonesian Government, as it would infringe the principle of national sovereignty.

In October 1996 Indonesia and Malaysia agreed to submit disputed claims to the islands of Ligitan and Sipadan to the ICJ, and in August 1997 the two countries agreed to postpone talks on the issue of the islands, pending a ruling by the Court. In December 2002 the ICJ awarded the islands to Malaysia; both countries had earlier stated that they would abide by the Court's

decision, thus bringing an end to the dispute. The forced repatriation in early 1998 of thousands of Indonesian workers from Malaysia as a result of the regional economic crisis placed a strain on relations between the two countries. Relations were further strained in October when the Indonesian Government condemned the treatment received in custody by the former Malaysian Deputy Prime Minister and Minister of Finance, Anwar Ibrahim (see the chapter on Malaysia), breaking with a tradition amongst ASEAN countries of non-interference in the internal affairs of other member countries. In May 2002 Indonesia signed a trilateral security pact with Malaysia and the Philippines enabling the signatories to exchange intelligence and launch joint police operations in an attempt to combat terrorism in the region; Cambodia and Thailand later also acceded to the agreement. In August relations with Malaysia were also affected by Malaysia's introduction of stringent anti-immigration laws, which resulted in the forced deportation of many illegal immigrants, most of whom were Indonesian, and provoked protests outside the Malaysian embassy in Jakarta. However, relations generally remained cordial.

Meanwhile, in May 2002 President Megawati Sukarnoputri attracted criticism when she attended celebrations in Timor-Leste to mark the territory's official accession to nation status; in February Indonesia and East Timor had agreed to establish full diplomatic relations following independence. In July the newly appointed President of Timor-Leste, Xanana Gusmão, visited Indonesia; during his stay he met with President Megawati, and the two leaders discussed the possibility of compensation for Indonesian assets remaining in Timor-Leste and the extent of Indonesian assistance with which the new country would be provided. In October the first meeting of the Indonesia-Timor-Leste Joint Ministerial Commission for Bilateral Co-operation took place in Jakarta.

In March 1996 the USA ended a ban on military training for members of ABRI, which had been imposed after the Dili massacre in 1991. In early June 1997, however, it was announced that President Suharto had cancelled Indonesia's participation in US military training programmes in response to the recent condemnation by the US House of Representatives of abuses of human rights committed by Indonesian armed forces in East Timor; the planned purchase by Indonesia of a number of US military aircraft was also cancelled. In November 1999 the newly-appointed President of Indonesia, Abdurrahman Wahid, made an official visit to the USA. In October 2000, however, relations between Indonesia and the USA deteriorated markedly as the result of a combination of factors, including the perceived 'interference' in Indonesian domestic political affairs of the recently-appointed US ambassador to Indonesia, Robert Gelbard, US criticism of Indonesia's failure to control pro-Jakarta militias in West Timor following the murder of three UN workers by militia members in September, and Indonesian perceptions of US bias towards Israel in the Middle East conflict. In late October and early November Muslim groups rallied outside the US embassy in Jakarta, calling for *jihad*, threats were made against US citizens in Indonesia, US companies in the country were attacked and it was reported that the Indonesian Government had requested Gelbard's immediate removal and replacement. In late October the USA closed its embassy in Jakarta for two weeks, and in early November the US Government warned citizens to defer all non-essential travel to the archipelago. Relations between the two countries remained strained throughout much of 2001.

Following the terrorist attacks of 11 September 2001 on the USA (see the chapter on the USA), in the same month President Megawati became the first leader of a predominantly Muslim country to meet with President George W. Bush. In return for assurances that the US campaign against terror was not one against Islam, she affirmed Indonesia's condemnation of the attacks. However, in late September Dien Syamsuddin, Secretary-General of the Indonesian Ulama Council, urged Muslims around the world to unite and the nation not to support any US-led retaliation on Afghanistan and the terrorist Osama bin Laden. Following the commencement of air strikes against the Taliban regime in October, fundamentalist Muslims threatened violence if the Indonesian Government did not sever diplomatic relations with the USA. In October Front Pembela Islam (FPI—Islamic Defenders' Front) warned that if British and US citizens did not leave the country immediately their safety could not be guaranteed. (The FPI disbanded in November 2002, claiming that it did not wish to compound the damage to the reputation of the Islamic religion at what was a violent time for Indonesia.

However, it announced in early 2003 that it intended to re-form.) Later in the same month President Megawati, under pressure from Muslim groups and Vice-President Hamzah Haz, indirectly condemned the US attacks for the first time. Protests against the Afghan campaign continued in Jakarta and various regional centres.

In 2002 relations with the USA improved somewhat. In April the two countries held sensitive security talks, during which they discussed measures to combat terrorism and to strengthen civilian control over the armed forces; the talks were perceived to signify an important move towards the renewal of bilateral military ties. In July the US Congress approved legislation awarding US \$16m. to the Indonesian police forces; this included \$12m. for the establishment of a dedicated anti-terrorism unit and followed a vote by the Senate Appropriations Committee to remove all remaining restrictions on the provision of military training to Indonesia (the vote awaited approval by Congress). The proposed legislation for the resumption of military assistance did, however, include human rights conditions. In August, during a two-day visit to Indonesia, US Secretary of State Colin Powell guaranteed substantial financial aid to the country to fight the terrorist threat within its borders. During his stay Powell also announced the resumption of a training programme for Indonesian army officers at US military schools and \$50m. of funding for Indonesia's police and counter-terrorism units over a three-year period. The bombings in Bali in October were widely perceived to constitute a further justification for the strengthening of military links with the USA. However, in early 2003 bilateral relations were strained when the USA placed Indonesia on a list of countries of which citizens were required to register with the US immigration authorities if they visited the country. The Government stated its intention to file a protest against the decision, claiming that it was discriminatory. In the mean time, the US Senate rejected an amendment proposing that funding be withdrawn for the enrolment of Indonesians in US military training programmes until the Indonesian Government co-operated fully with the investigation into the murder of two US citizens in Papua in August 2002; the rejection signified continued progress in the restoration of normal military links between the two countries.

In September 1994 a 220-strong medical detachment from the Indonesian army joined the UN Protection Force in Bosnia and Herzegovina (UNPROFOR), in the first mission of its kind to Europe. Indonesia's international standing was further enhanced when, in January 1995, it replaced Pakistan as the non-permanent Asian representative on the UN Security Council for a period of two years. In October 1997 Indonesia proposed that two permanent seats for the representation of Asia be established on the Council. In October 1994 Indonesia underscored its pivotal regional role through hosting its fifth informal meeting to resolve peacefully the dispute over the conflicting claims of six Asian countries to sovereignty over parts of the South China Sea, particularly the Spratly Islands. Moreover, in November the Asia-Pacific Economic Co-operation (APEC, see p. 139) summit meeting took place in Bogor. Indonesia had been one of the founding members of APEC, which had been established in 1989. In October 2001 President Megawati Sukarnoputri travelled to Shanghai to attend her first APEC summit meeting as leader.

On 16 November 1994 the United Nations Convention on the Law of the Sea came into effect and immediately led to recognition of Indonesia's status as an archipelago and the country's sovereignty over all of the waters between its islands. Enforcement of the convention increased Indonesia's territorial waters by more than 3m. sq km.

In August 1995 Queen Beatrix of the Netherlands, the former colonial power in Indonesia, visited Indonesia (the first Dutch monarch to do so for 24 years) and spoke of her regret for the suffering caused by Dutch rule. Bilateral relations were strained from 1992, when Indonesia rejected Dutch aid because it was linked to progress on human rights.

In September and October 1997 President Suharto apologized to neighbouring countries when thick smog, caused by fires started in land-clearance operations in southern Sumatra and central and southern Kalimantan, affected Malaysia, Singapore and parts of the Philippines and Thailand. In late 1999 the newly-appointed President of Indonesia, Abdurrahman Wahid, made a tour of neighbouring ASEAN countries. In August 2001 President Megawati Sukarnoputri embarked on a tour of all ASEAN member states on her first overseas trip since her

assumption of the presidency. The trip duly affirmed Indonesia's close ties with the other ASEAN nations.

In October 1998 it was reported that Indonesia and Portugal were to open representative offices in each other's capital cities in January 1999. In May 1999 the two countries signed an agreement allowing for total independence for East Timor if the East Timorese people voted to reject autonomy proposals offered by the Indonesian Government in a UN-supervised referendum scheduled for August. In late December, with the issue of the status of East Timor resolved following a vote in favour of independence at the referendum in August, Indonesia and Portugal formally re-established full diplomatic relations.

In mid-2000 it was reported that President Wahid had expressed his desire to develop Indonesia's relations with Iraq and other Muslim countries. In June of the same year President Wahid made an official visit to Iran, and in October Indonesia and Pakistan signed a memorandum of understanding relating to the promotion of bilateral ties. In January 2001 the Prime Minister of India made a four-day visit to Indonesia, following a visit to India by President Wahid in February 2000.

Government

The highest authority of the State is the Majelis Permusyawaratan Rakyat (MPR—People's Consultative Assembly), with 700 members (reduced from 1,000 in 1999) who serve for five years. The MPR includes all 500 members of the Dewan Perwakilan Rakyat (DPR—House of Representatives), the country's legislative organ. The DPR has 38 members appointed from Tentara Nasional Indonesia (TNI—the Indonesian National Defence Forces) and 462 directly-elected representatives. The remaining 200 seats in the MPR comprise 135 members elected by provincial assemblies and 65 members appointed by the Komite Pemilihan Umum (General Election Committee). Executive power rests with the President, elected for five years by the MPR. He governs with the assistance of an appointed Cabinet, which is responsible to him. In August 2002 the MPR approved a series of amendments to the Constitution. These provided for: the direct election of the President and Vice-President; the termination of all non-elected representation in the DPR and MPR; and the creation of the Dewan Perwakilan Daerah (DPD—House of Representatives of the Regions) which, together with the DPR, would comprise the MPR. The changes were due to come into effect following the holding of the country's next national elections, scheduled to take place in 2004.

There are 30 provinces, and local government is through a three-tier system of provincial, regency and village assemblies. Each province is headed by a Governor, who is elected to a five-year term of office by the Provincial Assembly. Provincial Governors must be confirmed by the President, who also approves the election of the Governor of Jakarta, which is designated as a 'special district', as are Aceh and Yogyakarta.

Defence

In August 2002 the total strength of the armed forces was 297,000 men: army an estimated 230,000, navy 40,000 and air force 27,000. There were also paramilitary forces, comprising an estimated 195,000 police, 12,000 marine police and an estimated 40,000 trainees of KAMRA (People's Security). Military service is selective and lasts for two years. Defence expenditure for 2002 was budgeted at an estimated Rp. 9,800,000m.

Economic Affairs

In 2001, according to estimates by the World Bank, Indonesia's gross national income (GNI), measured at average 1999–2001 prices, was US \$144,731m., equivalent to \$680 per head (or \$2,940 per head on an international purchasing-power parity basis). During 1990–2001, it was estimated, the population increased at an average annual rate of 1.7%, while gross domestic product (GDP) per head increased, in real terms, by an average of 2.4% per year. Overall GDP increased, in real terms, by an average of 4.1% per year in 1990–2001. GDP increased by 4.9% in 2000 and by 3.3% in 2001.

Agriculture, forestry and fishing contributed 16.4% of GDP in 2001, and engaged 43.8% of the employed labour force in the same year. Principal crops for domestic consumption were rice, cassava and maize. Once self-sufficient in rice, Indonesia was obliged to import supplies during the 1990s. In the late 1990s Indonesia remained a major exporter of rubber and palm oil. Other principal cash crops were coffee, spices, tea, cocoa, tobacco, bananas, coconuts and sugar cane. In 1995 an estimated 61% of Indonesia's land area was covered by tropical rain forests. In 2001 there were demands for a tightening of controls on the exploitation of the country's natural resources owing to the prevalence of illegal and unsustainable practices, particularly in the forestry sector. In January 2003 a report published by the Environmental Investigation Agency (EIA) blamed the corruption endemic in Indonesia for the obstruction of efforts to prevent the widespread environmental damage caused by illegal logging practices. During 1990–2001, according to the World Bank, agricultural GDP increased by an estimated average of 1.8% per year. The GDP of the sector expanded by 1.7% in 2000 and by 0.6% in 2001.

Industry (including mining, manufacturing, construction and power) engaged 18.7% of the employed labour force in 2001 (including activities not adequately defined), and provided 46.5% of GDP in the same year. During 1990–2001, according to the World Bank, industrial GDP increased by an average of 5.2% per year. The GDP of the sector increased by 5.9% in 2000 and by 3.3% in 2001.

Mining engaged only 0.5% of the employed labour force in 2000, but contributed 13.6% of GDP in 2001. Indonesia's principal mineral resource is petroleum, and the country remained the world's leading exporter of liquefied natural gas in 1994. At the end of 2001 proven reserves of petroleum amounted to 5,000m. barrels, enough to sustain production at that year's level (averaging 1.41m. barrels per day) for approximately 10 years. In 2001 natural gas production was 62,900m. cu m, from proven reserves amounting to 262,000m. cu m, enough to sustain production at that year's level for less than 42 years. In the same year coal production was 56.9m. metric tons, from proven reserves of 5,370m. metric tons, sufficient to sustain production at that year's level for a further 58 years. With effect from 1 February 2003 Indonesia's petroleum production quota was set by the Organization of the Petroleum Exporting Countries (OPEC) at 1.27m. barrels per day. In 1992 Indonesia became the world's second largest producer of tin. Bauxite, nickel, copper, gold, silver and coal are also mined. During 1990–2001, according to the ADB, mining GDP increased by an average of 3.4% per year. The GDP of the sector increased by 5.1% in 2000 but decreased by 0.6% in 2001.

Manufacturing contributed 26.1% of GDP in 2001, and engaged 13.3% of the employed labour force in the same year. Apart from petroleum refineries, the main branches of the sector (in terms of output) in 1996 were food products (contributing 13.1% of the total), textiles (11.6%), transport equipment (8.7%) and electrical machinery (7.4%). According to the ADB, manufacturing GDP increased by an estimated average of 6.6% per year in 1990–2001. Manufacturing GDP increased by 6.1% in 2000 and by 4.3% in 2001.

During the 1980s Indonesia broadened the base of its energy supplies to include gas, coal, hydroelectricity and geothermal energy, in addition to the traditional dependence on petroleum. In 1999, of the total 84,611m. kWh of electricity produced, natural gas accounted for 36.5%, coal for 30.1%, petroleum for 19.0% and hydroelectricity for 11.1%. In 2001 imports of petroleum and its products comprised almost 17.7% of the value of merchandise imports.

Services (including trade, transport and communications, finance and tourism) provided an estimated 37.1% of GDP in 2001, and engaged 37.5% of the employed labour force in the same year. Tourism is normally one of the principal sources of foreign exchange, although following the terrorist attack on the tourist destination of Bali in October 2002 (see Recent History) it was feared that revenues from tourism might suffer significantly in subsequent years. In 2000 5.1m. tourists visited the country. This increased to 5.2m. in 2001. In 2000 revenue from tourism totalled US $5,749m., having increased from a total of $4,710 in 1999. According to the ADB, the GDP of the services sector expanded by an estimated average of 3.6% per year in 1990–2001. The sector's GDP increased by 5.2% in 2000 and by 4.4% in 2001.

In 2001 Indonesia recorded a visible trade surplus of US $22,695m. In the same year a surplus of $6,899m. was recorded on the current account of the balance of payments. In 2001 the principal source of imports (15.2%) and principal market for exports (23.1%) was Japan. Other major suppliers were the USA, Singapore, the Republic of Korea, the People's Republic of China and Australia; other major purchasers were the USA, Singapore, the Republic of Korea, the People's Republic of China and Taiwan. The principal exports in 2001 were petroleum and its products, plywood, rubber, shrimp and coffee. In the same year the principal imports were machinery,

mechanical appliances and electrical equipment, mineral and chemical products and textiles.

The budget for 2001/02 projected a deficit of Rp. 17,340,000m. Indonesia's total external debt stood at US $141,803m. at the end of 2000, of which $69,161m. was long-term public debt. In that year the cost of debt-servicing was equivalent to 25.3% of revenue from exports of goods and services. The annual rate of inflation averaged 16.0% in 1995–2002. Consumer prices rose by an average of 3.7% in 2000, by 11.5% in 2001 and by an estimated 11.9% in 2002. In 2001, according to the ADB, 8.1% of the labour force were unemployed. The level of underemployment remained very high.

Indonesia is a member of the Association of South East Asian Nations (ASEAN, see p. 146), the Asian Development Bank (ADB, see p. 146), the Asia-Pacific Economic Co-operation (APEC, see p. 139) forum, the Colombo Plan (see p. 339) and the Organization of the Petroleum Exporting Countries (OPEC, see p. 298). As a member of ASEAN, Indonesia signed an accord in January 1992, pledging to establish a free trade zone, to be known as the ASEAN Free Trade Area (AFTA), within 15 years (subsequently reduced to 10 years), beginning in January 1993. AFTA was formally established on 1 January 2002.

The Indonesian economy was particularly badly affected by the repercussions of the regional financial crisis from mid-1997 and by political instability. In 2001 the impeachment of President Wahid, combined with the IMF's continued refusal to release funds in support of the Government's economic reforms, led to a rapid downturn in the capital and currency markets. The accession of Megawati Sukarnoputri to the presidency in July 2001, however, seemed to restore a measure of political stability, which it was hoped would engender an economic revival. In September the IMF finally released a US $395m. loan to Indonesia after signing an agreement with the new President. The budget for 2002, revised in the aftermath of the terrorist attacks on the USA, focused on reducing the fiscal deficit to 2.5% of GDP through the introduction of taxation and civil service reforms, the increase of non-oil revenues and the implementation of an aggressive policy of privatization. Meanwhile, in October 2001, in an effort to reduce the Government's energy subsidies in line with IMF requirements, the House of Representatives approved legislation to liberalize the oil and gas sector by terminating the 30-year monopoly held by Pertamina, the state oil and gas company. At the annual meeting of the Consultative Group for Indonesia (CGI—a donor grouping chaired by the World Bank and incorporating IMF representatives) held in November 2001, donors pledged US $3,140m. for 2002. However, US $1,300m. of this aid was conditional upon the Government increasing its efforts to privatize state-owned assets, improve the legal system and revive the troubled banking sector. In 2002 Indonesia made significant progress towards reducing its budget deficit; it was estimated that this had fallen to under 2% of GDP. Some pressing reforms were also implemented within the financial sector, and the Government succeeded in transferring a major stake in the state telecommunications company, Indosat, to the private sector, consequently exceeding its privatization target for the year. In October the economy was placed under severe strain by the terrorist attack on the island of Bali (see Recent History). As well as severely affecting the tourism sector, the bombing served to exacerbate further the problem of declining foreign investment in the country; in 2002 foreign direct investment (FDI) was estimated at US $9,740m., a decrease of 35% compared with the previous year. Exports also continued to slow, affected by economic deceleration in the country's principal export markets—Japan, the USA and Singapore. According to official estimates, GDP increased by 3.7% in 2002, a figure higher than had been forecast. In 2003 speculation that the USA would lead an attack against Iraq contributed to fears of the effects of a decline in world petroleum production on both the domestic and regional economy. In January the Government implemented price rises on several fuel and utility tariffs in accordance with the reform programme recommended by the IMF and other international donors. However, in the face of widespread protests the increases were rescinded shortly afterwards. Meanwhile, the IMF announced that it had reached a new agreement with the Government concerning its ongoing reform programme; the arrangement would allow Indonesia to draw $450m. of the $1,800m. that remained available to it under the terms of the $5,000m. extended fund facility. However, it was thought likely, owing to increasing pressure within the Government, that the country would elect not to extend its involvement with the IMF upon the termination of the existing agreement at the end of 2003. At the CGI meeting held in early 2003 international donors pledged $2,700m. of budgetary support for the year. Indonesia's economic performance in 2003, however, remained dependent upon the continued implementation of reforms in the legal and judicial sector and the improvement of investment conditions. A growth rate of 3.5%–4% was forecast for the year.

Education

Education is mainly under the control of the Ministry of National Education, but the Ministry of Religious Affairs is in charge of Islamic religious schools at the primary level. In 1987 primary education, beginning at seven years of age and lasting for six years, was made compulsory. In 1993 it was announced that compulsory education was to be expanded to nine years. Secondary education begins at 13 years of age and lasts for six years, comprising two cycles of three years each. Primary enrolment in 1994 included 97% of children in the relevant age-group (males 99%; females 95%). In the same year enrolment at secondary level included 42% of the relevant population (males 45%; females 39%). In 1999/2000 there were 1,634 universities. In 1994 enrolment at tertiary level was equivalent to 11.1% of the relevant population (males 13.5%; females 8.6%). In 2000/01, according to provisional data, the Government allocated Rp. 13,433,000m., representing 3.7% of total expenditure, to education.

Public Holidays

2003: 1 January (New Year's Day), 1 February (Chinese New Year), 12 February* (Id al-Adha, Feast of the Sacrifice), 5 March* (Muharram, Islamic New Year), 18 April (Good Friday), 21 April (Easter Monday), 14 May* (Mouloud, Prophet Muhammad's Birthday), 15 May (Vesak Day), 29 May (Ascension Day), 17 August (Independence Day), 24 September* (Ascension of the Prophet Muhammad), 26 November* (Id al-Fitr, end of Ramadan), 25 December (Christmas Day).

2004: 1 January (New Year's Day), 22 January (Chinese New Year), 2 February* (Id al-Adha, Feast of the Sacrifice), 22 February* (Muharram, Islamic New Year), 9 April (Good Friday), 12 April (Easter Monday), 2 May* (Mouloud, Prophet Muhammad's Birthday), 20 May (Ascension Day), 2 June (Vesak Day), 17 August (Independence Day), 12 September* (Ascension of the Prophet Muhammad), 14 November* (Id al-Fitr, end of Ramadan), 25 December (Christmas Day).

* These holidays are dependent on the Islamic lunar calendar and may vary by one or two days from the dates given.

Weights and Measures

The metric system is in force.

Statistical Survey

Source (unless otherwise stated): Badan Pusat Statistik (Central Bureau of Statistics/Statistics Indonesia), Jalan Dr Sutomo 6–8, Jakarta 10710; tel. (21) 3507057; fax (21) 3857046; e-mail bpshq@bps.go.id; internet www.bps.go.id.

Note: Unless otherwise stated, figures for East Timor (now Timor-Leste, occupied by Indonesia between July 1976 and October 1999) are not included in the tables.

Area and Population

AREA, POPULATION AND DENSITY

Area (sq km)	1,922,570*
Population (census results)	
31 October 1990	178,631,196
30 June 2000	
Males	103,417,180
Females	102,847,415
Total	206,264,595
Density (per sq km) at 30 June 2000	107.3

* 742,308 sq miles.

ISLANDS

(population at 2000 census)*

	Area (sq km)	Population	Density (per sq km)
Jawa (Java) and Madura . . .	127,499	121,352,608	951.8
Sumatera (Sumatra)	482,393	43,309,707	89.8
Sulawesi (Celebes)	191,800	14,946,488	77.9
Kalimantan	547,891	11,331,558	20.7
Nusa Tenggara†	67,502	7,961,540	117.9
Bali	5,633	3,151,162	559.4
Maluku (Moluccas)	77,871	1,990,598	25.6
Papua‡	421,981	2,220,934	5.3
Total	1,922,570	206,264,595	107.3

* Figures refer to provincial divisions, each based on a large island or group of islands but also including adjacent small islands.

† Comprising most of the Lesser Sunda Islands, principally Flores, Lombok, Sumba, Sumbawa and part of Timor.

‡ Formerly Irian Jaya (West Papua).

PRINCIPAL TOWNS

(estimated population at 31 December 1996)

Jakarta (capital) . .	9,341,400	Malang	775,900
Surabaya	2,743,400	Padang	739,500
Bandung	2,429,000	Banjarmasin . .	544,700
Medan	1,942,000	Surakarta . . .	518,600
Palembang . . .	1,394,300	Pontianak . . .	459,100
Semarang	1,366,500	Yogyakarta	
		(Jogjakarta) . .	421,000
Ujung Pandang			
(Makassar) . . .	1,121,300		

Mid-2000 (UN estimates, '000 persons, incl. suburbs): Jakarta 11,018; Bandung 3,409; Surabaya 2,461; Medan 1,879; Palembang 1,422; Ujung Pandang 1,051 (Source: UN, *World Urbanization Prospects: The 2001 Revision*).

Mid-2001 (UN estimate, '000 persons, incl. suburbs): Jakarta 11,429 (Source: UN, *World Urbanization Prospects: The 2001 Revision*).

BIRTHS AND DEATHS

(UN estimates, annual averages)

	1985–90	1990–95	1995–2000
Birth rate (per 1,000) . . .	28.0	24.9	22.5
Death rate (per 1,000) . . .	9.3	8.3	7.5

Source: UN, *World Population Prospects: The 2000 Revision*.

Expectation of life (WHO estimates, years at birth): 65.9 (males 64.4; females 67.4) in 2001 (Source: WHO, *World Health Report*).

Birth rate (per 1,000): 22.9 in 1997; 22.8 in 1998; 22.4 in 1999 (Source: UN, *Statistical Yearbook for Asia and the Pacific*).

Death rate (per 1,000): 7.5 in 1997; 7.7 in 1998; 7.5 in 1999 (Source: UN, *Statistical Yearbook for Asia and the Pacific*).

ECONOMICALLY ACTIVE POPULATION
(persons aged 15 years and over)

	1999	2000*	2001
Agriculture, hunting, forestry and fishing	38,378,133	40,676,713	39,743,908
Mining and quarrying . . .	725,739	n.a.	n.a.
Manufacturing	11,515,955	11,641,756	12,086,122
Electricity, gas and water . .	188,321	n.a.	n.a.
Construction	3,415,147	3,497,232	3,837,554
Trade, restaurants and hotels .	17,529,099	18,489,005	17,469,129
Transport, storage and communications	4,206,067	4,553,855	4,448,279
Financing, insurance, real estate and business services . . .	633,744	882,600	1,127,823
Public services	12,224,654	9,574,009	11,003,482
Activities not adequately defined .	—	522,560†	1,091,120†
Total employed	88,816,859	89,837,730	90,807,417
Unemployed	6,030,319	5,813,231	8,005,031
Total labour force	94,847,178	95,650,961	98,812,448

* Excluding Maluku province.

† Includes mining and quarrying and electricity, gas and water.

Health and Welfare

KEY INDICATORS

Total fertility rate (children per woman, 2001)	2.4
Under-5 mortality rate (per 1,000 live births, 2001) . . .	45
HIV/AIDS (% of persons aged 15–49, 2001)	0.10
Physicians (per 1,000 head, 1994)	0.16
Hospital beds (per 1,000 head, 1994)	0.66
Health expenditure (2000): US $ per head (PPP) . . .	84
Health expenditure (2000): % of GDP	2.7
Health expenditure (2000): public (% of total) . . .	23.7
Access to water (% of persons, 2000)	76
Access to sanitation (% of persons, 2000) . . .	66
Human Development Index (2000): ranking . . .	110
Human Development Index (2000): value	0.684

For sources and definitions, see explanatory note on p. vi.

Agriculture

PRINCIPAL CROPS
('000 metric tons, incl. East Timor)

	1999	2000	2001
Rice (paddy)	50,866	51,898	50,096
Maize	9,204	9,677	9,165
Potatoes	924	977	1,000
Sweet potatoes	1,666	1,828	1,686
Cassava (Manioc)	16,438	16,089	16,158
Other roots and tubers* . . .	350	350	350
Sugar cane†	24,000	23,500	23,900
Dry beans*	900	900	900
Cashew nuts	88	90	80*
Soybeans	1,383	1,018	863
Groundnuts (in shell)† . . .	1,020	974	990
Coconuts	13,946†	13,891†	14,300*
Oil palm fruit*	31,250	34,750	38,500*
Cabbages	1,660	1,556†	1,750*
Tomatoes	324	315*	320*
Pumpkins, squash and gourds .	221†	250*	290*
Cucumbers and gherkins . .	432	450*	480*
Aubergines (Eggplants) . . .	300	300*	300*
Chillies and green peppers . .	497	510*	550*
Dry onions	938	773	1,000*
Garlic	62	59	60*
Green beans	172	175*	175*
Carrots	287	327	320*
Other vegetables*	1,429	1,451	1,493
Oranges	500	644	680*
Avocados	126	128*	130*
Mangoes	827	876	950*
Pineapples	317	360*	300*
Bananas	3,376	3,747	3,600*
Papayas	450	429	470*
Other fruits and berries* . .	1,557	1,540	1,740
Coffee (green)	493	495	377†
Cocoa beans	443	466	340†
Tea (made)	161	159	172*
Tobacco (leaves)	135	136	134
Natural rubber	1,604	1,610	1,650*

* FAO estimate(s).
† Unofficial figure(s).

Source: FAO.

LIVESTOCK
('000 head, incl. East Timor; year ending September)

	1999	2000	2001
Cattle	11,276	11,642	11,191
Sheep	7,226	7,427	7,294
Goats	12,701	12,585	12,456
Pigs	7,042	5,357	5,897
Horses	484	517	430
Buffaloes	2,504	2,405	2,287
Chickens	622,531	859,497	853,832
Ducks	27,552	28,076	29,905

Source: FAO.

LIVESTOCK PRODUCTS
('000 metric tons, incl. East Timor)

	1999	2000	2001
Beef and veal	309	351	339
Buffalo meat	48	46	42
Mutton and lamb	32	36	33
Goat meat	45	45	43
Pig meat*	550	413	463
Poultry meat	620	818	821
Cows' milk	436	498	505
Sheep's milk*	87	89	89
Goats' milk*	204	200	200
Hen eggs	525	642	641
Other poultry eggs . . .	116	120	125*
Wool: greasy*	22	22	22
Cattle and buffalo hides* . .	57	56	55
Sheepskins*	7	8	8
Goatskins*	10	10	10

Note: Figures for meat refer to inspected production only, i.e. from animals slaughtered under government supervision.
* FAO estimate(s).
Source: FAO.

Forestry

ROUNDWOOD REMOVALS
('000 cubic metres, excluding bark)

	1999	2000	2001
Sawlogs, veneer logs and logs for sleepers:			
Coniferous .	300	—	—
Non-coniferous .	33,000	27,000	27,000
Pulpwood .	3,248	3,248*	3,248*
Other industrial wood* .	3,249	3,249	3,249
Fuel wood* .	90,417	88,981	85,712
Total .	130,214	122,478	119,209

* FAO estimate(s).
Source: FAO.

SAWNWOOD PRODUCTION
('000 cubic metres, including railway sleepers)

	1999	2000	2001
Coniferous (softwood) .	125	—	—
Broadleaved (hardwood).	6,500	6,500	6,400
Total .	6,625	6,500	6,400

Source: FAO.

Fishing

('000 metric tons, live weight)

	1998	1999	2000
Capture .	3,964.9	3,986.9	4,140.0
Scads .	277.6	261.1	261.3
Goldstripe sardinella .	174.7	162.7	163.5
Bali sardinella .	154.0	89.3	92.7
'Stolephorus' anchovies .	166.8	163.1	165.2
Kawakawa .	236.7	236.1	251.5
Skipjack tuna .	227.1	244.8	270.8
Indian mackerels .	204.8	201.5	203.5
Aquaculture .	629.8	749.3	788.5
Common carp .	109.9	168.9	180.2
Milkfish .	158.7	209.8	217.2
Total catch .	4,594.7	4,736.2	4,928.5

Note: Figures exclude aquatic plants ('000 metric tons): 47.5 (capture 7.5, aquaculture 40.0) in 1998; 49.8 (capture 7.8, aquaculture 42.0) in 1999; 223.1 (capture 17.9, aquaculture 205.2) in 2000. Also excluded are crocodiles, recorded by number rather than by weight. The number of crocodiles caught was: 11,647 in 1998; 7,661 in 1999; 10,387 in 2000.
Source: FAO, *Yearbook of Fishery Statistics*.

Mining

('000 metric tons, unless otherwise indicated)

	1998	1999	2000
Crude petroleum (million barrels)‡	568.2	547.6	516.1
Natural gas (million cubic metres)	84,333	86,863	82,334
Bauxite .	1,055	1,116	1,551
Coal .	61,146	72,618	76,800§
Nickel*.	74.1	89.1	98.2
Copper* .	780.8	766.0	1,012.1
Tin ore (metric tons)* .	53,959	47,754	51,629
Gold (kg)† .	124,018	127,184	124,596
Silver (kg)† .	348,987	288,200	255,578

* Figures refer to the metal content of ores and concentrates.
† Including gold and silver in copper concentrate.
‡ Including condensate.
§ Estimate.

Source: US Geological Survey.

Industry

SELECTED PRODUCTS
('000 metric tons, unless otherwise indicated)

	1996	1997	1998
Refined sugar .	2,564	n.a.	1,793
Cigarettes (million) .	n.a.	220,157	271,177
Veneer sheets ('000 cubic metres) .	50	50	1,110
Plywood ('000 cubic metres) .	9,575	9,600	7,015
Newsprint .	267	390	478
Other printing and writing paper .	1,236	1,510	1,855
Other paper and paperboard*†	2,618	2,922	3,154
Nitrogenous fertilizers*†‡ .	2,986	2,993	2,899
Jet fuel .	1,167	990	1,150†
Motor spirit (petrol) .	7,155	7,950	7,302†
Naphthas .	1,673	929	522†
Kerosene .	6,894	6,159	6,956†
Gas-diesel oil .	14,400†	12,275†	13,423†
Residual fuel oils .	10,200†	12,000†	11,560†
Lubricating oils .	240†	220†	211†
Liquefied petroleum gas.	3,179	2,945	2,344†
Rubber tyres ('000)§ .	n.a.	23,388	25,701
Cement .	24,648	20,702	22,344†
Aluminium (unwrought)‖¶ .	223.2	219.4	133.4
Tin (unwrought, metric tons)†‖¶ .	48,960	52,577	54,000
Radio receivers ('000) .	n.a.	4,177	n.a.
Passenger motor cars ('000)[1] .	n.a.	42	6
Electric energy (million kWh)† .	78,117	84,096	90,027
Gas from gasworks (terajoules) .	29,528	20,134	26,715†

1999: Veneer sheets ('000 cubic metres) 927; Plywood ('000 cubic metres) 4,437; Newsprint ('000 metric tons) 532; Other printing and writing paper ('000 metric tons) 2,733; Cement ('000 metric tons) 24,024†.

* Data from FAO.
† Provisional or estimated production.
‡ Production in terms of nitrogen.
§ For road motor vehicles, excluding bicycles and motorcycles.
‖ Primary metal production only.
¶ Data from *World Metal Statistics*.
[1] Vehicles assembled from imported parts.

Source: mainly UN, *Industrial Commodity Statistics Yearbook*.

Palm oil ('000 metric tons): 4,899 in 1996; 5,385 in 1997; 5,902 in 1998; 6,250 (unofficial figure) in 1999; 7,050 (unofficial figure) in 2000; 7,950 (unofficial figure) in 2001 (Source: FAO).

Raw sugar (centrifugal, '000 metric tons): 2,160 in 1996; 2,187 in 1997; 1,846 in 1998; 1,494 in 1999; 1,575 in 2000; 1,635 in 2001 (Source: FAO).

Finance

CURRENCY AND EXCHANGE RATES

Monetary Units
  100 sen = 1 rupiah (Rp.)

Sterling, Dollar and Euro Equivalents (31 December 2002)
  £1 sterling = 14,409.5 rupiah
  US \$1 = 8,940.0 rupiah
  €1 = 9,375.4 rupiah
  100,000 rupiah = £6.940 = \$11.186 = €10.666

Average Exchange Rate (rupiah per US \$)
  2000   8,421.8
  2001   10,260.9
  2002   9,311.2

BUDGET

('000 million rupiah, year ending 31 March)

Revenue	1998/99	1999/2000	2000/01*
Tax revenue	147,600	183,281	196,720
Taxes on income, profits, etc.† .	97,313	118,164	94,462
Individual	52,995	15,571	19,146
Corporate‡	41,368	99,638	70,463
Domestic taxes on goods and services	38,750	55,453	78,254
General sales, turnover or VAT	27,803	33,087	55,863
Excises	7,733	10,381	17,394
Taxes on international trade. .	6,936	5,035	9,568
Import duties	2,306	4,177	9,026
Export duties	4,630	858	542
Non-tax revenue	9,781	15,330	111,121
Entrepreneurial and property income	6,281	10,292	15,834
Other	1,967	3,347	92,787
Total	157,381	198,611	307, 841
Capital revenue	31	62	35

Expenditure	1998/99	1999/2000	2000/01*
General public services . . .	16,148	11,425	16,607
Defence	8,955	8,576	10,673
Public order and safety . . .	3,080	4,453	7,400
Education	11,918	14,349	13,433
Health	3,889	5,186	4,542
Social security and welfare . . .	9,220	12,006	30,766
Housing and community amenities	23,435	33,787	4,726
Recreational, cultural and religious affairs	2,992	3,347	2,257
Economic affairs and services . .	22,164	23,250	12,747
Agriculture, hunting, forestry and fishing	11,511	8,610	4,652
Transportation and communication	6,395	5,580	3,709
Other economic affairs and services	2,481	5,509	858
Other	72,297	109,494	255,886
Interest payments	31,264	42,910	—
Total	174,097	225,874	359,038
Current expenditure	114,412	170,684	n.a.
Capital expenditure	59,686	55,190	n.a.

* Figures are provisional.

† Prior to 1999, tax on income, profits, etc. could not be broken into its components, and almost all income tax was classified as taxes paid by individuals.

‡ Prior to 2000, natural resources oil and gas revenue were classified as corporate income tax.

Source: IMF, *Government Finance Statistics Yearbook*.

INTERNATIONAL RESERVES

(US $ million at 31 December)

	2000	2001	2002
Gold*	766	772	1,076
IMF special drawing rights . . .	32	16	19
Reserve position in IMF	190	183	198
Foreign exchange	28,280	27,048	30,284
Total	29,268	28,019	31,577

* Valued at market-related prices.

Source: IMF, *International Financial Statistics*.

MONEY SUPPLY

('000 million rupiah at 31 December)

	2000	2001	2002
Currency outside banks	72,370	76,342	80,659
Demand deposits at deposit money banks	82,241	97,746	106,558
Total money (incl. others) . .	160,923	175,110	188,008

Source: IMF, *International Financial Statistics*.

COST OF LIVING

(Consumer Price Index; base: 1996 = 100)*

	1999	2000	2001
Food (incl. beverages)	242.5	249.0	267.1
Non-food	177.3	190.2	213.4
All items	202.7	210.3	234.5

* Excluding East Timor (now Timor-Leste) since November 1999.

Source: Asian Development Bank, *Key Indicators of Developing Asian and Pacific Countries*.

NATIONAL ACCOUNTS

('000 million rupiah at current prices)

National Income and Product

	1996	1997	1998
Domestic factor incomes* . . .	505,939	596,310	952,855
Consumption of fixed capital . .	26,628	31,385	49,479
Gross domestic product (GDP) at factor cost . .	532,567	627,695	1,002,334
Indirect taxes, *less* subsidies . .	—	—	—
GDP in purchasers' values . .	532,567	627,695	1,002,334
Net factor income from abroad . .	−14,271	18,355	−53,895
Gross national product (GNP) .	518,296	609,340	948,439
Less Consumption of fixed capital .	26,628	31,385	49,479
National income in market prices	491,668	577,955	898,960

* Compensation of employees and the operating surplus of enterprises. The amount is obtained as a residual.

Source: UN, *National Accounts Statistics*.

Expenditure on the Gross Domestic Product

	1999	2000	2001
Government final consumption expenditure	72,631	90,780	110,837
Private final consumption expenditure	813,183	867,997	999,266
Increase in stocks*	−96,461	−81,385	−56,820
Gross fixed capital formation . .	221,472	268,669	310,909
Total domestic expenditure . .	1,010,825	1,146,061	1,364,192
Exports of goods and services . .	390,560	542,992	612,482
Less Imports of goods and services	301,654	407,036	485,700
GDP in purchasers' values . .	1,099,732	1,282,018	1,490,974
GDP at constant 1993 prices .	379,352	397,934	411,132

* Figures obtained as a residual.

Source: Asian Development Bank, *Key Indicators of Developing Asian and Pacific Countries*.

Gross Domestic Product by Economic Activity

	1999	2000	2001
Agriculture, forestry and fishing .	215,687	218,301	244,381
Mining and quarrying	109,925	176,640	202,680
Manufacturing	285,874	335,339	389,321
Electricity, gas and water . . .	13,429	15,072	17,286
Construction	67,616	76,091	84,045
Trade, hotels and restaurants . .	175,835	194,910	239,959
Transport, storage and communications	55,190	64,550	79,825
Finance, insurance, real estate and business services	71,220	79,477	92,459
Public administration	56,745	69,460	81,851
Other services	48,210	52,177	59,167
Total	1,099,732	1,282,018	1,490,974

Source: Asian Development Bank, *Key Indicators of Developing Asian and Pacific Countries*.

BALANCE OF PAYMENTS
(US $ million)

	1999	2000	2001
Exports of goods f.o.b.	51,242	65,406	57,364
Imports of goods f.o.b.	−30,598	−40,366	−34,669
Trade balance	20,644	25,040	22,695
Exports of services	4,599	5,213	5,500
Imports of services	−11,573	−15,011	−15,880
Balance on goods and services	13,670	15,242	12,315
Other income received	1,891	2,456	2,004
Other income paid	−11,690	−11,529	−8,940
Balance on goods, services and income	3,871	6,169	5,379
Current transfers received	1,914	1,816	1,520
Current balance	5,785	7,985	6,899
Direct investment abroad	−72	−150	−125
Direct investment from abroad	−2,745	−4,550	−3,278
Portfolio investment liabilities	−1,792	−1,909	−243
Other investment liabilities	−1,332	−1,287	−3,968
Net errors and omissions	2,128	3,637	700
Overall balance	1,972	3,726	−15

Source: IMF, *International Financial Statistics*.

External Trade

PRINCIPAL COMMODITIES
(distribution by SITC, US $ million)

Imports c.i.f.	1996	1997	1998
Food and live animals	3,926.6	2,979.8	2,611.7
Cereals and cereal preparations	2,002.5	1,106.1	1,567.9
Rice	766.4	109.0	861.2
Crude materials (inedible) except fuels	3,441.3	2,958.8	2,349.1
Textile fibres and waste	1,261.3	1,034.0	976.0
Mineral fuels, lubricants, etc.	3,775.0	4,142.0	2,752.4
Crude petroleum oils, etc.	1,519.0	1,467.1	1,058.3
Refined petroleum products	2,086.2	2,451.7	1,611.7
Gas oils	963.6	1,173.1	893.2
Chemicals and related products	5,876.9	5,768.9	4,030.0
Organic chemicals	2,226.8	2,222.9	1,491.5
Basic manufactures	6,844.7	6,715.4	4,671.0
Textile yarn, fabrics, etc.	1,288.4	1,172.9	1,036.6
Iron and steel	2,370.8	2,286.4	1,478.6
Machinery and transport equipment	17,458.6	17,499.8	9,902.9
Power-generating machinery and equipment	1,968.6	1,877.0	1,154.5
Machinery specialized for particular industries	4,118.4	3,959.4	2,702.2
General industrial machinery, equipment and parts	3,629.2	3,682.3	2,394.3
Telecommunications and sound equipment	1,766.3	1,778.8	504.8
Other electrical machinery, apparatus, etc.	1,868.4	2,110.7	1,228.4
Road vehicles and parts*	2,673.5	2,593.0	940.0
Parts and accessories for cars, buses, lorries, etc.*	1,359.5	1,297.2	388.0
Total (incl. others)	42,928.5	41,679.8	27,336.9

Exports f.o.b.	1997	1998	1999
Food and live animals	3,531.4	3,717.4	3,643.8
Fish, crustaceans and molluscs	1,619.4	1,614.4	1,526.3
Coffee, tea, cocoa and spices	1,285.1	1,516.3	1,288.5
Crude materials (inedible) except fuels	4,357.8	3,719.2	3,396.6
Ores and concentrates of non-ferrous base metals	1,718.2	1,453.3	1,451.6
Mineral fuels, lubricants, etc.	13,153.9	9,429.4	11,191.3
Petroleum, petroleum products, etc.	6,822.4	4,264.3	5,528.6
Crude petroleum oils, etc.	5,480.0	3,348.6	4,517.3
Petroleum gases, etc., in the liquefied state	4,840.1	3,815.5	4,357.0
Animal and vegetable oils, fats and waxes	2,282.1	1,520.7	1,825.9
Fixed vegetable oils, fluid or solid, crude, refined or purified	2,174.9	1,152.1	1,674.4
Chemicals and related products	1,869.4	2,086.6	2,354.9
Basic manufactures	9,778.8	8,832.6	11,125.4
Wood and cork manufactures (excl. furniture)	4,445.3	2,714.4	3,306.6
Veneers, plywood, etc.	3,729.1	2,207.2	2,515.8
Plywood of wood sheets	3,410.6	2,077.9	2,256.3
Paper, paperboard, etc.	939.6	1,439.9	1,975.3
Textile yarn, fabrics, etc.	2,268.9	2,358.0	3,028.6
Machinery and transport equipment	4,620.0	4,654.6	5,271.6
Telecommunications and sound equipment	1,752.8	1,360.5	1,468.1
Miscellaneous manufactured articles	6,876.0	6,603.6	8,171.7
Clothing and accessories (excl. footwear)	2,952.8	2,681.2	3,914.9
Footwear	1,477.2	1,156.7	1,541.1
Jewellery, goldsmiths' and silversmiths' wares, etc.	703.4	1,661.7	174.2
Total (incl. others)	53,443.6	48,847.5	48,665.5

* Excluding tyres, engines and electrical parts.

Source: UN, *International Trade Statistics Yearbook*.

PRINCIPAL TRADING PARTNERS
(US $ million)*

Imports c.i.f.	1999	2000	2001
Australia	1,460.4	1,693.8	1,814.2
Canada	421.2	638.3	356.6
China, People's Republic	1,242.2	2,022.0	1,842.6
France	371.6	400.0	396.9
Germany	1,398.5	1,244.7	1,300.5
Hong Kong	227.5	342.4	257.4
Italy	276.9	345.1	407.5
Japan	2,913.3	5,397.3	4,689.4
Korea, Republic	1,330.1	2,082,6	2,209.4
Malaysia	605.6	1,128.8	n.a.
Netherlands	346.7	434.4	343.9
Singapore	2,525.9	3,788.6	3,147.0
Taiwan	784.1	1,269.7	1,071.1
Thailand	933.4	1,109.1	n.a.
United Kingdom	511.2	557.3	643.0
USA	2,839.0	3,390.3	3,207.6
Total (incl. others)	24,003.3	33,514.8	30,962.1

Exports f.o.b.	1999	2000	2001
Australia	1,484.8	1,519.4	1,844.8
Belgium/Luxembourg	696.5	840.6	n.a.
China, People's Republic	2,008.9	2,767.7	2,200.6
France	503.2	718.3	662.6
Germany	1,233.9	1,443.1	1,296.9
Hong Kong	1,330.0	1,554.1	1,290.3
Italy	655.5	757.8	621.9
Japan	10,397.2	14,415.2	13,010.1
Korea, Republic	3,319.8	4,317.9	3,772.4
Malaysia	1,335.9	1,971.8	n.a.
Netherlands	1,543.6	1,837.4	1,498.2
Philippines	694.7	819.5	n.a.
Singapore	4,930.5	6,562.4	5,363.8
Spain	741.6	932.2	n.a.
Taiwan	1,757.5	2,378.3	2,188.0
Thailand	812.7	1,026.5	n.a.
United Kingdom	1,176.1	1,507.9	1,383.1
USA	6,896.5	8,475.4	7,748.7
Total (incl. others)	48,665.4	62,124.0	56,320.9

* Imports by country of production; exports by country of consumption. Figures include trade in gold.

Transport

RAILWAYS
(traffic)

	1998	1999	2000
Passengers embarked (million)	170	187	192
Passenger-km (million)	16,340*	n.a.	n.a.
Freight loaded ('000 tons)	18,129	19,302	19,545
Freight ton-km (million)	5,368*	n.a.	n.a.

* Estimate.

Source: Indonesian State Railways.

ROAD TRAFFIC
(motor vehicles registered at 31 December)

	1998*	1999	2000†
Passenger cars	2,769,375	2,897,803	3,038,913
Lorries and trucks	1,586,721	1,628,531	1,707,134
Buses and coaches	626,680	644,667	666,280
Motorcycles	12,628,991	13,053,148	13,563,017

* Including East Timor (now Timor-Leste).
† Preliminary figures.

Source: State Police of Indonesia.

SHIPPING

Merchant Fleet
(registered at 31 December)

	1999	2000	2001
Number of vessels	2,369	2,480	2,528
Displacement ('000 grt)	3,241.5	3,384.2	3,613.1

Source: Lloyd's Register-Fairplay, *World Fleet Statistics*.

Sea-borne Freight Traffic
('000 metric tons)

	1999	2000	2001*
International:			
Goods loaded	139,340	141,528	143,750
Goods unloaded	43,477	45,040	46,659
Domestic:			
Goods loaded	113,633	127,740	163,685
Goods unloaded	122,368	137,512	138,667

* Preliminary figures.

CIVIL AVIATION
(traffic on scheduled services)

	1997	1998	1999
Kilometres flown (million)	199	155	122
Passengers carried ('000)	12,937	9,603	8,047
Passenger-km (million)	23,718	15,974	14,544
Total ton-km (million)	2,797	1,826	1,560

Source: UN, *Statistical Yearbook*.

Tourism

FOREIGN TOURIST ARRIVALS

Country of Residence	1999	2000	2001
Australia	531,211	459,994	397,982
Germany	169,083	151,897	159,881
Japan	606,102	643,794	611,314
Korea, Republic	220,440	213,762	212,233
Malaysia	440,212	475,845	484,692
Netherlands	86,022	105,109	114,656
Singapore	1,332,877	1,427,886	1,477,132
Taiwan	349,247	356,436	391,696
United Kingdom	138,296	161,662	189,027
USA	151,763	176,379	177,869
Total (incl. others)	4,727,520	5,064,217	5,153,620

Receipts from tourism (US $ million): 4,331 in 1998; 4,710 in 1999; 5,749 in 2000 (Source: World Tourism Organization).

Communications Media

	1999	2000	2001
Television receivers ('000 in use)	30,000	31,700	n.a.
Telephones ('000 main lines in use)	6,080.2	6,662.6	7,949.3
Mobile cellular telephones ('000 subscribers)	2,221.0	3,669.3	5,303.0
Personal computers ('000 in use)	1,900	2,100	2,300
Internet users ('000)	900	2,000	4,000

Facsimile machines (estimated number in use, 1997): 185,000.

Radio receivers ('000 in use, 1997): 31,500 (Source: UN, *Statistical Yearbook*).

Daily newspapers (1998): Number: 172; Average circulation: 4,713,000 (Source: UN, *Statistical Yearbook*).

Non-daily newspapers (1998): Number: 433; Average circulation: 7,838,000 (Source: UN, *Statistical Yearbook*).

Source (unless otherwise indicated): International Telecommunication Union.

Education

(2001/02)

	Institutions	Teachers	Pupils and Students
Primary schools	148,516	1,164,808	25,850,849
General junior secondary schools	20,842	476,827	7,466,458
General senior secondary schools	7,785	224,149	3,024,176
Vocational senior secondary schools	4,522	139,359	2,027,464
Universities*	1,634	194,828	3,126,307

* Figures from 1999/2000.

Source: Ministry of National Education.

Adult literacy rate (UNESCO estimates): 86.9% (males 91.8%; females 82.0%) in 2000 (Source: UN Development Programme, *Human Development Report*).

Directory

The Constitution

Indonesia had three provisional Constitutions: in August 1945, February 1950 and August 1950. In July 1959 the Constitution of 1945 was re-enacted by presidential decree. The General Elections Law of 1969 supplemented the 1945 Constitution, which has been adopted permanently by the Majelis Permusyawaratan Rakyat (MPR—People's Consultative Assembly). Amendments made to the Constitution in 2001 and 2002 were to take effect in 2004, when Indonesia was scheduled to hold its next general election. The following is a summary of the Constitution's main provisions, with subsequent amendments:

GENERAL PRINCIPLES

The 1945 Constitution consists of 37 articles, four transitional clauses and two additional provisions, and is preceded by a preamble. The preamble contains an indictment of all forms of colonialism, an account of Indonesia's struggle for independence, the declaration of that independence and a statement of fundamental aims and principles. Indonesia's National Independence, according to the text of the preamble, has the state form of a Republic, with sovereignty residing in the People, and is based upon five fundamental principles, the *pancasila*:
1. Belief in the One Supreme God.
2. Just and Civilized Humanity.
3. The Unity of Indonesia.
4. Democracy led by the wisdom of deliberations (*musyawarah*) and consensus among representatives.
5. Social Justice for all the people of Indonesia.

STATE ORGANS

Majelis Permusyawaratan Rakyat—MPR (People's Consultative Assembly)

Sovereignty is in the hands of the People and is exercised in full by the MPR as the embodiment of the whole Indonesian People. The MPR is the highest authority of the State, and is to be distinguished from the legislative body proper (Dewan Perwakilan Rakyat, see below), which is incorporated within the MPR. The bicameral MPR, with a total of 700 members (reduced from 1,000 in 1999), is composed of the members of the DPR and the DPD (see below). Elections to the MPR are held every five years. The MPR sits at least once every five years, and its primary competence is to determine the Constitution and the broad lines of the policy of the State and the Government. It also inaugurates the President and Vice-President, who are responsible for implementing that policy. All decisions are taken unanimously in keeping with the traditions of *musyawarah*.

The President

The highest executive of the Government, the President, holds office for a term of five years and may be re-elected once. As Mandatory of the MPR he must execute the policy of the State according to the Decrees determined by the MPR during its Fourth General and Special Sessions. In conducting the administration of the State, authority and responsibility are concentrated in the President. The Ministers of the State are his assistants and are responsible only to him. The President and Vice-President are to be directly elected on a single ticket (until November 2001 the MPR had exercised the power to elect them). If no candidate succeeds in obtaining more than one-half of the votes cast in a general election, a second round of voting shall be held. The President and Vice-President may be dismissed by the MPR on the proposal of the Dewan Perwakilan Rakyat if it is proven that he/she has either violated the law or no longer meets the requirements of his/her office. The President may not freeze or dissolve the Dewan.

Dewan Perwakilan Rakyat (House of Representatives)

The legislative branch of the State, the Dewan Perwakilan Rakyat, sits at least once a year. Its members are all directly elected. Every statute requires the approval of the Dewan. Members of the Dewan have the right to submit draft bills which require ratification by the President, who has the right of veto. In times of emergency the President may enact ordinances which have the force of law, but such Ordinances must be ratified by the Dewan during the following session or be revoked.

Dewan Perwakilan Daerah—DPD (House of Representatives of the Regions)

The Dewan Perwakilan Daerah is the second chamber of the MPR. Its members are directly elected from every province. Each province has an equal number of members and total membership of the DPD is no more than one-third of the total membership of the DPR. The DPD sits at least once a year. It may propose to the DPR Bills relating to regional autonomy, the relationship between central and local government, the formation, expansion and merger of regions, the management of natural and other economic resources, and the financial balance between the centre and the localities. It may also participate in the discussion of such Bills and oversee the implementation of regional laws, as well as the State Budget, taxation, education and religion.

Dewan Pertimbangan Agung—DPA (Supreme Advisory Council)

The DPA is an advisory body assisting the President who chooses its members from political parties, functional groups and groups of prominent persons.

Mahkamah Agung (Supreme Court)

The judicial branch of the State, the Supreme Court and the other courts of law (public courts, religious courts, military tribunals, administrative courts and a Constitutional Court) are independent of the Executive in exercising their judicial powers. There is an independent Judicial Commission which is authorized to propose candidates for appointment as justices of the Supreme Court and to ensure the good behaviour of judges. Its members are appointed and dismissed by the President with the approval of the DPR.

Badan Pemeriksa Keuangan (Supreme Audit Board)

Controls the accountability of public finance, enjoys investigatory powers and is independent of the Executive. Its findings are presented to the Dewan.

The Government

HEAD OF STATE

President: MEGAWATI SUKARNOPUTRI (inaugurated 23 July 2001).
Vice-President: HAMZAH HAZ.

CABINET
(April 2003)

Co-ordinating Minister for Political Affairs, Security and Social Welfare: Gen. (retd) SUSILO BAMBANG YUDHOYONO.

Co-ordinating Minister for the Economy, Finance and Industry: DORODJATUN KUNTJORO-JAKTI.

Co-ordinating Minister for People's Welfare: JUSUF KALLA.

Minister of Home Affairs and Regional Autonomy: Lt-Gen. (retd) HARI SABARNO.

Minister of Foreign Affairs: HASSAN WIRAYUDA.

Minister of Defence: MATORI ABDUL DJALIL.

Minister of Maritime Affairs and Fisheries: ROCHIMIN DAHURI.

Minister for Justice and Human Rights Affairs: YUSRIL IHZA.

Minister of Finance and State Enterprises Development: BOEDIONO.

Minister of Industry and Trade: RINI SUWANDI.

Minister of Agriculture: Prof. Dr Ir BUNGARAN SARAGIH.

Minister of Forestry: M. PRAKOSA.

Minister of Energy and Mineral Resources: Dr Ir PURNOMO YUSGIANTORO.

Minister of Transportation and Telecommunication: Lt-Gen. (retd) AGUM GUMELAR.

Minister of Manpower and Transmigration: JACOB NUWA WEA.

Minister of National Education: ABDUL MALIK FAJAR.

Minister of Health: Dr AHMAD SUYUDI.

Minister of Social Affairs: BACHTIAR CHAMSYAH.

Minister of Religious Affairs: SAID AQIEL MUNAWAR.

Minister of Resettlement and Regional Infrastructure Development: SOENARNO.

Minister of State for Culture and Tourism: Drs I. GDE ARDIKA.

Minister of State for Research and Technology: HATTA RAJASA.

Minister of State for Co-operatives and Small- and Medium-Sized Businesses: ALIMARWAN HANAN.

Minister of State for the Environment: NABIEL MAKARIM.

Minister of State for Women's Empowerment: Sri REDJEKI SOE-MARYOTO.

Minister of State for Administrative Reform: FEISAL TAMIN.

Minister of State for State Enterprises: LAKSAMANA SUKARDI.

Minister of State for Communications and Information: SYAMSUL MU'ARIF.

Minister of State for Eastern Indonesian Development: MANUEL KAISIEPO.

Minister of State for National Development Planning: KWIK KIAN GIE.

Officials with the rank of Minister of State:

Attorney-General: MUHAMMAD ABDUL RACHMAN.

State Secretary: BAMBANG KESOWO.

MINISTRIES

Office of the President: Instant Merdeka, Jakarta; tel. (21) 3840946.

Office of the Vice-President: Jalan Merdeka Selatan 6, Jakarta; tel. (21) 363539.

Office of the Attorney-General: Jalan Sultan Hasanuddin 1, Kebayoran Baru, Jakarta; tel. (21) 7221377; fax (21) 7392576; e-mail kejagung@kejaksaan.go.id; internet www.kejaksaan.go.id.

Office of the Cabinet Secretary: Jalan Veteran 18, Jakarta Pusat; tel. (21) 3810973.

Office of the Co-ordinating Minister for Political Affairs, Security and Social Welfare: Jalan Medan Merdeka Barat 15, Jakarta 10110; tel. (21) 3849453; fax (21) 3450918.

Office of the Co-ordinating Minister for the Economy, Finance and Industry: Jalan Taman Suropati 2, Jakarta 10310; tel. (21) 3849063; fax (21) 334779.

Office of the State Secretary: Jalan Veteran 17, Jakarta 10110; tel. (21) 3849043; fax (21) 3452685; internet www.ri.go.id.

Ministry of Agriculture and Forestry: Jalan Harsono R.M. 3, Gedung D-Lantai 4, Ragunan, Pasar Minggu, Jakarta Selatan 12550; tel. (21) 7822638; fax (21) 7816385; e-mail eko@deptan.go.id; internet www.deptan.go.id.

Ministry of Defence: Jalan Medan Merdeka Barat 13–14, Jakarta Pusat; tel. (21) 3456184; fax (21) 3440023; e-mail postmaster@dephan.go.id; internet www.dephan.go.id.

Ministry of Finance and State Enterprises Development: Jalan Lapangan Banteng Timur 2–4, Jakarta 10710; tel. (21) 3814324; fax (21) 353710; internet www.depkeu.go.id.

Ministry of Foreign Affairs: Jalan Taman Pejambon 6, Jakarta 10410; tel. (21) 3441508; fax (21) 3805511; e-mail guestbook@dfa-deplu.go.id; internet www.deplu.go.id.

Ministry of Health and Social Welfare: Jalan H. R. Rasuna Said, Block X5, Kav. 4–9, Jakarta 12950; tel. (21) 5201587; fax (21) 5203874; e-mail webadmin@depkes.go.id; internet www.depkes.go.id.

Ministry of Home Affairs and Regional Autonomy: Jalan Merdeka Utara 7–8, Gedung Utama Lt. 4, Jakarta Pusat 10110; tel. (21) 3842222; fax (21) 372812; e-mail dpod@indosat.net.id; internet www.depdagri.go.id.

Ministry of Industry and Trade: Jalan Jenderal Gatot Subroto, Kav. 52–53, 2nd Floor, Jakarta Selatan; tel. (21) 5256458; fax (21) 5229592; e-mail men-indag@dprin.go.id; internet www.deprin.go.id.

Ministry of Justice and Human Rights Affairs: Jalan H. R. Rasuna Said, Kav. 4–5, Kuningan, Jakarta Pusat; tel. (21) 5253004; fax (21) 5253095; internet www.depkehham.go.id.

Ministry of Manpower and Transmigration: Jalan Jenderal Gatot Subroto, Kav. 51, Jakarta Selatan 12950; tel. (21) 5255683; fax (21) 515669; internet www.nakertrans.go.id.

Ministry of Mines and Mineral Resources: Jalan Merdeka Selatan 18, Jakarta 10110; tel. (21) 3804242; fax (21) 3847461; e-mail pulahta@setjen.dpe.go.id; internet www.dpe.go.id.

Ministry of National Education: Jalan Jenderal Sudirman, Senayan, Jakarta Pusat; tel. (21) 5731618; fax (21) 5736870; internet www.depdiknas.go.id.

Ministry of Religious Affairs: Jalan Lapangan Banteng Barat 3–4, Jakarta Pusat; tel. (21) 3811436; fax (21) 380836; internet www.depag.go.id.

Ministry of Transportation and Telecommunication: Jalan Merdeka Barat 8, Jakarta 10110; tel. (21) 3811308; fax (21) 3451657; e-mail pusdatin@rad.net.id; internet www.dephub.go.id.

Office of the Minister of State for Co-operatives and Small- and Medium-Sized Businesses: Jalan H. R. Rasuna Said, Kav. 3–5, POB 177, Jakarta Selatan 12940; tel. (21) 5204366; fax (21) 5204383; internet www.depkop.go.id.

Office of the Minister of State for the Environment: Jalan D. I. Panjaitan, Kebon Nanas Lt. II, Jakarta 134110; tel. (21) 8580103; fax (21) 8580101; internet www.bapedal.go.id.

Office of the Minister of State for Research and Technology: BPP Teknologi II Bldg, Jalan M. H. Thamrin 8, Jakarta Pusat 10340; tel. (21) 3169166; fax (21) 3101952; e-mail webmstr@ristek.go.id; internet www.ristek.go.id.

Office of the Minister of State for Women's Affairs: Jalan Medan Merdeka Barat 15, Jakarta 10110; tel. (21) 3805563; fax (21) 3805562; e-mail birum@menperta.go.id.

OTHER GOVERNMENT BODIES

Dewan Pertimbangan Agung (DPA) (Supreme Advisory Council): Jalan Merdeka Utara 15, Jakarta; tel. (21) 362369; internet www.dpa.go.id; Chair. Gen. (retd) ACHMAD TIRTOSUDIRO; Sec.-Gen. SUTOYO.

Badan Pemeriksa Keuangan (BPK) (Supreme Audit Board): Jalan Gatot Subroto 31, Jakarta; tel. (21) 584081; internet www.bpk.go.id; Chair. Prof. Dr SATRIO BUDIHARDJO JUDONO; Vice-Chair. Drs BAMBANG TRIADJI.

Legislature

MAJELIS PERMUSYAWARATAN RAKYAT (MPR)
(People's Consultative Assembly)

Jalan Jendral Gatot Subroto 6, Jakarta 10270; tel. (21) 5715268; fax (21) 5715611; e-mail kotaksurat@mpr.go.id; internet www.mpr.go.id.

The Majelis Permusyawaratan Rakyat (MPR—People's Consultative Assembly) consists of the 500 members of the Dewan Perwakilan Rakyat (House of Representatives) and 200 other appointees (reduced from 500 in 1999), including regional delegates and representatives of various professions. In late 2002 the Constitution was amended to provide for the direct election of all members of the MPR at the next general election, scheduled to be held in 2004. The MPR was to be a bicameral institution comprising the Dewan Perwakilan Rakyat and the Dewan Perwakilan Daerah (House of Representatives of the Regions).

Speaker: Dr AMIEN RAIS.

	Seats
Members of the Dewan Perwakilan Rakyat	500
Regional representatives	135
Professional representatives	65
Total	700

Dewan Perwakilan Rakyat
(House of Representatives)

Jalan Gatot Subroto 16, Jakarta; tel. (21) 586833; e-mail humas-dpr@dpr.go.id; internet www.dpr.go.id.

Following the election of June 1999 the Dewan Perwakilan Rakyat (House of Representatives) comprised 500 members; of these, 462 were directly elected (increased from 425) and 38 were nominated by the President from the armed forces (reduced from 75). In 2002 the Constitution was amended to provide for the direct election of all members of the Dewan at the next general election, scheduled to be held in 2004. The role of the armed forces in the Dewan was thus to be abolished.

Speaker: Ir AKBAR TANDJUNG.

General Election, 7 June 1999

	Seats
Partai Demokrasi Indonesia Perjuangan (PDI—P)	154
Partai Golongan Karya (Golkar)	120
Partai Persatuan Pembangunan (PPP)	59
Partai Kebangkitan Bangsa (PKB)	51
Partai Amanat Nasional (PAN)	35
Partai Bulan Bintang (PBB)	13
Partai Keadilan (PK)	6
Partai Keadilan dan Persatuan (PKP)	6
Partai Demokrasi Kasih Bangsa (PDKB)	3
Partai Nahdlatul Umat (PNU)	3
Partai Bhinneka Tunggal Ika	3
Partai Demokrasi Indonesia (PDI)	2
Others	7
Appointed members*	38
Total	500

*Members of the political wing of the Indonesian National Defence Forces (TNI).

Political Organizations

Prior to 1998, electoral legislation permitted only three organizations (Golkar, the PDI and PPP) to contest elections. Following the replacement of President Suharto in May 1998, political restrictions were relaxed and new parties were allowed to form (with the only condition being that all parties must adhere to the *pancasila* and reject communism); by early 1999, more than 200 new political parties were reported to have been established.

Barisan Nasional (National Front): Jakarta; f. 1998; committed to ensuring that Indonesia remains a secular state; Sec.-Gen. RACHMAT WITOELAR.

Chinese Indonesian Reform Party: Jakarta; e-mail lieus@parti.or.id; f. 1998.

Indonesian National Unity: Jakarta; f. 1995 by fmr mems of Sukarno's National Party; seeks full implementation of 1945 Constitution; Chair. SUPENI.

Indonesian Reform Party (PPI): Jakarta; f. 1998; Gen. Chair. CHANDRA KUWATLI; Sec.-Gen. Dr H. ACE MULYADI.

Islamic Indonesian Party (PII): Jakarta; f. 1998; Pres. SUUD BAJEBER; Sec.-Gen. SYAIFUL MUNIR.

National Brotherhood Foundation: Jakarta; f. 1995; Chair. KHARIS SUHUD.

New Indonesian National Party: Jakarta; f. 1998.

Partai Amanat Nasional (PAN) (National Mandate Party): c/o Dewan Perwakilan Rakyat, Jalan Gatot Subroto 16, Jakarta; f. 1998; aims to achieve democracy, progress and social justice, to limit the length of the presidential term of office and to increase autonomy in the provinces; Gen. Chair. Dr AMIEN RAIS; Sec.-Gen. FAISAL BASRI.

Partai Bhinneka Tunggal Ika (PBI): c/o Dewan Perwakilan Rakyat, Jalan Gatot Subroto 16, Jakarta.

Partai Bulan Bintang (PBB) (Cresent Moon and Star Party): c/o Dewan Perwakilan Rakyat, Jalan Gatot Subroto 16, Jakarta; f. 1998; Leader YUSRIL IHZA MAHENDRA.

Partai Demokrasi Indonesia (PDI) (Indonesian Democratic Party): Jalan Diponegoro 58, Jakarta 10310; tel. (21) 336331; fax (21) 5201630; f. 1973 by merger of five nationalist and Christian parties; Chair. SOERJADI (installed to replace Megawati Sukarnoputri as leader of the party in a government-orchestrated coup in 1996).

Partai Demokrasi Indonesia Perjuangan (PDI—P) (Indonesian Democratic Struggle Party): c/o Dewan Perwakilan Rakyat, Jalan Gatot Subroto 16, Jakarta; established by Megawati Sukarnoputri, fmr leader of the Partai Demokrasi Indonesia (PDI—see above), following her removal from the leadership of the PDI by the Government in 1996; Chair. MEGAWATI SUKARNOPUTRI.

Partai Demokrasi Kasih Bangsa (PDKB) (The Nation Compassion Democratic Party): Sekretariat, Kompleks Widuri Indah Blok A-4, Jalan Palmerah Barat 353, Jakarta Selatan 12210; tel. (21) 53673648; fax (21) 5330973; e-mail pdkb@pdkb.or.id; internet www.pdkb.or.id.

Partai Golongan Karya (Golkar) (Functional Group): Jalan Anggrek Nellimurni, Jakarta 11480; tel. (21) 5302222; fax (21) 5303380; f. 1964; reorg. 1971; 23m. mems (1999); Co-ordinator of Advisors Haji HARMOKO; Pres. and Chair. Ir AKBAR TANDJUNG; Sec.-Gen. BUDI HARSONO.

Partai Keadilan (PK) (Justice Party): c/o Dewan Perwakilan Rakyat, Jalan Gatot Subroto 16, Jakarta; e-mail partai@keadilan.or .id; internet www.keadilan.or.id; f. 1998; Islamic; Pres. Dr NUR MAHMUDI ISMA'IL; Sec.-Gen. LUTHFI HASAN ISHAAQ.

Partai Keadilan dan Persatuan (PKP) (Justice and Unity Party): c/o Dewan Perwakilan Rakyat, Jalan Gatot Subroto 16, Jakarta; internet www.pkp.or.id; f. 1999; Gen. Chair. EDI SUDRADJAT.

Partai Kebangkitan Bangsa (PKB) (National Awakening Party): Jakarta; e-mail fahmi201@yahoo.com; internet www.pkb.org; Islamic; f. 1998; Chair. of Exec. Council Kiai Haji MA'RUF AMIN; Chair. of Advisory Council Haji MATORI ABDUL JALIL.

Partai Kebangkitan Umat (PKU) (Islamic Awakening Party): c/o Dewan Perwakilan Rakyat, Jalan Gatot Subroto 16, Jakarta; f. 1998 by clerics and members of the Nahdlatul Ulama, with the aim of promoting the adoption of Islamic law in Indonesia.

Partai Nahdlatul Umat (PNU): c/o Dewan Perwakilan Rakyat, Jalan Gatot Subroto 16, Jakarta; Islamic party.

Partai Pembauran (Assimilation Party): Jakarta; f. 1998; Chinese.

Partai Persatuan Pembangunan (PPP) (United Development Party): Jalan Diponegoro 60, Jakarta 10310; tel. (21) 336338; fax (21) 3908070; e-mail dpp@ppp.or.id; internet www.ppp.or.id; f. 1973 by the merger of four Islamic parties; Leader HAMZAH HAZ; Sec.-Gen. ALI MARWAN HANAN.

Partai Rakyat Demokrasi (PRD) (People's Democratic Party): Jakarta; Chair. BUDIMAN SUJATMIKO.

Partai Tionghoa Indonesia (The Indonesian-Chinese Party): Jakarta; f. 1998; Chinese.

Partai Uni Demokrasi Indonesia (PUDI) (Democratic Union Party of Indonesia): Jakarta; e-mail sribintangpamungkas@e-mail .com; internet www.pudi.or.id; f. 1996; Chair. Sri BINTANG PAMUNGKAS.

Other groups with political influence include:

Ikatan Cendekiawan Muslim Indonesia (ICMI) (Association of Indonesian Muslim Intellectuals): Gedung BPPT, Jalan M. H. Thamrin 8, Jakarta; tel. (21) 3410382; e-mail nama_anda@icmi.or .id; internet www.icmi.or.id; f. 1990 with government support; Chair. ACHMAD TIRTOSUDIRO; Sec.-Gen. ADI SASONO.

Masyumi Baru: Jalan Pangkalan Asem 12, Cempaka Putih Ba, Jakarta Pusat; tel. (21) 4225774; fax (21) 7353077; Sec.-Gen. RIDWAN SAIDI.

Muhammadiyah: Jalan Menteng Raya 62, Jakarta Pusat; tel. (21) 3903024; fax (21) 3141582; internet www.muhammadiyah.or.id; second largest Muslim organization; f. 1912; 28m. mems; Chair. SYAFII MA'AIRF.

Nahdlatul Ulama (NU) (Council of Scholars): Jalan H. Agus Salim 112, Jakarta Pusat; tel. (21) 336250; largest Muslim organization; 30m. mems; Chair. AHMAD HASYIM.

Syarikat Islam: Jalan Taman Amir Hamzah Nomor 2, Jakarta; tel. (21) 31906037.

The following groups remain in conflict with the Government:

Gerakan Aceh Merdeka (GAM) (Free Aceh Movement): based in Aceh; f. 1976; seeks independence from Indonesia; Leader HASAN DI TIRO; Military Commdr MUZZAKIR MANAF.

National Liberation Front Acheh Sumatra: based in Aceh; f. 1989; seeks independence from Indonesia.

Organisasi Papua Merdeka (OPM) (Free Papua Movement): based in Papua; f. 1963; seeks unification with Papua New Guinea; Chair. MOZES WEROR; Leader KELLY KWALIK.

Presidium Dewan Papua (PDP) (Papua Presidium Council): based in Papua; internet www.westpapua.net; seeks independence from Indonesia; Chair. (vacant); Vice-Chair. TOM BEANAL.

Diplomatic Representation

EMBASSIES IN INDONESIA

Afghanistan: Jalan Dr Kusuma Atmaja 15, Jakarta; tel. (21) 3143169; fax (21) 335390; Ambassador Dr MOHAMMAD HAIDAR.

Algeria: Jalan H. R. Rasuna Said, Kav. 10-1, Kuningan, Jakarta 12950; tel. (21) 5254719; fax (21) 5254654; e-mail ambalyak@rad.net .id; Ambassador SOUFIANE MIMOUNI.

Argentina: Menara Mulia, Suite 1901, Jalan Jenderal Gatot Subroto Kav. 9–11, Jakarta 12930; tel. (21) 5265661; fax (21) 5265664; e-mail embargen@cbn.net.id; Ambassador JOSÉ LUIS MIGNINI.

Australia: Jalan H. R. Rasuna Said, Kav. C15–16, Kuningan, Jakarta 12940; tel. (21) 25505555; fax (21) 5227101; e-mail public-affairs-jakt@dfat.gov.au; internet www.austembjak.or.id; Ambassador DAVID RITCHIE.

Austria: Jalan Diponegoro 44, Jakarta 10310; tel. (21) 338101; fax (21) 3904927; e-mail jakarta-ob@bmaa.gv.at; internet www .austrian-embassy.or.id; Ambassador Dr BERNHARD ZIMBURG.

Bangladesh: Jalan Denpasar Raya 3, Block A-13, Kav. 10, Kuningan, Jakarta 12950; tel. (21) 5221574; fax (21) 5261807; e-mail bdootjak@dnet.net.id; internet www.bangladeshembassyjakarta.or .id; Ambassador NASIM FIRDAUS.

Belgium: Deutsche Bank Bldg, 16th Floor, Jalan Imam Bonjol 80, Jakarta 10310; tel. (21) 3162030; fax (21) 3162035; e-mail jakarta@ diplobel.org; Ambassador LUK DARRAS.

Bosnia and Herzegovina: Menara Imperium, 11th Floor, Suite D-2, Metropolitan Kuningan Super Blok, Kav. 1, Jalan H. R. Rasuna Said, Jakarta 12980; tel. (21) 83703022; fax (21) 83703029; Ambassador ZDRAVKO RAJIĆ.

Brazil: Menara Mulia, Suite 1602, Jalan Jenderal Gatot Subroto, Kav. 9, Jakarta 12930; tel. (21) 5265656; fax (21) 5265659; e-mail brasemb@rad.net.id; Ambassador JADIEL FERREIRA DE OLIVEIRA.

Brunei: Jalan Tanjung Karang 7, Jakarta Pusat; tel. (21) 31906080; fax (21) 31905070; Ambassador Dato' Haji MOHAMMAD AMIN BIN Haji ABDUL RAHIM.

Bulgaria: Jalan Imam Bonjol 34–36, Jakarta 10310; tel. (21) 39040489; fax (21) 3904049; e-mail bgemb.jkt@centrin.net.id; Ambassador GATYU GATEV.

Cambodia: 33 Jalan Kintamani Raya C-15, Jakarta 12950; tel. (21) 9192895; fax (21) 5202673; e-mail recjkt@cabi.net.id; Ambassador KHEM BUNNEANG.

Canada: World Trade Centre, 6th Floor, Jalan Jenderal Sudirman, Kav. 29–31, POB 8324/JKS, Jakarta 12920; tel. (21) 25507800; fax (21) 25507811; e-mail canadianembassy.jkrta@dfait-maeci.gc.ca; internet www.dfait-maeci.gc.ca/jakarta/; Ambassador FERRY DE KERCKHOVE.

Chile: Bina Mulia Bldg, 7th Floor, Jalan H. R. Rasuna Said, Kav. 10, Kuningan, Jakarta 12950; tel. (21) 5201131; fax (21) 5201955; e-mail emchijak@indosat.net.id; Ambassador SINCLAIR MANLEY JAMES.

China, People's Republic: Jalan Mega Kuningan 2, Karet Kuningan, Jakarta 12950; tel. (21) 5761038; fax (21) 5761034; e-mail enbsychn@cbn.net.id; internet www.chinaembassy-indonesia.or.id; Ambassador LU SHUMIN.

Colombia: Central Plaza Bldg, 16th Floor, Jalan Jenderal Sudirman, Kav. 48, Jakarta; tel. (21) 516446; fax (21) 5207717; e-mail ejakarta@minrelext.gov.co; Ambassador LUIS FERNANDO ANGEL.

Croatia: Menara Mulia Bldg, Suite 2101, Jalan Gatot Subroto, Kav. 9–11, Jakarta 12930; tel. (21) 5257822; fax (21) 5204073; e-mail croemb@rad.net.id; internet www.croatemb.or.id; Ambassador BORIS MITOVIĆ.

Cuba: Taman Puri, Jalan Opal, Blok K-1, Permata Hijau, Jakarta 12210; tel. (21) 5304293; fax (21) 53676906; e-mail cubaindo@cbn .net.id; Ambassador MIGUEL ANGEL RAMÍREZ RAMOS.

Czech Republic: Jalan Gereja Theresia 20, POB 1319, Jakarta Pusat 10350; tel. (21) 3904075; fax (21) 336282; e-mail jakarta@ embassy.mzv.cz; internet www.czech-embassy.or.id; Ambassador MILAN ŠARAPATKA.

Denmark: Menara Rajawali, 25th Floor, Jalan Mega Kuningan, Lot 5.1, Jakarta 12950; tel. (21) 5761478; fax (21) 5761535; e-mail jktamb@um.dk; internet www.emb-denmark.or.id; Ambassador MICHAEL STERNBERG.

Egypt: Jalan Teuku Umar 68, Jakarta 10350; tel. (21) 331141; fax (21) 3105073; e-mail egypt@indosat.net.id; Ambassador EZZAT SAAD.

Finland: Menara Rajawali, 9th Floor, Jalan Mega Kuningan, Kawasan Mega Kuningan, Jakarta 12950; tel. (21) 5761650; fax (21) 5761631; e-mail sanomat.jak@formin.fi; internet www.finembjak .com; Ambassador MATTI PULLINEN.

France: Jalan M. H. Thamrin 20, Jakarta 10350; tel. (21) 3142807; fax (21) 3143338; e-mail ambassade@ambafrance-id.org; internet www.ambafrance-indonesie.org; Ambassador HERVÉ LADSOUS.

Germany: Jalan M. H. Thamrin 1, Jakarta 10310; tel. (21) 3901750; fax (21) 3901757; e-mail germany@rad.net.id; internet www .deutschebotschaft-jakarta.or.id; Ambassador Dr GERHARD FULDA.

Greece: Plaza 89, 12th Floor, Suite 1203, Jalan H. R. Rasuna Said, Kav. X-7 No. 6, Kuningan, Jakarta 12540; tel. (21) 5207776; fax (21) 5207753; e-mail grembas@cbn.net.id; internet www.greekembassy .or.id; Ambassador ALEXIOS G. CHRISTOPOULOS.

Holy See: Jalan Merdeka Timur 18, POB 4227, Jakarta Pusat (Apostolic Nunciature); tel. (21) 3841142; fax (21) 3841143; e-mail vatjak@cbn.net.id; Apostolic Nuncio Most Rev. RENZO FRATINI (Titular Archbishop of Botriana).

Hungary: 36 Jalan H. R. Rasuna Said, Kav. X/3, Kuningan, Jakarta 12950; tel. (21) 5203459; fax (21) 5203461; e-mail huembjkt@rad.net .id; internet www.huembjkt.or.id; Ambassador GYÖRGY BUSZTIN.

India: Jalan H. R. Rasuna Said, Kav. S/1, Kuningan, Jakarta 12950; tel. (21) 5204150; fax (21) 5204160; e-mail eoiisi@indo.net.id; internet www.eoijakarta.or.id; Ambassador HEMANT KRISHAN SINGH.

Iran: Jalan Hos Cokroaminoto 110, Menteng, Jakarta Pusat 10310; tel. (21) 331391; fax (21) 3107860; e-mail irembjkt@indo.net.id; internet www.iranembassy.or.id; Ambassador ABDOLLAH ZIFAN.

Iraq: Jalan Teuku Umar 38, Jakarta 10350; tel. (21) 3904067; fax (21) 3904066; e-mail iraqembi@rad.net.id; Ambassador SA'DOON J. AL-ZUBAYDI.

Italy: Jalan Diponegoro 45, Jakarta 10310; tel. (21) 337445; fax (21) 337422; e-mail italemba@italambjkt.or.id; internet www.italambjkt .or.id; Ambassador FRANCESCO MARIA GRECO.

Japan: Menara Thamrin, 7th–10th Floors, Jalan M. H. Thamrin Kav. 3, Jakarta 10350; tel. (21) 324308; fax (21) 325460; internet www.id.emb-japan.go.jp; Ambassador YUTAKA IIMURA.

Jordan: Jalan Denpasar Raya, Blok A XIII, Kav. 1–2, Jakarta 12950; tel. (21) 5204400; fax (21) 5202447; e-mail jordanem@cbn.net .id; internet www.jordanembassy.or.id; Ambassador MOHAMED ALI DAHER.

Korea, Democratic People's Republic: Jalan H. R. Rasuna Said, Kav. X/5, Jakarta; tel. (21) 5210181; fax (21) 5210183; Ambassador JANG CHANG-CHON.

Korea, Republic: Jalan Jenderal Gatot Subroto 57, Jakarta Selatan; tel. (21) 5201915; fax (21) 5254159; e-mail koremb_in@ mofat.go.kr; Ambassador KIM JAE-SUP.

Kuwait: Jalan Denpasar Raya, Blok A XII, Kuningan, Jakarta 12950; tel. (21) 5202477; fax (21) 5204359; e-mail ami@ Kuwait-toplist.com; Ambassador JASEM M. J. AL-MUBARAKI.

Laos: Jalan Patra Kuningan XIV 1-A, Kuningan, Jakarta 12950; tel. (21) 5229602; fax (21) 5229601; e-mail laoemjkt@cabi.net.id; Ambassador LEUANE SOUMBHONKHAN.

Lebanon: Jalan YBR V 82, Kuningan, Jakarta 12950; tel. (21) 5253074; fax (21) 5207121; Ambassador NAZIH ACHOUR.

Libya: Jalan Pekalongan 24, Jakarta; tel. (21) 335308; fax (21) 335726; Chargé d'affaires a.i. TAJEDDIN A. JERBI.

Malaysia: Jalan H. R. Rasuna Said, Kav. X/6, Kuningan, Jakarta 12950; tel. (21) 5224947; fax (21) 5224974; e-mail mwjakarta@ indosat.net.id; Ambassador Datuk RASTAM MOHAMMAD ISA.

Mali: Jalan Mendawai III 18, Kebayoran Baru, Jakarta 12130; tel. (21) 7208472; fax (21) 7229589; e-mail ambamali@indosat.net.id; Ambassador AMADOU N'DIAYE.

Marshall Islands: Jalan Pangeran Jayakarta 115, Blok A-11, Jakarta Pusat 10730; tel. (21) 7248565; fax (21) 7248566; e-mail marshall@idola.net.id; Ambassador CARL L. HEINE.

Mexico: Menara Mulia Bldg, Suite 2306, Jalan Gatot Subroto, Kav. 9–11, Jakarta 12930; tel. (21) 5203980; fax (21) 5203978; e-mail embmexic@rad.net.id; Ambassador PEDRO GONZALES-RUBIO Sr.

Morocco: Suite 512, 5th Floor, South Tower, Kuningan Plaza, Jalan H. R. Rasuna Said C-11–14, Jakarta 12940; tel. (21) 5200773; fax (21) 5200586; e-mail sifamajakar@cbn.net.id; Ambassador M. ABDER-AHMAN DRISSI ALAMI.

Mozambique: Wisma GKBI, 37th Floor, Suite 3709, Jalan Jenderal Sudirman 28, Jakarta 10210; tel. (21) 5740901; fax (21) 5740907; e-mail embamoc@cbn.net.id; Ambassador GERALDO ANTONIO CHIRINZA.

Myanmar: Jalan Haji Agus Salim 109, Jakarta Selatan; tel. (21) 327684; fax (21) 327204; e-mail myanmar@cbn.net.id; Ambassador U KYAW MYINT.

Netherlands: Jalan H. R. Rasuna Said, Kav. S/3, Kuningan, Jakarta 12950; tel. (21) 5251515; fax (21) 5700734; e-mail jak-cdp@ minbuza.nl; internet www.netherlandsembassy.or.id; Ambassador RUDOLF JAN TREFFERS.

New Zealand: BRI II Bldg, 23rd Floor, Jalan Jenderal Sudirman, Kav. 44–46, Jakarta; tel. (21) 5709460; fax (21) 5709457; e-mail nzembjak@cbn.net.id; Ambassador CHRIS ELDER.

Nigeria: Jalan Tamam Patra XIV/11–11A, Kuningan Timur, POB 3649, Jakarta Selatan 12950; tel. (21) 5260922; fax (21) 5260924; e-mail embnig@centrin.net.id; Ambassador SAIDU MOHAMMED.

Norway: Menara Rajawali Bldg, 25th Floor, Kawasan Mega Kuningan, Jakarta 12950; tel. (21) 5761523; fax (21) 5761537; e-mail emb.jakarta@mfa.no; internet www.norwayemb-indonesia.org; Ambassador SJUR TORGERSEN.

Pakistan: Jalan Lembang 10, Menteng, Jakarta; tel. (21) 3144008; fax (21) 3103945; e-mail parepjkt@link.net.id; Ambassador Maj.-Gen. (retd) SYED MUSTAFA ANWER HUSAIN.

Panama: World Trade Centre, 8th Floor, Jalan Jenderal Sudirman, Kav. 29–31, Jakarta 12920; tel. (21) 5711867; fax (21) 5711933; e-mail panacon@pacific.net.id; Ambassador VIRGINIA WEDEN DE ACOSTA.

Papua New Guinea: Panin Bank Centre, 6th Floor, Jalan Jenderal Sudirman 1, Jakarta 10270; tel. (21) 7251218; fax (21) 7201012; e-mail kdujkt@cbn.net.id; Ambassador TARCY ERI.

Peru: Menara Rajawali Bldg, 12th Floor, Jalan Mega Kuningan, Lot 5.1, Kawasan Mega Kuningan, Jakarta 12950; tel. (21) 5761820; fax (21) 5761825; e-mail embaperu@cbn.net.id; Ambassador NILO FIG-UEROA CORTAVARRIA.

Philippines: Jalan Imam Bonjol 6–8, Jakarta 10310; tel. (21) 3155118; fax (21) 3151167; e-mail phjkt@indo.net.id; Ambassador RAFAEL E. SEGUIS.

Poland: Jalan H. R. Rasuna Said, Kav. X, Blok IV/3, Jakarta Selatan 12950; tel. (21) 2525948; fax (21) 2525958; e-mail plembjkt@net.id; Ambassador KRZYSZTOF SZUMSKI.

Portugal: Bina Mulia Bldg I, 7th Floor, Jalan H. R. Rasuna Said, Kav. X, Kuningan, Jakarta 12950; tel. (21) 5265103; fax (21) 5271981; e-mail porembjak@cbn.net.id; Ambassador ANA MARIA ROSA MARTINS GOMES.

Qatar: Jalan Taman Ubud I, No. 5, Kuningan Timur, Jakarta 12920; tel. (21) 5277751; fax (21) 5277754; e-mail jakarta@mofa.gov.qa; Ambassador ABDULLA MOHAMMED TALEB AL-MARI.

Romania: Jalan Mas Putih 29, Kompleks D, Permata Hijau, Jakarta Selatan; tel. (21) 5305073; fax (21) 5305074; e-mail romind@cbn.net.id; Ambassador GHEORGHE SAVUICA.

Russia: Jalan H. R. Rasuna Said, Kav. X-6, Jakarta; tel. (21) 5222912; e-mail rusembjkt@dnet.net.id; Ambassador VLADIMIR Y. PLOTNIKOV.

Saudi Arabia: Jalan M. T. Haryono, Kav. 27, Cawang Atas, Jakarta Timur; tel. (21) 8011533; fax (21) 3905864; e-mail idemb@mofa.gov.sa; Ambassador ELLSWORTH I. A. JOHN.

Serbia and Montenegro: Jalan Hos Cokroaminoto 109, Jakarta 10310; tel. (21) 3143560; fax (21) 3143613; e-mail ambajaka@rad.net.id; Ambassador VELJKO ČAGOROVIĆ.

Singapore: Jalan H. R. Rasuna Said, Blok X/4, Kav. 2, Kuningan, Jakarta 12950; tel. (21) 5201489; fax (21) 5201486; e-mail denpasar@pacific.net.id; internet www.mfa.gov.sg/jkt; Ambassador EDWARD LEE.

Slovakia: Jalan Prof. Mohammed Yamin 29, POB 1368, Jakarta Pusat; tel. (21) 3101068; fax (21) 3101180; e-mail slovemby@indo.net.id; Ambassador MILAN LAJČIAK.

South Africa: Suite 705, Wisma GKBI, Jalan Jenderal Sudirman 28, Jakarta 10210; tel. (21) 5740660; fax (21) 5740661; e-mail saembhom@mweb.co.id; internet www.saembassy-jakarta.or.id; Ambassador NORMAN M. MASHABANE.

Spain: Jalan H. Agus Salim 61, Jakarta 10350; tel. (21) 335937; fax (21) 325996; e-mail embespid@mail.mae.es; Ambassador DAMASO DE LARIO RAMIREZ.

Sri Lanka: Jalan Diponegoro 70, Jakarta 10320; tel. (21) 3161886; fax (21) 3107962; e-mail lankaemb@rad.net.id; Ambassador H. J. K. R. BANDARA.

Sudan: Wisma Bank Dharmala, 7th Floor, Suite 01, Jalan Jenderal Sudirman, Kav. 28, Jakarta 12920; tel. (21) 5212099; fax (21) 5212077; e-mail leen@cbn.net.id; Ambassador SIDIQ YOUSIF ABU-AGLA.

Sweden: Menara Rajawali Bldg, 9th Floor, Jalan Mega Kuningan, Lot 5.1, Kawasan Mega Kuningan, Jakarta 12950; POB 2824, Jakarta 10001; tel. (21) 5762690; fax (21) 5762691; e-mail sweden@cbn.net.id; internet www.swedemb-jakarta.com; Ambassador HARALD SANDBERG.

Switzerland: Jalan H. R. Rasuna Said, Kav. X-3/2, Kuningan, Jakarta Selatan 12950; tel. (21) 5256061; fax (21) 5202289; e-mail vertretung@jak.rep.admin.ch; internet www.swissembassy.or.id; Ambassador GEORGES MARTIN.

Syria: Jalan Karang Asem I/8, Jakarta 12950; tel. (21) 515991; fax (21) 5202511; Ambassador NADIM DOUAY.

Thailand: Jalan Imam Bonjol 74, Jakarta 10310; tel. (21) 3904052; fax (21) 3107469; e-mail thaijkt@indo.net.id; Ambassador CHAIYONG SATJIPANON.

Timor-Leste: Surya Bldg, Jalan Thamrin, Jakarta; Ambassador ARLINDO MARCAL.

Tunisia: Wisma Dharmala Sakti, 11th Floor, Jalan Jenderal Sudirman 32, Jakarta 10220; tel. (21) 5703432; fax (21) 5700016; e-mail embtun@uninet.net.id; Ambassador MAHMOUD BESSROUR.

Turkey: Jalan H. R. Rasuna Said, Kav. 1, Kuningan, Jakarta 12950; tel. (21) 5256250; fax (21) 5226056; e-mail cakabe@cbn.net.id; Ambassador FERYAL ÇOTUR.

Ukraine: WTC Bldg, 8th Floor, Jalan Jenderal Sudirman, Kav. 29–31, Jakarta 12084; tel. (21) 5211700; fax (21) 5211710; e-mail uaembas@rad.net.id; Chargé d'affaires a.i. SERGIY NIKSHICH.

United Arab Emirates: Jalan Prof. Dr Satrio, Kav. 16–17, Jakarta 12950; tel. (21) 5206518; fax (21) 5206526; e-mail uaeemb@rad.net.id; Ambassador MOHAMMED SULTAN AS-SOWAIDI.

United Kingdom: Jalan M. H. Thamrin 75, Jakarta 10310; tel. (21) 3156264; fax (21) 3926263; e-mail britem2@ibm.net.id; internet www.britain-in-indonesia.or.id; Ambassador RICHARD GOZNEY.

USA: Jalan Merdeka Selatan 4–5, Jakarta 10110; tel. (21) 34359000; fax (21) 3857189; e-mail jakconsul@state.gov; internet www.usembassyjakarta.org; Ambassador RALPH (SKIP) BOYCE.

Uzbekistan: Menara Mulia Bldg, Suite 2401, 24th Floor, Jalan Jenderal Gatot Subroto, Kav. 9–11, Jakarta 12930; tel. (21) 5222581; fax (21) 5222582; e-mail registan@indo.net.id.

Venezuela: Menara Mulia Bldg, 20th Floor, Suite 2005, Jalan Jenderal Gatot Subroto, Kav. 9–11, Jakarta Selatan 12930; tel. (21) 5227547; fax (21) 5227549; e-mail evenjakt@indo.net.id; Ambassador LUIS EDUARDO SOTO.

Viet Nam: Jalan Teuku Umar 25, Jakarta; tel. (21) 3100358; fax (21) 3100359; e-mail embvnam@uninet.net.id; Ambassador NGUYEN DANG QUANG.

Yemen: Jalan Yusuf Adiwinata 29, Menteng, Jakarta 10350; tel. (21) 3904074; fax (21) 3904946; e-mail yemenemb@rad.net.id; Ambassador Dr AHMAD SALIM AL-WAHISHI.

Judicial System

There is one codified criminal law for the whole of Indonesia. In December 1989 the Islamic Judicature Bill, giving wider powers to Shariah courts, was approved by the Dewan Perwakilan Rakyat (House of Representatives). The new law gave Muslim courts authority over civil matters, such as marriage. Muslims may still choose to appear before a secular court. Europeans are subject to the Code of Civil Law published in the State Gazette in 1847. Alien orientals (i.e. Arabs, Indians, etc.) and Chinese are subject to certain parts of the Code of Civil Law and the Code of Commerce. The work of codifying this law has started, but, in view of the great complexity and diversity of customary law, it may be expected to take a considerable time to achieve.

Supreme Court
(Mahkamah Agung)

Jalan Merdeka Utara 9–13, Jakarta 10110; tel. (21) 3843348; fax (21) 3811057; e-mail pansekjen@mari.go.id; internet www.mari.go.id.

The final court of appeal.

Chief Justice: Prof. BAGIR MANAN.

Deputy Chief Justice: H. TAUFIK.

High Courts in Jakarta, Surabaya, Medan, Makassar, Banda Aceh, Padang, Palembang, Bandung, Semarang, Banjarmasin, Menado, Denpasar, Ambon and Jayapura deal with appeals from the District Courts.

District Courts deal with marriage, divorce and reconciliation.

Religion

All citizens are required to state their religion. According to a survey in 1985, 86.9% of the population were Muslims, while 9.6% were Christians, 1.9% were Hindus, 1.0% were Buddhists and 0.6% professed adherence to tribal religions.

Five national religious councils—representing the Islamic, Catholic, Protestant, Hindu and Buddhist religious traditions—were established to serve as liaison bodies between religious adherents and the Government and to advise the Government on the application of religious principles to various elements of national life.

ISLAM

In 1993 nearly 90% of Indonesians were Muslims. Indonesia has the world's largest Muslim population.

Majelis Ulama Indonesia (MUI) (Indonesian Ulama Council): Komp. Masjid Istiqlal, Jalan Taman Wijaya Kesuma, Jakarta

10710; tel. (21) 3455471; fax (21) 3855412; internet www.mui.or.id; central Muslim organization; Chair. SAHAL MAHFUDZ; Sec.-Gen. DIEN SYAMSUDDIN.

CHRISTIANITY

Persekutuan Gereja-Gereja di Indonesia (Communion of Churches in Indonesia): Jalan Salemba Raya 10, Jakarta 10430; tel. (21) 3908119; fax (21) 3150457; e-mail pgi@bit.net.id; internet www .pgi.or.id; f. 1950; 70 mem. churches; Chair. Rev. Dr SULARSO SOPATER; Gen. Sec. Rev. Dr JOSEPH M. PATTIASINA.

The Roman Catholic Church

Indonesia comprises eight archdioceses and 26 dioceses. At 31 December 2000 there were an estimated 6,289,326 adherents in Indonesia (excluding the territory of East Timor), representing 3.3% of the population.

Bishops' Conference

Konferensi Waligereja Indonesia (KWI), Jalan Cut Meutia 10, POB 3044, Jakarta 10002; tel. (21) 336422; fax (21) 3918527; e-mail kwi@ parokinet.org.

f. 1973; Pres. Cardinal JULIUS RIYADI DARMAATMADJA (Archbishop of Jakarta).

Archbishop of Ende: Most Rev. ABDON LONGINUS DA CUNHA, Keuskupan Agung, POB 210, Jalan Katedral 5, Ndona-Ende 86312, Flores; tel. (381) 21176; fax (381) 21606; e-mail uskup@ende .parokinet.org.

Archbishop of Jakarta: Cardinal JULIUS RIYADI DARMAATMADJA, Keuskupan Agung, Jalan Katedral 7, Jakarta 10710; tel. (21) 3813345; fax (21) 3855681.

Archbishop of Kupang: Most Rev. PETER TURANG, Keuskupan Agung Kupang, Jalan Thamrin, Oepoi, Kupang 85111, Timor NTT; tel. (380) 826199; fax (380) 833331.

Archbishop of Makassar: Most Rev. JOHANNES LIKU ADA', Keuskupan Agung, Jalan Thamrin 5–7, Makassar 90111, Sulawesi Selatan; tel. (411) 315744; fax (411) 326674; e-mail pseupg@indosat .net.id.

Archbishop of Medan: Most Rev. ALFRED GONTI PIUS DATUBARA, Jalan Imam Bonjol 39, POB 1191, Medan 20152, Sumatra Utara; tel. (61) 4519768; fax (61) 4145745; e-mail mar39@indosat.net.id.

Archbishop of Merauke: Most Rev. JACOBUS DUIVENVOORDE, Keuskupan Agung, Jalan Mandala 30, Merauke 99602, Irian Jaya (Papua); tel. (971) 321011; fax (971) 321311.

Archbishop of Pontianak: Most Rev. HIERONYMUS HERCULANUS BUMBUN, Keuskupan Agung, Jalan A. R. Hakin 92A, POB 1119, Pontianak 78011, Kalimantan Barat; tel. (561) 732382; fax (561) 738785; e-mail kap@pontianak.wasantara.net.id.

Archbishop of Semarang: Most Rev. IGNATIUS SUHARYO HARDJOATMODJO, Keuskupan Agung, Jalan Pandanaran 13, Semarang 50231; tel. (24) 312276; fax (24) 414741; e-mail uskup@semarang.parokinet .org.

Other Christian Churches

Protestant Church in Indonesia (Gereja Protestan di Indonesia): Jalan Medan Merdeka Timur 10, Jakarta 10110; tel. (21) 3519003; fax (21) 34830224; consists of 10 churches of Calvinistic tradition; 2,789,155 mems, 3,841 congregations, 1,965 pastors (1998); Chair. Rev. Dr D. J. LUMENTA.

Numerous other Protestant communities exist throughout Indonesia, mainly organized on a local basis. The largest of these (1985 memberships) are: the Batak Protestant Christian Church (1,875,143); the Christian Church in Central Sulawesi (100,000); the Christian Evangelical Church in Minahasa (730,000); the Christian Protestant Church in Indonesia (210,924); the East Java Christian Church (123,850); the Evangelical Christian Church in Irian Jaya (Papua)—360,000); the Evangelical Christian Church of Sangir-Talaud (190,000); the Indonesian Christian Church/Huria Kristen Indonesia (316,525); the Javanese Christian Churches (121,500); the Kalimantan Evangelical Church (182,217); the Karo Batak Protestant Church (164,288); the Nias Protestant Christian Church (250,000); the Protestant Church in the Moluccas (575,000); the Simalungun Protestant Christian Church (155,000); and the Toraja Church (250,000).

BUDDHISM

All-Indonesia Buddhist Association: Jakarta.

Indonesian Buddhist Council: Jakarta.

HINDUISM

Hindu Dharma Council: Jakarta.

The Press

In August 1990 the Government announced that censorship of both the local and foreign press was to be relaxed and that the authorities would refrain from revoking the licences of newspapers that violated legislation governing the press. In practice, however, there was little change in the Government's policy towards the press. In June 1994 the Government revoked the publishing licences of three principal news magazines, *Tempo, Editor* and *DeTik*. Following the resignation of President Suharto in May 1998, the new Government undertook to allow freedom of expression. *DeTik* magazine subsequently resumed publication under the new name, *DeTak* in July; *Tempo* magazine resumed publication in October.

PRINCIPAL DAILIES

Bali

Harian Pagi Umum (Bali Post): Jalan Kepudang 67A, Denpasar 80232; internet www.balipost.co.id; f. 1948; daily (Indonesian edn), weekly (English edn); Editor K. NADHA; circ. 25,000.

Java

Angkatan Bersenjata: Jalan Kramat Raya 94, Jakarta Pusat; tel. (21) 46071; fax (21) 366870.

Bandung Post: Jalan Lodaya 38A, Bandung 40264; tel. (22) 305124; fax (22) 302882; internet www.bandung-post.com; f. 1979; Chief Editor AHMAD SAELAN; Dir AHMAD JUSACC.

Berita Buana: Jalan Tahah Abang Dua 33–35, Jakarta 10110; tel. (21) 5487175; fax (21) 5491555; internet www.beritabuana.net; f. 1970; relaunched 1990; Indonesian; circ. 150,000.

Berita Yudha: Jalan Letjenderal Haryono MT22, Jakarta; tel. (21) 8298331; f. 1971; Indonesian; Editor SUNARDI; circ. 50,000.

Bisnis Indonesia: Wisma Bisnis Indonesia, Jalan Letjenderal S. Parman, Kav. 12, Slipi, Jakarta 11480; tel. (21) 5305869; fax (21) 5305868; e-mail iklana@bisnis.co.id; internet www.bisnis.com; f. 1985; available online; Indonesian; Editor SUKAMDANI S. GITOSARDJONO; circ. 60,000.

Harian Berita Sore: Jakarta; e-mail edy@beritasore.com; internet www.beritasore.com; Indonesian.

Harian Indonesia (Indonesia Rze Pao): Jalan Toko Tiga Seberang 21, POB 4755, Jakarta 11120; tel. (21) 6295948; fax (21) 6297830; e-mail info@harian-indonesia.com; internet www.harian-indonesia .com; f. 1966; Chinese; Editor W. D. SUKISMAN; Dir HADI WIBOWO; circ. 42,000.

Harian Terbit: Jalan Pulogadung 15, Kawasan Industri Pulogadung, Jakarta 13920; tel. (21) 4602953; fax (21) 4602950; f. 1972; Indonesian; Editor H. R. S. HADIKAMAJAYA; circ. 125,000.

Harian Umum AB: CTC Bldg, 2nd Floor, Kramat Raya 94, Jakarta Pusat; f. 1965; official armed forces journal; Dir GOENARSO; Editor-in-Chief N. SOEPANGAT; circ. 80,000.

The Indonesia Times: Jalan Pulo Lentut 12, Jakarta Timur; tel. (21) 4611280; fax (21) 375012; e-mail info@webpacific.com; internet www.indonesiatimes.com; f. 1974; English; Editor TRIBUANA SAID; circ. 35,000.

Indonesian Observer: Wisma Indovision, 11th Floor, Jalan Raya Panjang Blok Z/III, Green Garden, Jakarta 11520; tel. (21) 5818855; fax (21) 58302414; internet www.indonesian-observer.com; f. 1955; English; independent; Editor TAUFIK DARUSMAN; circ. 25,000.

Jakarta Post: Jalan Palmerah Selatan 15, Jakarta 10270; tel. (21) 5300476; fax (21) 5492685; e-mail editorial@thejakartapost.com; internet www.thejakartapost.com; f. 1983; English; Chief Editor RAYMOND TORUAN; circ. 50,000.

Jawa Pos: Graha Pena Bldg, 4th and 5th Floors, Achmad Yani 88, Surabaya 60234; tel. (31) 8283333; fax (31) 8285555; internet www .jawapos.co.id; f. 1949; Indonesian; CEO DAHLAN ISKAN; circ. 120,000.

Jepara Pos: Jepara; internet www.jeparapos.com; Indonesian.

Kedaulatan Rakyat: Jalan P. Mangkubumi 40–42, Yogyakarta; tel. (274) 65685; fax (274) 63125; internet www.kr.co.id; f. 1945; Indonesian; independent; Editor IMAN SUTRISNO; circ. 50,000.

Kompas: Jalan Palmerah Selatan 26–28, Jakarta; tel. (21) 5483008; fax (21) 5305868; internet www.kompas.com; f. 1965; Indonesian; Editor Drs JAKOB OETAMA; circ. 523,453.

Media Indonesia Daily: Jalan Pilar Mas Raya, Kav. A–D, Kedoya Selatan, Kebon Jeruk, Jakarta 11520; tel. (21) 5812088; fax (21) 5812105; e-mail redaksi@mediaindonesia.co.id; internet www .mediaindo.co.id; f. 1989; fmrly Prioritas; Indonesian; Publr Surya Paloh; Editor Djafar H. Assegaff; circ. 2,000.

Merdeka: Jalan Raya Kebayoran Lama 17, Jakarta Selatan 12210; tel. (21) 5556059; fax (21) 5556063; f. 1945; Indonesian; independent; Dir and Chief Editor B. M. Diah; circ. 130,000.

Neraca: Jalan Jambrut 2–4, Jakarta; tel. (21) 323969; fax (21) 3101873.

Pelita (Torch): Jalan Jenderal Sudirman 65, Jakarta; f. 1974; Indonesian; Muslim; Editor Akbar Tanjung; circ. 80,000.

Pewarta Surabaya: Jalan Karet 23, POB 85, Surabaya; f. 1905; Indonesian; Editor Raden Djarot Soebiantoro; circ. 10,000.

Pikiran Rakyat: Jalan Asia-Afrika 77, Bandung 40111; tel. (22) 51216; internet www.pikiran-rakyat.com; f. 1950; Indonesian; independent; Editor Bram M. Darmaprawira; circ. 150,000.

Pos Kota: Yayasan Antar Kota, Jalan Gajah Mada 100, Jakarta 10130; tel. (21) 6290874; e-mail iklankilat@poskota.net; internet www.poskota.co.id; f. 1970; Indonesian; Editor H. Sofyan Lubis; circ. 500,000.

Republika: Jalan Warung Buncit Raya 37, Jakarta 12510; tel. (21) 7803747; fax (21) 7800420; internet www.republika.co.id; f. 1993; organ of ICMI; Chief Editor Parni Hadi.

Sinar Pagi: Jalan Letjenderal Haryono MT22, Jakarta Selatan.

Suara Karya: Jalan Bangka II/2, Kebayoran Baru, Jakarta Selatan 12720; tel. (21) 7192656; fax (21) 71790784; internet www .suarakarya-online.com; f. 1971; Indonesian; Editor Syamsul Basri; circ. 100,000.

Suara Merdeka: Jalan Pandanaran 30, Semarang 50241; tel. (24) 412660; fax (24) 411116; internet www.suaramerdeka.com; f. 1950; Indonesian; Publr Ir Budi Santoso; Editor Suwarno; circ. 200,000.

Suara Pembaruan: Jalan Dewi Sartika 136/D, Cawang, Jakarta 13630; tel. (21) 8013208; fax (21) 8007262; e-mail koransp@ suarapembaruan.com; internet www.suarapembaruan.com; f. 1987; licence revoked in 1986 as Sinar Harapan (Ray of Hope); Publr Dr Albert Hasibuan.

Surabaya Post: Jalan Taman Ade Irma Nasution 1, Surayaba; tel. (31) 45394; fax (31) 519585; internet www.surabayapost.co.id; f. 1953; independent; Publr Tuty Azis; Editor Imam Pujono; circ. 115,000.

Wawasan: Bapak Mahmud, Jalan Letjen Suprapto, Brigjen Katamso 1, Medan 20151; tel. (24) 4150858; fax (24) 4510025; e-mail waspada@waspada.co.id; internet www.waspada.co.id; f. 1986; Indonesian; Chief Editor H. Prabudi Said; circ. 65,000.

Kalimantan

Banjarmasin Post: Jalan Haryono MT 54–143, Banjarmasin; tel. (511) 54370; fax (511) 66123; e-mail bpost@Indomedia.com; internet www.indomedia.com/bpost/; f. 1971; Indonesian; Chief Editor H. Basuki Subianto; circ. 50,000.

Gawi Manuntung: Jalan Pangeran Samudra 97B, Banjarmasin; f. 1972; Indonesian; Editor M. Ali Sri Indradjaya; circ. 5,000.

Harian Umum Akcaya: Jalan Veteran 1, Pontianak.

Lampung Post: Jalan Pangkal Pinang, Lampung.

Manuntung: Jalan Jenderal Sudirman RT XVI 82, Balikpapan 76144; tel. (542) 35359; internet www.manuntung.co.id; largest newspaper in East Borneo.

Maluku

Pos Maluku: Jalan Raya Pattimura 19, Ambon; tel. (911) 44614.

Suara Maluku: Komplek Perdagangan Mardikas, Blok D3/11A, Ternate; tel. (911) 44590.

Papua

Berita Karya: Jayapura.

Cendrawasih Post: Jayapura; Editor Rustam Madubun.

Teropong: Jalan Halmahera, Jayapura.

Riau

Riau Pos: Pekanbaru, Riau; internet www.riaupos.com; circ. 40,000.

Sulawesi

Bulletin Sulut: Jalan Korengkeng 38, Lt II Manado, 95114, Sulawesi Utara.

Cahaya Siang: Jalan Kembang II 2, Manado, 95114, Sulawesi Utara; tel. (431) 61054; fax (431) 63393.

Fajar (Dawn): Makassar; circ. 35,000.

Manado Post: Manado Post Centre, Jalan Babe Palar 54, Manado; tel. (431) 855558; fax (431) 860398; internet www.mdopost.net.

Pedoman Rakyat: Jalan H. A. Mappanyukki 28, Makassar; f. 1947; independent; Editor M. Basir; circ. 30,000.

Suluh Merdeka: Jalan R. W. Mongsidi 4/96, POB 1105, Manado, 95110; tel. and fax (431) 866150.

Tegas: Jalan Mappanyukki 28, Makassar; tel. (411) 3960.

Wenang Post: Jalan R. W. Mongsidi 4/96, POB 1105, Manado 95115; tel. and fax (431) 866150; weekly.

Sumatra

Harian Analisa: Jalan Jenderal A. Yani 37–43, Medan; tel. (61) 326655; fax (61) 514031; internet www.analisadaily.com; f. 1972; Indonesian; Editor Soffyan; circ. 75,000.

Harian Haluan: Jalan Damar 59 C/F, Padang; f. 1948; Editor-in-Chief Rivai Marlaut; circ. 40,000.

Harian Umum Nasional Waspada: Jalan Brigjenderal 1 Katamso, Medan 20151; tel. (61) 4150858; fax (61) 4510025; e-mail waspada@indosat.net.id; internet www.waspada.co.id; f. 1947; Indonesian; Editor-in-Chief H. Prabudi Said.

Mimbar Umum: Merah, Medan; tel. (61) 517807; f. 1947; Indonesian; independent; Editor Mohd Lud Lubis; circ. 55,000.

Serambi Indonesia: Jalan T. Nyak Arief 159, Lampriek, Banda Aceh; e-mail serambi@indomedia.com; internet www.indomedia .com/serambi/.

Sinar Indonesia Baru: Jalan Brigjenderal Katamso 66, Medan 20151; tel. (61) 438150; e-mail redaksi@hariansib .com; internet www.hariansib.com; f. 1970; Indonesian; Chief Editor G. M. Panggabean; circ. 150,000.

Suara Rakyat Semesta: Jalan K. H. Ashari 52, Palembang; Indonesian; Editor Djadil Abdullah; circ. 10,000.

Waspada: Jalan Jenderal Sudirman, cnr Jalan Brigjenderal Katamso 1, Medan 20151; tel. (61) 550858; fax (61) 510025; f. 1947; Indonesian; Chief Editor Ani Idrus; circ. 60,000 (daily), 55,000 (Sunday).

PRINCIPAL PERIODICALS

Amanah: Jalan Garuda 69, Kemayoran, Jakarta; tel. (21) 410254; fortnightly; Muslim current affairs; Indonesian; Man. Dir Maskun Iskandar; circ. 180,000.

Berita Negara: Jalan Pertjetakan Negara 21, Kotakpos 2111, Jakarta; tel. (21) 4207251; fax (21) 4207251; f. 1951; 2 a week; official gazette.

Bobo: PT Gramedia, Jalan Kebahagiaan 4–14, Jakarta 11140; tel. (21) 6297809; fax (21) 6390080; f. 1973; weekly; children's magazine; Editor Tineke Latumeten; circ. 240,000.

Bola: Yayasan Tunas Raga, Jalan Palmerah Selatan 17, Jakarta 10270; tel. and fax (21) 5483008; internet www.bolanews.com; 2 a week; Tue. and Fri. sports magazine; Indonesian; Chief Editor Ian Situmorang; circ. 715,000.

Buana Minggu: Jalan Tanah Abang Dua 33, Jakarta Pusat 10110; tel. (21) 364190; weekly; Sunday; Indonesian; Editor Winoto Pararthō; circ. 193,450.

Business News: Jalan H. Abdul Muis 70, Jakarta 10160; tel. (21) 3848207; fax (21) 3454280; f. 1956; 3 a week (Indonesian edn), 2 a week (English edn); Chief Editor Sanjoto Sastromihardjo; circ. 15,000.

Citra: Gramedia Bldg, Unit 11, 5th Floor, Jalan Palmerah Selatan 24–26, Jakarta 10270; tel. (21) 5483008; fax (21) 5494035; e-mail citra@gramedia-majalah.com; internet www.tabloid-citra.com; f. 1990; weekly; TV and film programmes, music trends and celebrity news; Chief Editor H. Maman Suherman; circ. 239,000.

Depthnews Indonesia: Jalan Jatinegara Barat III/6, Jakarta 13310; tel. (21) 8194994; fax (21) 8195501; f. 1972; weekly; publ. by Press Foundation of Indonesia; Editor Sumono Mustoffa.

Dunia Wanita: Jalan Brigjenderal, Katamso 1, Medan; tel. (61) 4150858; fax (61) 4510025; e-mail waspada@indosat.net.id; f. 1949; fortnightly; Indonesian; women's tabloid; Chief Editor Dr Rayati Syafrin; circ. 10,000.

Economic Review: c/o Bank BNI, Strategic Planning Division, Jalan Jenderal Sudirman, Kav. 1, POB 2955, Jakarta 10220; tel. (21) 5728606; fax (21) 5728456; internet www.economicreview.net; f. 1966; 4 a year; English.

Ekonomi Indonesia: Jalan Merdeka, Timur 11–12, Jakarta; tel. (21) 494458; monthly; English; economic journal; Editor Z. Achmad; circ. 20,000.

Eksekutif: Jalan R. S. Fatmawati 20, Jakarta 12430; tel. (21) 7659218; fax (21) 7504018; e-mail eksek@pacific.net.id; internet www.pacific.net.id/eksekutif/.

Femina: Jalan H. R. Rasuna Said, Blok B, Kav. 32–33, Jakarta Selatan; tel. (21) 5209370; fax (21) 5209366; e-mail info@femina-online.com; internet www.femina-online.com; f. 1972; weekly; women's magazine; Publr Sofjan Alisjahbana; Editor Widarti Gunawan; circ. 130,000.

Forum: Kebayoran Centre, 12a–14, Jalan Kebayoran Baru, Welbak, Jakarta 12240; tel. (21) 7255625; fax (21) 7255645.

Gadis Magazine: Jalan H. R. Rasuna Said, Blok B, Kav. 32–33, Jakarta 12910; tel. (21) 5253816; fax (21) 5262131; e-mail gadis@indosat.net.id; internet www.gadis-online.com; f. 1973; every 10 days; Indonesian; teen lifestyle magazine; Editor-in-Chief Petty S. F. circ. 100,000.

Gamma: Jakarta; internet www.gamma.co.id; f. 1999 by fmr employees of *Tempo* and *Gatra*.

Gatra: Gedung Gatra, Jalan Kalibata Timur IV/15, Jakarta 12740; tel. (21) 7973535; fax (21) 79196923; e-mail gatra@gatra.com; internet www.gatra.com; f. 1994 by fmr employees of *Tempo* (banned 1994–1998); Gen. Man. and Editor-in-Chief Widi Yarmanto.

Gugat (Accuse): Surabaya; politics, law and crime; weekly; circ. 250,000.

Hai: Gramedia, Jalan Palmerah Selatan 22, Jakarta 10270; tel. (21) 5483008; fax (21) 6390080; f. 1973; weekly; youth magazine; Editor Arswendo Atmowiloto; circ. 70,000.

Indonesia Business News: Wisma Bisnis Indonesia, Jalan Letjenderal S. Parman, Kav. 12, Slipi, Jakarta 11410; tel. (21) 5304016; fax (21) 5305868; English.

Indonesia Business Weekly: Jalan Letjenderal S. Parman, Kav. 12, Slipi, Jakarta 11410; tel. (21) 5304016; fax (21) 5305868; English; Editor Taufik Darusman.

Indonesia Magazine: 20 Jalan Merdeka Barat, Jakarta; tel. (21) 352015; f. 1969; monthly; English; Chair. G. Dwipayana; Editor-in-Chief Hadely Hasibuan; circ. 15,000.

Intisari (Digest): Jalan Palmerah Selatan 24–26, Gedung Unit II, 5th Floor, Jakarta 10270; tel. (21) 5483008; fax (21) 53696525; e-mail intisari@gramedia-majalah.com; internet www.intisari-online.com; f. 1963; monthly; Indonesian; popular science, health, technology, crime and general interest; Editors Al. Heru Kustara, Irawati; circ. 141,000.

Jakarta Jakarta: Gramedia Bldg, Unit II, 5th Floor, Jalan Palmerah Selatan No. 24–26, Jakarta 10270; tel. (21) 5483008; fax (21) 5494035; f. 1985; weekly; food, fun, fashion and celebrity news; circ. 70,000.

Keluarga: Jalan Sangaji 11, Jakarta; fortnightly; women's and family magazine; Editor S. Dahono.

Majalah Ekonomis: POB 4195, Jakarta; monthly; English; business; Chief Editor S. Arifin Hutabarat; circ. 20,000.

Majalah Kedokteran Indonesia (Journal of the Indonesian Medical Asscn): Jalan Kesehatan 111/29, Jakarta 11/16; f. 1951; monthly; Indonesian, English.

Manglé: Jalan Lodaya 19–21, 40262 Bandung; tel. (22) 411438; f. 1957; weekly; Sundanese; Chief Editor Drs Oejang Darajatoen; circ. 74,000.

Matra: Grafity Pers, Kompleks Buncit Raya Permai, Kav. 1, Jalan Warung, POB 3476, Jakarta; tel. (21) 515952; f. 1986; monthly; men's magazine; general interest and current affairs; Editor-in-Chief (vacant); circ. 100,000.

Mimbar Kabinet Pembangunan: Jalan Merdeka-Barat 7, Jakarta; f. 1966; monthly; Indonesian; publ. by Dept of Information.

Mutiara: Jalan Dewi Sartika 136d, Cawang, Jakarta Timur; general interest; Publr H. G. Rorimpandey.

Nova: PT Gramedia, Gedung Unit II, Lantai V, Jalan Palmerah Selatan No. 24–26, Jakarta 10270; tel. (21) 5483008; fax (21) 5483146; weekly; Wed. women's interest; Indonesian; Editor Koes Sabandiyah; circ. 618,267.

Oposisi: Jakarta; weekly; politics; circ. 400,000.

Otomotif: Gramedia Bldg, Unit II, 5th Floor, Jalan Palmerah Selatan 24–26, Jakarta 10270; tel. (21) 5490666; fax (21) 5494035; e-mail iklanmjl@ub.net.id; f. 1990; weekly; automotive specialist tabloid; circ. 215,763.

Peraba: Bintaran Kidul 5, Yogyakarta; weekly; Indonesian and Javanese; Roman Catholic; Editor W. Kartosoeharsono.

Pertani PT: Jalan Pasar Minggu, Kalibata, POB 247/KBY, Jakarta Selatan; tel. (21) 793108; f. 1974; monthly; Indonesian; agricultural; Pres. Dir Ir Rusli Yahya.

Petisi: Surabaya; weekly; Editor Choirul Anam.

Rajawali: Jakarta; monthly; Indonesian; civil aviation and tourism; Dir R. A. J. Lumenta; Man. Editor Karyono Adhy.

Selecta: Kebon Kacang 29/4, Jakarta; fortnightly; illustrated; Editor Samsudin Lubis; circ. 80,000.

Simponi: Jakarta; f. 1994 by fmr employees of *DeTik* (banned 1994–98).

Sinar Jaya: Jakarta Selatan; fortnightly; agriculture; Chief Editor Ir Suryono Projopranoto.

Swasembada: Gedung Chandra Lt 2, Jalan M. H. Thamrin 20, Jakarta 10310; tel. (21) 3103316.

Tempo: Gedung Tempo, 8th Floor, Jalan H. R. Rasuna Said, Kav. C-17, Kuningan, Jakarta 12940; tel. (21) 5201022; fax (21) 5200092; internet www.tempo.co.id; f. 1971; weekly; Editor-in-Chief Bambang Harymurti.

Tiara: Gramedia Bldg, Unit 11, 5th Floor, Jalan Palmerah Selatan 24–26, Jakarta 10270; tel. (21) 5483008; fax (21) 5494035; f. 1990; fortnightly; lifestyles, features and celebrity news; circ. 47,000.

Ummat: Jakarta; Islamic; sponsored by ICMI.

NEWS AGENCIES

Antara (Indonesian National News Agency): Wisma Antara, 3rd, 19th and 20th Floors, 17 Jalan Merdeka Selatan, POB 1257, Jakarta 10110; tel. (21) 3802383; fax (21) 3840970; e-mail antara@antara.co.id; internet www.antara.co.id; f. 1937; 20 radio, seven television, 96 newspaper, eight foreign newspaper, seven tabloid, seven magazine, two news agency, nine embassy and seven dotcom subscribers in 2001; 26 brs in Indonesia, six overseas brs/correspondents; four bulletins in Indonesian and one in English; monitoring service of stock exchanges world-wide; photo service; Exec. Editor Heru Purwanto; Man. Dir Mohamad Sobary.

Kantorberita Nasional Indonesia (KNI News Service): Jalan Jatinegara Barat III/6, Jakarta Timur 13310; tel. (21) 811003; fax (21) 8195501; f. 1966; independent national news agency; foreign and domestic news in Indonesian; Dir and Editor-in-Chief Drs Sumono Mustoffa; Exec. Editor Harim Nurrochadi.

Foreign Bureaux

Agence France-Presse (AFP): Jalan Indramayu 18, Jakarta Pusat 10310; tel. (21) 3336082; fax (21) 3809186; Chief Correspondent Pascal Mallet.

Agenzia Nazionale Stampa Associata (ANSA) (Italy): Jalan Petogogan 1 Go-2 No, 13 Kompleks RRI, Kebayoran Baru, Jakarta Selatan; tel. (21) 7391996; fax (21) 7392247; Correspondent Herytno Pujowidagdo.

Associated Press (AP) (USA): Deutsche Bank Bldg, 14th Floor, No. 1403–1404, Jalan Imam Bonjol 80, Jakarta 10310; tel. (21) 39831269; fax (21) 39831270; e-mail gspencer@ap.org; Chief of Bureau Geoff Spencer.

Central News Agency Inc (CNA) (Taiwan): Jalan Gelong Baru Timur 1–13, Jakarta Barat; tel. and fax (21) 5600266; Bureau Chief Wu Pin-Chiang.

Informatsionnoye Telegrafnoye Agentstvo Rossii—Telegrafnoye Agentstvo Suverennykh Stran (ITAR—TASS) (Russia): Jalan Surabaya 7 Menteng, Jakarta Pusat 10310; tel. and fax (21) 3155283; e-mail ab1952@indosat.net.id; Correspondent Andrey Aleksandrovich Bytchkov.

Inter Press Service (IPS) (Italy): Gedung Dewan Pers, 4th Floor, Jalan Kebon Sirih 34, Jakarta 10110; tel. (21) 3453131; fax (21) 3453175; Chief Correspondent Abdul Razak.

Jiji Tsushin (Japan): Jalan Raya Bogor 109b, Jakarta; tel. (21) 8090509; Correspondent Marga Raharja.

Kyodo Tsushin (Japan): Skyline Bldg, 11th Floor, Jalan M. H. Thamrin 9, Jakarta 10310; tel. (21) 345012; Correspondent Masayuki Kitamura.

Reuters (United Kingdom): Wisma Antara, 6th Floor, Jalan Medan Merdeka Selatan 17, Jakarta 10110; tel. (21) 3846364; fax (21) 3448404; e-mail jerry.norton@reuters.com; internet www.reuters.com; Bureau Chief Jerry Norton.

United Press International (UPI) (USA): Wisma Antara, 14th Floor, Jalan Medan Merdeka Selatan 17, Jakarta; tel. (21) 341056; Bureau Chief John Hail.

Xinhua (New China) News Agency (People's Republic of China): Jakarta.

PRESS ASSOCIATIONS

Aliansi Jurnalis Indpenden (AJI) (Alliance of Independent Journalists): Jakarta; internet www.aji.or.id; f. 1994; unofficial; aims to promote freedom of the press; Sec.-Gen. AHMAD TAUFIK.

Persatuan Wartawan Indonesia (Indonesian Journalists' Asscn): Gedung Dewan Pers, 4th Floor, Jalan Kebon Sirih 34, Jakarta 10110; tel. (21) 353131; fax (21) 353175; f. 1946; government-controlled; 5,041 mems (April 1991); Chair. TARMAN AGAM; Gen. Sec. H. SOFJAN LUBIS.

Serikat Penerbit Suratkabar (SPS) (Indonesian Newspaper Publishers' Asscn): Gedung Dewan Pers, 6th Floor, Jalan Kebon Sirih 34, Jakarta 10110; tel. (21) 3459671; fax (21) 3862373; e-mail sps-pst@dnet.net.id; internet www.dnet.net.id/sps; f. 1946; Exec. Chair. Drs S. L. BATUBARA; Sec.-Gen. Drs AMIR E. SIREGAR.

Yayasan Pembina Pers Indonesia (Press Foundation of Indonesia): Jalan Jatinegara Barat III/6, Jakarta 13310; tel. (21) 8194994; f. 1967; Chair. SUGIARSO SUROYO, MOCHTAR LUBIS.

Publishers

JAKARTA

Aries Lima/New Aqua Press PT: Jalan Rawagelan II/4, Jakarta Timur; tel. (21) 4897566; general and children's; Pres. TUTI SUNDARI AZMI.

Aya Media Pustaka PT: Wijaya Grand Centre C/2, Jalan Dharmawangsa III, Jakarta 12160; tel. (21) 7206903; fax (21) 7201401; children's; Dir Drs ARIANTO TUGIYO.

PT Balai Pustaka: Jalan Gunung Sahari Raya 4, POB 1029, Jakarta 10710; tel. and fax (21) 3855733; e-mail bp1917@hotmail .com; internet www.balaiperaga.com; f. 1917; children's, school textbooks, literary, scientific publs and periodicals; Dir R. SISWADI.

Bhratara Niaga Media PT: Jalan Oto Iskandardinata III/29F, Jakarta 13340; tel. (21) 8502050; fax (21) 8191858; f. 1986; fmrly Bhratara Karya Aksara; university and educational textbooks; Man. Dir AHMAD JAYUSMAN.

Bina Rena Pariwara PT: Jalan Pejaten Raya 5-E, Pasar Minggu, Jakarta 12510; tel. (21) 7901931; fax (21) 7901939; e-mail hasanbas@softhome.net; f. 1988; financial, social science, economic, Islamic, children's; Dir Drs HASAN BASRI.

Bulan Bintang PT: Jalan Kramat Kwitang 1/8, Jakarta 10420; tel. (21) 3901651; fax (21) 3107027; f. 1954; Islamic, social science, natural and applied sciences, art; Pres. AMRAN ZAMZAMI; Man. Dir FAUZI AMELZ.

Bumi Aksara PT: Jalan Sawo Raya 18, Rawamanguu, Jakarta 13220; tel. (21) 4717049; fax (21) 4700989; f. 1990; university textbooks; Dir H. AMIR HAMZAH.

Cakrawala Cinta PT: Jalan Minyak I/12B, Duren Tiga, Jakarta 12760; tel. (21) 7990725; fax (21) 7974076; f. 1984; science; Dir Drs M. TORSINA.

Centre for Strategic and International Studies (CSIS): Jalan Tanah Abang III/23–27, Jakarta 10160; tel. (21) 3865532; fax (21) 3847517; e-mail csis@pacific.net.id; internet www.csis.or.id; f. 1971; political and social sciences; Dir Dr DAOED JOESOEF.

Cipta Adi Pustaka: Graha Compaka Mas Blok C 22, Jalan Cempaka Putih Raya, Jakarta Pusat; tel. (21) 4213821; fax (21) 4269315; f. 1986; encyclopedias; Dir BUDI SANTOSO.

Dian Rakyat PT: Jalan Rawagelas I/4, Kaw. Industri Pulo Gadung, Jakarta; tel. (21) 4604444; fax (21) 4609115; f. 1966; general; Dir H. MOHAMMED AIS.

Djambatan PT: Jalan Wijaya I/39, Jakarta 12170; tel. (21) 7203199; fax (21) 7227989; f. 1954; children's, textbooks, social sciences, fiction; Dir SJARIFUDIN SJAMSUDIN.

Dunia Pustaka Jaya: Jalan Rawa Bambu Rt. 003/07 38, Komp. BATAN, Pasar Minggu, Jakarta Selatan 12520; tel. (21) 7891875; fax (21) 3909320; f. 1971; fiction, religion, essays, poetry, drama, criticism, art, philosophy and children's; Man. A. RIVAI.

EGC Medical Publications: Jalan Agung Jaya III/2, Sunter Agung Podomoro, Jakarta 14350; tel. (21) 686351; fax (21) 686352; e-mail egc_arcan@hotmail.com; f. 1978; medical and public health, nursing, dentistry; Dir IMELDA DHARMA.

Elex Media Komputindo: Jalan Palmerah Selatan 22, Kompas–Gramedia Bldg, 6th Floor, Jakarta 10270; tel. (21) 53699059; fax (21) 5326219; e-mail elex@elexmedia.co.id; internet www.elexmedia .co.id; f. 1985; publishing (management, computing, software and merchandising); Dir AL. ADHI MARDHIYONO.

Erlangga PT: Kami Melayani II, Pengetahuan, Jalan H. Baping 100, Ciracas, Jakarta 13740; tel. (21) 8717006; fax (21) 8717011; e-mail erlprom@rad.net.id; internet www.erlangga.com; f. 1952; secondary school and university textbooks; Man. Dir GUNAWAN HUTAURUK.

Gaya Favorit Press: Jalan H. R. Rasuna Said, Blok B, Kav. 32–33, Jakarta 12910; tel. (21) 5209370; fax (21) 5209366; f. 1971; fiction, popular science and children's; Vice-Pres. MIRTA KARTOHADIPRODJO; Man. Dir WIDARTI GUNAWAN.

Gema Insani Press: Jalan Kalibata Utara II/84, Jakarta 12740; tel. (21) 7984391; fax (21) 7984388; e-mail gipnet@indosat.net.id; internet www.gemainsani.co.id; f. 1986; Islamic; Dir UMAR BASYARAHIL.

Ghalia Indonesia: Jalan Pramuka Raya 4, Jakarta 13140; tel. (21) 8584330; fax (21) 8502334; f. 1972; children's and general science, textbooks; Man. Dir LUKMAN SAAD.

Gramedia Widyasarana Indonesia: Jalan Palmerah Selatan 22, Lantai IV, POB 615, Jakarta 10270; tel. (21) 5483008; fax (21) 5300545; f. 1973; university textbooks, general non-fiction, children's and magazines; Gen. Man. ALFONS TARYADI.

Gunung Mulia PT: Jalan Kwitang 22–23, Jakarta 10420; tel. (21) 3901208; fax (21) 3901633; e-mail corp.off@bpkgm.com; internet www.bpkgm.com; f. 1951; general, children's, Christian; Pres. Dir ICHSAN GUNAWAN; Dir V. N. LEIMENA.

Hidakarya Agung PT: Jalan Kebon Kosong F/74, Kemayoran, Jakarta Pusat; tel. (21) 4241074; Dir MAHDIARTI MACHMUD.

Ichtiar: Jalan Majapahit 6, Jakarta Pusat; tel. (21) 3841226; f. 1957; textbooks, law, social sciences, economics; Dir JOHN SEMERU.

Indira PT: Jalan Borobudur 20, Jakarta 10320; tel. (21) 882754; f. 1953; general science and children's; Man. Dir BAMBANG P. WAHYUDI.

Kinta CV: Jalan Kemanggisan Ilir V/110, Pal Merah, Jakarta Barat; tel. (21) 5494751; f. 1950; textbooks, social science, general; Man. Drs MOHAMAD SALEH.

LP 3 ES: Jalan Letjen. S. Parman 81, Jakarta 11420; tel. (21) 5674211; fax (21) 5683785; e-mail lp3es@indo.net.id; f. 1971; general; Dir IMAM AHMAD.

Masagung Group: Gedung Idayu, Jalan Kwitang 13, POB 2260, Jakarta 10420; tel. (21) 3154890; fax (21) 3154889; f. 1986; general, religious, textbooks, science; Pres. H. ABDURRAHMAN MASAGUNG.

Midas Surya Grafindo PT: Jalan Kesehatan 54, Cijantung, Jakarta 13760; tel. (21) 8400414; fax (21) 8400270; f. 1984; children's; Dir Drs FRANS HENDRAWAN.

Mutiara Sumber Widya PT: Jalan Kramat II 55, Jakarta; tel. (21) 3926043; fax (21) 3160313; f. 1951; textbooks, Islamic, social sciences, general and children's; Pres. FADJRAA OEMAR.

Penebar Swadya PT: Jalan Gunung Sahari III/7, Jakarta Pusat; tel. (21) 4204402; fax (21) 4214821; agriculture, animal husbandry, fisheries; Dir Drs ANTHONIUS RIYANTO.

Penerbit Universitas Indonesia: Jalan Salemba Raya 4, Jakarta; tel. (21) 335373; f. 1969; science; Man. S. E. LEGOWO.

Pradnya Paramita PT: Jalan Bunga 8–8A, Matraman, Jakarta 13140; tel. (21) 8504944; e-mail pradnya@centrin.net.id; f. 1973; children's, general, educational, technical and social science; Pres. Dir WILLY LALUYAN.

Pustaka Antara PT: Jalan Taman Kebon Sirih III/13, Jakarta Pusat 10250; tel. (21) 3156994; fax (21) 322745; e-mail nacelod@cbn .net.id; f. 1952; textbooks, political, Islamic, children's and general; Man. Dir AIDA JOESOEF AHMAD.

Pustaka Binaman Pressindo: Bina Manajemen Bldg, Jalan Menteng Raya 9–15, Jakarta 10340; tel. (21) 2300313; fax (21) 2302047; e-mail pustaka@bit.net.id; f. 1981; management; Dir Ir MAKFUDIN WIRYA ATMAJA.

Pustaka Sinar Harapan PT: Jalan Dewi Sartika 136D, Jakarta 13630; tel. (21) 8093208; fax (21) 8091652; f. 1981; general science, fiction, comics, children's; Dir W.M. NAIDEN.

Pustaka Utma Grafiti PT: Jalan Utan Kayu 68EFG, Utan Kayu Utara, Jakarta 13120; tel. (21) 8567502; fax (21) 8573387; f. 1981; social sciences, humanities and children's books; Dir ZULKIFLY LUBIS.

Rajagrafindo Persada PT: Jalan Pelepah Hijau IV TN-1 14–15, Kelapa Gading Permai, Jakarta 14240; tel. (21) 4529409; fax (21) 4520951; f. 1980; general science and religion; Dir Drs ZUBAIDI.

Rineka Cipta PT: Blok B/5, Jalan Jenderal Sudirman, Kav. 36A, Bendungan Hilir, Jakarta 10210; tel. (21) 5737646; fax (21) 5711985; f. 1990 by merger of Aksara Baru (f. 1972) and Bina Aksara; general science and university texts; Dir Dr H. SUARDI.

Rosda Jayaputra PT: Jalan Kembang 4, Jakarta 10420; tel. (21) 3904984; fax (21) 3901703; f. 1981; general science; Dir H. ROZALI USMAN.

Sastra Hudaya: Jalan Kalasan 1, Jakarta Pusat; tel. (21) 882321; f. 1967; religious, textbooks, children's and general; Man. ADAM SALEH.

Tintamas Indonesia: Jalan Kramat Raya 60, Jakarta 10420; tel. and fax (21) 3911459; f. 1947; history, modern science and culture, especially Islamic; Man. MARHAMAH DJAMBEK.

Tira Pustaka: Jalan Cemara Raya 1, Kav. 10D, Jaka Permai, Jaka Sampurna, Bekasi 17145; tel. (21) 8841277; fax (21) 8842736; e-mail Tirapus@cbn.net.id; f. 1977; translations, children's; Dir ROBERT B. WIDJAJA.

Widjaya: Jalan Pecenongan 48C, Jakarta Pusat; tel. (21) 3813446; f. 1950; textbooks, children's, religious and general; Man. DIDI LUTHAN.

Yasaguna: Jalan Minangkabau 44, POB 422, Jakarta Selatan; tel. (21) 8290422; f. 1964; agricultural, children's, handicrafts; Dir HILMAN MADEWA.

Bandung

Alma'arif: Jalan Tamblong 48–50, Bandung; tel. (22) 4264454; fax (22) 4239194; f. 1949; textbooks, religious and general; Man. H. M. BAHARTHAH.

Alumni PT: Jalan Bukit Pakar Timur II/109, Bandung 40197; tel. (22) 2501251; fax (22) 2503044; f. 1968; university and school textbooks; Dir EDDY DAMIAN.

Angkasa: Jalan Merdeka 6, POB 1353 BD, Bandung 40111; tel. (22) 4204795; fax (22) 439183; Dir H. FACHRI SAID.

Armico: Jalan Madurasa Utara 10, Cigereleng, Bandung 40253; tel. (22) 5202234; fax (22) 5201972; f. 1980; school textbooks; Dir Ir ARSIL TANJUNG.

Citra Aditya Bakti PT: Jalan Geusanulun 17, Bandung 40115; tel. (22) 438251; fax (22) 438635; f. 1985; general science; Dir Ir IWAN TANUATMADJA.

Diponegoro Publishing House: Jalan Mohammad Toha 44–46, Bandung 40252; tel. and fax (22) 5201215; e-mail dpnegoro@indosat .net.id; f. 1963; Islamic, textbooks, fiction, non-fiction, general; Man. H. A. DAHLAN.

Epsilon Group: Jalan Marga Asri 3, Margacinta, Bandung 40287; tel. (22) 7567826; f. 1985; school textbooks; Dir Drs BAHRUDIN.

Eresco PT: Jalan Megger Girang 98, Bandung 40254; tel. (22) 5205985; fax (22) 5205984; f. 1957; scientific and general; Man. Drs ARFAN ROZALI.

Ganeca Exact Bandung: Jalan Kiaracondong 167, Pagauban, Bandung 40283; tel. (22) 701519; fax (22) 775329; f. 1982; school textbooks; Dir Ir KETUT SUARDHARA LINGGIH.

Mizan Pustaka PT: Jalan Yodkali 16, Bandung 40124; tel. (22) 7200931; fax (22) 7207038; e-mail info@mizan.com; internet www .mizan.com; f. 1983; Islamic and general books; Pres. Dir HAIDAR BAGIR; Man. Dir PUTUT WIDJANARKO.

Penerbit ITB: Jalan Ganesa 10, Bandung 40132; tel. and fax (22) 2504257; e-mail itbpress@bdg.centrin.net.id; f. 1971; academic books; Dir EMMY SUPARKA; Chief Editor SOFIA MANSOOR-NIKSOLIHIN.

Putra A. Bardin: Jalan Ganesya 4, Bandung; tel. (22) 2504319; f. 1998; textbooks, scientific and general; Dir NAI A. BARDIN.

Remaja Rosdakarya PT: Jalan Ciateul 34–36, POB 284, Bandung 40252; tel. (22) 5200287; fax (22) 5202529; textbooks and children's fiction; Pres. ROZALI USMAN.

Sarana Panca Karyam PT: Jalan Kopo 633 KM 13/4, Bandung 40014; f. 1986; general; Dir WIMPY S. IBRAHIM.

Tarsito PT: Jalan Guntur 20, Bandung 40262; tel. (22) 304915; fax (22) 314630; academic; Dir T. SITORUS.

Flores

Nusa Indah: Jalan El Tari, Ende 86318, Flores; tel. (0381) 21502; fax (0381) 22373; f. 1970; religious and general; Dir LUKAS BATMO-MOLIN.

Kudus

Menara Kudus: Jalan Menara 4, Kudus 59315; tel. (291) 371143; fax (291) 36474; f. 1958; Islamic; Man. CHILMAN NAJIB.

Medan

Hasmar: Jalan Letjenderal Haryono M. T. 1, POB 446, Medan 20231; tel. (61) 24181; f. 1962; primary school textbooks; Dir HAS-BULLAH LUBIS; Man. AMRAN SAID RANGKUTI.

Impola: Jalan H. M. Joni 46, Medan 20217; tel. (61) 711415; f. 1984; school textbooks; Dir PAMILANG M. SITUMORANG.

Madju: Jalan Amaliun 37, Medan 20215; tel. (61) 711990; fax (61) 717753; f. 1950; textbooks, children's and general; Pres. H. MOHAMED ARBIE; Man. Dir Drs ALFIAN ARBIE.

Masco: Jalan Sisingamangaraja 191, Medan 20218; tel. (61) 713375; f. 1992; school textbooks; Dir P. M. SITUMORANG.

Monora: Jalan Letjenderal Jamin Ginting 583, Medan 20156; tel. (61) 812667; fax (61) 812669; f. 1968; school textbooks; Dir CHAIRIL ANWAR.

Semarang

Aneka Ilmu: Jalan Raya Semarang Demak Km 8.5, Sayung, Demak; tel. (24) 6580335; fax (24) 6582903; e-mail aneka@semarang .wasantara.net.id; f. 1983; general and school textbooks; Dir H. SUWANTO.

Effhar COY PT: Jalan Dorang 7, Semarang 50173; tel. (24) 3511172; fax (24) 3551540; e-mail effhar_dahara@yahoo.com; f. 1976; general books; Dir H. DARADJAT HARAHAP.

Intan Pariwara: Jalan Beringin, Klaten Utara, Kotak Pos III, Kotif Klaten, Jawa-Tengah; tel. (272) 22441; fax (272) 22021; school textbooks; Pres. SOETIKNO.

Mandira PT: Jalan Letjenderal M. T. Haryono 501, Semarang 50241; tel. (24) 316150; fax (24) 415092; f. 1962; Dir Ir A. HARIYANTO.

Mandira Jaya Abadi PT: Jalan Letjenderal M. T. Haryono 501, Semarang 50241; tel. (24) 519547; fax (24) 542189; e-mail mjabadi@ indosat.net.id; f. 1981; Dir Ir A. HARIYANTO.

Solo

Pabelan PT: Jalan Raya Pajang, Kertasura KM 8, Solo 57162; tel. (271) 743975; fax (271) 714775; f. 1983; school textbooks; Dir AGUNG SASONGKO.

Tiga Serangkai PT: Jalan Dr Supomo 23, Solo; tel. (271) 714344; fax (271) 713607; f. 1977; school textbooks; Dir ABDULLAH.

Surabaya

Airlangga University Press: Kampus C, Jalan Mulyorejo, Surabaya; tel. (31) 5992246; fax (31) 5992248; e-mail aupsby@rad.net .id; academic; Dir Dr ARIFAAN RAZAK.

Bina Ilmu PT: Jalan Tunjungan 53E, Surabaya 60275; tel. (31) 5323214; fax (31) 5315421; f. 1973; school textbooks, Islamic; Pres. ARIEFIN NOOR.

Bintang: Jalan Potroagung III/41C, Surabaya; tel. (31) 3770687; fax (31) 3715941; school textbooks; Dir AGUS WINARNO.

Grip PT: Jalan Rungkut Permai II/C–11, Surabaya; tel. (31) 22564; f. 1958; textbooks and general; Man. SURIPTO.

Jaya Baya: Jalan Embong Malang 69H, POB 250, Surabaya 60001; tel. (31) 41169; f. 1945; religion, philosophy and ethics; Man. TADJIB ERMADI.

Sinar Wijaya: Jalan Raya Sawo VII/58, Bringin-Lakarsantri, Surabaya; tel. (31) 706615; general; Dir DULRADJAK.

Yogyakarta

Andi Publishers: Jalan Beo 38–40, Yogyakarta 55281; tel. (274) 561881; fax (274) 588282; e-mail andi_pub@indo.net.id; f. 1980; Christian, computing, business, management and technical; Dir J. H. GONDOWIJOYO.

BPFE PT: Jalan Gambiran 37, Yogyakarta 55161; tel. (274) 373760; fax (274) 380819; f. 1984; university textbooks; Dir Drs INDRIYO GITOSUDARMO.

Centhini Yayasan: Gg. Bekisar UH V/716 E–1, Yogyakarta 55161; tel. (274) 383148; f. 1984; Javanese culture; Chair. H. KARKONO KAMAJAYA.

Gadjah Mada University Press: Jalan Grafika 1, Campus UGM, Bulaksumur, Yogyakarta 55231; tel. (274) 902727; fax (274) 561037; f. 1971; university textbooks; Dir Drs H. SUKAMTO.

Indonesia UP: Gg. Bekisar UH V/716 E–1, Yogyakarta 55161; tel. (274) 383148; f. 1950; general science; Dir H. KARKONO KAMAJAYA.

Kanisius Publr: Jalan Cempaka 9, Deresan, POB 1125, Yogyakarta 55281; tel. (274) 588783; fax (274) 563349; e-mail office@ kanisius.co.id; internet www.kanisius.co.id; f. 1922; children's, textbooks, Christian and general; Man. E. SURONO.

Kedaulatan Rakyat PT: Jalan P. Mangkubumi 40–42, Yogyakarta; tel. (274) 2163; Dir DRONO HARDJUSUWONGSO.

Penerbit Tiara Wacana Yogya: Jalan Kaliurang KM 7, 8 Kopen 16, Banteng, Yogyakarta 55581; tel. and fax (274) 880683; f. 1986; university textbooks and general science; Dir SITORESMI PRABU-NINGRAT.

Government Publishing House

Balai Pustaka PT (Persero) (State Publishing and Printing House): Jalan Gunung Sahari Raya 4, Gedung Balai Pustaka, 7th Floor, Jakarta Pusat 10710; tel. (21) 3447003; fax (21) 3446555;

e-mail mail@balaiperaga.com; internet www.balaiperaga.com; history, anthropology, politics, philosophy, medical, arts and literature; Pres. Dir H. R. SISWADI IDRIS.

PUBLISHERS' ASSOCIATION

Ikatan Penerbit Indonesia (IKAPI) (Asscn of Indonesian Book Publishers): Jalan Kalipasir 32, Jakarta 10330; tel. (21) 3141907; fax (21) 3146050; e-mail sekretariat@ikapi.or.id; internet www.ikapi .or.id; f. 1950; 631 mems (Jan. 2000); Pres. MAKFUDIN WIRYA ATMAJA; Sec.-Gen. ROBINSON RUSDI; 496 mems (Aug. 2002).

Broadcasting and Communications

TELECOMMUNICATIONS

Directorate-General of Posts and Telecommunications (Postel): Gedung Sapta Pesona, Jalan Medan Merdeka Barat 17, Jakarta 10110; tel. (21) 3835912; fax (21) 3860754; e-mail admin@ postel.go.id; internet www.postel.go.id; Dir Gen. DJAMHARI SIRAT.

PT Indosat (Persero) Tbk: Jalan Medan Merdeka Barat 21, POB 2905, Jakarta 10110; tel. (21) 3802614; fax (21) 3458155; e-mail sant@indosat.com; internet www.indosat.com; telecommunications; partially privatized in 1994; 41.9% stake sold to Singapore Technologies Telemedia in 2002; Pres. WIDYA PURNAMA.

PT Satelit Palapa Indonesia (SATELINDO): Jalan Daan Mogot Km 11, Jakarta 11710; tel. (21) 5451745; fax (21) 5451748; e-mail webmaster@satelindo.co.id; internet www.satelindo.co.id; Pres. Dir JOHNY SWANDI SJAM.

PT Telekomunikasi Indonesia Tbk (TELKOM): Corporate Office, Jalan Japati No. 1, Bandung 40133; tel. (22) 4521510; fax (22) 440313; internet www.telkom.co.id; domestic telecommunications; 24.2% of share capital was transferred to the private sector in 1995; CEO ASMAN AKHIR NASUTION.

BROADCASTING

Regulatory Authority

Directorate-General of Radio, Television and Film: Jalan Merdeka Barat 9, Jakarta 10110; Dep. Dir M. ARSYAD SUBIK.

Radio

Radio Republik Indonesia (RRI): Jalan Medan Merdeka Barat 4–5, Jakarta 10110; tel. (21) 3846817; fax (21) 3457134; e-mail rri@ rrionline.com; internet www.rrionline.com; f. 1945; 49 stations; Dir SURYANTA SALEH; Dep. Dirs FACHRUDDIN SOEKARNO (Overseas Service), ABDUL ROCHIM (Programming), SUKRI (Programme Development), SAZLI RAIS (Administration), CHAERUL ZEN (News).

Voice of Indonesia: Jalan Medan Merdeka Barat 4–5, POB 1157, Jakarta; tel. (21) 3456811; international service provided by Radio Republik Indonesia; daily broadcasts in Arabic, English, French, German, Bahasa Indonesia, Japanese, Bahasa Malaysia, Mandarin, Spanish and Thai.

Television

In March 1989 Indonesia's first private commercial television station began broadcasting to the Jakarta area. In 1996 there were five privately-owned television stations in operation.

PT Cakrawala Andalas Televisi (ANTEVE): Gedung Sentra Mulia, 18th Floor, Jalan H. R. Rasuna Said, Kav. X-6 No. 8, Jakarta 12940; tel. (21) 5222086; fax (21) 5222087; e-mail ancorcom@uninet .net.id; internet www.anteve.uninet.net.id; f. 1993; private channel; broadcasting to 10 cities; Pres. Dir H. R. AGUNG LAKSONO; Gen. Man. CEO NENNY SOEMAWINATA.

PT Rajawali Citra Televisi Indonesia (RCTI): Jalan Raya Pejuangan 3, Kebon Jeruk, Jakarta 11000; tel. (21) 5303540; fax (21) 5493852; e-mail webmaster@rcti.co.id; internet www.rcti.co.id; f. 1989; first private channel; 20-year licence; Pres. Dir M. S. RALIE SIREGAR; Vice-Pres. ALEX KUMARA.

PT Surya Citra Televisi (SCTV): GRHA SCTV, 2nd Floor, Jalan Gatot Subroto, Kav. 21, Jakarta 12930; tel. (21) 5225555; fax (21) 5224777; e-mail pr@sctv.co.id; internet www.sctv.co.id; f. 1990; private channel broadcasting nationally; Pres. Dir Dr Ir AGUS MULYANTO.

PT CIPTA TPI: Jalan Pintu II—Taman Mini Indonesia Indah, Pondok Gede, Jakarta 13810; tel. (21) 8412473; fax (21) 8412470; e-mail info@tpi.co.id; internet www.tpi.co.id; f. 1991; private channel funded by commercial advertising; Pres. Dir SITI HARDIJANTI RUKMANA.

Televisi Republik Indonesia (TVRI): TVRI Senayan, Jalan Gerbang Pemuda, Senayan, Jakarta; tel. (21) 5733135; fax (21) 5732408; e-mail info@tvrisby.com; internet www.tvrisby.com; f. 1962; state-controlled; Pres. Dir HARI SULISTYONO.

Finance

(cap. = capital; auth. = authorized; p.u. = paid up; res = reserves; dep. = deposits; m. = million; brs = branches; amounts in rupiah)

BANKING

In December 1996 there were 9,276 banks, with 14,956 branches, in operation in Indonesia, including seven state commercial banks, 27 regional government banks, 164 private national banks and 41 foreign and joint-venture banks. At the end of March 1995 total bank deposits stood at 167,123,000m. rupiah. A programme of extensive reform of the banking sector was ongoing in 2003, under the auspices of the Indonesian Bank Restructuring Agency (IBRA, see Government Agencies, below).

Central Bank

Bank Indonesia: Jalan M. H. Thamrin 2, Pusat, Jakarta 10002; tel. (21) 2310408; fax (21) 2311058; e-mail humasbi@bi.go.id; internet www.bi.go.id; f. 1828; nationalized as central bank in 1953; cap. 2,606,000m., res 116,570,000m., dep. 322,904,000m. (Dec. 2000); Gov. Dr SYAHRIL SABIRIN; 42 brs.

State Banks

In late December 1997 the Government announced that four of the state-owned banks—Bank Bumi Daya, Bank Dagang Negara, Bank Ekspor Impor Indonesia and Bank Pembangunan Indonesia—were to merge; the four banks subsequently merged into a single new institution, PT Bank Mandiri, which was established in July 1999.

PT Bank Ekspor Indonesia (Persero): Gedung Brs Efek, Menara II Lt. 8, Jalan Sudirman, Kav. 52–53, Jakarta; tel. (21) 5154638; fax (21) 5154639; internet www.bexi.co.id.

PT Bank Mandiri (Persero): Plaza Mandiri, Jalan Jenderal Gatot Subroto, Kav. 36-38, Jakarta 12190; tel. (21) 5265045; fax (21) 5268246; internet www.bankmandiri.co.id; f. 1999; as a result of the merger of four state-owned banks—PT Bank Bumi Daya, PT Bank Dagang Negara, PT Bank Ekspor Impor Indonesia and PT Bank Pembangunan Indonesia; cap. 4,251m., res 175,219m., dep. 163,923m. (Dec. 2000); Pres. Commissioner BINHADI; Pres. Dir E. C. W. NELOE.

PT Bank Negara Indonesia (Persero) Tbk: Jalan Jenderal Sudirman, Kav. 1, BP 2955, Jakarta 10220; tel. (21) 2511946; fax (21) 2511221; e-mail hin@bni.co.id; internet www.bni.co.id; f. 1946; commercial bank; specializes in credits to the industrial sector; cap. 7,091,336m., res 57,505,154m., dep. 86,273,706m. (Dec. 2000); Pres. Dir SAIFUDDIEN HASAN; 585 local brs, 6 overseas brs.

PT Bank Rakyat Indonesia (Persero): Jalan Jenderal Sudirman, Kav. 44–46, BP 94, Jakarta 10210; tel. (21) 2510244; fax (21) 2500077; internet www.bri.co.id; f. 1895; present name since 1946; commercial and foreign exchange bank; specializes in agricultural smallholdings and rural development; state-owned; cap. 1,728,000m., res 29,341,025m., dep. 50,522,731m. (Dec. 2000); Pres. Dir DJOKOSANTOSO MOELJONO; 323 brs.

PT Bank Tabungan Negara (Persero): 10th Floor, Bank BTN Tower Bldg, Jalan Gajah Mada 1, Jakarta 10130; tel. (21) 6336789; fax (21) 6336704; e-mail webadmin@btn.co.id; internet www.btn.co .id; f. 1964; commercial bank; state-owned; cap. 15,093,540m., dep. 16,712,526m. (Dec. 2000); Chair. DARMIN NASUTION; 37 brs.

Commercial Banks

PT ANZ Panin Bank: Panin Bank Centre, Jalan Jenderal Sudirman (Senayan), Jakarta 10270; tel. (21) 5750300; fax (21) 5727447; internet www.anz.com/indonesia; f. 1990 as Westpac Panin Bank; 85%-owned by the Australia and New Zealand Banking Group Ltd; cap. 50,000m., dep. 972,000m. (Dec. 2000); Pres. Dir SCOTT ARMSTRONG.

Bank Artha Graha: Bank Artha Graha Tower, 5th Floor, Jalan Jenderal Sudirman, Kav. 52–53, Jakarta 12920; tel. (21) 5152168; fax (21) 5152162; e-mail agraha@rad.net.id; f. 1967; merged with PT Bank Arta Pratama in 1999; cap. 75,000m., dep. 340,344m. (Dec. 1993); Pres. Dir ANTON B. S. HUDYANA; Chair. LETJEN; 64 brs.

PT Bank Bali: Gedung Bank Bali, 19th Floor, Jalan Jenderal Sudirman, Kav. 27, Jakarta 12920; tel. (21) 5237899; fax (21) 2500811; internet www.bankbali.co.id; f. 1954; scheduled to merge with PT Bank Universal, PT Bank Prima Express, PT Bank Arthamedia and PT Bank Patriot by Dec. 2002; cap. 5,691,698m., res

201,598m., dep. 9,860,617m. (Dec. 2000); Pres. Commissioner I. NYOMAN SOEWANDA; 270 brs.

PT Bank Central Asia (BCA): Wisma BCA, 5th Floor, Jalan Jenderal Sudirman, Kav. 22–23, Jakarta 12920; tel. (21) 5711250; fax (21) 5701865; internet www.klikbca.com; f. 1957; placed under the supervision of the Indonesian Bank Restructuring Agency in May 1998; 51% share sold to Farallon Capital Management (USA) in March 2002; cap. 1,471,993m., res 4,814,280m., dep. 86,072,502m. (Dec. 2000); Chair. MUHAMMAD DJOEANA KOESOEMAHARDJA; 796 brs.

PT Bank Dagang Bali: Jalan Gajah Mada 2, Denpasar, Bali; tel. (361) 263736; fax (361) 231226; e-mail bdbBank@yahoo.com; f. 1970; cap. 51,000m., res 3,774m., dep. 1,112,303m. (Dec. 2000); Pres. Dir I. GUSTI MADE OKA; Chair. GUSTI AYU NYOMEN SAYANG.

PT Bank Danamon Indonesia Tbk: Wisma Bank Danamon, Jalan Jenderal Sudirman, Kav. 45, Jakarta 12930; tel. (21) 5770551; fax (21) 5770704; internet www.danamon.co.id; f. 1956; placed under the supervision of the Indonesian Bank Restructuring Agency in April 1998, merged with PT Bank Tiara Asia in July 2000, with PT Tamara Bank in August 2000, and with PT Bank Duta and PT Bank Nusa Nasional in September 2000; cap. 3,562,261m., res 32,994,432m., dep. 30,643,895m. (Dec. 2000); Chair. PETER B. STOCK; Pres. Dir ARWIN RASYID; 737 brs.

Bank Internasional Indonesia (BII): Plaza BII, Jalan M. H. Thamrin 51, Kav. 22, Jakarta 10350; tel. (21) 2300888; fax (21) 2301494; e-mail bii-info@idola.net.id; internet www.bii.co.id; cap. 13,054,731m., res 1,442,194m., dep. 28,784,389m. (Dec. 2000); Chair. RUSLI PRAKARSA; Pres. Dir HIROSHI TADANO; 249 brs.

PT Bank Mayapada Internasional: Arthaloka Bldg, Ground & 1st Floor, Jalan Jenderal Sudirman, Kav. 2, Jakarta 10220; tel. (21) 2511588; fax (21) 2511539; e-mail mayapada@bankmayapada.com; internet www.bankmayapada.com; f. 1989; cap. 164,145m., dep. 925,394m. (Dec. 2000); Chair. TAHIR; Pres. Dir HARYONO TJAHJARIJADI; 5 brs, 7 sub-brs.

PT Bank Mizuho Indonesia: Plaza B11, 24th Floor, Menara 2, Jalan M. H. Thamrin 51, Jakarta 10350; tel. (21) 3925222; fax (21) 3926354; fmrly PT Bank Fuji International Indonesia; f. 1989; cap. 144,375m., res 25,908m., dep. 1,431,883m. (Dec. 1998); Pres. Dir TAKAO ENDO.

PT Bank Muamalat Indonesia (BMI): Arthaloka Bldg, Jalan Jenderal Sudirman 2, Jakarta 10220; tel. (21) 2511414; fax (21) 2511453; internet www.muamalatbank.com; Indonesia's first Islamic bank; cap. 165,593m. (July 2000); Pres. Dir A. RIAWAN AMIN; Chair. ABBAS ADHAR.

PT Bank Niaga: Graha Niaga, Jalan Jenderal Sudirman, Kav. 58, Jakarta 12190; tel. (21) 2505252; fax (21) 2505205; e-mail caniaga@attglobal.net; internet www.bankniaga.com; f. 1955; cap. 359,270m., res 557,805m., dep. 12,614,890m. (Dec. 1999); Pres. Commissioner SUKANTO REKSOHADIPRODJO; Pres. Dir PETER B. STOCK; 96 brs.

PT Bank NISP Tbk: Jalan Taman Cibeunying Selatan 31, Jakarta 40114; tel. (22) 7234123; fax (22) 7100466; e-mail nisp@banknisp.com; internet www.banknisp.com; f. 1941; cap. 274,611m., dep. 2,740,549m. (Dec. 1999); Pres. Dir PRAMUKTI SURJAUDAJA; Chair. KARMAKA SURJANDAJA; 59 brs.

PT Bank Prima Express: Jalan Roa Malaka Selatan 67, Jakarta 11230; tel. (21) 6906377; fax (21) 6908606; e-mail primex@rad.net.id; f. 1956 as Bank Tani Nasional PT; scheduled to merge into PT Bank Bali by Dec. 2002; cap. 167,000m., res 484,071m., dep. 1,522,444m. (Dec. 2000); Chair. BUDI PURWANTO; Pres. MICHAEL HUTABARAT; 16 brs.

PT Bank Rabobank International Indonesia: Plaza 89, 9th Floor, Jalan H. R. Rasuna Said, Kav. X-7, Jakarta 12940; tel. (21) 2520876; fax (21) 2520875; internet www.rabobank.com; cap. 350,000m., res 2,741m., dep. 1,010,012m. (Dec. 1999); Pres. and Dir HANS WINKELMOLEN.

PT Bank Sumitomo Mitsui Indonesia: Summitmas II, 10th Floor, Jalan Jenderal Sudirman, Kav. 61–62, Jakarta 12069; tel. (21) 5227011; fax (21) 5227022; f. 1989; fmrly PT Bank Sumitomo Indonesia, merged with PT Bank Sakura Swadharma in April 2001; cap. 753,191m., dep. 2,050,876m. (Dec. 1999); Pres. Dir YOSHIRO MORIMOTO; 1 br.

PT Bank UFJ Indonesia: Bank Bali Bldg, 4th–5th Floors, Jalan Jenderal Sudirman, Kav. 27, Jakarta 12920; tel. (21) 2500401; fax (21) 2500410; f. 1989 as PT Sanwa Indonesia Bank; fmrly PT Bank Sanwa Indonesia; name changed as above Oct. 2001 following merger with PT Tokai Lippo Bank; cap. 817,449m., res 546,850m., dep. 2,635,793m. (Dec. 2002); Pres., Bd of Commrs MASATERU NAKAMURA; Pres. Dir MAKOTO KANEKO; 1 br., 4 sub-brs.

PT Bank Universal: Plaza Setiabudi, Atrium Bldg, 2nd Floor, Jalan H. R. Rasuna Said, Kav. 62, Jakarta 12920; tel. (21) 5210550; fax (21) 5210588; e-mail info@bankuniversal.co.id; internet www.bankuniversal.co.id; f. 1990; to merge into PT Bank Bali by Dec. 2002; cap. 849,196m., res 4,734,630m., dep. 9,099,995m. (Dec. 1999);

Pres. Dir STEPHEN Z. SATYAHADI; Chair. THEODORE PERMADI RACHMAT; 65 brs.

PT Hagabank: Jalan Abdul Muis 28, Jakarta 10160; tel. (21) 2312888; fax (21) 2312250; e-mail info@hagabank.com; internet www.hagabank.com; f. 1989; cap. 65,000m., res -939m., dep. 1,484,928m. (Dec. 2000); Pres. DANNY HARTONO; Chair. TIMOTY E. MARNANDUS.

PT Korea Exchange Bank Danamon: Suite 1201, 12th Floor, Wisma GKBI, Jalan Jenderal Sudirman, Kav. 28, Selatan, Jakarta; tel. (21) 5741030; fax (21) 5741032; e-mail kebd@idola.net.id; cap. 150,000m., dep. 542,739m. (Dec. 2000); Pres. NAM HAENG WAN; Chair. HONG YOUNG CHEUL.

PT Lippo Bank: Gedung Menara Asia, Jalan Raya Diponegoro 101, Lippo Karawaci, Tangerang 15810; tel. (21) 5460555; fax (21) 5460816; e-mail info_crc@lippobank.co.id; internet www.lippobank.co.id; f. 1948; cap. 811,494m., res 10,416,818m., dep. 18,938,719m. (Dec. 2000); Chair. MOCHTAR T. RIADY; Pres. Dir and CEO EDDY SINDORO; 310 brs.

PT Pan Indonesia Tbk (Panin Bank): Panin Bank Centre, 11th Floor, Jalan Jenderal Sudirman, Senayan, Jakarta 10270; tel. (21) 2700545; fax (21) 2700340; e-mail jasman@panin.co.id; internet www.panin.co.id; f. 1971; cap. 1,488,888m., res 1,082,472m., dep. 11,019,510m. (Dec. 2000); Chair. FUADY MOURAD; Pres. H. ROSTIAN SJAMSUDIN; 116 brs, 2 overseas brs.

PT Pesona Kriyadana: Jalan Pecenongan 84, POB 1471, Jakarta 10120; tel. (21) 3458103; fax (21) 3451617; f. 1974; fmrly Overseas Express Bank, Bank Utama; cap. 85,000m., res 16,039m., dep. 1,944,241m. (Dec. 1995); Chair. A. SUBOWO; Pres. Dir JANPIE SIAHAAN; 8 brs.

Foreign Banks

ABN AMRO Bank NV (Netherlands): Jalan Ir H. Juanda 23–24, POB 2950, Jakarta 10029; tel. (21) 2312777; fax (21) 2313222; internet www.abnamro.co.id; Man. C. J. DE KONING; 15 brs.

Bangkok Bank Public Company Ltd (Thailand): Jalan M. H. Thamrin 3, Jakarta 10110; POB 4165, Jakarta 11041; tel. (21) 2311008; fax (21) 3853881; f. 1968; Gen. Man. PRASARN TUNTASOOD.

Bank of America NA (USA): Jakarta Stock Exchange Bldg Tower 1, 22nd Floor, Jalan Jenderal Sudirman, Kav. 52–53, Jakarta 12190; POB 4931 JKTM, Jakarta 12049; tel. (21) 5158000; fax (21) 5158088; e-mail rahul.goswamy@bankofamerica.com; f. 1968; Man. Dir and Country Man. RAHUL GOSWAMY.

Bank of Tokyo-Mitsubishi Ltd (Japan): Midplaza Bldg, 1st–3rd Floors, Jalan Jenderal Sudirman, Kav. 10–11, POB 2711, Jakarta 10227; tel. (21) 5706185; fax (21) 5731927; e-mail pip@botm.co.id; internet www.btmjkt.com; Gen. Man. HIDEYUKI ABE.

Citibank NA (USA): Citibank Tower, Jalan Jenderal Sudirman, Kav. 54–55, Jakarta 12910; tel. (21) 52962277; fax (21) 52969303; internet www.citibank.co.id; f. 1912; Vice-Pres JAMES F. HUNT, EDWIN GERUNGAN, ROBERT THORNTON.

Deutsche Bank, AG (Germany): Deutsche Bank Bldg, Jalan Iman Bonjol 80, Jakarta 10310; POB 1135, Jakarta 10011; tel. (21) 3904792; fax (21) 335252; Gen. Man. HEINZ POEHLSEN.

Hongkong and Shanghai Banking Corpn Ltd (Hong Kong): 1st–5th Floors, World Trade Centre, Jalan Jenderal Sudirman, Kav. 29–31, Jakarta 12920; POB 2307, Jakarta 10023; tel. (21) 5246222; fax (21) 5211103; internet www.hsbc.co.id; CEO P. C. L. HOLBERTON; 6 brs.

The JP Morgan Chase Bank, NA (USA): Chase Plaza, 5th Floor, Jalan Jenderal Sudirman, Kav. 21, POB 311/JKT, Jakarta 12920; tel. (21) 5712213; fax (21) 5703690; Vice-Pres. and Sr Officer PETER NICE.

Standard Chartered Bank (United Kingdom): Wisma Standard Chartered Bank, Jalan Jenderal Sudirman, Kav. 33-A, Jakarta 10220; POB 57 JKWK, Jakarta 10350; tel. (21) 2513333; fax (21) 5721234; internet www.standardchartered.com/id/index.html; Chief Exec. DAVID HAWKINS; 5 brs.

Banking Association

The Association of Indonesian National Private Commercial Banks (Perhimpunan Bank-Bank Umum Nasional Swasta—PERBANAS): Jalan Perbanas, Karet Kuningan, Setiabudi, Jakarta 12940; tel. (21) 5223038; fax (21) 5223037; e-mail secretariat@perbanas.web.id; internet www.perbanas.web.id; f. 1952; 94 mems; Chair. GUNARNI SOEWORO; Sec.-Gen. WIBOWO NGASERIN.

STOCK EXCHANGES

At the end of January 2000 278 companies were listed on the Jakarta Stock Exchange, and market capitalization was 410,520,769m. rupiah. At the end of August 2002 there were 287 companies listed on the Jakarta Stock Exchange.

Bursa Paralel: PT Bursa Paralel Indonesia, Gedung Bursa, Jalan Medan Merdeka Selatan 14, Jakarta; tel. (21) 3810963; fax (21) 3810989; f. 1987.

Jakarta Stock Exchange (JSX): PT Bursa Efek Jakarta, Jakarta Stock Exchange Bldg, 4th Floor, Jalan Jenderal Sudirman, Kav. 52–53, Jakarta 12190; tel. (21) 5150515; fax (21) 5150330; e-mail webmaster@jsx.co.id; internet www.jsx.co.id; PT Bursa Efek Jakarta, the managing firm of the JSX, was transferred to the private sector in April 1992; 197 securities houses constitute the members and the shareholders of the exchange, each company owning one share; Pres. Dir ERRY FIRMANSYAH.

Surabaya Stock Exchange: 5th Floor, Gedung Medan Pemuda, Jalan Pemuda 27–31, Surabaya 60271; tel. (31) 5340888; fax (31) 5342888; e-mail helpdesk@bes.co.id; internet www.bes.co.id; f. 1989; Chair. NATAKOESOEMAH.

Regulatory Authority

Badan Pengawas Pasar Modal (BAPEPAM) (Capital Market Supervisory Agency): Jalan Medan Merdeka Selatan 14, Jakarta 10110; tel. (21) 365509; fax (21) 361460; Chair. BACELIUS RURU; Exec. Sec. M. IRSAN NASARUDIN.

INSURANCE

In August 1996 there were 163 insurance companies, comprising 98 non-life companies, 56 life companies, four reinsurance companies and five social insurance companies.

Insurance Supervisory Authority of Indonesia: Directorate of Financial Institutions, Ministry of Finance, Jalan Dr Wahidin, Jakarta 10710; tel. (21) 3451210; fax (21) 3849504; Dir SOPHAR L. TORUAN.

Selected Life Insurance Companies

PT Asuransi AIA Indonesia: Bank Panin Senayan, 7th and 8th Floors, Jalan Jenderal Sudirman, Senayan, Jakarta 10270; tel. (21) 5721388; fax (21) 5721389; f. 1975; Pres. Dir HARRY HARMAIN DIAH.

PT Asuransi Allianz Aken Life: Summitmas II, 20th Floor, Jalan Jenderal Sudirman, Kav. 61–62, Jakarta 12190; tel. (21) 2522470; fax (21) 2523246; e-mail general@allianz.co.id; internet www.allianz.co.id; Pres. Dir Dr PETER ENARES.

Asuransi Jiwa Bersama Bumiputera 1912: Wisma Bumiputera, Lt. 17–21, Jalan Jenderal Sudirman, Kav. 75, Jakarta 12910; tel. (21) 5703812; fax (21) 5712837; Pres. Drs H. SUGUARTO; Dir H. SURATNO HADISUWITO.

PT Asuransi Jiwa Buana Putra: Jalan Salemba Tengah 23, Jakarta Pusat; tel. (21) 3908835; fax (21) 3908810; f. 1974; Pres. SUBAGYO SUTJITRO; Dir H. M. FATHONI SUSILO.

PT Asuransi Jiwa Bumiputera John Hancock: Plaza Mashill, 7th Floor, Jalan Jenderal Sudirman, Kav. 25, Jakarta 12920; tel. (21) 5228857; fax (21) 5228819; e-mail iby@pacific.net.id; internet www.jhancock.co.id; life insurance and pension schemes; CEO DAVID W. COTTRELL.

PT Asuransi Jiwa Central Asia Raya: Wisma Asia, 10th–11th Floors, Jalan S. Parman, Kav. 79, Slipi, Jakarta 11420; tel. (21) 5637901; fax (21) 5637902; e-mail service@car.co.id; internet www.car.co.id; Man. Dir DJONNY WIGUNA.

PT Asuransi Jiwasraya (Persero): Jalan H. Juanda 34, Jakarta 10120; tel. (21) 3845031; fax (21) 3862344; e-mail asuransi@jiwasraya.co.id; internet www.jiwasraya.co.id; f. 1959; Pres. and CEO HERRIS B. SIMANDJUNTAK.

PT Asuransi Jiwa 'Panin Putra': Jalan Pintu Besar Selatan 52A, Jakarta 11110; tel. (21) 672586; fax (21) 676354; f. 1974; Pres. Dir SUJONO SOEPENO; Chair. NUGROHO TJOKROWIRONO.

PT Asuransi Jiwa Pura Nusantara: Wisma Bank Dharnala, Lt. 20–21, Jalan Jenderal Sudirman, Jakarta 12920; tel. (21) 5211990; fax (21) 5212001; Dir MURNIATY KARTONO.

PT Asuransi Lippo Life: Menara Matahari Lippo Life Bldg, Lt. 7, Jalan Bulevar Palem Raya 7, Lippo Karawaci, Tangerang 15811; tel. (21) 5475433; fax (21) 5475401; f. 1983; life insurance, pensions, healthcare.

PT Asuransi Panin Life: Panin Bank Plaza, 5th Floor, Jalan Palmerah Utara 52, Jakarta 11480; tel. (21) 5484870; fax (21) 5484570; Pres. NUGROHO TJOKROWIRONO; Dir SUJONO SUPENO.

Bumi Asih Jaya Life Insurance Co Ltd: Jalan Matraman Raya 165–167, Jakarta 13140; tel. (21) 2800700; fax (21) 8509669; e-mail baj@bajlife.com; f. 1967; Chair. P. SITOMPUL; Pres. VIRGO HUTAGALUNG.

Bumiputera 1912 Mutual Life Insurance Co: Wisma Bumiputera, 18th–21st Floors, Jalan Jenderal Sudirman, Kav. 75, Jakarta 12910; tel. (21) 2512154; fax (21) 2512172; e-mail spw@bumiputera.com; f. 1912; Pres. SUPARWANTO.

Koperasi Asuransi Indonesia: Jalan Iskandarsyah I/26, Jakarta; tel. (21) 7207879; fax (21) 7207451; Dir H. J. V. SUGIMAN.

Selected Non-Life Insurance Companies

PT Asuransi Bina Arta Tbk: Wisma Dharmala Sakti, 8th Floor, Jalan Jenderal Sudirman, Kav. 32, Jakarta 10220; tel. (21) 5708157; fax (21) 5708166; e-mail dharins@uninet.net.id; Pres. SUHANDA WIRAATMADJA; Vice-Pres. M. MULYATNO.

PT Asuransi Bintang Tbk: Jalan R. S. Fatmawati 32, Jakarta 12430; tel. (21) 7504872; fax (21) 7506197; e-mail bintang@asuransibintang.com; internet www.asuransibintang.com; f. 1955; general insurance; Pres. Dir ARIYANTI SULIYANTO.

PT Asuransi Buana Independen: Jalan Pintu Besar Selatan 78, Jakarta 11110; tel. (21) 6904331; fax (21) 6263005; Exec. Vice-Pres. SUSANTY PURNAMA.

PT Asuransi Central Asia: Wisma Asia, 12th–15th Floors, Jalan Letjen S. Parman, Kav. 79, Slipi, Jakarta 11420; tel. (21) 5637933; fax (21) 5638029; e-mail cust-aca@aca.co.id; internet www.aca.co.id; Pres. ANTHONY SALIM; Dir TEDDY HAILAMSAH.

PT Asuransi Danamon: Gedung Danamon Asuransi, Jalan H. R. Rasuna Said, Kav. C10, Jakarta 12920; tel. (21) 516512; fax (21) 516832; Chair. USMAN ADMADJAJA; Pres. Dir OTIS WUISAN.

PT Asuransi Dayin Mitra: Jalan Raden Saleh Raya, Kav. 1B–1D, Jakarta 10430; tel. (21) 3153577; fax (21) 39129; e-mail nuning@dayinmitra.co.id; internet www.dayinmitra.co.id; f. 1982; general insurance; Man. Dir LARSOEN HAKER.

PT Asuransi Indrapura: Jakarta; tel. (21) 5703729; fax (21) 5705000; f. 1954; Pres. Dir ROBERT TEGUH.

PT Asuransi Jasa Indonesia: Jalan Letjenderal M. T. Haryono, Kav. 61, Jakarta 12780; tel. (21) 7994508; e-mail jasindo@jasindo.co.id; internet www.jasindo.co.id; Pres. Dr Ir BAMBANG SUBIANTO; Dir AMIR IMAM POERO.

PT Asuransi Parolamas: Komplek Golden Plaza, Blok G 39–42, Jalan R. S. Farmawati 15, Jakarta 12420; tel. (21) 7508983; fax (21) 7506339; internet www.parolamas.co.id; Pres. TJUT RUKMA; Dir Drs SYARIFUDDIN HARAHAP.

PT Asuransi Ramayana: Jalan Kebon Sirih 49, Jakarta 10343; tel. (21) 337148; fax (21) 334825; f. 1956; Chair. R. G. DOERIAT; Pres. Dir F. WIDYASANTO.

PT Asuransi Tri Pakarta: Jalan Paletehan I/18, Jakarta 12160; tel. (21) 711850; fax (21) 7394748; Pres. Drs M. MAINGGOLAN; Dir HUSNI RUSTAM.

PT Asuransi Wahana Tata: Jalan H. R. Rasuna Said, Kav. 12, Jakarta 12920; tel. (21) 5203145; fax (21) 5203146; internet www.aswata.co.id; Chair. S. SUGIARSO; Pres. RUDY WANANDI.

PT Lloyd Indonesia: Jalan Tiang Bendera 34-1, Jakarta 11230; tel. (21) 677195; Dir JOHNY BASUKI.

Berdikari Insurance Company: Jalan Merdeka Barat 1, Jakarta 10002; tel. (21) 3841339; fax (21) 3440586; e-mail ho@berdikari-insurance.com; internet www.berdikari-insurance.com; Pres. HOTBONAR SINAGA.

PT Maskapai Asuransi Indonesia (MAI): Jalan Sultan Hasanuddin 53–54, Kebayoran Baru, Jakarta Selatan 12160; tel. (21) 7204250; fax (21) 7256980; e-mail ptmai@cbn.net.id; Pres. Dir J. TRI WAHONO.

PT Maskapai Asuransi Jasa Tania: Gedung Agro Bank, Lt. 4, Jalan Teuku Cik Ditiro 14, Jakarta 10350; tel. (21) 3101912; fax (21) 323089; Pres. H. R. SUTEDJIO; Dir Drs H. ABELLAH.

PT Maskapai Asuransi Timur Jauh: Jalan Medan Merdeka Barat 1, Jakarta Pusat; tel. (21) 370266; f. 1954; Pres. Dir BUSTANIL ARIFIN; Dirs V. H. KOLONDAM, SOEBAKTI HARSONO.

PT Pan Union Insurance: Panin Bank Plaza, Lt. 6, Jalan Palmerah Utara 52, Jakarta 11480; tel. (21) 5480669; fax (21) 5484047; e-mail paninins@cbn.net.id; Chair. CHANDRA R. GUNAWAN; Pres. NIZARWAN HARAHAP.

PT Perusahaan Maskapai Asuransi Murni: Jalan Roa Malaka Selatan 21–23, Jakarta Barat; tel. (21) 679968; f. 1953; Dirs HASAN DAY, HOED IBRAHIM, R. SOEGIATNA PROBOPINILIH.

PT Pool Asuransi Indonesia: Blok A–IV Utara, Jalan Muara Karang Raya 293, Jakarta 14450; tel. (21) 6621946; fax (21) 6678021; f. 1958; Pres. BAMBANG GUNAWAN TANUJAYA; Dir TANDJUNG SUSANTO.

PT Tugu Pratama Indonesia: Wisma Tugu I, Jalan H. R. Rasuna Said, Kav. C8-9, Jakarta 12940; tel. (21) 52961777; fax (21) 52961555; e-mail tpi@tugu.com; internet www.tugu.com; f. 1981; general insurance; Chair. AINUN NA'IM; Pres. BAHDER MUNIR SJAMSOEDDIN.

Joint Ventures

PT Asuransi AIU Indonesia: Panin Bank Bldg, 3rd Floor, Jalan Jenderal Sudirman, Senayan, Jakarta 10270; tel. (21) 5720888; fax (21) 5703759; Pres. Dir PETER MEYER; Dirs SWANDI KENDY, GUNAWAN TJIU.

PT Asuransi Jayasraya: Jalan M. H. Thamrin 9, Jakarta; tel. (21) 324207; Dirs SUPARTONO, SADAO SUZUKI.

PT Asuransi Jiwa EKA Life: Wisma EKA Jiwa, 9th Floor, Jalan Mangga Dua Raya, Jakarta 10730; tel. (21) 6257808; fax (21) 6257837; e-mail cs@ekalife.co.id; internet www.ekalife.co.id; Pres. Dir HENRY C. SURYANAGA.

PT Asuransi Mitsui Marine Indonesia: Menara Thamrin, 14th Floor, Jalan M. H. Thamrin, Kav. 3, Jakarta 10340; tel. (21) 2303432; fax (21) 2302930; internet www.mitsuimarine.co.id; Pres. Dir S. AOSHIMA; Vice-Pres. PUTU WIDNYANA.

PT Asuransi Royal Indrapura: Jakarta Stock Exchange Bldg, 29th Floor, Jalan Jenderal Sudirman, Kav. 52–53, Jakarta 12190; tel. (21) 5151222; fax (21) 5151771; Pres. Dir Ir MINTARTO HALIM; Man. Dir MORAY B. MARTIN.

Insurance Association

Dewan Asuransi Indonesia (Insurance Council of Indonesia): Jalan Majapahit 34, Blok V/29, Jakarta 10160; tel. (21) 363264; fax (21) 354307; f. 1957; Chair. MUNIR SIAMSOEDDIN; Gen. Sec. SOEDJIWO.

Trade and Industry

GOVERNMENT AGENCIES

Agency for Strategic Industries (BPIS): Jakarta; f. 1989; co-ordinates for production of capital goods.

Badan Pengkajian dan Penerapan Teknologi (BPPT) (Agency for the Assessment and Application of Technology): Jalan M. H. Thamrin 8, Jakarta 10340; tel. (21) 3162222; e-mail webmaster@bppt.go.id; internet www.bppt.go.id.

Badan Penyehatan Perbankan Nasional (BPPN) (Indonesian Bank Restructuring Agency—IBRA): Wisma Danamon Aetna Life, Lantai 15, Jalan Jenderal Sudirman, Kav. 45–46, Jakarta 12930; tel. (21) 5770952; fax (21) 5772301; e-mail bppncare@bppn.go.id; internet www.bppn.go.id; f. 1998 to restructure the banking sector; Chair. SYAFRUDDIN TUMENGGUNG; Sr Dep. Chair. ARWIN RASYID.

Badan Tenaga Nuklir Nasional (BATAN) (National Nuclear Energy Agency): Jalan Kuningan Barat, Mampang Prapatan, Jakarta 12710; tel. (21) 5251109; fax (21) 5251110; e-mail humas@batan.go.id; internet www.batan.go.id.

Badan Urusan Logistik (BULOG) (National Logistics Agency): Jalan Jenderal Gatot Subroto 49, POB 2345, Jakarta 12950; tel. and fax (21) 5256482; e-mail rotu03@bulog.go.id; internet www.bulog.go.id; Chair. WIDJANARKO PUSPOYO.

National Agency for Export Development (NAFED): Jalan Gajah Mada 8, Jakarta 10310; tel. (21) 3841082; fax (21) 6338360; e-mail nafed@nafed.go.id; internet www.nafed.go.id.

National Economic Council: Jakarta; f. 1999; 13-member council formed to advise the President on economic policy; Chair. EMIL SALIM; Sec.-Gen. Sri MULYANI INDRAWATI.

DEVELOPMENT ORGANIZATIONS

Badan Koordinasi Penanaman Modal (BKPM) (Investment Co-ordinating Board): Jalan Jenderal Gatot Subroto 44, POB 3186, Jakarta 12190; tel. (21) 5252008; fax (21) 5254945; e-mail sysadm@bkpm.go.id; internet www.bkpm.go.id; f. 1976; Chair. THEO F. TOEMION.

Badan Perencanaan Pembangunan Nasional (Bappenas) (National Planning Development Board): Jalan Taman Suropati 2, Jakarta 10310; tel. (21) 336207; fax (21) 3145374; e-mail admin@bappenas.go.id; internet www.bappenas.go.id; formulates Indonesia's national economic development plans; Chair. KWIK KIAN GIE.

Commercial Advisory Foundation in Indonesia (CAFI): Jalan Probolinggo 5, Jakarta 10350; tel. (21) 3156013; fax (21) 3156014; f. 1958; information, economic regulations bulletin, consultancy and translation services; Chair. JOYCE SOSROHADIKOESOEMO; Man. Dir LEILA RIDWAN SOSROHADIKOESOEMO.

CHAMBER OF COMMERCE

Kamar Dagang dan Industri Indonesia (KADIN) (Indonesian Chamber of Commerce and Industry): Chandra Bldg, 3rd–5th Floors, Jalan M. H. Thamrin 20, Jakarta 10350; tel. (21) 324000; fax (21) 3150241; f. 1969; 27 regional offices throughout Indonesia; Chair. Ir ABURIZAL BAKRIE; Sec.-Gen. Ir IMAN SUCIPTO UMAR.

INDUSTRIAL AND TRADE ASSOCIATIONS

Association of Indonesian Automotive Industries (GAIKINDO): Jalan H. O. S. Cokroaminoto 6, Jakarta 10350; tel. (21) 3102754; fax (21) 332100.

Association of Indonesian Beverage Industries (ASRIM): Jalan M. Ikhwan Mais 8, Jakarta Pusat; tel. (21) 3841222; fax (21) 3842294.

Association of Indonesian Coal Industries (ABBI): Perum Batu Bara Bldg, Jalan Supomo 10, Jakarta Selatan; tel. (21) 8295608.

Association of Indonesian Coffee Exporters (AICE): Jalan R. P. Soeroso 20, Jakarta 10330; tel. (21) 3106765; fax (21) 3144115; Chair. OESMAN SOEDARGO.

Association of Indonesian Heavy Equipment Industries (HINABI): c/o PT Traktor Nusantara, Jalan Pulogadung 32, Jakarta 13930; tel. (21) 4703932; fax (21) 4713940.

Association of Indonesian Tea Producers (ATI): Jalan Pulombangkeng 15, Kebayoran Baru, Jakarta 72110; tel. (21) 7260772; fax (21) 7205810; e-mail indotea@indosat.net.id; internet www.indotea.org.

Association of State-Owned Companies: CTC Bldg, Jalan Kramat Raya 94–96, Jakarta; tel. (21) 346071; co-ordinates the activities of state-owned enterprises; Pres. ODANG.

Electric and Electronic Appliance Manufacturers' Association: Jalan Pangeran, Blok 20/A-1D, Jakarta; tel. (21) 6480059.

GINSI (Importers' Asscn of Indonesia): Oil Center Bldg, 1st Floor, Jalan M. H. Thamrin 55, Jakarta 10350; tel. (21) 39837395; fax (21) 39837394; f. 1956; 2,921 mems (1996); Chair. AMIRUDIN SAUD; Sec.-Gen. MUSTAFA KEMAL.

Indonesian Cocoa Association (AKI): Jalan Brawijaya VII/5, Kebayoran Baru, Jakarta 12160; tel. (21) 771721; fax (21) 7203487.

Indonesian Cement Association: Graha Purnayudha, Jalan Jenderal Sudirman, Jakarta; tel. (21) 5207603; fax (21) 5207188.

Indonesian Exporters' Federation: Menara Sudirman, 8th Floor, Jalan Jenderal Sudirman, Kav. 60, Jakarta 12190; tel. (21) 5226522; fax (21) 5203303; Chair. HAMID IBRAHIM GANIE.

Indonesian Footwear Association (APRISINDO): Gedung Langlang Asia Ruang A, Jalan Daan Mogot 151, Jakarta Barat 11510; tel. (21) 5664157; fax (21) 5604671; e-mail aprisindo@vision.net.id; Chair. ANTON J. SUPIT.

Indonesian Furniture Industry and Handicraft Association (ASMINDO): Jalan Pegambiran 5A, 3rd Floor, Rawamangun Jakarta 13220; tel. (21) 47864028; fax (21) 47864031; e-mail asmindo@indo.net.id; internet www.furniture-indonesia.com/asmindo; Chair. DJALAL KAMAL.

Indonesian Nutmeg Exporters' Association: Jalan Hayam Wuruk 103, Jakarta; tel. (21) 6297432.

Indonesian Palm Oil Producers' Association: Jalan Pulo Mas IIID/1, Jakarta; tel. (21) 4892635; Chair. NUKMAN NASUTION.

Indonesian Precious Metals Association: Jalan Wahid Hasyim 45, Jakarta; tel. (21) 3841771.

Indonesian Pulp and Paper Association: Jalan Cimandiri 6, Jakarta 10330; tel. (21) 326084; fax (21) 3140168.

Indonesian Textile Association (API): Panin Bank Centre, 3rd Floor, Jalan Jenderal Sudirman 1, Jakarta Pusat 10270; tel. (21) 7396094; fax (21) 7396341; f. 1974; Sec.-Gen. DANANG D. JOEDONAGORO.

Indonesian Tobacco Association: Jalan H. Agus Salim 85, Jakarta 10350; tel. (21) 3140627; fax (21) 325181; Pres. H. A. ISMAIL.

Masyarakat Perhutanan Indonesia (MPI) (Indonesian Forestry Community): Gedung Manggala Wanabakti, 9th Floor, Wing B/Blok IV, Jalan Jenderal Gatot Subroto, Jakarta Pusat 10270; tel. (21) 5733010; fax (21) 5732564; f. 1974; nine mems; Pres. M. HASAN.

National Board of Arbitration (BANI): Menara Kadin Indonesia, 29th Floor, Jalan H. R. Rasuna Said, Kav. 2–3, Jakarta 12950; tel. and fax (21) 5274716; e-mail bani-arb@indo.net.id; f. 1977; resolves company disputes; Chair. Prof. H. PRIYATNA ABDURRASYID.

Rubber Association of Indonesia (Gapkindo): Jalan Cideng Barat 62A, Jakarta; tel. (21) 3846813; fax (21) 3846811; e-mail karetind@indosat.net.id; Exec. Dir SUHARTO HONGGOKUSUMO.

Shippers' Council of Indonesia: Jalan Kramat Raya 4–6, Jakarta; Pres. R. S. PARTOKUSUMO.

UTILITIES

Electricity

PT Perusahaan Umum Listrick Negara (PLN): Jalan Trunojoyo, Blok M1/135, Kebayaran Baru, Jakarta Selatan 12160; tel. (21) 7261875; fax (21) 7204929; e-mail webmaster@pln.co.id; internet www.pln.co.id; state-owned electricity co; Pres. EDDIE WIDYONO.

Gas

PT Perusahaan Pertambangan Minyak dan Gas Bumi Negara (PERTAMINA): Jalan Medan Merdeka Timur Ia, Jakarta 10110; tel. (21) 3815111; fax (21) 363585; internet www.pertamina .com; f. 1957; state-owned petroleum and natural gas mining enterprise; Pres. Dir and CEO BAIHAKI HAKIM.

Perusahaan Gas Negara (PGN) (Public Gas Corporation): Jakarta; e-mail webmaster@pgn.co.id; internet www.pgn.co.id; monopoly of domestic gas distribution; Pres. Dir W. M. P. SIMANDJUNTAK.

Water

PDAM DKI Jakarta (PAM JAYA): Jalan Penjernihan 11, Pejompongan, Jakarta 10210; tel. (21) 5704250; fax (21) 5711796; f. 1977; responsible for the water supply systems of Jakarta; Pres. Dir Ir H. MUZAHIEM MOKHTAR.

PDAM Kodya Dati II Bandung: Jalan Badaksinga 10, Bandung 40132; tel. (22) 2509030; fax (22) 2508063; e-mail pdambdg@elga.net .id; f. 1974; responsible for the water supply and sewerage systems of Bandung; Pres. Dir Ir SOENITIYOSO HADI PRATIKTO.

PDAM Tirtanadi Medan: Jalan Sisingamangaraja 1, Medan 20212; tel. (61) 571666; fax (61) 572771; f. 1979; manages the water supply of Medan and nearby towns and cities; Man. Dir Ir KUMALA SIREGAR.

CO-OPERATIVES

In 1996 there were 48,391 primary and secondary co-operatives in Indonesia; membership of primary co-operatives was 27,006,000 in the same year.

Indonesian Co-operative Council (DEKOPIN): Jakarta; Pres. Sri EDY SWASONO.

TRADE UNIONS

Serikat Buruh Sejahtera Indonesia (SBSI) (Indonesian Prosperity Trade Union Central Board): Jakarta; f. 1998; application for official registration rejected in May 1998; 1,228,875 mems in 168 branches in 27 provinces throughout Indonesia; Gen. Chair. MUCHTAR PAKPAHAN; Gen. Sec. SUNARTY.

Federasi Serikat Pekerja Seluruh Indonesia (FSPSI) (Federation of All Indonesian Trades Unions): Jalan Raya Pasar Minggu Km 17 No. 9, Jakarta 12740; tel. (21) 7974359; fax (21) 7974361; f. 1973; renamed 1995; sole officially recognized National Trade Union Centre; comprises 18 national industrial unions; 5.1m. mems in February 1999; Gen. Chair. JACOB NUWA WEA; Gen. Sec. SJUKUR SARTO.

Transport

Directorate General of Land Transport and Inland Waterways: Ministry of Transportation and Telecommunication, Jalan Medan Merdeka Barat 8, Jakarta 10110; tel. (21) 3456332; fax (21) 3451657; Dir-Gen. SOEJONO.

RAILWAYS

There are railways on Java, Madura and Sumatra, totalling 6,458 km in 1996, of which 125 km were electrified.

In 1995 a memorandum of understanding was signed by a consortium of European, Japanese and Indonesian companies for the construction of a subway system in Jakarta. However, in 2002 construction had not yet begun owing to the Government's inability to fund the project, which was expected to cost US $1,500m. to implement.

Perusahan Umum Kereta Api (PERUMKA): Jalan Perintis Kermedekaan 1, Bandung 40117, Java; tel. (22) 430031; fax (22) 430062; six regional offices; transferred to the private sector in 1991; Chief Dir Drs ANWAR SUPRIADI.

ROADS

There is an adequate road network on Java, Sumatra, Sulawesi, Kalimantan, Bali and Madura, but on most of the other islands traffic is by jungle track or river boat. In 1997 the road network in Indonesia totalled 342,700 km; 27,357 km were main roads and

40,490 km were secondary roads. About 158,670 km of the network were paved.

Directorate General of Highways: Ministry of Public Works, Jalan Pattimura 20, Kebayoran Baru, Jakarta Selatan 12110; tel. (21) 7262805; fax (21) 7260769; Dir-Gen. Ir SURYATIN SASTROMIJOYO.

SHIPPING

The Ministry of Communications controls 349 ports and harbours, of which the four main ports of Tanjung Priok (near Jakarta), Tanjung Perak (near Surabaya), Belawan (near Medan) and Makassar (formerly Ujung Pandang, in South Sulawesi) have been designated gateway ports for nearly all international shipping to deal with Indonesia's exports and are supported by 15 collector ports. Of the ports and harbours, 127 are classified as capable of handling oceangoing shipping.

Directorate General of Sea Communications: Ministry of Communications, Jalan Medan Merdeka Barat 8, Jakarta 10110; tel. (21) 3456332; Dir-Gen. SOENTORO.

Indonesian National Ship Owners' Association (INSA): Jalan Gunung Sahari 79, Jakarta Pusat; tel. (21) 414908; fax (21) 416388; Pres. H. HARTOTO HADIKUSUMO.

Shipping Companies

Indonesian Oriental Lines, PT Perusahaan Pelayaran Nusantara: Jalan Raya Pelabuhan Nusantara, POB 2062, Jakarta 10001; tel. (21) 494344; Pres. Dir A. J. SINGH.

PT Jakarta Lloyd: Jalan Agus Salim 28, Jakarta Pusat 10340; tel. (21) 331301; fax (21) 333514; f. 1950; services to USA, Europe, Japan, Australia and the Middle East; Pres. Dir Drs M. MUNTAQA.

PT Karana Line: Jalan Kali Besar Timur 30, POB 1081, Jakarta 11110; tel. (21) 6907381; fax (21) 6908365; Pres. Dir BAMBANG EDIYANTO.

PT Pelayaran Bahtera Adhiguna (Persero): Jalan Kalibesar Timur 10–12, POB 4313, Jakarta 11043; tel. (21) 6912613; fax (21) 6901450; f. 1971; Pres. H. DJAJASUDHARMA.

PT Pelayaran Nasional Indonesia (PELNI): Jalan Angkasa 18, Jakarta; tel. (21) 4211921; fax (21) 491623; internet www.pelni.com; state-owned; national shipping co; Pres. Dir ISNOOR HARYANTO.

PT Pelayaran Samudera Admiral Lines: Jalan Gunung Sahari 79–80, Jakarta 10610; POB 1476, Jakarta 10014; tel. (21) 4247908; fax (21) 4206267; e-mail admiral@uninet.net.id; Pres. Dir DJOKO SOETOPO.

PT (Persero) Pann Multi Finance: Pann Bldg, Jalan Cikini IV 11, POB 3377, Jakarta 10330; tel. (21) 322003; fax (21) 322980; state-controlled; Pres. Dir W. NAYOAN; Dir HAMID HADIJAYA.

PT Perusahaan Pelayaran Gesuri Lloyd: Gesuri Lloyd Bldg, Jalan Tiang Bendera IV 45, Jakarta 11230; tel. (21) 6904000; fax (21) 6904190; e-mail gesuri@indosat.net.id; internet www.gesuri.co .id; f. 1963; Pres. FRANKIE NURIMBA.

PT Perusahaan Pelayaran 'Nusa Tenggara': Kantor Pusat, Jalan Raya Pelabuhan Benoa, POB 3069, Denpasar 80222, Bali; tel. (361) 723608; fax (361) 722059; e-mail ntship@indo.net.id; Man. Dir KETUT DERESTHA.

PT Perusahaan Pelayaran Samudera 'Samudera Indonesia': Jalan Kali Besar Barat 43, POB 1244, Jakarta; tel. (21) 671093; fax (21) 674242; Chair. and Dir SOEDARPO SASTROSATOMO; Exec. Dir RANDY EFFENDI.

PT Perusahaan Pelayaran Samudera Trikora Lloyd: Bank Bumi Daya Bldg, 2nd and 3rd Floors, Jalan Malaka 1, Jakarta 11230; POB 4076, Jakarta 11001; tel. (21) 6907751; fax (21) 6907757; f. 1964; Pres. Dir GANESHA SOEGIHARTO; Man. Dir P. R. S. VAN HEEREN.

PT Perusahaan Pertambangan Minyak dan Gas Bumi Negara (PERTAMINA): Directorate for Shipping, Harbour and Communication, Jalan Yos Sudarso 32–34, POB 327, Tanjung Priok, Jakarta; tel. (21) 4301086; fax (21) 4301492; state-owned; tanker services; Pres. and Chair. Dr IBNU SUTOWO.

CIVIL AVIATION

The first stage of a new international airport, the Sukarno-Hatta Airport, at Cengkareng, near Jakarta, was opened in 1985, to complement Halim Perdanakusuma Airport, which was to handle charter and general flights only. A new terminal was opened at Sukarno-Hatta in 1991, vastly enlarging airport capacity. Construction of an international passenger terminal at the Frans Kaisepo Airport, in Papua (then Irian Jaya), was completed in 1988. Other international airports include Ngurah Rai Airport at Denpasar (Bali), Polonia Airport in Medan (North Sumatra), Juanda Airport, near Surabaya (East Java), Sam Ratulangi Airport in Manado (North Sulawesi) and Hasanuddin Airport, near Makassar (formerly Ujung Pandang, South Sulawesi). There are a total of 72 airports, six of which are capable of accommodating wide-bodied aircraft. Domestic air services link the major cities, and international services are provided by the state airline, PT Garuda Indonesia, by its subsidiary, PT Merpati Nusantara Airlines, and by numerous foreign airlines. In December 1990 it was announced that private airlines equipped with jet-engined aircraft would be allowed to serve international routes.

In 2000 the Government announced a policy of liberalization for the airline industry. This led to a dramatic increase in the number of airlines operating in Indonesia; in July 2002 Indonesia had 25 domestic airlines, compared to five in 2000. Of these, only 16 new companies had begun operations by July 2002.

Directorate-General of Air Communications: Jalan Arief Rahman Hakim 3, Jakarta 10340; tel. (21) 3914235; fax (21) 3914239; Dir-Gen. ZAINUDDIN SIKADO.

Awair International: Graha Aktiva Bldg, Jalan H. R. Rasuna Said, Jakarta; tel. and fax (21) 5203598; internet www.awairlines.com; f. 2000; scheduled domestic passenger services from Jakarta; Pres. YASSIR ISMAIL.

Bayu Indonesia Air (BYU): Jalan Bikatamsu 29E, Jakarta; tel. (21) 4515588; fax (21) 4515777; f. 1975; international services; Man. Dir PERMADI WIRATANUNINGRAT.

PT Bouraq Indonesia Airlines (BOU): Jalan Angkasa 1–3, POB 2965, Kemayoran, Jakarta 10720; tel. (21) 6288815; fax (21) 6008729; internet www.bouraq.com; f. 1970; private company; scheduled regional and domestic passenger and cargo services linking Jakarta with points in Java, Borneo, Sulawesi, Bali, Timor and Tawau (Malaysia); Pres. Dir DANNY SUMENDAP.

Carstensz Papua Airlines (CPA): Papua; f. 2002; domestic services.

Citilink: Jakarta; internet www.ga-citilink.com; f. 2001; subsidiary of PT Garuda Indonesia; provides shuttle services between domestic destinations.

Deraya Air Taxi (DRY): Terminal Bldg, 1st Floor, Rm 150/HT, Halim Perdanakusuma Airport, Jakarta 13610; tel. (21) 8093627; fax (21) 8095770; internet www.boedihardjogroup.com; scheduled and charter passenger and cargo services to domestic and regional destinations; Pres. Dir SITI RAHAYU SUMADI.

Dirgantara Air Service (DAS): POB 6154, Terminal Bldg, Halim Perdanakusuma Airport, Rm 231, Jakarta 13610; tel. (21) 8093372; fax (21) 8094348; charter services from Jakarta, Barjarmas and Pontianak to destinations in West Kalimantan; Pres. MAKKI PERDANAKUSUMA.

PT Garuda Indonesia: Garuda Indonesia Bldg, Jalan Merdeka Selatan 13, Jakarta 10110; tel. (21) 2311801; fax (21) 2311962; internet www.garuda.co.id; f. 1949; state airline; operates scheduled domestic, regional and international services to destinations in Europe, the USA, the Middle East, Australasia and the Far East; Pres. and CEO INDRA SETIAWAN.

Indonesia Air Transport (IAT) (IDA): Pondok Cabe Aerodrome, POB 2485, Jakarta; tel. (21) 7490213; fax (21) 7491287; charter passenger and cargo services to domestic, regional and international destinations; f. 1968; Man. Dir AZMAR MUALIM.

Indonesian Airlines: Jakarta; f. 1999; domestic services; Pres. RUDY SETYOPURNOMO.

Lion Mentari Airlines: Gedung Jaya, 7th Floor, Jalan M. H. Thamrin 12, Jakarta 10340; tel. (21) 331838; fax (21) 327808; internet www.lionairlines.com; f. 1999; domestic and international services; Pres. Dir RUSDI KILANA.

PT Mandala Airlines: Jalan Tomang Raya, Kav. 35–37, Jakarta 11440; tel. (21) 4206646; fax (21) 4249491; internet www.mandala.co.id; f. 1969; privately-owned; scheduled regional and domestic passenger and cargo services; Pres. and Dir GUNADI SUGOTO.

PT Merpati Nusantara Airlines: Jalan Angkasa, Blok 15, Kav. 2–3, Jakarta 10720; tel. (21) 6546789; fax (21) 6540620; e-mail lt13@indosat.net.id; internet www.merpati.co.id; f. 1962; subsidiary of PT Garuda Indonesia; domestic and regional services to Australia and Malaysia; Chair. MUCHTARUDIN SIREGAR; Pres. WAHYU HIDAYAT.

Pelita Air Service: Jalan Abdul Muls 52–56A, Jakarta 10160; tel. (21) 2312030; fax (21) 2312216; internet www.pelita-air.co.id; f. 1970; domestic services; Pres. Dir SOERATMAN.

PT Star Air: Jalan Gunung Sahari Raya 57 A-B, POB 4724, Jakarta Pusat10610; tel. (21) 4222622; fax (21)4249538; e-mail prstarair@cbn.net.id; f. 2000; scheduled domestic passenger services; Pres. Dir ALE SUGIARTO.

Sumut Airlines: North Sumatra; f. 2002; domestic services.

Tourism

Indonesia's tourist industry is based mainly on the islands of Java, famous for its volcanic scenery and religious temples, and Bali, renowned for its scenery and Hindu-Buddhist temples and religious festivals. Lombok, Sumatra and Sulawesi are also increasingly popular. Domestic tourism within Indonesia has also increased significantly. In 2001 5.2m. foreign tourists visited Indonesia, compared with 5.1m. in 2000 and 4.7m. in 1999. Tourist receipts totalled US $5,749m. in 2000. Following the terrorist attack on Bali in October 2002 (see Recent History) it was feared that the tourist industry would be significantly affected. However, in 2003 early indications suggested that the industry could make a full recovery by the end of that year as tourists began to return to the area.

Department of Culture and Tourism: Jalan Medan Merdeka Barat 16–19, Jakarta Pusat; tel. (21) 3838805; fax (21) 3848245; internet www.indonesiatourisminfo.com; f. 1957; Chair. I. GEDE ARDIKA.

Indonesia Tourism Promotion Board: Wisma Nugra Santana, 9th Floor, Jalan Jenderal Sudirman 7–8, Jakarta 10220; tel. (21) 5704879; fax (21) 5704855; e-mail itpb@cbn.net.id; internet www.goindo.com; private body; promotes national and international tourism; Chair. PONTJO SUTOWO; CEO GATOT SOEMARTONO.

IRAN

Introductory Survey

Location, Climate, Language, Religion, Flag, Capital

The Islamic Republic of Iran lies in western Asia, bordered by Azerbaijan and Turkmenistan to the north, by Turkey and Iraq to the west, by the Persian (Arabian) Gulf and the Gulf of Oman to the south, and by Pakistan and Afghanistan to the east. The climate is one of great extremes. Summer temperatures of more than 55°C (131°F) have been recorded, but in the winter the great altitude of much of the country results in temperatures of −18°C (0°F) and below. The principal language is Farsi (Persian), spoken by about 50% of the population. Turkic-speaking Azerbaijanis form about 27% of the population, and Kurds, Arabs, Balochis and Turkomans form less than 25%. The great majority of Persians and Azerbaijanis are Shi'ite Muslims, while the other ethnic groups are mainly Sunni Muslims. There are also small minorities of Christians (mainly Armenians), Jews and Zoroastrians. The Bahá'í faith, which originated in Iran, has been severely persecuted. The national flag (proportions 4 by 7) comprises three unequal horizontal stripes, of green, white and red, with the emblem of the Islamic Republic of Iran (the stylized word Allah) centrally positioned in red, and the inscription 'Allaho Akbar' ('God is Great') written 11 times each in white Kufic script on the red and green stripes. The capital is Tehran.

Recent History

Iran, called Persia until 1935, was formerly a monarchy, ruled by a Shah (Emperor). In 1927 Reza Khan, a Cossack officer, seized power in a military coup, and was subsequently elected Shah, adopting the title Reza Shah Pahlavi. In 1941 British and Soviet forces occupied Iran, and the Shah (who favoured Nazi Germany) was forced to abdicate in favour of his son, Muhammad Reza Pahlavi. British and US forces left Iran in 1945, but Soviet forces remained in the north-west of the country (Azerbaijan province) until 1946. The United Kingdom retained considerable influence through the Anglo-Iranian Oil Co, which controlled much of Iran's extensive petroleum reserves. In March 1951, however, the Majlis (National Consultative Assembly) approved the nationalization of the petroleum industry, despite British and other Western opposition. The leading advocate of nationalization, Dr Muhammad Mussadeq, who became Prime Minister in May 1951, was deposed in August 1953 in a military *coup d'état*, engineered by the US and British intelligence services.

The Shah gradually increased his personal control of government following the coup, assuming dictatorial powers in 1963 with the so-called 'White Revolution'. Large estates were redistributed to small farmers, and women were granted the right to vote in elections, provoking opposition from landlords and the conservative Muslim clergy. In 1965 Prime Minister Hassan Ali Mansur was assassinated, reportedly by a follower of Ayatollah Ruhollah Khomeini, a fundamentalist Shi'ite Muslim leader strongly opposed to the Shah. (Khomeini had been deported in 1964 for his opposition activities, and was living in exile in Iraq.) Amir Abbas Hoveida held the office of Prime Minister until 1977.

Between 1965 and 1977 Iran enjoyed political stability and considerable economic growth, based on substantial petroleum revenues which funded a high level of expenditure on defence equipment and infrastructure projects. From late 1977, however, public opposition to the regime increased dramatically, largely in response to a declining economy and the repressive nature of the Shah's rule. By the end of 1978 anti-Government protests were widespread, involving both left-wing and liberal opponents of the Shah, as well as Islamist activists. The most effective opposition came from supporters of Ayatollah Khomeini, who was now based in France. The growing unrest forced the Shah to leave Iran in January 1979. Khomeini arrived in Tehran on 1 February and effectively took power 10 days later. A 15-member Islamic Revolutionary Council was formed to govern the country, in co-operation with a Provisional Government, and on 1 April Iran was declared an Islamic republic. Supreme authority was vested in the Wali Faqih, a religious leader (initially Khomeini) appointed by the Shi'ite clergy. Executive power was to be vested in a President, to which post

Abolhasan Bani-Sadr was elected in January 1980, with some 75% of the votes cast. Elections to a 270-member Majlis (National—later Islamic—Consultative Assembly) took place in two rounds in March and May. The Islamic Republican Party (IRP), which was identified with Khomeini and traditionalist Muslims, won some 60 seats, but subsequently increased its support base.

In November 1979 Iranian students seized 63 hostages at the US embassy in Tehran. The original purpose of the siege was in support of a demand for the return of the Shah (then in the USA) to Iran to face trial. The Shah died in Egypt in July 1980, by which time Iran had made other demands, notably for a US undertaking not to interfere in its affairs. Intense diplomatic activity finally resulted in the release of the 52 remaining hostages in January 1981.

The hostage crisis had forced the resignation of the moderate Provisional Government, and during 1980 it became clear that a rift was developing between President Bani-Sadr and his moderate allies on the one hand, and the IRP and traditionalist elements on the other. Clashes between supporters of the two groups escalated in June 1981 into sustained fighting between members of the Mujahidin-e-Khalq (an Islamist guerrilla group which supported Bani-Sadr) and troops of the Revolutionary Guard Corps. The Majlis voted to impeach the President, who was subsequently dismissed by Khomeini. Bani-Sadr fled to France, as did the leader of the Mujahidin, Massoud Rajavi. A presidential election in July resulted in victory for the Prime Minister, Muhammad Ali Rajani, who was himself replaced by Muhammad Javar Bahunar. Meanwhile, conflict between the Mujahidin-e-Khalq and government forces intensified. In August both the President and Prime Minister were killed in a bomb attack attributed to the Mujahidin. A further presidential election, held in October, was won by Hojatoleslam Ali Khamenei. Mir Hussein Moussavi was appointed Prime Minister.

Two ministers resigned and three more were dismissed in August 1983. The outgoing ministers were right-wing 'bazaaris', members of the merchant class, who opposed policies of nationalization and land reform advocated by technocrats in the Government. Moussavi's attempts to implement such economic reforms were continually obstructed by the predominantly conservative, clerical Majlis. Elections to the second Majlis in April and May 1984 resulted in a clear win for the IRP. The elections were boycotted by the sole opposition party to have a degree of official recognition, Nehzat-e Azadi-ye Iran (Liberation Movement of Iran), led by Dr Mehdi Bazargan (who had been Prime Minister of the Provisional Government from February to November 1979), in protest at the allegedly undemocratic conditions prevailing in Iran.

Three candidates, including the incumbent, contested the August 1985 presidential election. The Council of Guardians (responsible for the supervision of elections) had rejected almost 50 others, among them Bazargan, who opposed the continuation of the war with Iraq (see below). Khamenei was elected President for a second four-year term, with 85.7% of the votes cast. Despite some opposition in the Majlis, Hussein Moussavi was reconfirmed as Prime Minister in October.

For most of the 1980s Iran's domestic and foreign policy was dominated by the war with Iraq. In September 1980, ostensibly to assert a claim of sovereignty over the disputed Shatt al-Arab waterway, Iraqi forces invaded Iran along a 500-km front, apparently anticipating a rapid military victory. The Iranian military offered strong resistance, and began a counter-offensive in early 1982; by June Iraq had been forced to withdraw from Iranian territory, and Iranian troops subsequently entered Iraq. A conflict of attrition thus developed, characterized by mutual offensives and targeting each other's petroleum reserves, installations and transhipment facilities. From 1984 Iraq began attacking tankers using Iran's Kharg Island oil terminal, in the Persian (Arabian) Gulf, and Iran retaliated by targeting Saudi Arabian and Kuwaiti tankers in the Gulf. Despite subsequent efforts by the UN to establish a basis for peace negotiations, Iran insisted that only the removal of the Iraqi President, Saddam

Hussain, in conjunction with agreement by Iraq to pay war reparations, could bring an end to the hostilities.

Although Iran was virtually diplomatically isolated by the war, in late 1986 it emerged that the USA, despite its active discouragement of arms sales to Iran by other countries, had begun secret negotiations with the country in 1985 and had made shipments of weapons, allegedly in exchange for Iranian assistance in securing the release of US hostages held by Shi'ite groups in Lebanon, and an Iranian undertaking to relinquish involvement in international terrorism. Meanwhile, Iran had begun to attack Kuwaiti shipping, and neutral vessels using Kuwait, in retaliation for Kuwait's support for Iraq. In mid-1987 the USA agreed to reregister 11 Kuwaiti tankers under its own flag, thus entitling them to US naval protection. The United Kingdom, France, the Netherlands, Belgium and Italy subsequently dispatched minesweepers to the Gulf region.

Iraq recaptured the Faw peninsula (which Iran had taken two years earlier) in April 1988, forcing the Iranian military to withdraw across the Shatt al-Arab. In June Iraq retook Majnoun Island and the surrounding area (which had been captured by Iran in 1984). In July an Iran Air passenger flight, allegedly mistaken for an attacking fighter jet, was shot down by a US aircraft carrier in the Strait of Hormuz; all 290 passengers and crew were killed. In that month Iraqi troops crossed into Iranian territory for the first time since 1986, and the last Iranian troops on Iraqi territory were dislodged. On 18 July 1988 Iran unexpectedly announced its unconditional acceptance of UN Security Council Resolution 598, adopted one year earlier. This urged an immediate cease-fire, the withdrawal of military forces to international boundaries, and the co-operation of Iran and Iraq in mediation efforts to achieve a peace settlement. More than 1m. people were estimated to have been killed in the eight-year conflict. A cease-fire came into effect on 20 August, and UN-sponsored peace negotiations began shortly afterwards in Geneva, Switzerland. In the same month a UN Iran-Iraq Military Observer Group (UNIIMOG) was deployed in the region. However, the negotiations soon became deadlocked in disputes regarding the sovereignty of the Shatt al-Arab, the exchange of prisoners of war, and the withdrawal of armed forces to within international boundaries. Hopes of a comprehensive peace settlement were raised by a meeting of the Iranian and Iraqi Ministers of Foreign Affairs in Geneva in July 1990, but were swiftly overshadowed by Iraq's invasion of Kuwait at the beginning of August. Saddam Hussain sought an immediate, formal peace with Iran, accepting all the claims that Iran has pursued since the declaration of a cease-fire (including the reinstatement of the Algiers Agreement of 1975, dividing the Shatt al-Arab waterway), and Iraq immediately began to redeploy troops from its border with Iran to Kuwait. Prisoner exchanges took place, and in September 1990 Iran and Iraq restored diplomatic relations. In February 1991 the withdrawal of all armed forces to internationally recognized boundaries was confirmed by UNIIMOG, whose mandate was terminated shortly afterwards.

Iran denounced Iraq's invasion of Kuwait, and observed the economic sanctions imposed by the UN on Iraq. However, it was unequivocal in its condemnation of the deployment of the US-led multinational force in the Gulf region. Relations between Iran and Iraq deteriorated after the liberation of Kuwait in February 1991. Iran protested strongly against the suppression of the Shi'a-led rebellion in southern and central Iraq, and the accompanying destruction of Shi'a shrines in the region, and renewed its demand for the resignation of Saddam Hussain. Iraq, in turn, accused Iran of supporting the rebellion. Thus, there was little further progress in implementing the terms of Resolution 598 until October 1993, when high-level bilateral talks were reported to have recommenced on the exchange of remaining prisoners of war. (See below for further details of Iran's relations with Iraq.)

Elections to the Majlis in April and May 1988 apparently provided a stimulus to 'reformist' elements in the Government (identified with Hashemi Rafsanjani, since 1980 the Speaker of the Majlis, and Prime Minister Moussavi) by producing an assembly strongly representative of their views. (The elections were the Islamic Republic's first not to be contested by the IRP, which had been dissolved in 1987.) In June 1988 Rafsanjani was re-elected as Speaker and Moussavi was overwhelmingly endorsed as Prime Minister. In February 1989, however, Ayatollah Khomeini referred explicitly to a division in the Iranian leadership between 'reformers' (who sought a degree of Western participation in Iran's post-war reconstruction) and 'conservatives' (who opposed such involvement), and declared that he

would never permit the 'reformers' to prevail. His intervention was reportedly prompted by Rafsanjani's decision to contest the presidential election scheduled for mid-1989. A number of prominent 'reformers', among them Ayatollah Ali Hossein Montazeri (who had been designated as successor to Khomeini by the Council of Experts in 1985), subsequently resigned from the Iranian leadership.

Ayatollah Khomeini died on 3 June 1989. In an emergency session on 4 June the Council of Experts elected President Khamenei to succeed Khomeini as Iran's spiritual leader (Wali Faqih). The presidential election, scheduled for mid-August, was brought forward to 28 July, to be held simultaneously with a referendum on proposed amendments to the Constitution. Both 'conservatives' and 'reformers' within the leadership apparently united in support of Rafsanjani's candidacy for the presidency, and Rafsanjani (opposed only by a 'token' candidate) secured an overwhelming victory, with 95.9% of the votes cast. A similar proportion of voters approved the constitutional amendments, the most important of which was the abolition of the post of Prime Minister (and a consequent increase in power for the President).

President Rafsanjani appointed a Government balancing 'conservatives', 'reformers' and technocrats, and its endorsement by the Majlis, in August 1989, was viewed as a mandate for Rafsanjani to conduct a more conciliatory policy towards the West, despite the opposition of certain 'conservative' elements. Large-scale protests against food shortages and high prices in early 1990 demonstrated the urgent need for economic reform. In October, with the co-operation of Ayatollah Khamenei, Rafsanjani was able to prevent the election of many powerful 'conservatives' to the Council of Experts. Elections to the fourth Majlis were held in April and May 1992. Of those who applied to contest the elections, about one-third (mostly considered to be opponents of Rafsanjani) were disqualified by the Council of Guardians. Thus an estimated 70% of the newly-elected deputies were, broadly speaking, pro-Rafsanjani. However, while the President appeared to have succeeded in marginalizing the 'conservatives', he remained constrained, not least by the fact that economic reform was lowering the living standards of the traditional constituency of the Islamic regime, the urban lower classes. Serious rioting reported in several cities at this time was attributed by some observers to dissatisfaction with the Government's economic programme.

The extent to which Rafsanjani had lost popular support became clear when he stood for re-election to the presidency in June 1993. Competing against three ostensibly 'token' candidates, Rafsanjani received 63.2% of the votes from a low electoral turn-out of 56%. An attempt was made on Rafsanjani's life at a rally in Tehran in February 1994, responsibility for which was later claimed by the self-styled 'Free Officers of the Revolutionary Guards'. The influence of Rafsanjani's opponents in the Majlis in seeking to modify the Government's economic reform programme was evident when in May the Government indicated that it would proceed more cautiously with a plan to reduce economic subsidies applied to basic commodities. In November, after almost a year of debate, the Majlis approved the Government's second five-year economic plan.

In August 1995 the official news agency cited members of the special commission for monitoring political parties as stating that political parties, associations and groups were free to conduct political activities in Iran on condition that they honoured the country's Constitution. It was reported subsequently, however, that Nehzat-e Azadi had been refused formal registration as a political party, despite its hitherto quasi-legal status. Earlier in the month representatives of Nehzat-e Azadi had criticized new electoral legislation granting the Council of Guardians the power to approve election candidates. In December Iranian officials reportedly indicated that political parties would be authorized to contest future elections.

Elections to the fifth Majlis in March and April 1996 provided an important measure of the shifting balance of power between 'reformers', or 'liberals', and 'conservatives' in Iranian politics. The first round of voting produced results in some 140 of the total 270 seats; turn-out by voters was put at about 77%. Candidates of the Servants of Iran's Construction, a new pro-Rafsanjani faction, were reported to have won some 70% of the seats. However, the 'conservative' Society of Combatant Clergy, with the unofficial patronage of Ayatollah Khamenei, claimed that its candidates had achieved an equally conclusive victory. After the second round of voting unofficial sources suggested that the Society of Combatant Clergy would command the loyalty of 110–120 deputies in the new Majlis, and the Servants of Iran's Construction that of 90–100 deputies.

In March 1997 Rafsanjani was appointed Chairman of the Council to Determine the Expediency of the Islamic Order (which arbitrates in disputes between the Majlis and the Council of Guardians) for a further five-year term, indicating that he would continue to play an influential role in political life upon the imminent expiry of his presidential mandate. (Rafsanjani was reappointed as head of the Expediency Council in March 2002.) In early May the Council of Guardians approved four candidatures for that month's presidential election, rejecting 234. Initial expectations were that Ali Akbar Nateq Nouri, the Majlis Speaker (who was favoured by the Society of Combatant Clergy), would secure an easy victory, but in the days prior to the election Sayed Muhammad Khatami (a presidential adviser and former Minister of Culture and Islamic Guidance) emerged as a strong contender. Regarded as a 'liberal', Khatami—supported by the Servants of Iran's Construction as well as by intellectuals, professionals, women's and youth groups—took some 69.1% of the total votes cast, ahead of Nateq Nouri, with 24.9%. The rate of participation by voters was more than 88%. (Nouri was re-elected Speaker of the Majlis in June.)

Taking office in August 1997, President Khatami emphasized his commitment to fostering sustained and balanced growth in the political, economic, cultural and educational spheres, as well as freedom of and respect for the individual and rights of the nation, in the context of the rule of law. In foreign affairs, the President undertook to promote the principle of mutual respect, but pledged that Iran would stand up to any power seeking to subjugate Iranian sovereignty. Notable among the 'moderate' appointees in Khatami's first Council of Ministers were Ata'ollah Mohajerani (a former Vice-President) as Minister of Culture and Islamic Guidance, and Abdollah Nuri as Minister of the Interior (a post he had previously held in 1989–93). Kamal Kharrazi (hitherto Iran's ambassador to the UN) replaced the veteran Ali Akbar Velayati as Minister of Foreign Affairs, while Qorbanali Dorri Najafabadi became Minister of Information. Hassan Habibi was retained by Khatami as First Vice-President. Six further Vice-Presidents included Masumeh Ebtekar, who, as Vice-President and Head of the Organization for the Protection of the Environment, was the first woman to be appointed to such a senior government post since the Islamic Revolution. In November Khatami appointed a new Committee for Ensuring and Supervising the Implementation of the Constitution.

In the months following his election, President Khatami appeared conciliatory towards the West, and also urged more tolerance of dissent in Islamic societies among groups who remained 'within the framework of law and order'. Khamenei, meanwhile, continued to denounce the West's military and cultural ambitions, particularly those of the USA and Israel. The divergent messages of Iran's political and spiritual leaders were widely interpreted by Western commentators as indicative of conflict between the country's 'moderate' and 'conservative' factions. Within Iran, however, it was frequently emphasized that there was no such rift, and Khamenei denounced reports of tensions within the regime as Western propaganda. None the less, the arrest on corruption charges of Gholamhossein Karbaschi, the mayor of Tehran and a popular 'moderate', in April 1998 was widely interpreted as particularly illustrative of the extent of rivalries. Karbaschi's detention, which was denounced by several government members, was apparently the culmination of investigations into the conduct of municipal affairs, as a result of which several of the mayor's aides had already been arrested. At a rally held by supporters of Karbaschi at the University of Tehran, clashes between 'moderate' and 'conservative' students reportedly resulted in about 100 arrests. Karbaschi was freed from detention, pending trial, and in May it was reported that the Ministry of the Interior had authorized the registration of the Servants of Iran's Construction as a political party (styled the Servants of Construction Party), with Karbaschi as its Secretary-General. Following a televised trial, Karbaschi was sentenced in July to five years' imprisonment and required to pay a fine of IR 1,000m., having been convicted of embezzlement, squandering state property and mismanagement (but acquitted of bribery charges). In December the custodial sentence was reduced on appeal to two years and a 20-year prohibition from holding public office was reduced to 10 years. A further appeal failed to overturn Karbaschi's conviction, and he began his prison term in May 1999. However, he received a presidential pardon and was released in January 2000 (shortly before the legislative elections).

In June 1998, meanwhile, as Karbaschi's trial proceeded, the Majlis voted to dismiss Abdollah Nuri as Minister of the Interior. Impeachment had been initiated by a group of 'conservative' deputies who charged that Nuri had made provocative statements via the media and questioned his support for Karbaschi. (Nuri had criticized the 'conservative' Head of the Judiciary, Ayatollah Muhammad Yazdi, for what he alleged to be the persecution of the mayor). The minister's opponents further maintained that he had permitted dissident rallies and had also failed to counter unrest involving supporters of Ayatollah Montazeri (once Khomeini's designated successor, now linked to 'reformist' elements within the clergy) in late 1997. Khatami, who had opposed Nuri's impeachment, appointed Abdolvahed Musavi-Lari (also regarded as a relative 'moderate') to the Ministry of the Interior, and later named Nuri as Vice-President in charge of Development and Social Affairs. In August 1998 it was reported that Khamenei had ceded control of the police forces to Musavi-Lari. (Under the Constitution, the forces are under the jurisdiction of the Wali Faqih, but by convention responsibility is transferred to the Minister of the Interior; however, Khamenei had declined to accord Nuri control of the police.)

During 1998 the Khatami administration apparently moved to formalize its support base. In addition to the registration of the Servants of Construction as a political party, the Islamic Iran Solidarity Party was authorized by the Ministry of the Interior early in the year. Vice-President Masumeh Ebtekar was among the leaders of the Islamic Iran Participation Front, inaugurated in December. However, at elections to the Council of Experts in October, 'conservatives' retained overwhelming control of the assembly, with an estimated 60% of the 86 seats being won by candidates of the 'radical' right wing; candidates of a 'centrist' grouping apparently associated with ex-President Rafsanjani took about 10% of the seats.

The Minister of Information, Qorbanali Dorri Najafabadi, resigned in February 1999, after it was admitted that agents of his ministry had (allegedly without his knowledge) been responsible for the murders of several intellectuals and dissident writers (among them Dariush Foruhar, leader of the unauthorized but officially tolerated Iranian People's Party) in late 1998. He was replaced by Ali Yunesi, who had led an investigative commission into the murders. In June 1999 it was reported that a former deputy minister of information, who had been one of four intelligence agents arrested and charged in connection with the crimes, had committed suicide while in custody.

Iran's first local government elections since the Islamic Revolution took place in February 1999, when some 60% of the electorate voted for 200,000 council seats. The elections resulted in considerable success for 'reformist' candidates, notably in Tehran, Shiraz and Esfahan; 'conservatives' secured control of councils in their traditional strongholds of Qom and Mashad. Marked successes were recorded by female candidates, who won some 300 seats. In subsequent weeks 'conservative' elements challenged the election of many 'reformist' councillors: among those whose victories were overturned was former Minister of the Interior Abdollah Nuri. Meanwhile, it was reported that the process of electing a successor to Karbaschi as mayor of Tehran was being hampered by opponents of the 'reformists', and it was not until June that Morteza Alviri, an adviser to Khatami, was chosen to head the city.

In April 1999 the Mujahidin-e-Khalq claimed responsibility for the assassination, in Tehran, of the deputy chief of staff of the armed forces, Lt-Gen. Ali Sayyad Shirazi. In the same month Mohsen Kadivar, a prominent 'reformist' cleric, was sentenced to 18 months' imprisonment by the Special Clerical Court. Kadivar, who had openly questioned the validity of one of the central tenets of post-Revolutionary Iran, had been arrested in February on charges of disseminating false information and confusing public opinion. In May an attempt by 'conservatives' in the Majlis to impeach the Minister of Culture and Islamic Guidance, Ata'ollah Mohajerani (a close associate of Khatami), was narrowly defeated. Mohajerani was accused by his detractors of failing, notably through his relatively liberal policy towards the media, to uphold revolutionary and Islamic principles.

The issue of press censorship had, meanwhile, increasingly become a focus of the political rivalries between 'conservatives' and 'reformists'. During 1998 several prominent journals had been closed, and their journalists prosecuted, and Ayatollah Khamenei had personally sought action against publications that he perceived as abusing freedom of speech to weaken Islamic beliefs. In July 1999 the Majlis endorsed draft amendments to legislation governing the press that would curb the activities of 'liberal' publications. Immediately *Salam*, a 'reformist' newspaper with close links to President Khatami, was ordered by the Special Clerical Court to close. The newspaper had recently published a document produced by the deputy information minister whose suicide had been reported in June (see above) advocating stricter controls on the 'reformist' media. The new press restrictions provoked what were reportedly the most serious street disturbances in Tehran since the Revolution. The day after the closure of *Salam* was ordered, a small demonstration by students at the University of Tehran was dispersed with considerable violence by police. Hours later security forces, aided by militant vigilantes of the Ansar-e Hezbollah, raided student dormitories; the authorities later stated that one student had been killed, although students claimed that there had been as many as eight deaths. Five days of rioting ensued in Tehran and other cities before the protests were quelled, with some 1,400 arrests made, by security forces and right-wing vigilantes. The Supreme Council for National Security (led by Khatami) announced that two senior police officials had been dismissed, and that the Chief of Police, Brig.-Gen. Heyedat Loftian, whose removal from office had been sought by the protesters, had been reprimanded. In August Loftian reportedly informed the Majlis that as many as 100 police-officers had been arrested for their role in the campus raid. At the end of August it was announced that Tehran's chief of police had been dismissed, while Brig.-Gen. Loftian was himself dismissed by Khamenei in June 2000. In July of that year the former Tehran chief of police and 17 co-defendants were acquitted on charges arising from the police invasion of student dormitories in July 1999; two police-officers received custodial sentences, having been convicted on relatively minor charges.

Meanwhile, in early August 1999 the ban on *Salam* was extended to five years, and the journal's publisher (who had in late July been convicted on charges including defamation and publication of a classified document) was given a suspended 42-month prison sentence, and also fined and banned from publishing for three years. Also in August Muhammad Yazdi was succeeded, upon retirement, as Head of the Judiciary by Ayatollah Mahmoud Hashemi Shahrudi. Yazdi was immediately appointed to the influential Council of Guardians. In September it was reported that four alleged leaders of the July riots had been sentenced to death (although the death sentences were commuted to 15 years' imprisonment in April 2000); 45 defendants were given custodial terms and fined, and a further 20 were acquitted. Abdollah Nuri was brought before the Special Clerical Court in October 1999, accused in his capacity as editor of the 'liberal' *Khordad* daily of insulting Islamic sanctities, publishing reports contrary to religious fundamentals, and refuting the values of Ayatollah Khomeini. Many observers regarded the charges against Nuri as a clear attempt to prevent his standing in the forthcoming elections to the Majlis, where, if elected, he was likely to be a strong contender for the post of Speaker. In November Nuri was convicted on 15 charges and sentenced to five years' imprisonment; he was also fined IR 15m., and the closure of *Khordad* was ordered. An appeal lodged with the Supreme Court was rejected in January 2000, on the grounds that the court had no constitutional authority to overturn a verdict of the Special Clerical Court. However, it was reported in November 2002 that Nuri had been pardoned by Ayatollah Khamenei following the sudden death of his brother, Ali Reza Nuri, a 'reformist' deputy who had achieved success in the 2000 general election (see below).

As anticipated, the process of scrutinizing candidates by the Council of Guardians, in preparation for elections to the Majlis scheduled for February 2000, resulted in the disqualification of many known 'reformist' candidates, on grounds principally of disloyalty to Islam, to Iran's Constitution or spiritual leader. ('Conservative' deputies had in late 1999 introduced legislation giving the Council extensive powers to vet election candidates.) Nevertheless, while there were indications, as lesser-known 'reformist' candidates were approved by the Guardians, that the sixth Majlis might include sufficient numbers of 'liberals' and 'moderates' to present the first real challenge to the 'conservative' majority, the extent of the success achieved by 'reformist' and 'moderate' candidates of the Islamic Iran Participation Front and the Servants of Construction was not widely pre-

dicted. An estimated 80% of Iran's registered electorate participated in the poll on 18 February 2000. Among those who secured notable victories were Muhammad Reza Khatami (brother of the President and head of the Participation Front's political bureau), Jamileh Kadivar (the wife of Ata'ollah Mohajerani and sister of dissident cleric Mohsen Kadivar) and Ali Reza Nuri. 'Conservative' candidates, meanwhile, were overwhelmingly defeated in Mashad, Esfahan, Shiraz and Tabriz. There was a marked increase in the proportion of Majlis seats won by women, while the number of clerics in the new assembly declined. The Council of Guardians ordered the recount of almost one-third of the votes cast in Tehran, following allegations of irregularities; however, Ayatollah Khamenei intervened to prevent a complete recount of ballots for all 30 of the capital's seats. Principal among those whose election was initially in doubt was former President Rafsanjani; however, Rafsanjani resigned his Tehran seat in late May, thereby relinquishing his ambition to become the new Speaker of the Majlis. Meanwhile, a second round of voting, for 66 undecided seats, proceeded on 5 May (having been postponed from April by the Council of Guardians). At the end of May the incoming Majlis elected Mahdi Karrubi, the candidate of the Servants of Construction, as Speaker, a post which he had previously held in 1989–92.

The outcome of the first round of legislative voting appeared to exacerbate the struggle for political dominance between 'conservative' and 'reformist' elements. While the opening, in late February 2000, of the trial of 20 police-officers and security officials (among them the former Tehran chief of police), on charges of involvement in the attacks on students that had preceded the violent unrest of July 1999, was interpreted as an expression of the State's likely response to acts of provocation by forces that might seek to foment further unrest, 'conservative' elements of the Revolutionary Guards Corps issued an apparent warning in April 2000 that a 'reformist' victory would not be tolerated. For its part, the judiciary pursued its actions against the 'reformist' press: a new press law, endorsed by the outgoing, 'conservative'-controlled Majlis, made criticism of the Constitution illegal and increased judicial powers to close newspapers. The Majlis also approved legislation effectively depriving the legislature of authority to call to account security organizations under Khamenei's control. In March Sayed Hajjarian, a prominent 'reformer', presidential adviser and manager of the daily *Sobh Emruz*, was seriously wounded in a gun attack which some claimed had been perpetrated by forces linked to the intelligence service. In May five men were found guilty of having attempted the assassination and sentenced to terms of imprisonment ranging from three to 15 years; three others were acquitted.

By mid-2000 it was estimated that 'reformist' or 'liberal' deputies held some 200 seats in the new Majlis, with the remaining 90 occupied by 'conservatives'. (In November the Majlis decided to hold by-elections in mid-2001—the time of the scheduled presidential election—for 18 seats where the results of earlier voting had been annulled.) However, while 'reformist' deputies acted swiftly to draft legislation to replace the previous year's restrictive press law, as well as proposals to curb the powers of the Council of Guardians, Muhammad Reza Khatami, who was elected in mid-June 2000 to the position of First Deputy Speaker of the Majlis, indicated that change would proceed at a moderate pace. At the end of July the Islamic Iran Participation Front elected Muhammad Reza Khatami as its Secretary-General.

In August 2000 Ayatollah Khamenei issued a decree instructing the new Majlis not to debate proposed amendments to the press law (which would make it more difficult for the judiciary to imprison journalists), on the grounds that such reforms would endanger state security and religious faith. Khamenei's intervention to block the 'reformist'-sponsored legislation appeared to sanction a more vigorous campaign against the 'liberal' interests in subsequent months. At the end of August a police-officer was killed, and about 100 people were injured, in four days of violent clashes between 'pro-reform' students and Ansar-e Hezbollah militants in the western town of Khorramabad. The confrontations occurred as two 'reformists', including the dissident cleric Mohsen Kadivar, were prevented by the militants from addressing an annual student congress. (Kadivar had been released from prison in July, although he had been informed of the possibility of indictment on further 'yet unknown' political charges.) In November the Council of Guardians rejected for a second time the proposed amendments to the press law, which were thus submitted for jurisdiction by the Council to Determine the Expediency of the

Islamic Order. It was reported in that month that some 30 'pro-reform' publications had been closed down by the authorities since April, some of which had reopened under new names to seek to overcome previous closures. Meanwhile, in September Khamenei dismissed the uncompromising chief of security police, Brig.-Gen. Muhammad Reza Naqdi, after a number of officers under his command were convicted of torture.

President Khatami implemented a number of important changes within the state administration at this time, merging and restructuring several state organizations and ministries. In December 2000 Khatami officially accepted the resignation (submitted in October) of Ata'ollah Mohajerani, the 'liberal' Minister of Culture and Islamic Guidance (whom 'conservatives' in the Majlis had attempted to impeach in 1999). Mohajerani was redesignated Chairman of the Organization for the Dialogue of Civilizations, while Ahmad Masjed Jame'i, reputedly more of a 'conservative' than Mohajerani, was confirmed as the new Minister of Culture and Islamic Guidance in January 2001.

In November 2000 the trial opened in Tehran of a group of prominent 'reformists', accused of 'acting against national security and propagandizing against the regime' through their attendance at a conference on Iranian political reform, held in Berlin, Germany, in April. Among the accused were a dissident cleric, Hassan Yousefi Eshkevari (whose separate trial before the Special Clerical Court in October on charges including apostasy had provoked considerable controversy), the 'reformist' politician Jamileh Kadivar, and a well-known investigative journalist, Akbar Ganji. The severity of the sentences, pronounced in mid-January 2001, against seven of the defendants, who were condemned to custodial terms of between four and 10 years, was denounced by 'reformist' politicians within Iran. Ganji received the maximum prison term, followed by five years' internal exile, having been found guilty of harming national security, propagandizing against the regime, possessing secret documents and committing offences against senior officials. Three others received suspended sentences, while six (including Kadivar) were acquitted. Appeals were immediately lodged by all those convicted, resulting in a dramatic reduction in the sentences of five of the prisoners by a Tehran court of appeal in December. Meanwhile, the outcome of Eshkevari's trial had not been disclosed, although there were unconfirmed reports that he had been sentenced to death. (It was reported in October 2002 that Eshkevari had been sentenced to seven years' imprisonment resulting from his participation in the Berlin conference.) A focus of Ganji's investigations in recent months had been the deaths of dissident intellectuals in late 1998 (see above). While the journalist had amassed what he alleged was evidence of the involvement of senior 'conservatives' in the murders, the authorities maintained that the assassinations had been instigated by 'rogue' agents of the Ministry of Information. The trial of 18 people, including senior intelligence officers, accused of involvement in the murders began, in camera, before a military court in Tehran in late December 2000. (The court had recently announced that former Minister of Information Najafabadi had no case to answer.) At the end of January 2001 three intelligence agents were condemned to death, having been convicted of perpetrating the killings; five received life sentences, and seven others custodial terms of up to 10 years (the other defendants were acquitted). However, in mid-August the Supreme Court ordered a retrial of the 15 agents. In late January 2003 it was reported that two of the agents had had their death sentences commuted to terms of life imprisonment; of those given life sentences, two now received prison terms of 10 years, while seven of the agents were given gaol terms of between two and 10 years. The remaining agents were to have their cases reviewed.

Meanwhile, in January 2001 the trial began of Mustafa Tajzadeh, the 'reformist' Deputy Minister of the Interior whom Khatami had chosen to monitor the forthcoming presidential election; Tajzadeh was accused of vote-rigging in the 2000 Majlis elections and of incitement to violence in Khorramabad in August of that year. In protest against his trial, more than 150 Majlis deputies signed a letter accusing the judiciary of harassing political and social activists, and insisting that the Majlis must be permitted to exercise its rights of supervision and investigation. In March 2001 Tajzadeh was convicted of involvement in electoral fraud and given a one-year prison sentence; he was banned from supervising elections for six years and from holding a government post for 39 months. However, in July Tajzadeh was reportedly acquitted of charges of electoral fraud. In late March and early April 2001 police detained more than 40 leading 'moderates', including relatives and close associates of

Mehdi Bazargan—the founder of Nehzat-e Azadi—as well as members of the movement, on charges of conspiring to overthrow the Islamic regime; many deputies condemned the action as illegal, and President Khatami publicly criticized the arrests. In May Akbar Ganji was cleared by a court of appeal of all the charges on which he had been convicted in January other than that of propagandizing against the regime; Ganji's sentence was reduced to a six-month prison term, and he was duly released. In July, however, after the prosecution objected to the initial verdict, a further appeal found Ganji guilty of having threatened national security, and the journalist was given a six-year custodial sentence.

In December 2000 the Council of Guardians declared that the presidential election would take place on 8 June 2001. Uncertainty at this time as to whether Khatami would seek re-election had been heightened in November 2000, when the President had stated publicly that he had been unable to enforce the rights and freedoms enshrined in the Constitution, and had failed to prevent the judiciary's punitive actions against the 'reformist' press and 'liberal' activists. Under growing pressure from 'reformist' deputies, Khatami did, however, declare his candidacy on 4 May 2001, just two days before the deadline for the registration of presidential candidates. In mid-May the Council of Guardians endorsed the candidature of 10 people from a total of 814 potential candidates (including 45 women). Although no 'conservative' candidate was officially endorsed by senior 'hardline' clerics, several independent 'conservatives' stood for election, including the Minister of Defence and Logistics, Rear-Adm. Ali Shamkhani, and Ahmed Tavakkoli, previously Minister of Labour and Social Affairs.

As had been widely predicted, on 8 June 2001 Khatami was re-elected as President, winning some 76.9% of the total votes cast, compared to 15.6% for his closest rival, Ahmed Tavakkoli. Moreover, Khatami became the first Iranian President to win a greater number of votes for his second term than for his first, although the rate of participation by voters (at around 67%) was considerably lower than the 88% recorded in 1997. Khatami's victory in Iran's eighth presidential election was seen as a public endorsement of his reform programme, and the President-elect pledged to continue his efforts to introduce a greater level of democracy and government accountability to Iran, and to improve economic conditions. In the weeks following the election it appeared that Khatami might be assisted in this task by an apparent widening of the divisions between moderate 'conservatives' and their more 'hardline' colleagues. Nevertheless, it soon became apparent that the 'ultra-conservatives' were unwilling to cede control of the Council of Guardians to 'reformist' supporters of Khatami. On 5 August Khatami's scheduled inauguration was postponed after the 'reformist' Majlis refused to approve two of the judiciary's 'conservative' nominees to the Council of Guardians. Ayatollah Khamenei requested, to the strenuous 'reformist' opposition, that the dispute be resolved by the 'conservative'-dominated Council to Determine the Expediency of the Islamic Order. Two days later, however, the Majlis finally endorsed the two candidates, following a ruling that candidates did not require the support of a majority of deputies in order to be elected to the Council of Guardians. Khatami was duly sworn in for a second presidential term on 8 August. In mid-August he presented his 20-member Council of Ministers to the Majlis, which approved the list later in the month. There were only five new ministerial appointments, including Tahmasb Mazaheri as the Minister of Economic Affairs and Finance. The composition of the new Government was criticized both by 'conservatives' for being too liberal and by 'reformists' for not being sufficiently bold. A few days later Khatami appointed Muhammad Reza Aref, formerly head of the Organization of Administration and Planning, as First Vice-President (in place of Hassan Ibrahim Habibi, who had resigned in July).

The judiciary's campaign against 'pro-reform' activists intensified following Khatami's re-election. Mass arrests, public floggings and even public executions—ordered ostensibly to reduce crime and encourage greater morality—were interpreted by many observers as a deliberate attempt by the 'ultra-conservatives' to defy the President's proposals to introduce social and political reform. In September 2001 Hossein Loqmanian, a 'reformist' deputy in the Majlis, lost his appeal against a custodial sentence imposed in October 2000 after Loqmanian had condemned in a parliamentary speech the closure by the press court of several 'pro-reform' publications. Sentenced to 10 months' custody, he became the first serving member of the Majlis to be imprisoned since 1979 (under the Constitution deputies are granted parliamentary immunity); meanwhile, four other 'reformist' deputies awaited the results of appeals against similar sentences, while several others faced charges for speeches they had made to the Iranian assembly. The imprisonment of Loqmanian in December 2001 provoked strong protests both from his constituents in the western city of Hamedan and from other 'liberal' deputies who, in January 2002, staged a brief boycott of the Majlis in a protest led by the Speaker, Mahdi Karrubi. The parliamentary boycott apparently resulted in a rare victory for the 'pro-reform' lobby as Loqmanian was swiftly pardoned by Ayatollah Khamenei and duly released. Meanwhile, it was reported in September 2001 that all six Kurdish deputies in the Majlis had resigned, amid claims of official discrimination against Iran's Kurdish community. There was serious rioting in Tehran and other cities in October, when protests related to two international football matches descended into violent demands for political change; some protesters attacked government buildings, and hundreds of arrests were made. Several Iranian officials accused foreign opposition groups of having incited the violence by means of satellite television broadcasts.

In November 2001 trial proceedings, held in camera, began of more than 30 members of the banned Nehzat-e Azadi movement who had been arrested earlier in the year on charges including acting against national security and plotting to overthrow the Islamic regime. Among the defendants—in what was reported to be the largest political trial in Iran since 1979—were two former ministers and a former mayor of Tehran. Custodial sentences of up to 10 years were handed down to 33 of the activists by the Revolutionary Court in late July 2002, and Nehzat-e Azadi was officially banned. A second trial of 15 other opposition activists (mostly academics and writers) commenced in early January 2002; the defendants were accused of anti-State activities and of seeking to encourage student unrest. An economic corruption trial was also instigated in late January, in which a number of state officials were thought to be implicated. Meanwhile, in late November 2001 the Council to Determine the Expediency of the Islamic Order rejected a bill to amend the electoral law that proposed a reduction in the power of the Council of Guardians to vet and disqualify electoral candidates. The new legislation had been proposed by 'reformist' deputies after the Council rejected about 60 of their candidates in the approach to by-elections due to be held in the province of Golestan. Also in November the Minister of Oil, Bijan Namdar-Zangeneh, was summoned to court by the judiciary, reportedly to answer charges of mismanagement of petroleum revenues and the granting of contract awards to an affiliate of Iran's national oil company. President Khatami's position became even more difficult in early December after the Minister of Industries and Mines, Eshaq Jahangiri, and the Governor of the Central Bank, Dr Mohsen Nourbakhsh, had also appeared in court (the charges against them were undisclosed). During December at least 60 'pro-reform' deputies were asked to appear before various courts, while several publications were ordered to close. In that month a UN human rights committee adopted a resolution voicing concern at the state of human rights in Iran, citing in particular the high number of executions and public floggings that had recently been ordered.

Iran's Deputy Foreign Minister for Education and Research, Sadegh Kharrazi, was forced to resign in April 2002, amid speculation that he had made contact with US officials. There was a renewed clamp-down on the 'pro-reform' movement by the judiciary in May, with the closure ordered of two 'liberal' newspapers. The Tehran judiciary warned journalists in late May that they would be committing a criminal offence by publishing any article that favoured dialogue between Iranian and US representatives. In early June Mahdi Karrubi was re-elected as Speaker of the Majlis for a further 12 months. Behzad Nabavi became First Deputy Speaker of the assembly, replacing Muhammad Reza Khatami, who assumed Nabavi's previous role as Second Deputy Speaker. The crack-down against Iranian 'liberals' appeared to be intensified in July. The authorities declared a ban on any rallies and protests organized to commemorate the third anniversary of the violent clashes that had occurred between students and the security forces in 1999. However, several hundred protesters were reported to have defied the ban in Tehran, resulting in sporadic clashes between protesters demanding political reform on the one side and security forces and 'right-wing' elements on the other. A prominent 'reformist' cleric in Esfahan, Ayatollah Jalaleddin Taheri, announced his resignation the following day, launching a strong

attack against Iran's 'conservative' religious establishment, citing its poor management of the country and official corruption. Taheri also demanded the release from house arrest of the dissident cleric, Ayatollah Montazeri. (A close ally of Ayatollah Khamenei was named as Taheri's replacement in mid-September 2002.) In mid-July 2002 the 'left-wing' Participation Front threatened to withdraw its co-operation with the Government and Majlis if 'hardliners' continued to block social and political reforms. In late July Mohsen Mirdamadi, a Majlis deputy and publisher of the Participation Front's *Norouz*, Iran's main 'pro-reform' newspaper, had a six-month gaol term handed down in May for propagandizing against the Islamic regime confirmed by a court of appeal. Mirdamadi was also fined and banned from involvement in press activities for four years, and his publication was closed down for six months. (He had alleged in an article published in *Norouz* to have information that Tehran had held secret talks with the USA.) More than 30 other 'reformists' were also imprisoned during that month. In August and September at least three 'pro-reform' newspapers were banned by the authorities.

During September 2002 President Khatami presented draft legislation to the Majlis which was aimed at reducing the powers of Iran's 'ultra-conservative' establishment in order to accelerate the President's reform programme. The first bill, presented early in the month, envisaged transferring the rights of the Council of Guardians to approve or disqualify electoral candidates to the Ministry of the Interior. The second bill, issued in late September, proposed granting Khatami wider powers to enforce adherence to the terms of the Constitution by the judiciary and other government departments, in an attempt to prevent practices such as politically motivated trials being held in camera and the closure of 'reformist' newspapers. Both bills required approval by the Majlis and the Council of Guardians prior to becoming law; 'liberal' deputies threatened to resign *en masse* if the Council blocked the reforms. However, the 'pro-reform' movement suffered a setback in early October when Behrouz Geranpayeh, director of a research institute affiliated to the 'reformist'-led Ministry of Culture and Islamic Guidance, was arrested on charges including publishing 'inappropriate' information, acting against national security and passing information to foreign intelligence agencies, and the institute was closed down by the authorities. The action came after a recent poll commissioned by the Majlis and published by Geranpayeh's research institute showed that a large majority of Iranians favoured the resumption of a political dialogue with the USA. During late 2002 a number of other officials, including a 'liberal' parliamentarian and the head of Iran's state news agency, also faced charges in connection with alleged Western influence at Iranian polling institutes. In early November another such organization was closed and its directors were arrested; they included Abbas Abdi, a journalist and leading member of the 'left-wing' Islamic Iran Participation Front.

Meanwhile, in early November 2002 the first of President Khatami's reform bills, concerning the vetting of electoral candidates, received preliminary approval by the Majlis. Four days later the second draft bill, relating to violations of the Constitution, was approved by parliament. However, at the same time a prominent 'reformist' academic, writer and close ally of the President, Hashem Aghajari, was handed down a death sentence by a court in the western city of Hamedan, having been found guilty of apostasy for a speech he had made to a university audience in June, in which he questioned the divine authority of the Islamic clergy and advocated reform within the religious establishment. (On other charges, Aghajari was sentenced to eight years in prison and 74 lashes, as well as receiving a 10-year teaching ban.) Aghajari was arrested in August and tried in camera. The severity of the sentence was widely condemned by academics, 'liberals' and even moderate 'conservatives', and led to several weeks of student protests—the largest witnessed in Iran since 1999. In mid-November 2002 Ayatollah Khamenei intervened in the worsening crisis by requesting that the judiciary initiate an urgent review of the case. However, this did not prevent further 'pro-reform' protests by students in Tehran, which resulted in clashes with members of a 'hardline' militia who were calling for Aghajari's execution. It was reported in late November that four students who had instigated the recent protests had been arrested on charges of acting against national security. In early December Aghajari's lawyers filed an appeal against his conviction. Meanwhile, the trial began in Tehran of three leading Iranian pollsters—including Behrouz Geranpayeh and Abbas Abdi—who were accused of espionage and of fabricating opinion polls. Abdi was sentenced to eight years' imprisonment in early February 2003, having been found guilty of selling information to a US polling institute, while another researcher received a nine-year term; Geranpayeh awaited a verdict. (In late December 2002 a 'reformist' Majlis deputy and former minister was charged with the misuse of state funds in relation to financial assistance he had given to Geranpayeh's institute.) Further demonstrations were staged in Tehran in early December by students demanding the release of Hashem Aghajari, some of whom also sought the resignation of the Head of the Judiciary. A number of arrests were reported to have been made. In the second week of December Hussain Mir-Muhammad Sadeghi, the official spokesman for the judiciary, resigned his post, reportedly citing dissatisfaction over the 'politicization' of the judiciary and Aghajari's death sentence. With the divide between 'hardliners' and 'reformists' apparently growing, there was a widespread belief that the 'conservative' establishment was preparing a serious crack-down against the 'liberal' movement, possibly by declaring a state of emergency. In mid-February 2003 Hashem Aghajari was ordered to face a retrial by the court in Hamedan that had issued the initial verdict. Meanwhile, in January 2003 the judiciary ordered the closure of two independent newspapers. In mid-January Tehran's municipal council was dissolved by the Ministry of the Interior and its mayor, Muhammad Hassan Malek-Madani, was removed from his post and reportedly given a short gaol term, following a series of disagreements between council members. The action, coming only weeks before nation-wide municipal elections, was widely seen as a setback for 'reformists'. At the end of January the dissident cleric, Ayatollah Montazeri, was released from house arrest, following reports that a 'conservative' daily newspaper, *Resalat*, had joined the 'pro-reform' lobby in demanding his release. (Some reports claimed that the authorities feared that the Ayatollah, who was said to be in poor health, could become a focus for the Iranian opposition movement should he die while under house arrest.)

Initial results of voting in Iran's second local government elections since the Islamic Revolution, held in late February 2003, indicated a heavy defeat for President Khatami's Islamic Iran Participation Front by candidates of the 'conservative' wing. Electoral turn-out was reported to have been extremely low (at some 39%), as some 'moderate' voters appeared to have boycotted the poll in protest at Khatami's failure to secure vital political reforms. 'Conservative' candidates were said to have secured 14 out of the 15 seats on the council in Tehran (where electoral turn-out was as low as 15%).

Relations with the USA since the end of the Iran–Iraq War have continued to be characterized by mutual suspicion. The USA, alleging that Iran is pursuing a programme of military expansion, has expressed particular concern over the nature of nuclear co-operation between the People's Republic of China, Russia and Iran, and has sought to persuade Iran's Western allies to reduce economic and technical assistance to, and direct investment in, the country. Iran maintains that it is not engaged in the development of weapons of mass destruction, while the Chinese and Russian Governments have strenuously denied involvement in non-civilian nuclear projects in Iran. In May 1994 US pressure was evident when the World Bank announced that it would approve no new loans to Iran in the foreseeable future. In July the USA accused Iran of being responsible for bomb attacks against Jewish targets in the United Kingdom and Argentina in an attempt to disrupt the Middle East peace process. (A former Iranian intelligence agent alleged in July 2002 that Iranian agents had plotted and carried out the bombing in Buenos Aires with the backing of the Iranian Government, although Iranian officials have persistently denied the claims.)

In April 1995 US efforts to isolate Iran internationally culminated in the announcement that all US companies and their overseas subsidiaries would be banned from investing in, or trading with, Iran. It was subsequently conceded that US oil companies active in the Caucasus and Central Asia would be allowed to participate in exchange deals with Iran in order to facilitate the marketing of petroleum from countries of the former USSR. Russia refused to support the embargo, but announced in May that it would henceforth separate the civilian and military components of an agreement to supply Iran with a nuclear reactor, to be constructed at Bushehr. In mid-1996 the US Congress approved legislation (termed the Iran-Libya Sanctions Act—ILSA) to penalize companies operating in US markets that were investing US $40m. (subsequently amended to

$20m.) or more in energy projects in prescribed countries deemed to be sponsoring terrorism. Like the embargo imposed on Iran in 1995, however, these so-called secondary economic sanctions received little international support. In December 1996 Iran and Russia concluded an extensive co-operation agreement. In September 1997, furthermore, a consortium comprising French, Malaysian and Russian energy companies signed a contract with the Iranian National Oil Company to invest some $2,000m. in the development of natural gas reserves in Iranian waters of the Persian Gulf. Threats of sanctions were effectively averted in May 1998, when the US Administration agreed to waive penalties for which the Secretary of State deemed the companies involved to be liable. This decision apparently facilitated further foreign investment in Iran, most notably in hydrocarbons projects, in 1998–2002.

Khatami's election to the Iranian presidency in mid-1997 prompted speculation regarding prospects for an improvement in relations with the USA and other Western countries. A notable development was the designation by the USA, in October, of the opposition Mujahidin-e-Khalq as one of 30 proscribed terrorist organizations. In December Khatami expressed his desire to engage in a 'thoughtful dialogue' with the American people. In what was interpreted as a major concession, US President Bill Clinton stated subsequently that the USA would not require Iran (or any other Islamic state) to modify its attitude towards the Middle East peace process. The cautious *rapprochement* continued in January 1998, when Khatami made a widely publicized address, via a US television news network, emphasizing the need for Iran to develop closer cultural links with the USA; that he did not urge direct political dialogue was generally interpreted as a compromise between 'moderates' in his administration and the regime's 'conservatives', most notably Khamenei, who continued vociferously to reject the possibility of any normalization of relations with the USA.

The announcement, in July 1998, that Iran had successfully test-fired a new ballistic missile, *Shehab-3*, capable of striking targets at a distance of 1,300 km, caused renewed tensions. (The missile could potentially target Israel and also US forces in the Gulf.) US concerns regarding what it perceived as Iran's efforts to acquire weapons of mass destruction remained a principal cause of mutual suspicion, and there was continuing evidence of efforts by the Clinton Administration to block trading agreements deemed to assist Iran's military programme. Ukraine had announced, following a visit by the US Secretary of State in March, that it would not proceed with an agreement to supply turbines for the Bushehr reactor; however, Russia, stating that the Bushehr plant was in conformity with standards prescribed by the International Atomic Energy Agency (IAEA) for the prevention of nuclear weapons' proliferation, subsequently declared its willingness to provide the equipment.

The USA was among countries to condemn the arrest, revealed in mid-1999, of 13 Jews in Shiraz and Esfahan, on charges of espionage on behalf of Israel and the USA. In July 2000, after a closed trial in Shiraz, 10 of the defendants were convicted and given custodial sentences of between four and 13 years; however, in September their sentences were reduced on appeal to terms of between two and nine years. Although it was reported in February 2001 that further appeals had been rejected by the Supreme Court, all the Jews had been released by late April 2003. Meanwhile, in September 1999 the US House of Representatives approved non-proliferation legislation requiring the imposition of sanctions against any country aiding Iran in the development of weapons of mass destruction. Furthermore, while the Clinton Administration continued to extend the prospect of further co-operation, indications that this might be contingent upon Iranian assistance in investigations into the bombing of a US military housing complex in al-Khobar, Saudi Arabia, in 1996 (see below) were not well received in Iran, which had consistently denied involvement. In October, none the less, the opposition National Council of Resistance was designated by the USA as a terrorist organization.

Addressing the American-Iranian Council in Washington, DC, in March 2000, US Secretary of State Madeleine Albright announced an end to restrictions on imports from Iran of several non-hydrocarbons items. This substantive step towards the normalization of relations was in recognition of what the US Administration regarded as trends towards democracy under President Khatami. Albright furthermore offered what amounted to an apology for the role played by the USA in the *coup d'état* of 1953, as well as for US support for Iraq in the Iran–

Iraq War. Such concessions were, however, accompanied by the assertion that Iran had done little to modify its support for what Albright termed international terrorism and its efforts to develop nuclear weaponry. In April 2000 the USA imposed sanctions on the Iranian Ministry of Defence and on three industrial organizations, alleging that they had been involved in the transfer of missile technology; Iran denied the claims. Despite US objections, in May the World Bank approved the release of two loans to Iran (the first new lending since 1994—see Economic Affairs, below). Open meetings and other contacts involving Iranian and US officials at the UN Millennium Summit in New York in September 2000 appeared to reinforce expectations of a further *rapprochement*. However, relations between Iran and the USA deteriorated in June 2001 after 14 men (13 Saudi Arabians and one Lebanese) were indicted *in absentia* by the US Government, having been charged in connection with the bomb attack at al-Khobar in 1996. Although no Iranians were among the accused, US officials reiterated allegations that members of the Iranian Government were behind the bombing. Despite early indications that the new Administration of President George W. Bush, inaugurated in January 2001, was reviewing US policy on sanctions, in early August the Bush Administration confirmed that ILSA was to be extended for a further five years (although the legislation allowed for a presidential review in 2003). In July 2001 the USA had, for the second time since May, blocked Iran's bid to enter negotiations regarding membership of the World Trade Organization; an Iranian application was again vetoed by the USA in February 2002.

President Khatami was swift to offer his condolences to the American nation following the suicide bombings in New York and Washington, DC, on 11 September 2001. However, as the USA initiated a campaign against the al-Qa'ida (Base) organization of its chief suspect, Osama bin Laden—the Saudi Arabian-born radical Islamist based in Afghanistan—Khatami asserted that the international community should act under the auspices of the UN in order to eradicate terrorism. Although Ayatollah Khamenei also condemned the terrorist attacks, he and Iran's 'conservative' press warned against any large-scale US military offensive targeting the Taliban regime and al-Qa'ida militants in Afghanistan. Iranians strongly condemned the commencement of hostilities in early October, and the Government emphasized that it would not lend any military assistance (including the use of Iranian airspace) to the US-led campaign. However, in mid-October details emerged of a secret agreement between Iran and the USA whereby Iran would offer assistance to any US military personnel either shot down or forced to land within its borders, provided that the USA respect Iran's territorial integrity. There were also reports that Iran might be sharing intelligence with the USA. Iranian and US officials held UN-sponsored talks in Geneva in that month to discuss the composition of a future Afghan government. Yet, despite an apparent shift in bilateral relations, in 2001 Iran continued to head the US Administration's list of states deemed to be 'most active' in sponsoring terrorism.

Early in 2002, and again in subsequent months, the Iranian administration was swift to deny accusations by the USA that it was permitting fleeing al-Qa'ida and Taliban fighters to cross the Afghan border into Iran. Relations deteriorated abruptly at the end of January, when, in his annual State of the Union address, the US President referred to Iran as forming (together with Iraq and the Democratic People's Republic of Korea) an 'axis of evil', explicitly accusing Iran of aggressively pursuing the development of weapons of mass destruction and of 'exporting terror'. Bush's remarks were denounced in the strongest terms by 'moderates' and 'conservatives' in the Iranian leadership, with Khatami accusing his US counterpart of 'war-mongering'. The Minister of Foreign Affairs, Kamal Kharrazi, subsequently cancelled a planned visit to New York. In May President Khatami, in an address to the Majlis, urged 'reformist' deputies not to attempt to hold discussions with US officials. In the same month the US Department of State again designated Iran as the world's 'most active' sponsor of terrorism, and US officials reiterated their claims that Russia was assisting Iran in the manufacture of nuclear weapons. In late July the US Administration was angered by Russia's conclusion of a development and co-operation accord with Iran, which reportedly involved the construction of additional reactors at the Bushehr nuclear plant. Iran did, nevertheless, accept an offer of humanitarian aid from the USA following a major earthquake in the northwest of the country in late June 2002. However, the deterio-

ration in Iranian–US relations was evident when, towards the end of July, President Khatami openly condemned US plans to use military force to bring about 'regime change' in Iraq, warning that such action posed a serious risk to regional stability. At the end of the month Iran was reported to have placed its armed forces and Revolutionary Guards on alert in preparation for any US-led military action. In late October Kamal Kharrazi declared that, in the event of 'regime change' in Iraq, Iran strongly opposed any post-war Iraqi government being imposed by the USA. In mid-December Iran again denied allegations made by US officials that they had evidence of Iran's secret involvement in the manufacture of nuclear weapons. Iran has persistently maintained that its nuclear programme is required to meet domestic energy demands rather than for military purposes. However, the USA condemned the announcement made in early February 2003 that Iran was to extract recently discovered deposits of uranium in order to produce nuclear fuel. Inspectors from the UN and the IAEA began an assessment of Iran's nuclear programme later in the month.

The European Union (EU, see p. 199) pursued a policy of 'critical dialogue' with Iran during the 1990s, despite US pressure as well as tensions between Iran and certain EU states. Notably, a lengthy period of strained relations with the United Kingdom developed after Ayatollah Khomeini issued a *fatwa* (edict) in February 1989, imposing a death penalty against a British writer, Salman Rushdie, for material deemed offensive to Islam in his novel *The Satanic Verses*. 'Critical dialogue' was suspended in April 1997, after a German court ruled that the Iranian authorities had ordered the assassination of four prominent members of the dissident Democratic Party of Iranian Kurdistan in Berlin in September 1992. Germany announced the withdrawal of its ambassador to Tehran and expelled four Iranian diplomats, while other EU members similarly withdrew their representatives. Although EU governments swiftly agreed a return of their ambassadors, Iran's reluctance to readmit the German envoy prevented the normalization of relations for several months. Khatami's installation as President and the subsequent appointment of a new Council of Ministers in August 1997 apparently eased tensions, and in November a compromise arrangement was finally reached allowing the readmission of all EU ambassadors. In February 1998, furthermore, EU ministers responsible for foreign affairs effectively resumed 'critical dialogue' by an agreement to resume senior-level ministerial contacts with Iran. Following a meeting between Kharrazi and the British Secretary of State for Foreign and Commonwealth Affairs, Robin Cook, at the UN headquarters in New York in September, the Iranian Minister of Foreign Affairs confirmed that the Iranian Government had no intention of threatening the life of Rushdie or anyone associated with his work, nor would it encourage or assist any attempt to do so; the Government also dissociated itself from any reward offered in connection with the *fatwa*. However, 'conservative' clerics maintained that the *fatwa* issued by Ayatollah Khomeini was irrevocable, and the Qom-based 15 Khordad Foundation subsequently increased its financial reward offered for the writer's murder. Relations between Iran and the United Kingdom were, none the less, upgraded to ambassadorial level in May 1999. President Khatami became the first Iranian head of state to visit the West since the Islamic Revolution when, in March of that year, he travelled to Italy and the Vatican; in September President Thomas Klestil of Austria made the first visit to Iran by an EU head of state since 1979. In July 2000 a visit to Germany by President Khatami provoked widespread protests by Iranian dissidents resident there. Kharrazi, meanwhile, had visited the United Kingdom in January 2000. However, a visit to Iran by his British counterpart, scheduled for May, was delayed until July and was again postponed in late June, shortly before the anticipated delivery of sentences in the Shiraz espionage trial (see above), although British officials denied that these and subsequent cancellations were linked to events in Iran. An official visit to Tehran by Cook's successor, Jack Straw, which had been scheduled for November 2001, was brought forward to late September following the suicide attacks on the USA in that month; the purpose of Straw's visit was primarily to request Iran's support for a US-led military campaign in Afghanistan (see above). Straw visited Iran again in late November, as part of an official tour of Afghanistan's neighbours aimed at consolidating support for an interim Afghan 'national unity' government, under UN auspices. Meanwhile, during September 2001 the most high-level discussions since 1979 were held between Iranian and EU representatives in Brussels and later Tehran;

both sides were reportedly keen for the swift commencement of negotiations towards a trade and economic co-operation accord. A setback occurred in February 2002, when Iran formally rejected the United Kingdom's nomination for its new British ambassador to Tehran (accusing the diplomat of being an agent of the British intelligence service); the status of Iran's ambassador to Britain was subsequently downgraded to that of chargé d'affaires. However, the dispute was resolved in late September when Tehran accepted the nomination of a new British ambassador. In mid-June 2002 EU ministers of foreign affairs, meeting in Luxembourg, had agreed to initiate negotiations with Iran regarding a trade and co-operation agreement later that year, provided that the accord be linked with consideration of political issues (notably human rights and terrorism); the talks began in Brussels in mid-December. In early October 2002 Jack Straw visited Iran as part of a wider tour of the Middle East which was intended to garner support for a possible US-led military campaign to oust the regime of Saddam Hussain in Iraq. Kamal Kharrazi visited the United Kingdom in early February 2003 for talks with British officials concerning the Iraqi crisis; Kharrazi was reported to have emphasized the desire of the Iranian leadership to avert a war between Iraq and the West.

Relations between Iran and Saudi Arabia were frequently strained after the Islamic Revolution of 1979. A period of particularly hostile relations, following the deaths of 275 Iranian pilgrims as a result of fierce clashes with Saudi security forces in the Islamic holy city of Mecca during the *Hajj* (annual pilgrimage) in July 1987 culminated in the suspension of diplomatic relations in April 1988. Links were restored in March 1991. Allegations of Iranian involvement in the bombing of a US military housing complex at al-Khobar, Saudi Arabia, in June 1996 again strained relations for several months. However, the installation of a new Iranian Government in August 1997 facilitated further *rapprochement*. There was considerable speculation that the improvement in relations reflected the desire of the two countries, as the region's principal petroleum producers, to co-operate in maintaining world oil prices and in efforts to curtail over-production by members of the Organization of the Petroleum Exporting Countries (OPEC, see p. 298). An Iranian delegation led by former President Rafsanjani began a 10-day visit to Saudi Arabia in February 1998, at the end of which the formation of a joint ministerial committee for bilateral relations was announced, and several co-operation agreements were signed following a visit to Iran by the Saudi Minister of State for Foreign Affairs in May. The signing of a Saudi-Iranian security agreement was announced in April 2001.

The Khatami administration has also sought improved relations with Saudi Arabia's fellow members of the Co-operation Council for the Arab States of the Gulf (Gulf Co-operation Council—GCC, see p. 175), although a long-standing territorial dispute with the United Arab Emirates (UAE) remains to be resolved. In March 1992 Iran occupied those parts of the Abu Musa islands and the Greater and Lesser Tunbs that had remained under the control of the emirate of Sharjah since the original occupation in 1971. In December 1994 the UAE announced its intention to refer the dispute to the International Court of Justice in The Hague, Netherlands. In early 1995 Iran was reported to have deployed air defence systems on Abu Musa and the Greater and Lesser Tunbs, prompting the USA to warn of a potential threat to shipping. In November talks between Iran and the UAE aimed at facilitating ministerial-level negotiations on the disputed islands ended in failure. Relations deteriorated further in the first half of 1996, after Iran opened an airport on Abu Musa and a power station on Greater Tunb. In 1997 the UAE protested that Iran was repeatedly violating the emirates' territorial waters. Talks in March were inconclusive, and in June the UAE protested to Iran and the UN at Iran's construction of a pier on Greater Tunb. Following a meeting with the UAE's Minister of Foreign Affairs during the eighth conference of the Organization of the Islamic Conference (OIC, see p. 295), held in Tehran in December 1997, President Khatami emphasized his willingness to discuss bilateral issues directly with President Zayed bin Sultan an-Nayhan of the UAE. Although the latter was said to be cautious about Iran's attempts at *rapprochement*, in the following month UAE officials expressed willingness to enter into negotiations. None the less, both countries continued to assert their sovereignty over the three areas.

Iran hosts one of the largest refugee populations in the world. At the beginning of 2002, according to provisional data published by the office of the UN High Commissioner for Refugees (UNHCR), there were 2,558,305 refugees in the country, of whom 2,355,427 were from Afghanistan and 202,878 from Iraq. All of the refugees in Iran were reported to be receiving UNHCR assistance.

Victories achieved by the Sunni fundamentalist Taliban in the Afghan civil war in September 1996 prompted Iran, which supported the Government of President Burhanuddin Rabbani, to express fears for its national security, and to accuse the USA of interference in Afghanistan's internal affairs. In June 1997 the Taliban accused Iran of espionage and ordered the closure of the Iranian embassy in Kabul and the withdrawal of all Iranian diplomats. Iran retaliated by halting all trade across its land border with Afghanistan, prompting Taliban protests that the ban violated international law. In August 1998 10 Iranian diplomats and an Iranian journalist based in the city of Mazar-i-Sharif were reported to have been captured and killed by Taliban militia. By mid-September, as it emerged that nine of the missing Iranian nationals had been murdered by Taliban fighters as they stormed Mazar-i-Sharif, 500,000 Iranian troops had reportedly been placed on full military alert in readiness for open conflict with Afghanistan. In an attempt to defuse the crisis, in October the Taliban agreed to free all Iranian prisoners being held in Afghanistan and to punish those responsible for the killing of the nine Iranian diplomats. Following the terrorist attacks on the USA in September 2001, as the USA began preparations for military action against al-Qa'ida and its Taliban hosts, Iran closed its eastern border with Afghanistan and sent a large contingent of troops there in order to prevent a further influx of Afghan refugees. In the following month, however, when the US-led military action began, Iran reportedly agreed to the establishment of eight refugee camps within its borders to provide shelter for some 250,000 Afghan refugees. Although Iran refused to give military assistance to the US-led coalition, it actively supported the Western-backed opposition forces, collectively known as the United National Islamic Front for the Salvation of Afghanistan (the Northern Alliance), and welcomed their swift victory over the Taliban. In early 2002 the Iranian authorities and UNHCR were co-operating in establishing registration centres for refugees wishing to return to Afghanistan; exit points were to be constructed at three points along the Iran–Afghanistan border in preparation for the commencement of voluntary repatriations. A programme for voluntary returns under UNHCR auspices was inaugurated by the Iranian and Afghan authorities in early April, although UNHCR put the number of 'spontaneous' repatriations prior to that date at 57,000. Some 500,000 refugees were said to have returned from Iran to Afghanistan by the end of January 2003 and the remainder were expected to be repatriated by 2004. In mid-August 2002 President Khatami became the first Iranian Head of State to visit Afghanistan for 40 years. Meanwhile, it was reported in that month that Iran had, in June, extradited 16 Saudis believed to be al-Qa'ida militants who had fled the Afghan conflict. In early November, moreover, Iranian officials declared that the authorities had arrested and extradited some 250 people suspected of having links with al-Qa'ida (allegedly including a son of the group's leader, Osama bin Laden).

In September 1997 Iraq opened a border crossing with Iran, thereby permitting, for the first time since the outbreak of the Iran–Iraq War, Iranian pilgrims to visit Shi'ite Muslim shrines on its territory. At the end of the month, however, Iranian aircraft violated the air exclusion zone over southern Iraq in order to bomb two bases of the Mujahidin-e-Khalq in that country (prompting Iraqi aircraft also to enter the zone). Vice-President Taha Yassin Ramadan of Iraq, attending December's OIC conference in Tehran, was the most senior Iraqi official to visit Iran since 1979. President Khatami subsequently expressed the hope that problems between the two countries could be resolved 'through negotiation and understanding'. During a visit to Iran by Iraq's Minister of Foreign Affairs in January 1998, it was agreed to establish joint committees with the aim of expediting prisoner exchanges, facilitating pilgrimages for Iranians to traditional Shi'a shrines in Iraq, and addressing other contentious issues. Exchanges of prisoners of war and the remains of troops killed in the 1980–88 conflict were reported at intervals in 1998–2003, despite periodic mutual accusations of failure to comply with obligations in this respect. In August 1999, according to Iranian statistics, some 55,438 Iranian and 39,417 Iraqi detainees had been exchanged since 1981. In October 2000 Kharrazi became the first Iranian Minister of Foreign Affairs to visit Iraq for a decade, and the two countries agreed to reactivate a 1975 border and security agreement that had been in abeyance since 1980. In November 2000 a bilateral transport and communications accord was signed. However, there were unconfirmed reports in October that Iran's Supreme Council for National Security was to suspend all high-level contacts with the Iraqi Government, following a series of mortar attacks on targets in Tehran apparently perpetrated by the Mujahidin-e-Khalq. Tensions between the two sides increased in April 2001 when Iran launched a heavy missile attack against Iraqi military bases used by the organization, apparently in response to repeated attacks by that group on Iranian targets. By early 2002, however, a general thaw in bilateral relations was evident, despite a protest lodged with the UN by Iraq in June stating that Iran was continuing to violate agreements reached at the end of the Iran–Iraq war. It was reported in September that Iran had made preparations for the provision of humanitarian assistance to Iraqi refugees along their joint border in the event of a US-led military campaign to remove the regime of Saddam Hussain. Discussions held between the Iraqi Minister of Foreign Affairs, Naji Sabri, and Kharrazi in Tehran in early February 2003 resulted in demands by several Iranian deputies for the impeachment of Kharrazi; the deputies claimed that many issues of contention between the two sides remained unresolved.

Closer relations were developed with Turkey during the 1990s, despite periodic tensions arising particularly from Turkish allegations of Iranian support for the Kurdish separatist Kurdistan Workers' Party (Partiya Karkeren Kurdistan—PKK, now Congress for Freedom and Democracy in Kurdistan—KADEK) in its conflict with the armed forces in south-eastern Turkey (q.v.). In 1997 Iran was a founder member of the Istanbul-based Developing Eight (D-8, see p. 339) group of Islamic countries. Meanwhile, considerable political and economic advantage has been perceived arising from Iran's potential as a transit route for hydrocarbons from the former Soviet republics of Central Asia, and since the early 1990s Iran has sought to strengthen its position in Central Asia through bilateral economic, security and cultural agreements as well as institutions such as the Tehran-based Economic Co-operation Organization (see p. 192). Relations between Iran and Azerbaijan—already tense owing to disagreement over a contested section of the Caspian Basin—deteriorated in July 2001, when Iran ordered a gunship into the disputed waters in order to prevent foreign companies from undertaking oil exploration there. A summit meeting of the five littoral states (Iran, Russia, Azerbaijan, Kazakhstan and Turkmenistan) held in April 2002 failed to resolve the dispute regarding the legal status of the Caspian.

In March 2001 Russia pledged to assist Iran with the completion of the nuclear plant at Bushehr (see above), with the first reactor scheduled to open by 2004. In May 2001 Russia reportedly agreed to supply Iran with advanced ship-borne cruise missiles. The two countries signed a military co-operation pact in October, believed to amount to annual sales to Iran of Russian weapons worth some US $300m. In July 2002 Russia and Iran concluded a draft 10-year development and co-operation accord, which was reported to include the construction of a further three nuclear reactors at the Bushehr plant.

Government

Legislative power is vested in the Islamic Consultative Assembly (Majlis), with 290 members. The chief executive of the administration is the President. The Majlis and the President are both elected by universal adult suffrage for a term of four years. A 12-member Council of Guardians supervises elections and ensures that legislation is in accordance with the Constitution and with Islamic precepts. The Council to Determine the Expediency of the Islamic Order, created in February 1988 and formally incorporated into the Constitution in July 1989, rules on legal and theological disputes between the Majlis and the Council of Guardians. The executive, legislative and judicial wings of state power are subject to the authority of the Wali Faqih (supreme religious leader).

Iran is divided into 28 provinces, each with an appointed Governor.

Defence

In August 2002 Iran's regular armed forces totalled an estimated 520,000: army 325,000, Revolutionary Guard Corps (Pasdaran Inqilab) some 125,000, navy 18,000, air force around 52,000. There were some 350,000 army reserves. Paramilitary forces comprised an estimated 300,000 volunteers of the Basij and some 40,000 under the command of the Ministry of the

Interior. There is a 21-month period of compulsory military service. Defence expenditure for the Iranian year ending 20 March 2003 was budgeted at IR 32,700,000m.

Economic Affairs

In 2001, according to estimates by the World Bank, Iran's gross national income (GNI), measured at average 1999–2001 prices, was US $112,855m., equivalent to $1,750 per head (or $6,230 per head on an international purchasing-power parity basis). During 1990–2001, it was estimated, the population increased at an average annual rate of 1.6%, while gross domestic product (GDP) per head increased, in real terms, by an average of 2.6% per year. Overall GDP increased at an average annual rate of 4.2% in 1990–2001. Excluding adjustment for terms of trade, GDP increased by an estimated 5.2% in 2000/01 (Iranian year to March), and by some 5.0% in 2001/02.

Agriculture (including forestry and fishing) contributed an estimated 12.8% of GDP in 2000/01. About 23.5% of the employed labour force were engaged in agriculture at the time of the 1996 census. The principal cash crops are fresh and dried fruit and nuts, which accounted for some 12.8% of non-petroleum export earnings in 2000/01. The principal subsistence crops are wheat, barley, sugar beet and sugar cane. Imports of cereals comprised some 9.7% of the value of total imports in 2000/01. Agricultural GDP increased by an average of 2.8% per year between 1991/92 and 2000/01; the sector's GDP declined by an estimated 9.4% in 1999/2000 (owing to the effects of the worst drought for three decades), but increased by some 2.8% in 2000/01 and by about 4.7% in 2001/02.

Industry (including mining, manufacturing, construction and power) contributed an estimated 39.7% of GDP in 2000/01, and engaged 31.2% of the employed labour force at the 1996 census. During 1991/92–2000/01 industrial GDP increased by an average of 3.0% per year; growth was estimated at 5.2% in 1999/2000, and at 9.1% in 2000/01.

Mining (including petroleum refining) contributed an estimated 22.7% of GDP in 2000/01, although the sector engaged only 0.8% of the working population in 1996. Metal ores are the major non-hydrocarbon mineral exports, and coal, magnesite and gypsum are also mined. The sector is dominated by the hydrocarbons sector, which contributed an estimated 22.1% of GDP in 2000/01. At the end of 2001 Iran's proven reserves of petroleum were estimated at 89,700m. barrels, sufficient to maintain the 2001/02 level of production—averaging 3.44m. barrels per day (b/d)—for almost 65 years. However, since 1999 several important discoveries of petroleum have been made, leading to estimates that reserves might be closer to 130,000m. barrels. With effect from February 2003, Iran's production quota within the Organization of the Petroleum Exporting Countries (OPEC, see p. 298) was 3.59m. b/d. Iran's reserves of natural gas (23,000,000m. cu m at the end of 2001) are the second largest in the world, after those of Russia. The GDP of the mining sector increased by an average of 0.8% per year in 1991/92–2000/01; mining GDP was estimated to have declined by 3.8% in 1999/2000, but to have increased by 9.4% in 2000/01.

Manufacturing (excluding petroleum refining) contributed about 12.7% of GDP in 2000/01, and engaged 17.8% of the employed labour force in 1996. The most important sectors, in terms of value added, are textiles, food processing and transport equipment. The sector's GDP increased by an average of 5.0% per year in 1991/92–2000/2001, with growth estimated at 7.7% in 2000/01 and at 10.0% in 2001/02.

Principal sources of energy are natural gas (providing around 76.5% of total electricity production in 1999) and petroleum (some 19.0% in the same year). Imports of mineral fuels and lubricants comprised just 2.4% of the value of total imports in 2000/01. The first phase of Iran's South Pars offshore gasfield (an extension of Qatar's North Field) was brought on stream in January 2003.

The services sector contributed an estimated 47.6% of GDP in 2000/01, and engaged 45.3% of the employed labour force in 1996. During 1991/92–2000/01 the GDP of the services sector increased by an average of 4.3% per year; the sector's GDP increased by an estimated 4.7% in 2000/01, and by some 4.6% in 2001/02.

According to provisional figures, in the year ending March 2002 Iran recorded a visible trade surplus of US $5,578m., and there was a surplus of $5,256m. on the current account of the balance of payments. In 2000/01 the principal source of imports was Germany (which supplied 10.5% of total imports); other major suppliers included the United Arab Emirates (UAE), Russia and Italy. The principal markets for exports in 1999/2000 were Japan and the United Kingdom (which took, respectively, 16.5% and 15.4% of total exports); the UAE, Italy and the Republic of Korea were also important markets for Iranian exports. Other than petroleum and natural gas, Iran's principal exports in 2000/01 were carpets, pistachios and other nuts and fruits, and iron and steel. Exports of petroleum and gas comprised 87.4% of the value of total exports in 2000/01. The principal imports in that year were machinery and transport equipment, basic manufactures, chemicals, and food and live animals.

For the financial year ending 20 March 2000 Iran recorded a budget surplus estimated at IR 4,301,000m., equivalent to 1.0% of GDP. Iran's total external debt was US $7,953m. at the end of 2000, of which $3,812m. was long-term public debt. In that year the cost of debt-servicing was equivalent to 11.4% of the value of exports of goods and services. The annual rate of inflation averaged 24.0% in 1990/91–2000/01. Consumer prices increased by an average of 12.6% in 2000/01 and by 11.4% in 2001/02. Some 16% of the total labour force were estimated to be unemployed in 2001/02.

Iran is a member of OPEC, of the Economic Co-operation Organization (ECO, see p. 192), of the Developing Eight (D-8, see p. 339) group of Islamic countries, and was admitted to the Group of 15 developing countries (G-15) in mid-2000.

Notable weaknesses in the Iranian economy include the Government's dependence on revenue from the petroleum sector, high rates of unemployment and inflation, and disparities in the distribution of income. Additional strain has, moreover, been placed on domestic resources by the presence in Iran of some 2.5m. refugees from Afghanistan and Iraq. A major emphasis of the Third Five Year Development Plan (TFYDP), which took effect in March 2000, was to be the reduction of Iran's dependence on the oil sector as the principal generator of wealth. President Khatami advocated as fundamental to the Plan the restructuring of the state portfolio and the elimination of monopolies, together with wide-ranging tax reforms. A priority was to be job-creation, with a target of some 765,000 new posts annually. Growth under the plan was forecast at some 6% annually, and major new oil and gas discoveries from 1999 enhanced confidence that the Plan's ambitious objectives might be realized. Moreover, the installation in mid-2000 of a new Majlis with a 'reformist' majority was expected to expedite Khatami's economic liberalization measures, although despite being elected to a second presidential term in June 2001, Khatami continued to encounter strong opposition to reform from 'conservatives' within the Islamic regime. Despite strong growth in 2000/01, largely reflecting the high level of petroleum export earnings (following the recovery in international oil prices from mid-1999), and while inflation and unemployment were reported to be at their lowest levels for some years, the implementation of vital structural reforms proceeded slowly. The TFYDP allowed for the private ownership of banks for the first time since the Revolution; by early 2003 three private banks had been authorized to commence operations and the Government declared its intention to privatize all banks except Bank Melli Iran. Meanwhile, in late 2002 the granting of licences to private insurance firms was announced, leading to the creation of Iran's first such company in February 2003. In addition, a return to international capital markets was achieved, with two Eurobond issues totalling €1,000m. being issued during 2002, while the introduction of a unified exchange rate for the rial in March of that year was expected to ease inflationary pressures. Meanwhile, a stabilization fund was established in March 2000, into which were paid petroleum revenues exceeding budgeted income; one-half of its value was to be reserved for use in the event of a future decline in international oil prices below budgeted levels, while the remainder was intended for private sector development and export promotion. In spite of ongoing efforts by the USA to deter foreign investment in the Iranian economy (see Recent History), high petroleum prices have resulted in enhanced foreign interest in important new petroleum and natural gas schemes, and the Khatami administration's economic programme was further strengthened in May 2000 by a decision by the World Bank (also despite US objections) to resume lending for the first time since 1994. Iran received a further World Bank loan in December 2002. A new foreign

investment law passed by the Expediency Council in May 2002 resulted in government approval for the first foreign take-over of an Iranian company. Assisted by buoyant oil revenues, real GDP showed sustained growth in 2001/02, and the Government forecast steady economic growth for 2002/03. The draft budget for 2003/04, announced in December 2002, anticipated increased spending on defence and infrastructural investment, as well as a further injection of funds into job creation schemes. World petroleum prices were extremely high in early 2003, amid considerable political and economic uncertainty brought about by the crisis in Iraq (see Recent History). Although vital economic reforms have taken place under President Khatami, Iran remains heavily dependent on revenue from the oil sector, and there is a need to accelerate the privatization of state-owned enterprises and to attract higher levels of foreign investment in order to provide employment for a rapidly expanding population.

Education

Primary education is officially compulsory, and is provided free of charge, for five years between six and 10 years of age, although this has not been fully implemented in rural areas. Secondary education, from the age of 11, lasts for up to seven years, comprising a first cycle of three years and a second of four years. In 1996 the total enrolment at primary and secondary schools was equivalent to 86% of the school-age population (90% of boys; 83% of girls). In 1996 primary enrolment included 90% of children in the relevant age-group (91% of boys; 88% of girls), while enrolment at secondary schools was equivalent to 59% of the appropriate age-group. There are 37 universities, including 16 in Tehran. According to official sources, there were some 759,870 students enrolled at Iran's public colleges and universities in 2001/02, in addition to the 806,639 students enrolled at the Islamic Azad University. Budgetary expenditure on education by the central Government in the financial year 2000/01 was IR 24,031,000m. (18.8% of total spending).

Public Holidays

The Iranian year 1382 runs from 21 March 2003 to 19 March 2004, and the year 1383 from 20 March 2004 to 19 March 2005.
2003: 3 January*† (Martyrdom of Imam Sadeq), 19 January* (Birth of Imam Reza), 11 February (Victory of the Islamic Revolution), 12 February* (Qorban, Feast of the Sacrifice), 20 February* (Qadir-e-Khom), 13 March* (Tasooay-e-Hosseini), 14 March* (Ashooray-e-Hosseini), 20 March (Day of Oil Industry Nationalization), 21–25 March‡ (Nowrooz, Iranian New Year), 1 April (Islamic Republic Day), 2 April (Sizdah-bedar, 13th and final day of Nowrooz celebrations), 12 April* (Qiyam-e-Khoonin), 22 April* (Arbain-e-Hosseini), 30 April* (Flight of Prophet Muhammad), 14 May* (Birth of Prophet Muhammad), 19 May* (Birth of Imam Ali), 4 June (Death of Imam Khomeini), 10 September* (Mabas), 24 September* (Birth of Imam Mahdi), 17 November* (Martyrdom of Imam Ali), 26 November* (Fetr, end of Ramadan), 24 December*† (Martyrdom of Imam Sadeq).

2004: 7 January* (Birth of Imam Reza), 2 February* (Qorban, Feast of the Sacrifice), 8 February* (Qadir-e-Khom), 11 February (Victory of the Islamic Revolution), 1 March* (Tasooay-e-Hosseini), 2 March* (Ashooray-e-Hosseini), 20 March (Day of Oil Industry Nationalization), 20–24 March‡ (Nowrooz, Iranian New Year), 31 March* (Qiyam-e-Khoonin), 1 April (Islamic Republic Day), 2 April (Sizdah-bedar, 13th and final day of Nowrooz celebrations), 10 April* (Arbain-e-Hosseini), 18 April* (Flight of Prophet Muhammad), 2 May* (Birth of Prophet Muhammad), 7 May* (Birth of Imam Ali), 4 June (Death of Imam Khomeini), 29 August* (Mabas), 12 September* (Birth of Imam Mahdi), 5 November* (Martyrdom of Imam Ali), 14 November* (Fetr, end of Ramadan), 12 December* (Martyrdom of Imam Sadeq).

* These holidays are dependent on the Islamic lunar calendar and may vary by one or two days from the dates given.
† This festival will occur twice within the same Gregorian year.
‡ This festival begins on the date of the Spring Equinox.

Weights and Measures

The metric system is in force, but some traditional units are still in general use.

Statistical Survey

The Iranian year runs from 21 March to 20 March

Source (except where otherwise stated): Statistical Centre of Iran, POB 14155-6133, Dr Fatemi Ave, Tehran 14144; tel. (21) 8965061; fax (21) 8963451; e-mail sci@sci.or.ir; internet www.sci.or.ir ; Bank Markazi Jomhouri Islami Iran (Central Bank), POB 15875-7177, 144 Mirdamad Blvd, Tehran; tel. (21) 3110231; fax (21) 3115674; e-mail g.secdept@cbi.ir; internet www.cbi.ir.

Area and Population

AREA, POPULATION AND DENSITY

Area (sq km)	1,648,043*
Population (census results)†	
1 October 1991	55,837,163
25 October 1996	
Males	30,515,159
Females.	29,540,329
Total	60,055,488
Population (official estimate at mid-year)	
2000	63,663,942
2001	64,528,162
2002	65,540,224
Density (per sq km) at mid-2002	39.8

* 636,313 sq miles.

† Excluding adjustment for underenumeration.

PROVINCES
(mid-2002)*

Province (Ostan)	Area (sq km)†	Population (estimates)	Density (per sq km)	Provincial capital
Tehran (Teheran) . .	19,196	11,689,301	608.9	Tehran (Teheran)
Markazi (Central). .	29,406	1,300,778	44.2	Arak
Gilan	13,952	2,310,033	165.6	Rasht
Mazandaran . . .	23,833	2,742,885	115.1	Sari
Azarbayejan-e-Sharqi (East Azerbaijan) .	45,481	3,378,242	74.3	Tabriz
Azarbayejan-e-Gharbi (West Azerbaijan) .	37,463	2,774,804	74.1	Orumiyeh
Bakhtaran (Kermanshah) . .	24,641	1,962,176	79.6	Bakhtaran
Khuzestan . . .	63,213	4,506,816	71.3	Ahvaz
Fars.	121,825	4,135,251	33.9	Shiraz
Kerman . . .	181,714	2,215,376	12.2	Kerman
Khorasan . . .	302,966	6,094,888	20.1	Mashhad
Esfahan . . .	107,027	4,316,767	40.3	Esfahan
Sistan and Baluchestan. .	178,431	2,086,170	11.7	Zahedan
Kordestan (Kurdistan) . .	28,817	1,492,007	51.8	Sanandaj
Hamadan . . .	19,547	1,718,627	87.9	Hamadan
Chaharmahal and Bakhtiyari . .	16,201	794,077	49.0	Shahr-e-Kord
Lorestan . . .	28,392	1,671,706	58.9	Khorramabad
Ilam.	20,150	550,971	27.3	Ilam
Kohgiluyeh and Boyerahmad .	15,563	627,517	40.3	Yasuj
Bushehr . . .	23,168	796,639	34.4	Bushehr
Zanjan	21,841	936,985	42.9	Zanjan
Semnan . . .	96,816	563,959	5.8	Semnan
Yazd	73,467	841,370	11.5	Yazd
Hormozgan . .	71,193	1,235,816	17.4	Bandar Abbas
Ardebil. . . .	17,881	1,204,410	67.4	Ardebil
Qom.	11,237	971,280	86.4	Qom
Qazvin . . .	15,491	1,066,317	68.8	Qazvin
Golestan . . .	20,893	1,555,058	74.4	Gorgan
Total	1,629,807	65,540,224	40.2	—

* On 1 January 1997 the legislature approved a law creating a new province, Qazvin (with its capital in the city of Qazvin), by dividing the existing province of Zanjan. In June 1997 the Council of Ministers approved draft legislation to establish another new province, Golestan (with its capital in the city of Gorgan), by dividing the existing province of Mazandaran.

† Excluding inland water (totalling 18,236 sq km).

PRINCIPAL TOWNS
(population at 1996 census)

Tehran (Teheran the capital) . .	6,758,845		Rasht	417,748
Mashad (Meshed) .	1,887,405		Hamadan	401,281
Esfahan (Isfahan) .	1,266,072		Kerman	384,991
Tabriz	1,191,043		Arak	380,755
Shiraz	1,053,025		Ardabil (Ardebil). .	340,386
Karaj	940,968*		Yazd	326,776
Ahwaz	804,980		Qazvin.	291,117
Qom	777,677		Zanjan.	286,295
Bakhtaran			Sanandaj	277,808
(Kermanshah) . .	692,986		Bandar-e-Abbas . .	273,578
Orumiyeh	435,200		Khorramabad . . .	272,815
Zahedan	419,518		Eslamshahr (Islam Shahr) . .	265,450

* Including towns of Rajayishahr and Mehrshahr. Estimated population of Mehrshahr at 1 October 1994 was 413,299 (Source: UN, *Demographic Yearbook*).

Mid-2000 (UN estimate, incl. suburbs): Mashhad 1,990,000; Esfahan 1,381,000; Tabriz 1,274,000; Shiraz 1,124,000; Karaj 1,044,000; Qom 888,000; Ahvaz 871,000.

Mid-2001 (UN estimate, incl. suburbs): Tehran 7,038,000.

Source: UN, *World Urbanization Prospects: The 2001 Revision.*

BIRTHS AND DEATHS
(UN estimates, annual averages)

	1985–90	1990–95	1995–2000
Birth rate (per 1,000)	40.1	31.4	23.5
Death rate (per 1,000)	8.2	6.4	5.3

Source: UN, *World Population Prospects: The 2000 Revision.*

Expectation of life (WHO estimates, years at birth): 68.6 (males 66.4; females 71.1) in 2001 (Source: WHO, *World Health Report*).

1999 (incomplete registration): Registered live births 1,177,557 (birth rate 18.8 per 1,000); Registered deaths 374,838 (death rate 6.0 per 1,000) (Source: UN, *Population and Vital Statistics Report*).

Marriages: 611,073 in 1999; 646,498 in 2000; 640,710 in 2001.

ECONOMICALLY ACTIVE POPULATION
(persons aged 6 years and over, 1996 census)

	Males	Females	Total
Agriculture, hunting and forestry .	3,024,380	294,156	3,318,536
Fishing	38,418	309	38,727
Mining and quarrying . . .	115,185	4,699	119,884
Manufacturing	1,968,806	583,156	2,551,962
Electricity, gas and water supply .	145,239	5,392	150,631
Construction	1,634,682	15,799	1,650,481
Wholesale and retail trade; repair of motor vehicles, motorcycles and personal and household goods	1,804,143	38,146	1,842,289
Hotels and restaurants	82,293	2,485	84,778
Transport, storage and communications	955,271	17,541	972,792
Financial intermediation . . .	139,286	13,586	152,872
Real estate, renting and business activities	137,039	12,051	149,090
Public administration and defence; compulsory social security . .	1,519,449	98,651	1,618,100
Education	581,597	459,459	1,041,056
Health and social work	184,242	118,897	303,139
Other community, social and personal service activities . .	183,246	41,159	224,405
Private households with employed persons	57,037	4,933	61,970
Extra-territorial organizations and bodies	660	220	880
Central departments and offices .	30,389	2,563	32,952
Activities not adequately defined .	204,808	52,220	257,028
Total employed	12,806,170	1,765,402	14,571,572

Unemployed ('000 persons, 1996 census): 1,455 (males 1,183; females 272).

1997/98 ('000 persons): Total employed 14,803; Unemployed 2,037; Total labour force 16,840.

1998/99 ('000 persons): Total employed 14,897; Unemployed 2,415; Total labour force 17,312.

Health and Welfare

KEY INDICATORS

Total fertility rate (children per woman, 2001)	2.9
Under-5 mortality rate (per 1,000 live births, 2001) . . .	42
HIV/AIDS (% of persons aged 15–49, 2001)	<0.10
Physicians (per 1,000 head, 1996)	0.85
Hospital beds (per 1,000 head, 1996)	1.6
Health expenditure (2000): US $ per head (PPP)	258
Health expenditure (2000): % of GDP	5.5
Health expenditure (2000): public (% of total)	46.3
Access to water (% of persons, 2000)	95
Access to sanitation (% of persons, 2000)	81
Human Development Index (2000): ranking	98
Human Development Index (2000): value	0.721

For sources and definitions, see explanatory note on p. vi.

Agriculture

PRINCIPAL CROPS
('000 metric tons)

	1999	2000	2001
Wheat	8,673.2	8,087.8	9,458.6
Rice (paddy)	2,348.2	1,971.5	1,990.2
Barley	1,999.0	1,686.0	2,423.1
Maize	1,155.7	1,119.7	1,064.2
Potatoes	3,433.1	3,658.0	3,485.8
Sugar cane	2,235.9	2,367.0	3,195.4
Sugar beet	5,548.3	4,332.2	4,649.0
Dry beans	182.7	180.9	144.0
Chick-peas	164.6	242.4	268.8
Lentils	62.7	78.3	104.4
Almonds	95.9	89.6	97.1
Walnuts	142.9	140.6	168.0
Pistachios	131.2	304.0	112.4
Soybeans (Soya beans) . . .	80.4	94.4*	104.9*
Cottonseed*	265	290	262
Cabbages†	200	220	260
Lettuce†	40	80	90
Tomatoes	3,490.5	3,191.0	3,009.5
Pumpkins, squash and gourds . .	717	524	500†
Cucumbers and gherkins . .	1,367.4	1,342.0	1,300.0†
Aubergines (Eggplants)† . . .	160	130	100
Chillies and green peppers† . .	80	90	100
Dry onions	1,676.9	1,343.6	1,419.3
Garlic†	50	50	70
Other vegetables	1,696*	1,884*	1,850†
Oranges	1,866.2	1,843.6	1,878.5
Tangerines, mandarins, clementines and satsumas . .	760.5	676.5	710.0
Lemons and limes	972.0	1,032.5	1,038.8
Other citrus fruits	160.6*	118.1*	142.6†
Apples	2,137.0	2,141.7	2,353.4
Pears	161.9	185.9	190.8
Apricots	240.7	262.4	282.9
Cherries (incl. sour)	270.1	265.2	269.1
Peaches and nectarines . . .	317.5	280.0†	270.0†
Plums	133.3	142.6	143.1
Grapes	2,342.1	2,405.2	2,516.7
Watermelons	2,178.7	1,650.0	1,815.7
Cantaloupes and other melons . .	1,054.7	994.0	1,000.0†
Figs	70.1	78.2	71.2
Dates	908.3	869.6	875.0
Cotton (lint)*	145	160	125
Tea (made)*	80.0	66.8	68.5

* Unofficial figure(s).
† FAO estimate(s).

Source: FAO.

LIVESTOCK
('000 head, year ending September)

	1999	2000	2001
Horses*	120	150	150
Mules	173†	175*	175*
Asses	1,554†	1,600*	1,600*
Cattle	8,047	8,270	8,500
Buffaloes	474	491	507
Camels	143	144	146
Sheep	53,900	53,900	53,900
Goats	25,757	25,757	25,757
Chickens (million)*	220	250	260

* FAO estimate(s).
† Unofficial figure.

Source: FAO.

LIVESTOCK PRODUCTS

('000 metric tons)

	1999	2000	2001
Beef and veal	286.0	268.8	274.1
Buffalo meat*	10.7	11.1	11.4
Mutton and lamb	293.0	326.2	332.6
Goat meat	104.0	103.0*	101.5*
Chicken meat	725.0	803.0	792.4
Turkey meat*	15	15	15
Other meat*	10.5	10.4	10.4
Cows' milk	4,403.0	4,760.0	4,865.9
Buffaloes' milk	214.0	216.2	221.0
Sheep's milk	549.0	288.8	295.2
Goats' milk	354.2	358.0	365.9
Cheese*	207.6	218.5	222.7
Butter and ghee*	139.4	140.1	143.2
Hen eggs	570.0	579.0	580.7
Honey	24.5	25.3	26.6
Wool (greasy)	73.9	75.0*	75.0*
Cattle hides*	41.0	38.7	39.4
Sheepskins*	54.9	61.2	62.4
Goatskins*	18.6	18.4	18.1

* FAO estimate(s).

Source: FAO.

Forestry

ROUNDWOOD REMOVALS

('000 cubic metres, excl. bark)

	1999	2000	2001
Sawlogs, veneer logs and logs for sleepers	310	319	319*
Pulpwood	394	488	488*
Other industrial wood . . .	256	253	253*
Fuel wood	189	54	264*
Total	1,149	1,114	1,324

* FAO estimate.

Source: FAO.

SAWNWOOD PRODUCTION

('000 cubic metres, incl. railway sleepers)

	1998	1999	2000
Total (all broadleaved)	129	96	106

2001: Production as in 2000 (FAO estimate).

Source: FAO.

Fishing

('000 metric tons, live weight)

	1998	1999	2000
Capture	367.2	387.2	411.5
Silver carp	11.6	14.4	25.8
Other cyprinids	19.6	10.8	17.0
Caspian shads	85.0	95.0	78.0
Clupeoids	9.7	13.0	15.0
Skipjack tuna	6.7	16.6	20.1
Longtail tuna	19.7	23.5	41.4
Yellowfin tuna	21.5	26.9	15.7
Aquaculture	33.2	31.8	40.6
Silver carp	16.4	13.8	17.0
Total catch	400.4	419.0	452.1

Source: FAO, *Yearbook of Fishery Statistics*.

Production of caviar (metric tons, year ending 20 March): 281 in 1988/89; 310 in 1989/90; 233 in 1990/91.

Mining

CRUDE PETROLEUM

('000 barrels per day, year ending 20 March)

	1999/2000	2000/01	2001/02
Total production	3,373	3,661	3,441

NATURAL GAS

(million cu metres, year ending 20 March)*

	1999/2000	2000/01	2001/02†
Consumption (domestic)‡ . . .	58,700	62,800	67,200
Flared	13,500	13,800	13,300
Regional uses and wastes . . .	7,800	6,600	5,500
Total production	80,000	83,200	86,500

* Excluding gas injected into oil wells.

† Estimates.

‡ Includes gas for household, commercial, industrial, generator and refinery consumption.

Source: IMF, *Islamic Republic of Iran: Statistical Appendix* (September 2002).

OTHER MINERALS

('000 metric tons, unless otherwise indicated, year ending 20 March)

	1998/99	1999/2000	2000/01*
Iron ore: gross weight . . .	10,536	10,776	11,000
Iron ore: metal content*	5,200	5,300	5,400
Copper concentrates† . . .	128	131	120
Bauxite	336	912	400
Lead concentrates†	11	11*	15
Zinc concentrates* †	80	80	85
Manganese ore‡	101.4	104.1	105.0
Chromium concentrates§ . . .	313.9	311.2	310.0
Molybdenum concentrates (metric tons)* †	1,400	1,600	1,600
Silver (metric tons)†	19	21	22
Gold (kilograms)†	856	930	950
Bentonite	83.3	65.0	70.0
Kaolin	582.5	837.3	800.0
Other clays*	450	400	450
Magnesite	109.6	141.1	141.0
Fluorspar (Fluorite)	25.9	18.4	20.0
Feldspar	185.7	239.8	240.0
Barite (Barytes)	187.7	183.9	185.0
Salt (unrefined)	1,912	1,600	1,600
Gypsum (crude)	11,843	10,834	11,000
Pumice and related materials* . .	150	150	150
Mica (metric tons)	1,084	1,425	2,000
Talc	27	25*	25
Turquoise (kilograms) . . .	6,000	20,000*	20,000

* Estimated production.

† Figures refer to the metal content of ores and concentrates.

‡ Figures refer to gross weight. The estimated metal content (in '000 metric tons) was: 30.5 in 1998/99; 32.0 in 1999/2000; 32.0 in 2000/01.

§ Figures refer to gross weight. The estimated chromic oxide content (in '000 metric tons) was: 138 in 1998/99; 137 in 1999/2000; 137 in 2000/01.

Source: US Geological Survey.

Hard coal (provisional figure, '000 metric tons, year ending 20 March): 1,169 in 1998/99 (Source: UN, *Industrial Commodity Statistics Yearbook*).

Industry

PETROLEUM PRODUCTS
('000 metric tons, year ending 20 March)

	1996/97	1997/98	1998/99
Liquefied petroleum gas* . . .	3,750	3,730	3,920
Naphtha	692	679	1,871*
Motor spirit (petrol)	7,643	7,893	9,025*
Aviation gasoline	78	99	96*
Kerosene*	4,655	4,700	4,750
White spirit*	300	320	320
Jet fuel*	1,300	1,325	1,350
Gas-diesel (distillate fuel) oil . .	15,500	16,000	16,850
Residual fuel oils*	18,500	19,000	19,500
Lubricating oils*	650	675	695
Petroleum bitumen (asphalt)* . .	2,806	2,839	2,841

* Provisional or estimated figure(s).

Source: UN, *Industrial Commodity Statistics Yearbook.*

OTHER PRODUCTS
(year ending 20 March)

	1996/97	1997/98	1998/99
Refined sugar ('000 metric tons)* .	832	1,055	1,050
Cigarettes (million)*	11,860	10,304	14,335
Paints ('000 metric tons)* . . .	33	39	41
Cement ('000 metric tons)† . .	17,703	18,349	20,049
Refrigerators ('000)*	756	702	1,104
Telephone sets ('000)* . . .	224	248	318
Radios and recorders ('000) . .	56	76	127
Television receivers ('000)* . . .	453	751	769
Footwear (million pairs)* . . .	28.3	27.3	22.4
Carpets and rugs ('000 sq m)* . .	59,487	84,457	85,163

* Figures refer to production in manufacturing establishments with 10 workers or more.

† Figures refer to production in large-scale manufacturing establishments with 50 workers or more.

Source: UN, *Industrial Commodity Statistics Yearbook.*

Production of Electricity (million kWh, year ending 20 March): *Ministry of Energy*: 85,825 in 1996/97; 92,310 in 1997/98; 97,863 in 1998/99; 107,207 in 1999/2000; 115,156 in 2000/01; 124,275 in 2001/02. *Private Sector*: 5,026 in 1996/97; 5,434 in 1997/98; 5,550 in 1998/99; 5,389 in 1999/2000; 5,624 in 2000/01.

Finance

CURRENCY AND EXCHANGE RATES

Monetary Units
100 dinars = 1 Iranian rial (IR)

Sterling, Dollar and Euro Equivalents (31 December 2002)
£1 sterling = 12,817.0 rials
US $1 = 7,952.0 rials
€1 = 8,339.2 rials
100,000 Iranian rials = £7.802 = $12.576 = €11.992

Average Exchange Rate (rials per US $)
2000   1,764.43
2001   1,753.56
2002   6,906.96

Note: In March 1993 the former multiple exchange rate system was unified, and since then the exchange rate of the rial has been market-determined. The foregoing information on average exchange rates refers to the base rate, applicable to receipts from exports of petroleum and gas, payments for imports of essential goods and services, debt-servicing costs and imports related to large national projects. There was also an export rate, set at a mid-point of US $1 = 3,007.5 rials in May 1995, which applied to receipts from non-petroleum exports and to all other official current account transactions not effected at the base rate. In addition, a market rate was determined by transactions on the Tehran Stock Exchange: at 31 January 2002 it was US $1 = 7,924 rials. The weighted average of all exchange rates (rials per US $, year ending 20 December) was: 3,206 in 1997/98; 4,172 in 1998/99; 5,731 in 1999/2000. A new unified exchange rate, based on the market rate, took effect from 21 March 2002.

BUDGET
('000 million rials, year ending 20 March)*

Revenue	1999/2000	2000/01	2001/02†
Oil and gas revenues	44,487	59,448	68,653
Non-oil revenues	59,404	61,673	88,833
Taxation	38,757	33,298	45,389
Income and wealth taxes . .	15,432	18,129	25,416
Corporate taxes . . .	10,049	11,295	15,766
Public corporations . .	4,944	4,899	7,266
Private corporations . .	5,105	6,396	8,500
Taxes on wages and salaries	2,469	3,413	5,000
Taxes on other income . .	2,914	3,421	4,650
Import taxes	5,806	7,948	11,276
Customs duties	3,046	4,158	7,150
Order registration fees . .	2,532	3,480	3,700
Taxes on consumpton and sales	16,367	5,765	5,899
Non-tax revenues	9,072	11,895	20,727
Services and sales of goods .	4,982	6,615	9,270
Other revenues‡	4,090	5,279	11,457
Special revenues	11,575	16,481	22,717
Total	**103,891**	**121,122**	**157,486**

Expenditure§	1998/99	1999/2000	2000/2001†
General services	6,469	8,457	12,047
National defence	8,144	9,472	17,390
Social services	31,150	37,558	45,733
Education	16,344	19,656	24,031
Health and nutrition . . .	3,694	4,007	5,004
Social security and welfare . .	6,686	8,464	10,195
Other social services . . .	4,426	5,431	6,503
Economic services	13,921	20,359	14,210
Agriculture	1,592	2,104	2,515
Water resources	1,444	2,407	3,914
Petroleum, fuel and power . .	6,803	10,470	707
Transport and communication .	3,157	4,300	4,601
Other economic services . .	927	1,078	2,473
Other expenditure‡	11,259	17,084	21,856
Sub-total	**70,943**	**92,929**	**111,236**
Current	53,518	67,987	84,866
Capital	17,425	24,942	26,370
Foreign exchange obligations . .	5,077	1,993	—
Special expenditures	8,931	11,575	16,481
Total	**84,951**	**106,497**	**127,717**

2001/02 (approved budget, '000 million rials): Total expenditure and net lending 141,155 (current expenditure 104,538).

* Figures refer to the consolidated accounts of the central Government, comprising the General Budget, the operations of the Social Security Organization and special (extrabudgetary) revenue and expenditure.
† Forecasts.
‡ Including operations of the Organization for Protection of Consumers and Producers, a central government unit with its own budget.
§ Excluding lending minus repayments ('000 million rials): −187 in 1998/99.

INTERNATIONAL RESERVES
(US $ million at 31 December)*

	1993	1994	1995
Gold (national valuation) . . .	229.1	242.2	251.9
IMF special drawing rights . .	144.0	142.9	133.6
Total	**373.1**	**385.1**	**385.5**

* Excluding reserves of foreign exchange, for which no figures are available since 1982 (when the value of reserves was US $5,287m.).

IMF special drawing rights (US $ million at 31 December): 344.8 in 1996; 330.1 in 1997; 1.6 in 1998; 139.0 in 1999; 348.5 in 2000; 336.1 in 2001; 364.3 in 2002.

Source: IMF, *International Financial Statistics.*

MONEY SUPPLY
('000 million rials at 20 December)

	2000	2001	2002
Currency outside banks . . .	20,020	21,840	25,945
Non-financial public enterprises' deposits at Central Bank . . .	7,859	4,552	5,401
Demand deposits at commercial banks	74,291	99,275	123,963
Total money	102,170	125,667	155,309

Source: IMF, *International Financial Statistics.*

COST OF LIVING
(Consumer Price Index in urban areas, year ending 20 March; base: 1997/98 = 100)

	1999/2000	2000/01	2001/02
Food, beverages and tobacco . .	152.7	166.3	178.5
Clothing	112.1	121.8	127.4
Housing, fuel and light	143.4	169.8	201.8
All items (incl. others)	141.8	159.7	177.9

NATIONAL ACCOUNTS
('000 million rials at current prices, year ending 20 March)

National Income and Product

	1998/99	1999/2000*	2000/01*
Domestic factor incomes† . . .	236,575.5	330,803.5	463,081.5
Consumption of fixed capital . .	80,070.7	94,083.1	116,193.0
Gross domestic product (GDP) at factor cost . . .	316,646.2	424,886.6	579,274.5
Indirect taxes . . . . . . } *Less* Subsidies . . . . . . }	438.1	1,480.8	2,775.8
GDP in purchasers' values . .	317,084.3	426,367.4	582,050.3
Factor income from abroad . } *Less* Factor income paid abroad . }	580.7	56.4	-2,764.9
Gross national product (GNP)	317,665.0	426,423.8	579,285.4
Less Consumption of fixed capital	80,070.7	94,083.1	116,193.0
National income in market prices	237,594.3	332,340.7	463,092.4

* Provisional figures.

† Compensation of employees and the operating surplus of enterprises.

Expenditure on the Gross Domestic Product

	1998/99	1999/2000	2000/01*
Government final consumption expenditure	50,460.6	65,412.4	83,795.0
Private final consumption expenditure	180,345.1	225,100.0	263,936.4
Increase in stocks	1,894.7	-10,299.9	-17,268.3
Gross fixed capital formation . .	96,298.5	121,287.0	157,555.6
Statistical discrepancy	-6,225.0	—	—
Total domestic expenditure . .	322,773.9	401,499.5	488,018.7
Exports of goods and services .	44,884.7	89,193.8	188,897.1
Less Imports of goods and services	50,574.3	64,326.0	94,865.5
GDP in purchasers' values . .	317,084.3	426,367.3	582,050.3
GDP at constant 1990/91 prices†	45,222.7	48,483.0	52,875.6

* Provisional figures.

† Including adjustment for changes in terms of trade ('000 million rials): -2,407.6 in 1998/99; -601.8 in 1999/2000; 811.3 in 2000/01.

Gross Domestic Product by Economic Activity

	1998/99	1999/2000*	2000/01*
Agriculture, hunting, forestry and fishing	52,501.4	60,407.2	74,725.5
Mining and quarrying†	1,914.0	2,577.4	3,412.4
Manufacturing†	72,532.6	122,049.0	204,003.5
Electricity, gas and water . . .	3,509.8	4,250.9	4,969.2
Construction	12,262.7	16,815.0	20,009.9
Trade, restaurants and hotels . .	55,041.8	67,939.3	83,916.1
Transport, storage and communications	25,033.4	29,768.8	36,249.0
Financial and monetary institutions	4,790.6	7,027.7	10,206.9
Real estate, specialized and professional services	44,881.6	55,928.2	68,321.5
Government services	39,876.3	51,588.7	66,045.6
Other services	8,407.8	11,751.6	13,784.7
Sub-total	320,752.0	430,103.8	585,644.3
Less Imputed bank service charge .	4,105.6	5,217.2	6,370.2
GDP at basic prices	316,646.4	424,886.6	579,274.5
Indirect taxes (net)	438.1	1,480.8	2,775.8
GDP in purchasers' values . .	317,084.5	426,367.4	582,050.3

* Provisional figures.

† Refining of petroleum is included in mining and excluded from manufacturing.

BALANCE OF PAYMENTS
(US $ million, year ending 20 March)

	1999/2000	2000/01*	2001/02*
Exports of goods f.o.b. . . .	21,030	28,461	23,716
Petroleum and gas.	17,089	24,280	19,339
Non-petroleum and gas exports .	3,941	4,181	4,377
Imports of goods f.o.b.	-13,433	-15,086	-18,136
Trade balance	7,597	13,375	5,578
Exports of services	1,215	1,201	1,848
Imports of services	-2,456	-2,397	-3,217
Balance on goods and services	6,356	12,179	4,209
Other income received	181	215	456
Other income paid	-473	-370	-231
Balance on goods, services and income	6,064	12,024	4,434
Unrequited transfers (net) . . .	525	610	822
Current balance	6,589	12,634	5,256
Long-term capital (net)	-3,342	-3,218	1,623
Short-term capital (net)	-2,552	-1,355	-2,754
Net errors and omissions . . .	1,150	-1,532	816
Overall balance	1,845	6,529	4,941

* Provisional figures.

External Trade

PRINCIPAL COMMODITIES
(US $ million, year ending 20 March)

Imports c.i.f. (distribution by SITC)*	1998/99	1999/2000	2000/01
Food and live animals	1,583	1,953	1,977
Cereals and cereal preparations	878	1,319	1,390
Crude materials (inedible) except fuels	596	648	707
Animal and vegetable oils and fats	654	516	417
Vegetable oils and fats	633	499	408
Chemicals	1,774	1,894	2,027
Chemical elements and compounds	458	470	460
Plastic, cellulose and artificial resins	413	391	428
Basic manufactures	2,520	2,213	3,185
Iron and steel	1,287	1,173	1,819
Machinery and transport equipment	6,348	4,785	5,172
Non-electric machinery	3,501	3,021	2,976
Electrical machinery, apparatus, etc.	1,521	961	1,085
Transport equipment	1,326	803	1,111
Miscellaneous manufactured articles	538	305	447
Total (incl. others)	14,323	12,683	14,347

* Including registration fee, but excluding defence-related imports.

Exports f.o.b.*	1998/99	1999/2000	2000/01
Agricultural and traditional goods	1,412.3	1,478.0	1,345.0
Carpets	570.1	691.2	581.2
Fruit and nuts (fresh and dried)	591.9	517.3	447.9
Pistachios	416.0	315.1	311.3
Industrial manufactures	1,588.2	1,847.7	2,061.8
Chemical products	139.7	83.3	692.7
Iron and steel	138.6	219.4	274.3
Hydrocarbons (gas)	183.4	150.7	203.4
Total	3,013.3	3,362.0	3,486.4

* Excluding exports of petroleum and gas (US $ million): 9,933 in 1998/99; 17,089 in 1999/2000; 24,226 in 2000/01.

PRINCIPAL TRADING PARTNERS
(US $ million, year ending 20 March)

Imports c.i.f.	1998/99	1999/2000	2000/01
Argentina	632	131	304
Australia	358	298	403
Austria	267	304	277
Belgium	899	597	426
Brazil	472	681	538
Canada	311	531	477
China, People's Republic	655	613	565
France	556	685	617
Germany	1,660	1,382	1,504
India	204	199	254
Indonesia	139	111	156
Italy	1,188	901	856
Japan	1,005	590	684
Kazakhstan	87	132	345
Korea, Republic	687	708	737
Netherlands	362	213	270
Russia	549	532	920
Singapore	106	100	155
Spain	410	341	343
Sweden	148	120	310
Switzerland	326	336	327
Thailand	162	214	228
Turkey	272	228	233
United Arab Emirates	759	769	1,154
United Kingdom	574	439	510
Total (incl. others)	14,323	12,683	14,347

Exports f.o.b.	1997/98	1998/99	1999/2000*
Azerbaijan	213.4	132.6	n.a.
Belgium	236.0	176.6	115
Brazil	351.7	81.1	n.a.
China, People's Republic	543.4	350.3	771
France	683.9	444.5	576
Germany	427.5	434.2	472
Greece	988.9	651.2	810
Hong Kong	248.5	n.a.	n.a.
India	530.9	364.6	718
Italy	1,630.9	1,122.3	1,500
Japan	2,787.3	2,060.2	3,479
Korea, Republic	1,280.2	648.0	1,349
Russia	250.0	111.2	n.a.
Singapore	694.5	513.8	858
Spain	633.7	431.3	n.a.
Sweden	220.1	173.0	n.a.
Taiwan	376.1	308.8	n.a.
Thailand	252.1	n.a.	n.a.
Turkey	545.9	497.1	723
United Arab Emirates	775.4	885.3	1,584
United Kingdom	3,037.2	2,204.0	3,238
Total (incl. others)	18,380.8	13,118.0	21,030

* Figures are rounded.

Transport

RAILWAYS
(traffic)

	1999	2000	2001
Passenger-km (million)	6,451	7,128	8,043
Freight ton-km (million)	14,082	14,179	14,613

ROAD TRAFFIC
(estimates, motor vehicles in use)

	1994	1995	1996
Passenger cars	1,636,000	1,714,000	1,793,000
Buses and coaches	n.a.	n.a.	55,457
Lorries and vans	626,000	657,000	180,154
Motorcycles and mopeds	2,262,000	2,380,500	2,565,585

1997: Buses and coaches 54,108; Lorries and vans 177,774.

1998: Buses and coaches 52,075; Lorries and vans 178,040.

Source: International Road Federation, *World Road Statistics*.

SHIPPING

Merchant Fleet
(registered at 31 December)

	1999	2000	2001
Number of vessels	380	395	389
Displacement ('000 grt)	3,546.2	4,234.4	3,943.6

Source: Lloyd's Register-Fairplay, *World Fleet Statistics*.

International Sea-borne Freight Traffic
('000 metric tons)

	1994	1995	1996
Goods loaded	128,026	132,677	140,581
Crude petroleum and petroleum products	123,457	127,143	134,615
Goods unloaded	20,692	22,604	27,816
Petroleum products	6,949	7,240	7,855

CIVIL AVIATION
(traffic on scheduled services)

	1997	1998	1999
Kilometres flown (million) . . .	70	68	63
Passengers carried ('000) . .	9,804	9,303	8,277
Passenger-km (million)	8,963	8,539	7,852
Total ton-km (million) . . .	901	856	799

Source: UN, *Statistical Yearbook*.

Tourism

FOREIGN TOURIST ARRIVALS

Country of nationality	1997	1998	1999
Afghanistan	69,728	125,189	146,322
Armenia	17,793	11,758	13,743
Azerbaijan.	264,564	383,123	447,797
Bahrain	14,918	14,322	16,740
Kuwait.	17,191	26,472	30,941
Pakistan	111,556	115,431	134,917
Russia	34,296	10,191	11,911
Saudi Arabia	16,770	21,093	24,654
Turkey.	70,108	160,959	188,130
Total (incl. others)	739,711	1,007,597	1,320,690*

* Including 147,000 of unspecified nationality.

Source: World Tourism Organization, *Yearbook of Tourism Statistics*.

Total arrivals: 1,341,762 in 2000; 1,402,160 in 2001.

Tourism receipts (US $ million): 351 in 1997; 464 in 1998; 586 in 1999; 671 in 2000.

Communications Media

	1999	2000	2001
Television receivers ('000 in use) .	10,300	10,400	n.a.
Telephones ('000 main lines in use)	8,371.2	9,486.3	10,005.5
Mobile cellular telephones ('000 subscribers).	490.5	962.6	1,484.8
Personal computers ('000 in use)	3,500	n.a.	4,500
Internet users ('000)	100	250	402
Book production*:			
titles.	20,642	23,305	31,660.
copies ('000)	105,687	117,785	162,674

Radio receivers ('000 in use): 17,400 in 1998.

Facsimile machines (number in use)† 30,000 in 1994.

Daily newspapers (1996): (number) 32; average circulation 1,651,000.

Periodicals (number): 623 in 1995.

* Including pamphlets.
† Twelve months ending March following the year stated.

Sources: mostly International Telecommunication Union; UNESCO, *Statistical Yearbook*; UN, *Statistical Yearbook*.

Education

(2000/01)

	Institutions	Teachers	Students Males	Females	Total
Pre-primary	7,382	97,529	142,538	144,365	286,903
Primary	69,149	314,654	4,175,849	3,792,588	7,968,437
Secondary:					
general*	42,079	337,912	4,814,139	4,276,799	9,090,938
teacher training . .	82	1,018	7,757	6,584	14,321
Higher	n.a.	n.a.	828,404	744,918	1,573,322

* Including evening classes.

2001/02 (secondary higher level): 1,566,509 students (798,076 males; 768,433 females).

Adult literacy rate (UNESCO estimates): 76.3% (males 83.2%; females 69.3%) in 2000 (Source: UNDP, *Human Development Report*).

Directory

The Constitution

A draft constitution for the Islamic Republic of Iran was published on 18 June 1979. It was submitted to a 'Council of Experts', elected by popular vote on 3 August, to debate the various clauses and to propose amendments. The amended Constitution was approved by a referendum on 2–3 December 1979. A further 45 amendments to the Constitution were approved by a referendum on 28 July 1989.

The Constitution states that the form of government of Iran is that of an Islamic Republic, and that the spirituality and ethics of Islam are to be the basis for political, social and economic relations. Persians, Turks, Kurds, Arabs, Balochis, Turkomans and others will enjoy completely equal rights.

The Constitution provides for a President to act as chief executive. The President is elected by universal adult suffrage for a term of four years. Legislative power is held by the Majlis (Islamic Consultative Assembly), with 290 members (effective from the 2000 election) who are similarly elected for a four-year term. Provision is made for the representation of Zoroastrians, Jews and Christians.

All legislation passed by the Islamic Consultative Assembly must be sent to the Council for the Protection of the Constitution (Article 94), which will ensure that it is in accordance with the Constitution and Islamic legislation. The Council for the Protection of the Constitution consists of six religious lawyers appointed by the Faqih (see below) and six lawyers appointed by the High Council of the Judiciary and approved by the Islamic Consultative Assembly. Articles 19–42 deal with the basic rights of individuals, and provide for equality of men and women before the law and for equal human, political, economic, social and cultural rights for both sexes.

The press is free, except in matters that are contrary to public morality or insult religious belief. The formation of religious, political and professional parties, associations and societies is free, provided they do not negate the principles of independence, freedom, sovereignty and national unity, or the basis of Islam.

The Constitution provides for a Wali Faqih (religious leader) who, in the absence of the Imam Mehdi (the hidden Twelfth Imam), carries the burden of leadership. The amendments to the Constitution that were approved in July 1989 increased the powers of the Presidency by abolishing the post of Prime Minister, formerly the Chief Executive of the Government.

The Government

SUPREME RELIGIOUS LEADER

Walih Faqih: Ayatollah Sayed Ali Khamenei.

HEAD OF STATE

President: Hojatoleslam Dr Sayed Muhammad Khatami (assumed office 3 August 1997; re-elected 8 June 2001).

First Vice-President: Muhammad Reza Aref.

Vice-President in charge of Legal and Parliamentary Affairs: Hojatoleslam Muhammad Ali Abtahi.

Vice-President and Head of the Iranian Atomic Energy Organization: Gholamreza Aghazadeh.

Vice-President and Head of the Organization for the Protection of the Environment: MASSOUMEH EBTEKAR.

Vice-President and Head of the Physical Education Organization: MOHSEN MEHRALIZADEH.

Vice-President and Head of the Management and Planning Organization: MUHAMMAD SATTARIFAR.

Advisers to the President with the rank of Vice-President: MUHAMMAD BAQERIAN, MUHAMMAD ALI NAJAFI.

COUNCIL OF MINISTERS
(April 2003)

Minister of Foreign Affairs: KAMAL KHARRAZI.

Minister of Education: MORTEZA HAJI.

Minister of Culture and Islamic Guidance: AHMAD MASJED JAME'I.

Minister of Intelligence and Security: Hojatoleslam ALI YUNESI.

Minister of Commerce: MUHAMMAD SHARI'ATMADARI.

Minister of Health: MASSOUD PEZESHKIAN.

Minister of Posts, Telegraphs and Telecommunications: AHMAD MO'TAMEDI.

Minister of Justice: Hojatoleslam MUHAMMAD ISMAÏL SHOUSHTARI.

Minister of Defence and Logistics: Rear-Adm. ALI SHAMKHANI.

Minister of Roads and Transport: AHMAD KHORRAM.

Minister of Science, Research and Technology: MOSTAFA MO'IN.

Minister of Industries and Mines: ESHAQ JAHANGIRI.

Minister of Labour and Social Affairs: SAFDAR HOSSEINI.

Minister of the Interior: Hojatoleslam SAYED ABDOLVAHED MUSAVI-LARI.

Minister of Agricultural Jihad: MAHMUD HOJJATI.

Minister of Housing and Urban Development: ALI ABD AL-ALIZADEH.

Minister of Energy: HABIBOLLAH BITARAF.

Minister of Oil: BIJAN NAMDAR ZANGENEH.

Minister of Economic Affairs and Finance: TAHMASB MAZAHERI.

Minister of Co-operatives: ALI SOUFI.

MINISTRIES

Office of the President: Palestine Ave, Azerbaijan Intersection, Tehran; e-mail khatami@president.ir; internet www.president.ir.

Ministry of Agricultural Jihad: 20 Malaei Ave, Vali-e-Asr Sq., Tehran; tel. (21) 8895354; fax (21) 8904357; e-mail webinfo@asid.moa.or.ir; internet www.moa.or.ir.

Ministry of Commerce: Vali-e-Asr Ave, Tehran; tel. (21) 8893620; fax (21) 896504; e-mail irantradepoint@irtp.com; internet www.irtp.com.

Ministry of Co-operatives: 16 Bozorgmehr St, Vali-e-Asr Ave, Tehran 14169; tel. (21) 6400938; fax (21) 6498440; e-mail pub_int@icm.gov.ir.

Ministry of Culture and Islamic Guidance: Baharestan Sq., Tehran; tel. (21) 32411; fax (21) 3117535; e-mail ershad@neda.net; internet www.farhang.gov.ir.

Ministry of Defence and Logistics: Shahid Yousuf Kaboli St, Sayed Khandan Area, Tehran; tel. (21) 21401; fax (21) 864008; e-mail vds@isiran.com.

Ministry of Economic Affairs and Finance: No. 61, Neiestan 7, Pasdaran, Tehran; tel. (21) 2553401; fax (21) 2581933; e-mail economicaffairs@hotmail.com; internet www.economicaffairs.ir.

Ministry of Education: Si-e-Tir St, Emam Khomeini Sq., Tehran; tel. (21) 32421; fax (21) 675503.

Ministry of Energy: North Palestine St, Tehran; tel. (21) 890001; fax (21) 8801995; e-mail webmaster@moe.or.ir; internet www.moe.or.ir.

Ministry of Foreign Affairs: Shahid Abd al-Hamid Mesri St, Ferdowsi Ave, Tehran; tel. (21) 3211; fax (21) 3212763; e-mail matbuat@mfa.gov.ir; internet www.mfa.gov.ir.

Ministry of Health and Medical Education: POB 15655-415, 371 Dr Shariati Ave, Averezi Station, Tehran 16139; tel. (21) 767631; fax (21) 7676733; e-mail webmaster@hbi.dmr.or.ir; internet www.hbi.dmr.or.ir.

Ministry of Housing and Urban Development: Shahid Khoddami St, Vanak Sq., Tehran; tel. (21) 877711; fax (21) 8776634; e-mail hud@icic.gov.ir.

Ministry of Industries and Mines: POB 1416, Somayeh St, Tehran 15996; tel. (21) 8807026; fax (21) 8807031; e-mail minister@mim.gov.ir; internet www.mim.gov.ir.

Ministry of Intelligence and Security: POB 16765-1947, Tehran; tel. (21) 233031; fax (21) 23305.

Ministry of the Interior: Jahad Sq., Fatemi St, Tehran; tel. (21) 61311; fax (21) 650912.

Ministry of Justice: Panzdah-e-Khordad Sq., Tehran; tel. (21) 8191; fax (21) 3113143.

Ministry of Labour and Social Affairs: Azadi Ave, Tehran; tel. (21) 930050; fax (21) 931066.

Ministry of Oil: Hafez St, Taleghani Ave, Tehran; tel. (21) 6152738; fax (21) 6152823; e-mail webmaster@nioc.org; internet www.nioc.org.

Ministry of Posts, Telegraphs and Telecommunications: POB 11365-931, Dr Shariati Ave, Tehran 16314; tel. (21) 864796; fax (21) 866023; e-mail webmaster@195.146.32.12; internet www.iranpac.net.ir.

Ministry of Roads and Transport: 49 Taleghani Ave, Spahbod Gharani St, Tehran; tel. (21) 6460583; fax (21) 6407991.

Ministry of Science, Research and Technology: POB 15875-4375, Central Bldg, Ostad Nejatollahi Ave, Tehran; tel. (21) 8891065; fax (21) 8827234; e-mail oise@msrt.gov.ir; internet www.msrt.gov.ir.

President and Legislature

PRESIDENT

Election, 8 June 2001

Candidates	Votes	%
Sayed Muhammad Khatami	21,656,476	76.9
Ahmed Tavakkoli	4,387,112	15.6
Ali Shamkhani	737,051	2.6
Abdollah Jasbi	259,759	0.9
Mahmoud Kashani	237,660	0.8
Hassan Ghafuri-Fard	129,155	0.5
Mansur Razavi	114,616	0.4
Shahabeddin Sadr	60,546	0.2
Ali Falahian	55,225	0.2
Moustafa Hashemi-Taba	27,949	0.1
Invalid votes	493,740	1.8
Total	**28,159,289**	**100.0**

MAJLIS-E-SHURA-E ISLAMI—ISLAMIC CONSULTATIVE ASSEMBLY

A first round of voting in elections to the sixth Majlis took place on 18 February 2000; and a second, for 66 undecided seats, on 5 May. Successful candidates in both rounds of voting were, for the most part, associated with either the 'conservative' tendency or its 'reformist' counterpart that are generally held to characterize Iranian political life. However, a significant number of independent candidates, who might ally themselves with either of the two principal tendencies, also contested the elections successfully. The sixth Majlis was notable as the first in which 'reformist' or 'liberal' candidates were estimated to have gained a working majority.

Speaker: Hojatoleslam MAHDI KARRUBI.

First Deputy Speaker: BEHZAD NABAVI.

Second Deputy Speaker: MUHAMMAD REZA KHATAMI.

SHURA-YE ALI-YE AMNIYYAT-E MELLI—SUPREME COUNCIL FOR NATIONAL SECURITY

Formed in July 1989 to co-ordinate defence and national security policies, the political programme and intelligence reports, and social, cultural and economic activities related to defence and security. The Council is chaired by the President and includes two representatives of the Wali Faqih, the Head of the Judiciary, the Speaker of the Majlis, the Chief of Staff, the General Command of the Armed Forces, the Minister of Foreign Affairs, the Minister of the Interior, the Minister of Information and the Head of the Plan and Budget Organization.

MAJLIS-E KHOBREGAN—COUNCIL OF EXPERTS

Elections were held on 10 December 1982 to appoint a Council of Experts which was to choose an eventual successor to the Wali Faqih (then Ayatollah Khomeini) after his death. The Constitution provides for a three- or five-man body to assume the leadership of the country if there is no recognized successor on the death of the Wali Faqih. The Council comprises 86 clerics. Elections to a third term of the Council were held on 23 October 1998.

Speaker: Ayatollah ALI MESHKINI.

First Deputy Speaker: Hojatoleslam ALI AKBAR HASHEMI RAFSANJANI.

Second Deputy Speaker: Ayatollah IBRAHIM AMINI NAJAFABADI.

Secretaries: Hojatoleslam HASSAN TAHERI-KHORRAMABADI, Ayatollah QORBANALI DORRI NAJAFABADI.

SHURA-E-NIGAHBAN—COUNCIL OF GUARDIANS

The Council of Guardians, composed of six qualified Muslim jurists appointed by Ayatollah Khomeini and six lay Muslim lawyers, appointed by the Majlis from among candidates nominated by the Head of the Judiciary, was established in 1980 to supervise elections and to examine legislation adopted by the Majlis, ensuring that it accords with the Constitution and with Islamic precepts.

Chairman: Ayatollah AHMAD JANNATI.

SHURA-YE TASHKHIS-E MASLAHAT-E NEZAM—COUNCIL TO DETERMINE THE EXPEDIENCY OF THE ISLAMIC ORDER

Formed in February 1988, by order of Ayatollah Khomeini, to arbitrate on legal and theological questions in legislation passed by the Majlis, in the event of a dispute between the latter and the supervisory Council of Guardians. Its permanent members, defined in March 1997, are Heads of the Legislative, Judiciary and Executive Powers, the jurist members of the Council of Guardians and the Minister or head of organization concerned with the pertinent arbitration. Four new members were appointed to the Expediency Council in March 2002, when Rafsanjani was reappointed as Chairman.

Chairman: Hojatoleslam ALI AKBAR HASHEMI RAFSANJANI.

HEY'AT-E PEYGIRI-YE QANUN ASASI VA NEZARAT BAR AN—COMMITTEE FOR ENSURING AND SUPERVISING THE IMPLEMENTATION OF THE CONSTITUTION

Formed by President Khatami in November 1997; members are appointed for a four-year term. Two new members were appointed to the Committee in April 2002.

Members: Dr GUDARZ EFTEKHAR-JAHROMI, MUHAMMAD ISMAÏL SHOUSHTARI, HASHEM HASHEMZADEH HERISI, Dr HOSSEIN MEHRPUR, Dr MUHAMMAD HOSSEIN HASHEMI, MUHAMMAD ALI ABTAHI.

Political Organizations

Numerous political organizations were registered in the late 1990s, following the election of President Khatami, among them several political tendencies that had formed within the Majlis. The following organizations appeared to have achieved considerable success at elections to the sixth Majlis in early 2000:

Chekad-e Azadandishan (Freethinkers' Front).

Hezb-e E'tedal va Towse'eh (Moderation and Development Party).

Hezb-e Hambastegi-ye Iran-e Islami (Islamic Iran Solidarity Party).

Hezb-e Kargozaran-e Sazandegi (Servants of Construction Party): Sec.-Gen. GHOLAMHOSSEIN KARBASCHI.

Jam'iyat-e Isargaran (Society of Self-sacrificing Devotees).

Jebbeh-ye Masharekat-e Iran-e Islami (Islamic Iran Participation Front): Leader (vacant).

Majma'-e Niruha-ye Khat-e Imam (Assembly of the Followers of the Imam's Line).

Most of the following organizations are opposed to the Iranian Government:

Ansar-e Hezbollah (Helpers of the Party of God): f. 1995; youth movement; seeks to gain access to the political process for religious militants.

Democratic Party of Iranian Kurdistan: POB 102, Paris 75623, France; e-mail pdkiran@club-internet.fr; internet www.pdk-iran .org; f. 1945; seeks autonomy for Kurdish area; mem. of the National Council of Resistance; 54,000 mems; Sec.-Gen. MUSTAPHA HASSANZADEH.

Fedayin-e-Khalq (Warriors of the People): urban Marxist guerrillas; Spokesman FARRAKH NEGAHDAR.

Fraksion-e Hezbollah: f. 1996 by deputies in the Majlis who had contested the 1996 legislative elections as a loose coalition known as the Society of Combatant Clergy; Leader ALI AKBAR HOSSAINI.

Hezb-e-Komunist Iran (Communist Party of Iran): POB 70445, 107 25 Stockholm, Sweden; e-mail cpi@cpiran.org; internet www .cpiran.org; f. 1979 by dissident mems of Tudeh Party; Sec.-Gen. 'AZARYUN'.

Komala: e-mail webmaster_komala@yahoo.se; internet www .komala.org; f. 1969; Kurdish wing of the Communist Party of Iran; Marxist-Leninist; First Sec. IBRAHIM ALIZADEH.

Marze Por-Gohar (Glorious Frontiers Party): POB 111, 1351 Westwood Blvd, Los Angeles, CA 90024, USA; tel. (510) 217–3982; e-mail info@marzeporgohar.org; internet www.marzeporgohar.org; f. 1998; ; nationalist party advocating secular democracy in Iran; Leader ROOZBEH FARAHANIPOUR.

Mujahidin-e-Khalq (Holy Warriors of the People): Islamic guerrilla group; since June 1987 comprising the National Liberation Army; mem. of the National Council of Resistance; Leaders MASSOUD RAJAVI, MARYAM RAJAVI (in Baghdad, 1986–).

National Democratic Front: e-mail ndfi@azadi-iran.org; internet www.azadi-iran.org; f. March 1979; Leader HEDAYATOLLAH MATINE-DAFTARI (in Paris, January 1982–).

National Front (Union of National Front Forces): comprises Iran Nationalist party, Iranian Party, and Society of Iranian Students; Leader Dr KARIM SANJABI (in Paris, August 1978–).

Nehzat-e Azadi-ye Iran (Liberation Movement of Iran): e-mail mizan@nehzateazadi.org; internet www.nehzateazadi.org; f. 1961; emphasis on basic human rights as defined by Islam; Gen. Sec. Dr IBRAHIM YAZDI; Principal Officers Prof. SAHABI, S. SADR, Dr SADR; Eng. SABAGHIAN; Eng. TAVASSOLI.

Pan-Iranist Party: e-mail email@paniranism.org; internet www .paniranism.org; extreme right-wing; calls for a Greater Persia; Leader Dr MOHSEN PEZESHKPOUR.

Sazmane Peykar dar Rahe Azadieh Tabaqe Kargar (Organization Struggling for the Freedom of the Working Class): Marxist-Leninist.

Tudeh Party (Party of the Masses): e-mail mardom@ tudehpartyiran.org; internet www.tudehpartyiran.org; f. 1941; declared illegal 1949; came into open 1979, banned again April 1983; First Sec. Cen. Cttee ALI KHAVARI.

The **National Council of Resistance (NCR)** was formed in Paris in October 1981 by former President Abolhasan Bani-Sadr and the Council's current leader, Massoud Rajavi, the leader of the Mujahidin-e-Khalq in Iran. In 1984 the Council comprised 15 opposition groups, operating either clandestinely in Iran or from exile abroad. Bani-Sadr left the Council in 1984 because of his objection to Rajavi's growing links with the Iraqi Government. The French Government asked Rajavi to leave Paris in June 1986 and he is now based in Baghdad, Iraq. On 20 June 1987 Rajavi, Secretary of the NCR, announced the formation of a National Liberation Army (10,000–15,000-strong) as the military wing of the Mujahidin-e-Khalq. There is also a National Movement of Iranian Resistance, based in Paris. Dissident members of the Tudeh Party founded the Democratic Party of the Iranian People in Paris in February 1988. A new pro-reform party, **Will of the Iranian Nation** (Leader Hakimi Pour), was founded in February 2001.

Diplomatic Representation

EMBASSIES IN IRAN

Afghanistan: Dr Beheshti Ave, Corner of 4th St, Pakistan St, Tehran; tel. (21) 8735600; Ambassador AHMAD MOSHAHED.

Albania: Tehran; Ambassador GILANI SHEHU.

Algeria: Tehran; Ambassador ABD AL-QADER HAJJAR.

Angola: Tehran; Ambassador MANUEL BERNARDO DE SOUSA.

Argentina: POB 15875-4335, 3rd and 4th Floor, 7 Argentina Sq., Tehran; tel. (21) 8718294; fax (21) 8712583; e-mail alvarez951@ yahoo.com; Chargé d'affaires ERNESTO CARLOS ALVAREZ.

Armenia: 1 Ostad Shahriar St, Razi St, Jomhouri Islami Ave, Tehran 11337; tel. (21) 674833; fax (21) 670657; e-mail armembiran@www.dci.co.ir; Ambassador YAHAN BAIBOURDIAN.

Australia: POB 15875-4334, No. 13, 23rd St, Khaled Eslamboli Ave, Tehran 15138; tel. (21) 8724456; fax (21) 8720484; e-mail dfat-tehran@dfat.gov.au; internet www.iran.embassy.gov.au; Ambassador JEREMY R. NEWMAN.

Directory

Austria: 3rd Floor, 78 Argentine Sq., Tehran; tel. (21) 8710753; fax (21) 8710778; e-mail teheran-ob@bmaa.gov.at; Ambassador Dr MICHAEL STIGELBAUER.

Azerbaijan: 10 Malek St, Dr Shariati Ave, Tehran; tel. (21) 2280063; fax (21) 2284929; e-mail azaremb@www.dci.co.ir; Ambassador ABBASALI K. HASANOV.

Bahrain: 248 Africa Ave, Cnr of Zoubin Alley, Tehran; tel. (21) 8773383; fax (21) 8779112; e-mail bahmanama@neda.net; internet www.inet.com; Ambassador KAMAL SALEH AS-SALEH.

Bangladesh: POB 11365-3711, Gandhi Ave, 5th St, Building No. 14, Tehran; tel. (21) 8772979; fax (21) 8778295; e-mail banglaemb@irtp.com; Ambassador ABDOLLAH AL-HASSAN.

Belarus: No. 18, Ghem-Magham Farahani Ave, 6th St, Ground Floor, Tehran; tel. (21) 8731601; Ambassador LEONID RACHKOV.

Belgium: POB 11365-115, 3 Babak Alley, Shabdiz St, Shahid Fayyaz Bakhsh Ave, Tehran 19659; tel. (21) 2009507; e-mail teheran@diplobel.org; Ambassador GUILLAUME METTEN.

Bosnia and Herzegovina: No. 485, Aban Alley, 4th St, Iran Zamin Ave, Shahrak-e-Ghods, Tehran; tel. (21) 8092728; Ambassador IBRAHIM EFENDIĆ.

Brazil: Vanak Sq., 58 Vanak St, Tehran 19918-44959; tel. (21) 8035175; fax (21) 8083348; e-mail emb_brazil@yahoo.com; Ambassador CESARIO MELANTONIO NETO.

Brunei: 60 Babak Bahrami St, Jordan Ave, Tehran 19687; tel. (21) 8784238; fax (21) 8783381; e-mail bneiran@yahoo.com; Ambassador Haji ISHAAQ BIN HAJI ABDULLAH.

Bulgaria: POB 11365-7451, Vali-e-Asr Ave, Dr Abbaspour Ave, Nezami-e-Ganjavi St, No. 82, Tehran; tel. (21) 8775662; e-mail bulgr .tehr@neda.net; Ambassador DUBROV GEORGIEV.

Burkina Faso: Tehran; tel. (21) 2225292.

Canada: POB 11365-4647, 57 Shahid Sarafraz St, Ostad Motahhari Ave; tel. (21) 8732623; fax 8733202; e-mail teran@dfait-maeci.gc.ca; Ambassador PHILIP M. KINNON.

Chad: Tehran.

Chile: Tehran; Ambassador JUAN GABRIEL VALDES.

China, People's Republic: 13 Narenjestan 7th, Pasdaran Ave, Tehran; tel. (21) 2291242; fax (21) 2291243; e-mail emchnir@neda .net; Ambassador LIU ZHENTANG.

Colombia: 5 Faryar St, Hedayat St, Darrous, Tehran; tel. (21) 2541981; e-mail emteh@apadana.com; Ambassador RAFAEL CANAL SANDOVAL.

Congo, Democratic Republic: Tehran; tel. (21) 222190; Chargé d'affaires N'DJATE ESELE SASA.

Côte d'Ivoire: Tehran; Ambassador TIETI ROCH D'ASSOMTION.

Croatia: No. 25, 1st Behestan, Pasdaran St, Tehran; tel. (21) 2589923; fax (21) 2549199; e-mail croatia@istn.irost.com; Chargé d'affaires a.i. TOLUŠIĆ MIJO.

Cuba: 10 Taban Alley, Naft-e-Jonobi, Mirdamad, Tehran; tel. (21) 2257809; e-mail embacub.iran@apadana.com; Ambassador JOSÉ RAMÓN RODRIGUES.

Cyprus: 55 Shahid Sartip Reza Saeidi, Farmanieh Ave, Tehran; tel. (21) 2299795; fax (21) 2299794; Ambassador STAVROS LOIZIDES.

Czech Republic: POB 11365-4457, Mirza-ye Shirazi Ave, Ali Mirza Hassani Ave, No. 15, Tehran; tel. (21) 8716720; fax (21) 8717858; e-mail teheran@embassy.mzv.cz; Chargé d'affaires a.i. MARTIN KLEPETKO.

Denmark: POB 19395-5358, 18 Dashti Ave, Tehran 19148; tel. (21) 2601363; fax (21) 2030007; e-mail thramb@um.dk; internet www .inet.uni2.dk/home/ambadane.teheran; Ambassador JØRGEN REIMERS.

Ethiopia: 38 Tehran; tel. (21) 2289338; Ambassador MOHAMMED HASAN KAHIM.

Finland: POB 19395–1733, Tehran; tel. (21) 2230979; fax (21) 2210948; e-mail finlandiran@hotmail.com; Ambassador YRJÖ KARINEN.

France: 85 Neauphle-le-Château Ave, Tehran; tel. (21) 6706018; e-mail ambafrance.teheran@kanoon.net; Ambassador FRANÇOIS NICOULLAUD.

Gambia: Tehran; Ambassador MANGOM MUKHTAR CEESAY.

Georgia: POB 19575-379, Elahiyeh, Tehran; tel. (21) 2211470; fax (21) 2206848; e-mail georgia@apadana.com; Ambassador JEMSHID GIUNASHVILI.

Germany: POB 11365-179, 320–324 Ferdowsi Ave, Tehran; tel. (21) 3114111; fax (21) 3119883; e-mail fmst@tehe.auswaertiges-amt.de; Ambassador Dr RÜDIGER REYELS.

Ghana: Tehran; Ambassador Mr AL-HASSAN.

Greece: POB 11365-8151, Africa Ave, Esfandiar St, No. 43, Tehran; tel. (21) 2050533; fax (21) 2057431; e-mail embgreece1@safineh.net; Ambassador HARALAMBOS KOUGEVETOPOULOS.

Guinea: POB 11365-4716, Dr Shariati Ave, Malek St, No. 10, Tehran; tel. (21) 7535744; fax (21) 7535743; e-mail ambaguinee_thr@hotmail.com; Ambassador ALPHA IBRAHIMA SOW.

Holy See: Apostolic Nunciature, POB 11365-178, Razi Ave, No. 97, Neauphle-le-Château Ave, Tehran; tel. (21) 6403574; fax (21) 6419442; e-mail apnun-thr@parsonline.net; Apostolic Nuncio Most Rev. ANGELO MOTTOLA (Titular Archbishop of Cercina).

Hungary: POB 6363-19395, Darrous, Hedayat Sq, Shadloo St, No. 15, Tehran; tel. (21) 2550460; fax (21) 2550503; e-mail huembthr@neda.net; Ambassador Dr ISTVÁN VÁSÁRY.

India: POB 15875-4118, 46 Mir-Emad St, Cnr of 9th St, Dr Beheshti Ave, Tehran; tel. (21) 8755103; fax (21) 8755973; e-mail indemteh@dpimail.net; internet www.indianembassy-tehran.com; Ambassador S. K. ARORA.

Indonesia: POB 11365-4564, Ghaem Magham Farahani Ave, No. 210, Tehran; tel. (21) 8716865; Ambassador BAMBANG SUDARSONO.

Iraq: Karamian Alley, No. 17, Pol-e-Roomi, Dr Shariati Ave, Tehran; tel. (21) 2218386; Chargé d'affaires ABD AS-SATTAR AR-RAWI.

Ireland: Bonbast Nahid St, North Kamranieh Ave, No. 9, Tehran 19369; tel. (21) 2297918; fax (21) 2286933; e-mail irelembteh@padisar.net; Ambassador THOMAS O. BOLSTER.

Italy: POB 11365-7863, 81 Neauphle-le-Château Ave, Tehran; tel. (21) 6726955; fax (21) 6726961; e-mail itaembtehe@kanoon.net; Ambassador RICCARDO SESSA.

Japan: POB 11365-814, Bucharest Ave, Corner of 5th St, Tehran; tel. (21) 8713396; Ambassador TAKEKAZU KAWAMURA.

Jordan: 47 Armaghan Sharghi St, Africa Ave, Tehran; tel. (21) 8082466; fax (21) 8090734; e-mail jordanembteh@neda.net; Ambassador Dr BASSAM ALI AL-OMOUSH.

Kazakhstan: Darrus, Hedayat St, Masjed Alley, No. 4, Tehran; tel. (21) 2565933; fax (21) 2546400; e-mail kazembir@apadana.com; Ambassador TULEGEN ZHUKEYEV.

Kenya: 60 Hormoz Satari St, Africa Ave, Tehran; tel. (21) 2270795; fax (21) 2270160; e-mail kenemteh@irtp.com; Ambassador HASSAN MUHAMMAD SALEH BAQA.

Korea, Democratic People's Republic: 349 Vahid Dastjerdi Ave, Africa Ave, Tehran; tel. (21) 2223341; Ambassador KIM JONG NAM.

Korea, Republic: No. 37, Ahmad Ghasir Ave, Tehran; tel. (21) 8731389; fax (21) 8737917; e-mail korth@dpi.net.ir; Ambassador LI SUNG-CHOOL.

Kuwait: No. 323/2, Vahid Dastjerdi Ave, Tehran; tel. (21) 8785997; Ambassador AHMAD AZ-ZAFIRI.

Kyrgyzstan: POB 19579-3511, Bldg 12, 5th Naranjestan Alley, Pasdaran St; tel. (21) 2830354; fax (21) 2281720; e-mail krembiri@kanoon.net; Ambassador MEDET SADYRKULOV.

Laos: Tehran; Ambassador CHANPHENG SIHAPHOM.

Lebanon: No. 31, Shahid Kalantari St, Ghantari Ave, Tehran; tel. (21) 8908451; fax (21) 8907345; Ambassador ADNAN MANSOUR.

Libya: Ostad Motahhari Ave, No. 163, Tehran; tel. (21) 8742572; Ambassador ALI MARIA.

Macedonia, former Yugoslav republic: No. 7, 4th Alley, Khaled Eslamboli Ave, Tehran; tel. (21) 8720810; Chargé d'affaires CVETKO SOFKOVSKI.

Malaysia: 72 Fereshteh Ave, Tehran; tel. (21) 2009275; fax (21) 2009143; e-mail mwtehran@neda.net; Ambassador MEZLAN MOHAMMAD.

Mexico: POB 15875-4636, No. 41, Golfam St, Africa Ave, Tehran; tel. (21) 2057586; fax (21) 2225375; e-mail embamex@apadana.com; Ambassador ANTONIO DUEÑAS PULIDO.

Mongolia: Tehran; Ambassador L. KHASHOAT.

Morocco: Tehran; tel. (21) 2059707; fax (21) 2051872; e-mail ambas .du.maroc@tavana.net; Ambassador JAMAL EDDINE GHAZI.

Mozambique: Tehran; Ambassador MURADE ISAC MIGUIGY MURARGY.

Myanmar: Tehran; Ambassador U SAW HLAING.

Namibia: Tehran; Ambassador MWAILEPENI T. P. SHITILIFA.

Nepal: Tehran; Ambassador Gen. ARJUN NARSING RONA.

Netherlands: POB 11365-138, Darrous, Shahrzad Blvd, Kamasaie St, 1st East Lane, No. 33, Tehran 19498; tel. (21) 2567005; fax (21) 2566990; e-mail nlambiran@dpi.net.ir; Ambassador R. A. MOLLINGER.

New Zealand: POB 15875-4313, 34 North Golestan Complex, Cnr of 2nd Park Alley and Sosan St, Aghdasiyeh St, Niavaran, Tehran;

tel. (21) 2800289; fax (21) 2831673; e-mail newzealand@mavara .com; Ambassador NIELS HOLM.

Niger: Tehran.

Nigeria: No. 11, 31st St, Khalid Eslamboli Ave, Tehran; tel. (21) 8774936; e-mail ngrembtehran@yahoo.com; Ambassador ADO SANUSI.

Norway: POB 19395-5398, Lavasani Ave 201, Tehran; tel. (21) 2291333; fax (21) 2292776; e-mail emb.tehran@mfa.no; Ambassador OLE KRISTIAN HOLTHE.

Oman: No. 12, Tandis Alley, Africa Ave, Tehran; tel. (21) 2056831; Chargé d'affaires a.i. RASHID BIN MUBARAK BIN RASHID AL-ODWALI.

Pakistan: Dr Fatemi Ave, Jamshidabad Shomali, Mashal St, No. 1, Tehran; tel. (21) 934332; e-mail pareptehran@yahoo.com; Ambassador JAVID HUSSEIN.

Peru: Tehran; Ambassador LUIS HERNÁNDEZ ORTIZ.

Philippines: POB 19395-4797, No. 13, Mahyar St, Africa Ave, Tehran; tel. (21) 2047802; fax (21) 2046239; e-mail tehranpe@dfa .gov.ph; Ambassador RODRIGO ARAGON.

Poland: Africa Ave, Piruz St, No. 1/3, Tehran; tel. (21) 8787262; e-mail ambrpri@sokhan.net; Ambassador WITOLD SMIDOWSKI.

Portugal: No. 13, Rouzbeh Alley, Darrous, Hedayat St, Tehran; tel. (21) 2543237; fax (21) 2552668; e-mail portugal@sr.co.ir; Ambassador Dr JOSÉ MANUEL DA COSTA ARSÉNIO.

Qatar: POB 11365-5631, Africa Ave, Golazin Ave, Parke Davar, No. 4, Tehran; tel. (21) 2051255; fax (21) 2056023; Ambassador ALI ABDULLAH ZAID AL-MAHMOOD.

Romania: Fakhrabad Ave 12, Baharestan Ave, Tehran; tel. (21) 7539041; fax (21) 7535291; e-mail ambrotehran@parsonline.net; Ambassador NICOLAE STAN.

Russia: 39 Neauphle-le-Château Ave, Tehran; tel. (21) 6701161; e-mail russembassy@apadana.com; Ambassador ALEKSANDR MARYASOV.

Saudi Arabia: No. 1, Niloufar, Boustan, Pasdaran Ave, Tehran; tel. (21) 2050081; fax (21) 2050083; Ambassador JAMIL BIN ABDULLAH AL-JISHI.

Senegal: Tehran; tel. (21) 8783596; Ambassador E. MBAKEH.

Serbia and Montenegro: POB 11365–118, Vali-e-Asr, Fereshteh Ave, Bossni Alley, No. 12, Tehran 19659; tel. (21) 2044126; fax (21) 2044978; e-mail yuembth1@neda.net; Chargé d'affaires VLADIMIR KEREČKI.

Sierra Leone: No. 10, Malek St, Off Dr Shariati Ave, Tehran; tel. (21) 7502819.

Slovakia: Tehran; tel. (21) 2271058; fax (21) 2271057; Ambassador YAN YOURSA.

Slovenia: Narenjestan 8th Alley, Pasdaran Ave, Tehran; tel. (21) 2802223; fax (21) 2282131; e-mail vte@mzz-dkp.sigov.si.

Somalia: 20 Sohail St, Dr Shariati Ave, Tehran; tel. (21) 8796509.

South Africa: POB 11365-7476, 5 Yekta St, Vali-e-Asr Ave, Tehran; tel. (21) 2702866; fax (21) 2716191; e-mail saemb@neda.net; Ambassador MZOLISI MABUDE.

Spain: 76 Sarv St, Africa Ave, Tehran; tel. (21) 8714575; fax (21) 8724581; e-mail embespir@mail.mae.es; Ambassador LEOPOLDO STAMPA PIÑEIRO.

Sri Lanka: 28 Golazin St, Africa Ave, Tehran; tel. (21) 2052688; fax (21) 2052149; e-mail emblanka@afranet.com; Chargé d'affaires a.i. OMAR KAMIL.

Sudan: No. 39, Babak B'ahrami Alley, Zafar St, Africa Ave, Tehran; tel. (21) 8781183; fax (21) 295008; Ambassador HAMED ALI MOHAMMAD AT-TINAY.

Sweden: POB 19575-458, 2 Nastaran St, Pasdaran Ave, Tehran; tel. (21) 2296802; fax (21) 2296451; e-mail ambassaden.teheran@ foreign.ministry.se; Ambassador STEEN HOHWÜ-CHRISTENSEN.

Switzerland: POB 19395-4683, 13/1 Boustan Ave, Elahieh, 19649 Tehran; tel. (21) 2008333; fax (21) 2006002; e-mail vertretung@teh .rep.admin.ch; Ambassador TIM GULDIMANN.

Syria: 19 Iraj St, Africa Ave, Tehran; tel. (21) 2052780; e-mail syrambir@www.dci.co.ir; Ambassador Dr TURKI MUHAMMAD SAQR.

Tajikistan: Tehran; Ambassador RAMAZAN MIRZOYEV.

Tanzania: Tehran.

Thailand: POB 11495-111, Baharestan Ave, Parc Amin ed-Doleh, No. 4, Tehran; tel. (21) 7531433; fax (21) 7532022; e-mail thairan@ bkk2000.org; Ambassador MAHADI WIMANA.

Tunisia: No. 12, Shahid Dr Lavasani, Tehran; tel. (21) 2704161; Ambassador MOLADI AS-SAKERI.

Turkey: Ferdowsi Ave, No. 337, Tehran; tel. (21) 3925619; fax (21) 3117928; e-mail tctahranbe@parsonline.net; Ambassador SELAHATTIN ALPAR.

Turkmenistan: No. 39, 5th Golestan St, Pasdaran Ave, Tehran; tel. (21) 2542178; Ambassador MURAT NAZAROV.

Ukraine: 101 Vanak St, Vanak Sq., Tehran; tel. (21) 8034119; fax (21) 8007130; e-mail emb_ir@mfa.gov.ua; Ambassador VADYM PRYMACHENKO.

United Arab Emirates: POB 19395-4616, No. 355, Vahid Dastjerdi Ave, Vali-e-Asr Ave, Tehran; tel. (21) 8781333; fax (21) 8789084; e-mail uae_emb_thr@universalmail.com; Ambassador KHALIFA SHAHEEN AL-MERREE.

United Kingdom: POB 11365-4474, 198 Ferdowsi Ave, Tehran 11344; tel. (21) 6705011; fax (21) 6708021; e-mail britemb@neda.net; internet www.britishembassy.gov.uk/iran; Ambassador RICHARD DALTON.

Uruguay: 45 Shabnam Alley, Atefi Shargi St, Africa Ave, Tehran; tel. (21) 2052030; e-mail uruter@chapar.net; Ambassador JOSÉ LOUISE.

Uzbekistan: No. 6, Nastaran Alley, Boostan St, Pasdaran Ave; tel. (21) 2299158; Ambassador ILHAM AKRAMOV.

Venezuela: POB 15875-4354, No. 26, Tandis St, Africa Ave, Tehran; tel. (21) 8715185; fax (21) 2053677; e-mail embeveneziran@ chapar.net; Ambassador VALDMAR RODRÍGUEZ.

Viet Nam: 155 Feresteh St, Vali-e-Asr Ave, Tehran; tel. (21) 2949247; fax (21) 2047350; e-mail sqvn.iran@mail.dci.co.ir; Ambassador NGO VAN QUANG.

Yemen: Tehran; tel. (21) 2048619; e-mail yem.emb.ir@neda.net; Ambassador ABDOLQAVI AR-RYANI.

Judicial System

In August 1982 the Supreme Court revoked all laws dating from the previous regime which did not conform with Islam; in October all courts set up prior to the Islamic Revolution were abolished. In June 1987 Ayatollah Khomeini ordered the creation of clerical courts to try members of the clergy opposed to government policy. A new system of *qisas*(retribution) was established, placing the emphasis on swift justice. Islamic codes of correction were introduced in 1983, including the dismembering of a hand for theft, flogging for fornication and violations of the strict code of dress for women, and stoning for adultery. In 1984 there were 2,200 judges. The Supreme Court has 16 branches.

Head of the Judiciary: Ayatollah SAYED MAHMOUD HASHEMI SHAHRUDI.

SUPREME COURT

Chief Justice: Hojatoleslam MUHAMMAD MUHAMMADI GUILANI.

Prosecutor-General: Hojatoleslam ABD AN-NABI NAMAZI.

Religion

According to the 1979 Constitution, the official religion is Islam of the Ja'fari sect (Shi'ite), but other Islamic sects, including Zeydi, Hanafi, Maleki, Shafe'i and Hanbali, are valid and will be respected. Zoroastrians, Jews and Christians will be recognized as official religious minorities. According to the 1996 census, there were 59,788,791 Muslims, 78,745 Christians (mainly Armenian), 27,920 Zoroastrians and 12,737 Jews in Iran.

ISLAM

The great majority of the Iranian people are Shi'a Muslims, but there is a minority of Sunni Muslims. Persians and Azerbaijanis are mainly Shi'ite, while the other ethnic groups are mainly Sunni.

CHRISTIANITY

The Roman Catholic Church

At 31 December 2000 there were an estimated 25,000 adherents in Iran, comprising 10,000 of the Armenian Rite, 10,000 of the Latin Rite and 5,000 of the Chaldean Rite.

Armenian Rite

Bishop of Esfahan: NECHAN KARAKEHEYAN, Armenian Catholic Bishopric, POB 11365-445, Khiaban Ghazzali 22, Tehran; tel. (21) 6707204; fax (21) 8715191.

Chaldean Rite

Archbishop of Ahvaz: HANNA ZORA, Archbishop's House, POB 61956, Naderi St, Ahvaz; tel. (61) 224980.

Archbishop of Tehran: RAMZI GARMOU, Archevêché, Enghelab St, Sayyed Abbas Mousavi Ave 91, Tehran 15819; tel. (21) 8823549; fax (21) 8308714.

Archbishop of Urmia (Rezayeh) and Bishop of Salmas (Shahpour): THOMAS MERAM, Khalifagari Kaldani Katholiq, POB 338, Orumiyeh 57135; tel. (441) 222739; fax (441) 236031; e-mail catholic@mail.dci.co.ir.

Latin Rite

Archbishop of Esfahan: IGNAZIO BEDINI, Consolata Church, POB 11365-445, 75 Neauphle-le-Château Ave, Tehran; tel. (21) 6703210; fax (21) 6724947; e-mail ispahan.latinorum@ravan.com.

The Anglican Communion

Anglicans in Iran are adherents of the Episcopal Church in Jerusalem and the Middle East, formally inaugurated in January 1976.

Bishop in Iran and President of the Episcopal Church in Jerusalem and the Middle East: Rt Rev. IRAJ KALIMI MOTTAHEDEH, St Luke's Church, POB 81465-135, Abbas-abad Rd, Esfahan; tel. (31) 2331435; fax (31) 2334675; e-mail bishraj@chavoosh.com; diocese founded 1912.

Presbyterian Church

Synod of the Evangelical (Presbyterian) Church in Iran: Assyrian Evangelical Church, Khiaban-i Hanifnejad, Khiaban-i Aramanch, Tehran; Moderator Rev. ADEL NAKHOSTEEN.

ZOROASTRIANS

There are almost 28,000 Zoroastrians, a remnant of a once widespread sect. Their religious leader is Moubad.

OTHER COMMUNITIES

Communities of Armenians, and somewhat smaller numbers of Jews, Assyrians, Greek Orthodox Christians, Uniates and Latin Christians are also found as officially recognized faiths. The Bahá'í faith, which originated in Iran, has about 300,000 Iranian adherents, although at least 10,000 are believed to have fled since 1979 in order to escape persecution. The Government banned all Bahá'í institutions in August 1983.

The Press

Tehran dominates the media, as many of the daily papers are published there, and the bi-weekly, weekly and less frequent publications in the provinces generally depend on the major metropolitan dailies as a source of news. A press law announced in August 1979 required all newspapers and magazines to be licensed and imposed penalties of imprisonment for insulting senior religious figures. Offences against the Act will be tried in the criminal courts. Under the Constitution the press is free, except in matters that are contrary to public morality, insult religious belief or slander the honour and reputation of individuals. Since the late 1990s the press has been the target of an intense judicial campaign to curb its freedoms.

PRINCIPAL DAILIES

Abrar (Rightly Guided): Tehran; tel. (21) 8848270; fax (21) 8849200; internet www.abrar.ws; f. 1985 after closure of *Azadegan* by order of the Prosecutor-General; morning; Farsi; circ. 75,000.

Aftab-e-Yazd (Sun of Yazd): POB 13145-1134, Tehran; tel. (21) 6495833; fax (21) 6495835; e-mail info@aftabnews.net; f. 2000; Farsi; pro-reform; Chief Editor MOJTABA VAHEDI; circ. 100,000.

Alik: POB 11365-953, Jomhouri Islami Ave, Alik Alley, Tehran 11357; tel. (21) 8768567; fax 8760994; e-mail alikmail@hyenet.net; internet www.alikonline.com; f. 1931; afternoon; Armenian; political and literary; Propr A. AJEMIAN; circ. 3,400.

Bahar (Spring): Tehran; Man. Dir SAYED POR-AZIZI; (Publication suspended in 2003).

Entekhab: 12 Noorbakhsh Ave, Vali-e-Asr Ave, Tehran; tel. (21) 8893954; fax (21) 8893951; e-mail public-relations@entekhab-daily .com; internet www.entekhab-daily.com; Farsi; Man. Dir TAHA HASHEMI.

Ettela'at (Information): Ettela'at Bldg, Mirdamad Ave, South Naft St, Tehran 15499; tel. (21) 29999; fax (21) 2258022; e-mail ettelaat@ ettelaat.com; internet www.ettelaat.com; f. 1925; evening; Farsi; political and literary; operates under the direct supervision of

Wilayat-e-Faqih (religious jurisprudence); Editor SAYED MAHMOUD DO'AYI; circ. 500,000.

Fath (Victory): POB 19395-7475, Tehran; pro-reform; Man. Dir YADOLLAH ESLAMI; Publication suspended in 2000.

Golestan-e Iran: f. 2002; reformist newspaper aimed at Iranian youth; Publisher MOHSEN SAZEGARA; (Publication suspended in Sept. 2002).

Hayat-e No (New Life): 50 North Sohrvardi Ave, Tehran; tel. (21) 8747437; fax (21) 8766373; internet www.aria.ws/hayateno; f. 2000; Farsi; pro-reform; Man. Dir SAYED HADI KHAMENEI; (Publication suspended in 2003).

Iran News: POB 15115-658, 41 Lida St, Vali-e-Asr Ave, North of Vanak Sq., Tehran 19697; tel. (21) 8880231; fax (21) 8786475; e-mail info@irannewsdaily.com; internet www.irannewsdaily.com; f. 1994; English; Man. Editor SHIRZAD BOZORGMEHR; circ. 35,000.

Kayhan (Universe): POB 11365-9631, Ferdowsi Ave, Tehran 11444; tel. (21) 3110251; fax (21) 3111120; e-mail kayhan@ofogh.net; internet www.kayhannews.com; f. 1941; evening; Farsi; political; also publishes *Kayhan International* (f. 1959; daily; English; Editor Hamid Najafi), *Kayhan Arabic* (f. 1980; daily; Arabic), *Kayhan Persian*(f. 1942; daily; Persian), *Kayhan Havaie* (f. 1950; weekly for Iranians abroad; Farsi), *Zan-e-Ruz* (Woman Today; f.1964; weekly; Farsi), *Kayhan Varzeshi* (World of Sport; f. 1955; weekly; Farsi), *Kayhan Bacheha* (Children's World; f. 1956; weekly; Farsi), *Kayhan Farhangi* (World of Culture; f. 1984; monthly; Farsi); owned and managed by Mostazafin Foundation from October 1979 until 1 January 1987, when it was placed under the direct supervision of Wilayat-e-Faqih (religious jurisprudence); Chief Editor HOSSEIN SHARIATMADARI; circ. 350,000.

Khorassan: Mashhad; Head Office: Khorassan Daily Newspapers, 14 Zohre St, Mobarezan Ave, Tehran; f. 1948; Propr MUHAMMAD SADEGH TEHERANIAN; circ. 40,000.

Khordad: Tehran; pro-reform; Publication suspended in 1999.

Neshat: Tehran; pro-reform; Man. Dir MASHALLAH SHAMSOLVAEZIN; Publication suspended in 1999.

Rahnejat: Darvazeh Dowlat, Esfahan; political and social; Propr N. RAHNEJAT.

Ressallat (The Message): POB 11365-777, 53 Ostad Nejatollahi Ave, Tehran; tel. (21) 8902642; fax (21) 8900587; e-mail info@ resalat-news.com; internet www.resalat-news.com; f. 1985; organ of right-wing group of the same name; political, economic, social; Propr Ressallat Foundation; Man. Dir SAYED MORTEZA NABAVI; circ. 100,000.

Salam: 2 Shahid Reza Nayebi Alley, South Felestin St, Tehran; tel. (21) 6495831; fax (21) 6495835; f. 1991; Farsi; political, cultural, economic, social; Editor MUHAMMAD MUSAVI KHOIENI; Closure ordered in July 1999.

Sobh Emruz: Tehran; pro-reform; Man. SAYED HAJJARIAN; Publication suspended in 2000.

Tehran Times: POB 14155–4843, 32 Bimeh Alley, Ostad Nejatollahi Ave, Tehran; tel. (21) 8810293; fax (21) 8808214; e-mail webmaster@tehrantimes.com; internet www.tehrantimes.com; f. 1979; English; independent; Man. Dir PARVIZ ESMAEILI.

PRINCIPAL PERIODICALS

Acta Medica Iranica: Bldg No. 8, Faculty of Medicine, Tehran Medical Sciences Univ., Poursina St, Tehran 14174; tel. and fax (21) 8962510; e-mail acta@sina.tums.ac.ir; internet www.tums.ac.ir; f. 1960; quarterly; English; Editors-in-Chief A. R. DEHPOUR, M. SAMINI; circ. 2,000.

Akhbar-e-Pezeshki: 86 Ghaem Magham Farahani Ave, Tehran; weekly; Farsi; medical; Propr Dr T. FORUZIN.

Ashur: Ostad Motahhari Ave, 11-21 Kuhe Nour Ave, Tehran; tel. (21) 622117; f. 1969; Assyrian; monthly; Founder and Editor Dr W. BET-MANSOUR; circ. 8,000.

Auditor: 77 Ferdowsi Ave North, Tehran; quarterly; financial and managerial studies.

Ayandeh: POB 19575-583, Niyavaran, Tehran; tel. (21) 283254; fax (21) 6406426; monthly; Iranian literary, historical and book review journal; Editor Prof. IRAJ AFSHAR.

Bulletin of the National Film Archive of Iran: POB 5158, Baharestan Sq., Tehran 11365; tel. 311242; f. 1989; English periodical; Editor M. H. KHOSHNEVIS.

Daneshmand (The Knowledgeable): POB 15875-3646, Tehran; tel. (21) 8883148; f. 1963; monthly; Farsi; scientific and technical magazine; Editor-in-Chief A. R. KARAMI.

Daneshkadeh Pezeshki: Faculty of Medicine, Tehran Medical Sciences University; tel. (21) 6112743; fax (21) 6404377; f. 1947; 10 a year; medical magazine; Propr Dr HASSAN AREFI; circ. 1,500.

Donaye Varzesh: Khayyam Ave, Ettela'at Bldg, Tehran; tel. (21) 3281; fax (21) 3115530; weekly; sport; Editor G. H. SHABANI; circ. 200,000.

The Echo of Iran: POB 14155-1168, 4 Hourtab Alley, Hafez Ave, Tehran; tel. (21) 6468114; fax (21) 6464790; e-mail support@ echoiran.com; internet www.echoiran.com; f. 1952; monthly; English; news, politics and economics; Editor J. BEHROUZ.

Echo of Islam: POB 14155-3899, Tehran; tel. (21) 8897663; fax (21) 8902725; e-mail echoofislam@itf.org.ir; internet www.itf.org.ir; monthly; English; published by the Islamic Thought Foundation; Man. Dir ALI AKBAR ZIAIE; Editor-in-Chief HAMID TEHRANI.

Economic Echo: POB 14155-1168, 4 Hourtab Alley, Hafez Ave, Tehran; tel. (21) 6468114; fax (21) 6464790; e-mail support@ echoiran.com; internet www.echoiran.com; f. 1998; English.

Ettela'at Elmi: 11 Khayyam Ave, Tehran; tel. (21) 3281; fax (21) 3115530; f. 1985; fortnightly; Farsi; sciences; Editor Mrs GHASEMI; circ. 75,000.

Ettela'at Haftegi: 11 Khayyam Ave, Tehran; tel. (21) 311238; fax (21) 3115530; f. 1941; general weekly; Farsi; Editor F. JAVADI; circ. 150,000.

Ettela'at Javanan: POB 15499-51199, Ettela'at Bldg, Mirdamad Ave, South Naft St, Tehran; tel. (21) 29999; fax (21) 2258022; f. 1966; weekly; Farsi; youth; Editor M. J. RAFIZADEH; circ. 120,000.

Farhang-e-Iran Zamin: POB 19575-583, Niyavaran, Tehran; tel. (21) 283254; annual; Farsi; Iranian studies; Editor Prof. IRAJ AFSHAR.

Film International, Iranian Film Quarterly: POB 11365-875, Tehran; tel. (21) 6709373; fax (21) 6719971; e-mail filmmag@ apadana.com; f. 1993; quarterly; English; Pres. and Man. Dir MASSOUD MEHRABI; circ 12,000.

Iran Tribune: POB 111244, Tehran; internet www.irantribune .com; monthly; English.

Iran Who's Who: POB 14155, 4 Hourtab Alley, Hafez Ave, Tehran; tel. (21) 6468114; fax (21) 6464790; e-mail support@echoiran.com; internet www.echoiran.com; annual; English; Editor KARAN BEHROUZ.

Iranian Cinema: POB 5158, Baharestan Sq., Tehran 11365; tel. 311242; f. 1985; annual; English; Editor B. REYPOUR.

JIDA: 94 West Piroozi St, Nasr Place, Tehran 14477; tel. (21) 8269591; fax 8269592; e-mail info@idaweb.org; internet www .idaweb.org; f. 1963; four a year; journal of the Iranian Dental Association; Editor-in-Chief Dr MUHAMMAD MOSHREF.

Kayhan Bacheha (Children's World): Shahid Shahsheragi Ave, Tehran; tel. (21) 310251; f. 1956; weekly; Editor AMIR HOSSEIN FARDI; circ. 150,000.

Kayhan Varzeshi (World of Sport): Ferdowsi Ave, Tehran; tel. (21) 310251; f. 1955; weekly; Dir MAHMAD MONSETI; circ. 125,000.

Mahjubah: Tehran; tel. (21) 8000067; fax (21) 8001453; e-mail tjamshid@chamran.ut.ac.ir; Islamic family magazine; published by the Islamic Thought Foundation; Editor-in-Chief TURAN JAMSHIDIAN.

Music Iran: Tehran; f. 1951; monthly; Editor BAHMAN HIRBOD; circ. 7,000.

Negin: Vali-e-Asr Ave, Adl St 52, Tehran; monthly; scientific and literary; Propr and Dir M. ENAYAT.

Salamate Fekr: M.20, Kharg St, Tehran; tel. (21) 223034; f. 1958; monthly; organ of the Mental Health Soc. Editors Prof. E. TCHEHRAZI, ALI REZA SHAFAI.

Soroush: POB 15875-1163, Soroush Bldg, Motahhari Ave, Mofatteh Crossroads, Tehran; tel. and fax and fax (21) 8847602; e-mail cultural@soroushpress.com; internet www.soroushpress.com; f. 1972; one weekly magazine; four monthly magazines, one for women, two for adolescents and one for children; one quarterly review of philosophy; all in Farsi; Editor-in-Chief ALI AKBAR ASHARI.

Vaqt: weekly; Farsi; pro-reform; Publication suspended in Sept. 2002.

Zan-e-Ruz (Woman Today): Ferdowsi Ave, Tehran; tel. (21) 3911570; fax (21) 3911569; e-mail kayhan@istn.irost.com; internet www.irost.com/kayhan; f. 1964; weekly; women's; circ. over 60,000. (Closure ordered April 1999.).

PRESS ASSOCIATION

Association of Iranian Journalists: No. 87, 7th Alley, Shahid Kabkanian St, Keshavarz Blvd, Tehran; tel. (21) 8954796; fax (21) 8963539; e-mail secretary@aoij.org; internet www.aoij.org; Gen. Sec. KARIM ARGHANDEHPOUR.

NEWS AGENCIES

Islamic Republic News Agency (IRNA): POB 764, 873 Vali-e-Asr Ave, Tehran; tel. (21) 8902050; fax (21) 8905068; e-mail irna@irna .com; internet www.irna.com; f. 1936; Man. Dir Dr ABDOLLAH NASSERI TAHERI.

Foreign Bureaux

Agence France-Presse (AFP): POB 15115-513, Office 207, 8 Vanak Ave, Vanak Sq., Tehran 19919; tel. (21) 8777509; fax (21) 8886289; Correspondent CHRISTOPHE DE ROQUEFEUIL.

Agenzia Nazionale Stampa Associata (ANSA) (Italy): Tehran; tel. (21) 276930; Chief of Bureau LUCIANO CAUSA.

Informatsionnoye Telegrafnoye Agentstvo Rossii— Telegrafnoye Agentstvo Suverennykh Stran (ITAR—TASS) (Russia): Kehyaban Hamid, Kouche Masoud 73, Tehran.

Kyodo Tsushin (Japan): No. 23, First Floor, Couche Kargozar, Couche Sharsaz Ave, Zafar, Tehran; tel. (21) 220448; Correspondent MASARU IMAI.

Reuters (UK): POB 15875-1193, Tehran; tel. (21) 847700.

Xinhua (New China) News Agency (People's Republic of China): Tehran; tel. (21) 241852; Correspondent CHEN MING.

Publishers

Amir Kabir Book Publishing and Distribution Co: POB 11365-4191, Jomhouri Islami Ave, Esteghlal Sq., Tehran; tel. (21) 6463487; fax (21) 390752; f. 1948; historical, social, literary and children's books; Dir H. ANWARY.

Avayenoor Publications: 31 Roshan Alley, Vali-e-Asr Ave, Tehran; tel. (21) 8899001; fax (21) 8907452; e-mail info@avayenoor .com; internet www.avayenoor.com; f. 1988; sociology, politics and economics; Editor-in-Chief Sayed MOHAMMAD MIRHOSSEINI.

Ebn-e-Sina: Meydane 25 Shahrivar, Tehran; f. 1957; educational publishers and booksellers; Dir EBRAHIM RAMAZANI.

Echo Publishers & Printers: POB 14155-1168, 4 Hourtab Alley, Hafez Ave, Tehran; tel. (21) 6468114; fax (21) 6464790; e-mail support@echoiran.com; internet www.echoiran.com; politics, economics and current affairs.

Eghbal Printing & Publishing Organization: 15 Booshehr St, Dr Shariati Ave, Tehran; tel. (21) 768113; f. 1903; Man. Dir DJAVAD EGHBAL.

Iran Chap Co: Mirdamad Ave, South Naft St, Tehran; tel. (21) 29999; fax (21) 2258022; e-mail iranchap@ettelaat.com; internet www.ettelaat.com; f. 1966; newspapers, books, magazines, bookbinding, colour printing and engraving; Man. Dir M. DOAEI.

Iran Exports Publication Co Ltd: POB 14335-746, 27 Eftekhar St, Vali-e-Asr Ave, Tehran 15956; tel. (21) 8801800; fax (21) 8900547; f. 1987; business and trade.

Ketab Sara: POB 15745-733, Tehran 15117; tel. (21) 8716104; fax (21) 8712479; e-mail ketab-sara@neda.net.ir; Chair. SADEGH SAMII.

Khayyam: Tehran; Dir MUHAMMAD ALI TARAGHI.

Majlis Press: Ketab-Khane Majlis-e-Showray-e Eslami No. 1 and the Documentation Centre, POB 11365-866, Baharestan Sq., Tehran; Ketab-Khane Majlis-e-Showray-e Eslami No. 2, Imam Khomeini Ave, Tehran 13174; tel. (21) 3130919; fax (21) 3124339; e-mail frelations@majlislib.com; internet www.majlislib.org; tel. (21) 6135335; fax (21) 3124339; f. 1923; f. 1950; library, museum and documentation centre of the Islamic Consultative Assembly; arts, humanities, social sciences, politics, Iranian and Islamic studies; Dir SAYED MUHAMMAD ALI AHMADI ABHARI.

Sahab Geographic and Drafting Institute: POB 11365-617, 30 Somayeh St, Hoquqi Crossroads, Dr Ali Shariati Ave, Tehran 16517; tel. (21) 7535907; fax (21) 7535876; maps, atlases, and books on geography, science, history and Islamic art; Man. Dir MUHAMMAD REZA SAHAB.

Scientific and Cultural Publications Co: Ministry of Science, Research and Technology, Tehran; tel. (21) 8048037; f. 1974; Iranian and Islamic studies and scientific and cultural books; Pres. SAYED JAVAD AZHARS.

Soroush Press: POB 15875-1163, Soroush Bldg, Motahhari Ave, Mofatteh Crossroads, Tehran; tel. and fax (21) 8847602; e-mail cultural@soroushpress.com; internet www.soroushpress.com; part of Soroush Publication Group, the publications dept of Islamic Republic of Iran Broadcasting; publishes books, magazines and multimedia products on a wide range of subjects; Man. Dir ALI AKBAR ASHARI.

Tehran University Press: 16th St, North Karegar St, Tehran; tel. (21) 8012076; fax (21) 8012077; e-mail press@ut.ac.ir; internet press .ut.ac.ir; f. 1944; university textbooks; Man. Dir Dr MOHAMMAD SHEKARCIZADEH.

Broadcasting and Communications

TELECOMMUNICATIONS

Telecommunications Company of Iran (TCI): POB 3316–17, Dr Ali Shariati Ave, Tehran; tel. (21) 8429595; fax (21) 8405055; Chair. and Man. Dir Dr ALIREZA BAHRAMPOUR.

BROADCASTING

Islamic Republic of Iran Broadcasting (IRIB): POB 19395-3333, Vali-e-Asr Ave, Jame Jam St, Tehran; tel. (21) 21961; fax (21) 2045056; e-mail webmaster@irib.com; internet www.irib.com; semi-autonomous authority, affiliated with the Ministry of Culture and Islamic Guidance; non-commercial; operates five national television and three national radio channels, as well as local provincial radio stations throughout the country; Dir-Gen. Dr ALI LARIJANI.

Radio

Radio Network 1 (Voice of the Islamic Republic of Iran): there are three national radio channels: Radio Networks 1 and 2 and Radio Quran, which broadcasts recitals of the Quran (Koran) and other programmes related to it; covers whole of Iran and reaches whole of Europe, the Central Asian republics of the CIS, whole of Asia, Africa and part of USA; medium-wave regional broadcasts in local languages; Arabic, Armenian, Assyrian, Azerbaijani, Balochi, Bandari, Dari, Farsi, Kurdish, Mazandarani, Pashtu, Turkoman, Turkish and Urdu; external broadcasts in English, French, German, Spanish, Turkish, Arabic, Kurdish, Urdu, Pashtu, Armenian, Bengali, Russian and special overseas programme in Farsi; Hebrew service introduced in 2002; 53 transmitters.

Television

Television (Vision of the Islamic Republic of Iran): 625-line, System B; Secam colour; two production centres in Tehran producing for two networks and 28 local TV stations.

Finance

(cap. = capital; res = reserves; dep. = deposits; brs = branches; m. = million; amounts in rials)

BANKING

Banks were nationalized in June 1979 and a revised commercial banking system was introduced consisting of nine banks (subsequently expanded to 10). Three banks were reorganized, two (Bank Tejarat and Bank Mellat) resulted from mergers of 22 existing small banks, three specialize in industry and agriculture and one, the Islamic Bank (now Islamic Economy Organization), set up in May 1979, was exempt from nationalization. The tenth bank, the Export Development Bank, specializes in the promotion of exports. A change-over to an Islamic banking system, with interest (forbidden under Islamic law) being replaced by a 4% commission on loans, began on 21 March 1984. All short- and medium-term private deposits and all bank loans and advances are subject to Islamic rules. A partial liberalization of the banking sector is planned by the Khatami administration, and the establishment of three private banks was authorized in 2001.

Although the number of foreign banks operating in Iran has fallen dramatically since the Revolution, some 30 are still represented.

Central Bank

Bank Markazi Jomhouri Islami Iran (Central Bank): POB 15875-7177, 144 Mirdamad Blvd, Tehran; tel. (21) 3110231; fax (21) 3115674; e-mail g.secdept@cbi.ir; internet www.cbi.ir; f. 1960; Bank Markazi Iran until Dec. 1983; issuing bank, government banking; cap. 350,000m., res 360,832m., dep. 106,239,671m. (March 2001); Gov. (vacant).

Commercial Banks

Bank Eqtesad-e Novin (Modern Economic Bank): Tehran; private bank; granted operating licence in 2001; Pres. FARID ZIAOLMOLKI.

Bank Keshavarzi (Agricultural Bank): POB 14155-6395, 129 Patrice Lumumba Ave, Jalal al-Ahmad Expressway, Tehran 14454; tel. (21) 8250135; fax (21) 8262313; e-mail info@agri-bank.com; internet www.agri-bank.com; f. 1979 by merger; state-owned; cap.

2,752,792m., res 3,310m., dep. 16,976,304m. (March 2002); Chair. and Man. Dir Dr JALAL RASOULOF; 1,700 brs.

Bank Mellat (Nation's Bank): Head Office Bldg, 327 Taleghani Ave, Cnr Forsat St, Tehran 15817; tel. (21) 82962004; fax (21) 82962700; e-mail mellat@mellatbank.com; f. 1980 by merger of 10 fmr private banks; state-owned; cap. 1,239,000m., res 42,823m., dep. 38,285,211m. (March 2001); Chair. and Man. Dir S. MANOUCHEHRI; 1,949 brs in Iran, 6 abroad.

Bank Melli Iran (The National Bank of Iran): POB 11365-171, Ferdowsi Ave, Tehran; tel. (21) 3231; fax (21) 3912813; e-mail inter@bankmelli-iran.com; internet www.bankmelli-iran.com; f. 1928; present name since 1943; state-owned; cap. 2,260,000m., res 52,775m., dep. 84,612,092m. (March 2001); Chair. and Man. Dir VALIOLLAH SEIF; 2,998 brs in Iran, 21 abroad.

Bank Refah Kargaran (Workers' Welfare Bank): POB 15815/1866, 40 Mollasadra Ave, Northern Shiraz St, Tehran 19917; tel. (21) 8042926; fax (21) 8041394; e-mail info@bank-refah.com; internet www.bank-refah.com; f. 1960; state-owned; cap. 95,000m., res 50,359m., dep. 6,937,916m. (March 2001); Chair. and Man. Dir Dr PAHVIZ AHMADI; 461 brs.

Bank Saderat Iran (The Export Bank of Iran): POB 15745-631, Bank Saderat Tower, 43 Somayeh Ave, Tehran; tel. (21) 8306091; fax (21) 8839539; e-mail saderat@emirates.net.ae; internet www .bank-saderat-iran.com; f. 1952; state-owned; cap. 1,887,000m., res 42,470m., dep. 53,996,383m. (March 2001); Chair. and Man. Dir AHMAD HATAMI YAZD; 3,254 brs in Iran, 24 abroad.

Bank Sepah: POB 9569, Imam Khomeini Sq., Tehran 11364; tel. (21) 3111091; fax (21) 2255267; e-mail info@banksepah.com; internet www.banksepah.com; f. 1925; nationalized in June 1979; cap. 1,052,000m., total assets 31,748,706m. (Dec. 2001); Chair. and Man. Dir Dr ALIREZA SHIRANI; 1,629 brs in Iran, 4 abroad.

Bank Tejarat (Commercial Bank): POB 11365-5416, 130 Taleghani Ave, Nejatoullahie, Tehran 15994; tel. (21) 8901257; fax (21) 8828215; e-mail webmaster@tejarat-bank.com; internet www .tejarat-bank.com; f. 1979 by merger of 12 banks; state-owned; cap. 1,231,120m., res 60,364m., dep. 33,061,406m. (March 2001); Chair. and Pres. SAYED ALI MILANI; 2,056 brs in Iran, 3 abroad.

Islamic Economy Organization (formerly Islamic Bank of Iran): Ferdowsi Ave, Tehran; f. 1980; cap. 2,000m.; provides interest-free loans and investment in small industry.

Karafarin Bank: No. 6, Ahmad Ghasir Ave, Tehran 15137; tel. (21) 8550316; fax (21) 8550624; e-mail info@karafinbank.com; internet www.karafarinbank.com; f. 1999 as Karafarin Credit Institute; converted into private bank in 2001; cap. 200,000m. (March 2002); Chair. MOHSEN KHALILI-ARAGHI; Man. Dir PARVIZ AGHILI; 6 brs.

Parsian Bank: Tehran; private bank; granted operating licence in 2001; Pres. BAHRAM FATHALI.

Development Banks

Bank Sanat va Madan (Bank of Industry and Mine): POB 15875-4459, 593 Hafiz Ave, Tehran; tel. (21) 8903271; fax (21) 8899294; e-mail webmaster@iran-bim.com; internet www.iran-bim.com; f. 1979 as merger of the following: Industrial Credit Bank (ICB), Industrial and Mining Development Bank of Iran (IMDBI), Development and Investment Bank of Iran (DIBI), Iranian Bankers Investment Company (IBICO); cap. 1,613,000m., res 64,000m., total assets 5,264,000m. (2000); Chair. and Man. Dir ABDORAHMAN NADIMI BOUSHEHRI.

Export Development Bank of Iran: POB 15875-5964, 2 Gandhi Ave, Tehran 15167; tel. (21) 8725140; fax (21) 8716979; e-mail kohzadi@edbi-iran.com; internet www.edbi-iran.com; f. 1991; cap. 1,120,000m., res 17,420m., dep. 368,103m. (August 2001); Chair. and Man. Dir Dr NOWROOZ KOHZADI; 26 brs.

Housing Bank

Bank Maskan (Housing Bank): POB 11365-5699, 247 Ferdowsi Ave, Tehran; tel. (21) 675021; fax (21) 673262; f. 1980; state-owned; cap. 140,000m., dep. 7,996,390m., total assets 9,838,667m. (March 2000); provides mortgage and housing finance; 630 brs; Chair. and Man. Dir AHMAD FARSHCHIAN.

Regulatory Authority

Supreme Council of Banks: Tehran; comprises two bankers and five ministerial appointees; regulates internal affairs of all Iranian banks; Chair. Dr HOSSEIN NEMAZI.

STOCK EXCHANGE

Tehran Stock Exchange: 228 Hafez Ave, Tehran 11389; tel. (21) 6708385; fax (21) 6710111; e-mail int.dept@tse.or.ir; internet www .tse.or.ir; f. 1966; Sec.-Gen. SAYED AHMAD MIR MOTAHARI.

INSURANCE

The nationalization of insurance companies was announced in June 1979.

Bimeh Alborz (Alborz Insurance Co): POB 4489-15875, Alborz Bldg, 234 Sepahboad Garani Ave, Tehran; tel. (21) 8903201; fax (21) 8803771; f. 1959; state-owned insurance company; all types of insurance; Man. Dir ALI FATHALI.

Bimeh Asia (Asia Insurance Co): POB 15815-1885, Asia Insurance Bldg, 297-299 Taleghani Ave, Tehran; tel. (21) 8800951; fax (21) 8898113; f. 1959; all types of insurance; Man. Dir MASOUM ZAMIRI; 6 brs.

Bimeh Dana (Dana Insurance Co): 25 Fifteenth Ave, Gandi St, Tehran 15178; tel. (21) 8770971; fax 8770812; f. 1988; life, personal accident and health insurance; Chair. and Man. Dir Dr ALI FARHANDI.

Bimeh Iran (Iran Insurance Co): POB 14155-6363, Dr Fatemi Ave, No. 107, Tehran; tel. (21) 6704346; fax (21) 6712646; e-mail info@bimeh-iran.com; internet www.bimeh-iran.com; f. 1935; all types of insurance; Chair. and Man. Dir ALI MOUSA REZA.

Bimeh Markazi Iran (Central Insurance of Iran): POB 19395-5588, 72 Africa Ave, Tehran 19157; tel. (21) 2050001; fax (21) 2054099; e-mail cent-ir@kanoon.net; f. 1971; supervises the insurance market and tariffs for new types of insurance cover; the sole state reinsurer for domestic insurance companies, which are obliged to reinsure 50% of their direct business in life insurance and 25% of business in non-life insurance with Bimeh Markazi Iran; Pres. ABDOLNASSER HEMMATI.

Trade and Industry

CHAMBER OF COMMERCE

Iran Chamber of Commerce, Industries and Mines: 254 Taleghani Ave, Tehran; tel. (21) 8846031; fax (21) 8825111; e-mail info@iccim.org; internet www.iccim.org; supervises the affiliated 32 Chambers in the provinces; Pres. ALI NAGHI KHAMOUSHI.

INDUSTRIAL AND TRADE ASSOCIATIONS

National Iranian Industries Organization (NIIO): POB 14155-3579, 133 Dr Fatemi Ave, Tehran; tel. (21) 656031-40; fax (21) 658070; f. 1979; owns 400 factories in Iran.

National Iranian Industries Organization Export Co (NECO): POB 14335-589, No. 8, 2nd St, Ahmad Ghasir Ave, Tehran 15944; tel. (21) 8733564; fax (21) 8732586.

STATE HYDROCARBONS COMPANIES

Iranian Offshore Oil Co (IOOC): POB 15875-4546, 339 Dr Beheshti Ave, Tehran; tel. (21) 8714102; fax (21) 8717420; wholly owned subsidiary of NIOC; f. 1980; development, exploitation and production of crude petroleum, natural gas and other hydrocarbons in all offshore areas of Iran in the Persian (Arabian) Gulf and the Caspian Sea; Chair. M. AGAZADEH; Dir S. A. JALILIAN.

National Iranian Gas Co (NIGC): Tehran; tel. (21) 8133347; e-mail pajohesh@nigc.org; internet www.nigc.org; Dir S. H. NAJIBI.

National Iranian Oil Co (NIOC): POB 1863, Taleghani Ave, Tehran; tel. (21) 6152738; fax (21) 6152823; e-mail webmaster@nioc.org; internet www.nioc.org; state organization controlling all 'upstream' activities in the petroleum and natural gas industries; incorporated April 1951 on nationalization of petroleum industry to engage in all phases of petroleum operations; in February 1979 it was announced that, in future, Iran would sell petroleum direct to the petroleum companies, and in September 1979 the Ministry of Oil assumed control of the National Iranian Oil Company; Chair. of Board BIJAN NAMDAR ZANGENEH (Minister of Oil); Man. Dir SAYED MAHDI MIR MOEZI.

National Iranian Oil Refining and Distribution Co (NIORDC): POB 15815-3499, NIORDC Bldg, 140 Ostad Nejatollahi Ave, Tehran 15989; tel. (21) 8801001; fax (21) 6152142; f. 1992 to assume responsibility for refining, pipeline distribution, engineering, construction and research in the petroleum industry from NIOC; Chair. and Man. Dir GHOLAMREZA AQAZADEH.

CO-OPERATIVES

Central Organization for Co-operatives of Iran: Ministry of Co-operatives, 16 Bozorgmehr St, Vali-e-Asr Ave, Tehran 14169; tel. (21) 6400938; fax (21) 6417041; e-mail min-coops@www.dci.co.ir; f. 1993; 15m. mems in 55,000 co-operative societies.

Central Organization for Rural Co-operatives of Iran (CORC): Vali-e-Asr Ave, Tehran 15948; e-mail smmirm@yahoo.com; internet www.ircorc.org; f. 1963; educational, technical, commercial and credit assistance to rural co-operative societies and unions; Chair. and Man. Dir SAYED MUHAMMAD MIRMUHAMMADI.

Transport

RAILWAYS

Iranian Islamic Republic Railways: POB 13185-1498, Shahid Kalantari Bldg, Railway Sq., Tehran 13165; tel. (21) 5641600; fax (21) 5650532; e-mail info@irirw.com; internet www.irirw.com; f. 1934; affiliated with Ministry of Roads and Transport; Pres. Deputy Minister of Roads and Transport; Pres. MOHAMMAD SAID NEJAD.

In 1999 the Iranian railway system comprised 6,300 km of standard 1,435 mm gauge, 146 km of electrified lines, and 94 km of wide 1,676 mm gauge. The railway network was estimated to comprise 7,156 km of mainline track in 2001. The system includes the following main routes:

Trans-Iranian Railway: runs 1,392 km from Bandar Turkman on the Caspian Sea in the north, through Tehran, and south to Bandar Imam Khomeini on the Persian (Arabian) Gulf.

Southern Line: links Tehran to Khorramshahr via Qom, Arak, Dorood, Andimeshk and Ahvaz; 937 km.

Northern Line: links Tehran to Gorgan via Garmsar, Firooz Kooh and Sari; 499 km.

Tehran–Kerman Line: via Kashan, Yazd and Zarand; 1,106 km.

Tehran–Tabriz Line: linking with the Azerbaijan Railway; 736 km.

Tabriz–Djulfa Electric Line: 146 km.

Garmsar–Meshed Line: connects Tehran with Mashhad via Semnan, Damghan, Shahrud and Nishabur; 812 km. A line is under construction to link Mashhad with Sarakhs on the Turkmen border. A 768-km line linking Mashhad with Bafq is also under construction.

Qom–Zahedan Line: when completed will be an intercontinental line linking Europe and Turkey, through Iran, with India. Zahedan is situated 91.7 km west of the Baluchistan frontier, and is the end of the Pakistani broad gauge railway. The section at present links Qom to Kerman via Kashan, Sistan, Yazd, Bafq and Zarand; 1,005 km. A branch line from Sistan was opened in 1971 via Esfahan to the steel mill at Zarrin Shahr; 112 km. A broad-gauge (1,976-mm) track connects Zahedan and Mirjaveh, on the border with Pakistan; 94 km.

Zahedan–Quetta (Pakistan) Line: 685 km; not linked to national network.

Ahvaz–Bandar Khomeini Line: connects Bandar Khomeini with the Trans-Iranian railway at Ahvaz; this line is due to be double-tracked; 112 km.

Azerbaijan Railway: extends from Tabriz to Djulfa (146.5 km), meeting the Caucasian railways at the Azerbaijani frontier. Electrification works for this section have been completed and the electrified line was opened in April 1982. A standard gauge railway line (139 km) extends from Tabriz (via Sharaf–Khaneh) to the Turkish frontier at Razi.

Bandar Abbas–Bafq: construction of a 730-km double-track line to link Bandar Abbas and Bafq commenced in 1982. The first phase, linking Bafq to Sirjan (260 km), was opened in May 1990, and the second phase was opened in March 1995. The line provides access to the copper mines at Sarcheshmeh and the iron ore mines at Gole-Gohar.

Bafq–Chadormalou: a 130-km line connecting Bafq to the Chadormalou iron-ore mines is under construction.

Chadormalou–Tabas: a 220-km line is under construction.

A passenger service running from Dushanbe (Tajikistan) to Tehran, via Uzbekistan and Turkmenistan, was scheduled to begin in 2001.

Underground Railway

In May 1995 the Tehran Urban and Suburban Railway Co concluded agreements with three Chinese companies for the completion of the Tehran underground railway, on which work had originally commenced in 1977. It was reported that about 80% of the work on two lines (one, 34 km in length, running north to south, and a second, 20 km in length, running east to west) had been completed. A 31-km suburban line, linking Tehran with the satellite city of Karaj, was inaugurated in February 1999, while phased sections of the urban lines were to enter service from the end of that year.

Tehran Urban and Suburban Railway Co (Metro): POB 4661, 37 Mir Emad St, Tehran 15878; tel. (21) 8740110; fax (21) 8740114;

e-mail info@tehranmetro.com; Chair. and Man. Dir MOHSEN HASHEMI.

ROADS

In 1998 there were an estimated 167,157 km of roads, including 890 km of motorways, 24,940 km of highways, main or national roads and 68,238 km of secondary or regional roads; about 56% of the road network was paved. There is a paved highway (A1, 2,089 km) from Bazargan on the Turkish border to the Afghanistan border. The A2 highway runs 2,473 km from the Iraqi border to Mir Javeh on the Pakistan border.

Ministry of Roads and Transport: see Ministries, above.

INLAND WATERWAYS

Principal waterways:

Lake Rezaiyeh (Lake Urmia): 80 km west of Tabriz in North-West Iran; and Karun river flowing south through the oilfields into the Shatt al-Arab, thence to the head of the Persian Gulf near Abadan.

Lake Rezaiyeh: From Sharafkhaneh to Golmankhaneh there is a twice-weekly service of tugs and barges for transport of passengers and goods.

Karun River: Regular cargo service is operated by the Meso-potamia-Iran Corpn Ltd. Iranian firms also operate daily motor-boat services for passengers and goods.

SHIPPING

Persian (Arabian) Gulf: The main oil terminal is at Kharg Island. The principal commercial non-oil ports are Bandar Shahid Rajai (which was officially inaugurated in 1983 and handles 9m. of the 12m. tons of cargo passing annually through Iran's Gulf ports), Bandar Khomeini, Bushehr, Bandar Abbas and Chah Bahar. A project to develop Bandar Abbas port, which predates the Islamic Revolution and was originally to cost IR 1,900,000m., is now in progress. Khorramshahr, Iran's biggest port, was disabled in the war with Iraq, and Bushehr and Bandar Khomeini also sustained war damage, which has restricted their use. In August 1988 the Iranian news agency (IRNA) announced that Iran was to spend US $200m. on the construction of six 'multi-purpose' ports on the Arabian and Caspian Seas, while ports which had been damaged in the war were to be repaired.

Caspian Sea: Principal ports Bandar Anzali (formerly Bandar Pahlavi) and Bandar Nowshahr.

Ports and Shipping Organization: 751 Enghelab Ave, Tehran; tel. (21) 8809280; fax (21) 8804100; internet www.ir-pso.com; affiliated with Ministry of Roads and Transport; Pres. AHMAD DONYAMALI.

Principal Shipping Companies

Iran Marine Services Co: Iran Marine Services Bldg, 151 Mirdamad Blvd, Tehran 19116; tel. (21) 2222249; fax (21) 2276203; e-mail imsco@neda.net; Chair. and Man. Dir ALIREZA HAJI BABAEI.

Irano–Hind Shipping Co: POB 15875-4647, 18 Sedaghat St, Vali-e-Asr Ave, Tehran; tel. (21) 2058095; fax (21) 2057739; joint venture between the Islamic Republic of Iran and the Shipping Corpn of India; Chair. AHAD MUHAMMADI.

Islamic Republic of Iran Shipping Lines (IRISL): POB 15875-4646, 675 North East Corner of Vali-e-Asr Sq., Tehran; tel. (21) 8893801; fax (21) 8308555; e-mail e-it@irisl.net; internet www.irisl.net; f. 1967; affiliated to the Ministry of Commerce; liner services in the Middle East, Europe, the USA, Far East and Central Asia; Chair. and Man. Dir Eng. ALI ASHRAF AFKHAMI.

National Iranian Tanker Co (NITC): POB 19395-4834, 67–68 Atefis St, Africa Ave, Tehran; tel. (21) 2229093; fax (21) 2228065; Chair. and Man. Dir MUHAMMAD SOURI.

CIVIL AVIATION

The two main international airports are Mehrabad (Tehran) and Abadan. An international airport was opened at Esfahan in July 1984 and the first international flight took place in March 1986. Work on a new international airport, 40 km south of Tehran, abandoned in 1979, resumed in the mid-1980s, and work on three others, at Tabas, Ardebil and Ilam was under way in mid-1990. The airports at Urumiyeh, Ahvaz, Bakhtaran, Sanandaj, Abadan, Hamadan and Shiraz were to be modernized and smaller ones constructed at Lar, Lamard, Rajsanjan, Barm, Kashan, Maragheh, Khoy, Sirjan and Abadeh. In early 1995 the Economic Co-operation Organization (ECO) agreed to establish a regional airline (Eco Air), based in Tehran. Construction of the Imam Khomeini International Airport in Tehran, anticipated to be one of the largest airports in the world, began in the late 1990s. The first phase of the project was completed in early 2001, and the airport was expected to be fully operational by 2003.

Civil Aviation Organization (CAO): Tehran; affiliated with Ministry of Roads and Transport; Head ASGHAR KETABCHI.

Iran Air (Airline of the Islamic Republic of Iran): POB 13185-755, Iran Air Bldg, Mehrabad Airport, Tehran; tel. (21) 9116689; fax (21) 6003248; internet www.iranair.co.ir; f. 1962; serves the Middle East and Persian (Arabian) Gulf area, Europe, Asia and the Far East; scheduled for part-privatization; Chair. and Man. Dir DAVOOD KESHAVARZIAN.

Iran Air Tours: 191 Motahhari Ave, Dr Moffateh Rd, Tehran 15879; tel. (21) 8758390; fax (21) 8755884; e-mail info@iranairtours.com; internet www.iranairtours.com; f. 1992; serves Middle East; Chair. MAHDI SADEGHI.

Iran Aseman Airlines: POB 141748, Mehrabad Airport, Tehran 13145-1476; tel. (21) 6484198; fax (21) 6404318; internet www.iran-aseman-airlines.com; f. 1980 as result of merger of Air Taxi Co (f. 1958), Pars Air (f. 1969), Air Service Co (f. 1962) and Hoor Asseman; domestic routes and charter services; Man. Dir ALI ABEDZADEH.

Kish Air: POB 19395-4639, 215 Africa Ave, Tehran 19697; tel. (21) 4665639; fax (21) 4665221; f. 1991; under the auspices of the Kish Development Organization; serves Persian Gulf area, Frankfurt, London and Paris; Pres. Capt. YADOLLAH KHALILI.

Mahan Air: POB 14515-411, Mahan Tower, 21 Azadegan St, Tehran; tel. (21) 4076081; fax (21) 4070404; e-mail international@mahanair.ir; internet www.mahanairlines.com; f. 1991; domestic routes and charter services between Europe and the Middle East; Man. Dir HAMID ARABNEJAD.

Saha Airline: POB 13445-956, Karadj Old Rd, Tehran 13873; tel. (21) 6696200; fax (21) 6698016; f. 1990; operates passenger and cargo charter domestic flights and services to Europe, Asia and Africa; Man. Dir Capt. A. SAEDI.

Tourism

Tourism was adversely affected by political upheaval following the Revolution. Iran's chief attraction for tourists is its wealth of historical sites, notably Esfahan, Rasht, Tabriz, Susa and Persepolis. Some 1,402,160 international tourist arrivals were recorded in 2001, compared with 326,048 in 1994. Receipts from tourism in 2000 totalled US $671m. Tourism centres are currently administered by the State, through the Ministry of Culture and Islamic Guidance, although in late 1997 the ministry indicated its intention to transfer all tourism affairs to the private sector.

Iran National Tourist Organization (INTO): Tehran; e-mail rrahmani@wanadoo.fr; internet perso.wanadoo.fr/rrahmani; f. 1979; affiliated with Ministry of Culture and Islamic Guidance; Man. Dir ABDOLLAH HOSSEINI.

Iran Touring and Tourism Organization (ITTO): e-mail info@itto.org; internet www.itto.org.

IRAQ

Introductory Survey

Location, Climate, Language, Religion, Flag, Capital

The Republic of Iraq is an almost land-locked state in western Asia, with a narrow outlet to the sea on the Persian (Arabian) Gulf. Its neighbours are Iran to the east, Turkey to the north, Syria and Jordan to the west, and Saudi Arabia and Kuwait to the south. The climate is extreme, with hot, dry summers, when temperatures may exceed 43°C (109°F), and cold winters, especially in the highlands. Summers are humid near the Persian Gulf. The official language is Arabic, spoken by about 80% of the population; about 15% speak Kurdish, while there is a small Turkoman-speaking minority. Some 95% of the population are Muslims, of whom more than 50% belong to the Shi'i sect. However, the Baath regime that came to power in 1968 was dominated by members of the Sunni sect. The national flag (proportions 2 by 3) has three equal horizontal stripes, of red, white and black, with three five-pointed green stars on the central white stripe. The inscription 'Allahu Akhbar' ('God is Great') was added to the flag in January 1991. The capital is Baghdad.

Recent History

Iraq was formerly part of Turkey's Ottoman Empire. During the First World War (1914–18), when Turkey was allied with Germany, the territory was captured by British forces. In 1920 Iraq was placed under a League of Nations mandate, administered by the United Kingdom. In 1921 Amir Faisal ibn Hussain, a member of the Hashimi (Hashemite) dynasty of Arabia, was proclaimed King of Iraq, and his brother, Abdullah, was proclaimed Amir (Emir) of neighbouring Transjordan (later renamed Jordan), also administered by the United Kingdom under a League of Nations mandate. The two new monarchs were sons of Hussain (Hussein) ibn Ali, the Sharif of Mecca, who had proclaimed himself King of the Hijaz (now part of Saudi Arabia) in 1916. The British decision to nominate Hashemite princes to be rulers of Iraq and Transjordan was a reward for Hussain's co-operation in the wartime campaign against Turkey. After prolonged negotiations, a 25-year Anglo-Iraqi Treaty of Alliance was signed in 1930. The British mandate ended on 3 October 1932, when Iraq became fully independent.

During its early years the new kingdom was faced with Kurdish revolts (1922–32) and with border disputes in the south. The leading personality in Iraqi political life under the monarchy was Gen. Nuri as-Said, who became Prime Minister in 1930 and held the office for seven terms over a period of 28 years. He strongly supported Iraq's close links with the United Kingdom and with the West in general. After the death of King Faisal I in 1933, the Iraqi monarchy remained pro-British in outlook, and in 1955 Iraq signed the Baghdad Pact, a British-inspired agreement on collective regional security. However, following the overthrow of King Faisal II (the grandson of Faisal I) during a military revolution on 14 July 1958, which brought to power a left-wing nationalist regime headed by Brig. (later Lt-Gen.) Abd al-Karim Kassem, the 1925 Constitution was abolished, the legislature was dissolved, and in March 1959 Iraq withdrew from the Baghdad Pact. Kassem, who had maintained a precarious and increasingly isolated position, opposed by pan-Arabists, Kurds and other groups, was assassinated in February 1963 in a coup by members of the armed forces. The new Government of Col (later Field Marshal) Abd as-Salem Muhammad Aref was more pan-Arab in outlook, and sought closer relations with the United Arab Republic (Egypt). Following his death in March 1966, President Aref was succeeded by his brother, Maj.-Gen. Abd ar-Rahman Muhammad Aref, who was ousted on 17 July 1968 by members of the Arab Renaissance (Baath) Socialist Party. Maj.-Gen. (later Field Marshal) Ahmad Hassan al-Bakr, a former Prime Minister, became President and Prime Minister, and supreme authority was vested in the Revolutionary Command Council (RCC), of which President al-Bakr was Chairman.

On 16 July 1979 the Vice-Chairman of the RCC, Saddam Hussain, who had long exercised real power in Iraq, replaced al-Bakr as RCC Chairman and as President of Iraq. Shortly afterwards several members of the RCC were executed for their alleged part in a coup plot. The suspicion of Syrian involvement in the attempted putsch resulted in the suspension of discussions concerning political and economic union between the two countries. (A bitter rivalry had developed after a younger generation of Baathists seized power in Syria in 1970; however, there had been some improvement in bilateral relations in late 1978, when President Hafiz al-Assad of Syria visited Baghdad.)

During 1979 the Iraqi Communist Party broke away from the National Progressive Front (NPF), an alliance of Baathists, Kurdish groups and Communists, claiming that the Baathists were conducting a 'reign of terror'. In February 1980 Saddam Hussain announced a National Charter, reaffirming the principles of non-alignment. In June elections took place (the first since the 1958 revolution) for a 250-member, legislative National Assembly; these were followed in September by the first elections to a 50-member Kurdish Legislative Council in the Kurdish Autonomous Region (which had been established in 1970).

Saddam Hussain retained his positions as Chairman of the RCC and Regional Secretary of the Baath Party following its Regional Congress in June 1982. A subsequent purge throughout the administration consolidated his control. Kurdish rebels became active in northern Iraq, occasionally supporting Iranian forces in the war with Iraq (see below). Another threat was posed by the Supreme Council of the Islamic Revolution in Iraq (SCIRI), formed in the Iranian capital, Tehran, in November 1982 by the exiled Shi'ite leader Muhammad Baqir al-Hakim. None the less, the majority of Iraq's Shi'ite community was not attracted by the fundamentalist Islamism of Ayatollah Khomeini of Iran, remaining loyal to Iraq and its Sunni President, while Iranian-backed militant groups (such as the Shi'ite fundamentalist Ad-Da'wa al-Islamiya group, which made numerous attempts to assassinate Saddam Hussain) were ineffective.

In the second half of the 1980s Saddam Hussain consolidated his control over the country and secured the loyalty of Iraq's Shi'ite community. In 1988, as a reward for its role in the war against Iran, the President announced political reforms, including the introduction of a multi-party system, and in January 1989 declared that these would be incorporated into a new permanent constitution. In April 1989 elections took place to the 250-seat National Assembly, in which one-quarter of the candidates were members of the Baath Party and the remainder either independent or members of the NPF. More than 50% of the newly-elected deputies were reported to be Baathists. In July the National Assembly approved a new draft Constitution, under the terms of which a 50-member Consultative Assembly was to be established; both institutions would assume the duties of the RCC, which was to be abolished after a presidential election.

During the 1980s representatives of Iraq's 2.5m.–3m. Kurds demanded greater autonomy. Resources were repeatedly diverted from the war with Iran to control Kurdish insurgency in the north-east of the country. Saddam Hussain sought an accommodation with the Kurds, and a series of discussions began in December 1983, after a cease-fire had been agreed with Jalal Talabani, the leader of the Patriotic Union of Kurdistan (PUK). The talks did not, however, include the other main Kurdish group, the Kurdistan Democratic Party (KDP), led by Masoud Barzani. Negotiations collapsed in May 1984, and armed conflict resumed in Kurdistan in January 1985 between PUK guerrillas and government troops, with Kurdish and Iranian forces repeatedly collaborating in raids against Iraqi military and industrial targets.

During February 1988 KDP and PUK guerrillas (assisted by Iranian forces) made inroads into government-controlled territory in Iraqi Kurdistan. In March the Iraqi Government retaliated by using chemical weapons against the Kurdish town of Halabja. In May the KDP and the PUK announced the formation of a coalition of six organizations to continue the struggle for Kurdish self-determination and to co-operate militarily with Iran. The cease-fire in the Iran–Iraq War in August allowed Iraq to launch a new offensive to overrun guerrilla bases near the borders with Iran and Turkey, again allegedly employing chemical weapons. Kurdish civilians and fighters fled across the borders, and by mid-September there were reported to be more than 200,000 Kurdish refugees in Iran and Turkey. In that month, with the army effectively in control of the border with Turkey, the Iraqi Government offered a full amnesty to all Iraqi Kurds inside and outside the country, excluding only Jalal Talabani. It also began to evacuate inhabitants of the Kurdish Autonomous Region to the interior of Iraq, as part of a plan to create a 30-km uninhabited 'security zone' along the whole of Iraq's border with Iran and Turkey. By October 1989, despite international censure of the evacuation programme, the 'security zone' was reported to be in place, prompting the PUK to announce a nation-wide urban guerrilla campaign against the Government. In September elections had proceeded to the legislative council of the Kurdish Autonomous Region.

Relations with Iran, precarious for many years, descended into full-scale war in September 1980. Iraq had become increasingly dissatisfied with the 1975 Algiers Agreement, which had defined the southern border between Iran and Iraq as the midpoint of the Shatt al-Arab waterway, and also sought the withdrawal of Iranian forces from Abu Musa and the Tunb islands, which Iran had occupied in 1971. The Iranian Revolution of 1979 exacerbated these grievances, and conflict soon developed as Iran accused Iraq of encouraging Arab demands for autonomy in Iran's Khuzestan ('Arabistan') region. Suspicion within Iraq's Sunni leadership of Shi'ite Iran under Ayatollah Khomeini was fuelled by Iranian backing for the SCIRI and other Iraqi groups opposed to Saddam Hussain. Border tensions in mid-1980 escalated into more extensive fighting after Iran ignored Iraqi demands for the withdrawal of Iranian forces from the border area of Zain ul-Qos, in Diala governorate, which Iraq maintained should have been returned under the 1975 agreement. In September 1980 Iraq abrogated the Algiers Agreement and its forces advanced into Iran. Fierce Iranian resistance led to military deadlock until mid-1982, when Iranian counter-offensives led to the retaking of the port of Khorramshahr and the withdrawal of Iraqi troops from territory occupied in 1980. In July 1982 the Iranian army crossed into Iraq.

In 1984 the balance of military power in the war with Iran moved in Iraq's favour, and its financial position improved as the USA and the USSR provided aid. Iraq and the USA reestablished full diplomatic relations (which had been severed by Iraq following the Arab–Israeli war of 1967) in November 1984.

From early 1988 Iraqi forces began to recapture land occupied by Iran, and in July they crossed into Iran for the first time since 1986. In that month Iran announced its unconditional acceptance of UN Security Council Resolution 598, and by August a UN-monitored cease-fire was in force. However, negotiations on the full implementation of the Resolution had made little progress by the time of Iraq's invasion of Kuwait in August 1990, at which point Saddam Hussain abruptly sought a formal peace agreement with Iran—accepting all the claims that Iran had pursued since the cease-fire, including the reinstatement of the Algiers Agreement of 1975. (For a fuller account of the 1980–88 Iran–Iraq War and of subsequent relations between the two countries, see the chapter on Iran.)

In mid-1990 the Iraqi Government criticized countries (principally Kuwait and the United Arab Emirates—UAE) that had persistently produced petroleum in excess of the quotas imposed by the Organization of the Petroleum Exporting Countries (OPEC, see p. 298). Iraq also accused Kuwait of violating the Iraqi border in order to secure petroleum resources, and demanded that Kuwait waive Iraq's debt repayments. In July, on the eve of an OPEC ministerial meeting in Geneva, Switzerland, Iraq mustered troops on its border with Kuwait. Direct negotiations between Iraq and Kuwait, with the aim of resolving their disputes over territory and Iraq's war debt, failed. On 2 August Iraqi forces invaded Kuwait, taking control of the country and establishing a provisional 'free government', and on 8 August Iraq announced its formal annexation of Kuwait. The UN Security Council unanimously adopted, on the day of the invasion, Resolution 660, demanding the immediate and unconditional withdrawal of Iraqi forces from Kuwait. Subsequent resolutions imposed mandatory economic sanctions against Iraq and occupied Kuwait (No. 661), and declared Iraq's annexation of Kuwait to be null and void (No. 662). On 7 August, at the request of King Fahd of Saudi Arabia, the US Government dispatched troops and aircraft to Saudi Arabia, in order to secure the country's border with Kuwait against a possible Iraqi attack: other countries quickly lent their support to what was

designated 'Operation Desert Shield', and a multinational force was formed to defend Saudi Arabia. Meanwhile, at a meeting of the League of Arab States (the Arab League, see p. 260) on the day after the invasion, 14 of the 21 members condemned the invasion and demanded an unconditional withdrawal by Iraq; one week later 12 member states voted to send an Arab deterrent force to the region of the Persian (Arabian) Gulf. However, there were widespread demonstrations of popular support for Iraq, notably among the Palestinian population of Jordan and in the Maghreb states.

Diplomatic efforts to achieve a peaceful solution to the Gulf crisis all foundered on Iraq's refusal to withdraw its forces from Kuwait. In November 1990 the UN Security Council adopted a resolution (No. 678) authorizing member states to use 'all necessary means' to enforce the withdrawal of Iraqi forces from Kuwait if they had not left by 15 January 1991. 'Operation Desert Storm'—in effect, war with Iraq—began on the night of 16–17 January, with air attacks on Baghdad by the multinational force. The Iraqi air force offered little effective resistance, and by the end of January the allied force had achieved air supremacy. Iraq launched *Scud* missiles against Saudi Arabia and Israel, but considerable diplomatic pressure was brought to bear upon Israel to prevent it from retaliating—which, since it would have been politically impossible for any Arab state to fight alongside Israel against Iraq, would have severely undermined the multinational force. In February Iraq formally severed diplomatic relations with Egypt, France, Italy, Saudi Arabia, Syria, the United Kingdom and the USA. In that month two Soviet-sponsored peace plans were accepted by Iraq but rejected by the US-led coalition (on the grounds that the proposals did not comply with UN Security Council resolutions on unconditional withdrawal from Kuwait). During the night of 23–24 February the multinational force began a ground offensive for the liberation of Kuwait: Iraqi troops were quickly defeated and surrendered in large numbers. A cease-fire was declared by the US Government on 28 February. Iraq agreed to renounce its claim to Kuwait, to release prisoners of war, and to comply with all pertinent UN Security Council resolutions. Resolution 687, adopted in April, provided for the establishment of a commission to demarcate the border between Iraq and Kuwait. The resolution also linked the removal of sanctions imposed on Iraq following its invasion of Kuwait to the elimination of non-conventional weaponry, to be certified by a UN Special Commission (UNSCOM), and also required that Iraq accept proposals for the establishment of a war reparation fund to be derived from Iraqi petroleum reserves.

Within Iraq the war was followed by domestic unrest: in March 1991 rebel forces, including Shi'ite Muslims and disaffected soldiers, were reported to have taken control of Al-Basrah (Basra) and other southern cities, although the rebellion was soon crushed by troops loyal to Saddam Hussain. In the north Kurdish separatists overran a large area of Kurdistan. The various Kurdish factions, allied since 1988 in the Kurdistan Iraqi Front (KIF), claimed that the objective of the northern insurrection was the full implementation of a 15-article peace plan concluded between Kurdish leaders and the Iraqi Government in 1970. Lacking military support from the multinational force, the Kurdish guerrillas were unable to resist the onslaught of the Iraqi armed forces, which were redeployed northwards as soon as they had crushed the uprising in southern Iraq, and an estimated 1m.–2m. Kurds fled before the Iraqi army across the northern mountains into Turkey and Iran. UN Security Council Resolution 688, adopted in April 1991, condemned the repression of Iraqi civilians, most recently in the Kurdish-populated areas, and insisted that Iraq allow immediate access by international humanitarian organizations to all those in need of assistance. This allowed the institution of an international repatriation and relief effort—co-ordinated by a multinational task force, designated 'Provide Comfort', which was immediately established in south-east Turkey to provide relief to displaced persons and to enforce the security both of the refugees and of the humanitarian effort in designated 'safe havens' on Iraqi territory north of latitude 36°N. A second phase of 'Operation Provide Comfort', which began in July, had only a limited role in humanitarian operations (responsibility for which had been assumed by the UN, under the terms of a memorandum of understanding with the Iraqi Government), its role being principally to deter further Iraqi aggression against the Kurds.

A second air exclusion zone, south of latitude 32°N, was established by France, Russia, the United Kingdom and the USA in August 1992, with the aim of protecting southern Iraqi

Shi'ite communities and the inhabitants of Iraq's southern marshlands. In December a combat aircraft shot down an Iraqi fighter which had allegedly entered the exclusion zone, and subsequent Iraqi military activity within the zone provoked air attacks by Western forces on targets in southern and northern Iraq in January 1993. (A ban imposed by the Iraqi Government on UN flights into the country was cited as further justification for the attacks.) Following the deployment of Iraqi armed forces close to the northern exclusion zone in May, the USA warned Iraq that it might suffer military reprisals in the event of any incursion into the Kurdish-held north. In June the USA launched an attack against intelligence headquarters in Baghdad, in retaliation for Iraq's role in an alleged conspiracy to assassinate former US President George Bush in Kuwait in April. In July Iraqi armed forces were reported to have renewed the Government's offensive against the inhabitants of the marshlands of southern Iraq. In May 1996 government forces launched a major offensive against the Shi'a opposition and tribes in Basra governorate; by the end of the year there were armed clashes between Iraqi security forces and the Shi'a opposition throughout the southern regions. In April 1998 the Iran-based SCIRI claimed that a renewed offensive against the Shi'a opposition in southern Iraq had resulted in the execution of some 60 Shi'ites during March.

Meanwhile, in April 1991 the PUK leader, Jalal Talabani, announced that President Saddam Hussain had agreed in principle to implement the provisions of the Kurdish peace plan of 1970. However, negotiations subsequently became deadlocked over the delineation of the Kurdish Autonomous Region, in which Kurdish groups wished the city of Kirkuk to be included. In October, in the absence of any negotiated agreement on an 'autonomous Kurdistan', the Iraqi Government withdrew all services from the area, effectively subjecting it to an economic blockade. The KIF proceeded to organize elections, in May 1992, to a 105-member Iraqi Kurdistan National Assembly, and for a paramount Kurdish leader. The outcome of voting, in which virtually the entire electorate (of some 1.1m.) participated, was that the KDP and the PUK were entitled to an almost equal number of seats. None of the smaller Kurdish parties achieved representation, and the KDP and the PUK subsequently agreed to share equally the seats in the new Assembly. The election for an overall Kurdish leader was deemed inconclusive, with Masoud Barzani, the leader of the KDP, receiving 47.5% of the votes cast, and Jalal Talabani 44.9%.

In December 1993 armed conflict broke out between militants of the PUK and the Islamic League of Kurdistan (or Islamic Movement of Iraqi Kurdistan—IMIK). Following mediation by the Iraqi National Congress (INC—a broad coalition of opposition groups), the two parties signed a peace agreement in February 1994. However, more serious armed conflict between partisans of the PUK and KDP led, in May, to the division of the northern Kurdish-controlled enclave into two zones. Peace accords concluded by the two parties in June, November and December all proved short-lived. In January 1995 Saddam Hussain offered to mediate in the dispute, prompting Western concern that the conflict might provide the Iraqi regime with a pretext to reassert control over the north. In June the IMIK withdrew from the INC, and in July there was renewed fighting between PUK and KDP forces, as a result of which scheduled elections to the Iraqi Kurdistan National Assembly were postponed. Peace negotiations under US auspices began in Dublin, Ireland, in August 1995 but collapsed in the following month. Subsequent discussions in the Iranian capital in October led to the signing of an agreement by the KDP and the PUK to hold elections to the Iraqi Kurdistan National Assembly in May 1996.

Tensions had been heightened in early and mid-1995 as Turkish armed forces attacked bases of the Kurdistan Workers' Party (Partiya Karkeren Kurdistan—PKK, now Congress for Freedom and Democracy in Kurdistan—KADEK) in the Kurdish enclave of northern Iraq. Moreover, Turkey's continued support for the KDP in its efforts to expel PKK fighters from the enclave was believed by some observers to have encouraged the PUK to seek support from Iran. The USA and Turkey were concerned at reports in late 1995 that the armed wing of the Iranian-based SCIRI had begun to deploy inside the Kurdish enclave. None the less, in February 1996 Turkey and NATO agreed to continue 'Operation Provide Comfort', which had become controversial in Turkey owing to the presence of PKK bases in the enclave.

In early 1996 the PUK leader, Jalal Talabani, offered to participate in peace negotiations with the KDP, and to take part

in new elections to the Iraqi Kurdistan National Assembly. Meanwhile, the USA continued to seek to mediate an agreement between the KDP and the PUK on the demilitarization of the Irbil (Arbil) region. However, hostilities between the two sides escalated in August, as the PUK contested the KDP's monopoly of duties levied on Turkish traders. At the end of the month the deployment of Iraqi armed forces inside the Kurdish area of northern Iraq, where they assisted KDP forces in retaking the PUK-held Kurdish towns of Arbil and As-Sulaimaniya (Sulaimaniya), provoked a new international crisis. In September the USA unilaterally launched retaliatory 'limited' air-strikes on air defence and communications targets in southern Iraq, and extended the southern air exclusion zone from latitude 32°N to latitude 33°N (thereby incorporating some southern suburbs of Baghdad). Turkey, which had refused to allow the use of its air bases for the US operation, deployed some 20,000 troops to reinforce its border with Iraq. Also in September the KDP captured the towns of Degala, Koy Sinjaq and Sulaimaniya, thereby gaining control of all three Kurdish provinces. The Iraqi Government subsequently announced the restoration of Iraqi sovereignty over Kurdistan, and offered an amnesty to its Kurdish opponents. In late September the KDP formed a KDP-led coalition administration comprising, among others, the IMIK, the Kurdistan Communist Party and representatives of the northern Assyrian and Turkoman communities. In October PUK fighters were reported to have recaptured much of the territory they had ceded to the KDP, and to be approaching the town of Arbil, having regained control of Sulaimaniya and Halabja. The PUK claimed that it would not, however, attempt to recapture Arbil because the town remained under the protection of Iraqi armed forces. Concern that Iran's alleged involvement in the conflict would provoke direct Iraqi intervention in the north prompted renewed diplomatic efforts on the part of the USA and Turkey, and US-sponsored peace talks in Ankara, Turkey, in late October resulted in a truce agreement.

A new air surveillance programme, 'Northern Watch', began in January 1997, following the termination of 'Operation Provide Comfort'. The new operation, based in south-east Turkey, was to be conducted by British, Turkish and US forces: France had announced that it would not participate, since the 'Northern Watch' mandate contained no provision for the supply of humanitarian aid.

In March 1997 the KDP withdrew from the US-sponsored peace negotiations. Although the KDP and the PUK continued to affirm their commitment to the pursuit of peace, each accused the other of violating the cease-fire. In May as many as 50,000 Turkish troops entered northern Iraq, where, apparently in co-operation with the KDP, they launched a major offensive against PKK bases. The incursion was condemned by Iraq and by Iran and Syria. The UN Secretary-General, Kofi Annan, demanded the withdrawal of Turkish troops from the area, expressing concern that their presence might obstruct the supply of food to the Kurdish enclave. Some 15,000 Turkish troops, again supported by KDP units, launched a further offensive against PKK bases in northern Iraq in September. Diplomatic efforts on the part of Turkish, British and US representatives failed to defuse escalating tensions between the Kurdish parties, and in mid-October, as Turkey began to withdraw its armed forces from northern Iraq, the PUK launched its strongest military assault against the KDP for a year, targeting several strategic points along the 1996 cease-fire line. The KDP alleged that the offensive had been orchestrated by Iran and conducted with PKK support. PUK and KDP representatives subsequently attended US-led negotiations in Turkey, resulting in a new cease-fire. However, fighting resumed later in the month; assertions by the PUK that Turkey was assisting the KDP, which claimed to have regained most of the territory lost to the PUK during the recent hostilities, were denied by the Turkish Government, which insisted that its military campaign was directed solely against the PKK. By mid-1998 a fragile cease-fire between the PUK and the KDP appeared to be enduring, and the two organizations agreed to exchange prisoners and to seek to co-operate in other areas. In September the USA brokered a formal peace agreement between the two parties: the accord, signed in Washington, DC, by Masoud Barzani on behalf of the KDP and Jalal Talabani for the PUK, provided for Kurdish legislative elections in 1999 (these did not take place, however), a unified regional administration, the sharing of local revenues, an end to hostilities and co-operation in implementing the 'oil-for-food' programme (see below) to benefit the Kurdish population. A new Kurdish coalition government was appointed by the Iraqi Kurdistan National Assembly in December 1999, reportedly comprising members of the KDP, the Kurdistan Independent Labour Party, the Assyrian Democratic Movement and the Turkoman community.

Meanwhile, some 7,000 Turkish troops were reported to have crossed into northern Iraq in February 1998, as the crisis between the Iraqi Government and the UN regarding weapons inspections deepened (see below), in order to prevent an influx of Kurdish refugees into south-east Turkey in the event of US air-strikes against Iraqi territory. In February 1999 the capture by Turkish forces, in Nairobi, Kenya, of the PKK leader, Abdullah Öcalan (see the chapter on Turkey), provoked demonstrations by Kurds in northern Iraq; some 4,000 Turkish troops again entered the territory in pursuit of PKK sympathizers. In November PKK fighters were reported to have attacked positions held by the KDP, and late in the month Iraq accused Turkey of having strengthened its forces in northern Iraq. In December Turkey accused Iraq of lending support to the PKK.

Following Iraq's defeat by the US-led coalition forces, Saddam Hussain strengthened his control over the country by placing family members and close supporters in the most important government positions. In September 1991 the Baath Party held its 10th Congress—the first such Congress since 1982—at which Saddam Hussain was re-elected Secretary-General of the Party's powerful Regional Command. Saddam Hussain attempted to bolster his domestic popularity through continued defiant rhetoric and confrontation with the UN over the dispatching of UN inspectors to monitor the elimination of Iraq's weapons of mass destruction, as stipulated by UN Security Council Resolution 687 (adopted in April 1991). In May 1994, confronted by a deepening economic crisis, Saddam Hussain personally assumed the post of Prime Minister. In January 1995 a comprehensive reorganization of military ranks took place, apparently the consequence of an unsuccessful military *coup d'état* in that month. In March another attempted coup—organized this time by the former head of Iraqi military intelligence and supported by Kurdish insurgents in the north and Shi'ite rebels in the south—was reported to have been suppressed. A further reorganization of military personnel resulted in the appointment of a new Chief of the General Staff in April. Reports of a mutiny by the armed forces at the Abu Ghraid army base, near Baghdad, in June were strongly denied by the Government. However, it appeared that an uprising had been organized by members of the Sunni Dulaimi clan, with the support of the élite 14 July battalion of the Iraqi army. A new Minister of Defence and a new Chief of the General Staff were appointed in July. In an apparent attempt to re-establish domestic and international recognition of Saddam Hussain's mandate, a meeting of the RCC was convened in September at which an interim amendment of the Constitution was approved whereby the elected Chairman of the RCC would automatically assume the Presidency of the Republic, subject to the approval by the National Assembly and endorsement by national plebiscite. Saddam Hussain's candidature was duly approved by the Assembly, and the referendum proceeded on 15 October, at which 99.96% of the votes cast (in a turn-out of 99.47%) endorsed the President's continuing in office. The result of the referendum was declared null and void in a statement issued by nine Iraqi opposition groups. In December 1996 Saddam Hussain's elder son, Uday, sustained serious injuries in an assassination attempt. Both the Sunni Dulaimi clan and Ad-Da'wa al-Islamiya claimed responsibility for the attack, although it was widely reported that the shooting was engineered by a former army officer whose uncle had been executed in 1990 after denouncing the Iraqi regime. In March 1997 an Iraqi opposition source alleged that Saddam Hussain had ordered the execution of 197 prisoners in retaliation for the attack on his son. In the previous month it had been reported that the President's younger son, Qusay, had twice been targeted by assassins, but had escaped injury on both occasions.

The first elections to the Iraqi National Assembly since 1989 took place in March 1996, when 689 candidates (all of whom had received the prior approval of a government selection committee) contested 220 of the Assembly's 250 seats: the remaining 30 seats were reserved for representatives of the Autonomous Regions of Arbil, D'hok and Sulaimaniya and were filled by presidential decree. An estimated 90% of Iraq's electorate participated in the elections, which were denounced by the INC, based in London, United Kingdom, and other groups opposed to the Government.

Reports emerged in late 1997 that a number of senior military officers and Baath Party members had been executed, as had an estimated 800 prisoners suspected of belonging to opposition organizations. Many senior Baath Party officials were reportedly replaced as part of a political purge apparently organized in order to dilute the influence of increasingly powerful provincial party groups.

UN human rights monitors were banned from Iraq after 1992, following critical reports by the Special Rapporteur of the UN Commission on Human Rights, Max van der Stoel. During 1998 van der Stoel later denounced the assassination of two senior Shi'a religious leaders, Ayatollah Murtada al-Burujirdi and Grand Ayatollah Mirza Ali al-Gharawi, killed in April and June respectively; and expressed fears that the murders were part of a systematic attack on the independent leadership of Iraq's Shi'a Muslims. The Iraqi Government denied any involvement in the murders, attributing them instead to 'malicious foreign-based elements'. In a report submitted in November the UN Special Rapporteur accused the Iraqi Government of continuing with a policy of forcibly deporting Kurds from the Kirkuk region, and, elsewhere, identified the plight of internally displaced persons as one of Iraq's most pressing humanitarian concerns. In February 1999 the killing of the leader of Iraq's Shi'a community, Grand Ayatollah Muhammad Sadiq as-Sader, provoked demonstrations in Baghdad and other cities. Despite claims by the INC that the unrest marked the beginning of an uprising against the Iraqi regime, it was reported that the demonstrations had been brutally suppressed by units of the Sunni-dominated Iraqi Special Republican Guard. In April the Iraqi authorities announced that four men had been executed for the murder of the Grand Ayatollah.

Several Western-based Arabic newspapers reported in early 2000 that the Iraqi authorities had foiled a coup attempt: accounts of the circumstances surrounding the alleged plot varied, with some sources claiming that about 40 officers of the Republican Guard had been executed for their part in an attempt to assassinate Saddam Hussain.

Elections took place on 27 March 2000 for 220 seats in the National Assembly. Official results stated that 165 seats had been won by members of the Baath Party, and the remaining 55 elective seats by independent candidates; a further 30 independents were nominated by the Government to fill the seats reserved for representatives of the Kurdish areas of the north, where the Iraqi authorities stated it was impossible to organize elections since the region remained 'occupied' by the USA. Saddam Hussain's elder son, Uday, was elected to the legislature for the first time, having reportedly received the highest number of votes of any candidate. Some 88.6% of the eligible electorate were said to have participated in the polls. The new National Assembly was inaugurated in April, when Sa'adoun Hammadi, who had held the office since 1996, was re-elected as Speaker. Throughout 2000 there was speculation that Saddam Hussain's son Qusay, who had reportedly been appointed deputy commander of the army and commander of the northern military region, had become the Iraqi leader's designated successor. Western-based media claimed in September and again in January 2001 that Saddam Hussain was in poor health, although the Iraqi authorities denied such reports.

In early May 2000 the SCIRI claimed to have perpetrated a rocket attack on presidential offices in Baghdad, in which there were said to have been a number of casualties; it was reported that Saddam Hussain had been scheduled to meet with his sons there at the time of the attack. In mid-July 2001 the SCIRI again claimed to have launched rocket assaults against a number of official targets in Baghdad, in reprisal for attacks on Shi'a religious leaders: most recently, a leading Shi'a cleric, Grand Ayatollah Sayed Hussain Bahr al-'Ulum, had died in what some considered to be suspicious circumstances in An-Najaf. Meanwhile, in March the Iraqi authorities had attributed a bomb explosion in Baghdad, in which two people were killed, to a US-backed 'terrorist' group.

In mid-May 2001 Saddam Hussain was re-elected Secretary-General of the Baath Party Command at the organization's 12th Regional Congress, while speculation that the Iraqi leader's son Qusay was being prepared as his successor was further fuelled by his election to the party Command and by his subsequent appointment as a deputy commander of the party's military section. Significant changes to the Council of Ministers were made from April, when Deputy Prime Minister Tareq Aziz assumed the foreign affairs portfolio on an interim basis: the outgoing Minister of Foreign Affairs, Muhammad Saeed as-Sahaf, became Minister of Information. Naji Sabri, formerly Iraq's ambassador to Austria, was appointed to the new position of Minister of State for Foreign Affairs, and was formally promoted to the post of Minister of Foreign Affairs in early August. In late May the Minister of Irrigation, Mahmoud Diyab al-Ahmad, was appointed acting Minister of the Interior, in place of Muhammad Ziman Abd ar-Razzaq, while Muhammad Hamzah az-Zubaydi was removed from the office of Deputy Prime Minister. Mahmoud Diyab al-Ahmad was confirmed as Minister of the Interior in late June, while Rasul Abd al-Hussain as-Swadi became the Minister of Irrigation. Presidential decrees issued in early and late July respectively elevated the Head of the Presidential Office, Ahmad Hussain Khudayyir, and the Minister of Military Industrialization, Abd at-Tawab Mullah Huweish, to the rank of Deputy Prime Minister. Samir Abd al-Aziz an-Najim was appointed acting Minister of Oil in early January 2003, following the dismissal from the post of Gen. Amir Muhammad Rashid.

Meanwhile, in mid-August 2002 the National Assembly unanimously endorsed the nomination of President Saddam Hussain to face a national referendum on his remaining in office for a further seven-year term. The referendum was duly held on 15 October, at which the President was officially reported to have received 100% of the votes. A general amnesty for prisoners held in Iraqi gaols was subsequently announced by the authorities; however, opposition groups maintained that there were still thousands of political prisoners in Iraq.

Issues of the maintenance of sanctions originally imposed under UN Security Council Resolution 661 and of Iraqi non-compliance with its obligations under Resolution 687 with regard to its weapons capabilities remained inextricably linked in the decade following the Gulf conflict. Security Council Resolution 692, adopted in May 1991, provided for the establishment of the UN Compensation Commission (UNCC) for victims of Iraqi aggression (both governments and individuals), to be financed by a levy (subsequently fixed at 30%) on Iraqi petroleum revenues. In August the Security Council adopted Resolution 706 (subsequently approved in Resolution 712 in September), proposing that Iraq should be allowed to sell petroleum worth up to US $1,600m. over a six-month period, the revenue from which would be paid into an escrow account controlled by the UN. Part of the sum thus realized was to be made available to Iraq for the purchase of food, medicines and supplies for essential civilian needs. Iraq rejected the terms proposed by the UN for the resumption of exports of petroleum, and in February 1992 withdrew from further negotiations. In October the UN Security Council adopted Resolution 778, permitting the confiscation of oil-related Iraqi assets to the value of up to $500m.

UN Security Council Resolution 707, adopted in August 1991, condemned Iraq's failure to comply with UN weapons inspectors, and demanded that Iraq disclose details of all non-conventional weaponry, that it allow members of UNSCOM and of the International Atomic Energy Agency (IAEA) unrestricted access to necessary areas and records, and that it halt all nuclear activities. Resolution 715, adopted in October, established the terms under which UNSCOM was to inspect Iraq's weapons capabilities. In October 1993 the Iraqi Government agreed to UN demands that it should release details of its weapons suppliers, and in November accepted the provisions for long-term weapons-monitoring contained in Resolution 715. However, it was clear by the end of the year that neither the Security Council nor the US Administration would be willing to allow even a partial easing of sanctions until Iraq had demonstrated a sustained commitment to the dismantling of its weapons systems. Moreover, the USA reiterated that Iraq must first also comply with all other relevant UN resolutions, recognize the newly demarcated border with Kuwait, and cease the repression of its Kurdish and southern Shi'ite communities.

In February 1994 the head of UNSCOM, Rolf Ekeus, stated, following talks with senior Iraqi officials, that Iraq had agreed to co-operate with UN weapons inspectors under Resolution 715. Thereafter, the Iraqi Government engaged in a campaign of diplomacy to obtain the removal of economic sanctions, and in July the first signs emerged of a division within the UN Security Council regarding their continuation. Russia, France and the People's Republic of China favoured acknowledging Iraq's increased co-operation with UN agencies, but were unable to obtain the agreement of the other permanent members of the Council—the USA and the United Kingdom. Tensions mounted in October when, as Ekeus announced that a system for monitoring Iraqi defence industries was ready to begin operating, there was a large movement of Iraqi forces towards the border with Kuwait, apparently to draw attention to Iraq's demands for

swift action to ease the sanctions. The US and British military responded by deploying additional naval vessels and forces to the region, and Iraqi forces began to withdraw northward. The Security Council adopted a resolution (No. 949) demanding the immediate withdrawal of all Iraqi forces recently transferred to southern Iraq, and stipulating that Iraq must not 'utilize its military or any other forces in a hostile or provocative manner to threaten its neighbours or the UN operations in Iraq'. In November the Iraqi National Assembly voted to recognize Kuwait within the border defined by the UN in April 1992.

In January 1995 the UN Secretary-General, Boutros Boutros-Ghali, offered to resume dialogue with Iraq on a partial removal of the economic sanctions. The UN Security Council subsequently renewed the sanctions for a further 60 days, although France and Russia reportedly favoured a partial easing of sanctions, provided that Iraq co-operated fully with UN weapons inspections. The sanctions were renewed for a further 60 days in March. Iraqi attempts to secure an end to the sanctions had suffered a serious reverse from February, when the head of UNSCOM announced that the Iraqi authorities had failed satisfactorily to account for material (known to have been imported in 1988) used in the manufacture of biological weapons. In April 1995 the Iraqi Government rejected as a violation of its sovereignty a revised UN proposal (contained in Security Council Resolution 986) for the partial resumption of exports of Iraqi petroleum to generate funds for humanitarian supplies under what was designated an 'oil-for-food' programme. Economic sanctions were renewed in July, and continued to be renewed at 60-day intervals.

In January 1996 it was announced that talks between the UN and Iraq on the sale of Iraqi petroleum, on the basis of Resolution 986, were to recommence. In May Iraq accepted the UN's terms governing a resumption of crude petroleum sales. At the insistence of the USA and the United Kingdom, the terms stipulated that Iraq should not be involved in the distribution to the Kurdish governorates of humanitarian aid purchased with funds realized. The memorandum of understanding signed by Iraq and the UN permitted Iraq to sell some 700,000 barrels per day (b/d) of petroleum over a period of six months, after which the UN would review the situation before deciding whether sales should continue for a further six months. Of every US $1,000m. realized through the sales, $300m. would be paid into the UN reparations fund; $30m.–$50m. would contribute to the costs of UN operations in Iraq; and $130m.–$150m. would go towards funding UN humanitarian operations in Iraq's Kurdish governorates. Remaining revenues would be used for the purchase and distribution, under close UN supervision, of humanitarian goods in Iraq. Iraq heralded the memorandum of understanding as the beginning of the dismantling of the sanctions regime, while the UN emphasized that the embargo on sales of Iraqi petroleum would not be fully revoked until all the country's weapons of mass destruction had been accounted for and destroyed.

The head of UNSCOM had reported to the Security Council his concern that Iraq might still be engaged in the development of prohibited weapons systems, and might be concealing biological missile warheads from the UN inspectorate. Incidents of non-co-operation between the Iraqi authorities and UN weapons inspection teams were reported at intervals. In July the UN Security Council sanctions committee announced procedures governing renewed sales of Iraqi petroleum; however, these terms required unanimous approval by the UN Security Council, and their endorsement was delayed by the USA's insistence on more stringent monitoring. A revised version was approved in August. In September, however, the implementation of Resolution 986 was postponed indefinitely, in response to the deployment of Iraqi armed forces inside the Kurdish 'safe haven' in northern Iraq (see above).

In October 1996 UNSCOM rejected Iraq's 'full, final and complete disclosures on its weapons programmes'. The USA was reported at this time to have granted its approval for the opening of an escrow account with the New York branch of the Banque Nationale de Paris, but the implementation of Resolution 986 was now dependent on the satisfaction of the UN Secretary-General with stability in northern Iraq and the approval by the UN sanctions committee of a formula fixing the value of Iraqi crude petroleum to be sold. Despite signs of renewed co-operation, in April 1997 Rolf Ekeus reiterated concerns that Iraq was not fully co-operating with UNSCOM weapons inspectors. In June the Security Council accused Iraq of obstructing inspection flights over Iraqi territory; Iraq subsequently denied UNSCOM access to three military sites. The UN reported renewed co-operation by Iraq in July, following the inauguration of Richard Butler as the new head of UNSCOM. In October, however, Butler's initial report to the UN Security Council asserted that although some progress had been made in inspecting Iraqi missiles, Iraq had failed to produce a credible account of its biological, chemical and nuclear warfare programmes and was continuing to hinder UNSCOM's work. Subsequently, within the UN Security Council, the USA and the United Kingdom proposed a resolution to prohibit Iraqi officials considered to be responsible for obstructing weapons inspections from leaving the country. France and Russia objected to the draft resolution but approved a revised version whereby a travel ban would be imposed on Iraqi officials in April 1998 should non-co-operation with UNSCOM continue. Meanwhile, Iraq's RCC criticized the high proportion of UNSCOM personnel supplied by the USA, demanding that these should leave the country by 5 November 1997; the deadline was subsequently extended by one week, in order to allow a UN mission to travel to Baghdad to attempt to resolve the dispute. When negotiations failed, the Security Council unanimously adopted a resolution (No. 1137) that immediately activated the travel ban on Iraqi officials. The resolution also stipulated that Iraq should retract its decision to expel US personnel and stated that further Iraqi intransigence regarding weapons inspections would result in the suspension of the 60-day sanctions review until April 1998 and might even provoke military action. Iraq refused to withdraw its demand, and US weapons inspectors were forced to leave the country. In response to the escalating crisis, the USA and the United Kingdom ordered military reinforcements to the region. Tensions appeared to ease in mid-November, however, after Russia's Minister of Foreign Affairs assured Iraq that his country would continue to promote the removal of economic sanctions on condition that Iraq complied with Resolution 1137. UNSCOM weapons inspectors were permitted to return to Iraq soon afterwards, but renewed Iraqi co-operation with UNSCOM was short-lived, as Iraqi officials refused to allow UNSCOM the unconditional access which it sought to areas designated as presidential palaces.

The confrontation over weapons inspections deepened in January 1998, when Iraq prohibited inspections by an UNSCOM team led by a former US marine officer, Scott Ritter, claiming that Ritter was spying for the US Central Intelligence Agency (CIA); the inspection team subsequently left Iraq. Meanwhile, the UN Security Council issued a statement deploring Iraq's failure to provide UNSCOM with 'full, unconditional and immediate access to all sites'. It was evident, none the less, that while the USA and United Kingdom continued to advocate increased coercion with regard to Iraq, the People's Republic of China, France and Russia were more amenable to the offsetting US dominance within UNSCOM. Richard Butler returned to Iraq, where he apparently agreed to Russian proposals to include experts from each of the permanent members of the Security Council, and from Germany, in forthcoming technical talks with Iraqi officials on the subject of weapons production records, thereby 'diluting' the presence of US personnel. However, Iraq maintained that it would be prepared to discuss UNSCOM access only following completion of the technical talks. The USA, supported by the United Kingdom, indicated that it was prepared to respond militarily to Iraq's continued non-co-operation, and the US Secretary of State, Madeleine Albright, and Secretary of Defense, William Cohen, led US diplomatic efforts to secure international support for possible military action against Iraq. However, China, France and Russia opposed the use of force. In view of threatened air-strikes against Iraq, Russia's Deputy Minister of Foreign Affairs held extensive talks with Iraqi officials in Baghdad in late January and early February. The Russian President, Boris Yeltsin, maintained that Russia would veto any Security Council resolution authorizing military attacks on Iraq, and warned that US military strikes could have serious international repercussions. Furthermore, it became apparent that there was little regional support for military action against Iraq: only Kuwait announced its approval of force if diplomatic efforts should fail; Saudi Arabia and Bahrain refused to authorize military attacks from their territories, while Egypt and Syria notably signalled their disapproval of military strikes against Iraq. Meanwhile, senior representatives of the Arab League, Russia, Turkey and France met in Baghdad in early February in an attempt to defuse the crisis. In mid-February the five permanent members of the UN Security Council approved a compromise formula whereby a group of diplomats, specially appointed by the UN Secretary-General in consultation with experts from UNSCOM and the IAEA, would be allowed unconditional and unrestricted access to the eight so-called presidential sites. The Secretary-General, Kofi Annan, travelled to Baghdad in order to discuss the compromise, which was accepted by Iraq following a meeting between Annan and Saddam Hussain; a new memorandum of understanding governing inspections was subsequently signed by the Deputy Prime Minister, Tareq Aziz, and Kofi Annan, thus averting the immediate threat of military action. In March the UN Security Council unanimously approved a resolution (No. 1154) endorsing the memorandum of understanding and warning of 'extreme consequences' should Iraq renege on the agreement. Inspection teams returned to Iraq shortly afterwards, and members of the special group began visiting the presidential sites later in the month. In April, in his six-monthly report to the Security Council, the head of UNSCOM concluded that there had been no progress in the disarmament verification process since October 1997, and that the destruction of Iraq's chemical and biological weapons was incomplete. Iraq, however, insisted that all of its weapons of mass destruction had been destroyed and urged the complete and comprehensive removal of sanctions. US and British opposition frustrated Russian attempts to secure a vote on a draft resolution proposing an end to weapons inspections, in view of an IAEA report concluding that it had failed to uncover evidence of a nuclear weapons programme in Iraq, and in late April the UN Security Council, in response to Butler's report, voted not to review the sanctions in force against Iraq. The USA began in May to withdraw military reinforcements deployed in the region at the height of the inspections crisis.

Richard Butler visited Baghdad in June 1998, where during talks with Tareq Aziz significant progress was reportedly made on plans for the verification of Iraqi disarmament and the eventual removal of sanctions. Later in the month the UNSCOM head was said to have informed the UN Security Council that US military tests on weaponry dismantled as part of the inspection process had shown that Iraq had loaded missile warheads with a chemical weapon component prior to the Gulf conflict. (Subsequent tests on the samples by French and Swiss scientists reportedly disclosed evidence of a decontaminant used to destroy agents of biological warfare.) The IAEA again reported in July that it had no evidence that Iraq was concealing nuclear weapons, but considered that Iraq lacked 'full transparency' in its disclosures to inspectors. In August negotiations between Butler and Aziz collapsed: Iraq rejected proposals for the acceleration of the inspection programme, apparently insisting that UNSCOM should report to the Security Council that Iraq had eliminated its weapons of mass destruction, and reiterated demands for a restructuring of UNSCOM to overcome the perceived US dominance. Iraq suspended arms inspections, and Saddam Hussain announced new terms and conditions for their resumption, including the establishment of a new executive bureau to supervise UNSCOM's operations. This effectively halted inspections of new sites, while UNSCOM continued existing monitoring without the co-operation of the Iraqi authorities. The UN Security Council voted later in August to renew the sanctions regime for a further 60 days, but in September unanimously adopted a resolution (No. 1194) condemning Iraq's action of the previous month, demanding that Iraq co-operate fully with UNSCOM, and suspending indefinitely the review of the sanctions regime. The Iraqi Government announced in response that it was halting all co-operation with UNSCOM indefinitely. Meanwhile, the apparent desire of the US Administration to avoid a confrontation such as that earlier in the year prompted the resignation of Scott Ritter from UNSCOM.

Reporting to the Security Council in October 1998, Richard Butler asserted that while Iraq was close to fulfilling its obligations with regard to missiles and chemical weapons programmes, UNSCOM remained concerned about the country's capacity for biological warfare. At the end of the month Iraq announced the suspension of all co-operation with UNSCOM until the UN Security Council cancelled the sanctions regime, dismissed Butler as head of UNSCOM, and restructured the inspectorate so as to ensure its neutrality. (UNSCOM inspectors were not expelled, however, and the IAEA was to be permitted to continue its operations in Iraq.) In early November the Security Council unanimously adopted a British-drafted resolution (No. 1205) demanding that Iraq immediately and unconditionally resume co-operation with UNSCOM. US and British military enforcements were again dispatched to the Gulf region to prepare for possible air-strikes against Iraqi targets. Egypt, Saudi Arabia and Syria, while they opposed the threat of force, urged Iraq to resume co-operation. In mid-November Iraq declared that UNSCOM would be permitted unconditionally to resume the weapons inspection programme, and inspectors subsequently returned to Iraq.

However, Iraq's relations with UNSCOM deteriorated once again in early December 1998, after a weapons inspection team conducting a new series of what were termed 'surprise' or 'challenge' inspections was denied access to the Baath Party headquarters in Baghdad. In a report to the UN Security Council in mid-December, Butler assessed that Iraq had failed to comply with its undertaking of the previous month regarding full co-operation with UNSCOM, and on the night of 16–17 December, following the withdrawal from Iraq of UNSCOM and IAEA personnel, the USA and the United Kingdom commenced a campaign of air-strikes against Iraqi targets; the operation, designated 'Desert Fox' was terminated on 20 December, with US and British forces claiming to have caused significant damage to Iraqi military installations. France, Russia and China contended that the military action had been undertaken without UN Security Council authorization; however, the USA and United Kingdom maintained that Resolution 1154, adopted in March, provided sufficient legitimacy. Following the attacks, Iraq, which accused the head of UNSCOM of having deliberately provided the US and British Governments with a pretext for military action, remained implacably opposed to the resumption of weapons inspections. In January 1999 US and Iraqi fighter aircraft clashed in the air exclusion zone over southern Iraq, while ground-launched attacks on US aircraft engaged in policing the zone (in retaliation for which US aircraft launched attacks on Iraqi defence sites) apparently indicated that Iraq was pursuing a more confrontational policy of refusing to recognize the exclusion zone. In late February and early March US and British forces undertook further air attacks on Iraqi military sites in response to alleged violations of the air exclusion zone, and in retaliation for further alleged ground-launched attacks. The Iraqi authorities claimed that on at least one occasion civilian targets had been attacked. In March the People's Republic of China urged the USA and the United Kingdom to halt the air-strikes against Iraq, claiming, as did Russia, that the exclusion zones were illegal since they had never been authorized by the UN. By mid-1999 US and British aircraft had reportedly made more than 200 multi-missile air-strikes against Iraq since mid-December 1998. US and British aircraft continued to attack Iraqi air defence targets during the second half of 1999, throughout 2000, and into 2001.

The new US Administration of George W. Bush, which assumed office in January 2001, swiftly demonstrated its resolve to maintain an uncompromising stance with regard to Iraq. In mid-February US and British fighter aircraft launched their first attack since Operation Desert Fox of December 1998 on air defence targets near Baghdad, in what the US President described as a 'routine mission' to enforce the northern and southern air exclusion zones. In justification of the assaults, the USA and United Kingdom cited a recent increased threat to their military aircraft operating in the exclusion zones from Iraqi missile defences. Iraq protested that the air-strikes had targeted residential areas of Baghdad, while there were Western media reports that three people had been killed in the initial attacks. In mid-June 2001 Iraq protested that 23 people had been killed by a bomb dropped on a football field outside Al-Mawsil (Mosul—within the northern exclusion zone); the USA and United Kingdom denied involvement, asserting that any deaths had been caused by Iraqi anti-aircraft shells. US and British military aircraft launched air-strikes against Iraqi air defence installations in the northern and southern exclusion zones during August–November 2001 and in early September 2002, in response to what they claimed were continuing Iraqi attacks on allied aircraft patrolling the zones; Iraqi officials reported that a number of civilians had died in the raids.

Meanwhile, the campaign of air-strikes conducted against Iraqi targets in December 1998 was regarded as marking the collapse of UNSCOM's mission. In January 1999, in order to establish the basis for a new approach to Iraq, the UN created three panels—to consider the question of Iraq's disarmament, to examine the issue of Kuwaiti prisoners of war, and to review the humanitarian situation—which reported in March. The panel on disarmament proposed the reform of UNSCOM, in order to reduce the dominance of the USA and the United Kingdom; however, the panel concluded that there were outstanding issues in almost every weapons category and urged a reinforced, continuous monitoring and verification programme. Iraq was deemed by the second panel not to have supplied adequate information to the UN regarding the fate of Kuwaiti prisoners of war. The humanitarian panel reported that Iraq had fallen into deep poverty since 1991, and recommended, *inter alia*, that the country should be permitted to export as much oil as possible in order to finance purchases under the oil-for-food programme. Iraq denounced the proposals of all three panels, declaring that they provided pretexts for continued aggression by the country's enemies.

Diplomatic initiatives undertaken by the Netherlands and the United Kingdom from early 1999 with the aim of drafting a proposal—acceptable to all the permanent members of the Security Council—to establish a successor body to UNSCOM culminated, in December, in the adoption by the Security Council of a resolution (No. 1284) that modified the regime in force for monitoring Iraqi weapons systems. Under the new resolution UNSCOM was to be replaced by a UN Monitoring, Verification and Inspection Commission (UNMOVIC). The resolution provided for the suspension of the economic sanctions in force against Iraq for renewable 120-day periods, provided that Iraq co-operated fully with the new weapons inspectorate and the IAEA throughout such periods. The resolution also effectively removed restrictions on the maximum amount of petroleum that Iraq was permitted to sell under the oil-for-food programme. Resolution 1284 was not approved unanimously, with the People's Republic of China, France and Russia, together with Malaysia (a non-permanent member) abstaining. Iraq immediately responded that it would not co-operate with UNMOVIC—although it was notable that the Government did not categorically reject the resolution. In January 2000 the Security Council unanimously endorsed the appointment of Hans Blix, a former Director-General of the IAEA, as head of UNMOVIC. (The UN Secretary-General's proposed appointment of Rolf Ekeus, Butler's predecessor as head of UNSCOM, to chair the new inspectorate had been opposed by Iraq, and China, Russia and France had formally objected to the nomination.) Meanwhile, IAEA personnel undertook the first routine inspection of Iraqi facilities since their withdrawal in December 1998.

In his first report to the UN Security Council, submitted in March 2000, Blix emphasized that, should Iraq permit the return of weapons inspectors, UNMOVIC would resume 'challenge' inspections of Iraqi sites. In the same month Iraq's Deputy Prime Minister, Tareq Aziz, decisively rejected the terms of Resolution 1284. In subsequent months the Iraqi Government repeated at frequent intervals that it would never admit UNMOVIC to enter the country. In early March 2001 it was reported that a recent UNMOVIC assessment had concluded that Iraq might still have the ability to build and use biological and chemical weapons, and might possess stocks of mustard gas, biological weapons and anthrax, as well as having the capability to deliver *Scud* missiles.

Exports of Iraqi crude petroleum, under the terms of Resolution 986, recommended in December 1996, whereupon Turkish officials reported that Iraq was pumping 350,000 b/d of crude petroleum through the Kirkuk–Yumurtalik pipeline. The first supplies of food purchased with the revenues from these exports arrived in Iraq in March 1997. In June the oil-for-food agreement was extended for a further six months, but Iraq suspended its petroleum exports shortly afterwards, protesting that it had not received sufficient humanitarian aid from the UN. Iraq submitted a new distribution plan, which was approved by the UN, and exports of petroleum recommenced in August. In December the UN renewed the sales agreement for another six months, but the following day exports were again halted at the behest of Iraq, which again criticized the UN for inefficient delivery of humanitarian supplies. Exports of petroleum resumed in January 1998, following UN approval of a new distribution plan drafted by Iraq. In February the UN Security Council raised the maximum permitted revenue from exports of petroleum to US $5,200m. in the six months to the end of July, of which Iraq would be permitted to spend some $3,550m. on humanitarian goods. The remainder would be used to finance reparations and UN operations in the country. However, Iraq stated that without the rehabilitation of its oil sector it would be unable to export more than $4,000m.-worth of oil every six months. In March UN technicians assessed that Iraq was currently able to export oil to the value of only $3,000m. every six months, and that it would only be able to maintain this level of exports if it was allowed to import essential spare parts. Accordingly, the UN Secretary-General requested the Security Council to allow Iraq to divert $300m. of oil revenues in order to carry out repairs to oil production facilities, and to reduce the value of permitted Iraqi exports under the revised agreement to $4,000m. every six months; Iraq was required to submit a new aid distribution programme before the revised agreement could take effect. The new plan, which was submitted in May and approved by the UN Secretary-General at the end of the month, provided for oil sales worth $4,500m. over the following six months, of which $3,100m. was to be allocated for humanitarian supplies and urgent infrastructural repairs, while the remainder would finance war reparations. In June the UN Security Council approved a resolution allowing Iraq to purchase spare parts to the value of $300m. for the oil sector. In November the Security Council renewed the oil-for-food agreement, allowing Iraq to sell $5,200m.-worth of oil over six months.

The oil-for-food programme was extended for a sixth phase in May 1999. In October the UN Security Council unanimously adopted a resolution (No. 1242) permitting Iraq to sell $3,040m.-worth of oil in addition to the quota agreed in May, to compensate for a severe shortfall in oil revenues in the two previous sale periods (partly owing to low world petroleum prices). However, Iraq's request to spend a further $300m. on equipment for the oil industry was not granted. In November, as the six-month sale period expired, Iraq rejected a proposal by the Security Council that the oil-for-food programme should be extended for a further two weeks, pending the revision of the programme's terms of reference. Iraq then temporarily suspended its exports of oil, causing world prices to rise to their highest levels since 1990. In December 1999 the Security Council voted unanimously to extend the oil-for-food programme for a further six months. In March 2000, in response to a report in which Kofi Annan recommended that Iraq be allowed to purchase increased quantities of parts and equipment to offset permanent damage to its oil industry, the UN Security Council unanimously approved a resolution permitting Iraq to make such purchases to the value of $600m. over six months. The oil-for-food programme was extended for further six-month periods in June and December. Prior to the latter extension, Iraq had briefly suspended petroleum exports, causing a sharp increase in international oil prices, in a dispute with the UN regarding pricing. Under the ninth phase of the oil-for-food programme, Iraq was to be allocated a maximum of $525m. for the local costs of maintaining the oil industry.

In February 2000 both the UN Humanitarian Co-ordinator in Iraq (responsible for the oil-for-food programme), Hans von Sponeck, and the head of World Food Programme operations in the country, Jutta Burghardt, resigned in protest at the hardship inflicted on the Iraqi people by the continuing sanctions regime. (The previous UN food co-ordinator, Denis Halliday, had resigned in 1998 after similarly denouncing the failure of the sanctions regime). Tun Myat, who took up office as UN Humanitarian Co-ordinator in Baghdad in April 2000, rejected criticism of the oil-for-food programme but undertook to try to improve its management. Throughout 2000 there was evidence of continued polarization among the five permanent members of the UN Security Council regarding the maintenance of the sanctions regime, while there were reports that Kofi Annan might himself favour a move towards so-called 'smarter' sanctions—targeting specific individuals rather than the entire Iraqi population. Furthermore, the international community became increasingly vocal in its condemnation of the humanitarian consequences of a decade of sanctions. In March, in spite of the objections of the UN sanctions committee, a British parliamentarian led an aid mission by road from the Jordanian capital, Amman, to Baghdad, delivering medicines to the headquarters of the Iraqi Red Crescent Society, and in April a member of the Italian and European parliaments chartered an aircraft from Amman to Baghdad, in direct contravention of the UN embargo on air travel to Iraq. In August President Hugo Chávez Frías of Venezuela became the first democratically elected head of state to visit Iraq since the Gulf conflict (in his capacity as Chairman of the OPEC Conference), travelling overland from Iran in order to avoid violating the air embargo. In September medical personnel and members of the French cultural and sporting establishment made a much-publicized three-day visit to Iraq, aboard an aircraft chartered by a French non-governmental organization: the French authorities insisted

that the flight did not require prior authorization by the UN sanctions committee since its mission was humanitarian.

Meanwhile, following the reopening in August 2000 of Baghdad's Saddam International airport (for the first time since 1991), several foreign airlines announced their intention to begin commercial scheduled flights to Iraq: notable among these was the Russian carrier Aeroflot, which signed a memorandum of understanding with the Iraqi authorities in October 2000 (no date was specified for the resumption of flights), while the Egyptian President, Hosni Mubarak, stated that he would not object to the resumption of flights from Egypt should any private airline choose to operate services. In August a rail link between Baghdad and Aleppo, Syria, was reopened after an interval of some 20 years. Furthermore, in November Iraq began to transport crude petroleum to Syria, via a pipeline not used since the early 1980s (the oil-for-food agreement permitted oil exports only via two designated outlets); the new route was assessed as having the capacity to more than double Iraqi oil sales from their existing level of 150,000 b/d.

In September 2000 the UN Security Council approved the payment to Kuwait of US $15,900m. in compensation for lost production and sales of petroleum as a result of the 1990–91 occupation. However, it was agreed to reduce the levy on Iraq's petroleum revenues destined for reparations under the oil-for-food programme from 30% to 25%: France and Russia had hitherto delayed a decision by the UNCC on the payment, and earlier in September Russia warned of its inclination to oppose Kuwaiti claims to reparations unless the levy on Iraqi oil revenues was reduced to 20%.

While Saddam Hussain insisted that the sanctions regime was beginning to disintegrate, and the Iraqi leader appeared to be deriving considerable political capital from the increasing international concern at the very evident humanitarian suffering that had resulted from more than a decade of sanctions, the new US Administration under President George W. Bush, who assumed office in January 2001, emphasized its commitment to ensuring the maintenance of the sanctions regime pending the full implementation of Resolution 1284. The new US Secretary of State, Colin Powell, swiftly undertook to secure implementation of a revised sanctions regime, with a view to resolving humanitarian concerns, by means of allowing the direct sale or supply to Iraq of most consumer goods without prior UN approval, while at the same time maintaining strict controls on the supply to Iraq of goods with potential military applications. Supporters of so-called 'smart' sanctions considered that these would have the effect of countering smuggling (of oil out of, and goods into, Iraq), as well as the divisions within the Security Council and delays in approving import contracts at the UN that had severely undermined the credibility of oil-for-food in recent years. The ninth phase of the oil-for-food programme was extended for a further month from the beginning of June 2001, to allow further consideration of a British-drafted initiative on 'smart' sanctions, which had US approval but was opposed, among the permanent members of the Security Council, by the People's Republic of China, France and Russia. In protest at the 'smart' sanctions scheme, Iraq swiftly suspended exports under oil-for-food, and urged other OPEC members not to increase production to compensate for the shortfall in supply. Intensive diplomatic activity in subsequent weeks resulted in the endorsement by China and France of a compromise list of items that Iraq would be unable to import under the new system (China's acceptance being secured by the USA's agreement to release sales contracts to the value of some US $90m. that it had been delaying within the UN sanctions committee). However, Russia maintained its threat to veto the British resolution, after its counter-initiative to defer a decision on 'smart' sanctions for a further six-months—whereby Resolution 1284 would be revised to allow a suspension of sanctions if Iraq agreed to readmit UN weapons inspectors—was rejected by other Security Council members. Thus, the United Kingdom withdrew its resolution, and in early July the Security Council unanimously adopted Resolution 1360, extending the oil-for-food regime for a further five months. Iraq resumed oil exports under the UN programme one week later.

In late November 2001, shortly before the end of the 10th phase, Minister of Foreign Affairs Naji Sabri emphasized that Iraq would end participation in oil-for-food if 'smart' sanctions revisions were adopted; he also reiterated that weapons inspectors would not be permitted to return to Iraq. Implementation of 'smart' sanctions was effectively deferred for a further six-month period when, at the end of November, the Security

Council unanimously approved Resolution 1382—essentially a compromise whereby Russia agreed to adopt an annexed list of embargoed items with military and civilian purposes before the expiry of the new (11th) phase, while the USA consented to review Resolution 1284. In early 2002 it was reported that the UN's recently imposed policy of assessing the export price for Iraqi oil retroactively, which had deprived Iraq of the opportunity to negotiate prices with brokers, had resulted in a decline in exports from 2.2m. b/d in December 2001 to 1.5m. b/d in January 2002. Meanwhile, Benon Sevan, the Executive Director of the Iraq Programme, expressed what he termed 'grave concern' in early January at an unprecedented surge in delays, amounting in value to almost US $5,000m., at the UN sanctions committee. In mid-May the Security Council adopted Resolution 1409, extending the oil-for-food programme for a further six months (the 12th phase) while implementing a mechanism to accelerate the processing of contracts not subject to inclusion on the Goods Review List. Earlier in May Iraq resumed exports under oil-for-food, which it had suspended a month earlier in protest against the USA's perceived failure to act to end Israel's military offensive against the Palestinian territories. In late November the UN Security Council adopted Resolution 1443, extending the 12th phase of the oil-for-food programme for a further nine days, amid disagreement concerning the issue of the Goods Review List: Russia and other council members were reported to have rejected US attempts to extend the list of prohibited goods. Resolution 1447 of early December extended the programme for a further six months (the 13th phase), while Resolution 1454, approved at the end of that month, expanded the list of goods subject to review to include certain items with a potential military use. In mid-March 2003, immediately prior to the start of the US-led military campaign in Iraq (see below), the UN announced a temporary suspension of the oil-for-food programme. However, amid a sharp deterioration in the living conditions of Iraqi citizens following the outbreak of hostilities, at the end of March the UN Security Council adopted Resolution 1472, granting the Secretary-General, Kofi Annan, the authority to implement existing contracts and to facilitate the delivery of aid for an initial 45-day period. The Security Council voted in late April to extend the Secretary-General's mandate until the beginning of June.

From late 2001, and especially after the defeat of the Taliban regime in Afghanistan (q.v.), speculation increased that the USA might extend its 'war on terror' to seek to remove the regime of Saddam Hussain. Although Iraq had strenuously denied any involvement in the September suicide attacks against New York and Washington, DC, and the majority of analysts contended that there was little likelihood of a link between the Iraqi regime and the al-Qa'ida (Base) network of Osama bin Laden, the Saudi Arabian-born fundamentalist Islamist alleged by the USA to have orchestrated the attacks, Iraq was noted for its failure to condemn the atrocities. In response to demands by George W. Bush that Iraq must readmit UN inspectors to prove that it was not developing weapons of mass destruction, or otherwise be 'held accountable', the Iraqi authorities denounced US 'arrogance' and stated that Iraq would not 'bow to threats', reiterating that UN sanctions should first be ended and the air exclusion zones revoked. Tensions were heightened in late January 2002 when, in his State of the Union address, President Bush assessed Iraq as forming what he termed an 'axis of evil' (with Iran and the Democratic People's Republic of Korea) seeking to develop weapons of mass destruction, specifically accusing Iraq of plotting to develop anthrax, nerve gas and nuclear weapons. The USA reacted with extreme caution to the announcement in early February that the Secretary-General of the Arab League had conveyed to Kofi Annan a message from Saddam Hussain stating Iraq's willingness to resume talks at the UN 'without preconditions', after a one-year hiatus; it remained the position of the USA that weapons inspectors should return to Iraq exclusively according to Security Council terms. It was subsequently confirmed that the UN Secretary-General was to meet with Naji Sabri in New York in early March (with the head of UNMOVIC, Hans Blix, also in attendance), for talks focusing on implementation of pertinent Security Council resolutions adopted since 1990, including the return to Iraq of weapons inspectors. The day before the meeting the USA presented new evidence to a committee of the Security Council purportedly showing that Iraq was violating UN sanctions and developing weapons capabilities. Shortly after the March meeting Vice-President Taha Yassin Ramadan accused the USA and United Kingdom of seeking to manufacture a new

crisis around the issue of weapons inspections as a pretext for renewed military attacks against Iraq. Further talks in early May and early July were reported to have ended with no substantive progress regarding the return of weapons inspectors.

In January 2002, meanwhile, the office of the UN High Commissioner for Human Rights reported that Andreas Mavrommatis, who had succeeded Max van der Stoel as Special Rapporteur on human rights in Iraq two years previously, had been invited to visit Iraq: his visit would be the first by a Special Rapporteur in a decade. In his annual report issued in April 2001 Mavrommatis had accused Iraq of perpetrating 'all-pervasive repression' and widespread terror.

In early August 2002 the UN Security Council declined an offer by the Iraqi Government to resume negotiations on the return of weapons inspectors, stating that Iraq should not impose any preconditions on the resumption of inspections. At the same time the USA continued to give clear signals that it intended to intervene to bring about 'regime change' in Baghdad, pursuing attempts to secure a UN resolution that would authorize military action, while indicating that the USA would be prepared to act unilaterally. Both US and British officials greeted with scepticism Iraq's declaration, made on 16 September, of its willingness to readmit weapons inspectors 'without conditions'; however, the People's Republic of China, France and Russia cautiously welcomed the move. In late September the British Government published a dossier outlining its case against the regime of Saddam Hussain and the perceived threat posed by Iraq's 'illicit weapons programmes' to the security of both the West and the Middle East. Shortly afterwards the US Secretary of Defense, Donald Rumsfeld, reiterated US claims that Iraq had provided assistance in the training of al-Qa'ida militants. Talks between Iraqi and UN officials were held in Vienna, Austria, at the end of September. Following the discussions, at the beginning of October Hans Blix stated that Iraq had agreed to allow inspectors 'unconditional and unrestricted access' to all relevant sites, but that no new agreement had been reached concerning access to Iraq's presidential palaces. (The memorandum of understanding signed by the UN and Iraq in February 1998 placed restrictions on such inspections.) The USA and United Kingdom were keen for the Security Council to approve a new resolution that would strengthen the mandate under which the UN inspectors were to operate. China, France and Russia all maintained that—in the event of Iraq's failure to comply with the terms of a future resolution concerning Iraqi disarmament—a second UN resolution should be passed prior to any military action being taken against the Iraqi regime. The UN Secretary-General, Kofi Annan, was also said to favour a 'two-step' approach. In mid-October 2002 President Bush signed a resolution adopted by the US Congress authorizing the use of force, if necessary unilaterally, to disarm Saddam Hussain's regime. On 8 November, after a compromise had been reached between the five permanent members, the UN Security Council unanimously adopted Resolution 1441, which demanded, *inter alia*, that Iraq permit weapons inspectors from UNMOVIC and the IAEA unrestricted access to sites suspected of holding illegal weapons (including the presidential palaces) and required the Iraqi leadership to make a full declaration of its chemical, biological, nuclear and ballistic weapons, as well as related materials used in civilian industries, within 30 days. The resolution warned that this represented a 'final opportunity' for Baghdad to comply with its disarmament obligations under previous UN resolutions, affirming that Iraq would face 'serious consequences' in the event of non-compliance with the UN inspectors or of any 'false statements and omissions' in its weapons declaration. Despite an initial rejection of Resolution 1441 by the Iraqi National Assembly on 12 November, on the following day the RCC announced its formal and unconditional acceptance of the terms of the resolution. Iraqi officials, however, repeatedly stated that they did not possess any weapons of mass destruction. Personnel from UNSCOM and the IAEA resumed weapons inspections in Iraq on 27 November.

Iraq presented UNMOVIC officials with a 12,000-page declaration of its weapons programmes on 7 December 2002. In mid-December the USA stated that Iraq was in 'material breach' of UN Resolution 1441 since it had failed to give a complete account of its weapons capabilities, citing in particular Iraq's failure to account for stocks of biological weapons such as anthrax. The United Kingdom also expressed its disappointment at the declaration. Meanwhile, both Hans Blix and the IAEA head, Muhammad el-Baradei, affirmed to the UN Security

Council that their inspectors required a greater level of co-operation from Iraqi officials. In early January 2003 Saddam Hussain accused the UN inspectorate of espionage. In mid-January UNMOVIC personnel reported the discovery of several empty chemical warheads to the south of Baghdad; the weapons had reportedly not been included in Iraq's December declaration, although it was unclear as to whether they constituted a significant discovery. Meanwhile, it was reported that some Arab states (including Saudi Arabia and Egypt) were attempting to persuade Saddam Hussain either to stand down or go into exile—suggestions that were immediately dismissed by Iraqi officials. At an emergency summit meeting of the Arab League in Cairo, Egypt, at the beginning of March, the UAE was reported to have presented a plan for the Iraqi President to stand down, and later in the month the King of Bahrain was said to have offered asylum to Saddam Hussain in order to avert an imminent war.

During January 2003 the USA and United Kingdom ordered a massive deployment of troops to the Gulf region, while asserting that a conflict was not inevitable if Iraq complied with the UN's disarmament terms. Both the French and German Governments, meanwhile, were vociferous in their opposition to military action and advocated an extension of the UN inspectors' mandate. In late January the foreign ministers of Turkey, Syria, Iran, Jordan, Egypt and Saudi Arabia attended a conference in Istanbul, Turkey, at the end of which they issued a joint communiqué urging Iraq to co-operate fully with UN inspectors in order to avoid a new conflict in the region. On 27 January, 60 days after the resumption of UN weapons inspections in Iraq (as stipulated under Resolution 1441), Hans Blix and Muhammad el-Baradei briefed the UN Security Council on the progress of inspections. El-Baradei stated that IAEA inspectors had found no evidence that Iraq had restarted its nuclear weapons programme, but requested more time for the organization to complete its research. Hans Blix, for his part, claimed that there was no evidence that Iraq had destroyed known stocks of illegal chemical and long-range ballistic weapons, and announced that he was sceptical about Baghdad's willingness to disarm. Following the briefing, the British Secretary of State for Foreign and Commonwealth Affairs, Jack Straw, declared Iraq to be in 'material breach' of Resolution 1441. As the likelihood of a US-led military response to the crisis increased, at the end of January eight European countries (including the United Kingdom, Italy and Spain) signed a joint statement expressing support for the USA's stance with regard to Iraq. In February the British Prime Minister, Tony Blair, under pressure from his electorate and members of his own Labour Party, accelerated his efforts to secure a second UN Security Council resolution authorizing a US-led campaign in Iraq should inspectors from UNMOVIC continue to report Baghdad's non-compliance. President Bush asserted at this time that, although he favoured the adoption of a second resolution, Resolution 1441 had given the USA the authority to disarm Iraq, if necessary by military means. The US Secretary of State, Colin Powell, had, on 5 February, presented to the Security Council what the USA claimed to be overwhelming evidence of Iraq's possession of weapons of mass destruction, its attempts to conceal such weapons from the UN inspectorate and its links with international terrorism, including the al-Qa'ida network. Despite signs of progress being reported by Hans Blix in his report on UNMO-VIC's inspections to the Security Council on 14 February—Iraqi officials had submitted new documents relating to banned materials, had announced an easing of restrictions governing the questioning by UN inspectors of Iraqi scientists, and had agreed to allow aerial reconnaissance flights over Iraq—the UNMOVIC chief stated that the inspections should continue, in order to determine whether Iraq did possess undeclared weapons of mass destruction.

On 24 February 2003 the USA, the United Kingdom and Spain presented a draft resolution to the UN Security Council effectively authorizing a US-led military campaign against Saddam Hussain's regime, in response to Baghdad's failure to disarm peacefully. The resolution stated that a deadline of 17 March would be set, by which time Iraq should prove that it was disarming; however, no specific mention was made of consequent military action in the event of the deadline not being met by Baghdad, apparently in an effort by the US-led coalition to persuade France, Russia and China not to exercise their right of veto. Officials from France, Russia and Germany responded to the draft resolution by presenting an alternative proposal involving an extended timetable of weapons inspections in order

to avert a war. At the beginning of March the Turkish parliament voted to allow US military aircraft to use Turkish airspace in the event of a campaign being waged against the Iraqi regime; however, the parliament rejected a plan for US forces to use Turkey's military bases, even for refuelling their aircraft. A few days later the Russian Minister of Foreign Affairs, Igor Ivanov, stated that any US-led military action without UN authorization would constitute a violation of the UN Charter. (France and Russia had by this time pledged to veto a second resolution authorizing the use of force to disarm Saddam Hussain.) On 12 March Tony Blair proposed six new conditions that Iraq must meet in order to prove that it was serious about disarmament: this was seen as an attempt at a compromise that might encourage wavering countries in the Security Council to support an amended resolution. The British proposals came a day after President Bush had rejected a suggested 45-delay postponement of any decision to go to war by six countries which had the power to influence the Security Council vote. On 15 March, in anticipation of a probable US-led invasion, Iraq's RCC issued a decree dividing the country into four military commands, under the overall leadership of Saddam Hussain. On the following day a summit meeting was held in the Azores, Portugal, between George W. Bush, Tony Blair and the Spanish Prime Minister, José Maria Aznar. Several commentators described the Azores summit as a 'council of war'. On 17 March the USA, the United Kingdom and Spain withdrew their draft resolution from the UN, demonstrating that the resolution's co-sponsors had realized the unlikelihood of winning UN support for military action; they stated that they reserved the right to take their own action to ensure Iraqi disarmament. On the same day President Bush issued an ultimatum giving Saddam Hussain and his two sons 48 hours to leave Baghdad or face military action. The Iraqi National Assembly rejected the ultimatum. UN weapons inspectors, humanitarian aid workers and UNIKOM observers along the Kuwait–Iraq border were subsequently withdrawn from Iraq.

Shortly after the expiry of President Bush's 48-hour deadline, on 19 March 2003 US and British armed forces launched a 'broad and concerted campaign' (code-named 'Operation Iraqi Freedom') to oust the regime of Saddam Hussain. An initial wave of air-strikes against a number of sites in the suburbs of Baghdad, apparently aimed at leading members of the Iraqi regime (including the President himself), apparently failed to achieve their target. Meanwhile, US-led coalition forces crossed into Iraq from Kuwait and began a steady advance towards the capital. At the same time a concerted campaign of massive air-strikes was launched against the key symbols of the Iraqi regime in and around Baghdad, including selected military bases, communications sites, government buildings and broadcasting headquarters. Government and military sites in other prominent Iraqi cities were targeted by the US-led coalition in subsequent days. The US and British forces adopted a simultaneous campaign of distributing leaflets and broadcasting radio messages, in an effort to persuade Iraqi citizens to abandon their support for the Baath regime: their declared intention was that Operation Iraqi Freedom would precipitate the disintegration of the regime 'from within'. British troops were principally engaged in securing towns in southern Iraq, including Iraq's second city of Basra, after the US-led coalition had seized control of the key southern port of Umm Qasr and the Al-Faw Peninsular. It was the intention of the USA and the United Kingdom that the Shi'a Muslim population of Basra would quickly initiate an uprising against the regime of Saddam Hussain, as had occurred following the Gulf war in 1991. Although fighting between US-led troops and Iraqi armed forces was often intense, resistance from the Iraqi army and from a number of *fedayeen* (martyrs) and volunteers from other Arab countries was generally lighter than had been anticipated by the allies. Moreover, there were widespread reports of Iraqi soldiers surrendering to the advancing forces. Shortly after the commencement of Operation Iraqi Freedom, in late March 2003 US forces had opened a second front in the Kurdish-controlled regions of northern Iraq, where Kurdish forces joined US troops in targeting bases of Ansar al-Islam. Fears that Turkey might exploit the situation to stage a mass deployment of its forces initially proved to be unfounded.

At an emergency summit meeting of Arab League states in Cairo on 24 March 2003, representatives of the 17 member states in attendance (with the exception of Kuwait) issued a resolution condemning the US-led invasion of Iraq and demanding the withdrawal of all foreign forces from Iraqi territory. Although the USA and the United Kingdom persistently maintained that they were seeking to avoid targeting civilian infrastructure, there was considerable anger in the Arab world and elsewhere at the reports of high numbers of civilian casualties as a result of the conflict. By 7 April US armed forces had entered central Baghdad, including its presidential palaces. The expected strong resistance from Saddam Hussain's élite Republican Guard did not materialize, and the disintegration of the Baath regime appeared to be complete on 9 April when crowds of Iraqis staged street demonstrations denouncing Saddam Hussain and destroying images and statues of the Iraqi President. Kurdish militias gained control of the northern town of Kirkuk on 10 April, while the town of Mosul was seized by Kurdish and US forces on the following day. The seizure by US troops of Saddam Hussain's birthplace and power base, Tikrit (to the north of Baghdad), on 14 April was widely viewed as the last strategic battle of the US-led campaign to remove the regime of Saddam Hussain.

Although it was unclear as to where leading members of the Iraqi regime, particularly Saddam Hussain and his sons, had fled—if indeed they were still alive—the US-led coalition began, in early April 2003, to turn its attention to preparations for the establishment of an Iraqi Interim Authority (initially under the leadership of retired US army general Jay Garner, Director of the USA's Office for Reconstruction and Humanitarian Assistance in Iraq), which was to administer the country for a transitional period prior to the eventual holding of democratic elections and the formation of a new Iraqi Government. As a number of leading Iraqi dissidents returned to the country, a US-sponsored conference of opposition groups was held near An-Nasiriyah (Nasiriya) in southern Iraq on 15 April. (The SCIRI boycotted the meeting owing to the leading role played by the USA in the discussions.) Participants at the conference agreed a 13-point resolution outlining their expectations for Iraq's future political development, which included the formal dissolution of the Baath Party and the need to create a democratic government based on the rule of law and excluding divisions along ethnic or tribal lines. Iraq was to retain the right to decide its leaders, which should not be imposed by a foreign power. However, it quickly became apparent that the immediate task of regaining military and civil control over the country would be an extremely challenging one, as widespread looting, arson and lawlessness initially replaced the firm control of Saddam Hussain's regime in many Iraqi cities. On 11 April the USA had issued a 'most wanted' list of 55 members of the deposed regime whom it sought to arrest: on 25 April the former Deputy Prime Minister, Tareq Aziz, surrendered to US forces, becoming the 12th Iraqi official on the list to be taken into US custody. Other leading figures in the former regime were detained by coalition forces in subsequent weeks. On 1 May President Bush officially declared an end to 'major combat operations' in Iraq. A few days later it was reported that a US diplomat, Paul Bremer, had been appointed as 'civilian administrator' in Iraq, in place of Jay Garner.

In September 2000 Iraq reiterated allegations that Kuwait was stealing Iraqi petroleum by drilling in an area near the Iraq–Kuwait border. Iraq also accused both Kuwait and Saudi Arabia of inflicting (through the maintenance of the sanctions regime) suffering on the Iraqi population, and alleged that Saudi Arabia was appropriating Iraqi petroleum transported under the oil-for-food programme. In September and October reports of Iraqi troop movements near the Iraq–Kuwait demilitarized zone prompted Kuwait to reinforce security arrangements in the border area. None the less, a general improvement was perceived in Iraq's relations with other Arab states from late 2000. In October Iraq was represented at a summit meeting of the Arab League for the first time since 1990, as RCC Vice-President Izzat Ibrahim attended the emergency session convened in Cairo, Egypt, to discuss the Israeli–Palestinian crisis that had erupted at the end of September 2000. Saddam Hussain (to whom an invitation had been issued for the first time since the Gulf crisis) was represented by senior officials of the Iraqi Government at the Arab League summit held in Amman, Jordan, in late March 2001. The summit was considered as having made the most comprehensive effort hitherto in addressing divisions arising from the Gulf conflict. None the less, a draft resolution presented by the Iraqi delegation urging an end to UN sanctions and a resumption of civilian flights failed to secure adoption, owing to Iraq's unwillingness to accede to a requirement of a specific guarantee that Iraq would not repeat the invasion of 1990: Iraq contended that it had already

done sufficient to make clear its recognition of Kuwait's territorial integrity. Meanwhile, in November 2000 the Jordanian Prime Minister, Ali Abu ar-Ragheb, became the highest ranking Arab leader to visit Iraq since the Gulf crisis.

In the context of a long-standing commitment to establish a regional common market under the auspices of the Council of Arab Economic Unity (see p. 178), plans for a quadripartite free-trade zone encompassing Iraq, Egypt, Libya and Syria were advanced following a meeting of the Council held in Baghdad in early June 2001. In the previous month Iraq had participated with Jordanian, Moroccan and Tunisian representatives in a meeting in Agadir, Morocco, at which the four countries agreed to establish a free-trade zone. In mid-August the Syrian Prime Minister, Muhammad Mustafa Mero, leading a ministerial and commercial delegation, became the most senior Syrian official to visit Iraq for two decades; Mero made a further visit in early December.

The extent of Iraq's rehabilitation among the majority of Arab states was particularly evident as, from the latter part of 2001, speculation increased regarding potential US-led military action against Iraq. Leaders of influential Arab states, among them Egypt, Jordan and Syria, all expressed particular concern at the likely consequences should the Bush Administration's campaign be directed against any Arab state, warning against exacerbating tensions in a region under great strain because of the Israeli–Palestinian crisis. During talks with a senior representative of the Qatari ruling family in early January 2002, Saddam Hussain issued an appeal to Arab states to set aside their differences, referring specifically to the need to improve relations with Kuwait and Saudi Arabia; later in the month Iraq reportedly announced its preparedness to allow a delegation from Kuwait to visit Iraq to verify that no Kuwaiti prisoners of war were being held (Kuwait continued to assert that Iraq was detaining at least 90 Kuwaiti nationals). At the Arab League summit held in Beirut, Lebanon, in late March it was announced that Kuwait and Iraq had reached agreement on the resolution of outstanding differences (see the chapter on Kuwait). In May Iraq notified the UN of its intention to return to Kuwait the official documents and archives removed during the 1990–91 occupation. Meanwhile, in mid-January 2002 Amr Moussa became the first Secretary-General of the Arab League to visit Baghdad since the Gulf conflict, subsequently conveying to the UN Secretary-General Saddam Hussain's willingness to resume talks (see above).

In October 1998 the US Congress approved the Iraq Liberation Act, permitting the US President to provide up to US $97m. in military assistance to Iraqi opposition groups in exile. In April 1999 11 opposition groups gathered in London, United Kingdom, where they undertook to reform the moribund INC and to prepare by July a plan of campaign against Saddam Hussain's regime. Although representatives of the two main Kurdish factions, the KDP and the PUK, attended the meeting, the SCIRI and the Iraqi Communist Party did not participate. Two new organizations were created at the meeting: a collegiate leadership of seven members (six members were nominated, with the remaining place reserved for a representative of the SCIRI), and a five-member committee charged with contacting all opposition groups. In November, delegates to a national assembly of the INC, held in New York, USA, elected a 65-member central council and a new, seven-member collegiate leadership. Several INC leaders meanwhile relocated to the USA, with a view to lobbying US support for the Iraqi opposition movement.

Following the September 2001 suicide attacks against the USA, elements within the Iraqi opposition were swift to draw attention to what they alleged to be the Baghdad regime's links with terrorism (although the UN Secretary-General notably asserted in late 2001 that he had seen no evidence connecting the Iraqi Government with the attacks). In late September the PUK launched an offensive against bases of the Islamic Unity Movement of Kurdistan and the Jund al-Islam (Army of Islam) at Halabja, claiming that the latter group, formed at the beginning of September, had links with the Iraqi intelligence services and had received training and funds from al-Qa'ida. In mid-December a delegation from the US Department of State, led by Ryan Crocker, Deputy Assistant Secretary for Near Eastern Affairs, visited northern Iraq on what was widely interpreted as a mission to assess the situation in the Kurdish areas in anticipation of possible military action against the regime in Baghdad. The USA was apparently keen to resolve outstanding differences between the PUK and the KDP, regarding unity among the Kurdish groups as a prerequisite for fostering any internal revolt against Saddam Hussain; US officials had reportedly been concerned at recent contacts between the KDP and the Iraqi Government. Meanwhile, there was considerable speculation that the Iraqi opposition movement was too disparate to form an effective political force against the incumbent regime, with key elements beset by rivalries. Furthermore, both the KDP and the PUK emphasized concerns at the likelihood of reprisals against civilians in the north should the USA launch a military assault against Baghdad. None the less, ongoing speculation that the USA would be likely to seek to use the northern areas in the event of a campaign to overthrow Saddam Hussain apparently prompted the Iraq leader to seek a dialogue with Kurdish groups. In mid-March 2002, in a speech commemorating the anniversary of the 1970 agreement which had accorded a degree of autonomy for the Kurdish regions, Saddam Hussain urged Iraqi Kurds to postpone their aspirations in view of the threats against Iraq, offering to discuss improvements to autonomy provisions. Both Syria and Turkey were particularly concerned at the potential ascendance of Iraqi Kurdish groups should Saddam Hussain be overthrown, although, visiting these countries in March 2002, the PUK leader, Jalal Talabani, gave assurances that Iraq's Kurdish groups had no intention of establishing their own state. The presence in the Syrian capital at the same time of Izzat Ibrahim prompted suggestion that Syria might attempt to mediate between the Iraqi Government and the Kurdish groups. It was reported in early April that Barham Salih, the head of the PUK administration in Sulaimaniya, had survived an assassination attempt. In early October, following renewed discussions between the PUK and the KDP, a transitional joint session of the Iraqi Kurdistan National Assembly was convened in Arbil—the first meeting of the assembly since 1994. In mid-December 2002 representatives from a large number of Iraqi opposition groups met in London, United Kingdom, and agreed to the formation of a 65-member committee to formulate a unified position in anticipation of a possible US-led military campaign to remove the regime of Saddam Hussain. A US-sponsored conference of Iraqi opposition parties was held in Salah ad-Din, in Kurdish-controlled northern Iraq, in late February 2003, at which delegates elected a leadership council of six members (including leaders of the KDP, PUK, SCIRI and INC). In late March, on the eve of the conflict in Iraq, opposition groups met with US and Turkish officials in Ankara, Turkey, and reportedly agreed to work towards the establishment of a 'fully representative and democratic government' in Iraq to replace the current regime.

Government

Prior to the ousting of the regime of Saddam Hussain by the US-led coalition in early April 2003 (see Recent History), Iraq was divided into 18 governorates (including three Autonomous Regions). In the immediate aftermath of the war in Iraq, a US-appointed Iraqi Interim Authority was expected to govern the country for a transitional period prior to the holding of democratic elections and the formation of a new Iraqi Government.

Defence

Military service is compulsory for all men at the age of 18 years, and lasts between 18 months and two years, extendable in wartime. In August 2002 the armed forces totalled an estimated 389,000 regular members: the army had an estimated total strength of 350,000 (including an estimated 100,000 recalled reserves); the air force had a strength of some 20,000, the navy an estimated 2,000, and an air defence command an estimated strength of 17,000. Paramilitary forces comprised security troops, border guards and *fedayeen* ('martyrs'), with strengths estimated, at 15,000, 9,000 and 18,000–20,000. Defence expenditure in 2001 was estimated at US $1,400m.

Economic Affairs

In 1999, according to estimates by the UN's Economic and Social Commission for Western Asia (ESCWA), Iraq's gross domestic product (GDP), measured in current prices, was ID 5,591,768m. In terms of US dollars, GDP was $4,142.1m. ($184 per head) in 1999. Real GDP growth was estimated at 15% in 1998 and 8% in 1999. Over the period 1990–2001 the population increased by an average of 2.5% per year, according to estimates by the World Bank.

Agriculture (including forestry and fishing) contributed 29.1% of GDP in 1999, compared with 15.3% in 1989—i.e. prior to the invasion of Kuwait. An estimated 9.6% of the labour force were employed in agriculture in 2001. Dates are the principal cash crop. Other crops include wheat, barley, tomatoes, melons and oranges. Production of eggs, milk and poultry meat is also important. During 1990–2001, according to FAO data, agricultural production declined by an average of 3.8% per year; however, output increased by 8.0% in 2001. Output of cereals fell from 3.45m. metric tons in 1990 to an estimated 1.54m. metric tons in 2001.

Industry (including mining, manufacturing, construction and power) employed 19.1% of the labour force in 1987; the sector provided 10.3% of GDP in 1999 (compared with 37.9% in 1989).

Mining (including production of crude petroleum and gas) employed 1.3% of the labour force in 1987. The sector contributed less than 0.1% of GDP in 1994 (compared with 17.9% in 1989), and by 1995 its contribution was negative. Iraq had proven reserves of 112,500m. barrels of petroleum at the end of 2001, as well as 3,110,000m. cu m of natural gas. Reserves of phosphates, sulphur, gypsum and salt are also exploited.

Manufacturing employed 7.4% of the labour force in 1987, and contributed 0.7% of GDP in 1995 (compared with 12.3% in 1989). Measured by the value of output, chemical, petroleum, coal, rubber and plastic products accounted for 35.2% of manufacturing activity in 1986. Other important branches of the sector in that year were food products (providing 15.8% of manufacturing output), non-metallic mineral products (12.6%) and textiles (6.1%). In the immediate aftermath of the war with the multinational force in 1991, all of Iraq's electrically-powered installations were reported to have ceased functioning, as a result of the destruction of power plants, etc. By late 1991 a drastic decline in industrial output had been observed, with further hundreds of industrial projects having ceased, owing to the continued trade embargo, and a consequent steep rise in unemployment.

Energy is derived principally from petroleum, which accounted for an estimated 98.0% of total electricity generation in 1999.

The services sector employed 67.2% of the labour force in 1987, and contributed 60.6% of GDP in 1999 (compared with 46.7% in 1989).

In 1996, according to the *Middle East Economic Digest* of London, Iraq recorded a trade surplus of US $300m. In that year, according to the same source, the current account of the balance of payments was estimated to be in balance. Crude petroleum was by far the most important export before the imposition of economic sanctions (see below). According to the IMF, the value of Iraq's imports in 2001 was ID 1,611.4m.

In a six-month emergency reconstruction budget, announced in mid-1991, planned expenditure in the general consolidated budget was reduced from ID 14,596m. to ID 13,876m., while investment budget expenditure was reduced from ID 2,340m. to ID 1,660m. The Iraqi Government estimated that, at 1 January 1991, its total external debt stood at ID 13,118m. (US $42,320m.); and that the servicing of the debt over the period 1991–95 would cost ID 23,388m. ($75,450m.). These estimates did not, however, take into account loans made to Iraq during the Iran–Iraq War by Saudi Arabia and Kuwait. The *Middle East Economic Digest* estimated that in 1996 the average rate of inflation was 450%, compared with inflation averaging 24.4% per year in 1985–89.

Iraq is a member of the Arab Fund for Economic and Social Development (see p. 136), the Council of Arab Economic Unity (see p. 178), the Organization of Arab Petroleum Exporting Countries (see p. 292), the Organization of the Petroleum Exporting Countries (see p. 298) and the Arab Co-operation Council (see p. 338).

Under the terms of UN Resolution 986, instituting the so-called oil-for-food programme whereby supply and distribution of humanitarian and consumer goods to Iraq and the sale of Iraqi petroleum are monitored by the UN, Iraq was initially permitted to sell petroleum to the value of US $2,000m. over a six-month period (subsequently extended). Of this, only about $1,200m. was available to the Iraqi Government, exclusively for the purchase of humanitarian goods under UN supervision. In February 1998 the UN Security Council increased the maximum permitted revenue from exports of petroleum to $5,200m. in the six months to 31 July. This increase was subsequently renewed, but Iraq was not able to take full advantage of it owing to the urgent need for rehabilitation of parts of its oil production sector. In June the Security Council accordingly adopted a resolution permitting Iraq to import equipment to the value of $300m. for the sector. In late 1998 it was estimated that Iraq's oil production capacity was declining by 4%–6% annually, and revenues were further undermined by the decline in international prices for petroleum. In October 1999 the UN Security Council adopted a resolution permitting Iraq to sell additional oil valued at $3,040m., while in December the Security Council effectively removed restrictions on the value of Iraqi petroleum exports. In March 2000 the Security Council unanimously approved a resolution permitting Iraq to make further purchases of parts and equipment for the oil industry to the value of $600m. over six months. The oil-for-food programme was extended for further six-month periods in June and December. Under this last (ninth) phase, Iraq was to be allocated a maximum of $525m. for the local costs of maintaining the oil industry. The ninth phase was extended for a further month from the beginning of June 2001, to allow the Security Council to debate an initiative on so-called 'smart' sanctions. The proposed revision of the sanctions regime would allow the direct sale or supply to Iraq of most consumer goods without prior UN approval, while at the same time maintaining strict controls on the supply to Iraq of goods with potential military applications. It was intended that such reforms would address the humanitarian degradation that had resulted from more than a decade of sanctions, while 'unblocking' contracts awaiting UN approval under existing oil-for-food regulations and also reducing smuggling of oil from, and goods into, Iraq: by this time Iraq was estimated to be procuring some $1,000m. annually outside the control of the sanctions administration. After the Security Council failed to reach agreement on 'smart' sanctions, a 10th phase of the existing programme was approved in July, and an 11th in November. A 12th phase under a modified mechanism was approved in May 2002 and extended for a further nine days from late November. A 13th phase of the oil-for-food programme was approved in early December. (For further details regarding changes to the oil-for-food programme during late 2002 and early 2003, see Recent History). In early 2003 industry sources estimated Iraq's oil production capacity to be around 2.8m. b/d; capacity prior to the Gulf crisis of 1990–91 was in the region of 3.5m. b/d.

According to an official UN report compiled in March 1991, Iraq's war with the multinational force 'wrought near apocalyptic results on the economic infrastructure', relegating Iraq to a 'pre-industrial age but with all the disabilities of post-industrial dependency on an intensive use of energy and technology'. The damage to the infrastructure has been reflected in every sector, with recovery undoubtedly obstructed by more than a decade of international sanctions. The failure of irrigation and drainage systems, owing to lack of fuel and spare parts, compounded by the inability of farmers to obtain pesticides and fertilizers, have resulted in very poor harvests, while reduced production of animal feed has resulted in a significant decrease in livestock and livestock products. The consequences for the Iraqi population of the resultant food shortages have been particularly severe. Upon his resignation in September 1998, the first co-ordinator of the UN oil-for-food programme, instituted in 1996, estimated that 4,000–5,000 Iraqi children were dying each month as a result of contaminated water supplies, poor sanitation, malnutrition and inadequate health facilities. His successor resigned in February 2000, as did the head of World Food Programme operations, in protest at what they considered to be the consequences of the sanctions regime and the inadequacy of the humanitarian programme to meet the basic requirements of the Iraqi people. In August 1999 a report by the UN Children's Fund (UNICEF) claimed that infant mortality rates in areas under Iraqi government control had more than doubled since the imposition of economic sanctions in 1990. UNICEF claimed that in some parts of Iraq that were outside government control infant mortality rates had fallen. (Iraqi claims that the increases were the result of the sanctions

regime were countered by the US Administration, which accused the Iraqi authorities of inadequate ordering and distribution of supplies.) A report issued by the International Committee of the Red Cross in February 2000 stated that infant mortality had risen threefold since the imposition of sanctions. In late February 2003, as a US-led military campaign to oust the regime of Saddam Hussain appeared to be imminent, a leaked UN document reportedly warned that such a conflict could lead to 'a humanitarian emergency of proportions well beyond the capacity of UN agencies and other aid organizations'. After hostilities began in late March, economists began to turn their attention to the prospects for Iraq's economy in a 'post-Saddam Hussain era' and, more immediately, to the costs involved in the reconstruction of Iraqi infrastructure after more than a decade of sanctions and the subsequent war damage, as well as to the repayment of Iraq's massive external debts. With the prospect that 'regime change' would result in the removal of economic sanctions, it appeared likely that foreign investment would, in the long term, flow into Iraq, particularly for the reconstruction of the oil industry.

Education

Education is provided free of charge, and primary education, beginning at six years of age and lasting for six years, has been made compulsory in an effort to reduce illiteracy. Enrolment at primary schools of children in the relevant age-group reached 100% in 1978, but the proportion had fallen to 76% by 1995 (males 81%; females 71%). Secondary education begins at 12 years of age and lasts for up to six years, divided into two cycles of three years each. Enrolment at secondary schools in 1995 was equivalent to 42% of children in the appropriate age-group (males 51%; females 32%). There are 47 teacher-training institutes, 19 technical institutes and eight universities. In the 1991/92 academic year 46,250 students were reported to have enrolled in courses of higher education. Following the change of regime in Iraq in April 2003, a comprehensive reform of the country's education system was anticipated.

Public Holidays*

2003: 1 January (New Year's Day), 6 January (Army Day), 8 February (14 Ramadan Revolution, anniversary of the 1963 *coup d'état*), 12 February† (Id al-Adha, Feast of the Sacrifice), 5 March† (Islamic New Year), 14 March† (Ashoura), 14 May† (Mouloud, Birth of Muhammad), 14 July (Republic Day, anniversary of the 1968 *coup d'état*), 17 July (Baath Revolution Day), 8 August (Peace Day, anniversary of the cease-fire announcement in the war with Iran), 24 September† (Leilat al-Meiraj, ascension of Muhammad), 26 November† (Id al-Fitr, end of Ramadan).

2004: 1 January (New Year's Day), 6 January (Army Day), 2 February† (Id al-Adha, Feast of the Sacrifice), 8 February (14 Ramadan Revolution, anniversary of the 1963 *coup d'état*), 22 February† (Islamic New Year), 2 March† (Ashoura), 2 May† (Mouloud, Birth of Muhammad), 14 July (Republic Day, anniversary of the 1968 *coup d'état*), 17 July (Baath Revolution Day), 8 August (Peace Day, anniversary of the cease-fire announcement in the war with Iran), 12 September† (Leilat al-Meiraj, ascension of Muhammad), 14 November† (Id al-Fitr, end of Ramadan).

* Public holidays in Iraq are likely to change as a result of the removal of Saddam Hussain's regime in early 2003.

† These holidays are dependent on the Islamic lunar calendar and may vary by one or two days from the dates given.

Weights and Measures

The metric system is in force. Local measurements are also used, e.g. 1 meshara or dunum = 2,500 sq m (0.62 acre).

IRAQ

Statistical Survey

Statistical Survey

Source (unless otherwise indicated): Central Statistical Organization, Ministry of Planning, Karradat Mariam, ash-Shawaf Sq., Baghdad; tel. (1) 537-0071.

Area and Population

AREA, POPULATION AND DENSITY*

Area (sq km)	438,317†
Population (census results)	
17 October 1987	16,335,199
17 October 1997	
Males	10,940,764
Females	11,077,219
Total	22,017,983
Density (per sq km) in October 1997	50.2

* No account has been taken of the reduction in the area of Iraq as a result of the adjustment to the border with Kuwait that came into force on 15 January 1993.

† 169,235 sq miles. This figure includes 924 sq km (357 sq miles) of territorial waters but excludes the Neutral Zone, of which Iraq's share is 3,522 sq km (1,360 sq miles). The Zone lies between Iraq and Saudi Arabia, and is administered jointly by the two countries. Nomads move freely through it but there are no permanent inhabitants.

GOVERNORATES
(population at 1987 census)

	Area*(sq km)	Population	Density (per sq km)
Nineveh	37,698	1,479,430	39.2
Salah ad-Din	29,004	726,138	25.0
At-Ta'meem	10,391	601,219	57.9
Diala	19,292	961,073	49.8
Baghdad	5,159	3,841,268	744.6
Al-Anbar	137,723	820,690	6.0
Babylon	5,258	1,109,574	211.0
Karbala	5,034	469,282	93.2
An-Najaf	27,844	590,078	21.2
Al-Qadisiya	8,507	559,805	65.8
Al-Muthanna	51,029	315,816	6.2
Thi-Qar	13,626	921,066	67.6
Wasit	17,308	564,670	32.6
Maysan	14,103	487,448	34.6
Al-Basrah (Basra) . . .	19,070	872,176	45.7
Autonomous Regions:			
D'hok	6,120	293,304	47.9
Irbil (Arbil)	14,471	770,439	53.2
As-Sulaimaniya (Sulaimaniya) . .	15,756	951,723	60.4
Total	437,393	16,335,199	37.3

* Excluding territorial waters (924 sq km).

PRINCIPAL TOWNS
(population at 1987 census)

Baghdad (capital) . .	3,841,268	As-Sulaimaniya (Sulaimaniya) . .	364,096
Al-Mawsil (Mosul) .	664,221	An-Najaf	309,010
Irbil (Arbil) . . .	485,968	Karbala	296,705
Kirkuk	418,624	Al-Hillah (Hilla) . .	268,834
Al-Basrah (Basra) . . .	406,296	An-Nasiriyah (Nasiriya) . . .	265,937

Source: Thomas Brinkhoff, *City Population* (internet www.citypopulation.de).

Mid-2000 (UN estimate, incl. suburbs): Mosul 1,131,000 (Source: UN, *World Urbanization Prospects: The 2001 Revision*).

Mid-2001 (UN estimate, incl. suburbs): Baghdad 4,958,000 (Source: UN, *World Urbanization Prospects: The 2001 Revision*).

BIRTHS AND DEATHS
(UN estimates, annual averages)

	1985–90	1990–95	1995–2000
Birth rate (per 1,000)	40.3	38.4	36.5
Death rate (per 1,000)	7.2	10.4	9.9

Source: UN, *World Population Prospects: The 2000 Revision*.

Registered live births (incomplete registration, 1992): 502,415 (birth rate 27.4 per 1,000).

Registered deaths (incomplete registration, 1990): 76,683 (death rate 4.4 per 1,000).

Expectation of life (WHO estimates, years at birth): 60.7 (males 58.7; females 62.9) in 2001 (Source: WHO, *World Health Report*).

ECONOMICALLY ACTIVE POPULATION*
(persons aged 7 years and over, 1987 census)

	Males	Females	Total
Agriculture, forestry and fishing .	422,265	70,741	493,006
Mining and quarrying	40,439	4,698	45,137
Manufacturing	228,242	38,719	266,961
Electricity, gas and water . .	31,786	4,450	36,236
Construction	332,645	8,541	341,186
Trade, restaurants and hotels . .	191,116	24,489	215,605
Transport, storage and communications	212,116	12,155	224,271
Financing, insurance, real estate and business services . . .	16,204	10,811	27,015
Community, social and personal services	1,721,748	233,068	1,954,816
Activities not adequately defined .	146,616	18,232	167,848
Total labour force	3,346,177	425,904	3,772,081

* Figures exclude persons seeking work for the first time, totalling 184,264 (males 149,938, females 34,326), but include other unemployed persons.

Source: ILO, *Yearbook of Labour Statistics*.

Mid-2001 (estimates in '000): Agriculture, etc. 633; Total 6,568 (Source: FAO).

Health and Welfare

KEY INDICATORS

Total fertility rate (children per woman, 2001)	4.9
Under-5 mortality rate (per 1,000 live births, 2001) . .	133
HIV/AIDS (% of persons aged 15–49, 2001) . . .	<0.10
Physicians (per 1,000 head, 1998)	0.55
Hospital beds (per 1,000 head, 1998)	1.45
Health expenditure (2000): US $ per head (PPP) . . .	573
Health expenditure (2000): % of GDP	3.7
Health expenditure (2000): public (% of total)	59.9
Access to water (% of persons, 2000)	85
Access to sanitation (% of persons, 2000)	79
Human Development Index (2000): value	0.567*

* Based on incomplete information.

For sources and definitions, see explanatory note on p. vi.

Agriculture

PRINCIPAL CROPS
('000 metric tons)

	1999	2000	2001
Wheat	800*	300†	900*
Rice (paddy)	180†	60†	90*
Barley*	500	400	500
Maize	112†	53*	50*
Potatoes†	300	200	200
Sugar cane	68†	65*	65†
Dry broad beans† . . .	17	10	10
Sunflower seed*	66	66	65
Sesame seed*	14	14	14
Olives†	12	10	11
Cabbages†	16	12	12
Lettuce†	26	20	20
Tomatoes†	650	500	500
Cauliflower†	25	19	19
Pumpkins, squash and gourds†	46	35	35
Cucumbers and gherkins† .	260	215	215
Aubergines (Eggplants)† . .	115	85	85
Chillies and green peppers† . .	24	18	18
Dry onions †	55	40	40
Green broad beans† . . .	80	60	60
String beans†	70	50	50
Okra†	115	85	85
Other vegetables†	264	194	194
Oranges†	300	270	270
Tangerines, mandarins, clementines and satsumas† .	39	37	37
Lemons and limes†	15	14	14
Apples†	80	75	75
Apricots†	25	22	22
Peaches and nectarines† . .	22	20	20
Plums†	28	27	27
Grapes†	290	265	265
Watermelons†	400	380	380
Canteloupes and other melons† .	210	195	195
Figs†	15	13	13
Dates*	438	600	650
Other fruits and berries† . . .	70	68	68

* Unofficial figure(s).
† FAO estimate(s).
Source: FAO.

LIVESTOCK
(estimates, '000 head, year ending September)

	1998	1999	2000*
Horses	48	46	47
Mules	13	11	11
Asses	385	375	380
Cattle	1,320	1,325	1,350
Buffaloes	64	64	65
Camels	8	8	8
Sheep	6,700	6,750	6,780
Goats	1,500	1,550	1,600
Poultry	13,000	22,000	23,000

* FAO estimates.

2001: Livestock numbers as in 2000 (FAO estimates).
Source: FAO.

LIVESTOCK PRODUCTS
(FAO estimates, '000 metric tons)

	1999	2000	2001
Beef and veal	45.4	45.5	45.5
Buffalo meat	2.1	2.1	2.1
Mutton and lamb	20.2	20.2	20.0
Goat meat	8.3	8.4	8.4
Poultry meat	49	50	50
Cows' milk	300	290	290
Buffaloes' milk	26.4	26.6	26.6
Sheep's milk	156.5	157.5	157.5
Goats' milk	53.6	53.9	53.9
Cheese	29.9	29.8	29.8
Butter	7.7	7.6	7.6
Hen eggs	9.5	14.0	14.0
Wool (greasy)	12.8	13.0	13.0
Cattle and buffalo hides . . .	5.3	5.3	5.0
Sheepskins	3.8	3.8	3.8
Goatskins	1.7	1.8	1.7

Source: FAO.

Forestry

ROUNDWOOD REMOVALS
(FAO estimates, '000 cubic metres, excl. bark)

	1999	2000	2001
Sawlogs, veneer logs and logs for sleepers	25	25	25
Other industrial wood . . .	34	34	34
Fuel wood	51	51	52
Total	110	110	111

Source: FAO.

SAWNWOOD PRODUCTION
('000 cu m, incl. railway sleepers)

	1996	1997	1998
Total (all broadleaved)	8	8	12

1999–2001: Annual production as in 1998 (FAO estimates).
Source: FAO.

Fishing

('000 metric tons, live weight)

	1998	1999	2000
Capture	22.6	24.6	20.8
Common carp	2.3	2.2	1.8*
Other cyprinids	1.7	5.7	4.8*
Other freshwater fishes . .	5.1	3.6	3.1*
Marine fishes	13.5	13.1	11.1*
Aquaculture (Common carp) . .	7.5	2.2	1.7
Total catch	30.1	26.8	22.5

* FAO estimate.
Source: FAO, *Yearbook of Fishery Statistics.*

Mining

(estimates, '000 metric tons, unless otherwise indicated)

	1999	2000	2001
Crude petroleum ('000 barrels) . .	915*	937	860
Natural gas (million cu m) . . .	7,000	7,500	7,000
Native sulphur	98	98	98
Phosphate rock	300	200	100
Salt (unrefined)	300	300	300

* Reported figure.
Source: US Geological Survey.

Industry

SELECTED PRODUCTS
(estimates, '000 metric tons, unless otherwise indicated)

	1996	1997	1998
Naphtha	482	489	505
Motor spirit (petrol)	2,927	2,968	3,066
Kerosene	977	991	1,023
Jet fuel	541	549	567
Gas-diesel (distillate fuel) oil	6,608	6,701	6,921
Residual fuel oils	7,495	7,601	7,850
Lubricating oils	220	223	230
Paraffin wax	86	87	90
Petroleum bitumen (asphalt)	451	457	472
Liquefied petroleum gas:			
from natural gas plants	1,590	1,620	1,650
from petroleum refineries	600	610	610
Cement*	1,600	1,700	2,000
Electric energy (million kWh)	29,050	29,561	30,346

* Data from the US Geological Survey.

Cigarettes: 5,794 million in 1992.

Footwear (excluding rubber): 4,087,000 pairs in 1992.

Source: UN, *Industrial Commodity Statistics Yearbook*.

Cement (estimate, '000 metric tons): 2,000 in 1999–2001 (Source: US Geological Survey).

Electric energy (net, million kWh): 27,971 in 1999; 31,746 in 2000; 36,009 in 2001 (Source: US Energy Information Administration).

Finance

CURRENCY AND EXCHANGE RATES

Monetary Units
1,000 fils = 20 dirhams = 1 Iraqi dinar (ID)

Sterling, Dollar and Euro Equivalents (31 December 2002)
£1 sterling = 501.04 fils
US $1 = 310.86 fils
€1 = 326.00 fils
100 Iraqi dinars = £199.58 = $321.69 = €306.75

Exchange Rate: From February 1973 to October 1982 the Iraqi dinar was valued at US $3.3862. Since October 1982 it has been valued at $3.2169. The dinar's average value in 1982 was $3.3513. The aforementioned data refer to the official exchange rate. There is, in addition, a special rate for exports and also a free-market rate. The unofficial exchange rate was estimated at $1 = 1,281 dinars in December 2002.

BUDGET ESTIMATES
(ID million)

Revenue	1981	1982
Ordinary	5,025.0	8,740.0
Economic development plan	6,742.8	7,700.0
Autonomous government agencies	7,667.8	n.a.
Total	19,434.9	n.a.

Petroleum revenues (estimates, US $ million): 9,198 in 1981; 10,250 in 1982; 9,650 in 1983; 10,000 in 1984; 11,900 in 1985; 6,813 in 1986; 11,300 in 1987.

Expenditure	1981	1982
Ordinary	5,025.0	8,740.0
Economic development plan	6,742.0	7,700.0
Autonomous government agencies	7,982.4	n.a.
Total	19,750.2	n.a.

1991 (ID million): General consolidated state budget expenditure 13,876; Investment budget expenditure 1,660.

INTERNATIONAL RESERVES
(US $ million at 31 December)

	1975	1976	1977
Gold	168.0	166.7	176.1
IMF special drawing rights	26.9	32.5	41.5
Reserve position in IMF	31.9	31.7	33.4
Foreign exchange	2,500.5	4,369.8	6,744.7
Total	2,727.3	4,600.7	6,995.7

IMF special drawing rights (US $ million at 31 December): 132.3 in 1981; 81.9 in 1982; 9.0 in 1983; 0.1 in 1984; 7.2 in 1987.

Reserve position in IMF (US $ million at 31 December): 130.3 in 1981; 123.5 in 1982.

Note: No figures for gold or foreign exchange have been available since 1977.

Source: IMF, *International Financial Statistics*.

COST OF LIVING
(Consumer Price Index; base: 1990 = 100)

	1991*
Food	363.9
Fuel and light	135.4
Clothing	251.1
Rent	107.0
All items (incl. others)	286.5

* May to December only.

Source: ILO, *Yearbook of Labour Statistics*.

NATIONAL ACCOUNTS
(UN estimates, ID million at current prices)

National Income and Product

	1997	1998	1999
Compensation of employees	1,375,121	1,674,787	1,976,037
Operating surplus	2,250,234	2,740,763	3,234,182
Domestic factor incomes	3,625,355	4,415,550	5,210,219
Consumption of fixed capital	394,464	480,426	566,896
Gross domestic product (GDP) at factor cost	4,019,819	4,895,976	5,777,115
Indirect taxes	63,041	76,852	90,705
Less Subsidies	192,231	234,042	276,052
GDP in purchasers' values	3,890,629	4,738,786	5,591,768

Source: UN, Economic and Social Commission for Western Asia, *National Accounts Studies of the ESCWA Region* (2000).

Expenditure on the Gross Domestic Product

	1997	1998	1999
Government final consumption expenditure	754,429	845,432	954,275
Private final consumption expenditure	2,948,725	3,563,417	4,175,437
Increase in stocks	−35,053	−19,129	−12,144
Gross fixed capital formation	262,740	398,560	511,801
Total domestic expenditure	3,930,841	4,788,280	5,629,369
Exports of goods and services	408,281	548,090	752,336
Less Imports of goods and services	448,493	597,584	789,937
GDP in purchasers' values	3,890,629	4,738,786	5,591,768
GDP at constant 1995 prices	2,874,396	3,305,556	3,570,000

Source: UN, Economic and Social Commission for Western Asia, *National Accounts Studies of the ESCWA Region* (2000).

Gross Domestic Product by Economic Activity

	1997	1998	1999
Agriculture, hunting, forestry and fishing	1,288,408	1,520,236	1,671,103
Mining and quarrying. . . . }	219,181	324,882	429,180
Manufacturing . . . . . }			
Electricity, gas and water. . .	13,649	20,396	26,105
Construction	68,691	104,203	135,717
Trade, restaurants and hotels .	983,907	1,200,120	1,402,469
Transport, storage and communications	721,414	837,382	940,650
Finance, insurance and real estate*	334,554	424,240	566,095
Government, community, social and personal services† . . .	361,081	428,618	573,640
Sub-total	3,990,885	4,860,077	5,744,949
Less Imputed bank service charge	100,256	121,291	153,191
GDP in purchasers' values .	3,890,629	4,738,786	5,591,768

* Including imputed rents of owner-occupied dwellings.

† Including private non-profit services to households, domestic services of households and import duties.

Source: UN, Economic and Social Commission for Western Asia, *National Accounts Studies of the ESCWA Region* (2000).

External Trade

PRINCIPAL COMMODITIES
(ID million)

Imports c.i.f.	1976	1977*	1978
Food and live animals . .	159.6	154.0	134.5
Cereals and cereal preparations .	70.0	79.9	74.9
Sugar, sugar preparations and honey	37.2	24.1	10.2
Crude materials (inedible) except fuels	33.7	20.5	25.1
Chemicals	58.5	47.4	58.7
Basic manufactures . . .	293.3	236.7	285.2
Textile yarn, fabrics, etc. . . .	44.3	69.4	72.7
Iron and steel	127.5	44.3	73.2
Machinery and transport equipment.	557.4	625.8	667.4
Non-electric machinery . . .	285.4	352.5	368.1
Electrical machinery, apparatus, etc.	106.9	120.2	160.5
Transport equipment	165.2	153.1	138.8
Miscellaneous manufactured articles.	33.2	49.4	51.7
Total (incl. others)	1,150.9	1,151.3	1,244.1

* Figures are provisional. Revised total is ID 1,323.2 million.

Total imports (official estimates, ID million): 1,738.9 in 1979; 2,208.1 in 1980; 2,333.8 in 1981.

Total imports (IMF estimates, ID million): 6,013.0 in 1981; 6,309.0 in 1982; 3,086.2 in 1983; 3,032.4 in 1984; 3,285.7 in 1985; 2,773.0 in 1986; 2,268.7 in 1987; 2,888.8 in 1988; 3,077.1 in 1989; 2,028.5 in 1990; 131.5 in 1991; 187.3 in 1992; 165.6 in 1993; 155.0 in 1994; 206.9 in 1995; 176.7 in 1996; 353.1 in 1997; 568.2 in 1998; 642.7 in 1999; 1,033.2 in 2000; 1,611.4 in 2001 (Source: IMF, *International Financial Statistics*).

Total exports (ID million): 5,614.6 (crude petroleum 5,571.9) in 1977; 6,422.7 (crude petroleum 6,360.5) in 1978; 12,522.0 (crude petroleum 12,480.0) in 1979.

Exports of crude petroleum (estimates, ID million): 15,321.3 in 1980; 6,089.6 in 1981; 5,982.4 in 1982; 5,954.8 in 1983; 6,937.0 in 1984; 8,142.5 in 1985; 5,126.2 in 1986; 6,988.9 in 1987; 7,245.8 in 1988 (Source: IMF, *International Financial Statistics*).

Exports of crude petroleum under UN-administered oil-for-food programme (six-month phases, unless otherwise indicated, beginning December 1996, US $ million): first 2,150; second 2,125; third 2,085; fourth 3,027; fifth 3,947; sixth* 7,402; seventh 8,302†; eighth 9,564; ninth (seven months to the end of June 2001) 5,638; 10th (five months beginning July 2001) 5,350; 11th 4,589; 12th 5,639; 13th 4,413.

* Iraq was permitted to export additional petroleum to the value of US $3,000m. under the sixth phase.

† UN Security Council Resolution 1284, adopted in December 1999, removed restrictions on the amount of petroleum that Iraq was permitted to export under the oil-for-food programme. Source: UN Office of the Iraq Programme.

PRINCIPAL TRADING PARTNERS
(US $ million)

Imports c.i.f.	1988	1989	1990
Australia	153.4	196.2	108.7
Austria.	n.a.	1.1	50.9
Belgium-Luxembourg . . .	57.6	68.2	68.3
Brazil	346.0	416.4	139.5
Canada	169.9	225.1	150.4
China, People's Republic . . .	99.2	148.0	157.9
France.	278.0	410.4	278.3
Germany	322.3	459.6	389.4
India	32.3	65.2	57.5
Indonesia	38.9	122.7	104.9
Ireland.	150.4	144.9	31.6
Italy	129.6	285.1	194.0
Japan	533.0	621.1	397.2
Jordan	164.3	210.0	220.3
Korea, Republic	98.5	123.9	149.4
Netherlands	111.6	102.6	93.8
Romania	113.3	91.1	30.1
Saudi Arabia	37.2	96.5	62.5
Spain	43.4	129.0	40.5
Sri Lanka	50.1	33.5	52.3
Sweden	63.0	40.6	64.8
Switzerland	65.7	94.4	126.6
Thailand	22.3	59.2	68.9
Turkey	874.7	408.9	196.0
USSR	70.7	75.7	77.9
United Kingdom	394.6	448.5	322.1
USA	979.3	1,001.7	658.4
Yugoslavia	154.5	182.0	123.1
Total (incl. others)	5,960.0	6,956.2	4,833.9

Exports f.o.b.	1988	1989	1990*
Belgium-Luxembourg	147.5	249.6	n.a.
Brazil	1,002.8	1,197.2	n.a.
France	517.4	623.9	0.8
Germany	122.0	76.9	1.7
Greece	192.5	189.4	0.3
India	293.0	438.8	14.7
Italy	687.1	549.7	10.6
Japan	712.1	117.1	0.1
Jordan	28.4	25.2	101.6
Netherlands	152.9	532.3	0.2
Portugal	120.8	125.8	n.a.
Spain	370.0	575.7	0.7
Turkey	1,052.6	1,331.0	83.5
USSR	835.7	1,331.7	8.9
United Kingdom	293.1	167.0	4.4
USA	1,458.9	2,290.8	0.2
Yugoslavia	425.4	342.0	10.4
Total (incl. others)	10,268.3	12,333.7	392.0

* Excluding exports of most petroleum products.

Source: UN, *International Trade Statistics Yearbook*.

Transport

RAILWAYS
(traffic)

	1995*	1996†	1997†
Passenger-km (million) . . .	2,198	1,169	1,169
Freight ton-km (million) . . .	1,120	931	956

* Source: UN, *Statistical Yearbook*.

† Source: Railway Gazette International, *Railway Directory*.

ROAD TRAFFIC
(estimates, '000 motor vehicles in use)

	1995	1996
Passenger cars	770.1	773.0
Buses and coaches	50.9	51.4
Lorries and vans.	269.9	272.5
Road tractors.	37.2	37.2

Source: IRF, *World Road Statistics*.

SHIPPING

Merchant Fleet
(registered at 31 December)

	1999	2000	2001
Number of vessels	98	99	91
Total displacement ('000 grt) . .	510.6	511.0	240.6

Source: Lloyd's Register-Fairplay, *World Fleet Statistics.*

CIVIL AVIATION
(revenue traffic on scheduled services)

	1991	1992	1994*
Kilometres flown (million) . . .	0	0	0
Passengers carried ('000) . . .	28	53	31
Passenger-km (million)	17	35	20
Freight ton-km (million) . . .	0	3	2

* Figures for 1993 unavailable.

Source: UN, *Statistical Yearbook.*

Tourism

ARRIVALS AT FRONTIERS OF VISITORS FROM ABROAD*

Country of nationality	1998	1999	2000
Afghanistan	392	250	1,041
India	1,523	4,893	3,092
Iran	35,234	20,849	69,155
Lebanon	2,536	780	8
Pakistan	2,833	2,063	2,985
Total (incl. others)	44,885	30,328	78,457

* Including same-day visitors.

Source: World Tourism Organization, *Yearbook of Tourism Statistics.*

Tourism receipts (US $ million): 13 in 1998.

Communications Media

	1997	1998	1999
Radio receivers ('000 in use) . .	4,850	n.a.	n.a.
Television receivers ('000 in use) .	1,750	1,800	1,850
Telephones ('000 main lines in use)	651	650	675*

* Estimate.

Daily newspapers (1996): number 4; average circulation 407,000.

Sources: UN, *Statistical Yearbook*; International Telecommunication Union.

Education

(1995/96)

	Institu-tions	Teachers	Students Males	Students Females	Students Total
Pre-primary . . .	571	4,841	43,889	41,135	85,024
Primary	8,145	145,455	1,602,071	1,301,852	2,903,923
Secondary:					
general	n.a.	52,393	631,457	406,025	1,037,482
teacher training .	n.a.	1,392	9,414	14,120	23,534
vocational . . .	n.a.	8,511	81,917	17,488	99,405

Source: UNESCO, *Statistical Yearbook.*

Adult literacy rate (UNESCO estimates): 55.9% in 2000 (Source: UNDP, *Human Development Report*).

Directory

As a result of the US-led military campaign to oust the regime of Saddam Hussain in March–April 2003, buildings occupied by a number of government ministries and other institutions were reported to have been damaged or destroyed.

The Constitution

A new constitution was expected to be adopted following the ousting of the regime of Saddam Hussain in April 2003.

The following are the principal features of the Provisional Constitution, issued on 22 September 1968:

The Iraqi Republic is a popular democratic and sovereign state. Islam is the state religion.

The political economy of the State is founded on socialism.

The State will protect liberty of religion, freedom of speech and opinion. Public meetings are permitted under the law. All discrimination based on race, religion or language is forbidden. There shall be freedom of the Press, and the right to form societies and trade unions in conformity with the law is guaranteed.

The Iraqi people is composed of two main nationalities: Arabs and Kurds. The Constitution confirms the nationalistic rights of the Kurdish people and the legitimate rights of all other minorities within the framework of Iraqi unity.

The highest authority in the country is the Council of Command of the Revolution (or Revolutionary Command Council—RCC), which will promulgate laws until the election of a National Assembly. The Council exercises its prerogatives and powers by a two-thirds' majority.

Two amendments to the Constitution were announced in November 1969. The President, already Chief of State and Head of the Government, also became the official Supreme Commander of the Armed Forces and President of the RCC. Membership of the latter body was to increase from five to a larger number at the President's discretion.

Earlier, a Presidential decree replaced the 14 local government districts by 16 governorates, each headed by a governor with wide powers. In April 1976 Tikrit (Salah ad-Din) and Karbala became separate governorates, bringing the number of governorates to 18, although three of these are designated Autonomous Regions.

The 15-article statement which aimed to end the Kurdish war was issued on 11 March 1970. In accordance with this statement, a form of autonomy was offered to the Kurds in March 1974, but some of the Kurds rejected the offer and fresh fighting broke out. The new Provisional Constitution was announced in July 1970. Two amendments were introduced in 1973 and 1974, the 1974 amendment stating that 'the area whose majority of population is Kurdish shall enjoy autonomy in accordance with what is defined by the Law'.

The President and Vice-President are elected by a two-thirds' majority of the Council. The President, Vice-President and members of the Council will be responsible to the Council. Vice-Presidents and Ministers will be responsible to the President.

Details of a new, permanent Constitution were announced in March 1989. The principal innovations proposed in the permanent Constitution, which was approved by the National Assembly in July 1990, were the abolition of the RCC, following a presidential election, and the assumption of its duties by a 50-member Consultative Assembly and the existing National Assembly; and the incorporation of the freedom to form political parties. The new, permanent Constitution is to be submitted to a popular referendum for approval.

In September 1995 an interim constitutional amendment was endorsed by the RCC whereby the elected Chairman of the RCC will assume the Presidency of the Republic subject to the approval of the National Assembly and endorsement by national referendum.

In July 1973 President Bakr announced a National Charter as a first step towards establishing the Progressive National Front. A National Assembly and People's Councils are features of the Charter. A law to create a 250-member National Assembly and a 50-member Kurdish Legislative Council was adopted on 16 March 1980, and the two Assemblies were elected in June and September 1980 respectively.

The Government

Following the removal of the regime of Saddam Hussain by the US-led coalition in early April 2003, an Iraqi Interim Authority was to be established to govern the country for a transitional period prior to the eventual holding of general elections and the formation of a new Iraqi Government.

MINISTRIES

Office of the President: Presidential Palace, Karradat Mariam, Baghdad; e-mail press@uruklink.net; internet www.uruklink.net.

Ministry of Agriculture: Khulafa St, Khullani Sq., Baghdad; tel. (1) 887-3251.

Ministry of Awqaf (Religious Endowments) and Religious Affairs: North Gate, St opp. College of Engineering, Baghdad; tel. (1) 888-9561.

Ministry of Defence: North Gate, Baghdad; tel. (1) 888-9071.

Ministry of Education: POB 258, An-Nidhal St, Baghdad; tel. (1) 886-0000; e-mail moe@uruklink.net; internet www.uruklink.net/moe.

Ministry of Finance: Khulafa St, nr ar-Russafi Sq., Baghdad; tel. (1) 887-4871.

Ministry of Foreign Affairs: opp. State Org. for Roads and Bridges, Karradat Mariam, Baghdad; tel. (1) 537-0091; e-mail foreign@uruklink.net; internet www.uruklink.net/mofa.

Ministry of Health: Khulafa St, Khullani Sq., Baghdad; tel. (1) 887-1881; e-mail health@uruklink.net; internet www.uruklink.net/health.

Ministry of Industry and Minerals: An-Nidhal St, nr Sa'adoun Petrol Station, Baghdad; tel. (1) 887-2006.

Ministry of Information: nr an-Nusoor Sq., fmrly Qasr as-Salaam Bldg, Baghdad; tel. (1) 551-4333; e-mail iraqinfo@uruklink.net; internet www.uruklink.net/iraqinfo.

Ministry of Oil: POB 19244, Zayouna, Baghdad; tel. (1) 817-7000; fax (1) 886-9432; e-mail oil@uruklink.net; internet www.uruklink.net/oil.

Ministry of Planning: POB 8001, Karradat Mariam, ash-Shawaf Sq., Baghdad; tel. and fax (1) 885-3653; e-mail plan@uruklink.net.

Ministry of Trade: Khulafa St, Khullani Sq., Baghdad; tel. (1) 887-2682; e-mail trade@uruklink.net; internet www.uruklink.net/trade/eindex.htm.

Ministry of Transport and Communications: nr Martyr's Monument, Karradat Dakhil, Baghdad; tel. (1) 776-6041.

Legislature

NATIONAL ASSEMBLY

Speaker: Dr SA'ADOUN HAMMADI.

Elections to the 220 elective seats of the fifth National Assembly took place on 27 March 2000. According to official results, candidates of the ruling Baath Party successfully contested 165 of the Assembly's seats, while independent candidates were returned to the remaining 55 elective seats. The remaining 30 seats of the Assembly that are reserved for representatives of the Kurdish Autonomous Regions were filled by government-appointed independents. A new legislature was expected to be established as a result of the removal of the regime of Saddam Hussain in April 2003.

Kurdish Autonomous Regions

The efforts of successive Iraqi administrations to address the grievances and aspirations of the Kurdish population by conferring limited autonomy on the Kurdish-inhabited regions began to be formalized in 1970 (under the terms of a 15-article accord providing for the creation of a unified autonomous area comprising the administrative departments of As-Sulaimaniya (Sulaimaniya), D'hok and Irbil (Arbil), and the Kurdish sector of the city of Kirkuk, and the establishment of a 50-member Kurdish Legislative Council), but have consistently fallen short of the, often disparate, demands and expectations of various Iraqi Kurd political parties and interest groups. Following the recapture of Kuwait from Iraqi forces by a multinational military coalition, in early 1991, a designated 'safe haven' north of latitude 36°N (encompassing much of the Kurdish territories) was imposed by the coalition partners. Renewed negotiations between the Iraqi Government (under Saddam Hussain) and Kurdish groups stalled over the status of Kirkuk, and in October 1991 the central Government withdrew all services from the region, effectively severing all economic and administrative support. In May 1992 the Kurdish Iraqi Front (KIF), an alliance of several Kurdish factions—including the two largest, the Patriotic Union of Kurdistan (PUK) and the Kurdistan Democratic Party (KDP)—established in 1988, organized elections to a new 105-member Iraqi Kurdistan National Assembly (see below). The results of a poll to select a Kurdish leader, conducted at the same time, were deemed inconclusive. Bitter factional disputes, including armed conflict between elements of the KDP and the PUK, subsequently led to the effective disintegration of the KIF, and thwarted attempts to consolidate Kurdish regional autonomy. In September 1996 the Iraqi Government announced the restoration of full Iraqi sovereignty over the Kurdish areas, but the KDP, which, under Masoud Barzani, had established the predominant influence in the region, announced the composition of a coalition administration for the territories (excluding the PUK, with which it was still in open conflict), to be based in Arbil, later in the same month. In September 1998 the USA brokered a formal peace agreement between representatives of the PUK and the KDP in Washington, DC, which provided for a unified regional administration, the sharing of local revenues and co-operation in implementing the UN-sponsored 'oil-for-food' programme. Fresh legislative elections, scheduled to take place in 1999 under the terms of the Washington agreement, were subsequently postponed. In December 1999 the KDP, still led by Barzani, announced the composition of a new 25-member coalition administration (comprising the KDP, the Iraqi Communist Party, the Assyrian Movement, the Independent Workers' Party of Kurdistan, the Islamic Union and independents—internet www.krg.org/about/cabinet.asp) for the areas under its control (principally the departments of Arbil and D'hok). Municipal elections (to select 571 officials) were conducted in the KDP-administered region in May 2001; according to official KDP sources, KDP candidates received 81% of votes cast, and the rate of voter participation was recorded at 79%. Negotiations between representatives of the KDP and the PUK for the full implementation of the Washington accord were held during 2002, and resulted in the resumption of a transitional joint session of the Iraqi Kurdistan National Assembly in October of that year (see below).

IRAQI KURDISTAN NATIONAL ASSEMBLY

In May 1992, negotiations with the Iraqi Government over the full implementation of the 1970 accord on Kurdish regional autonomy having stalled, the KIF organized elections to a 105-member Iraqi Kurdistan National Assembly, in which almost the entire electorate of 1.1m. participated, unilaterally. The KDP and the PUK were the only parties to achieve representation in the new Assembly and subsequently agreed to share seats equally (50 seats each—five having been reserved for two Assyrian Christian parties). The subsequent disintegration of the KIF and prolonged armed conflict between elements of the KDP and the PUK prevented the Assembly from becoming properly instituted, although the KDP attempted to incorporate the legislature into the administration of the territories under its control in the late 1990s and early 2000s, retaining the name of the Assembly and continuing to appoint officials (Jawhar N. Salem and Farsat A. Abdullah were serving as President and Secretary, respectively, in August 2002). Relations between the KDP and the PUK were generally improved following the Washington agreement of September 1998, and in August 2002 it was reported that representatives of the two parties had agreed to the inauguration of a transitional joint parliamentary session (with representation based on the results of the May 1992 elections) before the end of the year: an agreement to this effect was signed on 8 September 2002. On 4 October a joint session of the Iraqi Kurdistan National Assembly was convened for the first time since 1996. At a further session held on 12 November 2002, a joint committee was established with the aim of preparing for parliamentary elections, scheduled to be held in Iraqi Kurdistan within nine months.

Political Organizations

National Progressive Front: Baghdad; f. July 1973, when Arab Baath Socialist Party and Iraqi Communist Party signed a joint manifesto agreeing to establish a comprehensive progressive national and nationalistic front. In 1975 representatives of Kurdish parties and organizations and other national and independent forces joined the Front; the Iraqi Communist Party left the National Progressive Front in mid-March 1979; Sec.-Gen. NAIM HADDAD (BAATH).

Arab Baath Socialist Party: POB 6012, al-Mansour, Baghdad; revolutionary Arab socialist movement founded in Damascus in 1947; has ruled Iraq since July 1968, and between July 1973 and March 1979 in alliance with the Iraqi Communist Party in the National Progressive Front; Founder MICHEL AFLAQ; Regional

Command Sec.-Gen. Saddam Hussain; Dep. Regional Command Sec.-Gen. Izzat Ibrahim; 18-mem. Regional Command; approx. 100,000 mems.

Kurdistan Revolutionary Party: f. 1972; succeeded Democratic Kurdistan Party; admitted to National Progressive Front 1974; Sec.-Gen. Abd as-Sattar Taher Sharef.

There are several illegal opposition groups, including:

Ad-Da'wa al-Islamiya (Voice of Islam): f. 1968; based in Tehran; mem. of the Supreme Council of the Islamic Revolution in Iraq (see below); guerrilla group; Leader Sheikh al-Assefie.

Iraqi Communist Party: Baghdad; f. 1934; became legally recognized in July 1973 on formation of National Progressive Front; left National Progressive Front March 1979; proscribed as a result of its support for Iran during the Iran–Iraq War; First Sec. Hamid Majid Moussa.

Umma (Nation) Party: f. 1982, in opposition to Saddam Hussain's regime; Leader Saad Saleh Jabr.

Principal Kurdish Parties

Kurdistan Democratic Party (KDP): European Office (Germany), 10749 Berlin, POB 301516; tel. (30) 79743741; fax (30) 79743746; e-mail kdpeurope@t-online.de; internet www.kdp.pp.se; f. 1946; seeks to protect Kurdish rights and promote Kurdish culture and interests through regional political and legislative autonomy, as part of a federative republic; Pres. Masoud Barzani; Vice-Pres. Ali Abdullah.

Patriotic Union of Kurdistan (PUK): European Office (Germany), 10502 Berlin, POB 210213; tel. (30) 34097850; fax (30) 34097849; e-mail pukoffice@pukq.de; internet www.puk.org; f. 1975; seeks to protect and promote Kurdish rights and interests through self-determination; Pres. Jalal Talabani.

There is also a breakaway element of the Arab Baath Socialist Party represented on the Iraqi National Joint Action Cttee (see below); the Democratic Gathering (Leader Saleh Doublah); the Iraqi Socialist Party (ISP; Leader Gen. Hassan an-Naquib); the Socialist Party of Kurdistan (SPK; f. 1975; Leader Rassoul Marmand); the Kurdistan Toilers' Party (KTP; f. 1985; Leader Qadir Aziz), a breakaway faction of the SPK; the United Socialist Party of Kurdistan (USPK; Leader Mahmoud Osman), a breakaway group from the PUK; the Kurdistan People's Democratic Party (KPDP; Leader Sami Abd ar-Rahman); the Kurdish Workers' Party (PKK); the Islamic League of Kurdistan (ILK, also known as the Islamic Movement of Iraqi Kurdistan—IMIK); the Islamic Union; the Islamic Unity Movement of Kurdistan (IUMK); Jund al-Islam (a militant Islamist faction of the IUMK; f. 2001; Leader Abu Abdullah ash-Shafi'i); Ansar al-Islam (f. 2002 by merger of Islah group and Jund al-Islam; Leader Mullah Krekar); the Kurdish Hezbollah (Party of God; f. 1985; Leader Sheikh Muhammad Khaled), a breakaway group from the KDP and a member of the Supreme Council of the Islamic Revolution in Iraq (SCIRI), which is based in Tehran under the leadership of the exiled Iraqi Shi'ite leader, Hojatoleslam Muhammad Baqir al-Hakim, and has a military wing, the Badr Brigade; the Iraqi National Accord (INA; based in Amman, Jordan; Leader Ayad Allawi); the Constitutional Monarchy Movement (based in the United Kingdom), which supports the claim to the Iraqi throne of Sharif Ali bin al-Hussain, cousin to the late King Faisal II; the Bet-Nahrain Democratic Party, which is seeking the creation of an autonomous state for Assyrians in Bet-Nahrain; and Hizb al-Watan, or Homeland Party (Leader Mishaan al-Jubouri).

Various alliances of political and religious groups have been formed to oppose the regime of Saddam Hussain in recent years. They include the Kurdistan Iraqi Front (KIF; f. 1988), an alliance of the KDP, the PUK, the SPK, the KPDP and other, smaller Kurdish groups, which subsequently disintegrated; the Iraqi National Joint Action Cttee, formed in Damascus in 1990 and grouping together the SCIRI, the four principal Kurdish parties belonging to the KIF, Ad-Da'wa al-Islamiya, the Movement of the Iraqi Mujahidin (based in Tehran; Leaders Hojatoleslam Muhammad Baqir al-Hakim and Said Muhammad al-Haidari), the Islamic Movement in Iraq (Shi'ite group based in Tehran; Leader Sheikh Muhammad al-Kalisi), Jund al-Imam (Imam Soldiers; Shi'ite; Leader Abu Zaid), the Islamic Action Organization (based in Tehran; Leader Sheikh Taqi Modaressi), the Islamic Alliance (based in Saudi Arabia; Sunni; Leader Abu Yasser al-Alousi), the Independent Group, the Iraqi Socialist Party, the Arab Socialist Movement, the Nasserite Unionist Gathering and the National Reconciliation Group. In September 1992 the KPDP, the SPK and the Kurdish Democratic Independence Party were reported to have merged to form the Kurdistan Unity Party (KUP).

The Iraqi National Congress (INC), based in London, United Kingdom, has sought to unite the various factions of the opposition. At a conference held in London in April 1999 a new collegiate leadership, under Salah esh-Sheikhli of the INA, was appointed. In November some 300 delegates to a national assembly, held in New York, USA, elected a 65-member central council and a new, seven-member collegiate leadership (Ayad Allawi, INA; Riyad al-Yawar, independent; Sharif Ali bin al-Hussain, Constitutional Monarchy Movement; Ahmad Chalabi, independent; Sheikh Muhammad Muhammad Ali, independent; Dr Latif Rashid, PUK; Hoshyar az-Zibari, KDP). Several leading members of the INC, including Ahmad Chalabi, have relocated to the USA.

Diplomatic Representation

EMBASSIES IN IRAQ

A number of countries closed their diplomatic missions in Baghdad in mid-March 2003, shortly before the US-led coalition began its military campaign to oust the regime of Saddam Hussain. However, some diplomatic missions reopened following the end of hostilities in April.

Algeria: 13/14/613 Hay ad-Daoudi, Baghdad; tel. (1) 543-4137; fax (1) 542-5829; Chargé d'affaires Moncef Benhaddid.

Armenia: 929/7/27 Hay Babel, Baghdad; tel. and fax (1) 718-9853; Chargé d'affaires Mourad Mkhitarian.

Bahrain: 41/6/605, Hay al-Mutanabi, Baghdad; tel. (1) 541-0841; fax (1) 541-2027; Chargé d'affaires Hassan al-Ansari.

Bangladesh: 6/14/929 Hay Babel, Baghdad; tel. (1) 719-0068; fax (1) 718-6045; Ambassador Muhammad Fazlur Rahma.

Belarus: 47/5/929 Hay Babel, Baghdad; tel. and fax (1) 719-5565; Chargé d'affaires Igor Syrets.

Bulgaria: 12/25/624 al-Ameriya, Baghdad; tel. (1) 556-8197; fax (1) 556-4182; Chargé d'affaires Venelin Lazarov.

Chad: 12/32/611 Hay ad-Daoudi, Baghdad; tel. (1) 542-3588; fax (1) 541-3449; Ambassador Ousman Kalibou Bella.

China, People's Republic: POB 15097, 624 New Embassy Area, Hitteen Quarter, Baghdad; tel. (1) 556-7880; fax (1) 556-7879; Ambassador Zhang Weiqiu.

Cuba: 8/29/923 Hay Babel, Baghdad; tel. (1) 717-0899; fax (1) 718-0701; Ambassador Héctor Estrada Acosta.

Czech Republic: 37/11/601 al-Mansour, Baghdad; tel. (1) 541-7136; fax (1) 543-0275; Chargé d'affaires Miroslav Belica.

Djibouti: 21/8/605 Hay al-Mutanabi, Baghdad; tel. (1) 541-3805; fax (1) 542-5002; Ambassador Idriss Ahmad Chirwa.

Egypt: 53a/11/601 al-Mansour, Baghdad; tel. (1) 543-0572; fax (1) 542-5839; e-mail egypt@uruklink.net; Ambassador Hussein az-Zughbi.

Germany: 40/2/929 Hay Babel, Baghdad; tel. (1) 719-2039; Chargé d'affaires a.i. Claude Robert Ellner.

Greece: 63/13/913 Hay Babel, Baghdad; tel. (1) 718-2433; fax (1) 718-8729; Chargé d'affaires Garilides Nikolaos.

Holy See: Apostolic Nuncio Most Rev. Fernando Filoni (Titular Archbishop of Volturno (Resident in Amman, Jordan)).

Hungary: POB 2065, 43/4/609 al-Mansour, Hay al-Mutanabi, Baghdad; tel. (1) 543-2956; fax (1) 541-4766; Chargé d'affaires András Nagy.

India: 6/25/306 Hay al-Maghrib, Baghdad; tel. (1) 422-2014; fax (1) 422-9549; Ambassador R. Dayakar.

Indonesia: POB 420, 906/02/77 Hay al-Wahda, Baghdad; tel. (1) 719-8677; fax (1) 719-8680; e-mail kombgd@warkaa.net; Ambassador Dachlan Abdul Hamied.

Iran: 35/19/222 Hay as-Salehiya, Baghdad; tel. (1) 885-3714; fax (1) 884-3033; Ambassador Ali Reza Haqiqian.

Japan: 50/21/929 Hay Babel, Baghdad; tel. (1) 776-6791; Chargé d'affaires Masahi Kono.

Jordan: 145/49/617 Hay al-Andalus, Baghdad; tel. (1) 541-2892; fax (1) 541-2009; e-mail jordan@uruklink.net; Ambassador Hmroud al-Qatarnah.

Libya: 21/11/601 al-Mansour, Hay al-Amerat, Baghdad; tel. (1) 541-8590; fax (1) 541-7398; Head of the Libyan People's Bureau Ibrahim Muhammad Abu Khaza.

Malaysia: POB 1275, 17/22/915 Jadiriyah, Hay al-Jamiyah, Baghdad; tel. (1) 776-6388; fax (1) 717-3619; e-mail mwiraq@uruklink.net; Ambassador Abdul Latif bin Awang.

Morocco: POB 6039, 27/11/601 al-Mansour, Baghdad; tel. (1) 542-1779; fax (1) 542-3030; Ambassador Muhammad Auragh.

Nigeria: 43/11/601 al-Mansour, Baghdad; tel. (1) 541-3133; fax (1) 543-4513; Ambassador Ibrahim Mohammed.

Oman: 2/5/613 Hay al-Andalus, Baghdad; tel. (1) 451-8198; fax (1) 541-3617; Chargé d'affaires AMIR BIN HAMID AL-HAJRI.

Pakistan: 14/7/609 al-Mansour, Baghdad; tel. (1) 542-5343; fax (1) 542-8707; Ambassador MANZAR SHAFIQ.

Philippines: 4/22/915 al-Jadriyah, Hay al-Jamiyah, Baghdad; tel. (1) 776-2696; fax 719-3228; e-mail bipe@uruklink.net; Ambassador REYNALDO B. PARUNGAO.

Poland: 22–24/60/904 Hay al-Wihda, Baghdad; tel. (1) 719-0297; fax (1) 719-0296; Ambassador ANDRZEJ BIERA.

Portugal: Baghdad.

Qatar: 114/15/611 Hay ad-Daoudi, Baghdad; tel. (1) 542-1954; fax (1) 542-9056; Chargé d'affaires HAMAD BIN MUHAMMAD BIN MUBARAK AL-KHALIFA.

Romania: 4/31/929 Hay Babel, Baghdad; tel. (1) 776-2860; fax (1) 776-7553; Chargé d'affaires EMILIAN ION.

Russia: 4/5/605 Hay al-Mutanabi, Baghdad; tel. (1) 541-4749; fax (1) 543-4462; Ambassador VLADIMIR TITORENKO.

Serbia and Montenegro: 16/35/923 Hay Babel, Baghdad; tel. (1) 776-7887; fax (1) 717-1069; e-mail embyugag@uruklink.net; Ambassador ENES KARABEGOVIĆ.

Slovakia: 94/28/923 Hay Babel, Baghdad; tel. (1) 776-7367; fax (1) 776-7368; Chargé d'affaires a.i. JOZEF MARÉFKA.

Somalia: 609/10/10 al-Mansour, Baghdad; tel. (1) 541-0088; fax (1) 541-6697; Ambassador ISSA ALI MOHAMMED.

Spain: POB 2072, 1/3/609 al-Mansour, Baghdad; tel. (1) 542-4827; fax (1) 541-9857; Chargé d'affaires (vacant).

Sri Lanka: 20–21/34/611 Hay al-Andalus, al-Mansour, Baghdad; tel. (1) 543-9986; fax (1) 543-9965; Ambassador MOHAMED MOHIDEEN AMANUL FARUK.

Sudan: 32/1/609 al-Mansour, Baghdad; tel. (1) 542-7982; fax (1) 542-5287; e-mail sudan@uruklink.net; Ambassador BUSHRA ESH-SHEIKH DAFALLA.

Thailand: POB 6062,18/18/601, al-Mansour, Baghdad; tel. (1) 541-8798; fax (1) 541-2618; Ambassador TAWATCHAI PIYARAT.

Tunisia: 1/49/617 Hay al-Andalus, Baghdad; tel. (1) 542-0602; fax (1) 542-8585; Ambassador HADI BEN NASR.

Turkey: 7/1/301 al-Waziriyah, Baghdad; tel. (1) 422-0022; fax (1) 422-8353; Ambassador (vacant).

Ukraine: 20/1/609 al-Mansour, Baghdad; tel. and fax (1) 542-6677; Chargé d'affaires VALENTIN NOVYKOV.

United Arab Emirates: 81/34/611 Hay al-Andalus (ad-Daoudi), Baghdad; tel. (1) 543-9174; fax (1) 543-9093; Chargé d'affaires AHMAD ABDULLAH BIN SAYEED.

Venezuela: 5/79/611 Hay ad-Daoudi, Baghdad; tel. and fax (1) 541-6133; e-mail evenik@uruklink.net; Ambassador JORGE RONDON UZCATEGUI.

Viet Nam: 71/34 Hay al-Andalus, Baghdad; tel. and fax (1) 541-1388; e-mail vietnam@uruklink.net; Ambassador NGUYEN VAN LINH.

Yemen: 4/36/904 Hay al-Wahada, Baghdad; tel. (1) 718-6682; fax (1) 717-2318; Ambassador ABD AL-MALIK SAID ABDO.

Note: France, Italy and Switzerland maintain interest sections or liaison offices in Baghdad; US interests are represented by the embassy of Poland.

Judicial System

Courts in Iraq consist of the following: The Court of Cassation, Courts of Appeal, First Instance Courts, Peace Courts, Courts of Sessions, *Shari'a* Courts and Penal Courts.

The Court of Cassation: This is the highest judicial bench of all the Civil Courts; it sits in Baghdad, and consists of the President and a number of vice-presidents and not fewer than 15 permanent judges, delegated judges and reporters as necessity requires. There are four bodies in the Court of Cassation, these are: (*a*) the General body, (*b*) Civil and Commercial body, (*c*) Personal Status body, (*d*) the Penal body.

Courts of Appeal: The country is divided into five Districts of Appeal: Baghdad, Al-Mawsil (Mosul), Al-Basrah (Basra), Al-Hillah (Hilla), and Kirkuk, each with its Court of Appeal consisting of a president, vice-presidents and not fewer than three members, who consider the objections against the decisions issued by the First Instance Courts of first grade.

Courts of First Instance: These courts are of two kinds: Limited and Unlimited in jurisdiction.

Limited Courts: deal with Civil and Commercial suits, the value

of which is 500 Iraqi dinars and less; and suits, the value of which cannot be defined, and which are subject to fixed fees. Limited Courts consider these suits in the final stage and they are subject to Cassation.

Unlimited Courts: consider the Civil and Commercial suits irrespective of their value, and suits the value of which exceeds 500 Iraqi dinars with first grade subject to appeal.

First Instance Courts consist of one judge in the centre of each *Liwa*, some *Qadhas* and *Nahiyas*, as the Minister of Justice judges necessary.

Courts of Sessions: There is in every District of Appeal a Court of Sessions which consists of three judges under the presidency of the President of the Court of Appeal or one of his vice-presidents. It considers the penal suits prescribed by Penal Proceedings Law and other laws. More than one Court of Sessions may be established in one District of Appeal by notification issued by the Minister of Justice mentioning therein its headquarters, jurisdiction and the manner of its establishment.

Shari'a Courts: A *Shari'a* Court is established wherever there is a First Instance Court; the Muslim judge of the First Instance Court may be a *Qadhi* to the *Shari'a* Court if a special *Qadhi* has not been appointed thereto. The *Shari'a* Court considers matters of personal status and religious matters in accordance with the provisions of the law supplement to the Civil and Commercial Proceedings Law.

Penal Courts: A Penal Court of first grade is established in every First Instance Court. The judge of the First Instance Court is considered as penal judge unless a special judge is appointed thereto. More than one Penal Court may be established to consider the suits prescribed by the Penal Proceedings Law and other laws.

One or more Investigation Court may be established in the centre of each *Liwa* and a judge is appointed thereto. They may be established in the centres of *Qadhas* and *Nahiyas* by order of the Minister of Justice. The judge carries out the investigation in accordance with the provisions of Penal Proceedings Law and the other laws.

There is in every First Instance Court a department for the execution of judgments presided over by the Judge of First Instance if a special president is not appointed thereto. It carries out its duties in accordance with the provisions of Execution Law.

Religion

ISLAM

About 95% of the population are Muslims, more than 50% of whom are Shi'ite. The Arabs of northern Iraq, the Bedouins, the Kurds, the Turkomans and some of the inhabitants of Baghdad and Basra are mainly of the Sunni sect, while the remaining Arabs south of the Diyali belong to the Shi'i sect.

CHRISTIANITY

There are Christian communities in all the principal towns of Iraq, but their principal villages lie mostly in the Mosul district. The Christians of Iraq comprise three groups: (*a*) the free Churches, including the Nestorian, Gregorian and Syrian Orthodox; (*b*) the churches known as Uniate, since they are in union with the Roman Catholic Church, including the Armenian Uniates, Syrian Uniates and Chaldeans; (*c*) mixed bodies of Protestant converts, New Chaldeans and Orthodox Armenians.

The Assyrian Church

Assyrian Christians, an ancient sect having sympathies with Nestorian beliefs, were forced to leave their mountainous homeland in northern Kurdistan in the early part of the 20th century. The estimated 550,000 members of the Apostolic Catholic Assyrian Church of the East are now exiles, mainly in Iraq, Syria, Lebanon and the USA. Their leader is the Catholicos Patriarch, His Holiness MAR DINKHA IV.

The Orthodox Churches

Armenian Apostolic Church: Primate of the Armenian Diocese of Iraq, POB 2280, Younis as-Saba'awi Sq., Baghdad; tel. (1) 815-1853; fax (1) 815-1857; Archbishop AVAK ASADOURIAN; 10 churches (four in Baghdad); 18,000 adherents, mainly in Baghdad.

Syrian Orthodox Church: about 12,000 adherents in Iraq.

The Greek Orthodox Church is also represented in Iraq.

The Roman Catholic Church

Armenian Rite

At 31 December 2000 the archdiocese of Baghdad contained an estimated 2,000 adherents.

Archbishop of Baghdad: (vacant), 27/903 Archevêché Arménien

Catholique, Karrada Sharkiya, POB 2344, Baghdad; tel. (1) 719-1827.

Chaldean Rite

Iraq comprises the patriarchate of Babylon, five archdioceses (including the patriarchal see of Baghdad) and five dioceses (all of which are suffragan to the patriarchate). Altogether, the Patriarch has jurisdiction over 21 archdioceses and dioceses in Iraq, Egypt, Iran, Lebanon, Syria, Turkey and the USA, and the Patriarchal Vicariate of Jerusalem. At 31 December 2000 there were an estimated 220,573 Chaldean Catholics in Iraq (including 155,000 in the archdiocese of Baghdad).

Patriarch of Babylon of the Chaldeans: His Beatitude RAPHAËL I BIDAWID, POB 6112, Patriarcat Chaldéen Catholique, Baghdad; tel. (1) 887-9604; fax (1) 884-9967.

Archbishop of Arbil: Most Rev. YACOUB DENHA SCHER, Archevêché Catholique Chaldéen, Ainkawa, Arbil; tel. (665) 27463.

Archbishop of Baghdad: the Patriarch of Babylon (see above).

Archbishop of Basra: Most Rev. DJIBRAIL KASSAB, Archevêché Chaldéen, POB 217, Ashar-Basra; tel. (40) 210323.

Archbishop of Kirkuk: Most Rev. ANDRÉ SANA, Archevêché Chaldéen, POB 490, Kirkuk; tel. (50) 213978.

Archbishop of Mosul: Most Rev. PAULOS FARAJ RAHHO, Archevêché Chaldéen, POB 757, Mayassa, Mosul; tel. (60) 762022; fax (60) 772460.

Latin Rite

The archdiocese of Baghdad, directly responsible to the Holy See, contained an estimated 2,500 adherents at 31 December 2000.

Archbishop of Baghdad: Most Rev. JEAN BENJAMIN SLEIMAN, Archevêché Latin, Hay al-Wahda—Mahallat 904, rue 8, Imm. 44, POB 35130, 12906 Baghdad; tel. (1) 719-9537; fax (1) 717-2471.

Melkite Rite

The Greek-Melkite Patriarch of Antioch (GRÉGOIRE III LAHAM) is resident in Damascus, Syria.

Patriarchal Exarchate of Iraq: Asfar St, Karrada Sharkiya, Baghdad; tel. (1) 719-1082; 600 adherents (31 December 1995); Exarch Patriarchal GEORGES EL-MURR.

Syrian Rite

Iraq comprises two archdioceses and the Patriarchal Exarchate of Basra; there were an estimated 55,700 adherents at 31 December 2000.

Archbishop of Baghdad: Most Rev. ATHANASE MATTI SHABA MATOKA, Archevêché Syrien Catholique, 1/2/903 Baghdad; tel. (1) 719-1850; fax (1) 719-0168.

Archbishop of Mosul: Most Rev. BASILE GEORGES CASMOUSSA, Archevêché Syrien Catholique, Hosh al-Khan, Mosul; tel. (60) 762160; fax (60) 771439.

The Anglican Communion

Within the Episcopal Church in Jerusalem and the Middle East, Iraq forms part of the diocese of Cyprus and the Gulf. Expatriate congregations in Iraq meet at St George's Church, Baghdad (Hon. Sec. GRAHAM SPURGEON). The Bishop in Cyprus and the Gulf is resident in Cyprus.

JUDAISM

Unofficial estimates assess the present size of the Jewish community at 2,500, almost all residing in Baghdad.

OTHERS

About 30,000 Yazidis and a smaller number of Turkomans, Sabians and Shebeks reside in Iraq.

Sabian Community: An-Nasiriyah (Nasiriya); 20,000 adherents; Mandeans, mostly in Nasiriya; Head Sheikh DAKHIL.

Yazidis: Ainsifni; 30,000 adherents; Leader TASHIN BAIK.

The Press

DAILIES

Al-Baath ar-Riyadhi: Baghdad; sports; Propr and Editor UDAY SADDAM HUSSAIN.

Babil (Babylon): Baghdad; internet www.iraq2000.com/babil; f. 1991; Propr and Editor UDAY SADDAM HUSSAIN.

Baghdad Observer: POB 624, Karantina, Baghdad; tel. (1) 416-9341; f. 1967; English; state-sponsored; Editor-in-Chief NAJI AL-HADITHI; circ. 22,000.

Al-Iraq: POB 5717, Baghdad; internet www.uruklink.net/al-iraq; f. 1976; Kurdish; formerly *Al-Ta'akhi*; organ of the National Progressive Front; Editor-in-Chief SALAHUDIN SAEED; circ. 30,000.

Al-Jumhuria (The Republic): POB 491, Waziriya, Baghdad; internet www.uruklink.net/jumhuriya; f. 1963; refounded 1967; Arabic; Editor-in-Chief SAMI MAHDI; circ. 150,000.

Al-Qadisiya: Baghdad; internet www.uruklink.net/qadissiya; organ of the army.

Ar-Riyadhi (Sportsman): POB 58, Jadid Hassan Pasha, Baghdad; internet www.iraq2000.com/alryadhi; f. 1971; Arabic; published by Ministry of Youth; circ. 30,000.

Tariq ash-Sha'ab (People's Path): as-Sa'adoun St, Baghdad; Arabic; organ of the Iraqi Communist Party; Editor ABD AR-RAZZAK AS-SAFI.

Ath-Thawra (Revolution): POB 2009, Aqaba bin Nafi's Sq., Baghdad; tel. (1) 719-6161; internet www.uruklink.net/thawra; f. 1968; Arabic; organ of Baath Party; Editor-in-Chief HAMEED SAEED; circ. 250,000.

WEEKLIES

Alif Baa (Alphabet): Baghdad; tel. (1) 886-2948; fax (1) 538-1296; internet www.uruklink.net/alef-ba; Arabic and English; Editor-in-Chief AMIR AL-HILOU; circ. 33,000.

Al-Idaa'a wal-Television (Radio and Television): Iraqi Broadcasting and Television Establishment, Karradat Mariam, Baghdad; tel. (1) 537-1161; radio and television programmes and articles; Arabic; Editor-in-Chief KAMIL HAMDI ASH-SHARQI; circ. 40,000.

Majallati: Children's Culture House, POB 8041, Baghdad; Arabic; children's newspaper; Editor-in-Chief RAAD BENDER; circ. 35,000.

Ar-Rased (The Observer): Baghdad; Arabic; general.

Sabaa Nisan: Baghdad; f. 1976; Arabic; organ of the General Union of the Youth of Iraq.

Sawt al-Fallah (Voice of the Peasant): Karradat Mariam, Baghdad; f. 1968; Arabic; organ of the General Union of Farmers Societies; circ. 40,000.

Waee ul-Ummal (The Workers' Consciousness): Headquarters of General Federation of Trade Unions in Iraq, POB 2307, Gialani St, Senak, Baghdad; Arabic; Iraq Trades Union organ; Chief Editor KHALID MAHMOUD HUSSEIN; circ. 25,000.

PERIODICALS

Afaq Arabiya (Arab Horizons): POB 2009, Aqaba bin Nafi's Sq., Baghdad; monthly; Arabic; literary and political; Editor-in-Chief Dr MOHSIN J. AL-MUSAWI.

Al-Aqlam (Pens): POB 4032, Adamiya, Baghdad; tel. (1) 443-3644; f. 1964; monthly; Arabic; literary; Editor-in-Chief Dr ALI J. AL-ALLAQ; circ. 7,000.

Bagdad: Dar al-Ma'mun for Translation and Publishing, POB 24015, Karradat Mariam, Baghdad; tel. (1) 538-3171; fortnightly; French; cultural and political.

Al-Funoon al-Ida'iya (Fields of Broadcasting): Cultural Affairs House, Karradat Mariam, Baghdad; quarterly; Arabic; supervised by Broadcasting and TV Training Institute; engineering and technical; Chief Editor MUHAMMAD AL-JAZA'RI.

Gilgamesh: Dar al-Ma'mun for Translation and Publishing, POB 24015, Karradat Mariam, Baghdad; tel. (1) 538-3171; quarterly; English; cultural.

Hurras al-Watan: Baghdad; Arabic.

L'Iraq Aujourd'hui: POB 2009, Aqaba bin Nafi's Sq., Baghdad; f. 1976; bi-monthly; French; cultural and political; Editor NADJI AL-HADITHI; circ. 12,000.

Iraq Oil News: POB 6178, al-Mansour, Baghdad; tel. (1) 541-0031; f. 1973; monthly; English; publ. by the Information and Public Relations Div. of the Ministry of Oil.

The Journal of the Faculty of Medicine: College of Medicine, University of Baghdad, Jadiriya, Baghdad; tel. (1) 93091; f. 1935; quarterly; Arabic and English; medical and technical; Editor Prof. YOUSUF D. AN-NAAMAN.

Al-Maarif an-Naftiah: Oil Institute, POB 4836, Waziriya, Baghdad; f. 2001; monthly; Arabic; Editor-in-Chief SHARIF MUTSIN AL-HADITHI.

Majallat al-Majma' al-'Ilmi al-'Iraqi (Journal of the Academy of Sciences): POB 4023, Waziriya, Baghdad; tel. (1) 422-1733; fax (1) 425-4523; f. 1950; quarterly; Arabic; scholarly magazine on Arabic Islamic culture; Editor-in-Chief Dr NAJIH M. K. AR-RAWI.

Majallat ath-Thawra az-Ziraia (Magazine of Iraq Agriculture): Baghdad; quarterly; Arabic; agricultural; published by the Ministry of Agriculture.

Al-Maskukat (Coins): Dept of Antiquities and Heritage, Karkh, Salihiya St, Baghdad; tel. (1) 884-0875; f. 1969; annually; numismatics; Chair. of Ed. Board RABI' AL-QAISI.

Al-Masrah wal-Cinema: Iraqi Broadcasting, Television and Cinema Establishment, Salihiya St, Baghdad; monthly; Arabic; artistic, theatrical and cinema.

Al-Mawrid: POB 2009, Aqaba bin Nafi's Sq., Baghdad; f. 1971; monthly; Arabic; cultural.

Al-Mu'allem al-Jadid: Ministry of Education, al-Imam al-A'dham St, A'dhamaiya, nr Antar Sq., Baghdad; tel. (1) 422-2594; f. 1935; quarterly; Arabic; educational, social, and general; Editor-in-Chief KHALIL I. HAMASH; circ. 190,000.

Sawt at-Talaba (The Voice of Students): al-Maghreb St, Waziriya, Baghdad; internet www.iraq2000.com/talaba; f. 1968; monthly; Arabic; organ of National Union of Iraqi Students; circ. 25,000.

As-Sina'a (Industry): POB 5665, Baghdad; every 2 months; Arabic and English; publ. by Ministry of Industry and Minerals; Editor-in-Chief ABD AL-QADER ABD AL-LATIF; circ. 16,000.

Sumer: Dept of Antiquities and Heritage, Karkh, Salihiya St, Baghdad; tel. (1) 884-0875; f. 1945; annually; archaeological, historical journal; Chair. of Ed. Board RABI' AL-QAISI.

Ath-Thaquafa (Culture): Place at-Tahrir, Baghdad; f. 1970; monthly; Arabic; cultural; Editor-in-Chief SALAH KHALIS; circ. 5,000.

Ath-Thaquafa al-Jadida (The New Culture): Baghdad; f. 1969; monthly; pro-Communist; Editor-in-Chief SAFA AL-HAFIZ; circ. 3,000.

At-Turath ash-Sha'abi (Popular Heritage): POB 2009, Aqaba bin Nafi's Sq., Baghdad; monthly; Arabic; specializes in Iraqi and Arabic folklore; Editor-in-Chief LUTFI AL-KHOURI; circ. 15,000.

Al-Waqai al-Iraqiya (Official Gazette of Republic of Iraq): Ministry of Justice, Baghdad; f. 1922; Arabic and English weekly editions; circ. Arabic 4,000, English 400; Dir HASHIM N. JAAFER.

PRESS ORGANIZATIONS

The General Federation of Journalists: POB 6017, Baghdad; tel. (1) 541-3993.

Iraqi Journalists' Union: POB 14101, Baghdad; tel. (1) 537-0762.

NEWS AGENCIES

Iraqi News Agency (INA): POB 3084, 28 Nissan Complex—Baghdad, Sadoun; tel. (1) 8863024; e-mail ina@uruklink.net; internet www.uruklink.net/iraqnews; f. 1959; Dir-Gen. UDAI EL-TAIE.

Foreign Bureaux

Agence France-Presse (AFP): POB 190, Apt 761-91-97, Baghdad; tel. (1) 551-4333; Correspondent FAROUQ CHOUKRI.

Agenzia Nazionale Stampa Associata (ANSA) (Italy): POB 5602, Baghdad; tel. (1) 776-2558; Correspondent SALAH H. NASRAWI.

Associated Press (AP) (USA): Hay al-Khadra 629, Zuqaq No. 23, Baghdad; tel. (1) 555-9041; Correspondent SALAH H. NASRAWI.

Deutsche Presse-Agentur (dpa) (Germany): POB 5699, Baghdad; Correspondent NAJHAT KOTANI.

Informatsionnoye Telegrafnoye Agentstvo Rossii—Telegrafnoye Agentstvo Suverennykh Stran (ITAR—TASS) (Russia): 67 Street 52, Alwiya, Baghdad; Correspondent ANDREI OSTALSKY.

Reuters (UK): House No. 8, Zuqaq 75, Mahalla 903, Hay al-Karada, Baghdad; tel. (1) 719-1843; Correspondent SUBHY HADDAD.

Xinhua (New China) News Agency (People's Republic of China): al-Mansour, Adrus District, 611 Small District, 5 Lane No. 8, Baghdad; tel. (1) 541-8904; Correspondent ZHU SHAOHUA.

Publishers

National House for Publishing, Distribution and Advertising: Ministry of Information, POB 624, al-Jumhuriyah St, Baghdad; tel. (1) 425-1846; f. 1972; publishes books on politics, economics, education, agriculture, sociology, commerce and science in Arabic and other Middle Eastern languages; sole importer and distributor of newspapers, magazines, periodicals and books; controls all advertising activities, inside Iraq as well as outside; Dir-Gen. M. A. ASKAR.

Afaq Arabiya Publishing House: POB 4032, Adamiya, Baghdad; tel. (1) 443-6044; fax (1) 444-8760; publisher of literary monthlies,

Al-Aqlam and *Afaq Arabiya*, periodicals, *Foreign Culture, Art, Folklore* and cultural books; Chair. Dr MOHSIN AL-MUSAWI.

Dar al-Ma'mun for Translation and Publishing: POB 24015, Karradat Mariam, Baghdad; tel. (1) 538-3171; publisher of newspapers and magazines including: the *Baghdad Observer* (daily newspaper), *Bagdad* (monthly magazine), *Gilgamesh* (quarterly magazine).

Al-Hurriyah Printing Establishment: Karantina, Sarrafia, Baghdad; tel. (1) 69721; f. 1970; largest printing and publishing establishment in Iraq; state-owned; controls *Al-Jumhuriyah* (see below).

Al-Jamaheer Press House: POB 491, Sarrafia, Baghdad; tel. (1) 416-9341; fax (1) 416-1875; f. 1963; publisher of a number of newspapers and magazines, *Al-Jumhuriyah, Baghdad Observer, Alif Baa, Yord Weekly*; Pres. SAAD QASSEM HAMMOUDI.

Al-Ma'arif Ltd: Mutanabi St, Baghdad; f. 1929; publishes periodicals and books in Arabic, Kurdish, Turkish, French and English.

Al-Muthanna Library: Mutanabi St, Baghdad; f. 1936; booksellers and publishers of books in Arabic and oriental languages; Man. ANAS K. AR-RAJAB.

An-Nahdah: Mutanabi St, Baghdad; politics, Arab affairs.

Kurdish Culture Publishing House: Baghdad; f. 1976; attached to the Ministry of Information.

Ath-Thawra Printing and Publishing House: POB 2009, Aqaba bin Nafi's Sq., Baghdad; tel. (1) 719-6161; f. 1970; state-owned; Chair. (vacant).

Thnayan Printing House: Baghdad.

Broadcasting and Communications

TELECOMMUNICATIONS

Iraqi Telecommunications and Posts: POB 2450, Karrada Dakhil, Baghdad; tel. (1) 718-0400; fax (1) 718-2125; Dir-Gen. Eng. MEZHER M. HASAN.

BROADCASTING

State Enterprise for Communications and Post: f. 1987 from State Org. for Post, Telegraph and Telephones, and its subsidiaries.

State Organization for Broadcasting and Television: Broadcasting and Television Bldg, Salihiya, Karkh, Baghdad; tel. (1) 537-1161.

Iraqi Broadcasting and Television Establishment: Salihiya, Baghdad; tel. (1) 884-4412; fax (1) 541-0480; f. 1936; radio broadcasts began 1936; home service broadcasts in Arabic, Kurdish, Syriac and Turkoman; foreign service in French, German, English, Russian, Azeri, Hebrew and Spanish; Dir-Gen. SABAH YASEEN.

Radio

Idaa'a Baghdad (Radio Baghdad): f. 1936; 22 hours daily.

Idaa'a Sawt al-Jamahir: f. 1970; 24 hours.

Other stations include **Idaa'a al-Kurdia Idaa'a al-Farisiya** (Persian).

Radio Iraq International: POB 8145, Baghdad.

Television

Baghdad Television: Ministry of Information, Iraqi Broadcasting and Television Establishment, Salihiya, Karkh, Baghdad; tel. (1) 537-1151; f. 1956; government station operating daily on two channels for 9 hours and 8 hours respectively; Dir-Gen. Dr MAJID AHMAD AS-SAMARRIE.

Kirkuk Television: f. 1967; government station; 6 hours daily.

Mosul Television: f. 1968; government station; 6 hours daily.

Basra Television: f. 1968; government station; 6 hours daily.

Missan Television: f. 1974; government station; 6 hours daily.

Kurdish Television: f. 1974; government station; 8 hours daily.

There are 18 other TV stations operating in the Iraqi provinces.

Finance

(cap. = capital; dep. = deposits; res = reserves; brs = branches; m. = million; amounts in Iraqi dinars)

All banks and insurance companies, including all foreign companies, were nationalized in July 1964. The assets of foreign companies were taken over by the State. In May 1991 the Government announced its decision to end the State's monopoly in banking, and by mid-1992 three private banks had commenced operations.

BANKING

Central Bank

Central Bank of Iraq: POB 64, Rashid St, Baghdad; tel. (1) 816-5171; fax (1) 816-6321; e-mail cbi@uruklink.net; f. 1947 as National Bank of Iraq; name changed as above 1956; has the sole right of note issue; cap. and res 125m. (Sept. 1988); Gov. ISSAM RASHID HUWEISH; brs in Mosul and Basra.

Nationalized Commercial Banks

Rafidain Bank: New Banks St, Baghdad; tel. (1) 415-8001; f. 1941; state-owned; cap. 2,000m., res 1,702.3m., dep. 453,678m., total assets 503,145.1m. (Dec. 1998); Pres. DHIA HABIB AL-KHAYYOON; 152 brs in Iraq, 9 brs abroad.

Rashid Bank: BOP 7177, Haifa St, Baghdad; tel. (1) 885-3411; f. 1988; state-owned; cap. 1,000m., res 1.5m., dep. 236.1m. (1999); Chair. and Gen. Man. FAIQ M. AL-OBAIDY; 133 brs.

Private Commercial Banks

Bank of Baghdad: POB 3192 Alwiya, Al-Karada St, Baghdad; tel. (1) 717-5007; fax (1) 717-5006; e-mail bankdad@uruklink.net; f. 1992; cap. 1,750m. Chair. MUNIB K. AS-SIKOUTI.

Commercial Bank of Iraq SA: POB 5639, 13/14/904 Al-Wahda St, Baghdad; tel. (1) 707-0049; fax (1) 718-4312; e-mail commerce@uruklink.net; f. 1992; cap. 1,800m. Chair. MUHAMMAD H. DRAGH.

Specialized Banks

Al-Ahli Bank for Agricultural Investment and Financing: Al-Huria Sq., Al-Ahh, Baghdad.

Agricultural Co-operative Bank of Iraq: POB 2421, Rashid St, Baghdad; tel. (1) 886-4768; fax (1) 886-5047; f. 1936; state-owned; cap. 295.7m., res 14m., dep. 10.5m., total assets 351.6m. (Dec. 1988); Dir-Gen. HDIYA H. AL-KHAYOUN; 32 brs.

Industrial Bank of Iraq: POB 5825, as-Sinak, Baghdad; tel. (1) 887-2181; fax (1) 888-3047; f. 1940; state-owned; cap. 59.7m., dep. 77.9m. (Dec. 1988); Dir-Gen. BASSIMA ABD AL-HADDI ADH-DHAHIR; 5 brs.

Investment Bank of Iraq: POB 3724, 102/91/24 Hay as-Sadoon, Alwiya, Baghdad; tel. (1) 718-4624; fax (1) 719-8505; f. 1993; cap. 300m., res 39.2m. (Dec. 1998); Chair. THAMIR R. SHAIKHLY; Man. Dir MOWAFAQ HASAN MAHMOOD.

Iraqi Islamic Bank SA: POB 940, Al-Kahiay, Bab Al-Muathem, Baghdad; tel. (1) 414-0694.

Iraqi Middle East Investment Bank: POB 10379, Bldg 65, Hay Babel, 929 Arasat al-Hindiya, Baghdad; tel. (1) 717-3745; f. 1993; cap., res and dep. 3,254.8m. (1998).

Real Estate Bank of Iraq: POB 8118, 29/222 Haifa St, Baghdad; tel. (1) 885-3212; fax (1) 884-0980; f. 1949; state-owned; gives loans to assist the building industry; cap. 800m., res 11m., total assets 2,593.6m. (Dec. 1988); acquired the Co-operative Bank in 1970; Dir-Gen. ABD AR-RAZZAQ AZIZ; 18 brs.

INSURANCE

Iraq Life Insurance Co: POB 989, Aqaba bin Nafi's Sq., Khalid bin al-Waleed St, Baghdad; tel. (1) 719-2184; fax (1) 719-2606; f. 1959; state-owned; Chair. and Gen. Man. WALID SALIH ABD AL-WAHAB.

Iraq Reinsurance Co: POB 297, Aqaba bin Nafi's Sq., Khalid bin al-Waleed St, Baghdad; tel. (1) 719-5131; fax (1) 791497; f. 1960; state-owned; transacts reinsurance business on the international market; total assets 93.2m. (1985); Chair. and Gen. Man. K. M. AL-MUDARIES.

National Insurance Co: POB 248, National Insurance Co Bldg, Al-Khullani St, Baghdad; tel. (1) 885-3026; fax (1) 886-1486; f. 1950; cap. 20m. all types of general and life insurance, reinsurance and investment; Chair. and Gen. Man. MUHAMMAD HUSSAIN JAAFAR ABBAS.

STOCK EXCHANGE

Capital Market Authority: Baghdad; Chair. MUHAMMAD HASSAN FAG EN-NOUR.

Trade and Industry

CHAMBERS OF COMMERCE

Federation of Iraqi Chambers of Commerce: Mustansir St, Baghdad; tel. (1) 886-1811; fax (1) 886-0283; f. 1969; all Iraqi Chambers of Commerce are affiliated to the Federation; Chair. ZUHAIR A. AL-YOUNIS; Sec.-Gen. FALIH A. AS-SALEH.

INDUSTRIAL AND TRADE ASSOCIATIONS

In 1987 and 1988, as part of a programme of economic and administrative reform, to increase efficiency and productivity in industry and agriculture, many of the state organizations previously responsible for various industries were abolished or merged, and new state enterprises or mixed-sector national companies were established to replace them.

Military Industries Commission (MIC): Baghdad; attached to the Ministry of Defence; Chair. (vacant).

State enterprises include the following:

Iraqi State Enterprise for Cement: f. 1987 by merger of central and southern state cement enterprises.

National Co for Chemical and Plastics Industries: Dir-Gen. RAJA BAYYATI.

The Rafidain Co for Building Dams: f. 1987 to replace the State Org. for Dams.

State Enterprise for Battery Manufacture: f. 1987; Dir-Gen. ADEL ABBOUD.

State Enterprise for Construction Industries: f. 1987 by merger of state orgs for gypsum, asbestos, and the plastic and concrete industries.

State Enterprise for Cotton Industries: f. 1988 by merger of State Org. for Cotton Textiles and Knitting, and the Mosul State Org. for Textiles.

State Enterprise for Drinks and Mineral Water: f. 1987 by merger of enterprises responsible for soft and alcoholic drinks.

State Enterprise for the Fertilizer Industries: f. by merger of Basra-based and central fertilizer enterprises.

State Enterprise for Import and Export: f. 1987 to replace the five state orgs responsible to the Ministry of Trade for productive commodities, consumer commodities, grain and food products, exports and imports.

State Enterprise for Leather Industries: f. 1987; Dir-Gen. MUHAMMAD ABD AL-MAJID.

State Enterprise for Sugar Beet: f. 1987 by merger of sugar enterprises in Mosul and Sulaimaniya.

State Enterprise for Textiles: f. 1987 to replace the enterprise for textiles in Baghdad, and the enterprise for plastic sacks in Tikrit.

State Enterprise for Tobacco and Cigarettes.

State Enterprise for Woollen Industries: f. by merger of state orgs for textiles and woollen textiles and Arbil-based enterprise for woollen textiles and women's clothing.

AGRICULTURAL ORGANIZATIONS

The following bodies are responsible to the Ministry of Agriculture:

State Agricultural Enterprise in Dujaila.

State Enterprise for Agricultural Supplies: Dir-Gen. MUHAMMAD KHAIRI.

State Enterprise for Developing Animal Wealth.

State Enterprise for Fodder.

State Enterprise for Grain Trading and Processing: Dir-Gen. ZUHAIR ABD AR-RAHMAN.

State Enterprise for Poultry (Central and Southern Areas).

State Enterprise for Poultry (Northern Area).

State Enterprise for Sea Fisheries: POB 260, Basra; Baghdad office: POB 3296, Baghdad; tel. (1) 92023; fleet of 3 fish factory ships, 2 fish carriers, 1 fishing boat.

PEASANT SOCIETIES

General Federation of Peasant Societies: Baghdad; f. 1959; has 734 affiliated Peasant Societies.

EMPLOYERS' ORGANIZATION

Iraqi Federation of Industries: Iraqi Federation of Industries Bldg, al-Khullani Sq., Baghdad; f. 1956; 6,000 mems; Pres. HATAM ABD AR-RASHID.

PETROLEUM AND GAS

Ministry of Oil: POB 19244, Zayouna, Baghdad; tel. (1) 817-7000; fax (1) 886-9432; e-mail oil@uruklink.net; internet www.uruklink .net/oil; merged with INOC in 1987; affiliated cos: Oil Marketing Co, Oil Projects Co, Midland Refineries Co, Oil Exploration Co, Oil Products Distribution Co, Gas Filling Co, Petroleum Pipelines Co, Iraqi Drilling Co, South Oil Co, South Refineries Co, North Oil Co, North Refineries Co, North Gas Co, South Gas Co, Iraqi Oil Tankers Co, Research and Development Centre.

Iraq National Oil Co (INOC): POB 476, al-Khullani Sq., Baghdad; tel. (1) 887-1115; f. in 1964 to operate the petroleum industry at home and abroad; when Iraq nationalized its petroleum industry, structural changes took place in INOC, and it became solely responsible for exploration, production, transportation and marketing of Iraqi crude petroleum and petroleum products. INOC was merged with the Ministry of Oil in 1987, and the functions of some of the organizations under its control were transferred to newly-created ministerial departments or to companies responsible to the ministry.

UTILITIES

Electricity

State Enterprise for Generation and Transmission of Electricity: f. 1987 from State Org. for Major Electrical Projects; Dir SALAH YUSUF KUZAYR.

TRADE UNIONS

General Federation of Trade Unions of Iraq (GFTU): POB 3049, Tahrir Sq., Rashid St, Baghdad; tel. (1) 887-0810; fax (1) 886-3820; f. 1959; incorporates six vocational trade unions and 18 local trade union federations in the governorates of Iraq; the number of workers in industry is 536,245, in agriculture 150,967 (excl. peasants) and in other services 476,621 (1986); GFTU is a member of the International Confederation of Arab Trade Unions and of the World Federation of Trade Unions; Pres. FADHIL MAHMOUD GHAREB.

Union of Teachers: Al-Mansour, Baghdad; Pres. Dr ISSA SALMAN HAMID.

Union of Palestinian Workers in Iraq: Baghdad; Sec.-Gen. SAMI ASH-SHAWISH.

There are also unions of doctors, pharmacologists, jurists, artists, and a General Federation of Iraqi Women (Chair. MANAL YOUNIS).

Transport

RAILWAYS

Iraq's railway lines extend over some 2,339 km. A line covers the length of the country, from Rabia, on the Syrian border, via Mosul, to Baghdad (534 km), and from Baghdad to Basra and Umm Qasr (608 km), on the Persian (Arabian) Gulf. A 404-km line links Baghdad, via Radi and Haditha to Husaibah, near the Iraqi–Syrian frontier. Baghdad is linked with Arbil via Khanaqin and Kirkuk, and a 252-km line (designed to serve industrial projects along its route) runs from Kirkuk via Baiji to Haditha. A 638-km line runs from Baghdad, via al-Qaim (on the Syrian border), to Akashat (with a 150-km line linking the Akashat phosphate mines and the fertilizer complex at al-Qaim). As well as the internal service, there is a regular international service between Baghdad and İstanbul, Turkey. Passenger rail services between Mosul and Aleppo, Syria, resumed in August 2000 after an interruption of almost 20 years. It was reported in mid-2001 that international contractors were submitting bids to revise and develop earlier plans for a 'loop' railway project for Baghdad.

State Enterprise for Iraqi Railways: Baghdad Central Station Bldg, Damascus Sq., Baghdad; tel. (1) 543-4404; fax (1) 884-0480; fmrly the Iraqi Republic Railways, under the supervision of State Org. for Iraqi Railways; re-formed as a State Enterprise in 1987, under the Ministry of Transport and Communications; Dir-Gen. GHASSAN ABD AR-RAZAQ AL-ANI.

New Railways Implementation Authority: POB 17040, al-Hurriya, Baghdad; tel. (1) 537-0021; responsible for development of railway network; Sec.-Gen. R. A. AL-UMARI.

ROADS

At the end of 1999, according to estimates by the International Road Federation, Iraq's road network extended over 45,550 km, of which approximately 38,400 km were paved.

The most important roads are: Baghdad–Mosul–Tel Kotchuk (Syrian border), 521 km; Baghdad–Kirkuk–Arbil–Mosul-Zakho (border with Turkey), 544 km; Kirkuk–Sulaimaniya, 160 km; Baghdad–Hilla–Diwaniya–Nasiriya–Basra, 586 km; Baghdad-Kut-Nasirya, 186 km; Baghdad–Ramadi–Rurba (border with Syria), 555 km; Baghdad–Kut–Umara–Basra–Safwan (border with Kuwait), 660 km; Baghdad–Baqaba–Kanikien (border with Iran). Most sections of the six-lane 1,264-km international Express Highway, linking Safwan (on the Kuwaiti border) with the Jordanian and Syrian borders, had been completed by June 1990. Studies have been completed for a second, 525-km Express Highway, linking Baghdad and Zakho on the Turkish border. A complex network of roads was constructed behind the war front with Iran in order to facilitate the movement of troops and supplies during the 1980–88 conflict.

Iraqi Land Transport Co: Baghdad; f. 1988 to replace State Organization for Land Transport; fleet of more than 1,000 large trucks; Dir Gen. AYSAR AS-SAFI.

Joint Land Transport Co: Baghdad; joint venture between Iraq and Jordan; operates a fleet of some 750 trucks.

State Enterprise for Implementation of Expressways: f. 1987; Dir-Gen. FAIZ MUHAMMAD SAID.

State Enterprise for Passenger Transport: Dir-Gen. THABIT MAHMUD GHARIB.

State Enterprise for Roads and Bridges: POB 917, Karradat Mariam, Karkh, Baghdad; tel. (1) 32141; responsible for road and bridge construction projects under the Ministry of Housing and Construction.

SHIPPING

The ports of Basra and Umm Qasr are usually the commercial gateway of Iraq. They are connected by various ocean routes with all parts of the world, and constitute the natural distributing centre for overseas supplies. The Iraqi State Enterprise for Maritime Transport maintains a regular service between Basra, the Gulf and north European ports. There is also a port at Khor az-Zubair, which came into use during 1979.

At Basra there is accommodation for 12 vessels at the Maqal Wharves and accommodation for seven vessels at the buoys. There is one silo berth and two berths for petroleum products at Muftia and one berth for fertilizer products at Abu Flus. There is room for eight vessels at Umm Qasr. There are deep-water tanker terminals at Khor al-Amaya and Faw for three and four vessels respectively. The latter port, however, was abandoned during the early part of the Iran–Iraq War.

For the inland waterways, which are now under the control of the General Establishment for Iraqi Ports, there are 1,036 registered river craft, 48 motor vessels and 105 motor boats.

General Establishment for Iraqi Ports: Maqal, Basra; tel. (40) 413211; f. 1987, when State Org. for Iraqi Ports was abolished; Dir-Gen. ABD AR-RAZZAQ ABD AL-WAHAB.

State Enterprise for Iraqi Water Transport: POB 23016, Airport St, al-Furat Quarter, Baghdad; f. 1987, when State Org. for Iraqi Water Transport was abolished; responsible for the planning, supervision and control of six nat. water transportation enterprises, incl.:

> **State Enterprise for Maritime Transport (Iraqi Line):** POB 13038, al-Jadiriya al-Hurriya Ave, Baghdad; Basra office: 14 July St, POB 766, Basra; tel. (1) 776-3201; f. 1952; Dir-Gen. JABER Q. HASSAN; Operations Man. M. A. ALI.

Shipping Company

Arab Bridge Maritime Navigation Co: Aqaba, Jordan; tel. (03) 316307; fax (03) 316313; f. 1987; joint venture by Egypt, Iraq and Jordan to improve economic co-operation; an expansion of the company that established a ferry link between the ports of Aqaba, Jordan, and Nuweibeh, Egypt, in 1985; cap. US $6m. Chair. NABEEH AL-ABWAH.

CIVIL AVIATION

There are international airports near Baghdad, at Bamerni, and at Basra. Baghdad's airport, previously named Saddam International Airport, reopened in August 2000, after refurbishment necessitated by damage sustained during the war with the multinational force in 1991. However, international air links have been virtually halted by the UN embargo imposed in 1990. Internal flights, connecting Baghdad to Basra and Mosul, recommenced in November 2000. In early April 2003 the capital's airport was renamed Baghdad International Airport by US forces during their military campaign to oust the regime of Saddam Hussain.

National Co for Civil Aviation Services: al-Mansour, Baghdad; tel. (1) 551-9443; f. 1987 following the abolition of the State Organization for Civil Aviation; responsible for the provision of aircraft, and for airport and passenger services.

Iraqi Airways Co: Baghdad International Airport; tel. (1) 887-2400; fax (1) 887-5808; f. 1948; Dir-Gen. AYAD ABD AL-KARIM HAMAM.

Tourism

In 2000 an estimated 78,457 tourists visited Iraq. Tourist receipts in 1998 were estimated at US $13m.

Iraq Tourism Board: Baghdad; e-mail iraqmail@uruklink.net; internet www.uruklink.net/tourism.

IRELAND

Introductory Survey

Location, Climate, Language, Religion, Flag, Capital

The Republic of Ireland consists of 26 of the 32 counties that comprise the island of Ireland. The remaining six counties, in the north-east, form Northern Ireland, which is part of the United Kingdom. Ireland lies in the Atlantic Ocean, about 80 km (50 miles) west of Great Britain. The climate is mild and equable, with temperatures generally between 0°C (32°F) and 21°C (70°F). Irish is the official first language, but its use as a vernacular is now restricted to certain areas, collectively known as the Gaeltacht, mainly in the west of Ireland. English is universally spoken. Official documents are printed in English and Irish. The vast majority of the inhabitants profess Christianity: of these about 95% are Roman Catholics and 5% Protestants. The national flag (proportions 1 by 2) consists of three equal vertical stripes, of green, white and orange. The capital is Dublin.

Recent History

The whole of Ireland was formerly part of the United Kingdom. In 1920 the island was partitioned, the six north-eastern counties remaining part of the United Kingdom, with their own government. In 1922 the 26 southern counties achieved dominion status, under the British Crown, as the Irish Free State. The dissolution of all remaining links with Great Britain culminated in 1937 in the adoption of a new Constitution, which gave the Irish Free State full sovereignty within the Commonwealth. Formal ties with the Commonwealth were ended in 1949, when the 26 southern counties became a republic. The partition of Ireland remained a contentious issue, and in 1969 a clandestine organization, calling itself the Provisional Irish Republican Army (IRA—see Northern Ireland, Vol. II), initiated a violent campaign to achieve reunification.

In the general election of February 1973, the Fianna Fáil party, which had held office, with only two interruptions, since 1932, was defeated. Jack Lynch, who had been Prime Minister since 1966, resigned, and Liam Cosgrave formed a coalition between his own party, Fine Gael, and the Labour Party. The Irish Government remained committed to power-sharing in the six counties, but opposed any British military withdrawal from Northern Ireland (see Northern Ireland, Vol. II).

Following the assassination of the British Ambassador to Ireland by the Provisional IRA in July 1976, the Irish Government introduced stronger measures against terrorism. Fianna Fáil won the general election of June 1977 and Jack Lynch again became Prime Minister. Lynch resigned as Prime Minister in December 1979 and was succeeded by Charles Haughey. In June 1981, following an early general election, Dr Garret FitzGerald became Prime Minister in a coalition Government between his own party, Fine Gael, and the Labour Party. However, the rejection by the Dáil (the lower house of the legislature) of the coalition's budget proposals precipitated a further general election in February 1982. Haughey was returned to power, with the support of three members of the Workers' Party and two independents. The worsening economic situation, however, made the Fianna Fáil Government increasingly unpopular, and in November Haughey lost the support of the independents over proposed reductions in public expenditure. In the subsequent general election Fianna Fáil failed to gain an overall majority, and in December FitzGerald took office as Prime Minister in a coalition with the Labour Party.

During 1986 FitzGerald's coalition lost support, partly due to the formation of a new party, the Progressive Democrats, by disaffected members of Fianna Fáil. In June a controversial government proposal to end a 60-year constitutional ban on divorce was defeated by national referendum, and shortly afterwards, as a result of a series of defections, the coalition lost its parliamentary majority. In January 1987 the Labour Party refused to support Fine Gael's budget proposals envisaging reductions in planned public expenditure, and the coalition collapsed. Fianna Fáil, led by Haughey, won 81 of the 166 seats in the Dáil at the general election held in February. Fianna Fáil formed a minority Government, which commenced upon a programme of unprecedented economic austerity.

Prior to the general election of June 1989 Fine Gael and the Progressive Democrats concluded an electoral pact to oppose Fianna Fáil. Although the Haughey administration had achieved significant economic improvements, severe reductions in public expenditure and continuing problems of unemployment and emigration adversely affected Fianna Fáil's electoral support, and it obtained only 77 of the 166 seats in the Dáil, while Fine Gael won 55 seats and the Progressive Democrats six seats.

At the end of June 1989 the Dáil reconvened to elect the Prime Minister. The Progressive Democrats voted in favour of Alan Dukes, the leader of Fine Gael, in accordance with their pre-election pact, and Haughey was defeated by 86 votes to 78. However, Dukes and Dick Spring, the leader of the Labour Party, also failed to be elected and, after nearly four weeks of negotiations, Fianna Fáil formed an 'alliance' with the Progressive Democrats; two of the latter's members were included in a new Cabinet. In mid-July Haughey became Prime Minister in a Fianna Fáil–Progressive Democrats coalition.

In October 1991 the Government defeated a motion of 'no confidence', which had been introduced following a series of financial scandals involving public officials, by 84 votes to 81.. Although members of Fianna Fáil were critical of Haughey's management of these affairs, they were reluctant to precipitate a general election, owing to the party's decline in popularity. The narrow government victory was secured with the support of the Progressive Democrats, following an agreement between Fianna Fáil and the Progressive Democrats on a programme of tax reforms. In November 1991, however, a group of Fianna Fáil deputies proposed a motion demanding Haughey's removal as leader of the party. Albert Reynolds, the Minister for Finance and a former close associate of Haughey, and Padraig Flynn, the Minister for the Environment, announced their intention of supporting the motion, and were immediately dismissed from office. In the event the attempt to depose Haughey was defeated by a substantial majority of the Fianna Fáil parliamentary grouping.

In January 1992 allegations arose that, contrary to his previous denials, Haughey had been aware of the secret monitoring, in 1982, of the telephone conversations of two journalists perceived to be critical of the Government. The Progressive Democrats made their continued support of the Government (without which a general election would have been necessary) conditional on Haughey's resignation. In February 1992 Reynolds was elected as leader of Fianna Fáil and assumed the office of Prime Minister, following Haughey's resignation. Reynolds extensively reshuffled the Cabinet, but retained the two representatives of the Progressive Democrats, in an attempt to preserve the coalition Government.

In June 1992 the leader of the Progressive Democrats, Desmond O'Malley, criticized Reynolds' conduct as Minister for Industry and Commerce in a parliamentary inquiry, which had been established in June 1991 to investigate allegations of fraud and political favouritism in the beef industry during 1987–88. In October 1992, in his testimony to the inquiry, the Prime Minister accused O'Malley of dishonesty. Following Reynolds' refusal to withdraw the allegations, in early November the Progressive Democrats left the coalition, and the Government was defeated on the following day in a motion of 'no confidence', proposed in the Dáil by the Labour Party. It was subsequently announced that a general election was to take place on 25 November, concurrent with three constitutional referendums on abortion. Fianna Fáil suffered a substantial loss of support, securing only 68 of the 166 seats in the Dáil and Fine Gael also obtained a reduced number of seats, taking only 45. In contrast, the Labour Party attracted substantial support, more than doubling its number of seats, to 33, while the Progressive Democrats increased their representation to 10 seats. In the referendums on abortion two of the proposals (on the right to seek an abortion in another European Community (EC—now European Union—EU, see p. 199), state and the right to information on abortion services abroad) were approved by about two-thirds of the votes cast. The third proposal—on the substantive issue of abortion, permitting the operation only in cases where the life (not merely the health) of the mother was threatened—was rejected, also by a two-thirds' majority.

Since no party had secured an overall majority in the general election, an extended period of consultations ensued, during which the four major parties negotiated on the composition of a governing coalition. In January 1993 Fianna Fáil and the Labour Party reached agreement on a joint policy programme and formed a coalition Government, which took office on 12 January. Reynolds retained the premiership, while Spring received the foreign affairs portfolio, as well as the post of Deputy Prime Minister.

In November 1994 serious differences arose within the coalition Government over the insistence by Fianna Fáil that the Attorney-General, Harry Whelehan, be appointed to a senior vacancy that had arisen in the High Court. Although such promotions accorded with past precedent, Whelehan's conservative record on social issues was unacceptable to the Labour Party, whose specific objection to Whelehan's appointment was based on his alleged obstruction of the processing of an extradition warrant for a Roman Catholic priest sought by the authorities in Northern Ireland on charges of the sexual abuse of children. It was alleged by the Labour Party that the transfer of Whelehan to the presidency of the High Court was intended by Fianna Fáil to protect him from public accountability for his conduct as Attorney-General. However, Reynolds and the Fianna Fáil members of the Cabinet approved the appointment in the absence of the Labour Party ministers. On 15 November Reynolds admitted to the Dáil that there was no satisfactory explanation for the delay in processing the extradition warrant, but denied that the matter affected the suitability of Whelehan for judicial office. Reynolds subsequently conceded that there had been unnecessary delays in the extradition procedure, and that Whelehan's promotion had been ill-advised. The Labour Party withdrew from the coalition, and the Government resigned. Reynolds, while remaining as Prime Minister of a 'caretaker' Government, relinquished the Fianna Fáil leadership on 19 November and was succeeded by the Minister for Finance, Bertie Ahern. Whelehan, meanwhile, resigned as President of the High Court.

The desire of all the major political parties to avoid an immediate general election led to protracted efforts to form a new coalition administration. Discussions between Spring and Ahern, however, failed to produce an agreement. Following extensive negotiations between the Labour Party and other parties, a new coalition, led by John Bruton, who had assumed the leadership of Fine Gael in late 1990, and with Spring as the Deputy Prime Minister and Minister for Foreign Affairs, took office on 15 December 1994. A third coalition partner, the Democratic Left, obtained the social welfare portfolio.

In November 1995 a referendum on the termination of the constitutional ban on divorce resulted in a narrow majority (50.3% to 49.7%) in favour of legalizing the dissolution of marriage. The first divorce under the revised constitutional arrangements was granted in January 1997 (although legislation to implement the reform did not come into effect until February).

In November 1996 the Minister for Transport, Energy and Communications, Michael Lowry, resigned following allegations that he had received personal financial gifts from an Irish business executive, Ben Dunne. During 1997 an inquiry into other political donations by Dunne, chaired by Justice Brian McCracken, revealed that payments totalling some IR£1.3m. had been made to the former Irish Prime Minister, Charles Haughey, during his term in office. Haughey later admitted the allegations, although he insisted that he had no knowledge of the donations until he resigned the premiership; however, McCracken's report, published in August, condemned Haughey's earlier misleading evidence given to the tribunal and recommended further legal investigation. The Government, at that time led by Bertie Ahern of Fianna Fáil following a general election (see below), endorsed the results of the inquiry and agreed to establish a new tribunal to investigate further payments made to politicians and the sources of specific 'offshore' bank accounts that had been used by Haughey. In December 1998 it was revealed that a tax liability on some IR£2m. of personal financial gifts received by Haughey, including those made by Dunne, had been cancelled by the Revenue Commission. Opposition criticism of the decision intensified following the disclosure that the tax appeals commissioner responsible for the concession was Ahern's brother-in-law. Ahern, however, denied that he had influenced the decision.

In May 1997 the Prime Minister called a general election, relying on strong economic growth figures and the negative impact of allegations concerning financial donations to Haughey to secure victory for Fine Gael's coalition with the Labour Party and Democratic Left, despite public opinion polls revealing a significant shortfall in support for the Government over the opposition Fianna Fáil. In the election on 6 June none of the main political parties secured an overall majority in the Dáil. Fine Gael increased its representation to 54 seats, having won 27.9% of the first-preference votes cast, while Fianna Fáil secured 77 seats with 39.3% of the votes. Support for the Labour Party, however, declined substantially and the party won just 17 seats. Sinn Féin won its first ever seat in the Dáil at the election. Bruton conceded that he could not form a majority coalition administration, and Ahern, the Fianna Fáil leader, undertook to form a new government, in alliance with the Progressive Democrats, who had won four parliamentary seats, and with the support of independents. A new administration, with Ahern as Prime Minister, was formally approved in the Dáil at the end of June.

In September 1997 the President, Mary Robinson, a liberal human rights lawyer, who had been elected President in November 1990, as an independent candidate with the support of the Labour Party and the Workers' Party, resigned her position in order to assume her new functions as the United Nations High Commissioner for Human Rights. In the ensuing presidential election, conducted on 30 October 1997, the Fianna Fáil candidate, Dr Mary McAleese, won 45.2% of the first-preference votes cast, compared with 29.3% for Mary Banotti of Fine Gael. McAleese was inaugurated on 11 November, and became the country's first President to be from Northern Ireland. In early November Spring resigned as leader of the Labour Party, owing to his party's poor electoral performances; he was replaced by Ruairí Quinn.

During 2000 independent judicial inquiries investigating corruption among politicians implicated many senior political figures. In January at a tribunal chaired by Justice Michael Moriarty, which was continuing the work of the McCracken inquiry, the revelation that Denis Foley, a Fianna Fáil deputy, had held up to IR£100,000 in 'offshore' accounts prompted Foley's eventual resignation from the Fianna Fáil parliamentary party. In late May Foley was suspended from the Dáil for 14 days for breach of parliamentary procedure after admitting he had failed to declare that he held money in such accounts before voting on a motion to extend the terms of reference to the McCracken inquiry (see above) into payments to politicians. Meanwhile, in mid-April Frank Dunlop, a political lobbyist and former government press secretary, admitted to an inquiry into planning irregularities in Dublin, headed by Justice Fergus Flood, that in 1991 he had paid a total of IR£112,000 to 15 Dublin county councillors on behalf of a property developer in order to ensure a favourable decision. Dunlop also testified that Fine Gael leader, Bruton, was aware that a member of Fine Gael had demanded IR£250,000 from Dunlop to secure that member's vote in favour of the decision. Furthermore, Bruton was also accused by Liam Lawlor, a Fianna Fáil deputy, who himself admitted that he had received political contributions from Dunlop for 'legitimate electoral purposes', of benefiting from the decision. Bruton vehemently denied both accusations and both Fianna Fáil and Fine Gael launched internal investigations to ascertain whether any of their members had received such payments.

Upon resumption of the Flood inquiry in mid-May 2000, Dunlop claimed that a current Fianna Fáil deputy had received 'ongoing' payments for his assistance with planning matters. Fine Gael concurrently revealed the results of its internal investigation into the matter and disclosed that it was satisfied that, except in the case of three of its current members where evidence was inconclusive, any payments received by Fine Gael members had not influenced their voting intentions. In late May the Moriarty tribunal heard that between 1979 and 1996 Haughey had received payments totalling IR£8.5m., a much larger figure than had previously been acknowledged, and it was announced that Haughey would appear before the tribunal in July as a witness. In early June Lawlor, who had resigned from the Dáil's Members' Interests Committee in April, resigned from Fianna Fáil following the publication of a report by the party's Standards in Public Life Committee, which described him as 'unco-operative and contradictory' in his dealings with its investigation. In late June separate criminal proceedings against Haughey were indefinitely postponed after a Dublin court ruled that pre-trial publicity, including remarks made by the Deputy Prime Minister, Mary Harney, would prevent Haughey from receiving a fair hearing. In July Haughey duly appeared before the Moriarty tribunal and continued to give evidence to the inquiry during late 2000 despite mounting fears regarding his health. In mid-January 2001 Lawlor was sentenced to three months' imprisonment for failing to comply with a High Court order to give evidence regarding the use of his credit cards to the Flood tribunal. Lawlor was released after serving seven days of the sentence but subsequently resigned from several parliamentary commissions.

Meanwhile, in late June 2000, just days after the Fianna Fáil candidate was comprehensively defeated at a parliamentary by-election, the Fianna Fáil-Progressive Democrats coalition narrowly defeated a motion of 'no confidence', which had been proposed by the opposition, by 84 votes to 80. On the day prior to the defeat of the motion Ahern had appeared before the Moriarty tribunal and had faced accusations that he and other senior party members had withheld details of an internal party investigation into political donations in 1996 from the inquiry.

In late 2000 the Government and employers' organizations came under increasing pressure from trade unions to review the Programme for Prosperity and Fairness (a pay agreement negotiated by trade unions, businesses and the Government in March) as rising inflation threatened to eradicate the benefits of salary increases agreed under the programme. Several unions organized industrial action in protest at the lack of government action, most notably the Association of Secondary Teachers in Ireland (ASTI), which had denounced the PPF as inadequate. ASTI members staged a series of strikes, which severely disrupted classes and forced the closure of several schools. In early December the Irish Congress of Trade Unions (ICTU) executive endorsed compensatory measures to offset the impact of inflation, which had been negotiated by unions and businesses. However, negotiations between the Government and ASTI members broke down later that month: ASTI members recommenced industrial action in mid-January 2001, but agreed to suspend their strike during negotiations with the Labour Court, which began later that month. However, the Labour Court's ruling that teachers had a 'sustainable case' for a significant pay rise, which was issued in mid-March, failed to satisfy ASTI members, who subsequently staged a one-day strike, prompting public criticisms from both Ahern and the Labour Court. Meanwhile, in late January Fine Gael deputies passed a motion of 'no confidence' in their leader Bruton, who resigned as leader of the party with immediate effect. He was replaced the following month by Michael Noonan, a former Minister for Health and Children.

Discussions between the Government, the Labour Court and ASTI in March 2001 resulted in the publication of revised Labour Court proposals, which reiterated that ASTI members would still have to submit their claims for a pay increase to the national benchmarking body, but also brought forward the convention of the body to June 2002. The recommendations did, however, propose that all teachers involved in the dispute who ensured school programmes were completed by end of the 2000/01 school year receive payment of IR£1,750. Delegates at ASTI's annual conference in April 2001 overwhelmingly approved a motion to reject the Labour Court's recommendations, although they voted against renewed strike action and instead threatened to impose a policy of non co-operation with extra-curricular activities. In early May, while concurrently ruling out a ban on examination supervision, ASTI's 17,000 members narrowly rejected the Labour Court proposals and it was subsequently announced that, from September, ASTI members would no longer carry out voluntary supervision and substitution duties in schools. Discussions with the Government continued but the offer of substantial supplementary payment for supervision and substitution duties was rejected, and in October ASTI members voted in favour of withdrawing from supervision and substitution work. Further negotiations in late 2001 between the Government and ASTI failed to bring an end to the impasse, although ASTI deferred the issuing of a directive regarding withdrawal. However, following a continued lack of progress, on 4 March 2002 ASTI members ceased all substitution and supervision duties. In July the benchmarking body recommended a pay increase of 13% for teachers and in November ASTI members voted to accept the Government's offer of €37 per hour for supervision and substitution duties. However, in January 2003 the ASTI Central Executive Committee announced that it would reballot its members after a

number of senior ASTI officials claimed that they had been misled about the exact details of the agreement. In March the acceptance of the government offer was again approved (by 59% of those who voted) and ASTI's President insisted that the Government should make arrangements for the immediate implementation of the substitution and supervision scheme in schools and arrange for the payment of arrears due to ASTI members for supervision and substitution work carried out in the 2001/2002 school year.

The inquiries headed by Justices Moriarty and Flood continued to hear evidence during 2001–03. In late March 2001 it was revealed that Lawlor had still not complied fully with the High Court order that he produce comprehensive documents and records of his financial transactions to the Flood tribunal. In late July Lawlor was again sentenced to seven days' imprisonment for his ongoing failure satisfactorily to assist the tribunal and was ordered to pay a further fine of IR£5,000 and legal costs of £100,000. Lawlor was also informed that he was required to make a full disclosure of his financial affairs to the Flood tribunal by early September or face further punishment. Lawlor maintained that he had co-operated as fully as possible with the tribunal and appealed against the sentence in the Supreme Court; however, in mid-December the Supreme Court upheld the High Court's verdict and Lawlor was ordered to serve the seven-day prison term. In late January 2002 lawyers for the Flood tribunal informed the High Court of Lawlor's 'very significant and continuing failure' to meet his obligations to the tribunal, and in early February Lawlor was sentenced to one month's imprisonment and also fined €12,500. He announced that he would not appeal against the sentence and again maintained that he had co-operated as fully as possible with the inquiry.

In March 2001 investigations by the Flood tribunal into the financial conduct of Ray Burke, a former Fianna Fáil minister, who had resigned as Minister for Foreign Affairs in October 1997, revealed that Burke had acted illegally by holding money in offshore accounts in the 1980s while a minister, and by transferring money to and from bank accounts held abroad without requesting permission from the Central Bank (as the law stipulated). He also admitted that he had on previous occasions misled the Dáil about his financial affairs. Furthermore, in mid-May 2001 the tribunal heard that Burke made representations to the Chairman of the Revenue Commissioners on behalf of a construction company while he was Minister for Industry and Commerce in 1989, and later in May 2001 the owners of the construction firm retracted their previous statement that IR£125,000 paid to Burke came from fundraising events and admitted that the money actually originated from offshore accounts related to their company. They were also subsequently unable to substantiate their claim that Burke had paid them for a property on land owned by them. In addition, their insistence that the company had paid up to £250,000 into Fianna Fáil accounts were refuted by lawyers for the party, who stated that the (now deceased) person to whom they alleged the funds had been donated had never been employed by the party. In mid-November the inquiry discovered three further accounts used by Burke, which he had previously failed to disclose, and heard that the construction company may have made payments to Burke totalling as much as £400,000. The hearing was adjourned later that month, and in February 2002 it was announced that it was unlikely that the tribunal would produce any findings before the general election, which was scheduled to be held on 17 May. In June 2001 Justice Flood requested that extra staff be appointed to the tribunal to cope with the increasing workload, and, although the Government agreed to the request the following month, it was not until mid-February 2002 that the appointments were confirmed. This prompted opposition parties to accuse the Government of deliberately delaying the appointments to avoid any further publication of Fianna Fáil involvement in cases of corruption immediately prior to the general election.

In September 2002 Justice Flood issued the second interim report into the tribunal's findings thus far in which, most notably, he stated that Burke had received several 'corrupt payments' totalling up to IR£200,000 between 1974 and 1989. A number of prominent figures implicated in the proceedings were criticized for failing to co-operate fully with the tribunal and, following the publication of the report, the director of Fianna Fáil's election campaigns tendered his resignation. It was anticipated that criminal proceedings against 15 people, including Burke, would be instigated in 2003, and Ahern came under intense political pressure regarding his decision to appoint Burke as Minister for Foreign Affairs in 1997. The tribunal, which was expected to sit for a further three years, recommenced hearings in November, when Dunlop alleged that nine Dublin county councillors had received payments totalling IR£25,000 in order to secure the favourable rezoning of land owned by Jackson Way, a British property company in which Lawlor had a significant stake. All those implicated in the scandal denied any wrongdoing and in December Jackson Way announced that it would no longer co-operate with the tribunal.

In mid-March 2001 Haughey finished giving evidence to the Moriarty tribunal; however, shortly afterwards he was admitted to hospital having suffered a near-fatal heart attack. It was subsequently announced that it was unlikely he would give any further evidence to the inquiry. In March 2003 Haughey agreed to pay the Irish Revenue Commissioners €5m. in settlement of his outstanding tax liabilities resulting from undisclosed payments made to him between 1979 and 1996, which were subsequently discovered by the Moriarty tribunal. Meanwhile, in May 2001 investigations by the tribunal into the award of a Global Standard for Mobiles (GSM) licence in May 1996 to the Esat Digifone consortium revealed that the Fine Gael party and in particular Lowry, then Minister for Transport, Energy and Communications. Lowry was linked to four payments made in 1996 of some IR£800,000 involving the Chairman of Esat Digifone, Denis O'Brien; £33,000 of this was transferred by a party fundraiser to Fine Gael's accounts, disguised as a personal donation. In June 2001 the tribunal heard evidence that O'Brien had indicated to Barry Maloney, the former Chief Executive of Esat Digifone, in November 1996 that he had made payments of £200,000 in relation to the GSM licence and that £100,000 of this sum had gone to Lowry; both Lowry and O'Brien denied that such a payment occurred. It was subsequently revealed, however, that O'Brien's then accountant, Aidan Phelan, transferred a total of £150,000 in July and August 1996 to an offshore account held on O'Brien's behalf. In October £147,000 was paid from this account into an offshore account in Lowry's name. In July 2001 Phelan denied that he had made payments, including a £420,000 loan to enable Lowry to buy property in England, on behalf of O'Brien and maintained that O'Brien had no knowledge of the transactions. Lowry gave evidence to the tribunal in late October and again denied that he had acted improperly with regard to the award of the licence and stated that he did not disclose the loan to him by Phelan as he did not believe it was relevant. The inquiry continued its work, largely in private, during 2002, and further investigations were expected to be carried out during 2003.

In early June 2001 the removal of all references to the death penalty from the Constitution along with the prohibition of any future legislation allowing capital punishment, and the ratification of the Rome Statute, which provided for the establishment of an International Criminal Court for crimes against humanity, were approved at separate referendums, by 62.1% and 64.2% of the electorate, respectively. However, at a third concurrently-held referendum on the ratification of the Treaty of Nice, which proposed changes to the future size of the European Commission and the European Parliament as well as changes in the number of votes allocated to each member state prior to the enlargement of the EU from 2003, 53.9% of those who voted rejected the endorsement of the treaty, resulting in an embarrassing reverse for the Government, which had urged a vote in favour of the treaty. The referendum was also marred by an extremely low voter participation rate of just 34.8%. The defeat was attributed to fears that ratification of the treaty would result in Irish participation in the EU's rapid reaction force, thus undermining Ireland's neutrality, and concerns that Ireland would receive reduced funding and assistance from the EU.

The Government suffered a further reverse when, at a referendum on abortion held in early March 2002, 50.4% of the electorate voted against proposed changes, which would have removed the constitutional protection accorded by the Supreme Court to the lives of suicidal pregnant women wishing to terminate their pregnancies, and would have made abortion a criminal offence, punishable by 12 years' imprisonment. The rate of voter participation remained low, however, at just 42.9%.

At the general election held on 17 May 2002 Fianna Fáil won 41.5% of the first-preference votes cast, increasing its parliamentary representation to 81 seats (from 77 in 1997), and thus only narrowly failing to achieve an overall majority in the Dáil. Fine Gael suffered a significant loss of support, winning just 31 seats (compared with 54 in 1997) and 22.5% of the votes. The

Progressive Democrats and Sinn Féin increased their representation to eight seats (with 4.0% of the votes cast) and five seats (6.5%), respectively, while the Green Party obtained six seats (3.8%). The official rate of participation, at 63.0%, was the lowest to be recorded at an Irish general election. Following Fine Gael's poor performance at the election, Michael Noonan announced his resignation as party leader and in early June he was succeeded by Enda Kelly. Also in early June Fianna Fáil and the Progressive Democrats successfully concluded their discussions on the formation of a new coalition Government. Ahern was duly re-elected Prime Minister, with Harney continuing as his deputy. Ahern appointed five new ministers to the Cabinet and also created several new ministries. The new Government immediately announced that one of its main priorities was to hold a second referendum on the Treaty of Nice.

At the EU Heads of State summit meeting held in Seville, Spain, in June 2002 the Irish Government successfully secured support for a declaration which formally stated that Ireland's participation in the rapid reaction force would be limited to those operations with a UN mandate, approved by the Government and sanctioned by the Dáil. For their part, Ireland's EU partners issued a complementary declaration reiterating that neither the Treaty of Nice nor previous EU treaties compromised Ireland's traditional neutrality and that no member state envisaged the rapid reaction force as a future European Army. In September the Irish Government announced that a second constitutional referendum which, as well as providing for the final ratification of the Treaty of Nice, would now explicitly prohibit Irish participation in any future common European defence force, would take place on October 19. At the referendum 62.9% of those who voted approved the ratification of the Treaty of Nice, with voter turnout recorded at 49.5% of the electorate. The endorsement was welcomed by most European Governments

In January 2003 the Irish Supreme Court issued a ruling that declared that non-national parents of Irish-born children and their non-national siblings were not entitled to live in Ireland by virtue of having an Irish-born child. The ruling was passed after appeals were launched by Nigerian and Czech nationals who had been issued with deportation orders, despite having given birth to children in Ireland. The Minister for Justice swiftly allayed fears that this would lead to mass deportations of non-EU immigrant parents of children born in the country; it was officially estimated that some 10,000 applications for residency on the basis of having given birth to a child in Ireland were outstanding at the time of the ruling.

In mid-March 2003 a government-supported motion to continue to allow US armed forces, who were engaged in military action against Iraq, to use Shannon Airport and Irish airspace was approved by 77 votes to 60 in the Dáil. A number of deputies, in particular the Fine Gael leader, Kelly, had voiced their vehement opposition to the motion as they feared that Ireland's traditional neutrality would be compromised as a result.

Consultations between the United Kingdom and Ireland on the future of Northern Ireland resulted in November 1985 in the signing of the Anglo-Irish Agreement, which provided for regular participation in Northern Ireland affairs by the Irish Government on political, legal, security and cross-border matters. The involvement of the Government of Ireland was to be through an Intergovernmental Conference. The Agreement maintained that no change in the status of Northern Ireland would be made without the assent of the majority of its population. The terms of the Agreement were approved by both the Irish and the British Parliaments, despite strong opposition by many Protestants in Northern Ireland.

Under the provisions of the Anglo-Irish Agreement, the Irish Government pledged co-operation in the implementation of new measures to improve cross-border security, in order to suppress IRA operations. It also promised to participate in the European Convention on the Suppression of Terrorism, which it signed in February 1986 and ratified in December 1987, when legislation amending the 1965 Extradition Act came into effect. In the same month the Government introduced controversial measures (without consulting the British Government) granting the Irish Attorney-General the right to approve or reject warrants for extradition of suspected IRA terrorists to the United Kingdom. In January 1988, however, the Irish Supreme Court ruled that members of the IRA could not be protected from extradition to Northern Ireland on the grounds that their offences were politically motivated. Nevertheless, in December the Irish Attorney-

General refused to grant the extradition of an alleged terrorist who had been repatriated to Ireland in November, following a similar refusal by the Belgian authorities. The Irish decision was based on allegations that the accused man would not receive a fair trial in the United Kingdom because publicity had prejudiced his case.

Relations between the Irish and British Governments in 1988 were also strained when Irish confidence in the impartiality of the British legal system was severely undermined by proposed legislation to combat terrorism in Northern Ireland and by the decision, in January, not to prosecute members of the Royal Ulster Constabulary (RUC) allegedly implicated in a policy of shooting terrorist suspects, without attempting to apprehend them, in Northern Ireland in 1982. Difficult relations with the United Kingdom did not, however, present a threat to the Anglo-Irish Agreement, and the co-ordination between the Garda Síochána (Irish police force) and the RUC, established under the agreement, resulted in an unprecedentedly high level of co-operation on cross-border security. In February 1989 a permanent joint consultative assembly, comprising 25 British and 25 Irish MPs, was established. The representatives were selected in October. The assembly's meetings, the first of which began in February 1990, were to take place twice a year, alternately in Dublin and London.

In July 1990 Desmond Ellis, an IRA member who had been charged with terrorist offences in the United Kingdom, lost his appeal against extradition in the High Court in Dublin. It was the first case to be considered under the 1987 Extradition Act, based on the European Convention on the Suppression of Terrorism. In November the Supreme Court upheld the ruling, and Ellis, was extradited to stand trial in the United Kingdom. In November 1991 the Supreme Court also upheld the extradition to the United Kingdom of an IRA member convicted of murder, who had escaped from detention in Belfast.

In January 1990 the British Secretary of State for Northern Ireland, Peter Brooke, launched an initiative to convene meetings between representatives from the major political parties in Northern Ireland, and the British and Irish Governments, to discuss devolution in Northern Ireland. In response to demands from Northern Ireland's Unionist parties, the Irish and British Governments publicly stated that they were prepared to consider an alternative to the Anglo-Irish Agreement. In March the Irish Supreme Court rejected an attempt by Ulster Unionists to have the Anglo-Irish Agreement declared contrary to Ireland's Constitution, which claims jurisdiction over Northern Ireland. In May the Unionists agreed to hold direct discussions with the Irish Government, a concession previously withheld because it lent credence to the Irish claim to a right to be involved in Northern Ireland's affairs. Disagreement remained, however, on the timing and conditions of Ireland's entry to the talks. Following extensive negotiations, discussions between the Northern Ireland parties, which were a prelude to the inclusion of the Irish Government, commenced in June 1991. They were suspended several times but did reach the inclusion of the Irish Government in April and September 1992. The principal point of contention was the Unionists' demand that Ireland hold a referendum on Articles 2 and 3 of its Constitution, which lay claim to the territory of Northern Ireland. Ireland was unwilling to make such a concession except as part of an overall settlement. With no progress made on this question, nor on the subject of Ireland's role in the administration of Northern Ireland, the negotiations formally ended in November, and the Anglo-Irish Conference, which had been temporarily suspended, resumed.

At the end of October 1993 the new Irish Prime Minister, Albert Reynolds and his British counterpart, John Major, issued a joint statement setting out the principles on which future negotiations were to be based. The statement emphasized the precondition that Sinn Féin permanently renounce violence before being admitted to the negotiations. In December the Prime Ministers made a joint declaration, known as the 'Downing Street Declaration', which provided a specific framework for a peace settlement. The Declaration referred to the possibility of a united Ireland and accepted the legitimacy of self-determination, but insisted on majority consent within Northern Ireland. While the Sinn Féin and Unionist parties considered their response to the Declaration, Reynolds received both groups' conditional support for his proposal to establish a 'Forum for Peace and Reconciliation', which was to encourage both sides to end violent action.

In April 1994 the IRA declared a temporary cease-fire over the Easter period. Despite a subsequent resumption of operations negotiations culminated in an announcement on 31 August by the IRA that it had ceased all military operations. This was followed in October by a similar suspension on the part of its counterpart loyalist organizations. In late 1994 and early 1995 the Irish authorities granted early release to more than 15 prisoners convicted of IRA terrorist offences. Inter-governmental talks were maintained, resulting in the publication, in February 1995, of a 'Joint Framework' document, in which the Irish Government undertook to support the withdrawal of the Republic's constitutional claim to jurisdiction over Northern Ireland. The document's proposals, which included detailed arrangements for cross-border institutions and economic programmes which would operate on an all-island basis see Northern Ireland, were stated by the British Government to be intended to provide a basis for public discussion and not as a definitive statement of government policy.

During 1995 the Irish Government expressed its increasing concern at the delay in initiating substantive all-party negotiations on the formulation of a permanent settlement of the conflict in Northern Ireland, largely owing to the insistence of the British Government that the IRA decommission its weapons as a precondition to such talks. Joint proposals in August by the British and Irish Governments for the formation of an international panel to consider the merits of decommissioning paramilitary weaponry in Northern Ireland received the full support of the US Government; the international panel, under the chairmanship of George Mitchell (a former US Senator), began work in December. Its findings, announced in January 1996, recommended that the decommissioning of arms should take place in parallel with all-party talks, and that their destruction should be monitored by an independent commission. The British and Irish Governments accepted the recommendations of the report, but new controversy arose over proposals by the British Cabinet to hold elections for a Northern Ireland assembly, which was to provide the framework for all-party negotiations. Although broadly acceptable to Unionist interests, this plan was rejected outright by Northern Ireland's Social Democratic and Labour Party (SDLP) and Sinn Féin, and declared unacceptable by the Irish Government.

In February 1996, following a bomb explosion in London, the IRA announced that the cease-fire had been terminated. The British and Irish Governments suspended official contacts with Sinn Féin, pending acceptable assurances that the IRA had discontinued all violence. Multi-party meetings, which commenced in June without Sinn Féin participation, were overshadowed in July by violent confrontations in Northern Ireland between the RUC and nationalists opposed to the routing of loyalist parades through predominantly nationalist districts. The Irish Government formally protested to the British Government over the conduct of the RUC, both in failing to re-route the processions and in its methods of suppressing the ensuing public disorders. In May 1997 a meeting of the Irish Prime Minister, Bruton with the newly elected British premier, Anthony (Tony) Blair, and the new Secretary of State for Northern Ireland, Dr Marjorie Mowlam, generated speculation that significant progress could be achieved in furthering a political agreement. In June the two Governments announced a new initiative to proceed with the decommissioning of paramilitary weapons, on the basis of the Mitchell report, at the same time as pursuing political negotiations for a constitutional settlement. In early July the newly elected Irish Prime Minister, Bertie Ahern, confirmed his commitment to the peace initiative during a meeting with Blair in London, and declared his support for the efforts of the British administration to prevent violence during the sectarian marching season in Northern Ireland. On 19 July the IRA announced a restoration of its cease-fire. A few days later the Irish and British Governments issued a joint statement that all-party negotiations would commence in mid-September with the participation of Sinn Féin. At the same time, however, the Unionist parties rejected the measures for weapons decommissioning that had been formulated by the two Governments. At the end of July the Irish Government restored official contacts with Sinn Féin and resumed the policy of considering convicted IRA activists for early release from prison.

In September 1997 Sinn Féin endorsed the so-called Mitchell principles, which committed participants in the negotiations to accepting the outcome of the peace process and renouncing violence as a means of punishment or resolving problems, providing for the party's participation in all-party talks when they resumed in the middle of that month. However, the Unionist parties failed to attend the opening session of the talks, owing partly to a statement by the IRA undermining Sinn Féin's endorsement of the Mitchell principles. A procedural agreement to pursue negotiations in parallel with the decommissioning of weapons (which was to be undertaken by a separate commission, the Independent International Commission on Decommissioning (IICD), led by Gen. John de Chastelain of Canada) was signed by all the main parties later in September. Substantive negotiations commenced in October but were adjourned in mid-December without agreement on an agenda for the next session of discussions. In mid-January 1998 the two Governments published a document outlining a framework for negotiations and specified that they hoped to achieve a settlement by May.

In March 1998 Mitchell set a deadline of 9 April for the conclusion of the peace talks. On 10 April the two Governments and eight political parties involved in the talks signed a comprehensive political accord, the Good Friday (or Belfast) Agreement, at Stormont Castle. Immediately thereafter the two Governments signed a new British-Irish Agreement, replacing the Anglo-Irish Agreement of November 1985, committing them to put the provisions of the multi-party agreement into effect, subject to approval of the Good Friday Agreement by a referendum to be held in the whole of Ireland in May. The peace settlement provided for changes to the Irish Constitution and to British constitutional legislation to enshrine the principle that a united Ireland could be achieved only with the consent of the majority of the people of both Ireland and Northern Ireland. Under the terms of the Good Friday Agreement the new Northern Ireland Assembly was to have devolved legislative powers over areas of social and economic policy, while security, justice, taxation and foreign policy were to remain under the authority of the British Government. Executive authority was to be discharged by an Executive Committee, comprising a First Minister, Deputy First Minister and as many as 10 ministers of government departments. The Assembly, which was to be elected in June, was to operate in transitional mode, without legislative or executive powers, until the establishment of the North/South and British-Irish institutions. In addition, provision was made for the release of paramilitary prisoners affiliated to organizations that established a complete and unequivocal cease-fire. All qualifying prisoners were to be released within two years of the commencement of the scheme, which was due to begin in June. The decommissioning of paramilitary weapons was to be completed within two years of the approval by referendum of the Good Friday Agreement. On 22 April the Dáil overwhelmingly approved the peace agreement. At referendums held simultaneously on 22 May the people of Ireland and Northern Ireland voted in support of the Good Friday Agreement. In Ireland 94.4% voted in favour of the agreement, while in Northern Ireland 71.1% voted to approve the accord.

Elections to the 108-member Northern Ireland Assembly were conducted on 25 June 1998; the Assembly convened for the first time in July. and elected the leader of the Ulster Unionist Party (UUP), David Trimble, as Northern Ireland's First Minister to head the Executive Committee. The peace process was threatened with disruption by sectarian violence in July and by the detonation of an explosive device in August in Omagh, Northern Ireland; the device was planted by a Republican splinter group, the Real IRA. Later that month Ahern announced a series of anti-terrorist measures, including restrictions on the right to silence and an extension to the maximum period of detention allowable for suspected terrorists, in an effort to facilitate convictions against terrorists based in Ireland

Progress in the peace process continued to be obstructed throughout late 1998 by a dispute between Unionists and Sinn Féin concerning the decommissioning of paramilitary weapons, with Trimble insisting that the admittance of Sinn Féin representatives to the Executive Committee be conditional on progress in the demilitarization of the IRA. As a result of the dispute the deadlines for the formation both of the Executive Committee and the North/South body (specified as 21 October by the Good Friday Agreement), and for the devolution of powers to the new Northern Ireland institutions (envisaged for 10 March 1999) were not met. Despite strenuous efforts to end the impasse, a new April deadline was also not met. An 'absolute' deadline for the devolution of powers was subsequently set for 30 June 1999, after which date, Blair asserted, he would suspend the Northern Ireland Assembly if agreement had not been reached. On 25 June the two Prime Ministers presented a compromise plan which envisaged the immediate establishment of the Executive Committee prior to the surrender of para-

military weapons, with the condition that Sinn Féin guarantee that the IRA complete decommissioning by May 2000. Negotiations continued beyond the June deadline but effectively collapsed in mid-July and a review of the peace process, headed by George Mitchell, began in early September. In November Mitchell succeeded in producing an agreement providing for the devolution of powers to the Executive Committee. The agreement followed a statement by the IRA that it would appoint a representative to enter discussions with the IICD. At a meeting of the ruling council of the UUP held in late November Trimble persuaded his party to vote in favour of the agreement. On 29 November 1999 the Northern Ireland Assembly convened to appoint the 10-member Executive Committee. On 2 December power was officially transferred from Westminster to the new Northern Ireland Executive at Stormont Castle. On the same day, in accordance with the Good Friday Agreement, the Irish Government removed from the Constitution the Republic's territorial claim over Northern Ireland.

In mid-December 1999 the Cabinet of the Republic attended the inaugural meeting, in Armagh, of the North/South Ministerial Council. The British-Irish Council met for the first time later that month. However, in late January 2000 Sinn Féin leader, Gerry Adams, dismissed the possibility of imminent IRA decommissioning and a report by the IICD confirmed that there had been no disarmament. With the prospect of the collapse of the peace process the British and Irish Governments engaged in intensive negotiations. On 1 February the IRA released a statement giving assurances that its cease-fire would not be broken and expressing support for the peace process. On 4 February the IRA were given until 11 February to begin decommissioning. However, it failed to comply and legislation came into effect on that day suspending the new executive, legislative and co-operative institutions and returning Northern Ireland to direct rule. The IRA subsequently announced its withdrawal from discussions with the IICD, raising serious doubts about the future of its cease-fire. In addition, Adams refused to participate in any further review of the peace process until the suspended institutions had been restored. At a republican rally held at the end of February Adams announced that Sinn Féin had abandoned its special role of attempting to persuade the IRA to decommission.

Direct talks between the Irish and British Governments and the principle parties resumed in early May 2000 with the British Government pledging to restore the Northern Ireland institutions on 22 May and postpone the deadline for decommissioning until June 2001 subject to a commitment by the IRA on the arms issue. On 6 May 2000 the IRA responded by offering to 'initiate a process that will completely and verifiably put arms beyond use'. On 30 May power was once again transferred from Westminster to the new Northern Ireland institutions. In November the British House of Lords approved legislation, which would enable members of the Irish Parliament to stand for election to the Northern Ireland Assembly as well as to the British lower chamber of Parliament, the House of Commons, but prohibited the holding of office in both Northern Ireland and the Republic of Ireland.

The issue of IRA weapons decommissioning continued severely to threaten the peace process during 2001 (see chapter on Northern Ireland). Prior to the general election held in the United Kingdom in early June, Trimble had announced his intention to resign as First Minister on 1 July, thus precipitating the collapse of the Northern Ireland institutions, if there was no independently confirmed decommissioning of weapons by the IRA by that date. Despite intensive efforts by Ahern and Blair to avert Trimble's resignation, on 1 July Trimble stood down from his post; Sir Reg Empey, the Minister of Enterprise, Trade and Investment assumed the role of acting First Minister. In mid-July Ahern and Blair convened talks, which were attended by representatives of all pro-agreement parties; however, they ended without achieving a breakthrough. Nevertheless, the two Prime Ministers announced that they would formulate a package of non-negotiable proposals to be tabled to the pro-agreement parties, which they expected would bring an end to the impasse. The joint British-Irish proposals were announced in early August but did not meet with the approval of the major political parties, and on 10 August the British Government suspended the Northern Ireland Assembly for 24 hours in order to delay the necessity to appoint a new First Minister for a further six weeks. Following the temporary suspension the IRA retracted its earlier offer to put arms 'beyond use', citing the British Government's willingness to suspend the Northern Irish institutions as unacceptable.

The Assembly was again suspended on 22 September 2001 as the deadlock between the major parties continued, and on 8 October, following the defeat of a Unionist motion to exclude Sinn Féin members from the Executive, Trimble announced that he would withdraw the three UUP ministers from the Executive. On 18 October the UUP ministers duly resigned along with two DUP ministers; five days later, however, the IRA announced that it had begun a process of putting arms beyond use in accordance with stipulations of the IICD and later that day the IICD revealed that it had witnessed the 'significant' disposal of IRA weapons. On 24 October Trimble renominated the UUP ministers to the Executive thus preventing the institution's collapse and the following day the two DUP ministers also retook their posts. Trimble subsequently received permission from the UUP executive council to reassume the position of First Minister; however, in early November he failed to secure a majority of both Nationalists and Unionists in favour of his re-election after two members of his own party voted against him. Following the redesignation of three members of the Alliance Party as Unionists, Trimble was finally re-elected First Minister, with Mark Durkan (who replaced John Hume as leader of the SDLP in November) as his deputy. A legal challenge by the DUP, which aimed to enforce the holding of fresh elections to the Assembly, had earlier been rejected.

The alleged IRA involvement in the theft of documents from Special Branch offices in Belfast in March 2002 and the discovery, in June, of an IRA intelligence database listing details of more than 200 judges, politicians and members of the security forces provoked Unionist demands that Sinn Féin ministers be removed from the power-sharing Executive and further 'crisis' meetings between the British and Irish Governments. In mid-July 2002 the IRA issued an apology for the deaths and injuries of 'non-combatants' caused as a result of its actions over the previous 30 years. The sincerity of the apology was questioned by Trimble and senior Unionists were sceptical that the IRA remained committed to the peace process in the light of continued sectarian violence in Belfast, for which the UUP maintained that the IRA was primarily responsible. In early July during talks between the British and Irish Governments and the pro-Agreement parties in Belfast, Trimble had implied that UUP ministers would resign from the Executive by the end of that month if the IRA did not clearly demonstrate its commitment to a 'full transition from violence to democracy'. He had also appealed to the British and Irish Governments to take stronger action against paramilitary groups and warned that the British Government risked losing public support for the Good Friday Agreement unless the ever-deteriorating situation in the province was resolved. In September the UUP Council announced that it would withdraw UUP ministers from the Northern Ireland Executive on 18 January 2003 if the IRA and Sinn Féin had not demonstrated it had completed its transition to democracy and non-violence.

In early October 2002 Northern Ireland was once again plunged into political crisis after Sinn Féin's offices at the Northern Ireland Assembly were raided by police, who, as part of a major investigation into intelligence-gathering by Republicans, suspected that the IRA had infiltrated the Northern Ireland Office and gained access to large numbers of confidential documents, including Reid's correspondence, highly sensitive intelligence material and details of members of the security forces and the prison service. Among a number of people detained by the police was Sinn Féin's Head of Administration, who was charged with possession of documents likely to be of assistance to terrorist organizations. Trimble accused Sinn Féin of a 'massive political conspiracy' and threatened to withdraw from the Executive unless the British Government proposed the expulsion of Sinn Féin from the Assembly. Emergency talks between the British and Irish Governments and the Northern Ireland political leaders followed, however, Blair's demands for IRA concessions on the arms issue were not met. On 11 October the two DUP ministers resigned from the Executive, and on 14 October Reid suspended the Assembly and returned Northern Ireland to direct rule. In a joint statement, Blair and Ahern announced that the devolved institutions would only be restored if Sinn Féin ended its link with paramilitary organizations and Blair subsequently called on the IRA to disband itself. Later that month the IRA announced that it had suspended all contact with the IICD and claimed that the British Government was to blame for the current crisis having failed to honour its commitments under the Good Friday Agreement.

Talks aimed at resolving the impasse continued between the major parties during late 2002 and early 2003, however, relations between Unionists and Nationalists were further strained in November 2002 by the arrest of a Roman Catholic civil servant, who had worked in the offices of both Trimble and Durkan, linked to the earlier suspected IRA infiltration of the Northern Ireland Office. In December Trimble walked out of multi-party talks in Belfast in protest at the leaking of a confidential Irish government document which stated that the IRA was still 'actively engaged in training, targeting, recruiting and acquiring small quantities of weapons'. Further talks in January and February 2003 were overshadowed by a severe escalation of the feud between rival loyalist paramilitary organizations in Belfast, in which two senior members of the UDA were killed. In March Ahern and Blair announced that the elections to the Northern Ireland Assembly would be postponed until 29 May. In April US President George W. Bush met with Blair in the province to discuss the progress of the US-led military campaign to oust the regime of Saddam Hussein in Iraq and subsequently held talks with Ahern and the pro-Agreement parties at which he urged their leaders to 'seize the opportunity for peace'. Despite these efforts, plans to publish proposals for reinstating the Northern Ireland institutions were abandoned just days later after the IRA failed to respond to the British Government's demand for a definitive cessation of paramilitary activities and in early May Blair postponed the elections until late 2003.

Ireland became a member of the EC (now the EU) in 1973. In May 1987 the country affirmed its commitment to the EC when, in a referendum, 69.9% of Irish voters supported adherence to the Single European Act, which provided for closer economic and political co-operation between EC member-states (including the creation of a single Community market by 1993). In December 1991, during the EC summit conference at Maastricht, in the Netherlands, Ireland agreed to the far-reaching Treaty on European Union. Ireland secured a special provision within the Treaty (which was signed by all parties in February 1992), guaranteeing that Ireland's constitutional position on abortion would be unaffected by any future EC legislation. The four major political parties in Ireland united in support of the ratification of the Treaty prior to a referendum on the issue, which took place in June. Despite opposition, from both pro- and anti-abortion campaigners, to the special provision within the Treaty and the threat to Ireland's neutrality inherent in the document's proposals for a common defence policy, ratification of the Treaty was endorsed by 68.7% of the votes cast (57.3% of the electorate participated in the referendum). In a referendum conducted in May 1998, 62% of Irish voters endorsed the Amsterdam Treaty, which had been signed by EU ministers in October 1997, amending the Treaty on European Union.

Government

Legislative power is vested in the bicameral National Parliament, comprising the Senate (with restricted powers) and the House of Representatives. The Senate (Seanad Éireann) has 60 members, including 11 nominated by the Prime Minister (Taoiseach) and 49 indirectly elected for five years. The House of Representatives (Dáil Éireann) has 166 members (Teachtaí Dála), elected by universal adult suffrage for five years (subject to dissolution) by means of the single transferable vote, a form of proportional representation.

The President (Uachtarán) is the constitutional Head of State, elected by direct popular vote for seven years. Executive power is effectively held by the Cabinet, led by the Prime Minister, who is appointed by the President on the nomination of the Dáil. The President appoints other Ministers on the nomination of the Prime Minister with the previous approval of the Dáil. The Cabinet is responsible to the Dáil.

Defence

At 1 August 2002 the regular armed forces totalled 10,460. The army comprised 8,500, the navy 1,100 and the air force 860. There was also a reserve of 14,800. Defence was allocated IR£707m. in the 2001 budget. Military service is voluntary.

Economic Affairs

In 2001, according to estimates by the World Bank, Ireland's gross national income (GNI), measured at average 1999–2001 prices, was US $88,385m., equivalent to $23,060 per head (or $27,460 on an international purchasing-power parity basis).

During 1990–2001, it was estimated, the population increased at an average annual rate of 0.8%, while gross domestic product (GDP) per head increased, in real terms, by an average of 6.2% per year. Overall GDP increased, in real terms, at an average annual rate of 7.1% in 1990–2001; it grew by 11.5% in 2000 and by 6.7% in 2001.

Agriculture (including forestry and fishing) contributed an estimated 3.7% of GDP (at factor cost) in 2001. An estimated 6.9% of the working population were employed in the sector in 2002. Beef and dairy production dominate Irish agriculture (in 2001 meat and meat preparations accounted for 1.7% of total exports while dairy products and birds' eggs accounted for 1.2%). Principal crops include barley, sugar beet, potatoes and wheat. Agricultural GDP increased by an average of 0.5% per year during 1991–97, and by an estimated 1.4% in 1997.

Industry (comprising mining, manufacturing, construction and utilities) provided an estimated 40.1% of GDP in 2001, and employed an estimated 27.7% of the working population in 2002. Industrial GDP increased by an average of 9.6% per year during 1991–97; it grew by 16.2% in 1995, by 8.3% in 1996 and by an estimated 15.2% in 1997.

Mining (including quarrying and turf production) provided employment to 0.4% of the working population in 1997. Ireland possesses substantial deposits of lead-zinc ore and recoverable peat, both of which are exploited. Natural gas, mainly from the Kinsale field, and small quantities of coal are also extracted. A significant natural gas deposit discovered in 1999 was expected to yield sufficient gas to meet more than one-half of the country's current average demand. Offshore reserves of petroleum have been located and several licences awarded to foreign-owned enterprises to undertake further exploration. During 1980–90 mining production decreased by an annual average of 1.7%.

Manufacturing was estimated to employ 20.3% of the working population in 1997. The manufacturing sector comprises many high-technology, largely foreign-owned, capital-intensive enterprises. The electronics industry accounted for 32.6% of the value of exports in 1996. During 1992–96 manufacturing production increased by an average of 10.1% per year.

Electricity is derived principally from coal, which provided 34.5% of total requirements in 1999, while natural gas provided 31.9% and petroleum 28.3%. In 2000 imports of mineral fuels were 4.1% (by value) of total merchandise imports.

Service industries (including commerce, finance, transport and communications, and public administration) contributed an estimated 56.2% of GDP in 2001, and employed an estimated 65.4% of the working population in 2002. The financial sector is of increasing importance to Ireland. An International Financial Services Centre in Dublin was opened in 1990; by September 1999 more than 485 companies were participating in the Centre, many of which were foreign concerns attracted by tax concessions offered by the Irish Government. Tourism is one of the principal sources of foreign exchange. Revenue from the tourism and travel sector amounted to an estimated IR£2,888m. in 2000. The GDP of the services sector increased by an average of 4.3% per year during 1991–97, and by an estimated 6.2% in 1997.

In 2001, according to IMF statistics, Ireland recorded a visible trade surplus of US $30,003m. while there was a deficit of $1,043m. on the current account of the balance of payments. In 2001 the principal source of imports (35.4%) was the United Kingdom; other major sources were the USA (15.2%) and Germany (6.2%). The United Kingdom was also the principal market for exports (24.0%); other major purchasers were the USA (17.0%), Germany (12.7%) and France (6.1%). In 1999 principal imports included office equipment and other electrical machinery, chemical products, road vehicles and parts and other manufactured items. Principal exports included electronic goods, chemicals and food and live animals.

In 2001 there was a budgetary surplus of €2,104.3m. (equivalent to 1.8% of GDP). At the end of 2001 Ireland's total national debt was estimated to be IR£28,499m. The annual rate of inflation averaged 2.7% in 1990–2001. The rate decreased from 5.6% in 2000 to 4.9% in 2001, and again to 4.7% in 2002. An estimated 4.2% of the labour force were unemployed in 2002, compared with 10.3% in 1997.

Ireland became a member of the European Community (EC—now European Union—EU, see p. 199) in 1973, and of the EC's Exchange Rate Mechanism (ERM, see p. 225) in 1979.

Between 1995 and 2000 the Irish economy enjoyed an unprecedentedly high rate of growth with GDP increasing by an average of 9.7% per year. This was attributable to a number of factors including prudent fiscal and monetary management, an expanding, well-qualified labour force and social partnership agreements between the Government, businesses and trade unions, providing for guaranteed pay rises in return for productivity and 'no strike' agreements. In addition government policies offering financial incentives to foreign-owned enterprises resulted in a substantial increase in direct foreign investment and expansion in the financial services and electronic manufacturing industries. However, the Irish economy suffered a number of reverses in the early 2000s, experiencing reduced growth and a sharp increase in the rate of inflation as the outbreak of foot-and-mouth disease adversely affected the agriculture and tourism industries and the world-wide economic slowdown reduced levels of foreign investment. A rise in unemployment was recorded in late 2001—the first increase in five years—and GDP growth predictions for 2003 were revised downwards to just 3.0%, compared with 11.5% in 2000. In late 2002 the Government announced a number of budgetary reductions in public expenditure totalling some €900m. and the Government was expected to run a budget deficit in 2003 for the first time since 1996, for which the Minister of Finance blamed the continued weakness of the international economy. Unemployment averaged more than 5% during 2002 with further increases predicted in 2003 as a result of planned reductions in the number of civil servants, and inflation, which remains at more than double the EU average, was predicted to reach 5.1% in that year. Furthermore, economic forecasters warned of the risks of a potential loss of competitiveness for the Irish economy. Despite initial pessimism, the renewal of the social partnership agreement appeared increasingly likely to take place in 2003, however, proposed pay increases under the Sustaining Progress programme were expected to place a further strain on the Government's finances.

Education

The State in Ireland has constitutional responsibility for the national education system. Irish schools are owned, not by the State, but by community groups, traditionally religious groups. It is in general an aided system: the State does not itself operate the schools (with a few minor exceptions) but assists other bodies, usually religious, to do so.

Education in Ireland is compulsory for nine years between six and 15 years of age. Primary education may begin at the age of six and lasts for six years. Aided primary schools account for the education of 98.5% of children in the primary sector, who attend until the age of 12, when they transfer to a post-primary school. Post-primary education lasts for up to six years, comprising a junior cycle of three years and a senior cycle of two or three years. The Junior Certificate examination is taken after three years in post-primary (second-level) education. By 1997 some 92% of 16-year-olds were participating in full-time, post-compulsory education. In 1999/2000 there were 16 technical colleges providing a range of craft, technical, professional and other courses. There are four universities: the University of Dublin (Trinity College); the National University of Ireland (comprising the University Colleges of Cork, Dublin and Galway); and the Dublin City University and the University of Limerick (former National Institutes of Higher Education, which obtained university status in 1989).

In the 2002 budget €4,717.2m. (equivalent to 14.8% of total expenditure) was allocated to education.

Public Holidays

2003: 1 January (New Year), 17 March (St Patrick's Day), 18 April (Good Friday), 21 April (Easter Monday), 5 May (May Day Holiday), 2 June (June Bank Holiday), 4 August (August Bank Holiday), 27 October (October Bank Holiday), 25–26 December (Christmas).

2004: 1 January (New Year), 17 March (St Patrick's Day), 9 April (Good Friday), 12 April (Easter Monday), 3 May (May Day Holiday), 7 June (June Bank Holiday), 2 August (August Bank Holiday), 25 October (October Bank Holiday), 25–26 December (Christmas).

Weights and Measures

The metric system of weights and measures is the primary system in force, but the imperial system is still used in a number of limited activities.

Statistical Survey

Source (unless otherwise stated): Central Statistics Office, Skehard Rd, Cork; tel. (21) 359000; fax (21) 359090; e-mail information@cso.ie; internet www .cso.ie.

Area and Population

AREA, POPULATION AND DENSITY

Area (sq km)	70,273*
Population (census results)	
28 April 1996	3,626,087
28 April 2002†	
Males	1,945,187
Females	1,972,149
Total	3,917,336
Population (preliminary estimates at April)	
1999	3,744,700
2000	3,786,900
2001	3,838,900
Density (per sq km) at April 2002	55.7

* 27,133 sq miles.
† Provisional results.

ADMINISTRATIVE DIVISIONS
(Provisional results, 2002 census)

Province/County	Area (sq km)	Population	Density (per sq km)
Connaught	17,711	464,050	26.2
Galway	6,148	208,826	34.0
Leitrim	1,590	25,815	10.2
Mayo	5,586	117,428	21.0
Roscommon . . .	2,548	53,803	21.1
Sligo	1,838	58,178	31.7
Leinster	19,801	2,105,449	106.3
Carlow	897	45,845	51.1
Dublin	922	1,122,600	1,217.6
Kildare	1,695	163,995	96.8
Kilkenny	2,073	80,421	38.8
Laoighis	1,720	58,732	34.1
Longford	1,091	31,127	28.5
Louth	826	101,802	123.2
Meath	2,342	133,936	57.2
Offaly	2,001	63,702	31.8
Westmeath	1,840	72,027	39.1
Wexford	2,367	116,543	49.2
Wicklow	2,027	114,719	56.6
Munster	24,674	1,101,266	44.6
Clare	3,450	103,333	30.0
Cork	7,500	448,181	60.0
Kerry	4,807	132,424	27.5
Limerick	2,756	175,529	63.7
Tipperary	4,305	140,281	32.6
Waterford	1,857	101,518	54.7
Ulster (part)	8,088	246,571	30.5
Cavan	1,932	56,416	29.2
Donegal	4,861	137,383	28.3
Monaghan	1,295	52,772	40.8
Total	70,273	3,917,336	55.7

PRINCIPAL TOWNS
(provisional population at 2002 census)

Dublin (capital) . .	1,122,600	Limerick	54,100
Cork	123,300	Waterford	44,600
Galway	65,800		

BIRTHS, MARRIAGES AND DEATHS

	Registered live births		Registered marriages		Registered deaths	
	Number	Rate (per 1,000)	Number	Rate (per 1,000)	Number	Rate (per 1,000)
1994 . .	47,929	13.4	16,621	4.6	30,744	8.6
1995 . .	48,530	13.5	15,604	4.3	31,494	8.8
1996 . .	50,390	13.9	16,174	4.5	31,514	8.7
1997 . .	52,311	14.3	15,631	4.3	31,605	8.6
1998 . .	53,551	14.5	16,783	4.5	31,352	8.5
1999 . .	53,354	14.2	18,526	4.9	31,683	8.5
2000 . .	54,239	14.3	19,168	5.1	31,115	8.2
2001 . .	57,882	15.1	19,246	5.0	29,812	7.8

Expectation of life (WHO estimates, years at birth): 76.5 (males 73.8; females 79.2) in 2001 (Source: WHO, *World Health Report*).

IMMIGRATION AND EMIGRATION
(preliminary figures)

Immigrants
('000)

Nationality and Country	2000	2001	2002
United Kingdom	16.4	15.5	13.1
Other EU	9.8	8.7	8.5
USA and Canada	4.6	4.4	4.1
Rest of the world	11.5	17.5	21.8
Total	42.3	46.2	47.5

Emigrants
('000)

Nationality and Country	2000	2001	2002
United Kingdom	6.3	5.3	5.1
Other EU	4.3	4.1	3.5
USA and Canada	3.2	2.3	3.5
Rest of the world	8.5	8.1	6.6
Total	22.3	19.9	18.8

ECONOMICALLY ACTIVE POPULATION
(estimates, '000 persons, quarterly (March–May) labour force survey)

	2000	2001	2002
Agriculture, forestry and fishing .	130.9	120.1	120.7
Mining and quarrying			
Manufacturing	309.9	317.1	302.9
Electricity, gas and water . . .			
Construction	166.3	180.2	181.1
Wholesale and retail trade . .	235.8	247.8	245.9
Hotels and restaurants . . .	109.0	104.8	104.8
Transport, storage and			
communications	100.8	110.4	110.2
Financial and other business			
services	212.1	218.3	229.1
Public administration and			
defence	77.8	80.4	89.2
Education and health	234.7	245.2	267.0
Other services	93.4	92.3	99.0
Total employed	1,670.7	1,716.5	1,749.9
Males	989.9	1,013.9	1,017.2
Females	680.8	702.5	732.7
Total unemployed	74.9	65.4	77.2

Health and Welfare

KEY INDICATORS

Total fertility rate (children per woman, 2001)	2.0
Under-5 mortality rate (per 1,000 live births, 2001) . .	6
HIV/AIDS (% of persons aged 15–49, 2001)	0.11
Physicians (per 1,000 head, 1998)	2.19
Hospital beds (per 1,000 head, 1997)	3.7
Health expenditure (2000): US $ per head (PPP)	1,944
Health expenditure (2000): % of GDP	6.7
Health expenditure (2000): public (% of total)	75.8
Human Development Index (2000): ranking	18
Human Development Index (2000): value	0.925

For sources and definitions, see explanatory note on p. vi.

Agriculture

PRINCIPAL CROPS
('000 metric tons)

	1999	2000	2001
Wheat	597	706	760
Oats	136	128	121
Barley	1,278	1,129	1,276
Potatoes	559	395	400*
Sugar beet	1,712	1,840	1,700*

* FAO estimate.

Source: FAO.

LIVESTOCK
('000 head)

	1998	1999	2000
Cattle	7,640	7,387	7,037
Sheep	8,312	7,925	6,892
Pigs	1,819	1,787	1,722

LIVESTOCK PRODUCTS
('000 metric tons)

	1999	2000	2001
Beef and veal	644	577	579
Mutton and lamb	90	83	78
Pig meat	249	226	238
Poultry meat	111	116	116*
Cows' milk	5,121	5,160	5,345
Butter	135	135	129
Cheese	105	102	127
Dry milk (excl. whey) . . .	130†	127†	134*
Hen eggs	32	34†	37†
Cattle hides*	74	66	66
Sheepskins*	17	17	15

* FAO estimate(s).
† Unofficial figure.

Source: FAO.

Forestry

ROUNDWOOD REMOVALS
('000 cubic metres, excluding bark)

	1999	2000	2001
Sawlogs, veneer logs and logs for sleepers	1,531	1,759	1,939
Pulpwood	966	961	500
Fuel wood	11	10	15
Total	2,508	2,730	2,454

SAWNWOOD PRODUCTION
('000 cubic metres, including railway sleepers)

	1999	2000	2001
Coniferous (softwood) . . .	804	886	920
Broadleaved (hardwood) . .	7	2	6
Total	811	888	925

Source: FAO, *Yearbook of Forest Products*.

Fishing

SEA FISH
(landings in metric tons)

	1998	1999	2000
European plaice	1,731	1,424	1,029
Atlantic cod	5,294	3,860	2,928
Haddock	6,572	4,898	5,812
Megrim	3,383	3,162	3,364
Whiting	7,762	7,643	6,505
Dogfish	2,403	1,645	1,361
Atlantic herring	58,248	45,334	42,114
Atlantic mackerel	67,310	59,609	70,183
Horse mackerel	74,253	58,201	55,438
Total fish (incl. others) . .	294,898	250,695	242,962
Crabs	7,970	8,550	10,295
Norway lobster (Dublin Bay prawn)	3,998	4,603	4,077
Mussels	5,660	8,563	n.a.
Total shellfish (incl. others*) . .	25,266	28,534	29,520
Total catch	320,163	279,230	272,482

* Excludes oysters, clams and farmed mussels.

INLAND FISH
(catch in metric tons)

	1998	1999	2000
Atlantic salmon	624	515	621
Total catch (incl. others) . .	895	775	881

Mining

('000 metric tons, unless otherwise indicated)

	1999	2000	2001
Natural gas (terajoules) . . .	44,587	n.a.	n.a.
Lead*	44.1	66.2	50.1
Zinc*	199.3	229.2	287.9

* Figures refer to the metal content of ores mined.

Peat ('000 metric tons, excluding peat for horticultural use): 4,767 in 1992; 3,288 in 1993.

Industry

SELECTED PRODUCTS
('000 metric tons, unless otherwise indicated)

	1996	1997	1998
Flour	190	195	n.a.
Margarine	54	48	33
Cigarettes (million)	7,500	4,605	6,452
Woven woollen fabrics (sq m) .	900,000	900,000	800,000
Motor spirit (petrol) . . .	379	452	468
Distillate fuel oils	765	1,000	1,112*
Residual fuel oils	793	1,022	1,099*
Electric energy (million kWh) . .	18,845	19,551	20,485

* Estimate.

Source: mainly UN, *Industrial Commodity Statistics Yearbook*.

1999: Electric energy 21,278 million kWh; Cigarettes (million) 6,176.

2000: Electric energy 22,920 million kWh; Cigarettes (million) 6,855.

2001: Electric energy 24,403 million kWh; Cigarettes (million) 7,918.

Finance

CURRENCY AND EXCHANGE RATES

Monetary Units

100 cent = 1 euro (€)

Sterling and Dollar Equivalents (31 May 2002)

£1 sterling = 1.537 euros
US $1 = 0.9536 euros
100 euros = £65.06 sterling = $104.87

Average Exchange Rate (euros per US $)

2000   1.0854
2001   1.1175
2002   1.0626

Note: The national currency was formerly the Irish pound (or punt). From the introduction of the euro, with Irish participation, on 1 January 1999, a fixed exchange rate of €1 = 78.7564 pence was in operation. Euro notes and coins were introduced on 1 January 2002. The euro and local currency circulated alongside each other until 9 February, after which the euro became the sole legal tender.

BUDGET

(million euros)

Revenue	2000	2001*	2002†
Current revenue	34,692	37,434	41,089
Taxes on income and wealth . .	13,088	14,113	15,365
Social insurance and health contributions	4,380	4,940	5,385
Taxes on expenditure	13,626	14,020	15,212
Gross trading and investment income	1,147	1,527	2,212
Capital revenue	2,227	2,586	2,463
Taxes on capital	998	1,025	926
Total	36,919	40,020	43,552

Expenditure	2000	2001*	2002†
Current expenditure	27,135	31,919	35,579
Subsidies	785	1,358	1,018
National debt interest . . .	2,138	1,883	2,082
Current transfer payments to residents	9,552	11,336	12,812
Current transfer payments to rest of the world. . . .	677	837	1,188
Current expenditure on goods and services (including depreciation)	6,526	7,838	8,802
Current expenditure on goods and services by local authorities	7,458	8,668	9,678
Capital expenditure	5,075	6,484	7,136
Gross physical capital formation	3,839	5,081	5,686
Total	32,211	38,403	42,715

* Provisional.
† Forecast.

INTERNATIONAL RESERVES

(US $ million at 31 December)

	2000	2001	2002
Gold*	48	49	60
IMF special drawing rights . .	48	55	66
Reserve position in IMF . . .	329	336	469
Foreign exchange	4,983	5,196	4,879
Total	5,408	5,636	5,474

* Eurosystem valuation.

Source: IMF, *International Financial Statistics*.

MONEY SUPPLY

(million euros at 31 December)

	2000	2001	2002
Currency issued	5,368	4,704	4,278*
Demand deposits at banking institutions	15,117	18,871	19,671

* Total currency put into circulation by the Central Bank of Ireland was 6,583 million euros.

Source: IMF, *International Financial Statistics*.

COST OF LIVING

(Consumer Price Index; base: November 1996 = 100)

	1999	2000	2001
Food	109.6	113.7	121.2
Alcoholic drink	108.7	114.0	119.5
Tobacco	112.7	130.5	133.9
Clothing and footwear . . .	81.1	76.5	73.8
Fuel and light	100.8	109.9	112.5
Housing	91.5	100.0	115.9
Durable household goods . . .	99.7	100.0	101.3
Other goods	105.7	109.7	114.9
Transport	105.3	114.0	115.5
Services and related expenditure .	109.7	116.0	121.8
All items	104.8	110.7	116.1

NATIONAL ACCOUNTS

(million euros at current prices)

National Income and Product

	1999	2000	2001†
Gross domestic product at factor cost	79,747	90,979	102,394
Net factor income from the rest of the world*	−13,218	−14,976	−17,677
Gross national product at factor cost	66,529	76,003	84,717
Less Consumption of fixed capital .	8,768	10,280	11,465
Net national product at factor cost	57,761	65,723	73,252
of which:			
Compensation of employees . .	36,474	41,811	47,254
Other domestic income . .	21,287	23,912	25,998
Indirect taxes, less subsidies . .	10,998	12,799	12,995
Net national product at market prices	68,759	78,522	86,247
Consumption of fixed capital . .	8,768	10,280	11,465
Gross national product at market prices	76,552	87,932	96,802
Less Net factor income from the rest of the world*	−13,218	−14,976	−17,677
Gross domestic product at market prices	89,770	102,910	114,479
Balance of exports and imports of goods and services*	12,373	14,035	16,877
Available resources	77,397	88,874	97,602
of which:			
Private consumption expenditure	44,361	50,330	55,144
Government consumption expenditure	11,347	12,880	15,288
Gross fixed capital formation .	21,323	24,767	26,670
Increase in stocks	402	590	279
Statistical discrepancy . . .	−36	307	221

* Excludes transfers between Ireland and the rest of the world.
† Preliminary figures.

Gross Domestic Product by Economic Activity
(at factor cost)

	1999	2000	2001*
Agriculture, forestry and fishing .	3,545	3,777	3,969
Mining, manufacturing, electricity, gas, water and construction . .	33,347	38,593	42,734
Public administration and defence.	2,945	3,220	3,563
Transport, communications and trade.	12,470	14,124	16,224
Other services	30,522	35,144	40,162
Sub-total	82,529	94,858	106,650
Adjustment for financial services .	−3,117	−3,571	−4,036
Discrepancy	36	−307	−221
Total	79,448	90,980	102,393

* Preliminary.

BALANCE OF PAYMENTS
(US $ million)

	1999	2000	2001
Exports of goods f.o.b.	68,540	73,433	78,371
Imports of goods f.o.b.	−44,284	−48,017	−48,369
Trade balance	24,256	25,416	30,003
Exports of services	15,522	16,788	20,194
Imports of services	−26,637	−28,745	−34,853
Balance on goods and services	13,142	13,459	15,344
Other income received . . .	24,442	29,973	28,697
Other income paid	−38,484	−44,974	−45,562
Balance on goods, services and income	−899	−1,542	−1,520
Current transfers received . .	5,308	4,304	4,295
Current transfers paid	−4,055	−3,355	−3,818
Current balance	354	−593	−1,043
Capital account (net) . . .	593	1,097	598
Direct investment abroad . . .	−6,102	−3,983	−5,405
Direct investment from abroad. .	18,615	22,778	9,865
Portfolio investment assets . . .	−82,813	−78,817	−108,535
Portfolio investment liabilities .	67,377	80,255	91,128
Financial derivatives assets .	n.a.	416	−867
Financial derivatives liabilities .	n.a.	−42	919
Other investment assets . . .	−38,545	−41,048	−12,101
Other investment liabilities . .	37,576	29,343	25,033
Net errors and omissions . . .	972	−9,284	803
Overall balance	−1,973	121	395

Source: IMF, *International Financial Statistics*.

External Trade

PRINCIPAL COMMODITIES
(distribution by SITC, million euros)

Imports c.i.f.	1999	2000	2001
Food and live animals . . .	2,555.9	2,825.7	3,060.3
Mineral fuels, lubricants, etc. .	1,294.1	2,299.7	2,206.9
Petroleum and petroleum products	1,007.6	1,926.2	1,718.0
Chemicals and related products	4,931.9	6,105.2	6,370.7
Organic chemicals	1,466.9	1,669.4	1,554.0
Medicinal and pharmaceutical products.	1,124.4	1,525.4	1,914.7
Basic manufactures	3,806.9	4,350.6	4,400.3
Machinery and transport equipment.	22,820.6	29,739.5	30,177.0
Office machines and automatic data-processing equipment . .	8,368.1	11,363.2	12,196.0
Parts and accessories for office machines, etc.	4,002.2	5,845.5	6,999.8
Telecommunications and sound equipment	2,074.1	2,880.9	3,131.6
Other electrical machinery, apparatus, etc.	5,192.9	7,048.4	7,541.9
Road vehicles and parts (excl. tyres, engines and electrical parts) .	2,984.5	4,053.5	3,197.6
Passenger motor cars (excl. buses).	2,160.2	3,067.4	2,302.2
Miscellaneous manufactured articles	4,891.2	5,893.0	6,189.4
Total (incl. others)*	44,327.1	55,908.8	57,177.5

* Including transactions not classified by commodity.

Exports f.o.b.	1999	2000	2001
Food and live animals . . .	5,483.6	5,948.4	5,725.7
Chemicals and related products	21,168.7	27,360.5	32,274.6
Organic chemicals	11,394.1	16,897.5	17,121.7
Organo-inorganic and heterocyclic compounds . .	9,691.2	15,577.2	15,686.7
Heterocyclic compounds (incl. nucleic acids)	8,892.3	14,435.5	14,429.9
Machinery and transport equipment.	26,193.2	34,011.7	37,922.7
Office machines and automatic data-processing equipment . .	15,152.0	19,616.8	22,393.9
Automatic data-processing machines and units. . . .	9,044.0	10,678.0	11,199.0
Parts and accessories for automatic-data processing equipment.	6,040.9	8,811.4	10,798.4
Electrical machinery, apparatus, etc.	5,135.8	7,916.0	9,222.8
Miscellaneous manufactured articles	7,638.5	8,863.9	8,781.6
Total (incl. others)*	66,956.2	83,888.9	92,523.3

* Including transactions not classified by commodity.

PRINCIPAL TRADING PARTNERS
(million euros)*

Imports c.i.f.	1999	2000	2001
Belgium-Luxembourg . . .	590.5	902.3	839.9
China, People's Republic . . .	656.0	900.4	1,709.2
France	1,820.9	2,576.9	2,810.9
Germany	2,751.4	3,336.2	3,525.6
Italy	927.1	1,253.1	1,160.7
Japan	2,542.2	2,635.2	2,004.0
Korea, Republic	801.9	1,291.0	797.4
Netherlands	1,335.8	1,778.0	1,924.7
Singapore	1,721.8	2,027.0	1,357.2
Taiwan.	911.6	1,011.9	1,073.4
United Kingdom	14,626.5	17,613.2	20,266.2
USA	7,383.7	9,148.5	8,711.9
Total (incl. others)	44,327.1	55,908.8	57,177.5

Exports f.o.b.		1999	2000	2001
Belgium-Luxembourg	. . . .	3,491.8	4,113.2	4,428.2
France .	. . . . .	5,636.4	6,342.6	5,614.7
Germany .	. . . .	7,995.8	9,414.7	11,718.7
Italy .	. . . . .	2,532.0	3,316.8	3,312.9
Japan .	. . . . .	1,959.0	3,122.9	3,266.2
Malaysia .	. . . .	824.2	753.6	1,140.2
Netherlands	. . . .	4,155.6	4,687.0	4,277.2
Spain .	. . . . .	1,830.6	2,123.8	2,276.5
Sweden .	. . . .	1,094.3	1,336.1	1,307.2
Switzerland	. . . .	1,618.3	2,033.2	2,811.9
United Kingdom .	. . .	14,690.2	18,869.8	22,160.9
USA .	. . . . .	10,336.8	14,227.8	15,695.6
Total (incl. others)	. . . .	66,956.2	83,888.9	92,523.3

* Imports by country of origin; exports by country of final destination.

Transport

RAILWAYS
(traffic, '000)

		1999	2000	2001
Passengers carried	. . . .	32,765	31,721	34,206
Passenger train-km .	. . .	11,140	10,580	12,356
Freight tonnage .	. . . .	2,901	2,707	2,612
Freight train-km .	. . . . .	4,215	3,933	4,133

ROAD TRAFFIC
(licensed motor vehicles at 31 December)

		1998	1999	2000
Passenger cars	. . . .	1,196,901	1,269,245	1,319,250
Lorries and vans .	. . .	170,866	188,814	205,575
Buses and coaches	. . .	17,353	19,640	20,594
Motorcycles and mopeds	. . .	24,398	26,677	30,638

SHIPPING

Merchant Fleet
(registered at 31 December)

		1999	2000	2001
Number of vessels	. . . .	153	172	193
Total displacement (grt) .	. . .	218,882	248,236	300,289

Source: Lloyd's Register-Fairplay, *World Fleet Statistics*.

Sea-borne Freight Traffic
('000 metric tons)*

		1999	2000	2001
Goods loaded .	. . . . .	12,202	13,594	13,161
Goods unloaded .	. . . .	30,726	31,679	32,634

* Figures refer to vessels engaged in both international and coastal trade.

CIVIL AVIATION*

		1999	2000	2001
Passengers carried ('000)	. . .	16,492	17,932	18,514
Freight (incl. mail) carried (tons) .		202,412	214,315	202,050
Total aircraft movements	. . .	264,947	284,456	284,267
scheduled	. . . . . .	172,686	188,912	193,329
non-scheduled	. . . . .	24,937	25,573	27,235

* Figures refer to traffic at Dublin, Cork and Shannon airports.

Tourism

FOREIGN TOURIST ARRIVALS BY ORIGIN
('000)*

		1999	2000	2001
Great Britain .	. . . . .	3,558	3,633	3,541
France .	. . . . . .	281	296	285
Germany .	. . . . .	303	320	288
Netherlands	. . . . .	139	184	184
Other continental Europe	. .	609	668	606
USA .	. . . . . .	861	956	844
Canada .	. . . . .	82	93	70
Other areas	. . . . .	233	260	262
Total	. . . .	6,068	6,409	6,081

* Excluding visitors from Northern Ireland and excursionists.

Communications Media

	1999	2000	2001
Television licences ('000 in use) .	1,037.8	965.0†	n.a.
Telephone lines ('000 in use) . .	1,634.1	1,737.8	1,860.0
Mobile cellular telephones ('000 subscribrs)	1,655	2,490	2,800
Personal computers ('000 in use) .	1,180	1,360	1,500
Internet users ('000)	679	784	895
Daily newspapers	6	6	6

* Sales of licences.
† To November 2000.

1996: Non-daily newspapers 77 (estimated circulation 1,561,000).

1997 (estimates): Radio receivers 2,550,000 in domestic use; Television receivers 1,470,000 in domestic use; Facsimile machines 100,000 (estimated number in use).

Source: UNESCO, *Statistical Yearbook* and International Telecommunication Union.

Education

(2000/01)

	Institutions	Teachers (full-time)	Students (full-time)
National schools* . . .	3,286	22,850	439,560
Secondary schools . .	419	12,476	197,376
Vocational schools . . .	247	5,788	96,842
Comprehensive schools .	16	518	8,258
Community schools . . .	69	2,653	42,908
Teacher (primary and home economics) training colleges	5	56	960
Technology colleges† . .	16	3,347	48,360
Universities and other Higher Education Authority Institutions .	10	3,507	69,254
Other aided institutions‡ .	3	71	1,417

* National schools are state-aided primary schools.
† Comprising 14 Institutes of Technology, Tipperary Institute, and the Hotel Training and Catering College, Killybegs, Co Donegal.
‡ Refers to the National College of Ireland, Mater Dei Institute and the Pontifical College, Maynooth, Co Kildare.

Directory

The Constitution

The Constitution took effect on 29 December 1937. Ireland became a republic on 18 April 1949. The following is a summary of the Constitution's main provisions:

TITLE OF THE STATE

The title of the State is Éire or, in the English language, Ireland.

NATIONAL STATUS*

The Constitution declares that Ireland is a sovereign, independent, democratic State. It affirms the inalienable, indefeasible and sovereign right of the Irish nation to choose its own form of government, to determine its relations with other nations, and to develop its life, political, economic and cultural, in accordance with its own genius and traditions.

The Constitution applies to the whole of Ireland, but, pending the reintegration of the national territory, the laws enacted by the Parliament established by the Constitution have the same area and extent of application as those of the Irish Free State.

THE PRESIDENT

At the head of the State is the President, elected by direct suffrage, who holds office for a period of seven years. The President, on the advice of the Government or its head, summons and dissolves Parliament, signs and promulgates laws and appoints judges; on the nomination of the Dáil, the President appoints the Prime Minister (Taoiseach) and, on the nomination of the Prime Minister with the previous approval of the Dáil, the President appoints the other members of the Government. The supreme command of the Defence Forces is vested in the President, its exercise being regulated by law.

In addition, the President has the power to refer certain Bills to the Supreme Court for decision on the question of their constitutionality; and also, at the instance of a prescribed proportion of the members of both Houses of Parliament, to refer certain Bills to the people for decision at a referendum.

The President, in the exercise and performance of certain of his or her constitutional powers and functions, has the aid and advice of a Council of State.

PARLIAMENT

The Oireachtas, or National Parliament, consists of the President and two Houses, viz. a House of Representatives, called Dáil Éireann, and a Senate, called Seanad Éireann. The Dáil consists of 166 members, who are elected for a five-year term by adult suffrage on the system of proportional representation by means of the single, transferable vote. Of the 60 members of the Senate, 11 are nominated by the Prime Minister, six are elected by the universities, and 43 are elected from five panels of candidates established on a vocational basis, representing: national language and culture, literature, art, education and such professional interests as may be defined by law for the purpose of this panel; agriculture and allied interests, and fisheries; labour, whether organized or unorganized; industry and commerce, including banking, finance, accountancy, engineering and architecture; and public administration and social services, including voluntary social activities.

A maximum period of 90 days is afforded to the Senate for the consideration or amendment of Bills sent to that House by the Dáil, but the Senate has no power to veto legislation.

EXECUTIVE

The Executive Power of the State is exercised by the Government, which is responsible to the Dáil and consists of not fewer than seven and not more than 15 members. The head of the Government is the Prime Minister.

FUNDAMENTAL RIGHTS

The State recognizes the family as the natural, primary and fundamental unit group of Society, possessing inalienable and imprescriptible rights antecedent and superior to all positive law. It acknowledges the right to life of the unborn and, with due regard to the equal right to life of the mother, guarantees in its laws to defend and vindicate that right. It acknowledges the right and duty of parents to provide for the education of their children, and, with due regard to that right, undertakes to provide free education. It pledges itself also to guard with special care the institution of marriage.

The Constitution contains special provision for the recognition and protection of the fundamental rights of citizens, such as personal liberty, free expression of opinion, peaceable assembly, and the formation of associations and unions.

Freedom of conscience and the free practice and profession of religion are, subject to public order and morality, guaranteed to every citizen. No religion may be endowed or subjected to discriminatory disability. Since December 1972, when a referendum was taken on the issue, the Catholic Church has no longer enjoyed a special, privileged position.

SOCIAL POLICY

Certain principles of social policy intended for the general guidance of Parliament, but not cognizable by the courts, are set forth in the Constitution. Among their objects are the direction of the policy of the State towards securing the distribution of property so as to subserve the common good, the regulation of credit so as to serve the welfare of the people as a whole, the establishment of families in economic security on the land, and the right to an adequate means of livelihood for all citizens.

The State pledges itself to safeguard the interests, and to contribute where necessary to the support, of the infirm, the widow, the orphan and the aged, and shall endeavour to ensure that citizens shall not be forced by economic necessity to enter occupations unsuited to their sex, age or strength.

AMENDMENT OF THE CONSTITUTION

No amendment to the Constitution can be effected except by the decision of the people given at a referendum.

* Under the terms of the Good Friday Agreement, signed in April 1998 and approved by referendum in May, provision was made for a change to the Constitution to enshrine the principle that a united Ireland could be achieved only with the agreement and consent of the majority of the people of both Ireland and Northern Ireland. Accordingly, Articles 2 and 3 of the Constitution, which lay claim to the territory of Northern Ireland, were removed on 2 December 1999.

The Government

HEAD OF STATE

Uachtarán (President): Dr MARY McALEESE (assumed office 11 November 1997).

THE CABINET
(April 2003)

A coalition of Fianna Fáil (FF) and the Progressive Democrats (PD).

Taoiseach (Prime Minister): BERTIE AHERN (FF).

Tánaiste (Deputy Prime Minister) and Minister for Enterprise, Trade and Employment: MARY HARNEY (PD).

Minister for Defence: MICHAEL SMITH (FF).

Minister for Agriculture and Food: JOE WALSH (FF).

Minister for Finance: CHARLES McCREEVY (FF).

Minister for Foreign Affairs: BRIAN COWEN (FF).

Minister for Education and Science: NOEL DEMPSEY (FF).

Minister for Communications, Marine and Natural Resources: DERMOT AHERN (FF).

Minister for Arts, Sport and Tourism: JOHN O'DONOGHUE (FF).

Minister for Health and Children: MICHEÁL MARTIN (FF).

Minister for Transport: SEAMUS BRENNAN (FF).

Minister for Justice, Equality and Law Reform: MICHAEL McDOWELL (PD).

Minister for the Environment and Local Government: MARTIN CULLEN (FF).

Minister for Community, Rural and Gaeltacht Affairs: EAMONN Ó'CUIV (FF).

Minister for Social and Family Affairs: MARY COUGHLAN (FF).

In addition there are 17 Ministers of State

MINISTRIES

Office of the President: Áras an Uachtaráin, Phoenix Park, Dublin 8; tel. (1) 6171000; fax (1) 6171001; e-mail webmaster@aras .irlgov.ie; internet www.irlgov.ie/aras.

Department of the Taoiseach: Government Bldgs, Upper Merrion St, Dublin 2; tel. (1) 6624888; fax (1) 6789791; e-mail pressoffice@taoiseach.gov.ie; internet www.taoiseach.gov.ie.

Department of Agriculture and Food: Agriculture House, Kildare St, Dublin 2; tel. (1) 6072000; fax (1) 6616263; e-mail info@agriculture.gov.ie; internet www.gov.ie/daff.

Department of Arts, Sports and Tourism: Kildare St, Dublin 2; tel. (1) 6313800; fax (1) 6611201; internet www.gov.ie/arts-sports-tourism.

Department of Communications, Marine and Natural Resources: Leeson Lane, Dublin 2; tel. (1) 6199200; fax (1) 6618214; e-mail contact@marine.gov.ie; internet www.marine.gov.ie.

Department of Community, Rural and Gaeltacht Affairs: Dún Aimhirgin, 43–49 Mespil Rd, Dublin 4; tel. (1) 6473000; fax (1) 6670826; e-mail eolas@pobail.ie; internet www.pobail.ie.

Department of Defence: Parkgate, Infirmary Rd, Dublin 7; tel. (1) 8042000; fax (1) 6703399; e-mail webmaster@defence.irlgov.ie; internet www.gov.ie/defence.

Department of Education and Science: Marlborough St, Dublin 1; tel. (1) 8734700; fax (1) 8892367; e-mail webmaster@educ.irlgov.ie; internet www.education.ie.

Department of Enterprise, Trade and Employment: Kildare St, Dublin 2; tel. (1) 6312121; fax (1) 6312827; e-mail erinfo@entemp.ie; internet www.entemp.ie.

Department of the Environment and Local Government: Custom House, Dublin 1; tel. (1) 8882000; fax (1) 8882888; e-mail press-office@environ.irlgov.ie; internet www.environ.ie.

Department of Finance: Government Bldgs, Upper Merrion St, Dublin 2; tel. (1) 6767571; fax (1) 6789936; e-mail webmaster@finance.irlgov.ie; internet www.irlgov.ie/finance.

Department of Foreign Affairs: 80 St Stephen's Green, Dublin 2; tel. (1) 4780822; fax (1) 4781484; e-mail library1@iveagh.irlgov.ie; internet www.irlgov.ie/iveagh.

Department of Health and Children: Hawkins House, Hawkins St, Dublin 2; tel. (1) 6354000; fax (1) 6354001; e-mail queries@health.irlgov.ie; internet www.doh.ie.

Department of Justice, Equality and Law Reform: 72–76 St Stephen's Green, Dublin 2; tel. (1) 6028202; fax 6615461; e-mail info@justice.ie; internet www.justice.ie.

Department of Social and Family Affairs: Áras Mhic Dhiarmada, Store St, Dublin 1; tel. (1) 7043860; fax (1) 7043870; e-mail press.office@welfare.ie; internet portal.welfare.ie.

Department of Transport: 44 Kildare St, Dublin 2; tel. (1) 6041089; fax (1) 6041185; e-mail minister@dpe.ie; internet www.gov.ie/tec.

Legislature

OIREACHTAS (NATIONAL PARLIAMENT)

Parliament comprises two Houses—Dáil Éireann (House of Representatives), with 166 members (Teachtaí Dála), elected for a five-year term by universal adult suffrage, and Seanad Éireann (Senate), with 60 members serving a five-year term, of whom 11 are nominated by the Taoiseach (Prime Minister) and 49 elected (six by the universities and 43 from specially constituted panels).

Dáil Éireann

Ceann Comhairle (Chairman): Dr RORY O'HANLON (Fianna Fáil).

Leas-Cheann Comhairle (Deputy Chairman): SÉAMUS PATTISON (Labour Party).

General Election, 17 May 2002

Party	Votes*	% of votes*	Seats
Fianna Fáil .	770,846	41.49	81
Fine Gael .	417,653	22.48	31
Labour Party .	200,138	10.77	21
Progressive Democrats .	73,628	3.96	8
Green Party.	71,480	3.85	6
Sinn Féin .	121,039	6.51	5
Others .	203,329	10.94	14
Total .	1,788,985	100.00	166

*The election was conducted by means of the single transferable vote. Figures refer to first-preference votes.

Seanad Éireann

Cathaoirleach (Chairman): RORY KIELY (Fianna Fáil).

Leas-Chathaoirleach (Deputy Chairman): PADDY BURKE (Fine Gael).

Election, July 2002 (11 non-affiliated members nominated)

Party	Seats at election
Fianna Fáil .	30
Fine Gael .	15
Independents .	5
Labour Party .	5
Progressive Democrats .	4
Others .	1

Political Organizations

Christian Solidarity Party: 73 Deepark Rd, Mount Merrion, Co Dublin; tel. (1) 2121037; fax (1) 2880051; e-mail comharcriostai@eircom.net; Pres. and Leader Dr GERARD CASEY; Nat. Sec. PATRICK SMYTH.

Comhaontas Glas (Green Party): 5A Upper Fownes St, Temple Bar, Dublin 2; tel. (1) 6790012; fax (1) 6797168; e-mail info@greenparty.ie; internet www.greenparty.ie; fmrly The Ecology Party; advocates a humane, ecological society, freedom of information and political decentralization; Pres. JOHN GORMLEY; Leader TREVOR SARGENT.

Communist Party of Ireland: James Connolly House, 43 East Essex St, Dublin 2; tel. and fax (1) 6711943; e-mail cpi@indigo.ie; internet www.communistpartyofireland.ie; f. 1933; advocates a united, socialist, independent Ireland; Chair. JAMES STEWART; Gen. Sec. EUGENE McCARTAN.

Fianna Fáil (Republican Party): 65–66 Lower Mount St, Dublin 2; tel. (1) 6761551; fax (1) 6785690; e-mail info@fiannafail.ie; internet www.fiannafail.ie; f. 1926; centrist; Pres. and Leader BERTIE AHERN; Gen. Sec. MARTIN MACKIN.

Fine Gael (United Ireland Party): 51 Upper Mount St, Dublin 2; tel. (1) 6198444; fax (1) 6625046; e-mail finegael@finegael.com; internet www.finegael.ie; f. 1933; centrist; Pres. and Leader ENDA KELLY; Gen. Sec. TOM CURRAN.

The Labour Party: 17 Ely Place, Dublin 2; tel. (1) 6612615; fax (1) 6612640; e-mail head_office@labour.ie; internet www.labour.ie; f. 1912; merged with Democratic Left (f. 1992) in 1999; Leader PAT RABBITE; Gen. Sec. MIKE ALLEN.

Muintir na hÉireann Pairti: 58 The Palms, Roebuck Rd, Dublin 14; tel. and fax (1) 2831484; e-mail muintir@indigo.ie; f. 1995; Christian conservative; Leader RICHARD GREENE.

Progressive Democrats: 25 South Frederick St, Dublin 2; tel. (1) 6794399; fax (1) 6794757; e-mail info@progressivedemocrats.ie; internet www.progressivedemocrats.ie; f. 1985 by fmr mems of Fianna Fáil; affiliated to the Liberal parties of Europe; Pres. MICHAEL McDOWELL; Chair. JOHN MINIHAN; Leader MARY HARNEY; Gen. Sec. JOHN HIGGINS.

Sinn Féin (Ourselves Alone): 44 Parnell Sq., Dublin 1; tel. (1) 8726100; fax (1) 8783595; e-mail sfadmin@eircom.net; internet www.sinnfein.ie; f. 1905; advocates the termination of British rule in Northern Ireland; seeks the establishment of a democratic socialist republic in a reunified Ireland; Pres. GERRY ADAMS; Chair. MITCHEL McLAUGHLIN.

The Workers' Party: 23 Hill St, Dublin 1; tel. (1) 8740716; fax (1) 8748702; e-mail wpi@indigo.ie; internet www.workers-party.org; f. 1905; fmrly Sinn Féin The Workers' Party; aims to establish a unitary socialist state on the island of Ireland; Pres. SEAN GARLAND; Gen. Sec. JOHN LOWRY.

Diplomatic Representation

EMBASSIES IN IRELAND

Argentina: 15 Ailesbury Drive, Dublin 4; tel. (1) 2691546; fax (1) 2600404; e-mail argembsy@indigo.ie; Ambassador VICTOR E. BEAUGÉ.

Australia: Fitzwilton House, 2nd Floor, Wilton Terrace, Dublin 2; tel. (1) 6645300; fax (1) 6785185; e-mail austremb.dublin@dfat.gov.au; internet www.australianembassy.ie; Ambassador Dr JOHN HERRON.

Austria: 15 Ailesbury Court, 93 Ailesbury Rd, Dublin 4; tel. (1) 2694577; fax (1) 2830860; e-mail dublin-ob@bmaa.gv.at; Ambassador Dr HARALD MILTNER.

Belgium: 2 Shrewsbury Rd, Dublin 4; tel. (1) 2692082; fax (1) 2838488; e-mail dublin@diplobel.org; Ambassador O. QUINAUX.

Brazil: 5th Floor, Europa House, Harcourt St, Dublin 2; tel. (1) 4756000; fax (1) 4751341; e-mail irlbra@iol.ie; Ambassador ARMANDO SÉRGIO FRAZÃO.

Bulgaria: 22 Burlington Rd, Dublin 4; tel. (1) 6603293; fax (1) 6603915; e-mail bgemb@eircom.net; Chargé d'affaires a.i. PETER POPTCHEV.

Canada: 65–68 St Stephen's Green, Dublin 2; tel. (1) 4174100; fax (1) 4174101; e-mail dubln@dfait-moeci.gc.ca; internet www.Canada .ie; Ambassador MARK J. MOHER.

China, People's Republic: 40 Ailesbury Rd, Dublin 4; tel. (1) 2691707; fax (1) 2839938; Ambassador SHA HAILAIN.

Cyprus: 71 Lower Leeson St, Dublin 2; tel. (1) 6763060; fax (1) 6763099; e-mail embassyofcyprusdub@eircom.net; Ambassador ANDREAS KAKOURIS.

Czech Republic: 57 Northumberland Rd, Ballsbridge, Dublin 4; tel. (1) 6681135; fax (1) 6681660; e-mail dublin@embassy.mzv.cz; internet www.mfa.cz/dublin; Ambassador PETR KOLÁŘ.

Denmark: 121–122 St Stephen's Green, Dublin 2; tel. (1) 4756404; fax (1) 4784536; e-mail embassy@denmark.ie; internet www .denmark.ie; Ambassador K. ERIK TYGESEN.

Egypt: 12 Clyde Rd, Ballsbridge, Dublin 4; tel. (1) 6606566; fax (1) 6683745; e-mail embegypt@indigo.ie; Ambassador ASHRAF RASHED.

Estonia: Riversdale House, St Ann's, Ailsesbury Rd, Dublin 4; tel. (1) 2696730; fax (1) 2196731; e-mail asjur@gofree.indigo.ie; Chargé d'affaires a.i. KRISTA KILVET.

Finland: Russell House, Stokes Place, St Stephen's Green, Dublin 2; tel. (1) 4781344; fax (1) 4783727; e-mail pekka.oinonen@forming .fi; Ambassador PEKKA OINONEN.

France: 36 Ailesbury Rd, Ballsbridge, Dublin 4; tel. (1) 2601666; fax (1) 2830178; Ambassador GABRIEL DE REGNAULD DE BELLESCIZE.

Germany: 31 Trimleston Ave, Booterstown, Blackrock, Co Dublin; tel. (1) 2693011; fax (1) 2693946; e-mail germany@indigo.ie; Ambassador Dr GOTTFRIED HAAS.

Greece: 1 Upper Pembroke St, Dublin 2; tel. (1) 6767254; fax (1) 6618892; e-mail dubgremb@tinet.ie; Ambassador MARIA ZOGRAFOU.

Holy See: 183 Navan Rd, Dublin 7 (Apostolic Nunciature); tel. (1) 8380577; fax (1) 8380276; e-mail nuncioirl@eircom.net; Apostolic Nuncio Most Rev. GIUSEPPE LAZZAROTTO (Titular Archbishop of Numana).

Hungary: 2 Fitzwilliam Place, Dublin 2; tel. (1) 6612902; fax (1) 6612880; e-mail Hungarian.embassy@eircom.net; Ambassador Dr GÉZA PÁLMAI.

India: 6 Leeson Park, Dublin 6; tel. (1) 4970843; fax (1) 4978074; e-mail eoidubln@indigo.ie; Ambassador PRABHAKAR MENON.

Iran: 72 Mount Merrion Ave, Blackrock, Co Dublin; tel. (1) 2880252; fax (1) 2834246; Ambassador SEYED HOSSEIN MIRFAKHAR.

Israel: 122 Pembroke Rd, Dublin 4; tel. (1) 2309400; fax (1) 2309446; e-mail info@dublin.mfa.gov.il; internet www.mfa.gov.il; Ambassador DANIEL MEGIDDO.

Italy: 63–65 Northumberland Rd, Dublin 4; tel. (1) 6601744; fax (1) 6682759; e-mail info@italianembassy.ie; internet www .italianembassy.ie; Ambassador Dr ALBERTO SCHEPISI.

Japan: Nutley Bldg, Merrion Centre, Nutley Lane, Dublin 4; tel. (1) 2028300; fax (1) 2838726; e-mail general@japanembassy.ie; Ambassador TAKESHI KAGAMI.

Korea, Republic: Clyde House, 15 Clyde Rd, Ballsbridge, POB 2101, Dublin 4; tel. (1) 6608800; fax (1) 6608716; Ambassador KI HO CHANG.

Mexico: 43 Ailesbury Rd, Dublin 4; tel. (1) 2600699; fax (1) 2600411; e-mail embasmex@indigo.ie; Ambassador Dr AGUSTÍN BASAVE-BENÍTEZ.

Morocco: 53 Raglan Rd, Ballsbridge, Dublin 4; tel. (1) 6609449; fax (1) 6609468; e-mail sifamdub@indigo.ie; Chargé d'affaires a.i. AÏCHA EL KABBAJ.

Netherlands: 160 Merrion Rd, Dublin 4; tel. (1) 2693444; fax (1) 2839690; e-mail info@netherlandsembassy.ie; internet www .netherlandsembassy.ie; Ambassador JACOBUS VAN DER VELDEN.

Nigeria: 56 Leeson Park, Dublin 6; tel. (1) 6604366; fax (1) 6604092; Ambassador ELIAS NATHAN.

Norway: 34 Molesworth St, Dublin 2; tel. (1) 6621800; fax (1) 6621890; e-mail emb.dublin@mfa.no; internet www.norway.ie; Ambassador LIV MØRCH FINBORUD.

Poland: 5 Ailesbury Rd, Dublin 4; tel. (1) 2830855; fax (1) 2698309; e-mail polembas@iol.ie; internet www.polishembassy.ie; Ambassador WITOLD SOBKÓW.

Portugal: Knocksinna House, Knocksinna, Foxrock, Dublin 18; tel. (1) 2894416; fax (1) 2892849; e-mail ptembassydublin@tinet.ie; Ambassador FERNANDO D'OLIVEIRA NEVES.

Romania: 47 Ailesbury Rd, Dublin 4; tel. (1) 2692852; fax (1) 2692122; e-mail romemb@iol.ie; Chargé d'affaires a.i. Dr GEORGE MAIOR.

Russia: 186 Orwell Rd, Dublin 14; tel. (1) 4922048; fax (1) 4923525; e-mail russiane@indigo.ie; Ambassador VLADIMIR OLEGOVICH RAKHMANIN.

Slovakia: 20 Clyde Rd, Ballsbridge, Dublin 4; tel. (1) 6600012; fax (1) 6600014; e-mail slovak@iol.ie; Chargé d'affaires a.i. VLADIMÍR HALGAŠ.

South Africa: Alexandra House, Earlsfort Terrace, Dublin 2; tel. (1) 6615553; fax (1) 6615590; e-mail information@saedublin.com; Ambassador MELANIE VERWOERD.

Spain: 17A Merlyn Park, Dublin 4; tel. (1) 2691640; fax (1) 2691854; Ambassador ENRIQUE PASTOR DE GANA.

Sweden: 13–17 Dawson St, Dublin 2; tel. (1) 6715822; fax (1) 6796718; e-mail swedembdublin@eircom.net; Ambassador NILS DAAG.

Switzerland: 6 Ailesbury Rd, Dublin 4; tel. (1) 2186382; fax (1) 2830344; e-mail vertretung@dub.rep.admin.ch; internet www .swissembassy.ie; Ambassador ERIC PFISTER.

Turkey: 11 Clyde Rd, Dublin 4; tel. (1) 6685240; fax (1) 6685014; e-mail turkemb@iol.ie; Ambassador AHMET BERKI DIBEK.

United Kingdom: 29 Merrion Rd, Dublin 4; tel. (1) 2053700; fax (1) 2053885; internet www.britishembassy.ie; Ambassador STUART ELDON.

USA: 42 Elgin Rd, Ballsbridge, Dublin 4; tel. (1) 6687777; fax (1) 6689946; internet www.usembassy.ie; Ambassador RICHARD J. EGAN.

Judicial System

Justice is administered in public by judges appointed by the President on the advice of the Government. The judges of all courts are completely independent in the exercise of their judicial functions. The jurisdiction and organization of the courts are dealt with in the Courts (Establishment and Constitution) Act, 1961, and the Courts (Supplemental Provisions) Acts, 1961 to 1981.

Attorney-General: RORY BRADY.

SUPREME COURT

An Chúirt Uachtarach
(The Supreme Court)

Four Courts, Dublin 7; tel. (1) 8886000; fax (1) 8732332; internet www.courts.ie.

Consisting of the Chief Justice and seven other judges, has appellate jurisdiction from all decisions of the High Court. The President of Ireland may, after consultation with the Council of State, refer a bill that has been passed by both Houses of the Oireachtas (other than a money bill or certain others), to the Supreme Court to establish whether it or any other provisions thereof are repugnant to the Constitution. The President of the High Court is *ex officio* an additional Judge of the Supreme Court.

Chief Justice: RONAN KEANE.

Judges: SUSAN DENHAM, JOHN MURRAY, BRIAN MCCRACKEN, HUGH GEOGHEGAN, CATHERINE MCGUINNESS, ADRIAN HARDIMAN, NIAL FENNELLY, JOSEPH FINNEGAN.

COURT OF CRIMINAL APPEAL

The Court of Criminal Appeal, consisting of the Chief Justice or an ordinary judge of the Supreme Court and two judges of the High Court, deals with appeals by persons convicted on indictment, where leave to appeal has been granted. The Court has jurisdiction to review a conviction or sentence on the basis of an alleged miscarriage of justice. The Director of Public Prosecutions may appeal against an unduly lenient sentence. The decision of the Court of Criminal Appeal is final unless the Court or Attorney-General or the Director of Public Prosecutions certifies that a point of law involved should, in the public interest, be taken to the Supreme Court.

HIGH COURT

An Ard-Chúirt
(The High Court)

Four Courts, Dublin 7; tel. (1) 8886592; fax (1) 8725669; internet www.courts.ie.

Consists of the President of the High Court and 27 ordinary judges (this number may be increased to 28 in the case of a serving High Court judge being appointed President of the Law Reform Commission), has full original jurisdiction in, and power to determine, all matters and questions whether of law or fact, civil or criminal. The High Court on circuit acts as an appeal court from the Circuit Court. The Central Criminal Court sits as directed by the President of the High Court to try criminal cases outside the jurisdiction of the Circuit Court. The duty of acting as the Central Criminal Court is assigned, for the time being, to a judge of the High Court. The Chief Justice and the President of the Circuit Court are *ex officio* additional Judges of the High Court.

President: JOSEPH FINNEGAN.

Master of the High Court: EDMUND HONOHAN.

Judges: MELLA CARROLL, RICHARD JOHNSON, VIVIAN LAVAN, PAUL J. P. CARNEY, DECLAN BUDD (also President of the Law Reform Commission), DERMOT KINLEN, MARY LAFFOY, MICHAEL MORIARTY, PETER KELLY, THOMAS C. SMYTH, DIARMUID B. D. O'DONOVAN, PHILIP O'SULLIVAN, KEVIN C. O'HIGGINS, JOHN QUIRKE, MATTHEW P. SMITH, NICHOLAS KEARNS, IARFHLAITH O'NEILL, AINDRIAS O'CAOIMH, RODERICK MURPHY, DANIEL HERBERT, PAUL BUTLER, LIAM MCKECHNIE, HENRY ABBOTT, EAMON DE VALERA, MARY GEOGHEGAN FINLAY, MICHAEL PEART, BARRY WHITE, PAUL GILLIGAN.

CIRCUIT AND DISTRICT COURTS

The civil jurisdiction of the Circuit Court is limited to €100,000 in contract and tort and in actions founded on hire-purchase and credit-sale agreements and to a rateable value of €254 in equity, and in probate and administration, but where the parties consent the jurisdiction is unlimited. In criminal matters the Court has jurisdiction in all cases except murder, rape, treason, piracy and allied offences. One circuit court judge is permanently assigned to each of the circuits outside Dublin with the exception of Cork, which has three judges. Dublin has 10 permanent judges. In addition there are eight permanently unassigned judges. The President of the District Court is *ex officio* an additional Judge of the Circuit Court. The Circuit Court acts as an appeal court from the District Court, which has a summary jurisdiction in a large number of criminal cases where the offence is not of a serious nature. In civil matters the District Court has jurisdiction in contract and tort (except slander, libel, seduction, slander of title, malicious prosecution and false imprisonment) where the claim does not exceed €20,000 and in actions founded on hire-purchase and credit-sale agreements.

All criminal cases, except those dealt with summarily by a judge in the District Court, are tried by a judge and a jury of 12 members. Juries are also used in some civil cases in the High Court. In a criminal case 10 members of the jury may, in certain circumstances, agree on a verdict, and in a civil case the agreement of nine members is sufficient.

President of the Circuit Court: ESMOND SMYTH.

President of the District Court: PETER A. SMITHWICK.

Religion

CHRISTIANITY

The organization of the churches takes no account of the partition of Ireland into two separate political entities; both the Republic of Ireland and Northern Ireland are subject to a unified ecclesiastical jurisdiction. The Roman Catholic Primate of All Ireland and the Church of Ireland (Protestant Episcopalian) Primate of All Ireland have their seats in Northern Ireland, at Armagh, and the head-quarters of the Presbyterian Church in Ireland is at Belfast, Northern Ireland.

At 31 December 2000 adherents of the Roman Catholic Church represented some 77% of the population. In late 2000 there were some 281,000 adherents of the Presbyterian Church and 55,701 of the Methodist Church. In 2000 there were some 346,000 adherents of the Church of Ireland.

Irish Council of Churches: Inter-Church Centre, 48 Elmwood Ave, Belfast, BT9 6AZ, Northern Ireland; tel. (28) 90382750; fax (28) 90664160; e-mail icpep@aol.com; internet www.irishchurches.org; f. 1922; present adopted 1966; 12 mem. churches; Pres. Rev. HERRON (Church of Ireland); Gen. Sec. Dr R. D. STEVENS.

The Roman Catholic Church

Ireland (including Northern Ireland) comprises four archdioceses and 22 dioceses.

Archbishop of Armagh and Primate of All Ireland: Most Rev. SEÁN B. BRADY, Ara Coeli, Cathedral Rd, Armagh, BT61 7QY, Northern Ireland; tel. (28) 3752-2045; fax (28) 3752-6182; e-mail admin@aracoeli.com; internet www.archdioceseofarmagh.org.

Archbishop of Cashel and Emly: Most Rev. DERMOT CLIFFORD, Archbishop's House, Thurles, Co Tipperary; tel. (504) 21512; fax (504) 22680; e-mail cashelemly@eircom.net.

Archbishop of Dublin and Primate of Ireland: Cardinal DESMOND CONNELL, Archbishop's House, Drumcondra, Dublin 9; tel. (1) 8373732; fax (1) 8369796.

Archbishop of Tuam: Most Rev. MICHAEL NEARY, Archbishop's House, St Jarlath's, Tuam, Co Galway; tel. (93) 24166; fax (93) 28070; e-mail archdiocesetuam@eircom.net.

Numerous Roman Catholic religious orders are strongly established in the country. These play an important role, particularly in the spheres of education, health and social welfare.

Church of Ireland
(The Anglican Communion)

Ireland (including Northern Ireland) comprises two archdioceses and 10 dioceses.

Central Office of the Church of Ireland

Church of Ireland House, Church Ave, Dublin 6; tel. (1) 4978422; fax (1) 4978821; e-mail office@rcbdub.org; internet www.ireland .anglican.org/rcb.html.

346,000 mems (2000); Chief Officer and Sec. to the Representative Church Body D. C. REARDON.

Archbishop of Armagh and Primate of All Ireland and Metropolitan: Most Rev. Lord EAMES, The See House, Cathedral Close, Armagh, BT61 7EE, Northern Ireland; tel. (28) 37527144; fax (28) 37527823; e-mail archbishop@armagh.anglican.org.

Archbishop of Dublin and Primate of Ireland and Metropolitan: Most Rev. JOHN R. W. NEILL, The See House, 17 Temple Rd, Milltown, Dublin 6; tel. (1) 4977849; fax (1) 4976355; e-mail archbishop@dublin.anglian.org.

Orthodox Churches

Greek Orthodox Church in Ireland: Sacred Church of the Annunciation, 46 Arbour Hill, Dublin 7; Pres. Very Rev. Dr IRENEU IOAN CRACIUN.

Russian Orthodox Church in Ireland: Flat 2; Fransiss St, Dublin 8; tel. (1) 8748469; e-mail michaelgogoleff@sourozh.org; internet ireland.ru/orthodox; Priest of Parish Fr MICHAEL GOGOLEFF.

Other Christian Churches

Association of Baptist Churches in Ireland: 19 Ballinderry Rd, Lisburn, BT28 2SA, Northern Ireland; tel. (28) 9266-9366; fax (28) 9266-9377; e-mail abcini@aol.com; internet www.baptistireland.org; Pres. S WEIR; Sec. Pastor W. COLVILLE.

Church of Jesus Christ of Latter-day Saints (Mormon): The Willows, Glasnevin, Dublin 11; tel. (1) 8306899; fax (1) 8304638.

Lutheran Church in Ireland: Lutherhaus, 24 Adelaide Rd, Dublin 2; tel. and fax (1) 6766548; e-mail lutheranchurch@eircom .net; Pres. Pastor Rev. FRITZ-GERT MAYER.

Methodist Church in Ireland: 1 Fountainville Ave, Belfast, BT9 6AN, Northern Ireland; tel. (28) 9032-4554; fax (28) 9023-9467; e-mail secretary@irishmethodist.org; internet www.irishmethodist .org; Sec. Rev. EDMUND T. I. MAWHINNEY.

Moravian Church in Ireland: 25 Church Rd, Gracehill, Ballymena, BT42 2NL, Northern Ireland; tel. (28) 2565-3141; internet www.moravian.org.uk; f. 1749; Chair. of Conf. Rev. V. D. LAUNDER.

Non-Subscribing Presbyterian Church of Ireland: Central Hall, 41 Rosemary St, Belfast, Northern Ireland; tel. (28) 9084-3592; Clerk to Gen. Synod Rev. NIGEL PLAYFAIR.

Presbyterian Church in Ireland: Church House, Fisherwick Place, Belfast, BT1 6DW, Northern Ireland; tel. (28) 9032-2284; fax (28) 9023-6609; e-mail info@presbyterianireland.org; internet www .presbyterianireland.org; Moderator of Gen. Assembly Rev. Dr RUSSELL BIRNEY; Clerk of Assembly and Gen. Sec. Very Rev. Dr S. HUTCHINSON.

The Religious Society of Friends: Swanbrook House, Bloomfield Ave, Morehampton Rd, Dublin 4; tel. and fax (1) 6683684; internet www.ipag.com/quakers; Registrar VALERIE O'BRIEN.

Salvation Army: POB 2098, Dublin Central Mission, Lower Abbey St, Dublin 1; tel. (1) 8740987; fax (1) 8747478; Divisional Dir Capt. HOWARD RUSSELL.

BAHÁ'Í FAITH

National Spiritual Assembly: 24 Burlington Rd, Dublin 4; tel. (1) 6683150; fax (1) 6689632; e-mail nsairl@iol.ie; internet www.bahai.ie.

ISLAM

The Muslim population of the Republic of Ireland was enumerated at 3,875 in the 1991 census. The number of adherents was estimated to total 9,000 in 1996, inclusive of Northern Ireland.

Islamic Cultural Centre of Ireland: 19 Roebuck Rd, Clonskeagh, Dublin 14; tel. (1) 2080000; fax (1) 2080001; e-mail iccislam@eircom.net; internet www.iccislam.ie; f. 1996; Dir Dr NOOH AL-KADDO, Imam Sheikh HUSSEIN HALAWA.

Islamic Foundation of Ireland: 163 South Circular Rd, Dublin 8; tel. (1) 4533242; fax (1) 4532785; e-mail ifi@indigo.ie; f. 1959; religious, cultural, educational and social organization; Imam YAHYA MUHAMMAD AL-HUSSEIN.

JUDAISM

The Jewish community was estimated to number 1,200 in 1996.

Chief Rabbi: Dr YAAKOV PEARLMAN, Herzog House, Zion Rd, Rathgar, Dublin 6; tel. (1) 4923751; fax (1) 4924680; e-mail irishcom@iol.ie.

The Press

A significant feature of the Irish press is the number of weekly newspapers published in provincial centres.

DAILIES

Cork

Evening Echo: 1–6 Academy St, Cork; tel. (21) 4272722; fax (21) 4275112; e-mail echo.ed@eecho.ie; f. 1892; Editor MAURICE GUBBINS; circ. 28,822.

Irish Examiner: Academy St, POB 21, Cork; tel. (21) 272722; fax (21) 275112; e-mail features@examiner.ie; internet www.examiner.ie; f. 1841; Editor TIM VAUGHAN; circ. 57,000.

Dublin

Dublin Daily: 18 Fairview, Dublin 3; tel. (1) 8536000; fax (1) 8536030; e-mail info@dublindaily.com; internet www.dublindaily.ie; f. 2002; Editor LIAM HAYES.

Evening Herald: Independent House, 90 Middle Abbey St, Dublin 1; tel. (1) 8731666; fax (1) 8731787; e-mail herald.news@independent.ie; f. 1891; Editor GERARD O'REGAN; circ. 115,000.

Irish Independent: Independent House, 90 Middle Abbey St, Dublin 1; tel. (1) 7055333; fax (1) 8720304; internet www.independent.ie; f. 1905; Editor VINCENT DOYLE; circ. 170,000.

The Irish Times: 10–16 D'Olier St, POB 74, Dublin 2; tel. (1) 6792022; fax (1) 6793910; e-mail itemail@irish-times.com; internet www.ireland.com; f. 1859; Editor GERALDINE KENNEDY; circ. 119,252.

The Star: Star House, 62A Terenure Rd North, Dublin 6; tel. (1) 4901228; fax (1) 4902193; Editor GERARD O'REAGAN; circ. 85,000.

PRINCIPAL WEEKLY NEWSPAPERS

An Phoblacht/Republican News: 58 Parnell Sq., Dublin 1; tel. (1) 8733611; fax (1) 8733074; e-mail aprn@irlnet.com; internet www.irlnet.com/aprn; f. 1970; Editor MARTIN SPAIN; circ. 20,000.

Anglo-Celt: Anglo-Celt Pl., Cavan; tel. (49) 4331100; fax (49) 4332280; internet www.unison.ie/anglo_celt; f. 1846; Fri. Editor J. F. O'HANLON; circ. 16,000.

Argus: Park St, Dundalk, Co Louth; tel. (42) 9331500; fax (42) 9331643; internet www.unison.ie/the_argus; f. 1835; Thurs. Editor KEVIN MULLIGAN; circ. 11,230.

Clare Champion: Barrack St, Ennis, Co Clare; tel. (65) 6828105; fax (65) 6820374; e-mail editor@clarechampion.ie; internet www.clarechampion.ie; f. 1903; Thurs. Editor GERRY COLLISON; circ. 20,000.

Connacht Tribune: 15 Market St, Galway; tel. (91) 536222; fax (91) 567970; e-mail sales@connacht-tribune.ie; internet www.connacht-tribune.ie; f. 1909; Fri. Editor J. CUNNINGHAM; circ. 29,900.

Connaught Telegraph: Ellison St, Castlebar, Co Mayo; tel. (94) 21711; fax (94) 24007; e-mail conntel@tinet.ie; internet www.con-telegraph.ie; f. 1828; Wed. Editor TOM GILLESPIE; circ. 16,000.

Donegal Democrat: Pier 1, Quay St, Donegal, Co Donegal; tel. (73) 40160; fax (73) 40161; e-mail donegal.democrat@mgn.ie; f. 1919; Tues. and Thurs. Editor MARTIN McGINLEY; circ. 18,000.

Drogheda Independent: 9 Shop St, Drogheda, Co Louth; tel. (41) 9838658; fax (41) 9834271; internet www.unison.ie/drogheda_independent; f. 1884; Thurs. Editor PAUL MURPHY; circ. 14,000.

Dundalk Democrat: 3 Earl St, Dundalk, Co Louth; tel. (42) 9334058; fax (42) 9331399; e-mail dundalkdemo@tinet.ie; f. 1849; Sat. Editor PETER E. KAVANAGH; circ. 16,000.

Dungarvan Leader and Southern Democrat: 78 O'Connell St, Dungarvan, Co Waterford; tel. (58) 41203; fax (58) 45301; e-mail dungarvanleader@cablesurf.com; Wed. Editor COLM J. NAGLE; circ. 13,000.

Dungarvan Observer and Munster Industrial Advocate: Shandon, Dungarvan, Co Waterford; tel. (58) 41205; fax (58) 41559; e-mail info@dungarvanobserver.com; Editor JAMES A. LYNCH; circ. 11,000.

Echo and South Leinster Advertiser: Mill Park Rd, Enniscorthy, Co Wexford; tel. (54) 33231; fax (54) 33506; f. 1902; Wed. Editor JAMES GAHAN; circ. 22,000.

The Guardian: The People Newspapers Ltd, Castle Hill, Enniscorthy, Co Wexford; tel. (54) 33833; fax (54) 35910; e-mail dasherin@hotmail.com; f. 1881; Wed. Man. Dir G. WALSH; circ. 36,000.

Ireland on Sunday: 50 City Quay, Dublin 2; tel. (1) 4179800; fax (1) 4179830; e-mail p.drury@irelandonsunday.com; internet www.irelandonsunday.com; acquired by Associated Newspapers in 2001; Editor PAUL DRURY; circ. 53,053.

Iris Oifigiuil (Official Irish Gazette): 51 St Stephen's Green, Dublin 2; tel. (1) 6476838; fax (1) 6476842; f. 1922; Editor MICK DUNNE.

The Kerryman/The Corkman: Clash Industrial Estate, Tralee, Co Kerry; tel. (66) 21666; fax (66) 21608; e-mail kerryman@indigo.ie; internet www.unison.ie/corkman; f. 1904; Thurs. Editor GERARD COLLERAN; circ. 35,000.

Kilkenny People: 34 High St, Kilkenny; tel. (56) 21015; fax (56) 21414; e-mail info@kilkennypeople.ie; internet www.kilkennypeople.ie; f. 1892; weekly; Editor SEAN HURLEY; circ. 17,000.

Leinster Express: Dublin Rd, Portlaoise, Co Laois; tel. (502) 21666; fax (502) 20491; e-mail lexpress@indigo.ie; internet www.unison.ie/leinster_express; f. 1831; weekly; Man. Editor TEDDY FENNELLY; circ. 18,500.

Leinster Leader: 19 South Main St, Naas, Co Kildare; tel. (45) 897302; fax (45) 897647; e-mail iain@iol.ie; internet www.unison.ie/leinster_leader; f. 1880; Wed. Editor MICHAEL SHEERAN; circ. 15,000.

Leitrim Observer: St George's Terrace, Carrick-on-Shannon, Co Leitrim; tel. (78) 20025; fax (78) 20112; e-mail editor@leitrimobserver.ie; internet www.unison.ie/leitrim_observer; f. 1889; Wed. Editor CLAIRE CASSERLY; circ. 10,000.

Limerick Chronicle: 54 O'Connell St, Limerick; tel. (61) 315233; fax (61) 314804; e-mail lkleader@iol.ie; f. 1766; Tues. Editor BRENDAN HALLIGAN; circ. 8,500.

Limerick Leader: 54 O'Connell St, Limerick; tel. (61) 214500; fax (61) 314804; e-mail admin@limerick-leader.ie; internet www.limerick-leader.ie; f. 1889; 4 a week; Editor BRENDAN HALLIGAN; circ. 29,000 (weekend edn).

Limerick Post: Rutland St, Limerick; tel. (61) 413322; fax (61) 417684; e-mail news@limerickpost.ie; internet www.limerickpost.ie; f. 1986; Thurs. Editor BILLY RYAN; circ. 39,500.

Longford Leader: Market Sq., Longford; tel. (43) 45241; fax (43) 41489; e-mail ads@longford-leader.iol.ie; internet www.longford-leader.ie; f. 1897; Wed. Editor EUGENE McGEE; circ. 13,500.

Longford News: Earl St, Longford; tel. (43) 45627; fax (43) 41549; e-mail info@longford-news.iol.ie; internet www.unison.ie/longford_news; Wed. Editor PAUL HEALY; circ. 24,000.

Mayo News: The Fairgreen, Westport, Co Mayo; tel. (98) 25311; fax (98) 26108; e-mail mayonews@anu.ie; internet www.mayonews.ie; f. 1892; Wed. Man. Editor SEÁN STAUNTON; circ. 35,000.

Meath Chronicle and Cavan and Westmeath Herald: 12 Market Sq., Navan, Co Meath; tel. (46) 79600; fax (46) 23565; e-mail info@meath-chronicle.ie; internet www.meath-chronicle.ie; f. 1897; Sat. Editor KEN DAVIS; circ. 18,000.

Midland Tribune: Emmet St, Birr, Co Offaly; tel. (509) 20003; fax (509) 20588; e-mail midtrib@iol.ie; internet www.unison.ie/midland_tribune; f. 1881; Wed. Editor JOHN O'CALLAGHAN; circ. 16,000.

The Munster Express: 37 The Quay and 1–3 Hanover St, Waterford; tel. (51) 872141; fax (51) 873452; e-mail munster@iol.ie; internet www.munster-express.ie; f. 1859; 2 a week; Editor K. J. WALSH; circ. 19,000.

Nationalist and Leinster Times: 42 Tullow St, Carlow; tel. (503) 70100; fax (503) 31442; e-mail news@leinster-times.ie; f. 1883; weekly; Editor E. COFFEY; circ. 17,000.

Nationalist Newspaper: Queen St, Clonmel, Co Tipperary; tel. (52) 22211; fax (52) 72528; f. 1890; Thurs. Editor TOM CORR; circ. 16,439.

The Northern Standard: The Diamond, Monaghan; tel. (47) 81867; fax (47) 72257; e-mail garysmyth@eircom.net; f. 1839; Fri. Editor MARTIN SMYTH; circ. 15,000.

Offaly Express: Bridge St, Tullamore, Co Offaly; tel. (506) 21744; fax (506) 51930; e-mail lexpress@indigo.ie; internet www.rmbi.ie; weekly; Editor JOHN WHELAN; circ. 18,000 (with Leinster Express).

Roscommon Champion: Abbey St, Roscommon; tel. (903) 25051; fax (903) 25053; e-mail roscommonchampion@tinet.ie; internet homepage.tinet.ie/~roscommonchampion; f. 1927; weekly; Editor PAUL HEALY; circ. 10,000.

Roscommon Herald: Boyle, Co Roscommon; tel. (79) 62622; fax (79) 62926; e-mail roherald@indigo.ie; internet www.unison.ie/roscommon_herald; f. 1859; weekly; Editor CHRISTINA MCHUGH; circ. 17,000.

Sligo Champion: Wine St, Sligo; tel. (71) 9169222; fax (71) 9169040; e-mail editor@sligochampion.ie; internet www.sligochampion.com; f. 1836; Wed. Editor S. FINN; circ. 14,824.

Southern Star: Ilen St, Skibbereen, Co Cork; tel. (28) 21200; fax (28) 21071; e-mail info@southernstar.ie; f. 1889; Sat. Editor LIAM O'REGAN; circ. 16,000.

Sunday Business Post: 80 Harcourt St, Dublin 2; tel. (1) 6026000; fax (1) 6796496; e-mail sbpost@iol.ie; internet www.thepost.ie; Editor TED HARDING; circ. 55,080.

Sunday Independent: Independent House, 90 Middle Abbey St, Dublin 1; tel. (1) 7055333; fax (1) 7055779; e-mail sunday.letters@independent.ie; internet www.independent.ie; f. 1905; Editor AENGUS FANNING; circ. 334,000.

Sunday Tribune: 15 Lower Baggot St, Dublin 2; tel. (1) 6314300; fax (1) 6615302; e-mail editorial@tribune.ie; internet www.tribune.ie; f. 1980; Editor PADDY MURRAY; circ. 86,000.

Sunday World: Newspaper House, 18 Rathfarnham Rd, Terenure, Dublin 6; tel. (1) 4063500; fax (1) 4901838; e-mail news@sundayworld.com; internet www.sundayworld.com; f. 1973; Editor COLM MACGINTY; circ. 308,786.

Tipperary Star: Friar St, Thurles, Co Tipperary; tel. (504) 21122; fax (504) 21110; e-mail info@tipperarystar.ie; internet www.tipperarystar.ie; f. 1909; Wed. Editor MICHAEL DUNDON; circ. 10,000.

Tuam Herald: Dublin Rd, Tuam, Co Galway; tel. (93) 24183; fax (93) 24478; e-mail editor@tuamherald.ie; internet www.unison.ie_tuamherald; f. 1837; Wed. Editor DAVID BURKE; circ. 11,000.

Tullamore Tribune: Church St, Tullamore, Co Offaly; tel. (506) 21152; fax (506) 21927; e-mail tulltrib@eircom.net; internet www.tullamoretribune.ie; f. 1978; Wed. Editor G. J. SCULLY; circ. 10,000.

Waterford News & Star: 25 Michael St, Waterford; tel. (51) 874951; fax (51) 855281; e-mail editor@waterford-news.ie; internet www.waterford-news.ie; f. 1848; Thurs. Editor P. DOYLE; circ. 16,000.

Western People: Francis St, Ballina, Co Mayo; tel. (96) 21188; fax (96) 70208; e-mail info@westernpeople.ie; internet www.westernpeople.ie; f. 1883; Tues. Editor TERENCE REILLY; circ. 24,000.

Westmeath Examiner: 19 Dominick St, Mullingar, Co Westmeath; tel. (44) 48426; fax (44) 40640; e-mail news@westmeathexaminer.ie; internet www.westmeath-examiner.ie; f. 1882; weekly; Man. Dir MARTIN NALLY; circ. 14,000.

Wicklow Times: 1 Eglinton Rd, Bray, Co Wicklow; tel. (1) 2869111; fax (1) 2869074; e-mail wicklowtimes@tinet.ie; fortnightly; Man. Editor SHAY FITZMAURICE; cir. 30,500.

SELECTED PERIODICALS

Banking Ireland: 50 Fitzwilliam Sq., Dublin 2; tel. (1) 6764587; fax (1) 6619781; f. 1898; quarterly; journal of the Inst. of Bankers in Ireland; Editor GERRY LAWLOR; circ. 15,500.

Books Ireland: 11 Newgrove Ave, Dublin 4; tel. (1) 2692185; fax (1) 2604927; e-mail booksi@eircom.net; Editor JEREMY ADDIS.

Business & Finance: 50 Fitzwilliam Sq., Dublin 2; tel. (1) 6764587; fax (1) 6619781; e-mail belenos@tinet.ie; internet www.businessandfinance.ie; f. 1964; weekly; Man. Editor JOHN MCGEE; circ. 11,000.

History Ireland: POB 695, James's St PO, Dublin 8; tel. (1) 4535730; fax (1) 4533234; e-mail info@historyireland.com; internet www.historyireland.com; quarterly; Jt Editors HIRAM MORGAN, TOMMY GRAHAM.

Hot Press: 13 Trinity St, Dublin 2; tel. (1) 2411500; fax (1) 2411538; e-mail info@hotpress.ie; internet www.hotpress.com; fortnightly; music, leisure, current affairs; Editor NIALL STOKES; circ. 21,000.

In Dublin: 6–7 Camden Place, Dublin 2; tel. (1) 4784322; fax (1) 4781055; f. 1976; fortnightly; listings and reviews of entertainments, restaurants; also news and current affairs; Editor DECLAN LAW; circ. 16,000.

Ireland Afloat: 2 Lower Glenageary Rd, Dún Laoghaire, Co Dublin; tel. (1) 2846161; fax (1) 2846192; e-mail info@afloat.ie; internet www.afloat.ie; monthly; sailing and boating; Man. Editor DAVID O'BRIEN; circ. 10,000.

Ireland's Own: Channing House, Rowe St, Wexford; tel. (53) 40140; fax (53) 40192; e-mail irelands.own@peoplenews.ie; f. 1902; weekly; family interest; Editors PHILIP MURPHY, SEAN NOLAN; circ. 50,000.

The Irish Catholic: 55 Lower Gardiner St, Dublin 1; tel. (1) 8555619; fax (1) 8364805; e-mail icn@indigo.ie; weekly; Editor DAVID QUINN; circ. 32,500.

Irish Computer: CPG House, Glenageary Office Park, Dún Laoghaire, Co Dublin; tel. (1) 2847777; fax (1) 2847584; e-mail bskelly@cpg.ie; internet www.irishcomputer.com; f. 1977; monthly; Editor BRIAN SKELLY; circ. 8,000.

Irish Farmers' Journal: Irish Farm Centre, Bluebell, Dublin 12; tel. (1) 4199500; fax (1) 4520876; e-mail editdept@farmersjournal.ie; internet www.farmersjournal.ie; f. 1948; weekly; Editor MATTHEW DEMPSEY; circ. 75,000.

Irish Field: 11–15 D'Olier St, POB 711, Dublin 2; tel. (1) 6758000; fax (1) 6793029; e-mail irish-field@irish-times.ie; f. 1870; weekly; horse racing, breeding and equine leisure; Man. Editor VALENTINE LAMB; circ. 11,788.

Irish Historical Studies: c/o Dept of Modern History, Trinity College, Dublin 2; tel. (1) 6081020; e-mail wvaughan@tcd.ie; 2 a year; Editor Dr DAVID HAYTON.

Irish Journal of Medical Science: Royal Academy of Medicine in Ireland, 6 Kildare St, Dublin 2; tel. (1) 6623706; fax (1) 6611684; e-mail journal@rami.ie; internet www.iformix.com; f. 1832; quarterly; organ of the Royal Academy of Medicine; Editor THOMAS WALSH.

Irish Law Times: Round Hall Sweet & Maxwell, 43 Fitzwilliam Place, Dublin 2; tel. (1) 6625301; fax (1) 6625302; e-mail terri.mcdonnell@roundhall.ie; f. 1983; 20 a year; Editor DAVID BOYLE.

Irish Medical Journal: 10 Fitzwilliam Place, Dublin 2; tel. (1) 6767273; fax (1) 6612758; e-mail imj@imj.ie; internet www.imj.ie; 10 a year; journal of the Irish Medical Org. Editor Dr JOHN MURPHY; circ. 8,000.

The Irish Skipper: Taney Hall, Eglinton Terrace, Dublin 14; tel. (1) 2960000; fax (1) 2960383; e-mail gill@irishskipper.net; internet www.irishskipper.net; f. 1964; monthly; journal of the commercial fishing and aquaculture industries; Editor GILLIAN MILLS.

Irish Tatler: 2 Clanwilliam Court, Lower Mount St, Dublin 2; tel. (1) 2405367; fax (1) 6619757; monthly; Editor VANESSA HARRIS.

Irish University Review: Rm J211, University College, Belfield, Dublin 4; fax (1) 7161174; e-mail anne.fogarty@ucd.ie; 2 a year; literature, history, fine arts, politics, cultural studies; Editor Dr ANNE FOGARTY.

Magill: Campden Place, Dublin 2; tel. (1) 4784322; fax (1) 4784544; e-mail magill@hobson.com; internet www.magill.ie; monthly; current affairs; Editor NIALL STANAGE.

Modern Woman Nationwide: Market Square, Navan, Co Meath; tel. (46) 79600; fax (46) 23565; f. 1984; monthly; Editor MARGOT DAVIS.

Motoring Life: Cyndale Enterprises Ltd, 48 North Great George's St, Dublin 1; tel. (1) 8780444; fax (1) 8787740; f. 1946; monthly; Editor KEVIN FENIX; circ. 9,000.

PC Live!: Prospect House, 3 Prospect Rd, Glasnevin, Dublin 9; tel. (1) 8824444; fax (1) 8300888; e-mail info@scope.ie; internet www.techcentral.ie; monthly; computers and the internet; Editor STEPHEN CAWLEY; circ. 18,000.

Phoenix: 44 Lower Baggot St, Dublin 2; tel. (1) 6611062; fax (1) 6624532; e-mail phoenix@indigo.ie; internet www.phoenix-magazine.com; f. 1983; fortnightly; news and comment; Editor PADDY PRENDIVILLE; circ. 22,000.

Poetry Ireland Review (Éigse Éirann): Upper Yard, Dublin Castle, Dublin 2; tel. (1) 6714632; fax (1) 6714634; e-mail poetry@iol.ie; Editor MICHAEL SMITH.

RTE Guide: Radio Telefís Éireann, Donnybrook, Dublin 4; tel. (1) 2083146; fax (1) 2083085; internet www.rteguide.ie; weekly; programmes of the Irish broadcasting service; Editor RAY WALSH; circ. 145,921.

Studies: 35 Lower Leeson St, Dublin 2; tel. (1) 6766785; fax (1) 6762984; e-mail studies@s-j.ie; internet www.studiesirishreview.com; f. 1912; quarterly review of letters, history, religious and social questions; Editor Fr FERGUS O'DONOGHUE; S.J.

U Magazine: 2 Clanwilliam Court, Lower Mount St, Dublin 2; tel. (1) 2405300; fax (1) 6619757; e-mail letters@umagazine.ie; f. 1979; monthly; Editor FIONNUALA MCCARTHY; circ. 20,750.

Woman's Way: 2 Clanwilliam Court, Lower Mount St, Dublin 2; tel. (1) 6623158; fax (1) 6628719; e-mail ltaylor@smurfit-comms.ie; f. 1963; weekly; Editor LUCY TAYLOR; circ. 67,000.

The Word: Divine Word Missionaries, 3 Pembroke Rd, Dublin 4; tel. (1) 6606646; e-mail wordeditor@eircom.net; f. 1953; monthly; Catholic general interest; Editor (vacant); circ. 24,500.

NEWS AGENCIES

Ireland International News Agency: 51 Wellington Quay, Dublin 2; tel. (1) 6712442; fax (1) 6796586; e-mail iina@eircom.net; Man. Dir DIARMAID MACDERMOTT.

Foreign Bureaux

Agenzia Nazionale Stampa Associata (ANSA) (Italy): 56 Greenfield Park, Knocklyon, Dublin 24; tel. (1) 4941389; fax (1) 4941300; e-mail enzo@iol.ie; Bureau Chief ENZO FARINELLA.

Informatsionnoye Telegrafnoye Agentstvo Rossii—Telegrafnoye Agentstvo Suverennykh Stran (ITAR—TASS) (Russia): 59 Glenbrook Park, Dublin; tel. (1) 2885513; Chief of Bureau EVGENY KLESHKOV.

Reuters Ireland: Kestrel House, Clanwilliam Place, Lower Mount St, Dublin 2; tel. (1) 5001550; fax (1) 5001551; Chief Correspondent KEITH WEIR.

Rossiiskoye Informatsionnoye Agentstvo—Novosti (RIA—Novosti) (Russia) is also represented.

PRESS ORGANIZATIONS

National Newspapers of Ireland: Clyde Lodge, 15 Clyde Rd, Dublin 4; tel. (1) 6689099; fax (1) 6689872; e-mail nni@cullencommunications.ie; internet www.nni.ie; Chair. GAVIN O'REILLY; Co-ordinating Dir FRANK CULLEN.

Regional Newspapers Association of Ireland: Sheridan House, 33 Parkgate St, Dublin 8; tel. (1) 6779049; fax (1) 6779144; e-mail michelle@rnan.ie; internet www.rnan.ie; f. 1917; 37 mems; Pres. NIALL TOWNSEND; CEO NEVILLE GALLOWAY.

Publishers

Anvil Books Ltd: 45 Palmerston Rd, Dublin 6; tel. (1) 4973628; fax (1) 4968263; f. 1964; Irish history and biography, folklore, children's fiction (10 years and above); Dirs R. DARDIS, M. DARDIS.

Attic Press Ltd: Crawford Business Park, Crosses Green, Cork; tel. (21) 4321725; fax (21) 4315329; e-mail corkunip@ucc.ie; internet www.corkuniversitypress.com; imprint of Cork University Press; Dirs SARA WILBOURNE, Prof. DES CLARKE.

Boole Press Ltd: 19 Silchester Rd, Glenageary, Co Dublin; e-mail jmiller@tcd.ie; f. 1979; scientific, technical, medical, scholarly; Man. Dir Dr J. MILLER.

Butterworth Ireland Ltd: 26 Upper Ormond Quay, Dublin 7; tel. (1) 8728514; fax (1) 8731378; e-mail ircustomer@butterworths.co.uk; internet www.butterworths.ie; taxation and law; Chair. P. VIRK.

Comhairle Bhéaloideas Éireann (Folklore of Ireland Council): c/o Dept of Irish Folklore, University College, Belfield, Dublin 4; tel. (1) 693244; Editor Prof. SÉAMUS O'CATHÁIN.

Cork University Press: Crawford Business Park, Crosses Green, Cork; tel. (21) 4902980; fax (21) 4315329; e-mail corkunip@ucc.ie; internet www.corkuniversitypress.com; f. 1925; academic; Man. Dir SARA WILBOURNE.

Dominican Publications: 42 Parnell Sq., Dublin 1; tel. (1) 8731355; fax (1) 8731760; e-mail dompubs@iol.ie; internet www.dominicans.ie/dompubs; f. 1897; religious affairs in Ireland and the developing world, pastoral-liturgical aids; Man. Rev. AUSTIN FLANNERY.

Dundalgan Press (W. Tempest) Ltd: Francis St, Dundalk, Co Louth; tel. (42) 9334013; fax (42) 9332351; e-mail info@dundalgen.ie; f. 1859; history and biography; Man. Dir GERARD GORMLEY.

C J Fallon: POB 1054, Lucan Rd, Palmerstown, Dublin 20; tel. (1) 6166400; fax (1) 6166499; e-mail info@cjfallon.ie; internet www.cjfallon.ie; f. 1927; educational; Man. Dir H. J. MCNICHOLAS.

Four Courts Press: 7 Maples St, Dublin 8; tel. (1) 4534668; fax (1) 4534672; e-mail info@four-courts-press.ie; internet www.four-courts-press.ie; f. 1970; philosophy, theology, Celtic and Medieval studies, art, literature, modern history; Dirs MICHAEL ADAMS, MARTIN HEALY, GERARD O'FLAHERTY.

Gallery Press: Loughcrew, Oldcastle, Co Meath; tel. and fax (49) 8541779; e-mail gallery@indigo.ie; f. 1970; poetry, plays, prose by Irish authors; Editor PETER FALLON.

Gill and Macmillan Ltd: Hume Ave, Park West, Dublin 12; tel. (1) 5009500; fax (1) 5009597; e-mail sales@gillmacmillan.ie; internet www.gillmacmillan.ie; f. 1968; literature, biography, history, mind, body and spirit, social sciences, current affairs, popular fiction and textbooks; Man. Dir M. H. GILL.

Goldsmith Press: Newbridge, Co Kildare; tel. (45) 433613; fax (45) 434648; e-mail de@lol.ie; internet www.irishpoems.com; f. 1972; poetry, Irish art, plays, foreign language, general; Dirs DESMOND EGAN, VIVIENNE ABBOTT.

Irish Academic Press: 44 Northumberland Rd, Dublin 4; tel. (1) 6688244; fax (1) 6686769; e-mail info@iap.ie; internet www.iap.ie; f. 1974; academic, mainly history and Irish studies; Dirs FRANK CASS, MICHAEL ZAIDNER, STEWART CASS; Man. Editor RACHEL MILOTTE.

Lilliput Press: 62/63 Sitric Rd, Arbour Hill, Dublin 7; tel. (1) 6711647; fax (1) 6711233; e-mail info@lilliputpress.ie; internet www.lilliputpress.ie; ecology and environment, literary criticism, biography, Irish history, general; Publr ANTONY FARRELL.

Mentor Books: 43 Furze Rd, Sandyford Industrial Estate, Dublin 18; tel. (1) 2952112; fax (1) 2952114; e-mail all@mentorbooks.ie; internet www.mentorbooks.ie; adult and children's fiction and non-fiction, educational; Man. Dir DANIEL MCCARTHY.

Mercier Press Ltd: Douglas Village, Cork; tel. (21) 4899858; fax (21) 4899887; e-mail books@mercierpress.ie; internet www.mercierpress.ie; f. 1946; Irish folklore, history, literature, fiction, politics, humour, religious; Chair. GEORGE EATON; Man. Dir JOHN F. SPILLANE.

O'Brien Press Ltd: 20 Victoria Rd, Rathgar, Dublin 6; tel. (1) 4923333; fax (1) 4922777; e-mail books@obrien.ie; internet www.obrien.ie; f. 1974; biography, history, sport, Celtic, politics, travel, crime, children's; Man. Dir MICHAEL O'BRIEN.

Poolbeg Press Ltd: 123 Baldoyle Industrial Estate, Dublin 13; tel. (1) 8321477; fax (1) 8321430; e-mail poolbeg@poolbeg.com; internet www.poolbeg.com; f. 1976; general, poetry, politics, children's; Man. Dir PHILIP MACDERMOTT.

Round Hall Ltd: 43 Fitzwilliam Place, Dublin 2; tel. (1) 6625301; fax (1) 6625302; e-mail info@roundhall.ie; internet www.roundhall.ie; law books and journals; Dir ELANOR MCGARRY.

Royal Irish Academy (Acadamh Ríoga na hÉireann): 19 Dawson St, Dublin 2; tel. (1) 6762570; fax (1) 6762346; e-mail admin@ria.ie; internet www.ria.ie; f. 1785; humanities and sciences; Pres. M. E. F. RYAN; Exec. Sec. PATRICK BUCKLEY; Editor RACHEL MCNICHOLL.

Sáirséal-Ó Marcaigh: 13 Bóthar Chríoch Mhór, Dublin 11; tel. and fax (1) 8378914; books in Irish; Dirs AINGEAL Ó MARCAIGH, CAOIMHÍN Ó MARCAIGH.

Sporting Books: 4 Sycamore Rd, Mount Merrion, Co Dublin; tel. (1) 2887914; fax (1) 2885779; sports; Publr RAYMOND SMITH.

Town House/Country House: Trinity House, Charleston Rd, Dublin 6; tel. (1) 4972399; fax (1) 4970927; e-mail books@townhouse.ie; fiction, biography, art, environmental, general; Dirs TREASA COADY, JIM COADY.

Veritas Publications: 7–8 Lower Abbey St, Dublin 1; tel. (1) 8788177; fax (1) 8786507; e-mail publications@veritas.ie; internet www.veritas.ie; f. 1900; religious and educational; Dir MAURA HYLAND.

Wolfhound Press: 68 Mountjoy Sq., Dublin 1; tel. (1) 8740354; fax (1) 8720207; internet www.wolfhound.ie; f. 1974; literature, biography, art, children's, fiction, history; Publr SÉAMUS CASHMAN.

Woodtown Music Publications Ltd: Teach an Dáma, Stráid an Dáma, Dublin 2; tel. and fax (1) 6793664; f. 1966; original works by Irish composers; Chair. GARECH DE BRÚN.

Government Publishing House

Stationery Office: Government Publications, 51 St Stephen's Green, Dublin 2; tel. (1) 6476849; fax (1) 6476843.

PUBLISHERS' ASSOCIATION

Irish Book Publishers' Association: 43–44 Temple Bar, Dublin 2; tel. (1) 6707393; fax (1) 6707642; e-mail info@publishingireland.com; internet www.publishingireland.com; f. 1970; 54 mems; Pres. FERGAL TOBIN; Exec. Dir ORLA MARTIN.

Broadcasting and Communications

TELECOMMUNICATIONS

Office of the Director of Telecommunications Regulation: Abbey Court, Irish Life Centre, Lower Abbey St, Dublin 1; tel. (1) 8049600; fax (1) 8049680; internet www.odtr.ie; f. 1997 as the regulatory authority for Ireland's postal and telecommunications sectors; issues licences to service providers; manages the interconnection of telecommunications networks; approves equipment and oversees national telephone numbering; Dir ETAIN DOYLE.

Cable and Wireless Ltd: 1 Airton Rd, Tallaght, Dublin 24; tel. (1) 4346333; fax (1) 4346339; e-mail info@candw.ie; internet www.candw.ie; independent telecommunications services provider; supplies telecommunications equipment including video-conferencing systems and paging devices; Man. Dir EDDIE BRENNAN; Gen. Man. PAT MACGRATH.

Eircell Vodafone: Unit 9, Richview Office Park, Dublin 14; tel. (1) 2037777; fax (1) 2037778; e-mail custcare@eircell.ie; internet www.eircell.ie; a subsidiary of Vodafone Ltd (UK), providing national mobile telecommunications services; CEO PAUL DONOVAN.

eircom plc: St Stephen's Green West, Dublin 2; tel. (1) 6714444; fax (1) 6716916; e-mail press-office@eircom.ie; internet www.eircom.ie; f. 1984; fmrly Telecom Éireann; nationalized body responsible for the provision of national and international telecommunications services, including mobile services; partially privatized in 1999, acquired by Valentia Telecommunications Ltd in September 2001; Chair. Sir ANTHONY O'REILLY; CEO Dr PHILIP NOLAN.

eircom net: Unit B, East Point Business Park, Fairview, Dublin 3; tel. (1) 7010011; fax (1) 7010185; e-mail info@eircom.net; internet www.eircom.net; f. 1996 to provide internet services to both business and private customers; Gen. Man. FINTAN LAWLEE.

O2: 76 Lower Baggot St, Dublin 2; tel. (1) 6095000; e-mail customercare@o2.ie; internet www2.o2.ie; f. 1997 as ESAT Digiphone; private telecommunications company; purchased by British Telecommunications PLC in Jan. 2000; renamed as above in May 2002; CEO DANUTA GRAY.

BROADCASTING

The Radio and Television Act of 1988 provided for the establishment of an independent television station, an independent national radio service and a series of local radio stations (see below).

Broadcasting Commission of Ireland (BCI): Marine House, Clanwilliam Place, Dublin 2; tel. (1) 6760966; fax (1) 6760948; e-mail info@bci.ie; internet www.bci.ie; f. 1988 as the Independent Radio and Television Commission; renamed as above in 2001 following the introduction of the 2001 Broadcasting Act; established by the Govt to ensure the creation, licensing, development and monitoring of independent broadcasting in Ireland; also responsible for the licensing of new digital, cable, multi-mode digital and satellite television services, as well as the development of codes of programming and advertising standards for television and radio services and the provision of a secretariat to the Broadcasting Complaints Commission; operations are financed by levies paid by franchised stations; Chair. CONOR J. MAGUIRE; CEO MICHAEL O'KEEFFE.

Broadcasting Complaints Commission: 2–5 Warrington Place, Dublin 2; tel. (1) 6761097; f. 1997; responsible for acting upon complaints relating to material broadcast by RTE and independent broadcasting stations; Chair. OONAH McCRANN.

Radio

Radio Telefís Éireann (RTE): Donnybrook, Dublin 4; tel. (1) 2083111; fax (1) 2083080; internet www.rte.ie; national broadcasting corpn; f. 1960; financed by net licence revenue and sale of advertising time, which is limited to 10% of transmission time; governed by Authority of nine mems, appointed by the GOA; operates six radio networks, Radio 1 (news, music, drama and variety shows), 2FM (popular music), Lyric FM (music, arts and culture), Raidió na Gaeltachta (see below), Radio OneWorld (multicultural programmes), and Radio Ceolnet (an internet only channel broadcasting traditional Irish music); Chair. of Authority PATRICK J. WRIGHT; Dir-Gen. BOB COLLINS; Dir of Programmes (Radio) ADRIAN MOYNES.

Raidió na Gaeltachta: Casla, Connemara, Co Galway; tel. (91) 506677; fax (91) 506666; e-mail rnag@rte.ie; internet www.rnag.ie; f. 1972; broadcasts 168 hours per week in Irish language; financed by RTE; Controller TOMAS MAC CONIOMAIRE.

100-102 Today FM: Today FM House, 124 Upper Abbey St, Dublin 1; tel. (1) 8049000; fax (1) 8049099; e-mail 100-102@todayfm.com; internet www.todayfm.com; f. 1998; national, independent station; Chair. JOHN McCOLGAN; CEO WILLIE O'REILLY.

Dublin's 98 FM: The Malt House, Grand Canal Quay, Dublin 2; tel. (1) 6708989; fax (1) 6708969; e-mail info@98fm.ie; internet www.98fm.ie; provides news service to independent local radio stations under contract from the BCI; CEO DAN HEALY; Head of News JOHN KEOGH.

There are also local radio stations operating under the supervision of the Independent Radio and Television Commission.

Television

Radio Telefís Éireann (RTE): see above; operates three television channels: RTE 1, Network 2 and TG4—an Irish language television service began transmissions in November 1996; Chair. of Authority PATRICK J. WRIGHT; Dir-Gen. BOB COLLINS; Dir of Programmes (Television) and Dir of News CATHAL GOAN; Dir of Digital Media EUGENE MURRAY.

TV3: Dublin; e-mail info@tv3; internet www.tv3.ie; f. 1998; first national, commercial, independent television network; Chair. JAMES MORRIS; Man. Dir and CEO RICK HETHERINGTON; Dir of Programming MATTHEW SALWAY; Dir of News ANDREW HANLON.

Finance

(cap. = capital; p.u. = paid up; res = reserves; dep. = deposits; m. = million; brs = branches; amounts in Irish pounds (IR£) or euros (€) unless otherwise stated)

BANKING

Ireland participates in the European System of Central Banks, which consists of the European Central Bank and the national central banks of all 15 EU Member States.

Central Bank

Bank Ceannais na hÉireann (Central Bank of Ireland): POB 559, Dame St, Dublin 2; tel. (1) 6716666; fax (1) 6716561; e-mail en@centralbank.ie; internet www.centralbank.ie; f. 1942; bank of issue; cap. and res €2,882m., dep. €9,181m. (Dec. 2000); Gov. JOHN HURLEY; Dir-Gen. LIAM BARRON.

Principal Banks

ACCBANK PLC: Charlemont Place, Dublin 2; tel. (1) 4184000; fax (1) 4184444; e-mail info@accbank.ie; internet www.accbank.ie; f. 1927; state-owned; provides banking services to personal customers, small businesses, farmers and corporate entities; total assets €3,065m. (Dec. 1999); Chair. P. O'CONNOR; CEO C. DARLING; 49 brs.

AIB Capital Markets PLC: AIB International Centre, IFSC, Dublin 1; tel. (1) 8740222; fax (1) 6795933; e-mail grouppa@iol.ie; internet www.aib.ie/capitalmarkets; f. 1966; merchant banking and investment management; cap. p.u. IR£8m., dep. IR£1,105m. (Dec. 1997); Man. Dir COLM E. DOHERTY; 3 brs.

AIB Group: POB 452, Bankcentre, Ballsbridge, Dublin 4; tel. (1) 6600311; fax (1) 6604715; e-mail aibtoday@aib.ie; internet www.aibgroup.com; f. 1966; fmrly Allied Irish Banks PLC; cap. €291m., res €2,020m., dep. €72,813m. (Dec. 2002); Chair. DERMOT GLEESON; CEO MICHAEL D. BUCKLEY; over 1,000 brs and offices.

Anglo Irish Bank Corporation PLC: 18–21 St Stephen's Green, Dublin 2; tel. (1) 6162000; fax (1) 6611852; e-mail anglo@iol.ie; internet www.angloirishbank.ie; f. 1964; cap. €91.1m., res €50m., dep. €9,852.3m. (Sept. 2000); Chair. PETER MURRAY; CEO TIARNAN O'MAHONEY; 9 brs.

Ansbacher Bankers Ltd: 18–21 St Stephen's Green, Dublin 2; tel. (1) 6613699; fax (1) 6618408; f. 1950; wholly-owned subsidiary of Anglo Irish Bank Corporation PLC; Chair. SEÁN P. FITZPATRICK.

Bank of Ireland Asset Management: 26 Fitzwilliam Place, Dublin 2; tel. (1) 6616433; fax (1) 6616688; e-mail biaminfo@biam.boi.ie; internet www.biam.ie; f. 1966; investment management; CEO WILLIAM R. COTTER.

Bank of Ireland Group: Lower Baggot St, Dublin 2; tel. (1) 6615933; fax (1) 6615671; e-mail careline@boimail.com; internet www.bankofireland.ie; f. 1783; cap. €679m., res €3,521m., dep. €63,694m. (March 2002); Gov. LAURENCE CROWLEY; CEO MICHAEL D. SODEN; 484 brs.

Bank of Scotland (Ireland) Ltd: Canada House, 65–68 St Stephen's Green, Dublin 2; tel. (1) 4083500; fax (1) 4083656; e-mail info@bankofscotland.ie; internet www.bankofscotland.ie; f. 1965 as Equity Bank Ltd, name changed as above in 2000; cap. and res €105.8m., dep. €1,878.9m. (Feb. 2001); Chair. PHIL FLYNN; Chief Exec. MARK DUFFY; 2 brs.

Barclays Bank PLC: 47/48 St Stephen's Green, Dublin 2; tel. (1) 6611777; fax (1) 6623141; internet www.barclays.com; total assets IR£ 569m. (Dec. 1996); Man. Dir BILL HANDLEY.

Bear Stearns Bank PLC: Harcourt Centre, Charlotte Way, Dublin 2; tel. (1) 4026200; fax (1) 4026237; e-mail plambert@bear.com; internet www.bearstearns.com; f. 1996; cap. US $1.0m., res US $94.0m., dep. US $2,765.4m. (Nov. 2000); Chair. PASCAL LAMBERT.

BNP Paribas Dublin: 5 George's Dock, Dublin 1; tel. (1) 6125000; fax (1) 6125100; e-mail dublin.desk@bnpparibas.com; Chair. J. P. BERNARD; Gen. Man. F. VAN DEN BOSCH.

BW Bank Ireland PLC: POB 4566, 6 George's Dock, IFSC, Dublin 1; tel. (1) 6701812; fax (1) 6701817; e-mail info@bwbank.ie; internet www.bw-bank.com; f. 1994; cap. €6.7m., res €127.9m., dep. €2,662.5m. (Dec. 2000); Chair. DIETER MAIER; Man. Dir BRYAN HIGGINS.

CIBC World Markets Ireland Ltd: 28 North Wall Quay, IFSC, Dublin 1; tel. (1) 6624400; fax (1) 6624371; f. 1994 as CIBC Wood Grundy Ireland Ltd; cap. US $0.5m., res US $397.5m. (Oct. 2001); Chair. and CEO IAN LETCHFORD.

Commerzbank International (Ireland): POB 7616, Commerzbank House, Guild St, IFSC, Dublin 1; tel. (1) 6491200; fax (1) 6491299; f. 1998; cap. €153.4m. (Dec. 2000); Chair. JÜRGEN LEMMER; Man. Dirs JOHN BOWDEN, STEPHAN WURM.

DePfa-Bank Europe PLC: International House, 3 Harbourmaster Pl., IFSC, Dublin 1; tel. (1) 6071600; fax (1) 8290213; e-mail information@depfa.com; internet www.depfa.com; cap. €593m., total assets €44,962m. (Dec. 2001); Chair. GERHARD E. BRUCKERMANN; Man. Dir DERMOT CAHILLANE.

Dresdner Bank (Ireland) PLC: La Touche House, IFSC, Dublin 1; tel. (1) 8181100; fax (1) 8181500; e-mail dbirl@dresdner-bank.ie; f. 1995; subsidiary of Allianz (AG), Germany; cap. €26.0m., res €229.5m., dep. €1,603.0m. (Dec. 2001); Chair. WOLFGANG BAERTZ; Man. Dirs WERNER SCHWANBERG, THOMAS KIEFER.

DZ Bank Ireland PLC: Trade Centre, IFSC, Dublin 1; tel. (1) 6700715; fax (1) 8290298; e-mail info@dzbank.ie; f. 1994 as SGZ (Ireland) PLC, name changed in 2001; cap. €153.4., dep. €1,930.5m. (Dec. 2000); Man. Dirs ANDREAS NEUGEBAUER, MARK JACOB.

Guinness and Mahon (Ireland) Ltd: 56–59 St Stephen's Green, Dublin 2; tel. (1) 7095200; fax (1) 7095210; internet www.gmbank.ie; f. 1836; wholly-owned subsidiary of Irish Life and Permanent PLC; cap. and res IR£5.7m., dep. IR£69.3m. (Dec. 1996); Chair. and Man. Dir BRIAN MCCONNELL.

ICC Bank PLC: 72–74 Harcourt St, Dublin 2; tel. (1) 4155555; fax (1) 6717797; e-mail info@icc.ie; internet www.icc.ie; f. 1933; privatized in 2000; industrial and commercial financing; cap. €46.9m., res €5.7m., dep. €3,508.1m. (Oct. 2000); Chair. PHIL FLYNN; Man. Dir MICHAEL QUINN; 6 brs.

IIB Bank Ltd: 91 Merrion Sq., Dublin 2; tel. (1) 6619744; fax (1) 6785034; e-mail info@iib-bank.ie; internet www.iib-bank.ie; f. 1973; subsidiary of Kredietbank NV, Belgium; merchant banking; cap. €79.7m., res €185.7m., dep. €7,509.9m. (Dec. 2000); Chair. PATRICK C. MCEVOY; CEO EDWARD A. MARAH; 1 br.

Irish Life and Permanent PLC: Lower Abber St, Dublin 1; tel. (1) 6615577; fax (1) 6615828; e-mail info@irishpermanent.ie; internet www.irishpermanent.ie; f. 1884 as Irish Temperance Building Society, name changed in 1999; cap €92.3m., res €2,741.4m., dep. €10,625.3m. (Dec. 2000); Chair. ROY DOUGLAS; CEO DAVID WENT; 94 brs.

Lombard & Ulster Banking Ltd: Ulster Bank Group Centre, George's Quay, Dublin 2; tel. (1) 6085000; fax (1) 6085001; e-mail info@lombard.ie; internet www.lombard.ie; f. 1971; subsidiary of Ulster Bank Ltd; cap. p.u. IR£2.8m. (Dec. 1996); Chair. M. RAFFERTY; CEO B. KINGSTON; 13 brs.

JP Morgan Bank (Ireland) PLC: Chase Manhattan House, IFSC, Dublin 1; tel. (1) 6123000; fax (1) 6123123; internet www.chase.com; f. 1968; cap. US $8.3m., res US $43.8m., dep. US $483.8m. (Dec. 1999); in Sept. 2000 Chase Manhattan and J. P. Morgan agreed to merge to form J. P. Morgan Chase and Co, name changed as above in October 2001; Man. Dir FRANK GAYNOR; 1 br.

National Irish Bank Ltd: International House, 3 Harbourmaster Pl., IFSC, Dublin 1; tel. (1) 4385000; fax (1) 4385198; internet www.nib.ie; f. 1986; subsidiary of National Australia Group; cap. €62.6m., res €30.8m., dep. €3,003.9m. (Dec. 2001); Chair. Sir DAVID FELL; CEO DONALD PRICE; 59 brs.

Pfizer International Bank Europe: La Touche House, IFSC, Dublin 1; tel. (1) 6700277; fax (1) 6700466; f. 1985; cap.

US $410,000., dep. US $61.9m. (Nov. 2000); Man. Dir B. MICHAEL SENIOR.

Rabobank Ireland PLC: George's Dock House, IFSC, Dublin 1; tel. (1) 6076100; fax (1) 6701724; e-mail liz.mansfield@dub.rabobank .com; internet www.rabobank-ireland.ie; f. 1994; corporate and investment banking; owned by Rabobank Nederland; cap. €6.4m., res €338.1m., dep. €15,792.0m. (Dec. 2000); Chair. WOUTER J. KOLFF; Man. Dir FERGUS MURPHY.

Rheinhyp Bank Europe PLC: POB 4343, Commerzbank House, Guild St, IFSC, Dublin 1; tel. (1) 6491600; fax (1) 6491659; e-mail rheinhyp@indigo.ie; f. 1994 as RHEINHYP Europe PLC, name changed in 1995; cap. €7.5m., res €95.8m., dep. €2,738.3m., (Dec. 2001); Chair. Dr KARSTEN VON KÖLLER; Man. Dir CHRISTIAN FERCHLAND.

Sanpaolo IMI Bank Ireland PLC: AIB Trade Centre, IFSC, Custom House Dock, Dublin 1; tel. (1) 8290500; fax (1) 8290280; e-mail sanpaoloirl@sanpaolo.ie; f. 1987; cap. US $7.5m., res US $407.4m., dep. US $262.5m. (Dec. 2000); Chair. MARIO TROMBETTI; Man. Dir GIUSEPPE SCARABOSIO.

Ulster Bank Ltd: 33 College Green, Dublin 2; tel. (1) 6777623; fax (1) 6775035; subsidiary of National Westminster Bank PLC (United Kingdom); cap. and res IR£115.9m., dep. IR£7,767.2m. (Dec. 1997); Chair. Sir GEORGE QUIGLEY; CEO M. J. WILSON; 205 brs.

Ulster Bank Markets Ltd: Ulster Bank Group Centre, George's Quay, Dublin 2; tel. (1) 6084000; fax (1) 6084288; e-mail admin@ ulsterbank.com; internet www.ulsterbank.com; f. 1973; subsidiary of Ulster Bank Ltd; total assets IR£5,061m. (Nov. 1998); Chair. MARTIN RAFFERTY; CEO PATRICK M. MCMAHON.

UniCredito Italiano Bank (Ireland) PLC: La Touche House, IFSC, Dublin 1; tel. (1) 6702000; fax (1) 6702100; e-mail enquiry@ creditodublin.ie; internet www.unicredito.ie; f. 1996 as Credito Italiano Bank (Ireland) PLC, name changed in 1999; cap. €7.8m., res €405.4m., dep. €4,170.3m. (Dec. 2000); Chair. BRIAN J. HILLERY; Man. Dir FRANCO SCHEPES.

Westdeutsche Landesbank (Ireland) PLC: 2 Harbourmaster Place, IFSC, Dublin 1; tel. (1) 6127199; fax (1) 6127107; e-mail info@ westlb.ie; f. 1978 as Standard Chartered Bank Ireland Ltd, name changed in 1996; cap. €17.7m., res €278.0m., dep €3,559.0m. (Dec. 2000); Chair. Dr W. A. PRAUTZSCH; Man. Dir T. KAISER.

Savings Banks

An Post Savings and Investments: College House, Townsend St, Dublin 2; tel. (1) 7057000; fax (1) 7057636; internet www.anpost.ie; f. 1861; dep.€4,500m. (Dec. 2001); Chief Exec. JOHN HYNES; 1,356 brs.

TSB Bank: TSB Corporate Centre, Blackrock, Co Dublin; tel. (1) 2124000; fax (1) 2124001; e-mail info@tsbbank.ie; internet www .tsbbank.ie; f. 1992; total assets IR£2,028.1m. (Dec. 1999); Chair. FINBARR GOLDEN; CEO HARRY W. LORTON; 80 brs.

Banking Associations

The Institute of Bankers in Ireland: Nassau House, Nassau St, Dublin 2; tel. (1) 6793311; fax (1) 6793504; e-mail info@instbank.ie; internet www.institute-of-bankers.com; f. 1898; 19,000 mems; Pres. AIDAN BRADY; CEO ANTHONY WALSH.

Irish Bankers' Federation: Nassau House, Nassau St, Dublin 2; tel. (1) 6715311; fax (1) 6796680; e-mail ibf@ibf.ie; internet www.ibis .ie; more than 50 mems; Dir-Gen. JAMES A. BARDON.

STOCK EXCHANGE

The Irish Stock Exchange: 28 Anglesea St, Dublin 2; tel. (1) 6174200; fax (1) 6776045; e-mail info@ise.ie; internet www.ise.ie; f. 1799 as the Dublin Stock Exchange; amalgamated in 1973 with the United Kingdom stock exchanges to form The International Stock Exchange of the United Kingdom and the Republic of Ireland; separated from The International Stock Exchange in 1995; operates independently under the supervision of the Central Bank of Ireland; Chair. D. KINGSTON; CEO TOM HEALY; 99 mems.

SUPERVISORY BODY

In February 2001 the Government announced its intention to establish a single regulatory authority for financial services. Under the umbrella of the Central Bank of Ireland and Financial Services Authority, the Irish Financial Services Regulatory Authority will be responsible for the regulation of banking practices and other financial services in addition to overseeing consumer protection. It was expected to be established in mid-2003. The Government also approved the establishment of the Irish Monetary Authority to handle the implementation of monetary policy and which will report to the European Central Bank.

Irish Financial Services Regulatory Authority: POB 559, Dame St, Dublin 2; tel. (1) 4344592; fax (1) 4344060; e-mail info@

ifsra.ie; internet www.ifsra.ie; Chair. BRIAN PATTERSON; Chief Exec. LIAM O'REILLY.

INSURANCE

Principal Companies

AXA PMPA Insurance Ltd: Wolfe Tone House, Wolfe Tone St, Dublin 1; tel. (1) 8726444; fax (1) 8726536; internet www.axa.ie; f. 1967; CEO JOHN O'NEILL.

Canada Life Assurance (Ireland) Ltd: Canada Life House, Temple Rd, Blackrock, Co Dublin; tel. (1) 2102000; fax (1) 210220; internet www.canadalife.ie; f. 1903; Man. Dir TOM BARRY.

Eagle Star Insurance: Eagle Star House, Ballsbridge Park, Dublin 2; tel. (1) 6770666; fax (1) 6670644; internet www.eaglestar.ie; f. 1919; Man. Dir IAN C. STUART.

Eagle Star Life Assurance Co (Ireland) Ltd: Eagle Star House, Frascati Rd, Blackrock, Co Dublin; tel. (1) 2831301; fax (1) 2831578; e-mail customerservices@eaglestarlife.ie; internet www .eaglestarlife.ie; f. 1950; Man. Dir M. J. BRENNAN.

Hansard Europe Ltd: POB 43, Enterprise House, Frascati Rd, Blackrock, Co Dublin; tel. (1) 2112800; fax (1) 2112850; e-mail heladmin@hansard.com; internet www.hansard.com.

Hibernian Group PLC: Haddington Rd, Dublin 4; tel. (1) 6078000; fax (1) 6608730; internet www.hibernian.ie; f. 1908; life and general; Chair. J. P. CULLITON; CEO P. J. McGORRIAN.

Irish Life and Permanent PLC: Irish Life Centre, Lower Abbey St, Dublin 1; tel. (1) 7042000; fax (1) 7041900; e-mail customer .sales@irishlife.ie; internet www.irishlife.ie; f. 1939; financial services; merger with Lloyds TSB pending; Chair. CONOR McCARTHY; Man. Dir DAVID WENT.

Lifetime Assurance Co Ltd: Lifetime House, Lower Baggot St, Dublin 2; tel. (1) 7039500; fax (1) 6620811; e-mail info@lifetime.ie; internet www.lifetime.ie; f. 1987; life; Chair. HENRY J. BYRNE; Man. Dir ROY KEENAN.

New Ireland Assurance Co PLC: 11–12 Dawson St, Dublin 2; tel. (1) 6172000; fax (1) 6172800; e-mail info@newireland.ie; internet www.newireland.ie; f. 1924; Chair. and Man. Dir JOHN F. CASEY.

Royal & SunAlliance: 13–17 Dawson St, Dublin 2; tel. (1) 6771851; fax (1) 6717625; e-mail talktous@royalsunalliance.ie; internet www .royalsunalliance.ie; Gen. Man. PAUL DONALDSON.

Standard Life Assurance Co: 90 St Stephen's Green, Dublin 2; tel. (1) 6397000; fax (1) 6397262; e-mail marketing@standardlife.ie; internet www.standardlife.ie; f. 1834; life assurance, pensions, investments and annuities; Gen. Man. R. O'RIORDAN.

Zurich Insurance Co: Eagle Star House, Ballsbridge Park, Ballsbridge, Dublin 4; tel. (1) 6670666; fax (1) 6670644; internet www .zurich.com; owned by Eagle Star Insurance; property, liability, motor; CEO IAN STUART.

Insurance Associations

Insurance Institute of Ireland: 39 Molesworth St, Dublin 2; tel. (1) 6772582; fax (1) 6772621; e-mail iii@iol.ie; internet www .insurance-institute.ie; f. 1885; Pres. PAUL DONALDSON; CEO DENIS HEVEY; 5,000 mems.

Irish Brokers' Association: 87 Merrion Sq., Dublin 2; tel. (1) 6613067; fax (1) 6619955; e-mail iba@iol.ie; internet www .irishbrokers.com; Pres. PAT TREACY; 600 mems.

Irish Insurance Federation: Insurance House, 39 Molesworth St, Dublin 2; tel. (1) 6761820; fax (1) 6761943; e-mail fed@iif.ie; internet www.iif.ie; Pres. IAN C. STUART; CEO MICHAEL KEMP.

Professional Insurance Brokers' Association (PIBA): 32 Greenmount Office Park, Harolds Cross, Dublin 6W; tel. (1) 4020250; fax (1) 4736920; e-mail info@piba.ie; internet www.piba.ie; CEO DIARMUID KELLY.

Trade and Industry

GOVERNMENT AGENCIES

An Post (The Post Office): General Post Office, Dublin 1; tel. (1) 7057000; fax (1) 8723553; e-mail press-office@anpost.ie; internet www.anpost.ie; f. 1984; provides national postal, savings and agency services through c. 1,800 outlets; Chair. STEPHEN O'CONNOR; CEO JOHN HYNES.

FÁS—Foras Áiseanna Saothair (State Training and Employment Authority): 27–33 Upper Baggot St, Dublin 4; tel. (1) 6070500; fax (1) 6070600; e-mail info@fas.ie; internet www.fas.ie; f. 1988; responsible for the provision of specific skills training, apprenticeships and traineeships, employment programmes provided by a network of 70 nation-wide, local and regional centres; supports co-operative and community enterprise; offers an industrial advisory service; public recruitment service at all levels of occupations; Chair. BRIAN GEOGHEGAN; Dir-Gen. RODY MOLLOY.

FORFÁS: Wilton Park House, Wilton Place, Dublin 2; tel. (1) 6073000; fax (1) 6073030; e-mail info@forfas.ie; internet www.forfas .ie; f. 1993 to provide advice and to co-ordinate national industrial and technological policy; co-ordinates Enterprise Ireland and IDA Ireland (see below); Chair. PETER CASSELLS; Chief Exec. JOHN TRAVERS.

National Economic and Social Council (NESC): , 16 Parnell Sq., Dublin 1; tel. (1) 8146390; fax (1) 8146358; e-mail info@nesc.ie; internet www.nesc.ie; f. 1973; analyses and reports on strategic issues relating to the efficient development of the economy and the achievement of social justice; Dir Dr RORY O'DONNELL.

DEVELOPMENT ORGANIZATIONS

Enterprise Ireland: Wilton Park House, Wilton Place, Dublin 2; tel. (1) 8082000; fax (1) 8082020; e-mail client.service@ enterprise-ireland.com; internet www.enterprise-ireland.com; f. 1998; combines the activities of the fmr An Bord Tráchtála, Forbairt and the in-company training activities of FÁS (see above); Chair. PATRICK J. MOLLOY; CEO DAN FLINTER.

IDA Ireland: Wilton Park House, Wilton Place, Dublin 2; tel. (1) 6034000; fax (1) 6034040; e-mail idaireland@ida.ie; internet www .idaireland.com; f. 1993; government agency with national responsibility for securing new investment from overseas in manufacturing and international services and for encouraging existing foreign enterprises in Ireland to expand their businesses; Chair. JOHN DUNNE; CEO SEAN DORGAN.

Irish Productivity Centre: 4B–5 Blanchardstown Corporate Park, Dublin 15; tel. (1) 8227125; fax (1) 8227116; e-mail ipc@ipc.ie; internet www.ipc.ie; aims to increase industrial productivity in Ireland; its council is composed of representatives from the Irish Business and Employers' Confed. and the Irish Congress of Trade Unions in equal numbers; offers consultancy services and practical assistance to Irish cos; CEO TOM McGUINNESS.

Teagasc (Agriculture and Food Development Authority): 19 Sandymount Ave, Dublin 4; tel. (1) 6376000; fax (1) 6688023; e-mail info@ hq.teagasc.ie; internet www.teagasc.ie; f. 1988; provides advisory, research, educational and training services to agri-food sector and rural communities; Chair. Dr TOM O'DWYER; Nat. Dir JIM FLANAGHAN.

CHAMBERS OF COMMERCE

The Chambers of Commerce of Ireland: 22 Merrion Sq., Dublin 2; tel. (1) 6612888; fax (1) 6612811; e-mail info@chambersireland.ie; internet www.chambersireland.ie; f. 1923; represents c. 10,000 businesses and 40 direct corporate mems; Pres. MONICA LEECH; Chief Exec. SIMON NUGENT.

Cork Chamber of Commerce: Fitzgerald House, Summerhill North, Cork; tel. (21) 4509044; fax (21) 4508568; e-mail info@ corkchamber.ie; internet www.corkchamber.ie; f. 1819; Pres. JOHN CASHELL; Chief Exec. MICHAEL GEARY.

Dublin Chamber of Commerce: 7 Clare St, Dublin 2; tel. (1) 6130800; fax (1) 6766043; e-mail info@dubchamber.ie; internet www .dubchamber.ie; f. 1783; Pres. PETER WEBSTER.

INDUSTRIAL AND TRADE ASSOCIATIONS

Construction Industry Federation: Construction House, Canal Rd, Dublin 6; tel. (1) 4066000; fax (1) 4966953; e-mail cif@cif.ie; internet www.cif.ie; 33 asscns representing 3,000 mems; Pres. FRANK McCAFFREY; Dir-Gen. LIAM B. KELLEHER.

Irish Creamery Milk Suppliers' Association (ICMSA): John Feely House, Dublin Rd, Limerick; tel. (61) 314677; fax (61) 315737; e-mail icmsa@eircom.net; f. 1950; Pres. PAT O'ROURKE; Gen. Sec. CIARAN DOLAN.

Irish Farmers' Association (IFA): Irish Farm Centre, Bluebell, Dublin 12; tel. (1) 4500266; fax (1) 4551043; e-mail ifapress@indigo .ie; internet www.ifa.ie; Pres. JOHN DILLON; Gen. Sec. MICHAEL BERKEREY.

Irish Fishermen's Organisation Ltd: Cumberland House, Fenian St, Dublin 2; tel. (1) 6612400; fax (1) 6612424; internet www .irishfish@eircom.net; f. 1974; representative body for Irish commercial fishermen; Chair. J. V. MADDOCK; Sec.-Gen. J. F. DOYLE.

Irish Grain and Feed Association: 18 Herbert St, Dublin 2; tel. (1) 6760680; fax (1) 6616774; e-mail igfa@cereal.iol.ie; Pres. M. MURPHY; Dir S. A. FUNGE.

EMPLOYERS' ORGANIZATIONS

Irish Business and Employers' Confederation (IBEC): Confederation House, 84–86 Lower Baggot St, Dublin 2; tel. (1) 6051500; fax (1) 6381500; e-mail info@ibec.ie; internet www.ibec.ie; f. 1993; represents c. 7,000 cos and orgs; Pres Maurice Pratt; Dir-Gen. Turlough O'Sullivan.

Irish Exporters' Association: 28 Merrion Sq., Dublin 2; tel. (1) 6612182; fax (1) 6612315; e-mail iea@irishexporters.ie; internet www.irishexporters.ie; f. 1951; Pres. Brian Ranalow; CEO John Whelan.

UTILITIES

Electricity

An Coimisiún um Rialáil Leictreachais (Commission for Electricity Regulation—CER): Plaza House, Belgard Rd, Tallaght, Dublin 24; tel. (1) 4000800; fax (1) 4000850; e-mail info@cer.ie; internet www.cer.ie; f. 1999; under the Electricity Regulation Act of 1999; responsible for licensing and regulating the generation and supply of electricity and authorizing construction of new generating plants; Commissioner Tom Reeves.

Electricity Supply Board: Lower Fitzwilliam St, Dublin 2; tel. (1) 6765831; fax (1) 6760727; internet www.esb.ie; f. 1927; reorg. 1988; operates 26 generating stations and manages the transmission and distribution of Ireland's electricity; Chair. Tadhg O'Donoghue; CEO Padraig McManus.

Gas

Bord Gáis Éireann (BGE) (The Irish Gas Board): POB 51, Gasworks Rd, Co Cork; tel. (21) 4534000; fax (21) 4534001; internet www.bordgais.com; f. 1976; natural gas transmission and distribution; Chair. Ed O'Connell; CEO Gerry Walsh.

Water

Dept of the Environment: Custom House, Dublin 1; tel. (1) 8882479; fax (1) 8882576; e-mail press-office@environ.irlgov.ie; internet www.environ.ie; responsiblity for water supply.

CO-OPERATIVES

Irish Co-operative Organisation Society Ltd: 84 Merrion Sq., Dublin 2; tel. (1) 6764783; fax (1) 6624502; f. 1894 to co-ordinate the co-operative movement; three operating divisions; offices in Dublin, Cork, Sligo and Brussels, Belgium; Pres. Dessie Boylan; Dir-Gen. John Tyrrell; mems: 130 co-operatives representing c. 175,000 farmers.

Irish Dairy Board: Grattan House, Lower Mount St, Dublin 2; tel. (1) 6619599; fax (1) 6612778; e-mail idb@idb.ie; internet www.idb.ie; f. 1961; reorg. 1973 as a famers' co-operative; principal exporter of Irish dairy products; Chair. Thomas Cleary; Man. Dir Noel Cawley.

TRADE UNIONS

Central Organization

Irish Congress of Trade Unions (ICTU): 31–32 Parnell Sq., Dublin 1; tel. (1) 8897777; fax (1) 8872012; e-mail congress@ictu.ie; internet www.ictu.ie; f. 1894; represents 745,127 workers in 61 affiliated unions in the Republic and Northern Ireland (1999); Gen. Sec. David Begg.

Principal Trade Unions Affiliated to the ICTU

*Amalgamated Transport and General Workers' Union: Transport House, 102 High St, Belfast, Northern Ireland, BT1 2DL; tel. (28) 9023-2381; fax (28) 9024-0133; internet tgwu.org.uk; Irish Regional Sec. Michael O'Reilly; 46,750 mems (2002).

Association of Higher Civil and Public Servants: 4 Warner's Lane, Dartmouth Rd, Dublin 6; tel. (1) 6686077; fax (1) 6686380; e-mail info@ahcps.ie; internet www.ahcps.ie; Gen. Sec. S. O'Riordáin; 2,700 mems (2002).

*Association of Teachers and Lecturers: c/o University of Ulster, 11b Coleraine Campus, Coleraine; internet www.askatl.org.uk; Irish Rep. E. Rodgers; 2,600 mems (2002).

Building and Allied Trades' Union: Arus Hibernia, 13 Blessington St, Dublin 7; tel. (1) 8301911; fax (1) 8304869; internet www.batu.ie; Gen. Sec. Patrick O'Shaughnessy; 10,020 mems (2002).

Civil, Public & Services Union: 19–20 Adelaide Rd, Dublin 2; tel. (1) 6765394; fax (1) 6762918; e-mail bhoran@cpsu.ie; internet www.cpsu.ie; Gen. Sec. B. Horan; 13,600 mems (2002).

Communications Workers' Union: Áras Ghaibréil, 575 North Circular Rd, Dublin 1; tel. (1) 8366388; fax (1) 8365582; e-mail info@

cwu.ie; internet www.cwu.ie; f. 1922; Gen. Sec. Con Scanlon; 19,600 mems (2002).

Electricity Supply Board Officers' Association: 43 East James's Place, Lower Baggot St, Dublin 2; tel. (1) 6767444; fax (1) 6789226; f. 1959; Gen. Sec. Willie Cremins; 2,200 mems (2002).

Federated Union of Government Employees: 32 Parnell Sq., Dublin 1; tel. (1) 8787057; 1,300 mems (2002).

*Graphical, Paper and Media Union: 10 The Anchorage, Charlotte Quay, Dublin 6; tel. (1) 6632048; fax (1) 6632022; e-mail gpmu@eircom.net; internet www.gpmu.org.uk; Irish Rep. E. A. Kirkpatrick; 7,427 mems (2002).

Guinness Staff Union: 107 James's St, Dublin 8; tel. (1) 4536700; Gen. Sec. S. Mackell.

Irish Bank Officials' Association: 93 St Stephen's Green, Dublin 2; tel. (1) 4755908; fax (1) 4780567; e-mail iboa@eircom.net; internet www.iboa.ie; Gen. Sec. Larry Broderick; 13,319 mems (2002).

Irish Federation of University Teachers: 11 Merrion Sq., Dublin 2; tel. (1) 6610910; fax (1) 6610909; e-mail ifut@eircom.net; internet www.ifut.ie; Gen. Sec. Daltún Ó'Ceallaigh; 1,595 mems (2002).

Irish Medical Organization: Graphic House, 10 Fitzwilliam Place, Dublin 2; tel. (1) 6767273; fax (1) 6612758; e-mail imo@imo.ie; internet www.imo.ie; CEO George McNeice; 5,209 mems (2002).

Irish Municipal, Public and Civil Trade Union (IMPACT): Nerney's Court, Dublin 1; tel. (1) 8171500; fax (1) 8171501; e-mail rnolan@impact.ie; internet www.impact.ie; f. 1991; Gen. Sec. Peter McLoone; 45,000 mems (2002).

Irish National Teachers' Organization: 35 Parnell Sq., Dublin 1; tel. (1) 8722533; fax (1) 8722462; e-mail info@into.ie; internet www.into.ie; f. 1868; Gen. Sec. Joe O'Toole; 30,174 mems (2002).

Irish Nurses' Organization: 11 Fitzwilliam Place, Dublin 2; tel. (1) 6760137; fax (1) 6610466; e-mail ino@ino.ie; internet www.ino.ie; Gen. Sec. Liam Doran; 27,718 mems (2002).

MANDATE: 9 Cavendish Row, Dublin 1; tel. (1) 8746321; fax (1) 8729581; e-mail mandate@mandate.ie; internet www.mandate.ie; f. 1994; Gen. Sec. Owen Nulty; 38,386 mems (2002).

*National Union of Journalists (Irish Executive Council): Liberty Hall, 9th Floor, Dublin 1; tel. (1) 8053258; fax (1) 8749250; e-mail liberty.hall@nuj.ie; internet indigo.ie/~nujdub; Gen. Sec. Eoin Ronayne; 4,713 mems (2002).

Prison Officers' Association: 18 Merrion Sq., Dublin 2; tel. (1) 6625495; Gen. Sec. John Clinton; 3,250 mems (2002).

Public Service Executive Union: 30 Merrion Sq., Dublin 2; tel. (1) 6767271; fax (1) 6615777; e-mail info@pseu.ie; internet www.pseu.ie; f. 1890; Gen. Sec. Dan Murphy; 9,000 mems (2002).

Services, Industrial Professional and Technical Union (SIPTU): Liberty Hall, Dublin 1; tel. (1) 8585300; e-mail gensec@siptu.ie; internet www.siptu.ie; f. 1990; Gen. Pres. Des Geraghty; Vice-Pres. Jack O'Connor; Gen. Sec. John McDonnell; 206,871 mems (2002).

Teachers' Union of Ireland: 73 Orwell Rd, Rathgar, Dublin 6; tel. (1) 4922588; fax (1) 4922953; e-mail tui@tui.ie; internet www.tui.ie; f. 1955; Gen. Sec. James Dorney; 11,477 mems (2002).

Technical, Engineering and Electrical Union: 5 Cavendish Row, Dublin 1; tel. (1) 8747047; fax (1) 8747048; e-mail info@teeu.ie; internet www.teeu.ie; f. 1992; Gen. Sec. Owen Wills; 35,685 mems (2003).

*Transport Salaried Staffs' Association: Nerney's Court, off Temple St, Dublin 1; tel. (1) 8743467; fax (1) 8745662; e-mail enquiries@tssa.ie; internet www.tssa.ie; f. 1897; Sec. Rodger Hannon; 1,869 mems (2002).

*Ulster Teachers' Union: 94 Malone Rd, Belfast BT9 5HP; tel. (28) 9066-2216; e-mail office@utu.edu; internet www.utu.edu; Gen. Sec. Ray Calvin; 6,045 mems (2002).

*Union of Construction, Allied Trades and Technicians: 56 Parnell Sq. West, Dublin 1; tel. (1) 8731599; internet www.ucatt.org.uk; Regional Sec. Jim Moore; 14,170 mems (2000).

* These unions have their head office in the United Kingdom. Membership figures relate jointly to the Republic of Ireland and Northern Ireland.

Unions not Affiliated to the ICTU

Association of Secondary Teachers, Ireland (ASTI): ASTI House, Winetavern St, Dublin 8; tel. (1) 6040160; fax (1) 6719280; e-mail info@asti.ie; internet www.asti.ie; Pres. P. J. Sheehy; Gen. Sec. Charlie Lennon; 16,500 mems (2000).

Chartered Institute of Journalists (Irish Region): EETPU Section, 5 Whitefriars, Aungier St, Dublin 2; tel. (1) 4784141; fax (1)

4750131; e-mail wims@journalism.com; internet www.cioj.dircon.co
.uk; Chair. (Ireland) JAMES WIMS.

National Bus and Rail Union: 54 Parnell Sq., Dublin 1; tel. (1)
8730411; fax (1) 8730137; e-mail nbru@eircom.net; Gen. Sec. LIAM
TOBIN.

Transport

Córas Iompair Éireann (CIE) (The Irish Transport Co): Heuston
Station, Dublin 8; tel. (1) 6771871; fax (1) 7032276; f. 1945; reorg.
1986; state corpn operating rail and road transport services; three
operating cos: Iarnród Éireann (Irish Rail), Bus Éireann (Irish Bus)
and Bus Átha Cliath (Dublin Bus); Chair. Dr JOHN LYNCH.

RAILWAYS

In 1999 there were 1,872 km of track, of which 37 km were electrified. Railway services are operated by Iarnród Éireann.

Iarnród Éireann (Irish Rail): Connolly Station, Dublin 1; tel. (1)
8363333; fax (1) 8364760; e-mail info@irishrail.ie; internet www
.irishrail.ie; f. 1987; division of CIE; Chair. MICHAEL P. MCDONNELL;
Man. Dir JOE MEAGHER.

INLAND WATERWAYS

The Grand and Royal Canals and the canal link into the Barrow
Navigation system are controlled by CIE. The Grand Canal and
Barrow are open to navigation by pleasure craft, and the rehabil-
itation and restoration of the Royal Canal is proceeding. The River
Shannon, which is navigable from Limerick to Lough Allen, includes
stretches of the Boyle, Suck, Camlin, and Inny Rivers, the Erne
Navigation, and the Shannon-Erne Waterway. The total length of
Irish navigable waterways is about 700 km. A further 10 km of the
Suck and Boyle Rivers were due to be opened to navigation in
1998/99.

ROADS

At 31 December 2000 there were an estimated 92,500 km of roads,
of which 2,739 km were national primary roads and 2,686 were
national secondary roads. About 94% of all roads were surfaced.

National Roads Authority: St Martin's House, Waterloo Rd,
Dublin 4; tel. (1) 6602511; fax (1) 6680009; e-mail info@nra.ie;
internet www.nra.ie; f. 1994; responsible for the planning, supervision and maintenance of nat. road network; Chair. LIAM CON-
NELLAN; CEO MICHAEL TOBIN.

SHIPPING

The principal sea ports are Dublin, Dún Laoghaire, Cork, Waterford,
Rosslare, Limerick, Foynes, Galway, New Ross, Drogheda, Dundalk,
Fenit and Whiddy Island.

Arklow Shipping Ltd: North Quay, Arklow, Co Wicklow; tel. (402)
39901; fax (402) 39902; e-mail chartering@asl.ie; internet www.asl
.ie; Man. Dir JAMES S. TYRELL; 9 carriers.

Irish Continental Group PLC: Ferryport, Alexandra Rd, POB 19,
Dublin 1; tel. (1) 6075628; fax (1) 8552268; e-mail info@icg.ie;
internet www.icg.ie; controls Irish Ferries, operating passenger
vehicle and roll-on/roll-off freight ferry services between Ireland, the
United Kingdom and continental Europe; Chair. THOMAS TONER;
Man. Dir EAMONN ROTHWELL.

Irish Ferries: Ferryport, Alexandra Rd, POB 19, Dublin 1; tel. (1)
8552222; fax (1) 8552272; e-mail info@irishferries.ie; internet www
.irishferries.ie; drive-on/drive-off car ferry and roll-on/roll-off freight
services between Ireland, the United Kingdom and continental
Europe, operating up to 109 sailings weekly; Group Man. Dir E.
ROTHWELL.

Stena Line: Ferry Terminal, Dún Laoghaire Harbour, Co Dublin;
tel. (1) 2047700; fax (1) 2047620; e-mail info.ie@stenaline.com;
internet www.stenaline.com; services between Dún Laoghaire and
Dublin Port and Holyhead including high-speed catamaran, Rosslare and Fishguard, Belfast and Stranraer, passengers, drive-
on/drive-off car ferry, roll-on/roll-off freight services.

Associations

Irish Chamber of Shipping: 5 Clanwilliam Sq., Grand Canal
Quay, Dublin 2; tel. (1) 6618211; fax (1) 6618270; e-mail bks@iol.ie;
Pres. ALEX MULLIN; Dir B. W. KERR.

Irish Ship Agents' Association: Ormonde House, 26 Harbour
Row, Cobh, Co Cork; tel. (21) 4813180; fax (21) 4811849; e-mail
isaa@eircom.net; Pres. JOHN DUNDON; Sec.-Gen. Lt-Commdr LIAM
SMITH.

CIVIL AVIATION

There are international airports at Shannon, Dublin, Cork and
Knock (Horan International), but only Shannon and Knock are used
for transatlantic flights. In 2000 Dublin, Shannon and Cork handled
13.8m., 2.4m., and 1.7m. passengers, respectively. The national
airline is Aer Lingus.

Aer Rianta (Irish Airports Authority): Dublin Airport, Dublin; tel.
(1) 8141111; fax (1) 8445113; internet www.aer-rianta.com; state-
controlled; responsible for the management and development of
Dublin, Shannon and Cork airports; also operates seven hotels in
Ireland and manages duty-free retail shops in several overseas
locations; Chair. NOEL HANLON; CEO JOHN BURKE.

Airlines

Aer Arann: Dublin Airport, Co. Dublin; tel. (1) 8145240; fax (1)
8145250; e-mail info@skyroad.com; internet www.skyroad.com.

Aer Lingus Group PLC: Dublin Airport, Dublin; tel. (1) 8862222;
fax (1) 8863832; internet www.aerlingus.com; f. 1936; reorg. 1993;
state-owned; domestic and international scheduled services; Chair.
TOM MULCAHY; CEO WILLIE WALSH.

Aer Turas Teoranta: Corballis Park, Dublin Airport, Dublin; tel.
(1) 8444131; fax (1) 8446049; e-mail aerturasdublin@tinet.ie; f. 1962;
world-wide cargo and passenger charter services; Chair. JOHN J.
HARNETT; CEO PATRICK J. COUSINS.

Ryanair: Dublin Airport, Dublin; tel. (1) 8121212; fax (1) 8121213;
internet www.ryanair.com; f. 1985; scheduled and charter passenger
services to European destinations; Chair. DAVID BONDERMAN; CEO
MICHAEL O'LEARY.

Tourism

Intensive marketing campaigns have been undertaken in recent
years to develop new markets for Irish tourism. In addition to many
sites of historic and cultural interest, the country has numerous
areas of natural beauty, notably the Killarney Lakes and the west
coast. In 2001 a total of 6.08m. foreign tourists (excluding residents
of Northern Ireland and excursionists) visited the Republic.

Bord Fáilte Éireann (Irish Tourist Board): Baggot St Bridge,
Dublin 2; tel. (1) 6024000; fax (1) 6024100; e-mail user@bordfailte.ie;
internet www.ireland.ie; f. 1955; Chair. NOEL MCGINLEY; Chief Exec.
NIALL REDDY (acting).

Dublin Regional Tourism Authority Ltd: Suffolk St, Dublin 2;
tel. (1) 6057700; fax (1) 6057757; e-mail reservations@dublintourism
.ie; internet www.visitdublin.com; Chair. MICHAEL FLOOD; CEO
FRANK MAGEE.

Irish Tourist Industry Confederation: 17 Longfod Terrace, Mon-
kstown, Co Dublin; tel. (1) 2844222; fax (1) 2804218; e-mail itic@
eircom.net; internet www.itic.ie; represents all major commercial
tourism interests; Chair. TONY KELLY; CEO BRENDAN LEAHY.

Irish Travel Agents' Association: Heaton House, 3rd Floor, 32
South William St, Dublin 2; tel. (1) 6794089; fax (1) 6719897; e-mail
info@itaa.ie; internet www.itaa.ie; f. 1971; 370 mems; Pres. TONY
BRAZIL; CEO BRENDAN MORAN.

Tourism Ireland: f. 2001 to promote jointly the Republic of Ireland
and Northern Ireland as a tourist destination; Chair. ANDREW
COPPEL; Chief Exec. PAUL O'TOOLE.

ISRAEL

Introductory Survey

Location, Climate, Language, Religion, Flag, Capital

The State of Israel lies in western Asia, occupying a narrow strip of territory on the eastern shore of the Mediterranean Sea. The country also has a narrow outlet to the Red Sea at the northern tip of the Gulf of Aqaba. All of Israel's land frontiers are with Arab countries, the longest being with Egypt to the west and with Jordan to the east. Lebanon lies to the north, and Syria to the north-east. The climate is Mediterranean, with hot, dry summers, when the maximum temperature in Jerusalem is generally between 30°C and 35°C (86°F to 95°F), and mild, rainy winters, with a minimum temperature in the city of about 5°C (41°F). The climate is sub-tropical on the coast but more extreme in the Negev Desert, in the south, and near the shores of the Dead Sea (a lake on the Israeli–Jordanian frontier), where the summer temperature may exceed 50°C (122°F). The official language of Israel is Hebrew, spoken by about two-thirds of the population, including most Jews. About 15% of Israeli residents, including Muslim Arabs, speak Arabic (which is also the language spoken by the inhabitants of the Occupied Territories and the Palestinian Autonomous Areas), while many European languages are also spoken. About 77% of the population profess adherence to Judaism, the officially recognized religion of Israel, while about 15% are Muslims. The national flag (proportions 8 by 11) has a white background, with a six-pointed blue star composed of two overlapping triangles (the 'Shield of David') between two horizontal blue stripes near the upper and lower edges. Although the Israeli Government has designated the city of Jerusalem (part of which is Jordanian territory annexed by Israel in 1967) as the country's capital, this is not recognized by the UN, and most foreign governments maintain their embassies in Tel-Aviv.

Recent History

The Zionist movement, launched in Europe in the 19th century, aimed at the re-establishment of an autonomous community of Jews in their historical homeland of Palestine (the 'Promised Land'). The growth of Zionism was partly due to the insecurity felt by Jewish minorities in many European countries as a result of racial and religious discrimination and persecution, known as anti-semitism.

Palestine, long inhabited by Arabs, became a part of Turkey's Ottoman Empire in the 16th century. During the First World War the Arabs under Ottoman rule rebelled. Palestine was occupied by British forces in 1917–18, when the Turks withdrew. In November 1917 the British Foreign Secretary, Arthur Balfour, declared British support for the establishment of a Jewish national home in Palestine, on condition that the rights of 'the existing non-Jewish communities' there were safeguarded. This so-called Balfour Declaration was confirmed by the governments of other countries then at war with Turkey. British occupation of Palestine continued after the war, when the Ottoman Empire was dissolved. In 1920 the territory was formally placed under British administration by a League of Nations mandate, which incorporated the Balfour Declaration. British rule in Palestine was hampered by the conflict between the declared obligations to the Jews and the rival claims of the indigenous Arab majority. In accordance with the mandate, Jewish settlers were admitted to Palestine (whose population in 1919 was almost entirely Arab), but only on the basis of limited annual quotas. There was serious anti-Jewish rioting by Arabs in 1921 and again in 1929. However, attempts to restrict immigration led to Jewish-sponsored riots in 1933. The extreme persecution of Jews by Nazi Germany caused an increase in the flow of Jewish immigrants, both legal and illegal, which intensified the unrest in Palestine. In 1937 a British proposal to establish separate Jewish and Arab states, while retaining a British-mandated area, was accepted by most Zionists but rejected by the Arabs, and by the end of that year hostilities between the two communities had descended into open conflict. A British scheme offering eventual independence for a bi-communal Palestinian state was postponed because of the Second World War. During the war the Nazis caused the deaths of an estimated 6m. Jews in central and eastern Europe, more than

one-third of the world's total Jewish population. The enormity of the Holocaust greatly increased international sympathy for Jewish claims to a homeland in Palestine.

After the war there was strong opposition by Palestinian Jews to continued British occupation. Numerous terrorist attacks were made by Jewish groups against British targets. In November 1947 the UN approved a plan for the partition of Palestine into two states, one Jewish (covering about 56% of the area) and one Arab. The plan was, however, rejected by Arab states and by Palestinian Arab leaders. Meanwhile, the conflict between the two communities in Palestine escalated into full-scale war.

On 14 May 1948 the United Kingdom terminated its Palestine mandate, and Jewish leaders immediately proclaimed the State of Israel, with David Ben-Gurion as Prime Minister. Although the new state had no agreed frontiers, it quickly received wide international recognition. Neighbouring Arab countries sent forces into Palestine in an attempt to crush Israel. Fighting continued until January 1949, when cease-fire agreements left Israel in control of 75% of Palestine, including West Jerusalem. The de facto territory of Israel was thus nearly one-third greater than the area assigned to the Jewish State under the UN partition plan. Most of the remainder of Palestine was controlled by Jordanian forces. This area, known as the West Bank (or, to Israelis, as Judaea and Samaria), was annexed by Jordan in December 1949 and fully incorporated in April 1950.

By the end of the British mandate the Jewish population of Palestine was about 650,000 (or 40% of the total). The new State of Israel encouraged further Jewish immigration: the Law of Return, adopted in July 1950, established a right of immigration for all Jews, and resulted in a rapid influx of Jewish settlers. Many former Arab residents of Palestine, meanwhile, had become refugees in neighbouring countries, mainly Jordan and Lebanon. About 400,000 Arabs had evacuated their homes prior to May 1948, and a similar number fled subsequently. In 1964 exiled Palestinian Arabs formed the Palestine Liberation Organization (PLO), with the aim, at that time, of overthrowing Israel.

Israel launched an attack on Egypt in October 1956, occupying the Gaza Strip (part of Palestine under Egyptian occupation since 1949) and the Sinai Peninsula. After pressure from the UN and the USA, Israeli forces evacuated these areas in 1957, when a UN Emergency Force (UNEF) was established in Sinai. In 1967 the United Arab Republic (Egypt) secured the withdrawal of UNEF from its territory. Egyptian forces immediately reoccupied the garrison at Sharm esh-Sheikh, near the southern tip of Sinai, and closed the Straits of Tiran to Israeli shipping, effectively (as in 1956) blockading the Israeli port of Eilat. In retaliation, Israeli forces attacked Egypt, Jordan and Syria, swiftly making substantial territorial gains. The so-called Six-Day War left Israel in possession of all Jerusalem, the West Bank area of Jordan, the Sinai Peninsula in Egypt, the Gaza Strip and the Golan Heights in Syria. East Jerusalem was almost immediately integrated into the State of Israel, while the other conquered areas were regarded as Occupied Territories.

Ben-Gurion resigned in June 1963 and was succeeded by Levi Eshkol. Three of the parties in the ruling coalition merged to form the Israel Labour Party in 1968. On the death of Eshkol in 1969, Golda Meir was elected Prime Minister. A cease-fire between Egypt and Israel was arranged in August 1970, but other Arab states and Palestinian guerrilla (mainly PLO) groups continued hostilities. Another Arab–Israeli war began on 6 October 1973, as Arab forces invaded Israeli-held territory on Yom Kippur (the Day of Atonement), the holiest day of the Jewish year. Egyptian forces crossed the Suez Canal and reoccupied part of Sinai, while Syrian troops launched an offensive on the Golan Heights. Having successfully countered these advances, Israel made cease-fire agreements with Egypt and Syria on 24 October.

Gen. Itzhak Rabin succeeded Golda Meir as Prime Minister of a Labour Alignment coalition in 1974. In May 1977 the Labour Alignment was defeated in a general election, and the Likud (Consolidation) bloc, led by Menachem Begin of the Herut

(Freedom) Party, formed a Government with the support of minority parties.

In November 1977 the Egyptian President, Anwar Sadat, visited Israel, indicating tacit recognition of the Jewish State. In September 1978 President Jimmy Carter of the USA, President Sadat and Prime Minister Begin met at the US presidential retreat at Camp David, Maryland, and concluded two agreements: a 'framework for peace in the Middle East', providing for autonomy for the West Bank and Gaza Strip after a transitional period of five years; and a 'framework for the conclusion of a peace treaty between Egypt and Israel'. In February 1980 Egypt became the first Arab country to grant diplomatic recognition to Israel. However, approval by the Israeli Knesset (parliament) in that year of legislation stating explicitly that Jerusalem should be forever the undivided capital of Israel, and Israel's formal annexation of the Golan Heights in 1981, subsequently impeded prospects of agreement on Palestinian autonomy.

Israel's phased withdrawal from Sinai was completed in April 1982. In June Israeli forces, under 'Operation Peace for Galilee', advanced through Lebanon and surrounded West Beirut, trapping 6,000 PLO fighters. Egypt withdrew its ambassador from Tel-Aviv in protest. Diplomatic efforts resulted in the evacuation of 14,000–15,000 PLO and Syrian fighters from Beirut to various Arab countries. In September Lebanese Phalangists massacred Palestinian refugees in the Sabra and Chatila camps in Beirut. An official Israeli inquiry found that its leaders were indirectly responsible through negligence; Gen. Ariel Sharon was forced to resign as Minister of Defence. Talks between Israel and Lebanon culminated in an agreement, in May 1983, declaring an end to hostilities and envisaging the withdrawal of all foreign forces from Lebanon within three months. Syria rejected this, leaving some 30,000 troops and 7,000 PLO fighters in the Beka'a valley and northern Lebanon. Israel thus refused to withdraw its troops, although these were redeployed south of Beirut in September, and were reduced from 30,000 to 10,000 by the end of the year.

The Government's prestige had been damaged by the Beirut massacre and by a capitulation to wage demands by Israeli doctors. In August 1983 Itzhak Shamir succeeded Begin as leader of the Likud bloc and Prime Minister. However, economic difficulties further undermined the Government, and the Labour Party forced a general election in July 1984. Neither the Labour Alignment nor Likud could form a viable coalition, so President Chaim Herzog invited the Labour leader, Shimon Peres, to form a government of national unity with Likud.

Responsibility for policing the occupied southern area of Lebanon fell increasingly on the Israeli-controlled 'South Lebanon Army' (SLA). Israel's own forces completed a withdrawal in June 1985, leaving a narrow buffer zone on the Lebanese side of the border effectively controlled by the SLA. During 1986 rocket attacks on settlements in northern Israel were resumed by Palestinian guerrillas. Israel responded with air assaults on Palestinian targets in southern Lebanon. Meanwhile, the Shi'ite fundamentalist Hezbollah intensified attacks on SLA positions within the buffer zone. The conflict escalated following the abduction, in July 1989, of a local Shi'a Muslim leader by Israeli agents; and again in February 1992, after the assassination by the Israeli air force of the Hezbollah Secretary-General, Sheikh Abbas Moussawi.

From 1984 numerous attempts were made to resolve the most urgent problem in the Middle East—the desire of Palestinians for an independent state. There was virtual deadlock because the PLO would not recognize Israel's right to exist, while Israel refused to participate in direct talks with the PLO, which it regarded as a terrorist organization. Repeated proposals by King Hussein of Jordan for an international peace conference were rejected by Israel, on the grounds that this would involve a PLO delegation. In December 1987 demonstrations and civil disobedience against Israeli rule in the Gaza Strip intensified and spread to the other Occupied Territories. Israeli attempts to crush the *intifada* (uprising) were condemned by world opinion for their severity.

In July 1988 King Hussein abrogated Jordan's legal and administrative responsibilities in the West Bank, and declared that he would no longer represent the Palestinians in any international conference on the Palestinian question. This undermined Israel's Palestine policy, and strengthened the PLO's negotiating position as the sole legitimate representative of the Palestinian people. In November the PLO declared an independent Palestinian State (notionally the West Bank and Gaza Strip), and endorsed UN Security Council Resolution 242

(of November 1967), thereby implicitly granting recognition to Israel. In December Yasser Arafat, the Chairman of the PLO, stated explicitly that the Palestine National Council accepted two States, a Palestinian State and a Jewish State, Israel. He presented a peace initiative, including proposals for a UN-sponsored international conference, the establishment of a UN peace-keeping force to supervise Israel's withdrawal from the Occupied Territories, and a comprehensive settlement based on UN Security Council Resolutions 242 and 338 (of October 1973). The USA refused to accept the PLO proposals, but it did open a dialogue with the organization. However, Prime Minister Itzhak Shamir (the Likud leader had assumed the Israeli premiership in October 1986, in accordance with the 1984 coalition agreement) would not negotiate, distrusting the PLO's undertaking to abandon violence. Instead, he appeared to favour the introduction of limited self-rule for the Palestinians of the West Bank and Gaza, as outlined in the 1978 Camp David accords. At the general election in November 1988 neither Likud nor Labour secured enough seats in the Knesset to form a viable coalition, leading to another Government of national unity being formed under Shamir, with Shimon Peres as Deputy Prime Minister and Minister of Finance.

In April 1989 Shamir presented a peace proposal that would include a reaffirmation by Egypt, Israel and the USA of the Camp David accords, and plans for the holding of free democratic elections in the West Bank and Gaza for Palestinian delegates who could negotiate self-rule under Israeli authority. The proposals, precluding direct talks with the PLO, were unacceptable to the PLO, which did not consider that elections could establish the basis for a political settlement. In September, none the less, President Hosni Mubarak of Egypt invited clarification of Shamir's plans and offered to convene an Israeli-Palestinian meeting in Cairo. This was rejected by Likud ministers, on the grounds that it would entail direct contact with PLO delegates. In November Israel provisionally accepted a proposal by the US Secretary of State, James Baker, for a preliminary meeting to discuss the holding of elections in the West Bank and Gaza, on condition that Israel would not be required to negotiate with the PLO and that the talks would concern only Israel's election proposals. However, the PLO continued to demand a direct role, and the Baker initiative foundered.

The fragile Likud-Labour coalition was endangered in early 1990 by disputes and dismissals, and in March the Knesset adopted a motion of 'no confidence' in Prime Minister Shamir. Shimon Peres was unable to form a new coalition, and in June, after several weeks of political bargaining, Shamir formed a new Government—a narrow, right-wing coalition of Likud and five small parties, with three independent members of the Knesset. In a policy document Shamir emphasized the right of Jews to settle in all parts of 'Greater Israel', his opposition to the creation of an independent Palestinian state, and his refusal to negotiate with the PLO—or with any Palestinians other than those resident in the Occupied Territories (excluding East Jerusalem).

In March 1990 US President George Bush opposed the granting to Israel of a loan of some US \$400m. for the housing of Soviet Jewish immigrants, since Israel would not guarantee to refrain from constructing new settlements in the Occupied Territories. Violence erupted throughout Israel and the Territories in May. The PLO's refusal to condemn the violence caused the USA to suspend its dialogue with the organization and to veto a UN Security Council resolution urging that international observers be dispatched to the Occupied Territories. In June Shamir invited President Hafiz al-Assad of Syria to peace negotiations, and the UN Secretary-General's special envoy also visited Israel for discussions. However, Shamir rejected US proposals for direct talks between Israeli and Palestinian delegations.

Iraq's invasion of Kuwait in August 1990 brought about an improvement in US-Israeli relations: it was imperative, if a coalition of Western and Arab powers opposed to Iraq was to be maintained, that Israel should not become actively involved in the conflict. In October some 17 Palestinians were shot dead by Israeli police, following clashes with Jewish worshippers. International outrage at the shootings resulted in a UN Security Council vote to send an investigative mission, although Israel agreed only to receive a UN emissary. Iraqi missile attacks on Israel in January 1991, shortly after the US-led multinational force had begun its offensive against Iraq, threatened the cohesion of the force. US diplomatic efforts, and the installation in

Israel of US air defence systems, averted an immediate Israeli response. Meanwhile, widespread support for Iraq among Palestinians increased the Israeli Government's insistence that Shamir's 1989 peace plan could be the only basis for dialogue.

In March 1991 President Bush identified the resolution of the Arab–Israeli conflict as a priority of his Administration. By August intensive diplomacy by US Secretary of State James Baker had secured the agreement of the Israeli, Syrian, Egyptian, Jordanian and Lebanese Governments, and of Palestinian representatives, to attend a regional peace conference, the terms of reference for which would be a comprehensive peace settlement based on UN Security Council Resolutions 242 and 338. An initial, 'symbolic' session was held in Madrid, Spain, in October. However, subsequent talks soon became deadlocked over procedural issues. Israel, wary of making any gesture that might be construed as recognition of Palestinian independence, repeatedly questioned the status of the Palestinian-Jordanian delegation and the right of the Palestinian component to participate separately in negotiations; furthermore, Israel's refusal to end construction of new settlements in the Occupied Territories continually jeopardized the peace process. In February 1992, immediately prior to the fourth session of peace talks, to be held in Washington, DC, Baker demanded a complete halt to Israel's settlement-building programme as a precondition for the granting of loan guarantees to the value of US $10,000m. for the housing of Jewish immigrants from the former USSR.

In December 1991 the Government's majority in the Knesset was reduced when the Minister of Agriculture (a member of the right-wing nationalist Tzomet Party) resigned in protest at the Prime Minister's opposition to electoral reform. The majority was lost entirely in January 1992, when two other right-wing nationalist groups, Moledet and Tehiya, left the coalition. Their withdrawal was a deliberate attempt to obstruct the third session of the Middle East peace conference, in Moscow, Russia, where delegates had begun to address the granting of transitional autonomy to Palestinians in the West Bank and Gaza Strip. A general election was subsequently scheduled for June, with Itzhak Shamir heading a minority administration meanwhile.

A fifth round of negotiations was held in Washington, DC, in April 1992. Procedural issues were resolved, and, during talks with the Palestinian component of the Palestinian-Jordanian delegation, Israeli representatives presented proposals for the holding of municipal elections in the West Bank and Gaza, and for the transfer of control of health-care provision there to Palestinian authorities. The Palestinian delegation did not reject the proposals outright, although they fell far short of the Palestinians' aim of full legislative control of the Occupied Territories. No progress was made between Israeli and Syrian officials on the issue of the Golan Heights.

In May 1992 the first multilateral negotiations between the parties to the Middle East peace conference commenced; however, the sessions were boycotted by Syria and Lebanon, considering them futile until progress had been made in the bilateral negotiations. Various combinations of delegations in several cities attended discussions concerning regional economic co-operation, arms control, water resources, environmental issues and Palestinian refugees. Israel boycotted the meetings on Palestinian refugees and regional economic development after the USA approved Palestinian proposals to allow exiles (i.e. non-residents of the Occupied Territories) to be included in the Palestinian delegations to these two sessions.

In the June 1992 general election the Labour Party won 44 of the 120 seats in the Knesset, and Likud 32. Meretz—an alliance of Ratz, Shinui and the United Workers' Party, which had won 12 seats—confirmed its willingness to form a coalition government with Labour. However, even with the support of the two Arab parties—the Democratic Arab Party and Hadash—which together held five seats in the Knesset, such a coalition would have a majority of only two votes over the so-called 'right bloc' (Likud, Tzomet, Moledet and Tehiya) and the religious parties which had allied themselves with Likud in the previous legislature. Itzhak Rabin (who had replaced Shimon Peres as Chairman of the Labour Party earlier in the year) was accordingly obliged to solicit support among the religious parties. His Government, presented to the Knesset in July, was an alliance of Labour, Meretz and the ultra-orthodox Shas; the coalition held a total of 62 Knesset seats, and also commanded the unofficial support of the two Arab parties.

Most international observers regarded the installation of the Labour-led coalition as having improved the prospects of the

Middle East peace process. However, at the conclusion of a sixth round of bilateral negotiations between Israeli, Syrian, Lebanese and Palestinian-Jordanian delegations in September 1992, no breakthrough was reported. In October, in a clear gesture of support for the new Government, the USA granted Israel the loan guarantees that it had hitherto withheld. Multilateral negotiations on regional economic co-operation, in which an Israeli delegation participated, took place in Paris, France, in that month; a seventh round of bilateral negotiations convened in Washington in October–November, and multilateral talks on the issue of refugees were held in Ottawa, Canada, in November. Nevertheless, no tangible progress was achieved.

An eighth round of bilateral negotiations between Israeli and Arab delegations commenced in Washington in December 1992. However, the talks were quickly overtaken by events in the Occupied Territories (where there had been several weeks of violent confrontations between Palestinians and the Israeli security forces), which led to the withdrawal of the Arab participants. In mid-December, in response to the deaths in the Territories of five members of the Israeli security forces, and to the abduction and murder by the Islamic Resistance Movement (Hamas) of an Israeli policeman, the Government ordered the deportation to Lebanon of 413 alleged Palestinian supporters of Hamas. The Lebanese authorities refused to co-operate in this action, leaving the deportees stranded in the territory between Israel's self-declared southern Lebanese security zone and Lebanon proper. The expulsions provoked international outrage, and intense diplomatic pressure was placed on Israel to revoke the deportation order. The UN Security Council unanimously approved a resolution (No. 799) condemning the deportations and demanding the return of the deportees to Israel. At the end of December the Israeli Government asserted that only 10 of the deportees had been unjustifiably expelled and would be permitted to return. Meanwhile, the Palestinian delegation to the eighth round of bilateral negotiations indicated that it would not resume talks until all of the deportees had been readmitted to Israel. In February 1993 the Israeli Government reportedly indicated its willingness to allow about 100 of the deportees to return, but insisted that the remainder should serve a period of exile lasting at least until the end of the year. The ninth round of bilateral negotiations was formally suspended; although the Security Council welcomed the Israeli Government's decision to permit the return of 100 deportees, Palestinian delegates insisted on full implementation of Resolution 799 as a precondition for resumed discussions. In March, amid a sharp escalation in violence between Palestinians and Israeli security forces in the West Bank and Gaza, Israel sealed off the territories indefinitely.

The suspended ninth round of bilateral negotiations in the Middle East peace process resumed in Washington in April 1993. The Palestinian delegation apparently agreed to attend the sessions following pressure by Arab governments, and after Israel had agreed to allow Faisal Husseini, the nominal leader of the Palestinian delegation, to participate. (Israel had previously refused this concession because Husseini was a resident of East Jerusalem, the status of which Israel regarded as distinct from that of the West Bank, the Gaza Strip and the Golan Heights.) Israel was also reported to have undertaken to halt punitive deportations, and, with the USA, to have reaffirmed its commitment to Resolutions 242 and 338 as the terms of reference for the peace process. However, no substantive progress was achieved during the talks.

In May 1993 Ezer Weizman was inaugurated as President; Weizman, leader of the Yahad party, had been elected by the Knesset in March. Also in March Binyamin Netanyahu was chosen to replace Shamir as the Likud leader.

At the 10th round of bilateral negotiations, convened in Washington in June 1993, the participants agreed to establish a committee charged with the drafting of a statement of principles concerning Palestinian self-rule in the Occupied Territories—now regarded as the key element in the Middle East peace process. In July Israeli armed forces mounted the most intensive air and artillery attacks on targets in Lebanon since 'Operation Peace for Galilee' in 1982, in retaliation for attacks by Hezbollah fighters on settlements in northern Israel.

The opening of the 11th round of bilateral negotiations, in Washington at the end of August 1993, was eclipsed by an unexpected breakthrough in discussions between Israel and the PLO, which culminated in the signing, on 13 September, of a Declaration of Principles on Palestinian Self-Rule in the Occupied Territories. The agreement, which entailed mutual recognition by Israel and the PLO, had been elaborated during a series of secret negotiations mediated by Norwegian diplomacy (and therefore became known as the Oslo accords). The Declaration of Principles established a detailed timetable for Israel's disengagement from the Occupied Territories, and stipulated that a permanent settlement of the Palestinian question should be in place by December 1998. From 13 October 1993 Palestinian authorities were to assume responsibility for education and culture, health, social welfare, direct taxation and tourism in the Gaza Strip and the Jericho area of the West Bank, and a transitional period of Palestinian self-rule was to begin on 13 December.

Although Prime Minister Rabin secured ratification of the Declaration of Principles, and of Israel's recognition of the PLO, by the Knesset on 23 September 1993, there was widespread opposition to it from right-wing Israelis. The PLO Central Council, meeting in the Tunisian capital, approved the accord on 11 October. However, the conclusion of the agreement aggravated divisions in the Palestinian liberation movement. Within the PLO some senior officials, hitherto loyal to Yasser Arafat's leadership, now declared their opposition to him, while dissident groups, such as the Democratic Front for the Liberation of Palestine (DFLP), denounced the Declaration of Principles as treason. Meanwhile, the reaction to the agreement by the other Arab Governments engaged in peace negotiations with Israel was mixed. King Hussein of Jordan welcomed it, and immediately agreed an agenda for direct discussions with Israel; this was also ratified by the Knesset on 23 September. Talks took place in Washington between Crown Prince Hassan of Jordan and Shimon Peres, Israel's Minister of Foreign Affairs, in October. Despite reports of subsequent secret negotiations, King Hussein insisted, during visits to Egypt and Syria in November, that Jordan would not conclude a separate peace agreement with Israel. Lebanon, meanwhile, feared that the divisions provoked by the Declaration of Principles within the Palestinian movement might lead to renewed conflict on Lebanese territory. It remained unclear whether Syria—which neither condemned nor welcomed the agreement—would continue to support those Palestinian groups opposed to Arafat's position.

Also in September 1993 the resignation of Aryeh Der'i of the ultra-orthodox Shas as Minister of the Interior, following allegations of corruption, provoked the withdrawal from the Government of other Shas ministers, thus reducing the coalition to an alliance between the Labour Party and Meretz (and the Government's majority in the Knesset to only two). Protracted negotiations failed to achieve the return of Shas to the Government and, in July 1994, were superseded by a coalition agreement signed with Yi'ud, a breakaway group from the Tzomet Party.

Itzhak Rabin and Yasser Arafat held their first meeting in the context of the Declaration of Principles in Cairo on 6 October 1993. A joint PLO-Israeli liaison committee subsequently met on 13 October, with delegations headed, respectively, by Mahmud Abbas and Shimon Peres; the committee was to meet frequently to monitor the implementation of the accord. A technical committee also held three meetings during October in the Egyptian resort of Taba: its task was to define the precise details of Israel's military withdrawal from the Gaza Strip and Jericho, scheduled to take place between 13 December 1993 and 13 April 1994. However, it proved impossible satisfactorily to negotiate the details of Israel's withdrawal by December 1993, largely because of a failure to agree on security arrangements for border crossings between the Gaza Strip and Jericho, and Jordan and Egypt.

Following meetings in Damascus between US Secretary of State Warren Christopher and Syria's President Assad and Minister of Foreign Affairs, Farouk ash-Shara', in December 1993, Syria announced its willingness to resume bilateral talks with Israel. In January 1994 Israel appeared to indicate, tentatively, that it might be prepared to execute a full withdrawal from the Golan Heights in return for a comprehensive peace agreement with Syria; it was reported subsequently that the Government would put the issue to a referendum before making such a withdrawal. Bilateral negotiations between Israeli and Syrian delegations resumed in Washington later that month.

In February 1994 Israel and the PLO reached an agreement to share control of the two future international border crossings. Security arrangements for Jewish settlers in the Gaza Strip had also reportedly been decided, whereby three access routes to settlements were to remain under Israeli control. However, the boundaries of the Jericho enclave remained undefined. Talks

followed regarding the implementation of the first stage of Palestinian autonomy in the Gaza Strip and Jericho; the size, structure and jurisdiction of a future Palestinian police force; control of sea and air space; and the delineation of the Jericho enclave. In April Israel and the PLO signed an agreement concerning economic relations between Israel and the autonomous Palestinian entity during the five-year period leading to self-rule. Meeting in Cairo, on 4 May the two parties signed an accord detailing arrangements for Palestinian self-rule in the Gaza Strip and Jericho. The accord provided for Israel's military withdrawal from these areas, and for the deployment there of a 9,000-strong Palestinian police force. A nominated Palestinian (National) Authority (PA) was to assume the responsibilities of the Israeli military administration in Gaza and Jericho, although Israeli authorities were to retain control in matters of external security and foreign affairs. Elections for a Palestinian Council, which, under the terms of the Oslo accords, were to have taken place in Gaza and the West Bank in July, were now postponed until October. Israel's military withdrawal from Gaza and Jericho was completed on 13 May, and on 17 May the PLO formally assumed control of the Israeli Civil Administration's departments there. On 26–28 May the PA held its inaugural meeting in Tunis, defining a political programme and distributing ministerial portfolios. Arafat made a symbolic return to Gaza City on 1 July—his first visit for 25 years—and the PA was formally inaugurated in Jericho on 5 July. Meanwhile, negotiations continued with Israel on the extension of Palestinian authority, the redeployment of Israeli armed forces in the West Bank and the holding of Palestinian elections. In August Israel and the PLO signed an agreement extending the authority of the PA to include education, health, tourism, social welfare and taxation.

On 25 July 1994 Israel and Jordan signed a joint declaration formally ending the state of war between them and further defining arrangements for future bilateral negotiations. In September Itzhak Rabin announced details of a plan for a partial withdrawal of Israeli armed forces from the occupied Golan Heights, after which a three-year trial period of Israeli-Syrian 'normalization' would ensue. The proposals were rejected by President Assad; however, the Syrian leader did state his willingness to work towards peace with Israel. In late September Rabin and King Hussein held talks in Aqaba, Jordan, with the aim of devising a timetable for a full Israeli-Jordanian peace treaty. Also in that month Morocco, closely followed by Tunisia, became the second and third Arab states to establish diplomatic ties with Israel, and the six members of the Co-operation Council for the Arab States of the Gulf (the Gulf Co-operation Council, see p. 175) also decided to revoke the subsidiary elements of the Arab economic boycott of Israel.

A World Bank-sponsored conference of international donors, held in Paris in September 1994, collapsed almost immediately, owing to a dispute between Israel and the Palestinians over Palestinian investment plans to fund projects in East Jerusalem. Israel regarded such plans as compromising negotiations on the final status of Jerusalem which, under the terms of the Declaration of Principles, were not due to begin before May 1996. Meeting in Oslo, Norway, shortly afterwards, Arafat and Peres negotiated a 15-point agreement aimed at accelerating economic aid to the PA. Later in September 1994 Arafat and Rabin met at the Erez crossing point between Gaza and Israel to discuss the future Palestinian elections in the West Bank and Gaza Strip. The PLO reportedly sought to elect a 100-member Palestinian Council, while Israel insisted that its size should be restricted to 25 members. Israel rejected Arafat's proposal for elections on 1 November as unrealistic; it was, however, agreed to meet again in October to negotiate a compromise. At the same time, Arafat agreed to 'take all measures' to prevent attacks on Israeli targets by opponents of the Oslo process. In late September, however, Rabin approved a plan to build some 1,000 new housing units at a Jewish settlement just inside the West Bank, in an apparent reversal of the moratorium he had imposed on construction in 1992. The PLO claimed that this contravened the Declaration of Principles. In early October 1994 Hamas claimed responsibility for an attack in Jerusalem in which an Israeli soldier and a Palestinian civilian died. On the same day another Israeli soldier was abducted by Hamas fighters near Tel-Aviv, who subsequently demanded that Israel release the detained Hamas spiritual leader, Sheikh Ahmad Yassin, and other Palestinian prisoners in exchange for his life. Despite Palestinian action to detain some 300 Hamas members in the Gaza Strip, the kidnapped soldier was killed in the West

Bank in mid-October. Shortly afterwards an attack by a Hamas suicide bomber in Tel-Aviv, in which 22 people died, prompted Israel to close its borders with the Palestinian territories.

On 26 October 1994 Israel and Jordan signed a formal peace treaty, defining their common border and providing for a normalization of relations. The peace treaty was denounced by the Syrian Government, all elements of Palestinian opinion, and by some Islamists in Jordan.

In November 1994 a member of another militant Palestinian organization, Islamic Jihad, was killed in a car bomb attack in Gaza. The attack was blamed on the Israeli security forces by many Palestinians opposed to the Oslo accords. Three Israeli soldiers were subsequently killed in a suicide bombing in the Gaza Strip, for which Islamic Jihad claimed responsibility. It became clear that Israel's security concerns would continue to delay the redeployment of its armed forces in the West Bank and the holding of Palestinian elections, as Rabin stated, in December, that the elections would either have to take place in the continued presence of Israeli forces, or be postponed for a year. In January 1995 a suicide bombing (responsibility for which was claimed by Islamic Jihad) at Beit Lid, in which 21 Israeli soldiers and civilians died, seriously jeopardized the peace process. The Government again closed Israel's borders with the West Bank and Gaza, and postponed the planned release of some 5,500 Palestinian prisoners. An emergency meeting of the leaders of Egypt, Israel, Jordan and the PLO was convened in Cairo early the following month; the summit's final communiqué condemned acts of terror and violence, and expressed support for the Declaration of Principles and the wider peace process. US President Bill Clinton subsequently held a meeting in Washington involving the Israeli and Egyptian Ministers of Foreign Affairs and the PA Minister of Planning and Economic Co-operation, after which Shimon Peres reportedly stated that any further expansion of Palestinian self-rule in the West Bank was conditional upon real progress by the PA in suppressing terrorism. On 9 February, meanwhile, Israeli armed forces completed their withdrawal from Jordanian territories, in accordance with the bilateral peace treaty concluded in October 1994.

In March 1995 Arafat and Peres agreed, at talks in Gaza, to adopt 1 July as the date by which an agreement on the expansion of Palestinian self-rule in the West Bank should be concluded. Later in March it was announced that Israel and Syria had agreed to resume peace negotiations for the first time since February 1994. In May 1995 Syria and Israel were reported to have concluded a 'framework understanding on security arrangements', intended to facilitate discussions on security issues. Peres subsequently indicated that Israel had proposed that its forces should withdraw from the Golan Heights over a four-year period; Syria, however, had insisted that the withdrawal be effected over 18 months.

In June 1995 one of the most prominent members of Likud, David Levy (who had opposed Netanyahu's election as party leader in 1993), announced that he was to form a new party to contest the legislative elections scheduled for 1996. The division was reportedly the result of Levy's opposition to new selection procedures within Likud for general election candidates. Levy's new political movement, Gesher, was formally inaugurated later in June 1995.

Despite intensive negotiations, it proved impossible to conclude an agreement on the expansion of Palestinian self-rule in the West Bank by the target date of 1 July 1995. The principal obstacles remained the question of precisely to where Israeli troops in the West Bank would redeploy, and the exact nature of security arrangements for some 130,000 Jewish settlers who were to remain there. In August Hamas claimed responsibility for a suicide bomb attack on a bus in Jerusalem, which killed six people. (Two suicide bombings in Gaza in April 1995, in which seven Israeli soldiers died, had reportedly led to the arrest by Palestinian police of up to 300 members of Hamas and Islamic Jihad, which claimed responsibility for the attacks.) On 28 September the Israeli-Palestinian Interim Agreement on the West Bank and the Gaza Strip was finally signed by Israel and the PLO. Its main provisions were the withdrawal of Israeli armed forces from a further six West Bank towns (Nablus, Ramallah, Jenin, Tulkaram, Qalqilya and Bethlehem), and a partial redeployment from the town of Hebron; national Palestinian legislative elections to an 82-member Palestinian Council and for a Palestinian Executive President; and the release, in three phases, of Palestinians detained by Israel. In anticipation of a violent reaction against the Interim Agreement by so-called

'rejectionist' groups within the Occupied Territories, Israel immediately sealed its borders with the West Bank and Gaza. Meanwhile, right-wing elements within Israel also denounced the agreement.

On 4 November 1995 Itzhak Rabin was assassinated in Tel-Aviv by a Jewish student opposed to the peace process, in particular the Israeli withdrawal from the West Bank. The assassination caused a further marginalization of those on the extreme right wing of Israeli politics who had advocated violence as a means of halting the Oslo process, and provoked criticism of the opposition Likud, which, it was widely felt, had not sufficiently distanced itself from such extremist elements. The Minister of Foreign Affairs, Shimon Peres, was, with the agreement of Likud, invited to form a new government. The members of the outgoing administration—Labour, Meretz and Yi'ud—subsequently signed a new coalition agreement, and the Cabinet was formally approved by the Knesset in late November. In February 1996 Peres announced that elections to the Knesset and—for the first time—the direct election of the Prime Minister would take place in May 1996.

In spite of Rabin's assassination, Israeli armed forces completed their withdrawal from the West Bank town of Jenin on 13 November 1995, and in December they withdrew from Tulkaram, Nablus, Qalqilya, Bethlehem and Ramallah. With regard to Hebron, Israel and the PA signed an agreement transferring jurisdiction in some 17 areas of civilian affairs from Israel to the PA. At talks with Arafat at Erez in December, Peres confirmed that Israel would release some 1,000 Palestinian prisoners before the impending Palestinian elections.

Peace negotiations between Israel and Syria resumed in December 1995 in Maryland, USA, followed by a second round in January 1996. Also in January King Hussein made a public visit to Tel-Aviv, during which Israel and Jordan signed a number of agreements relating to the normalization of economic and cultural relations.

Palestinian legislative and presidential elections were held in late January 1996, leading in principle to the final stage of the peace process, when Palestinian and Israeli negotiators would address such issues as Jerusalem, the rights of Palestinian refugees, the status of Jewish settlements in the Palestinian territories, and the extent of that autonomy. In February and March, however, more than 50 Israelis died as a result of suicide bomb attacks in Jerusalem, Ashkelon and Tel-Aviv, and talks were suspended. Israel again ordered the indefinite closure of its borders with the Palestinian territories, and demanded that the PA suppress the activities of Hamas and Islamic Jihad in the areas under its control. A hitherto unknown group, the 'Yahya Ayyash Units', claimed responsibility for the attacks, to avenge the assassination—allegedly by Israeli agents—of Ayyash, a leading Hamas activist, in January 1996. Yasser Arafat, now the elected Palestinian President, condemned the bombings, and in late February more than 200 members of Hamas were reported to have been detained by Palestinian security forces. The attacks led Israel to impose even more stringent security measures, notably asserting the right of its armed forces to enter PA-controlled areas when Israeli security was at stake. Furthermore, an agreement to redeploy troops from Hebron by 20 March was rescinded. For their part, the Palestinian authorities reportedly outlawed the armed wings of Hamas, Islamic Jihad and other paramilitary groups.

The suicide bombings also undermined the talks taking place between Israeli and Syrian representatives in the USA, and in March 1996 the Israeli negotiators returned home. Syria and Lebanon both declined an invitation to attend the so-called 'Summit of Peacemakers', held at the Egyptian resort of Sharm esh-Sheikh in that month, at which some 27 Heads of State expressed their support for the Middle East peace process and pledged to redouble their efforts to combat terrorism. In April Israel and Turkey signed a number of military co-operation agreements, a development condemned by Syria as a threat to its own security and to that of all Arab and Islamic countries.

In April 1996 Israeli armed forces began a sustained campaign of intense air and artillery attacks on alleged Hezbollah positions in southern Lebanon and the southern suburbs of Beirut. The declared aim of the Israeli operation (code-named 'Grapes of Wrath') was to achieve the complete cessation of rocket attacks by Hezbollah on settlements in northern Israel. Some 400,000 Lebanese were displaced northwards, after the Israeli military authorities warned that they would be endangered by the offensive against Hezbollah. Moreover, the shelling by Israeli forces of a base of the UN peace-keeping force at Qana resulted in the deaths of more than 100 Lebanese civilians who had been sheltering there, and of four UN peace-keepers. A cease-fire 'understanding' took effect in late April, after more than two weeks of hostilities. This was effectively a compromise confining the conflict to the area of the security zone in southern Lebanon, recognizing both Hezbollah's right to resist Israeli occupation and Israel's right to self-defence; the 'understanding' also envisaged the establishment of an Israel-Lebanon Monitoring Group (ILMG), comprising Israel, Lebanon, Syria, France and the USA, to supervise the cease-fire.

Israel welcomed the decision of the Palestine National Council (PNC) in late April 1996 to amend the Palestinian National Charter (or PLO Covenant), removing all clauses demanding the destruction of Israel: the Israeli Government had demanded that the Covenant be amended as a precondition for participation in the final stage of peace negotiations with the PLO.

No party gained an outright majority of the 120 seats in the elections to the Knesset, held on 19 May 1996, but the Likud leader, Binyamin Netanyahu, achieved a marginal victory over Peres in the direct election for the Prime Minister. Prior to the legislative election a formal alliance between Likud, the Tzomet Party and Gesher had been announced. This alliance secured 32 seats, and Labour 34. The success of the ultra-orthodox Shas and the National Religious Party (NRP), with 10 seats and nine, respectively, was the key factor in determining that the new Government would be formed by Likud. Some 79.7% of the electorate participated in the polls. Netanyahu proceeded to sign agreements between the Likud alliance and Shas, the NRP, Israel B'Aliyah, United Torah Judaism and the Third Way, to form a coalition that would command the support of 66 deputies in the Knesset. Moledet also agreed to support the Government, but did not formally enter the coalition. The new Government received the approval of the Knesset in mid-June. Its statement of policy excluded the possibility of granting Palestinian statehood or, with regard to Syria, of relinquishing *de facto* sovereignty of the occupied Golan Heights. Moreover, Netanyahu reportedly postponed further discussion of the withdrawal of Israeli armed forces from the West Bank town of Hebron—where they provided security for some 400 Jewish settlers—and reiterated his refusal to meet the Palestinian President. In July the likely stance of the new Government was underlined by the incorporation into the Cabinet, as Minister of Infrastructure, of Ariel Sharon—who had played a leading role in the creation and expansion of Jewish settlements in the West Bank. The PA organized a short general strike at the end of the month, in protest at the refusal of the Israeli authorities to allow Palestinian Muslims to participate in Friday prayers at the al-Aqsa Mosque in East Jerusalem, and at a decision by the new Government to expand existing Jewish settlements in the West Bank.

The election of a Likud-led Government thus appeared to have particularly grave implications for the future of Israeli-Palestinian peace negotiations. In late May 1996 a joint meeting, in Gaza, of the Palestinian Cabinet and the Executive Committee of the PLO urged the incoming Israeli Government to implement all previous agreements and to commence the final stage of peace talks. In late June, in response to Likud's electoral victory, a summit meeting of all Arab leaders (with the exception of Iraq) was convened in Cairo. The meeting's final communiqué reiterated Israel's withdrawal from all occupied territories (including East Jerusalem) as a basic requirement for a comprehensive Middle East peace settlement. Netanyahu and Arafat did in fact meet in September, at the Erez crossing point, when they confirmed their commitment to the implementation of the Interim Agreement.

In September 1996 it was announced that Israel's Ministry of Defence had approved plans to construct some 1,800 new homes at existing Jewish settlements in the West Bank, causing many observers to conclude that the new Israeli Government had effectively halted the peace process by either abandoning or postponing many of the commitments inherited from its predecessor. Violent confrontations erupted between Palestinian security forces and civilians and the Israeli armed forces, in which at least 50 Palestinians and 18 Israelis were killed and hundreds wounded. The direct cause of the disturbances was attributed to the decision of the Israeli Government to open the north end of the Hasmonean tunnel running beneath the al-Aqsa Mosque in Jerusalem, although it appeared to be the inevitable culmination of Palestinian frustration at Israel's failure to implement agreements previously signed with the PA. Amid fears of a new Palestinian *intifada*, the Israeli military authorities declared a state of emergency in the Gaza Strip and

the West Bank, and threatened military intervention to suppress the disturbances. A special session of the UN Security Council was convened, and intense international diplomacy facilitated a crisis summit in Washington hosted by US President Clinton and attended by Netanyahu, Arafat and King Hussein of Jordan. The meeting reportedly achieved nothing, but in October it was announced that, following further US mediation, Israel had agreed to resume negotiations on the partial withdrawal of its armed forces from Hebron. Netanyahu subsequently stated that once this issue had been settled Israel would reopen its borders with the West Bank and Gaza—which had remained closed since February—and move quickly towards seeking a final settlement with the Palestinians.

In January 1997 Israel and the PA finally concluded an agreement on the withdrawal of Israeli armed forces from Hebron. The principal terms of the accord were that Israeli forces should withdraw from 80% of the town within 10 days, and that the first of three subsequent redeployments from the West Bank should take place six weeks after the signing of the agreement, and the remaining two by August 1998. With regard to security arrangements for Jewish settlers in central Hebron, Palestinian police patrols would be armed only with pistols in areas close to the Jewish enclaves, while joint Israeli-Palestinian patrols would secure the heights above the enclaves. The 'final status' negotiations on borders, the Jerusalem issue, Jewish settlements and Palestinian refugees were to commence within two months of the signing of the Hebron agreement. As guarantor of the agreement, the USA undertook to obtain the release of Palestinian prisoners, and to ensure that Israel continued to engage in negotiations for a Palestinian airport in the Gaza Strip and on safe passage for Palestinians between the West Bank and Gaza. The USA also undertook to ensure that the PA would continue to combat terrorism, complete the revision of the Palestinian National Charter and consider Israeli requests to extradite Palestinians suspected of involvement in attacks in Israel.

While the conclusion of the Hebron agreement marked the first significant progress in the peace process since Netanyahu's election as Prime Minister, negotiations with Syria remained suspended. In January 1997 Netanyahu urged Syria to exert pressure on Hezbollah to cease hostilities in Israel's security zone in southern Lebanon. In February, however, he denied speculation that Israel was considering a unilateral withdrawal from the zone, which had intensified as a result of the deaths, in a helicopter accident, of 73 Israeli soldiers travelling to southern Lebanon.

Progress achieved through the agreement on Hebron was severely undermined in February 1997, when Israel announced that it was to proceed with the construction of 6,500 housing units at Har Homa (Jabal Abu Ghunaim in Arabic) in East Jerusalem. Tensions escalated in the following month, after Israel decided unilaterally to withdraw its armed forces from only 9% of the West Bank. Arafat denounced the decision and King Hussein accused Netanyahu of intentionally destroying the peace process. Increasing anti-Israeli sentiment reportedly motivated a Jordanian soldier to murder seven Israeli schoolgirls in Nayarim, an enclave between Israel and Jordan. Israeli intransigence over the Har Homa settlement prompted Palestinians to abandon the 'final status' talks, scheduled to begin on 17 March, and on the following day construction at the site began. Riots among Palestinians erupted immediately, and shortly afterwards Hamas carried out a bomb attack in Tel-Aviv, killing four people. In response, the Israeli Government again ordered the closure of Israel's borders with the West Bank and Gaza Strip (although they were reopened at the end of April). In late March the League of Arab States (the Arab League, see p. 260) voted to resume its economic boycott of Israel, suspend moves to establish diplomatic relations, and withdraw from multilateral peace talks. (Jordan, the PA and Egypt were excluded from the resolution, owing to their binding bilateral agreements with Israel.) Meeting with US President Clinton in Washington in early April, Netanyahu reiterated that he would not suspend the settlement programme. During May the USA's chief Middle East negotiator, Dennis Ross, failed to achieve any progress towards a resumption of peace talks despite a nine-day mediation attempt.

Meanwhile, in April 1997 police investigators recommended that the Prime Minister be charged with fraud and breach of trust for his appointment, in January, of Roni Bar-On as Attorney-General. Bar-On had resigned within 12 hours of his appointment after it was alleged that his promotion had been made in order to facilitate a plea bargain for Aryeh Der'i, leader of the Shas party, who was the subject of separate corruption charges. It was suggested that, in return for Bar-On's appointment, Der'i had pledged his party's support for the Cabinet's decision regarding the withdrawal from Hebron. In May Der'i was indicted for obstruction of justice, but charges against Netanyahu were dismissed owing to lack of evidence. However, the Prime Minister's authority was further undermined by the subsequent resignation of the Minister of Finance, Dan Meridor. In June Ehud Barak, a former government minister and army chief of staff, was elected to replace Peres as Labour Party Chairman.

In June 1997 the US House of Representatives voted in favour of recognizing Jerusalem as the undivided capital of Israel and of transferring the US embassy there, from Tel-Aviv. The decision coincided with violent clashes between Palestinian civilians and Israeli troops in both Gaza and Hebron. Meanwhile, Yasser Arafat, fearing Israeli reoccupation of Hebron, assigned 200 police-officers to patrol the area.

In July 1997 the USA brokered an agreement between Israel and the PA to resume peace talks the following month. At the end of July, however, on the eve of a planned visit to Israel by Dennis Ross, two Hamas suicide bombers killed 14 civilians and wounded more than 150 others in Jerusalem. Ross cancelled his visit and Israel suspended payment of tax revenues to the PA and again closed off the Gaza Strip and the West Bank. Netanyahu insisted that the restrictions would remain until the Palestinians demonstrated a commitment to combat terrorism. Arafat subsequently convened a forum of Palestinian groups, during which he publicly embraced Hamas leaders and urged them, together with Islamic Jihad, to unite with the Palestinian people against Israeli policies. Israel reopened borders with the West Bank and Gaza in early September, but restrictions were reimposed three days later after suicide bombings in West Jerusalem killed eight people and injured at least 150 others. The security crisis cast doubt on the viability of a planned visit by US Secretary of State Madeleine Albright in mid-September. However, Albright's visit was positively received; Israel released further Palestinian assets (one-third of tax revenues owed to the PA had been released in August), while the Palestinians announced the closure of 17 institutions affiliated to Hamas. In early October Netanyahu and Arafat met for the first time in eight months. Israel announced plans to release further dues to the PA and to reopen the sealed borders. However, Israel failed to participate in a second round of negotiations, scheduled for that month, aimed at accelerating the 'final status' talks, and Netanyahu stated that further redeployments would not take place until Palestinians made further efforts to combat terrorism.

Renewed hostilities erupted in northern Israel in August 1997 after Hezbollah launched a rocket attack on civilians in Kiryat Shmona. The attack, made in retaliation for raids by Israeli commandos in which five Hezbollah members were killed, prompted further air-strikes by Israel in southern Lebanon. Violence escalated, with the shelling by the SLA of the Lebanese port of Sidon resulting in at least six deaths. Domestic pressure for an Israeli withdrawal from southern Lebanon increased after 12 Israeli marines, allegedly on a mission to assassinate Shi'ite leaders, were killed south of Sidon in September.

Meanwhile, relations between Jordan and Israel deteriorated in September 1997, after members of the Israeli intelligence force, Mossad, attempted to assassinate a Hamas leader, Khalid Meshaal, in Amman. In an attempt to preserve relations, intensive negotiations took place between Netanyahu, Crown Prince Hassan of Jordan and US officials. Several agreements regarding the release of prisoners ensued: in October Israel freed the Hamas spiritual leader, Sheikh Ahmad Yassin, in return for the release by Jordan of two Mossad agents arrested in connection with the attack on Meshaal; a further 12 Mossad agents were expelled by the Jordanian authorities following the release of 23 Jordanian and 50 Palestinian prisoners by Israel.

Bilateral negotiations between Israel and the PA resumed in November 1997. Israel offered to decelerate its construction of Jewish settlements in return for Palestinian approval of a plan to delay further redeployments of Israeli troops from the West Bank. At the same time, the Israeli Government announced plans to build 900 new housing units in the area. This virtual stalemate in the peace process prompted several Arab states to boycott the Middle East and North Africa economic conference, held in Doha, Qatar, in mid-November, which an Israeli delegation was scheduled to attend. Separate peace talks involving

Albright, Netanyahu and Arafat were inconclusive. At the end of November the Israeli Cabinet agreed in principle to a partial withdrawal from the West Bank, but specified neither its timing nor its scale. Conflicting opinions within the Cabinet meant that Netanyahu failed to produce a conclusive redeployment plan to present at talks with Albright in Paris in December; furthermore, the Israeli Government had recently prevented PA officials from conducting a census in East Jerusalem. Israeli and PA officials none the less demonstrated their commitment to peace by signing a security memorandum.

In late 1997 divisions within the coalition Government obliged Netanyahu, in order to secure passage in the Knesset of the 1998 budget vote (effectively a demonstration of confidence in the Prime Minister), to grant concessions to various parties, in particular to right-wing members of the coalition. In January 1998 David Levy, the Gesher leader, withdrew from the Government, citing dissatisfaction with the budget and with the slow rate of progress in the peace talks. Gesher's departure reduced Netanyahu's majority to only two votes, although the budget secured the approval of the Knesset, and Netanyahu subsequently survived a vote of 'no-confidence'. Meanwhile, Netanyahu announced that he would not make any further decisions regarding the peace process until the Palestinians had demonstrated further efforts to combat terrorism, reduced their security forces from 40,000 to 24,000 and amended their National Charter to recognize Israel's right to exist. The Israeli premier again failed, in January 1998, to present a plan of redeployment in talks with President Clinton in Washington. Netanyahu did express interest in a US proposal to withdraw troops from at least 10% of the land in several stages, but this was decisively rejected by Arafat. At the end of February Arafat also rejected Netanyahu's appeals for a peace summit, stating that he would hold talks only after Israel had agreed to further redeployment and had fully implemented existing agreements. Progress had been further frustrated in early February, when the Ministry of the Interior approved plans to construct a new 132-home Jewish settlement in East Jerusalem.

Addressing the Knesset in March 1998, UN Secretary-General Kofi Annan urged Israel to end 'provocative acts' towards the Palestinians, including the building of Jewish settlements. Meanwhile, the US Special Co-ordinator to the Middle East, Dennis Ross, visited the region, briefing Netanyahu, Arafat and Egypt's President Mubarak on a US peace proposal whereby Israel would redeploy from 13.1% of the West Bank over a 12-week period in exchange for specific security guarantees from the Palestinians. The proposal failed to revive the peace process, however, with Israel reportedly agreeing only to a phased redeployment from 9% of the territory. Violence had recently re-erupted on the West Bank, after three Palestinians were killed by Israeli soldiers near Hebron. Moreover, the assassination—allegedly by the Israeli secret services—of a senior Hamas official in late March precipitated widespread protests among Palestinians. Netanyahu warned that the risk of reprisal attacks on Israeli citizens would prevent further redeployments of Israeli troops from the Occupied Territories.

In April 1998 Netanyahu and President Mubarak held their first meeting (in Cairo) since May 1997. President Mubarak reportedly advised Netanyahu to 'respond positively' to the US peace initiative. However, the Israeli Prime Minister rejected the proposal, which was publicly accepted by Arafat the following day. In May 1998 US Secretary of State Albright conducted separate rounds of talks with Netanyahu and Arafat in London, United Kingdom, with the aim of reviving negotiations on redeployments. The talks were inconclusive, and further meetings held in Washington later that month similarly failed to achieve a breakthrough. Meanwhile, celebrations to commemorate the 50th anniversary of the founding of the State of Israel provoked widespread rioting in the Occupied Territories.

In May 1998 the UN Committee Against Torture ruled for a second successive year that interrogation methods used by the Israeli security service, Shin Bet, were in contravention of the 1984 UN Convention against Torture and Other Cruel, Inhuman or Degrading Treatment or Punishment (which Israel had ratified in 1991). Shortly afterwards proceedings began at the Israeli Supreme Court in an unprecedented appeal case, brought by Palestinian detainees and two human rights groups, questioning the legality of Shin Bet's use of torture. (In September 1999 the Supreme Court ruled that the use of 'physical force' by Shin Bet during the interrogation of suspects was illegal. The ruling invalidated a 1987 decision that allowed the use of 'moderate physical pressure' against those accused of plotting terrorist attacks against Israel. Details of a report compiled by the State Comptroller in 1995 concerning Shin Bet's interrogation methods during the first Palestinian *intifada* were published in early 2000. The report acknowledged that Palestinian prisoners had been 'systematically tortured' and that guide-lines allowing 'moderate physical pressure' had been exceeded.)

Details of the US peace plan were published in the Israeli newspaper *Ha'aretz* in June 1998. Although several Jewish settler groups threatened a campaign of civil disobedience in protest at any further redeployments from the West Bank, it became apparent that Netanyahu was under increasing pressure to accept the US initiative. Public opinion was reportedly shifting in favour of further redeployments, and in late June President Weizman (who had been elected for a second presidential term in March) angered Netanyahu by publicly demanding the dissolution of the Knesset and early elections so that Israelis might choose the future direction of peace talks. Meanwhile, further controversy arose when the Cabinet approved Netanyahu's draft plan whereby the municipal boundaries of Jerusalem would be extended to incorporate seven West Bank Jewish settlements—to create a 'Greater Jerusalem' covering six times the current area of the city. Arab leaders accused Netanyahu of seeking formally to annex parts of the West Bank, and the UN Security Council urged Israel to abandon the proposals. Arafat stated that the peace process was 'completely deadlocked', and that Palestinians could make no further concessions beyond those outlined in the US plan.

The first substantive senior-level meetings for several months between Israeli and Palestinian negotiators took place in Jerusalem in July 1998. However, Arafat withdrew his delegates in protest at what he described as Israel's 'obscure formulations' on the US peace plan. Israel had reportedly offered a compromise package, proposing redeployment from 10%, and partial redeployment from 3%, of the West Bank. By the end of August there were indications that the so-called '10+3' plan might lead to a revival of peace negotiations; however, the assassination of a settler rabbi in Hebron increased tensions on the West Bank. In September Israel again closed its borders with the West Bank and Gaza, following warnings of imminent terrorist attacks in retaliation for the fatal shooting, by Israeli troops, of two leading Hamas members. Nevertheless, a US-mediated meeting between Netanyahu and Arafat held in Washington at the end of the month resulted in an agreement by the two leaders to attend a peace summit in mid-October, with the aim of finalizing agreement on further Israeli redeployments.

In July 1998, meanwhile, the Labour Party (supported by some members of Netanyahu's coalition) secured a preliminary vote seeking the dissolution of the Knesset and early elections. In October Ariel Sharon was redesignated Minister of Foreign Affairs and National Infrastructure. (Netanyahu had assumed the foreign affairs portfolio following David Levy's resignation in January.) Sharon's promotion was interpreted as an attempt by Netanyahu to secure the support of right-wing nationalists and settler groups, since he was known to be opposed to redeployment from a further 13% of the West Bank.

On 23 October 1998, after nine days of intensive talks with President Clinton at the Wye Plantation, Maryland, USA, Netanyahu and Arafat signed an agreement that effectively outlined a three-month timetable for the implementation of the 1995 Interim Agreement and signalled the commencement of 'final status' talks, which should have begun in May 1996. The signing of this Wye River Memorandum, which broke a 19-month stalemate in the Israeli-Palestinian track of the Middle East peace process, was achieved despite a Palestinian grenade attack in Beersheba, in which at least 60 people were injured. With the mediation of Clinton and King Hussein of Jordan, Israel agreed to redeploy its troops from 13.1% of the West Bank, while the PA agreed to intensify measures to prevent terrorism and to rewrite the Palestinian National Charter. In an effort to reassure Jewish settler groups in the West Bank, who protested against the 'land-for-security' deal, Netanyahu gave assurances that the construction of 1,025 new homes at the Har Homa settlement would proceed. On 11 November, after the postponement of four scheduled meetings (due to a bombing by Islamic Jihad in Jerusalem and Israeli fears of further terrorist attacks), the Israeli Cabinet approved the Wye Memorandum by a majority of eight votes to four. Netanyahu subsequently reiterated that a number of conditions would first have to be met by the Palestinians (primarily an annulment of clauses in the Palestinian National Charter demanding Israel's destruction),

and threatened effective Israeli annexation of areas of the West Bank if a Palestinian state were to be declared on 4 May 1999. (Arafat continued to reassert his right to declare a Palestinian state on the expiry date of the interim stage defined in Oslo, an act Netanyahu claimed would fundamentally violate the Oslo accords.) In mid-November 1998 Arafat retracted a previous warning that the PLO would renew its armed struggle against Israel. On 17 November the Knesset ratified the Wye Memorandum by 75 votes to 19. Three days later the Israeli Government implemented the first stage of renewed redeployment from the West Bank, also releasing 250 Palestinian prisoners and signing a protocol allowing for the opening of an international airport at Gaza.

During December 1998 it became increasingly evident that divisions within Netanyahu's coalition over implementation of the Wye Memorandum were making government untenable. Attempts to avoid an early general election by offering to reappoint David Levy to the Government were frustrated when the Gesher leader refused the terms proposed by Netanyahu, and the administration effectively collapsed when the Minister of Finance, Yaacov Ne'eman, announced his resignation. Shortly afterwards the Knesset voted to hold elections to the legislature and premiership in the spring of 1999. Netanyahu's leadership was challenged by senior members of his own party, including Binyamin Begin, who left Likud to form the New Herut party. In January 1999 Netanyahu dismissed Itzhak Mordechai as Minister of Defence, appointing Moshe Arens in his place. Speculation that Mordechai had been intending to leave Likud was apparently confirmed when he launched the new Centre Party.

Meanwhile, unrest in the West Bank and Gaza increased prior to a visit by President Clinton in December 1998. Palestinians demonstrated in support of almost 700 prisoners who began a nine-day hunger-strike to protest against Israel's failure to honour commitments made at Wye Plantation to release Palestinians detained on political charges. Clinton attended a session of the PNC, at which the removal from the Palestinian National Charter of all clauses seeking Israel's destruction was reaffirmed. At a meeting between Clinton, Arafat and Netanyahu at the Erez check-point, Netanyahu reiterated accusations that the Palestinians had not adequately addressed their security commitments and announced that he would not release Palestinian prisoners considered to have 'blood on their hands'. Netanyahu also repeated his demand that Arafat renounce his intention to declare Palestinian statehood in May 1999. Arafat, for his part, reasserted demands for a moratorium on the construction of Jewish settlements in disputed territory. Following the meeting, Netanyahu announced that the second phase of Israeli troop deployment envisaged by the Wye Memorandum, scheduled for 18 December, would not be undertaken. The Knesset subsequently voted to suspend implementation of the Wye Memorandum, thereby effectively suspending the peace process. In late December Arafat freed the Hamas spiritual leader, Sheikh Ahmad Yassin, from house arrest, prompting further Israeli claims that agreed anti-terrorism measures were not being implemented.

In January 1999 it was reported that the US Secretary of State would refuse to meet Ariel Sharon during a visit to the USA, owing to US frustration with Israel's 'freezing' of peace negotiations. The stalemate appeared likely to continue as violent clashes between Israelis and Palestinians again erupted in the West Bank. The US Administration threatened to withhold US $1,200m. promised to Israel to fund its redeployment in the West Bank unless it complied with the terms of the Wye Memorandum. For several months President Clinton refused to hold a private meeting with Netanyahu, while agreeing to meet Arafat in March to discuss his threatened unilateral declaration of statehood on 4 May; following intense international pressure, the declaration was postponed at the end of April. Meanwhile, relations between Israel and the European Union (EU) deteriorated, owing to continuing disagreement over Likud's settlement programme and the status of Jerusalem. In March 1999 the EU strongly condemned Israeli instructions to foreign delegations not to visit the PLO's *de facto* headquarters in Jerusalem. Earlier in March the EU had provoked condemnation from Israeli officials by reaffirming that it regarded Jerusalem as a *corpus separatum* (in accordance with UN Resolution 181), which was outside Israeli sovereignty.

Although in March 1998 Ariel Sharon announced publicly that Israel still planned to assassinate the Hamas leader Khalid Meshaal, the conclusion of several bilateral trade agreements indicated an improvement in Israeli-Jordanian relations. In

April King Hussein and the Israeli Prime Minister met for the first time since the assassination attempt which had strained relations in 1997. In December 1998 Israel agreed to allow foreign airlines en route to Jordan to use Israeli airspace. There was widespread apprehension about the future of Israel's relations with Jordan following the death, in February 1999, of King Hussein (whose funeral was attended by Netanyahu). Nevertheless, the Israeli Government expected 'continuity' in bilateral relations under Jordan's new King Abdullah. In September Israel commended the Jordanian authorities for their arrest of Khalid Meshaal and two other Hamas leaders. King Abdullah made his first official visit to Israel in April 2000.

Hostilities between Israeli forces and Hezbollah in southern Lebanon persisted throughout 1998. In that year some 23 Israeli soldiers were killed, and there was increasing pressure on Netanyahu, even from some Likud ministers, for a unilateral withdrawal from the territory. On 1 April the Israeli Security Cabinet voted unanimously to adopt UN Resolution 425 (which called for an immediate withdrawal of Israeli troops from all Lebanese territory), provided that the Lebanese army gave security guarantees. However, both Lebanon and Syria demanded an unconditional withdrawal. In June the first Israeli-Lebanese exchange of prisoners and bodies since July 1996 took place. Fighting escalated when, in August 1998, Hezbollah launched rocket attacks on northern Israel in retaliation for an Israeli helicopter attack in which a senior Lebanese military official died. Seven Israeli soldiers died in two attacks in November, leading Netanyahu to curtail a European tour in order to hold an emergency cabinet meeting on a possible withdrawal. In December an Israeli air attack in which eight Lebanese civilians were killed provoked condemnation from the ILMG, which declared it to be a violation of the cease-fire 'understanding' reached in April 1996. Following several Hezbollah attacks, in January 1999 Netanyahu reiterated previous warnings that in the event of further attacks, Israeli troops would target Lebanese infrastructure. In February three Israeli army officers were killed during fighting with Hezbollah. A few days later the commander of the Israeli army unit for liaison with the SLA became the most senior Israeli officer to be killed in southern Lebanon since 1982. Israel responded with its heaviest air raids against Lebanon since the 1996 'Grapes of Wrath' operation, prompting fears of another major conflict. However, Israel's Minister of Defence stated that Israel had no intention of escalating the conflict as long as Syria refrained from encouraging Hezbollah rocket attacks on northern Israel.

In July 1998 it had been reported that Israel and Syria might resume talks on the disputed Golan Heights, on the basis of a French initiative whereby Israel would accept a 'land-for-peace' formula in return for Syrian acceptance of Israel's security needs. However, in late July the Knesset approved preliminary legislation seeking a majority parliamentary vote and a referendum before Israel would withdraw from the territory; the vote was condemned in Syria. Tensions between the two countries increased in September when Israel publicly stated its intention to enter a military alliance with Turkey.

By the time of the general election, held on 17 May 1999, Netanyahu and Ehud Barak were the only remaining candidates for the premiership. Following a decision by Itzhak Mordechai to transfer his support to Barak, who in March had established the 'One Israel' movement (including Gesher and the moderate Meimad party), victory for the Labour leader seemed certain. Barak was elected Prime Minister with 56.1% of the total votes cast. In the elections to the Knesset, Barak's One Israel alliance secured 26 seats, while Likud's strength declined from 32 seats to 19. Shas, meanwhile, increased its representation to 17 seats. (In April the Shas leader, Aryeh Der'i, had been sentenced to four years' imprisonment, having been found guilty of bribery, fraud and breach of public trust; his sentence was suspended pending appeal, enabling him to campaign in the elections.) The new Knesset contained an unprecedented 15 factions. Some 78.8% of the electorate were reported to have voted. Netanyahu subsequently resigned from both the Knesset and the Likud leadership, and in September Ariel Sharon was elected as Likud's new Chairman.

Although Ehud Barak had received a clear mandate to form a government that would attempt to revive the stalled Middle East peace process, Israel's Prime Minister-elect committed himself only to seek a formula for regional peace. Barak stated that he would observe four 'security red lines' concerning negotiations with the Palestinians: Jerusalem would remain under Israeli sovereignty; there would be no return to the pre-1967

borders; most West Bank settlers would remain in settlements under Israeli sovereignty; and no 'foreign armies' would be based west of the Jordan river. Following complex negotiations, Barak forged a broad coalition of the Centre Party, Shas, Meretz, Israel B'Aliyah and the NRP (talks with Likud having collapsed), which was endorsed by the Knesset in early July 1999. Barak himself took the defence portfolio, granting the foreign affairs ministry to David Levy; Itzhak Mordechai was made one of three Deputy Prime Ministers, while Shimon Peres became Minister of Regional Co-operation.

In July 1999 the Speaker of the Palestinian Legislative Council became the first senior Palestinian official to address the Knesset. Meanwhile, Barak held a series of summit meetings with Arab and European leaders, culminating in discussions with US President Clinton in mid-July. The first direct talks between the new Israeli premier and Yasser Arafat were held at the Erez check-point in Gaza on 11 July, during which both leaders reaffirmed their commitment to peace. In late July, however, PA negotiators were angered when Barak expressed the desire to combine the Israeli land withdrawals agreed under the terms of the Wye Memorandum with 'final status' negotiations, although Israel later agreed to withdraw its demand to postpone further redeployments.

In early September 1999, during a visit to the region by US Secretary of State Albright, Barak and Arafat travelled to Egypt for talks at Sharm esh-Sheikh. On 4 September the two leaders signed the Sharm esh-Sheikh Memorandum (or Wye Two accords), which outlined a revised timetable for implementation of the outstanding provisions of the original Wye Memorandum in order to facilitate the resumption of 'final status' talks: a new target date—13 September 2000—was set for the conclusion of a comprehensive 'final status' settlement, with a framework agreement to be in place by 13 February. (One important change was the reduction, to 350, of the number of Palestinian prisoners to be released by Israel.) Although the success of the deal was immediately threatened by two suicide bomb attacks in northern Israel, on 8 September the Knesset ratified the Wye Two accords. The following day Israel released some 200 Palestinian prisoners, and on 10 September a further 7% of the West Bank was transferred to Palestinian civilian control. A ceremony marking the launch of 'final status' negotiations between Israel and the PA was held at the Erez check-point on 13 September, and a few days later it was reported that Barak and Arafat had held a secret meeting to discuss an agenda for such talks. Meanwhile, Israel signed an agreement with the USA to purchase 50 F-16 fighter aircraft. A further 151 Palestinian prisoners were released from Israeli custody in mid-October. On 25 October a southern 'safe passage' for Palestinians travelling between Gaza and Hebron was finally opened, under the terms of the Wye Memorandum.

In September 1999 Netanyahu and his wife were questioned by police following allegations, published in the daily *Yediot Aharanot*, that they had charged extensive private work on their residence to the Prime Minister's Office while Netanyahu was in power. Further allegations of the misuse of public funds emerged, and in October police reportedly seized several official gifts from Netanyahu's home and offices. (In March 2000 the police recommended that Netanyahu should stand trial on charges of bribery, fraud, breach of trust and obstruction of justice, and that his wife should be charged with fraud and theft; however, the Attorney-General announced in September that no prosecution would be brought against the Netanyahus, owing to insufficient evidence.)

In September 1999 Shas and Likud announced that they were to co-ordinate their policies on issues of national importance; however, Shas (which was embroiled in a dispute with its coalition partners over the allocation of funds for Shas' education proposals) denied rumours that the party was about to join the opposition. Meanwhile, Eliyahu Yishai, the Minister of Labour and Social Affairs, replaced Aryeh Der'i (who had resigned the leadership in June) as Chairman of Shas.

In the autumn of 1999 Barak encountered severe criticism by left-wing groups and Palestinians over his Government's apparent intention to continue to approve the expansion of Jewish settlements in the West Bank. (Since coming to power, the Government had issued tenders for some 2,600 new homes in such settlements.) Barak subsequently angered settler groups with a ruling that several of the 42 'outpost settlements' established in the West Bank under the Likud Government had been built illegally; 12 of the 'outposts' were dismantled in October.

In October 1999 Mauritania became the third member of the Arab League (after Egypt and Jordan) to establish full diplomatic relations with Israel. In early November Arafat, Barak and US President Clinton held talks in Oslo, Norway. Representatives of Israel and the PA commenced talks on 'final status' issues on 8 November in the West Bank city of Ramallah; further rounds of talks were held during November and December. Prior to the discussions, three bombs had exploded in the Israeli town of Netanya, wounding at least 33 people. (Although no group claimed responsibility for the bombings, they followed an alleged warning by the military wing of Hamas of an escalation of violence in protest at Israeli settlement policies.) The redeployment of Israeli armed forces from a further 5% of the West Bank (due on 15 November) was delayed owing to a dispute over which areas were to be transferred. In December Barak and Arafat met on Palestinian territory for the first time. At the end of the month Israel released some 26 Palestinian 'security' prisoners as a 'goodwill' gesture.

On 6–7 January 2000 Israeli troops withdrew from a further 5% of the West Bank. However, Israel subsequently announced the postponement of a third redeployment, agreed under Wye Two (and scheduled for 20 January), until Barak had returned from talks with Syrian representatives in the USA (see below). Meanwhile, a bomb explosion in northern Israel was believed to have been carried out by Palestinian militants. In early February PA officials suspended peace negotiations with Israel, following the decision by the Israeli Cabinet to withdraw its armed forces from a sparsely populated 6.1% of the West Bank. The redeployment from a further 6.1% of the West Bank took place on 21 March (Israel had on the previous day released 15 Palestinian prisoners), facilitating an official resumption of 'final status' talks. In that month a ruling by Israel's Supreme Court that the allocation of state-owned land on the basis of religion, nationality or ethnicity was illegal allowed Israeli Arabs to purchase land for the first time.

Meanwhile, in May 1999 senior Israeli commanders in southern Lebanon for the first time urged an immediate Israeli withdrawal. (Prime Minister-elect Barak had made a pre-election pledge to recall Israeli troops from Lebanon by July 2000.) In June 1999 the SLA completed a unilateral withdrawal from the Jezzine enclave. Later that month Barak was reportedly angered when the outgoing Netanyahu administration launched a series of air attacks on Lebanon, destroying Beirut's main power station and other infrastructure, in response to Hezbollah rocket attacks on northern Israel. In July Barak confirmed that he would propose to his Cabinet a unilateral withdrawal from Lebanon if no peace accord had been reached (in the context of an agreement with Syria over the Golan Heights) within one year. In December Israel apologized for an attack in which some 18 Lebanese schoolchildren were injured. The incident followed an increase in Hezbollah military action after the announcement of a resumption of Israeli-Syrian peace negotiations (see below). In late December Israel and Syria reached an 'understanding in principle' to limit the fighting in southern Lebanon; the informal cease-fire did not endure, however, and in late January 2000 a senior SLA commander became the first Israeli soldier to be killed there for five months. At the end of January the deaths of another three of its soldiers led Israel to declare that peace talks with Syria would not resume until Syria took action to restrain Hezbollah. Attacks by Hezbollah escalated none the less, and in February Israel retaliated with a massive series of bombing raids on Lebanese infrastructure. Israel announced a unilateral withdrawal from the 1996 'cease-fire' agreement, and there were renewed fears of a major conflict. Following the killing of three Israeli soldiers by Hezbollah in the same month, the Israeli Security Cabinet approved wide powers for the Prime Minister to order immediate retaliatory bombing raids in Lebanon.

In January 2000 a criminal investigation began into the financial affairs of the Israeli President, Ezer Weizman, following allegations that he had accepted some US $450,000 in undeclared donations from a French businessman while serving as a member of the Knesset. Despite demands for his resignation, Weizman insisted that no favours had been granted in return for the donations. In April the police declared that Weizman would not be prosecuted, owing to a lack of evidence. Weizman had announced that he would retire prior to the expiry of his second term of office in 2003, citing ill health; after the police investigation failed completely to exonerate him, the President stated in May 2000 that he would resign on 10 July. Also in January the State Comptroller accused the One Israel

campaign team for the 1999 general election of serious financial irregularities. The Attorney-General subsequently ordered a criminal investigation into the financial activities of One Israel and several other parties; One Israel was required to pay a fine of NIS 13.5m. In March 2000 Itzhak Mordechai took a leave of absence from the Government pending a police investigation into allegations that he had sexually harassed a female ministry employee. Mordechai denied the claims, but in May he was arraigned on three charges of sexual harassment; he subsequently resigned as leader of the Centre Party, in which post he was succeeded by the Minister of Tourism, Amnon Lipkin-Shahak. In March 2001 Mordechai was found guilty of committing indecent assault against two of the women; he subsequently received an 18-month suspended sentence.

A third round of 'final status' discussions opened in Eilat on 30 April 2000. The talks began acrimoniously, as Palestinian negotiators denounced a recent decision by the Israeli Government to approve construction of 174 new housing units in the West Bank. Maps presented by Israeli officials to the PA in early May, defining Barak's interpretation of a future Palestinian state, were firmly rejected by the Palestinians. Two days later Barak and Arafat held a crisis meeting in Ramallah, at which Barak proposed that Israel transfer to full PA control three Arab villages situated close to Jerusalem, on condition that the third West Bank redeployment (scheduled for June) was postponed until after the conclusion of a final peace settlement. The Knesset approved the transfer in mid-May. The decision prompted the threatened withdrawal from the Government, should the transfer take place, of the NRP, while Jewish settlers held a mass demonstration in Jerusalem. Meanwhile, protests by Palestinians in support of a hunger-strike by Palestinians held in Israeli gaols escalated into a 'day of rage' on 15 May. Three days of violent gun battles in the West Bank between Israeli forces, Palestinian police and civilians resulted in the deaths of some seven Palestinians, while several Israelis were injured. In late May Barak ordered an end to 'secret' talks between Israeli and Palestinian officials in Stockholm, Sweden, after an Israeli child was seriously injured in a petrol bomb attack near Jericho. Barak also announced that an Israeli withdrawal from the Arab villages would not be implemented until the PA took appropriate measures to curb the unrest. By early June, however, Barak appeared to be willing to resume peace negotiations, after the PA arrested several Palestinians believed to have been responsible for the recent violence. Later in the month Israel released three Palestinian prisoners as a 'goodwill' gesture.

A major political crisis developed in June 2000 when One Israel's largest coalition partner, the right-wing Shas, threatened to withdraw from the Government unless its demands regarding the peace process and the funding of its religious schools were met. After Barak capitulated to most of the party's demands, the four Shas ministers withdrew their resignations, thereby averting the collapse of the coalition; however, the return of Shas to the Government led to the departure of the two Meretz ministers, the Minister of Education, Yossi Sarid, and the Minister of Industry and Trade, Ran Cohen, both strong supporters of the Oslo peace process. In early July the former Shas leader, Aryeh Der'i, received a three-year term of imprisonment, having lost his appeal against conviction on bribery and fraud charges; he began his sentence in September.

In early July 2000 Bill Clinton invited Barak and Arafat to attend a peace summit at the US presidential retreat at Camp David, in an attempt to reach a framework agreement for a final settlement. Immediately prior to the summit the Israeli Government was severely weakened when the three right-wing parties (Israel B'Aliyah, the NRP and Shas) withdrew from the coalition, in protest at what they perceived to be Barak's readiness to concede more Israeli territory to the PA. Barak was left without six Cabinet ministers (including the Minister of the Interior, Natan Sharansky) and narrowly survived a 'no confidence' motion in the Knesset. President Clinton opened the Camp David talks on 11 July, and, although no accord had been reached by their scheduled close on 19 July, he persuaded Israeli and Palestinian negotiators to remain at Camp David. However, despite intensive mediation efforts, the summit ended on 25 July without agreement. Progress had reportedly been made concerning the borders of a future Palestinian entity and on the issue of Palestinian refugees. It had none the less proved impossible for the two sides to reach a compromise regarding the future status of Jerusalem. Barak had apparently offered the PA municipal authority over certain parts of East Jerusalem and access to Islamic holy sites in the Old City, although Israel would retain full sovereignty. Arafat, meanwhile, had continued to demand a Palestinian state with East Jerusalem as its capital and sovereignty over the Islamic holy sites. In the summit's final communiqué both sides vowed to continue the pursuit of a 'final status' settlement and to avoid 'unilateral actions'—thereby implying that Arafat would not declare a Palestinian state on 13 September. Nevertheless, the failure of the Camp David talks led to fears of renewed violence in the West Bank and Gaza.

In the presidential election held on 31 July 2000, the little-known Moshe Katsav of Likud unexpectedly defeated Barak's nominee, Shimon Peres, by 63 votes to 57 in a second round of Knesset voting (neither candidate having secured an outright majority in the first). Katsav was duly sworn in as the eighth President of Israel on 1 August, to serve an exceptional seven-year term. Immediately after the election Barak survived another 'no confidence' motion. However, in early August the Minister of Foreign Affairs, David Levy, announced his resignation, citing disagreements with Barak over the peace process (Levy had notably refused to attend the Camp David summit). The Minister of Public Security, Shlomo Ben-Ami, was subsequently appointed acting Minister of Foreign Affairs. (He was confirmed in this post in November.)

At the end of July 2000 Clinton stated that the USA was considering the relocation of its embassy from Tel-Aviv to Jerusalem, apparently reviving this issue to express US frustration at what it regarded as Palestinian intransigence regarding the city's status. Israeli and Palestinian officials none the less resumed talks in an attempt to restart the peace process, and the PA came under mounting international pressure to postpone a unilateral declaration of independence on 13 September. (Shortly before that date the Palestinian legislature voted to delay such a declaration for an indefinite period.) Meanwhile, in early August there were clashes between Muslims and Jews in Jerusalem, after Jewish extremists attempted to invade the al-Aqsa Mosque. In mid-August it was reported that Barak had for the first time hinted at offering statehood to the Palestinians. During that month Israeli security services claimed to have uncovered a number of Palestinian 'terrorist squads', and more than 20 alleged militants, some of whom were believed to have links with the Saudi Arabian-born leader of the militant Islamist al-Qa'ida (Base) network, Osama bin Laden, were arrested.

In late September 2000 Barak and Arafat met, at the Israeli premier's home, for the first time since the Camp David summit. However, the resumption of contacts was swiftly overshadowed by a serious escalation of violence between Palestinians and Israelis in the West Bank and Gaza Strip, which threatened to bring a complete halt to the Middle East peace process and led to increased fears that a conflict might once again engulf the region. On 28 September a highly controversial visit by Likud leader Ariel Sharon to the Temple Mount/Haram ash-Sharif compound in Jerusalem (the site of the Dome of the Rock and the al-Aqsa Mosque) provoked violent protests by stone-throwing Palestinians, which quickly spread throughout the Palestinian territories. For the first time Israeli Arabs clashed with security forces within Israel. The Israeli Government received international criticism for the severity of its response to the renewed Palestinian uprising—widely termed the al-Aqsa *intifada*. On 7 October the UN Security Council issued a resolution condemning the 'excessive use of force' employed by Israeli security forces against Palestinian demonstrators. Intensive diplomatic efforts aimed at restoring calm, particularly by Egypt, the USA and France, failed to end the violent confrontations (which within a month had claimed at least 140 lives—all but eight of them Palestinian—and wounded thousands more). Israel responded by closing the borders of the Palestinian territories and Gaza airport. Barak emphasized to Arafat his intention to suspend the peace process if the Palestinian unrest continued, and demanded that Arafat re-arrest about 60 militant Islamists who had recently been freed from Palestinian detention. Arafat, for his part, demanded an international inquiry into the causes of the violence. The crisis escalated in mid-October after Israeli forces launched rocket attacks on the headquarters of Arafat's Fatah movement in Ramallah and other PA offices, in response to the murder of two Israeli army reservists by a Palestinian crowd. Following mediation by the UN Secretary-General, on 16–17 October an emergency summit meeting between Barak and Arafat was convened by President Clinton and hosted by President Mubarak at Sharm esh-Sheikh, at which the Israelis and Palestinians agreed what the US President termed 'immediate concrete measures' to end the fighting (including the formation of an international fact-finding commission to investigate the causes of the conflict). However, violence intensified, and on 22 October Barak announced that Israel was to take a 'time-out' from the peace process. This declaration came as Barak undertook discussions with Likud on the formation of a 'national unity' government prior to the reconvening of the Knesset for the new parliamentary term; no compromise was reached, however, reportedly owing to Ariel Sharon's demand for a veto on all decisions relating to national security. Barak's decision formally to suspend Israel's participation in the peace process was precipitated by the final communiqué issued by Arab leaders after an emergency summit of the Arab League held in Cairo on 21–22 October, declaring that Israel bore full responsibility for the recent violence. Morocco, Tunisia and Oman announced that they had severed diplomatic relations with Israel, and Qatar broke off ties in November.

A suicide bomb attack perpetrated by Islamic Jihad on an Israeli military target in Gaza at the end of October 2000 apparently signalled a new campaign of violence by militant Palestinian organizations, and led the Israeli army to declare a new strategy of targeting for assassination the leaders of such groups, as well as senior Fatah commanders, whom it held responsible for 'terrorist' actions. (Israeli officials referred to this new policy as 'initiated attacks' or 'targeted killings'.) In early November the Israeli Minister of Regional Co-operation, Shimon Peres, held crisis talks with Arafat in Gaza, at which the two sides were reported to have agreed a fragile 'cease-fire' based on the provisions agreed the previous month at Sharm esh-Sheikh. The truce was broken almost immediately, however, when a car bomb exploded in Jerusalem, killing two Israelis; Islamic Jihad claimed responsibility for the attack, while Barak held the PA responsible through the recent release of dozens of Islamist militants. Arafat, meanwhile, requested US support in his appeal to the UN to provide an international peace-keeping force to protect Palestinians in the Occupied Territories. In mid-November Israel effectively imposed a complete economic blockade of the Palestinian areas, in an effort to overcome increasing concerns over its national security. Later in the month the explosion of a bomb close to a bus carrying Israeli schoolchildren (as a result of which two people died and several children were injured) provoked public outrage and led Israel to launch further air raids against Fatah targets in Gaza. Egypt responded by announcing that it was recalling its ambassador from Tel-Aviv; in early April 2002 Egypt suspended all direct contact with the Israeli Government, other than diplomatic channels aimed at restoring peace in the region.

It was reported at the end of November 2000 that the PA had rejected a partial peace plan put forward by Barak, whereby Israel would effect further troop redeployments from the West Bank in exchange for a postponement of discussions concerning the remaining 'final status' issues. Although US-brokered talks between Israeli and Palestinian negotiators resumed in December, in an effort to achieve a framework peace settlement prior to the expiry of Clinton's presidential term in late January 2001, the differences between the two sides remained apparently unbreachable. The outgoing US President had reportedly proposed a far-reaching deal which included granting the PA sovereignty over Islamic holy sites in the Old City of Jerusalem, while the area (also comprising the Temple Mount) would remain under Israeli control. However, the talks stalled in late December 2000 following the deaths of two Israelis in bomb explosions in Tel-Aviv and the Gaza Strip.

Meanwhile, in early December 2000 a US-led investigative committee—the Sharm esh-Sheikh Fact-Finding Committee or Mitchell Committee (its chairman was a former US senator, George Mitchell)—began conducting its research into the Israeli–Palestinian violence, which by now increasingly involved fighting between Jewish settlers and Palestinians in the West Bank and Gaza. In mid-December five Palestinian policemen were killed by Israeli security forces during a gun battle in the Gaza Strip. At the end of the month an extremist Jewish settler leader and a senior Fatah official were both shot dead in the West Bank. In early January 2001 three bombs exploded in the northern Israeli town of Netanya, wounding more than 40 people. Discussions between Israeli and PA representatives resumed in Taba, Egypt, in mid-January but were broken off a few days later, after the killing of a Jewish settler in the Gaza Strip—which resulted in revenge attacks on Palestinians by right-wing settlers. Renewed attempts at breaking the deadlock in the peace process had failed by early February, when Israelis turned their attention to the election for the premiership.

At the end of November 2000 Barak unexpectedly called early prime ministerial elections for 2001, in an apparent attempt to secure his increasingly beleaguered Government. The date of the premiership election was subsequently set for February 2001 (ahead of legislative elections due in May 2003). The Likud leader, Ariel Sharon, immediately declared his candidacy for the premiership, as did Netanyahu (against whom corruption charges had recently been abandoned). The former Prime Minister urged the Knesset either to amend electoral legislation that prevents non-members standing for election, or to vote for the assembly's dissolution and force general elections; however, Netanyahu withdrew from the premiership contest in December, after the Knesset voted against its own dissolution. Barak had formally resigned the premiership in early December, and was immediately chosen as the Labour Party's candidate. Despite the widely held belief that the Minister of Regional Co-operation, Shimon Peres, was the only Labour politician likely to present a viable challenge to Sharon, Barak insisted that he would contest, and win, the election for Prime Minister.

However, the premiership election, held on 6 February 2001, resulted in an overwhelming victory for Ariel Sharon of Likud, with 62.4% of the votes cast; the rate of participation was 62.3% of registered voters. Barak's defeat was compounded by the effective loss of the Israeli Arab vote—as the Arab parties had urged their supporters to boycott or abstain in the poll—and was interpreted as a decisive rejection of the Oslo peace process by the majority of Israelis. Sharon, whose principal election pledge had been to restore domestic and regional stability, immediately sought the formation of a broadly-based government of national unity, essentially in an effort to secure a political base in the Knesset (where Likud held only 19 of the 120 seats). Immediately following his defeat, meanwhile, Barak (who remained Prime Minister in a 'caretaker' capacity pending the appointment of a new cabinet) announced his resignation as Labour leader, leaving the party—already bitterly divided over the issue of participation in a Sharon government—in disarray. Barak later declared that he would not enter a government of national unity under Sharon (although he advised the Labour Party to finalize a coalition deal with Likud) and was to withdraw from political life 'for some time'. In late February Labour's Central Committee voted to join a coalition administration, despite the objections of certain prominent members of the party. This enabled Sharon to conclude coalition agreements principally with the religious and right-wing parties, and the 'national unity' Government was approved by the Knesset in early March. The 26-member Cabinet (reportedly the largest in Israel's history) included the ultra-orthodox Shas (whose leader, Eliyahu Yishai, became Deputy Prime Minister and Minister of the Interior), Israel B'Aliyah (Natan Sharansky's appointment as Deputy Prime Minister and Minister of Construction and Housing was particularly well received in the Occupied Territories) and the extreme right-wing Haichud Haleumi-Israel B'Aitainu bloc.

While Israel's new Minister of Defence, Binyamin Ben-Eliezer of the Labour Party, was known for his uncompromising stance, the appointment of Shimon Peres as Deputy Prime Minister and Minister of Foreign Affairs was a cause for cautious optimism for those who wished to see a revival of the Middle East peace process. However, there was considerable uncertainty regarding the prospects for a continuation of the Oslo process under Ariel Sharon, and without the active involvement of the Administration of Bill Clinton (whose term of office as US President had come to an end in January 2001): the new US Administration under George W. Bush chose initially to disengage itself from Arab–Israeli affairs in terms of its Middle East policy. Following his election victory, Sharon underlined his hard-line stance by affirming that he was not prepared to resume negotiations with the PA from their point of suspension in January. In the weeks after the election Hamas and other militant Palestinian groups intensified their campaign against Israeli military and civilian targets. In late February, during an official tour of the Middle East, the new US Secretary of State, Colin Powell, held talks with Prime Minister-elect Sharon, at which a demand by Powell that Israel end its blockade on the West Bank and Gaza Strip and deliver overdue tax transfers to the PA was refused by Sharon, who stated that the Palestinians should first halt all attacks against Israelis. In late March Sharon travelled to Washington for discussions with the US President. Mean-

while, Israel reinforced its closure of the Occupied Territories in a further effort to prevent attacks by Palestinian organizations. At the end of March Israel responded to the deaths of three settler children by launching military strikes against Palestinian military bases in Gaza City and Ramallah. Also in late March Arab League heads of state, meeting in the Jordanian capital, resolved *inter alia* to reinstate the 'secondary' economic boycott of Israel.

It was announced in early April 2001 that the Israeli Government had issued tenders for the construction of a further 708 Jewish housing units in the West Bank. The Palestinian *intifada* intensified in the middle of that month when Israel took unprecedented action in response to a Palestinian mortar attack on the Israeli town of Sderot. Israeli armed forces imposed road blockades which effectively divided the Gaza Strip into three sections, and sent tanks and bulldozers into the Gazan town of Beit Hanun. This represented Israel's first armed incursion into territory that it had transferred to PA control under the terms of the Oslo accords. However, amid heavy pressure from the US Administration (which described the occupation of Beit Hanun as 'excessive and disproportionate'), Israel withdrew its forces less than 24 hours later. Discussions between Israeli and PA security officials resumed in mid-April, but were unsuccessful as the cycle of revenge attacks continued. Nevertheless, hopes of an end to the Israeli–Palestinian conflict and a resumption of the Oslo peace talks were raised amid a revival of the so-called 'Egyptian-Jordanian initiative' or Taba plan. The initiative, based on the fragile understanding reached at Sharm esh-Sheikh in October 2000, required that the situation on the ground be restored to that prior to the start of the al-Aqsa *intifada*. It also stipulated that negotiations be resumed from the point at which they stalled in January 2001, and that Israel agree to halt its settlement programme in the Occupied Territories. Sharon stated in late April that Israel would endorse the Taba plan provided that the PA cease its demand for a complete 'freeze' on the construction of Jewish settlements; he also demanded the total cessation of Palestinian violence prior to the resumption of peace talks.

Israeli officials admitted in mid-May 2001 that the killing of five Palestinian police-officers in the West Bank had been 'accidental'. A few days later, following a Hamas suicide bombing in Netanya (in which five Israelis died), Israel deployed US-made F-16 fighter aircraft to shell security targets in the West Bank towns of Nablus and Ramallah, killing a number of Palestinians. In late May the Arab League and the Organization of the Islamic Conference (OIC, see p. 295) both urged member states to suspend all 'political' contacts with Israel. Meanwhile, the Sharm esh-Sheikh Fact-Finding Committee published its recommendations relating to the causes of the Israeli–Palestinian clashes. The so-called Mitchell Report referred to the visit of Ariel Sharon to the Islamic holy sites in September 2000 as 'provocative', but declined to single out for blame either Sharon or the PA leadership (which Israeli officials had accused of having orchestrated the violence). The Mitchell Report also demanded that Arafat undertake further measures to curb Palestinian 'terrorist' attacks, and called on Israel to end its economic blockade of the West Bank and Gaza Strip and to halt its settlement expansion programme. At the beginning of June 21 Israelis were killed, and more than 100 injured, in an attack by a Palestinian suicide bomber at a Tel-Aviv discothèque. The US Administration had recently undertaken diplomatic attempts to reactivate Israeli-Palestinian peace talks, and in early June the Director of the US Central Intelligence Agency (CIA), George Tenet, was dispatched to the region by President Bush. On 12 June proposals for a comprehensive cease-fire, brokered by Tenet, were approved by Israel and the PA; however, although Israel began to implement provisions made under the terms of the cease-fire to pull back troops from PA-controlled towns and to ease the economic blockade, the murder of two West Bank settlers by Palestinian gunmen and the killing of two Israeli soldiers in a suicide bombing in the Gaza Strip again hindered moves towards peace. During discussions in Washington with George W. Bush at the end of June, Sharon reportedly demanded 10 days of 'total calm' before Israel would implement the provisions of the Tenet plan. However, the PA rejected the terms of the US initiative, stating that the agreement favoured Israel.

In early July 2001 Israel's 'inner' Security Cabinet voted to accelerate its strategy of 'targeted killings' of leading Palestinians alleged to have orchestrated 'terrorist' acts against Israeli citizens. There were reports that some right-wing members of the Sharon Government even advocated the assassination of Yasser Arafat. However, the international community, in particular the UN, continued to denounce such a policy, which the PA claimed was in contravention of the 12 June cease-fire provisions. The Israeli Government also attracted strong criticism from other foreign Governments when, in early July, it ordered the destruction of several Palestinian homes in the Gaza Strip and East Jerusalem which were deemed to be 'illegal'. Amid an intensification of reciprocal attacks in the Occupied Territories, Egypt's President Mubarak convened a meeting in Cairo between Arafat and the Israeli Deputy Prime Minister and Minister of Foreign Affairs, Shimon Peres. In mid-July the USA indicated for the first time that it would support the deployment of an international peace-keeping force in the Territories, although Israel continued to oppose such a move. Meanwhile, on several occasions during late 2001 Israel ordered its forces into PA-controlled towns—among them Hebron, Bethlehem, Jenin and Beit Jala—where violent clashes between Israelis and Palestinians were taking place. At the end of the month two leading Hamas members, alleged by Israel to have been involved in the Tel-Aviv nightclub bombing, were killed during an air raid on Hamas media offices in Nablus. The massive Israeli strikes, in which at least six other Palestinians died, led the Hamas leadership to threaten that henceforth it would target senior Israeli politicians. In early August the Israeli administration published a 'most wanted' list of seven Palestinians whom it alleged to be prominent in the preparation of 'terrorist attacks'. Only days later at least 15 Israelis (including six children) were killed, and up to 100 injured, by a Palestinian suicide bomber at a Jerusalem restaurant. The Israeli Government responded to the bombing by taking temporary control of Orient House, the *de facto* headquarters of the PA in East Jerusalem. At the end of August Abu Ali Moustafa, leader of the Popular Front for the Liberation of Palestine (PFLP), was killed by Israeli security forces at the party's offices in Ramallah. In early September the PFLP claimed responsibility for four bomb attacks in Jerusalem, while another suicide bombing was also carried out there. The attacks prompted Israel to launch further raids against alleged Palestinian militants, and it was reported that the Israeli Ministry of Defence was drafting proposals to establish a military 'buffer zone' inside the West Bank in order to prevent further Palestinian attacks within Israel. A few days later a man believed to be an Israeli Arab carried out a suicide bomb attack in northern Israel, killing himself and three other Israeli citizens.

Meanwhile, in early September 2001 the election for the Labour Party leadership proved inconclusive when one of the two candidates, the Minister of Defence, Binyamin Ben-Eliezer, alleged that Knesset Speaker Avraham Burg (who had won a narrow victory) had engaged in vote-rigging. Ben-Eliezer initiated legal proceedings against the outcome of the ballot, and following a second election in late December was named as the new Labour leader. At the end of September a report released by the State Comptroller raised doubts about the legality of certain donations made to Ariel Sharon and his campaign team in the approach to the premiership election. In early October the Attorney-General ordered a criminal investigation into the alleged violation of campaign funding regulations; the Prime Minister and his son, Omri (who had managed Sharon's campaign), were both questioned by police. In mid-November Sharon was obliged to repay what had been found to be an illegal donation received by his campaign team.

International attention was abruptly distracted from the al-Aqsa *intifada* and its suppression after the massive suicide attacks apparently perpetrated by members of the al-Qa'ida group against New York and Washington, DC, on 11 September 2001. Initial fears that supposed evidence of the involvement of militant Islamists in the attacks would motivate Israel to escalate its military campaign against Palestinian targets appeared to be realized. The attacks on the USA accelerated US and EU efforts to urge Israel and the PA to effect a lasting cease-fire. However, Sharon demanded that he would not meet Arafat until the Palestinian leader could bring about 48 hours of 'complete quiet'. In late September Shimon Peres was finally granted permission by Sharon to hold talks with Yasser Arafat in the Gaza Strip, at which the two sides agreed to reactivate the cease-fire provisions brokered by CIA Director Tenet in June, and to implement the recommendations of the Mitchell Committee. However, by the time of the first anniversary of the outbreak of the al-Aqsa *intifada* on 28 September, there appeared to be little hope for an end to the Israeli–Palestinian

violence (which had led to the deaths of at least 600 Palestinians and more than 160 Israelis thus far). In early October two young Jewish settlers were killed by Hamas militants in Gaza. Israel responded by launching military strikes against Palestinian targets in Gaza City and sending troops into PA-controlled areas of Gaza and the West Bank; moreover, Israeli forces were granted the requisite powers to resume 'initiated attacks' against Palestinians deemed to be involved in 'terrorist' actions. Following further attacks by Palestinian militants within Israel in early October, crisis talks were convened between Peres and two senior PA officials, Saeb Erakat and Ahmad Quray (Abu Ala). The PA negotiators accused Israel of having violated the recent cease-fire, while Israel repeated demands that Arafat arrest Palestinian militants in order to end the bloodshed.

In mid-October 2001 the right-wing Haichud Haleumi-Israel B'Aitainu bloc withdrew from the governing coalition in protest at the Sharon administration's decision to pull back Israeli armed forces from the West Bank town of Hebron and at plans to ease the blockade on the Palestinian areas; the Minister of National Infrastructure, Avigdor Lieberman, and the hard-line Minister of Tourism, Rechavam Ze'evi, both resigned. Two days later (on the day that the ministers' resignations were to take effect) Ze'evi was assassinated at an hotel in Arab East Jerusalem by a militant of the PFLP, which claimed that the killing was in retaliation for the recent assassination of its leader. Following the murder of Ze'evi—who was the first Israeli cabinet minister to be assassinated by an Arab militant—the Haichud Haleumi-Israel B'Aitainu bloc maintained its presence in the Government, with Lieberman retaining his post and Benyamin Elon subsequently being named as the new Minister of Tourism. Sharon, meanwhile, suspended all contacts with the PA and declared that he held Arafat personally responsible for the minister's death. The Israeli Government also decided to reverse its recent moves to ease the economic restrictions on Palestinians in the West Bank and Gaza, and demanded that the PA immediately extradite the PFLP militants implicated in the assassination. A number of PFLP activists were subsequently detained by the PA, and the group's military wing was reportedly banned from operating in PA-controlled territory. In mid-October Israeli armed forces entered six Palestinian towns in the West Bank (including Ramallah, Jenin, Nablus and Bethlehem) and killed a leading member of Arafat's Fatah movement.

As the Israeli–Palestinian conflict escalated, US and European leaders urged Ariel Sharon not to carry out his threat to 'go to war' with the PA. In late October 2001, amid reports that some Labour ministers were openly critical of the Government's recent military actions in the West Bank and the resultant deaths of many Palestinian civilians, US officials urged Israel to pull back its troops from PA-controlled areas. Discussions took place between Israeli, Palestinian and US security officials at the end of the month; the Israeli representatives declared their terms for a staged withdrawal of troops from the six West Bank towns. Israeli forces duly withdrew from Bethlehem and Beit Jala, despite the continuing violence. (Five Israelis—four of them women—were shot dead in two separate incidents in the Israeli coastal town of Hadera.) However, Sharon announced that the withdrawal from the remaining four towns would not take place until the PA arrested more Islamist militants. In early November a Palestinian gunman, believed to be a member of Islamic Jihad, opened fire on a bus in Jerusalem, killing two Israelis and wounding more than 40 others. Sharon cancelled a scheduled visit to the USA, citing as his reason Israel's 'security situation'. However, it was reported that US officials were set to criticize the Israeli Government for its failure to co-operate in US attempts to ease tensions in the Middle East while the USA pursued its international 'war on terror'. Also in early November several thousand Israelis held a peace rally in Tel-Aviv on the occasion of the sixth anniversary of the murder of Itzhak Rabin. Meanwhile, the Knesset voted to revoke the parliamentary immunity of its most prominent Arab Israeli member, Azmi Bishara, in order that Bishara could answer charges of supporting terrorism against Israel and of undermining the Jewish State. The action followed comments made by Bishara in support of the Lebanese resistance organization, Hezbollah, and after he had assisted a group of Arab Israelis to visit their families in Syria. Trial proceedings against Bishara began in early December.

An EU delegation which visited Israel in mid-November 2001 failed to persuade Sharon to end his demand for a seven-day period without violence prior to the resumption of peace talks with the Palestinians and the redeployment of Israeli armed forces from PA-controlled territory. Later in that month both the UN Committee Against Torture and the human rights group Amnesty International issued warnings to Israel regarding the continuing use of torture by its security forces during the interrogation of Palestinian detainees; the UN also criticized Israel's policy of 'extra-judicial killing'. In late November the USA renewed diplomatic efforts to restart the Oslo peace process, following further Palestinian assaults on Jewish settlers and Israeli soldiers, and an Israeli rocket attack on Palestinian security positions in Gaza. The USA sent its two special envoys to the Middle East, William Burns and Anthony Zinni (the former had been named Assistant Secretary of State for Near Eastern Affairs in May, while Zinni's appointment had been made earlier in November), to the region in an attempt to broker a new cease-fire. However, hopes for a breakthrough were dimmed when Israel announced that it had appointed a hard-line former army general, Meir Dagan, as its chief negotiator in talks with US and PA representatives. At the end of November, while Sharon travelled to the USA for discussions with President Bush, Islamic Jihad claimed responsibility for a suicide bomb attack in Hadera in which at least three people died.

In early December 2001 the Israeli–Palestinian crisis witnessed a considerable escalation: in a single weekend some 25 Israelis were killed, and scores wounded, in suicide bombings perpetrated by Palestinian extremists in Haifa and Jerusalem, in retaliation for the killing of a Hamas leader. Four Palestinian gunmen were also killed in the West Bank town of Jenin. Sharon cut short his official visit to the USA, and Israel launched heavy military strikes against Palestinian security targets in the Occupied Territories; two of Arafat's helicopters were destroyed in one Israeli raid. The PA was reported to have arrested at least 100 Hamas and Islamic Jihad members in the aftermath of the weekend attacks; however the US Government urged Arafat to do more to end the violence. Although Israeli military action continued, especially in the Gaza Strip, senior Israeli and Palestinian security officials resumed talks a few days later. Israel escalated its military operations in the Territories in mid-December after 10 Israelis had died in a bomb attack in the West Bank. The Government responded to a speech by Arafat (in which he ordered militant groups to end their armed campaign against Israelis and pledged to arrest the perpetrators of the violence) by demanding 'concrete action' from the PA. Israeli armed forces staged a 'tactical' withdrawal from areas around Nablus and Ramallah to permit Arafat's security forces to arrest wanted Palestinian militants. However, Arafat remained confined to his headquarters in Ramallah after Israel imposed a travel ban on the Palestinian leader.

Anthony Zinni returned to the Middle East in early January 2002. Prior to the US Special Adviser's four-day visit to Israel, the Israeli administration ordered the partial withdrawal of its forces from some West Bank towns and the easing of certain restrictions against Palestinians there. Meanwhile, it was announced that Israeli forces in the Red Sea had intercepted a freighter ship, the *Karine-A*, claimed by Israel to be carrying a large consignment of Iranian-made heavy weaponry destined for the Gaza Strip, to be used by Palestinians in their *intifada* against Israel. Israeli and US officials claimed to have evidence of the PA's involvement in the trafficking of arms into the Occupied Territories. Arafat instituted an internal inquiry into the *Karine-A* affair, although he denied any knowledge of the shipment. Shortly afterwards, following a brief period of relative calm in Israel and the Occupied Territories, four Israeli soldiers were killed by Hamas gunmen in the Gaza Strip. Israel retaliated with force, even destroying the runway at Gaza airport. In mid-January Israeli forces assassinated a leader of Fatah's military wing, the Al-Aqsa Martyrs' Brigade, provoking retaliatory attacks by that organization in Hadera and Jerusalem in which six Israelis died. Israeli forces proceeded to tighten the blockade around Arafat's Ramallah offices. In late January four Palestinians were killed in an alleged raid on a Hamas cell in Nablus. At the end of the month Sharon approved a security plan involving the physical 'separation' of Jerusalem from the West Bank, in order to prevent attacks by Palestinian Islamist groups on Israeli territory.

By February 2002 there were reports that Sharon's popularity among the Israeli electorate was dwindling. Moreover, in that month at least 250 Israeli army reservists signed a petition stating their refusal to serve in the Occupied Territories. The Council for Peace and Security—which includes many senior reserve officers—urged the Government to redeploy its forces from most of the West Bank and Gaza. Sharon also received vociferous criticism from Palestinian and EU leaders when he declared his regret for not having 'liquidated' Yasser Arafat during the hostilities in Lebanon in 1982. In early February 2002 Sharon reportedly rejected new proposals for a peace settlement drafted by Shimon Peres and the Speaker of the Palestinian legislature, Ahmad Quray. Meanwhile, it appeared that Palestinian militants were increasingly targeting their attacks against the Israeli military and Jewish settlers in the Territories. In mid-February six Israeli soldiers died in a Palestinian assault on their West Bank check-point—this was the most serious attack on Israeli military forces since the start of the al-Aqsa *intifada*. The violence escalated significantly at this time, with the death toll rising on both sides as Israeli forces responded to Palestinian armed attacks on Israelis by launching heavy air-strikes against Ramallah and Gaza.

In early March 2002 the UN Security Council adopted Resolution 1397, affirming its 'vision' of both Israeli and Palestinian states 'within secure and recognized borders'. However, Israel rejected a peace initiative put forward by Crown Prince Abdullah of Saudi Arabia at the Arab League summit held in Beirut in late March, since the proposals required Israel to withdraw from all Arab lands occupied since 1967, in exchange for Arab recognition of the State of Israel and the normalization of relations. Towards the end of March 2002 a Hamas suicide bombing at a Passover celebration in Netanya resulted in the deaths of 29 Israelis, while some 140 were injured in the attack. The so-called 'Passover massacre' led the Israeli Government, on 29 March, to initiate a massive campaign of military incursions into West Bank towns—code-named 'Operation Defensive Shield'—with the declared aim of dismantling the Palestinian 'terrorist infrastructure' in order to prevent future suicide attacks against Israeli citizens. Yasser Arafat's presidential compound at Ramallah was surrounded by Israeli troops, leaving the Palestinian leader effectively isolated. At the end of the month the UN Security Council, meeting in emergency session, issued Resolution 1402 expressing 'grave concern' at the escalation of violence in Israel and the Palestinian territories. Egypt announced in early April that it was suspending all diplomatic relations with Israel except those that 'serve the Palestinian cause'. During the first two weeks of April intense fighting between the Israeli army and Palestinian militias occurred in the Jenin refugee camp—considered by Israel to be a base for Palestinian militants opposed to the Oslo accords. (A suicide bomber from Jenin had recently killed 15 Israelis at a café in Haifa.) Some 23 Israeli soldiers were reportedly killed in ambushes and gun battles at the Jenin camp, while Palestinian sources claimed that over 100 Palestinians had died in the fighting. Although a UN fact-finding mission had been scheduled to start investigations into Palestinian allegations that the Israeli army had committed war crimes at Jenin at the end of April, in early May the UN team was disbanded, following repeated refusals by Israel to accept both its composition and mandate. Meanwhile, in mid-April 2002 US Secretary of State Powell arrived in Israel in an attempt to negotiate an Israeli-Palestinian cease-fire, and the Bush Administration repeated demands for Israel to withdraw from PA-controlled towns. Although Israel did subsequently redeploy its forces from most areas of the West Bank, in late April Israeli troops continued to surround Arafat's presidential compound in Ramallah, as well as part of Bethlehem. Sharon demanded that the siege in Ramallah would continue until the PA handed over five men suspected of involvement in the assassination of Rechavam Ze'evi, as well as a militant believed to have plotted the shipment of weapons to Gaza, aboard the *Karine-A* freighter ship. The Palestinian leader was freed by the Israeli authorities at the beginning of May, after the PA agreed to hand over the prisoners: four of the men were convicted of direct involvement in Ze'evi's murder by an *ad hoc* Palestinian court inside the Ramallah compound and sentenced to various terms of imprisonment. (For further details of events in the West Bank and Gaza Strip in March–May 2002, see the chapter on the Palestinian Autonomous Areas.)

The right-wing Haichud Haleumi-Israel B'Aitainu bloc withdrew from the governing coalition in early March 2002, in protest against recent concessions made towards the Palestinians. However, the Government was strengthened a month later by the appointment of David Levy of Gesher and two ministers from the NRP as ministers without portfolio. In late May Sharon dismissed four Shas ministers who had failed to support emergency economic measures; Shas's fifth minister resigned in protest at the action. However, the four dismissed ministers were reinstated by Sharon in early June, having agreed to support the Government's amended economic package.

The Central Committee of Likud voted in early May 2002 to categorically reject the creation of a Palestinian state; the vote was widely considered to be a reverse for Ariel Sharon, who had always publicly accepted the possibility of Palestinian independence. As Palestinian militants continued to launch suicide bombings against Israeli citizens, in mid-June Israel was reported to have begun the construction of an electrified 'security' fence, which would eventually extend the length of its border with the West Bank, in an effort to prevent Palestinian militants from infiltrating Israeli territory to perpetrate further attacks. Despite international diplomatic efforts aimed at securing a new round of peace talks between Israel and the PA, and reports of a potential US initiative involving the creation of an 'interim' Palestinian state, there was a marked increase in violence at this time: in response to a series of suicide attacks against Israeli citizens by Palestinian militants (in which a large number of Israelis died), Israel again ordered its armed forces into several towns in the West Bank and Gaza. This latest offensive, code-named 'Operation Determined Path', again included an Israeli military blockade on Arafat's headquarters in Ramallah. At the end of June Israeli forces began the removal of a small number of settler 'outposts' deemed to be illegal. Meanwhile, there were reports that a senior commander of Hamas' military wing had been killed by Israeli troops in Nablus; Israel alleged that he was a prominent bomb-maker, who had been responsible for attacks such as the Passover bombing in Netanya. By early July almost all of the West Bank was again reoccupied, after Israel had called up further army reservists. At this time the Israeli Cabinet agreed to support an amendment to the Israeli Lands Law that would ban Arab Israelis from living in new homes built on Israeli state land; the bill awaited the approval of the Knesset. In early July senior-level talks were resumed between Israel and the PA, while the Quartet group (comprising the USA, Russia, the UN and EU) held discussions in London, United Kingdom, in a bid to re-activate the Oslo peace process. In the second week of July a new Israeli army Chief of Staff, Lt-Gen. Moshe Ya'alon, was named as a replacement to Shaul Mofaz.

Violence again appeared to be on the increase when several Israelis died in an attack on a bus near a Jewish settlement in the West Bank in mid-July 2002, for which three Palestinian militant groups all claimed responsibility. The increased violence came as new peace talks were convened by the Quartet group. Israel responded to the renewed Palestinian assaults by shooting dead a suspected militant and by 'freezing' plans to ease some of the restrictions imposed on Palestinians living in the Territories. Shortly afterwards, Israeli forces in the Nablus refugee camp detained a number of relatives of two suspected Palestinian militants and announced plans to deport some of them to the Gaza Strip. The announcement attracted strong criticism from human rights organizations; however, in early September the Israeli Supreme Court ruled that the expulsion of militants' relatives was legitimate. Meanwhile, tensions increased between Israelis and Palestinians in late July, when an Israeli air-strike on a residential building in Gaza City resulted in the deaths of up to 15 Palestinans (including several children). The Israeli raid had achieved its aim of assassinating a leader of Hamas' military wing. However, the civilian deaths were condemned by both the PA and the international community, leading Israeli officials to express 'regret' at the loss of civilian lives. Following international (and especially US) pressure, Israel moved to ease the restrictions in the West Bank and Gaza, and Sharon pledged to release some of the tax revenues owed to the PA. The Gaza air-strike precipitated a new round of violence, however, with four Jewish settlers being killed near Hebron towards the end of July. Israel responded by ordering tanks into the Gaza Strip. However, at the end of the month at least seven Israelis were killed in a suicide bomb attack at the Hebrew University in Jerusalem; Hamas claimed responsibility for the blast. Also at this time one of the Ministers without Portfolio, David Levy of Gesher, resigned from Sharon's coalition, owing to disagreement over the Prime Minister's style of government. There were at least 15 further Israeli fatalities in early August as a result of attacks by militant Palestinians. The Israeli Government responded by ordering a total ban on freedom of movement for Palestinians in most West Bank cities.

The UN again called on Israel to withdraw immediately from PA-controlled territory, referring to the serious humanitarian situation there. The PA accused Israel of reneging on a recent pledge to pull its troops out of PA-administered towns and villages. The focus of much of Israel's military campaign during late August was the Gaza Strip, where a number of leading militants and civilians were killed. Israel and the PA agreed at this time to implement a security plan (termed the 'Gaza, Bethlehem First' plan) whereby Israel would withdraw from the Gaza Strip and Bethlehem, in return for Palestinian security guarantees and a crack-down on militants. Israel began to withdraw its forces from Bethlehem on the following day; however, violence continued throughout the Territories and further talks were cancelled. Following further Palestinian civilian deaths, in early September Israel announced that it would launch an inquiry into the circumstances of the deaths. Later in the month a landmark decision by the Israeli Ministry of the Interior revoked the citizenship of an Arab Israeli who was accused of assisting Palestinian militants in plotting suicide attacks against Israelis. The situation deteriorated further in mid-September, with two suicide bombings in Um al-Fahm and Tel-Aviv. Israeli forces entered Arafat's Ramallah compound once again in mid-September, and began the systematic destruction of buildings there, in a stated attempt to force the surrender of some 20 Palestinian militants believed by the Israeli authorities to be sheltering there. Israel asserted that Arafat, who was sheltering in the only building that remained standing within two days of the reoccupation, was not a target, but that a decision had been taken to 'isolate' the PA leader following the suicide attacks. In late October trial proceedings began against a senior Bedouin officer in the Israeli army, who was accused of selling Israeli military secrets to Hezbollah. Meanwhile, there were reports during that month that the USA was assisting Israel with preparations to strengthen its military defences against a possible attack by Iraq, as the prospect of a US-led campaign to oust the regime of Saddam Hussain increased.

Elections to the Knesset were held on 28 January 2003, despite being originally scheduled for May 2003. The elections had been called in early November 2002 after the Labour Party withdrew from Sharon's governing coalition at the end of October, following Labour's opposition to funds being allocated to Jewish settlements in the West Bank in the 2003 budget. Ariel Sharon and his Likud party won a resounding victory over the left-wing parties at the polls, securing 40 seats in the Knesset; however, the electoral turn-out (at under 68%) was reported to have been the lowest in Israel's history. Following lengthy discussions (during which Sharon attempted to persuade the Labour leader, Amram Mitzna, to join a new 'government of national unity' with Likud), a new coalition Government was announced on 28 February 2003. The Cabinet was composed of Likud, the secularist Shinui party, and the right-wing and religious NRP, Haichud Haleumi and Israel B'Aliyah parties. (Mitzna had declared that Labour would only join the Government on the condition that Sharon agreed to close Jewish settlements in the Gaza Strip and to resume peace talks with the PA.) The former Likud premier, Binyamin Netanyahu, became the Minister of Finance, while the Shinui and NRP leaders were both appointed as Deputy Prime Ministers. Reuven Rivlin was named as the new Speaker of the Knesset. In early May Amram Mitzna announced his resignation as Labour leader; his successor was expected to be chosen in July.

Meanwhile, in late December 2002 Yasser Arafat announced a postponement of Palestinian legislative and presidential elections, which had originally been scheduled for January 2003; the Palestinian leader declared that it would be impossible to hold elections while many towns in the West Bank remained under Israeli occupation. President Bush announced in mid-April 2003 that he would publish the Quartet-sponsored 'road map' for achieving peace in the Middle East once the new Palestinian Prime Minister, Mahmoud Abbas (Abu Mazen)—who had been appointed in mid-March—had announced a new Cabinet. A new Palestinian administration was duly endorsed by the Palestinian legislature on 29 April. On the following day the USA presented both the Israeli and Palestinian Prime Ministers with copies of the 'road map'.

In early March 2000 the Israeli Cabinet voted unanimously to withdraw its forces from southern Lebanon by 7 July, even in the absence of a peace agreement with Syria. The Lebanese Government responded by demanding that Israel also depart from a small area on the Syrian border known as Shebaa Farms. In mid-April Israel released 13 Lebanese prisoners who had been detained without trial for more than a decade, apparently as 'bargaining chips' for Israeli soldiers missing in Lebanon. Fighting between Israeli troops and Hezbollah intensified in May, and there were fears that further violence might follow an Israeli withdrawal after it was announced that Israel would not disarm the SLA. On 23 May Israel's Security Cabinet voted to accelerate the withdrawal of its remaining troops from southern Lebanon. By this date Hezbollah had taken control of about one-third of the territory following the evacuation by the SLA of outposts transferred to its control by the Israeli army; moreover, mass defections from the SLA were reported. Meanwhile, Lebanese citizens stormed the al-Khiam prison in the security zone and freed 144 inmates. The rapid departure of all Israeli forces from southern Lebanon was completed on 24 May, nearly six weeks before Barak's original July deadline. Israeli public opinion generally welcomed an end to the occupation, since about 900 Israelis had been killed in southern Lebanon since 1978. After the withdrawal several thousand SLA members and their families fled across the border into northern Israel. In mid-June 2000 the UN Security Council confirmed that Israel had completed its withdrawal from Lebanon in compliance with UN Resolution 425. UNIFIL's mandate was extended for a six-month period at the end of July (by which time UNIFIL personnel were patrolling the area vacated by Israeli forces, monitoring the line of withdrawal and providing humanitarian assistance), and again at the end of January 2001. Further six-month extensions of UNIFIL's mandate were announced in July of that year, in January and July 2002, and again at the end of January 2003.

Hezbollah reaffirmed in mid-2000 that it would pursue its armed campaign against Israel until Shebaa Farms was returned to Lebanese control. The al-Aqsa *intifada*, which erupted in late September, precipitated renewed operations by Hezbollah against the Israeli army. In early October three Israeli soldiers were kidnapped on the border with Lebanon by Hezbollah militants demanding the release of Arab prisoners held in Israel. One week later an Israeli army reservist was also captured by Hezbollah. Tensions escalated at the end of November when an Israeli soldier was killed by a Hezbollah bomb in Shebaa Farms; Israel responded by launching air raids on suspected Hezbollah targets. Another Israeli soldier was killed in a Hezbollah missile attack near Shebaa Farms in mid-February 2001. In mid-April Israeli helicopter gunships attacked a Syrian radar base in central Lebanon (in which at least one Syrian soldier died), in retaliation for the recent killing by Hezbollah of an Israeli soldier in Shebaa Farms. Israel launched a further raid on a Syrian radar station in eastern Lebanon in early July. In late July 2001 the UN announced that it would permit Israeli and Lebanese officials to view a censored copy of a video-cassette made by a UN peace-keeper in Lebanon, which Israel claimed would offer vital information relating to the three soldiers kidnapped by Hezbollah in late 2000. However, at the end of October 2001 Israeli military officials declared that the soldiers were 'almost certainly' dead.

Syria had welcomed the election of Ehud Barak to the Israeli premiership in May 1999. In July, at the inauguration of his Cabinet, Barak undertook to negotiate a bilateral peace with Syria, based on UN Resolutions 242 and 338: this was interpreted as a signal of his intention to return most of the occupied Golan Heights in exchange for peace and normalized relations. On 20 July Syria ordered a 'cease-fire' with Israel. However, it was not until December that the two sides agreed to a resumption of negotiations from the point at which they had broken off in 1996, reportedly as a result of diplomatic efforts by US President Clinton and secret meetings between Israeli and Syrian officials. The Knesset subsequently approved the decision to resume talks, while Barak reasserted that any agreement concluded with Syria would be put to a national referendum. Clinton inaugurated peace negotiations between Barak and the Syrian Minister of Foreign Affairs, Farouk ash-Shara', in Washington, DC, on 15 December 1999. The talks commenced amid rising tensions in southern Lebanon, and resulted only in an agreement to resume discussions in January 2000. Barak, meanwhile, was encountering growing opposition in Israel to a possible return of the Golan Heights to Syria. In late December 1999 Israel and Syria agreed an informal 'cease-fire' to curb hostilities in Lebanon. Barak and ash-Shara' attended further discussions (in which President Clinton played an active role) on 3–10 January 2000 in Shepherdstown, West Virginia. As a preliminary to the talks it was agreed that four committees would be established to discuss simultaneously the issues of borders, security, normalization of relations and water sharing. As further discussions proved inconclusive, the US Administration presented a 'draft working document' to both sides, as the basis for a framework agreement. However, Syria announced that it required a commitment from Israel to withdraw from the Golan Heights before negotiations could resume. Israel, meanwhile, demanded the personal involvement of President Hafiz al-Assad in the peace process. In early January a huge demonstration was held in Tel-Aviv by Israelis opposed to any withdrawal from the Golan Heights, while Israel B'Aliyah and the NRP threatened to leave Barak's coalition in any such event. On 17 January talks between Israel and Syria, which had been scheduled to reconvene two days later, were postponed indefinitely. Despite the intensification of the conflict in southern Lebanon (see above), and a Knesset vote in early March to change the majority required in the event of a referendum on an Israeli withdrawal from the Golan Heights from 50% of participants to 50% of the registered electorate, hopes of an imminent breakthrough in the Syrian track of the peace process were raised by the announcement, later in March, that Presidents Clinton and Assad were to meet in Geneva, Switzerland. However, the talks, on 26 March, broke down after only three hours, when it became apparent that the US President had no new Israeli proposals to offer to Syria regarding its demand for a full and unconditional withdrawal from the Golan Heights. In early April Barak declared that the Israeli Government would resume the construction of Jewish settlements in the Golan Heights (following a declared suspension prior to the December 1999 talks). The prospect of further peace-making initiatives between Israel and Syria was further distanced by the death of President Assad in early June 2000, although Assad's second son, Bashar —who assumed the Syrian presidency in July—promised a continuation of his father's policies towards Israel. The Israeli-Syrian track remained deadlocked following the election of Ariel Sharon as Israel's premier. Despite reports in January 2002 that the Israeli Minister of Defence, Binyamin Ben-Eliezer, had informed the Syrian leadership that Israel would be willing to resume peace negotiations provided that there were no pre-conditions, by early 2003 the possibility of a swift resumption of talks appeared remote (especially as the USA increasingly referred to Syria as a possible target in President Bush's 'war on terror').

Government

Supreme authority in Israel rests with the Knesset (Assembly), with 120 members elected by universal suffrage for four years (subject to dissolution), on the basis of proportional representation. The President, a constitutional Head of State, is elected by the Knesset for five years. (Moshe Katsav, who assumed the presidency in August 2000, was exceptionally elected for a seven-year term.) Executive power lies with the Cabinet, led by a directly-elected Prime Minister. The Cabinet takes office after receiving a vote of confidence in the Knesset, to which it is responsible. Ministers are usually members of the Knesset, but non-members may be appointed.

The country is divided into six administrative districts. Local authorities are elected at the same time as elections to the Knesset. There are 31 municipalities (including two Arab towns), 115 local councils (46 Arab and Druze) and 49 regional councils (one Arab) comprising representatives of 700 villages.

Defence

The Israel Defence Forces consist of a small nucleus of commissioned and non-commissioned regular officers, a contingent enlisted for national service, and a large reserve. Men are enlisted for 36 months of military service (excluding officers, who serve for 48 months), and women for 24 months. Military service is compulsory for Jews and Druzes, but voluntary for Christians, Circassians and Muslims. Total regular armed forces in August 2002 numbered an estimated 161,500 (including 107,500 conscripts), comprising an army of 120,000, a navy estimated at 6,500 and an air force of 35,000; full mobilization to 586,500 can be quickly achieved with reserves of 425,000. State expenditure on defence in 2002 was estimated at NIS 43,700m.

Economic Affairs

In 2000, according to estimates by the World Bank, Israel's gross national income (GNI), measured at average 1998–2000 prices, was US $104,128m., equivalent to $16,710 per head (or $19,330 per head on an international purchasing-power parity basis). During 1990–2000, it was estimated, the population increased at an average annual rate of 6.0%, while gross domestic product

(GDP) per head increased, in real terms, by an average of 4.4% per year. Overall GDP increased, in real terms, at an average annual rate of 10.6% in 1990–2000; growth was 3.0% in 1999 and 6.8% in 2000. However, negative growth was recorded in both 2001 and 2002.

Agriculture (including hunting, forestry and fishing) contributed 1.8% of GDP in 2000, and in 2001 engaged 1.9% of the employed labour force. Most agricultural workers live in large co-operatives (*kibbutzim*), of which there were 267 at December 1998, or co-operative smallholder villages (*moshavim*), of which there were 454. Israel is largely self-sufficient in foodstuffs. Citrus fruits constitute the main export crop. Other important crops are vegetables (particularly tomatoes and potatoes), wheat, melons and grapes. The export of exotic fruits, winter vegetables and flowers has increased significantly in recent years. Poultry, livestock and fish production are also important. According to FAO data, agricultural output increased at an average annual rate of 0.3% in 1990–2001; production increased by 1.8% in 2000, but declined by 0.5% in 2001.

Industry (comprising mining, manufacturing, construction and power) contributed 24.3% of GDP in 2000, and engaged 23.5% of the employed labour force in 2001. The State plays a major role in all sectors of industry, and there is a significant co-operative sector. Industrial production increased by an average of 5.9% annually in 1988–95.

The mining and manufacturing sectors together contributed 17.6% of GDP in 2000, and engaged 17.5% of the employed labour force in 2001; mining and quarrying employed about 0.2% of the working population in 1997. Israel has small proven reserves of petroleum (of some 3.9m. barrels), from which less than 500 barrels per day are currently produced; however, in 1999 potential new reserves were discovered in central Israel and off the southern coast. Some natural gas is also produced, and significant offshore gas discoveries were made in the south in 1999 and 2000. Phosphates, potash, bromides, magnesium and other salts are mined, and Israel is the world's largest exporter of bromine. Gold, in potentially commercial quantities, was discovered in 1988.

Manufacturing employed 19.3% of the working population in 1997. The principal branches of manufacturing, measured by gross revenue, in 1996 were food products, beverages and tobacco (accounting for 17.4% of the total), chemical, petroleum and coal products (15.0%), electrical machinery (12.1%), metal products (11.1%), scientific, photographic, optical equipment, etc. (8.0%), paper, publishing and printing (6.5%), textiles and clothing (5.6%), non-metallic mineral manufactures (5.4%), rubber and plastic products (5.1%) and non-electrical machinery (5.0%).

Energy is derived principally from coal (accounting for 67.3% of total electricity output in 1999) and imported petroleum (32.6% in 1999); however, it is intended that natural gas should eventually become Israel's principal energy source. Imports of mineral fuels comprised 8.0% of the total value of imports in 2002.

Services contributed 75.2% of GDP in 2000, and engaged 74.6% of the employed labour force in 2001. Tourism is an important source of revenue, although the sector has been severely damaged by regional instability and a series of bomb attacks carried out by militant Islamist groups in recent years. In 2000 some 2.4m. tourists visited Israel and receipts from tourism totalled US $3,859m. However, the significant upsurge in violence from September 2000 has once again deterred many foreign visitors, resulting in hotel closures, redundancies and a reduction in air travel. Tourist arrivals decreased to some 1.2m. in 2001, and to an estimated 0.9m. in 2002. Receipts from tourism in 2001 were US $2,460m. Financial services are also important: banking, insurance, real estate and business services together contributed 30.9% of GDP in 2000, and employed 15.6% of the working population in 2001.

In 2001 Israel recorded a visible trade deficit of US $3,264m., and there was a deficit of $1,852m. on the current account of the balance of payments. Excluding trade with the West Bank and Gaza Strip, in 2002 the principal source of imports was the USA, which supplied 18.5% of imports to Israel; other major suppliers were the Belgo-Luxembourg Economic Union (BLEU), Germany, the United Kingdom and Switzerland. The USA was also the principal market for exports, taking 40.3% of Israeli exports in that year; other important purchasers were the BLEU, Hong Kong, the United Kingdom and Germany. Israel is the world's largest supplier of polished diamonds. The principal exports in 2002 were basic manufactures (chiefly non-metallic mineral

manufactures), machinery and transport equipment, chemicals and related products, and miscellaneous manufactured articles. The principal imports in that year were basic manufactures (mainly non-metallic mineral manufactures), machinery and transport equipment, chemicals and related products, and miscellaneous manufactured articles.

In 2000 there was an overall budgetary deficit (excluding net allocation of credit) of NIS 2,800m. (equivalent to 0.6% of GDP). Government revenue each year normally includes some US $3,000m. in economic and military aid from the USA. At 31 December 2000 Israel's gross foreign debt amounted to $64,877m., of which $27,762m. was government debt. During 1990–2001 consumer prices rose at an average annual rate of 8.7%. Annual inflation averaged 1.1% in both 2000 and 2001. The unemployment rate was reported to be in excess of 10% in 2002.

The most significant factor affecting the Israeli economy in the 1990s was the mass influx of Jews from the former USSR, which led to a substantial increase in the population, additional flexibility in the labour market and growth in construction. In 1996, however, a period of economic slowdown began, reflecting an end to the demand boom and reduced tourism revenues following an increase in Islamist violence. In May 1998 foreign-exchange restrictions were ended, allowing the shekel to become fully convertible. After the Government of Ehud Barak was elected in mid-1999 and the Middle East peace process was revived, the economy entered a period of revival, with a significant improvement in business activity and increased foreign investment. Moreover, inflation declined to its lowest level since 1967. The strong rate of economic growth in 2000 was led by the success of Israel's high-technology sector. However, in the fourth quarter of 2000 the economic boom ended as a new *intifada* by Palestinians in the West Bank and Gaza dramatically reduced foreign investment and tourism revenues, while the global economic downturn had a particularly detrimental effect on high-tech companies. The negative growth in the Israeli economy in 2001 was reported to have been the first contraction since 1953; negative growth was also recorded in 2002, and in March 2003 the IMF described the Israeli economy as being 'in the midst of a deep recession'. Following the deregulation of the domestic telecommunications market and the privatization of Bank Hapoalim—Israel's largest bank—in 2000, the Government of Ariel Sharon defined its own privatization programme in May 2001, including the proposed sale of its controlling stake in Bank Leumi. However, privatization and other structural reforms have proceeded slowly while the Government has concentrated its efforts on political and military matters. Should discussions regarding both the Palestinian and Syrian tracks of the (currently stalled) Middle East peace process eventually result in a comprehensive, and enduring, regional peace settlement, Israel would be in a far better position to achieve its long-term economic growth potential.

Education

Israel has high standards of literacy and advanced educational services. Free, compulsory education is provided for all children between five and 15 years of age; in early 1999 legislation was passed allowing for the introduction of free education for pre-primary children. Primary education is provided for all those between five and 10 years of age. There is also secondary, vocational and agricultural education. Post-primary education comprises two cycles of three years. Enrolment at primary and secondary schools in 1995 was equivalent to 93% of children aged six to 17 (primary 98%; secondary 88%). There are six universities, one institute of technology (the Technion) and one institute of science (the Weizmann Institute), which incorporates a graduate school of science. In 2001 budgetary expenditure on education by the central Government was forecast at NIS 31,271m. (13.9% of total spending).

Public Holidays

The Sabbath starts at sunset on Friday and ends at nightfall on Saturday. The Jewish year 5764 begins on 27 September 2003, and the year 5675 on 16 September 2004.
2003: 17–23 April (Pesach, Passover—public holidays on first and last days of festival), 7 May (Yom Ha'atzmaut, Independence Day), 6 June (Shavuot, Feast of Weeks), 27–28 September (Rosh Hashanah, Jewish New Year), 6 October (Yom Kippur, Day of Atonement), 11–17 October (Succot, Feast of the Tabernacles).
2004: 6–12 April (Pesach, Passover—see 2003), 26 April (Yom Ha'atzmaut, Independence Day), 26 May (Shavuot, Feast of

Weeks), 16–17 September (Rosh Hashanah, Jewish New Year), 25 September (Yom Kippur, Day of Atonement), 30 September–6 October (Succot, Feast of the Tabernacles).

(The Jewish festivals and fast days commence in the evening of the dates given.)

Islamic holidays are observed by Muslim Arabs, and Christian holidays by the Christian Arab community.

Weights and Measures

The metric system is in force.
1 dunum = 1,000 sq metres.

Statistical Survey

Source: Central Bureau of Statistics, POB 13015, Hakirya, Romema, Jerusalem 91130; tel. 2-6592037; fax 2-6521340; e-mail yael@cbs.gov.il; internet www.cbs.gov.il.

Area and Population

AREA, POPULATION AND DENSITY

Area (sq km)	
Land	21,671
Inland water	474
Total	22,145*
Population (*de jure*; census results)†	
4 June 1983	4,037,620
4 November 1995	
Males	2,738,175
Females.	2,810,348
Total	5,548,523
Population (*de jure*; official estimates at mid-year)†	
2000	6,282,300
2001	6,433,500
2002	6,568,500
Density (per sq km) at mid-2002†	296.6

* 8,550 sq miles. Area includes East Jerusalem, annexed by Israel in June 1967, and the Golan sub-district (1,154 sq km), annexed by Israel in December 1981.

† Including the population of East Jerusalem and Israeli residents in certain other areas under Israeli military occupation since June 1967. Beginning in 1981, figures also include non-Jews in the Golan sub-district, an Israeli-occupied area of Syrian territory. Census results exclude adjustment for underenumeration.

31 December 2002 (*de jure*, official estimate): Population 6,640,100.

POPULATION BY RELIGION

(31 December 2001)

	Number	%
Jews	5,025,000	77.25
Muslims	1,004,600	15.44
Christians	138,500	2.13
Druze	106,300	1.63
Unclassified	230,900	3.55
Total *	**6,505,200**	**100.00**

* Excluding Lebanese not classified by religion (3,600 at 31 December 2001).

30 June 2002: Jews 5,322,400.

DISTRICTS

(31 December 2001)

	Area (sq km)*	Population†	Density (per sq km)
Jerusalem‡	652	777,400	1,192.3
Northern§	4,478	1,105,500	246.9
Haifa.	863	830,200	962.0
Central	1,276	1,502,100	1,177.2
Tel-Aviv	171	1,160,700	6,787.7
Southern	14,231	924,600	65.0
Total	**21,671**	**6,300,500**	**290.7**

* Excluding lakes, with a total area of 474 sq km.

† Excluding Israelis residing in Jewish localities in the West Bank and Gaza Strip, totalling 208,300.

‡ Including East Jerusalem, annexed by Israel in June 1967.

§ Including the Golan sub-district (area 1,154 sq km, population 35,400 at 31 December 2001), annexed by Israel in December 1981.

PRINCIPAL TOWNS

(estimated population at 31 December 2001)

Jerusalem (capital)*.	670,000		Petach-Tikva . . .	170,700
Tel-Aviv—Jaffa . .	358,800		Holon	166,200
Haifa	272,200		Netanya . . .	163,700
Rishon LeZiyyon . .	207,900		Bene Beraq . .	139,000
Ashdod . . .	181,100		Bat Yam . . .	135,500
Beersheba. . .	177,900		Ramat Gan . . .	127,400

* The Israeli Government has designated the city of Jerusalem (including East Jerusalem, annexed by Israel in June 1967) as the country's capital, although this is not recognized by the UN.

BIRTHS, MARRIAGES AND DEATHS*

	Registered live births		Registered marriages		Registered deaths	
	Number	Rate (per 1,000)	Number	Rate (per 1,000)	Number	Rate (per 1,000)
1995 .	116,886	21.1	35,990	6.5	35,348	6.4
1996 .	121,333	21.3	36,081	6.3	34,647	6.1
1997 .	124,478	21.4	37,611	6.5	36,106	6.2
1998 .	130,080	21.8	40,137	6.7	36,953	6.2
1999 .	131,936	21.5	40,236	6.6	37,247†	6.1†
2000 .	136,390	21.7	38,894	6.4	37,618†	6.0†
2001 .	136,638	21.2	32,694	n.a.	37,149†	5.8†
2002† .	139,360	21.2	n.a.	n.a.	38,163	5.8

* Including East Jerusalem.
† Provisional figure(s).

Expectation of life (WHO estimates, years at birth): 78.5 (males 76.1; females 80.9) in 2001 (Source: WHO, *World Health Report*).

IMMIGRATION*

	1999	2000	2001
Immigrants:			
on immigrant visas	70,586	55,736	39,571
on tourist visas†	6,104	4,428	3,974
Potential immigrants:			
on potential immigrant visas . .	18	12	6
on tourist visas†	58	16	29
Total	**76,766**	**60,192**	**43,580**

* Excluding immigrating citizens (3,226 in 1999; 3,372 in 2000; 2,930 in 2001) and Israeli residents returning from abroad.

† Figures refer to tourists who changed their status to immigrants or potential immigrants.

2002: Immigrants and potential immigrants 33,564.

ECONOMICALLY ACTIVE POPULATION

(sample surveys, '000 persons aged 15 years and over, excluding armed forces)*

	1999	2000	2001
Agriculture, hunting, forestry and fishing	49.6	47.9	43.0
Industry†	389.8	396.6	394.2
Electricity, gas and water supply	19.2	19.3	19.5
Construction	120.3	116.4	116.7
Wholesale and retail trade; repair of motor vehicles, motorcycles and personal and household goods	281.6	295.6	299.8
Hotels and restaurants	90.1	101.7	96.8
Transport, storage and communications	135.6	144.9	149.2
Financial intermediation	73.7	73.2	74.7
Real estate, renting and business activities	224.7	258.7	277.2
Public administration and defence; compulsory social security	116.2	119.9	126.6
Education	267.8	272.4	283.7
Health and social work	211.9	213.6	225.1
Other community, social and personal service activities	99.2	106.4	107.9
Private households with employed persons	40.1	34.7	38.1
Extra-territorial organizations and bodies	1.8	1.3	1.6
Not classifiable by economic activity	14.6	18.5	16.3
Total employed	2,136.7	2,221.2	2,270.5
Unemployed	208.5	213.8	233.1
Total labour force	2,345.3	2,435.1	2,503.3
Males	1,285.1	1,323.4	1,357.3
Females	1,060.2	1,111.6	1,146.0

* Figures are estimated independently, so the totals may not be the sum of the component parts.

† Comprising mining and quarrying, and manufacturing.

Source: ILO, *Yearbook of Labour Statistics*.

Health and Welfare

KEY INDICATORS

Total fertility rate (children per woman, 2001)	2.8
Under-5 mortality rate (per 1,000 live births, 2001)	6
HIV/AIDS (% of persons aged 15–49, 2001)	0.10
Physicians (per 1,000 head, 1998)	3.85
Hospital beds (per 1,000 head, 1995)	5.98
Health expenditure (2000): US $ per head (PPP)	2,338
Health expenditure (2000): % of GDP	10.9
Health expenditure (2000): public (% of total)	75.9
Human Development Index (2000): ranking	22
Human Development Index (2000): value	0.896

For sources and definitions, see explanatory note on p. vi.

Agriculture

PRINCIPAL CROPS

('000 metric tons)

	1999	2000	2001
Wheat	29.0	94.0	159.6
Maize	80.1*	79.8*	87.0†
Potatoes	369.2	363.1	380.3
Olives	23.2	56.0	26.0
Cottonseed	39.6	26.9	n.a.
Cabbages	48.7	46.0	49.6
Lettuce	37.4	37.8	38.9
Tomatoes	574.6	462.0	399.3
Cucumbers and gherkins	108.3	104.5	104.5†
Aubergines (Eggplants)	61.1	43.3	43.3†
Chillies and green peppers	102.3	90.7	100.0
Dry onions	92.6	106.5	79.0
Carrots	65.0	73.3	75.1
Other vegetables	230.1*	216.7*	214.0†
Watermelons	369.2	370.1	420.0†
Cantaloupes and other melons	73.8	68.6	68.6†
Bananas	117.8	87.5	100.1
Oranges	203.5	250.5	201.1
Tangerines, mandarins, clementines and satsumas	127.6	135.8	91.0
Grapefruit and pomelo	372.2	324.4	325.3
Apples	127.5	102.5	92.1
Peaches and nectarines	45.8	58.2	49.8
Grapes	85.0	101.8	118.5
Avocados	55.9	81.3	85.9
Other fruits and berries†	166.5	193.1	177.0

* Unofficial figure.

† FAO estimate(s).

Source: FAO.

LIVESTOCK

('000 head, year ending September)

	1999	2000	2001
Cattle	395	395	390
Pigs*	122	141	150
Sheep	350	380	389
Goats	75	62	63
Chickens	27,340	27,923	30,000*
Geese*	1,400	1,400	1,400
Turkeys	4,900	4,785	5,000*
Ducks*	200	200	200

* FAO estimate(s).

Source: FAO.

LIVESTOCK PRODUCTS

('000 metric tons)

	1999	2000	2001
Beef and veal	46.4	51.6	56.5
Mutton and lamb*	5.4	5.4	5.4
Pig meat	8.7	10.8	11.6
Chicken meat*	189	201	204
Goose meat†	5.1	5.1	5.1
Turkey meat*	86	90	90
Cows' milk	1,194.0	1,186.4	1,211.2
Sheep's milk	18.5	19.4	21.0
Goats' milk	14.5	11.3	12.9
Cheese	96.7	99.7	102.1†
Butter	7.9	7.4	7.5†
Hen eggs	91.8	87.9	84.7
Honey	3.0	2.6	3.0
Cattle hides†	4.8	5.3	5.3

* Unofficial figures.

† FAO estimate(s).

Source: FAO.

Forestry

ROUNDWOOD REMOVALS

('000 cubic metres, excl. bark)

	1999	2000	2001
Sawlogs, veneer logs and logs for sleepers	36*	28†	11†
Pulpwood	32*	22†	7†
Other industrial wood	32*	22†	7†
Fuel wood	13*	8†	2†
Total	113	81	27

* FAO estimate.
† Unofficial figure.
Source: FAO.

Fishing

('000 metric tons, live weight)

	1998	1999	2000
Capture	6,300	5,884	5,818
Carps, barbels, etc.	1,396	1,302	1,333
Aquaculture	18,556	18,777	20,098
Common carp	7,172	7,062	6,281
Tilapias	6,696	6,410	7,059
Gilthead seabream	1,643	2,210	2,511
Flathead grey mullet	1,476	1,542	1,661
Total catch	24,856	24,661	25,916

Note: Figures exclude crocodiles and alligators, recorded by number rather than weight. The number of American alligators caught was: 401 in 1998; 425 in 1999; n.a. in 2000.

Source: FAO, *Yearbook of Fishery Statistics*.

Mining

('000 metric tons, unless otherwise indicated)

	1999	2000	2001
Crude petroleum ('000 barrels)	29.4	25.0	25.0*
Natural gas (million cu m)	10.7	9.7	9.5*
Kaolin	20.0	13.0	13.3*
Phosphate rock†	4,128	4,110	3,511
Potash salts‡	1,702	1,748	1,774
Salt (unrefined)	538	526	537*
Gypsum (crude)	140	130	133

* Estimated production.
† Figures refer to beneficiated production. The phosphoric acid content (in '000 metric tons) was: 1,310 in 1999; 1,305 in 2000; 1,115 in 2001.
‡ Figures refer to K_2O content.
Source: US Geological Survey.

Industry

SELECTED PRODUCTS

('000 metric tons, unless otherwise indicated)

	1992	1993	1994
Refined vegetable oils (metric tons)	56,463	57,558	45,447
Margarine	35.1	33.8	24.7
Wine ('000 litres)	12,373	12,733	n.a.
Beer ('000 litres)	51,078	58,681	50,750
Cigarettes (metric tons)	5,742	5,525	5,638
Newsprint (metric tons)	0	247	0
Writing and printing paper (metric tons)	66,334	65,426	65,790
Other paper (metric tons)	32,368	30,446	28,985
Cardboard (metric tons)	92,072	95,108	103,142
Rubber tyres ('000)	892	854	966
Ammonia (metric tons)	41,072	n.a.	n.a.
Ammonium sulphate (metric tons)	12,444	n.a.	n.a.
Sulphuric acid	138	n.a.	n.a.
Chlorine (metric tons)	33,912	35,241	37,555
Caustic soda (metric tons)	29,459	29,851	32,765
Polyethylene (metric tons)	128,739	144,147	126,979
Paints (metric tons)	58,963	57,429	53,260
Cement	3,960	4,536	4,800
Commercial vehicles (number)	852	836	1,260
Electricity (million kWh)	24,731	26,042	28,327

1996 ('000 metric tons, unless otherwise indicated): Cigarettes (metric tons) 4,793; Chlorine 35; Paints 58.0 (Source: UN, *Industrial Commodity Statistics Yearbook*).

1997: Rubber tyres ('000) 792 (Source: UN, *Monthly Bulletin of Statistics*).

2000: Commercial vehicles (number) 373 (Source: International Road Federation, *World Road Statistics*).

2001 ('000 metric tons, unless otherwise indicated): Margarine 29.8; Wine (FAO estimate, '000 litres) 7,500; Beer (FAO estimate, '000 litres) 65,000; Writing and printing paper (FAO estimate) 95 (Source: FAO). Caustic soda (estimate) 44.9; Cement (estimate) 6,900 (Source: US Geological Survey). Electric energy (million kWh) 43,800 (Source: UN, *Monthly Bulletin of Statistics*).

Finance

CURRENCY AND EXCHANGE RATES

Monetary Units

100 agorot (singular: agora) = 1 new sheqel (plural: sheqalim) or shekel (NIS)

Sterling, Dollar and Euro Equivalents (31 December 2002)

£1 sterling = NIS 7.635
US $1 = NIS 4.737
€1 = NIS 4.968
NIS 100 = £13.10 = $21.11 = €20.13

Average Exchange Rate (NIS per US $)

2000	4.0773
2001	4.2057
2002	4.7378

STATE BUDGET
(NIS million)

Revenue*	1999	2000	2001
Tax revenue†	148,222	169,539	171,532
Taxes on income, profits and			
capital gains	62,087	77,433	77,511
Companies	12,622	18,308	17,443
Individuals	45,483	54,035	55,735
Other unallocated taxes on			
income	3,982	5,090	4,333
Social security contributions . .	24,266	27,028	29,027
Employees	13,768	15,394	16,548
Employers	7,141	8,034	9,073
Taxes on payroll and work force .	4,180	4,608	4,729
Domestic taxes on goods and			
services	54,153	57,503	57,353
General sales, turnover or			
value-added tax . . .	45,883	48,994	48,666
Excises	6,519	6,595	6,601
Non-tax revenue	24,965	25,197	23,844
Entrepreneurial and property			
income	11,079	8,614	6,869
Administration fees, charges and			
nonind. sales	12,382	15,220	15,486
Total	173,187	194,736	195,376

Expenditure‡	1999	2000	2001
General public services	4,115	4,920	5,114
Defence	34,021	36,185	38,380
Public order	6,853	7,419	8,137
Education	27,829	28,236	31,271
Health	27,160	28,023	30,179
Social security and welfare . . .	51,270	56,441	62,759
Housing and community amenities	6,490	6,347	6,765
Economic affairs and services . .	12,481	12,248	12,791
Mining, manufacturing and			
construction	4,464	4,035	3,781
Transport and communications .	3,942	4,621	5,075
Other expenditure	25,297	27,207	27,155
Interest payments	22,956	25,140	25,207
Adjustment	476	−260	−216
Total	197,954	208,603	224,287
Current	185,614	197,305	211,936
Capital	11,940	11,378	12,351

* Excluding grants received from abroad (NIS million): 12,327 in 1999; 11,957 in 2000; 11,534 in 2001.

† Excluding fees, classified as non-tax revenue.

‡ Expenditure excludes the central Government's lending minus repayments (NIS million): −3,742 in 1999; −5,929 in 2000; −107 in 2001.

Source: IMF, *Government Finance Statistics Yearbook*.

2001 (draft budget, NIS million): Total revenue 245,813; Total expenditure 245,813 (Source: Ministry of Finance).

2002 (provisional budget, NIS million): Total revenue 191,254; Total expenditure 205,115 (Source: Ministry of Finance).

2003 (provisional budget, NIS million): Total revenue 197,614; Total expenditure 212,952 (Source: Ministry of Finance).

CENTRAL BANK RESERVES
(US $ million at 31 December)

	2000	2001	2002
Gold*	0.0	0.0	0.0
IMF special drawing rights . .	1.1	1.7	4.6
Reserve position in IMF . . .	117.1	197.8	413.3
Foreign exchange	23,163.0	23,179.1	23,658.4
Total	23,281.2	23,378.6	24,076.3

* Valued at SDR 35 per troy ounce.

Source: IMF, *International Financial Statistics*.

MONEY SUPPLY
(NIS million at 31 December)

	1999	2000	2001
Currency outside banks . . .	12,178	12,347	14,580
Demand deposits at deposit money			
banks	17,933	18,537	23,053
Total money (incl. others) . . .	30,263	31,030	37,796

Source: IMF, *International Financial Statistics*.

COST OF LIVING
(Consumer Price Index, annual averages; base: 1990 = 100)

	1999	2000	2001
Food (incl. beverages)	218.1	223.2	228.9
Electricity, gas and other fuels . .	228.0	242.1	243.1
Clothing (incl. footwear) . . .	150.4	150.2	144.5
Rent	370.4	362.4	376.5
All items (incl. others)	245.8	248.6	251.4

Source: ILO, *Yearbook of Labour Statistics*.

NATIONAL ACCOUNTS
(NIS million at current prices)

National Income and Product

	1998	1999	2000
Gross domestic product (GDP) at			
market prices	405,021	443,048	480,780
Compensation of employees (net) }	−14,269	−21,155	−27,149
Property income (net) . . . . }			
Gross national income (GNI) .	390,752	421,893	453,631
Less Consumption of fixed			
capital	55,875	61,845	63,856
Net national income . . .	334,877	360,048	389,775
Current transfers from abroad .	25,974	29,693	30,655
Less Current transfers paid			
abroad	2,329	3,355	3,793
Net national disposable			
income	358,522	386,386	416,637

Source: UN, *National Accounts Statistics*.

Expenditure on the Gross Domestic Product

	1998	1999	2000
Final consumption expenditure .	333,378	362,776	388,800
Households	216,326	235,176	253,573
Non-profit institutions serving			
households	4,863	5,326	5,850
General government . . .	112,189	122,275	129,378
Gross capital formation . . .	85,850	97,849	97,447
Gross fixed capital formation .	85,921	92,555	92,051
Changes in inventories . .	−72	5,293	5,396
Total domestic expenditure . .	419,228	460,625	486,247
Exports of goods and services .	122,169	151,180	184,173
Less Imports of goods and services	136,375	168,757	189,640
GDP in market prices . . .	405,022	443,048	480,780
GDP at constant 1995 prices .	316,296	324,855	346,990

Source: UN, *National Accounts Statistics*.

Gross Domestic Product by Economic Activity

	1998	1999	2000
Agriculture, hunting, forestry and fishing	7,470	7,154	7,502
Manufacturing, mining and quarrying	63,851	70,733	74,846
Electricity, gas and water supply .	6,797	7,382	8,093
Construction	22,006	21,118	20,383
Wholesale, retail trade, repair of motor vehicles, motorcycles and personal and household goods; hotels and restaurants . .	35,024	39,373	42,832
Transport, storage and communications	30,634	32,276	34,181
Financial intermediation; real estate, renting and business activities	103,876	114,360	131,422
Public administration and defence; compulsory social security . .	31,637	33,941	35,872
Education	28,649	31,105	33,707
Health and social work . . .	19,302	21,152	23,229
Other community, social and personal services	14,354	16,515	18,782
Statistical discrepancy	−3,200	−4,204	−5,458
Sub-total	360,400	390,905	425,391
Less Financial intermediation services indirectly measured .	8,300	5,943	6,534
Gross value added in basic prices	352,100	384,962	418,857
Taxes on products	54,877	60,409	64,170
Less Subsidies on products . .	1,955	2,323	2,245
GDP in market prices . . .	405,021	443,048	480,780

Source: UN, *National Accounts Statistics.*

BALANCE OF PAYMENTS
(US $ million)

	1999	2000	2001
Exports of goods f.o.b.	25,577	30,947	27,678
Imports of goods f.o.b.	−30,041	−34,036	−30,942
Trade balance	−4,464	−3,089	−3,264
Exports of services	11,447	15,181	11,991
Imports of services	−10,708	−12,529	−12,563
Balance on goods and services	−3,726	−437	−3,836
Other income received . . .	2,553	3,353	3,545
Other income paid	−8,420	−11,360	−7,959
Balance on goods, services and income	−9,592	−8,443	−8,251
Current transfers received . .	7,125	7,483	7,531
Current transfers paid . . .	−809	−1,015	−1,132
Current balance	−3,277	−1,974	−1,852
Capital account (net) . . .	569	455	681
Direct investment abroad . .	−933	−2,859	−1,135
Direct investment from abroad.	2,873	4,524	3,224
Portfolio investment assets .	−830	−2,139	−1,199
Portfolio investment liabilities . .	1,499	4,361	656
Other investment assets . . .	−3,948	−2,854	−2,850
Other investment liabilities . .	3,379	1,950	1,194
Net errors and omissions . .	677	−1,591	1,477
Overall balance	9	−128	196

Source: IMF, *International Financial Statistics.*

External Trade

PRINCIPAL COMMODITIES
(US $ million)*

Imports c.i.f.†	2000	2001	2002
Food and live animals . . .	1,534.2	1,543.8	1,535.4
Mineral fuels, lubricants, etc. .	3,251.6	2,721.6	2,654.4
Petroleum, petroleum products, etc.	3,219.0	2,702.0	2,625.3
Chemicals and related products	3,230.5	3,169.0	3,261.2
Basic manufactures	10,682.2	9,227.6	10,691.4
Non-metallic mineral manufactures	7,229.4	6,056.0	7,646.2
Machinery and transport equipment.	12,431.3	11,931.4	10,436.6
General industrial machinery, equipment and parts . . .	1,178.2	1,126.2	1,140.6
Office machines and automatic data-processing machines . .	1,716.9	1,410.4	1,279.2
Telecommunications and sound equipment	1,667.0	1,431.6	1,365.2
Other electrical machinery, apparatus, etc.	3,599.7	3,373.0	2,787.2
Road vehicles and parts‡ . .	2,315.8	2,171.9	1,891.4
Other transport equipment and parts‡	493.6	1,038.7	703.0
Miscellaneous manufactured articles	3,217.9	3,224.7	2,974.2
Total (incl. others)	35,749.5	33,303.2	33,106.3

Exports f.o.b.	2000	2001	2002
Chemicals and related products	4,042.5	4,159.4	4,539.6
Organic chemicals	999.4	990.7	1,126.3
Medical and pharmaceutical products.	428.8	638.4	927.0
Basic manufactures	11,365.9	10,513.4	12,070.4
Non-metallic mineral manufactures	9,727.5	8,857.9	10,436.9
Machinery and transport equipment.	11,133.3	9,986.9	8,639.7
Telecommunications and sound equipment	4,256.3	3,610.7	2,768.2
Other electrical machinery, apparatus, etc.	3,556.0	3,192.8	2,813.2
Road vehicles and other transport equipment and parts‡. .	982.5	1,025.0	1,101.5
Miscellaneous manufactured articles.	3,174.8	2,948.6	2,775.6
Professional, scientific and controlling instruments, etc. .	934.7	921.2	849.8
Total (incl. others)	31,403.8	29,060.9	29,467.0

* The data exclude trade with the West Bank and the Gaza Strip. Including such transactions, the value of total trade (in US $ million) was: Imports c.i.f. (excl. military goods) 36,029.9 in 2000; 33,642.8 in 2001; n.a. in 2002; Exports f.o.b. 32,938.6 in 2000; 30,408.5 in 2001; n.a. in 2002.

† Figures exclude military goods. After deducting net returned imports, the value of total imports (in US $ million), excluding trade with the West Bank and the Gaza Strip, was: 31,404.2 in 2000; 35,449.2 in 2001; n.a. in 2002 (Source: IMF, *International Financial Statistics*).

‡ Data on parts exclude tyres, engines and electrical parts.

PRINCIPAL TRADING PARTNERS
(US $ million)*

Imports (excl. military goods) c.i.f.	2000	2001	2002
Belgium-Luxembourg . . .	3,565.2	2,655.0	3,056.9
Canada	340.7	285.4	375.5
China, People's Republic . . .	602.3	737.3	793.3
France	1,157.6	1,254.0	1,186.9
Germany	2,673.2	2,614.8	2,347.8
Hong Kong	898.3	805.6	1,194.1
India	534.8	429.5	653.2
Italy	1,720.7	1,651.3	1,530.5
Japan	1,186.7	1,011.8	782.0
Korea, Republic	650.0	523.7	512.4
Netherlands	1,436.7	1,353.7	1,177.9
Russia	472.6	507.1	519.9
South Africa	287.1	345.9	234.8
Spain	685.3	673.6	637.8
Sweden	414.1	422.6	313.6
Switzerland-Liechtenstein . . .	1,918.3	1,774.7	2,075.2
Taiwan	570.8	430.4	368.6
Turkey	586.5	683.3	813.7
United Kingdom	2,714.6	2,208.5	2,226.8
USA	6,645.5	6,704.6	6,134.1
Total (incl. others)	35,749.5	33,303.2	33,106.3

			2002
Australia	226.5	235.6	2002
Belgium-Luxembourg . . .	1,877.5	1,573.9	1,868.9
Brazil	320.0	392.1	321.9
Canada	283.3	288.4	295.6
China, People's Republic . . .	261.6	349.6	423.9
France	747.4	712.7	648.9
Germany	1,521.4	1,288.1	1,028.2
Hong Kong	1,383.7	1,254.4	1,372.9
India	557.0	473.5	619.8
Italy	803.6	766.3	688.8
Japan	838.7	800.4	649.4
Korea, Republic	396.2	322.4	319.9
Malaysia	732.4	615.9	291.4
Netherlands	898.7	829.6	915.6
Philippines	386.5	245.6	96.5
Singapore	327.3	261.9	277.1
Spain	436.1	506.5	398.7
Switzerland-Liechtenstein . . .	501.6	343.4	383.7
Taiwan	407.5	330.5	333.4
Thailand	341.4	330.8	393.3
Turkey	434.4	316.5	378.2
United Kingdom	1,358.4	1,219.5	1,151.8
USA	11,733.6	11,111.9	11,868.0
Total (incl. others)	31,403.8	29,060.9	29,467.0

* Imports by country of purchase; exports by country of destination. The totals exclude trade with the West Bank and the Gaza Strip (US $ million): Imports c.i.f. 308 in 2000; 238 in 2001; n.a. in 2002; Exports f.o.b. 1,631 in 2000; 1,163 in 2001; n.a. in 2002.

Transport

RAILWAYS
(traffic)

	1999	2000	2001
Freight ton-km (million) . . .	1,128	1,173	1,098
Passenger-km (million) . . .	529	781	961

ROAD TRAFFIC
(motor vehicles in use at 31 December)

	1999	2000	2001
Private passenger cars	1,316,765	1,396,947	1,460,851
Taxis	13,836	14,806	15,163
Minibuses	16,240	16,476	16,752
Buses and coaches	11,303	11,849	11,897
Lorries, vans and road tractors .	292,038	309,987	326,428
Special service vehicles . . .	3,932	3,993	4,068
Motorcycles and mopeds . . .	75,643	77,472	79,736

SHIPPING

Merchant Fleet
(registered at 31 December)

	1999	2000	2001
Number of vessels	52	49	48
Displacement ('000 grt) . . .	728.4	611.7	611.4

Source: Lloyd's Register of Shipping, *World Fleet Statistics*.

International Sea-borne Freight Traffic
('000 metric tons)

	1999	2000	2001
Goods loaded	12,875	13,866	13,287
Goods unloaded*	28,750	29,197	29,695

* Including traffic between Israeli ports.

CIVIL AVIATION
(traffic on scheduled services)

	1997	1998	1999
Kilometres flown (million) . . .	75	79	86
Passengers carried ('000) . . .	3,754	3,699	4,033
Passenger-km (million) . . .	11,776	12,418	13,515
Total ton-km (million) . . .	2,195	2,241	2,259

Source: UN, *Statistical Yearbook*.

Tourism

TOURIST ARRIVALS
('000)*

Country of residence	1999	2000	2001†
Canada	51.4	55.0	34.2
France	194.9	202.4	129.3
Germany	181.0	176.0	65.5
Italy	146.7	171.4	25.0
Jordan	59.8	77.9	24.6
Netherlands	90.4	91.3	43.3
Russia	55.4	35.9	55.8
Spain	35.1	65.6	11.8
Ukraine	27.9	38.0	33.5
United Kingdom	195.5	201.2	140.2
USA	515.2	488.5	266.2
Total (incl. others)	2,312.3	2,416.8	1,195.7

* Excluding arrivals of Israeli nationals residing abroad.
† Provisional figures.

2002: Tourist arrivals (provisional) 862,000.

Tourism receipts (US $ million): 3,971 in 1999; 3,859 in 2000; 2,460 in 2001.

Communications Media

	1999	2000	2001
Television receivers ('000 in use)	2,000	2,100	n.a.
Telephones ('000 main lines in use)	2,877	3,021	3,100
Mobile cellular telephones ('000 subscribers).	2,880	4,400	5,260
Personal computers ('000 in use)	1,360	1,590	1,600
Internet users ('000)	800	1,270	1,500

Radio receivers (1997): 3,070,000 in use.

Facsimile machines (1995): 140,000 in use.

Book production (1998): 2,317 titles.

Daily newspapers (1996): 34 titles (estimated circulation 1,650,000 copies).

Non-daily newspapers (1988): 80 titles.

Other periodicals (1985): 807 titles.

Sources: International Telecommunication Union; UNESCO, *Statistical Yearbook*; UN, *Statistical Yearbook*.

Education

(2001/02, unless otherwise indicated)

	Schools	Pupils	Teachers
Jewish			
Kindergarten	n.a.	295,000	n.a.
Primary schools	1,770	552,762	44,106†
Intermediate schools.	502	191,927	25,635*
Secondary schools	1,064	284,549	37,922*
Vocational schools.	104	119,395	n.a.
Agricultural schools	2	3,321	n.a.
Teacher training colleges	46	30,761	n.a.
Others (handicapped)	188	9,517	4,300‡
Arab			
Kindergarten	n.a.	70,000	n.a.
Primary schools	393	195,733	9,830†
Intermediate schools.	112	52,338	4,398*
Secondary schools	159	54,876	4,413*
Vocational schools.	16	16,017	n.a.
Agricultural schools	—	557	n.a.
Teacher training colleges	3	3,061	n.a.
Others (handicapped)	40	2,161	604‡

* 1999/2000 figure.
† 1997/98 figure.
‡ 1996/97 figure.

Adult literacy rate (UNESCO estimates): 94.6% (males 96.8%; females 92.4%) in 2000 (Source: UN Development Programme, *Human Development Report*).

Directory

The Constitution

There is no written constitution. In June 1950 the Knesset voted to adopt a state constitution by evolution over an unspecified period. A number of laws, including the Law of Return (1950), the Nationality Law (1952), the State President (Tenure) Law (1952), the Education Law (1953) and the 'Yad-va-Shem' Memorial Law (1953), are considered as incorporated into the state Constitution. Other constitutional laws are: The Law and Administration Ordinance (1948), the Knesset Election Law (1951), the Law of Equal Rights for Women (1951), the Judges Act (1953), the National Service and National Insurance Acts (1953), and the Basic Law (The Knesset) (1958). The provisions of constitutional legislation that affect the main organs of government are summarized below:

THE PRESIDENT
The President is elected by the Knesset for a maximum of two five-year terms.*

Ten or more Knesset members may propose a candidate for the Presidency.

Voting will be by secret ballot.

The President may not leave the country without the consent of the Government.

The President may resign by submitting his resignation in writing to the Speaker.

The President may be relieved of his duties by the Knesset for misdemeanour.

The Knesset is entitled to decide by a two-thirds majority that the President is too incapacitated owing to ill health to fulfil his duties permanently.

The Speaker of the Knesset will act for the President when the President leaves the country, or when he cannot perform his duties owing to ill health.

* Moshe Katsav was elected to the presidency on 31 July 2000 for a seven-year term of office.

THE KNESSET
The Knesset is the parliament of the state. There are 120 members.

It is elected by general, national, direct, equal, secret and proportional elections.

Every Israeli national of 18 years or over shall have the right to vote in elections to the Knesset unless a court has deprived him of that right by virtue of any law.

Every Israeli national of 21 and over shall have the right to be elected to the Knesset unless a court has deprived him of that right by virtue of any law.

The following shall not be candidates: the President of the State; the two Chief Rabbis; a judge (shofet) in office; a judge (dayan) of a religious court; the State Comptroller; the Chief of the General Staff of the Defence Army of Israel; rabbis and ministers of other religions in office; senior state employees and senior army officers of such ranks and in such functions as shall be determined by law.

The term of office of the Knesset shall be four years.

The elections to the Knesset shall take place on the third Tuesday of the month of Marcheshvan in the year in which the tenure of the outgoing Knesset ends.

Election day shall be a day of rest, but transport and other public services shall function normally.

Results of the elections shall be published within 14 days.

The Knesset shall elect from among its members a Chairman and Vice-Chairman.

The Knesset shall elect from among its members permanent committees, and may elect committees for specific matters.

The Knesset may appoint commissions of inquiry to investigate matters designated by the Knesset.

The Knesset shall hold two sessions a year; one of them shall open within four weeks after the Feast of the Tabernacles, the other within four weeks after Independence Day; the aggregate duration of the two sessions shall not be less than eight months.

The outgoing Knesset shall continue to hold office until the convening of the incoming Knesset.

The members of the Knesset shall receive a remuneration as provided by law.

THE GOVERNMENT
The Government shall tender its resignation to the President immediately after his election, but shall continue with its duties until the formation of a new government. After consultation with representatives of the parties in the Knesset, the President shall charge one of the members with the formation of a government. The Government shall be composed of a Prime Minister (directly elected from May 1996, but from 2003 to revert to the previous system of election on a party basis) and a number of ministers from among the Knesset members or from outside the Knesset. After it has been chosen, the Government shall appear before the Knesset and shall be considered as formed after having received a vote of confidence. Within seven days of receiving a vote of confidence, the Prime Minister and the other ministers shall swear allegiance to the State of Israel and its Laws and undertake to carry out the decisions of the Knesset.

The Government

HEAD OF STATE

President: MOSHE KATSAV (took office 1 August 2000).

THE CABINET
(April 2003)

A coalition of Likud, Shinui, Haichud Haleumi, the National Religious Party (NRP) and Israel B'Aliyah.

Prime Minister and Minister of Communications and of Religious Affairs: ARIEL SHARON (Likud).

Deputy Prime Minister and Minister of Foreign Affairs: SILVAN SHALOM (Likud).

Deputy Prime Minister and Minister of Industry and Trade: EHUD OLMERT (Likud).

Deputy Prime Minister and Minister of Justice: YOSEF (TOMMY) LAPID (Shinui).

Minister of the Interior: AVRAHAM PORAZ (Shinui).

Minister of Defence: Lt-Gen. SHAUL MOFAZ.

Minister of Labour and Social Affairs: ZEVULUN ORLEV (NRP).

Minister of Health: DAN NAVEH (Likud).

Minister of the Environment: YEHUDITH NAOT (Shinui).

Minister of Education, Culture and Sport: LIMOR LIVNAT (Likud).

Minister of Public Security: TZACHI HANEGBI (Likud).

Minister of Finance: BINYAMIN NETANYAHU (Likud).

Minister of Immigrant Absorption: TZIPI LIVNI (Likud).

Minister of National Infrastructure: JOSEPH PARITZKY (Shinui).

Minister of Agriculture and Rural Development: YISRAEL KATZ (Likud).

Minister of Transport: AVIGDOR LIEBERMAN (Haichud Haleumi).

Minister of Science and Technology: ELIEZER SANDBERG (Shinui).

Minister of Construction and Housing: EFRAIM EITAM (NRP).

Minister of Tourism: BINYAMIN ELON (Haichud Haleumi).

Minister without Portfolio, responsible for Jerusalem, Social and Diaspora Affairs: NATAN SHARANSKY (Israel B'Aliyah).

Minister without Portfolio in the Ministry of Finance: MEIR SHEETRIT (Likud).

Ministers without Portfolio: GIDEON EZRA (Likud), UZI LANDAU (Likud).

MINISTRIES

Office of the Prime Minister: POB 187, 3 Rehov Kaplan, Kiryat Ben-Gurion, Jerusalem 91919; tel. 2-6705511; fax 2-6512631; e-mail webmaster@pmo.gov.il; internet www.pmo.gov.il.

Ministry of Agriculture and Rural Development: POB 30, 14 Arnia St, Hakirya, Tel-Aviv 50200; tel. 3-9485561; fax 3-9485870; e-mail webmaster@moag.gov.il; internet www.moag.gov.il.

Ministry of Communications: 23 Jaffa St, Jerusalem 91999; tel. 2-6706320; fax 2-6706372; internet www.moc.gov.il.

Ministry of Construction and Housing: POB 18110, Kiryat Hamemshala (East), Jerusalem 91180; tel. 2-5847654; fax 2-5847250; e-mail webmaster@moch.gov.il; internet www.moch.gov.il.

Ministry of Defence: Kaplan St, Hakirya, Tel-Aviv 67659; tel. 3-5692010; fax 3-6916940; e-mail public@mod.gov.il; internet www.mod.gov.il.

Ministry of Education: POB 292, 34 Shivtei Israel St, Jerusalem 91911; tel. 2-5602222; fax 2-5602752; e-mail info@education.gov.il; internet www.education.gov.il.

Ministry of the Environment: POB 34033, 5 Kanfei Nesharim St, Givat Shaul, Jerusalem 95464; tel. 2-6553745; fax 2-6553752; e-mail ori@sviva.gov.il; internet www.sviva.gov.il.

Ministry of Finance: POB 13191, 1 Rehov Kaplan, Kiryat Ben-Gurion, Jerusalem 91008; tel. 2-5317111; fax 2-5637891; e-mail webmaster@mof.gov.il; internet www.mof.gov.il.

Ministry of Foreign Affairs: Hakirya, Romema, Jerusalem 91950; tel. 2-5303111; fax 2-5303367; e-mail ask@israel-info.gov.il; internet www.mfa.gov.il.

Ministry of Health: POB 1176, 2 Ben-Tabai St, Jerusalem 91010; tel. 2-6705705; fax 2-6796267; e-mail yonit.mor@moh.health.gov.il; internet www.health.gov.il.

Ministry of Immigrant Absorption: POB 13061, 13 Rehov Kaplan, Kiryat Ben-Gurion, Jerusalem 91006; tel. 2-6752696; fax 2-5618138; e-mail info@moia.gov.il; internet www.moia.gov.il.

Ministry of Industry and Trade: POB 299, 30 Rehov Agron, Jerusalem 94190; tel. 2-6220661; fax 2-6222412; e-mail dover@moit.gov.il; internet www.tamas.gov.il.

Ministry of the Interior: POB 6158, 2 Rehov Kaplan, Kiryat Ben-Gurion, Jerusalem 91008; tel. 2-6701411; fax 2-6701628; e-mail pniot@moin.gov.il; internet www.moin.gov.il.

Ministry of Justice: POB 1087, 29 Rehov Salahadin, Jerusalem 91010; tel. 2-6466666; fax 2-6287757; e-mail pniot@justice.gov.il; internet www.justice.gov.il.

Ministry of Labour and Social Affairs: POB 915, 2 Rehov Kaplan, Kiryat Ben-Gurion, Jerusalem 91008; tel. 2-6752311; fax 2-6752803; e-mail sar@molsa.gov.il.

Ministry of National Infrastructure: Ala Bldg, 216 Jaffa St, Jerusalem; e-mail pniot@mmi.gov.il; internet www.mni.gov.il; also responsible for:

> **Israel Lands Administration:** POB 2600, 6 Shamai St, Jerusalem 94631; tel. 2-6208422; fax 2-6234960; e-mail pniot@mmi.gov.il; internet www.mmi.gov.il.

Ministry of Public Security: POB 18182, Bldg 3, Kiryat Hamemshala (East), Jerusalem 91181; tel. 2-5308003; fax 2-5847872; e-mail dover@mops.gov.il.

Ministry of Regional Co-operation: 8 Shaul Hamelech Blvd, Tel-Aviv 64733; tel. 3-6086111; fax 3-6086126; e-mail m_r_c@netvision.net.il; internet www.mrc.gov.il.

Ministry of Religious Affairs: POB 13059, 7 Kanfei Nesharim St, Jerusalem 95464; tel. 2-5311182; fax 2-6513679; e-mail dover@religions.gov.il; internet www.religions.gov.il.

Ministry of Science and Technology: POB 49100, Kiryat Hamemshala, Hamizrachit, Bldg 3, Jerusalem 91490; tel. 2-5411100; fax 2-5811613; e-mail nps@most.gov.il; internet www.most.gov.il.

Ministry of Tourism: POB 1018, 24 Rehov King George, Jerusalem 91009; tel. 2-6754811; fax 2-6253407; e-mail pniot@tourism.gov.il; internet www.tourism.gov.il.

Ministry of Transport: Klal Bldg, 97 Jaffa St, Jerusalem 91000; tel. 2-6228211; fax 2-6228693; e-mail pniot@mot.gov.il; internet www.mot.gov.il.

Legislature

KNESSET

Speaker: REUVEN RIVLIN.

General Election, 28 January 2003

Party	Valid votes cast	% of valid votes	Seats
Likud.	925,279	29.4	40
Labour–Meimad . . .	455,183	14.5	19
Shinui	386,535	12.3	15
Shas	258,879	8.2	11
Haichud Haleumi	173,973	5.5	7
Meretz	164,122	5.2	6
National Religious Party .	132,370	4.2	6
United Torah Judaism . .	135,087	4.3	5
Hadash	93,819	3.0	3
Am Ehad	86,808	2.8	3
Balad	71,299	2.3	3
United Arab List . . .	65,551	2.1	2
Total (incl. others) . . .	3,148,364*	100.0	120

*Excluding 52,409 invalid votes.

Prior to the January 2003 general election, pre-1996 legislation was restored according to which the Prime Minister is not directly elected. As leader of Likud, the incumbent premier, Ariel Sharon, was duly returned as Israel's Prime Minister.

Political Organizations

Agudat Israel: POB 513, Jerusalem; tel. 2-385251; fax 2-385145; orthodox Jewish party; stands for strict observance of Jewish religious law; Leaders AVRAHAM SHAPIRO, MENACHEM PORUSH.

Agudat Israel World Organization (AIWO): POB 326, Hacherut Sq., Jerusalem 91002; tel. 2-5384357; fax 2-5383634; f. 1912 at

Congress of Orthodox Jewry, Kattowitz, Germany (now Katowice, Poland), to help solve the problems facing Jewish people worldwide; more than 500,000 mems in 25 countries; Chair. Rabbi J. M. ABRA-MOWITZ (Jerusalem); Secs Rabbi MOSHE GEWIRTZ, Rabbi CHAIM WEINSTOCK.

Am Ehad (One Nation): tel. 3–6950644; internet www.am1.org.il; Workers' and pensioners' party affiliated to Histadrut trade union federation; Leader AMIR PERETZ.

Balad (National Democratic Alliance): f. 1999; united Arab party; Leader AZMI BISHARA.

Council for Peace and Security: f. 1988 by four retd Israeli generals; Maj.-Gen. AHARON YARIV, Maj.-Gen. ORI ORR, Brig.-Gen. YORAM AGMON, Brig.-Gen. EPHRAIM SNEH; Moshe Amirav of Shinui a founder mem. aims: an Israeli withdrawal from the Occupied Territories in return for a peace treaty with the Arab nations.

Degel Hatora: 103 Rehov Beit Vegan, Jerusalem; tel. 2-6438106; fax 2-6418967; f. 1988 as breakaway from Agudat Israel; orthodox Western Jews; Chair. AVRAHAM RAVITZ.

Democratic Arab Party (DAP): Nazareth; tel. 6-6560937; fax 6-6560938; e-mail dap@g-ol.com; f. 1988; aims: to unify Arab political forces so as to influence Palestinian and Israeli policy; international recognition of the Palestinian people's right to self-determination; the withdrawal of Israel from all territories occupied in 1967, including East Jerusalem; the DAP also aims to achieve full civil equality between Arab and Jewish citizens of Israel, to eliminate discrimination and improve the social, economic and political conditions of the Arab minority in Israel; Dir MUHAMMAD DARAWSHE.

Gush Emunim (Bloc of the Faithful): f. 1967; engaged in unauthorized establishment of Jewish settlements in the Occupied Territories; Leader Rabbi MOSHE LEVINGER.

Hadash (Democratic Front for Peace and Equality—Communist Party of Israel): POB 26205, Tel-Aviv 61261; tel. 3-6293944; fax 3-6297263; e-mail info@hadash.org.il; internet www.hadash.org.il; descended from the Socialist Workers' Party of Palestine (f. 1919); renamed Communist Party of Palestine 1921, Communist Party of Israel (Maki) 1948; pro-Soviet anti-Zionist group formed New Communist Party of Israel (Rakah) 1965; Jewish Arab membership; aims for a socialist system in Israel, a lasting peace between Israel and the Arab countries and the Palestinian Arab people, favours full implementation of UN Security Council Resolutions 242 and 338, Israeli withdrawal from all Arab territories occupied since 1967, formation of a Palestinian Arab state in the West Bank and Gaza Strip (with East Jerusalem as its capital), recognition of national rights of State of Israel and Palestinian people, democratic rights and defence of working class interests, and demands an end to discrimination against Arab minority in Israel and against oriental Jewish communities; Gen. Sec. (Hadash) MUHAMMAD BARAKEH; Gen. Sec. (Communist Party) MUHAMMAD NAFAH.

Haichud Haleumi (National Unity): internet www.leumi.org.il; f. 1999; right-wing coalition comprising Herut, Moledet and Tekuma parties; in February 2000 Herut withdrew from the coalition, which subsequently merged with Israel B'Aitainu; Leaders Rabbi BINYAMIN (BENNY) ELON, AVIGDOR LIEBERMAN.

Herut (Freedom): 55 Hamasger St, Tel-Aviv; tel. 3–5621521; fax 3–5618699; e-mail herut@herut.org.il; internet www.herut.org.il; f. 1948; reconstituted 1998; right-wing nationalist party; opposed to further Israeli withdrawal from the Occupied Territories; Leader MICHAEL KLEINER.

Israel B'Aitainu (Israel Is Our Home): internet www.beytenu.org.il; f. 1999; right-wing immigrant party, formed as a rival to Israel B'Aliyah; Leader AVIGDOR LIEBERMAN.

Israel B'Aliyah: f. 1995; campaigns for immigrants' rights; Leader NATAN SHARANSKY.

Israel Labour Party: POB 62033, Tel-Aviv 61620; tel. 3-6899444; fax 3-6899420; e-mail inter@havoda.org.il; f. 1968 as a merger of the three Labour groups, Mapai, Rafi and Achdut Ha'avoda; a Zionist democratic socialist party; Chair. (vacant); Sec.-Gen. OPHIR PINES-PAZ.

Kahane Chai (Kahane Lives): 111 Agripas St, Jerusalem; tel. 2-231081; f. 1977 as 'Kach' (Thus); right-wing religious nationalist party; advocates creation of a Torah state and expulsion of all Arabs from Israel and the annexation of the Occupied Territories; Leader (vacant).

Likud (Consolidation): 38 Rehov King George, Tel-Aviv 61231; tel. 3-5630666; fax 3-5282901; internet www.likud.org.il; f. September 1973; fmrly a parliamentary bloc of Herut (Freedom; f. 1948; Leader Itzhak Shamir; Sec.-Gen. Moshe Arens), the Liberal Party of Israel (f. 1961; Chair. Avraham Sharir), Laam (For the Nation) (f. 1976; fmrly led by Yigael Hurwitz, who left the coalition to form his own party, Ometz, before the 1984 general election), Ahdut (a one-man faction, Hillel Seidel), Tami (f. 1981; represents the interests of

Sephardic Jews; Leader Aharon Uzan), which joined Likud in June 1987, and an independent faction (f. 1990; Leader Itzhak Modai), which formed the nucleus of a new Party for the Advancement of the Zionist Idea; Herut and the Liberal Party formally merged in August 1988 to form the Likud-National Liberal Movement; aims: territorial integrity (advocates retention of all the territory of post-1922 mandatory Palestine); absorption of newcomers; a social order based on freedom and justice, elimination of poverty and want; development of an economy that will ensure a decent standard of living; improvement of the environment and the quality of life; Leader of Likud ARIEL SHARON.

Meimad: internet www.meimad.org.il; moderate Jewish party; Leader Rabbi MICHAEL MELCHIOR.

Meretz (Vitality): Tel-Aviv; tel. 3-6360111; fax 3-5375107; e-mail information@meretz.org.il; internet www.meretz.org.il; an alliance of Ratz, Shinui and the United Workers' Party; stands for civil rights, electoral reform, welfarism, Palestinian self-determination, separation of religion from the state and a halt to settlement in the Occupied Territories; Leader (vacant).

Moledet (Homeland): 14 Rehov Yehuda Halevi, Tel-Aviv; tel. 3-654580; internet www.moledet.org.il; f. 1988; right-wing nationalist party; aims: the expulsion ('transfer') of the 1.5m. Palestinians living in the West Bank and Gaza Strip; united with Tehiya—Zionist Revival Movement in June 1994 as the Moledet—the Eretz Israel Faithful and the Tehiya; Leader Rabbi BINYAMIN (BENNY) ELON.

Movement for the Advancement of the Zionist Idea (MAZI): f. 1990 as breakaway group of Likud; Leader ITZHAK MODAI.

National Religious Party (NRP): Jerusalem; tel. 2-377277; fax 2-377757; f. 1902 as the Mizrachi Organization within the Zionist Movement; present name adopted in 1956; stands for strict adherence to Jewish religion and tradition, and strives to achieve the application of religious precepts of Judaism in everyday life; it is also endeavouring to establish a Constitution for Israel based on Jewish religious law (the Torah); 126,000 mems; Leader EFRAIM EITAM; Sec.-Gen. ZEVULUN ORLEV.

New Liberal Party: Tel-Aviv; f. 1987 as a merger of three groups: Shinui-Movement for Change (f. 1974 and restored 1978, when Democratic Movement for Change split into two parties; centrist; Leader Amnon Rubinstein), the Centre Liberal Party (f. 1986 by members of the Liberal Party of Israel; Leader Itzhak Berman), and the Independent Liberal Party (f. 1965 by seven Liberal Party of Israel Knesset mems, after the formation of the Herut Movement and Liberal Party of Israel bloc; 20,000 mems; Chair. Moshe Kol; Gen. Sec. Nissim Eliad); Leaders AMNON RUBINSTEIN, ITZHAK BERMAN, MOSHE KOL.

Poale Agudat Israel: f. 1924; working-class Orthodox Judaist party; Leader Dr KALMAN KAHANE.

Political Zionist Opposition (Ometz): f. 1982; one-man party; YIGAEL HURWITZ.

Progressive List for Peace: 5 Simtat Lane, Nes Tziona, Tel-Aviv; tel. 3-662457; fax 3-659474; f. 1984; Jewish-Arab; advocates recognition of the PLO and the establishment of a Palestinian state in the West Bank and Gaza Strip; Leader MUHAMMAD MI'ARI.

Ra'am: Arab party; Leader ABD AL-MALIK DEHAMSHE.

Ratz (Civil Rights and Peace Movement): 21 Tchernihovsky St, Tel-Aviv 63291; tel. 3-5254847; fax 3-5255008; f. 1973; concerned with human and civil rights, opposes discrimination on basis of religion, gender or ethnic identification and advocates a peace settlement with the Arab countries and the Palestinians; Leader Mrs SHULAMIT ALONI.

Shas (Sephardic Torah Guardians): Beit Abodi, Rehov Hahida, Bene Beraq; tel. 3-579776; f. 1984 by splinter groups from Agudat Israel; ultra-orthodox Jewish party; Spiritual Leader Rabbi OVADIA YOSEF; Leader ELIYAHU YISHAI.

Shinui (Change): POB 20533, 100 Ha' Hashmonaim St, Tel-Aviv 67133; tel. 3-5620118; fax 3-5620139; e-mail shinui@shinui.org.il; internet www.shinui.org.il; f. 1974 as a new liberal party; combines an anti-religious coercion policy with a free-market economic philosophy; Leaders YOSEF (TOMMY) LAPID, AVRAHAM PORAZ.

Third Way: f. 1995; opposed to any transfer of the Golan Heights to Syria; Leader AVIGDOR KAHALANI.

Tiqva (Hope): f. 1999; campaigns for rights of new immigrants from former USSR; Leader ALEX TENCHER.

Tzomet (Crossroads): 22 Rehov Huberman, Tel-Aviv; tel. 3-204444; f. 1988; right-wing nationalist party; breakaway group from Tehiya party; Leader RAFAEL EITAN.

United Arab List: Arab party affiliated to Labour Party.

United Torah Judaism: electoral list of four minor ultra-orthodox parties (Moria, Degel Hatora, Poale Agudat Israel, Agudat Israel) formed, prior to 1992 election, to overcome the increase in election threshold from 1% to 1.5% and help to counter the rising influence of the secular Russian vote; contested 1999 election comprised of Degel Hatora and Agudat Israel.

United Workers' Party (Mapam): POB 1777, 2 Homa U'Migdal St, Tel-Aviv; tel. 3-6360111; fax 3-5375107; f. 1948; left-wing socialist-Zionist Jewish-Arab party; grouped in Labour-Mapam Alignment with Israel Labour Party from January 1969 until Sept. 1984 when it withdrew in protest over Labour's formation of a Government with Likud; member of the Socialist International; 77,000 mems; Chair. CHANAN EREZ; Sec.-Gen. VICTOR BLIT.

Yahad (Together): f. 1984; advocates a peace settlement with the Arab peoples and the Palestinians; joined the Labour Party parliamentary bloc in January 1987.

Yi'ud: f. 1994; breakaway group from the Tzomet Party.

Diplomatic Representation

EMBASSIES IN ISRAEL

Argentina: Apt 3, Medinat Hayeudim 85, Herzliya Business Park, Herzliya; tel. 9-9702743; fax 9-9702748; e-mail embarg@netvision.net.il; Ambassador GREGORIO JOSÉ DUPONT.

Australia: Beit Europa, 4th Floor, 37 Shaul Hamelech Blvd, Tel-Aviv 64928; tel. 3-6950451; fax 3-6968404; Ambassador ROSS BURNS.

Austria: Beit Crystal, 12 Hahilazon, Ramat-Gan, Tel-Aviv 52522; tel. 3-6120924; fax 3-7510716; e-mail autambta@netvision.net.il; Ambassador Dr KURT HENGL.

Belarus: 2 Rehov Kaufman, Tel-Aviv 68012; tel. 3-5102236; fax 3-5102235; Ambassador MIKHAIL FARFEL.

Belgium: 12 Hahilazon, Ramat-Gan, Tel-Aviv 52522; tel. 3-6138130; fax 3-6138160; e-mail telaviv@diplobel.org; Ambassador WILFRIED GEENS.

Bolivia: Toyota Bldg, 65 Rehov Yigal Alon, 13A/2, Tel-Aviv 67443; tel. 3-5621992; fax 3-5621990; e-mail embolivia-telaviv@emb.co.il; Ambassador Dr VÍCTOR TORRES ACHA.

Brazil: 2 Rehov Kaplan, Beit Yachin, 8th Floor, Tel-Aviv 64734; tel. 3-6919292; fax 3-6916060; Ambassador JOSÉ NOGUEIRA FILHO.

Bulgaria: 4th Floor, Leonardo da Vinci St, Tel-Aviv 64733; tel. 3-6961361; fax 3-6961430; e-mail bgemtlv@hotmail.com; Ambassador Prof. TSANKO YABLANSKI.

Cameroon: Tel-Aviv; tel. 3-5298401; fax 3-5298249; Chargé d'affaires a.i. HENRI ETOUNDI ESSOMBA.

Canada: 3 Nirim St, Tel-Aviv; tel. 3-6363300; fax 3-6363385; Ambassador MICHAEL D. BELL.

Chile: 4 Rehov Kaufman, Tel-Aviv 68012; tel. 3-5102751; fax 3-5100102; e-mail echileil@inter.net.il; Ambassador SALLY BENDERSKY SCHACHNER.

China, People's Republic: POB 6067, 222 Ben Yehuda St, Tel-Aviv 61060; tel. 3-5467277; fax 3-5467311; e-mail chnemb@isdn.net.il; Ambassador PAN ZHALIN.

Colombia: 52 Rehov Pinkas, Apt 26, Tel-Aviv 62261; tel. 3-5461717; fax 3-5461404; e-mail emcolis@netvision.net.il; Ambassador DAVID DE LA ROSA PEREZ.

Congo, Democratic Republic: Apt 5, 60 Hei Be'Iyar, Kikar Hamedina, Tel-Aviv 62198; tel. 3-452681; Ambassador Gen. ELUKI MONGA AUNDU.

Costa Rica: 13 Rehov Diskin, Apt 1, Kiryat Wolfson, Jerusalem 92473; tel. 2-5666197; fax 2-5632591; e-mail emcri@netmedia.net.il; Ambassador RODRIGO X. CARRERAS.

Côte d'Ivoire: South Africa Bldg, 25 Bezalel St, Ramat-Gan, Tel-Aviv 52521; tel. 3-6126677; fax 3-6126688; e-mail ambacita@netvision.net.il; Ambassador LÉON H. KACOU ADOM.

Cyprus: 14th Floor, Top Tower, Dizengoff Centre, 50 Dizengoff St, Tel-Aviv 64322; tel. 3-5250212; fax 3-6290535; e-mail cyprus@netvision.net.il.

Czech Republic: POB 16361, 23 Rehov Zeitlin, Tel-Aviv 61664; tel. 3-6918282; fax 3-6918286; e-mail telaviv@embassy.mzv.cz; internet www.mfa.cz/telaviv; Ambassador DANIEL KUMERMANN.

Denmark: POB 21080, 23 Rehov Bnei Moshe, Tel-Aviv 61210; tel. 3-5442144; fax 3-5465502; e-mail tlvamb@um.dk; internet www.dk-embassy.org.il; Ambassador HANS MICHAEL KOFOED-HANSEN.

Dominican Republic: 19 Soutine St, Tel-Aviv 64684; tel. 3-5277073; fax 3-5277074; e-mail embajdom@netvision.net.il; Ambassador Dr MANUEL MORALES-LAMA.

Ecuador: Asia House, 4 Rehov Weizman, Tel-Aviv 64239; tel. 3-6958764; fax 3-6913604; e-mail mecuaisr@infolink.net.il; Ambassador LEONARDO RUILOVA.

Egypt: 54 Rehov Bazel, Tel-Aviv 62744; tel. 3-5464151; fax 3-5441615; e-mail egypem.ta@zahav.net.il; Chargé d'affaires Dr IHAH ESH-SHARIF (Ambassador withdrawn in Nov. 2000).

El Salvador: POB 4005, Jerusalem 91039; tel. 2-6728411; fax 2-6733641; e-mail embasal@inter.net.il; internet www.el-salvador.org.il; Ambassador ERNESTO ARRIETA PERALTA.

Ethiopia: 48 Darech Petach Tikva, Tel-Aviv 66184; tel. 3-6397831; fax 3-6397837; e-mail ethembis@netvision.net.il; Ambassador FIT ZEWDIE OTTORO.

Finland: POB 39666, 40 Einstein St, Tel-Aviv 69101; tel. 3-7440303; fax 3-7440314; e-mail sanomat.tel@formin.fi; Ambassador PASI PATOKALLIO.

France: 112 Tayelet Herbert Samuel, Tel-Aviv 63572; tel. 3-5208300; fax 3-5208342; e-mail diplomatie@ambafrance-il.org; internet www.ambafrance-il.org; Ambassador JACQUES HUNTZINGER.

Germany: POB 16038, 19th Floor, 3 Rehov Daniel Frisch, Tel-Aviv 61160; tel. 3-6931313; fax 3-6969217; e-mail ger_emb@netvision.net.il; internet www.germanemb.org.il; Ambassador RUDOLF DRESSLER.

Greece: 3 Daniel Frisch St, Tel-Aviv 64731; tel. 3-6953060; fax 3-6951329; e-mail gremil@netvision.net.il; Ambassador PANAYOTIS ZOGRAFOS.

Guatemala: Ackerstein Bldg, 103 Medinat Hayeudim, Herzliya Pituach, Herzliya B. 46130; tel. 9-9577335; fax 9-9518506; Ambassador MARCO TULIO ZÚÑIGA.

Haiti: Tel-Aviv 64336; tel. 3-280285; Ambassador FRANCK M. JOSEPH.

Holy See: POB 19199, Jerusalem 91191; tel. 2-6282298; fax 2-6281880; e-mail vatge@netvision.net.il; Apostolic Nuncio Mgr PIETRO SAMBI (Titular Archbishop of Belcastro).

Honduras: Zohar Tal 1, Herziya Pituach, Tel-Aviv 46741; tel. 9-9577686; fax 9-9577457; e-mail honduras@netvision.net.il; Ambassador FRANCISCO ZEPEDA ANDINO.

Hungary: 18 Rehov Pinkas, Tel-Aviv 62661; tel. 3-5466860; fax 3-5468968; Ambassador Dr JÁNOS HÓVÁRI.

India: 4 Rehov Kaufman, Tel-Aviv; tel. 3-5101431; fax 3-5101434; e-mail indemtel@indembassy.co.il; Ambassador R. S. JASSAL.

Ireland: 17th Floor, The Tower, 3 Daniel Frisch St, Tel-Aviv 64731; tel. 3-6964166; e-mail telaviv@iveagh.irlgov.ie; Ambassador PATRICK HENNESSY.

Italy: Asia House, 4 Rehov Weizman, Tel-Aviv 64239; tel. 3-6964223; fax 3-6918428; e-mail italemb@netvision.net.il; internet www.italian-embassy-israel.org; Ambassador GIAN PAOLO CAVARAI.

Japan: Asia House, 4 Rehov Weizman, Tel-Aviv 64239; tel. 3-6957292; fax 3-6910516; Ambassador HIROSHI SHIGETA.

Jordan: 14 Abba Hillel, Ramat-Gan, Tel-Aviv 52506; tel. 3-7517722; fax 3-7517712; e-mail jordanembassy@barak.net.il; Chargé d'affaires a.i. Dr MAZEN TAL.

Kazakhstan: 185 Rehov Hayarkon, Tel-Aviv 63453; tel. 3-5236776; fax 3-5239045; e-mail embacy@internet-zahav.net; Ambassador BYRGANYM AITIMOVA.

Korea, Republic: 38 Sderot Chen, Tel-Aviv 64166; tel. 3-6963244; fax 3-6963243; Ambassador LEE CHANG-HO.

Latvia: 9 Marmorek St, Tel-Aviv 64254; tel. 3-6869544; fax 3-6869543; e-mail latvembi@netvision.net.il; Ambassador JĀNIS LOVNIKS.

Liberia: 6 Shimon Frug, Ramat-Gan, Tel-Aviv 524282; tel. 3-728525; Ambassador Maj. SAMUEL B. PEARSON, Jr.

Lithuania: 14th Floor, Top Tower, Dizengoff Centre, Tel-Aviv 64332; tel. 3-5288514; fax 3-5257265; e-mail lrambizr@netvision.net.il; Ambassador ALFONSAS EIDINTAS.

Mauritania: Tel-Aviv; Ambassador AHMAD OULD TEGUEDDI.

Mexico: 25 Hamered St, 5th Floor, Trade Tower, Tel-Aviv 68125; tel. 3-5163938; fax 3-5163711; e-mail embamex@netvision.net.il; Ambassador ANDRES VALENCIA BENAVIDE.

Myanmar: 26 Rehov Hayarkon, Tel-Aviv 68011; tel. 3-5170760; fax 3-5171440; e-mail teltaman@classnet.co.il; Ambassador U TIN WIN.

Netherlands: Asia House, 4 Rehov Weizman, Tel-Aviv 64239; tel. 3-6910036; fax 3-6910071; e-mail tel-cdp@minbuza.nl; Ambassador H. R. R. V. FROGER.

Nigeria: POB 3339, 34 Gordon St, Tel-Aviv 61030; tel. 3-5222144; fax 3-5237886; Ambassador E. EGBARA.

Norway: POB 17575, 40 Einstein St, Tel-Aviv 69101; tel. 3-7441490; fax 3-7441498; e-mail norambta@netvision.net.il; Ambassador MONA JUUL.

Panama: 10 Rehov Hei Be'Iyar, Kikar Hamedina, Tel-Aviv 62998; tel. 3-6960849; fax 3-6910045; Ambassador Prof. PAULINO C. ROMERO.

Peru: 37 Rehov Hamarganit, Shikun Vatikin, Ramat-Gan, Tel-Aviv 52584; tel. 3-6135591; fax 3-7512286; e-mail emperu@netvision.net .il; Ambassador NICOLAS RONCAGLIOLO.

Philippines: POB 50085, 13th Floor, Textile Centre Bldg, 2 Rehov Kaufman, Tel-Aviv 68012; tel. 3-5175263; fax 3-5102229; e-mail filembis@netvision.net.il; Ambassador ROSALINDA DE PERIO-SANTOS.

Poland: 16 Soutine St, Tel-Aviv 64684; tel. 3-5240186; fax 3-5237806; e-mail embpol@netvision.net.il; Ambassador MACIEJ KOZŁOWSKI.

Portugal: 12th Floor, 3 Daniel Frisch St, Tel-Aviv 64731; tel. 3-6956373; fax 3-6956366; e-mail eptel@netvision.net.il; Ambassador ANTÓNIO TÂNGER CORRÊA.

Romania: 24 Rehov Adam Hacohen, Tel-Aviv 64585; tel. 3-5230066; fax 3-5247379; e-mail ambtaviv@zahav.net.il; Ambassador VALERIA MARIANA STOICA.

Russia: 120 Rehov Hayarkon, Tel-Aviv 63573; tel. 3-5226736; fax 3-5226713; e-mail amb_ru@mail.netvision.net.il; internet www.israel .mid.ru; Ambassador GENNADII TARASOV.

Serbia and Montenegro: Iderot Shaul Hamelech 8, Tel-Aviv 64733; tel. 3-6938412; fax 3-6938411; Chargé d'affaires a.i. MIRKO STEFANOVIĆ.

Slovakia: POB 6459, 37 Jabotinsky St, Tel-Aviv 61064; tel. 3-5440066; fax 3-5449144; Ambassador Dr MAROŠ ŠEFČOVIČ.

Slovenia: Tel-Aviv; Ambassador PETER TOS.

South Africa: POB 7138, 16th Floor, Top Tower, 50 Dizengoff St, Tel-Aviv 61071; tel. 3-5252566; fax 3-5253230; e-mail saemtel@isdn .net.il; internet www.safis.co.il; Ambassador JOHANN MARX.

Spain: Dubnov Tower, 3 Rehov Daniel Frisch, 18th Floor, Tel-Aviv 64731; tel. 3-6965218; fax 3-6965217; Ambassador CARLOS BÁRCENA PORTOLÉS.

Sweden: Asia House, 4 Rehov Weizman, Tel-Aviv 64239; tel. 3-6958111; fax 3-6958116; e-mail swembtlv@trendline.co.il; internet www.swedishembassy.co.il; Ambassador ANDERS LIDÉN.

Switzerland: 228 Rehov Hayarkon, Tel-Aviv 63405; tel. 3-5464455; fax 3-5464408; e-mail vertretung@tel.rep.admin.ch; internet www .eda.admin.ch/telaviv; Ambassador ERNST ITEN.

Thailand: Tel-Aviv; Ambassador DOMEDEJ BUNNAG.

Turkey: 202 Rehov Hayarkon, Tel-Aviv 63405; tel. 3-5241101; fax 3-5241390; e-mail turqua2@netvision.net.il; internet www .turkishembassy-telaviv.org; Ambassador FERIDUN SINIRLIOGLU.

Ukraine: 50 Yirmiyagu, Tel-Aviv 62594; tel. 3-6040242; fax 3-6042512; e-mail embukr@netvision.net.il; internet www .ukraine-embassy.co.il; Ambassador (vacant).

United Kingdom: 192 Rehov Hayarkon, Tel-Aviv 63405; tel. 3-7251222; fax 3-5243313; e-mail webmaster.telaviv@fco.gov.uk; internet www.britemb.org.il; Ambassador SHERARD COWPER-COLES.

USA: POB 26180, 1 Ben Yahuda St, Tel-Aviv; tel. 3-5103822; fax 3-5103828; e-mail webmaster@usembassy-israel.org.il; internet usembassy-israel.org.il; Ambassador DANIEL C. KURTZER.

Uruguay: Tel-Aviv 62261; tel. 3-440411; Ambassador JOSÉ LUÍS POMBO.

Venezuela: Textile Center, 2 Rehov Kaufman, 16th Floor, Tel-Aviv 61500; tel. 3-5176287; fax 3-5176210; Chargé d'affaires JORGE MENDEZ MONTILLA.

The Jewish Agency for Israel

POB 92, Jerusalem 91000; tel. 2-6202222; fax 2-6202303; e-mail elibir@jazo.org.il; internet www.jafi.org.il.

Organization: The governing bodies are the Assembly which determines basic policy, the Board of Governors which sets policy for the Agency between Assembly meetings and the Executive responsible for the day-to-day running of the Agency.

Chairman of Executive: SALLAI MERIDOR.

Chairman of Board of Governors: ALEX GRASS.

Director-General: AHARON ABRAMOWITZ.

Secretary-General: ILAN RUBIN.

Functions: According to the Agreement of 1971, the Jewish Agency undertakes the immigration and absorption of immigrants in Israel, including absorption in agricultural settlement and immigrant housing; social welfare and health services in connection with immigrants; education, youth care and training; neighbourhood rehabilitation through project renewal.

Budget (2000): US $376m.

Judicial System

The law of Israel is composed of the enactments of the Knesset and, to a lesser extent, of the acts, orders-in-council and ordinances that remain from the period of the British Mandate in Palestine (1922–48). The pre-1948 law has largely been replaced, amended or reorganized, in the interests of codification, by Israeli legislation. This legislation generally follows a pattern which is very similar to that operating in England and the USA.

Attorney-General: ELYAQIM RUBENSTEIN.

CIVIL COURTS

The Supreme Court

Sha'arei Mishpat St, Kiryat David Ben-Gurion, Jerusalem 91950; tel. 2-6759666; fax 2-6759648; e-mail marcia@supreme.court.gov.il; internet www.court.gov.il.

This is the highest judicial authority in the state. It has jurisdiction as an Appellate Court over appeals from the District Courts in all matters, both civil and criminal (sitting as a Court of Civil Appeal or as a Court of Criminal Appeal). In addition it is a Court of First Instance (sitting as the High Court of Justice) in actions against governmental authorities, and in matters in which it considers it necessary to grant relief in the interests of justice and which are not within the jurisdiction of any other court or tribunal. The High Court's exclusive power to issue orders in the nature of *habeas corpus, mandamus*, prohibition and *certiorari* enables the court to review the legality of and redress grievances against acts of administrative authorities of all kinds and religious tribunals.

President of the Supreme Court: AHARON BARAK.

Deputy President of the Supreme Court: SHLOMO LEVIN.

Justices of the Supreme Court: DORIT BEINISCH, JACOB TÜRKEL, MISHAEL CHESHIN, TOVA STRASBERG-COHEN, THEODORE OR, ELIYAHU MAZZA, ITZHAK ENGLAND, DALIA DORNER, ELIEZER RIVLIN, EDMOND E. LEVY, AYALA PROCACCIA.

Registrars: Judge MICHAL AGMON, Attorney HAGIT MACK-KALMANO-WITCH.

The District Courts: There are five District Courts (Jerusalem, Tel-Aviv, Haifa, Beersheba, Nazareth). They have residual jurisdiction as Courts of First Instance over all civil and criminal matters not within the jurisdiction of a Magistrates' Court, all matters not within the exclusive jurisdiction of any other tribunal, and matters within the concurrent jurisdiction of any other tribunal so long as such tribunal does not deal with them. In addition, the District Courts have appellate jurisdiction over appeals from judgments and decisions of Magistrates' Courts and judgments of Municipal Courts and various administrative tribunals.

Magistrates' Courts: There are 29 Magistrates' Courts, having criminal jurisdiction to try contraventions, misdemeanours and certain felonies, and civil jurisdiction to try actions concerning possession or use of immovable property, or the partition thereof whatever may be the value of the subject matter of the action, and other civil claims not exceeding one million shekels.

Labour Courts: Established in 1969. Regional Labour Courts in Jerusalem, Tel-Aviv, Haifa, Beersheba and Nazareth, composed of judges and representatives of the public. A National Labour Court in Jerusalem. The Courts have jurisdiction over all matters arising out of the relationship between employer and employee or parties to a collective labour agreement, and matters concerning the National Insurance Law and the Labour Law and Rules.

RELIGIOUS COURTS

The Religious Courts are the courts of the recognized religious communities. They have jurisdiction over certain defined matters of personal status concerning members of their respective communities. Where any action of personal status involves persons of different religious communities the President of the Supreme Court decides which Court will decide the matter. Whenever a question arises as to whether or not a case is one of personal status within the exclusive jurisdiction of a Religious Court, the matter must be referred to a Special Tribunal composed of two Justices of the Supreme Court and the President of the highest court of the religious community concerned in Israel. The judgments of the Religious Courts are executed by the process and offices of the Civil Courts. Neither these Courts nor the Civil Courts have jurisdiction to dissolve the marriage of a foreign subject.

Jewish Rabbinical Courts: These Courts have exclusive jurisdiction over matters of marriage and divorce of Jews in Israel who are Israeli citizens or residents. In all other matters of personal status they have concurrent jurisdiction with the District Courts.

Muslim Religious Courts: These Courts have exclusive jurisdiction over matters of marriage and divorce of Muslims who are not foreigners, or who are foreigners subject by their national law to the jurisdiction of Muslim Religious Courts in such matters. In all other matters of personal status they have concurrent jurisdiction with the District Courts.

Christian Religious Courts: The Courts of the recognized Christian communities have exclusive jurisdiction over matters of marriage and divorce of members of their communities who are not foreigners. In all other matters of personal status they have concurrent jurisdiction with the District Courts.

Druze Courts: These Courts, established in 1963, have exclusive jurisdiction over matters of marriage and divorce of Druze in Israel, who are Israeli citizens or residents, and concurrent jurisdiction with the District Courts over all other matters of personal status of Druze.

Religion

JUDAISM

Judaism, the religion of the Jews, is the faith of the majority of Israel's inhabitants. On 31 December 2001 Judaism's adherents totalled 5,025,000, equivalent to 77.25% of the country's population. Its basis is a belief in an ethical monotheism.

There are two main Jewish communities: the Ashkenazim and the Sephardim. The former are the Jews from Eastern, Central, or Northern Europe, while the latter originate from the Balkan countries, North Africa and the Middle East.

There is also a community of about 10,000 Falashas (Ethiopian Jews) who have been airlifted to Israel at various times since the fall of Emperor Haile Selassie in 1974.

The supreme religious authority is vested in the Chief Rabbinate, which consists of the Ashkenazi and Sephardi Chief Rabbis and the Supreme Rabbinical Council. It makes decisions on interpretation of the Jewish law, and supervises the Rabbinical Courts. There are 8 regional Rabbinical Courts, and a Rabbinical Court of Appeal presided over by the two Chief Rabbis.

According to the Rabbinical Courts Jurisdiction Law of 1953, marriage and divorce among Jews in Israel are exclusively within the jurisdiction of the Rabbinical Courts. Provided that all the parties concerned agree, other matters of personal status can also be decided by the Rabbinical Courts.

There are 195 Religious Councils, which maintain religious services and supply religious needs, and about 405 religious committees with similar functions in smaller settlements. Their expenses are borne jointly by the state and the local authorities. The Religious Councils are under the administrative control of the Ministry of Religious Affairs. In all matters of religion, the Religious Councils are subject to the authority of the Chief Rabbinate. There are 365 officially appointed rabbis. The total number of synagogues is about 7,000, most of which are organized within the framework of the Union of Israel Synagogues.

Head of the Ashkenazi Community: The Chief Rabbi YONA METZGER.

Head of the Sephardic Community: Jerusalem; tel. 2-5313131 The Chief Rabbi SHLOMO AMAR.

Two Jewish sects still loyal to their distinctive customs are:

The Karaites: a sect which recognizes only the Jewish written law and not the oral law of the Mishna and Talmud. The community of about 12,000, many of whom live in or near Ramla, has been augmented by immigration from Egypt.

The Samaritans: an ancient sect mentioned in 2 Kings xvii, 24. They recognize only the Torah. The community in Israel numbers about 500; about one-half of this number live in Holon, where a Samaritan synagogue has been built, and the remainder, including the High Priest, live in Nablus, near Mt Gerazim, which is sacred to the Samaritans.

ISLAM

The Muslims in Israel are mainly Sunnis, and are divided among the four rites of the Sunni sect of Islam: the Shafe'i, the Hanbali, the Hanafi and the Maliki. Before June 1967 they numbered approx.

175,000; in 1971, approx. 343,900. On 31 December 2001 the total Muslim population of Israel was 1,004,600.

Mufti of Jerusalem: POB 19859, Jerusalem; tel. 2-283528; Sheikh ABD AL-QADIR ABIDIN (also Chair. Supreme Muslim Council for Jerusalem); The Palestinian National Authority also claims the right to appoint the Mufti of Jerusalem and has named Sheikh Akram Sa'id Sabri as its choice.

There was also a total of 106,300 Druzes in Israel at 31 December 2001.

CHRISTIANITY

The total Christian population of Israel (including East Jerusalem) at 31 December 2001 was 138,500.

United Christian Council in Israel: POB 116, Jerusalem 91000; tel. 2-6714351; fax 2-6721349; e-mail kopp@galanet.net; f. 1956; 28 mems (churches and other bodies); Chair. CHARLES KOPP.

The Roman Catholic Church

Armenian Rite

The Armenian Catholic Patriarch of Cilicia is resident in Beirut, Lebanon.

Patriarchal Exarchate of Jerusalem: POB 19546, Via Dolorosa 36, Jerusalem 91190; tel. 2-6284262; fax 2-6272123; f. 1885; about 425 adherents (2000); Exarch Patriarchal GEORGES KHAZZOUM.

Chaldean Rite

The Chaldean Patriarch of Babylon is resident in Baghdad, Iraq.

Patriarchal Exarchate of Jerusalem: Chaldean Patriarchal Vicariate, POB 20108, 7 Chaldean St, Saad and Said Quarter, Jerusalem 91200; tel. 2-6284519; fax 2-6274614; Exarch Patriarchal Mgr PAUL COLLIN.

Latin Rite

The Patriarchate of Jerusalem covers Palestine, Jordan and Cyprus. At 31 December 2000 there were an estimated 77,000 adherents.

Bishops' Conference: Conférence des Evêques Latins dans les Régions Arabes, Notre Dame of Jerusalem Center, POB 20531, Jerusalem 91204; tel. 2-6288554; fax 2-6288555; e-mail evcat@palnet.com; f. 1967; Pres. His Beatitude MICHEL SABBAH (Patriarch of Jerusalem).

Patriarchate of Jerusalem: Patriarcat Latin, POB 14152, Jerusalem 91141; tel. 2-6282323; fax 2-6271652; e-mail latinpat@actcom.co.il; internet www.lpj.org; Patriarch His Beatitude MICHEL SABBAH; Vicar-General for Jerusalem KAMAL HANNA BATHISH (Titular Bishop of Jericho); Vicar-General for Israel GIACINTO-BOULOS MARCUZZO (Titular Bishop of Emmaus Nicopolis); Vicariat Patriarcal Latin, Street 6191/3, Nazareth 16100; tel. 4-6554075; fax 4-6452416; e-mail latinpat@rannet.com.

Maronite Rite

The Maronite community, under the jurisdiction of the Maronite Patriarch of Antioch (resident in Lebanon), has about 7,000 members.

Patriarchal Exarchate of Jerusalem: Maronite Patriarchal Exarchate, POB 14219, 25 Maronite Convent St, Jaffa Gate, Jerusalem 91141; tel. 2-6282158; fax 2-6272821; about 504 adherents (2000); Exarch Patriarchal Mgr PAUL NABIL SAYAH (also the Archbishop of Haifa and the Holy Land).

Melkite Rite

The Greek-Melkite Patriarch of Antioch and all the East, of Alexandria and of Jerusalem (Grégoire III Laham) is resident in Damascus, Syria.

Patriarchal Vicariate of Jerusalem

Patriarcat Grec-Melkite Catholique, POB 14130, Porte de Jaffa, Jerusalem 91141; tel. 2-6271968; fax 2-6286652; e-mail gcpjer@p-ol.com.

About 3,300 adherents (2000); Protosyncellus Archim. MTANIOS HADDAD (resident in Rome).

Archbishop of Akka (Acre): Most Rev. PIERRE MOUALLEM, Archevêché Grec-Catholique, POB 279, 33 Hagefen St, 31002 Haifa; tel. 4-8523114; fax 4-8520798.

65,200 adherents at 31 December 2001.

Syrian Rite

The Syrian Catholic Patriarch of Antioch is resident in Beirut, Lebanon.

Patriarchal Exarchate of Jerusalem: Vicariat Patriarcal Syrien Catholique, POB 19787, 6 Chaldean St, Jerusalem 91191; tel. 2-6282657; fax 2-6284217; e-mail stjossc@l-ol.com; about 10,298 adherents (Dec. 2000); Exarch Patriarchal Mgr GRÉGOIRE PIERRE MELKI.

The Armenian Apostolic (Orthodox) Church

Patriarch of Jerusalem: TORKOM MANOOGIAN, St James's Cathedral, Jerusalem; tel. 2-6264853; fax 2-6264862.

The Greek Orthodox Church

The Patriarchate of Jerusalem contains an estimated 260,000 adherents in Israel, the Occupied Territories, Jordan, Kuwait, the United Arab Emirates and Saudi Arabia.

Patriarch of Jerusalem: IRINEOS I, POB 19632-633, Greek Orthodox Patriarchate St, Old City, Jerusalem; tel. 2-6271657; fax 2-6282048.

The Anglican Communion

Episcopal Church in Jerusalem and the Middle East: POB 19122, St George's Cathedral Close, Jerusalem; tel. 2-6271670; fax 2-6273847; e-mail ediosces@netvision.net.il; Bishop The Rt. Rev. RIAH ABU AL-ASSAL.

Other Christian Churches

Other denominations include the Coptic Orthodox Church (700 members), the Russian Orthodox Church, the Ethiopian Orthodox Church, the Romanian Orthodox Church, the Baptist Church, the Lutheran Church and the Church of Scotland.

The Press

Tel-Aviv is the main publishing centre. Largely for economic reasons, no local press has developed away from the main cities; hence all papers regard themselves as national. Friday editions, issued on Sabbath eve, are increased to as much as twice the normal size by special weekend supplements, and experience a considerable rise in circulation. No newspapers appear on Saturday.

Most of the daily papers are in Hebrew, and others appear in Arabic, English, French, Polish, Yiddish, Hungarian, Russian and German. The total daily circulation is 500,000–600,000 copies, or 21 papers per hundred people, although most citizens read more than one daily paper.

Most Hebrew morning dailies have strong political or religious affiliations. *Hatzofeh*, for example, is affiliated to the National Religious Party. Most newspapers depend on subsidies from political parties, religious organizations or public funds. The limiting effect on freedom of commentary entailed by this party press system has provoked repeated criticism. There are around 400 other newspapers and magazines including some 50 weekly and 150 fortnightly; over 250 of them are in Hebrew, the remainder in 11 other languages.

The most influential and respected daily, for both quality of news coverage and commentary, is *Ha'aretz*. This is the most widely read of the morning papers, exceeded only by the popular afternoon press, *Ma'ariv* and *Yedioth Aharonoth*. The *Jerusalem Post* gives detailed and sound news coverage in English.

The Israeli Press Council (Chair. ITZHAK ZAMIR), established in 1963, deals with matters of common interest to the Press such as drafting the code of professional ethics which is binding on all journalists.

The Daily Newspaper Publishers' Association represents publishers in negotiations with official and public bodies, negotiates contracts with employees and purchases and distributes newsprint.

DAILIES

Al Anba (The News): Jerusalem Publications Ltd, POB 428, 37 Hillel St, Jerusalem; f. 1968; circ. 10,000.

Globes: POB 5126, Rishon le Zion 75150; tel. 3-9538888; fax 3-9525971; e-mail mailbox@globes.co.il; internet www.globes.co.il; f. 1983; evening; Hebrew; business, economics; CEO AMI EVEN; Editor-in-Chief HAGGAI GOLAN; circ. 40,000.

Ha'aretz (The Land): POB 233, 21 Salman Schocken St, Tel-Aviv 61001; tel. 3-5121110; fax 3-6815859; e-mail iht@haaretz.co.il; internet www.haaretz.co.il; f. 1918; morning; Hebrew; liberal, independent; Editor HANOCH MARMARI; circ. 65,000 (weekdays), 75,000 (weekends).

Hadashot (The News): 108 Igal Alon St, Tel-Aviv; tel. 3-5120555; fax 3-5623084; late morning; Hebrew.

Hamodia (The Informer): POB 1306, Yehuda Hamackabbi 5, Jerusalem 91012; tel. 2-5389255; fax 2-5389108; e-mail english@hamodia.co.il; morning; Hebrew; also publishes weekly English-language edition; organ of Agudat Israel; Editors M. A. DRUCK, H. M. KNOPF; circ. 35,000.

Hatzofeh (The Watchman): POB 2045, 66 Hamasger St, Tel-Aviv; tel. 3-5622951; fax 3-5621502; e-mail hazofe@zahav.net.il; internet www.hazofe.co.il; f. 1938; morning; Hebrew; organ of the National Religious Party; Editor GONEN GINAT; circ. 60,000.

Israel Nachrichten (News of Israel): POB 35248, 49 Tschlenow St, Tel-Aviv 66048; tel. 3-5372059; fax 3-6877142; f. 1974; morning; German; Editor ALICE SCHWARZ-GARDOS; circ. 20,000.

Al-Itihad (Unity): POB 104, Haifa; tel. 4-511296; fax 4-511297; f. 1944; Arabic; organ of Hadash; Editor AHMAD SA'AD; circ. 60,000.

The Jerusalem Post: POB 81, Romema, Jerusalem 91000; tel. 2-5315666; fax 2-5389527; e-mail jpedt@jpost.co.il; internet www.jpost.com; f. 1932; morning; English; independent; Pres. PAUL STASZEWSKI; Editor CARL SCHRAG; circ. 30,000 (weekdays), 50,000 (weekend edition); there is also a weekly international edition, circ. 70,000, and a weekly French-language edition, circ. 7,500.

Le Journal d'Israël: Tel-Aviv; tel. 3-33188; f. 1971; French; independent; Chief Editor J. RABIN; circ. 10,000; also overseas weekly selection; circ. 15,000.

Letzte Nyess (Late News): Tel-Aviv; tel. 3-35815; f. 1949; morning; Yiddish; Editor S. HIMMELFARB; circ. 23,000.

Ma'ariv (Evening Prayer): 2 Carlebach St, Tel-Aviv 61200; tel. 3-5632111; fax 3-5610614; f. 1948; mid-morning; Hebrew; independent; published by Modiin Publishing House; Editor OFER NIMRODI; circ. 160,000 (weekdays), 270,000 (weekends).

Mabat: 8 Toshia St, Tel-Aviv 67218; tel. 3-5627711; fax 3-5627719; f. 1971; morning; Hebrew; economic and social; Editor S. YARKONI; circ. 7,000.

Nasha Strana (Our Country): 52 Harakeret St, Tel-Aviv 67770; tel. 3-370011; fax 3-5371921; f. 1970; morning; Russian; Editor S. HIMMELFARB; circ. 35,000.

Al-Quds (Jerusalem): POB 19788, Jerusalem; tel. 2-6272663; fax 2-6272657; e-mail info@alquds.com; internet www.alquds.com; f. 1968; Arabic; Founder and Publr MAHMOUD ABU ZALAF; Gen. Man. Dr MARWAN ABU ZALAF; circ. 55,000.

Ash Shaab (The People): POB 19154, Jerusalem; tel. 2-289881.

Shearim (The Gates): POB 11044, 64 Frishman St, Tel-Aviv; tel. 3-242126; organ of the Poale Agudat Israel Party.

Uj Kelet: 49 Tchlenor St, Tel-Aviv; tel. 3-5371395; fax 3-377142; f. 1918; morning; Hungarian; independent; Editor D. DRORY; circ. 20,000.

Viata Noastra: 49 Tchlenor St, Tel-Aviv 61351; tel. 3-5372059; fax 3-6877142; e-mail erancourt@shani.co.il; f. 1950; morning; Romanian; Editor GEORGE EDRI; circ. 30,000.

Yated Ne'eman: POB 328, Bnei Brak; tel. 3-6170800; fax 3-6170801; e-mail let-edit@yatedneman.co.il; f. 1986; morning; religious; Editors Y. ROTH, N. GROSSMAN; circ. 25,000.

Yedioth Aharonoth (The Latest News): 2 Yehuda and Noah Mozes St, Tel-Aviv 61000; tel. 3-6972222; fax 3-6953950; f. 1939; evening; Hebrew; independent; Editor-in-Chief MOSHE VARDI; circ. 300,000, Friday 600,000.

WEEKLIES AND FORTNIGHTLIES

Aurora: Aurora Ltd, POB 18066, Tel-Aviv 61180; tel. 3-5625216; fax 3-5625082; e-mail aurora@aurora-israel.co.il; internet www.aurora-israel.co.il; f. 1963; weekly; Spanish; for Spanish-speakers in Israel and abroad; Pres. ARIE AVIDOR; circ. 20,000.

Bama'alah: 120 Kibbutz Gabuyot St, Tel-Aviv; tel. 3-6814488; fax 3-6816852; Hebrew; journal of the young Histadrut Movement; Editor ODED BAR-MEIR.

Bamahane (In the Camp): Military POB 1013, Tel-Aviv; f. 1948; military, illustrated weekly of the Israel Armed Forces; Hebrew; Editor-in-Chief YOSSEF ESHKOL; circ. 70,000.

Ethgar (The Challenge): 75 Einstein St, Tel-Aviv; twice weekly; Hebrew; Editor NATHAN YALIN-MOR.

Al Fajr (The Dawn): POB 19315, Jerusalem; tel. 2-271649; fax 2-273521; f. 1980; weekly; Editor-in-Chief MANNA SINIORA.

Glasul Populurui: Tel-Aviv; weekly of the Communist Party of Israel; Romanian; Editor MEÏR SEMO.

Harefuah (Medicine): POB 3566, 35 Jabotinsky St, Ramat-Gan 52136; tel. 3-6100444; fax 3-5751616; f. 1920; fortnightly journal of the Israeli Medical Association; Hebrew with English summaries; an English publication, IMAJ, has also been published since 1999; Editor Y. SHOENFELD; circ. 16,000.

Hotam: Al-Hamishmar House, Choma U'Migdal St, Tel-Aviv; Hebrew.

Al-Hurriya (Freedom): 38 King George St, Tel-Aviv; Arabic weekly of the Herut Party.

Illustrirte WeltWoch: Tel-Aviv; f. 1956; weekly; Yiddish; Editor M. KARPINOVITZ.

Information Week: POB 1161, 13 Yad Harutzim St, Tel-Aviv 61116; tel. 3-6385858; fax 3-6889207; e-mail world@pc.co.il; internet www.people-and-computers.co.il; weekly; Man. Dirs DAHLIA PELED, PELI PELED; Editor-in Chief PELI PELED.

The Israeli Tourist Guide Magazine: Tourist Guide Communications Ltd, POB 53333, Tel-Aviv 61533; tel. 3-5168282; fax 3-5168284; e-mail ishchori@touristguide.co.il; internet www.touristguide.co.il; f. 1994; weekly; Publisher and Editor ILAN SHCHORI; circ. 10,000.

Jerusalem Post International Edition: POB 81, Romema, Jerusalem 91000; tel. 2-5315666; fax 2-5389527; e-mail jpedt@jpost.co.il; internet www.jpost.co.il; f. 1959; weekly; English; overseas edition of the Jerusalem Post (q.v.); circ. 70,000 to 106 countries.

Jerusalem Report: POB 1805, Jerusalem 91017; tel. 2-5315440; fax 2-5379489; e-mail jrep@jreport.co.il; internet www.jrep.com; f. 1990; bi-weekly; English; Publr and Editor DAVID HOROVITZ; published by *Jerusalem Report Publications*; circ. 65,000 worldwide.

The Jerusalem Times: POB 20185, Jerusalem; tel. 2-6264883; fax 2-6264975; e-mail tjt@jerusalem-times.net; internet www.jerusalem-times.net; f. 1994; weekly; English; Editor HANNA SINIORA.

Kol Ha'am (Voice of the People): Tel-Aviv; f. 1947; Hebrew; organ of the Communist Party of Israel; Editor B. BALTI.

Laisha (For Women): POB 28122, 35 Bnei Brak St, Tel-Aviv 67132; tel. 3-6386969; fax 3-6386933; f. 1946; Hebrew; women's magazine; Editor MIRIAM NOFECH-MOSES; circ. 150,000.

Ma'ariv Lanoar: POB 20020, 2 Carlebach St, Tel-Aviv 67132; tel. 3-5632525; fax 3-5632030; e-mail maariv_lanoar@maariv.co.il; f. 1957; weekly for teenagers; Hebrew; Editor DANA BEN-NAFTALI; circ. 100,000.

MB (Mitteilungsblatt): POB 1480, Tel-Aviv 61014; tel. 3-5164461; fax 3-5164435; f. 1932; German monthly journal of the Irgun Olei Merkas Europa (The Association of Immigrants from Central Europe); Editor Prof. PAUL ALSBERG.

Otiot: Jerusalem; tel. 2-895097; fax 2-895196; f. 1987; weekly for children; English; Editor URI AUERBACH.

People and Computers: POB 11616, 13 Yad Harutzim St, Tel-Aviv 61116; tel. 3-6385888; fax 3-6889207; e-mail world@enet.co.il; internet www.enet.co.il; f. 1981; weekly; Hebrew; information technology; CEOs PELI PELED, DAHLIA PELED; circ. 15,000.

Reshumot: Ministry of Justice, POB 1087, 29 Rehov Salahadin, Jerusalem 91010; f. 1948; Hebrew, Arabic and English; official government gazette.

Sada at-Tarbia (The Echo of Education): published by the Histadrut and Teachers' Association, POB 2306, Rehovot; f. 1952; fortnightly; Arabic; educational; Editor TUVIA SHAMOSH.

As-Sinnarah: Nazareth; internet www.asennara.com; twice weekly; for Christian and Muslim Arabs in the region; Arabic; Editor-in-Chief LUFTI MASH'UR.

OTHER PERIODICALS

Ariel: the Israel Review of Arts and Letters: Cultural and Scientific Relations Division, Ministry of Foreign Affairs, Jerusalem; Distributor: Youval Tal Ltd, POB 2160, Jerusalem 91021; Editorial Office: 214 Jaffa Road, Jerusalem 94383; tel. 2-6248897; fax 2-6245434; e-mail magariel@netvision.net.il; internet www.israel-mfa.gov.il; tel. 2-6432147; fax 2-6437502; f. 1962; quarterly review of all aspects of culture in Israel; regular edns in English, Spanish, French, German, Arabic and Russian; occasional edns in other languages; Editor ASHER WEILL; circ. 30,000.

Asakim Vekalkala (Business and Economics): POB 20027, 84 Ha' Hashmonaim St, Tel-Aviv 61200; tel. 3-5631010; fax 3-5619025; monthly; Hebrew; Editor ZVI AMIT.

Bitaon Heyl Ha'avir (Israel Air Force Magazine): Military POB 01560, Zahal; tel. 3-5694153; fax 3-5695806; e-mail iaf@inter.net.il; internet www.iaf.org.il; f. 1948; bi-monthly; Hebrew; Dep. Editor U. ETSION; Editor-in-Chief MERAV HALPERIN; circ. 30,000.

Al-Bushra (Good News): POB 6228, Haifa 31061; tel. 4-8385002; fax 4-8371612; f. 1935; monthly; Arabic; organ of the Ahmadiyya movement; Editor MUSA ASA'AD O'DEH.

Business Diary: Haifa; f. 1947; weekly; English, Hebrew; shipping movements, import licences, stock exchange listings, business failures, etc. Editor G. ALON.

Challenge: POB 41199, Jaffa 61411; tel. 3-6839145; fax 3-6839148; e-mail oda@netvision.net.il; internet www.hanitzotz.com/challenge; f. 1989; magazine on the Israeli–Palestinian conflict, published by Hanitzotz Publishing House; bi-monthly; English; Editor-in-Chief RONI BEN EFRAT; Editor LIZ LEYH LEVAC; circ. 1,000.

Christian News from Israel: 30 Jaffa Rd, Jerusalem; f. 1949; half-yearly; English, French, Spanish; issued by the Ministry of Religious Affairs; Editor SHALOM BEN-ZAKKAI; circ. 10,000.

Diamond Intelligence Brief: POB 3441, Silver Bldg, 7 Abba Hillel St, Ramat-Gan, Tel-Aviv 52133; tel. 3–5750196; fax 3–5754829; e-mail office@tacy.co.il; f. 1985; Publr CHAIM EVEN-ZOHAR.

Divrei Haknesset: c/o The Knesset, Jerusalem; f. 1949; Hebrew; records of the proceedings of the Knesset; published by the Government Printer, Jerusalem; Editor DVORA AVIVI (acting); circ. 350.

Eastern Mediterranean Tourism and Travel: Israel Travel News Ltd, POB 3251, Tel-Aviv 61032; tel. 3-5251646; fax 3-5251605; f. 1979; monthly; English; circ. 19,515.

The Easy Way to do Business with Israel: POB 20027, Tel-Aviv; tel. 3-5612444; fax 3-5612614; published by Federation of Israeli Chambers of Commerce; Editor Y. SHOSTAK.

Eitanim (Popular Medicine): POB 16250, Merkez Kupat Holim, Tel-Aviv 62098; f. 1948; Hebrew; monthly; circ. 20,000.

Folk un Zion: POB 7053, Tel-Aviv 61070; tel. 3-5423317; f. 1950; bi-monthly; current events relating to Israel and World Jewry; Editor MOSHE KALCHHEIM; circ. 3,000.

Frei Israel: POB 8512, Tel-Aviv; progressive monthly; published by Asscn for Popular Culture; Yiddish.

Hamizrah Hehadash (The New East): Israel Oriental Society, The Hebrew University, Mount Scopus, Jerusalem 91905; tel. 2-5883633; e-mail ios49@hotmail.com; f. 1949; annual of the Israel Oriental Society; Middle Eastern, Asian and African Affairs; Hebrew with English summary; Editors HAIM GERBER, ELIE PODEH; circ. 1,500–2,000.

Hamionai (The Hotelier): Tel-Aviv; f. 1962; monthly of the Israel Hotel Assoc; Hebrew and English; Editor Z. PELTZ.

Hapraklit (Law): POB 14152, 8 Wilson St, Tel-Aviv 61141; tel. 3-5614695; fax 3-561476; f. 1943; quarterly; Hebrew; published by the Israel Bar Assoc; Editor-in-Chief A. POLONSKI; Editor ARNAN GAVRIELI; circ. 7,000.

Hassadeh: POB 40044, 8 Shaul Hamelech Blvd, Tel-Aviv 61400; tel. 3-6929018; fax 3-6929979; f. 1920; monthly; review of Israeli agriculture; English and Hebrew; Publr GUY KING; Editor NAAMA DOTAN; circ. 13,000.

Hed Hagan: 8 Ben Saruk St, Tel-Aviv 62969; tel. 3-6922958; f. 1935; quarterly; Hebrew; educational; Editor MIRIAM SNAPIR; circ. 9,000.

Hed Hahinukh: 8 Ben Saruk St, Tel-Aviv 62969; tel. 3-5432911; fax 3-5432928; f. 1926; monthly; Hebrew; educational; published by the Israeli Teachers' Union; Editor DALIA LACHMAN; circ. 40,000.

Historia: POB 4179, Jerusalem 91041; tel. 2-5650444; fax 2-6712388; e-mail shazar@shazar.org.il; f. 1998; Hebrew, with English summaries; general history; published by the Historical Society of Israel; Editors STEVEN ASCHHEIM, MICHAEL HEYD, RANON KATZOFF, SHULAMIT SHAHAR.

Internet World (Israel): POB 1161, 13 Yad Harutzim St, Tel-Aviv 61116; tel. 3-6385858; fax 3-6889207; e-mail benrun@netvision.net.il; internet www.people-and-computers.co.il; 24 a year; computers and information technology; Man. Dirs DAHLIA PELED, PELI PELED; Editor-in-Chief PELI PELED.

Israel Agritechnology Focus: 8 Twersky St, Tel-Aviv 61574; tel. 3-5628511; fax 3-5628512; f. 1993; quarterly; farming technology, agricultural company and investment news; Editor NICKY BLACKMAN.

Israel Economist: 6 Hazanowitz St, Jerusalem; tel. 2-234131; fax 2-246569; f. 1945; monthly; English; independent; political and economic; Editor BEN MOLLOV; Publisher ISRAEL KELMAN; also publishes *Keeping Posted*(diplomatic magazine), *Mazel and Brucha*(jewellers' magazine); annuals: *Travel Agents' Manual, Electronics, International Conventions in Israel, Arkia, In Flight*, various hotel magazines.

Israel Environment Bulletin: Ministry of the Environment, POB 34033, 5 Kanfei Nesharim St, Jerusalem 95464; tel. 2-6553777; fax 2-6535937; internet www.environment.gov.il; f. 1973; Editor SHOSHANA GABBAY; circ. 3,500.

Israel Exploration Journal: POB 7041, 5 Avida St, Jerusalem 91070; tel. 2-6257991; fax 2-6247772; e-mail ies@vms.huji.ac.il; internet www.hum.huji.ac.il/ies; f. 1950; bi-annual; English; general and biblical archaeology, ancient history and historical geography of Israel and the Holy Land; Editors S. AHITUV, MIRIAM TADMOR; circ. 2,500.

Israel Export: POB 57500, 8 Twersky St, Tel-Aviv 61574; tel. and fax 3-5628512; f. 1993; annual; Editor NAOYA NAKAMURA.

Israel Export News: Tel-Aviv; tel. 3-5142947; f. 1949; bi-monthly; English; commercial and economic; published by Israel Export Institute; Dir of Media Dept DANI BLOCH.

Israel Journal of Chemistry: POB 35409, Jerusalem 91352; tel. 2-6522226; fax 2-6522277; e-mail laserpages@netmedia.net.il; internet www.sciencefromisrael.com; f. 1951; quarterly; published by Laser Pages Publishing Ltd; Editor Prof. H. LEVANON.

Israel Journal of Earth Sciences: POB 35409, Jerusalem 91352; tel. 2-6522226; fax 2-6522277; e-mail laserpages@netmedia.net.il; internet www.sciencefromisrael.com; f. 1951; quarterly; published by Laser Pages Publishing Ltd; Editors Prof. ALAN MATTHEWS, Dr AHUUA ALMOGI.

Israel Journal of Mathematics: POB 39099, Jerusalem 91390; tel. 2-6586660; fax 2-5633370; e-mail magnes@vms.huji.ac.il; f. 1951; monthly, four vols of three issues per year; published by Magnes Press; Editor Prof. G. KALAI.

Israel Journal of Medical Sciences: Jerusalem; tel. 2-5817727; fax 2-5815722; f. 1965; monthly; Editor-in-Chief Prof. MOSHE PRYWES; circ. 5,500.

Israel Journal of Plant Sciences: POB 35409, Jerusalem 91352; tel. 2-6522226; fax 2-6522277; e-mail laserpages@netmedia.net.il; internet www.sciencefromisrael.com; f. 1951 as *Israel Journal of Botany*; quarterly; published by Laser Pages Publishing Ltd; Editor Prof. A. M. MAYER.

Israel Journal of Psychiatry and Related Sciences: Gefen Publishing House Ltd, POB 36004, Jerusalem 91360; tel. 2-5380247; fax 2-5388423; e-mail info@gefenpublishing.com; internet www.israelbooks.com; f. 1963; quarterly; Editor-in-Chief Dr DAVID GREENBERG.

Israel Journal of Veterinary Medicine: POB 3076, Rishon Le-Zion 75130; tel. 9-7419929; fax 9-7431778; e-mail ivma@internet-zahav.net; internet www.isrvma.org; f. 1943; formerly *Refuah Veterinarith*; quarterly of the Israel Veterinary Medical Asscn; Editors G. SIMON, I. GLAS.

Israel Journal of Zoology: POB 35409, Jerusalem 91352; tel. 2-6522226; fax 2-6522277; e-mail laserpages@netmedia.net.il; internet www.sciencefromisrael.com; f. 1951; quarterly; published by Laser Pages Publishing Ltd; Editors Prof. ALAN DEGEN, Prof. MICHA ILAN, Prof. ORA MANHEIM.

Israel Law Review: Faculty of Law, The Hebrew University of Jerusalem, Mount Scopus, Jerusalem 91905; tel. 2-5882520; fax 2-5882565; e-mail msilr@mscc.huji.ac.il; f. 1965; quarterly; published by the Israel Law Review Association.

Israel Press Service: POB 33188, Jerusalem 91330; tel. 2-6419783; fax 2-6439377; e-mail junes@netvision.net.il; internet www.israel-press-service.co.il; f. 1956; English; Zionist; Editor JUNE SPITZER.

Israel-South Africa Trade Journal: Tel-Aviv; f. 1973; bi-monthly; English; commercial and economic; published by Israel Publications Corpn Ltd; Man. Dir Z. PELTZ.

Israels Aussenhandel: Tel-Aviv; tel. 3-5280215; f. 1967; monthly; German; commercial; published by Israel Periodicals Co Ltd; Editor PELTZ NOEMI; Man. Dir ZALMAN PELTZ.

Al-Jadid (The New): POB 104, Haifa; f. 1951; literary monthly; Arabic; Editor SALEM JUBRAN; circ. 5,000.

Journal d'Analyse Mathématique: f. 1955; 2 vols per year; published by Magnes Press; Editor Prof. L. ZALCMAN.

Kibbutz Trends: Yad Tabenkin, Ramat Efal 52960; tel. 3-5301217; fax 3-5346376; e-mail yadtab@inter.net.il; f. 1991; bi-annual; English language journal on kibbutz; Editors IDIT PAZ, NEIL HARRIS, ROCHELLE MASS; circ. 1,500.

Leshonenu: Academy of the Hebrew Language, POB 3449, Jerusalem 91034; tel. 2-6493555; fax 2-5617065; e-mail acad2u@vms.huji.ac.il; internet www.hebrew-academy.huji.ac.il; f. 1929; 4 a year; for the study of the Hebrew language and cognate subjects; Editor M. BAR-ASHER.

Leshonenu La'am: Academy of the Hebrew Language, POB 3449, Jerusalem 91034; tel. 2-6493555; fax 2-5617065; e-mail acad2u@vms.huji.ac.il; internet www.hebrew-academy.huji.ac.il; f. 1945; 4 a year; popular Hebrew philology; Editors M. FLORENTIN, D. TALSHIR, Y. OFER.

Lilac: Nazareth; internet www.lilac-m.com; f. 2000; monthly; Arabic; Israel's first magazine for Arab women.

Ma'arachot (Campaigns): POB 7026, Hakirya, 3 Albert Mendler St, Tel-Aviv 61070; tel. 3-5694345; fax 3-5694343; f. 1939; military and political bi-monthly; Hebrew; periodical of Israel Defence Force; Editors HAGGAI GOLAN, EFI MELZER; circ. 20,000.

Magallati (My Magazine): POB 28049, Tel-Aviv; tel. 3-371438; f. 1960; bi-monthly children's magazine; circ. 3,000.

Melaha Vetaassiya (Trade and Industry): Tel-Aviv; f. 1969; bi-monthly review of the Union of Artisans and Small Manufacturers of Israel; Hebrew; Man. Dir Z. PELTZ; circ. 8,500.

M'Lakha V'ta Asiya (Israel Industry): POB 11587, 40 Rembrandt St, Tel-Aviv; monthly; published by Israel Publications Corporation Ltd; circ. 8,500.

Moznaim (Balance): POB 7098, Tel-Aviv; tel. 3-6953256; fax 3-6919681; f. 1929; monthly; Hebrew; literature and culture; Editors ASHER REICH, AZRIEL KAUFMAN; circ. 2,500.

Nekuda: Hebrew; organ of the Jewish settlers of the West Bank and Gaza Strip.

New Outlook: 9 Gordon St, Tel-Aviv 63458; tel. 3-5236496; fax 3-5232252; f. 1957; bi-monthly; Israeli and Middle Eastern Affairs; dedicated to the quest for Arab-Israeli peace; Editor-in-Chief CHAIM SHUR; Senior Editor DAN LEON; circ. 10,000.

News from Within: POB 31417, Jerusalem; tel. 2-6241159; fax 2-6253151; e-mail nfw@alt-info.org; internet www.alternativenews.org; monthly; joint Israeli-Palestinian publication; political, economic, social and cultural; publ. by the Alternative Information Centre.

OTOT: 10 Beit Shamai, Tel-Aviv; tel. 3-5615310; fax 3-5615281; e-mail igud@inter.net.il; f. 1975; monthly; Hebrew; advertising, marketing and communications; Editor-in-Chief YAIR FELDMANN; Editor RAYA RUBIN; circ. 4,000.

PC Magazine (Israel): PC Media, POB 11438, 13 Yad Harutzim St, Tel-Aviv 61114; tel. 3-6385810; fax 3-6889207; e-mail editor@pc.co.il; f. 1992; monthly; Hebrew; information on personal computers; Man. Dirs DAHLIA PELED, YEHUDA ELYADA; Editor-in-Chief YEHUDA ELYADA; circ. 13,500.

Proche-Orient Chrétien: POB 19079, Jerusalem 91190; tel. 2-6283285; fax 2-6280764; e-mail poc@steanne.org; f. 1951; quarterly on churches and religion in the Middle East; circ. 1,000.

Publish Israel: Tel-Aviv; tel. 3-5622744; fax 3-5621808; e-mail olamot@inter.net.il; f. 1998; six times a year; magazine for printers and publishers; Gen. Man. DAN SHEKEL; circ. 12,000.

The Sea: POB 33706, Hane'emanim 8, Haifa; tel. 4-529818; every six months; published by Israel Maritime League; review of marine problems; Pres. M. POMROCK; Chief Editor M. LITOVSKI; circ. 5,000.

Shituf (Co-operation): POB 7151, 24 Ha'arba St, Tel-Aviv; f. 1948; bi-monthly; Hebrew; economic, social and co-operative problems in Israel; published by the Central Union of Industrial, Transport and Service Co-operative Societies; Editor L. LOSH; circ. 12,000.

Shivuk (Marketing): POB 20027, Tel-Aviv 61200; tel. 3-5631010; fax 3-5612614; monthly; Hebrew; publ. by Federation of Israeli Chambers of Commerce; Editor SARA LIPKIN.

Sinai: POB 642, Jerusalem 91006; tel. 2-6526231; fax 2-6526968; f. 1937; Hebrew; Torah science and literature; Editor Rabbi YOSEF MOVSHOVITZ.

As-Sindibad: POB 28049, Tel-Aviv; tel. 3-371438; f. 1970; children's monthly; Arabic; Man. JOSEPH ELIAHOU; Editor WALID HUSSEIN; circ. 8,000.

Terra Santa: POB 14038, Jaffa Gate, Jerusalem 91140; tel. 2-6272692; fax 2-6286417; e-mail cicts@netmedia.net.il; f. 1921; every two months; published by the Custody of the Holy Land (the official custodians of the Holy Shrines); Italian, Spanish, French, English and Arabic editions published in Jerusalem, by the Franciscan Printing Press, German edition in Munich, Maltese edition in Valletta.

WIZO Review: Women's International Zionist Organization, 38 Sderot David Hamelech Blvd, Tel-Aviv 64237; tel. 3-6923805; fax 3-6923801; e-mail wreview@wizo.org; internet www.wizo.org; f. 1947; English edition (quarterly), Spanish and German editions (two a year); Editor HILLEL SCHENKER; circ. 20,000.

World Fellowship of the Israel Medical Asscn (Mif'al Haverut Hutz): POB 3604, 2 Twin Towers, 35 Jabotinsky St, Ramat Gan 52136; tel. 3-6100424; fax 3-6133274; e-mail ingrid@ima.org.il; internet www.ima.org.il/wf; quarterly; English.

The Youth Times: POB 54065, Jerusalem; tel. 2-2343428; fax 2-2343430; e-mail pyalara@pyalara.org; internet www.pyalara.org; f. 1998; monthly; Arabic and English; Editor-in-Chief HANIA BITAR.

Zion: POB 4179, Jerusalem 91041; tel. 2-5650444; fax 2-6712388; e-mail shazar@shazar.org.il; f. 1935; quarterly; published by the Historical Society of Israel; Hebrew, with English summaries; research in Jewish history; Editors I. ETKES, A. OPPENHEIMER, Y. KAPLAN; circ. 1,000.

Zraim: POB 40027, 7 Dubnov St, Tel-Aviv; tel. 3-691745; fax 3-6953199; f. 1953; Hebrew; journal of the Bnei Akiva (Youth of Tora Va-avoda) Movement; Editor URI AUERBACH.

Zrakor: Haifa; f. 1947; monthly; Hebrew; news digest, trade, finance, economics, shipping; Editor G. ALON.

PRESS ASSOCIATIONS

Daily Newspaper Publishers' Asscn of Israel: POB 51202, 74 Petach Tikva Rd, Tel-Aviv 61200; fax 3-5617938; safeguards professional interests and maintains standards, supplies newsprint to dailies; negotiates with trade unions, etc. mems all daily papers; affiliated to International Federation of Newspaper Publishers; Pres. SHABTAI HIMMELFARB; Gen. Sec. BETZALEL EYAL.

Foreign Press Asscn: Beit Sokolov, 4 Kaplan St, Tel-Aviv; tel. 3-6916143; fax 3-6961548; e-mail fpa@netvision.net.il; internet www.fpa.org.il; Chair. DAN PERRY.

Israel Association of the Periodical Press (IAPP): 93 Arlozorof St, Tel-Aviv 62098; tel. 3-6921238; fax 3-6960155; e-mail lavied@arg.huji.ac.il; Chair. DAVID LAVIE.

Israel Press Asscn: Sokolov House, 4 Kaplan St, Tel-Aviv.

NEWS AGENCIES

ITIM (The Israeli News Agency): 10 Tiomkin St, Tel-Aviv; tel. 3-5601011; fax 3-5605190; e-mail noy@itim.co.il; internet www.itim.co.il; f. 1950; Editor-in-Chief HAIM NOY.

Jewish Telegraphic Agency (JTA): Israel Bureau, Jerusalem Post Bldg, Romema, Jerusalem 91000; tel. 2-610579; fax 2-536635; Dir DAVID LANDAU.

Palestine Press Service: Salah ad-Din St, East Jerusalem; Proprs IBRAHIM QARA'EEN, Mrs RAYMONDA TAWIL; only Arab news agency in the Occupied Territories.

Foreign Bureaux

Agence France-Presse: POB 1507, 206 Jaffa Rd, Jerusalem 91014; tel. 2-5373243; fax 2-5373873; e-mail afpjer@netvision.net.il; Correspondent LUC DE BAROCHEZ.

Agencia EFE (Spain): POB 37190, 18 Hilel St, Jerusalem 91371; tel. 2-6242038; fax 2-6242056; e-mail postigocarmen@hotmail.com; Correspondent CARMEN POSTIGO.

Agenzia Nazionale Stampa Associata (ANSA) (Italy): 30 Dizengoff St, Tel-Aviv 64332; 9 Lloyd George St, Jerusalem 93110; tel. 3-6299319; fax 3-5250302; e-mail ansnews@netvision.net.il; Bureau Chief STEFANO POSCIA; Correspondent GIORGIO RACCAH.

Associated Press (AP) (USA): POB 13172, 206 Jaffa Rd, Jerusalem 91131; tel. 2-5385577; fax 2-5376083; Chief of Bureau DAN PERRY.

Deutsche Presse-Agentur (dpa) (Germany): 30 Ibn Gvirol St, Tel-Aviv 64078; tel. 3-6959007; fax 3-6969594; e-mail dpatlv@trendline.co.il; Correspondents Dr HEINZ-RUDOLF OTHMERDING, JEFF ABRAMOVITZ.

Jiji Tsushin-Sha (Japan): 9 Schmuel Hanagld, Jerusalem 94592; tel. 2-232553; fax 2-232402; Correspondent HIROKAZU OIKAWA.

Kyodo News Service (Japan): Tel-Aviv; tel. 3-6958185; fax 3-6917478; Correspondent HAJIME OZAKI.

Reuters (UK): 38 Hamasger St, Tel-Aviv 67211; Jerusalem Capital Studios (JCS) 206 Jaffa Rd, Jerusalem 91131; tel. 3-5372211; fax 3-5372045; tel. 2-5370502; fax 2-5374241; Chief of Bureau PAUL HOLMES.

United Press International (UPI) (USA): 138 Petach Tikva Rd, Tel-Aviv; Bureau Man. BROOKE W. KROEGER; Bureau Man. in Jerusalem LOUIS TOSCANO.

Informatsionnoye Telegrafnoye Agentstvo Rossii—Telegrafnoye Agentstvo Suverennykh Stran (ITAR—TASS) (Russia) is also represented.

Publishers

Achiasaf Ltd: POB 8414, Netanya 42504; tel. 9-8851390; fax 9-8851391; e-mail info@achiasaf.co.il; internet www.achiasaf.co.il; f. 1933; general; Man. Dir MATAN ACHIASAF.

Am Oved Publishers Ltd: POB 470, 22 Mazeh St, Tel-Aviv 61003; tel. 3-6291526; fax 3-6298911; e-mail info@am-oved.co.il; internet www.am-oved.co.il; f. 1942; fiction, non-fiction, reference books, school and university textbooks, children's books, poetry, classics, science fiction; Man. Dir YARON SADAN.

'Amihai' Publishing House Ltd: POB 8448, 19 Yad Harutzim St, Netanya Darom 42505; tel. 9-8859099; fax 9-8853464; e-mail oron@idc.ac.il; f. 1948; fiction, general science, linguistics, languages, arts; Dir YITZHAK ORON.

Arabic Publishing House: 93 Arlozorof St, Tel-Aviv; tel. 3-6921674; f. 1960; established by the Histadrut; periodicals and books; Gen. Man. GASSAN MUKLASHI.

Ariel Publishing House: POB 3328, Jerusalem 91033; tel. 2-6434540; fax 2-6436164; e-mail elysch@netvision.net.il; f. 1976; history, archaeology, religion, geography, folklore; CEO ELY SCHILLER.

Astrolog Publishing House: POB 11231, Hod Hasharon 45111; tel. 9-7412044; fax 9-7442714; e-mail sarabm@netvision.net.il; f. 1994; general non-fiction, religion, alternative medicine; Man. Dir SARA BEN-MORDECHAI.

Bitan Publishers A. S. Media International Ltd: POB 3068, Ramat-Hasharon 47130; tel. 3-6040089; fax 3-6136588; f. 1965; aeronautics, biography, child development, fiction, educational, literature and literary criticism, mysteries, leisure, travel, women's studies, self-help books; Man. A. BITAN.

Carta, The Israel Map and Publishing Co Ltd: POB 2500, 18 Ha'uman St, Industrial Area, Talpiot, Jerusalem 91024; tel. 2-6783355; fax 2-6782373; e-mail cartaben@netvision.net.il; internet www.holyland-jerusalem.com; f. 1958; the principal cartographic publisher; Pres. and CEO SHAY HAUSMAN.

Dvir Publishing Co Ltd: POB 22383, 32 Schocken St, Tel-Aviv; tel. 3-6812244; fax 3-6826138; e-mail info@zmora.co.il; internet www.zmora.co.il; f. 1924; literature, science, art, education; Publr OHAD ZMORA.

Rodney Franklin Agency: POB 37727, 53 Mazeh St, Tel-Aviv 65789; tel. 3-5600724; fax 3-5600479; e-mail rodney@netvision.net.il; f. 1974; exclusive representative of various British, other European, US and Canadian publishers; Dir RODNEY FRANKLIN.

Gefen Publishing House Ltd: POB 36004, 6 Hatzvi St, Jerusalem 91360; tel. 2-5380247; fax 2-5388423; e-mail info@gefenpublishing.com; internet www.israelbooks.com; f. 1981; the largest publisher of English-language books; also publishes wide range of fiction and non-fiction; CEOs ILAN GREENFIELD, DROR GREENFIELD.

Globes Publishers: POB 18041, 127 Igal Alon St, Tel-Aviv 67443; tel. 3-6979797; fax 3-6910334; internet www.globes.co.il.

Gvanim: POB 11138, 29 Bar-Kochba St, Tel-Aviv 61111; tel. 3-5281044; fax 3-5283648; e-mail traklinm@zahav.net.il; f. 1992; poetry, belles lettres, fiction; Man. Dir MARITZA ROSMAN.

Hakibbutz Hameuchad Publishing House Ltd: POB 1432, Bnei Brak, Tel-Aviv 51114; tel. 3-5785810; fax 3-5785811; e-mail bruria@kibutz-poalim.co.il; f. 1940; general; Dir UZI SHAVIT.

Hanitzotz A-Sharara Publishing House: POB 41199, Jaffa 61411; tel. 3-6839145; fax 3-6839148; e-mail oda@netvision.net.il; internet www.hanitzotz.com; 'progressive' booklets and publications in Arabic, Hebrew and English.

Hed Arzi (Ma'ariv) Publishing Ltd: 3A Yoni Netanyahu St, Or-Yehuda, Tel-Aviv 60376; tel. 3-5383333; fax 3-6343205; e-mail shimoni@hed-arzi.co.il; f. 1954 as Sifriat-Ma'ariv Ltd; later known as Ma'ariv Book Guild Ltd; general; Man. Dir and Editor-in-Chief ITZIK GLIK.

Hod-Ami—Computer Books Ltd: POB 6108, Herzliya 46160; tel. 9-9564716; fax 9-9571582; e-mail info@hod-ami.co.il; internet www.hod-ami.co.il; f. 1984; computer science; CEO ITZHAK AMIHUD.

Intermedia Publishing Enterprises Ltd (IPE): POB 2121, 23 Hataas St, Kefar-Sava 44641; tel. 9-5608501; fax 9-5608513; e-mail freed@inter.net.il; f. 1993; business, education, English as a second language, journalism, health, nutrition, mathematics, medicine, philosophy, self-help; Man. Dir ARIE FRIED.

Israeli Music Publications Ltd: POB 7681, Jerusalem 94188; tel. 2-6251370; fax 2-6241378; e-mail khanukaev@pop.isracom.net.il; f. 1949; books on music, dance and musical works; Dir of Music Publications SERGEI KHANUKAEV.

Jerusalem Center for Public Affairs: 13 Tel Hai St, Jerusalem 92107; tel. 2-5619281; fax 2-5619112; e-mail jcenter@jcpa.org; internet www.jcpa.org; f. 1976; Jewish political tradition; publishes the Jewish Political Studies Review.

The Jerusalem Publishing House Ltd: POB 7147, 39 Tchernechovski St, Jerusalem 91071; tel. 2-5636511; fax 2-5634266; e-mail jphgagi@netvision.net.il; f. 1967; biblical research, history, encyclopedias, archaeology, arts of the Holy Land, cookbooks, guidebooks, economics, politics; Dir SHLOMO S. GAFNI; Man. Editor RACHEL GILON.

The Jewish Agency—Department of Jewish Zionist Education: POB 10615, Jerusalem 91104; tel. 2-6202629; fax 2-6204122; e-mail bookshop@jazo.org.il; f. 1945; education, Jewish philosophy, studies in the Bible, children's books published in Hebrew, English, French, Spanish, German, Swedish and Portuguese; Hebrew teaching material.

Jewish History Publications (Israel 1961) Ltd: POB 1232, 29 Jabotinsky St, Jerusalem 92141; tel. 2-5632310; f. 1961; encyclopedias, World History of the Jewish People series; Chair. ALEXANDER PELI.

Karni Publishers Ltd: 32 Zalman Schocken St, Tel-Aviv 66556; tel. 3-6812244; fax 3-6826138; e-mail info@zmora.co.il; internet www.zmora.co.il; f. 1951; biography, fiction, poetry, children's and educational books; Publr OHAD ZMORA.

Keter Publishing House Ltd: POB 7145, Givat Shaul B, Jerusalem 91071; tel. 2-6557822; fax 2-6536811; e-mail info@keter-books .co.il; internet www.keter-books.co.il; f. 1959; original and translated works of fiction, encyclopedias, non-fiction, guidebooks and children's books; publishing imprints: Israel Program for Scientific Translations, Keter Books, Domino, Encyclopedia Judaica; Man. Dir YIPHTACH DEKEL.

Kinneret Publishing House: 14 Habanai St, Holon 58850; tel. 3-5582252; fax 3-5582255; e-mail kinbooks@netvision.net.il; f. 1980; child development and care, cookery, dance, educational, humour, non-fiction, music, home-care, psychology, psychiatry, travel; Man. Dir YORAM ROS.

Kiryat Sefer: Tel-Aviv 65812; tel. 3-5660188; fax 3-5100227; f. 1933; concordances, dictionaries, textbooks, maps, scientific books; Dir AVRAHAM SIVAN.

Laser Pages Publishing Ltd: POB 35409, Merkaz Sapir 6/36, Givat Shaul, Jerusalem 91352; tel. 2-6522226; fax 2-6522277; e-mail laserpages@netmedia.net.il; internet www.sciencefromisrael.com; scientific journals.

LB Publishing Co: POB 32056, Jerusalem 91000; tel. and fax 2-5664637; f. 1993; history, regional issues, religion; Pres. LILI BREZINER.

Magnes Press: The Hebrew University, POB 39099, Jerusalem 91390; tel. 2-6586656; fax 2-5633370; e-mail magnes@vms.huji.ac.il; f. 1929; biblical studies, Judaica, and all academic fields; Dir DAN BENOVICI.

MAP-Mapping and Publishing Ltd (Tel-Aviv Books): POB 56024, 17 Tchernikhovski St, Tel-Aviv 61560; tel. 3-6210500; fax 3-5257725; e-mail info@mapa.co.il; internet www.mapa.co.il; f. 1985; maps, atlases, travel guides, textbooks and reference books; Man. Dir DANI TRACZ; Editor-in-Chief MOULI MELTZER.

Rubin Mass Ltd: POB 990, 7 Ha-Ayin-Het St, Jerusalem 91009; tel. 2-6277863; fax 2-6277864; e-mail rmass@barak.net.il; internet www.id-knowledge.com/mas; f. 1927; Hebraica, Judaica, export of all Israeli books and periodicals; Dir OREN MASS.

Ministry of Defence Publishing House: 107 Ha' Hashmonaim St, Tel-Aviv 67133; tel. 3-5655900; fax 3-5655994; e-mail publish@ attmail.com; internet www.modpublishing.co.il; f. 1939; military literature, Judaism, history and geography of Israel; Dir JOSEPH PERLOVITZ.

M. Mizrachi Publishing House Ltd: 106 Allenby St, Tel-Aviv 65815; tel. 3-5601579; fax 3-5660274; f. 1960; children's books, fiction, history, medicine, science; Dirs MEIR MIZRACHI, ISRAEL MIZRACHI.

Mosad Harav Kook: POB 642, 1 Maimon St, Jerusalem 91006; tel. 2-6526231; fax 2-6526968; f. 1937; editions of classical works, Torah and Jewish studies; Dir Rabbi YOSEF MOVSHOVITZ.

Otsar Hamoreh: c/o Israel Teachers' Union, 8 Ben Saruk, Tel-Aviv 62969; tel. 3-6922983; fax 3-6922988; f. 1951; educational; Man. Dir JOSEPH SALOMAN.

PC Media: POB 11438, 13 Yad Harutzim St, Tel-Aviv 61114; tel. 3-6385810; fax 3-6889207; e-mail pcmedia@pc.co.il; internet www .zdnet.co.il; information technology; Man. Dir DAHLIA PELED.

Alexander Peli Jerusalem Publishing Co Ltd: POB 1232, 29 Jabotinsky St, Jerusalem 92141; tel. 2-5632310; f. 1961; encyclopedias such as the Standard Jewish Encyclopedia, history, the arts, educational material; Chair. ALEXANDER PELI.

Schocken Publishing House Ltd: POB 2316, 24 Nathan Yelin Mor St, Tel-Aviv 67015; tel. 3-5610130; fax 3-5622668; e-mail lind:schocken.co.il; f. 1938; general; Dir Mrs RACHELI EDELMAN.

Shalem Press: 22AHatzfira St, Jerusalem 93102; tel. 2-5662202; e-mail shalem@shalem.org.il; internet www.shalem.org.il; f. 1994; economics, political science, history, philosophy, cultural issues.

Shikmona Publishing Co Ltd: POB 7145, Givat Shaul B, Jerusalem 91071; tel. 2-6557822; fax 2-6536811; e-mail info@keter-books .co.il; internet www.keter-books.co.il; f. 1965; Zionism, archaeology, art, guidebooks, fiction and non-fiction; Man. Dir YIPHTACH DEKEL.

Sifriat Poalim: POB 1432, Bnei Brak, Tel-Aviv 51114; tel. 3-5785810; fax 3-5785811; e-mail avram@kibutz-poalim.co.il; internet www.dbook.co.il/images/poalim/default.html; f. 1939; general literature; Gen. Man. AVRAM KANTOR.

Sinai Publishing: 72 Allenby St, Tel-Aviv 65812; tel. 3-5163672; fax 3-5176783; f. 1853; Hebrew books and religious articles; Dir MOSHE SCHLESINGER.

Steinhart-Katzir: POB 8333, Netanya 42505; tel. 9-8854770; fax 9-8854771; e-mail mail@haolam.co.il; internet www.haolam.co.il; f. 1991; travel; Man. Dir OHAD SHARAV.

Tcehrikover Publishers Ltd: 12 Hasharon St, Tel-Aviv 66185; tel. 3-6870621; fax 3-6874729; e-mail barkay@inter.net.il; education, psychology, economics, psychiatry, literature, literary criticism, essays, history geography, criminology, art, languages, management; Man. Editor S. TCHERIKOVER.

Yachdav United Publishers Co Ltd: POB 20123, 29 Carlebach St, Tel-Aviv 67132; tel. 3-5614121; fax 3-5611996; e-mail info@tbpai .co.il; f. 1960; educational; Chair. EPHRAIM BEN-DOR; Exec. Dir AMNON BEN-SHMUEL.

Yavneh Publishing House Ltd: 4 Mazeh St, Tel-Aviv 65213; tel. 3-6297856; fax 3-6293638; e-mail publishing@yavneh.co.il; f. 1932; general; Dir NIRA PREISKEL.

Yeda Lakol Publications Ltd: POB 1232, 29 Jabotinsky St, Jerusalem 92141; tel. 2-5632310; f. 1961; encyclopedias, Judaica, the arts, educational material, children's books; Chair. ALEXANDER PELI.

Yedioth Ahronoth Books: POB 53494, 3 Mikunis St, Tel-Aviv 61534; tel. 3-7683333; fax 3-7683300; e-mail info@ybook.co.il; f. 1952; non-fiction, politics, Jewish religion, health, music, dance, fiction, education; Man. Dir DOV EICHENWALD; Editor-in-Chief ALIZA ZIGLER.

S. Zack and Co: 31 Beit Hadfus St, Jerusalem 95483; tel. 2-6537760; fax 2-6514005; e-mail zackpublishers@bezeqint.net; f. 1930; fiction, science, philosophy, Judaism, children's books, educational and reference books, dictionaries; Dir MICHAEL ZACK.

PUBLISHERS' ASSOCIATION

The Book Publishers' Association of Israel: POB 20123, 29 Carlebach St, Tel-Aviv 67132; tel. 3-5614121; fax 3-5611996; e-mail info@tbpai.co.il; internet www.tbpai.co.il; f. 1939; mems: 84 publishing firms; Chair. SHAI HAUSMAN; Man. Dir AMNON BEN-SHMUEL.

Broadcasting and Communications

TELECOMMUNICATIONS

Barak I.T.C.: Cibel Industrial Park, 15 Hamelacha St, Rosh Ha'ayin 48091; tel. 3-9001900; fax 3-9001800; internet www .barak-online.net; f. 1998; Chair. MAIR LAISER; Pres. and CEO AVI PATIR.

Bezeq—The Israel Telecommunication Corpn Ltd: POB 1088, 15 Hazvi St, Jerusalem 91010; tel. 2-5395503; fax 2-5000410; e-mail bzq.spk@attmail.com; internet www.bezeq.co.il; 54.6% state-owned; scheduled for full privatization in 2002; launched own cellular network, Pelephone Communications Ltd, in 1986; total assets US $4,837m. (Dec. 1997); Chair. ISRAEL TAPOOHI; Pres. and CEO AMI EREL.

Pelephone Communications Ltd: 33 Hagvura St, Givatayim, Tel-Aviv 53483; tel. 3-5728881; fax 3-5728111; internet www .pelephone.co.il; Pres. and CEO YIGAL BAR-YOUSSEF.

Cellcom Israel: POB 3164, 3 Hagalim Blvd, Herzlia Pituach, Herzlia B, Netanya 46131; tel. 9-9599599; fax 9-9599700; internet www.cellcom.co.il; f. 1994; mobile telecommunications operator; Chair. S. PIOTRKOWSKY; Pres. and CEO JACOB PERRY.

ECI Telecom Ltd: POB 3038, 30 Hasivim St, Petach Tikva, Tel-Aviv 49133; tel. 3-9266555; fax 3-9266500; internet www.ecitele .com; Chair. JONATHON B. KOLBER; Pres. and Gen. Man. DAVID RUBNER.

Partner Communications Co Ltd: POB 435, Rosh Ha'ayin, Tel-Aviv 48103; tel. 3-9054888; fax 3-9054999; mobile telecommunications operator; f. 1998, when obtained licence to operate Israel's first GSM system; CEO AMIKAM COHEN; Man. Dir E. COHEN.

Vocal Tec: Tel-Aviv; Gen. Man. DORON SINGER.

BROADCASTING

Radio

Israel Broadcasting Authority (IBA)(Radio): POB 28080, Jerusalem 91280; tel. 2-240124; fax 2-257034; internet www.iba.org.il; f. 1948; state-owned station in Jerusalem with additional studios in Tel-Aviv and Haifa. IBA broadcasts six programmes for local and overseas listeners on medium, shortwave and VHF/FM in 16 languages; Hebrew, Arabic, English, Yiddish, Ladino, Romanian, Hungarian, Moghrabi, Persian, French, Russian, Bucharian, Georgian, Portuguese, Spanish and Amharic; Chair. MICHA YINON; Dir-Gen. URI PORAT; Dir of Radio (vacant); Dir External Services VICTOR GRAJEWSKY.

Galei Zahal: MPOB 01005, Zahal; tel. 3-5126666; fax 3-5126760; e-mail galatz@glz.co.il; internet www.glz.co.il; f. 1950; Israeli Defence Force broadcasting station, Tel-Aviv, with studios in Jerusalem; broadcasts news, current affairs, music and cultural programmes on medium-wave and FM stereo, 24-hour in Hebrew; Dir ISACK TUNIK.

Kol Israel (The Voice of Israel): POB 1082, 21 Heleni Hamalka, Jerusalem 91010; tel. 2-6248715; fax 2-5383173; internet www .artificia.com/html/news.cgi; broadcasts music, news, and multilingual programmes for immigrants in Hebrew, Arabic, French and English on medium wave and FM stereo; Dir and Prog. Dir AMNON NADAV.

Television

Israel Broadcasting Authority (IBA): POB 7139, Jerusalem 91071; tel. 2-5301333; fax 2-292944; internet www.iba.org.il; broadcasts began in 1968; station in Jerusalem with additional studios in Tel-Aviv; one colour network (VHF with UHF available in all areas); one satellite channel; broadcasts in Hebrew, Arabic and English; Dir-Gen URI PORAT; Dir of Television YAIR STERN; Dir of Engineering RAFI YEOSHUA.

The Council of Cable TV and Satellite Broadcasting: 23 Jaffa Rd, Jerusalem 91999; tel. 2-6702210; fax 2-6702273; e-mail inbard@ moc.gov.il; Chair. DORIT INBAR.

Israel Educational Television: Ministry of Education, 14 Klausner St, Tel-Aviv; tel. 3-6415270; fax 3-6427091; f. 1966 by Hanadiv (Rothschild Memorial Group) as Instructional Television Trust; began transmission in 1966; school programmes form an integral part of the syllabus in a wide range of subjects; also adult education; Gen. Man. AHUVA FAINMESSE; Dir of Engineering S. KASIF.

Second Channel TV and Radio Administration: 3 Kanfi Nesharim St, POB 34112, Jerusalem 95464; tel. 2-6556222; fax 2-6556287; e-mail channel2@netvision.net.il; f. 1991; Chair. Prof. GIDEON DORON; Man. Dir NACHMAN SHAI.

In 1986 the Government approved the establishment of a commercial radio and television network to be run in competition with the state system.

Finance

(cap. = capital; dep. = deposits; m. = million; res = reserves; brs = branches; amounts in shekels)

BANKING

During 1991–98 the Government raised some US $3,995m. through privatization and the issuance of shares and convertible securities in the banking sector.

Central Bank

Bank of Israel: POB 780, Bank of Israel Bldg, Kiryat Ben-Gurion, Jerusalem 91007; tel. 2-6552211; fax 2-6528805; e-mail webmaster@ bankisrael.gov.il; internet www.bankisrael.gov.il; f. 1954 as the Central Bank of the State of Israel; cap. 60m., res –14,552m., dep. 103,269m. (Dec. 2000); Gov. DAVID KLEIN; 2 brs.

Principal Israeli Banks

Arab-Israel Bank Ltd: POB 27, Nesher 20300; tel. 4-8308222; fax 4-8308250; internet www.bank-aravi-israeli.co.il; total assets 3,198.4m., dep. 2,873.4m. (Dec. 1999); subsidiary of Bank Leumi le-Israel BM; Chair. D. EFRIMA; Gen. Man. Y. AZRAD.

Bank Hapoalim: POB 27, 50 Rothschild Blvd, Tel-Aviv 66883; tel. 3-5673333; fax 3-5607028; e-mail international@bnhp.co.il; internet www.bankhapoalim.co.il; f. 1921 as the Workers' Bank, name changed as above 1961; American-Israel Bank merged into the above 1999; privatized in June 2000; total assets 240,250m., dep. 205,729m. (Dec. 2001); Chair. SHLOMO NEHAMA; 364 brs in Israel and abroad.

Bank of Jerusalem Ltd: POB 2255, 2 Herbert Samuel St, Jerusalem 91022; tel. 2-6706211; fax 2-6246793; e-mail webmaster@ bankjerusalem.co.il; internet www.bankjerusalem.co.il; private bank; total assets 6,057m., dep. 5,463m. (Dec. 2001); Chair. DAVID BLUMBERG; Man. Dir and Gen. Man. DAVID BARUCH.

Bank Leumi le-Israel BM: POB 2, 24–32 Yehuda Halevi St, Tel-Aviv 65546; tel. 3-5148111; fax 3-5661872; internet www.bankleumi .com; f. 1902 as Anglo-Palestine Co; renamed Anglo-Palestine Bank 1930; reincorporated as above 1951; 41.73% state-owned; total assets 234,261m., dep. 204,589m. (Dec. 2001); Chair. EITAN RAFF; Pres., CEO and Gen. Man. GALIA MAOR; 229 brs in Israel and abroad.

Euro-Trade Bank Ltd: POB 37318, 2 Yavne St, Tel-Aviv 61372; tel. 3-6216806; fax 3-6209062; e-mail info@eurotrade.co.il; internet www.eurotrade.co.il; f. 1953; renamed Israel Building Bank Ltd 1978; name changed as above 1993; total assets 261,274m., dep. 208,932m. (Dec. 2000); Chair. of Bd ZELEKHA SHLOMO; Man. Dir JOSEPH PINCHASOF.

First International Bank of Israel Ltd: POB 29036, Shalom Mayer Tower, 9 Ahad Ha'am St, Tel-Aviv 62251; tel. 3-5196111; fax 3-5100316; e-mail yuval@fibimail.co.il; internet www.fibi.co.il; f. 1972 by merger between Foreign Trade Bank Ltd and Export Bank Ltd; total assets 64,996m., cap. 3,142m., dep. 57,223m. (June 2001); Chair. SHLOMO PIOTRKOWSKY; Man. Dir and CEO DAVID GRANOT; 90 brs.

Industrial Development Bank of Israel Ltd: POB 33580, Asia House, 4 Weizman St, Tel-Aviv 61334; tel. 3-6972727; fax 3-6972893; internet www.idbi.co.il; f. 1957; 61% state-owned; total assets 12,839.4m., dep. 11,599.6m. (Dec. 2000); Chair. SHLOMO BOROCHEV; Gen. Man. YEHOSHUA ICHILOV.

Investec Bank (Israel) Ltd: POB 677, 38 Rothschild Blvd, Tel-Aviv 61006; tel. 3-5645645; fax 3-5645210; e-mail irroni@igb.co.il; internet www.investec.co.il; f. 1934 as Palestine Credit Utility Bank Ltd, renamed Israel General Bank Ltd 1964; ownership transferred to Investec Bank Ltd (South Africa) in 1996; name changed to Investec Clali Bank Ltd 1999, and as above 2001; total assets 5,856.7m., dep. 5,278.8m. (Dec. 1999); Chair. HUGH SYDNEY HERMAN; Man. Dir and CEO JONATHON IRRONI; 3 brs.

Israel Continental Bank Ltd: POB 37406, 65 Rothschild Blvd, Tel-Aviv 61373; tel. 3-5641616; fax 3-6200399; f. 1974; capital held jointly by Bank Hapoalim BM (63.3%) and Bank für Gemeinwirtschaft AG (36.7%); total assets 1,982.8m., dep. 1,671.7m. (Dec. 2001); Chair. AMIRAM SIVAN; Man. Dir P. HOREV; 3 brs.

Israel Discount Bank Ltd: 27 Yehuda Halevi St, Tel-Aviv 65136; tel. 3-5145555; fax 3-5145346; e-mail contact@discountbank.net; internet www.discountbank.net; f. 1935; 57.09% state-owned; cap. 98m., dep. 123,810m. (Sept. 2002); Chair. ARIE MIENTKAVICH; some 138 brs in Israel and abroad.

Leumi Industrial Development Bank Ltd: POB 2, 13 Ahad Haam St, Tel-Aviv 61000; tel. 3-5149951; fax 3-5149897; e-mail michaelz@bll.co.il; f. 1944; subsidiary of Bank Leumi le-Israel BM; cap. and res 100.1m. (Dec. 2001); Chair. B. NAVEH; Gen. Man. MICHAEL ZIV.

Maritime Bank of Israel Ltd: POB 29373, 35 Ahad Ha'am St, Tel-Aviv 61293; tel. 3-5642222; fax 3-5642323; e-mail sap_mat@ netvision.net.il; internet www.sapanut.co.il; f. 1962; total assets 1,257.1m., cap. 6.0m., res 237.4m., dep. 883.0m. (Dec. 2001); Chair. SHIMON TOPOR; CEO and Gen. Man. DAVID LEVINSON.

Mercantile Discount Bank Ltd: POB 1292, 103 Allenby Rd, Tel-Aviv 61012; tel. 3-7105550; fax 3-7105532; e-mail fec@mdb.co.il; internet www.mercantile.co.il; f. 1971 as Barclays Discount Bank Ltd; by Barclays Bank International Ltd and Israel Discount Bank Ltd to incorporate Israel brs of Barclays; Israel Discount Bank Ltd became the sole owner in February 1993; name changed as above April 1993; absorbed Mercantile Bank of Israel Ltd in 1997; total assets 13,734m., cap. 48m., dep. 12,539m. (Dec. 2000); Chair. of Bd ARIE MIENTKAVICH; Gen. Man. Prof. SHALOM JOSEF HOCHMAN; 67 brs.

Union Bank of Israel Ltd: POB 2428, 6–8 Ahuzat Bayit St, Tel-Aviv 65143; tel. 3-5191111; fax 3-5191274; internet www.unionbank .co.il; f. 1951; 18.4% state-owned; total assets 22,100m., dep. 19,411m. (Dec. 2001); Chair. Z. ABELES; CEO and Gen. Man. B. OSHMAN; 28 brs.

United Mizrahi Bank Ltd: POB 309, Tel-Aviv 61002; tel. 3-5679433; fax 3-5679121; e-mail umb_ifts@mizrahi.co.il; internet www.mizrahi.co.il; f. 1923 as Mizrahi Bank Ltd; 1969 absorbed Hapoel Hamizrahi Bank Ltd and name changed as above; absorbed Finance and Trade Bank Ltd in 1990; 1.23% state-owned; total assets 68,760m., dep. 62,842m. (Dec. 2000); Pres. and CEO VICTOR MEDINA; 101 brs.

Mortgage Banks

Discount Mortgage Bank Ltd: POB 2844, 16–18 Simtat Beit Hashoeva, Tel-Aviv 61027; tel. 3-5643311; fax 3-5661704; f. 1959; subsidiary of Israel Discount Bank Ltd; cap. p.u. 1.3m., res 463.6m. (Dec. 1997); Chair. ARIE MIENTKAVICH; Man. M. ELDAR.

First International Mortgage Bank Ltd.: 39 Montefiore St, Tel-Aviv 65201; tel. 3-5643311; fax 3-5643321; f. 1922 as the Mortgage and Savings Bank, name changed as above 1996; subsidiary of First International Bank of Israel Ltd; cap. and res 334m. (Dec. 1996); Chair. SHLOMO PIOTRKOWSKY; Man. Dir P. HAMO; 50 brs.

Leumi Mortgage Bank Ltd: POB 69, 31–37 Montefiore St, Tel-Aviv 65201; tel. 3-5648444; fax 3-5648334; f. 1921 as General Mortgage Bank Ltd; subsidiary of Bank Leumi le-Israel BM; total assets 26,155m., dep. 23,830m. (Dec. 2000); Chair. A. ZELDMAN; Gen. Man. R. ZABAG; 9 brs.

Mishkan-Hapoalim Mortgage Bank Ltd: POB 1610, 2 Ibn Gvirol St, Tel-Aviv 61015; tel. 3-6970505; fax 3-6961379; f. 1950; subsidiary of Bank Hapoalim BM; total assets 8,289m., dep. 10,268.3m. (Dec. 1993); Chair. M. OLENIK; Man. Dir A. KROIZER; 131 brs.

Tefahot, Israel Mortgage Bank Ltd: POB 93, 9 Heleni Hamalka St, Jerusalem 91902; tel. 2-6755222; fax 2-6755344; f. 1945; subsidiary of United Mizrahi Bank Ltd; total assets 27,442m., cap. and res 1,446m. (Dec. 2000); Chair. REUVEN ADLER; Man. Dir CHAIM FREILICHMAN; 50 brs.

STOCK EXCHANGE

The Tel-Aviv Stock Exchange: 54 Ahad Ha'am St, Tel-Aviv 65202; tel. 3-5677411; fax 3-5105379; e-mail spokesperson@tase.co.il; internet www.tase.co.il; f. 1953; Chair. Prof. YAIR E. ORGLER; Gen. Man. SAUL BRONFELD.

INSURANCE

The Israel Insurance Assen lists 15 member companies; a selection of these are listed below, as are some non-members.

Ararat Insurance Co Ltd: Ararat House, 13 Montefiore St, Tel-Aviv 65164; tel. 3-640888; f. 1949; Co-Chair. AHARON DOVRAT, PHILIP ZUCKERMAN; Gen. Man. PINCHAS COHEN.

Aryeh Insurance Co of Israel Ltd: 9 Ahad Ha'am St, Tel-Aviv 65251; tel. 3-5141777; fax 3-5179339; e-mail rubens@aryeh-ins.co.il; f. 1948; Pres. RUBEN SHARONI; Chair. AVIGDOR KAPLAN.

Clal Insurance Co Ltd: POB 326, 46 Petach Tikva Rd, Tel-Aviv 66184; tel. 3-6387777; fax 3-6387676; e-mail avigdork@clal-ins.co.il; f. 1962; Pres. and CEO AVIGDOR KAPLAN; Man. Dir RIMON BEN-SHAOUL.

Eliahu Insurance Co Ltd: 2 Ibn Gvirol St, Tel-Aviv 64077; tel. 3-6920911; fax 3-6956995; e-mail ofer@eliahu.com; Chair. OFER ELIAHU.

Hassneh Insurance Co of Israel Ltd: POB 805, 115 Allenby St, Tel-Aviv 61007; tel. 3-5649111; f. 1924; Man. Dir M. MICHAEL MILLER.

Israel Phoenix Assurance Co Ltd: 30 Levontin St, Tel-Aviv 61020; tel. 3-7141111; fax 3-5666902; e-mail vardab@phoenix.co.il; internet www.phoenix.co.il; f. 1949; CEO BAR-KOCHVA BEN-GERA; Chair. of Bd JOSEPH D. HACKMEY.

Menorah Insurance Co Ltd: Menorah House, 15 Allenby St, Tel-Aviv 65786; tel. 3-7107777; fax 3-7107402; e-mail anat-by@bezeqint.net; f. 1935; Chair. MENACHEM GUREWITZ; Gen. Man. SHABTAI ENGEL.

Migdal Insurance Co Ltd: POB 37633, 26 Sa'adiya Ga'on St, Tel-Aviv 67135; tel. 3-5637637; fax 3-5610220; e-mail sarav@migdal-group.co.il; internet www.migdal.co.il; part of Bank Leumi Group; f. 1934; Chair. AHARON FOGEL; CEO IZZY COHEN.

Palglass Palestine Plate Glass Insurance Co Ltd: Tel-Aviv 65541; f. 1934; Gen. Man. AKIVA ZALZMAN.

Sahar-Zion Insurance Co Ltd: 3 Abba Hillel St, Ramat-Gan, Tel-Aviv; tel. 3-7547777; fax 3-7547800; e-mail mukya@sahar-zion.co.il; f. 1949; Chair. GIDEON HAMBURGER.

Samson Insurance Co Ltd: POB 33678, Avgad Bldg, 5 Jabotinsky St, Ramat-Gan, Tel-Aviv 52520; tel. 3-7521616; fax 3-7516644; f. 1933; Chair. E. BEN-AMRAM; Gen. Man. GIORA SAGI.

Sela Insurance Co Ltd: Tel-Aviv; tel. 3-61028; f. 1938; Man. Dir E. SHANI.

Shiloah Insurance Co Ltd: 3 Abba-Hillel St, Ramat-Gan, Tel-Aviv 52118; tel. 3-7547777; fax 3-7545100; e-mail y_hamburger@harel-hamishmar.co.il; f. 1933; Chair. YAIR HAMBURGER; Gen. Man. Dr S. BAMIRAH.

Trade and Industry

CHAMBERS OF COMMERCE

Federation of Bi-National Chambers of Commerce and Industry with and in Israel: POB 50196, 29 Hamered St, Tel-Aviv 61500; tel. 3-5173261; fax 3-5173283; federates: Israel-British Chamber of Commerce; Australia-Israel Chamber of Commerce; Chamber of Commerce and Industry Israel-Asia; Chamber of Commerce Israel-Belgique-Luxembourg; Canada-Israel Chamber of Commerce and Industry; Israel-Denmark Chamber of Commerce; Chambre de Commerce Israel-France; Chamber of Commerce and Industry Israel-Germany; Camera di Commercio Israeli-Italia; Israel-Japan Chamber of Commerce; Israel-Latin America, Spain and Portugal Chamber of Commerce; Netherlands-Israel Chamber of Commerce; Israel-Greece Chamber of Commerce; Israel-Bulgaria Chamber of Commerce; Israel-Ireland Chamber of Commerce; Handelskammer Israel-Schweiz; Israel-South Africa Chamber of Commerce; Israel-Sweden Chamber of Commerce; Israel-Hungary Chamber of Commerce; Israel-Romania Chamber of Commerce;

Israel-Russia Chamber of Commerce; Israel-Poland Chamber of Commerce; Israel-Austria Chamber of Commerce; Israel-Ukraine Chamber of Commerce; Israel-Africa Chamber of Commerce; Israel-Jordan Chamber of Commerce; Israel-Egypt Chamber of Commerce; Israel-Morocco Chamber of Commerce; Israel-Moldova Chamber of Commerce; Israel-Norway Chamber of Commerce; Israel-Slovakia Chamber of Commerce; Israel-Portugal Chamber of Commerce; Israel-Finland Chamber of Commerce; Israel-Kazakhstan Chamber of Commerce; Israel-Turkey Chamber of Commerce; Israel-Thailand Chamber of Commerce; Chair. G. PROPPER.

Federation of Israeli Chambers of Commerce: POB 20027, 84 Ha 'Hashmonaim St, Tel-Aviv 67011; tel. 3-5631010; fax 3-5619025; e-mail chamber@tlv-chamber.org.il; internet www.tlv-chamber.org.il; co-ordinates the Tel-Aviv, Jerusalem, Haifa and Beersheba Chambers of Commerce; Pres. URIEL LYNN.

Haifa Chamber of Commerce and Industry (Haifa and District): POB 33176, 53 Haatzmaut Rd, Haifa 31331; tel. 4-8626364; fax 4-8645428; e-mail main@haifachamber.org.il; internet www.haifachamber.com; f. 1921; 700 mems; Pres. E. MELAMUD; S. GANTZ; Man. Dir D. MAROM.

Israel-British Chamber of Commerce: POB 50321, 29 Hamered St, Tel-Aviv 61502; tel. 3-5109424; fax 3-5109540; e-mail isrbrit@netvision.net.il; f. 1951; 350 mems; Chair. AMNON DOTAN; Exec. Dir FELIX KIPPER.

Jerusalem Chamber of Commerce: POB 2083, Jerusalem 91020; tel. 2-6254333; fax 2-6254335; e-mail jerccom@inter.net.il; internet www.jerccom.co.il; f. 1908; c. 300 mems; Pres. SHMULIK SEMMEL.

Tel-Aviv Chamber of Commerce: POB 20027, 84 Ha 'Hashmonaim St, Tel-Aviv 61200; tel. 3-5631010; fax 3-5619025; e-mail chamber@chamber.org.il; internet www.chamber.org.il; f. 1919; 2,500 mems; Pres. URIEL LYNN.

INDUSTRIAL AND TRADE ASSOCIATIONS

Agricultural Export Co (AGREXCO): Tel-Aviv; state-owned agricultural marketing organization; Dir-Gen. AMOTZ AMIAD.

The Agricultural Union: Tel-Aviv; consists of more than 50 agricultural settlements and is connected with marketing and supplying organizations, and Bahan Ltd, controllers and auditors.

The Centre for International Agricultural Development Cooperation (CINADCO): POB 30, Beit Dagan 50200; tel. 3-9485776; fax 3-9485761; e-mail cinadco@moag.gov.il; shares agricultural experience through the integration of research and project development; runs specialized training courses, advisory missions and feasibility projects in Israel and abroad; Dir ZVI HERMAN.

Citrus Marketing Board: POB 80, Beit Dagan 50250; tel. 3-9683811; fax 3-9683838; e-mail cmbi@netvision.net.il; internet www.online.co.il/cmbi; f. 1942; the central co-ordinating body of citrus growers and exporters in Israel; represents the citrus industry in international organizations; licenses private exporters; controls the quality of fruit; has responsibility for Jaffa trademarks; mounts advertising and promotion campaigns for Jaffa citrus fruit worldwide; carries out research and development of new varieties of citrus fruit, and 'environmentally friendly' fruit; Chair. D. KRITCHMAN; Gen. Man. M. DAVIDSON.

Farmers' Union of Israel: POB 209, 8 Kaplan St, Tel-Aviv; tel. 3-69502227; fax 3-6918228; f. 1913; membership of 7,000 independent farmers, citrus and winegrape growers; Pres. PESACH GRUPPER; Dir-Gen. SHLOMO REISMAN.

Flower Board of Israel: 2 Kaplan St, Tel-Aviv 64734; e-mail fbi@fbi.org.il; internet www.fbi.org.il.

Fruit Board of Israel: POB 20117, 119 Rehov Ha 'Hashmonaim, Tel-Aviv 61200; tel. 3-5632929; fax 3-5614672; e-mail fruits@fruit.org.il; internet www.fruit.org.il; Dir-Gen. DANY BRUNER.

General Assen of Merchants in Israel: Tel-Aviv; the organization of retail traders; has a membership of 30,000 in 60 brs.

Israel Cotton Production and Marketing Board Ltd: POB 384, Herzlia B 46103; tel. 9-9509493; fax 9-9509159; e-mail mali@cotton.co.il.

Israel Diamond Exchange Ltd: POB 3222, Ramat-Gan, Tel-Aviv; tel. 3-5760211; fax 3-5750652; e-mail judi@isde.co.il; f. 1937; production, export, import and finance facilities; net exports (2002) US $5,200m. Pres. SHMUEL SCHNITZER.

Israel Export Institute: POB 50084, 29 Hamered St, Tel-Aviv 68125; tel. 3-5142830; fax 3-5142902; e-mail library@export.gov.il; internet www.export.gov.il; Dir-Gen. ISRAEL SHOTLAND.

Israel Journalists' Assen: 4 Kaplan St, Tel-Aviv 64734; tel. 3-6956141; Man. Dir TUVIA SAAR.

Kibbutz Industries' Assen: 8 Rehov Shaul Hamelech, Tel-Aviv 64733; tel. 3-6955413; fax 3-6951464; e-mail kiakia@netvision.co.il;

liaison office for marketing and export of the goods produced by Israel's kibbutzim; Pres. GIORA MASAD.

Manufacturers' Asscn of Israel: POB 50022, Industry House, 29 Hamered St, Tel-Aviv 61500; tel. 3-5198787; fax 3-5162026; e-mail gendiv@industry.org.il; internet www.industry.org.il; 1,700 mem. enterprises employing nearly 85% of industrial workers in Israel; Pres. ODED TYRAH.

National Federation of Israeli Journalists: POB 7009, 4 Kaplan St, Tel-Aviv 64734; tel. 3-6956141; fax 3-6951438.

UTILITIES

The Israel Electric Corporation Ltd and the **Mekorot (Israel National Water Co)** are two of Israel's largest state-owned companies, with total assets valued at US $10,832m. and US $1,978m., respectively, at the end of 1997.

Israel Electric Corporation Ltd (IEC): POB 8810, 2 Ha 'Haganah St, Haifa 31086; tel. 4-8548148; fax 4-8538149; internet www .israel-electric.co.il; Chair. GAD YA'ACOBI.

Mekorot (Israel National Water Co): 9 Lincoln St Development, Tel-Aviv 61201; tel. 3-6230806; fax 3-6230598; e-mail akanarek@ mekorot.co.il; internet www.mekorot.co.il.

The Histadrut

Histadrut (General Federation of Labour in Israel): 93 Arlozorof St, Tel-Aviv 62098; tel. 3-6921513; fax 3-6921512; e-mail histint@ netvision.net.il; f. 1920.

The General Federation of Labour in Israel, the Histadrut, is the largest labour organization in Israel. It strives to ensure the social security, welfare and rights of workers, and to assist in their professional advancement, while endeavouring to reduce the divisions in Israeli society. Membership of the Histadrut is voluntary, and open to all men and women of 18 years of age and above who live on the earnings of their own labour without exploiting the work of others. These include the self-employed and professionals, as well as housewives, students, pensioners and the unemployed. Workers' interests are protected through a number of occupational and professional unions affiliated to the Histadrut (see below). The organization operates courses for trade unionists and new immigrants, as well as apprenticeship classes. It maintains an Institute for Social and Economic Issues and the International Institute, one of the largest centres of leadership training in Israel, for students from Africa, Asia, Latin America and Eastern Europe, which includes the Levinson Centre for Adult Education and the Jewish-Arab Institute for Regional Co-operation. Attached to the Histadrut is Na'amat, a women's organization which promotes changes in legislation, operates a network of legal service bureaux and vocational training courses, and runs counselling centres for the treatment and prevention of domestic violence.

Chair.: AMIR PERETZ.

Secretary-General: HAIM RAMON.

ORGANIZATION

In 1989 the Histadrut had a membership of 1,630,000. In addition some 110,000 young people under 18 years of age belong to the Organization of Working and Student Youth, a direct affiliate of the Histadrut.

All members take part in elections to the Histadrut Convention (Veida), which elects the General Council (Moetsa) and the Executive Committee (Vaad Hapoel). The latter elects the 41-member Executive Bureau (Vaada Merakezet), which is responsible for day-to-day implementation of policy. The Executive Committee also elects the Secretary-General, who acts as its chairman as well as head of the organization as a whole and chairman of the Executive Bureau. Nearly all political parties are represented on the Histadrut Executive Committee.

The Executive Committee has the following departments: Trade Union, Organization and Labour Councils, Education and Culture, Social Security, Industrial Democracy, Students, Youth and Sports, Consumer Protection, Administration, Finance and International.

TRADE UNION ACTIVITIES

Collective agreements with employers fix wage scales, which are linked with the retail price index; provide for social benefits, including paid sick leave and employers' contributions to sick and pension and provident funds; and regulate dismissals. Dismissal compensation is regulated by law. The Histadrut actively promotes productivity through labour management boards and the National Productivity Institute, and supports incentive pay schemes.

There are unions for the following groups: clerical workers, building workers, teachers, engineers, agricultural workers, technicians, textile workers, printing workers, diamond workers, metal

workers, food and bakery workers, wood workers, government employees, seamen, nurses, civilian employees of the armed forces, actors, musicians and variety artists, social workers, watchmen, cinema technicians, institutional and school staffs, pharmacy employees, medical laboratory workers, X-ray technicians, physiotherapists, social scientists, microbiologists, psychologists, salaried lawyers, pharmacists, physicians, occupational therapists, truck and taxi drivers, hotel and restaurant workers, workers in Histadrut-owned industry, garment, shoe and leather workers, plastic and rubber workers, editors of periodicals, painters and sculptors and industrial workers.

Histadrut Trade Union Department: Dir SHLOMO SHANI.

ECONOMIC ACTIVITIES AND SOCIAL SERVICES

These include Hevrat Haovdim (employing 260,000 workers in 1983), Kupat Holim (the Sick Fund, covering almost 77% of Israel's population), seven pension funds, and Na'amat (see above).

Other Trade Unions

General Federation of West Bank Trade Unions: Sec.-Gen. SHAHER SAAD.

Histadrut Haovdim Haleumit (National Labour Federation): 23 Sprintzak St, Tel-Aviv 64738; tel. 3-6958351; fax 3-6961753; e-mail nol@netvision.net.il; f. 1934; 220,000 mems; CEO ITZHAK RUSSO.

Histadrut Hapoel Hamizrahi (National Religious Workers' Party): 166 Ibn Gvirol St, Tel-Aviv 62023; tel. 3-5442151; fax 3-5468942; 150,000 mems in 85 settlements and 15 kibbutzim; Sec.-Gen. ELIEZER ABTABI.

Histadrut Poale Agudat Israel (Agudat Israel Workers' Organization): POB 11044, 64 Frishman St, Tel-Aviv; tel. 3-5242126; fax 3-5230689; has 33,000 members in 16 settlements and 8 educational insts.

Transport

RAILWAYS

Freight traffic consists mainly of grain, phosphates, potash, containers, petroleum and building materials. Rail service serves Haifa and Ashdod ports on the Mediterranean Sea, while a combined rail-road service extends to Eilat port on the Red Sea. Passenger services operate between the main towns: Nahariya, Haifa, Tel-Aviv and Jerusalem. In 1988 the National Ports Authority assumed responsibility for the rail system, creating the Ports and Railways Authority. It was decided in 1996 that Israel Railways should become a separate state concern, although this has not yet occurred. A US $1,400m. light railway network in Jerusalem was expected to be launched in 2004.

Israel Railways (IR): POB 18085, Central Station, Tel-Aviv 61180; tel. 3-6937401; fax 3-6937480; internet www.israrail.org.il; in 2001 the total length of railway line was 684 km; Dir-Gen. AMOS UZANI; Gen. Man. EHUD HADAR.

Underground Railway

Haifa Underground Funicular Railway: 122 Hanassi Ave, Haifa 34633; tel. 4-8376861; fax 4-8376875; e-mail funicular@netvision .net.il; opened 1959; 2 km in operation; Man. AVI TELLEM.

ROADS

In 2001 there were 16,563 km of paved roads, of which 9,508 km were urban roads, 5,523 km were non-urban roads and 1,532 km were access roads.

Ministry of Transport: Public Works Dept, Klal Bldg, 97 Jaffa St, Jerusalem 91000; tel. 2-6228211; fax 2-6228693; e-mail pniot@mot .gov.il; internet www.mot.gov.il.

SHIPPING

At 31 December 2001 Israel's merchant fleet consisted of 48 vessels amounting to 611,396 grt.

Haifa and Ashdod are the main ports in Israel. The former is a natural harbour, enclosed by two main breakwaters and dredged to 45 ft below mean sea-level. In 1965 the deep water port was completed at Ashdod which had a capacity of about 8.6m. tons in 1988.

The port of Eilat is Israel's gateway to the Red Sea. It is a natural harbour, operated from a wharf. Another port, to the south of the original one, started operating in 1965.

Israel Ports and Railways Authority (PRA): POB 20121, 74 Menachem Begin Rd, Tel-Aviv 61201; tel. 3-5657000; fax 3-5617142; e-mail dovf@israports.org.il; internet www.israports.org.il; f. 1961 to plan, build, develop, maintain and operate Israel's commercial ports and Israel Railways. A contract to expand Ashdod port was awarded in mid-2000, involving 1,900 m of new cargo and container quays, a breakwater extension and hinterland development; the first ship was scheduled to be handled at the new facilities in 2004. A proposed extension to Haifa port was also under way. Cargo traffic in 2001 amounted to 32m. tons; Chair. GAD YAACOBI; Dir-Gen. AMOS RON.

Ofer (Ships Holding) Ltd: POB 1755, 2 Hanamal St, Haifa 31016; tel. 4-8610610; fax 4-8675666; e-mail ops@oferb.co.il; runs cargo and container services; operates some 18 vessels; Chair. Y. OFER; Man. Dir E. ANGEL.

ZIM Israel Navigation Co Ltd: POB 1723, 7–9 Pal-Yam Ave, Haifa 31000; tel. 4-8652111; fax 4-8652956; e-mail zimpress@zim.co.il; internet www.zim.co.il; f. 1945; international integrated transportation system providing door-to-door services around the world; operates about 80 vessels; estimated total cargo carried: 1,500,000 TEUs in 2002; Chair. U. ANGEL; Pres. and CEO Dr YORAM SEBBA.

CIVIL AVIATION

Israel Airports Authority: Ben-Gurion International Airport, Tel-Aviv; tel. 3-9710101; fax 3-9712436; internet www.ben-gurion-airport.co.il; Chair. TSVI SHALOM; Dir-Gen. GABRIEL OFFIR.

El Al Israel Airlines Ltd: POB 41, Ben-Gurion International Airport, Tel-Aviv 70100; tel. 3-9716111; fax 3-9716040; internet www.elal.com; f. 1948; 100% state-owned, but scheduled for privatization; total assets US $980m. (Dec. 1997); daily services to most capitals of Europe; over 20 flights weekly to New York; services to the USA, Canada, China, Egypt, India, Kenya, South Africa, Thailand and Turkey; scheduled for privatization; Chair. MICHAEL LEVY; Pres. AMOS SHAPIRA.

Arkia Israeli Airlines Ltd: POB 39301, Dov Airport, Tel-Aviv 61392; tel. 3-6902222; fax 3-6991512; e-mail income@arkia.co.il; internet www.arkia.co.il; f. 1980 by merger of Kanaf-Arkia Airlines and Aviation Services; scheduled passenger services linking Tel-Aviv, Jerusalem, Haifa, Eilat, Rosh Pina, Kiryat Shmona and Yotveta; charter services to European destinations; Chair. YIGAL ARNON; Pres. and CEO Prof. ISRAEL BOROVICH.

Tourism

In 2002 an estimated 862,000 tourists visited Israel, compared with some 1,195,700 in 2001. Tourist receipts in 2001 totalled US $2,460m.

Ministry of Tourism: POB 1018, 24 Rehov King George, Jerusalem 91009; tel. 2-6754811; fax 2-6253407; e-mail pniot@tourism.gov.il; internet www.tourism.gov.il; Dir-Gen. DAVID LITVAK.

Occupied Territories

THE GOLAN HEIGHTS

Location, Climate

The Golan Heights, a mountainous plateau which formed most of Syria's Quneitra Province (1,710 sq km) and parts of Dera'a Province, was occupied by Israel after the 1967 Arab–Israeli War. Following the Disengagement Agreement of 1974, Israel continued to occupy some 70% of the territory (1,176 sq km), valued for its strategic position and abundant water resources (the headwaters of the Jordan river have their source on the slopes of Mount Hermon). The average height of the Golan is approximately 1,200 m above sea-level in the northern region and about 300 m above sea-level in the southern region, near Lake Tiberias (the Sea of Galilee). Rainfall ranges from about 1,000 mm per year in the north to less than 600 mm per year in the southern region.

Administration

Prior to the Israeli occupation, the Golan Heights were incorporated by Syria into a provincial administration of which the city of Quneitra, with a population at the time of 27,378, was capital. The disengagement agreement that was mediated by US Secretary of State Henry Kissinger in 1974 (after the 1973 Arab–Israeli War) provided for the withdrawal of Israeli forces from Quneitra. Before they withdrew, however, Israeli army engineers destroyed the city. In December 1981 the Israeli Knesset enacted the Golan Annexation Law, whereby Israeli civilian legislation was extended to the territory of Golan, now under the administrative jurisdiction of the Commissioner for the Northern District of Israel. The Arab-Druze community of the Golan immediately responded by declaring a strike and appealed to the UN Secretary-General to force Israel to rescind the annexation decision. At the seventh round of multilateral talks between Israeli and Arab delegations in Washington,

DC, USA, in August 1992, the Israeli Government of Itzhak Rabin for the first time accepted that UN Security Council Resolution 242, adopted in 1967, applied to the Golan Heights. In January 1999 the Knesset passed legislation which stated that any transfer of land under Israeli sovereignty (referring to the Golan Heights and East Jerusalem) was conditional on the approval of at least 61 of the 120 Knesset members and of the Israeli electorate in a subsequent national referendum. Following the election of Ehud Barak as Israel's Prime Minister in May 1999, peace negotiations between Israel and Syria were resumed in mid-December. However, in January 2000 the talks were postponed indefinitely after Syria demanded a written commitment from Israel to withdraw from the Golan Heights. In July 2001 Israel's recently elected premier, Ariel Sharon, stated that he would be prepared to resume peace talks with Syria; however, Sharon also declared that the Israeli occupation of the Golan was 'irreversible'. The withdrawal of Israel from the disputed territory is one of Syria's primary objectives in any future peace agreement with Israel. Peace negotiations between Israel and Syria had not resumed by mid-2003.

Demography and Economic Affairs

As a consequence of the Israeli occupation, an estimated 93% of the ethnically diverse Syrian population of 147,613, distributed across 163 villages and towns and 108 individual farms, was expelled. The majority were Arab Sunni Muslims, but the population also included Alawite and Druze minorities and some Circassians, Turcomen, Armenians and Kurds. Approximately 9,000 Palestinian refugees from the 1948 Arab–Israeli War also inhabited the area. At the time of the occupation, the Golan was a predominantly agricultural province, 64% of the labour force being employed in agriculture. Only one-fifth of the population resided in the administrative centres. By 1991 the Golan Heights had a Jewish population of about 12,000 living in 21 Jewish settlements (four new settlements had been created by the end of 1992), and a predominantly Druze population of some 16,000 living in the only six remaining villages, of which Majd ash-Shams is by far the largest. According to official figures, at the end of 2001 the Golan Heights had a total population of 35,400 (including 15,100 Jews, 17,700 Druze and 1,800 Muslims). The Golan Heights have remained largely an agricultural area, and although many Druze now work in Israeli industry in Eilat, Tel-Aviv and Jerusalem, the indigenous economy relies almost solely on the cultivation of apples, for which the area is famous. The apple orchards benefit from a unique combination of fertile soils, abundance of water and a conducive climate.

EAST JERUSALEM

Location

Greater Jerusalem includes Israeli West Jerusalem (99% Jewish), the Old City and Mount of Olives, East Jerusalem (the Palestinian residential and commercial centre), Arab villages declared to be part of Jerusalem by Israel in 1967 and Jewish neighbourhoods constructed since 1967, either on land expropriated from Arab villages or in areas requisitioned as 'government land'. Although the area of the Greater Jerusalem district is 627 sq km, the Old City of Jerusalem covers just 1 sq km.

Administration

Until the 1967 Arab–Israeli War, Jerusalem had been divided into the new city of West Jerusalem—captured by Jewish forces in 1948 —and the old city, East Jerusalem, which was part of Jordan. Israel's victory in 1967, however, reunited the city under Israeli control. Two weeks after the fighting had ended, on 28 June, Israeli law was applied to East Jerusalem and the municipal boundaries were extended by 45 km (28 miles). Jerusalem had effectively been annexed. Israeli officials, however, still refer to the 'reunification' of Jerusalem.

Demography and Economic Affairs

In June 1993 the Deputy Mayor of Jerusalem, Avraham Kahila, declared that the city now had 'a majority of Jews', based on population forecasts which estimated the Jewish population at 158,000 and the Arab population at 155,000. For the Israeli administration this signified the achievement of a long-term objective. Immediately prior to the June 1967 Arab–Israeli War, East Jerusalem and its Arab environs had an Arab population of approximately 70,000, and a small Jewish population in the old Jewish quarter of the city. By contrast, Israeli West Jerusalem had a Jewish population of 196,000. As a result of this imbalance, in the Greater Jerusalem district as a whole the Jewish population was in the majority even prior to the occupation of the whole city in 1967. Israeli policy following the occupation of East Jerusalem and the West Bank consisted of encircling the eastern sector of the city with Jewish settlements. In contrast to the more politically sensitive siting of Jewish settlements in the old Arab quarter of Jerusalem, the Government of Itzhak Rabin concentrated on the outer circle of settlement building. Official statistics for the end of 1998 reported that Greater Jerusalem had a total population of 633,700, of whom 433,600 (68%) were Jews. At the end of 2001 the city's population was 670,000. The Jerusalem Institute for Israel Studies estimates that the Arab population of Greater Jerusalem is increasing at a rate three times greater than the Jewish population.

The Old City, within the walls of which are found the ancient quarters of the Jews, Christians, Muslims and Armenians, has a population of approximately 25,500 Arabs and 2,600 Jews. In addition, there are some 600 recent Jewish settlers in the Arab quarter.

Many imaginative plans have been submitted with the aim of finding a solution to the problem of sharing Jerusalem between Arabs and Jews, including the proposal that the city be placed under international trusteeship, under UN auspices. However, to make the implementation of such plans an administrative as well as a political quagmire, the Israeli administration, after occupying the whole city in June 1967, began creating 'facts on the ground'. Immediately following the occupation, all electricity, water and telephone grids in West Jerusalem were extended to the east. Roads were widened and cleared, and the Arab population immediately in front of the 'Wailing Wall' was forcibly evicted. Arabs living in East Jerusalem became 'permanent residents' and could apply for Israeli citizenship if they wished (in contrast to Arabs in the West Bank and Gaza Strip). However, few chose to do so. None the less, issued with identity cards (excluding the estimated 25,000 Arabs from the West Bank and Gaza living illegally in the city), the Arab residents were taxed by the Israeli authorities, and their businesses and banks became subject to Israeli laws and business regulations. Now controlling approximately one-half of all land in East Jerusalem and the surrounding Palestinian villages (previously communally, or privately, owned by Palestinians), the Israeli authorities allowed Arabs to construct buildings on only 10%–15% of the land in the city; and East Jerusalem's commercial district has been limited to three streets.

Since the 1993 signing of the Declaration of Principles on Palestinian Self-Rule, the future status of Jerusalem and the continuing expansion of Jewish settlements in East Jerusalem have emerged as two of the most crucial issues affecting the peace process. In May 1999 the Israeli Government announced its refusal to grant Israeli citizenship to several hundred Arabs living in East Jerusalem, regardless of their compliance with the conditions stipulated under the Citizenship Law. In October, however, Israel ended its policy of revoking the right of Palestinians to reside in Jerusalem if they had spent more than seven years outside the city. Moreover, the Israeli Government announced in March 2000 that Palestinian residents of Jerusalem who had had their identity cards revoked could apply for their restoration.

At the Camp David talks held between Israel and the Palestinian (National) Authority (PA) in July 2000, the issue of who would have sovereignty over East Jerusalem in a future 'permanent status' agreement proved to be the principal obstacle to the achievement of a peace deal. It was reported in late July that the Israeli Government had offered the PA municipal autonomy over certain areas of East Jerusalem (including access to the Islamic holy sites), although sovereignty would remain in Israeli hands; the proposals were rejected by Yasser Arafat. In late September 2000 the holy sites of East Jerusalem were the initial focal point of a renewed uprising by Palestinians against the Israeli authorities, which became known as the al-Aqsa *intifada* and which continued into mid-2003. At the end of April, however, there was some expectation of a resumption of Israeli-Palestinian discussions with a view to resolving the Jerusalem issue, following the USA's publication of a 'road map' for achieving peace in the Middle East.

ITALY
Introductory Survey

Location, Climate, Language, Religion, Flag, Capital

The Italian Republic comprises a peninsula, extending from southern Europe into the Mediterranean Sea, and a number of adjacent islands. The two principal islands are Sicily, to the south-west, and Sardinia, to the west. The Alps form a natural boundary to the north, where the bordering countries are France to the north-west, Switzerland and Austria to the north and Slovenia to the north-east. The climate is temperate in the north and Mediterranean in the south, with mild winters and long, dry summers. The average temperature in Rome is 7.4°C (45.3°F) in January and 25.7°C (78.3°F) in July. The principal language is Italian. German and Ladin are spoken in the Alto Adige region on the Austrian border, and French in the Valle d'Aosta region (bordering France and Switzerland), while in southern Italy there are Greek-speaking and Albanian minorities. A language related to Catalan is spoken in north-western Sardinia. Almost all of the inhabitants profess Christianity: more than 90% are adherents of the Roman Catholic Church. There is freedom of expression for other Christian denominations and for non-Christian religions. The national flag (proportions 2 by 3) has three equal vertical stripes, of green, white and red. The capital is Rome.

Recent History

The Kingdom of Italy, under the House of Savoy, was proclaimed in 1861 and the country was unified in 1870. Italy subsequently acquired an overseas empire, comprising the African colonies of Eritrea, Italian Somaliland and Libya. Benito Mussolini, leader of the Fascist Party, became Prime Minister in October 1922 and assumed dictatorial powers in 1925–26. Relations between the Italian State and the Roman Catholic Church, a subject of bitter controversy since Italy's unification, were codified in 1929 by a series of agreements, including the Lateran Pact, which recognized the sovereignty of the State of the Vatican City (q.v.), a small enclave within the city of Rome, under the jurisdiction of the Pope. Under Mussolini, Italian forces occupied Ethiopia in 1935–36 and Albania in 1939. Italy supported the fascist forces in the Spanish Civil War of 1936–39, and from June 1940 supported Nazi Germany in the Second World War. In 1943, however, as forces from the allied powers invaded Italy, the fascist regime collapsed. In July of that year King Victor Emmanuel III dismissed Mussolini, and the Fascist Party was dissolved.

In April 1945 German forces in Italy surrendered and Mussolini was killed. In June 1946, following a referendum, the monarchy was abolished and Italy became a republic. Until 1963 the Partito della Democrazia Cristiana (DC—Christian Democratic Party) held power unchallenged, while industry expanded rapidly, supported by capital from the USA. By the early 1960s, however, public discontent was increasing, largely owing to low wage rates and a lack of social reform. In the general election of 1963 the Partito Comunista Italiano (PCI—Italian Communist Party), together with other parties of the extreme right and left, made considerable gains at the expense of the DC. During the next decade there was a rapid succession of mainly coalition Governments, involving the DC and one or more of the other major non-communist parties.

Aldo Moro's coalition Government of the DC and the Partito Repubblicano Italiano (PRI—Italian Republican Party), formed in November 1974, resigned in January 1976, following the withdrawal of support by the Partito Socialista Italiano (PSI—Italian Socialist Party). After the failure of a minority DC administration, general elections to both legislative chambers took place in June, at which the PCI won 228 seats in the 630-member Camera dei Deputati (Chamber of Deputies). The DC remained the largest party, but could no longer govern against PCI opposition in the legislature. However, the DC continued to insist on excluding the PCI from power, and in July formed a minority Government, with Giulio Andreotti as Prime Minister. He relied on the continuing abstention of PCI deputies to introduce severe austerity measures in response to the economic crisis. In January 1978 the minority Government was forced to resign under pressure from the PCI, which wanted more active participation in government (the PCI had for several months been allowed to participate in policy-making but had no direct role in government), although Andreotti subsequently formed a new, almost identical Government, with PCI support. In May of the same year Aldo Moro was murdered by the Brigate Rosse (Red Brigades) terrorist group. (In June 2000 a suspected former member of the Brigate Rosse was arrested in France in connection with Moro's murder.) In July 1978 Alessandro Pertini was inaugurated as Italy's first socialist head of state, succeeding Giovanni Leone, who had resigned as President in the previous month in response to allegations of corruption.

The Andreotti administration collapsed in January 1979, when the PCI withdrew from the official parliamentary majority. A new coalition Government, formed by Andreotti in March, lasted only 10 days before being defeated on a vote of 'no confidence'. Following elections in June, at which its representation in the Camera dei Deputati declined to 201 seats, the PCI returned to the role of opposition. In August Francesco Cossiga, a former Minister of the Interior, formed a minority 'government of truce', composed of the DC, the Partito Liberale Italiano (PLI—Italian Liberal Party) and the Partito Socialista Democratico Italiano (PSDI—Italian Social Democratic Party), relying on the abstention of the PSI to remain in office. However, the new Government was continually thwarted by obstructionism in Parliament. In April 1980 Cossiga formed a majority coalition, comprising members of the DC, the PRI and the PSI. The exclusion of the PCI prompted a concerted effort on the part of its deputies in the legislature to defeat the new Government, and in September the Government resigned after losing a vote on its economic programme. A four-party coalition Government assembled by Arnaldo Forlani, the Chairman of the DC, was beset with allegations of corruption, and in turn was forced to resign in May 1981, after it became known that more than 1,000 of Italy's foremost establishment figures belonged to a secret masonic lodge, P-2 ('Propaganda Due'), which had extensive criminal connections both in Italy and abroad. The lodge was linked with many political and financial scandals and with right-wing terrorism, culminating in 1982 with the collapse of one of Italy's leading banks, Banco Ambrosiano, and the death (later deemed to be murder) of its President, Roberto Calvi. In April 1992 Carlo De Benedetti, formerly one of Italy's most prominent financiers, and Licio Gelli, the former head of P-2, were convicted (along with more than 30 other defendants) on charges relating to the Banco Ambrosiano scandal. (Six years later De Benedetti was cleared on appeal of the fraud charges, while Gelli's 12–year prison sentence was confirmed by the Supreme Court.)

In June 1981 Senator Giovanni Spadolini, leader of the PRI, formed a five-party coalition Government, thus becoming the first non-DC Prime Minister since 1946. Spadolini resigned in November 1982, following a dispute over economic policy. Amintore Fanfani, a former DC Prime Minister, formed a new, four-party coalition in December. This administration lasted until the PSI withdrew its support in April 1983. A general election was held in June, at which the DC lost considerable support, winning only 32.9% of the votes for the Camera dei Deputati. The PSI increased its share of the votes to 11.4%, and its leader, Bettino Craxi, was subsequently appointed Italy's first socialist Prime Minister, at the head of a five-party coalition. This Government lost a vote of confidence in the Camera dei Deputati in June 1986, thus bringing to an end Italy's longest administration (1,060 days) since the Second World War. Craxi resigned, and President Francesco Cossiga (who had succeeded Alessandro Pertini as head of state in July 1985) nominated the former DC Prime Minister, Giulio Andreotti, to attempt to form a new government. However, the refusal of other parties to support Andreotti led to Craxi's return to power in July, on condition that he transfer the premiership to a DC member in March 1987. Craxi accordingly submitted his resignation, and that of his Government, at that time. After several unsuccessful attempts to form a coalition, a general election was held in June, at which the DC obtained 34.3% of the votes cast and the PSI increased its share to 14.3%. With 26.6% of the votes, the PCI suffered its worst post-war electoral result, and lost 21 seats in the Camera dei Deputati. Giovanni Goria, a DC member and the former Minister of the Treasury, became Prime Minister of a five-party coalition Government. By the end of the year, however, the Government had lost considerable support. Goria offered his resignation in November (following the withdrawal of the PLI from the coalition) and again in February 1988, but it was rejected both times by President Cossiga; Goria finally resigned in March. Ciriaco De Mita, the Secretary-General of the DC, formed a coalition with the same five parties that had served in Goria's administration. In May the Government's decision to grant a measure of autonomy to the Alto Adige region (Südtirol), on the north-eastern border with Austria, prompted a series of bombings, perpetrated by German-speaking extremists in the region.

Severe criticism by Craxi of De Mita's premiership led to the collapse of the coalition Government in May 1989. In June President Cossiga nominated De Mita to form a new government, but he was unsuccessful and it was not until late July that the coalition partners of the outgoing Government agreed to form a new administration, with Andreotti as Prime Minister. De Mita resigned from the presidency of the DC in February 1990, following an internal party dispute. His supporters, who together constituted a left-wing alliance within the DC, also withdrew from party posts, but pledged their continued support for the Government. Andreotti resigned the premiership in March 1991, accused by the PSI of failing to implement effectively policies on key issues. President Cossiga none the less nominated Andreotti to form a new government (Italy's 50th since the Second World War). The new Government comprised the same coalition partners as the outgoing administration, other than the PRI (whose members had rejected the portfolios they had been allocated).

From late 1989, meanwhile, the PCI, which had suffered a recent series of electoral reverses, began a process of transforming itself from a communist into a mass social democratic party. In early 1991 the party was renamed the Partito Democratico della Sinistra (PDS—Democratic Party of the Left). A minority of members of the former PCI refused to join the PDS, and in May they formed the Rifondazione Comunista (RC—Reconstructed Communism).

In September 1991, apparently in response to widespread nationalist fervour in parts of Eastern Europe, German-speaking separatists from the Alto Adige region made demands for greater autonomy from Italy. In the same month the Union Valdôtaine, the nationalist party governing the Aosta Valley (on the borders of France and Switzerland), announced that it was planning a referendum on secession. In January 1992 the Italian Government, in an attempt to end a long-standing dispute with Austria over the Alto Adige area, agreed to grant further autonomy to the region. Demands for greater autonomy were also made in Sardinia, following a resurgence of activism by militant separatists there.

In February 1992 President Cossiga dissolved the legislature and announced that a general election would take place on 5 April. The election campaign was marred by the murder of Salvatore Lima, an associate of Andreotti (see below). At the election, support for the DC was reduced to less than 30% of votes cast. The PDS won 16.1% of votes cast for the Camera dei Deputati, while the PSI received 13.6%. The Lega Nord (Northern League), an increasingly vocal grouping of regionalist parties which denounced the 'southern hegemony' of the central Government, led by Umberto Bossi, performed well in northern Italy, as did a new anti-Mafia political party, La Rete per il Partito Democratico (Democratic Network Party), in the south. Andreotti announced his resignation following the election, as did Cossiga (whose mandate was not due to expire until July). In May Cossiga was succeeded by Oscar Luigi Scalfaro, the newly elected President of the Camera dei Deputati. In the following month Giuliano Amato, of the PSI, was appointed Prime Minister. The new Council of Ministers comprised mainly members of the PSI and DC, with the remaining portfolios being allocated to the PSDI, PLI and non-party politicians.

A corruption scandal uncovered in Milan in 1992 assumed wider implications in subsequent months. It was alleged that politicians (mainly of the PSI and DC) and government officials had accepted bribes in exchange for the awarding of large public contracts. Among those accused of corruption was senior PSI official Gianni De Michelis, a former Minister of Foreign Affairs. The Amato Government's credibility was seriously undermined in February 1993 when the Minister of Justice, Claudio Martelli

of the PSI, was obliged to resign, after being placed under formal investigation for alleged complicity in the 1982 collapse of Banco Ambrosiano. Shortly afterwards Craxi resigned as Secretary-General of the PSI, although he continued to deny accusations of fraud. (He was replaced by Giorgio Benvenuto, formerly General Secretary of the Unione Italiana del Lavoro trade union and Director-General of the Ministry of Finance; Benvenuto in turn resigned in May, after the party rejected his proposals for reform, and was replaced by Ottaviano del Turco.) The Prime Minister's difficulties were compounded by the resignation of four senior ministers in February and March 1993. Also in March, five DC politicians, including Andreotti, were placed under investigation over their alleged links with the Mafia. The Government's position became increasingly untenable, but President Scalfaro prevailed upon Amato to remain in office until impending referendums on constitutional reform had taken place.

Nation-wide referendums proceeded in April 1993 on a number of proposed changes to the Constitution, including an amendment providing for the election by majority vote of 75% of the 315 elective seats in the upper legislative chamber, the Senato (Senate—the remainder would be elected under a system of proportional representation); the end of state funding of political parties; and the establishment of an environmental regulator. These amendments, intended to prevent electoral malpractice and, in particular, interference by organized crime, were overwhelmingly approved. (In August Parliament approved a similar system for elections to the Camera dei Deputati.)

Amato resigned as Prime Minister shortly after the referendums, and Carlo Azeglio Ciampi was subsequently invited by President Scalfaro to form a new government. Ciampi, hitherto Governor of the Bank of Italy, was the first non-parliamentarian to be appointed to the premiership. His proposed coalition, chosen without consultation with party leaders, comprised the four parties of the outgoing administration, but also included the PDS, the PRI and the Federazione dei Verdi (Green Party). The PDS and the Federazione dei Verdi immediately withdrew their ministers from the coalition, in protest at the new administration's refusal to revoke Craxi's parliamentary immunity from prosecution, although both continued to support Ciampi's Government. In May 1993 the Camera dei Deputati voted overwhelmingly to abolish parliamentary immunity in cases of corruption and serious crime; while the Senato approved the removal of Andreotti's parliamentary immunity, to allow investigations into his alleged association with the Mafia, although his arrest remained prohibited. In May the PLI elected Raffaele Costa, the Minister of Transport, to succeed Renato Altissimo as party Secretary-General, following Altissimo's arrest on corruption charges in March. Meanwhile, investigations began in April into the activities of former DC Prime Minister Arnaldo Forlani. In May corruption investigations extended to encompass politicians of the PDS and PRI, as arrests of leading political and business figures multiplied. In August the Camera dei Deputati voted to allow Craxi to be investigated by magistrates on four charges of corruption. In the following month Diego Curto, head of Milan's commercial court, became the first member of the judiciary to be investigated in connection with the corruption scandals. At the end of the month Andreotti was charged with having provided the Sicilian Mafia (Cosa Nostra) with political protection in exchange for votes in Sicily, and with complicity in the murder of an investigative journalist who had allegedly discovered evidence linking Andreotti with the Mafia. (He was acquitted of both charges in late 1999; however, in November 2002 his acquittal was overturned by an appeals court—see below.) In November 1993 Senator Giuseppe Leoni, a founding member of the Lega Nord, resigned after a judicial inquiry was initiated into the illegal funding of his electoral campaign.

Ciampi resigned in January 1994, in response to parliamentary divisions over the timing of a general election. Scalfaro dissolved the legislature, but requested that Ciampi remain in office until the forthcoming elections in March. In late January Silvio Berlusconi, the principal shareholder in and former manager of the media-based Fininvest, Italy's third largest private business group, announced the formation of a right-wing organization, Forza Italia (Come on, Italy!), to contest the elections. The liberal wing of the DC, whose mainstream was now discredited by corruption scandals, relaunched itself as the centrist Partito Popolare Italiano (PPI—Italian People's Party). In subsequent weeks, parties of the left, right and centre sought to form alliances capable of securing a majority in the Camera dei

Deputati; seven parties—including the PDS, RC, the Federazione dei Verdi and La Rete—formed I Progressisti (the Progressives); the Polo per le Libertà e del Buon Governo (hereafter referred to as the Polo per le Libertà—known in English as the Freedom Alliance), was formed by the Lega Nord, Forza Italia and the Alleanza Nazionale (AN—National Alliance, a new party led by Gianfranco Fini and incorporating members of the neo-fascist Movimento Sociale Italiano-Destra Nazionale—MSI-DN—Italian Social Movement-National Right), under the leadership of Berlusconi; the centre-right Patto per l'Italia (Pact for Italy), comprised Mario Segni's Patto Segni and the PPI. The election campaign intensified against a background of judicial investigations and mutual accusations of media bias and malpractice, while Berlusconi's popularity increased markedly—despite the arrest of a number of senior Fininvest executives on suspicion of financial malpractice. The Polo per le Libertà alliance won an outright majority in the Camera dei Deputati, obtaining 366 of the 630 seats, and was only three seats short of an outright majority in the elections to the Senato, winning 156 of the 315 seats. The Progressisti took 213 seats in the Camera dei Deputati and 122 seats in the Senato, while the Patto per l'Italia won only 46 and 31 seats respectively. In spite of the success of the right-wing alliance, major differences divided its constituent parties. Berlusconi selected his own candidates for the usually non-partisan posts of President of the Camera dei Deputati and President of the Senato, using the threat of calling new elections to ensure that these were elected in the second round of voting. In late April Berlusconi was invited by President Scalfaro to form a government. The new Council of Ministers, announced in May, included five members of the AN, including Roberto Maroni of the Lega Nord as Minister of the Interior and two members of the neo-fascist MSI-DN. Forza Italia won 30.6% of the votes at elections to the European Parliament held in June. The PDS won only 19.1% of the votes, and its leader, Achille Occhetto, resigned and was replaced by Massimo D'Alema in July.

In July 1994 Bettino Craxi and the former Deputy Prime Minister and Minister of Justice, Claudio Martelli, were both sentenced (Craxi to eight-and-a-half years' imprisonment) for fraudulent bankruptcy in relation to the collapse of Banco Ambrosiano in 1982. Craxi, who claimed to be too ill to return for trial from his residence in Tunisia, was sentenced *in absentia*. (In July 1995 two international warrants were issued for his arrest, and when he failed to return to Italy he was formally declared a fugitive from justice.) Also in July 1994 the arrest of two Fininvest employees on charges of bribing the finance police (Guardi di Finanza), together with ongoing controversy regarding the appropriateness of the extent of the Prime Minister's media holdings, fuelled concern about Berlusconi's continued involvement in Fininvest. In November Berlusconi was placed under investigation for bribery. In the following month Antonio Di Pietro, the most high-profile magistrate in Milan and one of the most popular public figures in Italy, resigned in protest at increasing government interference in the work of the Milanese judiciary. The failure of the Prime Minister to resolve his conflict of business and political interests, together with the growing tension between the Government and the judiciary, undermined the integrity of the Government and precipitated the disintegration of the coalition. Berlusconi resigned in order to avoid probable defeat in three votes of 'no confidence' proposed by the Lega Nord and opposition parties. In January 1995 Lamberto Dini, the Minister of the Treasury and a former Director-General of the Bank of Italy, was invited to form an interim government. Dini appointed a Council of Ministers comprised of technocrats, and pledged to hold elections once he had implemented a programme to improve public finances, reform the state pension system, introduce new regional electoral laws, and establish controls on media ownership and its use during electoral campaigns. In March it was formally announced that Berlusconi was to be subject to further investigation on charges of financial irregularities. Moreover, his Polo per le Libertà was defeated by the centre-left parties in nine of the 15 regional elections held in April, despite obtaining 40.7% of the votes cast (compared with 40.5% won by parties of the centre-left).

New political alliances emerged during 1995 in preparation for legislative elections. In January the MSI-DN was officially disbanded and most of its members were absorbed in the AN. The AN leader, Gianfranco Fini, distanced the party from its neo-fascist past, denouncing racism and anti-Semitism, in an attempt to widen support. The PSI had been dissolved in No-vember 1994 and reformed as the Socialisti Italiani (Italian Socialists), under the leadership of Enrico Bosselli. Divisions within the Lega Nord led to the formation of a breakaway group in February 1995 under the leadership of Roberto Maroni, who was in favour of an alliance with Berlusconi. In the same month Romano Prodi, a respected business executive, offered to lead the centre-left parties to challenge Berlusconi in the forthcoming elections. In March the PPI rejected a proposed alliance with Berlusconi, deposing its leader, Rocco Buttiglione, in favour of Gerardo Bianco; Buttiglione subsequently founded a new centre-right party, the Cristiani Democratici Uniti (CDU—United Christian Democrats). In July the PDS formally endorsed Prodi as leader of the centre-left electoral alliance, subsequently named L'Ulivo (The Olive Tree).

In June 1995 12 referendums were held on issues including media ownership, trade union and electoral reform, retailing and crime. Significantly, the majority of the voters who participated in the referendums on media ownership approved the retention of laws permitting an individual to own more than one commercial television channel and preserving the existing monopoly on television advertising. Furthermore, the majority of voters supported the partial privatization of the state-owned RAI broadcasting company, control of which had become increasingly contentious since the resignation of its directorate in mid-1994 in protest at increased government control over appointments. Another important outcome was the endorsement of proposed restrictions on trade unions' powers of representation, effectively reducing the dominance of the three largest trade union federations.

In October 1995 the Minister of Justice, Filippo Mancuso, refused to resign from the Council of Ministers despite a successful motion of 'no confidence' in him, which had been prompted by his allegedly ruthless vendetta against anti-corruption magistrates in Milan. Since Dini was constitutionally unable to remove a minister from office without submitting the Government's resignation, Scalfaro intervened and revoked Mancuso's mandate, appointing Dini as interim Minister of Justice. Dini's administration remained precarious, however, and shortly afterwards Berlusconi allied himself with Mancuso and proposed a motion of 'no confidence' in the Government, claiming the support of the RC. The Government narrowly defeated the motion, after having forged an agreement whereby RC deputies abstained from the vote on condition that Dini resign as Prime Minister by the end of the year. Dini's resignation, submitted in late December, was, however, rejected by President Scalfaro, who asked the Prime Minister to remain in office pending a parliamentary debate to resolve the political crisis and determine the future of the Government. In January 1996 the AN tabled a resolution demanding Dini's resignation, which it was expected to win with the support of parties of the extreme left. Scalfaro was thus obliged to accept Dini's resignation, which he submitted prior to the vote. In February, following an unsuccessful attempt by Antonio Maccanico, a former Chairman of Italy's powerful merchant bank Mediobanca, to form a government, Scalfaro dissolved Parliament and asked Dini to remain as interim Prime Minister until a general election in April. In October 1995, meanwhile, all 22 defendants were convicted in a trial concerning illegal funding of political parties. Among those convicted were former Prime Ministers Craxi, who was sentenced *in absentia* to four years' imprisonment, and Forlani, sentenced to 28 months' custody; Umberto Bossi of the Lega Nord received a suspended sentence.

At the legislative elections, held in April 1996, Romano Prodi's L'Ulivo alliance (dominated by the PDS, but also including the PPI and Dini's newly formed, centrist Rinnovamento Italiano, RI—Italian Renewal) narrowly defeated the Polo per le Libertà, securing 284 of the 630 seats in the Camera dei Deputati and 157 of the 315 elective seats in the Senato; the Polo per le Libertà won 246 seats in the Camera dei Deputati and 116 seats in the Senato. Both the Lega Nord and the RC, neither of which had allied with any grouping, increased their parliamentary representation, respectively obtaining 59 and 35 seats in the Camera dei Deputati and 27 and 10 seats in the Senato. President Scalfaro invited Prodi to form a government; Prodi announced his intention to introduce educational and constitutional reforms, reduce unemployment, address the contentious issue of media ownership and persevere with a policy of economic austerity. Massimo D'Alema, the influential General Secretary of the PDS, elected not to serve in the new Council of Ministers; however, his second-in-command, Walter Veltroni, was appointed Deputy Prime Minister. Prodi's Government was endorsed by votes of confidence in the Camera dei Deputati and in the Senato in May. Although the RC agreed to support the Government in the vote of confidence in the Camera dei Deputati, its Secretary-General, Fausto Bertinotti, emphasized that his party could express only 'conditional confidence' in the new administration, and on several occasions in subsequent months the Government was obliged to accede to RC demands in return for that party providing crucial parliamentary support.

In May 1996 Umberto Bossi of the Lega Nord announced the formation of an 11-member 'Government of the Independent Republic of Padania' (a territory comprising the regions of Liguria, Emilia-Romagna, Lombardy, Piedmont and the Veneto). The concept of the creation of a 'Republic of Padania' was generally regarded with scepticism, although many inhabitants of the northern regions were in favour of greater local autonomy. The Lega Nord fared relatively poorly in key northern cities at local elections in June, however, and in September Bossi's credibility was damaged further by the expulsion from the party of Irene Pivetti (a highly-regarded Lega Nord member and former President of the Camera dei Deputati) for publicly supporting a less extreme policy of local autonomy. In addition, a well-publicized rally in Venice to mark the formal independence of 'Padania' was attended by only 50,000 people, compared with some 150,000 people who participated in an anti-secession demonstration held concurrently in Milan. Shortly afterwards Bossi was placed under investigation, and his offices were searched for anti-constitutional material.

Meanwhile, former magistrate Antonio Di Pietro was alleged to have abused his position within the judiciary to extort favours and to have attempted to discredit Berlusconi to further his own political ambitions. In March 1996, after a court in Brescia dismissed charges against Di Pietro, Berlusconi's brother, Paolo, and Cesare Previti, a former Minister of Defence and a lawyer for Fininvest, were placed under investigation for allegedly attempting to discredit him. Although Di Pietro had been appointed Minister of Public Works in May, by November he had resigned from the post, in protest at renewed investigations into his affairs. In December the Court of Review ruled that raids on Di Pietro's home and offices by the finance police (suspected of seeking vengeance on Di Pietro for his earlier investigations into their affairs) were 'unjustified and illegitimate'. Paolo Berlusconi and Cesare Previti were acquitted in January 1997. In November 1996 Romano Prodi was himself placed under investigation for alleged abuse of office while head of the state holding company Istituto per la Ricostruzione Industriale (Iri) during 1993–94; the Prime Minister dismissed the allegations and pledged to co-operate fully with the inquiry.

In July 1996 the Government had presented draft legislation on media reform that, apparently adopting a lenient interpretation of a ruling on the issue by the Constitutional Court, would allow Berlusconi's Mediaset organization to convert one of its three television channels to cable or satellite (or else reduce its share of the terrestrial audience) rather than to divest it. The draft legislation also envisaged the establishment of a telecommunications and media regulator, while the RAI broadcasting group would be obliged to convert one of its channels to a regional network. However, the reforms failed to receive parliamentary approval prior to the late August deadline set by the Constitutional Court, and, in the absence of new legislation, the Court ruled that its recommendation to reduce the proportion of television companies held by any one group from 25% to 20% would take effect. It consequently announced that it would block the transmission of one of Mediaset's channels as of 22 December. In early December Massimo D'Alema, who had increasingly been acknowledged as the principal strategist in the Government, secured the postponement of the Constitutional Court's decision to enforce its broadcasting ruling and, in addition, indicated that the Government might support the introduction of judicial reforms that could result in extensive plea-bargaining in corruption cases—thereby successfully exploiting Berlusconi's vulnerability with regard to both media legislation and to judicial investigations into his affairs (see below). In return, Berlusconi agreed to co-operate with the Government and support the rapid conversion of numerous decrees into law. (In September the Constitutional Court had ruled that the widespread practice of renewing decrees without substantially altering their content was illegal; it declared that decrees issued by the Prodi administration, as well as those inherited from previous Governments, would no longer be renewable.) In January 1997 the co-operation of the Polo per le Libertà enabled the Senato to approve the creation of a 70-

member bicameral commission on constitutional reform, with D'Alema as its elected President. In June the commission presented its recommendations, which included a directly-elected President, a reduction in the size of the Camera dei Deputati and the Senato, and greater regional financial autonomy. Referendum procedures were also to be amended following the invalidation of several referendums due to low participation.

In October 1997 the RC announced that it would oppose the 1998 budget, thus leaving the Government without a legislative majority. Following the failure of negotiations in which the Secretary-General of the RC, Fausto Bertinotti, demanded policy changes in exchange for continued support, Prodi offered his resignation to Scalfaro. He remained as caretaker Prime Minister, and a one-year political pact was subsequently announced that included significant concessions from Bertinotti, who agreed to the adoption of measures to secure qualification for European economic and monetary union (EMU—see Economic Affairs), while Prodi was obliged to compromise on pension reform. Scalfaro thereupon formally rejected Prodi's resignation, and the Prime Minister won a parliamentary vote of confidence.

In December 1997 Berlusconi and four associates were convicted on charges of false accounting with regard to the purchase of a film group in 1988; they were ordered to pay fines, but 16-month prison sentences were quashed. Later in December 1997 Berlusconi and Cesare Previti were ordered to stand trial on charges relating to allegations that they had accumulated funds with the intention of bribing judges. In two separate trials in July 1998 Berlusconi was convicted of bribing tax inspectors involved in Fininvest audits and of making illicit payments, via Fininvest, to Craxi and the PSI in 1991. The prescribed custodial sentences (of 33 months and 28 months, respectively) were not, however, to be enforced as the former Prime Minister (who was awaiting trial on several further charges) was protected by parliamentary immunity. In the same month warrants were issued for the arrest of 113 people on corruption charges, among them local administration officials and 20 members of the finance police. Further allegations against Berlusconi were uncovered in August when a witness in an unrelated corruption trial accused him of money-laundering on behalf of the Mafia; Berlusconi strenuously denied the charge. In November legislation, adopted in 1997, that effectively favoured defendants in Mafia trials by disallowing testimony given before the start of legal proceedings was overturned.

In May 1997 the Lega Nord organized a referendum to determine the level of popular support for 'Padania'. Despite media reports that participation levels had been low, Umberto Bossi claimed that 5m. people had voted, of whom 99% supported an independent 'Republic of Padania'. In local elections in April the Lega Nord had suffered a sharp decline in support, losing control of Gorizia, Pavia and Mantua. In October elections to a 200-seat constituent assembly in the 'Republic of Padania', organized by the Lega Nord, were contested by 63 parties. In January 1998 Bossi received a one-year suspended prison sentence for inciting criminal acts during a Lega Nord meeting in 1995; in July 1998 he received a second sentence, of seven months, for resistance to authority and offensive behaviour.

In June 1998 the Camera dei Deputati approved legislation endorsing the admission to the North Atlantic Treaty Organization (NATO, see p. 271) of Hungary, Poland and the Czech Republic. The vote, which had become an issue of confidence in the Prodi Government as the RC (on which the coalition relied in parliamentary votes) opposed the eastward expansion of the alliance and thus withdrew its support, was carried with the support of the new, centrist Unione Democratica per la Repubblica (UDR—Democratic Union for the Republic, led by former President Francesco Cossiga) and with the abstention of Forza Italia. Inter-party talks on the proposed constitutional reforms collapsed earlier that month without any agreement, the principal area of contention being the issue of presidential powers. Berlusconi, in particular, opposed any alteration of the presidential mandate and demanded greater reform of the judiciary, including a curb on the power of the magistrates. There was a further political crisis in October, when the RC again withdrew its support for the Government on the issue of the 1999 budget. The Government lost an ensuing confidence motion by one vote, and Prodi was forced to resign. Following an unsuccessful attempt by Prodi to form a new government, the leader of the Democratici di Sinistra (DS, as the PDS had been renamed), Massimo D'Alema, was asked to assume the premiership. D'Alema announced the formation of a coalition Government, composed of members of the DS, the Federazione dei Verdi, the Partito dei Comunisti Italiani (PdCI), the UDR, the PPI, the Socialisti Democratici Italiani (SDI—Italian Democratic Socialists) and RI.

In May 1999 former Prime Minister Carlo Azeglio Ciampi was elected to succeed Scalfaro as President of the Republic. Giuliano Amato, latterly Minister of Institutional Reforms, succeeded Ciampi as Minister of the Treasury and of the Budget. In that month, Massimo D'Antona, an adviser to the Minister of Employment and Social Welfare, Antonio Bassolino, was shot dead. Responsibility was claimed by the Brigate Rosse (the terrorist grouping had been believed inactive since the late 1980s), which cited D'Antona's involvement in formulating a series of liberalizing labour reforms, together with Italy's involvement in the NATO action in Kosovo (see below). (In May 2000 a trade union employee, Alessandro Geri, was arrested and subsequently charged with complicity in D'Antona's murder; his case was dismissed, however, in December 2002.) In June 1999 Bassolino resigned in order to devote himself to his role as Mayor of Naples. Municipal and provincial elections in June resulted in a number of defeats for the governing coalition, most notably in the leftist stronghold of Bologna, where a right-wing candidate was elected Mayor for the first time since 1945; elections to the European Parliament earlier in the month also showed increased support for right-wing parties.

Meanwhile, in March 1999 Berlusconi was acquitted on charges of tax fraud; his 1998 conviction for making illicit payments to Craxi and the PSI was overturned in October 1999. In the following month, however, Berlusconi was ordered to stand trial in two cases involving charges of bribery and false accounting; in one of the cases former Minister of Defence Cesare Previti was also to stand trial on a charge of perverting the course of justice. Meanwhile, in June a new trial had been ordered against Craxi on charges of illegal party financing, and in November a Milan court ruled that Craxi could return to Italy from exile in Tunisia for medical treatment and serve his sentence under house arrest rather than in prison. However, Craxi maintained that he would not return to Italy unless he received an official pardon, and he died in exile in January 2000.

Prime Minister D'Alema tendered his resignation in December 1999, following several months of tension within the governing coalition which had culminated in the withdrawal of support by an alliance of parties including the SDI and the UDR. D'Alema was asked by Ciampi to form a new government, and forged a new coalition of parties of the left and centre, including I Democratici per l'Ulivo (The Democrats for the Olive Tree), founded earlier in the year by Romano Prodi, and the Unione Democratici per l'Europa (UDEUR—Union of Democrats for Europe). At regional elections held in April 2000, however, the new centre-left coalition was defeated by a centre-right alliance composed of Berlusconi's Forza Italia and Bossi's Lega Nord: the centre-right won 51% of the vote and eight regions, compared with 45% of the votes and seven regions for the centre-left. In an attempt to avert a general election, which would follow his predicted defeat in a parliamentary confidence motion, D'Alema resigned. The Minister of Treasury and the Budget, former Prime Minister Giuliano Amato, was appointed in his place, and a new, eight-party centre-left Government was sworn in in late April. A low turn-out (32%) at seven referendums in May on measures including the abolition of proportional representation in legislative elections rendered them invalid and was interpreted by opposition parties as reflecting a lack of support for the new Government; demands were made by Berlusconi for Amato to stand down.

Also in May 2000, at a first appeal, Berlusconi was acquitted of one charge of bribing tax inspectors involved in Fininvest audits on which he had been convicted in 1998; the appeals court also invoked the statute of limitations (on the grounds that too much time had elapsed since the perpetration of the crimes) to overturn his convictions on three similar counts. In June 2000 Berlusconi was further acquitted at a pre-trial hearing of bribery charges relating to his acquisition of the Mondadori publishing company in 1991.

In September 2000 Prime Minister Amato announced that he would stand down as leader of the centre-left alliance in advance of the next parliamentary elections, scheduled to take place in May 2001, in favour of the Mayor of Rome, Francesco Rutelli of I Democratici per l'Ulivo. Amato considered that Rutelli's growing popularity among the Italian electorate would increase the centre-left coalition's chances of defeating Berlusconi's centre-right alliance at the elections. Rutelli was endorsed as

the centre-left's official candidate for Prime Minister in October, and he stood down as Mayor of Rome in early January 2001 to concentrate on the election campaign. Also in September 2000 Lombardy's Regional Council announced that it was to hold a referendum, in tandem with the parliamentary elections, on the possible transfer of certain powers (including health, education, trade, and law and order) from the national capital, Rome, to the regional capital, Milan. The move, though supported by the Lega Nord and Forza Italia, was strongly condemned by Amato and by the AN. In October Piedmont's administration in turn announced its intention to hold a referendum on possible devolution, while the President of the Veneto Regional Council, Giancarlo Galan, a member of Forza Italia, called for a referendum to be held on proposals that the region be granted sovereignty over its 'foreign policy', immigration laws, tax collection, education and health. However, the Government asserted in November that referendums could be declared only by central Government.

Berlusconi's Casa delle Libertà (House of Freedoms) alliance won a decisive victory over the L'Ulivo alliance at the general election, held on 13 May 2001, securing majorities in both legislative chambers. The Casa delle Libertà won 177 seats in the Senato (compared with the 128 held by L'Ulivo), and 368 in the Camera dei Deputati (compared with 242 for L'Ulivo). In the elections to the lower house the Casa delle Libertà took 49.4% of the total votes cast for the seats allocated by proportional representation. Berlusconi's Forza Italia won the largest share of the vote by a single party, with 29.4%; within L'Ulivo, the DS obtained 16.6% of votes cast, thus remaining the second largest party in Parliament, and Rutelli's Margherita alliance (including I Democratici per l'Ulivo, the PPI, UDEUR and RI) 14.5%. The AN secured 12.0% of the vote, but Bossi's Lega Nord did not perform as well as expected, winning just 3.9% of votes cast, compared with 10.1% in the 1996 legislative elections. Berlusconi was appointed Prime Minister by President Ciampi, and his coalition Government—composed of Forza Italia, the AN, Lega Nord, the CDU, the Centro Cristiano Democratico (Christian Democratic Centre—CCD) and independents, was named on 10 June. The AN leader, Gianfranco Fini, became Deputy Prime Minister. The appointment of Bossi as Minister without Portfolio, with responsibility for Reforms and Devolution, and of two other reputedly extremist Lega Nord members (Roberto Castelli as Minister of Justice and Roberto Maroni as Minister of Labour and Welfare) was condemned by opposition parties on the grounds that this gave the Lega Nord responsibility for the sensitive issue of immigration. Berlusconi's new Government was endorsed in confidence votes in both chambers of Parliament later in June. Meanwhile, despite its defeat in the general election, at mayoral elections in late May L'Ulivo retained control of the cities of Rome, Naples and Turin. Former Deputy Prime Minister Walter Veltroni was elected Mayor of Rome.

The issue of apparent conflict of interest between Berlusconi's political role and business interests was heightened by the general election. Berlusconi's new position as Prime Minister placed him in effective control of the state broadcasting company, RAI, and this, coupled with his ownership of the media company Fininvest (which operates Italy's principal private television concern, Mediaset), potentially gave him control over the majority of the Italian television network. Prior to the May 2001 election Berlusconi had apparently contradicted earlier indications that, should he become premier, he would relinquish a significant proportion of his media interests—stating that he had no intention of selling any part of Fininvest but that he would introduce legislation addressing conflict of interest. In late April the leader of the small Partito Radicale, Emma Bonino, had undertaken a six-day hunger strike in protest at what she claimed was the broadcast media's disregard of smaller political parties in the election campaign.

A parliamentary inquiry into alleged police brutality was ordered by the Government in late July 2001 after serious rioting in Genoa earlier that month around the summit meeting of the Group of Eight (G-8) industrialized nations. One person was shot dead by a police-officer during clashes between anti-capitalist protesters and security forces, and an estimated 300 (among them some 70 members of the security forces) were injured. Some 93 people were arrested, many of whom were reportedly beaten and severely injured, following a police raid on the temporary headquarters of the Genoa Social Forum, the non-violent organization that had organized the protests. Despite assertions by the security forces that their actions had been justified and appropriate, all but one of those arrested in the raid were released without charge. Italy's chief of police later admitted that he believed excessive violence had been used during the riots, and three senior police commanders were subsequently dismissed from their posts by the Minister of Internal Affairs, Claudio Scajola. In early August Scajola himself survived a motion of 'no confidence' in respect of the security forces' handling of the G-8 riots. The official report into the G-8 riots, published in September, effectively absolved the security forces of any wrongdoing, and asserted that the protester's death and the widespread violence and material damage arising from the incidents in Genoa had not prevented the G-8 summit's success.

In early August 2001 a bomb was detonated at a court building in Venice, prior to a visit later that day by Berlusconi and the Minister of Infrastructure and Transport, Pietro Lunardi. Later that month another bomb explosion occurred at the offices of the Lega Nord near Padua. Responsibility for the bombings was claimed by a number of extremist groups, including one purporting to be associated with the Brigate Rosse. Also in that month legislation to decriminalize fraud associated with false accounting was approved by the Camera dei Deputati despite opposition claims that Berlusconi, who faced a number of ongoing investigations into his accounting practices, was personally motivated. Furthermore, in October legislation was adopted by the Senato which altered regulations governing the use of evidence in criminal cases. Opposition parties protested that Berlusconi would directly benefit from the new regulations, which were likely to invalidate legal proceedings against himself and former Minister of Defence Cesare Previti in respect of allegations that they had bribed judges in return for a favourable court judgment over the sale of a state-owned food company, SME Meridionale. Prior to the trial's commencement, in January 2002, an attempt by the Minister of Justice, Roberto Castelli, to remove one of the three judges on the case caused public and judicial consternation. Castelli asserted that he had been trying to honour a transfer request by the judge; however, the judge was reinstated, thereby allowing the trial to proceed. In October 2001 Italy's Supreme Court of Appeal overturned Berlusconi's 1998 conviction on charges of bribing tax inspectors in exchange for favourable audits of Fininvest.

At a referendum held in early October 2001 a proposal to devolve certain powers to Regional Councils was overwhelmingly approved by participants, although the electoral turn-out was only 34%; the constitutional amendment would grant greater legislative powers to the regions, increasing local control over areas including taxation, education, health and agriculture, while the central Government would remain in charge of the national police forces, defence, treasury and foreign policy.

Berlusconi's continued popularity was apparently confirmed in November 2001 when the Forza Italia candidate at Palermo's mayoral election won 56.1% of votes cast, compared with only 23.3% won by the candidate for L'Ulivo. However, the resignation of the Minister of Foreign Affairs, Renato Ruggiero, in early January 2002 exposed severe divisions within the Government over European policy. Ruggiero's resignation was prompted by comments made by three other ministers expressing their disapproval of the new European currency, the euro—notes and coins of which had come into circulation on 1 January. As an independent, Ruggiero failed to receive the support of Berlusconi, who stated that he himself was responsible for Italy's foreign policy; Berlusconi subsequently assumed the foreign affairs portfolio on an interim basis. Opposition members, heads of state of other countries of the European Union (EU, see p. 199) and the President of the European Commission, Romano Prodi, expressed their disappointment at Ruggiero's resignation. Berlusconi, meanwhile, reiterated Italy's commitment to full participation within the EU.

In February 2002 Berlusconi announced his intention to transfer to private ownership two of the three state-owned RAI television channels. The planned privatization was heavily criticized by opposition members as well as by the outgoing President of RAI, Roberto Zaccaria; the new President, Antonio Baldassare, was labelled as partisan by Rutelli of L'Ulivo, but claimed impartiality. At the end of April a 'conflict of interest' bill was passed in the Camera dei Deputati, following a 'walk-out' by all of the L'Ulivo deputies. The legislation prohibited a figure in public office from actively running a company, but did not forbid ownership, thus permitting Berlusconi's continued possession of Mediaset. (The bill was passed by the Senato in

July, eliciting a demand by President Ciampi for a law guaranteeing pluralism in the media.)

In mid-March 2002 Marco Biagi, an adviser to the Minister of Labour and Welfare, Roberto Maroni, was shot dead in Bologna. Responsibility for the assassination was claimed by a faction of the Brigate Rosse, which cited Biagi's key role in the drafting of controversial new labour legislation as the motive for the shooting. Nation-wide protests against the proposed legislation, which would ease employers' restrictions on the employment and dismissal of workers, led to a general strike, organized by Italy's three largest trade unions, in mid-April, despite an appeal by the Government that the protest be abandoned in the wake of the murder. A Patto per l'Italia (Pact for Italy), was signed on 5 July between the Government and two major trade unions, the Confederazione Italiana Sindacati Lavoratori (CISL) and the Unione Italiana del Lavoro (UIL), which agreed to increase the flexibility of the labour market while allowing for the reintroduction of concertation. The accord, however, caused a split in the trade union movement (and consequently the affiliations of the political left), through the exclusion of the Confederazione Generale Italiana del Lavoro (CGIL), Italy's largest trade union. Claudio Scajola, the Minister of Internal Affairs, who had faced criticism for the lack of protection given to Biagi, resigned in early July amid pressure from the opposition following an ill-judged remark about the murder victim. Scajola was replaced by Giuseppe Pisanu, the erstwhile Minister without Portfolio with responsibility for the Implementation of the Government Programme. However, protests against the labour-market reform, led by the CGIL, continued.

Meanwhile, prior to local elections in mid-2002 the PPI, RI and I Democratici per l'Ulivo merged into a single electoral coalition within L'Ulivo, entitled Democrazia è Libertà—La Margherita (Democracy is Freedom—The Daisy Party), without UDEUR. The first round of local elections in May seemed to confirm the strength of the centre-right coalition, comprising Forza Italia, AN, Lega Nord and Marco Follini's Unione Democraticocristiana e di Centro (UDC—Christian Democratic and Centrist Union). However, the second round in early June saw the coalition suffer surprise defeats in nine out of 11 major cities, including Piacenza and Verona (in which Berlusconi had personally campaigned), following a concerted effort by L'Ulivo, in alliance with Fausto Bertinotti's RC and Antonio Di Pietro's Italia dei Valori (Italy of Values). The defeats were widely viewed as a statement of general public uncertainty about Berlusconi's Government one year after its election. During July Berlusconi shocked commentators by announcing his interest in running for the presidency and resigning his post as Prime Minister, should the Constitution be altered to give the presidential mandate greater power along the lines of France; the revelation was soon followed by Berlusconi's announcement that he would continue as Minister of Foreign Affairs in the face of opposition within his coalition for his favoured candidate, Franco Frattini. In August Romano Prodi broached the possibility of an early return to politics in an attempt to reunite the centre-left before the general election in 2006.

Following the rejection of an appeal by Berlusconi in May 2002 to have his bribery trial (see above) moved from Milan, several bills proposing judicial reform provoked controversy in the legislature and the judiciary. Proposed reforms, including the nomination of magistrates by the Minister of Justice rather than by an independent body, precipitated a judges' strike in late June. A Trial Bill, which would allow a process to be rescheduled and relocated if there was 'legitimate suspicion' of prosecutorial bias on the part of the judge, aroused concern that Berlusconi would make use of the new legislation in a corruption trial involving himself and former Minister for Defence Cesare Previti, scheduled for September 2002, in order to delay the trial beyond the statute of limitations (he failed to have the trial relocated in November 2002). Nevertheless, the bill was passed by the Senate amid 'walk-outs' by the opposition at the beginning of August; members of the centre-right coalition were alleged to have voted electronically for absent colleagues, which elicited large-scale street protests against Berlusconi's judicial policies in September. The bill was subsequently passed by the Camera dei Deputanti in November, again amid widespread opposition protest.

Meanwhile, further concerns about Berlusconi's influence over the news media were engendered in August 2002 by the dismissal of an anti-Berlusconi television journalist at RAI, who had been subject to earlier accusations of bias by Berlusconi; this followed an attempt during May to pass legislation forcing four allegedly 'one-sided' television programmes off the air. Berlusconi's actions aroused anger from the opposition and from journalism organizations, who accused the Prime Minister of threatening freedom of speech and of acting with political motivation. (Berlusconi's problems were compounded in November with the resignation of three RAI directors in protest at government interference.) In March 2003 Lucia Annunziata became the first female President of RAI following the resignation of both Baldassare and his successor.

On 15 October 2002 a constitutional amendment was approved allowing Italy's long-exiled royal family to return to the country. Also in October, a second general strike, led by the CGIL, was staged in protest against the Government's budget proposals for 2003, which, it was estimated, could lead to 260,000 job losses. An earthquake in San Giuliano di Puglia on 31 October, with a final death toll of 30 people, including 27 school-children, was followed in November by a volcanic eruption of Mount Etna. These events stimulated wide-scale discussion of local accountability and the culture of corruption surrounding the construction industry; an official inquiry was instigated. During late November a Devolution Bill, which would allow regional control over education, the health service and the police, was put forward by Umberto Bossi of Lega Nord; although the opposition tabled 1,600 amendments in an effort to derail the bill, Berlusconi threatened a vote of confidence if the bill was not passed. Bossi created splits in the ruling coalition, however, when he attacked President Ciampi for seeking assurance that the bill would not threaten national unity. Bossi's determination to withdraw the Lega Nord from the coalition if the bill was blocked coincided with a similar threat from the UDC, which cited its lack of influence within the alliance. The Devolution Bill was subsequently passed in early December. In mid-November Franco Frattini was appointed Minister of Foreign Affairs, ending 10 months of interim control of that portfolio by Berlusconi. Later that month an appeals court in Palermo overturned the previous acquittal of Giulio Andreotti on charges of conspiracy to murder a journalist in 1979, and sentenced the former Prime Minister to 24 years' imprisonment; the sentence aroused widespread condemnation of the judicial system by politicians, including Berlusconi. A verdict was expected during 2003 on a separate charge of collusion.

In January 2003, after a further bid to relocate the his bribery trial was rejected by the Supreme Court, Berlusconi announced the possible reintroduction of immunity from prosecution for MPs (removed after the corruption scandal of 1992), which aroused opposition protest. He also confirmed that he would complete his mandate as Prime Minister even if found guilty in the trial, which was due to finish in late 2003. The immunity legislation was proposed in early May following the conviction of Cesare Previti on bribery charges in connection with the purchase of Mondadori; Previti was sentenced to 11 years' imprisonment.

Despite mass trials of Mafia suspects in the late 1980s, the Italian Government continued to experience problems in dealing with organized crime. In 1992 the murders of Salvatore Lima, a Sicilian politician and member of the European Parliament, Giovanni Falcone, a prominent anti-Mafia judge, and that of his colleague, Paolo Borsellino, provoked renewed public outrage, and later that year, following an increase in the powers of the police and the judiciary, hundreds of suspects were detained. In January 1993 the capture of Salvatore Riina, the alleged head of the Sicilian Mafia, was regarded as a significant success in the Government's campaign against organized crime. In 1993 the judiciary mounted a campaign to seize Mafia funds, and in the course of the year several suspects, alleged to be leading figures in the world of organized crime, were arrested. Among these were Paolo Benedetto, regarded as the leader of the Mafia in Catania, Giuseppe Pulvirenti, alleged to be another principal figure of the Mafia in Eastern Sicily, and Michele Zaza, the alleged head of the Camorra, based in Naples. A sudden increase in Mafia-related violence in Sicily during 1995 was largely attributed to attempts to intimidate potential informers. Numerous alleged mafiosi were arrested, including Leoluca Bagarella, the alleged head of the Sicilian Mafia. In November of that year Francesco Musotto, a senior politician in Palermo and an ally of Berlusconi, was arrested and charged with assisting high-ranking members of the Sicilian Mafia to evade capture over a four-year period. Following the arrests of a number of senior mafiosi in 1996, in March 1997 more than 70 alleged members of the Mafia were arrested in Sicily and later that month a further 70 suspected members of the Calabrian

Mafia were detained. In July troops were dispatched to Naples to assist the security forces, owing to violent territorial disputes between rival Mafia groups. In September 24 influential members of the Mafia, including Salvatore Riina, were sentenced to life imprisonment for their part in the murder of Giovanni Falcone. Several senior Mafia figures were arrested in 1998, including Vito Vitale, the alleged head of the Mafia in Trapani, Sicily, and Francesco Schiavone, the leader of the Camorra. During the year more than 100 people were arrested on suspicion of having links with the Mafia, and in March the Government voted unanimously to oust a junior minister following allegations that he had links with the Mafia. In July 18 people, including Salvatore Riina, were convicted of complicity in the murder of Salvatore Lima in 1992; this constituted Riina's 13th sentence of life imprisonment. In January 1999 D'Alema announced that the army was to return to Sicily to assist in operations against the Mafia, only six months after its withdrawal had been completed (troops had been installed following the murders of Paolo Borsellino and Giovanni Falcone in 1992); some 500 troops were to guard public buildings, thereby allowing police to concentrate on countering organized crime. In April 1999 an official of the treasury ministry was arrested on charges of external complicity with the Mafia; he was the first serving government member to be taken into preventive detention. Further arrests were made during 1999, and in December 17 Mafia members were sentenced to life imprisonment for the murder of Borsellino. In January 2000 Riina was sentenced to life imprisonment for, amongst other charges, the bombing of the Uffizi Gallery in Florence in May 1993 in which six people were killed. Emergency measures were decreed in November 2000 in an attempt to prevent the early release from prison of those accused of Mafia-related crimes. The laws followed the discharge, on technical grounds, of 10 detainees accused of involvement in murders attributed to the Mafia. Magistrates were granted greater powers in determining the length of preventive detention for suspects and a ban on plea-bargaining was introduced. In February 2001 Vincenzo Virga, the financial head of the Sicilian Mafia, who had been in hiding since 1994, was arrested. Benedetto Spera, reputedly the closest colleague of the head of the Sicilian Mafia, Bernardo Provenzano, had also been arrested at the end of January; Spera had been convicted *in absentia* for his role in the 1992 murders of Giovanni Falcone and Paolo Borsellino. In April 2001 Riina, along with six others, was sentenced to 30 years' imprisonment for the murder, in 1979, of a journalist, Mario Francese. Organized crime continued to be problematic during Berlusconi's second tenure of the premiership. In July 2002 a member of Forza Italia was arrested at a Cosa Nostra summit meeting in Sicily. Meanwhile, although a murder charge was dropped against Berlusconi in May, the trial of his close friend, and one of the founders of Forza Italia, Marcello dell'Utri, on charges of Mafia collusion continued in Palermo throughout 2002. Berlusconi, who was expected to be questioned over possible connections between Fininvest and the Mafia, pleaded his right to silence in July, cancelled two meetings with judges in September and October, and again pleaded silence in November. Bernardo Provenzano's closest accomplice, Antonino Giuffre, was arrested in April 2002 near Palermo; his testimony was used in the trials of Andreotti (see above) and dell'Utri. In December Giuffre directly implicated Berlusconi in the bribing of the Mafia for votes in Sicily in 1993.

Italy's foreign policy has traditionally been governed by its firm commitment to Europe, notably through its membership of the European Community (EC—now EU) and NATO.

In July 1991, following the escalation of hostilities in the neighbouring Yugoslav republic of Slovenia, the Italian Government temporarily deployed military personnel in the north-east of Italy and reinforced border posts in the region. Italy gave firm support to the EC's efforts to find a peaceful solution to the Yugoslav crisis. In May 1992 the Italian Government was obliged to declare a state of emergency, following an influx of thousands of refugees from Bosnia and Herzegovina. The victory of Berlusconi's right-wing alliance in the general election in March 1994 was met with unease by the European Parliament due to the neo-fascist element of the grouping. In May Italy was refused a place on the international 'Contact Group' formed to facilitate a cease-fire in Bosnia and Herzegovina, following alleged statements by AN members reviving claims to territories of the former Yugoslavia. In July relations between Italy and Slovenia deteriorated, following a threat by the Italian Government to veto Slovenian membership of the EU if some form of non-monetary compensation were not given to the ethnic Italians who were dispossessed when Slovenia (then part of the former Yugoslavia) was awarded the Italian territory of Istria under the post-1945 peace settlement. Slovenia subsequently conceded that legislation would be amended to allow foreign nationals to acquire property in Slovenia, and in March 1995 the Italian Government withdrew its veto on Slovenian negotiations to become a member of the EU. In February 1998 Italy and Slovenia agreed a set of compensation measures for those Italians expelled from Slovenia at the end of the Second World War.

In May 1995 a contingent of some 500 troops was deployed along Italy's south-eastern coast in an attempt to halt a sudden influx of illegal immigrants, primarily from Albania and Montenegro. It was estimated that as many as 10,000 foreign nationals had entered Italy illegally via this route during the previous six months. Controversial legislation was approved in November restricting immigration and imposing harsh sanctions on illegal immigrants. As a result of the deteriorating political situation within Albania, large numbers of refugees arrived in Italy throughout 1997, and in March a state of emergency was declared for three months. Following a visit by Prodi, an Italian-led multi-national peace-keeping force, known as Operation Alba, was deployed in Albania in April, with a three-month mandate to facilitate the distribution of humanitarian aid. In June Italy was forced to recall two successive ambassadors to Albania, following comments that they were alleged to have made regarding the Albanian political situation. At the end of July, at an international conference in Rome, it was decided that Italian security aid to Albania would continue after the withdrawal of the international force and that co-operation on border control would be extended until October. At the end of August it was announced that the repatriation of refugees would be delayed until November. In October it was agreed to establish a joint office to combat organized crime, and in December Italy and Albania signed an aid agreement.

Following Italy's accession to the EU's Schengen Agreement on cross-border travel in late October 1997, large numbers of refugees, mainly Turkish and Iraqi Kurds, began arriving in southern Italy, provoking concern from Italy's EU partners. These concerns were partially alleviated by the initial approval, in November, of a bill designed to facilitate the deportation of illegal immigrants. However, the concerns resurfaced in January 1998, following comments by President Scalfaro, who proclaimed that Italy had an 'open arms' policy towards refugees. On 1 April 1998 the Schengen Agreement, which had previously only been applicable to air travel between Italy and the other EU member states, was fully implemented, opening the borders with Austria and France. In order to comply with the terms of the agreement, a new law had been promulgated in February, providing for the detention, prior to forcible repatriation, of illegal immigrants; previously they had been given unenforced expulsion orders and released. In August the discovery of ambiguities in the new immigration law, which would enable immigrants to be released if their country of origin could not be determined, led to renewed fears of a 'flood' of immigrants. In February 1999 legislation was approved allowing for the detention of illegal immigrants arriving in Italy without making an asylum application; previously they had been given 15 days to leave before being expelled, and it was considered many used this period to find employment in the 'black' economy and go into hiding. In March 2002 a state of emergency was declared following the arrival of 1,000 Kurdish refugees in Sicily; conflict arose within the Government between the Minister of the Interior, Claudio Scajola, who was prepared to offer asylum and Umberto Bossi, who wanted the refugees ejected and demanded stricter immigration controls. Berlusconi voiced concern over the rise in the level of immigration into Italy, and in early June legislation was passed allowing for the fingerprinting of non-EU nationals and requiring residence permits to be renewed every two years.

In March 1999, as the conflict in the Serbian province of Kosovo deepened (see the chapter on Serbia and Montenegro), Italian bases were used for NATO bombing raids on Yugoslavia. However, political opinion within Italy was strongly in favour of a diplomatic solution, and the Camera dei Deputati overwhelmingly endorsed a motion urging the reopening of negotiations and an immediate suspension of the bombing. In early April the RC threatened to withdraw from the Government unless there was an unconditional end to the NATO action; D'Alema averted a crisis in May by proposing a compromise resolution seeking the suspension of the bombing raids only if a UN Security Council resolution to end the conflict was achieved with Russian and Chinese backing. In April the Senato had approved the deployment of 2,000 Italian troops in Albania to aid the humanitarian mission, although they refused to sanction any military ground intervention in Yugoslavia; by mid-1999 some 5,500 Italians had been deployed in Kosovo as part of a NATO contingent in the region. In March Italy had launched a programme of humanitarian aid for Kosovan refugees in Albania, and a large number of Kosovan refugees also arrived in Italy. However, in July Italy announced that as the conflict in Kosovo had ended, those arriving from the region would no longer be accorded refugee status, but would be regarded as illegal immigrants. In early January 2001 the Minister of Defence, Sergio Mattarella, requested that NATO impose a temporary ban on the use of depleted uranium (DU) as a weapons component, following alleged evidence that deaths of veterans of NATO operations in the Balkans, including a number of former Italian military personnel, were linked to exposure to DU. NATO subsequently announced that a full examination of the use of DU weapons would be undertaken.

The deployment of some 2,700 Italian troops to assist military efforts as part of the US-led 'campaign against terror', following the September 2001 suicide attacks on New York and Washington, DC, was approved by the Italian Parliament in November. Comments made by Prime Minister Berlusconi in September that were widely interpreted as a declaration of Western superiority over the Islamic world were condemned by opposition members and foreign leaders, as well as by the League of Arab States and other international organizations. Berlusconi later issued an apology, claiming that his remarks had been taken out of context. An investigation into the existence of terrorist cells possibly connected with the al-Qa'ida (Base) organization headed by the Saudi-born dissident Osama bin Laden led to a number of arrests in Italy in 2002–03. In January 2003 28 Pakistani citizens were arrested on charges of terrorist activities following the discovery of maps and explosives at a residential address in Naples; this followed the arrest of five Moroccans on similar charges. In early 2003 Berlusconi's increasing political allegiance with the so-called 'coalition of the willing' (the group of powers, including the USA, the United Kingdom and Spain, which was in favour of military action against the regime of Saddam Hussein in Iraq), gave rise to massive nation-wide protests on 15 February. Official estimates numbered the marchers in Rome at 650,000; however, other sources placed the figure at up to 3m. Similar large-scale protests were staged in Milan. At the onset of armed conflict in Iraq in March, the anti-war movement in the Italy gained momentum, with the trade unions organizing a general strike on 20 March, and protests in Rome continuing on a daily basis. The Italian Government offered the USA the use of Italy's bases and airspace for logistical purposes, but not for direct attacks. In addition, following a request by the US authorities, Italy was the first EU country to expel a number of Iraqi diplomatic staff, although the embassy remained open. Several arson attacks on US and NATO vehicles were reported during March. Discontent at Berlusconi's stance on the conflict in Iraq deepened following the discovery of a large munitions dump at the US Army's Camp Darby near Livorno and the deployment in northern Iraq of 1,000 US troops that had been stationed in Italy.

Government

Under the 1948 Constitution, legislative power was held by the bicameral Parliament, elected by universal suffrage for five years (subject to dissolution) on the basis of proportional representation. A referendum held in April 1993 supported the amendment of the Constitution to provide for the election of 75% of the members of the Senato (Senate) by a simple plurality and the remainder under a system of proportional representation, and provided for further electoral reform. In August the Parlamento (Parliament) approved a similar system for elections to the Camera dei Deputati (Chamber of Deputies). The Senato has 315 elected members (seats allocated on a regional basis) and 10 life Senators. The Camera dei Deputati has 630 members. The minimum voting age is 25 years for the Senato and 18 years for the Camera dei Deputati. The two houses have equal power.

The President of the Republic is a constitutional Head of State elected for seven years by an electoral college comprising both Houses of Parliament and 58 regional representatives. Executive power is exercised by the Council of Ministers. The Head of State appoints the President of the Council (Prime Minister) and, on the latter's recommendation, other ministers. The Council is responsible to Parliament.

The country is divided into 20 regions, of which five (Sicily, Sardinia, Trentino-Alto Adige, Friuli-Venezia Giulia and Valle d'Aosta) enjoy a special status. There is a large degree of regional autonomy. Each region has a Regional Council elected every five years by universal suffrage and a Giunta regionale responsible to the regional council. The Regional Council is a legislative assembly, while the Giunta holds executive power. The regions are subdivided into a total of 95 provinces.

Defence

Italy has been a member of the North Atlantic Treaty Organization (NATO, see p. 271) since 1949. In August 2002 it maintained armed forces totalling 216,800 (conscripts numbered an estimated 70,200), comprising an army of 128,000, a navy of 38,000 and an air force of 50,800. There were also paramilitary forces numbering 254,300 men (including 111,800 Carabinieri). Military service lasts 10 months in all the services. However, in 1999 the Government approved a draft law phasing out military conscription by 2006 and introducing women soldiers. The law, which would replace the current defence force with a professional army of some 190,000, was approved by the legislature in June 2000. The 2002 state budget allocated €19,000m. to defence.

Economic Affairs

In 2001, according to estimates by the World Bank, Italy's gross national income (GNI), measured at average 1999–2001 prices, was US $1,226,385m., equivalent to $19,470 per head (or $24,340 per head on an international purchasing-power parity basis). During 1990–2001, it was estimated, the population increased at an average rate of 0.2% per year, while Italy's gross domestic product (GDP) per head increased, in real terms, by an average of 1.4% per year. Overall GDP increased, in real terms, at an average annual rate of 1.6% in 1990–2001; growth in 2001 was 1.8%.

Agriculture (including forestry and fishing) contributed 2.5% of GDP and engaged 4.5% of the employed labour force in 2001. The principal crops are sugar beet, maize, grapes, wheat and tomatoes. Italy is a leading producer and exporter of wine. According to the World Bank, during 1990–2000 the real GDP of the agricultural sector increased at an average rate of 2.0% per year. Real agricultural GDP increased by 5.8% in 1999, but declined by 2.1% in 2000.

Industry (including mining, manufacturing, construction and power) contributed 29.5% of GDP in 2000; 31.9% of the employed labour force were engaged in industrial activities in that year. In 1990–2000 industrial GDP increased, in real terms, at an average annual rate of 1.2% per year. Real industrial GDP increased by 0.7% in 1999 and by 3.3% in 2000.

The mining sector contributed just 0.5% of GDP and engaged only 0.3% of the employed labour force in 2000. The major product of the mining sector is petroleum (reserves of which were estimated at 600m. barrels at the end of 2000, sufficient to sustain production, at that year's level of 90,000 barrels per day, for 19 years), followed by rock salt, talc, fluorspar and barytes. Italy also has reserves of lignite, lead and zinc. Reserves of epithermal gold in Sardinia were discovered in 1996. Average annual growth in the GDP of the mining sector was negligible in 1990–2000; mining GDP declined by 1.1% in 1999 and by 4.6% in 2000.

Manufacturing contributed 18.8% of GDP in 2001; 20.5% of the employed labour force were engaged in the sector in that year. The most important branches of manufacturing in 1994, measured by gross value of output, were non-electric machinery (accounting for 12.2% of the total), metals and metal products (11.7%), food products (10.5%), chemical products (9.0%) and refined petroleum products (8.1%). In 1990–2000 the GDP of the manufacturing sector increased, in real terms, at an average annual rate of 1.3%, according to the World Bank. Manufacturing GDP increased by 0.7% in 1999 and by 2.8% in 2000.

More than 80% of energy requirements are imported. In 1999 35.2% of requirements were derived from petroleum; coal-fired electricity generating stations provided 10.9%, natural gas-fired stations provided 33.6%, and hydroelectric power stations provided 17.5%. In 2000 imports of mineral fuels and lubricants accounted for 9.9% of the value of total imports.

Services engaged 62.8% of the employed labour force in 2000 and accounted for 67.6% of GDP in that year. Tourism is an important source of income, and in 2001 a total of 35.8m. foreigners visited Italy, an increase of some 1.8% compared with 2000. Tourism receipts totalled €28,962m. in 2001. The combined GDP of the services sector increased, in real terms, at an

estimated average rate of 1.8% per year in 1990–2000. Services GDP increased by 1.5% in 1999 and by 3.1% in 2000.

In 2001 Italy recorded a visible trade surplus of US $15,862m., and a deficit of $163m. on the current account of the balance of payments. In 2002 the principal source of imports (17.8%) was Germany; other major suppliers were France (11.3%), the Netherlands (5.9%) and the United Kingdom (5.0%). Germany was also the principal market for exports (13.7%); other major purchasers in that year were France (12.2%), the USA (9.7%), the United Kingdom (6.9%) and Spain (6.3%). In 2002 Italy's fellow members of the European Union (EU, see p. 199) purchased 38.6% of its exports. The principal exports in 2002 were machinery and transport equipment, basic manufactures, chemicals and related products, and clothing and footwear. The principal imports were machinery and transport equipment, basic manufactures, chemicals and related products, and food and live animals.

The budgetary deficit for 1998 was equivalent to 3.5% of annual GDP. At the end of 1999 Italy's total accumulated government debt was equivalent to 110.5% of annual GDP. The annual rate of inflation averaged 3.7% in 1990–2000; consumer prices increased by an annual average of 2.8% in 2000 and 2.7% in 2001. As a percentage of the total labour force, unemployment was 9.5% in 2001.

Italy is a member of the EU, the Organisation for Economic Co-operation and Development (OECD, see p. 277), and the Central European Initiative (see p. 349).

Italy has long-term structural problems, principally the underdevelopment of the southern part of the country, a low level of agricultural productivity, and heavy dependence on imported energy supplies. From mid-1995 government economic policy was directed towards meeting the economic convergence criteria for European economic and monetary union (EMU). Despite a continuing high level of public debt, Italy was among the first countries to adopt the single European currency, the euro, in January 1999. In February 2000 it was announced that the gas market was to be liberalized by January 2003 to comply with EU regulations, ending the monopoly held by the principal producer and distributor of gas and petroleum, Eni. The privatization programme proceeded with the partial sale of government stakes in Eni and Enel (electricity), although in early 2002 Enel still owned some 80% of the generating capacity (in late 2002, in an attempt to reduce public debt, the Government was considering a merger of the gas and power branches of Eni and Enel). The programme had been accelerated in an attempt to make up a shortfall in revenue needed to meet debt reduction pledges, following the sale of third-generation mobile telephone licences held in October 2000, which generated less income than had been expected. In July 2001 the new Government of Silvio Berlusconi announced a five-year economic reform programme which aimed to achieve a balanced public-sector budget by 2003. The plan, which contained a number of measures for reducing public expenditure, was instigated following concerns expressed by the EU over the country's high budget deficit. The budget for 2002 significantly reduced government spending in all departments except defence (funds for which remained unaltered owing to Italy's security commitments following the September 2001 attacks on the USA), as part of plans to ensure a budget deficit equivalent to 0.5% of GDP in 2002. By July 2002, however, the Government had been forced to abandon this target, while predictions placed the deficit at 2.1% of GDP (or 2.3%, according to IMF estimates); the predictions for 2003 were likewise altered to a deficit of 0.8% of GDP, and the EU warned Italy not to renege on its commitment to a balanced budget by 2004. Berlusconi's electoral commitment to tax reductions, while largely overlooked in 2002, figured significantly in the 2003 budget, with reductions in low-income and corporate taxes totalling €5,600m. An IMF report in October 2002, however, criticized the 2003 budget for the implementation of one-off measures to reduce deficits without the introduction of the necessary structural reforms to lower expenditure on health, pensions and public administration. The 2003 budget was also criticized by the Central Bank and by the employers' association CONFINDUSTRIA, which predicted a GDP growth rate of 2.0% rather than 2.3% and claimed that the budget neglected the poorer South. Following the approval of legislation in June 2002, part of Italy's national heritage was to be privatized under a new state agency, Patrimonio dello Stato. In December 2002 the State sold its last remaining shares in Telecom Italia SpA in an attempt to pay off growing debt. In January 2003 the Banca d'Italia exchanged a debt of €39,400m., thus reducing the public-debt-to-GDP ratio from 3.5% to 1.7%, well under the 3% threshold demanded by the EU, but increasing long-term debt. The Government was accused of lack of commitment to the EU's Growth and Stability Pact. The economic disparity between the north and the south persists, with unemployment levels in southern regions at 21% in 2000, compared with less than 5% in the north. Furthermore, the forthcoming enlargement of the EU to include countries of central and eastern Europe is likely to be to the detriment of those regions in Italy benefiting from special regional development status within the Union, since income per head in much of the southern parts of the country will exceed 75% of the EU average, the key criterion.

Education

Education is free and compulsory between the ages of six and 15 years, comprising five years of primary education, three years of lower secondary education and one year of higher secondary education. The curricula of all Italian schools are standardized by the Ministry of Education, Universities and Scientific Research. After primary school, for children aged six to 11 years, the pupil enters the lower secondary school (scuola media unificata). An examination at the end of three years leads to a lower secondary school certificate (Diploma di Licenza della Scuola Media), which gives access to all higher secondary schools, of which only the first year is compulsory. Pupils wishing to enter a classical lycée (liceo classico) must also pass an examination in Latin.

Higher secondary education is provided by classical, artistic, linguistic and scientific lycées, training schools for elementary teachers and technical and vocational institutes (industrial, commercial, nautical, etc.). After five years at a lycée, the student sits an examination for the higher secondary school certificate (Diploma di Esame di Stato), which allows automatic entry into any university or non-university institute of higher education. Special four-year courses are provided at the teachers' training schools and the diploma obtained permits entry to a special university faculty of education, the magistero, and a few other faculties. The technical institutes provide practical courses that prepare students for a specialized university faculty.

Following the approval of educational reforms in March 2003, an eight-year first cycle, comprising five years of primary education (scuola primaria) and three years of secondary education (scuola secondaria di I grado), was to culminate in a diploma (Esame di Stato); this was to qualify the student for entrance to a four-year second cycle at either a lycée or vocational instution, concluding in a fifth year specifically directed towards higher education. A further Esame di Stato would then lead to either university or non-university higher education.

In 1999 the total enrolment at primary schools was equivalent to 101% of all children in the relevant age-group (females 101%; males 102%), while the comparable ratio for secondary enrolment was 93% (females 91%; males 95%). In 2000 2.8m. children were enrolled in primary education, and 4.3m. were enrolled in secondary education.

In 2000 65.2% of students taking school-leaving examinations enrolled at university, 25% of whom left their courses during their first year. In 2002 there were 1.67m. students in higher education in Italy; the largest universities were La Sapienza in Rome (with 170,000 students) and Bologna (100,000 students). In 2001/02 there were 776 university instutions, including 52 state universities. Following the introduction of university reforms, courses last for a three-year cycle, followed by a two-year specialized cycle. Study allowances are awarded to students according to their means and merit; however, 90% of parents pay fees. In 2001 government expenditure on education (including higher education) was €41,000m. (equivalent to 10.5% of total government expenditure).

Public Holidays

2003: 1 January (New Year's Day), 6 January (Epiphany), 21 April (Easter Monday), 25 April (Liberation Day), 1 May (Labour Day), 15 August (Assumption), 1 November (All Saints' Day), 8 December (Immaculate Conception), 25 December (Christmas Day), 26 December (St Stephen).

2004: 1 January (New Year's Day), 6 January (Epiphany), 12 April (Easter Monday), 26 April (for Liberation Day), 3 May (for Labour Day), 15 August (Assumption), 1 November (All Saints' Day), 8 December (Immaculate Conception), 25 December (Christmas Day), 26 December (St Stephen).

There are also numerous local public holidays, held on the feast day of the patron saint of each town.

Weights and Measures

The metric system is in force.

Statistical Survey

Source (unless otherwise stated): Istituto Nazionale di Statistica, Via Cesare Balbo 16, 00184 Rome; tel. (06) 46731; fax (06) 46733101; e-mail dipdiff@istat.it; internet www.istat.it.

Area and Population

AREA, POPULATION AND DENSITY

Area (sq km)	301,338*
Population (census results)	
20 October 1991	56,778,031
21 October 2001 (provisional)	
Males	27,260,953
Females	29,044,615
Total	56,305,568
Population (official estimates at 1 January)†	
2000	57,679,895
2001	57,844,017
2002	57,943,355
Density (per sq km) at 1 January 2002	192.3

* 116,346 sq miles.

† Not revised to take account of the October 2001 census results.

REGIONS

(at census of 21 October 2001, preliminary results)

Region	Area (sq km)	Population	Regional capital(s)	Population of capital*
Abruzzo	10,798	1,244,226	L'Aquila	63,121
Basilicata	9,992	595,727	Potenza	69,295
Calabria	15,080	1,993,274	Catanzaro	93,540
Campania	13,595	5,652,492	Napoli (Naples)	993,386
Emilia-Romagna	22,124	3,960,549	Bologna	369,955
Friuli-Venezia Giulia	7,855	1,180,375	Trieste	209,520
Lazio	17,207	4,976,184	Roma (Rome)	2,459,776
Liguria	5,421	1,560,748	Genova (Genoa)	603,560
Lombardia (Lombardy)	23,861	8,922,463	Milano (Milan)	1,182,693
Marche	9,694	1,476,184	Ancona	100,402
Molise	4,438	316,548	Campobasso	46,860
Piemonte (Piedmont)	25,399	4,166,442	Torino (Turin)	857,433
Puglia	19,362	3,983,487	Bari	312,452
Sardegna (Sardinia)	24,090	1,599,511	Cagliari	158,351
Sicilia (Sicily)	25,708	4,866,202	Palermo	652,640
Toscana (Tuscany)	22,997	3,460,835	Firenze (Florence)	352,227
Trentino-Alto Adige	13,607	937,107	Bolzano (Bozen)†	93,079
			Trento (Trent, Trient)†	104,844
Umbria	8,456	815,588	Perugia	148,575
Valle d'Aosta	3,263	119,356	Aosta	33,926
Veneto	18,392	4,490,586	Venezia (Venice)	266,181

* Measured by population of *comune*.

† Joint regional capitals.

PRINCIPAL TOWNS

(population at census of 21 October 2001, measured by *comune*, preliminary results)

Roma (Rome, the capital)	2,459,776	Livorno (Leghorn)	148,143
Milano (Milan)	1,182,693	Foggia	146,072
Napoli (Naples)	993,386	Salerno	144,078
Torino (Turin)	857,433	Reggio nell' Emilia	141,383
Palermo	652,640	Ravenna	138,204
Genova (Genoa)	603,560	Ferrara	130,461
Bologna	369,955	Rimini	128,301
Firenze (Florence)	352,227	Siracusa (Syracuse)	121,000
Bari	312,452	Monza	117,068
Catania	306,464	Pescara	115,197
Venezia (Venice)	266,181	Sassari	112,959
Verona	243,474	Bergamo	110,690
Messina	236,621	Latina	108,711
Trieste	209,520	Forlí	108,363
Padova (Padua)	203,350	Vicenza	106,069
Taranto	201,349	Trento (Trent, Trient)	104,844
Brescia	187,865	Terni	103,964
Reggio di Calabria	179,384	Novara	101,921
Modena	175,442	Ancona	100,402
Prato	170,388	Piacenza	95,132
Cagliari	158,351	Udine	94,759
Parma	156,172	Catanzaro	93,540
Perugia	148,575	Bolzano (Bozen)	93,079

BIRTHS, MARRIAGES AND DEATHS

	Registered live births		Registered marriages		Registered deaths	
	Number	Rate (per 1,000)	Number	Rate (per 1,000)	Number	Rate (per 1,000)
1994	527,406	9.2	285,112	5.0	548,081	9.6
1995	525,609	9.2	290,009	5.1	566,690	9.7
1996	528,103	9.2	278,611	4.9	554,576	9.7
1997	528,901*	9.2	277,738	4.8	561,207	9.6
1998†	515,439	9.0	276,570	4.8	569,418	9.9
1999†	523,463	9.1	275,250	4.8	565,838	9.8
2000†	543,039	9.4	280,488	4.9	560,241	9.7
2001*	544,550	9.4	269,949	4.7	544,094	9.4

* Estimate(s).

† Provisional figures.

Expectation of life (WHO estimates, years at birth): 79.3 (males 76.2; females 82.2) in 2001 (Source: WHO, *World Health Report*).

IMMIGRATION AND EMIGRATION

Immigrants

Origin*	1997	1998
European Union (EU)	19,911	19,235
Non-EU European	51,341	60,298
Albania	13,724	12,463
Russia	—	10,731
former Yugoslavia	6,745	13,079
Africa	13,021	19,493
Morocco	5,185	8,325
Middle East and Asia	15,116	27,666
India	2,061	3,267
Sri Lanka	1,563	3,066
North America	7,310	6,616
USA	6,754	5,954
Central and South America	14,849	16,426
Brazil	4,015	4,055
Oceania	910	982
Total (incl. others)	123,824	153,353

* Refers to country of immigrants' last permanent residence.

Source: Ministry of Internal Affairs.

Emmigrants:

Destination	1994	1995	1996
Belgium	3,845	2,177	1,870
France	5,181	3,371	3,448
Germany	21,407	10,816	10,805
Switzerland	10,449	4,560	5,149
United Kingdom	3,515	2,787	3,666
Other European countries	6,380	6,780	8,049
Argentina	1,936	1,592	1,478
Brazil	636	641	770
Canada	1,082	693	706
USA	4,135	3,043	3,939
Venezuela	632	433	484
Oceania	866	692	656
Other countries	5,484	5,718	6,590
Total	65,548	43,303	47,610

Total: 46,273 in 1997; 76,483 in 1999.

ECONOMICALLY ACTIVE POPULATION

(annual averages, '000 persons aged 15 years and over)

	1999	2000	2001
Agriculture, hunting and forestry	1,089	1,071	1,084
Fishing	45	49	42
Mining and quarrying	70	64	64
Manufacturing	4,928	4,918	4,907
Electricity, gas and water supply	176	167	162
Construction	1,575	1,618	1,707
Wholesale and retail trade; repair of motor vehicles, motorcycles and personal and household goods	3,308	3,377	3,416
Hotels and restaurants	739	814	880
Transport, storage and communications	1,133	1,190	1,180
Financial intermediation	671	662	659
Real estate, renting and business activities	1,336	1,478	1,550
Public administration and defence; compulsory social security	1,943	1,942	1,987
Education	1,445	1,467	1,520
Health and social work	1,289	1,288	1,321
Other community, social and personal service activities	898	905	939
Private households with employed persons	201	196	193
Extra-territorial organizations and bodies	17	20	20
Total employed	20,864	21,225	21,634
Unemployed	2,669	2,495	2,267
Total labour force	23,533	23,720	23,901
Males	14,596	14,640	14,640
Females	8,937	9,080	9,261

Source: ILO.

Health and Welfare

KEY INDICATORS

Total fertility rate (children per woman, 2001)	1.2
Under-5 mortality rate (per 1,000 live births, 2001)	6
HIV/AIDS (% of persons aged 15–49, 2001)	0.37
Physicians (per 1,000 head, 1997)	5.54
Hospital beds (per 1,000 head, 1999)	5.5
Health expenditure (2000): US $ per head (PPP)	2,040
Health expenditure (2000): % of GDP	8.1
Health expenditure (2000): public (% of total)	73.7
Human Development Index (2000): ranking	20
Human Development Index (2000): value	0.913

For sources and definitions, see explanatory note on p. vi.

Agriculture

PRINCIPAL CROPS
('000 metric tons)

	1999	2000	2001
Wheat	7,743	7,464	6,510
Rice (paddy)	1,427	1,186	1,273
Barley	1,313	1,262	1,134
Maize	10,017	10,138	10,513
Oats	331	318	315
Sorghum	202	219	215
Potatoes	2,072	2,050	2,010
Sugar beet	14,505	12,370	11,107
Almonds (in the shell)	104	119	113
Hazelnuts (Filberts)	118	99	119
Soybeans (Soya beans)	893	904	895
Olives	3,765	2,821	2,894
Sunflower seed	444	467	425
Cabbages	523	483	519
Artichokes	472	515	505
Lettuce	938	938*	966
Tomatoes	7,129	7,650	6,529
Cauliflowers	448	500	490
Pumpkins, squash and gourds	363	366	424
Aubergines (Eggplants)	303	319	358
Chillies and green peppers	304	346	392
Dry onions	460	440	426
Green beans	204	214	219
Carrots	510	588	591
Strawberries	178	139	184
Watermelons	496	505	507
Cantaloupes and other melons	502	529	510*
Grapes	9,362	8,870	8,988
Kiwi fruit	325	353	382
Oranges	1,732	1,876	1,857
Lemons and limes	544	610	574
Tangerines, mandarins, clementines and satsumas	595	593	613
Apples	2,368	2,241	2,341
Pears	819	942	963
Peaches and nectarines	1,767	1,654	1,708
Apricots	212	218	194
Cherries†	122	148	117
Plums	189	188	177
Tobacco	131	126	130

* FAO estimate.
† Unofficial figure(s).

Source: FAO.

LIVESTOCK
('000 head, year ending September)

	1999	2000	2001
Horses*	288	280	285
Mules*	10	10	10
Asses*	23	23	23
Cattle	7,150	7,162	7,211
Buffaloes	170	200	190
Pigs	8,225	8,414	8,329
Sheep	10,770	11,017	11,089
Goats	1,365	1,397	1,375
Chickens*	106,000	100,000	100,000
Turkeys*	25,000	23,000	25,000
Rabbits*	67,000	67,000	67,000

* FAO estimates.

Source: FAO.

LIVESTOCK PRODUCTS
('000 metric tons)

	1999	2000	2001
Beef and veal	1,164	1,154	1,133
Mutton and lamb	70	66	60
Pig meat	1,472	1,489	1,510
Horse meat	50	50*	51*
Poultry meat	1,177†	1,140†	1,156*
Rabbit meat	221†	221*	221*
Cows' milk†	11,736	11,741	10,700
Buffaloes' milk	158†	158*	158*
Sheeps' milk*	850	850	850
Goats' milk	140†	140*	140*
Butter†	105	101	105
Cheese	982	1,011	1,093
Hen eggs	768†	768*	722†
Cattle hides (fresh)* . . .	145	143	141

* FAO estimate(s).
† Unofficial figure(s).

Source: FAO.

Forestry

ROUNDWOOD REMOVALS
('000 cubic metres, excl. bark)

	1998	1999	2000
Sawlogs, veneer logs and logs for sleepers	2,572	2,120	2,062
Pulpwood	705	930	708
Other industrial wood . . .	1,090	1,163	879
Fuel wood	5,183	6,925	5,680
Total	9,550	11,138	9,329

SAWNWOOD PRODUCTION
('000 cubic metres, incl. railway sleepers)

	1998	1999	2000
Coniferous (softwood) . . .	700	730	750
Broadleaved (hardwood) . . .	900	900	840
Total	1,600	1,630	1,590

Source: FAO.

Fishing
('000 metric tons, live weight)

	1998	1999	2000
Capture	315.6	294.2	299.9
European hake	13.2	9.8	9.2
European pilchard	36.4	28.9	25.8
European anchovy	44.4	39.8	50.7
Mediterranean mussel . .	39.0	37.9	42.0
Striped venus	28.8	36.5	34.1
Aquaculture	246.6	246.4	213.5
Rainbow trout	48.0	44.0	44.5
Mediterranean mussel . .	90.0	92.0	94.0
Clams	48.8	50.0	53.0
Total catch	562.2	540.5	513.5

Note: Figures exclude aquatic plants ('000 metric tons): 5.0 (capture 2.0; aquaculture 3.0) in 1998; 5.0 (capture 2.0; aquaculture 3.0) in 1999; 5.0 (capture 2.0; aquaculture 3.0) in 2000.

Source: FAO, *Yearbook of Fishery Statistics*.

Mining
('000 metric tons, unless otherwise indicated)

	1999	2000†	2001
Crude petroleum	5,049.4	4,499.4	4,045.4
Natural gas (million cu m)*† . .	18,500	18,500	18,000
Manganese	0.9	1.0	0.8
Lead‡	9.7	4.9	4.0
Gold (kilograms)*‡	600	791	503
Fluorspar (Fluorite) . . .	46.9	67.8	26.2
Barite (Barytes)	24.5	11.3	10.8
Feldspar	2,493.8	2,851.3	3,092.4
Bentonite	562.7	636.6	579.0
Kaolin	295.9	284.1	286.1
Salt: Marine*†§	600	600	600
Salt: Rock	3,338.2	3,339.8	3,281.3
Loam rock	13,962.6	14,663.8	13,973.9
Gypsum	1,382.7	1,523.9	1,545.3
Pumice*†‖	600	600	600
Pozzolan*†	4,000	4,000	4,000
Talc and steatite	123.5	121.1	126.9

* Source: US Geological Survey.
† Estimate(s).
‡ Metal content of ores and concentrates.
§ Excluding production from Sardinia and Sicily, estimated at 200,000 tons per year.
‖ Including pumiceous lapilli.

Industry

SELECTED PRODUCTS
('000 metric tons, unless otherwise indicated)

	1999	2000	2001
Natural methane gas (million cu m)	17,635.2	16,379.6	15,442.3
Wine*	5,807.3	5,408.8	5,286.0
Cotton yarn	239.3	254.2	249.2
Cotton woven fabrics . . .	198.4	210.1	214.7
Wood pulp, mechanical . . .	365.8	353.6	335.9
Newsprint	837.7	871.9	852.4
Other printing and writing paper .	2,131.2	2,183.3	2,098.9
Sulphuric acid at 50° Bé . . .	1,627.2	1,676.4	1,581.2
Nitric acid at 36° Bé . . .	816.4	1,052.5	996.1
Caustic soda	810.0	833.4	n.a.
Washing powders and detergents .	2,100.3	2,234.2	2,032.6
Jet fuels	2,655.5	2,752.5	2,607.8
Benzene	20,591.3	20,875.4	20,887.9
Motor gasoline	34,407.0	33,890.9	36,755.9
Naphthas	3,273.4	3,459.3	3,165.2
Gas-diesel oil	15,676.1	14,349.2	13,490.6
Bitumen	2,719.7	2,686.0	2,925.2
Coke	4,931.5	4,885.1	4,738.5
Tyres for road motor vehicles . .	391.5	387.4	385.1
Glass bottles and other containers of common glass	2,674.9	2,852.0	2,899.2
Cement	36,826.6	38,302.3	38,964.9
Pig iron	10,664.5	11,176.1	10,562.4
Steel	24,780.4	26,622.6	26,526.2
Rolled iron	23,463.4	24,300.6	23,854.7
Other iron and steel-finished manufactures	3,277.9	3,002.0	3,109.8
Iron alloys and *spiegel-eisen* special pig irons	92.9	127.4	102.5
Aluminium, unwrought, primary .	205.6	189.8	187.5
Zinc, unwrought, primary . . .	162.3	170.3	178.6
Refrigerators for household use ('000 units)	6,581.9	6,987.0	6,844.3
Washing machines for household use ('000 units)	7,367.2	8,185.8	8,333.5
Passenger motor cars ('000 units) .	1,384.3	1,422.3	1,271.8
Lorries (Trucks) ('000 units) . .	288.0	313.2	304.6
Motorcycles, scooters etc. ('000 units)	949.0	1,004.7	633.1
Bicycles ('000 units)	916.6	828.9	711.8
Hydroelectric power (million kWh)†	51.8	50.9	n.a.
Thermoelectric power (million kWh)†	209.1	220.5	n.a.

* Data from FAO.
† Net production.

Finance

CURRENCY AND EXCHANGE RATES

Monetary Units
100 cent = 1 euro (€)

Sterling, Dollar and Euro Equivalents (31 December 2002)
£1 sterling = 1.5370 euros
US $1 = 0.9536 euros
100 euros = £65.06 = $104.87

Average Exchange Rate (euros per US $)
2000 1.0854
2001 1.1175
2002 1.0626

Note: The national currency was formerly the Italian lira (plural: lire). From the introduction of the euro, with Italian participation, on 1 January 1999, a fixed exchange rate of €1 = 1,936.27 lire was in operation. Euro notes and coins were introduced on 1 January 2002. The euro and local currency circulated alongside each other until 28 February, after which the euro became the sole legal tender. Some of the figures in this Survey are still in terms of Italian lire.

STATE BUDGET
('000 million euros, forecasts)

Revenue	2000	2001
Taxation	301.4	326.7
Other current revenue	23.6	21.9
Capital revenue	2.1	2.3
Total	327.1	350.8

Expenditure	2000	2001
General public services	69.4	68.4
Defence	12.9	15.2
Public order and safety	17.6	18.8
Economic affairs	47.2	50.8
Environmental protection	1.8	1.7
Housing and community amenities	1.9	1.7
Health	27.8	36.6
Recreation, culture and religion	10.2	11.6
Education	40.6	41.0
Social protection	62.3	64.3
Interest payments	76.0	78.7
Total	367.7	389.0

Source: Ministry of Economy and Finance, Rome.

INTERNATIONAL RESERVES
(US $ million at 31 December)*

	2000	2001	2002
Gold†	21,493	21,796	27,019
IMF special drawing rights	238	297	108
Reserve position in IMF	2,906	3,217	3,907
Foreign exchange	22,423	20,905	24,588
Total	47,059	46,215	55,622

* Excluding deposits made with the European Monetary Institute (now the European Central Bank).
† Valued at market-related prices.

Source: IMF, *International Financial Statistics*.

MONEY SUPPLY
(million euros at 31 December)

	2000	2001	2002
Currency issued	76,416	65,888	65,530*
Demand deposits at banking institutions	410,650	449,750	492,720

* Currency put into circulation by the Banca d'Italia was 71,263 million euros.

Source: IMF, *International Financial Statistics*.

COST OF LIVING
(Consumer Price Index; base: 1995 = 100)

	1999	2000	2001
Food (incl. non-alcoholic beverages)	105.8	107.5	111.9
Alcohol and tobacco	118.1	119.6	122.6
Rent and utilities	112.5	119.0	122.6
Clothing (incl. footwear)	111.6	114.1	117.4
Household goods	109.4	111.4	113.7
Health services	113.5	116.7	119.4
Transport	109.9	114.3	116.1
Communications	99.3	95.7	93.7
Education	109.8	112.5	116.1
Hotels, restaurants and public services	113.0	116.7	121.3
All items (incl. others)	110.0	112.8	115.9

NATIONAL ACCOUNTS
(million euros at current prices)

National Income and Product

	1999	2000	2001
Compensation of employees	451,505	473,782	497,121
Operating surplus	357,716	376,096	395,277
Domestic factor incomes	809,221	849,878	892,398
Consumption of fixed capital	145,457	153,652	161,187
Gross domestic product (GDP) at factor cost	954,678	1,003,530	1,053,585
Indirect taxes	172,171	180,189	182,390
Less Subsidies	18,352	18,952	19,281
GDP in purchasers' values	1,108,497	1,164,767	1,216,694
Net factor income received from abroad	−6,438	−8,059	−5,458
Gross national product	1,102,059	1,156,617	1,211,236
Less Consumption of fixed capital	145,457	153,561	161,188
National income in market prices	956,602	1,003,056	1,050,048
Other current transfers abroad (net)	−4,439	−3,947	−5,193
National disposable income	952,162	999,110	1,044,856

Expenditure on the Gross Domestic Product

	1999	2000	2001
Government final consumption expenditure*	204,748	217,508	230,226
Private final consumption expenditure	661,737	698,745	726,695
Increase in stocks	7,099	6,180	−711
Gross fixed capital formation	212,100	230,952	240,987
Total domestic expenditure	1,085,684	1,153,385	1,197,197
Exports of goods and services	283,064	330,337	343,975
Less Imports of goods and services	260,251	318,956	324,478
GDP in purchasers' values	1,108,497	1,164,767	1,216,694
GDP at constant 1995 prices	984,567	1,012,802	1,030,782

* Including non-profit institutions serving households.

Gross Domestic Product by Economic Activity

	1999	2000	2001
Agriculture, forestry and fishing	30,324	29,857	30,754
Manufacturing	211,179	221,484	228,533
Electricity, gas and water supply	29,002	29,372	30,783
Construction	49,337	52,033	55,584
Commerce, hotels and public commercial concerns	171,254	180,476	191,246
Transport and communications	75,307	78,193	81,089
Financial intermediation, insurance, real estate, renting and business activities*	261,071	282,268	298,950
Public administration and defence; compulsory social security	57,234	57,926	60,896
Other community, social and personal service activities	141,120	148,682	156,989
Sub-total	1,025,826	1,080,291	1,134,825
Import duties	122,569	127,824	128,461
Less Imputed bank service charge	39,898	43,348	46,593
GDP in purchasers' values	1,108,497	1,164,767	1,216,694

* Including imputed rents of owner-occupied dwellings.

BALANCE OF PAYMENTS
(US $ million)

	1999	2000	2001
Exports of goods f.o.b.	235,856	240,473	242,430
Imports of goods f.o.b.	−212,420	−230,925	−226,568
Trade balance	23,437	9,549	15,862
Exports of services	58,788	56,566	57,548
Imports of services	−57,707	−55,601	−57,345
Balance on goods and services	24,517	10,504	16,605
Other income received	46,361	38,671	38,649
Other income paid	−57,411	−50,680	48,929
Balance on goods, services and income	13,467	−1,506	5,785
Current transfers received	16,776	15,797	16,176
Current transfers paid	−22,132	−20,073	22,125
Current balance	8,111	−5,781	−163
Capital account (net)	2,964	−2,879	846
Direct investment abroad	−6,723	−12,077	−21,758
Direct investment from abroad.	6,943	13,176	14,874
Portfolio investment assets	−129,624	−80,263	−36,167
Portfolio investment liabilities	104,607	57,020	29,329
Financial derivatives assets	161	744	−2,277
Financial derivatives liabilities	1,709	1,588	1,839
Other investment assets	−33,573	242	717
Other investment liabilities	39,085	27,074	10,233
Net errors and omissions	−1,711	−1,355	1,940
Overall balance	−8,051	3,247	−588

Source: IMF, *International Financial Statistics.*

External Trade

Note: Figures refer to the trade of Italy, San Marino and the Vatican City.

PRINCIPAL COMMODITIES
(distribution by SITC, million euros)

Imports c.i.f.	2000	2001	2002*
Food and live animals	23,607	24,969	25,820
Crude materials (inedible) except fuels	14,490	13,929	12,561
Mineral fuels, lubricants, etc.	24,993	24,206	23,205
Petroleum, petroleum products, etc.	23,293	20,627	19,627
Crude petroleum oils, etc.	18,522	16,526	15,193
Chemicals and related products	31,476	32,391	33,251
Organic chemicals	7,597	7,380	7,374
Basic manufactures	40,064	39,998	37,641
Textile yarn, fabrics, etc.			
Iron and steel.	9,126	8,840	8,431
Machinery and transport equipment.	85,994	87,576	85,478
General industrial machinery, equipment and parts	9,512	9,570	9,264
Office machines and automatic data-processing equipment	9,193	8,698	7,884
Telecommunications and sound equipment	8,806	8,402	7,869
Other electrical machinery, apparatus, etc.	13,223	12,903	11,540
Road vehicles and parts†	28,122	30,062	31,327
Passenger motor cars (excl. buses).	18,863	20,753	21,778
Miscellaneous manufactured articles.	25,869	27,646	28,070
Clothing and accessories (excl. footwear)	6,647	7,478	7,969
Total (incl. others)	258,207	263,757	256,887

Exports f.o.b.	2000	2001	2002*
Food and live animals	12,788	12,975	12,951
Chemicals and related products	24,557	26,439	27,630
Basic manufactures	53,642	55,856	53,429
Textile yarn, fabrics, etc.	13,036	13,582	12,737
Non-metallic mineral manufactures	8,813	8,955	8,692
Machinery and transport equipment.	100,049	103,000	99,505
Machinery specialized for particular industries	17,009	17,881	17,055
General industrial machinery and equipment	21,998	23,199	23,093
Electrical machinery, apparatus, etc.	15,854	16,024	15,574
Road vehicles and parts†	21,054	20,978	20,401
Passenger motor cars (excl. buses).	7,857	7,438	7,040
Miscellaneous manufactured articles.	54,849	57,925	55,512
Furniture and parts	9,175	9,495	9,155
Clothing and accessories (excl. footwear)	14,491	15,877	15,316
Total (incl. others)	260,413	272,990	265,365

* Provisional.
† Data on parts exclude tyres, engines and electrical parts.

PRINCIPAL TRADING PARTNERS
(million euros)*

Imports c.i.f.	2000	2001	2002
Algeria.	5,629	5,344	4,254
Austria.	6,049	6,471	6,921
Belgium	10,461	11,544	11,203
China, People's Republic	7,028	7,484	8,307
France.	29,682	29,648	28,987
Germany.	45,471	47,077	45,613
Ireland.	3,508	3,592	3,550
Japan.	6,421	6,278	5,321
Libya.	6,384	5,466	4,908
Netherlands	15,401	16,588	15,080
Romania.	2,564	3,371	3,815
Russia.	8,336	8,536	7,915
Spain.	10,769	11,180	11,762
Sweden.	3,819	3,521	3,440
Switzerland	8,447	9,604	9,725
Turkey.	2,210	3,030	2,941
United Kingdom.	14,185	13,540	12,868
USA.	13,517	12,892	12,507
Total (incl. others)	258,207	263,757	256,887

Exports f.o.b.	2000	2001	2002
Austria.	5,804	5,928	5,811
Belgium.	7,208	8,300	8,121
China, People's Republic	2,380	3,275	4,018
France.	33,196	33,691	32,275
Germany.	39,558	40,096	36,305
Greece.	5,414	5,394	5,519
Hong Kong	3,269	3,277	3,089
Hungary.	2,432	2,988	2,725
Japan.	4,338	4,705	4,493
Netherlands	6,965	7,280	6,794
Poland.	3,845	4,243	4,278
Portugal.	3,612	3,652	3,268
Romania.	2,672	3,363	3,613
Russia.	2,521	3,539	3,801
Spain.	16,355	16,955	16,824
Sweden.	2,631	2,542	2,534
Switzerland	8,627	9,840	9,361
Turkey.	4,646	3,923	4,073
United Kingdom.	18,036	18,474	18,312
USA.	26,659	26,243	25,854
Total (incl. others)	260,413	272,990	265,365

* Imports by country of production; exports by country of consumption.

Transport

STATE RAILWAYS
(traffic)

	1999	2000	2001
Passenger journeys ('000) . .	431,503	478,141	472,807
Passenger-km (million) . .	40,971	47,133	46,675
Freight ton-km (million) . . .	23,781	27,537	24,995

ROAD TRAFFIC
(vehicles in use at 31 December)

	1997	1998*	1999
Passenger motor cars . . .	30,741,953	31,370,765	31,953,247
Buses and coaches	84,177	84,822	85,509
Goods vehicles	3,169,538	3,548,589	3,217,060

* Source: International Road Federation, *World Road Statistics*.

SHIPPING

Merchant Fleet
(registered at 31 December)

	1999	2000	2001
Number of vessels	1,389	1,457	1,476
Displacement ('000 grt) . . .	8,048	9,049	9,655

Source: Lloyd's Register-Fairplay, *World Fleet Statistics*.

International Sea-borne Freight Traffic

	1994	1995	1996
Vessels entered ('000 nrt) . . .	180,175	181,733	190,910
Vessels cleared ('000 nrt) . . .	91,288	96,505	160,757
Goods loaded ('000 metric tons) .	50,247	48,250	59,218
Goods unloaded ('000 metric tons).	226,220	234,120	248,063

1997 ('000 nrt): Vessels entered 226,977; Vessels cleared 132,532.

1998 ('000 nrt): Vessels entered 250,830; Vessels cleared 152,655.

Source: UN, *Statistical Yearbook* and *Monthly Bulletin of Statistics*.

2000 ('000 metric tons): Goods loaded 131,484; Goods unloaded 315,155.

CIVIL AVIATION
(traffic on scheduled services)

	1995	1996	1997
Kilometres flown (million) . . .	260	293	326
Passengers carried ('000) . . .	23,396	25,868	27,241
Passenger-km (million)	33,264	36,140	37,734

1998: Kilometres flown (million): 344; Passengers carried ('000) 28,037; Passenger-km (million) 38,122; Total ton-km (million) 5,261 (Source: UN, *Statistical Yearbook*).

Tourism

TOURIST ARRIVALS BY COUNTRY OF ORIGIN

	1999	2000	2001
Austria	1,698,170	1,808,161	1,892,431
Belgium	691,242	717,427	797,377
France	2,329,845	2,792,552	2,854,117
Germany	8,848,933	9,532,149	9,764,800
Japan	1,875,139	1,617,442	1,575,472
Netherlands	1,020,015	1,263,448	1,374,043
Spain	878,716	1,098,396	1,089,041
Switzerland	1,355,157	1,396,829	1,479,268
United Kingdom	2,076,710	2,244,639	2,446,173
USA	3,746,399	4,044,252	3,740,545
Total (incl. others)	31,845,086	35,107,475	35,753,822

Tourism receipts (million euros): 26,724 in 1999; 29,919 in 2000; 28,962 in 2001.

Source: partly World Tourism Organization, *Yearbook of Tourism Statistics*.

Communications Media

	1999	2000	2001
Telephones ('000 main lines in use)	26,502	27,153	27,133
Mobile cellular telephones ('000 in use)	30,296	42,246	48,698
Personal computers ('000 in use) .	9,000	10,300	11,300
Internet users ('000)	8,200	12,200	16,000
Television receivers ('000 in use) .	28,200	28,300	n.a.

Facsimile machines ('000 in use): 1,800 in 1997.

Radio receivers ('000 in use): 50,500 in 1997.

Book production (titles): 35,236 in 1996.

Daily newspapers (1996): Titles 78; Average circulation 5,960,000.

Non-daily newspapers (1995): Titles 274; Average circulation 2,132,000.

Sources: mainly UNESCO, *Statistical Yearbook*; International Telecommunication Union.

Education

(2000/01, provisional)

	Schools	Teachers	Students
Pre-primary	25,041	128,972	1,576,456
Primary	18,854	287,344	2,810,259
Secondary:			
Scuola Media	7,906	209,829	1,776,950
Secondaria Superiore . . .	6,637	307,279	2,565,029
of which:			
Technical*	2,966	139,392	1,113,794
Vocational*	1,690	68,957	507,125
Teacher training*	762	22,317	200,305
Art Licei*	312	13,481	93,429
Classical, linguistic and scientific Licei*	2,158	68,854	747,107
Higher†	74	54,856	1,702,575

* Data refer to the 1995/96 academic year.
† Data refer to the 2001/02 academic year.
Source: partly, Ufficio di Statistica, Ministero dell'Instruzione, dell'Università e della Ricerca.

Adult literacy rate (UNESCO estimates): 98.4% (males 98.9%; females 98.0%) in 2000 (Source: UN Development Programme, *Human Development Report*).

Directory

The Constitution*

The Constitution of the Italian Republic was approved by the Constituent Assembly on 22 December 1947 and came into force on 1 January 1948 (and was amended in April 1993). The fundamental principles are declared in Articles 1–12, as follows:

Italy is a democratic republic based on the labour of the people.

The Republic recognizes and guarantees as inviolable the rights of its citizens, either as individuals or in a community, and it expects, in return, devotion to duty and the fulfilment of political, economic and social obligations.

All citizens shall enjoy equal status and shall be regarded as equal before the law, without distinction of sex, race, language or religion, and without regard to the political opinions which they may hold or their personal or social standing.

It shall be the function of the Republic to remove the economic and social inequalities which, by restricting the liberty of the individual, impede the full development of the human personality, thereby reducing the effective participation of the citizen in the political, economic and social life of the country.

The Republic recognizes the right of all citizens to work and shall do all in its power to give effect to this right.

The Republic, while remaining one and indivisible, shall recognize and promote local autonomy, fostering the greatest possible decentralization in those services which are administered by the State, and subordinating legislative methods and principles to the exigencies of decentralized and autonomous areas.

The State and the Catholic Church shall be sovereign and independent, each in its own sphere. Their relations shall be governed by the Lateran Pact (Patti Lateranensi), and any modification in the pact agreed upon by both parties shall not necessitate any revision of the Constitution.

All religious denominations shall have equal liberty before the law, denominations other than the Catholic having the right to worship according to their beliefs, in so far as they do not conflict with the common law of the country.

The Republic shall do all in its power to promote the development of culture and scientific and technical research. It shall also protect and preserve the countryside and the historical and artistic monuments which are the inheritance of the nation.

The juridical system of the Italian Republic shall be in conformity with the generally recognized practice of international law. The legal rights of foreigners in the country shall be regulated by law in accordance with international practice.

Any citizen of a foreign country who is deprived of democratic liberty such as is guaranteed under the Italian Constitution, has the right of asylum within the territory of the Republic in accordance with the terms of the law, and his extradition for political offences will not be granted.

Italy repudiates war as an instrument of offence against the liberty of other nations and as a means of resolving international disputes. Italy accepts, under parity with other nations, the limitations of sovereignty necessary for the preservation of peace and justice between nations. To that end, it will support and promote international organizations.

The Constitution is further divided into Parts I and II, in which are set forth respectively the rights and responsibilities of the citizen and the administration of the Republic.

PART I

Civic Clauses

Section I (Articles 13–28). The liberty of the individual is inviolable and no form of detention, restriction or inspection is permitted unless it be for juridical purposes and in accordance with the provisions of the law. The domicile of a person is likewise inviolable and shall be immune from forced inspection or sequestration, except according to the provisions of the law. Furthermore, all citizens shall be free to move wheresoever they will throughout the country, and may leave it and return to it without let or hindrance. Right of public meeting, if peaceful and without arms, is guaranteed. Secret organizations of a directly or indirectly political or military nature are, however, prohibited.

Freedom in the practice of religious faith is guaranteed.

The Constitution further guarantees complete freedom of thought, speech and writing, and lays down that the Press shall be entirely free from all control or censorship. No person may be deprived of civic or legal rights on political grounds.

The death penalty is not allowed under the Constitution except in case of martial law. The accused shall be considered 'not guilty' until he is otherwise proven. All punishment shall be consistent with humanitarian practice and shall be directed towards the re-education of the criminal.

Ethical and Social Clauses

Section II (Articles 29–34). The Republic regards the family as the fundamental basis of society and considers the parents to be responsible for the maintenance, instruction and education of the children. The Republic shall provide economic assistance for the family, with special regard to large families, and shall make provision for maternity, infancy and youth, subject always to the liberty and freedom of choice of the individuals as envisaged under the law.

Education, the arts and science shall be free, the function of the State being merely to indicate the general lines of instruction. Private entities and individuals shall have the right to conduct educational institutions without assistance from the State, but such non-state institutions must ensure to their pupils liberty and instruction equal to that in the state schools. Institutions of higher culture, universities and academies shall be autonomous within the limitations prescribed by the law.

Education is available to all and is free and obligatory for at least eight years. Higher education for students of proven merit shall be aided by scholarships and other allowances made by the Republic.

Economic Clauses

Section III (Articles 35–47). The Republic shall safeguard the right to work in all its aspects, and shall promote agreement and co-operation with international organizations in matters pertaining to the regulation of labour and the rights of workers. The rights of Italian workers abroad shall be protected.

All workers shall be entitled to remuneration proportionate to the quantity and quality of their work, and in any case shall be ensured of sufficient to provide freedom and a dignified standard of life for themselves and their families.

The maximum working hours shall be fixed by law, and the worker shall be entitled to a weekly day of rest and an annual holiday of nine days with pay.

Women shall have the same rights and, for equal work, the same remuneration as men. Conditions of work shall be regulated by their special family requirements and the needs of mother and child. The work of minors shall be specially protected.

All citizens have the right to sickness, unemployment and disability maintenance.

Liberty to organize in trade unions is guaranteed and any union may register as a legal entity, provided it is organized on a democratic basis. The right to strike is admitted within the limitations of the relevant legislation.

Private enterprise is permitted in so far as it does not run counter to the well-being of society nor constitute a danger to security, freedom and human dignity.

Ownership of private property is permitted and guaranteed within the limitations laid down by the law regarding the acquisition, extent and enjoyment of private property. Inheritance and testamentary bequests shall be regulated by law.

Limitation is placed by law on private ownership of land and on its use, with a view to its best exploitation for the benefit of the community.

The Republic recognizes the value of mutual co-operation and the right of the workers to participate in management.

The Republic shall encourage all forms of saving, by house purchase, by co-operative ownership and by investment in the public utility undertakings of the country.

Political Clauses

Section IV (Articles 48–54). The electorate comprises all citizens, both men and women, who have attained their majority. Voting is free, equal and secret, and its exercise is a civic duty. All citizens have the right to associate freely together in political parties, and may also petition the Chambers to legislate as may be deemed necessary.

All citizens of both sexes may hold public office on equal terms.

Defence of one's country is a sacred duty of the citizen, and military service is obligatory within the limits prescribed by law†. Its fulfilment shall in no way prejudice the position of the worker nor hinder the exercise of political rights. The organization of the armed forces shall be imbued with the spirit of democracy.

All citizens must contribute to the public expenditure, in proportion to their capacity.

All citizens must be loyal to the Republic and observe the terms of the law and the Constitution.

PART II

Sections I, II and III (Articles 55–100). These sections are devoted to a detailed exposition of the Legislature and legislative procedure of the Republic.

Parliament shall comprise two Chambers, namely the Camera dei Deputati (Chamber of Deputies) and the Senato (Senate of the Republic).

The Camera dei Deputati is elected by direct universal suffrage, the number of Deputies being 630. All voters who on the day of the elections are 25 years of age, may be elected Deputies.

Three-quarters of the seats are allocated on the basis of a simple plurality and the remaining one-quarter by proportional representation.

The Senato is elected on a regional basis, the number of eligible Senators being 315. No region shall have fewer than seven Senators. Valle d'Aosta has only one Senator.

Three-quarters of the seats are allocated on the basis of a simple plurality and the remaining one-quarter by proportional representation.

The Camera dei Deputati and the Senato are elected for five years.

The term of each House cannot be extended except by law and only in the case of war.

Members of Parliament shall receive remuneration fixed by law.

The President of the Republic must be a citizen of at least 50 years of age and in full enjoyment of all civic and political rights. The person shall be elected for a period of seven years (Articles 84–85).

The Government shall consist of the President of the Council and the Ministers (Consiglio dei Ministri) who themselves shall form the Council. The President of the Council, or Prime Minister, shall be nominated by the President of the Republic, who shall also appoint the ministers on the recommendation of the Prime Minister (Article 92).

Section IV (Articles 101–113). Sets forth the judicial system and procedure.

Section V (Articles 114–133). Deals with the division of the Republic into regions, provinces and communes, and sets forth the limits and extent of autonomy enjoyed by the regions. Under Article 131 the regions are enumerated as follows:

Piemonte (Piedmont)	Marche
Lombardia (Lombardy)	Lazio
Veneto	Abruzzo
Liguria	Molise
Emilia-Romagna	Campania
Toscana (Tuscany)	Puglia
Umbria	Basilicata
Calabria	Trentino-Alto Adige‡
Sicilia (Sicily)‡	Friuli-Venezia Giulia‡
Sardegna (Sardinia)‡	Valle d'Aosta‡

*In June 1997 a parliamentary commission on constitutional reform, which had been established in January, announced its recommendations, which included: a directly-elected President for a six-year term with responsibility for foreign and defence policy; a reduction of the Camera dei Deputati from 630 to 400 members and of the Senato from 315 to 200 members; greater financial autonomy for the regions; and a second round of voting for seats allocated on the basis of a simple plurality. The recommendations required approval by both the Camera dei Deputati and the Senato prior to endorsement at a national referendum.

† In October 2000 the Senato approved a bill to end compulsory military service by 2006, to be replaced by a voluntary system.

‡ These five regions have a wider form of autonomy, based on constitutional legislation specially adapted to their regional characteristics (Article 116). Each region shall be administered by a Regional Council, in which is vested the legislative power and which may make suggestions for legislation to the Chambers, and the Giunta regionale, which holds the executive power (Article 121).

The final articles provide for the establishment of the Corte Costituzionale to deal with constitutional questions and any revisions that may be found necessary after the Constitution has come into operation.

The Government

HEAD OF STATE

President of the Republic: Carlo Azeglio Ciampi (inaugurated 18 May 1999).

COUNCIL OF MINISTERS
(April 2003)

A coalition of Forza Italia (FI), Alleanza Nazionale (AN), Lega Nord, Cristiani Democratici Uniti (CDU), Centro Cristiano Democratico (CCD) and Independents (Ind.).

Prime Minister: Silvio Berlusconi (FI).

Deputy Prime Minister: Gianfranco Fini (AN).

Minister of Foreign Affairs: Franco Frattini (FI).

Minister of Internal Affairs: Giuseppe Pisanu (FI).

Minister of Justice: Roberto Castelli (Lega Nord).

Minister of Economy and Finance: Giulio Tremonti (FI).

Minister of Productive Activities: Antonio Marzano (FI).

Minister of Education, Universities and Scientific Research: Letizia Moratti (Ind.).

Minister of Labour and Social Affairs: Roberto Maroni (Lega Nord).

Minister of Defence: Antonio Martino (FI).

Minister of Agriculture and Forestry: Giovanni Alemanno (AN).

Minister of the Environment and Land Management: Altero Matteoli (AN).

Minister of Infrastructure and Transport: Pietro Lunardi (Ind.).

Minister of Health: Girolamo Sirchia (Ind.).

Minister of Culture: Giuliano Urbani (FI).

Minister of Communications: Maurizio Gasparri (AN).

Ministers without Portfolio:

Public Function: Luigi Mazzella (Ind.).

European Union Affairs: Rocco Buttiglione (CDU).

Technological Innovation: Lucio Stanca (Ind.).

Regional Affairs: Enrico La Loggia (FI).

Equal Opportunities: Stefania Prestigiacomo (FI).

Italians in the World: Mirko Tremaglia (AN).

Reforms and Devolution: Umberto Bossi (Lega Nord).

Relations with Parliament: Carlo Giovanardi (CCD).

MINISTRIES

Office of the President: Palazzo del Quirinale, 00187 Roma; tel. (06) 46991; fax (06) 46992384.

Office of the Prime Minister: Palazzo Chigi, Piazza Colonna 370, 00186 Roma; tel. (06) 67791; fax (06) 6783998; internet www.palazzochigi.it.

Ministry of Agriculture and Forestry: Via XX Settembre, 00187 Roma; tel. (06) 46651; fax (06) 4742314; internet www.politicheagricole.it.

Ministry of Communications: Viale America 201, 00144 Roma; tel. (06) 54441; fax (06) 5407728; e-mail mincom@tin.it; internet www.comunicazioni.it.

Ministry of Culture: Via del Collegio Romano 27, 00186 Roma; tel. (06) 67231; internet www.beniculturali.it.

Ministry of Defence: Via XX Settembre 8, 00187 Roma; tel. (06) 4882126; fax (06) 4747775; internet www.difesa.it.

Ministry of Economy and Finance: Viale Europa 242, 00144 Roma; tel. (06) 59971; fax (06) 5910993; internet www.finanze.it.

Ministry of Education, Universities and Scientific Research: Viale Trastevere 76A, 00153 Roma; tel. (06) 58491; fax (06) 5803381; internet www.istruzione.it.

Ministry of the Environment and Land Management: Via Cristoforo Colombo 44, 00144 Roma; tel. (06) 70361; fax (06) 6790130; internet www.minambiente.it.

Ministry of Foreign Affairs: Piazzale della Farnesina 1, 00194 Roma; tel. (06) 36911; fax (06) 3236210; e-mail info@mincomes.it; internet www.esteri.it.

Ministry of Health: Piazzale dell'Industria 20, 00144 Roma; tel. (06) 59941; fax (06) 59647749; internet www.sanita.it.

Ministry of Infrastructure and Transport: Piazza della Croce Rossa 1, 00161 Roma; tel. (06) 44101; fax (06) 8415693; internet www.infrastrutturetrasporti.it.

Ministry of Internal Affairs: Piazzale del Viminale, 00184 Roma; tel. (06) 4651; fax (06) 4741717; internet www.mininterno.it.

Ministry of Justice: Via Arenula 71, 00186 Roma; tel. (06) 68851; fax (06) 6875419; e-mail staff@giustizia.it; internet www.giustizia.it.

Ministry of Labour and Social Affairs: Via Veneto 56, 00187 Roma; tel. (06) 48161; fax (06) 48161441; e-mail capo.gabinetto@ minwelfare.it; internet www.minwelfare.it.

Ministry of Productive Activities: Viale Boston 25, 00144 Roma; tel. (06) 59931; e-mail info@mincomes.it; internet www.mincomes.it.

Legislature

PARLAMENTO
(Parliament)

Senato
(Senate)

President: MARCELLO PERA.

General Election, 13 May 2001

Parties/Alliances	Percentage of votes for seats elected by proportional representation*	Total seats
Casa delle Libertà†	42.5	177
L'Ulivo and Südtiroler Volkspartei (SVP)‡	38.7	128
Rifondazione Comunista	5.0	3
Democrazia Europea	3.2	2
Lista Di Pietro	3.4	1
Lista Bonino	2.0	—
Movimento Sociale—Fiamma Tricolore	1.0	—
Others	4.2	4
Total§	100.0	315

* Figures refer to seats elected by proportional representation (25% of the total); percentages for the remaining 75% of seats, elected by majority vote, are not available.
† Centre-right grouping including Forza Italia, the Alleanza Nazionale (AN), the Centro Cristiano Democratico (CCD), the Cristiani Democratici Uniti (CDU), the Lega Nord per l'Indipendenza della Padania, and the Nuovo Partito Socialista Italiano.
‡ Centre-left alliance comprising the Democratici di Sinistra (DS), the Partito Popolare Italiano (PPI), the Rinnovamento Italiano (RI), the Federazione dei Verdi (FV), the Partito dei Comunisti Italiani (PdCI), the Democratici per l'Ulivo, the Socialisti Democratici Italiani (SDI) and the Unione Democratici per l'Europa (UDEUR).
§ In addition to the 315 elected members, there are 10 life members.

Camera dei Deputati
(Chamber of Deputies)

President: PIER FERDINANDO CASINI.

General Election, 13 May 2001

Parties/Alliances	Percentage of votes for seat selected by proportional representation*	Total seats
Casa delle Libertà	49.4	368
Forza Italia	29.4	
Alleanza Nazionale (AN)	12.0	
Lega Nord	3.9	
Biancofiore†	3.2	
Nuovo Partito Socialista Italiano	0.9	
L'Ulivo	35.0	242
Democratici di Sinistra (DS)	16.6	
Partito dei Comunisti Italiani (PdCI)	1.7	
Margherita‡	14.5	
Girasole§	2.2	
Rifondazione Comunista	5.0	11
Lista Di Pietro	3.9	—
Democrazia Europea	2.4	—
Lista Bonino	2.3	—
Movimento Sociale—Fiamma Tricolore	0.4	—
Others	1.6	1
L'Ulivo—Südtiroler Volkspartei (SVP)	—	8
Total	100.0	630

* Figures refer to seats elected by proportional representation (25% of the total); percentages for the remaining 75% of seats, elected by majority vote, are not available.
† Coalition of the Cristiani Democratici Uniti (CDU) and the Centro Cristiano Democratico (CCD).
‡ Coalition of the Partito Popolare Italiano (PPI), the Unione Democratici per l'Europa (UDEUR) and Rinnovamento Italiano.
§ Coalition of the Federazione dei Verdi and the Socialisti Democratici Italiani (SDI).

Political Organizations

Alleanza Nazionale (AN) (National Alliance): Via della Scrofa 39, 00186 Roma; tel. (06) 688171; fax (06) 688172; e-mail ufficiostampa@ alleanzanazionale.it; internet www.alleanzanazionale.it; f. 1994; in early 1995 absorbed the neo-fascist Movimento Sociale Italiano-Destra Nazionale (MSI-DN, f. 1946); Sec.-Gen. GIANFRANCO FINI; 400,000 mems.

Associazione Riformatori per l'Europa (Association of Reformists for Europe): Largo A. Sarti 4, 00196 Roma; tel. (06) 36001070; fax (06) 36001231; Spokesman GIORGIO BENVENUTO.

Cattolici Liberali (Liberal Catholics): Piazza San Salvatore in Lauro 15, 00186 Roma; tel. (06) 68805651; fax (06) 68805706; Pres. ALBERTO MICHELINI.

Centro Cristiano Democratico (CCD) (Christian-Democratic Centre): Via dei Due Macelli 66, 00182 Roma; tel. (06) 69791001; fax (06) 6795940; e-mail amministrazione@ccd.it; internet www.ccd.it; f. 1994; Pres. MARCO FOLLINI; Pres. DEL CONSIGLIO NAZIONALE, SANDRO FONTANA.

Il Centro-Unione Popolare Democratica (The Popular Democratic Centre-Union): Piazza C. Battisti 30, 38100 Trento; tel. and fax (0461) 260416; f. 1998; Pres. RENZO GUBERT.

Coalizione Cristiana (Christian Coalition): Via U. Bassi 20, 00152 Roma; tel. (06) 58340843; fax (06) 58179926; e-mail consorzio .esteuropa@flashnet.it; Gen. Sec. DEMETRIO ERRIGO.

Coordinamento Nazionale dei Repubblicani per l'Unità della Sinistra Democratica (National Co-ordination of Republicans for the Unity of the Democratic Left): Via del Tritone 62c, 00187 Roma; tel. and fax (06) 69940909; Gen. Sec. GIORGIO BOGI.

Cristiani Democratici Uniti (CDU) (United Christian Democrats): Piazza del Gesù 46, 00186 Roma; tel. (06) 6775204; fax (06) 6785956; e-mail buttiglione@cdu.it; internet www.cdu.it; f. 1995; after split with Partito Popolare Italiano; advocates centre-right policies; Sec.-Gen. ROCCO BUTTIGLIONE.

Cristiano Democratici Europei (CDE) (European Christian Democrats): Via dei Pontefici 3, 00186 Roma; tel. (06) 68199913; fax (06) 68134196; Pres. ALESSANDRO MELUZZI; Gen. Sec. STEFANO PEDICA.

I Democratici per l'Ulivo (The Democrats for the Olive Tree): Piazza SS Apostoli 73, Roma; tel. (06) 695191; fax (06) 69781764; internet www.democraticiperlulivo.it; f. 1999; Pres. ARTURO PARISI.

Democratici di Sinistra (DS) (Democrats of the Left): Via Nazionale 75, 00184 Roma; tel. (06) 67111; fax (06) 6711596; e-mail posta@ democraticidisinistra.it; internet www.dsonline.it; f. 1921 as the Partito Comunista Italiano (PCI) (Italian Communist Party); name changed to Partito Democratico della Sinistra 1991; name changed as above 1998; advocates a democratic and libertarian society; Pres. MASSIMO D'ALEMA; Gen. Sec. PIERO FASSINO; approx. 1.4m. mems.

Democrazia è Libertà—La Margherita (Democracy is Liberty—The White Ox-Eye Daisy): Via Poli 29, 00187, Roma; e-mail organizzativo@margheritaonline.it; internet www .margheritaonline.it; f. 2002 as sub-coalition of L'Ulivo; comprising I Democratici per l'Ulivo, the Partito Popolare Italiano and Rinnovamento Italiano; Pres. FRANCESCO RUTELLI; Dir FRANCO MARINI.

Federalisti (The Federalists): Via P. Micca 4, 21047 Saronno; tel. and fax (02) 96700677; Pres. DACIRIO GHIDORZI GHIZZI.

Federazione dei Liberali Italiani (Federation of Italian Liberals): Via Laurina 20, 00187 Roma; tel. and fax (06) 32110200; e-mail liberali@luda.livorno.it; Pres. VALERIO ZANONE; Gen. Sec. RAFAELLO MORELLI.

Federazione dei Verdi (Verdi) (Green Party): Via Antonio Salandra 6, 00187 Roma; tel. (06) 4203061; fax (06) 42004600; e-mail federazione@verdi.it; internet www.verdi.it; f. 1986; advocates environmentalist and anti-nuclear policies; branch of the European Green movement; Pres. ALFONSO PECORARO SCANIO; Hon. Pres. GRAZIA FRANCESCATO.

Forum Popolare Federalista per l'Assemblea Costituente (People's Federalist Forum for the Constituent Assembly): Piazza Rondanini 29, 00186 Roma; tel. and fax (06) 6872055; Spokesman PAOLO BAMPO.

Forza Italia (FI) (Come on, Italy!): Via dell'Umiltà 36, 00187 Roma; tel. (06) 67311; fax (06) 6788255; e-mail lettere@forza-italia.it; internet www.forza-italia.it; f. 1993; advocates principles of market economy; Leader SILVIO BERLUSCONI.

Italia dei Valori—Lista Di Pietro (Italy of Values—Di Pietro List): Via Milano 14, 21052 Busto Arsizio; tel. (0331) 624412; fax (0331) 325161; e-mail dipietro@antoniodipietro.org; internet www .antoniodipietro.org; Pres. ANTONIO DI PIETRO.

Italia Democratica (Democratic Italy): Viale Col di Lana 12, 20136 Milano; tel. (02) 8392338; fax (02) 8356459; e-mail italiademocratica@virgilio.it; internet www.italiademocratica.it; Gen. Sec. NANDO DELLA CHIESA.

Lega Autonomia Veneta—Lega delle Regioni (League for the Autonomy of Veneto—League for the Regions): Via Rossarol 22, 30175 Marghera; tel. and fax (041) 935736; e-mail venetonordest@ hotmail.com; Gen. Sec. MARIO RIGO.

Lega Nord per l'Indipendenza della Padania (Northern League for the Independence of Padania): Via C. Bellerio 41, 20161 Milano; tel. (02) 66234236; fax (02) 66234402; e-mail webmaster@leganord .org; internet www.leganord.org; f. 1991; advocates federalism and transfer of control of resources to regional govts; in 1996 declared the 'Independent Republic of Padania'; opposes immigration; Pres. LUCIANO GASPERINI; Sec. UMBERTO BOSSI.

Movimento Cristiano-Sociali (Christian-Social Movement): Piazza Adriana 5, 00193 Roma; tel. (06) 68300537; fax (06) 68300539; e-mail movcs@tin.it; internet www.cristianosociali.it; Pres. DOMENICO LUCÀ; National Co-ordinator GIORGIO TONINI.

Movimento dei Comunisti Unitari (Movement of Unitary Communists): Via della Colonna Antonina 41, 00186 Roma; tel. (06) 6790293; fax (06) 6788498; e-mail mc5300@mclink.it; internet www .comunisti.org; Gen. Sec. FAMIANO CRUCIANELLI.

Movimento Federalista (Federalist Movement): Via Soperga 39, 20127 Milano; tel. (02) 26826465; fax (02) 26826788; e-mail federalisti@movimentofederalista.it; internet www .movimentofederalista.it; f. 1993; Sec. UMBERTO GIOVINE.

Movimento Italiano Democratico (Italian Democratic Movement): Via del Tritone 61, 00187 Roma; tel. (06) 6796912; fax (06) 6796915; Pres. SERGIO BERLINGUER; Gen. Sec. CARMELO PUJIA.

Movimento Sociale–Fiamma Tricolore (Social Movement of the Tricolour Flame): Via Simon de Saint Bon 89, 00195 Roma; tel. (06) 3701756; fax (06) 3720376; e-mail fiamma@msifiammatric.it; internet www.msifiammatric.it; f. 1996; electoral alliance incorporating former mems of neo-fascist Movimento Sociale Italiano-Destra Nazionale; Nat. Sec. LUCA ROMAGNOLI.

Movimento per l'Ulivo (Movement for the Olive Tree alliance): Largo Pietro di Brazzà 26, 00187 Roma; tel. (06) 6990200; fax (06) 69920457; e-mail scrivi@perlulivo.it; internet www.perlulivo.it; Gen. Sec. MARINA MAGISTRELLI.

Movimento Unitario Pensionati—Uomini Vivi (Unitary Pensioners Movement—Living Men): Via Boezio 17, 00193 Roma; tel. (06) 6878628; fax (06) 6878697; Pres. GIUSEPPE POLINI; Sec. BALILLA TATA.

Nuovo Partito Socialista Italiano (New Italian Socialist Party): Via dei Pontefici 3, 00186 Roma; tel. (06) 68892583; fax (06) 6892000; internet www.nuovopsi.com; Sec. GIANNI DE MICHELIS.

Partito Autonomista Trentino Tirolese (PATT) (Autonomist Party of Trent and the Tyrol): Piazza Silvio Pellico 5, 38100, Trento; tel. (0461) 986633; fax (0461) 986417; e-mail info@patt.tn.it; internet www.patt.tn.it; Pres. RUDI OSS.

Partito dei Comunisti Italiani (PdCI) (Party of Italian Communists): Piazza Augusto Imperatore 32, 00186 Roma; tel. (06) 686271; fax (06) 68627230; e-mail direzionenazionale@comunisti-italiani.it; internet www.comunisti-italiani.it; f. 1998; Chair. ARMANDO COSSUTTA.

Partito Liberal (Liberal Party): Via del Corso 117, 00187, Roma; tel. (06) 69549041; fax (06) 6787511; internet www.partitoliberale.it; Pres. PROF. CARLA MARTINO.

Partito Popolare Italiano (PPI) (Italian People's Party): Piazza del Gesù 46, 00186 Roma; tel. (06) 699591; fax (06) 69959324; e-mail uffstampa@pronet.it; internet www.popolari.it; f. 1994 as the successor to the Partito della Democrazia Cristiana (DC) (Christian Democrat Party f. 1943); while extending its appeal to voters of all classes, the party attempts to maintain a centre position; Sec.-Gen. PIERLUIGI CASTAGNETTI.

Partito Repubblicano Italiano (PRI) (Italian Republican Party): Corso Vittorio Emanuele 326, 00186 Roma; tel. (06) 6865044; fax (06) 6893002; e-mail ufficiostampapri@yahoo.it; internet www.pri.it; f. 1897; followers of the principles of Mazzini (social justice in a modern free society) and modern liberalism; Pres. GIORGIO LA MALFA; Gen. Sec. FRANCESCO NUCARA; 110,000 mems.

Partito della Rifondazione Comunista (PRC) (Reconstructed Communism): Viale del Policlinico 131, 00161 Roma; tel. (06) 441821; fax (06) 44182282; e-mail direzione.prc@rifondazione.it; internet www.rifondazione.it; f. 1991 by former members of the Partito Comunista Italiano (Italian Communist Party); Sec.-Gen. FAUSTO BERTINOTTI.

Partitu Sardu—Partito Sardo d'Azione (Sardinian Action Party): Via Roma 231, 09123 Cagliari; tel. (070) 657599; fax (070) 657779; internet www.psdaz-ichnos.com; Pres. LORENZO PALERMO; Sec. GIACOMO SANNA.

Patto Segni Liberaldemocratici (Segni's Pact—Liberal Democrats): Via Belsiana 100, 00187 Roma; tel. (06) 6780840; fax (06) 6789890; e-mail edpatto@tin.it; internet www.mariosegni.it; f. 1993; liberal party, advocating institutional reform; Leader MARIO SEGNI.

Pensionati Nord (Pensioners of the North): Via Silvio Pellico 8, 20121 Milano; tel. (02) 866593; fax (02) 8057079; e-mail pensionati .nord@tiscalinet.it; Sec. ROBERTO BERNARDELLI.

Pour la Vallée d'Aoste (For the Aosta Valley): Via Festaz 47, 11100 Aosta; tel. and fax (0165) 41055; Pres. CESARE DUJANY; Sec. ILARIO LANIVI.

Radicali Italiani: Roma; e-mail d.capezzone@agora.it; internet www.radicali.it; f. 2001 as il Partito Radicale; Gen. Sec. DANIELE CAPEZZONE.

Riforme e Libertà (Reforms and Freedom): Via Cornaggia 9, 20123 Milano; e-mail liberta@pobox.com; internet www.liberta.com; Pres. GUILIO SAVELLI.

Rinnovamento Italiano (Italian Renewal): Via di Ripetta 142, 00186 Roma; tel. (06) 68808380; fax (06) 68808480; e-mail informa@ rinnovamento.it; internet www.rinnovamento.it; f. 1996; centrist; Leader Prof. LAMBERTO DINI.

Socialisti Democratici Italiani (SDI) (Italian Democratic Socialists): Piazza S. Lorenzo in Lucina 26, 00186 Roma; tel. (06) 68307666; fax (06) 68307659; e-mail socialisti@socialisti.org; internet www.socialisti.org; f. 1892 as Partito Socialista Italiano (PSI); in 1966 merged with the Social Democratic Party to form the United Socialist Party, but in 1969 the Social Democrats broke away; name changed to Socialisti Italiani in 1994; in 1998 re-merged with Social Democratic Party, name changed as above; centre-left; it adheres to the Socialist International and believes that socialism is inseparable from democracy and individual freedom; Pres. ENRICO BOSSELLI.

Socialisti Riformisti Sicilia: Palermo; internet www.psi2000.it; f. 2001; left-wing Sicilian party; Pres. ANTONIO MATASSO.

Südtiroler Volkspartei (SVP) (South Tyrol People's Party): Brennerstrasse 7A, 39100 Bozen/Bolzano; tel. (0471) 304000; fax (0471) 981473; e-mail info@svpartei.org; internet www.svpartei.org; regional party of the German and Ladin-speaking people in the South Tyrol; Pres. SIEGFRIED BRUGGER; Gen. Sec. THOMAS WIDMANN.

L'Ulivo (The Olive Tree): Piazza SS. Apostoli 55, 00187 Roma; tel. (06) 696881; fax (06) 69380442; e-mail info@ulivo.it; internet www .ulivo.it; f. 1995; centre-left alliance comprising the Democratici di Sinistra (formerly the Partito Democratico della Sinistra), the Partito Popolare Italiano, the Südtiroler Volkspartei, the Unione Democratica, the Lista Romano Prodi, the Rinnovamento Italiano and the Federazione dei Verdi; Leader FRANCESCO RUTELLI.

Union Autonomista Ladina (Autonomist Ladin Movement): Via Pilat 8, 38039 Vigo di Fassa; tel. (0462) 763396; fax (0462) 763407; Pres. GINO FONTANA; Sec. GIUSEPPE DETOMAS.

Union Valdôtaine (Aosta Valley Union): Ave. des Maquisards 27/29, 11100 Aosta; tel. (0165) 235181; fax (0165) 364289; internet www.unionvaldotaine.org; Pres. AUGUSTE ROLLANDIN.

Unione Democratici per l'Europa (UDEUR)—Popolari per l'Europa (Union of Democrats for Europe): Largo Arenula 34, 00186 Roma; tel. (06) 684241; fax (06) 68210615; e-mail udeur@udeur.org; internet www.udeur.org; f. 1999; Pres. MARIDA DENTAMARO; Sec. CLEMENTE MASTELLA.

Unione Democraticocristiana e di Centro (Democratic Christian and Centrist Union): Corso Vitorio Emanuele 326, 00186, Roma; tel. (06) 6872544; fax (06) 6872543; e-mail info@sergiodantoni .it; internet www.democraziaeuropea.it; f. 2002; Pres. SERGIO D'ANTONI.

Unione Liberale di Centro (Centre-Liberal Union): Via del Tritone 62c, 00187 Roma; tel. and fax (06) 69921932; Gen. Sec. RAFFAELE COSTA; Pres. PIERLUIGI FLORIO.

Unione per la Repubblica (Union for the Republic): Via Cicerone 44, 00193 Roma; tel. (06) 36003745; fax (06) 32609549; Sec. ANGELO SANZA; Pres. FRANCESCO COSSIGA.

Veneti d'Europa (Inhabitants of the Veneto region for Europe): Viale della Navigazione Interna 23, 35129 Padua; tel. (049) 7800702; fax (049) 7803077; internet www.ligafronteveneto.org; Pres. FABRIZIO COMENCINI; Gen. Sec. ETTORE BEGGIATO.

Diplomatic Representation

EMBASSIES IN ITALY

Afghanistan: Via Nomentana, 120, 00161 Roma; tel. (06) 8611009; fax (06) 86322939; Chargé d'affaires a.i. MOSTAPHA ZAHER.

Albania: Via Asmara 3–5, 00199 Roma; tel. (06) 8621214; fax (06) 86216005; Ambassador PELLUMB XHUFI.

Algeria: Via Barnaba Oriani 26, 00197, Roma; tel. (06) 80687620; fax (06) 8083436; Ambassador MOKHTAR REGUIEG.

Angola: Via Filippo Bernardini 21, 00165 Roma; tel. (06) 39366902; fax (06) 634960; Ambassador BOAVENTURA DA SILVA CARDOSO.

Argentina: Piazza dell'Esquilino 2, 00185 Roma; tel. (06) 4742551; fax (06) 4819787; Ambassador ELSA DIANA ROSA KELLY.

Armenia: Via dei Colli della Farnesina 174, 00194 Roma; tel. (06) 3296638; fax (06) 3297763; e-mail gaghikb@tin.it; internet www .space.tin.it/associazioni/gbaghdas; Ambassador GAGHIK BAGHDAS-SARIAN.

Australia: Via Alessandria 215, 00198 Roma; tel. (06) 852721; fax (06) 85272300; e-mail info-rome@dfat.gov.au; internet www .australian-embassy.it; Ambassador MURRAY A. COBBAN.

Austria: Via G. B. Pergolesi 3, 00198 Roma; tel. (06) 8440141; fax (06) 8543286; e-mail rom-ob@bmaa.gv.at; internet www.austria.it; Ambassador ALFONS KLOSS.

Bangladesh: Via Antonio Bertoloni 14, 00197 Roma; tel. (06) 8078541; fax (06) 8084853; Ambassador MOHAMMAD ZIAUDDIN.

Belarus: Via delle Alpi Apuane 16, 00141 Roma; tel. (06) 8208141; fax (06) 82002309; Chargé d'affaires VLADIMIR KONDRATOV.

Belgium: Via dei Monti Parioli 49, 00197 Roma; tel. (06) 3609511; fax (06) 3226935; Ambassador JAN WILLEMS.

Bolivia: Via Brenta 2A, Int.18, 00198 Roma; tel. (06) 8841001; fax (06) 8840740; Chargé d'affaires a.i. MIREYA SOFIA DURAN ROSALE.

Bosnia and Herzegovina: Piazzale Clodio 12, int. 17/18, 00195 Roma; tel. (06) 39742817; fax (06) 39030567; e-mail ambasciatabosnia@libero.it; Ambassador LUKSA SOLJAN.

Brazil: Palazzo Pamphili, Piazza Navona 14, 00186 Roma; tel. (06) 683981; fax (06) 6867858; internet www.web.tin.it/brasile; Ambassador ANGELO ANDREA MATARAZZO.

Bulgaria: Via Pietro Paolo Rubens 21, 00197 Roma; tel. (06) 3224640; fax (06) 3226122; e-mail bgamb.roma@tin.it; Ambassador NIKOLA KALOUDOV.

Burkina Faso: Via Alessandria 26, 00198 Roma; tel. (06) 44250052; fax (06) 44250042; internet www.airafrique.it/burkinafaso.htm; Ambassador MAMADOU SOSSOKO.

Cameroon: Via Siracusa 4–6, 00161 Roma; tel. (06) 44291285; fax (06) 44291323; Ambassador MICHAEL TABONG KIMA.

Canada: Via G. B. de Rossi 27, 00161 Roma; tel. (06) 445981; fax (06) 44598760; e-mail rome@dfaitmaeci.gc.ca; internet www.canada .it; Ambassador ROBERT R. FOWLER.

Cape Verde: Via Giosuè Carducci 4, 00181 Roma; tel. (06) 4744678; fax (06) 4744643; Chargé d'affaires a.i. ARNALDO DELGADO.

Chile: Via Po 23, 00198 Roma; tel. (06) 844091; fax (06) 8841452; e-mail embachile.italia@flashnet.it; Ambassador JOSÉ GOÑI CAR-RASCO.

China, People's Republic: Via Bruxelles 56, 00198 Roma; tel. (06)8413458; fax (06) 85352891; Ambassador CHENG WENDONG.

Colombia: Via Giuseppe Pisanelli 4, 00196 Roma; tel. (06) 3612131; fax (06) 3225798; e-mail eroma@minrelext.gov.co; Ambassador FABIO VALENCIA COSSIO.

Congo, Democratic Republic: Via Barberini 3, 00187 Roma; tel. (06) 42010779; fax (06) 7480240; Ambassador EDOUARD UMBA ILUNGA.

Congo, Republic: Via Ombrone 8–10, 00198 Roma; tel. (06) 5567732; fax (06) 41400218; Ambassador MAMADOU KAMARA DEKAMO.

Costa Rica: Via Bartolomeo Eustachio 22, 00161 Roma; tel. (06) 44251042; fax (06) 44251048; internet www.mix.it/utenti/embcosta; Ambassador MANUEL HERNÁNDEZ GUTIÉRREZ.

Côte d'Ivoire: Via Guglielmo Saliceto 8, 00161 Roma; tel. (06) 44231129; fax (06) 44292531; Chargé d'affaires a.i. RICHARD GBAKA ZADY.

Croatia: Via Luigi Bodio 74–76, 00191 Roma; tel. (06) 36307650; fax (06) 36303405; e-mail ambasada-rh@mclink.it; Ambassador DRAGO KRALJEVIĆ.

Cuba: Via Licinia 7, 00153 Roma; tel. (06) 5717241; fax (06) 5745445; internet www.elabora95.it/ambasciatadicuba; Ambassador MARÍA DE LOS ANGELES FLÓREZ PRIDA.

Cyprus: Via Francesco Denza 15, 00197 Roma; tel. (06) 8088365; fax (06) 8088338; e-mail emb.rome@flashnet.it; Ambassador ALEXANDROS N. ZENON.

Czech Republic: Via dei Gracchi 322, 00192 Roma; tel. (06) 3244459; fax (06) 3244466; e-mail rome@embassy.mzv.cz; internet www.mzv.cz; Ambassador HANA ŠEVČÍKOVÁ.

Denmark: Via dei Monti Parioli 50, 00197 Roma; tel. (06) 3200441; fax (06) 3610290; e-mail ambadane@iol.it; Ambassador GUNNAR RIBERHOLDT.

Dominican Republic: Via Pisanelli 1, int. 8, 00196 Roma; tel. (06) 6004377; fax (06) 6004380; Ambassador LEONARDO MATOS BERRIDO.

Ecuador: Via Antonio Bertoloni 8, 00197 Roma; tel. (06) 8076272; fax (06) 8078209; e-mail mecuroma@flashnet.it; Ambassador ARTURO GANGOTENA GUARDERAS.

Egypt: Villa Savoia, Via Salaria 267, 00199 Roma; tel. (06) 8440191; fax (06) 8554424; Ambassador HELMY ABDELHAMID SALEH BEDER.

El Salvador: Via G. Castellini 13, 00197 Roma; tel. (06) 8076605; fax (06) 8079726; Ambassador MARIA EULALIA JIMÉNEZ.

Equatorial Guinea: Via Adelaide Ristori, 9/B-13, 00197, Roma; tel. and fax (06) 8078989; Chargé d'affaires a.i. ABDEL AZIZ SOUMAH.

Eritrea: Via Boncompagni 16B, 00187 Roma; tel. (06) 42741293; fax (06) 42086806; e-mail segretaria@embassyoferitrea.it; Ambassador AMDEMICAEL KAHSAI.

Estonia: Viale Liegi 28, int. 5, 00198 Roma; tel. (06) 8440751; fax (06) 844075119; e-mail saatkond@rooma.vm.ee; Ambassador JURI SEILENTHAL.

Ethiopia: Via Andrea Vesalio 16–18, 00161 Roma; tel. (06) 4402602; fax (06) 4403676; Ambassador Dr MENGISTU HULLUKA.

Finland: Via Lisbona 3, 00198 Roma; tel. (06) 852231; fax (06) 8540362; e-mail ambasciata.di.finlandia@interbusiness.it; internet www.finland.it/info/ambasciata/ambasciata.htm; Ambassador DIETER VITZTHUM.

France: Piazza Farnese 67, 00186 Roma; tel. (06) 686011; fax (06) 68601360; internet www.france-italia.it; Ambassador LOÏC HENNE-KINE.

Gabon: Via Mercalli 25, 00197 Roma; tel. (06) 80691390; fax (06) 80691504; Ambassador VINCENT BOULÉ.

Georgia: Palazzo Pierret, Piazza di Spagna 20, 00187 Roma; tel. (06) 69941972; fax (06) 69941942; Ambassador RUSSADAN LORTKIPA-NIDZE.

Germany: Via San Martino della Battaglia 4, 00185 Roma; tel. (06) 49213; fax (06) 4452672; internet www.ambgermania-roma.it; Ambassador KLAUS NEUBERT.

Ghana: Via Ostriana 4, 00199 Roma; tel. (06) 8391200; fax (06) 610270; e-mail ghembrom@rdn.net; Ambassador DR KOFI DSANE-SELBY.

Greece: Via Mercadante 36, 00198 Roma; tel. (06) 8537551; fax (06) 8415927; e-mail gremroma@tin.it; internet www.greekembassy.it; Ambassador CONSTANTIN YEROCOSTOPOULOS.

Guatemala: Via dei Colli della Farnesina 128, 00194 Roma; tel. (06) 36307392; fax (06) 3291639; e-mail embaguate.ita@flashnet.it; Chargé d'affaires a.i. EMILIO RENÉ MALDONADO GULARTE.

Haiti: Via di Villa Patrizi 7/7A, 00161 Roma; tel. (06) 44254106; fax (06) 44254208; e-mail amb.haiti@micanet.net; Ambassador ROGER PERODIN.

Holy See: Via Po 27–29, 00198 Roma; tel. (06) 8546287; fax (06) 8549725; Apostolic Nuncio Most Rev. PAOLO ROMEO (Titular Archbishop of Vulturia).

Honduras: Via Giambattista Vico 40, 00196 Roma; tel. (06) 3207236; fax (06) 3207973; e-mail embhon@tin.it; Ambassador LUIS ARMANDO BOTAZZI SUÁREZ.

Hungary: Via dei Villini 12-16, 00161 Roma; tel. (06) 4402032; fax (06) 4403270; e-mail huembit@tin.it; internet www.huembit.it; Ambassador ENIKŐ GYŐRI.

India: Via XX Settembre 5, 00187 Roma; tel. (06) 4884642; fax (06) 4819539; Ambassaor SIDDHARTH SINGH.

Indonesia: Via Campania 55, 00187 Roma; tel. (06) 4200911; fax (06) 4880280; Ambassador FREDDY NUMBERI.

Iran: Via Nomentana 361, 00162 Roma; tel. (06) 86328485; fax (06) 86328492; e-mail embassiran_rome@hotmail.com; Ambassador BAHRAM GHASEMI.

Ireland: Piazza di Campitelli 3, 00186 Roma; tel. (06) 6979121; fax (06) 6792354; Ambassador JOHN F. COGAN.

Israel: Via Michele Mercati 12, 00197 Roma; tel. (06) 36198500; fax (06) 36198555; e-mail info-coor@roma.mfa.gov.il; internet roma.mfa .gov.il; Ambassador EHUD GOL.

Japan: Via Quintino Sella 60, 00187 Roma; tel. (06) 487991; fax (06) 4873316; internet www.it.emb-japan.go.jp; Ambassador AKIRA HAY-ASHI.

Jordan: Via G. Marchi 1B, 00161 Roma; tel. (06) 86205303; fax (06) 8606122; e-mail joroma@inwind.it; Ambassador OMAR A.M. RIFAI.

Kazakhstan: Piazza Farnese 101, int. 3, 00186 Roma; tel. (06) 68808640; fax (06) 68891360; e-mail kazakhstan.emb@agora.stm.it; Ambassador BYRGANYM AITIMOVA.

Kenya: Via Archimede 164, 00197 Roma; tel. (06) 8082714; fax (06) 8082707; Chargé d'affaires a.i. BRUCE MISOGA MADETE.

Korea, Democratic People's Republic: Via Ludovico di Savoia 23, 00185 Roma; tel. (06) 77209094; fax (06) 77209111; Ambassador CHOE TAEK-SAN.

Korea, Republic: Via Barnaba Oriani 30, 00197 Roma; tel. (06) 8088820; fax (06) 80687794; Ambassador SONG YOUNG-HO.

Kuwait: Via Archimede 124-126, 00197 Roma; tel. (06) 8078415; fax (06) 8076651; Ambassador ABDULA AS SULEIMAN AL-GANAIE.

Latvia: Viale Liegi 42, 00198 Roma; tel. (06) 8841227; fax (06) 8841239; e-mail embassy.italy@mfa.gov.la; Ambassador JĀNIS LŪSIS.

Lebanon: Via Giacomino Carissimi 38, 00198 Roma; tel. (06) 8537211; fax (06) 8411794; e-mail lamba@rmnet.it; internet www .geocities.com/CapitolHill/Lobby/5290; Chargé d'affaires a.i. FADI HAJJALI.

Lesotho: Via Serchio 8, 00198 Roma; tel. (06) 8542496; fax (06) 8542527; e-mail les.rome@flashnet.it; Ambassador RACHEL R. MATHABO NTSINYI.

Liberia: Via A. Vivaldi 15, 00199 Roma; tel. (06) 86329034; fax (06) 86384898; e-mail liberiaembassy@hotmail.com; Ambassador LILY BEHNA.

Libya: Via Nomentana 365, 00162 Roma; tel. (06) 86320951; fax (06) 86205473; e-mail liberiaembassy@hotmail.com; internet allaboutliberia.com; Ambassador LILY BEHNA.

Lithuania: Viale di Villa Grazioli 9, 00198 Roma; tel. (06) 8559052; fax (06) 8559053; e-mail info@ltemb.it; Ambassador EDMINAS BAG-DONAS.

Luxembourg: Via S. Croce in Gerusalemme 90, 00185 Roma; tel. (06) 77201177; fax (06) 77201055; Ambassador JEAN FALTZ.

Macedonia, former Yugoslav republic: Viale Bruxelles 73–75, 00198 Roma; tel. (06) 84241109; fax (06) 84241131; e-mail repmaced@ats.it; Ambassador MIRIE RUSANI.

Madagascar: Via Riccardo Zandonai 84A, 00194 Roma; tel. (06) 36307797; fax (06) 3294306; Chargé d'affaires a.i. SOLOFONIAINA RANIARAMANANA.

Malaysia: Via Nomentana 297, 00162 Roma; tel. (06) 8415764; fax (06) 8555040; Ambassador SHAMSUDDIN BIN ABDULLAH.

Mali: Via Antonio Bosio 2, 00161 Roma; tel. (06) 44254068; fax (06) 44254029; e-mail amb.malirome@tiscalinet.it; Ambassador IBRAHIM BOCAR DAGA.

Malta: Lungotevere Marzio 12, 00186 Roma; tel. (06) 6879990; fax (06) 6892687; e-mail maltaembassy.rome@gov.mt; internet www .foreign.gov.mt; Ambassador EDWARD MELILLO.

Mauritania: Via Giovanni Paisiello 26, 00198 Roma; tel. (06) 85351530; fax (06) 85351441; Ambassador HAMOUD OULD ELY.

Mexico: Via Lazzaro Spallanzani 16, 00161 Roma; tel. (06) 441151; fax (06) 4403876; e-mail ofna.prensa@emexitalia.it; internet www .target.it/messico; Ambassador RAFAEL TOVAR Y DE TERESA.

Moldova: Via Montebello 8, 00185 Roma; tel. (06) 47824400; fax (06) 47881092; Ambassador VALENTIN CIUMAC.

Monaco: Via Bertoloni 36, 00197 Roma; tel. (06) 8083361; fax (06) 8077692; Ambassador HENRI FISSORE.

Morocco: Via Lazzaro Spallanzani 8, 00161 Roma; tel. (06) 4402524; fax (06) 4402695; Ambassador AZIZ MEKOUAR.

Mozambique: Via Filippo Corridoni 14, 00195 Roma; tel. (06) 37514852; fax (06) 37514699; Chargé d'affaires a.i. FRANCISCO ELIAS PAULO CIGARRO.

Myanmar: Via Gioacchino Rossini 18, 00198 Roma; tel. (06) 8549374; fax (06) 8413167; e-mail meroma@tiscali.it; Ambassador U KHIN MAUNG AYE.

Netherlands: Via Michele Mercati 8, 00197 Roma; tel. (06) 3221141; fax (06) 3221440; e-mail nlgovrom@tin.it; internet www .olanda.it; Ambassador RONALD HENRY LOUDON.

New Zealand: Via Zara 28, 00198 Roma; tel. (06) 4417171; fax (06) 4402984; e-mail nzemb.rom@flashnet.it; internet www.nzembassy .com/italy; Ambassador PETER ROBERT BENNETT.

Nicaragua: Via Brescia 16, 00198 Roma; tel. (06) 8413471; fax (06) 8841695; Ambassador JOSÉ CUADRA CHAMORRO.

Niger: Via Antonio Baiamonti 10, 00195 Roma; tel. (06) 3729013; fax (06) 37518017; Ambassador ADAMOU CHEKOU.

Nigeria: Via Orazio 14–18, 00193 Roma; tel. (06) 6896243; fax (06) 6832528; Ambassador ETIM JACK OKPOYO.

Norway: Via delle Terme Deciane 7, 00153 Roma; tel. (06) 5717031; fax (06) 57170316; Ambassador GEIR GRUNG.

Oman: Via della Camilluccia 625, 00135 Roma; tel. (06) 36300517; fax (06) 3296802; Ambassador YAHYA BIN ABDULLAH BIN SALIM AL-IRAIMY.

Pakistan: Via della Camilluccia 682, 00135 Roma; tel. (06) 36301775; fax (06) 36301936; e-mail pareprom@linet.it; Ambassador ZAFAR A. HILALY.

Panama: Viale Regina Margherita 239, 00198 Roma; tel. (06) 44252173; fax (06) 44252237; Ambassador ROBERTO ALFARO ESTRI-PEAUT.

Paraguay: Viale Castro Pretorio 116, 00185 Roma; tel. (06) 44704684; fax (06) 4461119; Ambassador LILIA ROMERO PEREIRA.

Peru: Via Siacci 4, 00197 Roma; tel. (06) 80691510; fax (06) 80691777; e-mail amb.peru@agora.stm.it; Ambassador HUGO PALMA.

Philippines: Viale delle Medaglie d'Oro 112-114, 00136 Roma; tel. (06) 39746621; fax (06) 39740872; e-mail ph1@agora.it; Ambassador PHILIPPE J. LHUILLIER.

Poland: Via Pietro Paolo Rubens 20, 00197 Roma; tel. (06) 3224455; fax (06) 3217895; Ambassador MICHAŁ RADLICKI.

Portugal: Viale Liegi 21–23, 00198 Roma; tel. (06) 844801; fax (06) 8417404; e-mail embptroma@virgilio.it; Ambassador VASCO VALENTE.

Qatar: Via Antonio Bosio 14, 00161 Roma; tel. (06) 44249450; fax (06) 44245273; Ambassador ALI FAHAD ASH-SHAHAWANI AL-HAJERI.

Romania: Via Nicolò Tartaglia 36, 00197 Roma; tel. (06) 8084529; fax (06) 8084995; e-mail amdiroma@libero.it; internet www.roembit .org; Ambassador SERBAN STATI.

Russia: Via Gaeta 5, 00185 Roma; tel. (06) 4941680; fax (06) 491031; Ambassador NIKOLAI NIKOLAYEVICH SPASSKII.

San Marino: Via Eleonora Duse 35, 00197 Roma; tel. (06) 8072511; fax (06) 8070072; Ambassador BARBARA PARA.

Saudi Arabia: Via G. B. Pergolesi 9, 00198 Roma; tel. (06) 844851; fax (06) 8551781; e-mail ambasciata.saudita@arabia-saudita.it; internet www.arabia-saudita.it; Ambassador MUHAMMAD BIN NAWAF BIN ABD AL-AZIZ AL-SAUD.

Senegal: Via Giulia 66, 00186 Roma; tel. (06) 6872381; fax (06) 68219294; e-mail ambasenequiri@tiscali.it; Ambassador MOMAR GUEYE.

Serbia and Montenegro: Via dei Monti Parioli 20, 00197 Roma; tel. (06) 3200805; fax (06) 3200868; e-mail darfj@flashnet.it; Ambassador MIODRAG LEKIĆ.

Slovakia: Via dei Colli della Farnesina 144, 00194 Roma; tel. (06) 367151; fax (06) 36715265; e-mail amb.slovac@virgilio.it; Ambassador JOZSEF MIKLOŠKO.

Slovenia: Via Leonardo Pisano 10, 00197 Roma; tel. (06) 80914310; fax (06) 8081471; e-mail vri@mzz-dkp.gov.si; Ambassador VOJKO VOLK.

South Africa: Via Tanaro 14, 00198 Roma; tel. (06) 852541; fax (06) 85254300; e-mail sae2@sudafrica.it; internet www.sudafrica.it; Ambassador ANTHONY LE CLERK MONGALO.

Spain: Palazzo Borghese, Largo Fontanella Borghese 19, 00186 Roma; tel. (06) 6840401; fax (06) 6872256; e-mail ambespit@correo .es; Ambassador JOSÉ DE CARVAJAL SALIDO.

Sri Lanka: Via Adige 2, 00198 Roma; tel. (06) 8554560; fax (06) 84241670; e-mail mc7785@mclink.it; Ambassador THELMUTH HARRIS WILHELM WOUTERSZ.

Sudan: Via Lazzaro Spallanzani 24, 00161 Roma; tel. (06) 4403071; fax (06) 4402358; Ambassador ANDREW MAKUR THOU.

Sweden: Piazza Rio de Janeiro 3, 00161 Roma; tel. (06) 441941; fax (06) 44194760; Ambassador ROLF GORAN KRISTOFFER BERG.

Switzerland: Via Barnaba Oriani 61, 00197 Roma; tel. (06) 809571; fax (06) 8088510; Ambassador ALEXEI LAUTENBERG.

Syria: Piazza dell'Ara Coeli 1, 00186 Roma; tel. (06) 674980; fax (06) 6794989; Chargé d'affaires a.i. NABILA CHAALAN.

Tanzania: Via Cesare Beccaria 88, 00196 Roma; tel. (06) 36005234; fax (06) 3216611; e-mail ambassador@tanzania-gov.it; internet www .tanzania-gov.it; Ambassador COSTA RICKY MAHALU.

Thailand: Via Nomentana 132, 00162 Roma; tel. (06) 86204381; fax (06) 86208399; e-mail thai.em.rome@pn.itnet.it; Ambassador VIKROM KOOMPIROCHANA.

Tunisia: Via Asmara 7, 00199 Roma; tel. (06) 8603060; fax (06) 86218204; Ambassador MOHAMED JEGHAM.

Turkey: Via Palestro 28, 00185 Roma; tel. (06) 4469933; fax (06) 4941526; Ambassador NECATI UTKAN.

Uganda: Via Ennio Quirino Visconti 8, 00193 Roma; tel. (06) 3225220; fax (06) 3213688; Ambassador VINCENT KIRABOKYAMARIA.

Ukraine: Via Guido d'Arezzo 9, 00198 Roma; tel. (06) 8412630; fax (06) 8547539; Ambassador BORYS GUDYAMA.

United Arab Emirates: Via della Camilluccia 492, 00135 Roma; tel. (06) 36306100; fax (06) 36306155; Ambassador MUHAMMAD FAHD ABDULRAHMAN ADH-DHAIM.

United Kingdom: Via XX Settembre 80A, 00187 Roma; tel. (06) 42200001; fax (06) 42202347; e-mail info@rome.mail.fco.gov.uk; internet www.britain.it; Ambassador JOHN SHEPHERD.

USA: Via Vittorio Veneto 119A, 00187 Roma; tel. (06) 46741; fax (06) 46742356; internet www.usembassy.it; Ambassador MELVIN F. SEMBLER.

Uruguay: Via Vittorio Veneto 183-5°, 00187 Roma; tel. (06) 4821776; fax (06) 4823695; e-mail emb.uruguay@agora.it; Ambassador CARLOS ALEJANDRO BARROS OREIRO.

Uzbekistan: Via Tolmino 12, 00198 Roma; tel. (06) 8542456; fax (06) 8541020; e-mail uzbembass@libero.it; internet www .uzbekistanitalia.com; Chargé d'affaires a.i. KHURSHID M. BABASHEV.

Venezuela: Via Nicolò Tartaglia 11, 00197 Roma; tel. (06) 8079797; fax (06) 8084410; e-mail embaveit@iol.it; internet users.libero.it/ embaveit; Ambassador FERNANDO GERBASI.

Viet Nam: Via Clitunno 34–36, 00198 Roma; tel. (06) 8543223; fax (06) 8548501; e-mail suquanvn@tin.it; Ambassador LE VINH THU.

Yemen: Viale Regina Margherita 1, 00196 Roma; tel. (06) 8416711; fax (06) 8416801; Chargé d'affaires a.i. MUHAMMAD SALEH AHMED AL-HELALY.

Zimbabwe: Via Virgilio 8, 00193 Roma; tel. (06) 68308282; fax (06) 68308324; e-mail zimrome@tiscalinet.it; Ambassador MARY MARGARET MUCHADA.

Judicial System

The Constitutional Court was established in 1956 and is an autonomous constitutional body, standing apart from the judicial system. Its most important function is to pronounce on the constitutionality of legislation both subsequent and prior to the present Constitution of 1948. It also judges accusations brought against the President of the Republic or ministers.

At the base of the system of penal jurisdiction are the Preture (District Courts), where offences carrying a sentence of up to four years' imprisonment are tried. Above the Preture are the Tribunali (Tribunals) and the Corti di Assise presso i Tribunali (Assize Courts attached to the Tribunals), where graver offences are dealt with. From these courts appeal lies to the Corti d'Appello (Courts of Appeal) and the parallel Corti di Assise d'Appello (Assize Courts of Appeal). Final appeal may be made, on juridical grounds only, to the Corte Suprema di Cassazione.

Civil cases may be taken in the first instance to the Giudici Conciliatori (Justices of the Peace), Preture or Tribunali, according to the economic value of the case. Appeal from the Giudici Conciliatori lies to the Preture, from the Preture to the Tribunali, from the Tribunali to the Corti d'Appello, and finally, as in penal justice, to the Corte Suprema di Cassazione on juridical grounds only.

Special divisions for cases concerning labour relations are attached to civil courts. Cases concerned with the public service and its employees are tried by Tribunali Amministrativi Regionali and the Consiglio di Stato. Juvenile courts have criminal and civil jurisdiction.

A new penal code was introduced in late 1989.

Consiglio Superiore della Magistratura (CSM)
Piazza dell'Indipendenza 6, 00185 Roma; tel. (06) 444911; internet www.csm.it.

f. 1958; supervisory body of judicial system; 27 mems.

President: The President of the Republic

CONSTITUTIONAL COURT

Corte Costituzionale
Palazzo della Consulta, Piazza del Quirinale 41, 00187 Roma; tel. (06) 4698560; fax (06) 4885239; e-mail segretaria.generale@ cortcostituzionale.it; internet www.cortecostituzionale.it.

Consists of 15 judges, one-third appointed by the President of the Republic, one-third elected by Parliament in joint session, one-third by the ordinary and administrative supreme courts.

President: RICCARDO CHIEPPA.

ADMINISTRATIVE COURTS

Consiglio di Stato
Palazzo Spada, Piazza Capo di Ferro 13, 00186 Roma; tel. (06) 68271; fax (06) 6827534.

Established in accordance with Article 10 of the Constitution; has both consultative and judicial functions.

President: ALBERTO DE ROBERTO.

Corte dei Conti
Via Antonio Baiamonti 25, 00195 Roma; and Via Barberini 38, Roma; tel. (06) 38761; fax (06) 38763477; e-mail uric@corteconti.it; internet www.corteconti.it.

Functions as the court of public auditors for the State.

President: FRANCESCO STADERINI.

SUPREME COURT OF APPEAL

Corte Suprema di Cassazione
Palazzo di Giustizia, 00193 Roma; tel. (06) 68831; fax (06) 6883420. Supreme court of civil and criminal appeal.

First President: ANDREA VELA.

Religion

More than 90% of the population of Italy are adherents of the Roman Catholic Church. Under the terms of the Concordat formally ratified in June 1985, Roman Catholicism was no longer to be the state religion, compulsory religious instruction in schools was abolished and state financial contributions reduced. The Vatican City's sovereign rights as an independent state, under the terms of the Lateran Pact of 1929, were not affected.

Several Protestant churches also exist in Italy, with a total membership of about 50,000. There is a small Jewish community, and in 1987 an agreement between the State and Jewish representatives recognized certain rights for the Jewish community, including the right to observe religious festivals on Saturdays by not attending school or work. In March 2000 Jehovah's Witnesses and Buddhism were officially recognized as religions by the Italian legislature.

CHRISTIANITY

The Roman Catholic Church
For ecclesiastical purposes, Italy comprises the Papal See of Rome, the Patriarchate of Venice, 60 archdioceses (including six directly responsible to the Holy See), 157 dioceses (including seven within the jurisdiction of the Pope, as Archbishop of the Roman Province, and 17 directly responsible to the Holy See), two territorial prelatures (including one directly responsible to the Holy See) and seven territorial abbacies (including four directly responsible to the Holy See). Almost all adherents follow the Latin rite, but there are two dioceses and one abbacy (all directly responsible to the Holy See) for Catholics of the Italo-Albanian (Byzantine) rite.

Bishops' Conference
Conferenza Episcopale Italiana, Circonvallazione Aurelia 50, 00165 Roma; tel. (06) 663981; fax (06) 6623037; e-mail segrgen@ chiesacattolica.it; internet www.chiesacattolica.it.

f. 1965; Pres. HE Cardinal CAMILLO RUINI (Vicar-General of Rome); Sec.-Gen. Mons GIUSEPPE BETORI.

Primate of Italy, Archbishop and Metropolitan of the Roman Province and Bishop of Rome: His Holiness Pope JOHN PAUL II.

Patriarch of Venice: Most Rev. ANGELO SCOLA.

Archbishops:

Acerenza
Most Rev. MICHELE SCANDIFFIO.

Agrigento
Most Rev. CARMELO FERRARO.

Amalfi-Cava de'Tirreni
Most Rev. ORAZIO SORICELLI.

Ancona-Osimo
Most Rev. FRANCO FESTORAZZI.

Bari-Bitonto
Most Rev. FRANCESCO CACUCCI.

Benevento
Most Rev. SERAFINO SPROVIERI.

Bologna
HE Cardinal GIACOMO BIFFI.

Brindisi-Ostuni
Most Rev. ROCCO TALUCCI.

Cagliari
Most Rev. OTTORINO PIETRO ALBERTI.

Camerino-San Severino Marche
Most Rev. ANGELO FAGIANI.

Campobasso-Boiano
Most Rev. ARMANDO DINI.

Capua
Most Rev. BRUNO SCHETTINO.

Catania
Most Rev. SALVATORE GRISTINA.

Catanzaro-Squillace
Most Rev. ANTONIO CILIBERTI.

Chieti-Vasto
Most Rev. EDOARDO MENICHELLI.

Cosenza-Bisignano
Most Rev. GIUSEPPE AGOSTINO.

Crotone-Santa Severina
Most Rev. ANDREA MUGIONE.

Fermo
Most Rev. GENNARO FRANCESCHETTI.

Ferrara-Comacchio
Most Rev. CARLO CAFFARRA.

Florence
Most Rev. ENNIO ANTONELLI.

Foggia-Bovino
Most Rev. DOMENICO UMBERTO D'AMBROSIO.

Gaeta
Most Rev. PIER LUIGI MAZZONI.

Genoa
Most Rev. TARCISIO BERTONE.

Gorizia
Most Rev. DINO DE ANTONI.

Lanciano-Ortona
Most Rev. CARLO GHIDELLI.

L'Aquila
Most Rev. GIUSEPPE MOLINARI.

Lecce
Most Rev. COSMO FRANCESCO RUPPI.

Lucca
Most Rev. BRUNO TOMMASI.

Manfredonia-Vieste-San Giovanni Rotondo
(vacant).

Matera-Irsina
(vacant).

Messina-Lipari-Santa Lucia del Mela
Most Rev. GIOVANNI MARRA.

Milan
HE Cardinal DIONIGI TETTAMANZI.

Modena-Nonantola
Most Rev. BENITO COCCHI.

Monreale
Most Rev. CATALDO NARO.

Naples
HE Cardinal MICHELE GIORDANO.

Oristano
Most Rev. PIER GIULIANO TIDDIA.

Otranto
Most Rev. DONATO NEGRO.

Palermo
HE Cardinal SALVATORE DE GIORGI.

Perugia-Città della Pieve
Most Rev. GIUSEPPE CHIARETTI.

Pesaro
Most Rev. ANGELO BAGNASCO.

Pescara-Penne
Most Rev. FRANCESCO CUCCARESE.

Pisa
Most Rev. ALESSANDRO PLOTTI.

Potenza-Muro Lucano-Marsico Nuovo
Most Rev. AGOSTINO SUPERBO.

Ravenna-Cervia
Most Rev. GIUSEPPE VERUCCHI.

Reggio Calabria-Bova
Most Rev. VITTORIO LUIGI MONDELLO.

Rossano-Cariati
Most Rev. ANDREA CASSONE.

Salerno-Campagna-Acerno
Most Rev. GERARDO PIERRO.

Sant'Angelo dei Lombardi-Conza-Nusco-Bisaccia
Most Rev. SALVATORE NUNNARI.

Sassari
Most Rev. SALVATORE ISGRÓ.

Siena-Colle di Val d'Elsa-Montalcino
Most Rev. ANTONIO BUONCRISTIANI.

Sorrento-Castellammare di Stabia
Most Rev. FELICE CECE.

Spoleto-Norcia
Most Rev. RICCARDO FONTANA.

Syracuse
Most Rev. GIUSEPPE COSTANZO.

Taranto
Most Rev. BENIGNO LUIGI PAPA.

Trani-Barletta-Bisceglie
Most Rev. GIOVANNI BATTISTA PICHIERRI.

Trento
Most Rev. LUIGI BRESSAN.

Turin
HE Cardinal SEVERINO POLETTO.

Udine
Most Rev. PIETRO BROLLO.

Urbino-Urbania-Sant'Angelo in Vado
Most Rev. FRANCESCO MARINELLI.

Vercelli
Most Rev. ENRICO MASSERONI.

Azione Cattolica Italiana (ACI) (Italian Catholic Action): Via Aurelia 481, 00193 Roma; tel. (06) 6631545; fax (06) 6621256; in Italy there are numerous apostolic lay organizations, prominent among which is Italian Catholic Action, which has a total membership of 1m. National Presidency is the supreme executive body and co-ordinator of the different branches of Catholic Action; Pres. Dott.ssa PAOLA BIGNARDI; Sec.-Gen. Ing. GILBERTO ZOFFOLI.

Protestant Churches

Federazione delle Chiese Evangeliche in Italia (Federation of the Protestant Churches in Italy): Via Firenze 38, 00184 Roma; tel. (06) 4825120; fax (06) 4828728; e-mail fcei@fcei.it; the Federation was formed in 1967; total mems more than 50,000; Pres. Dott. GIANNI LONG; Sec. Dr RENATO MAIOCCHI; includes the following organizations:

Chiesa Evangelica Luterana in Italia (Lutheran Church): Via Toscana 7, 00187 Roma; tel. (06) 4880394; fax (06) 4874506; e-mail decanato@elki-celi.org; Dean JÜRGEN ASTFALK; 20,100 mems.

Esercito della Salvezza (Salvation Army): Via degli Apuli 39, 00185 Roma; tel. (06) 4463912; fax (06) 490078; e-mail pascalads@hotmail.com; internet www.esercitodellasalvezza.org; Officer Commanding for Italy Maj. MASSIMO PAONE; 19 regional centres.

Opera per le Chiese Evangeliche Metodiste in Italia (Board of the Evangelical Methodist Churches in Italy): Via Firenze 38, 00184 Roma; tel. (06) 4743695; fax (06) 47881267; e-mail metodismo@tin.it; f. 1861; merged with Waldensian Church 2002; Pres. Pastor MASSIMO AQUILANTE; 4,000 mems.

Tavola Valdese (Waldensian Church): Via Firenze 38, 00184 Roma; tel. (06) 4745537; fax (06) 47885308; e-mail moderatore@chiesavaldese.org; internet www.chiesavaldese.org; Moderator GIANNI GENRE; Sec.-Treas. ROSELLA PANZIRONI; 27,465 mems.

Unione Cristiana Evangelica Battista d'Italia (Italian Baptist Union): Piazza San Lorenzo in Lucina 35, 00186 Roma; tel. (06) 6876124; fax (06) 6876185; e-mail ucebit@tin.it; f. 1873; Pres. ALDO CASONATO; 5,000 mems.

Associated Organization

Seventh-day Adventists: Lungotevere Michelangelo 7, 00192 Roma; tel. (06) 3609591; fax (06) 36095952; e-mail uicca@avventisti.org; internet www.avventisti.org; f. 1929; represents 90 communities in Italy and Malta; Supt LUCIO ALTIN; Sec. IGNAZIO BARBUSCIA.

JUDAISM

The number of Jews was estimated at 30,000 in 1997.

Union of Italian Jewish Communities: Lungotevere Sanzio 9, 00153 Roma; tel. (06) 5803667; fax (06) 5899569; f. 1930; represents 21 Jewish communities in Italy; Pres. AMOS LUZZATTO; Chief Rabbi of Rome Dr. RICCARDO DI SEGNI.

Rabbinical Council: Chief Rabbi Prof. GIUSEPPE LARAS (Via Guastalla 19, Milano), Rabbi SHALOM BACHBOUT (c/o UCEI, Lungotevere Sanzio 9, Roma); Chief Rabbi ALBERTO SOMEKH (Ptta. Primo Levi 12, Torino).

BAHÁ'Í FAITH

Assemblea Spirituale Nazionale: Via Stoppani 10, 00197 Roma; tel. (06) 8079647; fax (06) 8070184; e-mail segreteria@bahai.it; internet www.bahai.it; mems resident in 420 localities.

The Press

Relative to the size of Italy's population, the number of daily newspapers is rather small (78 in 1996). The average total circulation of daily newspapers in 1996 was 5,960,000 copies per issue; sales in the north and centre of the country accounted for 80% of this figure, and those in the south for 20%.

Rome and Milan are the main press centres. The most important national dailies are *Corriere della Sera* in Milan and Rome and *La Repubblica* in Rome, followed by Turin's *La Stampa*, *Il Sole 24 Ore* in Milan, the economic and financial newspaper with the highest circulation in Europe, *Il Messaggero* in Rome, *Il Resto del Carlino* in Bologna, *La Nazione* in Florence, and *Il Giornale* and *Il Giorno*, which circulate mainly in the north.

In 1993 there were about 10,000 periodical titles, with a combined annual circulation of some 4,036m. Many illustrated weekly papers and magazines maintain very high levels of circulation, with *TV Sorrisi e Canzoni* and *Famiglia Cristiana* enjoying the highest figures. Other very popular general-interest weeklies are *Gente* and *Oggi*. Among the serious and influential magazines are *Panorama* and *L'Espresso*.

PRINCIPAL DAILIES

Ancona

Il Corriere Adriatico: Via Berti 20, 60126 Ancona; tel. (071) 4581; fax (071) 42980; e-mail corriere.adriatico@fastnet.it; f. 1860; Dir SESTO EGIDI; circ. 29,349.

Bari

La Gazzetta del Mezzogiorno: Viale Scipione l'Africano 264, 70124 Bari; tel. (080) 5470200; fax (080) 5470488; internet www.gdmland.it; f. 1887; independent; Man. Dir PASQUALE PATRUNO; circ. 82,398.

Il Quotidiano di Bari: Piazza Aldo Moro 31, 70121 Bari; tel. (080) 5240473; fax (080) 5245486; Dir LUCIANO VENTURA.

Bergamo

L'Eco di Bergamo: Viale Papa Giovanni XXIII 118, 24121 Bergamo; tel. (035) 386111; fax (035) 386217; e-mail redazione@eco.bg.it; internet www.eco.bg.it; f. 1880; Catholic; Man. Dr ETTORE ONGIS; circ. 59,114.

Il Nuovo Giornale di Bergamo: Vis S. Bernardino 120, 24126 Bergamo; tel. (035) 4243161; fax (035) 4243160; Dir SERGIO CARRARO.

Bologna

Il Resto del Carlino: Via Enrico Mattei 106, 40138 Bologna; tel. (051) 6006111; fax (051) 536111; internet www.ilrestodelcarlino.it; f. 1885; independent; Dir MARCO LEONELLI; circ. 250,000.

Bolzano/Bozen

Alto Adige: Via Volta 10, 39100 Bozen; tel. (0471) 904111; fax (0471) 9042663; e-mail altoadi@tin.it; internet www.altoadige.it; f. 1945; independent; Dir GIAMPAOLO VISETTI; circ. 55,000.

Dolomiten: Via del Vigneto/Weinbergweg 7, 39100 Bozen; tel. (0471) 925111; fax 925440; e-mail dolomiten@athesia.it; internet www.dolomiten.it; f. 1882; independent; German language; Dir Dr TONI EBNER; circ. 56,623.

Il Mattino dell'Alto Adige: Via Dante 5, 39100 Bozen; tel. (0471) 978478; fax (0471) 990729; internet www.ilmattinobz.it; f. 1988; Dir PAOLO GHEZZI; circ. 4,000.

Brescia

Bresciaoggi Nuovo: Via Eritrea 20a, 25126 Brescia; tel. (030) 2294260; fax (030) 2294229; internet www.bresciaoggi.it; f. 1974; Dir MAURIZIO CATTANEO; circ. 19,000.

Il Giornale di Brescia: Via Solferino 22, 25121 Brescia; tel. (030) 37901; fax (030) 292226; f. 1945; Editor GIAN BATTISTA LANZANI; Man. Dir FRANCESCO PASSERINI GLAZEL; circ. 70,000.

Cagliari

L'Unione Sarda: Viale Regina Elena 12, 9100 Cagliari; tel. (070) 60131; fax (070) 6013306; e-mail unione@unionesarda.it; internet www.unionesarda.it; f. 1889; independent; Man. ANTONANGELO LIORI; circ. 97,000.

Catania

La Sicilia: Viale Odorico da Pordenone 50, 95126 Catania; tel. (095) 330544; fax (095) 336466; e-mail teee-lasicilia@ctonline.it; internet www.lasicilia.it; f. 1945; independent; Man. Dott. MARIO CIANCIO SANFILIPPO; circ. 80,000.

Como

Corriere di Como: Via Vittorio Emanuele II 115, 22100 Como; tel. (031) 337788; fax (031) 3377823; e-mail redazione@corrierecomo.it; internet www.corrieredicomo.it; Dir MARIO RAPISARDA.

La Provincia di Como: Via Pasquale Paoli 21, 22100 Como; tel. (031) 582311; fax (031) 505003; e-mail laprovincia@laprovincia.it; f. 1892; independent; Dir ALESSANDRO SALLUSTI; circ. 56,000.

Cremona

La Provincia di Cremona: Via delle Industrie 2, 26100 Cremona; tel. (0372) 4981; fax (0372) 28487; internet www.cremonaonline.it; f. 1947; independent; Pres. MARIO MAESTRONI; Man. Dir ENRICO PIRONDINI; circ. 23,560.

Ferrara

La Nuova Ferrara: Via Baruffaldi 22, 44100 Ferrara; tel. (0532) 214211; fax (0532) 247689; internet www.lanuovaferrara.it; f. 1989; independent; Man. Dir VALENTINO PESCI; circ. 18,788.

Foggia

Foggia Sera: Corso Roma 204b, 71100 Foggia; tel. (0881) 632259; fax (0881) 661534; Dir MATTEO TATTARELLA.

Il Quotidiano di Foggia: Corso Roma 204b, 71100 Foggia; tel. (0881) 686967; fax (0881) 777812; Dir MATTEO TATTARELLA.

Florence

La Nazione: Via Ferdinando Paolieri 2, 50121 Firenze; tel. (055) 87951; fax (055) 2478207; internet www.lanazione.it; f. 1859; independent; Dir UMBERTO CECCHI; circ. 200,000.

Genoa

L'Avvisatore Marittimo: Piazza Piccapietra 21, 16121 Genova; tel. (010) 545341; fax (010) 5453436; e-mail avvmar@tin.it; internet www.avvmar.it; f. 1919; shipping and financial; Editor SANDRO GRIMALDI; circ. 5,000.

Corriere Mercantile: Via Archimede 169/R, 16142 Genova; tel. (010) 53691; fax (010) 504148; f. 1824; political and financial; independent; Editor MIMMO ANGELI; circ. 16,000.

Il Secolo XIX: Piazza Piccapietra 21, 16122 Genova; tel. (010) 53881; fax (010) 5388388; e-mail amministrazione@ilsecoloxix.it; internet www.ilsecoloXIX.it; f. 1886; independent; Dir ANTONIO DI ROSA; circ. 179,360.

Lecce

Quotidiano di Lecce, Brindisi e Taranto: Via dei Mocenigo 25–29, 73100 Lecce; tel. (0832) 3382000; fax (0832) 338244; f. 1979; Dir GIANCARLO MINICUCCI; circ. 26,502.

Leghorn/Livorno

Il Tirreno: Viale Alfieri 9, 57124 Livorno; tel. (0586) 220111; fax (0586) 220717; e-mail iltirreno@petrurianet.it; internet www.iltirreno.it; f. 1978; independent; Dir SANDRA BONSANTI; circ. 91,595.

Lodi

Il Cittadino: Via Paolo Gorini 34, 26900, Lodi; tel. (0371) 544200; fax (0371) 544201; e-mail redazione@ilcittadino.it; internet www.ilcittadino.it; f. 1890; Dir FERRUCCIO PALLAVERA; circ. 14,200.

Mantua

Gazzetta di Mantova: Via Fratelli Bandiera 32, 46100 Mantova; tel. (0376) 3031; fax (0376) 303263; internet www.gazzettadimantova.it; f. 1664; independent; Man. SERGIO VARALDI; circ. 45,000.

Messina

Gazzetta del Sud: Uberto Bonino 15c, 98124 Messina; tel. (090) 2261; fax (090) 2936359; internet www.gazzettadelsud.it; f. 1952; independent; Dir NINO CALARCO; circ. 70,000.

Milan

Avvenire: Piazza Carbonari 3, 20125 Milano; tel. (02) 67801; fax (02) 6780208; internet www.avvenire.it; f. 1968; Catholic; Man. Dir DINO BOFFO; circ. 138,000.

Corriere della Sera: Via Solferino 28, 20121 Milano; tel. (02) 6339; fax (02) 29009668; internet www.corriere.it; f. 1876; independent; contains weekly supplement, *Sette*; Dir FERRUCCIO DE BORTOLI; circ. 886,832.

Il Foglio Quotidiano: Largo Corsua dei Servi 3, 20122 Milano; tel. (02) 7712951; fax (02) 781378; e-mail lettere@ilfoglio.it; internet www.ilfoglio.it; Dir GIULIANO FERRARA.

La Gazzetta dello Sport: RCS Editoriale Quotidiani SpA, Via Solferino 28, 20121 Milano; tel. (02) 6339; fax (02) 29009668; e-mail gasport@rcs.it; internet www.gazzetta.it; f. 1896; sport; Dir CANDIDO CANNAVÒ; circ. 426,000.

Il Giornale: Via Gaetano Negri 4, 20123 Milano; tel. (02) 85661; fax (02) 72023859; e-mail segreteria@ilgiornale.it; f. 1974; independent, controlled by staff; Editor MAURIZIO BELPIETRO; circ. 350,000.

Il Giorno: Via Stradivari 4, 20131 Milano; tel. (02) 277991; fax (02) 27799537; e-mail ilgiorno@ilgiorno.it; internet www.ilgiorno.it; Chief Editor GABRIELE CANE; circ. 255,377.

Italia Oggi: Classe Editori, Via M. Burigozzo 5, 20122 Milano; tel. (02) 58219256; e-mail italiaoggi@class.it; internet www.italiaoggi.it; ; economic daily.

MF (MilanoFinanza): Classe Editori, Via M. Burigozzo 5, 20122 Milano; internet www.milanofinanza.it; economic daily.

Il Sole 24 Ore: Via Paolo Lomazzo 52, 20154 Milano; tel. (02) 30221; fax (02) 312055; internet www.ilsole24ore.com; f. 1865; financial, political, economic; Dir GUIDO GENTILI; circ. 417,153.

Modena

Nuova Gazzetta di Modena: Via Ricci 56, 41100 Modena; tel. (059) 247311; fax (059) 226533; internet www.nuovagazzettadimodena.it; Dir ANTONIO MASCOLO; circ. 16,500.

Naples

Corriere del Mezzogiorno: Vico II san Nicola alla dogana 9, 80133 Napoli; tel. (081) 7602001; fax (081) 5802779; internet www.corrieredelmezzogiorno.it; Dir MARCO DEMARCO.

Il Denaro: Piazza dei Martiri 58, 80121 Napoli; tel. (081) 421900; fax (081) 422212; e-mail denaro@denaro.it; internet www.ildenaro.it; economic daily; Dir ALFONSO RUFFO.

Il Giornale di Napoli: Piazzetta Matilde Serao 19, 80133 Napoli; tel. (081) 497200; fax (081) 497227; e-mail gdn@itb.it; internet dns.itb.it/gdn/; f. 1985; Editor ROBERTO TUMBARELLO; circ. 11,000.

Il Mattino: Soc Ed Edime Spa, Via Chiatamone 65, 80121 Napoli; tel. (081) 7947111; fax (081) 7947288; internet www.ilmattino.it; f. 1892; reformed 1950; independent; Dir PAOLO GRALDI; Editor MARINO LONGONI; circ. 200,000.

Padua

Il Mattino di Padova: Via Pelizzo 3, 35128 Padua; tel. (049) 8083411; fax (049) 8079067; internet www.mattinopadova.it; f. 1978; Dir ALBERTO STATERA; circ. 30,082.

Palermo

Giornale di Sicilia: Via Lincoln 21, 90122 Palermo; tel. (091) 6627111; fax (091) 6627280; internet www.gds.it; f. 1860; independent; Man. GIOVANNI PEPI; circ. 66,415.

Parma

Gazzetta di Parma: Via Emilio Casa 5A, 43100 Parma; tel. (0521) 2251; fax (0521) 285515; e-mail gazzpr@tin.it; internet www.gazzettadiparma.it; f. 1735; Dir GIULIANO MOLOSSI; circ. 56,000.

Pavia

La Provincia Pavese: Viale Canton Ticino 16–18, 27100 Pavia; tel. (0382) 434511; fax (0382) 473875; e-mail info@laprovincia.pv.it; internet www.laprovincia.pv.it; f. 1866; independent; Man. ENRICO GRAZIOLI; circ. 25,000.

Perugia

Corriere dell'Umbria: Via Pievaiola km 5700, 06100 Perugia; tel. (075) 52731; fax (075) 5273259; internet www.corr.it; f. 1983; independent; Editor FEDERICO FIORAVANTI; circ. 23,000.

Pescara

Il Centro: Corso Vittorio Emanuele 372, 65100 Pescara; tel. (085) 20521; fax (085) 4212460; e-mail ilcentro@micso.it; internet www.ilcentro.it; f. 1986; independent; Dir ANTONIO DEL GIUDICE; circ. 30,000.

Piacenza

Libertà: Via Benedettine 68, 29100 Piacenza; tel. (0523) 393939; fax (0523) 393962; e-mail area.prestampa@liberta; internet www.liberta.it; f. 1883; Dir GAETANO RIZZUTO; circ. 40,000.

Reggio Emilia

Gazzetta di Reggio: Via Isonzo 72/A-B, 42100 Reggio Emilia; tel. (0552) 501511; fax (0522) 517301; internet www.gazzettadireggio.it; f. 1860; Man. LUIGI CARLETTI; circ. 19,563.

Rimini

Corriere di Romagna: Piazza Tre Martiri 43a, 47900 Rimini; tel. (0541) 354111; fax (0541) 351499; Editor CLAUDIO CASALI.

Rome

Il Corriere dello Sport: Piazza Indipendenza 11B, 00185 Roma; tel. (06) 49921; fax (06) 4992690; f. 1924; Editor MARIO SCONCERTI; circ. 239,249.

Europa: Roma; f. 2003; organ of the Margherita coalition, replacing Il Popolo, which ceased operations Jan. 2003; Dir NIN RIZZO NERVO.

Il Giornale d'Italia: Società Editrice Esedra Srl, Via Parigli 11, 00185 Roma; tel. (06) 474901; fax (06) 4883435; e-mail g.italia@tiscalinet.it; f. 1901; Man. PAOLO FRAIOLI; Editor MATTIAS MAINIERO; circ. 70,000.

Liberazione: Viale del Policlinico 131, 00161 Roma; tel. (06) 441831; fax (06) 44183247; organ of the Partito della Rifondazione Comunista; Dir ALESSANDRO CURZI.

Il Manifesto: Via Tomacelli 146, 00186 Roma; tel. (06) 687191; fax (06) 68719573; e-mail redazione@ilmanifesto.it; internet www.ilmanifesto.it; f. 1971; splinter communist; Dir RICCARDO BARENGHI; circ. 55,000.

Il Messaggero: Via del Tritone 152, 00187 Roma; tel. (06) 47201; fax (06) 4720300; e-mail posta@ilmessaggero.it; internet www.ilmessaggero.it; f. 1878; independent; Dir PAOLO GAMBESCIA; Editor F.G. CALTAGIRONE; circ. 369,000.

L'Opinione: Via del Corso 117, 00186 Roma; tel. (06) 69200880; fax (06) 6787573; internet www.opinione.it; f. 1977; independent; Man. Editor ARTURO DIACONALE; circ. 5,000.

La Repubblica: Gruppo Editoriale L'Espresso Div. La, Piazza dell'Indipendenza 11B, 00185 Roma; tel. (06) 49821; fax (06) 49822923; e-mail larepubblica@repubblica.it; internet www .repubblica.it; f. 1976; left-wing; Editor EZIO MAURO; circ. 616,700.

Il Riformista: Via della Scrofula 57, Roma; tel. (06) 684361; internet www.ilriformista.it; Dir ANTONIO POLITO.

Secolo d'Italia: Via della Scrofa 43, 00186 Roma; tel. (06) 68899221; fax (06) 6861598; f. 1951; organ of the AN; Editor GENNARO MALGIERI; circ. 15,000.

Il Tempo: L'Editrice Romana SpA, Piazza Colonna 366, 00187 Roma; tel. (06) 675881; fax (06) 6758869; internet www.iltempo.it; f. 1944; right-wing; Editor GIAN PAOLO CRESCI; circ. 85,000.

L'Unità: Via dei Due Macelli 23/13, 00187 Roma; tel. (06) 699961; fax (06) 69996359; e-mail unitaedi@unita.it; internet www.unita.it; f. 1924; Dir PAOLO GAMBESCIR; circ. 100,000.

Salerno

La Città: Corso Garibaldi 215, 84100 Salerno; tel. (089) 245111; fax (089) 245236; internet www.lacittadisalerno.kataweb.it; Dir MAURIZIO DE LUCA.

Sassari

La Nuova Sardegna: Via Porcellana 9, 7100 Sassari; tel. (079) 222400; fax (079) 236293; internet www.lanuovasardegna.it; f. 1891; independent; Editor LIVIO LIUZZI; circ. 78,000.

Taranto

Corriere del Giorno di Puglia e Lucania: Piazza Maria Immacolata 30, 74100 Taranto; tel. (099) 4553111; fax (099) 4538322; f. 1947; Editor ROBERTO ANTONIO RASCHILLA; circ. 12,000.

Trent

l'Adige: Via Missioni Africane 17, 38100 Trento; tel. (0461) 886111; fax (0461) 886263; internet www.ladige.it; f. 1945; independent; Dir Dott. PAOLO GHEZZI; circ. 30,000.

Treviso

La Tribuna di Treviso: Corso del Popolo 42, 31100 Treviso; tel. (0422) 417611; fax (0422) 579212; internet www.tribunatreviso.it; f. 1978; independent; Editor Dr ALBERTO STATERA; circ. 20,000.

Trieste

Il Piccolo (Giornale di Trieste): Via Guido Reni 1, 34123 Trieste; tel. (040) 3733111; fax (040) 3733283; e-mail piccolo@ilpiccolo.it; internet www.ilpiccolo.it; f. 1881; independent; Man. Dr MARIO QUAIA; circ. 60,000.

Primorski Dnevnik: Via dei Montecchi 6, 34137 Trieste; tel. (040) 7786300; fax (040) 772418; e-mail redakcija@primorski.it; internet www.primorski.it; f. 1945; Slovene; Editor-in-Chief BOJAN BREZIGAR; circ. 10,000.

Turin

La Stampa: Via Marenco 32, 10126 Torino; tel. (011) 656811; fax (011) 655306; e-mail lettere@lastampa.it; internet www.lastampa.it; f. 1867; independent; Dir MARCELLO SORGI; circ. 410,000.

Udine

Il Messaggero Veneto: Viale Palmanova 290, 33100 Udine; tel. (0432) 5271; fax (0432) 523072; e-mail messven@messaggeroveneto .it; internet www.messaggeroveneto.it; f. 1946; Editor SERGIO GERVASUTTI; circ. 60,000.

Varese

La Prealpina: Viale Tamagno 13, 21100 Varese; tel. (0332) 275700; fax (0332) 275701; e-mail prealpina@betanet.it; internet www .laprealpinagiorn.it; f. 1888; Dir GIGI GERVASUTTI; circ. 40,000.

Venice

Il Gazzettino: Via Torino 110, 30172 Venice-Mestre; tel. (041) 665111; fax (041) 665386; internet www.gazzettino.it; f. 1887; independent; Dir LUIGI BACIALLI; circ. 139,000.

La Nuova Venezia: Castello 5620, Campo San Lio, 30122 Venezia; tel. (041) 5074611; fax (041) 958856; e-mail nuova@nuovavenezia.it; internet www.nuovavenezia.it; Dir ALBERTO STATERA; circ. 11,000.

Verona

L'Arena: Viale del Lavoro 11, 37036, San Martino Buon Albergo, Verona; tel. (045) 8094899; fax (045) 597966; internet www.larena .it; f. 1866; independent; Editor-in-Chief ADRIANO PAGANELLA; Man. Dir Ing. ALESSANDRO ZELGER; circ. 68,000.

Vicenza

Il Giornale di Vicenza: Viale S. Lazzaro 89, 36100 Vicenza; tel. (0444) 396311; fax (0444) 396333; internet www.ilgiornaledivicenza .it; f. 1945; Editor NINO ALLIONE; circ. 50,000.

SELECTED PERIODICALS

Fine Arts, etc.

Abitare: Via Ventura, 5, 20134 Milano; tel. (02) 210581; fax (02) 21058316; e-mail redazione@abitare.it; internet www.abitare.it; f. 1962; monthly; architecture and design; in Italian and English; Editor RENATO MINETTO; Dir ITALO LUPI.

Casabella: Via Trentacoste 7, 20134 Milano; tel. (02) 215631; fax (02) 21563260; e-mail casabella@mondadori.it; f. 1938; 10 a year; architecture and interior design; Editor FRANCESCO DAL CO; circ. 43,000.

Domus: Via Achille Grandi 5/7, 20089 Rozzano, Milano; tel. (02) 824721; fax (02) 82472386; e-mail domus@edidomus.it; internet www.edidomus.it; f. 1928; 11 a year; architecture, interior design and art; Editor Dr G. MAZZOCCHI; circ. 53,000.

Graphicus: Casa Editrice ProFashion, Viale Espinasse 141, 20156 Milano; tel. (02) 3024121; fax (02) 30039400; internet www .eurographicus.com; f. 1911; 10 a year; printing and graphic arts; circ. 7,200.

L'Illustrazione Italiana: Via Nino Bixio 30, 20129 Milano; tel. (02) 2043941; fax (02) 2046507; f. 1873; quarterly; fine arts; Editor MASSIMO CAPRARA.

Interni: Via D. Trentacoste 7, 20134 Milano; tel. (02) 215631; fax (02) 26410847; e-mail interni@mondadori.it; internet www .internimagazine.it; monthly; interior decoration and design; Editor GILDA BOJARDI; circ. 40,000.

Lotus International: Via Santa Marta 19A, 20123 Milano; tel. (02)45475745; fax (02) 45475746; e-mail lotus@editorialelotus.it; f. 1963; quarterly; architecture, town-planning; Editor PIERLUIGI NICOLIN.

Rivista Italiana di Musicologia: Leo S. Olschki, Viuzzo del Pozzetto, 50126 Firenze; tel. (055) 6530684; fax (055) 6530214; e-mail celso@olschki.it; internet www.olschki.it/riviste/rivmusic.htm; f. 1966; twice a year; musicology; Editor ENRICO FUBINI.

Il Saggiatore Musicale: Leo S. Olschki, Viuzzo del Pozzetto, 50126 Firenze; tel. (055) 6530684; fax (055) 6530214; e-mail saggmus@ muspe.unibo.it; internet www.muspe.unibo.it/period/saggmus; f. 1994; twice a year; musicology; Dir GIUSEPPINA LA FACE BIANCONI.

Storia dell'Arte: Roma; tel. (0361) 3729220; fax (0361) 3251055; e-mail webmaster@storiadellarte.com; internet www.storiadellarte .com; f. 1969; quarterly; art history; Dirs MAURIZIO CALVESI, ORESTE FERRARI, ANGIOLA M. ROMANINI; circ. 1,200.

Studi Musicali: Leo S. Olschki, Viuzzo del Pozzetto, 50126 Firenze; tel. (055) 6530684; fax (055) 6530214; e-mail celso@olschki.it; internet www.olschki.it/riviste/stmusic.htm; f. 1972; twice a year; musicology; Editor AGOSTINO ZIINO.

General, Literary and Political

Archivio Storico Italiano: Leo S. Olschki, Viuzzo del Pozzetto, 50126 Firenze; tel. (055) 6530684; fax (055) 6530214; e-mail celso@ olschki.it; internet www.storia.unifi.it/asidspt/ASI/apertura.htm; f. 1842; quarterly; history; Editor GIULIANO PINTO.

Belfagor: Leo S. Olschki, Viuzzo del Pozzetto, 50126 Firenze; tel. (055) 6530684; fax (055) 6530214; e-mail celso@olschki.it; internet www.olschki.it/riviste/belfagor.htm; f. 1946; every 2 months; historical and literary criticism; Editor CARLO FERDINANDO RUSSO; circ. 2,500.

La Bibliofilia: Leo S. Olschki, Viuzzo del Pozzetto, 50126 Firenze; tel. (055) 6530684; fax (055) 6530214; e-mail celso@olschki.it; internet www.olschki.it/riviste/bibliof.htm; f. 1899; every 4 months; bibliography, history of printing; Editor LUIGI BALSAMO.

Diario: Via Melzo 9, 20129, Milano; tel. (02) 2771181; fax (02) 2046261; e-mail redazione@diario.it; internet www.diario.it; weekly; general interest; Dir ENRICO DEAGLIO.

L'Espresso: Via Po 12, 00198 Roma; tel. (06) 84781; fax (06) 8550246; e-mail segred@espresso.it; internet www.espressoedit.it; weekly; independent left; political; illustrated; Dir DANIELA HAMAUI; circ. 450,000.

Famiglia Cristiana: Via Giotto 36, 20145 Milano; tel. (02) 48071; fax (02) 48008247; e-mail famigliacristiana@stpauls.it; internet www.famigliacristiana.it; f. 1931; weekly; Catholic; illustrated; Dir ANTONIO SCIORTINO; circ. 862,600.

Francofonia: Leo S. Olschki, Viuzzo del Pozzetto, 50126 Firenze; tel. (055) 6530684; fax (055) 6530214; e-mail francofonia@lingue .unibo.it; internet www.olschki.it/riviste/francof.htm; f. 1981; twice a year; French language; Editor ADRIANO MARCHETTI.

Gazzetta del Lunedì: Via Archimede 169/R, 16142 Genova; tel. (010) 53691; fax (010) 504148; f. 1946; weekly; political; Dir GEROLAMO ANGELI; circ. 83,315.

Gente: Viale Sarca 235, 20126 Milano; tel. (02) 27751; f. 1957; weekly; illustrated political, cultural and current events; Editor Dott. RENDINI; circ. 758,440.

Giornale della Libreria: Via Bergonzoli 1/5, 20122 Milano; tel. (02) 28315996; fax (02) 28315906; e-mail bibliografica@bibliografica .it; f. 1888; monthly; organ of the Associazione Italiana Editori; bibliographical; Editor FEDERICO MOTTA; circ. 5,000.

Lettere Italiane: Leo S. Olschki, POB 66, 50100 Firenze; tel. (055) 6530684; fax (055) 6530214; e-mail celso@olschki.it; internet www .olschki.it/riviste/lettital.htm; f. 1949; quarterly; literary; Dirs VITTORE BRANCA, CARLO OSSOLA.

Mondo Economico: Via Paolo Lomazzo 51, 20154 Milano; tel. (02) 3492451; fax (02) 316905; f. 1946; weekly; economics, business, finance; Editor ENRICO SASSOON; circ. 85,752.

Il Mulino: Strada Maggiore 37, 40125 Bologna; tel. (051) 222419; fax (051) 6486014; e-mail ilmulino@mulino.it; internet www.mulino .it/ilmulino; f. 1951; every 2 months; culture and politics; Dir ALESSANDRO CAVALLI; Editor-in-Chief BRUNO SIMILI.

Oggi: Via Angelo Rizzoli 2, 20132 Milano; tel. (02) 25841; fax (02) 27201485; f. 1945; weekly; topical, literary; illustrated; Dir PAOLO OCCHIPINTI; circ. 760,038.

Panorama: Arnoldo Mondadori Editore SpA, Via Marconi 27, 20090 Segrate, Milano; tel. (02) 75421; fax (02) 75422769; e-mail panorama@mondadori.it; internet www.mondadori.com/panorama; f. 1962; weekly; current affairs; Dir CARLO ROSSELLA; circ. 200,000.

Il Pensiero Politico: Leo S. Olschki, Viuzzo del Pozzetto, 50126 Firenze; tel. (055) 6530684; fax (055) 6530214; e-mail penspol@unipg .it; internet www.olschki.it/riviste/penspol.htm; f. 1968; every 4 months; political and social history; Editor VITTOR IVO COMPARATO.

Rassegna Storica Toscana: Leo S. Olschki, Viuzzo del Pozzetto, 50126 Firenze; tel. (055) 6530684; fax (055) 6530214; e-mail rogari@ unifi.it; internet www.olschki.it/riviste/rasstor.htm; f. 1955; twice a year; Tuscan history; Editors FRANCESCO ADORNO, SANDRO ROGARI.

Rivista di Storia della Filosofia: Via de Togni 7, 20123 Milano; tel. (02) 8052538; fax (02) 8053948; e-mail riviste@francoangeli.it; internet www.francoangeli.it/riviste; f. 1946; quarterly; philosophy.

Scuola e Didattica: Via Luigi Cadorna 11, 25124 Brescia; tel. (030) 2993245; e-mail sdid@lascuola.it; internet www.lascuola.it; f. 1955; 19 a year; education; Editor GIUSEPPE VICO; circ. 40,000.

Selezione dal Reader's Digest: Via Lorenzini 4, 20139 Milano; tel. 800 351090; fax (02) 61293407; e-mail readerd@tin.it; internet www .selezionerd.it; monthly; Editor-in-Chief CLAUDIO PINA (acting); circ. 521,432.

Visto: Via Rizzoli 4, 20132 Milano; tel. (02) 25843961; fax (02) 25843907; f. 1989; illustrated weekly review; Editor-in-Chief PINO BELLERI; circ. 342,850.

Zett-Die Ganze Woche: Weinbergweg 7, 39100 Bozen; tel. (0471) 200400; fax (0471) 200462; e-mail zett@athesia.it; f. 1989; German language; circ. 34,000.

Religion

Città di Vita: Piazza Santa Croce 16, 50122 Firenze; tel. and fax (055) 242783; e-mail cittadivita@dada.it; internet www.casa.dada.it/ cittadivita; f. 1946; every 2 months; cultural review of religious research in theology, art and science; Dir P. M. GIUSEPPE ROSITO; circ. 2,000.

La Civiltà Cattolica: Via di Porta Pinciana 1, 00187 Roma; tel. (06) 6979201; fax (06) 69792022; e-mail civcatt@laciviltacattolica.it; internet www.laciviltacattolica.it; f. 1850; fortnightly; Catholic; Editor GIAN PAOLO SALVINI; circ. 17,000.

Humanitas: Via G. Rosa 71, 25121 Brescia; tel. (030) 46451; fax (030) 2400605; e-mail redazione@morcelliana.it; f. 1946; every 2 months; religion, philosophy, science, politics, history, sociology, literature, etc. Dir ILARIO BERTOLETTI.

Protestantesimo: Via Pietro Cossa 42, 00193 Roma; tel. (06) 3207055; fax (06) 3201040; e-mail fvt.protest@chiesavaldese.org; internet www.chiesavaldese.org/facolta/protestantesimo; f. 1946;

quarterly; theology and current problems, book reviews; Dir Prof. SERGIO ROSTAGNO.

La Rivista del Clero Italiano: Largo Gemelli 1, 20123 Milano; tel. (02) 72342370; fax (02) 72342974; e-mail redazione.vp@mi.unicatt .it; internet www.vitaepensiero.it; f. 1920; monthly; Dir BRUNO MAGGIONI; circ. 4,300.

Rivista di Storia della Chiesa in Italia: Piazza San Giovanni in Laterano 4, 00184 Roma; tel. and fax (06) 69886176; e-mail rsci@pul .it; internet www.vitaepensiero.it; f. 1947; twice a year; Editor AGOSTINO PARAVICINI BAGLIANI.

Rivista di Storia e Letteratura Religiosa: Leo S. Olschki, Viuzzo del Pozzetto, 50126 Firenze; tel. (055) 6530684; fax (055) 6530214; e-mail celso@olschki.it; internet www.olschki.it/riviste/rivrelig.htm; f. 1965; every 4 months; religious history and literature; Dir MARIO ROSA.

Science and Technology

L'Automobile: Viale Regina Margherita 290, 00198 Roma; tel. (06) 441121; fax (06) 44231160; e-mail lea.srl@iol.it; f. 1945; monthly; motor mechanics, tourism; Dir PAOLO BASILI; circ. 1,083,210.

Gazzetta Medica Italiana Archivio per le Scienze Mediche: Edizioni Minerva Medica, Corso Bramante 83–85, 10126 Torino; tel. (011) 678282; fax (011) 674502; e-mail minervamedica@ minervamedica.it; internet www.minervamedica.it; six a year; medical science; Dir ALBERTO OLIARO; circ. 2,900.

Il Nuovo Medico d'Italia: Via Monte Oliveto 2, 00141 Roma; tel. (06) 87185017; fax (06) 87185017; e-mail numedi@tiscalinet.it; internet www.numedi.it; monthly; medical science; Editor-in-Chief Dott. MARIO BERNARDINI.

Minerva Medica: Corso Bramante 83–85, 10126 Torino; tel. (011) 678282; fax (011) 674502; e-mail minervamedica@minervamedica.it; internet www.minervamedica.it; 10 a year; medical science; Dir ALBERTO OLIARO; circ. 4,900.

Monti e Boschi: Via Goito 13, 40126 Bologna; tel. (051) 65751; e-mail mb@gce.it; internet www.gce.it; f. 1949; every 2 months; ecology and forestry; Publr Edagricole; Editor UMBERTO BAGNARESI; circ. 16,700.

Motor: Piazza Antonio Mancini 4G, 00196 Roma; tel. (06) 3233195; fax (06) 3233309; e-mail info@rivistamotor.com; internet www .rivistamotor.com; f. 1940; monthly; motor mechanics; Dir S. FAVIA DEL CORE; circ. 35,500.

Newton: Via Angelo Rizzoli 2, 20132, Milano; internet www.newton .rcs.it; f. 1997; monthly; popular science; Dir GIORGIO RIVIECCIO; circ. 138,555.

Nuncius: Leo S. Olschki, Viuzzo del Pozzetto, 50126 Firenze; tel. (055) 6530684; fax (055) 6530214; e-mail ciardi@imss.fi.it; internet http://galileo.imss.firenze.it/pubblic/inuncius.html; f. 1976; twice a year; history of science; Dir PAOLO GALLUZZI.

Physis: Leo S. Olschki, Viuzzo del Pozzetto, 50126 Firenze; tel. (055) 6530684; fax (055) 6530214; e-mail guidocimino@uniroma1.it; internet www.olschki.it/riviste/physis.htm; f. 1959; twice a year; history of science; Editor GUIDO CIMINO.

Rivista Geografica Italiana: Via S. Gallo 10, 50129 Firenze; tel. (055) 2757956; fax (055) 2757956; e-mail vecchio@unifi.it; f. 1894; quarterly geographical review; Editors PAOLO DOCCIOLI, LEONARDO ROMBAI, BRUNO VECCHIO.

Women's Publications

Amica: Via Angelo Rizzoli 2, 20132 Milano; tel. (02) 2588; f. 1962; monthly; Dirs MARIA LAURA RODOTA, EMANUELA TESTORI; circ. 292,269.

Anna: Via Civitavecchia 102, Milano; tel. (02) 25843213; f. 1932; weekly; Editor M. VENTURI; circ. 291,784.

Confidenze: Arnoldo Mondadori Editore SpA, Via Mondadori 1, 20090 Segrate, Milano; tel. (02) 75421; fax (02) 75422806; e-mail cassinoni@mondadori.it; f. 1946; weekly; Dir LAURA PAVESE; circ. 229,825.

Cosmopolitan Italia: Arnoldo Mondadori Editore SpA, Via Marconi 27, 20090, Segrate, Milano; internet home.mondadori.com/ cosmopolitan; monthly; Dir CINZIA FELICETTI.

Donna Moderna: Arnoldo Mondadori Editore SpA, Via Marconi 27, 20090 Segrate, Milano; internet www.donnamoderna.com; monthly; Dir PATRIZIA AVOLEDO.

Gioia: Viale Sarca 235, 20126 Milano; tel. (02) 66191; fax (02) 66192717; e-mail gioia@rusconi.it; f. 1937; weekly; Dir VERA MONTANARI; circ. 297,516.

Grazia: Arnoldo Mondadori Editore SpA, Via Mondadori 1, 20090 Segrate, Milano; tel. (02) 75422390; fax (02) 75422515; e-mail grazia@mondadori; f. 1938; weekly; Dir CARLA VANNI; circ. 379,820.

Intimità della Famiglia: Piazza Aspromonte 13, 20131 Milano; tel. (02) 706421; fax (02) 70642306; e-mail intimita@quadratum.it; internet www.quadratum.it; weekly; published by Quadratum; Dir ANNA GIUSTI; circ. 424,946.

Vogue Italia: Piazza Castello 27, 20121 Milano; tel. (02) 85611; fax (02) 870686; internet www.vogue.com; monthly; Editor FRANCA SOZZANI; circ. 73,773.

Miscellaneous

Annali della Classe di Lettere e Filosofia: Scuola Normale Superiore, Piazza dei Cavalieri 7, 56100 Pisa; tel. (050) 509111; fax (050) 563513; e-mail publ_lettere@sns.it; internet www.sns.it; f. 1873; quarterly; archaeology, art history, philosophy, philology, history, literature; Editor ENRICO CASTELNUOVO; circ. 1,200.

Capital: Via Angelo Rizzoli 2, 20132, Milano; f. 1979; monthly; men's lifestyle, economics, technology; Dir GIOVANNI IOZZIA; circ. 90,199.

Cooperazione Educativa: La Nuova Italia, Via dei Piceni 16, 00185 Roma; tel. (06) 4457228; fax (06) 4460386; f. 1952; monthly; education; Dir MIRELLA GRIEG.

Dove: Via Angelo Rizzoli 2, 20132, Milano; f. 1991; monthly; lifestyle and travel; Dir VALERIA TEGAMI; circ. 106,807.

Gambero Rosso: GRH SpA, Via Angelo Bargoni 8, 00153, Roma; tel. (06) 5852121; fax (06) 58310170; e-mail gambero@gamberorosso.it; internet www.gamberorosso.it; f. 1986; monthly; food and wine; Dir STEFANO BONILLI.

Lares: Leo S. Olschki, Viuzzo del Pozzeto, 50126 Firenze; tel. (055) 6530684; fax (055) 6530214; e-mail laresredazione@libero.it; internet www.olschki.it/riviste/lares.htm; f. 1912; quarterly; folklore; Editor PIETRO CLEMENTE.

Il Maestro: Clivo di Monte del Gallo 48, 00165 Roma; tel. (06) 634651; fax (06) 39375903; e-mail a.i.m.c@flashnet.it; internet www.aimc.it; f. 1945; monthly; Catholic teachers' magazine; Dir GIUSEPPE DESIDERI; circ. 40,000.

Max: Via Angelo Rizzoli 2, 20132, Milano; internet www.max.rcs.it; f. 1985; monthly; men's lifestyle; Dir GIUSEPPE DI PIAZZA; circ. 147,836.

Quattroruote: Via Gianni Mazzocchi 1/3, 20089 Rozzano, Milano; tel. (02) 824721; fax (02) 57500416; e-mail quattroruote@edidomus.it; internet www.edidomus.it; f. 1956; motoring; monthly; Editor RAFAELE LAURENZI; circ. 662,000.

NEWS AGENCIES

AdnKronos: Via Ripetta 73, 00186 Roma; tel. (06) 324961; fax (06) 32002204; internet www.adnkronos.it; Dir-Gen. MARIA ROSARIA BELLIZZI DE MARCO.

Agenzia Giornalistica Italia (AGI): Via Cristoforo Colombo 98, 00147 Roma; tel. (06) 519961; fax (06) 51996201; e-mail info@agi.it; internet www.agi.it; Gen. Man. NICOLA LAINÉ.

Agenzia Nazionale Stampa Associata (ANSA): Via della Dataria 94, 00187 Roma; tel. (06) 67741; fax (06) 69797383; e-mail webmaster@ansa.it; internet www.ansa.it; f. 1945; 22 regional offices in Italy and 90 brs all over the world; service in Italian, Spanish, French, English; Pres. BORIS BIANCHERI; CEO and Man. Dir GIUSEPPE CERBONE; Gen. Man. PIERLUIGI MAGNASCHI.

Asca: Via Due Macelli 23, 00187 Roma; tel. (06) 69792911; fax (06) 6783555; e-mail segreteria@asca.it; internet www.asca.it; Dir CLAUDIO SONZOGNO.

Documentazioni Informazioni Resoconti (Dire): Via Abruzzi 3, 00187 Roma; tel. (06) 4203811; fax (06) 42012689; e-mail dire@dire.it; internet www.dire.it; Dir ADRIANO PANICCIA.

Inter Press Service International Association (IPS): Via Panisperna 207, 00184 Roma; tel. (06) 485692; fax (06) 4827112; e-mail romaser@ips.org; internet www.ips.org; f. 1964; international daily news agency; Dir-Gen. PATRICIA A. MADE.

Foreign Bureaux

Agencia EFE (Spain): Via dei Canestrari 5, 00186 Roma; tel. (06) 6834087; fax (06) 6874918; e-mail eferoma@efe.it; Bureau Chief JAIME ANTONIO CASTILLO ARROYO.

Agence France-Presse (AFP): Piazza SantiApostoli 66, 00187 Roma; tel. (06) 6793588; fax (06) 6793623; e-mail afp-rome@afp.com; internet www.afp.com; Bureau Chief PATRICK CRAMPONT.

Associated Press (AP) (USA): Piazza Grazioli 5, 00186 Roma; tel. (06) 6798382; fax (06) 6790103; internet www.ap.org/italia; Bureau Chief DENNIS F. REDMONT.

Česká tisková kancelář (ČTK) (Czech Republic): Via di Vigna Stelluti 150/13, 00191 Roma; tel. (06) 3270777.

Deutsche Presse-Agentur (dpa) (Germany): Via della Mercede 33, Int. 15, 00187 Roma; tel. (06) 6789810; fax (06) 6841598; Bureau Chief PEER MEINERT.

Informatsionnoye Telegrafnoye Agentstvo Rossii (ITAR—TASS) (Russia): Viale dell'Umanesimo 172, 00144 Roma; tel. (06) 5912882; fax (06) 5926800; e-mail romatass@mail.com; Correspondents OLEG OSSIPOV, ALEXEI BULGAKOV.

Kyodo Tsushin (Japan): Roma; tel. (06) 8440709; internet home.kyodo.co.jp; Bureau Chief KATSUO UEDA.

Magyar Távirati Iroda (MTI) (Hungary): Roma; tel. (06) 8441309; internet homewww.mti.hu; Correspondent ISTVÁN GÓZON.

Reuters (United Kingdom): Viale Fulvio Testi 280, 20126 Milano; tel. (02) 66129508; fax (02) 66118167; Editor NELSON GRAVES.

United Press International (UPI) (USA): Via della Mercede 55, 00187 Roma; tel. (06) 6795747; fax (06) 6781540; Correspondent CHARLES RIDLEY.

Xinhua (New China) News Agency (People's Republic of China): Via Bruxelles 59, 00198 Roma; tel. (06) 865028; fax (06) 8450575; Bureau Chief HUANG CHANGRUI.

CNA (Taiwan) and Jiji Tsushin (Japan) are also represented.

PRESS ASSOCIATIONS

Associazione della Stampa Estera in Italia: Via della Umiltà 83c, 00187 Roma; tel. (06) 675911; fax (06) 67591262; e-mail segreteria@stampa-estera.it; internet www.stampa-estera.it; foreign correspondents' asscn; Pres. ERIC JOZSEF; Sec. AHMAD RAFAT.

Federazione Italiana Editori Giornali (FIEG): Via Piemonte 64, 00187 Roma; tel. (06) 4881683; fax (06) 4871109; e-mail fiegroma@iol.it; internet www.fieg.it; f. 1950; association of newspaper publishers; Pres. LUCA CORDERO DI MONTEZEMOLO; 268 mems.

Federazione Nazionale della Stampa Italiana: Corso Vittorio Emanuele II 349, 00186 Roma; tel. (06) 6833879; fax (06) 6871444; internet www.fnsi.it; f. 1877; 17 affiliated unions; Pres. FRANCO SIDDI; Sec.-Gen. PAOLO SERVENTI LONGHI; 16,000 mems.

Unione Stampa Periodica Italiana (USPI): Viale Bardanzellu 95, 00155 Roma; tel. (06) 4071388; fax (06) 4066859; e-mail uspi@uspi.it; internet www.uspi.it; Pres. MARIO NEGRI; Gen. Sec. FRANCESCO SAVERIO VETERE; 4,500 mems.

Publishers

There are more than 300 major publishing houses and many smaller ones.

Bologna

Gruppo Calderini Edagricole: Via Goito 13, 40126 Bologna; tel. (051) 65751; fax (051) 6575800; e-mail sede@gce.it; internet www.gce.it; group includes Calderini (f. 1960; art, sport, electronics, mechanics, university and school textbooks, travel guides, nursing, architecture) and Edagricole (f. 1935; agriculture, veterinary science, gardening, biology, textbooks); Pres. Prof. GIORGIO AMADEI; Man. Dir GIOVANNA VILLANI PERDISA.

Nuova Casa Editrice Licinio Cappelli GEM SrL: Via Farini 14, 40124 Bologna; tel. (051) 239060; fax (051) 239286; f. 1848; medical science, history, politics, literature, textbooks; Chair. and Man. Dir MARIO MUSSO.

Editrice CLUEB: Via Marsala 31, 40126 Bologna; tel. (051) 220736; fax (051) 237758; e-mail clueb@clueb.com; internet www.clueb.com; f. 1959; education, arts, business, history, literature; Man. Dir LUIGI GUARDIGLI.

Società Editrice Il Mulino: Strada Maggiore 37, 40125 Bologna; tel. (051) 256011; fax (051) 256034; e-mail info@mulino.it; internet www.mulino.it; f. 1954; politics, history, philosophy, social sciences, linguistics, literary criticism, law, music, theatre, psychology, economics, journals; Gen. Man. GIOVANNI EVANGELISTI.

Zanichelli Editore SpA: Via Irnerio 34, 40126 Bologna; tel. (051) 293111; fax (051) 249782; e-mail zanichelli@zanichelli.it; internet www.zanichelli.it; f. 1859; educational, history, literature, philosophy, mathematics, science, technical books, law, psychology, architecture, reference books, dictionaries, atlases, earth sciences, linguistics, medicine, economics, etc. Chair. and Gen. Man. FEDERICO ENRIQUES; Vice-Chair. and Man. Dir LORENZO ENRIQUES.

Brescia

Editrice La Scuola SpA: Via Cadorna 11, Brescia; tel. (030) 29931; fax (030) 2993299; e-mail lascuola@tin.it; internet www.lascuola.it; f. 1904; educational magazines, educational textbooks, audiovisual aids and toys; Chairs. Dott. Ing. Luciano Silveri; Dott. Ing. Giorgio Raccis; Man. Dir Rag. Giuseppe Covone.

Florence

Casa Editrice Bonechi: Via dei Cairoli 18B, 50131 Firenze; tel. (055) 576841; fax (055) 5000766; e-mail bonechi@bonechi.it; internet www.bonechi.it; f. 1973; art, travel, cooking, CD-Rom; Pres. Giampaolo Bonechi.

Cremonese: Borgo Santa Croce 17, 50122 Firenze; tel. (055) 2476371; fax (055) 2476372; e-mail cremonese@ed-cremonese.it; internet www.ed-cremonese.it; f. 1929; history, reference, engineering, science, textbooks, architecture, mathematics, aviation; Chair. Alberto Stianti.

Giunti Gruppo Editoriale: Via Bolognese 165, 50139 Firenze; tel. (055) 50621; fax (055) 5062298; f. 1839; art, psychology, literature, science, law; Man. Dir Marcino Montanarini.

Casa Editrice Felice Le Monnier: Via A. Meucci 2, 50015 Grassina, Firenze; tel. (055) 64910; fax (055) 643983; e-mail monnier@tin.it; f. 1836; academic and cultural books, textbooks, dictionaries; Man. Dirs Dott. Vanni Paoletti; Dott. Guglielmo Paoletti; Dott. Simone Paoletti.

La Nuova Italia Editrice SpA: Via Ernesto Codignola 1, 50018 Firenze; tel. (055) 75901; fax (055) 7590208; f. 1926; biography, psychology, philosophy, philology, education, history, politics, belles-lettres, art, music and science; Man. Dirs Federico Codignola, Carmelo Sambugar.

Casa Editrice Leo S. Olschki: CP 66, 50100 Firenze; tel. (055) 6530684; fax (055) 6530214; e-mail celso@olschki.it; internet www.olschki.it; f. 1886; reference, periodicals, textbooks, humanities; Man. Alessandro Olschki.

Vallecchi Editore SpA: Via Maragliano 6 int., 50144, Firenze; tel. (055) 324761; e-mail gangemi@vallechi.it; internet www.vallecchi.it; f. 1913; art, fiction, literature, essays, media; Editorial Dir Umberto Croppi.

Genoa

Casa Editrice Marietti SpA: Via Vittorio Pisani,, Genova; tel. (010) 6984226; fax (010) 667092; e-mail marietti1820@split.it; f. 1820; liturgy, theology, fiction, history, politics, literature, philosophy, art, children's books; Editor Carla Villata.

Milan

Adelphi Edizioni SpA: Via S. Giovanni sul Muro 14, 20121 Milano; tel. (02) 725731; fax (02) 89010337; f. 1962; classics, philosophy, biography, music, art, psychology, religion and fiction; Pres. Roberto Calasso.

Editrice Ancora: Via G. B. Niccolini 8, 20154 Milano; tel. (02) 3456081; fax (02) 34560866; e-mail editrice@ancora-libri.it; internet www.ancora-libri.it; f. 1934; religious, educational; Dir Gilberto Zini.

Franco Angeli Srl: Viale Monza 106, CP 17130, 20127 Milano; tel. (02) 2827651; fax (02) 2891515; f. 1956; general; Man. Dir Franco Angeli.

Bramante Editrice: Viale Bianca Maria 19, 20122 Milano; tel. (02) 760759; fax (02) 780904; f. 1958; art, history, encyclopaedias, natural sciences, interior decoration, arms and armour, music; Chair. Dott. Guido Ceriotti.

Feltrinelli SpA: Via Andegari 6, 20121 Milano; tel. (02) 808346; f. 1954; fiction, juvenile, science, technology, textbooks, poetry, art, music, history, literature, political science, philosophy, reprint editions of periodicals; Chair. Inge Feltrinelli; Man. Dir Giuseppe Antonini.

Garzanti Editore: Via Gasparotto 1, 20124 Milano; tel. (02) 674161; fax (02) 67416292; internet www.garzanti.it; f. 1938; literature, poetry, science, art, history, politics, encyclopaedias, dictionaries, scholastic and children's books; Chair. Giovanni Merlini; Gen. Man. Marco Bendinelli.

Casa Editrice Libraria Ulrico Hoepli: Via Hoepli 5, 20121 Milano; tel. (02) 864871; fax (02) 8052886; f. 1870; grammars, art, technical, scientific and school books, encyclopaedias; Chair. Ulrico Hoepli; Man. Dir Gianni Hoepli.

Longanesi e C. SpA: Corso Italia 13, 20122 Milano; tel. (02) 80206620; fax (02) 72000306; f. 1946; art, history, philosophy, fiction; Pres. S. Passigli; Man. Dir S. Mauri.

Massimo: Viale Bacchiglione 20A, 20139 Milano; tel. (02) 55210800; fax (02) 55211315; f. 1950; fiction, biography, history, social science, philosophy, pedagogy, theology, school texts; Chair. Cesare Crespi.

Arnoldo Mondadori Editore SpA: Via Mondadori 1, 20090 Segrate, Milano; tel. (02) 75421; fax (02) 75422302; internet www .mondadori.com; f. 1907; books, magazines and online publishing; Pres. Marina Berlusconi.

Edizioni Bruno Mondadori: Via Archimede 23, 20129 Milano; tel. (02) 748231; fax (02) 74823362; f. 1946; investment activity in publishing companies; Chair. Roberta Mondadori; Man. Dir Roberto Gulli; Dir Agostino Cattaneo.

Gruppo Ugo Mursia Editore SpA: Via M. Gioia 45, 20124, Milano; tel. (02) 67378500; fax (02) 67378605; e-mail info@mursia .com; internet www.mursia.com; f. 1955; general fiction and non-fiction, reference, art, history, nautical books, philosophy, biography, sports, children's books; Gen. Man. Fiorenza Mursia.

RCS Libri SpA: Via Mecenate 91, 20138 Milano; tel. (02) 50951; fax (02) 5065361; internet www.rcs.it/libri; f. 1947; juveniles, education, textbooks, reference, literature, art books; Chair. Gaetano Mele; CEO Gianni Vallardi.

> **Bompiani:** e-mail ; internet www.rcs.it/rcslibri/bompiani; f. 1929; modern literature, biographies, theatre, science, art, history, classics, dictionaries, pocket books; Dir Mario Andreose.

> **Etas Srl:** technical periodicals and books; Man. Dir Dott. Giorgio Orsi.

> **Rizzoli:** internet www.rcs.it/rcslibri/rizzoli; f. 1929; newspapers, magazines and books; Dir-Gen. Giovanni Ungarelli; Man. Dir Giorgio Fattori.

> **Sonzogno:** internet www.rcs.it/rcslibri/sonzogno; f. 1861; fiction, non-fiction, illustrated, manuals; Dir Mario Andreose.

Riccardo Ricciardi Editore SpA: c/o Arnoldo Mondadori Editore, Via Mondadori 1, 20090 Segrate, Milano; tel. (02) 75421; f. 1907; classics, philology, history, literature; Gen. Man. Gian Arturo Ferrari.

Casa Ricordi SpA: Via Berchet 2, 20121 Milano; tel. (02) 88812206; fax (02) 88812212; f. 1808; academic, art, music; Chair. Gianni Babini; Man. Dir Mimma Guastoni.

Rusconi Libri Srl: Milano; tel. (02) 66191; fax (02) 66192758; f. 1969; non-fiction including history, biography, music, philosophy, archaeology, religion, needlecraft, embroidery and art; Pres. Alberto Rusconi; Editorial Dir Alberto Conforti.

Il Saggiatore: Via Melzo 9, 20129 Milano; tel. (02) 29403460; fax (02) 29513061; e-mail diritti@saggiatore.it; internet www.saggiatore .it; art, fiction, social sciences; Pres. Luca Formenton.

Adriano Salani Editore Srl: Corso Italia 13, 20122 Milano; tel. (02) 80206624; fax (02) 72018806; e-mail salani@salani.it; internet www.salani.it; f. 1988; fiction, children's books; Editor Mariagrazia Mazzitelli.

Edizioni San Paolo: Piazza Soncino 5, 20092 Cinisello Balsamo—Milan; tel. (02) 660751; fax (02) 66075211; e-mail sanpaoloedizioni@ stpauls.it; internet www.sanpaolo.org.it; f. 1914; religious; Gen. Man. Vincenzo Santarcangelo.

SEDES SpA-Ghisetti e Corvi Editori: Corso Concordia 7, 20129 Milano; tel. (02) 76006232; fax (02) 76009468; e-mail sedes.spa@gpa .it; internet www.sedes.gpa.it; f. 1937; educational textbooks.

Selezione dal Reader's Digest: Camuzzi Editoriale, SpA, Via Lorenzini 4, 20139 Milano; fax (02) 61293497; e-mail reader@tin.it; internet www.selezionerd.it; f. 1948; Reader's Digest, educational, reference, general interest; Man. Dir Charles J. Lobkowicz.

Sugarco Edizioni Srl: Via Fermi 9, 21040, Camago (VA); tel. (0331) 985511; fax (0331) 985385; f. 1957; fiction, biography, history, philosophy, guidebooks, Italian classics; Chair. Prof. Sergio Cigada; Gen. Man. Oliviero Cigada.

Casa Editrice Luigi Trevisini: Via Tito Livio 12, 20137 Milano; tel. (02) 5450704; fax (02) 55195782; e-mail trevisini@trevisini.it; internet www.trevisini.it; f. 1849; school textbooks; Dirs Luigi Trevisini, Giuseppina Trevisini.

Vita e Pensiero: Largo A. Gemelli 1, 20123 Milano; tel. (02) 72342370; fax (02) 72342974; f. 1914; publisher to the Catholic University of the Sacred Heart; cultural, scientific books and magazines; Dir Sergio Zaninelli.

Naples

Idelson Gnocchi Editore Srl: Via Alcide De Gasperi 55, 80133 Napoli; tel. (081) 5524733; fax (081) 5518295; e-mail idelgno@tin.it; internet www.idelson-gnocchi.com; f. 1908; medicine, psychology, biology; CEO Guido Gnocchi.

Liguori Editore Srl: Via Posillipo 394, 80123 Napoli; tel. (081) 7206111; fax (081) 7206244; e-mail liguori@liguori.it; internet www .liguori.it; f. 1949; linguistics, mathematics, engineering, economics, law, history, philosophy, sociology; Man. Dir Dott. Guido Liguori.

Edizioni Scientifiche Italiane SpA: Via Chiatamone 7, 80121 Napoli; tel. (081) 7645443; fax (081) 7646477; e-mail info@esispa

.com; internet www.esispa.com; f. 1945; law, economics, literature, arts, history, science; Pres. PIETRO PERLINGIERI.

Novara

Instituto Geografico De Agostini SpA: Via Giovanni da Verrazano 15, 28100 Novara; tel. (0321) 4241; fax (0321) 471286; e-mail ufficio.stampa@deagostini.it; internet www.deagostini.it; geography, maps, encyclopaedias, dictionaries, art, literature, textbooks, science; Chair. ANTONIO BELLONI; CEOs PIETRO BOROLI, GIANNI CRESPI.

Padua

CEDAM (Casa Editrice Dr A. Milani): Via Jappelli 5/6, 35121 Padua; tel. (049) 8239111; fax (049) 8752900; e-mail info@cedam.com; internet www.cedam.com; f. 1903; law, economics, political and social sciences, engineering, science, medicine, literature, philosophy, textbooks; Dirs ANTONIO MILANI, CARLO PORTA, FRANCESCO GIORDANO.

Libreria Editrice Gregoriana: Via Roma 82, 35122 Padua; tel. (049) 8758455; e-mail l.gregoriana@mclink.it; f. 1922; *Lexicon Totius Latinitatis*, religion, philosophy, psychology, social studies; Dir DON GIANCARLO MINOZZI.

Piccin Nuova Libraria SpA: Via Altinate 107, 35121 Padua; tel. (049) 655566; fax (049) 8750693; e-mail info@piccinonline.com; internet www.piccinonline.com; f. 1980; scientific and medical textbooks and journals; Man. Dir Dott. MASSIMO PICCIN.

Palermo

Editrice Ciranna: Via G. Besio 143, 90145, Palermo; tel. (091) 224499; fax (091) 311064; e-mail info@ciranna.it; internet www.ciranna.it; f. 1940; school textbooks; Man. Dir LIDIA FABIANO.

Rome

Armando Armando Srl: Viale Trastevere 236, 00153 Roma; tel. (06) 5806420; fax (06) 5818564; e-mail armando@palomar.it; internet www.armando.it; f. 1950; philosophy, psychology, social sciences, languages, ecology, education; Man. Dir ENRICO JACOMETTI.

Edizioni d'Arte di Carlo E. Bestetti & C. Sas: Roma; tel. (06) 6790174; f. 1947; art, architecture, industry; Man. Dir CARLO BESTETTI.

AVE (Anonima Veritas Editrice): Via Aurelia 481, 00165 Roma; tel. (06) 6631545; fax (06) 6620207; f. 1935; theology, sociology, pedagogy, psychology, essays, learned journals, religious textbooks; Pres. ARMANDO OBERTI.

Vito Bianco Editore: Roma; tel. (06) 8443151; fax (06) 8417595; various, especially marine publications; Chair. Dott. VITO BIANCO.

Edizioni Borla Srl: Via delle Fornaci 50, 00165 Roma; tel. (06) 39376728; fax (06) 39376620; e-mail borla@edizioni-borla.it; internet www.edizioni-borla.it; f. 1863; religion, philosophy, psychoanalysis, ethnology, literature; Man. Dir VINCENZO D'AGOSTINO.

Bulzoni Editore—Le edizioni universitarie d'Italia: Via dei Liburni 14, 00185 Roma; tel. (06) 4455207; fax (06) 4450355; f. 1969; science, arts, fiction, textbooks; Man. Dir MARIO BULZONI.

Edizioni Europa: Via G.B. Martini 6, 00198 Roma; tel. (06) 8449124; f. 1944; essays, literature, art, history, politics, music, economics; Chair. Prof. PIER FAUSTO PALUMBO.

Hermes Edizioni Srl: Via Flaminia 109, 00196 Roma; tel. (06) 3201656; fax (06) 3236277; e-mail info@ediz-mediterranee.com; internet www.ediz-mediterranee.com; f. 1979; alternative medicine, astrology, nature, dietetics, sports; Gen. Man. GIOVANNI CANONICO.

Jandi Sapi Editori Srl: Via Crescenzio 62, 00193 Roma; tel. (06) 68805515; fax (06) 6832612; e-mail info@jandisapi.com; internet www.jandisapi.com; f. 1941; industrial and legal publications, art books.

Giuseppe Laterza e Figli SpA: Via di Villa Sacchetti 17, 00197 Roma; tel. (06) 3218393; fax (06) 3223853; f. 1885; belles-lettres, biography, reference, religion, art, classics, history, economics, philosophy, social science; Editorial Dirs ALESSANDRO LATERZA, GIUSEPPE LATERZA.

Edizioni Lavoro: Via G.M. Lancisi 25, 00161 Roma; tel. (06) 44251174; fax (06) 44251177; e-mail direz.edizionilavoro@tiscalinet.it; f. 1982; history, politics, political philosophy, sociology, religion, Islamic, African, Arab and Caribbean literature; Chair. PIETRO GELARDI; Man. Dir LIONELLA CARPITA.

Edizioni Mediterranee Srl: Via Flaminia 109, 00196 Roma; tel. (06) 3201656; fax (06) 3236277; e-mail info@ediz-mediterranee.com; internet www.ediz-mediterranee.com; f. 1979; esoterism, parapsychology, hobbies, martial arts.

Guida Monaci SpA: Via Salaria 1319, 00138 Roma; tel. (06) 8887777; fax (06) 8889996; e-mail guida.monaci@italybygm.it; internet www.italybygm.it; f. 1870; commercial and industrial, financial, administrative and medical directories; Dir Ing. GIANCARLO ZAPPONINI.

Fratelli Palombi Srl: Via dei Gracchi 181–185, 00192 Roma; tel. (06) 3214150; fax (06) 3214752; e-mail flli.palombi@mail.sth.it; f. 1914; history, art, etc. of Rome; Man. Dir Dott. MARIO PALOMBI.

Angelo Signorelli: Via Falconieri 84, 00152 Roma; tel. (06) 5314942; fax (06) 531492; f. 1912; science, general literature, textbooks; Man. Dirs GIORGIO SIGNORELLI, GILBERTA ALPA.

Società Editrice Dante Alighieri Srl: Via Timavo 3, 00195 Roma; tel. (06) 3725870; fax (06) 37514807; e-mail dante-alighieri@libero.it; f. 1928; school textbooks, science and general culture; Pres. and Man. Dir SILVANO SPINELLI.

Edizioni Studium: Via Cassiodoro 14, 00193 Roma; tel. (06) 6865846; fax (06) 6875456; e-mail edizionistudium@libero.it; f. 1927; philosophy, literature, sociology, pedagogy, religion, economics, law, science, history, psychology; periodical *Studium*.

Stresa

Edizioni Rosminiane Sodalitas Sas: Centro Internazionale di Studi Rosminiani, Corso Umberto I 15, 28838 Stresa; tel. (0323) 30091; fax (0323) 31623; e-mail edizioni@rosmini.it; internet www.rosmini.it; f. 1925; philosophy, theology, *Rivista Rosminiana* (quarterly); Dir Prof. PIER PAOLO OTTONELLO.

Turin

Bollati Boringhieri Editore: Corso Vittorio Emanuele II 86, 10121 Torino; tel. (011) 5591711; fax (011) 543024; e-mail info@bollatiboringhieri.it; internet www.bollatiboringhieri.it; f. 1957; history, economics, natural sciences, psychology, social and human sciences, fiction and literary criticism; Chair. ROMILDA BOLLATI.

Giulio Einaudi Editore SpA: Via Umberto Biancamano 2, CP 245, 10121 Torino; tel. (011) 56561; fax (011) 542903; internet www.einaudi.it; f. 1933; fiction, classics, general; Chair. ROBERTO CERATI; Gen. Man. VITTORIO BO.

G. Giappichelli Editore Srl: Via Po 21, 10124 Torino; tel. (011) 8153511; fax (011) 8125100; e-mail editoriale@giappichelli.com; internet www.giappichelli.it; f. 1921; university publications on law, economics, politics and sociology.

Lattes S. e C. Editori SpA: Via Confienza 6, 10121 Torino; tel. (011) 5625335; fax (011) 5625070; f. 1893; technical, textbooks; Pres. CATERINA BOTTARI LATTES; Man. Dir RENATA LATTES.

Levrotto e Bella, Libreria Editrice Universitaria: Via Pigafetta Antonio 2/E, 10129, Torino; tel. (011) 5097367; fax (011) 504025; e-mail info@levrotto-bella.net; internet shop.levrotto-bella.net; f. 1911; university textbooks; Man. Dir Dott. ELISABETTA GUALINI.

Loescher: Via Vittorio Amedeo II 18, 10121 Torino; tel. (011) 5654111; fax (011) 5625822; e-mail loescher@inrete.it; f. 1867; school textbooks, general literature, academic books; Chair. LORENZO ENRIQUES.

Edizioni Minerva Medica: Corso Bramante 83–85, 10126 Torino; tel. (011) 678282; fax (011) 674502; e-mail minmed@tin.it; internet www.minervamedica.it; medical books and journals; Pres. ALBERTO OLIARO.

Petrini Editore: Strada del Portone 179, 10095 Grugliasco, Torino; tel. (011) 2098768; fax (011) 2098710; e-mail petrini@petrini.it; internet www.petrini.it; f. 1872; school textbooks.

Rosenberg & Sellier: Via Andrea Doria 14, 10123 Torino; tel. (011) 8127808; fax (011) 8127820; f. 1883; philology, social sciences, philosophy, linguistics, dictionaries, scientific journals; Chair. and Man. Dir UGO GIANNI ROSENBERG.

Società Editrice Internazionale SpA (SEI): Corso Regina Margherita 176, 10152 Torino; tel. (011) 52271; fax (011) 5211320; e-mail sei@seieditrice.com; f. 1908; textbooks, religion, history, education, multimedia; Head of Editorial Dept ULISSE JACOMUZZI.

Unione Tipografico-Editrice Torinese (UTET): Corso Raffaello 28, 10125 Torino; tel. (011) 2099111; fax (011) 2099394; e-mail utet@utet.it; internet www.utet.it; f. 1791; university and specialized editions on history, geography, art, literature, economics, law, sciences, encyclopaedias, dictionaries, etc. Pres. Prof. ANTONIO BELLONI.

Venice

Alfieri Edizioni d'Arte: Venezia; tel. (041) 5223323; f. 1939; modern art, Venetian art, architecture, periodicals; Chair. GIORGIO FANTONI; Gen. Man. MASSIMO VITTA ZELMAN.

Marsilio Editori: Marittima, Fabbricato 205, 30135 Venezia; tel. (041) 2406511; fax (041) 5238352; e-mail info@marsilioeditori.it;

internet www.marsilioeditori.it; f. 1961; fiction, non-fiction, history of art, catalogues, cartography; Man. Dirs Dott. EMANUELA BASSETTI, Prof. CESARE DE MICHELIS.

Verona

Giorgio Bertani Editore Srl: Verona; tel. (045) 8011345; fax (045) 8350402; f. 1973; politics, literature, anthropology, sociology, theatre, cinema, geography, humanities, history of Verona and Veneto, psychology, cultural journals; Man. Dir MARIO QUARANTA; Editorial Dir GIORGIO BERTANI.

Arnoldo Mondadori Editore: Via Arnoldo Mondadori 15, 37131 Verona; tel. (045) 934602; fax (045) 934566; e-mail forestan@ mondadori.it; f. 1912; children and young adults' books; Man. Dir MARGHERITA FORESTAN.

Vicenza

Neri Pozza Editore SpA: Contrà Oratorio dei Servi 21, 36100 Vicenza; tel. (0444) 320787; fax (0444) 324613; e-mail info@ neripozza.it; internet www.neripozza.it; f. 1946; art, fiction, history, politics; Pres. SILVIO FORTUNA; Dir GIUSEPPE RUSSO.

Government Publishing House

Istituto Poligrafico e Zecca dello Stato: Piazza Verdi 10, 00198 Roma; tel. (06) 85082391; fax (06) 85084135; e-mail editoriale@ipzs .it; internet www.ipzs.it; f. 1928; art, literary, scientific, technical books and reproductions; Chair. Dott. MICHELE TEDESCHI; Man. Dir Dott. LAMBERTO GABRIELLI.

PUBLISHERS' ASSOCIATION

Associazione Italiana Editori (AIE): Via delle Erbe 2, 20121 Milano; tel. (02) 86463091; fax (02) 89010863; e-mail aie@aie.it; internet www.aie.it; f. 1869; Pres. FEDERICO MOTTA; Dir IVAN CECCHINI.

Broadcasting and Communications

L'Autorità per le Garanzie nelle Communicazioni (AGC): Centro Direzionale, Isola B5, 80143 Napoli; tel. (081) 7507111; fax (081) 7507616; e-mail info@agcom.it; internet www.agcom.it; Italian Communications Regulatory Authority; Pres. ENZO CHELI.

TELECOMMUNICATIONS

Telecom Italia SpA: Piazza Affari 2, 20123 Milano; internet www .telecomitalia.it; Italy's leading telecommunications operator; merged with Società Finanziaria Telefonica SpA in 1997; controlling stake owned by Pirelli SpA; Chair. MARCO TRONCHETTI PROVERA; co-CEOs ENRICO BONDI, CARLO BUORA.

Telecom Italia Mobile SpA (TIM): Via Luigi Rizzo 22, 00136 Roma; tel. (06) 39001; internet www.tim.it; f. 1995; after split from Telecom Italia SpA; Italy's leading mobile telecommunications operator; Chair. ENRICO BONDI.

Tiscali SpA: Viale Trento 39, 09123 Cagliari; tel. (070) 46011; Chair. RENATO SORU.

Vodafone Omnitel S.p.A.: Via Caboto 15, 20094 Milano; tel. (02) 41431; internet www.omnitel.it; f. 1995; operates mobile network; Chief Exec. CHRISTOPHER GENT.

WIND Telecomunicazioni SpA: Via Cesare Giulio Viola 48, 00148 Roma; tel. (06) 83111; internet www.wind.it; f. 1997; Chair. JEAN-YVES GOUIFFES; CEO TOMMASO POMPEI.

BROADCASTING

Radio

In April 1975 legislation was adopted to ensure the political independence of Radiotelevisione Italiana (RAI). The state monopoly on broadcasting was abolished in 1976; more than 2,100 private local radio stations had begun broadcasting by 1995.

Radiotelevisione Italiana (RAI): Viale Mazzini 14, 00195 Roma; tel. (06) 38781; fax (06) 3725680; e-mail webmaster@rai.it; internet www.radio.rai.it; f. 1924; a public share capital company; programmes comprise the national programme (general), Second Programme (recreational), Third Programme (educational); there are also regional programmes in Italian and in the languages of ethnic minorities; the foreign and overseas service (Radio Roma) broadcasts in 27 languages; Pres. LUCIA ANNUZIATA; Dir-Gen. FLAVIO CATTANEO.

Rundfunk Anstalt Südtirol (RAS): Europaallee 164A, 39100 Bozen; tel. (0471) 546666; fax (0471) 200378; e-mail info@ras.bz.it; internet www.ras.bz.it; f. 1975; relays television and radio broad-

casts from Germany, Austria and Switzerland to the population of South Tyrol; Pres. HELMUTH HENDRICH; Man. Dir KLAUS GRUBER.

Television

Sixteen private stations have nation-wide networks. In 1995 there were about 900 privately-operated television stations, mostly offering a local service.

Gruppo Mediaset: Piazza SS. Giovanni e Paolo 8, 00184, Roma; tel. (06) 770801; or Palazzo Cigni, Milano 2, 20090, Segrate, Milano; tel. (02) 21021; f. 1993; operates the TV channels Canale 5, Italia 1 and Retequattro; and the telecommunications company Albacom, SpA; owned by Fininvest; Pres. FEDELE CONFALONIERI; Vice-Pres. SILVIO BERLUSCONI.

Gruppo Telepiù: Via Piranesi 46,, Milano; tel. (02) 700271; fax (02) 70027201; internet www.telepiu.it; f. 1991; operates pay digital channels Tele+Bianco, Tele+Nero, Tele+Grigio, Tele+ 16/9 and Tele+ 30; 80.1% owned by News Corpn, 19.9% owned by Telecom Italia following purchase from Vivendi in 2002; expected to be merged with Stream and renamed Sky Italia; Pres. EMANUEL GOUT.

Radiotelevisione Italiana (RAI): Viale Mazzini 14, 00195 Roma; tel. (06) 38781; fax (06) 3226070; e-mail rai-tv@rai.it; internet www .rai.it; f. 1924; operates three channels, RAI Uno, RAI Due and RAI Tre; also broadcasts local programmes in Italian and in German for the Alto Adige; Pres. ANTONIO BALDASSARRE; Dir-Gen. AGOSTINO SACCÀ.

Rundfunk Anstalt Südtirol (RAS): see Radio.

Finance

(cap. = capital; res = reserves; dep. = deposits; m. = million; brs = branches; amounts in lire or euros (€))

The number of banks in Italy fell during the 1990s, from 1,156 in 1990 to 921 in 1998, owing to an increasing number of mergers. In 1990 a programme of privatization of state-controlled banks was initiated and in November 1999 the last state-controlled bank was divested. There are more than 100 private banks, and a large number of co-operative and savings banks (*banche popolari, casse di risparmio, casse rurali*) of widely ranging size and importance. In addition, there are some 90 specialized credit institutions which provide medium-and long-term finance, together with other services outside the scope of the banks.

BANKING

Central Bank

Banca d'Italia: Via Nazionale 91, 00184 Roma; tel. (06) 47921; fax (06) 47922983; internet www.bancaditalia.it; f. 1893; cap. €0.2m., res €12,742.0m., dep. €47,994.0m. (Dec. 2001); since 1926 the Bank has had the sole right to issue notes in Italy; Gov. ANTONIO FAZIO; Dir-Gen. VINCENZO DESARIO; 99 brs.

Major Commercial Banks

Banca Agricola Mantovana SpA: Corso Vittorio Emanuele 30, 46100 Mantua; tel. (0376) 3111; fax (0376) 313566; e-mail intl.rel@ bam.it; internet www.bam.it; f. 1871; cap. €449.9m., res €366.9m., dep. €9,384.2m. (Dec. 2001); Chair. PIERMARIA PACCHIONI; Gen. Man. GIUSEPPE MENZI; 287 brs.

Banca Antonveneta SpA: Piazzetta Turati 2PiazP, 35131 Padua; tel. (049) 6991111; fax (049) 6991605; e-mail esterbap@tin.it; internet www.antonveneta.it; f. 1893 as Antoniana; July 1996 merged with Banca Popolare di Veneta Scarl; name changed September 2001; cap. €698.1m., res €1,957.5m., dep. €31,071.4m. (Dec. 2001); Chair ANTONIO CEOLA; Gen. Man. ENRICO PERNICE; 596 brs.

Banca Carige SpA (Cassa di Risparmio di Genova e Imperia): Via Cassa di Risparmio 15, 16123 Genova; tel. (010) 5792041; fax (010) 5794000; e-mail carige@carige.it; internet www.carige.it; f. 1846; cap. €1,017.5m., res €310.2m., €9,751.3 (Dec. 2001); Chair. Prof. FAUSTO CUOCOLO; Gen. Man. Dott. GIOVANNI BERNESCHI; 246 brs.

Banca Carime SpA: Viale Crati, 87100, Cosenza; tel. (0984) 8011; fax (0984) 806988; internet www.carime.it; cap. €829.7, res €9.6m. dep. €8,210.9m. (Dec. 2000); Chair. TOMMASO CARTONE; Man. Dir GIAMPIERO AULETTA ARMENISE.

Banca d'Intermediazione Mobiliare IMI SpA: Corso Matteotti 6, 20121, Milano; tel. (02) 77511; fax (02) 77512030; internet www.bancaimi.it; f. 1974 as Imisigeco Sim SpA; name changed as above 1998; cap. €180.0m., res €172.2m., dep. €12,316.2m. (Dec. 2001); Chair. and Pres. GIAN FRANCO MATTEI; Man. Dir CARLO CORRADINI.

Banca Lombarda e Piemontese SpA: Via Cefalonia 62, 25175 Brescia; tel. (030) 24331; fax (030) 2433509; e-mail info@ bancalombarda.com; internet www.bancalombarda.it; f. 1998; by merger of Banca San Paolo di Brescia SpA into CAB SpA; cap. €280.4m., res €800m., dep. €21,208.6m. (Dec. 2000); Chair. GINO TROMBI; Gen. Man. BRUNO DEGRANDI.

Banca Monte dei Paschi di Siena SpA: Piazza Salimbeni 3, 53100 Siena; tel. (0577) 294111; fax (0577) 294313; e-mail mps@mps .it; internet www.mps.it; f. 1472; joint stock company; cap. €1,356.1m., res €3,426.6m., dep. €55,679.4m. (Dec. 2001); Chair. PIERLUIGI FABRIZI; CEO and Gen. Man. VINCENZO DE BUSTIS; 999 brs.

Banca Nazionale del Lavoro SpA: Via Vittorio Veneto 119, 00187 Roma; tel. (06) 47021; fax (06) 47026646; e-mail press.bnl@bnl.it; internet www.bnl.it; f. 1913; cap. €1,073.9m., res €2,323.4m., dep. €70,536.4m. (Dec. 2001); Pres. Dr LUIGI ABETE; Man. DAVIDE CROFF; 706 brs.

Banca Popolare Commercio e Industria Scarl: POB 10167, Via della Moscova 33, 20121 Milano; tel. (02) 62751; fax (02) 62755640; e-mail intbkg@bpci.it; internet www.bpci.it; f. 1888; cap. €252.5m., res €443.6m., dep. €11,568.2m. (Dec. 2001); Chair. and Man. Dir GIUSEPPE VIGORELLI; Gen. Man. GIAMPIERO AULETTA; 164 brs.

Banca Popolare di Bergamo-Credito Varesino Scarl: Piazza Vittorio Veneto 8, 24122 Bergamo; tel. (035) 392111; fax (035) 392480; e-mail info@bpb.it; internet www.bpb.it; f. 1869; co-operative bank; cap.€407.6m., res€1,432.6m., dep. €20,656.1m. (June 2002); Chair. E. ZANETTI; CEO and Gen. Man. G. CATTANEO; 651 brs.

Banca Popolare dell'Emilia Romagna Scarl: Via San Carlo 8/20, 41100 Modena; tel. (059) 2021111; fax (059) 220537; e-mail relest@bper.it; internet www.bper.it; f. 1867; cap. €199.5m., res. €891.4m., dep. €13,419.3m. (Dec. 2001); Chair. Avv. FAUSTO BATTINI; Gen. Man. Dott. GUIDO LEONI; 251 brs.

Banca Popolare di Lodi Scarl: Via Polenghi Lombardo 13, 26900 Lodi; tel. (0371) 580111; fax (0371) 580762; e-mail v.manzoni@bpl .gruppobipielle.it; internet www.gruppobipielle.it; f. 1864; cap. €360.9m., res €1,284.0m., €12,862.1m. (Dec. 2001); Chair. GIOVANNI BENEVENTO; CEO GIANPIERO FIORANI; 368 brs.

Banca Popolare di Milano Scarl: Piazza F. Meda 4, 20121 Milano; tel. (02) 77001; fax (02) 77002993; e-mail bipiemme@bpm.it; internet www.bpm.it; f. 1865; cap. €1,152m., res €1,016m., dep. €23,385m. (Dec. 2001); Pres. ROBERTO MAZZOTTA; Gen. Man. ERNESTO PAOLILLO; 482 brs.

Banca Popolare di Sondrio Scarl: Piazza Garibaldi 16, 23100 Sondrio; tel. (0342) 528111; fax (0342) 528204; internet www.popso .it; f. 1871; cap. €412.7m., res €279.9m., dep. €7,374.8m. (Dec. 2001); Chair. and CEO PIERO MELAZZINI; 172 brs.

Banca Popolare di Vicenza Scparl: Via Battaglione Framarin 18, 36100 Vicenza; tel. (0444) 339111; fax (0444) 329364; e-mail info@popvi.it; internet www.popolarevicenza.it; f. 1866; cap. €154.2m., res €1,348.6m., dep. €7,576.9m. (Dec. 2001); Chair. GIOVANNI ZONIN; Gen. Man. DIVO GRONCHI; 284 brs.

Banca Regionale Europea Spa: Via Monte di Pietà 7, 20121 Milano; tel. (02) 721211; fax (02) 865413; e-mail breestero@tin.it; internet www.brebanca.it; cap. 850,000m. lire, res 449,958m. lire, dep. 11,460,770m. lire (Dec. 2000); Chair. MARIO CERA; Gen. Man. PIERLUIGI GARDELLA; 250 brs.

Banca di Roma: Viale Umberto Tupini 180, I-00144, Roma; tel. (06) 54451; fax (06) 54453154; e-mail web@bancaroma.it; internet www .bancaroma.it; f. 2002 as result of reorganization of Capitalia; cap. €1,374.1m., res €4,198.7m., dep. €77,057.2m. (Dec. 2001); Chair. BERARDINO LIBONATI; Man. Dir PIETRO LOCATI; 1,281 brs.

Banca Toscana SpA: Via Leone Pancaldo 4, 50127 Firenze; tel. (055) 43911; fax (055) 4360061; e-mail international.dept@ bancatoscana.it; internet www.bancatoscana.it; f. 1904; cap. €381.2m., res €711.7m., dep. €13,472.4m. (Dec. 2001); Pres. PAOLO MOTTURA; Gen. Man. and CEO PIERO FARRONI; 330 brs.

Banco di Brescia SpA: Corso Martiri della Libertà 13, 25100, Brescia; tel. (030) 29921; fax (030) 2992470; e-mail info@ bancodibrescia.com; internet www.bancodibrescia.com; f. 1999; cap. 812,500m. lire, res 460,122m. lire, dep. 24,599,201m. lire (Dec. 2000); Chair. GINO TROMBI; Gen. Man. COSTANTINO VITALI.

Banco di Napoli SpA: Via Toledo 177–178, 80132 Napoli; tel. (081) 7911111; fax (081) 7924400; e-mail relest@bancodinapoli.it; internet www.bancodinapoli.it; f. 1539; chartered public institution; cap. €1,035.9m., res €319.9m., dep. €25,186.1m. (Dec. 2001); Chair. FEDERICO PEPE; Man. Dir AMADIO LAZZARINI; 757 brs.

Banco Popolare di Verona e Novara Scrl: Piazza Nogara 2, POB 509, 37100 Verona; tel. (045) 8675111; fax (045) 8675474; internet www.bpv.it; f. 2002 by merger of Banco Popolare di Verona—Banco S. Geminiano e S. Prospero and Banco Popolare di Novara; cap. €1,331.8m., res €1,443.5m., dep. €41,624.7m. (June. 2002); Pres. Prof. CARLO FRATTA PASINI; Man.Dir MASSIMO MINOLFI; 372 brs.

Banco di Sardegna SpA: Viale Umberto 36, 07100 Sassari; tel. (079) 226000; fax (079) 226015; internet www.bancosardegna.it; f.

1953; cap. €127.8m., res €607.4m., dep. €9,234.4m. (Dec. 2001); Chair. Prof. ANTONIO SASSU; Gen. Man. NATALINO OGGIANO; 235 brs.

Banco di Sicilia SpA: Via Generale Magliocco 1, 90141 Palermo; tel. (091) 6081111; fax (091) 6085051; internet www.bancodisicilia .it; f. 1860; cap. €1,235.5m., res €74.8m., dep. €22,634.8m. (Dec. 2001); Chair. and Pres. SABINO CASSESE; Gen. Man. CESARE CALETTI; 566 brs.

BIPOP-CARIRE SpA: Via Leonardo da Vinci 74, 25122 Brescia; tel. (030) 39931; fax (030) 396313; e-mail info@bipop.it; internet www.bipop.it; f. 1999; by merger of Banca Popolare di Brescia and Cassa di Risparmio di Reggio Emilia; owned by Capitalia SpA; due to merge with Banca di Roma in 2003; cap. 871,035.6m. lire, res 1,200,173.4m. lire, dep. 22,219,299m. lire (Dec. 2000); Chair. FRANCESCO SPINELLI; Gen. Man. GIORGIO BRAMBILLA; 69 brs.

Cassa di Risparmio di Firenze SpA: Via Bufalini 4/6, 50122 Firenze; tel. (055) 26121; fax (055) 679986; e-mail estero@carifirenze .it; internet www.carifirenze.it; f. 1829; cap. 1,086,236m. lire, res 427,387m. lire, dep. 18,440,349m. lire (Dec. 2001); Chair. and Pres. AURELIANO BENEDETTI; Gen. Man. LINO MOSCATELLI; 270 brs and agencies.

Cassa di Risparmio di Padova e Rovigo SpA: POB 1088, Corso Garibaldi 22/26, 35122 Padua; tel. (049) 8368111; fax (049) 8368540; e-mail mk@cariparo.it; internet www.cariparo.it; f. 1822; cap. 534,666m. lire, res 1,467,656.7m.lire, dep. 22,094,238.4m. lire (Dec. 2000); Pres. ORAZIO ROSSI; Man. Dir PIO BUSSOLOTTO; 231 brs.

Cassa di Risparmio di Parma e Piacenza SpA: Via Università l, 43100 Parma; tel. (0521) 912111; fax (0521) 912976; internet www .cariprpc.it; f. 1860; cap. €500.0m., res €218,4m., dep. €11,047.3 (Dec. 2001); Chair. GIUSEPPE CONTINO; Gen. Man. and CEO BENIAMINO ANSELMI; 300 brs.

Cassa di Risparmio in Bologna SpA (CARISBO): Via Farini 22, 40124 Bologna; tel. (051) 6454111; fax (051) 6454366; internet www .carisbo.it; f. 1837; cap. €450m., res €105.0m. (January 2001); Chair. GIANGUIDO SACCHI MORSIANI; Gen. Man. PAOLO LELLI; 184 brs.

Credito Bergamasco SpA: Largo Porta Nuova 2, 24122 Bergamo; tel. (035) 393111; fax (035) 393144; e-mail dip.internazionale@ creberg.it; internet www.creberg.it; f. 1891; cap. €185.2m., res €439.1m., dep. €8,387.6m. (Dec. 2001); Pres. CESARE ZONCA; Gen. Man. FRANCO MENINI; 215 brs.

Credito Emiliano SpA (CREDEM): Via Emilia S. Pietro 4, 42100 Reggio-Emilia; tel. (0522) 582111; fax (0522) 433969; e-mail intmil@ credem.it; internet www.credem.it; f. 1910; cap. €272.5m., res €327.6m., dep. €10,670m. (Dec. 2001); Pres. GIORGIO FERRARI; Gen. Man. ADOLFO BIZZOCCHI; 416 brs.

Deutsche Bank SpA: Via Borgogna 8, 20122 Milano; tel. (02) 40241; fax (02) 40242636; internet www.deutsche-bank.it; f. 1918 as Banca dell'Italia Meridionale; in 1923 name changed to Banca d'America e d'Italia SpA, and as above in 1994; cap. €310.7m. (Dec. 2002), res €622.8m., dep. €9,289.1m. (Dec. 2001); Pres. GIANNI TESTONI; Man. Dir THOMAS RUESCHEN; 253 brs.

IntesaBci SpA: Via Monte di Pietà 8, 20121 Milano; tel. (02) 88441; fax (02) 88443638; internet www.intesabci.it; f. 2001 by merger of Cariplo, Banco Ambrosiano Veneto and Banca Commerciale Italiana; cap. €3,489m., res €9,645.7m., dep. €250,634.9m. (Dec. 2001); Chair. GIOVANNI BAZOLI; CEOs CORRADO PASSERA, CHRISTIAN MERLE; 3,637 brs.

MCC SpA: Via Piemonte 51, 00187 Roma; tel. (06) 47911; e-mail mcc@mcc.it; internet www.mcc.it; f. 1952 as Mediocredito Centrale; changed name as above in 2002; owned by Capitalia banking group; cap. €475.1m. (Dec. 2001); Chair. FRANCO CARRARO; CEO MATTEO ARPE.

SANPAOLO IMI SpA: Piazza San Carlo 156, 10121 Torino; tel. (011) 5551; e-mail investor.relation@sanpaoloimi.com; internet www.sanpaoloimi.com; f. 1563 as a foundation; merged with Istituto Mobiliare Italiano SpA 1998; name changed as above in 1999; cap. €3,932.4m., res €2,648.8m., dep. €79,176.1m. (Dec. 2001); Chair. RAINER STEFANO MASERA; Man. Dirs PIO BUSSOLOTTO, LUIGI MARANZANA, ALFONSO IOZZO; 2,180 brs.

UniCredito Italiano SpA: Piazza Cordusio, 20123 Milano; tel. (02) 88621; fax (02) 88623034; e-mail info@unicredito.it; internet www .unicredito.it; f. 1870; cap. €2,523.2m., res €5,491.0m., dep. €161,065.0m. (Dec. 2001); Chair. CARLO SALVATORI; CEO ALESSANDRO PROFUMO; 973 brs.

FINANCIAL INSTITUTIONS

CENTROBANCA (Banca Centrale di Credito Popolare) SpA: Corso Europa 16, 20122 Milano; tel. (02) 77811; fax (02) 784372; e-mail comunica@centrobanca.it; internet www.centrobanca.it; f. 1946; central organization for medium- and long-term operations of Banche Popolari (co-operative banks) throughout Italy; cap.

€336.0m., res €126.9m., dep. €7,591.6m. (Dec. 2001); Pres. TANCREDI BIANCHI; Gen. Man. GIAN GIACOMO FAVERIO.

Dexia Crediop SpA: Via XX Settembre 30, 00187 Rome; tel. (06) 47711; fax (06) 47715952; e-mail contact@dexia-crediop.it; internet www.dexia-crediop.it; f. 1919; newly incorporated 1996; name changed from Crediop SpA in May 2001; cap. €450.2m., res €30.4m., dep. €15,919.6m (Dec. 2001); Man. Dir GÉRARD BAYOL; Sec.-Gen. ALBERTO MARI.

EFIBANCA (Ente Finanzario Interbancario SpA): Via Po 28–32, 00198 Roma; tel. (06) 85991; fax (06) 8599250; e-mail rel.esterne@efispa.it; internet www.efibancaspa.it; f. 1939; cap. 316,113m. lire; res 352,121.9m. lire; dep. 11,264,280.9m. lire; Chair. PIETRO RASTELLI; Gen. Man. VALERIO LATTANZI; 8 brs.

ICCRI Banca Federale Europea SpA: Via Boncompagni 71h, 00187 Roma; tel. (06) 47151; fax (06) 47153579; internet www.iccri.it; f. 1919 as Istituto di Credito delle Casse di Risparmio Italiane, name changed in 1999; cap. 1,040,468.8m.lire, res 281,073.4m. lire, dep. 10,501,599.8m. lire (Dec. 2000); Chair. Prof. DINO PIERO GIARDA; Gen. Man. Dr MARCO BELLINZONI.

INTERBANCA SpA: Corso Venezia 56, 20121 Milano; tel. (02) 77311; fax (02) 784321; internet www.interbanca.it; f. 1961; cap. €148.7m., res €243.3m., dep. €7,199.6m. (Dec. 2001); Chair. ANTONIO CEOLA; Man. Dir GIORGIO CIRLA; Gen. Man. MAURO GAMBARO; 11 brs.

Istituto Centrale delle Banche di Credito Cooperativo (ICCREA SpA): Via Torino 146, 00184 Roma; tel. (06) 47161; fax (06) 4747155; f. 1963; cap. 400,000m., res 14,150m., dep. 8,931,934m. (Dec. 1999); Pres. GIORGIO CLEMENTI; Gen. Man. ALFREDO NERI; 5 brs.

Mediobanca—Banca di Credito Finanziario SpA: Piazzetta Enrico Cuccia 1, 20121 Milano; tel. (02) 88291; fax (02) 8829367; internet www.mediobanca.it; f. 1946; cap. €331.7m., res €2,949.9m., dep. €18,258.9m. (June 2001); Chair. FRANCESCO CINGANO; Man. Dir VINCENZO MARANGHI.

BANKERS' ORGANIZATIONS

Associazione Bancaria Italiana: Piazza del Gesù 49, 00186 Roma; tel. (06) 67671; fax (06) 6767437; e-mail abi@abi.it; internet www.abi.it; f. 1919; advocates the common interests of the banking industry; Pres. MAURIZIO SELLA; Gen. Man. Dott. GIUSEPPE ZADRA; membership (1,003 mems) is comprised of the following institutions: banks authorized to gather savings from the general public and exercise credit business as well as to perform other financial activities; brs and representative offices of foreign banks; asscns of banks or financial intermediaries; financial intermediaries engaging in one or more of the activities subject to mutual recognition under the Second Banking Directive or other financial activities subject to public prudential supervison.

Associazione fra le Casse di Risparmio Italiane: POB 7221, Viale di Villa Grazioli 23, 00198 Roma; tel. (06) 855621; fax (06) 8540192; internet www.acri.it; f. 1912; Chair. Dott. GIUSEPPE GUZZETTI; Gen. Man. STEFANO MARCHETTINI.

Associazione fra gli Istituti Regionali di Mediocredito (ASSIREME): Piazza della Marina 1, 00196 Roma; tel. (06) 3225150; fax (06) 3225135; Pres. Prof. ANGELO CALOIA; Gen. Man. Dott. ANTONIO DE VITO.

Associazione Italiana per il Factoring: Via Cerva 9, 20122 Milano; tel. (02) 76020127; fax (02) 76020159; e-mail posta.assifact@tiscalinet.it; internet www.assifact.it; Pres. Dott. FRANCO ROSSO; Sec.-Gen. Prof. ALESSANDRO CARRETTA.

Associazione Nazionale Banche Private (ASSBANK): Via Cosimo del Fante 7, 20122 Milano; tel. (02) 5821261; fax (02) 58212650; e-mail assbank@assbank.it; internet www.assbank.it; Pres. Dott. Prof. TANCREDI BIANCHI.

Associazione Nazionale fra le Banche Popolari: Piazza Venezia 11, 00187 Roma; tel. (06) 695351; Pres. Prof. SIRO LOMBARDINI; Dir-Gen. Dott. GIORGIO CARDUCCI.

Associazione Nazionale fra gli Istituti di Credito Agrario (ANICA): Roma; tel. (06) 8077506; fax (06) 8077506; f. 1946; Pres. Prof. GIUSEPPE GUERRIERI; Sec.-Gen. Dott. ERNESTO DE MEDIO.

Associazione Italiana delle Società ed Enti di Gestione Mobiliare ed Immobiliare: Via in Lucina 17, 00186, Roma; tel. (06) 6840591; fax (06) 6893262; e-mail info.roma@assogestioni.it; internet www.assogestioni.it; f. 1984; Pres. Prof. GUIDO CAMMARANO; Sec.-Gen. FABIO GALLI.

Associazione Italiana Leasing (ASSILEA): Piazza di Priscilla 4, 00199 Roma; tel. (06) 86211271; fax (06) 86211214; e-mail info@assilea.it; internet www.assilea.it; Pres. Dott. ANTONIO DATTOLO; Dir-Gen. Ing. FABRIZIO MARAFINI.

STOCK EXCHANGES

Commissione Nazionale per le Società e la Borsa (CONSOB) (Commission for Companies and the Stock Exchange): Via Isonzo 19, 00198 Roma; tel. (06) 84771; f. 1974; regulatory control over cos quoted on stock exchanges, convertible bonds, unlisted securities, insider trading, all forms of public saving except bank deposits and mutual funds; Chair. LUIGI SPAVENTA; there are 10 stock exchanges, of which the following are the most important:

Genoa: Borsa Valori, Via G. Boccardo 1, Genova; tel. (010) 590920; f. 1855; Pres. LUCIANO GAMBAROTTA.

Borsa Italiana (Italian Stock Exchange): Piazza degli Affari 6, 20123 Milano; tel. (02) 72426207; fax (02) 72426279; e-mail info@borsaitalia.it; internet www.borsaitalia.it; Pres. ANGELO TANTAZZI; Dir-Gen. MASSIMO CAPUANO.

Naples: Borsa Valori, Palazzo Borsa, Piazza Bovio, Napoli; tel. (081) 269151; Pres. GIORGIO FOCAS.

Rome: Borsa Valori, Via dei Burro 147, 00186 Roma; tel. (06) 6792701; f. 1821; Pres. ALBERTO BORTI.

Turin: Borsa Valori, Torino; tel. (011) 547743; fax (011) 5612193; f. 1850; Pres. Dott. FRANCO CELLINO.

INSURANCE

Alleanza Assicurazioni SpA: Viale Luigi Sturzo 35, 20154 Milano; tel. (02) 62961; fax (02) 653718; e-mail info@alleanzaassicurazioni.it; f. 1898; life insurance; subsidiary of Assicurazioni Generali (q.v.); cap. €423.1m. (December 1999); Chair. Dott. SANDRO SALVATI.

Allianz Subalpina SpA: Via Alfieri 22, 10121 Torino; tel. (011) 5161431; fax (011) 5627246; f. 1928; cap. 40,910.6m. lire (Dec. 1998); Chair. Dott. GIULIO BASEGGIO; Man. Dir Dott. ROBERTO GAVAZZI.

Assicuratrice Edile SpA: Via A. De Togni 2, 20123 Milano; tel. (02) 480411; fax (02) 48041292; e-mail cauzioni@assedile.it; internet www.assedile.it; f. 1960; cap. 16,000m. lire (Jan. 2000); Chair. CHRISTIAN HUOT; Man. Dir ANTOINE NINU.

Assicurazioni Generali SpA: Piazza Duca degli Abruzzi 2, 34132 Trieste; tel. (040) 671111; fax (040) 671600; internet www.generali.com; f. 1831; cap. €1,275.7m. (2002); Chair. ANTOINE BERNHEIM; Gen. Man. GIOVANNI PERISSINOTTO.

Le Assicurazioni d'Italia (ASSITALIA) SpA: Corso d'Italia 33, 00198 Roma; tel. (06) 84831; fax (06) 84833142; f. 1923; cap. 150,000m. lire (Dec. 1990); Pres. Avv. PIER LUIGI CASSIETTI; Gen. Man. Prof. Avv. VINCENZO MUNGARI.

BNC Assicurazioni SpA: Via S. Martino della Battaglia 4, 00185 Roma; tel. (06) 44761; fax (06) 44763343; f. 1927; cap. 157,360m. lire (Dec. 1996); Pres. Dott. LUCA A. BERTOLA; Dir-Gen. Dott. RICCARDO ROMUSSI.

Compagnia Assicuratrice Unipol SpA: Via Stalingrado 45, 40128 Bologna; tel. (051) 6097111; fax (051) 375349; f. 1961; cap. 261,680m. lire (Sept. 1999); Chair. GIOVANNI CONSORTE; Vice-Chair. IVANO SACCHETTI.

Compagnia di Assicurazioni di Milano SpA: Strada 6, Pal. A13, Assago Milanofiori, 20090, Milano; tel. (02) 82291; fax (02) 82292389; f. 1825; cap. 175,333m. lire (Dec. 1996); Pres. Dott. AMATO MOLINARI; Dir-Gen. Ing. LUCIANO PASQUALI.

Dival Vita SpA: Piazza Erculea 13, 20122 Milano; tel. (02) 85751; fax (02) 8575266; f. 1975; cap. 175,000m. lire (Dec. 1996); Pres. Dott. GIULIO BASEGGIO; Dir-Gen. ENZO ZENI.

FATA (Fondo Assicurativo Tra Agricoltori) SpA: Via Urbana 169/A, 00184 Roma; tel. (06) 47651; fax (06) 4871187; f. 1927; cap. 20,000m. lire (Dec. 1990); Chair. GIANCARLO BUSCARINI; Man. Dir FRANCO RIZZI.

La Fiduciaria: Via A. Finelli 8, 40126 Bologna; tel. (051) 6307011; fax (051) 243030; f. 1970; cap. 11,508m. lire (June 1992); Chair. JEAN PAUL GALBRUN; Man. Dir Dott. Ing. SERGIO BEDINI.

La Fondiaria Assicurazioni SpA: Piazza della Libertà 6, 50129 Firenze; tel. (055) 47941; fax (055) 476026; f. 1879; cap. 390,160m. lire (1996); merged with SAI SpA in 2002 to form FONDIARIA-SAI SpA; Pres. PAOLO FERRO-LUZZI; CEO ROBERTO GAVAZZI.

Istituto Nazionale delle Assicurazioni SpA (INA): Via Sallustiana 51, 00187 Roma; tel. (06) 47221; fax (06) 47224559; internet www.gruppoina.it; f. 1912; Chair. Dott. SERGIO SIGLIENTI; Man. Dir LINO BENASSI.

ITAS, Istituto Trentino-Alto Adige per Assicurazioni: Via Mantova 67, 38100 Trento; tel. (0461) 891702; fax (0461) 980297; e-mail itas.direzione@gruppoitas.it; internet www.gruppoitas.it; f. 1821; cap. €40m. (Dec. 2001); Chair. Dott. EDO BENEDETTI; Gen. Man. Dott. ETTORE LOMBARDO.

Levante Norditalia Assicurazioni SpA: Viale Certosa 222, 20156 Milano; tel. (02) 30761; fax (02) 3086125; f. 1963; cap. €102.5m. (Dec.

2000); Pres. Dr. GIOVANNI BERNESCHI; Man. Dir Dr. FERDINANDO MENCONI.

Lloyd Adriatico SpA: Largo Ugo Irneri 1, 34123 Trieste; tel. (040) 77811; fax (040) 7781311; f. 1936; cap. €60m. (Dec. 2000); Chair. Dott. HELMUT PERLET; Vice-Chair. Dott. GIOVANNI GABRIELLI; Man. Dir Dott. ENRICO TOMASO CUCCHIANI.

Lloyd Italico Assicurazioni SpA: Via Fieschi 9, 16121 Genova; tel. (010) 53801; fax (010) 592856; e-mail info@lloydadriatico.it; internet www.lloydadriatico.it; f. 1983; cap. 61,500m. lire (Dec. 1990); Chair. Dott. ENRICO TOMASO CUCCHIANI; Man. Dir GIORGIO E. FUSELLI.

Mediolanum Vita SpA: Palazzo Meucci, Via Francesco Sforza 15, 20080 Basiglio; tel. (02) 90491; fax (02) 90492427; f. 1972; cap. 170,000m. lire (Dec. 1996); Pres. Dott. ALFREDO MESSINA.

Meieaurora Assicurazioni SpA: Corso di Porta Vigentina 9, 20122, Milano; tel. (02) 59922205; fax (02) 59922561; e-mail marketing@meieaurora.it; internet www.meieaurora.it. f. 2001 by merger of Meie Assicurazioni SpA and Aurora Assicurazioni SpA; cap. €2,595m. res. €2,438m. (Sept. 2002.); Gen. Man. Dott. GIAMPIERO GELMI.

La Nationale Assicurazioni SpA: Piazza del Porto di Ripetta 1, 00186 Roma; tel. (06) 682801; fax (06) 6834089; f. 1962; cap. 30,000m. lire (1992); Pres. JEAN PAUL GALBRUN; Vice-Pres. PIER UGO ANDREINI.

Nuova Tirrena SpA: Via Massimi 158, 00136 Roma; tel. (06) 30181; fax (06) 30183613; f. 1929; cap. €142.6m. Pres. Rag. FRANCESCO TORRI; Dir-Gen. Dott. LUCIANO BECCHIO.

RAS, SpA (Riunione Adriatica di Sicurtà): Corso Italia 23, 20122 Milano; tel. (02) 72161; f. 1838; merged with Lavoro & Sicurtà, SpA, in 1999; cap. €437.8m. Chair. Dott. GIUSEPPE VITA; Man. Dir Dott. MARIO GRECO.

SAI (Società Assicuratrice Industriale SpA): Corso Galileo Galilei 12, 10126 Torino; tel. (011) 65621; fax (011) 6562685; f. 1921; merged with La Fondiaria Assicurazioni SpA in 2002 to form FONDIARIA-SAI SpA; cap. 165,000m. lire (Dec. 1990); Chair. Dott. Ing. JONELLA LIGRESTI; CEO CARLO CIANI.

SARA Assicurazioni SpA: Via Po 20, 00198 Roma; tel. (06) 84751; fax (06) 8475223; f. 1924; cap. 60,750m. lire (June 1994); Chair. ROSARIO ALESSI; Gen. Man. Dott. MARCO ROCCA.

Società Cattolica di Assicurazione: Lungadige Cangrande 16, 37126 Verona; tel. (045) 8391111; fax (045) 8391112; f. 1896; cap. 78,150m. lire (June 1994); Chair. Ing. GIULIO BISOFFI; Gen. Man. Dott. EZIO PAOLO REGGIA.

Società Italiana Cauzioni SpA (SIC): Via Crescenzio 12, 00193 Roma; tel. (06) 688121; fax (06) 6874418; e-mail sic.dirgen@gerlingncm.com; internet www.sic-spa.it; f. 1948; cap. €20m. (Dec. 2001); Chair. BERND MEYER; Man. Dir GIORGIO CIMAGALLI.

Società Reale Mutua di Assicurazioni: Via Corte d'Appello 11, 10122 Torino; tel. (011) 431111; fax (011) 4350966; e-mail webmaster@realmutua.it; internet www.realmutua.it; f. 1828; total assets 8,195,584m. lire (1998); Chair. CARLO ALBANI CASTELBARCO VISCONTI; Gen. Man. Dott. PIERO CASTELLI.

Toro Assicurazioni SpA: Via Arcivescovado 16, 10121 Torino; tel. (011) 51631; fax (011) 543587; f. 1833; cap. 159,510m. lire (Dec. 1998); Chair. BENEDETTO SALAROLI; Man. Dir Rag. FRANCESCO TORRI.

UAP Italiana SpA: Via Leopardi 15, 20123 Milano; tel. (02) 480841; fax (02) 48084331; f. 1956; cap. 8,211m. lire (Dec. 1990); Chair. and Man. Dir Dott. PIERRE MERCIER.

Swiss Re Italia SpA: Via dei Giuochi Istmici 40, 00194 Roma; tel. (06) 323931; fax (06) 36303398; e-mail srit-communicazione@swissre.com; internet www.swissre.com; f. 1922; cap. €100m. (Dec. 2001); Chair. Avv. BERARDINO LIBONATI; Man. Dir ANTONIO SOLARI.

Universo Assicurazioni SpA: Via del Pilastro 52, 40127 Bologna; tel. (051) 6371111; fax (051) 6371401; f. 1972; cap. 62,500m. lire (Dec. 1990); Chair. Dott. GIUSEPPE SOLINAS; Gen. Man. Dott. GIORGIO DI GIANSANTE.

Vittoria Assicurazioni SpA: Via Caldera 21, 20153 Milano; tel. (02) 482191; fax (02) 48203693; e-mail direzione@vittoriaassicurazioni.it; internet www.vittoriaassicurazioni.com; f. 1921; cap. €30m. (Dec. 2000); Chair. Prof. LUIGI GUATRI; Man. Dir Rag. ROBERTO GUARENA.

Winterthur Assicurazioni SpA: Piazza Missori 2, 20122 Milano; tel. (02) 85471; fax (02) 8547701; f. 1919; cap. 223,000m. lire (Dec. 1996); Pres. Dott. LUIGO CAPÈ; Dir-Gen. Dott. FABRIZIO RINDI.

INSURANCE ASSOCIATION

Associazione Nazionale fra le Imprese Assicuratrici (ANIA): Piazza S. Babila 1, 20122 Milano; tel. (02) 77641; fax (02) 780870; e-mail info@ania.it; f. 1944; Pres. Dott. ALFONSO DESIATA; Dir-Gen. Dott. MARIO ORIO; 210 mems.

Trade and Industry

GOVERNMENT AGENCIES

Autorità garante della concorrenza e del mercato (Regulatory authority for competition and markets): Via Liguria 26, 00187 Roma; tel. (06) 481621; fax (06) 48162256; e-mail antitrust@agcm.it; internet www.agcm.it; Pres. GIUSEPPE TESAURO; Sec.-Gen. RITA CICCONE.

Istituto Nazionale per il Commercio Estero (ICE) (National Institute for Foreign Trade): Via Liszt 21, 00144 Roma; tel. (06) 59921; fax (06) 59926899; e-mail ice@ice.it; internet www.ice.it; f. 1919; govt agency for the promotion of foreign trade; Chair. and CEO Prof. BENIAMINO QUINTIERI.

CHAMBERS OF COMMERCE

Unione Italiana delle Camere di Commercio, Industria, Artigianato e Agricoltura (Italian Union of Chambers of Commerce, Industry, Crafts and Agriculture): Piazza Sallustio 21, 00187 Roma; tel. (06) 47041; f. 1954 to promote the development of chambers of commerce, industry, trade and agriculture; Pres. CARLO SANGALLI; Sec.-Gen. GIUSEPPE TRIPOLI.

INDUSTRIAL AND TRADE ASSOCIATIONS

Confederazione Generale dell'Industria Italiana (CONFINDUSTRIA) (General Confederation of Italian Industry): Viale dell'Astronomia 30, 00144 Roma; tel. (06) 59031; fax (06) 5919615; e-mail confindustria@confindustria.it; internet www.confindustria.it; f. 1910; re-established 1944; mems: 107 territorial asscns and 110 branch asscns, totalling 111,000 firms and 4.5m. employees; office in Brussels; Pres. ANTONIO D'AMATO; Dir-Gen. STEFANO PARISI.

Principal Affiliated Organizations

Associazione degli Industriali della Birra e del Malto (Brewers): Viale di Val Fiorita 90, 00144 Roma; tel. (06) 543932; fax (06) 5912910; e-mail birra.viva@assobirra.it; internet www.assobirra.it; f. 1946; Pres. Dott. HARALD FUCHS; Dir Dott. FILIPPO TERZAGHI.

Associazione Industrie per l'Aerospazio, i Sistemi e la Difesa (AIAD) (Aerospace, Systems and Defence Industries): Via Nazionale 54, 00184 Roma; tel. (06) 4880247; fax (06) 4827476; e-mail aiad@aiad.it; internet www.aiad.it; f. 1947; Pres. Ing. REMO PERTICA; Sec.-Gen. CARLO FESTUCCI.

Associazione Italiana delle Industrie della Filiera Tessile Abbigliamento (SISTEMA MODA ITALIA) (Clothing and Knitwear Manufacturers): Viale Sarca 223, 20123 Milano; tel. (02) 66103391; fax (02) 66103670; e-mail info@sistemamodaitalia.it; internet www.sistemamodaitalia.it; f. 1945; produces weekly, fortnightly and annual periodicals; Pres. Dott. VITTORIO GIULINI; Dir Dott. PIERO COSTA.

Associazione Italiana Industrie Prodotti Alimentari (AIIPA) (Food Manufacturers): Corso di Porta Nuova 34, 20121 Milano; tel. (02) 654184; fax (02) 654822; e-mail info@aiipa.it; internet www.aiipa.it; f. 1946; Pres. Dott. DEMETRIO CORNO; Dir Dott. GIOVANNI FRANCO CRIPPA; 300 mems.

Associazione Italiana Tecnico Economica del Cemento (AITEC) (Cement): Piazza G. Marconi 25, 00144 Roma; tel. (06) 54210237; fax (06) 5915408; e-mail aitec@aitecweb.com; f. 1959; Pres. GIACOMO MARAZZI; Dir Dott. Ing. DOMENICO BURATTINI.

Associazione Mineraria Italiana (ASSOMINERARIA) (Italian Oil and Mining Industry): Via delle Tre Madonne 20, 00197 Roma; tel. (06) 8073045; fax (06) 8073385; e-mail info@assomineraria.org; internet www.assomineraria.org; f. 1144; Pres. Dott. Ing. STEFANO CAO; Dir-Gen. Dott. ANDREA KETOFF; 100 mems.

Associazione Nazionale Costruttori Edili (ANCE) (Builders): Via Guattani 16, 00161 Roma; tel. (06) 845671; fax (06) 44232832; e-mail info@ance.it; internet www.ance.it; f. 1946; Pres. Dott. Ing. CLAUDIO DE ALBERTIS; Man. Dir CARLO FERRONI; mems: 19,000 firms in 101 provincial and 20 regional asscns.

Associazione Nazionale delle Fonderie (ASSOFOND) (Foundries): Via Copernico 54, 20090 Trezzano Sul Naviglio; tel. (02) 48400967; fax (02) 48401282; e-mail info@assofond.it; internet www.assofond.it; f. 1948; Pres. EMILIO CREMONA; Dir PAOLO PONZINI.

Associazione Nazionale dell'Industria Farmaceutica (FARM-INDUSTRIA) (Pharmaceutical Industry): Largo del Nazareno 3/8, 00187 Roma; tel. (06) 675801; fax (06) 6786494; e-mail farmindustria@farmindustria.it; internet www.farmindustria.it; f. 1978; Pres. Dott. GIAN PIETRO LEONI; 222 mem. firms.

Associazione Nazionale fra Industrie Automobilistiche (ANFIA) (Motor Vehicle Industries): Corso Galileo Ferraris 61, 10128 Torino; tel. (011) 5546505; fax (011) 545986; e-mail anfia@anfia.it; internet www.anfia.it; f. 1912; Pres. Dott. CARLO SINCERI; Dir-Gen. Dott. EMILIO DI CAMILLO; 260 mems.

Associazione Nazionale Italiana Industrie Grafiche, Cartotecniche e Trasformatrici (ASSOGRAFICI) (Printing and Paper-Converting Industries): Piazza Conciliazione 1, 20123 Milano; tel. (02) 4981051; fax (02) 4816947; e-mail info@assografici.it; internet www.assografici.it; f. 1946; Pres. Ing. EMANUELE PIOVANO; Gen. Dir Dott. CLAUDIO COVINI; 1,200 mems.

Federazione delle Associazioni Nazionali dell'Industria Meccanica Varia ed Affine (ANIMA) (Federation of the Italian Associations of Mechanical and Engineering Industries): Via L. Battistotti Sassi 11/B, 20133 Milano; tel. (02) 73971; fax (02) 7397316; e-mail anima@anima-it.com; internet www.anima-it.com; f. 1945; Pres. Dott. Ing. SAVINO RIZZIO; Dir Dott. Ing. ENRICO MALCOVATI; 1,500 mems.

Federazione Italiana Industriali Produttori Esportatori ed Importatori di Vini, Acquaviti, Liquori, Sciroppi, Aceti ed Affini (FEDERVINI) (Producers, Importers and Exporters of Wines, Brandies, Liqueurs, Syrups, Vinegars and Allied Products): Via Mentana 2B, 00185 Roma; tel. (06) 4941630; fax (06) 4941566; e-mail federvini@federvini.it; internet www.federvini.it; f. 1917; Pres. PIERO MASTROBERARDINO; Dir-Gen. FEDERICO CASTELLUCCI.

Federazione Nazionale dell'Industria Chimica (FEDER-CHIMICA) (Chemical Industry): Via Giovanni da Procida 11, 20149 Milano; tel. (02) 345651; fax (02) 34565310; e-mail federchimica@federchimica.it; internet www.federchimica.it; f. 1945; Pres. Dott. GIORGIO SQUINZI; Dir Dott. CLAUDIO BENEDETTI.

Federazione Nazionale Imprese Elettrotecniche ed Elettroniche (ANIE) (Electrotechnic and Electronic Companies): Via Gattamelata 34, 20149 Milano; tel. (02) 32641; fax (02) 3264212; e-mail info@anie.it; internet www.anie.it; Pres. Dott. Ing. RENZO TANI; Dir. ROBERTO TARANTO.

Unione Industriali Pastai Italiani (UNIPI) (Pasta Manufacturers): Via Po 102, 00198 Roma; tel. (06) 8543291; fax (06) 8415132; e-mail unipi@unipi-pasta.it; internet www.unipi-pasta.it; f. 1968; Pres. Dott. MARIO RUMMO; Dir RAFFAELLO RAGAGLINI.

Unione Nazionale Cantieri e Industrie Nautiche ed Affini (UCINA) (Italian Marine Industry Association): Piazzale Kennedy 1, 16129 Genova; tel. (010) 5769811; fax (010) 5531801; e-mail ucina@ucina.it; internet www.ucina.it; Pres. Dott. PAOLO VITELLI; Sec.-Gen. Dott. Ing. LORENZO POLLICARDO.

Unione Petrolifera (Petroleum Industries): Via Giorgione 129, 00147 Roma; tel. (06) 5423651; fax (06) 59602925; e-mail info@unionepetrolifera.it; internet www.unionepetrolifera.it; f. 1948; Pres. Dott. PASQUALE DE VITA; Dir-Gen. Dott. PIETRO DE SIMONE; 28 mems.

Others

Associazione Nazionale Comuni Italiani (ANCI): Via dei Prefetti 46, 00186 Roma; tel. (06) 680091; fax (06) 68009202; e-mail baroni@anci.it; internet www.anci.it; Pres. Dott. LEONARDO DOMENICI; Dir-Gen. Dott. FABIO MELILLI.

Associazione Nazionale fra i Concessionari del Servizio di Riscossione del Tributi (ASCOTRIBUTI) (Services relating to Collection of Payments): Via Parigi 11, 00185 Roma; tel. (06) 485764; fax (06) 4740422; Pres. RICCARDO TRIGLIA; Dir-Gen. Dott. GERARDO CHIRO.

Associazione Sindacale per le Aziende Petrochimiche e Collegate a Partecipazione Statale (State-controlled Petrochemical Cos): Roma; tel. (06) 67341; fax (06) 6734242; f. 1960; draws up labour and union contracts and represents the cos in legal matters; Pres. Avv. GUIDO FANTONI; Vice-Pres. and Dir-Gen. Dott. MODESTINO FUSCO.

Associazione fra le Società Italiane per Azioni (ASSONIME) (Limited Cos): Piazza Venezia 11, 00187 Roma; tel. (06) 695291; fax (06) 6790487; e-mail assonime@assonime.it; internet www.assonime.it; f. 1911; Pres. VITTORIO MERLONI; Dir-Gen. Prof. STEFANO MICOSSI.

Confederazione Generale della Agricoltura Italiana (CONFAGRICOLTURA) (General Agricultural): Corso Vittorio Emanuele II 101, 00186 Roma; tel. (06) 68521; fax (06) 68308578; e-mail immco@mail.confagricoltura.it; internet www.confagricoltura.it; f. 1945; Pres. Dott. AUGUSTO BOCCHINI; Dir-Gen. VITO BIANCO.

CONFCOMMERCIO—Confederazione Generale Italiana del Commercio, del Turismo, dei Servizi e delle Piccole e Medie Industrie (Commerce, Tourism, Services and Small and Medium-sized Industry): Piazza G.G. Belli 2, 00153 Roma; tel. (06) 58661; fax (06) 5809425; e-mail confcommercio@confcommercio.it; internet www.confcommercio.it; f. 1946; Pres. Dott. SERGIO BILLÈ; Sec.-Gen. Dott. GIUSEPPE CERRONI.

Confederazione Italiana della Piccola e Media Industria Privata (CONFAPI) (Small and Medium Private Industry): Via della Colonna Antonina 52, 00186 Roma; tel. (06) 690151; fax (06) 6791488; e-mail mail@confapi.org; internet www.confapi.org; f. 1947; Pres. ROBERTO RADICE; Dir-Gen. Dott. SANDRO NACCARELLI; 55,000 mems.

Confederazione Italiana della Proprietà Edilizia (CONFEDILIZIA) (Property and Building): Via Borgognona 47, 00187 Roma; tel. (06) 6793489; fax (06) 6793447; e-mail roma@confedilizia.it; internet www.confedilizia.it; Pres. Avv. CORRADO SFORZA FOGLIANI; Sec.-Gen. Avv. GIORGIO SPAZIANI TESTA.

Delegazione Sindacale Industriale Autonoma della Valle d'Aosta (Autonomous Industrial Delegation of the Valle d'Aosta): Via G. Elter 6, 11100 Aosta; Pres. Dott. ETTORE FORTUNA; Sec. Dott. ROBERTO ANSALDO.

Federazione delle Associazioni Italiane Alberghi e Turismo (FEDERALBERGHI) (Hotels and Tourism): Via Toscana 1, 00187 Roma; tel. (06) 42741151; fax (06) 42871197; f. 1950; Pres. AMATO RAMONDETTI; Gen. Man. ALESSANDRO CIANELLA; 30,000 mems.

UNAPACE: Via Ombrone 2G, 00198 Roma; tel. (06) 8537281; fax (06) 85356431; internet www.unapace.it; f. 1946; represents the interests of concerns producing and/or offering electricity; Pres. Dott. Ing. GIORDANO SERENA; Dir-Gen. FRANCESCO DE LUCA.

UTILITIES

Autorità per l'Energia Elettrica e il Gas: Piazza Cavour 5, 20121 Milano; tel. (02) 655651; fax (02) 29014219; e-mail milano@autorita.energia.it; internet www.autorita.energia.it; regulatory authority; Pres. PIPPO RANCI.

Electricity

Edison, SpA: Foro Buonaparte 31, 20121, Milano; tel. (02) 62221; e-mail infoweb@edison.it; internet www.edison.it; f. 1884; as Società Generale Italiana di Elettricità Sistema Edison; upon privatization in electricity industry in 1963 merged with Montecatini; changed name as above in 1991; electricity and natural gas; 76% owned by Italenergia; Chair. UMBERTO QUADRINO; CEO GIULIO DEL NINNO.

Enel, Spa: Via le Regina Margherita 137, 00198 Roma; tel. (06) 85091; fax (06) 85092162; internet www.enel.it; f. 1962 to generate and distribute electrical power and natural gas in Italy; 34.5% privatized in 1999; further divestment of government stake planned for 2003; Chair. PIERO GNUDI; CEO PAULO SACRONI.

Gas

In February 2000 the Government announced that the gas market was to be liberalized by January 2003 to comply with European Union regulations.

Italgas, SpA: Via XX Settembre 41, 10121, Torino; internet www.italgas.it; 40.9% owned by Snam; supplies 6.7m customers; Pres. ALBERTO MEOMARTINI; Vice-Pres. and Man. Dir GIACOMO VITALI.

Linde Gas Italia, Srl: Via Guido Rossa 3, 20010 Arluno, Milano; tel. (02) 903731; fax (02) 90373500; internet www.linde-gas.it.

Snam Rete Gas: Piazza Vanoni 1, 20097 San Donato Milanese; tel. (02) 5201; fax (02) 52043226; internet www.snamretegas.it; subsidiary of Ente Nazionale Idrocarburi (Eni), fmrly Rete Gas Italia, fmrly Snam; transports natural gas; Pres. and CEO SALVATORE RUSSO.

TRADE UNIONS

There are three main federations of Italian trade unions, CGIL, CISL and UIL, all of which have close ties with political parties. The CGIL was formerly dominated by the Partito Comunista Italiano (Italian Communist Party, now the Democratici di Sinistra—Democrats of the Left), the CISL has links with the Partito Popolare Italiano (Italian Popular Party, formerly Partito della Democrazia Cristiana (Christian Democrat Party)) and the UIL is associated with the socialists.

National Federations

Confederazione Autonoma Italiana del Lavoro (CONFAIL): Viale Abruzzi 38, 20131 Milano; tel. (02) 29404554; fax (02) 29525692; e-mail info@confail.org; internet www.confail.org; Gen. Sec. EVANGELISTA ZACCARIA.

Confederazione Autonoma Sindacati Artigiani (CASARTI-GIANI): Via Flaminio Ponzio 2, 00153 Roma; tel. (06) 5758081; f. 1958; federation of artisans' unions and regional and provincial asscns; Pres. GIACOMO BASSO.

Confederazione Generale Italiana dell'Artigianato (CON-FARTIGIANATO) (Artisans): Via di S. Giovanni in Laterano 152, 00184 Roma; tel. (06) 703741; fax (06) 70452188; e-mail confartigianato@confartigianato.it; internet www.confartigianato .it; f. 1945; independent; 170 mem. unions; 600,000 associate enterprises; Pres. LUCIANO PETRACCHI.

Confederazione Generale Italiana del Lavoro (CGIL) (General Confederation of Italian Labour): Corso d'Italia 25, 00198 Roma; tel. (06) 84761; fax (06) 8845683; e-mail segreteria.cofferati@mail.cgil.it; internet www.cgil.it; f. 1944; federation of 15 federations; Sec.-Gen. GIUGLELMO EPIFANI; Dir-Gen. ACHILLE PASSONI; 5,402,408 mems.

Confederazione Italiana Dirigenti di Azienda (CIDA): Via Nazionale 75, 00184 Roma; tel. (06) 4888241; fax (06) 4873994; e-mail dirigenti@tin.it; internet www.cida.it; federation of six managers' unions; Pres. Dott. GIAN PAOLO CARROZZA; Sec.-Gen. Dott. GIOVANNI CARDEGNA.

Confederazione Italiana Lavoratori Democratici Indipendenti (CILDI): Via dell'Impruneta 15, 00192 Roma; tel. (06) 5002444; fax (06) 5003196; Gen. Sec. VINCENZO CACI.

Confederazione Italiana Lavoratori Liberi (CONFIL): Via di Campo Marzio 46, 00186 Roma; tel. (06) 6872508; fax (06) 6872509; Gen. Sec. FRANCESCO BRUNETTI.

Confederazione Italiana dei Professionisti ed Artisti (CIPA) (Artists and the Liberal Professions): Via S. Nicola da Tolentino 21, 00187 Roma; tel. (06) 461849; federation of 19 unions; Pres. Rag. SERGIO SPLENDORI.

Confederazione Italiana Sindacati Addetti ai Servizi (CISAS): Via Sapri 6, 00185 Roma; tel. (06) 4466618; fax (06) 4466617; internet www.cisas.org; Gen. Sec. ONOFRIO DANIELLO.

Confederazione Italiana dei Sindacati Autonomi Lavoratori (CISAL): Viale Giulio Cesare 21, 00192 Roma; tel. (06) 3207941; fax (06) 3212521; internet www.cisal.org; f. 1957; affiliated to Confédération Européenne des Syndicats Indépendants; federation of 45 unions; Sec.-Gen. GIUSEPPE CARBONE; 1,500,000 mems.

Confederazione Italiana Sindacati Lavoratori (CISL): Via Po 21, 00198 Roma; tel. (06) 84731; fax (06) 8413782; e-mail cisl@cisl.it; internet www.cisl.it; 8413782; f. 1950; affiliated to the International Confederation of Free Trade Unions and the European Trade Union Confederation; federation of 14 unions; Sec.-Gen. SAVINO PEZZOTTA; 4,084,000 mems.

Confederazione Nazionale dell'Artigianato e delle Piccole Imprese (CNA): Via G. A. Guattani 13, 00161 Roma; tel. (06) 441881; fax (06) 44249513; e-mail cna@cna.it; internet www.cna.it; provincial asscns; Pres. IVAN MALAVDSI; Gen. Sec. Dott. GIAN CARLO SANGALLI.

Confederazione dei Sindacati Autonomi dei Lavoratori (CONFSAL): Viale Trasevere 60, 00153 Roma; tel. (06) 5852071; fax (06) 5818218; e-mail info@confsal.it; internet www.confsal.it; Sec.-Gen. Prof. MARCO PAULO NIGI.

Confederazione Unitaria Quadri (CUQ): Via XX Settembre 58, 10121 Torino; tel. (011) 5612042; fax (011) 5620362; e-mail confquadri@tin.it; Pres. CARLO CAPELLARO.

Confederazione Unitaria Sindacati Autonomi Lavoratori (CUSAL): Via di Campo Marzio 46, 00186 Roma; tel. (06) 6872508; fax (06) 6872509; Pres. DOMENICO MANNO; Gen. Sec. FRANCESCO BRUNETTI.

Coordinamento Sindacale Autonomo (CSA): Via Avicenna 40, 00146 Roma; tel. (06) 5585292; fax (06) 5576903; Gen. Man. ANTONIO MARRONE.

Federazione fra le Associazioni ed i Sindacati Nazionali dei Funzionari Direttivi, Dirirenti e delle Elevate Professionalità della Pubblica Amministrazione (DIRSTAT): Via Ezio 12, 00192 Roma; tel. (06) 3211535; fax (06) 3212690; e-mail dirstat@ dirstat.it; internet www.dirstat.it; f. 1948; federation of 33 unions and asscns of civil-service executives and officers; Sec.-Gen. ARCANGELO D'AMBROSIO; Treas. Dott. SERGIO DI DONNA.

Unione Generale del Lavoro (UGL): Via Margutta 19, 00187 Roma; tel. (06) 324821; fax (06) 324820; e-mail ugl@ugl.it; internet www.ugl.it; f. 1950 as CISNAL, name changed as above 1995; upholds traditions of national syndicalism; federation of 64 unions, 77 provincial unions; Gen. Sec. STEFANO CETICA; 2,137,979 mems.

Unione Italiana del Lavoro (UIL): Via Lucullo 6, 00187 Roma; tel. (06) 4753210; fax (06) 4753295; e-mail segretariagenerale@uil.it; internet www.uil.it; f. 1950; socialist, social democrat and republican; affiliated to the International Confederation of Free Trade Unions and European Trade Union Confederation; 18 national trade union federations and 108 provincial union councils; Gen. Sec. LUIGI ANGELETTI; 1,758,729 mems.

Unione Italiana Quadri (UNIONQUADRI): Via A. Gramsci 34, 00197 Roma; tel. (06) 3611683; fax (06) 3225558; e-mail uquadri@tin .it; internet www.unionquadri.it; Pres. CORRADO ROSSITTO; Sec. ANTONIO DIONESALVI.

Principal Unions

Banking and Insurance

Federazione Autonoma Bancari Italiana (FABI) (Bank, Tax and Finance Workers): Via Tevere 46, 00198 Roma; tel. (06) 8415751; fax (06) 8559220; f. 1948; independent; Sec.-Gen. GIANFRANCO STEFFANI; 69,000 mems.

Federazione Autonoma Lavoratori Casse di Risparmio Italiane (FALCRI) (Savings Banks Workers): Via Mercato 5, Milano; Via Carducci 4, Roma; tel. (02) 86460536; Sec.-Gen. DAVIDE CATTANEO.

Federazione Italiana Bancari e Assicuratori (FIBA): Via Modena 5, 00184 Roma; tel. (06) 4741245; fax (06) 4746136; internet www.fiba.it; affiliated to the CISL; Gen. Sec. ELIGIO BONI; 58,980 mems.

Federazione Italiana Sindacale Lavoratori Assicurazioni Credito (Employees of Credit Institutions): Via Vicenza 5A, 00184 Roma; tel. (06) 448841; fax (06) 4457356; e-mail fisac@fisac.it; internet www.fisac.it; affiliated to the CGIL; Sec.-Gen. MARCELLO TOCCO; 60,000 mems.

Federazione Nazionale Assicuratori (FNA) (Insurance Workers): Via Vincenzo Monti 25, Milano; Via Val Montebello 104, Roma; independent; Pres. LUIGI FERAZZI; Sec.-Gen. EZIO MARTONE.

Unione Italiana Lavoratori Credito e Assicurazioni (UILCA) (Credit and Assurance Co Workers): Via Lombardia 30, 00187 Roma; tel. (06) 4872132; fax (06) 484704; affiliated to the UIL; Sec.-Gen. ELIO PORINO; 37,453 mems.

Building and Building Materials

Federazione Autonoma Italiana Lavoratori Cemento, Legno, Edilizia ed Affini (FAILCLEA) (Workers in Cement, Wood, Construction and Related Industries): c/o CISAL, Viale Giulio Cesare 21, 00192 Roma; affiliated to the CISAL; Sec. ENZO BOZZI.

Federazione Italiana Lavoratori Costruzioni a Affini (FILCA) (Building Industries' Workers): Via del Viminale 43, 00184, Roma; tel. (06) 4870634; fax (06) 4818884; e-mail federazione_filca@cisl.it; internet www.filca.cisl.it; f. 1955; affiliated to the CISL; Sec.-Gen. CESARE REGENZI; 188,009 mems.

Federazione Italiana Lavoratori Legno, Edili, Industrie Affini ed Estrattive (FILLEA) (Wood-workers, Construction Workers and Allied Trades): Via G. B. Morgagni 27, 00161 Roma; tel. (06) 441141; fax (06) 44235849; e-mail fillea@mail.cgil.it; internet www.cgil.it/fillea; affiliated to the CGIL; Sec.-Gen. FRANCO MARTINI; 434,154 mems.

Federazione Nazionale Costruzioni (Construction): Lungotevere Sanzio 5, Roma; tel. (06) 585511; fax (06) 5815184; affiliated to the UGL; Sec. EGIDIO SANGUE.

Federazione Nazionale Lavoratori Edili Affini e del Legno (FeNEAL) (Builders and Woodworkers): Via Alessandria 171, 00198 Roma; tel. (06) 8547393; fax (06) 8547423; affiliated to the UIL; Sec.-Gen. FRANCO MARABOTTINI; 106,698 mems.

Chemical, Mining and Allied Industries

Federazione Lavoratori Energia Risorse Chimica Affini (FLERiCA) (Chemical and Allied Workers): Via Bolzano 16, Roma; tel. (06) 85565415; fax (06) 85565414; e-mail federazione@flerica.cisl .it; internet flerica.cisl.it; affiliated to the CISL; Sec.-Gen. ANTONINO SCALFARO.

Federazione Nazionale Chimici (Chemicals): Via Manin 53, Roma; tel. (06) 4742703; fax (06) 4746051; affiliated to the UGL; Sec. DOMENICO SCOPELLITI.

Unione Italiana Lavoratori Chimici, Energia e Manufatturiero (UILCEM) (Chemicals, Energy and Manufacturing Workers): Via Bolzano 16, 00198 Roma; tel. (06) 85565305; fax (06) 8417002; e-mail uilcem@uil.it; affiliated to the UIL; Sec.-Gen. ROMANO BELLISSIMA; 84,649 mems.

Clothing and Textiles

Federazione Italiana Lavoratori Tessili Abbigliamento, Calzaturieri (FILTEA) (Textile and Clothing Workers and Shoe Manufacturers): Via Leopoldo Serra 31, 00153 Roma; tel. (06) 581380; fax (06) 5803182; e-mail filtea@uni.net; internet www.uni.net/filtea; f. 1966; affiliated to the CGIL; Gen. Sec. AGOSTINO MEGALE; 150,000 mems.

Federazione Italiana dei Lavoratori Tessili e Abbigliamento **(FILTA-CISL):** Via Salaria 30, 00198, Roma; tel. (06) 8416361; fax (06) 8417544; e-mail fltnazio@tin.it; internet www.cisl.it.filta; affiliated to the CISL; Gen. Sec. AUGUSTA RESTELLI; 125,084 mems.

Unione Italiana Lavoratori Tessili, Abbigliamento e Calzaturieri (UILTA): Via del Viminale 43, 00184 Roma; tel. (06) 4883486; fax (06) 4819421; e-mail uilta.roma@libero.it; affiliated to the UIL; Sec.-Gen. PASQUALE ROSSETTI.

Engineering and Metallurgy

Federazione Impiegati Operai Metallurgici (FIOM-CGIL) (Metalworkers): Corso Trieste 36, 00198 Roma; tel. (06) 852621; fax (06) 85303079; e-mail fiom@cgil.it; internet www.cgil.it/fiom; f. 1902; affiliated to the CGIL; Sec. CLAUDIO SABATTINI; 400,000 mems.

Federazione Italiana Metalmeccanici (FIM) (Metal Mechanic Workers): C.so Trieste. 36, 00198, Roma; tel. (06) 852621; fax (06) 85262464; internet www.cisl.it/fim; f. 1951; affiliated to the CISL; Sec.-Gen. GIORGIO CAPRIOLI; 190,000 mems.

Federazione Nazionale Metalmeccanici: Via Amadeo 23, Roma; tel. (06) 4741808; fax (06) 4881236; affiliated to the UGL; Sec. DOMENICO FRESILLI.

Sindacato Nazionale Ingegneri Liberi Professionisti Italiana (SNILPI) (Liberal Professionals-Engineers): Via Salaria 292, 00199 Roma; Pres. Dott. Ing. LUIGI LUCHERINI; Sec.-Gen. Dott. Ing. GIUSEPPE MILONE.

Unione Italiana Lavoratori Metalmeccanici (UILM) (Metalworkers): Corso Trieste 36, 00198 Roma; tel. (06) 852621; fax (06) 85262203; e-mail uilm@uil.it; f. 1950; affiliated to the UIL; Sec.-Gen. TONINO REGAZZI; 100,534 mems.

Food and Agriculture

Confederazione Italiana Agricoltori (CIA) (Farmers): Via Mariano Fortuny 20, 00196 Roma; tel. (06) 32687302; fax (06) 32687308; e-mail segreteriacentrale@cia.it; internet www.cia.it; independent; Pres. MASSIMO PACETTI; Vice-Pres. MASSIMO BELLOTTI.

Confederazione Italiana Dirigenti, Quadri e Impiegati dell' Agricoltura (CONFEDERDIA): Viale Beethoven 48, 00144 Roma; tel. (06) 5912808; fax (06) 5915014; e-mail confederdia@confederdia.it; internet www.confederdia.it; Pres. LUCIANO BOZZATO; Gen. Sec. TOMMASO BRANDONI.

Confederazione Nazionale Coltivatori Diretti (Coldiretti) (Small-holders): Via XXIV Maggio 43, 00187 Roma; tel. (06) 46821; fax fax (06) 4682305; e-mail coldiretti@coldiretti.it; internet www.coldiretti.it; independent; Pres. PAOLO BEDONI; Sec.-Gen. Dott. FRANCO PASQUALI; mems: 18 regional federations, 98 provincial federations.

Federazione Italiana Salariati Braccianti Agricoli e Maestranze Specializzate (FISBA) (Permanent Unskilled and Skilled Agricultural Workers): Via Tevere 20, 00198 Roma; tel. (06) 8415455; f. 1950; Sec. ALBINO GORINI; 347,265 mems.

Federazione Lavoratori dell'Agroindustria (Workers in the Agricultural Industry): Via Leopoldo Serra 31, 00153 Roma; tel. (06) 585611; fax (06) 5580585; e-mail flai@mail.cgil.it; internet www.cgil.it/flai; f. 1988; affiliated to the CGIL; Sec.-Gen. GIANFRANCO BENZI; 438,000 mems.

Unione Coltivatori Italiana (UCI) (Farmers): Via in Lucina 10, 00186 Roma; tel. (06) 6871043; Pres. VINCENZO PANDOVINO.

Unione Generale Coltivatori (UGC): Via Tevere 44, 00198 Roma; tel. (06) 8552383; fax (06) 8553891; affiliated to the CISL; Pres. GAVINO DERUDA; 151,625 mems.

Unione Italiana Lavoratori Agroalimentari (UILA-UIL) (Food Workers): Via Savoia 80, 00198 Roma; tel. (06) 85301610; fax (06) 85303253; e-mail uila@uil.it; affiliated to the UIL; Sec. STEFANO MANTEGAZZA.

Unione Italiana Mezzadri e Coltivatori Diretti (UIMEC) (Land Workers): Via Reno 30, 00198, Roma; tel. (06) 85304428; fax (06) 85357571; e-mail uimec@uil.it; affiliated to the UILA-UIL; Pres. GIOVANBATTISTA AIUTO; 100,000 mems.

Medical

Confederazione Italiana Sindacati Medici Dirigenti (COSMED) (Doctors): c/o Anaao Assomed, via Barberini 3, 00187 Roma; tel. (06) 4820154; fax (06) 48903523; Man. SERAFINO ZUCCHELLI.

Federazione Italiana Servizi Territoriali (FIST) (Hospital and Regional Municipal Workers' Unions): Via Lancisi 25, 00161 Roma; tel. (06) 4425981; fax (06) 44230114; e-mail fist@cisl.it; internet www.mclink.it/com/fist; affiliated to the CISL; Sec.-Gen. ERMENEGILDO BONFANTI; 250,000 mems.

Federazione Nazionale Medici (Doctors): Via Amendola 7, Roma; tel. (06) 4870444; fax (06) 4874323; e-mail federmed@flashnet.it; affiliated to the UGL; Sec.-Gen. GIOVANNI PALOMBI.

Public Services

Confederazione dei Quadri Direttivi e Dirigenti della Funzione Pubblica (CONFEDIR) (Public Office Managers): Arco dei Banchi 8, 00186 Roma; tel. and fax (06) 68803688; Gen. Sec. ROBERTO CONFALONIERI.

Federazione Lavoratori Aziende Elettriche Italiane (FLAEI) (Workers in Italian Electrical Undertakings): Via Salaria 83, 00198 Roma; tel. (06) 8440421; fax (06) 8548458; e-mail nazionale@flaei.org; internet www.flaei.org; f. 1948; affiliated to the CISL; Sec. ARSENIO CAROSI; 32,000 mems.

Federazione Lavoratori del Pubblico Impiego (FPI) (Public-Sector Workers): Via Po 102, 00198 Roma; tel. (06) 852381; e-mail fpi@interbusiness.it; internet www.fpi.cisl.it; affiliated to the CISL; Sec.-Gen. RINO TARELLI.

Federazione Nazionale Energia (Energy): Via Filiberto 125, Roma; tel. (06) 7005935; fax (06) 7003451; affiliated to the UGL; Sec. LUIGI DE NARDIS.

Federazione Nazionale Enti Locali (Employees of Local Authorities): Via Amendola 5, Roma; tel. (06) 4743418; fax (06) 4743853; affiliated to the UGL; Sec. GUIDO ANDERSON.

Federazione Nazionale Enti Pubblici (Public Employees): Via del Corea 13, Roma; tel. (06) 59056508; fax (06) 3226052; f. 1962; affiliated to the UGL; Gen. Sec. GIANFRANCO SCHETTINO.

Federazione Nazionale Lavoratori Funzione Pubblica: Via Leopoldo Serra 31, 00153 Roma; tel. (06) 585441; fax (06) 5836970; e-mail fp@cgil.it; internet www.cgil.it/fp; affiliated to the CGIL, Public Services International, and European Public Services Union (EPSU); Sec.-Gen. LAIMER ARMUZZI.

Federazione Nazionale Lavoratori Energia (Gas, Water and Electricity): Via Piemonte 32, 00187 Roma; tel. (06) 4620091; fax 4824246; e-mail fnle@mail.cgil.it; internet www.cgil.it/fnle; affiliated to the CGIL; Sec. GIACOMO BERNI; 72,000 mems.

Federazione Nazionale Sanità (Sanitary Workers): Via Farini 16, Roma; tel. (06) 4814678; fax (06) 4814651; affiliated to the UGL; Sec. SALVATORE GALIZIA.

Unione Italiana Lavoratori Federazione Poteri Locali (UIL FPL) (Local Authority Employees): Via di tor Fiorenza 35, 00199 Roma; tel. (06) 865081; fax (06) 86508235; e-mail segreteria@uilfpl.org; internet www.uilfpl.org; affiliated to the UIL; Gen. Sec. CARLO FIORDALISO; 89,179 mems.

Unione Italiana Lavoratori degli Organi Costituzionali (Employees of Constitutional Bodies): Via del Corso 173, 00186 Roma; tel. (06) 67609118; fax (06) 67604890; affiliated to the UIL; Sec.-Gen. SILVANO SGREVI.

Unione Italiana Lavoratori Pubblico Amministrazione (UILPA) (Public Office Workers): Via Emilio Lepido 46, 00175 Roma; tel. (06) 71588888; fax (06) 71582046; e-mail uilpa@uil.it; affiliated to the UIL; Sec.-Gen. SALVATORE BOSCO; 67,702 mems.

Unione Italiana Lavoratori Sanità (UIL Sanità) (Sanitary Workers): Via Nemorense 18, 00199 Roma; tel. (06) 8550164; fax (06) 8416777; e-mail uilsanità@uil.it; affiliated to the UIL; Sec.-Gen. CARLO FIORDALISO; 98,669 mems.

Teachers

Cisl-Scuola (School Teachers): Via Bargoni 8, 00153 Roma; tel. (06) 583111; fax (06) 5881713; affiliated to the CISL; Sec.-Gen. DANIELA COLTURANI.

Cisl-Università (University Teachers): Via Rovereto 11, 00198 Roma; tel. (06) 8840772; fax (06) 8844977; e-mail info@cisluniversita.it; internet www.cisluniversita.it; affiliated to the CISL; Sec.-Gen. ANTONIO MARSILIA.

Federazione Italiana Scuola Università e Ricerca (University Teachers): Via S. Croce in Gerusalemme 107, 00185 Roma; tel. (06) 757941; affiliated to the CISL; Gen. Sec MARIO GIOVANNI GAROFALO; 184,235 mems.

Federazione Nazionale Scuola ed Università (School and University Teachers): Via Manin 53, Roma; tel. (06) 4741200; fax (06) 4874738; affiliated to the UGL; Sec. ORESTE TOFANI.

Sindacato Nazionale Scuola (School Teachers): Via Leopoldo Serra 31, Roma; tel. (06) 585480; e-mail mail@cgilscuola.it; internet www.cgilscuola.it; affiliated to the CGIL; 97,149 mems (1997).

Unione Italiana Lavoratori Scuola (UIL Scuola) (School Workers): Via Marino Laziale 44, 00179 Roma; tel. (06) 7846941; fax (06) 7842858; e-mail uilscuola@uil.it; internet www.uil.it/uilscuola; affiliated to the UIL; Sec.-Gen. MASSIMO DI MENNA; 59,402 mems.

Tourism and Entertainment

Federazione Informazione Spettacolo e Telecomunicazioni (FISTEL) (Actors, Artists and Media Workers): Via Palestro 30,

00185 Roma; tel. (06) 492171; fax (06) 4457330; affiliated to the CISL; Sec.-Gen. FULVIO GIACOMASSI; 43,388 mems.

Federazione Italiana Lavoratori Commercio Albergo Mensa e Servizi (FILCAMS) (Hotel and Catering Workers): Via Leopoldo Serra 31, 00153 Roma; tel. (06) 5885102; fax (06) 5885323; f. 1960; affiliated to the CGIL; Sec.-Gen. ALDO AMORETTI; 189,000 mems.

Federazione Italiana Personale Aviazione Civile (Aviation Employees): Via Ostiense 224, Roma; affiliated to the CGIL; Sec. PIERRO TORINO.

Federazione Italiana Sindacati Addetti Servizi Commerciali Affini e del Turismo (FISASCAT-CISL) (Commercial and Tourist Unions): Via Livenza 7, 00198 Roma; tel. (06) 8541042; fax (06) 8558057; internet www.fisascat.it; Sec.-Gen. GIANNI BARATTA; 153,900 mems.

Federazione Nazionale Informazione e Spettacolo (Actors, Artists and Media Workers): Via Margutta 19, Roma; tel. (06) 324821; fax (06) 323420; affiliated to the UGL; Sec. GIANNI IMPROTA.

Sindacato Attori Italiani (SAI) (Actors): Via Ofanto 18, 00198 Roma; tel. (06) 8411288; fax (06) 8546780; e-mail sai-slc@cgil.it; internet www.cgil.it/sai-slc; affiliated to the CGIL; Pres. MASSIMO GHINI; Sec.-Gen. MASSIMO CESTARO.

Unione Italiana Lavoratori Turismo Commercio e Servizi (UILTuCS): Via Nizza, 154, 00198, Roma; tel. (06) 84242268; fax (06) 84242292; e-mail info@uiltucs.it; internet www.uiltucs.it; f. 1977; affiliated to the UIL; Gen. Sec. BRUNO BOCO; 75,042 mems.

Transport and Telecommunications

Federazione Italiana Lavoratori Postelegrafonici (Filpt) (Postal, Telegraph and Telephone Workers): Piazza Verdi 5,, Ferrara; tel. (05) 32783111; affiliated to the CGIL; division of Sindacato Lavoratori Comunicazione; Sec. GIUSEPPE MASTRACCHI; 35,000 mems.

Federazione Italiana Trasporti: Settore Marittimi (Italian Maritime): Roma; tel. (06) 4689216; fax (06) 4825233; internet www.fit.cisl.it.mare_co.htm; affiliated to the International Transport Workers' Federation; Gen. Sec. REMODI FIORE.

Federazione Italiana Lavoratori dei Trasporti (FILT-CGIL): Via G. B. Morgagni 27, 00161 Roma; tel. (06) 442961; fax (06) 44293313; e-mail filt@mail.cgil.it; affiliated to the CGIL; Sec. GUIDO ABBADESSA.

Federazione Italiana Trasporti (FIT): Via di San Giovanni in Laterano 98, 00184 Roma; tel. (06) 7726581; fax (06) 77205994; e-mail fit_reg_lazio@cisl.it (Lazioregion); internet www.fitcisl-lazio.com (Lazioregion); f. 1950; affiliated to the CISL; National Sec. LUIGI VAGLICA; 40,000 mems.

Federazione Nazionale Comunicazioni (Communications): Via Volturno 40, Roma; tel. (06) 4746714; fax (06) 49384693; affiliated to the UGL; Sec. SERAFINO CABRAS.

Federazione Nazionale Trasporti (Transport): Via Margutta 19, Roma; tel. (06) 324821; fax (06) 3232420; affiliated to the UGL; Sec. PAOLO SEGARELLI.

Federazione dei Sindacati Dipendenti Aziende di Navigazione (FEDERSINDAN): Roma; independent; Sec.-Gen. Dott. GIUSEPPE AURICCHIO.

Sindacato Lavoratori Communicazione (SLC) (Communications Workers): Piazza Sallustio 24, 00187 Roma; tel. (06) 421071; fax (06) 4824325; e-mail slc.sal@mail.cgil.it; internet www.cgil.it/slc; affiliated to the CGIL; Gen. Sec. FULVIO FAMMONI.

SLP—Federazione Lavoratori Poste e Appalti (Postal Workers): Via dell'Esquilino 38, 00185 Roma; internet www.slp-cisl.it; affiliated to the CISL; Sec.-Gen. ANTONINO SORGI.

UIL TRASPORTI (Transport Workers): Via Salaria 44, 00198 Roma; tel. (06) 852511; fax (06) 85350502; e-mail uiltrasporti@uil.it; affiliated to the UIL; Sec. SANDRO DEGNI; 103,687 mems.

Unione Italiana Lavoratori della Comunicazione (UILCOM) (Media and Telecommunications): Via Belisario 7, 00187 Roma; tel. (06) 42744102; fax (06) 42744897; e-mail uilcom@uilcom.it; affiliated to the UIL; Sec.-Gen. BRUNO DI COLA.

Unione Italiana Lavoratori Postelegrafonici (UILPOST) (Post, Telegraph and Telephone Workers): Via Sallustiana 15, 00187 Roma; tel. (06) 4871213; fax (06) 4814403; e-mail uilpost@uil.it; affiliated to the UIL; Sec.-Gen. PAOLO TULLO; 30,853 mems.

Miscellaneous

Federazione Nazionale Pensionati (FNP) (Pensioners): Via Castelfidardo 47, 00185 Roma; tel. (06) 448811; fax (06) 4452608; e-mail andrea.pellicari@fnp.cisl.it; internet fnp.cisl.it; f. 1952; affiliated to the CISL; Sec. CARMELO MUSCOLIMO; 1,180,000 mems.

Federazione Nazionale Pensionati dell'Unione Generale del Lavoro (Pensioners): Via Margutta 19, 00187 Roma; tel. (06)

32482248; fax (06) 3612027; internet www.pensionatiugl.it; affiliated to the UGL; Sec. CORRADO MANNUCCI.

Federazione Nazionale Terziario (Service Sector Workers): Via Farini 62, 00185, Roma; tel. (06) 4820754; fax (06) 4820702; affiliated to the UGL; Sec. RENATA POLVERINI.

Sindacato Pensionati Italiani SPI-Cgil (Pensioners): Via Frentani 4A, 00185 Roma; tel. (06) 444811; fax (06) 4440941; e-mail spi@mail.cgil.it; f. 1948; affiliated to the CGIL; Sec.-Gen. ELISABETTA LEONE; 2, 757,010 mems.

Unione Italiana Lavoratori Pensionati (UILP) (Pensioners): Via Po 162, 00198 Roma; tel. (06) 852591; fax (06) 8548632; e-mail segreteria@uilpensionati.it; internet www.uilpensionati.it; affiliated to the UIL; Sec.-Gen. SILVANO MINIATI; 429,697 mems.

Co-operative Unions

Associazione Generale delle Cooperative Italiane (AGCI): Via A. Bargoni, 00153 Roma; tel. (06) 583271; fax (06) 58327210; e-mail info@agci.it; internet www.agci.it; f. 1952; Pres. MAURIZIO ZAFFI.

Confederazione Cooperative Italiane (CONFCOOPERATIVE): Borgo S. Spirito 78, 00193 Roma; tel. (06) 680001; fax (06) 6868595; e-mail confcooperative@confcooperative.it; internet www.confcooperative.it; f. 1919; federation of co-operative unions; Pres. LUIGI MARINO; Sec.-Gen. VINCENZO MANNINO.

Lega Nazionale delle Cooperative e Mutue (National League of Co-operative and Friendly Societies): Via Guattani 9, 00161 Roma; tel. (06) 84439391; fax (06) 84439370; e-mail presidenza@legacoop.it; internet www.legacoop.it; f. 1886; nine affiliated unions; Pres. IVANO BARBERINI.

Unione Nazionale Cooperative Italiane: Via San Sotero 32, 00165 Roma; tel. (06) 39366729; fax (06) 39375080; e-mail uncinazionale@mclink.it; internet www.uncinazionale.it; Pres. LUCIANO D'ULIZIA.

Transport

Direzione Generale della Motorizzazione Civile e del Trasporti in Concessione: Via Giuseppe Caraci 36, 00157 Roma; tel. (06) 41581; fax (06) 41582211; controls road transport and traffic, and public transport services (railways operated by private cos, motor-buses, trolley-buses, funicular railways and inland waterways); Dir-Gen. Dott. GIORGIO BERRUTI.

RAILWAYS

The majority of Italian lines are controlled by an independent state-owned corporation. In 1999 the total length of the network was 16,198 km, of which 10,688 km were electrified. Apart from the state railway system there are 24 local and municipal railway companies, many of whose lines are narrow gauge. There are metro systems in Rome, Milan and Naples; a metro system is also planned for Turin. A high-speed service is planned on the following routes: Rome–Milan–Turin, Naples–Rome, Milan–Genoa and Milan–Venice. In 1991 TAV, a semi-private company for the creation of a high-speed train network, was established; from 1998 it was wholly-owned by Ferrovie dello Stato. Work on the following lines was to be completed by 2006: Naples–Rome and Rome–Milan. In January 2001 it was announced that plans had been approved for the construction of a 52-km rail tunnel under the Alps linking France with Italy. Due to be completed in 2015, the tunnel was to be part of a new high-speed rail link between Turin and Lyons in France.

Ferrovie dello Stato SpA: Piazza della Croce Rossa 1, 00161 Roma; tel. (06) 84903758; fax (06) 84905186; e-mail info@fs-on-line.it; internet www.fs-on-line.it; Pres. C. DEMATTÈ; Man. Dir GIANCARLO CIMOLI.

ROADS

In 1999 there were an estimated 479,688 km of roads in Italy, including 6,621 km of motorway, 46,009 km of major roads and 114,909 km of secondary roads. All the *autostrade* (motorways) are toll roads except for the one between Salerno and Reggio Calabria and motorways in Sicily. By law the National Road Board is responsible for the planning, construction and management of the motorway network. Plans were approved in 2001 for the construction of a 3.89km bridge linking Sicily to the Italian mainland; the bridge was to be completed over a seven-year period starting in 2005.

Autostrade SpA: Via Alberto Berganini 50, 00159 Roma; tel. (06) 43631; fax (06) 43634090; e-mail info@autostrade.it; internet www.autostrade.it; maintenance and management of motorway network; CEOs VITO GAMBERALE, GIANMARIA GROS PIETRO.

Ente Nazionale per le Strade (National Road Board): Via Monzambano 10, 00185 Roma; tel. (06) 44461; f. 1928 as Azienda Nazionale Autonoma delle Strade, name changed as above 1995;

responsible for the administration of state roads and their improvement and extension; Pres. GIUSEPPE D'ANGIOLINO.

SHIPPING

In 2001 the Italian merchant fleet (1,476 vessels) had a displacement of 9,655,000 grt.

Direzione Generale della Marina Mercantile: Via dell'Arte 16, 00144 Roma.

Genoa

Costa Crociere: Via Gabriele D'Annunzio 2, 16121 Genova; tel. (010) 54831; fax (010) 5483290; passenger and cargo service; Mediterranean–North, Central and South America; Caribbean cruises; Chair. NICOLA COSTA.

'Garibaldi' Società Cooperativa di Navigazione Srl: Piazza Dante 8, 16121 Genova; tel. (010) 581635; fax (010) 5702386; f. 1918; tanker and cargo services; Pres. GIAN FRANCO VIALE.

'Italia di Navigazione' SpA: Torre WTC, Via de Marini 1, Genova; tel. (010) 24021; fax (010) 2402386; e-mail bo@italialine.it; internet www.italialine.it; f. 1932; freight services to Mediterranean, and North, South and Central America; Chair. ANTONIO D'AMICO; CEO CESARE D'AMICO.

Messina, Ignazio and C. SpA: Via G. d'Annunzio 91, 16121 Genova; tel. (010) 53961; fax (010) 5396264; e-mail info@messinaline.it; internet www.messinaline.it; services to Arabian Gulf, India, Pakistan, Nigeria, North, East, South and West Africa, Libya and Near East, Red Sea, Malta, Europe; Chair. GIANFRANCO MESSINA.

Naples

Garolla Fratelli SpA: Pontile Falvio Giola 45, 80133 Napoli; tel. (081) 5534477; Chair. R. GAROLLA; Dirs F. GAROLLA, C. GAROLLA.

Fratelli Grimaldi Armatori: Via M. Campodisola 13, 80133 Napoli; tel. (081) 205466; passenger, cargo, containers and tramp to Europe, Middle East, South, Central and North America; Dirs M. GRIMALDI, G. GRIMALDI, A. GRIMALDI, U. GRIMALDI.

Tirrenia di Navigazione SpA: Head Office: Palazzo Sirignano, Rione Sirignano 2, 80121 Napoli; tel. (081) 7201111; fax (081) 7201441; ferry services to Sardinia, Sicily, North Africa; part of Gruppo Tirrenia di Navigazione; Man. Dir and Dir-Gen. FRANCO PECORINI.

Palermo

Sicilia Regionale Marittima SpA (SIREMAR): Calata Marinai d'Italia, Porto, Palermo; tel. (091) 6021111; fax (091) 6021221; e-mail siremar@infovoce24.it; internet www.siremar.it; owned by Gruppo Tirrenia di Navigazione; ferry services; Pres. Dott GIUSEPPE RAVERA; Man. Dir CARLO COSTA.

Sicula Oceanicas SA (SIOSA): Via Mariano Stabile 179, 90139 Palermo; tel. (091) 217939; f. 1941; cruises, passenger and cargo; Italy to North Europe, South, Central, North America; Dir G. GRIMALDI.

Rome

D'Amico Fratelli, SpA: Via Liguria 36, 00187 Roma; tel. (06) 4671; fax (06) 4871914; e-mail damiship@damicofratelli.it; internet www.damicofratelli.it; dry cargo and tankers; Pres. GIUSEPPE D'AMICO; Gen. Man. CARLO CAMELI.

Trieste

Fratelli Cosulich SpA: Piazza S. Antonio 4, 34122 Trieste; tel. (040) 6797111; fax (040) 630844; f. 1854; shipowners and shipping agents; domestic network and cargo to Near East, Red Sea, Hong Kong, Singapore, New York and Zürich; Chair. and Man. Dir GEROLIMICH COSULICH.

Lloyd Triestino di Navigazione SpA: Palazzo della Marineria, Passeggio S. Andrea 4, 34123 Trieste; tel. (040) 3180111; fax (040) 3180296; e-mail headoffice@ts.lloydtriestino.it; internet www.lloydtriestino.it; f. 1836; cargo services by container to South Africa, Australasia and Far East, plus trans-Pacific services; privatized 1998; Pres. PIER LUIGI MANESCHI; Vice-Pres. GEORGE HSU; Man. Dir BRONSON HSIEH.

Navigazione Montanari SpA: Corso Italia 31, 34122 Trieste; fax (0721) 830430; e-mail giovannip@navmont.com; internet www.navmont.com; f. 1889; cargo services to Mediterranean, Northern Europe, USA and Far East.

Venice

Adriatica di Navigazione SpA: Zattere 1411, CP 705, 30123 Venezia; tel. (041) 781861; fax (041) 781818; e-mail adrnav@interbusiness.it; internet www.adriatica.it; f. 1937; owned by Gruppo Tirrenia di Navigazione; passenger services from Italy, Albania, Croatia and Yugoslavia; Pres. GIORGIO GROSSO; Man. Dir ANTONIO CACUCCI.

SHIPPING ASSOCIATION

Confederazione Italiana Armatori (CONFITARMA): Piazza SS. Apostoli 66, 00187 Roma; tel. (06) 674811; fax (06) 69783726; e-mail confitarma@confitarma.it; internet www.confitarma.it; f. 1901; shipowners' asscn; Pres. GIOVANNI MONTANARI; Dir-Gen. LUIGI PERISSICH; 140 mems.

CIVIL AVIATION

National Airline

Alitalia (Linee Aeree Italiane): Viale Alessandro Marchetti 111, 00148 Roma; tel. (06) 65621; fax (06) 7093065; internet www.alitalia.com; f. 1946; state-owned; domestic and international services throughout Europe and to Africa, North and South America, the Middle East, the Far East and Australia; Chair. FAUSTO CERETI; CEO FRANCESCO MENGOZZI.

Other Airlines

Air Dolomiti: Via Senatore Augusto Tambarin 36, 34077 Ronchi dei Legionari; tel. (0481) 477711; fax (0481) 474540; internet www.airdolimiti.it; f. 1989; main regional airline in northern Italy; Pres. and CEO ALCIDE LEALI.

Air Europe: Via Carlo Noè 3, 21013 Gallarate, Varese; tel. (0331) 713111; fax (0331) 713850; e-mail marketing@aireurope.it; internet www.aireurope.it; f. 1988; international charter flights; Chair. LUPO RATTAZZI; Man. Dir ISABELLA ANTONELLO.

Air One: Via Sardegna 14, 00187 Roma; tel. (06) 478761; fax (06) 4820399; internet www.flyairone.it; f. 1983 as Aliadriatica, adopted current name in 1995; private co; domestic flights; Chair. GIOVANNI SEBASTIANI; Pres. CARLO TOTO.

Air Sicilia: Via G. La Rosa 21, 95041 Caltagirone; tel. (0993) 26714; fax (0916) 25510; internet www.airsicilia.it; f. 1994; operates domestic and international scheduled services throughout Europe; Chair. ARMANDO CRISPINO.

Alpi Eagles: c/o Valecenter, Via Enrico Mattei 1/98, 30020 Marcon; tel. (041) 5997777; fax (041) 5997707; e-mail info@alpieagles.com; internet www.alpieagles.com; f. 1979; privately-owned regional carrier operating scheduled passenger services within Italy and to some European destinations; Pres. PAOLO SINIGAGLIA.

Azzurra Air: Via Pietro Paleocapa 3d, 24122 Bergamo; tel. (035) 4160311; fax (035) 4160300; e-mail info@azzurraair.it; internet www.azzurraair.it; f. 1995; scheduled and chartered European flights; CEO DOMINIC R. ATTARD.

Gandalfair: Via Aeroporto 13, Orio al Serio, 24050 Bergamo; tel. (035) 4595011; fax (035) 4595083; e-mail info@gandalfair.it; internet www.gandalfair.it; f. 1998; private airline operating scheduled services aimed at business travellers; Chair. CARLO PERETTI.

Meridiana SpA: Aeroporto Costa Smeralda, Olbia, 07026 Sardinia; tel. (0789) 52821; fax (0789) 52972; e-mail relazioni.clienti@meridiana.it; internet www.meridiana.it; f. 1963 as Alisarda, renamed 1991; scheduled and charter services throughout Italy and Europe; Chair. FRANCO TRIVI; CEO GIOVANNI SEBASTIANI.

Tourism

A great number of tourists are attracted to Italy by its Alpine and Mediterranean scenery, sunny climate, Roman archaeological remains, medieval and Baroque churches, Renaissance towns and palaces, paintings and sculpture and famous opera houses. Each of the 95 provinces has a Board of Tourism; there are also about 300 Aziende Autonome di Cura, Soggiorno e Turismo, with information about tourist accommodation and health treatment, and about 2,000 Pro Loco Associations concerned with local amenities. In 2001 a total of 35.8m. foreign visitors (including excursionists) arrived in Italy; tourist receipts totalled €28,962m. in that year.

Compagnia Italiana Turismo: Via Nazionale 196, 00184 Roma; tel. (06) 48787252; fax (06) 4819120; internet www.citonline.it.

Direzione Generale per il Turismo: Ministero della Attivitá Produttive, Via della Ferratella in Laterano 51, 00184 Roma; tel. (06) 7732431; fax (06) 77209808; e-mail a.m.guzzardi@virgilio.it; Dir-Gen. Ing. FRANCO VITALE.

Ente Nazionale Italiano per il Turismo (ENIT) (Italian State Tourist Board): Via Marghera 2, 00185 Roma; tel. (06) 49711; fax (06) 4463379; e-mail sedecentrale@enit.it; internet www.enit.it; f. 1919; Chair. AMEDEO OTTAVIANI; Dir-Gen. PIERGIORGIO TOGNI.

JAMAICA

Introductory Survey

Location, Climate, Language, Religion, Flag, Capital

Jamaica is the third largest island in the Caribbean Sea, lying 145 km (90 miles) to the south of Cuba and 160 km (100 miles) to the south-west of Haiti. The climate varies with altitude, being tropical at sea-level and temperate in the mountain areas. The average annual temperature is 27°C (80°F) and mean annual rainfall is 198 cm (78 ins). The official language is English, although a local patois is widely spoken. The majority of the population belong to Christian denominations, the Church of God being the most numerous. The national flag (proportions 1 by 2) consists of a diagonal yellow cross on a background of black (hoist and fly) and green (above and below). The capital is Kingston.

Recent History

Jamaica, a British colony from 1655, was granted internal self-government in 1959, and full independence, within the Commonwealth, was achieved on 6 August 1962. Jamaica formed part of the West Indies Federation between 1958 and 1961, when it seceded, following a referendum. The Federation was dissolved in May 1962. The two dominant political figures after the Second World War were the late Sir Alexander Bustamante, leader of the Jamaica Labour Party (JLP), who retired as Prime Minister in 1967, and Norman Manley, a former Premier and leader of the People's National Party (PNP), who died in 1969. The JLP won the elections of 1962 and 1967 but, under the premiership of Hugh Shearer, it lost the elections of February 1972 to the PNP, led by Michael Manley, the son of Norman Manley. Michael Manley advocated democratic socialism and his Government put great emphasis on social reform and economic independence.

The early 1970s were marked by escalating street violence and crime, with gang warfare rife in the deprived areas of Kingston. More than 160 people were killed in the first half of 1976, and in June the Government declared a state of emergency (which remained in force until June 1977). Despite the unrest, high unemployment and severe economic stagnation, the PNP was returned to power in December 1976 with an increased majority. By January 1979, however, there was again widespread political unrest, and violent demonstrations signalled growing discontent with the Manley administration. In February 1980, in the context of a worsening economic crisis, Manley rejected the stipulation of the International Monetary Fund (IMF) that economic austerity measures be undertaken, as a condition of its making further loans to Jamaica. He called a general election to seek support for his economic policies and his decision to end dependence on the IMF. The electoral campaign was one of the most violent in Jamaica's history. In the October election the JLP received about 57% of the total votes and won 51 of the 60 seats in the House of Representatives. Edward Seaga, the leader of the JLP, became Prime Minister; he supported closer political and economic links with the USA and the promotion of free enterprise. Seaga severed diplomatic relations with Cuba in October 1981, and secured valuable US financial support for the economy. Negotiations on IMF assistance were resumed.

In November 1983, before the completion of a new electoral roll, Seaga announced that an election would take place in mid-December. Only four days were allowed for the nomination of candidates, and the PNP, unable to present candidates at such short notice, refused to participate and declared the elections void. The JLP, opposed in only six constituencies (by independent candidates), won all 60 seats in the House of Representatives and formed a one-party legislature.

Devaluations of the Jamaican dollar and the withdrawal of food subsidies provoked demonstrations and sporadic violence in 1984, as the prices of foodstuffs and energy increased by between 50% and 100%. Despite government attempts to offset the effects of these economic austerity measures, imposed at the instigation of the IMF, unemployment, together with the consequences of illicit trading in drugs, contributed to a rise in the incidence of crime and violence, especially in Kingston. In 1985 another increase in fuel prices precipitated further violent demonstrations in the capital and industrial unrest in the public sector. In May 1986 Seaga defied recommendations by the IMF and other aid agencies, and introduced an expansionary budget for 1986/87, in an attempt to stimulate economic growth.

Municipal elections took place in July 1986, having been postponed three times. The PNP obtained control of 11 of the 13 municipalities in which polling took place, winning 57% of the total votes. A significant increase in drugs-related violence in 1987 prompted the Government to announce more severe punishments for drugs-related offences.

In September 1988 Jamaica was struck by 'Hurricane Gilbert', the most damaging storm in the country's recorded history. More than 100,000 homes were destroyed, while the economy, particularly the agriculture sector, was severely disrupted. Seaga's successful efforts to secure international aid won him some initial support, but this soon declined, particularly following controversy over the alleged preferential allocation of relief resources to JLP supporters.

After a brief, and relatively peaceful, campaign, a general election took place in February 1989. The PNP received about 56% of the votes cast, thereby securing 45 of the 60 seats in the House of Representatives. Manley, who had developed a more moderate image during his years in opposition, again became Prime Minister. The Government conceded the necessity for a devaluation of the Jamaican dollar, which was announced in October. Unusually for Jamaican politics, the two main parties achieved a limited consensus on the pursuit of an economic policy of austerity, despite its unpopularity. There was also agreement that further action should be taken against the drugs trade. The Government was particularly anxious to prevent the use of Jamaican shipping and aviation for the smuggling of illegal drugs, and demanded increased security measures, despite the consequent impediment to normal trade movements.

New economic adjustment measures (including a further devaluation of the Jamaican dollar) were adopted in January 1990, in order to secure another IMF stand-by arrangement. In June a five-year economic development plan was announced, as part of the Government's programme of deregulation and reform. However, the cost of living continued to rise, prompting industrial unrest in late 1991.

In December 1991 controversy surrounding the waiving of taxes worth some US $30m. that were owed to Jamaica by an international petroleum company, Shell, resulted in the resignation of Horace Clarke, the Minister of Mining and Energy, and Percival Patterson, the Deputy Prime Minister, amid opposition allegations of corruption and misconduct. Patterson requested not to be included in the new Cabinet (which was reorganized following the scandal), but remained as Chairman of the PNP. In March 1992 Manley announced his resignation, owing to ill health, from the premiership and from the presidency of the PNP. Patterson was subsequently elected as Manley's successor by members of the PNP, and was appointed Prime Minister at the end of the month.

During 1992 there was a marked increase in violent crime, much of which appeared to be politically motivated. Speculation that the Government would organize an early general election intensified in the first few months of 1993, following reports that public support for the JLP had diminished considerably. Patterson's PNP duly secured 52 of the 60 seats in the House of Representatives at a general election contested on 30 March 1993. The scale of the PNP victory was widely attributed to the success of Patterson's populist overtures to the island's majority population of African origin, and a perceived shift in political influence away from the capital, traditionally a power base of the JLP (which won the remaining eight seats). In April Patterson announced plans to reform and modernize the electoral system. However, allegations of electoral malpractice and demands by the JLP for an official inquiry into suspected procedural abuses were rejected by the PNP, prompting the JLP to boycott the official opening of Parliament later in the month. By February 1994 attempts at electoral reform had been undermined by the resignation of the Chairman of the Electoral Advisory Committee (EAC), and by the failure of the EAC to appoint a new Director of Elections. Demands for constitutional and electoral reform continued, and the JLP repeatedly accused the Government of seeking to delay progress towards any such reforms. Proposals drafted in late 1994 recommended the establishment of a permanent electoral commission to supervise elections, the publication of a revised register of voters every six months, and rules governing political campaigning and the nomination of candidates. An electronic voter registration system was installed in 1996 and new electoral rolls were completed in late 1997.

Industrial relations deteriorated in 1994, and there was further industrial unrest in 1995, as workers in both the public and private sectors argued for large pay increases to compensate for high rates of inflation. Meanwhile, the country's poor economic performance (particularly its high inflation rate and increasing trade deficit) and an increase in violent crime in Kingston compounded widespread dissatisfaction with the Government.

In early 1995 widespread dissatisfaction with the leadership of Edward Seaga of the JLP was reported among party members. However, Seaga survived an attempt to remove him as leader of the party in March, and in September the party leadership dismissed the main critics of Seaga as prospective parliamentary candidates for the JLP. In October Bruce Golding, who had resigned as Chairman of the JLP in February after disagreements with Seaga, announced the formation of a political party, the National Democratic Movement (NDM). The NDM, which aimed to achieve constitutional reform, including the introduction of an elected, executive president, gathered support from former members of both the JLP and the PNP.

In an effort to stabilize the economy, and, in particular, to address the problem of continuing industrial unrest, in 1996 the Government sought the agreement of a 'social contract' with trade unions and the private sector. In return for a commitment to increase its efforts to reduce inflation, the Government hoped to secure an undertaking from the labour organizations to moderate their wage demands. In July the Government implemented a 60% increase in the minimum wage. However, efforts to establish a 'social contract' continued to be frustrated during 1997 owing to trade union intransigence concerning demands for salary increases.

A general election was held on 18 December 1997, at which the PNP won 56% of the votes cast and 50 of the 60 seats in the House of Representatives. The JLP obtained 39% of the votes and secured 10 seats, but the NDM, which won 5% of the votes, failed to gain parliamentary representation. It was estimated that 67% of the electorate participated in the election. Patterson, who was subsequently sworn in as Prime Minister for a third consecutive term, appointed a new Cabinet in January 1998 and announced plans for Jamaica to become a republic within five years.

Local elections, which had been repeatedly postponed since 1993 following allegations of electoral malpractice, finally took place in September 1998. The PDP secured control of all 13 local councils, one of which had previously been controlled by the JLP. The NDM, which had called for the introduction of further electoral reforms in order to prevent procedural abuses, did not contest the elections, while Seaga resigned from the JLP leadership for three months in protest at the party's decision to contest the elections; Seaga opposed the decision on the grounds of possible electoral malpractice.

In 1998 and 1999 there were many public protests against police actions and the deepening economic crisis, several of which resulted in riots. The continuing unrest led to the imposition of a curfew in Kingston in October 1998. In the same month a firebomb attack was made on Parliament although no-one was hurt. There was further unrest in April 1999 following the announcement made in the 1999/2000 budget proposals of a significant increase in the price of diesel. The JLP and NDM, while initially helping to organize the protests, disassociated themselves from the subsequent violence, in which eight people were killed and many businesses were burnt or looted. The Government later agreed to reduce the proposed increase. In July the authorities announced that army personnel were to be deployed on patrols in greater Kingston in an attempt to combat the high incidence of criminal activity, the majority of which was reportedly related to drugs-trafficking. In October the British Government announced that it would contribute £2.9m. in grant assistance towards a programme to reform and modernize the Jamaican police force. In early September 2000 the Jamaican Government announced the establishment of a specialized police unit to combat organized crime. In October 2000 an

investigation was initiated in response to widespread allegations of corruption in the police force, which included involvement in drugs-trafficking and the illicit recording of ministerial telephone conversations.

In July 1999 the JLP's central executive voted to suspend the party's deputy leader, Mike Henry. Henry, who was replaced by Dwight Nelson, had been accused of publicly criticizing Seaga earlier in the year. In November the recently-established pressure group, Citizens for Civil Society (CCS), organized a demonstration to protest at what it termed Seaga's 'ineffective' leadership of the opposition and to demand his resignation. In the same month the CCS staged a protest march to demand the dismissal of the Minister of National Security and Justice, Keith (K. D.) Knight, whom the CCS held responsible for the country's high crime rate, and that of the Minister of Finance and Planning, Dr Omar Davies, whom the CCS accused of mishandling the economy. The country's police federation, however, indicated its support for Knight, while Prime Minister Patterson criticized the CCS's tactic of organizing protest marches, which he claimed diverted the attention of the security forces from their anti-crime activities.

Despite the measures implemented by the Government in the previous year, confrontations between the police and various sectors of the community continued in 2001. In March the killing of seven young men in the Kingston suburb of Braeton during a police raid provoked accusations of excessive brutality by the police force. The human rights organization Amnesty International claimed that the Jamaican police force had the one of the highest records for the execution of its own citizens in the world. In 2000 the police had shot dead 140 suspected criminals. Furthermore, in July conflict broke out between police and rival PNP and JLP factions in Kingston, reportedly caused by an exchange of gunfire between police and a group of civilians during a weapons patrol. Following three days of fighting, in which 25 people were reported to have been killed, units of the Jamaica Defence Force were deployed to restore order. Seaga alleged that the violence had been deliberately instigated by the PNP in suburbs where the JLP had influence, in an attempt to damage the credibility of his party. Nevertheless, in August the leaders of the two political parties held a meeting to discuss ways of reducing crime and violence in the suburbs. It was proposed that a crime committee would be established, to be led jointly by the Minister of National Security and the JLP's Spokesman on National Security.

A Commission of Inquiry into the July disturbances opened in September 2001, chaired by a Canadian former chief justice, Julius Alexander Isaac. The Commission was to investigate the conduct of the security forces during the unrest and to consider evidence of criminal activity in the area in the months preceding the violence, specifically the significance of drugs- and weapons-trafficking. The Commission was also to make proposals on ways of preventing further civil unrest. Seaga and the JLP's team of lawyers refused to co-operate with the Commission of Inquiry on several occasions. In October JLP lawyers walked out of the Commission in protest at the judge's refusal to allow them to cross-examine witnesses, and in January 2002 Seaga declined to testify before the Court, expressing his doubt as to the effectiveness of the Inquiry. Meanwhile, the sporadic outbreaks of violence in the Kingston suburbs continued during the remainder of 2001 and into 2002. In October 2001 the Government was forced to deploy army, air and coastguard units to suppress unrest, and in January 2002 seven people were shot dead by as many as 30 gunmen in a suburb known to be a traditional stronghold of the PNP, leading to accusations that the killings were politically motivated. In July 2002 the Commission of Inquiry cleared the security forces of any misconduct, concluding that there was no evidence to suggest that neither soldiers nor police had used excessive brutality to quell the unrest. The rate of violent crime continued to rise throughout 2002.

The social unrest and the perceived decline in popularity of the PNP prompted the Prime Minister to reorganize the Government in October 2001. Keith (K. D.) Knight, Minister of National Security and Justice for the previous 13 years, was appointed Minister of Foreign Affairs and Foreign Trade. The previous Minister of Foreign Affairs, Paul Robertson, had resigned in order to co-ordinate the PNP's election campaign (elections were constitutionally due by the end of 2002). Dr Peter Phillips, hitherto Minister of Transportation and Works, was appointed Minister of National Security and given the task of thoroughly reviewing the country's security systems. Arnold J. Nicholson, was given the justice portfolio, in addition to his duties as Attorney-General. The post of Deputy Prime Minister, from which Seymour Mullings had retired to become Ambassador to the USA in August, remained vacant. One of Phillips' first acts as Minister of National Security Minister was to propose legislation that would give the police the power to wiretap the telephones of individuals thought to be involved in the illegal trafficking of drugs and weapons. The legislation was approved by Parliament in late January 2002. Other proposed measures to reduce crime included the extension of the death penalty to crimes that involved drugs-trafficking. The Inter-American Development Bank (IDB, see p. 239) approved a US $160m. loan to the Government to help in the fight against crime in September 2001.

In October 2001 record levels of torrential rain and high winds caused by 'Hurricane Michelle' caused severe damage, estimated at US $30m., to eastern Jamaica. The Government subsequently announced a relief programme worth US $23.9m for the region. In February 2002, in an attempt to improve the transparency of the financial sector, the Government amended the 1964 Money Laundering Act to include money transfer and remittance companies in the clause relating to financial institutions. Henceforth, financial institutions would be required to report all suspicious transactions exceeding US $50,000.

In May 2002 the Minister of Water and Housing, Karl Blythe, was forced to resign following the results of an inquiry into his ministry's land redistribution programme, which had revealed poor budget management, fraud and cronyism. Similar accusations of mismanagement had been directed at Ministry of Industry, Commerce and Technology in March, although the minister, Philip Paulwell, retained his job.

In September 2002 the Prime Minister announced that legislative elections would be held on 16 October and Parliament was dissolved. The two main parties had already begun preparations for elections; if re-elected, the PNP pledged to reduce the country's debt from the current 140% of GDP to 100% by 2005, while the JLP campaign focused on protecting the future of tourism in Jamaica and the provision of free secondary education. Although both parties vowed to work together to halt the rise in violence, some 11 murders were committed during the months preceding the ballot. At the elections the PNP were re-elected for a fourth consecutive term, receiving 52.2% of votes cast, although its majority in the House of Representatives was reduced by 14 seats to 34. The JLP won 47.2% of votes and the remaining 26 seats. Voting was deemed to have been fair and democratic by an international delegation, led by former US President Jimmy Carter, which oversaw the process.

Patterson was sworn in as premier on 23 October 2002 and became the first Jamaican Prime Minister to swear allegiance to the people and Constitution of Jamaica, rather than to the British monarch, in accordance with new legislation introduced in August. He subsequently formed a new Cabinet, retaining most of the members of the previous administration. Seaga held a meeting with Patterson in which he outlined a number of proposals for reform, including the appointment of an independent Governor-General for Jamaica and a restructuring of the police force.

In December 2002 the armed forces and police began a joint offensive on crime. The Government also revived a previously debated proposal to extend capital punishment to drugs-related crimes and to replace the British Privy Council with a Caribbean Court of Justice (see below) as the final court of appeal, thereby removing the Privy Council's ability to commute death sentences to life imprisonment. Over 1,000 murders were reported in 2002 and extended use of capital punishment gained increasing popular support. Some units of the police force and human rights organizations, however, demanded the dismissal of Reneto Adams, the head of the Crime Management Unit amid allegations of human rights abuses by his staff. In February 2003 the Minister of Finance, Omar Davies, survived a motion of 'no confidence' proposed by the opposition, following his admission that he had authorized increased government spending during the 2002 electoral campaign in an attempt to gain favour with the electorate.

A decision reached in November 1993 by the Judicial Committee of the Privy Council in the United Kingdom (in its capacity as the final court of appeal for the Jamaican legal system) to commute to life imprisonment the death sentences imposed on two Jamaicans in 1979, in recognition of their prolonged suffering in anticipation of execution, threw doubt on the legal position of many similarly-sentenced prisoners in Jamaica and other Caribbean Commonwealth countries, given the recommendation of the Judicial Committee that all executions not effected within five years of sentencing should be subject to review, with a recommendation for commutation. In January 1998 Jamaica withdrew from a UN treaty that had hitherto allowed prisoners sentenced to death to appeal for a review by the UN Commission on Human Rights and later that year it also withdrew from the Organization of American States' Inter-American Court of Human Rights. In February 2001, following legislative approval in November 2000, Patterson and 10 other Caribbean leaders signed an agreement to establish a Caribbean Court of Justice, based in Trinidad and Tobago. The Court was to replace the Privy Council as the final court of appeal, and would allow for the executions of convicted criminals. The JLP opposed the move, and demanded that a referendum be held on the issue.

In January 2003 the British Government introduced new legislation requiring all Jamaican visitors to the United Kingdom to carry visas. The British Foreign and Commonwealth Office maintained that the measure was necessary to reduce the number of visitors who absconded on arrival in the United Kingdom. The Jamaican Government expressed its disappointment with the decision but took no further action.

Relations between Jamaica and the USA have been hampered by persistent demands by the USA for the eradication of Jamaica's marijuana crop. In May 1997, after months of negotiation, the two countries concluded a counter-narcotics agreement, permitting US drugs-enforcement agents to pursue suspected drugs-traffickers in Jamaican airspace and territorial waters. In August 1999 a Jamaican delegation visited the USA to discuss the prospect of increasing US assistance in measures aimed at combating crime.

Government

The Head of State is the British monarch, who is represented locally by the Governor-General, who is appointed on the recommendation of the Prime Minister in consultation with the Leader of the Opposition. The Governor-General acts, in almost all matters, on the advice of the Cabinet.

Legislative power is vested in the bicameral Parliament: the Senate, with 21 appointed members, and the House of Representatives, with 60 elected members. Thirteen members of the Senate are appointed by the Governor-General on the advice of the Prime Minister and eight on the advice of the Leader of the Opposition. Members of the House are elected by universal adult suffrage for five years (subject to dissolution). Executive power lies with the Cabinet. The Prime Minister is appointed from the House of Representatives by the Governor-General, and is the leader of the party that holds the majority of seats in the House of Representatives. The Cabinet is responsible to Parliament.

Defence

In August 2002 the Jamaica Defence Force consisted of 2,830 men on active service, including an army of 2,500, a coastguard of 190 and an air wing of 140 men. There are reserves of some 953. Defence expenditure in 2002 was budgeted at J $1,800m.

Economic Affairs

In 2001, according to estimates by the World Bank, Jamaica's gross national income (GNI), measured at average 1999–2001 prices, was US $7,264m., equivalent to US $2,490 per head (or US $2,720 per head on an international purchasing-power parity basis). During 1990–2001, it was estimated, the population increased at an average rate of 1.0% per year, while gross domestic product (GDP) per head was estimated to have increased, in real terms, by an average of 0.3% per year. Overall GDP increased, in real terms, at an average annual rate of 1.2% in 1990–2001; growth in 2001 was 1.7%.

Agriculture (including forestry and fishing) contributed an estimated 6.5% of GDP in 2001, and engaged an estimated 21.0% of the economically active population in 2000. The principal cash crops are sugar cane (sugar accounted for an estimated 5.1% of total export earnings in 2000/01), bananas, coffee, citrus fruit and cocoa. The cultivation of vegetables, fruit and rice is being encouraged, in an attempt to reduce imports and diversify agricultural exports. According to the World Bank, agricultural GDP increased at an average annual rate of 2.4% in 1990–2000; according to central bank figures, the sector decreased by 10.9% in 2000, but grew by an estimated 5.2% in 2001.

Industry (including mining, manufacturing, public utilities and construction) contributed an estimated 31.3% of GDP in

2001, and engaged an estimated 17.4% of the economically active population in 2000. According to the World Bank, industrial GDP declined at an average rate of 0.5% per year in 1990–2000. The sector declined by 0.4% in 1999, but grew by 0.2% in 2000.

Mining and quarrying contributed an estimated 4.2% of GDP in 2001, but engaged only 0.5% of the active labour force in 2000. Mining is the principal productive sector of the economy, and in 2000/01 bauxite and its derivative, alumina (aluminium oxide), accounted for an estimated 47.9% of total export earnings. Bauxite, of which Jamaica is one of the world's leading producers, is the major mineral mined, but there are also reserves of marble, gypsum, limestone, silica and clay. Bauxite production fell slightly in 2000, to 11.1m. metric tons, but was expected to increase in 2001. Alumina output rose to 3.6m. tons in 2000; production was forecast to rise further in 2001. In March 2001 the mining of gold began.

Manufacturing contributed an estimated 13.2% of GDP in 2001, and engaged some 7.5% of the active labour force in 2000. Much of the activity in the sector is dependent upon the processing of sugar and bauxite. The export of garments, mainly to the USA, became increasingly important in the late 20th century, providing an estimated 11.4% of total value of export earnings in 2000. According to the central bank, manufacturing GDP decreased at an average annual rate of 1.6% during 1990–2001; however, the sector increased by 0.9% in 2000 and by a further estimated 0.6% in 2001.

Energy is derived principally from imported hydrocarbon fuels. Most of Jamaica's petroleum requirements are fulfilled by imports from Venezuela and Mexico. In 2001 fuel imports accounted for 17.5% of the total value of merchandise imports. In March 2001 the Government sold 80% of the country's electricity company, Jamaica Public Service Co, to the US-based Mirant Corporation. In mid–2002 the Government announced plans to replace fuel oil as the country's main source of fuel with liquified natural gas by 2005/6. It was estimated that the project would cost some US $250m., most of which the Government hoped would be funded by private-sector investment.

The services sector contributed an estimated 62.1% of GDP in 2001, and engaged some 61.5% of the active labour force in 2000. The principal earner of foreign exchange is tourism. Total visitors reached an estimated 2.3m. in 2000/01. The largest proportion of tourists is from the USA (69.7% in 1999). Expenditure by tourists totalled an estimated US $1,395m. in 2000/01. According to the World Bank, the GDP of the services sector increased at an average annual rate of 2.4% in 1990–2000. The sector decreased by 0.8% in 1999, but increased by 7.4% in 2000.

In 2001 Jamaica recorded a visible trade deficit of US $1,618.2m., and there was a deficit of US $788.4m. on the current account of the balance of payments. In 2000 the principal source of imports (44.8%) was the USA. Other major suppliers in that year were Trinidad and Tobago, Japan and Venezuela. In that year the USA was also the principal market for exports (39.2%), while the United Kingdom, Canada and Norway were among other important purchasers. The principal exports in 2001 were bauxite and alumina. Foods, including sugar and bananas, were also important export commodities, as well as garments. The principal imports in 2001 were machinery and transport equipment and mineral fuels and lubricants. The illegal production of hemp (marijuana) is also believed to generate significant export revenue.

In the financial year ending 31 March 2001 Jamaica's overall budget deficit was estimated at J $9,282m., equivalent to 2.6% of GDP. Total external debt in 2000 was US $4,287m., of which US $3,475m. was long-term public debt. In that year the cost of debt-servicing was equivalent to 14.1% of earnings from exports of goods and services. The average annual rate of inflation was 23.0% in 1990–2001, and stood at 7.0% in 2001. Some 15.5% of the labour force were unemployed in 2000.

Jamaica is a founding member of the Caribbean Community and Common Market (CARICOM, see p. 155) and of the IDB (see p. 239).

The Jamaican economy was impeded in the 1990s by persistent fiscal imbalances and a high rate of inflation. A crisis in the financial sector in 1995–96 led to a costly state intervention in troubled banks and insurance companies that resulted in an increased fiscal deficit (reaching the equivalent of some 12% of GDP in 1998). Considerable progress was none the less made in reforming the financial sector in the late 1990s, while the

Government continued to implement a policy of privatization of state assets and of increased trade liberalization. In the late 1990s bauxite and alumina production rose significantly, although weak international market prices meant that the sector's improved productivity did not create increased revenue. Following the re-opening of the US-owned Kaiser Aluminium bauxite refinery in late 2000, the industry was expected to resume shipments of some 400,000 metric tons per year. The sugar and coffee industries were both affected by aberrant climatic conditions and a lack of investment. Despite the adverse conditions, the Government's stringent monetary policy succeeded in reducing the rate of increase in consumer prices from 31% in 1995/96 to 7.0% in 2001. Although a lower inflation rate resulted in lower wage demands, industrial unrest increased and the Patterson Government was criticized for inhibiting economic growth. GDP declined annually, in real terms, in 1996–99; however, growth resumed in 2000 and continued in 2001. In 1999 the Government's announcement of a significant rise in the price of diesel in order to increase revenue from taxation prompted widespread protests, estimated to have cost the economy between J $10,250m. and J $14,250m., thereby revealing the extent to which the Jamaican economy remained highly vulnerable to domestic and external pressures. In 2000 Jamaica entered into a Staff Monitored Programme (SMP) with the IMF, with the aim of encouraging foreign investment. In 2001 the economy grew by 1.7%. The main reasons for the lack of significant growth were thought to be the continuing social unrest, the reduction in the number of tourists to the island following the terrorist attacks in the USA in September, and the damage to crops and infrastructure caused by 'Hurricane Michelle' in the following month. US nationals made up the largest group of tourists by nationality; it was estimated that the number of US visitors declined by 28.5% in the period after 11 September, compared with 2000. In late September the Government announced that an extra US $8m. would be allocated to the tourism sector. However, it also predicted that tax relief granted to businesses in the tourist industry and the decrease in customs revenue would contribute to an increased budget deficit in 2002. A modest growth of 0.2% was forecast for 2002, mainly owing to a recession in the agricultural sector caused by heavy rains in July and August and to a continued downturn in the number of tourists visiting the island. While increasing taxes on property, increased expenditure on national security and a growing tax evasion problem meant that the budget deficit for 2003 was expected to be 8.4% of GDP. In November 2002 the World Bank approved a loan to fund financial-sector reform and improvements to infrastructure and the education system.

Education

Primary education is compulsory in certain districts, and free education is ensured. The education system (which begins at six years of age) consists of a primary cycle of six years, followed by two secondary cycles of three and four years, respectively. In 1999/2000 enrolment at primary schools included 94.20% of children in the relevant age-group (males 94.32%; females 94.08%), while enrolment at secondary schools was equivalent to only 74.72% of children in the appropriate age-group (males 73.13%; females 76.34%). Higher education is provided by technical colleges and by the University of the West Indies, which has five faculties situated at its Mona campus in Kingston. Education was declared the first priority for special attention in the 1999/2000 budget proposals. Government expenditure on education during the financial year 2000/01 was estimated to be some J $21,628m., representing 16.0% of total budgetary expenditure.

Public Holidays

2003: 1 January (New Year's Day), 5 March (Ash Wednesday), 18 April (Good Friday), 21 April (Easter Monday), 23 May (Labour Day), 3 August (Emancipation Day), 4 August (Independence Day), 20 October (National Heroes Day), 25 December (Christmas Day), 26 December (Boxing Day).

2004: 1 January (New Year's Day), 25 February (Ash Wednesday), 29 March (Good Friday), 9 April (Easter Monday), 23 May (Labour Day), 1 August (Emancipation Day), 2 August (Independence Day), 18 October (National Heroes' Day), 25 December (Christmas Day), 26 December (Boxing Day).

Weights and Measures

Both the imperial and the metric systems are in use.

Statistical Survey

Sources (unless otherwise stated): Statistical Institute of Jamaica, 9 Swallowfield Rd, Kingston 5, Jamaica; tel. 926-2175; fax 926-4859; e-mail statinja@infochan.com; internet www.statinja.com ; Jamaica Information Service, 58a Half Way Tree Rd, POB 2222, Kingston 10, Jamaica; tel. 926-3740; fax 926-6715; e-mail jis@jis.gov.jm; internet www.jis.gov.jm; Bank of Jamaica, Nethersole Pl., POB 621, Kingston, Jamaica; tel. 922-0752; fax 922-0854; e-mail info@boj.org.jm; internet www.boj.org.jm.

Area and Population

AREA, POPULATION AND DENSITY

Area (sq km)	10,991*
Population (census results)	
8 June 1982	2,205,507
7 April 1991	
Males	1,134,386
Females	1,180,093
Total	2,314,479
Population (official estimates at 31 December)	
1999	2,590,400
2000	2,604,800
2001	2,621,100
Density (per sq km) at 31 December 2001	238.5

* 4,243.6 sq miles.

PARISHES

	Area (sq km)	Population (estimates, 1999)	Parish capitals (with population at 1991 census)
Kingston	22 }	707,400	Kingston M.A. (587,798)
St Andrew	431 }		
St Thomas	743	91,400	Morant Bay (9,185)
Portland	814	79,400	Port Antonio (13,246)
St Mary	611	112,900	Port Maria (7,651)
St Ann	1,213	162,000	St Ann's Bay (10,518)
Trelawny	875	72,700	Falmouth (7,245)
St James	595	176,100	Montego Bay (83,446)
Hanover	450	67,900	Lucea (6,002)
Westmoreland	807	137,900	Savanna La Mar (16,553)
St Elizabeth	1,212	148,900	Black River (3,675)
Manchester	830	183,000	Mandeville (39,430)
Clarendon	1,196	227,100	May Pen (46,785)
St Catherine	1,192	409,500	Spanish Town (92,383)
Total	10,991	2,576,200	—

Source: Thomas Brinkoff, *City Population* (internet www.citypopulation.de).

PRINCIPAL TOWNS
(population at census of 7 April 1991)

Kingston (capital)	587,798	Montego Bay	83,446
Spanish Town	92,383	May Pen	46,785
Portmore	90,138	Mandeville	39,430

Source: Thomas Brinkoff, *City Population* (internet www.citypopulation.de).

BIRTHS, MARRIAGES AND DEATHS*

	Registered live births		Registered marriages		Registered deaths	
	Number	Rate (per 1,000)	Number	Rate (per 1,000)	Number	Rate (per 1,000)
1992	56,276	23.5	13,042	5.6	13,225	5.5
1993	58,627	24.0	14,352	5.9	13,927	5.7
1994	57,404	23.2	15,171	6.1	13,503	5.5
1995	57,607	23.0	16,515	6.6	12,776	5.1
1996	59,194	23.4	19,170	7.6	16,926	6.7
1997	59,385	23.3	21,502	8.4	15,087	5.9
1998	56,937	22.1	24,131	9.4	15,967	6.2
1999	56,911	22.0	26,871	10.4	17,353	6.7

2000: Birth rate 20.7; Death rate 6.3.

2001: Birth rate 21.2; Death rate 6.6.

* Data are tabulated by year of registration rather than by year of occurrence.

Source: partly UN, *Demographic Yearbook*.

Expectation of life (WHO estimates, years at birth): 72.7 (males 71.0; females 74.5) in 2001 (Source: WHO, *World Health Report*).

ECONOMICALLY ACTIVE POPULATION
('000 persons aged 14 years and over)

	1998	1999	2000
Agriculture, forestry and fishing	203.8	200.0	195.7
Mining and quarrying	5.6	5.5	4.6
Manufacturing	84.1	79.0	69.6
Electricity, gas and water	6.5	6.5	6.3
Construction	79.7	77.9	81.5
Trade, restaurants and hotels	205.4	205.4	206.3
Transport, storage and communications	54.9	61.8	59.4
Financing, insurance, real estate and business services	56.8	52.5	53.1
Community, social and personal services	255.5	259.6	254.8
Activities not adequately defined	1.3	4.3	2.3
Total employed	953.6	943.9	933.5

Unemployed ('000 persons aged 10 years and over): 175.0 in 1998; 175.2 in 1999; 171.8 in 2000.

Source: ILO.

Health and Welfare

KEY INDICATORS

Total fertility rate (children per woman, 2001)	2.4
Under-5 mortality rate (per 1,000 live births, 2001)	20
HIV/AIDS (% of persons aged 15–49, 2001)	1.22
Physicians (per 1,000 head, 1996)	1.40
Hospital beds (per 1,000 head, 1996)	2.12
Health expenditure (2000): US $ per head (PPP)	208
Health expenditure (2000): % of GDP	5.5
Health expenditure (2000): public (% of total)	47.0
Access to water (% of persons, 2000)	71
Access to sanitation (% of persons, 2000)	84
Human Development Index (2000): ranking	86
Human Development Index (2000): value	0.742

For sources and definitions, see explanatory note on p. vi.

Agriculture

PRINCIPAL CROPS
('000 metric tons)

	1999	2000	2001
Sweet potatoes	25.0	21.1	25.0
Yams	195.7	147.7	157.6
Other roots and tubers*	55.3	30.9	42.4
Sugar cane	2,313	2,025	2,400†
Coconuts*	170	170	170
Cabbages	27.2	19.3	22.5
Tomatoes	21.6	20.9	24.1
Pumpkins, squash and gourds	33.8	34.7	35.0*
Carrots	24.7	19.9	20.2
Other vegetables*	79.9	70.8	73.5
Bananas*	130	130	130
Plantains*	25.0	27.0	29.0
Oranges*	140	140	140
Lemons and limes*	24	24	24
Grapefruit and pomelo*	42	42	42
Pineapples	19.3	20.3	20.4
Other fruit*	104.5	98.5	104.5

* FAO estimate(s).
† Unofficial figure.

Source: FAO.

LIVESTOCK
(FAO estimates, '000 head, year ending September)

	1999	2000	2001
Horses	4	4	4
Mules	10	10	10
Asses	23	23	23
Cattle	400	400	400
Pigs	180	180	180
Sheep	1	1	1
Goats	440	440	440
Chickens	11,000	11,000	11,000

Source: FAO.

LIVESTOCK PRODUCTS
('000 metric tons)

	1999	2000	2001
Beef and veal	14.7	14.0	13.4
Goat meat*	1.7	1.7	1.7
Pig meat	6.9	6.6	6.4
Chicken meat	72.9	77.1	83†
Cows' milk*	28	29	29
Hen eggs*	7.6	5.8	5.8
Honey*	1	1	1
Cattle hides*	1.4	1.3	1.3

* FAO estimates.
† Unofficial figure.

Source: FAO.

Forestry

ROUNDWOOD REMOVALS
('000 cubic metres, excl. bark)

	1997	1998	1999
Sawlogs, veneer logs and logs for sleepers	129	132	132
Other industrial wood	150	150	150
Fuel wood*	524	547	572
Total	804	830	855

* FAO estimates.

2000: Production as in 1999 (FAO estimates).

Source: FAO.

SAWNWOOD PRODUCTION
('000 cubic metres, incl. railway sleepers)

	1996	1997	1998
Coniferous (softwood)	3	3	3
Broadleaved (hardwood)	61	62	63
Total	64	65	66

1999–2001: Annual production as in 1998 (FAO estimates).

Source: FAO.

Fishing

('000 metric tons, live weight)

	1998	1999	2000
Capture	6.6	8.5	5.7
Marine fishes	4.2	6.3	4.6
Caribbean spiny lobster	0.2	0.3	0.5
Stromboid conchs	1.7	1.4	—
Aquaculture*	3.4	4.2	4.5
Nile tilapia	3.4	4.1	4.5
Total catch*	10.0	12.7	10.2

* FAO estimates.

Source: FAO, *Yearbook of Fishery Statistics*.

Mining

('000 metric tons)

	1998	1999	2000
Bauxite*	12,646	11,688	11,127
Alumina	3,440	3,570	3,600
Crude gypsum	154.5	235.9	330.4
Salt	15.6	19.1	19.1

* Dried equivalent of crude ore.

Source: US Geological Survey.

Industry

SELECTED PRODUCTS

	1998	1999	2000
Edible oil ('000 litres)	14,038	15,976	n.a.
Flour (metric tons)	135,859	130,885	n.a.
Sugar (metric tons)	182,761	201,319	179,381
Molasses (metric tons)	97,865	85,120	63,185
Rum ('000 litres)	22,171	19,709	19,836
Beer and stout ('000 litres)	66,933	65,573	n.a.
Animal feed (metric tons)	191,765	232,351	n.a.
Fertilizers (metric tons)	27,918	43,897	n.a.
Fuel oil ('000 litres)	399,018	284,967	560,583
Asphalt ('000 litres)	3,708	5,508	n.a.
Gasoline (petrol) ('000 litres)	146,224	86,683	184,013
Kerosene, turbo and jet fuel ('000 litres)	52,690	41,397	99,684
Auto diesel oil ('000 litres)	150,109	102,336	221,342
Cement ('000 metric tons)	588,001	503,053	n.a.
Concrete ('000 cu. metres)	n.a.	116,535	107,030

2001: Sugar 205,300 metric tons; Rum and alchohol 23,102,000 litres; Diesel and fuel oils 744.1m. litres; Gasoline 166.1m. litres; Cement 545,000 metric tons.

Electrical energy (million kWh): 6,480 in 1998 (Source: UN, *Industrial Commodity Statistics Yearbook*).

Finance

CURRENCY AND EXCHANGE RATES

Monetary Units
100 cents = 1 Jamaican dollar (J $)

Sterling, US Dollar and Euro Equivalents (31 December 2002)
£1 sterling = J $81.818
US $1 = J $50.762
€1 = J $53.234
J $1,000 = £12.22 = US $19.70 = €18.79

Average Exchange Rate (J $ per US $)
2000   42.701
2001   45.996
2002   48.416

BUDGET*
(J $ million, year ending 31 March)

Revenue†	1999	2000	2001
Tax revenue	74,634	84,659	90,985
Taxes on income, profits and			
capital gains	32,185	35,456	35,495
Individual	16,681	16,386	19,750
Corporate	9,051	8,825	6,680
Domestic taxes on goods and			
services	29,451	34,285	38,561
General sales, turnover or			
value-added taxes . . .	26,392	30,717	34,625
Taxes on international trade .	6,919	7,503	8,501
Other current revenue . . .	22,777	29,260	27,423
Entrepreneurial and property			
income	8,626	9,875	9,954
Administrative fees, non-			
industrial and incidental			
sales	6,606	8,260	9,365
Fines and forfeits	2,590	2,891	2,808
Capital revenue	601	5,063	4,595
Total	98,012	118,982	123,004

Expenditure	1999	2000	2001
General public services	11,164	26,992	13,698
Defence	1,802	1,896	2,212
Public order and safety	8,143	8,677	10,693
Education	17,470	4,877	21,628
Health	7,048	3,743	8,222
Social security and welfare . . .	1,182	1,697	1,295
Housing and community amenities	2,565	2,572	2,741
Recreational, cultural and religious			
affairs and services	167	260	276
Economic affairs and services . .	10,689	11,969	11,258
Agriculture, forestry, fishing and			
hunting	2,327	2,048	2,291
Transport and communications .	3,383	3,576	3,577
Other purposes	52,278	60,245	63,500
Total expenditure	112,506	122,929	135,523
Current‡	97,945	105,461	120,192
Capital	14,561	17,468	15,331

* Figures refer to consolidated accounts of the central Government.
† Excluding grants received (J $ million): 797 in 1999; 3,236 in 2001.
‡ Including interest payments (J $ million): 41,911 in 1999; 43,335 in 2000; 51,550 in 2001.

Source: IMF, *Government Finance Statistics Yearbook* .

INTERNATIONAL RESERVES
(US $ million, at 31 December)

	2000	2001	2002
IMF special drawing rights . .	0.1	1.5	0.9
Foreign exchange	1,053.6	1,899.4	1,644.6
Total	1,053.7	1,900.9	1,645.5

Source: IMF, *International Financial Statistics.*

MONEY SUPPLY
(J $ million at 31 December)

	2000	2001	2002
Currency outside banks . . .	17,607	18,783	20,399
Demand deposits at commercial			
banks	30,289	35,359	38,920
Total money	47,897	54,142	58,319

Source: IMF, *International Financial Statistics.*

COST OF LIVING
(Consumer Price Index; base: 1990 = 100)

	1998	1999	2000
Food (incl. beverages) . . .	794.2	812.4	869.3
Fuel and household supplies . .	793.9	841.4	907.5
Clothing (incl. footwear) . .	846.4	885.1	932.3
Rent and household operation . .	512.0	843.7	1,015.5
All items (incl. others)	797.5	845.0	914.0

2001 (base: 1990 = 100): Food (incl. beverages) 899.3; All items (incl. others) 978.0.

Source: ILO.

NATIONAL ACCOUNTS
(J $ million at current prices)

Expenditure on the Gross Domestic Product

	1999	2000	2001
Government final consumption			
expenditure	48,633	53,570	55,710
Private final consumption			
expenditure	196,641	223,341	245,990
Increase in stocks	237	575	562
Gross fixed capital formation . .	73,531	90,338	107,118
Total domestic expenditure . .	319,042	377,824	409,380
Exports of goods and services . .	124,754	146,163	148,477
Less Imports of goods and services	149,721	184,815	199,821
GDP in purchasers' values . .	294,076	329,171	358,036
GDP at constant 1986 prices .	19,472	19,602	19,940

Source: IMF, *International Financial Statistics.*

Gross Domestic Product by Economic Activity

	1999	2000	2001
Agriculture, forestry and fishing .	20,552	21,327	22,888
Mining and quarrying	12,013	13,827	14,820
Manufacturing	39,043	42,212	46,554
Electricity and water	10,246	12,877	14,125
Construction	27,667	30,963	34,763
Wholesale and retail trade . . .	59,694	66,984	71,590
Transport, storage and			
communication	29,415	32,206	37,809
Finance and insurance services . .	22,030	25,019	21,577
Real estate and business services .	17,676	19,330	21,563
Producers of government services .	34,045	37,104	40,296
Household and private non-profit			
services	1,657	2,010	2,100
Other services	20,768	23,017	23,863
Sub-total*	294,808	327,874	351,948
Value-added tax	19,743	22,132	23,337
Less Imputed bank service charge .	20,475	20,835	17,249
GDP in purchasers' values . .	294,076	329,171	358,036

* Totals may not be equal to the sum of component parts, owing to rounding.

BALANCE OF PAYMENTS
(US $ million)

	1999	2000	2001
Exports of goods f.o.b.	1,499.1	1,562.8	1,454.4
Imports of goods f.o.b.	−2,685.6	−3,004.3	−3,072.6
Trade balance	−1,186.5	−1,44.5	−1,618.2
Exports of services	1,978.4	2,025.8	1,900.7
Imports of services	−1,323.0	−1,442.1	−1,519.2
Balance on goods and services	−531.1	−857.9	−1,236.7
Other income received	165.8	193.1	218.2
Other income paid	−498.3	−543	−656
Balance on goods, services and income	−863.6	−1,207.8	−1,674.5
Current transfers received	757.9	969.4	1,062.7
Current transfers paid	−110.6	−148.6	176.6
Current balance	−216.3	−287	−788.4
Capital account (net)	−10.9	2.2	−22.3
Direct investment abroad	−94.9	−74.3	−89
Direct investment from abroad	523.7	468.4	613.9
Portfolio investment (assets)	−3.7	−70.0	−39.3
Portfolio investment liabilities	8.6	5.9	69.7
Other investment assets	−122.7	−95.5	−215.5
Other investment liabilities	−216.2	619.5	1,320.7
Net errors and omissions	−4.0	−49.2	15.2
Overall balance	−136.4	518.4	865.0

Source: IMF, *International Financial Statistics*.

External Trade

PRINCIPAL COMMODITIES
(J $ million)

Imports c.i.f.	1999	2000	2001
Foods	17,969.5	19,231.7	21,899.8
Mineral fuels and lubricants	16,421.5	27,961.3	27,122.6
Chemicals	13,351.1	16,141.4	17,264.8
Manufactured goods	17,313.0	19,029.4	21,446.8
Machinery and transport equipment	25,801.6	32,220.8	40,512.3
Misc. manufactured articles	17,272.4	19,377.0	18,142.0
Total (incl. others)	115,690.2	141,986.7	154,799.3

Exports f.o.b.	1999	2000	2001
Foods	9,369.2	9,619.7	10,260.2
Beverages and tobacco	2,194.8	2,557.0	2,219.6
Crude materials (excl. fuels)	26,850.2	31,604.9	34,011.5
Chemicals	1,800.0	2,900.9	3,009.3
Misc. manufactured articles	6,440.7	6,650.5	4,348.9
Total (incl. others)	47,369.2	53,829.0	54,845.7

PRINCIPAL TRADING PARTNERS
(US $ million)

Imports c.i.f.	1998	1999	2000
Canada	95	97	98
Guyana	29	29	33
Japan	200	179	192
Trinidad and Tobago	230	289	320
United Kingdom	115	96	98
USA	1,523	1,437	1,431
Venezuela	46	53	125
Total (incl. others)	2,992	2,960	3,192

Exports f.o.b.	1998	1999	2000
Canada	151	136	133
Japan	17	22	30
Norway	88	80	119
Trinidad and Tobago	16	15	22
United Kingdom	159	154	149
USA	52	461	509
Total (incl. others)	1,316	1,246	1,300

Source: IMF, *Jamaica: Statistical Appendix* (June 2001).

Transport

RAILWAYS
(traffic)

	1988	1989	1990
Passenger-km ('000)	36,146	37,995	n.a.
Freight ton-km ('000)	115,076	28,609	1,931

Source: Jamaica Railway Corporation.

ROAD TRAFFIC
('000 motor vehicles in use)

	1995	1996	1997
Passenger cars	104.0	120.7	156.8
Commercial vehicles	49.1	52.8	56.1

Source: UN, *Statistical Yearbook*.

SHIPPING

Merchant Fleet
(registered at 31 December)

	1999	2000	2001
Number of vessels	9	9	7
Total displacement ('000 grt)	3.6	3.6	23.1

Source: Lloyd's Register-Fairplay, *World Fleet Statistics*.

International Sea-borne Freight Traffic
(estimates, '000 metric tons)

	1989	1990	1991
Goods loaded	7,711	8,354	8,802
Goods unloaded	5,167	5,380	5,285

Source: Port Authority of Jamaica.

CIVIL AVIATION
(traffic on scheduled services)

	1997	1998	1999
Kilometres flown (million)	22	23	35
Passengers carried ('000)	1,400	1,454	1,670
Passenger-km (million)	2,677	2,961	3,495
Total ton-km (million)	264	293	377

Source: UN, *Statistical Yearbook*.

Tourism

VISITOR ARRIVALS BY COUNTRY OF ORIGIN

	1998	1999	2000
Canada	109,802	100,338	107,492
USA	829,330	870,019	942,561
United Kingdom	116,552	124,930	135,338
Total (incl. others)	1,225,287	1,248,397	1,322,690

Source: World Tourism Organization, *Yearbook of Tourism Statistics*.

Total visitors ('000): 2,277 in 2000/01*.

Total expenditure (US $ million): 1,276 in 1999/2000; 1,395* in 2000/01.

* Preliminary figures (Source: IMF, *Jamaica: Statistical Appendix* (June 2001)).

Communications Media

	1999	2000	2001
Telephones ('000 main lines in use)	487.3	511.7	512.6
Mobile cellular telephones ('000 subscribers)	144.4	367.0	700.0
Personal computers ('000 in use)	110	110*	130*
Internet users ('000)	60.0	60.0*	100.0

Radio receivers ('000 in use): 1,215 in 1997.

Television receivers ('000 in use): 500 in 2000.

Facsimile machines (number in use): 1,567 in 1992†.

Daily newspapers: 3 in 1996 (circulation 158,000).

* Estimate(s).

† Year ending 1 April.

Sources: International Telecommunication Union; UN, *Statistical Yearbook*; UNESCO, *Statistical Yearbook*.

Education

	Institutions	Teachers	Students
Pre-primary*	1,681	4,158†	133,687†
Primary‡	—	9,512†	293,863†
Secondary§	—	10,931	235,071
Tertiary‖.	1	418	8,191

* Figures for 1990/91.

† Public sector only.

‡ Figures for 1996/97.

§ Figures for 1992/93.

‖ Figures for 1995/96.

Source: UNESCO, *Statistical Yearbook*.

Adult literacy rate (UNESCO estimates): 86.9% (males 82.9%; females 90.7%) in 2000 (Source: UN Development Programme, *Human Development Report*).

Directory

The Constitution

The Constitution came into force at the independence of Jamaica on 6 August 1962. Amendments to the Constitution are enacted by Parliament, but certain entrenched provisions require ratification by a two-thirds' majority in both chambers of the legislature, and some (such as a change of the head of state) require the additional approval of a national referendum.

HEAD OF STATE

The Head of State is the British monarch, who is locally represented by a Governor-General, appointed by the British monarch, on the recommendation of the Jamaican Prime Minister in consultation with the Leader of the Opposition party.

THE LEGISLATURE

The Senate or Upper House consists of 21 Senators, of whom 13 will be appointed by the Governor-General on the advice of the Prime Minister and eight by the Governor-General on the advice of the Leader of the Opposition. (Legislation enacted in 1984 provided for eight independent Senators to be appointed, after consultations with the Prime Minister, in the eventuality of there being no Leader of the Opposition.)

The House of Representatives consists of 60 elected members called Members of Parliament.

A person is qualified for appointment to the Senate or for election to the House of Representatives if he or she is a citizen of Jamaica or other Commonwealth country, of the age of 21 or more and has been ordinarily resident in Jamaica for the immediately preceding 12 months.

THE PRIVY COUNCIL

The Privy Council consists of six members appointed by the Governor-General after consultation with the Prime Minister, of whom at least two are persons who hold or who have held public office. The functions of the Council are to advise the Governor-General on the exercise of the Royal Prerogative of Mercy and on appeals on disciplinary matters from the three Service Commissions.

THE EXECUTIVE

The Prime Minister is appointed from the House of Representatives by the Governor-General, and is the leader of the party that holds the majority of seats in the House of Representatives. The Leader of the party is voted in by the members of that party. The Leader of the Opposition is voted in by the members of the Opposition party.

The Cabinet consists of the Prime Minister and not fewer than 11 other ministers, not more than four of whom may sit in the Senate. The members of the Cabinet are appointed by the Governor-General on the advice of the Prime Minister.

THE JUDICATURE

The Judicature consists of a Supreme Court, a Court of Appeal and minor courts. Judicial matters, notably advice to the Governor-General on appointments, are considered by a Judicial Service Commission, the Chairman of which is the Chief Justice, members being the President of the Court of Appeal, the Chairman of the Public Service Commission and three others.

CITIZENSHIP

All persons born in Jamaica after independence automatically acquire Jamaican citizenship and there is also provision for the acquisition of citizenship by persons born outside Jamaica of Jamaican parents. Persons born in Jamaica (or persons born outside Jamaica of Jamaican parents) before independence who immediately prior to independence were citizens of the United Kingdom and colonies also automatically become citizens of Jamaica.

Appropriate provision is made which permits persons who do not automatically become citizens of Jamaica to be registered as such.

FUNDAMENTAL RIGHTS AND FREEDOMS

The Constitution includes provisions safeguarding the fundamental freedoms of the individual, irrespective of race, place of origin, political opinions, colour, creed or sex, subject only to respect for the rights and freedoms of others and for the public interest. The fundamental freedoms include the rights of life, liberty, security of the person and protection from arbitrary arrest or restriction of movement, the enjoyment of property and the protection of the law, freedom of conscience, of expression and of peaceful assembly and association, and respect for private and family life.

The Government

Head of State: HM Queen Elizabeth II (succeeded to the throne 6 February 1952).

Governor-General: Sir Howard Felix Hanlan Cooke (appointed 1 August 1991).

PRIVY COUNCIL OF JAMAICA

Kenneth Smith, Donald Mills, Dennis Lalor, James Kerr, Elsa Leo Rhynie, Headley Cunningham.

CABINET
(April 2003)

Prime Minister: Percival James Patterson.

Deputy Prime Minister: (vacant).

Minister of Finance and Planning: Dr Omar Davies.

Minister of Labour and Social Security: Horace Dalley.

Minister of Industry and Tourism: Aloun N'Dombet-Assamba.

Minister of Local Government: Portia Simpson-Miller.

Minister of National Security: Dr Peter Phillips.

Minister of Justice and Attorney-General: Arnold J. Nicholson.

Minister of Agriculture: Roger Clarke.

Minister of Foreign Affairs and Foreign Trade: Keith D. Knight.

Minister of Mining and Energy: Anthony Hylton.

Minister of Health: JOHN JUNOR.

Minister of Education, Youth and Culture: MAXINE HENRY-WILSON.

Minister of Transport and Works: ROBERT PICKERSGILL.

Minister of Water and Housing: DONALD BUCHANAN.

Minister of Commerce, Science and Technology: PHILLIP PAULWELL.

Minister of Land and the Environment: DEAN PEART.

Minister of Information and Leader of Government Business: BURCHELL WHITEMAN.

Minister of Development: PAUL ROBERTSON.

MINISTRIES

Office of the Governor-General: King's House, Hope Rd, Kingston 10; tel. 927-6424.

Office of the Prime Minister: Jamaica House, 1 Devon Rd, POB 272, Kingston 10; tel. 927-9941; fax 929-0005; e-mail pmo@opm.gov .jm.

Ministry of Agriculture: Hope Gardens, POB 480, Kingston 6; tel. 927-1731; fax 977-1879; internet www.moa.gov.jm.

Ministry of Commerce, Science and Technology: PCJ Bldg, 36 Trafalgar Rd, Kingston 10; tel. 929-8990; fax 960-1623; e-mail admin@mct.gov.jm; internet www.mct.gov.jm.

Ministry of Development: tel. 927-9941.

Ministry of Education, Youth and Culture: 2a National Heroes Circle, Kingston 4; tel. 922-1400; fax 922-1837; internet www.moec .gov.jm.

Ministry of Finance and Planning: 30 National Heroes Circle, Kingston 4; tel. 922-8600; fax 922-7097; e-mail info@mof.gov.jm; internet www.mof.gov.jm.

Ministry of Foreign Affairs and Foreign Trade: 21 Dominica Dr., POB 624, Kingston 5; tel. 926-4220; fax 929-5112; e-mail mfaftjam@cwjamaica.com; internet www.mfaft.gov.jm.

Ministry of Health: Oceana Hotel Complex, 2–4 King St, Kingston; tel. 967-1092; fax 967-7293; internet www.moh.gov.jm.

Ministry of Labour and Social Security: 1F North St, POB 10, Kingston; tel. 922-3904; fax 924-9560; e-mail manpower@minlab .gov.jm; internet www.minlab.gov.jm.

Ministry of Land and the Environment: 1 Devon Rd, Kingston 6; tel. 929-8880; fax 929-7349; e-mail mehsys@hotmail.com.

Ministry of Local Government, Community Development and Sport: 85 Hagley Park Rd, Kingston 10; tel. 754-0994; fax 960-0725; internet www.mlgycd.gov.jm.

Ministry of Justice: Kingston; tel. 906-2416; fax 922-5109.

Ministry of Mining and Energy: PCJ Bldg, 36 Trafalgar Rd, Kingston 10; tel. 926-9170; fax 968-2082; e-mail hmme@cwjamaica .com; internet www.minesandgeologyjamaica.com.

Ministry of National Security: Mutual Life Bldg, North Tower, 2 Oxford Rd, Kingston 5; tel. 906-4909; fax 906-1724; e-mail information@mnsj.gov.jm; internet www.mnsj.gov.jm.

Ministry of Industry and Tourism: 64 Knutsford Blvd, Kingston 5; tel. 920-4956; fax 920-4944; e-mail optm@cwjamaica.com.

Ministry of Transport and Works: 1c–1f Pawsey Place, Kingston 5; tel. 754-1900; fax 927-8763; e-mail ps@mtw.gov.jm; internet www .mtw.gov.jm.

Ministry of Water and Housing: 7th Floor, Island Life Bldg, 6 St Lucia Ave, Kingston 5; tel. 754-0971; fax 754-0975; e-mail genefa@ cwjamaica.com.

Legislature

PARLIAMENT

Houses of Parliament: Gordon House, Duke St, Kingston; tel. 922-0200.

Senate

President: SYRINGA MARSHALL-BURNETT.

Vice-President: NOEL MONTEITH.

The Senate has 20 other members.

House of Representatives

Speaker: VIOLET NEILSON.

Deputy Speaker: O'NEIL T. WILLIAMS.

General Election, 16 October 2002

	% of votes cast	Seats
People's National Party (PNP)	52.2	34
Jamaica Labour Party (JLP)	47.2	26
Total (incl. others)	100.0	60

Political Organizations

Jamaica Labour Party (JLP): 20 Belmont Rd, Kingston 5; tel. 929-1183; fax 968-0873; e-mail info@thejlp.com; internet www.thejlp .com; f. 1943; supports free enterprise in a mixed economy and close co-operation with the USA; Leader EDWARD SEAGA; Deputy Leader OLIVIA ('BABSY') GRANGE.

Jamaican Alliance for National Unity (JANU): Kingston; f. 2002.

Jamaica Alliance Movement (JAM): Kingston; f. 2002.

National Democratic Movement (NDM): 72 Half Way Tree Rd, Kingston 10; e-mail mail@ndmjamaica.net; internet www .ndmjamaica.net; f. 1995; advocates a clear separation of powers between the central executive and elected representatives; supports private investment and a market economy; Pres. HYACINTH BENNETT; Chair. BRASCOE LEE.

Natural Law Party: c/o 21st Century Integrated Medical Centre, Shop OF3, Overton Plaza, 49 Union St, Montego Bay; tel. 971-9107; fax 971-9109; e-mail nlp@cwjamaica.com; internet www .natural-law-party.org/jamaica/; f. 1996; Leader Dr. LEO CAMPBELL.

People's National Party (PNP): 89 Old Hope Rd, Kingston 5; tel. 978-1337; fax 927-4389; internet www.pnpjamaica.com; f. 1938; socialist principles; affiliated with the National Workers' Union; Leader PERCIVAL J. PATTERSON; Gen. Sec. MAXINE HENRY-WILSON; First Vice-Pres. PETER PHILLIPS.

Republican Party of Jamaica (RPJ): Kingston; Leader DENZIL TAYLOR.

United People's Party (UPP): 6 Trinidad Terrace, Kingston 5; tel. 929-6429; e-mail uppjam@cwjamaica.com; internet www .uppjamaica.com; f. 2001; Pres. ANTOINETTE HAUGHTON CARDENAS; Gen. Sec. HORACE MATTHEWS.

In 1999 a pressure group, **Citizens for a Civil Society** (CCS), was formed by DARYL VAZ to lobby the Government on specific issues. Another pressure group, **Jamaicans for Justice**, headed by Dr CAROLYN GOMES, was formed in 2001.

Diplomatic Representation

EMBASSIES AND HIGH COMMISSIONS IN JAMAICA

Argentina: 6th Floor, Dyoll Bldg, 40 Knutsford Blvd, Kingston 5; tel. 926-5588; fax 926-0580; e-mail fejama@mrecic.gov.ar; Ambassador GONZALO FERNÁNDEZ MEDRANO.

Brazil: PCMB Bldg, 3rd Floor, 64 Knutsford Blvd, Kingston 5; tel. 929-8607; fax 929-1259; e-mail brasking@infochan.com; Ambassador CYRO CARDOSO.

Canada: 3 West Kings House Rd, POB 1500, Kingston 10; tel. 926-1500; e-mail kngtn@dfait-maeci.gc.ca; High Commissioner JOHN M. ROBINSON.

Chile: Island Life Centre, 5th Floor, South 6th St, Lucia Ave, Kingston; tel. 968-0260; fax 968-0265; e-mail chilejam@cwjamaica .com; Ambassador FERNANDO PARDO HUERTA.

China, People's Republic: 8 Seaview Ave, Kingston 10; tel. 927-0850; Ambassador LI SHANGSHENG.

Colombia: Victoria Mutual Bldg, 3rd Floor, 53 Knutsford Blvd, Kingston 5; tel. 929-1702; fax 929-1701; Ambassador FRANCIS JAMES KENT.

Costa Rica: Belvedere House, Beverly Dr., Kingston 5; tel. 927-5988; fax 978-3946; e-mail cr_emb_jam@hotmail.com; Chargé d'affaires a.i. MARCIA WATSON LOCKWOOD.

Cuba: 9 Trafalgar Rd, Kingston 5; tel. 978-0931; fax 978-5372; e-mail embacuba@cwjamaica.com; Ambassador JOSÉ FRANCISCO PIEDRA RENCURRELL.

France: 13 Hillcrest Ave, POB 93, Kingston 6; e-mail frenchembassy@cwjamaica.com; internet ambafrance-jm.org; Ambassador PIERRE-ANTOINE BERNIARD.

Germany: 10 Waterloo Rd, POB 444, Kingston 10; tel. 926-6728; fax 929-8282; e-mail germanemb@cwjamaica.com; Ambassador Dr CHRISTIAN HAUSMANN.

Haiti: 2 Monroe Rd, Kingston 6; tel. 927-7595; fax 978-7638; Ambassador JEAN-GABRIEL AUGUSTIN.

Honduras: 35 Hall Crescent, Aylsham, Kingston 8; tel. 931-5248; fax 931-1790; e-mail emhonjam@kasnet.com; Ambassador CARLOS AUGUSTO MATUTE RIVERA.

India: 4 Retreat Ave, POB 446, Kingston 6; tel. 927-0486; fax 978-2801; High Commissioner OM PRAKASH GUPTA.

Japan: Mutual Life Centre, North Tower, 6th Floor, 2 Oxford Rd, Kingston 10; tel. 929-3338; fax 968-1373; Ambassador TAKASHI MATSUMOTO.

Mexico: PCJ Bldg, 36 Trafalgar Rd, Kingston 10; tel. 926-6891; fax 929-7995; e-mail mexico.j@cwjamaica.com; Ambassador BENITO ANDIÓN SANCHO.

Netherlands: Victoria Mutual Bldg, 53 Knutsford Blvd, Kingston 5; tel. 926-2026; fax 926-1248; e-mail rnekst@cwjamaica.com; Chargé d'affaires a.i. G.C.H. KERSTEN.

Nigeria: 5 Waterloo Rd, Kingston 10; tel. 926-6400; fax 968-7371; e-mail nhckingston@mail-infochan.com; High Commissioner FLORENTINA ADENIKE UKONGA.

Panama: 1 St Lucia Ave, Spanish Court, Office 26, Kingston 5; tel. 968-2928; fax 960-1618; Chargé d'affaires JOSÉ DE JESÚS MARTÍNEZ.

Russia: 22 Norbrook Dr., Kingston 8; tel. 924-1048; Ambassador NIKOLAI VLADIMIR.

Spain: 9th Floor, The Towers, Kingston 5; tel. 929-6710; e-mail jamesp@jamweb.net; Ambassador RAFAEL JOVER.

Trinidad and Tobago: First Life Bldg, 3rd Floor, 60 Knutsford Blvd, Kingston 5; tel. 926-5730; fax 926-5801; e-mail t&thckgn@infochan.com; High Commissioner DENNIS FRANCIS.

United Kingdom: 28 Trafalgar Rd, POB 575, Kingston 10; tel. 510 0700; fax 510 0737; e-mail bhckingston@cwjamaica.com; internet www.fco.gov.uk; High Commissioner PETER MATHERS.

USA: Mutual Life Centre, 2 Oxford Rd, Kingston 5; tel. 929-4850; Ambassador SUE MCCOURT COBB.

Venezuela: Petroleum Corpn of Jamaica Bldg, 3rd Floor, 36 Trafalgar Rd, Kingston 10; tel. 926-5510; fax 926-7442; Ambassador ROCIO MANIERO.

Judicial System

The Judicial System is based on English common law and practice. Final appeal is to the Judicial Committee of the Privy Council in the United Kingdom, although in 2001 the Jamaican Government signed an agreement to establish a Caribbean Court of Justice to fulfil this function.

Justice is administered by the Privy Council, Court of Appeal, Supreme Court (which includes the Revenue Court and the Gun Court), Resident Magistrates' Court (which includes the Traffic Court), two Family Courts and the Courts of Petty Sessions.

Judicial Service Commission: Office of the Services Commissions, 63–67 Knutsford Blvd, Kingston 5; advises the Governor-General on judicial appointments, etc. chaired by the Chief Justice.

Attorney-General: ARNOLD J. NICHOLSON.

SUPREME COURT
(Public Building E, 134 Tower St, POB 491, Kingston; tel. 922-8300; fax. 967-0669; e-mail webmaster@sc.gov.jm; internet www.sc.gov.jm)

Chief Justice: LENSLEY H. WOLFE.

Senior Puisne Judge: LLOYD B. ELLIS.

Master: CHRISTINE MCDONALD.

Registrar: AUDRE LINDO.

COURT OF APPEAL
(POB 629, Kingston; tel. 922-8300)

President: I.X. FORTE.

Registrar: G. P. LEVERS.

Religion

CHRISTIANITY
There are more than 100 Christian denominations active in Jamaica. According to the 1982 census, the largest religious bodies were the Church of God, Baptists, Anglicans and Seventh-day Adventists. Other denominations include the Methodist and Congregational Churches, the Ethiopian Orthodox Church, the Disciples of Christ, the Moravian Church, the Salvation Army and the Society of Friends (Quakers).

Jamaica Council of Churches: 14 South Ave, Kingston 10; tel. 926-0974; e-mail jchurch@yahoo.com; f. 1941; 10 member churches and three agencies; Pres. Rev. STANLEY CLARKE; Gen. Sec. NORMAN MILLS.

The Anglican Communion
Anglicans in Jamaica are adherents of the Church in the Province of the West Indies, comprising eight dioceses. The Archbishop of the Province is the Bishop of the North East Caribbean and Aruba. The Bishop of Jamaica, whose jurisdiction also includes Grand Cayman (in the Cayman Islands), is assisted by three suffragan Bishops (of Kingston, Mandeville and Montego Bay). The 1982 census recorded 154,548 Anglicans.

Bishop of Jamaica: Rt Rev. ALFRED C. REID, Church House, 2 Caledonia Ave, Kingston 5; tel. 952-4963; fax 952-2933.

The Roman Catholic Church
Jamaica comprises the archdiocese of Kingston in Jamaica (also including the Cayman Islands), and the dioceses of Montego Bay and Mandeville. At 31 December 2000 the estimated total of adherents in Jamaica and the Cayman Islands was 116,130, representing about 4.5% of the total population. The Archbishop and Bishops participate in the Antilles Episcopal Conference (currently based in Port of Spain, Trinidad and Tobago).

Archbishop of Kingston in Jamaica: Most Rev. EDGERTON ROLAND CLARKE, Archbishop's Residence, 21 Hopefield Ave, POB 43, Kingston 6; tel. 927-9915; fax 927-4487; e-mail rcabkgn@cwjamaica.com.

Other Christian Churches
Assembly of God: Evangel Temple, 3 Friendship Park Rd, Kingston 3; tel. 928-2728; Pastor WILSON.

Baptist Union: 6 Hope Rd, Kingston 10; tel. 926-7820; fax 968-7832; e-mail jbuaid@mail.infochan.com; internet www.jbu.org.jm; Pres. Rev. NEVILLE CALLAM; Gen. Sec. Rev. KARL JOHNSON.

Church of God in Jamaica: 35a Hope Rd, Kingston 10; tel. 927-8128; 400,379 adherents (1982 census).

First Church of Christ, Scientist: 17 National Heroes Circle, C.S.O., Kingston 4.

Methodist Church (Jamaica District): 143 Constant Spring Rd, POB 892, Kingston 8; tel. and fax 924-2560; e-mail jamaicamethodist@cwjamaica.com; f. 1789; 15,820 mems; Pres. Rev. PHILIP G.O'B. ROBINSON; Synod Sec. Rev. CATHERINE L. GALE.

Moravian Church in Jamaica: 3 Hector St, POB 8369, Kingston 5; tel. 928-1861; fax 928-8336; e-mail moravianchja@colis.com; internet www.jol.com.jm/moravian; f. 1754; 30,000 mems; Pres. Rev. STANLEY G. CLARKE.

Seventh-day Adventist Church: 56 James St, Kingston; tel. 922-7440; f. 1901; 150,722 adherents (1982 census); Pastor Rev. E.H. THOMAS.

United Church in Jamaica and the Cayman Islands: 12 Carlton Cres., POB 359, Kingston 10; tel. 926-8734; fax 929-0826; f. 1965 by merger of the Congregational Union of Jamaica (f. 1877); and the Presbyterian Church of Jamaica and Grand Cayman to become United Church of Jamaica and Grand Cayman; merged with Disciples of Christ in Jamaica in 1992 when name changed as above; 20,000 mems; Gen. Sec. Rev. MAITLAND EVANS.

RASTAFARIANISM
Rastafarianism is an important influence in Jamaican culture. The cult is derived from Christianity and a belief in the divinity of Ras (Prince) Tafari Makonnen (later Emperor Haile Selassie) of Ethiopia. It advocates racial equality and non-violence, but causes controversy in its use of 'ganja' (marijuana) as a sacrament. The 1982 census recorded 14,249 Rastafarians (0.7% of the total population). Although the religion is largely unorganized, there are some denominations.

Royal Ethiopian Judah Coptic Church: Kingston; not officially incorporated, on account of its alleged use of marijuana; Leader ABUNA S. WHYTE.

BAHÁ'Í FAITH

National Spiritual Assembly: 208 Mountain View Ave, Kingston 6; tel. 927-7051; fax 978-2344; incorporated in 1970; 6,300 mems resident in 368 localities.

ISLAM

At the 1982 census there were 2,238 Muslims.

JUDAISM

The 1991 census recorded 250 Jews.

United Congregation of Israelites: Kingston; tel. 927-7948; fax 978-6240; f. 1655; c. 250 mems; Spiritual Leader and Sec. ERNEST H. DE SOUZA; Pres. WALLACE R. CAMPBELL.

The Press

DAILIES

Daily Gleaner: 7 North St, POB 40, Kingston; tel. 922-3400; fax 922-2058; e-mail feedback@jamaica-gleaner.com; internet www .jamaica-gleaner.com; f. 1834; morning; independent; Chair. and Man. Dir OLIVER CLARKE; Editor-in-Chief WYVOLYN GAGER; circ. 50,000.

Daily Star: 7 North St, POB 40, Kingston; tel. 922-3400; fax 922-6223; e-mail feedback@jamaica-gleaner.com; internet www .jamaica-gleaner.com; f. 1951; evening; Editor-in-Chief WYVOLYN GAGER; Editor LEIGHTON LEVY; circ. 45,000.

Jamaica Herald: 86 Hagley Park Rd, Kingston 10; tel. 937-7304; Man. Editor FRANKLIN MCKNIGHT.

Jamaica Observer: 2 Fagan Ave, Kingston 8; tel. 931-5188; fax 931-5190; internet www.jamaicaobserver.com; f. 1993; Chair. GORDON 'BUTCH' STEWART; CEO Dr GEORGE T. PHILLIP.

PERIODICALS

Caribbean Challenge: 55 Church St, POB 186, Kingston; tel. 922-7878; fax 922-6969; f. 1957; monthly; religious; Editor JOHN KEANE; circ. 17,000.

Caribbean Shipping: Creative Communications Inc, Kingston; tel. 968-7279; fax 926-2217; 2 a year.

Catholic Opinion: St Michael's Theological Centre, Golding Ave, POB 198, Kingston 7; tel. 702-2337; fax 702-2199; e-mail rcabkgn@ cwjamaica.com; 6 a year; religious; Editor Rev. MICHAEL LEWIS.

Children's Own: 7 North St, POB 40, Kingston; tel. 922-3400; fax 922-6223; e-mail feedback@jamaica-gleaner.com; internet www .jamaica-gleaner.com; weekly during term time; Editor-in-Chief WYVOLYN GAGER; circ. 120,000.

Inquirer: 7–11 West St, Kingston; tel. 922-3952; weekly; current affairs.

Jamaica Churchman: 2 Caledonia Ave, Kingston 5; tel. 926-6608; quarterly; Editor BARBARA GLOUDON; circ. 7,000.

Jamaica Journal: 4 Camp Rd, Kingston 4; tel. 929-4048; fax 926-8817; f. 1967; 3 a year; literary, historical and cultural review; publ. by Instit. of Jamaica Publs Ltd; Man. Dir PATRICIA ROBERTS; Editor LEETA HEARNE.

The Siren: 1 River Bay Rd, PO Box 614, Montego Bay, St James; tel. 952-0997; f. 1990; weekly.

Sunday Gleaner: 7 North St, POB 40, Kingston; tel. 922-3400; fax 922-6223; e-mail feedback@jamaica-gleaner.com; internet www .jamaica-gleaner.com; weekly; Editor-in-Chief WYVOLYN GAGER; circ. 100,000.

Sunday Herald: 17 Morwood Ave, Kingston 10; tel. 906-7572; fax 908-4044; e-mail sunherald@cwjamaica.com; internet www .sunheraldjamaica.com; f. 1997; weekly; Exec. Editor R. CHRISTENE KING; circ. 20,000.

Sunday Observer: 2 Fagan Ave, Kingston 8; tel. 931-5188; fax 931-5190; internet www.jamaicaobserver.com; weekly; Chair. GORDON 'BUTCH' STEWART; CEO Dr GEORGE T. PHILLIP.

Swing: 102 East St, Kingston; f. 1968; monthly; entertainment and culture; Editor ANDELL FORGIE; circ. 12,000.

The Vacationer: POB 614, Montego Bay; tel. 952-6006; f. 1987; monthly; Man. Editor EVELYN L. ROBINSON; circ. 8,000.

The Visitor Vacation Guide: 82 Barnett St, POB 1258, Montego Bay; tel. 952-5253; fax 952-6513; weekly; Editor LLOYD B. SMITH.

Weekend Star: 7 North St, POB 40, Kingston; tel. 922-3400; fax 922-6223; e-mail feedback@jamaica-gleaner.com; internet www

.jamaica-gleaner.com; f. 1951; weekly; Editor-in-Chief WYVOLYN GAGER; Editor LOLITA TRACEY-LONG; circ. 80,000.

The Western Mirror: 82 Barnett St, POB 1258, Montego Bay; tel. 952-5253; fax 952-6513; e-mail westernmirror@mail.infochan.com; f. 1980; 2 a week; Man. Dir and Editor LLOYD B. SMITH; circ. 16,000.

West Indian Medical Journal: Faculty of Medical Sciences, University of the West Indies, Kingston 7; tel. 927-1214; fax 927-1846; e-mail wimj@uwimona.edu.jm; f. 1951; quarterly; Editor EVERARD N. BARTON; circ. 2,000.

PRESS ASSOCIATION

Press Association of Jamaica (PAJ): Kingston; tel. 926-7584; f. 1943; 240 mems; Pres. DESMOND ALLEN; Sec. MONICA DIAS.

Foreign Bureaux

Associated Press (USA), Caribbean Media Corpn and Inter Press Service (Italy) are represented in Jamaica.

Publishers

Jamaica Publishing House Ltd: 97 Church St, Kingston; tel. 967-3866; fax 922-5412; e-mail jph@jol.com.jm; f. 1969; wholly-owned subsidiary of Jamaica Teachers' Asscn; educational, English language and literature, mathematics, history, geography, social sciences, music; Chair. WOODBURN MILLER; Man. ELAINE R. STENNETT.

Kingston Publishers Ltd: 7 Norman Road, Suite 10, LOJ Industrial Complex, Kingston CSO; tel. 928-8898; fax 928-5719; f. 1970; educational textbooks, general, travel, atlases, fiction, non-fiction, children's books; Chair. L. MICHAEL HENRY.

Western Publishers Ltd: 82 Barnett St, POB 1258, Montego Bay; tel. 952-5253; fax 952-6513; e-mail westernmirror@mail.infochan .com; f. 1980; Man. Dir and Editor-in-Chief LLOYD B. SMITH.

Government Publishing House

Jamaica Printing Services: 77 Duke St, Kingston; tel. 967-2250; Chair. EVADNE STERLING; Man. RALPH BELL.

Broadcasting and Communications

TELECOMMUNICATIONS

The telecommunications sector was to become fully liberalized on 1 March 2003. The sector was regulated by the Office of Utilities Regulation (see Utilities).

Cable & Wireless Jamaica Ltd: 7 Cecilio Ave, Kingston 10; tel. 926-9450; fax 929-9530; f. 1989; in 1995 merged with Jamaica Telephone Co Ltd and Jamaica International Telecommunications Ltd, name changed as above 1995; 79% owned by Cable & Wireless; Pres. E. MILLER.

Cellular One Caribbean: Kingston; mobile cellular telephone operator; licence granted Dec. 1999.

Centennial Digital (Jamaica) Ltd: Kingston; f. 2001; mobile cellular telephone operator; Chief Operations Officer JIM BENEDA.

Digicel: Kingston; mobile cellular telephone operator; owned by Irish consortium, Mossel (Jamaica) Ltd; f. 2001; Chair. DENIS O'BRIEN.

Mossel (Jamaica) Ltd: Kingston; mobile cellular telephone operator consortium.

BROADCASTING

Television

CVM Television: 69 Constant Sprint Rd, Kingston 10; tel. 931-9400; fax 931-9417; e-mail apatterson@cvmtv.com; internet www .cvmtv.com.

Love Television: Kingston; f. 1997; religious programming; owned by religious Media Ltd.

Television Jamaica Limited (TVJ): 5–9 South Odeon Ave, POB 100, Kingston 10; tel. 926-5620; fax 929-1029; e-mail tvjadmin@ cwjamaica.com; internet www.radiojamaica.com; f. 1959 as Jamaica Broadcasting Corporation; privatized 1997, name changed as above; island-wide VHF transmission 24 hrs a day; Gen. Man. MARCIA FORBES.

Radio

Educational Broadcasting Service: Multi-Media Centre, 37 Arnold Road, Kingston 4; tel. 922-9370; f. 1964; radio broadcasts during school term; Pres. OUIDA HYLTON-TOMLINSON.

Independent Radio: 6 Bradley Ave, Kingston 10; tel. 968-4880; fax 968-9165; commercial radio station; broadcasts 24 hrs a day on FM; Gen. Man. NEWTON JAMES.

IRIE FM: Coconut Grove, POB 282, Ocho Rios, St Ann; tel. 974-5051; fax 968-8332; f. 1991; commercial radio station; plays only reggae music.

Island Broadcasting Services Ltd: 41b Half Way Tree Rd, Kingston 5; tel. 929-1344; fax 929-1345; commercial; broadcasts 24 hrs a day on FM; Exec. Chair. NEVILLE JAMES.

KLAS-FM 89: 81 Knutsford Blvd, Kingston 5; f. 1991; commercial radio station.

Love 101 FM: Kingston; f. 1997; commercial radio station, broadcasts religious programming on FM; owned by Religious Media Ltd.

Radio Jamaica Ltd (RJR): Broadcasting House, 32 Lyndhurst Rd, POB 23, Kingston 5; tel. 926-1100; fax 929-7467; e-mail rjr@ radiojamaica.com; internet www.radiojamaica.com; f. 1947; commercial, public service; three channels.

    FAME FM: broadcasts on FM, island-wide 24 hrs a day; Exec. Producer FRANCOIS ST. JUSTE.

    Radio 2 FM: broadcasts on FM, island-wide 24 hrs a day; Media Services Man. DONALD TOPPING.

    RJR Supreme '94: broadcasts on AM and FM, island-wide 24 hrs a day; Exec. Producer NORMA BROWN-BELL.

ZIP 103 FM: 1b Derrymore Rd, Kingston 10, Jamaica; tel. 929-6233; fax 960-0523; f. 2002; commercial radio station.

Other stations broadcasting include Hot 102 FM, Power 106 FM, Roots FM and TBC FM.

Finance

(cap. = capital; p.u. = paid up; res = reserves; dep. = deposits;
m. = million; brs = branches; amounts in Jamaican dollars)

BANKING

Central Bank

Bank of Jamaica: Nethersole Place, POB 621, Kingston; tel. 922-0752; fax 922-0854; e-mail info@boj.org.jm; internet www.boj.org.jm; f. 1960; cap. 4.0m., res 869.6m., dep. 47,044.2m. (Dec. 1999); Gov. DERICK MILTON LATIBEAUDIÈRE.

Commercial Banks

Bank of Nova Scotia Jamaica Ltd (Canada): Scotiabank Centre Bldg, cnr Duke and Port Royal Sts, POB 709, Kingston; tel. 922-1000; fax 924-9294; f. 1967; cap. 1,463.6m., res 5,850.9m., dep. 62,435.4m. (Dec. 2000); Chair. BRUCE R. BIRMINGHAM; Man. Dir WILLIAM E. CLARKE; 36 brs.

Citibank, NA (USA): 63–67 Knutsford Blvd, POB 286, Kingston 5; tel. 926-3270; fax 929-3745.

FirstCaribbean International Bank Ltd (Canada/United Kingdom): 23–27 Knutsford Blvd, POB 762, Kingston 5; tel. 929-9310; fax 929-7751; internet www.firstcaribbeanbank.com; 43.5% owned by Canadian Imperial Bank of Commerce and Barclays Bank PLC; cap. 96.7m., res 832.4m., dep. 14,665.0m. (Oct. 2001); Chair. MICHAEL MANSOOR; CEO CHARLES PINK; 12 brs.

National Commercial Bank Jamaica Ltd: 'The Atrium', 32 Trafalgar Rd, POB 88, Kingston 10; tel. 929-9050; fax 929-8399; internet www.jncb.com; f. 1977; merged with Mutual Security Bank in 1996; cap. 5,701.0m., res 2,122.2m., dep. 58,579.0m. (Sept. 2000); Chair. Hon. OLIVER F. CLARKE; Man. Dir CHRISTOPHER J. LOWE; 33 brs.

Union Bank of Jamaica Ltd: 17 Dominica Dr., Kingston 5; tel. 960-1350; fax 960-2332; f. 2000; by merger of Citizens Bank Ltd, Eagle Commercial Bank Ltd, Island Victoria Bank Ltd, and Workers' Savings and Loan Bank; bought by the Royal Bank of Trinidad and Tobago in 2001; Chair. Dr OWEN JEFFERSON; Man. Dir MICHAEL E. A. WRIGHT; 6 brs.

Development Banks

Development Bank of Jamaica Ltd: 11a–15 Oxford Rd, POB 466, Kingston 5; tel. 929-4010; fax 929-6055; e-mail dbank@cwjamaica .com; replaced Jamaica Development Bank; f. 1969; provides funds for medium- and long-term devt-orientated projects in the agricultural, tourism, industrial, manufacturing and services sectors

through financial intermediaries; Chair. RITA HUMPHRIES-LEWIN; Man. Dir KINGSLEY THOMAS.

Jamaica Mortgage Bank: 33 Tobago Ave, POB 950, Kingston 5; tel. 929-6350; fax 968-5428; f. 1971 by the Jamaican Govt and the US Agency for Int. Devt; govt-owned statutory org. since 1973; intended to function primarily as a secondary market facility for home mortgages and to mobilize long-term funds for housing devts in Jamaica; also insures home mortgage loans made by approved financial institutions, thus transferring risk of default on a loan to the Govt; Chair. PETER THOMAS; Man. Dir EVERTON HANSON.

Trafalgar Development Bank: The Towers, 3rd Floor, 25 Dominica Dr., Kingston 5; tel. 929-4760; e-mail tdbhrgen@cwjamaica .com.

Other Banks

National Export-Import Bank of Jamaica Ltd: 48 Duke St, POB 3, Kingston; tel. 922-9690; fax 922-9184; e-mail eximjam@cwjamaica .com; internet www.eximbankja.com; replaced Jamaica Export Credit Insurance Corpn; finances import and export of goods and services; Chair. Dr OWEN JEFFERSON; Deputy Chair. PAUL THOMAS.

National Investment Bank of Jamaica Ltd: 11 Oxford Rd, POB 889, Kingston 5; tel. 960-9691; fax 920-0379; e-mail nibj@infochan .com; Chair. DAVID COORE; Pres. Dr GAVIN CHEN.

Banking Association

Jamaica Bankers' Association: POB 1079, Kingston; tel. 929-9050; fax 929-8399; Pres. PETER MOSES.

Financial Sector Adjustment Company

FINSAC Ltd: 76 Knutsford Blvd, POB 54, Kingston 5; tel. 906-1809; fax 906-1822; e-mail info@finsac.com; internet www.finsac.com; f. 1997; state-owned; intervenes in the banking and insurance sectors to restore stability in the financial sector.

STOCK EXCHANGE

Jamaica Stock Exchange Ltd: 40 Harbour St, Kingston; tel. 967-3271; fax 922-6966; internet www.jamstockex.com; f. 1968; 42 listed cos (2002); Chair. ROY JOHNSON; Deputy Chair. AUDREY RICHARDS; Gen. Man. C. WAIN ITON.

INSURANCE

Office of the Superintendent of Insurance: 51 St Lucia Ave, POB 800, Kingston 5; tel. 926-1790; fax 968-4346; f. 1972; regulatory body; Superintendent ERROL MCLEAN (acting).

Jamaica Association of General Insurance Companies: 3-3A Richmond Ave, Kingston 10; tel. 929-8404; e-mail jagic@cwjamaica .com; internet www.jagonline.com; Man. GLORIA M. GRANT; Chair. LESLIE CHUNG.

Principal Companies

British Caribbean Insurance Co Ltd: 36 Duke St, POB 170, Kingston; tel. 922-1260; fax 922-4475; internet www.bcicdirect.com; f. 1962; general insurance; Gen. Man. LESLIE W. CHUNG.

First Life Insurance Group: 60 Knutsford Blvd, Kingston 5; tel. 926-3700; fax 929-8523; e-mail info@firstlife.com.jm; internet www .firstlife.com.jm; division of the Pan-Jamaican Investment Trust Group; all branches.

General Accident Insurance Co Jamaica Ltd: 58 Half Way Tree Rd, Kingston 10; tel. 929-8451; fax 929-1074; e-mail genac@ cwjamaica.com; internet www.genac.com; f. 1981; Gen. Man. SHARON E. DONALDSON.

Globe Insurance Co of the West Indies Ltd: 19 Dominica Dr., POB 401, Kingston 5; tel. 926-3720; fax 929-2727; e-mail admin@ globeins.com; internet www.globeins.com; Man. Dir R. E. D. THWAITES.

Guardian Holdings: Kingston; internet www.guardianholdings .com; pension and life policies.

Insurance Co of the West Indies Ltd (ICWI): 2 St Lucia Ave, POB 306, Kingston 5; tel. 926-9182; fax 929-6641; Chair. DENNIS LALOR; CEO KENNETH BLAKELEY.

Island Life Insurance Co: 6 St Lucia Ave, Kingston 5; tel. 968-6874; e-mail ceo@islandlife-ja-com.jm; 64% owned by Barbados Mutual Life Assurance Co; 26% owned by FINSAC with Life of Jamaica Ltd in 2001.

Jamaica General Insurance Co Ltd: 9 Duke St, POB 408, Kingston; tel. 922-6420; fax 922-2073; Man. Dir A. C. LEVY.

Life of Jamaica Ltd: 28–48 Barbados Ave, Kingston 5; tel. 929-8920; fax 929-4730; f. 1970; life and health insurance, pensions; 76%

owned by Barbados Mutual Life Assurance Co merged with Island Life Insurance Co in 2001; Pres. R. D. WILLIAMS.

NEM Insurance Co (Jamaica) Ltd: NEM House, 9 King St, Kingston; tel. 922-1460; fax 922-4045; fmrly the National Employers' Mutual General Insurance Asscn; Gen. Man. NEVILLE HENRY.

Trade and Industry

GOVERNMENT AGENCIES

Jamaica Commodity Trading Co Ltd: Kingston; f. 1981 as successor to State Trading Corpn; oversees all importing on behalf of state; Chair. DAVID GAYNAIR; Man. Dir ANDREE NEMBHARD.

Jamaica Information Service (JIS): 58a Half Way Tree Rd, POB 2222, Kingston 10; tel. 926-3741; fax 920-7427; e-mail jis@jis.gov.jm; internet www.jis.gov.jm; f. 1963; information agency for govt policies and programmes, ministries and public sector agencies; CEO CARMEN E. TIPLING.

DEVELOPMENT ORGANIZATIONS

Agricultural Development Corpn (ADC) Group of Companies: Mais House, Hope Rd, POB 552, Kingston; tel. 977-4412; fax 977-4411; f. 1989; manages and develops breeds of cattle, provides warehousing, cold storage, offices and information for exporters and distributors of non-traditional crops and ensures the proper utilization of agricultural lands under its control; Chair. Dr ASTON WOOD; Gen. Man. DUDLEY IRVING.

Coffee Industry Development Co: Marcus Garvey Dr., Kingston 15; tel. 923-5645; fax 923-7587; e-mail cofeboard-jam@cwjamaica .com; f. 1981 to implement coffee devt and rehabilitation programmes financed by international aid agencies; Sec. JOYCE CHANG.

Jamaica Promotions Corpn (JAMPRO): 35 Trafalgar Rd, Kingston 10; tel. 929-7190; fax 960-8082; e-mail jampro@investjamaica .com; f. 1988; by merger of Jamaica Industrial Development Corpn, Jamaica National Export Corpn and Jamaica Investment Promotion Ltd; trade and investment promotion agency; Pres. PATRICIA FRANCIS; Chair. JOSEPH A. MATALON.

National Development Agency Ltd: Kingston; tel. 922-5445.

Planning Institute of Jamaica: 8 Ocean Blvd, Kingston Mall; tel. 967-3690; fax 967-3688; e-mail doccen@mail.colis.com; f. 1955 as the Central Planning Unit; adopted current name in 1984; monitoring performance of the economy and the social sector; publishing of devt plans and social surveys; Dir-Gen. WESLEY HUGHES.

Urban Development Corpn: The Office Centre, 8th Floor, 12 Ocean Blvd, Kingston; tel. 922-8310; fax 922-9326; f. 1968; responsibility for urban renewal and devt within designated areas; Chair. Dr VINCENT LAWRENCE; Gen. Man. IVAN ANDERSON.

CHAMBERS OF COMMERCE

Associated Chambers of Commerce of Jamaica: 7–8 East Parade, POB 172, Kingston; tel. 922-0150; f. 1974; 12 associated Chambers of Commerce; Pres. RAY CAMPBELL.

Jamaica Chamber of Commerce: 7–8 East Parade, POB 172, Kingston; tel. 922-0150; fax 924-9056; e-mail jamcham@cwjamaica .com; internet www.jcc.org.jm; f. 1779; 450 mems.

INDUSTRIAL AND TRADE ASSOCIATIONS

Cocoa Industry Board: Marcus Garvey Dr., POB 1039, Kingston 15; tel. 923-6411; fax 923-5837; e-mail cocoajam@cwjamaica.com; f. 1957; has statutory powers to regulate and develop the industry; owns and operates four central fermentaries; Chair. JOSEPH SUAH; Man. and Sec. NABURN NELSON.

Coconut Industry Board: 18 Waterloo Rd, Half Way Tree, Kingston 10; tel. 926-1770; fax 968-1360; f. 1945; 9 mems; Chair. R. A. JONES; Gen. Man. JAMES S. JOYLES.

Coffee Industry Board: Marcus Garvey Dr., POB 508, Kingston 15; tel. 923-5850; fax 923-7587; e-mail cibcommercial@cwjamaica .com; internet www.jamaicancoffee.gov.jm; f. 1950; 9 mems; has wide statutory powers to regulate and develop the industry; Chair. RICHARD DOWNER; CEO GONZALO HERNÁNDEZ.

Jamaica Bauxite Institute: Hope Gardens, POB 355, Kingston 6; tel. 927-2073; fax 927-1159; f. 1975; adviser to the Govt in the negotiation of agreements, consultancy services to clients in the bauxite/alumina and related industries, laboratory services for mineral and soil-related services, Pilot Plant services for materials and equipment testing, research and development; Chair. CARLTON DAVIS.

Jamaica Export Trading Co Ltd: 6 Waterloo Rd, POB 645, Kingston 10; tel. 929-4390; fax 926-1608; e-mail jetcoja@infochan.com; f.

1977; export trading in non-traditional products, incl. spices, fresh produce, furniture, garments, processed foods, minerals, etc. Chair. JOSEPH A. MATALON; Man. Dir HERNAL HAMILTON.

Sugar Industry Authority: 5 Trevennion Park Rd, POB 127, Kingston 5; tel. 926-5930; fax 926-6149; e-mail sia@cwjamaica.com; f. 1970; statutory body under portfolio of Ministry of Agriculture; responsible for regulation and control of sugar industry and sugar marketing; conducts research through Sugar Industry Research Institute; Exec. Chair. DERICK HEAVEN.

Trade Board: 107 Constant Spring Rd, Kingston 10; tel. 969-0478; Admin. JEAN MORGAN.

EMPLOYERS' ORGANIZATIONS

All-Island Banana Growers' Association Ltd: Banana Industry Bldg, 10 South Ave, Kingston 4; tel. 922-5492; fax 922-5497; f. 1946; 1,500 mems (1997); Chair. BOBBY POTTINGER; Sec. I. CHANG.

All-Island Jamaica Cane Farmers' Association: 4 North Ave, Kingston Gardens, Kingston 4; tel. 922-3010; fax 922-2077; e-mail allcane@cwjamaica.com; f. 1941; registered cane farmers; 27,000 mems; Chair. ABIJAH B. BUCHANAN; Man. ADITER MILLER.

Banana Export Co (BECO): 1a Braemar Ave, Kingston 10; tel. 927-3402; fax 978-6096; f. 1985 to replace Banana Co of Jamaica; oversees the devt of the banana industry; Chair. Dr MARSHALL HALL.

Citrus Growers' Association Ltd: Kingston; f. 1944; 13,000 mems; Chair. IVAN H. TOMLINSON.

Jamaica Association of Sugar Technologists: c/o Sugar Industry Research Institute, Kendal Rd, Mandeville; tel. 962-2241; fax 962-1288; e-mail maureenwil@hotmail.com; f. 1936; 275 mems; Pres. GILBERT THORNE; Sec. Dr MAUREEN R. WILSON.

Jamaica Exporters' Association (JEA): 13 Dominica Dr., POB 9, Kingston 5; tel. 960-1675; fax 960-1465; e-mail sbed@cwjamaica .com; internet www.exportjamaica.org; Pres. KARL JAMES; Exec. Dir PAULINE GRAY.

Jamaica Livestock Association: Newport East, POB 36, Kingston; tel. 922-7130; fax 923-5046; e-mail jlapurch@cwjamaica.com; internet www.jlatd.com; f. 1941; 7,584 mems; Chair. Dr JOHN MASTERTON; Man. Dir and CEO HENRY J. RAINFORD.

Jamaica Manufacturers' Association Ltd: 85a Duke St, Kingston; tel. 922-9205; e-mail jma@toj.com; internet www .jma.com.jm; f. 1947; 400 mems; Pres. CLARENCE CLARK.

Jamaica Producers' Group Ltd: 6a Oxford Rd, POB 237, Kingston 5; tel. 926-3503; fax 929-3636; e-mail cosecretary@jpjamaica .com; f. 1929; fmrly Jamaica Banana Producers' Asscn; Chair. C. H. JOHNSTON; Man. Dir Dr MARSHALL HALL.

Private Sector Organization of Jamaica (PSOJ): 39 Hope Rd, POB 236, Kingston 10; tel. 927-6238; fax 927-5137; federative body of private business individuals, cos and asscns; Pres. Hon. OLIVER F. CLARK; Exec. Dir GRETA BOGUES.

Small Businesses' Association of Jamaica (SBAJ): 2 Trafalgar Rd, Kingston 5; tel. 927-7071; fax 978-2738; Pres. ALBERT GRAY; Exec. Dir ESME L. BAILEY.

Sugar Manufacturing Corpn of Jamaica Ltd: 5 Trevennion Park Rd, Kingston 5; tel. 926-5930; fax 926-6149; established to represent the sugar manufacturers in Jamaica; deals with all aspects of the sugar industry and its by-products; provides liaison between the Govt, the Sugar Industry Authority and the All-Island Jamaica Cane Farmers' Assoc; 9 mems; Chair. CHRISTOPHER BOVELL; Gen. Man. DERYCK T. BROWN.

UTILITIES

Regulatory Authority

Office of Utilities Regulation (OUR): PCJ Resource Centre, 3rd Floor, 36 Trafalgar Rd, Kingston 10; tel. 929-6672; fax 929-3635; e-mail office@our.org.jm; internet www.our.org.jm; f. 1995; regulates provision of services in the following sectors: water, electricity, telecommunications, public passenger transportation, sewerage; Dir-Gen. WINSTON HAY.

Electricity

Jamaica Public Service Co (JPSCo): Dominion Life Bldg, 6 Knutsford Blvd, POB 54, Kingston 5; tel. 926-3190; fax 968-5341; e-mail media@jpsco.com; internet www.jpsco.com; responsible for the generation and supply of electricity to the island; 80% sold to Mirant Corpn (USA) in March 2001; Chair. J. R. HARRIS; Pres. and CEO CHARLES MATTHEWS.

Water

National Water Commission: 4a Marescaux Rd, Kingston 5; tel. 929-3540; internet www.nwcjamaica.com; f. 1980; statutory body;

provides potable water and waste water services; Chair. PETER BUNTING.

Water Resources Authority: Hope Gardens, POB 91, Kingston 7; tel. 927-0077; fax 977-0179; e-mail wra@colis.com; internet www .wra-ja.org; f. 1996; manages, protects and controls allocation and use of water supplies; Man. Dir BASIL FERNANDEZ.

TRADE UNIONS

Bustamante Industrial Trade Union (BITU): 98 Duke St, Kingston; tel. 922-2443; fax 967-0120; f. 1938; HUGH SHEARER; Gen. Sec. GEORGE FYFFE; 60,000 mems.

National Workers' Union of Jamaica (NWU): 130–132 East St, POB 344, Kingston 16; tel. 922-1150; e-mail nwyou@cwjamaica.com; f. 1952; affiliated to the International Confederation of Free Trade Unions, etc. Pres. CLIVE DOBSON; Gen. Sec. LLOYD GOODLEIGH; 10,000 mems.

Trades Union Congress of Jamaica: 25 Sutton St, POB 19, Kingston; tel. 922-5313; fax 922-5468; affiliated to the Caribbean Congress of Labour and the International Confederation of Free Trade Unions; Pres. E. SMITH; Gen. Sec. HOPETON CRAVEN; 20,000 mems.

Principal Independent Unions

Caribbean Union of Teachers: 97 Church St, Kingston; tel. 922-1385; fax 922-3257; e-mail jta@cwjamaica.com; Pres. COLIN GREENE; Gen. Sec. ADOLPH CAMERON.

Industrial Trade Union Action Council: 2 Wildman St, Kingston; Pres. RODERICK FRANCIS; Gen. Sec. KEITH COMRIE.

Jamaica Federation of Musicians' and Artistes' Unions: POB 1125, Montego Bay 1; tel. 952-3238; f. 1958; Pres. HEDLEY H. G. JONES; Sec. CARL AYTON; 2,000 mems.

Jamaica Local Government Officers' Union: c/o Public Service Commission, Knutsford Blvd, Kingston 5; Pres. E. LLOYD TAYLOR.

Jamaica Teachers' Association: 97 Church St, Kingston; tel. 922-1385; fax 922-3257; e-mail jta@cwjamaica.com; Pres. PAUL ADAMS.

Jamaica Union of Public Officers and Public Employees: 4 Northend Place, Kingston 10; tel. 929-1354; Pres. FITZROY BRYAN; Gen. Sec. NICKELLOH MARTIN.

Jamaica Workers' Union: 3 West Ave, Kingston 4; tel. 922-3222; fax 967-3128; Pres. CLIFTON BROWN; Gen. Sec. MICHAEL NEWTON.

Union of Schools, Agricultural and Allied Workers (USAAW): 2 Wildman St, Kingston; tel. 967-2970; f. 1978; Pres. DWAYNE BARNETT.

Union of Technical, Administrative and Supervisory Personnel: 108 Church St, Kingston; tel. 922-2086; Pres. ANTHONY DAWKINS; Gen. Sec. REG ENNIS.

United Portworkers' and Seamen's Union: Kingston.

United Union of Jamaica: 35a Lynhurst Rd, Kingston; tel. 960-4206; Pres. JAMES FRANCIS; Gen. Sec. WILLIAM HASFAL.

University and Allied Workers' Union (UAWU): 50 Lady Musgrave Rd, Kingston; tel. 927-7968; fax 927 9931; e-mail jacisera@cwjamaica.com; affiliated to the (WPJ); Pres. Prof. TREVOR MUNROE. There are also some 30 associations registered as trade unions.

Transport

RAILWAYS

There are about 339 km (211 miles) of railway, all standard gauge, in Jamaica. Most of the system is operated by the Jamaica Railway Corpn, which is subsidized by the Government. The main lines are from Kingston to Montego Bay, and Spanish Town to Ewarton and Port Antonio. Passenger services were suspended in 1992; operations were scheduled to resume in 2003. There are four railways for the transport of bauxite.

Jamaica Railway Corpn (JRC): 142 Barry St, POB 489, Kingston; tel. 922-6620; fax 922-4539; f. 1845 as Jamaica Railway Co, the earliest British colonial railway; transferred to JRC in 1960; govt-owned, but autonomous, statutory corpn until 1990, when it was partly leased to Alcan Jamaica Co Ltd (subsequently West Indies Alumina Co) as the first stage of a privatization scheme; 207 km of railway; Chair. W. TAYLOR; Gen. Man. OWEN CROOKS.

Alcoa Railroads: Alcoa Minerals of Jamaica Inc, May Pen PO; tel. 986-2561; fax 986-2026; 43 km of standard-gauge railway; transport of bauxite; Supt RICHARD HECTOR; Man. FITZ CARTY (Railroad Operations and Maintenance).

Kaiser Jamaica Bauxite Co Railway: Discovery Bay PO, St Ann; tel. 973-2221; 25 km of standard-gauge railway; transport of bauxite; Gen. Man. TIM DAMON.

ROADS

Jamaica has a good network of tar-surfaced and metalled motoring roads. According to estimates by the International Road Federation, there were an estimated 18,700 km of roads in 1999, of which 70.1% were paved. In 2001 a consortium of two British companies, Kier International and Mabey & Johnson, was awarded a contract to supply the materials for and construct six road bridges in Kingston and Montego Bay, and a further 20 bridges in rural areas. In the same year the Inter-American Development Bank approved a US $24.5m. loan to improve road maintenance. In March 2002 construction of the first part of a 230 km highway system linking major cities was scheduled to begin.

SHIPPING

The principal ports are Kingston, Montego Bay and Port Antonio. The port at Kingston has four container berths, and is a major transhipment terminal for the Caribbean area. Jamaica has interests in the multinational shipping line WISCO (West Indies Shipping Corpn—based in Trinidad and Tobago). Services are also provided by most major foreign lines serving the region. In September 2001 a US $100m. plan to expand Kingston's container terminal was announced.

Port Authority of Jamaica: 15–17 Duke St, Kingston; tel. 922-0290; fax 924-9437; e-mail pajmktg@infochan.com; internet www .seaportsofjamaica.com; f. 1966; Govt's principal maritime agency; responsible for monitoring and regulating the navigation of all vessels berthing at Jamaican ports, for regulating the tariffs on public wharves, and for the devt of industrial Free Zones in Jamaica; Pres. and Chair. NOEL HYLTON.

Kingston Free Zone Co Ltd: 27 Shannon Dr., POB 1025, Kingston 15; tel. 923-5274; fax 923-6023; f. 1976; subsidiary of Port Authority of Jamaica; management and promotion of an export-orientated industrial free trade zone for cos from various countries; Gen. Man. OWEN HIGGINS.

Montego Bay Export Free Zone: c/o Port Authority of Jamaica, 15–17 Duke St, Kingston; tel. 922-0290.

Shipping Association of Jamaica: 4 Fourth Ave, Newport West, POB 1050, Kingston 15; tel. 923-3491; fax 923-3421; e-mail jfs@jashipco.com; internet www.seaportsofjamaica.com; f. 1939; 63 mems; an employers' trade union which regulates the supply and management of stevedoring labour in Kingston; represents members in negotiations with govt and trade bodies; Pres. GRANTLEY STEPHENSON; Gen. Man. MARJORY KENNEDY.

Principal Shipping Companies

Jamaica Freight and Shipping Co Ltd (JFS): 80–82 Second St, Port Bustamante, POB 167, Kingston 13; tel. 923-9371; fax 923-4091; e-mail cshaw@toj.com; cargo services to and from the USA, Caribbean, Central and South America, the United Kingdom, Japan and Canada; Exec. Chair. CHARLES JOHNSTON; Man. Dir GRANTLEY STEPHENSON.

Portcold Ltd: 122 Third St, Newport West, Kingston 13; tel. 923-7425; fax 923-5713; Chair. and Man. Dir ISHMAEL E. ROBERTSON.

CIVIL AVIATION

There are two international airports linking Jamaica with North America, Europe, and other Caribbean islands. The Norman Manley International Airport is situated 22.5 km (14 miles) outside Kingston. The Donald Sangster International Airport is 5 km (3 miles) from Montego Bay. A J $800m. programme to expand and improve the latter was under consideration.

Airports Authority of Jamaica: Victoria Mutual Bldg, 53 Knutsford Blvd, POB 567, Kingston 5; tel. 926-1622; fax 929-8171; e-mail aaj@cwjamaica.com; internet www.aaj.com.jm. Chair. DENNIS MORRISON; Pres. EARL RICHARDS.

Civil Aviation Authority: 4 Winchester Rd, Kingston 10; tel. 960-3948; fax 920-0194; e-mail jcivav@cwjamaica.com; internet www .jcaa.gov.jm.

Air Jamaica Ltd: 72–76 Harbour St, Kingston; tel. 922-3460; fax 922-0107; internet www.airjamaica.com; f. 1968; privatized in 1994, 45% reacquired by the Govt in 2001; services within the Caribbean and to Canada (in asscn with Air Canada), the USA and the United Kingdom; Chair. GORDON 'BUTCH' STEWART; CEO CHRISTOPHER ZACCA.

Air Jamaica Express: Tinson Pen Aerodrome, Kingston 11; tel. 923-6664; fax 937-3807; internet www.airjamaica.com/express; previously known as Trans-Jamaican Airlines; internal services between Kingston, Montego Bay, Negril, Ocho Rios and Port Antonio and services to the Cayman Islands, the Bahamas, the

Dominican Republic and Cuba; Chair. GORDON 'BUTCH' STEWART; Man. Dir PAULO MOREIRA.

Air Negril: Post Office 1, POB 477, Montego Bay; tel. 940-7741; fax 940-6491; e-mail airnegril@mail.com; internet www.airnegril.com; domestic charter services.

Tourism

Tourists, mainly from the USA, visit Jamaica for its beaches, mountains, historic buildings and cultural heritage. In 2000 there were an estimated 1,322,690 visitors (excluding cruise-ship passengers). Tourist receipts were estimated to be US $1,395m. in 2000/01. In 2001 there were some 24,007 rooms in all forms of tourist accommodation.

Jamaica Tourist Board (JTB): ICWI Bldg, 2 St Lucia Ave, Kingston 5; tel. 929-9200; fax 929-9375; internet www.jamaicatravel.com; f. 1955; a statutory body set up by the Govt to develop all aspects of the tourist industry through marketing, promotional and advertising efforts; Chair. ADRIAN ROBINSON; Dir of Tourism FAY PICKERSGILL.

Jamaica Hotel and Tourist Association (JHTA): 2 Ardenne Rd, Kingston 10; tel. 926-2796; fax 929-1054; e-mail info@jhta.org; internet www.jobsnmore.com; f. 1961; trade asscn for hoteliers and other cos involved in Jamaican tourism; Pres. JOSEF FORSTMAYR; Exec. Dir CAMILLE NEEDHAM.

JAPAN

Introductory Survey

Location, Climate, Language, Religion, Flag, Capital

Japan lies in eastern Asia and comprises a curved chain of more than 3,000 islands. Four large islands, named (from north to south) Hokkaido, Honshu, Shikoku and Kyushu, account for about 98% of the land area. Hokkaido lies just to the south of Sakhalin, a large Russian island, and about 1,300 km (800 miles) east of Russia's mainland port of Vladivostok. Southern Japan is about 150 km (93 miles) east of the Republic of Korea. Although summers are temperate everywhere, the climate in winter varies sharply from cold in the north to mild in the south. Temperatures in Tokyo range from –6°C (21°F) to 30°C (86°F). Typhoons and heavy rains are common in summer. The language is Japanese. The major religions are Shintoism and Buddhism, and there is a Christian minority. The national flag (proportions 7 by 10) is white, with a red disc (a sun without rays) in the centre. The capital is Tokyo.

Recent History

Following Japan's defeat in the Second World War, Japanese forces surrendered in August 1945. Japan signed an armistice in September, and the country was placed under US military occupation. A new democratic constitution, which took effect from May 1947, renounced war and abandoned the doctrine of the Emperor's divinity. Following the peace treaty of September 1951, Japan regained its independence on 28 April 1952, although it was not until 1972 that the last of the US-administered outer islands were returned to Japanese sovereignty.

In November 1955 rival conservative groups merged to form the Liberal-Democratic Party (LDP). Nobusuke Kishi, who became Prime Minister in February 1957, was succeeded by Hayato Ikeda in July 1960. Ikeda was replaced by Eisaku Sato in November 1964. Sato remained in office until July 1972, when he was succeeded by Kakuei Tanaka.

Tanaka's premiership was beset by problems, leading to his replacement by Takeo Miki in December 1974. Tanaka was subsequently accused of accepting bribes from the Marubeni Corporation, and he was arrested in July 1976. The LDP lost its overall majority in the House of Representatives (the lower house of the Diet) at a general election held in December 1976. Miki resigned and was succeeded by Takeo Fukuda. However, Masayoshi Ohira defeated Fukuda in the LDP presidential election of November 1978, and replaced him as Prime Minister in December. Ohira was unable to win a majority in the lower house at elections in October 1979. In May 1980 the Government was defeated in a motion of 'no confidence', forcing the dissolution of the lower house. Ohira died before the elections in June, when the LDP won 284 of the 511 seats, despite obtaining only a minority of the votes cast. In July Zenko Suzuki, a relatively little-known compromise candidate, was elected President of the LDP, and subsequently appointed Prime Minister. In November 1981 Suzuki reorganized the Cabinet, distributing major posts among the five feuding LDP factions. The growing factionalism of the LDP and the worsening economic crisis prompted Suzuki's resignation as Prime Minister and LDP President in October 1982. He was succeeded by Yasuhiro Nakasone.

At elections in June 1983 for one-half of the seats in the House of Councillors (the upper house of the Diet), a new electoral system was used. Of the 126 contested seats, 50 were filled on the basis of proportional representation. As a result, two small parties entered the House of Councillors for the first time. The LDP increased its strength from 134 to 137 members in the 252-seat chamber. This result was seen as an endorsement of Nakasone's policies of increased expenditure on defence, closer ties with the USA and greater Japanese involvement in international affairs.

In October 1983 the former Prime Minister, Kakuei Tanaka, was found guilty of accepting bribes. However, Tanaka refused to relinquish his legislative seat (he had already resigned from the LDP). The opposition parties therefore led a boycott of the Diet, forcing Nakasone to call a premature general election in December 1983. The Komeito (Clean Government Party), the Democratic Socialist Party (DSP) and the Japan Socialist Party (JSP) gained seats, at the expense of the Communists and the New Liberal Club (NLC). The LDP, which had performed badly in the election, formed a coalition with the NLC (which had split from the LDP over the Tanaka affair in 1976) and several independents. Nakasone remained President of the LDP, after promising to reduce Tanaka's influence. Following the trial of Tanaka, reforms were introduced, whereby cabinet members were required to disclose the extent of their personal assets.

Nakasone called another premature general election for July 1986, which coincided with elections for one-half of the seats in the House of Councillors. In the election to the House of Representatives, the LDP obtained its highest level of electoral support since 1963, and won a record 304 of the 512 seats. The increased LDP majority was achieved largely at the expense of the JSP and the DSP, thus enabling the LDP to dispense with its coalition partner, the NLC (which disbanded in August and rejoined the LDP). In September the leaders of the LDP agreed to alter by-laws to allow party presidents one-year extensions beyond the normal limit of two terms of two years each. Nakasone was thus able to retain the posts of President of the LDP and Prime Minister until October 1987.

In July 1987 the Secretary-General of the LDP, Noboru Takeshita, left the Tanaka faction, with 113 other members, and announced the formation of a major new grouping within the ruling party. In the same month Tanaka's political influence was further weakened when the Tokyo High Court upheld the decision, taken in 1983, declaring him guilty of accepting bribes. (In February 1995 this ruling was upheld by the Supreme Court.)

In October 1987 Nakasone nominated Takeshita as his successor. The Diet was convened and Takeshita was formally elected as Prime Minister in November. In the new Cabinet, Takeshita maintained a balance among the five major factions of the LDP, retaining only two members of Nakasone's previous Cabinet, but appointing four members of the Nakasone faction to senior ministerial posts (including Nakasone's staunch ally, Sosuke Uno, as Minister of Foreign Affairs).

The implementation of a programme of tax reforms was one of the most important issues confronting Takeshita's Government. In June 1988 the proposed introduction of a new indirect tax (a general consumption tax, or a form of value-added tax) aroused widespread opposition. In the same month the Prime Minister and the LDP suffered a serious set-back when several leading figures in the party, including Nakasone, Shintaro Abe, Kiichi Miyazawa and Takeshita himself, were alleged to have been indirectly involved in share-trading irregularities with the Recruit Cosmos Company. In November, shortly after the LDP had agreed to establish a committee to investigate the Recruit scandal, the House of Representatives approved proposals for tax reform (which constituted the most wide-ranging revision of the tax system for 40 years). Three cabinet ministers and the Chairman of the DSP were subsequently forced to resign, owing to their alleged involvement in the Recruit affair.

In January 1989 Emperor Hirohito, who had reigned since 1926, died after a long illness, thus ending the Showa era. He was succeeded by his son, Akihito, and the new era was named Heisei ('achievement of universal peace').

In April 1989, as the allegations against politicians widened to include charges of bribery and malpractice, Takeshita announced his resignation. He was subsequently found to have accepted donations worth more than 150m. yen from the Recruit organization. Takeshita nominated Sosuke Uno as his successor. Uno was elected Prime Minister by the Diet on 2 June; a new Cabinet was appointed on the same day. Uno thus became the first Japanese Prime Minister since the foundation of the LDP not to command his own political faction. In May, following an eight-month investigation undertaken by the LDP's special committee, public prosecutors indicted 13 people. Nakasone resigned from his faction and from the LDP, assuming responsibility for the Recruit affair, but did not relinquish his seat in the Diet.

Within a few days of Uno's assumption of office, a Japanese magazine published allegations of sexual impropriety involving the Prime Minister, which precipitated demands for his resignation. Serious losses suffered by the LDP in Tokyo's municipal elections in July 1989 further discredited Uno. As a result of a considerable increase in support for the JSP, led by Takako Doi, the LDP lost its majority in the upper house for the first time in its history. Uno's offer to resign was accepted by the LDP, which in August chose the relatively unknown Toshiki Kaifu, a former Minister of Education, to replace Uno as the party's President and as the new Prime Minister. Although the House of Councillors' ballot rejected Kaifu as the new Prime Minister in favour of Takako Doi, the decision of the lower house was adopted, in accordance with stipulations embodied in the Constitution. This was the first time in 41 years that the two houses of the Diet had disagreed over the choice of Prime Minister. In October Kaifu was re-elected as President of the LDP for a further two-year term.

At a general election held in February 1990, the LDP was returned to power with an unexpectedly large measure of support, securing 275 of the 512 seats in the lower house. In December Toshiyuki Inamura, a former cabinet minister, resigned from the LDP after charges of large-scale tax evasion and complicity in a new stock-manipulation scandal were brought against him. A prison sentence with hard labour, which he received in November 1991, was regarded as a deterrent to other politicians from engaging in financial corruption. In January 1991 the JSP changed its English name to the Social Democratic Party of Japan (SDPJ) and Makato Tanabe later replaced Takako Doi as Chairman of the party. In September senior LDP officials forced Kaifu to abandon proposals for electoral reform and the Takeshita faction of the LDP subsequently withdrew its support for the Prime Minister. Sponsored by the faction, the former Minister of Finance, Kiichi Miyazawa, was elected President of the LDP in October, and in November the Diet endorsed his appointment as Prime Minister. New allegations of involvement in the Recruit affair, publicized by the SDPJ in December 1991, seriously undermined Miyazawa's position.

In early 1992 public disgust at official corruption was registered at two prefectural by-elections to the upper house, when the LDP lost seats, which had previously been considered secure, to Rengo-no-kai (the political arm of RENGO, the trade union confederation). However, the anti-Government alliance, which had supported Rengo-no-kai, disintegrated in May over the issue of the authorization of Japanese involvement in UN peace-keeping operations. Members of the SDPJ attempted to obstruct the vote in the lower house by submitting their resignations *en masse*. The Speaker, however, ruled that these could not be accepted during the current Diet session. The successful passage through the Diet of the legislation on international peace-keeping improved the Government's standing, and in elections to the upper house in July the LDP won 69 of the 127 seats contested. The SDPJ, by contrast, lost 25 of its 46 seats; the Komeito increased its total strength from 20 to 24 seats, but Rengo-no-kai failed to win any seats, owing to the dissolution of the informal coalition it had facilitated between the SDPJ and the DSP. The Japan New Party (JNP), founded only two months prior to the election by LDP dissidents, secured four seats. A formal split within the Takeshita faction took place in December 1992. The new faction was to be led nominally by Tsutomu Hata, the Minister of Finance, although it was widely recognized that Ichiro Ozawa held the real power in the grouping.

Electoral reform was a major political issue in the first half of 1993. While the LDP favoured a single-member constituency system, the opposition parties proposed various forms of proportional representation. The LDP's lack of a majority in the upper house rendered it unable to enforce any reforms without the agreement of the opposition parties. Within the LDP itself there was conflict over whether or not to compromise with opposition parties. In June the lower house adopted a motion of 'no confidence' against the Government, after the LDP refused to modify its reform proposals to meet opposition demands. Numerous LDP members opposed the Government or abstained. The Ozawa-Hata group, comprising 44 former LDP members, immediately established a new party, the Shinseito (Japan Renewal Party, JRP), in order to contest the forthcoming general election. Another new party, the New Party Sakigake, was also formed by LDP Diet members. In the election to the House of Representatives, held in July, the LDP won 223 of the 511 seats, and was thus 33 seats short of a majority. Miyazawa resigned as Prime Minister and a coalition Government was formed. On 6 August Morihiro Hosokawa, the leader of the JNP,

was elected Prime Minister, defeating the new President of the LDP, Yohei Kono.

In late 1993 three senior politicians, Noboru Takeshita, Ichiro Ozawa and Kishiro Nakamura (a former Minister of Construction), were implicated in a scandal involving payments from construction companies in return for awarding building contracts. Ozawa claimed that the payments were legal, since none had exceeded 1.5m. yen. In January 1994 the Public Prosecutor's office began investigations into bribery allegations against Nakamura and Hideo Watanabe, the former Minister of Posts and Telecommunications.

In November 1993 four items of electoral reform legislation were passed by a majority of 270 to 226 votes in the House of Representatives (they were opposed by the LDP). In January 1994, however, the reform bills were defeated in the upper house, but Hosokawa, (who had threatened to resign if the legislation were not passed), subsequently reached agreement with the LDP on modifications to the reform bills (see below).

Hosokawa resigned as Prime Minister in April 1994. Tsutomu Hata was subsequently appointed Prime Minister, at the head of a minority Government that excluded the SDPJ and the New Party Sakigake. Hata was obliged to resign in June, however, owing to his continued failure to command a viable majority in the Diet, and a new coalition of the SDPJ, the LDP and the New Party Sakigake took office. Tomiichi Murayama, the leader of the SDPJ, became Prime Minister, and Kono was appointed Deputy Prime Minister and Minister of Foreign Affairs.

In July 1994 Murayama recognized the constitutional right to the existence of Japan's Self-Defence Forces (SDF, the armed forces), thereby effectively contradicting official SDPJ policy on the issue. (The SDPJ amended its policy to accord with Murayama's statement in September.) In December nine opposition parties, including the JNP, the JRP, the DSP and the Komeito, amalgamated to form a new political party, the Shinshinto (New Frontier Party, NFP). A faction of Komeito remained outside the new party and was renamed Komei. Kaifu, the former LDP Prime Minister, was elected leader of the NFP; Ozawa was appointed Secretary-General.

The creation of the NFP was widely perceived to be a response to the approval by the Diet in November 1994 of the electoral reform bills first proposed in 1993, which appeared to favour larger political parties. Under the terms of the new law, the House of Representatives was to be reduced to 500 seats, comprising 300 single-seat constituencies and 200 seats determined by proportional representation; the proportional-representation base was to be divided into 11 regions, and a party would qualify for a proportional-representation seat if it received a minimum of 2% of the vote; donations amounting to 500,000 yen annually per private sector corporation to individual politicians were permitted, but this was to be phased out after five years; restrictions on corporate donations would be subsidized by the State; door-to-door campaigning was to be permitted and an independent body would draw up new electoral boundaries. In June 1995 the first distribution of public money to political parties took place.

In January 1995 a massive earthquake in the Kobe region caused thousands of deaths and serious infrastructural damage. The Government was severely criticized for the poor co-ordination of the relief operation. In March a poisonous gas, sarin, was released into the Tokyo underground railway system, killing 12 people and injuring more than 5,000. A religious sect, Aum Shinrikyo, was accused of perpetrating the attack. Following a further gas attack in Yokohama in April, a number of sect members were detained by the authorities. In June Shoko Asahara, the leader of Aum Shinrikyo, was indicted on a charge of murder. The trial of Asahara opened in April 1996. In September Asahara and two other members of the sect were instructed to pay some US $7.3m. in compensation to victims of the Tokyo incident.

Participation in the elections to the House of Councillors, held in July 1995, was low. With one-half of the 252 seats being contested, the LDP won only 49 seats, the SDPJ 16 and the New Party Sakigake three, whereas the NFP, benefiting from the support of the Soka Gakkai religious organization, won 40 seats. In September Ryutaro Hashimoto, the Minister of International Trade and Industry, was elected leader of the LDP, after Yohei Kono announced that he would not seek re-election.

Conflict in the Diet escalated between February and June 1995 over government plans, announced in June 1994, to issue a resolution to commemorate the 50th anniversary of the ending of the Second World War. The resolution was to constitute an apology to countries whose citizens had suffered from the actions of the Japanese army during the war. The New Party Sakigake threatened to withdraw from the coalition if an apology were not made, while a group of 160 LDP Diet members, led by Seisuke Okuno, objected to the definition of Japan as an aggressor. A resolution was finally passed in June 1995, despite a boycott of the vote by the NFP.

In December 1995 Toshiki Kaifu was succeeded by Ichiro Ozawa as leader of the NFP. In January 1996 Tomiichi Murayama resigned as Prime Minister; he was, however, re-elected Chairman of the SDPJ. The LDP leader, Ryutaro Hashimoto, was elected Prime Minister on 11 January. A coalition Cabinet, largely dominated by the LDP, was formed.

In March 1996 the New Socialist Party (NSP) was formed by left-wing defectors from the SDPJ. Osamu Yatabe was elected Chairman of the NSP and Tetsuo Yamaguchi was appointed Secretary-General. In mid-1996, in an attempt to strengthen their electoral bases, particularly in the new single-member districts, there was a further realignment of political parties. In August Shoichi Ide and Hiroyuki Sonoda were elected Leader and Secretary-General, respectively, of the New Party Sakigake following the resignations of Masayoshi Takemura and Yukio Hatoyama. Hatoyama left the party and founded the Democratic Party of Japan (DPJ), with other dissident members of the New Party Sakigake and individual members of the SDPJ and NFP.

A general election was held in October 1996. The LDP won 239 of the 500 seats in the House of Representatives, while the NFP secured 156, the DPJ 52, the Japan Communist Party (JCP) 26, the SDPJ 15, and the New Party Sakigake two seats. Four deputies, who were elected as independents, subsequently formed a new party called the 21st Century. In November Ryutaro Hashimoto was re-elected Prime Minister, and formed the first single-party Cabinet since 1993.

Soon after the election several government ministers and party leaders were implicated in various official corruption scandals. In December 1996 the former Prime Minister, Tsutomu Hata, left the NFP and formed a new party, called Taiyoto (Sun Party), together with 12 other dissident NFP members. In late December Takako Doi was formally appointed Chairwoman of the SDPJ (she had been acting Chairwoman since the dissolution of the House of Representatives in September).

In early 1997 the Government established several commissions, charged with devising a comprehensive programme of administrative and economic reforms. A reduction in government bureaucracy and public expenditure was envisaged, and details of a series of financial deregulation measures were announced in February, including the transfer of the Ministry of Finance's supervisory role to an independent agency in mid-1998. The Government's management of the nuclear programme was comprehensively reviewed, following two accidents at plants in December 1995 and March 1997. Allegations that a further 11 unreported radiation leaks had occurred over the previous three years heightened public disquiet.

In mid-1997 Hosokawa resigned from the NFP, reportedly owing to dissatisfaction with Ozawa's leadership. (In December Hosokawa formed a new party—From Five.) In addition, the NFP lost all of its seats in elections to the Tokyo Metropolitan Assembly, held in July. The LDP and the JCP, by contrast, increased their representation in the Assembly. By September the LDP had regained its majority in the House of Representatives, following a series of defections by members of the NFP. In December a much-reduced NFP was dissolved. Six new parties were founded by former NFP members, Ozawa and his supporters forming the Liberal Party (LP), and a significant political realignment thus took place. In January 1998 six opposition parties, including the DPJ, formed a parliamentary group, Minyuren, which constituted the largest opposition bloc in the Diet. In March the parties comprising Minyuren agreed on their integration into the DPJ, formally establishing a new DPJ, with Naoto Kan as its President, in the following month.

Meanwhile, during 1997 various circumstances, including continuing financial corruption, an increase in the rate of the unpopular consumption tax, a decrease in public expenditure and the collapse of several prominent financial institutions, together with the threat of further bankruptcies, contributed to the development of an economic crisis. The Government announced a series of measures designed to encourage economic growth, including a reduction in taxes and, in a major reversal of policy, the use of public funds to support the banking system. In January 1998 the Diet reconvened earlier than scheduled, in order to approve the budget for 1998/99, as well as supple-

mentary budget proposals incorporating the tax reductions. In late January 1998 two senior officials from the Ministry of Finance were arrested on suspicion of accepting bribes from banks. The Minister of Finance, Hiroshi Mitsuzuka, resigned, accepting full moral responsibility for the affair. As more banks and other financial institutions became implicated in the bribery scandal, the central bank initiated an internal investigation into its own operations. In March the Governor resigned after a senior bank executive was arrested amid further allegations of bribery. Trials of those implicated in the financial scandals took place in 1998 and 1999. A number of financial deregulation measures took effect on 1 April 1998, as part of Japan's 'Big Bang' reform process. The economy continued to stagnate, however, and Hashimoto's administration was widely criticized for its slow reaction to the crisis. In June the SDPJ and the New Party Sakigake withdrew from their alliance with the ruling LDP.

The LDP performed poorly in elections for one-half of the seats in the House of Councillors in July 1998, retaining only 44 of its 61 seats contested, while the DPJ won 27 seats, increasing its representation to 47 seats, and the JCP became the third-largest party in the upper house, taking 15 seats. Hashimoto resigned as Prime Minister and President of the LDP and was succeeded by Keizo Obuchi, hitherto Minister for Foreign Affairs. Obuchi was elected Prime Minister on 30 July.

Although Obuchi's Government was designated an 'economic reconstruction' Cabinet, doubts arose about its commitment to comprehensive reform. Kiichi Miyazawa, the former Prime Minister, was appointed Minister of Finance. In his inaugural policy speech, Obuchi announced the establishment of an Economic Strategy Council and promised substantial tax cuts. As Japan's economic situation worsened, political disputes over banking reform dominated the following months, with the Government reluctant to commit itself to the closure of failing banks. Following weeks of negotiations, in October 1998 the Diet approved banking legislation that included provisions for the nationalization of failing banks, as demanded by the opposition.

Shinto Heiwa and Komei merged in November 1998 to form New Komeito, which thus became the second-largest opposition party. Also in that month Fukushiro Nukaga, the Director-General of the Defence Agency, resigned from the Government to assume responsibility for a procurement scandal involving his agency. In mid-November the LDP and the Liberal Party (LP) reached a basic accord on the formation of a coalition, which would still remain short of a majority in the upper house. In January 1999 agreement was reached on coalition policies, including measures to reduce the influence of bureaucrats on the legislative process. The Cabinet was reorganized to include the LP, the leader of which, Ichiro Ozawa, had refused a cabinet position. At the end of January the Government adopted an administrative reform plan, which aimed to reduce further the number of cabinet ministers and public servants and to establish an economic and fiscal policy committee. Draft legislation on the implementation of the plan was introduced in the Diet in April.

At local elections in April 1999, 11 of the 12 governorships contested were won by the incumbents, all standing as independents. At the gubernatorial election for Tokyo, the convincing victory of Shintaro Ishihara, a nationalist writer and a former Minister of Transport under the LDP (although now unaffiliated), was regarded as an embarrassment for the ruling party. Ishihara immediately provoked controversy, making inflammatory comments about the 1937 Nanjing massacre and criticizing the Chinese Government, which responded angrily, prompting the Japanese Government to distance itself publicly from the new Governor's remarks. In November the Chinese Government also expressed its concern regarding an unofficial visit by Ishihara to Taiwan, which had recently suffered a major earthquake. Ishihara also angered the People's Republic of China by visiting Taiwan in May 2000 for the inauguration of the latter's new President, Chen Shui-bian, despite having refused an invitation to visit China as part of celebrations to mark the anniversary of the establishment of relations between Beijing and Tokyo.

In June 1999 the Government voted to grant official legal status to the *de facto* national flag (*Hinomaru*) and anthem (*Kimigayo*), despite considerable opposition owing to their association with Japan's militaristic past. The necessary legislation became effective in mid-August, following approval by the Diet. Meanwhile, in July New Komeito agreed to join the ruling LDP-LP coalition, giving the Government a new majority in the upper house and expanding its control in the lower house to more than 70% of the seats. Negotiations on policy initiatives proved difficult, however, owing to differences over a number of contentious issues such as constitutional revision and New Komeito's opposition to a reduction in the number of seats in the lower house, as favoured by the LP. Obuchi was re-elected President of the LDP in September. Naoto Kan was replaced as President of the DPJ by Yukio Hatoyama, hitherto Secretary-General of the party.

At the end of September 1999 a serious accident at a uranium-processing plant at Tokaimura severely undermined public confidence in the safety of Japan's nuclear industry. Furthermore, in November it was revealed that 15 of 17 nuclear facilities recently inspected by government officials had failed to meet legal health and safety standards. In December the Diet enacted legislation aimed at preventing accidents and improving procedures. In February 2000 the Government announced that 439 people had been exposed to radiation in the Tokaimura accident, far more than the 69 recorded in the initial report. Two workers from the plant subsequently died from radiation exposure. In September 2000 compensation was agreed for the victims of the accident. Former staff at the plant were arrested in October and charged with negligence resulting in death. In November 2000 the plant was authorized to be reopened.

A new Cabinet was appointed in October 1999. Notably, Michio Ochi was appointed Chairman of the Financial Reconstruction Commission. The LP and New Komeito each received one cabinet post. A basic accord on coalition policy included an agreement to seek a reduction in the number of seats in the House of Representatives, initially by 20 and subsequently by a further 30. A Vice-Minister at the Defence Agency resigned shortly after being appointed, following widespread criticism of his suggestion that Japan should arm itself with nuclear weapons. Obuchi, whose judgement in the affair was questioned, subsequently apologized to the nation in a speech to the Diet.

Trials continued in 1997–99 of members of Aum Shinrikyo, the cult accused of perpetrating the sarin gas attack on the Tokyo underground railway system in March 1995. In September 1999 Masato Yokoyama, a leading member of the cult, became the first of those accused to receive the death sentence. In late 1999 Aum Shinrikyo issued a series of statements in an apparent attempt to avert any restriction on the cult or seizure of its assets. The leaders of the cult announced a suspension of all external activities from October, and in December acknowledged its culpability for a number of crimes, including the 1995 gas attack. Moreover, in January 2000 the cult announced that it was changing its name to Aleph and renouncing its leader, Shoko Asahara, who was still being tried for his part in the gas attack. In February, following a police raid on Aum Shinrikyo premises, it was revealed that a number of major companies and government agencies had placed orders for computer software with a firm believed to be major source of revenue for the cult; the Defence Agency subsequently announced that it was to abandon software purchased from the company for use by the SDF.

In December 1999 a political crisis was averted when Ozawa was persuaded not to withdraw the LP from the ruling coalition, as he had threatened, over a delay in the proposal of legislation to reduce the number of seats in the lower house. The ruling parties had earlier agreed also to postpone the consideration of a proposal to expand Japan's participation in UN peace-keeping activities. In early 2000 the ruling coalition approved the controversial legislation on the reduction in seats through the Diet, despite an opposition boycott, which continued for some two weeks. Multi-party committees were established in both houses in January, which were to review the Constitution over a period of five years. In late February Michio Ochi was forced to resign from the Cabinet over remarks that suggested he would be lenient on banking reform.

Discord within the coalition increased, and in April 2000 the LP withdrew from the Government; 26 members of the LP formed the New Conservative Party—NCP (Hoshuto). Keizo Obuchi, however, suffered a stroke and went into a coma from which he never regained consciousness. The Government was criticized for not releasing the news of Obuchi's condition (it was not reported in the media for at least 24 hours) even though the country had effectively been without a premier. Chief Cabinet Secretary Mikio Aoki became Acting Prime Minister, claiming that Obuchi had specifically asked him to fulfil the role, but the LDP elected Yoshiro Mori, the Secretary-General, as party

President; he was subsequently elected Prime Minister by both houses of the Diet. Mori immediately affirmed his commitment to the economic and political reform initiatives of his predecessor and formed a coalition with New Komeito and the NCP. All ministers from the Obuchi administration were retained. Both Seiroku Kajiyama (a former Chief Cabinet Secretary) and Noboru Takeshita, the former Prime Minister, announced their retirement from politics and from the LDP; both men died shortly afterwards. Former Prime Minister Ryutaro Hashimoto was appointed head of the Takeshita faction of the LDP, which had been led by Obuchi.

Following his appointment as Prime Minister, Mori made a number of controversial public statements, expressing imperialist views. Although forced to issue apologies, he did not retract his remarks. In the general election held on 25 June 2000 the number of seats in the House of Representatives was reduced from 500 to 480. The LDP won the most seats, although its representation was reduced to 233 and many of its key political figures, including current and former cabinet ministers, lost their seats, particularly in metropolitan areas. The DPJ increased its representation to 127 seats, New Komeito won 31 seats, the LP 22 seats, the NCP 20 seats and the SDPJ 19 seats. The LDP benefited from the electoral system, which gave rural areas (where the LDP had strong support) disproportionately high representation. Tradition and family connections remained important, with two candidates (the brother of Noboru Takeshita and the daughter of Keizo Obuchi) winning seats despite their lack of political experience. The participation rate was 62.5%. Although remaining in power, the LDP faced serious problems, among the most prominent of which related to the suitability of its leadership, Mori having made numerous political gaffes and public errors of protocol. Nevertheless, Mori was returned as Prime Minister and announced the composition of his new Cabinet in July.

Meanwhile, in February 2000 Governor Ishihara of Tokyo proposed that a tax be levied on major banks based on the size of their business rather than their profits; he was criticized by the central Government, which had previously been the only body able to introduce taxes. Ishihara attracted criticism from the foreign residents of Tokyo, and from neighbouring countries, in April when, in an address to members of the SDF, he blamed foreign residents for a number of serious crimes and referred to them as *sangokujin*, a derogatory wartime term for people from Taiwan and Korea.

In October 2000 an amendment to the voting system, under which electors would choose to vote either for a party or for an individual candidate, was proposed by the governing coalition. The opposition strongly criticized the proposed changes and, following the Government's insistence that they be passed through the Diet, commenced a boycott of proceedings. The bill was approved in the House of Representatives despite the boycott, which lasted 18 days and ended following an agreement between the Government and the opposition to debate the proposed legislation in the House of Representatives. It was enacted in late October. Meanwhile, Juro Saito resigned as President of the House of Councillors, owing to his failure successfully to mediate in the dispute. He was replaced by the former Minister of Education, Yutaka Inoue.

Corruption was a major issue throughout 2000, particularly the taking of bribes, revelations of which resulted in several resignations. Among the most serious incidents was a 'cash for questions' scandal involving an insurance company. One LDP member resigned and another was arrested in connection with the affair in November, and in January 2001 Fukushiro Nukaga, the Minister of State for Economy, Industry and Information Technology, resigned, having earlier admitted that he had accepted bribes from the firm. An LDP ally of Yoshiro Mori, Masakuni Murakami, was implicated in the case and arrested in March. In October 2000 Hidenao Nakagawa, Minister of State, Chief Cabinet Secretary, Director-General of the Okinawa Development Agency and Minister in Charge of Information Technology, resigned after it was alleged, *inter alia*, that he had links to a right-wing activist. In the following month the former Minister of Construction, Eiichi Nakao, acknowledged in court that he had taken bribes in 1996 in exchange for the allocation of public works contracts.

The high incidence of corruption further undermined Mori, and during October 2000 the Prime Minister came under increasing pressure to resign after it was alleged in a magazine that some years previously he had been arrested for violation of an anti-prostitution law. Mori denied the allegation and sued the publication for libel. Later that month, during a meeting with Tony Blair, the British Prime Minister, Mori reportedly suggested that the Democratic People's Republic of Korea could release Japanese hostages (see below) to a third country in order to avoid any admission of their existence. Harsh criticism ensued, and subsequent attempts to mitigate the situation, by claiming that the remarks referred to an episode from the past, proved unsuccessful. In mid-November the opposition launched a motion of 'no confidence' in the Prime Minister. Furthermore, LDP member Koichi Kato publicly criticized Mori and declared himself ready to form a government. The Prime Minister won the vote, however, following threats by the party leadership that rebels voting against Mori would be expelled from the LDP. In early December, Mori suffered a set-back when his strong ally, Hiromu Nonaka, resigned as Secretary-General of the LDP and retired from politics. His nominated successor, Makoto Koga, subsequently assumed the role.

Meanwhile, in November 2000 Fusako Shigenobu, the founder of the extremist left-wing Japanese Red Army which had been responsible for a number of terrorist attacks during the 1970s, was arrested in Tokyo. She was detained on suspicion of the seizure of the French embassy in The Hague, The Netherlands, in 1974 and subsequently indicted on various related charges. A number of other members had been repatriated from several countries since 1995, and now faced trials for terrorism. Japan hoped to obtain the extradition from the Democratic People's Republic of Korea, in return for economic aid, of more Red Army members, who had hijacked a Japanese aircraft and forced it to fly to Pyongyang in 1970 (later being granted political asylum there).

A major cabinet reorganization was effected in December 2000, and substantial changes were made to the government structure. The number of ministries was to be reduced from 23 to 13, mainly through mergers, and various state agencies were absorbed into the newly created Cabinet Office. (Legislation providing for these changes had been approved in June 1998.) The new structure was not fully implemented until January 2001, following an administrative reform. Notable appointments to the new Cabinet included the leader of the largest LDP faction and former Prime Minister, Ryutaro Hashimoto, and Hakuo Yanagisawa, the former Director-General of the Financial Reconstruction Commission. The former was appointed Minister of State for the Development of Okinawa and the Settlement of the Northern Territories, and the latter became Minister of State for Financial Affairs. Both men were well-respected and enjoyed considerable political support, and their appointment was seen as an attempt by Mori to strengthen his position. During December 2000, however, photographs showing the Prime Minister in the company of an alleged gangster and convicted murderer were published. In the same month, and again in January 2001, senior officials of the party were implicated in a bribery scandal (see above), resulting in the resignations of the Minister of State for the Economy, Industry and Information Technology, Fukushiro Nukaga, and the LDP leader in the House of Councillors, Masakuni Murakami, amongst others. Mori won another vote of confidence in March, but in early April announced his intention to resign.

In late April 2001 Junichiro Koizumi, a former Minister of Health and Welfare, unexpectedly defeated two other candidates, including Ryutaro Hashimoto, to secure the presidency of the ruling LDP and thus the post of Prime Minister. Koizumi owed his victory to a change in party election rules that allowed a greater influence of local and ordinary party members in selecting the President. He subsequently reorganized the Cabinet, largely ignoring LDP factional politics, and appointed a number of reformists, including Makiko Tanaka, daughter of former Prime Minister Kakuei Tanaka, as Japan's first woman Minister of Foreign Affairs; Heizo Takenaka, an economics professor, as Minister of State for Economy, Industry and Information Technology; and Nobuteru Ishihara as Minister of State for Administrative Reform. However, there were concerns that the relatively unknown new Minister of Finance, Masajuro Shiokawa, lacked the authority necessary to bring about economic and financial reforms. At the same time, Koizumi also reshuffled the LDP's senior leadership, appointing his ally Taku Yamasaki as Secretary-General, and Taro Aso as Chairman of the Policy Research Council. Immediately after taking office, Koizumi attained a record popularity rating of above 80%, leading to hopes that he would use his popularity to secure the passage of difficult economic reforms against the wishes of his more reluctant party. In addition to according priority to eco-

nomic reform, Koizumi also sought to introduce direct elections for the post of Prime Minister, and upgrade the status of the SDF into that of a full army, a move that would involve changing Article 9 of the Constitution, whereby Japan renounces the use of war. This, coupled with his stated intention to pay an official visit in August to the Yasukuni Shrine, a controversial war memorial, led to fears in neighbouring countries of a growth of nationalism in Japan. In May 2001 the Government issued an apology and agreed to pay compensation to 127 leprosy victims (who had been forcibly isolated for years) following a ruling by a provincial court. Koizumi's refusal to challenge the ruling was seen as a sign of greater political openness. The Government also approved the construction of a new nuclear power plant for the first time since the Tokaimura accident in September 1999, thereby ending a hiatus in the country's nuclear programme.

In June 2001 the Government finally announced an economic reform programme, drafted by Minister for Economy Takenaka. The plan consisted of the privatization of special public institutions, a review of regulatory economic laws, the strengthening of insurance functions, improving human resources, including assistance to business entrepreneurs, revitalizing urban areas, promoting regional autonomy and a reduction of public-works projects. Despite his warnings of economic hardship ahead, Koizumi's high popularity was a major factor behind the LDP's gains in the Tokyo assembly elections in late June. Veteran members of the LDP, particularly the Hashimoto faction, however, remained opposed to Koizumi's reforms. By early July, Koizumi had already retreated from his earlier long-held plan to privatize the post office savings system.

Elections to the House of Councillors were held on 29 July 2001, and Koizumi's personal popularity enabled the LDP to make gains. Of the 121 seats being contested, the LDP won 64, bringing its total in the upper chamber to 110, a net gain of eight seats. The opposition DPJ won 26 seats, raising its strength to 60 seats, a net gain of 13 seats, while New Komeito won 23 seats, a net gain of one seat. The elections were widely seen as a test for Koizumi's reformist agenda and as a victory for the LDP after years of declining popularity. Koizumi was re-elected unopposed for a further two-year term as LDP President in early August.

Koizumi aroused controversy in mid-August 2001 when he made an official visit to the Yasukuni Shrine to honour Japan's war dead. He sought to diminish the controversy by visiting two days before the anniversary of Japan's surrender in the Second World War, but nevertheless drew both domestic and international criticism. Left-wingers opposed the visit on principle, while right-wingers denounced Koizumi for bringing forward his visit to placate critics.

In September 2001 the terrorist attacks on the USA again raised the subject of the role of Japan's military, with Koizumi apparently using the USA's war against the Taliban regime of Afghanistan to expand the role of the SDF. The Diet in late October approved new legislation for the overseas deployment of the SDF in a non-combat support role, and in late November Japan deployed warships to the Indian Ocean, in the biggest such deployment since the Second World War (see below). The Japanese people strongly supported logistical assistance to the USA, but there remained considerable public opposition to amending Article 9. Amid the worsening economic situation, meanwhile, the Government in September introduced emergency stimulus measures to counter rising unemployment, the deteriorating situation in the corporate sector and the banking crisis. Also in September, the Government confirmed the country's first case of BSE-infected cattle, giving rise to widespread public concern and a decline in beef consumption. In late October the Government proclaimed Japanese beef to be safe for consumption; however, a second infected cow was discovered in late November.

By November 2001 Koizumi was in dispute with Minister of Foreign Affairs Tanaka over bureaucratic reform in her ministry, her occasional failure to meet visiting foreign dignitaries and her absence from two major international forums. Koizumi had meanwhile formed a new 'foreign policy taskforce' to deal more efficiently with international affairs. There was increasing speculation about a cabinet reorganization, with members of the LDP's Hashimoto faction keen to modify reforms and regain ministerial posts. Koizumi had in previous months indicated his willingness to work with the opposition DPJ if the LDP continued to block his reforms; later in the month more than 50 LDP legislators formed a group aimed at stalling them.

Also in November 2001, hundreds of people filed lawsuits against Koizumi over his visit to the Yasukuni Shrine, claiming that he had violated the constitutional separation of religion and state. In early December Princess Masako, wife of Crown Prince Naruhito, finally gave birth to her first child, Princess Aiko. However, the Constitution forbade females from succeeding to the 'Chrysanthemum Throne', leading to calls for an amendment to the rules at a future date, a suggestion that was strongly supported by the public. The last female ruler had been Empress Gosakuramachi in the late 1700s.

In mid-December 2001 the Government agreed to abolish 17 public corporations and transfer 45 others (of a total of 163) to the private sector; it also showed signs of addressing the problems of the banking sector. Koizumi's major reform of privatizing the postal savings system, however, was further delayed. Meanwhile, the opposition DPJ itself experienced divisions, between those who favoured co-operation with Koizumi and his reforms (including the President of the DPJ, Yukio Hatoyama), and those who favoured greater co-operation with other opposition parties. The latter group was led by DPJ Deputy President Takahiro Yokomichi, who in late November held meetings with the Liberal Party leader, Ichiro Ozawa, and the SDPJ leader, Takako Doi. The DPJ had failed to make a significant impact against the LDP during the ongoing economic crisis.

By the beginning of 2002 had failed to deliver tangible economic results, and there was considerable uncertainty regarding his ability to do so. Shizuka Kamei, a senior LDP official, accused Koizumi of damaging the economy in order to push through his reform agenda, highlighting the stiff resistance within the LDP. In the first week of January Koizumi appointed two members of the Hashimoto faction as vice-ministers, in a bid to placate his main opponents. At the end of the month Koizumi dismissed his Minister of Foreign Affairs, Makiko Tanaka, following months of disputes over reform within the ministry, which had delayed the passage of a supplementary budget through the Diet. Tanaka had been one of the most popular politicians in the country, and her dismissal was regarded as a victory for LDP veterans and as a set-back for reform. She was replaced by Yoriko Kawaguchi, hitherto Minister of the Environment, after former UN High Commissioner for Refugees Sadako Ogata turned down the post. In March the LDP suffered a reverse as one Diet member, Muneo Suzuki, was accused of exerting pressure on officials of the Ministry of Foreign Affairs to limit bids for a construction project to companies from within his own parliamentary constituency, and Saburo Sato, a former aide to LDP faction leader Koichi Kato, was arrested on suspicion of tax evasion. Suzuki resigned in disgrace from the LDP in mid-March, as did Kato, who also resigned from his seat in the Diet in early April. In March former Prime Minister Ryutaro Hashimoto, one of the most influential men in the LDP, underwent heart surgery, forcing him to halt temporarily his political activities

The LDP suffered further set-backs in April 2002 when its candidates lost the election for the mayoralty of Yokohama, and a by-election in Niigata Prefecture. In Yokohama, an independent young reformist, Hiroshi Nakada, defeated the incumbent Hidenobu Takahide, who had the support of both the LDP and opposition parties. The electoral defeats, and Koizumi's unscheduled visit to the Yasukuni Shrine in late April, led to renewed criticism of the Prime Minister. In early May Yutaka Inoue, a former President of the House of Councillors and a member of the LDP, resigned from the party owing to allegations of bribery. At the same time, opponents of Koizumi within the LDP were increasingly holding discussions with Shintaro Ishihara, the Governor of Tokyo, with a view to replacing the Prime Minister with the latter.

In June 2002 the LDP suspended Makiko Tanaka from the party for a two-year period owing to her failure to co-operate with an investigation into the misuse of state funds at the Ministry of Foreign Affairs. Tanaka relinquished her seat in the Diet in early August, thereby ending her political career. Also in June Muneo Suzuki was arrested on bribery charges. Meanwhile, the sitting session of the Diet was extended until July in order for Koizumi to draft legislation for reforms to the postal service, as well as health, and defence and security sectors, which were opposed by considerable elements within the LDP. In July Koizumi was forced to accept a compromise with anti-reformist LDP elements over his plans to reform the postal service—a key promise that he had made when seeking the post of Prime Minister a year earlier. Meanwhile, in the middle of that month the Governor of Nagano Prefecture, Yasuo Tanaka, was ousted by the prefectural assembly owing to his policies of reducing major public works projects, which were often used by

local politicians to generate political support. Tanaka, a former novelist, was one of an increasing number of independent, reformist candidates who had been elected to prefectural governorships as a protest against traditional political parties. However, he was overwhelmingly re-elected to the post of Governor in September 2002, in what was seen as a victory for reformist forces.

In August 2002 the Government introduced a controversial new database that stored personal data of all citizens. Civil liberty groups immediately opposed the scheme on the grounds that it inveighed on personal privacy. Thousands of people protested against the system, and several municipalities refused to join the scheme.

In late September Koizumi implemented a long-expected cabinet reorganization, dismissing the Minister of State for the Financial Services Agency, Hakuo Yanagisawa, and appointing the Minister of State for Economic and Fiscal Policy, Heizo Takenaka, to concurrently hold that post. The portfolios for agriculture, defence, disaster management, environment, food safety, and Okinawa and the Northern Territories, were also replaced. It was widely believed that the reallocation of portfolios came in support of a plan by the Governor of the Bank of Japan, Masaru Hayami, to shore up the ailing banking sector by buying poorly-performing shares owned by commercial banks—a proposal opposed by Yanagisawa. Plans to reform the banking sector also created tensions between the LDP and its two coalition partners, New Komeito and the NCP. At the end of October a tripartite committee of the ruling coalition published a banking-sector reform plan that was far less radical than that sought by Takenaka, who had urged the nationalization of major banks to prevent their collapse. The political wrangling over how to revive Japan's economy and reform the banking system continued throughout the remainder of 2002. Despite the political tensions, the LDP in late October won five out of seven by-elections, strengthening the reputation of Prime Minister Koizumi following his visit to North Korea in September (see below). At the same time Japan witnessed its first political assassination since 1960, when a member of the DPJ, Koki Ishii, a known campaigner against corruption, was stabbed to death.

In early December 2002 the opposition DPJ elected Naoto Kan as its President, replacing Yukio Hatoyama, who had himself been re-elected to a third term as party President in late September. Hatoyama was forced to resign after the failure of secret attempts to merge the party with the smaller opposition LP, led by Ichiro Ozawa. Katsuya Okada, Kan's main rival for the DPJ presidency, was appointed secretary-general. Kan had previously led the DPJ during 1997–99, and although his leadership was expected to strengthen the opposition, analysts noted that the DPJ had hitherto failed to make a significant impact against the ruling LDP. Four DPJ members of the Diet, led by former party Vice-President Hiroshi Kumagai, resigned from the party in late December and joined the ruling coalition's NCP; the President of that party, Takeshi Noda, resigned in favour of Kumagai.

In mid-January 2003 Junichiro Koizumi visited the Yasukuni Shrine for the third time since becoming Prime Minister, once again prompting criticism within Japan as well as in the region. Also at that time Emperor Akihito underwent surgery for prostate cancer, his duties being temporarily transferred to Crown Prince Naruhito. In late February Toshihiko Fukui, a long-serving official at the Bank of Japan, was appointed Governor. His conservative background, however, raised concerns that he would not bring about radical reforms to the banking sector.

In early March 2003 the Governor of Tokyo, Shintaro Ishihara, announced that he would seek re-election in April, ending months of speculation that he might form a new political party in order to challenge Koizumi. Ishihara's announcement was welcomed by Koizumi, since the Governor had been seen as the Prime Minister's most serious rival, and had been holding discussions with Shizuka Kamei, an LDP faction leader who was Koizumi's main opponent within the party. However, the LDP was, in early March, embarrassed by the arrest of one of its Diet members over the illicit management of political donations. At the end of the month the Minister of Agriculture, Forestry and Fisheries, Tadamori Oshima, resigned over a series of financial scandals concerning his aides—the wife of one having committed suicide days earlier. Oshima was the first minister in Koizumi's Cabinet to resign over a funding scandal, and further weakened public faith in party politics. He was replaced by Yoshiyuki Kamei.

The 15th unified quadrennial local elections, comprising gubernatorial elections in 11 prefectures (including Tokyo), one city mayoral election, and local assembly elections in 44 prefectures and 12 cities, were held in mid-April 2003. In Tokyo, Governor Ishihara was overwhelmingly re-elected, and pledged to use his position to campaign for reform in the country as a whole. Three other incumbent governors were also re-elected, and it was noted that independent candidates performed strongly or won posts in several prefectures, at the expense of traditional political parties. Turn-out in the gubernatorial elections was a record low of 52.6%, however. The LDP won 1,309 of 2,634 local seats contested, an improvement on the 1,288 seats it had won four years earlier. By-elections for three seats in the House of Representatives and one seat in the House of Councillors were held in late April; the LDP won three seats and the DPJ one seat.

In late April 2003 the LDP announced that it aimed to amend the Constitution explicitly to state the legitimacy of the SDF and to expand its role in international peacekeeping and collective self-defence. In mid-May the House of Representatives approved new legislation granting the Government and the SDF greater powers to act in the event of an attack on Japan.

From the mid-1990s Japan's growing trade surplus with the USA became a matter of increasing concern for the US authorities. In October 1994 trade agreements in three of the four main areas under bilateral discussion were signed. Negotiations concerning the automobile trade resulted in the signing of an agreement with the USA in June 1995. However, an increase in the export of Japanese vehicles to the USA in 1997, and a concomitant rise in the US trade deficit with Japan, caused growing tension between the two countries. Negotiations in April and June focused on trade issues. In September an agreement to reform Japanese port operations was concluded shortly after the USA imposed large fines on Japanese companies for employing restrictive harbour practices. Negotiations on increased access to airline routes were successfully concluded in January 1998. However, relations were again strained by trade disputes in 1998, with Japan's high tariffs on rice, in the forestry and fisheries sectors, and low-priced steel exports being of particular concern to the USA. Tension also arose over the USA's repeated criticism that Japan was not doing enough to stimulate its own economy and alleviate the Asian economic crisis. During a visit to Japan in November 1998, President Clinton urged the Government rapidly to implement measures to encourage domestic demand, reform the banking sector and liberalize its markets. Meanwhile, Japan's trade surplus with the USA continued to increase, and in 1998 reached its highest level since 1987. In May 1999, during a visit by Prime Minister Obuchi to the USA (the first such official state visit in 12 years), Clinton praised Obuchi's efforts to promote economic recovery and welcomed Japanese plans for further deregulation in several sectors. Meanwhile, a dispute over Japanese steel exports had escalated. A ruling, in April 1999, by the US Department of Commerce that Japan had 'dumped' hot-rolled steel into the US market was endorsed, in June, by the US International Trade Commission, and punitive duties were subsequently imposed. In November Japan announced its intention to bring a complaint before the World Trade Organization (WTO) against the US ruling. Relations between the two countries deteriorated in mid-2000, following the expansion by Japan of its hunting of whales as part of a 'scientific research' programme. The USA subsequently banned Japan from future access to its territorial waters and threatened to impose sanctions on Japanese food imports. Japan warned that if any such sanctions were imposed, it would take the dispute to the WTO. The International Whaling Commission refused a bid by Japan to hold its next meeting in the country.

Together with trade issues, Japan's bilateral security arrangements with the USA, concluded by treaty in 1951, continued to be the focus of US-Japanese relations. The treaty granted the use of military bases in Japan to the USA, in return for a US commitment to provide military support to Japan in the event of external aggression. In January 1992, the 'Tokyo declaration on the US-Japan global partnership' was issued, whereby the two countries undertook to co-operate in promoting international security and prosperity. In February 1993 Japan and the USA reaffirmed their security relationship, with the USA agreeing to protect Japan from the threat posed by potential nuclear proliferation around the world.

The presence of the US forces in Japan provoked much debate in the mid-1990s. In November 1995 three US servicemen were arrested and subsequently imprisoned for the rape of a schoolgirl in Okinawa. Considerable civil unrest ensued and legal proceedings were initiated against the Governor of Okinawa, Masahide Ota, following his refusal to renew the leases for US military installations in the region. Protracted negotiations between the two countries resulted in the USA agreeing, in December 1996, to release 21% of the land used for US military purposes in Okinawa, and to build a floating offshore helicopter base to replace the air base at Futenma. In April 1997 it was proposed to relocate several of the US bases to other prefectures. In December, in a non-binding referendum held in Nago, Okinawa, to assess public opinion concerning the construction of the offshore helicopter base, the majority of voters rejected the proposal, prompting the resignation of the Mayor of Nago. Governor Ota stated his opposition to the proposed base, a position also adopted by the new Mayor, elected in February 1998. In November 1998 Keiichi Inamine defeated Ota in the Okinawa gubernatorial elections. Inamine, who had been supported by the LDP, presented an alternative solution, proposing that a military-commercial airport be built in northern Okinawa and leased to the USA for a period of 15 years. In December 1998 a US military site was the first of the 11 bases to be returned under the 1996 agreement. In December 1999 Inamine's proposal for the relocation of the Futenma air base was approved by both the local authorities and the Japanese Government, with the Henoko district of Nago chosen as the site for the new airport; at the same time funding was allocated for a 10-year development plan for northern Okinawa. Negotiations with the US Government, which opposed any time limit on its use of the airport, took place in October 2000; no progress was made.

In September 1997 revised Guidelines for Japan-US Defense Co-operation (first compiled in 1978) were issued. The Guidelines envisaged enhanced military co-operation between the USA and Japan, not only on Japanese territory, but also in situations in unspecified areas around Japan. In April 1998 the LDP Government approved legislation on the implementation of the revised Guidelines, which was enacted in May 1999, prompting criticism from China and Russia. Its approval was ensured by an agreement between the LDP, the LP, and New Komeito to exclude a clause that would have allowed the inspection of unidentified foreign ships by the SDF, with the aim of enforcing economic sanctions. In August 1999 the Japanese Government formally approved a memorandum of understanding with the USA stipulating details of joint technical research on the development of a theatre missile defence system, which aims to detect and shoot down incoming ballistic missiles within a 3,000-km radius. The Defence Agency estimated that Japan would have to allocate up to 30,000m. yen to the controversial research project over a five-year period.

From 1982 Japan remained under pressure from the USA to increase its defence expenditure and to assume greater responsibility for security in the Western Pacific area. In December 1990 the Government announced a new five-year programme to develop the country's defence capability. The new programme also envisaged that Japan would assume a greater share of the cost of maintaining the US troops stationed in Japan. In November 1995 the Cabinet approved a new national defence programme, which envisaged a 20% reduction in troops and confirmed Japan's security co-operation with the USA. In November 2000 the Japanese House of Representatives approved a five-year agreement, to commence in April 2001, to reduce host nation spending for US forces stationed in Japan. Although the administration of US President George W. Bush favoured stronger links with Japan than its predecessor, relations between Japan and the USA briefly deteriorated in February 2001 when a Japanese trawler sank, killing the entire crew, following a collision with a US submarine, the *Greenville*, off Hawaii. The revelation that a civilian had been at the controls of the submarine at the time caused fury in Japan, as did reports that Yoshiro Mori had insisted on finishing a game of golf before dealing with the situation. The USA subsequently appointed the navy's second-in-command as a special envoy to Japan, who travelled to Tokyo at the end of the month to apologize in person and to brief the Japanese Prime Minister on the progress of investigations into the accident. The captain of the submarine also apologized to the families of those who had died, but resentment over the US military presence in Japan remained. In April the USA announced that the captain would not be court-martialled. Also in that month, Japan banned US nuclear submarines from visiting its ports after the US Navy failed to give prior notification of such a visit, as required. The

Japanese victims of the submarine collision, and their relatives, accepted US $13m. in compensation from the US Navy in November 2002.

In May 2001 US Deputy Secretary of State Richard Armitage urged even stronger relations with Japan and a greater Japanese participation in regional security, a view shared by Koizumi. In June Minister of Foreign Affairs Tanaka stated that Japan needed to become more independent of the USA. Tanaka also expressed doubts about the USA's planned 'national missile defense' (NMD) system, and the Director-General of the Defence Agency, Gen Nakatani, stated that any Japanese missile defence programme would be separate from the USA's plan. Koizumi held talks with President Bush at Camp David, USA, in late June–early July, but the summit meeting was marred by the news that a woman in Okinawa had allegedly been raped by a US serviceman; he was later surrendered to the Japanese authorities. Meanwhile, Japan and the USA disagreed over how to reduce global 'greenhouse gas' emissions, following the USA's withdrawal of support for the Kyoto Treaty in early 2001. The disagreements threatened to nullify the treaty.

Following the terrorist attacks on the USA in September 2001, Japan immediately pledged co-operation with the USA's 'war on terrorism', including military support within the framework of Japan's Constitution. Koizumi visited Washington, DC, later that month and announced that Japan would assist in the gathering of intelligence, the delivery of supplies and of medical and humanitarian relief. The requisite legislation was approved by the Diet, and in November Japan deployed several warships and 1,500 personnel to the Indian Ocean in this capacity; however, Japanese forces were still forbidden to participate in combat activities. At this time, several Japanese companies signed a deal with a US firm to build air defence systems for Japan's military.

President Bush visited Japan in February 2002 and praised Koizumi, urging him to reform the country's economy. Disagreements remained, however, over the USA's description of North Korea as part of an 'axis of evil' and over measures to reduce global warming. Japan pursued a policy of engagement with North Korea, while the USA adopted a more sceptical attitude to that country. None the less, Japan, along with South Korea, sought to encourage the USA to support Koizumi's visit to the North in September 2002 (see below). However, the USA adopted a harder line towards North Korea after it allegedly admitted to pursuing a secret nuclear-weapons programme, in October 2002. In early November 2002 the Japanese Government extended the deployment of its Maritime Self-Defense Force vessels in the Indian Ocean in support of the USA's 'war on terrorism'. In mid-December, at the request of the USA, Japan dispatched an advanced *Aegis* destroyer to the region, its highest-profile deployment to date. Meanwhile, in November Keiichi Inamine was re-elected Governor of Okinawa, having strongly campaigned in preceding months for a significant reduction in US troops stationed on the island.

There were signs in 2002 that Japan was gradually moving to reduce its dependency on the USA for its security. During that year Japan launched four H-IIA rockets as part of its civilian space programme, but analysts noted that the rocket could be put to military use. In addition, several politicians indicated that Japan could eventually develop nuclear weapons if the country felt threatened. In February 2003 the Defence Agency revealed that it had considered the possibility of developing nuclear weapons in 1995, but decided against such a move. In March 2003 Japan launched its first spy satellites, aiming to improve its independent intelligence-gathering capabilities.

In mid–December 2002 Japan and the USA held a meeting of defence and foreign ministers in Tokyo on outstanding security issues. In addition to seeking an early resolution of the crisis over North Korea's nuclear weapons programme, the two countries moved closer to agreement on the deployment of a joint-missile shield, which, the USA anticipated, would be deployed by 2008. In February 2003 the Government stated that the two countries would begin joint training of ballistic missile interception off the coast of Hawaii for two years, beginning in 2004. A final decision on whether to deploy such a system would then be made in 2005. Meanwhile, Koizumi gave President Bush his full support for the USA's war against Iraq, which commenced in late March 2003, despite strong opposition from the Japanese public. However, Japan would not provide any financial, logistical or military support to the USA in Iraq.

Stability in East and South-East Asia remained a vital consideration in Japanese foreign policy, since Japan continued to depend on Asia for much of its foreign trade, including imports of raw materials. Despite the signing of a treaty of peace and friendship with the People's Republic of China in 1978, relations deteriorated in the late 1980s after China expressed concern at Japan's increased defence expenditure and its more assertive military stance. Japanese aid to China was suspended in June 1989, following the Tiananmen Square massacre in Beijing, and was not resumed until November 1990. Relations between the two countries were strengthened by the visits to China by Emperor Akihito in October 1992, the first-ever Japanese imperial visit to China, and by Prime Minister Hosokawa in March 1994. However, in August of that year Japan announced the suspension of economic aid to China, following renewed nuclear testing by the Chinese Government. The provision of economic aid was resumed in early 1997, following the declaration of a moratorium on Chinese nuclear testing.

In July 1996 Japan's relations with both China and Taiwan were strained when a group of nationalists, the Japan Youth Federation, constructed a lighthouse and war memorial on the Senkaku Islands (or Diaoyu Islands in Chinese), a group of uninhabited islands situated in the East China Sea, to which all three countries laid claim. The situation was further aggravated in September by the accidental drowning of a Hong Kong citizen during a protest near the islands against Japan's claim. In October a flotilla of small boats, operated by activists from Taiwan, Hong Kong and Macao, raised the flags of China and Taiwan on the disputed islands. The Japanese Government sought to defuse tensions with China and Taiwan by withholding official recognition of the lighthouse; it did not, however, condemn those who had constructed the controversial buildings. In May 1997 China expressed serious concern, when a member of the Japanese Diet landed on one of the disputed islands. The Japanese Government distanced itself from the action.

In September 1997 Hashimoto visited China to commemorate the 25th anniversary of the normalization of relations between the two countries. China expressed concern at the revised US-Japanese security arrangements, following a statement by a senior Japanese minister that the area around Taiwan might be covered under the new guidelines. Procedures for the removal of chemical weapons, deployed in China by Japanese forces during the Second World War, were also discussed. During a visit to Japan by the Chinese Premier, Li Peng, in November, a bilateral fisheries agreement was signed. In November 1998, during a six-day state visit by President Jiang Zemin, Obuchi and Jiang issued (but declined to sign) a joint declaration on friendship and co-operation, in which Japan expressed deep remorse for past aggression against China. China, however, was reported to be displeased by the lack of a written apology, and remained concerned at the implications of US-Japanese defence arrangements regarding Taiwan. A subsequent US-Japanese agreement to initiate joint technical research on the development of a theatre missile defence system, followed by the Japanese Diet's approval, in May 1999, of legislation on the implementation of the revised US-Japanese defence guidelines (see above), provoked severe criticism from China, despite Japan's insistence that military co-operation with the USA was purely defensive. In July a meeting in Beijing between Obuchi and the Chinese Premier, Zhu Rongji, resulted in the formalization of a bilateral agreement on China's entry to the WTO, following several months of intense negotiations on the liberalization of trade in services. In August 2000 China withdrew permission for the Japanese Minister of Transport, Hajime Morita, to visit the People's Republic in September, owing to scheduling difficulties with Chinese officials. The Japanese media, however, attributed the Chinese change of attitude to a recent visit by Morita to a shrine honouring Japan's war dead, including those convicted of war crimes. Zhu Rongji visited Japan in October, and admitted that his failure to demand an apology for the host country's wartime conduct had attracted criticism in China.

In April 2001 a trade dispute broke out between China and Japan after the latter, seeking to protect its domestic manufacturers, imposed tariffs on imports of Chinese mushrooms, leeks and rushes. China responded by introducing tariffs on Japanese consumer goods, leading to further disputes, which persisted throughout the rest of 2001. China was further angered by Japan's decision to allow former Taiwanese President Lee Teng-hui to visit the country in May. These disagreements led to a postponement of a visit to Japan by former Chinese Premier Li Peng. Meanwhile, China reacted angrily to Koizumi's visit to the Yasukuni Shrine, and a senior official of the Chinese Ministry of Foreign Affairs urged Japan to take 'visible action' to renounce its militaristic past. Koizumi travelled to China in early October, when he visited the Marco Polo Bridge (the site of a clash between China and Japan that led to full-scale war in 1937) and apologized for Japan's past crimes in China. The visit was also aimed at reassuring Beijing about Japan's support for the USA's 'war on terrorism', and bilateral relations subsequently improved, although Chinese concerns about Tokyo's military deployment remained. In November China and Japan, along with the Republic of Korea, agreed to hold regular meetings of their ministers of finance and of foreign affairs in order to foster closer co-operation. However, in late December 2001 a state-supported Chinese newspaper criticized Japan for allowing the yen to depreciate, a move that might curb Chinese exports.

In March 2002 Makiko Tanaka, the former Minister of Foreign Affairs, visited China to mark 30 years of diplomatic relations between the two countries. (Her father, Kakuei Tanaka, had overseen the restoration of relations in 1972.) Li Peng visited Japan in early April, stating that he was optimistic about improving bilateral relations. However, Koizumi's second visit to the Yasukuni Shrine in late April was condemned by China, as was a third visit to the shrine in January 2003. Tensions remained in Japan's relations with China. In April 2002 the leader of the opposition Liberal Party, Ichiro Ozawa, warned that Japan was capable of developing thousands of nuclear warheads in response to China's military build-up, if necessary. In May Japan strongly protested against the entry by Chinese security forces into the Japanese consulate in Shenyang, China, to remove several North Koreans who had sought refuge there. China responded that Japanese officials had consented to the move. The dispute was resolved when both sides allowed the North Koreans to travel to South Korea via a third country. The confrontation raised mutual suspicions, although in June China allowed Japan to salvage an alleged North Korean spy vessel from its territorial waters.

Although China had, in October 2001, invited Japanese Crown Prince Naruhito and Crown Princess Masako to visit China to mark the occasion of the 30th anniversary, in September 2002, of the establishment of diplomatic relations, the royal couple did not attend the ceremonies. None the less, in late 2002 Japan and China were increasingly seeking to forge a tripartite free-trade agreement with South Korea, and Koizumi held discussions with Jiang Zemin at the APEC summit meeting in Mexico in October. Tokyo hoped that Beijing would use its influence with North Korea to bring about a peaceful resolution to the diplomatic crisis surrounding the latter's nuclear weapons programme. In February 2003 China agreed to allow a Japanese escapee from North Korea to travel to Japan after she sought asylum at the Japanese consulate in Shenyang. Several other such cases were subsequently reported.

In January 1993, meanwhile, Prime Minister Miyazawa toured four member countries of the Association of South East Asian Nations (ASEAN, see p. 146), during which he advocated an expansion of political and economic co-operation in the region. A visit by Prime Minister Hashimoto to ASEAN countries in January 1997 aimed to strengthen economic and security relations with the member countries. During 1998 Japan was widely criticized for its slow response to the Asian economic crisis. Japan's proposals for an 'Asian Monetary Fund' to stabilize the region were rejected by the USA and IMF, fearing a loss of influence in debtor countries. The weakness of the Japanese currency adversely affected financial markets throughout Asia, undermining efforts to stimulate regional economic recovery. As a result of increasing international pressure, in October the Japanese Government announced a US $30,000m. aid 'package' for Asian countries. In November the USA and Japan presented a joint initiative for growth and economic recovery in Asia, and in the following month Japan pledged further aid, to be disbursed over a three-year period. In January 2000 Prime Minister Obuchi visited Cambodia, Laos and Thailand. In April Japan proposed that its coast guard participate in joint anti-piracy patrols in the Melaka (Malacca) Straits (lying between Indonesia and Malaysia) with other regional navies, but was prevented from doing so following Chinese objections. In May Japan provided Myanmar with a substantial aid programme, aimed at building closer bilateral ties. Also in May, Singapore agreed to allow Japan to use its military bases for evacuating its citizens from crisis locations, and for regional peace-keeping missions, the first agreement of its kind between Japan and another country. In April 2001 Japan provided another aid programme for Myanmar, despite a

de facto international moratorium on such aid owing to the repressive nature of the country's ruling military junta. In October Japan reached a comprehensive free-trade agreement with Singapore, and in January 2002 Prime Minister Koizumi visited Indonesia, Malaysia, the Philippines, Singapore and Thailand. Japan's influence in South-East Asia largely depended on its aid and investment programmes, both of which were being curtailed owing to Japan's economic problems. In April 2002 Koizumi also visited Viet Nam, East Timor (now Timor-Leste), Australia and New Zealand, and in November he attended the ASEAN summit meeting in Phnom-Penh, Cambodia, where he signed an agreement to develop a comprehensive economic partnership with ASEAN members within 10 years—including the possible formation of a Japan-ASEAN free-trade area. Japan had hitherto established bilateral free-trade agreements with several ASEAN members, but not with the organization as a whole. In February 2003 the Secretary-General of ASEAN, Ong Keng Yong, urged Japan to develop political, security, and cultural co-operation with the organization.

Attempts to establish full diplomatic relations with the Democratic People's Republic of Korea (DPRK) in early 1991 were hindered by North Korean demands for financial reparations for the Japanese colonization of the country during 1910–45 and by the DPRK's refusal to allow International Atomic Energy Agency inspectors access to its nuclear facilities. Relations improved in 1995 and 1996 after Japan provided emergency aid to the DPRK when serious food shortages were reported. Concerns that the DPRK had developed a missile capable of reaching Japanese territory resulted in the suspension of food aid in mid-1996, but, following bilateral negotiations in August 1997, at which it was agreed to reopen discussions aimed at restoring full diplomatic relations, provision of food aid resumed in October. Agreement was also reached concerning the issue of visits to relatives in Japan by the estimated 1,800 Japanese nationals resident in the DPRK. The first such visits took place in November. However, food aid and normalization talks were suspended in mid-1998, following the testing by the DPRK of a suspected missile over Japanese territory. Tensions were exacerbated in March 1999, when two suspected North Korean spy ships, which had infiltrated Japanese waters, were pursued and fired on by Japanese naval forces. In mid-1999 it was reported that Japanese components had been used by the DPRK for the construction of weapons and other military equipment. Relations improved following the DPRK's agreement with the USA, in September, to suspend its reported plans to test a new long-range missile. In October, following unofficial talks between Japanese and North Korean government officials in Singapore, Japan lifted a ban on charter flights to the DPRK. In December the Japanese Government announced that it would resume the provision of food aid. Later that month intergovernmental preparatory talks on re-establishing diplomatic relations were held in Beijing, after Japanese and North Korean Red Cross officials reached an agreement on humanitarian issues. Most notably, the Red Cross organization of the DPRK promised to urge its Government to co-operate in an investigation into the fate of some 10 missing Japanese nationals, believed by the Japanese Government to have been abducted by North Korean agents in the 1970s and 1980s. Full negotiations on the establishment of diplomatic relations were held in April 2000, and several further rounds of talks took place during the year, despite an announcement by Japan in September that normal bilateral relations would not be restored until the cases of Japanese citizens allegedly abducted by North Korean agents had been solved. In October, however, a further round of negotiations took place in Beijing, China. Meanwhile, in September the long-delayed third series of visits to their homeland by the Japanese wives of North Korean men took place. In February 2001 Pyongyang again reiterated the need for compensation from Japan. In early May Japan expelled Kim Jong Nam, the son of North Korean leader Kim Jong Il, and Jong Nam's wife, son and a second woman, when they attempted to enter the country on false passports. The DPRK was one of several Asian countries that condemned Junichiro Koizumi's visit to the Yasukuni Shrine in August. In November Japanese police arrested Kan Young Kwan, an executive of the Japan-based, pro-North Korean organization, *Chongryon*, on charges of misappropriating funds through local credit unions. The incident highlighted the sometimes-illegal activities of the North Korean community in Japan.

In late December 2001 Japan's coast guard sank a suspected North Korean spy vessel after it had been expelled from Japan's exclusive economic zone. The DPRK condemned the incident, but denied any involvement. Japanese coast guard forces searched the sunken vessel in May 2002, and raised it in September of that year. Japan's concerns had been heightened in early 2002 when US President Bush referred to North Korea as one of three countries forming an 'axis of evil', comments that Japan viewed as inconsistent with aims of reducing regional tensions.

In an unexpected diplomatic move, Junichiro Koizumi visited Pyongyang in mid-September 2002, becoming the first incumbent Japanese Prime Minister to do so. His one-day visit, during which he held discussions with Kim Jong Il, was dominated by the latter's admission that North Korean agents had abducted 12 Japanese citizens in the 1970s and 1980s, of whom five were still alive. The remainder were said to have died of natural causes, although suspicions remained that they might have been executed, after Pyongyang failed to locate their graves. Kim apologized for the incidents, but attributed them to rogue elements within the security services. The admission led to a hardening of attitudes against North Korea among the Japanese public, with some sources indicating that the total number of Japanese abductees might be as high as 100. The surviving captives were temporarily allowed to return to Japan in mid-October, although they had to leave behind any spouses or children. The Japanese authorities, however, refused to allow them to return to North Korea after the visit. Despite this, representatives from the two countries held the first round of resumed discussions on the restoration of normal diplomatic relations in Malaysia at the end of October, but failed to make any progress.

Japan became alarmed in October 2002 after North Korean representatives allegedly admitted to visiting US officials that Pyongyang was pursuing a secret nuclear weapons programme. Koizumi announced that Japan would halt further economic co-operation with North Korea until the issues of the abducted Japanese citizens and the nuclear programme were resolved. Pyongyang's admission led to increased co-operation between Japan and the USA over how to resolve the crisis, with Japan moving closer to participating in a missile shield with the USA (see above). Pyongyang warned Japan that it would abandon its moratorium on missile-testing if normalization talks failed to make any progress. In separate incidents in late February and early March 2003 North Korea test-launched two short-range ground-to-ship missiles in the Sea of Japan, and in early April tested a third missile in the Yellow Sea. However, it refrained from testing longer-range ballistic missiles, which Tokyo considered a threat to its security. The director-general of Japan's Defence Agency warned North Korea that Japan could conduct a pre-emptive strike on North Korean missile facilities if necessary.

Relations with the Republic of Korea were strained during 1996–98 for various reasons, principally concerning territorial and fishing disputes. Relations improved, however, during a four-day state visit by the South Korean President, Kim Dae-Jung, to Japan in October 1998, when a joint declaration was signed, in which Japan apologized for the suffering inflicted on the Korean people during Japanese colonial rule. Japan also pledged substantial aid to the Republic of Korea to stimulate economic recovery. In November the two countries concluded negotiations on the renewal of their bilateral fisheries agreement, which came into effect in January 1999. An agreement to modify some of the terms of the accord was reached in March 1999, following a series of differences over its implementation. Increased co-operation was emphasized during a visit by Obuchi to the Republic of Korea later that month, when both countries agreed to strengthen bilateral economic relations, and Japan pledged further aid. In August, Japan and the Republic of Korea held their first joint military exercises since the Second World War, in the Tsushima Straits. Prime Minister Mori visited Seoul in May 2000, where he advocated closer bilateral ties and pledged support for the inter-Korean summit meeting held in June.

Relations between Japan and the Republic of Korea deteriorated in 2001, however, following Tokyo's official endorsement of a new history school textbook, which minimized the suffering of Chinese and Koreans during Japanese occupation. In early April the Republic of Korea recalled its ambassador, cancelled planned exchanges in protest and demanded 35 revisions to the text. In July Japan stated that there would be no revisions, further inflaming public opinion in Korea. This anger was exacerbated in August when Prime Minister Koizumi visited the Yasukuni Shrine, leading to many protests. In October Koizumi visited Seoul and apologized for past crimes and suffering under Japanese rule; however, he was forced to cancel a visit to the National Assembly, owing to hostility against him there. In November Japan and the Republic of Korea, along with China, agreed to establish regular contacts between their ministers of finance and foreign affairs. In late March 2002 Koizumi again visited South Korea and discussed the possibility of establishing a free trade pact, as well as Japan's policy towards North Korea.

Along with China and North Korea, South Korea condemned Koizumi's visits to the Yasukuni Shrine in late April 2002 and mid-January 2003. However, Koizumi and Kim Dae-Jung in late March agreed to begin discussions on a possible bilateral free-trade agreement, and at the end of May Koizumi attended the opening ceremony of the 2002 football World Cup in Seoul. Also in attendance was Prince Takamado (who died in November 2002) and his wife, who were making the first official visit to South Korea by a member of the Imperial family. The football tournament, a major source of prestige to both countries, passed by without incident. Any remaining mutual hostility between the two countries was overshadowed in 2002 by the need for co-operation in engaging with the North. In December 2002 Koizumi and South Korean President-elect Roh Moo-Hyun agreed to form a united front when dealing with the North. Koizumi subsequently attended Roh's inauguration in late February 2003, and the two were expected to continue efforts towards reaching a free-trade agreement.

The actions of the Japanese army in the Second World War proved to be a contentious issue from the mid-1990s, both domestically and in Japan's relations with neighbouring Asian countries, in the context of the 50th anniversary, in August 1995, of the surrender of Japanese forces. In November 1994 an international ruling that Asian women, used for sexual purposes by the Japanese army during the Second World War ('comfort women'), should receive compensation was rejected by the Japanese Government, which insisted that the issue of reparation payments to individuals had been fully covered under the terms of the peace treaty of 1951. Japan also applied this policy to claims for compensation made by former prisoners of war belonging to the Allied forces. In February 1995 Prime Minister Murayama publicly acknowledged that Japan was responsible, in part, for the post-war division of the Korean peninsula. He was forced to retract the statement, however, following bitter controversy in the Diet. In June a resolution was passed apologizing for Japanese actions in the war, despite considerable disagreement in the Diet. However, countries whose citizens had been prisoners of the Japanese army criticized the resolution as being insufficiently explicit. In August 1996 the first compensation payments, accompanied by a letter of apology from Prime Minister Hashimoto, were made from a private fund to four Philippine victims, who had been used as 'comfort women' during the war. The majority of groups representing South Korean victims refused to accept payment from the fund, demanding that compensation be forthcoming from official, rather than private, sources. In April 1998, however, a Japanese district court ordered the Government to pay compensation to three former 'comfort women' from the Republic of Korea. Another group of South Korean 'comfort women' was refused the right to compensation by the Japanese High Court in November 2000. In late 1999 a lawsuit was filed in the US state of California against several large Japanese corporations on behalf of former prisoners of war and civilians from various countries, who alleged that the companies had profited from their forced labour during the Second World War. In November 2000 one of these corporations agreed to pay compensation to Chinese forced labourers used during the War. There were fears among Japan's neighbours that the emergence of Junichiro Koizumi as Prime Minister marked the emergence of a more nationalistic Japan. Tokyo's endorsement of a high school textbook that played down Japan's atrocities in Asia during the 1930s and 1940s, and Koizumi's visit to the Yasukuni Shrine in 2001, 2002 and 2003, were widely condemned in the region, especially in China and the Koreas (see above). In July 2002 a court in Hiroshima rejected a compensation claim by five Chinese labourers who had been brought to Japan during the Second World War, but acknowledged that the men had been forcibly brought to the country. At the same time Koizumi and his Cabinet agreed to donate 10% of their annual salary to a fund designed to compensate former 'comfort women'. In August a Tokyo court rejected a compensation claim by 180 Chinese for damages inflicted in biological warfare during the 1930s and 1940s, but acknowledged that Japan had, in fact, waged such warfare in

China at that time. This was corroborated by a former member of Japan's biological warfare division, who testified to such crimes at the trial. Historians estimated that 300,000 Chinese had been killed by Japanese biological warfare schemes.

Japan's relations with Russia have been dominated by the issue of the Northern Territories, four small islands situated close to Hokkaido, which were annexed in 1945 by the USSR. Both countries claim sovereignty over the islands, and there has been no substantial progress towards resolving the situation since 1956, when Japan and the USSR resumed diplomatic relations. In February 1992 a joint Japanese-Russian working group began discussions about a prospective peace treaty (formally ending the Second World War), and meetings on the issue took place in 1992 and 1993. However, relations between the two countries deteriorated, following the disposal of nuclear waste in Japanese waters by Russian ships in November, and Russia's decision, in August 1994, to open fire on Japanese vessels, that were alleged to have been fishing in Russian waters. Bilateral negotiations over the status of the disputed territory opened in March 1995. In November 1996 Japan indicated that it was prepared to resume the disbursement of an aid 'package', withheld since 1991, and in May 1997 the Japanese Government abandoned its opposition to Russia's proposed membership of the G-7 group. Russian plans for joint development of the mineral and fishing resources of the disputed territory were followed, in July, by an outline agreement on the jurisdiction of the islands. Later in that month a new diplomatic policy was forged, based on 'trust, mutual benefit and long-term prospects'. At an informal summit meeting in November, the two parties agreed to work towards the conclusion of a formal peace treaty by the year 2000. Negotiations resulted in the conclusion of a framework fisheries agreement in December 1997. The Japanese Government offered considerable financial aid to Russia during a visit by President Yeltsin to Japan in April 1998, and agreement was reached on the expansion of economic co-operation. In November Prime Minister Obuchi and Yeltsin signed a joint declaration on bilateral relations in Moscow. During Obuchi's visit Yeltsin reportedly submitted proposals on the resolution of the territorial dispute, in response to suggestions made by Hashimoto in April. Although it had been agreed that the contents of the proposals should not be made public, it was widely reported that both countries still claimed sovereignty over the islands, with Japan advocating a transitional period of Russian administrative control. Agreement was reached on the establishment of subcommissions to examine issues of border delimitation and joint economic activity on the disputed islands. However, little progress was achieved by the subcommissions during 1999. In September Japan agreed to resume lending to Russia, which had been suspended since the Russian Government had effectively devalued the rouble and defaulted on some of its debts in mid-1998. At the same time an accord was concluded on improved access to the disputed islands for former Japanese inhabitants. Negotiations achieved little progress during 2000, a major obstacle being the issue of how many of the islands should be returned. Despite Russian President Vladimir Putin's repudiation of Japan's claim to any of the islands during his first official visit to Tokyo in September, Russia subsequently offered to abide by a 1956 declaration that it would relinquish two of the islands after the signature of a peace treaty, but Japan initially rejected this partial solution. Meanwhile, in November 2000 a former Japanese naval officer on trial in Tokyo admitted spying for Russia. There was outrage in Japan at the fact that the crime carried possible punishments that were perceived as being extremely lenient in relation to the severity of the offence.

In March 2001 Prime Minister Mori met President Putin in Irkutsk, Russia, and discussed the future of the islands; however, no new agreements were reached. Nevertheless, in April Japanese and Russian military leaders agreed to improve bilateral military co-operation. In May Prime Minister Koizumi adopted a harder stance than his predecessor, and demanded that all four islands be relinquished, a position rejected by Russia. Prime Minister Koizumi met Putin at the Group of Eight summit meeting in July, amid Japanese anger that Russia had permitted South Korean vessels to fish off the islands. The ongoing disputes meant that no agreement was reached on developing a Japan-Russia-Europe transport corridor, and in August Koizumi warned of serious damage to relations with Russia if the fishing dispute were not resolved. Hopes for 'two-track' negotiations (dealing with two of the four islands separately from the other two) seemed in doubt in January 2002;

however, in February both sides agreed to continue talks. Japanese officials met their Russian counterparts on the margins of the G–8 summit meeting and the Asian security summit in Brunei in mid-2002, and both sides expressed a willingness to expand relations in all fields. By late 2002 Koizumi was increasingly seeking Russia's assistance in persuading North Korea to abandon its nuclear weapons programme. In early January 2003 Koizumi visited Moscow and held a summit meeting with Putin, during which the two agreed to engage North Korea. Koizumi also visited the Russian Far East, where he met regional leaders. Both Japan and Russia were keen to build a 3,800-km pipeline that would transport petroleum from Angarsk, in Siberia, to Nakhodka on Russia's Pacific coast, from where it could be shipped to Japan. The cost, estimated at US $5,000m., was considered a prohibitive factor, but the scheme would reduce Japan's dependency on Middle Eastern supplies.

The Japanese Government criticized India and Pakistan for conducting nuclear tests in mid-1998, and in response suspended grants of non-humanitarian aid and loans to both countries. A series of missile tests carried out by India and Pakistan in April 1999 again provoked criticism from Japan. Following a visit to India by the Japanese Prime Minister in August 2000, differences over nuclear testing were set aside in favour of enhanced security, defence and research co-operation between Japan and India, which continued during 2001. Indian Prime Minister Vajpayee visited Japan in December, the first such visit since 1992. In addition to security issues, the two countries discussed closer co-operation in their software and computer industries.

In January 2002 Japan hosted an international conference on the reconstruction of Afghanistan, and emerged as the largest single donor, pledging some US $500m. over two-and-a-half years. During 2002 and early 2003 Japan also sought to bring a lasting peace settlement to Sri Lanka, and pledged to continue overseas development assistance to the war-ravaged island.

In November 2000 the Peruvian President, Alberto Fujimori, arrived in Tokyo from where he submitted his resignation by fax, following increasing allegations of domestic corruption. In December Japan announced that Fujimori possessed dual nationality as his father had been a Japanese citizen, and that he was therefore entitled to remain indefinitely in the country. In March 2001, however, the Peruvian authorities charged Fujimori with criminal abuse of power and requested his extradition. Japan refused, despite Peruvian warnings of serious consequences if the former President did not return. Fujimori remained in Japan throughout 2002, refusing to co-operate with members of a Peruvian Truth and Reconciliation Commission who visited Japan. In March 2003 Japan refused to extradite Fujimori, despite Interpol's issue of a warrant for his arrest.

In September 1990 Japan contributed to the international effort to force an unconditional Iraqi withdrawal from Kuwait. A controversial LDP-sponsored Peace Co-operation Bill, which provided for the dispatch to the Persian (Arabian) Gulf area of some 2,000 non-combatant personnel, was withdrawn in November after it encountered severe political opposition. In January 1991, following repeated US demands for a greater financial commitment to the resolution of the Gulf crisis (and a swifter disbursement of moneys already pledged), the Japanese Government announced plans substantially to increase its contribution and to provide aircraft for the transport of refugees in the region. Opposition to the proposal was again vociferous. The Government secured the support of several centrist parties, by pledging that any financial aid from Japan would be employed in a 'non-lethal' capacity, and legislation to approve the new contribution was adopted by the Diet in March.

Japan's urgent need for new oil supplies prompted the visit to the country in October 2000 of the Iranian President, Muhammad Khatami, the first by an Iranian Head of State since that country's revolution of 1979. The trip culminated in Japan's acquisition of negotiation rights over the world's largest undeveloped oilfield, Azadegan field, in Iran. In July 2001 the Minister of Economy, Trade and Industry visited Iran, Kuwait, Saudi Arabia and the United Arab Emirates, in order to promote Japan's oil interests in the Middle East.

In June 1992 controversial legislation to permit the SDF to participate in UN peace-keeping operations was approved. Their role, however, was to be confined to logistical and humanitarian tasks, unless a special dispensation from the Diet were granted. In September members of the SDF were dispatched to serve in the UN Transitional Authority in Cambodia (UNTAC).

Japanese troops participated in further UN peace-keeping operations in Mozambique, in 1993, and, under Japanese command, on the Rwandan–Zairean border, in 1994. Legislation was approved in November 1994 to enable Japanese forces to be deployed overseas if the Government believed the lives of Japanese citizens to be at risk. In September Japan reiterated its desire to be a permanent member of the UN Security Council, particularly in view of its status as the world's largest donor of development aid and the second largest contributor (after the USA) to the UN budget. In October 1996 the UN General Assembly voted to allocate to Japan a non-permanent seat on the Security Council, to be held for a two-year period from January 1997. In the late 1990s the Japanese Government was campaigning for a greater proportion of senior-level positions within the UN to be allocated to Japanese personnel. Draft legislation on an expansion of SDF participation in UN peace-keeping operations was to be considered by the Japanese Diet in 2000. In November of that year Japan's announcement that it hoped to reduce expenditure on its foreign aid programme by 3% in 2001/02 prompted concern from the UN. Japan intensified its campaign to obtain a permanent seat on the UN Security Council in January 2001, when Yoshiro Mori visited South Africa, Kenya and Nigeria, on the first ever trip by a serving Japanese Prime Minister to sub-Saharan Africa. He hoped to obtain support for the bid in return for economic assistance.

In November 2001 Japan announced plans to send 700 SDF members to East Timor as part of the international peace-keeping force. The force consisted mostly of engineers, and the first contingent arrived in March 2002. In February 2002 the Japanese Government planned to revise the 1992 law on peace-keeping missions, in order to allow the dispatch of the SDF without the consent of those in conflict following a UN request, and for SDF personnel to be equipped with more powerful weapons, rather than purely defensive ones.

Government

Under the Constitution of 1947, the Emperor is Head of State but has no governing power. Legislative power is vested in the bicameral Diet, comprising the House of Representatives (lower house), whose members are elected for a four-year term, and the House of Councillors (upper house), members of which are elected for six years, one-half being elected every three years. The House of Representatives comprises 480 seats—300 single-seat constituencies and 180 determined by proportional representation—and there are 252 seats in the House of Councillors. The number of seats in the House of Representatives was reduced from 500 for the 2000 elections; the reduction was in the number of seats determined by proportional representation. There is universal suffrage for all adults from 20 years of age. Executive power is vested in the Cabinet, which is responsible to the Diet. The Emperor appoints the Prime Minister (on designation by the Diet), who appoints the other Ministers in the Cabinet.

Japan has 47 prefectures, each administered by an elected Governor.

Defence

Although the Constitution renounces war and the use of force, the right of self-defence is not excluded. Japan maintains ground, maritime and air self-defence forces. Military service is voluntary. The USA provides equipment and training staff and also maintains bases in Japan. US forces in Japan totalled 38,450 at 1 August 2002. The total strength of the Japanese Self-Defence Forces at 1 August 2002 was some 239,900: army 148,200, navy 44,400, air force 45,4600 and central staff 1,700. Government expenditure on defence under revised projections for the 2002/03 general account budget was 4,956,000m. yen.

Economic Affairs

In 2001, according to estimates by the World Bank, Japan's gross national income (GNI), measured at average 1999–2001 prices, was US $4,574,164m., equivalent to $35,990 per head (or $27,430 per head on an international purchasing-power parity basis). During 1990–2001, it was estimated, the population increased by an average annual of 0.3%, while gross domestic product (GDP) per head increased, in real terms, by an average of 1.0% per year. Overall GDP increased, in real terms, by an average annual rate of 1.3% in 1990–2001; in 2001 GDP contracted by 0.4%.

In 2001 agriculture (including forestry and fishing) contributed 1.3% of GDP, and engaged 4.9% of the employed labour force in that year. The principal crops are rice, potatoes, cabbages, sugar beets, and citrus fruits. During 1990–2001 according to official sources, agricultural GDP declined, in real terms, at an average rate of 3.0% annually. Compared with the previous year, however, the sector's GDP increased by 0.4% in 2001.

Industry (including mining, manufacturing, construction and utilities) contributed 29.4% of GDP in 2001, and engaged 30.5% of the employed labour force in that year. During 1990–2001, according to official sources, industrial GDP decreased at an average annual rate of only 0.1%. Following an increase of 4.7% in 2000, however, during 2001 industrial output decreased by 4.0%.

Mining and quarrying contributed 0.1% of GDP in 2001 and engaged less than 0.1% of the employed labour force in that year. While the domestic output of limestone and sulphur is sufficient to meet domestic demand, all of Japan's requirements of bauxite, crude petroleum and iron ore, and a high percentage of its requirements of copper ore and coking coal are met by imports. The GDP of the mining sector contracted by an average annual rate of 3.3% in 1990–2001. Compared with the previous year, however, mining GDP rose by 2.8% in 2001.

In 2001 manufacturing contributed 19.8% of GDP, and in that year 20.0% of the employed labour force were engaged in the sector. Manufacturing GDP increased by an average of 0.6% per year in 1990–2001, expanding by 5.5% in 2000 compared with the previous year, but decreasing by 4.9% in 2001. The most important branches of manufacturing are machinery and transport equipment, electrical and electronic equipment, and iron and steel.

Japan imports most of its energy requirements, with imports of petroleum and petroleum products comprising 20.4% of the value of total imports in 2000. Nuclear energy accounted for 30.0% of electricity output in 1999, natural gas 22.1%, and coal 21.2%. The remainder of electricity output was generated by petroleum and hydroelectric power. There are proposals to construct a further 20 nuclear reactors by 2010. In October 2000 Japan secured negotiation rights over the world's largest undeveloped oilfield, in Iran.

The services sector contributed 69.3% of GDP in 2001, and engaged 64.6% of the employed labour force in that year. The GDP of the services sector increased by an average of 2.4% annually in 1990–2001, expanding by 2.5% in 2001 compared with the previous year. Tourist receipts, totalling US $3,374m. in 2000, are an important source of revenue.

In 2001 Japan recorded a trade surplus of US $70,214m., and there was a surplus of $89,280m. on the current account of the balance of payments. In 2001 the principal source of imports was the USA (18.1%), which was also the principal market for exports (30.0%). Other major suppliers in that year were the People's Republic of China (16.6%), Australia, the Republic of Korea and Taiwan. Other major purchasers of Japanese exports were China (7.7%), the Republic of Korea, Taiwan and Hong Kong. The principal imports in 2001 were machinery and transport equipment, miscellaneous manufactured articles, petroleum and petroleum products, food and live animals, and basic manufactures. The principal exports in that year were non-electric and electrical machinery, and transport equipment.

On the general account budget, projections for the financial year ending 31 March 2003 envisaged that both revenue and expenditure would stand at 81,230,000m. yen., with government bond issues accounting for 30,000,000m. yen of revenue. The budget for 2003/04 projected expenditure of 81,790,000m. yen, an increase of 0.7% compared with the previous year. The annual rate of inflation averaged 0.8% in 1990–2000. Consumer prices declined by 0.3% in 1999 and by 0.6% in 2000, continuing to decrease in 2001 and 2002. The rate of unemployment was 5.5% of the labour force in February 2003.

Japan is a member of the Asia-Pacific Economic Co-operation (APEC, see p. 139) forum, the Asian Development Bank (ADB, see p. 143), the Organisation for Economic Co-operation and Development (OECD, see p. 277), the Colombo Plan (see p. 339) and the World Trade Organization (WTO, see p. 323).

Following a period of rapid economic expansion in the 1980s, Japan underwent a period of prolonged economic stagnation, including several recessions, during the 1990s. This resulted from the collapse of asset prices and the end of the so-called 'bubble economy'. A number of economic stimulus 'packages' failed to generate recovery, but initially limited the extent of the deceleration. Despite some signs of improvement during 1999 and the first half of 2000, in 2001 the Japanese economy moved into recession once again. Consumer demand remained depressed, in part because declining prices encouraged consumers to wait for further price reductions. By December 2001 the unemployment rate had reached its highest level since the Second World War, amid fears that it could rise further as restructuring continued to lead to job losses. By early 2003, however, unemployment had stabilized at 5.5%. Political instability and a lack of confidence in the Government's commitment to reform contributed to the Japanese stock market's decline, and in early March 2003 the benchmark Nikkei index declined to its lowest level for over 20 years, falling to below 8,000 points —a decrease of 80% from its peak in December 1989. The concurrent economic deceleration in the USA limited Japan's ability to implement an export-led recovery, and also had an indirect adverse effect on Japan's regional trade, as other Asian countries reliant on extensive export revenue from the USA found their purchasing power for Japanese goods reduced. In the financial sector consolidation was widespread in 2000–02, and bankruptcies of high-profile organizations continued. The banking system remained troubled by bad loans in 2001–02, with an estimated 81,540,000m. yen of such loans having been cancelled between 1992 and March 2002. In September 2002 the Government announced plans to buy back shares in Japanese banks that had been sold by the institutions in order to cover losses from bad loans, and in late 2002 plans to reform the banking sector, including the possible nationalization of several major banks, were blocked by anti-reformist elements within the LDP. None the less, the Government committed itself to halving the ratio of non-performing loans by 2005. On becoming Prime Minister in April 2001, Junichiro Koizumi had pledged to introduce major structural reforms, to address the problem of the country's debt burden, to compel the closure of businesses with excessive bad debts and to transfer the state-managed postal savings system to the private sector. However, he faced immense opposition to such plans from elements within his own party, which had strong ties with vested interest groups. Furthermore, the yen declined to its lowest point against the US dollar for three years in December 2001, having lost almost 13% of its value since January, as Japan sought to boost exports. Although GDP was initially said to have increased at an annual rate of 5.7% during the first quarter of 2002, this was later revised to a contraction of 0.1% at an annualized rate. Second quarter growth was 1.9% at an annualized rate. By early 2002 Japan's public debt had risen to the equivalent of almost 140% of GDP, in part owing to the series of massive economic stimulus 'packages' the Government had introduced in its attempts to revitalize the economy. As a result, in May 2002 Moody's, the international credit-ratings agency, reduced Japan's sovereign rating to the same level as that of Botswana and Latvia. In August Koizumi revealed plans for only limited tax cuts, greatly disappointing the business community. Meanwhile, Japan faced renewed international pressure to combat deflation, forecast at –0.8% in 2003 and –0.6% in 2004. A modified reform plan was announced in October 2002, but was criticized for its lack of boldness and a specific timeframe. The Government announced a supplementary budget of 3,000m. yen in November, half of which would be spent on public works and the remainder on social security. Additional fears arose from a decrease in exports —traditionally a source of growth in Japan's economy—in 2002.

Meanwhile, preliminary figures indicated that GDP had increased by 0.5% (2.2% at an annualized rate) in the last quarter of 2002, bolstered by a temporary revival of exports and consumer spending, yielding overall growth in 2002 at 0.3%. There were fears that the commencement of the USA's war against Iraq in March 2003 would raise petroleum prices and precipitate a global economic slowdown, both of which would adversely affect Japan's economic growth, originally forecast at 0.4%–0.5% in 2003.

Education

A kindergarten (*yochien*) system provides education for children aged between three and five years of age, although the majority of kindergartens are privately controlled. Education is compulsory between the ages of six and 15. Elementary education, which begins at six years of age, lasts for six years. Lower secondary education lasts for a further three years. In 2000 more than 11.4m. children aged six to 15 were enrolled in compulsory education, while 4.2m. of those aged 15 to 18 received upper secondary education. Upper secondary schools provide a three-year course in general topics, or a vocational course in subjects such as agriculture, commerce, fine art and technical studies. There are four types of institution for higher education. Universities (*daigaku*) offer a four-year degree course, as well as postgraduate courses. In 2001 there were 669 graduate schools and universities in Japan. Junior colleges (*tanki-daigaku*) provide less specialized two- to three-year courses. In 2001 there were 559 junior colleges in Japan. Both universities and junior colleges offer facilities for teacher-training. Colleges of technology (*koto-senmon-gakko*), of which there were 62 in 2001, offer a five-year specialized training. Since 1991 colleges of technology have been able to offer short-term advanced courses. Special training colleges (*senshu-gakko*) offer advanced courses in technical and vocational subjects, lasting for at least one year. Initial forecasts for the 1999/2000 general account budget envisaged government expenditure of 6,473,100m. yen on education and science.

Public Holidays

2003: 1 January (New Year's Day), 15 January (Coming of Age Day), 11 February (National Foundation Day), 20 March (Vernal Equinox Day), 29 April (Greenery Day), 3 May (Constitution Memorial Day), 5 May (Children's Day), 20 July (Marine Day), 15 September (Respect for the Aged Day), 23 September (Autumnal Equinox), 14 October (Sports Day), 3 November (Culture Day), 23 November (Labour Thanksgiving Day), 23 December (Emperor's Birthday).

2004: 1 January (New Year's Day), 15 January (Coming of Age Day), 11 February (National Foundation Day), 20 March (Vernal Equinox Day), 29 April (Greenery Day), 3 May (Constitution Memorial Day), 5 May (Children's Day), 20 July (Marine Day), 15 September (Respect for the Aged Day), 23 September (Autumnal Equinox), 14 October (Sports Day), 3 November (Culture Day), 23 November (Labour Thanksgiving Day), 23 December (Emperor's Birthday).

Weights and Measures

The metric system is in force.

Statistical Survey

Source (unless otherwise stated): Statistics Bureau and Statistics Center, Ministry of Public Management, Home Affairs, Posts and Telecommunications, 19-1, Wakamatsu-cho, Shinjuku-ku, Tokyo 162-8668; tel. (3) 3202-1111; fax (3) 5273-1181; e-mail webmaster@stat.go.jp; internet www.stat.go.jp.

Area and Population

AREA, POPULATION AND DENSITY

Area (sq km)	377,864*
Population (census results)†	
1 October 1995	125,570,246
1 October 2000	
Males	62,110,764
Females.	64,815,079
Total	126,925,843
Population (official estimates at mid-year)	
2000	126,870,000
2001	127,130,000
2002	127,450,000
Density (per sq km) at mid-2002	337.3

* 145,894 sq miles.

† Excluding foreign military and diplomatic personnel and their dependants.

PRINCIPAL CITIES

(population at census of 1 October 2000)*

Tokyo (capital)† . .	8,130,408	Utsunomiya . . .	443,787
Yokohama . . .	3,426,506	Nishinomiya . . .	438,129
Osaka	2,598,589	Oita	436,490
Nagoya	2,171,378	Kurashiki	430,239
Sapporo . . .	1,822,300	Yokosuka . . .	428,836
Kobe	1,493,595	Nagasaki	423,163
Kyoto	1,467,705	Gifu	402,748
Fukuoka	1,341,489	Hirakata	402,586
Kawasaki . . .	1,249,851	Toyonaka . . .	391,732
Hiroshima . . .	1,126,282	Wakayama . . .	386,501
Kitakyushu‡ . . .	1,011,491	Fujisawa	379,151
Sendai	1,008,024	Fukuyama . . .	378,793
Chiba	887,163	Machida	377,546
Sakai	792,034	Nara	366,196
Kumamoto . . .	662,123	Toyohashi . . .	364,868
Okayama	626,534	Iwaki	360,143
Sagamihara . . .	605,555	Nagano	360,117
Hamamatsu . . .	582,120	Asahikawa . . .	359,526
Kagoshima . . .	552,099	Takatsuki . . .	357,440
Funabashi . . .	550,079	Toyota	351,068
Hachioji . . .	536,000	Suita	347,938
Higashiosaka . . .	515,055	Okazaki	336,570
Niigata	501,378	Koriyama	334,845
Urawa	484,834	Takamatsu . . .	332,866
Himeji	478,312	Kawagoe	330,737
Matsuyama . . .	473,397	Kochi	330,613
Shizuoka . . .	469,679	Tokorozawa . . .	330,152
Amagasaki . . .	466,161	Kashiwa	327,868
Matsudo . . .	464,836	Toyama	325,693
Kawaguchi . . .	459,952	Akita	317,563
Kanazawa. . . .	456,434	Koshigaya. . . .	308,277
Omiya	456,164	Miyazaki	305,777
Ichikawa . . .	448,553	Naha	301,107

* Except for Tokyo, the data for each city refer to an urban county (*shi*), an administrative division which may include some scattered or rural population as well as an urban centre.

† The figure refers to the 23 wards (*ku*) of the old city. The population of Tokyo-to (Tokyo Prefecture) was 12,059,237.

‡ Including Kokura, Moji, Tobata, Wakamatsu and Yahata (Yawata).

Source: UN, *Demographic Yearbook*.

BIRTHS, MARRIAGES AND DEATHS*

	Registered live births		Registered marriages†		Registered deaths	
	Number	Rate (per 1,000)	Number	Rate (per 1,000)	Number	Rate (per 1,000)
1993 .	1,188,282	9.6	792,658	6.4	878,532	7.1
1994 .	1,238,328	10.0	782,738	6.3	875,933	7.1
1995 .	1,187,064	9.6	791,888	6.4	922,139	7.4
1996 .	1,206,555	9.7	795,080	6.4	896,211	7.2
1997 .	1,191,665	9.5	775,651	6.2	913,402	7.3
1998 .	1,203,147	9.6	784,595	6.3	936,484	7.5
1999 .	1,177,669	9.4	762,011	6.1	982,031	7.8
2000 .	1,190,547	9.5	798,138	6.4	961,653	7.7
2001 .	1,170,662	9.3	799,999	6.4	970,331	7.7

* Figures relate only to Japanese nationals in Japan.

† Data are tabulated by year of registration rather than by year of occurrence.

Expectation of life (WHO estimates, years at birth): 81.4 (males 77.9; females 84.7) in 2001 (Source: WHO, *World Health Report*).

ECONOMICALLY ACTIVE POPULATION*

(annual averages, '000 persons aged 15 years and over)

	2000	2001	2002
Agriculture and forestry . . .	2,970	2,860	2,680
Fishing and aquaculture . . .	290	270	280
Mining and quarrying	50	50	50
Manufacturing	13,210	12,840	12,220
Electricity, gas and water . . .	340	340	340
Construction	6,530	6,320	6,180
Wholesale and retail trade and restaurants	14,740	14,730	14,380
Transport, storage and communications	4,140	4,070	4,010
Financing, insurance, real estate and business services	2,480	2,400	2,410
Community, social and personal services (incl. hotels)	17,180	17,680	18,040
Government (not elsewhere classified)	2,140	2,110	2,170
Activities not adequately defined .	390	450	540
Total employed.	64,460	64,120	63,300
Unemployed	3,200	3,400	3,590
Total labour force	67,660	67,520	66,890
Males	40,140	39,920	39,560
Females	27,530	27,600	27,330

* Figures are rounded to the nearest 10,000 persons.

Health and Welfare

KEY INDICATORS

Total fertility rate (children per woman, 2001).	1.4
Under-5 mortality rate (per 1,000 live births, 2001) . . .	4
HIV/AIDS (% of persons aged 15–49, 2001).	<0.10
Physicians (per 1,000 head, 1996)	1.93
Hospital beds (per 1,000 head, 1999)	16.4
Health expenditure (2000): US $ per head (PPP)	2,009
Health expenditure (2000): % of GDP	7.8
Health expenditure (2000): public (% of total)	76.7
Human Development Index (2000): ranking	9
Human Development Index (2000): value	0.933

For sources and definitions, see explanatory note on p. vi.

Agriculture

PRINCIPAL CROPS
('000 metric tons)

	1999	2000	2001
Wheat	583.1	688.2	699.9
Rice (paddy)	11,468.8	11,863.0	11,320.0
Barley	205.3	214.3	206.4
Potatoes	2,963.0	2,898.0	2,959.0
Sweet potatoes	1,008.0	1,073.4	1,063.0
Taro (Coco yam)	247.7	230.5	218.1
Yams	193.0	201.2	200.0*
Other roots and tubers	75.0	76.0*	76.0*
Sugar cane	1,571.0	1,395.0	1,482.0†
Sugar beets	3,787.0	3,673.0	3,793.0
Dry beans	102.0	103.5	94.6
Soybeans (Soya beans)	187.2	235.0	290.6
Cabbages	2,550.0	2,485.0	2,472.0
Lettuce	540.5	537.2	553.8
Spinach	329.0	316.4	319.3
Tomatoes	768.7	806.3	797.6
Cauliflowers	115.9	114.7	115.0*
Pumpkins, squash and gourds	265.6	253.6	227.5
Cucumbers and gherkins	765.9	766.7	735.0
Aubergines (Eggplants)	473.2	476.9	448.0
Chillies and green peppers	165.1	171.4	159.3
Green onions and shallots	532.3	537.0	526.9
Dry onions	1,205.0	1,247.0	1,259.0
Green beans	62.0	63.9	63.9*
Carrots	676.7	681.7	690.3
Green corn	294.0	300.0*	300.0*
Mushrooms	70.5	67.2	67.2
Other vegetables	3,022.0	2,900.0†	2,900.0†
Watermelons	595.3	580.6	573.2
Cantaloupes and other melons	317.0	315.0*	315.0*
Grapes	242.0	237.5	225.4
Apples	927.7	799.6	930.0
Pears	415.7	424.3	397.0
Peaches and nectarines	158.1	174.6	175.8
Plums	119.1	121.2	123.7
Oranges†	111.0	102.0	102.0
Tangerines, mandarins, clementines and satsumas	1,447.0	1,143.0	1,281.0
Other citrus fruit	258.0	260.0*	260.0*
Persimmons	286.0	278.8	281.8
Strawberries	203.1	205.3	208.6
Other fruits and berries*	81.9	81.2	84.6
Tea (made)	88.5	85.0	84.5†
Tobacco (leaves)	64.7	60.8	60.6†

* FAO estimate(s).
† Unofficial figure(s).

Source: FAO.

LIVESTOCK
('000 head at 30 September)

	1999	2000	2001
Horses*	25	25	25
Cattle	4,658	4,588	4,530
Pigs	9,879	9,806	9,785
Sheep*	12	11	11
Goats*	33	35	35
Poultry	296,250	295,792	292,437

* FAO estimates.

Source: FAO.

LIVESTOCK PRODUCTS
('000 metric tons)

	1999	2000	2001
Beef and veal	540.4	530.4	460.2
Pig meat	1,275.7	1,255.1	1,242.3
Poultry meat	1,211.3	1,195.4	1,183.9
Cows' milk	8,459.7	8,497.0	8,301.0
Butter	85.5	87.6	79.5
Cheese	123.7	126.2	123.4
Hen eggs	2,539.4	2,540.1	2,549.9
Cattle hides (fresh)*	34.0	33.0	29.0

* FAO estimates.

Source: FAO.

Forestry

ROUNDWOOD REMOVALS
('000 cubic metres, excl. bark)

	1999	2000	2001
Sawlogs, veneer logs and logs for sleepers	13,402	12,936	11,948
Pulpwood	4,994	4,717	3,826
Other industrial wood	341	334	334*
Fuel wood	308	134*	129*
Total	19,045	18,121	16,237

* FAO estimate.

Source: FAO.

SAWNWOOD PRODUCTION
('000 cubic metres, incl. railway sleepers)

	1999	2000	2001
Coniferous (softwood)	17,270	16,479	14,974
Broadleaved (hardwood)	682	615	511
Total	17,952	17,094	15,485

Source: FAO.

Fishing

('000 metric tons, live weight)

	1998	1999	2000
Capture	5,263.4	5,201.8	4,989.4
Chum salmon (Keta or Dog salmon)	206.6	182.9	165.8
Alaska (Walleye) pollock	316.0	382.4	300.0
Atka mackerel	241.0	169.5	165.1
Pacific saury (Skipper)	145.0	141.0	216.5
Japanese jack mackerel	311.3	211.1	246.0
Japanese pilchard (sardine)	167.1	351.2	149.6
Japanese anchovy	470.6	484.2	381.0
Skipjack tuna (Oceanic skipjack)	385.4	287.3	341.4
Chub mackerel	511.2	381.9	346.2
Yesso scallop	287.8	299.6	304.3
Japanese flying squid	180.7	237.3	337.3
Aquaculture	766.8	759.3	762.8
Pacific cupped oyster	199.5	205.3	221.3
Yesso scallop	226.1	216.0	210.7
Total catch	6,030.2	5,961.1	5,752.2

Note: Figures exclude aquatic plants ('000 metric tons): 640.6 (capture 116.9, aquaculture 523.7) in 1998; 676.9 (capture 120.9, aquaculture 556.0) in 1999; 647.9 (capture 119.0, aquaculture 528.9) in 2000. Also excluded are aquatic mammals (generally recorded by number rather than by weight), pearls, corals and sponges. The number of whales and dolphins caught was: 13,884 in 1998; 17,729 in 1999; 17,889 in 2000 (including FAO estimate for toothed whales) (figures include whales caught during the Antarctic summer season beginning in the year prior to the year stated). The catch of other aquatic mammals (in '000 metric tons) was: 1.2 in 1998; 1.7 in 1999; 1.8 in 2000. For the remaining categories, catches (in kilograms) were: Pearls 29.1 in 1998, 24.8 in 1999, 30.1 in 2000; Corals (including FAO estimates) 6.9 in 1998, 5.2 in 1999, 9.1 in 2000; Sponges (FAO estimates) 4.0 in 1998–2000.

Source: FAO, *Yearbook of Fishery Statistics*.

Mining

('000 metric tons, unless otherwise indicated)

	1998	1999	2000
Hard coal	3,663	3,906	3,149
Zinc ore*	68	64	64
Iron ore†	2	2	2
Silica stone	16,236	15,548	15,578
Limestone	183,955	180,193	185,569
Copper ore (metric tons)*	1,070	1,038	1,211
Lead ore (metric tons)*	6,198	6,074	8,835
Gold ore (kg)*	8,601	9,405	8,400
Crude petroleum ('000 barrels)	4,982	4,592	4,654
Natural gas (million cu m)	2,301	2,280	2,453

* Figures refer to the metal content of ores.
† Figures refer to gross weight. The estimated iron content is 54%.

Source: US Geological Survey.

Industry

SELECTED PRODUCTS

('000 metric tons, unless otherwise indicated)

	1997	1998	1999
Refined sugar	2,311	n.a.	n.a.
Cotton yarn—pure (metric tons)	169,141	160,381	157,941
Cotton yarn—mixed (metric tons)	14,378	13,046	13,059
Woven cotton fabrics—pure and mixed (million sq m)	917	842	774
Flax, ramie and hemp yarn (metric tons)	1,411	682	998
Linen fabrics ('000 sq m)	4,039	3,070	3,577
Woven silk fabrics—pure and mixed ('000 sq m)	55,381	40,440	34,564
Wool yarn—pure and mixed (metric tons)	62,439	46,637	41,997
Woven woollen fabrics—pure and mixed ('000 sq m)[1]	246,966	212,862	199,058
Rayon continuous filaments (metric tons)	43,374	40,127	33,980
Acetate continuous filaments (metric tons)	29,900	27,762	24,204
Rayon discontinuous fibres (metric tons)	110,796	96,611	77,294
Acetate discontinuous fibres (metric tons)[2]	76,036	71,989	80,536
Woven rayon fabrics—pure and mixed (million sq m)[1]	416.3	361	325
Woven acetate fabrics—pure and mixed (million sq m)[1]	39.4	28	27
Non-cellulosic continuous filaments (metric tons)	736,476	683,458	664,280
Non-cellulosic discontinuous fibres (metric tons)	825,847	803,558	754,033
Woven synthetic fabrics (million sq m)[1, 3]	2,040.6	1,743	1,581
Leather footwear ('000 pairs)[4]	47,573	42,573	37,546
Mechanical wood pulp	1,674	1,598	1,474
Chemical wood pulp[5]	9,812	9,390	9,497
Newsprint	3,192.3	3,265	3,295
Other printing and writing paper	11,092.4	10,887	11,330
Other paper	3,983	3,704	3,769
Paperboard	12,746.8	12,031	12,338
Synthetic rubber	1,591.9	1,520	1,577
Motor vehicle tyres ('000)	170,800	166,956	171,083
Rubber footwear ('000 pairs)	19,052	13,954	12,775
Ethylene—Ethene	7,416.1	7,076	7,687
Propylene—Propene	5,408.6	5,101	5,520
Benzene—Benzol	4,502.0	4,203	4,459
Toluene—Toluol	1,418.7	1,349	1,488
Xylenes—Xylol	4,634.0	4,340	4,641
Ethyl alcohol—95% (kilolitres)	283,319	265,027	263,633
Sulphuric acid—100%	6,828	6,739	6,493
Caustic soda—Sodium hydroxide	4,391	4,252	4,345
Soda ash—Sodium carbonate	801.2	722	722
Ammonium sulphate	1,779.8	1,618	1,716
Nitrogenous fertilizers (a)[6]	854	762	751
Phosphate fertilizers (b)[6]	472	422	399
Liquefied petroleum gas	5,904	4,777	4,871

— continued	1997	1998	1999
Naphtha (million litres)	19,234	18,003	17,978
Motor spirit—Gasoline (million litres)[7]	53,534	55,316	56,316
Kerosene (million litres)	27,620	27,685	26,669
Jet fuel (million litres)	9,224	10,526	10,451
Gas oil (million litres)	48,153	46,071	44,536
Heavy fuel oil (million litres)	74,297	71,782	69,305
Lubricating oil (million litres)	2,833	2,630	2,693
Petroleum bitumen—Asphalt	5,886	5,492	5,596
Coke-oven coke	41,224	39,568	36,473
Cement	91,938	81,328	80,120
Pig-iron	78,519	74,981	74,520
Ferro-alloys[8]	1,004.4	903	847
Crude steel	104,545	93,548	94,192
Aluminium—unwrought: primary	363	309	311
Electrolytic copper	1,278.7	1,277	342
Refined lead—unwrought (metric tons)	227,953	227,571	227,122
Electrolytic, distilled and rectified zinc—unwrought (metric tons)	603,112	607,899	633,383
Calculating machines ('000)	3,238	2,705	2,402
Video disk players ('000)	1,214.5	171	43
Television receivers ('000)[9]	6,672	5,569	3,444
Merchant vessels launched ('000 grt)	9,963	10,563	n.a.
Passenger motor cars ('000)	8,491.4	8,056	8,100
Lorries and trucks ('000)	2,421.4	1,937	1,746
Motorcycles, scooters and mopeds ('000)	2,675.7	2,636	2,252
Cameras ('000)	12,275	11,977	10,326
Watches and clocks ('000)[10]	541,070	594,963	552,269
Construction: new dwellings started ('000)	1,387.0	n.a.	1,223.5
Electric energy (million kWh)[11]	1,037,938	1,046,288	n.a.

[1] Including finished fabrics.
[2] Including cigarette filtration tow.
[3] Including blankets made of synthetic fibres.
[4] Sales.
[5] Including pulp prepared by semi-chemical processes.
[6] Figures refer to the 12 months ending 30 June of the year stated and are in terms of (a) nitrogen, 100%, and (b) phosphoric acid, 100%.
[7] Including aviation gasoline.
[8] Including silico-chromium.
[9] Figures refer to colour television receivers only.
[10] Including watch and clock movements.
[11] Twelve months beginning 1 April of the year stated.

Source: partly UN, *Industrial Commodity Statistics Yearbook*.

Finance

CURRENCY AND EXCHANGE RATES

Monetary Units
100 sen = 1 yen

Sterling, Dollar and Euro Equivalents (31 December 2002)
£1 sterling = 193.25 yen
US $1 = 119.90 yen
€1 = 125.74 yen
1,000 yen = £5.175 = $8.340 = €7.953

Average Exchange Rate (yen per US $)
2000 107.77
2001 121.53
2002 125.39

BUDGET

('000 million yen, year ending 31 March)*

Revenue	2000/01†	2001/02‡	2002/03‡
Tax and stamp revenues	50,713	47,948	46,816
Individual income tax	18,789	17,807	15,831
Corporation tax	11,747	10,258	11,174
Consumption tax	9,822	9,767	9,825
Liquor tax	1,816	1,765	1,735
Stamp revenue	1,532	1,429	1,444
Government bond issues	33,004	30,000	30,000
Total (incl. others)	93,361	86,903	81,230

Expenditure‡	2000/01	2001/02	2002/03
Defence	4,936	4,955	4,956
Social security	16,767	17,555	18,280
Public works	9,431	9,435	8,424
Servicing of national debt§ . . .	21,965	17,171	16,671
Interest payments	10,743	n.a.	n.a.
Transfer of local allocation tax to local governments	14,930	16,823	17,011
Total (incl. others)	84,987	82,652	81,230

* Figures refer only to the operations of the General Account budget. Data exclude transactions of other accounts controlled by the central Government: two mutual aid associations and four special accounts (including other social security funds).
† Revised forecasts.
‡ Initial forecasts.
§ Including the repayment of debt principal and administrative costs.

Source: Ministry of Finance, Tokyo.

INTERNATIONAL RESERVES
(US $ million at 31 December)

	2000	2001	2002
Gold*	1,119	1,082	1,171
IMF special drawing rights . . .	2,437	2,377	2,524
Reserve position in IMF	5,253	5,051	7,203
Foreign exchange	347,212	387,727	387,727
Total	356,021	396,237	462,357

* Valued at SDR 35 per troy ounce.

Source: IMF, *International Financial Statistics.*

MONEY SUPPLY
('000 million yen at 31 December)

	2000	2001	2002
Currency outside banks	61,947	66,676	71,338
Demand deposits at deposit money banks	185,911	215,109	276,651
Total money	247,858	281,785	347,989

Source: IMF, *International Financial Statistics.*

COST OF LIVING
(Consumer Price Index; average of monthly figures; base: 2000 = 100)

	1999	2001	2002
Food (incl. beverages)	102.0	99.4	98.6
Housing	99.8	100.2	100.1
Rent	99.6	100.4	100.4
Fuel, light and water charges . .	98.4	100.6	99.4
Clothing and footwear	101.1	97.8	95.6
Miscellaneous	100.4	99.8	100.0
All items	100.7	99.3	98.4

NATIONAL ACCOUNTS
('000 million yen at current prices)

National Income and Product

	1999	2000	2001
Compensation of employees . . .	276,420.6	278,620.7	275,634.9
Operating surplus	91,841.0	94,879.2	85,870.2
Domestic factor incomes . . .	368,261.6	373,499.9	361,505.1
Consumption of fixed capital . .	95,713.8	98,532.6	98,602.2
Statistical discrepancy	7,690.1	5,043.1	4,235.3
Gross domestic product (GDP) at factor cost	471,665.5	477,075.6	464,342.6
Indirect taxes	43,416.7	42,620.0	42,406.4
Less Subsidies	4,394.9	4,217.8	4,146.6
GDP in purchasers' values . .	510,687.3	515,477.9	502,602.3
Factor income received from abroad	11,141.9	12,197.5	13,716.0
Less Factor income paid abroad .	4,802.0	5,247.5	5,174.3
Gross national product (GNP) .	517,027.2	522,427.9	511,144.0
Statistical discrepancy	−7,690.1	−5,043.1	−4,235.3
Less Consumption of fixed capital .	95,713.8	98,532.6	98,602.2
National income in market prices	413,623.3	418,852.2	408,306.6
Other current transfers, net . .	−927.5	−745.8	−498.1
National disposable income . .	412,695.8	418,106.3	407,808.5

Expenditure on the Gross Domestic Product

	1999	2000	2001
Government final consumption expenditure	83,365.5	86,946.4	88,645.1
Private final consumption expenditure	287,364.7	286,107.0	285,708.9
Increase in stocks	−1,781.1	966.8	−1,799.8
Gross fixed capital formation . .	133,909.7	135,261.8	126,178.9
Total domestic expenditure . .	502,858.8	509,282.0	498,733.1
Exports of goods and services . .	52,151.4	55,632.4	52,272.5
Less Imports of goods and services	44,322.9	49,436.6	48,403.3
GDP in purchasers' values* . .	510,687.3	515,477.9	502,602.3
GDP at constant 1995 prices .	523,981.7	539,215.3	531,569.0

* Including adjustment.

Gross Domestic Product by Economic Activity

	1999	2000	2001
Agriculture, hunting, forestry and fishing	7,582.9	7,109.9	6,973.0
Mining and quarrying	655.1	661.8	662.6
Manufacturing	110,991.2	112,114.0	104,230.8
Electricity, gas and water . . .	14,423.7	14,218.2	14,494.8
Construction	38,494.6	37,936.3	35,762.3
Wholesale and retail trade . . .	73,100.1	70,070.2	70,524.6
Transport, storage and communications	32,935.5	32,619.5	32,161.5
Finance and insurance	30,223.2	31,119.0	33,636.9
Real estate*	65,129.6	66,342.2	67,383.8
Public administration	27,121.3	27,525.5	28,027.4
Other government services . . .	18,749.7	19,025.1	19,094.8
Other business, community, social and personal services	100,725.6	103,751.9	104,719.8
Private non-profit services to households	9,976.9	9,342.8	9,357.5
Sub-total	530,109.6	531,836.5	527,029.8
Import duties	2,940.9	3,165.0	3,242.9
Less Imputed bank service charge .	23,850.4	23,204.1	25,754.6
Less Consumption taxes for gross capital formation	3,308.3	3,533.7	3,545.8
Statistical discrepancy	3,224.0	5,113.2	6,483.0
GDP in purchasers' values . .	509,115.9	513,376.8	507,455.4

* Including imputed rents of owner-occupied dwellings.

BALANCE OF PAYMENTS
(US $ million)

	1999	2000	2001
Exports of goods f.o.b.	403,694	459,513	383,592
Imports of goods f.o.b.	−280,369	−342,797	−313,378
Trade balance	123,325	116,716	70,214
Exports of services	60,998	69,238	64,515
Imports of services	−115,158	−116,864	−108,249
Balance on goods and services	69,165	69,091	26,480
Other income received	188,272	206,935	190,823
Other income paid	−138,432	−149,313	−120,118
Balance on goods, services and			
income	119,004	126,713	97,185
Current transfers received . . .	6,212	7,381	6,152
Current transfers paid	−18,350	−17,211	−14,056
Current balance	106,865	116,883	89,280
Capital account (net)	−16,467	−9,259	−2,869
Direct investment abroad . . .	−22,267	−31,534	−38,497
Direct investment from abroad. .	12,308	8,227	6,191
Portfolio investment assets . . .	−154,410	−83,362	−106,788
Portfolio investment liabilities . .	126,929	47,387	60,503
Financial derivatives assets . .	−12,426	−2,996	15,063
Financial derivatives liabilities .	17,535	1,100	−15,158
Other investment assets . . .	266,340	−4,148	46,588
Other investment liabilities . .	−265,117	−10,211	−17,550
Net errors and omissions . . .	16,966	16,869	3,724
Overall balance	76,256	48,955	40,487

Source: IMF, *International Financial Statistics*.

JAPANESE DEVELOPMENT ASSISTANCE
(net disbursement basis, US $ million)*

	1999	2000	2001
Official:			
Bilateral assistance:			
Grants	5,539	5,678	4,742
Grant assistance	2,340	2,100	1,904
Technical assistance . . .	3,199	3,578	2,837
Loans	4,959	4,090	2,716
Total	10,498	9,768	7,458
Contributions to multilateral			
institutions	4,888	3,740	2,389
Total	15,386	13,508	9,847
Other official flows:			
Export credits	−755	−1,239	−427
Equities and other bilateral			
assets, etc.	7,242	−3,709	−447
Transfers to multilateral			
institutions	1,231	−252	19
Total	7,718	−5,200	−854
Total official	23,104	8,308	8,993
Private flows:			
Export credits	−2,292	−799	−384
Direct investment and others .	7,882	2,874	6,473
Bilateral investment in			
securities, etc.	−4,546	702	−354
Transfers to multilateral			
institutions	−4,114	−52	−355
Grants from private voluntary			
agencies	261	231	235
Total private	−2,809	2,956	5,615
Grand total	20,295	11,264	14,608

* Excluding aid to Eastern Europe.

External Trade

PRINCIPAL COMMODITIES
(million yen)

Imports c.i.f.	1999	2000	2001
Food and live animals . . .	5,040,063	4,966,400	5,250,600
Fish and fish preparations* . .	1,647,257	1,650,088	1,626,474
Crude materials (inedible)			
except fuels	2,550,759	2,642,000	2,586,100
Mineral fuels, lubricants, etc.	5,646,300	8,316,600	8,523,700
Petroleum and petroleum products	3,696,152	5,772,043	5,621,462
Crude and partly refined			
petroleum	3,040,166	4,818,853	4,718,360
Gas (natural and manufactured) .	1,314,922	1,934,747	2,125,873
Chemicals	2,636,936	2,855,000	3,101,100
Machinery and transport			
equipment.	11,045,403	12,924,000	13,215,900
Non-electric machinery	3,753,000	n.a.	n.a.
Office machines	2,259,548	2,904,233	2,764,027
Thermionic valves, tubes, etc. .	1,532,974	2,139,923	1,909,535
Miscellaneous manufactured			
articles.	n.a.	n.a.	n.a.
Clothing (excl. footwear) . . .	1,855,506	2,115,377	2,318,293
Total (incl. others)†	35,268,008	40,938,423	42,415,533

* Including crustacea and molluscs.

† Including re-imports not classified according to kind.

Exports f.o.b.	1999	2000	2001
Chemicals	3,503,000	3,804,700	3,738,800
Basic manufactures . . .	n.a.	n.a.	n.a.
Iron and steel.	1,533,471	1,600,262	1,649,543
Machinery and transport			
equipment.	32,508,684	35,594,800	32,895,700
Non-electric machinery	10,151,195	11,096,400	10,229,500
Power-generating machinery .	1,514,557	1,635,451	1,720,184
Office machines	3,057,154	3,094,226	2,820,710
Automatic data-processing			
machines	1,647,785	1,600,555	1,535,273
Electrical machinery, apparatus,			
etc.	11,564,384	13,670,200	11,533,300
Thermionic valves, tubes, etc. .	3,726,048	4,575,803	3,647,382
Electronic integrated circuits .	2,307,400	2,933,751	2,372,424
Transport equipment	10,793,105	10,828,200	11,132,900
Road motor vehicles and parts* .	7,094,811	6,930,054	7,210,812
Passenger cars (excl. buses) .	6,226,149	6,123,022	6,421,641
Parts for cars, buses, lorries,			
etc.*	1,636,732	1,864,212	1,880,380
Miscellaneous manufactured			
articles.	n.a.	n.a.	n.a.
Scientific instruments, watches,			
etc.	2,403,965	2,772,590	2,629,101
Scientific instruments and			
photographic equipment .	2,240,592	2,625,666	2,504,480
Total (incl. others)†	47,547,556	51,654,198	48,979,244

* Excluding tyres, engines and electrical parts.

† Including re-exports not classified according to kind.

Source: Ministry of Finance.

PRINCIPAL TRADING PARTNERS
(million yen)*

Imports c.i.f.	1999	2000	2001
Australia	1,456,995	1,595,908	1,755,871
Canada	900,255	938,485	941,469
China, People's Republic	4,875,385	5,941,358	7,026,677
France	699,010	691,297	750,358
Germany	1,307,034	1,371,925	1,505,798
Indonesia	1,429,002	1,766,187	1,805,632
Iran	355,989	577,787	609,819
Ireland	335,491	399,108	441,373
Italy	572,892	572,761	654,978
Korea, Republic	1,824,286	2,204,703	2,088,356
Kuwait	342,975	538,281	538,096
Malaysia	1,241,390	1,562,726	1,561,324
Philippines	603,437	776,247	778,879
Qatar	392,382	632,000	731,801
Russia	428,543	493,791	468,419
Saudi Arabia	944,329	1,531,277	1,496,299
Singapore	618,188	693,625	653,684
Switzerland	382,292	354,262	399,228
Taiwan	1,455,915	1,930,161	1,722,643
Thailand	1,008,226	1,142,346	1,260,472
United Arab Emirates	1,001,012	1,599,649	1,559,855
United Kingdom	674,111	709,180	729,016
USA	7,639,510	7,778,861	7,671,481
Total (incl. others)	35,268,008	40,938,423	42,415,533

Exports f.o.b.	1999	2000	2001
Australia	961,664	923,830	933,178
Belgium	569,822	564,615	555,798
Canada	788,693	805,939	797,113
China, People's Republic	2,657,428	3,274,448	3,763,723
France	775,731	803,801	758,786
Germany	2,121,636	2,155,178	1,896,740
Hong Kong	2,507,213	2,929,696	2,826,044
Indonesia	551,041	817,745	777,704
Italy	578,147	624,309	584,615
Korea, Republic	2,606,234	3,308,751	3,071,871
Malaysia	1,264,899	1,496,627	1,337,217
Mexico	500,173	561,557	496,995
Netherlands	1,367,273	1,356,814	1,393,132
Panama	775,000	695,408	586,630
Philippines	996,864	1,105,654	995,303
Singapore	1,854,167	2,243,914	1,786,059
Taiwan	3,276,252	3,874,042	2,942,227
Thailand	1,284,801	1,469,397	1,442,488
United Kingdom	1,616,321	1,598,434	1,474,989
USA	14,605,315	15,355,867	14,711,055
Total (incl. others)	47,547,556	51,654,198	48,979,244

* Imports by country of production; exports by country of last consignment.

Transport

RAILWAYS
(traffic)

	1998	1999	2000
National railways:			
Passengers (million)	8,760	8,720	8,670
Passenger-km (million)	242,810	240,795	240,659
Freight ('000 tons)	19,724	18,673	18,976
Freight ton-km (million)	n.a.	22,270	21,860
Private railways:			
Passengers (million)	13,250	13,030	12,980
Passenger-km (million)	388,939	385,101	384,442
Freight ('000 tons)	17,739	17,513	17,923
Freight ton-km (million)	n.a.	270	280
Total:			
Passengers (million)	22,013,767	21,750,274	21,646,752
Passenger-km (million)	388,938	385,101	384,441
Freight ('000 tons)	37,463	36,186	36,899
Freight ton-km (million)	n.a.	22,540	22,140

ROAD TRAFFIC
('000 motor vehicles owned, year ending 31 March)

	1999/2000	2000/01	2001/02
Passenger cars	42,056	42,365	42,528
Buses and coaches	236	236	234
Trucks, incl. trailers	8,266	8,106	7,907
Special use vehicles	1,386	1,431	1,430
Heavy use vehicles	321	323	325
Light two-wheeled vehicles	1,288	1,308	1,334
Light motor vehicles	21,030	21,755	22,513
Total	74,583	75,525	76,271

SHIPPING

Merchant Fleet
(registered at 31 December)

	1999	2000	2001
Number of vessels	8,462	8,012	7,924
Total displacement ('000 grt)	17,063	15,257	16,653

Source: Lloyd's Register-Fairplay, *World Fleet Statistics*.

International Sea-borne Traffic

	1998	1999	2000
Vessels entered:			
Number	63,950	65,593	n.a.
Total displacement ('000 net tons)	425,193	446,482	n.a.
Goods ('000 metric tons):			
Loaded	100,905	101,995	101,727
Unloaded	730,217	748,855	787,987

CIVIL AVIATION
(traffic on scheduled services)

	1998	1999	2000
Kilometres flown (million)	1,328	1,367	1,422
Passengers carried ('000)	189,578	198,728	205,106
Passenger-km (million)	232,280	245,124	256,428
Total ton-km (million)	8,538	9,263	9,800

Source: UN, *Statistical Yearbook*.

Tourism

FOREIGN TOURIST ARRIVALS
(excl. Japanese nationals resident abroad)

Country of Nationality	1998	1999	2000
Australia	123,681	135,303	147,393
Canada	106,884	106,734	119,168
China, People's Republic	267,180	294,937	351,788
Germany	86,194	87,132	88,309
Hong Kong	356,861	252,870	243,149
Korea, Republic	724,445	942,674	1,064,390
Philippines	82,346	93,346	112,182
Taiwan	843,088	931,411	912,814
United Kingdom	181,533	182,894	192,930
USA	666,700	697,630	725,954
Total (incl. others)	4,106,057	4,437,863	4,757,146

Receipts from tourism (US $ million): 3,742 in 1998; 3,428 in 1999; 3,374 in 2000.

Communications Media

	1999	2000	2001
Television receivers ('000 in use) .	91,000	92,000	n.a.
Telephones ('000 main lines in use)	70,530.0	74,343.6	76,000.0
Mobile cellular telephones ('000			
subscribers).	56,845.6	66,784.4	72,795.9
Personal computers ('000 in use)	36,300	40,000	44,400
Internet users ('000)	27,060	47,080	57,900
Book production:			
titles.	65,026	65,065	n.a.
copies (million).	1,368	1,420	n.a.
Daily newspapers:			
number	121	122	124
circulation ('000 copies) . . .	72,218	n.a.	53,681

Radio receivers ('000 in use): 120,500 in 1997.

Facsimile machines ('000 in use): 16,000 in 1997.

Sources: Foreign Press Center, *Facts and Figures of Japan*; UNESCO, *Statistical Yearbook*; UN, *Statistical Yearbook*; International Telecommunication Union.

Education

(2001)

	Institutions	Teachers	Students
Elementary schools	23,964	408,000	7,297,000
Lower secondary schools . . .	11,191	255,000	3,992,000
Upper secondary schools . . .	5,479	267,000	4,062,000
Colleges of technology	62	4,000	57,000
Junior colleges	559	16,000	289,000
Graduate schools and universities	669	153,000	2,766,000

Directory

The Constitution

The Constitution of Japan was promulgated on 3 November 1946 and came into force on 3 May 1947. The following is a summary of its major provisions, with subsequent amendments:

THE EMPEROR

Articles 1–8. The Emperor derives his position from the will of the people. In the performance of any state act as defined in the Constitution, he must seek the advice and approval of the Cabinet, though he may delegate the exercise of his functions, which include: (i) the appointment of the Prime Minister and the Chief Justice of the Supreme Court; (ii) promulgation of laws, cabinet orders, treaties and constitutional amendments; (iii) the convocation of the Diet, dissolution of the House of Representatives and proclamation of elections to the Diet; (iv) the appointment and dismissal of Ministers of State, the granting of amnesties, reprieves and pardons, and the ratification of treaties, conventions or protocols; (v) the awarding of honours and performance of ceremonial functions.

RENUNCIATION OF WAR

Article 9. Japan renounces for ever the use of war as a means of settling international disputes.

Articles 10–40 refer to the legal and human rights of individuals guaranteed by the Constitution.

THE DIET

Articles 41–64. The Diet is convened once a year, is the highest organ of state power and has exclusive legislative authority. It comprises the House of Representatives (480 seats—300 single-seat constituencies and 180 determined by proportional representation) and the House of Councillors (247 seats). The members of the former are elected for four years whilst those of the latter are elected for six years and election for approximately one-half of the members takes place every three years. If the House of Representatives is dissolved, a general election must take place within 40 days and the Diet must be convoked within 30 days of the date of the election. Extraordinary sessions of the Diet may be convened by the Cabinet when one-quarter or more of the members of either House request it. Emergency sessions of the House of Councillors may also be held. A quorum of at least one-third of the Diet members is needed to carry out parliamentary business. Any decision arising therefrom must be passed by a majority vote of those present. A bill becomes law having passed both Houses, except as provided by the Constitution. If the House of Councillors either vetoes or fails to take action within 60 days upon a bill already passed by the House of Representatives, the bill becomes law when passed a second time by the House of Representatives, by at least a two-thirds majority of those members present.

The Budget must first be submitted to the House of Representatives. If, when it is approved by the House of Representatives, the House of Councillors votes against it or fails to take action on it within 30 days, or failing agreement being reached by a joint committee of both Houses, a decision of the House of Representatives shall be the decision of the Diet. The above procedure also applies in respect of the conclusion of treaties.

THE EXECUTIVE

Articles 65–75. Executive power is vested in the Cabinet, consisting of a Prime Minister and such other Ministers as may be appointed. The Cabinet is collectively responsible to the Diet. The Prime Minister is designated from among members of the Diet by a resolution thereof.

If the House of Representatives and the House of Councillors disagree on the designation of the Prime Minister, and if no agreement can be reached even through a joint committee of both Houses, provided for by law, or if the House of Councillors fails to make designation within 10 days, exclusive of the period of recess, after the House of Representatives has made designation, the decision of the House of Representatives shall be the decision of the Diet.

The Prime Minister appoints and may remove other Ministers, a majority of whom must be from the Diet. If the House of Representatives passes a no-confidence motion or rejects a confidence motion, the whole Cabinet resigns, unless the House of Representatives is dissolved within 10 days. When there is a vacancy in the post of Prime Minister, or upon the first convocation of the Diet after a general election of members of the House of Representatives, the whole Cabinet resigns.

The Prime Minister submits bills, reports on national affairs and foreign relations to the Diet. He exercises control and supervision over various administrative branches of the Government. The Cabinet's primary functions (in addition to administrative ones) are to: (a) administer the law faithfully; (b) conduct State affairs; (c) conclude treaties subject to prior (or subsequent) Diet approval; (d) administer the civil service in accordance with law; (e) prepare and present the budget to the Diet; (f) enact Cabinet orders in order to make effective legal and constitutional provisions; (g) decide on amnesties, reprieves or pardons. All laws and Cabinet orders are signed by the competent Minister of State and countersigned by the Prime Minister. The Ministers of State, during their tenure of office, are not subject to legal action without the consent of the Prime Minister. However, the right to take that action is not impaired.

Articles 76–95. Relate to the Judiciary, Finance and Local Government.

AMENDMENTS

Article 96. Amendments to the Constitution are initiated by the Diet, through a concurring vote of two-thirds or more of all the members of each House and are submitted to the people for ratification, which requires the affirmative vote of a majority of all votes cast at a special referendum or at such election as the Diet may specify.

Amendments when so ratified must immediately be promulgated by the Emperor in the name of the people, as an integral part of the Constitution.

Articles 97–99 outline the Supreme Law, while Articles 100–103 consist of Supplementary Provisions.

The Government

HEAD OF STATE

His Imperial Majesty Akihito, Emperor of Japan (succeeded to the throne 7 January 1989).

THE CABINET
(April 2003)

A coalition of the Liberal Democratic Party (LDP), New Conservative Party (NCP) and New Komeito. All ministers were members of the LDP, unless otherwise specified.

Prime Minister: JUNICHIRO KOIZUMI.

Minister of Public Management, Home Affairs, Posts and Telecommunications: TORANOSUKE KATAYAMA.

Minister of Justice: MAYUMI MORIYAMA.

Minister of Foreign Affairs: YORIKO KAWAGUCHI (non-politician).

Minister of Finance: MASAJURO SHIOKAWA.

Minister of Education, Culture, Sports, Science and Technology: ATSUKO TOYAMA (non-politician).

Minister of Health, Labour and Welfare: CHIKARA SAKAGUCHI (New Komeito).

Minister of Agriculture, Forestry and Fisheries: YOSHIYUKI KAMEI.

Minister of Economy, Trade and Industry: TAKEO HIRANUMA.

Minister of Land, Infrastructure and Transport: CHIKAGE OGI (NCP).

Minister of the Environment: SHUNICHI SUZUKI.

Minister responsible for Disaster Prevention: YOSHITADA KONOIKE.

Minister of State and Chief Cabinet Secretary (Gender Equality): YASUO FUKUDA.

Minister of State and Chairman of the National Public Safety Commission: SADAKAZU TANIGAKI.

Minister of State and Director-General of the Defence Agency: SHIGERU ISHIBA.

Minister of State for Development of Okinawa and Northern Territories Affairs, Science and Technology Policy: HIROYUKI HOSODA.

Minister of State (Financial Services Agency and Economic and Fiscal Policy): HEIZO TAKENAKA (non-politician).

Minister of State (Administrative Reform, Regulatory Reform): NOBUTERU ISHIHARA.

MINISTRIES

Imperial Household Agency: 1-1, Chiyoda, Chiyoda-ku, Tokyo 100-8111; tel. (3) 3213-1111; fax (3) 3282-1407; e-mail information@kunaicho.go.jp; internet www.kunaicho.go.jp.

Prime Minister's Office: 1-6-1, Nagata-cho, Chiyoda-ku, Tokyo 100-8968; tel. (3) 3581-2361; fax (3) 3581-1910; internet www.kantei .go.jp.

Cabinet Office: 1-6-1, Nagata-cho, Chiyoda-ku, Tokyo 100-8914; tel. (3) 5253-2111; internet www.cao.go.jp.

Ministry of Agriculture, Forestry and Fisheries: 1-2-1, Kasumigaseki, Chiyoda-ku, Tokyo 100-8950; tel. (3) 3502-8111; fax (3) 3592-7697; e-mail white56@sc.maff.go.jp; internet www.maff.go.jp.

Ministry of Disaster Prevention: Tokyo.

Ministry of Economy, Trade and Industry: 1-3-1, Kasumigaseki, Chiyoda-ku, Tokyo 100-8901; tel. (3) 3501-1511; fax (3) 3501-6942; e-mail webmail@meti.go.jp; internet www.meti.go.jp.

Ministry of Education, Culture, Sports, Science and Technology: 3-2-2, Kasumigaseki, Chiyoda-ku, Tokyo 100-8959; tel. (3) 5253-4111; fax (3) 3595-2017; internet www.mext.go.jp.

Ministry of the Environment: 1-2-2, Kasumigaseki, Chiyoda-ku, Tokyo 100-8975; tel. (3) 3581-3351; fax (3) 3502-0308; e-mail moe@eanet.go.jp; internet www.env.go.jp.

Ministry of Finance: 3-1-1, Kasumigaseki, Chiyoda-ku, Tokyo 100-8940; tel. (3) 3581-4111; fax (3) 5251-2667; e-mail info@mof.go .jp; internet www.mof.go.jp.

Ministry of Foreign Affairs: 2-11-1, Shiba-Koen, Minato-ku, Tokyo 105-8519; tel. (3) 3580-3311; fax (3) 3581-2667; e-mail webmaster@mofa.go.jp; internet www.mofa.go.jp.

Ministry of Health, Labour and Welfare: 1-2-2, Kasumigaseki, Chiyoda-ku, Tokyo 100-8916; tel. (3) 5253-1111; fax (3) 3501-2532; internet www.mhlw.go.jp.

Ministry of Justice: 1-1-1, Kasumigaseki, Chiyoda-ku, Tokyo 100-8977; tel. (3) 3580-4111; fax (3) 3592-7011; e-mail webmaster@moj .go.jp; internet www.moj.go.jp.

Ministry of Land, Infrastructure and Transport: 2-1-3, Kasumigaseki, Chiyoda-ku, Tokyo 100-8918; tel. (3) 5253-8111; fax (3) 3580-7982; e-mail webmaster@mlit.go.jp; internet www.mlit.go.jp.

Ministry of Public Management, Home Affairs, Posts and Telecommunications: 2-1-2, Kasumigaseki, Chiyoda-ku, Tokyo 100-8926; tel. (3) 5253-5111; fax (3) 3504-0265; internet www.soumu .go.jp.

Defence Agency: 5-1 Ichigaya, Honmura-cho, Shinjuku-ku, Tokyo 162-8801; tel. (3) 3268-3111; e-mail info@jda.go.jp; internet www.jda .go.jp.

Financial Services Agency: 3-1-1 Kasumigaseki, Chiyoda-ku, Tokyo 100-8967; tel. (3) 3506-6000; internet www.fsa.go.jp.

National Public Safety Commission: 2-1-2, Kasumigaseki, Chiyoda-ku, Tokyo 100-8974; tel. (3) 3581-0141; internet www.npsc .go.jp.

Legislature

KOKKAI
(Diet)

The Diet consists of two Chambers: the House of Councillors (upper house) and the House of Representatives (lower house). The members of the House of Representatives are elected for a period of four years (subject to dissolution). Following the enactment of reform legislation in December 1994, the number of members in the House of Representatives was reduced to 500 (from 511) at the general election of October 1996. Further legislation was enacted in February 2000, reducing the number of members in the House of Representatives to 480, comprising 300 single-seat constituencies and 180 seats determined by proportional representation. For the House of Councillors, which has 247 members (following legislation enacted in October 2000: previously the membership had been 252), the term of office is six years, with approximately one-half of the members elected every three years.

House of Councillors

Speaker: HIROYUKI KURATA.

Party	Seats after elections*	
	12 July 1998	29 July 2001
Liberal-Democratic Party	102	110
Democratic Party of Japan	47	60
Komei†	22	23
Japanese Communist Party	23	20
Social Democratic Party of Japan	13	8
Liberal Party	12	8
New Conservative Party	—	5
New Party Sakigake‡	3	—
Kaikaku (Reform) Club	3	—
Dai-Niin Club	1	—
Independents	26	8
Other parties	—	5
Total	252	247

*Approximately one-half of the seats are renewable every three years. At the 2001 election 48 of the 121 seats were allocated on the basis of proportional representation.
†Renamed New Komeito in November 1998 following merger with Shinto Heiwa.
‡Dissolved October 1998; new party (Party Sakigake) formed; absorbed by Democratic Party of Japan in March 2001.

House of Representatives

Speaker: TAMISUKE WATANUKI.

General Election, 25 June 2000

Party	Seats
Liberal-Democratic Party	233
Democratic Party of Japan	127
New Komeito	31
Liberal Party	22
Japanese Communist Party	20
Social Democratic Party of Japan	19
New Conservative Party	7
Independents and others	21
Total	480

Political Organizations

The Political Funds Regulation Law provides that any organization wishing to support a candidate for an elective public office must be registered as a political party. There are more than 10,000 registered parties in the country, mostly of local or regional significance.

21st Century: 1-7-1, Nagata-cho, Chiyoda-ku, Tokyo; tel. (3) 3581-5111; f. 1996 by four independent mems of House of Representatives; Chair. HAJIME FUNADA.

Dai-Niin Club: Rm 531, Sangiin Kaikan, 2-1-1, Nagata-cho, Chiyoda-ku, Tokyo 100-0014; tel. (3) 3508-8531; e-mail info@niinkuraba.gr.jp; successor to the Green Wind Club (Ryukufukai), which originated in the House of Councillors in 1946–47.

Democratic Party of Japan (DPJ): 1-11-1, Nagata-cho, Chiyoda-ku, Tokyo 100-0014; tel. (3) 3595-9988; e-mail democrat@smn.co.jp; internet www.dpj.or.jp; f. 1998 by the integration into the original DPJ (f. 1996) of the Democratic Reform League, Minseito and Shinto Yuai; advocates a cabinet formed and controlled by the people; absorbed Party Sakigake in March 2001; Pres. NAOTO KAN; Sec.-Gen. KATSUYA OKADA.

Japanese Communist Party (JCP): 4-26-7, Sendagaya, Shibuya-ku, Tokyo 151-8586; tel. (3) 3403-6111; fax (3) 3746-0767; e-mail intl@jcp.jp; internet www.jcp.or.jp; f. 1922; 400,000 mems (2002); Chair. of Cen. Cttee TETSUZO FUWA; Chair. of Exec. Cttee KAZUO SHII.

Kaikaku (Reform) Club: Sabo Kaikan Bldg, 2-7-5, Hirakawa-cho, Chiyoda-ku, Tokyo 102-0093; tel. (3) 5211-3331; f. 1997; Pres. TATSUO OZAWA.

Liberal Party (LP): Kokusai Kogyo Bldg, 2-2-12, Akasaka, Minato-ku, Tokyo 107-0052; tel. (3) 5562-7111; fax (3) 5562-7122; internet www.jiyuto.or.jp; f. 1998; Pres. ICHIRO OZAWA; Sec.-Gen. HIROHISA FUJII.

Liberal-Democratic Party—LDP (Jiyu-Minshuto): 1-11-23, Nagata-cho, Chiyoda-ku, Tokyo 100-8910; tel. (3) 3581-6211; e-mail koho@ldp.jimin.or.jp; internet www.jimin.jp/; f. 1955; advocates the establishment of a welfare state, the promotion of industrial development, the improvement of educational and cultural facilities and constitutional reform as needed; 2,369,252 mems (2001); Pres. JUNICHIRO KOIZUMI; Sec.-Gen. TAKU YAMASAKI; Chair. of Gen. Council MITSUO HORIUCHI; Chair of Policy Research Council TARO ASO.

New Conservative Party—NCP (Hoshuto): 2-7-5, Hirakawa-cho, Chiyoda-ku, Tokyo 102-0093; tel. (3) 5212-5111; fax (3) 5212-4111; internet www.hoshushintoh.com; f. 2000; by 26 fmr mems of the LP; Pres. HIROSHI KUMAGAI; Sec.-Gen. TOSHIHIRO NIKAI.

New Komeito: 17, Minami-Motomachi, Shinjuku-ku, Tokyo 160-0012; tel. (3) 3353-0111; internet www.komei.or.jp/; f. 1964 as Komeito, renamed as Komei 1994 following defection of a number of mems to the New Frontier Party (Shinshinto, dissolved Dec. 1997); absorbed Reimei Club Jan. 1998; renamed as above Nov. 1998 following merger of Komei and Shinto Heiwa; advocates political moderation, humanism and globalism, and policies respecting 'dignity of human life'; 350,000 mems (2001); Representative TAKENORI KANZAKI; Sec.-Gen. TETSUZO FUYUSHIBA.

New Socialist Party: Sanken Bldg, 6th Floor, 4-3-7, Hatchobori, Chuo-ku, Tokyo 104-0032; tel. (3) 3551-3980; e-mail honbu@sinsyakai.or.jp; internet www.sinsyakai.or.jp; f. 1996 by left-wing defectors from SDPJ; opposed to US military bases on Okinawa and to introduction in 1996 of new electoral system; seeks to establish an ecological socio-economic system; Chair. TATSUKUNI KOMORI; Sec.-Gen. KEN-ICHI UENO.

Sangiin Club: Tokyo; f. 1998; Leader MOTOO SHIINA.

Social Democratic Party of Japan—SDPJ (Shakai Minshuto): 1-8-1, Nagata-cho, Chiyoda-ku, Tokyo 100-0014; tel. (3) 3580-1171; fax (3) 3580-0691; e-mail sdpjmail@omnics.co.jp; internet www.sdp.or.jp; f. 1945 as the Japan Socialist Party (JSP); adopted present name in 1996; seeks the establishment of collective non-aggression

and a mutual security system, including Japan, the USA, the CIS and the People's Republic of China; 115,000 mems (1994); Chair. TAKAKO DOI; Sec.-Gen. SADAO FUCHIGAMI.

Diplomatic Representation

EMBASSIES IN JAPAN

Afghanistan: Olympia Annex Apt 503, 6-31-21, Jingumae, Shibuya-ku, Tokyo 150-0001; tel. (3) 3407-7900; fax (3) 3400-7912; Chargé d'affaires a.i. RAHMATULLAH AMIR.

Algeria: 2-10-67, Mita, Meguro-ku, Tokyo 153-0062; tel. (3) 3711-2661; fax (3) 3710-6534; e-mail ambalgto@twics.com; Ambassador BOUDJEMAA DELMI.

Angola: 2-10-24 Daizawa, Setagaya-ku, Tokyo 155-0032; tel. (3) 5430-7879; fax (3) 5712-7481; e-mail angolamd@s3.ocv.ne.jp.

Argentina: 2-14-14, Moto Azabu, Minato-ku, Tokyo 106-0046; tel. (3) 5420-7101; fax (3) 5420-7109; internet www.embargentina.or.jp; Ambassador ALFREDO VICENTE CHIARADIA.

Australia: 2-1-14, Mita, Minato-ku, Tokyo 108-8361; tel. (3) 5232-4111; fax (3) 5232-4149; internet www.australia.or.jp; Ambassador JOHN MCCARTHY.

Austria: 1-1-20, Moto Azabu, Minato-ku, Tokyo 106-0046; tel. (3) 3451-8281; fax (3) 3451-8283; e-mail austria@gol.com; internet www.austria.or.jp; Ambassador HANS DIETMAR SCHWEISGUT.

Bangladesh: 4-15-15, Meguro, Meguro-ku, Tokyo 153-0063; tel. (3) 5704-0216; fax (3) 5704-1696; Ambassador S. M. RASHED AHMED.

Belarus: 4-14-12, Shirogane K House, Shirogane, Minato-ku, Tokyo 108-0072; tel. (3) 3448-1623; fax (3) 3448-1624; e-mail belarus@japan.co.jp; Ambassador PETR K. KRAVCHANKA.

Belgium: 5, Niban-cho, Chiyoda-ku, Tokyo 102-0084; tel. (3) 3262-0191; fax (3) 3262-0651; e-mail tokyo@diplobel.org; Ambassador Baron PATRICK NOTHOMB.

Bolivia: Kowa Bldg, No. 38, Room 804, 4-12-24, Nishi Azabu, Minato-ku, Tokyo 106-0031; tel. (3) 3499-5441; fax (3) 3499-5443; e-mail emboltk@interlink.or.jp; Ambassador EUDORO GALINDO ANZE.

Bosnia and Herzegovina: 3-4 Rokuban-cho, Chiyoda-ku, Tokyo 102-0085; tel. (3) 3556-4151.

Brazil: 2-11-12, Kita Aoyama, Minato-ku, Tokyo 107-0061; tel. (3) 3404-5211; fax (3) 3405-5846; internet www.brasemb.or.jp; Ambassador FERNANDO GUIMARÃES REIS.

Brunei: 6-5-2, Kita Shinagawa, Shinagawa-ku, Tokyo 141-0001; tel. (3) 3447-7997; fax (3) 3447-9260; Ambassador P. S. N. YUSUF.

Bulgaria: 5-36-3, Yoyogi, Shibuya-ku, Tokyo 151-0053; tel. (3) 3465-1021; fax (3) 3465-1031; e-mail bulemb@gol.com; Ambassador PETAR ANDONOV.

Burkina Faso: Apt 301, Hiroo Glisten Hills, 3-1-17, Hiroo, Shibuya-ku, Tokyo 150-0012; tel. (3) 3400-7919; fax (3) 3400-6945; Ambassador W. RAYMOND EDOUARD OUÉDRAOGO.

Burundi: 6-5-3, Kita-Shinagawa, Shinagawa-ku, Tokyo 141; tel. (3) 3443-7321; fax (3) 3443-7720; Ambassador GABRIEL NDIHOKUBWAYO.

Cambodia: 8-6-9, Akasaka, Minato-ku, Tokyo 107-0052; tel. (3) 5412-8521; fax (3) 5412-8526; e-mail aap33850@hkg.odn.ne.jp; Ambassador ING KIETH.

Cameroon: 3-27-16, Nozawa, Setagaya-ku, Tokyo 154-0003; tel. (3) 5430-4381; fax (3) 5430-6489; e-mail ambacamtokyo@gol.com; Chargé d'affaires a.i. MBELLA MBELLA LEJEUNE.

Canada: 7-3-38, Akasaka, Minato-ku, Tokyo 107-8503; tel. (3) 5412-6200; fax (3) 5412-6249; internet www.canadanet.or.jp; Ambassador ROBERT G. WRIGHT.

Chile: Nihon Seimei Akabanebashi Bldg, 8th Floor, 3-1-14, Shiba, Minato-ku, Tokyo 105-0014; tel. (3) 3452-7561; fax (3) 3452-4457; e-mail embajada@chile.or.jp; internet www2.tky.3web.ne.jp/~oficomtc/main.htm; Ambassador DEMETRIO INFANTE.

China, People's Republic: 3-4-33, Moto Azabu, Minato-ku, Tokyo 106-0046; tel. (3) 3403-3380; fax (3) 3403-3345; internet www.china-embassy.or.jp; Ambassador WU DAWEI.

Colombia: 3-10-53, Kami Osaki, Shinagawa-ku, Tokyo 141-0021; tel. (3) 3440-6451; fax (3) 3440-6724; internet www.colombianembassy.org/html/homejp.htm; Ambassador RICARDO GUTIÉRREZ.

Congo, Democratic Republic: Harajuku Green Heights, Room 701, 3-53-17, Sendagaya, Shibuya-ku, Tokyo 151-0051; tel. (3) 3423-3981; fax (3) 3423-3984; Chargé d'affaires NGAMBANI ZI-MIZELE.

Costa Rica: Kowa Bldg, No. 38, Room 901, 4-12-24, Nishi Azabu, Minato-ku, Tokyo 106-0031; tel. (3) 3486-1812; fax (3) 3486-1813; Chargé d'affaires a.i. ANA LUCÍA NASSAR SOTO.

Côte d'Ivoire: 2-19-12, Uehara, Shibuya-ku, Tokyo 151-0064; tel. (3) 5454-1401; fax (3) 5454-1405; e-mail ambacijp@gol.com; Chargé d'affaires a.i. THOMAS A. YAPO.

Croatia: 3-3-100, Hiroo, Shibuya-ku, Tokyo 150-0012; tel. (3) 5469-3014; fax (3) 5469-3015; e-mail veltok@hpo.net; Ambassador DRAGO BOVAČ.

Cuba: 1-28-4 Higashi-Azabu, Minato-ku, Tokyo 106-0044; tel. (3) 5570-3182; internet www.cyborg.ne.jp/~embcubaj; Ambassador ERNESTO MELÉNDEZ BACHS.

Czech Republic: 2-16-14, Hiroo, Shibuya-ku, Tokyo 150-0012; tel. (3) 3400-8122; fax (3) 3400-8124; e-mail tokyo@embassy.mzv.cz; internet embassy.kcom.ne.jp/czech; internet www.mzv.cz; Ambassador KAREL ZEBRAKOVSKY.

Denmark: 29-6, Sarugaku-cho, Shibuya-ku, Tokyo 150-0033; tel. (3) 3496-3001; fax (3) 3496-3440; e-mail embassy.tokyo@denmark.or.jp; internet www.denmark.or.jp; Ambassador POUL HOINESS.

Djibouti: 5-18-10, Shimo Meguro, Meguro-ku, Tokyo 153-0064; tel. (3) 5704-0682; fax (3) 5725-8305; Ambassador RACHAD AHMED SALEH FARAH.

Dominican Republic: Kowa Bldg, No. 38, Room 904, 4-12-24, Nishi Azabu, Minato-ku, Tokyo 106-0031; tel. (3) 3499-6020; fax (3) 3499-2627.

Ecuador: Kowa Bldg, No. 38, Room 806, 4-12-24, Nishi Azabu, Minato-ku, Tokyo 106-0031; tel. (3) 3499-2800; fax (3) 3499-4400; internet www.embassy-avenue.or.jp/ecuador/index-j.htm; Ambassador MARCELO AVILA.

Egypt: 1-5-4, Aobadai, Meguro-ku, Tokyo 153-0042; tel. (3) 3770-8022; fax (3) 3770-8021; internet embassy.kcom.ne.jp/egypt/index.html; Ambassador Dr MAHMOUD KAREM.

El Salvador: Kowa Bldg, No. 38, 8th Floor, 4-12-24, Nishi Azabu, Minato-ku, Tokyo 106-0031; tel. (3) 3499-4461; fax (3) 3486-7022; e-mail embesal@gol.com; Ambassador RICARDO PAREDES-OSORIO.

Estonia: Akasaka Royal Office Bldg, 3rd Floor, 6-9-17, Akasaka, Minato-ku, Tokyo 107; tel. (3) 5545-7171; fax (3) 5545-7172; e-mail embassy.tokyo@mfa.ee; Ambassador MARK SINISOO.

Ethiopia: 3-4-1, Takanawa, Minato-ku, Tokyo 108-0074; tel. (3) 5420-6860; fax (3) 5420-6866; e-mail ethioemb@gol.com; Ambassador MAHDI AHMED.

Fiji: Noa Bldg, 14th Floor, 2-3-5, Azabudai, Minato-ku, Tokyo 106-0041; tel. (3) 3587-2038; fax (3) 3587-2563; e-mail fijiemb@hotmail.com; Ambassador Ratu TEVITA MOMOEDONU.

Finland: 3-5-39, Minami Azabu, Minato-ku, Tokyo 106-8561; tel. (3) 5447-6000; fax (3) 5447-6042; e-mail info@finland.or.jp; internet www.finland.or.jp; Ambassador EERO KALEVI SALOVAARA.

France: 4-11-44, Minami Azabu, Minato-ku, Tokyo 106-8514; tel. (3) 5420-8800; fax (3) 5420-8917; e-mail ambafrance.tokyo@diplomatie.fr; internet www.ambafrance-jp.org; Ambassador MAURICE GOURDAULT-MONTAGNE.

Gabon: 1-34-11, Higashigaoka, Meguro-ku, Tokyo 152-0021; tel. (3) 5430-9171; Ambassador VINCENT BOULÉ.

Germany: 4-5-10, Minami Azabu, Minato-ku, Tokyo 106-0047; tel. (3) 5791-7700; fax (3) 3473-4243; e-mail germtoky@ma.rosenet.ne.jp; internet www.germanembassy-japan.org; Ambassador HENRIK SCHMIEGLOW.

Ghana: 1-5-21, Nishi Azabu, Minato-ku, Tokyo 106-0031; tel. (3) 5410-8631; fax (3) 5410-8635; e-mail mission@ghanaembassy.or.jp; internet www.ghanaembassy.or.jp; Ambassador Dr BARFUOR ADJEI-BARWUAH.

Greece: 3-16-30, Nishi Azabu, Minato-ku, Tokyo 106-0031; tel. (3) 3403-0871; fax (3) 3402-4642; e-mail greekemb@gol.com; Ambassador KYRIAKOS RODOUSSAKIS.

Guatemala: Kowa Bldg, No. 38, Room 905, 4-12-24, Nishi Azabu, Minato-ku, Tokyo 106-0031; tel. (3) 3400-1830; fax (3) 3400-1820; e-mail embguate@twics.com; Ambassador ANTONIO ROBERTO CASTELLANOS LÓPEZ.

Guinea: 12-9, Hachiyama-cho, Shibuya-ku, Tokyo 150-0035; tel. (3) 3770-4640; fax (3) 3770-4643; e-mail ambagui-tokyo@gol.com; Chargé d'affaires a.i. JEAN-PIERRE DIAWARA.

Haiti: Kowa Bldg, No. 38, Room 906, 4-12-24, Nishi Azabu, Minato-ku, Tokyo 106; tel. (3) 3486-7096; fax (3) 3486-7070; Ambassador MARCEL DURET.

Holy See: Apostolic Nunciature, 9-2, Sanban-cho, Chiyoda-ku, Tokyo 102-0075; tel. (3) 3263-6851; fax (3) 3263-6060; Apostolic Nuncio Most Rev. AMBROSE B. DE PAOLI (Titular Archbishop of Lares).

Honduras: Kowa Bldg, No. 38, Room 802, 8th Floor, 4-12-24, Nishi Azabu, Minato-ku, Tokyo 106-0031; tel. (3) 3409-1150; fax (3) 3409-0305; e-mail honduras@interlink.or.jp; Ambassador EDGARDO SEVILLA IDIÁQUEZ.

Hungary: 2-17-14, Mita, Minato-ku, Tokyo 108-0073; tel. (3) 3798-8801; fax (3) 3798-8812; e-mail huembtio@attmail.com; internet www2.gol.com/users/huembtio; Ambassador Dr ZOLTÁN SÜDY.

India: 2-2-11, Kudan Minami, Chiyoda-ku, Tokyo 102-0074; tel. (3) 3262-2391; fax (3) 3234-4866; internet embassy.kcom.ne.jp/embnet/india.html; Ambassador SIDDHARTH SINGH.

Indonesia: 5-2-9, Higashi Gotanda, Shinagawa-ku, Tokyo 141-0022; tel. (3) 3441-4201; fax (3) 3447-1697; Ambassador SOEMADI D. M. BROTODININGRAT.

Iran: 3-10-32, Minami Azabu, Minato-ku, Tokyo 106-0047; tel. (3) 3446-8011; fax (3) 3446-9002; internet www2.gol.com/users/sjei/indexjapanese.html; Ambassador ALI MAJEDI.

Iraq: 8-4-7, Akasaka, Minato-ku, Tokyo 107-0052; tel. (3) 3423-1727; fax (3) 3402-8636; Chargé d'affaires a.i. MUHSIN M. ALI.

Ireland: Ireland House, 2-10-7, Kojimachi, Chiyoda-ku, Tokyo 102-0083; tel. (3) 3263-0695; fax (3) 3265-2275; internet www.embassy-avenue.jp/ireland/; Ambassador PÁDRAIG MURPHY.

Israel: 3, Niban-cho, Chiyoda-ku, Tokyo 102-0084; tel. (3) 3264-0911; fax (3) 3264-0791; e-mail israel@gol.com; internet www.israelembassy-tokyo.com; Ambassador YITZHAK LIOR.

Italy: 2-5-4, Mita, Minato-ku, Tokyo 108-8302; tel. (3) 3453-5291; fax (3) 3456-2319; e-mail itembtky@gol.com; internet sunsite.sut.ac.jp/embitaly; Ambassador GABRIELE MENEGATTI.

Jamaica: Toranomon Yatsuka Bldg, 2nd Floor, 1-1-11, Atago, Minato-ku, Tokyo 105-0002; tel. (3) 3435-1861; fax (3) 3435-1864; e-mail secrat@jamaicaemb.or.jp; Ambassador Dr EARL A. CARR.

Jordan: Chiyoda House, 4th Floor, 2-17-8, Nagata-cho, Chiyoda-ku, Tokyo 100-0014; tel. (3) 3580-5856; fax (3) 3593-9385; internet www2.giganet.net/private/users/emb-jord; Ambassador SAMIR NAOURI.

Kazakhstan: 5-9-8 Himonya, Meguro-ku, Tokyo 152-0023; tel. (3) 3791-5273.

Kenya: 3-24-3, Yakumo, Meguro-ku, Tokyo 152-0023; tel. (3) 3723-4006; fax (3) 3723-4488; e-mail kenrepj@ma.kcom.ne.jp; internet embassy.kcom.ne.jp/kenya; Ambassador MARY DONDE ODINGA.

Korea, Republic: 1-2-5, Minami Azabu, Minato-ku, Tokyo 106-0047; tel. (3) 3452-7611; fax (3) 5232-6911; internet www.mofat.go.kr/embassy_htm/asia/japan/japanese/jp_japan; Ambassador CHO SE-HYUNG.

Kuwait: 4-13-12, Mita, Minato-ku, Tokyo 108-0073; tel. (3) 3455-0361; fax (3) 3456-6290; internet kuwait-embassy.or.jp; Ambassador Sheikh AZZAM MUBARAK SABAH AL-SABAH.

Laos: 3-3-22, Nishi Azabu, Minato-ku, Tokyo 106-0031; tel. (3) 5411-2291; fax (3) 5411-2293; Ambassador SOUKTHAVONE KEOLA.

Lebanon: Chiyoda House, 5th Floor, 2-17-8, Nagata-cho, Chiyoda-ku, Tokyo 100-0014; tel. (3) 3580-1227; fax (3) 3580-2281; e-mail ambaliba@japan.co.jp; Ambassador JAAFAR MOAWI.

Liberia: Sugi Terrace 201, 3-13-11, Okusawa, Setagaya-ku, Tokyo 158; tel. (3) 3726-5711; fax (3) 3726-5712; Chargé d'affaires a.i. HARRY TAH FREEMAN.

Libya: 10-14, Daikanyama-cho, Shibuya-ku, Tokyo 150-0034; tel. (3) 3477-0701; fax (3) 3464-0420; Secretary of the People's Bureau SULAIMAN ABU BAKER BADI (acting).

Lithuania: Rm. 401, 7-11-12 Roppongi, Minato-ku, Tokyo 106-0032; tel. (3) 5414-3433; fax (3) 5414-3434; e-mail lithemb@gol.com; internet www2.gol.com/users/lithemb.

Luxembourg: Niban-cho TS Bldg, 4th Floor, 2-1, Niban-cho, Chiyoda-ku, Tokyo 102-0084; tel. (3) 3265-9621; fax (3) 3265-9624; internet www.luxembourg.or.jp; Ambassador PIERRE GRAMEGNA.

Madagascar: 2-3-23, Moto Azabu, Minato-ku, Tokyo 106; tel. (3) 3446-7252; fax (3) 3446-7078; Ambassador CYRILLE FIDA.

Malawi: Takanawa-Kaisei Bldg, 7th Floor, 3-4-1, Takanawa, Minato-ku, Tokyo 108-0074; tel. (3) 3449-3010; fax (3) 3449-3220; e-mail malawi@mx1.ttcn.ne.jp; internet embassy.kcom.ne.jp/malawi; Ambassador BRIGHT S. M. MANGULAMA.

Malaysia: 20-16, Nanpeidai-cho, Shibuya-ku, Tokyo 150-0036; tel. (3) 3476-3840; fax (3) 3476-4971; e-mail maltokyo@kln.gov.my; Ambassador Dato' MARZUKI MOHAMMAD NOOR.

Marshall Islands: Meiji Park Heights 101, 9-9, Minamimoto-machi, Shinjuku-ku, Tokyo 106; tel. (3) 5379-1701; fax (3) 5379-1810; Ambassador MACK T. KAMINAGA.

Mauritania: 5-17-5, Kita Shinagawa, Shinagawa-ku, Tokyo 141-0001; tel. (3) 3449-3810; fax (3) 3449-3822; Ambassador BA ALIOU IBRA.

Mexico: 2-15-1, Nagata-cho, Chiyoda-ku, Tokyo 100-0014; tel. (3) 3581-1131; fax (3) 3581-4058; e-mail embamex@twics.com; internet www.embassy-avenue.jp/mexico/index; Ambassador CARLOS DE ICAZA.

Micronesia: Reinanzaka Bldg, 2nd Floor, 1-14-2, Akasaka, Minato-ku, Tokyo 107-0052; tel. (3) 3585-5456; fax (3) 3585-5348; e-mail fsmemb@fsmemb.or.jp; Ambassador ALIK L. ALIK.

Mongolia: Pine Crest Mansion, 21-4, Kamiyama-cho, Shibuya-ku, Tokyo 150-0047; tel. (3) 3469-2088; fax (3) 3469-2216; e-mail embmong@gol.com; internet www.embassy.avenue.jp/mongolia/index-j.htm; Ambassador JAMBYU BATJARGAL.

Morocco: Silva Kingdom Bldg, 5th–6th Floors, 3-16-3, Sendagaya, Shibuya-ku, Tokyo 151-0051; tel. (3) 3478-3271; fax (3) 3402-0898; Ambassador SAAD EDDIN TAIB.

Mozambique: 6th Floor, 3-12-17 Mita, Minato-ku, Tokyo 105-0014; tel. (3) 5419-0973; Chargé d'affaires a.i. ARTUR JOSSEFA JAMO.

Myanmar: 4-8-26, Kita Shinagawa, Shinagawa-ku, Tokyo 140-0001; tel. (3) 3441-9291; fax (3) 3447-7394; Ambassador U SOE WIN.

Nepal: 7-14-9, Todoroki, Setagaya-ku, Tokyo 158-0082; tel. (3) 3705-5558; fax (3) 3705-8264; e-mail nepembjp@big.or.jp; internet www.nepal.co.jp/embassy.html; Ambassador KEDAR BHAKTA MATHEMA.

Netherlands: 3-6-3, Shiba Koen, Minato-ku, Tokyo 105-0011; tel. (3) 5401-0411; fax (3) 5401-0420; e-mail nlgovtok@oranda.or.jp; internet www.oranda.or.jp; Ambassador EGBERT F. JACOBS.

New Zealand: 20-40, Kamiyama-cho, Shibuya-ku, Tokyo 150-0047; tel. (3) 3467-2271; fax (3) 3467-2278; e-mail nzemb.tky@mail.com; internet www.nzembassy.com./japan; Ambassador PHILIP GIBSON.

Nicaragua: Kowa Bldg, No. 38, Room 903, 9th Floor, 4-12-24, Nishi Azabu, Minato-ku, Tokyo 106; tel. (3) 3499-0400; fax (3) 3499-3800; Ambassador Dr HARRY BODÁN-SHIELDS.

Nigeria: 5-11-17, Shimo-Meguro, Meguro-ku, Tokyo 153-0064; tel. (3) 5721-5391; fax (3) 5721-5342; internet www.crisscross.com/users/nigeriaemb/home.htm; Ambassador EMMANUEL OSEIMIEGHA OTIOTIO.

Norway: 5-12-2, Minami Azabu, Minato-ku, Tokyo 106-0047; tel. (3) 3440-2611; fax (3) 3440-2620; e-mail emb.tokyo@mfa.no; internet www.norway.or.jp; Ambassador ODD FOSSEIDBRÅTEN.

Oman: 2-28-11, Sendagaya, Shibuya-ku, Tokyo 151-0051; tel. (3) 3402-0877; fax (3) 3404-1334; e-mail omanemb@gol.com; Ambassador MOHAMMED ALI AL-KHUSAIBY.

Pakistan: 2-14-9, Moto Azabu, Minato-ku, Tokyo 106-0046; tel. (3) 3454-4861; fax (3) 3457-0341; e-mail pakemb@gol.com; Ambassador TOUQIR HUSSAIN.

Palau: Rm 201, 1-1, Katamachi, Shinjuku-ku, Tokyo 160-0001; tel. (3) 3354-5500; Ambassador MASAO SALVADOR.

Panama: Kowa Bldg, No. 38, Room 902, 4-12-24, Nishi Azabu, Minato-ku, Tokyo 106-0031; tel. (3) 3499-3741; fax (3) 5485-3548; e-mail panaemb@gol.com; internet www.embassy-avenue.jp/panama/index-j.html; Ambassador JOSÉ A. SOSA.

Papua New Guinea: Mita Kokusai Bldg, Room 313, 3rd Floor, 1-4-28, Mita, Minato-ku, Tokyo 108; tel. (3) 3454-7801; fax (3) 3454-7275; Ambassador AIWA OLMI.

Paraguay: 3-12-9, Kami-Osaki, Shinagawa-ku, Tokyo 141-0021; tel. (3) 5485-3101; fax (3) 5485-3103; e-mail embapar@gol.com; internet www.embassy-avenue.jp/paraguay/index-j.htm; Ambassador Dr MIGUEL A. SOLANO LÓPEZ.

Peru: 4-4-27, Higashi, Shibuya-ku, Tokyo 150-0011; tel. (3) 3406-4243; fax (3) 3409-7589; e-mail 1-tokio@ma.kcom.ne.jp; Ambassador JUAN AURICH MONTERO (acting).

Philippines: 5-15-5, Roppongi, Minato-ku, Tokyo 106-8537; tel. (3) 5562-1600; e-mail phpjp@gol.com; internet www.rptokyo.org; Ambassador ROMEO ABELARDO ARGUELLES.

Poland: 4-5-14, Mita, Minato-ku, Tokyo 108-0074; tel. (3) 3280-2881; Ambassador JERZY POMIANOWSKI.

Portugal: Kamiura-Kojimachi Bldg, 5th Floor, 3-10-3, Kojimachi, Chiyoda-ku, Tokyo 102-0083; tel. (3) 5212-7322; fax (3) 5226-0616; e-mail embportj@ma.kcom.ne.jp; internet www.pnsnet.co.jp/users/cltembpt; Ambassador MANUEL GERVÁSIO DE ALMEIDA LEITE.

Qatar: 2-3-28, Moto-Azabu, Minato-ku, Tokyo 106-0046; tel. (3) 5475-0611; Ambassador RIYADH ALI AL-ANSARI.

Romania: 3-16-19, Nishi Azabu, Minato-ku, Tokyo 106-0031; tel. (3) 3479-0311; fax (3) 3479-0312; e-mail romembjp@gol.com; internet www2.gol.com/users/romembjp/; Ambassador ION PASCU.

Russia: 2-1-1, Azabu-dai, Minato-ku, Tokyo 106-0041; tel. (3) 3583-4224; fax (3) 3505-0593; internet www.embassy-avenue.jp/russia/index-j.html; Ambassador ALEKSANDR N. PANOV.

Rwanda: Kowa Bldg, No. 38, 4-12-24, Nishi Azabu, Minato-ku, Tokyo 106; tel. (3) 3486-7801; fax (3) 3409-2434; Ambassador MATANGUHA ZEPHYR.

Saudi Arabia: 1-8-4, Roppongi, Minato-ku, Tokyo 106-0032; tel. (3) 3589-5241; fax (3) 3589-5200; Ambassador MOHAMED BASHIR KURDI.

Senegal: 1-3-4, Aobadai, Meguro-ku, Tokyo 153-0042; tel. (3) 3464-8451; fax (3) 3464-8452; e-mail senegal@senegal.jp; Ambassador GABRIEL ALEXANDRE SAR.

Serbia and Montenegro: 4-7-24, Kita-Shinagawa, Shinagawa-ku, Tokyo 140-0001; tel. (3) 3447-3571; fax (3) 3447-3573; e-mail embtokyo@twics.com; internet www.twics.com/~embtokyo/home.htm; Chargé d'affaires a.i. NEMANJA JOVIĆ.

Singapore: 5-12-3, Roppongi, Minato-ku, Tokyo 106-0032; tel. (3) 3586-9111; fax (3) 3582-1085; Ambassador LIM CHIN BENG.

Slovakia: POB 35, 2-16-14, Hiroo, Shibuya-ku, Tokyo 150-8691; tel. (3) 3400-8122; fax (3) 3406-6215; e-mail zutokio@twics.com; internet www.embassy-avenue.jp/slovakia/index-j.html; Ambassador JÚLIUS HAUSER.

Slovenia: 7-5-15, Akasaka, Minato-ku, Tokyo 107-0052; tel. (3) 5570-6275; fax (3) 5570-6075; Chargé d'affaires a.i. BERNARD ŠRAJNET.

South Africa: 414 Zenkyoren Bldg, 4th Floor, 2-7-9, Hirakawa-cho, Chiyoda-ku, Tokyo 102-0093; tel. (3) 3265-3366; fax (3) 3265-1108; e-mail sajapan@rsatk.com; internet www.rsatk.com; Ambassador KARAMCHUND MACKERDHUJ.

Spain: 1-3-29, Roppongi, Minato-ku, Tokyo 106-0032; tel. (3) 3583-8531; fax (3) 3582-8627; e-mail embspjp@mail.mae.es; Ambassador JUAN LEÑA CASAS.

Sri Lanka: 2-1-54, Takanawa, Minato-ku, Tokyo 108-0074; tel. (3) 3440-6911; fax (3) 3440-6914; e-mail lankaemb@sphere.ne.jp; internet www.embassy-avenue.jp/srilanka/index.html; Ambassador KARUNATILAKA AMUNUGAMA.

Sudan: 2-7-11, Shirogane, Minato-ku, Tokyo 108-0072; tel. (3) 3280-3161; Ambassador Dr AWAD MURSI TAHA.

Sweden: 1-10-3-100, Roppongi, Minato-ku, Tokyo 106-0032; tel. (3) 5562-5050; fax (3) 5562-9095; e-mail ambassaden.tokyo@foreign.ministry.se; internet www.sweden.or.jp; Ambassador KRISTER KUMLIN.

Switzerland: 5-9-12, Minami Azabu, Minato-ku, Tokyo 106-8589; tel. (3) 3473-0121; fax (3) 3473-6090; e-mail vertretung@tok.rep.admin.ch; internet www.eda.admin.ch/Tokyo; Ambassador JACQUES REVERDIN.

Syria: Homat Jade, 6-19-45, Akasaka, Minato-ku, Tokyo 107-0052; tel. (3) 3586-8977; fax (3) 3586-8979; Chargé d'affaires a.i. HAMZAH HAMZAH.

Tanzania: 4-21-9, Kami Yoga, Setagaya-ku, Tokyo 158-0098; tel. (3) 3425-4531; fax (3) 3425-7844; e-mail tzrepjp@gol.com; Ambassador ELLY E. E. MTANGO.

Thailand: 3-14-6, Kami Osaki, Shinagawa-ku, Tokyo 141-0021; tel. (3) 3447-2247; fax (3) 3442-6750; e-mail thaitke@crisscross.com; Ambassador CHAWAT ARTHAYUKTI.

Tunisia: 3-6-6, Kudan-Minami, Chiyoda-ku, Tokyo 102-0074; tel. (3) 3511-6622; fax (3) 3511-6600; Ambassador SALAH HANNACHI.

Turkey: 2-33-6, Jingumae, Shibuya-ku, Tokyo 150-0001; tel. (3) 3470-5131; fax (3) 3470-5136; e-mail embassy@turkey.jp; internet www.turkey.jp; Ambassador YAMAN BAŞKUT.

Uganda: 4-10-1, Himonya, Meguro-ku, Tokyo 152-0003; tel. (3) 3715-1097; e-mail ugabassy@crisscross.com.

Ukraine: 3-15-6, Nishi Azabu, Minato-ku, Tokyo 106-0046; tel. (3) 5474-9770; fax (3) 5474-9772; e-mail ukremb@rose.ocn.ne.jp; internet ukremb-japan.gov.ua; Ambassador YURIY KOSTENKO.

United Arab Emirates: 9-10, Nanpeidai-cho, Shibuya-ku, Tokyo 150-0036; tel. (3) 5489-0804; fax (3) 5489-0813; e-mail uae-emb@onyx.dti.ne.jp; Ambassador AHMED ALI HAMAD ALMUALLA.

United Kingdom: 1, Ichiban-cho, Chiyoda-ku, Tokyo 102-8381; tel. (3) 5211-1100; fax (3) 5275-3164; e-mail embassy@fco.gov.uk; internet www.uknow.or.jp; Ambassador Sir STEPHEN GOMERSALL.

USA: 1-10-5, Akasaka, Minato-ku, Tokyo 107-8420; tel. (3) 3224-5000; e-mail ustkyecn@ppp.bekkoame.or.jp; internet usembassy.state.gov/tokyo/wwwhjmain.html; Ambassador HOWARD H. BAKER.

Uruguay: Kowa Bldg, No. 38, Room 908, 4-12-24, Nishi Azabu, Minato-ku, Tokyo 106-0031; tel. (3) 3486-1888; fax (3) 3486-9872; Ambassador ZULMA GUELMAN.

Uzbekistan: 5-11-8, Shimo-Meguro, Meguro-ku, Tokyo 153-0064; tel. (3) 3760-5625.

Venezuela: Kowa Bldg, No. 38, Room 703, 4-12-24, Nishi Azabu, Minato-ku, Tokyo 106-0031; tel. (3) 3409-1501; fax (3) 3409-1505; e-mail embavene@interlink.or.jp; internet sunsite.sut.ac.jp/embassy/venemb/embvenez.html; Ambassador Dr CARLOS ENRIQUE NONES.

Viet Nam: 50-11, Moto Yoyogi-cho, Shibuya-ku, Tokyo 151-0062; tel. (3) 3466-3313; fax (3) 3466-3391; Ambassador NGUYEN TAM CHIEN.

Yemen: Kowa Bldg, No. 38, Room 807, 4-12-24, Nishi Azabu, Minato-ku, Tokyo 106-0031; tel. (3) 3499-7151; fax (3) 3499-4577; Chargé d'affaires a.i. ABDULRAHMAN M. AL-HOTHI.

Zambia: 1-10-2, Ebara, Shinagawa-ku, Tokyo 142-0063; tel. (3) 3491-0121; fax (3) 3491-0123; e-mail shulamusakanya@hotmail .com; Chargé d'affaires a.i. SHULA-PATRICK MUSAKANYA.

Zimbabwe: 5-9-10, Shiroganedai, Minato-ku, Tokyo 108; tel. (3) 3280-0331; fax (3) 3280-0466; e-mail zimtokyo@chive.ocn.ne.jp; Ambassador Dr ANDREW H. MTETWA.

Judicial System

The basic principles of the legal system are set forth in the Constitution, which lays down that judicial power is vested in the Supreme Court and in such inferior courts as are established by law, and enunciates the principle that no organ or agency of the Executive shall be given final judicial power. Judges are to be independent in the exercise of their conscience, and may not be removed except by public impeachment, unless judicially declared mentally or physically incompetent to perform official duties. The justices of the Supreme Court are appointed by the Cabinet, the sole exception being the Chief Justice, who is appointed by the Emperor after designation by the Cabinet.

The Court Organization Law, which came into force on 3 May 1947, decreed the constitution of the Supreme Court and the establishment of four types of lower court—High, District, Family (established 1 January 1949) and Summary Courts. The constitution and functions of the courts are as follows:

SUPREME COURT

4-2, Hayabusa-cho, Chiyoda-ku, Tokyo 102-8651; tel. (3) 3264-8111; fax (3) 3221-8975; internet www.courts.go.kp.

This court is the highest legal authority in the land, and consists of a Chief Justice and 14 associate justices. It has jurisdiction over Jokoku (Jokoku appeals) and Kokoku (Kokoku appeals), prescribed in codes of procedure. It conducts its hearings and renders decisions through a Grand Bench or three Petty Benches. Both are collegiate bodies, the former consisting of all justices of the Court, and the latter of five justices. A Supreme Court Rule prescribes which cases are to be handled by the respective Benches. It is, however, laid down by law that the Petty Bench cannot make decisions as to the constitutionality of a statute, ordinance, regulation, or disposition, or as to cases in which an opinion concerning the interpretation and application of the Constitution, or of any laws or ordinances, is at variance with a previous decision of the Supreme Court.

Chief Justice: SHIGERU YAMAGUCHI.

Secretary-General: YUKIO HORIGOME.

LOWER COURTS

High Court

A High Court conducts its hearings and renders decisions through a collegiate body, consisting of three judges, though for cases of insurrection the number of judges must be five. The Court has jurisdiction over the following matters:

Koso appeals from judgments in the first instance rendered by District Courts, from judgments rendered by Family Courts, and from judgments concerning criminal cases rendered by Summary Courts.

Kokoku appeals against rulings and orders rendered by District Courts and Family Courts, and against rulings and orders concerning criminal cases rendered by Summary Courts, except those coming within the jurisdiction of the Supreme Court.

Jokoku appeals from judgments in the second instance rendered by District Courts and from judgments rendered by Summary Courts, except those concerning criminal cases.

Actions in the first instance relating to cases of insurrection.

Presidents: TOKUJI IZUMI (Tokyo), YOSHIO OKADA (Osaka), REISUKE SHIMADA (Nagoya), TOYOZO UEDA (Hiroshima), TOSHIMARO KOJO (Fukuoka), FUMIYA SATO (Sendai), KAZUO KATO (Sapporo), FUMIO ARAI (Takamatsu).

District Court

A District Court conducts hearings and renders decisions through a single judge or, for certain types of cases, through a collegiate body of three judges. It has jurisdiction over the following matters:

Actions in the first instance, except offences relating to insurrection, claims where the subject matter of the action does not exceed 900,000 yen, and offences liable to a fine or lesser penalty.

Koso appeals from judgments rendered by Summary Courts, except those concerning criminal cases.

Kokoku appeals against rulings and orders rendered by Summary Courts, except those coming within the jurisdiction of the Supreme Court and High Courts.

Family Court

A Family Court handles cases through a single judge in case of rendering judgments or decisions. However, in accordance with the provisions of other statutes, it conducts its hearings and renders decisions through a collegiate body of three judges. A conciliation is effected through a collegiate body consisting of a judge and two or more members of the conciliation committee selected from among citizens.

It has jurisdiction over the following matters:

Judgment and conciliation with regard to cases relating to family as provided for by the Law for Adjudgment of Domestic Relations.

Judgment with regard to the matters of protection of juveniles as provided for by the Juvenile Law.

Actions in the first instance relating to adult criminal cases of violation of the Labour Standard Law, the Law for Prohibiting Liquors to Minors, or other laws especially enacted for protection of juveniles.

Summary Court

A Summary Court handles cases through a single judge, and has jurisdiction in the first instance over the following matters:

Claims where the value of the subject matter does not exceed 900,000 yen (excluding claims for cancellation or change of administrative dispositions).

Actions which relate to offences liable to a fine or lesser penalty, offences liable to a fine as an optional penalty, and certain specified offences such as habitual gambling and larceny.

A Summary Court cannot impose imprisonment or a graver penalty. When it deems proper the imposition of a sentence of imprisonment or a graver penalty, it must transfer such cases to a District Court, but it can impose imprisonment with labour not exceeding three years for certain specified offences.

Religion

The traditional religions of Japan are Shintoism and Buddhism. Neither is exclusive, and many Japanese subscribe at least nominally to both. Since 1945 a number of new religions (Shinko Shukyo) have evolved, based on a fusion of Shinto, Buddhist, Daoist, Confucian and Christian beliefs. In 1995 there were some 184,000 religious organizations registered in Japan, according to the Ministry of Education.

SHINTOISM

Shintoism is an indigenous religious system embracing the worship of ancestors and of nature. It is divided into two cults: national Shintoism, which is represented by the shrines; and sectarian Shintoism, which developed during the second half of the 19th century. In 1868 Shinto was designated a national religion and all Shinto shrines acquired the privileged status of a national institution. Complete freedom of religion was introduced in 1947, and state support of Shinto was prohibited. In the mid-1990s there were 81,307 shrines, 90,309 priests and 106.6m. adherents.

BUDDHISM

World Buddhist Fellowship: Hozenji Buddhist Temple, 3-24-2, Akabane-dai, Kita-ku, Tokyo; Rev. FUJI NAKAYAMA.

CHRISTIANITY

In 1993 the Christian population was estimated at 1,050,938.

National Christian Council in Japan: Japan Christian Centre, 2-3-18-24, Nishi Waseda, Shinjuku-ku, Tokyo 169-0051; tel. (3) 3203-0372; fax (3) 3204-9495; e-mail ncc-j@jca.apc.org; internet www.jca.apc.org/ncc-j; f. 1923; 14 mems (churches and other bodies), 19 assoc. mems; Chair. REIKO SUZUKI; Gen. Sec. Rev. TOSHIMASA YAMAMOTO.

The Anglican Communion

Anglican Church in Japan (Nippon Sei Ko Kai): 65, Yarai-cho, Shinjuku-ku, Tokyo 162-0805; tel. (3) 5228-3171; fax (3) 5228-3175;

e-mail general-sec.po@nskk.org; internet www.nskk.org; f. 1887; 11 dioceses; Primate of Japan Most Rev. JAMES T. UNO (Bishop of Kita-Kanto); Gen. Sec. LAURENCE Y. MINABE; 57,878 mems (2001).

The Orthodox Church

Japanese Orthodox Church (Nippon Haristosu Seikyoukai): Holy Resurrection Cathedral (Nicolai-Do), 4-1-3, Kanda Surugadai, Chiyoda-ku, Tokyo 101; tel. (3) 3291-1885; fax (3) 3291-1886; e-mail ocj@gol.com; three dioceses; Archbishop of Tokyo, Primate and Metropolitan of All Japan Most Rev. DANIEL; 24,821 mems.

Protestant Church

United Church of Christ in Japan (Nihon Kirisuto Kyodan): Japan Christian Center, Room 31, 2-3-18, Nishi Waseda, Shinjuku-ku, Tokyo 169-0051; tel. (3) 3202-0541; fax (3) 3207-3918; e-mail ecumeni-c@uccj.org; f. 1941; union of 34 Congregational, Methodist, Presbyterian, Reformed and other Protestant denominations; Moderator Rev. SEISHI OJIMA; Gen. Sec. Rev. NOBORU TAKEMAE; 200,627 mems (2000).

The Roman Catholic Church

Japan comprises three archdioceses and 13 dioceses, and the Apostolic Prefecture of Karafuto. There were an estimated 511,063 adherents at 31 December 2001.

Catholic Bishops' Conference of Japan (Chuo Kyogikai)

2-10-10, Shiomi, Koto-ku, Tokyo 135-8585; tel. (3) 5632-4411; fax (3) 5632-4457; e-mail info@cbcj.catholic.jp; internet www.cbcj.catholic .jp.
Pres. Most Rev. AUGUSTINE JUN-ICHI NOMURA (Bishop of Nagoya).

Archbishop of Nagasaki: Most Rev. FRANCIS XAVIER KANAME SHIMA-MOTO, Archbishop's House, 1-1, Hashiguchi-machi, Nagasaki-shi, Nagasaki-ken 852-8114; tel. (95) 843-4188; fax (95) 843-4322.

Archbishop of Osaka: Most Rev. LEO JUN IKENAGA, Archbishop's House, 2-24-22, Tamatsukuri, Chuo-ku, Osaka 540-0004; tel. (6) 6941-9700; fax (6) 6946-1345.

Archbishop of Tokyo: Most Rev. PETER TAKEO OKADA, Archbishop's House, 3-16-15, Sekiguchi, Bunkyo-ku, Tokyo 112-0014; tel. (3) 3943-2301; fax (3) 3944-8511; e-mail peter2000@nifty.com.

Other Christian Churches

Japan Baptist Convention: 1-2-4, Minami Urawa, Saitama-shi, Saitama 336-0017; tel. (48) 883-1091; fax (48) 883-1092; f. 1947; Gen. Sec. Rev. MAKOTO KATO; 33,165 mems (March 2002).

Japan Baptist Union: 2-3-18, Nishi Waseda, Shinjuku-ku, Tokyo 169-0051; tel. (3) 3202-0053; fax (3) 3202-0054; e-mail generalsecretary@jbu.or.jp; f. 1958; Moderator KUNIHIKO AMANO; Gen. Sec. KAZUO OYA; 4,615 mems.

Japan Evangelical Lutheran Church: 1-1, Sadohara-cho, Ichi-gaya-shi, Shinjuku-ku, Tokyo 162-0842; tel. (3) 3260-8631; fax (3) 3268-3589; e-mail s-matsuoka@jelc.or.jp; internet www.jelc.or.jp; f. 1893; Moderator Rev. MASATOSHI YAMANOUCHI; Gen. Sec. Rev. SHU-NICHIRO MATSUOKA; 21,967 mems (2000).

Korean Christian Church in Japan: Room 52, Japan Christian Center, 2-3-18, Nishi Waseda, Shinjuku-ku, Tokyo 169-0051; tel. (3) 3202-5398; fax (3) 3202-4977; e-mail kccj@kb3.so-net.ne.jp; f. 1909; Moderator LEE BYUNG-KU; Gen. Sec. PARK SOO-KIL; 7,119 mems (2002).

Among other denominations active in Japan are the Christian Catholic Church, the German Evangelical Church and the Tokyo Union Church.

OTHER COMMUNITIES

Bahá'í Faith

The National Spiritual Assembly of the Bahá'ís of Japan: 7-2-13, Shinjuku, Shinjuku-ku, Tokyo 160-0022; tel. (3) 3209-7521; fax (3) 3204-0773; e-mail nsajpn@tka.att.ne.jp; internet www.bahaijp .org.

Judaism

Jewish Community of Japan: 3-8-8 Hiro, Shibuya-ku, Tokyo 150-0012; tel. (3) 3400-2559; e-mail jccjapan@gol.com; internet www .jccjapan.or.jp; Leader Rabbi ELLIOTT M. MARMON.

Islam

Islam has been active in Japan since the late 19th century. There is a small Muslim community, maintaining several mosques, including those at Kobe, Nagoya, Chiba and Isesaki, the Arabic Islamic Institute and the Islamic Center in Tokyo. The construction of Tokyo Central mosque was ongoing in 1999.

Islamic Center, Japan: 1-16-11, Ohara, Setagaya-ku, Tokyo 156-0041; tel. (3) 3460-6169; fax (3) 3460-6105; e-mail islamcpj@ islamcenter.or.jp; internet www.islamcenter.or.jp; f. 1965; Chair. Dr SALIH SAMARRAI.

The New Religions

Many new cults have emerged in Japan since the end of the Second World War. Collectively these are known as the New Religions (Shinko Shukyo), among the most important of which are Tenrikyo, Omotokyo, Soka Gakkai, Rissho Kosei-kai, Kofuku-no-Kagaku, Agonshu and Aum Shinrikyo. (Following the indictment on charges of murder of several members of Aum Shinrikyo, including its leader, Shoko Asahara, the cult lost its legal status as a religious organization in 1996. In January 2000 the cult announced its intention to change its name to Aleph. At that time it named a new leader, Tatsuko Muraoka.)

Kofuku-no-Kagaku (Institute for Research in Human Happiness): Tokyo; f. 1986; believes its founder to be reincarnation of Buddha; 8.25m. mems; Leader RYUHO OKAWA.

Rissho Kosei-kai: 2-11-1, Wada Suginami-ku, Tokyo 166-8537; tel. (3) 3380-5185; fax (3) 3381-9792; internet www.kosei-kai.or.jp; f. 1938; Buddhist lay organization based on the teaching of the Lotus Sutra, active inter-faith co-operation towards peace; Pres. Rev. Dr NICHIKO NIWANO; 6.3m. mems with 245 brs world-wide (2000).

Soka Gakkai: 32, Shinano-machi, Shinjuku-ku, Tokyo 160-8583; tel. (3) 5360-9830; fax (3) 5360-9885; e-mail webmaster@sokagakkai .info; internet sokagakkai.info; f. 1930; society of lay practitioners of the Buddhism of Nichiren; membership of 8.21m. households (2000); group promotes activities in education, international cultural exchange and consensus-building towards peace, based on the humanist world view of Buddhism; Hon. Pres. DAISAKU IKEDA; Pres. EINOSUKE AKIYA.

The Press

In December 2000 there were 122 daily newspapers in Japan. Their average circulation was the highest in the world, and the circulation per head of population was also among the highest, at 573 copies per 1,000 inhabitants in 1999. The large number of weekly news journals is a notable feature of the Japanese press. At December 1998 a total of 2,763 periodicals were produced, 85 of which were weekly publications. Technically the Japanese press is highly advanced, and the major newspapers are issued in simultaneous editions in the main centres.

The two newspapers with the largest circulations are the *Yomiuri Shimbun* and *Asahi Shimbun*. Other influential papers include *Mainichi Shimbun, Nihon Keizai Shimbun, Chunichi Shimbun* and *Sankei Shimbun*.

NATIONAL DAILIES

Asahi Shimbun: 5-3-2, Tsukiji, Chuo-ku, Tokyo 104-8011; tel. (3) 3545-0131; fax (3) 3545-0358; internet www.asahi.com; f. 1879; also published by Osaka, Seibu and Nagoya head offices and Hokkaido branch office; Pres. SHINICHI HAKOSHIMA; Dir and Exec. Editor MASAO KIMIWADA; circ. morning 8.3m., evening 4.1m.

Mainichi Shimbun: 1-1-1, Hitotsubashi, Chiyoda-ku, Tokyo 100-8051; tel. (3) 3212-0321; fax (3) 3211-3598; internet www.mainichi .co.jp; f. 1882; also published by Osaka, Seibu and Chubu head offices, and Hokkaido branch office; Pres. AKIRA SAITO; Man. Dir and Editor-in-Chief MASATOU KITAMURA; circ. morning 4.0m., evening 1.7m.

Nihon Keizai Shimbun: 1-9-5, Otemachi, Chiyoda-ku, Tokyo 100-8066; tel. (3) 3270-0251; fax (3) 5255-2661; internet www.nikkei.co .jp; f. 1876; also published by Osaka head office and Sapporo, Nagoya and Seibu branch offices; Pres. TAKUHIKO TSURUTA; Dir and Man. Editor YASUO HIRATA; circ. morning 3.0m., evening 1.7m.

Sankei Shimbun: 1-7-2, Otemachi, Chiyoda-ku, Tokyo 100-8077; tel. (3) 3231-7111; internet www.sankei.co.jp; f. 1933; also published by Osaka head office; Man. Dir and Editor NAGAYOSHI SUMIDA; circ. morning 2.0m., evening 905,771.

Yomiuri Shimbun: 1-7-1, Otemachi, Chiyoda-ku, Tokyo 100-8055; tel. (3) 3242-1111; e-mail webmaster@yomiuri.co.jp; internet www .yomiuri.co.jp; f. 1874; also published by Osaka, Seibu and Chubu head offices, and Hokkaido and Hokuriku branch offices; Pres. and Editor-in-Chief TSUNEO WATANABE; circ. morning 10.2m., evening 4.3m.

PRINCIPAL LOCAL DAILIES

Tokyo

Daily Sports: 1-20-3, Osaki, Shinagawa-ku, Tokyo 141-8585; tel. (3) 5434-1752; f. 1948; morning; Man. Dir HIROHISA KARUO; circ. 400,254.

The Daily Yomiuri: 1-7-1, Otemachi, Chiyoda-ku, Tokyo 100-8055; tel. (3) 3242-1111; f. 1955; morning; Man. Editor TSUTOMU YAMAGUCHI; circ. 51,421.

Dempa Shimbun: 1-11-15, Higashi Gotanda, Shinagawa-ku, Tokyo 141-8790; tel. (3) 3445-6111; fax (3) 3444-7515; f. 1950; morning; Pres. TETSUO HIRAYAMA; Man. Editor TOSHIO KASUYA; circ. 298,000.

Hochi Shimbun: 4-6-49, Kohnan, Minato-ku, Tokyo 108-8485; tel. (3) 5479-1111; internet www.yomiuri.co.jp/hochi/home.htm; f. 1872; morning; Pres. MASARU FUSHIMI; Man. Editor TATSUE AOKI; circ. 755,670.

The Japan Times: 4-5-4, Shibaura, Minato-ku, Tokyo 108-8071; tel. (3) 3453-5312; internet www.japantimes.co.jp; f. 1897; morning; English; Chair. and Pres. TOSHIAKI OGASAWARA; Dir and Editor-in-Chief YUTAKA MATAEBARA; circ. 61,929.

The Mainichi Daily News: 1-1-1, Hitotsubashi, Chiyoda-ku, Tokyo 100-8051; tel. (3) 3212-0321; f. 1922; morning; English; also publ. from Osaka; Man. Editor TETSUO TOKIZAWA; combined circ. 49,200.

Naigai Times: 1-1-15, Ariake, Koto-ku, Tokyo 135-0063; tel. (3) 5564-7021; fax (3) 5564-1022; e-mail info@naigai-times.co.jp; f. 1949; evening; Pres. MITSUGU ONDA; Vice-Pres. and Editor-in-Chief KENICHIRO KURIHARA; circ. 410,000.

Nihon Kaiji Shimbun (Japan Maritime Daily): 5-19-2, Shimbashi, Minato-ku, Tokyo 105-0004; tel. (3) 3436-3221; internet www.jmd.co.jp; f. 1942; morning; Man. Editor OSAMI ENDO; circ. 55,000.

Nihon Kogyo Shimbun: 1-7-2, Otemachi, Chiyoda-ku, Tokyo 100-8125; tel. (3) 3231-7111; internet www.jij.co.jp; f. 1933; morning; industrial, business and financial; Man. Editor YOSHIMI KURA; circ. 408,444.

Nihon Nogyo Shimbun (Agriculture): 2-3, Akihabara, Taito-ku, Tokyo 110-8722; tel. (3) 5295-7411; fax (3) 3253-0980; f. 1928; morning; Man. Editor YASUNORI INOUE; circ. 423,840.

Nihon Sen-i Shimbun (Textile and Fashion): 13-10, Nihombashi-kobunacho, Chuo-ku, Tokyo 103-0024; tel. (3) 5649-8711; f. 1943; morning; Man. Editor KIYOSHIGE SEIRYU; circ. 116,000.

Nikkan Kogyo Shimbun (Industrial Daily News): 1-8-10, Kudan-kita, Chiyoda-ku, Tokyo 102-8181; tel. (3) 3222-7111; fax (3) 3262-6031; internet www.nikkan.co.jp; f. 1915; morning; Man. Editor HIDEO WATANABE; circ. 533,145.

Nikkan Sports News: 3-5-10, Tsukiji, Chuo-ku, Tokyo 104-8055; tel. (3) 5550-8888; fax (3) 5550-8901; internet www.nikkansports.com; f. 1946; morning; Man. Editor YUKIHIRO MORI; circ. 993,240.

Sankei Sports: 1-7-2, Otemachi, Chiyoda-ku, Tokyo 100-8077; tel. (3) 3231-7111; internet www.xusxus.com; f. 1963; morning; Man. Editor YUKIO INADA; circ. 809,245.

Shipping and Trade News: Tokyo News Service Ltd, Tsukiji Hamarikyu Bldg, 5-3-3, Tsukiji, Chuo-ku, Tokyo 104-8004; tel. (3) 3542-6511; fax (3) 3542-5086; internet www.tvguide.or.jp; f. 1949; English; Man. Editor TAKASHI INOUE; circ. 15,000.

Sports Nippon: 2-1-30, Etchujima, Koto-ku, Tokyo 135-8735; tel. (3) 3820-0700; internet www.mainichi.co.jp/suponichi/; f. 1949; morning; Man. Editor SUSUMU KOMURO; circ. 929,421.

Suisan Keizai Shimbun (Fisheries): 6-8-19, Roppongi, Minato-ku, Tokyo 106-0032; tel. (3) 3404-6531; fax (3) 3404-0863; f. 1948; morning; Man. Editor KOSHI TORINOUMI; circ. 61,000.

Tokyo Chunichi Sports: 2-3-13, Kohnan, Minato-ku, Tokyo 108-8010; tel. (3) 3471-2211; f. 1956; evening; Head Officer TETSUO TANAKA; circ. 330,431.

Tokyo Shimbun: 2-3-13, Kohnan, Minato-ku, Tokyo 108-8010; tel. (3) 3471-2211; fax (3) 3471-1851; internet www.tokyo-np.co.jp; f. 1942; Man. Editor KATSUHIKO SAKAI; circ. morning 655,970, evening 354,191.

Tokyo Sports: 2-1-30, Etchujima, Koto-ku, Tokyo 135-8721; tel. (3) 3820-0801; f. 1959; evening; Man. Editor YASUO SAKURAI; circ. 1,321,250.

Yukan Fuji: 1-7-2, Otemachi, Chiyoda-ku, Tokyo 100-8077; tel. (3) 3231-7111; fax (3) 3246-0377; internet www.zakzak.co.jp; f. 1969; evening; Man. Editor MASAMI KATO; circ. 268,984.

Osaka District

Daily Sports: 1-18-11, Edobori, Nishi-ku, Osaka 550-0002; tel. (6) 6443-0421; f. 1948; morning; Man. Editor TOSHIAKI MITANI; circ. 562,715.

The Mainichi Daily News: 3-4-5, Umeda, Kita-ku, Osaka 530-8251; tel. (6) 6345-1551; f. 1922; morning; English; Man. Editor KATSUYA FUKUNAGA.

Nikkan Sports: 5-92-1, Hattori-kotobuki-cho, Toyonaka 561-8585; tel. (6) 6867-2811; internet www.nikkansports.com/osaka; f. 1950; morning; Man. Editor KATSUO FURUKAWA; circ. 513,498.

Osaka Shimbun: 2-4-9, Umeda, Kita-ku, Osaka 530-8279; tel. (6) 6343-1221; internet www.osakanews.com; f. 1922; evening; Man. Editor KAORU YURA; circ. 88,887.

Osaka Sports: Osaka Ekimae Daiichi Bldg, 4th Floor, 1-3-1-400, Umeda, Kita-ku, Osaka 530-0001; tel. (6) 6345-7657; f. 1968; evening; Head Officer KAZUOMI TANAKA; circ. 470,660.

Sankei Sports: 2-4-9, Umeda, Kita-ku, Osaka 530-8277; tel. (6) 6343-1221; f. 1955; morning; Man. Editor MASAKI YOSHIDA; circ. 552,519.

Sports Nippon: 3-4-5, Umeda, Kita-ku, Osaka 530-8278; tel. (6) 6346-8500; f. 1949; morning; Man. Editor HIDETOSHI ISHIHARA; circ. 477,300.

Kanto District

Chiba Nippo (Chiba Daily News): 4-14-10, Chuo, Chuo-ku, Chiba 260-0013; tel. (43) 222-9211; internet www.chibanippo.co.jp; f. 1957; morning; Man. Editor NOBORU HAYASHI; circ. 190,187.

Ibaraki Shimbun: 2-15, Kitami-cho, Mito 310-8686; tel. (292) 21-3121; internet www.ibaraki-np.co.jp; f. 1891; morning; Pres. and Editor-in-Chief TADANORI TOMOSUE; circ. 117,240.

Jomo Shimbun: 1-50-21, Furuichi-machi, Maebashi 371-8666; tel. (272) 54-9911; internet www.jomo-news.co.jp; f. 1887; morning; Man. Editor MUTSUO ODAGIRI; circ. 296,111.

Joyo Shimbun: 2-7-6, Manabe, Tsuchiura 300-0051; tel. (298) 21-1780; internet www.tsukuba.com; f. 1948; morning; Pres. MINEO IWANAMI; Man. Editor AKIRA SAITO; circ. 88,700.

Kanagawa Shimbun: 6-145, Hanasaki-cho, Nishi-ku, Yokohama 220-8588; tel. (45) 411-2222; internet www.kanagawa-np.co.jp; f. 1890; morning; Man. Editor NOBUYUKI CHIBA; circ. 238,203.

Saitama Shimbun: 6-12-11, Kishi-cho, Urawa 336-8686; tel. (48) 862-3371; internet www.saitama-np.co.jp; f. 1944; morning; Man. Editor YOTARO NUMATA; circ. 162,071.

Shimotsuke Shimbun: 1-8-11, Showa, Utsunomiya 320-8686; tel. (286) 25-1111; internet www.shimotsuke.co.jp; f. 1884; morning; Man. Dir and Editor-in-Chief EISUKE TODA; circ. 306,072.

Tohoku District
(North-east Honshu)

Akita Sakigake Shimpo: 1-1, San-no-rinkai-machi, Akita 010-8601; tel. (18) 888-1800; fax (188) 23-1780; internet www.sakigake.co.jp; f. 1874; Man. Editor SHIGEAKI MAEKAWA; circ. 263,246.

Daily Tohoku: 1-3-12, Shiroshita, Hachinohe 031-8601; tel. (178) 44-5111; f. 1945; morning; Man. Editor TOKOJU YOSHIDA; circ. 104,935.

Fukushima Mimpo: 13-17, Ota-machi, Fukushima 960-8602; tel. (245) 31-4111; internet www.fukushima-minpo.co.jp; f. 1892; Pres. and Editor-in-Chief TSUTOMU HANADA; circ. morning 308,353, evening 9,489.

Fukushima Minyu: 4-29, Yanagi-machi, Fukushima 960-8648; tel. (245) 23-1191; internet www.minyu; f. 1895; Man. Editor KENJI KANNO; circ. morning 201,414, evening 6,066.

Hokuu Shimpo: 3-2, Nishi-dori-machi, Noshiro 016-0891. (185) 54-3150; f. 1895; morning; Chair. KOICHI YAMAKI; circ. 31,490.

Ishinomaki Shimbun: 2-1-28, Sumiyoshi-machi, Ishinomaki 986; tel. (225) 22-3201; f. 1946; evening; Man. Editor MASATOSHI SATO; circ. 13,050.

Iwate Nichi-nichi Shimbun: 60, Minamishin-machi, Ichinoseki 021-8686; tel. (191) 26-5114; internet www.isop.ne.jp/iwanichi; f. 1923; morning; Pres. TAKESHI YAMAGISHI; Man. Editor SEIICHI WATANABE; circ. 59,850.

Iwate Nippo: 3-7, Uchimaru, Morioka 020-8622; tel. (196) 53-4111; internet www.iwate-np.co.jp; f. 1876; Man. Editor TOKUO MIYAZAWA; circ. morning 230,073, evening 229,815.

Kahoku Shimpo: 1-2-28, Itsutsubashi, Aoba-ku, Sendai 980-8660; tel. (22) 211-1111; fax (22) 224-7947; internet www.kahoku.co.jp; f. 1897; Exec. Dir and Man. Editor MASAHIKO ICHIRIKI; circ. morning 503,318, evening 133,855.

Mutsu Shimpo: 2-1, Shimo-shirogane-cho, Hirosaki 036-8356; tel. (172) 34-3111; f. 1946; morning; Man. Editor YUJI SATO; circ. 53,500.

Shonai Nippo: 8-29, Baba-cho, Tsuruoka 997-8691; tel. (235) 22-1480; f. 1946; morning; Pres. TAKAO SATO; Man. Editor MASAYUKI HASHIMOTO; circ. 19,100.

To-o Nippo: 78, Kanbayashi, Yatsuyaku, Aomori 030-0180; tel. (177) 39-1111; internet www.toonippo.co.jp; f. 1888; Exec. Dir YOSHIO WAJIMA; Man. Editor TAKAO SHIOKOSHI; circ. morning 262,532, evening 258,590.

Yamagata Shimbun: 2-5-12, Hatagomachi, Yamagata 990-8550; tel. (236) 22-5271; internet www.yamagata-np.co.jp; f. 1876; Man. Editor TOSHINOBU SHIONO; circ. morning 213,057, evening 213,008.

Yonezawa Shimbun: 3-3-7, Monto-cho, Yonezawa 992-0039; tel. (238) 22-4411; f. 1879; morning; Man. Dir and Editor-in-Chief MAKOTO SATO; circ. 13,750.

Chubu District
(Central Honshu)

Chubu Keizai Shimbun: 4-4-12, Meieki, Nakamura-ku, Nagoya 450-8561; tel. (52) 561-5215; f. 1946; morning; Man. Editor NORIMITSU INAGAKI; circ. 97,000.

Chukyo Sports: Chunichi Kosoku Offset Insatsu Bldg, 4-3-9, Kinjo, Naka-ku, Nagoya 460-0847; tel. (52) 982-1911; f. 1968; evening; circ. 289,430; Head Officer OSAMU SUETSUGU.

Chunichi Shimbun: 1-6-1, San-no-maru, Naka-ku, Nagoya 460-8511; tel. (52) 201-8811; internet www.chunichi.ne.jp; f. 1942; Man. Editor NOBUAKI KOIDE; circ. morning 2.7m., evening 748,635.

Chunichi Sports: 1-6-1, San-no-maru, Naka-ku, Nagoya 460-8511; tel. (52) 201-8811; f. 1954; evening; Head Officer YASUHIKO AIBA; circ. 631,429.

Gifu Shimbun: 10, Imakomachi, Gifu 500-8577; tel. (582) 64-1151; internet www.jic-gifu.or.jp/np; f. 1881; Exec. Dir and Man. Editor TADASHI TANAKA; circ. morning 170,176, evening 31,775.

Higashi-Aichi Shimbun: 62, Torinawate, Shinsakae-machi, Toyohashi 441-8666; tel. (532) 32-3111; f. 1957; morning; Man. Editor YOSHIYUKI SUZUKI; circ. 52,300.

Nagano Nippo: 3-1323-1, Takashima, Suwa 392-8611; tel. (266) 52-2000; f. 1901; morning; Man. Editor ETSUO KOIZUMI; circ. 73,000.

Nagoya Times: 1-3-10, Marunouchi, Naka-ku, Nagoya 460-8530; tel. (52) 231-1331; f. 1946; evening; Man. Editor NAOKI KITO; circ. 146,137.

Shinano Mainichi Shimbun: 657, Minamiagata-machi, Nagano 380-8546; tel. (26) 236-3000; fax (26) 236-3197; internet www.shinmai.co.jp; f. 1873; Man. Editor SEIICHI INOMATA; circ. morning 469,801, evening 55,625.

Shizuoka Shimbun: 3-1-1, Toro, Shizuoka 422-8033; tel. (54) 284-8900; internet www.sbs-np.co.jp; f. 1941; Man. Editor HISAO ISHIHARA; circ. morning 730,746, evening 730,782.

Yamanashi Nichi-Nichi Shimbun: 2-6-10, Kitaguchi, Kofu 400-8515; tel. (552) 31-3000; internet www.sannichi.co.jp; f. 1872; morning; Man. Editor KATSUHITO NISHIKAWA; circ. 205,758.

Hokuriku District
(North Coastal Honshu)

Fukui Shimbun: 1-1-14, Haruyama, Fukui 910-8552; tel. (776) 23-5111; internet www.fukuishimbun.co.jp; f. 1899; morning; Man. Editor KAZUO UCHIDA; circ. 202,280.

Hokkoku Shimbun: 2-5-1, Korinbo, Kanazawa 920-8588; tel. (762) 63-2111; internet www.hokkoku.co.jp; f. 1893; Man. Editor WATARU INAGAKI; circ. morning 328,532, evening 97,051.

Hokuriku Chunichi Shimbun: 2-7-15, Korinbo, Kanazawa 920-8573; tel. (762) 61-3111; internet www.hokuriku.chunichi.co.jp; f. 1960; Man. Editor KANJI KOMIYA; circ. morning 116,719, evening 12,820.

Kitanippon Shimbun: 2-14, Azumi-cho, Toyama 930-8680; tel. (764) 45-3300; internet www.kitanippon.co.jp; f. 1884; Dir and Man. Editor MINORU KAWATA; circ. morning 223,033, evening 29,959.

Niigata Nippo: 772-2, Zenku, Niigata 950-1189; tel. (25) 378-9111; internet www.niigata-nippo.co.jp; f. 1942; Dir and Man. Editor MICHIEI TAKAHASHI; circ. morning 496,567, evening 66,836.

Toyama Shimbun: 5-1, Ote-machi, Toyama 930-8520; tel. (764) 91-8111; internet www.toyama.hokkoku.co.jp; f. 1923; morning; Man. Editor SACHIO MIYAMOTO; circ. 42,988.

Kinki District
(West Central Honshu)

Daily Sports: 1-5-7, Higashikawasaki-cho, Chuo-ku, Kobe 650-0044; tel. (78) 362-7100; morning; Man. Editor TAKASHI HIRAI.

Ise Shimbun: 34-6, Honmachi, Tsu 514-0831; tel. (592) 24-0003; internet www.isenp.co.jp; f. 1878; morning; Man. Editor FUJIO YAMAMOTO; circ. 100,550.

Kii Minpo: 100, Akizucho, Tanabe 646-8660; tel. (739) 22-7171; internet www.agara.co.jp; f. 1911; evening; Man. Editor KAZUSADA TANIGAMI; circ. 38,165.

Kobe Shimbun: 1-5-7, Higashikawasaki-cho, Chuo-ku, Kobe 650-8571; tel. (78) 362-7100; internet www.kobe-np.co.jp; f. 1898; Man. Editor MASAO MAEKAWA; circ. morning 545,854, evening 268,787.

Kyoto Shimbun: 239, Shoshoi-machi, Ebisugawa-agaru, Karasuma-dori, Nakagyo-ku, Kyoto 604-8577; tel. (75) 241-5430; internet www.kyoto-np.co.jp; f. 1879; Man. Editor OSAMU SAITO; circ. morning 505,723, evening 319,313.

Nara Shimbun: 606, Sanjo-machi, Nara 630-8686; tel. (742) 26-1331; internet www.nara-shimbun.com; f. 1946; morning; Dir and Man. Editor HISAMI SAKAMOTO; circ. 118,064.

Chugoku District
(Western Honshu)

Chugoku Shimbun: 7-1, Dobashi-cho, Naka-ku, Hiroshima 730-8677; tel. (82) 236-2111; fax (82) 236-2321; e-mail denshi@hiroshima-cdas.or.jp; internet www.chugoku-np.co.jp; f. 1892; Man. Editor NOBUYUKI AOKI; circ. morning 734,589, evening 85,089.

Nihonkai Shimbun: 2-137, Tomiyasu, Tottori 680-8678; tel. (857) 21-2888; internet www.nnn.co.jp; f. 1976; morning; Man. Editor KOTARO TAMURA; circ. 101,768.

Okayama Nichi-Nichi Shimbun: 6-30, Hon-cho, Okayama 700-8678; tel. (86) 231-4211; f. 1946; evening; Man. Dir and Man. Editor TAKASHI ANDO; circ. 45,000.

San-In Chuo Shimpo: 383, Tono-machi, Matsue 690-8668; tel. (852) 32-3440; f. 1882; morning; Man. Editor MASAMI MOCHIDA; circ. 172,605.

Sanyo Shimbun: 2-1-23, Yanagi-machi, Okayama 700-8634; tel. (86) 231-2210; internet www.sanyo.oni.co.jp; f. 1879; Man. Dir and Man. Editor TAKAMASA KOSHIMUNE; circ. morning 454,263, evening 71,200.

Ube Jiho: 3-6-1, Kotobuki-cho, Ube 755-8557; tel. (836) 31-1511; f. 1912; evening; Exec. Dir and Man. Editor KAZUYA WAKI; circ. 42,550.

Yamaguchi Shimbun: 1-1-7, Higashi-Yamato-cho, Shimonoseki 750-8506; tel. (832) 66-3211; internet www.minato-yamaguchi.co.jp; f. 1946; morning; Man. Editor SHOICHI SASAKI; circ. 84,000.

Shikoku Island

Ehime Shimbun: 1-12-1, Otemachi, Matsuyama 790-8511; tel. (899) 35-2111; internet www.ehime-np.co.jp; f. 1876; morning; Man. Editor RYOJI YANO; circ. 319,522.

Kochi Shimbun: 3-2-15, Honmachi, Kochi 780-8572; tel. (888) 22-2111; internet www.kochinews.co.jp; f. 1904; Dir and Man. Editor KENGO FUJITO; circ. morning 233,319, evening 146,276.

Shikoku Shimbun: 15-1, Nakano-cho, Takamatsu 760-8572; tel. (878) 33-1111; internet www.shikoku-np.co.jp; f. 1889; morning; Man. Editor JUNJI YAMASHITA; circ. 208,816.

Tokushima Shimbun: 2-5-2, Naka-Tokushima-cho, Tokushima 770-8572; tel. (886) 55-7373; fax (866) 54-0165; internet www.topics.or.jp; f. 1944; Dir and Man. Editor HIROSHI MATSUMURA; circ. morning 253,184, evening 52,203.

Hokkaido Island

Doshin Sports: 3-6, Odori-nishi, Chuo-ku, Sapporo 060-8711; tel. (11) 241-1230; internet douspo.aurora-net.or.jp; f. 1982; morning; Pres. KOSUKE SAKAI; circ. 139,178.

Hokkai Times: 10-6, Nishi, Minami-Ichijo, Chuo-ku, Sapporo 060; tel. (11) 231-0131; f. 1946; Man. Editor KOKI ITO; circ. morning 120,736.

Hokkaido Shimbun: 3-6, Odori-nishi, Chuo-ku, Sapporo 060-8711; tel. (11) 221-2111; internet www.aurora.co.jp; f. 1942; Man. Editor RYOZO ODAGIRI; circ. morning 1.2m., evening 740,264.

Kushiro Shimbun: 7-3, Kurogane-cho, Kushiro 085-8650; tel. (154) 22-1111; internet www.hokkai.or.jp/senshin/index.html; f. 1946; morning; Man. Editor YUTAKA ITO; circ. 55,686.

Muroran Mimpo: 1-3-16, Hon-cho, Muroran 051-8550; tel. (143) 22-5121; internet www.muromin.mnw.jp; f. 1945; Man. Editor TSUTOMO KUDO; circ. morning 60,300, evening 52,500.

Nikkan Sports: 3-1-30, Higashi, Kita-3 jo, Chuo-ku, Sapporo 060-0033; tel. (11) 242-3900; fax (11) 231-5470; internet www.kita-nikkan.co.jp; f. 1962; morning; Pres. SATOSHI KATO; circ. 160,355.

Tokachi Mainichi Shimbun: 8-2, Minami, Higashi-Ichijo, Obihiro 080-8688; tel. (155) 22-2121; fax (155) 25-2700; internet www .tokachi.co.jp; f. 1919; evening; Dir and Man. Editor TOSHIAKI NAKAHASHI; circ. 89,264.

Tomakomai Mimpo: 3-1-8, Wakakusa-cho, Tomakomai 053-8611; tel. (144) 32-5311; internet www.tomamin.co.jp; f. 1950; evening; Dir and Man. Editor RYUICHI KUDO; circ. 60,676.

Yomiuri Shimbun: 4-1, Nishi, Kita-4 jo, Chuo-ku, Sapporo 060-8656; tel. (11) 242-3111; f. 1959; Head Officer TSUTOMO IKEDA; circ. morning 261,747, evening 81,283.

Kyushu Island

Kagoshima Shimpo: 7-28, Jonan-cho, Kagoshima 892-8551; tel. (99) 226-2100; internet www.kagoshimashimpo.com; f. 1959; morning; Dir and Man. Editor JUNSUKE KINOSHITA; circ. 39,330.

Kumamoto Nichi-Nichi Shimbun: 172, Yoyasu-machi, Kumamoto 860-8506; tel. (96) 361-3111; internet www.kumanichi.co.jp; f. 1942; Man. Editor HIROSHI KAWARABATA; circ. morning 389,528, evening 101,795.

Kyushu Sports: Fukuoka Tenjin Center Bldg, 2-14-8, Tenjin-cho, Chuo-ku, Fukuoka 810-0001; tel. (92) 781-7401; f. 1966; morning; Head Officer HIROSHI MITOMI; circ. 449,850.

Minami Nippon Shimbun: 1-9-33, Yojirou, Kagoshima 890-8603; tel. (99) 813-5001; fax (99) 813-5016; e-mail tuusin@po.minc.ne.jp; internet www.minaminippon.co.jp; f. 1881; Man. Editor KEITEN NISHIMURA; circ. morning 401,938, evening 27,959.

Miyazaki Nichi-Nichi Shimbun: 1-1-33, Takachihodori, Miyazaki 880-8570; tel. (985) 26-9315; internet www.the-miyanichi.co.jp; f. 1940; morning; Man. Editor MASAAKI MINAMIMURA; circ. 236,083.

Nagasaki Shimbun: 3-1, Mori-machi, Nagasaki 852-8601; tel. (958) 44-2111; internet www.nagasaki-np.co.jp; f. 1889; Dir and Man. Editor SADAKATSU HONDA; circ. morning 200,128.

Nankai Nichi-Nichi Shimbun: 10-3, Nagahama-cho, Naze 894-8601; tel. (997) 53-2121; internet www.amami.or.jp/nankai; f. 1946; morning; Man. Editor TERUMI MATSUI; circ. 24,038.

Nishi Nippon Shimbun: 1-4-1, Tenjin, Chuo-ku, Fukuoka 810-8721; tel. (92) 711-5555; internet www.nishinippon.co.jp; f. 1877; Exec. Dir and Man. Editor TAKAMICHI TAMAGAWA; circ. morning 834,800, evening 188,444.

Nishi Nippon Sports: 1-4-1, Tenjin, Chuo-ku, Fukuoka 810; tel. (92) 711-5555; f. 1954; Man. Editor KENJI ISHIZAKI; circ. 184,119.

Oita Godo Shimbun: 3-9-15, Funai-machi, Oita 870-8605; tel. (975) 36-2121; internet www.oita-press.co.jp; f. 1886; Dir and Man. Editor MASAKATSU TANABE; circ. morning 245,257, evening 245,227.

Okinawa Times: 2-2-2, Kumoji, Naha 900-8678; tel. (98) 860-3000; internet www.okinawatimes.co.jp; f. 1948; Dir and Man. Editor MASAO KISHIMOTO; circ. morning 204,420, evening 204,420.

Ryukyu Shimpo: 1-10-3, Izumizaki, Naha 900-8525; tel. (98) 865-5111; internet www.ryukyushimpo.co.jp; f. 1893; Man. Editor TOMOKAZU TAKAMINE; circ. 200,936.

Saga Shimbun: 3-2-23, Tenjin, Saga 840-8585; tel. (952) 28-2111; fax (952) 29-4829; internet www.saga-s.co.jp; f. 1884; morning; Man. Editor TERUHIKO WASHIZAKI; circ. 138,079.

Yaeyama Mainichi Shimbun: 614, Tonoshiro, Ishigaki 907-0004; tel. (9808) 2-2121; internet www.cosmos.ne.jp/~mainichi; f. 1950; morning; Exec. Dir and Man. Editor YOSHIO UECHI; circ. 14,500.

WEEKLIES

An-An: Magazine House, 3-13-10, Ginza, Chuo-ku, Tokyo 104-03; tel. (3) 5545-7050; fax (3) 3546-0034; f. 1970; fashion; Editor MIYOKO YODOGAWA; circ. 650,000.

Asahi Graphic: Asahi Shimbun Publishing Dept, 5-3-2, Tsukiji, Chuo-ku, Tokyo 104-11; tel. (3) 3545-0131; f. 1923; pictorial review; Editor KIYOKAZU TANNO; circ. 120,000.

Diamond Weekly: Diamond Inc, 1-4-2, Kasumigaseki, Chiyoda-ku, Tokyo 100; tel. (3) 3504-6250; f. 1913; economics; Editor YUTAKA IWASA; circ. 78,000.

Focus: Shincho-Sha, 71, Yaraicho, Shinjuku-ku, Tokyo 162; tel. (3) 3266-5271; fax (3) 3266-5390; politics, economics, sport; Editor KAZUMASA TAJIMA; circ. 850,000.

Friday: Kodan-Sha Co Ltd, 2-12-21, Otowa, Bunkyo-ku, Tokyo 112; tel. (3) 5395-3440; fax (3) 3943-8582; current affairs; Editor-in-Chief TETSU SUZUKI; circ. 1m.

Hanako: Magazine House, 3-13-10, Ginza, Chuo-ku, Tokyo 104-03; tel. (3) 3545-7070; fax (3) 3546-0994; f. 1988; consumer guide; Editor KOJI TOMONO; circ. 350,000.

Nikkei Business: Nikkei Business Publications Inc, 2-7-6, Hirakawa-cho, Chiyoda-ku, Tokyo 102-8622; tel. (3) 5210-8101; fax (3) 5210-8520; internet www.nikkeibp.co.jp; f. 1969; Editor-in-Chief HIROTOMO NOMURA; circ. 350,000.

Shukan Asahi: Asahi Shimbun Publishing Dept, 5-3-2, Tsukiji, Chuo-ku, Tokyo 104-8011; tel. (3) 3545-0131; f. 1922; general interest; Editor-in-Chief AKIRA KATO; circ. 482,000.

Shukan Bunshun: Bungei-Shunju Ltd, 3-23, Kioicho, Chiyoda-ku, Tokyo 102; tel. (3) 3265-1211; fax (3) 3234–3964; general interest; Editor SEIGO KIMATA; circ. 800,000.

Shukan Gendai: Kodan-Sha Co Ltd, 2-12-21, Otowa, Bunkyo-ku, Tokyo 112; tel. (3) 5395-3438; fax (3) 3943-7815; f. 1959; general; Editor-in-Chief TETSU SUZUKI; circ. 930,000.

Shukan Josei: Shufu-To-Seikatsu Sha Ltd, 3-5-7, Kyobashi, Chuo-ku, Tokyo 104; tel. (3) 3563-5130; fax (3) 3563-2073; f. 1957; women's interest; Editor HIDEO KIKUCHI; circ. 638,000.

Shukan Post: Shogakukan Publishing Co Ltd, 2-3-1, Hitotsubashi, Chiyoda-ku, Tokyo 101-01; tel. (3) 3230-5951; f. 1969; general; Editor NORIMICHI OKANARI; circ. 696,000.

Shukan Shincho: Shincho-Sha, 71, Yarai-cho, Shinjuku-ku, Tokyo 162-8711; tel. (3) 3266-5311; fax (3) 3266-5622; f. 1956; general interest; Editor HIROSHI MATSUDA; circ. 521,000.

Shukan SPA: Fuso-Sha Co, 1-15-1, Kaigan, Minato-ku, Tokyo 105; tel. (3) 5403-8875; f. 1952; general interest; Editor-in-Chief TOSHIHIKO SATO; circ. 400,000.

Shukan ST: Japan Times Ltd, 4-5-4, Shibaura, Minato-ku, Tokyo 108-0023; tel. (3) 3452-4077; fax (3) 3452-3303; e-mail shukanst@ japantimes.co.jp; f. 1951; English and Japanese; Editor MITSURU TANAKA; circ. 150,000.

Shukan Yomiuri: Yomiuri Shimbun Publication Dept, 1-2-1, Kiyosumi, Koto-ku, Tokyo 135; tel. (3) 5245-7001; f. 1938; general interest; Editor SHINI KAGEYAMA; circ. 453,000.

Sunday Mainichi: Mainichi Newspapers Publishing Dept, 1-1-1, Hitotsubashi, Chiyoda-ku, Tokyo 100-51; tel. (3) 3212-0321; fax (3) 3212-0769; f. 1922; general interest; Editor KENJI MIKI; circ. 237,000.

Tenji Mainichi: Mainichi Newspapers Publishing Dept, 3-4-5, Umeda, Osaka; tel. (6) 6346-8386; fax (6) 6346-8385; f. 1922; in Japanese braille; Editor TADAMITSU MORIOKA; circ. 12,000.

Weekly Economist: Mainichi Newspapers Publishing Dept, 1-1-1, Hitotsubashi, Chiyoda-ku, Tokyo 100-51; tel. (3) 3212-0321; f. 1923; Editorial Chief NOBUHIRO SHUDO; circ. 120,000.

Weekly Toyo Keizai: Toyo Keizai Inc, 1-2-1, Hongoku-cho, Nihombashi, Chuo-ku, Tokyo 103-8345; tel. (3) 3246-5655; fax (3) 3270-0159; e-mail sub@toyokeizai.co.jp; internet www.toyokeizai.co.jp; f. 1895; business, economics, finance, and corporate information; Editor TOSHIKI OTA; circ. 62,000.

PERIODICALS

All Yomimono: Bungei-Shunju Ltd, 3-23, Kioicho, Chiyoda-ku, Tokyo 102; tel. (3) 3265-1211; fax (3) 3239-5481; f. 1930; monthly; popular fiction; Editor KOICHI SASAMOTO; circ. 95,796.

Any: 1-3-14, Hirakawa-cho, Chiyoda-ku, Tokyo 102; tel. (3) 5276-2200; fax (3) 5276-2209; f. 1989; every 2 weeks; women's interest; Editor YUKIO MIWA; circ. 380,000.

Asahi Camera: Asahi Shimbun Publishing Dept, 5-3-2, Tsukiji, Chuo-ku, Tokyo 104-8011; tel. (3) 3545-0131; fax (3) 5565-3286; f. 1926; monthly; photography; Editor HIROSHI HIROSE; circ. 90,000.

Balloon: Shufunotomo Co Ltd, 2-9, Kanda Surugadai, Chiyoda-ku, Tokyo 101; tel. (3) 3294-1132; fax (3) 3291-5093; f. 1986; monthly; expectant mothers; Dir MARIKO HOSODA; circ. 250,000.

Brutus: Magazine House, 3-13-10, Ginza, Chuo-ku, Tokyo 104-03; tel. (3) 3545-7000; fax (3) 3546-0034; f. 1980; every 2 weeks; men's interest; Editor KOICHI TETSUKA; circ. 250,000.

Bungei-Shunju: Bungei-Shunju Ltd, 3-23, Kioicho, Chiyoda-ku, Tokyo 102-8008; tel. (3) 3265-1211; fax (3) 3221-6623; internet bunshun.topica.ne.jp; f. 1923; monthly; general; Pres. MASARU SHIRAISHI; Editor KIYONDO MATSUI; circ. 656,000.

Business Tokyo: Keizaikai Bldg, 2-13-18, Minami-Aoyama, Minato-ku, Tokyo 105; tel. (3) 3423-8500; fax (3) 3423-8505; f. 1987; monthly; Dir TAKUO IDA; Editor ANTHONY PAUL; circ. 125,000.

Chuokoron: Chuokoron-Shinsha Inc, 2-8-7, Kyobashi, Chuo-ku, Tokyo 104–8320; tel. (3) 3563-2751; fax (3) 3561-5926; f. 1887; monthly; general interest; Chief Editor MICHIKAZU KOHNO; circ. 90,000.

Croissant: Magazine House, 3-13-10, Ginza, Chuo-ku, Tokyo 104-03; tel. (3) 3545-7111; fax (3) 3546-0034; f. 1977; every 2 weeks; home; Editor MASAAKI TAKEUCHI; circ. 600,000.

Fujinkoron: Chuokoron-Sha Inc, 2-8-7, Kyobashi, Chuo-ku, Tokyo 104; tel. (3) 3563-1866; fax (3) 3561-5920; f. 1916; women's literary monthly; Editor YUKIKO YUKAWA; circ. 185,341.

Geijutsu Shincho: Shincho-Sha, 71, Yarai-cho, Shinjuku-ku, Tokyo 162-8711; tel. (3) 3266-5381; fax (3) 3266-5387; e-mail geishin@shinchosha.co.jp; f. 1950; monthly; fine arts, music, architecture, films, drama and design; Editor-in-Chief KAZUHIRO NAGAI; circ. 50,000.

Gendai: Kodan-Sha Ltd, 2-12-21, Otowa, Bunkyo-ku, Tokyo 112; tel. (3) 5395-3517; fax (3) 3945-9128; f. 1966; monthly; cultural and political; Editor SHUNKICHI YABUKI; circ. 250,000.

Ginza: Magazine House, 3-13-10, Ginza, Chuo-ku, Tokyo 104-8003; tel. (3) 3545-7080; fax (3) 3542-6375; internet webmaster.magazine .co.jp; f. 1997; monthly; women's interest; Editor MIYOKO YODOGAWA; circ. 250,000.

Hot-Dog Press: Kodan-Sha Ltd, 2-12-21, Otowa, Bunkyo-ku, Tokyo 112-01; tel. (3) 5395-3473; fax (3) 3945-9128; every 2 weeks; men's interest; Editor ATSUHIDE KOKUBO; circ. 650,000.

Ie-no-Hikari (Light of Home): Ie-no-Hikari Asscn, 11, Ichigaya Funagawaramachi, Shinjuku-ku, Tokyo 162-8448; tel. (3) 3266-9013; fax (3) 3266-9052; e-mail hikari@mxd.meshnet.or.jp; internet www.mediagalaxy.co.jp/ienohikarinet; f. 1925; monthly; rural and general interest; Pres. SHUZO SUZUKI; Editor KAZUO NAKANO; circ. 928,000.

Japan Company Handbook: Toyo Keizai Inc, 1-2-1, Nihombashi Hongoku-cho, Chuo-ku, Tokyo 103-8345; tel. (3) 3246-5621; fax (3) 3246-5473; e-mail sub@toyokeizai.co.jp; internet www.toyokeizai.co .jp; f. 1974; quarterly; English; Editor MASAKI HARA; total circ. 100,000.

Jitsugyo No Nihon: Jitsugyo No Nihon-Sha Ltd, 1-3-9, Ginza, Chuo-ku, Tokyo 104; tel. (3) 3562-1967; fax (3) 2564-2382; f. 1897; monthly; economics and business; Editor TOSHIO KAWAJIRI; circ. 60,000.

Junon: Shufu-To-Seikatsu Sha Ltd, 3-5-7, Kyobashi, Chuo-ku, Tokyo 104; tel. (3) 3563-5132; fax (3) 5250-7081; f. 1973; monthly; television and entertainment; circ. 560,000.

Kagaku (Science): Iwanami Shoten Publishers, 2-5-5, Hitotsubashi, Chiyoda-ku, Tokyo 102; tel. (3) 5210-4070; fax (3) 5210-4073; f. 1931; Editor NOBUAKI MIYABE; circ. 29,000.

Kagaku Asahi: Asahi Shimbun Publishing Dept, 5-3-2, Tsukiji, Chuo-ku, Tokyo 104-8011; tel. (3) 5540-7810; fax (3) 3546-2404; f. 1941; monthly; scientific; Editor TOSHIHIRO SASAKI; circ. 105,000.

Keizaijin: Kansai Economic Federation, Nakanoshima Center Bldg, 6-2-27, Nakanoshima, Kita-ku, Osaka 530-6691; tel. (6) 6441-0101; fax (6) 6443-5327; internet www.kankeiren.or.jp; f. 1947; monthly; economics; Editor M. YASUTAKE; circ. 2,600.

Lettuce Club: SS Communications, 11-2, Ban-cho, Chiyoda-ku, Tokyo 102; tel. (3) 5276-2151; fax (3) 5276-2229; f. 1987; every 2 weeks; cookery; Editor MITSURU NAKAYA; circ. 800,000.

Money Japan: SS Communications, 11-2, Ban-cho, Chiyoda-ku, Tokyo 102; tel. (3) 5276-2220; fax (3) 5276-2229; internet www.sscom .co.jp/money; f. 1985; monthly; finance; Editor TOSHIO KOBAYASHI; circ. 500,000.

Popeye: Magazine House, 3-13-10, Ginza, Chuo-ku, Tokyo 104-8003; tel. (3) 3545-7160; fax (3) 3545-9026; f. 1976; every 2 weeks; fashion, youth interest; Editor KATSUMI NAMAIZAWA; circ. 320,000.

President: President Inc, Bridgestone Hirakawacho Bldg, 2-13-12, Hirakawa-cho, Chiyoda-ku, Tokyo 102; tel. (3) 3237-3737; fax (3) 3237-3748; internet www.president.co.jp; f. 1963; monthly; business; Editor KAYOKO ABE; circ. 263,308.

Ray: Shufunotomo Co Ltd, 2-9, Kanda Surugadai, Chiyoda-ku, Tokyo 101; tel. (3) 3294-1163; fax (3) 3291-5093; f. 1988; monthly; women's interest; Editor TATSURO NAKANISHI; circ. 450,000.

Ryoko Yomiuri: Ryoko Yomiuri Publications Inc, 2-2-15, Ginza, Chuo-ku, Tokyo 104; tel. (3) 3561-8911; fax (3) 3561-8950; f. 1966; monthly; travel; Editor TETSUO KINUGAWA; circ. 470,000.

Sekai: Iwanami Shoten Publishers, 2-5-5, Hitotsubashi, Chiyoda-ku, Tokyo 101; tel. (3) 5210-4141; fax (3) 5210-4144; internet www .iwanami.co.jp/sekai; f. 1946; monthly; review of world and domestic affairs; Editor ATSUSHI OKAMOTO; circ. 120,000.

Shinkenchiku: Shinkenchiku-Sha Co Ltd, 2-31-2, Yushima, Bunkyo-ku, Tokyo 113-8501; tel. (3) 3811-7101; fax (3) 3812-8229; e-mail ja-business@japan-architect.co.jp; internet www .japan-architect.co.jp; f. 1925; monthly; architecture; Editor YASUHIRO TERAMATSU; circ. 87,000.

Shiso (Thought): Iwanami Shoten Publishers, 2-5-5, Hitotsubashi, Chiyoda-ku, Tokyo 101-8002; tel. (3) 5210-4055; fax (3) 5210-4037; e-mail shiso@iwanami.co.jp; internet www.iwanami.co.jp/shiso; f. 1921; monthly; philosophy, social sciences and humanities; Editor KIYOSHI KOJIMA; circ. 20,000.

Shosetsu Shincho: Shincho-Sha, 71, Yarai-cho, Shinjuku-ku, Tokyo 162-8711; tel. (3) 3266-5241; fax (3) 3266-5412; internet www .shincho.net/magazines/shosetsushincho; f. 1947; monthly; literature; Editor-in-Chief TSUYOSHI MENJO; circ. 80,000.

Shufunotomo: Shufunotomo Co Ltd, 2-9, Kanda Surugadai, Chiyoda-ku, Tokyo 101; tel. (3) 5280-7531; fax (3) 5280-7431; f. 1917; monthly; home and lifestyle; Editor KYOKO FURUTO; circ. 450,000.

So-en: Bunka Publishing Bureau, 4-12-7, Hon-cho, Shibuya-ku, Tokyo 151; tel. (3) 3299-2531; fax (3) 3370-3712; f. 1936; fashion monthly; Editor KEIKO SASAKI; circ. 270,000.

NEWS AGENCIES

Jiji Tsushin (Jiji Press Ltd): Shisei-Kaikan, 1-3, Hibiya Park, Chiyoda-ku, Tokyo 100-8568; tel. (3) 3591-1111; e-mail info@jiji.co .jp; internet www.jiji.com; f. 1945; Pres. MASATOSHI MURAKAMI; Man. Dir and Man. Editor MASAKI SUGIURA.

Kyodo Tsushin (Kyodo News): 2-2-5, Toranomon, Minato-ku, Tokyo 105-8474; tel. (3) 5573-8081; fax (3) 5573-2268; e-mail kokusai@kyodonews.jp; internet http://home.kyodo.co.jp; f. 1945; Pres. TOYOHIKO YAMANOUCHI; Man. Editor TOSHIEI KOKUBU.

Radiopress Inc: R-Bldg Shinjuku, 5F, 33-8, Wakamatsu-cho, Shinjuku-ku, Tokyo 162-0056; tel. (3) 5273-2171; fax (3) 5273-2180; e-mail rptokyo@oak.ocn.ne.jp; f. 1945; provides news from China, the former USSR, Democratic People's Repub. of Korea, Viet Nam and elsewhere to the press and govt offices; Pres. YOSHITOMO TANAKA.

Sun Telephoto: Palaceside Bldg, 1-1-1, Hitotsubashi, Chiyoda-ku, Tokyo 100-0003; tel. (3) 3213-6771; e-mail webmaster@suntele.co.jp; internet www.suntele.co.jp; f. 1952; Pres. KOZO TAKINO; Man. Editor KIYOSHI HIRAI.

Foreign Bureaux

Agence France-Presse (AFP): Asahi Shimbun Bldg, 11th Floor, 5-3-2, Tsukiji, Chuo-ku, Tokyo 104-0045; tel. (3) 3545-3061; fax (3) 3546-2594; Bureau Chief PHILIPPE RIES.

Agencia EFE (Spain): Kyodo Tsushin Bldg, 9th Floor, 2-2-5, Toranomon, Minato-ku, Tokyo 105-0001; tel. (3) 3585-8940; fax (3) 3585-8948; Bureau Chief CARLOS DOMÍNGUEZ.

Agenzia Nazionale Stampa Associata (ANSA) (Italy): Kyodo Tsushin Bldg, 9th Floor, 2-2-5, Toranomon, Minato-ku, Tokyo 105-0001; tel. (3) 3584-6667; fax (3) 3584-5114; Bureau Chief ALBERTO ZANCONATO.

Antara (Indonesia): Kyodo Tsushin Bldg, 9th Floor, 2-2-5, Toranomon, Minato-ku, Tokyo 105-0001; tel. (3) 3584-4234; fax (3) 3584-4591; Correspondent MARIA ANDRIANA.

Associated Press (AP) (USA): Asahi Shimbun Bldg, 11th Floor, 5-3-2, Tsukiji, Chuo-ku, Tokyo 104-0045; tel. (3) 3545-5902; fax (3) 3545-0895; internet www.ap.org; Bureau Chief MYRON L. BELKIND.

Central News Agency (Taiwan): 3-7-3-302, Shimo-meguro, Meguro-ku, Tokyo 153-0064; tel. (3) 3495-2046; fax (3) 3495-2066; Bureau Chief CHANG FANG MIN.

Deutsche Presse-Agentur (dpa) (Germany): Nippon Press Center, 3rd Floor, 2-2-1, Uchisaiwai-cho, Chiyoda-ku, Tokyo 100-0011; tel. (3) 3580-6629; fax (3) 3593-7888; Bureau Chief LARS NICOLAYSEN.

Informatsionnoye Telegrafnoye Agentstvo Rossii—Telegrafnoye Agentstvo Suverennykh Stran (ITAR—TASS) (Russia): 1-5-1, Hon-cho, Shibuya-ku, Tokyo 151-0071; tel. (3) 3377-0380; fax (3) 3378-0606; Bureau Chief VASILII GOLOVNIN.

Inter Press Service (IPS) (Italy): 1-15-19, Ishikawa-machi, Ota-ku, Tokyo 145-0061; tel. (3) 3726-7944; fax (3) 3726-7896; Correspondent SUVENDRINI KAKUCHI.

Magyar Távirati Iroda (MTI) (Hungary): 1-3-4-306, Okamoto, Setagaya-ku, Tokyo 157-0076; tel. (3) 3708-3093; fax (3) 3708-2703; Bureau Chief JÁNOS MARTON.

Reuters (UK): Shuwa Kamiya-cho Bldg, 5th Floor, 4-3-13, Toranomon, Minato-ku, Tokyo 105-0001; tel. (3) 3432-4141; fax (3) 3433-2921; Editor WILLIAM SPOSATO.

Rossiiskoye Informatsionnoye Agentstvo—Novosti (RIA-Novosti) (Russia): 3-9-13 Higashi-gotanda, Shinagawa-ku, Tokyo 141-0022; tel. (3) 3441-9241; fax (3) 3447-8443; e-mail riatokyo@ma .kcom.ne.jp; Bureau Chief VIATCHESLAV BANTINE.

United Press International (UPI) (USA): Ferrare Bldg, 4th Floor, 1-24-15, Ebisu, Shibuya-ku, Tokyo 150-0013; tel. (3) 5421-1333; fax (3) 5421-1339; Bureau Chief RUTH YOUNGBLOOD.

Xinhua (New China) News Agency (People's Republic of China): 3-35-23, Ebisu, Shibuya-ku, Tokyo 150-0013; tel. (3) 3441-3766; fax (3) 3446-3995; Bureau Chief WANG DAJUN.

Yonhap (United) News Agency (Republic of Korea): Kyodo Tsushin Bldg, 2-2-5, Toranomon, Minato-ku, Tokyo 105-0001; tel. (3)

3584-4681; fax (3) 3584-4021; f. 1945; Bureau Chief Moon Young Shik.

PRESS ASSOCIATIONS

Foreign Correspondents' Club of Japan: 20th Floor, 1-7-1, Yuraku-cho, Chiyoda-ku, Tokyo 100-0006; tel. (3) 3211-3161; fax (3) 3211-3168; e-mail yoda@fccj.or.jp; internet www.fccj.or.jp; f. 1945; 193 companies; Pres. Hans van der Lugt; Man. Seishi Yoda.

Foreign Press Center: Nippon Press Center Bldg, 6th Floor, 2-2-1, Uchisaiwai-cho, Chiyoda-ku, Tokyo 100-0011; tel. (3) 3501-3401; fax (3) 3501-3622; internet www.nttls.co.jp/fpc; f. 1976; est. by the Japan Newspaper Publrs' and Editors' Asscn and the Japan Fed. of Economic Orgs; provides services to the foreign press; Pres. Yoshio Hatano; Man. Dir Masahiko Ishizuka.

Nihon Shinbun Kyokai (The Japan Newspaper Publishers and Editors Asscn): Nippon Press Center Bldg, 2-2-1, Uchisaiwai-cho, Chiyoda-ku, Tokyo 100-8543; tel. (3) 3591-3462; fax (3) 3591-6149; e-mail s_intl@pressnet.or.jp; internet www.pressnet.or.jp; f. 1946; mems include 154 companies (112 daily newspapers, 4 news agencies and 38 radio and TV companies); Chair. Tsuneo Watanabe; Man. Dir and Sec.-Gen. Shigemi Murakami.

Nihon Zasshi Kyokai (Japan Magazine Publishers Asscn): 1-7, Kanda Surugadai, Chiyoda-ku, Tokyo 101-0062; tel. (3) 3291-0775; fax (3) 3293-6239; f. 1956; 85 mems; Pres. Haruhiko Ishikawa; Sec. Genya Inui.

Publishers

Akane Shobo Co Ltd: 3-2-1, Nishikanda, Chiyoda-ku, Tokyo 101-0065; tel. (3) 3263-0641; fax (3) 3263-5440; f. 1949; juvenile; Pres. Masaharu Okamoto.

Akita Publishing Co Ltd: 2-10-8, Iidabashi, Chiyoda-ku, Tokyo 102-8101; tel. (3) 3264-7011; fax (3) 3265-5906; f. 1948; social sciences, history, juvenile; Chair. Sadao Akita; Pres. Sadami Akita.

ALC Press Inc: 2-54-12, Eifuku, Suginami-ku, Tokyo 168-0064; tel. (3) 3323-1101; fax (3) 3327-1022; e-mail menet@alc.co.jp; internet www.alc.co.jp; f. 1969; linguistics, educational materials, dictionary, juvenile; Pres. Terumaro Hiramoto.

Asahi Shimbun Publications Division: 5-3-2, Tsukiji, Chuo-ku, Tokyo 104-8011; tel. (3) 3545-0131; fax (3) 5540-7682; f. 1879; general; Pres. Muneyuki Matsushita; Dir of Publications Hisao Kuwashima.

Asakura Publishing Co Ltd: 6-29, Shin Ogawa-machi, Shinjuku-ku, Tokyo 162-8707; tel. (3) 3260-0141; fax (3) 3260-0180; e-mail edit@asakura.co.jp; internet www.asakura.co.jp; f. 1929; natural science, medicine, social sciences; Pres. Kunizo Asakura.

Baifukan Co Ltd: 4-3-12, Kudan Minami, Chiyoda-ku, Tokyo 102-8260; tel. (3) 3262-5256; fax (3) 3262-5276; f. 1924; engineering, natural and social sciences, psychology; Pres. Itaru Yamamoto.

Baseball Magazine-Sha: 3-10-10, Misaki-cho, Chiyoda-ku, Tokyo 101-8381; tel. (3) 3238-0081; fax (3) 3238-0106; internet www.bbm-japan.com; f. 1946; sports, physical education, recreation, travel; Chair. Tsuneo Ikeda; Pres. Tetsuo Ikeda.

Bijutsu Shuppan-Sha Ltd: Inaoka Kudan Bldg, 6th Floor, 2-36, Kanda Jimbo-cho, Chiyoda-ku, Tokyo 101-8417; tel. (3) 3234-2151; fax (3) 3234-9451; f. 1905; fine arts, graphic design; Pres. Atsushi Oshita.

Bonjinsha Co Ltd: 1-3-13, Hirakawa-cho, Chiyoda-ku, Tokyo 102-0093; tel. (3) 3263-3959; fax (3) 3263-3116; f. 1973; Japanese language teaching materials; Pres. Hisamitsu Tanaka.

Bungeishunju Ltd: 3-23, Kioi-cho, Chiyoda-ku, Tokyo 102-8008; tel. (3) 3265-1211; fax (3) 3239-5482; internet www.bunshun.co.jp; f. 1923; fiction, general literature, recreation, economics, sociology; Dir Masaru Shiraishi.

Chikuma Shobo: Komuro Bldg, 2-5-3, Kuramae, Taito-ku, Tokyo 111-8755; tel. (3) 5687-2671; fax (3) 5687-1585; e-mail webinfo@chikumashobo.co.jp; internet www.chikumashobo.co.jp; f. 1940; general literature, fiction, history, juvenile, fine arts; Pres. Akio Kikuchi.

Child-Honsha Co Ltd: 5-24-21, Koishikawa, Bunkyo-ku, Tokyo 112-8512; tel. (3) 3813-3785; fax (3) 3813-3765; e-mail ehon@childbook.co.jp; internet www.childbook.co.jp; f. 1930; juvenile; Pres. Yoshiaki Shimazaki.

Chuokoron-Shinsha Inc: 2-8-7, Kyobashi, Chuo-ku, Tokyo 104-8320; tel. (3) 3563-1261; fax (3) 3561-5920; f. 1886; philosophy, history, sociology, general literature; Pres. Jin Nakamura.

Corona Publishing Co Ltd: 4-46-10, Sengoku, Bunkyo-ku, Tokyo 112-0011; tel. (3) 3941-3131; fax (3) 3941-3137; e-mail info@coronasha.co.jp; internet www.coronosha.co.jp; f. 1927; electronics business publs; Pres. Tatsumi Gorai.

Dempa Publications Inc: 1-11-15, Higashi Gotanda, Shinagawa-ku, Tokyo 141-0022; tel. (3) 3445-6111; fax (3) 3445-6101; f. 1950; electronics, personal computer software, juvenile, trade newspapers; Pres. Tetsuo Hirayama.

Diamond Inc: 6-12-17, Jingumae, Shibuya-ku, Tokyo 150-8409; tel. (3) 5778-7203; fax (3) 5778-6612; e-mail mitachi@diamond.co.jp; internet www.diamond.co.jp; f. 1913; business, management, economics, financial; Pres. Yutaka Iwasa.

Dohosha Ltd: TAS Bldg, 2-5-2, Nishikanda, Chiyoda-ku, Tokyo 101-0065; tel. (3) 5276-0831; fax (3) 5276-0840; e-mail intl@doho-sha.co.jp; internet www.doho-sha.co.jp; f. 1997; general works, architecture, art, Buddhism, business, children's education, cooking, flower arranging, gardening, medicine.

Froebel-Kan Co Ltd: 6-14-9, Honkomagome, Bunkyo-ku, Tokyo 113-8611; tel. (3) 5395-6614; fax (3) 5395-6639; e-mail info-e@froebel-kan.co.jp; internet www.froebel-kan.co.jp; f. 1907; juvenile, educational; Pres. Mamoru Kitabayashi; Dir Mitsuhiro Tada.

Fukuinkan Shoten Publishers Inc: 6-6-3, Honkomagome, Bunkyo-ku, Tokyo 113-8686; tel. (3) 3942-2151; fax (3) 3942-1401; f. 1952; juvenile; Pres. Shiro Tokita; Chair. Katsumi Sato.

Gakken Co Ltd: 4-40-5, Kamiikedai, Ota-ku, Tokyo 145-8502; tel. (3) 3726-8111; fax (3) 3493-3338; f. 1946; juvenile, educational, art, encyclopaedias, dictionaries; Pres. Kazuhiko Sawada.

Graphic-sha Publishing Co Ltd: 1-9-12, Kudan Kita, Chiyoda-ku, Tokyo 102-0073; tel. (3) 3263-4318; fax (3) 3263-5297; e-mail info@graphicsha.co.jp; internet www.graphicsha.co.jp; f. 1963; art, design, architecture, manga techniques, hobbies; Pres. Seiichi Sugaya.

Gyosei Corpn: 4-30-16, Ogikubo, Suginami-ku, Tokyo 167-8088; tel. (3) 5349-6666; fax (3) 5349-6677; e-mail business@gyosei.co.jp; internet www.gyosei.co.jp; f. 1893; law, education, science, politics, business, art, language, literature, juvenile; Pres. Motoo Fujisawa.

Hakusui-Sha Co Ltd: 3-24, Kanda Ogawa-machi, Chiyoda-ku, Tokyo 101-0052; tel. (3) 3291-7821; fax (3) 3291-7810; f. 1915; general literature, science and languages; Pres. Kazuaki Fujiwara.

Hayakawa Publishing Inc: 2-2, Kanda-Tacho, Chiyoda-ku, Tokyo 101-0046; tel. (3) 3252-3111; fax (3) 3254-1550; f. 1945; science fiction, mystery, autobiography, literature, fantasy; Pres. Hiroshi Hayakawa.

Heibonsha Ltd: 2-29-4 Hakusan, Bunkyo-ku, Tokyo 112-0001; tel. (3) 3818-0641; fax (3) 3818-0754; internet www.heibonsha.co.jp; f. 1914; encyclopaedias, art, history, geography, literature, science; Pres. Naoto Shimonaka.

Hirokawa Publishing Co: 3-27-14, Hongo, Bunkyo-ku, Tokyo 113-0033; tel. (3) 3815-3651; fax (3) 5684-7030; f. 1925; natural sciences, medicine, pharmacy, nursing, chemistry; Pres. Setsuo Hirokawa.

Hoikusha Publishing Co: 1-6-12, Kawamata, Higashi, Osaka 577-0063; tel. (6) 6788-4470; fax (6) 6788-4970; internet www.hoikusha.co.jp; f. 1947; natural science, juvenile, fine arts, geography; Pres. Yuki Imai.

Hokuryukan Co Ltd: 3-8-14, Takanawa, Minato-ku, Tokyo 108-0074; tel. (3) 5449-4591; fax (3) 5449-4950; e-mail hk-ns@mk1.macnet.or.jp; internet www.macnet.or.jp/co/hk-ns; f. 1891; natural science, medical science, juvenile, dictionaries; Pres. Hisako Fukuda.

The Hokuseido Press: 3-32-4, Honkomagome, Bunkyo-ku, Tokyo 113-0021; tel. (3) 3827-0511; fax (3) 3827-0567; e-mail info@hokuseido.com; f. 1914; regional non-fiction, dictionaries, textbooks; Pres. Masazo Yamamoto.

Ie-No-Hikari Association: 11, Funagawara-cho, Ichigaya, Shinjuku-ku, Tokyo 162-8448; tel. (3) 3266-9000; fax (3) 3266-9048; e-mail hikari@mxd.meshnet.or.jp; internet www.mediagalaxy.co.jp/ienohikarinet; f. 1925; social science, agriculture; Chair. Shuzo Suzuki; Pres. Katsuro Kawaguchi.

Igaku-Shoin Ltd: 5-24-3, Hongo, Bunkyo-ku, Tokyo 113-8719; tel. (3) 3817-5610; fax (3) 3815-4114; e-mail info@igaku-shoin.co; internet www.igaku-shoin.co.jp; f. 1944; medicine, nursing; Pres. Yu Kanehara.

Institute for Financial Affairs Inc (KINZAI): 19, Minami-Moto-machi, Shinjuku-ku, Tokyo 160-8519; tel. (3) 3358-1161; fax (3) 3359-7947; e-mail JDI04072@nifty.ne.jp; internet www.kinzai.or.jp; f. 1950; finance and economics, banking laws and regulations, accounting; Pres. Masateru Yoshida.

Ishiyaku Publishers Inc: 1-7-10, Honkomagome, Bunkyo-ku, Tokyo 113-8612; tel. (3) 5395-7600; fax (3) 5395-7606; internet www.ishiyaku.co.jp; f. 1921; medicine, dentistry, rehabilitation, nursing, nutrition and pharmaceutics; Pres. Katsuji Fujita.

Iwanami Shoten, Publishers: 2-5-5, Hitotsubashi, Chiyoda-ku, Tokyo 101-8002; tel. (3) 5210-4000; fax (3) 5210-4039; e-mail rights@

iwanami.co.jp; internet www.iwanami.co.jp; f. 1913; natural and social sciences, humanities, literature, fine arts, juvenile, dictionaries; Pres. NOBUKAZU OTSUKA.

Japan Broadcast Publishing Co Ltd: 41-1, Udagawa-cho, Shibuya-ku, Tokyo 150-8081; tel. (3) 3464-7311; fax (3) 3780-3353; e-mail webmaster@npb.nhk-grp.co.jp; internet www.nhk-grp.co.jp/npb; f. 1931; foreign language textbooks, gardening, home economics, sociology, education, art, juvenile; Pres. TATSUO ANDO.

Japan External Trade Organization (JETRO): 2-2-5, Toranomon, Minato-ku, Tokyo 105-8466; tel. (3) 3582-5511; fax (3) 3587-2485; internet www.jetro.go.jp; f. 1958; trade, economics, investment.

Japan Publications Trading Co Ltd: 1-2-1, Sarugaku-cho, Chiyoda-ku, Tokyo 101-0064; tel. (3) 3292-3751; fax (3) 3292-0410; e-mail jpt@po.iijnet.or.jp; internet www.jptco.co.jp; f. 1942; general works, art, health, sports; Pres. SATOMI NAKABAYASHI.

The Japan Times Ltd: 4-5-4, Shibaura, Minato-ku, Tokyo 108-0023; tel. (3) 3453-2013; fax (3) 3453-8023; e-mail jt-books@kt.rim.or.jp; internet bookclub.japantimes.co.jp; f. 1897; linguistics, culture, business; Pres. TOSHIAKI OGASAWARA.

Japan Travel Bureau Inc: Shibuya Nomura Bldg, 1-10-8, Dogenzaka, Shibuya-ku, Tokyo 150-8558; tel. (3) 3477-9521; fax (3) 3477-9538; internet www.jtb.co.jp; f. 1912; travel, geography, history, fine arts, languages; Vice-Pres. MITSUMASA IWATA.

Jimbun Shoin: 9, Nishiuchihata-cho, Takeda, Fushimi-ku, Kyoto 612-8447; tel. (75) 603-1344; fax (75) 603-1814; e-mail edjimbun@mbox.kyoto-inet.or.jp; internet www.jimbunshoin.co.jp; f. 1922; general literature, philosophy, fiction, social science, religion, fine arts; Pres. MUTSUHISA WATANABE.

Kadokawa Shoten Publishing Co Ltd: 2-13-3, Fujimi, Chiyoda-ku, Tokyo 102-0071; tel. (3) 3238-8611; fax (3) 3238-8612; f. 1945; literature, history, dictionaries, religion, fine arts, books on tape, compact discs, CD-ROM, comics, animation, video cassettes, computer games; Pres. TSUGUHIKO KADOKAWA.

Kaibundo Publishing Co Ltd: 2-5-4, Suido, Bunkyo-ku, Tokyo 112-0005; tel. (3) 5684-6289; fax (3) 3815-3953; e-mail LED04737@nifty.ne.jp; f. 1914; marine affairs, natural science, engineering, industry; Pres. YOSHIHIRO OKADA.

Kaiseisha Publishing Co Ltd: 3-5, Ichigaya Sadohara-cho, Shinjuku-ku, Tokyo 162-8450; tel. (3) 3260-3229; fax (3) 3260-3540; e-mail foreign@kaiseisha.co.jp; internet www.kaiseisha.co.jp; f. 1936; juvenile; Pres. MASAKI IMAMURA.

Kanehara & Co Ltd: 2-31-14, Yushima, Bunkyo-ku, Tokyo 113-8687; tel. (3) 3811-7185; fax (3) 3813-0288; f. 1875; medical, agricultural, engineering and scientific; Pres. SABURO KOMURO.

Kenkyusha Ltd: 2-11-3, Fujimi, Chiyoda-ku, Tokyo 102-8152; tel. (3) 3288-7711; fax (3) 3288-7821; e-mail hanbai@kenkyusha.co.jp; internet www.kenkyusha.co.jp; f. 1907; bilingual dictionaries, books on languages; Pres. KUNIKATSU ARAKI.

Kinokuniya Co Ltd: 5-38-1, Sakuragaoka, Setagaya-ku, Tokyo 156-8691; tel. (3) 3439-0172; fax (3) 3439-0173; e-mail publish@kinokuniya.co.jp; internet www.kinokuniya.co.jp; f. 1927; humanities, social science, natural science; Pres. OSAMU MATSUBARA.

Kodansha International Ltd: 1-17-14, Otowa, Bunkyo-ku, Tokyo 112-8652; tel. (3) 3944-6492; fax (3) 3944-6323; e-mail sales@kodansha-intl.co.jp; f. 1963; art, business, cookery, crafts, gardening, language, literature, martial arts; Pres. SAWAKO NOMA.

Kodansha Ltd: 2-12-21, Otowa, Bunkyo-ku, Tokyo 112-8001; tel. (3) 5395-3574; fax (3) 3944-9915; f. 1909; fine arts, fiction, literature, juvenile, comics, dictionaries; Pres. SAWAKO NOMA.

Kosei Publishing Co Ltd: 2-7-1, Wada, Suginami-ku, Tokyo 166-8535; tel. (3) 5385-2319; fax (3) 5385-2331; e-mail dharmaworld@kosei-shuppan.co.jp; internet www.kosei-shuppan.co.jp; f. 1966; general works, philosophy, religion, history, pedagogy, social science, art, juvenile; Pres. TEIZO KURIYAMA.

Kyoritsu Shuppan Co Ltd: 4-6-19, Kohinata, Bunkyo-ku, Tokyo 112-8700; tel. (3) 3947-2511; fax (3) 3947-2539; e-mail kyoritsu@po.iijnet.or.jp; internet www.kyoritsu-pub.co.jp; f. 1926; scientific and technical; Pres. MITSUAKI NANJO.

Maruzen Co Ltd: 3-9-2, Nihombashi, Chuo-ku, Tokyo 103-8244; tel. (3) 3272-0521; fax (3) 3272-0693; internet www.maruzen.co.jp; f. 1869; general works; Pres. SEISHIRO MURATA.

Medical Friend Co Ltd: 3-2-4, Kudan Kita, Chiyoda-ku, Tokyo 102-0073; tel. (3) 3264-6611; fax (3) 3261-6602; f. 1947; medical and allied science, nursing; Pres. KAZUHARU OGURA.

Minerva Shobo: 1, Tsutsumi dani-cho, Hinooka, Yamashina-ku, Kyoto 607-8494; tel. (75) 581-5191; fax (75) 581-0589; e-mail info@minervashobo.co.jp; internet www.minervashobo.co.jp; f. 1948; general non-fiction and reference; Pres. KEIZO SUGITA.

Misuzu Shobo Ltd: 5-32-21, Hongo, Bunkyo-ku, Tokyo 113-0033; tel. (3) 3815-9181; fax (3) 3818-8497; f. 1947; general, philosophy, history, psychiatry, literature, science, art; Pres. KEIJI KATO.

Morikita Shuppan Co Ltd: 1-4-11, Fujimi, Chiyoda-ku, Tokyo 102-0071; tel. (3) 3265-8341; fax (3) 3264-8709; e-mail info@morikita.co.jp; internet www.morikita.co.jp; f. 1950; natural science, engineering; Pres. HAJIME MORIKITA.

Nakayama-Shoten Co Ltd: 1-25-14, Hakusan, Bunkyo-ku, Tokyo 113-8666; tel. (3) 3813-1100; fax (3) 3816-1015; e-mail eigyo@nakayamashoten.co.jp; internet www.nakayamashoten.co.jp; f. 1948; medicine, biology, zoology; Pres. TADASHI HIRATA.

Nanzando Co Ltd: 4-1-11, Yushima, Bunkyo-ku, Tokyo; tel. (3) 5689-7868; fax (3) 5689-7869; e-mail info@nanzando.com; internet www.nanzando.com; medical reference, paperbacks; Pres. HAJIME SUZUKI.

Nigensha Publishing Co Ltd: 2-2, Kanda Jimbo-cho, Chiyoda-ku, Tokyo 101-8419; tel. (3) 5210-4733; fax (3) 5210-4723; e-mail sales@nigensha.co.jp; internet www.nigensha.co.jp; f. 1953; calligraphy, fine arts, art reproductions, cars, watches; Pres. TAKAO WATANABE.

Nihon Keizai Shimbun Inc, Publications Bureau: 1-9-5, Otemachi, Chiyoda-ku, Tokyo 100-0004; tel. (3) 3270-0251; fax (3) 5255-2864; f. 1876; economics, business, politics, fine arts, video cassettes, CD-ROM; Pres. TOYOHIKO KOBAYASHI.

Nihon Vogue Co Ltd: 3-23, Ichigaya Honmura-cho, Shinjuku-ku, Tokyo 162-8705; tel. (3) 5261-5139; fax (3) 3269-8726; e-mail asai@tezukuritown.com; internet www.tezukuritown.com; f. 1954; quilt, needlecraft, handicraft, knitting, decorative painting, pressed flowers; Pres. NOBUAKI SETO.

Nippon Jitsugyo Publishing Co Ltd: 3-2-12, Hongo, Bunkyo-ku, Tokyo 113-0033; tel. (3) 3814-5651; fax (3) 3818-2723; e-mail int@njg.co.jp; internet www.njg.co.jp; f. 1950; business, management, finance and accounting, sales and marketing; Chair. and CEO YOICHIRO NAKAMURA.

Obunsha Co Ltd: 78, Yarai-cho, Shinjuku-ku, Tokyo 162-0805; tel. (3) 3266-6000; fax (3) 3266-6291; internet www.obunsha.co.jp; f. 1931; textbooks, reference, general science and fiction, magazines, encyclopaedias, dictionaries; software; audio-visual aids; CEO FUMIO AKAO.

Ohmsha Ltd: 3-1, Kanda Nishiki-cho, Chiyoda-ku, Tokyo 101-8460; tel. (3) 3233-0641; fax (3) 3233-2426; e-mail kaigaika@ohmsha.co.jp; internet http://www.ohmsha.co.jp/index_e.htm; f. 1914; engineering, technical and scientific; Pres. SEIJI SATO; Dirs M. MORI, O. TAKEO.

Ondorisha Publishers Ltd: 11-11, Nishigoken-cho, Shinjuku-ku, Tokyo 162-8708; tel. (3) 3268-3101; fax (3) 3235-3530; f. 1945; knitting, embroidery, patchwork, handicraft books; Pres. HIDEAKI TAKEUCHI.

Ongaku No Tomo Sha Corpn (ONT): 6-30, Kagurazaka, Shinjuku-ku, Tokyo 162-0825; tel. (3) 3235-2111; fax (3) 3235-2119; internet www.ongakunotomo.co.jp; f. 1941; compact discs, videograms, music magazines, music books, music data, music textbooks; Pres. JUN MEGURO.

PHP Institute Inc: 11, Kitanouchi-cho, Nishikujo, Minami-ku, Kyoto 601-8411; tel. (75) 681-4431; fax (75) 681-9921; internet www.php.co.jp; f. 1946; social science; Pres. MASAHARU MATSUSHITA.

Poplar Publishing Co Ltd: 5, Suga-cho, Shinjuku-ku, Tokyo 160-8565; tel. (3) 3357-2216; fax (3) 3351-0736; e-mail henshu@poplar.co.jp; internet www.poplar.co.jp; f. 1947; children's; Pres. HARUO TANAKA.

Sanseido Co Ltd: 2-22-14, Misaki-cho, Chiyoda-ku, Tokyo 101-8371; tel. (3) 3230-9411; fax (3) 3230-9547; f. 1881; dictionaries, educational, languages, social and natural science; Chair. HISANORI UENO; Pres. TOSHIO GOMI.

Sanshusha Publishing Co Ltd: 1-5-34, Shitaya, Taito-ku, Tokyo 110-0004; tel. (3) 3842-1711; fax (3) 3845-3965; e-mail maeda_k@sanshusha.or.jp; internet www.sanshusha.co.jp; f. 1938; languages, dictionaries, philosophy, sociology, electronic publishing (CD-ROM); Pres. KANJI MAEDA.

Seibundo-Shinkosha Co Ltd: 3-3-1, Hongo, Bunkyo-ku, Tokyo 113-0033; tel. (3) 5800-5775; fax (3) 5800-5773; f. 1912; technical, scientific, design, general non-fiction; Pres. MINORU TAKITA.

Sekai Bunka Publishing Inc: 4-2-29, Kudan-Kita, Chiyoda-ku, Tokyo 102-8187; tel. (3) 3262-5111; fax (3) 3221-6843; internet www.sekaibunka.com; f. 1946; history, natural science, geography, education, art, literature, juvenile; Pres. TSUTOMU SUZUKI.

Shincho-Sha Co Ltd: 71, Yarai-cho, Shinjuku-ku, Tokyo 162-8711; tel. (3) 3266-5411; fax (3) 3266-5534; e-mail shinchosha@webshincho.com; internet www.webshincho.com; f. 1896; general literature, fiction, non-fiction, fine arts, philosophy; Pres. TAKANOBU SATO.

Shinkenchiku-Sha Co Ltd: 2-31-2, Yushima, Bunkyo-ku, Tokyo 113-8501; tel. (3) 3811-7101; fax (3) 3812-8229; e-mail ja-business@japan-architect.co.jp; internet www.japan-architect.co.jp; f. 1925; architecture; Pres. NOBUYUKI YOSHIDA.

Shogakukan Inc: 2-3-1, Hitotsubashi, Chiyoda-ku, Tokyo 101-8001; tel. (3) 3230-5526; fax (3) 3288-9653; internet www .shogakukan.co.jp; f. 1922; juvenile, education, geography, history, encyclopaedias, dictionaries; Pres. MASAHIRO OHGA.

Shokabo Publishing Co Ltd: 8-1, Yomban-cho, Chiyoda-ku, Tokyo 102-0081; tel. (3) 3262-9166; fax (3) 3262-7257; e-mail info@shokabo.co.jp; internet www.shokabo.co.jp; f. 1895; natural science, engineering; Pres. TATSUJI YOSHINO.

Shokokusha Publishing Co Ltd: 25, Saka-machi, Shinjuku-ku, Tokyo 160-0002; tel. (3) 3359-3231; fax (3) 3357-3961; e-mail eigyo@shokokusha.co.jp; f. 1932; architectural, technical and fine arts; Pres. TAKESHI GOTO.

Shueisha Inc: 2-5-10, Hitotsubashi, Chiyoda-ku, Tokyo 101-8050; tel. (3) 3230-6320; fax (3) 3262-1309; f. 1925; literature, fine arts, language, juvenile, comics; Pres. and CEO TAMIO KOJIMA.

Shufunotomo Co Ltd: 2-9, Kanda Surugadai, Chiyoda-ku, Tokyo 101-8911; tel. (3) 5280-7567; fax (3) 5280-7568; e-mail international@shufunotomo.co.jp; internet www.shufunotomo.co.jp; f. 1916; domestic science, fine arts, gardening, handicraft, cookery and magazines; Pres. KUNIHIKO MURAMATSU.

Shunju-Sha: 2-18-6, Soto-Kanda, Chiyoda-ku, Tokyo 101-0021; tel. (3) 3255-9614; fax (3) 3255-9370; f. 1918; philosophy, religion, literary, economics, music; Pres. AKIRA KANDA; Man. RYUTARO SUZUKI.

Taishukan Publishing Co Ltd: 3-24, Kanda-Nishiki-cho, Chiyoda-ku, Tokyo 101-8466; tel. (3) 3294-2221; fax (3) 3295-4107; internet www.taishukan.co.jp; f. 1918; reference, Japanese and foreign languages, sports, dictionaries, audio-visual aids; Pres. KAZUYUKI SUZUKI.

Tankosha Publishing Co Ltd: 19-1, Miyanishi-cho Murasakino, Kita-ku, Kyoto 603-8691; tel. (75) 432-5151; fax (75) 432-0273; e-mail tankosha@magical.egg.or.jp; internet tankosha.topica.ne.jp; f. 1949; tea ceremony, fine arts, history; Pres. YOSHITO NAYA.

Teikoku-Shoin Co Ltd: 3-29, Kanda Jimbo-cho, Chiyoda-ku, Tokyo 101-0051; tel. (3) 3262-0834; fax (3) 3262-7770; e-mail kenkyu@teikokushoin.co.jp; f. 1926; geography, atlases, maps, textbooks; Pres. MUTSUO SHIRAHAMA.

Tokai University Press: 2-28-4, Tomigaya, Shibuya-ku, Tokyo 151-8677; tel. (3) 5478-0891; fax (3) 5478-0870; f. 1962; social science, cultural science, natural science, engineering, art; Pres. TATSURO MATSUMAE.

Tokuma Shoten Publishing Co Ltd: 1-1-16, Higashi Shimbashi, Minato-ku, Tokyo 105-8055; tel. (3) 3573-0111; fax (3) 3573-8788; e-mail info@tokuma.com; internet www.tokuma.com; f. 1954; Japanese classics, history, fiction, juvenile; Pres. YASUYOSHI TOKUMA.

Tokyo News Service Ltd: Tsukiji Hamarikyu Bldg, 5-3-3, Tsukiji, Chuo-ku, Tokyo 104; tel. (3) 3542-6511; fax (3) 3545-3628; f. 1947; shipping, trade and television guides; Pres. T. OKUYAMA.

Tokyo Shoseki Co Ltd: 2-17-1, Horifune, Kita-ku, Tokyo 114-8524; tel. (3) 5390-7513; fax (3) 5390-7409; internet www.tokyo-shoseki.co .jp; f. 1909; textbooks, reference books, cultural and educational books; Pres. YOSHIKATSU KAWAUCHI.

Tokyo Sogen-Sha Co Ltd: 1-5, Shin-Ogawa-machi, Shinjuku-ku, Tokyo 162-0814; tel. (3) 3268-8201; fax (3) 3268-8230; f. 1954; mystery and detective stories, science fiction, literature; Pres. YASUNOBU TOGAWA.

Tuttle Publishing Co Inc: Yaekari Bldg, 3rd Floor, 5-4-12 Osaki, Shinagawa-ku, Tokyo 141-0032; tel. (3) 5437-0171; fax (44) 5437-0755; e-mail tuttle@gol.com; internet www.tuttlepublishing.com; f. 1948; books on Japanese and Asian religion, history, social science, arts, languages, literature, juvenile, cookery; Pres. ERIC OEY.

United Nations University Press: 5-53-70, Jingumae, Shibuya-ku, Tokyo 150-8925; tel. (3) 3499-2811; fax (3) 3499-2828; e-mail sales@hq.unu.edu; internet www.unu.edu/unupress; f. 1975; social sciences, humanities, pure and applied natural sciences; Rector HANS J. H. VAN GINKEL.

University of Tokyo Press: 7-3-1, Hongo, Bunkyo-ku, Tokyo 113-8654; tel. (3) 3811-0964; fax (3) 3815-1426; e-mail info@utp.or.jp; f. 1951; natural and social sciences, humanities; Japanese and English; Chair. MASARU NISHIO; Man. Dir TADASHI YAMASHITA.

Weekly Toyo Keizai: 1-2-1, Nihombashi, Hongoku-cho, Chuo-ku, Tokyo 103-8345; tel. (3) 3246-5655; fax (3) 3231-0906; e-mail sub@toyokeizai.co.jp; internet www.toyokeizai.co.jp; f. 1895; economics, business, finance and corporate, information; Pres. HIROSHI TAKAHASHI.

Yama-Kei Publishers Co Ltd: 1-1-33, Shiba-Daimon, Minato-ku, Tokyo 105-0012; tel. (3) 3436-4021; fax (3) 3438-1949; f. 1930; natural science, geography, mountaineering; Pres. YOSHIMITSU KAWASAKI.

Yohan: 3-14-9, Okubo, Shinjuku-ku, Tokyo 169-0072; tel. (3) 3208-0181; fax (3) 3209-0288; internet www.yohan.co.jp; f. 1963; social science, language, art, juvenile, dictionary; Pres. MASANORI WATANABE.

Yuhikaku Publishing Co Ltd: 2-17, Kanda Jimbo-cho, Chiyoda-ku, Tokyo 101-0051; tel. (3) 3264-1312; fax (3) 3264-5030; f. 1877; social sciences, law, economics; Pres. TADATAKA EGUSA.

Yuzankaku Shuppan: 2-6-9, Fujimi, Chiyoda-ku, Tokyo 102; tel. (3) 3262-3231; fax (3) 3262-6938; e-mail yuzan@cf.mbn.or.jp; internet www.nepto.co.jp/yuzankaku; f. 1916; history, fine arts, religion, archaeology; Pres. KEIKO NAGASAKA.

Zoshindo Juken Kenkyusha Co Ltd: 2-19-15, Shinmachi, Nishi-ku, Osaka 550-0013; tel. (6) 6532-1581; fax (6) 6532-1588; e-mail zoshindo@mbox.inet-osaka.or.jp; internet www.zoshindo.co.jp; f. 1890; educational, juvenile; Pres. AKITAKA OKAMATO.

Government Publishing House

Government Publications' Service Centre: 1-2-1, Kasumigaseki, Chiyoda-ku, Tokyo 100-0013; tel. (3) 3504-3885; fax (3) 3504-3889.

PUBLISHERS' ASSOCIATIONS

Japan Book Publishers Association: 6, Fukuro-machi, Shinjuku-ku, Tokyo 162-0828; tel. (3) 3268-1301; fax (3) 3268-1196; internet www.jbpa.or.jp; f. 1957; 499 mems; Pres. TAKAO WATANABE; Exec. Dir TOSHIKAZU GOMI.

Publishers' Association for Cultural Exchange, Japan: 1-2-1, Sarugaku-cho, Chiyoda-ku, Tokyo 101-0064; tel. (3) 3291-5685; fax (3) 3233-3645; e-mail office@pace.or.jp; internet www.pace.or.jp; f. 1953; 135 mems; Pres. Dr TATSURO MATSUMAE; Man. Dir YASUKO KORENAGA.

Broadcasting and Communications

TELECOMMUNICATIONS

International Digital Communications: 5-20-8, Asakusabashi, Taito-ku, Tokyo 111; tel. (3) 5820-5080; fax (3) 5820-5363; f. 1985; 53% owned by Cable and Wireless Communications (UK); Pres. SIMON CUNNINGHAM.

Japan Telecom Co Ltd: 4-7-1, Hatchobori, Chuo-ku, Tokyo 104-8508; tel. (3) 5540-8417; fax (3) 5540-8485; internet www .japan-telecom.co.jp; 30% owned by alliance of British Telecommunications PLC (UK) and American Telegraph and Telephone Corpn (USA); Chair. HARUO MURAKAMI; Pres. BILL MORROW.

KDDI Corpn: KDDI Bldg, 2-3-2, Nishi Shinjuku, Shinjuku-ku, Tokyo 163-03; tel. (3) 3347-7111; fax (3) 3347-6470; internet www .kddi.com; f. 2000; by merger of DDI Corpn, Kokusai Denshin Denwa Corpn (KDD) and Nippon Idou Tsushin Corpn (IDO); major international telecommunications carrier; Chair. JIRO USHIO; Pres. TADASHI ONODERA.

Nippon Telegraph and Telephone Corpn: 2-3-1, Otemachi, Chiyoda-ku, Tokyo 100-0004; tel. (3) 5359-2122; e-mail hyamada@yamato.ntt.jp; operates local, long-distance and international services; largest telecommunications co in Japan; Chair. SHIGEO SAWADA; Pres. JUN-ICHIRO MIYAZU.

NTT DoCoMo: 2-11-1 Nagatacho, Chiyoda-ku, Tokyo 100-6150; tel. (3) 5156-1111; fax (3) 5156-0271; internet www.nttdocomo.com; f. 1991; operates mobile phone network; Pres. KEIJI TACHIKAWA.

Tokyo Telecommunication Network Co Inc: 4-9-25, Shibaura, Minato-ku, Tokyo 108; tel. (3) 5476-0091; fax (3) 5476-7625.

KDDI, Digital Phone and Digital TU-KA also operate mobile telecommunication services in Japan.

BROADCASTING

NHK (Japan Broadcasting Corporation): 2-2-1, Jinnan, Shibuya, Tokyo 150-8001; tel. (3) 3465-1111; fax (3) 3469-8110; e-mail webmaster@www.nhk.or.jp; internet www.nhk.or.jp; f. 1925; fmrly Nippon Hose Kyokai, NHK (Japan Broadcasting Corpn); Japan's sole public broadcaster; operates five TV channels (incl. two terrestrial services—general TV and educational TV, two digital satellite services—BS-1 and BS-2 and a digital Hi-Vision service—HDTV), three radio channels, Radio 1, Radio 2, and FM Radio, and three worldwide services, NHK World TV, NHK World Premium and NHK World Radio Japan; headquarters in Tokyo, regional headquarters in Osaka, Nagoya, Hiroshima, Fukuoka, Sendai, Sapporo and Matsuyama; Pres. KATSUJI EBISAWA.

National Association of Commercial Broadcasters in Japan (NAB-J): 3-23, Kioi-cho, Chiyoda-ku, Tokyo 102-8577; tel. (3) 5213-7727; fax (3) 5213-7730; internet www.nab.or.jp; f. 1951; asscn of 201 companies (133 TV cos, 110 radio cos). Among these companies, 42 operate both radio and TV, with 664 radio stations and 8,315 TV stations (incl. relay stations). Pres. SEIICHIRO UJIIE; Exec. Dir AKIRA SAKAI.

In June 2000 there were a total of 99 commercial radio broadcasting companies and 127 commercial television companies operating in Japan.

Some of the most important companies are:

Asahi Hoso—Asahi Broadcasting Corpn: 2-2-48, Ohyodominami, Kita-ku, Osaka 531-8501; tel. (6) 6458-5321; fax (6) 6458-3672; internet www.asahi.co.jp; Pres. TOSHIHARU SHIBATA.

Asahi National Broadcasting Co Ltd—TV Asahi: 1-1-1, Roppongi, Minato-ku, Tokyo 106-8001; tel. (3) 3587-5412; fax (3) 3438-9696; internet www.tv-asahi.co.jp; f. 1957; Pres. KUNIO ITO.

Bunka Hoso—Nippon Cultural Broadcasting, Inc: 1-5, Wakaba, Shinjuku-ku, Tokyo 160-8002; tel. (3) 3357-1111; fax (3) 3357-1140; internet www.joqr.co.jp; f. 1952; Pres. SHIGEKI SATO.

Chubu-Nippon Broadcasting Co Ltd: 1-2-8, Shinsakae, Naka-ku, Nagoya 460-8405; tel. (052) 241-8111; internet hicbc.com.co.jp; Pres. KEN-ICHI YOKOYAMA.

Fuji Television Network, Inc: 2-4-8, Daiba, Minato-ku, Tokyo 137-8088; tel. (3) 5500-8888; fax (3) 5500-8027; internet www.fujitv.co.jp; f. 1959; Pres. HISASHI HIEDA.

Kansai TV Hoso (KTV)—Kansai: 2-1-7, Ogimachi, Kita-ku, Osaka 530-8408; tel. (6) 6314-8888; internet www.ktv.co.jp; Pres. MICHIO IZUMA.

Mainichi Hoso (MBS)—Mainichi Broadcasting System, Inc: 17-1, Chayamachi, Kita-ku, Osaka 530-8304; tel. (6) 6359-1123; fax (6) 6359-3503; internet mbs.co.jp; Pres. MASAHIRO YAMAMOTO.

Nippon Hoso—Nippon Broadcasting System, Inc: 2-4-8, Daiba, Minato-ku, Tokyo 137-8686; tel. (3) 5500-1234; internet www.1242.com; f. 1954; Pres. MICHIYASU KAWAUCHI.

Nippon TV Hoso-MO (NTV)—Nippon Television Network Corpn: 14, Niban-cho, Chiyoda-ku, Tokyo 102-8004; tel. (3) 5275-1111; fax (3) 5275-4501; internet www.ntv.co.jp; f. 1953; Pres. SEIICHIRO UJIIE.

Okinawa TV Hoso (OTV)—Okinawa Television Broadcasting Co Ltd: 1-2-20, Kumoji, Naha 900-8588; tel. (988) 63-2111; fax (988) 61-0193; internet www.otv.co.jp; f. 1959; Pres. BUNKI TOMA.

Radio Tampa—Nihon Short-Wave Broadcasting Co: 1-9-15, Akasaka, Minato-ku, Tokyo 107-8373; tel. (3) 3583-8151; fax (3) 3583-7441; internet www.tampa.co.jp; f. 1954; Pres. TAMIO IKEDA.

Ryukyu Hoso (RBC)—Ryukyu Broadcasting Co: 2-3-1, Kumoji, Naha 900-8711; tel. (98) 867-2151; fax (98) 864-5732; internet www.rbc-ryukyu.co.jp; f. 1954; Pres. YOSHIO ISHIGAKE.

TV Osaka (TVO)—Television Osaka, Inc: 1-2-18, Otemae, Chuo-ku, Osaka 540-8519; tel. (6) 6947-0019; fax (6) 6946-9796; internet www.tv-osaka.co.jp; f. 1982; Pres. MAKOTO FUKAGAWA.

TV Tokyo (TX)—Television Tokyo Channel 12 Ltd: 4-3-12, Toranomon, Minato-ku, Tokyo 105-8012; tel. (3) 3432-1212; fax (3) 5473-3447; internet www.tv-tokyo.co.jp; f. 1964; Pres. YUTAKA ICHIKI.

Tokyo –Hoso (TBS)—Tokyo Broadcasting System, Inc: 5-3-6, Akasaka, Minato-ku, Tokyo 107-8006; tel. (3) 3746-1111; fax (3) 3588-6378; internet www.tbs.co.jp/index.html; f. 1951; Chair. HIROSHI SHIHO; Pres. YUKIO SUNAHARA.

Yomiuri TV Hoso (YTV)—Yomiuri Telecasting Corporation: 2-2-33, Shiromi, Chuo-ku, Osaka 540-8510; tel. (6) 6947-2111; internet www.ytv.co.jp; f. 1958; 20 hrs colour broadcasting daily; Pres. TOMONARI DOI.

Satellite, Cable and Digital Television

In addition to the two broadcast satellite services that NHK introduced in 1989, a number of commercial satellite stations are in operation. Cable television is available in many urban areas, and in 1996/97 there were some 12.6m. subscribers to cable services in Japan. Satellite digital television services, which first became available in 1996, are provided by Japan Digital Broadcasting Services (f. 1998 by the merger of PerfecTV and JSkyB) and DirecTV. Terrestrial digital services were scheduled to be introduced by 2000.

Finance

(cap. = capital; p.u. = paid up; res = reserves; dep. = deposits; m. = million; brs = branches; amounts in yen)

BANKING

Japan's central bank and bank of issue is the Bank of Japan. More than one-half of the credit business of the country is handled by 136 private commercial banks, seven trust banks and three long-term credit banks, collectively designated 'All Banks'. At October 1998 the private commercial banks had total assets of 641,000,000m. yen, the trust banks had total assets of 62,000,000m. yen and the long-term credit banks had total assets of 72,000,000m. yen.

Of the former category, the most important are the city banks, of which there are 10, some of which have a long and distinguished history, originating in the time of the *zaibatsu*, the private entrepreneurial organizations on which Japan's capital wealth was built before the Second World War. Although the *zaibatsu* were abolished as integral industrial and commercial enterprises during the Allied Occupation, the several businesses and industries that bear the former *zaibatsu* names, such as Mitsubishi, Mitsui and Sumitomo, continue to operate and to give each other mutual assistance through their respective banks and trust corporations.

Among the commercial banks, the Bank of Tokyo-Mitsubishi specializes in foreign-exchange business, while the Industrial Bank of Japan finances capital investment by industry. Shinsei Bank and Nippon Credit Bank also specialize in industrial finance; the work of these three privately-owned banks is supplemented by the government-controlled Development Bank of Japan.

The Government has established a number of other specialized institutions to provide services that are not offered by the private banks. Thus the Japan Bank for International Cooperation advances credit for the export of heavy industrial products and the import of raw materials in bulk. A Housing Loan Corporation assists firms in building housing for their employees, while the Agriculture, Forestry and Fisheries Finance Corporation provides loans to the named industries for equipment purchases. Similar services are provided for small enterprises by the Japanese Finance Corporation for Small Business.

An important financial role is played by co-operatives and by the many small enterprise institutions. Each prefecture has its own federation of co-operatives, with the Central Co-operative Bank of Agriculture and Forestry as the common central financial institution. This bank also acts as an agent for the government-controlled Agriculture, Forestry and Fisheries Finance Corporation.

There are also two types of private financial institutions for small business. There were 342 Credit Co-operatives, with total assets of 22,000,000m. yen, and 400 Shinkin Banks (credit associations), with total assets of 113,000,000m. yen at October 1998, which lend only to members. The latter also receive deposits.

The most common form of savings is through the government-operated Postal Savings System, which collects small savings from the public by means of the post office network. Total deposits amounted to 248,000,000m. yen in November 1998. The funds thus made available are used as loan funds by government financial institutions, through the Ministry of Finance's Trust Fund Bureau.

Clearing houses operate in each major city of Japan, and total 182 institutions. The largest are those of Tokyo and Osaka.

In June 1998 the Financial Supervisory Agency was established to regulate Japan's financial institutions.

Central Bank

Nippon Ginko (Bank of Japan): 2-1-1, Hongoku-cho, Nihombashi, Chuo-ku, Tokyo 100-8630; tel. (3) 3279-1111; fax (3) 5200-2256; internet www.boj.or.jp; f. 1882; cap. and res 2,831,600m., dep. 41,823,400m. (March 2002); Gov. TOSHIHIKO FUKUI; Dep. Govs TOSHIRO MUTO, KAZUMASA IWATA; 33 brs.

Principal Commercial Banks

Asahi Bank Ltd: 1-1-2, Otemachi, Chiyoda-ku, Tokyo 100-8106; tel. (3) 3287-2111; fax (3) 3212-3484; internet www.asahibank.co.jp; f. 1945 as Kyowa Bank Ltd; merged with Saitama Bank Ltd (f. 1943) in 1991; adopted present name in 1992; to merge with Daiwa Bank in 2002; cap. 403,380m., res 914,252m., dep. 26,357,595m. (March 2001); Chair. TADASHI TANAKA; Pres. TATSURO ITOH; 424 brs.

Ashikaga Bank Ltd: 4-1-25, Sakura, Utsunomiya, Tochigi 320-8610; tel. (286) 22-0111; e-mail ashigin@ssctnet.or.jp; internet www.ashikagabank.co.jp; f. 1895; cap. 132,446m., res 98,934m., dep. 5,083,099m. (March 2000); Chair. YOSHIO YANAGITA; Pres. SHIN IIZUKA; 140 brs.

Bank of Fukuoka Ltd: 2-13-1, Tenjin, Chuo-ku, Fukuoka 810-8727; tel. (92) 723-2131; fax (92) 711-1746; f. 1945; cap. 58,657m., res 272,349m., dep. 5,805,102m. (March 2000); Chair. KIYOSHI TERAMOTO; Pres. RYOJI TSUKUDA; 189 brs.

Bank of Tokyo-Mitsubishi Ltd: 2-7-1, Marunouchi, Chiyoda-ku, Tokyo 100-8388; tel. (3) 93240-1111; fax (3) 93240-4197; internet www.btm.co.jp; f. 1996 as a result of merger between Bank of Tokyo Ltd (f. 1946) and Mitsubishi Bank Ltd (f. 1880); specializes in international banking and financial business; cap. 785,970m., res 1,391,469m., dep. 62,606,410m. (March 2001); Chair. SATORU KISHI; Pres. SHIGEMITSU MIKI; 805 brs.

Bank of Yokohama Ltd: 3-1-1, Minatomirai, Nishi-ku, Yokohama, Kanagawa 220-8611; tel. (45) 225-1111; fax (45) 225-1160; e-mail iroffice@hamagin.co.jp; internet www.boy.co.jp; f. 1920; cap. 184,800m., res 183,399m., dep. 9,192,156m. (March 2002); Pres. and CEO SADAAKI HIRASAWA; 185 brs.

Chiba Bank Ltd: 1-2, Chiba-minato, Chuo-ku, Chiba 260-8720; tel. (43) 245-1111; e-mail 27528400@people.or.jp; internet www .chibabank.co.jp; f. 1943; cap. 106,888m., res 194,702m., dep. 6,870,950m. (March 2000); Chair. TAKASHI TAMAKI; Pres. TSUNEO HAYAKAWA; 163 brs.

Dai-Ichi Kangyo Bank Ltd: 1-1-5, Uchisaiwai-cho, Chiyoda-ku, Tokyo 100-0011; tel. (3) 3596-1111; fax (3) 3596-2179; internet www .dkb.co.jp; f. 1971; jt holding co established with Fuji Bank Ltd and Nippon Kogyo Ginko in September 2000, prior to full merger by early 2002; cap. 858,784m., res 1,519,755m., dep. 40,012,121m. (March 2000); Pres. and CEO KATSUYUKI SUGITA; 353 brs.

Daiwa Bank Ltd: 2-2-1, Bingo-machi, Chuo-ku, Osaka 540-8610; tel. (6) 6271-1221; internet www.daiwabank.co.jp; f. 1918 to merge with Asahi Bank in 2002; cap. 465,158m., res 452,813m., dep 12,772,280m. (March 2001); Chair. TAKASHI KAIHO; Pres. YASUHISA KATSUTA; 182 brs.

Fuji Bank Ltd: 1-5-5, Otemachi, Chiyoda-ku, Tokyo 100-0004; tel. (3) 3216-2211; internet www.fujibank.co.jp; f. 1880; jt holding co with Dai-Ichi Kangyo Bank Ltd and Nippon Kogyo Ginko established Sept. 2000, prior to full merger by early 2002; cap. 1,039,543m., res 1,239,276m., dep. 38,961,618m. (March 2000); Chair. TORU HASHIMOTO; Pres. YOSHIRO YAMAMOTO; 293 brs.

Hachijuni Bank: 178-8 Okada, Nagano-shi, Nagano 380-8682; tel. (26) 227-1182; fax (26) 226-5077; internet www.82bank.co.jp; f. 1931; cap. 52,243m., res 74,745m., dep. 5,137,760m. (March 2000); Pres. MINORU CHINO.

Hokuriku Bank Ltd: 1-2-26, Tsutsumichodori, Toyama 930-8637; tel. (764) 237-111; fax (764) 915-908; e-mail kokusaibu@hokugin.co .jp; internet www.hokugin.co.jp; f. 1877; cap. 120,842m., res 145,857m., dep. 5,440,960m. (March 2000); Pres. SHINICHIRO INUSHIMA; 191 brs.

Japan Net Bank: internet www.japannetbank.co.jp; f. 2000; Japan's first internet-only bank.

Joyo Bank Ltd: 2-5-5, Minamimachi, Mito-shi, Ibaraki 310-0021; tel. (29) 231-2151; fax (29) 255-6522; e-mail joyointl@po.net-ibaraki .ne.jp; internet www.joyobank.co.jp; f. 1935; cap. 85,113m., res 326,961m., dep. 6,340,849m. (March 2001); Chair. TORANOSUKE NISHINO; Pres. ISAO SHIBUYA; 186 brs.

North Pacific Bank: 3-11 Odori Nishi, Chuo-ku, Sapporo 060-8661; tel. (11) 261-1416; fax (11) 232-6921; f. 1917 as Hokuyo Sogo Bank Ltd; assumed present name in 1989; cap. 49,223m., res 71,088m., dep 5,153,501m. (March 2001); Chair. MASANAO TAKEI; Pres. IWAO TAKAMUKI.

Shizuoka Bank Ltd: 1-10, Gofuku-cho, Shizuoka 420-8760; tel. (54) 261-3131; fax (54) 344-0090; internet www.shizuokabank.co.jp; f. 1943; cap. 90,845m., res 207,804m., dep. 7,129,226m. (Dec. 2002); Chair. SOICHIRO KAMIYA; Pres. YASUO MATSUURA; 199 brs.

Sumitomo Mitsui Banking Corpn: 1-2 Yurakucho, Chiyoda-ku, Tokyo 100-0006; tel. (3) 2501-1111; internet www.smbc.co.jp; f. 1895; merged with Sakura Bank Ltd in April 2001 and assumed present name; cap. 752,848m., res 764,376m., dep. 52,651,617m. (March 2001); Chair. AKISHIGE OKADA; Pres. YOSHIFUMI NISHIKAWA; 351 brs.

UFJ Bank Ltd: 3-5-6, Fushimi-machi, Chuo-ku, Osaka-shi, Osaka; internet www.ufj.co.jp; f. April 2001 following merger of Sanwa Bank, Tokai Bank, and Toyo Trust and Banking (see above); cap. 1,000,000m. (Dec. 2001); dep. 51,107,000m. (Sept. 2001); Pres. MASASHI TERANISHI.

Principal Trust Banks

Chuo Mitsui Trust and Banking Co Ltd: 3-33-1, Shiba, Minato-ku, Chuo-ku, Tokyo 105-8574; tel. (3) 5232-3331; fax (3) 5232-8864; internet www.chuomitsui.co.jp; f. 1962 as Chuo Trust and Banking Co Ltd, name changed as above in 2000, following merger with Mitsui Trust and Banking Co Ltd; cap. 170,966m., res 166,803m., dep. 3,594,827m. (March 2000); Chair. HISAO MURAMOTO; Pres. KIICHIRO FURUSAWA; 169 brs.

Mitsubishi Trust and Banking Corporation: 2-11-1 Nagatacho, Chiyoda-ku, Tokyo 100-8212; tel. (3) 3212-1211; fax (3) 3519-3367; internet www.mitsubishi-trust.co.jp; f. 1927; absorbed Nippon Trust Bank Ltd and Tokyo Trust Bank Ltd in Oct. 2001; cap. 292,794m., res 562,883m., dep. 11,359,018m. (March 2001); Chair. TOYOSHI NAKANO; Pres. AKIO UTSUMI; 54 brs.

Sumitomo Trust and Banking Co Ltd: 4-5-33, Kitahama, Chuo-ku, Osaka 540-8639; tel. (6) 6220-2121; fax (6) 6220-2043; e-mail ipda@sumitomotrust.co.jp; internet www.sumitomotrust.co.jp; f. 1925; cap. 283,985m., res 302,861m., dep. 9,782,090m. (March 2001); Chair. HITOSHI HURAKAMI; Pres. ATSUSHI TAKAHASHI; 57 brs.

UFJ Trust Bank: 1-4-3, Marunouchi, Chiyoda-ku, Tokyo 100-0005; tel. (3) 3287-2211; fax (3) 3201-1448; f. 1959 as Toyo Trust and Banking; merged with Sanwa Bank Ltd and Tokai Bank Ltd in April 2001 to form UFJ Holdings Ltd (see above); cap. 280,471m., res 263,357m., dep. 3,952,347m. (March 2000); Pres. YASUKUNI DOI; 56 brs.

Yasuda Trust and Banking Co Ltd: 1-2-1, Yaesu, Chuo-ku, Tokyo 103-8670; tel. (3) 3278-8111; fax (3) 3281-6947; internet www.ytb.co .jp; f. 1925; cap. 337,231m., res 13,905m., dep. 4,549,580m. (March 2001); Pres. and CEO HIROAKI ETOH; 50 brs.

Long-Term Credit Banks

Aozora: 1-13-10, Kudan-kita, Chiyoda-ku, Tokyo 102-8660; tel. (3) 3263-1111; fax (3) 3265-7024; e-mail sora@aozora.co.jp; internet www.aozora.co.jp; f. 1957; nationalized Dec. 1998, sold to consortium led by Softbank Corpn in Aug. 2000; fmrly The Nippon Credit Bank, name changed as above 2001; cap. 419,781m., res 33,333m., dep. 4,650,510m. (March 2001); Pres. and CEO HIROSHI MARUYAMA; Man. Exec. Dir YUJI INAGAKI; 17 brs.

Nippon Kogyo Ginko (The Industrial Bank of Japan Ltd): 1-3-3, Marunouchi, Chiyoda-ku, Tokyo 100-8210; tel. (3) 3214-1111; fax (3) 3201-7643; internet www.ibjbank.co.jp; f. 1902; jt holding co with Dai-Ichi Kangyo Bank Ltd and Fuji Bank Ltd established in Sept. 2000, prior to full merger by early 2002; medium- and long-term financing; cap. 673,605m., res 650,501m., dep. 28,041,940m. (March 1999); Pres. and CEO MASAO NISHIMURA; 23 domestic brs, 20 overseas brs.

Shinsei Bank Ltd: 2-1-8, Uchisaiwai-cho, Chiyoda-ku, Tokyo 100-8501; tel. (3) 5511-5111; fax (3) 5511-5505; internet www .shinseibank.co.jp; f. 1952 as The Long-Term Credit Bank of Japan; nationalized Oct. 1998, sold to Ripplewood Holdings (USA), renamed as above June 2000; cap. 180,853m., res 305,343m., dep. 7,595,821m. (March 2001); Chair. MASAMOTO YASHIRO; 23 brs.

Co-operative Bank

Shinkin Central Bank: 3-8-1, Kyobashi, Chuo-ku, Tokyo 104-0031; tel. (3) 3563-4111; fax (3) 3563-7553; internet www.shinkin.co .jp; f. 1950; cap. 290,998m., res 494,202m., dep. 22,116,995m. (March 2001); Chair. YUKIHIKO NAGANO; Pres. YASUTAKA MIYAMOTO; 17 brs.

Principal Government Credit Institutions

Agriculture, Forestry and Fisheries Finance Corporation: Koko Bldg, 1-9-3, Otemachi, Chiyoda-ku, Tokyo 100-0004; tel. (3) 3270-2261; e-mail intl@afc.go.jp; internet www.afc.go.jp; f. 1953; finances mainly plant and equipment investment; Gov. TOSHIHIKO TSURUOKA; Dep. Gov. SHIGEO OHARA; 22 brs.

Development Bank of Japan: 1-9-1, Otemachi, Chiyoda-ku, Tokyo 100-0004; tel. (3) 3244-1770; fax (3) 3245-1938; e-mail safukus@dbj.go.jp; internet www.dbj.go.jp; f. 1951 as the Japan Development Bank; renamed Oct. 1999 following consolidation with the Hokkaido and Tohoku Development Finance Public Corpn; provides long-term loans; subscribes for corporate bonds; guarantees corporate obligations; invests in specific projects; borrows funds from Govt and abroad; issues external bonds and notes; provides market information and consulting services for prospective entrants to Japanese market; cap. 1,122,286m. (March 2002), res 455,768m. (March 1999), dep. 15,096,100m. (March 1998); Gov. TAKESHI KOMURA; Dep. Govs NORITADA TERASAWA, TAKASHI MATSUKAWA; 10 domestic brs, 6 overseas brs.

Housing Loan Corporation: 1-4-10, Koraku, Bunkyo-ku, Tokyo 112-8570; tel. (3) 3812-1111; fax (3) 5800-8257; internet www.jyukou .go.jp; f. 1950 to provide long-term capital for the construction of housing at low interest rates; cap. 97,200m. (1994); Pres. SUSUMU TAKAHASHI; Vice-Pres. HIROYUKI ITOU; 12 brs.

Japan Bank for International Cooperation (JBIC): 1-4-1, Otemachi, Chiyoda-ku, Tokyo 100-8144; tel. (3) 5218-3101; fax (3) 5218-3955; internet www.jbic.go.jp; f. 1999 by merger of The Export-Import Bank of Japan (f. 1950) and The Overseas Economic Co-operation Fund (f. 1961); governmental financial institution, responsible for Japan's external economic policy and co-operation activities; cap. 6,679,944m. (March 2000); Gov. KYOSUKE SHINOZAWA.

Japan Finance Corporation for Small Business: Koko Bldg, 1-9-3, Otemachi, Chiyoda-ku, Tokyo 100-0004; tel. (3) 3270-1271; internet www.jfs.go.jp; f. 1953 to promote long-term growth and development of small businesses by providing the necessary funds and information on their use in accordance with national policy; cap. 433,715m. (Jan. 2002); wholly subscribed by Govt; Gov. TOMIO TSUTSUMI; Vice-Gov. SOHEI HIDAKA; 58 brs.

National Life Finance Corporation: Koko Bldg, 1-9-3, Otemachi, Chiyoda-ku, Tokyo 100-0004; tel. (3) 3270-1361; internet www .kokukin.go.jp; f. 1999 following consolidation of The People's Finance Corpn (f. 1949 to provide business funds, particularly to small enterprises unable to obtain loans from banks and other private financial institutions) and the Environmental Sanitation Business Finance Corpn (f. 1967 to improve sanitary facilities); cap. 290,771m. (March 2000); Gov. MAMORU OZAKI; Dep. Gov. MASAAKI TSUCHIDA; 152 brs.

Norinchukin Bank (Central Co-operative Bank for Agriculture, Forestry and Fisheries): 1-13-2, Yuraku-cho, Chiyoda-ku, Tokyo 100; tel. (3) 3279-0111; fax (3) 3218-5177; internet www.nochubank .or.jp; f. 1923; main banker to agricultural, forestry and fisheries co-operatives; receives deposits from individual co-operatives, federations and agricultural enterprises; extends loans to these and to local govt authorities and public corpns; adjusts excess and shortage of funds within co-operative system; issues debentures, invests funds and engages in other regular banking business; cap. 1,124,999m., res 723,455m., dep. 47,245,076m. (March 2001); Pres. HIROFUMI UENO; Dep. Pres. HIROHISA ISHIHARA; 39 brs.

Shoko Chukin Bank (Central Co-operative Bank for Commerce and Industry): 2-10-17, Yaesu, Chuo-ku, Tokyo 104-0028; tel. (3) 3272-6111; fax (3) 3272-6169; e-mail JDK06560@nifty.ne.jp; internet www.shokochukin.go.jp; f. 1936 to provide general banking services to facilitate finance for smaller enterprise co-operatives and other organizations formed mainly by small- and medium-sized enterprises; issues debentures; cap. 474,865m., res 24,410m., dep. 12,947,345m. (March 2000); Pres. YUKIHARU KODAMA; Dep. Pres. SHIGENORI SHIODA; 99 brs.

Other government financial institutions include the Japan Finance Corpn for Municipal Enterprises, the Small Business Credit Insurance Corpn and the Okinawa Development Finance Corpn.

Principal Foreign Banks

In March 1999 there were 88 foreign banks operating in Japan.

ABN AMRO Bank NV (Netherlands): Atago Green Hills MORI Tower, 32nd Floor, 2-5-1, Atago, Minato-ku, Tokyo 105-6231; tel. (3) 5405-6500; fax (3) 5405-6900; Br. Man. ATSUSHI WATANABE.

Bangkok Bank Public Co Ltd (Thailand): Bangkok Bank Bldg, 2-8-10, Nishi Shinbashi, Minato-ku, Tokyo 105-0003; tel. (3) 3503-3333; fax (3) 3502-6420; Senior Vice-Pres. and Gen. Man. (Japan) THAWEE PHUANGKETKEOW; br. in Osaka.

Bank of America NA: Sanno Park Tower, 15th Floor, 2-11-1, Nagatacho, Chiyoda-ku, Tokyo 100-6115; tel. (3) 3508-5800; fax (3) 3508-5811; Sr Vice-Pres. and Regional Man. Japan, Australia and Korea ARUN DUGGAL.

Bank of India: Mitsubishi Denki Bldg, 2-2-3, Marunouchi, Chiyoda-ku, Tokyo 100-0005; tel. (3) 3212-0911; fax (3) 3214-8667; e-mail boitok@gol.com; CEO (Japan) P. SIVARAMAN; br. in Osaka.

Bank Negara Indonesia (Persero): Rm 117-18, Kokusai Bldg, 3-1-1, Marunouchi, Chiyoda-ku, Tokyo 100-0005; tel. (3) 3214-5621; fax (3) 3201-2633; e-mail tky-br@ptbni.co.jp; Gen. Man. SURYO DANISWORO.

Bank One NA (USA): Hibiya Central Bldg, 7th Floor, 1-2-9, Nishi Shimbashi, Minato-ku, Tokyo 105; tel. (3) 3596-8700; fax (3) 3596-8744; Sr Vice-Pres. and Gen. Man. YOSHIO KITAZAWA.

Barclays Bank PLC (UK): Urbannet Otemachi Bldg, 15th Floor, 2-2-2, Otemachi, Chiyoda-ku, Tokyo 100-0004; tel. (3) 3276-5100; fax (3) 3276-5085; CEO ANDY SIMMONDS.

Bayerische Hypo- und Vereinsbank AG (Germany): Otemachi 1st Sq. East Tower, 17th Floor, 1-5-1, Otemachi, Chiyoda-ku, Tokyo 100-0004; tel. (3) 3284-1341; fax (3) 3284-1370; Exec. Dirs Prof. PETER BARON, KENJI AKAGI.

BNP Paribas (France): Tokyo Sankei Bldg, 22rd Floor, 1-7-2, Otemachi, Chiyoda-ku, Tokyo 100-0004; tel. (3) 5290-1000; fax (3) 5290-1111; internet www.bnpparibas.co.jp; CEO (Japan) ERIC MARTIN; Representative in Japan HIROAKI INOUE; br. in Osaka.

Citibank NA (USA): Pan Japan Bldg, 1st Floor, 3-8-17, Akasaka Minato-ku, Tokyo 107; tel. (3) 3584-6321; fax (3) 3584-2924; Country Corporate Officer MASAMOTO YASHIRO; 20 brs.

Commerzbank AG (Germany): Nippon Press Center Bldg, 2nd Floor, 2-2-1, Uchisaiwai-cho, Chiyoda-ku, Tokyo 100-0011; tel. (3) 3502-4371; fax (3) 3508-7545; Gen. Man. NORIO YATOMI.

Crédit Agricole Indosuez (France): Indosuez Bldg, 3-29-1, Kanda Jimbo-cho, Chiyoda-ku, Tokyo 101; tel. (3) 3261-3001; fax (3) 3261-0426; Sr Country Exec. FRANÇOIS BEYER.

Deutsche Bank AG (Germany): Sanno Park Tower, 2-11-1 Nagatacho, Chiyoda-ku, Tokyo 100-6170; tel. (3) 5156-4000; fax (3) 5156-6070; CEO and Chief Country Officer JOHN MACFARLANE; brs in Osaka and Nagoya.

The Hongkong and Shanghai Banking Corpn Ltd (Hong Kong): HSBC Bldg, 3-11-1, Nihombashi, Chuo-ku, Tokyo 103-0027; tel. (3) 5203-3000; fax (3) 5203-3108; CEO NORMAN A. WILSON; br. in Osaka.

International Commercial Bank of China (Taiwan): Togin Bldg, 1-4-2, Marunouchi, Chiyoda-ku, Tokyo 100; tel. (3) 3211-2501; fax (3) 3216-5686; Sr Vice-Pres. and Gen. Man. SHIOW-SHYONG LAI; br. in Osaka.

JP Morgan Chase Bank (USA): Akasaka Park Bldg, 11th–13th Floors, 5-2-20, Akasaka, Minato-ku, Tokyo 107; tel. (3) 5570-7500; fax (3) 5570-7960; Man. Dir and Gen. Man. NORMAN J. T. SCOTT; br. in Osaka.

Korea Exchange Bank (Republic of Korea): Shin Kokusai Bldg, 3-4-1, Marunouchi, Chiyoda-ku, Tokyo 100; tel. (3) 3216-3561; fax (3) 3214-4491; f. 1967; Acting Gen. Man. CHO YOUNG-HYO; brs in Osaka and Fukuoka.

Lloyds TSB Bank PLC (UK): Akasaka Twin Tower New Bldg, 2-11-7, Akasaka, Minato-ku, Tokyo 107; tel. (3) 3589-7700; fax (3) 3589-7722; Principal Man. (Japan) G. M. HARRIS.

Morgan Guaranty Trust Co of New York (USA): Akasaka Park Bldg, 5-2-20, Akasaka, Minato-ku, Tokyo 107-6151; tel. (3) 5573-1100; Man. Dir TAKESHI FUJIMAKI.

National Bank of Pakistan: S. K. Bldg, 3rd Floor, 2-7-4, Nishi Shimbashi, Minato-ku, Tokyo 105; tel. (3) 3502-0331; fax (3) 3502-0359; f. 1949; Gen. Man. ZIAULLAH KHAN.

Oversea-Chinese Banking Corpn Ltd (Singapore): Akasaka Twin Tower, 15th Floor, 2-17-22, Akasaka, Minato-ku, Tokyo 107-0052; tel. (3) 5570-3421; fax (3) 5570-3426; Gen. Man. ONG SING YIK.

Société Générale (France): Ark Mori Bldg, 1-12-32, Akasaka, Minato-ku, Tokyo 107-6014; tel. (3) 5549-5800; fax (3) 5549-5809; Chief Operating Officer SHOZO NURISHI; br. in Osaka.

Standard Chartered Bank (UK): 21st Floor, Sanno Park Tower, 2-11-1, Nagata-cho, Chiyoda-ku, Tokyo 100-6155; tel. (3) 5511-1200; fax (3) 5511-9333; Chief Exec. (Japan) JULIAN WYNTER.

State Bank of India: 352 South Tower, Yuraku-cho Denki Bldg, 1-7-1, Yuraku-cho, Chiyoda-ku, Tokyo 100-0006; tel. (3) 3284-0085; fax (3) 3201-5750; e-mail sbitok@gol.com; internet www.sbijapan.com; CEO J. K. SINHA; br. in Osaka.

UBS AG: Urbannet Otemachi Bldg, 2-2-2, Otemachi, Chiyoda-ku, Tokyo 100-0004; tel. (3) 5201-8585; fax (3) 5201-8099; Man. MITSURU TSUNEMI.

Union de Banques Arabes et Françaises (UBAF) (France): Sumitomo Jimbocho Bldg, 8th Floor, 3-25, Kanda Jimbocho, Chiyoda-ku, Tokyo 101-0051; tel. (3) 3263-8821; fax (3) 3263-8820; e-mail antoine.homsy@ubaf.fr; Gen. Man. (Japan) ANTOINE R. HOMSY; br. in Osaka.

WestLB AG (Germany): Fukoku Seimei Bldg, 2-2-2, Uchisaiwaicho, Chiyoda-ku, Tokyo 100-0011; tel. (3) 5510-6200; fax (3) 5510-6299; Man. Dir and Gen. Man. MICHAEL KRAMER.

Bankers' Associations

Japanese Bankers Association: 1-3-1, Marunouchi, Chiyoda-ku, Tokyo 100-8216; tel. (3) 3216-3761; fax (3) 3201-5608; internet www .zenginkyo.or.jp; f. 1945; fmrly Federation of Bankers Associations of Japan; 140 full mems, 46 associate mems, 72 special mems; Chair. MASASHI TERANISHI.

Tokyo Bankers Association, Inc: 1-3-1, Marunouchi, Chiyoda-ku, Tokyo 100-8216; tel. (3) 3216-3761; fax (3) 3201-5608; f. 1945; 116 mem. banks; conducts the above Association's administrative business; Chair. MASASHI TERANISHI; Vice-Chair. MASARI UGAI.

National Association of Labour Banks: 2-5-15, Kanda Surugadai, Chiyoda-ku, Tokyo 101-0062; tel. (3) 3295-6721; fax (3) 3295-6752; Pres. TETSUEI TOKUGAWA.

Regional Banks Association of Japan: 3-1-2, Uchikanda, Chiyoda-ku, Tokyo 101-0047; tel. (3) 3252-5171; fax (3) 3254-8664; f. 1936; 64 mem. banks; Chair. SADAAKI HIROSAWA.

Second Association of Regional Banks: 5, Sanban-cho, Chiyoda-ku, Tokyo 102-0075; tel. (3) 3262-2181; fax (3) 3262-2339; f. 1989; fmrly National Asscn of Sogo Banks; 65 commercial banks; Chair. MASANAO TAKEI.

STOCK EXCHANGES

Fukuoka Securities Exchange: 2-14-2, Tenjin, Chuo-ku, Fukuoka 810-0001; tel. (92) 741-8231; internet www.fse.or.jp; Pres. FUBITO SHIMOMURA.

Hiroshima Stock Exchange: 14-18, Kanayama-cho, Naka-ku, Hiroshima 730-0022; tel. (82) 541-1121; f. 1949; 20 mems; Pres. MASARU NANKO.

Jasdaq Market: 1-14-8 Nihombashi-Ningyocho, Chuo-ku, Tokyo 103-0013; tel. (3) 5641-1818; internet www.jasdaq.co.jp.

Kyoto Securities Exchange: 66, Tachiuri Nishimachi, Shijodori, Higashitoin Higashi-iru, Shimogyo-ku, Kyoto 600-8007; tel. (75) 221-1171; Pres. IICHI NAKAMURA.

Nagoya Stock Exchange: 3-3-17, Sakae, Naka-ku, Nagoya 460-0008; tel. (52) 262-3172; fax (52) 241-1527; e-mail kikaku@nse.or.jp; internet www.nse.or.jp; f. 1949; Pres. HIROSHI FUJITA; Sr Exec. Dir KAZUNORI ISHIMOTO.

Nasdaq Japan Market: 23rd Floor, Akasaka, Minato-ku, Tokyo 107-6023; tel. (3) 5563-8210; internet www.nasdaq-japan.com.

Niigata Securities Exchange: 1245, Hachibancho, Kami-Okawa-maedori, Niigata 951-8068; tel. (252) 222-4181; Pres. KYUUZOU NAKATA.

Osaka Securities Exchange: 1-6-10, Kitahama, Chuo-ku, Osaka 541-0041; tel. (6) 4706-0875; fax (6) 6231-2639; internet www.ose.or .jp; f. 1949; 103 regular mems, 5 special participants; Chair. HIR-OTARO HIGUCHI; Pres. GORO TATSUMI.

Sapporo Securities Exchange: 5-14-1, Nishi, Minami Ichijo, Chuo-ku, Sapporo 060-0061; tel. (11) 241-6171; Pres. YOSHIRO ITOH.

Tokyo Stock Exchange Inc: 2-1, Nihombashi, Kabuto-cho, Chuo-ku, Tokyo 103-8220; tel. (3) 3666-0141; fax (3) 3662-0547; internet www.tse.or.jp; f. 1949; 114 participants (incl. 22 foreign partic-ipants) (Dec. 2001); Pres. and CEO MASAAKI TSUCHIDA; Exec. Vice-Pres. and CFO YOSHIMASA YAMASHITA.

Supervisory Body

The Securities and Exchange Surveillance Commission: 3-1-1, Kasumigaseki, Chiyoda-ku, Tokyo 100; tel. (3) 3581-7868; fax (3) 5251-2136; f. 1992 for the surveillance of securities and financial futures transactions; Chair. TOSHIHIRO MIZUHARA.

INSURANCE

Principal Life Companies

Aetna Heiwa Life Insurance Co Ltd: 3-2-16, Ginza, Chuo-ku, Tokyo 104-8119; tel. (3) 3563-8111; fax (3) 3374-7114; f. 1907; Pres. BARRY S. HALPERN.

American Family Life Assurance Co of Columbus AFLAC Japan: Shinjuku Mitsui Bldg, 12th Floor, 2-1-1, Nishishinjuku, Shinjuku-ku, Tokyo 163-0456; tel. (3) 3344-2701; fax (3) 0424-41-3001; f. 1974; Chair. YOSHIKI OTAKE; Pres. HIDEFUMI MATSUI.

American Life Insurance Co (Japan): 1-1-3, Marunouchi, Chiyoda-ku, Tokyo 100-0005; tel. (3) 3284-4111; fax (3) 3284-3874; f. 1972; Chair. HIROSHI FUJINO; Pres. SEIKI TOKUNI.

Aoba Life Insurance Co Ltd: 3-6-30, Aobadai, Meguro-ku, Tokyo 153-8523; tel. (3) 3462-0007; fax (3) 3780-8169; Pres. TAKASHI KASA-GAMI.

Asahi Mutual Life Insurance Co: 1-7-3, Nishishinjuku, Shin-juku-ku, Tokyo 163-8611; tel. (3) 3342-3111; fax (3) 3346-9397; internet www.asahi-life.co.jp; f. 1888; Pres. YUZURU FUJITA.

AXA Insurance Holding Co Ltd: 1-2-19 Higashi, Shibuya-ku, Tokyo 150-8020; tel. (3) 3407-6210; fax (3) 5466-7131; internet www .axa.co.jp; Pres. and CEO MICHAEL W. SHORT.

Cardif Assurance Vie: 3-25-2, Toranomon, Minato-ku, Tokyo 105-0001; tel. (3) 5776-6230; fax (3) 5776-6236; f. 2000; Pres. ATSUSHI SAKAUCHI.

Chiyoda Mutual Life Insurance Co: 2-19-18, Kamimeguro, Meguro-ku, Tokyo 153-8611; tel. (3) 5704-5111; fax (3) 3719-6605; internet www.chiyoda-life.co.jp; f. 1904; declared bankrupt October 2000; Pres. REIJI YONEYAMA.

Chiyodakasai EBISU Life Insurance Co Ltd: Ebisu MF Bldg, 6th Floor, 4-6-1, Ebisu Shibuya-ku, Tokyo 150-0013; tel. (3) 5420-8282; fax (3) 5420-8273; f. 1996; Pres. SHIGEJI MINOSHIMA.

Daido Life Insurance Co: 1-2-1, Edobori Nishi-ku, Osaka City, Osaka 550-0002; tel. (6) 6447-6111; fax (6) 6447-6315; f. 1902; Pres. NAOTERU MIYATO.

Daihyaku Mutual Life Insurance Co: 3-1-4, Shibuya, Shibuya-ku, Tokyo 150-8670; tel. (3) 3498-2294; fax (3) 3400-9313; e-mail kikaku@daihyaku-life.co.jp; internet www.daihyaku-life.co.jp; f. 1914; declared bankrupt June 2000; Pres. MITSUMASA AKIYAMI.

Dai-ichi Mutual Life Insurance Co: 1-13-1, Yuraku-cho, Chiyoda-ku, Tokyo 100-8411; tel. (3) 3216-1211; fax (3) 5221-8139; f. 1902; Chair. TAKAHIDE SAKURAI; Pres. TOMIJIRO MORITA.

Dai-Tokyo Happy Life Insurance Co Ltd: Shinjuku Square Tower, 17th Floor, 6-22-1, Nishishinjuku, Shinjuku-ku, Tokyo 163-1131; tel. (3) 5323-6411; fax (3) 5323-6419; f. 1996; Pres. HITOSHI HASUNUMA.

DIY Life Insurance Co Ltd: 5-68-2, Nakano, Nakano-ku, Tokyo 164-0001; tel. (3) 5345-7603; fax (3) 5345-7608; f. 1999; Pres. HITOSHI KASE.

Fuji Life Insurance Co Ltd: 1-18-17, Minamisenba, Chuo-ku, Osaka-shi 542-0081; tel. (6) 6261-0284; fax (6) 6261-0113; f. 1996; Pres. YOSHIAKI YONEMURA.

Fukoku Mutual Life Insurance Co: 2-2-2, Uchisaiwai-cho, Chiyoda-ku, Tokyo 100-0011; tel. (3) 3508-1101; fax (3) 3597-0383; f. 1923; Chair. TAKASHI KOBAYASHI; Pres. TOMOFUMI AKIYAMA.

GE Edison Life Insurance Co: Shibuya Markcity, 1-12-1, Dogen-zaka, Shibuya-ku, Tokyo 150-8674; tel. (3) 5457-8100; fax (3) 5457-8017; Chair. MICHAEL D. FRAIZER; Pres. and CEO K. RONE BALDWIN.

Gibraltar Life Insurance Co Ltd: 4-4-1, Nihombashi, Hongoku-cho, Chuo-ku, Tokyo 103-0021; tel. (3) 3270-8511; fax (3) 3231-8276; internet www.gib-life.co.jp; f. 1947; fmrly Kyoei Life Insurance Co Ltd, declared bankrupt Oct. 2000; Pres. KAZUO MAEDA.

ING Life Insurance Co Ltd: 26th Floor, New Otani Garden Court, 4-1, Kioi-cho, Chiyoda-ku, Tokyo 102-0094; tel. (3) 5210-0300; fax (3) 5210-0430; f. 1985; Pres. MAKOTO CHIBA.

Koa Life Insurance Co Ltd: 3-7-3, Kasumigaseki, Chiyoda-ku, Tokyo 100-0013; tel. (3) 3593-3111; fax (3) 5512-6651; internet www .koa.co.jp; f. 1996; Pres. AKIO OKADA.

Kyoei Kasai Shinrai Life Insurance Co Ltd: J. City Bldg, 5-8-20, Takamatsu, Nerima-ku, Tokyo 179-0075; tel. (3) 5372-2100; fax (3) 5372-7701; f. 1996; Pres. YOSHIHIRO TOKUMITSU.

Manulife Life Insurance Co: 4-34-1, Kokuryo-cho, Chofu-shi, Tokyo 182-8621; tel. (3) 2442-7120; fax (3) 2442-7977; e-mail trevor_matthews@manulife.com; internet www.manulife.co.jp; f. 1999; fmrly Manulife Century Life Insurance Co; Pres. and CEO TREVOR MATTHEWS.

Meiji Life Insurance Co: 2-1-1, Marunouchi, Chiyoda-ku, Tokyo 100-0005; tel. (3) 3283-8111; fax (3) 3215-5219; internet www .meiji-life.co.jp; f. 1881 to merge with Yasuda Mutual Life Insurance Co in April 2004; Chair. KENJIRO HATA; Pres. RYOTARO KANEKO.

Mitsui Mirai Life Insurance Co Ltd: Mitsui Kaijyo Nihombashi Bldg, 1-3-16, Nihombashi, Chuo-ku, Tokyo 103-0027; tel. (3) 5202-2811; fax (3) 5202-2997; f. 1996; Pres. KATSUYA WATANABE.

Mitsui Mutual Life Insurance Co: 1-2-3, Otemachi, Chiyoda-ku, Tokyo 100-8123; tel. (3) 3211-6111; fax (3) 5252-7265; internet www .mitsui-seimei.co.jp; f. 1927; Chair. KOSHIRO SAKATA; Pres. AKIRA MIYAKE.

Nichido Life Insurance Co Ltd: 4-2-3, Toranomon, Minato-ku, Tokyo 105-0001; tel. (3) 5403-1700; fax (3) 5403-1707; f. 1996 to merge with Tokio Marine Life Insurance Co in 2002; Pres. YOSHIAKI MIYAMOTO.

NICOS Life Insurance Co Ltd: Hongo MK Bldg, 1-28-34, Hongo, Bunkyo-ku, Tokyo 113-8414; tel. (3) 5803-3111; fax (3) 5803-3199; internet www.nicos-life.co.jp; f. 1986; Pres. RENE MULLER.

Nippon Fire Partner Life Insurance Co Ltd: 3-4-2, Tsukiji, Chuo-ku, Tokyo 104-8407; tel. (3) 5565-8080; fax (3) 5565-8365; f. 1996; Pres. HIRONOBU HARA.

Nippon Life Insurance Co (Nissay): 3-5-12, Imabashi, Chuo-ku, Osaka 541-8501; tel. (6) 6209-4500; e-mail hosokawa15560@nissay .co.jp; internet www.nissay.co.jp; f. 1889; Chair. JOSEI ITOH; Pres. IKUO UNO.

Orico Life Insurance Co Ltd: Sunshine 60, 26th Floor, 3-1-1, Higashi Ikebukuro, Toshima-ku, Tokyo 170-6026; tel. (3) 5391-3051; fax (3) 5391-3060; f. 1990; Chair. HIROSHI ARAI; Pres. TAKASHI SATO.

ORIX Life Insurance Corpn: Shinjuku Chuo Bldg, 5-17-5, Shin-juku, Shinjuku-ku, Tokyo 160-0022; tel. (3) 5272-2700; fax (3) 5272-2720; f. 1991; Chair. SHOGO KAJINISHI; Pres. SHINOBU SHIRAISHI.

Prudential Life Insurance Co Ltd: 1-7, Kojimachi, Chiyoda-ku, Tokyo 102-0083; tel. (3) 3221-0961; fax (3) 3221-2305; f. 1987; Chair. KIYOFUMI SAKAGUCHI; Pres. ICHIRO KONO.

Saison Life Insurance Co Ltd: Sunshine Sixty Bldg, 39th Floor, 3-1-1, Higashi Ikebukuro, Toshima-ku, Tokyo 170-6067; tel. (3) 3983-6666; fax (3) 2980-0598; internet www.saison-life.co.jp; f. 1975; Chair. and Pres. TOSHIO TAKEUCHI.

Skandia Life Insurance Co (Japan) Ltd: 5-6-6, Hiroo, Shibuya-ku, Tokyo 150-0012; tel. (3) 5488-1500; fax (3) 5488-1501; f. 1996; Pres. and CEO IAIN MESSENGER.

Sony Life Insurance Co Ltd: 1-1-1, Minami-Aoyama, Minato-ku, Tokyo 107-8585; tel. (3) 3475-8811; fax (3) 3475-8914; Chair. TSUNAO HASHIMOTO; Pres. KEN IWAKI.

Sumitomo Life Insurance Co: 7-18-24, Tsukiji, Chuo-ku, Tokyo 104-8430; tel. (3) 5550-1100; fax (3) 5550-1160; f. 1907; Chair. TOSHIOMI URAGAMI; Pres. KOICHI YOSHIDA.

Sumitomo Marine Yu-Yu Life Insurance Co Ltd: 2-27-1, Shin-kawa, Chuo-ku, Tokyo 104-0033; tel. (3) 5541-3111; fax (3) 5541-3976; f. 1996; Pres. KATSUHIRO ISHII.

T & D Financial Life Insurance Co: 1-5-2, Uchisaiwai-cho, Chiyoda-ku, Tokyo 100-8555; tel. (3) 3504-2211; fax (3) 3593-0785; f. 1895; fmrly Tokyo Mutual Life Insurance Co; Pres. OSAMU MIZUYAMA.

Taisho Life Insurance Co Ltd: 1-9-1, Yurakucho, Chiyoda-ku, Tokyo 100-0006; tel. (3) 3281-7651; fax (3) 5223-2299; f. 1913; Pres. GEN SHIMURA.

Taiyo Mutual Life Insurance Co: 2-11-2, Nihombashi, Chuo-ku, Tokyo 103-0027; tel. (3) 3272-6211; fax (3) 3272-1460; Pres. MASAHIRO YOSHIIKE.

Tokio Marine Life Insurance Co Ltd: Tokio Marine New Bldg, 1-2-1, Marunouchi, Chiyoda-ku, Tokyo 100-0005; tel. (3) 5223-2111; fax (3) 5223-2165; internet www.tokiomarine-life.co.jp; f. 1996 to merge with Nichido Life Insurance Co in 2002; Pres. SUKEAKI OHTA.

Yamato Mutual Life Insurance Co: 1-1-7, Uchisaiwai-cho, Chiyoda-ku, Tokyo 100-0011; tel. (3) 3508-3111; fax (3) 3508-3118; f. 1911; Pres. KEIJI NONOMIYA.

Yasuda Kasai Himawari Life Insurance Co Ltd: 2-1-1, Nishi-Shinjuku, Shinjuku-ku, Tokyo 163-0434; tel. (3) 3348-7011; fax (3) 3346-9415; f. 1981; fmrly INA Himawari Life Insurance Co Ltd; Chair. (vacant); Pres. MAKOTO YOSHIDA.

Yasuda Mutual Life Insurance Co: 1-9-1, Nishi-Shinjuku, Shin-juku-ku, Tokyo 169-8701; tel. (3) 3342-7111; fax (3) 3349-8104; f. 1880 to merge with Meiji Life Insurance Co in April 2004; Chair. YUJI OSHIMA; Pres. MIKIHIKO MIYAMOTO.

Zurich Life Insurance Co Ltd: Shinanomachi Rengakan, 35, Shinanomachi, Shinjuku-ku, Tokyo 160-0016; tel. (3) 5361-2700; fax (3) 5361-2728; f. 1996; Pres. KENICHI NOGAMI.

Principal Non-Life Companies

ACE Insurance: Arco Tower, 1-8-1, Shimomeguro, Meguro-ku, Tokyo 153-0064; tel. (3) 5740-0600; fax (3) 5740-0608; internet www .ace-insurance.co.jp; f. 1999; Chair. FUMIO TOKUHIRA; Pres. TAKASHI OHKAWA.

Allianz Fire and Marine Insurance Japan Ltd: MITA N. N. Bldg, 4th Floor, 4-1-23, Shiba, Minato-ku, Tokyo 108-0014; tel. (3) 5442-6500; fax (3) 5442-6509; e-mail admin@allianz.co.jp; internet www.allianz.co.jp; f. 1990; Chair. HEINZ DOLLBERG; Pres. ALEXANDER ANKEL.

The Asahi Fire and Marine Insurance Co Ltd: 2-6-2, Kaji-cho, Chiyoda-ku, Tokyo 101-8655; tel. (3) 3254-2201; fax (3) 3254-2296; e-mail asahifmi@blue.ocn.ne.jp; f. 1951; Pres. MORIYA NOGUCHI.

AXA Non-Life Insurance Co Ltd: Ariake Frontier Bldg, Tower A, 3-1-25, Ariake Koto-ku, Tokyo 135-0063; tel. (3) 3570-8900; fax (3) 3570-8911; f. 1998; Pres. GUY MARCILLAT.

The Chiyoda Fire and Marine Insurance Co Ltd: 1-28-1, Ebisu, Shibuya-ku, Tokyo 150-8488; tel. (3) 5424-9288; fax (3) 5424-9382; bought by Dai-Tokyo Fire and Marine Insurance Co in 2000, to combine in April 2001; f. 1897; Pres. KOJI FUKUDA.

The Daido Fire and Marine Insurance Co Ltd: 1-12-1, Kumoji, Naha-shi, Okinawa 900-8586; tel. (98) 867-1161; fax (98) 862-8362; f. 1971; Pres. MUNEMASA URA.

The Daiichi Mutual Fire and Marine Insurance Co: Ochano-mizu-Kyoun-Building, 2-2 Kanda Surugadai, Chiyoda-ku, Tokyo 101-0062; tel. (3) 3518-6727; fax (3) 3518-6732; f. 1949; dissolved March 2001.

The Dai-ichi Property and Casualty Insurance Co Ltd: 1-2-10, Hirakawa-cho, Chiyoda-ku, Tokyo 102-0093; tel. (3) 5213-3124; fax (3) 5213-3306; f. 1996; Pres. TSUYOSHI SHINOHARA.

The Dai-Tokyo Fire and Marine Insurance Co Ltd: 3-25-3, Yoyogi, Shibuya-ku, Tokyo 151-8530; tel. (3) 5371-6122; fax (3) 5371-6248; internet www.daitokyo.index.or.jp; f. 1918; bought Chiyoda Fire and Marine Insurance Co in 2000; Chair. HAJIME OZAWA; Pres. AKIRA SESHIMO.

The Dowa Fire and Marine Insurance Co Ltd: St Luke's Tower, 8-1, Akashi-cho, Chuo-ku, Tokyo 104-8556; tel. (3) 5550-0254; fax (3) 5550-0318; internet www.dowafire.co.jp; f. 1944; Chair. MASAO OKA-ZAKI; Pres. SHUICHIRO SUDO.

The Fuji Fire and Marine Insurance Co Ltd: 1-18-11, Minami-senba, Chuo-ku, Osaka 542-8567; tel. (6) 6271-2741; fax (6) 6266-7115; internet www.fujikasai.co.jp; f. 1918; Pres. YASUO ODA.

The Japan Earthquake Reinsurance Co Ltd: Kobuna-cho, Fuji Plaza, 4th Floor, 8-1, Nihombashi, Kobuna-cho, Chuo-ku, Tokyo 103-0024; tel. (3) 3664-6107; fax (3) 3664-6169; e-mail kanri@ nihonjishin.co.jp; f. 1966; Pres. KAZUMOTO ADACHI.

JI Accident & Fire Insurance Co Ltd: A1 Bldg, 20-5, Ichiban-cho, Chiyoda-ku, Tokyo 102-0082; tel. (3) 3237-2045; fax (3) 3237-2250; internet www.jihoken.co.jp; f. 1989; Pres. TSUKASA IMURA.

The Kyoei Mutual Fire and Marine Insurance Co: 1-18-6, Shimbashi, Minato-ku, Tokyo 105-8604; tel. (3) 3504-2335; fax (3) 3508-7680; e-mail reins.intl@kyoeikasai.co.jp; internet www .kyoeikasai.co.jp; f. 1942; Chair. HIDEJI SUZUKI; Pres. WATARU OZAWA.

Meiji General Insurance Co Ltd: 2-11-1, Kanda-tsukasa-cho, Chiyoda-ku, Tokyo 101-0048; tel. (3) 3257-3141; fax (3) 3257-3295; e-mail nobuo.shimoda@meiji-life.co.jp; internet meiji-general.aaapc .co.jp; f. 1996; Pres. SEISUKE ADACHI.

Mitsui Marine and Fire Insurance Co Ltd: 3-9, Kanda Sur-ugadai, Chiyoda-ku, Tokyo 101-8011; tel. (3) 3259-3111; fax (3) 3291-5467; internet www.mitsuimarine.co.jp; f. 1918; Pres. TAKEO INO-KUCHI.

Mitsui Seimei General Insurance Co Ltd: 2-1-1, Toranomon, Minato-ku, Tokyo 105-0001; tel. (3) 3224-2830; fax (3) 3224-2677; f. 1996; Pres. KIYOSHI MATSUOKA.

The Nichido Fire and Marine Insurance Co Ltd: 5-3-16, Ginza, Chuo-ku, Tokyo 104-0061; tel. (3) 3289-1066; fax (3) 3574-0646; e-mail nichido@mu2.so-net.ne.jp; internet www.mediagalaxy.co.jp/ nichido; f. 1914; Chair. IKUO EGASHIRA; Pres. TAKASHI AIHARA.

The Nipponkoa Insurance Co Ltd: 3-7-3, Kasumigaseki, Chiyoda-ku, Tokyo 100-8965; tel. (3) 3593-3111; fax (3) 3593-5388; internet www.nipponkoa.co.jp; f. 1892; fmrly The Nippon Fire and Marine Insurance Co Ltd before merging with The Koa Fire and Marine Insurance Co Ltd; Pres. and CEO KEN MATSUZAWA.

The Nissan Fire and Marine Insurance Co Ltd: 2-9-5, Kita-Aoyama, Minato-ku, Tokyo 107-8654; tel. (3) 3746-6516; fax (3) 3470-1308; e-mail webmas@nissan-ins.co.jp; internet www .nissan-ins.co.jp; f. 1911; Chair. FUMIYA KAWATE; Pres. RYUTARO SATO.

Nissay General Insurance Co Ltd: Shinjuku NS Bldg, 25th Floor, 2-4-1, Nishi-Shinjuku, Shinjuku-ku, Tokyo 163-0888; tel. (3) 5325-7932; fax (3) 5325-8149; f. 1996; Pres. TADAO NISHIOKA.

The Nisshin Fire and Marine Insurance Co Ltd: 2-3 Kanda Surugadai, Chiyoda-ku, Tokyo 100-8329; tel. (3) 5282-5534; fax (3) 5282-5582; e-mail nisshin@mb.infoweb.ne.jp; internet www .nisshinfire.co.jp; f. 1908; Pres. MICHIO NODA.

Saison Automobile and Fire Insurance Co Ltd: Sunshine 60 Bldg, 3-1-1, Higashi Ikebukuro, Toshima-ku, Tokyo 170-6068; tel. (3) 3988-2572; fax (3) 3980-7367; internet www.ins-saison.co.jp; f. 1982; Pres. TOMONORI KANAI.

Secom General Insurance Co Ltd: 2-6-2, Hirakawa-cho, Chiyoda-ku, Tokyo 103-8645; tel. (3) 5216-6129; fax (3) 5216-6149; internet www.secom-sonpo.co.jp; Pres. SEIJI YAMANAKA.

Sony Assurance Inc.: Aromia Square 11/F, 5-37-1, Kamata, Ota-ku, Tokyo 144-8721; tel. (3) 5744-0300; fax (3) 5744-0480; internet www.sonysonpo.co.jp; f. 1999; Pres. SHINIEH YAMAMOTO.

The Sumi-Sei General Insurance Co Ltd: Sumitomo Life Yot-suya Bldg, 8-2, Honshio-cho, Shinjuku-ku, Tokyo 160-0003; tel. (3) 5360-6229; fax (3) 5360-6991; f. 1996; Chair. HIDEO NISHIMOTO; Pres. HIDEKI ISHII.

The Sumitomo Marine and Fire Insurance Co Ltd: 2-27-2, Shinkawa, Chuo-ku, Tokyo 104-8252; tel. (3) 3297-6663; fax (3) 3297-6882; internet www.sumitomomarine.co.jp; f. 1944; Chair. TAKASHI ONODA; Pres. HIROYUKI UEMURA.

The Taisei Fire and Marine Insurance Co Ltd: 4-2-1, Kudan-Kita, Chiyoda-ku, Tokyo 102-0073; tel. (3) 3222-3096; fax (3) 3234-4073; e-mail saiho@taiseikasai.co.jp; internet www.taiseikasai.co.jp; f. 1950; Pres. ICHIRO OZAWA.

Taiyo Fire and Marine Insurance Co Ltd: 7-7, Niban-cho, Chiyoda-ku, Tokyo 102-0084; tel. (3) 5226-3117; fax (3) 5226-3133; f. 1951; Chair. YUJI YAMASHITA; Pres. TSUNAIE KANIE.

The Toa Reinsurance Co Ltd: 3-6, Kanda Surugadai, Chiyoda-ku, Tokyo 101-8703; tel. (3) 3253-3177; fax (3) 3253-5298; f. 1940; Dir TAKAYA IMASHIMIZU.

The Tokio Marine and Fire Insurance Co Ltd (Tokio Kaijo): 1-2-1, Marunouchi, Chiyoda-ku, Tokyo 100-8050; tel. (3) 3285-1900; fax (3) 5223-3040; internet www.tokiomarine.co.jp; f. 1879; Chair. SHUNJI KONO; Pres. KOUKEI HIGUCHI.

The Yasuda Fire and Marine Insurance Co Ltd: 1-26-1, Nishi-Shinjuku, Shinjuku-ku, Tokyo 160-8338; tel. (3) 3349-3111; fax (3) 5381-7406; internet www.yasuda.co.jp; f. 1887; Chair. KOICHI ARIYOSHI; Pres. HIROSHI HIRANO.

The Yasuda General Insurance Co Ltd: Shinjuku MAYNDS Tower, 29th Floor, 2-1-1, Yoyogi, Shibuya-ku, Tokyo 151-0053; tel.

(3) 5352-8129; fax (3) 5352-8213; e-mail uwdept@mx7.mesh.ne.jp; f. 1996; Chair. Shigeo Fujino; Pres. Ieji Yoshioka.

The Post Office also operates life insurance and annuity plans.

Insurance Associations

Japan Trade and Investment Insurance Organization (Boeki Hoken Kiko): 6th Floor, 2-8-6, Nishi-Shinjuku, Minato-ku, Tokyo 105-0003; tel. (3) 3580-0321; internet www.jtio.or.jp; Pres. Yukio Otsu.

The Life Insurance Association of Japan (Seimei Hoken Kyokai): New Kokusai Bldg, 3-4-1, Marunouchi, Chiyoda-ku, Tokyo 100-0005; tel. (3) 3286-2652; fax (3) 3286-2630; internet www.seiho.or.jp; f. 1908; 42 mem. cos; Chair. Shinichi Yokoyama; Senior Man. Dir Shigeru Suwa.

The Marine and Fire Insurance Association of Japan Inc (Nihon Songai Hoken Kyokai): Non-Life Insurance Bldg, 2-9, Kanda Awaji-cho, Chiyoda-ku, Tokyo 101-8335; tel. (3) 3255-1437; fax (3) 3255-1234; e-mail kokusai@sonpo.or.jp; internet www.sonpo.or.jp; f. 1946; 25 mems; (Dec. 2002); Chair. Kunio Ishihara; Exec. Dir Eiji Nishiura.

Non-Life Insurance Rating Organization of Japan: 1-9, Kanda-nishikicho, Chiyoda-ku, Tokyo 101-0054; tel. (3) 3233-4762; fax (3) 3295–9301; e-mail service@grp.nliro.or.jp; internet www.nliro.or.jp; f. 1964; 44 mems (Dec. 2002); Chair. Akio Morishima; Senior Exec. Dir. Masahiro Ishii.

Trade and Industry

CHAMBERS OF COMMERCE AND INDUSTRY

The Japan Chamber of Commerce and Industry (Nippon Shoko Kaigi-sho): 3-2-2, Marunouchi, Chiyoda-ku, Tokyo 100-0005; tel. (3) 3283-7851; fax (3) 3216-6497; e-mail info@jcci.or.jp; internet www.jcci.or.jp/home-e; f. 1922; the cen. org. of all chambers of commerce and industry in Japan; mems 521 local chambers of commerce and industry; Chair. Kosaku Inaba; Pres. Shoichi Tanimura.

Principal chambers include:

Kobe Chamber of Commerce and Industry: 6-1, Minatojima-nakamachi, Chuo-ku, Kobe 650-8543; tel. (78) 303-5806; fax (78) 306-2348; e-mail info@kcci.hyogo-iic.ne.jp; f. 1878; 12,700 mems; Chair. Hiroshi Ohba; Pres. Hiroshi Miyamichi.

Kyoto Chamber of Commerce and Industry: 240, Shoshoi-cho, Ebisugawa-agaru, Karasumadori, Nakakyo-ku, Kyoto 604-0862; tel. (75) 212-6450; fax (75) 251-0743; e-mail kyoto@kyo.or.jp; f. 1882; 13,008 mems; Chair. Kazuo Inamori; Pres. Osamu Kobori.

Nagoya Chamber of Commerce and Industry: 2-10-19, Sakae, Naka-ku, Nagoya, Aichi 460-8422; tel. (52) 223-5722; fax (52) 232-5751; f. 1881; 20,622 mems; Chair. Seitaro Taniguchi; Pres. Yoshiki Kobayashi.

Naha Chamber of Commerce and Industry: 2-2-10, Kume Naha, Okinawa; tel. (98) 868-3758; fax (98) 866-9834; e-mail cci-naha@cosmos.ne.jp; f. 1927; 4,874 mems; Chair. Akira Sakima; Pres. Kosei Yonemura.

Osaka Chamber of Commerce and Industry: 2-8, Hommachi-bashi, Chuo-ku, Osaka 540-0029; tel. (6) 6944-6400; fax (6) 6944-6248; e-mail intl@osaka.cci.or.jp; internet www.osaka.cci.or.jp; f. 1878; 35,069 mems; Chair. Wa Tashiro; Pres. Takao Ohno.

Tokyo Chamber of Commerce and Industry: 3-2-2, Marunouchi, Chiyoda-ku, Tokyo 100-0005; tel. (3) 3283-7756; fax (3) 3216-6497; e-mail webmaster@tokyo-cci.or.jp; f. 1878; 118,642 mems; Chair. Kosaku Inaba; Pres. Shoichi Tanimura.

Yokohama Chamber of Commerce and Industry: Sangyo Boueki Center Bldg, 8th Floor, Yamashita-cho, Naka-ku, Yokohama 231-8524; tel. (45) 671-7400; fax (45) 671-7410; e-mail info@yokohama-cci.or.jp; f. 1880; 14,965 mems; Chair. Masayoshi Takanashi; Pres. Namio Oba.

INDUSTRIAL AND TRADE ASSOCATIONS

General

The Association for the Promotion of International Trade, Japan (JAPIT): 1-26-5, Toranomon, Minato-ku, Tokyo; tel. (3) 3506-8261; fax (3) 3506-8260; f. 1954 to promote trade with the People's Repub. of China; 700 mems; Chair. Yoshio Nakata; Pres. Yoshio Sakurauchi.

Industry Club of Japan: 1-4-6, Marunouchi, Chiyoda-ku, Tokyo; tel. (3) 3281-1711; f. 1917 to develop closer relations between industrialists at home and abroad and promote expansion of Japanese

business activities; c. 1,600 mems; Pres. Gaishi Hiraiwa; Exec. Dir Kouichirou Shinno.

Japan Commercial Arbitration Association: Taishoseimei Hibiya Bldg, 1-9-1, Yurakucho, Chiyoda-ku, Tokyo 100-1006; tel. (3) 3287-3061; fax (3) 3287-3064; e-mail info@jcaa.or.jp; internet www.jcaa.or.jp; f. 1950; 1,012 mems; provides facilities for mediation, conciliation and arbitration in international trade disputes; Pres. Nobuo Yamaguchi.

Japan External Trade Organization (JETRO): 2-2-5, Toranomon, Minato-ku, Tokyo 105-8466; tel. (3) 3582-5511; fax (3) 3582-5662; e-mail seh@jetro.go.jp; internet www.jetro.go.jp; f. 1958; information for international trade, investment, import promotion, exhibitions of foreign products; Chair. and CEO Osamu Watanabe; Pres. Hiroshi Tsukamoto.

Japan Federation of Smaller Enterprise Organizations (JFSEO) (Nippon Chusokigyo Dantai Renmei): 2-8-4, Nihombashi, Kayaba-cho, Chuo-ku, Tokyo 103-0025; tel. (3) 3669-6862; f. 1948; 18 mems and c. 1,000 co-operative socs; Pres. Masataka Toyoda; Chair. of Int. Affairs Seiichi Ono.

Japan General Merchandise Exporters' Association: 2-4-1, Hamamatsu-cho, Minato-ku, Tokyo; tel. (3) 3435-3471; fax (3) 3434-6739; f. 1953; 40 mems; Pres. Tadayoshi Nakazawa.

Japan Productivity Center for Socio-Economic Development (JPC-SED) (Shakai Keizai Seisansei Honbu): 3-1-1, Shibuya, Shibuya-ku, Tokyo 150-8307; tel. (3) 3409-1112; fax (3) 3409-1986; f. 1994 following merger between Japan Productivity Center and Social Economic Congress of Japan; 10,000 mems; concerned with management problems and research into productivity; Chair. Sugiichiro Watari; (acting); Pres. Yasuo Sawama.

Keizai Doyukai (Japan Association of Corporate Executives): Palace Bldg, 8th Floor, 1-1-1, Marunouchi, Chiyoda-ku, Tokyo 100-0005; tel. (3) 3211-1271; fax (3) 3212-3774; e-mail contact@doyukai.or.jp; internet www.doyukai.or.jp; f. 1946; mems: c. 1,400; corporate executives concerned with national and international economic and social policies; Chair. Yotaro Kobayashi.

Nihon Boeki-Kai (Japan Foreign Trade Council, Inc): World Trade Center Bldg, 6th Floor, 2-4-1, Hamamatsu-cho, Minato-ku, Tokyo 105-6106; tel. (3) 3435-5952; fax (3) 3435-5969; e-mail mail@jftc.or.jp; internet www.jftc.or.jp; f. 1947; 192 mems; Chair. Kenji Miyahara; Exec. Man. Dir Keisuke Takanashi; Man. Dir Hisao Ikegami.

Chemicals

Federation of Pharmaceutical Manufacturers' Associations of Japan: Tokyo Yakugyo Bldg, 2-1-5, Nihombashi Honcho, Chuo-ku, Tokyo 103-0023; tel. (3) 3270-0581; fax (3) 3241-2090; Pres. Tadashi Suzuki.

Japan Chemical Industry Association: Tokyo Club Bldg, 3-2-6, Kasumigaseki, Chiyoda-ku, Tokyo 100-0013; tel. (3) 3580-0751; fax (3) 3580-0764; internet www.nikkakyo.org; f. 1948; 266 mems; Pres. Akio Kosai.

Japan Cosmetic Industry Association: Hatsumei Bldg, 2-9-14, Toranomon, Minato-ku, Tokyo 105-0001; tel. (3) 3502-0576; fax (3) 3502-0829; f. 1959; 687 mem. cos; Chair. Reijiro Kobayashi.

Japan Gas Association: 1-15-12, Toranomon, Minato-ku, Tokyo 105-0001; tel. (3) 3502-0116; fax (3) 3502-3676; f. 1947; Chair. Shinichiro Ryoki; Vice-Chair. and Sr Man. Dir Koshiro Goda.

Japan Perfumery and Flavouring Association: Saeki No. 3 Bldg, 3rd Floor, 37 Kandakon-cho, Chiyoda-ku, Tokyo 101-0035; tel. and fax (3) 3526-7855; f. 1947; Chair. Tokajiro Hasegawa.

Photo-Sensitized Materials Manufacturers' Association: JCII Bldg, 25, Ichiban-cho, Chiyoda-ku, Tokyo 102-0082; tel. (3) 5276-3561; fax (3) 5276-3563; f. 1948; Pres. Masayuki Muneyuki.

Fishing and Pearl Cultivation

Japan Fisheries Association (Dainippon Suisankai): Sankaido Bldg, 1-9-13, Akasaka, Minato-ku, Tokyo 107-0052; tel. (3) 3585-6683; fax (3) 3582-2337; internet www.suisankai.or.jp; Pres. Hiroya Sano.

Japan Pearl Export and Processing Co-operative Association: 3-7, Kyobashi, Chuo-ko, Tokyo; f. 1951; 130 mems.

Japan Pearl Exporters' Association: 122, Higashi-machi, Chuo-ku, Kobe; tel. (78) 331-4031; fax (78) 331-4345; e-mail jpeakobe@lime.ocn.ne.jp; internet www.japan-pearl.com; f. 1954; 56 mems; Pres. Hideo Kanai.

Paper and Printing

Japan Federation of Printing Industries: 1-16-8, Shintomi, Chuo-ku, Tokyo 104; tel. (3) 3553-6051; fax (3) 3553-6079; Pres. Hiromichi Fujita.

Japan Paper Association: Kami Parupu Bldg, 3-9-11, Ginza, Chuo-ku, Tokyo 104-8139; tel. (3) 3248-4801; fax (3) 3248-4826; internet www.jpa.gr.jp; f. 1946; 54 mems; Chair. MASAO KOBAYASHI; Pres. KIYOSHI SAKAI.

Japan Paper Exporters' Association: Kami Parupu Bldg, 3-9-11, Ginza, Chuo-ku, Tokyo 104-8139; tel. (3) 3248-4831; fax (3) 3248-4834; e-mail japex@green.an.egg.or.jp; f. 1952; 37 mems; Chair. KENTARO NAGAOKA.

Japan Paper Importers' Association: Kami Parupu Bldg, 3-9-11, Ginza, Chuo-ku, Tokyo 104-8139; tel. (3) 3248-4832; fax (3) 3248-4834; e-mail japim@yacht.ocn.ne.jp; f. 1981; 27 mems; Chair. NOBUO KATSUMATA.

Japan Paper Products Manufacturers' Association: 4-2-6, Kotobuki, Taito-ku, Tokyo; tel. (3) 3543-2411; f. 1949; Exec. Dir KIYOSHI SATOH.

Mining and Petroleum

Asbestos Cement Products Association: Takahashi Bldg, 7-10-8, Ginza, Chuo-ku, Tokyo; tel. (3) 3571-1359; f. 1937; Chair. KOSHIRO SHIMIZU.

Japan Cement Association: Hattori Bldg, 1-10-3, Kyobashi, Chuo-ku, Tokyo 104-0031; tel. (3) 3561-8632; fax (3) 3567-8570; f. 1948; 20 mem. cos; Chair. KAZUTSUGU HIRAGA; Exec. Man. Dir HIROFUMI YAMASHITA.

Japan Coal Association: Hibiya Park Bldg, 1-8-1, Yuraku-cho, Chiyoda-ku, Tokyo 100; tel. (3) 3271-3481; fax (3) 3214-0585; Chair. TADASHI HARADA.

Japan Mining Industry Association: Shuwa Toranomon Bldg, No. 3, 1-21-8 Toranomon, Minato-ku, Tokyo 105-0001; tel. (3) 3502-7451; fax (3) 3591-9841; f. 1948; 60 mem. cos; Chair. AKIRA NISHIKAWA; Pres. A. SHINOZAKI; Dir-Gen. H. HIYAMA.

Japan Petrochemical Industry Association: 2nd Floor, 2-1-1, Uchisaiwai-cho, Chiyoda-ku, Tokyo 100-0011; tel. (3) 3501-2151; internet www.jpca.or.jp; Chair. MITSUO OHASHI.

Japan Petroleum Development Association: Keidanren Bldg, 1-9-4, Otemachi, Chiyoda-ku, Tokyo 100; tel. (3) 3279-5841; fax (3) 3279-5844; f. 1961; Chair. TAMOTSU SHOYA.

Metals

Japan Aluminium Association (JAA): Tsukamoto-Sozan Bldg, 4-2-15, Ginza, Chuo-ku, Tokyo 104-0061; tel. (3) 3538-0221; fax (3) 3538-0233; f. 1999 by merger of Japan Aluminium Federation and Japan Light Metal Association; Chair. SHIGESATO SATO.

Japan Brass Makers' Association: 1-12-22, Tsukiji, Chuo-ku, Tokyo 104-0045; tel. (3) 3542-6551; fax (3) 3542-6556; e-mail jbmajwcc@copper-brass.gr.jp; internet www.copper-brass.gr.jp; f. 1948; 62 mems; Pres. S. SATO; Man. Dir J. HATANO.

Japan Iron and Steel Exporters' Association: Tekko Kaikan Bldg, 3-2-10, Nihombashi Kayaba-cho, Chuo-ku, Tokyo 103-0025; tel. (3) 3669-4818; fax (3) 3661-0798; f. 1953; mems 17 mfrs, 27 dealers; Chair. AKIRA CHIHAYA.

The Japan Iron and Steel Federation: Keidanren Bldg, 1-9-4, Otemachi, Chiyoda-ku, Tokyo 100-0004; tel. (3) 3279-3612; fax (3) 3245-0144; internet www.jisf.or.jp; f. 1948; Chair. AKIRA CHIHAYA.

Japan Stainless Steel Association: Tekko Bldg, 3-2-10, Nihombashi Kayaba-cho, Chuo-ku, Tokyo 103; tel. (3) 3669-4431; fax (3) 3669-4431; e-mail yabe@jssa.gr.jp; internet www.jssa.gr.jp; Pres. MIKIO KATOH; Exec. Dir TAKEO YABE.

The Kozai Club: Tekko Bldg, 3-2-10, Nihombashi Kayaba-cho, Chuo-ku, Tokyo 103-0025; tel. (3) 3669-4815; fax (3) 3667-0245; f. 1947; mems 39 mfrs, 69 dealers; Chair. AKIRA CHIHAYA.

Steel Castings and Forgings Association of Japan (JSCFA): Uchikanda DNK Bldg, 2-15-2, Uchikanda, Chiyoda-ku, Tokyo 101-0047; tel. (3) 3255-3961; fax (3) 3255-3965; e-mail jscfa@aqua.famille.ne.jp; f. 1972; mems 48 cos, 54 plants; Exec. Dir SADAO HARA.

Machinery and Precision Equipment

Electronic Industries Association of Japan: 3-2-2, Marunouchi, Chiyoda-ku, Tokyo 100-0005; tel. (3) 3213-5861; fax (3) 3213-5863; e-mail pao@eiaj.or.jp; internet www.eiaj.or.jp; f. 1948; 540 mems; Chair. FUMIO SATO.

Japan Camera Industry Association: JCII Bldg, 25, Ichibancho, Chiyoda-ku, Tokyo 102-0082; tel. (3) 5276-3891; fax (3) 5276-3893; internet www.photo-jcia.gr.jp; f. 1954; Pres. MASATOSHI KISHIMOTO.

Japan Clock and Watch Association: Kudan Sky Bldg, 1-12-11, Kudan-kita, Chiyoda-ku, Tokyo 102-0073; tel. (3) 5276-3411; fax (3) 5276-3414; internet www.jcwa.or.jp; Chair. HIROSHI HARUTA.

Japan Electric Association: 1-7-1, Yuraku-cho, Chiyoda-ku, Tokyo 100-0006; tel. (3) 3216-0551; fax (3) 3214-6005; f. 1921; 4,610 mems; Pres. TATSUO KAWAI.

Japan Electric Measuring Instruments Manufacturers' Association (JEMIMA): 1-9-10, Toranomon, Minato-ku, Tokyo 105-0001; tel. (3) 3502-0601; fax (3) 3502-0600; e-mail watanabe@jemima.or.jp; internet www.jemima.or.jp; 125 mems; Sec. Gen. KATSUHIKO WATANABE.

Japan Electrical Manufacturers' Association: 2-4-15, Nagata-cho, Chiyoda-ku, Tokyo 100-0014; tel. (3) 3581-4841; fax (3) 3593-3198; internet www.jema-net.or.jp; f. 1948; 245 mems; Chair. TAIZO NISHIMURO.

Japan Energy Association: Houwa Mita Tsunasaka Bldg, 2-7-7, Mita, Minato-ku, Tokyo 108-0073; tel. (3) 3451-1651; fax (3) 3451-1360; e-mail common@jea-wec.or.jp; internet www.jea-wec.or.jp; f. 1950; 142 mems; Chair. SHIGE-ETSU MIYAHARA; Exec. Dir HAJIME MURATA.

Japan Machine Tool Builders' Association: Kikai Shinko Bldg, 3-5-8, Shiba Koen, Minato-ku, Tokyo 105-0011; tel. (3) 3434-3961; fax (3) 3434-3763; f. 1951; 112 mems; Chair. TOYO KATO; Exec. Dir S. ABE.

Japan Machinery Center for Trade and Investment (JMC): Kikai Shinko Bldg, 3-5-8, Shiba Koen, Minato-ku, Tokyo 105-0011; tel. (3) 3431-9507; fax (3) 3436-6455; Pres. ISAO YONEKURA.

The Japan Machinery Federation: Kikai Shinko Bldg, 3-5-8, Shiba Koen, Minato-ku, Tokyo 105-0011; tel. (3) 3434-5381; fax (3) 3434-2666; f. 1952; Pres. SHOICHI SADA; Exec. Vice-Pres. SHINICHI NAKANISHI.

Japan Machinery Importers' Association: Koyo Bldg, 8th Floor, 1-2-11, Toranomon, Minato-ku, Tokyo 105-0001; tel. (3) 3503-9736; fax (3) 3503-9779; f. 1957; 94 mems; Pres. ISAO YONEKURA.

Japan Microscope Manufacturers' Association: c/o Olympus Optical Co Ltd, 2-43-2, Hatagaya, Shibuya-ku, Tokyo 151-0072; tel. (3) 3377-2139; fax (3) 3377-2139; e-mail jmma@olympus.co.jp; f. 1954; 31 mems; Chair. T. SHIMOYAMA.

Japan Motion Picture Equipment Industrial Association: Kikai Shinko Bldg, 3-5-8, Shiba Koen, Minato-ku, Tokyo 105; tel. (3) 3434-3911; fax (3) 3434-3912; Pres. MASAO SHIKATA; Gen. Sec. TERUHIRO KATO.

Japan Optical Industry Association: Kikai Shinko Bldg, 3-5-8, Shiba Koen, Minato-ku, Tokyo 105-0011; tel. (3) 3431-7073; f. 1946; 200 mems; Chair. SHIGEO ONO; Exec. Dir M. SUZUKI.

The Japan Society of Industrial Machinery Manufacturers: Kikai Shinko Bldg, 3-5-8, Shiba Koen, Minato-ku, Tokyo 105-0011; tel. (3) 3434-6821; fax (3) 3434-4767; e-mail obd@jsim.or.jp; internet www.jsim.or.jp; f. 1948; 213 mems; Exec. Man. Dir KOJI FUJISAKI; Pres. KENTARO AIKAWA.

Japan Textile Machinery Association: Kikai Shinko Bldg, Room 310, 3-5-8, Shiba Koen, Minato-ku, Tokyo 105; tel. (3) 3434-3821; fax (3) 3434-3043; f. 1951; Pres. JUNICHI MURATA.

Textiles

Central Raw Silk Association of Japan: 1-9-4, Yuraku-cho, Chiyoda-ku, Tokyo; tel. (3) 3214-5777; fax (3) 3214-5778.

Japan Chemical Fibers Association: Seni Kaikan, 3-1-11, Nihombashi-Honcho, Chuo-ku, Tokyo 103-0023; tel. (3) 3241-2311; fax (3) 3246-0823; internet www.fcc.co.jp/JCFA; f. 1948; 41 mems, 9 assoc. mems; Pres. KATSUHIKO HIRAI; Dir-Gen. KUNIO YAGI.

Japan Cotton and Staple Fibre Weavers' Association: 1-8-7, Nishi-Azabu, Minato-ku, Tokyo; tel. (3) 3403-9671.

Japan Silk Spinners' Association: f. 1948; 95 mem. firms; Chair. ICHIJI OHTANI.

Japan Spinners' Association: Mengyo Kaikan Bldg, 2-5-8, Bingo-machi, Chuo-ku, Osaka 541-0051; tel. (6) 6231-8431; fax (6) 6229-1590; e-mail spinas@cotton.or.jp; internet www.jsa-jp.org/; f. 1948; Exec. Dir HARUTA MUTO.

Transport Machinery

Japan Association of Rolling Stock Industries: Awajicho Suny Bldg, 1-2, Kanda-Sudacho, Chiyoda-ku, Tokyo 101-0041; tel. (3) 3257-1901.

Japan Auto Parts Industries Association: 1-16-15, Takanawa, Minato-ku, Tokyo 108-0074; tel. (3) 3445-4211; fax (3) 3447-5372; e-mail japiaint@green.am.egg.or.jp; f. 1948; 530 mem. firms; Chair. TSUNEO ISHIMARU; Exec. Dir K. SHIBASAKI.

Japan Automobile Manufacturers Association, Inc (JAMA): Otemachi Bldg, 1-6-1, Otemachi, Chiyoda-ku, Tokyo 100-0004; tel. (3) 5219-6660; fax (3) 3287-2073; e-mail kaigai_tky@mta.jama.or.jp;

internet www.jama.or.jp; f. 1967; 14 mem. firms; Chair. YOSHIHIDE MUNEKUNI; Pres. TAKAO SUZUKI.

Japan Bicycle Manufacturers' Association: 1-9-3, Akasaka, Minato-ku, Tokyo 107; tel. (3) 3583-3123; fax (3) 3589-3125; f. 1955.

Japan Ship Exporters' Association: Nippon-Zaidan Bldg, 1-15-16, Toranomon, Minato-ku, Tokyo 105-0001; tel. (3) 3502-2094; fax (3) 3508-2058; e-mail postmaster@jsea.or.jp; 38 mems; Exec. Man. Dir YUICHI WATANABE.

Japanese Marine Equipment Association: Kaiyo Senpaku Bldg, 15-16, Toranomon, Minato-ku, Tokyo 105-0001; tel. (3) 3502-2041; fax (3) 3591-2206; e-mail info@jsmea.or.jp; internet www.jsmea.or.jp; f. 1956; 240 mems; Pres. TADAO YAMAOKA.

Japanese Shipowners' Association: Kaiun Bldg, 2-6-4, Hirakawa-cho, Chiyoda-ku, Tokyo 102-0093; tel. (3) 3264-7171; fax (3) 3262-4760; Pres. KENTARO KAWAMURA.

Shipbuilders' Association of Japan: 1-15-16, Toranomon, Minato-ku, Tokyo 105-0001; tel. (3) 3502-2010; fax (3) 3502-2816; internet www.sajn.or.jp; f. 1947; 21 mems; Chair. TOSHIMICHI OKANO.

Society of Japanese Aerospace Companies Inc (SJAC): Toshin-Tameike Bldg, 2nd Floor, 1-1-14, Akasaka, Minato-ku, Tokyo 107-0052; tel. (3) 3585-0511; fax (3) 3585-0541; e-mail miwa-shuichi@sjac.or.jp; internet www.sjac.or.jp; f. 1952; reorg. 1974; 117 mems, 41 assoc. mems; Chair. TOSHIFUMI TAKEI; Pres. TAKATOSHI HOSOYA.

Miscellaneous

Communications Industry Association of Japan (CIA-J): Sankei Bldg, 1-7-2, Otemachi, Chiyoda-ku, Tokyo 100-0004; tel. (3) 3231-3005; fax (3) 3231-3110; e-mail admin@ciaj.or.jp; internet www.ciaj.or.jp; f. 1948; non-profit org. of telecommunications equipment mfrs; 236 mems; Chair. TADASHI SEKIZAWA; Pres. YUTAKA HAYASHI.

Japan Canners' Association: Yurakucho Denki Bldg, 1-7-1, Yuraku-cho, Chiyoda-ku, Tokyo 100-0006; tel. (3) 3213-4751; fax (3) 3211-1430; Pres. KEINOSUKE HISAI.

Japan Hardwood Exporters' Association: Matsuda Bldg, 1-9-1, Ironai, Otaru, Hokkaido 047; tel. (134) 23-8411; fax (134) 22-7150; 7 mems.

Japan Lumber Importers' Association: Yushi Kogyo Bldg, 3-13-11, Nihombashi, Chuo-ku, Tokyo 103; tel. (3) 3271-0926; fax (3) 3271-0928; f. 1950; 130 mems; Pres. SHOICHI TANAKA.

Japan Plastics Industry Federation: Kaseihin-Kaikan, 5-8-17, Roppongi, Minato-ku, Tokyo 106-0032; tel. (3) 3586-9761; fax (3) 3586-9760; internet www.jpif.gr.jp; Chair. AKIO SATO.

Japan Plywood Manufacturers' Association: Meisan Bldg, 1-18-17, Nishi-Shimbashi, Minato-ku, Tokyo 105; tel. (3) 3591-9246; fax (3) 3591-9240; f. 1965; 92 mems; Pres. HIROSHI INOUE.

Japan Pottery Manufacturers' Federation: Toto Bldg, 1-1-28, Toranomon, Minato-ku, Tokyo; tel. (3) 3503-6761.

The Japan Rubber Manufacturers Association: Tobu Bldg, 1-5-26, Moto Akasaka, Minato-ku, Tokyo 107-0051; tel. (3) 3408-7101; fax (3) 3408-7106; f. 1950; 125 mems; Pres. YASUO TOMINAGA.

Japan Spirits and Liquors Makers' Association: Koura Dai-ichi Bldg, 7th Floor, 1-1-6, Nihonbashi-Kayaba-cho, Chuo-ku, Tokyo 103; tel. (3) 3668-4621.

Japan Sugar Import and Export Council: Oshima Bldg 1–3, Nihonbashi Koamicho, Chuo-ku, Tokyo; tel. (3) 3571-2362; fax (3) 3571-2363; 16 mems.

Japan Sugar Refiners' Association: 5-7, Sanban-cho, Chiyoda-ku, Tokyo 102; tel. (3) 3288-1151; fax (3) 3288-3399; f. 1949; 17 mems; Sr Man. Dir KATSUYUKI SUZUKI.

Japan Tea Exporters' Association: 17, Kitaban-cho, Shizuoka, Shizuoka Prefecture 420-0005; tel. (54) 271-3428; fax (54) 271-2177; e-mail japantea2000@ybb.ne.jp; 33 mems.

Japan Toy Association: 4-22-4, Higashi-Komagata, Sumida-ku, Tokyo 130; tel. (3) 3829-2513; fax (3) 3829-2549; Chair. MAKOTO YAMASHINA.

Motion Picture Producers' Association of Japan, Inc: Tokyu Ginza Bldg, 2-15-2, Ginza, Chuo-ku, Tokyo 104-0061; tel. (3) 3547-1800; fax (3) 3547-0909; e-mail eiren@mc.neweb.ne.jp; internet www2.neweb.ne.jp/wd/eiren; Pres. ISAO MATSUOKA.

EMPLOYERS' ORGANIZATION

Japan Business Federation (JBF) (Keidanren Kaikan): 1-9-4, Otemachi, Chiyoda-ku, Tokyo 100-8188; tel. (3) 5204-1920; fax (3) 5204-1943; e-mail intlab@keidanren.or.jp; internet www.keidanren.or.jp; f. 2002 by merger of Keidanren (f. 1946) and Nikkeiren (f. 1948); 1,540 mem. asscns; Chair. HIROSHI OKUDA; Dir-Gen. RYUKOH WADA.

UTILITIES

Electricity

Chubu Electric Power Co Inc: 1, Higashi-Shincho, Higashi-ku, Nagoya 461-8680; tel. (52) 951-8211; fax (52) 962-4624; internet www.chuden.co.jp; Chair. KOHEI ABE; Pres. HIROJI OTA.

Chugoku Electric Power Co Inc: 4-33, Komachi, Naka-ku, Hiroshima 730-8701; tel. (82) 241-0211; fax (82) 523-6185; e-mail angel@inet.energia.co.jp; internet www.energia.co.jp; f. 1951; Chair. SHITOMI TAKASU; Pres. SHIGEO SHIRAKURA.

Hokkaido Electric Power Co Inc: internet www.hepco.co.jp; Chair. KAZUO TODA; Pres. SEIJI IZUMI.

Hokuriku Electric Power Co Inc: internet www.rikuden.co.jp.

Kansai Electric Power Co Inc: 3-3-22, Nakanoshima, Kita-ku, Osaka 530-8270; tel. (6) 6441-8821; fax (6) 6441-8598; e-mail postmaster@kepco.co.jp; internet www.kepco.co.jp; Chair. YOSHIHISA AKIYAMA; Pres. H. ISHIKAWA.

Kyushu Electric Power Co Inc: 2-1-82, Watanabe-dori, Chuo-ku, Fukuoka 810-8726; tel. (92) 726-1649; fax (92) 731-8719; internet www.kyuden.co.jp; Chair. MICHISADA KAMATA.

Shikoku Electric Power Co Inc: 2-5, Marunouchi, Takamatsu 760-8573; tel. (878) 21-5061; fax (878) 26-1250; e-mail postmaster@yonden.co.jp; internet www.yonden.co.jp; Chair. HIROSHI YAMAMOTO; Pres. KOZO KONDO.

Tohoku Electric Power Co Inc: 3-7-1, Ichiban-cho, Aoba-ku, Sendai 980; tel. (22) 225-2111; fax (22) 222-2881; e-mail webmaster@tohoku-epco.co.jp; internet www.tohoku-epco.co.jp; Chair. TERUYUKI AKEMA; Pres. TOSHIAKI YASHIMA.

Tokyo Electric Power Co Inc: 1-1-3, Uchisaiwai-cho, Chiyoda-ku, Tokyo 100; tel. (3) 3501-8111; fax (3) 3592-1795; internet www.tepco.co.jp; Chair. SHOH NASU; Pres. N. MINAMI.

Gas

Osaka Gas Co Ltd: e-mail intlstaff@osakagas.co.jp; internet www.osakagas.co.jp.

Toho Gas Co Ltd: 19-18, Sakurada-cho, Atsuta-ko, Nagoya 456; tel. (52) 871-3511; internet www.tohogas.co.jp; f. 1922; Chair. SUSUMU OGAWA; Pres. SADAHIKO SIMIZU.

Tokyo Gas Co Inc: 1-5-20, Kaigan, Minato-ku, Tokyo 105; tel. (3) 3433-2111; fax (3) 5472-5385; internet www.tokyo-gas.co.jp; f. 1885; Chair. HIROSHI WATANABE; Pres. H. UEHARA.

CO-OPERATIVE ORGANIZATION

Nikkenkyo (Council of Japan Construction Industry Employees' Unions): Moriyama Bldg, 1-31-16, Takadanobaba, Shinjuku-ku, Tokyo 169; tel. (3) 5285-3870; fax (3) 5285-3879; Pres. NOBORU SEKIGUCHI.

TRADE UNIONS

A feature of Japan's trade union movement is that the unions are usually based on single enterprises, embracing workers of different occupations in that enterprise. In June 1994 there were 32,581 unions; union membership stood at 12.5m. workers in 1996. In November 1989 the two largest confederations, SOHYO and RENGO, merged to form the Japan Trade Union Confederation (JTUC—RENGO).

Japanese Trade Union Confederation (JTUC–RENGO): 3-2-11, Kanda Surugadai, Chiyoda-ku, Tokyo 101-0062; tel. (3) 5295-0550; fax (3) 5295-0548; e-mail jtuc-kokusai@sv.rengo-net.or.jp; internet www.jtuc-rengo.or.jp; f. 1989; 7.5m. mems; Pres. KIYOSHI SASAMORI.

Principal Affiliated Unions

Ceramics Rengo (All-Japan Federation of Ceramics Industry Workers): 3-11, Heigocho, Mizuho-ku, Nagoya-shi, Aichi 467; tel. (52) 882-4562; fax (52) 882-9960; 30,083 mems; Pres. TSUNEYOSHI HAYAKAWA.

Chain Rokyo (Chain-store Labour Unions' Council): 3rd Floor, 2-29-8, Higashi-ikebukuro, Toshima-ku, Tokyo 170; tel. (3) 5951-1031; fax (3) 5951-1051; 40,015 mems; Pres. TOSHIFUMI HIRANO.

Denki Rengo (Japanese Electrical, Electronic & Information Union): Denkirengo Bldg, 1-10-3, Mita, Minato-ku, Tokyo 108-8326; tel. (3) 3455-6911; fax (3) 3452-5406; internet www.jeiu.or.jp; f. 1953; 688,436 mems; Pres. NOBUAKI KOGA.

Denryoku Soren (Federation of Electric Power Related Industry Workers' Unions of Japan): TDS Mita 7-13, 3rd Floor, Mita 2-Chome, Minato-ku, Tokyo 108-0073; tel. (3) 3454-0231; fax (3) 3798-1470; e-mail info@denryokusoren.or.jp; internet www.denryokusoren.or.jp; 255,278 mems; Pres. NORIO TSUMAKI.

Dokiro (Hokkaido Seasonal Workers' Union): Hokuro Bldg, Kita 4, Nishi 12, Chuo-ku, Sapporo, Hokkaido 060; tel. (11) 261-5775; fax (11) 272-2255; 19,063 mems; Pres. YOSHIZO ODAWARA.

Gomu Rengo (Japanese Rubber Workers' Union Confederation): 2-3-3, Mejiro, Toshima-ku, Tokyo 171; tel. (3) 3984-3343; fax (3) 3984-5862; 60,070 mems; Pres. YASUO FURUKAWA.

Hitetsu Rengo (Japanese Metal Mine Workers' Union): Gotanda Metalion Bldg, 5-21-15, Higashi-gotanda, Shinagawa-ku, Tokyo 141; tel. (3) 5420-1881; fax (3) 5420-1880; 23,500 mems; Pres. SHOUZOU HIMENO.

Insatsu Roren (Federation of Printing Information Media Workers' Unions): Yuai-kaikan, 7th Floor, 2-20-12, Shiba, Minato-ku, Tokyo 105-0014; tel. (3) 5442-0191; fax (3) 5442-0219; 22,303 mems; Pres. HIROFUMI NAKABAYASHI.

JA Rengo (All-Japan Agriculture Co-operative Staff Members' Union): 964-1, Toyotomicho-mikage, Himeji-shi, Hyogo 679-21; tel. and fax (792) 64-3618; 2,772 mems; Pres. YUTAKA OKADA.

Japan Federation of Service and Distributive Workers Unions: New State Manor Bldg, 3rd Floor, 2-23-1, Yoyogi, Shibuya-ku, Tokyo 151-0053; tel. (3) 3370-4121; fax (3) 3370-1640; internet www.jsd-union.org; 170,000 mems; Pres. MITSUO NAGUMO.

Jichi Roren (National Federation of Prefectural and Municipal Workers' Unions): 1-15-22, Oji-honcho, Kita-ku, Tokyo 114; tel. and fax (3) 3907-1584; 5,728 mems; Pres. NOBUO UENO.

Jichiro (All-Japan Prefectural and Municipal Workers' Union): Jichiro Bldg, 1, Rokubancho, Chiyoda-ku, Tokyo 102-0085; tel. (3) 3263-0263; fax (3) 5210-7422; internet www.jichiro.gr.jp; f. 1951; 1,004,000 mems; Pres. MORISHIGE GOTO.

Jidosha Soren (Confederation of Japan Automobile Workers' Unions): U-Life Center, 1-4-26, Kaigan, Minato-ku, Tokyo 105-8523; tel. (3) 3434-7641; fax (3) 3434-7428; internet www.jaw.or.jp; f. 1972; 728,000 mems; Pres. YUJI KATO.

Jiunro (Japan Automobile Drivers' Union): 2-3-12, Nakameguro, Meguro-ku, Tokyo 153; tel. (3) 3711-9387; fax (3) 3719-2624; 1,958 mems; Pres. SADAO KANEZUKA.

JR-Rengo (Japan Railway Trade Unions Confederation): TOKO Bldg, 9th Floor, 1-8-10, Nihonbashi-muromachi, Chuo-ku, Tokyo 103; tel. (3) 3270-4590; fax (3) 3270-4429; 78,418 mems; Pres. KAZUAKI KUZUNO.

JR Soren (Japan Confederation of Railway Workers' Unions): Meguro-satsuki Bldg, 3-2-13, Nishi-gotanda, Shinagawa-ku, Tokyo 141-0031; tel. (3) 3491-7191; fax (3) 3491-7192; internet www.jr-souren.com; 87,000 mems; Pres. YUJI ODA.

Jyoho Roren (Japan Federation of Telecommunications, Electronic Information and Allied Workers): Zendentsu-rodo Bldg, 3-6, Kanda Surugadai, Chiyoda-ku, Tokyo 101-0062; tel. (3) 3219-2231; fax (3) 3253-3268; 265,132 mems; Pres. KAZUO SASAMORI.

Kagaku League 21 (Japanese Federation of Chemistry Workers' Unions): Senbai Bldg, 5-26-30, Shiba, Minato-ku, Tokyo 108-8389; tel. (3) 3452-5591; fax (3) 3454-7464; internet www.jec-u.com; formed by merger of Goka Roren and Zenkoku Kagaku; 104,000 mems; Pres. KATUTOSHI KATO.

Kagaku Soren (Japanese Federation of Chemical Workers' Unions): Kyodo Bldg, 7th Floor, 2-4-10, Higashi-shimbashi, Minato-ku, Tokyo 105; tel. (3) 5401-2268; fax (3) 5401-2263; Pres. HIROKAZU IWASAKI.

Kaiin Kumiai (All-Japan Seamen's Union): 7-15-26, Roppongi, Minato-ku, Tokyo 106-0032; tel. (3) 5410-8330; fax (3) 5410-8336; internet www.jsu.or.jp; 35,000 mems; Pres. SAKAE IDEMOTO.

Kamipa Rengo (Japanese Federation of Pulp and Paper Workers' Unions): 2-12-4, Kita Aoyama, Minato-ku, Tokyo 107-0061; tel. (3) 3402-7656; fax (3) 3402-7659; 50,858 mems; Pres. TUNEO MUKAI.

Kensetsu Rengo (Japan Construction Trade Union Confederation): Yuai Bldg, 7th Floor, 2-20-12, Shiba, Minato-ku, Tokyo 105; tel. (3) 3454-0951; fax (3) 3453-0582; 13,199 mems; Pres. MASAYASU TERASAWA.

Kinzoku Kikai (National Metal and Machinery Workers' Unions of Japan): 6-2, Sakuraokacho, Shibuya-ku, Tokyo 150-0031; tel. (3) 3463-4231; fax (3) 3463-7391; f. 1989; 205,082 mems; Pres. MASAOKI KITAURA.

Kokko Soren (Japan General Federation of National Public Service Employees' Unions): 1-2-1, Kasumigaseki, Chiyoda-ku, Tokyo 100; tel. (3) 3508-4990; fax (3) 5512-7555; 40,370 mems; Pres. MARUYAMA KENZO.

Koku Domei (Japanese Confederation of Aviation Labour): Nikko-kiso Bldg, 2nd Floor, 1-6-3, Haneda-kuko, Ota-ku, Tokyo 144; tel. (3) 3747-7642; fax (3) 3747-7647; 16,310 mems; Pres. KATSUMI UTAGAWA.

Kokuzei Roso (Japanese Confederation of National Tax Unions): R154, Okurasho Bldg, 3-1-1, Kasumigaseki, Chiyoda-ku, Tokyo 100; tel. (3) 3581-2573; fax (3) 3581-3843; 40,128 mems; Pres. TATSUO SASAKI.

Kotsu Roren (Japan Federation of Transport Workers' Unions): Yuai Bldg, 3rd Floor, 2-20-12, Shiba, Minato-ku 105-0014; tel. (3) 3451-7243; fax (3) 3454-7393; 97,239 mems; Pres. SHIGEO MAKI.

Koun-Domei (Japanese Confederation of Port and Transport Workers' Unions): 5-10-2, Kamata, Ota-ku, Tokyo 144-0052; tel. (3) 3733-5285; fax (3) 3733-5280; f. 1987; 1,638 mems; Pres. SAKAE IDEMOTO.

Leisure Service Rengo (Japan Federation of Leisure Service Industries Workers' Unions): Zosen Bldg, 4th Floor, 3-5-6, Misaki-cho, Chiyoda-ku, Tokyo 101-0061; tel. (3) 3230-1724; fax (3) 3239-1553; 47,601 mems; Pres. HIROSHI SAWADA.

NHK Roren (Federation of All-NHK Labour Unions): NHK, 2-2-1, Jinnan, Shibuya-ku, Tokyo 150; tel. (3) 3485-6007; fax (3) 3469-9271; 12,526 mems; Pres. YASUZO SUDO.

Nichirinro (National Forest Workers' Union of Japan): 1-2-1, Kasumigaseki, Chiyoda-ku, Tokyo 100; tel. (3) 3580-8891; fax (3) 3580-1596; Pres. KOH IKEGAMI.

Nikkyoso (Japan Teachers' Union): Japan Education Hall, 2-6-2, Hitotsubashi, Chiyoda-ku, Tokyo 101-0003; tel. (3) 3265-2171; fax (3) 3230-0172; internet www.jtu-net.or.jp; f. 1947; 400,000 mems; Pres. NAGAKAZU SAKAKIBARA.

Rosai Roren (National Federation of Zenrosai Workers' Unions): 2-12-10, Yoyogi, Shibuya-ku, Tokyo 151; tel. (3) 3299-0161; fax (3) 3299-0126; 2,091 mems; Pres. TADASHI TAKACHI.

Seiho Roren (National Federation of Life Insurance Workers' Unions): Tanaka Bldg, 3-19-5, Yushima, Bunkyo-ku, Tokyo 113-0034; tel. (3) 3837-2031; fax (3) 3837-2037; 414,021 mems; Pres. YOHTARU KOHNO.

Seiroren (Labour Federation of Government Related Organizations): Hasaka Bldg, 4th-6th Floors, 1-10-3, Kanda-ogawacho, Chiyoda-ku, Tokyo 101; tel. (3) 5295-6360; fax (3) 5295-6362; Chair. MITSURU WATANABE.

Sekiyu Roren (Japan Confederation of Petroleum Industry Workers' Union): NKK Bldg, 7th Floor, 2-18-2, Nishi-shinmbashi, Minato-ku, Tokyo 105; tel. (3) 3578-1315; fax (3) 3578-3455; 28,807 mems; Pres. HIROSHI MOCHIMARU.

Sen'i Seikatsu Roren (Japan Federation of Textile Clothing Workers' Unions of Japan): Katakura Bldg, 3-1-2, Kyobashi, Chuo-ku, Tokyo 104; tel. (3) 3281-4806; fax (3) 3274-3165; 4,598 mems; Pres. KATSUYOSHI SAKAI.

Shigen Roren (Federation of Japanese Metal Resources Workers' Unions): Roppongi Azeria Bldg, 1-3-8, Nishi-azabu, Minato-ku, Tokyo 106; tel. (3) 3402-6666; fax (3) 3402-6667; Pres. MINORU TAKAHASHI.

Shin Unten (F10-Drivers' Craft Union): 4th Floor, 3-25-6, Negishi, Taito-ku, Tokyo 110; tel. (3) 5603-1015; fax (3) 5603-5351; 4,435 mems; Pres. SHOHEI SHINOZAKI.

Shinkagaku (National Organization of All Chemical Workers): MF Bldg, 2nd Floor, 2-3-3, Fujimi, Chiyoda-ku, Tokyo 102; tel. (3) 3239-2933; fax (3) 3239-2932; 8,400 mems; Pres. HISASHI YASUI.

Shinrin Roren (Japanese Federation of Forest and Wood Workers' Unions): 3-28-7, Otsuka, Bunkyo-ku, Tokyo 112; tel. (3) 3945-6385; fax (3) 3945-6477; 13,928 mems; Pres. ISAO SASAKI.

Shitetsu Soren (General Federation of Private Railway Workers' Unions): 4-3-5, Takanawa, Minato-ku, Tokyo 108-0074; tel. (3) 3473-0166; fax (3) 3447-3927; f. 1947; 160,000 mems; Pres. RYOICHI IKEMURA.

Shokuhin Rengo (Japan Federation of Foods and Tobacco Workers' Unions): Hiroo Office Bldg, 8th Floor, 1-3-18, Hiroo, Shibuya-ku, Tokyo 150; tel. (3) 3446-2082; fax (3) 3446-6779; f. 1991; 116,370 mems; Pres. SHIGERU MASUDA.

Shokuhin Rokyo (Food Industry Workers' Union Council—FIWUC): ST Bldg, 6th Floor, 4-9-4, Hatchobori, Chuo-ku, Tokyo 104; tel. (3) 3555-7671; fax (3) 3555-7760; Pres. TAROU FUJIE.

Sonpo Roren (Federation of Non-Life Insurance Workers' Unions of Japan): Kanda MS Bldg, 4th Floor, 27, Kanda-higashimatsushitacho, Chiyoda-ku, Tokyo 101; tel. (3) 5295-0071; fax (3) 5295-0073; Pres. KUNIO MATSUMOTO.

Tanro (Japan Coal Miners' Union): Hokkaido Rodosha Bldg, 2nd Floor, Kita-11, Nishi-4, Kita-ku, Sapporo-shi, Hokkaido 001; tel. (11) 717-0291; fax (11) 717-0295; 1,353 mems; Pres. KAZUO SAKUMA.

Tanshokukyo (Association of Japan Coal Mining Staff Unions): 2-30, Nishiminatomachi, Omuta-shi, Fukuoka 836; tel. (944) 52-3883; fax (944) 52-3853; Pres. KEIZO UMEKI.

Tekko Roren (Japan Federation of Steel Workers' Unions): I&S Riverside Bldg, 4th Floor, 1-23-4, Shinkawa, Chuo-ku, Tokyo 104-

0033; tel. (3) 3555-0401; fax (3) 3555-0407; internet www .tekko-roren.or.jp; 135,000 mems; Pres. TAKESHI OGINO.

Tokei Roso (Statistics Labour Union Management and Co-ordination Agency): 19-1, Somucho, Wakamatsucho, Shinjuku-ku, Tokyo 162; tel. (3) 3202-1111; fax (3) 3205-3850; Pres. TOSHIAKI MAGARA.

Toshiko (The All-Japan Municipal Transport Workers' Union): 3-1-35, Shibaura, Minato-ku, Tokyo 108; tel. (3) 3451-5221; fax (3) 3452-2977; 43,612 mems; Pres. SHUNICHI SUZUKI.

Ui Zensen (Japanese Federation of Textile, Chemical, Food, Commercial, Service and General Workers' Unions): 4-8-16, Kudanminami, Chiyoda-ku, Tokyo 102-0074; tel. (3) 3288-3723; fax (3) 3288-3728; e-mail kokusai@uizensen.or.jp; internet www.uizensen .or.jp; f. 2002 by merger of CSG Rengo and Zensen Domei; 1,986 affiliates; 790,289 mems; (Jan. 2003); Pres. TSUYOSHI TAKAGI.

Unyu Roren (All-Japan Federation of Transport Workers' Union): Zennittsu Kasumigaseki Bldg, 5th Floor, 3-3-3, Kasumigaseki, Chiyoda-ku, Tokyo 100-0013; tel. (3) 3503-2171; fax (3) 3503-2176; f. 1968; 143,084 mems; Pres. KAZUMARO SUZUKI.

Zeikan Roren (Federation of Japanese Customs Personnel Labour Unions): 3-1-1, Kasumigaseki, Chiyoda-ku, Tokyo 100; tel. and fax (3) 3593-1788; Pres. RIKIO SUDO.

Zen Insatsu (All-Printing Agency Workers' Union): 3-59-12, Nishigahara, Kita-ku, Tokyo 114; tel. (3) 3910-7131; fax (3) 3910-7155; 5,431 mems; Chair. TOSHIO KATAKURA.

Zen Yusei (All-Japan Postal Labour Union): 1-20-6, Sendagaya, Shibuya-ku, Tokyo 151; tel. (3) 3478-7101; fax (3) 5474-7085; 77,573 mems; Pres. NOBUAKI IZAWA.

Zenchuro (All-Japan Garrison Forces Labour Union): 3-41-8, Shiba, Minato-ku, Tokyo 105; tel. (3) 3455-5971; fax (3) 3455-5973; Pres. EIBUN MEDORUMA.

Zendensen (All- Japan Electric Wire Labour Union): 1-11-6, Hatanodai, Shinagawa-ku, Tokyo 142; tel. (3) 3785-2991; fax (3) 3785-2995; Pres. NAOKI TOKUNAGA.

Zen-eien (National Cinema and Theatre Workers' Union): Hibiya Park Bldg, 1-8-1, Yurakucho, Chiyoda-ku, Tokyo 100; tel. (3) 3201-4476; fax (3) 3214-0597; Pres. SADAHIRO MATSUURA.

Zengin Rengo (All-Japan Federative Council of Bank Labour Unions): R904, Kyodo Bldg, 16-8, Nihonbashi-Kodenmacho, Chuoku, Tokyo 103; tel. and fax (3) 3661-4886; 32,104 mems; Pres. KIKUO HATTORI.

Zenjiko Roren (National Federation of Automobile Transport Workers' Unions): 3-7-9, Sendagaya, Shibuya-ku, Tokyo 151; tel. (3) 3408-0875; fax (3) 3497-0107; Pres. OSAMU MIMASHI.

Zenkairen (All-Japan Shipping Labour Union): Shinbashi Ekimae Bldg, No. 1, 8th Floor, 2-20-15, Shimbashi, Minato-ku, Tokyo 105; tel. (3) 3573-2401; fax (3) 3573-2404; Chair. MASAHIKO SATO.

Zenkin Rengo (Japanese Federation of Metal Industry Unions): Yuai Bldg, 5th Floor, 2-20-12, Shiba, Minato-ku, Tokyo 105-0014; tel. (3) 3451-2141; fax (3) 3452-0239; f. 1989; 310,818 mems; Pres. MITSURO HATTORI.

Zenkoku Gas (Federation of Gas Workers' Unions of Japan): 5-11-1, Omori-nishi, Ota-ku, Tokyo 143; tel. (3) 5493-8381; fax (3) 5493-8216; 31,499 mems; Pres. AKIO HAMAUZU.

Zenkoku Keiba Rengo (National Federation of Horse-racing Workers): 2500, Mikoma, Miho-mura, Inashiki-gun, Ibaragi 300-04; tel. (298) 85-0402; fax (298) 85-0416; Pres. TOYOHIKO OKUMURA.

Zenkoku Nodanro (National Federation of Agricultural, Forestry and Fishery Corporations' Workers' Unions): 1-5-8, Hamamatsucho, Minato-ku, Tokyo 105; tel. (3) 3437-0931; fax (3) 3437-0681; 26,010 mems; Pres. SHIN-ICHIRO OKADA.

Zenkoku Semento (National Federation of Cement Workers' Unions of Japan): 5-29-2, Shimbashi, Minato-ku, Tokyo 105; tel. (3) 3436-3666; fax (3) 3436-3668; Pres. KIYONORI URAKAWA.

Zenkoku-Ippan (National Council of General Amalgamated Workers' Unions): Zosen Bldg, 5th Floor, 3-5-6, Misakicho, Chiyoda-ku, Tokyo 101-0061; tel. (3) 3230-4071; fax (3) 3230-4360; 54,708 mems; Pres. YASUHIKO MATSUI.

Zenkyoro (National Race Workers' Union): Nihon Kyoiku Kaikan, 7th Floor, 2-6-2, Hitotsubashi, Chiyoda-ku, Tokyo 101; tel. (3) 5210-5156; fax (3) 5210-5157; 24,720 mems; Pres. SHIMAKO YOSHIDA.

Zennitto (Japan Painting Workers' Union): Shin-osaka Communication Plaza, 1st Floor, 1-6-36, Nishi-miyahara, Yodogawa-ku, Osaka-shi, Osaka 532; tel. (6) 6393-8677; fax (6) 6393-8533; Pres. SEIICHI UOZA.

Zenrokin (Federation of Labour Bank Workers' Unions of Japan): Nakano Bldg, 3rd Floor, 1-11, Kanda-Awajicho, Chiyoda-ku, Tokyo 101; tel. (3) 3256-1015; fax (3) 3256-1045; Pres. EIICHI KAKU.

Zensuido (All-Japan Water Supply Workers' Union): 1-4-1, Hongo, Bunkyo-ku, Tokyo 113; tel. (3) 3816-4132; fax (3) 3818-1430; 33,522 mems; Pres. KAZUMASA KATO.

Zentanko (National Union of Coal Mine Workers): Yuai Bldg, 6th Floor, 2-20-12, Shiba, Minato-ku, Tokyo 105; tel. (3) 3453-4721; fax (3) 3453-6457; Pres. AKIRA YASUNAGA.

Zentei (Japan Postal Workers' Union): 1-2-7, Koraku, Bunkyo-ku, Tokyo 112-0004; tel. (3) 3812-4260; fax (3) 5684-7201; internet www .zentei.or.jp; 156,784 mems; Pres. MASAYUKI ISHIKAWA.

Zenzohei (All-Mint Labour Union): 1-1-79, Temma, Kita-ku, Osaka-shi, Osaka 530; tel. and fax (6) 6354-2389; Pres. CHIKASHI HIGUCHI.

Zenzosen-kikai (All-Japan Shipbuilding and Engineering Union): Zosen Bldg, 6th Floor, 3-5-6, Misakicho, Chiyoda-ku, Tokyo 101; tel. (3) 3265-1921; fax (3) 3265-1870; Pres. YOSHIMI FUNATSU.

Zosen Juki Roren (Japan Confederation of Shipbuilding and Engineering Workers' Unions): Yuai Kaikan Bldg, 4th Floor, 2-20-12, Shiba, Minato-ku, Tokyo 105-0014; tel. (3) 3451-6783; fax (3) 3451-6935; e-mail zosenjuki@mth.biglobe.ne.jp; 111,405 mems; Pres. MASAYUKI YOSHII.

Transport

RAILWAYS

Japan Railways (JR) Group: 1-6-5, Marunouchi, Chiyoda-ku, Tokyo 100-0005; tel. (3) 3215-9649; fax (3) 3213-5291; internet www .japanrail.com; fmrly the state-controlled Japanese National Railways (JNR); reorg. and transferred to private-sector control in 1987; the high-speed Shinkansen rail network consists of the Tokaido line (Tokyo to Shin-Osaka, 552.6 km), the Sanyo line (Shin-Osaka to Hakata, 623.3 km), the Tohoku line (Tokyo to Morioka, 535.3 km) and the Joetsu line (Omiya to Niigata, 303.6 km). The 4-km link between Ueno and Tokyo stations was opened in June 1991. The Yamagata Shinkansen (Fukushima to Yamagata, 87 km) was converted in 1992 from a conventional railway line. It is operated as a branch of the Tohoku Shinkansen with through trains from Tokyo, though not at full Shinkansen speeds. In 1997 the total railway route length was about 36,634 km.

Central Japan Railway Co: Yaesu Center Bldg, 1-6-6, Yaesu, Chuo-ku, Tokyo 103-8288; tel. (3) 3274-9727; fax (3) 5255-6780; internet www.jr-central.co.jp; f. 1987; also operates travel agency services, etc. Chair. HIROSHI SUDA; Pres. YOSHIYUKI KASAI.

East Japan Railway Co: 2-2-2, Yoyogi, Shibuya-ku, Tokyo 151-8578; tel. (3) 5334-1151; fax (3) 5334-1110; internet www.jreast.co .jp; privatized in 1987; Pres. MUTSUTAKE OTSUKA.

Hokkaido Railway Co: West 15-chome, Kita 11-jo, Chuo-ku, Sapporo 060-8644; tel. (11) 700-5717; fax (11) 700-5719; e-mail keieki@jrhokkaido.co.jp; internet www.jrhokkaido.co.jp; Chair. YOSHIHIRO OHMORI; Pres. SHINICHI SAKAMOTO.

Japan Freight Railway Co: 2-3-19, Koraku, Bunkyo-ku, Tokyo 112-0004; tel. (3) 3816-9722; internet www.jrfreight.co.jp; Chair. MASASHI HASHIMOTO; Pres. YASUSHI TANAHASHI.

Kyushu Railway Co: 3-25-21, Hakataekimae, Hakata-ku, Fukuoka 812-8566; tel. (92) 474-2501; fax (92) 474-9745; internet www.jrkyushu.co.jp; Chair. K. TANAKA; Pres. S. ISHIHARA.

Shikoku Railway Co: 8-33, Hamano-cho, Takamatsu, Kagawa 760-8580; tel. (87) 825-1622; fax (87) 825-1623; internet www .jr-shikoku.co.jp; Chair. HIROATSU ITO; Pres. TOSHIYUKI UMEHARA.

West Japan Railway Co: 2-4-24, Shibata, Kita-ku, Osaka 530-8341; tel. (6) 6375-8981; fax (6) 6375-8919; e-mail wjr01020@mxy .meshnet.or.jp; internet www.westjr.co.jp; scheduled for privatization in 2001; Chair. MASATAKA IDE; Pres. SHOJIRO NANYA.

Other Principal Private Companies

Hankyu Corpn: 1-16-1, Shibata, Kita-ku, Osaka 530-8389; tel. (6) 6373-5092; fax (6) 6373-5670; e-mail koho@hankyu.co.jp; internet www.hankyu.co.jp; f. 1907; links Osaka, Kyoto, Kobe and Takarazuka; Chair. KOHEI KOBAYASHI; Pres. T. OHASHI.

Hanshin Electric Railway Co Ltd: 1-1-24, Ebie, Fukushima-ku, Osaka 553; tel. (6) 6457-2123; f. 1899; Chair. S. KUMA; Pres. M. TEZUKA.

Keihan Electric Railway Co Ltd: 1-2-27, Shiromi, Chuo-ku, Osaka 540; tel. (6) 6944-2521; fax (6) 6944-2501; internet www .keihan.co.jp; f. 1906; Chair. MINORU MIYASHITA; Pres. A. KIMBA.

Keihin Express Electric Railway Co Ltd: 2-20-20, Takanawa, Minato-ku, Tokyo 108-8625; tel. (3) 3280-9120; fax (3) 3280-9199; internet www.keikyu.co.jp; f. 1899; Chair. ICHIRO HIRAMATSU; Pres. M. KOTANI.

Keio Electric Railway Co Ltd: 1-9-1, Sekido, Tama City, Tokyo 206-8052; tel. (42) 337-3106; fax (42) 374-9322; internet www.keio.co .jp; f. 1913; Chair. K. KUWAYAMA; Pres. H. NISHIYAMA.

Keisei Electric Railway Co Ltd: 1-10-3, Oshiage, Sumida-ku, Tokyo 131; tel. (3) 3621-2242; fax (3) 3621-2233; internet www.keisei .co.jp; f. 1909; Chair. (vacant); Pres. M. SATO.

Kinki Nippon Railway Co Ltd: 6-1-55, Uehommachi, Tennoji-ku, Osaka 543-8585; tel. (6) 6775-3444; fax (6) 6775-3468; internet www .kintetsu.co.jp; f. 1910; Chair. WA TASHIRO; Pres. AKIO TSUJI.

Nagoya Railroad Co Ltd: 1-2-4, Meieki, Nakamura-ku, Nagoya-shi 450; tel. (52) 571-2111; fax (52) 581-6060; e-mail info@meitetsu .co.jp; internet www.meitetsu.co.jp; Chair. S. TANIGUCHI; Pres. S. MINOURA.

Nankai Electric Railway Co Ltd: 5-1-60, Namba, Chuo-ku, Osaka 542; tel. (6) 6644-7121; internet www.nankai.co.jp; Pres. SHIGERU YOSHIMURA; Vice-Pres. K. OKAMOTO.

Nishi-Nippon Railroad Co Ltd: 1-11-17, Tenjin-cho, Chuo-ku, Fukuoka 810; tel. (92) 761-6631; fax (92) 722-1405; internet www .nnr.co.jp; serves northern Kyushu; Chair. H. YOSHIMOTO; Pres. G. KIMOTO.

Odakyu Electric Railway Co Ltd: 1-8-3, Nishi Shinjuku, Shinjuku-ku, Tokyo 160; tel. (3) 3349-2151; fax (3) 3346-1899; internet www.odakyu-group.co.jp; f. 1948; Chair. TATSUZO TOSHIMITSU; Pres. M. KITANAKA.

Sanyo Electric Railway Co Ltd: 3-1-1, Oyashiki-dori, Nagata-ku, Kobe 653; tel. (78) 611-2211; Pres. T. WATANABE.

Seibu Railway Co Ltd: 1-11-1, Kasunokidai, Tokorozawa-shi, Saitama 359; tel. (429) 26-2035; fax (429) 26-2237; internet www .seibu-group.co.jp/railways; f. 1894; Pres. YOSHIAKI TSUTSUMI.

Tobu Railway Co Ltd: 1-1-2, Oshiage, Sumida-ku, Tokyo 131-8522; tel. (3) 3621-5057; internet www.tobu.co.jp; f. 1897; Chair. KAICHIRO NEZU; Pres. TAKASHIGE UCHIDA.

Tokyo Express Electric Railway (Tokyu) Co Ltd : 5-6, Nanpeidai-cho, Shibuya-ku, Tokyo 150; tel. (3) 3477-6111; fax (3) 3496-2965; e-mail public@tokyu.co.jp; internet www.tokyu.co.jp; f. 1922; Pres. S. SHIMUZU.

Principal Subways, Monorails and Tunnels

Subway services operate in Tokyo, Osaka, Kobe, Nagoya, Sapporo, Yokohama, Kyoto, Sendai and Fukuoka. A subway was being planned for Kawasaki by 2010. Most subway lines operate reciprocal through-services with existing private railway lines which connect the cities with suburban areas.

The first commercial monorail system was introduced in 1964 with straddle-type cars between central Tokyo and Tokyo International Airport, a distance of 13 km. Monorails also operate in other cities, including Chiba, Hiroshima, and Kitakyushu.

In 1985 the 54-km Seikan Tunnel (the world's longest undersea tunnel), linking the islands of Honshu and Hokkaido, was completed. Electric rail services through the tunnel began operating in March 1988.

Fukuoka City Subway: Fukuoka Municipal Transportation Bureau, 2-5-31, Daimyo, Chuo-ku, Fukuoka 810-0041; tel. (92) 732-4107; fax (92) 721-0754; internet subway.city.fukuoka.jp; 2 lines of 17.8 km open; Dir KENNICHIROU NISHI.

Kobe Rapid Transit: 6-5-1, Kanocho, Chuo-ku, Kobe 650; tel. (78) 331-8181; 22.7 km open; Dir YASUO MAENO.

Kyoto Rapid Transit: 48, Bojocho Mibu, Nakakyo-ku, Kyoto 604; tel. (75) 822-9115; fax (75) 822-9240; 26.4 km open; Chair. T. TANABE.

Nagoya Subway: Transportation Bureau City of Nagoya , Nagoya City Hall, 3-1-1, Sannomaru, Naka-ku, Nagoya 460-8508; tel. (52) 972-3824; fax (52) 972-3849; internet www.kotsu.city.nagoya.jp; 78.2 km open (2001); Dir-Gen. TAKAYASU TSUKAMOTO.

Osaka Monorail: 5-1-1, Higashi-machi, Shin-Senri, Toyonakashi, Osaka 565; tel. (6) 871-8280; fax (6) 871-8284; 113.5 km open; Gen. Man. S. OKA.

Osaka Underground Railway: Osaka Municipal Transportation Bureau, 1-11-53, Kujominami, Nishi-ku, Osaka 550; tel. (6) 6582-1101; fax (6) 6582-7997; f. 1933; 120 km open in 1998; the 6.6 km computer-controlled 'New Tram' service began between Suminoe-koen and Nakafuto in 1981; a seventh line between Kyobashi and Tsurumi-ryokuchi was opened in 1990; Gen. Man. HARUMI SAKAI.

Sapporo Transportation Bureau: Higashi, 2-4-1, Oyachi, Atsubetsu-ku, Sapporo 004; tel. (11) 896-2708; fax (11) 896-2790; f. 1971; 3 lines of 48 km open in 1993/94; Dir T. IKEGAMI.

Sendai City Subway: Sendai City Transportation Bureau, 1-4-15, Kimachidori, Aoba-ku, Sendai-shi, Miyagi-ken 980-0801; tel. (22) 224-5502; fax (22) 224-6839; internet www.comminet.or.jp/~kotsu-s; 15.4 km open; Dir T. IWAMA.

Tokyo Metropolitan Government (TOEI) Underground Railway: Bureau of Transportation, Tokyo Metropolitan Government, 2–8–1 Nishi-Shinjuku, Tokyo 163–8001; tel. (3) 5320–6026; internet www.kotsu.metro.tokyo.jp; operates four underground lines, totalling 105 km.

Tokyo Underground Railway (TEITO): Teito Rapid Transit Authority (TRTA), 3-19-6, Higashi Ueno, Taito-ku, Tokyo 110-0015; tel. (3) 3837-7046; fax (3) 3837-7048; internet www.tokyometro.go .jp; f. 1941; operates nine lines; Pres. YASUTOSHI TSUCHISAKA; 183.2 km open (March 2003).

Yokohama Rapid Transit: Municipal Transportation Bureau, 1-1, Minato-cho, Naka-ku, Yokohama 231-80; tel. (45) 671-3201; fax (45) 664-3266; 40.4 km open; Dir-Gen. MICHINORI KISHIDA.

ROADS

In December 1999 Japan's road network extended to an estimated 1,161,894 km, including 6,455 km of motorways and 53,685 km of highways. In May 1999 work was completed on a 29-year project to construct three routes, consisting of a total of 19 bridges, between the islands of Honshu and Shikoku across the Seto inland sea, at a cost of some US $25,000m.

There is a national omnibus service, 60 publicly-operated services and 298 privately-operated services.

Japan Highway Public Corpn: 3-3-2, Kasumigaseki, Chiyoda-ku, Tokyo 100-8979; tel. (3) 3506-0111; privatization plans announced in Dec. 2001.

SHIPPING

Shipping in Japan is subject to the supervision of the Ministry of Transport. At 31 December 2001 the Japanese merchant fleet (7,924 vessels) had a total displacement of 16,653,028 grt. The main ports are Tokyo, Yokohama, Nagoya and Osaka. The rebuilding of the port at Kobe, severely damaged by an earthquake in January 1995, was completed in 1997.

Principal Companies

Daiichi Chuo Kisen Kaisha: Dowa Bldg, 3-7-13, Toyoi, Koto-ku, Tokyo 103-8271; tel. (3) 5634-2276; fax (3) 5634-2262; f. 1960; liner and tramp services; Pres. MAHIKO SAOTOME.

Iino Kaiun Kaisha Ltd: Iino Bldg, 2-1-1, Uchisaiwai-cho, Chiyoda-ku, Tokyo 100; tel. (3) 3506-3037; fax (3) 3508-4121; f. 1918; cargo and tanker services; Chair. T. CHIBA; Pres. A. KARINO.

Kansai Kisen KK: Osaka Bldg, 3-6-32, Nakanoshima, Kita-ku, Osaka 552; tel. (6) 6574-9131; fax (6) 6574-9149; f. 1942; domestic passenger services; Pres. TOSHIKAZU EGUCHI.

Kawasaki Kisen Kaisha Ltd (K Line): 1-2-9, Nishi Shimbashi, Minato-ku, Tokyo 105-8421; tel. (3) 3595-5082; fax (3) 3595-5001; e-mail otaki@email.kline.co.jp; internet www.kline.co.jp; f. 1919; containers, cars, LNG, LPG and oil tankers, bulk carriers; Chair. of Bd I. SHINTANI; Exec. Vice-Pres. Z. WAKABAYASHI.

Nippon Yusen Kaisha (NYK) Line: 2-3-2, Marunouchi, Chiyoda-ku, Tokyo 100-0005; tel. (3) 3284-5151; fax (3) 3284-6361; e-mail prteam@jp.nykline.com; internet www.nykline.com; f. 1885; merged with Showa Line Ltd in 1998; world-wide container, cargo, pure car and truck carriers, tanker and bulk carrying services; Chair. JIRO NEMOTO; Pres. KENTARO KAWAMURA.

Nissho Shipping Co Ltd: 33, Mori Bldg, 7th Floor, 3-8-21, Toranomon, Minato-ku, Tokyo 105; tel. (3) 3438-3511; fax (3) 3438-3566; f. 1943; Pres. MINORU IKEDA.

OSK Mitsui Ltd: Shosen Mitsui Bldg, 2-1-1, Toranomon, Minato-ku, Tokyo 105-91; tel. (3) 3587-7092; fax (3) 3587-7734; f. 1942; merged with Navix Line Ltd in 1999; world-wide container, liner, tramp, and specialized carrier and tanker services; Chair. SUSUMU TEMPORIN; Pres. MASAHURU IKUTA.

Ryukyu Kaiun KK: 1-24-11, Nishi-machi, Naha, Okinawa 900; tel. (98) 868-8161; fax (98) 868-8561; cargo and passenger services on domestic routes; Pres. M. AZAMA.

Taiheiyo Kaiun Co Ltd: Mitakokusai Bldg, 23rd Floor, 1-4-28, Minato-ku, Tokyo 100; tel. (3) 5445-5805; fax (3) 5445-5806; f. 1951; cargo and tanker services; Pres. SANROKURO YAMAJI.

CIVIL AVIATION

There are international airports at Tokyo (Haneda and Narita), Osaka, Nagoya and Fukuoka. In 1991 the Government approved a plan to build five new airports, and to expand 17 existing ones. This project was expected to take five years to complete and to cost US $25,000m. There are proposals to build new airports at Shizuoka, Nagoya and Kobe. In September 1994 the world's first offshore international airport (Kansai International Airport) was opened in Osaka Bay, and a second runway was due for completion in 2007. In April 2002 a second runway was opened at Narita. In

December 2001 plans were approved for a fourth runway at Haneda. Chubu, Kansai, and Narita airports were scheduled to be privatized in 2004. At March 1999 a total of 85 airports were in operation.

Air Do: 6, Nishi, Kita 5, Chuo-ku, Sapporo; tel. (11) 252-5533; fax (11) 252-5580; e-mail postbear@airdo.co.jp; internet www.airdo.co .jp; f. 1996; domestic service between Tokyo and Sapporo; Pres. AKIRA NAKAMURA.

Air Nippon: 3-5-10, Haneda Airport, Ota-ku, Tokyo 144-0041; tel. (3) 5756-4710; fax (3) 5756-4788; internet www.air-nippon.co.jp; f. 1974; fmrly Nihon Kinkyori Airways; international and domestic passenger services; Pres. and CEO YUZURU MASUMOTO.

All Nippon Airways (ANA): 3-5-10 Haneda Airport, Ota-ku, Tokyo 144-0041; tel. (3) 5756-5675; fax (3) 5756-5679; internet www.ana.co .jp; f. 1952; operates domestic passenger and freight services; scheduled international services to the Far East, Australasia, the USA and Europe; charter services world-wide; Pres. and CEO KICHISABURO NOMURA.

Hokkaido Air System: Hokkadama-cho Airport, Sapporo-shi, Shigashi-ku, Sapporo 063; tel. (11) 781-1247; fax (11) 784-1716; internet www.hac-air.co.jp; f. 1997; domestic services on Hokkaido; Pres. TAKESHI KANDI.

JALways Co Ltd: JAL Bldg, 18th Floor, 2-4-11, Higashi-Shinagawa, Shinagawa-ku, Tokyo 140-8647; tel. (3) 5460-6830; fax (3) 5460-6839; e-mail jazgz@jaz.jalgroup.or.jp; internet www.jalways.co .jp; f. 1990; subsidiary of JAL; domestic and international scheduled and charter services; Chair. JIRO SAGARA; Pres. YUKIO OHTANI.

Japan Air Commuter: 8-2-2, Fumoto, Mizobe-cho, Aira-gun, Kagoshima 899-64; tel. (995) 582151; fax (995) 582673; e-mail info@ jac.co.jp; internet www.jac.co.jp; f. 1983; subsidiary of Japan Air System; domestic services; Chair. YOSHITOMI ONO.

Japan Air System: JAS M1 Bldg, 3-5-1, Haneda Airport, Ota-ku, Tokyo 144-0041; tel. (3) 5756-4022; fax (3) 5473-4109; internet www .jas.co.jp; f. 1971; domestic and international services; plans to coordinate services with Northwest Airlines (USA) announced in 1995; merging with JAL in late 2002 to form Japan Airlines System; Chair. TAKESHI MASHIMA; Pres. HIROMI FUNABIKI.

Japan Airlines Co Ltd (JAL) (Nihon Koku Kabushiki Kaisha): JAL Bldg, 2-4-11, Higashi-Shinagawa, Shinagawa-ku, Tokyo 140; tel. (3) 5460-3121; fax (3) 5460-3936; internet www.jal.co.jp; f. 1951; fully transferred to private-sector control in 1987; domestic and international services to Australasia, the Far East, North America, South America and Europe; merging with Japan Air System in late 2002 to form Japan Airlines System; Pres. ISAO KANEKO.

Japan Asia Airways Co: JAL Bldg, 19th Floor, 2-4-11. Higashi-shinagawa, Shinagawa-ku, Tokyo 140-0002; tel. (3) 5460-7285; fax (3) 5460-7286; e-mail jaabz@jaa.jalgroup.or.jp; internet www .japanasia.co.jp; f. 1975; subsidiary of JAL; international services from Tokyo, Osaka, Nagoya and Okinawa to Hong Kong and Taiwan; Chair. TEIICHI KURIBAYASHI; Pres. OSAMU IGARASHI.

Japan TransOcean Air: 3-24, Yamashita-cho, Naha-shi, Okinawa 900; tel. (988) 572112; fax (988) 582581; internet www.jal.co.jp/jta; f. 1967; present name since 1993; subsidiary of JAL; inter-island service in Okinawa; Chair. KEIICHI INAMINE; Pres. MICHIO OKUNO.

Nakanihon Airlines (NAL): Nagoya Airport, Toyoyama-cho, Nishikasugai-gun, Aichi 480-0202; tel. (568) 285405; fax (568) 285417; internet www.nals.co.jp; f. 1988; regional and domestic services; Pres. AKIRA HIRABAYASHI.

Skymark Airlines: World Trade Center, Bldg 3F, 2-4-1, Hamamatsucho, Minato-ku, Tokyo 105-6103; tel. (3) 5402-6767; fax (3) 5402-6770; e-mail info@skymark.co.jp; internet www.skymark.co.jp; f. 1997; domestic services; Chair. HIDEO SAWADA; Pres TAKASHI IDE.

Tourism

The ancient capital of Kyoto, pagodas and temples, forests and mountains, traditional festivals and the classical Kabuki theatre are some of the many tourist attractions of Japan. In 2000 there were 4,757,000 foreign visitors to Japan, and receipts from tourism totalled US $3,374m.

Department of Tourism: 2-1-3, Kasumigaseki, Chiyoda-ku, Tokyo 100; tel. (3) 3580-4488; fax (3) 3580-7901; f. 1946; a dept of the Ministry of Transport; Dir-Gen. KIMITAKA FUJINO.

Japan National Tourist Organization: Tokyo Kotsu Kaikan Bldg, 2-10-1, Yuraku-cho, Chiyoda-ku, Tokyo 100-0006; tel. (3) 3216-1901; fax (3) 3216-1846; internet www.jnto.go.jp; Pres. HIDEAKI MUKAIYMA.

Japan Travel Bureau Inc: 1-6-4, Marunouchi, Chiyoda-ku, Tokyo 100-0005; tel. (3) 3284-7028; f. 1912; 10,297 mems; Chair. I. MATSU-HASHI; Pres. R. FUNAYAMA.

JORDAN

Introductory Survey

Location, Climate, Language, Religion, Flag, Capital

The Hashemite Kingdom of Jordan is an almost land-locked state in western Asia. It is bordered by Israel and the Palestinian Autonomous Areas to the west, by Syria to the north, by Iraq to the east and by Saudi Arabia to the south. The port of Al-Aqabah (Aqaba), in the far south, gives Jordan a narrow outlet to the Red Sea. The climate is hot and dry. The average annual temperature is about 15°C (60°F) but there are wide diurnal variations. Temperatures in Amman are generally between −1°C (30°F) and 32°C (90°F). More extreme conditions are found in the valley of the River Jordan and on the shores of the Dead Sea (a lake on the Israeli–Jordanian frontier), where the temperature may exceed 50°C (122°F) in summer. The official language is Arabic. More than 90% of the population are Sunni Muslims, while there are small communities of Christians and Shi'i Muslims. The national flag (proportions 1 by 2) has three equal horizontal stripes, of black, white and green, with a red triangle, containing a seven-pointed white star, at the hoist. The capital is Amman.

Recent History

Palestine (including the present-day West Bank of Jordan) and Transjordan (the East Bank) were formerly parts of Turkey's Ottoman Empire. During the First World War (1914–18), when Turkey was allied with Germany, the Arabs under Ottoman rule rebelled. British forces, with Arab support, occupied Palestine and Transjordan in 1917–18, when the Turks withdrew. British occupation continued after the war, when the Ottoman Empire was dissolved. In 1920 Palestine and Transjordan were formally placed under British administration by a League of Nations mandate. In 1921 Abdullah ibn Hussein, a member of the Hashimi (Hashemite) dynasty of Arabia, was proclaimed Amir (Emir) of Transjordan. In the same year his brother, Faisal, became King of neighbouring Iraq. The two new monarchs were sons of Hussein ibn Ali, the Sharif of Mecca, who had proclaimed himself King of the Hejaz (now part of Saudi Arabia) in 1916. The British decision to nominate Hashemite princes to be rulers of Iraq and Transjordan was a reward for Hussein's co-operation in the wartime campaign against Turkey.

Under the British mandate Transjordan (formally separated from Palestine in 1923) gained increasing autonomy. In 1928 the United Kingdom acknowledged the nominal independence of Transjordan, while retaining certain financial and military powers. Amir Abdullah followed a generally pro-British policy and supported the Allied cause in the Second World War (1939–45). The mandate was terminated on 22 March 1946, when Transjordan attained full independence. On 25 May Abdullah was proclaimed King, and a new Constitution took effect.

When the British Government terminated its mandate in Palestine in May 1948, Jewish leaders there proclaimed the State of Israel. Palestinian Arabs, however, with military support from Arab states, opposed Israeli claims and hostilities continued until July. Transjordan's forces occupied about 5,900 sq km of Palestine, including East Jerusalem, and this was confirmed by the armistice with Israel in April 1949. In June the country was renamed Jordan, and in April 1950, following a referendum, King Abdullah formally annexed the West Bank territory, which contained many Arab refugees from Israeli-held areas.

In July 1951 King Abdullah was assassinated in Jerusalem by a Palestinian belonging to an extremist Islamist organization. Abdullah was succeeded by his eldest son, Talal ibn Abdullah, hitherto Crown Prince. However, in August 1952, because of Talal's mental incapacity, the crown passed to his son, Hussein ibn Talal, then 16 years of age. King Hussein formally came to power in May 1953.

In March 1956, responding to Arab nationalist sentiment, King Hussein dismissed the British army officer who had been Chief of Staff of the British-equipped and -financed Arab Legion (the Jordanian armed forces) since 1939. Jordan's treaty relationship with the United Kingdom was ended in March 1957, and British troops completed their withdrawal from Jordan in July.

The refugee camps in the West Bank became the centre of Palestinian resistance to Israel, and during the 1950s there were numerous attacks on Israeli territory by groups of Palestinian *fedayeen* ('martyrs'). In September 1963 the creation of a unified 'Palestinian entity' was approved by the Council of the League of Arab States (the Arab League, see p. 260), and the first Palestinian congress was held in the Jordanian sector of Jerusalem in May–June 1964, at which it was agreed to form the Palestine Liberation Organization (PLO), which would be financed by the Arab League and would recruit military units to form a Palestine Liberation Army (PLA). The principal Palestinian guerrilla organization within the PLO was the Palestine National Liberation Movement, known as Fatah ('Conquest'), led from 1968 by Yasser Arafat. However, King Hussein regarded the establishment of the PLO as a threat to Jordanian sovereignty, and from the outset refused to allow the PLA to train in Jordan or the PLO to levy taxes from Palestinian refugees residing in his country.

In April 1965 Hussein nominated his brother Hassan ibn Talal to be Crown Prince. During the Six-Day War of June 1967 Israel made substantial military gains, including possession of the whole of Jerusalem (which was incorporated into Israel) and the West Bank; the latter became an Israeli 'administered territory'. The influx of Palestinian refugees into the East Bank bolstered the strength of the PLO, whose continued armed raids on the Israeli-administered territories challenged the personal authority of King Hussein and the sovereignty of the Jordanian Government. King Hussein responded by expelling the guerrilla groups, after a civil war which lasted from September 1970 to July 1971. Aid to Jordan from Kuwait and other wealthy Arab states, suspended after the expulsion of the Palestinian fighters, was only restored following Jordan's military support for Syria during the Arab–Israeli War of October 1973. At an Arab summit meeting in Rabat, Morocco, in October 1974 King Hussein supported a unanimous resolution recognizing the PLO as the 'sole legitimate representative of the Palestinian people' and granting the organization the right to establish an independent national authority on any piece of Palestinian land to be liberated.

In November 1974, as a response to this resolution, both chambers of the Jordanian National Assembly (which had equal representation for the East and West Banks) approved constitutional amendments that empowered the King to dissolve the Assembly and to postpone elections for up to 12 months. The Assembly was dissolved later that month, although it was briefly reconvened in February 1976, when it approved a constitutional amendment giving the King power to postpone elections indefinitely and to convene the Assembly as required. A royal decree of April 1978 provided for the creation of a National Consultative Council, with 60 members appointed for a two-year term by the King, on the Prime Minister's recommendation, to debate proposed legislation.

A proposal put forward by US President Ronald Reagan in September 1982 for an autonomous Palestinian authority on the West Bank, in association with Jordan, was rejected by Yasser Arafat following talks with King Hussein. In January 1984, however, the King responded by dissolving the National Consultative Council and recalling the National Assembly for the first time since 1967—in effect creating the kind of Palestinian forum envisaged by the Reagan initiative. Israel allowed the surviving West Bank deputies to attend the Assembly, which approved constitutional amendments enabling elections to be held in the East Bank, while West Bank deputies would be chosen by the Assembly itself. After discussions with the PLO leader in January 1984 on a joint Palestinian-Jordanian peace initiative, King Hussein's proposals for negotiations, based on UN Security Council Resolution 242 (the resolution, adopted in November 1967, sought to return the region's territorial boundaries to the pre-Six-Day War status, but incorporated implicit recognition of an Israeli state), met with a non-committal response from the Palestine National Council (PNC), which convened in Amman in November 1984. President Hosni Mubarak of Egypt gave his support to Hussein's proposals, following the resumption of diplomatic relations between the two countries in September. In February 1985 King Hussein and Yasser Arafat announced the terms of a Jordanian-Palestinian agreement, proposing a confederated state of Jordan and Palestine to be reached through the convening of a conference of all concerned parties in the Middle East, including the PLO.

In July 1985 Israel rejected a list of seven Palestinians, five of whom were members of the PLO or had links with the PNC, whom King Hussein had presented to the USA as candidates for a joint Jordanian-Palestinian delegation to preliminary peace talks. Further progress was hampered by a series of terrorist incidents in which the PLO was implicated, thereby giving Israel further cause to reject the PLO as a credible partner in peace negotiations. King Hussein came under increasing pressure to advance the peace process, if necessary without PLO participation. In September President Reagan revived his 1984 plan to sell military equipment to the value of some US $1,900m. to Jordan. The proposal was approved by the US Congress on the condition that Jordan enter into direct talks with Israel before 1 March 1986. However, such talks were obstructed by a gradual *rapprochement* between Jordan and Syria, both of which supported a Middle East peace settlement through an international conference, having recently rejected 'partial and unilateral' solutions.

Frustrated by the lack of co-operation from Yasser Arafat in advancing the aims of the Jordanian-PLO peace initiative, King Hussein publicly severed political links with the PLO on 19 February 1986. Arafat was subsequently ordered to close his main PLO offices in Jordan by 1 April. The PLO's activities were henceforth to be restricted even further, and a number of Fatah officers loyal to Arafat were expelled. In July the Jordanian authorities closed all 25 Fatah offices in Amman; only 12 bureaux belonging to the PLO remained.

Despite the termination of political co-ordination with the PLO, Jordan continued to reject Israeli requests for direct peace talks that excluded a form of PLO representation. However, Jordan's subsequent efforts to strengthen its influence in the Israeli-occupied territories (Occupied Territories), and to foster a Palestinian constituency there independent of Arafat's PLO, coincided with Israeli measures to grant a limited autonomy to Palestinians in the West Bank. In March 1986 the Jordanian House of Representatives approved a draft law increasing the number of seats in the House from 60 to 142 (71 seats each for the East and West Banks), thereby providing for greater representation for West Bank Palestinians in the National Assembly. In August, with Israeli support, Jordan announced a five-year development plan, valued at US $1,300m., for the West Bank and Gaza Strip; the plan was condemned by Arafat and West Bank Palestinians as representing a normalization of relations with Israel. Support for Arafat among Palestinians in the Occupied Territories, and in Jordan, was consolidated as he re-established himself at the head of a reunified PLO at the 18th session of the PNC in April 1987 (when the Jordanian-PLO accord of 1985 was formally abrogated).

In May 1987, following secret meetings with King Hussein, the Israeli Minister of Foreign Affairs, Shimon Peres, claimed to have made significant progress on the crucial issue of Palestinian representation at a Middle East peace conference, and to have the consent of Egypt, Jordan and the USA to convene a conference involving the five permanent members of the UN Security Council and a delegation of Palestinians who rejected terrorism and accepted Security Council Resolutions 242 and 338 (the latter defined the terms of immediate peace following the 1973 Arab–Israeli war) as the basis for negotiations. The Jordanian Prime Minister, Zaid ar-Rifai, confirmed his country's willingness to participate in a joint Jordanian-Palestinian delegation including the PLO, provided that the organization complied with the stated conditions. However, Israel's Prime Minister, Itzhak Shamir, reiterated his alternative proposal of direct regional talks excluding the PLO, and Peres failed to secure the support of a majority of the Israeli Cabinet for his proposals.

At the first full meeting of the Arab League for eight years, convened in Amman in November 1987, King Hussein pursued an agenda of greater Arab unity in support of Iraq in its war with Iran. Prior to the summit, Jordan restored full diplomatic relations with Libya (severed in 1984), which had modified its support for Iran. However, King Hussein's appeal for Egypt to be restored to membership of the League (suspended following the peace treaty with Israel in 1979) was resisted by Libya and Syria, although 11 Arab states subsequently re-established

diplomatic relations. Jordan also announced the resumption of co-operation with the PLO.

These achievements were soon overshadowed by the Palestinian *intifada* (uprising), which erupted in the West Bank and Gaza Strip in December 1987, in protest at the continued Israeli occupation and the seemingly indifferent attitude of Arab League states to the Palestinians' plight. The *intifada*, and the Israelis' increasingly violent response, increased international support for the PLO and Palestinian national rights. At an extraordinary meeting of the Arab League held in the Algerian capital in June 1988, King Hussein gave the *intifada* his unconditional support and insisted that the PLO must represent the Palestinians at any future peace conference. Furthermore, in accordance with agreements reached at the meeting, Jordan cancelled the West Bank development plan and severed its legal and administrative links with the territory. Jordan's disengagement from the West Bank effectively rendered a proposal put forward earlier in the year by the US Secretary of State, George Shultz, for an international peace conference excluding the PLO or a joint Jordanian-Palestinian delegation, redundant.

On 15 November 1988 the PNC, meeting in Algiers, proclaimed the establishment of an independent State of Palestine and, for the first time, endorsed UN Security Council Resolution 242 as a basis for a Middle East peace settlement, thus implicitly recognizing Israel. Jordan and 60 other countries recognized the new state. Addressing a special session of the UN General Assembly in Geneva, Switzerland, in December, Arafat renounced violence on behalf of the PLO. The USA subsequently opened a dialogue with the PLO, making it more probable that Israel would have to do likewise.

In April 1989 there was rioting in several cities, after the Jordanian Government imposed sizeable price increases on basic goods and services. The riots led to the resignation of Zaid ar-Rifai (the Prime Minister since 1985) and his Cabinet. Field Marshal Sharif Zaid ibn Shaker, a cousin of the King who had been Commander-in-Chief of the Jordanian Armed Forces in 1976–88, was appointed to head a new Government. While King Hussein refused to make any concessions regarding the price increases, he announced that a general election would be held for the first time since 1967. The election to the 80-seat House of Representatives, which proceeded in November 1989, was contested by 647 candidates, mostly independents, as the ban on political parties (in force since 1963) remained. However, the Muslim Brotherhood was able to present candidates for election, owing to its legal status as a charity. At the election the Muslim Brotherhood won 20 seats, while as many as 14 seats were won by independent Islamist candidates who supported the Brotherhood. The strength of support for opposition candidates was unexpected, especially since a disproportionately large number of seats had been assigned to rural areas from which the Government had traditionally drawn most support. In December King Hussein appointed Mudar Badran as Prime Minister, a post he had previously held in 1976–79 and 1980–84. The Muslim Brotherhood declined participation in the new Cabinet after its demand for the education portfolio was rejected. However, the Government included three independent Muslim deputies and three 'leftists', all of whom were regarded as members of the opposition. In January 1990 Badran pledged to abolish martial law (which had been suspended in December 1989) within four to six months, and to liberalize the judicial system.

Meanwhile, in January 1990 Badran announced the abolition of the anti-communism law (in force since 1954). In April King Hussein appointed a 60-member commission, under the chairmanship of former premier Ahmad Ubeidat, to devise a national charter that would legalize political parties. The commission's draft national charter was approved by the King in January 1991, and further endorsed by Hussein and leading political figures in June. Also in January the Cabinet was reorganized to include five members of the Muslim Brotherhood.

Iraq's invasion of Kuwait in August 1990, and the consequent imposition of economic sanctions by the UN against Iraq, had a profound impact on Jordan: Iraq was its principal trading partner, and Jordan relied on supplies of Iraqi petroleum. Although King Hussein condemned the Iraqi invasion, he was slow to do so, and advocated an 'Arab' solution to the crisis. There was considerable support for the Iraqi President, Saddam Hussain, among the Jordanian population, particularly among Palestinians. King Hussein was critical of the US-led deployment of multinational military forces in Saudi Arabia and the Persian (Arabian) Gulf, and in the closing months of 1990 he visited numerous Middle East and other capitals in an attempt to avert a war. Jordan's response to the Gulf crisis prompted the USA to review its military and economic assistance to Jordan and led to a deterioration in Jordan's relations with Egypt and Saudi Arabia, both of which contributed to the US-led force. However, diplomatic relations between Jordan and Iran were re-established (having been severed in 1981).

In the early stages of the Gulf crisis Jordan experienced the additional problem of a large-scale influx of refugees from Iraq and Kuwait, many of whom were seeking passage through Jordan in order to return to the Indian sub-continent and South East Asia. Large numbers of Jordanian nationals also returned from the Gulf region. Some 300,000 of these expatriates remained in Jordan after the liberation of Kuwait in February 1991, fearing reprisals in Kuwait, where most Jordanian and Palestinian residents were regarded by the authorities as collaborators with the Iraqi occupation forces.

In the months following the Gulf War Jordan concentrated on attempts to revive its shattered economy and on improving relations with its Arab neighbours, particularly Saudi Arabia. In response to Jordanian co-operation in the arrest of a Saudi dissident in Amman, Saudi Arabia revoked a ban on the entry of Jordanian transport vehicles into its territory, and trade between Jordan and Saudi Arabia was resumed. However, high-level ministerial contacts were not renewed until mid-1995.

Meanwhile, Jordan secured the approval of the USA by agreeing to join with a Palestinian delegation at the Middle East peace conference which opened in Madrid, Spain, in October 1991. Subsequent talks in Washington, DC, and Moscow, Russia, between the Israeli and the joint Jordanian-Palestinian delegations remained deadlocked with regard to substantive issues until September 1993, when Israel and the PLO agreed to a declaration of principles regarding Palestinian self-rule in the Occupied Territories. On the signing of the Declaration of Principles, which King Hussein welcomed, the Jordanian-Palestinian delegation was disbanded, and Jordan and Israel concluded an agreement that defined the agenda for subsequent bilateral negotiations within the context of the Middle East peace conference. The talks were to address the following issues: refugees and displaced persons; security; water resources; the demarcation of the border between Jordan and Israel; and future bilateral co-operation.

In 1991 Jordan and the PLO had agreed on the principle of confederation between Jordan and whatever Palestinian entity ultimately emerged from the Middle East peace process; and in July 1993 Jordan and the PLO agreed to form six committees to discuss relations between Jordan and the Occupied Territories during a period of transitional Palestinian self-rule. Within the terms of the Declaration of Principles, however, Jordan was formally excluded from the discussion of some of the issues—henceforth to be dealt with bilaterally by Israeli and Palestinian authorities—which the committees had already begun to address. Jordan was also to be invited to participate in a joint Israeli-Palestinian Liaison Committee to determine procedures for the return of Palestinians displaced from the West Bank and Gaza in 1967. However, Jordan stated its unwillingness to join such a committee, since it had not been consulted about its establishment. In January 1994, after King Hussein had twice warned that Jordan might otherwise pursue its own agenda in the ongoing peace talks with Israel, the PLO agreed to sign a comprehensive economic co-operation agreement with Jordan, and to establish a joint committee to co-ordinate financial policy in the Palestinian territories. In the same month Jordan signed a draft security accord with the PLO. Yasser Arafat visited Amman immediately following the signing of the Cairo Agreement on the Gaza Strip and Jericho by Israel and the PLO in May (see the chapter on Israel), but King Hussein reportedly remained disappointed at the PLO's failure to liaise fully with Jordan in the peace process.

On 25 July 1994 King Hussein and the Israeli Prime Minister, Itzhak Rabin, meeting in the US capital, signed the Washington Declaration, which formally ended the state of war that had existed between Jordan and Israel since 1948. In October 1994 the two countries signed a full peace treaty settling outstanding issues of contention between them and providing, *inter alia*, for the establishment of diplomatic relations and for talks on economic and security co-operation. The official normalization of relations between Jordan and Israel had been completed by 18 January 1996. In Jordan the peace treaty was opposed by Islamist militants, and it was also criticized by Syria. The PLO leadership complained that the treaty undermined Palestinian

claims to sovereignty over Jerusalem. None the less, in January 1995 the PLO and Jordan signed an agreement regulating relations between Jordan and the Palestinian Autonomous Areas with regard to economic affairs, finance, banking, education, transport, telecommunications, information and administration. At the same time, the PLO acknowledged Jordan's custodianship of the Muslim holy places in Jerusalem for as long as Jordan recognized and supported Palestinian claims to sovereignty over East Jerusalem.

Meanwhile, in June 1991 Taher al-Masri was appointed to replace Mudar Badran as Prime Minister. However, in the period preceding the opening of the National Assembly in December, it became clear that al-Masri could not command majority support in the legislature; he was forced to resign in November, whereupon Sharif Zaid ibn Shaker again assumed the premiership. An extraordinary session of the House of Representatives was convened in June 1992 to debate new laws regarding political parties and the press. In July the House adopted legislation whereby, subject to certain conditions, political parties were formally legalized. In May King Hussein appointed Abd as-Salam al-Majali, the head of the Jordanian delegation to the Middle East peace conference, to the premiership; his Government was regarded as a transitional administration pending legislative elections to be held before November 1993.

In August 1993 King Hussein unexpectedly dissolved the House of Representatives, provoking criticism from some politicians who had expected the House to debate proposed amendments to Jordan's electoral law. Changes in voting procedures at the general election were announced by the King in that month: voters were to be allowed to cast one vote only, rather than, as before, multiple votes equal to the number of candidates contesting a given constituency. Some 68% of the electorate were reported to have participated in Jordan's first multi-party general election, held on 8 November. By far the largest number of deputies returned to the House of Representatives were independent centrists loyal to the King. The Islamic Action Front (IAF, the political wing of the Muslim Brotherhood), which emerged as the second largest party in the legislature, maintained that the new electoral law had prevented it from winning more seats. A new Senate was appointed by the King on 18 November, and a new Cabinet, led by al-Majali, was announced in December. Al-Majali was dismissed in January 1995, whereupon Sharif Zaid ibn Shaker once again assumed the premiership at the head of an extensively reorganized Cabinet. Islamist and left-wing groups failed to win significant popular support at municipal elections held in July, most elected candidates being largely pro-Government or independent. The IAF attributed its poor performance to a low level of voter participation, and to official harassment of its members during the campaign.

King Hussein implemented a further extensive cabinet reshuffle in February 1996, appointing Abd al-Karim al-Kabariti, hitherto Minister of Foreign Affairs, as Prime Minister. (Kabariti retained the foreign affairs portfolio, and also assumed responsibility for defence.) In August rioting erupted in southern Jordan after the Government imposed a sharp increase on the price of bread. The unrest quickly spread to other parts of the country, including impoverished areas of the capital, and was regarded as the greatest challenge to the King's rule since the rioting over fuel prices in 1989. King Hussein responded by suspending the legislature and deploying the army in order to suppress the worst disturbances. In December 1996 the Government announced its commitment to certain reforms of electoral legislation before the next general election. Kabariti was unexpectedly dismissed by Hussein in March 1997, reportedly as a result of disagreement over issues relating to Jordan's policies towards Israel. Abd as-Salam al-Majali again assumed the premiership, taking the defence portfolio in the new Cabinet.

In July 1997 the IAF announced its intention to boycott the forthcoming parliamentary elections, in protest at what it regarded as the Government's overly concessionary policies towards Israel and at recent restrictive amendments to press legislation. Several other parties also boycotted the polls. Many of the 524 candidates at the elections, which took place on 4 November, were independents or tribal leaders campaigning on local issues. In all, 62 of the 80 seats in the new House of Representatives were won by pro-Government candidates (including two members of the recently-formed National Constitutional Party); 10 seats were secured by nationalist and left-wing candidates, and eight by independent Islamists. The overall level of voter participation was reported to have been 54.6%, and was declared by the Government to be an endorsement of the country's electoral system and of the policies of King Hussein. However, there were reports that the level of turn-out was only 20% in some districts of Amman, and that the majority of Jordan's Palestinians had not voted. A new Senate was appointed by the King on 22 November. The Government was reorganized in February 1998. In July widespread public discontent arising from severe water shortages and the contamination of water supplies in Amman prompted the resignation of the Minister of Water and Irrigation. In August Fayez at-Tarawneh was appointed Prime Minister, in place of al-Majali (who had also been criticized with regard to the water crisis); a new Cabinet was subsequently named.

Meanwhile, in July 1998 King Hussein began to undergo treatment for cancer in the USA. In August he issued a royal decree transferring responsibility for certain executive duties to his brother, Crown Prince Hassan. On King Hussein's return to Jordan in January 1999, amid official assurances that his health had been restored, the King prompted renewed speculation about the royal succession by appointing Crown Prince Hassan as his 'deputy'. On 24 January King Hussein issued a royal decree naming his eldest son, Abdullah, as Crown Prince of Jordan. Although Hassan had been regent since 1965, King Hussein was said to have been dissatisfied with his brother's handling of Jordanian affairs during his absence, in particular his attempts to intervene in military matters. King Hussein had also accused his brother's supporters of slandering his immediate family, fuelling rumours that serious divisions had emerged within the royal family. Two days later the King left Jordan for emergency treatment in the USA, following a rapid deterioration in his health. King Hussein returned to Amman on 5 February 1999 and was pronounced dead on 7 February. The Crown Prince was sworn in, as King Abdullah ibn al-Hussein of Jordan, the same day. Prince Hamzeh ibn Hussein, the late King's youngest son, became the new Crown Prince.

In March 1999 King Abdullah announced the formation of a new Cabinet. Abd ar-Raouf ar-Rawabdeh, a former Deputy Prime Minister and mayor of Amman, replaced Fayez at-Tarawneh as Prime Minister and Minister of Defence; Abd al-Karim al-Kabariti was appointed Chief of the Royal Court. Ar-Rawabdeh's Cabinet retained eight ministers from the outgoing administration, including those responsible for the key portfolios of the interior, finance and foreign affairs, although several ministers regarded as loyal to Prince Hassan were replaced. King Abdullah charged ar-Rawabdeh with implementing what he termed 'fundamental reforms', including a strengthening of the rule of law and further democratization, as well as economic reforms to address the serious problems of poverty and unemployment in Jordan. Opposition groups expressed cautious loyalty to the new King. The Muslim Brotherhood urged an open dialogue with the Government, and its political wing, the IAF, indicated that it would participate in municipal elections scheduled for July. However, the IAF declined to join the Popular Participation Bloc, a new grouping of 13 leftist, Baathist and pan-Arab parties subsequently formed to contest the elections, owing to a disagreement regarding each party's quota of candidates.

Although in March 1999 King Abdullah had, under a recent amnesty law, released almost 500 prisoners, in April the Arab Human Rights Organization in Jordan criticized the Government for an increase in human rights violations, including arrests of journalists and harsh treatment of prisoners held in detention centres. Nevertheless, censorship of the foreign press was revoked in that month, and in June the Government agreed to amend part of the controversial Press and Publications Law in order to ease certain restrictions on journalists.

The final results of municipal elections held in July 1999 indicated that independent and tribal candidates had secured the most seats. Islamists too were successful in their traditional urban strongholds: the IAF, which notably increased its presence on the Amman municipal council, announced subsequently that it would contest the general election due in 2001 if the electoral law was amended. The overall level of voter participation was around 59%; voting in some areas was marred by violence, in which two people died. In September the Government agreed in principle to some of the opposition's demands regarding electoral reform; these included an increase in the number of seats in the House of Representatives from 80 to 120, and the division of the country into 80 electoral districts.

In December 1999 King Abdullah appointed an Economic Consultative Council to supervise implementation of the Five-Year Plan for 1999–2003. In January 2000 Abd al-Karim al-Kabariti, a long-standing rival of ar-Rawabdeh, resigned as Chief of the Royal Court for unspecified reasons. He was replaced by former premier Fayez at-Tarawneh. A reorganization of the Government followed shortly afterwards: the new Cabinet, which included seven new ministers, was dominated by technocrats and supporters of the Prime Minister, and the key ministries remained unchanged. In February the Deputy Prime Minister and Minister of Planning, Dr Rima Khalaf al-Hunaidi, announced her resignation, owing to alleged differences with the Government regarding economic reforms; Dr Taleb ar-Rifai was appointed to succeed her in May. Also in February, meanwhile, a parliamentary committee charged with investigating allegations of corruption made against ar-Rawabdeh and his son Issam (both had been accused of having sought a US $20m. bribe from a Gulf businessman in return for securing approval to build a tourism complex in Jordan) cleared both the Prime Minister and his son of any wrongdoing. Later that month a majority of deputies in the House of Representatives submitted a petition to the Speaker, Abd al-Hadi al-Majali, demanding the implementation of *Shari'a* (Islamic) law in order to reduce corruption and nepotism in public office.

In April 2000 a group of deputies in the House of Representatives, among them al-Majali and the Chairman of the Economic and Finance Committee, Ali Abu ar-Ragheb, urged King Abdullah to dismiss the ar-Rawabdeh Government for its failure to implement reforms and safeguard public freedoms, and demanded the establishment of a 'parliamentary government' of deputies. At the same time opposition groups accused the Government of using excessive force in controlling public dissent. Although the King responded by expressing his confidence in the Prime Minister, in June Abdullah dismissed ar-Rawabdeh, appointing the more liberal ar-Ragheb in his place. A new Cabinet was duly appointed, including nine Palestinians and three Islamists together with several ministers from the outgoing administration. A leading member of the IAF, Abd ar-Rahim al-Akour, was named as Minister of Municipal, Rural and Environmental Affairs, which led the IAF to suspend his party membership. King Abdullah stated that the priorities of the new Government were to end corruption, to introduce electoral legislation prior to the parliamentary elections scheduled for late 2001, and to accelerate the economic reform programme. In August 2000 the King was said to have called for the formation of a royal committee whose task would be to implement a 'drastic review' of the country's judicial system. Former Prime Ministers Ahmad Ubeidat and Taher al-Masri established a new political bloc, the Arab Democratic Front, in September.

In mid-January 2001 the Government was forced to reverse a decision to increase fuel prices, following opposition from deputies who cited the widespread deterioration in living standards. In March–April King Abdullah convened a National Economic Forum, with the participation of both public- and private-sector organizations; delegates at the conference concluded that task forces should be created to reform agriculture, education, administration and financial services.

In late January 2001 an Anti-Normalization Committee, composed of trade union activists opposed to Jordan's peace treaty with Israel, issued a list of more than 60 organizations and public figures deemed to have links with Israel (for further details, see below). A shorter list of 'normalizers' had been published two months previously. Several prominent members of the Committee, including its leader, Ali Abu as-Sukkar, were subsequently arrested by the Jordanian authorities, provoking condemnation by the Muslim Brotherhood. All the trade unionists were released on bail at the end of February, pending trial.

On 23 April 2001 King Abdullah exercised his constitutional right to extend the current term of the House of Representatives by two years. There was some speculation that the King's decision to postpone legislative elections—scheduled for November—had been taken in an attempt to prevent Islamist opposition parties (which were highly critical of the Government's policies towards Israel) from presenting a serious challenge to his leadership. On 16 June the King ordered the dissolution of the House, which had been sitting in extraordinary session since April, and effected a Cabinet reshuffle involving 11 new ministerial appointments (but excluding the key portfolios). The following day King Abdullah set the Government the task of drafting amendments to the electoral law within one month. On 22 July the King approved the new electoral legislation, which provided for the redrawing of electoral boundaries (the number of constituencies was to rise from 21 to 44) in order to increase the number of seats in the House of Representatives from 80 to 104, and a reduction of the age of eligibility to vote from 19 years to 18. The Muslim Brotherhood threatened to boycott the forthcoming parliamentary elections, in view of the Government's failure to meet its demand for the reintroduction of an 'electoral list' system. Critics of the amendments also complained that they failed to address the issue of under-representation in the legislature of Jordanians of Palestinian origin. Nevertheless, the new law did provide for the formation of special committees whose task would be to monitor the electoral process. Shortly afterwards it was reported that the November elections were to be postponed until late 2002 for technical reasons. At the end of August 2001 legislation was enacted imposing a ban on public gatherings and demonstrations. At the King's request, in late October Prime Minister ar-Ragheb effected a minor reorganization of the Cabinet; the changes included the abolition of the Ministries of Information and of Youth and Sports, which were to be replaced by independent higher councils. (However, the former ministry was still in existence in mid-2003). On 23 November 2001 King Abdullah appointed a new 40-member Senate upon the expiry of its term.

Meanwhile, in early October 2001, following the suicide attacks on the USA (see below), King Abdullah issued a royal decree amending Jordan's penal code in order to strengthen counter-terrorism measures; he also imposed tougher penalties on those found guilty of 'publication crimes'.

In mid-January 2002 Prime Minister ar-Ragheb again submitted the resignation of his Government, but was asked by King Abdullah to form a new administration capable of initiating economic and social reforms prior to parliamentary elections (now expected by November). A new Cabinet was named shortly afterwards; seven new ministers joined the Government, including Marwan al-Muasher as Minister of Foreign Affairs and Qaftan al-Majali as Minister of the Interior. In late January the King suffered one of the most serious challenges to his rule when two days of violent clashes erupted between protesters and security forces in Ma'an, following the death of a local youth in police custody. The authorities stated that the boy had died of natural causes, although demonstrators alleged that he had been the victim of police brutality. One policeman died in the violence, and several others were injured. The Government later announced that two investigations had been launched to determine the causes of both the adolescent's death and the subsequent riots. Also in late January details emerged of a massive investigation by the authorities into a case of alleged corruption and fraud involving several members of the Jordanian establishment (some of whom were close associates of the King). In mid-May Toujan al-Faisal, once the country's only female legislator, was handed down an 18-month prison sentence by the State Security Court, having been found guilty of seditious libel; however, al-Faisal received a royal pardon in late June.

King Abdullah announced in mid-August 2002 that legislative elections would be postponed until 2003, owing to the continuing instability in the region. A limited reorganization of the Cabinet was effected in late September 2002: the most significant change was the promotion of the Minister of Justice, Faris an-Nabulsi, to a new post of Deputy Prime Minister. In early November security forces in Ma'an carried out a large-scale operation aimed at detaining a local Islamist cleric, Muhammad Shalabi (or 'Abu Sayyaf') and his supporters, whom the Government claimed had played an important role in January's riots. Many observers believed that the security operation was linked to the recent assassination of a US diplomat (see below). At least three civilians and two police-officers were reportedly killed during the week-long campaign; however, despite the security forces making a large number of arrests, Abu Sayyaf apparently evaded capture. Renewed clashes between police and local gunmen later in November resulted in another civilian death in Ma'an. At the end of the month the Government announced that it would henceforth have the authority to disband any trade union-affiliated committee opposed to the normalization of relations with Israel. A limited reshuffle of the Cabinet took place in early January 2003, following the resignation of the Minister of Tourism and Antiquities, Taleb ar-Rifai. The tourism portfolio was given to the Minister of Transport, Nader ad-Dahabi, while the Minister of State for Administrative Development, Muhammad ath-Thneibat, was also to head the newly formed Ministry of the Environment. King Abdullah approved amendments to draft electoral legislation on 9 February: the amendments, which were to take effect from the next general election, increased the number of seats in the House of Representatives from 104 to 110, in order to provide a quota of six seats for female legislators. In early March the King effected several changes to the composition of the Royal Court, including the appointment of a former army general and minister of state, Yousuf ad-Dalabeeh, as Chief of the Royal Court, in place of Fayez at-Tarawneh. The King also appointed Faisal al-Fayez to the new government post of Minister of the Royal Court.

Meanwhile, in September 1997 relations with Israel were severely undermined when the head of the political bureau of the Palestinian Islamist group Hamas, Khalid Meshaal, was the victim of an assassination attempt in Amman by agents of the Israeli intelligence service, Mossad. Intensive negotiations involving Crown Prince Hassan, Israeli Prime Minister Binyamin Netanyahu and US officials resulted in an agreement in October whereby Israel freed the Hamas spiritual leader, Sheikh Ahmad Yassin, in return for Jordan's release of two Mossad agents arrested in connection with the attack on Meshaal. A further 12 Mossad agents were expelled from Jordan following the release from Israeli custody of 23 Jordanian and 50 Palestinian detainees. The Mossad chief, Danny Yatom, resigned in February 1998 and was replaced by Ephraim Halevy, who had played an important role in the negotiations leading to the 1994 peace treaty between Israel and Jordan. The two countries signed several bilateral trade agreements in March 1998, and in the following month King Hussein met with Netanyahu for the first time since the attempt on Meshaal's life; in March, however, the Israeli Minister of National Infrastructure, Ariel Sharon, had angered Jordan by stating publicly that Israel still intended to kill Meshaal (although Sharon later retracted his remarks). King Hussein's mediation at the US-brokered peace summit held between Israel and the Palestinian (National) Authority (PA) in October was crucial to the signing of the Wye Memorandum (see the chapter on Israel). In December Israel agreed to open its airspace to foreign airlines *en route* for Jordan.

Upon his accession in February 1999 King Abdullah assured Israel that he would pursue his father's commitment to the Middle East peace process. None the less, Netanyahu's first official visit to Amman, in late February, was largely overshadowed by recent comments made by the Israeli premier to the effect that Jordan intended to strengthen its links with Iraq at the expense of improving relations with Israel. In July Abdullah held talks with the new Israeli Prime Minister, Ehud Barak; discussions reportedly focused on ways to revive the peace process. The King welcomed the reactivation of the stalled Wye Memorandum by the signing (to which he was a witness) of the Sharm esh-Sheikh Memorandum (Wye Two—see the chapter on Israel) by Barak and Arafat in September 1999.

There was considerable speculation at the time of the Wye Two agreement that recent efforts to bring an end to Hamas' political activities in Jordan had been motivated by a consensus among the Jordanian, Palestinian, Israeli and US authorities on the need to contain potential Islamist opposition to a revival of the peace process. In August 1999 the Jordanian security forces closed down Hamas offices in Amman, on the grounds that these were being used by foreign groups for illegal political activities. The home of the Hamas bureau chief, Khalid Meshaal, was also raided, while some 15 Hamas officials were detained and arrest warrants issued for a further five of the organization's leaders. In September three of the five (including Meshaal and the Hamas spokesman, Ibrahim Ghosheh) were arrested on their return to Amman from Iran, on charges of involvement in illicit political activities and the illegal possession of firearms. Further charges were brought against Meshaal and Ghosheh in October. In November another senior Hamas official was arrested, amid reports that the organization had rejected an offer by the Jordanian Government to release the detained activists provided that they agreed to cease all political activity and that their leaders left the country. Later in the month the Jordanian authorities released some 24 Hamas officials, including four leaders (among them Meshaal and Ghosheh) who were immediately flown to Qatar. An appeal against this effective deportation, lodged by the four men at Jordan's Higher Court of Justice in January 2000, was rejected in June. In November, during talks with Khalid Meshaal in Qatar, Jordan's Prime Minister, Ali Abu ar-Ragheb, reportedly reiterated the conditions under which the Hamas leaders would be allowed to return to Jordan. The Jordanian authorities granted permission for Ibrahim Ghosheh to enter the country in June 2001, after he had agreed to end his involvement with Hamas.

Meanwhile, in December 1999 16 people were arrested on charges of plotting attacks against US and Israeli tourist targets in Jordan. The detainees were alleged to be members of the al-Qa'ida (Base) organization, under the command of the Saudi-born militant Islamist, Osama bin Laden. Trial proceedings began against the 16 in Amman in May 2000; 12 further alleged al-Qa'ida members were tried *in absentia*. In September six of the defendants were sentenced to death, having been convicted of charges including membership of al-Qa'ida and the manufacture of explosives; 16 were condemned to various terms of imprisonment, while six defendants were acquitted. The Jordanian authorities arrested a number of suspected Islamist extremists in July 2000, apparently in response to a warning that the US embassy in Amman was vulnerable to attacks by militant groups; in September four of the defendants received the death sentence. In February 2002 a Jordanian-US national, Raed Hijazi, was sentenced to death, having been found guilty of several charges relating to the alleged terrorist plot in late 1999; however, he was cleared of any involvement with al-Qa'ida. (After an appeals court ordered a retrial of Hijazi's case in early October 2002, claiming that there had been insufficient evidence to convict him, the death sentence was upheld by the State Security Court in early January 2003.) At the end of February 2002 at least two people were killed in an attack in Amman on a car belonging to the wife of a senior anti-terrorism police-officer who had played a prominent role in the original trial of the 28 al-Qa'ida suspects. There were reports in early July that 10 Jordanians (most of whom were of Palestinian origin) had been arrested by the authorities in Amman between April and June, on suspicion of plotting to launch terrorist attacks against US and Israeli targets in the country. All the suspects were acquitted of the terrorism charges by a military court in late January 2003, although eight of them received short prison sentences in connection with firearms offences.

King Abdullah postponed his first visit to Israel in February 2000, apparently in protest at recent Israeli bombing raids against infrastructure targets in Lebanon (although Jordanian officials cited the lack of progress in the Middle East peace process). Abdullah finally visited Israel in April, when he held brief discussions with Ehud Barak regarding the peace process, as well as water management and other bilateral issues. In advance of the Israeli-Palestinian peace talks held at the US presidential retreat at Camp David, Maryland, in July, Prime Minister ar-Ragheb emphasized that the Jordanian Government would not accept any more Palestinian refugees and that it supported their right of return to their homeland. (Recent reports had implied that Jordan was being considered as a possible home for those displaced persons currently in refugee camps in Lebanon.) In December 2002 there were 1,698,271 Palestinian refugees in Jordan and a further 639,448 in the West Bank registered with the UN Relief and Works Agency for Palestine Refugees in the Near East (UNRWA). Meanwhile, in August 2000 King Abdullah reiterated that Jordan would not accept Israeli or international sovereignty over the Islamic holy sites in East Jerusalem, an issue that had been a major obstacle to progress at Camp David.

King Abdullah participated in the intense diplomatic efforts aimed at restoring peace in the region following the outbreak of violence in the West Bank and Gaza in late September 2000 (see the chapters on Israel and the Palestinian Autonomous Areas). In mid-October the King attended a US-brokered summit meeting between Ehud Barak and Yasser Arafat in Sharm esh-Sheikh, Egypt. As violence between Palestinians and Israeli security forces escalated, Jordan came under growing pressure from other Arab states to sever diplomatic ties with Israel, while large-scale public demonstrations against Israeli and US policies towards the new Palestinian uprising (often termed the al-Aqsa *intifada*) were held in Amman and at Jordan's refugee camps. One 'anti-normalization' protest held in early October resulted in violent confrontations between protesters and police. The Government subsequently issued a ban on public demonstrations, and several protesters were detained (although many were later released). Meanwhile, Jordan delayed the dispatch of its new ambassador to Israel, in response to the deteriorating situation in the West Bank and Gaza; also in October 30 parliamentary deputies signed a petition demanding the expulsion of the Israeli ambassador in Amman. In late October Jordanian police used tear gas and water cannons to disperse thousands of protesters who had gathered on Jordan's border

with the West Bank in support of the right of return for Palestinian refugees. In November the Israeli Vice-Consul in Amman was injured in a gun attack by militant Islamists; another Israeli diplomat was wounded in a similar attack in December. In late November, meanwhile, King Abdullah appealed to the USA to intervene in order to halt 'Israeli aggressive practices' which threatened to destroy the prospects for achieving peace in the Middle East. Abdullah expressed his hope that the peace process would continue following the election of the uncompromising Ariel Sharon as Israeli Prime Minister in early February 2001, and appealed to the new US Administration under President George W. Bush to engage actively in efforts to bring an end to the violence. Later in that month King Abdullah urged the USA to exert pressure on Israel to end its economic blockade on the Palestinian areas.

The convening of a summit meeting of Arab League heads of state in Amman in late March 2001 reflected Jordan's prominent role in diplomatic efforts to resolve the Israeli–Palestinian conflict. At the summit Arab leaders pledged to transfer funds to the PA as part of a US $1,000m. fund established in late 2000. Jordan and Egypt both refused to return their ambassadors to Tel-Aviv in protest at Israeli military actions against the Palestinians, although they did not proceed to a formal suspension of diplomatic relations. (Egypt did, however, downgrade its relations with Israel in April 2002.) The summit's final communiqué —termed the Amman Declaration—repeated demands for Israel to withdraw its armed forces from all occupied territory. It was reported at the end of March 2001 that a joint Egyptian-Jordanian initiative for Middle East peace had been submitted to European Union (EU) and US officials in an attempt to encourage Israel and the PA to revive negotiations. King Abdullah held further discussions with President Bush in Washington, DC, in early April. Fears among Jordanians that the violence in the Occupied Territories might spread to Jordan were heightened in August when an Israeli businessman in Amman was murdered by a militant Islamist.

Further mass demonstrations were held in Jordanian cities and Palestinian refugee camps during late March and April 2002, after public anger had been fuelled by Israel's reoccupation of Palestinian-controlled population centres in the West Bank. Many unlicensed rallies only ended after considerable use of force by Jordanian anti-riot police, who resorted to tear gas, water cannons and beatings. Several protesters demanded that Jordan sever diplomatic ties with Israel. In early April Jordan was reported to be considering the expulsion of Israel's ambassador to Amman, in protest against continuing Israeli military action in the Palestinian territories. In mid-April the Jordanian Minister of Foreign Affairs, Marwan al-Muashar, held talks with Yasser Arafat at his besieged compound in Ramallah, in an apparent demonstration of solidarity with the Palestinian leader. Moreover, in that month the Jordanian authorities began to deliver large consignments of humanitarian aid from Jordan and other Arab states to the West Bank.

Jordan's relations with the USA in the early 1990s were frequently strained by US allegations of Jordanian assistance to Iraq in circumventing the UN trade embargo, as well as Jordan's vocal criticism of US-led policies towards Iraq. In July 1993 the USA reportedly informed Jordan that it must make payments to the UN Compensation Fund for Kuwait if it continued to receive deliveries of petroleum from Iraq. In September, however, US President Bill Clinton announced that some US $30m. in economic and military aid to Jordan was to be released in recognition of the country's enforcement of sanctions against Iraq and of its role in the Middle East peace process. In early 1994 renewed tensions emerged with the USA over the Jerusalem issue and the US-led naval blockade of Jordan's only port at Aqaba. In August 1995, as King Hussein formally severed political ties with Iraq (see below), Clinton promised to support Jordan in the event of any threat to its security; however, the USA failed to persuade Jordan to sever all economic links with Iraq. In January 1996 the USA offered Jordan $300m. in military assistance, and an expansion of bilateral military co-operation was announced in March. In June 1997 the USA pledged $100m. in economic aid to Jordan, reportedly in recognition of Jordan's contributions to the regional peace process; an assistance fund was established in August. In the same month Jordan signed a debt-rescheduling agreement with the USA, in accordance with a deal reached in May by members of the 'Paris Club' of Western official creditors to reschedule approximately $400m. of Jordanian debt. During a visit to Washington, DC, in March 1998 King Hussein reiterated demands that the USA exert pressure on Israel to make concessions over the West Bank; Hussein also proposed that Jordan participate in future negotiations between US and Iraqi officials.

In May 1999 King Abdullah began a three-week tour of the USA and several European capitals. Prior to the visit, the King had announced that, in anticipation of a summit of leaders of the Group of Eight (G-8) industrialized countries, due to be held in Germany in June, he would be seeking US support for an agreement by Western countries to write off as much as 50% of Jordan's debt. He achieved some success when, in late May (two days after a meeting with President Clinton) the 'Paris Club' agreed to reschedule about US $800m. of Jordanian debt; in June the G-8 leaders recommended arrangements for debt-reduction for Jordan. In mid-2000 King Abdullah held a series of meetings with President Clinton and senior US officials to discuss the Middle East peace process and bilateral trade. During a visit by the King to Washington, DC, in late October, Jordan and the USA signed a free-trade agreement involving the reciprocal removal of all customs duties by 2010. The deal was fully implemented in early December 2001.

King Abdullah strongly condemned the September 2001 suicide attacks against New York and Washington, DC, for which the USA held Osama bin Laden's al-Qa'ida network principally responsible, and the King swiftly affirmed Jordan's commitment to the proposed US-led 'war on terror'. Jordanian armed forces joined US and European forces when, from early October, they launched military strikes against al-Qa'ida bases and the Sunni fundamentalist Taliban regime in Afghanistan (which was believed to be harbouring bin Laden). However, Abdullah emphasized that the international community must simultaneously renew efforts to resolve the Israeli–Palestinian conflict. He also warned persistently that any extension of the US-led military action to target any Arab country, such as Iraq, would undermine the international campaign. In April 2002 certain sections of Jordan's business community called on the Government to boycott US products, in protest against perceived US support for Israeli aggression in the West Bank (see above). In July King Abdullah warned that Jordan would not allow its territory to be used by US troops to launch a military attack aimed at ousting the regime of Saddam Hussain in Iraq, and Jordanian officials denied reports in late September that the Government had agreed to allow US forces to use Jordanian military bases in return for a guaranteed supply of cheap oil during a potential disruption to Iraq's oil supplies. In early October the USA was said to have pledged a further US $85m. to Jordan, apparently in an effort to secure the country's support during a possible US-led military campaign in Iraq and to enable the Jordanian economy to withstand the consequences of a war.

At the end of October 2002 a senior US diplomat, Laurence Foley, became the first Western official to be assassinated in Jordan. The killing of Foley was widely believed to demonstrate a growing antipathy among a large section of the Jordanian population to the USA, owing in large part to the policies adopted by the Bush Administration with regard to the Israeli–Palestinian conflict and to Iraq. The Jordanian security forces detained a large number of suspected Islamic militants following the assassination. In mid-December two alleged members of al-Qa'ida—one Jordanian and the other Libyan—were arrested on suspicion of involvement in Foley's murder. In early February 2003 Jordanian officials confirmed that the USA was to provide an anti-missile defence system to Jordan in the event of a conflict in Iraq; the kingdom had received six F-16 fighter aircraft from the US military in late January. A large public demonstration against probable US military action in Iraq, held in Amman in early February, was the first such protest to be licensed by the authorities for several months.

After August 1995, when Jordan granted political asylum to the two sons-in-law of the Iraqi President, Saddam Hussain, and their wives (see the chapter on Iraq), King Hussein became more openly critical of the Iraqi regime, although Jordan continued to provide Iraq with a crucial external economic link. In December 1997 Jordan recalled its chargé d'affaires in Baghdad and expelled a number of Iraqi diplomats from Jordan in protest at the execution of four Jordanians by the Iraqi authorities. Later in that month, however, the two countries signed an agreement whereby Iraq was to supply 4.8m. metric tons of crude petroleum and refined petroleum products to Jordan in 1998. In January of that year more than 50 Jordanian detainees were released by Iraq.

In response to critical confrontations between Iraq and the UN during 1998 over the issue of weapons inspections, Jordan indicated that it would not allow its territory or airspace to be used for air-strikes against Iraq. King Hussein consistently advocated a resolution of the crises by diplomatic means, whilst urging Iraq to comply with all pertinent UN resolutions. This position allowed Jordan to improve its relations with some Arab states, notably Egypt. Jordan strongly condemned the air-strikes carried out against Iraq by US and British forces in December, and in early 1999 the Jordanian National Assembly voted in favour of an end to the UN embargo against Iraq.

King Abdullah made attempts to improve Jordan's relations with Iraq following his accession in February 1999. However, in June 2000 Jordan condemned the execution by Iraq of a Jordanian national charged with spying for the US Central Intelligence Agency (CIA). Tensions were eased somewhat following a visit to Amman in mid-July by Iraqi Vice-President Taha Yassin Ramadan. In November Prime Minister ar-Ragheb undertook an official visit to Iraq—the first visit by a Jordanian premier since 1991—and the two states agreed to increase the value of their trade agreement from US $300m. in 2000 to $450m. in 2001. Jordan condemned the air-strikes launched on Baghdad by US and British forces in February 2001. By mid-2001 Jordan was increasingly concerned that the proposed imposition of so-called 'smart' sanctions against Iraq (the initiative, supported principally by the USA and United Kingdom, was under debate at the UN Security Council—see the chapter on Iraq) would result in the loss of its oil supply from Iraq, in addition to its main regional export market. However, although Jordanian officials declared publicly their opposition to 'smart' sanctions, they were said to have privately assured Western governments that they accepted the policy. The Iraqi leadership, meanwhile, threatened to halt trade with any government that assisted in the implementation of the sanctions regime. In June Royal Jordanian Airline resumed scheduled flights to Iraq for the first time since 1990. At senior-level discussions held in Amman in early January 2002, Iraq and Jordan renewed their oil protocol and also agreed to the creation of a free-trade zone.

Following discussions held in London, United Kingdom, between the British Prime Minister, Tony Blair, and King Abdullah in late February 2003, the two leaders issued a joint statement calling on the Iraqi regime to comply with the terms of UN Security Council Resolution 1441 (see the chapter on Iraq), but stating that both Jordan and the United Kingdom favoured a peaceful solution to the crisis regarding Iraqi disarmament. King Abdullah had asserted in early February that the dispute regarding Iraq's alleged non-compliance with UN weapons inspectors should only be resolved under the umbrella of the UN. During early 2003 Jordan was said to be taking measures to prevent an influx of Iraqi refugees into the kingdom in the event of a US-led military campaign to remove Saddam Hussain from power. Following the outbreak of hostilities in Iraq in mid-March, it was reported in early April that two Iraqi terrorist squads had recently been detained in Jordan, after allegedly plotting to poison a reservoir used by US troops and to bomb a hotel frequented by Western journalists and military officials; three Iraqi diplomats were expelled from Jordan in late March after being implicated in the alleged poisoning plot.

President Hafiz al-Assad of Syria led a high-level Syrian delegation at King Hussein's funeral in February 1999, since when Jordan's relations with Syria have improved significantly. It was announced in May that Syria would supply Jordan with water in order to ease the summer drought. In June Jordan refused to participate in joint Turkish-Israeli naval exercises, scheduled for the following month; similar exercises in 1998 had provoked a diplomatic crisis with Syria. In August 1999 the first senior Syrian delegation for almost a decade visited Amman for a session of the Jordanian-Syrian Higher Committee; the meeting resulted in an accord that officials hoped might double the volume of bilateral trade. Later in the month Syria reportedly agreed to end the ban (imposed in 1994) on the free circulation of Jordanian newspapers and publications. King Abdullah made an unscheduled visit to Syria in July 1999, amid Jordanian concerns that any peace agreement concluded by Israel and Syria could damage the Palestinians' position and effectively isolate them in future negotiations. None the less, following the brief resumption of Israeli-Syrian peace talks in December, Abdullah urged Israel to make concessions to Syria in order to increase the likelihood of a bilateral settlement being reached. The King attended the funeral of President Assad in June 2000, and acted swiftly to forge close relations with the new Syrian President, Bashar al-Assad. In November Syria confirmed that it had upgraded its diplomatic representation in Amman to ambassadorial status, and the Syrian state airline resumed regular flights to Amman after a hiatus of more than 20 years. The Syrian authorities declared in January 2001 that all Jordanian prisoners held in Syria would soon be released. In late August 2002 Jordan and Syria signed an agreement under which Syria was to provide Jordan with water to ease Jordan's water shortages.

Meanwhile, King Abdullah sought to strengthen relations with other Arab states. His first major foreign visit was to Egypt for talks with President Mubarak in March 1999. (Jordan and Egypt had signed an agreement in December 1998 providing for the establishment of a free-trade zone by 2005.) During April 1999 the new King visited a number of Middle Eastern countries, including Kuwait. Jordan's embassy there had been re-opened in March of that year, following the restoration of full diplomatic relations between the two countries (which had been severed in 1990), and in September 1999 the *rapprochement* was apparently confirmed as King Abdullah again visited Kuwait. Kuwait subsequently announced an end to a nine-year ban on the sale of Jordanian newspapers. In October Kuwait returned an ambassador to Amman, the post having been vacant since the Gulf crisis. Abdullah became the first Jordanian monarch to visit Lebanon for more than 30 years when, in September 1999, he held discussions with senior Lebanese officials regarding the Middle East peace process and bilateral issues (including a planned free trade agreement). Jordan's relations with Qatar deteriorated in early August 2002, after the Jordanian authorities announced a ban on broadcasts in Jordan by the Al-Jazeera television station following criticism of the Government's foreign policy. The Jordanian authorities responded by summoning the Qatari ambassador and later withdrawing its ambassador to Qatar. In late October a Jordanian journalist employed by Qatari state television received a death sentence from a court in Qatar, having been convicted of espionage.

Government

Jordan is a constitutional monarchy. Legislative power is vested in a bicameral National Assembly: the Senate (House of Notables) has 40 members, appointed by the King for eight years (one-half of the members retiring every four years), while the House of Representatives (House of Deputies) has 80 members, elected by universal adult suffrage for four years. Legislation adopted in July 2001 increased membership of the lower house to 104, with effect from the next general election. Further legislation passed in February 2003 raised membership of the House of Representatives to 110 (again with effect from the next election), in order to provide a quota of six seats for female legislators. Executive power is vested in the King, who governs with the assistance of an appointed Council of Ministers, responsible to the Assembly.

There are eight administrative provinces, of which three have been occupied by Israel since June 1967.

Defence

The total strength of the Jordanian armed forces in August 2002 was 100,240. The army had 84,700 men, the air force 15,000 and the navy (coastguard) an estimated 540. Reserve forces numbered 35,000 (30,000 in the army). Paramilitary forces numbered an estimated 45,000 men, comprising a Civil Militia of some 35,000 and a Public Security Force of an estimated 10,000. Military service is based on selective conscription. Defence expenditure in 2002 was estimated at JD 720m.

Economic Affairs

In 2001, according to estimates by the World Bank, the East Bank of Jordan's gross national income (GNI), measured at average 1999–2001 prices, was US $8,786m., equivalent to $1,750 per head (or $4,080 per head on an international purchasing-power parity basis). During 1990–2001, it was estimated, the population increased at an average annual rate of 4.3%, while the East Bank's gross domestic product (GDP) per head increased, in real terms, by an average of 0.7% per year. Overall GDP increased, in real terms, by an average annual rate of 5.0% in 1990–2001; growth was 4.0% in 2000 and 4.2% in 2001.

Agriculture (including hunting, forestry and fishing) contributed about 2.1% of Jordan's GDP in 2001. An estimated 4.1% of the country's labour force were employed in the sector in that year. The principal cash crops are vegetables, fruit and nuts, which accounted for about 7.6% of export earnings in 2002.

Wheat production is also important. During 1990–2001 the sector's GDP decreased at an average annual rate of 0.2%. Agricultural GDP declined by 20.4% in 1999, owing to severe drought in that year, but increased by 6.3% in 2000.

Industry (including mining, manufacturing, construction and power) provided an estimated 24.1% of GDP in 2001, when about 21.9% of the country's active labour force were employed in the sector. During 1990–2001 industrial GDP increased by an average of 4.8% per year. The sector's GDP increased by 4.8% in 1999 and by 4.7% in 2000.

Mining and quarrying contributed an estimated 2.8% of GDP in 2001. The sector employed about 1.5% of the total labour force in that year. Phosphates and potash are the principal mineral exports, together accounting for around 15.2% of total export earnings in 2002. Jordan also has reserves of oil-bearing shale, but exploitation of this resource is at present undeveloped. The GDP of the mining sector declined by an estimated 5.9% in 1998.

Manufacturing provided an estimated 14.8% of GDP in 2001, and engaged some 12.1% of the employed labour force in that year. In 1997 the most important branches of manufacturing, measured by gross value of output, were food, beverages and tobacco (accounting for 25.3% of the total), refined petroleum products (17.4%), chemicals (11.0%), non-metallic mineral products (9.1%) and metal products (7.2%). Manufacturing GDP increased by an average of 5.3% per year in 1990–2001; the sector recorded growth of 5.8% in 1999 and 5.7% in 2000.

Energy is derived principally from imported petroleum, but attempts are being made to develop alternative sources of power, including wind and solar power. In 1999 petroleum provided 89.4% of total electricity production, while natural gas accounted for 10.4%. Imports of mineral fuels comprised some 15.5% of the total value of imports in 2002. Following an agreement signed in mid-2001, Egyptian gas was to be supplied to Jordan via a proposed high-capacity pipeline from mid-2003.

Services accounted for some 73.8% of Jordan's GDP in 2001. In that year an estimated 74.1% of the total employed labour force were engaged in the service sector. During 1990–2001 the GDP of the service sector increased by an average of 4.7% per year. Services GDP increased by 3.2% in 1999 and by 2.2% in 2000.

In 2001 Jordan recorded a visible trade deficit of US $2,007.0m., and there was a deficit of $4.1m. on the current account of the balance of payments. In 2002 Iraq was the main source of imports (with 15.6% of the total) and was also the principal market for exports (with 19.9% of the total). Other major trading partners in that year were Germany, the USA and the People's Republic of China. The principal exports in 2002 were miscellaneous manufactured articles, chemicals and minerals, while the principal imports were machinery and transport equipment, basic manufactures, and mineral fuels and lubricants.

In 1999 there was a budget deficit of JD 223.6m., equivalent to 4.2% of GDP in that year. Jordan's external debt totalled US $8,226m. at the end of 2000, of which US $7,055m. was long-term public debt. In that year the cost of debt-servicing was equivalent to 11.4% of the value of exports of goods and services. The annual rate of inflation averaged 4.0% in 1990–2000. Consumer prices increased by an annual average of 1.8% in both 2001 and 2002. Unemployment was officially put at 14.7% of the labour force in 2001, but unofficially estimated to be 20%–30%.

Jordan is a member of the Council of Arab Economic Unity (see p. 178), the Arab Co-operation Council (see p. 338), the Arab Monetary Fund (see p. 138) and the World Trade Organization (WTO, see p. 323). In September 1999 the Jordanian parliament ratified the Jordanian-European Partnership Agreement (signed with the EU in November 1997), which provides for the creation of a duty-free zone and the abolition of import duties by 2010.

Since the early 1990s the Jordanian economy has been constrained by a heavy burden of foreign debt and by the loss, owing to the imposition of UN sanctions, of its vital Iraqi market. Nevertheless, the conclusion of a peace treaty with Israel in 1994, as well as the recent improvement in relations with other Arab states, has created new opportunities in tourism, transport, banking and trade. Exports from Jordan to the USA were expected to rise considerably following the conclusion of a bilateral free-trade agreement which took effect in late 2001. Jordan has implemented an IMF-supported adjustment and reform programme with the aim of reducing state intervention in industry and, through privatization, raising funds to support the repayment of foreign debt. In order to encourage foreign investment, all foreign-exchange restrictions were revoked in June 1997. By early 2001 the restructuring of a number of state enterprises was under way, notably in the utilities, transport and telecommunications sectors. Jordan is deemed to have brought its external debt under control, a process facilitated by a series of debt-relief measures by Western creditors in the late 1990s and early part of this century; however, the IMF has recommended a faster pace of structural reform and the introduction of new banking legislation. In November 2001 the Government announced a two-year social and economic programme involving a new programme of large-scale industrial privatization, the receipts from which are to be used to fund vital education, health and development projects. It was reported in early 2003 that the programme had achieved considerable success thus far. Meanwhile, a value-added tax was introduced in 2001, while in January 2002 a new income tax law reduced the tax burden on private companies in an effort to encourage competition. In December of that year the WTO agreed to exempt Jordanian exports from income tax for a five-year period. In January 2001 the Aqaba region was accorded the status of a Special Economic Zone, which was officially inaugurated in May; the Government hoped that the zone would attract investment worth US $6,000m. and create as many as 70,000 new jobs by 2020. Meanwhile, the economic growth rate was deemed to be insufficient to reduce unemployment and raise living standards. The 1999–2003 Plan forecast GDP growth reaching 6% by 2003; however, growth remained at around 4% in both 2000 and 2001. GDP growth was expected to be in the region of 5% in 2002. Since September 2000 the impact on regional security of the Israeli–Palestinian conflict has hampered efforts by the Jordanian Government to attract foreign investment, and has had a particularly detrimental effect on Jordan's tourist and banking sectors. Moreover, the conflict in Iraq during March–April 2003 was expected to be especially damaging to the Jordanian economy; the war seemed likely to have a profound impact on the trade, tourism and transport sectors in particular, and would almost certainly deter foreign investment into the country, at least in the short term.

Education

Primary education, beginning at six years of age, is free and compulsory. This 10-year preparatory cycle is followed by a two-year secondary cycle. UNRWA provides schooling for Palestinian refugees. In 2001, at the primary level, there were 50,562 teachers and 1,173,314 pupils. At the secondary level (including both general and vocational education) there were 14,280 teachers and 173,755 pupils in that year. There were 6,036 teachers and 153,965 pupils engaged in higher education in 2001. Education in Jordan was provided at 4,999 schools and 22 institutions of higher education in that year. Budgetary expenditure on education by the central Government in 1997 was JD 245.1m. (14.6% of total spending).

Public Holidays

2003: 15 January (Arbor Day), 30 January (King Abdullah's Birthday), 12 February* (Id al-Adha, Feast of the Sacrifice), 5 March* (Muharram, Islamic New Year), 22 March (Arab League Day), 14 May* (Mouloud, Birth of Muhammad), 25 May (Independence Day), 9 June (King Abdullah's Accession), 24 September* (Leilat al-Meiraj, Ascension of Muhammad), 14 November (the late King Hussein's Birthday), 26 November* (Id al-Fitr, end of Ramadan).

2004: 15 January (Arbor Day), 30 January (King Abdullah's Birthday), 2 February* (Id al-Adha, Feast of the Sacrifice), 22 February* (Muharram, Islamic New Year), 22 March (Arab League Day), 2 May* (Mouloud, Birth of Muhammad), 25 May (Independence Day), 9 June (King Abdullah's Accession), 12 September* (Leilat al-Meiraj, Ascension of Muhammad), 14 November (the late King Hussein's Birthday) (Id al-Fitr, end of Ramadan*).

*These holidays are dependent on the Islamic lunar calendar and may vary by one or two days from the dates given.

Weights and Measures

The metric system is in force. In Jordan the dunum is 1,000 sq m (0.247 acre).

Statistical Survey

Source: Department of Statistics, POB 2015, Amman; tel. (6) 5300700; fax (6) 5300710; e-mail stat@dos.gov.jo; internet www.dos.gov.jo.

Area and Population

AREA, POPULATION AND DENSITY
(East Bank only)

Area (sq km)	89,342*
Population (census results)	
10–11 November 1979	2,100,019
10 December 1994	
Males	2,160,725
Females.	1,978,733
Total	4,139,458
Population (official estimates at 31 December)	
1999	4,900,000
2000	5,039,000
2001	5,182,000
Density (per sq km) at 31 December 2001	58.0

* 34,495 sq miles.

GOVERNORATES
(East Bank only; estimated population at 31 December 2001)

	Area (sq km)	Population	Density (per sq km)
Amman	8,231	1,971,750	239.6
Irbid	1,621	924,470	570.3
Az-Zarqa (Zarqa). . . .	4,080	815,130	199.8
Al-Balqa	1,076	339,940	315.9
Al-Mafraq	26,435	238,890	9.0
Al-Karak (Kerak). . .	3,217	208,315	64.8
Jarash (Jerash) . . .	402	152,350	379.0
Madaba	2,008	132,140	65.8
Ajloun	412	115,040	279.2
Al-Aqabah (Aqaba) . . .	6,583	101,050	15.4
Ma'an	33,163	104,160	3.1
At-Tafilah	2,114	78,765	37.3
Total	**89,342**	**5,182,000**	**58.0**

PRINCIPAL TOWNS
(population at 1994 census)

Amman (capital). .	969,598	Al-Baq'ah . . .	58,592
Az-Zarqa (Zarqa). .	350,849	As-Salt	56,458
Irbid	208,329	Madaba	55,749
Ar-Rusayfah (Russeifa) . .	137,247	Ar-Ramtha . . .	55,022
Wadi as-Sir . . .	89,104	Suwaylih	53,250
Al-Aqabah (Aqaba) .	62,773		

Source: Thomas Brinkhoff, *City Population* (internet www.citypopulation.de).

Population at 31 December 2001 (including suburbs): Amman 1,766,155; Zarqa 447,122; Irbid 257,795; Russeifa 227,544.

BIRTHS, MARRIAGES AND DEATHS

(East Bank only)*

	Registered live births		Registered marriages		Registered deaths	
	Number	Rate (per 1,000)	Number	Rate (per 1,000)	Number	Rate (per 1,000)
1994 . .	140,444	34.5	36,132	8.9	12,290	3.0
1995 . .	141,319	33.5	35,501	8.4	13,018	3.1
1996 . .	142,404	32.6	34,425	7.9	13,302	3.0
1997 . .	130,633	28.4	37,278	8.1	13,190	2.9
1998 . .	133,714	28.0	39,376	8.3	13,552	5.0
1999 . .	135,300†	28.0	39,443†	8.0	13,900†	5.0
2000 . .	143,800†	28.0	45,600†	9.0	14,600†	5.0
2001 . .	143,000†	28.0	49,800†	9.7	16,200†	5.0

* Data are tabulated by year of registration rather than by year of occurrence. Registration of births and marriages is reported to be complete, but death registration is incomplete. Figures exclude foreigners, but include registered Palestinian refugees.
† Figures are rounded.

Expectation of life (years at birth): 70.8 (males 68.6; females 73.5) in 2001 (Source: WHO, *World Health Report*).

ECONOMICALLY ACTIVE POPULATION

(Jordanians only)

	1990	1991	1992
Agriculture	38,266	40,848	44,400
Mining and manufacturing . . .	53,468	56,856	61,800
Electricity and water	6,815	7,176	6,600
Construction	51,895	54,096	60,000
Trade	52,944	56,856	63,000
Transport and communications. .	44,557	48,576	52,200
Financial and insurance services .	16,774	17,664	19,800
Social and administrative services	259,478	269,928	292,200
Total employed	524,197	552,000	600,000
Unemployed	106,000	128,000	106,000
Total civilian labour force . .	630,197	680,000	706,000

Source: Ministry of Labour, *Annual Report*.

2001 (% of total): Agriculture 4.1; Mining and quarrying 1.5; Manufacturing 12.1; Electricity, gas and water supply 1.5; Construction 6.8; Wholesale and retail trade 18.0; Hotels and restaurants 2.5; Transport, storage and communications 10.0; Financial intermediation 2.1; Real estate, renting and business activities 3.7; Public administration 15.9; Education 11.4; Health and social work 4.5; Other community activities 5.5; Private households with employed persons 0.3; Extra-territorial organizations and bodies 0.2.

Health and Welfare

KEY INDICATORS

Total fertility rate (children per woman, 2001)	4.4
Under-5 mortality rate (per 1,000 live births, 2001) . . .	33
HIV/AIDS (% of persons aged 15–49, 2001)	<0.10
Physicians (per 1,000 head, 1997)	1.66
Hospital beds (per 1,000 head, 1997)	1.8
Health expenditure (2000): US $ per head (PPP)	325
Health expenditure (2000): % of GDP	8.1
Health expenditure (2000): Public (% of total)	51.8
Access to water (% of persons, 2000)	96
Access to sanitation (% of persons, 2000)	99
Human Development Index (2000): Ranking	99
Human Development Index (2000): Value	0.717

For sources and definitions, see explanatory note on p. vi.

Agriculture

PRINCIPAL CROPS

(East Bank only; '000 metric tons)

	1999	2000	2001
Wheat	9.3	25.4	19.3
Barley	4.9	12.1	17.3
Maize	12.3	18.8	15.0*
Potatoes	96.3	97.1	101.3
Olives	38.3	134.3	65.8
Cabbages	34.5	12.0	11.3
Lettuce	13.2	11.6	10.9
Tomatoes	293.3	354.3	310.2
Cauliflowers	48.6	26.3	18.7
Pumpkins, squash and gourds . .	35.8	49.5	45.0*
Cucumbers and gherkins . . .	66.3	132.9	140.0*
Aubergines (Eggplants) . . .	43.7	35.7	32.0*
Chillies and green peppers . . .	22.8	22.0	21.3
Green onions and shallots . . .	7.6	19.6	18.0*
Dry onions	27.6	47.3	23.5
Green beans	11.2	14.1	13.1
Green broad beans	6.7	9.1	13.9
Other vegetables	55.1	65.9	50.9*
Watermelons	120.7	35.0	34.3
Cantaloupes and other melons . .	21.4	34.0	32.0*
Bananas	36.4	20.8	24.3
Oranges	18.0	39.6	32.1
Tangerines, mandarins, clementines and satsumas . .	33.3	49.4	61.1
Lemons and limes	23.9	28.7	34.2
Apples	31.0	37.5	37.1
Peaches and nectarines	11.6	8.2	11.9
Grapes	18.2	23.9	27.0
Other fruits and berries	29.0	27.0	26.3*

* FAO estimate.

Source: FAO.

LIVESTOCK

(East Bank only; '000 head, year ending September)

	1999	2000	2001
Horses*	4	4	4
Mules*	3	3	3
Asses*	18	18	18
Cattle	65	65	67
Camels*	18	18	18
Sheep	1,934	1,896	1,869
Goats	641	640	534
Chickens	23,000	23,500	23,750

* FAO estimates.

Source: FAO.

LIVESTOCK PRODUCTS

(East Bank only; '000 metric tons)

	1999	2000	2001
Beef and veal	3.9	3.4	3.6
Mutton and lamb	13.4	9.3	6.0
Goat meat	3.4	2.0	2.8
Poultry meat	110.8	118.7	117.4
Cows' milk	140.6	161.8	162.8
Sheeps' milk	20.5	31.3	28.7
Goats' milk	12.0	11.5	16.8
Cheese*	2.3	3.5	3.2
Hen eggs	48.0	45.8	54.5
Greasy wool	2.7*	2.1*	1.8
Sheepskins*	113.2	93.5	80.4
Goatskins*	31	19	26

* FAO estimate(s).

Source: FAO.

Forestry

ROUNDWOOD REMOVALS
(estimates, '000 cubic metres, excluding bark)

	1999	2000	2001
Industrial wood	4	4	4
Fuel wood	213	222	230
Total	217	226	234

Source: FAO.

Fishing

(metric tons, live weight)

	1998	1999	2000
Capture	470	510	550
Freshwater fishes	350	350	400
Tunas	70	96	90
Aquaculture	293	515	569
Tilapias	263	515	563
Total catch	763	1,025	1,119

Source: FAO, *Yearbook of Fishery Statistics*.

Mining

('000 metric tons, unless otherwise indicated)

	1999	2000	2001
Crude petroleum ('000 barrels)	14.6*	14.6*	14.6
Phosphate rock	6,014	5,526	5,843
Potash salts†	1,080	1,160	1,180*
Salt (unrefined)	279.1	311.2	321.0

* Estimate.

† Figures refer to the K_2O content.

Source: US Geological Survey.

Industry

SELECTED PRODUCTS
('000 barrels, unless otherwise indicated)

	1999	2000	2001
Liquefied petroleum gas	1,505	1,684	1,750*
Motor spirit (petrol)	4,685	4,957	5,160*
Kerosene	1,382	1,991	2,070*
Jet fuels	1,722	1,950	2,030*
Distillate fuel oils	8,222	10,001	10,400*
Other refinery products	830	688	690*
Phosphate fertilizers ('000 metric tons)	613.8	409.1	443.0*
Cement ('000 metric tons)	2,687	2,640	3,159
Electricity (million kWh)	6,456	7,056	7,200

* Estimate.

Nitrogenous fertilizers (nitrogen, metric tons): 121,000 in 1996.

Potassic fertilizers (potassic acid, metric tons): 987 in 1997.

Cigarettes (million): 2,652 in 1996.

Sources: US Geological Survey; UN, *Monthly Bulletin of Statistics*.

Finance

CURRENCY AND EXCHANGE RATES

Monetary Units
1,000 fils = 1 Jordanian dinar (JD)

Sterling, Dollar and Euro Equivalents (31 December 2002)
£1 sterling = JD 1.1428
US $1 = 709.0 fils
€1 = 743.5 fils
JD 100 = £87.51 = $141.04 = €134.49

Exchange Rate: An official mid-point rate of US $1 = 709 fils (JD1 = $1.4104) has been maintained since October 1995.

BUDGET
(East Bank only; JD million)*

Revenue†	2000	2001	2002‡
Taxation	961.9	996.4	1,000.3
Taxes on income and profits	161.0	195.4	196.2
Corporations	97.3	131.3	120.9
Individuals	37.9	38.4	39.8
Taxes on domestic transactions	520.2	554.4	564.5
General sales tax	464.5	502.7	510.7
Taxes on foreign trade	264.7	228.5	219.8
Customs duties	260.5	224.3	214.4
Other revenue	598.8	641.6	679.3
Licences	37.4	32.1	31.9
Fees	200.1	215.0	225.1
Interest and profits	140.7	136.4	136.6
Total	1,610.1	1,718.6	1,752.1

Expenditure§	2000	2001	2002‡
Wages and salaries	366.0	384.1	407.2
Purchases of goods and services	72.2	74.9	80.6
Interest payments	293.1	278.0	251.4
Other transfers	408.4	452.5	504.8
Pensions	268.6	290.9	320.2
Decentralized agencies	67.2	70.3	91.8
University and municipalities	43.0	55.0	44.0
Defence and security	531.2	537.0	551.3
Total	2,054.1	2,192.3	2,289.1
Current	1,718.3	1,788.5	1,852.3
Capital‖	335.8	403.8	436.8

* Figures represent a consolidation of the Current, Capital and Development Plan Budgets of the central Government. The data exclude the operations of the Health Security Fund and of other government agencies with individual budgets.

† Excluding foreign grants received (JD million): 240.2 in 2000; 249.4 in 2001; 277.4 in 2002.

‡ Preliminary figures.

§ Excluding lending minus repayments (JD million): −2.0 in 2000; −36.9 in 2001; n.a. in 2002.

‖ Includes overdue settlements and arrears on public sector.

Source: Central Bank of Jordan.

2003 (draft budget, JD million): Total revenue 2,125; Total expenditure 2,441 (Source: Ministry of Finance).

INTERNATIONAL RESERVES
(US $ million at 31 December)

	2000	2001	2002
Gold*	99.1	112.2	141.2
IMF special drawing rights	0.6	1.2	0.9
Foreign exchange	3,330.6	3,061.0	3,975.0
Total	3,430.3	3,174.4	4,117.1

* National valuation.

Source: IMF, *International Financial Statistics*.

MONEY SUPPLY
(JD million at 31 December)

	1999	2000	2001
Currency outside banks	1,106.6	1,239.9	1,202.4
Demand deposits at commercial banks	658.0	774.2	888.4
Total money (incl. others)	1,766.1	2,017.4	2,094.8

Source: IMF, *International Financial Statistics*.

COST OF LIVING
(Consumer Price Index; base: 1997 = 100)

	2000	2001	2002
Food (incl. beverages)	102.4	102.7	102.9
Clothing (incl. footwear)	110.0	111.3	110.6
Housing	104.0	105.9	108.3
Other goods and services	107.6	112.7	118.5
All items	104.4	106.3	108.2

Source: Central Bank of Jordan.

NATIONAL ACCOUNTS
(East Bank only; JD million at current prices)

Expenditure on the Gross Domestic Product

	1998	1999	2000
Government final consumption expenditure	1,367.0	1,386.7	1,421.6
Private final consumption expenditure	4,110.7	4,166.3	4,856.1
Increase in stocks	35.6	−106.6	64.0
Gross fixed capital formation	1,189.8	1,353.5	1,263.2
Total domestic expenditure	6,703.1	6,799.9	7,604.9
Exports of goods and services	2,515.7	2,505.4	2,507.0
Less Imports of goods and services	3,608.7	3,537.9	4,109.5
GDP in purchasers' values	5,610.1	5,767.4	6,002.4
GDP at constant 1994 prices	5,027.4	5,181.5	5,399.8

Gross Domestic Product by Economic Activity

	1999	2000*	2001*
Agriculture, hunting, forestry and fishing	115.9	116.7	115.9
Mining and quarrying	163.8	157.4	156.9
Manufacturing	750.2	792.0	828.7
Electricity and water	129.4	134.6	135.1
Construction	207.1	203.9	227.2
Wholesale and retail trade, restaurants and hotels	543.2	602.5	650.5
Transport, storage and communications	762.2	831.6	876.7
Finance, insurance, real estate and business services	990.5	1,071.2	1,136.2
Government services	995.7	1,079.1	1,112.7
Other community, social and personal services	224.3	242.9	265.0
Private non-profit services to households	57.4	63.2	73.5
Domestic services of households	7.9	9.7	9.2
Sub-total	4,947.6	5,304.8	5,587.6
Less Imputed bank service charge	93.5	108.5	116.6
GDP at factor cost	4,854.1	5,196.3	5,471.0
Indirect taxes, *less* subsidies	913.2	795.8	787.8
GDP in purchasers' values	5,767.3	5,992.1	6,258.8

* Preliminary figures.

BALANCE OF PAYMENTS
(US $ million)

	1999	2000	2001
Exports of goods f.o.b.	1,831.9	1,899.3	2,294.4
Imports of goods f.o.b.	−3,292.0	−4,073.6	−4,301.4
Trade balance	−1,460.1	−2,174.3	−2,007.0
Exports of services	1,701.7	1,636.7	1,481.7
Imports of services	−1,698.0	−1,722.6	−1,725.0
Balance on goods and services	−1,456.4	−2,260.2	−2,250.3
Other income received	467.6	670.1	648.5
Other income paid	−479.7	−535.4	−461.4
Balance on goods, services and income	−1,468.6	−2,125.5	−2,063.1
Current transfers received	2,154.9	2,461.5	2,361.8
Current transfers paid	−281.4	−277.4	−302.8
Current balance	404.9	58.5	−4.1
Capital account (net)	90.3	64.9	21.6
Direct investment abroad	−4.5	−4.7	−7.9
Direct investment from abroad	158.0	786.6	100.3
Other investment assets	−41.9	146.4	26.8
Other investment liabilities	609.5	600.1	580.3
Net errors and omissions	28.7	315.6	80.0
Overall balance	1,249.0	1,826.6	625.3

Source: IMF, *International Financial Statistics*.

External Trade

PRINCIPAL COMMODITIES
(distribution by SITC, JD '000)

Imports c.i.f.	2000	2001	2002*
Food and live animals	529,895	524,323	485,091
Crude materials (inedible) except fuels	103,790	106,101	105,825
Mineral fuels, lubricants, etc.	508,811	495,376	545,724
Crude petroleum	373,131	385,871	412,855
Chemicals	349,603	379,414	397,804
Basic manufactures	493,722	666,575	682,685
Machinery and transport equipment	931,114	938,668	873,928
Miscellaneous manufactured articles	180,806	204,985	246,318
Total (incl. others)	3,259,404	3,453,729	3,531,482

Exports f.o.b.	2000	2001	2002*
Food and live animals	116,422	135,530	151,029
Vegetables, fruit and nuts	71,849	94,393	116,847
Crude materials (inedible) except fuels	249,306	250,165	252,137
Phosphates	90,864	90,485	96,593
Potash	138,061	138,334	136,605
Animal and vegetable oils and fats	44,731	42,735	66,742
Chemicals	347,161	345,135	389,151
Phosphoric acid	73,687	37,012	61,709
Medical and pharmaceutical products	110,875	129,716	142,569
Polishing and cleaning preparations and perfume materials	34,813	33,490	52,136
Fertilizers	59,768	61,099	63,959
Basic manufactures	113,619	168,795	153,427
Paper and cardboard	39,427	50,084	33,159
Machinery and transport equipment	69,253	122,826	99,515
Miscellaneous manufactured articles	131,497	264,262	395,490
Clothing	75,916	203,851	343,081
Total (incl. others)	1,080,817	1,352,371	1,538,104

* Preliminary figures.

Source: Central Bank of Jordan.

PRINCIPAL TRADING PARTNERS
(countries of consignment, JD million)

Imports c.i.f.	2000	2001	2002*
Argentina	69.7	73.0	69.5
Australia	46.6	52.9	39.7
Belgium-Luxembourg	39.3	30.5	44.6
China, People's Republic	125.6	168.6	233.6
Egypt	30.9	36.6	53.6
France	124.0	131.8	147.0
Germany	375.2	317.1	326.5
India	45.6	52.1	57.9
Indonesia	42.1	42.3	55.7
Iraq	483.9	485.6	549.3
Italy	118.7	114.0	124.2
Japan	127.8	124.1	111.7
Korea, Republic	116.7	99.6	91.4
Lebanon	27.6	31.5	30.2
Malaysia	37.0	34.1	36.7
Netherlands	52.5	47.8	65.4
Russia	51.3	42.5	22.1
Saudi Arabia	106.2	111.0	99.4
Spain	31.9	59.7	44.5
Sweden	24.5	56.6	34.1
Switzerland	39.3	40.1	38.5
Syria	31.8	47.1	68.4
Taiwan	38.6	60.2	77.4
Turkey	64.3	86.4	85.8
United Arab Emirates	34.9	41.7	54.8
United Kingdom	148.3	124.3	131.5
USA	322.0	280.7	254.1
Total (incl. others)	3,259.4	3,453.7	3,531.5

Exports f.o.b.	2000	2001	2002*
Bahrain	10.6	13.0	14.3
China, People's Republic	33.0	29.5	32.4
Egypt	16.9	14.9	10.6
Germany	4.5	16.8	8.8
India	172.2	145.3	162.1
Indonesia	20.0	21.0	13.5
Iraq	100.1	299.4	306.7
Israel	55.3	72.9	86.3
Kuwait	19.5	24.8	26.3
Lebanon	24.1	27.7	33.0
Malaysia	14.8	16.7	13.5
Pakistan	24.4	18.1	21.8
Qatar	15.2	17.8	19.1
Saudi Arabia	92.0	95.6	104.4
Syria	16.5	25.6	46.6
Turkey	10.0	8.9	13.0
United Arab Emirates	47.6	58.9	58.7
United Kingdom	8.0	14.8	6.1
USA	44.8	164.6	289.7
Total (incl. others)	1,080.8	1,352.4	1,538.1

* Preliminary figures.

Source: Central Bank of Jordan.

Transport

RAILWAYS
(traffic)

	1998	1999	2000
Passenger-km (million)	2.0	2.5	2.1
Freight ton-km (million)	596	585	348

ROAD TRAFFIC
(motor vehicles in use at 31 December)

	1998	1999	2000
Passenger cars	191,940	203,503	245,357
Buses and coaches	10,104	9,962	9,839
Lorries and vans	101,343	94,028	102,531
Motorcycles and mopeds	271	311	273

SHIPPING

Merchant Fleet
(registered at 31 December)

	1999	2000	2001
Number of vessels	10	9	10
Displacement (grt)	42.1	41.8	42.1

Source: Lloyd's Register-Fairplay, *World Fleet Statistics.*

International Sea-borne Freight Traffic
('000 metric tons)

	1998	1999	2000
Goods loaded	7,308	7,476	7,188
Goods unloaded	5,340	5,376	5,364

Source: UN, *Monthly Bulletin of Statistics.*

CIVIL AVIATION
(traffic on scheduled services)

	1997	1998	1999
Kilometres flown (million)	40	35	36
Passengers carried ('000)	1,353	1,187	1,252
Passenger-km (million)	4,900	4,065	4,195
Total ton-km (million)	721	596	579

Source: UN, *Statistical Yearbook.*

Passengers carried ('000): 1,343.4 in 2000; 1,236.3 in 2001.

Tourism

ARRIVALS BY NATIONALITY
('000)*

	1999	2000	2001
Egypt	270.4	215.0	325.1
Iraq	358.0	330.2	417.5
Israel	125.5	136.7	185.4
Kuwait	73.8	58.1	80.5
Saudi Arabia	609.2	471.1	602.7
Syria	939.3	898.6	1,127.2
Turkey	78.2	59.4	70.7
USA	100.5	99.2	59.1
Total (incl. others)	3,315.2	3,019.6	2,366.3

* Including pilgrims and excursionists (same-day visitors). The total number of tourist arrivals (in '000) was: 1,357.8 in 1999; 1,426.9 in 2000; 1,477.7 in 2001.

Source: partly World Tourism Organization, *Yearbook of Tourism Statistics.*

2002 ('000 arrivals): Egypt 354.8; Iraq 391.6; Saudi Arabia 687.4; Syria 1,364.0; USA 58.3 (Source: Central Bank of Jordan).

Tourism receipts (JD million): 564.0 in 1999; 512.4 (preliminary figure) in 2000; 496.1 (preliminary figure) in 2001 (Source: Central Bank of Jordan).

Communications Media

(East Bank only)

	1999	2000	2001
Television receivers ('000 in use)	540	560	n.a.
Telephones ('000 main lines in use)	565.3	620.0	660.0
Mobile cellular telephones ('000 subscribers)	118.4	388.9	745.5
Personal computers ('000 in use)	90	150	170
Internet users ('000)	120.0	127.3	212.0

1996: Book production (titles) 511.

1997: Radio receivers ('000 in use) 1,660.

1998: Facsimile machines ('000 in use) 51.6; Daily newspapers (titles) 8, (average circulation) 352,000 copies; Non-daily newspapers (titles) 13; Periodicals (titles) 270, (average circulation) 148,000 copies.

Sources: International Telecommunication Union; UNESCO, *Statistical Yearbook*; UN, *Statistical Yearbook*.

Education

(East Bank, 2001, unless otherwise indicated)

	Schools	Teachers	Pupils
Pre-primary	1,165	3,878	83,777
Primary	2,708	50,562	1,173,314
Secondary: general	912	11,254	129,894
Secondary: vocational	214	3,026	43,861
Higher	22	6,036	153,965
of which universities*	n.a.	3,982	89,010

* 1996/97 figures.

Adult literacy rate (UNESCO estimates): 89.7% (males 95.1%; females 83.9%) in 2000 (Source: UNDP, *Human Development Report*).

Directory

The Constitution

The revised Constitution was approved by King Talal I on 1 January 1952.

The Hashemite Kingdom of Jordan is an independent, indivisible sovereign state. Its official religion is Islam; its official language Arabic.

RIGHTS OF THE INDIVIDUAL

There is to be no discrimination between Jordanians on account of race, religion or language. Work, education and equal opportunities shall be afforded to all as far as is possible. The freedom of the individual is guaranteed, as are his dwelling and property. No Jordanian shall be exiled. Labour shall be made compulsory only in a national emergency, or as a result of a conviction; conditions, hours worked and allowances are under the protection of the state.

The Press, and all opinions, are free, except under martial law. Societies can be formed, within the law. Schools may be established freely, but they must follow a recognized curriculum and educational policy. Elementary education is free and compulsory. All religions are tolerated. Every Jordanian is eligible for public office, and choices are to be made by merit only. Power belongs to the people.

THE LEGISLATIVE POWER

Legislative power is vested in the National Assembly and the King. The National Assembly consists of two houses: the Senate and the House of Representatives.

THE SENATE

The number of Senators is one-half of the number of members of the House of Representatives. Senators must be unrelated to the King, over 40, and are chosen from present and past Prime Ministers and Ministers, past Ambassadors or Ministers Plenipotentiary, past Presidents of the House of Representatives, past Presidents and members of the Court of Cassation and of the Civil and *Shari'a*Courts of Appeal, retired officers of the rank of General and above, former members of the House of Representatives who have been elected twice to that House, etc... They may not hold public office. Senators are appointed for four years. They may be reappointed. The President of the Senate is appointed for two years.

THE HOUSE OF REPRESENTATIVES

The members of the House of Representatives are elected by secret ballot in a general direct election and retain their mandate for four years. General elections take place during the four months preceding the end of the term. The President of the House is elected by secret ballot each year by the Representatives. Representatives must be Jordanians of over 30, they must have a clean record, no active business interests, and are debarred from public office. Close relatives of the King are not eligible. If the House of Representatives is dissolved, the new House shall assemble in extraordinary session not more than four months after the date of dissolution. The new House cannot be dissolved for the same reason as the last.

GENERAL PROVISIONS FOR THE NATIONAL ASSEMBLY

The King summons the National Assembly to its ordinary session on 1 November each year. This date can be postponed by the King for two months, or he can dissolve the Assembly before the end of its three months' session. Alternatively, he can extend the session up to a total period of six months. Each session is opened by a speech from the throne.

Decisions in the House of Representatives and the Senate are made by a majority vote. The quorum is two-thirds of the total number of members in each House. When the voting concerns the Constitution, or confidence in the Council of Ministers, 'the votes shall be taken by calling the members by name in a loud voice'. Sessions are public, though secret sessions can be held at the request of the Government or of five members. Complete freedom of speech, within the rules of either House, is allowed.

The Prime Minister places proposals before the House of Representatives; if accepted there, they are referred to the Senate and finally sent to the King for confirmation. If one house rejects a law while the other accepts it, a joint session of the House of Representatives and the Senate is called, and a decision made by a two-thirds majority. If the King withholds his approval from a law, he returns it to the Assembly within six months with the reasons for his dissent; a joint session of the Houses then makes a decision, and if the law is accepted by this decision it is promulgated. The Budget is submitted to the National Assembly one month before the beginning of the financial year.

THE KING

The throne of the Hashemite Kingdom devolves by male descent in the dynasty of King Abdullah ibn al-Hussein. The King attains his majority on his eighteenth lunar year; if the throne is inherited by a minor, the powers of the King are exercised by a Regent or a Council of Regency. If the King, through illness or absence, cannot perform his duties, his powers are given to a Deputy, or to a Council of the Throne. This Deputy, or Council, may be appointed by Iradas (decrees) by the King, or, if he is incapable, by the Council of Ministers.

On his accession, the King takes the oath to respect and observe the provisions of the Constitution and to be loyal to the nation. As Head of State he is immune from all liability or responsibility. He approves laws and promulgates them. He declares war, concludes peace and signs treaties; treaties, however, must be approved by the National Assembly. The King is Commander-in-Chief of the navy, the army and the air force. He orders the holding of elections; convenes, inaugurates, adjourns and prorogues the House of Representatives. The Prime Minister is appointed by him, as are the President and members of the Senate. Military and civil ranks are also granted, or withdrawn, by the King. No death sentence is carried out until he has confirmed it.

MINISTERS

The Council of Ministers consists of the Prime Minister, President of the Council, and of his ministers. Ministers are forbidden to become members of any company, to receive a salary from any company, or to participate in any financial act of trade. The Council of Ministers is entrusted with the conduct of all affairs of state, internal and external.

The Council of Ministers is responsible to the House of Representatives for matters of general policy. Ministers may speak in either House, and, if they are members of one House, they may also vote in that House. Votes of confidence in the Council are cast in the House of Representatives, and decided by a two-thirds majority. If a vote of 'no confidence' is returned, the ministers are bound to resign. Every newly-formed Council of Ministers must present its programme to the House of Representatives and ask for a vote of confidence. The House of Representatives can impeach ministers, as it impeaches its own members.

AMENDMENTS

Two amendments were passed in November 1974 giving the King the right to dissolve the Senate or to take away membership from any of its members, and to postpone general elections for a period not to exceed a year, if there are circumstances in which the Council of Ministers feels that it is impossible to hold elections. A further amendment in February 1976 enabled the King to postpone elections indefinitely. In January 1984 two amendments were passed, allowing elections 'in any part of the country where it is possible to hold them' (effectively, only the East Bank) and empowering the National Assembly to elect deputies from the Israeli-held West Bank.

The Government

HEAD OF STATE: King ABDULLAH IBN AL-HUSSEIN (succeeded to the throne on 7 February 1999).

CABINET*
(April 2003)

Prime Minister and Minister of Defence: Eng. ALI ABU AR-RAGHEB.

Deputy Prime Minister and Minister of Justice: FARIS AN-NABULSI.

Minister of the Interior: QAFTAN AL-MAJALI.

Minister of National Economy and Minister of State: SAMER AT-TAWIL.

Minister of Awqaf (Religious Endowments) and Islamic Affairs: Dr AHMAD HILAYEL.

Minister of Health: Dr WALID AL-MA'ANI.

Minister of Foreign Affairs: MARWAN AL-MUASHER.

Minister of Finance: Dr MICHEL MARTO.

Minister of Labour: MUZAHIM AL-MUHAISIN.

Minister of Public Works and Housing: Eng. HOSNI ABU GHEIDA.

Minister of Energy and Mineral Resources: MUHAMMAD ALI AL-BATAYNEH.

Minister of Education: Dr KHALID TOUQAN.

Minister of Higher Education and Scientific Research: Dr MUHAMMAD HAMDAN.

Minister of Municipal and Rural Affairs: Dr ABD AR-RAZZAQ TBEISHAT.

Minister of Culture: HAIDAR MAHMOUD.

Minister of Agriculture: TARRAD AL-FAYEZ.

Minister of Industry and Trade: SALAH AL-BASHIR.

Minister of Planning: Dr BASSEM AWADALLAH.

Minister of Water and Irrigation: Dr HAZEM AN-NASSER.

Minister of Social Development: Dr RUWAIDAH MA'AITAH.

Minister of Information and Communications Technology: Dr FAWWAZ HATIM AZ-ZU'BI.

Minister of Transport and of Tourism and Antiquities: NADER AD-DAHABI.

Minister of the Environment and Minister of State for Administrative Development: Dr MUHAMMAD ATH-THNEIBAT.

Minister of the Royal Court: FAISAL AL-FAYEZ.

Minister of State for Foreign Affairs: SHAHER BAK.

Minister of State for Cabinet Affairs: MOUSTAFA AL-QAISI.

Minister of State for Political Affairs and Information: Dr MUHAMMAD AFFASH AL-ADWAN.

* The Head of Intelligence and the Governor of the Central Bank also have full ministerial status.

MINISTRIES

Office of the Prime Minister: POB 80, Amman; tel. (6) 4641211; fax (6) 4642520; e-mail pmic@pm.gov.jo; internet www.pm.gov.jo.

Ministry of Agriculture: POB 2099, Amman; tel. (6) 5686151; fax (6) 5686310; e-mail agri@moa.gov.jo; internet www.moa.gov.jo.

Ministry of Awqaf (Religious Endowments) and Islamic Affairs: POB 659, Amman; tel. (6) 5666141; fax (6) 5602254.

Ministry of Culture: POB 6140, Amman; tel. (6) 5696218; fax (6) 5696598; e-mail info@culture.gov.jo; internet www.culture.gov.jo.

Ministry of Defence: POB 80, Amman; tel. (6) 4641211; fax (6) 4642520.

Ministry of Development Affairs: POB 1577, Amman; tel. (6) 4644361; fax (6) 4648825.

Ministry of Education: POB 1646, Amman 11118; tel. (6) 5607181; fax (6) 5666019; e-mail moe@amra.nic.gov.jo; internet www.moe.gov.jo.

Ministry of Energy and Mineral Resources: POB 2310, Amman; tel. (6) 5863326; fax (6) 5818336; e-mail memr@amra.nic.gov.jo; internet www.nic.gov.jo/memr/memr.html.

Ministry of Finance: POB 85, Amman 11118; tel. (6) 4636321; fax (6) 4643132; e-mail webmaster@mof.gov.jo; internet www.mof.gov .jo.

Ministry of Foreign Affairs: POB 35217, Amman 11180; tel. (6) 5735150; fax (6) 5735163; e-mail inquiry@mfa.gov.jo; internet www .mfa.gov.jo.

Ministry of Health: POB 86, Amman; tel. (6) 5665131; fax (6) 5665232; e-mail info@moh.gov.jo; internet www.moh.gov.jo.

Ministry of Industry and Trade: POB 2019, Amman; tel. (6) 5607191; fax (6) 5603721; e-mail info@mit.gov.jo; internet www.mit .gov.jo.

Ministry of Information and Communications Technology: POB 9903, Amman 11191; tel. (6) 5859001; fax (6) 5825262; e-mail cio@mopc.gov.jo; internet www.mopc.gov.jo/moict.htm.

Ministry of the Interior: POB 100, Amman; tel. (6) 4638849; fax (6) 5606908.

Ministry of Justice: POB 6040, Amman; tel. (6) 4653533; fax (6) 4643197; e-mail moj@amra.nic.gov.jo.

Ministry of Labour: POB 8160, Amman; tel. (6) 5607481; fax (6) 5667193; internet www.mol.gov.jo.

Ministry of Municipal and Rural Affairs: POB 1799, Amman; tel. (6) 4641393; fax (6) 4640404.

Ministry of Planning: POB 555, Amman 11118; tel. (6) 4641460; fax (6) 4649341; e-mail mop@mop.gov.jo; internet www.mop.gov.jo.

Ministry of Public Works and Housing: POB 1220, Amman; tel. (6) 5850470; fax (6) 5857590; e-mail mhpw@amra.nic.gov.jo.

Ministry of Social Development: POB 6720, Amman; tel. (6) 5931391; fax (6) 5932645; e-mail mosd@mosd.gov.jo ; internet www .mosd.gov.jo.

Ministry of Tourism and Antiquities: POB 224, Amman 11118; tel. (6) 4642311; fax (6) 4648465; e-mail tourism@mota.gov.jo; internet www.mota.gov.jo.

Ministry of Transport: POB 35214, Amman; tel. (6) 5518111; fax (6) 5527233; e-mail mot1@go.com.jo.

Ministry of Water and Irrigation: POB 2412, Amman 5012; tel. (6) 5680100; fax (6) 5680075; e-mail info@mwi.gov.jo; internet www .mwi.gov.jo.

Legislature

MAJLIS AL-UMMA
(National Assembly)

Senate

Speaker: ZAID AR-RIFAI.

The Senate (House of Notables) consists of 40 members, appointed by the King. A new Senate was appointed by the King on 22 November 1997.

House of Representatives

Speaker: ABD AL-HADI AL-MAJALI.

General Election, 4 November 1997*

Party/Group	Seats
Pro-Government†	60
Independent nationalists and leftists	10
Independent Islamists	8
National Constitutional Party (NCP)	2
Total	**80**

*The 1997 general election was boycotted by all the principal opposition parties in Jordan, including the Islamic Action Front (which had emerged as the largest single party in the House of Representatives after the 1993 elections).
†Excluding NCP.
Note: On 22 July 2001 legislation was introduced whereby membership of the lower house was to be increased from 80 to 104, with effect from the next general election. Following amendments to draft electoral legislation ratified by the King on 9 February 2003, membership of the lower house was to be increased to 110 (again with effect from the next election); the six seats were to be reserved for female legislators.

Political Organizations

Political parties were banned before the elections of July 1963. In September 1971 King Hussein announced the formation of a Jordanian National Union, which was the only legal political organization. Communists, Marxists and 'other advocates of imported ideologies' were ineligible for membership. In March 1972 the organization was renamed the Arab National Union. In April 1974 King Hussein dissolved the executive committee of the Arab National Union, and accepted the resignation of the Secretary-General. In February 1976 the Cabinet approved a law abolishing the Union. A royal commission was appointed in April 1990 to draft a National Charter, one feature of which was the legalization of political parties. In January 1991 King Hussein approved the National Charter, which was formally endorsed in June. In July 1992 the House of Representatives adopted draft legislation which formally permitted the establishment of political parties, subject to certain conditions. In the same month a joint session of the Senate and the House of Representatives was convened to debate amendments to the new legislation, proposed by the Senate. The organizations that achieved representation in the general election of November 1993 were: the Islamic Action Front (Sec.-Gen. Dr Abd al-Latif Arabiyat; Dep. Sec.-Gen. Hamzeh Mansur); al-Mustaqbal (Future) Party (Sec.-Gen. Suleiman Arar); the Jordanian Arab Socialist Baath Party (Sec.-Gen. Tayseer Salameh al-Homsi); al-Yakatha (Reawakening) Party; al-Ahd (Pledge) Party; the Jordan National Alliance; the Jordan People's Democratic Party (Leader Taysir az-Zabri; Sec.-Gen. Salem Nahhas); the Jordan Social Democratic Party; and the Jordanian Arab Democratic Party. In May 1997 nine centre parties, including al-Ahd and the Jordan National Alliance, united to form the National Constitutional Party (NCP; Sec.-Gen. Abd al-Hadi al-Majali), which became Jordan's largest political grouping. The formation of the NCP, together with the establishment in 1996 of the Unionist Arab Democratic Party (a coalition of three leftist parties), reduced the total number of political parties from 24 to 14. In July 1997 the establishment of a new Jordanian party, the Popular Democratic Pan-Arab Movement, was announced. In May 1999 the Popular Participation Bloc was established to contest the municipal elections, held in July; it was a new grouping of 13 leftist, Baathist and pan-Arab parties. The formation of two new political parties was announced in late 1999: the New Generations Party (centrist green party; Leader Zahi Karim) and the Jordanian Arab New Dawn Party. In September 2000 a new political grouping, the Arab Democratic Front (Founders Ahmad Ubeidat, Taher al-Masri), was established. Two new political organizations were granted licences in late 2001: the Jordanian People's Committees Movement (moderate; Sec.-Gen. Khalid Shubaki) and the Jordan Rafah (Welfare) Party (Leader Muhammad Rijjal Shumali). In July 2001 the moderate Muslim Centrist Party was formed by dissidents of the Muslim Brotherhood and the Islamic Action Front.

Diplomatic Representation

EMBASSIES IN JORDAN

Algeria: POB 830375, Amman 11183; tel. (6) 4641271; fax (6) 4647957; Ambassador Bouteija Hadef.

Australia: POB 35201, Amman 11180; tel. (6) 5930246; fax (6) 5932160; e-mail ausemb@nets.com.jo; Ambassador John A. Tilemann.

Austria: POB 830795, Jabal Amman, Amman 11183; tel. (6) 4601101; fax (6) 4612725; e-mail amman-ob@bmaa.gv.at; internet www.bmaa.gv.at; Ambassador Dr Heinrich Querner.

Bahrain: POB 5220, Amman 11183; tel. (6) 5664148; fax (6) 5664190; Ambassador Muhammad Seif Jaber al-Msallam.

Belgium: POB 942, Amman 11118; tel. (6) 5932683; fax (6) 5930487; e-mail belgica@nol.com.jo; Ambassador Marc Do Schoutheete.

Bosnia and Herzegovina: POB 850836, Amman 11185; tel. (6) 5856921; fax (6) 5856923; e-mail bosnia@go.com.jo; Ambassador Jasko Lupi.

Brazil: POB 5497, Amman 11183; tel. (6) 4642183; fax (6) 4641328; e-mail jorbrem@go.com.jo; Ambassador Sergio Henrique Nabuco de Castro.

Brunei: POB 851752, Amman 11185; tel. (6) 5928021; fax (6) 5928024; e-mail bruneijo@go.com.jo; Ambassador Pehin Dato Hj Hussain bin Ahmad.

Bulgaria: POB 950578, Amman 11195; tel. (6) 5529391; fax (6) 5539393; Ambassador Nikolay Nikolov.

Canada: POB 815403, Amman 11180; tel. (6) 5666124; fax (6) 5689227; Ambassador Roderick Bell.

Chile: POB 830663, 28 Hussein Abu Ragheb St, Abdoun, Amman 11183; tel. (6) 5923360; fax (6) 5924263; e-mail echilejo@go.com.jo; Ambassador Alfredo Tapia.

China, People's Republic: POB 7365, Amman 11118; tel. (6) 5529167; fax (6) 5518713; e-mail poli@index.com.jo; Ambassador Chen Yonglong.

Czech Republic: POB 2213, Amman 11181; tel. (6) 5927051; fax (6) 5927053; e-mail amman@embassy.mzv.cz; internet www.mzv.cz/amman; Chargé d'affaires Tomas Lane.

Denmark: POB 222, 24 Sharih Abd-al Hamid Sharaf St, Shmeisani, Amman 11118; tel. (6) 5604644; fax (6) 5604664; e-mail dancons@kawar.com.jo; Ambassador Ole Wøhlers Olsen.

Egypt: POB 35178, Amman 11180; tel. (6) 5605175; fax (6) 5604082; e-mail egyptemb@joinnet.com.jo; Ambassador Muhammad Hijazi.

France: POB 5348, Amman 11183; tel. (6) 4641273; fax (6) 4659606; e-mail ambafr@joinnet.com.jo; internet www.ambafrance.org.jo; Ambassador Jean-Michel Casa.

Germany: POB 183, Benghazi St, Jabal Amman 11118; tel. (6) 5930351; fax (6) 5932887; e-mail germaemb@go.com.jo; Ambassador Dr Martin Schneller.

Greece: POB 35069, Amman 11180; tel. (6) 5672331; fax (6) 5696591; e-mail greekemb@nol.com.jo; Ambassador Ioannis Cambolis.

Holy See: POB 142916, Amman 11814; tel. (6) 5929934; fax (6) 5929931; e-mail nuntius@nol.com.jo; Apostolic Nuncio Most Rev. Fernando Filoni (Titular Archbishop of Volturno).

Hungary: POB 3441, Amman 11181; tel. (6) 5925614; fax (6) 5930836; e-mail huembamm@nol.com.jo; Ambassador Balazs Bokor.

India: POB 2168, Amman 11181; tel. (6) 4622098; fax (6) 4659540; e-mail indembjo@firstnet.com.jo; Ambassador M. Venkatraman.

Indonesia: POB 811784, South Um-Uthaina, 6th Circle, Amman 11181; tel. (6) 5538911; fax (6) 5528380; e-mail amman96@go.com.jo; Ambassador Edhimurti Sunoko.

Iran: POB 173, Amman 11118; tel. (6) 4641281; fax (6) 4641383; e-mail emb@go.com.jo; Ambassador Nosratollah Tajik.

Iraq: POB 2025, 1st Circle, Jabal Amman; tel. (6) 4623175; fax (6) 4619172; Ambassador Dr Sabah Yassein Ali.

Israel: POB 950866, Amman 11195; tel. (6) 5524680; fax (6) 5524689; e-mail isrem@go.com.jo; Ambassador David Dadon.

Italy: POB 9800, Jabal Luweibdeh, Amman 11191; tel. (6) 4638185; fax (6) 4659730; e-mail italemb1@go.com.jo; internet www.italembamman.org; Ambassador Stefano Jedrkiewicz.

Japan: POB 2835, Amman 11181; tel. (6) 5932005; fax (6) 5931006; e-mail mail@embjapan.org.jo; Ambassador Koichi Obata.

Korea, Democratic People's Republic: Amman; tel. (6) 5666349; Ambassador (vacant).

Korea, Republic: POB 3060, Amman 11181; tel. (6) 5930745; fax (6) 5930280; e-mail jordan@mofat.go.kr; Ambassador Kim Kyung-Keun.

Kuwait: POB 2107, Jabal Amman; tel. (6) 5675135; fax (6) 5699217; Ambassador Faysal al-Mesha'an.

Lebanon: POB 811779, Amman 11181; tel. and fax (6) 5929111; Ambassador Adib Alam ed-Din.

Morocco: POB 2175, Amman 11183; tel. (6) 5921771; fax (6) 5925185; Ambassador Moulay Mehdi Alaoui.

Netherlands: POB 94136, Amman 11194; tel. (6) 5930581; fax (6) 5930214; e-mail nlgovamm@index.com.jo; Ambassador Dr M. De Kwaasteniet.

Norway: POB 830510, Amman 11183; tel. (6) 5931646; fax (6) 5931650; e-mail emb.amman@mfa.no; Ambassador Sverre Stub.

Oman: POB 20192, Amman 11110; tel. (6) 5686155; fax (6) 5689404; Ambassador Hamad bin Hilal al-Ma'mari.

Pakistan: POB 1232, Amman 11118; tel. (6) 4622787; fax (6) 4611633; e-mail pakembjo@go.com.jo; Ambassador Tariq Fatemi.

Poland: POB 942050, Amman 11194; tel. (6) 5512593; fax (6) 5512595; e-mail polemb@nol.com.jo; Chargé d'affaires Mariusz Woźniak.

Qatar: POB 5098, Amman 11183; tel. (6) 5607311; fax (6) 5607350; e-mail qataremb@index.com.jo; Ambassador Sheikh Abd ar-Rahman bin Jassim bin Muhammad ath-Thani.

Romania: POB 2869, 33 Madina Munawwara St, Amman; tel. (6) 5813423; fax (6) 5812521; e-mail romania@accessme.com; Ambassador Vasile Sofineti.

Russia: POB 2187, Amman 11181; tel. (6) 4641158; fax (6) 4647448; e-mail russjo@nets.com.jo; Ambassador Ivanov Galitsin.

Saudi Arabia: POB 2132, 5th Circle, Jabal Amman; tel. (6) 5924154; fax (6) 5921154; Ambassador Abd ar-Rahman N. al-Ohaly.

Serbia and Montenegro: POB 5227, Amman 11183; tel. (6) 4647593; fax (6) 4647605; e-mail emb1@yugoembassy.index.com.jo; Ambassador Radonja Radović.

South Africa: POB 851508, Sweifieh 11185, Amman; tel. (6) 5921194; fax (6) 5920080; e-mail saembjor@index.com.jo; Ambassador Dr Vincent T. Zulu.

Spain: Zahran St, POB 454, Amman 11118; tel. (6) 4621369; fax (6) 4614173; e-mail embespjo@mail.mae.es; Ambassador Antonio López Martínez.

Sri Lanka: POB 830731, Amman 11183; tel. (6) 5820611; fax (6) 5820615; e-mail lankaemb@go.com.jo; Ambassador Kathan Marimuttu.

Sudan: POB 3305, Amman 11181; tel. (6) 5854500; fax (6) 5854501; e-mail sudani@firstnet.com.jo; Ambassador Sayed Jalal ed-Din el-Amin.

Sweden: POB 830536, 4th Circle, Amman 11183; tel. (6) 5931177; fax (6) 5930179; e-mail info@swe-embamman.org; internet www.swe-embamman.org; Ambassador Klas Gierow.

Switzerland: POB 5341, Amman 11183; tel. (6) 5931416; fax (6) 5930685; e-mail vertretung@amm.rep.admin.ch; Ambassador Rolf Bodenmüller.

Syria: POB 1733, Amman 11118; tel. (6) 4641935; fax (6) 4651945; Ambassador Abd al-Fattah Ammourah.

Tunisia: POB 17185, Amman 11195; tel. (6) 5674307; fax (6) 5605790; Ambassador Habib Kaabachi.

Turkey: POB 2062, Amman 11181; tel. (6) 4641251; fax (6) 4612353; e-mail ammanbe@nets.com.jo; Ambassador Ercan Özer.

United Arab Emirates: POB 2623, Amman 11181; tel. (6) 5934780; fax (6) 5932666; Ambassador Rahma Hussain R. Az-Za'abi.

United Kingdom: POB 87, Abdoun Amman 11118; tel. (6) 5923100; fax (6) 5923759; e-mail info@britain.org.jo; internet www.britain.org .jo; Ambassador Christopher Prentice.

USA: POB 354, Amman 11118; tel. (6) 5920101; fax (6) 5920163; e-mail administration@usembassy-amman.org.jo; Ambassador Edward William Gnehm, Jr.

Yemen: POB 3085, Amman 11181; tel. (6) 5923771; fax (6) 5923773; Ambassador Dr Ibrahim S. al-Adoof.

Judicial System

With the exception of matters of purely personal nature concerning members of non-Muslim communities, the law of Jordan was based on Islamic Law for both civil and criminal matters. During the days of the Ottoman Empire, certain aspects of Continental law, especially French commercial law and civil and criminal procedure, were introduced. Due to British occupation of Palestine and Transjordan from 1917 to 1948, the Palestine territory has adopted, either by statute or case law, much of the English common law. Since the annexation of the non-occupied part of Palestine and the formation of the Hashemite Kingdom of Jordan, there has been a continuous effort to unify the law.

Court of Cassation: The Court of Cassation consists of seven judges, who sit in full panel for exceptionally important cases. In most appeals, however, only five members sit to hear the case. All cases involving amounts of more than JD 100 may be reviewed by this Court, as well as cases involving lesser amounts and cases which cannot be monetarily valued. However, for the latter types of cases, review is available only by leave of the Court of Appeal, or, upon refusal by the Court of Appeal, by leave of the President of the Court of Cassation. In addition to these functions as final and Supreme Court of Appeal, the Court of Cassation also sits as High Court of Justice to hear applications in the nature of habeas corpus, mandamus and certiorari dealing with complaints of a citizen against abuse of governmental authority.

Courts of Appeal: There are two Courts of Appeal, each of which is composed of three judges, whether for hearing of appeals or for dealing with Magistrates Courts' judgments in chambers. Jurisdiction of the two Courts is geographical, with the Court for the Western Region (which has not sat since June 1967) sitting in Jerusalem and the Court for the Eastern Region sitting in Amman. The regions are separated by the Jordan river. Appellate review of the Courts of Appeal extends to judgments rendered in the Courts of First Instance, the Magistrates' Courts, and Religious Courts.

Courts of First Instance: The Courts of First Instance are courts of general jurisdiction in all matters civil and criminal except those specifically allocated to the Magistrates' Courts. Three judges sit in all felony trials, while only two judges sit for misdemeanour and civil cases. Each of the seven Courts of First Instance also exercises appellate jurisdiction in cases involving judgments of less than JD 20 and fines of less than JD 10, rendered by the Magistrates' Courts.

Magistrates' Courts: There are 14 Magistrates' Courts, which exercise jurisdiction in civil cases involving no more than JD 250 and in criminal cases involving maximum fines of JD 100 or maximum imprisonment of one year.

Religious Courts: There are two types of religious court The *Shari'a*Courts (Muslims): and the Ecclesiastical Courts (Eastern Orthodox, Greek Melkite, Roman Catholic and Protestant). Jurisdiction extends to personal (family) matters, such as marriage, divorce, alimony, inheritance, guardianship, wills, interdiction and, for the Muslim community, the constitution of Waqfs (Religious Endowments). When a dispute involves persons of different religious communities, the Civil Courts have jurisdiction in the matter unless the parties agree to submit to the jurisdiction of one or the other of the Religious Courts involved.

Each *Shari'a* (Muslim) Court consists of one judge (*Qadi*), while most of the Ecclesiastical (Christian) Courts are normally composed of three judges, who are usually clerics. *Shari'a*Courts apply the doctrines of Islamic Law, based on the Koran and the *Hadith*(Precepts of Muhammad), while the Ecclesiastical Courts base their law on various aspects of Canon Law. In the event of conflict between any two Religious Courts or between a Religious Court and a Civil Court, a Special Tribunal of three judges is appointed by the President of the Court of Cassation, to decide which court shall have jurisdiction. Upon the advice of experts on the law of the various communities, this Special Tribunal decides on the venue for the case at hand.

Religion

Over 80% of the population are Sunni Muslims, and the King can trace unbroken descent from the Prophet Muhammad. There is a Christian minority, living mainly in the towns, and there are smaller numbers of non-Sunni Muslims.

ISLAM

Chief Justice and President of the Supreme Muslim Secular Council: Sheikh Izzedin al-Khatib at-Tamimi.

Director of Shari'a Courts: Sheikh Subhi al-Muwqqat.

Mufti of the Hashemite Kingdom of Jordan: Sheikh Muhammad Abdo Hashem.

CHRISTIANITY

The Roman Catholic Church

Latin Rite

Jordan forms part of the Patriarchate of Jerusalem (see the chapter on Israel).

Vicar-General for Transjordan: Mgr Selim Sayegh (Titular Bishop of Aquae in Proconsulari), Latin Vicariate, POB 851379, Sweifieh, Amman 11185; tel. (6) 5929546; fax (6) 5920548; e-mail proffice@joinnet.com.jo.

Melkite Rite

The Greek-Melkite archdiocese of Petra (Wadi Musa) and Philadelphia (Amman) contained 31,300 adherents at 31 December 2000.

Archbishop of Petra and Philadelphia: Most Rev. GEORGES EL-MURR, Archevêché Grec-Melkite Catholique, POB 2435, Jabal Amman 11181; tel. (6) 4624757; fax (6) 4628560.

Syrian Rite

The Syrian Catholic Patriarch of Antioch is resident in Beirut, Lebanon.

Patriarchal Exarchate of Jerusalem: Mont Achrafieh, POB 510393, Rue Barto, Amman; e-mail stjossc@p-ol.com; Exarch Patriarchal Mgr GRÉGOIRE PIERRE MELKI.

The Anglican Communion

Within the Episcopal Church in Jerusalem and the Middle East, Jordan forms part of the diocese of Jerusalem. The President Bishop of the Church is the Bishop in Jerusalem (see the chapter on Israel).

Assistant Bishop in Amman: Rt Rev. Elia Khoury, POB 598, Amman.

Other Christian Churches

The Coptic Orthodox Church, the Greek Orthodox Church (Patriarchate of Jerusalem) and the Evangelical Lutheran Church in Jordan are also active.

The Press

Jordan Press Association (JPA): Amman; Pres. RAKAN AL-MAJALI; Vice-Pres. TARIQ MUMANI; Sec.-Gen. NIDAL MANSUR.

DAILIES

Al-Akhbar (News): POB 62420, Amman; f. 1976; Arabic; publ. by the Arab Press Co; Editor RACAN EL-MAJALI; circ. 15,000.

Arab Daily: Amman; f. 1999; English.

Al-Aswaq (Markets): POB 11117, Queen Rania St, Amman 11123; tel. (6) 5157690; fax (6) 5154390; e-mail alaswaq@nets.com.jo; f. 1992; Arabic; business; Man. Editor YAHYA MAHMOUD; Editor-in-Chief MUSTAFA ABU LIBDEH; circ. 40,000.

Ad-Dustour (The Constitution): POB 591, Amman 11118; tel. (6) 5664153; fax (6) 5667170; e-mail dustour@go.com.jo; internet www.addustour.com; f. 1967; Arabic; publ. by the Jordan Press and Publishing Co; owns commercial printing facilities; Chair. KAMEL ASH-SHERIF; Editor Dr NABIL ASH-SHARIF; Man. Dir SAIF ASH-SHARIF; circ. 70,000.

The Jordan Times: POB 6710, Amman 11118; tel. (6) 5696331; fax (6) 5696183; e-mail jotimes@jpf.com.jo; internet www.jordantimes.com; f. 1975; English; publ. by Jordan Press Foundation; Chief Editor ABDULLAH HASANAT; circ. 10,000.

Al-Mithaq (The Covenant): Amman; f. 1993; Arabic.

Ar-Rai (Opinion): POB 6710, Queen Rania St, Amman 11118; tel. (6) 5667171; fax (6) 5676581; e-mail alrai@jpf.com.jo; internet www.alrai.com; f. 1971; morning; Arabic; independent; publ. by Jordan Press Foundation; Chair. AHMAD ABD AL-FATTAH; Editor-in-Chief GEORGE HAWATMEH; circ. 100,000.

Sawt ash-Shaab (Voice of the People): POB 3037, Amman; tel. (6) 5667101; fax (6) 5667993; f. 1983; Arabic; Editor-in-Chief HASHEM KHAISAT; circ. 30,000.

WEEKLIES

Al-Ahali (The People): POB 9966, Amman; tel. (6) 691452; fax (6) 5686857; e-mail ahali@go.com.jo; internet www.hashd_ahalia.org; f. 1990; Arabic; publ. by the Jordan People's Democratic Party; Editor-in-Chief SALEM NAHHAS; circ. 5,000.

Akhbar al-Usbou (News of the Week): POB 605, Amman; tel. (6) 5677881; fax (6) 5677882; f. 1959; Arabic; economic, social, political; Chief Editor and Publr ABD AL-HAFIZ MUHAMMAD; circ. 50,000.

Al-Liwa' (The Standard): POB 3067, 2nd Circle, Jabal Amman 11181; tel. (6) 5642770; fax (6) 5656324; e-mail info@al-liwa.com; internet www.al-liwa.com; f. 1972; Arabic; Editor-in-Chief HASSAN AT-TAL; circ. 15,000.

Al-Majd (The Glory): POB 926856, Amman 11190; tel. (6) 5530553; fax (6) 5530352; f. 1994; Arabic; political; Editor FAHD AR-RIMAWI; circ. 8,000.

As-Sabah (The Morning): POB 2396, Amman; Arabic; circ. 6,000.

Shihan: POB 96-654, Amman; tel. (6) 5603585; fax (6) 5696183; e-mail shihan@go.com.jo; internet www.access2arabia.com/shihan; Arabic; Editor-in-Chief JIHAD MONANI; circ. 60,000.

The Star: POB 591, University St, Amman 11118; tel. (6) 5664153; fax (6) 5667170; e-mail star@addustour.com.jo; internet www.star.arabia.com; f. 1966 as The Jerusalem Star; resumed publication in Jordan in 1990; English and French; political, economic and cultural; publ. by the Jordan Press and Publishing Co; Publr and Editor-in-Chief OSAMA ASH-SHERIF; circ. 12,000.

PERIODICALS

Arabia Online: POB 91128, Amman 11191; tel. (6) 5154238; fax (6) 5154239; e-mail info@arabia.com; internet www.arabia.com; f. 1995; monthly; Arabic; information technology; Editor-in-Chief KHALDOON TABAZA.

Al-Ghad al-Iqtisadi: Media Services International, POB 9313, Amman 11191; tel. (6) 5645380; fax (6) 5648298; fortnightly; English; economic; Chief Editor RIAD AL-KHOURI.

Huda El-Islam (The Right Way of Islam): POB 659, Amman; tel. (6) 5666141; f. 1956; monthly; Arabic; scientific and literary; published by the Ministry of Awqaf and Islamic Affairs; Editor Dr AHMAD MUHAMMAD HULAYYEL.

Jordan: POB 224, Amman; f. 1969; published quarterly by Jordan Information Bureau, Washington; circ. 100,000.

Jordan Today: Media Services International, POB 9313, Amman 11191; tel. (6) 652380; fax (6) 648298; e-mail star@arabia.com; internet www.corp.arabia.com/JordanToday; f. 1995; monthly; English; tourism, culture and entertainment; Editor-in-Chief ZEID NASSER.

Military Magazine: Army Headquarters, Amman; f. 1955; quarterly; dealing with military and literary subjects; published by Armed Forces.

Royal Wings: POB 302, Amman; tel. (6) 5672872; fax (6) 5672527; bi-monthly; Arabic and English; magazine for Royal Jordanian Airline; circ. 40,000.

Shari'a: POB 585, Amman; f. 1959; fortnightly; Islamic affairs; published by Shari'a College; circ. 5,000.

World Travel Gazette (WTG): POB 658, Amman; tel. (6) 5665091; fax (6) 5667933; Arabic.

NEWS AGENCIES

Jordan News Agency (PETRA): POB 6845, Amman; tel. (6) 5644455; e-mail petra@petranews.gov.jo; internet www.petra.gov.jo; f. 1965; government-controlled; Dir-Gen. ABDULLAH AL-UTUM.

Foreign News Bureaux

Agence France-Presse (AFP): POB 3340, Amman 11181; tel. (6) 4642976; fax (6) 4654680; e-mail afp@globalone.com.jo; Bureau Man. Mrs RANDA HABIB.

Agenzia Nazionale Stampa Associata (ANSA) (Italy): POB 35111, Amman; tel. (6) 5644092.

Associated Press (AP) (USA): POB 35111, Amman 11180; tel. (6) 4614660; fax (6) 4614661; e-mail jhalaby@ap.org; Correspondent JAMAL HALABY.

Deutsche Presse Agentur (dpa) (Germany): POB 35111, Amman; tel. (6) 5623907.

Reuters (UK): POB 667, Amman; tel. (6) 5623776; fax (6) 5619231; Bureau Chief JACK REDDEN.

Central News Agency (Taiwan), Iraqi News Agency, Kuwait News Agency (KUNA), Middle East News Agency (Egypt), Qatar News Agency, Saudi Press Agency and UPI (USA) also maintain bureaux in Amman.

Publishers

Alfaris Publishing and Distribution Co: POB 9157, Amman 11191; tel. (6) 5605432; fax (6) 5685501; e-mail mkayyali@jonet.com; Dir MAHER SAID KAYYALI.

Aram Studies Publishing and Distribution House: POB 997, Amman 11941; tel. (6) 835015; fax (6) 835079; art, finance, health, management, science, business; Gen. Dir SALEH ABOUSBA.

Jordan Book Centre Co Ltd: POB 301, Al-Jubeiha, Amman 11941; tel. (6) 5151882; fax (6) 5152016; e-mail jbc@go.com.jo; f. 1982; fiction, business, economics, computer science, medicine, engineering, general non-fiction; Man. Dir J. J. SHARBAIN.

Jordan Distribution Agency Co Ltd: POB 375, Amman 11118; tel. (6) 4630191; fax (6) 4635152; e-mail jda@go.com.jo; internet www.jda-jo.com; f. 1951; history; Chair. and Gen. Man. RAJA ELISSA; Dir NADIA ELISSA.

Jordan House for Publication: POB 1121, Basman St, Amman; tel. (6) 24224; fax (6) 51062; f. 1952; medicine, nursing, dentistry; Man. Dir MURSI EL-ASHKAR.

Jordan Press and Publishing Co Ltd: POB 591, Amman 11118; tel. (6) 5664153; fax (6) 5667170; e-mail dustour@go.com.jo; f. 1967 by *Al-Manar* and *Falastin* dailies; publishes *Ad-Dustour* (daily), *Ad-Dustour Sport* (weekly) and *The Star* (English weekly); Chair. KAMEL ASH-SHARIF; Dir-Gen. SEIF ASH-SHERIF.

Jordan Press Foundation: POB 6710, Amman 11118; tel. (6) 5667171; fax (6) 5661242; e-mail alrai@jpf.com.jo; internet www.alrai.com.jo; f. 1971; publishes *Ar-Rai* (daily), the *Jordan Times* (daily) and *Hatem* (monthly for children); Chair. AHMAD ABD AL-FATAH; Gen. Dir NADER HORANI.

El-Nafa'es: POB 211511, Al-Abdali, Amman 11121; tel. (6) 5693940; fax (6) 5693941; e-mail alnafaes@hotmail.com; f. 1990; education, Islamic; CEO SUFYAN OMAR AL-ASHQR.

At-Tanwir al-Ilmi (Scientific Enlightenment Publishing House): POB 4237, Al-Mahatta, Amman 11131; tel. and fax (6) 4899619; e-mail taisir@yahoo.com; education, engineering, philosophy, science, sociology; Owner DR TAISIR SUBHI MAHMOUD.

Other publishers in Amman include: Dairat al-Ihsaat al-Amman, George N. Kawar, Al-Matbaat al-Hashmiya and The National Press.

Broadcasting and Communications

TELECOMMUNICATIONS

Telecommunications Regulatory Commission (TRC): POB 850967, Amman 11185; tel. (6) 5862020; fax (6) 5863641; e-mail webmaster@trc.gov.jo; internet www.trc.gov.jo; f. 1995; Dir-Gen. MAMOUN BALQAR.

Jordan Mobile Telephone Services Company (JMTS—Fastlink): POB 940821, 8th Circle, King Abdullah II St, Amman 11194; tel. (6) 5828100; fax (6) 5828200; e-mail info@fastlink.com.jo; internet www.jmts-fastlink.com; f. 1994; private co; since 1995 operates Jordan's first mobile telecommunications network; Pres. and CEO MICHAEL DAGHER.

Jordan Telecom: POB 1689, Amman 11118; tel. (6) 4606666; fax (6) 4606111; e-mail info@jtc.com.jo; internet www.jordantelecom.jo; f. 1971; formerly Jordan Telecommunications Corpn and then Jordan Telecommunications Co; 41.5% govt-owned; 58.5% privately-owned; Chair. Dr SHABIB AMMARI; CEO PIERRE MATTEI.

MobileCom: POB 851114, Amman 11185; internet www.mobilecom.jo; f. 1999; launched cellular telecommunications service in 2000; subsidiary of Jordan Telecom.

BROADCASTING

Radio and Television

Jordan Radio and Television Corporation (JRTV): POB 1041, Amman; tel. (6) 773111; fax (6) 751503; e-mail general@jrtv.gov.jo; internet www.jrtv.com; f. 1968; government TV station; broadcasts for 90 hours weekly in Arabic and English; in colour; advertising accepted; Dir-Gen. IHSAN RAMZI SHIKIM; Dir of Television NASSER JUDEH; Dir of Radio HASHIM KHURAYSAT.

Finance

(cap. = capital; dep. = deposits; m. = million; res = reserves; brs = branches; JD = Jordanian dinars)

BANKING

Central Bank

Central Bank of Jordan: POB 37, King Hussein St, Amman 11118; tel. (6) 4630301; fax (6) 4638889; e-mail redp@cbj.gov.jo; internet www.cbj.gov.jo; f. 1964; cap. JD 18m., res JD 59.3m., dep. JD 2,868.1m. (Dec. 2001); Gov. and Chair. Dr UMMAYA TOUKAN; Dep. Govs Dr AHMAD MOUSTAFA, SALEH AT-TAYEH.

National Banks

Arab Bank PLC: POB 950545, Shmeisani, Amman 11195; tel. (6) 5607231; fax (6) 5606793; e-mail international@arabbank.com.jo; internet www.arabbank.com; f. 1930; cap. JD 146.9m., res JD 2,161.8m., dep. JD 19,010.2m. (Dec. 2001); CEO and Dep. Chair. ABD AL-MAJID SHOMAN; Dep. Chair. and Pres. KHALID SHOMAN; 92 brs in Jordan, 87 brs abroad.

Bank of Jordan PLC: POB 2140, Shmeisani, Amman 11181; tel. (6) 5696277; fax (6) 5696291; e-mail boj@bankofjordan.com.jo; internet www.bankofjordan.com; f. 1960; cap. JD 21m., res JD 14.1m., dep. JD 553.8m. (Dec. 1999); Chair. TAWFIK SHAKER FAKHOURI; Gen. Man. MUHAMMAD JOMAH ALQASSIM; 64 brs.

Cairo Amman Bank: POB 950661, Cairo Amman Bank Bldg, Wadi Saqra St, Amman 11195; tel. (6) 4616910; fax (6) 4642883; e-mail cainfo@ca-bank.com.jo; internet www.ca-bank.com; f. 1960; cap. JD 20m., res JD 32.5m., dep. JD 754.0m. (Dec. 2001); Chair. KHALED AL-MASRI; Gen. Man. YAZID AL-MUFTI; 50 brs in Jordan, 19 brs in the Palestinian self-rule areas.

Export and Finance Bank: POB 941283, Issam Ajlouni St, Amman 11194; tel. (6) 5694250; fax (6) 5692062; e-mail info@efbank.com.jo; internet www.efbank.com.jo; f. 1995; cap. JD 25.3m., res JD 3.7m., dep. JD 132.7m. (Dec. 2001); Chair. and CEO MUHAMMAD ALI AL-HUSRY; Gen. Man. HAKOUB BANNAYAN (acting).

Jordan Gulf Bank: POB 9989, Shmeisani-Al Burj Area, Amman 11191; tel. (6) 5603931; fax (6) 5664110; e-mail jgb@jgbank.com.jo; internet www.jgbank.com.jo; f. 1977; cap JD 33m., res JD –0.1m., dep. JD 253.8m. (Dec. 1999); Chair. NABEEL YOUSUF BARAKAT; Gen. Man. THABET TAHER; 33 brs.

Jordan Islamic Bank for Finance and Investment: POB 926225, Shmeisani, Amman 11190; tel. (6) 5677377; fax (6) 5666326; e-mail jib@islamicbank.com.jo; internet www.jordanislamicbank.com; f. 1978; cap. JD 40m., res JD 11.8m., dep. JD 873.1m. (June 2002); Chair. MAHMOUD J. HASSOUBEH; Vice-Chair. and Gen. Man. MUSA ABD AL-AZIZ SHIHADEH; 67 brs.

Jordan Kuwait Bank: POB 9776, Amman 11191; tel. (6) 5688814; fax (6) 5687452; e-mail webmaster@jkbank.com.jo; internet www.jordan-kuwait-bank.com; f. 1976; cap. JD 35.3m., res JD 23.3m., dep. JD 583.9m. (Dec. 2001); Chair. and CEO ABD AL-KARIM AL-KABARITI; Gen. Man. MUHAMMAD YASSER AL-ASMAR; 19 brs.

Jordan National Bank PLC: POB 3103, Queen Noor St, Shmeisani, Amman 11181; tel. (6) 5622283; fax (6) 5622281; e-mail info@jnb.com.jo; internet www.ahli.com; f. 1955; cap. JD 42m., res JD 24.4m., dep. JD 1,248.4m. (Dec. 2001); Chair., CEO and Gen. Man. Dr RAJAI MOUASHER; CEO and Man. Dir WASEF AZAR; 49 brs in Jordan, 10 brs abroad.

Middle East Investment Bank: POB 560, 30 Prince Shaker bin Zeid St, Shmeisani, Amman 11118; tel. (6) 5695470; fax (6) 5693410; e-mail meibsg@meib.com; internet www.meib.com; f. 1981; cap. JD 15.9m., res JD 0.8m., dep. JD 36.0m. (Dec. 2001); Chair. HASSAN MANGO; Gen. Man. FADI JABRY; 13 brs.

Foreign Banks

Arab Banking Corpn: POB 926691, ABC Bldg, Al-Malekah Noor St, Shmeisani, Amman 11190; tel. (6) 5664183; fax (6) 5686291; e-mail info@arabbanking.com.jo; internet www.arabbanking.com.jo; f. 1990; cap. JD 20m., dep. JD 4.0m., dep. JD 234.0m., total assets JD 310.5m. (Dec. 2001); Chair. GHAZI M. ABD AL-JAWAD; Dep. CEO Dr ZIAD FARIZ; 16 brs.

Citibank NA (USA): POB 5055, Prince Muhammad St, Jabal Amman 11183; tel. (6) 4644065; fax (6) 4658693; internet www.citibank.com/jordan; f. 1974; cap. JD 5m., dep. JD 56.2m., total assets JD 75.4m. (Dec. 1992); Chair. and CEO JOHN S. REED; Gen. Man. SUHEIR AL-ALI; 3 brs.

Egyptian Arab Land Bank: POB 6729, Queen Noor St, Amman 11118; tel. (6) 5650180; fax (6) 5677574; e-mail ealb@arakari.com.jo; internet www.arakari.com.jo; f. 1976; wholly-owned by Government of Egypt; cap. JD 10m., dep. JD 103.3m., res JD 5.5m., total assets JD 136.1m. (Dec. 1997); Chair. ALAA AL-OUSSIYA; Gen. Man. SAMIR MAHDI; 19 brs in Jordan, 32 brs abroad.

HSBC Bank Middle East (United Kingdom): POB 925286, Khalid Bin Walid St, Jebel Hussein, Amman 11110; tel. (6) 5607471; fax (6) 5682047; f. 1889; cap. JD 5m., dep. JD 150m., total assets JD 169m. (Dec. 1994); Chair. Sir JOHN BOND; Gen. Man. ROBERT JAMES BRAY; 4 brs.

Islamic International Arab Bank: POB 925802, Amman 11190; tel. (6) 5694901; fax (6) 5694914; f. 1997; cap. JD 40m; Chair. ABD AL-HAMID SHOMAN; Gen. Man. JAMEEL AD-DASOQI; 9 brs.

Rafidain Bank (Iraq): POB 1194, Amman 11118; tel. (6) 4624365; fax (6) 4658698; f. 1941; cap. JD 5m., res JD 2.1m., dep. JD 31.4m. (Dec. 1992); Pres. and Chair. DHIA HABEEB AL-KHAYOON; Regional Man. MUHSEN ABD AL-HASSAN; 4 brs.

Standard Chartered Bank: POB 9997, Shmeisani, Amman 11191; tel. (6) 5607201; fax (6) 5624106; e-mail muntaser.dawwas@jo.standardchartered.com; internet www.standardchartered.com/jo; cap. JD 13m., dep. JD 200m., total assets JD 240m. (Dec. 2002); CEO ZAHID RAHIM; 7 brs.

Bank Al-Mashrek (Lebanon) also has a branch in Amman.

Specialized Credit Institutions

Agricultural Credit Corporation: POB 77, Amman; tel. (6) 5661105; fax (6) 5698365; e-mail agri-cc@nets.com.jo; f. 1959; cap. JD 24m., res JD 12.4m., total assets JD 125.1m. (Dec. 2000); Chair. MAHMOUD DUWAYRI; Dir-Gen. NIMER AN-NABULSI; 20 brs.

Arab Jordan Investment Bank: POB 8797, Arab Jordan Investment Bank Bldg, Shmeisani Commercial Area, Amman 11121; tel. (6) 5607126; fax (6) 5681482; e-mail info@ajib.com; internet www.ajib.com; f. 1978; cap. JD 20m., res JD 13.7m., dep. JD 248.4m. (Dec. 2001); Chair. and CEO ABD AL-KADER AL-QADI; 15 brs in Jordan, 1 br abroad.

Cities and Villages Development Bank: POB 1572, Amman 11118; tel. (6) 5668151; fax (6) 5668153; e-mail cvdb100@hotmail.com; f. 1979; cap. JD 25m., res JD 14.5m., total assets JD 66.5m. (Dec. 1998); Gen. Man. Dr IBRAHIM AN-NSOUR; 4 brs.

Housing Bank for Trade and Finance: POB 7693, Parliament St, Amman 11118; tel. (6) 5667126; fax (6) 5678121; e-mail quality@hbtf.com.jo; internet www.the-housingbank.com.jo; f. 1973; cap. JD 100m., res JD 149.1m., dep. JD 1,365.3m. (Dec. 2001); Chair. ZUHAIR KHOURI; Gen. Man. ABD AL-QADER DWEIK; 97 brs.

Industrial Development Bank: POB 1982, Zahran St, Amman 11118; tel. (6) 4642216; fax (6) 4647821; e-mail idb@indevbank.com.jo; internet www.indevbank.com.jo; f. 1965; cap. JD 24m., res JD 21.8m., dep. JD 44.7m. (Dec. 2000); Chair. MOFLEH AKEL; Gen. Man. MARWAN AWAD; 3 brs.

Jordan Co-operative Organization: POB 1343, Amman; tel. (6) 5665171; f. 1968; cap. JD 5.2m., dep. JD 11.5m., res JD 6.8m. (Nov. 1992); Chair. and Dir-Gen. JAMAL AL-BEDOUR.

Jordan Investment and Finance Bank (JIFBANK): POB 950601, Issam Ajlouni St, Shmeisani, Amman 11195; tel. (6) 5665145; fax (6) 5681410; e-mail souha@jifbank.com; internet www.jifbank.com; f. 1982 as Jordan Investment and Finance Corpn, name changed 1989; cap. JD 20m., res JD 5.9m., dep. JD 303.9m. (Dec. 2000); Chair. NIZAR JARDANEH; Man. Dir BASIL JARDANEH; 5 brs.

Jordan Investment Board (JIB): POB 893, Amman 11821; tel. (6) 5608400; fax (6) 5608416; e-mail info@jib.com.jo; internet www.jordaninvestment.com; Dir-Gen. REEM BADRAN.

Jordan Investment Corporation (JIC): Amman; state-owned; Dir-Gen. (vacant).

Social Security Corporation: POB 926031, Amman 11110; tel. (6) 4643000; fax (6) 4610014; f. 1978; Dir-Gen. Dr SAFWAN TOQAN.

Union Bank for Savings and Investment: POB 35104, Prince Shaker Bin Zeid St, Shmeisani, Amman 11180; tel. (6) 5607011; fax (6) 5666149; e-mail info@unionbankjo.com; internet www.unionbankjo.com; f. 1978 as Arab Finance Corpn, name changed 1991; cap. JD 20m., res 9.4m., dep. 269.4m. (Dec. 2001); Chair. and Gen. Man. ISAM AS-SALFITI; Dep. Gen. Man. AMMAR HADADDIN; 14 brs.

STOCK EXCHANGE

Amman Stock Exchange (ASE): POB 212466, Arjan, nr Ministry of the Interior, Amman 11121; tel. (6) 5664109; fax (6) 5664071; e-mail info@ase.com.jo; internet www.ase.com.jo; f. 1978 as Amman Financial Market; name changed March 1999; Chair. MUHAMMAD SALHEH HOURANI; Exec. Man. JALIL TARIF.

INSURANCE

Jordan Insurance Co Ltd: POB 279, Company's Bldg, 3rd Circle, Jabal Amman, Amman; tel. (6) 4634161; fax (6) 4637905; e-mail jicjo@go.com.jo; f. 1951; cap. JD 9.9m. Chair. KHALDUN ABU HASSAN; 7 brs (3 in Saudi Arabia, 3 in the United Arab Emirates, 1 in Lebanon).

Middle East Insurance Co Ltd: POB 1802, Al Kindy St, Um Uthaina 5th Circle, Jabal Amman, Amman; tel. (6) 5527100; fax (6) 5527801; e-mail meico@go.com.jo; internet www.meico.com.jo; f. 1963; cap. US $5.0m. Chair. SAMIR KAWAR; 1 br. in Saudi Arabia.

National Ahlia Insurance Co: POB 6156-2938, Sayed Qotub St, Shmeisani, Amman 11118; tel. (6) 5671169; fax (6) 5684900; e-mail natinsur@go.com.jo; internet www.nationalahlia.com; f. 1965; cap. JD 2m. Chair. MUSTAFA ABU-GOURA; Gen. Man. GHALEB ABU-GOURA.

United Insurance Co Ltd: POB 7521, United Insurance Bldg, King Hussein St, Amman; tel. (6) 4648513; fax (6) 4629417; e-mail uic@united.com.jo; internet www.1stjordan.net/united-insurance; f. 1972; all types of insurance; cap. JD 2m.; Gen. Man. TAISIR MASHAL.

There are 17 local and one foreign insurance company operating in Jordan.

Trade and Industry

DEVELOPMENT ORGANIZATIONS

Amman Development Corporation: POB 926621, Amman; tel. (6) 5629471; f. 1979; development of services in the Amman municipality by constructing and running real estate; industrial and other complexes; Dir Gen. SAMI AR-RASHID.

Jordan Valley Authority (JVA): POB 2769, Amman; tel. (6) 5689400; fax (6) 5689916; e-mail jvadewan2@mwi.gov.jo; f. 1977 as a governmental organization responsible for the integrated social and economic development of the Jordan Valley. Projects in Stage I of the Jordan Valley Development Plan were completed in 1979. In 1988 the JVA was incorporated into the Ministry of Water and Irrigation. By late 2000 completed infrastructure projects included 2,205 km of roads, 2,223 housing units, 90 schools, 15 health centres, 16 local government buildings, 4 marketing centres, 2 tomato paste factories, 1 cold storage facility and several workshops. Electricity is now provided to all towns and villages in the valley from the national network and potable water is supplied to them from tube wells. Many of the Stage II irrigation projects are now completed. These include the construction of the King Talal, Wadi Arab, Kafrein and Karamah dams; the extension of the King Abdullah Canal to total 110.5 km in length; the construction of major municipal water projects in Amman and Irbid; the construction and conversion of a surface irrigation system into a pressurized pipe system covering an irrigated area of 25,000 ha; the development of groundwater resources and subsurface drainage systems. Projects under way include the construction of the Al-Wehdeh, Tanour and Wala dams, as well as the Mujeb dam and diversion weir. Future developments in tourist and industrial infrastructure will include the development of the Dead Sea East shore, Christ's baptism site on the Jordan river, and industrial free zones; Sec.-Gen. AVEDIS SERPEKIAN.

CHAMBERS OF COMMERCE AND INDUSTRY

Amman Chamber of Commerce: POB 1800, Amman 11118; tel. (6) 5666151; e-mail aci@amra.nic.gov.jo; f. 1923; Pres. HAIDER MURAD; Sec.-Gen. MUHAMMAD AL-MUHTASSEB.

Amman Chamber of Industry: POB 1800, Amman; tel. (6) 5643001; fax (6) 5647852; e-mail aci@aci.org.jo; internet www.aci.org.jo; f. 1962; 7,500 industrial companies registered (1999); Pres. KHALDUN ABU HASSAN; Dir.-Gen. Dr MUHAMMAD SMADI.

Federation of the Jordanian Chambers of Commerce: POB 7029, Amman 11118; e-mail fjcc@nets.com.jo; internet www.fjcc.com; tel. (6) 5665492; fax (6) 5685997; f. 1955; Chair. HAIDAR MURAD; Sec.-Gen. AMIN HUSSEINI.

Professional Associations Council (PAC): Professional Associations Complex, Amman; Pres. HASHIM GHARAIBEH.

UTILITIES

Electricity

Jordanian Electric Power Company (JEPCO): POB 618, Amman 11118; tel. (6) 4636381; fax (6) 4648482; e-mail jepco@go.com.jo; privately-owned; Chair. ISSAM BDEIR; Gen. Man. Eng. MARWAN BUSHNAQ.

Central Electricity Generating Company (CEGCO): POB 2564, Amman 11953; tel. (6) 5356989; fax (6) 5357210; e-mail chairman@cegco.com.jo; internet www.cegco.com.jo; electricity generation; govt-owned; scheduled for privatization; Chair. Eng. ALI YOUSUF ENSOUR.

Electricity Distribution Company (EDCO): POB 2310, Orthodox St, 7th Circle, Jabal Amman; tel. (6) 5858615; fax (6) 5818336; e-mail info@nepco.com.jo; internet www.edco.com.jo; electricity distribution; govt-owned; scheduled for privatization.

National Electric Power Company (NEPCO): POB 2310, Amman 11118; tel. (6) 5858615; fax (6) 5818336; e-mail nepco@nepco.com.jo; internet www.nepco.com.jo; f. 1996; formerly Jordan Electricity Authority; electricity transmission; govt-owned; scheduled for privatization; Man. Dir Eng. MUHAMMAD AZZAM.

Water

Water Authority of Jordan (WAJ): Amman.

TRADE UNIONS

The General Federation of Jordanian Trade Unions: POB 1065, Amman; tel. (6) 5675533; f. 1954; 33,000 mems; member of Arab Trade Unions Confederation; Chair. KHALIL ABU KHURMAH; Gen. Sec. ABD AL-HALIM KHADDAM.

There are also a number of independent unions, including:

Drivers' Union: POB 846, Amman; tel. (6) 4765637; fax (6) 4765829; Sec.-Gen. MAHMOUD ABD AL-HADI HAMMAD.

Jordan Engineers' Association (JEA): POB 940188, Shmeisani, Amman; tel. (6) 5607616; fax (6) 5676933; e-mail info@jea.org.jo; internet www.jea.org.jo; f. 1958; Pres. AZZAM HUNEIDI; Sec.-Gen. ALI ABU AS-SUKKAR.

Union of Petroleum Workers and Employees: POB 1346, Amman; Sec.-Gen. BRAHIM HADI.

Transport

RAILWAYS

Aqaba Railways Corporation (ARC): POB 50, Ma'an; tel. (3) 2132114; fax (3) 2131861; e-mail arc@go.com.jo; f. 1975; length of track 292 km (1,050-mm gauge); scheduled for privatization; Dir-Gen. ABDULLAH KHAWALDIH.

Formerly a division of the Hedjaz–Jordan Railway (see below), the Aqaba Railway was established as a separate entity in 1972; it retains close links with the Hedjaz but there is no regular through traffic between Aqaba and Amman. It comprises the 169-km line south of Menzil (leased from the Hedjaz–Jordan Railway) and the 115-km extension to Aqaba, opened in October 1975, which serves phosphate mines at el-Hasa and Wadi el-Abyad.

Hedjaz–Jordan Railway: POB 4448, Amman; tel. (6) 4895414; fax (6) 4894117; e-mail hji@nets.com.jo; f. 1902; administered by the Ministry of Transport; length of track 496 km (1,050-mm gauge); Chair. NADER DAHABI; Dir-Gen. A. ABULAL-FEILAT.

This was formerly a section of the Hedjaz Railway (Damascus to Medina) for Muslim pilgrims to Medina and Mecca. It crosses the Syrian border and enters Jordanian territory south of Dera'a, and runs for approximately 366 km to Naqb Ishtar, passing through Az-Zarqa, Amman, Qatrana and Ma'an. Some 844 km of the line, from Ma'an to Medina in Saudi Arabia, were abandoned for more than 60 years. Reconstruction of the Medina line, begun in 1965, was scheduled to be completed in 1971 at a cost of £15m., divided equally between Jordan, Saudi Arabia and Syria. However, the reconstruction work was suspended at the request of the Arab states concerned, pending further studies on costs. The line between Ma'an and Saudi Arabia (114 km) is now completed, as well as 15 km in Saudi Arabia as far as Halet Ammar Station. A new 115-km extension to Aqaba (owned by the Aqaba Railway Corporation (see above)was opened in 1975. In 1987 a study conducted by Dorsch Consult (Federal Republic of Germany) into the feasibility of reconstructing the Hedjaz Railway to high international specifications to connect Saudi Arabia, Jordan and Syria concluded that the reopening of the Hedjaz line would be viable only if it were to be connected with European rail networks. In August 1999 an express rail link between Amman and the Syrian capital, Damascus, was inaugurated.

ROADS

Amman is linked by road with all parts of the kingdom and with neighbouring countries. All cities and most towns are connected by a two-lane paved road system. In addition, several thousand km of tracks make all villages accessible to motor transport. In 2000 the total road network of the East Bank of Jordan was an estimated 7,245 km: 2,911 km of main roads, 2,059 km of secondary roads (both types asphalted) and 2,275 km of other roads.

Joint Land Transport Co: Amman; joint venture of Govts of Jordan and Iraq; operates about 750 trucks.

Jordanian-Syrian Land Transport Co: POB 20686, Amman; tel. (6) 5661134; fax (6) 5669645; internet www.josyco@joinnet.com.jo; f. 1976; transports goods between ports in Jordan and Syria; Chair. and Gen. Man. HAMDI AL-HABASHNEH.

SHIPPING

The port of Aqaba is Jordan's only outlet to the sea and has more than 20 modern and specialized berths, and one container terminal (540 m in length). The port has 299,000 sq m of storage area, and is used for Jordan's international trade and regional transit trade (mainly with Iraq). There is a ferry link between Aqaba and the Egyptian port of Nuweibeh.

Jordanian Ports Corporation (JPC): POB 115, Aqaba 77110; tel. (3) 2014031; fax (3) 2016204; e-mail ports@amra.nic.gov.jo; Dir-Gen. Eng. ABDULLAH ABU ALIM.

Amman Shipping & Trading Co: POB 213083, 5th Floor, Al-Aqqad Trading Centre, Gardens St; tel. (6) 5514620; fax (6) 5532324.

Arab Bridge Maritime Co: Aqaba; f. 1987; joint venture by Egypt, Iraq and Jordan to improve economic co-operation; an extension of the company that established a ferry link between Aqaba and the Egyptian port of Nuweibeh in 1985; Chair. Eng. MUHAMMAD N. ALKOUSI; Dir Capt. BASSAM AL-KINJI.

Arrow Trans Shipping SA: POB 213083, 5th Floor, Aqad Complex Bldg, Wasfi at-Tal St, Amman 11121; tel. (6) 5512621; fax (6) 5532324; e-mail arrow@albitar.com; f. 1990; Gen. Man. MARWAN JAMAL ED-DIN BITAR.

Assaf Shipping Co SA: POB 2637, Irbid 21110; tel. (2) 7279117; fax (2) 7261329; e-mail reefer_assaf@yahoo.com.

Tawfiq Gargour & Fils: POB 419, 4th Floor, Da'ssan Commercial Centre, Wasfi at-Tal St, Amman; tel. (6) 5524142; fax (6) 5530512; e-mail tgf@tgf.com.jo; f. 1928; shipping agents and owners; Chair. JOHN GARGOUR; Man. Dir NADIM GARGOUR.

Hijazi & Ghosheh Co: POB 183292, Amman; tel. (6) 4886166; fax (6) 4886211.

International Ship Management Co Ltd (ISM): POB 941430, 2nd Floor, Noor Centre, Islam Abad St, Ar-Rabeiah, Amman 11194; tel. (6) 5512607; fax (6) 5532083; e-mail ism@go.com.jo; Gen. Man. MOUSTAFA MASSAD.

Jordan National Shipping Lines Co Ltd: POB 5406, Nasir Ben Jameel St, Wadi Saqra, Amman 11183; POB 557, Aqaba; tel. (6) 5511500; fax (6) 5515119; e-mail jnl@go.com.jo; internet www.jnsl-jo .com; tel. (3) 2018739; fax (3) 318738; 75% govt-owned; service from Antwerp, Bremen and Tilbury to Aqaba; daily passenger ferry service to Egypt; land transportation to destinations in Iraq and elsewhere in the region; Chair. MUHAMMAD SMADI; Gen. Man. Eng. AKEF ABU TAYEH.

Amin Kawar & Sons Co W.L.L.: POB 222, 24 Abd al-Hamid Sharaf St, Amman 11118; tel. (6) 5603703; fax (6) 5672170; e-mail kawar@kawar.com.jo; internet www.kawar.com.jo; chartering, forwarding and shipping line agents; Chair. TAWFIQ A. KAWAR; CEO RUDAIN T. KAWAR; Gen. Man. GHASSOUB F. KAWAR.

Al-Mansour Marine Transportation and Trading Co: POB 960359, Amman; tel. (6) 697958; fax (6) 702352.

Orient Shipping Co Ltd: POB 207, Amman 11118; tel. (6) 5641695; fax (6) 5651567.

Petra Navigation and International Trading Co Ltd: POB 8362, White Star Bldg, King Hussein St, Amman 11121; tel. (6) 5607021; fax (6) 5601362; e-mail petra@armoush.com.jo; general cargo, ro/ro and passenger ferries; Chair. MAJED ARMOUSH.

Salam International Transport and Trading Co: King Hussein St, Abdali, Amman 11121; tel. (6) 5607021.

Syrian-Jordanian Shipping Co: POB 148, rue Port Said, Latakia, Syria; tel. (41) 471635; fax (41) 470250; Chair. OSMAN LEBBADI.

PIPELINES

Two oil pipelines cross Jordan. The former Iraq Petroleum Co pipeline, carrying petroleum from the oilfields in Iraq to Haifa, has not operated since 1967. The 1,717-km (1,067-mile) pipeline, known as the Trans-Arabian Pipeline (Tapline), carries petroleum from the oilfields of Dhahran in Saudi Arabia to Sidon on the Mediterranean seaboard in Lebanon. Tapline traverses Jordan for a distance of 177 km (110 miles) and has frequently been cut by hostile action. Tapline stopped pumping to Syria and Lebanon at the end of 1983, when it was first due to close. It was later scheduled to close in 1985, but in September 1984 Jordan renewed an agreement to receive Saudi Arabian crude oil through Tapline. The agreement can be cancelled by either party at two years' notice.

CIVIL AVIATION

There are international airports at Amman and Aqaba. The Queen Alia International Airport at Zizya, 40 km south of Amman, was opened in 1983.

Jordan Civil Aviation Authority (JCAA): POB 7547, Amman; tel. (6) 4891401; fax (6) 4892065; e-mail info@jcaa.gov.jo; internet www.jcaa.gov.jo; f. 1950; Dir-Gen. Capt. JIHAD IRSHAID.

Royal Jordanian Airline: Head Office: POB 302, Housing Bank Commercial Centre, Shmeisani, Amman 11118; tel. (6) 5607300; fax (6) 5672527; e-mail rj@go.com.jo; internet www.rjair.com; f. 1963; partial privatization in Feb. 2001; scheduled and charter services to Middle East, North Africa, Europe, USA and Far East; Chair. WALID ASFOUR; Pres. and CEO SAMER MAJALI.

Arab Wings Co Ltd: POB 341018, Amman 11134; tel. (6) 4893901; fax (6) 4893158; e-mail info@arabwings.com.jo; internet www .arabwings.com.jo; f. 1975; subsidiary of Royal Jordanian; executive jet charter service, air ambulances, priority cargo; Man. Dir AHED QUNTAR.

Royal Wings Co Ltd: POB 314018, Amman 11134; tel. (6) 4875206; fax (6) 4875656; e-mail info@royalwings.com.jo; internet www .royalwings.com.jo; f. 1996; subsidiary of Royal Jordanian; operates scheduled and charter regional and domestic services; Man. Dir AHED QUNTAR.

Tourism

The ancient cities of Jarash (Jerash) and Petra, and Jordan's proximity to biblical sites, have encouraged tourism. The development of Jordan's Dead Sea coast is currently under way; owing to the Sea's mineral-rich waters, the growth of curative tourism is anticipated.

The Red Sea port of Aqaba is also undergoing a major programme of development, with a view to becoming a centre for diving holidays. In 2001 Jordan received some 2.4m. visitors (including pilgrims and excursionists). Income from tourism in that year was estimated at JD $496.1m.

Ministry of Tourism and Antiquities: POB 224, Amman 11118; tel. (6) 4642311; fax (6) 4648465; e-mail tourism@mota.gov.jo; internet www.mota.gov.jo; f. 1952; Minister of Tourism and Antiquities Dr TALEB AR-RIFAI; Sec.-Gen. SULTAN ABU JABER.

Jordan Tourism Board: POB 830688, Amman 11183; tel. (6) 5678294; fax (6) 5678295; e-mail jtb@nets.com.jo; internet www .see-jordan.com; f. 1997; Man. Dir MARWAN KHOURY.

INDEX OF INTERNATIONAL ORGANIZATIONS

(Main reference only)

A

Abdus Salam International Centre for Theoretical Physics (UNESCO), 107
ACP Secretariat, 234
ACP States, 234
ADB Institute—ADBI, 144
Aerospace Medical Association—AsMA, 359
AFESD, 136
Africa Reinsurance Corporation—Africa-Re, 129
African Accounting Council, 133
African Airlines Association, 393
African Association for Public Administration and Management—AAPAM, 348
African Bar Association, 354
African Capacity Building Foundation—ACBF, 338
African Centre for Monetary Studies—ACMS, 342
African Civil Aviation Commission—AFCAC, 133
African Commission on Agricultural Statistics (FAO), 79
African Commission on Human and People's Rights, 378
African Development Bank—ADB, 128
African Development Fund—ADF, 129
African Economic Community—AEC, 130
African Export-Import Bank—Afreximbank, 130
African Forestry and Wildlife Commission (FAO), 79
African Groundnut Council—AGC, 335
African Guarantee and Economic Co-operation Fund, 343
African Insurance Organization—AIO, 342
African Nuclear-Weapon Free Zone Treaty (Pelindaba Treaty), 82
African Oil Palm Development Association—AFOPDA, 335
African Organization of Cartography and Remote Sensing, 384
African Petroleum Producers' Association—APPA, 335
African Regional Centre for Technology, 384
African Regional Organization for Standardization, 388
African Social and Environmental Studies Programme, 376
African Society of International and Comparative Law—ASICL, 354
African Telecommunications Union, 363
African Timber Organization—ATO, 330
African Trade Insurance Agency—ATI (COMESA), 163
African Training and Research Centre in Administration for Development, 338
African Union, 130
Afro-Asian Peoples' Solidarity Organization—AAPSO, 348
Afro-Asian Rural Development Organization—AARDO, 338
AFTA, 147
Agence française de développement—AFD, 239
Agence Intergouvernementale de la Francophonie, 338
Agence Universitaire de la Francophonie—AUF, 344
Agency for the Prohibition of Nuclear Weapons in Latin America and the Caribbean, 348
AGFUND, 338
Agudath Israel World Organisation, 366
Aid to Displaced Persons and its European Villages, 378
AIESEC International, 395
AIIM International, 385
Airports Council International—ACI, 393
Al-Quds Fund (OIC), 295
ALADI, 259
All Africa Conference of Churches—AACC, 366
Alliance Internationale de Tourisme, 387
Alliance Israélite Universelle—AIU, 366
Alliance of Small Island States—AOSIS, 348
Amnesty International, 378
Andean Business Advisory Council, 136
Andean Community of Nations, 133
Andean Development Corporation, 136
Andean Labour Advisory Council, 136
Andrés Bello Agreement, 136
Anti-Slavery International, 378
ANZUS, 348
APEC, 139
APEC Business Advisory Council—ABAC, 140
Arab Academy for Science, Technology and Maritime Transport—AASTMT, 261
Arab Administrative Development Organization—ARADO, 261
Arab Air Carriers' Organization—AACO, 393

Arab Atomic Energy Agency—AAEA, 261
Arab Authority for Agricultural Investment and Development—AAAID, 338
Arab Bank for Economic Development in Africa, 261
Arab Centre for the Study of Arid Zones and Dry Lands—ACSAD, 261
Arab Co-operation Council, 338
Arab Co-operative Federation, 179
Arab Company for Drug Industries and Medical Appliances—ACDIMA, 179
Arab Company for Electronic Commerce, 179
Arab Company for Industrial Investment, 179
Arab Company for Livestock Development, 179
Arab Detergent Chemicals Company—ARADET, 293
Arab Drilling and Workover Company, 293
Arab Federation for Paper, Printing and Packaging Industries, 179
Arab Federation of Chemical Fertilizers Producers, 179
Arab Federation of Engineering Industries, 179
Arab Federation of Leather Industries, 179
Arab Federation of Petroleum, Mining and Chemicals Workers, 352
Arab Federation of Shipping, 179
Arab Federation of Textile Industries, 179
Arab Federation of Travel Agents, 179
Arab Fund for Economic and Social Development—AFESD, 136
Arab Fund for Technical Assistance to African Countries, 261
Arab Geophysical Exploration Services Company—AGESCO, 293
Arab Gulf Programme for the United Nations Development Organizations, 338
Arab Industrial Development and Mining Organization, 261
Arab Iron and Steel Union—AISU, 388
Arab Labour Organization, 261
Arab League, 260
Arab League Educational, Cultural and Scientific Organization—ALECSO, 261
Arab Maritime Petroleum Transport Company—AMPTC, 293
Arab Mining Company, 179
Arab Monetary Fund, 138
Arab Organization for Agricultural Development—AOAD, 261
Arab Permanent Postal Commission, 364
Arab Petroleum Investments Corporation—APICORP, 293
Arab Petroleum Services Company—APSCO, 293
Arab Petroleum Training Institute—APTI, 293
Arab Satellite Communications Organization—ARABSAT, 261
Arab Seaports Federation, 179
Arab Shipbuilding and Repair Yard Company—ASRY, 293
Arab Sports Confederation, 381
Arab States Broadcasting Union—ASBU, 261
Arab Steel Union, 179
Arab Sugar Federation, 179
Arab Telecommunications Union, 364
Arab Towns Organization—ATO, 376
Arab Trade Financing Program—ATFP, 139
Arab Union for Cement and Building Materials, 179
Arab Union for Information Technology, 179
Arab Union of Fish Producers, 179
Arab Union of Food Industries, 179
Arab Union of Hotels and Tourism, 179
Arab Union of Land Transport, 179
Arab Union of Railways, 179
Arab Union of the Manufacturers of Pharmaceuticals and Medical Appliances, 179
Arab Union of the Manufacturers of Tyres and Rubber Products, 179
Arab Well Logging Company—AWLCO, 293
Arctic Council, 338
ASEAN, 146
ASEAN Free Trade Area—AFTA, 147
ASEAN Regional Forum—ARF, 149
Asia and Pacific Commission on Agricultural Statistics (FAO), 79
Asia and Pacific Plant Protection Commission (FAO), 79
Asia-Europe Meeting—ASEM, 231
Asia Pacific Academy of Ophthalmology—APAO, 358
Asia-Pacific Broadcasting Union—ABU, 364

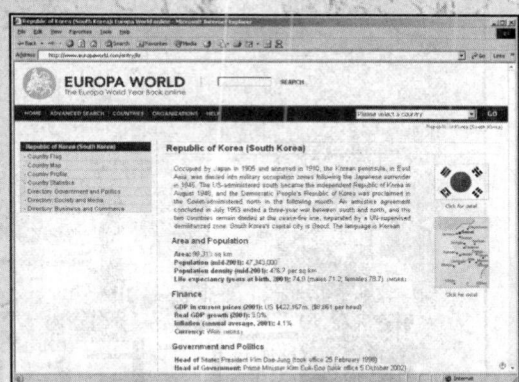

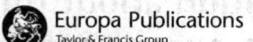

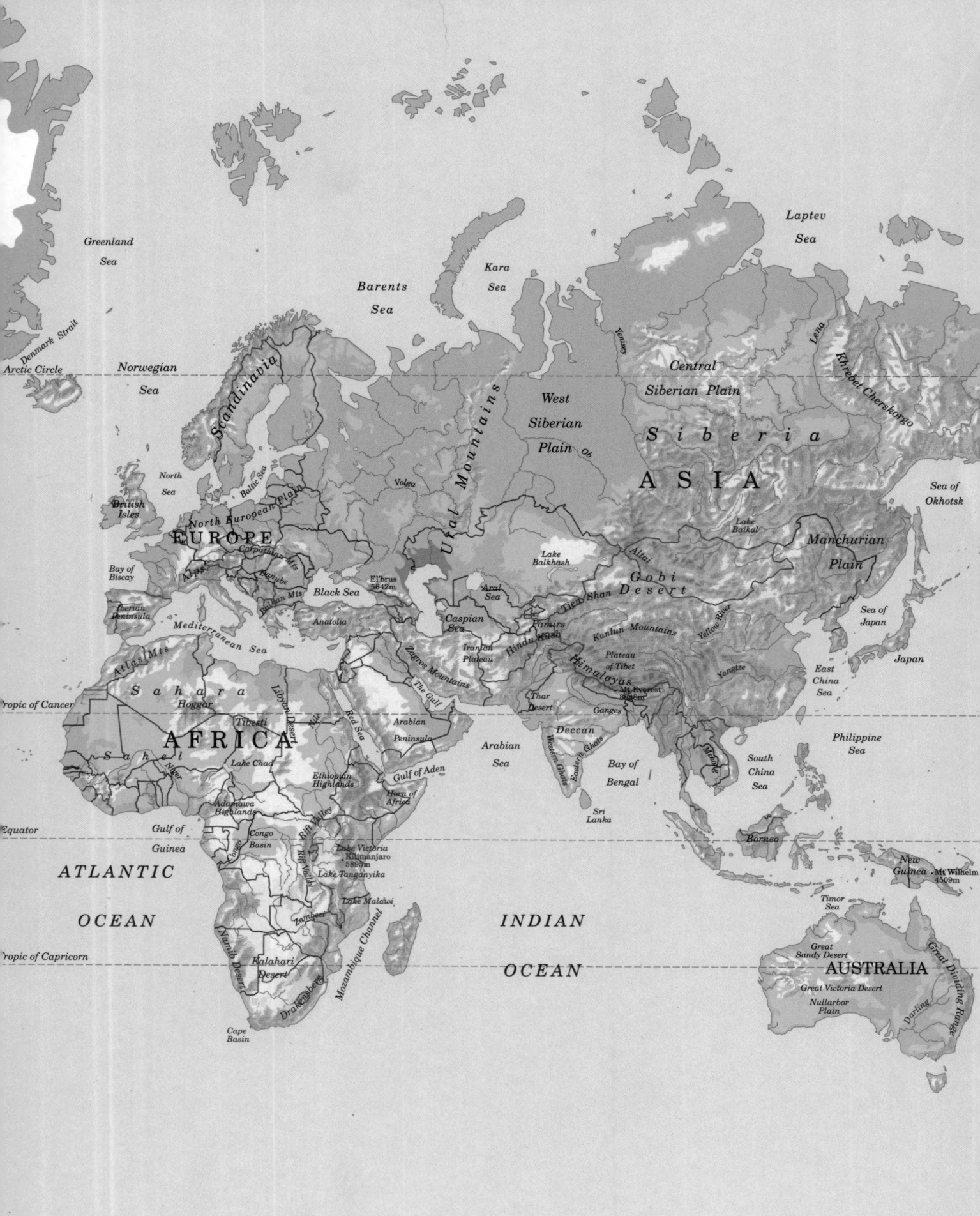

Greenland
Sea

Denmark Strait

Arctic Circle

*Norwegian
Sea*

*Barents
Sea*

*Kara
Sea*

*Laptev
Sea*

Scandinavia

North
Sea

Baltic Sea

*British
Isles*

Ural Mountains

*West
Siberian
Plain*

*Central
Siberian Plain*

Khrebet Cherskorgo

Lena

Yenisey

S i b e r i a

A S I A

*Sea of
Okhotsk*

North European Plain

EUROPE

Volga

Ob

*Lake
Baikal*

*Manchurian
Plain*

Carpathian Mts

*Bay of
Biscay*

Alps

Danube

Balkan Mts

Black Sea

*El'brus
5642m*

*Aral
Sea*

Altai

*Gobi
Desert*

*Sea of
Japan*

*Iberian
Peninsula*

*Caspian
Sea*

Tien Shan

Kunlun Mountains

Yellow River

Japan

Mediterranean Sea

Anatolia

Pamirs

Hindu Kush

*East
China
Sea*

Atlas Mts

Zagros Mountains

*Iranian
Plateau*

*Plateau
of Tibet*

Yangtze

The Gulf

Himalayas

Tropic of Cancer

S a h a r a

Hoggar

Libyan Desert

Tibesti

Nile

Red Sea

*Arabian
Peninsula*

*Arabian
Sea*

*Thar
Desert*

*Mt Everest
8848m*

Ganges

Deccan

Western Ghats

Eastern Ghats

Mekong

*South
China
Sea*

*Philippine
Sea*

AFRICA

S a h e l

Niger

Lake Chad

*Ethiopian
Highlands*

Gulf of Aden

*Horn of
Africa*

*Bay of
Bengal*

*Sri
Lanka*

*Adamawa
Highlands*

Equator

*Gulf of
Guinea*

*Congo
Basin*

Congo

Rift Valley

Lake Victoria

*Kilimanjaro
5895m*

Lake Tanganyika

Borneo

*New
Guinea*

*Mt Wilhelm
4509m*

ATLANTIC

Rift Valley

Lake Malawi

*Timor
Sea*

OCEAN

Zambezi

Mozambique Channel

INDIAN

Tropic of Capricorn

Namib Desert

*Kalahari
Desert*

Drakensberg

OCEAN

*Great
Sandy Desert*

Great Dividing Range

AUSTRALIA

Great Victoria Desert

*Nullarbor
Plain*

Darling

*Cape
Basin*

Antarctic Circle

A n t a r c t i c a